ENCARTA®
WORLD ENGLISH
DICTIONARY

ENCARTA
WORLD ENGLISH
DICTIONARY

BLOOMSBURY

A BLOOMSBURY REFERENCE BOOK
Created from the Bloomsbury Database of World English

First published in 1999 by
Bloomsbury Publishing Plc
38 Soho Square
London W1V 5DF

British Library Cataloguing in Publication Data
A CIP record for this book is available from the British Library.

ISBN 0 7475 4371 2

10 9 8 7 6 5 4 3 2 1

Typeset by Selwood Systems, Midsomer Norton, Bath
Printed in the United States of America

Contents

WORLD ENGLISH AND LANGUAGE CONSULTANTS

Robert Allen
Editor and lexicographer

David Blair
Senior Lecturer, Department of Linguistics, Macquarie University (Australia)

Robert B. Costello
Editor and lexicographer

Professor Nikolas Coupland
Centre for Applied English Language Studies, University of Wales (English in Wales)

Tony Deverson
Senior Lecturer, Department of English, University of Canterbury, New Zealand (New Zealand)

Dr Scott Delancey
Department of Linguistics, University of Oregon (Native American English)

Professor Margery Fee
Department of English, University of Vancouver; author, *Oxford Guide to Canadian Usage* (Canada)

Professor Joshua Fishman
City University of New York (Yiddish)

Jonathon Green
Author of a history of lexicography *Chasing the Sun: Dictionary-makers and the Dictionaries They Made*, and Britain's leading slang lexicographer; author of the *Cassell Dictionary of Slang* (A Brief History of Dictionaries and Dictionary-Makers)

Dr Eva Hertel
English Language and Linguistics, TU Chemnitz (East Africa)

Betty Kirkpatrick
Editor and lexicographer; editor, *Roget's Thesaurus*

Jacqueline Lam
Senior Lecturer, Hong Kong University of Science and Technology (Hong Kong)

Naomi C. Losch
Assistant Professor in Hawaiian, Department of Hawaiian and Indo-Pacific Languages, University of Hawaii at Manoa (Hawaiian English)

Dr Catherine Macafee
University of Aberdeen (Scottish, Northern Irish)

Rajend Mesthrie
Senior Lecturer, Department of Linguistics, University of Capetown (South Africa)

Mark Newbrook, PhD
Senior Lecturer, Department of Linguistics, Monash University (Malaysia and Singapore)

Dr Mark Sebba
Department of Linguistics, Lancaster University (UK Black English)

Professor Geneva Smitherman
University Distinguished Professor; Director, African American Language and Literacy Program; Director, 'My Brother's Keeper' Program, Department of English, Michigan State University (African American English)

Kamal Keskar Sridhar
Associate Professor, Department of Linguistics, State University of New York, Stony Brook (South Asia)

Dr Loreto Todd
Senior Lecturer, English Department, University of Leeds (Irish)

Professor Don Winford
Department of Linguistics, Ohio State University (Caribbean)

SUBJECT CONSULTANTS

Professor Clark Adams
Department of Wildlife and Fisheries Sciences, Texas A & M University (Hunting)

Michael Allaby
Writer and science consultant (Life Sciences)

Professor Christopher Arnison
Royal Agricultural College (Agriculture)

Dr Tallis Barker
(Music)

Dr Alan Barnard
University of Edinburgh (Anthropology)

Professor Joseph Bel Bruno
Dartmouth College, Hanover, New Hampshire (Chemistry)

Professor David Bjorklund
Department of Psychology, Florida Atlantic University (Psychology)

Professor Donald Black
College of Food and Natural Resources, University of Massachusetts (Agriculture)

Dr Sheila Blair
Editor for Islam and Central Asia, *The Dictionary of Art* (Arabic Words and Places)

Dr Clive Bloom
Middlesex University (Media)

Allan Brooks
Editor and writer; member, US Government technical committees (Engineering)

Charles Butcher
Specialist writer and editor (Chemical Engineering)

Edward Butcher
Editor (Currencies)

Colin Callander
Editor, *Golf Monthly* (Golf)

Col. John A. Calabro
Professor of English, US Military Academy, West Point (Military)

Professor Paul A. Carling
University of Lancaster (Geography)

Dr Christopher Chippendale
Museum of Archaeology and Anthropology, University of Cambridge (Archaeology)

Timothy Collings
Motor racing correspondent, Reuters and *Daily Telegraph* (Motor Sports)

Robert B. Costello
Editor and lexicographer (Computing/Foreign Words and Phrases)

Professor Helen Cowie
Roehampton Institute, London (Psychology)

Michael Crane
Director, British Isles Backgammon Association (Backgammon)

Dr Andrew Dalby
Honorary Librarian, Institute of Linguists, author, *Bloomsbury Dictionary of Languages* (Languages)

Robert Day
Chairman, Suffolk Advanced Motorcyclists Group (DIY, Motorcycles)

Col. Michael Dewar
Formerly Institute of Strategic Studies (Military)

Professor Robert Ditton
Department of Wildlife and Fisheries Sciences, Texas A & M University (Ecology)

Professor Bethany K. Dumas
Department of Linguistics, Language and Law, University of Tennessee (Law)

Dr Roy Evans
Formerly Faculty of Education, Roehampton Institute, London (Education)

Alan Ewert, PhD
University of Northern British Columbia (Mountaineering/Climbing)

Nancy Flynn
Cornell University (Botany)

Professor Bruce Ganem
Department of Chemistry, Cornell University (Chemistry)

Professor James Gramman
Department of Recreation, Park, and Tourism Sciences, Texas A & M University (Leisure)

Fayal Greene
Gardening writer and editor (Gardening)

Professor Lynne Goldstein
Professor and Chair, Department of Anthropology, Michigan State University; editor, *American Antiquity* (Anthropology and Archaeology)

Dr Jeremy Gray
Open University (Mathematics)

Steven Griffiths
UK civil servant (Transport/Environment)

Professor Trevor Griffiths
Programme Director, School of Arts and Humanities, University of North London (Theatre)

Andrew Howard
Middlesex University (Politics)

Alastair Hudson
Queen Mary and Westfield College, University of London (Law)

Philip Johansson
Naturalist and writer (Zoology)

Bridget Jones
Cookery editor and writer; member of the Guild of Food Writers (Food)

Professor Darlene Juschka
University of Toronto (World Religions)

David Kemp
VP and Euro Director, London, ABN-AMRO Bank N.V. (Currencies)

Alison Kervin
Editor, *Rugby World* (Rugby)

Professor Ira Konigsberg
University of Michigan, Ann Arbor; author, *Complete Film Dictionary* (Cinema)

Dr John Laurence
Boyce Thomson Institute, Cornell University (Botany)

Professor Bryan Lawson
School of Architecture, University of Sheffield (Architecture)

Professor Andrew Leclair
Newman Laboratory, Cornell University (Physics)

Becky Lee, PhD
Centre for Religion, University of Toronto (Christianity and the Bible)

Professor Franklin M. Loew
President, Becker College, Worcester, MA; formerly Dean of Veterinary Medicine, Tufts and Cornell Universities (Veterinary Science)

Alastair McIver
Editor, *Tennis World* (Tennis)

Jeffrey McQuain
Writer and researcher, *New York Times*; word columnist and researcher; author, *Power Language* and *Never Enough Words* (Politics)

Carolyn Marcus
Gardening writer and editor (Gardening)

Anthony Middleton
Formerly editor, RAF in-house publications service; formerly, Technical Publications Editor, GEC-Marconi (Engineering)

Mark Miller
Editor (Literature)

Martyn Moore
Editor, *Practical Photography* (Photography)

Philip D. Morehead
Chicago Lyric Opera (Music)

Professor David Morton
School of Biomedical Science and Ethics, University of Birmingham (Veterinary Science)

Professor Bruce Murphy
Faculty of Veterinary Medicine, University of Montreal (Biology)

Adrian Napper
formerly Dept of Architecture, Edinburgh College of Art (Building and Construction)

Susan North
Department of Textiles and Dress, Victoria and Albert Museum (Fashion)

Kathleen O'Grady
Trinity College, University of Cambridge (Religion and Mythology)

Professor Alex Orenstein
City University of New York (Philosophy)

Professor Anthony Pellegrini
Department of Educational Psychology, University of Minnesota (Education)

Michael Quinion
Lexicographer and editor (New Words)

John Ross
Writer and editor (Computing)

Dr Edward Ruddell
Department of Parks, Recreation, and Tourism, University of Utah (Martial Arts)

Richard Soffe
Seale-Hayne Faculty of Agriculture, Food and Land Use, University of Plymouth (Agriculture)

Professor Tony Spybey
Department of Sociology, Staffordshire University (Sociology)

Professor Peter N. Stearns
Dean, College of Humanities and Social Sciences, Carnegie Mellon University; author, *Encyclopedia of World History* (History)

Professor James M. Steele
School of Architecture, University of Southern California; author, *Architecture Today* (Architecture and Building)

Professor Robert Strong
Department of Economics, University of Maine (Finance)

Peter Timmer
University College London (Computing)

Dr Amos Turk
Professor Emeritus, Department of Chemistry, City College of New York (Chemical Engineering)

Dr Heather Valencia
University of Stirling (Judaism)

Michael J. Walsh
Librarian, Heythrop College, University of London (the Bible)

Rosemary Wilkinson
Freelance writer and editor (Crafts and Design)

Gillian Williams
Editor, *Ski and Board* magazine (Skiing)

John Williams
Sir Norman Chester Centre for Football Research, University of Leicester (Football)

Ellen Wohl
Associate Professor, Colorado State University (Geography)

Professor Philip C. Wright
University of New Brunswick (Business and Management)

Dr Robert Youngson
Author, *Royal Society of Medicine Encyclopedia of Family Health*, formerly consultant advisor on ophthalmology to the British Army (Medicine and Pharmacology)

EDITORIAL CONTRIBUTORS

LEXICOGRAPHERS

Sandra Anderson
Debra Bailey
David Barnett
Peter Blanchard
Jane Bradbury
Callum Brines
Pat Bulhosen
Dewayne Crawford
Steve Curtis
David A. Daniel
Dana Darby Johnson
George Davidson
Jessica Feinstein
Rosalind Fergusson
Scott Forbes
Lora Goldman
Jennifer Goss Duby
Alice Grandison
David Hallworth
Orin Hargraves
Ruth Hein
Archie Hobson
Lucy Hollingworth
Katy Isaacs
Stanley A. Kurzban
Barbara Kelly
Imogen Kerr
Rachel P. King
Virginia Klein

Paul Lagassé
Duncan Marshall
Patricia Marshall
Michael Mayor
Héloïse McGuinness
Martin Mellor
Sara Montgomery
Justyn Moulds
Michael Munro
Lynne Murphy
Claire Needler
Susan R. Norton
Dr Julia Penelope
Luisa Plaja
Julia B. Plier
Elaine Pollard
Deborah M. Posner
Jenny Roberts
Mairi Robinson
Jane Rogoyska
Howard Sargeant
Anne Seaton
Tom Shields
Martin Stark
Penny Stock
Fraser Sutherland
Katharine Turok
Dr Donald Watt
Holly Webber
Pamela White

SCIENCE AND TECHNICAL EDITORS

Rich Cutler
Pam England
Robert Hine
Ruth Koenigsberg
Alan D. Levy
Ann Marie Menting
Dr Ruth Salomon
James E. Shea
Martin Tolley

PRONUNCIATIONS

Dr Phillip Backley
Valerie Boulanger
C. Rodolfo Celis
Kimberley Farrar
Sharon Goldstein
Phil Harrison
Esther Hurrell
Bettina Isensee
Dinah Jackson
Nicholas Jones
Dr John M. Kirk
Rafal S. Konopka
Rima McKinzey
Scott Montgomery

Susan Rennie
Dr Mary Rigby
Susan Sharpe
Misty Shock

ETYMOLOGIES

Anna Berge
Titus Bicknell
Pietro Bortone
Anne Corlett
Dr Julia Cresswell
Dr Jim Girsch
Kerstin Hoge
Andrew Horton
Martha Mayou
Fred McDonald
Dr Robert Mory
Cerywss O'Hare
Joseph Patwell
Edward Pettit
Sean Pollack
Anne Seaton
Susan Shephard
Dr Susan Sigalas
Dr Roger Woodard
David M. Weeks, PhD
Jason Zerdin

ADDITIONAL CONTRIBUTORS

LANGUAGE ANALYSIS

Ruth Blackmore
Richard Breheny
Roland Chambers
Rosalind Combley
Alison Crann
Kay Cullen
Gill Francis
Elizabeth Manning
Diane Nicholls
Christina Rammell
Alison Renshaw
Laura Wedgeworth
Emily Young

PROOFREADERS

Stuart Fortey
Bruce Frost
Katherine Carson
Debra Goring
Isabel Griffiths
Margaret Hill
Ruth Hillmore

Margaret Jull Costa
Irene Lakhani
Laura Lawrie
Jill Leatherbarrow
Julie Marsh
Margaret Mullen
Paula Parish
Kathy Seed
John Wheelwright

EDITORIAL, KEYBOARDING, AND ADMINISTRATIVE ASSISTANCE

Charlotte Adams
Sara Al-Bader
Neil Atherton
Lanfranca Attanasio
Simon Beattie
Alistair Bruce
Joan Carpenter
Barry Day
    (Database Assistant)

Anna Degotardi
Sarah Faherty
Emma Harrison
Fiona Henderson
Angela Jackson
Andy Lacey
Una McGovern
Soraya Moeng
Fearghus Ó Conchúir
Elizabeth Partington
Melanie Poyo
James Randall
Lucy Reiter
Ian Ronayne
Ian Rowley
Walter Hepburne Scott
Laura Stoddart
Melanie Tate
Rachael Tuley
Kamala Wickramasinghe
Harriet Wynne Finch

Corpus material
Nigel Clifford

GEOGRAPHICAL AND BIOGRAPHICAL ENTRIES

Consultants
John Bowman, Editor-in-Chief, *Cambridge Dictionary of American Biography*

Maggy Hendry, Editor, *Macmillan Encyclopedia of Women* (revised edition)

Professor Howard Nenner, Department of History, Smith College, Consultant and associate editor, *New Dictionary of National Biography*

Sarah Waldram

Managing Editor
Stephen Adamson

Compilers and editors
Trevor Anderson
Richard Beatty
Ian Crofton
Duncan Brewer
Susan Johnson
Keith Lye
Richard O'Neill
Rebecca Palmer
Eileen Ramchandran
Theodore Rowland-
    Entwistle
Eleanor Stanley
Lucilla Watson

ILLUSTRATIONS

Coordinator
Gill Paul

Picture Researcher
Elaine Willis

Illustrators
Wendy Bramwell
Chris Lyon
Annabel Milne

Sylvie Rabbe
Beatriz Waller
David Wood

Tables
Jeffrey Petts
Ruth Bateson

Annotations
Andrew Clarke

Maps
Digital Wisdom
Publishing Ltd

Illustrations Assistants
Dawn Boulton
Elizabeth Geary

DESIGN

Jacket and Text Design
William Webb

Frontmatter Design
Simon Mercer,
Mercer Design

Foreword

Nigel Newton

THE NEED FOR A WORLD English dictionary became apparent to me after 16 years of living as an American in Britain and travelling around the world. It was clear in this period towards the end of the Cold War that the English language was gaining a level of adoption by non-native speakers which could never have been dreamt of by propagandists among the Cold Warriors themselves. English has become the preferred language of communication in the same way that so many propositions that have been around for a long time suddenly achieve widespread acceptance, in the same way as the idea that the Earth orbits the Sun, rather than the Sun orbiting the Earth, gained currency during the late seventeenth century.

The argument for a new English dictionary, using the world as its cultural perspective, is inescapable, as English can no longer be said to be the British language originally defined by James Murray in the first *Oxford English Dictionary* or the language of America that Noah Webster set out to define. Today English is the language of the world. What does this mean? It is interesting to note that in the current edition of a leading English dictionary the term 'imperial' is defined as 'of or relating to an empire: *Britain's imperial era*'. The **Encarta® World English Dictionary** defines the same term as 'concerning or involving an empire or its ruler'. The point is that a dictionary of the world's *lingua franca* in the third millennium should reflect a broad cultural perspective rather than the history of nations that once held power over others.

Our goal has been to create a dictionary of the world's language that will become the most widely used reference work in the world. In order to realize that vision, we assembled a partnership of publishers around the world. We have been fortunate in the great strength this partnership has given the project. We have worked with Microsoft who publish the Dictionary in electronic form, St. Martin's Press who publish the print edition in North America, Macmillan who publish the print edition in Australia and New Zealand, and other partners around the world.

In order to reflect the global stature of English, we recruited a team of over 320 lexicographers, editors, and special consultants to create, edit, and check the text of the Dictionary. They live in many different countries. This has brought to the text a global perspective that distinguishes this Dictionary from its rivals, and in it we have been able to reflect the many varieties of English around the world. We hope that this Dictionary will be responsible for increasing the awareness of many of the beautiful English words used in other places, for example 'tabanca', a word in Caribbean English which dates from the nineteenth century and is defined as 'a state of sadness resulting from unrequited or lost love'.

We also live in a multimedia age. This Dictionary is the first to be planned and created with the specific aim of being published in both book and electronic form at the same time. There are many people who will find the electronic edition of this Dictionary the most useful one. However, we know that the market for the print form of the Dictionary is still a large one. It has been observed that a book is a superior piece of mid-technology, rather like the bicycle, which has continued to flourish in the age of the car. Indeed, unless one's computer is already switched on, a dictionary in book form is probably the fastest random access device available.

The team of exceptional lexicographers who have created this Dictionary have been very excited to be contributing to a completely new information tool in the information age. On a recent visit to the exhibition of 'The Information Age' at the Smithsonian Museum of American History in Washington, DC, I was left in no doubt that communication and information are the best hope we have to avoid repeating the mistakes of history. The e-mails from ordinary citizens in Belgrade that currently appear on the CNN nightly news may not have ended the war in Yugoslavia, but they certainly contribute to an understanding of the perspective of both sides in a way which could not have happened in any previous world conflict. It is to be hoped that they may eventually contribute to its resolution. These e-mails are written in English.

Nigel Newton

When the world wants to communicate, especially if it wants to communicate or do business beyond its own borders, English tends to be the chosen means of communication. One century ago that language might have been French, and several centuries earlier it would have been Latin. Landmarks in the spread of English range from the decision by air traffic controllers in the 1950s to adopt English as their world language on the one hand, to the huge worldwide popularity of Hollywood movies and American TV shows on the other. The fact that almost 90 per cent of the world's Web pages are in English has a compounding effect with the explosive growth of the Internet.

World English demands its own dictionary. In the *Encarta World English Dictionary* we are not asserting the primacy of one form of English over another. We are celebrating the richness and diversity of the many varieties of English encountered in daily life. In today's global village, the influences on English from all over the world are intense. We read Canadian novels, some watch Australian soap operas on television, while American language and style dominate software programs. There are many brilliant dictionaries available already, but none which have been conceived with the specific goal of defining the global language of World English.

The *Encarta World English Dictionary* takes a new view of today's world language and will in years to come continue to reflect the changes and developments in the language.

Nigel Newton,
Chairman,
Bloomsbury Publishing Plc,
London,
18 May 1999

Introduction to the First Edition

Dr Kathy Rooney

THE ENGLISH LANGUAGE has changed. One in five of the world's population speaks English. Approximately 375 million people speak English as their first language. Over 375 million people speak English as their second language. English is the main international language of business, pop music, sport, advertising, academic conferences, travel, airports, air-traffic control, diplomacy, science, and technology. It is estimated that English is the language of over 80 percent of the information stored in the world's computers and 85 percent of Internet home pages, and that English is the first language of 68 percent of Web users.

The *Encarta World English Dictionary* is the first dictionary to be able to reflect this new world status of the English language, bringing together not only the two main spelling forms of the language (American English and British English), but also all the other main varieties of our language — from Canada, Australia, New Zealand, Africa, Asia, the Caribbean, and the Pacific Rim.

The Database from which the *Encarta World English Dictionary* is derived is the first dictionary database to have been written in both of the main spelling forms of English at the same time. This gives the Dictionary a truly world perspective. The great dictionaries of the past have all been firmly rooted in their specific cultural heritage — Oxford on the one hand, and, in the United States, the multitude of Websters on the other. In writing the *Encarta World English Dictionary* we have gone beyond such national boundaries and created a dictionary that accurately reflects the worldwide presence of the English language today. The Dictionary has been compiled by a team of over 320 dictionary editors (lexicographers), word-history experts (etymologists), pronunciation specialists (phoneticians), and over 120 special subject and World English consultants. Our team has been drawn from around the world and has included, for example a Canadian poet, the manager of a meditation centre in rural Maryland, and a telecommuting mother of twins from the Orkney Islands, off the northernmost coast of Scotland.

The *Encarta World English Dictionary* is first and foremost a dictionary of the modern English language. The audience for this dictionary is diverse, worldwide, encompassing a wide range of ages and backgrounds. It is also a multimedia audience, for the Dictionary is the first written with both print and electronic publications in view, and the first to be published simultaneously around the world and in both print and electronic formats. For this reason we have made the language of the definitions as natural as possible, and we have tried to avoid dictionary jargon where feasible. We have tried to create clear, informative, and readable definitions that our readers will understand without difficulty. Our goal has been to write our definitions in natural English, to use a level of vocabulary more accessible than the entry term, and to differentiate a word from its near-synonyms while making the user aware of any nuances that generally attach to a sense. Our definitions identify and focus clearly on the characteristics that distinguish and differentiate a word from related terms and include features that are picked up in similes and metaphorical usage.

Where other dictionaries might be described as literary, based on historical principles, or scientific, the *Encarta World English Dictionary* should be described as modern. Its focus is on the language needs of general dictionary users today. These needs encompass both the newest scientific and slang terms, and literary or historical language that users of the Dictionary may encounter in their reading. Our guiding principle has been to define the language that our readers are likely to encounter in their everyday lives.

There are in the region of one million words in the English language today, and this total continues to grow, especially in areas such as technology, science, popular culture, and business. The *Encarta World English Dictionary* gives a picture of the language today, and, as our Corpus grows, we will continue to monitor and expand the Dictionary to reflect new coinages and senses. The *Encarta World English Dictionary* has over 100,000 headwords (the words you look up), including

10,000 biographical and geographical entries, and over 3.5 million words of text.

Dictionary editors require hard data to make sure that the definitions they write are based on good linguistic evidence. For earlier dictionary writers such evidence has been garnered and stored on cards or slips of paper. In recent years the advent of the computer has meant that such cumbersome and time-consuming methods have been replaced by computerized corpora. A corpus is like a huge filing cabinet, filled with millions of words of real language (taken from fiction, nonfiction, and journalism, for example). Software developed specifically for this project has enabled our editors to call up examples of the use of any term at the touch of a computer key. The Corpus of World English was created specifically for the *Encarta World English Dictionary* and contains over 50 million words of English from around the world. The *Encarta World English Dictionary* is the first dictionary compiled for speakers of US English for which its editors have been able to use a corpus.

Computers have been vital not only in helping us find the evidence for our definitions but also in enabling us to communicate effectively with our far-flung team. This Dictionary is the first to have made maximum use of the Internet not only as a source of language evidence but also as a fundamental means of communication among members of the compilation team. Every evening from our offices we e-mailed our team batches of work. These were then returned to us by e-mail.

People use dictionaries to find out what words mean, and often these words are scientific or technical. However, many dictionaries define such terms in ways that can seem just as technical as the term itself. In writing the *Encarta World English Dictionary* we have tried to bring the same criteria of clarity and transparency to our scientific and technical definitions that have characterized our approach to other definitions. We have applied these criteria across all our specialized entries. In doing so, we combined the skills of our technical definers with contributions from our many

subject advisers who checked the accuracy of our definitions and patiently answered thousands of queries. Thus, the *Encarta World English Dictionary* tries to paint a word picture that the reader can understand by keeping use of specialist terminology to a minimum.

Our research has indicated that today's dictionary users want to find the information they are seeking quickly. In response to that need we have developed the 'quick definition' feature that is unique to this Dictionary. Quick definitions appear in small capital letters at all entries with more than one sense. They give a brief gloss of the headword for the user who does not want, or need, the full picture. They provide a thumbnail sketch rather than an analysis of the meaning. The quick definitions are also important in helping readers to navigate through the many senses of a long entry. When deciding on the order of sense categories, our general principle has been 'most frequent first, least frequent last' as judged by current usage and evidence from our Corpus of World English. This is to make certain that the most common senses occur early in the entry, to make the text of the Dictionary easy to use. We have, however, in some instances overridden this principle where more frequent senses clearly develop out of a less frequent (probably more technical) sense. Senses within the same part of speech are grouped together in an entry. Informal and slang senses usually come before dated or archaic senses but after stylistically neutral senses. In sense division, we have tried to strike a balance midway between broad and narrow categorization of senses. The primary consideration has always been ease of use by the reader. We have applied a similar priority when deciding which words and senses should be expanded by example phrases and sentences. We have tried to include these wherever they will help the reader grasp the meaning more easily.

The pronunciation system has been especially developed for the *Encarta World English Dictionary* to provide a system that speakers of English will find easy to decode. Rather than using the International Phonetic Alphabet (IPA), an excellent system for learners of our language, we felt that we should provide a more up-to-date system that our users, mainly speakers of the English language, would find easier to understand.

Language is a powerful tool, one that can hurt and offend. In writing the *Encarta World English Dictionary* we have been at pains to write definitions that convey the meaning of the word in an appropriately clear but sensitive way. Since the Dictionary is a snapshot of the language today, we include some terms that a few users may find offensive or even highly offensive. It has been our policy throughout to indicate clearly when such terms are likely to cause offence. A number of lexical entries labeled *offensive* or *taboo* must be defined as entries in any adult dictionary that attempts to cover the whole range of the language. However, in writing the Dictionary, we have tried to avoid sexist, ethnic, ethnocentric, ethnophobic, ageist, racist, or physiologically stereotypical language in the definitions, examples, and other elements of the text.

Since the English language has a fascinating history, we have paid particular attention to tracing the histories of words (**etymologies**). Our etymologies are written in clear language, avoiding symbols and abbreviations wherever possible. They show not only the origins of the word but also its relationship to other words and the reasons why the word has its particular origin. We have also included hundreds of extended word-history essays. In addition to extended paragraphs on word histories, we have included similar brief essays on usage, synonyms, World English, regional English, and cultural notes. The essays form a stepping stone from the Dictionary text into the wider world of cultural reference.

Writing the *Encarta World English Dictionary* has been a huge challenge. Over 320 people have worked on the project. I would like to thank all of them most sincerely for their commitment and dedication at all stages. I would also like to thank our international publishing partners who have shared with us the excitement of writing this completely new dictionary of the world's language — English.

Kathy Rooney
April 1999

How to use the *Encarta World English Dictionary*

Faye Carney

INTRODUCTION

A dictionary is a complex amalgam of different elements that relate to what users want from a dictionary – spelling, pronunciation, meaning, examples of use, advice on grammar or usage, and the explanation of the origins of a word. This section outlines briefly the different elements in the text, so that you can find what you want in the *Encarta World English Dictionary* quickly and easily.

THE PAGE

Guide Words

Each page has two **guide words** that show, on the left, the first **boldface** dictionary entry on that page, and, on the right, the last, so that you can quickly find the word you are looking for.

Pronunciation Key

Each double-page spread shows the **pronunciation key** along the foot of the page for ease of reference. (For full details on the **Pronunciation System**, see pp. xxi-xxii.)

Text Layout

The text is designed in three columns for maximum coverage and legibility. Important elements of the text appear in **boldface** type. Quick definitions appear in SMALL CAPITALS. Full definitions appear in roman type and examples and quotations in *italic type*.

Illustrations

Illustrations appear as close as possible to the entries to which they refer. Over 4,000 items are illustrated in this dictionary in more than 3,500 single and composite images and tables.

guide word – first entry ....

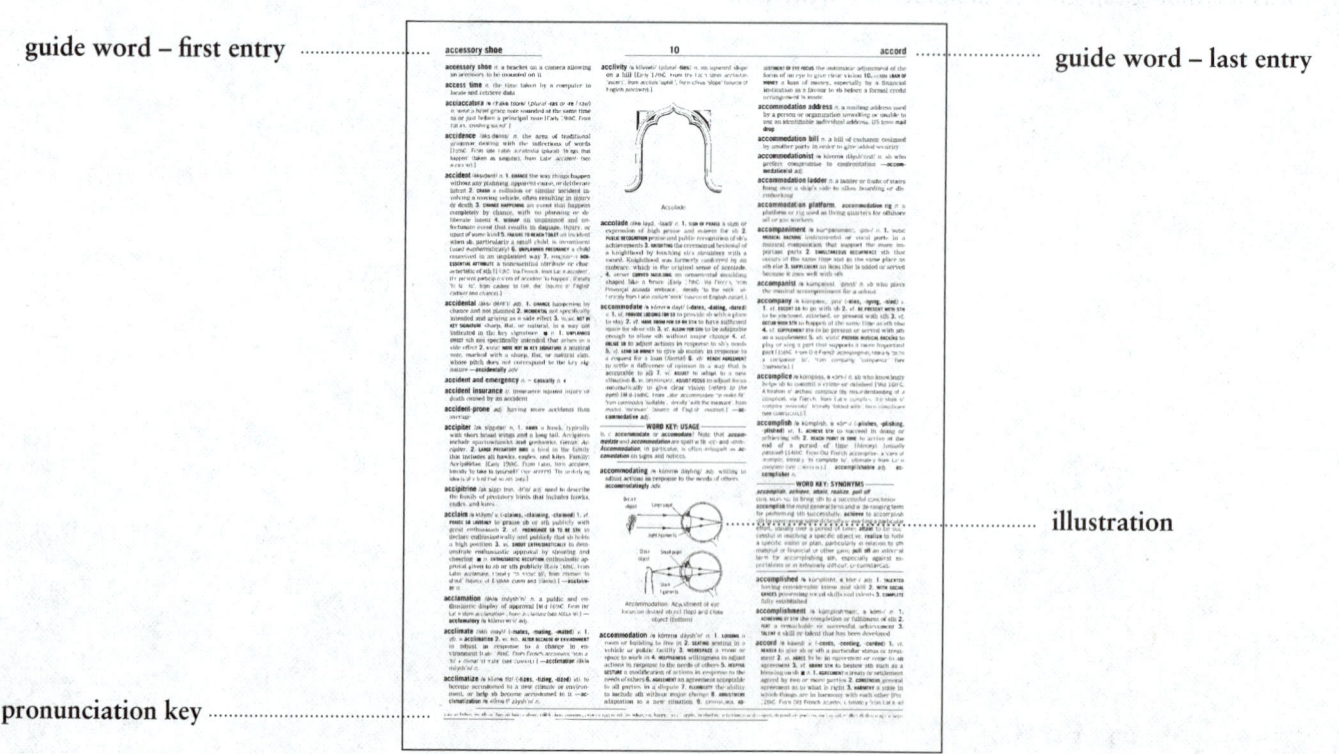

guide word – last entry

illustration

pronunciation key ....

THE TEXT

The text of a dictionary combines many different elements, which are explained briefly here.

Headwords

The *Encarta World English Dictionary* contains over 100,000 headwords (the words you look up), including approximately 10,000 entries about people and places – the biographical and geographical entries.

Alphabetical order

Headwords are listed in strict letter order, ignoring punctuation and other characters:

> **box bed** *n.*
> **boxboard** *n.*
> **box calf** *n.*
> **box camera** *n.*
> **box canyon** *n.*
> **boxcar** *n.*
> **box coat** *n.*
> **box elder** *n.*

Biographical and geographical entries are listed alphabetically. Wherever one name appears in more than one entry, the entries appear in alphabetical order following the comma:

> **Adams, Abigail**
> **Adams, Ansel**
> **Adams, Gerry**
> **Adams, Henry**
> **Adams, John**
> **Adams, John Quincy**
> **Adams, Samuel**

Phrasal verbs are listed with their root verb.

Words with the same spelling

Words with the same spelling (**homographs**) but with different pronunciations or origins (**etymologies**) are listed with superscript numbers to differentiate them. The order of these numbers broadly reflects usage and frequency.

bow[1] /bō/ *n.* **1.** LOOPED KNOT a knot in which the loops remain visible, e.g. in tied shoelaces or in ribbons used for decorating gifts or hair. ◊ **bow tie 2.** SPORTS, ARMS WEAPON FOR FIRING ARROWS a weapon used to fire arrows, consisting of a curved, flexible piece of wood and a taut string fastened to the two ends **3.** MUSIC ROD FOR PLAYING STRINGED INSTRUMENTS a rod with fibres tightly stretched between the two ends, used for playing stringed instruments **4.** CURVED SHAPE OR PART a rounded or semicircular shape, e.g. a part of a building or a loop in a river **5.** ARCHERY, HIST = **bowman**[1] (*literary*) **6.** = **rainbow** ■ **bows** *npl.* ARCHERY, HIST ARCHERS bowmen or archers considered as a group (*literary*) ■ *v.* (**bows, bowing, bowed**) **1.** *vti.* BEND STH INTO BOW SHAPE to bend, or bend sth, into a rounded or bow shape **2.** *vti.* MUSIC DRAW BOW ACROSS STRINGED INSTRUMENT to draw a bow across the strings of a stringed instrument **3.** *vt.* MUSIC INDICATE BOWING FOR MUSIC to mark a piece of music to indicate which notes are to be played with the bow moving in one direction across the strings and which are to be played with it moving in the opposite direction [Old English *boga*. Ultimately from a prehistoric Germanic word meaning 'to bend', which is also the ancestor of English *bow*[2], *bight*, and *bagel*.]

bow[2] /bow/ *v.* (**bows, bowing, bowed**) **1.** *vti.* BEND HEAD OR BODY FORWARD to bend the head forward, or to bend forward from the waist, as a signal of respect, greeting, consent, submission, or acknowledgment ○ *bowing her head in shame* **2.** *vti.* BEND STH OR DROOP to bend sth over so that it droops, or to be bent in this way ○ *branches bowed down with fruit.* **3.** *vi.* YIELD TO STH OR SB to accept sth and yield to it, often unwillingly ○ *bowed to the demands of pressure groups* ■ *n.* BENDING FORWARD OF UPPER BODY a bending forward of the upper part of the body to show respect, acknowledgment, subservience, courtesy,

or greeting [Old English *būgan* (source also of English *buxom*). Ultimately from an Indo-European word meaning 'to bend', which is also the ancestor of English *bow*[1].] ◊ **bow and scrape** to be excessively polite or attentive in an attempt to ingratiate yourself with sb

bow[3] /bow/ *n.* **1.** SHIPPING FRONT PART OF VESSEL the front section of a boat or other vessel **2.** ROWING PERSON IN BOW the rower closest to the front of a boat [Early 17thC. From Low German *boog* or Middle Dutch *boeg*.]

Pronunciation

Our pronunciation system has been developed specifically for the *Encarta World English Dictionary*. It relies on familiar combinations of letters of the alphabet, so that you can use it without constant reference to a table of explanations and symbols. The system is explained in full on pp. xxi-xxii.

Variant spellings

The Dictionary takes note wherever a word has more than one possible spelling **variant**. Such entries appear in boldface type following their headword. Variant spellings are cross-referred back to the entry where they are defined using an equals sign = .

falafel /fə láaf'l/, **felafel** *n.* a deep-fried ball of ground chickpeas seasoned with onions and spices, often eaten in pitta bread with salad and yogurt or tahini sauce. It was originally a Middle Eastern dish. [Mid-20thC. Via Egyptian Arabic *falāfil* from Arabic *fulful* 'pepper'.]

felafel *n.* = **falafel**

Inflections

Inflections are forms of words that are different from the headword. These include the principal tenses of verbs, the comparative and superlative forms of adjectives and adverbs, and irregular plurals of nouns. These forms are shown after the pronunciation where the inflection applies to the whole headword or at a specific sense or group of senses as appropriate.

gambol /gámb'l/ *vi.* (**-bols, -bolling, -bolled**) LEAP PLAYFULLY to leap or skip about playfully ■ *n.* PLAYFUL LEAPING an instance of leaping about playfully [Mid-16thC. Alteration of GAMBADE.]

gas /gass/ *n.* (*plural* **gases** *or* **gasses**) **1.** CHEM SUBSTANCE SUCH AS AIR a substance such as air that is neither a solid nor a liquid at ordinary temperatures and that has the ability to expand indefinitely **2.** UTIL, GEOL FOSSIL FUEL a combustible gaseous substance such as natural gas or coal gas, used as a fuel **3.** MIL, CRIMINOL GAS FOR POISONING OR ASPHYXIATING a gaseous mixture used as a poison, irritant, or asphyxiating agent **4.** PHARM ANAESTHETIC a gaseous substance used as an anaesthetic **5.** *US* AUTOMOT GASOLINE gasoline for internal-combustion engines **6.** *US* AUTOMOT CAR ACCELERATOR the pedal used for accelerating a motor vehicle (*informal*) ○ *step on the gas* **7.** *US* PHYSIOL FLATULENCE gaseous product of digestion (*informal*) **8.** MINING METHANE AND AIR the highly explosive product of methane combined with air **9.** SB OR STH ENTERTAINING sb or sth such as an experience that is very thrilling or entertaining (*informal*) **10.** NONSENSE meaningless empty talk (*informal*) ■ *v.* (**gases** *or* **gasses, gassing, gassed**) **1.** *vt.* TO HARM SB WITH GAS to attack, injure, or kill a person or animal with a poisonous, irritating, or asphyxiating gas **2.** *vi.* RELEASE GAS to give off gas or a gas **3.** *vi.* TALK IDLY to talk too much, especially about unimportant matters (*informal*) [Mid-17thC. From Dutch, coined by the Flemish chemist J. B. van Helmont (1577–1644), based on Greek *khaos* 'empty space' (source of English *chaos*).] —**gassing** *n.*

gateau /gáttō/ (*plural* **-teaux** /-tōz/), **gâteau** (*plural* **-teaux**) *n.* **1.** RICH CAKE a rich cake, usually consisting of several layers held together with a cream filling **2.** BAKED SAVOURY FOOD savoury food baked and served in a form resembling a cake [Mid-19thC. From French, 'cake'.]

fluffy /flúffi/ (**-ier, -iest**) *adj.* **1.** SOFT AND LIGHT consisting of sth soft and light to the touch such as wool or feathers **2.** DOWNY OR FEATHERY covered in sth soft and light to the touch such as down or feathers **3.** COOK SOFT AND LIGHT IN TEXTURE soft and light in texture because air has been beaten or whisked in —**fluffily** *adv.* —**fluffiness** *n.*

Important irregular inflections also appear as headwords in their own right:

> fora Plural of forum
>
> laid Past tense, past participle of lay

Parts of Speech

Parts of speech labels, in *italic type*, indicate the linguistic function of the headword. They are:

abbr.	abbreviation
adj.	adjective
adv.	adverb
aux. v.	auxiliary verb
conj.	conjunction
contr.	contraction
det.	determiner
interj.	interjection
modal v.	modal verb
n.	noun
npl.	plural noun
prefix	prefix
prep.	preposition
pron.	pronoun
symbol	symbol
suffix	suffix
tdmk.	trademark
v.	verb
vi.	intransitive verb
vr.	reflexive verb
vt.	transitive verb
vti.	transitive and intransitive verb

Abbreviations and Acronyms

Abbreviations and acronyms are grouped together according to their punctuation and their status as either an abbreviation or symbol. Our Corpus has shown that punctuation within abbreviations varies considerably. This Dictionary gives the most common form; important variants are also shown. Senses are ordered alphabetically.

> **q**[1] /kyoo/ (*plural* **q's**), **Q** (*plural* **Q's** *or* **Qs**) *n.* **1.** 17TH LETTER OF ENGLISH ALPHABET the 17th letter of the modern English alphabet **2.** SPEECH SOUND CORRESPONDING TO LETTER 'Q' the speech sound that corresponds to the letter 'Q' **3.** LETTER 'Q' WRITTEN a written representation of the letter 'Q'
>
> **q**[2] *symbol.* PHYS **1.** electric charge **2.** heat *n.* 1.
>
> **Q** *abbr.* **1.** CHESS queen **2.** MONEY quetzal
>
> **q.** *abbr.* **1.** quart **2.** quarter **3.** quarterly **4.** quarto **5.** question **6.** query **7.** quire **8.** MEASURE quintal
>
> **Q.** *abbr.* **1.** quartermaster **2.** quarto **3.** Quebec **4.** queen

When an abbreviation is more frequently used than its full form, we give the definition at the abbreviation:

> **DNA** *n.* a nucleic acid molecule in the form of a twisted double strand (**double helix**) that is the major component of chromosomes and carries genetic information. DNA, which is found in all living organisms except some viruses, is self-replicating and is responsible for passing along hereditary characteristics from one generation to the next. Full form **deoxyribonucleic acid**

Senses

Many words have more than one sense. The different senses are indicated by sense numbers that appear in **boldface** type. Senses are ordered according to usage and frequency; they are grouped according to part of speech (all noun senses together, all verb senses together, and so on).

The symbol (■) introduces a new part of speech within an entry.

> **radiant** /ráydiənt/ *adj.* **1.** SHOWING HAPPINESS expressing joy, energy, or good health in a pleasing way **2.** SHINING lit with a bright or glowing light **3.** PHYS IN RAY FORM used to describe light, heat, or other energy emitted in the form of waves or rays ○ *radiant heat* **4.** PHYS EMITTING RADIANT ENERGY emitting light, heat, or other energy in the form of waves or rays ■ *n.* **1.** ELEC ENG HEATING ELEMENT an element in a heater that gives out radiant heat **2.** ASTRON METEOR SHOWER'S POINT OF ORIGIN a point in space from which a meteor shower appears to originate [15thC. From Latin *radiant-*, the

present participle stem of *radiare* (See RADIATE).] —**radiantly** *adv.*

Undefined Terms (Runons)

At the end of many entries there are additional **boldface** entries that have no definitions. These are called undefined runons, and they consist of the headword plus a standard derivative suffix such as –*ly* or –*ness*, or the headword shown in another part of speech. They do not require definitions because they correlate almost exactly in meaning and usage with the main entry. Where appropriate, runons have been given pronunciations, for example where their stress pattern is different from that of the headword.

> **fluffy** /flúffi/ (**-ier, -iest**) *adj.* **1.** SOFT AND LIGHT consisting of sth soft and light to the touch such as wool or feathers **2.** DOWNY OR FEATHERY covered in sth soft and light to the touch such as down or feathers **3.** COOK SOFT AND LIGHT IN TEXTURE soft and light in texture because air has been beaten or whisked in —**fluffily** *adv.* —**fluffiness** *n.*

Where we have had evidence from our Corpus that a potential runon in fact has a different pattern of linguistic behaviour, that term has been defined fully.

Subject Labels

Many senses define terms belonging to specific subject areas. **Subject area labels** indicate the subject area to which a sense belongs. The subject labels signpost the different senses in an entry and help you find your way through it.

> **marking** /maárking/ *n.* **1.** ZOOL MARK OR MARKS a mark or pattern of marks that occurs naturally, e.g. on an animal's coat (*often used in the plural*) **2.** AIR AIRCRAFT IDENTIFYING MARK an identifying mark, usually a coloured symbol, on an aircraft (*often used in the plural*) **3.** EDUC ASSESSMENT AND GRADING OF WRITTEN WORK a teacher's correction and assessment of students' written work

Quick Definitions

The **quick definitions**, like subject labels, are designed to guide you through longer entries. They appear in SMALL CAPITALS and act as a brief summary of the full definition, so that you can easily find your way to the appropriate sense.

> **ease** /eez/ *n.* **1.** LACK OF DIFFICULTY lack of difficulty in doing or achieving sth ○ *defeated the challenger with ease* **2.** LACK OF AWKWARDNESS lack of awkwardness, stiffness, or self-consciousness in social situations ○ *He felt totally at ease with her.* **3.** COMFORT AND AFFLUENCE a comfortable and leisured state free from problems and restrictions, especially those caused by poverty ○ *a life of ease* **4.** RELAXATION a state of comfort and relaxation **5.** RELIEF FROM WORRY OR PAIN freedom or relief from worry or pain

Definitions

The definitions in the *Encarta World English Dictionary* explain the meaning of the sense clearly and comprehensibly and differentiate it from related terms and words meaning almost the same thing.

> **oasis** /ō áyssiss/ (*plural* **-ses** /-seez/) *n.* **1.** GEOG FERTILE LAND IN DESERT fertile ground in a desert where the level of underground water rises to or near ground level, where plants grow and travellers can replenish water supplies **2.** PLACE OR TIME OF RELIEF a place or period that gives relief from a troubling or chaotic situation

Specialist Terminology

The Dictionary includes as headwords the main specialized language you are likely to encounter in general publications and consumer magazines, as well as the principal terminology likely to be encountered by college students.

> **ligature** /líggəchər/ *n.* **1.** STH USED FOR TYING sth that is used for binding things or tying things up **2.** TYING PROCESS the process of binding sth or tying sth up **3.** BOND a unifying link or bond (*formal*) **4.** SURG SURGICAL THREAD FOR TYING OFF A DUCT a piece of surgical thread used to tie off a duct or blood vessel in order to cut off the supply of body fluid normally running through it **5.** PRINTING, LING CHARACTER CONSISTING OF JOINED

LETTERS a character or piece of type, e.g. æ, that consists of two or more letters joined together **6.** MUSIC = **tie** *n.* **8 7.** MUSIC SYMBOL IN MEDIEVAL MUSIC a symbol indicating a group of notes to be sung to one syllable in the notation of medieval music **8.** MUSIC REED-HOLDER ON WOODWIND INSTRUMENT on a woodwind instrument, a band, usually made of metal, that holds the reed to the mouthpiece [14thC. Via Old French from, ultimately, Latin *ligare* 'to bind' (see LIGAMENT).]

Dated and Archaic Language

The Dictionary includes usages that are no longer current but that you may encounter in works of literature, such as prominent obsolete, archaic, or dated terms.

> **jorum** /jáwrəm/, **joram** *n.* a large drinking bowl or its contents (*archaic*) [Mid-18thC. Origin uncertain: perhaps named after *Joram*, who took silver, gold, and brass vessels to King David (II Samuel 8:10).]

Examples

The *Encarta World English Dictionary* has thousands of illustrative examples that clarify the definitions and place them in context. These are drawn from our Corpus of World English.

The symbol [○] introduces examples.

> **narrow** /nárrō/ *adj.* **1.** SMALL IN WIDTH having a small width, especially in comparison to height or length ○ *a narrow gap* **2.** LIMITED IN SIZE limited or restricted in size or scope ○ *a narrow range of options* **3.** NARROW-MINDED limited and usually inflexible in outlook ○ *a narrow view of events* **4.** JUST ENOUGH FOR SUCCESS only just sufficient for success ○ *a narrow victory* ○ *a narrow escape*

Citations

The Dictionary also includes many quotations taken from written sources (**citations**) such as fiction, nonfiction, and journalism. These citations are drawn from our Corpus of World English.

> **entanglement** /in táng g'lmant/ *n.* **1.** COMPLICATED PERSONAL SITUATION a complicated situation involving two or more people **2.** CONFUSION confusion or a confused situation ○ *'He sat with his mouth full of toast and his eyes sparkling with mischief, watching my intellectual entanglement'.* (Arthur Conan Doyle, *The Valley of Fear*; 1915) **3.** TANGLED THING a mass of tangled objects

Word Origins

The principal aim of the word origins (**etymologies**) in the Dictionary is to present the etymology of the entries with as much accuracy as present-day knowledge will permit, in a way that is accessible and interesting to the general reader. Etymologies have as far as possible been written in plain English, with few abbreviations or technical terms. Where possible, etymologies include the date when the headword was first recorded, an account of the word's origin, and other relevant information likely to be of interest to readers. Many words have a story that is not obvious from the standard 'bare-bones' etymology. Where possible, we tell it.

> **nail** /nayl/ *n.*
> [Old English *nægl*. Ultimately from an Indo-European word denoting a fingernail or toenail that is also the ancestor of English *onyx* and *ungulate*. The meaning 'fastener' evolved in prehistoric Germanic.]

In writing the etymologies, we have put particular stress on three themes. Firstly, the etymological connections between English words, both the obvious and the more remote, such as that between *nail* and *onyx* above.

> **nautical** /náwtik'l/ *adj.* relating to sailors, ships, or seafaring [Mid-16thC. Via Latin from Greek *nautikos*, from *nautēs* 'sailor', from *naus* 'ship' (source of English *astronaut*, *nausea*, and *noise*).]

Secondly, where possible we explain any ultimate metaphor that underlies the meaning of a modern English word:

> **naive** /nī éev/, **naïve** *adj.*
> [Mid-17thC. From French *naïve*, feminine of *naïf*, from Latin *nativus* 'born' (source of English *native*). The underlying idea is of the innocence or gullibility of the newborn.]

Thirdly, we explain why a word is used with a particular meaning. This may be because of a development of meaning in English or in a source language, an association with a person or place, or some visual image or stereotype. We call these 'Why?' etymologies, since telling an interesting story is a key feature of the word histories in the Dictionary.

> **namby-pamby** /námbi pámbi/ *adj.* (*informal*) **1.** WEAK feeble, childish, and weak **2.** SILLY silly, sentimental, or overly sensitive ■ *n.* (*plural* **namby-pambies**) NAMBY-PAMBY PERSON sb who is considered weak or silly (*informal*) [Mid-16thC. Originally a mocking nickname for the English poet Ambrose Philips (1674–1749), who wrote feebly sentimental pastorals; based on *Amb*(*rose*).]

> **chortle** /cháwrt'l/ *n.* GLEEFUL LAUGH a noisy gleeful laugh ■ *vi.* (-tles, -tling, -tled) GIVE A CHORTLE to laugh in a noisy gleeful way [Late 19thC. Blend of CHUCKLE and SNORT, originated by Lewis CARROLL in *Through the Looking-Glass* (1872).] —**chortler** *n.*

> **graham flour** *n.* US unbolted whole-wheat flour [Named after Dr Sylvester *Graham* (1794–1851), an American dietary reformer]

We have also included additional interesting information about the word's origin or transmission into English, for example:

> **nainsook** /náynssŏŏk, nán-/ *n.* a lightweight cotton fabric used for babywear and lingerie, originally from India [Late 18thC. From Hindi *nainsukh*, literally 'pleasure to the eye'.]

See also Word Keys (pp. xix).

Function Words

Function words are grammatical words that include the common prepositions, adverbs, conjunctions, and pronouns (*up, down, at, so, what, when, many, such, a, the,* and so on); the modal verbs and auxiliaries; and verbs such as *come, do, get,* and *give*.

Speakers of a language rarely look up common senses of terms such as these. They tend to look up rare or archaic senses; technical and specialist senses, such as the nautical use of *after*; dialectal terms, or senses from other varieties of English, such as Irish *I'm after going to town*; senses that present a style or usage problem, such as *a* or *an* used before 'h'; least frequently of all, users might want to verify grammar points, for example whether *after* is an adverb or a preposition.

An introductory summary of the word's 'core', or central, meaning appears at the start of the entry. Remaining senses appear at sense records in the usual way, except that parts of speech may be combined at one sense. Senses are ordered by frequency.

> **no**[2] /nō/ CORE MEANING: a determiner used to indicate that there is not any or not one person or thing ○ *There is nothing within walking distance: no post office, no bank.* ○ *I had no choice in the matter.* ○ *They pay no attention to me.*
> *det.* **1.** NOT AT ALL used to indicate that sb or sth does not have any of the characteristic or identity mentioned ○ *She's no fool.* **2.** NOT not exceeding a particular amount or quality (*used with comparative adjectives and adverbs*) ○ *The issue was no less important to us than you.* [12thC. Shortening of NONE.]

Foreign Words and Phrases

Based on information in our Corpus of World English, foreign words and phrases are included in the A–Z list as entries if they have established English pronunciations and are used without being explained in contemporary literature, journalism, general writing, or general conversation.

> **jeu d'esprit** /zhŏ̌ de spreé/ (*plural* **jeux d'esprit** /zhŏ̌-/) *n.* a witticism, especially one that appears in a work of literature (*literary*) [Early 18thC. From French, literally 'game of spirit or wit'.]

Cross-References

The *Encarta World English Dictionary* contains two main types of cross-reference.

Direct cross-references

A direct cross-reference takes the place of a definition, and indicates that the information you need is given at another entry in the alphabetical sequence of headwords that has the same meaning.

> calif n. = caliph
> eminency n. = eminence n. 1
> call-in n. US = phone-in

The sign (=) refers from a variant to its main form. *Plural of, past tense of,* and so on refer from an inflected form to its root word. *Abbr. of, symbol for,* or *full form of* refer from an abbreviation or acronym or symbol to its full form, or vice versa.

Indirect cross-references

The symbol [⇨] indicates an indirect cross-reference to another entry where you will find additional relevant information:

> **carnivore** /ka'arni vawr/ *n.* **1.** FLESH-EATING ANIMAL an animal that eats other animals. ◊ **herbivore, omnivore**

Idioms and Phrases

Phrases and idioms are important lexical groups that are typically underrepresented in dictionaries. The *Encarta World English Dictionary* gives particular attention to such items.

> **carpet** /ka'arpit/ *n.* **1.** FLOOR COVERING thick fabric for covering a floor **2.** PIECE OF FLOOR COVERING a piece of thick, heavy fabric covering the floor of a room or area **3.** LAYER OR COVERING a layer or covering (*literary*) ○ *a carpet of snow* ■ *vt.* (-pets, -peting, -peted) **1.** COVER FLOOR WITH CARPET to cover a floor, or the floor of a room, with a carpet ○ *We could carpet every room in the house with the money she spent on that rug.* **2.** COVER to cover sth in a layer (*literary*) ○ *The valley was carpeted with flowers.* **3.** REPRIMAND to reprimand sb severely (*informal*) [14thC. Via Old French *carpite* or medieval Latin *carpita* from, ultimately, Latin *carpere* 'to pluck'. The underlying idea is of a cloth made from plucked or unravelled fabric.] ◇ **roll out the red carpet** to give a special welcome to a distinguished visitor ◇ **sweep sth under the carpet** to conceal or ignore sth that needs attention

Idioms and phrases are preceded by the symbol [◇].

Phrasal Verbs

The Dictionary gives phrasal verbs fuller treatment than they have traditionally received in dictionaries for native speakers. Phrasal verbs are verb-plus-particle combinations in which the total meanings are not literally the sum of the parts. They appear after the root form of the verb (**carry away** comes after **carry**, etc.).

> **carry away** *vt.* to make sb become less controlled, reasonable, or attentive by arousing his or her emotion or interest (*usually passive*) ○ *I was completely carried away by the beauty of it.*
> **carry back** *vt.* to transfer sth such as a tax credit so that it is calculated against the previous year's income
> **carry forward** *vt.* **1.** TRANSFER ITEM IN ACCOUNT OR CALCULATION to transfer an item to the next section or column in accounts or in a calculation **2.** TRANSFER STH TO NEXT YEAR to transfer sth, such as a tax credit or liability, so that it is calculated against the next year's income
> **carry off** *vt.* **1.** REMOVE SB OR STH to take sth or sb away with determination or purpose, or by force ○ *carried him off, kicking and screaming, to his crib* **2.** WIN to win a prize (*informal*) ○ *She carried off the award for best newcomer.* **3.** DO STH SUCCESSFULLY OR WELL to succeed in doing sth well or producing a good effect ○ *He was nervous about chairing the meeting, but carried it off in style.* ○ *It's a very sophisticated outfit, but she can't quite carry it off.*

Illustrations

The *Encarta World English Dictionary* illustrates over 4,000 items. The main function of the illustrations is to help the reader by adding to and complementing the text, providing additional context for the definition, and placing the definition in its context.

Style Level and Register

The Dictionary uses *italic* labels to indicate the stylistic level (register) and currency:

Currency

archaic	not used since before World War II
dated	used at some stage between 1945 and 1990 but no longer part of the current idiom

Register

literary	used in literature and poetry and for special effect, but not used in everyday contexts
formal	used in formal situations and formal writing, but inappropriate in everyday contexts
technical	marks specialist terms that have an everyday equivalent
informal	used in relaxed conversation or writing but avoided in more formal contexts; often has an innocuous or euphemistic feel
humorous	pompous or formal or dated terms typically used for humorous effect
disapproving	marks a derogatory attitude on the part of the speaker
slang	highly informal, completely inappropriate in formal contexts, and often with a crude edge
babytalk	used by adults when talking to young children and babies
nonstandard	not considered part of correct or educated usage, though current in spoken usage

Offensiveness

insult	a pejorative term that would be likely to insult or upset somebody if it is said directly to the person
offensive	likely to be offensive to many people, for example because it is racist or sexual
taboo	for classic taboo words referring to sex and bodily functions

Some lexical entries commonly regarded as offensive or taboo require inclusion in a dictionary of this size and scope. However, the editors have attempted to ensure that these and other offensive or potentially offensive lexical items and areas of reference are not used in the defining language and other elements of the text.

Words not universally regarded as offensive but likely to give offence in varying degrees are qualified accordingly: *often considered offensive, sometimes considered offensive,* and *offensive in some contexts.*

Offensive terms have been defined by a gloss rather than a substitutable definition.

World English and Regional Varieties of English

In the *Encarta World English Dictionary* we have attempted to give a world view of the English language. We have included information on the two main spelling forms of English – American and British – as well as reflecting words and patterns of usage from a world perspective:

> **caisse populaire** /késs póppyóo láir/ (*plural* **caisses populaires** /késs póppyóo láir/) *n. Quebec* in Quebec and other French-speaking parts of Canada, a financial institution resembling a credit union [From French]

> **Aotearoa** /áà ō tee ə rố ə/ *n. NZ* the preferred Maori name for New Zealand (*often used in combination*) ○ *Aotearoa-New Zealand*

The Dictionary uses the following *italic* labels to indicate the geographical area where a word is used:

ANZ	Australian and New Zealand English
Aus	Australian English
Can	Canadian English
Carib	Caribbean English
Hawaii	Hawaiian English
Hong Kong	Hong Kong English
Ireland	Irish English

Malaysia	Malaysian English
Midwest	Midwestern United States
N England	Northern England
NZ	New Zealand English
New England	New England
Northeast US	Northeastern United States
Northwest US	Northwestern United States
Quebec	Quebec
Rocky Mountains	Rocky Mountains
S Africa	South African English
S Asia	South Asian English
S Atlantic US	South Atlantic United States
S England	Southern England
Scotland	Scottish English
Singapore	Singapore
Southeast US	Southeastern United States
Southern US	Southern United States
Southwest US	Southwestern United States
UK	British English
US	American English
Wales	Welsh English
Western US	Western United States

Usage Notes

The Usage Notes serve one of three main purposes. They spell out useful syntactic information beyond the basic part of speech, for example *takes a singular verb*; they give information on the typical users of a word or phrase, for example *used mainly by children*; and they give information on the speaker's attitude or tone of voice, for example *often used ironically*.

> **nonproliferation** /nónprə líffə ráysh'n/ *n.* the practice of limiting the production or spread of sth, especially nuclear weapons (*often used before a noun*) ○ *nonproliferation agreements*

See also **Word Keys**.

Trademarks, Trade Names, and Proprietary Terms

The Dictionary includes words on the basis of their usage in the English language today. Words that are known to have current trademark or proprietary registrations have been given the part of speech *tdmk*.

Word Keys

The *Word Keys* are a feature of the *Encarta World English Dictionary* that has allowed the editors to provide more information on an aspect of a word than is possible within the scope of the standard dictionary entry.

Word History Essays

Over 400 word history essays give additional information of etymological or language-historical interest that is not directly relevant to the etymology of a particular headword, for example at *fluent*:

> ——— **WORD KEY: ORIGIN** ———
> The Latin word *fluere*, from which **fluent** is derived, is also the source of English *affluent, effluent, flu, fluctuate, fluid, fluorides, flush, fluvial, flux, influence, mellifluous,* and *superfluous*.

World English and Regional Essays

The World English coverage in the Dictionary is underpinned by a number of essays on specific varieties of English, both regional and from around the world:

> ——— **WORD KEY: REGIONAL NOTE** ———
> British dialects abound in words for ants, suggesting perhaps that they once played a bigger role in people's lives, and in those of country people in particular. Among the best-known synonyms are *emmets, muryans, nants, pismires, piss-annats,* and *pissy-beds,* a name they share with dandelions.

> ——— **WORD KEY: WORLD ENGLISH** ———
> The English language as used in the Caribbean region, also called *West Indian English*. The islands and coasts of the Caribbean, since their discovery by Columbus in 1492, have, since that time, been claimed, disputed, settled, and governed by the Spanish, Portuguese, French, British, Dutch, Danish, and Americans with obvious, long-term, varied effects on the languages spoken there. In the second half of the 20th century, most of the territories are independent, but colonization has created a complex inheritance. In such mainland areas as Belize and Guyana, indigenous languages survive, but not on the islands, and in all territories there is a complex continuum between the standard forms of English (American and British), Dutch, French, and Spanish on the one side and their creole varieties on the other. In general terms, the creoles mix European lexical items with varying degrees of African structural features. In most Anglo-Caribbean territories, although school-based standard English is the official language it is a minority form and, in states like Belize and Guyana, English mixes with a range of other languages. Apart from Barbados and Guyana, *Caribbean English* is usually non-rhotic (i.e., r is not pronounced in such words as art, door, worker).

Usage Essays

The Usage Essays complement the Usage Notes by providing more extended information on particularly thorny usage problems:

> ——— **WORD KEY: USAGE** ———
> **Meaning trap** The use of **scenario** in a generalized way to denote a projected or imagined sequence of events or set of circumstances (*an alternative scenario if the vote goes the other way*) is widely deprecated in dictionaries and books on usage, although it is hard to see why this figurative use of a word is to be rejected when so many others (such as *scene*) are accepted without comment. It is a useful word when the imagined events or circumstances can be regarded as a whole and are therefore directly comparable to the elements of a film or theatre plot.

Synonym Essays

The Synonym Essays help distinguish between words that are close in meaning:

> ——— **WORD KEY: SYNONYMS** ———
> ***necessary, essential, vital, indispensable, requisite, needed***
> CORE MEANING: used to describe sth that is required
> **necessary** used to describe sth that must be done or provided, or to indicate that sb's presence is required; **essential** used to emphasize that sth is necessary, for example because a process could not take place without it; **vital** a very emphatic word used to stress that sth is urgently necessary; **indispensable** literally suggesting sb who or sth that cannot be done without, but also often used simply to indicate that sth is desirable or useful; **requisite** a formal word used especially to suggest that sth has been made necessary by a particular circumstance; **needed** used to describe sth that is required or desired but implying less urgency than the other words in the group.

Cultural Notes

Cultural Notes are a unique feature in the Dictionary. They form a stepping-stone from a particular sense of a word to its wider cultural context. They typically refer to titles of books, movies, plays, and musical pieces, especially those that have passed into the language.

> ——— **WORD KEY: CULTURAL NOTE** ———
> ***The Crucible***, a play by US dramatist Arthur Miller (1953). Intended as a metaphor for the 'un-American' McCarthy hearings of the 1950s, is set in Salem, Massachusetts, in 1692 and describes how the social fabric of a small town is ripped apart when a group of young girls starts to denounce townsfolk to witch-hunters. It was made into a film by Nicholas Hytner in 1996.

> ——— **WORD KEY: CULTURAL NOTE** ———
> ***Picnic at Hanging Rock***, a novel by Australian author Joan Lindsay (1967). Set in turn-of-the-century Australia, it tells the story of the disappearance of three school girls during a St Valentine's Day picnic at Hanging Rock in Victoria. Although one girl reappears, the mystery is never explained. It was made into a film by Peter Weir in 1976.

Subject Labels for Specialist Areas

Label	Meaning
ACCESSORIES	Accessories (clothing)
ACCT	Accounting
ACOUSTICS	Acoustics
AERON	Aeronautics
AEROSP	Aerospace
AGRIC	Agriculture
AIR	Aircraft
AIR FORCE	Air Force
ALGEBRA	Algebra
ALTERN MED	Alternative Medicine
AMERICAN FOOTBALL	American Football
AMPHIB	Amphibians
ANAT	Anatomy
ANGLING	Angling
ANTHROP	Anthropology
ANTIQUES	Antiques
ARCHAEOL	Archaeology
ARCHERY	Archery
ARCHIT	Architecture
ARITH	Arithmetic
ARMS	Arms
ARMY	Armed Forces
ART	Art
ARTS	Arts
ASTROL	Astrology
ASTRON	Astronomy
ASTROPHYS	Astrophysics
AUTOMOT	Automotive
BACKGAMMON	Backgammon
BALLET	Ballet
BALLROOM	Ballroom Dancing
BANKING	Banking
BASEBALL	Baseball
BASKETBALL	Basketball
BETTING	Betting
BEVERAGES	Beverages
BIBLE	Biblical Terms
BIOCHEM	Biochemistry
BIOL	Biology
BIRDS	Birds and Ornithology
BOARD GAMES	Board Games
BOBSLEIGH	Bobsleighing
BOT	Botany
BOWLS	Bowls
BOXING	Boxing
BRIDGE	Bridge (card game)
BROADCAST	Broadcasting and Media
BUDDHISM	Buddhism
BUILDING	Building
BUSINESS	Business
CALENDAR	Calendar Terms
CARDS	Card Games
CARS	Cars
CELL BIOL	Cell Biology
CERAMICS	Ceramics and Pottery
CHEM	Chemistry
CHEM ELEM	Chemical Elements
CHEM ENG	Chemical Engineering
CHESS	Chess
CHR	Christianity
CINEMA	Cinema
CIV ENG	Civil Engineering
CLIMBING	Climbing
CLOTHES	Clothing and Costume
COINS	Coins and Coin Collecting
COLLECTING	Collecting
COLOURS	Colours
COMM	Commerce
COMM LAW	Commercial Law
COMMUNICATIONS	Communications
COMPASS	Compass points
COMP SCI	Computer science
COMPUT	Computers
CONSTR	Construction
COOK	Cookery
COSMETICS	Cosmetics
COSMOL	Cosmology
COUNSELLING	Counselling
CRAFT	Crafts
CRICKET	Cricket
CRIMINAL LAW	Criminal Law
CRIMINOL	Criminology
CRYSTALS	Crystals and Crystallography
CUE GAMES	Cue Games (eg billiards)
CYCLING	Cycling
DANCE	Dance
DARTS	Darts
DENT	Dentistry
DERMAT	Dermatology
DESIGN	Design
DIY	DIY and Home Maintenance
DRAWING	Drawing
DRESSAGE	Dressage
DRUGS	Drugs
EASTERN RELIG	Eastern Religions
ECOL	Ecology
ECON	Economics
EDUC	Education
ELEC	Electricity
ELEC ENG	Electrical Engineering
ELECTRON ENG	Electronic Engineering
EMBRYOL	Embryology
EMERGENCIES	Emergency Services
ENERGY	Energy
ENG	Engineering
ENVIRON	Environment
EQU	Equestrianism
ETHICS	Ethics
ETHNOL	Ethnology
FASHION	Fashion
FENCING	Fencing
FIN	Finance
FISHING	Fishing
FITNESS	Fitness
FOOD	Food
FOOD TECH	Food Technology
FOOTBALL	Football
FORESTRY	Forestry
FREEMASONRY	Freemasonry
FREIGHT	Freight
FUNGI	Fungi
FURNITURE	Furniture
GAMBLING	Gambling
GAMES	Games
GARDENING	Gardening
GENETICS	Genetics
GEOG	Geography
GEOL	Geology
GEOM	Geometry
GOLF	Golf
GRAM	Grammar
GYM	Gymnastics
GYN	Gynaecology
HAIR	Hairdressing
HEALTH	Health
HERALDRY	Heraldry
HIKING	Hiking
HIST	History
HOCKEY	Hockey
HORSE RACING	Horse racing
HOUSEHOLD	Household
HR	Human Resources
HUNT	Hunting
ICE SKATING	Ice Skating
ILLNESS	Illness
INDIAN RELIG	Indian Religions
INDUST	Industry
INSECTS	Insects
INSUR	Insurance
INTERNAT LAW	International Law
ISLAM	Islam
JOINERY	Joinery
JUDAISM	Judaism
JUD-CHR	Judaeo-Christian
KNITTING	Knitting
LACROSSE	Lacrosse
LANG	Languages
LAW	Law
LEGEND	Legend
LEISURE	Leisure
LIBRARIES	Libraries
LING	Linguistics
LITERAT	Literature
LOGIC	Logic
MAIL	Mail and postal services
MANAGEMT	Management
MANUF	Manufacturing
MAPS	Maps and Cartography
MARINE BIOL	Marine Biology
MARKETING	Marketing
MARTIAL ARTS	Martial Arts
MATH	Mathematics
MEASURE	Measurement
MECH ENG	Mechanical Engineering
MED	Medicine
METALL	Metallurgy
METEOROL	Meteorology
MICROBIOL	Microbiology
MIL	Military
MINERALS	Minerals and Mineralogy
MONEY	Currencies
MOTOR SPORTS	Motor Sports
MOTORCYCLES	Motorcycles
MOUNTAINEERING	Mountaineering
MUSIC	Music
MYTHOL	Mythology
NAUT	Nautical
NAVIG	Navigation
NAVY	Navy
NUCLEAR PHYS	Nuclear Physics
OBSTET	Obstetrics
OCEANOG	Oceanography
ONLINE	Online
OPHTHALMOL	Ophthalmology
OPTICS	Optics
PAINTING	Painting
PALAEONT	Palaeontology
PAPER	Paper manufacturing
PATHOL	Pathology
PENSIONS	Pensions
PEOPLES	Peoples
PHARM	Pharmacology
PHILOS	Philosophy
PHON	Phonetics
PHOTOGRAPHY	Photography
PHYS	Physics
PHYSIOL	Physiology
PLANTS	Plants
POETRY	Poetry
POL	Politics
PREHIST	Prehistory
PRESS	Press and Journalism
PRINTING	Printing
PROPERTY LAW	Property Law
PSYCHIAT	Psychiatry
PSYCHOANAL	Psychoanalysis
PSYCHOL	Psychology
PUBL	Publishing
PUBLIC ADMIN	Public Administration
QUANTUM PHYS	Quantum Physics
RACKET GAMES	Racket Games
RADIO	Radio
RAIL	Railways
RECORDING	Recording
RELIG	Religion
RIDING	Riding
RIFLE SHOOTING	Rifle Shooting
ROLLER SKATING	Roller Skating
ROWING	Rowing
RUGBY	Rugby
SAILING	Sailing
SCI	Science
SCOUTING	Scouting
SCULPTURE	Sculpture
SEISMOL	Seismology
SEW	Sewing
SHIPPING	Shipping
SHOWJUMPING	Showjumping
SKIING	Skiing
SOC SCI	Social Science
SOC WELFARE	Social Welfare
SOCCER	Soccer
SOCIOL	Sociology
SOFTBALL	Softball
SPACE TECH	Space Technology
SPORTS	Sport
STAMPS	Stamps
STATS	Statistics
STOCK EXCH	Stock Exchange
SURG	Surgery
SWIMMING	Swimming
TECH	Technology
TELECOM	Telecommunications
TENNIS	Tennis
TEXTILES	Textiles
THEATRE	Theatre
TIME	Time
TRANSP	Transport
TREES	Trees
TV	Television
UNIV	University
UTIL	Public Utilities
VET	Veterinary Medicine
VIDEO	Video
WINE	Wine and Winemaking
WOODWORK	Woodworking
WRESTLING	Wrestling
ZODIAC	Zodiac
ZOOL	Zoology

Labels for Varieties of Regional English and World English

Label	Meaning
ANZ	Australian and New Zealand English
Aus	Australian English
Can	Canadian English
Carib	Caribbean English
Hawaii	Hawaiian English
Hong Kong	Hong Kong English
Ireland	Irish English
Malaysia	Malaysian English
Midwest	Midwestern United States
N England	Northern England
NZ	New Zealand English
New England	New England
Northeast US	Northeastern United States
Northwest US	Northwestern United States
Quebec	Quebec
Rocky Mountains	Rocky Mountains
S Africa	South African English
S Asia	South Asian English
S Atlantic US	South Atlantic United States
S England	Southern England
Scotland	Scottish English
Singapore	Singapore
Southeast US	Southeastern United States
Southern US	Southern United States
Southwest US	Southwestern United States
UK	British English
US	American English
Wales	Welsh English
Western US	Western United States

Pronunciation Guide

Pronunciations in the *Encarta World English Dictionary* are given in a pronunciation system specially developed for the Dictionary. It relies on familiar combinations of letters of the alphabet so that it can be interpreted without constant reference to a table of explanations. The only symbol taken from outside the ordinary alphabet is the *schwa* /ə/, which stands for the sound represented by *a* in **approve** and **megabyte**. In the Dictionary the pronunciations follow the headword or sense number and appear between forward slashes / /.

Pronunciation Key

a	at
aa	father
aw	all
ay	day
air	hair
b, bb	but, ribbon
ch	chin
d, dd	do, ladder
ə	about, edible, item, common, circus
e	egg
ee	eel
f, ff	fond, differ
g, gg	go, giggle
h	hot
hw	when
i	it, happy, medium
ī	ice
j, jj	juice, pigeon
k	key, thick
l, ll	let, silly
m, mm	mother, hammer
n, nn	not, funny
ng	song
o	odd
ō	open
o͝o	good
oo	school
ow	owl
oy	oil
p, pp	pen, happy
r, rr	road, carry, hard
s, ss	say, lesson
sh	sheep
th	thin
th	this
t, tt	tell, butter
u	up
ur	urge
v, vv	very, savvy
w	wet
y	yes
z, zz	zoo, blizzard
zh	vision

´ over a vowel indicates the syllable with the strongest (primary) or medium (secondary) stress.

' before /l/, /m/, or /n/ shows that the consonant is syllabic (takes the function of a vowel).

I. Consonants

The following are used to describe the sound they usually stand for in ordinary spelling:
/b d f g h j k l m n p r s t v w y z/.

befriend	/bi frénd/
hug	/hug/
strap	/strap/
milk	/milk/
jazz	/jaz/
yes	/yess/

The following two-consonant combinations (**consonantal digraphs**) also denote the sound they stand for in ordinary spelling: /ch ng th/.

church	/church/
thing	/thing/
shop	/shop/

For the sound in 'the' (**voiced dental fricative**) we have used th:

mother	/múthər/
that	/that/

For the central sound in 'vision' (**voiced palatoalveolar fricative**) we use zh:

vision	/vízh'n/
pleasure	/plézhər/

Doubling

This Dictionary uses double consonants to show many sounds in the middle of words because English spelling normally doubles letters in these positions. Consonants are doubled when they are preceded by the stressed vowels /á, é, í, ó, ú, o͝o/ and followed by either a vowel or a syllabic consonant, or by /l, r, y, or w/:

rubber	/rúbbər/
petrol	/péttrəl/
travel	/trávv'l/
inward	/ínnwərd/
deputy	/déppyooti/
supposition	/súppə zísh'n/
teakettle	/teé kett'l/

In order to show clearly that /s/ is required, not /z/, we double the /s/ additionally at the end of a syllable and with voiced consonants:

face	/fayss/
miscue	/míss kyoo/
mincer	/mínssər/

But not with voiceless consonants:

wasp	/wosp/
first	/furst/
tax	/taks/

The consonant /k/ is not doubled:

flicker	/flíkər/
tackle	/ták'l/

There is no doubling of the two-consonant combinations /ch, sh, th, ng, th, zh/:

touching	/túching/
passion	/pásh'n/
rhythm	/ríth'm/
measure	/mézhər/
hanger	/hángər/

II. Vowels

The traditional short vowels /a, e, i, o, u/ denote the sounds they usually stand for in ordinary spelling:

cat	/kat/
head	/hed/
myth	/mith/
swan	/swon/
double	/dúbb'l/

For the short vowel as in 'put', we use /o͝o/:

good	/go͝od/
could	/ko͝od/
full	/fo͝ol/

For the weak vowel as in the first syllable of 'along' and the second syllable of 'butter' we use the symbol /ə/ (schwa):

along	/ə lóng/
butter	/búttər/
flattering	/fláttəring/

For the vowel in 'goose' and 'soup' we use /oo/:

food	/food/
move	/moov/
rude	/rood/

When this is preceded by a y-sound (**palatal semivowel**) we use /yoo/:

music	/myoozik/
acute	/ə kyoot/
sinuous	/sínnyoo əss/

In words such as 'sure' and 'pure' we have used /oor/ and /yoor/ respectively:

poor	/poor, pawr/
cure	/kyoor/
during	/dyoóring/

For the diphthongs in 'grey', 'flee', and 'boy', the respellings /ay/, /ee/, and /oy/ are used:

great	/grayt/
niece	/neess/
voice	/voyss/

For the diphthongs in 'high', 'low', and 'cow' we use /ī/, /ō/, and /ow/ respectively:

write	/rīt/
goat	/gōt/
micro	/míkrō/
loud	/lowd/
frown	/frown/

For the vowel of 'nurse', we use /ur/:

turn	/turn/
stern	/sturn/
first	/furst/

For the stressed vowel of 'father' we use /aa/:

father	/fa͞athər/
bravado	/brə va͞adō/

For the vowel of 'start' in words where there is an 'r' in the spelling, we use /aar/:

farm	/faarm/
starry	/sta͞ari/

We have used /aw/ for the vowel of 'thought':

thought	/thawt/
tall	/tawl/

For the vowel of 'north' in words where there is an 'r' in the spelling, we have used /awr/:

short	/shawrt/
war	/wawr/
sport	/spawrt/
story	/stáwri/

For the vowels in 'near' and 'square' we have used /eer/ and /air/ respectively:

beer	/beer/
beard	/beerd/
weary	/weéri/
declare	/di kláir/
scarce	/skairss/
vary	/váiri/

For the vowels in 'fire' and 'sour', we have used /Ir/ and /owr/:

inspire	/in spír/
virus	/vírəss/
shower	/shówr/
dowry	/dówri/

Consonants that take the place of a vowel in a syllable (syllabic consonants) are preceded by /'/:

apple	/ápp'l/
garden	/ga͞ard'n/
station	/stáysh'n/
dental	/dént'l/
rhythm	/ríth'm/

In the vowel at the end of words such as 'happy', we have used /i/. The same applies to vowels such as the central one in 'various':

happy	/háppi/
coffee	/kóffi/
various	/váiri əss/
radiate	/ráydi ayt/

III. Stress

Single syllable words (monosyllables) have no stress marks. In words with more than one syllable (polysyllables) we have indicated the primary stress with an acute accent:

another	/ə núthər/
collide	/kə líd/
cosmetic	/koz méttik/

We have used the acute accent to show secondary stress before the main stress (pretonic stresses).

seventeen	/sévv'n teén/
academic	/ákə démmik/

IV. When are pronunciations given?

The *Encarta World English Dictionary* shows pronunciations at headwords except where the headword is made up of separate or hyphenated words that are given pronunciations elsewhere in the Dictionary. Thus we include pronunciations for all entries that are different headwords with the same spelling (homographs) such as *bank* or *bow*. Capitalized forms of common nouns are not given a pronunciation unless they are geographical or biographical entries. In geographical and biographical entries where the names are repeated, the first occurrence only is given a pronunciation. Important variants in pronunciation are covered in the Dictionary, as are changes in pronunciation or stress in undefined entries (runons) and pronunciations of plural or other forms where the pronunciation or stress changes from that of the headword.

V. Spacing

As it is easier to work out the pronunciation of a word if longer respellings are broken up into easily processed pieces, we have inserted spaces within the respelling of a word in the following cases:

(i) before a stressed syllable or other syllable containing a strong vowel (which means, for this purpose, any vowel other than /ə i ŏ oo yoo o͞o/):

allow	/ə lów/
detect	/di tékt/
unknown	/ún nón/
celebrate	/séllə brayt/
cucumber	/kyo͞o kumbər/

(ii) between the elements of a compound in which each element retains its usual pronunciation:

bedtime	/béd tīm/
getaway	/gét ə way/

(iii) between any two successive vowel or diphthong symbols:

conveyance	/kən váy ənss/
chaos	/káy oss/

(iv) between /ur/ and a vowel or diphthong symbol:

furry	/fúr i/

(v) between /ng/ and a following /g/:

anger	/áng gər/

VI. Foreign pronunciations

In occasional cases — particularly proper names — we have used the following to indicate non-English sounds:

/hl/	as in Welsh Llangollen
/kh/	as in Scottish loch, German Bach, Spanish Gijón
/N/	to show nasalization of the preceding vowel as in the French pronunciation of **un bon vin blanc** /öN boN vaN blaaN/
/ö/	as in French boeuf, German schön
/ü/	as in French rue, German gemütlich

Abbreviations and symbols

b.	born	kmph	kilometres per hour	■	precedes new part of speech
C	century (in etymologies)	l	litre(s)		
cgs	centimetre-gram-second	lb	pound(s)	○	precedes illustrative example
cl	centilitre(s)	m	metre(s)		
d.	died	mi.	mile(s)	◇	precedes idiomatic phrase
cm	centimetre(s)	ml	millilitre(s)		
cu.	cubic	mm	millimetre(s)	=	precedes direct cross-reference
e.g.	for example	mph	miles per hour		
fl.	flourished	oz	ounce(s)	⇒	precedes cross-reference to related entry
fl.	fluid	pt	pint(s)		
ft	foot/feet	sb	somebody		
gal.	gallon(s)	sq.	square		
in.	inch(es)	sth	something		
kg	kilogram(s)	yd	yard(s)		
km	kilometre(s)				

History of the English Language – a brief overview

Main contributors:

Professor Christian J. Kay
Professor of English Language
University of Glasgow

Professor Lee Pederson
Charles Howard Candler
Professor of English Language
Emory University

Additional contribution:

Anne H. Soukhanov

THE FIRST PEOPLE to speak the language we now know as English began to arrive in the British Isles around 450 AD. They came from various parts of what are now Germany, Holland, and Denmark, speaking Germanic dialects that were to form the basis of English dialects in Britain. These people are collectively called the Anglo-Saxons, and their language is known as Anglo-Saxon or Old English. This language, first spoken by a few thousand people, is thus the ancestor of all the varieties of English spoken by millions around the world today.

Written records of Old English survive from the seventh century AD. At first sight their language may seem like a foreign language to speakers of Modern English. However, if you look at the following Old English sentence, and at its literal translation into Modern English below, you should see some of the connections between the two as well as the kinds of changes that have occurred.

Pæt hus feoll and hys hryre wæs mycel.

The house fell and its destruction was great.

Some of the words in this sentence have changed only slightly in spelling and pronunciation, like *hus* 'house' and *feoll* 'fall'; one word *and* has not changed at all. The Old English alphabet had letters that have disappeared from Modern English, such as [Þ], called 'thorn' and pronounced /th/, and [æ], called 'ash' and pronounced /a/. The Old English word *pæt* is thus the same as Modern English 'that', although its use was somewhat different. Other words, such as *hryre*, have disappeared altogether or survive only in some varieties, mainly in Scots; *mycel*, for example, survives as the Scottish *mickle*, meaning 'a little'.

This short example shows you two things. The first is that many of our most basic words come from Old English: words for things in the world around us, such as *earth*, *sun*, *moon*, and *stars*; words for relationships, such as *mother* and *father*; words for many physical and mental activities, such as *run*, *love*, and *think*. The second point is that English has changed considerably since Anglo-Saxon times, especially in its grammar and in the enormous growth of its vocabulary.

Languages change for two main reasons. The first of these is contact with other languages or varieties. The second, and often related, reason is changes in the social and cultural context in which speakers operate. The worldwide presence of the English language today bears testament not only to its shared heritage but also to the energetic independence of the many varieties that make up today's phenomenon of World English. Thus, twentieth-century speakers of English may speak any one of a number of varieties — for example American, Canadian, British, or Australian. These varieties have a long tradition of mutual interconnections and influence that we will trace briefly here.

Even before they came to England, the Germanic peoples had made contact with the Romans, borrowing such words as *cheese* and *copper*. In England they encountered the Celtic peoples, whose language is still spoken in parts of Ireland, Wales, and Scotland. Many Celtic placenames and geographical terms survive, as in *Dunedin*, the Celtic name for Anglo-Saxon Edinburgh. More important from the point of view of the general development of English were the waves of invasions by Scandinavian Vikings that started in the late eighth century. Some came simply to plunder, but others settled down. Unlike the Celts, their language was quite similar to that of the Anglo-Saxons, making communication between the two groups possible. They added many everyday words to English, such as *sky*, *egg*, and *law*, the verb *to take*, and the pronoun *they*. Grammatical changes, such as the *-s* ending in such forms as *she walks*, spread into English from Scandinavian areas.

By far the most important contact, however, was the Norman Conquest of 1066, when the Norman-French Duke William defeated the Anglo-Saxon King Harold at the Battle of Hastings and became King William I of England. French became the language of government, although the bulk of the population continued to speak English. As the Norman nobles took over the lands of their Anglo-Saxon predecessors, communication between French and English speakers became increasingly necessary, and, as in any bilingual situation, the languages influenced each other. By the end of this period, generally known as Middle English, English was much more recognizably the language we know today. Thus in the late fourteenth century, the poet Geoffrey Chaucer wrote of one of his characters:

He was a verray parfit gentil knyght.

He was a very perfect gentle knight.

The words *he*, *was*, *a*, and *knyght* are Old English in origin, but *verray*, *parfit*, and *gentil* were borrowed into English from French and from there can be traced back to Latin. *Knyght* has changed in meaning since Old English, where it meant a boy or servant, while the use of *gentle* to mean noble or courteous differs somewhat from its modern meaning. Such changes in the meanings of words are typical of the way languages develop. These Middle English borrowings from French show the beginnings of one of the most characteristic features of modern English — its large and varied vocabulary. French words come from many vocabulary areas, such as government, law, religion, the arts, and courtly life.

A magnifying glass shows a detail of 'The Wyf of Bathe' in a first edition of Chaucer's *Canterbury Tales*. Printed in 1477.

Sometimes words from both sources survive side by side, as with *kingly* (Old English) and *royal* (French). Sometimes their meanings are differentiated, as in *calf* (Old English) and *veal* (French), originally the animal, but developing to mean only the meat.

Because French and Latin were the official languages during the early Middle English period, English was slow to develop a standard form in speech or writing. There was considerable diversity in the way people spoke, and when English began to be written again, the scribes tended to write the words as they were pronounced. The spelling and grammar in their manuscripts can often help us reconstruct how people spoke in different regions.

From the point of view of Modern English, continuing changes in grammar are also significant. In Old English grammatical relationships between words were expressed mainly by changing their endings, as in many of the world's languages. This system began to break down through contact with Scandinavian speakers, whose language had the same system but different endings, and the process was accelerated by the contact with French. At the end of this process English began to move towards its present system of expressing such relationships largely through word order and the use of prepositions. It also lost its system of grammatical gender and began to develop the complex system of verb forms that we know today.

By the end of the Middle English period, generally put at around 1500, a more uniform written language was emerging, a development greatly assisted by the rapid spread of printed books at this time. The printers were less tolerant of spelling variation than the medieval scribes had been, and a standardized system began to emerge. Unfortunately for modern users of English, this system predated various changes in the pronunciation of vowels, especially a series known as the Great Vowel Shift. This situation led to apparently illogical spelling variations such as *make/maid*, *flood/food*, or *great/dream*; in the first pair, the vowels used to be pronounced differently, whereas in the others they were once the same.

Early Modern English saw major grammatical patterns being established. Shakespeare and his contemporaries in the late sixteenth century could use either older forms such as 'Why go you?' or 'He speaks not', or newer ones such as 'Why do you go?' and 'He does not speak'. They could choose between the older 'Thou goest, he goeth' or the more modern 'You go, he goes'. They could express wishes through the old subjunctive form, 'Long live the Queen', or the newer 'May the Queen live long'. In all these cases the older forms were in decline and died out as modern English progressed. At the same time, the verbal group developed, producing forms unavailable to Shakespeare, such as 'When are you going?' or 'He would have been surprised'.

Vocabulary has also continued to grow throughout Modern English. Partly as a result of the renaissance of learning in Europe, the Early Modern period saw an upsurge in Latin borrowings in order to develop terminologies for new approaches to subjects such as science, philosophy, and medicine. Formal prose styles developed, often favouring Latinate words above native ones: *fraternal* might be considered more elegant than the native *brotherly*, or *illuminate* preferred to *light up*. English thus acquired a multilayered vocabulary, able to express a concept at different stylistic levels. This process of borrowing, changing, or inventing words to accommodate new intellectual developments continues to this day, as can be seen from the vocabulary of industrialization in the nineteenth century or of computers or space travel in the twentieth into the twenty-first century.

During the Early Modern period English-speaking traders and adventurers were also setting out to explore the world, reaching the Americas, Africa, India, the Far East, and later Australia and New Zealand. Exotic objects were collected or described, and words such as *chocolate*, *wigwam*, *banana*, *gorilla*, *tea*, and *outback* were added to the language. Like their ancestors before them, some of the invaders settled down, thus laying the foundations of English as a world language and contributing to its continual development.

The same factors of contact and context underlie the process of linguistic change that formed American speech and writing. Through four centuries of cultural evolution, American English developed its distinctive pattern, reflecting the unique social experience of a people. As Horace Gregory explained in his preface to William Carlos Williams's *In the American Grain*, 'Our nationality which answers to the name of American is neither at the centre of a huge continent nor is it floating loosely around its East, West, and Tropical coastlines and harbours. It is a language.' The Colonial American period of the seventeenth century marked the settlements of the Atlantic Seaboard communities, the focal areas of major regional dialects: Northern (Boston 1630), Midland (Philadelphia 1701), Greater New York (New York

Title page of the original Bodleian copy of the First Folio edition of Shakespeare (1623).

City 1644), and Southern (Newport News 1621; Charleston 1670). All of these varieties began with the same energetic, fluid, and unsettled code called Early Modern English, but each American dialect selected somewhat differently among the alternatives provided in the source language. From these early options came such distinctive forms as Northern *broom, roof,* and *root,* and Midland *poke* ('sack'). With these English forms emerged the loanwords from Native American such as *moose, hickory, squash,* and *terrapin;* from Dutch *coleslaw, cruller, sleigh,* and *snoop;* and from French *bateau, portage, prairie,* and *rapids.*

The Frontier period of the eighteenth century extended American speech westwards to include the Old Frontier delimited by Pittsburgh in the northwest and Knoxville in the southwest. This period framed the greatest variety of cultural interaction and the most remarkable demographic movement in American history, including the settlement of the Interior South through the Shenandoah Valley and, later, of Kentucky and the Ohio Valley through the Cumberland Gap. This process carried Midland (East Pennsylvania) speech across the Appalachian Highlands to the Piedmont and then south and westwards. During this period, the German and Scotch-Irish influences combined with earlier French and Native American loans, especially along the Frontier. Familiar forms from this period reflect sources in German: *clook* 'brood hen', *flitch* 'fritter', *pannhas* 'scrapple', and *smearcase* 'cottage cheese'; and Scotch-Irish: *brickle* 'brittle', *donsie* 'sick, peaked', *redd up* 'clean up (the house)', and *scoot over* 'make room for'.

The nineteenth century began with the Louisiana Purchase and ended with the Spanish-American War. Between those events the divisiveness of Sectionalism emerged across the country, but, nowhere more ominously than in those conflicts that led to the American Civil War. But the isolation of the South had a profound impact on its dialects. Immediately after the Civil War technology developed equipment that made agriculture possible in the arid sections of the West and Southwest. The period also witnessed the rise of regional literature, from Harriet Beecher Stowe in the Northeast, George Washington Harris in the South Midlands of Tennessee, Joel Chandler Harris in the South, and Mark Twain in the West, a literary progression that began with local colourists and concluded with *The Adventures of Huckleberry Finn*. Interaction with Mexico began with the acquisition of Texas and much of the Southwest. Although Spanish loans appeared in the previous eras, the largest number occurred in the nineteenth and twentieth centuries. Among the earlier forms are Louisiana French *bayou, levee,* and *picayune;* and Spanish *buckaroo* (from *vaquero*), *lariat* (from *la reata*), *pronto,* and *stampede.*

The language of twentieth-century America combines the resources of its past with the factors of contact and context in an urban setting. Here, linguistic change reflects the reorganization of inner cities, from Boston to Los Angeles, involving the emergence of the rural Southern-based Black English and Latino dialects from several sources including Puerto Rico, Cuba, and Mexico. The process also involves a sharp contrast between rural and urban varieties, resulting in a national suburban speech community. This means that the language and culture of suburban New York, Chicago, and San Francisco have more in common with one another in speech and society than they have with any immediate rural communities. These developments explain the emergence of social dialects based on social class and caste. Although most of the old regional dialects endure, most have fewer speakers today as megalopolitan areas have emerged from Massachusetts to Washington, DC, or Gary, Indiana, through Chicago to Milwaukee, Wisconsin. Contrary to the assumption that it obliterates differences of language and culture, modern American urbanization expands and unifies communities by bringing together formerly discrete communities and suburbs. Such new social contexts make linguistic change inevitable.

The same patterns of a heritage gained from a country's first settlers, borrowings from local languages and peoples, and continuing development and change in response to geographical, cultural, social, and other factors characterize the continuing changes to the English language in its many manifestations today. Australian and New Zealand Englishes have been enriched by words from Aboriginal and Maori traditions; the English of South Asia bears testament to the many local languages and varied cultural heritage of that vast subcontinent. South Africa's Anglo-Dutch heritage yields a multiplicity of words from that dual background as well as from local languages. In the many territories of the Pacific Rim the same process has given rise to a continuing enrichment of English with new words and senses.

In the early years of a new millennium English can reasonably be regarded as the first worldwide *lingua franca* since Latin. This Dictionary has been written to reflect this phenomenon. It will fall to our dictionary editors to monitor the continuing development of the English language in its manifold forms around the world.

A Brief History of Dictionaries and Dictionary-Makers
Jonathon Green

THE FIRST DICTIONARY, a very distant ancestor of today's CD-ROMs and spellcheckers, was a list of words committed to a clay tablet around 2000 BC. The conquest of Sumeria (roughly in the region of today's Iraq) by the neighbouring territory Akkad required, as such things do, that the conquerors absorb the language of the conquered. In this case the Akkadians were particularly anxious to take on board the sophistication of the Sumerian legal system. So the tablets were filled with glossaries of legal, and soon other words offering the Sumerian term followed by the Akkadian term.

Such early compilations, however, remained isolated. It was only in the fourth century BC that the Greeks took up dictionary-making. They feared that the language of Homer was becoming 'dead', even to scholars, and began to compile glossaries of his more obscure vocabulary. This same process was repeated later by the Romans, who also were seeking to preserve the language of their 'dead' authorities and authors.

From then, through the scholars of Byzantium, of the Middle Ages, and of the Renaissance, the flow of dictionaries was maintained, mainly as bilingual glossaries that translated words from one language into another. One of the most ambitious was the *Calepine*, first created by the monk Ambrosio Calepino in 1502. Edition followed edition, and at its peak its massive folio pages encompassed words in no less than 11 discrete languages for every single entry.

Precursors to today's English dictionaries first appeared in the eighth century. Four glossaries (the *Corpus*, the *Leiden*, the *Epinal*, and the *Erfurt* (named after the libraries that now hold them) are each dedicated to translating the vocabulary of a single text and were written to give scholars access to what were seen as the harder words of specific, usually ecclesiastical texts, by translating the original Latin into Anglo-Saxon English.

Over subsequent centuries the production of such text-specific lists began to be amalgamated, offering scholars translations of more than one work in the same list. Such lists, it should be noted, were rudimentary. All these dictionaries — some 20 major works between 1440 and 1600 — were bilingual, the usual mix being Latin-English, although some involved European languages. One of these, John Florio's *A World of Words* (1598), introduced so many new English words in his translations that it provided a huge step in English dictionary-making in itself.

WORDS FOR WORD BOOKS

Among the titles given to word books have been an *abecedarium* (an alphabetical order), an *alveary* (beehive), a *catholicon* (cure-all), an *ortus* (garden), a *medulla* (marrow or pith), a *glossary*, a *manipulus* (a handful), a *sylva* (wood), a *promptuarium*, a *vocabulary*, and a *vulgar* (common thing).

By 1700 *dictionary*, from the medieval Latin *dictionarius*, a repertory of words, had won out, and ever since it has been the predominant term.

In 1604 the first dictionary that defined rather than translated words appeared. Robert Cawdrey's *Table Alphabeticall, Contayning and Teaching the True Writing and Understanding of Hard Usuall English Words* was the first true English-English dictionary. It contained barely 3,000 entries, and its goal was to explain the meanings of difficult words.

Cawdrey had many successors who formed major stages in the development of lexicography in English. Among the 'hard words' lexicographers were John Bullokar (in 1616), Henry Cockeram (1623), Thomas Blount (1656), Edward Philips (1658), and Elisha Coles, whose dictionary, appearing in 1676, would be the first mainstream English work to include slang (the dedicated collection of which had begun in Copland's *Hye Way to the Spittel House* in 1531). These were in response to the emergence in the seventeenth century of a middle class and thus a surge in literacy.

ALPHABETICAL ORDER

Early glossaries were usually based only on "A-order." This meant that all the words starting with the same letter were listed together, but with no attempt to refine the order further. It would take several centuries before full alphabetization was finally in place.

If the seventeenth century had reflected the expansion of literacy beyond the universities and churches, then the eighteenth reflected that of England itself beyond its own territorial borders. The century that saw the expansion and consolidation of the British colonies demanded new efforts to establish English as a major language, specifically as a rival to French. The creation in 1635 of the *Académie Française* and the publication in 1694 of its authoritative *Dictionnaire* prompted much comment across the Channel. Such literary figures as John Dryden, Robert Hooke, Daniel Defoe, and Jonathan Swift variously called for some form of English Academy and suggested that, if established, its primary task would be to produce a purified version of truly standard English.

These ruminations led in 1746 to the commissioning by a group of booksellers (who, as was the custom, were also publishers) of one Samuel Johnson, then best-known as an essayist and parliamentary writer for the *Gentleman's Magazine*, to prepare a *Dictionary of the English Language*. That dictionary, which appeared in 1755, represents a great turning point in English-language dictionary-making.

Lexicography is an ever developing craft, for the language does not reform and reappear mint-new in time for every successive lexicon. Johnson used his predecessors, especially Nathaniel Bailey, whose own major work, the *Universal Etymological English Dictionary*, published in 1730, provided massive assistance in compiling the basic word lists. Nor did Johnson invent any of the processes seen to such advantage in his work, namely etymology, illustrative citations, and basic guides to pronunciation. All of these had been attempted before, but Johnson brought them together and did so more skilfully than had ever been done before.

Samuel Johnson

Johnson did not, however, fix the language, as he and his publishers had once felt was feasible. Instead, recognizing reality, he would declare that such fantasies were 'the dreams of a poet doomed at last to wake a lexicographer' and that thus to pursue perfection was reminiscent of ancient tribes who would 'chace the sun, which, when they had reached the hill where he seemed to rest, was still beheld at the same distance from them'. Language changes and lexicographers, now as much as then, must reflect such changes in their work. Johnson's decision to accept such a reality has influenced the growth of English ever since.

In a nice twist of coincidence, the very first US dictionary, *The School Dictionary* (1798), was written by one Samuel Johnson, a teacher. And others would follow, among them titles from this Johnson and his co-editor the Reverend John Elliott (1800), from another preacher Caleb Alexander (1800), from Richard Coxe (1813) and, in 1807, from Sarah Rowson, a British actor who had quit London and gained a new reputation as a best-selling US novelist.

The first major US dictionary, Noah Webster's *American Dictionary of the English Language*, appeared in 1828. Webster was a New England schoolteacher whose *Blue Back Speller* (1788) sold an astounding 82 million copies within a century of its publication. He was a great pioneer of US English, as opposed to British English. For him the establishment of a national language, based upon but independent of its source, was as politically important as the American Revolution itself. In *Dissertations on the English Language* (1789), Webster wrote: 'Several circumstances render a future separation of the American tongue from the English necessary and unavoidable'. The spelling of such terms as *theater* for 'theatre' and *color* for 'colour' is Webster's legacy.

The *Oxford English Dictionary* (*OED*) is arguably still the world's greatest dictionary on historical principles (offering the usage, history, and development of a word as well as definition and etymology). Conceived in 1857, it would override a false start (in 1865) to begin once more in 1878 with the appointment of James Murray, a self-educated schoolteacher and philologist, as its editor. The first 352-page section, offering words from A to Ant, appeared in 1884 and the dictionary was eventually completed in 1928 after Murray's death.

With the exception of Webster, lexicography has never really been a solo craft. Even Johnson had his assistants, the eight 'harmless drudges' who did the basic work of compilation, while the *OED* lists dozens of individuals, from Murray's co-editors through to the ranks of subeditors and readers, all enlisted on the great work. Today's dictionaries, the products of publishers (whether academic or popular), are rarely associated with

Noah Webster

a single individual. Modern lexicography is in every sense a corporate endeavour — the hundreds of lexicographers enlisted for this project are typical. Such a finely tuned exercise may have sacrificed a degree of idiosyncrasy (after all, is not the decision by one individual to compile a dictionary, 'chasing the panting syllable' as one poet had it, somewhat eccentric in itself?), but has gained an infinity of expertise. It may be less romantic, but today's user wants accuracy and information first. And not only have dictionaries become available on computer, whether on a CD-ROM or online via the Internet, but computers are central to every stage of the production. The great dictionaries of the past

depended on armies of amateur readers, scanning texts for examples of usage. Today's compilers have the great corpora, literally 'bodies' of real language, available for consultation. Such a corpus was compiled for this Dictionary, ensuring that every nuance of a word's existence can be laid down, and backed up with illustrative quotations. Not only that, but the keyboarding of a great dictionary into a permanent, if evolving, database, renders the great consumers of the lexicographer's time — inserting new and updating old entries and inserting and verifying cross-references — infinitely simpler than the most sophisticated of pre-electronic systems could ever manage.

Perhaps the most important aspect of lexicographic change, and never more so than as illustrated here, is the change in the word list itself. All these earlier dictionaries tried to be language-specific; not so today. World English is the name of the modern game. This Dictionary, as users will find, has responded to that new situation in ways hitherto untried. Aimed at a worldwide audience, incorporating multinational expertise in its compilation and in the entries that have been produced, it is proof in itself of the extent to which English has long since burst through its territorial confines.

The lexicographer is not and never has been, in Johnson's ironic, now hackneyed phrase, a 'harmless drudge'. Lexicographers hold a strange position, employed in an unglamorous task, yet occupying a position of power and influence by virtue of defining what the words in our language mean. That those words, once confined to a small elite of scholars, are now the property of many differing millions and available in myriad variations is both a challenge and a reward to the dictionary-maker.

World English

Tom McArthur

AT THE TURNING POINT of a new century and millennium, English is the most used — and studied — language in the history of the human race. At the beginning of the twentieth century, it was already one of the foremost languages of the world, because it was the main language of both the British Empire and the United States of America. At that time it had significant competition from other widespread European languages such as French, German, Russian, and Spanish and, beyond Europe, from Mandarin Chinese, Arabic, and Swahili that all still belong, with English, in the prestigious club of world languages. However, since World War II, although all the other world languages have continued to be widely used, English has been alone in becoming — ever more notably with each passing decade — the sole universal language, the world's *lingua franca*.

Noting its growing role, scholars and other observers have for some time been giving distinctive labels to this runaway language. Increasingly, since occasional use in the 1930s, it has come most commonly to be known as 'World English' — whence the name of this dictionary. Since around 1980, this term has also been put into the plural, as 'World Englishes', so as to highlight proliferating varieties that are often called simply 'the Englishes', and, in Asia and Africa, 'the New Englishes'. Since at least the 1970s, the language complex has also been called 'International English', and, in the 1990s, the term 'Global English' has proved fashionable, to accompany and blend in with the current economic buzzword *globalization*.

Describing and cataloguing any language is difficult, but in the past the relatively limited scope and roles of the world's languages have allowed us to suppose that the grammars, dictionaries, and other works associated with them are comprehensive. But the scale and variety of present-day English do not permit any such comfortable illusion. Even the population statistics of World English are uncertain, ranging hazily from over three hundred million people who are assumed to be native speakers to over a billion users of English of all kinds, from the most informed and fluent to the most casual and halting. The unnumbered varieties and uses of this language (whether thought, spoken, written, typed, printed, broadcast, taped, telephoned, faxed, e-mailed, or disseminated on the World Wide Web) are so complex that no individual, group, or system can catch them all. Even the most extensive and flexible computer corpus currently imaginable cannot encompass all the registers and usages of the standard language, let alone all the rest.

Even so however, and paradoxically, there is a manifest need to say something as comprehensive as possible about World English, including its immense wealth of words, past, present, and potential. Although the task is fraught with difficulty, publishers of dictionaries must inevitably respond to the challenge, part of which is to acknowledge the nature and impact of the phenomenon being described, and this has been the primary goal of the *Encarta World English Dictionary*.

The *study* of English is an international industry. Tens of thousands of scholars and teachers engage in it throughout the world, instructing a student population of hundreds of millions while producing innumerable books, periodicals, dissertations, articles, reports, conference proceedings, class notes, textbooks, newsletters, and Internet materials. Their total output is more than any of them can digest; indeed, few will see — or even be informed about — every proceeding or document that touches on their special interests *within* the language and its literatures. But again, simply to say this and turn away is not enough. If anything, we now need more and better guidance and discrimination from the makers of dictionaries than ever in the past: the millennial challenge is to make even fuller, clearer, and more appropriate dictionaries of English, both benefiting from the technological revolution that has accompanied and helped drive the enlargement of English and acknowledging that English is larger than any of the communities in which it is used — and that members of those communities need to be fully aware of the nature

ENGLISH AROUND THE WORLD

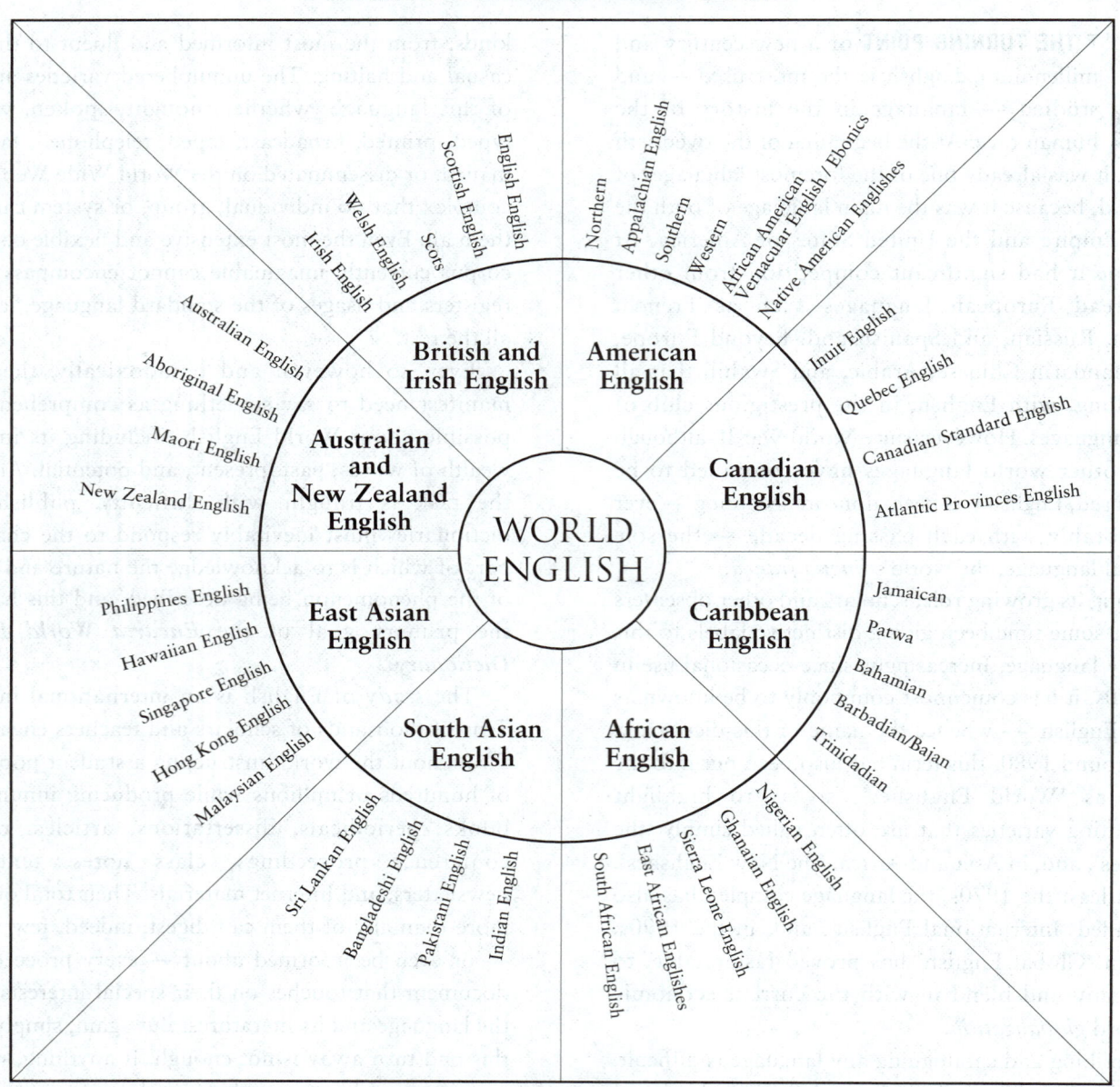

There are many varieties of World English; some of the main ones are included in this diagram.

of the international linguistic resource at their disposal.

One outcome of this unique and often unnerving state of affairs is that no one can even think today about who 'owns' the language or its many varieties. The English language has become a global resource. As such, it does not owe its existence — or its future — to any nation, group, or individual. Inasmuch as a language belongs to any individual or community, English is the possession of every individual and community that wishes to use it, wherever they are in the world. It is in effect as democratic and universal an institution as humankind has ever possessed.

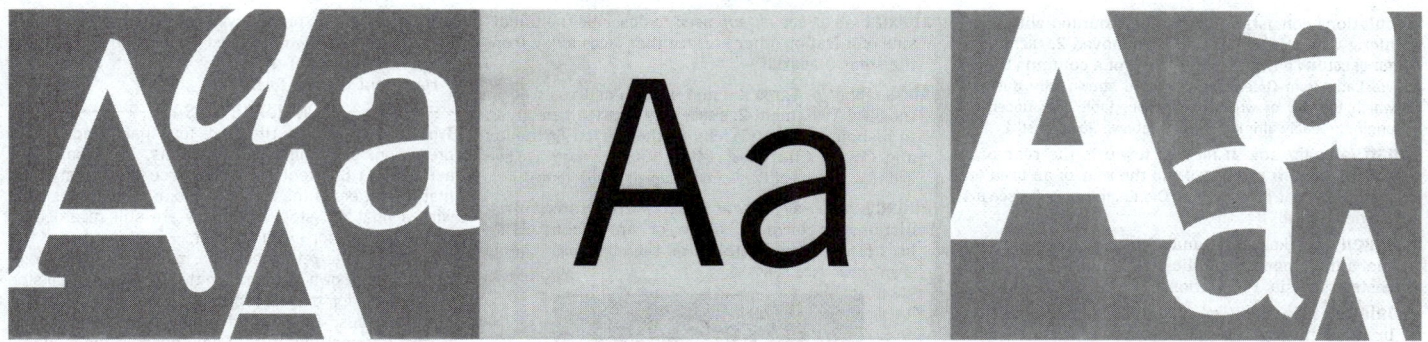

a[1] /ay/ (*plural* **as** *or* **a's**), **A** (*plural* **As** *or* **A's**) *n.* **1.** FIRST LETTER IN ENGLISH ALPHABET the first letter and first vowel of the alphabet in modern English, and in other languages that also use the Latin alphabet **2.** SOUND OF 'A' any speech sound represented by the letter 'a' **3.** 'A'-SHAPED OBJECT sth shaped like the capital letter 'A' **4.** LETTER 'A' WRITTEN a written representation of the letter 'a' **5.** CHESS FIRST VERTICAL ROW OF CHESSBOARD used to refer to the first vertical row of squares from the left on a chessboard ◇ **from A to B** from one place to another ◇ **from A to Z 1.** extremely thoroughly **2.** all the way from the beginning to the end

a[2] (*stressed*) /ay/; (*unstressed*) /ə/ CORE MEANING: a determiner, used before a singular countable noun to refer to one person or thing not previously known or specified, in contrast with 'the', referring to sb or sth known to the listener ○ *I need a new car.*
det. **1.** INDICATES A TYPE used before a noun to indicate that sb or sth has some of the same qualities as the person or thing mentioned ○ *a doormat* **2.** ONE used instead of 'one' with words of measurement ○ *a teaspoonful of salt* **3.** PER in each or in every ○ *twice a day* **4.** INDICATES SB NOT KNOWN PERSONALLY used to indicate sb not personally known, but known of ○ *There's a Mr. O'Flynn here to see you.* **5.** ANY used in negative structures to emphasize a complete absence of sth ○ *He doesn't have a hope!* [Old English, shortening of *ān* (see ONE)]

────── WORD KEY: USAGE ──────

a or **an?** *A* is the form of the indefinite article used before words that are pronounced with an initial consonant sound (even if the spelling does not begin with a consonant): *a banana; a hunk; a ewe.* *An* is used before words that begin with a vowel sound (even if an unpronounced consonant comes first): *an elephant; an heir.* The same rule regarding sound rather than spelling applies to abbreviations: *a CD* but *an LP.* The practice of using *an* before words beginning with *h* and an unstressed syllable (for example *an hotel, an historic occasion*) is falling out of use, and it is much more usual now to hear *a hotel* and *a historic occasion,* with the *h* sounded in each word.

a[3] *symbol.* PHYS acceleration

a[4] *abbr.* MEASURE are

A[1] /ay/ (*plural* **As** *or* **A's**) *n.* **1.** MUSIC 6TH NOTE IN C MAJOR the sixth note of a scale in C major. The A above middle C is often used to tune instruments and is standardized at a frequency of 440 hertz. **2.** MUSIC STH THAT PRODUCES AN A a string, key, or pipe tuned to produce the note A **3.** MUSIC SCALE BEGINNING ON A a scale or key that starts on the note A **4.** MUSIC WRITTEN SYMBOL OF A a graphic representation of the tone of A **5.** TOP GRADE the highest standing or grade ○ *solid As in her exams.* ◊ **alpha 6.** MED HUMAN BLOOD TYPE a human blood type of the ABO system, containing the A antigen. A person with this type of blood can donate to people of the same group or of the AB group, and can receive blood from people with this type or with type O.

A[2] *symbol.* **1.** COMPUT 10 (*used in hexadecimal notation*) **2.** PHYS mass number **3.** BIOCHEM adenine **4.** MEASURE ampere

A., **Å** *symbol.* angstrom

a- *prefix.* in a particular place, condition, or manner ○ *abed* ○ *adrift* ○ *aloud* [Old English, from *an*, an alternative for *on* (see ON)]

A1, **A-1**, **A-one** *adj.* **1.** TOP-NOTCH in excellent or first-rate condition (*informal*) **2.** FULLY SEAWORTHY used to describe a ship as being well equipped and in excellent condition [Mid-19thC. Originally from Lloyd's Register, an annual British shipping list; *A* indicated a hull in first-class condition, *1* that the ship was well provisioned and equipped.]

aa /áa aá/ *n.* solidified lava with a rough jagged surface and sharp angular features [Mid-19thC. From Hawaiian *a-'a.*]

AA *abbr.* Alcoholics Anonymous

AAA[1] *abbr.* **1.** Amateur Athletic Association **2.** Australian Association of Accountants

AAA[2] *abbr.* American Automobile Association

a.a.e. *abbr.* according to age and experience

aah /aa/ *interj.* EXPRESSING EMOTION used to express surprise, pleasure, satisfaction, or sympathy (*informal*) ■ *vi.* (**aahs, aahing, aahed**) SAY 'AAH' to say 'aah' (*informal*) ♦ **ooh** ■ *n.* UTTERANCE OF 'AAH' an exclamation of 'aah' expressing surprise, pleasure, satisfaction, or sympathy (*informal*) [Lengthened form of AH]

Aalto /áal taw/, **Alvar** (1898–1976) Finnish architect. He designed the Helsinki Hall of Culture (1958) and was noted for his use of organic materials and forms. Full name **Hugo Alvar Henrik Aalto**

AAM *abbr.* air-to-air missile

A & E *abbr.* MED accident and emergency

A & M *abbr.* (Hymns) Ancient and Modern

A & P *abbr.* NZ Agricultural and Pastoral

A & R *abbr.* artists and repertoire

Aardvark

aardvark /áard vaark/ *n.* a burrowing mammal with a long snout, powerful claws, long tongue, and heavy tail. It eats termites and is native to southern Africa. Latin name: *Orycteropus afer.* [Late 18thC. From Afrikaans, literally 'earth pig'.]

aardwolf /áard woolf/ (*plural* **-wolves** /-vz/) *n.* a striped nocturnal mammal related to the hyena that lives in southern Africa and feeds mainly on termites. Latin name: *Proteles cristatus.* [Mid-19thC. From Afrikaans, literally 'earth wolf'.]

Aarhus /áwr hooss, áar-/, **Århus** city, port, and seat of Aarhus county on the Jutland Peninsula and Aarhus bay in eastern Jutland, Denmark. Population: 213,826 (1996).

Aaron /áirən/ *n.* in the Bible, the first Jewish high priest and elder brother of Moses. With Moses, he led the Israelites out of Egypt but died before reaching the Promised Land.

Aaron's beard *n.* = **rose of Sharon** [Named after AARON, who had a long beard (see Psalms 133:2), because of the flower's prominent hairy stamens]

Aaron's rod *n.* a plant found in Asia, Europe, and North America that has tall smooth stems and yellow flowers, especially the great mullein [Named after the rod bearing the name of AARON, which was said to have flowered (see Numbers 17:8)]

A'asia *abbr.* Australasia

AAVE *abbr.* African American Vernacular English

Ab /ob/ *n.* in the Jewish calendar, the 11th month of the civil year and the fifth month of the religious year, falling in approximately July to August. It is 30 days long. US term **Av** [Late 18thC. From Hebrew *'āb.*]

AB[1] *abbr.* **1.** able-bodied seaman **2.** Alberta

AB[2] *n.* a human blood type of the ABO group, containing the A and B antigens. A person with this type of blood can donate to sb of the same group and receive blood from sb with this type or with type O, A, or B.

ab- *prefix.* away from, off ○ *aboral* [From Latin. Ultimately from an Indo-European base meaning 'off, away', which is also the ancestor of English *off, ebb,* and *post-.*]

aba /áb bə/ *n.* **1.** SYRIAN CLOTH a cloth made in Syria using hair from goats or camels **2.** MIDDLE EASTERN GARMENT a loose sleeveless outer garment worn by boys and men in the Middle East [Early 19thC. From Arabic *'abā.*]

ABA *abbr.* **1.** Amateur Boxing Association **2.** ABA, A.B.A. American Bar Association

abaca /ábbəkə/ *n.* **1.** PLANT YIELDING FIBRE a large plant from whose leaves Manila hemp is produced. It is related to the banana. Latin name: *Musa textilis.* **2.** = **Manila hemp** [Mid-18thC. Via Spanish from Tagalog *abaká.*]

abaci plural of **abacus**

aback /ə bák/ *adv.* **1.** WITH WIND PRESSING AGAINST SAILS with the wind blowing against the forward part of a sail or sails, so that a vessel cannot move ahead **2.** BACKWARDS backwards or towards the back (*archaic*) [Old English *on bæc* 'towards the back, backwards'] ◇ **taken aback** surprised and unsure how to react

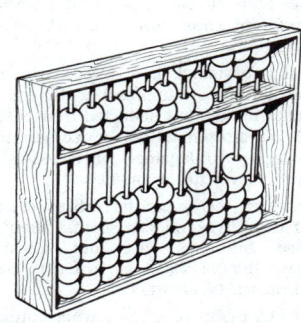

Abacus

abacus /ábəkəss/ (*plural* **-cuses** *or* **-ci** /-sī/) *n.* **1.** MATH COUNTING DEVICE a mechanical device for making calculations consisting of a frame mounted with rods along which beads or balls are moved **2.** ARCHIT **FLAT TOP OF COLUMN** a flat slab at the top of a column [14thC. Via Latin from Greek *abakos* 'board strewn with dust on which to draw or write' (later 'slab, table'), of uncertain origin: probably ultimately from Hebrew *ʼābāq* 'dust'.]

abaft /ə baáft/ *adv.* **AT THE REAR** towards the rear of a ship or boat ■ *prep.* **BEHIND** to the rear of an area on a ship or boat [14thC. From Old English *an* + *be* (see BY) + *æften* 'behind'.]

Abakan /aábə kaan/ city and administrative centre of the autonomous republic of Khakassa in north-eastern Russia. Population: 158,200 (1992 est.).

abalone /ábbə lṓ ni/ *n.* an edible sea mollusc that breathes through holes in its ear-shaped shell. The pearly interior of the shell is used for making jewellery. Genus: *Haliotis.* [Mid-19thC. Via American Spanish *abulón* from Shoshonean *aulun.*]

abampere /ab ám peer/ *n.* the centimetre-gram-second unit of electromagnetic current equal to ten amperes

abandon /ə bándən/ *v.* (**-dons, -doning, -doned**) **1.** *vt.* **LEAVE SB BEHIND** to leave sb or sth behind for others to look after, especially sb or sth meant to be a personal responsibility ○ *pets abandoned by their owners* **2.** *vt.* **LEAVE A PLACE BECAUSE OF DANGER** to leave a place or vehicle, especially for reasons of safety and without intending to return soon ○ *Drivers caught in the snowstorm had to abandon their vehicles.* **3.** *vt.* **RENOUNCE STH** to renounce or reject sth previously done or used ○ *The practice was abandoned long ago.* **4.** *vt.* **GIVE UP CONTROL OF STH** to surrender control of sth completely to sb else ○ *As troops closed in the town was abandoned to its fate.* **5.** *vt.* **HALT STH IN PROGRESS** to stop doing sth before it is completed, usually because of difficulty or danger **6.** *vt.* INSUR **GIVE UP TO INSURER** to surrender part of an insured property to the insurer in order to make a claim for total loss **7.** *vr.* **GIVE IN TO EMOTION** to give yourself over to a powerful emotion ○ *He abandoned himself to his grief.* ■ *n.* **LACK OF RESTRAINT** complete lack of inhibition or self-restraint [14thC. From Old French *abandoner,* from *a bandon,* literally 'under control', from, ultimately, Latin *bannum* 'proclamation'. The underlying idea is of giving up control.] —**abandonment** *n.*

abandoned /ə bándənd/ *adj.* **1. EMPTY** left empty because of not being used or lived in any more **2. ALONE** left alone without being cared for or supported **3. UNRESTRAINED** without restraint or self-control

abase /ə báyss/ (**abases, abasing, abased**) *vt.* to make sb feel belittled or degraded (*literary*) [14thC. From Old French *abaissier,* from *baissier* 'to lower', ultimately from Latin *bassus* 'short of stature'.] —**abasement** *n.* ◇ **abase yourself** to behave in a way that lowers your sense of dignity or self-esteem (*literary*)

abash /ə básh/ (**abashes, abashing, abashed**) *vt.* to make sb feel ashamed, embarrassed, or uncomfortable [14thC. From the Anglo-Norman stem *abaïss-,* from, ultimately, Old French *baïr* 'to astound'.] —**abashedly** /ə báshidli/ *adv.* —**abashment** *n.*

abate /ə báyt/ (**abates, abating, abated**) *v.* **1.** *vti.* **BECOME LESS** to lessen or make sth lessen gradually (*formal or literary*) **2.** *vti.* **END** to suppress or end a nuisance, act, or writ **3.** *vt.* FIN **REDUCE STH** to lower the amount or rate of sth such as a tax (*formal*) [13thC. From Old French *abatre* 'to beat down', from, ultimately, Latin *batt(u)ere* 'to fight or beat' (source of English *battle, combat,* and *debate*).]

abatement /ə báytmənt/ *n.* **1. REDUCING** the action of reducing, ending, or suppressing sth, e.g. noise **2.** FIN **DEDUCTION** an amount deducted from a full price or tax **3.** LAW **DECREASE IN LEGACY** a decrease in outlay from a legacy to legatees when assets are insufficient to cover full payment

abatis /ábbətiss, -tee/ (*plural* **-tis** or **-tises**) *n.* a rampart made of felled trees placed so that their bent or sharpened branches face out towards the enemy [Mid-18thC. From French, from Old French *abatre* 'to beat down, fell' (see ABATE).]

abattoir /ábbə twaar/ *n.* a place where animals are slaughtered for their meat and by-products [Early 19thC. From French, formed from *abattre* 'to fell', from Old French *abatre* (see ABATE). The underlying sense is 'place where things are knocked down'.]

abaxial /ab ák see əl/ *adj.* used to describe the underside of a leaf or other surface that faces away from the stem. ◊ **adaxial**

Abba /ábbə/ *n.* **1. GOD** a name used to address God in the New Testament **2. BISHOP OR PATRIARCH** a title given to bishops and patriarchs in the Syrian Orthodox and Coptic Churches [14thC. Via ecclesiastical Latin and New Testament Greek from Aramaic *'abbā* 'father'.]

abbacy /ábbəssi/ (*plural* **-cies**) *n.* the rank, jurisdiction, or term of office of an abbot or abbess [15thC. From ecclesiastical Latin *abbacia,* from the stem *abbat-* (see ABBOT).]

Claudio Abbado

Abbado /ə baádō/, **Claudio** (*b.* 1933) Italian conductor. He began his career with the La Scala Opera, Milan, Italy, but since 1989 has been artistic director of the Berlin Philharmonic Orchestra, Germany.

Abbas /ábbəss/ (566?–653) Arabian merchant. He was instrumental in spreading the tenets of Islam. The prophet Muhammad was his nephew.

Abbas I, Shah of Persia (1571–1629). A member of the Safavid dynasty, he ruled from 1588 until his death. Known as **Abbas the Great**

Abbasid /ə bássid, ábbə sid/ *n.* a member of a dynasty that ruled an Islamic empire from Baghdad from 750 to 1258. Descended from Muhammad's uncle, Abbas, they wielded little political power, but were great patrons of Islamic art and culture. —**Abbasid** *adj.*

abbatial /ə báysh'l/ *adj.* relating to an abbey, abbot, or abbess [Late 17thC. From French, or from medieval Latin *abbatialis,* both from the ecclesiastical Latin stem *abbat-* (see ABBOT).]

abbé /ábbay/ *n.* an abbot or member of a religious order in a French-speaking area [Mid-16thC. Via French from the ecclesiastical Latin stem *abbat-* (see ABBOT).]

abbess /ábbess/ *n.* the nun in charge of a convent [13thC. From Old French *abbesse,* ultimately from the ecclesiastical Latin stem *abbat-* (see ABBOT).]

Abbevillean /ab vílli ən/ *adj.* relating to or typical of early Lower Palaeolithic culture in Europe [Mid-20thC. From French *Abbevillien,* named after the town of *Abbeville* in northern France, where artefacts from this period were discovered.]

abbey /ábbi/ (*plural* **-beys**) *n.* **1. MONASTERY OR CONVENT** a building or buildings occupied by monks under an abbot or nuns under an abbess, especially the church building **2. CHURCH** a church that is or was used by a community of monks or nuns [13thC. From Old French *ab(b)eïe,* from, ultimately, the ecclesiastical Latin stem *abbat-* (see ABBOT).]

abbot /ábbət/ *n.* the monk in charge of a monastery [Pre-12thC. Via ecclesiastical Latin *abbat-,* stem of *abbas,* from, ultimately, Aramaic *'abbā* 'father'.] —**abbotship** *n.*

abbr., **abbrev.** *abbr.* abbreviation

abbreviate /ə breé vi ayt/ (**-ates, -ating, -ated**) *vt.* **1. SHORTEN WORD** to shorten a word by leaving out some of its letters or sounds **2. SHORTEN TEXT** to shorten a piece of text by cutting sections or paraphrasing it [15thC. From Latin *abbreviat-,* the past participle stem of *abbreviare* 'to shorten' (source of English *abridge*), from, ultimately, *brevis* 'short' (source of English *brief*).] —**abbreviator** *n.*

abbreviation /ə breévi áysh'n/ *n.* **1. REDUCED FORM** a shortened form of a word or phrase **2. REDUCTION** the shortening of a word or phrase to be used to represent the full form

WORD KEY: USAGE

Types of abbreviation There are four main kinds of abbreviation: shortenings, contractions, initialisms, and acronyms. **1** Shortenings of words usually consist of the first few letters of the full form and are sometimes spelt with a final full stop when they are still regarded as abbreviations, for example *cent.* = century, *foll.* = following (in page references). In many cases they form words in their own right, and in these cases the full stop is omitted, for example *gym* = gymnasium, *hippo* = hippopotamus. Such shortenings are often but not always informal in nature. Some become the standard forms, and the full forms are then regarded as formal or technical, for example *bus* = omnibus, *phone* = telephone, *pub* = public house, *zoo* = zoological garden. **2** Contractions are abbreviated forms in which letters from the middle of the full form have been omitted, for example *Dr* = doctor, *St* = saint. Practice varies with regard to adding a full stop, but in modern usage it is increasingly usual to omit it. Another kind of contraction is the type *can't* = cannot, *didn't* = did not, *you've* = you have, with an apostrophe marking the omission of letters. **3** Initialisms are made up of the initial letters of words and are pronounced as separate letters: *CIA* (or *C.I.A.*), *pm* (or *p.m.*), *US* (or *U.S.*). Practice again varies with regard to full stops, with current usage increasingly in favour of omitting them, especially when the initialism consists entirely of capital letters. **4** Acronyms are initialisms that have become words in their own right, and are pronounced as words rather than as a series of letters, for example *Aids, laser, scuba, UNESCO.* In many cases the acronym becomes the standard term and the full form is only used in explanatory contexts.

ABC[1] *n.* US term **ABCs 1. ALPHABET** the alphabet, especially when this also refers to the most basic aspects of reading and writing **2. BASIC READING AND WRITING** the most basic aspects of reading and writing **3. ESSENTIALS** the most basic facts or essential elements of a particular subject ○ *the ABC of building your own home* ◇ **as easy as ABC** extremely easy

ABC[2] *abbr.* **1.** Australian Broadcasting Company **2.** American Broadcasting Company

abcoulomb /ab koó lom/ *n.* the centimetre-gram-second unit of electrical charge equal to ten coulombs

ABCs *npl.* *US* = **ABC**

Abd al-Hamid /ab daal hámmid/ = **Abdul Hamid II**

Abd Allah /ab daálə/ (1846–99) Sudanese nationalist resistance leader who led the uprising against the Egyptian administration of the Sudan and was defeated by Lord Horatio Kitchener.

Abd-ar-Rahman Khan /ábdər rə maán kaán/, **emir of Afghanistan** (1844?–1901). During his rule (1880–1901) he helped to establish the Durand Line (1893), which fixed the Afghan-Indian border.

abdicate /áb di kayt/ (**-cates, -cating, -cated**) *v.* **1.** *vti.* **RESIGN POSITION** to give up a high office formally or officially, especially the throne **2.** *vt.* **NEGLECT A DUTY** to fail to fulfil a duty or responsibility ○ *The company seems to have abdicated all responsibility in this matter.* [Mid-16thC. From Latin *abdicat-,* the past participle stem of *abdicare* 'to renounce', from *dicare* 'to proclaim' (source of English *dedicate, indicate,* and *predicate*).] —**abdication** /áb di káysh'n/ *n.* —**abdicator** /áb di kaytər/ *n.*

abdomen /ábdəmən/ *n.* **1. BODY SECTION CONTAINING STOMACH** the part of the body of a vertebrate that contains the stomach, intestines, and other organs. In mammals it is situated between the pelvis and the thorax. **2. BELLY** the surface of the body of a vertebrate around the stomach **3. REAR PART OF INSECT** the elongated portion of the body of an arthropod, located behind the thorax. It is usually segmented. [Mid-16thC. From Latin, of unknown origin.]

abdominal /ab dómmin'l/ *adj.* **OF ABDOMEN** relating to, located in, or occurring in the abdomen ■ **abdominals** *npl.* **ABDOMINAL MUSCLES** the muscles that form the wall of the abdomen (*informal*) [Mid-18thC. From modern Latin *abdominalis*, from Latin *abdomen*.] —**abdominally** *adv*.

abducens nerve /ab dyóoss'nz-/ *n*. a nerve conveying impulses from the brain to the muscle that moves the eye laterally in its socket, one of a pair of cranial nerves [*Abducens* from modern Latin, literally 'leading out', from the present participle of *abducere* (see ABDUCT)]

abduct /əb dúkt/ (**-ducts, -ducting, -ducted**) *vt*. **1.** SNATCH SB AWAY to take sb away by force or deception **2.** PULL STH AWAY to pull sth, e.g. a muscle, away from the midpoint or midline of the body or of a limb. ◊ **adduct** [Early 17thC. From Latin *abduct-*, the past participle stem of *abducere* 'to lead out', from *ducere* 'to lead' (source of English *duct*, *conduct*, and *educate*).] —**abduction** /-dúksh'n/ *n*.

Abdul-Hamid II /áb dool hámmid/ (1842–1918) Ottoman sultan. He suspended the constitution (1877) and fought Western influences. He was deposed by the Young Turks' revolt (1909).

Abdullah /ab dúllə/, **King of Jordan** (b. 1962). He was commander of the Jordanian army's Special Forces and succeeded his father Hussein in 1999. Full name **Abdullah bin Hussein**

Abdul Rahman /ab dool raamən/, **Tunku** (1903–90) Malayan politician. He was the first prime minister of the Federation of Malaya (1957–63) and of Malaysia (1963–70).

abeam /ə beém/ *adv*. to or at the side of a ship, boat, or aircraft, especially at right angles to its length

abecedarian /áy bee see dáiri ən/ *n*. sb who is learning the basics of literacy or a subject [Early 17thC. From medieval Latin *abecedarium* 'book containing the alphabet', from, ultimately, the names of the first four letters of the alphabet.]

abed /ə béd/ *adv*. in or confined to bed (*archaic*)

Abednego /ə bédni gō/ *n*. in the Bible, one of Daniel's companions thrown into Nebuchadnezzar's furnace (Daniel 3:12–20)

Abel /áyb'l/ *n*. in the Bible, a shepherd and the second son of Adam and Eve, who was killed by his brother Cain (Genesis 4)

Abelard /ábbə laard/ (1079–1142) French philosopher and theologian. He was an influential teacher and writer on theology, ethics, and dialectics. His love affair with his pupil Héloïse scandalized her family, who ordered his castration. Both took religious orders. Their later correspondence became a literary classic.

abele /ə beél/ *n*. = **white poplar** [13thC. Directly or via Dutch *abeel* from Old French *a(u)bel*, from, ultimately, Latin *albus* 'white' (source of English *albino*, *albumen*, and *album*).]

Abeles /áyb'lz/, **Sir Peter** (b. 1924) Hungarian-born Australian business executive. He was a director of major national freight and airline corporations in Sydney, Australia. Full name **Sir Emil Herbert Peter Abeles**

abelia /ə beéli ə/ *n*. a shrub originally from eastern Asia but now widespread that has white, pink, or purple tubular flowers. Genus: *Abelia*. [Mid-19thC. From modern Latin, named after the English botanist Clarke Abel (1780–1826).]

Abelian group /ə beéli ən-/ *n*. an algebraic group in which the result of the operation is independent of the sequence of the operands, e.g. ab = ba or a+b = b+a [Mid-19thC. Named after the Norwegian mathematician Niels *Abel* (1802–29), whose research contributed to the concept.]

abelmosk /áyb'l mosk/ *n*. a tropical Asian plant of the mallow family with yellow-and-red flowers. Latin name: *Abelmoschus moschatus*. [Late 18thC. Via modern Latin *abelmoschus*, from Arabic *abu'l misk*, literally 'father of musk'.]

Abenaki /ab naaki, -naáki/ (*plural* **-ki** *or* **-kis**), **Abnaki** (*plural* **-ki** *or* **-kis**) *n*. a member of a Native American people who originally lived throughout New England and southeastern Canada, but who now live only in parts of Maine and southern Quebec [Early 18thC. Via French *Abénaqui* from Montagnais *ouabanâkionek* 'people of the eastern country'.] —**Abenaki** *adj*.

Abeokuta /áybi ō kóotə/ city and port in southwestern Nigeria. It is the capital of Ogun state. Population: 367,900 (1990 est.).

Aberdeen /ábbər deén/ **1.** city, port, and industrial centre in northeastern Scotland, located at the mouth of the rivers Dee and Don. It is known as the Granite City as many of its buildings are constructed of granite. Population: 217,260 (1996). **2.** council area in northeastern Scotland. Population: 218,220 (1993). Area: 186 sq. km/72 sq. mi. Official name **City of Aberdeen 3.** city and port in western Washington State, situated where the Chehalis River flows into Grays Harbor. Population: 16,598 (1996).

Aberdeen Angus (*plural* **Aberdeen Angus**) *n*. a cow belonging to a short-haired, black, hornless breed of beef cattle. US term **Angus** [Mid-19thC. Named after ABERDEENSHIRE and ANGUS.]

Aberdeenshire /ábbər deénshər/ Scottish administrative county since 1998, formerly in Grampian Region. The county headquarters are in Aberdeen. Area: 5,103 sq. km/1,971 sq. mi.

Aberdonian /ábbər dóni ən/ *n*. sb who lives in or was born or brought up in the city of Aberdeen

Aberfan /ábbər ván/ coalmining village in southern Wales, where in 1966 a landslide killed 144 people

abernethy /ábər néthi/ (*plural* **abernethies**) *n*. a crisp semisweet biscuit flavoured with caraway [Mid-19thC. Origin uncertain: probably named after the English physician John *Abernethy* (1764–1831).]

aberrant /ə bérrənt/ *adj*. deviating from what is normal or desirable [Mid-16thC. From Latin *aberrant-*, the present participle stem of *aberrare* (see ABERRATION).] —**aberrance** *n*. —**aberrantly** *adv*.

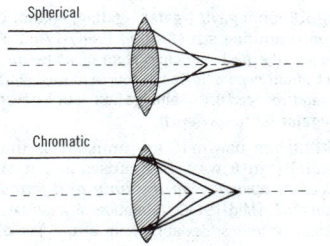

Aberration: Lenses with defects causing distorted image (top) and image with coloured edges (bottom)

aberration /ábbə ráysh'n/ *n*. **1.** DEVIATION a departure from what is normal or desirable ○ *in a moment of aberration* **2.** LAPSE a temporary departure from sb's normal mental state **3.** OPTICS OPTICAL DEFECT a defect in a lens or mirror, causing a distorted image or one with coloured edges **4.** ASTRON APPARENT DISPLACEMENT IN STAR'S POSITION a small periodic change in the apparent position of a star or other astronomical object, caused by the motion of the Earth around the Sun [Late 16thC. From the Latin stem *aberration-*, from *aberrare* 'to go astray', from *errare* 'to wander, err' (source of English *error* and *erratic*).] —**aberrational** *adj*.

Abertawe /ábbər tówi/ Welsh **Swansea**

Aberystwyth /ábbə rístwith, -rústwith/ seaside resort and university city in Ceredigion, Wales. Population: 11,154 (1991).

abet /ə bét/ (**abets, abetting, abetted**) *vt*. to assist sb to do sth, especially sth illegal [14thC. From Old French *abeter* 'to urge, stimulate', from *beter* 'to hound or drive on'. Originally 'to urge'; 'to assist' came from the legal phrase 'to aid and abet'.] —**abettor** *n*.

abeyance /ə báy ənss/ *n*. **1.** SUSPENSION temporary inactivity or non-operation ○ *a law that has fallen into abeyance* **2.** OWNERLESSNESS a condition in which legal ownership of an estate has not been established [Late 16thC. From Old French *abeance* 'expectation, desire', from *abaer* 'to desire', from *baer* 'to gape' (source of English *bay*), from medieval Latin *batare*.] —**abeyant** *adj*.

abfarad /ab fárrad, -fárrəd/ *n*. the centimetre-gram-second unit of electrical capacitance equal to 10^9 farads

abhenry /ab hénri/ (*plural* **-ries**) *n*. the centimetre-gram-second unit of electrical conductance equal to 10^{-9} of a henry

abhor /əb háwr/ (**-hors, -horring, -horred**) *vt*. to dislike or reject sth very strongly (*formal*) [15thC. From Latin *abhorrere* 'to shrink back in horror', from *horrere* 'to shudder', literally 'to bristle' (source of English *horrid* and *horror*).] —**abhorrer** *n*.

abhorrence /əb hórrənss/ *n*. **1.** AVERSION a feeling of loathing for or intense disapproval of sth **2.** OBJECT OF REPUGNANCE sb or sth that is loathed or detested ○ *The idea became an abhorrence to her.*

—————— **WORD KEY: SYNONYMS** ——————
See Synonyms at *dislike*.

abhorrent /əb hórrənt/ *adj*. **1.** REPUGNANT arousing strong feelings of repugnance or disapproval (*formal*) ○ *a practice abhorrent to all animal lovers* **2.** INCOMPATIBLE incompatible or conflicting with sth (*literary*)

Abib /a beéb/ *n*. the first month of the ancient Hebrew calendar, corresponding to Nisan in the modern Jewish calendar [Mid-16thC. From Hebrew *'ābīb* 'ear of corn'.]

abide /ə bíd/ (**abides, abiding, abode** /ə bód/ *or* **abided, abode** *or* **abided**) *v*. **1.** *vt*. TOLERATE STH to find sb or sth acceptable or bearable ○ *couldn't abide his superior attitude* **2.** *vt*. AWAIT STH to wait for sb or sth (*archaic*) **3.** *vi*. DWELL to live or reside in a place (*archaic*) **4.** *vt*. WITHSTAND STH to endure or withstand sth (*archaic*) [Old English *ābīdan* 'to wait for or expect', from *bīdan* 'to wait' (see BIDE).] —**abidance** *n*. —**abider** *n*.

abiding /ə bíding/ *adj*. permanent or long-lasting ○ *my abiding memory of her* —**abidingly** *adv*.

Abidjan /ábbi jaán/ city and cultural and commercial capital of the Côte d'Ivoire. Population: 2,700,000 (1990 est.).

abietic acid /ábbi éttik-/ *n*. a yellowish powder extracted from rosin and used in making varnishes, lacquers, and soaps. Formula: $C_{20}H_{30}O_2$. [*Abietic* from the Latin stem *abiet-* 'fir', from which rosin is obtained]

Abigail /ábbi gayl/ *n*. in the Bible, a woman who averted a hostile attack by David and his followers by taking provisions to them. She later married David. (1 Samuel 25)

ability /ə bílləti/ (*plural* **-ties**) *n*. **1.** BEING ABLE the capacity to do sth or perform successfully ○ *It has the ability to perform well on really rough terrain.* **2.** EXCEPTIONAL SKILL OR INTELLIGENCE a high degree of general skill or competence ○ *We need people of your ability.* **3.** TALENT a particular talent or acquired skill ○ *a student with great musical abilities* [14thC. Via Old French *ablete* from Latin *habilitas* 'suitability, aptness', from *habilis* (see ABLE). The underlying sense is of suitable or sufficient power to do sth.]

—————— **WORD KEY: SYNONYMS** ——————
ability, skill, competence, aptitude, talent, capacity, capability
CORE MEANING: the necessary skill, knowledge, or experience to do sth
ability the most general term, covering both natural and acquired skills or knowledge; **skill** proficiency gained through training or experience; **competence** the ability to do sth reasonably but not outstandingly well; **aptitude** a natural inclination towards a subject or area of activity; **talent** an unusual natural ability to do sth extremely easily or well; **capacity** ability that may not actually have been tested; **capability** the potential ability of a person or machine to do sth complex or demanding.

ab initio /áb i níshi ō/ *adv*. **1.** FROM THE BEGINNING from the beginning (*formal*) **2.** EDUC FROM SCRATCH without any previous knowledge or skill ○ *study Spanish ab initio* [Early 17thC. From Latin.]

abiogenesis /áy bī ō jénnəssiss/ *n*. the hypothesis that life can come into being from non-living materials [Late 19thC. From Greek *abios* 'without life', from *bios* 'life' + GENESIS.] —**abiogenetic** /áy bī ōjə néttik/ *adj*. —**abiogenetical** /-néttik'l/ *adj*. —**abiogenist** /áy bī ójjənist/ *n*.

abiosis /áy bī őssiss/ *n.* the state of not containing or supporting life

abiotic /áy bī óttik/ *adj.* **1.** ECOL **PHYSICAL NOT BIOLOGICAL** used to describe the physical and chemical aspects of an organism's environment **2.** BIOL **FREE OF LIVING THINGS** not containing or supporting life —**abiotically** *adv.*

abject /áb jekt/ *adj.* **1. MISERABLE** allowing no hope of improvement or relief **2. HUMBLE** extremely or excessively humble, e.g. in making an apology or request **3. DESPICABLE** utterly despicable or contemptible [15thC. From Latin *abjectus*, past participle of *abjicere* 'to throw away, reject', from *jacere* 'to throw' (source of English *eject, ejaculate,* and *trajectory*). The underlying sense is 'rejected'.] —**abjection** /ab jéksh'n/ *n.* —**abjectly** /áb jektli/ *adv.* —**abjectness** /-nəss/ *n.*

abjure /əb jóor/ (**-jures, -juring, -jured**) *vt.* **1. FORMALLY RENOUNCE STH** to give up a previously held belief, especially when this is done formally or solemnly **2. DENY YOURSELF STH** to abstain from, reject, or avoid sth (*literary*) [15thC. From Latin *abjurare*, 'to deny on oath', from *jurare* 'to swear'.] —**abjuration** /áb joor ráysh'n/ *n.* —**abjurer** /əb jóorər/ *n.*

Abkhaz /ab kaáz/ *n.* **1.** PEOPLES **MEMBER OF PEOPLE LIVING IN GEORGIA** a member of a people who live between the eastern shores of the Black Sea and the Great Caucasus Mountain range in Georgia **2.** LANG **CAUCASIAN LANGUAGE** a language spoken in northwestern Georgia, belonging to the Abkhaz-Adyghean group of languages. Abkhaz is spoken by between 80,000 and 100,000 people. [Mid-19thC. From *Abkhaz*, a territory in the Caucasus.] —**Abkhaz** *adj.*

Abkhazia /ab kaázi ə/ autonomous republic in northwestern Georgia, bordered to the north by Russia and to the southwest by the Black Sea. Area: 8,600 sq. km/3,320 sq. mi. Population: 537,500 (1990 est.).

abl. *abbr.* GRAM ablative

ablate /ə bláyt/ (**-lates, -lating, -lated**) *vt.* **1.** MED **REMOVE TISSUE** to remove diseased or unwanted tissue from the body by surgical or other means **2.** GEOL **MELT SNOW AND ICE** to remove or reduce snow and ice from a glacier by melting and evaporation [15thC. From Latin *ablat-*, the past participle stem of *auferre* (see ABLATIVE).]

ablation /ə bláysh'n/ *n.* **1.** MED **REMOVAL OF TISSUE** the removal of diseased or unwanted tissue from the body by surgical or other means **2.** SPACE TECH **MELTING OF SPACECRAFT'S OUTER SURFACE** the melting or erosion of the protective outer surface of a spacecraft during re-entry through the earth's atmosphere **3.** GEOL **MELTING OF SNOW AND ICE** the removal of snow and ice by melting and sublimation from a glacier or iceberg

ablative /ább lətiv/ *adj.* **GRAMMATICAL CASE** used to describe a case, used for nouns, pronouns, and adjectives in some inflected languages, that indicates the source, agent, or instrument of action of the verb ■ *n.* **ABLATIVE CASE OR WORD** the ablative case, or a word or form in this case [15thC. Directly or via French *ablatif* from Latin *ablativus*, from *ablatus*, past participle of *auferre* 'to carry away'. The case originally expressed 'direction from'.]

ablator /ə bláytər/ *n.* a heat shield on a spacecraft

ablaut /áb lowt/ *n.* in Indo-European languages, a regular change of vowels in a related series of words or forms, e.g. 'sing', 'sang', 'sung' [Mid-19thC. From German, from *ab* 'off' + *Laut* 'sound'.]

ablaze /ə bláyz/ *adj.* **1. ON FIRE** burning strongly **2. BRIGHTLY LIT** very brightly lit **3. SHOWING STRONG EMOTION** displaying great emotion or excitement, especially on the face

able /áyb'l/ (**abler, ablest**) *adj.* **1. IN A POSITION TO DO STH** physically or mentally equipped to do sth, especially because of circumstances and timing ○ *Were you able to reach her before she left?* **2. CAPABLE OR TALENTED** having the necessary resources or talent to do sth ○ *a very able administrator* [14thC. Via Old French *(h)able* from Latin *habilis* 'easy to hold or handle', from *habere* 'to have, to hold'.]

WORD KEY: SYNONYMS

See Synonyms at ***intelligent***.

-able *suffix.* **1.** capable of or fit for ○ *readable* **2.** tending to ○ *changeable* [From Latin *-abilis*] —**-ability** *suffix.*

able-bodied /-bóddid/ *adj.* healthy and physically strong

able-bodied seaman (*plural* **able-bodied seamen**) *n.* a member of a ship's crew, especially the crew of a merchant ship, who possesses basic skills and qualifications. ◊ **able rating**

abled /áyb'ld/ *adj.* having unrestricted physical or mental functions. ◊ **differently abled**

ableism /áyb'lizzəm/ *n.* discrimination in favour of those who are not considered to be physically or mentally challenged —**ableist** *adj., n.*

able rating *n.* in the Royal Navy, a non-commissioned sailor who possesses basic skills and qualifications

able seaman (*plural* **able seamen**) *n.* a member of a ship's crew who possesses basic skills and qualifications and ranks above an ordinary seaman and below a leading hand in the Royal Navy. ◊ **able rating**

abloom /ə blóom/ *adj.* blooming or flowering

ablution /ə blóosh'n/ *n.* **RITUAL WASHING** the ritual cleansing of a priest's hands or body, or of sacred vessels, during a religious ceremony ■ **ablutions** *npl.* **1. WASHING YOURSELF** the act of washing the hands or the whole of the body (*formal or humorous*) **2. WASHING FACILITIES** washing facilities in a military camp or base [14thC. Directly or via French from the Latin stem *ablution-*, from *abluere* 'to wash away, wash clean', from *luere* 'to wash' (source of English *dilute*).] —**ablutionary** *adj.*

ably /áybli/ *adv.* in a skilful or competent way

ABM *n., abbr.* antiballistic missile

Abnaki *n., adj.* = **Abenaki**

abnegate /ábni gayt/ (**-gates, -gating, -gated**) *vt.* to give up or renounce sth (*formal*) [Early 17thC. From Latin *abnegat-*, the past participle stem of *abnegare* 'to refuse, reject', from *negare* 'to deny' (source of English *deny, negative,* and *renegade*).] —**abnegation** /ábni gáysh'n/ *n.* —**abnegator** /ábni gaytər/ *n.*

abnormal /ab náwrm'l/ *adj.* unusual or unexpected, especially in a way that causes alarm or anxiety ○ *Doctors operated on the lung and found nothing abnormal.* [Mid-19thC. Alteration of ANORMAL, modelled on Latin *abnormis* 'deviating from a rule'.] —**abnormally** *adv.*

abnormality /áb nawr mállәti/ (*plural* **-ties**) *n.* **1. PHYSICAL OR MENTAL IRREGULARITY** an unusual variation from a normal structure or function of the mind or body ○ *The blood test detected no abnormalities.* **2. ABNORMAL CONDITION** deviation from the usual or expected condition

Abo /ábbō/ (*plural* **Abos**), **abo** (*plural* **abos**) *n. Aus* an offensive term for an Aboriginal (*slang offensive*) [Early 20thC. Shortening.] —**Abo** *adj.*

aboard /ə báwrd/ *adv., prep.* **1. ONTO A SHIP OR VEHICLE** on, onto, in, or into a ship, aeroplane, train, or other vehicle **2. INTO A GROUP** in or into an organization or group (*informal*)

abode[1] /ə bṓd/ *n.* (*literary*) **1. SB'S HOME** the house or other place where a particular person lives **2. STAY** a period of living somewhere [13thC. Formed from ABIDE; the underlying meaning is of staying, hence 'a place where sb stays'.] ◇ **of no fixed abode** having no permanent place in which to live (*formal*)

WORD KEY: SYNONYMS

See Synonyms at ***residence***.

abode[2] past participle, past tense of **abide**

abohm /ab ṓm/ *n.* the centimetre-gram-second unit of electrical resistance equal to 10^{-9} ohms

aboiteau /ábbwo tṓ/ (*plural* **aboiteaux** /-tṓ/) *n. Can* a sluice gate in a dike that prevents sea water from flowing in but allows flood water to flow out

abolish /ə bóllish/ (**-ishes, -ishing, -ished**) *vt.* to put an end to sth, e.g. a law ○ *'Critics of advertising usually forget that if it were eliminated or abolished, other methods would necessarily be substituted for it'.* (Daniel Starch, *Principles of Advertising*; 1923) [15thC. Via French *aboliss-*, the stem of *abolir*, from Latin *abolere* 'to destroy'.] —**abolishable** *adj.* —**abolisher** *n.* —**abolishment** *n.*

abolition /ábbə lísh'n/ *n.* **1. ACT OF OUTLAWING STH** the act of officially ending a law, regulation, or practice **2. abolition, Abolition ENDING OF SLAVERY** the official ending of the practice of slavery. In British territories the slave trade was abolished in 1807 and slavery in 1833. [Early 16thC. Directly or via French from the Latin stem *abolition-*, from abolere 'to destroy' (see ABOLISH).] —**abolitionary** *adj.*

abolitionist *n.* **1. abolitionist, Abolitionist OPPONENT OF SLAVERY** sb who campaigned against slavery during the 18th and 19th centuries **2. SB WHO SEEKS TO BAN STH** sb who supports the abolition of a practice, e.g. capital punishment —**abolitionism** *n.*

abomasum /ábbō máyssəm/ (*plural* **-sa** /-sə/) *n.* the fourth and final chamber of the multi-stomach digestive system of cattle and other ruminants, where enzymatic or true digestion takes place [Late 17thC. From the idea of being separate from the omasum.]

A-bomb *n.* an atom bomb [Mid-20thC. Contraction.]

abominable /ə bómminəb'l/ *adj.* **1. LOATHSOME** extremely repugnant or offensive **2. UNPLEASANT** of a very poor quality, or very unpleasant to experience [14thC. Via Old French from Latin *abominabilis*, from *abominari* 'to shun sth as being a bad omen', from *omen* 'omen'.] —**abominably** *adv.*

WORD KEY: ORIGIN

From the 14th to the 17th centuries ***abominable*** was often spelt *abhominable* because of a widely held belief that it was derived from Latin *ab hominem*, literally 'away from humankind', hence 'unnatural, beastly'. Shakespeare puns on this sense when Hamlet speaks of incompetent actors who 'imitate humanity abominably'.

Abominable Snowman *n.* = **yeti**

abominate /ə bómin ayt/ (**-nates, -nating, -nated**) *vt.* to dislike and disapprove of sb or sth intensely (*formal*) [Mid-17thC. From Latin *abominat-*, the past participle stem of *abominari* (see ABOMINABLE).] —**abominator** *n.*

abomination /ə bómmi náysh'n/ *n.* **1. STH HORRIBLE** an object of intense disapproval or dislike **2. STH SHAMEFUL** sth that is immoral, disgusting, or shameful **3. INTENSE DISLIKE** a feeling of intense dislike or disapproval towards sb or sth (*literary*)

aboriginal /ábbə ríjjinəl/ *adj.* **INDIGENOUS** existing from the earliest known times ○ *the aboriginal rainforest* ■ *n.* **ORIGINAL INHABITANT** a member of a people that has lived in an area from the earliest known times [Mid-17thC. Formed from *aborigines* (see ABORIGINE).] —**aboriginality** /ábbə rijji nálləti/ *n.* —**aboriginally** /-ríjjinəli/ *adv.*

WORD KEY: SYNONYMS

See Synonyms at ***native***.

Aboriginal *n.* **EARLY AUSTRALIAN** a member of any of the indigenous peoples that inhabited Australia before the arrival of European settlers ■ *adj.* **OF ABORIGINALS** relating to the earliest inhabitants of Australia

aborigine /ábbə ríjjini/ *n.* a person, animal, or plant that has lived in an area from the earliest known times [16thC. Back-formation from Latin *aborigines*, the pre-Roman inhabitants of Latium, from *ab origine* 'from the beginning'.]

Aborigine *n.* an Aboriginal inhabitant of Australia

aborning /ə báwrning/ *adv. US* while being born, created, or realized

abort /ə báwrt/ (**aborts, aborting, aborted**) *v.* **1.** *vti.* **REMOVE FOETUS** to remove an embryo or foetus from the womb in order to end a pregnancy **2.** *vi.* **HAVE MISCARRIAGE** to give birth to an embryo or foetus before its independent survival is possible. Survival is usually possible at 24 weeks for human foetuses, but may occur earlier. (*technical*) **3.** *vti.* **END PREMATURELY** to bring sth to an end or come to an end at an early stage **4.** *vti.* **ABANDON MISSION** to end a space flight or similar mission before it is completed **5.** *vti.* COMPUT **QUIT COMPUTER PROGRAM** to abandon a computer program, command, or operation before it has finished [Mid-16thC. From Latin *abort-*, the past participle stem of *aboriri* 'to miscarry', from *oriri* 'to come into being' (source of English *origin*).]

abortifacient /ə báwrti fáysh'nt/ *adj.* used to describe a drug or device that causes abortion —**abortifacient** *n.*

abortion /ə báwrsh'n/ *n.* **1.** OPERATION TO END PREGNANCY an operation or other intervention to end a pregnancy by removing an embryo or foetus from the womb **2.** MISCARRIAGE a miscarriage (*technical*) **3.** CANCELLATION the ending of a flight or mission before it is completed **4.** OFFENSIVE TERM sth so badly done or made that it is a complete failure (*offensive*)

abortionist /ə báwrsh'nist/ *n.* an offensive and disapproving term for sb who performs abortions, especially suggesting the illegality of the procedure

abortive /ə báwr tiv/ *adj.* **1.** UNSUCCESSFUL failing to reach completion **2.** BIOL DISRUPTED IN DEVELOPMENT used to describe an organ that has had its development terminated —**abortively** *adv.*

ABO system *n.* a system that classifies human blood by dividing it into the four groups A, B, AB, and O. Classification is based on the presence or absence of two chemical groups (**antigens**), A and B, on the red blood cells.

abound /ə bównd/ (**abounds, abounding, abounded**) *vi.* **1.** BE PLENTIFUL to be present in large numbers or quantities **2.** BE WELL SUPPLIED to contain sth in large numbers or amounts [14thC. Via Old French *abunder* from Latin *abundare* 'to overflow', from *undare* 'to surge', from *unda* 'wave' (source of English *inundate, redundant*, and *surround*).] —**abounding** *adj.* —**aboundingly** *adv.*

about /ə bówt/ CORE MEANING: a grammatical word that refers to different sides or aspects of sth from some point of orientation ○ (prep) *a book about a dog* ○ (adv) *There's a lot of laziness about.*

1. *prep.* IN CONNECTION WITH in connection with or relating to ○ *think about problems* **2.** *prep.* APPROXIMATELY close to in number, time, or degree ○ *inviting about 15 people* **3.** *prep.* DOING OR ATTENDING TO with or in an activity ○ *go about your business* **4.** *prep.* CLOSE BY placed, located, or happening close by or around ○ *frantic activity going on all about us* **5.** *prep.* AROUND around or on a place or person ○ *a red scarf about her neck* **6.** *adv., prep.* IN VARIOUS PLACES positioned here and there ○ *scattered about the house* **7.** *adv., prep.* IN DIFFERENT DIRECTIONS from place to place in different directions or in no particular direction ○ *children running about everywhere* **8.** *adv.* IN CIRCULATION available or in circulation ○ *there was never much money about* **9.** *adv.* INTO A REVERSED POSITION in or to the opposite direction ○ *the wrong way about* **10.** *adv.* ALL AROUND on every side of or all the way around ○ *'He proceeded to the banks of the Hudson, and looked about among the vessels'.* (Jules Verne, *Around the World in 80 Days*; 1873) **11.** *adv.* USED AS INTENSIFIER used to emphasize a statement, usually when expressing impatience or anger (*informal*) ○ *Well, it's about time you showed up!* **12.** *adv.* NAUT TO OPPOSITE TACK on or to the opposite tack [Old English *onbūtan* 'on or around the outside of', from *on* (see ON) + *būtan* (see BUT)] ◇ **be what sth** *or* **sb is (all) about** to be what sth or sb involves or has as a purpose (*informal*) ◇ **be about to** to be on the point of doing sth ○ *The game was about to start.* ◇ **not about to** used to emphasize that sb is certainly not going to do sth (*informal*) ○ *I'm not about to apologize!*

about-face *vi.* (**about-faces, about-facing, about-faced**), *n.* US = **about-turn**

about-ship (**about-ships, about-shipping, about-shipped**) *vi.* to turn to a new tack in sailing

about-turn *vi.* (**about-turns, about-turning, about-turned**) TURN AROUND to turn to face in the opposite direction (*usually used as a command*) ■ *n.* **1.** REVERSAL a sudden and complete reversal of a previous opinion or policy **2.** TURN a turn to face in the opposite direction

above /ə búv/ CORE MEANING: a grammatical word indicating a position directly overhead, on top of, or higher than sth ○ (prep) *The bird flew up above the trees.* ○ (adv) *gazing at the sky above*

1. *prep., adv.* MORE THAN greater than an amount or level ○ *100 pounds above the ideal body weight* **2.** *prep., adv.* SUPERIOR TO higher in status or power ○ *You can rise above your station.* **3.** *prep.* TOO GOOD FOR too good or important to be affected by or involved in sth ○ *They felt they were above small town gossip.* **4.** *prep.* BEYOND not subject to sth negative such as criticism or reproach ○ *'He wanted her to know that here too his conduct should be above suspicion'.* (George Eliot, *Middlemarch*; 1872) **5.** *prep.* IN POSITION OF HIGHER RESPECT in a position that is valued more or considered more important than other people or things ○ *We put the people above everything else.* **6.** *prep.* TOO DIFFICULT outside or beyond sb's understanding ○ *The lecture was completely above me.* **7.** *prep.* LOUDER THAN OTHER NOISE louder than or over another sound ○ *She couldn't hear him above the roar of the band.* **8.** *prep.* NORTH OF lying north of a place ○ *a small town just above London* **9.** *prep.* UPSTREAM FROM lying upstream from a place **10.** *adv., adj.* IN A PREVIOUS PLACE IN WRITING in a previous place, or further towards the top of the page in a piece of writing (*often used in hyphenated compounds*) ○ *using the information from the table above* **11.** *adv.* RELIG IN HEAVEN to or in heaven (*literary*) ○ *pray to God above* [Old English, from *an* (see ON) + *bufan* 'above', ultimately from an Indo-European root that is also the ancestor of English *up, open, eaves*, and *opal*] ◇ **above all** used to indicate the most important thing or the main point of a statement ◇ **get above yourself** to become conceited

aboveboard /ə búv báwrd/ *adj.* OPEN TO SCRUTINY honest, legal, and without deception ■ *adv.* **aboveboard, above board** OPENLY honestly, legally, and without deception [Late 16thC. Originally a gambling term indicating that the player's hands were above the *board* or gaming table and that nothing was being concealed.]

above-the-title *adj.* shown in film credits before the title is seen, and therefore in a starring role ○ *an above-the-title mention*

ab ovo /ab ṓvō/ *adv.* from the very beginning (*literary*) [Late 16thC. From Latin, literally 'from the egg'.]

abp, Abp *abbr.* archbishop

abracadabra /àbbrəkə dábbrə/ *interj.* MAGIC WORD a word spoken by magicians and conjurors supposedly to ensure the success of a trick ■ *n.* **1.** MAGIC SPELL a magical charm or spell **2.** GIBBERISH deliberately nonsensical language [Mid-16thC. Via Latin from, ultimately, Greek, possibly from abraxas, a series of letters with the value 365 (the days of the year) in numerological theory. Originally a cabbalistic word and formerly usedas a talisman or charm against fever.]

abrade /ə bráyd/ (**abrades, abrading, abraded**) *vti.* to wear sth away or be worn away by friction [Late 17thC. From Latin *abradere*, from *radere* 'to scrape' (source of English *erase, raze*, and *razor*).]

Abraham /áybrə ham/, **Abram** /áybrəm/ *n.* the first patriarch in the Bible who was asked by God to sacrifice his son, Isaac, and was rewarded for being prepared to do so. He is seen by Jewish people as the father of the Hebrews through his son Isaac, and by Muslims as the father of Arab peoples through his son Ishmael.

Abrahams /áybrə hamz/, **Harold** (1899–1978) British athlete. His victory in the 100 metres at the 1924 Paris Olympic Games was featured in the film *Chariots of Fire* (1981).

abranchiate /ay brángki ət/, **abranchial** *adj.* without gills

abrasion /ə bráyzh'n/ *n.* **1.** WEARING AWAY the process of wearing away by friction **2.** MED SCRAPED AREA OF SKIN an area on the skin, or some other surface of the body, that has been damaged by scraping or rubbing ○ *dental abrasion* **3.** GEOG WEARING AWAY OF ROCK the erosion of bedrock by continuous friction caused by rock fragments in water, wind, or ice [Mid-17thC. From the Latin stem *abrasion-*, from *abradere* (see ABRADE).]

abrasive /ə bráy siv/ *adj.* **1.** USING FRICTION using friction and roughness of texture to smooth or clean a surface ○ *an abrasive cleaner* **2.** HARSH IN MANNER aggressively direct and insensitive ■ *n.* SMOOTHING SUBSTANCE a substance used to smooth or polish a surface by grinding or scraping. Typical abrasives include sandpaper, pumice, and emery. [Mid-19thC. From Latin *abras-*, the past participle stem of *abradere* (see ABRADE).]

abreact /àbbri ákt/ (**-acts, -acting, -acted**) *vt.* to release unconscious tension by talking about or reliving the events that caused it —**abreaction** /-áksh'n/ *n.*

abreast /ə brést/ *adv.* IN LINE side by side and facing the front ■ *adj.* WELL INFORMED up to date with sth

abri /a brée/ *n.* a place of refuge or shelter, e.g. a dugout [Early 19thC. Via French from Latin *apricum* 'open place'.]

abridge /ə bríj/ (**abridges, abridging, abridged**) *vt.* **1.** SHORTEN STH to shorten a text, e.g. by cutting or summarizing it ○ *abridged for television in three episodes* **2.** CUT STH SHORT to reduce sth in scope or extent ○ *They abridged the meeting as best they could.* **3.** RESTRICT STH to deprive sb of rights or privileges (*archaic*) [14thC. Via Old French *abreg(i)er* from Latin *abbreviare* 'to shorten' (source of English *abbreviate*), from, ultimately, *brevis* 'short' (source of English *brief*).] —**abridgable** *adj.* —**abridged** *adj.* —**abridger** *n.*

abridgment /ə bríjmənt/, **abridgement** *n.* **1.** SHORTENED VERSION a shortened version of a novel, play, or other work **2.** ABRIDGING the process of abridging a work **3.** CURTAILMENT a curtailment or reduction of sth

abroach /ə brṓch/ *adj.* opened or tapped so that liquid can be drawn off

abroad /ə bráwd/ *adv.* **1.** AWAY FROM YOUR OWN COUNTRY in or to a foreign country or countries **2.** IN CIRCULATION in public or into general circulation **3.** EVERYWHERE over a wide area **4.** OFF TARGET wide of the mark (*literary*) **5.** *Ireland* NOT AT HOME out of your house or home ■ *n.* OTHER COUNTRIES foreign countries (*informal*) [Coined from A- + BROAD. The original sense was 'widely, over a wide area', hence 'away from home, in a foreign country'.]

abrogate /ábbrə gayt/ (**-gates, -gating, -gated**) *vt.* to repeal or abolish sth formally and publicly (*formal*) [Early 16thC. From Latin *abrogat-*, the past participle stem of *abrogare*, 'to repeal a law', from *rogare* 'to ask, to propose a law' (source of English *arrogant, interrogate*, and *prerogative*).] —**abrogation** /àbbrə gáysh'n/ *n.*

WORD KEY: SYNONYMS

See Synonyms at ***nullify***.

abrupt /ə brúpt/ *adj.* **1.** SUDDEN sudden and unexpected **2.** BRUSQUE brief and making no effort to be friendly **3.** STEEP with a sudden steep slope **4.** DISCONNECTED not passing smoothly from topic to topic **5.** GEOL PROJECTING used to describe a rock layer that is steeply inclined and stands out from surrounding rocks [Late 16thC. From Latin *abruptus* 'broken off, steep', past participle of *abrumpere* 'to break off', from *rumpere* 'to break' (source of English *disrupt, interrupt*, and *rupture*).] —**abruptly** *adv.* —**abruptness** *n.*

abruption /ə brúpsh'n/ *n.* the sudden breaking off of a part from a larger mass (*formal*) [Early 17thC. From the Latin stem *abruption-*, from *abrumpere* (see ABRUPT).]

Abruzzi /ə bróotsi/ agricultural region of central southern Italy consisting of the provinces of L'Aguila, Chieti, Pescara, and Teramo. Area: 10,794 sq. km/4,168 sq. mi. Population: 1,249,388 (1991).

abs /abz/ *npl.* the abdominal muscles, or exercises done to firm them (*informal*) [Late 20thC. Shortening.]

ABS[1] *n.* a type of strong plastic (**copolymer**) used for making moulded cases and car parts. Full form **acrylonitrile-butachene-styrene**

ABS[2] *abbr.* anti-lock braking system

Absalom /ábsseləm/ *n.* in the Bible, the third son of David, King of Israel. He rebelled against his father and was killed by Joab (2 Samuel 13–18).

abscess /áb sess/ *n.* PUS-FILLED CAVITY a pus-filled cavity resulting from inflammation and usually caused by bacterial infection ■ *vi.* (**-scesses, -scessing, -scessed**) FORM AN ABSCESS to form an abscess, or be the site where one develops [Mid-16thC. From Latin *abscessus*, from *abscedere* 'to go away (referring to bodily humours going away in the pus)', from *cedere* 'to go' (source of English *cede* and *ancestor*).] —**abscessed** *adj.*

abscisic acid /ab síssik-/ *n.* a plant hormone that promotes dormancy in buds and seeds, retardation of growth, and shedding of leaves, flowers, and fruits. Formula: $C_{15}H_{20}O_4$.

abscissa /ab síssə/ (*plural* **-sas** *or* **-sae** /-see/) *n.* the horizontal coordinate or x-coordinate of a point in a two-dimensional system of Cartesian coordinates. It is the distance from the vertical axis or y-axis measured along a line parallel to the horizontal axis or x-axis. ◊ **ordinate** [Late 17thC. From modern Latin *abscissa linea*, literally 'line cut off'.]

abscission /ab sísh'n/ *n.* **1. DETACHMENT OF PARTS FROM PLANTS** the natural process by which leaves or other parts are shed from a plant **2. CUTTING OFF** the act of suddenly cutting sth off [Early 17thC. From the Latin stem *abscission-*, from *abscindere* 'to cut off', from *scindere* 'to cut up or divide' (source of English *rescind*).]

abscond /əb skónd, ab-/ (**-sconds, -sconding, -sconded**) *vi.* **1. RUN AWAY** to run away secretly, especially in order to avoid arrest or prosecution **2. ESCAPE** to escape from a place of detention [Mid-16thC. From Latin *abscondere* 'to hide or put away', from *condere* 'to stow'. Originally 'to hide'; the underlying meaning is of making oneself scarce.] —**absconder** *n.*

abseil /áb sayl/ *vi.* (**-seils, -seiling, -seiled**) **DESCEND BY ROPE** to descend a steep slope or vertical face using a rope that is secured at the top and passed around the body. US term **rappel** ■ *n.* **DESCENT BY ABSEILING** a descent of a steep slope or vertical face by abseiling. US term **rappel** [Mid-20thC. From German *abseilen*, from *ab* 'down' + *Seil* 'rope'.] —**abseiler** *n.*

absence /ábs'nss/ *n.* **1. NOT BEING PRESENT** the fact of sb's not being in a particular place **2. TIME AWAY** a period during which sb is away **3. NONEXISTENCE** the lack or nonexistence of a particular quality or feature ○ *in the absence of any fresh information* [14thC. Via French from Latin *absentia*, from *abesse* (see ABSENT[1]).]

absent[1] /ábs'nt/ *adj.* **1. NOT PRESENT** not attending a place or event, especially when expected to ○ *absent from school* **2. INATTENTIVE** not paying attention [14thC. From Latin *absent-*, the present participle stem of *abesse*, literally 'to be away', from *esse* 'to be'.]

absent[2] /ab sént/ (**-sents, -senting, -sented**) *vr.* to stay away from or leave sth such as an event or occasion ○ *She absented herself from the gathering and went outside.* [14thC. Directly or via French *absenter* from Latin *absentare* 'to keep or be away', from *absent-* (see ABSENT[1]).]

absentee /ábs'n tée/ *n.* sb who is not present or not attending an event

absentee ballot *n.* = **postal vote**

absenteeism /ábs'n tee izzəm/ *n.* persistent absence from work or some other place without good reason

absentee landlord *n.* a landlord who lives away from the accommodation or land rented out, especially one who neglects the needs of tenants

absently /ábs'ntli/ *adv.* in an inattentive or absent-minded way

absent-minded *adj.* tending to be preoccupied or forgetful —**absent-mindedly** *adv.* —**absent-mindedness** *n.*

absent without leave *adj.* absent from military duties without permission, but not assumed to have deserted

absinthe /ábssinth/, **absinth** *n.* **1. TYPE OF DRINK** a highly alcoholic liqueur tasting of aniseed and made from wormwood and herbs. Absinthe is now banned in most Western countries because of its toxicity. **2.** = **wormwood** [Early 17thC. Via French from, ultimately, Greek *apsinthion* 'wormwood'; not of Indo-European origin.]

absolute /ábssə loot/ *adj.* **1. OUT-AND-OUT** used to emphasize the strength of the speaker's feeling on the subject ○ *an absolute fool* **2. UNBOUNDED** to the very greatest degree possible ○ *absolute confidence in her ability to win* **3. DESPOTIC** having total power and authority **4. TOTAL AND UNEQUIVOCAL** completely unequivocal and not capable of being viewed as partial or relative ○ *No absolute correlation has been established.* **5. INDEPENDENT AND UNMODIFIABLE** not dependent on or qualified by anything else ○ *absolute truth* **6.** GRAM **GRAMMATICALLY INDEPENDENT** not syntactically dependent on the main clause of a sentence, e.g. 'It being sunny' in the sentence 'It being sunny, they went to the pool' **7.** GRAM **WITHOUT DIRECT OBJECT** used without an explicit direct object. The usage of 'satisfy' is absolute in the sentence 'We aim to satisfy'. **8.** GRAM **USED AS NOUN** used without an explicit noun. 'The rich and the poor' are absolute adjectival uses. **9.** PHYS **MEASURED RELATIVE TO VACUUM** involving or relating to measurements made relative to the vacuum state **10.** PHYS **ACCORDING TO STANDARDIZED MEASURES** relating to or using fundamental units of length, time, mass, and charge **11.** PHYS **MEASURED RELATIVE TO ABSOLUTE ZERO** measured on or relating to a scale that has as its lowest temperature absolute zero, the point at which all molecular motion ceases **12.** LAW **FULL AND UNCONDITIONAL** complete and in no way conditional on any future evidence or behaviour **13.** LAW **OWNED OUTRIGHT** having unconditional ownership of a title or property, unrestricted by trusts or entails (*often used after a noun*) **14.** MATH **ALWAYS TRUE ALGEBRAICALLY** true for all values of a variable in an algebraic expression **15.** MATH **CONSTANT IN VALUE** not changing in value in varying mathematical expressions **16.** MATH **WITHOUT VARIABLES** not containing an algebraic variable ■ *n.* **1. UNQUESTIONABLE RULE** a principle or value that is held to be always true or valid **2. absolute, Absolute** PHILOS **ULTIMATE REALITY** in some schools of philosophy, the one ultimate reality that does not depend on anything, and is not relative to anything else [14thC. From Latin *absolutus* 'freed', the past participle of *absolvere* 'to set free' (see ABSOLVE). The underlying idea is of setting sth free from defect and making it complete.]

absolute ceiling *n.* the maximum height above sea level at which an aircraft can maintain horizontal flight

absolutely /ábssə lootli, -lóotli/ *adv.* **1. TOTALLY** used to give strong emphasis to what is being said **2. THAT'S RIGHT** used in speech or dialogue as an emphatic way of agreeing with the other speaker ○ *Absolutely!* **3. NOT IN RELATIVE WAY** in a way that is independent of circumstances and never variable or modified **4.** GRAM **WITH NO GRAMMATICAL OBJECT** used syntactically with an implied direct object or noun head **5.** LAW **UNCONDITIONALLY** with no conditions or restrictions, especially constitutional or legal ones

WORD KEY: USAGE

Some people dislike the use of ***absolutely*** to mean 'very' or 'completely' (*That is absolutely disgraceful.*) and regard it as an affectation. Even more controversial is its use to mean simply 'yes' or 'I agree with you'. It has some relevance of meaning in uses such as 'Do you like it?''Yes, absolutely', but has less to justify it when used with answers that are factual rather than judgmental: *'Have you been to Paris?''Yes, absolutely'.*

absolute majority (*plural* **absolute majorities**) *n.* the winning total of votes that amounts to more than half of the votes cast

absolute music *n.* music whose meaning is derived solely from the music itself and which does not evoke another source, e.g. a visual scene. ◊ **programme music**

absolute pitch *n.* **1. GOOD MUSICAL EAR** the ability to identify the pitch of a single note without reference to any other sound **2. PITCH MEASURED BY VIBRATION** the exact pitch a tone is expected to have, measured by its rate of vibrations per second

absolute temperature *n.* temperature derived from the laws of thermodynamics rather than being primarily derived from properties of substances

absolute value *n.* **1. NUMBER IGNORING PLUS OR MINUS SIGN** the magnitude of a number, irrespective of whether it is positive or negative. It is symbolized by placing the number within vertical bars, thus $|7| = |-7| = 7$. **2.** = **modulus**

absolute zero *n.* the temperature at which hypothetically all molecular motion ceases, equal to 0 degrees K and equivalent to -273.16°C or -459.69°F

absolution /ábssə lóosh'n/ *n.* **1. FORGIVENESS** forgiveness for sb's sins, especially in a Christian church **2. PRAYER OF FORGIVENESS** a spoken blessing used in a Christian church to grant absolution to sb [13thC. Via French from the Latin stem *absolution-* 'acquittal, perfection', from *absolvere* (see ABSOLVE).]

absolutism /ábssə lootizzəm/ *n.* **1.** POL **POLITICAL SYSTEM** a political system in which the power of a ruler is unchecked and absolute **2. STH ABSOLUTE** a standard, principle, or theory that is absolute **3.** PHILOS **THEORY OF OBJECTIVE VALUES** a philosophical theory in which values such as truth or morality are absolute and not conditional upon human perception **4.** CHR **PREDESTINATION** a strict form of the doctrine of predestination —**absolutist** *n., adj.*

absolve /əb zólv/ (**-solves, -solving, -solved**) *vt.* **1. PRONOUNCE SB BLAMELESS** to state publicly or officially that sb is not guilty and not to be held responsible **2. RELIEVE SB OF OBLIGATION** to release sb from an obligation or requirement **3. FORGIVE SB** to forgive sb's sins, especially in a Christian church service or sacrament [15thC. From Latin *absolvere* 'to set free', literally 'to loosen away', from *solvere* 'to loosen' (source of English *dissolve* and *soluble*).] —**absolvable** *adj.* —**absolver** *n.*

WORD KEY: SYNONYMS

See Synonyms at ***excuse***.

absorb /əb sáwrb, -záwrb/ (**-sorbs, -sorbing, -sorbed**) *vt.* **1. TAKE STH UP** to soak up a liquid or take in nutrients or chemicals gradually **2. NOT TRANSMIT STH** to take up light, noise, or energy and not transmit it at all **3. INCORPORATE STH INTO WHOLE** to incorporate sth into a larger entity in such a way that it loses much of its own identity **4. ADAPT** to adapt to changing situations without being adversely affected **5. REQUIRE STH IN QUANTITY** to require sth in considerable quantities, usually without the results being precisely itemizable ○ *absorbing a huge amount of money* **6. NOT PASS STH ON** to accept increased costs without passing them on to customers **7. TAKE STH IN MENTALLY** to see, read, or hear sth and realize its implications mentally **8. ENGROSS SB** to hold sb's attention or occupy sb's time completely [15thC. Via French *absorber* from Latin *absorbere* 'to swallow', from *sorbere* 'to suck in'.] —**absorbable** *adj.* —**absorber** *n.*

absorbance /əb sáwrbənss, -záwrb-/ *n.* the capacity of a substance to absorb radiation

absorbed /əb sáwrbd, -záwrbd/ *adj.* so interested in sth that all of the attention is focused on it —**absorbedly** /əb sáwrbidli, -záwrbidli/ *adv.*

absorbent /əb sáwrbənt, -záwrb-/ *adj.* **1. ABLE TO ABSORB LIQUID** capable of soaking up liquid **2. NONREFLECTIVE** capable of absorbing light, noise, or energy instead of reflecting it (*often used in combination*) [Early 18thC. From Latin *absorbent-*, the present participle stem of *absorbere* 'to swallow' (see ABSORB).] —**absorbency** *n.* —**absorbent** *n.*

absorbent cotton *n. US* = **cotton wool**

absorbing /əb sáwrbing, -záwrb-/ *adj.* occupying the attention completely —**absorbingly** *adv.*

absorptance /əb sáwrptənss, -záwrp-/ *n.* a measure of the ability of an object or substance to absorb radiant energy, equal to the ratio of the absorbed energy to the total energy reaching the object or substance. Symbol α [Mid-20thC. Formed from Latin *absorptus*, the past participle of *absorbere* 'to swallow' (see ABSORB).]

absorption /əb sáwrpsh'n, -záwrp-/ *n.* **1. PREOCCUPATION** a state in which the whole attention is occupied **2. SOAKING UP** the uptake of liquid into the fibres of a substance **3. NONREFLECTION** the ability of a substance to absorb light, noise, or energy, or the fact that it does so **4. INCORPORATION** the incorporation of sth into a larger group or entity **5.** PHYSIOL **ASSIMILATION BY THE BODY** the passage of material through the lining of the intestine into the blood or through a cell membrane into a cell **6.** PHYS **REDUCTION IN RADIATED ENERGY** the reduction in intensity of radiated energy within a medium caused by converting some or all of the energy into another form **7.** IMMUNOL **REMOVAL OF ANTIBODIES** the elimination of antibodies or antigens by the use of a chemical reagent [Late 16thC. From the Latin stem *absorption-*, from *absorptus*, the past participle of *absorbere* 'to swallow' (see ABSORB).] —**absorptive** *adj.*

absorption spectrum *n.* the pattern of dark bands that is seen when electromagnetic radiation passes through an absorbing medium and is observed with a spectroscope. It is the result of unequal absorption of the radiation as it passes through the medium.

abstain /əb stáyn/ (**-stains, -staining, -stained**) *vi.* **1. REFRAIN FROM STH** to choose deliberately not to do sth **2. NOT VOTE** not vote for or against a proposal when a vote is held [14thC. Via Old French *abstenir* from Latin *abstinere*, literally 'to hold yourself away', from *tenere* 'to hold' (source of English *tenant* and *continue*).] —**abstainer** *n.*

abstemious /əb stéemi əss/ *adj.* not indulging in or involving excessive eating or drinking [Early 17thC. From Latin *abstemius*, from *abs-* 'away from' + *temetum* 'intoxicating liquor', of unknown origin.] —**abstemiously** *adv.* —**abstemiousness** *n.*

a at; aa father; aw all; ay day; air hair; ə about, edible, item, common, circus; e egg; ee eel; hw when; i it, happy; ī ice; 'l apple; 'm rhythm; 'n fashion; o odd; ō open; ŏŏ good; oo pool; ow owl; oy oil; th thin; th this; u up; ur urge;

abstention /əb sténsh'n/ *n.* **1. NOT DOING STH** the deliberate choice not to do sth **2. NOT VOTING** a vote or voting neither for nor against a proposal [Early 16thC. From the late Latin stem *abstention-*, from *abstentus*, the past participle of *abstinere* (see ABSTAIN).]

abstinence /ábstinənss/ *n.* restraint from indulging a desire for sth pleasurable, e.g. alcohol or sexual relations [14thC. Via Old French from Latin *abstinentia*, from *abstinent-*, the present participle stem of *abstinere* (see ABSTAIN).] —**abstinent** *adj.* —**abstinently** *adv.*

abstract *adj.* /áb strakt/ **1. NOT CONCRETE** not relating to concrete objects but expressing sth that can only be appreciated intellectually **2. THEORETICAL** based on general principles or theories rather than on specific instances ○ *abstract arguments* **3. ARTS NON-REPRESENTATIONAL** not aiming to depict an object but composed with the focus on internal structure and form **4. MUSIC CONCEPTUAL** used to describe music that is intended to have no programmatic or emotional content **5. WITH IRREGULAR PATTERN** decorated with irregular areas of colour that do not represent anything concrete **6. IMPERSONAL** emotionally detached or distanced from sth ■ *n.* /áb strakt/ **1. PRINTED SUMMARY** a summary of a longer text, especially of an academic article **2. INTELLECTUAL CONCEPT** a concept or term that does not refer to a concrete object but that denotes a quality, an emotion, or an idea **3. ARTS ABSTRACT ARTWORK** a work of art, especially a painting, in an abstract style ■ *vt.* /əb strákt/ (**-stracts, -stracting, -stracted**) **1. CONCEPTUALIZE STH** to develop a line of thought from a concrete reality to a general principle or an intellectual idea **2. SUMMARIZE STH** to make a summary of the main points of an argument or some information **3. EXTRACT STH** to remove sth from a place, usually with some difficulty **4. STEAL STH** to steal sth by taking it unobtrusively (*used euphemistically*) **5. ENVIRON PUMP WATER** to remove water from a river or other source for industrial use [14thC. From Latin *abstractus*, the past participle of *abstrahere* 'to drag away', from *trahere* 'to drag' (source of English *tractor*, *trail*, and *treat*).] —**abstracter** /əb stráktər/ *n.* —**abstractly** /áb stráktli/ *adv.* —**abstractness** /áb straktnəss/ *n.*

abstracted /əb stráktid/ *adj.* **1. PREOCCUPIED** in deep thought and not concentrating on surroundings **2. TAKEN OUT OF STH** extracted or separated from sth —**abstractedly** *adv.* —**abstractedness** *n.*

abstract expressionism *n.* a school of painting, originating in New York in the 1940s, that combined abstract forms with spontaneity of artistic expression

abstraction /əb stráksh'n/ *n.* **1. PREOCCUPATION** a state in which sb is deep in thought and not concentrating on his or her surroundings **2. GENERALIZED CONCEPT** a generalized idea or theory developed from specific concrete examples of events **3. GENERALIZING PROCESS** the forming of general ideas or concepts from specific concrete examples **4. PHILOS CONCEPTUALIZATION** the philosophical process by which people develop concepts either from experience or from other concepts **5. ARTS ABSTRACT ART** an abstract painting or sculpture **6. EXTRACTION** the removal or theft of sth, usually with some difficulty **7. ENVIRON PUMPING WATER FROM RIVER** the pumping of water from a river or other source for industrial use

abstractionism /əb stráksh'nizzəm/ *n.* the principles and practice of abstract art —**abstractionist** *n.*

abstract music *n.* = absolute music

abstract noun *n.* a noun signifying a concept, quality, or other abstract idea

abstract of title *n.* a summary of the details about the ownership of a piece of land, including all conveyances and any burdens or charges on it

abstruse /əb strōoss/ *adj.* obscure and not easily understood [Late 16thC. Directly or via French from Latin *abstrusus*, the past participle of *abstrudere*, literally 'to thrust away', from *trudere* 'to thrust' (source of English *intrude*).] —**abstrusely** *adv.* —**abstruseness** *n.*

— **WORD KEY: SYNONYMS** —
See Synonyms at *obscure*.

absurd /əb súrd/ *adj.* **1. LUDICROUS** ridiculous because of being irrational, incongruous, or illogical ○ *an absurd notion* **2. MEANINGLESS** lacking any meaning

that would give purpose to life ■ *n.* **absurd, Absurd MEANINGLESSNESS** the condition of living in a meaningless universe where life has no purpose, especially as a concept in certain 20th-century philosophical movements. ◊ **Theatre of the Absurd** [Mid-16thC. Via French from Latin *absurdus* 'inharmonious', literally 'away from the (right) sound', from assumed *surdos* 'sound'.] —**absurdly** *adv.* —**absurdness** *n.*

absurdism /əb súrdizzəm/, **Absurdism** *n.* the idea that the universe is without meaning or rational order and that human beings, in attempting to find a sense of order, must come into conflict with the universe —**absurdist** *n., adj.*

absurdity /əb súrdəti/ (*plural* **-ties**) *n.* **1. LUDICROUSNESS** ridiculousness or silliness **2. STH LUDICROUS** sth that is that is irrational, incongruous, or illogical

ABTA /ábtə/ *abbr.* Association of British Travel Agents

Abu Bakr /ə bōō bákər/ (573–634) Arabian religious leader who was the first caliph of Islam. He was responsible for uniting Arabia and spreading Islam.

Abu Dhabi /ábboo dáabi/ capital of the United Arab Emirates, on the southern shore of the Persian Gulf. Population: 363,432 (1989).

Abuja /ə bōō jaa/ official capital of Nigeria since December 1991. It is located in the Federal Capital Territory in central Nigeria. Population: 305,900 (1992).

Abukir, Bay of /ábboo keer/, **Aboukir, Abū Qīr** a bay in the Nile Delta that was the site of Nelson's defeat of the French fleet in 1798

abundance /ə búndənss/ *n.* **1. LARGE AMOUNT** a more than plentiful quantity of sth **2. AFFLUENCE** a lifestyle with more than adequate material provisions **3. FULLNESS** a fullness of spirit that overflows **4. CHEM, GEOL RATE OF INCIDENCE** the extent to which an element is present in the earth or in rocks of a particular type **5. PHYS PROPORTION OF ISOTOPE ATOMS** the proportion of one isotope of an element, expressed by number of atoms, to the total quantity of the element [14thC. Via Old French from Latin *abundantia*, from *abundant-* (see ABUNDANT).]

abundant /ə búndənt/ *adj.* **1. PLENTIFUL** present in great quantities **2. WELL-SUPPLIED** providing a more than plentiful supply of sth **3. FOUND IN QUANTITY** existing in large quantities [14thC. From Latin *abundant-*, the present participle stem of *abundare* 'to overflow' (see ABOUND).] —**abundantly** *adv.*

abuse *n.* /ə bōōss/ **1. MALTREATMENT** the physical, sexual, or psychological maltreatment of a person or animal **2. IMPROPER USE** the illegal, improper, or harmful use of sth, or an illegal, improper, or harmful practice **3. INSULTS** insulting or offensive language **4. DRUG USE** the harmful or illegal non-medicinal use of drugs or alcohol ■ *v.* /ə byōōz/ (**abuses, abusing, abused**) **1.** *vt.* **MALTREAT SB** to maltreat a person or animal physically, sexually, or psychologically **2.** *vt.* **MISUSE STH** to use sth in an improper, illegal, or damaging way **3.** *vt.* **INSULT SB** to speak insultingly or offensively to sb **4.** *vr.* **MASTURBATE** to masturbate (*disapproving*) [15thC. Via French *abus* from Latin *abusus*, the past participle of *abuti* 'to use up, misuse', from *uti* 'to use'.]

— **WORD KEY: USAGE** —

abuse or **misuse**? Both as a verb and as a noun, *abuse* is more morally loaded than **misuse**; **alcohol misuse** is a factual statement about alcohol wrongly used, whereas **alcohol abuse** implies a judgment about the user. This difference has been greatly emphasized by the use of *abuse* (both noun and verb) with reference to violence or sexual acts committed against children; the alternative word **misuse** would be meaningless here.

— **WORD KEY: SYNONYMS** —
See Synonyms at *misuse*.

abuser /ə byōōzər/ *n.* **1. SB WHO MALTREATS ANOTHER** sb who physically, sexually, or psychologically maltreats a person or an animal **2. DRUG USER** sb who uses drugs or alcohol in a way that may be addictive, harmful, or illegal

Great Temple of Ramses II

Abu Simbel /ábboo símb'l/ *n.* the site of two carved rock temples in southern Egypt, built in the reign of Ramses II in the 13th century BC. They were moved to higher ground in the 1960s to avoid possible damage from the construction of the Aswan High Dam.

abusive /ə byōōssiv/ *adj.* **1. INSULTING** calculated to insult or offend sb ○ *abusive language* **2. HARMFUL** involving physical or psychological damage ○ *an abusive relationship* **3. IMPROPERLY USED** involving illegal, improper, or harmful activities ○ *using abusive methods to secure power* —**abusively** *adv.* —**abusiveness** *n.*

abut /ə bút/ (**abuts, abutting, abutted**) *vti.* to touch or be adjacent to sth along one side [15thC. Partly from Anglo-Latin *abuttare*, from *butta* 'ridge or strip of land'; partly from Old French *aboter* 'to aim at', from *boter* 'to strike', from Germanic.]

abutilon /ə byōōtilən/ *n.* a tropical plant or shrub of the mallow family with bell-shaped red, yellow, or white flowers. Genus: *Abutilon*. US term **flowering maple** [Late 16thC. Via modern Latin from Arabic *ubutilun*.]

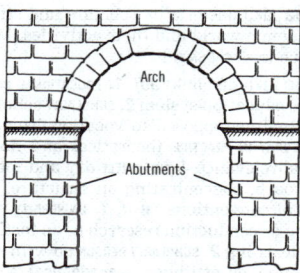
Arch
Abutments
Abutment

abutment /ə bútmənt/ *n.* **1. abutment, abuttal ADJACENCY** the immediate adjacency of two objects or pieces of land **2. abutment, abuttal MEETING POINT** the point at which two things abut **3. MAKING THINGS ABUT** the positioning of two things so that they abut **4. SUPPORT STRUCTURE** a structure that supports the end of a bridge or dam, or that bears the thrust of an arch or vault

abuttals /ə bútt'lz/ *npl.* the boundaries of a piece of land in relation to an adjoining piece of land

abuzz /ə búz/ *adj.* full of lively conversation or activity

abwatt /áb wot/ *n.* the centimetre-gram-second unit of electrical power, equal to one ten millionth (10^{-7}) of a watt

abysm /ə bízzəm/ *n.* a chasm, void, or other abyss (*archaic*) [14thC. Via Old French *abisme* from medieval Latin *abysmus*, an alteration of late Latin *abyssus* (see ABYSS).]

abysmal /ə bízm'l/ *adj.* **1. HORRIBLE** appallingly bad or extremely severe **2. VERY DEEP** similar to the great depth of an abyss **3. DEEP-SEA** extremely deep or found at extreme depths (*archaic*) —**abysmally** *adv.*

abyss /ə bíss/ *n.* **1. CHASM** a chasm or gorge so deep or vast that its extent is not visible **2. ENDLESS SPACE** sth that is immeasurably deep or infinite **3. TERRIBLE SITUATION** a situation of apparently unending awfulness **4. HELL** hell thought of as a bottomless pit [14thC. Via late Latin *abyssus* from Greek *abussos*, literally 'bottomless', from *bussos* 'bottom'. Ultimately from an Indo-European word that is also the ancestor of English *bathos*.]

abyssal /ə bíss'l/ *adj.* found in the very deepest areas of the oceans or on the deep ocean floor

Abyssinia /ábbə sínni ə/ *n.* former name for **Ethiopia** — **Abyssinian** *adj., n.*

Abyssinian cat *n.* a domestic cat belonging to a breed with dark brown or black markings on its short-haired brown coat

abyssopelagic /ə bíssō pə lájjik/ *adj.* relating to or living in the water just above the deep ocean floor [Ultimately from Greek *abussos* 'abyss' (see ABYSS) + *pelagikos* 'of the sea' (see PELAGIC)]

Ac *symbol.* actinium

AC *abbr.* **1.** ELEC ENG alternating current. ◊ DC **2.** ATHLETICS Athletic Club (*used in club names*) **3.** ante Christum **4.** BEVERAGES appellation contrôlée **5.** air conditioning

ac. *abbr.* acre

ac- *prefix.* = **ad-** (*used before c, k, and q*)

-ac *suffix.* person affected with a condition ○ *amnesiac* [Via modern Latin *-acus* from Greek *-akos*]

A/C *abbr.* **1.** A/C, a/c ACCT account **2.** A/C, a/c ACCT account current **3.** air conditioning

acacia /ə káyshə/ (*plural* **-cias** *or* **-cia**) *n.* **1.** FLOWERING TREE a tropical or subtropical shrub or tree that has small fluffy yellow globular flowers, narrow leaves, and dark fruit pods. Genus: *Acacia*. **2.** TREE LIKE TRUE ACACIA any tree or shrub like acacia proper, e.g. the locust **3.** = gum arabic [14thC. Via Latin from Greek *akakia*, of uncertain origin: perhaps from Egyptian.]

academe /ákə deem/ *n.* **1.** = academia **2.** ACADEMIC INSTITUTION a place of learning, especially a college or university [Late 16thC. Partly from Latin *academia*, and partly from its Greek source *Akademeia* (see ACADEMY).]

academia /ákə deémi ə/ *n.* scholars and students of the academic world and their activities [Mid-20thC. From Latin (see ACADEMY).]

academic /ákə démmik/ *adj.* **1.** EDUCATIONAL connected with the education system **2.** SCHOLARLY scholarly and intellectual, as opposed to vocational or practical **3.** IRRELEVANT IN PRACTICE theoretical and not of any practical relevance **4.** NOT LIVELY dry and intellectual in approach, concentrating on structure, form, or historical conventions ■ *n.* **1.** UNIVERSITY TEACHER sb teaching or conducting research at an institution of higher learning **2.** SCHOLARLY PERSON sb with scholarly background or attitudes —**academical** *adj.* —**academically** *adv.*

academicals /ákə démmik'lz/ *npl.* = academic dress

academic dress *n.* formal garments for students or university staff, usually including a gown and hood

academician /ə káddə mísh'n/ *n.* a member of an academy or society concerned with the arts or sciences

academicism /ákə démməsìzzəm/ *n.* artistry that relies on conventional techniques or emphasizes the formal aspects of an art form such as painting or poetry

academic year *n.* the annual cycle of teaching and study at an educational institution. It usually starts part way through the calendar year and is divided into sessions or terms

academism /ə káddəmìzzəm/ *n.* = academicism

academy /ə káddəmi/ (*plural* **-mies**) *n.* **1.** SOCIETY a formal society whose purpose is to promote a particular aspect of knowledge or culture **2.** SPECIALIZED SCHOOL an educational institution devoted to a particular subject **3.** SCHOOL NAME a secondary school, often a private one (*usually used in school names*) [Mid-16thC. Via Latin *academia* from Greek *Akademeia*, the school of philosophy founded by Plato, named after the park on the outskirts of Athens where he taught.]

Academy *n.* the school Plato founded to teach his philosophy

Academy Award *n.* an award given annually by the Academy of Motion Picture Arts and Sciences in the United States for work in film-making or acting. The statuette awarded is called an Oscar.

Acadia /ə káydi ə/ *n.* a former French colony in North America that comprised present-day New Brunswick, Nova Scotia, Prince Edward Island, and parts of Quebec and New England

Acadian /ə káydi ən/ *n.* **1.** SB FROM ACADIA one of the French settlers who colonized Acadia after 1604, most of whom were deported elsewhere in North America, especially to Louisiana, by the British authorities between 1755 and 1762 **2.** FRENCH CANADIAN LIVING IN MARITIMES a French-speaking inhabitant of the Canadian provinces of New Brunswick, Nova Scotia, or Prince Edward Island **3.** = Acadian French [Early 18thC] —**Acadian** *adj.*

Acadian French, **Acadian** *n.* Can the form of French spoken in the Canadian provinces of New Brunswick, Nova Scotia, and Prince Edward Island — **Acadian French** *adj.*

acalculia /áy kal kyoóli ə/ *n.* an inability, or the loss of the ability, to carry out basic arithmetic calculations [Early 20thC. Coined from A- 'not' + Latin *calculare* 'to calculate' (see CALCULATE) + -IA.]

acanthi plural of **acanthus**

acantho- *prefix.* thorn ○ *acanthopterygian* [From Greek *akanthos* 'thorn plant' (see ACANTHUS)]

acanthocephalan /ə kánthō séffələn/ *n.* = **spiny-headed worm** [Mid-19thC. Coined from ACANTHO- + Greek *kephalē* 'head' (see CEPHALO-).] —**acanthocephalan** *adj.*

acanthopterygian /ákən thoptə ríjji ən/ *n.* a fish with spiny-rayed fins and toothed scales. Mackerel, perch, and bass are acanthopterygians. Superorder: Acanthopterygii. [Mid-19thC. Ultimately from Greek *akantha* 'thorn' + *pterugion* 'fin', literally 'small wing', from *pterux* 'wing'.] —**acanthopterygian** *adj.*

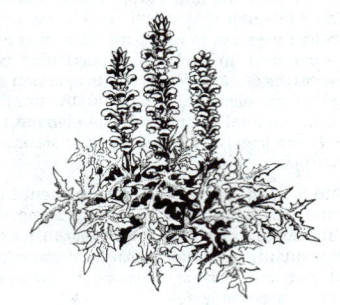

Acanthus

acanthus /ə kánthəss/ (*plural* **-thuses** *or* **-thi** /-ī/ *or* **-thus**) *n.* **1.** PLANTS PLANT WITH SPINY LEAVES a Mediterranean shrub or perennial plant with spiny leaves and white or purple flowers. Bear's breech is a variety of acanthus. Genus: *Acanthus*. **2.** ARCHIT LEAF DESIGN a design characteristic of the capital of a Corinthian column, representing acanthus leaves [Mid-16thC. Via Latin, from Greek *akanthos*, from Greek *akantha* 'thorn'.]

a cappella /áa kə péllə, ákə-/ *adv., adj.* without accompaniment from musical instruments [Late 19thC. From Italian *a cappella*, literally 'by the choir', that is, 'in the style of church music'.]

Acapulco /ákə poólkō/ seaport and resort on the Pacific coast in southern Mexico. Population: 592,187 (1990).

acari plural of **acarus**

acariasis /ákə rí əssiss/ *n.* infestation of the skin with mites

acarid /ákərid/ *n.* a mite or tick. Order: Acarina.

acaroid resin /ákəroyd-/, **acaroid gum** /ákəroyd-/ *n.* a red resin exuded by certain grass trees, used in making varnishes and coating paper

acarology /ákə rólləji/ *n.* the branch of zoology devoted to the study of mites and ticks —**acarologist** *n.*

acarophobia /ákərə fóbi ə/ *n.* abnormal fear of mites or ticks

acarus /ákərəss/ (*plural* **-ri** /-rī/) *n.* a mite or tick (*technical*) [Mid-17thC. Via modern Latin, from Greek *akari*

'mite', literally 'too short to cut, tiny', ultimately from the stem *kar-* 'to cut'.]

ACAS /áy kass/, **Acas** *n.* an organization that mediates between employers and workers or trade unions in industrial disputes. Full form **Advisory, Conciliation, and Arbitration Service**

acatalectic /áy katt'l éktik/ *adj.* METRICALLY COMPLETE having the full number of syllables in the final foot of a line of verse ■ *n.* METRICALLY COMPLETE VERSE a line of verse that has the full number of syllables in the final foot [Late 16thC. Via late Latin *acatalecticus* from Greek *akatalektos* 'complete', from *katalektos* 'incomplete'.]

acaudal /ay káwd'l/, **acaudate** /-dayt/ *adj.* without a tail (*technical*)

acaulescent /áy kaw léss'nt, ákaw-/ *adj.* with no stem or with a stem that is very short

acauline /ay káw lin, -līn/ *adj.* with no stem (*technical*)

acc. *abbr.* **1.** GRAM accusative **2.** ACCT account

ACCC *n., abbr.* Aus Australian Competition and Consumer Commission

accede /ək seéd/ (**-cedes, -ceding, -ceded**) *vi.* **1.** ASSENT to give consent or agreement to sth **2.** COME TO POWER to attain an important and powerful position **3.** SIGN TREATY to become a party to an international agreement or treaty [15thC. From Latin *accedere*, literally 'to come to', from *cedere* 'to come' (source of English *cease* and *ancestor*).] —**accedence** *n.* —**acceder** *n.*

accel. *abbr.* accelerando

accelerando /ak séllə rándō, ə chéllə-/ *adv., adj.* with gradually increasing speed (*used as a musical direction*) [Early 19thC. From Italian, 'accelerating'.]

accelerant /ək séllərənt/ *n.* **1.** = accelerator *n.* **3 2.** COMBUSTIBLE SUBSTANCE a substance that is used to intensify a fire

accelerate /ək séllə rayt/ (**-ates, -ating, -ated**) *vti.* **1.** GO FASTER to move increasingly quickly, or cause sth to move faster **2.** PROGRESS FASTER to happen or develop faster, or cause sth to happen or develop faster **3.** PHYS INCREASE VELOCITY to cause an increase in the velocity of sth, or experience an increase in velocity [Early 16thC. From Latin *acceleratus*, the past participle of *accelerare* 'to quicken', from *celer* 'quick' (source of English *celerity*).] —**accelerated** *adj.* —**accelerative** /-rətiv/ *adj.*

acceleration /ək séllə ráysh'n/ *n.* **1.** INCREASE IN VELOCITY the rate at which sth increases in velocity **2.** INCREASE IN RATE OF PROGRESS an increase in the rate at which sth happens or develops **3.** ACT OF ACCELERATING sth's accelerating, or the causing of sth to accelerate **4.** PHYS INCREASE IN VELOCITY the rate of increase in the velocity of sth. Symbol *a*

acceleration clause *n.* a clause in the terms of a loan or mortgage stipulating that payments must be made earlier in particular circumstances

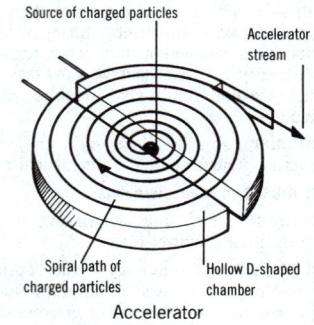

Accelerator

accelerator /ək séllə raytər/ *n.* **1.** SPEED-INCREASING CONTROL a pedal or other control mechanism used to cause a vehicle to increase speed **2.** NUCLEAR PHYS DEVICE FOR GIVING PARTICLES HIGH VELOCITIES a machine used to increase the velocity, and hence the kinetic energy, of subatomic particles or nuclei, usually in preparation for collision with a target **3.** CHEMICAL THAT SPEEDS UP REACTION a substance that increases the rate of a chemical reaction

accelerator card, **accelerator board** *n.* a circuit board that adds a faster central processing unit or a special coprocessor to a computer

accelerometer /ək séllə rómmitər/ *n.* an instrument or device for measuring acceleration

accent *n.* /áks'nt/ **1.** MANNER OF PRONUNCIATION a way of pronouncing words that indicates the place of origin or social background of the speaker **2.** INTONATION a way of using intonation or inflection to convey the speaker's mood or character **3.** STRESS ON SYLLABLE the prominence given to a syllable within a word or to a word within a phrase **4.** MARK ABOVE LETTER a symbol used in print or writing to indicate stress or the pronunciation of a vowel **5.** MAIN EMPHASIS an aspect of a situation, issue, or state of affairs that is emphasized ○ *the accent is on safety* **6.** CONTRASTING DETAIL a contrasting decorative feature used to add interest ○ *a blue room with green accents in the furnishings* **7.** STYLE a distinctive style that is characteristic of a particular person, region, or artistic school **8.** MUSIC STRESS ON NOTES stress placed on particular notes in a piece of music, or the symbol printed above the notes to indicate this stress **9.** MUSIC RHYTHM the rhythm of a piece of music, represented as the stress on the first beat of each bar **10.** MATH MATHEMATICAL SYMBOL a superscript symbol, ' or ", used to indicate a unit of measurement such as feet and inches respectively or minutes and seconds of an arc respectively ■ *vt.* /ak sént/ **(-cents, -centing, -cented) 1.** EMPHASIZE STH to stress sth, e.g. by pronouncing a word or syllable more prominently **2.** MARK STH WITH AN ACCENT to mark a letter, word, or sth else with a written or printed accent [Early 16thC. Via French, from Latin *accentus*, from *ad* 'to' + *cantus* 'singing' (source of English *cantor, chant,* and *incentive*), a literal translation of Greek *prosōidia* 'accompanied song'.]

WORD KEY: REGIONAL NOTE

An ***accent*** refers to a method of pronunciation and every speaker has one; a regional accent is often incorrectly referred to as a *dialect.* There is no single standard pronunciation for British English although, for centuries, an educated southeast English accent has been associated with privilege and prestige. Irish, Scottish, and West Country accents tend to be rhotic, that is, they pronounce the 'r' in 'dear' and 'warm'; most English and Welsh accents are non-rhotic.

accent lighting *n.* lighting that highlights an area or feature of a room, e.g. a painting or an alcove

accentor /ək séntər, -tawr/ *n.* a Eurasian and African songbird distinguished from a house sparrow by its thin finely pointed bill. Hedge sparrows are one type of accentor. Family: Prunellidae.

accentual /ək sénchoo əl/ *adj.* **1.** OF ACCENT involving or associated with accent or stress **2.** POETRY BASED ON STRESS employing a structure based on the number of stresses in a poetic line rather than on the number of syllables. ◊ **syllabic** —**accentually** *adv.*

accentuate /ək sénchoo ayt/ **(-ates, -ating, -ated)** *vt.* **1.** DRAW ATTENTION TO STH to make a feature of sth more noticeable **2.** STRESS STH to emphasize a syllable, word, or phrase when saying it [Mid-18thC. From medieval Latin *accentuatus*, the past participle of *accentuare* 'to emphasize', from Latin *accentus* (see ACCENT).] —**accentuation** /ək sénchoo áysh'n/ *n.*

accept /ək sépt/ **(-cepts, -cepting, -cepted)** *v.* **1.** *vt.* TAKE STH OFFERED to take sth that is offered, e.g. a gift or payment **2.** *vti.* SAY YES TO INVITATION to reply in the affirmative to an invitation **3.** *vt.* LAW, COMM AGREE TO TERMS to indicate formal agreement to the terms and conditions in a contract **4.** *vt.* ENDURE SITUATION to tolerate sth without protesting or attempting to change it **5.** *vt.* BELIEVE STH to acknowledge that sth is true **6.** *vt.* COME TO TERMS WITH STH to acknowledge a fact or truth and come to terms with it **7.** *vt.* ADMIT STH to admit the blame or responsibility for sth **8.** *vti.* TAKE ON DUTY to agree to take on a duty, responsibility, or position **9.** *vt.* PROCESS STH to be able to process sth or be operated by sth ○ *old machines that won't accept the new cards* **10.** *vt.* ALLOW SB TO JOIN to allow sb to join an organization or attend an institution **11.** *vt.* BE WELCOMING TO SB to treat sb as a member of a group or social circle **12.** *vt.* RECEIVE STH FOR REVIEW to receive sth such as a report for official action or review **13.** *vt.* AGREE TO MARRY SB to reply in the affirmative to a marriage proposal (*dated*) [14thC. Via French *accepter* from Latin *acceptare*, from *accipere*, literally 'to take to (yourself)', from *capere* 'to take' (source of English *catch* and *occupy*).]

acceptable /ək séptəb'l/ *adj.* **1.** ADEQUATE considered to be satisfactory **2.** APPROVED OF likely to gain sb's approval **3.** WELCOME likely to please the person who receives it (*usually modified by an adverb such as 'most' or 'quite'*) —**acceptability** /ək séptə bílləti/ *n.* —**acceptableness** /-b'lnəss/ *n.* —**acceptably** /ək séptəbli/ *adv.*

acceptable daily intake *n.* the highest daily intake level of a chemical that, if continued over the whole life of a person, appears to pose no health risk

acceptance /ək séptənss/ *n.* **1.** SAYING YES a written or verbal indication that sb agrees to an invitation **2.** TAKING OF A GIFT the willing receipt of a gift or payment **3.** WILLINGNESS TO BELIEVE willingness to believe that sth is true **4.** COMING TO TERMS WITH STH the realization of a fact or truth resulting in sb's coming to terms with it **5.** TOLERATION the tolerating of sth without protesting **6.** SOCIAL TOLERANCE willingness to treat sb as a member of a group or social circle **7.** POSITIVE RESPONSE TO APPLICATION an offer to allow sb to join an organization or attend an institution **8.** LAW, COMM AGREEMENT TO TERMS formal agreement, in writing or verbally, showing that sb assents to the terms and conditions in a contract **9.** COMM AGREEMENT TO PAY a formal agreement by a debtor to pay a draft or bill of exchange when it becomes payable

acceptant /ək séptənt/ *adj.* receiving sth willingly (*formal*)

acceptation /áksep táysh'n/ *n.* **1.** GENERAL ACCEPTANCE a generally favourable reception of sth **2.** ACCEPTED MEANING the sense in which a word or phrase is generally understood

accepted /ək séptid/ *adj.* widely used and recognized

accepter *n.* = **acceptor** *n.* 1, **acceptor** *n.* 2

accepting house (*plural* **accepting houses**) *n.* a financial institution that guarantees bills of exchange

acceptor /ək séptər/ *n.* **1. acceptor, accepter** COMM SB ACCEPTING DEBT sb who accepts liability for a bill of exchange **2. acceptor, accepter** ELECTRON ENG IMPURITY IMPROVING CONDUCTIVITY an impurity added to a semiconductor to increase its conductivity. The metallic element gallium is often used in this way. **3.** CHEM ATOM ACCEPTING ELECTRONS an atom or group of atoms that accepts electrons to form a coordinate bond during the formation of a chemical compound. ◊ **donor**

access /ák sess/ *n.* **1.** ENTRY OR APPROACH the possibility or means of entering or approaching a place **2.** OPPORTUNITY FOR USE the opportunity or right to experience or make use of sth **3.** RIGHT TO MEET SB the right or opportunity to meet sb **4.** OUTBURST a sudden strongly felt burst of emotion (*literary*) ○ *'With a sudden access of tenderness he flung his arm about me'.* (Rider Haggard, *She*; 1887) **5.** COMPUT RIGHT TO USE COMPUTER the right or ability to log on to a computer system or use a computer program ○ *software that allows network access* ■ *adj.* EDUC FOR UNQUALIFIED STUDENTS designed as a course of study for people without formal educational qualifications, in order to give them entry to higher education ■ *vt.* **(-cesses, -cessing, -cessed) 1.** ENTER PLACE to find a way or means of entering or approaching a place **2.** GET INFORMATION to have the opportunity or right to experience or make use of sth **3.** COMPUT CALL UP to retrieve data or a computer file ○ *the program can be accessed using the correct password* [14thC. Directly or via Old French *acces* from Latin *accessus*, the past participle of *accedere* 'to come near' (see ACCEDE).]

WORD KEY: USAGE

access or **accession**? The essential difference is that ***access*** refers to a right whereas ***accession*** refers to a process (and is normally used in the special ways mentioned). If you have ***access*** to a library you are allowed to use it, consult the books, and perhaps take them away. An ***accession*** to a library is a new book that has been bought for people with ***access*** to the library to use. ***Accession*** to the throne is the process by which an heir to the throne becomes king or queen. Somebody who wants to petition a new monarch would seek ***access*** to him or her after his or her ***accession***. You might have an ***access*** of strong feeling such as joy or anger, but you would have an ***accession*** of strength.

WORD KEY: USAGE

What things can you **access**? There is normally no problem with using ***access*** as a verb in computing contexts (although even this is objected to by some people), but there is more resistance to using it in general contexts such as accessing bank accounts or items of information.

accessary *n.* = **accessory**

WORD KEY: USAGE

See Usage note at ***accessory.***

access code *n.* a sequence of letters or numbers that have to be keyed in to allow sb access to sth such as a building or a telephone network

accessible /ək séssəb'l/ *adj.* **1.** EASILY REACHED easy to enter or reach physically **2.** EASILY UNDERSTOOD able to be appreciated or understood without specialist knowledge **3.** EASILY AVAILABLE able to be obtained, used, or experienced without difficulty **4.** APPROACHABLE not aloof and not difficult to talk to or meet **5.** SUSCEPTIBLE susceptible to or likely to be influenced by sth (*literary*) **6.** LOGIC OBSERVABLE FROM ANOTHER WORLD able to be referred to from another possible world, so that the truth value of statements about it can be given —**accessibility** /ək séssə bílləti/ *n.* —**accessibly** /-bli/ *adv.*

accession /ək sésh'n/ *n.* **1.** TAKING UP POSITION the assumption of an important position, usually a position of power **2.** INTERNAT LAW ACCEPTANCE OF TREATY the formal acceptance by a state of an international treaty or convention **3.** ASSENT agreement or consent, usually when given unwillingly **4.** SUDDEN MOOD a sudden and unexpected display of a particular mood or emotion (*literary*) **5.** ADDITION TO COLLECTION an item added to a collection **6.** LAW INCREASE TO PROPERTY addition to property by natural growth or by improvement **7.** LAW RIGHT TO INCREASE IN PROPERTY the right of an owner to add to a property by natural growth or improvement ■ *vt.* **(-sions, -sioning, -sioned)** CATALOGUE ADDITIONS TO COLLECTION to make a formal record of an addition to a collection —**accessional** *adj.*

WORD KEY: USAGE

See Usage note at ***access.***

accessorize /ək séssə rīz/ **(-izes, -izing, -ized), accessorise (-ises, -ising, -ised)** *v.* **1.** *vt.* PROVIDE WITH ACCESSORIES to fit accessories to sth **2.** *vti.* DECORATE AN OUTFIT to wear or use items such as gloves, hats, and handbags to complete an outfit of clothing

accessory /ək séssəri/, **accessary** *n.* (*plural* **-ries**) **1.** OPTIONAL PART an optional part that may be fitted to sth to perform an additional function or enhance performance **2.** FASHION ARTICLE an item of clothing that is worn or used for fashionable effect with an outfit ○ *'designers who create neckties as fashion accessories'* (*International Herald Tribune*; June 1997) **3.** LAW CRIMINAL HELPER sb who aids sb else to commit a crime or avoid arrest but who does not participate in the crime itself ■ *adj.* **1.** ADDITIONAL supplementary or subsidiary to the main thing **2.** LAW ASSISTING IN CRIME aiding a criminal act although not participating in the crime itself —**accessorial** /ák se sáwri əl/ *adj.* —**accessorily** /ək séssərəli/ *adv.* —**accessoriness** /-rinəss/ *n.*

WORD KEY: USAGE

accessory or **accessary**? ***Accessory*** is now the normal spelling in the two main meanings of the word, 'an extra attachment' and 'sb who is involved in a crime in addition to the person who commits the crime'. ***Accessary*** is an older spelling, and you will still find it used, especially in legal contexts.

accessory after the fact (*plural* **accessories after the fact**) *n.* sb who aids and abets sb who has committed a crime

accessory before the fact (*plural* **accessories before the fact**) *n.* sb who incites or aids sb to commit a crime but who is not present during the crime

accessory nerve *n.* the eleventh cranial nerve, associated with the pharynx and muscles in the throat, larynx, palate, neck, and back

accessory shoe *n.* a bracket on a camera allowing an accessory to be mounted on it

access time *n.* the time taken by a computer to locate and retrieve data

acciaccatura /ə cháke tòorə/ (*plural* **-ras** *or* **-re** /-ray/) *n.* MUSIC a brief grace note sounded at the same time as or just before a principal note [Early 19thC. From Italian, 'crushing sound'.]

accidence /áksidənss/ *n.* the area of traditional grammar dealing with the inflections of words [15thC. From late Latin *accidentia* (plural) 'things that happen' (taken as singular), from Latin *accident-* (see ACCIDENT).]

accident /áksidənt/ *n.* **1.** CHANCE the way things happen without any planning, apparent cause, or deliberate intent **2.** CRASH a collision or similar incident involving a moving vehicle, often resulting in injury or death **3.** CHANCE HAPPENING an event that happens completely by chance, with no planning or deliberate intent **4.** MISHAP an unplanned and unfortunate event that results in damage, injury, or upset of some kind **5.** FAILURE TO REACH TOILET an incident when sb, particularly a small child, is incontinent (*used euphemistically*) **6.** UNPLANNED PREGNANCY a child conceived in an unplanned way **7.** PHILOSOPHY NON-ESSENTIAL ATTRIBUTE a nonessential attribute or characteristic of sth [14thC. Via French, from Latin *accident-*, the present participle stem of *accidere* 'to happen', literally 'to fall to', from *cadere* 'to fall, die' (source of English *cadaver* and *chance*).]

accidental /áksi dént'l/ *adj.* **1.** CHANCE happening by chance and not planned **2.** INCIDENTAL not specifically intended and arising as a side effect **3.** MUSIC NOT IN KEY SIGNATURE sharp, flat, or natural, in a way not indicated in the key signature ◼ *n.* **1.** UNPLANNED EFFECT sth not specifically intended that arises as a side effect **2.** MUSIC NOTE NOT IN KEY SIGNATURE a musical note, marked with a sharp, flat, or natural sign, whose pitch does not correspond to the key signature —**accidentally** *adv.*

accident and emergency *n.* = casualty *n.* 4

accident insurance *n.* insurance against injury or death caused by an accident

accident-prone *adj.* having more accidents than average

accipiter /ak síppitər/ *n.* **1.** HAWK a hawk, typically with short broad wings and a long tail. Accipiters include sparrowhawks and goshawks. Genus: *Accipiter*. **2.** LARGE PREDATORY BIRD a bird in the family that includes all hawks, eagles, and kites. Family: Accipitidae. [Early 19thC. From Latin, literally 'to take to (yourself)' (see ACCEPT). The underlying idea is of a bird that seizes prey.]

accipitrine /ak síppi trin, -trīn/ *adj.* used to describe the family of predatory birds that includes hawks, eagles, and kites

acclaim /ə kláym/ *v.* (**-claims, -claiming, -claimed**) **1.** *vt.* PRAISE SB LAVISHLY to praise sb or sth publicly with great enthusiasm **2.** *vt.* PRONOUNCE SB TO BE STH to declare enthusiastically and publicly that sb holds a high position **3.** *vi.* SHOUT ENTHUSIASTICALLY to demonstrate enthusiastic approval by shouting and cheering ◼ *n.* ENTHUSIASTIC RECEPTION enthusiastic approval given to sb or sth publicly [Early 16thC. From Latin *acclamare*, literally 'to shout to', from *clamare* 'to shout' (source of English *claim* and *clamor*).] —**acclaimer** *n.*

acclamation /áklə máysh'n/ *n.* a public and enthusiastic display of approval [Mid-16thC. From the Latin stem *acclamation-*, from *acclamare* (see ACCLAIM).] —**acclamatory** /ə klámmətri/ *adj.*

acclimate /ákli mayt/ (**-mates, -mating, -mated**) *v.* **1.** *vti.* = acclimatize 2. **2.** *vi.* BIOL ALTER BECAUSE OF ENVIRONMENT to adjust in response to a change in environment [Late 18thC. From French *acclimater*, from *a-* 'to' + *climat* 'climate' (see CLIMATE).] —**acclimation** /áklə máysh'n/ *n.*

acclimatize /ə klímə tīz/ (**-tizes, -tizing, -tized**) *vti.* to become accustomed to a new climate or environment, or help sb become accustomed to it —**acclimatization** /ə klímə tī záysh'n/ *n.*

acclivity /ə klívvəti/ (*plural* **-ties**) *n.* an upward slope on a hill [Early 17thC. From the Latin stem *acclivitat-* 'ascent', from *acclivis* 'uphill', from *clivus* 'slope' (source of English *proclivity*).]

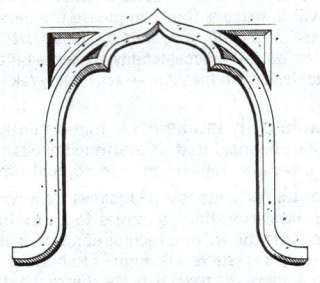

Accolade

accolade /ákə layd, -laad/ *n.* **1.** SIGN OF PRAISE a sign or expression of high praise and esteem for sb **2.** PUBLIC RECOGNITION praise and public recognition of sb's achievements **3.** KNIGHTING the ceremonial bestowal of a knighthood by touching sb's shoulders with a sword. Knighthood was formerly conferred by an embrace, which is the original sense of accolade. **4.** ARCHIT CURVED MOULDING an ornamental moulding shaped like a brace [Early 17thC. Via French, from Provençal *acolada* 'embrace', literally 'to the neck', ultimately from Latin *collum* 'neck' (source of English *collar*).]

accommodate /ə kómmə dayt/ (**-dates, -dating, -dated**) *v.* **1.** *vt.* PROVIDE LODGING FOR SB to provide sb with a place to stay **2.** *vt.* HAVE ROOM FOR SB OR STH to have sufficient space for sb or sth **3.** *vt.* ALLOW FOR STH to be adaptable enough to allow sth without major change **4.** *vt.* OBLIGE SB to adjust actions in response to sb's needs **5.** *vt.* LEND SB MONEY to give sb money in response to a request for a loan (*formal*) **6.** *vti.* REACH AGREEMENT to settle a difference of opinion in a way that is acceptable to all **7.** *vi.* ADJUST to adapt to a new situation **8.** *vi.* OPHTHALMOL ADJUST FOCUS to adjust focus automatically to give clear vision (*refers to the eyes*) [Mid-16thC. From Latin *accommodare* 'to make fit', from *commodus* 'suitable', literally 'with the measure', from *modus* 'measure' (source of English *modern*).] —**accommodative** *adj.*

— **WORD KEY: USAGE** —

Is it **accommodate** or **accomodate**? Note that **accommodate** and **accommodation** are spelt with -cc- and -mm-. **Accommodation**, in particular, is often misspelt as **accomodation** on signs and notices.

accommodating /ə kómmə dayting/ *adj.* willing to adjust actions in response to the needs of others —**accommodatingly** *adv.*

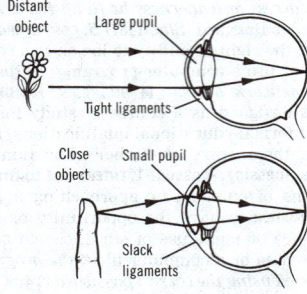

Accommodation: Adjustment of eye focus on distant object (top) and close object (bottom)

accommodation /ə kómmə dáysh'n/ *n.* **1.** LODGING a room or building to live in **2.** SEATING seating in a vehicle or public facility **3.** WORKSPACE a room or space to work in **4.** HELPFULNESS willingness to adjust actions in response to the needs of others **5.** HELPFUL GESTURE a modification of actions in response to the needs of others **6.** AGREEMENT an agreement acceptable to all parties in a dispute **7.** FLEXIBILITY the ability to include sth without major change **8.** ADJUSTMENT adaptation to a new situation **9.** OPHTHALMOL AD-

JUSTMENT OF EYE FOCUS the automatic adjustment of the focus of an eye to give clear vision **10.** COMM LOAN OF MONEY a loan of money, especially by a financial institution as a favour to sb before a formal credit arrangement is made

accommodation address *n.* a mailing address used by a person or organization unwilling or unable to use an identifiable individual address. US term **mail drop**

accommodation bill *n.* a bill of exchange cosigned by another party in order to give added security

accommodationist /ə kómmə dáysh'nist/ *n.* sb who prefers compromise to confrontation —**accommodationist** *adj.*

accommodation ladder *n.* a ladder or flight of stairs hung over a ship's side to allow boarding or disembarking

accommodation platform, **accommodation rig** *n.* a platform or rig used as living quarters for offshore oil or gas workers

accompaniment /ə kúmpənimənt, -pni-/ *n.* **1.** MUSIC MUSICAL BACKING instrumental or vocal parts in a musical composition that support the more important parts **2.** SIMULTANEOUS OCCURRENCE sth that occurs at the same time and in the same place as sth else **3.** SUPPLEMENT an item that is added or served because it goes well with sth

accompanist /ə kúmpənist, -pnist/ *n.* sb who plays the musical accompaniment for a soloist

accompany /ə kúmpəni, -pni/ (**-nies, -nying, -nied**) *v.* **1.** *vt.* ESCORT SB to go with sb **2.** *vt.* BE PRESENT WITH STH to be enclosed, attached, or present with sth **3.** *vt.* OCCUR WITH STH to happen at the same time as sth else **4.** *vt.* SUPPLEMENT STH to be present or served with sth as a supplement **5.** *vti.* MUSIC PROVIDE MUSICAL BACKING to play or sing a part that supports a more important part [15thC. From Old French *acompaignier*, literally 'to be a companion to', from *compaing* 'companion' (see COMPANION).]

accomplice /ə kúmpliss, ə kóm-/ *n.* sb who knowingly helps sb to commit a crime or misdeed [Mid-16thC. Alteration of archaic *complice* (by misunderstanding of *a complice*), via French, from Latin *complic-*, the stem of *complex* 'associate', literally 'folded with', from *complicare* (see COMPLICATE).]

accomplish /ə kúmplish, ə kóm-/ (**-plishes, -plishing, -plished**) *vt.* **1.** ACHIEVE STH to succeed in doing or achieving sth **2.** REACH POINT IN TIME to arrive at the end of a period of time (*literary*) (*usually passive*) [14thC. From Old French *acompliss-*, a stem of *acomplir*, literally 'to complete to', ultimately from Latin *complere* (see COMPLETE).] —**accomplishable** *adj.* —**accomplisher** *n.*

— **WORD KEY: SYNONYMS** —

accomplish, achieve, attain, realize, pull off
CORE MEANING: to bring sth to a successful conclusion
accomplish the most general term and wide-ranging term for performing sth successfully; **achieve** to accomplish sth by overcoming some difficulty or exerting a particular effort, usually over a period of time; **attain** to be successful in reaching a specific objective; **realize** to fulfil a specific vision or plan, particularly in relation to sth material or financial or other gain; **pull off** an informal term for accomplishing sth, especially against expectations or in extremely difficult circumstances.

accomplished /ə kúmplisht, ə kóm-/ *adj.* **1.** TALENTED having considerable talent and skill **2.** WITH SOCIAL GRACES possessing social skills and talents **3.** COMPLETE fully established

accomplishment /ə kúmplishmənt, ə kóm-/ *n.* **1.** ACHIEVING OF STH the completion or fulfilment of sth **2.** FEAT a remarkable or successful achievement **3.** TALENT a skill or talent that has been developed

accord /ə káwrd/ *v.* (**-cords, -cording, -corded**) **1.** *vt.* RENDER to give sb or sth a particular status or treatment **2.** *vi.* AGREE to be in agreement or come to an agreement **3.** *vt.* GRANT STH to bestow sth such as a blessing on sb ◼ *n.* **1.** AGREEMENT a treaty or settlement agreed by two or more parties **2.** CONSENSUS general agreement as to what is right **3.** HARMONY a state in which things are in harmony with each other [Pre-12thC. From Old French *acorder*, ultimately from Latin *ad* 'to' + *cord-*, the stem of *cor* 'heart' (source of English *cordial* and *quarry*).] ◇ **of your own accord** of your own free will ◇ **with one accord** together and with everyone agreeing (*formal*)

accordance /ə káwrd'nss/ *n.* **1.** CONSENSUS consensus as to the right course of action **2.** ADHERENCE TO CORRECT PROCESS conformity with specified procedures or actions **3.** BESTOWAL the bestowal of a particular status or treatment on sb or sth

accordant /ə káwrd'nt/ *adj.* in general harmony or agreement (*formal*) —**accordantly** *adv.*

according as *conj.* depending on whether, or corresponding to the extent to which

accordingly /ə káwrdingli/ *adv.* **1.** CORRESPONDINGLY in a way that is appropriate **2.** IN CONSEQUENCE in accordance with what has been said or with a principle or practice

accordion /ə káwrdi ən/ *n.* a musical instrument with a keyboard or buttons on one side, buttons on the other, and a middle section that is expanded and contracted to force air past metal reeds [Mid-19thC. From German *Akkordion*, from *Akkord* 'chord', from Italian *accordare* 'to tune (an instrument)'.]

accordion pleats *npl.* sharp pleats in a garment or piece of fabric, resembling the folds in the bellows of an accordion

accost /ə kóst/ (**-costs, -costing, -costed**) *vt.* to approach and stop sb in order to speak, especially in an aggressive, insistent, or suggestive way [Late 16thC. Via French from, ultimately, Latin *accostare* 'to adjoin', from *costa* 'rib, side' (source of English *coast*). The underlying sense is 'to be alongside'.]

accoucheur /ákoo shúr/ *n.* a male midwife or obstetrician (*archaic*) [Mid-18thC. From French, formed from *accoucher*, from *coucher* 'to lay down' (source of English *couch*).]

account /ə kównt/ *n.* **1.** REPORT a written or verbal report of sth **2.** EXPLANATION an explanation of sth that has happened, especially one given to sb in authority **3.** BANKING BANK ARRANGEMENT an arrangement in which a customer keeps money in a bank or building society and is offered certain services in exchange **4.** BANKING MONEY IN BANK the money that a customer keeps in a bank **5.** FIN FINANCIAL ARRANGEMENT an arrangement with a store, company, stockbroker, or other business, which provides certain financial services, e.g. credit **6.** RECORD OF FINANCES a regular printed statement of financial transactions conducted through an account **7.** STOCK EXCH PERIOD OF TRANSACTION the period during which transactions are made, usually lasting two weeks, and at the end of which settlements are made **8.** *US, Can* BUSINESS CUSTOMER a customer who has a regular business relationship with a company **9.** BUSINESS BUSINESS ON SB'S BEHALF an area of business handled by a company on behalf of another, e.g. advertising, design, or publicity **10.** IMPORTANCE importance, relevance, or value (*used mostly in negative constructions*) ■ **accounts** *npl.* ACCT LIST OF FINANCIAL INFORMATION a detailed list of everything that a company or individual earns or spends, kept primarily for tax purposes ■ *vt.* (**-counts, -counting, -counted**) CONSIDER to consider sth, sb, or yourself to have a specified quality (*dated*) [14thC. From Old French *aconte* 'a counting up', from *aconter*, from, ultimately, Latin *computare* 'to sum up' (source of English *computer*).] ◇ **by all accounts** according to what most people say ◇ **call sb to account** to demand that sb explains what he or she has done ◇ **give a good account of yourself** to do sth well, especially sth difficult ◇ **of no account** of no importance ◇ **on account** on credit ◇ **on account of** because of ◇ **on no account** for no reason, whatever the circumstances ◇ **on sb's account** out of concern for sb's well-being ◇ **take account of sth, take sth into account** to consider sth when making a decision ◇ **turn sth to good account** to use or deal with sth in a way that puts it to good use

account for *vt.* **1.** EXPLAIN to provide an explanation for sth ○ *And how do you account for the hole in the wall?* **2.** BE RESPONSIBLE FOR to be responsible for sth or be an important factor in sth ○ *Export sales account for at least half of our total business.* **3.** KILL OR DESTROY to be responsible for killing, destroying, or neutralizing sb or sth

accountable /ə kówntəb'l/ *adj.* **1.** RESPONSIBLE responsible to sb else or to others, or responsible for sth **2.** ABLE TO BE EXPLAINED capable of being explained (*formal*) —**accountability** /ə kówntə bílləti/ *n.* —**accountableness** /-b'lnəss/ *n.* —**accountably** /-bli/ *adv.*

accountancy /ə kówntənssi/ *n.* the work or profession of an accountant

accountant /ə kówntənt/ *n.* sb who is responsible for maintaining and checking the business records of an individual or organization and preparing reports for tax or other financial purposes

account day *n.* the day on which payments and deliveries that have been agreed on during the preceding two-week period are made

account executive *n.* sb employed by a company, especially in advertising or public relations, to handle all of the business of an individual client

accounting /ə kównting/ *n.* the activity, practice, or profession of maintaining and checking the business records of an individual or organization and preparing reports for tax or other financial purposes

accounts payable *npl. US, Can* a record that shows how much a firm owes suppliers for the purchase of supplies or services on credit

accounts receivable *npl. US, Can* a record that shows how much is owed to a company by customers who have purchased supplies or services on credit

accouter *vt.* US = **accoutre**

accouterment *n.* US = **accoutrement**

accoutre /ə kóotər/ (**-tres, -tring, -tred**) *vt.* to equip and clothe sb, especially for military purposes [Mid-16thC. Via French *accoutrer* 'to equip with sth, especially clothes', from, ultimately, assumed Latin *consutura* 'sewn together', from *sutura* 'sewn' (source of English *suture*).]

accoutrement /ə kóotrəmənt/ *n.* **1.** ACCESSORY an accessory or piece of equipment associated with a particular object, task, or role **2.** PIECE OF MILITARY EQUIPMENT a piece of military equipment carried by soldiers in addition to their standard uniform and weapons

Accra /ákrə/ capital of Ghana. It is located on the Gulf of Guinea in southeastern Ghana. Population: 953,500 (1990).

accredit /ə kréddit/ (**-its, -iting, -ited**) *vt.* **1.** GIVE OFFICIAL RECOGNITION TO SB officially to recognize a person or organization as having met a standard or criterion (*usually passive*) **2.** GIVE AUTHORITY to give sb the authority to perform a function (*usually passive*) **3.** APPOINT AS ENVOY to appoint sb as an envoy or ambassador representing his or her government or country **4.** *NZ* PASS FOR UNIVERSITY ENTRANCE to pass a student for entrance to university without having to sit an external examination [Early 17thC. From French *accréditer* 'to believe (firmly)', from *crédit* (see CREDIT).] —**accreditation** /ə kréddi táysh'n/ *n.*

accrete /ə kréet/ (**-cretes, -creting, -creted**) *vti.* to become bigger, or make sth become bigger, especially by adding to what is there or by two or more things growing together [Late 18thC. From Latin *accret-*, the past participle stem of *accrescere* from *crescere* 'to grow'.]

accretion /ə kréesh'n/ *n.* **1.** INCREASE an increase in size or amount as a result of sth accumulating or being added gradually, or sth accumulated in this way **2.** LAW ADDITION sth added to sth else, e.g. a fund or account, from an external source **3.** ASTRON ATTRACTION OF MATTER BY GRAVITY a process in which matter revolving around an astronomical object is gradually pulled in and added to the body's mass **4.** GEOL INCREASE IN LAND MASS a process by which a body of rock or a land mass increases in size as a result of material accumulating on or around it **5.** GEOL INCREASE IN SIZE OF CONTINENTS a process by which the size of a continent increases as a result of the moving together and deforming of tectonic plates —**accretionary** *adj.*

accrual /ə króo əl/ *n.* **1.** STH ACCRUED sth that has accrued **2.** PROCESS OF ACCRUING the process of accruing or of being accrued

accrual method *n.* a method of accounting that counts income or expenses at the time they are earned or incurred, irrespective of when money is received or paid out. ◊ **cash method**

accrue /ə króo/ (**-crues, -cruing, -crued**) *v.* **1.** *vi.* COME INTO SB'S POSSESSION to come into sb's possession, often over a period of time **2.** *vi.* INCREASE to increase in amount or value **3.** *vt.* GATHER TOGETHER to gather together an amount, especially over a period of time **4.** *vi.* LAW BECOME ENFORCEABLE to become legally enforceable (*refers to claims or rights*) [15thC. Via Anglo-Norman from, ultimately, Latin *accrescent-* (see ACCRETE).] —**accruement** *n.*

acct *abbr.* account

acculturate /ə kúlchə rayt/ (**-ates, -ating, -ated**) *v.* **1.** *vi.* TAKE ON OTHER CULTURE to absorb and assimilate the culture of another group of people or another individual **2.** *vt.* CHANGE CULTURE OF SB to change sb's cultural behaviour and thinking through contact with another culture [Mid-20thC. Back-formation from ACCULTURATION.] —**acculturative** *adj.*

acculturation /ə kúlchə ráysh'n/ *n.* **1.** CULTURAL CHANGE a change in the cultural behaviour and thinking of an individual or group through contact with another culture **2.** ABSORPTION OF CULTURE the process by which sb absorbs the culture of a society from birth onwards [Late 19thC. Coined from AC- + CULTURE + -ATION.] —**acculturational** *adj.*

accumulate /ə kyóomyoo layt/ (**-lates, -lating, -lated**) *vti.* to gather sth together or collect sth, or gather together or collect, over a period of time [15thC. From Latin *accumulat-*, the past participle stem of *accumulare* 'to heap up in addition', from *cumulus* 'heap'.] —**accumulable** /ə kyóomyooləb'l/ *adj.*

WORD KEY: SYNONYMS

See Synonyms at ***collect***.

accumulation /ə kyóomyoo láysh'n/ *n.* **1.** PROCESS OF GATHERING the process of gathering together and increasing in amount over a period of time **2.** COLLECTION OF THINGS a number of things that have collected or been collected over a period of time **3.** FIN GROWTH THROUGH INTEREST the growth of a sum by the addition of earned interest

accumulative /ə kyóomyoolətiv/ *adj.* **1.** TENDING TO ACCUMULATE tending to gather or collect things **2.** GROWING BY ADDITIONS growing by gradual additions —**accumulatively** *adv.* —**accumulativeness** *n.*

accumulator /ə kyóomyoo laytər/ *n.* **1.** BATTERY a rechargeable battery consisting of one or more cells for producing electrical energy from stored chemical energy. US term **storage battery 2.** COMPUT MEMORY FOR SHORT-TERM STORAGE a section of memory in a computer or calculator in which the results of a calculation are temporarily held **3.** BET ON SEVERAL RACES a bet made on a chosen number of horse races, with the stake and winnings from one race being automatically bet on the next

accuracy /ákyoorəssi/ *n.* **1.** CORRECTNESS the correctness or truthfulness of sth **2.** ABILITY TO AVOID ERRORS the ability to be precise and avoid errors

accurate /ákyoorət/ *adj.* **1.** CORRECT giving a correct or truthful representation of sth ○ *Their account of the incident was not entirely accurate.* **2.** FREE FROM ERRORS precise or free from errors ○ *an accurate typist* **3.** PROVIDING INFORMATION TO ACCEPTED STANDARD providing correct information in accordance with an accepted standard [Late 16thC. Via Latin *accuratus* 'done with care', from, ultimately, *cura* 'care' (source of English *curious*, *procure*, and *secure*).] —**accurately** *adv.* —**accurateness** *n.*

accursed /ə kúrssid, ə kúrst/, **accurst** /ə kúrst/ *adj.* (*archaic or literary*) **1.** DOOMED enduring the effects of a curse **2.** HORRIBLE horrible or hateful [12thC. Formed from *a-* 'on' (from Old English *ar-*) + CURSE.] —**accursedly** /ə kúrssidli/ *adv.* —**accursedness** /ə kúrssidnəss/ *n.*

accus. *abbr.* accusative

accusation /ákyoo záysh'n/ *n.* **1.** ALLEGATION a claim that sb has done sth illegal, wrong, or undesirable **2.** ACT OF ACCUSING the accusing of sb, or the state of having been accused of sth

accusative /ə kyóozətiv/ *n.* **1.** GRAMMATICAL CASE a grammatical case that identifies the direct object of a verb or certain other grammatical parts in some inflected languages and that affects nouns, pronouns, and adjectives **2. WORD OR PHRASE IN ACCUSATIVE** a word or phrase in the accusative ■ *adj*. **IN ACCUSATIVE** in or relating to the accusative [15thC. From Latin *accusativus*, from *accusare* (see ACCUSE). The grammatical meaning comes from a mistranslation of Greek *ptōsis aitiātikē* 'case denoting causation', as 'case denoting the accused'.] —**accusatively** *adv*.

accusatorial /ə kyoōzə táwri əl/, **accusatory** /-təri, ákyoō záytəri/ *adj*. **1. CLAIMING WRONGDOING** containing or suggesting a claim that sb has done sth wrong (*formal*) **2. LAW RELYING ON PROOF PROVIDED BY PROSECUTOR** used to describe a legal system in which the prosecution is required to provide proof beyond reasonable doubt against an accused person, with the evidence being assessed by an impartial judge and jury. ◊ **inquisitorial** —**accusatorially** *adv*.

accuse /ə kyoōz/ (-**cuses**, -**cusing**, -**cused**) *v*. **1.** *vti*. **CONFRONT AND BLAME** to confront sb with a charge of having done sth illegal, wrong, or undesirable **2.** *vt*. **LAW CHARGE** to charge sb formally with having committed a crime (*often passive*) [14thC. Via French, from Latin *accusare* 'to call sb to account', from *ad causa* 'to the (legal) case'. The underlying idea is to take sb to court.] —**accuser** *n*.

accused /ə kyoōzd/ *n*. the person or people being charged in a criminal case

accusing /ə kyoōzing/ *adj*. containing or suggesting a claim that sb has done sth wrong —**accusingly** *adv*.

accustom /ə kústəm/ (-**toms**, -**toming**, -**tomed**) *vt*. to make yourself or sb else become used to sth through frequent or prolonged contact or use [15thC. From Anglo-Norman *acustomer*, from *custume* 'habit' (see CUSTOM).]

accustomed /ə kústəmd/ *adj*. **1. USED TO STH** used to or familiar with sth **2. HABITUAL** habitual or usual

AC/DC *adj*. **1. ELEC POWERED BY BATTERY OR MAINS** able to be powered by battery or by connection to the mains. Full form **alternating current/direct current 2. BISEXUAL** bisexual (*slang offensive*) (*often used disapprovingly*)

ace /ayss/ *n*. **1. CARDS PLAYING CARD** a playing card that has a single mark on it, or the single mark itself **2. SINGLE-SPOTTED SIDE** a single-spotted side of a dice or domino, or the single spot itself **3. TENNIS WINNING SERVE** a serve that an opponent cannot reach **4. GOLF HOLE IN ONE** the hitting of a golf ball into a hole in one stroke, or a hole at which only one stroke was taken **5. AIR FORCE FIGHTER PILOT** a top fighter pilot, especially one who has shot down a number of enemy aircraft **6. SB WITH AN EXCEPTIONAL SKILL** sb who is outstandingly good at a particular activity, e.g. a sport (*informal*) **7. BEST FRIEND** sb who is a best friend (*slang*) ■ *vt*. (**aces**, **acing**, **aced**) **TENNIS BEAT WITH SERVE** to beat an opponent by serving an ace ■ *adj*. **EXCELLENT** excellent (*informal*) [14thC. Via French *as* from Latin, 'unit, unity'. Originally the lowest score, one, in dice; its connotations of 'excellence' come from the powerful status of the ace in cards.] ◇ **hold all the aces** to have all the advantages (*informal*) ◇ **within an ace of** very close to ◇ **have an ace up your sleeve** to have a concealed advantage

ACE[1] /ayss/ *n*. an enzyme causing high blood pressure. Its action can be controlled by drugs as a treatment for heart disease. [Late-20thC. Acronym of angiotensin-converting enzyme.]

ACE[2] *abbr*. **1.** Allied Command Europe **2.** Advisory Centre for Education

-acean *suffix*. = -aceous

ACE inhibitor *n*. a drug that counters the effects of an enzyme that causes high blood pressure

acentric /ay séntrik/ *adj*. **1. LACKING CENTRE** without a centre **2. WITHOUT CENTROMERE** used to describe a chromosome that lacks the structure at which the two arms of a chromosome join (**centromere**). ◊ **acrocentric, metacentric, telocentric**

-aceous, **-acean** *suffix*. resembling or related to ◇ *herbaceous* [Formed from modern Latin -*aceus*, from Latin]

acephalous /ay séffaləss/ *adj*. used to describe an animal that has no head [Mid-18thC. Via medieval Latin, from Greek *akephalos* 'without a head', from *kephalē* 'head' (see CEPHAL-).]

acer /áyssər/ *n*. a Eurasian and North American tree or shrub grown as an ornamental for its foliage. Genus: *Acer*.

acerbate /ássər bayt/ (-**bates**, -**bating**, -**bated**) *vt*. (*formal*) **1. ANNOY SB** to annoy or irritate sb **2. MAKE STH BITTER** to make sth taste bitter [Mid-18thC. From Latin *acerbat-*, the past participle stem of *acerbare* 'to make harsh', from *acerbus* (see ACERBIC).]

acerbic /ə sérbik/, **acerb** /ə sérb/ *adj*. bitter or sharp in tone, taste, or manner [Mid-19thC. Formed from Latin *acerbus* 'harsh', from, ultimately, an Indo-European word that is also the ancestor of English *acid*, *acne*, and *oxygen*.] —**acerbically** *adv*. —**acerbity** *n*.

acet- *prefix*. = **aceto-** (*used before vowels*)

acetabulum /ássi tábbyoōləm/ (*plural* -**la** /-lə/) *n*. **1. ANAT CAVITY ON HIPBONE** the curved cavity on the side of the hipbone where the end of the thighbone fits **2. ZOOL ROUND SUCKER** a round cup-shaped sucker found on flatworms, leeches, and molluscs such as the octopus [14thC. From Latin, literally 'a vinegar cup' but also used to mean 'a cup-shaped cavity', formed from *acetum* 'vinegar' (see ACETIC).] —**acetabular** *adj*.

acetal /ássi tal/ *n*. **1. COLOURLESS CHEMICAL SOLVENT** a colourless volatile liquid used in perfumes and as a solvent. Formula: $C_6H_{14}O_2$. **2. ORGANIC COMPOUND** an organic compound similar to acetal that contains a particular chemical group. Formula: $-CH(OR_1)OR_2$.

acetaldehyde /ássi táldi hīd/ *n*. a colourless volatile liquid with a distinctive smell, used in the manufacture of other chemicals, especially acetic acid, acetic anhydride, and butanol. Formula: C_2H_4O.

acetamide /ə séttə mīd, ássi tá-/ *n*. a white crystalline solid that absorbs water readily and is used in the manufacture of other chemicals. Formula: CH_3CONH_2.

acetaminophen /ə seétə mínnəfən, ássitə-/ *n*. US = **paracetamol**

acetanilide /ássi tánni līd/ *n*. a white crystalline compound used to relieve pain and reduce fever, and in manufacturing other chemicals, dyes, and rubber. Formula: C_8H_9NO. [Mid-19thC. Coined from ACETYL + ANILINE + -IDE.]

acetate /ássi tayt/ *n*. **1. DERIVATIVE OF ACETIC ACID** a salt or ester of acetic acid **2.** = **cellulose acetate 3. PRODUCT CONTAINING ACETATE** a product made of or containing acetate

acetic /ə seétik/ *adj*. containing, producing, or made from vinegar or acetic acid [Late 18thC. From French *acétique*, from Latin *acetum* 'vinegar'. Ultimately from the same Indo-European ancestor as English *acute*, *acrid*, and *acid*.]

acetic acid *n*. a colourless acid with a pungent odour that is the main component of vinegar and is used in manufacturing drugs, dyes, plastics, fibres, and other products. Formula: CH_3COOH. ◊ **glacial acetic acid**

acetic anhydride *n*. a colourless liquid with a pungent odour, used in the manufacture of aspirin and plastics

acetify /ə sétti fī/ (-**fies**, -**fying**, -**fied**) *vti*. to turn into, or cause sth to turn into, acetic acid or vinegar — **acetification** /ə séttifi káysh'n/ *n*. —**acetifier** /ə sétti fī ər/ *n*.

aceto-, **acet-** *prefix*. acetic acid ◇ *acetify* [From Latin *acetum* 'vinegar' (see ACETUM).]

acetone /ássitōn/ *n*. a colourless flammable liquid with a pleasant smell, widely used as a solvent for paints and nail polish, and in manufacturing chemicals. Formula: C_3H_6O.

acetone body *n*. = **ketone body**

acetophenetidin /ə seétō fə néttidin, ássitō-/ *n*. = **phenacetin**

acetous /ássitəss, ə seé-/ *adj*. like, containing, or producing acetic acid or vinegar [14thC. From late Latin *acetosus*, from Latin *acetum* 'vinegar' (see ACETIC).]

acetyl /ássi tīl, ə seé-/ *n*. relating to or containing the chemical group derived from acetic acid. Formula: CH_3CO-. —**acetylic** /ássi tíllik/ *adj*.

acetylate /ə sétti layt/ (-**lates**, -**lating**, -**lated**) *vt*. to introduce the acetyl group into a compound — **acetylation** /ə sétti láysh'n/ *n*.

acetylcholine /ássi tīl kṓ leen/ *n*. a white crystalline compound released from the ends of nerve fibres and involved in the transmission of nerve impulses. Formula: $C_7H_{17}NO_3$.

acetylcholinesterase /ássi tīl kōlin éstə rayz/ *n*. an enzyme, present in blood and some nerve endings, that aids the breakdown of acetylcholine and suppresses its stimulatory effect on nerves

acetyl coenzyme A, **acetyl CoA** *n*. a coenzyme derived from fatty acids, carbohydrates, and amino acids during metabolism

acetylene /ə sétti leen/ *n*. a colourless gaseous flammable hydrocarbon used in welding and in manufacturing chemicals. Formula: C_2H_2. —**acetylenic** /ə sétti lénnik/ *adj*.

acetylide /ə sétti līd/ *n*. any chemical compound derived from acetylene and containing a metal atom. Many of these compounds are very explosive.

acetylsalicylic acid /ássi tīl sálli síllik-/ *n*. the drug aspirin (*technical*)

acey-deucy /áyssi dyoóssi/ *n*. a version of backgammon in which a dice throw of one or two wins an additional turn [Formed from ACE and DEUCE]

ACGI *abbr*. Associate of the City and Guilds Institute

ach /aakh/ *interj*. *Scotland* used to express emotion, e.g. annoyance, surprise, or resignation, often as an introduction to saying sth [15thC. From Celtic.]

Achaea /ə keé ə/, **Achaia** /ə kī ə, ə káy ə/ *n*. **1. MODERN GREEK DEPARTMENT** an administrative department in modern Greece **2. ANCIENT GREEK PROVINCE** in ancient Greece, a province in the northern Peloponnese

Achaean /ə keé ən, ə káy ən/, **Achaian** *n*. **1. MEMBER OF ANCIENT HELLENIC PEOPLE** a member of an ancient Hellenic people thought to have founded the Mycenean civilization on the Peloponnese **2. SB FROM ACHAEA** sb who lives in or was born in the modern Greek department of Achaea —**Achaean** *adj*.

achalasia /ákə láyzi ə/ *n*. a failure of certain smooth muscle bands, e.g. in the gullet, to relax [Early 20thC. Coined from A- + Greek *khalasis* 'relaxation', from *khalan* 'to loosen'.]

achar /ə chaár/ *n*. a pungent pickle made of mango, lemon, and ginger, used in Indian cooking

acharya /ə chaári ə/ *n*. *S Asia* a learned religious teacher and guide

ache /ayk/ *vi*. (**aches**, **aching**, **ached**) **1. FEEL PAIN** to feel or be the site of a dull constant pain **2. YEARN** to yearn for the presence of sb or sth **3. WANT BADLY** to want sth very much (*informal*) ○ *aching to tell her the news* ■ *n*. **CONSTANT PAIN** a feeling of constant dull pain [Old English *æce* (noun), *acan* (verb), of uncertain origin: perhaps ultimately from an Indo-European word meaning 'fault'. The *ch* spelling arose from a mistaken association with Greek *akhos* 'pain'.]

—————— **WORD KEY: SYNONYMS** ——————

See Synonyms at *pain*.

Achebe /ə cháybi/, **Chinua** (*b*. 1930) Nigerian novelist. He is the author of *Things Fall Apart* (1958) and *Anthills of the Savannah* (1987).

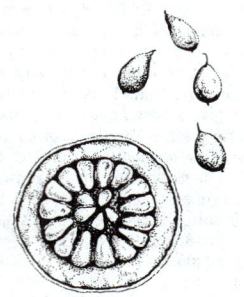

Achene: Cross-section of the fruit of the dog rose

achene /ə keén/, **akene** *n*. a dry single-seeded fruit that does not open to release its seed. Dandelions and sunflowers have achenes. [Mid-19thC. From modern Latin *achaenium*, literally 'not gaping', from Greek *khainein* 'to gape'.]

Acheron /ákərōn/ *n.* in Greek mythology, one of the rivers that ran through Hades

Acheson /áchəss'n/, **Dean** (1893–1971) US lawyer and statesman who was prominent in the development of the Truman Doctrine, the Marshall Plan, and NATO.

Acheulian /ə shōóli ən/ *n.* a period of the Palaeolithic era during which people made symmetrical stone hand axes [Early 20thC. Named after the French village of Saint-Acheul near Amiens in Picardy, where a large number of distinctive tools were found in the 19thC.] —**Acheulian** *adj.*

à cheval /áshə vál/ *adv.* used to describe a bet made on two adjacent numbers, e.g. in roulette or cards [From French, literally 'on horseback', used to mean 'with one foot on either side, astride'. Its use in betting comes from the risk being shared equally between two cards.]

achieve /ə chéev/ *vt.* (**achieves, achieving, achieved**) *vt.* to succeed in doing or gaining sth, usually with effort [14thC. From French *achever* 'to bring to an end, bring to a head', from *a chief*, literally 'to a head' (see CHIEF).] —**achievable** *adj.*

─── **WORD KEY: SYNONYMS** ───

See Synonyms at *accomplish*.

achieved /ə chéevd/ *adj. US* showing great skill or accomplishment

achievement /ə chéevmənt/ *n.* **1.** SUCCESS sth that sb has succeeded in doing, usually with effort **2.** FINISHING WELL the act or process of finishing sth successfully **3.** HERALDRY FULL COAT OF ARMS a full coat of arms that includes standing figures such as lions or unicorns (**supporters**), the family symbol (**crest**), and the family motto

achievement age *n.* the age at which a child should be able to perform a particular task successfully

achiever /ə chéevər/ *n.* **1.** SUCCESSFUL PERSON sb who is successful and motivated to go on being successful **2.** SB WHO DOES STH SUCCESSFULLY sb who succeeds in doing or gaining a particular thing

Achilles /ə kílleez/ *n.* in Greek mythology, the principal hero of the Trojan War, made invulnerable by being dipped in the river Styx as a baby by his mother, except for the heel she held him by. He killed the Trojan hero Hector before being fatally wounded in the heel with an arrow fired by Paris.

Achilles heel *n.* a weakness that seems small but makes sb fatally vulnerable

Achilles tendon *n.* the tendon that connects the heelbone to the calf muscles

achiral /ay kírəl/ *adj.* used to describe a molecule that does not have either left-handed or right-handed configuration (**chirality**)

achlorhydria /áy klaw hǐdri ə/ *n.* an absence of or reduction in hydrochloric acid in the gastric juice —**achlorhydric** *adj.*

achondrite /ay kón drīt/ *n.* a stony meteorite that does not contain rounded grains (**chondrules**) —**achondritic** /áy kon dríttik/ *adj.*

achondroplasia /áy kondrō pláyzi ə/ *n.* a genetic disorder in which cartilage fails to develop into bone at the early stages of development, resulting in dwarfism [Late 19thC. Coined from Greek *akhondros* 'without cartilage' + -PLASIA.] —**achondroplastic** /-plástik/ *adj.*

achromat /ákrə mat/ *n.* **1.** PHYS = **achromatic lens 2.** OPHTHALMOL = **monochromat** [Early 20thC. Back-formation from ACHROMATIC.]

achromatic /áykrō máttik/ *adj.* **1.** WITHOUT COLOUR without colour and therefore white, grey, or black in appearance **2.** PHYS WITHOUT SPECTRUM COLOURS able to reflect or refract light without spectral colour separation **3.** BIOL NOT EASILY STAINED used to describe cells not easily stained with standard dyes **4.** MUSIC WITHOUT SHARPS OR FLATS using a scale with no sharps or flats —**achromatically** *adv.* —**achromaticity** /áykrōmə tíssəti/ *n.* —**achromatism** /ə krómətízzəm/ *n.*

achromatic colour *n.* a colour with no hue or chromatic component

achromatic lens *n.* a composite lens in which two or more lenses with different properties are combined to prevent distortion (**chromatic aberration**)

achy /áyki/ (**-ier, -iest**) *adj.* feeling or being the site of a constant dull pain —**achiness** *n.*

acicula /ə síkyōólə/ (*plural* **-lae** /-lee/) *n.* a needle-shaped part, e.g. a spine, bristle, or crystal (*technical*) [Mid-19thC. From late Latin, literally 'little needle'.] —**aciculate** /ə síkyōó layt/ *adj.* —**aciculated** *adj.*

acid /ássid/ *n.* **1.** CHEM SOUR-TASTING SUBSTANCE a compound, usually water-soluble, that releases hydrogen ions when in solution. An acid reacts with a base to form a salt, has a pH less than 7, and turns blue litmus red. Acids are corrosive and have a sour taste. ◊ **alkali 2.** DRUGS = **LSD** (*slang*) **3.** SHARPNESS a sharp, bitter, or sarcastic quality in speech or writing ■ *adj.* **1.** RELATING TO AN ACID with the properties of or containing an acid **2.** SOUR-TASTING having a sour or sharp taste **3.** SHARP sharp, bitter, or sarcastic **4.** METEOROL POLLUTED used to describe rain or snow that contains dilute acid resulting from pollution **5.** GEOL HIGH IN SILICA used to describe igneous rocks that have a high silica content [Late 17thC. Directly or via French, from Latin *acidus*, from *acere* 'to be sour'.] —**acidly** *adv.*

─── **WORD KEY: ORIGIN** ───

The Indo-European word from which *acid* comes is also the ancestor of English *acacia, acme, acne, acrid, acrobat, acute, alacrity, eager, edge, oxygen,* and *vinegar.*

acid deposition *n.* a deposit of water vapour formed in the atmosphere, e.g. dew, rain, snow, hail or fog, that is high in acid content because of atmospheric pollution

acid drop *n.* a boiled sweet that has a sharp lemony taste

acid dye *n.* a dye created from an acidic solution

acidhead /ássid hed/ *n.* sb who takes the illegal drug LSD regularly (*slang*)

acid house *n.* a type of electronic dance music popular in the late 1980s, using hypnotic pulsating rhythms and associated with the use of the drug ecstasy

acidic /ə síddik/ *adj.* **1.** SOUR-TASTING sour or bitter in taste **2.** SARCASTIC sour, bitter, or sarcastic in manner or tone **3.** CHEM FORMING ACID IN WATER forming an acid in water

acidification /ə síddifi káysh'n/ *n.* the process of becoming acid, e.g. when soil or water is polluted by acid rain [Late 18thC]

acidify /ə síddi fī/ (**-fies, -fying, -fied**) *vti.* to turn sth acid, or become acid —**acidifiable** *adj.* —**acidifier** *n.*

acidimeter /ássi dímmitər/ *n.* an instrument for measuring the amount of acid in a solution —**acidimetric** /ássidi méttrik/ *adj.* —**acidimetry** /ássi dímmətri/ *n.*

acidity /ə síddəti/ (*plural* **-ties**) *n.* **1.** EXTENT TO WHICH STH IS ACID the concentration of an acid in a substance, often measured in terms of pH **2.** = **hyperacidity 3.** BEING ACID the quality or condition of being acid

acid jazz *n.* a mixture of funk, jazz, and soul music that first appeared in the 1980s

acidophil /ássi dōfil, ə síddōfil/, **acidophile** /ássi dō fīl, ə síddōfīl/ *n.* **1.** ACID-LOVING ORGANISM a microorganism or plant that flourishes in an acid environment **2.** BIOL CELL TAKING UP ACIDIC DYE a cell that stains readily with acidic dyes

acidophilic /ássidō fíllik/ *adj.* **1.** BIOL EASILY STAINED BY ACID DYE used to describe cells that are easily stained by an acid dye **2.** MICROBIOL, BOT FLOURISHING IN ACID ENVIRONMENT used to describe microorganisms or plants that flourish in an acid environment

acidophilus milk /ássi dóffiləss-/ *n.* milk fermented using bacterial cultures, used to treat digestive disorders

acid protease *n.* a protein-digesting enzyme that has maximum activity in the acid environment of the stomach

Acid rain: Detail of tree in Norway damaged by acid rain

acid rain *n.* rain that contains dilute acid derived from burning fossil fuels and that is potentially harmful to the environment

acid rock *n.* a type of electric rock music popular in the late 1960s, with instrumental effects and lyrics suggesting or promoting psychedelic experiences

acid test *n.* a decisive test that establishes the worth or credibility of sth [From the use of nitric acid to test gold]

─── **WORD KEY: USAGE** ───

An *acid test* is one that is definitive or conclusive: *The treatment accorded Russia by her sister nations in the months to come will be the acid test of their good will.* It was a vogue word of the 1920s, having been famously used by Woodrow Wilson, 28th President of the United States.

acidulate /ə síddyōó layt/ (**-lates, -lating, -lated**) *vti.* to make sth slightly acid, or become slightly acid —**acidulation** /ə síddyōó láysh'n/ *n.*

acidulous /ə síddyōóləss/ *adj.* **1.** SOUR-TASTING slightly sour in taste (*formal*) **2.** CUTTING cutting and sharp in speech or tone [Mid-18thC. Formed from Latin *acidulus*, from *acidus* (see ACID).]

acid-washed *adj. US* treated with chlorine acid to make the fabric look worn and washed-out and feel softer

ACII *abbr.* Associate of the Chartered Insurance Institute

acinus /ássinəss/ (*plural* **-ni** /ə seé nī/) *n.* **1.** SMALL GLANDULAR SAC a rounded sac, containing secretory cells, found at the ends of the ducts in an exocrine gland **2.** ANAT = **alveolus 3.** PART OF BLACKBERRY one of the small globes (**drupelets**) that make up an aggregate fruit such as a blackberry or raspberry [Mid-18thC. From Latin, 'berry growing in a cluster, kernel'.] —**acinar** *adj.* —**acinous** *adj.*

ack. *abbr.* acknowledge

ack-ack /ák ak/ *n.* (*informal*) **1.** ANTIAIRCRAFT GUN an antiaircraft gun **2.** ANTIAIRCRAFT FIRE antiaircraft fire [In military jargon ANTIAIRCRAFT was abbreviated to 'AA', which became 'ack-ack' from the use of 'ack' for the letter 'a' when spelling out messages]

ackee /ákee/ *n.* = **akee**

─── **WORD KEY: REGIONAL NOTE** ───

Ackee, used especially in the phrase ackee rice, has been introduced into British English by the Caribbean community. The flesh of the fruit is often eaten with rice and saltfish.

Ackerman steering /ákərmən-/ *n.* the steering system used in most motor vehicles, in which the wheels swivel at each end of the axle, instead of the whole axle beam swivelling at its central point

acknowledge /ək nóllij/ (**-edges, -edging, -edged**) *v.* **1.** *vti.* ADMIT STH to admit or accept that sth exists, is true, or is real **2.** *vti.* SHOW AWARENESS OF STH to respond to sth such as a greeting or message to show it has been noticed or received **3.** *vti.* SHOW APPRECIATION OF STH to show appreciation or express thanks for sth such as a letter or gift **4.** *vt.* RECOGNIZE STH LEGALLY to recognize or admit the existence, rights, or authority of sb or sth, especially in a legal context **5.** *vt.* THANK SB OFFICIALLY to give official or public recognition of the help sb has given or the work sb has done [15thC. Probably formed from KNOWLEDGE on the model of obsolete English *aknow* 'to recognize, acknowledge' (formed from KNOW).] —**acknowledgable** *adj.* —**acknowledger** *n.*

acknowledged /ək nóllijd/ *adj.* well-known or widely accepted as having a particular status

acknowledgment /ək nóllijmənt/, **acknowledgement** *n.* **1.** ACT OF ACKNOWLEDGING the act of acknowledging sth, or the condition of being acknowledged **2.** SIGN OF RECOGNITION a sign showing that sb has seen or heard sb else's greeting or presence **3.** INDICATION OF RECEIPT a letter or other message sent to say that sth has been received **4.** THANKS an expression of thanks or appreciation for sth **5.** OFFICIAL RECOGNITION official or public recognition of the help sb has given or the work sb has done ■ **acknowledgments** *npl.* AUTHOR'S THANKS a section at the beginning or end of a book or other piece of writing where an author thanks those who have helped

aclinic line /ay klínnik-/ *n.* = **magnetic equator** [*Aclinic* formed from Greek *aklinēs* 'not leaning', from *klinein* 'to lean']

ACLU *abbr.* American Civil Liberties Union

ACM *abbr.* air chief marshal

acme /ákmi/ *n.* the highest point of perfection or achievement [Late 16thC. From Greek *akmē*, literally 'highest point'. Ultimately from the same Indo-European ancestor that produced English *acid*, *edge*, and *oxygen*.]

acne /ákni/ *n.* a disease of the skin giving rise to blackheads and pimples on the face, neck, and shoulders. It often affects adolescents. [Mid-19thC. From Latin, a misreading of Greek *akmē* (see ACME).] —**acned** *adj.*

acoelomate /ə seélə mayt/ *n.* an organism such as a flatworm or jellyfish with no cavity (**coelom**) between its digestive tract and outer wall

acolyte /ákə līt/ *n.* **1.** RELIG ASSISTANT TO CLERIC sb, especially a young person, who assists a member of the clergy in the performance of rites **2.** ASSISTANT a follower or assistant ○ *the acolytes of this powerful leader* [14thC. Directly or via Old French, from ecclesiastical Latin *acolytus*, from Greek *akolouthos* 'follower', from *a-* 'together' + *keleuthos* 'path' (source of English *anacoluthon*).]

Aconcagua /ákən kágwə/ highest mountain in the Andes and in the western hemisphere, located in western Argentina near the Chilean border. Height: 6,960 m/22,834 ft.

aconite /ákə nīt/ *n.* **1.** PLANT WITH HOODED FLOWERS a plant with poisonous roots that grows in northern temperate regions and has purplish blue or white hooded flowers. Monkshood and wolfsbane are types of aconite. Genus: *Aconitum*. **2.** = **winter aconite 3.** EXTRACT OF PLANT ROOT an extract of the dried poisonous root of some aconite plants, used in the past as a drug [Mid-16thC. Directly or via French, from Latin *aconitum*, from Greek *akoniton*, of unknown origin.]

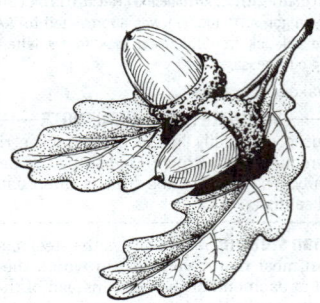

Acorn

acorn /áy kawrn/ *n.* the hard fruit of an oak tree, consisting of a smooth single-seeded nut that is set in a cup-shaped base and ripens from green to brown [Old English *æcern*, possibly formed from *æcer* 'open land' (source of English *acre*). The word was later interpreted as 'oak-corn', as if meaning 'fruit of the oak'.]

acorn barnacle *n.* a marine organism that attaches itself to rocks and catches food using tendrils that protrude from a hole in the top of its conical shell. Latin name: *Balanus balanoides*.

Acorn squash

acorn squash (*plural* **acorn squashes** *or* **acorn squash**) *n.* US an acorn-shaped winter squash with a ridged dark-green rind and yellow or orange flesh

acorn worm *n.* a small burrowing sea animal that looks like a worm and has an acorn-shaped snout that it uses to dig for food on the sea floor. Phylum: Chordata.

acouchi /ə koóshi/ (*plural* **-chis** *or* **-chies**), **acouchy** (*plural* **-chies**) *n.* an agile South American rodent similar to an agouti. Genus: *Myoprocta*. [Late 18thC. Via French, from Tupi.]

acoustic /ə koóstik/, **acoustical** /-stik'l/ *adj.* **1.** RELATING TO SOUND relating to, involving, or typical of sound, hearing, or the study of sound **2.** DESIGNED FOR USE WITH SOUND designed to control sound, absorb it, or carry it better **3.** MUSIC NOT AMPLIFIED used to describe music or a musical instrument that is not amplified electronically ■ *n.* = **acoustics** [Early 18thC. From Greek *akoustikos*, from *akouein* 'to hear', from the same Indo-European ancestor as English *hear* and *caution*.] —**acoustically** *adv.*

acoustician /əkoo stísh'n/ *n.* a specialist in the study of sound

acoustic nerve *n.* NERVE CONNECTING EAR TO BRAIN either of the eighth pair of cranial nerves, which convey impulses relating to hearing and balance from the inner ear to the brain

acoustics /ə koóstiks/ *n.* **1.** STUDY OF SOUND the scientific study of sound (*takes a singular verb*) ■ *npl.* **2.** SOUND-CARRYING ABILITY the characteristic way in which sound carries or can be heard within a particular enclosed space, e.g. an auditorium

acoustic tile *n.* a ceiling or wall tile designed to stop or diminish the transmission of sound

acoustoelectric /ə koósto i léktrik/ *adj.* = **electroacoustic** —**acoustoelectrically** *adv.*

ACP *n.* a group of over forty non-aligned developing countries with aid-related and economic links. Full form **African, Caribbean and Pacific** (**countries**)

acquaint /ə kwáynt/ (**-quaints**, **-quainting**, **-quainted**) *vt.* **1.** MAKE AWARE to make sb, or yourself, aware of or familiar with sth **2.** US INTRODUCE SB to introduce sb or make sb known to sb else (*dated or formal*) [13thC. Via French *acointier* 'to make known' from Latin *accognoscere* 'to know perfectly', from *cognoscere* 'to know' (source of English *cognition* and *quaint*).]

acquaintance /ə kwáyntənss/ *n.* **1.** SB KNOWN sb who is known slightly rather than intimately **2.** KNOWLEDGE knowledge, usually slight, of sb or sth **3.** PEOPLE SLIGHTLY KNOWN people who are known slightly but not well ○ *a wide circle of acquaintance* —**acquaintanceship** *n.* ◇ **have a nodding acquaintance with** sb *or* sth to know sb or sth slightly ◇ **make sb's acquaintance** to meet sb for the first time

acquainted /ə kwáyntid/ *adj.* **1.** FAMILIAR having some, often not very much, knowledge of sth **2.** KNOWN known to sb or to each other from a previous introduction

acquiesce /ákwi éss/ (**-esces**, **-escing**, **-esced**) *vi.* to agree to or comply with sth passively rather than expressing approval or support [Early 17thC. From Latin *acquiescere* 'to remain resting', hence 'to agree tacitly', from *quiescere* 'to rest' (source of English *coy* and *quiet*).] —**acquiescence** *n.* —**acquiescent** *adj.* —**acquiescently** *adv.*

——— **WORD KEY: SYNONYMS** ———
See Synonyms at *agree*.

acquire /ə kwír/ (**-quires**, **-quiring**, **-quired**) *vt.* **1.** GET STH to get or obtain possession of sth **2.** DEVELOP STH to learn or develop sth ○ *a habit I acquired in the Army* **3.** AEROSP LOCATE BY RADAR to locate an object such as an aircraft by the use of radar or another detector [15thC. Via Old French *acquerre* from Latin *acquirere* 'to get sth extra', from *quaerere* 'to try to get or obtain' (see QUERY).] —**acquirable** *adj.* —**acquired** *adj.* —**acquirer** *n.*

——— **WORD KEY: SYNONYMS** ———
See Synonyms at *get*.

acquired character, **acquired characteristic** *n.* a characteristic that an organism develops in response to its environment and that cannot be passed on to the next generation

acquired immune deficiency syndrome, **acquired immunodeficiency syndrome** *n.* full form of **Aids**

acquired taste *n.* a liking that develops for sth that seems unpleasant at first

acquirement /ə kwírmənt/ *n.* **1.** ACT OF ACQUIRING STH the act or process of acquiring sth **2.** LEARNED SKILL sth learned or attained, especially a skill

acquisition /ákwi zísh'n/ *n.* **1.** ACQUIRING act of acquiring sth **2.** NEW POSSESSION sth that has recently been bought or obtained **3.** SKILL DEVELOPMENT developing a new skill, practice, or way of doing things ○ *language acquisition* **4.** AEROSP LOCATING BY RADAR the location of an object such as an aircraft by the use of radar or some other detector ■ **acquisitions** *npl.* FIN COMPANY DEPARTMENT the department in a company responsible for taking over other businesses ○ *I work in acquisitions and mergers.* [14thC. From the Latin stem *acquisition-*, from *acquisit-*, the past participle stem of *acquirere* (see ACQUIRE).]

acquisitive /ə kwízzətiv/ *adj.* eager to acquire things, especially possessions [Mid-17thC. Formed from the Latin stem *acquisit-* (see ACQUIRE), on the model of French *acquisitif*.] —**acquisitively** *adv.* —**acquisitiveness** *n.*

acquit /ə kwít/ (**-quits**, **-quitting**, **-quitted**) *v.* **1.** LAW DECLARE INNOCENT to declare officially that sb is not guilty of a charge or accusation **2.** *vr.* BEHAVE to conduct yourself in a particular way ○ *The band acquitted itself well at the performance.* **3.** *vt.* FREE FROM OBLIGATION to free sb from a duty or obligation (*formal*) **4.** *vt.* REPAY to repay sth such as a debt (*formal*) [13thC. Via Old French from assumed Latin *acquitare*, literally 'to bring to rest', hence 'to set free', from *quies* 'quiet' (source of English *quiet* and *aquiesce*).] —**acquitter** *n.*

——— **WORD KEY: SYNONYMS** ———
See Synonyms at *excuse*.

acquittal /ə kwítt'l/ *n.* a judgment given by a court of law that sb is not guilty of a charge or accusation

acquittance /ə kwítt'ns/ *n.* release from a debt or obligation, or a written receipt or other record of this (*formal*)

acre /áykər/ *n.* UNIT OF AREA a unit of area used in some countries, including the United States and the United Kingdom, equal to 4,046.86 sq. m/4,840 sq. yd ■ **acres** *npl.* **1.** LAND land, especially a large amount of land **2.** LARGE AMOUNT a large amount or area of sth (*informal*) [Old English *æcer*. Ultimately probably 'area over which ploughing oxen can be driven in a day', from an Indo-European ancestor (source also of English *acorn* and *agriculture*) meaning 'to drive'.]

——— **WORD KEY: CULTURAL NOTE** ———
A Thousand Acres, a novel by US writer Jane Smiley (1991). A retelling of *King Lear* set in the American Midwest, it exposes the tragedies of alcoholism and emotional and environmental abuse behind the rural idyll of a family farm. The novel won the Pulitzer Prize in literature and a National Book Critics' Circle Award, and was made into a film in 1997.

Acre /áykər/ industrial seaport in northern Israel. Population: 39,100 (1982).

acreage /áykərij/ *n.* land, or an area of land, measured in acres

acre-foot (*plural* **acre-feet**) *n.* the volume of water that would cover an area of one acre to a depth of one foot, equivalent to 1,233.5 cu m/43,560 cu ft

acre-inch *n.* one-twelfth of an acre-foot, or the volume of water that would cover an area of one acre to a depth of one inch, equivalent to 102.8 cu m/3,630 cu ft

acrid /ákrid/ *adj.* **1.** UNPLEASANTLY PUNGENT unpleasantly strong and bitter in smell or taste **2.** BITTER sharp or bitter in tone or character [Early 18thC. Formed from the Latin stem *acri-* 'sharp, pungent', modelled on ACID (which has the same Indo-European ancestor).] —**acridity** /ə kríddəti/ *n.* —**acridly** /ákridli/ *adv.* —**acridness** /-nəss/ *n.*

acridine /ákri deen/ *n.* a colourless crystalline solid used in manufacturing dyes and pharmaceuticals. Formula: $C_{13}H_9N$. [Late 19thC. From German *Acridin*, from the Latin stem *acri-* (see ACRID).]

acriflavine /ákri fláy veen/ *n.* an orange-brown crystalline solid used in solution as an antiseptic. Formula: $C_{14}H_{14}N_3Cl$.

acrimonious /ákri mṓni əss/ *adj.* full of or displaying anger and resentment —**acrimoniously** *adv.* —**acrimoniousness** *n.*

acrimony /ákriməni/ *n.* bitterness and resentment, especially in speech, attitude, or tone [Mid-16thC. Directly or via French, from Latin *acrimonia*, from the stem *acri-* (see ACRID).]

acro- *prefix.* top, tip, height ○ *acrocentric* ○ *acrophobia* [From Greek *akros* 'extreme, topmost'. Ultimately from an Indo-European base meaning 'sharp, pointed', which is also the ancestor of English *edge, acute, acid,* and *acme.*]

acrobat /ákrə bat/ *n.* **1.** GYMNAST ENTERTAINER a performer of gymnastic feats as entertainment **2.** FACILE CHANGER OF OWN OPINIONS sb whose opinions or positions change readily to suit the circumstances [Early 19thC. Via French from, ultimately, Greek *akrobatos* 'walking on tiptoe', from *akros* (see ACRO-) + *bainein* 'to walk' (source of English *base* and *basis*).]

acrobatic /ákrə báttik/ *adj.* **1.** RELATING TO ACROBATICS relating to or involving acrobatics **2.** AGILE showing or demanding agility and energy —**acrobatically** *adv.*

acrobatics /ákrə báttiks/ *n.* (*takes a singular or plural verb*) **1.** GYMNASTICS the skill or performance routines of an acrobat **2.** ACTIVITY REQUIRING AGILITY an activity that requires great skill or agility **3.** VIRTUOSO PERFORMANCE performance of sth that is marked by virtuosic skill ○ *verbal acrobatics in her summing-up*

acrocentric /ákrō séntrik/ *adj.* used to describe a chromosome that has arms of unequal length because the structure at which the two arms join (**centromere**) is located towards one end. ◊ **acentric, telocentric**

acrocephaly /ákrō séffəli/ *n.* = **oxycephaly** —**acrocephalic** /ákrō sə fállik/ *adj.* —**acrocephalous** /-séffələss/ *adj.*

acrodont /ákrə dont/ *adj.* used to describe the teeth of some reptiles that have no roots and are joined to the jawbone, or reptiles with teeth of this type

acrolein /ə krṓli in/ *n.* a colourless poisonous pungent aldehyde used in manufacturing chemicals and pharmaceuticals. Formula: CH_2CHCHO.

acrolith /ákrō lith/ *n.* a statue, especially in ancient Greece, with only the hands, feet, and head made in stone, the body being wooden

acromegaly /ákrō méggəli/ *n.* a disease of adults that is caused by overproduction of growth hormones, resulting in abnormal enlargement of the bones of the hands, feet, jaw, nose, and ribs —**acromegalic** /ákrō mi gállik/ *adj.*

acromion /ə krṓmi ən/ (*plural* **-a** /-mi ə/) *n.* a bony projection from the outer end of the spine of the shoulder blade, to which the collarbone is attached [Late 16thC. From Greek *akrōmion*, from *akros* (see ACRO-) + *ōmos* 'shoulder'.]

acronym /ákrə nim/ *n.* a word formed from the initials or other parts of several words, e.g. 'NATO', from the initial letters of 'North Atlantic Treaty Organization' [Mid-20thC. Literally 'tip-name'.] —**acronymic** /ákrə nímmik/ *adj.* —**acronymous** /ə krónniməss/ *adj.*

WORD KEY: USAGE

See Usage note at ***abbreviation.***

acropetal /ə króppit'l/ *adj.* used to describe leaves or flowers that grow in order from the base of a plant or stem towards the apex. ◊ **basipetal** —**acropetally** *adv.*

acrophobia /ákrə fṓbi ə/ *n.* an abnormal fear of being in high places —**acrophobic** *adj.*

acropolis /ə króppəliss/ *n.* the fortified citadel of a city in ancient Greece [Early 17thC. From Greek *akropolis.*]

Acropolis /ə króppəliss/ *n.* the ancient citadel of Athens in Greece that was the religious focus of the city. It contains the remains of several classical temples, including the Parthenon.

acrosome /ákrō sōm/ *n.* a structure at the end of a sperm cell that releases enzymes to digest the cell membrane of an egg, enabling the sperm to penetrate the egg

across /ə króss/ CORE MEANING: a grammatical word indicating that sb or sth is on the opposite side of sth or moves or reaches from one side to the other ○ (prep) *I live across the street from you.* ○ (adv) *a bridge wide enough to walk across*

1. *prep.* ON OPPOSITE SIDE at or on the opposite side of sth ○ *across the road* **2.** *prep.* FROM ONE SIDE TO OTHER from one side of sth to the opposite side ○ *ran across the road* ○ *a bridge across the river* **3.** *prep.* IN SPITE OF BOUNDARIES in such a way that boundaries or borders are transcended ○ *united across cultures* **4.** *adj., adv.* SO AS TO CROSS STH in such a way as to intersect or form a cross with sth ○ *placed one board across the other* **5.** *prep.* THROUGHOUT all over sth or somewhere ○ *all across America* **6.** *adv.* AT OR TO OTHER SIDE at, on, or to the other side of sth ○ *Once we were across, we felt safe.* **7.** *adv.* MEASURED IN WIDTH as measured from one side of sth to the other ○ *about an inch across* **8.** *adv.* HORIZONTALLY ON CROSSWORD in a horizontal position in a crossword ○ *couldn't find the solution to 3 across.* ◊ **down** [13thC. Via Old French *à croix* or *en croix* 'transversely', literally 'at cross' or 'in cross', from Latin *crux* (see CROSS).]

across-the-board *adj., adv.* COMPREHENSIVE affecting everyone or everything equally or proportionally ■ *adj. US* WINNING IF PLACING IN A RACE wagering an equal amount to win if a horse or other competitor finishes first, second, or third

acrostic /ə króstik/ *n.* a number of lines of writing, especially a poem or word puzzle, in which particular letters, e.g. the first, in each line spell a word or phrase [Late 16thC. Via French *acrostiche* from Greek *akrostikhis*, from *akros* 'outermost' + *stikhos* 'line of verse' (formed from *steikhein* 'to go').] —**acrostically** *adv.*

acrylate resin /ákri layt-/ *n.* a resin derived from acrylic acid or other related acids and used in paints, sizing, adhesives, and plastics [*Acrylate* formed from ACRYLIC]

acrylic /ə kríllik/ *n.* **1.** SYNTHETIC FIBRE a synthetic textile fibre produced from acrylonitrile **2.** STH MADE WITH ACRYLIC ACID sth containing or made from acrylic acid **3.** PAINT a paint containing acrylate resin, used especially in painting pictures ■ *adj.* RELATING TO ACRYLIC ACID relating to, derived from, or containing acrylic acid

acrylic acid *n.* a colourless corrosive acid used in the manufacture of acrylate resins. Formula: $C_3H_4O_2$.

acrylic resin *n.* = **acrylate resin**

acrylonitrile /ákrilō nī́ trīl/ *n.* a colourless toxic liquid used in making acrylic fibres and resins, rubber, and thermoplastics. Formula: C_3H_3N. [Late 19thC. Coined from ACRYLIC + NITRILE.]

act /akt/ *n.* **1.** STH DONE sth that sb does **2.** DOING STH the action of carrying sth out **3.** PART OF PLAY one of the main sections of a play or other dramatic performance **4.** ONE OF SEVERAL PERFORMANCES a short performance, especially one that is part of a varied programme or show ○ *The next act is a barbershop quartet.* **5.** PERFORMER the performer or performers who take part in an act **6.** PERSONAL BEHAVIOUR sb's actions or behaviour considered as entertainment or used as an assessment of that person's worth (*informal*) ○ *a class act* **7.** PRETENCE behaviour that is intended to impress or deceive other people **8.** POL STATEMENT OF INSTRUCTION REGARDING LAW a record or statement of the decision made by a law-making or judicial body such as Parliament **9.** FORMAL RECORD a formal written record of the proceedings of a society, committee, or elected group **10.** PHILOS STH DONE INTENTIONALLY sth brought about by human will ■ *v.* (**acts, acting, acted**) **1.** *vi.* DO STH to do sth to change a situation, e.g. to solve a problem or prevent one arising **2.** *vti.* BEHAVE IN CERTAIN WAY to adopt a particular way of behaving ○ *You've been acting funny all morning.* ○ *Stop acting the fool.* ○ *'I even liked him when he was 'difficult' and official, because I thought I knew why he acted like that'.* (Paul Scott, *The Jewel in the Crown*; 1966) **3.** *vi.* PRETEND to behave in a way intended to impress or deceive other people **4.** *vi.* FUNCTION AS STH to serve a particular purpose or perform a particular function ○ *The ozone layer acts as a barrier against harmful radiation.* **5.** *vi.* REPLACE SB to be a substitute for sb or sth else ○ *Since the director cannot attend, his deputy will act for him.* **6.** *vi.* HAVE AN EFFECT to create, produce, or bring about an effect or result ○ *Once the medicine acts, you'll feel better.* **7.** *vti.* PLAY A ROLE to play the part of a character in a dramatic performance ○ *a chance to act Othello* **8.** *vi.* BE ACTOR to pursue a career in films or drama **9.** *vti.* PERFORM STH OR BE PERFORMED to stage a dramatic performance, or be capable of being staged ○ *The company will act a different play tomorrow night.* [14thC. Directly or via French *acte* from Latin *actus* and *actum* 'public transaction', both from the past participle stem of *agere* 'to do' (source of English *agent* and *prodigal*).] —**actable** *adj.* ◇ **a hard** *or* **tough act to follow** sb or sth that sets a standard difficult to reach by others who come later ◇ **catch sb in the act** to see or meet sb just as he or she is doing sth, especially sth wrong ◇ **clean up your act** to improve your behaviour ◇ **get in on the act** to join in sth in order to share in its success or profit (*informal*) ◇ **get your act together** to do sth to become more organized (*informal*)

WORD KEY: USAGE

act or **action**? Both ***act*** and ***action*** mean 'sth done', but ***action*** tends to emphasize the process of doing whereas ***act*** denotes the deed itself: *Terrorist action has increased. It was an act of terrorism.* ***Acts*** are more often associated with people, whereas ***actions*** can refer to machines (especially to denote the way a machine works).

act on, act upon *vt.* **1.** DO AS SUGGESTED to be guided by sb's advice or suggestion **2.** HAVE AN EFFECT to have an effect on sth

act out *vt.* **1.** PERFORM STH to perform sth or portray it in action **2.** PSYCHIAT MISBEHAVE TO EXPRESS FEELING to express a negative feeling or impulse by behaving in a socially unacceptable way

act up *vi.* to cause trouble or pain

ACT *abbr.* Australian Capital Territory ■ *abbr.* advance corporation tax

Actaeon /ak tée ən/ *n.* in Greek mythology, a hunter who was turned into a stag after inadvertently catching sight of the goddess Artemis bathing

ACTH *n.* a hormone produced by the pituitary gland that stimulates the adrenal cortex to produce steroid hormones. Full form **adrenocorticotrophic hormone**

actin /áktin/ *n.* a protein that is essential for cell movement and the maintenance of cell shape. It is a constituent of the structure of cells and muscle tissue and combines with myosin during muscle contraction. [Mid-20thC. Formed from Latin *actus* (see ACT).]

actin- *prefix.* = **actino-** (*used before vowels*)

actinal /áktənəl/ *adj.* **1.** RELATING TO MARINE ANIMAL'S MOUTH AREA used to describe the side of a marine animal such as a jellyfish or sea anemone from which the arms or tentacles radiate, or on which the mouth area is situated **2.** WITH TENTACLES with rays or tentacles

acting /ákting/ *n.* PERFORMING IN PLAYS the art, profession, or performance of an actor ■ *adj.* **1.** TEMPORARY carrying out certain duties or doing sb else's job temporarily ○ *the acting manager* **2.** WITH DIRECTIONS FOR STAGING including directions in a play's text to be used in staging a performance ○ *a copy of the acting edition of the play*

actinian /ak tínni ən/ *n.* a sea anemone (*technical*) [Late 19thC. Formed from modern Latin *Actinia*, genus name, from Greek *aktin-* 'ray', from its radial form.]

actinic /ak tínnik/ *adj.* relating to radiation such as ultraviolet radiation that produces a chemical effect —**actinically** *adv.*

actinide /ákti nīd/ *n.* chemical element in the series of radioactive elements beginning with actinium and ending with lawrencium [Mid-20thC. Formed from ACTINIUM, on the model of LANTHANIDE.]

actinism /áktinizzəm/ *n.* the property of radiation that makes it possible to effect photochemical changes

actinium /ak tínni əm/ *n.* a radioactive silvery-white metallic chemical element found in pitchblende, and used as a source of alpha rays. Symbol **Ac** [Early 20thC. Formed from the Greek stem *aktin-* 'ray'.]

actino-, **actin-** *prefix.* **1.** radial ○ *actinomorphic* **2.** radiation [From Greek *aktin-*, the stem of *aktis* 'ray of light']

actinolite /ak tínnə līt/ *n.* a green or greyish-green mineral consisting of calcium magnesium iron silicate. It is a member of the amphibole group.

actinomere /áktinō meer/ *n.* ZOOL = **antimere**

actinometer /ákti nómmitər/ *n.* a device for measuring the intensity of radiation, especially that from the sun —**actinometric** /áktinō méttrik/ *adj.* —**actinometry** /ákti nómmətri/ *n.*

actinomorphic /áktinō máwrfik/, **actinomorphous** /áktinō máwrfəss/ *adj.* spreading out symmetrically around a central point and so making identical halves when divided along any vertical axis. Tulips and starfish are actinomorphic. —**actinomorphy** *n.*

actinomycete /áktinō mī seet/ *n.* a rod-shaped or filamentous bacterium belonging to a large group that includes some that cause diseases and some that are the sources of antibiotics. Order: Actinomycetales. [Early 20thC. Back-formation from modern Latin *actinomycetes*, coined from ACTINO- + Greek *mukēs* 'fungus'.] —**actinomycetous** *adj.*

actinomycin /áktinō mīssin/ *n.* an antibiotic used mainly to treat childhood cancers

actinouranium /áktinōyoo ráyni əm/ *n.* the only naturally occurring radioactive isotope of uranium that is naturally fissile. It is used in nuclear reactors and weapons.

action /áksh'n/ *n.* **1. DOING STH TOWARD GOAL** the process of doing sth in order to achieve a purpose **2. STH DONE** sth that sb or sth does **3. MOVEMENT** the way sb or sth moves or works, or the movement itself ○ *the action of a piston* **4. VERVE** energetic activity ○ *a woman of action* **5.** LAW **LEGAL PROCEEDINGS** legal proceedings in a court to obtain compensation for sth or to enforce a right ○ *decided not to take action* **6. EVENTS** the important events in any form of narrative composition such as a novel or film **7. FUNCTION OR INFLUENCE** the way in which sth functions, or the effect it produces ○ *the action of water on stone* **8.** MIL **FIGHTING DURING WAR** a small battle, or the fighting that takes place during a war ○ *wounded in action* ○ *a campaign of brief actions* **9. EXCITING OR PROFITABLE ACTIVITY** involvement in sth that brings excitement, profit, or pleasure (*informal*) ○ *a piece of the action* **10. OPERATING MECHANISM** the operating parts of a mechanism or instrument, e.g. a watch or piano **11.** MUSIC **SPACE UNDER STRINGS** the space between the fingerboard and strings of a string instrument such as a violin or a guitar **12.** PHYS **FORCE** the force applied to a body **13.** PHYS **PROPERTY OF SYSTEM USED IN DYNAMICS** twice the average kinetic energy of a system in a given time multiplied by the time **14.** PHILOSOPHY **VOLUNTARY BEHAVIOUR** voluntary or intended behaviour, as opposed to forced behaviour ■ *interj.* CINEMA **START PERFORMING** a command from a film director telling actors to begin acting as filming has begun ■ *vt.* (**-tions, -tioning, -tioned**) **PUT PLAN INTO OPERATION** to put a plan into operation, or begin work on it

WORD KEY: USAGE

Can **action** be used as a verb? The use of ***action*** as a verb, as in *Criticism was levelled at the way the operation was actioned*, has crept into ordinary usage from business jargon. It is disliked by many people because they maintain, with good reason, that simpler words such as **do**, **achieve**, and **complete** are just as effective and a good deal less pretentious. The use is particularly unwelcome in cases such as **to action dismissal**, as in *Dismissal will be actioned if any employee violates this rule*, when a simple verb is available (*Any employee who violates this rule will be dismissed.*). It is always better to use the more straightforward word when this conveys the meaning just as well.

actionable /áksh'nəb'l/ *adj.* giving a basis for sb to take legal action

action chess *n.* = **speed chess**

actioner /áksh'nər/ *n.* a film that features a great deal of usually extreme action (*informal*) ○ *a made-for-TV actioner with a little-known cast*

action group *n.* a group of people formed to achieve some purpose, e.g. to support or oppose a proposal

action painting *n.* a technique used by artists of the Abstract Expressionism movement in which paintings are created by splashing, dripping, spattering, or smearing paint

action potential *n.* a temporary change in electrical potential that occurs between the inside and the outside of a nerve or muscle fibre when a nerve impulse is transmitted

action replay *n.* the reshowing of a brief part of a television film or tape of a sports event, often in slow motion. US term **instant replay**

action stations *npl.* MIL **POST FOR COMBAT** the posts assigned to people during or in readiness for combat. US term **battle stations** ■ *interj.* US term **battle stations** **1.** MIL **GO TO COMBAT POSTS** used as a command ordering people to take up the posts assigned to them during or in readiness for combat **2. GET READY** used to warn people to get ready to carry out their assigned tasks (*informal*)

activate /ákti vayt/ (**-vates, -vating, -vated**) *v.* **1.** *vt.* **MAKE STH ACTIVE** to make sth active, or set sth in motion **2.** *vi.* **BECOME ACTIVE** to become active or begin to operate **3.** *vt.* PHYS **MAKE STH RADIOACTIVE** to make sth radioactive **4.** *vt.* CHEM **MAKE STH REACTIVE** to increase the rate of a chemical reaction, e.g. by applying heat **5.** *vt.* CHEM **INCREASE POWER OF ADSORPTION** to treat a substance such as charcoal so as to increase its capacity for adsorption **6.** *vt.* PHYSIOL **PREPARE BY STIMULATION OR CONVERSION** to prepare an organ, body part, or body chemical for activity by stimulating it or converting an inactive form into one capable of action **7.** *vt.* INDUST **PURIFY WITH AIR** to purify sewage by aerating it —**activation** /ákti váysh'n/ *n.* —**activator** /-vaytər/ *n.*

activated alumina *n.* a highly adsorbent form of aluminium oxide, used to remove moisture from gases, to filter oil, and as a catalyst

activated carbon, **activated charcoal** *n.* a highly adsorbent powdered or granular form of carbon, used to purify liquids and gases through adsorption, to extract chemicals, to recover solvents, and as an antidote to some poisons

activated sludge *n.* aerated sewage containing microorganisms added to untreated sewage to purify it by accelerating its bacterial decomposition

activation energy *n.* the energy needed to make molecules of a substance take part in a chemical reaction

active /áktiv/ *adj.* **1. MOVING ABOUT** moving about, working, or doing sth as opposed to resting or sleeping **2. BUSY** full of or involved in busy activity ○ *an active life* **3. DOING STH** carrying out some action or process, or able to do so ○ *an active ingredient* **4. SHOWING ENERGY AND INVOLVEMENT** marked by involvement, energy, or action ○ *played an active part* **5. NEEDING AND USING ENERGY** requiring a lot of energy and movement ○ *active pastimes* **6.** GEOL **NOT EXTINCT** used to describe a volcano that is not extinct and still erupts occasionally **7.** GRAM **RELATING TO ROLE OF VERB'S SUBJECT** used to describe a verb whose subject is the person or thing performing the action described by the verb. ◊ **passive** **8.** ASTRON **SHOWING VARIABLE SURFACE FEATURES** used to describe the sun when it is displaying large numbers of dark patches (**sunspots**) and bright patches (**faculae**) and high variability in radio-wave emissions **9.** COMM **USED TO PRODUCE PROFIT** producing or being used to produce profits or dividends **10.** FIN **TRADING IN LARGE VOLUME** being bought and sold in large quantities **11.** FIN **INVOLVING FREQUENT TRADING** used to describe a form of portfolio management in which the manager adds value to the portfolio by frequent trades **12.** ELECTRON ENG **WITH POWER SOURCE** used to describe electronic networks and components that contain a power source and are capable of operating ■ *n.* GRAM **VERB VOICE** the active voice of a verb —**activeness** *n.*

WORD KEY: SYNONYMS

See Synonyms at ***busy***.

active duty, **active service** *n.* US full-time service in the armed forces with full pay and benefits

active immunity *n.* immunity generated by the production of antibodies within a body when it is exposed to antigens

active list *n.* a list of officers on or available for full duty

actively /áktivli/ *adv.* with determination, effort, and purpose ○ *'Naples – a city where 'pleasure' is actively cultivated'* (Henry James, *Roderick Hudson*; 1876)

active-matrix display *n.* a flat liquid-crystal display with high colour resolution that is particularly suited to use in laptop and notebook computers

active service *n.* **1. SOLDIERING IN OPERATIONAL AREA** service with the armed forces in an operational area **2.** *US* = **active duty**

active site *n.* the part of an enzyme or antibody molecule that reacts with the substance the enzyme acts on (**substrate**) or the substance that gives rise to the antibody (**antigen**)

active transport *n.* a process in which energy is used to move a chemical substance across a cellular membrane from a region of low concentration to a region of high concentration

active vocabulary (*plural* **active vocabularies**) *n.* the range of words that sb normally uses in speech or writing, as opposed to words he or she understands when used by others

activism /áktivizzəm/ *n.* vigorous and sometimes aggressive action in pursuing a political or social end —**activist** *n.*, *adj.* —**activistic** /ákti vístik/ *adj.*

activity /ak tívvəti/ (*plural* **-ties**) *n.* **1. STH SB DOES** sth that sb takes part in or does (*often used in the plural*) **2. PHYSICAL EXERCISE** energetic physical movement or exercise **3. STATE OF DOING STH** work, movement, or whatever sb or sth is doing ○ *Activity in the newsroom has reached fever pitch.* **4.** CHEM **MEASURE OF POTENTIAL FOR CHEMICAL REACTION** a measure of the ability of a chemical substance to undergo a chemical reaction **5. NATURAL PROCESS** a process or function that takes place naturally in a living organism ○ *activities such as eating or sleeping* **6.** EDUC **LEARNING EXPERIENCE** an educational exercise designed to provide direct experience of sth ○ *an activity to accompany the geography lesson* **7.** NUCLEAR PHYS **RADIOACTIVITY** radioactivity (*technical*) Symbol *A*

act of contrition *n.* a short prayer of penitence

act of faith *n.* an action motivated by belief in sth for which there is no concrete evidence

act of God *n.* a sudden uncontrollable event produced by natural forces, e.g. an earthquake or a tornado

actomyosin /áktō mī əssin/ *n.* a protein complex of actin and myosin that is found in muscle cells and that is partly responsible for muscular contraction

actor /áktər/ *n.* **1. PERFORMER IN PLAYS** sb who acts in plays, films, or television **2. SB WHO PRETENDS** sb who pretends to be sb else or to feel sth so as to impress or deceive

actress /áktrəss/ *n.* **1. PERFORMER IN PLAYS** a woman or girl who acts in plays, films, or television **2. WOMAN WHO PRETENDS** a woman or girl who behaves in a way intended to deceive or impress others

Acts of the Apostles *n.* the fifth book of the New Testament, in which the early history of the Christian church is described (*takes a singular verb*) See table at **Bible**

ACTU *abbr.* Australian Council of Trade Unions

actual /ákchoo əl, ákchəl/ *adj.* **1. REAL** real and existing as fact ○ *Is that her actual title?* **2. USED FOR EMPHASIS** used for emphasis, e.g. to stress that sb or sth being referred to is genuinely the person or thing involved ○ *This is the actual place where Wellington stood.* **3. EXISTING NOW** existing or occurring at the moment ○ *actual as opposed to projected income*

— **WORD KEY: USAGE** —

Actual should normally be used when it contrasts with some other condition such as 'ideal' or 'imagined' rather than as a mere intensifier often without any real meaning: *He wanted to know what actual damage had been done.* In this sentence **actual** could be removed without any significant change to the sense. But in the sentence *The actual total was much higher*, **actual** is legitimately used to mark a contrast with projected or estimated totals.

actuality /ákchoo álləti/ (*plural* **-ties**) *n.* **1. WHAT IN FACT IS** sth that is real, as opposed to what is expected, intended, or feared ○ *Let's deal with actualities.* **2. EVERYTHING THAT REALLY EXISTS OR HAPPENS** everything that does or could exist or happen in real life

actualize /ákchoo ə līz/ (**-izes, -izing, -ized**), **actualise** (**-ises, -ising, -ised**) *vt.* **1. MAKE REAL** to make sth real or actual, or make sth come about ○ *expectations actualized by deeds* **2. PORTRAY** to portray or represent sth realistically —**actualization** /ákchoo ə lī záysh'n/ *n.*

actually /ákchoo əli, ákchəli/ *adv.* used to emphasize that sth really is so or really exists, e.g. when it may be hard to believe or contrasts with what has already been said ○ *He's actually over 35, although he looks much younger.*

— **WORD KEY: USAGE** —

Actually, like *actual*, is used most effectively when it contrasts with what is theoretical or only apparent: *It sounds difficult but it's actually quite straightforward.* It is regarded as poor style to use it as a kind of sentence filler with no real meaning, although this is more acceptable in informal conversation, in which such fillers help to maintain the flow and balance of the sentence and to avoid bluntness: *Actually, I prefer her to her cousin.*

actuarial /ákchoo áiri əl/ *adj.* **1. RELATING TO CALCULATION OF RISK** relating to the statistical calculation of risk or life expectancy for insurance purposes **2. RELATING TO ACTUARIES** relating to actuaries and their work

actuarial science *n.* the branch of statistics that deals with the calculation of risk, life expectancy, and insurance premiums

actuary /ákchoo əri/ (*plural* **-ies**) *n.* a statistician who calculates insurance premiums, risks, dividends, and annuity rates

actuate /ákchoo ayt/ (**-ates, -ating, -ated**) *vt.* **1. MAKE ACT** to make sb act or behave in a certain way (*often used in the passive*) ○ *actuated by self-interest* **2. MAKE WORK** to make a device move or start working (*formal*) [Late 16thC. From medieval Latin *actuatus*, the past participle of *actuare* 'to cause sth to be done', from Latin *actus* (see ACT).] —**actuation** /ákchoo áysh'n/ *n.* —**actuator** /ákchoo aytər/ *n.*

ACT-UP /ákt up/ *n.* an Aids activist organization in the United States and United Kingdom. Full form **Aids Coalition To Unleash Power**

acuity /ə kyoo əti/ *n.* keenness of hearing, sight, or intellect [Mid-16thC. Directly or via French *acuité* from medieval Latin *acuitas*, from Latin *acuere* (see ACUTE).]

aculeate /ə kyoo li ət/ *adj.* **1. STINGING** used to describe an insect that has a sting **2. PRICKLY** used to describe a plant or plant part that has prickles [Mid-17thC. From Latin *aculeatus*, from *aculeus*, 'a small needle', from *acus* (see ACUTE).]

acumen /ákyoomən/ *n.* quick insight, or the ability to make quick accurate judgments of people or situations ○ *political acumen* [Late 16thC. From Latin, 'point, sharpness', formed from *acuere* 'to sharpen'.]

acuminate *adj.* /ə kyoominət/ used to describe leaves that taper to a sharp point [Late 16thC. From late Latin *acuminatus*, the past participle of *acuminare* 'to sharpen to a point', from *acumen* (see ACUMEN).]

acupressure /ákyoo preshər/ *n.* a form of alternative therapy similar to acupuncture that uses manual pressure rather than needles [Mid-19thC. 'Acu-' from ACUPUNCTURE.]

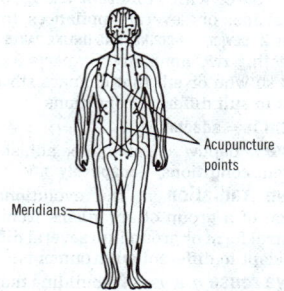

Acupuncture: Points and energy flow paths (meridians) in the human body

acupuncture /ákyoo pungkchər/ *n.* a method, originally from China, of treating disorders by inserting needles into the skin at points where the flow of energy is thought to be blocked (**meridians**) [Late 17thC. 'Acu-' from Latin *acus* 'needle'.] —**acupuncturist** *n.*

acute /ə kyoot/ *adj.* **1. VERY GREAT OR BAD** extremely serious, severe, or painful ○ *an acute financial crisis* **2. PERCEPTIVE** keenly perceptive and intelligent ○ *an acute grasp of foreign affairs* **3. SENSITIVE** very powerful and sensitive to detail ○ *acute eyesight* **4. GEOM LESS THAN 90°** used to describe an angle that is less than 90° **5. GEOM WITH ANGLES LESS THAN 90°** used to describe a triangle that has three internal angles of less than 90° **6. MED SEVERE AND OF SHORT DURATION** used to describe a disease that is brief, severe, and quickly comes to a crisis **7. BOT POINTED** used to describe leaves that end in a short narrow point ■ *n.* **acute, acute accent** LANG **MARK ABOVE LETTER** in some languages, a mark placed above a letter, as in *á* and *ó*, to show it is sounded in a particular way. In Spanish, the acute indicates a stressed syllable, as in *cupón*, in French a particular pronunciation of *e*, as in *blé*, and in classical Greek a vowel sounded at a higher pitch. [14thC. From Latin *acutus* (source of English *ague*), the past participle of *acuere* 'to sharpen', from *acus* 'needle' (source of English *acuity* and *cute*.] —**acutely** *adv.* —**acuteness** *n.*

acute arch *n.* = lancet arch

acute dose *n.* a fatal amount of radiation received over a short period

ACW *abbr.* aircraftwoman

acyclic /ay síklik, -síklik/ *adj.* **1. CHEM WITH ATOMS FORMING CHAIN STRUCTURE** having a molecular structure in which the atoms are arranged in a string whose ends do not meet (**open chain**) rather than being arranged in a ring **2. BOT WITH PARTS IN SPIRAL ARRANGEMENT** used to describe flowers that have their parts arranged in a spiral rather than a whorl

acyclovir /ay síklə veer/ *n.* an antiviral drug used to treat genital herpes and cold sores. It works by interfering with viral reproduction, thereby reducing infection.

acyl /áy síl/ *adj.* relating to or containing the chemical group derived from a carboxylic acid, e.g. the acetyl group

acylation /áy sī láysh'n/ *n.* the introduction of an acyl group into a chemical compound

ad[1] /ad/ *n.* an advertisement [Mid-19thC. Shortening.]

ad[2] *abbr.* TENNIS advantage

AD *abbr.* Alzheimer's disease

A.D., AD *adv.* used to indicate a date that is a specified number of years after the birth of Jesus Christ. Full form **anno Domini**. ◊ **CE, BC, BCE**

— **WORD KEY: USAGE** —

Before or after the date? Because of its meaning, AD is traditionally put before the numeral to which it relates, so that it makes grammatical sense if understood in its expanded form: AD *1453*. In practice, AD is often put after the numeral, being then understood as a word in its own right, and it is normally acceptable to put it after

the identification of a century, as in *the fifth century* AD.

ad-, ac-, af-, ag-, at-, ap- *prefix.* **1.** to, toward ○ *adsorb* ○ *advance* **2.** near ○ *adrenal* [From Latin *ad* 'toward, near'. Ultimately from an Indo-European word that is also the ancestor of English *at*.]

-ad *suffix.* to, toward ○ *cephalad* [From Latin *ad* (see AD-)]

Ada /áydə/ *n.* a high-level general-purpose programming language used for military and other complex programming applications. Ada programs are highly readable and therefore easy to maintain. [Late 20thC. Named after the English mathematician Augusta *Ada* Byron, Countess of Lovelace (1815–52).]

adage /ádij/ *n.* a traditional saying that expresses sth taken as a general truth ○ *'Oysters are said to be best in months containing the letter R, according to an old adage'.* (Barbara Sturm, *Living Page*; 1997) [Mid-16thC. Via French, from Latin *adagium*, from *ad* 'to' + a variant of *aio* 'I say'.]

adagio /ə daaji ō/ *adv.* **SLOWLY** slowly, but faster than lento (*used as a musical direction*) ■ *n.* (*plural* **adagios**) **MUSICAL PIECE** a movement or piece of music played or marked adagio [Late 17thC. From Italian, literally 'at ease'.] —**adagio** *adj.*

Adam /áddəm/ *n.* in the Bible, the first man, created by God ◇ **not know sb from Adam** to have never met or seen sb before ◇ **the old Adam** a natural tendency in people to do wrong

Adam /áddəm/, **Adolphe Charles** (1803–56) French composer who wrote sixty operas and the ballet *Giselle* (1841).

Adam, Robert (1728–92) British architect and interior designer who built grand neoclassical country and town houses, including Kenwood House (1768) and Osterley Park (1778).

adamant /áddəmənt/ *adj.* **SET IN OPINION** very determined and not influenced by appeals to reconsider ○ *'They did their best to persuade her, but Mother was adamant'.* (Gerald Durrell, *Birds, Beasts and Relatives*; 1969) ■ *n.* **LEGENDARY STONE** a extremely hard legendary stone, sometimes identified as diamond or lodestone (*archaic*) [Pre-12thC. Via Old French *adamaunt* and the Latin stem *adamant-* 'adamant, steel, diamond', from Greek *adamas*, literally 'unbreakable', from *daman* 'to break down'.] —**adamantly** *adv.*

adamantine /áddə mán tīn/ *adj.* (*literary*) **1. UNYIELDING** extremely hard or unyielding **2. HARD AND BRILLIANT** like a diamond in hardness and brilliance

Adamite /áddə mīt/ *n.* **1. HUMAN BEING** a human being regarded as a descendant of Adam **2. MEMBER OF RELIGIOUS GROUP** a member of a Christain religious group in 2nd-century North Africa whose members preferred not to wear clothes

Abigail Adams

Adams /áddəmz/, **Abigail** (1744–1818) US feminist. She married John Adams, second president of the United States. Her letters to him were published by her grandson.

Adams, Gerry (*b.* 1948) Northern Irish politician and president of Sinn Fein, the political wing of the Irish Republican Army. He was elected to the British Parliament (1983–92, 1997) but declined to take his seat.

John Adams

John Quincy Adams

Adams, John (1735–1826) US statesman and second president of the United States. He served from 1797 until 1801 and was one of the committee that drafted the Declaration of Independence (1776).

Adams, John Quincy (1767–1848) US statesman and sixth president of the United States. He served from 1825 until 1829. As secretary of state to President James Monroe (1817–25), he formulated the Monroe Doctrine opposing foreign intervention in the American continents.

Adams, Philip Andrew (b. 1939) Australian writer and film producer, chairman of the Australian Film Commission (1983–90). Published collections of his work include *The Unspeakable Adams* (1977).

Adam's apple *n.* the hard lump at the front of the throat formed by the thyroid cartilage of the larynx [From the belief that it results from the forbidden apple being stuck in Adam's throat]

Adam-Smith, Patsy (b. 1926) Australian writer and historian, author of *The Anzacs* (1978). Full name **Patricia Jean Adam-Smith**

Adam's needle *n.* a North American yucca cultivated for its spiny pointed leaves and spikes of white flowers. Latin name: *Yucca filamentosa*. [From the spines on its leaves, in allusion to Adam and Eve sewing fig leaves together to cover themselves (Genesis 3:7)]

adapt /ə dápt/ (adapts, adapting, adapted) *v.* 1. *vti.* CHANGE STH TO MEET REQUIREMENTS to change, or change sth, to suit different conditions or a different purpose ○ *adapted the novel for radio* 2. *vti.* ADJUST TO STH to make or become used to a new environment or different conditions 3. *vt.* REWRITE BOOK OR PLAY to rewrite a book or a play so that it can be made into a film or a television programme [15thC. Via French *adapter* and Latin *adaptare*, literally 'to fit to', from, ultimately, *aptus*, 'attached' (source of English *apt*).]

adaptable /ə dáptəb'l/ *adj.* 1. CHANGING EASILY able to adjust easily to changes and new conditions 2. ADJUSTABLE capable of being modified to suit different purposes or conditions ○ *adaptable for different voltages* —**adaptability** /ə dáptə bílləti/ *n.* —**adaptableness** /ə dáptəb'lnəss/ *n.*

adaptation /áddap táysh'n, -əp-/, **adaption** /ə dápsh'n/ *n.* 1. ADAPTING the process or state of changing to fit new circumstances or conditions, or the resulting change 2. STH ADAPTED TO FIT NEED sth that has been modified for a purpose ○ *a film adaptation of a novel* 3. BIOL CHANGE TO SUIT ENVIRONMENT the development of physical and behavioural characteristics that allow organisms to survive and reproduce in their habitats 4. PHYSIOL DIMINISHING SENSORY RESPONSE the di-minishing response of a sense organ to a sustained stimulus —**adaptational** *adj.* —**adaptationally** *adv.*

adapter /ə dáptər/, **adaptor** *n.* 1. ELECTRIC CONNECTOR a device used to connect an electrical appliance to a power source with a different voltage or a different plug shape, or several appliances to one mains socket 2. DEVICE FOR CONNECTING UNLIKE PARTS a device for connecting two nonmatching parts 3. SB OR STH THAT ADAPTS sb who or sth that changes sth or is able to adjust to suit different conditions

adaption *n.* = adaptation

adaptive /ə dáptiv/ *adj.* able to be adjusted for use in different conditions —**adaptively** *adv.*

adaptive radiation *n.* the evolutionary diversi-fication of a group of organisms from an original ancestral form or group into several different forms that adapt to different environments

adaptive reuse *n.* a use of a building that is different from its original or previous use, often involving conversion work

adaptor *n.* = adapter

Adar /ə daár/ *n.* in the Jewish calendar, the sixth month of the civil year and the twelfth month of the religious year. It is 29 or 30 days long. In leap years it is renamed Adar Rishon. [14thC. From Hebrew *ădār*.]

Adar Rishon /-ríshon/ *n.* in the Jewish calendar, the name given to the month of Adar during a leap year, when an additional month (**Adar Sheni**) follows it

Adar Sheni /-sháyni/ *n.* a 13th month added to the Jewish calendar after Adar in leap years. It is 29 days long. [*Sheni* from Hebrew *šēnî*, 'second']

adaxial /ad áksi əl/ *adj.* used to describe the upper side of a leaf or other surface that faces towards the stem. ◊ **abaxial**

ADC *abbr.* analogue-to-digital converter

Adcock /ád kok/, **Fleur** (b. 1934) New Zealand poet, author of *The Inner Harbour* (1979). Full name **Kareen Fleur Adcock**

ad court *n.* the left-hand side of a tennis court, from which alternate, odd points are played [From *ad* 'advantage']

add /ad/ (adds, adding, added) *v.* 1. *vt.* UNITE OR COMBINE THINGS to put sth into or join sth onto sth else ○ *I'll add your name to the list.* 2. *vti.* MATH FIGURE TOTAL to calculate the total of two or more numbers or amounts 3. *vt.* PUT IN INGREDIENT to mix in an ingredient that is part of a recipe ○ *Add six eggs to the flour.* 4. *vt.* INTRODUCE STH to give sth a particular quality or more of a particular quality ○ *The flowers add a touch of cheerfulness.* 5. *vi.* INTENSIFY STH to increase the effect of sth ○ *This adds to our problems.* 6. *vt.* SUPPLEMENT SPEECH OR WRITING to say or write sth else after you have written or said sth ○ *'Don't forget your umbrella', she added.* [14thC. From Latin *addere*, from *dare* 'to give' (source of English *data*, *edit*, and *vendor*).] —**addable** *adj.*

add up *v.* 1. *vti.* MAKE TOTAL to calculate the total of two or more numbers or amounts, or reach a total 2. *vi.* MAKE SENSE to make a sensible or believable story or explanation ○ *His story just doesn't add up.* 3. *vi.* FORM LARGE AMOUNT to make a large total or amount ○ *If everyone gives a little, it soon adds up.*

add up to *vt.* to amount to or result in a particular sum or thing

ADD *abbr.* attention deficit disorder

add. *abbr.* 1. addendum 2. MATH addition 3. address

addax /áddaks/ (plural **-daxes** or **-dax**) *n.* an antelope

Addax

that has long spiralling horns and lives in desert regions of North Africa. Latin name: *Addax naso-maculatus.* [Late 17thC. From Latin, from an African word.]

addend /áddend, ə dénd/ *n.* a number that is to be added [Late 17thC. Shortening of ADDENDUM.]

addendum /ə déndəm/ (plural **-da** /-də/) *n.* 1. STH ADDED sth that is or has been added 2. SUPPLEMENT a sup-plement to a book or magazine [Late 17thC. From Latin, formed from *addere* (see ADD).]

Adder

adder¹ /áddər/ *n.* sb or sth that adds, especially an electronic device that adds numbers

adder² /áddər/ *n.* a small venomous snake, common in Europe, that is dark grey with a black zigzag pattern on its back. It is the only snake found in the United Kingdom that has a poisonous bite. Latin name: *Vipera berus.* [Old English *næd(d)re* 'snake'. The initial *n* was lost when 'a nadder' was misanalysed as 'an adder'. Ultimately from an Indo-European word that also produced German *Natter* 'adder'.]

Adder's tongue

adder's tongue *n.* a fern found in the northern hemisphere that has a spore-bearing stalk at the base of a pointed frond. Genus: *Ophioglossum.* [From the resemblance of the stalk to a snake's tongue]

addict /áddikt/ *n.* 1. SB CRAVING A DRUG sb who is physio-logically or mentally dependent on a drug or other substance liable to have a damaging physiological or psychological effect 2. ENTHUSIAST sb who is devoted to sth ○ *soap opera addicts* [Mid-16thC. From Latin *addictus*, the past participle of *addicere* 'to award, devote', from *dicere* 'to say' (source of English *dictionary*, *dictate*, and *verdict*).]

addicted /ə díktid/ *adj.* 1. DEPENDENT physiologically or mentally dependent on tobacco, alcohol, or other substance 2. VERY ENTHUSIASTIC very interested in sth and devoting a lot of time to it ○ *addicted to football*

addiction /ə díksh'n/ *n.* 1. DRUG DEPENDENCE a state of physiological or psychological dependence on a sub-stance, especially an illegal drug or one liable to have a damaging effect 2. DEVOTION great interest in sth to which a lot of time is devoted

addictionology /ə díksh'n ólləji/ *n.* the study and treatment of addictions —**addictionologist** *n.*

addictive /ə díktiv/ *adj.* making sb an addict, or able or likely to do so —**addictively** *adv.*

addictive personality (plural **addictive personalities**) *n.* a personality predisposed towards becoming addicted to sth

add-in *n.* = add-on

Addington /áddington/, **Henry, 1st Viscount Sidmouth** (1757–1844) British statesman. He was prime minister from 1801 until 1821. He resigned after criticism of his conduct of the Napoleonic Wars.

Addis Ababa /áddiss ábbəbə/ capital of Ethiopia. Population: 1,912,500 (1990).

Addison, Joseph (1672–1719) English essayist and politician. An originator of the modern essay, he was cofounder (with Richard Steele) of *The Spectator* (1711).

Addison, Thomas (1793–1860) British physician who correctly ascribed the symptoms of Addison's disease to adrenal malfunction.

Addison's disease *n.* a wasting disease characterized by bronzing of the skin, low blood pressure, and weakness. It is caused by underactivity of the adrenal glands. [Mid-19thC. Named after Thomas ADDISON.]

addition /ə dísh'n/ *n.* **1.** PUTTING IN OR ON the act of adding sth onto or into sth else **2.** STH ADDED sth or sb that is added **3.** MATH CALCULATION the process of calculating the sum of two or more numbers or amounts **4.** CHEM CHEMICAL REACTION a chemical reaction in which a new compound is produced by the combination of two or more compounds ◊ *an addition-type reaction.* ◊ substitution [14thC. Directly or via French, from the Latin stem *addition-*, from *additus*, the past participle of *addere* (see ADD).] ◇ **in addition 1.** used to introduce an additional point or a relevant fact **2.** also ◇ **in addition to** as well as

additional /ə dísh'nəl/ *adj.* added on to sth else

additionality /ə díshə nálləti/ *n.* a principle of funding in the European Union by which funds for a project are only granted to a member state if the latter also contributes

additionally /ə dísh'nəli/ *adv.* **1.** FURTHER further to what has just been said ◊ *Additionally, each machine is checked hourly.* **2.** EVEN MORE to an even greater extent (*literary*) ◊ *'The atmosphere of the place was heavy and mouldy, being rendered additionally oppressive by the closing of the door which led into the church'.* (Wilkie Collins, *The Woman in White*; 1860) **3.** ALSO as well as

additional member system *n.* a method of voting in which votes are cast separately for parties and candidates and parties may be awarded extra seats according to their share of the total vote

additive /áddətiv/ *n.* STH ADDED sth added to sth else to alter or improve it in some way, e.g. to change the colour or texture of food ■ *adj.* INVOLVING ADDING STH involving or produced by addition or by the addition of sth (*formal*) [Late 16thC. From late Latin *additivus*, from *additus* (see ADDITION).]

additive identity (*plural* **additive identities**) *n.* a quantity that, when added to another, leaves it unchanged. For ordinary numbers this is zero.

additive inverse *n.* a number or quantity that gives zero when added to another. For example, the additive inverse of 3 is –3.

additive printing *n.* a process in printing in which colours are produced by adding proportionate amounts of three primary colours

addle /ádd'l/ (**-dles, -dling, -dled**) *vti.* **1.** BEFUDDLE to confuse or muddle sb, or become confused or muddled **2.** ROT to make sth rotten or spoiled [Old English *adela* 'filth, liquid manure'. Ultimately from a prehistoric Germanic word that is also the ancestor of Dutch *aal* 'liquid manure'.]

addlepated /ádd'l páytid/, **addlebrained** /-bráynd/, **addleheaded** /-héddid/ *adj.* with a mind that is muddled and confused (*dated informal*)

add-on, add-in *n.* a piece of equipment that can be added to another, e.g. a computer system, to expand its capabilities

address /ə dréss/ *n.* **1.** PHYSICAL LOCATION the number, street name, and other information that describes where a building is or where sb lives **2.** WRITTEN FORM OF ADDRESS the address of a person or organization when written on a letter or an item of mail **3.** FORMAL TALK a formal speech or report **4.** COMPUT NUMBER FOR LOCATION a number that specifies a location in a computer's memory **5.** STATEMENT FROM PARLIAMENT a statement of opinions or desires sent to the sovereign by either or both of the Houses of Parliament ■ **addresses** *npl.* COURTSHIP attention paid to sb that is intended as courtship (*archaic*) ■ *v.* (**-dresses, -dressing, -dressed**) **1.** *vt.* WRITE DIRECTIONS ON to write or print on an item of mail details of where it is to be delivered **2.** *vt.* SPEAK OR MAKE SPEECH TO to say sth to sb, or make a speech to an audience **3.** *vr.* BEGIN JOB to set about doing some task ◊ *'Through this program of action we address ourselves to putting our own national house in order'* (Franklin D. Roosevelt, *First Inaugural Address*; 1933) **4.** *vt.* DEAL WITH to face up to and deal with a problem or issue ◊ *failure to address the main issue* **5.** *vt.* SPORTS, DANCE FACE to move to face or stand facing a target in a sport or a partner in a dance ◊ *address the target* **6.** *vt.* GOLF AIM GOLF CLUB to take up the correct stance before hitting a golf shot ◊ *address the ball* [14thC. Via Old French *adresser* and assumed Vulgar Latin *addrictiare*, literally 'to direct to', from, ultimately, Latin *directus* (see DIRECT).]

addressable /ə dréssəb'l/ *adj.* capable of being dealt with or resolved (*formal*) —**addressability** /ə dréssə bílləti/ *n.*

addressee /áddre seé, ə dréss eé/ *n.* a person or organization to whom an item of mail is to be delivered

adduce /ə dyóoss/ (**-duces, -ducing, -duced**) *vt.* to offer sth as evidence, reason, or proof (*formal*) [15thC. From Latin *adducere* 'to bring forward', from *ducere* 'to lead' (source of English *abduct, duke*, and *seduce*).] —**adduceable** *adj.*

adduct /ə dúkt, a-/ *vt.* (**-ducts, -ducting, -ducted**) PULL TOWARDS AXIS to pull a leg or arm towards the central line of the body or a toe or finger towards the axis of a leg or arm. ◊ abduct ■ *n.* CHEMICAL COMPOUND a chemical compound formed by the combination of two or more different compounds or elements in an addition-type reaction [Mid-19thC. Back-formation from ADDUCTION, which came directly or via French from the Latin stem *adduction-*, from *adductus*, the past participle of *adducere* (see ADDUCE).] —**adduction** *n.* —**adductive** *adj.*

adductor /ə dúktər/ *n.* a muscle that pulls a leg or arm towards the central line of the body or a toe or finger towards the axis of a leg or arm [Early 17thC. From modern Latin, formed from Latin *adductus*, the past participle of *adducere* (see ADDUCE).]

-ade *suffix.* **1.** a sweetened drink ◊ *orangeade* **2.** an action ◊ *cannonade* [Via Old French from, ultimately, Latin *-ata*, feminine of *-atus* (see -ATE).]

Adelaide /ádd'l ayd/ city in southeastern Australia, situated on the Gulf of St Vincent. It was founded in 1836. Population: 978,100 (1996).

Aden /áyd'n/ **1.** former British colony and protectorate that became part of South Yemen in 1967 and is now part of Yemen. Area: 195 sq. km/75 sq. mi. **2.** port and second largest city of Yemen, situated on a peninsula that juts into the Gulf of Aden. Population: 562,000 (1995).

aden- *prefix.* = adeno- (*used before vowels*)

Adenauer /áddə now ər/, **Konrad** (1876–1967) German statesman and the first chancellor of the Federal Republic of Germany (1949–63). He led West Germany into NATO in 1955.

adenectomy /áddə néktəmi/ (*plural* **-mies**) *n.* the surgical removal of a gland

adenine /áddə neen/ *n.* a component of nucleic acids, energy-carrying molecules such as ATP, and certain coenzymes that carries hereditary information in DNA and RNA. Chemically, it is a purine base. Formula: $C_5H_5N_5$. Symbol **A**

adenitis /áddə nítiss/ *n.* inflammation of a gland or a lymph node

adeno-, aden- *prefix.* gland ◊ *adenovirus* [From Greek *adēn*. Ultimately related to Latin *inguen* 'groin' (source of English *inguinal*).]

adenocarcinoma /áddinō ka'arssi nōmə/ (*plural* **-mas** or **-mata** /-mətə/) *n.* **1.** MALIGNANT TUMOUR IN GLAND a malignant tumour in glandular tissue. Breast cancers are often adenocarcinomas. **2.** TUMOUR RESEMBLING GLAND a malignant tumour with cells arranged in patterns similar to those of a gland —**adenocarcinomatous** *adj.*

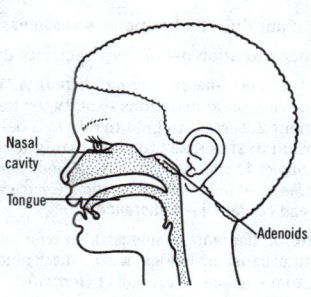

Adenoids

adenoid /áddə noyd/ *adj.* **1.** RELATING TO GLANDS relating to or similar to a gland **2.** CONCERNING LYMPHOID TISSUE relating to lymphoid tissue **3.** = adenoidal *adj.* 1 ■ **adenoids** *npl.* THROAT TISSUE a mass of tissue at the back of the throat. If they become enlarged, breathing can be restricted through the nose.

adenoidal /áddi nóyd'l/ *adj.* **1.** AFFECTED BY ENLARGED ADENOIDS displaying symptoms caused by enlarged adenoids, e.g. a nasal voice or breathing difficulties **2.** RELATING TO ADENOIDS used to describe the adenoids

adenoidectomy /áddi noy déktəmi/ (*plural* **-ies**) *n.* surgical removal of adenoids

adenoma /áddi nōmə/ (*plural* **-mas** or **-mata** /-mətə/) *n.* **1.** BENIGN TUMOUR IN GLAND a benign tumour in glandular tissue **2.** TUMOUR-LIKE GLAND a benign tumour with cells arranged in patterns similar to those found in a gland —**adenomatoid** *adj.*

adenopathy /áddi nóppəthi/ (*plural* **-nopathies**) *n.* a diseased condition, e.g. inflammation or enlargement, in a gland or lymph node

adenosine /ə dénnō seen/ *n.* a compound of adenine and a ribose that is a component of nucleic acids and energy-carrying molecules such as ATP. Formula: $C_{10}H_{13}N_5O_4$. [Early 20thC. A blend of ADENINE and RIBOSE.]

adenosine diphosphate full form of ADP

adenosine monophosphate /-monō fós fayt/ full form of AMP

adenosine triphosphatase /-trī fósfə tayz/ *n.* an enzyme occurring in living organisms that aids the breakdown of ATP into ADP with the release of energy that is used by cells

adenosine triphosphate full form of ATP

adenosis /áddi nōssiss/ *n.* **1.** ENLARGED OR ABNORMAL GLANDS the enlargement of a gland, or the abnormal formation of glandular tissue **2.** GLAND DISEASE any disease characterized by adenosis

adenovirus /áddinō vírəss/ *n.* a virus that causes respiratory infections in humans [From its occurrence in adenoid tissue when first discovered]

adenylate cyclase /ə dénnə layt-/, **adenyl cyclase** /áddənī'l-/ *n.* an enzyme involved in the formation of cyclic AMP from ATP

adept *adj.* /ə dépt/ SKILFUL highly proficient or expert ■ *n.* /ádd ept/ SKILLED PERSON sb who is highly proficient or expert at sth [Mid-17thC. From Latin *adeptus*, the past participle of *adipisci* 'to acquire', from *apisci* 'to pursue'. The underlying idea is of having acquired a skill.] —**adeptly** *adv.* —**adeptness** *n.*

adequate /áddikwət/ *adj.* **1.** ENOUGH sufficient in quality or quantity to meet a need **2.** JUST BARELY ENOUGH just barely sufficient in quality or quantity to meet a need or qualify for sth [Late 16thC. From Latin *adaequatus*, the past participle of *adaequare* 'to make equal, to match', from *aequus* 'even' (source of English *equal*).] —**adequacy** *n.* —**adequately** *adv.* —**adequateness** *n.*

—— **WORD KEY: SYNONYMS** ——
See Synonyms at **sufficient** and **enough**.

Ader /ə dáir/, **Clément** (1841–1926) French engineer who constructed a steam-powered aircraft and made the first heavier-than-air powered flight (1890).

à deux /aa dö́/ *adv., adj.* involving only two people and therefore private [Late 19thC. From French.]

ADH *abbr.* antidiuretic hormone. ▸ **vasopressin**

ADHD *abbr.* attention deficit hyperactivity disorder

adhere /əd héer/ (**-heres, -hering, -hered**) *vi.* **1.** OBEY to follow a rule or instructions exactly, or keep to an agreement **2.** SUPPORT to hold firmly to a belief, idea, or opinion **3.** STICK FIRMLY to stick firmly to a surface or an object [15thC. Directly or via French *adhérer* from Latin *adhaerere*, from *haerere* 'to stick' (source of English *cohere* and *hesitate*).] —**adherence** *n.*

adherent /əd héerənt/ *n.* SUPPORTER sb who supports a particular cause or leader ■ *adj.* STICKY able to stick firmly to a surface or an object (*formal*)

adhesion /əd héezh'n/ *n.* **1.** STICKING POWER the ability to stick firmly to sth **2.** NON-SLIPPINESS the ability to make firm contact with a surface without slipping **3.** SUPPORT loyal support for a cause or a leader **4.** PHYS INTERMOLECULAR ATTRACTION the intermolecular attraction between substances that are unlike and in surface contact, causing them to cling together **5.** JOINING OF BODY PARTS the joining of normally unconnected body parts by bands of fibrous tissue [15thC. Directly or via French, from the Latin stem *adhaesion-*, from *adhaes-*, the past participle stem of *adhaerere* (see ADHERE).]

adhesive /əd héessiv, -ziv/ *n.* GLUE a substance used to stick things together ■ *adj.* STICKY able to stick to sth or to stick things together [Late 17thC. Formed from the Latin stem *adhaes-* (see ADHESION).] —**adhesively** *adv.* —**adhesiveness** *n.*

ad hoc /ad hók/ *adj.* done or set up solely in response to a particular situation or problem and without considering wider issues ○ *ad hoc measures* [Mid-17thC. From Latin, 'to this'.] —**ad hoc** *adv.*

ad hocism /ad hókizzəm/ *n.* taking decisions or implementing measures according to the nature and needs of each specific case individually rather than on the basis of a set, well-thought-out policy (*disapproving*)

ad hominem /ad hómmi nem/ *adj.* **1.** APPEALING TO EMOTIONS appealing to people's emotions and prejudices rather than their ability to think (*formal*) **2.** *S Africa* FOR MERIT on the basis of personal merit ○ *ad hominem promotion* [Late 16thC. From Latin, 'to the person'.] —**ad hominem** *adv.*

ADI *abbr.* acceptable daily intake

adiabatic /áddi ə báttik/ *adj.* used to describe a thermodynamic process that happens without loss or gain of heat [Late 19thC. Formed from Greek *adiabatos* 'impassable', from *diabainein*, 'to go through' (source of English *diabetes*).] —**adiabatically** *adv.*

adiaphorism /áddi áffərizzəm/ *n.* especially in Protestant Christianity, the view that things not specifically forbidden by the Scriptures may be treated with indifference [Early 17thC. Formed from Greek *adiaphoros* 'indifferent'.] —**adiaphoristic** /áddi áffə rístik/ *adj.*

adieu /ə dyóo/ *interj., n.* (*plural* **adieux** /ə dyóoz/ or **adieus** /ə dyóoz/) used to say goodbye ○ *'...the more gentle adieus of her sisters were uttered without being heard'* (Jane Austen, *Pride And Prejudice*; 1813) [14thC. From French, literally '(I commend you) to God'.]

Adi Granth /áadi grúnt/ *n.* the principal Sikh scripture, which contains the teachings of the first five gurus and also poems and hymns [From Sanskrit *ādigrantha* literally 'first book', from *grantha* 'tying, work of literature']

ad infinitum /ádd infi nítəm/ *adv.* endlessly, or for so long as to seem endless [Early 17thC. From Latin, 'to infinity'.]

ad interim /ád íntərim/ *adv.* TEMPORARILY for the meantime ■ *adj.* TEMPORARY done or created for the meantime only [From Latin, literally 'to the meanwhile']

adios /áddi óss/ *interj.* used to say goodbye (*informal*) [Mid-19thC. From Spanish, literally 'to God' (see ADIEU).]

adipic acid /ə díppik-/ *n.* a white crystalline solid used in making nylon and in the production of other chemicals. Formula: $C_6H_{10}O_4$. [Mid-19thC. *Adipic* formed from the Latin stem *adip-* 'fat' (see ADIPO-), because the acid was originally made by oxidizing fats.]

adipo- *prefix.* fat, fatty ○ *adipocyte* [From Latin *adip-*, the stem of *adeps* 'fat', of unknown origin]

adipocere /áddi pō seer/ *n.* a brownish, waxy substance, consisting primarily of fatty acids, that is produced by postmortem chemical changes to body fat over time or as a result of prolonged immersion in water [Early 19thC. From French, from the Latin stem *adip-* (see ADIPO-) + French *cire* 'wax'.]

adipocyte /áddi pō sīt/ *n.* a cell that synthesizes and stores fat [Mid-20thC. Coined from modern Latin *adiposus* 'of fat' (from the Latin stem *adip-* 'animal fat') + -CYTE.]

adipose /áddi pōss/ *adj.* FATTY containing fat ■ *n.* FAT fat found in tissue just below the skin and surrounding major organs, acting as an energy reserve and providing insulation and protection [Mid-18thC. From modern Latin *adiposus* 'fatty'.] —**adiposeness** *n.* —**adiposity** /áddi póssəti/ *n.*

adipose tissue *n.* connective tissue in animal bodies that contains fat

adipsin /ay dípsin/ *n.* a protein that is believed to control appetite, and so is used to treat obesity [Late 20thC. Coined from *adipsia* 'abstaining from liquids'.]

Adirondack Mountains /áddə rón dak-/, **Adirondacks** mountain chain in northeastern New York State, known for spectacular scenery and recreational activities. The highest peak is Mount Marcy 1,629 m/5,344 ft.

adit /áddit/ *n.* a nearly horizontal shaft used for giving access to a mine or for drainage [Early 17thC. From Latin *aditus* 'approach, entrance', from the past participle of *adire* 'to go towards', from *ire* 'to go'.]

adj. *abbr.* **1.** GRAM adjective **2.** MATH adjoint **3.** adjunct **4.** BANKING, INSUR adjustment **5. adj., Adj.** MIL adjutant

adjacency /ə jáyss'nssi/ (*plural* **-cies**) *n.* **1.** STH ADJACENT sth that is near or adjoining **2.** BEING ADJACENT the state of being near or adjoining

adjacent /ə jáyss'nt/ *adj.* **1.** NEIGHBOURING near or close, especially adjoining **2.** MATH SHARING EDGES used to describe either a pair of vertices in a graph that have common edges, or a pair of edges in a graph that have a common vertex [15thC. From Latin *adjacent-*, the present participle stem of *adjacere* 'to lie near', from *jacere* 'to lie'.]

WORD KEY: USAGE

adjacent or **adjoining**? Two houses are said to be ***adjoining*** when they are next to each other with a common wall. ***Adjoining*** tables are next to each other end to end, forming one surface (they are, to use a more technical word, **contiguous**). ***Adjacent*** houses, on the other hand, can have a space between them or even be on opposite sides of the road, as long as there is nothing significant between them (for example another house) and they are close enough for you to pass easily from one to the other. ***Adjacent*** tables are next to each other but not necessarily touching. Note also that ***adjoining***, being a form of a verb, can govern an object (*the house adjoining ours*), whereas ***adjacent*** needs the addition of *to* (*the house adjacent to ours*).

adjacent angle *n.* either of the two angles that are formed by the intersection of two straight lines and lie on the same side of one line

adjectival /ájjik tív'l/ *adj.* **1.** USED AS ADJECTIVE relating to or functioning as an adjective **2.** LAW = **adjective** —**adjectivally** *adv.*

adjective /ájjiktiv/ *n.* WORD QUALIFYING NOUN a word that qualifies or describes a noun or pronoun ■ *adj.* **1.** ACTING AS ADJECTIVE relating to, forming, or functioning as an adjective **2.** LAW PRACTISED IN COURT relating to court practice and procedure rather than the principles of law [14thC. Via French *adjectif* from Latin *adjectivus*, from, ultimately, *adjicere*, literally 'to throw to', from *jacere* 'to throw'.] —**adjectively** *adv.*

adjective pronoun *n.* a pronoun acting as an adjective, e.g. 'what' in 'what day is it?'

adjoin /ə jóyn/ (**-joins, -joining, -joined**) *v.* **1.** *vti.* BORDER to be next to or share a common border with sth, especially an area of land ○ *The two properties adjoin.* **2.** *vt.* CONNECT to attach or add on sth (*archaic*) [14thC. Via Old French *ajoin-*, the stem of *ajoindre*, from Latin *adjungere* 'to join to', from *jungere* 'to join'.]

adjoining /ə jóyning/ *adj.* situated next to or touching sth or each other

WORD KEY: USAGE

See Usage note at ***adjacent.***

adjoint /ájjoynt/ *n.* a matrix formed from a given square matrix, each element being derived from its cofactors, the determinants of the given matrix obtained by removing the row and column containing the element [Late 16thC. From French, the past participle of *adjoindre* (see ADJOIN).]

adjourn /ə júrn/ (**-journs, -journing, -journed**) *v.* **1.** *vti.* POSTPONE PROCEEDINGS to suspend the business of a court, legislature, or committee temporarily or indefinitely, or become suspended temporarily or indefinitely ○ *The court adjourned at one o'clock.* **2.** *vti.* POSTPONE to postpone a meeting to another time, or become postponed **3.** *vt.* DEFER to defer a matter or an action to another time **4.** *vi.* MOVE AS GROUP to move together from one place to another **5.** *vi.* STOP WORKING to stop working (*informal*) [14thC. From Old French *ajourner*, from the phrase *à jorn (nomé)* 'to an (appointed) day'.]

adjournment /ə júrnmənt/ *n.* a temporary or indefinite cessation of the business of a court, legislature, or committee

adjournment debate *n.* in the British House of Commons, a debate on the motion that Parliament be adjourned, used as a formal device for raising other topics

Adjt *abbr.* adjutant

adjudge /ə júj/ (**-judges, -judging, -judged**) *vt.* **1.** MAKE DECLARATION ABOUT to judge sb or sth in a particular way ○ *She was adjudged to be an accomplished musician.* **2.** LAW DETERMINE JUDICIALLY to decide sth in a judicial proceeding **3.** LAW DECREE LEGALLY to pronounce sth by law **4.** GRANT MONEY IN JUDGMENT to make sb an award of damages or costs in a legal judgment [14thC. Via Old French *ajuger* from Latin *adjudicare* (see ADJUDICATE).]

adjudicate /ə jóodi kayt/ (**-cates, -cating, -cated**) *vti.* **1.** LAW DECIDE LEGALLY to reach a judicial decision on sth **2.** DECIDE ABOUT to make an official decision about a problem or dispute [Early 18thC. From Latin *adjudicat-*, the past participle stem of *adjudicare* 'to award in arbitration', from the stem *judic-* 'judge'.] —**adjudicative** /ə jóodikətiv/ *adj.* —**adjudicator** /-kaytər/ *n.*

adjudication /ə jóodi káysh'n/ *n.* **1.** PROCESS OF JUDGING the process of making an official decision about a problem, dispute, or competition **2.** COURT DECISION a judicial decision, sentence, or decree

adjunct /ájjungkt/ *n.* **1.** STH EXTRA ADDED ON sth inessential added to sth else **2.** ASSISTANT sb who assists and is subordinate to sb else **3.** GRAM INESSENTIAL PART OF SENTENCE a part of a sentence that is not the subject or predicate [Early 16thC. From Latin *adjunctus*, the past participle of *adjungere* (see ADJOIN).] —**adjunction** /ə júngksh'n/ *n.* —**adjunctive** *adj.*

adjuration /ájjoo ráysh'n/ *n.* **1.** FORMAL OATH a solemn oath **2.** SUPPLICATION an earnest appeal —**adjuratory** /ə jóorətəri, ájjoo ráy-/ *adj.*

adjure /ə jóor/ (**-jures, -juring, -jured**) *vt.* **1.** COMMAND SOLEMNLY to order sb to do sth, especially under oath **2.** MAKE APPEAL to make an earnest appeal to sb [14thC. From Latin *adjurare* 'to swear by oath', from *jurare* 'to swear' (see JURY).] —**adjurer** *n.*

adjust /ə júst/ (**-justs, -justing, -justed**) *v.* **1.** *vt.* CHANGE SLIGHTLY to make slight changes in sth to make it fit or function better **2.** *vti.* ADAPT TO NEW CIRCUMSTANCES to adapt to a new environment or condition **3.** *vt.* REARRANGE to put sth back in order, especially clothing, so that it is tidy **4.** *vt.* DECIDE AMOUNT OF MONEY OWED to decide what sums are payable in the settlement of an insurance claim [Early 17thC. Via obsolete French *adjuster* from assumed Vulgar Latin *adjuxtare* 'to put close to', from Latin *juxta* 'close' (source of English *juxtapose*).]

adjustable /ə jústəb'l/ *adj.* able to change or be changed slightly so as to fit or become more accurate —**adjustably** *adv.*

adjustable rate mortgage *n.* *US* = **variable rate mortgage**

adjuster /ə jústər/, **adjustor** n. US = loss adjuster

adjustment /ə jústmənt/ n. **1.** ACT OF BEING ADJUSTED the act of being or becoming adjusted **2.** SLIGHT CHANGE a slight change intended to make sth fit or function better **3.** DEVICE FOR ADJUSTING STH a device for adjusting sth

adjutant /ájjōtənt/ n. an officer who acts as an administrative assistant to a commanding officer [Early 17thC. From Latin *adjutant-*, the present participle stem of *adjutare*, literally 'to keep on helping' (source also of English *aid*), from *adjuvare* (see ADJUVANT).]

adjutant general (*plural* **adjutants general**) n. **1.** SENIOR MILITARY ADMINISTRATIVE OFFICER an army general responsible for administration and personnel **2.** GENERAL'S EXECUTIVE OFFICER an executive officer of an army general

Adjutant stork

adjutant stork n. a carrion-eating stork of Southeast Asia with a pink neck and soft white feathers on its underside. Latin name: *Leptoptilos dubius* and *Leptoptilos javanicus*. [From the similarity of its walk to that of a military staff officer]

adjuvant /ájjōovənt/ n. **1.** MED DRUG-ENHANCING AGENT a drug or agent added to another drug or agent to enhance its medical effectiveness **2.** MED ANTIGEN-ENHANCING DRUG a substance injected along with an antigen to enhance the immune response stimulated by the antigen **3.** HELPING AGENT sth that helps or assists ■ *adj.* SUPPLEMENTARY helping by supplementing [Late 16thC. Directly or via French, from Latin *adjuvant-*, the present participle stem of *adjuvare* 'to give help to', from *juvare* 'to help'.]

Adler /ádlər/, **Alfred** (1870–1937) Austrian psychiatrist who stressed the importance of the inferiority complex. His books include *The Neurotic Constitution* (1912).

ad lib /ád líb/ *adj.* = ad libitum ■ *adv.* **1.** = ad libitum **2.** OFF THE CUFF without any advance preparation [Early 19thC. Shortening of AD LIBITUM.]

ad-lib /ád líb/ *vti.* (**ad-libs, ad-libbing, ad-libbed**) IMPROVISE SPEECH OR PERFORMANCE to make up a speech or a musical or dramatic performance on the spot without a fixed text or score ■ *adj.* UNPLANNED improvised or made up on the spot ■ *n.* IMPROVISED REMARK IN PERFORMANCE sth said by an actor or other performer that is not in the script [Early 20th C. From AD LIB.] —**ad-libber** n.

ad libitum /ád líbbitəm/ *adj., adv.* to be performed at the discretion of the performer, or in a speed or style of the performer's choice [Early 17thC. From Latin, literally 'at your pleasure'.]

ad litem /ád lí tem/ *adj.* LAW appointed by a court to represent a minor [Mid-18thC. From Latin, literally 'for the purpose of a lawsuit'.]

Adm. *abbr.* **1.** Admiral **2.** Admiralty

adman /ád man/ (*plural* **-men** /-men/) n. sb who works in the advertising business (*informal*)

admass /ád mass/ n. the part of society that can be influenced by advertising or publicity [Mid-20thC. Coined by the English writer J. B. Priestley from AD + MASS.]

admeasure /ad mézhər/ (**-ures, -uring, -ured**) *vt.* to divide sth up to be shared out [14thC. Via Old French *amesurer* from medieval Latin *admensurare* 'to apply a measure to'.]

admin /ád min/ n. the administrative work involved in running a business or organization (*informal*) [Mid-20thC. Shortening.]

administer /əd mínnistər/ (**-ters, -tering, -tered**) v. **1.** *vti.* BE IN CHARGE OF to manage the affairs of a business, organization, or institution **2.** *vt.* DISPENSE to preside over the dispensation of sth ○ *He administered justice in the fairest possible manner.* **3.** *vt.* GIVE AS MEDICATION to give sb a measured amount of a medication, often also physically introducing it into the body **4.** *vt.* PERFORM AS MEDICAL PROCEDURE to apply a medical technique or procedure to sb **5.** *vt.* PERFORM AS RITUAL to carry out a set ritual or religious ceremony on behalf of an individual or group **6.** *vi.* SUPERVISE OATH-TAKING to oversee the taking of an oath by sb **7.** *vi.* LOOK AFTER SB to look after and tend to the needs of sb **8.** *vt.* ORGANIZE HANDOVER OF PROPERTY to manage the distribution of a deceased person's property in accordance with the law [14thC. Via Old French *aminister* from Latin *administrare* 'to serve, manage', from *ministrare* 'to serve'.] —**administrable** *adj.*

administrate /əd mínni strayt/ (**-trates, -trating, -trated**) *vti.* to oversee or organize the affairs of sth, especially a business, organization, or institution [Mid-16thC. From Latin *administrat-*, past participle stem of *administrare* (see ADMINISTER).]

administration /əd mínni stráysh'n/ n. **1.** MANAGEMENT OF BUSINESS the management of the affairs of a business or organization **2.** MANAGEMENT STAFF the staff of a business or institution whose task is to manage its affairs **3.** MANAGEMENT OF GOVERNMENT the management of public affairs or the affairs of a government **4.** STAFF OF GOVERNMENT a government's staff whose task is to manage its affairs **5.** TERM OF OFFICE the duration of a particular office, usually a political one **6.** GOVERNMENT a government, especially its executive branch **7.** LEGAL DISPOSAL OF ESTATE the disposal or management of a deceased person's estate or an estate held in trust **8.** ADMINISTERING STH TO SB the act of administering sth such as an oath, medicine, or sacrament **9.** STH ADMINISTERED sth that is administered to sb, especially an oath, medicine, or sacrament

administration order n. **1.** COURT ORDER a court order appointing sb to run a company in financial trouble, in order to return it to successful trading or to oversee the sale of its assets **2.** COURT ORDER FOR DEBT a court order appointing sb to administer the estate of a debtor

administrative /əd mínnistrətiv/ *adj.* relating to the administration of a business or organization —**administratively** *adv.*

administrative area n. a part of a country under the control of a particular local government administration

administrative law n. the area of law dealing with the affairs of agencies of the executive branch of a government, and with the judicial review of public bodies generally

administrative officer n. sb whose job is to carry out administrative tasks in an institution or a local or central government body, usually at a fairly junior level

administrator /əd mínni straytər/ n. **1.** MANAGER IN ORGANIZATION sb whose job is to administer the affairs of a business or organization **2.** MANAGER OF ESTATE sb appointed by a court to manage the estate of a deceased person, especially when there is no competent executor

admirable /ádmərəb'l/ *adj.* deserving to be admired [15thC. From Latin *admirabilis*, from *admirari* (see ADMIRE).] —**admirableness** n. —**admirably** *adv.*

admiral /ádmərəl/ n. **1.** NAVAL COMMANDER the officer in command of a navy or fleet **2.** SENIOR NAVAL OFFICER a naval rank above vice admiral and below Admiral of the Fleet **3.** NAVAL OFFICER a high-ranking naval officer entitled to fly a personal flag **4.** ADMIRAL'S FLAGSHIP an admiral's flagship (*archaic*) **5.** ZOOL BRIGHTLY COLOURED BUTTERFLY a brightly coloured butterfly of temperate regions. Family: Nymphalidae. ◊ **red admiral, white admiral** [13thC. Via French *amiral* from, ultimately, Arabic *amir-al*, literally 'commander of' in such phrases as *amir-al-bahr* 'commander of the sea'.] —**admiralship** n.

Admiral of the Fleet n. an officer holding the highest rank in the Royal Navy or the US Navy

admiralty /ádmərəlti/ (*plural* **-miralties**) n. the office or jurisdiction of an admiral

Admiralty n. a former UK government department that administered the affairs of the Navy

Admiralty Board n. the department of the British Ministry of Defence responsible for the administration of the Royal Navy

Admiralty Islands /ádmərəlti-/ island group in the Bismarck Archipelago, north of New Guinea in the western Pacific Ocean. Manus is the group's largest island. Area: 2,072 sq. km/829 sq. mi.

admiration /ádmə ráysh'n/ n. **1.** HIGH REGARD a feeling of pleasure, approval, and, often, surprise **2.** OBJECT OF HIGH REGARD sth or sb regarded with a feeling of pleasure, approval, and, often, surprise

— WORD KEY: SYNONYMS —
See Synonyms at *regard*.

admire /əd mír/ (**-mires, -miring, -mired**) *vt.* **1.** BE PLEASED BY to regard sb or sth with a feeling of pleasure, approval, and, often, surprise **2.** RESPECT to have a high opinion of sb or sth, e.g. a quality or attribute [Late 16thC. Directly or via French *admirer* from Latin *admirari* 'to wonder at', from *mirari* 'to wonder' (source of English *miracle*).]

admiring /əd míring/ *adj.* full of admiration for sb or sth —**admiringly** *adv.*

admissibility /əd míssə bílləti/ n. acceptability in court, usually during a trial

admissible /əd míssəb'l/ *adj.* **1.** ALLOWABLE allowed to be done **2.** ALLOWED TO COME IN able or deserving to enter **3.** ALLOWED TO BE GIVEN IN COURT accepted as evidence in court [Early 17thC. Directly or via French, from medieval Latin *admissibilis*, from the Latin stem *admiss-* (see ADMISSION).] —**admissibleness** n. —**admissibly** *adv.*

admission /əd mísh'n/ n. **1.** ENTRY the right, ability, or permission to enter **2.** FEE FOR ENTRY a fee paid for entrance to a place or event **3.** CONFESSION a confession to having committed a crime or having made a mistake **4.** DECLARATION an acknowledgment that sth is true [15thC. From the Latin stem *admission-*, from *admiss-*, the past participle stem of *admittere* (see ADMIT).]

— WORD KEY: USAGE —
admission or **admittance**? Both words mean 'permission or right to enter'. *Admission* is the more usual word, whereas **admittance** is largely restricted to formal or official contexts, for example signs and notices: *Admission is by ticket only. No admittance.* **Admission** is the only word of the two that can by itself mean 'the price charged for entrance' and that can be used before another noun in this meaning: *admission money*; *admission ticket*.

admissive /əd míssiv/ *adj.* granting or showing admission

admit /əd mít/ (**-mits, -mitting, -mitted**) v. **1.** *vti.* CONFESS to confess to having committed a crime or having made a mistake **2.** *vti.* ACKNOWLEDGE TRUTH to acknowledge that sth is true ○ *You must admit it is a tempting offer.* **3.** *vt.* ALLOW TO ENTER to allow sb or sth entrance or access ○ *'Admits one'* **4.** *vti.* OFFER POSSIBILITY to permit the possibility of sth ○ *Their conduct admits of only one explanation.* [14thC. From Latin *admittere*, literally 'to let go into', from *mittere* 'to let go'. The sense 'to confess' probably evolved from 'letting a confession enter your speech'.]

Admiral butterfly

admittance /əd mítt'ns/ n. **1.** PERMISSION TO GO IN permission or right to enter a place **2.** ENTRANCE TO PLACE physical entry to a place **3.** PHYS MEASURE OF FLOW

OF CURRENT the reciprocal of impedance, a measure of the ability of an electrical current to flow. Symbol *Y*

— **WORD KEY: USAGE** —

See Usage note at **admission.**

admittedly /əd míttidli/ *adv.* as must be acknowledged

admix /əd míks/ (-mixes, -mixing, -mixed) *vt.* to mix sth into sth else [Early 16thC. Origin uncertain: probably a back-formation from ADMIXTURE.]

admixture /əd míkschər/ *n.* **1. PRODUCT OF MIXING** sth produced by mixing sth into sth else **2. INGREDIENT** sth added to sth else by mixing **3. PROCESS OF MIXING INGREDIENTS** the mixing of sth into sth else [Early 17thC. Formed from MIXTURE.]

admonish /əd mónnish/ (-ishes, -ishing, -ished) *vt.* **1. REBUKE** to rebuke sb mildly but earnestly **2. ADVISE** to advise sb to do or, more often, not to do sth **3. REPRIMAND OFFICIALLY** in the UK police force, to reprimand an employee severely for misconduct [14thC. Anglicization of Old French *amonester* from assumed Vulgar Latin *admonere*, from Latin *monere* 'to warn' (source of English *monitor*).] —**admonisher** *n.*

admonishment /əd mónnishmənt/ *n.* in the UK police force, a severe reprimand to an employee for misconduct

admonition /ádmə nísh'n/ *n.* **1. REBUKE** a mild but earnest rebuke **2. ADVICE** advice for or against doing sth

admonitory /əd mónnitəri/ *adj.* **1. REBUKING** mildly reproving **2. ADVISORY** advising sb to do or not to do sth

ad nauseam /ad náwzi am/ *adv.* to an extreme or annoying extent [Mid-17thC. From Latin, literally 'to sickness'.]

adnexa /ad néksə/ *npl.* adjoining structural parts of the body [Late 19thC. From Latin, from, ultimately, *adnectere* 'to tie together', from *nectere* 'to tie'.] —**adnexal** *adj.*

adnominal /əd nómmin'l/ *n.* a word that modifies a noun [Mid-19thC. Formed from Latin *adnomen*, alteration of *agnomen* 'agnomen'.] —**adnominal** *adj.*

adnoun /ád nown/ *n.* an adjective that is used as a noun, e.g. 'meek' in 'Blessed are the meek' [Mid-18thC. Coined from AD- + NOUN, on the model of *adverb*.]

ado /ə doó/ *n.* excited activity or bother [14thC. Contraction of northern English dialect *at do*, a form of 'to do', from Old Norse *at* 'to' + DO.] ◇ **without further** or **more ado** without wasting any time

— **WORD KEY: CULTURAL NOTE** —

Much Ado About Nothing, a play by William Shakespeare (1598?). A comedy set in the court of the Duke of Messina in Sicily, it tells of the love of a soldier, Claudio, for the Duke's daughter, Hero, and the eventually unsuccessful attempts of Claudio's enemy, Don John, to prevent their marriage.

adobe /ə dóbi/ *n.* **1. EARTHEN BRICK** brick made from earth and straw and dried by the sun **2. BUILDING MADE OF ADOBE** a structure made with adobe bricks **3. EARTH THAT FORMS ADOBE** earth used to make adobe bricks [Mid-18thC. Via Spanish, from Arabic *at-tūb* 'the bricks'.]

adobe flat *n.* in the United States, a gently sloping plain of clay soil deposited by desert floods

adobo /ə dóbō/ (*plural* -**bos**) *n.* a Philippine dish of marinated meat or fish seasoned with vinegar, garlic, soy sauce, and spices [Mid-20thC. From Spanish.]

adolescence /áddə léss'nss/ *n.* **1. TIME PRECEDING ADULTHOOD** the period from puberty to adulthood in human beings **2. INTERMEDIATE STAGE OF DEVELOPMENT** the stage in the development of sth such as a civilization before its reaching maturity

adolescent /áddə léssn't/ *n.* **SB IN PERIOD PRECEDING ADULTHOOD** sb who has reached puberty but is not yet an adult ■ *adj.* **1. EXPERIENCING ADOLESCENCE** going through the period of adolescence ○ *adolescent males* **2. HAPPENING DURING ADOLESCENCE** typically occurring during the period of adolescence **3. IMMATURE** typical of sb who is immature [15thC. Via French, from Latin *adolescent-*, the present participle stem of *adolescere* 'to be nourished, grow up' (source also of English *adult*), from *alere* 'to nourish'.]

— **WORD KEY: SYNONYMS** —

See Synonyms at **young.**

Adonai /áddo ní/ *n.* a name used in Judaism to speak the unspeakable name of YHWH, God [14thC. From Hebrew *'ăḏōnay*.]

Adonic /ə dónnik/ *adj.* **1. OF CLASSICAL VERSE STYLE** used to describe a line in classical verse consisting of a dactyl followed by either a spondee or trochee **2. RELATING TO ADONIS** like or typical of Adonis ■ *n.* **CLASSICAL LINE OR POEM** an Adonic line or poem [Late 16thC. Via French, from medieval Latin *adonicus*, from Greek *Adōnis* 'ADONIS'.]

Adonis /ə dóniss/ *n.* **1. YOUNG MAN IN GREEK MYTHOLOGY** in Greek mythology, a handsome youth loved by Aphrodite and Persephone. He was killed while hunting boar, but was allowed by Zeus to divide his time between Aphrodite on earth and Persephone in the underworld. **2. HANDSOME YOUTH adonis, Adonis** an extremely handsome young man [Late 16thC. From Greek *Adōnis*, from, ultimately, Phoenician *æḏōnī* 'my lord'.]

adopt /ə dópt/ (**adopts, adopting, adopted**) *vt.* **1. LEGALLY RAISE ANOTHER'S CHILD AS YOUR OWN** to raise a child of other biological parents as if it were your own, in accordance with formal legal procedures **2. CHOOSE AND DECIDE TO USE** to take up sth such as a plan, idea, cause, or practice and use or follow it **3. TAKE OVER** to take over sth such as an idea that originated elsewhere and use it as your own **4. CHOOSE AS CANDIDATE** to choose sb as a political candidate **5. ASSUME WAY OF ACTING** to assume a particular attitude or way of behaving **6. START USING** to take on and use a new name or title **7. VOTE IN FAVOUR OF** to vote to accept sth such as a committee's decision or a parliamentary bill [15thC. Directly or via French *adopter* from Latin *adoptare* 'to choose for oneself', from *optare* 'to choose' (see OPT).] —**adoptable** *adj.* —**adopter** *n.*

— **WORD KEY: USAGE** —

adopted or **adoptive?** Parents who adopt a child have an *adopted* child, and the child has *adoptive* parents. It is easy to confuse these two words but it is important to remember the distinction.

adopted /ə dóptid/ *adj.* used to describe a child who has been adopted

adoptee /ə dóp teé/ *n.* a child who has been adopted

adoption /ə dópsh'n/ *n.* **1. LEGAL PROCEDURE FOR ADOPTING A CHILD** a formal legal process to adopt a child **2. INSTANCE OF ADOPTING SB OR STH** an instance of adopting sb or sth such as an idea, name, or attitude

adoption panel *n.* a committee set up by a local authority to make recommendations on proposed cases concerning the adoption of a child

adoptive /ə dóptiv/ *adj.* used to describe a parent who adopts a child or sb related to another by adoption

— **WORD KEY: USAGE** —

See Usage note at **adopt.**

adorable /ə dáwrəb'l/ *adj.* charming, lovable, and usually very attractive —**adorability** /ə dáwrə bílləti/ *n.* —**adorableness** /-b'lnəss/ *n.* —**adorably** /-əbli/ *adv.*

adoration /áddə ráysh'n/ *n.* **1. LOVE** great love and esteem **2. WORSHIP** religious worship of God, a god, or a spirit

adore /ə dáwr/ (**adores, adoring, adored**) *vt.* **1. LOVE DEEPLY** to love sb intensely **2. WORSHIP** to worship God, a god, or a spirit **3. LIKE VERY MUCH** to like sth or sb very much (*informal*) [14thC. Via Old French, from late Latin *adorare*, literally 'to pray to', from Latin *orare* 'to pray' (see ORATE).] —**adorer** *n.*

adoring /ə dáwring/ *adj.* showing love or admiration for sb —**adoringly** *adv.*

adorn /ə dáwrn/ (**adorns, adorning, adorned**) *vt.* **1. EMBELLISH** to add decoration or ornamentation to sth **2. ENHANCE** to add to the beauty or glory of sth or sb [14thC. Via Old French, from Latin *adornare* 'to embellish with ornaments', from *ornare* 'to embellish' (see ORNATE).] —**adorner** *n.*

adornment /ə dáwrnmənt/ *n.* **1. DECORATING** the act of adorning sth **2. STH DECORATIVE** a decorative item or material added to sth to make it more attractive

ADP[1] *n.* a chemical compound (**nucleotide**) in living organisms that is formed when another nucleotide (**ATP**) breaks down to release energy that is used by cells. Full form **adenosine diphosphate**

ADP[2] *abbr.* automatic data processing

Adrastea /ə drásti ə/ *n.* a small natural satellite of Jupiter, discovered in 1979

ad rem /ad rém/ *adv.* to the point or purpose [Late 16thC. From Latin, literally 'to the matter or business'.] —**ad rem** *adj.*

adren- *prefix.* = **adreno-** (*used before vowels*)

adrenal /ə dréen'l/ *adj.* **1. ON THE KIDNEYS** relating to or on the kidneys **2. RELATING TO ADRENAL GLANDS** used to describe parts or effects of the adrenal glands ■ *n.* = **adrenal gland** [Late 19thC. Coined from AD- + RENAL.] —**adrenally** *adv.*

adrenalectomy /ə dreenə léktəmi/ (*plural* -**mies**) *n.* the surgical removal of one or both of the adrenal glands

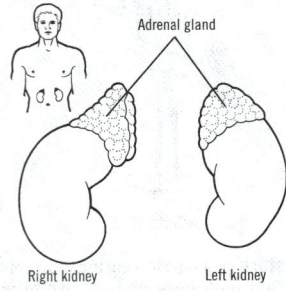

Adrenal glands

adrenal gland *n.* an endocrine gland located above each kidney. The inner part (**medulla**) of each gland secretes adrenalin and the outer part (**cortex**) secretes steroids.

adrenalin /ə drénnəlin/, **adrenaline** *n.* a hormone secreted in the adrenal gland that raises blood pressure, produces a rapid heartbeat, and acts as a neurotransmitter when the body is subjected to stress or danger (*often used informally*) ○ *get the adrenalin pumping* [Early 20thC. Coined from ADRENAL + -IN.]

— **WORD KEY: USAGE** —

adrenalin or **adrenaline?** In British English, the usual spelling is *adrenalin,* but *adrenaline* is also used. In American usage, *adrenaline* is the more usual spelling, and *Adrenalin* (with a capital initial letter) is a proprietary term for a commercial drug. An alternative term, especially in American English, is *epinephrine.*

adrenergic /áddrə núrjik/ *adj.* producing or activated by adrenalin or a similar substance —**adrenergically** *adv.*

adreno-, adren- *prefix.* pertaining to adrenaline or the adrenal glands ○ *adrenochrome* [Coined from AD- + RENAL, because the adrenal glands are next to the kidneys]

adrenocortical /ə dreenō káwrtik'l/ *adj.* involving, located in, or produced by the cortex of the adrenal glands

adrenocorticosteroid /ə dreenō káwrtikō steér oyd, -stérr oyd/ *n.* **1. HORMONE PRODUCED BY ADRENAL GLANDS** a steroid hormone obtained from the cortex of the adrenal glands **2. SYNTHETIC STEROID DRUG** a drug with similar physiological effects to the natural steroid produced by the cortex of the adrenal glands

adrenocorticotrophic /ə dreenō káwrtikō tróffik/, **adrenocorticotropic** /-tróppik/ *adj.* used to describe hormones or drugs that stimulate the cortex of the adrenal glands to produce corticosteroids

adrenocorticotrophic hormone *n.* full form of **ACTH**

adrenocorticotrophin /ə dreenō káwrtikō tróffin/, **adrenocorticotropin** /-tróppin/ *n.* = **ACTH**

adrenoleukodystrophy /ə dreenō loókə dístrəfi/ *n.* a hereditary disorder of the nervous system in boys that affects the adrenal glands

adrenolytic /ə dreenō líttik/ *adj.* **STOPPING ADRENALIN EFFECTS** blocking the action of the adrenergic nerves

a at; aa father; aw all; ay day; air hair; ə about, edible, item, common, circus; e egg; ee eel; hw when; i it, happy; ī ice; 'l apple; 'm rhythm; 'n fashion; o odd; ō open; oo good; oo pool; ow owl; oy oil; th thin; th this; u up; ur urge;

or inhibiting the response to adrenalin ■ *n.* INHIBITORY DRUG an adrenolytic drug or agent

Adriatic Sea /áydri áttik-/ arm of the Mediterranean Sea, east of Italy. Area: about155,000 sq.km/60,000 sq.mi.

adrift /ə drı́ft/ *adj., adv.* **1.** FLOATING WITHOUT DIRECTION floating freely without being steered in a particular direction **2.** WITHOUT PURPOSE living life without a goal **3.** OFF TARGET astray, off target, or amiss

adroit /ə dróyt/ *adj.* **1.** SKILFUL displaying physical or mental skill **2.** QUICK-WITTED able to react quickly in thought or actions [Mid-17thC. From French *à droit* 'by right, properly'. The meaning 'skilful' evolved from the idea of 'doing sth properly or well'.] —**adroitly** *adv.* —**adroitness** *n.*

adscititious /ádsi tíshəss/ *adj.* added to sth rather than being inherent or essential (*formal*) [Early 17thC. Formed from Latin *adscit-*, the past participle stem of *adsciscere* 'to admit, adopt'.]

ADSL *abbr.* asymmetrical digital subscriber line

adsorb /ad sáwrb, -záwrb/ (**-sorbs, -sorbing, -sorbed**) *vti.* to undergo or cause sth to undergo adsorption [Late 19thC. Back-formation from ADSORPTION.] —**adsorbable** *adj.*

adsorbate /ad sáwr bayt, -sáwrb-/ *n.* a substance that is adsorbed

adsorbent /ad sáwrbənt, -záwrbənt/ *adj.* CAPABLE OF ADSORBING able to adsorb ■ *n.* ADSORBING SUBSTANCE a substance capable of adsorbing

adsorption /ad sáwrpsh'n, -záwrp-/ *n.* the process by which a layer of atoms or molecules of a substance, usually a gas, is formed on the surface of a solid or liquid [Late 19thC. Blend of AD- and ABSORPTION.] —**adsorptive** *adj.*

adularia /áddyoǒ láiri ə/ *n.* a white or transparent variety of the mineral orthoclase, used as a gemstone. Formula: $KAlSi_3O_8$. [Late 18thC. Formed from French *adulaire*, from *Adula*, the name of mountains in the Swiss Alps where the mineral was first found.]

adulate /áddyoǒ layt/ (**-lates, -lating, -lated**) *vt.* to admire or flatter sb excessively [Mid-18thC. Back-formation from ADULATION.] —**adulator** *n.*

adulation /áddyoǒ láysh'n/ *n.* excessive flattery or admiration [14thC. Directly or via French, from the Latin stem *adulation-*, from *adulari* 'to flatter'.]

adulatory /áddyoǒ láytəri/ *adj.* excessively admiring and flattering

adult /áddult, ə dúlt/ *adj.* **1.** COMPLETELY GROWN fully developed and mature **2.** FOR SB MATURE involving, typical of, or meant for mature people **3.** UNSUITABLE FOR CHILDREN considered unsuitable for young people because of pornography, violence, or sexually explicit language ■ *n.* **1.** FULLY GROWN LIFE FORM a fully mature person, animal, plant, or other form of life **2.** SB LEGALLY AN ADULT sb who has reached the age of legal majority [Mid-16thC. From Latin *adultus*, the past participle of *adolescere* (see ADOLESCENT).] —**adultness** *n.*

adult child (*plural* **adult children**) *n.* sb who is an adult in age but, because of a psychiatric disorder, thinks and behaves more like a child

adulterant /ə dúltərənt/ *n.* sth that makes sth else less pure —**adulterant** *adj.*

adulterate /ə dúltə rayt/ *vt.* (**-ates, -ating, -ated**) MAKE IMPURE to make sth less pure by adding inferior or unsuitable elements or substances to it ■ *adj.* **1.** IMPURE made less pure **2.** = **adulterous** (*literary*) [Mid-16thC. From Latin *adulterat-*, the past participle stem of *adulterare* 'to change, corrupt, commit adultery', from *alterare* 'to alter' (see ALTER).] —**adulterative** /-rətiv/ *adj.*

adulteration /ə dúltə ráysh'n/ *n.* the act of making sth less pure by adding an inferior or unsuitable substance

adulterer /ə dúltərər/ *n.* sb who commits adultery [Early 16thC. Formed from earlier *adulter* 'to commit adultery', from Latin *adulterare* (see ADULTERATE).]

adulteress /ə dúltərəss/ *n.* a woman who commits adultery [Early 17thC. Via Old French *a(v)outresse* from *a(v)outrer* 'to commit adultery', from Latin *adulterare* (see ADULTERATE).]

adulterine /ə dúltərin/ *adj.* **1.** IMPURE characterized by adulteration **2.** BORN IN ADULTERY born from an adulterous relationship **3.** ILLEGAL not within the law

adulterous /ə dúltərəss/ *adj.* relating to or involved in adultery [Early 17thC. Formed from earlier *adulter* 'adulterer' from Latin *adulterare* (see ADULTERATE).] —**adulterously** *adv.*

adultery /ə dúltəri/ *n.* voluntary sexual relations between a married person and sb other than his or her spouse [15thC. Directly and via Old French *avout(e)rie* from Latin *adulterare* (see ADULTERATE).]

adulthood /áddult hoǒd, ə dúlt-/ *n.* the age or state of legal majority

adult-onset diabetes *n.* a form of diabetes mellitus that develops slowly in some adults as the body becomes unable to use insulin effectively

Adult Training Centre *n.* a local authority day centre at which adults with special needs gain work experience and learn social and life skills

adumbrate /áddum brayt/ (**-brates, -brating, -brated**) *vt.* **1.** SKETCHILY INDICATE to give an incomplete or faint outline or indication of sth **2.** FORESHADOW to give a vague indication or warning of sth to come **3.** CONCEAL to overshadow and obscure sth [Late 16thC. From Latin *adumbrat-*, the past participle stem of *adumbrare* 'to overshadow', from *umbra* 'shade'.] —**adumbration** /áddum bráysh'n/ *n.* —**adumbrative** /ad úmbrətiv/ *adj.* —**adumbratively** *adv.*

adv. *abbr.* **1.** adverb **2.** adverbial **3.** advertisement **4.** advisory

ad val. *abbr.* ad valorem

ad valorem /ád və láw rem/ *adj., adv.* in proportion to the value of sth [Late 17thC. From Latin.]

advance /əd vaánss/ *v.* (**-vances, -vancing, -vanced**) **1.** *vti.* MOVE AHEAD to move forward in position **2.** *vt.* SUGGEST to put sth forward as a proposal **3.** *vt.* GIVE BEFOREHAND to supply sth or part of sth, especially money, before it is due **4.** *vt.* LEND MONEY OR GOODS to supply money or goods on credit **5.** *vti.* RISE IN STATUS to rise in rank or position **6.** *vt.* BRING FORWARD IN TIME to make sth happen earlier than originally expected **7.** *vti.* PROGRESS to further the progress or improvement of sth, e.g. a cause, or undergo such progress or improvement **8.** *vti.* RISE IN AMOUNT to increase in price, rate, or amount ■ *n.* **1.** DEVELOPMENT a progress or improvement **2.** PAYMENT AHEAD OF TIME a sum of money paid before it is due **3.** MOVEMENT AHEAD a forward movement in position **4.** FRIENDLY APPROACH an approach made to sb in an attempt to form a relationship or come to an agreement (*often used in the plural*) **5.** PROVIDING STH BEFORE BEING PAID the act of supplying money or goods before payment is received **6.** STH RECEIVED BEFORE BEING PAID FOR a quantity of money or goods supplied before payment is made or repayments begin **7.** LOAN a loan of money **8.** PRICE RISE an increase in price or rate ■ *adj.* **1.** AHEAD OF TIME made, given, or sent ahead of time **2.** GOING IN FRONT going ahead of the main group [13thC. Via Old French *avancer* from assumed Vulgar Latin *abantiare*, from *abante* '(from) before', from Latin *ante* 'before'.] —**advancer** *n.* ◇ **in advance** before a particular event takes place

advance copy (*plural* **advance copies**) *n.* a copy of a book made available before the actual publication date

advance corporation tax *n.* a tax paid by any company that pays a dividend, calculated by deducting the basic rate of income tax from the grossed-up value of the dividend

advanced /əd vaánst/ *adj.* **1.** MORE HIGHLY DEVELOPED at a higher stage of development or progress than other similar people or things **2.** FAR ALONG at a point late in the progress or development of sth **3.** FUTURISTIC considered to be radical or ahead of its time

Advanced level *n.* full form of **A level**

advance guard *n.* a body of troops sent ahead of a main force to prepare an area for operations

advancement /əd vaánssmənt/ *n.* **1.** PROMOTION a promotion in rank or position **2.** ADVANCING an act or instance of moving ahead **3.** DEVELOPMENT an improvement or progress in sth **4.** LAW USE OF LEGACY BEFORE DUE the use of money from a legacy by or on behalf of its beneficiary before the person is strictly entitled to it

advance party (*plural* **advance parties**) *n.* **1.** MILITARY FORCE SENT ON AHEAD a group of soldiers or units sent ahead of a larger force to prepare an area for operations **2.** SMALL GROUP SENT AHEAD a small group sent on ahead of any main party, e.g. on an expedition

advance poll *n.* in Canada, an early vote held for voters who will be absent from their regular polling place on election day

advantage /əd vaántij/ *n.* **1.** SUPERIOR POSITION a superior or favourable position in relation to sb or sth **2.** FACTOR FAVOURING SB a circumstance or factor that places sb in a favourable position in relation to others ○ *These children have the advantage of a stable home.* **3.** PROFIT a benefit or gain ○ *Their mistakes in the race worked to our advantage.* **4.** TENNIS POINT AFTER DEUCE in tennis, the point scored after deuce ■ *vt.* (**-tages, -taging, -taged**) BENEFIT SB to put sb in a superior or favourable position in relation to other people [14thC. Alteration of Old French *avantage*, from *avant* 'before', from assumed Vulgar Latin *abante* (see ADVANCE).] ◇ **take advantage of sb** to use sb in a selfish way in order to achieve a personal benefit, usually by exploiting a weakness ◇ **take advantage of sth** to make use of sth that is available for personal benefit ◇ **to advantage** in a way that emphasizes the positive aspects of sb or sth

advantageous /ádvən táyjəss/ *adj.* **1.** GIVING AN ADVANTAGE giving an advantage **2.** USEFUL of use or benefit —**advantageously** *adv.* —**advantageousness** *n.*

advect /əd vékt/ (**-vects, -vecting, -vected**) *vt.* to transfer sth by advection [Mid-20thC. Back-formation from ADVECTION.]

advection /əd véksh'n/ *n.* the horizontal transfer of a property such as heat, caused by air movement [Early 20thC. From the Latin stem *advection-*, from *advehere* 'to carry to', from *vehere* 'to carry' (see VEHICLE).]

advent /ád vent/ *n.* the arrival of sth important or awaited

Advent *n.* the four-week period leading up to Christmas, beginning on the fourth Sunday before Christmas Day [Pre-12thC. From Latin *adventus* 'arrival', from, ultimately, *advenire*, literally 'to come to', from *venire* 'to come' (see VENUE).]

Advent calendar *n.* a large decorated card with numbered doors on it, one of which is opened each day from 1 to 24 December, revealing a picture

Adventist /ádvəntist/ *n.* a member of any of several Christian denominations, e.g. the Seventh-Day Adventists, who believe that the Second Coming of Jesus Christ is imminent —**Adventism** *n.*

adventitia /ád ven tíshi ə/ *n.* the outer covering of an organ or body part, especially that of a blood vessel [Late 19thC. From Latin, from the neuter plural of medieval Latin *adventitius* (see ADVENTITIOUS).]

adventitious /ádvən tíshəss/ *adj.* **1.** FROM OUTSIDE added from an outside and often unexpected source rather than intrinsic **2.** BIOL UNUSUALLY POSITIONED developing in an unusual position, as does, e.g., a root growing downward from a branch [Early 17thC. From medieval Latin *adventitius* 'coming from outside', alteration of Latin *adventicius*, from *adventus* (see ADVENT).] —**adventitiously** *adv.* —**adventitiousness** *n.*

adventive /əd véntiv/ *adj.* NOT INDIGENOUS used to describe a plant or animal found in an environment where it is not native and is not fully established ■ *n.* NON-INDIGENOUS PLANT OR ANIMAL an adventive plant or animal —**adventively** *adv.*

Advent Sunday *n.* the fourth Sunday before Christmas, marking the start of Advent. It is regarded as the beginning of the Christian ecclesiastical year.

adventure /əd vénchər/ *n.* **1.** EXCITING EXPERIENCE an exciting or extraordinary event or series of events **2.** BOLD UNDERTAKING an undertaking involving uncertainty and risk **3.** INVOLVEMENT IN BOLD UNDERTAKINGS the participation or willingness to participate in things that involve uncertainty and risk ○ *Where's your sense of adventure?* **4.** FINANCIAL SPECULATION a risky or speculative financial undertaking ■ *v.* (**-tures, -turing, -tured**) **1.** *vt.* RISK to risk sth **2.** *vt.* RISK SAYING to risk saying sth that other people may disagree with or find offensive **3.** *vi.* RISK DANGER to dare to go somewhere new or engage in sth dangerous [13thC. Via French *aventure* from Latin *adventurus* 'about to arrive', the future participle of *advenire* (see ADVENT). The sense 'exciting event' evolved from 'what arrives by chance' via 'hazardous undertaking'.]

adventure playground *n.* an outdoor play area for children with slides, climbing frames, ropes, and sometimes materials with which to build things

adventurer /əd vénchərər/ *n.* **1.** SB IN SEARCH OF ADVENTURE sb who takes part in exciting or risky activities **2.** SB PURSUING MONEY OR POSITION sb who uses unscrupulous means in order to gain wealth or social position **3.** SPECULATOR sb who seeks wealth through financial speculation

adventuresome /əd vénchərsəm/ *adj.* willing or eager to participate in risky or exciting activities —**adventuresomely** *adv.* —**adventuresomeness** *n.*

adventuress /əd vénchərəss/ *n.* a woman who uses unscrupulous means in order to gain wealth or social position (*dated*)

adventurism /əd vénchərizzəm/ *n.* **1.** FINANCIAL SPECULATION involvement in risky financial enterprises **2.** POLITICAL BRINKMANSHIP reckless intervention by one government in the affairs of another —**adventurist** *n.*

adventurous /əd vénchərəss/ *adj.* **1.** DARING willing or eager to participate in risky or exciting activities **2.** RISKY involving risk —**adventurously** *adv.* —**adventurousness** *n.*

adverb /ád vurb/ *n.* a word that modifies a verb, an adjective, another adverb, or a sentence, e.g. 'happily', 'very', or 'frankly' [15thC. Directly or via French, from Latin *adverbium*, which was modelled on Greek *epirrhēma* 'added word'.]

adverbial /ad vúrbi əl/ *adj.* RELATING TO ADVERB relating to or functioning as an adverb ■ *n.* ADVERB an adverb, or a phrase or clause that functions as an adverb —**adverbially** *adv.*

ad verbum /ad vúrbəm/ *adv.* word for word [From Latin, 'in accordance with the word']

adversarial /ád vur sáiri əl/ *adj.* **1.** RELATING TO ADVERSARIES relating to conflict or adversaries **2.** CONTESTING involving conflicting parties or interests, in relation to a legal proceeding. US term **adversary**

adversary /ádvərsəri/ *n.* (*plural* **-ies**) OPPONENT sb who opposes sb else in a conflict, contest, or debate ■ *adj.* US = **adversarial** [14thC. Via Old French, from Latin *adversarius* 'enemy', from *adversus* (see ADVERSE).]

— **WORD KEY: SYNONYMS** —
See Synonyms at *opponent*.

adversative /əd vúrssətiv/ *n.* a word, phrase, or clause that expresses opposition or contrast, e.g. 'but' or 'although' [Mid-16thC. Directly or via French, from late Latin *adversativus* 'opposed', from Latin *adversus* (see ADVERSE).] —**adversative** *adj.* —**adversatively** *adv.*

adverse /ád vurss, ad vúrss/ *adj.* **1.** ANTAGONISTIC acting with or characterized by opposition or antagonism **2.** HARMFUL creating unfavourable or undesirable results **3.** CONTRARY creating momentum in a direction opposite from that desired **4.** BOT FACING THE STEM used to describe a leaf or flower that faces the main stem [14thC. Via Old French, from Latin *adversus* 'turned against, hostile', from the past participle of *advertere* (see ADVERT[1]).] —**adversely** /ád vurssli/ *adv.* —**adverseness** *n.*

— **WORD KEY: USAGE** —
adverse or **averse**? Both words mean 'opposed' in different ways. *Adverse* is normally used before an abstract noun such as *circumstances* or *conditions* when these are unfavourable or likely to cause difficulties. *Averse* describes people who are disinclined to do sth or have a strong dislike that is specified by the word that follows *to*: *He was not averse to a bit of flattery*. *Averse* is never used attributively (ie before a noun), as *adverse* normally is.

adverse possession *n.* the possession or occupation of land or property without the owner's permission as a method of acquiring legal ownership

adversity /əd vúrssəti/ (*plural* **-ties**) *n.* **1.** MISFORTUNE hardship and suffering **2.** ADVERSE HAPPENING an extremely unfavourable experience or event

advert[1] /əd vúrt/ (**-verts**, **-verting**, **-verted**) *vi.* to call attention to or make reference to sth [15thC. Via Old French *advertir* 'to notice', from Latin *advertere* 'to turn towards', from *vertere* 'to turn'.]

advert[2] /ád vurt/ *n.* an advertisement (*informal*) [Mid-19thC. Shortening.]

advertence /əd vúrtənss/ *n.* the act of paying attention to or being mindful of sth

advertise /ádvər tīz/ (**-tises**, **-tising**, **-tised**) *v.* **1.** *vti.* PRAISE COMMERCIAL PRODUCT to publicize the qualities of a product, service, business, or event in order to encourage people to buy or use it **2.** *vti.* PUBLICLY ANNOUNCE AVAILABILITY OR NEED to publicize sth such as a job vacancy or item for sale in a newspaper or on the radio, television, or Internet ○ *advertise for a new flatmate* **3.** *vt.* TELL OTHERS ABOUT to make sth known to others [15thC. From Old French *advertiss-*, the stem of *advertir* (see ADVERT[1]). The meaning 'to publicize' evolved from 'to notice' via 'to warn' and 'to give notice of'.] —**advertiser** *n.*

advertisement /əd vúrtissmənt/ *n.* **1.** ACT OF ADVERTISING the act of advertising sth **2.** PUBLIC ANNOUNCEMENT a public announcement in a newspaper or on the radio, television, or Internet advertising sth such as a product for sale or an event

advertising /ádvər tīzing/ *n.* **1.** PUBLIC PROMOTION OF STH the promotion through public announcements in newspapers or on the radio, television, or Internet of sth such as a product, service, event, or vacancy in order to attract or increase interest in it **2.** BUSINESS OF PRODUCING ADVERTISEMENTS the business of producing advertisements **3.** ADVERTISEMENTS advertisements considered collectively

advertising agency (*plural* **advertising agencies**) *n.* a business that produces advertisements for its clients

advice /əd víss/ *n.* **1.** RECOMMENDATION ABOUT ACTION sb's opinion about what another person should do ○ *I followed her advice and changed jobs.* **2.** OFFICIAL INFORMATION formal or official information about sth, usually received from a distance (*often used in the plural*) [13thC. Via French *avis* 'opinion' from, ultimately, Latin *ad (meum) visum* 'in (my) view or opinion'; *visum* is the past participle of *videre* 'to see'.]

advice note *n.* a formal document from a supplier to a customer indicating that goods have been sent, usually giving details of quantity, price, and means of sending

advisable /əd vízəb'l/ *adj.* being a sensible or desirable thing to do —**advisability** /əd vízə bílləti/ *n.* —**advisableness** /-b'lnəss/ *n.* —**advisably** /-bli/ *adv.*

advise /əd víz/ (**-vises**, **-vising**, **-vised**) *v.* **1.** *vti.* OFFER ADVICE to offer advice to sb ○ *We were advised to leave.* **2.** *vt.* RECOMMEND to suggest or recommend sth ○ *'I have advised him to join a club or get a hobby but he is determined to feel sorry for himself'.* (Sue Townsend, *The Secret Diary of Adrian Mole Aged 13¾*; 1982) **3.** *vt.* INFORM to make sb aware of sth [14thC. Via Old French *aviser*, from *avis* 'opinion'. Ultimately from Latin *ad (meum) visum* (see ADVICE).]

— **WORD KEY: USAGE** —
advise = 'inform' The use of the verb *advise* to mean 'inform' is widely regarded as commercialese and is best avoided in general usage: *Please advise us of* [better: *tell us*] *your new address. I will advise them* [better: *inform them*] *of the new time of the meeting.*

— **WORD KEY: SYNONYMS** —
See Synonyms at *recommend*.

advisedly /əd vízidli/ *adv.* after careful consideration

advisee /əd ví zee/ *n.* sb who receives advice

adviser /əd vízər/, **advisor** *n.* **1.** GIVER OF ADVICE sb who gives advice **2.** SB ADVISING STUDENTS sb who advises students on academic matters such as course choices **3.** SUBJECT SPECIALIST a teacher who is a specialist in a particular subject and is appointed by an education authority to advise school heads and teachers on the teaching of that subject [Early 17thC. Formed from ADVISE.]

— **WORD KEY: USAGE** —
adviser or **advisor**? Both spellings are used for 'sb who gives advice'. *Adviser* is often regarded as more correct

because *-er* is the more usual suffix for newer words; *advisor* is common in the United States and is probably influenced by the form of the adjective *advisory* or the spelling of Latin *advisor*.

advisory /əd vízəri/ *adj.* **1.** GIVING ADVICE providing or of the nature of advice **2.** HAVING THE FUNCTION OF GIVING ADVICE having the function of giving advice, usually with the implication that the advice given need not be followed ■ *n.* US WARNING OF STH TO COME an advance notice of sth, e.g. a warning of impending severe weather ○ *traffic advisory*

advisory teacher *n.* = adviser

advocaat /ádvō kaa, -kaat/ *n.* an alcoholic beverage similar to eggnog, containing eggs, sugar, and brandy [Mid-20thC. From Dutch 'advocate', because it was supposed to help clear the throat.]

advocacy /ádvəkəssi/ (*plural* **-cies**) *n.* **1.** GIVING AID TO A CAUSE active verbal support for a cause or position **2.** GIVING DISADVANTAGED PEOPLE A VOICE support for people who are regarded as unable to speak up on their own behalf, e.g. people with a learning disability, so that their opinion is listened to [14thC. Via Old French *advocacie* from, ultimately, Latin *advocatus* (see ADVOCATE).]

advocate *vt.* /ádvə kayt/ (**-cates**, **-cating**, **-cated**) SUPPORT to support or speak in favour of sth ○ *a tireless advocate of social reform* ■ *n.* /ádvəkət, -kayt/ **1.** SB GIVING SUPPORT sb who supports or speaks in favour of sth **2.** HELPER sb who acts or intercedes on behalf of another **3.** LAW LEGAL REPRESENTATIVE sb, e.g. a lawyer, who pleads another's case in a legal forum **4.** LAW SCOTTISH BARRISTER the equivalent of an English barrister in Scotland [14thC. Via Old French *avocat* 'advocate' from, ultimately, *advocare* 'to call to', from Latin *vocare* 'to call' (source of English *vocation* and *revoke*).] —**advocator** *n.* —**advocatory** /ádvə káytəri, ádvəkətəri/ *adj.*

— **WORD KEY: SYNONYMS** —
See Synonyms at *recommend*.

Advocate Depute (*plural* **Advocates Depute**) *n.* a law officer in Scotland, appointed to prosecute cases on behalf of the Lord Advocate. The equivalent in the English and US legal systems is a public prosecutor.

advt *abbr.* advertisement

Adyghe /aádi gay, -gáy/, **Adygei** *n.* a language spoken in the northwestern region of the republic of Georgia, belonging to the Abkhaz-Adyghean group of languages. Adyghe is spoken by about 100,000 people. —**Adyghe** *adj.*

adytum /ádditəm/ (*plural* **-ta** /-tə/) *n.* the most sacred part in an ancient temple, restricted to priests [Early 17thC. Via Latin, from Greek *adutos*, literally 'not to be entered', from *duein* 'to enter'.]

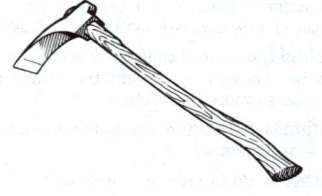

Adze

adze /adz/, **adz** *n.* a tool similar to an axe, with an arched blade set at right angles to the handle, used for trimming and shaping wood [Old English *adesa* or *eadesa*, of unknown origin]

adzuki bean /ad zóoki-/, **aduki bean** /ə dóoki-/, **azuki bean** /a zóoki-/ *n.* **1.** ASIAN BEAN PLANT a bean belonging to a species grown especially in China and Japan. Latin name: *Vigna angularis*. **2.** SWEET BEAN a small, slightly sweet, red-brown bean, the seed of the adzuki plant, used in sweet dishes in Asian cooking and in western vegetarian cooking [*Adzuki* from Japanese *azuki* 'red bean']

ae /ay/ *det.* Scotland a single (*literary*) [Variant of A]

AEA *abbr.* Atomic Energy Authority

aecidiospore *n.* = aeciospore

aecidium *n.* = aecium

aeciospore /éessi ə spawr/, **aecidiospore** /-síddi ō-/ *n.* a spore produced in the reproductive organ (**aecium**) of a rust fungus and containing two genetically distinct rust nuclei [Early 20thC. Coined from AECIUM + SPORE.]

aecium /éessi əm/ (*plural* **-a** /-ə/), **aecidium** /ee síddi əm/ (*plural* **-a** /-ə/) *n.* a cup-shaped reproductive organ (**fruiting body**) produced by some rust fungi in the tissue of their host plant, in which spores (**aeciospores**) are formed [Early 20thC. Via modern Latin, from Greek *aikia* 'injury'; from the harm caused by the fungi.]

aedes /ay eé deez/ (*plural* **-des**) *n.* a tropical and subtropical mosquito that can transmit serious diseases, e.g. yellow fever and dengue. Latin name: *Aedes aegypti*. [Early 20thC. From modern Latin, genus name, from Greek *aēdēs* 'unpleasant', because it carries diseases.]

aedile /eé dīl/ *n.* a magistrate in ancient Rome responsible for public works and buildings, games, markets, and the grain and water supplies [Mid-16thC. From Latin *aedilis*, from *aedes* 'building' (source of English *edifice*).]

AEEU *abbr.* Amalgamated Engineering and Electrical Union

Aegean Sea /i jeé ən-/ arm of the Mediterranean Sea containing numerous islands divided into three main groups, the Cyclades, Dodecanese, and Sporades. Area: about 179,000 sq. km/69,000 sq. mi.

aegis /éejiss/ *n.* in Greek mythology, the shield of Zeus or Athena [Early 17thC. Via Latin, from Greek *aigis* 'goatskin shield of Zeus.'] ◇ **under the aegis of sb** *or* **sth** with the support or protection of sb or sth (*formal*)

aegrotat /ī́grō tat, eégrō-, ee grṓ-/ *n.* **1.** MEDICAL EXEMPTION a certificate granted to a university student crediting the student with passing an examination missed because of illness **2.** EXAM PASS a degree or other qualification granted to a university student by an aegrotat [Late 18thC. From Latin, literally 'he or she is ill'.]

Aelfric /ǽlfrik/ (955?–1020?) Anglo-Saxon monk and writer. As Abbot of Eynsham from 1005 he wrote several works, including *Lives of the Saints* (990–992) and a Latin grammar.

Aeneas /i neé əss/ *n.* in Greek and Roman mythology, a Trojan hero who escaped after the fall of Troy and spent seven years travelling before settling near the site of Rome in Italy. His travels are the subject of Virgil's *Aeneid*.

Aeolia = Aeolis

aeolian /ee óli ən/ *adj.* GEOL carried or produced by the wind ○ *aeolian deposits* [Early 20thC. Formed from AEOLUS.]

Aeolian /ee óli ən/, **Eolian** *n.* **1.** MEMBER OF HELLENIC PEOPLE a member of an ancient Hellenic people who lived in Aeolis and Lesbos about 1100 BC **2.** LANG = Aeolic ▪ *adj.* **1.** OF AEOLIS relating to or typical of Aeolis, or its people or culture **2.** OF AEOLUS relating to Aeolus

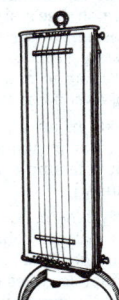

Aeolian harp: 18th-century French three-sided aeolian harp

aeolian harp, **Aeolian harp** *n.* a box-shaped musical instrument, a type of zither, with strings tuned in unison to produce their fundamental tones and harmonics when the wind blows over them [*Aeolian* formed from AEOLUS, from Greek *aiolos* 'fast-moving']

Aeolian Islands = Lipari Islands

Aeolic /ee ólik/, **Eolic** *n.* a dialect of Ancient Greek that was spoken mainly in Aeolis, Thessaly, and Boeotia —**Aeolic** *adj.*

Aeolis /eé ə liss/, **Aeolia** /ee óli ə/ ancient region on the northwestern coast of Asia Minor, settled by the Aeolian Greeks about 1100 BC

Aeolus /eé ə ləss/ *n.* in Greek mythology, the god of wind

aeon /eé ən, eé on/, **eon** *n.* **1.** VAST AMOUNT OF TIME a length of time that is too long to measure (*informal*) **2.** GEOL LONGEST UNIT OF GEOLOGICAL TIME a division of geological time comprising two or more eras [Mid-17thC. Via late Latin, from Greek *aiōn*, 'age, lifetime'.] —**aeonian** *adj.*

aer- *prefix.* = aero- (*used before vowels*)

aerate /áir rayt/ (**-ates**, **-ating**, **-ated**) *vt.* **1.** EXPOSE TO AIR to allow circulating air to reach or penetrate sth **2.** PUT GAS INTO A LIQUID to charge a liquid with a gas, especially with carbon dioxide when making fizzy drinks **3.** = oxygenate [Late 18thC. Formed from Latin *aer* 'air', from Greek *aēr* (see AERO-).] —**aeration** /air ráysh'n/ *n.* —**aerator** /áir raytər/ *n.*

aerenchyma /a réngkəmə/ *n.* the spongy tissue in some aquatic plants that keeps them afloat and helps in the exchange of gases [Late 19thC. Coined from Greek *aēr* 'air' + *egkhuma* 'infusion'.]

aeri- *prefix.* = aero-

aerial /áiri əl/ *adj.* **1.** RELATING TO AIR consisting of, typical of, or relating to the air **2.** IN AIR living, happening, or moving in the air ○ *a plant with aerial roots* **3.** LIGHT IN WEIGHT like the air in being light and insubstantial **4.** IMAGINARY existing only in the imagination **5.** INVOLVING AIRCRAFT done by or involving aircraft ○ *an aerial bombardment* ▪ *n.* **1.** METAL ROD FOR RADIO WAVES a metallic rod or wire for sending and receiving radio waves or microwaves. An aerial is attached to a radio or TV to improve the reception. US term **antenna 2.** HOCKEY HIGH BALL IN HOCKEY in hockey, a ball passed by being raised off the ground [Early 17thC. Formed from Latin *aerius*, from Greek *aerios*, from *aēr* 'air']

aerialist /áiri əlist/ *n.* an acrobat who performs on a tightrope or trapeze

aerial ladder *n.* US = turntable ladder

aerial perspective *n.* the use in painting of gradations in colour and definition to suggest distance

aerie *n.* US = eyrie

aeriform /áiri fawrm/ *adj.* **1.** GASEOUS existing as air or gas **2.** INSUBSTANTIAL having no substance or material form

aero /áirō/ *adj.* used in aircraft or aeronautics

aero-, **aeri-**, **aer-** *prefix.* **1.** air, atmosphere, gas ○ *aerodynamic* **2.** aviation ○ *aerospace* [From Greek *aēr* 'air']

aeroballistics /áirō bə lístiks/ *n.* the branch of ballistics that deals with projectiles fired or dropped from aircraft (*takes a singular verb*) —**aeroballistic** *adj.*

aerobatics /áirō báttiks/ *n.* the flying of an aircraft in daring manoeuvres, often as an entertainment (*takes a singular or plural verb*) [Early 20thC. Coined from AERO-, modelled on ACROBATICS.] —**aerobatic** *adj.*

aerobe /áirōb/ *n.* a microorganism that requires oxygen for metabolism [Late 19thC. Coined from AERO- + Greek *bios* 'life'.]

aerobic[1] /air rṓbik/ *adj.* **1.** NEEDING OXYGEN living or taking place only in the presence of oxygen **2.** GIVING OXYGEN having or providing oxygen [Late 19thC. Formed from French *aérobie*, coined by Louis Pasteur from Greek *aēr* 'air' + *bios* 'life'.] —**aerobically** *adv.*

aerobic[2] /air rṓbik/ *adj.* **1.** SPEEDING UP RESPIRATION increasing respiration and heart rates ○ *aerobic exercise* **2.** OF AEROBICS used in or relating to aerobics [Mid-20thC. From AEROBICS.]

aerobic respiration *n.* the breakdown of foodstuffs to create energy in a process that requires the presence of oxygen. ◊ **anaerobic respiration**

aerobics /air rṓbiks/ *n.* (*takes a singular or plural verb*) **1.** FITNESS EXERCISES an active exercise programme done to music, often in a class **2.** ACTIVITIES THAT SPEED UP RESPIRATION exercises, e.g. walking, jogging, bicycling, and swimming, that increase respiration and heart rates [Mid-20thC. Coined by Dr Kenneth H. Cooper from AEROBIC on the model of *gymnastics*.]

aerobiology /áirō bī ólləji/ *n.* the study of airborne biological materials and organisms, e.g. airborne allergens and disease-causing microorganisms —**aerobiological** /áirō bī ə lójjik'l/ *adj.* —**aerobiologically** /-lójjikli/ *adv.*

aerobiosis /áirō bī óssiss/ *n.* life in the presence of oxygen [Early 20thC. Via modern Latin from, ultimately, Greek (see AEROBIC).]

aerobraking *n.* = aerodynamic braking

aerodrome /áirō drōm/ *n.* a small airfield with limited facilities [Early 20thC. Coined from AERO- + DROME.]

aerodynamic /áirō dī námmik/ *adj.* **1.** OF AERODYNAMICS involving or typical of aerodynamics **2.** DESIGNED TO REDUCE AIR RESISTANCE designed to reduce air resistance, especially to increase fuel efficiency or maximum speed —**aerodynamically** *adv.*

aerodynamics /áirō dī námmiks/ *n.* STUDY OF OBJECTS MOVING THROUGH AIR the study of moving gases, especially the study of the forces experienced by objects moving through air (*takes a singular verb*) ▪ *npl.* AERODYNAMIC PROPERTIES the aerodynamic properties of an object (*takes a plural verb*) —**aerodynamicist** /-námmissist/ *n.*

aerodyne /áirō dīn/ *n.* an aircraft such as an aeroplane or helicopter that is heavier than air and whose lift in flight results from forces caused by its motion through the air [Early 20thC. Back-formation from AERODYNAMIC.]

aeroembolism /áirō émbəlizzəm/ *n.* = air embolism

aerofoil /áirō foyl/ *n.* a part of an aircraft's or other vehicle's surface, e.g. an aileron, wing, or propeller, that acts on the air to provide lift or control

aerogram /áirə gram/, **aerogramme** *n.* a letter designed for airmail consisting of a single sheet of lightweight paper that, once written on, can be folded and sealed to form an envelope [Late 19thC. Modelled on TELEGRAM.]

aerography /air róggrəfi/ *n.* the study of atmospheric conditions

aerolite /áirō līt/ *n.* a meteorite with a high silicate content [Early 19thC. Coined from AERO- + -LITE.] —**aerolitic** /áirō líttik/ *adj.*

aerology /air rólləji/ *n.* the study of the lower layers of the Earth's atmosphere —**aerologic** /áirə lójjik/ *adj.* —**aerological** /-lójjik'l/ *adj.* —**aerologist** /air rólləjist/ *n.*

aeromagnetic /áirō mag néttik/ *adj.* relating to the study or measurement of the earth's magnetic field from aircraft —**aeromagnetically** *adv.* —**aeromagnetics** *n.*

aeromechanics /áirō mi kánniks/ *n.* the study of gases in motion and in equilibrium, including the study of the mechanical effects of gases upon objects (*takes a singular verb*) —**aeromechanical** *adj.* —**aeromechanically** *adv.*

aeromedicine /áirō médss'n/ *n.* = aviation medicine —**aeromedical** /-méddik'l/ *adj.*

aerometeorograph /áirō meéti ərə graaf, -graf/ *n.* an instrument on board an aircraft that records temperature, atmospheric pressure, and humidity

aerometer /air rómmitər/ *n.* an instrument for measuring the mass or density of air or another gas [Late 18thC. From French *aéromètre*.]

aeronaut /áirə nawt/ *n.* sb who pilots, navigates, or is a passenger in an airship or balloon [Late 18thC. From French *aéronaute*, from *aéro-* (from Greek *aēr* 'air') + Greek *nautēs* 'sailor' (source of English *nautical* and *astronaut*).]

aeronautical /áirə náwtik'l/, **aeronautic** /-náwtik/ *adj.* relating to aircraft or their flight [Early 20thC. From French *aéronautique* (see AERONAUT).] —**aeronautically** *adv.*

aeronautics /áirə náwtiks/ *n.* the science, art, theory, and practice of designing, building, and operating aircraft (*takes a singular verb*)

aeroneurosis /áirō nyoŏ rṓssiss/ *n.* anxiety and fatigue in airline pilots brought on by prolonged periods of flying

aeropause /áirə pawz/ *n.* the part of the Earth's upper atmosphere above which air is too thin for aircraft to fly

aerophagy /air róffəji/, **aerophagia** /áirə fáyji ə, -fáyjə/ *n.* the abnormal spasmodic swallowing of air, a common cause of flatulence and belching [Late 19thC. Modelled on French *aérophagie*.]

aerophobia /áirə fṓbi ə/ *n.* an abnormal fear of draughts of air —**aerophobic** *adj.*

aerophyte /áirə fīt/ *n.* = **epiphyte**

aeroplane /áirə playn/ *n.* a vehicle with wings and a jet engine or propellers, that is heavier than air, and is able to fly [Late 19thC. From French *aéroplane*, from *aéro-* 'AERO-' + *-plane*, of uncertain origin: possibly from *plan* 'flat' or *planer* 'to soar', or from Greek *planos* 'wandering'.]

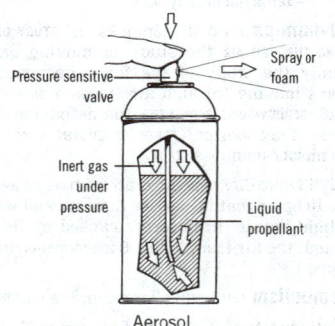
Aerosol

aerosol /áirə sol/ *n.* **1.** CONTAINER WITH GAS UNDER PRESSURE a small container holding a substance that can be dispensed under pressure by a propellant as a spray **2.** SUBSTANCE SPRAYED a substance held in a small container from which it can be dispensed under pressure by a propellant as a spray **3.** SUSPENSION OF PARTICLES IN GAS a suspension of solid or liquid particles in a gaseous medium

aerospace /áirə spayss/ *n.* ATMOSPHERE AND OUTER SPACE the Earth's atmosphere and outer space ■ *adj.* OF AIRCRAFT AND SPACECRAFT relating to the design, manufacture, and flight of vehicles or missiles that fly in and beyond the Earth's atmosphere

aerospace medicine *n.* the branch of medicine concerned with disorders associated with flight both inside and outside the Earth's atmosphere

aerostat /áirə stat/ *n.* a hot-air or gas-filled aircraft such as an airship or balloon [Late 18thC. From French *aérostat*, from *aéro-* 'AERO-' + Greek *statos* 'standing' (source of English *static*).] —**aerostatic** /áirə státtik/ *adj.*

aerostatics /áirə státtiks/ *n.* **1.** PHYS STUDY OF GASES IN EQUILIBRIUM the study of gases in equilibrium and objects in equilibrium in gases **2.** AEROSP STUDY OF DIRIGIBLES AND BALLOONS the science of aircraft that are lighter than air, e.g. dirigibles and balloons

aerothermodynamics /áirō thúrmō dī námmiks/ *n.* the study of the heat exchange between gases and solid objects, especially between air and aircraft flying at high velocity (*takes a singular verb*) —**aerothermodynamic** *adj.*

Aertex /áir teks/ *tdmk.* a trademark for an open-weave fabric, used for vests and sportswear

aery[1] /áiri/ (**-ier, -iest**) *adj.* insubstantial and unworldly [Late 16thC. From Latin *aerius*, ultimately derived from Greek *aēr* 'air' (source of English *air*).]

aery[2] *n.* = **eyrie**

Aesculapian /ēéskyoŏ láypi ən/ *adj.* relating to medicine and the healing arts [Early 17thC. Formed from Latin *Aesculapius*, the Roman god of medicine.]

aesculapian snake *n.* a long slender brown nonvenomous snake found in forests in Europe and western Asia. Latin name: *Elaphe longissima*. [From

the common depiction of Aesculapius (see AESCULAPIAN) in antiquity with such a snake]

Aesop /ēéssəp/ (*fl.* 6th century BC) Greek writer and reputedly a former slave. His fables were popularized by the Roman poet Phaedrus (1st century AD).

AEST *abbr.* Australian Eastern Standard Time

aesthesia /eess théezi ə/ *n.* the ability to feel or experience through the senses [Early 18thC. Via modern Latin from Greek *aisthēsis* 'perceiving', from *aisthesthai* 'to perceive' (see AESTHETIC).]

aesthete /ēés theet/ *n.* sb who has or affects a highly developed appreciation of beauty, especially in the arts [Late 19thC. Back-formation from AESTHETIC, modelled on ATHLETE.]

aesthetic /eess théttik, iss-/ *adj.* **1.** PHILOSOPHY RELATING TO AESTHETICS relating to the philosophical principles of aesthetics **2.** ARTS APPRECIATING BEAUTY sensitive to or appreciative of art or beauty **3.** ATTRACTIVE pleasing in appearance ■ *n.* SET OF PRINCIPLES a set of principles about art [Early 19thC. From Greek *aisthētikos* 'perceptual', from *aisthesthai* 'to perceive' (source of English *anaesthetic*, literally 'without feeling'). The sense 'relating to perception of beauty' evolved from 'perception'.] —**aesthetically** *adv.*

aesthetician /ēéssthə tísh'n, éss-/ *n.* a student or devotee of the principles of art or beauty

aestheticism /eess théttisizzəm, iss-/ *n.* **1.** DERIVATION OF MORAL PRINCIPLES FROM BEAUTY the philosophical doctrine that all moral principles are derived from beauty **2.** BELIEF IN IMPORTANCE OF AESTHETICS the belief that the principles of aesthetics are of the highest importance in the arts **3.** LOVE OF BEAUTY appreciation of and devotion to beauty

aestheticize /eess thétti sīz, iss-/ (**-cizes, -cizing, -cized**) *vt.* to show sth in its best or most artistic light

aesthetics /eess théttiks, iss-/ *n.* **1.** STUDY OF BEAUTY the branch of philosophy dealing with the study of aesthetic values such as the beautiful and the sublime (*takes a singular verb*) **2.** STUDY OF ART the study of the rules and principles of art (*takes a singular verb*) **3.** IDEA OF BEAUTY a particular idea of what is beautiful or artistic (*takes a singular or plural verb*) **4.** HOW STH LOOKS how sth looks, especially when considered in terms of how pleasing it is (*takes a singular or plural verb*) [Early 19thC. Via modern Latin *aesthetica*, from Greek *aisthētikos* (see AESTHETIC), perhaps modelled on ATHLETICS.]

aesthetic surgery *n.* = **cosmetic surgery**

aestival /ee stív'l, éstivl/ *adj.* relating to or happening during summer [14thC. Via Old French from Latin *aestivalis*, from *aestas* 'summer'. Ultimately from an Indo-European word meaning 'to burn'.]

aestivate /ēésti vayt, ésti-/ (**-vates, -vating, -vated**) *vi.* **1.** SPEND SUMMER SOMEWHERE to spend the summer in a particular place or activity (*formal*) **2.** BE DORMANT IN SUMMER to be dormant during the summer or during months of drought (*refers to animals, especially certain amphibians, reptiles, and insects*) [Early 17thC. From Latin *aestivat-*, the past participle stem of *aestivare*, from *aestivus* (see AESTIVAL).]

aestivation /ēésti váysh'n, ésti-/ *n.* **1.** PARTICULAR SUMMER ACTIVITY spending summer in a particular place or activity **2.** SUMMER DORMANCY dormancy in certain animals during the summer or months of drought **3.** ARRANGEMENT OF FLOWER BUD PARTS the arrangement of the sepals and petals in a flower bud

aether *n.* = **ether** n. 3, **ether** n. 4

aethereal *adj.* = **ethereal** (*literary archaic*)

aetiology /ēéti ólləji/, **etiology** *n.* **1.** STUDY OF CAUSES the philosophical investigation of causes and origins **2.** MED MEDICAL STUDY OF CAUSE OF DISEASE the study of the causes and origins of disease **3.** MED, BIOL CAUSE OF DISEASE the set of factors that contributes to the occurrence of a disease [Mid-16thC. Via Latin *aetiologia* from Greek *aitiologiā* 'statement of the cause', from *aitiā* 'cause'.] —**aetiologic** /ēéti ə lójjik/ *adj.* —**aetiologically** /-lójjikli/ *adv.* —**aetiologist** /ēéti ólləjist/ *n.*

Aetius /ēéti əss/, **Flavius** (390?–454) Roman general who ruled the Western empire for Valentinian III (425–455) and defeated Attila the Hun (451).

AEU *abbr.* Australian Education Union

AEW *abbr.* airborne early warning (aircraft)

AF *abbr.* **1.** air force **2.** Anglo-French **3.** audio frequency **4.** autofocus

Af. *abbr.* **1.** Africa **2.** African

af- *prefix.* = **ad-** (*used before f*)

afar /ə faár/ *adv.* FAR AWAY at, to, or from a great distance (*literary*) ■ *n.* PLACE FAR AWAY a great distance away [14thC. From A + FAR.]

AFB *abbr.* Air Force Base

AFC *abbr.* **1.** automatic flight control **2.** automatic frequency control

afeard /ə feérd/, **afeared** *adj.* afraid (*regional dated*) [Old English, the past participle of *afǣren* 'to frighten', from *fǣren* 'to fear']

afebrile /a feéb rīl, ay-/ *adj.* having no fever, or marked by absence of fever

affable /áffəb'l/ *adj.* good-natured, friendly and easy to talk to [15thC. Via French, from Latin *affabilis* 'easy to speak to', from *(af)fari* 'to speak (to)' (source of English *fable*, *fame*, and *fabulous*).] —**affability** /áffə bílləti/ *n.* —**affably** /-bli/ *adv.*

affair /ə faír/ *n.* **1.** BUSINESS MATTER a matter that has been attended to or that needs attention, especially business ○ *a family affair* **2.** OCCURRENCE an event or occurrence that has been referred to or is known about ○ *that odd affair at work last week* **3.** SOCIAL EVENT a social event **4.** STH OF A PARTICULAR KIND an object or item of a particular kind ○ *The house is a ramshackle affair.* **5.** SEXUAL RELATIONSHIP a sexual relationship between two people not married to each other **6.** SCANDALOUS INCIDENT an incident that attracts public attention or notoriety ○ *the Profumo affair* ■ **affairs** *npl.* BUSINESS TO ATTEND TO professional, public, or personal business [12thC. Via French, literally 'to do', from, ultimately, Latin *facere* (source of English *fact* and *fashion*).]

affaire /ə faír/ *n.* = **affair** [Early 20thC. Shortening of AFFAIRE DE COEUR.]

affaire de coeur /a faír də kúr/ (*plural* **affaires de coeur** /a faír də kúr/) *n.* a love affair or romantic attachment [Early 19thC. From French, literally 'affair of the heart'.]

affect[1] /ə fékt/ (**-fects, -fecting, -fected**) *vt.* **1.** INFLUENCE to act upon or have an effect on sb or sth **2.** MOVE EMOTIONALLY to move sb emotionally **3.** CAUSE DISEASE to infect or damage sb or sth with disease [14thC. From Latin *affect-*, the past participle stem of *afficere* 'to act on', from *facere* 'to do' (source of English *fact* and *fetish*).]

——— **WORD KEY: USAGE** ———

affect or **effect**? The first thing to notice is that **affect** is only a verb, whereas **effect** is a noun and verb. What causes confusion is that they are both pronounced the same way and have meanings that are closely related. If one thing *affects* another, it has an *effect* on it. Notice also that you can *affect* (cause a change in) people as well as things, but you can only *effect* (bring about) things. *The election effected major changes in the government.*

affect[2] /ə fékt/ (**-fects, -fecting, -fected**) *vt.* **1.** PRETEND TO BE to give the appearance or pretence of sth **2.** ADOPT STH to adopt a use, style, or manner as your own **3.** ACT LIKE SB to imitate sb else's style or character **4.** COME TO BE OR HAVE to assume a particular form or state ○ *affect a liquid state* [15thC. Directly or via French *affecter* from Latin *affectare* 'to strive for', from *affect-*, the past participle stem of *afficere* (see AFFECT[1]).] —**affecter** *n.*

affect[3] /áffekt, ə fékt/ *n.* an emotion or mood associated with an idea or action, or the external expression of such a feeling ○ *blunted affect* [Late 19thC. Via German *Affekt*.]

affectation /áffek táysh'n/ *n.* **1.** BEHAVIOUR INTENDED TO IMPRESS feigned or unnatural behaviour that is often meant to impress others **2.** ACT INTENDED TO IMPRESS an appearance or manner assumed or put on as a show or pretence, often to impress others [Mid-16thC. Directly or via French, from the Latin stem *affection-* 'influence', from *affectare* (see AFFECT[2]).]

affected /ə féktid/ *adj.* **1.** INFLUENCED BY STH acted upon or influenced by sth or sb **2.** MOVED EMOTIONALLY emotionally moved by sth **3.** INFECTED OR DAMAGED infected

a at; aa father; aw all; ay day; air hair; ə about, edible, item, common, circus; e egg; ee eel; hw when; i it, happy; ī ice; 'l apple; 'm rhythm; 'n fashion; o odd; ō open; oŏ good; oō pool; ow owl; oy oil; th thin; <u>th</u> this; u up; ur urge;

or damaged by disease **4.** TRYING TO IMPRESS behaving in an unnatural way intended to impress others **5.** INTENDED TO IMPRESS done or assumed with the intention of impressing others —**affectedly** *adv.* —**affectedness** *n.*

affecting /ə fékting/ *adj.* able to stir the emotions —**affectingly** *adv.*

affection /ə féksh'n/ *n.* FONDNESS fond or tender feeling towards sb or sth ■ **affections** *npl.* FEELINGS feelings of fondness or tenderness, sometimes as opposed to reason [12thC. Via Old French *affectation* 'emotion', from the Latin stem *affection-* 'inclination', from, ultimately, *afficere* (see AFFECT[1]).] —**affectional** *adj.* —**affectionally** *adv.*

WORD KEY: SYNONYMS

See Synonyms at ***love***.

affectionate /ə féksh'nət/ *adj.* having or showing affection [15thC. Directly or via French, from Latin *affectionatus* 'devoted', from the stem *affection-* (see AFFECTION).] —**affectionately** *adv.* —**affectionateness** *n.*

affective /ə féktiv/ *adj.* **1.** PSYCHOL OF EMOTIONAL EXPRESSION relating to an external expression of emotion associated with an idea or action **2.** = **affecting** [15thC. Via French *affectif* from late Latin *affectivus*, from Latin *affect-*, the past participle stem of *afficere* (see AFFECT[1]).] —**affectively** *adv.* —**affectivity** /àffek tívvəti/ *n.*

affective disorder *n.* a prolonged emotional disturbance, e.g. depression

affectless /ə féktləss/ *adj.* feeling or showing no emotion —**affectlessness** *n.*

Affenpinscher

affenpinscher /áffən pinshər/ *n.* a European breed of small dog with wiry hair and tufted muzzle [Early 20thC. From German, literally 'ape terrier'.]

afferent /áffərənt/ *adj.* used to describe nerves that carry impulses from the outer body towards the brain or spinal cord, or blood vessels that carry blood to an organ [Mid-19thC. From Latin, the present participle stem of *afferre* 'to bring towards'.] —**afferently** *adv.*

affettuoso /a féchoo ṓssō/ *adv., adj.* played or sung musically with feeling (*used as a musical direction*) [Early 18thC. From Italian, ultimately from Latin *affect-*, the past participle stem of *afficere* 'to act on' (see AFFECT[1]).]

affiance /ə fī́ ənss/ (**-ances, -ancing, -anced**) *vt.* to promise yourself or sb else in marriage to sb (*formal*) (*often passive*) [14thC. Via Old French *afiancer* from *afiance* 'trust', from, ultimately, medieval Latin *affidare* 'to trust' (source of English *affidavit*).]

affidavit /áffi dáyvit/ *n.* a written declaration made on oath before sb authorized to administer oaths, usually setting out the statement of a witness for court proceedings [Late 16thC. From medieval Latin, literally 'he or she has sworn', a form of *affidare* 'to trust, affirm', from, ultimately, *fidus* 'faithful' (source of English *fidelity*).]

affiliate *vti.* /ə fílli ayt/ (**-ates, -ating, -ated**) COMBINE ORGANIZATIONS to come, or bring a person or group, into a close relationship with another, usually larger, group ■ *n.* /ə fílli ət, -ayt/ ASSOCIATE a group that is closely connected with a larger group, or an individual who combines with others to form a group [Mid-18thC. From Latin *affiliare* 'to adopt as a son', from *filius* 'son' (source of English *filial*).] —**affiliated** /ə fílli aytid/ *adj.* —**affiliation** /ə fílli áysh'n/ *n.*

affiliation order *n.* a court order requiring a man adjudged to be the father of an illegitimate child to pay money towards its maintenance

affiliation proceedings *npl.* legal proceedings usually initiated by a woman seeking to prove that a certain man is the father of her illegitimate child, especially in order to claim monetary support from him (*technical*)

affine /áffīn/ *n.* **1.** MATH TYPE OF GEOMETRIC TRANSFORMATION a geometric transformation that maps points and parallel lines to points and parallel lines **2.** ANTHROP RELATIVE a relative by marriage [Early 20thC. From Latin *affinis* (see AFFINITY).] —**affinal** *adj.*

affined /ə fī́nd/ *adj.* joined by close relationship (*formal*)

affinity /ə fínnəti/ (*plural* **-ties**) *n.* **1.** FEELING OF IDENTIFICATION a natural liking for or inclination towards sb or sth, or a feeling of identification with sb or sth **2.** SB ATTRACTIVE sb to whom sb else is attracted **3.** CONNECTION a similarity or likeness that connects persons or things **4.** ANTHROP KINSHIP BY MARRIAGE a relationship by marriage rather than blood **5.** BIOL, LANG SIMILARITY IN STRUCTURE a similarity in structure between groups that may suggest a common origin **6.** CHEM LIKELIHOOD OF CHEMICAL REACTION a measure of the likelihood of a chemical reaction taking place between two substances **7.** IMMUNOL ANTIGEN-ANTIBODY ATTRACTION the attraction between an antigen and an antibody [14thC. Via Old French *afinité* 'close relationship' from, ultimately, Latin *affinis*, literally 'bordering on sth', from *finis* 'border' (source of English *finish* and *confine*).]

affinity card *n.* a credit card the use of which benefits a named charity or charities

affirm /ə fúrm/ (**-firms, -firming, -firmed**) *v.* **1.** *vti.* DECLARE POSITIVELY to declare positively that sth is true ○ *They affirmed their continued support for the initiative* **2.** *vt.* CONFIRM to confirm sth as binding or valid **3.** *vi.* LAW MAKE A FORMAL STATEMENT to make a statement formally but not under oath [13thC. Via Old French, from Latin *affirmare* 'to strengthen', from *firmus* 'firm' (source of English *firm* and *farm*).] —**affirmable** *adj.* —**affirmably** *adv.* —**affirmant** *n.* —**affirmer** *n.*

affirmation /áffər máysh'n/ *n.* **1.** ASSERTION OF TRUTH an assertion of truth **2.** STH SAID TO BE TRUE sth asserted as being true **3.** LAW FORMAL LEGAL DECLARATION a formal declaration acceptable in a court, usually made by sb who has a conscientious objection to taking an oath **4.** POSITIVE STATEMENT OF ACHIEVEMENT a positive statement asserting that a goal the speaker or thinker wishes to achieve is already happening ○ *Start the day by repeating 20 times the affirmation 'I am a non-smoker'.* [15thC. Directly or via French, from the Latin stem *affirmation-*, from *affirmare* (see AFFIRM).]

affirmative /ə fúrmətiv/ *adj.* **1.** TRUE confirming or asserting that sth is true **2.** INDICATING AGREEMENT indicating agreement or giving assent **3.** LOGIC RELATING TO A TYPE OF PROPOSITION relating to or being a categorical proposition in which the predicate's extension is contained partially or wholly within the subject, e.g. 'All humans are mammals' ■ *n.* **1.** POSITIVE ASSERTION a positive assertion **2.** WORD CONVEYING AGREEMENT a word or statement conveying agreement or approval **3.** *US* SIDE FOR A PROPOSITION the side in a debate that supports a proposition ■ *interj.* MIL YES a signal codeword expressing agreement or compliance —**affirmatively** *adv.*

affirmative action *n.* *US* = **positive discrimination**

affix *vt.* /ə fíks/ (**-fixes, -fixing, -fixed**) **1.** FASTEN TO STH ELSE to fasten sth to sth else **2.** ADD ON TO STH to add sth at the end of sth, e.g. a signature to a document **3.** ATTRIBUTE TO SB to ascribe sth, e.g. responsibility or blame, to sb ■ *n.* /áffiks/ **1.** LING PART ADDED TO A WORD a form added to the beginning, middle, or end of another word that creates a derivative word or inflection **2.** STH ATTACHED sth attached or added [Mid-16thC. Directly or via French *affixer* from medieval Latin *affixare*, literally 'to keep on fastening to', from Latin *affigere* 'to fasten to', from *figere* 'to fasten' (source of English *fix*).] —**affixable** /ə fíksəb'l/ *adj.* —**affixer** /ə fíksər/ *n.*

afflatus /ə fláytəss/ *n.* creative inspiration, usually thought of as divine (*literary*) [Mid-17thC. From Latin, literally 'act of blowing on', from, ultimately, *flare* 'to blow' (source of English *flatulent*). The underlying sense is of divine breath infusing a mortal being.]

afflict /ə flíkt/ (**-flicts, -flicting, -flicted**) *vt.* to cause severe mental or physical distress to sb [14thC. From Latin *afflict-*, the past participle stem of *affligere*, literally 'to strike down', hence 'to cause to suffer', from *fligere* 'to strike' (source of English *profligate*).] —**afflicter** *n.* —**afflictive** *adj.* —**afflictively** *adv.*

WORD KEY: USAGE

afflict or **inflict**? The chief difference is in the grammatical construction: you ***inflict*** sth unpleasant on sb, whereas you ***afflict*** sb (or, more usually, sb is ***afflicted***) with or by sth unpleasant. *The government will inflict a new hardship on students when it abolishes the maintenance grant. The population was afflicted with a series of food shortages.*

affliction /ə flíksh'n/ *n.* **1.** DISTRESS a condition of great physical or mental distress **2.** CAUSE OF DISTRESS sth that causes great physical or mental distress [14thC. Via Old French from the Latin stem *affliction-*, from *affligere* (see AFFLICT).]

affluence /áffloo ənss/ *n.* an abundance of material wealth [14thC. Via French, from Latin *affluentia*, from *affluent-*, the present participle stem of *affluere* (see AFFLUENT).]

affluent /áffloo ənt/ *adj.* WEALTHY having an abundance of material wealth ■ *n.* **1.** WEALTHY PEOPLE people who are financially well-off ○ *restaurants and clubs frequented by the affluent* **2.** GEOG STREAM FLOWING INTO ANOTHER a stream or river that flows into another [15thC. Via Old French, from, ultimately, Latin *affluere* 'to flow towards', from *fluere* 'to flow' (source of English *fluid*).] —**affluently** *adv.*

WORD KEY: CULTURAL NOTE

The Affluent Society, a book by US economist John Kenneth Galbraith (published 1958). One of Galbraith's most widely read works, it attacks what he views as the American obsession with production and material goods and urges greater government expenditure on the country's infrastructure and public services.

afflux /áffluks/ *n.* an inward flow or flow towards a point, especially of blood in the body [Early 17thC. From medieval Latin *affluxus*, from *affluere* (see AFFLUENT).]

afford /ə fáwrd/ (**-fords, -fording, -forded**) *vt.* **1.** BE ABLE TO BUY to be able to meet the cost of sth without unacceptable difficulty **2.** BE ABLE TO DO to be able to do or provide sth without unacceptable or disadvantageous consequences **3.** BE ABLE TO SPARE to be able to spare sth without unacceptable or disadvantageous consequences **4.** PROVIDE to supply or provide sth (*formal*) [Old English *geforþian* 'to accomplish', from *forþian* 'to further'. The sense 'to be able to buy' evolved from the idea of 'having enough money to accomplish sth'.]

affordable /ə fáwrdəb'l/ *adj.* able to be paid for, done, or spared without unacceptable difficulty or disadvantageous consequences —**affordability** /ə fáwrdə bíllәti/ *n.* —**affordably** /-bli/ *adv.*

afforest /ə fórrist/ (**-ests, -esting, -ested**) *vt.* to convert land not previously forested into forest by planting trees [Early 16thC. From medieval Latin *afforestare*, from *foresta* (partial source of English *forest*).] —**afforestation** /ə fórri stáysh'n/ *n.*

affray /ə fráy/ *n.* a fight or violent disturbance in a public place [14thC. Via Anglo-Norman *afrayer* 'to disturb' from assumed Vulgar Latin *exfridare*, literally 'to take out of peace'. Ultimately of prehistoric Germanic origin.]

affreightment /ə fráytmənt/ *n.* a contract hiring a vessel to carry goods by sea [Mid-18thC. Anglicization of French *affrètement*, from *affréter* 'to freight', from *fret* 'freight'.]

affricate /áffrikət/, **affricative** /ə fríkətiv/ *n.* a composite speech sound made up of a stop immediately followed by a fricative [Late 19thC. From Latin *affricat-*, the past participle stem of *affricare* 'to rub against', from *fricare* 'to rub' (source of English *friction*).] —**affricative** *adj.*

affright /ə frī́t/ *vt.* (**-frights, -frighting, -frighted**) FRIGHTEN to overwhelm sb with sudden fear (*archaic literary*) ■ *n.* TERROR sudden overpowering fear (*archaic literary*) [Late 16thC. Formed from the verb FRIGHT.] —**affrightment** *n.*

affront /ə frúnt/ *n.* **OPEN INSULT** an open insult or giving of offence to sb ▪ *vt.* (**-fronts, -fronting, -fronted**) **INSULT OPENLY** to insult or offend sb openly [14thC. Via Old French, from Vulgar Latin *affrontare* 'to strike in the face', from *ad frontem* 'to the face'.]

affusion /ə fyoōzh'n/ *n.* a form of baptism in which water is poured over sb's head [From Latin *affus-*, the past participle stem of *affundere* 'to pour on', from *fundere* 'to pour' (source of English *foundry*).]

afghan /áf gan, áfgən/ *n.* **1. BLANKET** a knitted or crocheted blanket or shawl, often with geometric designs **2. CARPET** a large carpet woven in a geometric design **3. CLOTHES SHEEPSKIN COAT** a sheepskin jacket or coat, fashionable in the 1960s and 1970s, usually embroidered and with the fleece left long around the edges as trimming [Early 18thC. From Pashto *afghāni* 'of Afghanistan'.]

Afghan *n.* **1. PEOPLES SB FROM AFGHANISTAN** sb who was born or brought up in Afghanistan, or who is a citizen of Afghanistan **2. LANG = Pashto 3. ZOOL = Afghan hound** ▪ *adj.* **OF AFGHANISTAN** relating to or typical of the Republic of Afghanistan, or its people or culture

Afghan hound

Afghan hound, Afghan (*unmarked inflection* **-ghans**) *n.* a tall dog with a long silky coat, belonging to a breed originally developed in Afghanistan as hunting dogs and sheepdogs

afghani /af gánni, -ga͞ani/ (*plural* **-is**) *n.* **1.** see table at **currency 2. COIN WORTH AN AFGHANI** a coin worth one afghani [Early 20thC. From Pashto *afghāni*.]

Afghanistan

Afghanistan /af gánni staan, -stan/ *former monarchy in southwestern Asia, which became a republic in 1973. Language: Pashto, Dari (Persian). Currency: Afghani. Capital: Kabul. Population: 23,738,085 (1997). Area: 652,225 sq. km/251,825 sq. mi.

Afghanistization /af gánni stī záysh'n/, **Afghanistisation** *n.* the process of becoming, or coming to be seen as, a remote and marginal place [Late 20thC. Formed from AFGHANISTAN, from the political and social disintegration there after the breakup of the Soviet Union.]

aficionada /ə físhə na͞adə, ə físsi ə-/ *n.* a woman who is enthusiastic and knowledgeable about sth

aficionado /ə físhə na͞adō, ə físsi ə-/ (*plural* **-dos**) *n.* **1. ENTHUSIAST** sb who is enthusiastic and knowledgeable about sth **2. BULLFIGHTING ENTHUSIAST** a devotee of bullfighting [Mid-19thC. Via Spanish, literally 'sb who likes sth', from, ultimately, the Latin stem *affection-* (see AFFECTION).]

afield /ə feeld/ *adv., adj.* **1. AWAY** distant from home or

customary surroundings **2. OFF THE POINT** off the point or subject

afikomen /a͞afi kómən/ *n.* in Judaism, the unleavened bread that completes the festive meal (**Seder**) on the first night of Passover [Late 19thC. Via Hebrew *aphīqōmān* from Greek, 'festival'.]

afire /ə fír/ *adj., adv.* **1. ABLAZE** on fire or blazing **2. PASSIONATE** passionately interested in sth

AFL *abbr.* Australian Football League

aflame /ə fláym/ *adj.* **1. ABLAZE** in flames or blazing **2. IMPASSIONED** highly aroused or impassioned

aflatoxin /áfflə tóksin/ *n.* a toxic compound produced by a mould fungus in agricultural crops, especially peanuts, and in animal feeds that have not been carefully stored. It can cause hepatitis and liver cancer. [Mid-20thC. Coined from modern Latin *Aspergillus flavus* + TOXIN.]

AFL-CIO *abbr.* American Federation of Labor and Congress of Industrial Organizations

afloat /ə flót/ *adj., adv.* **1. FLOATING ON WATER** floating on water **2. ON BOARD SHIP** on board ship or at sea **3. FLOODED** covered with water **4. DRIFTING PURPOSELESSLY** drifting without purpose or guidance **5. IN CIRCULATION** circulating among the public **6. FINANCIALLY SOLVENT** free of debt or financial problems

aflutter /ə flúttər/ *adj., adv.* **1. EXCITED** in a state of agitation or excitement **2. FLAPPING** flapping or waving, e.g. as a flag does in the breeze

AFNOR /áf nawr/ *abbr.* Association Française de Normalisation

afoot /ə foŏt/ *adj., adv.* **1. HAPPENING** in the process of happening **2. ON FOOT** on foot or by walking [13thC. Partly modelled on Old Norse *á fótum* 'on foot'.]

afore /ə fáwr/ *adv., prep., conj.* before (*regional*) [Old English *onforan*, from *foran* 'in front, before' (source also of English *before*).]

aforementioned /ə fáwr mensh'nd/ *adj.* **MENTIONED EARLIER** previously mentioned (*formal*) ▪ *n.* **THE PREVIOUSLY MENTIONED** the previously mentioned person or people (*formal*)

aforesaid /ə fáwr sed/ *adj.* previously named (*formal*)

aforethought /ə fáwr thawt/ *adj.* thought about or planned beforehand

a fortiori /ay fáwrti áwr ī, aa fáwrti áwree/ *adv.* for an even stronger reason [Early 17thC. From Latin, literally 'from the stronger (reason)', from *fortis* 'strong'.]

afoul /ə fówl/ *adj., adv.* **1. INTO CONFLICT** in or into trouble or conflict with sb or sth **2. ENTANGLED** entangled or in collision with sth

AFP *abbr.* **1.** alpha-foetoprotein **2.** Australian Federal Police

Afr. *abbr.* Africa ▪ *abbr.* African

afraid /ə fráyd/ *adj.* **1. FRIGHTENED** frightened or apprehensive about sth **2. RELUCTANT** feeling hesitation or disinclination towards sth **3. REGRETFUL** regretful that sth is or is not the case [14thC. Originally the past participle of AFFRAY, modelled on Anglo-Norman *affrayé*.]

───── **WORD KEY: CULTURAL NOTE** ─────

Who's Afraid of Virginia Woolf?, a play by American dramatist Edward Albee (1962). Albee's first full-length play examines the sour relationship between a middle-aged, underachieving academic and his embittered wife. A dinner party with a younger, not dissimilar, couple forces them to confront the reality of their past and present.

A-frame *adj.* **SHAPED LIKE A** built in the shape of a capital

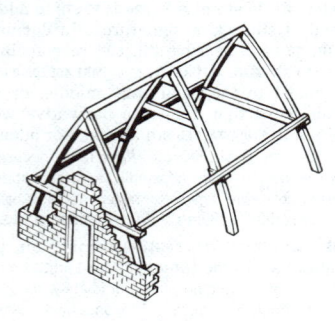

A-frame

letter A ▪ *n.* **A-SHAPED BUILDING** a building shaped like a capital letter A, with a triangular front and back and a roof that slopes to the ground forming the sides of the building

afreet /áffreet, ə frée t/, **afrit** *n.* an evil spirit or powerful monster in Arabian mythology [Late 18thC. From Arabic *afrīt*.]

afresh /ə frésh/ *adv.* once again, especially from the beginning

Africa /áffrikə/ the second largest continent, lying south of Europe with the Atlantic Ocean to the west and the Indian Ocean to the east. Population: 728,000,000 (1995). Area: 30,330,000 sq. km/11,699,000 sq. mi.

African /áffrikən/ *adj.* **OF AFRICA** relating to or typical of any of the countries of the African continent, or their peoples or cultures ▪ *n.* **1. SB FROM AFRICA** sb who was born or who lives in Africa **2. SB OF AFRICAN DESCENT** sb descended from any of the peoples of Africa [Pre-12thC. From Latin *Africanus*, from, ultimately, *Afri* 'the ancient inhabitants of North Africa'.]

African American *n.* an American of African descent —**African American** *adj.*

───── **WORD KEY: USAGE** ─────

African American, Afro-American, or **Black**? *African American* has vigorously overtaken *Afro-American* as a term descriptive of Black Americans. Similarly, *Chinese American* is now more common than *Sino-American*,, and *Italian American* than *Italo-American*. Unlike the others of these compounds, of course, *African American*, along with *Asian American*, refers to a continent, not a country. This lack of parallelism perhaps explains why *African American* and *Asian American* seldom appear in discussions of international relations, whereas both forms of the compounds that pair another country with the United States often do (*Franco-American dialogue* and *French-American friendship*). Other limitations on the use of *African American* have to do with the stress it lays on African heritage. Although Blacks with Caribbean or Hispanic backgrounds may be able to trace their ancestry to Africa, they do not necessarily regard themselves as *African Americans*, any more than the descendants of Spanish immigrants to Argentina consider themselves Spanish. *Black* is broader in application, referring as well to non-Americans. *People of colour* is broader still, referring to non-whites of whatever origin and nationality. *Coloured people* is redolent of other times or other places and is not recommended.

African American Vernacular English *n.* the variety of English spoken by many African Americans

───── **WORD KEY: WORLD ENGLISH** ─────

African American Vernacular English, or **AAVE**, is the term used by scholars for the widespread and varied African American usages also called *Ebonics, Afro-American English, American Black English, Black English, Black English Vernacular,* and *Black Vernacular English*. Originating in the pidgin of the slave trade and Plantation Creole in the US Southern states, African American Vernacular English considerably influenced US Southern English and, in the late 19th and the 20th centuries, spread by migration through much of the nation. It therefore has both rural and urban components. It has also come to be associated with the language of blues, jazz, and rap music.

As with African English, African American Vernacular English is "non-rhotic" or r-dropping: r is not pronounced in words such as *art, door,* and *worker*. Its other characteristics – some going back to similar features of African languages – are these: (1) the use of *d* and *t* instead of *th*, as in *dem* for *them* and *tree* for *three*; 2. *l*-dropping, as in *hep* for *help, sef* for *self,* and *too* for *tool*; (3) consonant reduction at the ends of some words (including tense endings), as in *wha* for *what, jus* for *just,* and *pas* for *past*; (4) use of *-n* for *-ing*, as in *runnin* for *running*; (5) multiple negatives, as in *no way nobody can do it*; (6) verb aspects marked for intermittent, momentary, or continuous action rather than tense per se, the tense time being apparent from the contexts, as in *he be laughin* for *he is always laughing* and *he run* for *he runs*; and (7) dropping of the verb *to be* in some constructions, as in *she sick* and *he gone* for *she is sick* and *he has gone*.

African American Vernacular English expressions have

───────────────────────────────

contributed to the rich texture of American English, these terms being typical: *yam* (sweet potato), *goober* (peanut), *okra*, *gumbo* (the soup and the river mud), *tote* (carry), *juke*, *mumbo jumbo*, *hey/hip*, and *boogie woogie*. All these are rooted in African languages. In its more urban settings, African American Vernacular English's contributions are also many, these few examples making the point: *dis* (to disrespect), *igg* (to ignore), *chill out* (to stop behaving stupidly), *'tude* (attitude), *the Man* (the police), *hang-up* (a problem), *rap* (to talk), *make it* (succeed), *kicks* (pleasure), and the sense of *bad* meaning variously 'good', 'extraordinary', and 'beautiful'. See also **African English**.

African buffalo (*plural* **African buffalos** or **African buffaloes** or **African buffalo**) *n.* a reddish-brown to black wild buffalo found in Africa. There are two species, the Cape buffalo and the smaller forest, or dwarf, buffalo. Latin name: *Synceros caffer* and *Synceros nanus*.

African daisy (*plural* **African daisies**) *n.* a plant with colourful flowers resembling large daisies. The name is used for several different plants originating in Africa.

Africander *n.* = **Afrikander**

African English *n.* the variety of English spoken in Africa

―――――**WORD KEY: WORLD ENGLISH**―――――
English, used in Africa since the 17th century, is currently the most widely employed language on the continent. Whereas the prime European colonial language in North Africa was French , the prime European colonial and missionary language south of the Sahara was English. At least two European languages are native to the continent: Afrikaans (an adaptation of Dutch) in southern Africa, and West African Pidgin English, which has written and printed forms in Sierra Leone (where it is known as Krio) and Cameroon (where it is known as Kamtok). English has come into close contact not only with many local languages but also with other widespread languages such as Arabic, Hausa , and Swahili , often resulting in hybrid usage. Scholars usually divide African English into three broad areas: West, East, and Southern Africa. African English is 'non-rhotic' (that is, r is not pronounced in words such as art, door and worker).

African greenheart (*plural* **African greenhearts** or **African greenheart**) *n.* a leguminous tree of African tropical forests that is the source of commercially important timber. Latin name: *Cylicodiscus gabunensis*.

Africanism /áfrikənizzəm/ *n.* a cultural characteristic typical of Africa or Africans, especially a linguistic feature, usually when found in a non-African language

Africanist /áfrikənist/ *n.* sb who specializes in African affairs, cultures, or languages

African lily (*plural* **African lilies**) *n.* = **agapanthus**

African mahogany (*plural* **African mahoganies**) *n.* **1.** AFRICAN TREE LIKE MAHOGANY an African tree that produces wood similar in appearance to that of tropical American mahogany. Genera: *Khaya* and *Entandrophragma*. **2.** WOOD LIKE MAHOGANY the hard wood of the African mahogany tree. It is used for making the same types of products as true mahogany, e.g. furniture.

African National Congress *n.* full form of **ANC**

African violet *n.* a tropical African plant grown as a

African violet

houseplant for its violet, white, or pink flowers and fleshy leaves. Genus: *Saintpaulia*.

Afrikaans /áffri káanss/ *n.* SOUTH AFRICAN LANGUAGE one of the 11 official languages of South Africa, also spoken in Namibia. It is descended from the Dutch spoken by 17th-century settlers. Afrikaans is spoken by about 10 million people. ■ *adj.* OF AFRIKANERS relating to or typical of the Afrikaner people, or their culture or language [Early 20thC. From Dutch 'African'.]

Afrikander /áffri kándər/, **Africander** *n.* **1.** AGRIC BREED OF S AFRICAN BEEF CATTLE a long-horned hump-backed animal with a reddish colour, belonging to a South African breed of beef cattle **2.** AGRIC BREED OF S AFRICAN SHEEP a sheep belonging to an indigenous South African breed **3.** PEOPLES AFRIKANER an Afrikaner (*archaic*) [Variant of AFRIKANER]

Afrikaner /áffri káanər/ *n.* AFRIKAANS-SPEAKING SOUTH AFRICAN a South African whose first language is Afrikaans, usually descended from 17th century settlers (**Boers**) ■ *adj.* OF AFRIKAANS-SPEAKING SOUTH AFRICANS relating to or typical of the Afrikaans-speaking population of South Africa [Early 19thC. From Afrikaans, formed from *Afrikaan* 'African person' on the model of *Hollander* 'Dutch person'.]

afrit *n.* = **afreet**

Afro /áffrō/ *n.* (*plural* **-ros**) HAIRSTYLE WITH TIGHT CURLS a hairstyle with rounded thick curls ■ *adj.* OF AFRICA of African origin or style [Mid-20thC. From AFRO-AMERICAN or AFRO-.]

Afro- *prefix.* Africa, African ◇ *Afro-Cuban* [From Latin *Afr-*, the stem of Afer 'an African']

Afro-American *n.*, *adj.* = **African-American**

Afro-Asian *adj.* relating to the continents of Africa and Asia or their peoples or shared cultural phenomena

Afro-Asiatic *n.* a family of more than 200 languages spoken across North Africa and the Middle East, consisting of the Semitic, Berber, Cushitic, Chadic, and Egyptian subfamilies. About 250 million people speak an Afro-Asiatic language. —**Afro-Asiatic** *adj.*

Afro-Caribbean *n.* sb of African descent who lives or used to live in the Caribbean, or whose family used to live there

Afro-Cuban *adj.* relating to Cuban culture as influenced by Africa, especially a style of jazz based on Cuban interpretations of African rhythms

afrormosia /áffrawr mốzi ə/ *n.* a hard wood, similar to teak, from tropical African trees [Mid-20thC. From modern Latin, from *Afro-* + *Ormosia*, genus name (from Greek *hormos* 'necklace', probably because the wood was used to make jewellery).]

aft /aaft/ *adv.*, *adj.* towards or at the rear of a ship, submarine, or aircraft [Early 17thC. Shortening of ABAFT.]

aft. *abbr.* afternoon

after /áaftər/ *prep.* **1.** LATER THAN later in time than **2.** BEHIND behind in order or place **3.** IN PURSUIT OF in pursuit of or looking for **4.** REGARDING about or regarding **5.** FOLLOWING FROM subsequent to and considering **6.** LIKE in imitation or in the manner of sb or sth **7.** AGREEING WITH in agreement with or in conformity to **8.** WITH THE SAME NAME AS with a name from that of a specified person or thing because of family relationships or respect **9.** *US* PAST THE HOUR OF past the hour of ■ *adv.* **1.** LATER later in time or place **2.** NAUT, AIR FURTHER BACK further towards the rear of a ship, submarine, or aircraft ■ *conj.* FOLLOWING A TIME WHEN following a time when, and sometimes as a result ■ *adj.* **1.** SUBSEQUENT later in time **2.** NAUT, AIR REAR nearer to the rear of a ship, submarine, or aircraft [Old English *æfter*. Assumed to be a comparative form, literally 'further away', from an Indo-European base meaning 'away, off' (ancestor also of English *off*).] ◇ **after all 1.** used to emphasize sth that should be taken into consideration in spite of what has happened or been said **2.** used to show that in the end sth happened, was done, or was recognized in spite of expectations to the contrary or efforts to prevent it

afterbeat /áaftər beet/ *n.* = **backbeat**

afterbirth /áaftər burth/ *n.* the placenta and foetal membranes expelled from the womb after a birth [Late 16thC. Perhaps modelled on German *Aftergeburt*.]

afterburner /áaftər burnər/ *n.* **1.** DEVICE FOR INCREASING JET'S THRUST a system for increasing the thrust of an aircraft jet engine by feeding fuel into the hot exhaust gases **2.** PART OF CAR EXHAUST a device in the exhaust system of an internal combustion engine for burning or catalytically destroying potentially harmful unburned or incompletely burned carbon compounds

aftercare /áaftər kair/ *n.* **1.** MED CARE AFTER LEAVING HOSPITAL care or support sb receives after leaving a hospital, prison, or psychiatric or other institution, often provided by a community nurse or social worker **2.** MED CARE AFTER ILLNESS care given in a hospital to a patient who is recovering from an illness or operation **3.** COMM UPKEEP OF PRODUCT PURCHASED the maintenance in good condition of a product after purchase, or a support service provided by a company to its customers to assist with this **4.** ENVIRON POLLUTION PREVENTION arrangements for preventing pollution from occurring after a potentially polluting activity such as landfill of waste has ended

afterdamp /áaftər damp/ *n.* gaseous fumes remaining in a mine after an explosion of firedamp

afterdeck /áaftər dek/ *n.* the part of the main open deck of a ship that extends from the bridge or midships to the stern

aftereffect /áaftər i fekt/ *n.* **1.** DELAYED RESULT an effect, usually unpleasant, that follows its cause after an interval of time ○ *The stock markets are still showing the aftereffects of last month's rise in interest rates.* **2.** PHYSIOL SECONDARY REACTION a secondary response that follows the primary response to a physiological stimulus **3.** PSYCHOL DELAYED REACTION a delayed reaction to a psychological stimulus

afterglow /áaftər glō/ *n.* **1.** LIGHT GLOW radiated light that remains visible after a source of light or energy has been removed, e.g. the glow sometimes seen in the sky after sunset **2.** GOOD FEELING a feeling of pleasure or a favourable impression that remains after a positive experience ○ *In the afterglow of the victory, we forgot our leading scorer had been injured.*

afterimage /áaftər immij/ *n.* a visual image that remains briefly after light stimulation has ended

afterlife /áaftər līf/ *n.* **1.** RELIG LIFE AFTER DEATH a form of existence believed to continue after death **2.** LATER STAGE OF LIFE the period of sb's life that follows a particular event ○ *Is there an afterlife for retired football players?*

aftermath /áaftə math, -maath/ *n.* **1.** PERIOD FOLLOWING BAD EVENT the consequences of an event, especially a disastrous one, or the period of time during which these consequences are felt ○ *in the aftermath of the war* **2.** SECOND CROP a second crop or growth of grass in the same season, after the first harvest or mowing [15thC. Literally 'grass that springs up after mowing', formed from *after* + obsolete *math* 'mowing'.]

―――――**WORD KEY: USAGE**―――――
aftermath = 'what comes after' When used figuratively, *aftermath* usually means either an event or circumstance that is unpleasant or unwelcome in itself or one that follows an unpleasant or unwelcome event such as war or disease: *The aftermath of the conflict was a time of confusion and recriminations.* The older literal meaning, 'a second mowing of grass, or the grass which grows again after the first mowing', does not carry any unfavourable implication. Some language purists insist that an *aftermath* should be the same kind of thing as the thing it comes after, but this is not the way the word is normally used.

aftermost /áaftər mōst/, **aftmost** /áaft mōst/ *adj.* nearest to the stern of a ship

afternoon /áaftər noón/ *n.* **1.** TIME DAYTIME BETWEEN MIDDAY AND EVENING the period of the day between noon or lunchtime, and evening **2.** LATTER PART a latter part of sth, especially of sb's life (*literary*) ■ *interj.* GREETING a greeting used to say 'good afternoon' (*informal*)

afternoons /áaftər noónz/ *adv.* during the afternoon, or every afternoon (*informal*)

afterpains /áaftər paynz/ *npl.* pains experienced by some women just after giving birth, similar to labour pains and caused by contractions of the womb

afterpiece /áaftər peess/ n. a short entertainment, usually comic, performed after a play

afters /áaftərz/ n. the sweet or dessert course of a meal (informal; takes a singular or plural verb) ○ What's for afters? [Early 20thC. Formed from after.]

aftersales /áaftə saylz/ adj. occurring or provided after the sale of a product

aftersensation /áaftər sen saysh'n/ n. any sense impression, e.g. an aftertaste or afterimage, that remains after the immediate stimulus has been removed

aftershave /áaftər shayv/ n. a liquid applied after shaving, to soothe and scent the skin of the face

aftershock /áaftər shok/ n. 1. SMALL EARTHQUAKE a small earthquake, usually one of several, that follows a larger one after a period of time 2. DELAYED REACTION a delayed psychological or physical reaction to a serious event or trauma

aftertaste /áaftər tayst/ n. 1. PERSISTING TASTE a taste left in the mouth by food or drink after swallowing 2. UNPLEASANT FEELING a feeling or sensation, especially an unpleasant one, left behind after an experience

afterthought /áaftər thawt/ n. 1. STH ADDED LATER sth not thought of, said, or done originally, but added afterwards 2. MUCH YOUNGER CHILD a child born several years after other children in the same family (humorous)

afterward /áaftərwərd/ adv. US = afterwards

afterwards /-wərdz/ adv. at a later time or after an event that has been mentioned previously ○ Let's have breakfast now and go skiing afterwards.

afterword /áaftər wurd/ n. a short concluding section added at the end of a literary work, which may be either an epilogue or a commentary of some kind

aftmost adj. = aftermost

AFV abbr. armoured fighting vehicle

Ag symbol. silver [Shortening of Latin argentum 'silver']

AG abbr. 1. Adjutant General 2. Attorney General

ag- prefix. = ad- (used before g)

aga /áagə/, **agha** n. used as a title for a military commander or important official in Islamic countries, especially during the Ottoman Empire ○ the Aga Khan [Mid-16thC. From Turkish aghā, literally 'chief, master, lord'.]

Aga /áagə/ tdmk. a trademark for a large iron stove used for both cooking and heating that includes two or more ovens to cook at different temperatures

Agadir /ággə deér/ port and city in Morocco, situated just south of the old city of Agadir, which was destroyed by an earthquake in 1960. Population: (greater city) 779,000 (1990).

again /ə gén, ə gáyn/ adv. 1. ANOTHER TIME at another time or on another occasion, repeating what has happened or been done before ○ I hope to come here again some day. 2. AS BEFORE to the place, person, or state where sb or sth was earlier ○ Will I ever be able to walk again? 3. IN ADDITION in addition to a previously mentioned quantity ○ You'll need all that and half as much again. 4. MOREOVER similarly and in addition (formal) ○ Again, that is something that the court must take into account. 5. IN RESPONSE in return or response (archaic) [Old English ongēan, literally 'in a direct line with, facing' or 'back to a starting point', from a prehistoric Germanic compound formed from the ancestor of German gegen 'against, towards'] ◇ **again and again** repeatedly

against /ə génst, ə gáynst/ CORE MEANING: a preposition indicating opposition to or conflict with sb or sth, either physically or intellectually ○ (prep) a battle against cancer
prep. 1. IN COMPETITION WITH with sb or sth as an opponent in a competitive situation, especially in sport ○ It's Australia against Sweden in the finals. 2. IN CONTACT WITH BY LEANING in a position such that part or all of sth touches another object or surface, by leaning or resting on the side of it rather than resting on top of it ○ I leaned against a tree. 3. INTO SUDDEN CONTACT OR COLLISION WITH so as to briefly touch or suddenly collide with a usually stationary object while in movement ○ banged his head against the beam 4. IN THE OPPOSITE DIRECTION OF in the opposite direction to the movement, angle, or position of sth or sb ○ to swim against the current 5. SEEN IN CONTRAST WITH seen in contrast with sth, e.g. a colour that is behind or surrounding sth ○ The dark green pines are lovely against the blue sky. 6. IN RELATION TO EVENTS in relation to, or contrasted with, a set of events or circumstances ○ Government actions makes sense against the background of rising tensions. 7. AS PROTECTION FROM in order to prevent or avoid sth, or to be protected from sth ○ vaccinate against disease 8. IN PAYMENT OF in partial or total payment of, or as a charge on ○ I'd like to put this money against the amount I owe you. 9. AS A DISADVANTAGE TO to the disadvantage of sb or sth ○ Will you hold it against me if I don't come to your party? 10. COMPARED WITH in comparison with sth ○ weighed the cost of hiring someone against that of promoting existing staff 11. CONTRARY TO contrary to or not approved or allowed by sth or sb ○ It's against the law. 12. IN PREPARATION FOR in preparation for sth, usually an expected unpleasant event (dated) ○ to save against hard times 13. OPPOSITE opposite to or facing sth (archaic) [14thC. Formed from earlier agenes (from Old English ongēan, the ancestor of AGAIN + the adverbial suffix -es) + -t, modelled on such words as amidst.]

Aga Khan III /áagə kaán/ (1877–1957) religious leader, born in Karachi, Pakistan. He was imam of the Ismaili Muslim religious group and president of the League of Nations Assembly (1937).

Aga Khan IV (b. 1936) Swiss-born Muslim leader. He became imam of the Ismaili religious group in 1957. Born **Karim al Hussaini Shah**

agama /ággəmə/ n. 1. SMALL LIZARD a small long-tailed, often colourful lizard native to tropical Africa and Asia. Genus: Agama. 2. = **agamid** [Late 18thC. Via modern Latin and Spanish from, probably, Carib mami 'lizard'.]

Agamemnon /ággə mém non/ n. the commander of the Greek army in the Trojan War. When Agamemnon returned from the war, he was murdered by his wife Clytemnestra and her lover Aegisthus. His death was later avenged by his son Orestes.

agamic /ə gámmik/, **agamous** /ə gámməss/ adj. used to describe an organism that multiplies asexually [Mid-19thC. Formed from Greek agamos 'unmarried', from gamos 'marriage'.] —**agamically** adv.

agamid /ággəmid/ n. a small long-tailed insect-eating lizard found in tropical regions of Africa and Asia. Family: Agamidae. [Late 19thC. From modern Latin Agamidae, family name, ultimately from agama (see AGAMA).]

agamogenesis /áy gamō jénnəssiss, ággəmō-/ n. asexual reproduction, e.g. by cell division or budding [Mid-19thC. Coined from Greek agamos 'unmarried' + -GENESIS.]

agamospermy /ággəmō spurmi/ n. the asexual formation of seeds without fertilization [Mid-20thC. Coined from Greek agamos 'not married' + SPERM + Y².]

agamous adj. = agamic

agapanthus /ággə pánthəss/ (plural **-thus** or **-thuses**) n. a South African plant of the lily family grown for its ball-shaped clusters of bluish or white funnel-shaped flowers. Genus: Agapanthus. US term **African lily** [Late 18thC. From modern Latin, formed from Greek agapē 'love' + anthos 'flower' (source of English anthology).]

agape¹ /ə gáyp/ adv., adj. (literary) 1. WIDE OPEN opened quite widely ○ The door to the room was agape. 2. OPEN-MOUTHED with the mouth wide open, usually in surprise or wonder

agape² /ággəpi/ n. 1. NON-SEXUAL LOVE love that is wholly selfless and spiritual 2. CHR CHRISTIAN LOVE selfless love felt by Christians for their fellow human beings 3. CHR CHRISTIAN COMMUNAL MEAL a communal meal held by a Christian community, especially in early Christian times, in commemoration of the Last Supper [Mid-17thC. From Greek agapē 'brotherly love'.]

agar /áygər, -gaar/, **agar-agar** n. 1. FOOD SETTING AGENT FROM SEAWEED an extract of seaweed in powder form used as a setting agent in vegetarian cooking and commercially as a thickener 2. BIOL GEL FOR GROWING MICROORGANISMS a gel culture medium based on a seaweed extract, widely used for growing micro-organisms in laboratories [Late 19thC. From Malay agar-agar 'jelly'.]

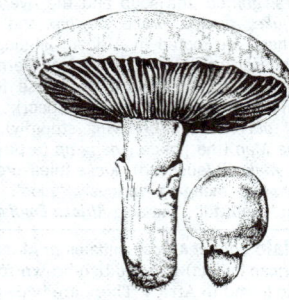
Agaric

agaric /ággərik, ə gárrik/ n. a fungus with a large cap resembling an umbrella with numerous radiating gills on the underside. Some types are edible and some are poisonous. Family: Agaricaceae. [15thC. Directly or via French, from Greek agarikum, from Greek agarikon 'tree fungus', of uncertain origin: perhaps named after Agaria in Sarmatia, an ancient region of eastern Europe.]

agarose /ággə röss, -röz/ n. a complex carbohydrate (**polysaccharide**) obtained from agar and used in chromatography and electrophoresis as a medium in which a substance being analysed can be separated into its component molecules

Aga saga n. a novel about middle class people, especially those living in the shire counties of Britain

Agassi /ággəssi/, **Andre** (b. 1970) US tennis player. He won Wimbledon in 1992 and gold in the Atlanta Olympics in 1996.

agate /ággət/ n. 1. TYPE OF CHALCEDONY a hard fine-grained form of chalcedony with variously coloured bands, markings, and areas of clouding, often used as a gemstone 2. TOY MARBLE a playing marble made of agate or of glass that looks like agate [Late 16thC. Via French, from, ultimately, Greek akhátēs, perhaps named after Achates, a river in Sicily.]

agateware /ággət wair/ n. decorative pottery made using a cross-section of layers of clay of contrasting colours

Agave

agave /ə gáyvi, ə gaávi, ággayv/ (plural **-ves** or **-ve**) n. a plant native to hot dry areas of North and South America that has spiny-edged leaves and a single tall stalk with clusters of flowers. Some species are grown as ornamentals, and others are grown for their fibre (**sisal**) and sap, which is used in making tequila and other alcoholic drinks. Genus: Agave. [Late 18thC. Via Latin, from Greek Agauē, the mother of Pentheus in Greek mythology, whose name meant literally 'illustrious' or 'brilliant'.]

AGC abbr. ELECTRON ENG automatic gain control

agcy abbr. agency

age /ayj/ n. 1. HOW OLD SB OR STH IS the length of time that sb or sth has existed, usually expressed in years 2. STAGE OF LIFE one of the stages or phases in the lifetime of sb or sth ○ She lived to a ripe old age. 3. LEGAL ADULTHOOD the age at which sb is legally considered as an adult 4. BEING OLD the state of being advanced in years ○ the wisdom of age 5. age, Age HISTORICAL ERA a period in history, especially a long period or one associated with and named after a distinctive characteristic, achievement, or influential person ○ *the space age* **6. age, Age** GEOL **GEOLOGICAL ERA** a relatively short division of recent geological time, shorter than an epoch ○ *the Ice Age* **7.** EDUC **LEVEL OF DEVELOPMENT** a level of development equivalent to that of an average person of the stated age ○ *a reading age of 7* **8. GENERATION** a generation of people (*literary*) ○ *the greatest writer of her age* ■ **ages** *npl.* **1. LONG TIME** a very long time (*informal*) **2. HISTORY** human history ○ *People have warred with one another throughout the ages.* ■ *v.* (**ages, ageing** *or* **aging, aged**) **1.** *vti.* **GROW OR CAUSE TO GROW OLD** to become old, develop the characteristics of being old, or cause sb or sth to become or seem old ○ *Too much sun ages the skin.* **2.** *vti.* FOOD **IMPROVE STH OVER TIME** to cause a food or wine to mature, develop a desired flavour, or become more tender, or to become improved in this way over time ○ *The wine is aged in oak barrels.* **3.** *vt.* ELECTRON ENG **STABILIZE STH THROUGH USE** to stabilize an electronic device by using it [13thC. Via Old French *aage* from the Latin stem *aetat-* 'period of life', ultimately from an Indo-European base that also produced English *aeon*.] ◇ **come of age** to reach the age when sb is legally considered an adult ◇ **of a certain age** no longer young (*humorous*)

-age *suffix.* **1.** action or result of an action ○ *breakage* ○ *coinage* **2.** collection of things ○ *signage* **3.** housing ○ *orphanage* **4.** condition, office ○ *brigandage* ○ *peerage* **5.** charge ○ *dockage* [Via French from assumed Vulgar Latin *-aticum*, formed from Latin *-aticus*, suffix forming adjectives]

aged /áyjid/ *adj.* **1. OLD** very advanced in years **2. OF PARTICULAR AGE** of the stated age ○ *a person aged 50* **3. IMPROVED WITH TIME** stored for a period of time in order to mature and produce the best flavour ○ *well-aged wine* **4. ERODED** showing evidence of advanced erosion ■ *npl.* **OLD PEOPLE** people of advanced years, especially those whose physical or mental health has diminished (*formal*) [15thC. Probably modelled on French *âgé* 'aged'.]

age discrimination *n.* discrimination against people because of their age, particularly in employment

age-grade *n.* ANTHROP a group of people in a society who are the same sex and approximately the same age. Age-grades and the relationships between them are an important part of the organization of certain cultures.

age group *n.* a group of people whose ages are approximately the same or fall within a stated range

ageing /áyjing/, **aging** *n.* **1. GROWING OLD** the process of growing old, especially of acquiring the physical and mental characteristics of old age **2. MATURING PROCESS** the natural or chemically assisted process of bringing foods to maturity or of making materials like wood appear older ■ *adj.* **BECOMING OLD** growing old or elderly ○ *caring for an ageing parent* ■ present participle of **age**

ageism /áyjizzəm/, **agism** *n.* discrimination or prejudice against people because of their age, particularly in employment —**ageist** *adj.*

ageless /áyjləss/ *adj.* **1. NOT BECOMING OLD** never growing or seeming to grow older **2. OF ALL GENERATIONS** not typical of or confined to a particular period of time ○ *the ageless search for the truth*

agency /áyjənssi/ (*plural* **-cies**) *n.* **1.** BUSINESS **COMPANY ACTING AS AGENT** an organization, especially a company, acting as the representative, agent, or subcontractor of a person or another company ○ *an employment agency* **2.** POL **GOVERNMENT ORGANIZATION** a division of a government or international organization that carries out administrative duties ○ *a United Nations agency* **3. SEPARATE PART OF UK CIVIL SERVICE** a part of the civil service in the United Kingdom that has some autonomy to deal with a particular aspect of administration such as issuing passports or benefits ○ *the Child Support Agency* **4. OFFICE OF AGENCY** the building or offices where an agency is located **5. ACTION OR OPERATION** the action, medium, or means by which sth is accomplished [Mid-17thC. From medieval Latin *agentia*, from the Latin stem *agent-* (see AGENT).]

agenda /ə jéndə/ *n.* **1. LIST OF THINGS TO DO** a formal list of things to be done in a particular order, especially a list of things to be discussed at a meeting **2. MATTERS NEEDING ATTENTION** the various matters that sb needs to deal with at a given time ○ *What's your agenda for today?* **3. SB'S PARTICULAR MOTIVE** an underlying personal viewpoint or bias ○ *Of course she's in favour, but then she has her own agenda.* ■ plural of **agendum** [Early 17thC. From Latin, the plural of *agendum* 'thing to be done', from *agere* 'to do' (see AGENT).] ◇ **set the agenda** to be the major influence or force affecting sth ○ *It is the environmental lobby that is setting the agenda in this round of negotiations.*

WORD KEY: USAGE

Is **agenda** singular or plural? Although ***agenda*** is strictly speaking a plural noun meaning 'items to be dealt with', the singular form ***agendum*** is not used, and ***agenda*** is used in the singular as if it were 'a list of things to be done', with a plural form ***agendas***: *The agenda for tomorrow's meeting has been changed. This item has appeared on a number of previous agendas.*

Agenda 21 *n.* the global environmental programme and statement of principles agreed at the Earth Summit in Rio de Janeiro in 1992

agendum /ə jéndəm/ (*plural* **-dums** *or* **-da** /-ə/) *n.* an item on an agenda (*formal*) [Early 17thC. From Latin (see AGENDA).]

agenesis /ay jénnəssiss/ *n.* the incomplete development or total absence of a body part ○ *ovarian agenesis*

agent /áyjənt/ *n.* **1.** BUSINESS **SB REPRESENTING ANOTHER** sb representing sb else in business, usually under contract, especially in buying and selling property or insurance, or in arranging work in entertainment or publishing **2. CAUSATIVE SUBSTANCE** sth, e.g. a chemical substance, organism, or natural force, that causes an effect ○ *a cleansing agent* **3. MEANS EFFECTING RESULT** the means by which an effect or result is produced ○ *As director you will be expected to be the main agent of change.* **4.** COMPUT **COMPUTER PROGRAM** a program that works automatically on routine tasks specified by a user, e.g. sorting e-mail or monitoring the Internet [15thC. From Latin *agent-*, the present participle stem of *agere* 'to drive, lead, act, do'.] —**agential** /ay jénsh'l/ *adj.*

WORD KEY: ORIGIN

The Latin word *agere* from which ***agent*** is derived is also the source of English *act, active, actual, agile, agitate, ambiguous, cachet, cogent, essay, exact, examine,* and *squat.*

agent-general (*plural* **agents-general**) *n.* a representative of a Canadian province or Australian state in a foreign country

Agent Orange *n.* a herbicide, now understood to be extremely toxic, that was sprayed from the air by the US military during the Vietnam War to defoliate the jungle and expose enemy forces [From the colour-coded orange stripe on the drums in which the toxin was stored]

agent provocateur /ázhoN prə vókə túr/ (*plural* **agents provocateurs** /ázhoN prə vókə túr/) *n.* sb employed to gain the trust of suspects and then tempt them to do sth illegal so that they can be arrested and punished [From French, literally 'provocative agent']

Age of Aquarius *n.* an astrological era in which increased spirituality and harmony is said to characterize people's lives

age of consent *n.* the age at which sb is legally old enough to consent to marriage or sexual intercourse

Age of Reason *n.* the period from the mid- to late 18th century during which there was an emphasis on rationalism in philosophy, religion, and society

age-old *adj.* dating from a very long time ago and still in existence

age pension *n. Aus* a social security payment made to men over 65 and women over 60

ageratum /ájjə ráytəm/ (*plural* **-tum** *or* **-tums**) *n.* a low-growing plant grown in gardens for its thick clusters of blue, white, or purplish flowers that almost hide the leaves. Genus: *Ageratum.* [Mid-16thC. Via modern Latin from, ultimately, Greek *agēratos* 'ageless, everlasting', from *gēras* 'old age' (source of English *geriatric*).]

Aggadah /əgə daá/ (*plural* **-doth** /-dáwt/) *n.* JUDAISM **1. RABBINIC LITERATURE ON BIBLICAL STORIES** those sections of the Talmud and other rabbinic literature dealing with biblical narrative and stories and legends on biblical themes, rather than with religious law and regulations **2.** = **Haggadah** *n.* **2**, **Haggadah** *n.* **3** [Mid-19thC. From Rabbinic Hebrew *haggādāh* 'tale', especially 'edifying tale'.]

aggiornamento /ə jáwrnə méntō/ *n.* the process of modernizing Roman Catholic Church ritual and policy [Mid-20thC. From Italian, from *aggiornare* 'to bring up to date', ultimately from Latin *diurnum* 'day'.]

agglomerate *vti.* /ə glómmə rayt/ (**-ates, -ating, -ated**) **1. FORM A MASS** to collect together into a mass **2.** GEOL **COLLECT IN ROUND MASS** to gather or accumulate sth in a roughly ball-shaped mass ■ *n.* /ə glómmərət/ **1. JUMBLED COLLECTION** a jumbled mass or collection of sth (*formal*) **2.** GEOL **VOLCANIC ROCK** rock produced by a volcanic eruption, consisting of fragments of different rock types, sizes, and shapes set in fine-grained solidified volcanic ash ■ *adj.* /ə glómmərət/ **IN ROUND MASS** gathered into or forming a rounded mass [Mid-17thC. From Latin *agglomerat-*, past participle stem of *agglomerare* 'to heap up', literally 'to wind or add onto a ball', ultimately from the stem *glomer-* 'ball' (source of English *conglomerate*).] —**agglomerative** /ə glómmərətiv, -raytiv/ *adj.* —**agglomerator** /-raytər/ *n.*

agglomeration /ə glómmə ráysh'n/ *n.* **1. JUMBLED MASS** a jumbled or confused mass of separate elements **2. GATHERING THINGS TO FORM MASS** the process of gathering things together to form a mass

agglutinate /ə glóoti nayt/ *vti.* (**-nates, -nating, -nated**) **1. ADHERE OR CAUSE STH TO ADHERE** to be joined or glued together, or cause things to stick to each other **2.** BIOL, IMMUNOL **CLUMP OR CAUSE CELLS TO CLUMP** to cause cells such as red blood cells or bacteria to form clumps, or stick together in clumps **3.** LING **FORM COMPOUND WORD** to combine simple words together without changing their form to make a new word, or be combined in a new word in this way ■ *n.* BIOL = **agglutination** *n.* **4** [Mid-16thC. From Latin *agglutinat-*, the past participle stem of *agglutinare* 'to fasten with glue', ultimately from *gluten* 'glue' (see GLUTEN).] —**agglutinability** /ə glóotinə bílləti/ *n.* —**agglutinable** /-əb'l/ *adj.* —**agglutinant** /-ənt/ *n., adj.*

agglutination /ə glóoti náysh'n/ *n.* **1. ADHESION** the gluing together or uniting of separate elements or objects **2. CLUMPED MASS** a group, clump, or mass formed by the gluing together or uniting of separate elements or objects **3.** BIOL, IMMUNOL **CLUMPING OF CELLS** the formation of clumps of cells, e.g. red blood cells or microorganisms, in the presence of particular antibodies ○ *platelet agglutination* **4.** BIOL **CELL CLUMP** clumps of cells, e.g. red blood cells or microorganisms, formed in the presence of particular antibodies **5.** LING **COMPOUND WORD FORMATION** the process of forming compound words, derivatives, or inflections by combining simple words or word components without alteration

agglutinative /ə glóotinətiv/ *adj.* **1. ABLE TO AGGLUTINATE** able or likely to agglutinate **2.** LING **FORMING WORDS BY AGGLUTINATION** forming words by combining simple words or word components without alteration ○ *an agglutinative language*

agglutinin /ə glóotinin/ *n.* a substance that causes cells to clump together, e.g. an antibody or lectin

agglutinogen /ágglóo tínnəjən/ *n.* an antigen responsible for the formation of a specific agglutinin

aggrade /ə gráyd/ (**-grades, -grading, -graded**) *vt.* to build up a land surface or stream bed through the natural deposition of material. ◊ **degrade** [Early 20thC. Back-formation from *aggradation*, from AG- + DEGRADATION.] —**aggradation** /ággrə dáysh'n/ *n.* —**aggradational** /-dáysh'nəl/ *adj.*

aggrandize /ə grán dīz, ággrən-/ (**-dizes, -dizing, -dized**), **aggrandise** (**-dises, -dising, -dised**) *vt.* **1. IMPROVE STATUS OF STH** to increase or improve the power, wealth, influence, or status of sb or sth, especially by deliberate plan **2. EXAGGERATE GREATNESS OF SB** to make sb or sth seem bigger or better than is actually the case, especially through exaggerated praise (*formal disapproving*) ○ *aggrandizing the value of her accomplishments* [Mid-17thC. From French *agrandiss-*, the stem of *agrandir*, from *grandir* 'to increase', ultimately from

Latin *grandis* 'great' (see GRAND).] —**aggrandizement** /ə grán dizmənt, -dīzmənt/ *n.* —**aggrandizer** /ə grán dīzər, ággrən-/ *n.*

aggravate /ággrə vayt/ (**-vates, -vating, -vated**) *vt.* **1.** **ANNOY SB** to irritate or anger sb, especially with a continuing or trivial annoyance (*informal*) **2.** **MAKE STH WORSE** to make sth that is already bad or serious worse or more severe [Mid-16thC. Probably via Old French, from Latin *aggravat-*, the past participle stem of *aggravare* 'to make heavier', ultimately from *gravis* 'heavy' (see GRAVE).] —**aggravating** *adj.* —**aggravatingly** *adv.* —**aggravator** *n.*

WORD KEY: USAGE

Can **aggravate** mean 'annoy'? The use of ***aggravate*** to mean 'annoy' or 'irritate' is still disliked by many people, despite a history of usage dating back to the 17th century: *We were aggravated by the continuous loud noise from the street. Their bad behaviour has been very aggravating.* Except in informal conversation it is usually better to use an alternative word such as **annoy**, **exasperate**, or **irritate**.

aggravated /ággrə vaytid/ *adj.* having features that make it a worse criminal offence ○ *aggravated assault*

aggravation /ággrə váysh'n/ *n.* **1.** **IRRITATION** a feeling of exasperation or irritation, especially when caused by a continuing problem **2.** **SOURCE OF IRRITATION** sb or sth that causes continuing exasperation, irritation, or trouble **3.** **WORSENING** the worsening of an already bad situation, or sth that or sb who makes a bad situation worse ○ *Exercising before you have fully recovered may lead to an aggravation of your condition.* **4.** **TROUBLE** annoyance or bother, often aggressive in nature (*informal*) ○ *I get a lot of aggravation from dissatisfied customers.*

aggregate *adj.* /ággrigət, -gayt/ **1.** **FORMING A TOTAL** collected together from different sources and considered as a whole (*formal*) **2.** GEOL **RESEMBLING ROCK** used to describe a mixture of minerals or rock fragments that resembles rock ○ *an aggregate structure* ■ *n.* /ággrigət, -gayt/ **1.** **SUM TOTAL** a total or whole made up of different parts from often disparate sources (*formal*) ○ *Her portfolio consisted of an aggregate of shares from different countries.* **2.** CONSTR **INGREDIENTS OF CONCRETE** broken stone, gravel, and sand used in road construction and, when mixed with cement and water, for making concrete **3.** GEOL **MINERAL MIXTURE RESEMBLING ROCK** a mixture of minerals or rock fragments that resembles rock ■ *v.* /ággri gayt/ (**-gates, -gating, -gated**) **1.** *vti.* **UNITE** to come together, or bring different things together, into a total, mass, or whole ○ *Aggregate the different totals to get the overall cost.* **2.** *vt.* MATH **ADD UP TO A NUMBER** to amount or add up to a particular number ○ *The company's earnings aggregate £175,000.* [15thC. From Latin *aggregat-*, past participle stem of *aggregare* 'to add to', literally 'to bring into the flock', ultimately from the stem *greg-* 'flock' (source also of English *gregarious*).] —**aggregately** /ággrigətli/ *adv.* —**aggregative** /-gətiv/ *adj.* —**aggregator** /-gaytər/ *n.* ◇ **in the aggregate** considered or taken together as a whole

aggregation /ággri gáysh'n/ *n.* a total or collection of different things added together, or the process of adding them together

aggress /ə gréss/ (**-gresses, -gressing, -gressed**) *vi.* to attack first, or begin a fight, argument, or war (*formal*) [Late 16thC. Via obsolete French *aggresser* from Latin *aggress-*, the past participle stem of *aggredi* 'to approach, attack', literally 'to walk to', from *gradi* 'to walk'.]

aggression /ə grésh'n/ *n.* **1.** **ATTACK** hostile action, especially a physical or military attack, directed against another person or country, often without provocation **2.** **HOSTILE ATTITUDE OR BEHAVIOUR** threatening behaviour or actions [Early 17thC. Directly or via French, from the Latin stem *aggression-*, from *aggress-* (see AGGRESS).]

aggressive /ə gréssiv/ *adj.* **1.** **LIKELY TO HARM** showing a readiness or having a tendency to attack or do harm to others **2.** **ATTACKING** attacking or taking action without provocation or without waiting for an enemy to make the first move **3.** **ASSERTIVE** characterized by or exhibiting determination, energy, and initiative ○ *an aggressive investment policy* **4.** MED **SPREADING QUICKLY** used to describe a disease process or pathological growth, e.g. a tumour, that is fast-growing or spreading to other parts of the body —**aggressively** *adv.* —**aggressiveness** *n.*

WORD KEY: USAGE

Aggressive or **assertive**? ***Aggressive*** normally implies hostility and even violence, and is best avoided when the meaning required is 'forceful' or 'assertive': *The sales team is encouraged to be assertive and use aggressive methods.*

WORD KEY: USAGE

One *g* or two? Note that the correct spelling of ***aggressive*** and ***aggression*** is with *-gg-* and *-ss-*.

aggressor /ə gréssər/ *n.* a person or country that attacks or starts a war, fight, or argument, often without being provoked [Mid-17thC. From late Latin, formed from *aggress-* (see AGGRESS).]

aggrieve /ə greév/ (**-grieves, -grieving, -grieved**) *vt.* **1.** **CAUSE DISTRESS TO SB** to cause sb pain, trouble, or distress (*formal*) **2.** LAW **INFLICT INJURY ON SB** to inflict an actionable injury on sb [13thC. Via Old French *agrever* 'to make heavier', from Latin *aggravare* (see AGGRAVATE). The modern spelling is modelled on *grieve*.]

aggrieved /ə greévd/ *adj.* **1.** **UPSET** distressed or angry because of being treated badly or unfairly **2.** LAW **WRONGED** suffering from injustice, especially a denial of legal rights ○ *Compensation was awarded to the aggrieved party.* —**aggrievedly** /ə greévidli/ *adv.* —**aggrievedness** /-nəss/ *n.*

aggro /ággrō/ *n.* (*slang*) **1.** **THREATENING BEHAVIOUR** threatening behaviour, especially trouble-making or fighting ○ *we don't want any aggro* **2.** **DIFFICULTY** trouble or difficulty ○ *He's having a lot of aggro with the garage.* [Mid-20thC. Shortening of AGGRAVATION or AGGRESSION.]

agha *n.* = **aga**

Agha Mohammad Khan /aágə mə hámməd kaán/, **Shah** (1742–97) Iranian ruler who was self-proclaimed Shah (1796–97). He founded the Qajar dynasty, which reigned from 1762 until 1925.

aghast /ə gaást/ *adj.* overcome with shock and dismay [13thC. From the past participle of obsolete *agast* 'to frighten', ultimately from Old English *gǣst* 'spirit, ghost' (source also of English *ghastly* and *ghost*).]

agile /ájjīl/ *adj.* **1.** **NIMBLE** able to move quickly and with suppleness, skill, and control **2.** **MENTALLY QUICK** able to think quickly and intelligently [Late 16thC. Via French, from Latin *agilis* 'that can be moved easily, nimble, quick', from *agere* 'to move, do' (see AGENT).] —**agilely** *adv.* —**agileness** *n.*

agility /ə jílləti/ *n.* **1.** **PHYSICAL NIMBLENESS** a combination of physical speed, suppleness, and skill **2.** **MENTAL ALERTNESS** a combination of mental quickness, alertness, and intelligence [15thC. Via French, from the Latin stem *agilitat-*, from *agilis* (see AGILE).]

agin /ə gín/ *prep.* against (*regional*)

aging *n.*, *adj.* = **ageing**

agio /ájji ō/ (*plural* **-os**) *n.* **1.** **CHARGE FOR EXCHANGING CURRENCY** an amount charged as a premium or percentage for changing one country's currency into another's **2.** **ALLOWANCE FOR FOREIGN CURRENCY** an allowance or discount given when paying in a foreign currency, to compensate for the costs of exchanging the currency [Late 17thC. Via Italian, from, ultimately, medieval Greek *allagion* 'exchange', from *allagē* 'change', from *allos* 'other'.]

agiotage /ájjətij/ *n.* **1.** **CURRENCY EXCHANGING** the business of exchanging currencies between countries **2.** **STOCK AND FOREIGN CURRENCY SPECULATION** speculation in stocks, securities, or foreign currencies [Late 18thC. From French, ultimately from Italian *agio* (see AGIO).]

agism *n.* = **ageism**

agitate /ájji tayt/ (**-tates, -tating, -tated**) *v.* **1.** *vt.* **MAKE SB ANXIOUS** to make sb feel anxious, nervous, or disturbed **2.** *vi.* **AROUSE PUBLIC INTEREST** to attempt to arouse public feeling, interest, or support for or against sth such as a cause **3.** *vt.* **MOVE STH VIOLENTLY** to cause sth to move vigorously or violently, e.g. by shaking or blowing it ○ *Agitate the mixture until the sediment is thoroughly dispersed.* [Late 16thC. From Latin *agitat-*, the past participle stem of *agitare* 'to move to and fro', from *agere* 'to drive, move'.] —**agitative** /ájjitətiv/ *adj.*

agitated /ájji taytid/ *adj.* anxious, nervous, or upset and unable to relax —**agitatedly** *adv.*

agitation /ájji táysh'n/ *n.* **1.** **ANXIETY** nervous anxiety **2.** **PUBLIC CAMPAIGNING** actions intended to arouse public feeling, interest, or support for or against sth such as a cause **3.** **SHAKING** vigorous or violent shaking, stirring, or other disturbance of sth, especially a liquid ○ *Observe the mixture after agitation.* —**agitational** *adj.*

agitato /ájji taátō/ *adj.*, *adv.* in a restless, tense, or excited manner (*used as a musical direction*) [Early 19thC. Via Italian, from, ultimately, Latin *agitat-* (see AGITATE).]

agitator /ájji taytər/ *n.* **1.** **SUPPORTER OF CAUSE** sb who attempts to arouse feeling or interest for or against sth, especially a political cause **2.** **APPARATUS CAUSING MOVEMENT** a machine or machine part that causes vigorous movement in a liquid or other substance

agitprop /ájjit prop/ *n.* **1.** **PROPAGANDA** political propaganda, especially pro-Communist, and especially when disseminated through literature, drama, music, or art **2.** **PROPAGANDIST ART** artistic work or works serving as a vehicle for political propaganda [Early 20thC. From Russian, from *agitatsiya* 'agitation' + *propaganda* 'propaganda'.]

Aglaia /ə glí ə, ə gláy ə/ *n.* in Greek mythology, one of the three Graces who lived on Mount Olympus and tended the goddess Aphrodite. Aglaia was the daughter of Zeus and Euronyme.

agleam /ə gleém/ *adj.* glowing, gleaming, or emitting a soft light (*literary*) ○ *She was laughing, her eyes agleam.*

aglet /ágglət/ *n.* **1.** **END OF SHOELACE** a plain or ornamental metal or plastic sheath covering the end of a shoelace or ribbon **2.** **METAL DECORATION FOR CLOTHING** a metallic ornament such as a stud, cord, or badge worn on clothing [15thC. From French *aiguillette* (see AIGUILLETTE).]

agley /ə gláy, ə glí, ə gleé/ *adv.*, *adj.* *Scotland, N England* awry or askew ○ *'The best laid schemes o' mice and men/ Gang aft agley'* (Robert Burns, *To a mouse*; 1785) [Late 18thC. Formed from A- + *gley* 'to squint' (of unknown origin).]

aglimmer /ə glímmər/ *adj.* glimmering with light (*literary*)

aglitter /ə glíttər/ *adj.* glittering or sparkling with light (*literary*)

agloo *n.* = **aglu**

aglow /ə glṓ/ *adj.* radiating light, warmth, excitement, or happy emotion

aglu /ágglooˈ/ (*plural* **-lus**), **agloo** (*plural* **-loos**) *n.* *Can* a breathing hole that a seal has made in sea ice [Late 19thC. From Inuktitut.]

aglycone /ə glíkōn/, **aglycon** /-kon/ *n.* a non-sugar compound that is produced from the reaction of a glycoside with water. Alcohols and phenols are aglycones. [Early 20thC. From German *Aglykon*, from Greek *glukus* 'sweet' (see GLUCOSE).]

AGM *abbr.* annual general meeting

agma /ágmə/ *n.* the symbol (ŋ) used to represent a velar nasal consonant, as in the final sound of 'long' or 'tank' [Mid-20thC. From Greek, 'fragment'.]

agnail /ág nayl/ *n.* = **hangnail** [Old English *angnægl*, formed from *ang-* 'narrow, painful' + *nægl* 'nail']

agnate /ág nayt/ *n.* **RELATIVE WITH SAME MALE ANCESTOR** a relative who is descended from a common male ancestor, especially through the male line (*formal*) ■ *adj.* (*formal*) **1.** **PATRILINEAL** patrilineal **2.** **RELATED** related or akin in any way [15thC. From Latin *agnatus*, literally 'born in addition', from Old Latin *gnatus*, the past participle of *gnasci* 'to be born' (source of English *innate* and *nativity*).] —**agnatic** /ag náttik/ *adj.* —**agnatically** /-náttikli/ *adv.* —**agnation** /ag náysh'n/ *n.*

Agni /úgni/ *n.* the Hindu god of fire [From Sanskrit, 'fire, the fire-god']

agnolotti /ánnyə lótti/ *npl.* small pieces of semicircular pasta stuffed with meat, cheese, or other filling and sealed at the edges [Late 20thC. From Italian dialect, an alteration of Italian *anellotto*, literally 'little ring'.]

agnomen /ag nṓm en/ (*plural* **-nomina** /-minə/) *n.* **1.** FOURTH NAME a fourth name that was occasionally bestowed on sb as an honour in ancient Rome **2.** NICKNAME a nickname (*literary*) [Mid-17thC. From Latin, literally 'additional name', from *(g)nomen* 'name'.]

agnosia /ag nṓzi ə/ *n.* the total or partial loss of the ability to recognize familiar people or objects, usually caused by brain damage [Early 20thC. From Greek *agnōsia*, literally 'lack of knowledge', from *gnōsis* 'knowledge'.]

agnostic /ag nóstik/ *n.* **1.** SB DENYING GOD'S EXISTENCE IS PROVABLE sb who believes that it is impossible to know whether or not God exists **2.** SB DENYING STH IS KNOWABLE sb who doubts that a particular question has a single correct answer or that a complete understanding of sth can be attained ○ *I'm an agnostic concerning the validity of modern educational methods.* [Mid-19thC. Coined (reputedly by the English biologist and religious sceptic T. H. Huxley (1825–95) in 1869, although an earlier use of the word has been recorded) from A- + GNOSTIC.] —**agnostic** *adj.* —**agnostically** *adv.*

agnosticism /ag nóstissizzəm/ *n.* the belief that it is impossible to know whether or not God exists

Agnus Dei /ágnòoss dáy ee/ *n.* **1.** LAMB WITH CROSS a lamb, usually depicted with a halo and holding a cross and banner, used as a symbol of Jesus Christ **2.** CHRISTIAN PRAYER a Christian prayer that begins in Latin with the words 'Agnus Dei', or 'Lamb of God', part of the liturgy of the Mass **3.** MUSIC MUSIC FOR AGNUS DEI PRAYER a musical setting of the Christian prayer beginning 'Agnus Dei' [15thC. From Latin, literally 'Lamb of God'.]

ago /ə gṓ/ *adv., adj.* before the present time ○ *He only left about five minutes ago.* [14thC. From the past participle of Old English *āgān* 'to go away, pass by', from *gān* 'to go'.]

WORD KEY: USAGE

ago and **since** If ***ago*** is used it should be followed by **that** and not **since** in a following clause: *It was several weeks ago that I saw them.* If ***ago*** is left out, then **since** is used: *It is several weeks since I saw them.* Note also that in sentences of this type, ***ago*** is preceded by a verb in the past tense (*was*) and **since** by a verb in the present tense.

agog /ə góg/ *adj.* intensely interested, excited, or eager ○ *agog at the new twist to the scandal* [15thC. Probably based on Old French *en gogues* 'enjoying yourself', literally 'in enjoyment'; the origin of *gogues* is unknown.]

-agog *suffix.* = **-agogue**

à gogo /ə gṓ gō/ *adj.* as much as anybody could want (*dated informal*) ○ *caviare à gogo* [Mid-20thC. From French, 'joyfully', from *en gogues* 'enjoying oneself' (see AGOG) by repeating the *go-*.]

-agogue, **-agog** *suffix.* substance promoting the flow of sth ○ *galactagogue* [Via French from, ultimately, Greek *agōgos* 'a drawing off', from *agein* 'to lead']

agon /ággōn, ágg on/ (*plural* **agones** /ə gṓ neez/) *n.* in ancient Greece, a festival featuring sports, musical, or theatrical competitions, e.g. the Olympic, Pythian, Nemean, and Isthmian games [Early 17thC. From Greek *agōn* 'contest', from *agein* 'to lead, conduct, celebrate'.]

agonal /ággənəl/ *adj.* involving intense pain, especially the pain or throes of death

agones plural of **agon**

agonise *vti.* = **agonize**

agonist /ággənist/ *n.* **1.** ANAT MUSCLE ACTING AGAINST ANOTHER a muscle whose action is balanced by that of another associated muscle. ◊ **antagonist 2.** BIOCHEM DRUG MIMICKING BODILY CHEMICAL a drug, hormone, or other substance that triggers a response in a particular body tissue or group of cells by binding to specific receptor molecules on or inside the cells. ◊ **antagonist 3.** COMPETITOR sb involved in a struggle, contest, or competition with sb else (*formal*) [Early 17thC. From Greek *agōnistēs* 'contestant, actor', from *agōn* (see AGON).]

agonistes /ággō nísteez/ *adj.* used after a name to indicate that sb is engaged in a fundamental struggle, especially a moral one (*literary*) [Late 17thC. From Greek *agōnistēs* (see AGONIST).]

agonistic /ággə nístik/, **agonistical** /ággə nístik'l/ *adj.* **1.** TRYING FOR EFFECT striving to achieve an effect but appearing contrived or exaggerated (*literary*) **2.** ARGUMENTATIVE tending to argue and eager to win an argument (*literary*) **3.** ZOOL AGGRESSIVE characteristic of aggressive interaction between individuals, usually of the same species [Mid-17thC. Via late Latin, from Greek *agōnistikos*, from *agōnistēs* (see AGONIST).] —**agonistically** *adv.*

agonize /ággə nīz/ (**-nizes, -nizing, -nized**), **agonise** (**-nises, -nising, -nised**) *v.* **1.** *vi.* SPEND TIME WORRYING to think about sth intensely and anxiously, usually in great detail and for a long time, before making a decision ○ *to agonize over the answer to every question* **2.** *vti.* SUFFER OR CAUSE SB PAIN to suffer, or cause sb to suffer, extreme pain or mental anguish **3.** *vi.* STRUGGLE to make a desperate or strenuous effort (*literary*) [Late 16thC. Directly or via French, from late Latin *agonizare*, modelled on Greek *agōnizesthai* 'to take part in a contest', from *agōn* (see AGON).]

agonized /ággə nīzd/, **agonised** *adj.* expressing or characterized by severe pain or anxiety ○ *an agonized scream* ○ *an agonized search for the missing person*

agonizing /ággə nīzing/, **agonising** *adj.* **1.** VERY PAINFUL extremely painful **2.** CAUSING DIFFICULTY OR UNPLEASANTNESS causing much difficulty or unpleasantness ○ *an agonizing decision* —**agonizingly** *adv.*

agony /ággəni/ (*plural* **-nies**) *n.* **1.** GREAT PAIN OR ANGUISH intense physical pain or mental anguish **2.** INTENSE EMOTION a consuming emotion ○ *in an agony of indecision* **3.** SUFFERING PRECEDING DEATH a period of struggle or suffering immediately preceding death (*archaic*) ○ *last agony* [14thC. Directly or via French, from Latin *agonia*, from Greek *agōnia* '(mental) struggle, anguish', from *agōn* 'contest' (see AGON).] ◇ **prolong the agony** to make a period of misfortune or anxiety last longer than necessary

agony aunt *n.* a woman who gives personal advice to readers in a regular column in a newspaper or magazine or to callers on a radio or television programme

agony column *n.* **1.** PUBLISHED PERSONAL ADVICE a regular column in a newspaper or magazine in which a columnist gives advice to readers who have written in about their personal problems **2.** ADVERTISEMENTS FOR MISSING PEOPLE a newspaper column of personal advertisements, usually inquiring about missing relatives or friends (*archaic*)

agony uncle *n.* a man who gives personal advice to readers in a regular column in a newspaper or magazine or to callers on a radio or television programme

agora[1] /ággərə/ (*plural* **-rae** /ággərī/ *or* **-ras**) *n.* an open space in a town where people gather, especially a marketplace in ancient Greece [Late 16thC. From Greek, 'marketplace, place of assembly', from *ageirein* 'to assemble'.]

agora[2] /ággə ráa/ (*plural* **-rot** /-rṓt/) *n.* **1.** see table at **currency 2.** COIN WORTH AN AGORA a coin worth one agora [Mid-20thC. From Hebrew *agōrāh* 'small coin'.]

agorae plural of **agora**[1]

agoraphobia /ággərə fṓbi ə/ *n.* a condition characterized by an irrational fear of public or open spaces [Late 19thC. Coined from Greek *agora* 'open place' (see AGORA[1]) + -PHOBIA.] —**agoraphobic** *adj., n.*

agorot plural of **agora**[2]

agouti /ə góoti/ (*plural* **-tis** *or* **-ties**) *n.* **1.** TROPICAL RODENT a tropical rodent native to Central and South America that is similar in size to a rabbit and has short ears and clawed feet. Genus: *Dasyprocta.* **2.** STRIPED FUR an irregularly striped pattern in the individual hairs of the fur of an agouti [Early 17thC. Via French or Spanish, from Tupi-Guarani *akutí*.]

agr. *abbr.* agriculture

Agra /áagrə/, **Āgra** city in Uttar Pradesh state, northern India. It is famous as the site of the Taj Mahal. Population: 955,674 (1991).

agranulocytosis /ə grányoōlō sī tṓssiss, ay-/ *n.* a serious and sometimes fatal acute illness characterized by a decrease in granular white blood cells, and lesions of the throat, gastrointestinal tract, and skin. The condition often occurs as a toxic effect of certain drugs. [Early 20thC. Coined from A- + GRANULOCYTE + -OSIS.]

agrapha /ággrəfə/ *npl.* sayings of Jesus Christ not recorded in the Bible but found in other early Christian writings [Late 19thC. From the plural of Greek *agraphon* 'unwritten'.]

agraphia /ə gráffi ə, ay-/ *n.* loss of the ability to write, resulting from neurological damage such as a brain lesion [Mid-19thC. Coined from A- + Greek *graphia* 'writing'.] —**agraphic** /ay gráffik/ *adj.*

agrarian /ə gráiri ən/ *adj.* **1.** OF LAND relating to land, especially its ownership and cultivation **2.** OF RURAL LIFE dominated by or relating to farming or rural life **3.** PRO-FARMER promoting the interests of farmers, especially in seeking a fairer or more equitable basis of land ownership ○ *an agrarian political party* ■ *n.* LAND REFORMER sb, often a member of an agrarian political movement, who believes in the fair distribution of land, especially the redistribution of large amounts of land owned by the rich [Early 17thC. Formed from Latin *agrarius*, from the stem *agr-* 'field' (see AGRICULTURE).]

agrarianism /ə gráiri ənizzəm/ *n.* a political movement or philosophy that promotes the interests of the farmer, especially the redistribution of land owned by the rich or by government

agree /ə grée/ (**agrees, agreeing, agreed**) *v.* **1.** *vi.* BE IN ACCORD to have the same opinion about sth as sb or each other ○ *Scientists don't agree about what causes these reactions.* **2.** *vi.* CONSENT to consent to or approve sth ○ *They agreed to a postponement.* **3.** *vi.* ADMIT AS TRUE to admit that sth is true ○ *I had to agree that the room looked better with a coat of paint.* **4.** *vti.* DECIDE to come to an understanding or reach a settlement regarding sth ○ *Do you think we can agree on a plan?* **5.** *vi.* BE CONSISTENT to be consistent in content, meaning, or characteristics with sth ○ *The witnesses' stories agree in most details with the accused's.* **6.** *vi.* BE SUITABLE to suit or be good for sb ○ *The climate doesn't agree with me.* **7.** *vt.* CAUSE TO CORRESPOND to make sth equal or consistent with sth else ○ *to agree the incomings with the outgoings* **8.** *vi.* LING MATCH GRAMMATICALLY to have the same grammatical number, case, person, or gender, especially in the same sentence [14thC. Via French *agréer* 'to please' from, ultimately, Latin *ad* 'to' + *gratus* 'pleasing'.]

WORD KEY: SYNONYMS

agree, consent, concur, acquiesce, assent

CORE MEANING: to accept an idea, plan, or proposed action that has been put forward

agree the most general and wide-ranging term; **consent** a slightly more formal term for ***agree***, also often used to mean to give formal permission to, and sometimes indicating willingness rather than enthusiasm; **concur** a formal term suggesting that sb has reached agreement independently, often regarding a statement or opinion; **acquiesce** a somewhat formal term that suggests a lack of enthusiasm and commitment, or an initial reluctance and reservation that may have been overcome by some form of external persuasion; **assent** the most formal term, indicating full support, often a statement or opinion.

agreeable /ə grée əb'l/ *adj.* **1.** PLEASING pleasing to the senses or to sb's taste ○ *The climate here is very agreeable.* **2.** FRIENDLY pleasant, friendly, and ready to please others ○ *an agreeable companion* **3.** WILLING TO COMPLY willing to consent to or consider sth ○ *If the committee is agreeable, you can start work straight away.* **4.** CONSISTENT consistent or in keeping with sth [14thC. From French, formed from *agréer* (see AGREE).] —**agreeability** /ə grée ə bílləti/ *n.* —**agreeably** /-b'li/ *adv.*

agreed /ə gréed/ *adj.* **1.** DETERMINED BY CONSENSUS previously decided and assented to by two or more people ○ *the agreed procedure* **2.** SHARING OPINION sharing the same view as sb else or others ○ *Are we all agreed on the proposal?* ■ *interj.* YES used to confirm agreement with sb else

agreement /ə gréemənt/ *n.* **1.** FORMAL CONTRACT a contract or arrangement, either written or verbal and sometimes enforceable by law **2.** ACT OR STATE OF AGREEING the reaching or sharing of the same opinion that sb or others hold ○ *Do we have your agreement on this issue?* **3.** CONSENSUS OF OPINION a situation in which

zh vision In foreign words: kh German Bach; aN French vin; aaN French blanc; ö German schön, French feu; öN French bon; öN French un; ü French rue Stress marks: ´ as in secret \sée̍k rət\; academic \ákə démmik\

everyone accepts the same terms or has the same opinion ○ *everyone is in agreement* **4.** CONSENT consent, or an answer of yes ○ *my parents' agreement to the marriage* **5.** GRAM **GRAMMATICAL CORRESPONDENCE** correspondence of the number, case, gender, or person of one word with that of another word, especially in the same sentence

agrestal /ə gréstʹl/ *adj.* used to describe a plant that grows on cultivated land or among crops [Mid-19thC. Formed from Latin *agrestis* 'of fields', from the stem *agr-* 'field' (see AGRICULTURE).]

agrestic /ə gréstik/ *adj.* (*literary*) **1.** RURAL rural or rustic **2.** CRUDE crude, uncouth, or unrefined [Early 17thC. Formed from Latin *agrestis* (see AGRESTAL).]

agri *prefix.* = **agro-**

agribusiness /ággri biznəss/ *n.* the operations and businesses that are associated with large-scale farming

agrichemical *n.* = **agrochemical**

Agricola /ə gríkələ/, **Gnaeus Julius** (37–93 BC) Roman colonial administrator and governor of Britain (78–84). He encouraged Romanization, and was recalled to Rome and retirement in 85 BC.

agricultural /ággri kúlchərəl/ *adj.* **1.** OF AGRICULTURE involving or relating to agriculture ○ *agricultural equipment* ○ *agricultural college* **2.** FARMING-CENTRED with farming as the dominant way of life ○ *one of the earliest agricultural communities* —**agricultural** *n.* —**agriculturally** *adv.*

agriculture /ággri kulchər/ *n.* the occupation or business of cultivating the land, producing crops, and raising livestock [15thC. Directly or via French, from Latin *agricultura*, from *agri* 'of the land' (from the stem *agr-* 'field, land') + *cultura* 'cultivation'.] —**agriculturist** /ággri kúlchərist/ *n.*

agrimony /ággriməni/ (*plural* **-ny** *or* **-nies**) *n.* **1.** PLANT WITH SPINY FRUITS a perennial plant that has compound leaves, spikes of small yellow flowers, and spiny fruits. Genus: *Agrimonia.* **2.** = **hemp agrimony** [Pre-12thC. Via Old French, from Latin *agrimonia*, a misreading of *argemonia*, from Greek *argemōnē* 'poppy'.]

Agrippa /ə gríppə/, **Marcus Vipsanius** (63–12 BC) Roman general and a principal aide of the Emperor Augustus. He won the naval battle of Actium (31 BC).

agro-, **agri-** *prefix.* **1.** soil ○ *agrology* **2.** agriculture ○ *agroindustrial* [From Latin *agri* (a form of *ager*) and Greek *agros* 'field'. Ultimately from an Indo-European word meaning 'field', which is also the ancestor of English *acre*.]

agrobiology /ággrō bī óllәji/ *n.* the branch of biology concerned with agricultural production, especially crop growth —**agrobiological** /ággrō bī ə lójjikʹl/ *adj.* —**agrobiologically** /-lójjikli/ *adv.* —**agrobiologist** /-óllәjist/ *n.*

agrochemical /ággrō kémmikʹl/, **agrichemical** /ággri-/ *n.* a chemical used in farming, e.g. a fertilizer or pesticide

agroforestry /ággrō fórristri/ *n.* **1.** AGRIC **FORESTRY COMBINED WITH FARMING** the method or practice of integrating the raising of trees into farming to provide fuel, fruits, forage, shelter for animals or crops, and other benefits **2.** FORESTRY **FORESTRY FOR TIMBER ONLY** forestry conducted purely to produce timber, without any regard for sporting or recreational pursuits

agroindustrial /ággrō in dústri əl/ *adj.* **1.** FOR AGRICULTURE AND INDUSTRY relating to the production or provision of materials needed by both agriculture and industry, e.g. water **2.** OF INDUSTRIAL AGRICULTURE used in, produced by, or involved in the industrial processing of agricultural products

agronomic /ággrə nómmik/, **agronomical** /-nómmikʹl/ *adj.* **1.** OF STUDY OF SOILS AND PLANTS relating to the scientific study of soil management, land cultivation, and crop production **2.** IMPORTANT FOR CROP QUALITY used to describe plant characteristics that are important during growth and development of a crop, e.g. height and stem strength

agronomics /ággrə nómmiks/ *n.* the branch of economics that is concerned with the use and productivity of land (*takes a singular verb*) [Mid-19thC. Coined from AGRO- + ECONOMICS.]

agronomy /ə grónnəmi/ *n.* the science of soil management, land cultivation, and crop production [Early 19thC. Via French *agronomie* from, ultimately, Greek *agronomos* 'overseer of land', from *agros* 'land' + *-nomos* 'dispensing, administering'.] —**agronomist** *n.*

aground /ə grównd/ *adj.*, *adv.* onto or on ground, especially a shore, a reef, rocks, or the bottom of shallow water

agt *abbr.* **1.** agent **2.** agreement

aguardiente /ág waardi énti/ *n.* rough brandy distilled in Spain, Portugal, or Latin America, sometimes flavoured with anise [Early 19thC. From Spanish, from *agua* 'water' + *ardiente* 'fiery'.]

ague /áy gyoo/ *n.* **1.** FEVER a feverish condition involving alternating hot, cold, and sweating stages, especially as a symptom of malaria **2.** ATTACK OF FEVER a fever or shivering fit (*archaic*) [14thC. Via French, from medieval Latin *acuta*, short for *febris acuta*, literally 'sharp fever'.] —**aguish** /áyg yoo ish/ *adj.* —**aguishly** *adv.* —**aguishness** *n.*

ah /aa/ *interj.* **1.** EXPRESSING EMOTION used to express emotions ranging from blissful contentment to acute discomfort to disgust, depending on the speaker's tone of voice. ◊ **aah 2.** EXPRESSING RECOGNITION used to express surprise or recognition and understanding ○ *Ah, I see.* ■ *vi.* SAY 'AH' to say 'ah.' ◆ **ooh** ■ *n.* UTTERANCE OF 'AH' an exclamation of 'ah' expressing any of various emotions

AH *adv.* used in the Muslim calendar to indicate the number of years from the Hegira (AD 622). Full form **anno Hegirae**

a.h. *abbr.* ampere-hour

aha /aa haá/ *interj.* used when discovering sth, especially to express triumphant satisfaction or excitement ○ *Aha, I caught you in the act!* [14thC. Formed from AH + HA.]

AHA *abbr.* alpha-hydroxy acid

ahead /ə héd/ *adv.*, *adj.* **1.** IN FRONT in front of sb or sth ○ *They are in the white car just ahead.* **2.** FORWARDS onwards or in a forward direction ○ *Keep walking straight ahead and it's on your left.* **3.** TO THE FUTURE in or into the future ○ *We expect more news in the weeks ahead.* **4.** EARLIER before or in advance of sth or sb ○ *You need to learn to plan ahead!* **5.** IN BETTER SHAPE in or into a more advanced or desirable state ○ *Our company is definitely ahead compared to competition.* **6.** IN FIRST PLACE in a winning position in a contest or competition ○ *They were ahead by 6 points to 4.* ◇ **ahead of 1.** in front of **2.** at an earlier time than **3.** in a more advanced or advantageous position than

ahem /ə hém/ *interj.* used in writing to indicate the sound of a quiet cough made to attract attention, express disapproval or doubt, or gain time [Mid-18thC. An imitation of the sound.]

Ahern /ə húrn/, **Bertie** (*b.* 1951) Irish politician who became leader of the Fianna Fáil political party in 1994 and was elected Taoiseach (prime minister) in 1997.

ahimsa /ə hím saa/ *n.* the Hindu, Buddhist, and Jainist philosophy of revering all life and refraining from harm to any living thing [Late 19thC. From Sanskrit, from *a-* 'without' + *hiṁsā* 'injury'.]

ahistorical /áy hi stórrikʹl/, **ahistoric** /áy hi stórrik/ *adj.* not concerned with or not taking into account history or historical development, especially when examining a phenomenon that changes over time

-aholic *suffix.* addicted to ○ *workaholic* [From ALCOHOLIC]

ahoy /ə hóy/ *interj.* **1.** EXPRESSING GREETING used by sailors to greet another ship or person or to attract attention ○ *Ahoy there!* **2.** REGISTERING A SIGHTING used by sailors to announce that sth, usually another ship or land, is in sight [Mid-18thC. Probably a blend of AHA and HOY.]

Ahriman /aárimən/ *n.* the spirit of evil in Zoroastrianism, and opponent of Ormadz [Via Persian, from, ultimately, Avestan *angrō mainiiuš* 'evil spirit']

Ahura Mazda /ə hoórə mázdə/ *n.* = **Ormazd** [From Avestan *ahurō mazdå*, literally 'wise lord']

AI *abbr.* **1.** artificial insemination **2.** artificial intelligence

aid /ayd/ *vti.* (**aids, aiding, aided**) GIVE HELP TO SB to provide sb or sth with help or with what is needed to achieve sth ○ *Better sewage systems aid in the fight against cholera.* ■ *n.* **1.** MONEY OR SUPPLIES financial or material assistance, e.g. that provided by a government or international organization, especially in times of crisis **2.** ASSISTANCE anything done or provided that assists sb or sth ○ *I wouldn't have made it without the aid of my friends.* **3.** SB OR STH HELPFUL sb or sth, e.g. a device, resource, or material, that helps or assists with sth ○ *visual aids such as maps* ○ *This book is an aid to surfing the Internet.* **4.** ASSISTANT an assistant or aide **5.** MOUNTAINEERING DEVICE TO AID CLIMBING any device that is used to help a climber ascend a cliff or mountain face **6.** HIST PAYMENT TO LORD a monetary payment by a vassal to an English feudal lord **7.** HIST SUBSIDY FOR ENGLISH KING a special subsidy formerly granted to the English king by parliament. Aids for extraordinary expenses were granted from the time of the Norman Conquest into the 18th century. [15thC. Via French, from Latin *adjutare* 'to help' (see ADJUTANT).] ◇ **aid and abet** to assist sb in commission of a crime ◇ **in aid of** in order to help or for a particular reason or purpose (*informal*)

AID *abbr.* **1.** Agency for International Development **2.** acute infectious disease **3.** artificial insemination by donor (*dated*)

aida /ī eédə/ *n.* a type of fabric used for cross-stitch that comes in different degrees of weave from coarse to fine, measured by the number of holes per inch [Origin unknown]

Aidan /áydʹn/, **St** (600?–651) Irish monk who became bishop of Northumbria (635) and founded the monastery of Lindisfarne.

aid climbing *n.* climbing mountains or rocks with the assistance of artificial aids such as pitons

aide /ayd/ *n.* **1.** ASSISTANT an assistant to sb in public office or to sb providing a professional service ○ *The letter was signed by one of the Prince's aides.* **2.** = **aide-de-camp** [Late 18thC. Shortening of AIDE-DE-CAMP.]

WORD KEY: SYNONYMS

See Synonyms at ***assistant***.

aide-de-camp /áyd də kaáN/ (*plural* **aides-de-camp** /áyd də kaáN/), **aide** /ayd/ *n.* a military officer acting as confidential assistant to a general or senior officer [Late 17thC. From French, literally 'camp assistant'.]

aide-mémoire /áyd mem waár/ (*plural* **aide-mémoire** /áyd mem waár/ *or* **aide-mémoires** *or* **aides-mémoire**) *n.* (*formal*) **1.** BRIEF SUMMARY a brief written summary or outline of the items on which agreement was reached in a meeting **2.** MEMORY AID sth, e.g. a mnemonic device, book, or document, that is an aid to remembering sth else [Mid-19thC. From French, literally 'help-memory'.]

Aids /aydz/, **AIDS** *n.* a disease of the immune system caused by infection with the retrovirus HIV, which destroys certain white blood cells and is transmitted through blood or bodily secretions such as semen. Patients lose the ability to fight infections, often resulting in death from secondary causes such as pneumonia or Kaposi's sarcoma. [Late 20thC. Acronym formed from *Acquired Immune Deficiency Syndrome.*]

Aids-related complex *n.* the set of symptoms associated with infection by HIV, including weight loss and fever

aid station *n.* *US* a military medical installation for troops in the field

aigrette /áy gret, ay grét/ *n.* **1.** PLUME OF FEATHERS a tuft of long upright plumes, especially the tail feathers of an egret, worn on the head or on a hat for decoration **2.** JEWELLERY RESEMBLING PLUME OF FEATHERS a piece of jewellery that resembles a plume of feathers, usually worn on the head or on a hat [Mid-17thC. From French, literally 'egret, heron' (see EGRET).]

Aiguille: Teton Mountains, Jackson Hole, Wyoming, United States

aiguille /ay gweél, ággweel/ n. a mountain peak or large rock that is tall and sharply pointed [Early 19thC. From French, literally 'needle'.]

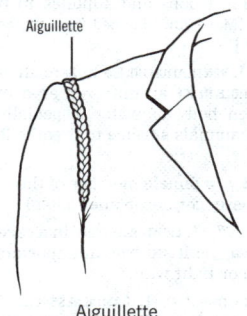

Aiguillette

aiguillette /áygwi lét/ n. a decorative cord worn on the shoulder of some military uniforms [Mid-16thC. From French, literally 'little needle', from *aiguille* 'needle'. The word originally denoted a metallic pin worn as an ornament.]

AIH abbr. artificial insemination by husband

aikido /ī keédō, íki-/ n. a martial art originating in Japan that is similar to judo but incorporates blows made with the hands and feet [Mid-20thC. From Japanese, literally 'way of coordinated breathing'.]

ail /ayl/ (ails, ailing, ailed) vt. to cause sth to be wrong with sb or sth, or cause sb to feel ill ○ *This soup is good for whatever ails you.* [Old English *eglian.* Ultimately from an Indo-European word meaning 'to be afraid or distressed', which is also the ancestor of English *awe*.]

ailanthus /ay lánthəss, ī-/ n. an Asian tree or shrub with long feathery leaves, winged fruit, and dense flower clusters. Tree of heaven is a type of ailanthus. Genus: *Ailanthus.* [Early 19thC. Via modern Latin, genus name, from Amboinese *ai lanto*, literally 'tree of heaven', influenced by plant names ending in *-anthus.*]

aileron /áylə ron/ n. a hinged flap on the trailing edge of an aircraft wing, used to control banking or rolling movements [Early 20thC. From French, literally 'small wing', from *aile* 'wing', from Latin *ala*.]

ailing /áyling/ adj. **1.** IN POOR CONDITION performing below an expected standard ○ *The nation's ailing steel industry.* **2.** ILL suffering from or weakened by an illness (dated)

ailment /áylmənt/ n. a mild illness or injury, especially a persistent one

— WORD KEY: SYNONYMS —
See Synonyms at *illness*.

Ailsa Craig /áylssə kráyg/ rocky islet in the Firth of Clyde, Scotland. Height: 340 m/1,114 ft.

ailurophile /ī loórə fíl, ī lyoórə/ n. sb who loves cats [Mid-20thC. Coined from Greek *ailuros* 'cat' + -PHILE.]

ailurophobe /ī loórə fōb, ī lyoórə-/ n. sb who hates or has an abnormal fear of cats [Early 20thC. Coined from Greek *ailuros* 'cat' + -PHOBE.] —**ailurophobia** /ī loórə fóbi ə, ī lyoórə-/ n.

aim /aym/ v. (aims, aiming, aimed) **1.** vi. PLAN TO DO STH to intend or plan to do sth **2.** vt. DIRECT A MESSAGE to target words, a message, an action, or a product at a particular person or group **3.** vti. POINT AN OBJECT to point a weapon or object or direct a blow at sb or sth ■ n. **1.** INTENTION a plan to do or achieve sth **2.** ACT OF AIMING an act or manner of aiming ○ *Take aim and fire.* **3.** SKILL IN AIMING skill at hitting a target ○ *Her aim was perfect.* **4.** DEGREE OF ACCURACY the level of accuracy of a weapon ○ *This pistol's aim is off.* **5.** TARGET sth at which a weapon or other object is aimed (*archaic*) [14thC. From Old French *esmer* 'to estimate' and *aesmer* 'to aim at', both ultimately from Latin *aestimare* (see ESTIMATE).]

aimless /áymləss/ adj. without purpose or direction —**aimlessly** adv. —**aimlessness** n.

aina /áá eenə/ n. Hawaii land or country [20thC. From Hawaiian *'āina.*]

ain't /aynt/ contr. a contraction of 'am not', 'is not', 'are not', 'have not', or 'has not' (*nonstandard*)

— WORD KEY: USAGE —
When can you say **ain't**? *Ain't* is one of the most informal verb contractions in English, and it is widely disliked because it is associated with uneducated speech of a kind that many people disfavour. It is slightly more acceptable as a contraction of *am not*, and in the form **ain't I?** is more common as a question in informal American English (*Ain't I right?*), whereas British English uses the form **aren't I?** or (more formally) **Am I not?** Otherwise *ain't* is best avoided, except in allusive phrases such as *You ain't seen nothing yet.*

Ainu /ī noo/ (*plural* **-nu** *or* **-nus**) n. **1.** MEMBER OF JAPANESE PEOPLE a member of a Japanese people who now live in the north of the Japanese island of Hokkaido, and on the Kuril Islands and the island of Sakhalin **2.** LANGUAGE OF NORTHERN JAPAN a language spoken in Hokkaido. It has proved impossible as yet to show a relationship between Ainu and any other language. [Early 19thC. From Ainu, 'person'.] —**Ainu** adj.

aioli /ī óli/ n. mayonnaise flavoured with garlic, used especially to garnish fish and vegetables [Early 20thC. Via French, from Provençal, formed from *ai* 'garlic' and *oli* 'oil'.]

air /air/ n. **1.** GASES FORMING ATMOSPHERE the mixture of gases, mainly nitrogen and oxygen, that forms the Earth's atmosphere **2.** ATMOSPHERE IN OPEN SPACE the atmosphere of an open space as opposed to that of an enclosed space ○ *in the open air* **3.** ATMOSPHERE WE BREATHE the particular atmosphere in a place or enclosed space ○ *fresh air* **4.** SKY the sky or the empty space above the earth ○ *it flew through the air and landed at our feet* **5.** TRAVEL IN AIRCRAFT travel in or transportation by aircraft (*often used before a noun*) ○ *sending the package by air* ○ *an air terminal* **6.** AURA an aura or particular quality ○ *an air of sadness about him* **7.** SB'S DISTINCTIVE QUALITY a distinctive quality in sb's appearance or manner ○ *her air of superiority* **8.** MUSIC MELODY a melody or tune, especially a light or cheerful one **9.** LIGHT WIND a very light wind ■ adj. OF ZODIAC SIGNS relating to the Aquarius, Gemini, or Libra signs of the zodiac ■ v. (**airs, airing, aired**) **1.** vti. BROADCAST OR BE BROADCAST to be broadcast or broadcast sth on radio or television ○ *aired in the spring* **2.** vt. MAKE KNOWN to express sth such as an opinion or complaint ○ *air your views* **3.** vti. EXPOSE TO AIR to be exposed to the air, or expose sth to the air in order to dry it, remove damp from it, cool it, or ventilate it [13thC. Partly via Old French and Latin, from Greek *aēr* 'atmosphere' (see AERO-), and partly via French, 'nature, place of origin', from Latin *ager* 'field' and *area* 'open space'.] ◇ **airs and graces** affected or pretentious behaviour ◇ **clear the air** to remove the tension, uncertainty, or misunderstanding from a situation ◇ **in the air** happening or about to happen ○ *The rumour is that a merger is in the air.* ◇ **off (the) air** not being broadcast on radio or television, e.g. because a person or programme has stopped or finished broadcasting ◇ **on (the) air** being broadcast on radio or television ◇ **take the air** to go for a walk (*formal*) ◇ **up in the air** undecided or uncertain ◇ **vanish into thin air** to disappear completely ◇ **walk** *or* **tread on air** to be extremely happy

AIR abbr. All India Radio

air bag n. **1.** SAFETY DEVICE a safety device in a car consisting of a bag that automatically inflates on impact to protect the occupant of the seat **2.** INFLATABLE RESCUE BAG a strong inflatable bag used to bring sunken items to the surface or by rescue workers to lift heavy machinery or debris under which sb is trapped

air base n. a place from which military aircraft operate

air bladder n. **1.** FISH'S BUOYANCY ORGAN an air-filled sac above the alimentary canal in most fishes that regulates buoyancy and, in some, aids in respiration **2.** AIR-FILLED SAC IN SEAWEED an air-filled sac that aids buoyancy in certain types of seaweed

airboat /áir bōt/ n. = **swamp boat** [So called because it is driven with a propellor and steered with a rudder like an aeroplane's]

airborne /áir bawrn/ adj. **1.** CARRIED BY AIR carried along by movements of air **2.** BY AIRCRAFT carried out or transported by aircraft **3.** IN FLIGHT in flight or in the air

air brake n. **1.** AIR-OPERATED BRAKE a brake operated by compressed air, especially in a heavy motor vehicle **2.** AIRCRAFT BRAKE a flap or small parachute on an aircraft operated to increase drag and thus slow the aircraft

airbrick /áir brik/ n. a brick with holes through it, incorporated in structures to increase ventilation

air bridge n. an air transport link between two places, especially where travel by land is not possible

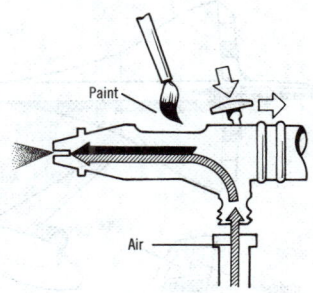

Airbrush

airbrush /áir brush/ n. PAINT SPRAYING DEVICE a device for spraying paint using compressed air ■ vt. (**-brushes, -brushing, -brushed**) PAINT WITH AIRBRUSH to paint on or alter or improve a picture using an airbrush ○ *The blemish had been airbrushed out.*

airburst /áir burst/ n. an explosion of a bomb, shell, or missile in the air

air chamber n. **1.** SPACE ENCLOSING AIR an enclosed space with air in it **2.** CHAMBER IN HYDRAULIC SYSTEM a chamber in a hydraulic system in which air expands and compresses to control the flow of a fluid

air chief marshal n. a senior officer in the British Royal Air Force and some other air forces, equivalent in rank to an admiral or general

air commodore n. a senior officer in the British Royal Air Force and some other air forces, equivalent in rank to a brigadier in the Army

air-condition (**air-conditions, air-conditioning, air-conditioned**) vt. to cool and control the humidity and purity of the air circulating in a building with an air conditioner —**air conditioned** adj.

air conditioner n. a device for cooling and controlling the humidity and purity of the air circulating in a building

air conditioning n. a system for cooling and con-

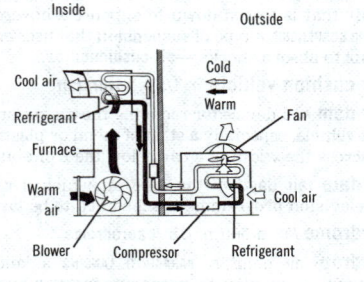

Air conditioning

trolling the humidity and purity of the air circulating in a building

air-cool (air-cools, air-cooling, air-cooled) vt. to cool sth, especially an engine, by a flow of air rather than a water system —**air-cooled** adj.

air corridor n. a specified route that aircraft should take through airspace in which flying is restricted

air cover n. the provision of an airborne defence for ground forces against an enemy air attack, or the aircraft providing the defence

aircraft /áir kraaft/ (plural -**craft**) n. any vehicle capable of flight

aircraft carrier n. a warship with a long flat deck designed to allow aircraft to take off and land on it

aircraftman /áir kraaftmən/ (plural -**men** /-mən/) n. a serviceman of the most junior rank in the British Royal Air Force

aircraftwoman /áir kraaft wo͞omən/ (plural -**en** /-wimin/) n. a servicewoman of the most junior rank in the British Royal Air Force

aircrew /áir kroo/ n. the pilot, navigator, and other crew members of an aircraft

land troops or supplies by parachute from an aircraft

air-dry v. (air-dries, air-drying, air-dried) DRY BY AIR to dry sth by exposing it to air ■ adj. TOTALLY DRY dry to the point where continued exposure to air will remove no further moisture

Airedale /áir dayl/, **Airedale terrier** n. a large terrier

Airedale

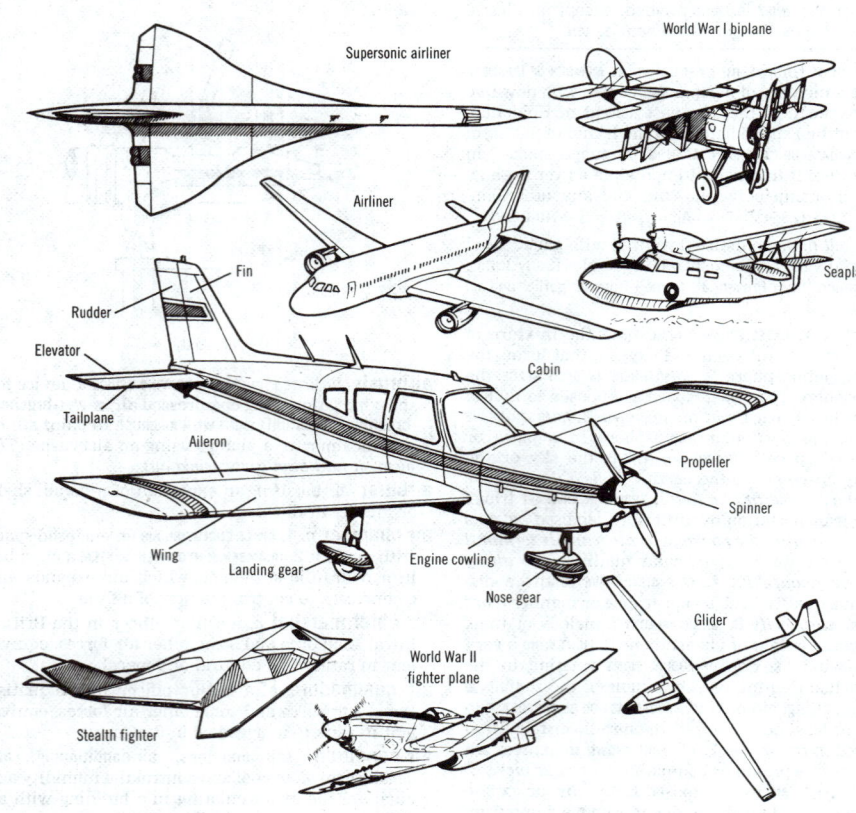

Supersonic airliner

World War I biplane

Airliner

Fin

Rudder

Elevator

Tailplane

Aileron

Cabin

Wing

Landing gear

Engine cowling

Nose gear

Propeller

Spinner

Seaplane

Glider

Stealth fighter

World War II fighter plane

Aircraft

air curtain n. a stream of air directed across a doorway, especially to prevent draughts

air cushion n. 1. AIR BENEATH HOVERCRAFT the pocket of air that is forced down to support a hovercraft 2. AIR SUSPENSION a type of suspension that uses enclosed air to absorb shocks —**air-cushioned** adj.

air cushion vehicle n. US = hovercraft

air dam n. a device for reducing the air resistance of a vehicle, especially a strip of metal or plastic fitted across the width of a car below the front bumper

airdate /áir dayt/ n. the date on which a radio or television programme is scheduled to be broadcast

airdrome /áir drōm/ n. US = aerodrome

airdrop /áir drop/ n. PARACHUTE LANDING a landing of troops or supplies by parachute from an aircraft ■ vt. (-drops, -dropping, -dropped) LAND BY PARACHUTE to

belonging to a breed with rough tan-coloured hair and a black patch on the back [Late 19thC. Named after the district of Airedale in West Yorkshire.]

air embolism n. the presence of air in a blood vessel resulting from injury, from moving too rapidly from high to lower atmospheric pressure, or from using a heart-lung machine during cardiopulmonary bypass

airfare /áir fair/ n. the price of a journey in an aircraft

airfield /áir feeld/ n. an area where aircraft can take off and land

airflow /áir flō/ n. a flow of air, especially around a moving vehicle

airfoil /áir foyl/ n. US = aerofoil

air force n. a military organization that uses aircraft in war, especially a branch of a nation's armed forces

Air Force One n. the official aeroplane of the President of the United States

airframe /áir fraym/ n. the whole body of an aircraft, apart from its engines [Mid-20thC. Coined from AIRCRAFT + FRAME.]

air gas n. = producer gas

airglow /áir glō/ n. a faint light observed in the night sky from low latitudes, caused by photochemical reactions generated by solar radiation in the upper atmosphere

air guitar n. an imaginary guitar held by sb pretending to play a real instrument, especially when miming to rock music (informal)

air gun n. a pistol or rifle that fires a projectile by releasing compressed air

airhead[1] /áir hed/ n. an unintelligent and superficial person (slang insult)

airhead[2] /áir hed/ n. an area in enemy territory captured and held by airborne forces and used when flying troops and supplies in or out of the territory [Mid-20thC. Formed from AIR, on the model of BEACHHEAD.]

air hole n. 1. VENTILATION HOLE a hole to allow the passage of air 2. HOLE IN ICE an unfrozen area in the surface of a frozen body of water, especially one where aquatic mammals surface to breathe 3. = **air pocket** n. 1

air hostess n. a female member of the cabin crew on a large passenger aeroplane (dated)

airily /áirili/ adv. 1. LIGHT-HEARTEDLY in a carefree or light-hearted way as if sth was unimportant 2. LIGHTLY in a delicate or light way

airiness /áirinəss/ n. 1. CASUALNESS carefree or light-hearted casualness 2. SPACIOUSNESS the quality of being spacious or having plenty of fresh air

airing /áiring/ n. 1. DRYING exposure to air or heat, especially for drying, removal of dampness, or ventilation 2. OUTING an outing in the open air 3. MAKING STH KNOWN the exposure to public attention of sb's opinions or ideas

airing cupboard n. a warm or heated cupboard where laundry can be aired or kept dry

air jacket n. 1. INSULATION an air-filled casing around a machine to insulate it against heat loss or gain 2. = **life jacket**

air-kiss (air-kisses, air-kissing, air-kissed) vt. greet sb by making a kissing gesture near to, but not actually making contact with, his or her cheek (informal) ○ The guests were welcomed in a flurry of air-kissing and delighted squeals. —**air-kiss** n.

air lane n. US a regular route used in air travel

air layering n. a plant propagation method in which a growing branch is cut or stripped of bark and the area wrapped in moist compost to encourage root formation

airless /áirləss/ adj. 1. WITH STALE AIR with stale rather than fresh air 2. WITHOUT AIR completely lacking any air 3. STILL without wind or movement of air

airlift /áir lift/ n. AIR TRANSPORT the transport of people or things by air, especially when alternative means cannot be used ■ vt. (-lifts, -lifting, -lifted) TRANSPORT BY AIR to transport people or things by air, especially when alternative means cannot be used

airline /áir līn/ n. 1. SYSTEM OF FLYING a system of commercial scheduled flights transporting people and goods, or a company that operates such a system 2. SOURCE OF AIR a tube through which air is passed under pressure

airliner /áir līnər/ n. a large passenger-carrying aircraft

airlock /áir lok/ n. 1. OBSTRUCTION IN FLOW OF LIQUID an obstruction to the flow of a liquid in a pipe, caused by a bubble of air 2. AIRTIGHT CHAMBER an airtight chamber between two areas of differing air pressure in which air pressure can be altered to match that of either area

airmail /áir mayl/ n. 1. SENDING OF MAIL BY AIR the system of transporting letters and parcels in aircraft 2. MAIL SENT BY AIR mail transported in aircraft ■ adj. SENT BY AIR sent by airmail ■ vt. (-mails, -mailing, -mailed)

SEND BY AIR to send sth, e.g. a letter or parcel, by airmail

airman /áirmən/ (*plural* **-men** /-mən/) *n.* **1. PILOT** a pilot, especially of a military aircraft **2. MEMBER OF AN AIR FORCE** an enlisted person in the United States Air Force, or the rank itself

air marshal *n.* a senior officer in the British Royal Air Force, equivalent in rank to a vice-admiral in the Royal Navy

air mass *n.* a large body of air with temperature, pressure, and moisture uniform throughout its mass but changed by the environment through which it passes

air mile *n.* = **nautical mile**

Air Miles *tdmk.* a trademark for points worth miles of free or discounted air travel issued by retailers and other businesses

air officer *n.* a senior officer in the British Royal Air Force with any rank above group captain

Air plant

air popper *n.* a container for cooking popcorn that uses heated air

airport /áir pawrt/ *n.* an area where civil aircraft may take off and land, especially one equipped with

CODES OF SELECTED INTERNATIONAL AIRPORTS

Code	City	Country	Airport
AKL	Auckland	New Zealand	*Auckland Intl.*
AMS	Amsterdam	Netherlands	*Schipol*
ATL	Atlanta	United States	*William B. Hartsfield Intl.*
BFS	Belfast	Northern Ireland	*Belfast Intl.*
BHX	Birmingham	England	*Birmingham*
BNE	Brisbane	Australia	*Brisbane Intl.*
CBR	Canberra	Australia	*Canberra*
CCU	Calcutta	India	*Dum Dum Intl.*
CDG	Paris	France	*Charles De Gaulle*
CGX	Chicago	United States	*O'Hare*
CHC	Christchurch	New Zealand	*Christchurch Intl.*
CMB	Colombo	Sri Lanka	*Katunayake*
CPT	Cape Town	South Africa	*Cape Town*
DAC	Dhaka	Bangladesh	*Zia Intl.*
DEL	Delhi	India	*Indira Ghandi Intl.*
DFW	Dallas/Fort Worth	United States	*Dallas/Fort Worth Intl.*
DUB	Dublin	Ireland	*Dublin*
DVX	Denver	United States	*Denver Intl.*
EWR	Newark	United States	*Newark Intl*
GLA	Glasgow	Scotland	*Glasgow*
HKG	Hong Kong	Hong Kong	*Kai-Tal Intl.*
JFK	New York	United States	*John F. Kennedy*
NB	Johannesburg	South Africa	*Johannesburg*
KHI	Karachi	Pakistan	*Quaid-E-Azam Intl*
KIN	Kingston	Jamaica	*Norman Manley*
KTP	Kingston	Jamaica	*Tinson*
LAX	Los Angeles	United States	*Los Angeles Intl.*
LGA	New York	United States	*La Guardia*
LGW	London	England	*Gatwick*
LHR	London	England	*Heathrow*
MAN	Manchester	England	*Manchester*
MEL	Melbourne	Australia	*Melbourne*
MIA	Miami	United States	*Miami*
PER	Perth	Australia	*Perth*
SEA	Seattle	United States	*Seattle-Tacoma Intl.*
SIN	Singapore	Singapore	*Singapore*
SYD	Sydney	Australia	*Kingsford Smith*
WAS	Washington	United States	*Dulles*
WLG	Wellington	New Zealand	*Wellington Intl.*
YMX	Montreal	Canada	*Mirabel Intl.*
YOW	Ottawa	Canada	*MacDonald-Cartier Intl.*
YUL	Montreal	Canada	*Dorval Intl.*
YVR	Vancouver	Canada	*Vancouver Intl.*
YYZ	Toronto	Canada	*Lester B. Pearson Intl.*

Airport

airpack /áir pak/ *n.* a device consisting of a portable supply of oxygen connected to a face mask that allows sb to enter an area where the air is unsafe to breathe

air piracy *n.* the hijacking of an aircraft in flight

air pistol *n.* a pistol that fires a projectile by releasing compressed air or another gas

airplane /áir playn/ *n.* US = **aeroplane**

air plant *n.* a plant that obtains nutrients and moisture from the air and rain, especially one grown as a houseplant for the novelty value of its requiring no soil or compost. ◊ **epiphyte**

airplay /áir play/ *n.* the playing on radio of a piece of recorded music

air pocket *n.* **1. DOWNWARD AIR CURRENT** a small area of lower air density or a downward air current that makes an aircraft abruptly lose height **2. AIR BUBBLE IN FLUID** an air bubble that impedes the flow of liquid or gas, e.g. in a pipe

surfaced runways and facilities for handling passengers and cargo

airpower /áir powər/ *n.* military capability in terms of combat power delivered from the air

air pressure *n.* = **atmospheric pressure**

air pump *n.* a device for compressing air or forcing it into or out of sth

air quality index (*plural* **air quality indexes** *or* **air quality indices**) *n.* a numerical scale that indicates how polluted the air is

air rage *n.* disruptive or aggressive behaviour by passengers aboard an aircraft that is liable to endanger the aircraft's safety

air raid *n.* an attack by aircraft on sth on the ground, especially a non-military target (*hyphenated when used before a noun*)

air rifle *n.* a rifle that fires a projectile by releasing compressed air or another gas

air sac *n.* **1.** = **alveolus**. **1 2. AIR-FILLED CAVITY IN BIRD** an air-filled cavity in a bird, formed as an extension of the respiratory system and growing into the bones, that aids respiration and decreases bone mass **3. RESPIRATION AID IN INSECT** a thin-walled bulge (**diverticulum**) that aids respiration, located in the tubes that transport air through the bodies of some insects

Air Scout *n.* a member of the Scout movement who belongs to a troop that goes flying or gliding

airscrew /áir skroo/ *n.* a propeller on an aircraft

air-sea rescue *n.* a rescue at sea in which aircraft are used

airship /áir ship/ *n.* an aircraft that is lighter than air, powered, and navigable

Barnaby's

Airship

airshow /áir shō/ *n.* a public exhibition at an airfield of aircraft in flight and on the ground

airsickness /áir siknəss/ *n.* motion sickness caused by air travel —**airsick** *adj.*

airside /áir sīd/ *n.* the area of an airport where the aircraft take off and land, load, or unload

air sock *n.* = **windsock**

airspace /áir spayss/ *n.* **1. SPACE ABOVE TERRITORY** the part of the atmosphere directly over an area of land or water, especially a part over which a state claims jurisdiction **2. FLYING SPACE** the space in the air that a flying aircraft occupies or needs to manoeuvre

air speed *n.* the speed of an aircraft in relation to the air through which it moves

air spray *n.* = **aerosol** n. 1, **aerosol** n. 2

air spring *n.* = **air cushion** n. 1

air station *n.* a small airfield with facilities for maintenance of aircraft

airstream /áir streem/ *n.* **1. WIND** a wind, especially one blowing at a high altitude **2.** = **airflow**

air strike *n.* an attack by aircraft on sth on the ground, especially an enemy position or formation [Late 20thC] —**airstrike** *vt.*

airstrip /áir strip/ *n.* a place for aircraft to take off and land that has no facilities and is often temporary

air stripping *n.* a technique for removing pollutants from water by breaking the water into minute particles

airt /áirt/ *n. Scotland* a direction or quarter, especially one of the cardinal compass points [15thC. Via Scottish Gaelic *aird* from Old Irish, 'point of the compass', of unknown origin.]

air taxi *n.* a small commercial aircraft used for brief flights between places that do not have regularly scheduled flights

air terminal *n.* a building in a city from which passengers are taken to an airport, or to which they are brought from an airport, by train or bus

air terrorism *n.* the use of actions such as skyjacking, aircraft bombing, and other terrorist acts in an attempt to achieve a political objective or get international publicity

airtight /áir tīt/ *adj.* **1. IMPERMEABLE BY AIR** not allowing air in or out **2. FLAWLESS** without flaws or vulnerable points

airtime /áir tīm/ *n.* **1. TIME ON AIR** the amount of time given to a programme or subject in radio or television broadcasting **2. TIME OF BROADCAST** the time at which an item is scheduled to be broadcast

air-to-air adj. moving or passing from one aircraft to another while in flight

air-to-surface adj. moving or passing from a flying aircraft to a point on the ground

air traffic n. the movement of aircraft in a particular area

air-traffic control n. the system or organization responsible for directing the movement of aircraft over a particular area, operated by ground staff in radio contact with pilots —**air traffic controller** n.

air vesicle n. an air-filled cavity between cells that assists buoyancy in certain aquatic plants, e.g. seaweed

air vice-marshal n. a senior officer in the British Royal Air Force, equivalent in rank to a rear admiral of the Royal Navy

airwaves /áir wayvz/ npl. radio waves as used in broadcasting

airway /áir way/ n. **1. AIR ROUTE** an air route, especially one used by regular commercial flights (often used in the plural) **2. Airways AIR TRANSPORT COMPANY** a company that operates a system of commercial flights (used in company names) **3. BREATHING PASSAGE** a passage for air from the nose or mouth to the lungs **4. TUBE TO KEEP AIRWAY OPEN** a device for keeping an unconscious person's airway open, incorporating a tube inserted into the throat **5. VENTILATION PASSAGE** a passage for ventilation in a mine or tunnel

airworthy /áir wùrthi/ adj. in good enough condition to be safe to fly [Early 19thC. Modelled on SEAWORTHY.] —**airworthiness** n.

airy /áiri/ (**-ier**, **-iest**) adj. **1. ROOMY** having plenty of space **2. VENTILATED** having plenty of fresh air **3. CAREFREE** carefree or lighthearted and unconcerned **4. ETHEREAL** ethereal or insubstantial **5. OF AIR** connected with, like, or taking place in the air **6. GRACEFUL** light and graceful in movement **7. HIGH IN THE AIR** at a great height in the sky

airy-fairy adj. fanciful or not grounded in reality (informal) [Mid-19thC. Perhaps originally in 'airy, fairy Lilian', in the poem Lilian by Alfred Tennyson.]

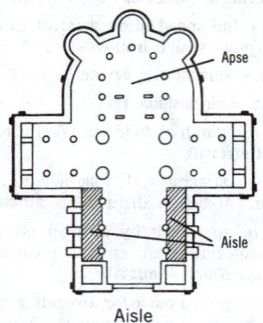

Aisle

aisle /íl/ n. **1. PASSAGEWAY BETWEEN SEATS** a passageway between areas of seating, especially in a church, theatre, or passenger vehicle **2. PASSAGEWAY BETWEEN GOODS** a passageway between stacks or displays of goods, especially in a supermarket or warehouse **3. DIVISION IN CHURCH** an area of a church separated from the nave or central area by pillars, especially one forming a passage between seats [14thC. Alteration of Old French ele 'wing', from Latin ala, under the influence of ISLE and, later, French aile 'wing'.] ◇ **rolling in the aisles** laughing very heartily

ait /ayt/ n. a small island, especially in a river (regional) [Old English īgep, literally 'small island', formed from īeg (see ISLAND)]

aitch /aych/ n. the letter 'h', or its sound [Mid-16thC. From French hache, via late Latin ach from Latin ah, an alteration of ha.]

—————— **WORD KEY: REGIONAL NOTE** ——————
Pronunciations involving h have been a source of problems for almost a thousand years. In parts of the English-speaking world, h is pronounced haitch, not aitch, and such a difference is often enough to distinguish Ulster Catholics from Protestants. In most other parts haitch

is thought to be an uneducated pronunciation. Dialect speakers have often been described as aitch-droppers, and so they 'appily 'and their 'ats to 'arry. The illogicality of some prejudices becomes clear when we realize that it is prestigious to drop the h in heir, honest, and hour.

Aix-en-Provence /ayks oN pro vóNss/ city in the Bouches-du-Rhône Department in the Provence-Alpes-Côte d'Azur Region of southeastern France. It was the first Roman settlement in Gaul. Population: 123,842 (1990).

AJA abbr. Australian Journalists' Association

Ajaccio /ə jáksi ṓ/ main port and capital of Corsica. Population: 59,318 (1990).

ajar /ə jaár/ adj., adv. neither shut nor wide open ◇ left the door ajar [Late 17thC. Formed from an obsolete word meaning 'turn', from Old English cierr. The underlying meaning is 'turning on its hinges'.]

Ajax /áy jaks/ n. in Greek mythology, a powerful warrior who fought in the Trojan War as leader of the Salaminian forces

AJK abbr. Australian Jockey Club

AK abbr. Alaska

a.k.a., **AKA** abbr. also known as

Akan /aá kaan/ (plural **Akan** or **Akans**) n. **1. PEOPLES MEMBER OF AFRICAN PEOPLE** a member of a people who live in southern Ghana, the southeastern Ivory Coast, and parts of Togo **2. LANGUAGE OF WESTERN AFRICA** a language spoken in Ghana and Ivory Coast, belonging to the Kwa group of Niger-Congo languages. Akan is spoken by about eight million people. [Late 17thC. From Twi akaŋ.] —**Akan** adj.

akaryote /áy kárri ṓt/ n. a cell that has no nucleus —**akaryotic** /ay kárri óttik/ adj.

Akee

akee /áki/ (plural **-ees** or **-ee**), **ackee** (plural **-kees** or **-kee**) n. **1. AFRICAN TREE** an evergreen tree of the soapberry family that is native to tropical western Africa and cultivated in the Caribbean and Florida for its fruit. Latin name: Blighia sapida. **2. FRUIT** the red pear-shaped fruit of the akee tree, edible when ripe but poisonous at other times and with poisonous seeds [Late 18thC. Origin uncertain: possibly from Kru.]

Akela /aa káylə/ n. the adult leader of a Cub Scout pack [Early 20thC. From Akela, the name of a wolf in Kipling's Jungle Book.]

akene n. = achene

Akhmatova /ákmə tṓvə/, **Anna** (1889–1966) Russian

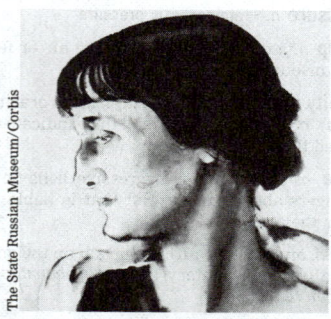

Anna Akhmatova: Detail of portrait (1928) by Nikolai Tyrsa

poet. She was a leading figure in an early 20th-century movement that advocated precision and brevity in poetic language. Pseudonym **Anna Andreyevna Gorenko**

Akihito /áki heé tṓ/, **Emperor of Japan** (b. 1933). He succeeded his father, Hirohito, in 1989.

Akimbo

akimbo /ə kímbṓ/ adj., adv. with the hands on the hips and the elbows turned outwards [14thC. Origin uncertain.]

akin /ə kín/ adj. **1. SIMILAR** similar or closely related to sth **2. RELATED** related by blood **3. WITH COMMON ORIGIN** used to describe languages that share a common origin or ancient forms

akinesia /áy ki neéssi ə, -kī-, á-/ n. the loss or reduction of the normal power of movement [Mid-19thC. From Greek 'lack of movement', from, ultimately, kinein 'to move' (see KINETIC).] —**akinetic** /áy ki néttik/ adj.

Akira Yoshimura /a keérə yóshi moórə/ (b. 1927) Japanese writer whose prize-winning novels and non-fiction works include Journey to the Stars (1966) and Von Siebold's Daughter (1978).

Akkad /á kad/ ancient region situated in central northern Mesopotamia that corresponds approximately to biblical Babylonia. It was most influential during the third millennium BC.

Akkadian /ə káydi ən/ n. **1. PEOPLES SB FROM AKKAD** sb who was born or lived in the ancient city or region of Akkad **2. LANG EXTINCT MIDDLE EASTERN LANGUAGE** the extinct Semitic language of Mesopotamia. It was written in cuneiform. [Mid-19thC. Formed from Akkad, a city in ancient Babylonia.] —**Akkadian** adj.

akrasia /ə kráyzi ə/ n. weakness of will, especially a failure to act according to a sense of moral obligation [From Greek, variant of akrateia, literally 'powerlessness', from kratos 'strength' (see -CRACY)] —**akratic** /ə kráttik/ adj.

Akron /ákrən/ city in northeastern Ohio noted for its rubber products. Population: 221,886 (1994).

Akubra /ə kúbrə/ tdmk. a trademark for a traditional Australian wide-brimmed hat, usually made of rabbit skin, and worn in the bush or country, particularly in outback areas

akvavit n. = aquavit

Al symbol. aluminium

AL abbr. **1.** Alabama **2.** Albania (international vehicle registration)

al. abbr. **1.** alcohol **2.** alcoholic

-al[1] suffix. relating to or characterized by ◇ delusional [Via French from Latin -alis]

-al[2] suffix. action, process ◇ disposal [Via Old French -aille from Latin -alia, neuter plural of -alis]

-al[3] suffix. aldehyde ◇ chloral [From ALDEHYDE]

à la /aá laa, állə/, **a la** prep. in the style of sb or sth [Late 16thC. From French, shortening of à la mode de 'in the fashion of'.]

Ala. abbr. Alabama

Alabama

Alabama /álle bámme/ state of the southeastern United States, bounded by Georgia, the Gulf of Mexico, Mississippi, and Tennessee. Capital: Montgomery. Population: 4,319,154 (1997). Area: 135,293 sq. km/52,237 sq. mi. —**Alabaman** adj., n. —**Alabamian** adj., n.

alabaster /álle baaster, -baster/ n. **1.** TYPE OF GYPSUM a type of gypsum, usually white or translucent, used for sculpture and decorative work **2.** TYPE OF CALCITE a hard semitranslucent type of calcite, which sometimes has bands ■ adj. OF ALABASTER made of alabaster, or white and translucent like alabaster [14thC. Via Old French, from, ultimately, Greek alabastros.]

à la carte /aá laa kaárt, álle-/, **a la carte** adj., adv. with each dish on a menu priced separately [Early 19thC. From French, literally 'by the menu'.]

alack /e lák/ interj. used to express regret (archaic or literary) [15thC. Formed from LACK, on the model of ALAS.]

alacrity /e lákreti/ n. promptness or eager and speedy readiness [Early 16thC. From Latin alacritas, formed from alacer 'lively'.] —**alacritous** adj.

Aladdin's cave /e láddinz-/ n. a suddenly discovered place containing great riches

al-Adha /ál aáde/ n. = **Eid-ul-Adha**

à la grecque /aá laa grék, állle-/, **a la grecque** adj. cooked in a sauce made with olive oil, lemon, usually wine, and herbs and served cold [From French, 'in the Greek style']

Alain-Fournier /állaN fóor nyay/ (1886–1914) French writer and journalist. He wrote one novel, Le Grand Meaulnes (1913), lyrical in style. He was killed in World War I. Pseudonym of **Henri-Alban Fournier**

à la king /aá laa kíng, álle-/, **a la king** /ál aa kíng/ adj. cooked in a cream sauce with peppers and mushrooms

Alamo /állemō/ chapel built at the San Antonio mission in Texas, in the United States, in 1744. It was besieged by Mexican forces in 1836 and all 182 Texan defenders were killed.

à la mode /aá laa mōd, állle-/, **a la mode** adj. in the latest fashion (dated) [Late 17thC. From French, literally 'in the style'.]

alanine /álle neen, -nīn/ n. a crystalline water-soluble amino acid that is a constituent of various proteins and can also be produced by humans and animals. Formula: $C_3H_7NO_2$. [Mid-19thC. From German Alanin, from Aldehyd 'aldehyde'.]

alannah /e lánne/ interj. Ireland used to address a child affectionately [Mid-19thC. From Irish a leanbh 'O child', from Old Irish lenab 'child'.]

alar /áyler/, **alary** /-ri/ adj. used to describe a part of an animal or plant that is shaped like a wing or is associated with such a part [Mid-19thC. From Latin alaris, from ala 'wing'.]

alarm /e laárm/ n. **1.** FEAR fear caused by perception of imminent danger **2.** WARNING DEVICE a device for giving a warning of danger **3.** SECURITY DEVICE a security device fitted to property, especially a house or car, to make a warning sound if a break-in or theft is attempted **4.** SOUND OF SECURITY OR WARNING DEVICE the sound made by a security or warning device **5.** = **alarm clock 6.** CALL TO ARMS a summons to prepare to fight (archaic) **7.** FENCING CHALLENGE MADE BY STAMPING a warning or challenge to a fencer made by stamping the leading foot ■ vt. (**alarms, alarming, alarmed**) **1.** FRIGHTEN to make sb frightened or apprehensive **2.** WARN to give sb warning of danger **3.** FIT WITH WARNING DEVICE to fit a building or vehicle with a security warning device [Early 16thC. Via French, from Italian all' arme 'to arms!'.] —**alarmed** adj.

alarm clock, **alarm** n. a clock that can be set to sound an alarm at a desired time, especially to wake sb

alarming /e laárming/ adj. frightening or disturbing —**alarmingly** adv.

alarmist /e laármist/ n. **1.** SB SPREADING FEAR sb who spreads unnecessary fear or warnings of danger **2.** SB EASILY SCARED sb who becomes afraid easily ■ adj. SPREADING FEAR liable to make people feel unnecessarily fearful or worried —**alarmism** n.

alarm reaction n. the initial response of a person or animal to stress, including an increased heart rate and hormonal activity

alarum /e lárrem, e laárem/ n. an alarm (archaic) [Variant of ALARM]

alas /e láss/ interj. EXPRESSING SORROW used to express sorrow or pity ■ adv. UNFORTUNATELY unfortunately or regrettably [13thC. Via French hélas from, ultimately, Latin lassus 'weary' (see LASSITUDE).]

Alas. abbr. Alaska

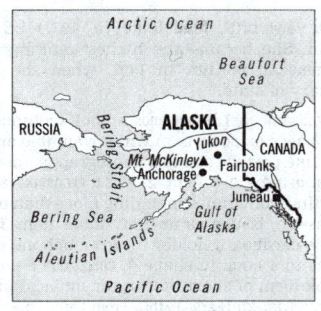
Alaska

Alaska /e láske/ US state of northwestern North America, bordered by Canada and the Pacific and Arctic oceans. Capital: Juneau. Population: 609,311 (1997). Area: 1,593,438 sq. km/615,230 sq. mi. —**Alaskan** adj., n.

Alaska Highway n. a road built in 1942 from Dawson Creek, British Columbia, to Fairbanks, Alaska. Former name **Alcan Highway**

Alaskan malamute n. = **malamute**

Alaska Range mountain range in southern Alaska, extending in a 640 km/400 mi. semicircle north of Anchorage. It includes the highest peak in North America, Mount McKinley 6,194 m/20,320 ft.

alastor /e lá stawr/ n. an avenging deity, frequently evoked in Greek tragedy [Late 16thC. From Greek, literally 'sb who is not forgotten', from lath-, the stem of lanthanesthai 'to forget' (see LANTHANUM).]

alate /áy layt/, **alated** /-laytid/ adj. used to describe insects with wings or seeds with parts resembling wings [Mid-17thC. From Latin alatus, from ala 'wing'.]

alb /alb/ n. a long white robe with long sleeves worn by priests [Pre-12thC. Via ecclesiastical Latin (vestis) alba 'white (garment)' from Latin albus 'white'.]

Alb. abbr. **1.** Albania ■ abbr. **2.** Albanian

Albacore

albacore /álbe kawr/ (plural **-core** or **-cores**) n. a large tuna with a long pectoral fin, found in the warm waters of the Atlantic and Pacific and used as a food fish. Latin name: Thunnus alalunga. [Late 16thC. From Portuguese albacor, of uncertain origin: possibly from Arabic al-bakrah 'young camel' or al-bakūra 'premature'.]

Alban /áwlben/, **St** (fl. 3rd century) Roman-born British martyr. A Roman soldier, he was converted to Christianity by a priest, and beheaded by the Roman authorities on the site of St Albans Abbey.

Albania

Albania /al báyni e/ republic in southeastern Europe, bordering the Adriatic Sea. A former Communist country, it became a parliamentary democracy in 1991. Language: Albanian. Currency: lek. Capital: Tirana. Population: 3,260,000 (1995). Area: 28,748 sq. km/11,100 sq. mi.

Albanian /al báyni en/ n. **1.** LANG LANGUAGE OF ALBANIA the official language of Albania, also spoken in parts of Serbia, Croatia, Macedonia, Italy, and Greece. A distinct branch of the Indo-European languages, Albanian is spoken by about four million people. **2.** PEOPLES SB FROM ALBANIA sb who was born or brought up in Albania, or who is a citizen of Albania ■ adj. OF ALBANIA relating to or typical of Albania, or its culture or people

Albany /áwlbeni/ coastal town in southwestern Western Australia, an important port and tourist destination. Population: 20,493 (1996).

Albatross

albatross /álbe tross/ (plural **-trosses** or **-tross**) n. **1.** LARGE SEABIRD a large long-winged seabird that inhabits cool southern oceans and spends most of its life in flight. Family: Diomedeidae. **2.** OPPRESSIVE BURDEN an oppressive burden or hindrance **3.** GOLF THREE BELOW PAR in golf, a score of three below par for a hole. US term **double eagle** [Late 17thC. Alteration (under the influence of Latin albus 'white') of Portuguese alcatraz, from Arabic al-ġaṭṭās 'the diver'.] ◇ **an albatross round sb's neck** a burden from which sb cannot escape

albedo /al beédō/ (plural **-dos**) n. the fraction of incident light that is reflected by an object, especially the Earth or another planet reflecting the Sun's light [Mid-19thC. Via ecclesiastical Latin, 'whiteness', from Latin albus 'white' (see ALB).]

albeit /awl bee it/ conj. used to add information that is different from what you have already said ○ a difficult, albeit rewarding job [14thC. Formed from ALL + BE + IT, meaning literally 'all though it may be'.]

Alberich /álberich/ n. in medieval German legend, king of the dwarves and guardian of the treasures of the Nibelung

Albers /álbərz, áwl-/, **Josef** (1888–1976) German painter and designer. He taught at the Bauhaus school of design. After 1933 he worked in the United States.

albert /álbərt/ *n.* a short chain used to attach a fob watch to a waistcoat [Mid-19thC. Named after Prince *Albert*, the Consort of Queen Victoria, who wore such a chain.]

Albert /álbərt/, **Prince, Prince Consort** (1819–61) German-born prince consort to Queen Victoria. A supporter of technological innovation and patron of the arts, he organized the Great Exhibition (1851). The proceeds enabled the building of several museums and the Royal Albert Hall (1871).

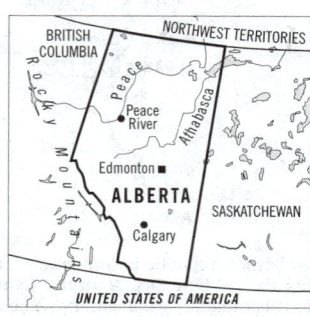
Alberta

Alberta /al búrtə/ Canada's westernmost Prairie Province and a leading producer of oil and natural gas. Capital: Edmonton. Population: 2,696,826 (1996). Area: 661,190 sq. km/255,287 sq. mi.

albertite /álbər tīt/ *n.* a solid black variety of bitumen found in oil-bearing rock strata [Mid-19thC. Named after *Albert* County, New Brunswick, in Canada, where it was originally found.]

Albertus Magnus /al búrtəss mágnəss/, **St** (1200?–80) German churchman and philosopher. He wrote on logic, natural, and moral sciences, and theology. He taught St Thomas Aquinas.

albescent /al béss'nt/ *adj.* becoming white or whitish [Early 18thC. Via the Latin stem *albescent-* from, ultimately, *albus* (see ALB).]

Albigenses /álbi jén seez/ *npl.* a heretical Christian religious group in southern France during the 12th and 13th centuries. They believed that everything in the material world is evil. [Early 17thC. From medieval Latin, formed from *Albiga*, the city of Albi in southern France, where the group originated.] —**Albigensian** *adj.* — **Albigensianism** *n.*

albinism /álbinizzəm/ *n.* congenital lack of normal pigmentation in the skin and hair of a person or animal or in the coloration of a plant —**albinistic** /álbi nístik/ *adj.*

Albino: Dwarf Russian hamsters with albino shown right

albino /al beenō/ *n.* (*plural* **-nos**) *n.* **1. PERSON OR ANIMAL LACKING PIGMENTATION** a person or animal whose skin and hair lack pigmentation and whose irises are pink because of a congenital condition (**albinism**) **2. PLANT LACKING NORMAL COLORATION** a plant that lacks normal coloration because of a congenital condition (**albinism**) [Early 18thC. Via Portuguese, from, ultimately, Latin *albus* 'white' (see ALB).] —**albinic** /al bínnik/ *adj.* — **albinotic** /álbi nóttik/ *adj.*

Albion /álbi ən/ ancient name for England or the island of Britain

albite /ál bīt/ *n.* a usually white form of feldspar consisting of sodium aluminium silicate, used in making glass and ceramics. Formula: $NaAlSi_3O_8$. [Early 19thC. Formed from Latin *albus* 'white' (see ALB).] —**albitic** /al bíttik/ *adj.*

ALBM *abbr.* air-launched ballistic missile

Madeleine Albright

Albright /áwl brīt/, **Madeleine** (*b.* 1937) US stateswoman. She became the highest-ranking woman in American politics in 1997, when she became secretary of state.

album /álbəm/ *n.* **1. BLANK BOOK** a book or binder with blank pages or pockets in which valuable or fragile items such as postage stamps, photographs, mementos, or autographs are kept **2. MUSIC RECORDING** a music recording, sometimes including more than one disk or cassette, issued as an individual item **3. RECORD HOLDER** a cardboard holder for gramophone records, similar to a book in shape **4. COLLECTION** a collection in book form of short literary or musical pieces or pictures (*dated*) [Early 17thC. From Latin, 'blank tablet', from *albus* 'white'.]

--- **WORD KEY: ORIGIN** ---

The Latin word *albus* from which **album** is derived is also the source of English *alb, albino, albumen, auburn,* and *daub.*

albumblatt /álbəm blat/ (*plural* **-blatts** or **-blätter** /-blettər/) *n.* a short light instrumental piece popular in the 19th century, usually bound together in a set with other similar pieces [From German, literally 'page from an album']

albumen /álbyoŏmin, al byoŏmin/ *n.* **1. WHITE OF EGG** the clear water-soluble protein that surrounds the yolk of an egg and provides nutrition for the embryo (*technical*) **2. EGG-WHITE PROTEIN** the protein component of egg white, which includes albumin [Late 16thC. From Latin, formed from *albus* 'white' (see ALB).]

albumin /álbyoŏmin, al byoŏmin/ *n.* a water-soluble protein coagulated by heat. Albumins are found in many animal and plant tissues, especially egg white, blood plasma, and milk.

albuminoid /al byoŏmi noyd/ *adj.* **LIKE ALBUMIN** resembling or having the characteristics of albumin ■ *n.* = scleroprotein —**albuminoidal** /al byoŏmi nóyd'l/ *adj.*

albuminous /al byoŏminəss/ *adj.* connected with, like, or containing albumin

albuminuria /al byoŏmi nyoŏri ə, ál byoŏmi-/ *n.* the presence of albumin in urine, usually an indication of kidney disease

Albuquerque /álbəbərki/ city and tourist resort on the Rio Grande and the largest city in New Mexico, United States. Population: 419,681 (1996).

Albury-Wodonga /áalbəri wo dóng gə/ urban area in southeastern Australia consisting of two towns: Albury and Wodonga. Population: 67,316 (1996).

Alcaic /al káy ik/ *adj.* **CONTAINING FOUR FOUR-FOOT LINES** in poetry, written in the metrical form of a stanza of four lines, each containing four feet ■ *n.* **POETRY TYPE** a poem or lines written in the Alcaic form (*often used in the plural*) [Mid-17thC. Via late Latin from, ultimately, Greek *Alkaios*, the lyric poet credited with inventing the form.]

alcaide /al kayd, -kídi/, **alcayde** *n.* **1. FORTRESS COMMANDER** a commander of a fortress in a Spanish-speaking area **2. PRISON GOVERNOR** a governor of a prison in a Spanish-speaking area [Early 16thC. Via Spanish, from Arabic *al-kā-'id* 'the commander'.]

alcalde /al káldi, -kaáldi/ *n.* the mayor or chief magistrate of a town in a Spanish-speaking area [Mid-16thC. Via Spanish, from Arabic *al-kāḍī* 'the judge'.]

Alcan Highway /ál kan/ *n.* former name for **Alaska Highway** [From *Alcan*, a contraction of *Alaska-Canada*]

Alcatraz /álkə traz/ island in San Francisco Bay, California, site of a federal prison from 1933 to 1963. It has been part of Golden Gate National Recreation Area since 1972.

alcayde *n.* = alcaide

alcazar /álkə zaár/ *n.* fortress or palace in Spain, especially one built by the Moors [Early 17thC. Via Spanish, from Arabic *al-kaṣr* 'the castle', ultimately from Latin *castrum* 'camp' (source also of English *castle*).]

Alcestis /al séstiss/ *n.* in Greek mythology, daughter of Pelias and wife of Admetus, King of Phaerae. She died to save her husband's life but was later rescued from Hades by Hercules.

alchemise *vt.* = alchemize

alchemist /álkəmist/ *n.* sb who practises alchemy — **alchemistic** /álkə místik/ *adj.*

--- **WORD KEY: CULTURAL NOTE** ---

The Alchemist, a play by Ben Jonson (1610). An energetic satire set in London, it tells the story of a servant, Face, and his friends Subtle and Doll Common. They pose as alchemists, convincing a series of gullible characters that they can help them attain wealth and happiness.

alchemize /álkə mīz/ (**-mizes, -mizing, -mized**), **alchemise** (**-mises, -mising, -mised**) *vt.* to transform sth into gold or into a much purer or brighter form by alchemy

alchemy /álkəmi/ *n.* **1. PREDECESSOR OF CHEMISTRY** an earlier and unscientific form of chemistry, seeking to transform base metals into gold and to discover a life-prolonging elixir, a universal cure for disease, and a universal solvent (**alkahest**) **2. TRANSFORMING OR ENCHANTING POWER** a power supposedly like alchemy, especially of enchantment or transformation [14thC. Via Old French *alquemie* and medieval Latin *alchimia* from Arabic *al-kīmiyā* 'the chemistry', ultimately from Greek *khēmeia*.] —**alchemic** /al kémmik/ *adj.* —**alchemical** *adj.*

ALCM *abbr.* air-launched cruise missile

Alcmene /alk meeni/ *n.* in Greek mythology, wife of Amphitryon. While her husband was away at war, Zeus visited Alcmene disguised as Amphitryon. She later gave birth to two sons, Hercules and Iphicles.

Alcock /áwl kok/, **Sir John William** (1892–1919) British aviator. With Arthur Brown, he made the first transatlantic flight, from Newfoundland to Ireland, which took 16 hours 27 minutes.

alcohol /álkə hol/ *n.* **1. LIQUID FOR DRINKS AND SOLVENTS** a colourless liquid, produced by the fermentation of sugar or starch, that is the intoxicating agent in fermented drinks and is used as a solvent. Formula: C_2H_5OH. **2. DRINKS WITH ALCOHOL** intoxicating drinks containing alcohol **3. ORGANIC COMPOUND** any organic compound containing one or more hydroxyl groups bound to carbon atoms [Mid-16thC. Via medieval Latin, 'fine powder, distilled essence of a substance', from Arabic *al-kuḥl* 'the antimony powder' (source of English *kohl*).]

alcoholic /álkə hóllik/ *adj.* **1. CONTAINING ALCOHOL** connected with or containing alcohol **2. CAUSED BY ALCOHOL** caused by alcohol consumption ○ *alcoholic dehydration* **3. ADDICTED TO ALCOHOL** addicted to drinking beverages containing alcohol ■ *n.* **ALCOHOL ADDICT** sb who is addicted to drinking alcohol

alcoholicity /álkə ho líssəti/ *n.* the amount of alcohol contained in sth

Alcoholics Anonymous *n.* an organization for alcoholics offering mutual support to members to help in overcoming their dependency

alcoholism /álkə holizzəm/ *n.* **1. ADDICTION TO ALCOHOL** dependence on alcohol to an extent that adversely affects behaviour and social or work function and produces withdrawal symptoms when intake is stopped or reduced **2. ALCOHOL POISONING** a physical disorder caused by the toxic effects of excessive alcohol consumption

alcopop /álkŏ pop/ *n.* a drink made up of a soft drink, e.g. lemonade, mixed with alcohol [Late 20thC. Coined from ALCOHOL + POP.]

Alcoran /álko raán/ *n.* = **Koran** —**Alcoranic** /álko ránnik/ *adj.*

Louisa May Alcott

Alcott /áwlkət/, **Louisa May** (1832–88) US novelist. Her novels include her most famous book, *Little Women* (1868), and its sequels.

alcove /álkŏv/ *n.* **1. INTERNAL RECESS** a recess in the wall of a room **2. EXTERNAL RECESS** a recess in an exterior wall, usually with a roof or some covering structure **3. SECLUDED PLACE** a shady or secluded place in a garden [Late 16thC. Via French *alcôve* and Spanish *alcoba* from Arabic *al-ḳubba* 'the vault, the arch'.]

Ald. *abbr.* alderman

Aldabra /al dábbrə/ group of four islands in the Seychelles in the Indian Ocean. Area: 154 sq. km/59 sq. mi.

Aldebaran /al débbərən/ *n.* the brightest star in the constellation Taurus and one of the brightest stars in the sky

Aldeburgh /áwldbərə/ seaside town in Suffolk, England. An annual music festival is held there. Population: 2,654 (1991).

aldehyde /áldi hīd/ *n.* a highly reactive organic compound produced by the oxidation of an alcohol and having a CHO group, especially acetaldehyde [Mid-19thC. Contraction of modern Latin *alcohol dehydrogenatum* 'dehydrogenated alcohol'.] —**aldehydic** /áldi híddik/ *adj.*

al dente /al dén tay, -dénti/ *adj.* cooked just long enough to be firm rather than soft [From Italian, literally 'to the tooth']

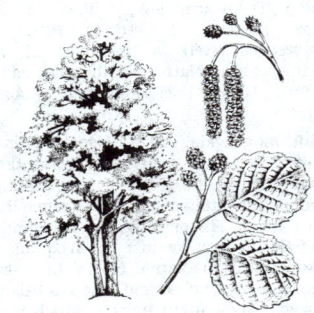

Alder

alder /áwldər/ *n.* **1. DECIDUOUS TREE** a deciduous tree or shrub with male catkins and cone-shaped fruits, common in wet places in northern temperate areas. Genus: *Alnus*. **2. WOOD OF THE ALDER** the wood of the alder tree, valuable for use in underwater structures as it resists rot when wet [Old English *alor*. Ultimately from an Indo-European base meaning 'reddish-brown', which is also the ancestor of English *elm* and *elk*.]

alderman /áwldər mən/ (*plural* **-men** /-mən/) *n.* **1. SENIOR COUNCIL MEMBER** a senior member of an English or Welsh local council before the local government reorganization of 1974 **2. MEMBER OF US TOWN LEGISLATING BODY** a member of the legislating body of a town or city in the United States or Canada **3. LOCAL GOVERNMENT MEMBER IN AUSTRALIA** a member of local gov-

ernment elected by the constituents of a municipality in Australia **4.** = **ealdorman** [Old English *ealdorman*, from *ealdor* 'an elder' + MAN] —**aldermanic** /áwldər mánnik/ *adj.* —**aldermancy** /áwldər mənssi/ *n.*

Aldermaston /áwldər maastən/ village in the county of Berkshire, England, the site of the Atomic Weapons Research Establishment

Alderney[1] /áwldərni/ third largest and most northerly of the Channel Islands. Population: 2,297 (1991). Area: 1,795 hectares/1,962 acres.

Alderney[2] *n.* a cow belonging to a breed of small dairy cattle originally from the Channel Islands

Aldershot /áwldər shot/ town and military centre in Hampshire, England. Population: 51,356 (1991).

Aldis lamp /áwldiss-/ *n.* a signalling device in the form of a portable lamp used to flash messages in Morse code [Early 20thC. Named after the British inventor A. C. W. *Aldis*, who designed it.]

Aldm. *abbr.* alderman

aldohexose /áldŏ héksŏss, -héksŏz/ *n.* a six-carbon sugar, e.g. glucose or mannose, that contains a CHO group [Early 20thC. Contraction of ALDEHYDE + HEXOSE.]

aldol /ál dol/ *n.* **1. LIQUID USED IN SOLVENTS AND PERFUMES** a colourless or pale yellow oily liquid used chiefly in making chemicals to accelerate the vulcanization of rubber, as a solvent, and in making perfumes. Formula: $C_4H_8O_2$. **2. ORGANIC COMPOUND** a colourless liquid formed by the condensation of acetaldehyde and used in organic synthesis and in denaturing alcohol

aldolase /áldə layss, -layz/ *n.* an enzyme that aids the breakdown of fructose [Mid-20thC. From German, coined from *Aldol* 'aldol' + -*ase* '-ase'.]

aldose /áldŏss, -dŏz/ *n.* a sugar (**monosaccharide**) that contains a CHO group

aldosterone /al dóstərōn/ *n.* a steroid hormone, secreted by the adrenal cortex, that controls the balance of salt and water in the body

aldosteronism /al dóstərənizzəm/ *n.* a condition caused by abnormally high secretion of aldosterone by the adrenal cortex, characterized by weakness, high blood pressure, and excessive fluid intake and urinary output

Aldrin /áwldrin/, **Buzz** (*b.* 1930) US astronaut. He was the second man to walk on the Moon (1969). Full name **Edwin Eugene Aldrin, Jr.**

ale /ayl/ *n.* **1. TYPE OF BEER** a type of beer, brewed from a cereal and originally distinguished from beer by the absence of hops **2.** = **beer 3.** *US* **ALCOHOLIC DRINK** an alcoholic drink made from rapidly fermented malt to which hops have been added [Old English *ealu*. From a prehistoric Germanic word possibly meaning 'intoxicating drink'.]

aleatory /áyli ətəri/ *adj.* **1. DEPENDING ON CHANCE** depending on chance or contingency **2. aleatory, aleatoric HAVING RANDOM NOTES** having the sequence of given notes or passages in a piece of music chosen at random by the performer or left to chance [Late 17thC. Via Latin *aleatorius* from, ultimately, *alea* 'dice', of unknown origin.]

alec /állik/, **aleck** *n. Aus* sb regarded as unintelligent and thoughtless (*slang*) [Early 20thC. Shortening of SMART ALEC.]

Alecto /ə léktō/ *n.* in Greek mythology, one of the three Furies. The others were Megaera and Tisiphone.

alee /ə lée/ *adv.*, *adj.* on or to the leeward side

alef *n.* = **aleph**

alegar /áyligər, ál-/ *n.* vinegar made from fermented ale [Mid-16thC. Formed from ALE, on the model of VINEGAR.]

alehouse /áyl howss/ *n.* **1. PUB** a pub (*dated*) **2. PLACE SELLING ALE** a place where ale was sold and served (*archaic*)

Alemanni /állə mánni, -maáni/ *npl.* a group of Germanic peoples who settled in areas around the Rhine, Main, and Danube rivers at the beginning of the fourth century AD [From Latin (source also of French *allemand* and Spanish *alemán* 'German'). Ultimately from a prehistoric Germanic word possibly meaning 'all the peoples'.]

Alemannic /állə mánnik/ *n.* **GERMAN DIALECTS** a group of High German dialects spoken in Alsace, Switzerland, and southwestern Germany ■ *adj.* **OF ALEMANNI** belonging to or typical of the Alemanni

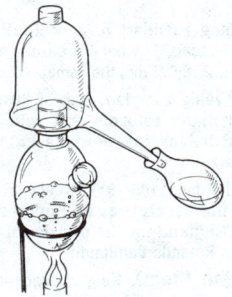

Alembic

alembic /ə lémbik/ *n.* an apparatus formerly used in distillation [14thC. Via Old French and medieval Latin *alembicus* from Arabic *al-'anbīk* 'the still', from Greek *ambix* 'cup'.]

aleph /állef, aá lef/, **alef** *n.* the first letter of the Hebrew alphabet, written as an apostrophe and pronounced as a glottal stop. See table at **alphabet** [14thC. Via Hebrew *'alep* from, ultimately, Canaanite *'alp* 'ox', which started with this sound.]

Aleppo /ə léppō/ city in northwestern Syria, northeast of Homs, an important centre on an ancient trade route to the East. Population: 1,542,000 (1994). Formerly **Beroea**

alert /ə lúrt/ *adj.* **1. WATCHFUL** watchful and ready to deal with whatever happens **2. MENTALLY LIVELY** clear-headed and responsive ■ *n.* **1. WARNING OF DANGER** an alarm or warning of danger **2. TIME OF DANGER** a period of time during which an alert remains in force ■ *v.* (**alerts, alerting, alerted**) **WARN** to make sb aware of possible dangers or difficulties ○ *Police have alerted the public to the danger.* [Late 16thC. Via French *alerte* from Italian *all'erta*, literally 'on the lookout'.] —**alertly** *adv.* —**alertness** *n.* ◇ **on red alert** prepared for any trouble or danger that may occur ◇ **on the alert** watchful and ready to deal with whatever happens

alethic /ə lée thik/ *adj.* relating to the philosophical concepts of truth and possibility and especially to the branch of logic that formalizes them [Late 20thC. Formed from Greek *alētheia* 'truth', from *alēthēs* 'true', literally 'not hidden'.]

aleurone /ə lyooʻrōn/, **aleuron** /-on/ *n.* a protein occurring as granules in various plants, especially in seeds [Mid-19thC. Alteration of Greek *aleuron* 'wheat flour'.] —**aleuronic** /állyoō-/ *adj.*

Aleut /álli oot, ə lyoot/ (*plural* **Aleut** *or* **Aleuts**) *n.* **1. PEOPLES MEMBER OF AN ALASKAN PEOPLE** a member of a Native North American people who live in the Aleutian Islands and southwestern coastal Alaska **2. LANG ESKIMO-ALEUT LANGUAGE** a Native North American language spoken in the Aleutian Islands and coastal parts of Alaska, belonging to the Eskimo-Aleut group. Only a few hundred people now speak Aleut. [Late 18thC. From Russian.] —**Aleut** *adj.*

Aleutian /ə loósh'n/ *adj.* relating to or typical of the Aleutian Islands, or their people or culture

Aleutian Islands chain of islands stretching westward for about 1,800 km/1,100 mi. from the tip of the Alaska Peninsula and separating the Pacific Ocean from the Bering Sea to the north

A level *n.* **1. SCHOOL EXAMINATION** the advanced level of any subject studied to gain a General Certificate of Education qualification in England, Wales, and Northern Ireland **2. EXAMINATION PASS** a pass in an examination in a subject studied at A level [Shortening of *Advanced level*]

alevin /álləvin/ *n.* a young salmon or trout with the yolk sac still attached [Mid-19thC. Via French, from assumed Vulgar Latin *allevamen*, literally 'sth that is raised', from Latin *levare* (see LEVER).]

alewife /áyl wīf/ (*plural* **-wives** /-wīvz/) *n.* **1. MIGRATING HERRING** a herring that migrates up rivers to spawn. It appears off the Atlantic coast of North America in early summer and can be eaten as food. Latin

Library of Congress

name: *Alosa pseudoharengus*. **2. WOMAN ALE-SELLER** a woman who sold ale, especially one who kept an alehouse (*archaic*) [14thC. From ALE + WIFE 'woman'. The application to the fish is perhaps an illusion to its large belly.]

alexander /állig zaándər/ *n.* a cocktail made from crème de cacao, sweet cream, and gin or brandy [Early 20thC. From the name *Alexander*.]

Alexander II /állig zaándər/, **Tsar of Russia** (1818–81). He enacted many reforms and sold the Russian lands in North America (now Alaska) to the United States in 1867.

Alexander III, Pope (1105?–81). He was pope from 1159 to 1181, during which time he imposed penance on Henry II of England for the murder of St Thomas à Becket. Born **Rolando Bandinelli**

Alexander (the Great), King of Macedonia (356–323 BC). He conquered most of the ancient world from Asia Minor to Egypt and India.

Alexander, William, Earl of Stirling (1567?–1640) Scots poet. Tutor to Prince Henry of Scotland, he later went to England on the accession of James I. His works include *Four Monarchicke Tragedies* (1664–67).

Alexander technique *n.* a method of improving the posture that involves developing awareness of it [Mid-20thC. Named after the Australian physiotherapist Frederick *Alexander* (1869–1955), who developed the technique.]

Alexandra /állig zaándrə/, **Empress of Russia** (1872–1918). The wife of Tsar Nicholas II, she was executed by the Bolsheviks at Ekaterinberg.

Alexandria /állig zaándri ə/ city and Mediterranean seaport in northern Egypt, on the delta of the River Nile. Founded by Alexander the Great in 332 BC, it was a major cultural centre of the ancient world, renowned for its library. Population: 3,380,000 (1992).

Alexandrian /állig zaándri ən/ *adj.* **1. OF ALEXANDER THE GREAT** of or relating to Alexander the Great **2. RELATING TO IDEAS IN EARLY ALEXANDRIA** relating to the literary, philosophical, and scientific theories and ideas in Alexandria during the 3rd century BC and later, when Alexandria was home to a famous library **3. SCHOLARLY BUT UNORIGINAL** scholarly and pedantic rather than creative or imaginative and original

Alexandrina /állig zan dreénə/ coastal lagoon in southeastern South Australia, situated at the mouth of the Murray River. Area: 680 sq. km/260 sq. mi.

alexandrine /állig zán drīn, -zaán-, -drin/ *n.* **1. ENGLISH VERSE FORM** in English poetry, a line of verse that has six iambic feet and usually a caesura after the third foot **2. FRENCH VERSE FORM** in French poetry, a line of verse that has twelve syllables and usually a caesura after the sixth syllable ■ *adj.* **LIKE OR IN ALEXANDRINES** typical of or written in alexandrines [Late 16thC. From French, named after the romance *Alexandre* about Alexander the Great, which was written in this metre.]

alexandrite /állig zán drīt, -zaán-/ *n.* a green chrysoberyl used as a gemstone [Mid-19thC. From German *Alexandrit*, named after *Alexander* II (1818–81), Tsar of Russia, because it was discovered on the day of his majority.]

alexia /ə léksi ə/ *n.* a loss of the ability to read, caused by a disorder of the central nervous system [Late 19thC. Coined from A- + Greek *lexis* 'speech' + -IA, under the influence of Latin *legere* 'to read'.]

alexin /ə léksin/ *n.* in biochemistry, a complement (*dated*) [Late 19thC. Via German, from Greek *alexein* 'to ward off'.]

Alexis Mikhailovich /ə léksiss mi kílə vich/, **Tsar of Russia** (1629–76). Ruling from 1654 to 1676, he legitimized serfdom (1649) and suppressed a peasant revolt (1671–71).

alf /alf/ *n. Aus* an unsophisticated person, especially an unsophisticated Australian (*informal*)

ALF *abbr.* Animal Liberation Front

Alfa *n., adj.* = **Alpha** [Variant of ALPHA]

alfalfa /al fálfə/ *n.* a European and Asian plant in the pea family, widely grown as a hay and forage crop.

Latin name: *Medicago sativa*. [Mid-19thC. Via Spanish, from Arabic *al-fasfasa*, literally 'the best kind of fodder'.]

Al Fatah /ál fáttə/ *n.* = **Fatah** [Late 20thC. From Arabic *al* 'the' + an acronym formed from Ḥ(arakat) T(aḥrīr) F(ilastīn) 'Movement for the Liberation of Palestine' (resembling *fataḥ* 'conquer').]

Alfieri /álfi áiri/, **Vittorio, Count** (1749–1803) Italian poet and dramatist. He wrote 28 plays, including *Cleopatra* (1775).

al-Fitr /al fíttər/ *n.* = **Eid-ul-Fitr**

Alfred (the Great) /álfrid/, **King of Wessex** (849–901). He reigned from 871, reconquering Danish territories in England. He also translated several Latin works into English.

alfredo /al fréddō/ *adj.* served with a rich sauce made from cream, butter, and Parmesan cheese [Late 20thC. Origin unknown.]

alfresco /al fréskō/ *adv.* **OUTDOORS** outdoors or in the open air ■ *adj.* **LOCATED OUTDOORS** taking place or located outdoors [Mid-18thC. From Italian, literally 'in the fresh (air)'.]

Alfven /al vén/, **Hannes Olof Gosta** (1908–95) Swedish theoretical physicist who worked on the harnessing of nuclear fusion power and was awarded the Nobel Prize in physics (1970).

alg. *abbr.* algebra

Alg. *abbr.* **1.** Algeria **2.** Algerian

alga /álgə/ (*plural* **-gae** /áljee, álgee/) *n.* a mainly aquatic photosynthetic organism that differs from plants in not having true leaves, roots, or stems and includes the seaweeds. Algae were once considered to be plants but are no longer classified as such. [Mid-16thC. From Latin, 'seaweed', of uncertain origin.] —**algal** /álgəl/ *adj.*

algal bloom *n.* an excessive growth of algae on or near the surface of water, occurring naturally or as a result of an oversupply of nutrients from organic pollution

Algarve /aal gaárv/ region in southern Portugal. Its coastline is the country's leading holiday area.

algebra /áljibrə/ *n.* **1. MATHEMATICS USING LETTERS AS SYMBOLS** a branch of mathematics in which symbols, usually letters of the alphabet, are used to represent unknown numbers and in doing so generalize arithmetic **2. STUDY OF MATHEMATICAL STRUCTURES** the study of structures in mathematics such as groups, rings, fields, and categories [Mid-16thC. Via Italian and medieval Latin from Arabic *al-jabr*, literally 'the reuniting', in the title of the treatise 'The science of reunion and equation', by the mathematician al-Khwarizmi.] —**algebraist** /álji bráyist/ *n.*

algebraic /álji bráyik/, **algebraical** /-bráyik'l/ *adj.* **1. RELATING TO ALGEBRA** involving or relating to algebra **2. USING ONLY FINITE NUMBERS OR OPERATIONS** relating to or using only finite numbers, expressions, and operations —**algebraically** *adv.*

Algeciras /álje seérəss/ port and resort near the southern tip of Spain. Population: 104,216 (1995).

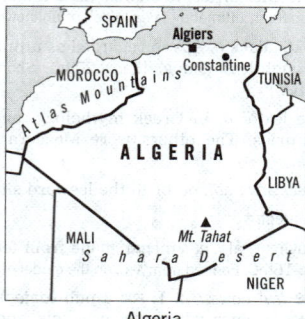

Algeria

Algeria /al jeérri ə/ country in northwestern Africa. It became independent from France in 1962. Language: Arabic. Currency: Algerian dinar. Capital: Algiers. Population: 29,830,371 (1997). Area: 2,381,741 sq. km/919,595 sq. mi. —**Algerian** *adj., n.*

algesia /al jeézi ə, -ssi ə/ *n.* sensitivity to or perception of pain [Formed from modern Latin *algesia* which was

formed from Greek *algesis* + modern Latin *ia*, suffix denoting a condition]

-algia *suffix.* pain ○ *neuralgia* [Formed from Greek *algos* 'pain', of uncertain origin]

algicide /álji sīd/ *n.* a substance that kills algae or prevents them from growing —**algicidal** /álji sīd'l/ *adj.*

algid /áljid/ *adj.* used to describe an episode during a severe fever when the patient's body temperature suddenly drops to an abnormally low level [Early 17thC. From Latin *algidus*, from *algere* 'to be cold'.] —**algidity** /al jíddəti/ *n.*

Algiers /al jeerz/ capital, chief port, and largest city of Algeria. Population: 2,168,000 (1995).

algin /áljin/ *n.* a viscous liquid, especially alginic acid or an alginate, obtained from seaweed and used as a thickener or emulsifier in the manufacture of plastics or in food [Late 19thC. Formed from ALGA + -IN, suffix denoting organic compounds (compare INSULIN).]

alginate /álji nayt/ *n.* a salt or ester of alginic acid. Alginates are often used as thickeners or emulsifiers in plastics or food.

alginic acid /al jínnik-/ *n.* an insoluble powdery acid obtained from brown seaweed and used in making food, pharmaceuticals, cosmetics, and textiles. Formula: $(C_6H_8O_6)_n$.

algo- *prefix.* pain ○ *algophobia* [From Greek *algos* 'pain', of uncertain origin]

algoid /ál goyd/ *adj.* resembling or relating to algae

ALGOL /ál gol/, **Algol** *n.* a high-level computer programming language that employs algebraic symbols and is designed for use in solving mathematical and scientific problems [Mid-20thC. Contraction of algorithm-oriented language.]

algolagnia /álgō lágni ə/ *n.* the attainment of sexual pleasure through inflicting or experiencing pain (*technical*) [Early 20thC. Formed from Greek *algos* 'pain' and *lagneia* 'lust'.] —**algolagnic** *adj.* —**algolagnist** *n.*

algology /al gólləji/ *n.* the branch of botany concerned with the scientific study of algae —**algological** /álgə lójjik'l/ *adj.* —**algologist** /-gólləjist/ *n.*

Algonkian *n.* = **Algonquian**

Algonkin *n.* = **Algonquin**

Algonquian /al góngki ən, -kwi-/ (*plural* **-an** *or* **-ans**), **Algonkian** /-ki-/ (*plural* **-an** *or* **-ans**) *n.* **1. LANG GROUP OF N AMERICAN LANGUAGES** a group of over thirty related North American languages that are, or used to be, spoken in central and eastern Canada, and parts of the central and eastern United States. Algonquian includes the languages of the Arapaho, Blackfoot, Cheyenne, Delaware, Fox, Ojibwa, Sauk, and Shawnee peoples. **2. PEOPLES MEMBER OF ALGONQUIAN-SPEAKING PEOPLE** a member of an Algonquian-speaking Native North American people [Late 19thC. Formed from ALGONQUIN.] —**Algonquian** *adj.*

Algonquin[1] /al góngkin, -kwin/, **Algonkin** /-kin/ (*plural* **-kin** *or* **-kins**) *n.* **1. PEOPLES MEMBER OF ABORIGINAL PEOPLE OF E CANADA** a member of a group of Aboriginal peoples living along the Ottawa and St Lawrence Rivers in eastern Canada. Historically, the Algonquin were allies of the French against the Iroquois. **2. LANG ALGONQUIAN LANGUAGE** a Native North American language spoken in Quebec and Ontario. About 3,000 people speak Algonquian dialects, which are closely related to Ojibwa. [Early 17thC. From Canadian French, of Algonquian origin.] —**Algonquin** *adj.*

Algonquin[2] /al góngkin, -kwin/ village in northeastern Illinois. Population: 18,019 (1996).

algophobia /álgə fóbi ə/ *n.* an abnormally intense fear of pain

algorism /álgərizzəm/ *n.* an algorithm (*dated*) [13thC. Via Old French and medieval Latin from Arabic *al-Ḵwārazmī*, name of the mathematician Abū Ja'far Muḥammad ibn Mūsā, (780?-850?), who introduced it to the West.]

algorithm /álgə rithəm/ *n.* **1. PROBLEM-SOLVING PROCEDURE** a logical step-by-step procedure for solving a mathematical problem in a finite number of steps, often involving repetition of the same basic operation **2. PROBLEM-SOLVING COMPUTER PROGRAM** a logical sequence of steps for solving a problem, often written out as a flow chart, that can be translated into a computer program [Late 17thC. Variant of ALGORISM, under the influence of Greek *arithmos* 'number'.] —**algorithmic** /álgə ríthmik/ *adj.*

Alhambra /al hámbrə/ citadel and palace in Granada, Spain, built for Moorish kings in the 12th and 13th centuries

Muhammad Ali

Ali /aa lí/, **Muhammad** (*b.* 1942) US boxer, three times world heavyweight champion (1964–71, 1974–78, 1978–80). Former name **Cassius Clay**

Alia /aáli ə/, **Ramiz** (*b.* 1925) Albanian politician who was president of Albania (1985–92).

alias /áyli əss/ *adv.* ALSO KNOWN AS otherwise or also known as ■ *n.* **1.** NAME TAKEN an assumed name **2.** COMPUT FILE OR DIRECTORY NAME a name assigned to file or directory, e.g. to make it more convenient to locate or manipulate [15thC. From Latin, 'otherwise'.]

alibi /álli bī/ *n.* (*plural* -**bis**) **1.** ACCUSED'S CLAIM OF HAVING BEEN ELSEWHERE a form of defence against an accusation in which the accused person claims to have been somewhere other than at the scene of the crime when the crime was committed **2.** SB USED TO ESTABLISH ALIBI sb or sth used to prove that sb else was elsewhere at the time that a crime was committed **3.** EXCUSE an explanation offered to justify sth (*informal*) ■ *vt.* (-**bis**, -**biing**, -**bied**) PROVIDE ALIBI FOR SB to provide an alibi or excuse for sb [Late 17thC. From Latin, 'elsewhere'.]

――――――― **WORD KEY: USAGE** ―――――――
alibi = 'excuse': *Alibi* should only be used informally in the weakened meaning 'excuse or pretext', because it has a precise legal meaning that is in danger of being compromised. In any case it often sounds silly and affected when used in this way. It is more natural word to use: *He used his illness as an excuse (not as an alibi) for leaving work early.*

Alicante /álli kánti/ city and port in southeastern Spain. Population: 276,526 (1995).

Alice band /álliss-/ *n.* a band of velvet or ribbon worn across the top of the head to hold the hair back off the face. So called because Alice is shown wearing one in the original illustrations to *Alice's Adventures in Wonderland* by Lewis Carroll.

Alice-in-Wonderland /állis in wúndər land/ *adj.* absurd, fantastic, or completely at odds with reality [Early 20thC. From the well-known fantasy by Lewis Carroll (1832–98), *Alice's Adventures in Wonderland* (1865).]

Alice Springs /álliss-/ town in the southern part of Australia's Northern Territory, a centre of tourism. Population: 25,585 (1991).

alicyclic /álli síklik, -sík-/ *adj.* used to describe organic compounds that have carbon atoms joined in a string (**open chain**) as well as in rings. ◊ **aliphatic** [Late 19thC. Blend of ALIPHATIC and CYCLIC.]

alien /áyli ən/ *n.* **1.** EXTRATERRESTRIAL BEING a being from another planet or another part of the universe, especially in works of science fiction **2.** LAW FOREIGN RESIDENT OF COUNTRY sb who is a citizen of a country other than the one in which he or she lives or happens to be **3.** OUTSIDER sb who does not belong to, is not accepted in, or does not feel part of a particular group or society ■ *adj.* **1.** STRANGE outside sb's normal or previous experience and seeming strange and sometimes threatening **2.** INCONSISTENT WITH STH not in keeping or totally incompatible with

the nature of sth or sb ○ *The idea was alien to her nature.* **3.** LAW FOREIGN not a citizen of, or not belonging to, the country in question **4.** EXTRATERRESTRIAL from another world or part of the universe, or involving or relating to extraterrestrial beings ■ *vt.* (-**ens**, -**ening**, -**ened**) LAW = **alienate** *v.* **4** [14thC. Via Old French or directly from Latin *alienus*, from *alius* 'other' (see ALIAS).]

alienable /áyli ənəb'l/ *adj.* capable of being transferred by a legal process to another owner —**alienability** /áyli ənə bílləti/ *n.*

alienate /áyli ə nayt/ (-**ates**, -**ating**, -**ated**) *vt.* **1.** MAKE SB UNFRIENDLY to cause sb to change his or her previously friendly or supportive attitude and become unfriendly, unsympathetic, or hostile ○ *His selfishness succeeded in alienating all of his friends.* **2.** MAKE SB FEEL DISAFFECTED to make sb feel that he or she does not belong to or share in sth, or is isolated from it (*often passive*) ○ *The long-term unemployed often feel alienated from society.* **3.** TURN STH AWAY to cause sth, especially sb's affections, to be directed at sb or sth else **4.** LAW TRANSFER OWNERSHIP TO SB to transfer the ownership of a property or right to sb [15thC. From Latin *alienat-*, the past participle stem of *alienare* 'to make sb else's, alienate' (see ALIEN).] —**alienator** *n.*

alienation /áyli ə náysh'n/ *n.* **1.** ESTRANGEMENT the process of causing sb to become unfriendly, unsympathetic, or hostile, or sb's estrangement from or unfriendly attitude towards sb else **2.** WITHDRAWN STATE a feeling of being isolated or withdrawn, or of not belonging to or sharing in sth ○ *prey to feelings of alienation* **3.** PSYCHOL FEELING OF UNREALITY a psychological condition in which sb comes to feel divorced from the objective world or parts of his or her own personality or feel that he or she is unreal **4.** LAW TRANSFER OF PROPERTY the transfer of property or a right to sb

alienee /áyli ə née/ *n.* sb to whom property or a right is transferred by a legal process

alienist /áyli ənist/ *n.* **1.** US PSYCHIATRIST IN LEGAL SYSTEM an expert witness, usually a psychiatrist, who is accepted by a court of law as qualified to assess the psychological state of people appearing in court **2.** PSYCHIATRIST a psychiatrist (*archaic*) [Mid-19thC. Via French, from, ultimately, Latin *alienare* 'to estrange, make irrational' (see ALIENATE).]

alienor /áyli ənər/ *n.* sb who transfers property or a right to sb else by a legal process

aliform /álli fawrm, áyli-/ *adj.* shaped like a wing (*technical*) [Early 18thC. Coined from Latin *ala* 'wing' (see ALA) + -FORM.]

Alighieri ◊ Dante

alight[1] /ə līt/ (**alights, alighting, alighted** *or* **alit** /ə lít/, **alighted** *or* **alit**) *vi.* **1.** GET OUT OF VEHICLE to step down from a vehicle onto the ground or a platform, or dismount from a horse or bicycle ○ *The VIPs alighted from their train.* **2.** LAND to land or settle after a flight ○ *A magpie alighted on a branch.* **3.** FIND BY CHANCE to happen to find, spot, or come to rest on sth ○ *to alight on a suitable candidate* [Old English *alíhtan*, from *a-* 'away, up, out', and *líhtan* 'to make lighter, lighten' (see LIGHT[1])]

alight[2] /ə līt/ *adj.* **1.** ON FIRE on fire or burning ○ *Try to keep the fire alight.* **2.** LIT UP lit up or full of light ○ *The sky was alight with fireworks.* **3.** FULL OF ENERGY filled with or radiating energy, excitement, interest, or pleasure ○ *His face was alight with joy.* [Old English *aliht* 'illuminated', past participle of *alihtan*, 'to light up' (see LIGHT[1])]

align /ə līn/ (**aligns, aligning, aligned**), **aline** (**alines, alining, alined**) *v.* **1.** *vt.* BRING STH INTO LINE to place sth in a line, or in an orderly spatial relationship, e.g. parallel, with sth else **2.** *vti.* BRING INTO CORRECT POSITION to bring sth, e.g. different parts of a machine or structure, into the correct position with respect to each other or sth else, or come into this position **3.** *vti.* DECLARE SUPPORT FOR SB OR STH to declare your support, or the support of sb or sth you represent, for a particular person, group, argument, or point of view ○ *The government aligned itself behind NATO.* ○ *The issue has aligned many citizens behind the candidate.* **4.** *vi.* FORM LINE to become arranged in a line [15thC. Via Old French *alignier* from, ultimately, Latin *linea* 'line'.] —**aligner** *n.*

alignment /ə línmənt/, **alinement** *n.* **1.** LINEAR OR ORDERLY ARRANGEMENT the arrangement of sth in a straight line or in an orderly position relative to sth else **2.** POSITIONING OF STH FOR PROPER PERFORMANCE the correct position or positioning of different components relative to one another, so that they perform properly ○ *the wheels are out of alignment* **3.** SUPPORT OR ALLIANCE support for, or a political alliance with, a particular person, group, or point of view ○ *shifting alignments within the legislature* **4.** GROUND PLAN a ground plan, especially one showing the course of a road or railway line **5.** ORDERING OF TYPE the ordering of lines of type relative to a margin or line ○ *Try changing the alignment from left to right.* ○ *The vertical alignment looks uneven.*

Aligoté /álli gố tay/ *n.* a white grape grown mainly in France, used for making wine, or a tart white wine made from this grape

alike /ə līk/ *adj.* SIMILAR similar in appearance or character ○ *They're so alike, it's difficult to tell them apart.* ■ *adv.* THE SAME in a similar or the same way ○ *The disaster affects young and old alike.* [Old English *gelíc* 'alike, similar'. Ultimately from a prehistoric Germanic word meaning 'body, form'.] —**alikeness** *n.*

aliment /állimənt/ *n.* STH THAT SUSTAINS sth that feeds, sustains, or supports sth else (*formal*) ■ *vt.* (-**ments**, -**menting**, -**mented**) SUPPORT to provide sustenance or support to sb or sth (*formal*) [15thC. Via French, from Latin *alimentum*, from *alere* 'to nourish'.] —**alimental** /álli mént'l/ *adj.* —**alimentally** /-mént'li/ *adv.*

alimentary /álli méntəri/ *adj.* (*formal*) **1.** OF FOOD OR NUTRITION relating to food or nutrition **2.** PROVIDING SUSTENANCE OR SUPPORT providing nourishment, sustenance, support, or maintenance

alimentary canal *n.* the tubular passage between the mouth and the anus, including the organs through which food passes for digestion and elimination as waste

alimentation /álli men táysh'n/ *n.* (*formal*) **1.** NOURISHMENT the providing of food or nourishment **2.** SUPPORT the providing of maintenance or support —**alimentative** /álli méntətiv/ *adj.*

alimony /állimƏni/ *n.* maintenance paid to a former spouse [Early 17thC. From Latin *alimonia* 'subsistence' (see ALIMENT).]

aline *vti.* = **align**

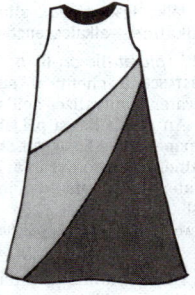

A-line

A-line *adj.* resembling the outline of the letter A, especially in a garment by flaring out from the top to the bottom ○ *an A-line dress*

alinement *n.* = **alignment**

aliphatic /álli fáttik/ *adj.* used to describe organic compounds that have carbon atoms linked in a string (**open chain**). ◊ **alicyclic** [Late 19thC. Formed from the Greek stem *aleiphat-* 'fat', because the term was originally applied to fatty acids (see LIPID).]

aliquant /állikwənt, -kwont/ *adj.* used to describe a number or quantity that cannot divide another number or quantity without leaving a remainder. ◊ **aliquot** [Late 17thC. From Latin *aliquantum* 'somewhat'.]

aliquot /álli kwot/ *adj.* DIVIDING INTO STH EXACTLY used to describe a number or quantity that will divide another number or quantity without leaving a remainder. ◊ **aliquant** ■ *n.* ALIQUOT PART an aliquot part, including fractional parts, e.g. $\frac{1}{3}$, $\frac{1}{4}$, or $\frac{1}{8}$ [Late 16thC. Via French, from Latin, 'a certain number'.]

A list *n.* the people most sought after or most in demand for any activity, e.g. as guests at social functions or for recruitment to a team or organization (*hyphenated when used before a noun*)

alit past tense and past participle of **alight**

aliterate /ay líttərət/ *n.* sb who, though usually able to read, is completely uninterested in reading and literature —**aliteracy** /ay líttərəssi/ *n.* —**aliterate** /-rət/ *adj.*

alive /ə lív/ *adj.* **1. LIVING** living, especially still living, and not dead **2. OF ALL PEOPLE LIVING** of all people currently living (*usually used with a superlative*) ○ *the luckiest person alive* **3. STILL IN EXISTENCE** still existing, continuing, or functioning ○ *The movement remained alive by going underground.* **4. STILL INTERESTING** still interesting, relevant, or vividly imaginable for people in the present day **5. FULL OF LIFE** full of energy and vigour, and with a zest for and interest in life **6. ANIMATED** active or animated, especially full of busy activity or a sense of excitement ○ *The place doesn't come alive till after midnight.* **7. SWARMING WITH STH** full of or swarming with people or animals ○ *The floor of the tent was alive with ants.* **8. AWARE OF STH** sensitive to or aware of things ○ *alive to the danger involved in the operation* **9.** = **live** [Old English *on life*, literally 'in life' (compare AFIRE)] —**aliveness** *n.* ◇ **alive and kicking** still active, healthy, or functioning vigorously (*humorous*)

WORD KEY: SYNONYMS

See Synonyms at ***living***.

aliyah /álli yaá/ *n.* **1. JEWISH IMMIGRATION INTO ISRAEL** immigration into Israel by Jews **2. READING FROM TORAH** the honour of being nominated to give a reading from the Torah [Mid-20thC. From Hebrew, literally 'ascent'.]

alizarin /ə lízzərin/ *n.* an orange-red or brownish-yellow crystalline compound, now made from coal tar but originally extracted from madder root, used as a dye and in making other dyes. Formula: $C_{14}H_8O_4$. [Mid-19thC. From French *alizarine*, probably ultimately from Arabic *alizari* 'madder'.]

al-Kadr *n.* = **Lailat-ul-Qadr**

alkahest /álkə hest/, **alcahest** *n.* a hypothetical universal solvent sought by alchemists [Mid-17thC. Coined by Paracelsus, in imitation of Arabic.] —**alkahestic** /álkə héstik/ *adj.*

alkalescent /álkə léss'nt/ *adj.* slightly alkaline or becoming alkaline —**alkalescence** *n.*

alkali /álkə lī/ (*plural* **-lis** *or* **-li**) *n.* **1. ACID-NEUTRALIZING CHEMICAL SUBSTANCE** a chemical substance that is soluble in water, neutralizes acids, and forms salts with them. An alkali has a pH above 7 and turns red litmus paper blue. **2. SOLUBLE SALT HARMFUL TO CROPS** a soluble mineral salt found in arid soils and some natural waters that is detrimental to agriculture [14thC. Via medieval Latin, from Arabic *al-kalī* 'ashes of saltwort', from which it was first obtained.]

alkali metal *n.* a metallic element belonging to the group comprising lithium, sodium, potassium, rubidium, caesium, and francium. Alkali metals are soft, white, and highly reactive, and their hydroxides are alkalis. Alkali metals also make up group 1 of the periodic table.

alkalimeter /álkə límmitər/ *n.* an instrument used for measuring the concentration of alkalis in a solution —**alkalimetry** *n.* —**alkalimetric** /álkəli méttrik/ *adj.* —**alkalimetrically** /-méttrik'li/ *adv.*

alkaline /álkə līn/ *adj.* having the properties of an alkali, or containing an alkali or alkalis

alkaline-earth metal, **alkaline earth** *n.* a metallic element belonging to the group comprising beryllium, magnesium, calcium, strontium, barium, and radium that makes up group 2 of the periodic table

alkalinity /álkə línnəti/ *n.* the concentration of alkali in a solution, measured in terms of pH

alkalize /álkə līz/ (**-lizes, -lizing, -lized**), **alkalise** (**-lises, -lising, -lised**) *vti.* to make sth alkaline, or become alkaline

alkaloid /álkə loyd/ *n.* a nitrogen-containing alkaline compound found in plants and used in medicines, drugs, or as a poison. Strychnine, nicotine, and quinine are alkaloids. [Early 19thC. Formed from ALKALI, because their chemical properties are similar to it.] —**alkaloidal** /álkə lóyd'l/ *adj.*

alkalosis /álkə lóssiss/ *n.* an abnormally high level of alkalinity in the blood, other body fluids, or body tissues, causing a high blood pH —**alkalotic** /álkə lóttik/ *adj.*

alkane /ál kayn/ *n.* an open-chain hydrocarbon compound with no carbon-to-carbon multiple bonds, belonging to a series whose members all have the same general chemical formula. Methane and ethane are alkanes. Formula: C_nH_{2n+2}.

alkanet /álkə net/ (*plural* **-nets** *or* **-net**) *n.* **1. EUROPEAN DYE PLANT** a European plant related to borage, with small blue flowers and red roots, from which a dye is extracted. Latin name: *Alkanna tinctoria.* **2. RED DYE** a red dye obtained from the roots of the alkanet plant **3. PLANT RELATED TO ALKANET** a bristly blue-flowered plant found in Europe, Asia, and Africa, related to alkanet. Genus: *Anchusa.* [14thC. Origin uncertain: probably from Old Spanish *alcaneta*, ultimately from Arabic *al-ḥinnā'* (see HENNA).]

alkene /ál keen/ *n.* an open-chain hydrocarbon compound containing one carbon-to-carbon double bond, belonging to a series whose members all have the same general chemical formula. Ethylene is an alkene. Formula: C_nH_{2n}.

alky /álki/ (*plural* **-kies**), **alkie** *n.* an offensive term for sb who is an (**alcoholic**) or who drinks to excess (*slang offensive*) [Mid-20thC. Shortening.]

alkyd /álkid/, **alkyd resin** *n.* a sticky resin that is prepared from phthalic acid and glycerol and becomes liquid or plastic when heated, used in paints and lacquer [Early 20thC. Coined from ALKYL + ACID.]

alkyl /ál kil/ *adj.* used to describe a hydrocarbon group derived from an alkane, e.g. the ethyl group [Late 19thC. From German, formed from *Alkohol* 'alcohol' + -YL.]

alkylation /álki láysh'n/ *n.* the addition of one or more alkyl groups to a chemical compound through replacement of a hydrogen atom

alkyne /ál kīn/ *n.* an open-chain hydrocarbon compound containing one carbon-to-carbon triple bond, belonging to a series whose members all have the same general chemical formula. Formula: C_nH_{2n-2}.

all /awl/ CORE MEANING: a grammatical word used to indicate that the whole of a particular thing, amount, group, or area is involved or affected ○ (det) *all men and all women* ○ (pron) *All of the computers are down.* ○ (pron) *All that glitters is not gold.*

1. *det.* **THE WHOLE OF** used to indicate that the whole of a particular amount, area, quantity, or thing is involved or affected ○ *All Europe was cold this winter.* **2.** *det.* **EVERY** every one of ○ *all men over 30* **3.** *det.* **ANY** any whatever (*used after a negative word such as 'refuse' or 'deny'*) ○ *Deny all connection with the plot.* **4.** *det.* **MOST** the greatest possible ○ *with all speed* **5.** *det.* **CHARACTERIZED BY** dominated in mood or character by sth (*informal*) ○ *He was all smiles.* **6.** *adv.* **VERY** very, completely, or totally (*informal*) ○ *I got all confused.* **7.** *pron.* **EVERY ONE OR THE WHOLE** the whole number or amount (*takes a plural verb*) ○ *All of us are going to the game.* **8.** *pron.* **EVERYTHING OR EVERYONE** the whole quantity or group ○ *All that glitters is not gold.* **9.** *n.* **SB'S BEST EFFORT** the greatest amount of sb's ability or effort (*literary*) ○ *He gave his all in the performance.* [Old English *eall*. From a prehistoric Germanic word meaning 'all', which is also the ancestor of English *also*.] ◇ **all along** from the start, or for the whole time that sth else was taking place ◇ **in all** when everything has been taken into account ◇ **all of** no less than (*informal*) ◇ **all square** in a situation where all debts and obligations to each other have been cleared and nobody owes anybody anything ◇ **all that** very, particularly, or to that extent (*informal; usually used in negative statements or questions*) ○ *I'm not all that worried about it.* ◇ **all the same 1.** nevertheless **2.** used to indicate that it is unimportant to the speaker which of two or more things is done or chosen ◇ **all there** fully alert, aware of what is going on, and able to handle it (*informal*) ◇ **all very well** used to indicate that there is some kind of objection or drawback, despite the fact that sb else is apparently satisfied with the situation ○ *That's all very well, but it's still my responsibility.* ◇ **be all over sb** to be extremely or excessively friendly or effusive towards sb (*informal*)

WORD KEY: USAGE

all or **all of**? There is a choice between ***all*** and ***all of*** when the following noun is qualified by *the, this, that, these, those*, or a possessive adjective such as *my* and *your*: *All my life I've wanted to be a singer. I've been a singer all of my life. All these things worried them. All of these things worried them.*

alla breve /állə bráyvi/ *n.* **TIME SIGNATURE BASED ON MINIMS** a time signature in music, represented by a C with a slash through it, specifying a beat of two or four minims to the bar. US term **cut time** ■ *adv.* **AT DOUBLE SPEED** at twice the normal speed (*used as a musical direction*) [From Italian, literally 'according to the breve'] —**alla breve** *adj.*

Allah /állə/ *n.* in Islam, the name of God [Late 16thC. From Arabic *'allāh*.]

all-American *adj.* **1. TYPICAL OF THE UNITED STATES** typical of the United States, its people, or their way of life, or representing them at their best **2.** SPORTS **BEST IN THE UNITED STATES** selected and honoured as the best amateur player or athlete in the United States in a particular position or event ○ *an all-American linebacker* **3. MADE OF US COMPONENTS** made up entirely of people from the United States, or of materials or components from the United States **4. OF ALL THE AMERICAS** including all the countries of North and South America or representatives from them ○ *an all-American agreement* ■ *n.* **1. BEST US ATHLETE** a player or athlete chosen as being the best in a position or event in the United States **2. TEAM OF BEST US PLAYERS** a team made up of US players or athletes selected for their excellence in a particular position or event

allantois /állən tō iss/ (*plural* **-ides** /állən tṓy deez/) *n.* a membranous sac that grows from the lower gut in mammal, bird, and reptile embryos. In mammals, it combines with the chorion to form the umbilical cord and placenta. [Mid-17thC. Via modern Latin from, ultimately, Greek *allantoeidēs* 'sausage-like', because of its shape.] —**allantoic** /állən tṓ ik/ *adj.*

allargando /állaar gándō/ *adv.* at a gradually slower tempo, with a broadening, stately sound (*used as a musical direction*) [Late 19thC. From Italian, literally 'broadening'.] —**allargando** *adj.*

all-around *adj.* US = **all-round**

allay /ə láy/ (**-lays, -laying, -layed**) *vt.* **1. CALM AN EMOTION OR WORRY** to calm a strong emotion, e.g. anger, or diminish and set at rest sb's fears or suspicions **2. RELIEVE PAIN** to relieve or reduce the severity of pain or a painful emotion [Old English *ālecgan* 'to lay aside' (see LAY). The meaning was influenced by Old French *aleger* 'to lighten' and *aleier* 'to moderate'.] —**allayer** *n.* —**allayment** *n.*

all-candidates meeting *n.* *Can* a public meeting during which all candidates for an elected office explain their policies and answer questions from the audience

all-choice *adj. US* used to describe a school system that allows people to choose a particular school to attend

all clear *n.* **1. SIGNAL THAT DANGER IS OVER** a signal that a period of danger is over, especially one sounded on a siren after an air raid **2. SIGNAL TO PROCEED** a signal or notification that sth may proceed ○ *We've got the all clear to start building.*

allegation /álli gáysh'n/ *n.* **1. UNPROVED ASSERTION** an assertion, especially relating to wrongdoing or misconduct on sb's part, that has yet to be proved or supported by evidence **2. ALLEGING** the alleging of sth, especially wrongdoing

allege /ə léj/ (**-leges, -leging, -leged**) *v.* **1.** *vti.* **ASSERT WITHOUT PROOF** to state or assert sth, especially to accuse sb of wrongdoing, without offering proof of it or with a view to proving it later ○ *The prosecutor alleged that Simmons knew about the planned hold-up.* **2.** *vti.* **GIVE STH AS REASON** to put sth forward as a reason or excuse for your actions or conduct (*formal*) ○ *He declined the invitation, alleging a prior* *appointment.* **3.** *vt.* **REFER TO STH** to cite or quote sth or sb as an authority (*archaic*) [14thC. Via Anglo-Norman 'to declare before a legal tribunal', from, ultimately, assumed Vulgar Latin *exlitigare* 'to clear of charges' (see LITIGATE).] —**allegeable** *adj.* —**alleger** *n.*

alleged /ə léjd/ *adj.* claimed but not yet proven to have taken place, have been committed, or be as described —**allegedly** /ə léjjidli/ *adv.*

WORD KEY: USAGE

alleged and **accused** ***Alleged*** is often used to describe a crime or wrongdoing and denotes uncertainty about whether it happened at all or whether a particular person is responsible for it: *The alleged fraud took place over a number of months.* It is also used to describe sb who is associated with a crime, not necessarily as the culprit: *The alleged victims all live in the suburbs.* In this use ***alleged*** differs from ***accused***, which is normally used with a neutral word: *The accused was remanded in custody.*

Allegheny /állə gayni/ river in Pennsylvania and New York, flowing north from its headwaters in Pennsylvania into New York before turning south again to join the Monongahela River at Pittsburgh to create the Ohio River. Length: 523 km/325 mi.

Allegheny Mountains, **Alleghenies** western mountain range of the Appalachian Mountains, in Pennsylvania, Maryland, West Virginia, and Virginia. The range is the divide between those rivers emptying into the Gulf of Mexico and those flowing into the Atlantic Ocean.

allegiance /ə léejənss/ *n.* **1. LOYALTY TO RULER OR STATE** a subject's or citizen's loyalty to a ruler or state, or the duty of obedience and loyalty owed by a subject or citizen **2. DEVOTED SUPPORT** loyalty to or support for a particular person, cause, or group ○ *The match was a treat for all fans, whatever their allegiance.* **3. FEUDAL OBLIGATION** the feudal obligation of vassals to their liege lord [14thC. Via Anglo-Norman, from Old French *ligeance*, from *lige* 'liege' (see LIEGE).] —**allegiant** *adj.*

allegorical /álli górrik'l/, **allegoric** /-górrik/ *adj.* **1. USING ALLEGORY** expressing sth through allegory, or intended to be understood as an allegory **2. TYPICAL OF ALLEGORY** used in or relating to allegory —**allegorically** *adv.*

allegorize /álligə rīz/ (**-rizes, -rizing, -rized**), **allegorise** (**-rises, -rising, -rised**) *v.* **1.** *vti.* **EXPRESS STH AS ALLEGORY** to express sth in the form of an allegory **2.** *vt.* **INTERPRET STH AS ALLEGORY** to interpret or treat sth as an allegory —**allegorization** /álligə rī záysh'n/ *n.* —**allegorizer** /álligə rīzər/ *n.*

allegory /álligəri/ (*plural* **-ries**) *n.* **1. SYMBOLIC WORK** a work in which the characters and events are to be understood as representing other things and symbolically expressing a deeper, often spiritual, moral, or political meaning **2. SYMBOLIC EXPRESSION OF MEANING IN STORY** the symbolic expression of a deeper meaning through a story or scene acted out by human, animal, or mythical characters ○ *the poet's use of allegory* **3. GENRE** allegories considered as a literary or artistic genre **4. SYMBOLIC REPRESENTATION** a symbolic representation of sth [14thC. Via Latin from, ultimately, Greek *allegorein*, literally 'to say otherwise', from *allos* 'other' and *agoreuein* 'to speak in public'.] —**allegorist** *n.*

allegretto /álli gréttō/ *adv.* **FAIRLY QUICKLY** at a fairly quick tempo (*used as a musical direction*) ■ *n.* (*plural* **-tos**) **PIECE OF MUSIC PLAYED ALLEGRETTO** a piece of music, or a section of a piece, played allegretto [Mid-18thC. From Italian, literally 'less than allegro'.] —**allegretto** *adj.*

allegro /ə láygrō, ə léggrō/ *adv.* **QUICKLY** at a quick and lively tempo (*used as a musical direction*) ■ *n.* (*plural* **-gros**) **PIECE OF MUSIC PALYED ALLEGRO** a piece of music, or a section of a piece, played allegro [Late 17thC. From Italian, literally 'lively'.] —**allegro** *adj.*

allele /ə léel/ *n.* one of two or more alternative forms of a gene, occupying the same position (**locus**) on paired chromosomes and controlling the same inherited characteristic [Mid-20thC. From German *Allel*, shortening of *Allelomorph* 'allelomorph'.] —**allelic** *adj.* —**allelism** *n.*

allelo- *prefix.* one another ○ *allelopathy* [From Greek *allēlon*, which was formed from *allos* 'other' (see ALLO-)]

allelochemical /ə léelə kémmik'l/ *n.* a chemical produced by one plant that is toxic to another

allelomorph /ə léelə mawrf, ə léllə-/ *n.* = **allele** [Early 20thC. Coined from the Greek stem *allēl-* 'one another' + -O- + -MORPH.] —**allelomorphic** /ə léelə máwrfik, ə léllə-/ *adj.* —**allelomorphism** /-fizzəm, ə léllə-/ *n.*

allelopathy /álli lóppəthi/ *n.* the release into the environment by one plant of a substance that inhibits the germination or growth of other potential competitor plants of the same or another species [Mid-20thC. Coined from the Greek stem *allēl-* 'one another' + -O- + -PATHY.] —**allelopathic** /ə léelə páthik, -léllə-/ *adj.*

allelotoxin /ə léelə tóksin/ *n.* = **allelochemical** [Late 20thC]

alleluia *interj., n.* = **hallelujah**

allemande /álli mand/ *n.* **1. MUSICAL MOVEMENT FORMING PART OF SUITE** a stately piece of music in moderate tempo and four-four time, often used as the opening movement of a baroque or classical suite **2. DANCE POPULAR IN 18C** a stately dance of German origin popular in France in the 18th century **3. DANCE MOVEMENT** a movement used in country dancing or square dancing that involves partners changing positions, often by interlinking arms [Late 17thC. From French, 'German'.]

all-embracing *adj.* including all or everything without discrimination

Allen /állən/, **Peter** (1944–92) Australian singer and songwriter. His songs include 'I Go to Rio' (1977). Real name **Peter Woolnough**

Allen, Woody (*b.* 1935) US film director, actor, screenwriter, playwright, and humorous essayist. His films include the Academy Award-winning *Annie Hall* (1977). Real name **Allen Stewart Konigsberg**

Allenby /állənbi/, **Edmund Henry Hynman, 1st Viscount** (1861–1936) British soldier who commanded the Third Army in France in World War I and took Jerusalem from the Turks (1917).

Allen key *n.* a tool in the form of an L-shaped rod, hexagonal in cross section, made in different sizes to turn corresponding sizes of Allen screws. US term **Allen wrench** [See ALLEN SCREW]

Allen screw *n.* a screw with a hexagonal recess in its head that allows it to be turned using an Allen key [Mid-20thC. Named after the *Allen* Manufacturing Company of Hartford, Connecticut in the United States.]

Allen wrench *n.* *US* = **Allen key** [See ALLEN SCREW]

allergen /állər jen, állərjən/ *n.* any substance that causes an allergic reaction —**allergenic** /állər jénnik/ *adj.*

allergic /ə lúrjik/ *adj.* **1. HAVING ALLERGY** having an allergy to a substance ○ *allergic to dust mites* **2. CAUSED BY ALLERGY** typical of or caused by an allergy ○ *an allergic reaction* **3. HAVING A DISLIKE** having a strong dislike for or aversion to sth or sb (*informal*) ○ *allergic to loud music*

allergist /állərjist/ *n.* a doctor who specializes in allergies and their treatment

allergy /állərji/ (*plural* **-gies**) *n.* **1. HYPERSENSITIVITY TO A SUBSTANCE** unusual sensitivity to a normally harmless substance that, when breathed in, ingested, or brought into contact with the skin, provokes a strong reaction from the person's body. The body is sensitized by the immune system's response to the first exposure to the substance, and the reaction takes place only upon subsequent exposures. **2. AVERSION** a strong dislike for or aversion to sth (*informal*) ○ *an allergy to washing* [Early 20thC. From German *Allergie*, from Greek *allos* 'other' (see ALLO-), on the model of *Energie* 'energy'.]

allethrin /a léthrin/ *n.* a clear or amber-coloured viscous liquid used as an insecticide. Formula: $C_{19}H_{26}O_3$. [Mid-20thC. Blend of ALLYL and PYRETHRIN.]

alleviate /ə léevi ayt/ (**-ates, -ating, -ated**) *vt.* to make sth, e.g. pain or hardship, more bearable or less severe ○ *Nothing could alleviate her despair.* [Early 16thC. From late Latin *alleviat-*, the past participle stem of *alleviare*, literally 'to lighten', from Latin *levis* 'light' (see LEVITY).] —**alleviation** /ə léevi áysh'n/ *n.* —**alleviative** /ə léevi ətiv/ *adj.* —**alleviator** /-aytər/ *n.* —**alleviatory** /ə léevi áytəri/ *adj.*

alley[1] /álli/ (*plural* **-leys**) *n.* **1. SMALL STREET** a short or narrow street, often in a poor neighbourhood **2. NARROW PASSAGE** a narrow passageway or lane, especially one running between or behind buildings **3. PATH IN GARDEN OR PARK** a path or walk in a garden or park, especially one between trees or shrubs **4.** = **bowling alley 5.** *US* TENNIS = **tramline** [14thC. From Old French *alee* 'a walk', ultimately from Latin *ambulare* (see AMBULATE).] ◇ **right up** *or* **down sb's alley** *US* completely suited to sb's interest, expertise, or line of work

alley[2] /álli/ *n.* a large playing marble [Early 18thC. Variant of *ally*, a shortening of ALABASTER, from which they were originally made.]

Alley /álli/, **Rewi** (1897–1987) New Zealand poet and translator, author of *Today and Tomorrow* (1975). He lived in China for sixty years, where he organized workers' cooperatives.

alley cat *n.* *US* **1. HOMELESS CAT** a homeless or stray cat, usually in poor condition or half wild, that lives on the streets **2. DISREPUTABLE PERSON** sb thought to resemble an alley cat, especially in being disreputable or fierce-tempered, or having loose morals

alley-oop /álli ŏop/ *interj.* **ENCOURAGEMENT ON GETTING UP** used as a word of encouragement when sb is getting up or being helped up, or sth is being lifted (*dated*) ■ *n.* (*plural* **alley-oops**) **1. TYPE OF MOVE IN BASKETBALL** a play in basketball in which a player jumps up to receive a pass over the basket and immediately puts the ball into the net from above **2. TYPE OF PASS IN BASKETBALL** a pass in basketball aimed to allow a player to jump up to receive it over the basket [Early 20thC. Coined from French *allez* 'come on!' + *houp* 'upsadaisy!'.]

alleyway /álli way/ *n.* an alley or narrow passageway

all-fired *adv.* *US* in an excessive or inordinate way (*informal*) ○ *Don't act so all-fired high and mighty.* [Early 19thC. Alteration of 'hell-fired'.]

All Fools' Day *n.* = **April Fools' Day**

all fours *n.* CARDS = **seven-up** ◇ **on all fours** crawling along or crouched down on the hands and knees ◇ **on all fours with** consistent or comparable with sth (*informal*)

all get-out ◇ **as** *or* **like all get-out** *US* as much, as fast, or as intensely or violently as is possible (*informal*)

all hail *interj.* a greeting, welcome, or shout of acclamation, usually addressed to a person of high rank or distinction (*archaic*)

Allhallows /awl hállōz/ (*plural* **-lows**), **Allhallowmas** /-hállōməss/ *n.* All Saints' Day (*archaic; takes a singular verb*) [Old English *ealra hálgena*, literally 'of all saints', from *hálga* 'saint', from *hálig* 'holy' (see HOLY)]

Allhallows' Eve *n.* Halloween (*archaic*)

allheal /áwl heel/ (*plural* **-heals** *or* **-heal**) *n.* a plant traditionally believed to have healing powers, e.g. valerian or selfheal

alliance /ə lī́ ənss/ *n.* **1. ASSOCIATION OF GROUPS WITH COMMON AIM** an association of two or more groups, individuals, or nations who agree to cooperate with one another to achieve a common goal **2. FORMING OF ALLIANCE** the establishment of or participation in an alliance with sb **3. MEMBERS OF ALLIANCE** the nations, individuals, or groups that make up an alliance ○ *the enemy alliance* **4. CLOSE RELATIONSHIP** a close relationship, based on the possession of similar aims or characteristics, between two or more people or things [13thC. From Old French *aliance*, from *alier* 'to ally' (see ALLY).]

allied /állīd, ə lī́d/ *adj.* **1. JOINED WITH OTHERS IN ALLIANCE** joined in an alliance with other nations, groups, or individuals by agreement or treaty **2. ASSOCIATED** having a close relationship or connection with each other ○ *allied banks* **3. OF SIMILAR TYPE** of a similar or related type ○ *sociology and allied studies*

alligator /álli gaytər/ *n.* **1.** (*plural* **-tors** *or* **-tor**) ZOOL **LARGE REPTILE** a large reptile that lives near water, has thick scaly skin, powerful jaws, a long tail, and a shorter and broader snout than a crocodile. There are two species of alligator, one found in the southern United States, the other found in China. Genus: *Alligator.* **2.** INDUST **LEATHER FROM ALLIGATOR SKIN** leather made from alligator skin **3. TOOL OR MACHINE WITH MOVABLE**

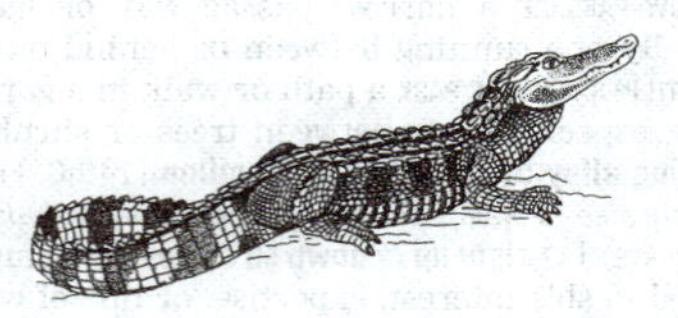

Alligator

JAW a tool or machine with a strong, movable, often toothed jaw for gripping or crushing [Mid-16thC. Alteration of Spanish *el lagarto*, literally 'the lizard', from Latin *lacertus* (source of English *lizard*).]

alligator clip *n. US* = **crocodile clip** [From the fact that it resembles an alligator's jaws]

alligator pear *n. US* = **avocado** [Mid-18thC. Alteration of American Spanish *aguacate* 'avocado', possibly because of the rough dark skin of some varieties.]

alligator snapping turtle, alligator snapper *n.* a large freshwater snapping turtle of the Gulf States of the United States. It is the largest North American freshwater turtle. Latin name: *Macroclemys temmincki.*

all-important *adj.* extremely or vitally important or necessary

all in *adj.* **1.** WITH EVERYTHING INCLUDED including everything, especially all costs (*hyphenated when used before a noun*) ○ *Is that the all-in price?* **2.** FATIGUED extremely tired ○ *We were all in by the time we got back to the hotel.*

all-inclusive *adj.* including or encompassing everything that is expected or appropriate

Allingham /állingəm/, **Margery** (1904–66) British writer. She produced a long series of detective novels, including *Tiger in the Smoke* (1952).

all-in wrestling *n.* a style of professional wrestling with relatively few restrictions on the permissible types of holds, blows, or throws ○ *an all-in wrestling tournament*

alliterate /ə lítti rayt/ (**-ates, -ating, -ated**) *v.* **1.** *vi.* BEGIN WITH SAME SOUND to begin words that are consecutive or close to each other with the same or a similar sound, or to contain alliteration **2.** *vti.* USE ALLITERATION to use alliteration in speaking or writing, or arrange words or construct sentences so as to achieve the effect of alliteration [Late 18thC. Back-formation from ALLITERATION.] —**alliterative** /ə líttirətiv/ *adj.* —**alliteratively** *adv.*

alliteration /ə lítti ráysh'n/ *n.* a poetic or literary effect achieved by using several words that begin with the same or a similar consonants, as in 'Whither wilt thou wander, wayfarer?' ◊ **assonance** [Early 17thC. Via medieval Latin from, ultimately, Latin *littera* 'letter' (see LETTER).]

all-night *adj.* lasting, open, or available throughout the night, or throughout a particular night ○ *an all-night rave*

allo- *prefix.* other, different, alternate ○ *allosteric* ○ *allophone* [From Greek *allos* 'other' (source of English *allegory* and *parallel*). Ultimately from an Indo-European word meaning 'other of more than two', which is also the ancestor of *else* and *alias*.]

Alloa /állō ə/ seaport on the River Forth in Scotland. It is an important engineering centre. Population: 18,842 (1991).

allocate /állə kayt/ (**-cates, -cating, -cated**) *vt.* **1.** GIVE OR EARMARK STH to give sth to a particular person, or set sth aside for a particular purpose, when dividing sth between different people or projects ○ *Each team member has been allocated a specific task.* **2.** SHARE OUT to share out or divide up sth between a number of different people or projects ○ *Much depends on how we allocate the time available for discussion.* [Mid-17thC. From medieval Latin *allocat-*, the past participle stem of *allocare*, literally 'to put in place' (see LOCUS).] —**allocable** /álləkəb'l/ *adj.* —**allocatable** /állə káytəb'l/ *adj.* —**allocator** /-kaytər/ *n.*

allocation /állə káysh'n/ *n.* **1.** ACT OF ALLOCATING the assignment or earmarking of sth ○ *allocation of duties* **2.** STH ALLOCATED a thing, amount, or share of sth allocated to sb or sth ○ *The department has already used its entire allocation.* **3.** ACCT SYSTEM OF DIVIDING INCOME AMONG DEPARTMENTS the system or practice of dividing a company's income and overheads among its various departments

allochthonous /ə lókthənəss/ *adj.* ◊ **autochthonous 1.** GEOL NOT IN ORIGINAL POSITION used to describe features of the landscape or elements of its geological structure that have been moved to their current position through tectonic forces **2.** BIOL INTRODUCED used to describe flora, fauna, or inhabitants that have moved to the region in which they are found from elsewhere [Early 20thC. Formed from Greek *allochthon*, from ALLO- + *khthōn* 'soil' + -OUS.]

allocution /állə kyoósh'n/ *n.* a formal speech or address, especially one that contains an authoritative statement on a subject or an exhortation to sb (*formal*) [Early 17thC. From the Latin stem *allocution-*, from *alloqui*, literally 'to speak to', from *loqui* 'to speak' (see LOQUACIOUS).]

allodium /ə lṓdi əm/ (*plural* **-lodia** /-ə/) *n.* land held by sb without any feudal obligation of rent, service, or other duty to an overlord [Early 17thC. Via medieval Latin, from an assumed Germanic compound word meaning 'all property'.] —**allodial** *adj.*

allogamy /ə lóggəmi/ *n.* the process of cross-fertilization in flowering plants —**allogamous** *adj.*

allogeneic /állō jə née ik/, **allogenic** /állō jénnik/ *adj.* used to describe tissues that are genetically different and therefore incompatible when transplanted [Mid-20thC. Coined from ALLO- + Greek *genea* 'race' (see GENEALOGY).] —**allogeneically** *adv.*

allograft /állō graaft/ *n.* a graft of tissue from one member of a species to a genetically different member of the same species. ◊ **homograft**

allograph /állə graaf, -graf/ *n.* **1.** STH WRITTEN ON SB'S BEHALF sth, especially a signature, written by one person on another's behalf **2.** GRAM REPRESENTATION OF PHONEME a letter or combination of letters that is one of a set that can be used to represent the same speech sound (**phoneme**), as, e.g., 's', 'ss', and 'c' in English

allomerism /ə lómmərizzəm/ *n.* a similarity in the structure of the crystals of substances that are chemically different —**allomerous** *adj.*

allometry /ə lómmətri/ *n.* measurement of the rate of growth of a part or parts of an organism relative to the growth of the whole organism. This rate determines the organism's final shape. —**allometric** /állə méttrik/ *adj.*

allomone /állə mōn/ *n.* a chemical substance produced by a plant in response to attack by other organisms [Late 20thC. Coined from ALLO- + PLANT HORMONE.]

allomorph /állə mawrf/ *n.* **1.** GRAM REPRESENTATION OF MORPHEME a letter or combination of letters that is part of a set used to represent the same basic grammatical element (**morpheme**) of a language, as, e.g., '-ed' and '-t' both form the English past tense **2.** VARIANT FORM OF CHEMICAL COMPOUND any of the differing crystalline forms of the same chemical compound or element, especially of a mineral [Mid-20thC. Coined from ALLO- + MORPHEME.] —**allomorphic** /állə máwrfik/ *adj.* —**allomorphism** /-fizzəm/ *n.*

allonym /állənim/ *n.* the name of another person, especially that of a significant historical figure, assumed by sb, especially a writer (*formal*) [Mid-19thC. From French *allonyme*, from Greek *allos* 'other' and *onoma* 'name'.] —**allonymous** /ə lónniməss/ *adj.* —**allonymously** /-məssli/ *adv.*

allopathy /ə lóppəthi/ *n.* the treatment of a disease by using remedies whose effects differ from those produced by that disease. This is the principle of mainstream medical practice, as opposed to that of homeopathy. —**allopath** /állə path/ *n.* —**allopathic** /állə páthik/ *adj.* —**allopathically** /-páthikli/ *adv.*

allopatric /állə páttrik/ *adj.* used to describe species or populations that do not interbreed because they are geographically isolated from one another [Mid-20thC. Coined from ALLO- + Greek *patra* 'homeland', from *patēr* 'father' (see PATRI-).] —**allopatrically** *adv.* —**allopatry** /ə lóppətri/ *n.*

allophane /állə fayn/ *n.* an amorphous mineral, hydrated aluminium silicate, that occurs in a variety of colours [Early 19thC. From Greek *allophanēs*, literally 'appearing otherwise' (because it changes colour when heated), from *allos* 'other' and *phainesthai* 'to appear' (see PHENOMENON).]

allophone /állə fōn/ *n.* one of the slightly differing forms that the same single speech sound (**phoneme**) can take [Mid-20thC. Coined from ALLO- + PHONEME.] —**allophonic** /állə fónnik/ *adj.* —**allophonically** /-fónnikli/ *adv.*

allopurinol /állō pyoóri nol/ *n.* a drug that reduces the level of the enzyme that produces uric acid in the blood, used in treating gout [Mid-20thC. Coined from ALLO- + PURINE.]

All-Ordinaries Index, All-Ords *informal n.* an index of the daily change in share prices on the Australian Stock Market, based on the average price change in the shares of a selection of top Australian companies

all-or-none *adj. US* functioning or taking effect either completely or not at all

all-or-nothing *adj.* **1.** INVOLVING COMPLETE SUCCESS OR FAILURE bound to result either in complete success or total failure, with no possibility of anything in between **2.** UNCOMPROMISING totally and uncompromisingly dedicated to the achievement of sth, or unwilling to accept anything less than all ○ *an all-or-nothing approach to negotiating*

allosaurus /állə sawrəss/ *n.* a very large carnivorous theropod dinosaur of the late Upper Jurassic period, fossil remains of which have been found in North America. Genus: *Allosaurus.* [Late 19thC. From modern Latin *Allosaurus*, genus name, from Greek *allos* 'other'+ *saurus* 'lizard'.]

allosteric /állō steérik/ *adj.* used to describe changes in the activity of proteins, especially enzymes, resulting from their combining with other substances at sites other than those where they are usually biochemically active —**allosterically** *adv.* —**allostery** /ə lóstəri/ *n.*

allot /ə lót/ (**-lots, -lotting, -lotted**) *vt.* **1.** GIVE AS SHARE to give sth to a sb as his or her share of what is available or what has to be done ○ *I was allotted the task of sweeping up.* **2.** EARMARK to earmark or reserve sth for a particular purpose ○ *alloting ten shelves to books* [15thC. From Old French *aloter*, from *lot* 'portion', of Germanic origin.] —**allotter** *n.*

allotment /ə lótmənt/ *n.* **1.** PLOT OF LAND a small plot of publicly owned land rented to a person for growing vegetables or flowers **2.** ALLOTTING OF STH the assignment or earmarking of sth ○ *the allotment of shares* **3.** STH ALLOTTED a thing, amount, or share allotted to sb or sth

allotransplant *vt.* /állō transs plaánt, -traanss-/ (**-plants, -planting, -planted**) TRANSPLANT BETWEEN GENETICALLY DIFFERENT INDIVIDUALS to transplant an organ or body tissue from one member of a species to a genetically different member of the same species ■ *n.* /állō tránss plaant, -traánss-/ STH TRANSPLANTED an organ or piece of body tissue transplanted from one member of a species to a genetically different member of the same species

allotrope /állə trōp/ *n.* one of several different forms in which a chemical element occurs, each of which differs in its physical properties but not in the kind of atoms in its composition. Diamonds and coal are allotropes of carbon. [Late 19thC. Formed from ALLO- + -TROPE.] —**allotropic** /állə tróppik/ *adj.* —**allotropically** /-tróppikli/ *adv.*

allotropism *n.* = **allotropy**

allotropous /ə lóttrəpəss/ *adj.* used to describe flowers in which the nectar is accessible to all species of insect

allotropy /ə lóttrəpi/, **allotropism** /ə lóttrəpizzəm/ *n.* the existence in more than one form (**allotrope**) of the same chemical element, each form differing in physical properties but having the same chemical properties

a at; aa father; aw all; ay day; air hair; ə about, edible, item, common, circus; e egg; ee eel; hw when; i it, happy; ī ice; 'l apple; 'm rhythm; 'n fashion; o odd; ō open; oŏ good; oo pool; ow owl; oy oil; th thin; th this; u up; ur urge;

all'ottava /állə taávə/ *adv.* to be played an octave higher or lower than written (*used as a musical direction*) [Early 19thC. From Italian, literally 'on the octave'.] —**all'ottava** *adj.*

allottee /ə lot ée/ *n.* sb to whom sth is allotted

all out *adv.* with maximum effort, at full power, or at top speed

all-out *adj.* **1.** GREATEST POSSIBLE involving the maximum possible effort or every available resource ○ *an all-out attempt to break the record* **2.** INVOLVING WHOLE WORKFORCE used to describe a strike involving the whole workforce

all over *adv.* (*informal*) **1.** EVERYWHERE everywhere **2.** STRESSING PARTICULAR ACTIONS OF SB used to stress that a particular description or action is utterly typical of the person or type of person stated ○ *That's Jackie all over: late again!*

all-over *adj.* covering the whole surface area of sth ○ *an all-over tan*

allow /ə lów/ (**-lows, -lowing, -lowed**) *v.* **1.** *vt.* LET SB DO STH to give permission for sth to happen or sb to do sth, or take no action or make no rule to prevent it ○ *I can't allow you to throw this chance away.* **2.** *vt.* LET SB ENTER OR BE PRESENT to let sb or sth enter or be present in a place ○ *Children are not allowed after nine o'clock.* **3.** *vt.* LET SB HAVE STH to let sb or yourself have sth, often a benefit or pleasure of some kind ○ *Allow yourself a few minutes to catch your breath.* **4.** *vt.* CREDIT SB MONEY FOR STH to give or credit sb with an amount of money as a discount or in exchange for sth ○ *How much will you allow on our old machine?* **5.** *vt.* ALLOCATE STH to set aside or make available sth such as a period of time or amount of material for a particular purpose ○ *Allow extra for shrinkage.* **6.** *vi.* MAKE PROVISION FOR STH to take sth into consideration or make provision for it when making a plan or decision ○ *The schedule doesn't allow for any delays.* **7.** *vt.* ADMIT to admit sth or accept it to be true or valid (*dated*) ○ *You must allow that it was rather harsh.* **8.** *vi.* PRESENT AS POSSIBLE to present sth as possible or reasonable (*formal*) ○ *The events allow of only one interpretation.* **9.** *vi. Southern US* SAY OR THINK to state or suppose ○ *He allowed it was time to go.* [14thC. Via Old French *allouer* from Latin *allaudare* 'to praise' and medieval Latin *allocare* 'to assign' (see ALLOCATE).] —**allowable** *adj.* —**allowably** *adv.* —**allowed** *adj.*

allowance /ə lówənss/ *n.* **1.** BUDGETED AMOUNT an amount of sth, especially money, given out at regular intervals or for a specific purpose ○ *a mileage allowance as well as expenses* **2.** *US* = **pocket money 3.** DISCOUNT money deducted from the selling price of sth by the seller as a discount or in exchange for sth **4.** FIN INCOME NOT TAXABLE an amount of a person's income that is exempt from taxation and is deducted from the total to be taxed ○ *the married person's allowance* **5.** EDUC SALARY SUPPLEMENT GIVEN TO TEACHER a salary supplement paid to a teacher for taking on extra duties or responsibilities **6.** TOLERATION the allowing of sth to happen, or the toleration of it **7.** MECH ENG AMOUNT OF VARIATION ALLOWED a small amount of variation permitted in the dimensions of closely fitting machine parts **8.** *US* SPORTS HANDICAP a handicap or advantage in certain sports ■ *vt.* (**-ances, -ancing, -anced**) **1.** *US* GIVE SB ALLOWANCE to restrict sb to a fixed regular amount of sth ○ *Members of the sales staff are allowanced for monthly expenses.* **2.** HAND STH OUT to supply sth, especially an amount of money, in limited amounts (*archaic*) ◇ **make allowance** *or* **allowances (for sb** *or* **sth) 1.** to take a charitable view of sb or sth and take mitigating circumstances into account **2.** to take sth into consideration when making a plan, decision, or judgment

allowedly /ə lówidli/ *adv.* admittedly or by general agreement ○ *Allowedly, the salary is modest.*

alloy *n.* /álloy/ **1.** METALL MIXTURE OF METALS a substance that is a mixture of two or more metals, or of a metal with a nonmetallic material **2.** DEBASING ADDITION sth that detracts from the value or quality of the thing it is added to or mixed with ○ *The film is weakened by the alloy of sentimentality.* **3.** BLEND any mixture, amalgam, or compound of different materials ■ *vt.* /ə lóy/ (**-loys, -loying, -loyed**) **1.** METALL MIX METALS to mix one metal with another, or mix a metal with a nonmetallic material **2.** DEBASE STH to detract from the quality, purity, or value of sth by being added to it or by adding an inferior material to it ○ *principles alloyed with cynicism* **3.** COMBINE STH to mix or combine different things [Mid-17thC. Via Old French dialect *allai* (noun) and *allayer* (verb) from, ultimately, Latin *alligare* 'to bind to' (see LIGATURE).]

WORD KEY: SYNONYMS

See Synonyms at ***mixture***.

all-points bulletin *n. US* a message broadcast to all police in a particular area, usually containing urgent information or a warning

all-purpose *adj.* suitable for a wide variety of uses

all right *adj.* **1.** SATISFACTORY generally good, satisfactory, or pleasing (*hyphenated when used before a noun*) ○ *Everything's going to be all right.* **2.** JUST ADEQUATE just about acceptable or adequate, but not very good ○ *The new job's all right, I guess.* **3.** UNINJURED not injured or unwell **4.** IN GOOD CONDITION in good condition or order, and not defective or damaged ■ *interj.* **1.** YES used to express agreement or approval ○ *'Will you come along?' 'All right'.* **2.** GREETING used as a greeting and friendly inquiry, meaning hello and how are you (*informal*) ■ *adv.* **1.** SATISFACTORILY in a generally good, satisfactory, or pleasing way ○ *My old drill still works all right.* **2.** CERTAINLY without any doubt ○ *He's his father's son all right.* ◇ **it's all right for some** some people are more privileged or have more advantages than others

WORD KEY: USAGE

Is it **all right** to use **alright**? No, only ***all right*** is correct. Some people think this one-word spelling is justified by the analogy of **already** and **altogether**, and that it is sometimes useful to be able to distinguish between ***all right*** and ***alright*** (just like **altogether** and **all together**): *The answers were alright (= satisfactory). The answers were all right (= all correct).* But ***alright*** has never been accepted as good usage.

all-round *adj.* **1.** WITH MANY ABILITIES able to do many things well, or useful in a number of different ways, not specialized ○ *the best all-round player for both attack and defence* **2.** ALL-INCLUSIVE broad or comprehensive in scope ○ *for all-round news coverage* **3.** IN ALL DIRECTIONS in all directions

all-rounder *n.* sb who is good at many different things, especially in sport

All Saints' Day, **All Saints** *n.* 1 November, the day in the Christian calendar set aside to celebrate the lives of saints

all-seater *adj.* providing seats for all spectators and no standing room ○ *an all-seater stadium*

all-singing-all-dancing *adj.* extraordinarily versatile or impressive (*informal humorous*)

All Souls' Day, **All Souls** *n.* 2 November, the day in the Roman Catholic Church calendar set aside for prayer for the souls of those who have died and are believed to be in purgatory

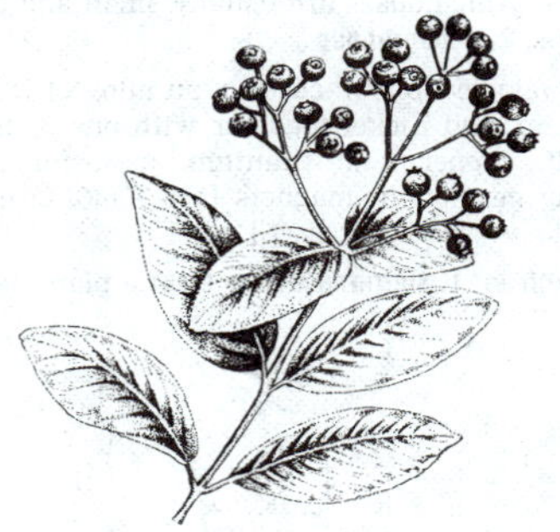

Allspice

allspice /áwl spīss/ *n.* **1.** (*plural* **-spices** *or* **-spice**) TREES TROPICAL TREE WITH AROMATIC BERRIES an evergreen tree from tropical America that is related to myrtle and has clusters of white flowers and aromatic berries. Latin name: *Pimenta dioica.* **2.** COOK SPICE the ground dried berries of the allspice tree, used as a spice [From the fact that it is thought to combine the flavours of cinnamon, cloves, and nutmeg]

all-star *adj.* MADE UP OF STAR PERFORMERS made up mainly or completely of very famous and talented performers or players ■ *n. US* MEMBER OF ALL-STAR TEAM a member of an all-star team

all-suite *adj.* used to describe a hotel room that has a sitting-room and kitchenette as well as the standard features of hotel accommodation

all-terrain bike *n.* a bicycle or motorcycle designed for use in open country as well as on roads

all-terrain vehicle *n.* a motor vehicle designed for use on rough, sandy, or marshy ground, as well as on roads. It usually has only one seat.

all-ticket *adj.* to which people are only admitted if they have a ticket bought in advance

all-time *adj.* having never yet been bettered, or the best, greatest, or most popular ever ○ *an all-time record for this distance*

all told *adv.* when everything or everyone is counted, included, or taken into account ○ *A dozen people made it, all told.* [TOLD in the early sense 'counted']

allude /ə lóod/ (**-ludes, -luding, -luded**) *vi.* to mention sth or sb, usually briefly, without giving a precise name or explicit identification but usually making clear by other means who or what is being referred to ○ *I presume you are alluding to the alleged financial discrepancy.* [Mid-16thC. From Latin *alludere*, literally 'to play to', formed from *ludere* 'to play' (see LUDICROUS).]

WORD KEY: USAGE

She alluded to her husband by name. This is a self-contradiction, because ***allude*** means 'to refer indirectly'. When the reference is direct, the word to use is **refer**. So if she mentioned 'the man at home looking after the children', she was ***alluding*** to her husband, whereas if she mentioned 'George' or 'my husband' directly, she was **referring** to him.

allure /ə lyóor, ə lóor/ *n.* HIGHLY ATTRACTIVE QUALITY an attractive or tempting quality possessed by sb or sth, often a glamorous and sometimes rather dangerous one ○ *They couldn't resist the allure of the big city.* ■ *vti.* (**-lures, -luring, -lured**) ATTRACT POWERFULLY to exert a very powerful and often dangerous attraction on sb [15thC. From Anglo-Norman *alurer*, Old French *aloirrier*, *aleurier*, literally 'to bring to the bait', from *leure* 'bait' (see LURE). Originally a term of falconry.] —**allurement** *n.*

alluring /ə lyóoring, ə lóoring/ *adj.* extremely attractive, tempting, or glamorous, and able to arouse strong desire in people —**alluringly** *adv.*

allusion /ə lóozh'n/ *n.* **1.** INDIRECT REFERENCE a reference that is made indirectly, subtly suggested, or implied ○ *a poem typical of its period in its use of classical allusions* **2.** ACT OF ALLUDING the act of making an indirect reference to sb or sth [Early 17thC. Directly or via French, from the late Latin stem *allusion-*, from Latin *allus-*, the past participle stem of *alludere* (see ALLUDE).]

WORD KEY: USAGE

allusion, delusion, or **illusion**? ***Allusion*** and ***illusion*** are the closest in sound but the furthest apart in meaning: an ***allusion*** is a process of alluding, that is an indirect reference to a person, thing, or event (*The story contained an allusion to his childhood in Africa*), whereas an ***illusion*** is a false or misleading impression or perception, either by the senses or by the mind: *The shimmering effect on a hot road is an optical illusion. By shutting himself in his room for hours he kept up an illusion of studying hard.* ***Illusion*** and ***delusion*** are similar in meaning, but ***delusion*** denotes sth sb falsely believes, often harmfully, rather than a wrong impression that sb receives: *Visitors often suffer under the delusion that the weather is always hot here.*

allusive /ə lóossiv/ *adj.* **1.** MAKING AN ALLUSION that makes or contains an indirect reference to sth or sb **2.** CHARACTERIZED BY ALLUSIONS characterized by the use of indirect references or subtle suggestion —**allusively** *adv.* —**allusiveness** *n.*

alluvia plural of **alluvium**

alluvial /ə lóovi əl/ *adj.* used to describe the environment, action, and sedimentary deposits of rivers or streams

alluvion /ə lo͞ovi ən/ *n.* **1.** MOVEMENT OF SEA AGAINST SHORE the flow or wash of the sea or other body of water against a shore **2.** FORMATION OF LAND the expansion of a land area through the build-up of alluvial deposits or the receding of a body of water [Mid-16thC. Via French, from the Latin stem *alluvion-*, from *alluvius* (see ALLUVIUM).]

alluvium /ə lo͞ovi əm/ *(plural -ums or -a /-vi ə/) n.* sediment deposited by running water, especially the type of soil formed in river valleys and deltas from material washed down by the river [Mid-17thC. From Latin, a form of *alluvius* 'washed against', from, ultimately, *lavere* 'to wash' (see LAVATORY).]

all-weather *adj.* usable in or able to stand up to all types of weather

ally /ə lɪ́, álli/ *v.* (**-lies, -lying, -lied**) **1.** *vti.* JOIN IN MUTUALLY SUPPORTIVE ASSOCIATION to join, or enlist sb, in an association with one or more other states, organizations, or individuals for mutual help and support or the achievement of a common purpose **2.** *vt.* AFFILIATE STH to connect sth with sth else through similarity or common features (*usually passive*) ○ *These plants are allied to lilies.* **3.** *vti.* CONNECT THROUGH MARRIAGE to connect individuals or families, or to form a connection with another individual or family, through marriage or a similar tie ■ *n.* (*plural* **-lies**) **1.** MEMBER OF ALLIANCE a person, group, or state that is joined in an association with another or others for mutual help and support or the achievement of a common purpose **2.** BIOL RELATED ORGANISM an organism that is closely related to another [14thC. Via Old French *al(e)ier* from Latin *alligare*, literally 'to bind to', from *ligare* 'to bind' (see LIGATE).]

allyl /álli, állɪ́/ *adj.* used to describe a chemical compound containing a chemical group consisting of three carbon and five hydrogen atoms. Formula: $C_3H_5–$. [Mid-19thC. Coined from Latin *allium* 'garlic' (because it was first obtained from garlic) + -YL.]

allyl alcohol *n.* a colourless, strong-smelling liquid that is used in the preparation of chemical products such as resins and plasticizers

Almagest /álmə jest/ *n.* **1.** ASTRONOMY TEXT a text on astronomy written by Ptolemy in the second century AD setting out his view of the universe with the Earth at its centre surrounded by spheres **2.** **Almagest, almagest** MEDIEVAL TREATISE ON ASTRONOMY an important medieval treatise on a subject, especially on astronomy, astrology, or alchemy [14thC. Via Old French from, ultimately, Arabic *al-mijistī*, literally 'the greatest', from Greek *megistē* 'greatest', superlative of *megas* 'great' (see MEGA-).]

alma mater /álmə máatər, -máytər/, **Alma Mater** *n.* the school, college, or university that sb formerly attended [From Latin, literally 'bounteous mother', a title given by the Romans to several goddesses associated with abundance]

almanac /áwlmə nak, álmə-/ *n.* **1.** CALENDAR an annual publication that includes a calendar for the year as well as astronomical information and details of anniversaries and events **2.** BOOK OF DATA an annually published book of information relating to a particular subject or activity ○ *a sports almanac* [14thC. From medieval Latin *almanac(h)*, of uncertain origin: perhaps from assumed Spanish Arabic *al-manākh*, literally 'the almanac'.]

almandine /álməndin, -dɪ́n/ *n.* a deep red garnet consisting of iron aluminium silicate, used as a gemstone. Formula: $Fe_3Al_2Si_3O_{12}$. [15thC. Via French, alteration of *alabandine*, from Latin *alabandina (gemma)* '(gem) of Alabanda', from *Alabanda*, city in Asia Minor where the gem was originally cut and polished.]

Alma-Tadema /álmə táddimə/, **Sir Lawrence** (1836–1912) Dutch-born British painter who specialized in scenes from classical antiquity, e.g. *Tarquinius Superbus* (1876).

Almaty /al máati/ city and former capital of Kazakhstan, in the southeastern part of the country, east of Bishkek in Kyrgyzstan. Population: 1,180,000 (1993). Former name **Alma-Ata**.

almighty /awl mɪ́ti/ *adj.* **1.** ALL-POWERFUL having supreme unquestionable power over everything ○ *the almighty dollar* **2.** EXTREME extreme or excessive of its kind (*informal*) ○ *an almighty falling-out* ■ *adv.* EXTREMELY to an extreme or excessive degree (*informal*) ○ *almighty rude* [Old English *ælmeahtig*, from *æl* 'completely' (see ALL) + *meahtig* 'mighty' (see MIGHTY)] — **almightiness** *n.*

Almighty *n.* God ○ *pray to the Almighty*

almirah /ál mɪ́rə/ *n.* S Asia a wardrobe, or chest of drawers

Almodóvar /álmə dóvər/, **Pedro** (b. 1951) Spanish film director who directed comedies such as *Women on the Verge of a Nervous Breakdown* (1988).

Almond

almond /áamənd, áalmənd/ *n.* **1.** NUT an edible, oval-shaped, brown-skinned nut that is widely used in cooking, particularly to flavour desserts, cakes, and biscuits **2.** SMALL TREE PRODUCING ALMONDS a small tree native to west Asia but widely cultivated, with pink flowers and green fruits containing a hard stone, the kernel of which is edible. Latin name: *Prunus dulcis*. **3.** ALMOND-SHAPED OBJECT sth oval and pointed in shape like an almond ■ *adj.* SHAPED LIKE AN ALMOND oval and pointed in shape like an almond [14thC. Via Old French *alemande*, *a(l)mande* from, ultimately, Greek *amugdalē*, of unknown origin.]

almoner /áamənər/ *n.* **1.** HOSPITAL SOCIAL WORKER in the past, sb attached to a hospital as a social worker for its patients **2.** GIVER OF MONEY AS CHARITY in former times, sb who distributed alms to the needy, especially on behalf of a church, monastery, or wealthy family [15thC. Alteration of obsolete *aumener*, which came via Old French *aumoner* from assumed late Latin *almosinarius*, from ecclesiastical Latin *eleemosynarius* 'connected with alms', from *eleemosyna* (see ALMS).]

almost /áwlmōst, awl mṓst/ *adv.* not exactly, not yet, or not in fact, but very close to being or happening as described ○ *I almost wrecked the car.*

alms /áamz/ *npl.* in former times, money or other assistance given to the poor as charity [Pre-12thC. Via assumed Vulgar Latin *alimosina* from ecclesiastical Latin *eleemosyna*, from Greek *eleēmosynē* 'compassionateness', from, ultimately, *eleos* 'compassion, mercy'.]

almshouse /áamz hows/ *(plural **-houses** /áamz howziz/) n.* **1.** HOME FOR POOR PEOPLE a house built and maintained by private charitable funds and intended as accommodation for a poor family or an old person or couple. Almshouses are usually small and built in groups. **2.** = **poorhouse**

alnico /álnikō/ *(plural **-coes**) n.* an alloy of iron, aluminium, and nickel together with one or more of cobalt, copper, and titanium, used for making strong permanent magnets [Mid-20thC. Coined from ALUMINIUM + NICKEL + COBALT.]

aloe /állō/ *n.* **1.** SOUTHERN AFRICAN PLANT a plant native to

Aloe

southern Africa that has fleshy toothed leaves and red or yellow flowers. Genus: *Aloe*. **2.** = **aloe vera** [14thC. Via Latin, from Greek *aloē*, probably of Asian origin. As ALOES pre-12thC.]

aloes /állōz/ *n.* (takes a singular verb) **1.** LAXATIVE MADE FROM ALOE a bitter-tasting laxative drug made from the leaves of some species of aloe **2.** **aloes, aloes wood** = **eaglewood**

aloe vera /-véerə/ *n.* **1.** MEDITERRANEAN PLANT a Mediterranean species of aloe. Latin name: *Aloe barbadensis*. **2.** SOOTHING PLANT EXTRACT an extract from the leaves of the aloe vera plant, used in drugs and cosmetics for its emollient and soothing qualities [From modern Latin, literally 'true aloe']

aloft /ə lóft/ *adv.* **1.** HIGH UP upwards, high up, or in a higher position **2.** IN OR INTO SHIP'S RIGGING in or into the rigging of a sailing ship [13thC. From Old Norse *á lopt(i)*, literally 'in the air', from *lopt* 'air, sky' (see LOFT).]

alogical /ay lójjik'l/ *adj.* that cannot be dealt with by, or has nothing to do with, logic [Late 17thC. Formed from A- 'not' + LOGICAL.] — **alogically** *adv.* — **alogicalness** *n.*

aloha /ə lṓ ə, aa lṓ haa/ *interj.* Hawaii used as a greeting or farewell [Early 19thC. From Hawaiian, literally 'love, affection'.]

aloha shirt *n.* US = **Hawaiian shirt**

aloin /állō in/ *n.* a bitter-tasting yellow crystalline derivative of aloe used in making laxative drugs [Mid-19thC. Coined from ALOE + -INE.]

alone /ə lṓn/ CORE MEANING: a grammatical word meaning without any other person or thing nearby ○ (adj) *I like to be alone sometimes.* ○ (adv) *wandering alone in the wilderness*
1. *adv.* WITHOUT HELP FROM OTHERS without help or support from anybody or anything else ○ *I can't do this job alone.* **2.** *adj.* UNIQUE IN SOME RESPECT used to describe the only one of a group to do, achieve, or think sth ○ *Am I alone in thinking this?* **3.** *adj.* DONE WITHOUT OTHERS carried out by sb or assigned to sb without the assistance or company of others **4.** *adv.*, *adj.* WITHOUT COMPANY without any other person or thing nearby or in attendance, for company, or to give assistance ○ *She left with the others but returned alone.* [13thC. From the phrase *all one* 'completely by oneself'.] — **aloneness** *n.*

along /ə lóng/ CORE MEANING: a preposition indicating that sth is situated or moves over all or part of the length of sth ○ *came racing along the path*
1. *prep.* PARALLEL WITH following a course or line parallel with or beside ○ *freighters sailing along the coastline* **2.** *prep.* SIMILAR TO in accordance with or similar to **3.** *adv.* FORWARDS forwards, onwards, or in a particular direction ○ *Move along there!* **4.** *adv.* WITH SB with you, with sb, or with the rest of the group when going somewhere ○ *I asked if I could come along.* ○ *Next time you come, bring your guitar along.* **5.** *adv.* AT OR TO A PLACE arriving at or coming or going to a particular place ○ *There'll be a bus along in a minute.* [14thC. From Old English *andlang*, literally 'against the long', from *lang* 'long'.] ◇ **along with** together with, or as well as

alongshore /ə lóng sháwr/ *adv.* BESIDE A SHORE near to, beside, or along a shore ○ *The water was too shallow to bring the ship alongshore.* ■ *adj.* BEING NEAR SHORE located on or near a shore or moving along a shore

alongside /ə lóng sɪ́d, ə lóng sɪ́d/ *prep.* **alongside, alongside of** BY THE SIDE OF close up against, near, or parallel to the side of ○ *pulled the boat alongside the pier* ■ *adv.* BY THE SIDE in or into a position along or by the side of sth

aloof /ə lo͞of/ *adj.* **1.** REMOTE IN MANNER uninvolved or unwilling to become involved with other people or events, often out of a sense of lofty superiority to them **2.** PHYSICALLY REMOTE physically distant or apart from sb or sth [Mid-16thC. Origin uncertain: probably from earlier *a luff* 'in a windward direction', hence 'away from the shore', modelled on Dutch *te loef*, the underlying idea being 'steering clear of sth'.] — **aloofly** *adv.* — **aloofness** *n.*

alopecia /állə peeshi ə, -peeshə/ *n.* loss or the absence of hair, especially from the human head [14thC. Via Latin, from Greek *alōpekia*, literally 'fox mange' (thought by the Greeks to resemble human baldness), from the stem *alōpek-* 'fox'.] —**alopecic** /álla peéshik/ *adj.*

aloud /ə lówd/ *adv.* **1.** AUDIBLY using an audible speaking voice ○ *reading aloud* **2.** LOUDLY in a loud voice ○ *cried aloud for mercy*

alp /alp/ *n.* **1.** HIGH MOUNTAIN a high mountain. ◊ **Alps 2.** SWISS MOUNTAIN PASTURE a high mountain pasture in Switzerland [15thC. Via French *Alpes* 'Alps' from Latin, from Greek *Alpeis.*]

ALP *n., abbr.* Australian Labor Party

Alpaca

alpaca /al pákə/ *n.* **1.** (plural **-as** or **-a**) S AMERICAN MAMMAL a domesticated, long-haired South American mammal of the camel family, related to the llama and similar in appearance. Latin name: *Lama pacos*. **2.** WOOL FROM ALPACA wool or cloth made from the long shaggy hair of the alpaca **3.** GLOSSY CLOTH a thin glossy fabric made from cotton, wool, or rayon to simulate cloth made from the wool of the alpaca [Late 18thC. Via Spanish, from Aymara *alpako*, from *pako* 'reddish-brown', from the colour of its hair.]

alpenglow /álpən glō/ *n.* a reddish glow on snow-covered mountain peaks at sunset or sunrise, caused by reflected weak sunlight. ◊ **afterglow** [Late 19thC. Partial translation of German *Alpenglühen*, literally 'glowing of the Alps'.]

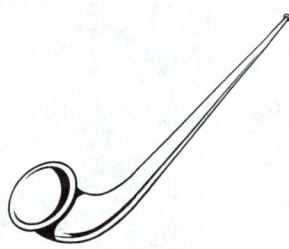
Alpenhorn

alpenhorn /álpən hawrn/, **alphorn** /álp-/ *n.* a traditional wooden wind instrument with a very long tube curving up at the end, originally blown by herders in the Swiss Alps to call cattle [Late 19thC. From German, literally 'horn of the Alps'.]

alpenstock /álpən stok/ *n.* a long staff with an iron spike at one end, used by mountain climbers until largely superseded by the ice axe [Early 19thC. From German, literally 'staff of the Alps'.]

alpestrine /al péstrin/ *adj.* used to describe a plant that grows at high altitudes [Late 19thC. Formed from Latin *alpestris* 'alpine', from *Alpes* (see ALP).]

alpha /álfə/, **alfa** *n.* **1.** 1ST LETTER OF GREEK ALPHABET the first letter of the Greek alphabet (A, α), represented in the English alphabet as 'a'. See table at **alphabet 2.** RADIO CODE WORD FOR LETTER 'A' the NATO phonetic alphabet code word for the letter 'A', used in international radio communications **3.** alpha, Alpha ASTRON BRIGHTEST STAR the brightest or main star in a constellation (*followed by the Latin genitive*) ○ *Alpha Centauri* **4.** EDUC HIGHEST MARK the highest mark in a system that uses Greek letters to grade examinations or pieces of academic work ■ *adj.* **1.** MOST IMPORTANT first or most important ○ *the alpha male in a group of chimpanzees* **2.** CHEM RELATING TO THE NEAREST ATOM used to describe the atom nearest to a

designated atom or group of atoms in an organic molecule **3.** CHEM RELATING TO THE MAJOR FORM OF ELEMENT used to describe the major form of a chemical element with more than one physical form (**allotrope**) [13thC. Via Latin, from Greek, from Hebrew or Phoenician *āleph* 'ox, leader', name of the first letter of the Phoenician and Hebrew alphabets, originally shaped to resemble an ox's head.]

alpha and omega *n.* **1.** BEGINNING AND END the beginning and end of sth **2.** MOST IMPORTANT PART the most important aspect of sth [From their being the first and last letters of the Greek alphabet]

alphabet /álfə bet/ *n.* **1.** LETTERS USED TO REPRESENT LANGUAGE a set of letters, usually listed in a fixed order, used in writing a language and representing its basic speech sounds ○ *the Cyrillic alphabet* **2.** SYMBOLS FOR COMMUNICATING a set of symbols representng units used in communication, especially speech sounds or words ○ *the alphabet in Braille* **3.** BASIC PRINCIPLES the basic principles of sth (*formal*) **4.** *Malaysia, Singapore* LETTER OF ALPHABET an individual letter of an alphabet [Early 16thC. Via late Latin *alphabetum* from Greek *alphabētos*, from Greek *alpha* and *bēta*, the first and second letters of the alphabet, taken as a name for the whole alphabet).]

alphabetical /álfə béttik'l/, **alphabetic** /álfə béttik/ *adj.* **1.** IN ORDER OF ALPHABET LETTERS arranged or listed in the customary order of the letters of the alphabet **2.** RELATING TO AN ALPHABET based on, typical of, or relating to an alphabet —**alphabetically** *adv.*

alphabetize /álfə bet īz/ (**-izes, -izing, -ized**), **alphabetise** (**-tises, -tising, -tised**) *vt.* **1.** PUT IN ALPHABETICAL ORDER to arrange words or items in alphabetical order **2.** PROVIDE WITH ALPHABET to provide a language with, or express sth in the form of, an alphabet —**alphabetization** /álfə bet ī záysh'n/ *n.* —**alphabetizer** /álfə bet īzər/ *n.*

alphabet soup *n.* **1.** SOUP CONTAINING PASTA LETTER SHAPES soup containing small pieces of pasta in the form of letters of the alphabet **2.** JUMBLE OF LETTERS a confusing mass of letters, especially a list of obscure abbreviations

alpha-blocker *n.* a drug used to treat high blood pressure and some other conditions, such as an enlarged prostate. The nervous stimulation that constricts blood vessels, and hence increases blood pressure, is blocked by such drugs.

alpha decay *n.* a radioactive decay process in which an alpha particle is emitted from a nucleus

alpha-foetoprotein *n.* a protein in the liver of a human foetus, the presence of which in abnormally high or low quantities in the amniotic fluid may indicate spina bifida or Down's syndrome

alpha-hydroxy acid *n.* an organic acid in which a hydroxyl acid is bonded to a carbon atom. Compounds of this type are frequently used as ingredients in skin care products.

alphanumeric /álfənyoo mérrik/, **alphanumerical** /álfənyoo mérrik'l/, **alphameric** /álfə mérrik/ *adj.* consisting of both letters and numbers or using both as symbols ○ *an alphanumeric code* [Mid-20thC. Blend of ALPHABET and NUMERIC.] —**alphanumerically** *adv.*

alpha particle *n.* a particle consisting of two neutrons and two protons that is identical to the helium nucleus and is emitted during certain radioactive transformations

alpha ray *n.* a stream of alpha particles

alpha-receptor *n.* a protein molecule in the membrane of a cell that specifically binds adrenaline, noradrenaline, or related substances and triggers a response, e.g. a nerve impulse, in the cell

alpha rhythm *n.* the pattern of electrical activity in the brain of sb awake but relaxed or drowsy, registering on an electroencephalograph at a reading between 8 and 13 hertz

alpha stock *n.* any of the 100–200 most profitable securities on the Stock Exchange

alpha test *n.* a first test on a new or upgraded piece of software or hardware, carried out by the manufacturer under laboratory conditions [From the idea of being 'first in a series', hence 'preliminary'] —**alpha-test** *vt.*

Alphege /álfij/, St, Archbishop of Canterbury (954–1012) English martyr. Captured by the Danes (1011), he was murdered for refusing to save himself at the expense of his tenants.

alphorn *n.* = alpenhorn

alpine /álp īn/ *adj.* **1.** TYPICAL OF HIGH MOUNTAINS relating to, typical of, or found in high mountains ○ *an alpine climate* **2.** BOT SITUATED OR GROWING ABOVE TREE LINE used to describe the zone of vegetation on high mountains between the tree line and snow line and any plant that grows in or originates from that zone **3.** USED IN MOUNTAINEERING used in or involving mountain climbing ■ *n.* MOUNTAIN PLANT a plant that originates from or can grow in the alpine zone on mountains, above the tree line [From Latin *alpinus*, from *Alpes* (see ALP)]

Alpine *adj.* **1.** GEOG OF THE ALPS relating to the Alps and those who live in them **2.** Alpine, alpine SKIING RELATING TO DOWNHILL SKIING used to describe competitive skiing on steep downhill courses, especially downhill and slalom events

alpine-style *adj.* used to describe a type of mountaineering in which the climbers carry all the necessary equipment with them on a single ascent to a mountain summit —**alpine-style** *adv.*

alpinist /álpinist/ *n.* a mountain climber, especially one who climbs in the Alps or mountains of similar height [Late 19thC. From French *alpiniste*, from Latin *alpinus* (see ALPINE).] —**alpinism** *n.*

Alps

Alps /alps/ mountain range in southern Europe, extending about 800 km/500 mi. from southeastern France to Austria. The highest peak is Mont Blanc. Height: 4,807 m/15,771 ft.

al-Quds /al kǒodz/ *n.* the Islamic name for Jerusalem, the third most important of the sacred sites of Islam

already /awl réddi, áwl redi/ CORE MEANING: an adverb indicating that sth has happened before now, or happened in the past before a particular time, or will have happened by or before a particular time in the future ○ *I already know what you're going to say.* ○ *She had already left when I arrived.*
adv. **1.** UNEXPECTEDLY EARLY by or at an earlier time than expected ○ *Have you finished already?* **2.** *US* USED TO GIVE EMPHASIS used after a command, exclamation, or other statement to give it emphasis or express exasperation (*informal*) ○ *Enough already!* [14thC. From the phrase *all ready* 'completely ready'; the meaning evolved via 'ready for sth' to 'beforehand'.]

alright /awl rīt, áwl rīt/ *adv.* SATISFACTORY generally good, satisfactory, or pleasing (*informal*) ■ *adj.* PLEASANT generally good, satisfactory, or pleasant (*informal*)

— WORD KEY: USAGE —
See Usage note at **allright**.

ALS *abbr.* amyotrophic lateral sclerosis

a.l.s. *abbr.* autograph letter, signed

Alsace /al sáss/ region and former province of France, situated west of the River Rhine. Capital: Strasbourg. Population: 1,642,000 (1990). Area: 8,280 sq. km/3,197 sq. mi.

Alsace-Lorraine /-lə ráyn/ area of France on the German border, now divided into two administrative regions, Alsace and Lorraine. The area was disputed by France and Germany between 1871 and 1945. Population: 3,930,100 (1990). Area: 31,827 sq. km/12,288 sq. mi.

MAJOR ALPHABETS OF THE WORLD

Phoenician 20 letters, no cases		Early Greek 21 letters, no cases		Hebrew 23 letters, no cases		Classical Roman 24 letters, capitals only	Modern Greek 24 letters[1]		Cyrillic 31 letters[2]		Modern Arabic 28 letters[3]	
Sound	Name	Sound	Name	Sound	Name		Sound	Name	Sound	Name	Sound	Name
ΚΚ	['] 'aleph	Ɐ	[a] alpha	א	['] 'aleph/alef	A	Αα	[a] alpha	Аа	[a]	ا	['] 'alif
99	[b] bēth	ꝺꝺ	[b] beta	ב	[b,bh] bēth	B	Ββ	[b] beta	Бб	[b]	ب ث ت	[b] bā
٦	[g] gaml, gimel	٦	[g] gamma	ג	[g,gh] gimel	C	Γγ	[g,n] gamma	Вв	[v]	ت ث ت	[t] tā
△△	[d] dag, dāleth	△	[d] delta	ד	[d,dh] dāleth	D	Δδ	[d] delta	Гг	[g]	ث ث ث	[t] thā
𐤄	[ḥ] hē	ꓱ	[ē] e (psilon)	ה	[h] hē	E	Εε	[e] epsilon	Дд	[d]	ج ج ج	[j] jīm
Υ	[w] wāw	ꓱ	[w] wau, digamma	ו	[w] wāw/vāv	F	Ζζ	[z] zēta	ЕеЁё	[e,ë][5]	ح ح ح	[ḥ] ḥā
Ι	[z] zayin	Ι	[z] zēta	ז	[z] zayin	G	Ηη	[ē] ēta	Жж	[zh]	خ خ خ	[kh] khā
𐤇	[ḥ] ḥēth	𐤇	[h,ē] ēta	ח	[ḥ] ḥeth	H	Θθ	[th] thēta	Зз	[z]	د د	[d] dāl
𐤆	[y] yōdh	𐤆	[i,y] iōta	ט	[t] ṭeth	I	Ιι	[i] iota	ИиЙй	[i][6]	ذ ذ	[dh] dhāl
↓↓	[k] kaph	Ɣ	[k] kappa	י	[y] yod/yodh	K	Κκ	[k] kappa	Кк	[k]	ر	[r] rā
CL	[l] lāmedh	Γ	[l] lambda	ךכ	[k,kh] kāph	L	Λλ	[l] lambda	Лл	[l]	ز	[z] zāy
ꟽ	[m] mēm	ꟽ	[m] mu	ל	[l] lāmedh	M	Μμ	[m] mu	Мм	[m]	س	[s] sīn
ꟿ	[n] naḥš, nūn	ꟿ	[n] nu	םמ	[m] mēm	N	Νν	[n] nu	Нн	[n]	ش	[sh] shīn
𐤎	[s] samekh	Ι	[ks] xi	ןנ	[n] nūn	O	Ξξ	[x] xi	Оо	[o]	ص	[s] ṣād
O	['] 'ayin	O	[ŏ] o (micron)	ס	[s] samekh	P	Οο	[o] omicron	Пп	[p]	ض	[d] ḍād
𐤏	[p] pē	Γ	[p] pi	ע	['] 'ayin	Q	Ππ	[p] pi	Рр	[r]	ط	[ṭ] ṭā
Φ	[q] qōph	Φ	[q] koppa	ףפ	[p,ph] pē	R	Ρρ	[r,rh] rhō	Сс	[s]	ظ	[z] ẓā
94	[r] rōsh, rēsh	Ρ	[r] rhō	ץצ	[s] sadhe/sade	S	Σσς	[s] sigma[4]	Тт	[t]	ع	['] 'ayn
W	[th,š] thann, shin	ꠦꠦ	[s] sigma	ק	[q] qōph	T	Ττ	[t] tau	Уу	[u]	غ	[ğ] ghayn
+Χ	[t] tāw	Τ	[t] tau	ר	[r] rēsh	V	Υυ	[y,u] upsilon	Фф	[f]	ف	[f] fā
		Υ	[ū,w] u (psilon)	שׂ	[ś] sin	X	Φφ	[ph] phi	Хх	[kh]	ق	[q] qāf
				שׁ	[šh] shin	Y	Χχ	[kh] chi/khi	Цц	[ts]	ك	[k] kāf
				ת	[t,th] tāv/tāw	Z	Ψψ	[ps] psi	Чч	[ch]	ل	[l] lām
							Ωω	[ō] ōmega	Шш	[sh]		[m] mīm
									Щщ	[shch]		[n] nūn
									Ъъ	["]		[h] hā
									Ыы	[y]		[w] wāw
									Ьь	[']		[y] yā
									Ээ	[e]		
									Юю	[yu]		
									Яя	[ya]		

Notes

1 In the modern Greek alphabet, each letter has an upper-case and lower-case form.
2 In the Cyrillic alphabet, each letter has an upper-case and lower-case form.
3 In the modern Arabic alphabet, each letter has between two and four forms each.
4 The Classical and modern Greek letter *sigma* has two lower-case forms.
5 The Cyrillic letter *e* has two forms, each with upper case and lower case.
6 The Cyrillic letter *i* has two forms, each with upper case and lower case.

Alsatian /al sáysh'n/ n. 1. ZOOL LARGE DOG a large power-ful dog belonging to a short-haired breed with erect ears, a face rather like a wolf's, and a brown and black coat. Alsatians are often used as police or guard dogs. US term **German shepherd 2.** SB FROM ALSACE sb who was born or who lives in Alsace ■ adj. FROM ALSACE from Alsace, or typical of Alsace or its people [Late 19thC. Formed from medieval Latin Alsatia 'Alsace'.]

alsike clover /ál sīk-, álsik-/ n. a European perennial clover with white or pink flowers, widely grown for forage. Latin name: Trifolium hybridum. [Mid-19thC. Named after Alsike, a town near Uppsala in Sweden, where it was first found.]

also /áwlsō/ adv. 1. IN ADDITION used to indicate that sth is true or is the case in addition ○ got his picture in the paper and also won a prize. ◊ too, as well 2. LIKEWISE OR SIMILARLY like or in the same way as sb or sth else ○ Her nephew was also called John. ○ When they withdraw their forces, we shall also withdraw ours. 3. MOREOVER and in addition to that (used to modify a whole sentence or clause) ○ Also, you must complete the task in one hour. [Old English ealswā, allswā. The main modern sense, 'in addition', evolved from 'just so, in exactly this way' via 'similarly'.]

also-ran n. 1. LOSING RUNNER a horse or other entrant in a race that does not finish in any of the winning places 2. LOSING COMPETITOR a losing entrant in any contest 3. SB UNIMPORTANT sb of little or no consequence or significance [Because newspaper racing results formerly listed horses that finished fourth or lower under the heading 'Also Ran']

alstroemeria /álstrə meéri ə/ (plural -as or -a) n. a tuberous South American plant of the amaryllis family, cultivated for its brightly and variously coloured flowers that last for a long time when cut. Genus: Alstroemeria. [Late 18thC. From modern Latin, genus name, named after Klas von Alstroemer (1736–96), Swedish naturalist.]

alt abbr. 1. alteration 2. alternate 3. altitude 4. alto

Alt abbr. Alt key

alt- prefix. = alto- (used before vowels)

Alta abbr. Alberta

Altaic /al táy ik/ n. a family of languages that consists of Turkic, Mongolic, and Tungusic. It is sometimes thought that Altaic languages form part of a wider Ural-Altaic family. [Mid-19thC. Named after the ALTAI MOUNTAINS.] —**Altaic** adj.

Altai Mountains /al tī-/ mountains in central Asia, on the Kazakhstan-Mongolia border, south of Russia and north of China

Altar: Roman Catholic Church altar

altar /áwltər/ n. 1. RAISED CEREMONIAL RELIGIOUS STRUCTURE a raised structure, typically a flat-topped rock or a table of wood or stone, or raised area where sac-rifices are offered or other religious ceremonies performed 2. COMMUNION TABLE the table or other raised structure in a Christian church on which the bread and wine of the Communion are prepared [Pre-12thC. From Latin altare, from altaria 'burnt offerings', from, probably, adolere 'to burn up'.] ◇ **lead sb to the altar** to marry sb (dated informal)

altar cloth n. a cloth covering for the top of a church altar, or sometimes for its top, front, and sides

altarpiece /áwltər peess/ n. a work of art placed above and behind an altar

altar rail n. a rail in front of a church altar separating the chancel from the rest of the church

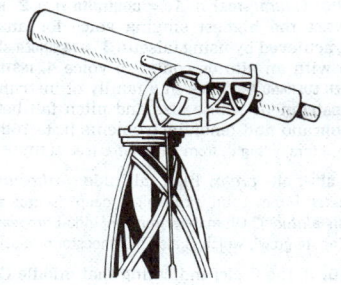

Altazimuth

altazimuth /al tázziməth/ n. 1. TELESCOPE an instrument, incorporating a telescope that can move vertically and horizontally, used to measure the altitude and azimuth of a celestial body 2. SURVEYING INSTRUMENT an instrument similar to a theodolite used in sur-veying to measure horizontal and vertical angles [Mid-19thC. Blend of ALTITUDE and AZIMUTH.]

alter /áwltər/ (-ters, -tering, -tered) v. 1. vti. CHANGE to make changes to sth or sb, or be changed or become different ○ We'll have to alter our plans. 2. vt. ADJUST GARMENT FOR BETTER FIT to make adjustments to a piece of clothing so that it fits better ○ The trousers are fine but the jacket will have to be altered. 3. vt. US, Aus CASTRATE to castrate or spay an animal (informal) [14thC. Via French, from late Latin alterare, from Latin alter 'other', source also of English alternate, altercation, and altruism.] —**alterability** /áwltərə bílliti/ n. —**alterable** /áwltərəb'l/ adj.

—— **WORD KEY: SYNONYMS** ——
See Synonyms at **change**.

alteration /áwltə ráysh'n/ n. 1. CHANGE a change, modi-fication, or adjustment made to sth 2. DIFFERENCE difference in sth resulting from change ○ I don't see any alteration in the patient's condition. 3. PROCESS OF CHANGING the process of changing sth or of being changed ○ undergoing alteration

altercate /áwltər kayt/ (-cates, -cating, -cated) vi. to engage in a heated argument or confrontation [Mid-16thC. From Latin altercat-, the past participle stem of altercari 'to dispute', from alter (see ALTER). The underlying idea is of taking turns speaking with another.]

altercation /áwltər káysh'n/ n. a heated argument, quarrel, or confrontation

alter ego /áwltər eegō/ (plural **alter egos**) n. 1. ALTERNATIVE PERSONALITY a second side to an individual's per-sonality, different from the one that most people know 2. VERY CLOSE FRIEND a very close and trusted friend [From Latin, literally 'other self', used by Cicero, a translation of Greek allos egō, heteros egō]

alternant /awl túrnənt/ adj. alternating (formal)

alternate v. /áwltər nayt/ (-nates, -nating, -nated) 1. vi. FOLLOW IN INTERCHANGING PATTERN to follow each other and take each other's place in a regular pattern of events ○ as night alternates with day 2. vi. FLUCTUATE to shift back and forth, especially regularly or constantly, between one state and another ○ Her mood al-ternates between elation and despair. 3. vt. ARRANGE THINGS IN INTERCHANGING PATTERN to arrange things, or cause things to happen, in a regular pattern in which one thing always follows the other ○ a design alternating black tiles with white 4. vi. BE AN UNDER-STUDY to act as an understudy for another performer ■ adj. /awl túrnət/ 1. ARRANGED IN ALTERNATING PATTERN arranged or happening in a regular pattern in which the one thing alternates with the other ○ alternate spells of sun and showers 2. EVERY OTHER every other or second of a series ○ They babysit for each other on alternate weekends. 3. BOT NOT ALIGNED used to describe flowers, buds, or leaves that are arranged singly and at different levels on either side of the stem of a plant, as opposed to being in pairs or groups ■ n. /awl túrnət/ US 1. SB WHO FILLS IN sb who acts as a substitute for sb else 2. = alternative n. 1 [Early 16thC. From Latin alternat-, the past participle stem of alternare 'to do one thing after another', from

alternus 'one after another', from alter (see ALTER).] —**alternateness** /awl túrnətnəss/ n.

—— **WORD KEY: USAGE** ——
alternate or **alternative**? **alternate** is usually an adjective: The window-cleaner comes every alternate Friday (or on alternate Fridays). **alternative** can be a noun or an adjective: If you want your windows cleaned, there is no alternative. We tried to find an alternative arrangement. **Alternate** is also a verb, and notice that the pronunciation is then different.

alternate angle n. one of a pair of angles on opposite sides and at opposite ends of a line that cuts two other lines

alternately /awl túrnətli/ adv. 1. INTERCHANGING by fol-lowing one immediately after the other in a regular repeated pattern or sequence 2. = alternatively

alternating current n. an electric current that regu-larly reverses direction

alternation /áwltər náysh'n/ n. 1. PROCESS OF ALTERNATING a process of change in which one thing follows, or is made to follow, another in a regular repeated pattern 2. LOGIC PROPOSITION a proposition of the form 'p or q', that is, either sentence 'p' is true or sentence 'q' is true

alternation of generations n. the existence in the life cycle of an organism of two or more alternating forms or reproductive modes, e.g. sexual and asexual cycles

alternative /awl túrnətiv/ n. 1. OTHER POSSIBILITY sth dif-ferent from, and able to serve as a substitute for, sth else ○ You could take the bus as an alternative to driving. 2. POSSIBILITY OF CHOOSING the possibility of choosing between two different things or courses of action ○ We gave you the alternative; you decided to stay. 3. OPTION either one of two, or one of several, things or courses of action to choose between ○ I can't decide which of the two alternatives is worse. ■ adj. 1. SERVING AS A BACKUP different and serving, or able to serve, as a substitute for sth else ○ There are alternative courses we can take. US term alternate 2. MUTUALLY EXCLUSIVE of which only one can be true, or only one can be used or chosen, or take place at any one time ○ There are two alternative theories as to why this phenomenon occurs. 3. UNCONVENTIONALLY NONTRADITIONAL outside the establishment or main-stream, and often presented as being less in-stitutionalized or conventional, or more natural or economical with resources ○ alternative methods of painting 4. LOGIC = disjunctive

alternative comedy n. any form of comedy char-acterized by subject matter and a style of pre-sentation deliberately made different from mainstream comedy —**alternative comedian** n.

alternative curriculum (plural **alternative curricula** or **alternative curriculums**) n. in England and Wales, any available course of study that is not included in the National Curriculum

alternative energy n. any form of energy obtained from the sun, wind, waves, or other natural re-newable source, in contrast to energy generated from fossil fuels

alternatively /awl túrnətivli/ adv. or instead of that ○ Alternatively, you could drive there.

alternative medicine n. the treatment of illness using remedies not considered part of mainstream medicine, e.g. homoeopathy or naturopathy

alternative vote n. a system of voting in which electors vote for several candidates in order of preference, their votes being transferred to the second choice if the first choice fails to receive a majority. This system of voting is used in Australia.

alternator /áwltər naytər/ n. a device that generates alternating current

altho /awl thó/ conj. US although (informal)

althorn /ált hawrn/ n. an alto brass wind instrument of either the saxhorn or the flügelhorn family, used mainly in brass or military bands [Mid-19thC. From German, literally 'alto horn', from Alt 'alto' + Horn 'horn'.]

although /awl thó/ conj. granting or in spite of the fact that ○ Although the children were sleepy, they

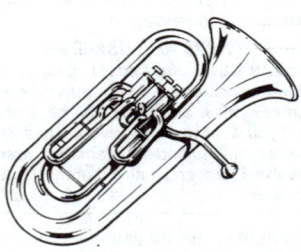

Althorn

kept watching the movie. [14thC. From ALL in the sense 'even' + THOUGH.]

WORD KEY: USAGE

although or **though**? In many uses **although** and **though** are interchangeable. **Although** is more usual when introducing a clause at the beginning of a sentence, but apart from this **though** is a generally more versatile word capable of occupying different positions in a sentence and having more grammatical flexibility. It is the only choice in the phrases **as though** and **even though**, and in the following types of use: *I don't like them, though. It is true though that they have been kind to us. The chair, though damaged, could still be used. We enjoyed the day out, cold though it was.*

---

alti- *prefix.* = alto-

altimeter /al tímmitər, álti meetər/ *n.* an instrument that shows height above sea level, especially one mounted in an aircraft and incorporating an aneroid barometer that senses differences in pressure caused by changes in altitude —**altimetric** /álti méttrik/ *adj.* —**altimetry** /álti méttri/ *n.*

altiplano /álti pla'anō/ (*plural* **-nos**) *n.* a high plateau, especially in Mexico or the Andes of South America [Early 20thC. From American Spanish, literally 'high plain'.]

Altiplano /álti pla'a nō/ area of the Andes Mountains extending from southwestern Bolivia to southern Peru. Height: about 3,650 m/12,000 ft.

altitude /álti tyood/ *n.* **1.** HEIGHT ABOVE SEA LEVEL the height of sth above a particular specified level, especially above sea level or the Earth's surface **2.** HIGH PLACE a place or region situated high above sea level (*often used in the plural*) **3.** GEOM DISTANCE in a geometrical figure, the perpendicular distance from the vertex to the base **4.** ASTRON ANGLE CELESTIAL BODY IS ABOVE HORIZON the angle of a celestial body above an observer's horizon, measured from the horizon along the circle passing through the object and the point above the observer **5.** HIGH RANK OR POSITION a high rank or high position in a society or group [14thC. From Latin *altitudo*, from *altus* 'high' (source of English *haughty*). Ultimately from an Indo-European word meaning 'to grow', the underlying idea being 'growing tall'.] —**altitudinal** /álti tyoódin'l/ *adj.*

altitude sickness *n.* a condition caused by low levels of oxygen in the air at high altitudes, resulting in nausea and breathlessness

Alt key /áwlt-/ *n.* a key on a computer keyboard that can be pressed together with another key to change the function of the latter

Altman /áwltmən/, **Robert** (b. 1925) US film director

Robert Altman

and screenwriter who is known for the films *M*A*S*H* (1970) and *The Player* (1992).

alto /áltō/ (*plural* **-tos**) *n.* **1.** = **contralto** *n.* **1 2.** HIGHEST MALE VOICE the highest singing voice for an adult male, achieved by using falsetto **3.** ALTO SINGER sb who sings with an alto or contralto voice **4.** INSTRUMENT BETWEEN SOPRANO AND TENOR in a family of instruments, the instrument whose size and pitch fall between the soprano and tenor instruments [Late 16thC. Via Italian, literally 'high', from Latin *altus* (see ALTITUDE).]

alto-, **alti-**, **alt-** *prefix.* high, altitude ○ *altocumulus, altimeter* [From Latin *altus* 'high, deep' (source also of English *altitude*). Ultimately from an Indo-European base meaning 'to grow', which is also the ancestor of *old*.]

alto clef *n.* the C clef indicating that middle C is on the third line of the stave

altocumulus /áltō kyoomyoóless/ (*plural* **-li** /-lī/) *n.* white or grey patchy cloud with a rounded outline

altogether /áwltə géthər, -geth-/ *adv.* **1.** WITH EVERYTHING INCLUDED when everything is included or taken into account ○ *Altogether, your bill comes to £75.99.* **2.** TOTALLY entirely or utterly ○ *I'm not altogether satisfied.* **3.** ON THE WHOLE considered as a whole ○ *Altogether, it's been a highly successful day.* [12thC. From ALL 'the whole group' + TOGETHER.] ◇ **in the altogether** naked (*informal*)

WORD KEY: USAGE

altogether or **all together**? The meanings are close and this causes confusion, but whereas **altogether** means 'completely' or 'in all' and is an adverb, **all together** means 'everyone together', that is 'all at the same place or time' and functions as an adjectival phrase. Usually the word *all* can be removed without affecting the grammar or the sense: *They arrived all together at nine. The plates are all together on a separate shelf.*

---

altoist /áltō ist/ *n.* a musician who plays an alto saxophone

alto-relievo /áltō ri leévō/ (*plural* **alto-relievos**), **alto-rilievo** (*plural* **alto-rilievos**) *n.* = **high relief** [Mid-17thC. From Italian *alto-rilievo*, literally 'high-relief'.]

altostratus /áltō straátəss, -sráytəss/ (*plural* **-ti** /-sráy tī/) *n.* greyish cloud in thin sheets or layers of uniform appearance, through which the Sun can be seen

altricial /al trísh'l/ *adj.* HELPLESS AND DEPENDENT used to describe birds or mammals that are helpless when young and dependent on their parents for food ■ *n.* ANIMAL PRODUCING HELPLESS YOUNG a bird or mammal that produces young that are unable to move or feed themselves without help [Late 19thC. Formed from modern Latin *Altrices* (former division of birds), plural of Latin *altrix* 'female nourisher', from *alere* 'to nourish'.]

altruism /áltroo izəm/ *n.* **1.** SELFLESSNESS an attitude or way of behaving marked by unselfish concern for the welfare of others **2.** BELIEF IN ACTING FOR OTHERS' GOOD the belief that acting for the benefit of others is right and good [Mid-19thC. Via French *altruisme* from Italian *altrui* 'that which belongs to other people', from, ultimately, Latin *alter* 'other'.] —**altruist** /áltroo ist/ *n.* —**altruistic** /áltroo ístik/ *adj.* —**altruistically** /-ístikli, -ístikəli/ *adv.*

ALU *abbr.* arithmetic logic unit

alula /ályoolə/ (*plural* **-lae** /-lə ə/) *n.* a bastard wing (*technical*) [Late 18thC. From modern Latin, literally 'little wing', formed from Latin *ala* 'wing'.] —**alular** *adj.*

alum /álləm/ *n.* **1.** COLOURLESS SOLID a colourless crystalline solid that turns white in air. It is used as an astringent, in water purification, to dress leather, and to make pigments and dyes. Formula: $KAl(SO_4)_2.12H_2O.$ **2.** COMPOUND STRUCTURALLY SIMILAR TO ALUM an inorganic chemical compound with a similar structure to that of alum [14thC. Via Old French, from Latin *alumen* (see ALUMINIUM).]

alumina /ə loómínə/ *n.* white or colourless aluminium oxide, found naturally as corundum and in bauxite. It is used as a catalyst and an abrasive, and in the manufacture of artificial sapphires and rubies. Formula: $Al_2O_3.$ [Late 18thC. Coined from the Latin stem *alumin-* (see ALUMINIUM), on the model of words such as SODA and MAGNESIA.]

aluminate /ə loómi nayt/ *n.* any salt of aluminium and a metallic oxide

aluminiferous /ə loómi nífferəss/ *adj.* that contains or is a source of alumina or aluminium

aluminise *vt.* = **aluminize**

aluminium /állə mínni əm/ *n.* a light metallic element that is silvery white, ductile, malleable, and resistant to corrosion. The commonest metal found in the Earth's crust, aluminium occurs naturally only in compounds such as bauxite. Symbol Al [Early 19thC. From Latin *alumin-*, the stem of *alumen* 'alum'. Coined by the British chemist Sir Humphrey Davy, who discovered the metal.]

aluminium foil *n.* aluminium in the form of a very thin sheet, used especially for wrapping food that is to be baked or roasted in an oven

aluminium hydroxide *n.* a white solid used as an antacid, catalyst, and drying agent, and in making glass and ceramics. Formula: $Al(OH)_3$ or $Al_2O_3.3H_2O.$

aluminium oxide *n.* = **alumina**

aluminium sulphate *n.* a white crystalline solid used in making paper and textiles and in water purification. Formula: $Al_2(SO_4)_3.$

aluminize /ə loómi nīz/ (**-nizes, -nizing, -nized**), **aluminise** (**-nises, -nising, -nised**) *vt.* to treat or coat sth with aluminium

aluminothermy /ə loómi nō thúrmi/ *n.* a process for extracting a metal from its oxide that involves burning the oxide together with aluminium powder

aluminous /ə loómínəss/ *adj.* **1.** RESEMBLING ALUMINIUM resembling aluminium or alum **2.** = **aluminiferous** [15thC. Formed from Latin *aluminosus*, from the stem *alumin-* (see ALUMINIUM).]

aluminum /ə loómínəm/ *n.* US = **aluminium**

alumna /ə lúmnə/ (*plural* **-nae** /-nī, -nee/) *n.* a female graduate or former student of a school, college, or university [Late 19thC. From Latin, feminine form of ALUMNUS.]

alumnus /ə lúmnəss/ (*plural* **-ni** /-nī, -nee/) *n.* a male graduate or former student of a school, college, or university [Mid-17thC. From Latin, literally 'pupil, fosterchild', formed from *alere* 'to nourish' (source of English *adolescent, adult*, and *alimony*).]

alunite /állyoo nīt/ *n.* a white, grey, or reddish mineral composed of hydrated potassium aluminium sulphate, formed by alteration of volcanic rocks and used in the production of fertilizers [Mid-19thC. From French, formed from *alun* 'alum' from, ultimately, Latin *alumen* (see ALUMINIUM).]

alveolar /álvi ōlər, al vee ələr/ *adj.* **1.** ANAT RELATING TO AIR SAC IN LUNG relating to the air sacs in the lungs (**alveoli**) **2.** ANAT RELATING TO THE JAWBONE relating to the part of the upper or lower jaw that contains the roots of the teeth **3.** PHON WITH TONGUE NEAR UPPER TEETH RIDGE used to describe a consonant that is sounded with the tongue touching or close to the ridge behind the teeth of the upper jaw ■ *n.* PHON ALVEOLAR CONSONANT an alveolar consonant, e.g. 't', 'd', or 's' in English —**alveolarly** *adv.*

alveolar ridge *n.* a hard ridge in the jaw immediately behind the roots of the teeth

alveolus /álvi ōləss, al vee ələss/ (*plural* **-li** /-lee, -lī/) *n.* **1.** AIR SAC IN LUNG a tiny thin-walled air sac found in large numbers in each lung, through which oxygen enters and carbon dioxide leaves the blood **2.** TOOTH SOCKET a socket in the jaw bone in which a tooth is rooted [Late 17thC. From Latin, literally 'little cavity', formed from *alveus* 'cavity', from *alvus* 'belly'.]

always /áwl wayz, -wiz/ *adv.* **1.** EVERY TIME OR CONTINUOUSLY used to indicate that sth happens or is done at all times, either continuously, repetitively, or on every occasion ○ *She's almost always late.* **2.** THROUGH ALL PAST OR FUTURE TIME throughout all past time or all future time, or for as long as anyone can remember and as long as anyone can foresee ○ *I will always love you.* **3.** IF NECESSARY if necessary, or if there is no other or no better option ○ *I could always stay an extra day if you need help.* [14thC. From Old English *ealne weg*, literally 'all the way', originally 'covering the complete distance', later 'perpetually'.] ◇ **for always** for all time

Alwyn /áwlwin/, **William** (1905–85) British composer who composed 60 film scores, including one of *Squadron Leader X* (1942). He also published *The Technique of Film Music* (1957).

alyssum /állissəm/ *n.* **1.** = **sweet alyssum 2. PLANT WITH YELLOW FLOWERS** a European perennial plant with oval, hairy, grey-green leaves and bright yellow flowers. Latin name: *Aurinia saxatilis*. US term **basket-of-gold** [Mid-16thC. Via modern Latin, genus name, from, ultimately, Greek *alysson* 'madwort' (a plant believed to cure rabies), formed from *alyssos*, literally 'without madness', from *lyssa* 'rabies'.]

Alzheimer's disease /álts hīmərz-/, **Alzheimer's** *n.* a degenerative disorder that affects the brain and causes senile dementia [Early 20thC. Named after Alois *Alzheimer* (1864–1915), German neurologist, who described it in 1907.]

am[1], **AM** *abbr.* amplitude modulation

am[2] (stressed) /am/; (unstressed) /əm/ *v.* 1st person present singular of **be** [Old English *eom*. Ultimately from an Indo-European verb meaning 'to be' (source also of French *être*).]

Am *abbr.* **1.** BIBLE Amos **2.** americium

AM *abbr.* **1.** anno mundi **2.** ante meridiem **3.** Artium Magister **4.** associate member **5.** Albert Medal

Am. *abbr.* American

a.m., **A.M.** *adj.*, *adv.* in the period between midnight and noon. Full form **ante meridiem**

AMA *abbr.* American Medical Association

Amadeus /ámmə dáyəss-/ large salt lake in the southern part of the Northern Territory, Australia. Area: 2,400 sq. km/927 sq. mi.

amah /áamə/ *n.* a children's nurse, female domestic servant, or office cleaner and attendant in the Far East [Mid-19thC. Via Portuguese *ama* 'nurse' from medieval Latin *amma* 'mother' (probably originally a nursery word).]

amalgam /ə málgəm/ *n.* **1.** MIXTURE a blend of two or more elements or characteristics **2.** DENT FILLING MATERIAL FOR TEETH a substance used as filling for tooth cavities, consisting of a paste of powdered mercury, silver, and tin that quickly hardens **3.** METALL MERCURY ALLOY an alloy of mercury and another metal [15thC. Directly or via French, from medieval Latin *amalgama*, of uncertain origin: probably ultimately from Greek *malagma* 'emollient', from, ultimately, *malakos* 'soft'. Originally in English, 'soft alloy'.]

───── WORD KEY: SYNONYMS ─────
See Synonyms at **mixture**.

amalgamate /ə málgə mayt/ (**-mates**, **-mating**, **-mated**) *vti.* **1.** COMBINE to combine two or more organizations or things into one unified whole, or join together to form one unified whole **2.** METALL ALLOY WITH MERCURY to alloy a metal with mercury, or be alloyed with mercury —**amalgamative** /ə málgəmətiv/ *adj.* —**amalgamator** /-maytər/ *n.*

amalgamation /ə málgə máysh'n/ *n.* **1.** COMBINING THINGS the process of amalgamating things into a unified whole **2.** RESULT OF COMBINING THINGS sth that is a combination of different things or results from their amalgamation **3.** COMM BUSINESS MERGER a combination of two or more business concerns so as to form one **4.** METALL METAL EXTRACTION FROM ORE a method of extracting a precious metal from an ore by using mercury to form an amalgam with the metal

Amalthea /ámmal thee ə/ *n.* a natural satellite of Jupiter, discovered in 1892

amandine /áamən deen, áamən déen, ámmən-/ *adj.* filled, cooked, or served with almonds [Mid-19thC. From French, formed from *amande* 'almond'.]

amantadine /ə mántə deen/ *n.* a drug used to combat viral infection, particularly certain types of influenza, and also to treat Parkinson's disease. It helps reduce the tremor of Parkinson's disease by promoting the release of dopamine in the brain. [Mid-20thC. Blend of AMINE and ADAMANTANE.]

amanuensis /ə mánnyoo énssiss/ (*plural* **-ses** /-én seez/) *n.* **1.** SCRIBE sb employed by an individual to write from his or her dictation or to copy manuscripts **2.** WRITER'S ASSISTANT a writer's assistant with research and secretarial duties [Early 17thC. From

Latin, formed from *a manu*, literally, 'by hand' (in the phrase *servus a manu* 'slave, servant with secretarial duties').]

amaranth /ámmə ranth/ (*plural* **-ranths** *or* **-ranth**) *n.* **1.** FLOWERING PLANT WITH DROOPING FLOWERHEADS a plant with long drooping heads of small green, red, or purple flowers. Some types are grown as a grain crop or as a leafy vegetable. Genus: *Amaranthus*. **2.** LEGENDARY FLOWER a flower, that, according to legend, never fades **3.** FOOD DYE a synthetic red food dye [Mid-16thC. Via either French *amarante* or modern Latin *amaranthus* from Latin *amarantus*, from Greek *amarantos*, literally 'not corruptible, not fading'.]

amaranthine /ámmə rán thīn, -thin/ *adj.* **1.** UNDYING undying or unfading, like the legendary amaranth (*literary*) **2.** DARK REDDISH-PURPLE of a dark reddish-purple colour

amaretto /ámmə réttō/ (*plural* **-tos**) *n.* an Italian almond-flavoured liqueur [Mid-20thC. From Italian, literally 'little bitter (one)', formed from *amaro* 'bitter', from Latin *amarus* (source of English *maraschino* and *morello*).]

Amarillo /ámmə ríllō/ city in northwestern Texas, near the centre of the Texas Panhandle. Population: 169,588 (1996).

Amaryllis

amaryllis /ámmə rílliss/ (*plural* **-lises** *or* **-lis**) *n.* **1.** SOUTHERN AFRICAN PLANT a southern African plant grown from a bulb for its large red, pink, or white trumpet-shaped flowers that appear facing in opposite directions at the head of a single stalk. Latin name: *Amaryllis belladonna*. **2.** TROPICAL AMERICAN PLANT a tropical American plant related to the southern African amaryllis. Genus: *Hippeastrum*. [Late 18thC. Via modern Latin from, ultimately, Greek *Amarullis*, name of a shepherdess in pastorals such as those of Theocritus, Virgil, and Ovid.]

amass /ə máss/ (**amasses**, **amassing**, **amassed**) *vti.* to gather things together or collect them over time until they form a large pile, collection, or fund, or accumulate or be collected in this way ○ *amassed a fortune in the 1950s* [15thC. From French *amasser*, from *masser* 'to gather into a mass', from, ultimately, Latin *massa* (see MASS).] —**amassable** *adj.* —**amasser** *n.* —**amassment** *n.*

───── WORD KEY: SYNONYMS ─────
See Synonyms at **collect**.

amateur /ámmətər, -choor/ *n.* **1.** SB DOING STH FOR PLEASURE sb who does or takes part in sth for pleasure rather than for pay ○ *a talented amateur golfer* **2.** UNSKILLED PERSON sb who has only limited skill in, or knowledge of, an activity ○ *Whoever handled your rewiring must have been an amateur.* **3.** SB WHO LOVES STH sb who loves or is greatly interested in sth (*literary*) ○ *She is an amateur of classical sculpture.* ■ *adj.* **1.** BY AMATEURS for, by, or consisting of amateurs **2.** NOT DONE WITH SKILL unskilful or unprofessional, or done in an unskilful or unprofessional way [Late 18thC. Via French, from Latin *amator* 'lover' from *amare* 'to love' (source of English *enamour*).]

amateurish /ámmətərish, -choor-/ *adj.* lacking the skill of a professional, or unskilfully or unprofessionally done —**amateurishly** *adv.* —**amateurishness** *n.*

amateurism /ámmətərizzəm, -choor-/ *n.* amateur status, participation by amateurs, or the principle that sth should reserved for amateurs ○ *one of the last bastions of true amateurism in sport*

amatol /ámmə tol/ *n.* an explosive made from ammonium nitrate and TNT and used in bombs [Early 20thC. Coined from AMMONIUM + TOLUENE.]

amatory /ámmətəri/, **amatorial** /ámmə táwri əl/ *adj.* relating to, involving, expressing, or typical of physical love ○ *amatory adventures* [Late 16thC. From Latin *amatorius*, from *amator* (see AMATEUR).]

amaurosis /ámmaw rṓssiss/ *n.* partial or complete blindness, especially when there is no obvious damage to the eye [Mid-17thC. From Greek *amaurōsis*, from *amauroun* 'to darken', from *amauros* 'dark'.] —**amaurotic** /ámmaw róttik/ *adj.*

amautik /ə mówtik/, **amauti** /-ti/ *n.* Can among the Inuit, a woman's jacket that has a fur-lined hood for carrying an infant or small child [From Inuktitut]

amaze /ə máyz/ *vt.* (**amazes**, **amazing**, **amazed**) **1.** FILL SB WITH WONDER to fill sb with wonder, astonishment, or extreme surprise ○ *We were amazed at the news.* **2.** BEWILDER SB to bewilder or stupefy sb (*archaic*) ■ *n.* AMAZEMENT a state of astonishment or bewilderment (*archaic*) [Old English *āmasian* 'to stupefy, stun' (source of English *maze*), of uncertain origin: perhaps from Old Norse] —**amazed** *adj.* —**amazedly** /ə máyzidli/ *adv.* —**amazedness** /-nəss/ *n.*

amazement /ə máyzmənt/ *n.* **1.** ASTONISHMENT a strong feeling of wonder or surprise at the extraordinariness of sth **2.** BEWILDERMENT bewilderment or confusion (*archaic*)

amazing /ə máyzing/ *adj.* **1.** CAUSING AMAZEMENT so extraordinary or wonderful as to be barely believable or cause extreme surprise ○ *an amazing escape* **2.** OUTSTANDING outstandingly good, skilful, or admirable (*informal*) ○ *an amazing concert* —**amazingly** *adv.*

amazon /ámmaz'n/ *n.* a parrot of tropical America that typically has green plumage. Genus: *Amazona*. [Late 19thC. Named after the AMAZON.]

Amazon[1] *n.* **1.** MYTHOLOGICAL WARRIOR in Greek mythology, a member of a group of women warriors who lived in Scythia or elsewhere at the northern limits of the world. They fought in the Trojan war on the side of Troy. **2. Amazon**, **amazon** STRONG WOMAN a tall, physically strong, or strong-willed woman —**Amazonian** /ámmə zṓni ən/ *adj.*

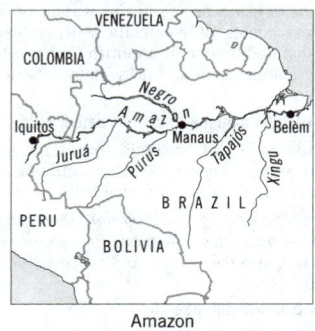

Amazon

Amazon[2] /ámmaz'n/ the world's second longest river. It flows east from northern Peru, traversing northern South America and emptying into the Atlantic Ocean in Brazil. Length: about 6,400 km/4,000 mi. —**Amazonian** *adj.*

Amazon dolphin *n.* a freshwater dolphin with a long snout found in the upper reaches of the Amazon and Orinoco rivers. Latin name: *Inia geoffrensis*.

amazonite /ámməzə nīt/ *n.* a green or bluish-green mineral, a form of microcline used as a gemstone [Named after the AMAZON[2], where similar green stones were formerly found]

Amb. *abbr.* ambassador

ambassador /am bássədər/ *n.* **1.** DIPLOMATIC REPRESENTATIVE a diplomatic official of the highest rank sent by one country as its long-term representative to another **2.** OFFICIAL REPRESENTATIVE sb who serves as an official representative of sth, e.g. a movement ○ *visiting this country as an ambassador for an organization dedicated to saving endangered species* **3.** UNOFFICIAL REPRESENTATIVE sb or sth regarded as an unofficial representative or a symbol of sth ○ *The swallow is an ambassador of spring.* [14thC. Via

French *ambassadeur* from Italian *ambasciator*, from, ultimately, Latin *ambactus* 'vassal', from a Gaulish word meaning 'servant' (source of English *embassy*).] —**ambassadorial** /am bássə dáwri əl/ *adj.* —**ambassadorship** /am bássədər ship/ *n.*

WORD KEY: CULTURAL NOTE

The Ambassadors, a novel by US writer Henry James (1903). Sometimes regarded as James's masterpiece, it tells the story of Lambert Strether, a middle-aged editor sent by his wealthy New England patron and fiancée to Paris to persuade her expatriate son Chad to return home.

ambassador at large (*plural* **ambassadors at large**) *n.* *US* an ambassador not assigned to one particular foreign country

ambassadress /am bássədrəss/ *n.* a woman who is an ambassador

amber /ámbər/ *n.* **1. YELLOW FOSSIL RESIN** a hard translucent fossil resin varying in colour from yellow to light brown, used for making jewellery and ornaments **2. BROWNY YELLOW COLOUR** a yellow to brown colour **3. SIGNAL FOR CAUTION** in a system of traffic signals, the yellow-coloured light that advises caution. A car at an amber must halt if it safely can, but a train may proceed with caution. ■ *adj.* **YELLOWISH-BROWN** of a yellowish-brown colour [14thC. Via French *ambre* from Arabic *anbar* 'ambergris', the original sense in English, from a perceived similarity between the two.]

amber fluid, **amber liquid, amber nectar** *n.* *Aus* beer (*informal*)

amber gambler *n.* a driver who takes risks by not stopping at traffic lights when they are at amber (*informal*)

ambergris /ámbər greess, -griss/ *n.* a grey waxy substance, consisting mainly of cholesterol, secreted from the intestines of the sperm whale. It is found floating in tropical waters or on beaches and is used in perfume-making. [15thC. From French *ambre gris*, literally 'grey amber'.]

amberjack /ámbər jak/ (*plural* **-jacks** *or* **-jack**) *n.* **1. ATLANTIC FISH** a large sea fish found in warm Atlantic waters that has golden markings. Genus: *Seriola.* **2. AUSTRALIAN FISH** a fish found in waters off the east and west coasts of Australia with a black-blue, yellow-banded body and a mouth that is a brilliant orange colour inside. Latin name: *Seriola purpurascens.*

amber liquid, **amber nectar** *n.* = **amber fluid**

amberoid /ámbə royd/, **ambroid** /-broyd/ *n.* a synthetic form of amber made by heating and compressing valueless small pieces of amber with other resins

ambi- *prefix.* both ○ *ambiversion* [From Latin *ambi* 'around, on both sides'. Ultimately from an Indo-European base that is also the ancestor of English *by, umlaut*, and *amphi-*.]

ambiance *n.* = **ambience**

ambidextrous /ámbi dékstrəss/ *adj.* **1. USING EITHER HAND** able to use either the right or the left hand with equal skill **2. SKILFUL IN MANY WAYS** very skilful and versatile [Mid-17thC. Formed from late Latin *ambidexter*, literally 'right-handed on both sides', formed from Latin *dexter* 'right-handed' (see DEXTROUS), from the traditional association of the right hand with skill.] —**ambidexterity** /ámbi dek stérrəti/ *n.* —**ambidextrously** /ámbi dék strəssli/ *adv.*

ambience /ámbi ənss, ámbi onss/, **ambiance** *n.* the typical atmosphere or mood of a place ○ *a restaurant with a welcoming ambience* [Mid-20thC. From French *ambiance*.]

ambient /ámbi ənt/ *adj.* **IN SURROUNDING AREA** in the immediately surrounding area ○ *ambient temperature* ■ *n.* **ambient, ambient music BACKGROUND MUSIC** a type of music that is usually instrumental and repetitive and often contains soothing electronic sounds. It is used to create an atmosphere of calm or relaxation. [Late 16thC. Directly or via French, from Latin *ambire*, literally 'to go round' (see AMBITION).]

ambiguity /ámbi gyóo əti/ (*plural* **-ties**) *n.* **1. DOUBT ABOUT MEANING** a situation in which sth can be understood in more than one way and it is not clear which meaning is intended **2. STATEMENT WITH MORE THAN ONE MEANING** an expression or statement that has more than one meaning

ambiguous /am bíggyoo əss/ *adj.* **1. HAVING MORE THAN ONE MEANING** having more than one possible meaning or interpretation ○ *an ambiguous response* **2. CAUSING UNCERTAINTY** causing uncertainty or confusion ○ *an ambiguous result* [Early 16thC. Formed from Latin *ambiguus* 'undecided', from *ambigere* 'to wander about', from *agere* 'to lead' (source of English *agent*).] —**ambiguously** *adv.* —**ambiguousness** *n.*

WORD KEY: USAGE

ambiguous or **ambivalent**? Both words describe uncertainty in understanding what sth or sb means. The principal difference is that ***ambivalent*** is used of people and their attitudes, whereas ***ambiguous*** refers to sth said or written. If people are ***ambivalent*** about disarmament, they are unsure about the advantages and disadvantages and cannot easily decide between the various arguments, whereas if a political leader makes an ***ambiguous*** statement about disarmament, then the statement has more than one possible meaning.

ambisexual /ámbi sékshoo əl/ *adj.* **1. OF BOTH SEXES** used to describe secondary sexual characteristics that are common to both sexes **2. ATTRACTED TO BOTH SEXES** sexually responsive or attracted to both sexes **3.** = **unisex** —**ambisexuality** /ámbi sékshoo álləti/ *n.*

ambisonics /ámbi sónniks/ *n.* a recording and reproduction system that uses separate channels and speakers to create the effect of being surrounded by sound (*takes a singular verb*) —**ambisonic** *adj.*

ambit /ámbit/ *n.* the scope, extent, or limits of sth ○ *within the ambit of the court's jurisdiction* [Late 16thC. From Latin *ambitus* 'circuit', from *ambire* (see AMBITION).]

ambit claim *n.* *Aus* a claim made to an arbitration authority by workers who expect to negotiate and therefore make extravagant initial demands

ambition /am bísh'n/ *n.* **1. DESIRE FOR SUCCESS** a strong feeling of wanting to be successful in life and achieve great things **2. AIM OR GOAL** an aim or objective that sb is trying to achieve [14thC. Via French, from Latin *ambitio*, from *ambire* 'to canvass for votes, go round', from *ire* 'to go' (source of English *exit*).]

ambitious /am bíshəss/ *adj.* **1. HAVING STRONG DESIRE FOR SUCCESS** having a strong desire to be successful in life **2. NEEDING GREAT EFFORT TO SUCCEED** sounding impressive but difficult to achieve because very high standards have been set or a great deal of work is required ○ *an ambitious plan to increase market share* **3. STRONGLY DESIROUS** with a strong desire to have or do sth ○ *ambitious to be the youngest person ever to win the championship* —**ambitiously** *adv.* —**ambitiousness** *n.*

ambivalence /am bívvələnss/ *n.* **1. CONFLICT OF IDEAS OR ATTITUDES** the presence of two opposing ideas, attitudes, or emotions at the same time **2. UNCERTAINTY** a feeling of uncertainty about sth due to a mental conflict [Early 20thC. From German *Ambivalenz*, which was modelled on *Äquivalenz* (see EQUIVALENCE).]

ambivalent /am bívvələnt/ *adj.* having mixed, uncertain, or conflicting feelings about sth

WORD KEY: USAGE

See Usage note at ***ambiguous.***

ambiversion /ámbi vúrsh'n/ *n.* a personality pattern that has characteristics of both introversion and extroversion —**ambivert** /ámbi vurt/ *n.*

amble /ámb'l/ *vi.* (**-bles, -bling, -bled**) **WALK SLOWLY** to walk slowly in a relaxed way ○ *'I took off shoes and socks and ambled along carrying them, enjoying the evening sun'.* (Dick Francis, *The Danger*; 1983) ■ *n.* **SLOW WALK** a slow and relaxed walk or style of walking [14thC. Via French *ambler* from Latin *ambulare* 'to walk'.] —**ambler** *n.*

amblyopia /ámbli ópi ə/ *n.* an impairment of the vision in one eye that is not caused by structural damage or physical defect [Early 18thC. Via modern Latin, from Greek *ambluōpia*, literally 'dim-sightedness'.] —**amblyopic** /ámbli óppik/ *adj.*

ambo /ámbō/ (*plural* **-bos** *or* **-bones** /am bṓ neez/) *n.* a stand or pulpit in early Christian churches from which the lessons or other parts of the service were read [Mid-17thC. Via medieval Latin from, ultimately, Greek *ambōn* 'raised edge (of a dish)'.]

ambones plural of **ambo**

ambroid *n.* BOT = **amberoid**

Ambrose /ámbrōz/, **St** (340?–397) Roman priest and theologian. As bishop of Milan from 374 he combatted Arianism and introduced much Greek theology to the West.

ambrosia /am brṓzi ə/ *n.* **1. FOOD OF THE GODS** in classical mythology, the food of the gods, which was supposed to make those who ate it immortal **2. STH DELICIOUS** a substance that tastes or smells delicious (*literary*) **3.** = **beebread 4. FRUIT AND COCONUT DISH** a dessert or salad made from oranges, bananas, and coconut [Mid-16thC. Via Latin, from Greek, from *ambrotos* 'immortal', from an archaic form of *brotos* 'mortal'.]

ambrosial /am brṓzi əl/, **ambrosian** /-zi ən/ *adj.* (*literary*) **1. DELICIOUS-TASTING** delightful to taste or smell **2. ASSOCIATED WITH GODS** associated with the gods —**ambrosially** *adv.*

ambry /ámbri/ (*plural* **-bries**), **aumbry** /áwmbri/ (*plural* **-bries**) *n.* **1. RECESS IN CHURCH** a small recess near the altar in a church, where sacred vessels are kept **2. SMALL CUPBOARD** a small cupboard or pantry (*archaic*) [14thC. Via French *armarie* from Latin *armarium* (see ARMOIRE).]

ambulacrum /ámbyoo láykrəm/ (*plural* **-ra** /-krə/) *n.* any one of the five radial areas on the underside of a starfish, sea urchin, or similar animal, along which the blood vessels and nerves run and through which the feet extend [Early 19thC. From Latin, 'avenue', formed from *ambulare* (see AMBULATE).] —**ambulacral** *adj.*

ambulance /ámbyoolənss/ *n.* a vehicle designed and equipped for carrying people to and from hospital [Mid-19thC. From French, from *hôpital ambulant* 'field hospital', literally 'walking hospital', from, ultimately, Latin *ambulare* (see AMBULATE).]

ambulance chaser *n.* a lawyer who, in order to earn large fees, seeks out accident victims and encourages them to claim heavy damages (*slang disapproving*) [Origin uncertain: probably from the late-19C practice of disreputable lawyers in New York City of commissioning ambulance drivers and police officers to inform them of accidents]

ambulant /ámbyoolənt/ *adj.* **1. TRAVELLING** moving around from place to place **2.** MED = **ambulatory** [Early 17thC. Via French from, ultimately, Latin *ambulare* (see AMBULATE).]

ambulate /ámbyoo layt/ (**-lates, -lating, -lated**) *vi.* to walk or move from one place to another (*formal*) [Early 17thC. From Latin *ambulat-*, the past participle stem of *ambulare* 'to walk' (source of English *alley, amble*, and *pram*).]

ambulatory /ámbyoo láytəri/ *adj.* **1. RELATING TO WALKING** relating to or equipped for walking (*formal*) **2. WALKING OR MOVING** walking or moving around, or done while walking or moving (*formal*) ○ *ambulatory activities* **3.** MED **MOBILE** used to describe a patient who is able to walk and does not have to be kept in bed **4.** LAW **REVOCABLE** able to be revoked ○ *an ambulatory will* ■ *n.* (*plural* **-ries**) ARCHIT **WALKWAY IN CHURCH OR CLOISTER** an aisle at the end of a choir or chancel in a church, or a covered walkway of a cloister —**ambulatorily** *adv.*

ambuscade /ámbə skáyd/ *n.* **AMBUSH SET** an ambush set for sb (*literary*) ■ *vt.* (**-cades, -cading, -caded**) **AMBUSH SB** to ambush sb (*literary*) [Late 16thC. Via French *embuscade* and Italian *imboscata* from, ultimately, assumed Vulgar Latin *imboscare* (see AMBUSH).]

ambush /ámbōōsh/ *n.* **1. SURPRISE ATTACK** an unexpected attack from a concealed position **2. CONCEALMENT BEFORE ATTACK** a concealment before a surprise attack ○ *They lay in ambush and waited for their victims.* **3. SB WAITING IN AMBUSH** one or more people concealed in order to make a surprise attack ■ *vt.* (**-bushes, -bushing, -bushed**) **ATTACK** to attack sb or sth suddenly from a concealed position [14thC. Via Old French *embusche* from, ultimately, assumed Vulgar Latin *imboscare*, literally 'to hide in a bush', from assumed *boscus* 'bush' (related to English *bush*).] —**ambusher** *n.*

AMDG to the greater glory of God. Abbr of **ad majorem dei gloriam**

a at; aa father; aw all; ay day; air hair; ə about, edible, item, common, circus; e egg; ee eel; hw when; i it, happy; ī ice; 'l apple; 'm rhythm; 'n fashion; o odd; ō open; ŏŏ good; oo pool; ow owl; oy oil; th thin; th this; u up; ur urge;

am dram /ám dram/ *n.* amateur dramatics (*informal*) [Shortening]

ameba *n.* = **amoeba**

amebiasis *n.* US = **amoebiasis**

amebic dysentery *n. US* = **amoebic dysentery**

ameliorate /ə mēeli ə rayt/ (**-rates, -rating, -rated**) *vti.* to improve sth or make it better (*formal*) [Mid-18thC. Alteration of MELIORATE (on the model of French *améliorer*).] —**ameliorable** /ə mēeli ərəb'l/ *adj.* —**ameliorative** /-raytiv/ *adj.* —**ameliorator** /-raytər/ *n.*

amelioration /ə mēeli ə ráysh'n/ *n.* **1.** PROCESS OF IMPROVEMENT the act of improving sth, or the process of getting better **2.** IMPROVEMENT MADE an improvement in sth or sb

amen /aá mén, áy-/ *interj.* **1.** SO BE IT said or sung at the end of a prayer or hymn to affirm its content **2.** EXPRESSING STRONG AGREEMENT used to express strong agreement ○ *amen to that* [Pre-12thC. Via late Latin and Greek, from Hebrew *'āmēn* 'truly', from *'āman* 'to confirm'.]

amenable /ə mēenəb'l/ *adj.* **1.** WILLING TO COOPERATE responsive to suggestion and likely to cooperate **2.** ACCOUNTABLE required to account for your behaviour to an authority **3.** LIABLE TO BE JUDGED likely or available to be tested or judged [Late 16thC. From Anglo-Norman, from Old French *amener*, literally 'to bring to', from, ultimately, Latin *minari* 'to threaten', from *minae* 'threats'.] —**amenability** /ə mēenə bílləti/ *n.* —**amenableness** /ə mēenəb'lnəss/ *n.* —**amenably** /-əbli/ *adv.*

amen corner /áy men-/ *n. US* **1.** SEATS FOR MOST DEVOUT the part of some Protestant churches where the most fervent worshippers sit **2.** ENTHUSIASTIC SUPPORTERS a group of supporters or followers who tend to agree with everything their leader says (*informal*) ○ *As usual, enthusiastic support for the bill came from the sponsoring senator's amen corner.* [From the practice of responding to the preacher's prayers by saying 'amen']

WORD KEY: USAGE

The term ***amen corner*** has traditionally been used in certain Protestant churches in the United States to describe the area set aside for members of the congregation who tend to make verbal responses, including the response *Amen.* By extension the term has come to mean, outside the world of religious worship, any area where strong support and high feeling are expressed on behalf of a speaker or performer.

amend /ə ménd/ (**amends, amending, amended**) *vt.* **1.** IMPROVE OR CORRECT STH to make changes to sth, especially a piece of text, in order to improve or correct it **2.** REVISE LEGISLATION to revise or alter formally a motion, bill, or constitution [13thC. Via French *amender* from, ultimately, Latin *emendare* 'to correct', from *menda* 'error' (source of English *emend* and *mendicant*).]

WORD KEY: USAGE

amend or **emend**? The normal word to use in general contexts is ***amend***. ***Emend*** is normally restricted to the correction of errors in a printed or written text. *The ambiguous wording at the beginning of the document needs amending (= changing to sth clearer). By emending two words (= suggesting alternatives for them because they may have been copied wrongly) it is possible to make the sentence intelligible.*

amendment /ə méndmənt/ *n.* **1.** ALTERATION TO STH a change, correction, or improvement to sth **2.** CHANGE TO LEGAL INSTRUMENT an addition or alteration to a motion, bill, or constitution **3.** PROCESS OF CHANGING OR IMPROVING STH the process of changing, correcting, or improving sth ○ *The bill was passed without amendment.*

amends /ə méndz/ *n.* sth done or given as compensation for a wrong (*takes a singular or plural verb*) ○ *a desire to make amends after the misunderstanding* ○ *No amends were forthcoming even after we proved that they were in the wrong.* [14thC. From Old French *amendes*, the plural of *amende* 'reparation', from *amender* (see AMEND).]

amenity /ə mēenəti/ (*plural* **-ties**) *n.* a useful or attractive feature or service, e.g. leisure facilities (*often used in the plural*) [14thC. Directly or via French *aménité* from Latin *amoenitas*, from *amoenus* 'pleasant'.]

amenorrhoea /áy menə rēe ə/, **amenorrhea** *n.* the abnormal absence or suppression of menstruation —**amenorrhoeic** *adj.*

ament /ə mént/, **amentum** /ə mént əm/ (*plural* **-ta**, /-tə/) *n.* BOT a catkin (*technical*) [Mid-18thC. From Latin *amentum* 'strap'.]

Amer. *abbr.* American

Amerasian /ámmə ráyzh'n/ *n.* SB OF AMERICAN AND ASIAN DESCENT sb of mixed American and Asian parentage ■ *adj.* OF MIXED PARENTAGE having mixed American and Asian parentage [Mid-20thC. A blend of AMERICAN and ASIAN.]

America /ə mérrikə/ **1.** **United States 2.** N, S, AND CENTRAL AMERICA a landmass comprising North America, South America, and Central America **3.** N AMERICA North America (*informal*) [Early 16thC. From *Americus*, Latinized form of the first name of *Amerigo* Vespucci (1454–1512), Italian navigator.]

WORD KEY: USAGE

Sensitivity trap: The use of ***America*** to mean North America is liable to cause offence to Canadians, and should be avoided.

American /ə mérrikən/ *n.* SB FROM UNITED STATES sb who was born in or is a citizen of the United States ■ *adj.* **1.** OF THE UNITED STATES relating to or typical of the United States, its people, its culture, or the form of English spoken there **2.** OF THE AMERICAN CONTINENT relating to or typical of North, South, and Central America [Mid-16thC. From modern Latin *Americanus*, from AMERICA.] —**Americanness** *n.*

Americana /ə mérri kaánə/ *n.* things from or about the United States, especially items that are valued by collectors (*takes a singular or plural verb*)

American chameleon *n.* = **anole**

American chestnut *n.* a North American deciduous tree with rough bark that produces catkins and prickly fruits. Almost annihilated by a blight, it is now found chiefly as shoots from old stumps. Latin name: *Castanea dentata.*

American eagle *n.* = **bald eagle**

American English *n.* the form of English that is spoken in the United States

WORD KEY: WORLD ENGLISH

With a population of over 260 million, the United States is the largest and most influential English-speaking country in the world, and English has been in use within its present borders for over 400 years. American English can be described in terms of three groups: (1) The dialect divisions Northern, Coastal Southern, Midland, and Western; (2) Distinctive urban varieties, as in New York and New Orleans; (3) Vernacular forms such as African American English and Jewish English. Because many (especially immigrant) Americans have at least one language other than English, they may casually mix English with those languages, as in the remark *Sometimes I start a sentence in English y termino en español* ('... and end in Spanish'). Spanish is the most prominent other language, and the hybrid variety *Spanglish* has distinctive forms in New York, Florida, Texas, California, and Puerto Rico. Although English is the administrative language of the nation, is culturally dominant, and is the statutory official language in many states, it is not statutory at the federal level – a situation that has engendered no small controversy.

The history of American English falls into three broad periods: (1) *Colonial* 1607–1776, dominated by British English norms; (2) *National* 1776–1898, exhibiting a vigorous and growing independence that included dictionaries and style guides; and (3) *International* 1898-, marked by a steadily increasing worldwide influence and prestige. American English tends to be nasal and, apart from three areas (eastern New England, New York City, and the Southern states), it is 'rhotic' (*r* is pronounced in words such as art, door, and worker) and 'retroflex' (*r* pronounced with the tip of the tongue curled back and raised). The spelling, punctuation, grammar, vocabulary, and idiom of standard American English have been established since the late 19th century; it differs in many ways from British English and other varieties, with the exception of Philippine English, which follows the US model, and Canadian English, which has features of both American English and British English). See ***African American Vernacular English, Canadian English, Hawaiian English, Philippine English.***

Although standard American and British English are similar, there are significant differences in pronunciation, grammar, and vocabulary. With pronunciation, the two Englishes differ chiefly in vowel quality, stress, and voice timbre. For example, Americans pronounce the *a* in words such as *ask, grass,* and *path* in a flat short manner, as in *gasoline*, whereas British English speakers use a broad *a*, as in *father*, when saying these words. American English speakers rather clearly articulate certain unaccented syllables, such as *-ary* in *secretary*, whereas British English speakers clip them to yield pronunciations such as *secret'ry.* American English often places stress on the first syllables of certain words, such as *laboratory* and *excess*, whereas British English moves the stress to medial or terminal positions, as in their pronunciations /lə bórrətri/ and /ek séss/. The reverse is also true with words such as *garage*, in which the US stress is on the last syllable, whereas the UK stress is on the first syllable. As for spelling, Americans use, for example, *aluminum, center, encyclopedia, color, fulfill*, and *tire* whereas British speakers use *aluminium, centre, encyclopaedia, colour, fulfil*, and *tyre.* In terms of vocabulary, the two Englishes can and do diverge markedly: American English uses *molasses, snow pea, truck stop,* and *zucchini*, while British English uses *treacle, mangetout, transport cafe*, and *courgette* for the same things. By preference or established convention, American English tends to prefer *store, defog, visor*, and *rooster*, while British English prefers *shop, demist, peak* and *cock.* American and British English are also set apart by sets of words sharing elements in common, yet being distinctively different words for the same things. American English speakers say *talk show, fish stick, substitute teacher*, and *moving van*, while speakers of British English say *chat show, fish finger, supply teacher*, and *removal van.* The two Englishes also have sets of words covering the same subject matter, yet not having the same specific meanings. A prime example is the food term *biscuit*, which, in British English, is the equivalent of US *cookie*, while *biscuit* in American English is a small, round, light pastry. Finally, there are words mutually exclusive to each English, based upon historical, social, and cultural differences: for example, *inside the Beltway* referring to people, opinions, and issues close to the nation's capital, is US English only, whereas *Questions in the Commons* or *Question Time*, the period when members of the British Parliament may question government ministers, is British English only. Finally, the idiomatic expressions used in both varieties of English can and do differ: *a tempest in a teapot* is American English; *a storm in a teacup* is British English.

American football *n.* a game played in the United States by two teams of 11 players who advance an oval ball by carrying or throwing (passing) it. Points are scored by carrying the ball across the opponent's goal line or by kicking it through open-topped goal posts. US term **football**

American Gothic (1930) by Grant Wood

American gothic, American Gothic *adj.* depicting or representing hard work, frugality, and conservative social attitudes associated with rural and small-town United States [Named after a 1930 painting by the Iowan painter Grant Wood (1892–1942), which depicts a dour farm couple and their surroundings]

American Indian *n.* a Native American (*dated*) — **American Indian** *adj.*

Americanise *vti.* = Americanize

Americanism /ə mérrikənizzəm/ *n.* **1.** US EXPRESSION OR FEATURE a word, phrase, or custom that originated in, or is regarded as characteristic of, the United States **2.** LOYALTY TO UNITED STATES strong affection or support for the United States

Americanist /ə mérrikənist/ *n.* **1.** AUTHORITY ON UNITED STATES an expert on the life, history, language, or culture of the United States **2.** SPECIALIST IN NATIVE AMERICAN LANGUAGES sb who is a student of or specialist in the languages and cultures of Native Americans

Americanize /ə mérrikə nīz/ (**-izes, -izing, -ized**), **Americanise** (**-ises, -ising, -ised**) *vti.* to give sth the form, style, or qualities associated with or used in the United States, or to take on such qualities —**Americanization** /ə mérrikə nī záysh'n/ *n.*

American kestrel *n.* = sparrow hawk *n.* 2

American plan *n. US* = full board

American Revised Version *n.* = American Standard Version

American Revolution *n.* = American War of Independence

American saddle horse *n.* a high-stepping saddle horse, originally bred in Kentucky and trained to walk, trot, canter, gallop, and pace

American Samoa US territory, consisting of a group of South Pacific islands, in the Samoan island chain. Pago Pago is the seat of government. Population: 59,566 (1996). Area: 200 sq. km/77 sq. mi.

American Sign Language *n.* a system of communication used by people with impaired hearing that uses signs made with the hands

American Standard Code for Information Interchange *n.* COMPUT full form of ASCII

American Standard Version *n.* a United States revision of the King James Bible, published in 1901

American War of Independence *n.* The war in which the American colonies won independence from Great Britain (1775–83). US term **American Revolution**

Americas /ə mérrikəss/ = America 2

americium /ámmə ríssi əm/ *n.* a white radioactive metallic chemical element used as a source of alpha particles to make other artificial radioactive elements. Symbol **Am** [Mid-20thC. Named after *America*, where it was first produced.]

Amerind /ámmərind/ *n.* a proposed grouping of languages, defined by some linguists as all those that were spoken in the Americas before the arrival of Europeans, except the Eskimo-Aleut and Na-Dené families

Amerindian /ámmə ríndi ən/ *n., adj.* a Native American (*dated*) [Late 19thC. A blend of AMERICAN and INDIAN.] —**Amerindic** /ámmə ríndik/ *adj.*

Ameslan /ámmə slan/ *n.* = American Sign Language [Late 20thC. Acronym.]

Ames test /áymz-/ *n.* a test used to determine the cancer-causing potential of a chemical or other agent by measuring its effect on bacteria [Late 20thC. Named after the US biochemist Bruce *Ames* (born 1928), who developed it.]

amethyst /ámməthist/ *n.* **1.** MINERALS VIOLET QUARTZ GEMSTONE a translucent violet variety of quartz used as a gemstone **2.** MINERALS PURPLE GEMSTONE a purple variety of sapphire used as a gemstone **3.** COLOURS BLUISH-PURPLE a bluish-purple colour ■ *adj.* **1.** MINERALS OF AMETHYST made of or containing amethyst **2.** COLOURS OF BLUISH-PURPLE COLOUR of a bluish-purple colour [13thC. Via Old French and Latin, from Greek *amethustos*, literally 'not intoxicating', from, ultimately, *methu* 'wine' (source of English *methyl*). From the belief that it prevented drunkenness.] —**amethystine** /ámmə thís tīn/ *adj.*

Amex /ámmeks/, **AMEX** *abbr.* American Stock Exchange

Amharic /am hárrik/ *n.* the official language of Ethiopia, belonging to the Semitic branch of Afro-Asiatic languages. Amharic is written in Ethiopic script. It has nearly 15 million native speakers, with as many more speaking it as a second lan-

guage. [Early 19thC. Formed from *Amhara*, the name of a province in northwestern Ethiopia.] —**Amharic** *adj.*

amiable /áymi əb'l/ *adj.* **1.** FRIENDLY AND PLEASANT friendly and pleasant to be with **2.** WITH FRIENDLY FEELINGS characterized by friendly feelings [14thC. Via French, from late Latin, *amicabilis* 'AMICABLE', influenced in meaning by French *aimable* 'lovable' (from Latin *amabilis*, from *amare* 'to love').] —**amiability** /áymi ə bílləti/ *n.* —**amiableness** /áymi əb'lnəss/ *n.* —**amiably** /-əbli/ *adv.*

amianthus /ámmi ánthəss/ *n.* a type of asbestos with thin silky fibres [Early 17thC. Via Greek *amiantos*, literally 'undefiled', from *miainein* 'to defile'.]

amicable /ámmikəb'l/ *adj.* characterized by or done in friendliness, without anger or bad feelings ○ *an amicable divorce* [15thC. From late Latin *amicabilis*, from Latin *amicus* 'friend' (source also of English *enemy*), from *amare* 'to love'.] —**amicability** /ámmikə bílləti/ *n.* —**amicableness** /ámmikəb'lnəss/ *n.* —**amicably** /-kəbli/ *adv.*

amice /ámmiss/ *n.* a length of white fabric worn by a Christian priest around the neck and shoulders [13thC. Origin uncertain: probably via Old French *amit* from Latin *amictus* 'cloak', from *amicire* 'to cover', from *iacere* 'to throw'.]

amicus curiae /ámikəs kyoóri ee/ (*plural* **amici curiae** /a mī́-/) *n.* sb who is not a party to a legal case but whose counsel provides information to the court on the legal issues involved [Early 17thC. From modern Latin, literally 'friend of the court'.]

amid /ə míd/, **amidst** /ə mídst/ *prep.* **1.** WITHIN OR AMONG surrounded by things or people ○ *a small lake amid the hills* **2.** WHILE STH IS HAPPENING used to indicate the circumstances or events around or accompanying sth ○ *I sat down amid roars of laughter.* [12thC. Formed from an earlier form of MIDDLE.]

amide /ámmīd/ *n.* **1.** ORGANIC DERIVATIVE OF AMMONIA any organic compound derived from ammonia, formed by the replacement of one or more hydrogen atoms with acyl groups **2.** INORGANIC DERIVATIVE OF AMMONIA any inorganic compound derived from ammonia and containing the NH_2 ion [Mid-19thC. Formed from AMMONIA.] —**amidic** /ə míddik/ *adj.*

amidships /ə mídships/ *adv., adj.* near or in the middle of a boat or ship

amidst *prep.* = amid

amigo /ə meegō/ (*plural* **-gos**) *n.* a friend (*used especially in Spanish-speaking regions*) [Mid-19thC. Via Spanish, from Latin *amicus* 'friend'.]

Idi Amin

Amin /aa meén/, **Idi** (*b.* 1925) Ugandan politician. Under his presidency (1971–79), approximately 70,000 Asians were expelled from Uganda, and up to 300,000 Ugandans were killed.

amine /ə meéen/ *n.* any organic derivative of ammonia formed by the replacement of hydrogen with one or more alkyl groups [Mid-19thC. Formed from AMMONIA.]

-amine *suffix.* amine ○ *tryptamine* [From AMINE.]

amino /ə meénō/ *adj.* used to describe a chemical compound containing the NH_2 group of atoms

amino- *prefix.* containing an NH_2 group combined with a nonacid radical ○ *aminophenol* [Formed from AMINE.]

amino acid *n.* an organic acid containing one or more amino groups, especially any of a group that make up proteins and are important to living cells.

Some can be synthesized by the body (**nonessential amino acids**) and others must be obtained through the diet (**essential amino acids**).

aminopeptidase /ə meénō pépti dayz, -dayss/ *n.* an enzyme bound to the lining of the small intestine, where it breaks down dietary peptides into amino acids

amir *n.* = emir

Amish /áamish/ *npl.* MEMBERS OF US PROTESTANT GROUP members of a Protestant group who migrated from Europe to the United States and Canada in the 18th century. The Amish seek to maintain a traditional rural way of life. ■ *adj.* OF THE AMISH relating to or typical of the Amish people or their culture [Late 19thC. Origin uncertain: probably from German *amisch*. Named after Jacob *Ammann* or *Amen*, a 17thC Swiss Mennonite preacher.]

amiss /ə míss/ *adj.* WRONG incorrect, inappropriate, or not as it should be ○ *We knew immediately from the disorder in the house that something was amiss.* ■ *adv.* INCORRECTLY incorrectly or inappropriately ○ *Things began to go amiss after she left.* [13thC. From Old Norse *á mis*, literally 'so as to miss'.] ◇ **not go** or **come amiss** to be welcome or useful ◇ **take sth amiss** to be upset or offended by sth, even though no offence was intended

amitosis /ámmi tóssiss/ *n.* cell division by simple division of the nucleus and cytoplasm, without the appearance of chromosomes [Late 19thC. Formed from MITOSIS.] —**amitotic** /ámmi tóttik/ *adj.*

amitriptyline /ámmi tríptə leen/ *n.* an antidepressant drug with sedative effects, also used to treat chronic pain

amity /ámməti/ *n.* friendliness and peaceful relations (*formal*) [15thC. Via French *amitié* from medieval Latin *amicitas*, from Latin *amicus* 'friend' (see AMICABLE).]

Amman /ə maán/ capital of the Hashemite Kingdom of Jordan, in the northwestern part of the country, northeast of the Dead Sea. Population: 1,000,000 (1994).

ammeter /ámmeetər/ *n.* an instrument used for measuring electric current in amperes [Late 19thC. Coined from AMPERE + -METER.]

ammo /ámmō/ *n.* ammunition (*informal*) [Early 20thC. Shortening.]

ammonia /ə móni ə/ *n.* **1.** PUNGENT GAS a colourless gas with a pungent odour that is highly soluble in water. It is used in refrigeration and in the manufacture of fertilizers, explosives, plastics, and other chemicals. Formula: NH_3. **2.** AMMONIA SOLUTION a solution of ammonia in water, used as a household cleaner and in the manufacture of a wide range of products including fertilizers and textiles [Late 18thC. From modern Latin, from Latin *sal ammoniacus*, literally 'salt of Ammon', from, ultimately, Greek *Ammōn* 'Ammon', an Egyptian god near whose temple ammonia and ammoniac were said to be obtained.]

ammoniac /ə móni ak/ *n.* a strong-smelling brownish-yellow gum resin obtained from an Asian plant of the carrot family, used in medicine and as a porcelain cement. = **ammoniacal** [14thC. Via French from, ultimately, Latin *ammoniacus* (see AMMONIA).]

ammoniacal /ámmə nī́ ək'l/, **ammoniac** *adj.* containing or resembling ammonia

ammoniate /ə móni ayt/ (**-ates, -ating, -ated**) *vt.* treat or combine sth with ammonia or an ammonia compound —**ammoniation** /ə móni áysh'n/ *n.*

ammonia water *n.* = ammonia *n.* 2

ammonite /ámmə nīt/ *n.* **1.** EXTINCT SEA ANIMAL an extinct marine mollusc with a flat partitioned spiral shell **2.** FOSSILIZED AMMONITE SHELL the fossilized shell of an ammonite [Mid-18thC. From modern Latin *ammonites*, from medieval Latin *cornu Ammonis*, literally 'horn of Ammon'. From its resemblance to a ram's horns, which characterize representations of the Egyptian god Ammon.] —**ammonitic** /ámmə níttik/ *adj.*

Ammonite /ámmə nīt/ *n.* a member of an ancient Semitic people in the Bible who lived between the Syrian desert and the Jordan River from the 13th to the 6th centuries BC. They were constant enemies of the Israelites. [Mid-16thC. From late Latin, from Hebrew '*Ammōn* 'Ammon (son of Lot)'.]

ammonium /ə móni əm/ *n.* relating to or containing the NH_4^+ ion derived from ammonia [Early 19thC. Formed from AMMONIA.]

ammonium carbonate *n.* a white crystalline solid that is used in smelling salts, baking powder, and dyeing. Formula: $(NH_4)_2CO_3$.

ammonium chloride *n.* a white crystalline solid that is used as a soldering flux, in dry batteries, and in medicine as an expectorant. Formula: NH_4Cl.

ammonium nitrate *n.* a colourless crystalline solid that is used as a fertilizer and in herbicides, insecticides, and explosives. Formula: NH_4NO_3.

ammonoid /ámmə noyd/ *n.* = **ammonite** *n.* 1 [Mid-19thC. From modern Latin *Ammonoidea*, order name, which was formed from *ammonites* 'ammonite'.]

ammunition /ámmyŏŏ nísh'n/ *n.* 1. BULLETS AND MISSILES bullets, shells, missiles, and other projectiles used as weapons 2. EXPLOSIVE MATERIAL bombs, grenades, and other explosive devices or substances used as weapons 3. SUPPORTING FACTS facts and information that can be used to support a point of view in an argument [Late 16thC. From French, an alteration (due to mistaking 'la munition' for 'l'amunition') of *munition* (see MUNITION).]

amnesia /am néezi ə/ *n.* loss of memory as a result of shock, injury, psychological disturbance, or medical disorder [Late 18thC. From Greek *amnēsia*, an alteration of *amnēstia* 'forgetfulness', from *amnēstos*, literally 'not remembered', from *mnasthai* 'to remember'.] —**amnesiac** /am néezi ak/ *n.*, *adj.* —**amnestic** /-néstik/ *adj.*

amnesty /ámnəsti/ *n.* (*plural* -ties) 1. PARDON a general pardon, especially for those who have committed political crimes 2. PROSECUTION-FREE PERIOD a period during which crimes can be admitted or illegal weapons handed in without prosecution ■ *vt.* (-ties, -tying, -tied) PARDON SB to grant amnesty to sb [Late 16thC. Via French from, ultimately, Greek *amnēstia* (see AMNESIA). The underlying idea is of forgetting a wrongdoing.]

Amnesty International *n.* an international human rights organization concerned with prisoners of conscience under any type of political regime

amnia plural of **amnion**

amnio /ámni ō/ (*plural* -os) *n.* an amniocentesis (*informal*) [Late 20thC. Shortening.]

amniocentesis /ámni ō sen téessiss/ (*plural* -ses /-seez/) *n.* a test performed to determine the health, sex, or genetic constitution of a foetus by taking a sample of amniotic fluid through a needle inserted into the womb of the mother [Mid-20thC. Coined from AMNION + Greek *kentēsis* 'pricking' (from *kentein* 'to prick').]

amniography /ámni óggrəfi/ *n.* an X-ray of the womb, taken after a substance that will be shown up by the X-rays has been injected into the bloodstream [Mid-20thC. Coined from AMNION + -GRAPHY.]

amnion /ámni ən/ (*plural* -ons or -a /-ni ə/) *n.* 1. INNER MEMBRANE SURROUNDING EMBRYO the inner of the two membranes enclosing the embryo of a bird, reptile, or mammal and its surrounding fluid. ◊ **chorion** 2. EMBRYO SAC the fluid-filled sac within which the embryo of a bird, reptile, or mammal develops [Mid-17thC. From Greek, 'caul', literally 'a small lamb', from *amnos* 'lamb'.] —**amniotic** /ámni óttik/ *adj.*

amniote /ámni ōt/ *n.* any vertebrate that develops from an embryo within an amnion, e.g. a bird, reptile, or mammal [Early 20thC. From modern Latin *Amniota*, from AMNION.]

amniotic fluid /ámni óttik-/ *n.* the fluid that surrounds a foetus while it is developing. It is the fluid that flows out in the 'breaking of the waters' before a baby is born.

amniotic sac *n.* = **amnion** *n.* 2

amoeba /ə méebə/ (*plural* -bae /ə méebee/ or -bas), **ameba** (*plural* -bas or -bae /-bee/) *n.* a single-celled organism found in water and in damp soil on land, and as a parasite of other organisms. Lacking a fixed form and supporting structures, an amoeba consists of a protoplasmic mass in a thin membrane, and forms temporary projections (**pseudopodia**) in order to move. Genus: *Amoeba*. [Mid-19thC. Via modern Latin, genus name, from Greek *amoibē* 'change',

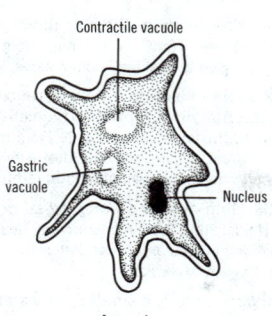

Contractile vacuole

Gastric vacuole

Nucleus

Amoeba

from *ameibein* 'to change'. From its changing shape.] —**amoebic** *adj.*

amoebiasis /ámmi bíəssiss/ *n.* an infection or disease affecting the bowel, caused by an amoeba *Entamoeba histolytica*

amoebic dysentery *n.* an inflammation of the colon causing diarrhoea of varying degrees of severity that results from infection by an amoeba *Entamoeba histolytica*

amok /ə mók/, **amuck** /ə múk/ *adj.* frenzied and out of control [Early 16thC. Directly or via Portuguese *am(o)uco* 'homicidally violent Malay' from Malay *amuk* 'fighting frenziedly'.] ◊ **run amok** to be or become out of control, especially in a frenzied way

among /ə múng/, **amongst** /-múngst/ CORE MEANING: a preposition indicating that sth or sb is surrounded by people, things, ideas, or circumstances ○ *You're among friends here.*
prep. 1. OF A GROUP of the stated group or class ○ *Her carvings are among the world's finest.* 2. IN A GROUP in or by the particular group stated ○ *a widely-held notion among physicists* 3. BETWEEN GROUP MEMBERS by, between, or to each person or thing in a group ○ *divided among six of us* 4. IN ADDITION TO in addition to other things or people ○ *The photos showed, among other things, a birthday party.* [Old English *on (ge)mong*, from *on* 'in' + *(ge)mong* 'crowd'. Ultimately from an Indo-European word that is also the ancestor of English *mingle* and *mongrel*.]

amontillado /ámmonti laádō/ (*plural* -dos) *n.* a pale medium-dry sherry from Spain [Early 19thC. From Spanish. Named after the Spanish town *Montilla*, where sherry of this type is made.]

amoral /ay mórrəl/ *adj.* 1. OUTSIDE SCOPE OF MORALITY not concerned with or amenable to moral judgments 2. WITHOUT MORAL STANDARDS not caring about good behaviour or morals —**amoralism** *n.* —**amorality** /áymo rálləti/ *n.* —**amorally** /ay mórrəli/ *adv.*

— WORD KEY: USAGE —
See Usage note at **immoral**.

amoretto /ámmə réttō/ (*plural* -ti /-rétti/) *n.* an artistic representation of a small naked boy or winged cherub as a symbol of love [Early 17thC. From Italian, literally 'a small cupid', from *amore* 'love', from Latin *amor* (see AMOROUS).]

amorist /ámmərist/ *n.* sb who writes about love or who is in love (*literary*) [Late 16thC. Formed from French *amour* 'love' or Latin *amor* (see AMOROUS).]

Amorite /ámmə rīt/ *n.* a member of an ancient Semitic people in the Bible who lived in Mesopotamia, Syria, and Palestine between approximately 2,600 and 1,200 BC [Mid-16thC. Formed from Hebrew *'ĕmōrī*, from, ultimately, Akkadian *Amurru(m)*, literally 'West', the name of the land inhabited by the Amorites.]

amoroso[1] /ámmə róssō/ *adv.*, *adj.* to be played or sung in a gentle loving way (*used as a musical direction*) [Late 18thC. Via Italian, from medieval Latin *amorosus* 'AMOROUS'.]

amoroso[2] /ámmə róssō/ (*plural* **amorosos**) *n.* a sweet dark sherry [Late 19thC. Via Spanish, from medieval Latin *amorosus* 'AMOROUS'.]

amorous /ámmərəss/ *adj.* showing or feeling romantic love or sexual attraction [14thC. Via Old French, from medieval Latin *amorosus*, from Latin *amor* 'love' (source of English *amateur*).] —**amorously** *adv.* —**amorousness** *n.*

amorphous /ə máwrfəss/ *adj.* 1. WITHOUT SHAPE without any clear shape, form, or structure 2. NOT CLASSIFIABLE not obviously belonging to any particular category or type 3. CHEM, GEOL WITHOUT CRYSTALLINE STRUCTURE without a crystalline structure [Mid-18thC. Via modern Latin, from Greek *amorphos*, literally 'without shape', from *morphē* 'shape'.] —**amorphously** *adv.* —**amorphousness** *n.*

amortisation *n.* = amortization

amortise *vt.* = amortize

amortization /ə máwr tī záysh'n/, **amortisation** *n.* the reduction of a debt by making payments in instalments or regular transfers, or the money used for this. ◊ **amortize** *v.* 2

amortize /ə máwr tīz/ (-tizes, -tizing, -tized), **amortise** (-tises, -tising, -tised) *vt.* 1. REDUCE DEBT BY INSTALMENTS to reduce a debt by making payments against the principal balance in instalments or regular transfers 2. WRITE OFF COST OF ASSET to write off the cost of an asset over a period of time in a statement of accounts 3. TRANSFER PROPERTY to transfer land or other assets to an ecclesiastical body (*archaic*) [14thC. Via the French stem *amortiss-* 'to alienate in mortmain' from assumed Vulgar Latin *admortire* 'to deaden', from the Latin stem *mort-* 'death'.] —**amortizable** *adj.*

Amos /áymoss/ HEBREW PROPHET a Hebrew prophet in the Bible who lived in the 8th century BC and delivered judgments against Judah, Samaria, and Israel ■ *n.* BOOK IN BIBLE a book of the Bible that contains the prophecies of Amos. See table at **Bible**

amount /ə mównt/ *n.* a quantity or degree of sth, considered as a unit or total [14thC. From Old French *amonter* 'to rise', from *amont* 'upwards', from Latin *ad montem*, literally 'to the mountain'.]

— WORD KEY: USAGE —
amount or **number**? *Amount* is normally used with singular forms of words or meanings that have no plural, that is so-called uncountable or mass nouns such as *cheese*, *happiness*, and *warfare*, whereas *number* is used with plural nouns such as *books*, *questions*, and *ships*. *a large amount of cheese. any amount of happiness. a large number of books. a good number of cheeses (= types of cheese). an excessive number of questions.* In everyday speech, *amount* is sometimes used when *number* is strictly called for: *a large amount of books.* This should be avoided in more formal speaking and writing.

amount to *vt.* 1. ADD UP TO to come to a particular total when added up 2. BE EQUIVALENT TO to be equivalent to sth ○ *Their statement amounts to nothing more than a slick evasion.*

amour /ə moŏr/ *n.* a love affair, especially one that is clandestine (*dated*) [14thC. Via French, from Latin *amor* 'love'.]

amour-propre /ámmoor própprə/ *n.* self-respect or estimation of your true worth (*formal*) [Late 18thC. From French, literally 'self-love'.]

Amoy /ə móy/ *n.* the dialect of Chinese spoken on the island of Xiamen and in neighbouring areas in southeastern China [Mid-19thC. Named after *Amoy* (XIAMEN).]

amp /amp/ *n.* 1. AMPERE an ampere 2. AMPLIFIER an amplifier (*informal*) [Late 19thC. Shortening.]

AMP *n.* a chemical compound (**nucleotide**) occurring in living organisms that is formed from another nucleotide, ATP, and affects the function of genes and enzymes. Full form **adenosine monophosphate**. ◊ **cyclic AMP**

amperage /ámpərij/ *n.* the number of amperes measured in an electric current

ampere /ám pair/ *n.* the basic unit of electric current in the SI system, equal to a current that produces a force of 2×10^{-7} newtons per metre between two parallel conductors in a vacuum. Symbol **A** [Late 19thC. Named after the French physicist André-Marie *Ampère* (1775–1836), who first distinguished between electrical current and voltage.]

ampere-hour *n.* a measure of quantity of electricity equal to the amount of electricity that passes in one hour through a conductor with a current of one ampere

ampersand /ámpər sand/ n. the symbol '&', meaning 'and' [Mid-19thC. From and per se and, literally '(the character) '&' by itself (means) and'. The character '&' itself is a conventionalized printed version of an abbreviation used for Latin et 'and'.]

amphetamine /am fétta meen/ n. a white crystalline compound, or any of its derivatives, formerly used as a stimulant of the central nervous system to treat conditions such as depression, and as an appetite suppressant. Excessive use of amphetamines can cause dangerous side effects and dependency. [Mid-20thC. Contraction of alpha-methyl-phenethylamine.]

amphi- prefix. both ○ amphibious [Via Latin from, ultimately, Greek amphi 'on both sides'. Ultimately from an Indo-European base that is also the ancestor of English by, umlaut, and ambi-.]

amphibian /am fíbbi ən/ n. **1.** LAND ANIMAL THAT BREEDS IN WATER a cold-blooded vertebrate that spends some time in water but must breed and develop into an adult in water. Frogs, salamanders, and toads are amphibians. Class: Amphibia. **2.** AIRCRAFT OR VEHICLE an aircraft or vehicle designed to operate on land or water ■ adj. = amphibious [Mid-19thC. Formed from modern Latin Amphibia, class name, from Greek amphibion 'amphibious being', from amphibios (see AMPHIBIOUS).]

amphibious /am fíbbi əss/ adj. **1.** LIVING ON LAND AND IN WATER used to describe an animal that lives in water during early development and on land as an adult **2.** ON LAND AND IN WATER taking place or operating both on land and in water ○ amphibious assault on the island ○ amphibious vehicles **3.** OF MIXED TYPE with two different qualities or features resulting in a mixed type [Mid-17thC. From Greek amphibios, literally 'living on both (land and water)', from bios 'life' (source of English biology).] —**amphibiously** adv. —**amphibiousness** n.

amphibole /ámfi bōl/ n. a hydrous silicate mineral containing aluminium, calcium, iron, magnesium, and sodium, singly or in combination. Hornblende, tremolite, and asbestos are amphiboles. [Early 19thC. From French, ultimately from Greek amphibolos 'ambiguous', literally 'throwing in both directions', from ballein 'to throw'; because the mineral is able to appear in a variety of forms.] —**amphibolic** /ámfi bóllik/ adj.

amphibolite /am fíbbə līt/ n. a metamorphic rock consisting mainly of amphibole with some plagioclase

amphibology /ámfi bólləji/ (plural -gies), **amphiboly** /am fíbbəli/ (plural -lies) n. a phrase or sentence that can be interpreted in two ways, usually because of the grammatical construction rather than the meanings of the words themselves. The phrase 'the boy on the chair with a broken leg' is an amphibology. [Late 16thC. From late Latin amphibologia 'ambiguity', coined from Latin amphibolia + Greek -logia 'speech'.] —**amphibological** /am fíbbə lójjik'l/ adj. —**amphibologically** /-lójjikli/ adv. —**amphibolous** /am fíbbələss/ adj.

amphibrach /ámfi brak/ n. a metrical foot of three syllables with the stress on the second syllable, or of one long syllable between two short syllables. The word 'contentment' and the phrase 'a mushroom' are amphibrachs. [Late 16thC. Via Latin amphibrachys from Greek amphibrakhus 'short on both sides', from brakhus 'short'.] —**amphibrachic** /ámfi brákik/ adj.

amphictyon /am fíkti ən/ n. a representative of an ancient Greek state or community at the council of a religious alliance (**amphictyony**) [Late 16thC. From Greek amphiktuones, originally amphiktiones 'nearby dwellers', from ktizein 'to settle, found'.]

amphictyony /am fíkti əni/ (plural -nies) n. a group of neighbouring states or communities in ancient Greece that shared responsibility for shrines and temples. The amphictyony maintaining the shrine of Apollo at Delphi is a famous example. —**amphictyonic** /am fíkti ónnik/ adj.

amphigory /ám figgəri/ (plural -ries), **amphigouri** /ámfí goori/ (plural -ris) n. a nonsensical piece of writing, usually in verse [Early 19thC. From French amphigouri, probably coined from Greek amphi- 'all around' and, perhaps, French allégorie 'allegory'.]

amphimacer /am fímməsser/ n. a metrical foot of three syllables with the stress on the first and third syllables, or of one short syllable between two long

syllables. The phrase 'happy days' is an amphimacer. [Late 16thC. Via Latin, from Greek amphimakros 'long on both sides', from makros 'long'.]

amphimixis /ámfi míksiss/ n. sexual reproduction involving the fusion of reproductive cells (**gametes**) from two organisms [Late 19thC. From modern Latin, coined from Greek amphi- 'on both sides' + mixis 'mingling', from mignunai 'to mix'.] —**amphimictic** /ámfi míktik/ adj.

amphioxus /ámfi óksəss/ (plural -i /-sī/ or -uses) n. = lancelet [Mid-19thC. From modern Latin, literally 'sharp at both sides', from Greek amphi- 'at both sides' + oxus 'sharp' (source of English oxygen).]

amphipod /ámfi pod/ n. a small freshwater or marine crustacean with a thin body and without a carapace. Order: Amphipoda. [Mid-19thC. Formed from modern Latin Amphipoda, order name, from Greek amphi- 'both' + pous 'foot', because there are two types of feet in this order.] —**amphipodous** /am fíppədəss/ adj.

amphiprostyle /ámfi prō stīl/ n. a classical temple or other building with a set of columns at each end but not at the sides [Early 18thC. Via French and Latin, from Greek amphiprostulos 'with pillars at both ends', from prostulos 'having pillars' (see PROSTYLE).]

amphisbaena /ámfiss beenə/ (plural -nae /-nee/ or -nas) n. **1.** LIZARD WITHOUT LEGS a legless lizard usually found in tropical America with a rounded tail resembling a second head. Family: Amphisbaenidae. **2.** MYTHOLOGICAL SERPENT in classical mythology, a poisonous snake that has a head at each end of its body, allowing it to move in either direction [14thC. Via Latin, from Greek amphisbaina, literally 'going both ways', from amphis 'both ways' + bainein 'to go'.] —**amphisbaenic** adj.

amphistylar /ámfi stīlər/ adj. used to describe a building, especially a classical temple, that has a set of columns on both ends or sides [19thC. Formed from AMPHI- + Greek stulos 'column'.]

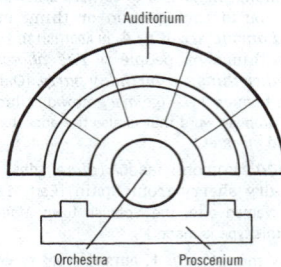

Amphitheatre

amphitheatre /ámfi theertər/ n. **1.** ARCHIT CIRCULAR BUILDING a round or oval building without a roof that has a central open space surrounded by tiers of seats, especially one used by the ancient Romans for public entertainments **2.** SPORT PLACE FOR SPORTS a large enclosure where sporting activities or public entertainments take place **3.** GEOL ROUND HOLLOW IN LAND a circular area of level ground surrounded by hills or rising ground, usually a natural feature of the landscape **4.** SEATING FOR SPECTATORS a gallery of seats arranged in semicircular tiers for the audience in a theatre or lecture room **5.** LECTURE ROOM a lecture hall or operating room where seating is arranged in semicircular tiers [Mid-14thC. Via Latin, from Greek amphitheatron, literally 'theatre on both sides' (because the typical classical Greek theatre had seating on one side only), from theatron 'theatre' (see THEATRE).] —**amphitheatric** /ámfithi áttrik/ adj. —**amphitheatrically** /ámfithi áttrikli/ adv.

amphora /ámfərə/ (plural -rae /-ree/ or -ras) n. a jar, usually made of clay, with a narrow neck and two handles, used by ancient Greeks and Romans for holding oil or wine [15thC. Via Latin from, ultimately, Greek amphiphoreus, from amphi- 'on both sides' + phoreus 'bearer', from pherein 'to bear', from its two handles.] —**amphoral** adj.

amphoteric /ámfə térrik/ adj. able to react chemically as either an acid or a base [Mid-19thC. Formed from Greek amphoteroi 'both of two', the comparative form of amphō 'both'.]

Amphora

ampicillin /ámpi síllin/ n. a semisynthetic form of penicillin, used especially in the treatment of respiratory infections [Mid-20thC. Blend of AMINO- and PENICILLIN.]

ample /ámp'l/ (-pler, -plest) adj. **1.** MORE THAN ENOUGH as much or as many as required, usually with some left over **2.** LARGE large, especially in physical size (often used euphemistically) [15thC. Via French, from Latin amplus 'large, plentiful'.] —**ampleness** n.

——— WORD KEY: SYNONYMS ———
See Synonyms at **sufficient** and **enough**.

amplexus /am pléksəss/ n. the mating posture of a pair of frogs or toads, in which the male clasps the female from behind during egg release and fertilization [Mid-20thC. From Latin, 'an embracing', from the past participle of amplecti 'to embrace'.]

amplicon /ámpli kón/ n. a nucleic acid fragment that is the product of the artificial large-scale reproduction of genetic material

amplification /ámpli fi káysh'n/ n. **1.** ENLARGEMENT OF STH the act or process of making sth larger, greater, or stronger **2.** PROCESS OF MAKING LOUDER the act or process of making sth louder **3.** ADDITION OF DETAIL the act or process of making a spoken or written account fuller or clearer **4.** DETAIL ADDED a detail, explanation, or illustration added to a spoken or written account to make it fuller or clearer **5.** ELECTRON ENG INCREASE IN SIGNAL MAGNITUDE the increase in the magnitude of a signal produced by an amplifier **6.** GENETICS GENE REPRODUCTION the artificial large-scale reproduction of genes or DNA sequences

amplifier /ámpli fī ər/ n. **1.** SOUND-INCREASING APPARATUS a device that makes sounds louder, especially one used to increase the sound level of musical instruments **2.** SIGNAL ENHANCER an electronic device that increases the magnitude of a signal, voltage, or current

amplify /ámpli fī/ (-fies, -fying, -fied) vti. **1.** INCREASE to become larger, greater, or stronger, or make sth such as an emotion or sensation become larger, greater, or stronger **2.** MAKE LOUDER to become louder, or make a sound become louder, by electronic or other means **3.** ADD DETAIL to make a spoken or written account fuller, clearer, or more detailed **4.** ELECTRON ENG INCREASE SIGNAL to increase the magnitude of a signal using an amplifier, or undergo such an increase [15thC. Via French amplifier from Latin amplificare 'to enlarge', from amplus 'large' (source of English ample) + fic-, a form of the stem of facere 'to make'.] —**amplifiable** adj.

——— WORD KEY: SYNONYMS ———
See Synonyms at **increase**.

amplitude /ámpli tyood/ n. **1.** LARGENESS a largeness in size, volume, or extent **2.** BREADTH a breadth of range **3.** ABUNDANCE an amount that is more than required **4.** PHYS DISTANCE FROM MEAN POINT the furthest distance that a vibrating or oscillating system such as a pendulum travels from a mean or zero point **5.** ELECTRON ENG SIGNAL'S MAXIMUM VALUE the maximum value of an alternating signal **6.** MATH ANGLE OF VECTOR REPRESENTING COMPLEX NUMBER the angle between a vector representing a complex number and the positive real axis [Mid-16thC. Via French, from Latin amplitudo 'size, greatness, grandeur', from amplus (see AMPLE).]

amplitude modulation n. the modulation of the amplitude of a radio wave in such a way as to encode the wave with audio or visual information

amply /ámpli/ *adv.* to a more than adequate degree

ampoule /ám pool, -pyool/, **ampule** *n.* a small sealed glass container that holds a measured amount of a medicinal substance to be injected [Early 20thC. Via French, from Latin *ampulla* (see AMPULLA).]

ampulla /am póollə/ (*plural* **-lae** /-lee/) *n.* **1.** VESSEL FOR HOLY LIQUID a small container for a consecrated substance, especially oil, water, or the wine used at the Christian Communion **2.** ANCIENT ROMAN BOTTLE a round two-handled bottle used by the ancient Romans to hold wine, oil, or perfume [Late 14thC. From Latin, literally 'little amphora', from *ampora*, a variant of *amphora* (see AMPHORA).]

amputate /ámpyoŏ tayt/ (**-tates, -tating, -tated**) *vti.* to cut off a limb or other appendage of the body, especially in a surgical operation [Mid-16thC. From Latin *amputat-*, the past participle stem of *amputare* 'to cut around', from *ambi-* 'around' + *putare* 'to cut'.] —**amputation** /ámpyoŏ táysh'n/ *n.* —**amputator** /ámpyoŏ taytər/ *n.*

amputee /ámpyoŏ tee/ *n.* sb who has had a limb or part of a limb cut off

amrita /am reétə/, **amreeta** *n.* **1.** DRINK BESTOWING IMMORTALITY in Hindu mythology, a substance prepared by the gods that makes those who drink it immortal **2.** IMMORTALITY immortality gained by drinking amrita [Late 18thC. From Sanskrit *amṛta*, literally 'without death', from *mṛta* 'death'.]

Amritsar /əm rítsər/ city in Punjab state in north-western India. It is a holy city for Sikhs. Population: 709,456 (1991).

Amsterdam /ámstər dam/ capital and commercial centre in the Netherlands, situated where the River Amstel flows into the Ijsselmeer. Population: 724,096 (1994).

amt *abbr.* amount

amu *abbr.* atomic mass unit

amuck *adj., adv.* = amok

Amu Darya /aǎ moo daǎryə/ river in central and western Asia flowing from the Pamir plateau towards the Aral Sea. Length: 2,540 km/1,580 mi.

amulet /ámmyoŏlət/ *n.* **1.** LUCKY JEWELLERY a piece of jewellery worn to provide protection against evil, injury, disease, or bad luck **2.** LUCKY OBJECT an ordinary object that is supposed to provide protection against bad luck or negative forces [Late 16thC. From Latin *amuletum*.]

Amun /aǎmən/ *n.* a supreme god of ancient Egypt. Amun was originally a local god of Thebes, but was elevated during the eighteenth dynasty.

Amundsen /ámmənds'n/, **Roald** (1872–1928) Norwegian explorer. He was the first person to reach the South Pole (1911).

Amur /ə múr/ river in east-central Asia that forms the boundary between Manchuria and Siberia before flowing north into the Tatar Strait. Length: 2,874 km/1,786 mi.

amuse /ə myooz/ (**amuses, amusing, amused**) *v.* **1.** *vti.* MAKE SB LAUGH to make sb smile or laugh or think that sth is funny **2.** *vt.* KEEP SB HAPPILY OCCUPIED to keep sb occupied or entertained by providing entertainment or an interesting task **3.** *vt.* DECEIVE SB BY DISTRACTION to distract sb's attention, usually in order to trick or deceive (*archaic*) [15thC. From French *amuser* 'to cause to stare stupidly', from *muser* 'to stare stupidly' (see MUSE). The modern senses evolved from 'to deceive' via 'to divert sb's attention'.] —**amused** *adj.*

—— **WORD KEY: ORIGIN** ——

The history of the word *amuse* is very similar to that of *distract* and *divert*: all three have moved from the notion of 'leading the mind astray' in a negative sense to the notion of 'entertainment'. In the case of *amuse* the earlier connotations have been entirely lost.

amusement /ə myoŏzmənt/ *n.* **1.** FEELING STH IS FUNNY the feeling that sth is funny or entertaining **2.** RECREATIONAL ACTIVITY an enjoyable activity such as a game, a hobby, or a form of entertainment **3.** RIDE OR GAME a ride, game, or other attraction found in an amusement park or arcade **4.** KEEPING HAPPILY OCCUPIED

the act of keeping sb or a group of people occupied or entertained

amusement arcade *n.* an indoor or covered area containing a variety of coin-operated machines for playing games or small-scale gambling. They are often found in shopping malls and at holiday resorts.

amusement park *n.* an outdoor area with a variety of mechanical rides, games, and other attractions that people pay to use

amusing /ə myooʒing/ *adj.* causing sb to smile or laugh or be amused, often in a subdued way — **amusingly** *adv.* —**amusingness** *n.*

amygdala /ə mígdələ/ (*plural* **-lae** /-lee/) *n.* an almond-shaped mass of grey matter, one in each hemisphere of the brain, associated with feelings of fear and aggression and important for visual learning and memory [Pre-12thC. Via Latin, from Greek *amugdalē* 'almond', the original sense in English.]

amygdalin /ə mígdəlin/, **amygdaline** /-lin, -leen/ *n.* a white crystalline bitter-tasting sugar derivative (**glycoside**) found in the seeds of many plants of the rose family such as apricots, almonds, and peaches [Mid-19thC. Coined from Latin *amygdala* 'almond' (see AMYGDALA) + -IN.]

amyl /ámmil, áy mīl/ *adj.* relating to or containing any of eight possible forms of a chemical group with the same basic formula. Formula: C_5H_{11}–. [Mid-19thC. Coined from Latin *amylum*, from Greek *amulon* 'finely ground meal', from, ultimately, *mulē* 'mill' + -YL.]

amyl- *prefix.* = amylo- (*used before vowels*)

amylaceous /ámmi láyshəss/ *adj.* having or resembling starch (*technical*)

amyl acetate *n.* a colourless volatile liquid that smells like pears. It is used as a flavouring and as a solvent for paints and lacquers. Formula: $CH_3CO_2C_5H_{11}$.

amyl alcohol *n.* a colourless alcohol, or a mixture of any of the eight related amyl alcohols, used in the synthesis of other chemicals and drugs and as a solvent. Formula: $C_5H_{12}O$.

amylase /ámmi layz, -layss/ *n.* an enzyme, found in plants, animal saliva, and pancreatic juice, that aids the conversion of starch and glycogen to simple sugars such as glucose

amyl nitrite *n.* a pale yellow fragrant liquid used mainly as an inhalant to dilate blood vessels in the treatment of angina pectoris. Formula: $C_5H_{11}NO_2$.

amylo-, **amyl-** *prefix.* starch ○ *amylosin* [From Latin *amylum* 'starch' (see AMYLUM)]

amyloid /ámmi loyd/ *n.* **1.** WAXY PROTEIN a waxy translucent substance composed of complex protein fibres and polysaccharides that is formed in body tissues in some degenerative diseases, e.g. Alzheimer's disease **2.** STARCHY SUBSTANCE a substance that resembles starch in composition or function ■ *adj.* STARCHY resembling a starch (*technical*)

amyloidosis /ámmi loy dóssiss/ *n.* a condition marked by the accumulation of a protein-based substance (**amyloid**) in the body's organs and tissues

amylopectin /ámmilō péktin/ *n.* an insoluble component of starch that is a carbohydrate polymer with a highly branched structure, high molecular weight, and an inability to gel readily in aqueous solution. ◊ **amylose**

amylopsin /ámmi lópsin/ *n.* an enzyme (**amylase**) found in pancreatic juice that aids the conversion of starch to maltose [Late 19thC. Coined from AMYLO- + TRYPSIN.]

amylose /ámmi lōz, -lōss/ *n.* a soluble component of starch that is an unbranched carbohydrate polymer formed of glucose units, with a tendency to form gels in aqueous solution. ◊ **amylopectin**

amyotonia /áy mī ə tóni ə/ *n.* an abnormal lack of muscle tension

amyotrophic lateral sclerosis /ə mí ə trófik-, -tróffik-/ *n.* a fatal degenerative disease of the nervous system marked by progressive muscle weakness and atrophy. It is a form of motor neurone disease.

amyotrophy /ámmi óttrəfi/ *n.* a degeneration of the muscles caused by nerve disease [Late 19thC. Coined from A- + MYO- + -TROPHY.]

an (*stressed*) /an/; (*unstressed*) /ən/ *det.* used instead of 'a', the indefinite article, in front of words with an initial vowel sound [Old English, a stressless form of the numeral *ān* 'one' (source also of English *a*)]

—— **WORD KEY: USAGE** ——
See Usage note at *a*.

an[2] /an, ən/, **an'** *conj.* if (*archaic*) [12thC. Reduced form of AND in the sense 'if'.]

AN *abbr.* Anglo-Norman

an. *abbr.* anno

an- *prefix.* = a- *prefix.* (*used before vowels*)

-an[1] *suffix.* **1.** of or relating to ○ *Minoan* ○ *agrarian* **2.** a person of or resembling a certain kind ○ *librarian* [Via Old French from Latin *-anus*, a suffix forming nouns and adjectives]

-an[2] *suffix.* an unsaturated carbon compound ○ *benzofuran* [Alteration of -ANE]

ana[1] /aǎnə/ (*plural* **-a** *or* **-as**) *n.* **1.** COLLECTION OF ITEMS a collection of things connected with a famous person, place, or period, especially spoken or written information, anecdotes, or sayings **2.** COLLECTIBLE ITEM an item in an ana

ana[2] /ánnə/ *adv.* of each of the ingredients specified in a medical prescription in equal amounts [From the Greek prefix *ana-* 'up, back, again', from the preposition and adverb *ana* 'up']

ana- *prefix.* **1.** up, upward ○ *anamorphic* **2.** back, backward, away ○ *anaphase* **3.** again ○ *anaplastic* [From Greek *ana*. Ultimately from an Indo-European word meaning 'on', which is also the ancestor of English *on*.]

-ana *suffix.* a collection of objects or information about a topic, person, or place ○ *Shakespeareana* [Via modern Latin from Latin, neuter plural of *-anus* 'pertaining to']

anabaptism /ánnə báptizzəm/ *n.* the advocacy of adult baptism on the grounds that only as adults can people responsibly accept and declare their faith [See ANABAPTISM]

Anabaptism *n.* the doctrines or beliefs of the Anabaptists [Mid-16thC. Via ecclesiastical Latin *anabaptismus* from Greek *anabaptismos* 'second baptism', from *baptismos* 'baptism'.]

Anabaptist /ánnə báptist/ *n.* a member of a 16th-century Protestant movement promoting the doctrine of adult baptism on the grounds that only adults can accept and declare their faith on their own behalf [Mid-16thC. From ecclesiastical Latin *anabaptista*, which was formed from Greek *ana-* 'again, afresh' + *baptistēs* 'baptizer' (see BAPTIZE).] —**Anabaptist** *adj.*

anabatic /ánnə báttik/ *adj.* used to describe winds that move or blow upwards during the daytime as warm air rises up mountain slopes. ◊ **katabatic** [Mid-20thC. From Greek *anabatikos* 'relating to mounting', from *anabainein* 'to go up, mount', from *bainein* 'to go'.]

anabolic /ánnə bóllik/ *adj.* used to describe a metabolic process in which energy is used to construct complex molecules from simpler ones [Late 19thC. Blend of ANA- and METABOLIC.]

anabolic steroid *n.* **1.** SYNTHETIC HORMONE a synthetic steroid hormone that increases muscle mass and strength. It is sometimes used by weightlifters and other athletes. **2.** HORMONE a naturally occurring hormone that promotes tissue growth

anabolism /ə nábbəlizzəm/ *n.* a metabolic process in which energy is used to construct complex molecules from simpler ones in the synthesis of needed compounds and tissues [Late 19thC. Blend of ANA- and METABOLISM.]

anabolite /ə nábbə līt/ *n.* a product or substance resulting from the metabolic process of anabolism

anabranch /ánnə brangk/ *n.* a stream that separates from a river and follows its own course before re-entering the same river further downstream [Mid-19thC. Blend of *anastomosing* (from ANASTOMOSE) and BRANCH.]

anachronism /ə nákrənizzəm/ *n.* **1.** CHRONOLOGICAL MISTAKE sth from a different period of time, e.g. a modern idea or invention wrongly placed in a historical setting in fiction or drama **2.** STH OUT OF TIME a person, thing, idea, or custom that seems to belong to a different time in history **3.** MAKING OF CHRONOLOGICAL MISTAKE the representation of sb or sth out of chronological order or in the wrong historical setting [Mid-17thC. Via French *anachronisme* from, ultimately, late Greek *anakhronizesthai*, literally 'to be timed backwards', from *khronos* 'time'.] —**anachronous** /ə nákrənəss/ *adj.* —**anachronously** *adv.*

anachronistic /ə nákrə nístik/ *adj.* **1.** CHRONOLOGICALLY WRONG belonging to a time other than the one being represented, especially in fiction or drama **2.** NOT APPROPRIATE TO THE TIMES out-of-date or inappropriate at the time in question —**anachronistically** *adv.*

anaclitic /ánnə klíttik/ *adj.* characterized by strong emotional dependence on a mother or other nurturing person, especially to the extent of exhibiting or causing serious developmental and psychological disturbances [Early 20thC. Formed from Greek *anaklitos* 'for reclining', from *anaklinein* 'to lean upon', from *klinein* 'to lean'.] —**anaclisis** /ánnə klíssiss/ *n.*

anacoluthon /ánnəkə lóo thon, -lóoth'n/ (*plural* **-tha** /-lóothə/) *n.* an instance of abandoning a grammatical construction in speech or writing before it is complete and continuing with another. The sentence 'The subject of the lecture was – I didn't really understand it' contains an anacoluthon. [Early 18thC. Via late Latin, from Greek *anakolouthon* 'illogicality, inconsistency', from *anakolouthos* 'not following', from *akolouthos* 'following' (source also of English *acolyte*).] —**anacoluthic** *adj.*

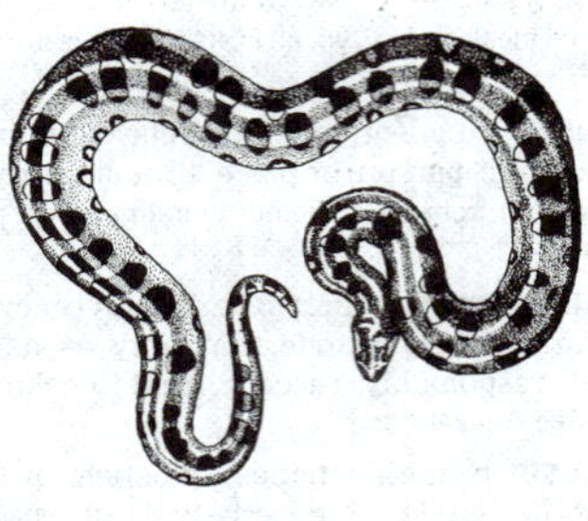

Anaconda

anaconda /ánnə kóndə/ *n.* a South American nonvenomous snake, the largest in the boa family, that lives in or near water and in trees. It can grow to a length of more than 9 m/30 ft. Latin name: *Eunectes murinus.* [Mid-18thC. Origin uncertain: perhaps from Sinhalese, an alteration of *henakandayā*, literally 'lightning snake'.]

Anacreon /ə nákri on/ (570?–478 BC) Greek lyric poet. He is well known for celebrating love and wine in his verse.

Anacreontic /ə nákri óntik/, **anacreontic** *adj.* WITH ANACREON'S STYLE OR THEMES written in the style or treating the subjects of the Greek poet Anacreon ■ *n.* TYPE OF POEM an Anacreontic poem [Early 17thC. Via Latin *Anacreonticus* from Greek *Anakreont-*, the stem of *Anakreōn* (see ANACREON).]

anacrusis /ánnə króossiss/ (*plural* **-ses** /-seez/) *n.* **1.** POETRY UNSTRESSED SYLLABLES one or more unstressed syllables at the beginning of a line of verse that are not considered part of the metrical pattern of the line **2.** MUSIC UNACCENTED NOTES one or more unaccented notes immediately before the first downbeat of a bar [Mid-19thC. Via modern Latin, from, ultimately, Greek *anakrouein* 'to strike up (a tune)', from *krouein* 'to strike'.] —**anacrustic** /ánnə krústik/ *adj.*

anadem /ánnə dem/ *n.* a garland or wreath worn on the head (*archaic or literary*) [Early 17thC. Via Latin, from Greek *anadēma* 'headband', from *anadeein* 'to bind up', from *deein* 'to bind' (source of English *diadem*).]

anadiplosis /ánnə di plóssiss/ (*plural* **-ses** /-seez/) *n.* the rhetorical repetition of the last word or words of one phrase or sentence at the beginning of the next. The sentence 'He was tormented by fears – fears that were soon to be realized' uses anadiplosis. [Late 16thC. Via Latin, from, ultimately, Greek *anadiploein*, literally 'to double back', from *diploein* 'to double'.]

anadromous /ə náddrəməss/ *adj.* used to describe fish such as salmon and shad that return from the sea to the rivers where they were born in order to breed. ◊ **catadromous** [Mid-18thC. Formed from Greek *anadromos* 'running up (a river from the sea)', from *dromos* 'a running'.]

anaemia /ə neémi ə/, **anemia** *n.* **1.** MED BLOOD DEFICIENCY a blood condition in which there are too few red blood cells or the red blood cells are deficient in haemoglobin, resulting in poor health **2.** WEAKNESS lack of vitality or courage [Early 19thC. Via modern Latin, from Greek *anaimia*, literally 'being without blood', from *haima* 'blood'.]

anaemic /ə neémik/, **anemic** *adj.* **1.** MED HAVING ANAEMIA having some form of anaemia **2.** SICK-LOOKING pale and not looking well **3.** WEAK lacking vitality, strength, or courage

anaerobe /ánnə rōb/ *n.* a microorganism that does not require oxygen for metabolism [Late 19thC. Back-formation from French *anaérobie* 'living without air', coined by Louis Pasteur, from Greek *an-* 'not' + French *aéro-* 'air' + Greek *bios* 'life'.]

anaerobic /ánnə rṓbik, án air-/ *adj.* **1.** NOT NEEDING OXYGEN living or taking place in the absence of oxygen, especially not requiring oxygen for metabolism **2.** LACKING OXYGEN having or providing no oxygen —**anaerobically** *adv.*

anaerobic process *n.* a chemical or biological process such as decay or decomposition that does not require oxygen. Such processes are often used to dispose of wastes while generating useful gases.

anaerobic respiration *n.* the production of energy from foodstuffs without the presence of oxygen. Anaerobic respiration occurs in some yeasts and bacteria, and in muscle tissue during strenuous exercise when oxygen is insufficient. ◊ **aerobic respiration**

anaerobiosis /ánnə rō bī óssiss, án air-/ *n.* life in the absence of free or atmospheric oxygen [Late 19thC. Coined from ANAEROBIC + -BIOSIS.] —**anaerobiotic** /ánnə rō bī óttik, án air-/ *adj.*

anaesthesia /ánnəss theézi ə/, **anesthesia** *n.* **1.** MED MEDICALLY INDUCED INSENSITIVITY TO PAIN induced loss of sensitivity to pain in all or a part of the body for medical reasons. Methods include drugs, acupuncture, and hypnosis. The procedure may render the patient unconscious (**general anaesthesia**) or merely numb a body part (**local anaesthesia**). **2.** MED LOSS OF SENSATION the loss of sensation caused by damage to a nerve **3.** APATHY a state of apathy or mindlessness [Early 18thC. Via modern Latin, from Greek *anaisthēsia*, literally 'lack of sensation', from *aisthēsis* 'feeling, sensation' (see AESTHETIC).]

anaesthesiologist *n.* = **anesthesiologist**

anaesthetic /ánnəss théttik/, **anesthetic** *n.* SUBSTANCE THAT DULLS PAIN a substance that reduces sensitivity to pain and may cause unconsciousness, especially a drug used in medicine ■ *adj.* PAIN-REDUCING relating to or producing loss of sensation and unconsciousness [Mid-19thC. Formed from Greek *anaisthētos*, literally 'without feeling', from *aisthētos* 'capable of feeling' (see AESTHETIC).] —**anaesthetically** *adv.*

anaesthetics /ánnəss théttiks/ *n.* the medical study and application of anaesthetic substances. US term **anesthesiology**

anaesthetise *vt.* = **anaesthetize**

anaesthetist /ə neésthətist/, **anesthetist** *n.* **1.** SENIOR DOCTOR SPECIALIZING IN ANAESTHETICS a senior doctor who specializes in administering anaesthetics. US term **anesthesiologist 2.** *US* QUALIFIED PERSON ADMINISTERING ANAESTHETICS sb qualified to administer anaesthetics, especially a nurse or technician

anaesthetize /ə neésthə tīz/ (**-tizes, -tizing, -tized**), **anesthetize** (**-tizes, -tizing, -tized**), **anaesthetise** /ə neésthətīz/ (**-tises, -tising, -tised**) *vt.* to administer an anaesthetic to sb —**anaesthetization** *n.*

anaglyph /ánnə glif/ *n.* **1.** CARVED DECORATION a decoration carved in low relief, so that the shape of the design projects only slightly from the background **2.** THREE-DIMENSIONAL PICTURE a three-dimensional visual effect created by dyeing each of two images a different colour, usually red and green, and then viewing them through complementary-coloured filters, one over each eye [Late 16thC. From Greek *anagluphē* 'low-relief sculpture', literally 'upwards carving', from *gluphein* 'to carve'.] —**anaglyphic** /ánnə glíffik/ *adj.* —**anaglyptic** /-glíptik/ *adj.*

Anaglypta /ánnə glíptə/ *tdmk.* a trademark for a thick embossed wallpaper

anagnorisis /ánnəg nórrississ/ (*plural* **-ses** /-seez/) *n.* in literature, especially Greek tragedy, the principal character's discovery or acknowledgment of some fact that leads to the resolution of the plot [Late 18thC. Via Latin, from Greek, 'recognition', formed from *anagnōrizein*, literally 'to know thoroughly', from *gnōrizein* 'to get knowledge of'.]

anagoge /ánnə gōji/, **anagogy** /ánnə gōji, -gogi/ (*plural* **-gies**) *n.* **1.** SPIRITUAL INTERPRETATION a spiritual or mystical interpretation of a word or passage, especially in a sacred text, in contrast to a literal or moral interpretation **2.** ALLEGORICAL INTERPRETATION IN BIBLE an allegorical interpretation of a passage in the Bible as an allusion to or foreshadowing of people or events in the New Testament [18thC. Via Latin, from Greek *anagōgē* 'reference', from *anagein*, literally 'to take back', from *agein* 'to take' (source of English *pedagogue*).] —**anagogic** /ánnə gójjik/ *adj.* —**anagogical** /-gójjik'l/ *adj.* —**anagogically** /ánnə gójjikli/ *adv.*

anagram /ánnə gram/ *n.* a word or phrase that contains all the letters of another word or phrase in a different order. 'Astronomers' is an anagram of 'no more stars'. [Late 16thC. Directly or via French *anagramme* from modern Latin *anagramma*, probably from Greek *anagrammatismos* 'transposition of letters', from *anagrammatizein* (see ANAGRAMMATIZE).] —**anagrammatic** /ánnə grə máttik/ *adj.* —**anagrammatically** /ánnəgrə máttikli/ *adv.*

anagrammatize /ánnə grámmə tīz/ (**-tizes, -tizing, -tized**), **anagrammatise** (**-tises, -tising, -tised**) *vt.* to rearrange the letters of a word or phrase to form a different word or phrase [Late 16thC. Origin uncertain: perhaps directly from Greek *anagrammatizein* 'to rearrange the letters of a word', from *gramma* 'letter'.]

Anaheim /ánnə hīm/ city in southwestern California. It is home to Disneyland. Population: 288,945 (1996).

anal /áyn'l/ *adj.* **1.** ANAT, ZOOL RELATING TO ANUS relating to or situated near the anus **2.** PSYCHOANAL RELATING TO CHILDHOOD INTEREST IN DEFECATION in Freudian theory, relating to a stage of childhood psychosexual development during which the focus is on the anal region and functions **3.** OBSESSIVELY SELF-CONTROLLED in Freudian theory, relating to adult personality traits, e.g. obsessive neatness, stubbornness, and meanness, that are considered to have originated during or be characteristic of the anal stage of development [Mid-18thC. From modern Latin *analis*, from *anus* 'ANUS'.] —**anally** *adv.*

anal. *abbr.* **1.** analogous **2.** analogy **3.** analysis **4.** analytic

analcime /ə nál seem/, **analcite** /-sīt/ *n.* a white or light-coloured mineral, a form of zeolite composed of hydrated silicate of sodium and aluminium and found in crystal form in igneous rock [Early 19thC. Via French, coined from Greek *analkimos*, literally 'not strong' (in reference to the mineral's weak electric current), from *alkimos* 'strong', from *alkē* 'strength'.] —**analcimic** /ánn'l símmik/ *adj.*

analects /ánnə lekts/, **analecta** /ánnə léktə/ *npl.* passages selected from one or more literary or philosophical works, especially when published as a collection [Early 17thC. Via Latin, from Greek *analekta* 'collected, or selected, things', from, ultimately, *analegein*, literally 'to gather up', from *legein* 'to gather'.] —**analectic** /ánnə léktik/ *adj.*

analemma /ánnə lémmə/ (*plural* **-mas** *or* **-mata** /-lémmətə/) *n.* a scale, found on some sundials and globes, that is shaped like a figure eight and marked to indicate the declination of the sun and to allow the calculation of apparent solar time [Mid-17thC. Via Latin, 'sundial, pedestal of a sundial', from Greek *analēmma* 'pedestal, support', from *analambanein* 'to take up, support', from *lambanein* 'to take'.]

analeptic /ánnə léptik/ *adj.* STIMULANT restorative or invigorating, especially after an illness ■ *n.* STIMULANT DRUG a drug that has a stimulating effect on the central nervous system [Mid-17thC. Via Latin, from Greek *analēptikos* 'restorative', from *analambanein* (see ANALEMMA).]

analgesia /ánn'l jéezi ə/ *n.* MED **1.** UNAWARENESS OF PAIN the lack of sensibility to pain while sb is conscious **2.** PAIN CONTROL treatment to control pain [Early 18thC. Via modern Latin, from Greek *analgēsia* 'lack of feeling, insensibility', from, ultimately, *algeein* 'to feel pain', from *algos* 'pain'.] —**analgetic** /ánn'l jéttik/ *adj.*

analgesic /ánn'l jéezik/ *adj.* PAIN-RELIEVING used to describe a type of medication that alleviates pain without loss of consciousness ■ *n.* PAIN-RELIEVING MEDICATION a type of medication that alleviates pain without loss of consciousness

anal intercourse *n.* = **sodomy**

analog /ánnə log/, **analogue** *n.* = **analogue** ■ *adj.* = **analogue** [Mid-20thC. Variant of ANALOGUE.]

analogical /ánnə lójjik'l/ *adj.* relating to or working by means of analogy [Late 16thC. Formed directly or via French *analogique* from Latin *analogicus*, from Greek *analogikos* (see ANALOGOUS).] —**analogically** *adv.*

analogise *vti.* = **analogize**

analogist /ə nálləjist/ *n.* sb who uses analogy as a form of reasoning, to provide an explanation, or to support an argument

analogize /ə nállə jīz/ (**-gizes, -gizing, -gized**), **analogise** (**-gises, -gising, -gised**) *v.* **1.** *vt.* DRAW COMPARISONS to compare two things that are similar in some respects, especially in order to explain sth or to support an argument **2.** *vi.* USE ANALOGY to make use of an analogy

analogous /ə nálləgəss/ *adj.* **1.** SIMILAR similar in some respects, allowing an analogy to be drawn **2.** BIOL EQUIVALENT BUT INDEPENDENTLY EVOLVED used to describe body parts and organs that have equivalent functions but that evolved independently of one another in different plants or animals. The wings of birds, bats, and insects, e.g., are analogous. [Mid-17thC. Via French *analogue* or Latin *analogus* from Greek *analogos*, from *analogon* 'in due ratio', from *ana* 'according to' + *logos* 'ratio'.] —**analogously** *adv.* —**analogousness** *n.*

WORD KEY: USAGE

Some things are more **analogous** than others. ***Analogous***, correctly used, should include a notion of **analogy**, that is of directly corresponding features: *The Commission has set up guidelines for broadcasters that are analogous to those for journalists.* It is better to avoid it when the comparison is only general and when more straightforward words such as **similar**, **equivalent**, **comparable**, or **corresponding** would serve as well: *The new system is analogous to that used in the electronics industry.*

analogue /ánnə log/ *n.* **1.** CORRESPONDING THING a thing, idea, or institution that is similar to or has the same function as another ○ *'They had no exact analogue for our word "home", any more than they had for our Roman-based "family".'* (Charlotte Perkins Gilman, *Herland*; 1915) **2.** BIOL EQUIVALENT BUT INDEPENDENTLY EVOLVED ORGAN a body part or organ that has an equivalent function to one in a different plant or animal but that evolved independently. The wings of birds, bats, and insects, e.g., are analogues. **3.** CHEM SIMILAR CHEMICAL a chemical with a similar structure to another but differing slightly in composition. US term **analog** *n.* **4.** FOOD FOOD SUBSTITUTE a food or dish made to resemble another by the substitution of inferior ingredients ■ *adj.* USING PHYSICAL REPRESENTATION relating to a system or device that represents data variation by a measurable physical entity. ◊ **digital** *adj.* 2. US term **analog** [Early 19thC. Via French, from Greek *analogon* (see ANALOGOUS).]

analogue clock *n.* a clock that shows the time by means of hands on a dial

analogue computer *n.* a computer that uses a variable physical quantity such as voltage to represent data

analogue recording, **analog recording** *n.* the recording of sound onto vinyl or tape by converting the audio waveform into analogous variations in shape or magnetization

analogue watch *n.* a watch that shows the time by means of hands on a dial

analogy /ə nálləji/ (*plural* **-gies**) *n.* **1.** COMPARISON a comparison between two things that are similar in some respects, often used to help explain sth or make it easier to understand **2.** SIMILARITY a similarity in some respects **3.** BIOL EQUIVALENCE BETWEEN INDEPENDENTLY EVOLVED PARTS equivalence in biological function between body parts or organs that have evolved independently in different plants and animals **4.** LOGIC FORM OF REASONING a form of logical inference, reasoning that if two things are taken to be alike in a particular way, they are alike in certain other ways **5.** LING STANDARDIZATION OF LINGUISTIC FORMS the development or production of linguistic forms and patterns that resemble those already predominating in a language [15thC. Via French *analogie* or Latin *analogia* from Greek *analogia* 'proportion', from *analogos* (see ANALOGOUS).]

analphabetic /án alfə béttik, an álfə-/ *adj.* **1.** NOT ALPHABETICAL not in alphabetical order (*formal*) **2.** ILLITERATE not knowing how to read or write (*formal*) **3.** NOT OF ALPHABET not belonging to or connected with an alphabet ■ *n.* **1.** PRINTING CHARACTER a typographical character used with the alphabet but lacking a place in the alphabetical order, e.g. a punctuation mark **2.** ILLITERATE PERSON sb who does not know how to read or write (*formal*) [Late 19thC. Formed from Greek *analphabētos* 'not knowing the alphabet', from *alphabētos* 'alphabet'.]

anal-retentive *adj.* = **anal** *adj.* 3 —**anal retention** *n.* —**anal-retentive** *n.* —**anal-retentiveness** *n.*

anal sex *n.* = **sodomy**

analysand /ə nálli sand/ *n.* sb who is undergoing psychoanalysis [Mid-20thC. Formed from ANALYSE, on the model of *operand*.]

analyse /ánnə līz/ (**-lyses, -lysing, -lysed**), **analyze** (**-lyzes, -lysing, -lysed**) *vt.* **1.** BREAK DOWN INTO COMPONENTS to find out what sth is made up of by identifying its constituent parts **2.** EXAMINE STRUCTURE to study or examine the structure of sth or how its constituent parts are put together **3.** STUDY CLOSELY to examine sth in great detail in order to understand it better or discover more about it **4.** GRAM EXPRESS BY USING FUNCTION WORDS to express grammatical relationships by using function words or word order rather than inflectional endings **5.** = **psychoanalyse** [Early 17thC. Origin uncertain: possibly a back-formation from ANALYSIS, or from French *analyse* 'analysis' used as a verb; in either case reinforced by French *analyser* 'to analyse'.] —**analysable** *adj.* —**analysation** /ánnə lī záysh'n/ *n.* —**analyser** /ánnə līzər/ *n.*

analysis /ə nálləssiss/ (*plural* **-ses** /-seez/) *n.* **1.** SEPARATION INTO COMPONENTS the separation of sth into its constituents in order to find out what it contains, to examine individual parts, or to study the structure of the whole **2.** LIST OF PARTS a statement giving details of all the constituent elements of sth and how they relate to each other **3.** CLOSE EXAMINATION the examination of sth in detail in order to understand it better or draw conclusions from it **4.** ASSESSMENT an assessment, description, or explanation of sth, usually based on careful consideration or investigation **5.** MATH BRANCH OF MATHEMATICS the branch of mathematics dealing with differential calculus, functions, and limits **6.** LING WAY OF EXPRESSING GRAMMATICAL RELATIONSHIPS the use of function words or word order, rather than inflectional forms, to express grammatical relationships in a language **7.** = **psychoanalysis** [Late 16thC. Via medieval Latin, from Greek *analusis* 'a breaking up into elements', from *analuein* 'to unloose, dissolve into elements', from *luein* 'to loosen'.] ◇ **in the final** *or* **last analysis** used to introduce or indicate a summary conclusion to a complex subject

analysis of variance *n.* the analysis of the difference in outcomes of an experiment to determine the factors contributing to the variations

analyst /ánnəlist/ *n.* **1.** EXPERT WHO EXAMINES STH sb with specialist knowledge or skill who studies or examines sth by separating it into its constituent elements and gives an assessment, description, or explanation of it **2.** = **psychoanalyst** [Mid-17thC. From French *analyste*, from *analyse* 'analysis' (see ANALYSE).]

analytic /ánnə líttik/, **analytical** /-líttik'l/ *adj.* **1.** OF ANALYSIS connected with or involving analysis **2.** USING ANALYSIS able or inclined to separate things into their constituent elements in order to study or examine them, draw conclusions, or solve problems **3.** LOGIC TRUE BY MEANING ALONE true by definition or by virtue of the meaning of the words used **4.** MATH DIFFERENTIABLE AT ALL POINTS IN DOMAIN used to describe a function of a complex variable that is differentiable at all points in its domain **5.** LING USING FUNCTION WORDS expressing grammatical relationships by means of function words or word order rather than inflections [Late 16thC. Via late Latin, from Greek *analutikos*, from *analuein* (see ANALYSIS).] —**analytically** *adv.*

analytical balance *n.* an accurate scales used in laboratories for weighing minute objects or quantities

analytical reagent *n.* a substance processed to be virtually free of impurities

analytic geometry, **analytical geometry** *n.* a branch of mathematics dealing with geometric properties using algebraic operations and notation to locate points within a coordinate system

analytic philosophy, **analytical philosophy** *n.* a 20th-century philosophy primarily concerned with resolving philosophical problems through the analysis and clarification of language

analytic psychology, **analytical psychology** *n.* a system of psychoanalysis based on the psychological theories of Carl Jung

analytics /ánnə líttiks/ *n.* the branch of logic involved with the analysis of propositions (*takes a singular or plural verb*)

analyze *vt.* US = **analyse**

anamnesis /án am néessiss/ (*plural* **-ses** /-seez/) *n.* the medical or psychiatric history of a patient, especially in the patient's own words [Late 16thC. From Greek, 'remembrance', from *anamimnēskein*, literally 'to call back to mind', from *mimnēskein* 'to call to mind'.]

anamnestic /án am néstik/ *adj.* showing a secondary immunological response to an antigen at some time after initial immunization [Early 18thC. From Greek *anamnēstikos*, ultimately from *anamimnēskein* (see ANAMNESIS).] —**anamnestically** *adv.*

anamorphic /ánnə máwrfik/ *adj.* relating to or producing image distortion caused by unequal magnification along different perpendicular axes

anamorphosis /ánnə mawr fóssiss, -máwrfəssiss/ (*plural* **-ses** /-seez/) *n.* **1.** DISTORTED IMAGE a distorted image or drawing of a distorted image that appears normal when viewed with or reflected from a special device **2.** IMAGING PROCESS the process of making distorted images by means of special mirrors or other devices [Mid-18thC. From Greek, 'transformation', from *anamorphoein*, literally 'to change shape again', from *morphoein* 'to change shape', from *morphē* 'shape'.]

Ananke /ə nángki/ *n.* a small natural satellite of Jupiter, discovered in 1951

anapaest /ánnə peest, -pest/, **anapest** *n.* a metrical foot of three syllables with the stress on the third syllable, or of two short syllables followed by a long syllable. The word 'unconcerned' and the phrase 'up the hill' are anapaests. [Late 16thC. Via Latin, from Greek *anapaistos* 'struck backwards' (from its being a reversed dactyl), the past participle of *anapaiein*, from *paiein* 'to strike'.] —**anapaestic** /ánnə péestik, -pést-/ *adj.*

anaphase /ánnə fayz/ *n.* a late stage of cell division during which chromosomes move to the poles of the spindle. ◊ **prophase, metaphase, telophase** [Late 19thC. Coined from Greek *ana-* 'up, back' + PHASE.]

anaphora /ə náffərə/ *n.* **1.** GRAM REFERRING BACK reference to a word or phrase used earlier, especially to avoid repeating the word or phrase by replacing it with sth else such as a pronoun. In the sentence 'I told Paul to close the door and he did so', the clause 'he did so' makes use of anaphora. **2.** REPETITION FOR EFFECT the use of the same word or phrase at the beginning of several successive clauses, sentences, lines, or verses, usually for emphasis or rhetorical effect. 'She didn't speak. She didn't stand. She didn't even look up when we came in' is an example of anaphora. (*formal*) **3.** CHR PART OF EUCHARIST the offering of the bread and wine at the Eucharist [Late 16thC. Via Latin, from Greek, 'reference, repetition', from *anapherein*, literally 'to carry back', from *pherein* 'to carry'.] —**anaphoric** /ánnə fórrik/ *adj.* —**anaphorically** /-fórrikli/ *adv.*

anaphoresis /ánnə fə reéssiss/ *n.* the movement towards the anode of suspended particles in solution

anaphrodisia /án affrə dízzi ə/ *n.* absence or reduction of sexual desire [20thC. From Greek, 'inability to inspire love', from *aphrodisios* 'relating to love' (see APHRODISIAC).]

anaphrodisiac /án affrə dízzi ak/ *adj.* **REDUCING SEXUAL DESIRE** tending to reduce sexual desire ■ *n.* **DRUG REDUCING SEXUAL DESIRE** a drug, herb, or other substance that reduces sexual desire [Early 19thC. Formed from Greek *aphrodisiakos* 'inspiring love, sexual' (see APHRODISIAC).]

anaphylactic /ánnəfi láktik/ *adj.* relating to or caused or characterized by extreme sensitivity to a substance **(anaphylaxis)** —**anaphylactically** *adv.*

anaphylactic shock *n.* a sudden severe and potentially fatal allergic reaction in sb sensitive to a particular substance, marked by a drop in blood pressure, difficulty in breathing, itching, and swelling

anaphylaxis /ánnəfi láksiss/ *n.* **1. EXTREME SENSITIVITY** extreme sensitivity to a particular substance such as a specific protein or drug **2.** = **anaphylactic shock** [Early 20thC. From modern Latin, coined from Greek *ana-* 'again' (because a substance is reintroduced) + *-phylaxis* 'guarding, watching'.] —**anaphylactoid** /ánnəfi lák toyd/ *adj.*

anaplasia /ánnə pláyzi ə/ *n.* the reversion of cells, usually within a tumour, to a simpler or less differentiated form

anaplastic /ánnə plástik/ *adj.* relating to or characterized by the loss of distinctive cell features **(anaplasia)**

anaptyxis /ánnap tíksiss/ *n.* the insertion of a weak vowel sound between two consonants in order to make a word or phrase easier to pronounce [Late 19thC. Via modern Latin, from Greek *anaptuxis* 'an unfolding', from *anaptussein* 'to unfold', from *ptussein* 'to fold'.]

anarch /án aark/ *n.* sb who supports or instigates anarchy (*archaic*) [Mid-17thC. Back-formation from ANARCHY.]

anarchic /an áarkik, ən-/, **anarchical** /-kik'l/ *adj.* **1. LAWLESS** showing no respect for established laws, rules, institutions, or authority **2. CHAOTIC** characterized by a lack of organization or control **3. ENCOURAGING ANARCHY** likely to cause the overthrow of a formal system of government or a breakdown of law and order —**anarchically** *adv.*

anarchism /ánnər kizzəm/ *n.* **1. DOCTRINE REJECTING GOVERNMENT** an ideology that rejects the need for a system of government in society and proposes its abolition **2. ACTIONS OF ANARCHISTS** behaviour intended to overthrow or weaken a society's formal system of government **3. RESISTANCE TO CONTROL** resistance to all forms of authority or control

anarchist /ánnərkist/ *n.* **1. SUPPORTER OF ANARCHISM** sb who rejects the need for a system of government in society and proposes its abolition **2. LAWLESS PERSON** sb who tries to overthrow a society's formal system of government or behaves in a generally lawless manner and encourages others to do the same (*disapproving*) —**anarchistic** /ánnər kístik/ *adj.*

anarchy /ánnərki/ *n.* **1. LACK OF GOVERNMENT** the absence of any formal system of government in a society **2. CHAOTIC SITUATION** a situation in which there is a total lack of organization or control [Mid-16thC. Via medieval Latin *anarchia*, from Greek *anarkhia*, from *anarkhos* 'without a ruler', from *arkhos* 'ruler'.]

anarthria /an áarthri ə/ *n.* the loss of the ability to articulate words [Late 19thC. Via modern Latin, from Greek, formed from *anarthros* 'inarticulate, disjointed', from *arthron* 'joint'.] —**anarthric** *adj.*

anarthrous /an áarthrəss/ *adj.* used or occurring without a definite or indefinite article [Early 19thC. Formed from Greek *anarthros*, literally 'not articulated', from *arthron* 'article, joint'.]

anasarca /ánnə saárkə/ *n.* the accumulation of watery fluid in connective tissue and cavities, resulting in swelling **(oedema)** [14thC. Via medieval Latin, from the Greek adjective *anasarx*, applied by the physician GALEN to dropsy, representing the phrase *ana sarka* 'throughout the flesh'.] —**anasarcous** *adj.*

Anastasia /ánnə stáyzi ə, -staázi ə/, **Grand Duchess** (1901–18). The daughter of Tsar Nicholas II, she died when the Bolsheviks executed the Romanovs (July 1918), but many women claimed to be her thereafter. Born **Anastasia Nikolaevna Romanovna**

anastigmat /an ástig mat, ánnə stíg mat/ *n.* a lens or combination of lenses free from astigmatism [Late 19thC. From German, a back-formation from *anastigmatisch* 'anastigmatic', from, ultimately, medieval Latin *stigmaticus* (see STIGMATIC).]

anastigmatic /ánnə stig máttik/ *adj.* used to describe a lens that is corrected for or free from astigmatism

anastomose /ə nástə mōz, -stə mōss/ (**-moses, -mosing, -mosed**) *vt.* to join blood vessels or other tubular parts in a surgical operation **(anastomosis)** [Late 17thC. Origin uncertain: probably a back-formation from ANASTOMOSIS, perhaps on the model of ANKYLOSE and METAMORPHOSE.]

anastomosis /ə nástə mṓssiss/ (*plural* **-ses** /-seez/) *n.* **1. NATURAL JOINT** the connection or place of connection of two or more parts of a natural branching system, e.g. of blood vessels, leaf veins, stems of woody plants, or rivers **2.** MED **SURGICAL UNION OF TUBULAR PARTS** the surgical union of two hollow organs, e.g. blood vessels or parts of the intestine, to ensure continuity of the passageway **3. NETWORK OF FUNGAL FILAMENTS** a fusion between fungal filaments **(hyphae)** to form a network [Early 17thC. Via modern Latin, from Greek, 'outlet, opening, interconnection of openings', from *anastomoein* 'to supply with a mouth or opening', from *stoma* 'mouth' (source also of English *stomach*).] —**anastomotic** /ə nástə móttik/ *adj.*

anastrophe /ə nástrəfi/ *n.* an alteration of the normal order of words or phrases in a grammatical construction, usually for rhetorical effect. Coleridge's 'The helmsman steered; the ship moved on; yet never a breeze up blew' ends with an anastrophe. [Mid-16thC. From Greek, 'a turning back, inversion', formed from *stroph-*, the stem of *strephein* 'to turn'.]

anat. *abbr.* **1.** anatomical **2.** anatomy

anatase /ánnə tayz/ *n.* a blue or yellowish-brown mineral consisting of titanium dioxide, which occurs in igneous rock [Early 19thC. Via French, from Greek *anatasis* 'extension' (from the elongated crystals), from, ultimately, *teinein* 'to stretch'.]

anathema /ə náthəmə/ *n.* **1. OBJECT OF LOATHING** sb or sth that is greatly disliked or detested and is therefore shunned **2.** RELIG **ECCLESIASTICAL CURSE** a curse from a religious authority that denounces sth or excommunicates sb **3. GENERAL CURSE** any forceful curse or denunciation **4.** RELIG **SB OR STH FORMALLY DENOUNCED** sb or sth cursed, denounced, or excommunicated by a religious authority [Early 16thC. Via ecclesiastical Latin, from Greek, 'sth devoted to evil', earlier 'sth devoted', variant of *anathēma* 'votive offering', from *anatithenai* 'to set up'.]

anathematize /ə náthəmə tīz/ (**-tizes, -tizing, -tized**), **anathematise** (**-tises, -tising, -tised**) *vti.* to formally curse, denounce, or excommunicate sb or sth [Mid-16thC. Via ecclesiastical Latin *anathematizare* 'to ban, curse' from Greek *anathematizein* 'to dedicate to evil', from *anathemat-*, the stem of *anathema* (see ANATHEMA).] —**anathematization** /ə náthəmə tī záysh'n/ *n.*

Anatolia /ánnə tṓli ə/ *n.* the Asian part of Turkey, forming the westernmost peninsula of Asia

Anatolian /ánnə tṓli ən/ *n.* **1.** PEOPLES **SB FROM ANATOLIA** sb who was born or who lives in Anatolia **2.** LANG **EXTINCT MIDDLE EASTERN LANGUAGE GROUP** a group of extinct languages spoken more than 3,000 years ago in central and western Turkey. They form a branch of the Indo-European language family. —**Anatolian** *adj.*

Anatolian Plateau /anə tṓli ən-/ mountainous region extending from Kurdistan to Turkey

anatomical /ánnə tómmik'l/, **anatomic** /-tómmik/ *adj.* relating to or showing the physical structure of animals or plants —**anatomically** *adv.*

anatomically correct *adj.* having an accurate representation of the genitals and other bodily details

anatomise *vt.* = **anatomize**

anatomist /ə náttəmist/ *n.* a student of or expert on the physical structure of animals or plants, especially the structure of the human body

anatomize /ə náttə mīz/ (**-mizes, -mizing, -mized**), **anatomise** (**-mises, -mising, -mised**) *vt.* **1.** = **dissect** *v.* 1 **2. ANALYSE IN DETAIL** to analyse or examine sth in great detail, thus revealing features that are not obvious —**anatomization** /ə náttə mī záysh'n/ *n.*

anatomy /ə náttəmi/ (*plural* **-mies**) *n.* **1. STUDY OF STRUCTURE OF BODY** the branch of science that studies the physical structure of animals, plants, and other organisms **2. PHYSICAL STRUCTURE OF ORGANISM** the physical structure, especially the internal structure, of an animal, plant, or other organism, or of any of its parts **3. BOOK ABOUT ANATOMY** a book or other written work about the physical structure of animals, plants, or other organisms **4. BODY** the human body (*informal*) **5. ANALYSIS** a detailed analysis of sth [14thC. Via French *anatomie* and late Latin *anatomia* from Greek *anatomē* 'cutting up' from, ultimately, *temnein* 'to cut' (source of English *atom*).]

WORD KEY: ORIGIN

From the 16th century to the early 19th century ***anatomy*** was used to mean 'skeleton', and in this sense it was often misanalysed as *an atomy*, as if the initial *an-* were the indefinite article: 'My bones...will be taken up smooth, and white, and bare as an atomy', Tobias Smollett (1755).

Anaxagoras /á nak sággərəss/ (500?–428 BC) Greek philosopher. He stated that matter was infinitely divisible and was the first person to explain solar eclipses.

Anaximander /ə náksi mándər/ (611?–547? BC) Greek philosopher. He put forward an evolutionary theory of the origins of life, claiming that human beings evolved from more primitive species.

Anaximenes /á nak símmə neez/ (570?–500? BC) Greek philosopher. He believed that the universe consisted of air or vapour in various stages of condensation, and that the movement of air changed the structure of physical objects.

ANC *n.* a South African political party founded in 1912 that fought against apartheid. It formed South Africa's first multiracial, democratically elected government in 1994. Full form **African National Congress**

ancestor /án sestər, ánsəstər/ *n.* **1. DISTANT RELATION SB IS DESCENDED FROM** sb from whom sb else is directly descended, especially sb more distant than a grandparent **2. FORERUNNER** a predecessor of sb, e.g. in the development of a certain art form **3.** BIOL **EARLIER SPECIES** an animal or plant from which a species has evolved **4. EARLIER MODEL** a device that was an earlier form of a modern invention or was used as a basis for developing it [14thC. Via Old French *ancestre* from Latin *antecessor*, literally 'sb who goes before', from *cess-*, the past participle stem of *cedere* (see CEDE).]

ancestral /an séstrəl/ *adj.* belonging to former generations of sb's family, or inherited from them [15thC. From Old French *ancestrel*, from *ancestre* (see ANCESTOR).] —**ancestrally** *adv.*

ancestress /án sess tress, ánssəs-/ *n.* a woman from whom sb is directly descended, especially sb more distant than a grandmother (*dated*)

ancestry /án sestri, ánsəs-/ *n.* sb's ancestors regarded as a line linking the modern generation to its past [14thC. Alteration of Old French *ancesserie*, from *ancessour*, from Latin *antecessor* (see ANCESTOR).]

Anchises /an kī́ seez/ *n.* in Greek and Roman mythology, a Trojan prince and the father of Aeneas by the goddess Aphrodite. In later life, Anchises was saved during the Greek sack of Troy when Aeneas carried him from the burning city on his back.

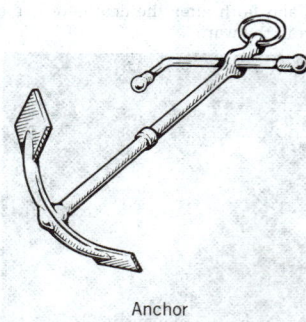

Anchor

anchor /ángkər/ n. 1. NAUT **DEVICE TO HOLD SHIP IN PLACE** a heavy, traditionally double-hooked, device for keeping a ship or floating object in place 2. **DEVICE KEEPING OBJECT IN PLACE** any device that keeps an object in place 3. **STH DEPENDABLE** sb who or sth that provides a sense of stability ○ *She was my anchor during the crisis.* 4. BROADCAST **PRESENTER OF NEWS PROGRAMME** a presenter on a news programme, providing links between the studio and reporters based outside. ◊ **anchorman, anchorwoman** 5. SPORTS **SB POSITIONED LAST** the team member who is responsible for the last leg in a relay race or who is at the back in a tug of war 6. MOUNTAINEERING **STH CLIMBER IS TIED TO** a rock feature, piton, or other feature to which a climber is tied ■ *adj.* ATTACHING used for securing or connecting sth ■ *vt.* (-chors, -choring, -chored) 1. **HOLD STH IN PLACE** to hold sth securely in place 2. BROADCAST **BE NEWS PROGRAMME'S PRESENTER** to be the presenter on a news programme [Pre-12thC. Via Latin *ancora* from Greek *agkura*. Ultimately from an Indo-European base meaning 'to bend, hook', which is also the ancestor of English *angle* and *ankle*.] ◊ **at anchor** held on the water by an anchor

anchorage /ángkərij/ n. 1. **PLACE TO HOLD BOATS SECURE** a place in or near a harbour where boats are moored 2. **CHARGE FOR ANCHORING BOAT** a charge for anchoring a boat in a harbour 3. **STH HOLDING OBJECT IN PLACE** any device used to hold an object in place 4. **ANCHORING** the securing of a ship with an anchor 5. **SECURITY** a source of stability, or a stable condition

Anchorage /ánkərij/ city and port in southern Alaska, at the eastern end of Cook Inlet. Population: 253,649 (1994).

anchorite /ángkə rīt/ n. sb who lives a life of prayer, either alone or as part of a religious community [15thC. Via medieval Latin *anc(h)orita* from, ultimately, ecclesiastical Greek *anakhōrētēs*, from Greek *anakhōrein*, literally 'to withdraw', from *ana-* 'away' + *khōrein* 'to move'.]

anchorman /ángkər man/ (*plural* **-men** /-men/) n. 1. SPORTS **MALE ANCHOR ON SPORTS TEAM** a man who is the anchor in a relay race or for a tug-of-war team 2. BROADCAST **MALE ANCHOR ON NEWS PROGRAMME** a man who is an anchor for a news programme

anchorperson /ángkər purss'n/ (*plural* **-persons** or **-people**) n. = anchor n. 4

anchorwoman /ángkər woŏmən/ (*plural* **-en** /-wimmin/) n. 1. SPORTS **WOMAN WHO ANCHORS SPORTS TEAM** a woman who is the anchor in a relay race or for a tug-of-war team 2. BROADCAST **WOMAN WHO PRESENTS NEWS PROGRAMME** a woman who is an anchor for a news programme

anchovy /ánchəvi, an chóvi/ (*plural* **-vies** or **-vy**) n. a small silvery edible sea fish that travels in large schools. It is widely used in Mediterranean cooking and is often sold salted and canned in oil. Family: Engraulidae. [Late 16thC. From Spanish *anchova*, of uncertain origin.]

ancien régime /aaN syaN ray zhee'm/ (*plural* **anciens régimes** /aaN syaN ray zhee'm/) n. 1. **PRE-REVOLUTIONARY FRENCH SOCIETY** the political and social system of France before the revolution of 1789 2. **FORMER SYSTEM** any former system or administration, or outmoded way of doing things [Late 18thC. From French, literally 'old regime'.]

ancient /áynshənt/ adj. 1. **OF DISTANT PAST** belonging to the distant past, especially to the time before the collapse of the Western Roman Empire in AD 476 2.

OLD very old ■ n. 1. **SB FROM PAST CIVILIZATION** sb who belonged to a civilization in the distant past 2. **SB OLD** a very mature or venerable person ■ **ancients** npl. 1. **PEOPLE OF ANCIENT WESTERN CIVILIZATIONS** the people who lived in one of the ancient civilizations, especially Greece and Rome 2. **ANCIENT GREEK AND ROMAN AUTHORS** the authors of ancient Greece and Rome, whose writings form the basis of the classics as a subject of study [14thC. Via French *ancien* from assumed Vulgar Latin *anteanus*, from Latin *ante* 'before'.] —**ancientness** n.

Ancient Greek n. the forms of the Greek language spoken from about 1500 BC to about AD 500

ancient history n. 1. **STUDY OF OLD CIVILIZATIONS** the study of the cultures of the distant past, especially those of Greece and Rome 2. **THINGS THAT HAPPENED IN PAST** things that happened a long time ago (*informal*)

ancient lights n. the legal right to receive daylight through windows (*takes a singular verb*)

Ancient Mariner n. sb who talks at length about subjects, often obsessively (*informal humorous*) [From the title of the poem by Samuel Taylor Coleridge]

ancient monument n. a building or part of a building, usually dating from at least medieval times, that is preserved and protected by law

Ancient of Days n. a name for God, used in the Authorized Version of the Bible (Daniel 7: 9) [Translation of Latin *antiquus dierum*]

ancillary /an síl̇əri/ adj. 1. **PROVIDING SUPPORT** providing support for sb or sth, e.g. nontechnical assistance to people who work in an industry or profession 2. **SUBORDINATE** in a position of lesser importance ■ n. (*plural* **-ies**) 1. **SUBORDINATE PART** a subordinate part or element, e.g. a branch of an organization 2. **NONTECHNICAL SUPPORT EMPLOYEE** a worker who provides nontechnical assistance or support to the core workers in an industry or profession [Mid-17thC. Formed from Latin *ancilla* 'handmaid', feminine of *anculus* 'manservant'.]

ancylostomiasis /ángki lōstə mī́ əsiss, ánssi-/, **ankylostomiasis** /ángki-/ n. a tropical disease caused by infestation of the small intestine by hookworms, with symptoms of anaemia and tiredness [Late 19thC. Formed from modern Latin *Ancyclostoma*, genus of hookworms, from Greek *agkulos* 'hooked' + *stoma* 'mouth'.]

and (*stressed*) /and/; (*unstressed*) /ənd, ən/ CORE MEANING: a conjunction used to indicate an additional thing, situation, or fact. 'And' in this case links words and phrases of the same grammatical value. ○ *a sister and two brothers* ○ *We need to clean the house and pack our suitcases.* ○ *switching back and forth between systems* conj. 1. **THEN** used to link two verbs or statements about events to indicate that the second follows the first ○ *Just add water and stir.* 2. **AS A RESULT** used to introduce a situation or event that is a consequence of sth just mentioned ○ *Their work was excellent and won several awards.* 3. **USED TO STRESS REPETITION OR CONTINUITY** used to link identical words or phrases in order to emphasize repetition or continuity ○ *It gets better and better.* 4. **PLUS** used to link two numbers or quantities to indicate that they are to be added together ○ *One and one are two.* 5. **BUT** used to introduce a contrasting statement ○ *Make sure you eat enough fruit and avoid refined sugar.* 6. **MOREOVER** used to introduce a statement that continues or adds weight to a statement just made ○ *Kim needed clothes, and I hadn't been paid in weeks.* 7. **USED TO CONNECT IDEAS** used to connect clauses or sentences, especially in spoken conversation ○ *I like Pierre, the head waiter, but the work's hard. And they pick on me sometimes.* 8. **INDICATES AN INFINITIVE VERB** used instead of 'to' before an infinitive verb, usually with verbs such as 'try', 'go', and 'come' (*informal*) ○ *I usually try and visit her once a week.* 9. **IF** used to introduce a conditional clause (*archaic*) ○ *and it please you* [Old English *and*, *ond* (related to Dutch *en* and German *und*)]

— **WORD KEY: USAGE** —

and at the beginning of a sentence The notion that **and** should not be used at the beginning of a sentence is a superstition arising from too literal an understanding of the 'joining' function of conjunctions: the same objection is also raised with regard to **but**. If it is overdone

the effect is of poor style, but this is not a matter of grammatical correctness, and the position of **and** at the beginning of a sentence can often be an effective way of drawing attention to what follows: *'You can't get away with this'*, he threatened. *And we knew he meant it. And I ate up all my vegetables.*

AND /and/ n. a word used in computer technology to link two or more items that must occur together [Mid-20thC. From AND.]

Andalusia /ándə loŏzi ə/ autonomous region of southern Spain bordered by the Mediterranean Sea and the Atlantic Ocean. It contains the historic cities of Seville, Granada, and Cadiz and many examples of Moorish architecture. Population: 6,940,522 (1991). Area: 87,268 sq. km/33,694 sq. mi. Spanish **Andalucía** —**Andalusian** adj., n.

andalusite /ándə loŏ sīt/ n. a hard mineral of various colours consisting of aluminium silicate. Some forms are used as gemstones. [Early 19thC. Named after ANDALUSIA, where the mineral was first found.]

Andaman Islands /ándəmən-/ northern part of the Indian union territory of the Andaman and Nicobar Islands, situated between the Bay of Bengal and the Andaman Sea. The Andaman Islands consist of five large islands and about 200 islets. Population: 240,089 (1991). Area: 6,475 sq. km/2,500 sq. mi.

andante /an dánti, -tay/ adj., adv. **SLOWLY** at a moderate musical tempo but slower than moderato (*used as a musical direction*) ■ n. **MUSIC PLAYED ANDANTE** a title given to certain musical pieces or movements that are to be played andante [Early 18thC. From Italian, 'walking', the present participle of *andare* 'to go, walk'.]

andantino /án dan tee nō/ adj., adv. **FAIRLY SLOWLY** at a moderate musical tempo slightly faster than andante (*used as a musical direction*) ■ n. (*plural* **-nos**) **MUSIC PLAYED ANDANTINO** a title given to certain musical pieces or movements that are to be played andantino [Early 19thC. From Italian, literally 'little andante'.]

Andersen /ándərs'n/, **Hans Christian** (1805–75) Danish writer. His fairy tales include 'The Snow Queen' (1844) and 'The Ugly Duckling' (1843).

Anderson, Elizabeth Garrett (1836–1917) English physician. Refused entry to medical school, she studied privately and gained her licence to practise in 1865.

Anderson /ándərsən/, **John** (1893–1962) Scottish-born Australian philosopher. He was professor of philosophy at the University of Sydney (1927–58), where his espousal of independent critical thinking influenced many local intellectuals.

Marian Anderson

Anderson, Marian (1897–1993) US contralto. She was the first Black singer to appear at the Metropolitan Opera in New York (1955).

Anderson, Philip W. (b. 1923) US physicist. He shared the Nobel Prize in physics in 1977.

Anderson shelter n. a small arch of corrugated metal designed to act as a shelter during air raids in World War II [Mid-20thC. Named after its designer, David A. Anderson, but popularly associated with Sir John Anderson, who was Home Secretary (1939–40) at the time it was adopted.]

Andersson /ándərs'n/, **Adolf** (1818–79) Prussian chess master. He won the first modern international tournament (1851). He used combination plays to force opponents into making immediate decisions.

Andes

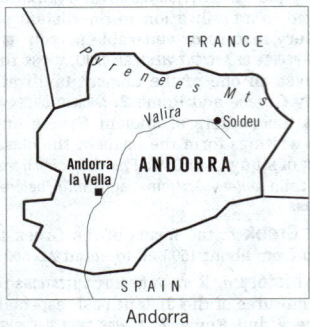
Andorra

Andromeda Galaxy: Photographed
from the Palomar Observatory,
California Institute of Technology

Andes /án deez/ huge South American mountain system that extends north to south along the western coast from Panama to Tierra del Fuego. It consists of several ranges and has its highest point at Aconcagua 6,960 m/22,835 ft. —**Andean** /ándi ən/ *adj.*, *n.*

andesine /ándi zeen, -zin/ *n.* a hard colourless mineral belonging to the feldspar group, an essential component of andesite [Because it is found in the Andes]

andesite /ándi zīt/ *n.* a fine-grained greyish volcanic rock characterized by feldspar minerals [Because it is found in the Andes] —**andesitic** /ándi zíttik/ *adj.*

Andhra Pradesh /ándrəprə désh/ Indian state, situated in the southeast of the country facing the Bay of Bengal. Capital: Hyderabad. Population: 71,800,000 (1994). Area: 275,045 sq. km/106,195 sq. mi.

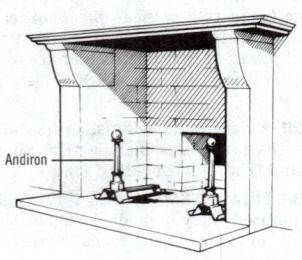
Andiron

andiron /ánd ī ərn/ *n.* either of a pair of metal stands used to hold logs in a fireplace [14thC. Alteration (influenced by IRON) of Old French *andier*, ultimately of Celtic origin.]

andolan /áán dōlən/ *n.* S Asia an angry protest or other act of opposition by a group of people

and/or /ánd áwr/ *conj.* a short way of saying that either or both of two options may be valid ○ *Bring mosquito netting and/or insect repellent.*

——— **WORD KEY: USAGE** ———
When to use **and/or**? *And/or* is a useful device to express three possibilities in a concise form: *A and/or B* gives the three possibilities A only, B only, or both A and B. On the other hand, it is not a particularly elegant expression and is usually more appropriate to legal and business usage. An alternative that is often preferable in general contexts is the type *A or B or both*.

Andorra /an dáwrə/ co-principality in the Pyrenees Mountains between France and Spain. Language: Catalan. Currency: French franc. Currency: Spanish peseta. Capital: Andorra la Vella. Population: 64,000 (1997). Area: 468 sq. km/181 sq. mi. —**Andorran** *adj.*, *n.*

Andorra la Vella /-lə véllə/ capital of the principality of Andorra. Population: 20,437 (1990).

andr- *prefix.* = **andro-** (*used before vowels*)

andradite /ándrə dīt/ *n.* a type of garnet consisting of calcium iron silicate of various colours. It is used as a gemstone. [Mid-19thC. Named after the Brazilian geologist and independence leader José Bonifácio de Andrada e Silva (1763?–1838).]

Andre /áán dray/, **Carl** (*b.* 1935) US sculptor. He is known for abstract minimalist sculptures made of mass-produced objects such as bricks and metal plates.

Andreotti /án dray ótti/, **Giulio** (*b.* 1919) Italian statesman. A Christian Democrat, he served three terms as Italian prime minister.

Andrew /án droo/, **Prince, Duke of York** (*b.* 1960). Second son of Queen Elizabeth II and Prince Philip, Duke of Edinburgh, he married Sarah Ferguson in 1986. They separated in 1992. Born **Andrew Albert Christian Edward**

Andrewes /án drooz/, **Lancelot** (1555–1626) English Anglican bishop and writer. He became Bishop of Winchester in 1619 and helped to translate the Authorized Version of the Bible.

Andrews, Julie (*b.* 1935) British-born US actor and singer. She made her Broadway debut in the musical *My Fair Lady* (1956) and starred in the popular films *Mary Poppins* (1964) and *The Sound of Music* (1965). Real name **Julia Elizabeth Wells**

andro-, **andr-** *prefix.* male, masculine ○ *androgen* [From Greek, formed from *andr-*, the stem of *anēr* 'man']

Androcles /ándrə kleez/ *n.* a legendary Roman slave who was forced to fight a lion, which spared his life after recognizing Androcles as the man who had once removed a thorn from its paw

androecium /an dreéssi əm/ (*plural* **-a** /-ə/) *n.* the set of stamens in a single flower [Mid-19thC. From modern Latin, from Greek *andro-* 'man, male' + *oikion* 'house'. The underlying sense is 'housing for the male part of the flower'.] —**androecial** /an dreéssi əl, an dreésh'l/ *adj.*

androgen /ándrəjən/ *n.* a natural or artificial steroid that acts as a male sex hormone. Androgens are responsible for the development of male sex organs and secondary sexual characteristics. Testosterone and androsterone are androgens. —**androgenic** /ándrə jénnik/ *adj.*

androgenize /an drójjə nīz/ (**-nizes**, **-nizing**, **-nized**), **androgenise** (**-nises**, **-nising**, **-nised**) *vt.* to cause a female to acquire some male sexual characteristics —**androgenization** /an drójjə nī záysh'n/ *n.*

androgyne /ándrə jīn/ *n.* **1.** ANDROGYNOUS PERSON sb who gives the impression of having both a male and a female sexual identity **2.** BOT = **hermaphrodite** [Mid-16thC. Via French and Latin from Greek *androgunos*, from *andro-* 'man' + *gunē* 'woman'.]

androgynous /an drójjənəss/ *adj.* **1.** BLENDING MASCULINE AND FEMININE neither male nor female in appearance but having masculine and feminine traits that give an impression of ambiguous sexual identity **2.** BOT WITH BOTH MALE AND FEMALE FLOWERS used to describe a plant species in which both male and female flowers occur in the same flower head **3.** = **hermaphrodite** [Early 17thC. Formed from Latin *androgynus* 'hermaphrodite' (see ANDROGYNE).] —**androgynously** *adv.* —**androgyny** *n.*

android /án droyd/ *n.* in science fiction, a robot that looks and behaves like a human being [Early 18thC. From modern Latin *androides*, from Greek *andro-*, the stem of *anēr* 'man'.]

Andromache /an drómməki/ *n.* in Greek mythology, a princess of Troy and the wife of Hector. She led the Trojan women throughout the Trojan War, and was celebrated in myth and literature for her dignity and faith after the deaths of her husband and son in the war.

Andromeda /an drómmidə/ *n.* **1.** MYTHOL WIFE OF PERSEUS in Greek mythology, the daughter of Cassiopeia, who was saved from a sea monster by her future husband, Perseus **2.** ASTRON CONSTELLATION IN NORTHERN HEMISPHERE a constellation in the northern hemisphere between the constellations of Cassiopeia and Pegasus. It contains a spiral galaxy, the (**Andromeda Galaxy**), that can be seen with the naked eye.

Andropov /an dróppov/, **Yuri** (1914–84) Soviet statesman. He was general secretary of the Communist Party of the Soviet Union from 1982. Full name **Yuri Vladimirovich Andropov**

androsterone /an dróstə rōn/ *n.* a steroid that is a weak male sex hormone, produced by the metabolism of other hormones such as testosterone, and normally present in both male and female urine. Formula: $C_{19}H_{30}O_2$. [Mid-20thC. Coined from ANDRO- + STEROL + -ONE.]

-andry *suffix.* **1.** The condition of having a particular number of males or husbands ○ *polyandry* **2.** The condition of having a particular number of stamens ○ *monandry* [From Greek *-andria*, from *andr-*, the stem of *anēr* 'man'] —**-androus** *suffix.*

-ane *suffix.* a saturated hydrocarbon ○ *methane* [Coined on the model of *-ene*, *-ine*, and *-one*, suffixes used in the names of other hydrocarbon derivatives]

anear /ə neér/ *prep.* NEAR near to (*archaic or literary*) ○ *'I wouldn't ever go anear that house again'* (Mark Twain, *The Adventures of Huckleberry Finn*; 1884) ■ *adv.* NEARBY nearby (*archaic or literary*)

anecdotal /ánnik dót'l/, **anecdotic** /ánnik dótik/ *adj.* **1.** BASED ON ANECDOTES OR HEARSAY consisting of or based on secondhand accounts rather than firsthand knowledge or experience or scientific investigation **2.** OF ANECDOTES relating to anecdotes or in the form of anecdotes —**anecdotally** *adv.*

anecdote /ánnik dōt/ *n.* a short personal account of an incident or event [Early 18thC. Directly or via French from modern Latin *anecdota*, from Greek *anekdota*, literally 'things unpublished', from *an-* 'not' + *ekdidonai*, 'to publish' (literally 'to give out').]

anecdotic *adj.* = **anecdotal**

anechoic /ánni kṓ ik/ *adj.* producing or characterized by few or no echoes

Aneirin /ə nírin/ (*fl.* early 6th century BC) Welsh court poet. He celebrated British heroes fallen in battle in his principal work *Y Gododdin*.

anemia *n.* = **anaemia**

anemic *adj.* = **anaemic**

anemo- *prefix.* wind ○ *anemography* [From Greek *anemos* 'wind'. Ultimately from an Indo-European base meaning 'to breathe', which is also the ancestor of English *animal* and *unanimous*.]

anemography /ánni móggrəfi/ *n.* the process of measuring wind speed

anemometer /ánni mómmitər/ *n.* an instrument that measures the force and direction of the wind

anemometry /ánni mómmətri/ *n.* the process of measuring the force and direction of the wind —**anemometrical** /ánnimə méttrik'l/ *adj.*

Anemone

anemone /ə némməni/ (*plural* **-nes** *or* **-ne**) *n*. **1.** BOT FLOWERING PLANT a perennial flowering plant of the buttercup family. Many anemone species grow wild and popular varieties are deep red, purple, and pink with black centres. Genus: *Anemone*. **2.** ZOOL ◆ **sea anemone** [Mid-16thC. Via Latin from Greek *anemōnē*, of uncertain origin.]

anemone fish *n*. a small colourful damselfish with stinging cells, found on tropical coral reefs in close association with sea anemones. Genus: *Amphiprion*.

anemophilous /ánni móffələss/ *adj*. used to describe a plant species that is pollinated by the wind — **anemophily** *n*.

anencephaly /án en séffəli/ *n*. the absence of all or a part of the brain and part of the skull at birth — **anencephalic** /án ensə fállik/ *adj*.

anergy /ánnərji/ *n*. decreased immunity or lack of immunity to an antigen [Late 19thC. From modern Latin *anergia*, from Greek *an-* 'without' + *ergon* 'work'.] — **anergic** /a núrjik/ *adj*.

aneroid /ánnə royd/ *adj*. not containing or using liquid [Mid-19thC. From French *anéroïde*, from Greek *a-* 'without' + *nēron* 'water, liquid'.]

aneroid barometer *n*. an instrument for indicating atmospheric pressure on a circular dial. You tap an aneroid barometer to ensure an up-to-date reading.

anesthesia *n*. = anaesthesia

anesthesiologist /ánnəss theezi ólləjist/, **anaesthesiologist** *n*. *US* = anaesthetist

anesthesiology /ánnəss theezi ólləji/, **anaesthesiology** *n*. *US* = anaesthetics

anesthetic *n*., *adj*. = anaesthetic

anesthetist *n*. = anaesthetist

anestrous *adj*. US = anoestrous

anestrus *n*. US = anoestrus

aneuploid /ánnyoo ployd/ *adj*. used to describe a cell or organism with fewer or more chromosomes than usual — **aneuploid** *n*. — **aneuploidy** *n*.

aneurysm /ánnyoorizzəm/, **aneurism** *n*. a fluid-filled sac formed when the wall of an artery abnormally dilates [From Greek *aneurusma* 'dilation, swelling', from *aneurunein* 'to widen out', from *ana-* 'through' + *eurus* 'wide'] — **aneurysmal** /ánnyoo rízm'l/ *adj*.

anew /ə nyóo/ *adv*. **1.** AGAIN again or once more **2.** IN NEW WAY in a new way or form that is unlike the previous one [14thC. From *a-* (an eroded form of *of*) + NEW; probably modelled on Old French *de neuf, de nouveau*.]

anfractuosity /án frakchoo óssəti/ (*plural* **-ties**) *n*. (*literary*) **1.** TWIST a twist or turn, e.g. in a road or in the plot of a novel **2.** TWISTINESS the twisting, turning nature of sth

anfractuous /an frákchoo əss/ *adj*. with much twisting and turning (*literary*) [Late 16thC. From late Latin *anfractuosus*, from late Latin *anfractus* 'bending', from *ambi-* 'around' + *fract-*, the past participle stem of *frangere* 'to break' (see FRANGIBLE).]

Angas /áng gəss/, **George Fife** (1789–1879) English-born Australian philanthropist. He encouraged the settlement of South Australia and raised money to found its capital, Adelaide.

angel /áynjəl/ *n*. **1.** RELIG HEAVENLY BEING a divine being who acts as a messenger of God. According to a medieval hierarchy, the nine classes of heavenly

being are, in ascending order, angels, archangels, principalities, powers, virtues, dominations, thrones, cherubim, and seraphim. **2.** PICTURE OF HEAVENLY BEING a picture of an angel as a human figure with wings **3.** KIND PERSON sb who is kind or beautiful (*informal*) **4.** GUARDIAN AND GUIDE a spirit that protects and offers guidance **5.** CHR MEMBER OF LOWEST ANGELIC ORDER a member of the lowest order of angels in the medieval Christian celestial hierarchy, ranked below archangels **6.** MONEY OLD ENGLISH COIN a gold coin that was a unit of currency in England from 1465 to the early 17th century [13thC. Via Old French from, ultimately, Greek *aggelos* 'messenger'.]

─── **WORD KEY: SYNONYMS** ───
See Synonyms at *backer*.

─── **WORD KEY: CULTURAL NOTE** ───
An Angel at My Table, the second volume of a three-part autobiography by New Zealand writer Janet Frame. It describes the author's commitment to a mental institution where she was erroneously diagnosed as schizophrenic. She narrowly avoided a leucotomy when a surgeon discovered she had published a collection of stories. The book was made into a film by Jane Campion in 1990.

angel cake *n*. a whitish light-textured cake with a delicate flavour, made with egg whites [From its light colour and texture, likened to the typically bright and ethereal conception of angels]

angel dust *n*. DRUGS the illegal hallucinogenic drug phencyclidine (*slang*) [From its white colour]

Angel Falls /áyng'l fáwlz/ *n*. the world's highest waterfall, located in southeastern Venezuela in the Guiana Highlands. Height: 979 m/3,212 ft.

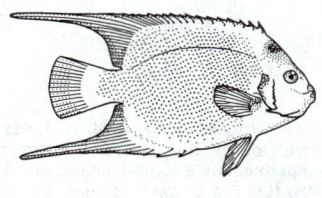

Angelfish

angelfish /áynjəl fish/ (*plural* **-fish** *or* **-fishes**) *n*. **1.** TROPICAL FRESHWATER FISH WITH STRIPED BODY a freshwater fish found in the tropical waters of South America. It has a broad striped body and large fins, and is often kept in aquariums. Latin name: *Pterophyllum scalare*. **2.** TROPICAL MARINE FISH a brightly coloured tropical marine fish that has a broad flat body. Family: Chaetodontidae and Pomocanthidae. **3.** = angel shark [Mainly from the fish's long wing-like fins]

angelic /an jéllik/, **angelical** /-jéllik'l/ *adj*. **1.** KINDLY very kind or beautiful **2.** OF ANGELS relating to angels — **angelically** *adv*. — **angelicalness** *n*.

angelica /an jéllikə/ (*plural* **-cas** *or* **-ca**) *n*. **1.** PLANTS TALL HOLLOW-STEMMED FLOWERING PLANT a tall hollow-stemmed flowering plant of the carrot family. Angelicas have white or greenish flowers and are found mainly in Europe and Asia. Genus: *Angelica*. **2.** COOK CANDIED STEMS OF ANGELICA PLANT the bright green, candied stems of the angelica plant, used to decorate cakes and biscuits [Early 16thC. From medieval Latin, short for *herba angelica*, literally 'angelic plant'; perhaps from its traditional use as a remedy for poison and contagion.]

angelical *adj*. = angelic

Angelico /an jélli kō/, **Fra** (1400?–55) Italian religious painter. He became a Dominican monk. He is noted for his frescoes in Florence, including the *Annunciation* and the *Coronation of the Virgin*. Born Guido di Pietro

Angel of Death *n*. = Azrael

angel of mercy *n*. sb who brings welcome assistance

Angel of the North *n*. a large metal sculpture by Antony Gormley of an angel, erected on a hill outside Gateshead, northeastern England, in 1997.

It has a wingspan of 54 m/177 ft and has been described as a symbol of renewal in a region undergoing social and economic change.

Maya Angelou

Angelou /ánjə loo/, **Maya** (*b*. 1928) US writer. Her novels and poetry are notable for their depiction of assertive African American women.

angel shark *n*. a small shark with a flat body, broad head, and enlarged pectoral fins, giving it the appearance of a ray. Genus: *Squatina*. [From its wing-like pectoral fins]

Angelus /ánjiləss/, **angelus** *n*. **1.** ROMAN CATHOLIC PRAYERS in the Roman Catholic Church, a set of prayers to commemorate the Annunciation and the Incarnation **2.** BELL ANNOUNCING ANGELUS a bell rung to announce the time for the Angelus [Mid-17thC. From Latin *Angelus domini* 'the angel of the Lord', the first words of the prayer.]

anger /áng gər/ *n*. GREAT ANNOYANCE a feeling of extreme annoyance ■ *vti*. (**-gers**, **-gering**, **-gered**) BECOME OR MAKE GREATLY ANNOYED to become or make sb extremely annoyed [13thC. From Old Norse *angr* 'trouble, sorrow'. Ultimately from an Indo-European base meaning 'tight, painful', which is also the ancestor of English *anxious*, *anguish*, *hangnail*, and *angina*.]

─── **WORD KEY: SYNONYMS** ───
anger, annoyance, indignation, rage, fury, ire, wrath
CORE MEANING: a feeling of strong displeasure in response to an assumed injury
anger the most general term; **annoyance** a feeling of irritation, milder or more fleeting than anger; **resentment** subdued anger caused by a sense of unfair treatment, and a powerlessness to remedy this; **indignation** anger based on a condemnation of sth considered wrong or unfair; **fury** an intense form of anger that suggests lack of control and potential to do violence; **rage** violent anger, more intense than fury; **ire** a literary term for anger; **wrath** a literary or formal term for strong anger, often with overtones of a desire for revenge.

─── **WORD KEY: CULTURAL NOTE** ───
Look Back in Anger, a play by John Osborne (1956). Seen at the time of its first performances as a landmark play that challenged the disaffection of many young people, this domestic drama focusses on Jimmy Porter, a working-class graduate who feels stifled by the middle-class family into which he has married and trapped by traditional social conventions.

Angers /óN zhay/ capital of Maine-et-Loire Department in the Pays de la Loire Region in western France. Population: 146,163 (1990).

Angevin /ánjəvin/ *n*. SB FROM ANJOU sb who was born in or lives in the Anjou region in southwestern France ■ *adj*. **1.** OF ANJOU relating to the Anjou region in France **2.** OF ANJOU AND PLANTAGENET DYNASTIES relating to the House of Anjou, especially the branch that includes the Plantagenet kings of England [Mid-17thC. Via French from medieval Latin *Andegavinus*, from *Andegavia* 'Anjou'.]

angina /an jínə/, **angina pectoris** /-péktəriss/ *n*. a medical condition in which lack of blood to the heart causes severe chest pains [Mid-16thC. From Latin, 'quinsy', an alteration (influenced by *angere* 'to squeeze') of Greek *agkhonē* 'strangling', from *agkhein* 'to squeeze, strangle'.]

angio- *prefix*. **1.** blood or lymph vessel ○ *angiogram* **2.** pericarp ○ *angiosperm* [Via modern Latin from Greek *aggeion* 'blood vessel', literally 'small vessel', from *aggos* 'vessel', of unknown origin]

angiocardiography /ánji ō kaardi óggrəfi/ *n.* X-ray examination of the heart and related blood vessels after a substance that will show up when X-rayed has been injected into the bloodstream —**angiocardiographic** /ánji ō kaardi ə gráffik/ *adj.*

angiogenesis /ánji ō jénnississ/ *n.* the formation of new blood vessels, e.g. in an embryo or as a result of a tumour

angiogram /ánji ō gram/ *n.* an X-ray photograph of a blood vessel

angiography /ánji ógrəfi/ *n.* X-ray examination of blood vessels after a substance that will show up when X-rayed has been injected into the bloodstream —**angiographic** /ánji ə gráffik/ *adj.*

angiology /ánji ólləji/ *n.* the branch of medicine that deals with blood vessels and the lymphatic system

angioma /ánji ṓmə/ (*plural* **-mas** *or* **-mata** /-mətə/) *n.* a benign tumour made up of blood or lymph vessels — **angiomatous** *adj.*

angiopathy /ánji óppəthi/ (*plural* **-thies**) *n.* a disease of the blood vessels or lymph vessels

angioplasty /ánji ō plasti/ (*plural* **-ties**) *n.* a surgical operation to clear a narrowed or blocked artery

angiosarcoma /ánji ō saar kṓmə/ *n.* a malignant tumour consisting of vascular cells, often in the liver

angioscope /ánji ə skṓp/ *n.* a long fine surgical viewing instrument threaded into a patient's blood vessels, to allow surgeons to observe and perform operations without large incisions [Late 20thC] — **angioscopy** /ánji óskəpi/ *n.*

angiosperm /ánji ō spurm/ *n.* a plant in which the sex organs are within flowers and the seeds are in a fruit. ◊ **gymnosperm** [Early 19thC. Coined from ANGIO- + Greek *sperma* 'seed'.]

angiotensin /ánji ō ténssin/ *n.* a hormone that causes blood pressure to rise, formed in the blood by a series of processes that can be influenced by drugs [Mid-20thC. Coined from ANGIO- + HYPERTENSION + -IN.]

Barnaby's

Angkor

Angkor /áng kawr/, **Ângkôr** ancient capital city of early Khmer civilization, now deserted but noted for its temples and monuments, built 850–900. It is in present-day northwestern Cambodia. Area: 13 sq. km/5 sq. mi.

angle¹ /áng g'l/ *n.* **1.** SPACE BETWEEN DIVERGING LINES the space between two diverging lines or planes, or a measure of the space **2.** FIGURE FORMED BY DIVERGING LINES a figure formed by two lines diverging from a common point or two planes diverging from a common line **3.** = **solid angle 4.** PART THAT STICKS OUT a projecting part of sth **5.** POSITION FOR VIEWING STH a position from which sb can look at sth ○ *a sculpture seen from three angles* **6.** WAY OF CONSIDERING STH a way of looking at a situation ○ *Consider the matter from this angle.* ■ *v.* (**-gles, -gling, -gled**) **1.** *vti.* DIRECT OR PLACE OBLIQUELY to direct or place sth obliquely, or move or be placed obliquely **2.** *vt.* PRESENT STH WITH BIAS to present sth with a particular audience in mind or in order to express a particular point of view **3.** *vi.* CHANGE DIRECTION SHARPLY to turn in a sharply different direction [14thC. Directly or via French from Latin *angulus* 'corner'. Ultimately from an Indo-European base meaning 'to bend, hook', which is also the ancestor of *angle²*, *ankle*, and *anchor*.]

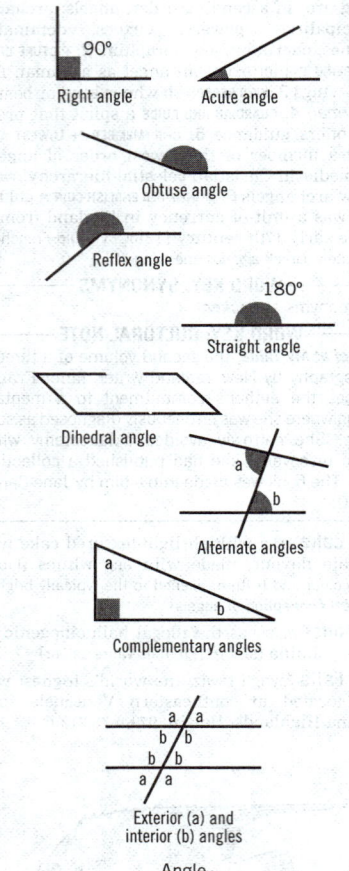

90°

Right angle   Acute angle

Obtuse angle

Reflex angle

180°

Straight angle

Dihedral angle

a *b* Alternate angles

a *b* Complementary angles

a/*a* *b*/*b* *b*/*b* *a*/*a*

Exterior (a) and interior (b) angles

Angle

angle² /áng g'l/ (**-gles, -gling, -gled**) *vi.* **1.** FISH WITH ROD to fish with a hook, line, and rod **2.** ATTEMPT TO GET STH to attempt to obtain a compliment or an advantage (*informal*) [Old English *angul* 'fishhook'. Ultimately from an Indo-European base meaning 'to bend, hook', which is also the ancestor of English *angle¹*, *ankle*, and *anchor*.]

Angle /áng g'l/ *n.* a member of a Germanic people who invaded and settled throughout eastern and northern England in the 5th and 6th centuries AD [Pre-12thC. From Latin *Angli*, literally 'people from *Angul*' in North Germany (source also of *English*), of Germanic origin; ultimately related to *angle¹*.]

angle bar *n.* = **angle iron**

angle bracket *n.* one of a pair of marks, < or >, used to enclose text

angle iron *n.* an iron or steel bar that is L-shaped in cross section

angle of attack *n.* the acute angle between the direction of airflow and the line linking the leading and trailing edges of an aircraft wing

angle of bank *n.* the angle between the lateral and horizontal axes of an aircraft in flight

angle of dip *n.* PHYS = **dip**

angle of incidence *n.* the angle between an incoming ray of light and the line perpendicular to the surface at the point of arrival

angle of reflection *n.* the angle between a reflected ray of light and the line perpendicular to the surface at the point of reflection

angle of refraction *n.* the angle between a refracted ray of light and the line perpendicular to the surface at the point of refraction

angle of repose *n.* the maximum slope or angle at which unconsolidated material such as sand can be made into a mound before it begins to slide

angle of yaw *n.* the acute angle between the direction in which an aircraft is flying and its own longitudinal axis

angle plate *n.* an L-shaped metal plate used to support a framework

Anglepoise /áng g'l poyz/ *tdmk.* a trademark for a desk lamp that uses the angle of the light to be adjusted without moving the base

angler /áng glər/ *n.* **1.** SB WHO GOES FISHING sb who fishes with a hook, line, and rod **2.** ZOOL = **anglerfish**

———— **WORD KEY: CULTURAL NOTE** ————
The Compleat Angler, a handbook by Izaak Walton (1653). Although presented as a discourse on fishing in the form of a dialogue between a fisherman, a hunter, and a fowler, the work's affectionate portrait of country life and its references to social issues transform it into a work of great literary and historical value.

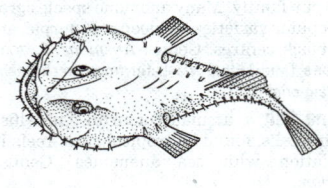

Anglerfish

anglerfish /áng glər fish/ (*plural* **-fish** *or* **-fishes**) *n.* a marine fish that uses a long dorsal fin extending over its mouth to attract prey. Order: Lophiiformes.

Anglesey /áng g'lssi/ island off the coast of northwestern Wales in the county of Gwynedd. Population: 67,200 (1995). Area: 620 sq. km/276 sq. mi.

anglesite /áng g'l sīt/ *n.* a colourless, white, or lightly tinted mineral consisting of lead sulphate

Anglian /áng gli ən/ *n.* LANG GROUP OF OLD ENGLISH DIALECTS a group of dialects of Old English that includes Mercian and Northumbrian. ◊ **Kentish, West Saxon** ■ *adj.* OF ANGLES relating to the Angles [Early 18thC. Formed from Latin *Angli* 'the Angles' (see ANGLE).]

Anglican /áng glikən/ *adj.* OF ANGLICAN CHURCH relating to the Anglican Church ■ *n.* MEMBER OF ANGLICAN CHURCH sb who belongs to an Anglican denomination [Early 17thC. Via medieval Latin *Anglicanus* 'English' from, ultimately, Latin *Angli* 'Angles' (see ANGLE); from its originally denoting the Church of England.]

Anglican Church, **Anglican Communion** *n.* a group of Christian churches including the Churches of England, Ireland, and Wales, and the Episcopal Church of Scotland

Anglicanism /áng glikənizzəm/ *n.* the doctrines of the Church of England and other Anglican churches

anglicise *vti.* = **anglicize**

Anglicism /áng gli sizzəm/, **anglicism** *n.* **1.** BRITISH ENGLISH WORD a term that is peculiar to British English as opposed to other varieties of English **2.** ENGLISH WORD IN FOREIGN LANGUAGE an English word or phrase used in a foreign language [Mid-17thC. Formed from medieval Latin *Anglicus* 'English' (see ANGLICAN).]

anglicize /áng gli sīz/, **Anglicize** (**-cizes, -cizing, -cized**), **anglicise** (**-cises, -cising, -cised**), **Anglicise** (**-cises, -cising, -cised**) *vti.* to become or make sb or sth more English [Early 18thC. Formed from medieval Latin *Anglicus* 'English' (see ANGLICAN).] —**anglicization** /áng gli sī záysh'n/ *n.*

angling /áng gling/ *n.* the sport of catching fish with a hook, line, and rod

Anglo /áng glṓ/ (*plural* **-glos**), **anglo** (*plural* **-glos**) *n.* (*informal*) **1.** *Aus* AUSTRALIAN OF BRITISH ORIGIN a derogatory term for an Australian citizen of British, Irish, or American origin **2.** *US* NON-HISPANIC WHITE PERSON an English-speaking white person in the United States who is not of Hispanic origin **3.** *Can* NON-FRENCH-SPEAKING CANADIAN an English-speaking person in Canada, especially in Quebec [Early 19thC. From ANGLO-.]

Anglo- *prefix*. England, the English ○ *Anglophile* [From Latin *Angli* 'Angles' (see ANGLE)]

Anglo-French *adj*. relating to the links that exist between France and the United Kingdom

Anglo-Indian *adj*. FROM INDIAN LANGUAGE introduced into English from an Indian language ■ *n*. **1.** SB WITH BRITISH AND INDIAN ANCESTRY sb of mixed English or British and Indian descent **2.** BRITISH PERSON RESIDENT IN INDIA an English or British person who has lived a long time in India, especially during the time when India was a British colony

Anglo-Irish *npl*. people of English descent who were born or live in Ireland —**Anglo-Irish** *adj*.

Anglo-Norman *adj*. HIST ENGLISH AND NORMAN connected with the 11th-century Norman conquerors of England ■ *n*. **1.** HIST NORMAN IN ENGLAND a Norman inhabitant of England after 1066 **2.** LANG FRENCH SPOKEN IN MEDIEVAL ENGLAND the form of Norman French spoken in medieval England

Anglophile /áng glō fīl/ *n*. sb who greatly admires England or the English —**Anglophilia** /áng glō fílli ə/ *n*. —**Anglophilic** /-fíllik/ *adj*.

Anglophobe /áng glō fṓb/ *n*. sb who hates England or the English —**Anglophobia** /áng glō fṓbi ə/ *n*. —**Anglophobic** /-fṓbik/ *adj*.

Anglophone /áng glə fṓn/ *n*. SPEAKER OF ENGLISH sb who speaks English, especially as a first language ■ *adj*. WHERE ENGLISH IS MOTHER TONGUE where English is spoken by most people as their first language

Anglo-Saxon *n*. **1.** PEOPLES MEMBER OF GERMANIC PEOPLE a member of one of the West Germanic peoples who settled in Britain from the fifth century AD and were dominant until 1066. They included the Angles, Saxons, and Jutes. **2.** LANG = Old English **3.** WHITE ENGLISH NATIVE SPEAKER sb who is white, speaks English as a first language, and has connections with an English-speaking country ■ *adj*. **1.** LANG FROM OLD ENGLISH used to describe a word in Modern English that comes from Old English **2.** OF ENGLISH SPEAKERS relating to white English speakers [Early 17thC. From modern Latin *Anglo-Saxones* 'Anglo-Saxons', a translation of Old English *Angulseaxe* 'English Saxon' (as opposed to one living on the continent of Europe)]

ang mo /áng mṓ/ (*plural* **ang mos**) *n*. *Malaysia, Singapore* an inhabitant of the West, especially western Europe or North America (*informal*) [From Hokkien, literally 'red hair']

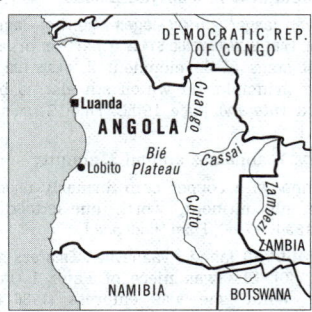
Angola

Angola /ang gṓlə/ republic in west-central Africa that gained its independence from Portugal in 1975. Language: Portuguese. Currency: kwanza. Capital: Luanda. Population: 10,548,000 (1997). Area: 1,246,700 sq. km/481,530 sq. mi. Official name **Republic of Angola** —**Angolan** *adj*., *n*.

angora /ang gáwrə/ *n*. **1.** SILKY-HAIRED ANIMAL a rabbit, goat, or cat belonging to a breed with long silky fur **2.** WOOL FROM ANGORA HAIR wool made from the hair of an angora goat or rabbit (*often used before a noun*) ◊ **mohair** [Early 19thC. From ANGORA.]

angostura /áng gə styóorə/, **angostura bark** *n*. the bitter aromatic bark of either of two South American citrus trees, used as a flavouring in bitters and formerly used medicinally to relieve fever [Named after the city of *Angostura* (Ciudad Bolívar) in Venezuela]

Angostura bitters *tdmk*. a trademark for a bitter-tasting flavouring for alcoholic drinks, made from herbs and spices

Angoulême /aaN goo lem/, Charles, Duc d' (1573–1650) French soldier and the illegitimate son of Charles IX. He commanded the siege of La Rochelle (1627).

angrily /áng grəli/ *adv*. **1.** WITH ANGER in a way that conveys extreme annoyance or displeasure **2.** STORM-ILY in a stormy threatening way

angry /áng gri/ (**-grier**, **-griest**) *adj*. **1.** FEELING VERY ANNOYED feeling extremely annoyed, often about an insult or a wrong **2.** EXPRESSING ANNOYANCE expressing extreme annoyance ○ '*Low growls and angry snarls assailed our ears on every side...*' (Edgar Rice Burroughs, *The Gods of Mars*; 1913) **3.** STORMY stormy-looking **4.** INFLAMED inflamed and painful-looking [14thC. Formed from ANGER.]

angry young man *n*. **1.** angry young man, Angry Young Man LITERAT, THEATRE REBELLIOUS WRITER a member of a group of British male writers in the 1950s who were hostile to authority. The setting for their works is typically working-class, and the central character typically a male loner. (*often used in the plural*) **2.** REBELLIOUS YOUNG MAN a young man who is hostile to authority

angst /angst/ *n*. **1.** PHILOSOPHY EXISTENTIALIST DREAD in existentialist philosophy, a feeling of dread arising from an awareness of free choice **2.** ANXIETY any feeling of dread or anxiety [Early 20thC. From German. Ultimately from an Indo-European base meaning 'tight, painful', which is also the ancestor of English *anguish* and *anger*.]

---- **WORD KEY: SYNONYMS** ----
See Synonyms at **worry**.

angstrom /áng strəm, -strom/, **angstrom unit** *n*. a unit of length equal to one ten-billionth of a metre (10^{-10} m), used to measure the wavelengths of electromagnetic radiations. Symbol **Å** [Late 19thC. Named after the Swedish physicist and astronomer Anders Jonas Ångström, (1814–84).]

Anguilla /ang gwíllə/ one of the Leeward Islands, in the West Indies. It is east of Puerto Rico. Area: 91 sq. km/35 sq. mi.

anguish /áng gwish/ *n*. EXTREME ANXIETY extreme anxiety or emotional torment ■ *vti*. (**-guishes**, **-guishing**, **-guished**) FEEL OR CAUSE SB ANGUISH to feel or cause to feel anguish [12thC. Via Old French *anguis* from, ultimately, Latin *angustia* 'narrow, tight'. Ultimately from an Indo-European base meaning 'tight, painful', which is also the ancestor of English *anxious*, *anger*, *hangnail*, and *angina*.]

anguished /áng gwisht/ *adj*. **1.** WITH ANGUISH feeling or showing extreme anxiety or torment **2.** CAUSING ANGUISH producing extreme anxiety or other torment

angular /áng gyóolər/ *adj*. **1.** THIN thin and bony **2.** AWKWARD AND UNGAINLY stiff, awkward, and ungainly **3.** SHARPLY DEFINED used to describe an object with a lot of angles **4.** MATH MEASURED BY ANGLES measured by an angle or rate of change of an angle [14thC. From Latin *angularis*, from *angulus* (see ANGLE[1]).]

angular acceleration *n*. the rate at which the rotation of a rotating body changes. Symbol α

angular displacement *n*. the angle through which sth has been rotated about an axis, usually measured in radians

angular frequency *n*. the frequency of a repeating rotation expressed in radians per second, or the frequency of an oscillation multiplied by 2π. Symbol ω

angularity /áng gyoo lárrəti/ (*plural* **-ties**) *n*. **1.** THIN BONY QUALITY the thin and bony appearance of sb's body **2.** SHARP ANGLE a sharp corner or angle (*often used in the plural*)

angular momentum *n*. the momentum that a body has due to its rotation about an axis, calculated as the product of its mass and its angular velocity. Symbol L

angular velocity *n*. the rate of rotation of a body around an axis. Symbol ω

Angus[1] /áng gəss/ (*plural* **-gus** *or* **-guses**) *n*. = **Aberdeen Angus**

Angus[2] /áng gəss/ historic Scottish county, revived in 1998. The county headquarters are in Forfar. Area: 2,535 sq. km/874 sq. mi.

anhidrotic /ánhi dróttik/ *n*. a medication or other agent that prevents or reduces sweating

anhinga /an híng gə/ (*plural* **-gas** *or* **-ga**) *n*. *US* BIRDS = **darter** [Mid-18thC. Via Portuguese from Tupi *áyinga*.]

anhydride /an hī drīd, -drid/ *n*. a chemical compound formed when water molecules are removed from another compound [Mid-19thC. Formed from AN-HYDROUS.]

anhydrite /an hī drīt/ *n*. a colourless or lightly tinted mineral consisting of anhydrous calcium sulphate, used in cement and fertilizers. Formula: $CaSO_4$. [Early 19thC. Formed from ANHYDROUS.]

anhydrous /an hídrəss/ *adj*. used to describe compounds that contain no water, or crystals that lack chemically bound water (**water of crystallization**) [Early 19thC. From Greek *anudros*, literally 'waterless', from *hudōr* 'water' (see HYDRO-)]

ani /áani/ (*plural* **anis** *or* **ani**) *n*. a black long-tailed bird of the cuckoo family that has a heavy arched bill and lives in tropical America. Anis lay eggs in a communal nest. Genus: *Crotophaga*. [Early 19thC. Via Spanish *aní* or Portuguese *ani* from Tupi *anū*.]

anicca /ánnikə/ *n*. in Buddhism, the cycle of birth, life, and death [Via Pali from Sanskrit *anitya-* 'not eternal', from *nitya-* 'constant, perpetual']

aniconic /án ī kónnik/ *adj*. used to describe images of gods that are not human or animal in form

anil /ánnil/ (*plural* **-ils** *or* **-il**) *n*. a West Indian shrub with small reddish-yellow flowers that is the source of indigo dye. Latin name: *Indigofera suffruticosa*. [Late 16thC. Via French, Portuguese, Arabic, and Persian from, ultimately, Sanskrit *nīla-* 'dark blue'.]

anile /ánnīl, áy-/ *adj*. typical of or resembling a woman of advanced years [Mid-17thC. From Latin *anilis*, from *anus* 'venerable woman'.]

aniline /ánnilin, -leen/ *n*. a colourless poisonous oily liquid that is used in the manufacture of dyes, resins, pharmaceuticals, and explosives. Formula: $C_6H_5NH_2$. [Mid-19thC. Formed from *anil* the indigo plant, because it was first obtained by distilling indigo with alkali.]

aniline dye *n*. a synthetic dye derived from aniline

anilingus /áyni líng gəss/ *n*. the practice of stimulating the anus with the tongue or mouth [Mid-20thC. From modern Latin, formed from *anus* 'anus', on the model of CUNNILINGUS.]

anima /ánnimə/ *n*. **1.** INNER SELF in Jungian psychology, the true inner self as opposed to the outer persona **2.** MALE'S FEMININE SIDE in Jungian psychology, the feminine aspect of the male personality [Early 20thC. From Latin, 'breath, soul, spirit' (source also of English *animate* and *unanimous*).]

animadversion /ánni mad vúrsh'n/ *n*. a critical comment or comments, especially those reproaching sb

animadvert /ánni mad vúrt, -məd-/ (**-verts**, **-verting**, **-verted**) *vi*. to comment critically or unfavourably [Mid-17thC. From Latin *animadvertere*, literally 'to turn the mind toward', from *animus* 'mind' + *advertere* 'to turn toward' (see ADVERT[1]).]

animal /ánnim'l/ *n*. **1.** LIVING ORGANISM WITH INDEPENDENT MOVEMENT a living organism that is distinguished from plants by independent movement and responsive sense organs **2.** MAMMAL a land mammal other than a human being **3.** BRUTISH PERSON sb who is vulgar or brutish (*informal*) **4.** INSTINCT-DRIVEN INNER SELF the instinctive inner self as opposed to the one subject to self-restraint **5.** PERSON OR THING any particular person or thing (*informal*) ■ *adj*. **1.** FROM ANIMALS derived from animals **2.** INSTINCTIVE belonging to the realm of instincts and urges [14thC. From Latin *animale*, from *animalis* 'living, breathing', from *anima* 'breath, life, soul' (see ANIMA).]

animal husbandry *n*. the branch of agriculture concerned with breeding and rearing farm animals

animalise *vt*. = animalize

animalism /ánnim'l,lizzəm/ *n*. **1.** THEORY OF HUMANS' NON-SPIRITUAL NATURE the theory that human beings are driven by physical appetites rather than spiritual needs **2.** PREOCCUPATION WITH PHYSICAL SIDE OF LIFE preoccupation with physical rather than spiritual needs **3.** TYPICAL ANIMAL BEHAVIOUR behaviour that is typical of animals —**animalistic** /ánnimə lístik/ adj.

animalist /ánnim'list/ n. **1.** SB PREOCCUPIED WITH PHYSICAL NEEDS sb who is preoccupied with physical rather than spiritual needs **2.** SB DENYING HUMANS' SPIRITUAL NATURE sb who holds that human beings are driven by physical appetites rather than spiritual needs **3.** ANIMAL RIGHTS SUPPORTER sb who believes in animal rights and is prepared to take part in militant action to protect them (informal)

animality /ánni málləti/ n. **1.** ANIMAL CHARACTERISTICS the characteristics of animals, as opposed to plants **2.** = **animalism** n. **2**

animalize /ánnimə līz/ (**-izes, -izing, -ized**), **animalise** (**-ises, -ising, -ised**) vt. to bring out sb's brutal or instinctive nature —**animalization** /ánnimə īt záysh'n/ n.

animal liberation n. the movement to free animals from human exploitation (often used before a noun)

animal magnetism n. sb's strong physical attractiveness (informal humorous)

animal protein n. animal tissue processed for commercial or industrial use

animal starch n. = glycogen

animal welfarist n. sb who believes in the rights of animals

animate vt. /ánni mayt/ (**-mates, -mating, -mated**) **1.** MAKE LIVELY to make sb or sth lively **2.** INSPIRE SB to rouse or inspire sb to take action or to have strong feelings **3.** PRESENT STH USING ANIMATION TECHNIQUES to present or record sth in the form of a sequence of moving still images **4.** MAKE SB ACTIVE to arouse sb or sth into activity **5.** CAUSE TO LIVE to bring sb or sth to life ■ adj. /ánni mət/ **1.** PHYSICALLY ALIVE in a physically live state, as opposed to being dead or inert **2.** FULL OF LIVELINESS full of liveliness or energy [14thC. From Latin animat-, the past participle stem of animare 'to give life to', from anima (see ANIMA).]

animated /ánni maytid/ adj. **1.** LIVELY OR BUSY full of liveliness or activity **2.** FILMED AS MOVING SEQUENCE OF STILLS in the form of a sequence of moving still images —**animatedly** adv.

animation /ánni máysh'n/ n. **1.** LIVELINESS liveliness in the way sb speaks or behaves **2.** PRODUCTION OF ANIMATED FILMS the making of films by photographing a sequence of slightly varying drawings or models so that they appear to move and change when the sequence is shown **3.** ANIMATED FILM OR FILMS a film or films consisting of a series of drawn, painted, or modelled scenes

animato /ánni máatō/ adj., adv. to be played in a lively animated manner (used as a musical direction) [Early 18thC. Via Italian from, ultimately, Latin animare (see ANIMATE).]

animator /ánnimaytər/ n. **1.** MAKER OF ANIMATED FILMS sb who makes animated films, or who provides a technical or artistic skill needed to produce animations **2.** SB OR STH ADDING LIVELINESS sb or sth that makes things lively, exciting, or interesting

animatronics /ánnimə trónniks/ n. the use of computer technology and a form of radio control to animate puppets or other models, e.g. for a film (takes a singular verb) [Late 20thC. A blend of ANIMATE and ELECTRONICS.] —**animatronic** adj.

animé /ánni may/ n. any of various resins from tropical American trees, used in varnishes and scents [Late 16thC. Via French from Tupi wana'ni.]

animism /ánnimizzəm/ n. **1.** BELIEF THAT NATURE HAS A SOUL the belief that things in nature, e.g. trees, mountains, and the sky, have souls or consciousness **2.** BELIEF IN ORGANIZING FORCE IN UNIVERSE the belief that a supernatural force animates and organizes the universe **3.** BELIEF IN EXISTENCE OF SEPARATE SPIRIT the belief that people have spirits that do or can exist separately from their bodies [Mid-19thC. Formed from Latin anima 'soul'.] —**animist** adj., n. —**animistic** /ánni místik/ adj.

animosity /ánni móssəti/ n. (plural **-ties**) a feeling or spirit of hostility and resentment [15thC. Directly or via French animosité from late Latin animositas 'spiritedness', from animosus 'spirited', from animus (see ANIMUS).]

animus /ánniməss/ n. **1.** HOSTILITY a feeling or display of animosity **2.** DISPOSITION an attitude or feeling that motivates sb's actions **3.** FEMALE PERSONALITY'S MALE SIDE in Jungian psychology, the masculine aspect of the female personality [Early 19thC. From Latin, 'mind, spirit'.]

anion /án ī ən/ n. a negatively charged ion, especially one that is attracted to an anode, either during electrolysis or within a vacuum tube [Mid-19thC. A blend of ANODE and ION.] —**anionic** /án ī ónnik/ adj. —**anionically** /-ónnikli/ adv.

anise /ánniss/ n. **1.** PLANT WITH LIQUORICE-FLAVOURED SEEDS an aromatic Mediterranean plant with liquorice-flavoured seeds (**aniseed**), used in medicines and for flavouring food and drink. Latin name: Pimpinella anisum. **2.** = **aniseed** [13thC. Via French anis and Latin anisum from Greek anison.]

aniseed /ánnis seed/ n. the liquorice-flavoured seeds of anise, used whole or in ground spice mixtures as a flavouring in foods, especially sweets and cakes, and in drinks, e.g. pastis and ouzo

aniseikonia /án ī sī kóni ə/ n. a defect in the lens of one eye that results in its seeing an image that differs in size and shape from the image seen by the other eye [Mid-20thC. Coined from ANIS- + Greek eikōn 'image' + -IA.]

anise seed n. = aniseed

anisette /ánni zét, -sét/ n. a sweet liqueur flavoured with aniseed [Mid-19thC. From French, literally 'a little anise', from anis 'ANISE'.]

aniso- prefix. differing, not equal ○ anisogamy [From Greek anisos, from an- 'not' + isos 'equal']

anisogamete /án ī sō gámmeet, -gə meet/ n. = heterogamete

anisogamy /án ī sóggəmi/ n. = heterogamy n. **1** —**anisogamic** /án īssə gámmik/ adj. —**anisogamous** /ánī sóggəməss/ adj.

anisole /ánni sōl/ n. a colourless liquid with a pleasant smell that is used as a solvent and a flavouring. Formula: $C_6H_5OCH_3$. [Mid-19thC. Coined from ANISE + -OLE.]

anisomeric /án īssō mérrik/ adj. used to describe a chemical compound that does not form structurally different molecules (**isomers**)

anisometric /á n īssō méttrik/ adj. **1.** ASYMMETRIC not isometric or symmetrical ○ an anisometric particle **2.** CRYSTALS SHAPED IRREGULARLY used to describe a crystal that does not have three perpendicular axes of equal length and is therefore not regular

anisometropia /án īssōmə trópi ə/ n. lack of balance between each eye's ability to refract light [Late 19thC. Coined from ANISO- + Greek metron 'measure' + -OPIA.] —**anisometropic** /án īssōmə tróppik/ adj.

anisotropic /án īssō tróppik/ adj. used to describe sth with physical properties that are different in different directions, e.g. crystals that are not symmetrical or regular, especially ones measuring differently along each of two or more axes —**anisotropically** /á nīssō tróppikli/ adv. —**anisotropism** /-sóttrəpizzəm/ n. —**anisotropy** /-sóttrəpi/ n.

Anjou[1] /aán zhoó, óN-/, **Anjou pear** n. a variety of pear with green skin and firm flesh [Named after ANJOU, where it was originally grown]

Anjou[2] /aán zhoó, óN-/ former province in western France in the lower Loire valley. Once part of the Plantagenet domain, it was claimed for France in 1481.

Ankara /ángkərə/ capital of Turkey, in the north-central part of the country, on the River Ankara, northwest of Adana and southeast of Bursa. Population: 2,782,200 (1994). Former name **Angora**

ankerite /ángkə rīt/ n. a white, grey, brown, or reddish mineral that resembles dolomite and contains calcium, magnesium, iron, and sometimes manganese [Mid-19thC. From German Ankerit. Named after its discoverer, the Austrian mineralogist M. J. Anker (1772–1843).]

ankh /angk/ n. a symbol consisting of a cross with a loop for the top extension and a short crossbar, used in ancient Egypt to signify life [Late 19thC. From Egyptian, literally 'life'.]

ankle /ángk'l/ n. **1.** JOINT BETWEEN FOOT AND LEG the joint that connects the bones of the leg with the highest bone in the foot **2.** SLIM PART OF LEG ABOVE ANKLE the slender part of the leg immediately above the ankle [14thC. From assumed Old Norse ankula, which replaced Old English anclēow (both related to English anchor and angle).]

anklebone /ángk'l bōn/ n. = talus[2] n.

ankle boot n. a boot that extends up to the ankle but not much beyond

ankle sock n. a sock that extends up to the ankle but not much past it. US term **anklet** n. **2**

anklet /ángklət/ n. **1.** ANKLE BRACELET a piece of jewellery or some other ornament worn round the ankle **2.** US = ankle sock

ankylosaur /ángkələ sawr/ n. a plant-eating dinosaur with short legs, a heavy thick-set body, and bony dorsal plates. It lived during the Cretaceous period. [Late 20thC. From modern Latin Ankylosaurus, genus name, from Greek agkulōsis (see ANKYLOSIS) + sauros 'lizard'.]

ankylose /ángkilōz, -lōss/ (**-loses, -losing, -losed**) vti. to fuse together and become stiff, or cause bones to fuse together and a joint to become stiff as a result of injury or disease. This is sometimes done surgically to relieve pain and allow injuries to heal. [Late 18thC. Back-formation from ANKYLOSIS.]

ankylosing spondylitis /ángkilōssing-, -lōzing-/ n. a disease of the spine that causes the vertebrae to form a solid inflexible column

ankylosis /ángki lōssiss/ (plural **-loses** /-lō seez/) n. **1.** FUSION OF BONES the fusion of the bones of a joint, often in an abnormal position as a result of disease or injury, or intentionally through surgery **2.** STIFFNESS OF JOINT BONES stiffness or immobility in a joint caused by bones fusing together as a result of disease or injury or arising from surgery to join one bone or part to another [Early 18thC. Via modern Latin from Greek agkulōsis 'stiffening of the joints', from agkuloun 'to bend', from agkulos 'bent'.] —**ankylotic** /ángki lóttik/ adj.

ankylostomiasis n. = ancylostomiasis

anlage /án laagə/ (plural **-lagen** /-gən/ or **-lages**) n. **1.** EMBRYOL PART IN EMBRYONIC STAGE a part or organ in its earliest stage of development **2.** BASIS FOR STH sth, often a principle, on which sth else is based or founded (literary) [Late 19thC. From German, literally 'layout'.]

ann. abbr. **1.** annals **2.** annual **3.** annuity

anna /ánnə/ n. a copper coin formerly used in the Indian subcontinent, worth one-sixteenth of a rupee [Early 17thC. From Hindi ānā.]

Anna Ivanovna /ánnə i vaánəvnə/, **Empress of Russia** (1693–1740). She was niece of Peter I (Peter the Great). While she was empress (1730–40), her German advisors actually administered the country.

annal /ánn'l/ n. a single entry in a record of historical events, or a record of the events of a single year in history (dated) [Early 17thC. Back-formation from ANNALS.]

annalist /ánn'list/ n. sb who compiles annals

annals /ánn'lz/ npl. **1.** ANNUAL RECORDS a record of events arranged chronologically by year **2.** RECORDED HISTORY history in general, as it is recorded in books and other documents ○ Her achievements have secured her place in the annals of our nation. **3.** LEARNED JOURNAL a periodical that records events and reports in a specific field of research [Mid-16thC. Directly or via French from Latin annales, from annalis (see ANNUAL).]

Annan /a nán, ánnən/, **Kofi** (b. 1938) Ghanaian statesman. He was elected Secretary General of the United Nations in 1997.

Annapolis /ə náppəliss/ capital of Maryland, situated near Chesapeake Bay. The US Naval Academy is here. Population: 33,234 (1996).

Annapurna /ánnə púrnə/ mountain in the Himalayan range in north-central Nepal, one of the world's highest peaks. Height: 8,078 m/26,504 ft.

Ann Arbor /an áarbər/ city in southeastern Michigan, home to the main campus of the University of Michigan. Population: 108,758 (1996).

annatto /ə náttō/ (*plural* **-tos**) *n.* **1.** INDUST **DYE FROM SEED-CASE PULP** a yellowish-red dye made from the pulp enclosing the seeds of a small tropical tree, used to colour fabric and food products **2.** TREES **SMALL FLOWERING TREE** a small tropical American tree with pink or red flowers and seeds encased in a pulpy substance used to make annatto dye. Latin name: *Bixa orellana.* [Early 17thC. From Carib.]

Anne /an/, **Queen of Great Britain and Ireland** (1665–1714). The daughter of James II, she inherited the throne from William III. She ruled from 1702 to 1714, and provided for the Hanoverian succession after her death.

Anne, the Princess Royal (*b.* 1950). Daughter of Queen Elizabeth II, she is also President of the Save the Children Fund.

anneal /ə néel/ *v.* **1.** *vti.* METALL, CRAFT **MAKE STH STRONGER THROUGH HEATING** to subject an alloy, metal, or glass to a process of heating and slow cooling to make it tougher and less brittle **2.** *vti.* CELL BIOL **SEPARATE STRANDS OF NUCLEIC ACID** to subject nucleic acid to a process of heating and cooling in order to separate strands **3.** *vt.* **MAKE STH MORE RESOLUTE** to make sth, especially an opinion, a feeling, or an intention, stronger, firmer, or more resolute (*literary*) [Old English *onǣlan*, from *ǣlan* 'to burn'. Originally in the meaning 'to set on fire'.]

annelid /ánnəlid/ *n.* an invertebrate organism with a flat body that is divided into segments. Earthworms and leeches are annelids. Phylum: Anelida. [Mid-19thC. From modern Latin *Annelida*, phylum name, from French *annelés* 'ringed', from, ultimately, Latin *an(n)ulus* (see ANNULUS).]

Anne of Austria, Queen of France (1601–66). She was the wife of Louis XIII of France and became queen regent for her son Louis XIV in 1643.

Anne of Cleves /-kleevz/, **Queen of England and Ireland** (1515–57). She married Henry VIII for religious expediency (1540). He divorced her the same year.

Anne of Denmark, Queen of England, Scotland, and Ireland (1574–1619). She married James I in 1589 and was the mother of Prince Henry and Charles I.

annex /ə néks/ *vt.* (**-nexes, -nexing, -nexed**) **1. ADD STH TO STH** to attach sth subsidiary to a larger thing (*usually passive*) ○ *The new pool will be annexed to the gymnasium.* **2. TAKE OVER TERRITORY** to take over territory and incorporate it into another political entity, e.g. a country or state **3. ATTACH A QUALITY TO STH** to add sth as a consequence, quality, or condition (*usually passive*) ○ *Annexed to his feeling of guilt was a sense of having let everybody down.* **4. STEAL** to take sth without permission (*informal*) ○ *He returned to find that his assistant had annexed his chair.* ■ *n. US* = **annexe** [14thC. Via French *annexer* from Latin *annectere* 'to tie together', from *nectere* 'to tie' (source of English *connect* and *nexus*).]

annexation /ánnek sáysh'n/ *n.* **1. ADDITION OF STH** the addition of sth to a larger whole **2. TAKING POSSESSION OF TERRITORY** the incorporation of a territory into another country, state, or other political entity **3. STH ADDED** sth that has been added to a larger whole, especially a territory that has been incorporated into another country or state —**annexational** *adj.* —**annexationism** *n.* —**annexationist** *n.*

annexe /ánneks/ *n.* US term **annex 1. AUXILIARY BUILDING** a building added onto another building or serving as an auxiliary building to a larger one **2. ATTACHED DOCUMENT** an appendix, epilogue, or other additional material attached to a larger document

Annigoni /ánni gṓni/, **Pietro** (1910–88) Italian painter who used traditional oil techniques to paint portraits, including those of President Kennedy (1961) and Queen Elizabeth II (1955 and 1970).

annihilate /ə nī ə layt/ (**-lates, -lating, -lated**) *v.* **1.** *vt.* **DESTROY STH** to destroy sth completely, especially so that it ceases to exist **2.** *vt.* **DEFEAT SB** to defeat sb easily and convincingly (*informal*) **3.** *vt.* **MAKE STH INVALID** to declare sth to be void or ineffective (*archaic*) **4.** *vi.* NUCLEAR PHYS **BE DESTROYED IN PARTICLE COLLISION** to be mutually destroyed when a particle collides with a corresponding antiparticle [Early 16thC. From late Latin *annihilat-*, the past participle stem of *annihilare* 'to reduce to nothing', from Latin *nihil* 'nothing' (source of English *nil*).] —**annihilable** /ə nī ələ b'l/ *adj.* —**annihilator** *n.*

annihilation /ə nī ə láysh'n/ *n.* **1. DESTRUCTION** the complete destruction of sth **2. DEFEAT OF OPPONENT** the complete and convincing defeat of an opponent (*informal*) **3.** NUCLEAR PHYS **DESTRUCTIVE COLLISION OF PARTICLE AND ANTIPARTICLE** the process in which a particle combines with its antiparticle, destroying both and releasing their energy in the form of radiation or other particles ○ *annihilation radiation*

anniversary /ánni v/ (*plural* **-ries** /rssəri/) *n.* **1. ANNUAL OBSERVATION OF PAST EVENT** a date that is observed on an annual basis because it is the same date as a remarkable event in a past year **2. ANNUAL RITUAL** a celebration or other commemorative ritual marking the date of a noteworthy event, often a wedding [13thC. Directly or via French *anniversaire* from medieval Latin *anniversarium*, from Latin *anniversarius* 'returning yearly', from *annus* 'year' + *versus*, the past participle of *vertere* 'to turn'.]

anno Domini /ánnō dómminī/ *adv.* full form of **AD** [Mid-16thC. From Latin, literally 'in the year of the Lord'.]

anno Hegirae /ánnō hə jīri/ *adv.* full form of **AH** [Late 19thC. From Latin, literally 'in the year of the Hegira'.]

annona /ə nṓnə/ (*plural* **-nas** *or* **-na**) *n.* any one of several tropical American and African trees from which fruits such as the cherimoya, custard apple, soursop, and sugar apple are obtained. Genus: *Annona.* [Via modern Latin and American Spanish from Arawak]

annotate /ánnə tayt/ (**-tates, -tating, -tated**) *vt.* to add critical or explanatory notes to a text (*usually passive*) [Mid-18thC. Via Latin *annotat-*, the past participle stem of *annotare* 'to note down', from, ultimately, *nota* 'mark' (source of English *note*).] —**annotative** *adj.* —**annotator** *n.*

annotation /ánnə táysh'n/ *n.* **1. ADDITION OF NOTES** the adding of explanatory or critical notes to a text **2. EXPLANATORY NOTE** an explanatory or critical comment that has been added to a text

announce /ə nówns/ (**-nounces, -nouncing, -nounced**) *vt.* **1. TELL STH PUBLICLY** to declare or report sth publicly **2. SAY STH** to say sth in a formal, forceful, or aggressive way **3. DECLARE ARRIVAL OF SB OR STH** to tell others formally that sb or sth has arrived **4. SIGNIFY OR FORETELL STH** to be a sign that sth has arrived or is imminent **5.** *US* **SERVE AS PRESENTER OF STH** to act as a presenter of sth, e.g. a television or radio show [15thC. Via French *annoncer* and Latin *annuntiare* from, ultimately, *nuntius* 'messenger' (source of English *nuncio*, *pronounce*, and *renounce*).]

announcement /ə nównssmənt/ *n.* **1. PUBLIC DECLARATION** a public statement giving people information or news, or the making of the statement **2. WRITTEN NOTICE** a formal written notice, often a card or newspaper item, giving the news of a birth, wedding, or other event

announcer /ə nównssər/ *n.* **1. SB MAKING ANNOUNCEMENTS** sb who makes public announcements, e.g. on a public address system at an airport or railway station **2.** BROADCAST **TV OR RADIO COMMENTATOR** sb who provides informative comment on sth, usually a television or radio commentator who gives news bulletins or programme information

annoy /ə nóy/ (**-noys, -noying, -noyed**) *v.* **1.** *vt.* **IRRITATE SB** to make sb feel impatient or angry **2.** *vt.* **HARASS SB** to harass or bother sb repeatedly **3.** *vi.* **BE IRRITATING** to be a source of irritation ○ *Barking dogs are bound to annoy.* [13thC. Via Old French *anoier* from late Latin *inodiare* 'to make loathsome', from Latin *in odio* 'in hatred'.]

WORD KEY: SYNONYMS

annoy, irritate, exasperate, vex, irk

CORE MEANING: to cause a mild degree of anger in sb

annoy to cause anything from slight impatience to anger in sb; **irritate** to annoy sb repeatedly or continuously, often over a period of time; **exasperate** to arouse strong impatience in sb by seeming to disregard his or her wishes; **vex** a more dated term than *annoy* suggesting distinct confusion or even mild distress; **irk** a more formal term suggesting that the annoyance is tiresome.

annoyance /ə nóy ənss/ *n.* **1. FEELING OF IRRITATION** feelings of mild anger and impatience **2. NUISANCE** sth that causes sb to be mildly angry or impatient ○ *Living in this neighbourhood is not without its annoyances.*

WORD KEY: SYNONYMS

See Synonyms at ***anger***.

annoying /ə nóy ing/ *adj.* causing mild anger or impatience —**annoyingly** *adv.*

annual /ánnyoo əl/ *adj.* **1. ONCE A YEAR** happening once a year **2. FOR PERIOD OF ONE YEAR** based on or accumulating over one year **3.** BOT **DYING AFTER ONE SEASON** used to describe a plant that flowers, produces seed, and dies in one growing season ■ *n.* **1.** BOT **PLANT THAT DIES AFTER ONE SEASON** a plant that flowers, produces seed, and dies in one growing season **2.** PUBL **YEARLY BOOK OR MAGAZINE** a book or magazine published once a year, especially one for children [14thC. Directly or via French *annuel* from late Latin *annualis*, a blend of Latin *annuus* and *annalis* 'yearly', from *annus* 'year'.]

annual general meeting *n.* a yearly gathering of members of an organization, at which officers are elected and the year's activities, including financial dealings, are discussed

annualize /ánnyoo ə līz/ (**-izes, -izing, -ized**), **annualise** (**-alises, -alising, -alised**) *vt.* **1. MAKE FIGURES APPLY TO A YEAR** to calculate or adjust figures so that they reflect a period of a year **2. DO STH YEARLY** to put sth on, or change sth to, a once-a-year schedule ○ *Let's annualize the newsletter.*

annually /ánnyoo əli/ *adv.* every year or once a year

annual report *n.* a document that outlines and analyses the activities, especially the financial dealings, of a company or other organization over the past year

Annual ring: Cross-section through pine log

annual ring *n.* = **growth ring**

annuitant /ə nyóo itənt/ *n.* sb who is entitled to receive an annuity

annuity /ə nyóo əti/ (*plural* **-ties**) *n.* **1. MONEY PAID AT REGULAR INTERVALS** an amount of money paid to sb yearly or at some other regular interval **2. INVESTMENT PAYING ANNUAL SUM** a type of investment that earns the investor a fixed amount of money each year for a number of years, often the investor's lifetime **3. CONTRACT FOR ANNUAL PAYMENT** the right to receive or the obligation to pay an annuity [15thC. Via French *annuité* from medieval Latin *annuitas*, from Latin *annuus* (see ANNUAL).]

annul /ə núl/ (**-nuls, -nulling, -nulled**) *vt.* **1.** LAW **MAKE STH INVALID** to render a legal document or agreement invalid **2.** RELIG **DECLARE MARRIAGE INVALID** to declare that a marriage was never a proper marriage in the eyes of the church, e.g. because one of the parties was not completely committed to it **3. DESTROY STH** to wipe out or destroy the effect or existence of sth ○ *not able to annul my fears* [14thC. Via Old French *anuller* from late Latin *annullare* 'to make into nothing', from Latin *nullus* 'nothing' (source of English *null*).]

WORD KEY: SYNONYMS

See Synonyms at ***nullify***.

annular /ánnyŏŏlər/ *adj.* shaped like or forming a ring [Late 16thC. Directly or via French *annulaire* from Latin *an(n)ularis*, from *an(n)ulus* (see ANNULUS).]

annular eclipse *n.* a solar eclipse in which all but the outermost rim of the sun is blocked by the moon, leaving a ring of sunlight visible round the moon

annular ligament *n.* a ring-shaped ligament that surrounds an ankle joint or a wrist joint and holds other ligaments in place

annulate /ányŏŏ layt/, **annulated** /ányoolaytid/ *adj.* with ring-shaped parts, or consisting of rings [Early 19thC. From Latin *an(n)ulatus*, from *an(n)ulus* (see ANNULUS).]

annulation /ánnyŏŏ láysh'n/ *n.* **1.** FORMATION OF RINGS the formation of rings or ring-shaped parts **2.** RING-SHAPED PART any part that is shaped like a ring

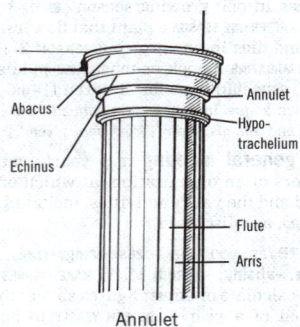

annulet /ánnyŏŏlət/ *n.* **1.** ARCHIT CIRCULAR MOULDING a ring-shaped moulding round a column **2.** HERALDRY CIRCULAR OBJECT ON SHIELD a ring-shaped object on a heraldic shield [Late 16thC. Formed from Latin *an(n)ulus* (see ANNULUS).]

annuli plural of **annulus**

annulment /ə núlmənt/ *n.* **1.** LAW VOIDING OF STH the process or result of making a legal document or agreement void or invalid **2.** RELIG RULING THAT MARRIAGE IS INVALID a ruling that a marriage was never a proper marriage in the eyes of the church

annulus /ánnyŏŏləss/ (*plural* -li /-lī/ *or* -luses) *n.* **1.** BIOL RING-SHAPED PART any ring-shaped part or arrangement of parts in a plant or animal, e.g. a growth ring on fish scales **2.** MATH AREA BETWEEN CONCENTRIC CIRCLES the area bounded by two concentric circles [Mid-16thC. From Latin *an(n)ulus*, literally 'a small ring', from *anus* 'ring'.]

annunciate /ə núnssi ayt/ (-ates, -ating, -ated) *vt.* to announce or proclaim sth (*archaic*) [14thC. From Latin *annuntiat-*, the past participle stem of *annuntiare* (see ANNOUNCE).]

annunciation /ə núnssi áysh'n/ *n.* the announcing of sth, or an announcement (*archaic*)

Annunciation (1513?) by Lucas Cranach the Elder

Annunciation *n.* **1.** GABRIEL'S VISIT TO MARY in the Bible, the archangel Gabriel's visit to the Virgin Mary to announce that she had been chosen to be the mother of Jesus Christ (Luke 1:26–38) **2.** CHRISTIAN FESTIVAL March 25, celebrated in the Christian calendar as the feast of the Annunciation

Annunciation Day *n.* = Lady Day

annunciator /ə núnssi aytər/ *n.* **1.** ANNOUNCER sb who makes announcements (*archaic*) **2.** ELEC ENG ELECTRONIC SIGNALLING DEVICE an electronic signalling device, e.g. a switchboard device that indicates the source of incoming telephone calls

annus horribilis /ánnəss hə ríbbiliss/ (*plural* anni horribiles /ánnī hə ríbbi layz/) *n.* a year of great unhappiness or misfortune (*formal*) [Late 20thC. From Latin, 'horrible year'.]

annus mirabilis /ánnəss mi ráabiliss/ (*plural* anni mirabiles /ánnī mi ráabi layz/) *n.* a year that is remarkable for its great events (*formal*) [Mid-17thC. From Latin, 'wonderful year'.]

anode /ánnŏd/ *n.* **1.** NEGATIVE TERMINAL the negative terminal of a battery **2.** POSITIVE ELECTRODE the positive electrode in an electrolytic cell [Mid-19thC. Formed from Greek *anodos*, literally 'way up', from *hodos* 'way'.]

anodize /ánnŏ dīz/ (-dizes, -dizing, -dized), **anodise** (-dises, -dising, -dised) *vt.* to coat a metal, e.g. aluminium, with a protective or decorative oxide by making the metal the anode of an electrolytic cell — **anodization** /ánnŏ dī záysh'n/ *n.*

anodontia /ánnə dónshə, -dónshi ə/ *n.* the abnormal absence of some or all teeth because the teeth have never developed [Late 19thC. Coined from AN- + -ODON-TIA.]

anodyne /ánnŏ dīn/ *adj.* **1.** PHARM PAINKILLING bringing relief from pain or discomfort **2.** SOOTHING serving to soothe, relax, or comfort (*literary*) ○ *the anodyne effects of a weekend in the mountains after a hard working week* **3.** BLAND harmless, inoffensive, or uncontroversial to the point of being dull (*literary*) ○ *a rather anodyne speech, given the nature of the crisis* ■ *n.* **1.** PHARM PAINKILLER a drug such as aspirin or codeine that relieves pain or distress **2.** COMFORTING THING sth that soothes, comforts, or relaxes (*literary*) [Mid-16thC. Via Latin from Greek *anodunos* 'without pain', from *odunē* 'pain'.]

anoestrous /an eestrəss/ *adj.* **1.** NOT ACTIVE SEXUALLY used to describe a female mammal that is inactive between breeding periods **2.** WITHOUT SEXUAL ACTIVITY used to describe the period of sexual inactivity between breeding periods in certain female mammals

anoestrus /an eestrəss/ *n.* the period of sexual inactivity between the breeding periods of certain female mammals

anoint /ə nóynt/ (anoints, anointing, anointed) *vt.* **1.** BLESS SB WITH OIL to rub oil or ointment on a part of sb's body, usually the head or feet, as part of a religious ceremony, e.g. in a Christian baptism **2.** ORDAIN SB to install sb officially or ceremonially in a position or office [14thC. Via Old French *enoint*, the past participle of *enoindre*, from Latin *inungere*, from *ungere* 'to smear' (source of English *ointment* and *unctuous*).] —**anointment** *n.*

anointing of the sick *n.* in the Roman Catholic Church, the sacrament of anointing people who are very ill, praying for their recovery, and offering confession and absolution of sins

anole /ə nő li/ *n.* any one of several tree-climbing, chiefly tropical lizards that can change colour. Genus: *Anolis*. [Early 18thC. Via modern Latin *Anolis*, genus name, from, ultimately, Carib *anoli*.]

anomalistic month /ə nómmə lístik-/ *n.* the average time taken by the Moon to orbit the Earth once, starting from the point in its orbit at which it is nearest the Earth, measured as 27.554 days

anomalistic year *n.* the time taken by the Earth to orbit the Sun once, starting from the point in its orbit at which the Earth is nearest the Sun, measured as 365.26 days

anomalous /ə nómmələss/ *adj.* **1.** ABNORMAL deviating from the norm or from what people expect ○ *We're getting anomalous readings on the heart monitor.* **2.** UNUSUAL strange and difficult to identify or classify ○ *'Individuals would occasionally give rise to new species having anomalous habits'.* (Charles Darwin, *On the Origin of Species*; 1859) [Mid-17thC. Formed from late Latin *anomalus*, from Greek *anōmalos* 'uneven', from *homalos* 'even'.]

anomaly /ə nómməli/ (*plural* -lies) *n.* **1.** IRREGULARITY sth that deviates from the norm or from expectations ○ *looking for anomalies in the patient's blood tests* **2.** PECULIARITY sth strange and difficult to identify or classify ○ *The space probe has encountered an anomaly.* **3.** ASTRON ANGLE IN PLANET'S ORBIT the angle between a planet's position, the Sun, and the point in the planet's orbit when it is closest to the Sun

anomic /ə nómmik/ *adj.* **1.** SOCIOL UNSTABLE BECAUSE OF MORAL BREAKDOWN unstable because moral and social codes have been eroded or abandoned ○ *an anomic society* **2.** PSYCHOL AFFECTED BY ALIENATION feeling alienated from society and disoriented by the perceived absence of a social or moral framework ■ *n.* PSYCHOL SB AFFECTED BY ALIENATION sb who feels a sense of alienation and disorientation as a result of the perceived absence of a social and moral framework

anomie /ánnŏmi/, **anomy** *n.* **1.** SOCIOL SOCIAL INSTABILITY instability in society caused by the erosion or abandonment of moral and social codes **2.** PSYCHOL SOCIAL ALIENATION a feeling of disorientation and alienation from society caused by the perceived absence of a supporting social or moral framework [Late 16thC. Via French from Greek *anomia* 'lawlessness', from *anomos* 'lawless', from *nomos* 'law'.]

anon /ə nón/ *adv.* (*archaic or literary*) **1.** ANOTHER TIME at an unspecified future time ○ *I'll see you anon.* **2.** SOON in a short while ○ *more of these grotesque escapades anon* [Old English *on ān*, literally 'in one']

anon. *abbr.* anonymous

anonym /ánnənim/ *n.* **1.** UNNAMED AUTHOR an author whose name is not known or not given **2.** PSEUDONYM a name used by sb to hide his or her identity **3.** PUBLICATION WITH UNNAMED AUTHOR a publication whose author is unnamed or unknown [Early 19thC. From French *anonyme* 'ANONYMOUS'.]

anonymity /ánnə nímməti/ (*plural* -ties) *n.* **1.** FREEDOM FROM IDENTIFICATION the state of not being known or identified by name, e.g. as the author or donor of sth **2.** LACK OF DISTINCTIVENESS a lack of distinctive features that makes things seem bland or interchangeable ○ *detested the anonymity of the city-centre hotels* **3.** UNNAMED PERSON sb who is unnamed or unacknowledged as the doer of sth **4.** STATE OF BEING UNNOTICED the state of blending into a crowd and going unnoticed ○ *I always preferred the anonymity of the big city.*

anonymous /ə nónniməss/ *adj.* **1.** UNNAMED whose name is not known or not given **2.** WITH NAME WITHHELD with the performer's, maker's, or creator's identity withheld **3.** INDISTINCTIVE lacking individuality or distinctiveness ○ *a quirkiness unsuited to an anonymous shopping mall* [Early 17thC. Formed from late Latin *anonymus*, from Greek *anōnumos* 'unnamed', from *onuma* 'name'.] —**anonymousness** *n.*

anonymous FTP *n.* a method of connecting to a computer on the Internet that allows files to be accessed and downloaded without needing a password

anonymously /ə nónniməssli/ *adv.* without being named or acknowledged

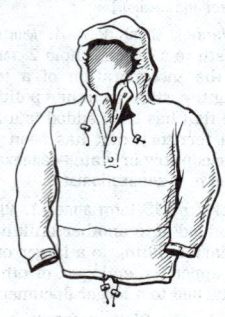

Anorak

anorak /ánnə rak/ *n.* **1.** HOODED WATERPROOF JACKET a warm thick waterproof hip-length jacket with a hood **2.** OBSESSIVE ENTHUSIAST a boring, unfashionable, or studious person, especially sb who is excessively devoted to a particular hobby or interest (*humorous*) ○ *You can be into something without becoming a* *total anorak about it.* [Early 20thC. From (Greenlandic) Inuit *annoraaq*.]

anorectic /ánnə réktik/ *adj.* **RELATING TO PATHOLOGICAL APPETITE LOSS** relating to, affected by, or causing pathological loss of appetite ■ *n.* **APPETITE-SUPPRESSING MEDICATION** a type of medication that suppresses the appetite, used in treating any disorder marked by overeating [Late 19thC. Formed from Greek *anorektos* 'without appetite', from *orexein* 'to desire'.]

anorexia /ánnə réksi ə/ *n.* **1.** = **anorexia nervosa** **2. CONTINUAL APPETITE LOSS** persistent loss of appetite [Late 16thC. Via modern Latin from Greek, 'lack of appetite', from *orexis* 'appetite', from *orexein* (see ANORECTIC).]

anorexia nervosa /-nur võssə/ *n.* an eating disorder, marked by an extreme fear of becoming overweight and leading to excessive dieting to the point of serious ill-health and sometimes death [From modern Latin, literally 'nervous anorexia']

anorexic /ánnə réksik/ *adj.* **1. OF ANOREXIA NERVOSA** relating to or affected by anorexia nervosa **2. VERY THIN** extremely thin, especially unhealthily or unattractively so (*informal*) ■ *n.* **SB WITH ANOREXIA** sb who is affected by loss of appetite or by anorexia nervosa

anorthite /ə náwr thīt/ *n.* a rare white, grey, or reddish-grey variety of the mineral feldspar, occurring mainly in igneous rocks and used in making glass and in ceramics. Formula: $CaAl_2Si_2O_8$. [Mid-19thC. Coined from AN- + ORTH- + -ITE. From its oblique crystals.] —**anorthitic** /ánnawr thíttik/ *adj.*

anorthosite /a náwrthə sīt/ *n.* a coarse-grained igneous rock comprising at least 90% feldspar [Mid-19thC. Formed from French *anorthose* 'type of feldspar', from Greek *anorthos*, literally 'not straight'. From its oblique crystals.] —**anorthositic** /a náwrthə síttik/ *adj.*

anosmia /a nózmi ə/ *n.* absence or loss of the sense of smell [Early 19thC. Coined from AN- + Greek *osmē* 'smell' + -IA.] —**anosmic** *adj.*

another /ə núthər/ *det.*, *pron.* **1. ONE MORE** an additional ○ *need another person to help* ○ *May I have another?* **1. ONE THAT IS DIFFERENT** sb who or sth that is completely separate or different from the one mentioned ○ *We need another accountant because ours is moving.* ○ *This one is too dark; I would prefer another.* **SOME OTHER** some other one, or any other one ◇ **another place** used by the House of Lords to refer to the House of Commons, and vice versa

A N Other /áy en/ *n.* an as-yet-unnamed person, e.g. in an incomplete list of participants or contributors

Anouilh /ánnoo ee/, **Jean** (1910–87) French dramatist. His plays include *Antigone* (1942), *Ring Round the Moon* (1947), and *Becket* (1959).

anovulant /a nóvvyoõlənt/ *n.* **DRUG PREVENTING OVULATION** a drug that prevents a woman from ovulating, e.g. a birth-control pill ■ *adj.* **PREVENTING OVULATION** used to describe a drug that prevents ovulation [Mid-20thC. Coined from AN- + OVULATE + -ANT.] —**anovulatory** /án ovvyoõ láytəri/ *adj.*, *n.*

anovulation /án ovvyoõ láysh'n/ *n.* the state of not ovulating because of a medical condition, suppression by drugs, or menopause

anoxaemia /ánnok seémi ə/ *n.* a deficiency of oxygen in the blood flowing through the arteries [Late 19thC. Coined from AN- + OX- + -AEMIA.] —**anoxaemic** *adj.*

anoxemia *n.* US = **anoxaemia**

anoxia /a nóksi ə/ *n.* = **hypoxia** [Mid-20thC. Coined from AN- + OX- + -IA.] —**anoxic** *adj.*

ans. *abbr.* answer

ansate /án sayt/ *adj.* with a handle or a part shaped like a handle [Late 19thC. From Latin *ansatus*, from *ansa* 'handle'.]

ansate cross *n.* = **ankh**

Ansermet /aáNsər may/, **Ernest** (1883–1969) Swiss conductor. He conducted Sergei Diaghilev's *Ballets Russes* (1918), and interpreted Igor Stravinsky and other 20th-century composers.

Ansett /ánssət/, **Sir Reginald Myles** (1909–81) Australian aviator and businessman. He was founder (1936) of Ansett Airways Ltd, now Ansett Airlines.

ANSI /ánssi/ *abbr.* American National Standards Institute

---

answer /aánssər/ *n.* **1. RESPONSE TO QUESTION** the information requested by a question **2. WAY OF SOLVING STH** the solution to a problem ○ *trying to find an answer to our ecological problems* **3. RESPONSE TO ACTION** a response to sth that sb says or does ○ *She had no answer to her opponent's lethal backhand.* **4. CORRESPONDING THING** sth designed to match or correspond to sth else **5. LAW PLEA IN COURT** a defendant's plea in response to a charge, lawsuit, or summons ■ *v.* (-swers, -swering, -swered) **1.** *vti.* **REPLY TO STH** to reply to sth written or spoken **2.** *vti.* **RESPOND TO CALL** to respond to a summons, e.g. a ringing telephone, a doorbell, or sb calling your name **3.** *vti.* **CORRESPOND TO STH** to match sth or correspond to it ○ *We haven't found anyone who answers to that description.* **4.** *vt.* **MEET A NEED** to fulfil a need or wish **5.** *vi.* **SERVE A PURPOSE** to be adequate in meeting a requirement or serving a purpose (*formal*) ○ *an upturned box that answers for a seat* **6.** *vt.* **LAW RESPOND TO CHARGE IN COURT** to offer a plea in response to a charge, lawsuit, or summons ○ *The defendant will now answer the charges.* [Old English *andswaru*. Ultimately from a prehistoric Germanic word meaning 'to swear against'. The underlying idea is of making a sworn statement rebutting a charge.] ◇ **be the answer to a maiden's prayer** to be exactly what is desired or sought after ◇ **know** *or* **have all the answers** to be admirably knowledgeable about a subject, or be irritatingly eager to demonstrate or claim superior knowledge

— **WORD KEY: SYNONYMS** —
answer, reply, response, rejoinder, retort, riposte
CORE MEANING: sth said, written, or done in acknowledgment of a question, remark, or other stimulus **answer** the most general term, used as an acknowledgment of, or reaction to, questions, letters, actions, and situations; **reply** a more restricted term than *answer*, used especially with reported speech; **rejoinder** a slightly more formal term than *reply*, used to indicate a considered reaction to a proposal, or a criticism or challenge a reply to a reply; **retort** a sharp reply, often to some form of criticism or accusation; **riposte** the most formal or literary term, used to indicate a quick or witty answer.

answer back *vti.* to reply to sb boldly or with impudence when silence is expected

answer for *vt.* **1. EXPLAIN MISTAKE OR FAULT** to give an excuse or explanation for a wrong that has been committed ○ *You'll have to answer for this broken window.* **2. GUARANTEE SB'S RELIABILITY** to give an assurance about sb's good character ○ *She can be trusted, but I can't answer for the rest of the team.*

answer to *vt.* to be obliged to give sb reasons for your behaviour, or be obliged to accept criticism or punishment from sb

answerable /aánssərəb'l/ *adj.* **1. ACCOUNTABLE** responsible for sth, or obliged to explain your actions to sb ○ *You're answerable to your boss for any losses you incur.* **2. SOLVABLE** having a possible solution or a correct response —**answerability** /aánssərə bílləti/ *n.* —**answerably** /aánssərəbli/ *adv.*

answerback /aánssər bak/ *n.* a response in a two-way radio transmission

answering machine *n.* a recording device that is connected to a telephone and can be activated to play a message to callers and record messages from them

answering service *n.* a business that receives telephone calls on behalf of other individuals and organizations and takes messages for them

ant /ant/ *n.* an insect that lives in complex well-organized colonies and is noted for its ability to carry objects heavier than itself. Male ants have wings, as do fertile females (**queens**) after mating. Family: Formicidae. [Old English *æmette*. Ultimately from a prehistoric Germanic word meaning 'to cut off', which also produced German *Ameise* 'ant'.] ◇ **have ants in your pants** to be excited or impatient about sth (*informal*)

— **WORD KEY: REGIONAL NOTE** —
British dialects abound in words for ants, suggesting perhaps that they once played a bigger role in people's lives, and in those of country people in particular. Among the best-known synonyms are *emmets, muryans, nants, pismires, piss-annats,* and *pissy-beds,* a name they share with dandelions.

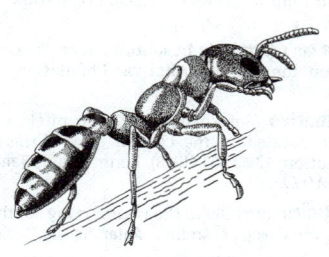

Ant (life size ×50)

ant. *abbr.* **1.** antiquarian **2.** antiquity **3.** antonym

Ant. *abbr.* Antarctica

ant- *prefix.* = **anti-** (*used before vowels*)

-ant *suffix.* **1.** performing a particular action ○ *desiccant* **2.** being in a particular state ○ *hesitant* [From Latin *-ant-*, the stem of *-ans*, a present participle ending] —**-ance** *suffix.* —**-ancy** *suffix.*

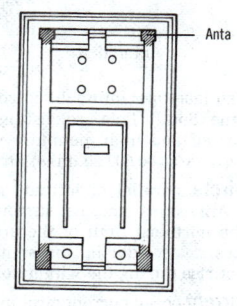

Anta

Anta

anta /ántə/ (*plural* **-tae** /ántī/) *n.* a thicker end of the side wall of a Greek temple that forms one side of a porch [Mid-18thC. Back-formation from Latin *antae* 'square pilasters'.]

antacid /an tássid/ *adj.* **NEUTRALIZING ACIDITY** preventing, counteracting, or neutralizing acidity, especially in the stomach ■ *n.* **ANTI-ACIDITY DRUG** a drug that reduces or neutralizes stomach acid

antae plural of **anta**

antagonise *vt.* = **antagonize**

antagonism /an tággənizzəm/ *n.* **1. HOSTILITY** hostility or hatred causing opposition and ill will **2. OPPOSITION** opposition between forces or principles ○ *the antagonism between good and evil* **3. PHYSIOL NEUTRALIZING INTERACTION** the interaction between two or more chemical substances in the body that diminishes the effect each of them has individually **4. PHYSIOL MUSCLE OPPOSITION** the opposing force that usually exists between pairs of muscles

antagonist /an tággənist/ *n.* **1. OPPONENT** sb or sth opposing or in conflict with another ○ *several antagonists locked in a power struggle* **2. ARTS CHARACTER IN CONFLICT WITH HERO** a major character in a book, play, or film whose values or behaviour are in conflict with those of the protagonist or hero **3. PHARM NEUTRALIZING AGENT** a substance, often a drug, that nullifies the effect another substance has on the body **4. PHYSIOL OPPOSING MUSCLE** a muscle that acts with and limits the action of another muscle

— **WORD KEY: SYNONYMS** —
See Synonyms at *opponent*.

antagonistic /an tággə nístik/ *adj.* showing or expressing hostility —**antagonistically** *adv.*

antagonize /an tággənīz/ (-nizes, -nizing, -nized), **antagonise** (-nises, -nising, -nised) *vt.* to cause a person or animal to be hostile [Mid-17thC. From Greek *antagōnizesthai*, literally 'to struggle against', from *agōnizesthai* 'to struggle', from *agōn* 'contest' (source of English *agony*).]

Antakya /an taákyə/ *city* in southern Turkey on the River Orontes. Founded in 301 BC, it was formerly known as Antioch and was the capital of the eastern

---

Roman Empire (64 BC – AD 260). Population: 124,443 (1990).

Antalya /an taályə/ city in southwestern Turkey, situated on the Gulf of Antalya. Population: 378,208 (1990).

Antananarivo /ántə nánnə reé vō/ capital of Madagascar, located in the central part of the island. Population: 1,052,835 (1993). Former name **Tananarive** (until 1977)

Antarctic /an taárktik/ n. the region lying south of the Antarctic Circle. ◊ **Arctic** —**Antarctic** adj.

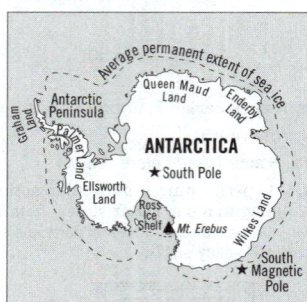

Antarctica

Antarctica /an taárktikə/ uninhabited continent surrounding the South Pole, consisting of an ice-covered plateau and high mountain peaks. Area: 14,245,000 sq. km/5,500,000 sq. mi. ◊ **Arctic**

Antarctic Circle parallel of latitude at 66° 30' S, encircling Antarctica and its surrounding seas, marking the northern limit of the area in which the sun does not set during the summer solstice and does not rise during the winter solstice

Antarctic Current ocean current circling Antarctica. Moving eastwards, it circulates water from one ocean to another.

Antarctic Ocean the waters that surround the South Pole and Antarctica, consisting of the waters of the southern Atlantic, Indian, and Pacific oceans. Depths exceed 6,000 m/20,000 ft.

ant bear n. = aardvark

ant cow n. an aphid that excretes a substance similar to honey (**honeydew**) that is eaten by certain ants

ante /ánti/ n. STAKE an amount a card player puts into the gambling pot before cards are dealt ■ vti. (**-tes, -teing, -ted** or **-teed, -ted** or **-teed**) CONTRIBUTE TO GAMBLING POT to place betting stakes before cards are dealt [Early 19thC. From Latin, literally 'before'.] ◊ **up the ante 1.** to increase the amount of money required to do or get sth (informal) **2.** to demand more, or try to get more from a situation (informal)
ante up vti. US to pay money that is due to be paid (informal) ○ We know you've got the cash, so ante up now!

ante- prefix. before, in front ○ antechamber [From Latin ante (source also of English ancient). Ultimately from an Indo-European base meaning 'front', which is also the ancestor of end, until, and anti-.]

Anteater

anteater /ánt eetər/ n. **1.** TROPICAL MAMMAL THAT FEEDS ON ANTS a long-snouted mammal of Central and South America that has no teeth but has long claws and a sticky tongue for catching prey, usually ants and

termites. Family: Myrmecophagidae. **2.** = **pangolin 3.** = **aardvark**

antebellum /ánti bélləm/ adj. preceding a war, or characteristic of the time preceding a war [Mid-19thC. From Latin ante bellum 'before the war'.]

antecede /ánti seéd/ (**-cedes, -ceding, -ceded**) vt. to precede sth in time or order ○ Economic depressions often antecede wars. [Early 17thC. From Latin antecedere, literally 'to go before', from cedere (see CEDE).]

antecedence /ánti seéd'nss/ n. an earlier position in time, order, or importance

antecedent /ánti seéd'nt/ n. **1.** THING COMING BEFORE sth that happened or existed before sth else ○ The book deals with the historical antecedents of the revolution. **2.** GRAM WORD THAT SUBSEQUENT WORD REFERS TO a word or phrase that a subsequent word refers back to. 'Mary' is the antecedent of 'her' in the sentence 'I'll give this to Mary if I see her'. **3.** LOGIC CLAUSE EXPRESSING CONDITION the first part of a conditional proposition, which states the condition and is the p component in a proposition phrased 'if p then q' ■ **antecedents** npl. **1.** ANCESTORS sb's ancestors **2.** SB'S HISTORY the events or circumstances in sb's past ○ He's done pretty well for himself, considering what we know of his antecedents. ■ adj. OCCURRING EARLIER IN TIME happening or existing before sth else (formal) ○ A high fever is usually an antecedent condition to other effects of the disease. [14thC. Directly or via French from Latin antecedent-, the present participle stem of antecedere (see ANTECEDE).] —**antecedently** adv.

antechamber /ánti chaymbər/ n. a small room leading into a larger main room and often used as a waiting area [Mid-17thC. From French antichambre, a translation of Italian anticamera, literally 'room in front'.]

antechoir /ánti kwīr/ n. an area at the entrance to the choir in a church, reserved for clergy and choir members

antedate /ánti dáyt/ vt. (**-dates, -dating, -dated**) **1.** OCCUR EARLIER THAN STH to exist or happen at an earlier date than sth else ○ These tapestries antedate the development of synthetic dyes. **2.** PUT EARLIER DATE ON STH to assign sth a date that is earlier than its true or original date ○ This vase was mistakenly antedated to the Ming dynasty. ■ n. EARLIER DATE a date assigned to sth that is earlier than its true or original date

antediluvian /ánti di loóvi ən/ adj. **1.** FROM TIME BEFORE FLOOD in or from the time before the biblical Flood **2.** OUTDATED extremely old-fashioned or out-of-date (informal) ○ a rather antediluvian notion of women's rights [Mid-17thC. Formed from Latin diluvium 'flood' (source of English deluge).]

—————— **WORD KEY: SYNONYMS** ——————
See Synonyms at **old-fashioned**.

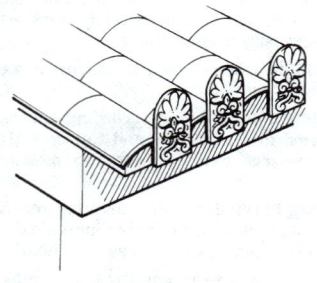

Antefix

antefix /ánti fiks/ (plural **-fixes** or **-fixa** /-fiksə/) n. an ornamental edging on the eaves of ancient buildings with tiled roofs that hides the joints of the roof tiles [Mid-19thC. From Latin antefixum, from antefigere 'to fasten before', from figere 'to fasten'.] —**antefixal** /ánti fíks'l/ adj.

antelope /ántəlōp/ (plural **-lopes** or **-lope**) n. a ruminant mammal with smooth brown or grey hair, two-toed hooves, and unbranched horns, native to Africa and southwestern Asia. Antelopes include the impala, springbok, and gazelles. Family: Bovidae. [15thC. Via Old French antelop 'mythical creature with sawlike horns

Antelope

said to live on the banks of the Euphrates' from, ultimately, medieval Greek antholops.]

antemeridian /ánti mə ríddi ən/ adj. relating to or taking place in the morning

ante meridiem /-mə ríddi əm/ adj., adv. full form of **a.m.** [Mid-16thC. From Latin, 'before noon'.]

antemortem /ánti máwrtəm/ adj. existing or happening before death (formal) [Late 19thC. From Latin ante mortem 'before death'.] —**ante mortem** adv.

antenatal /ánti náyt'l/ adj. existing or happening during pregnancy but before childbirth. US term **prenatal** —**antenatally** adv.

antenna /an ténnə/ (plural **-nae** /-nee/ or **-nas**) n. **1.** ZOOL THIN SENSOR ON ORGANISM'S HEAD a thin movable sensory organ found in pairs on the heads of some organisms, including insects and crustaceans **2.** INQUIRING SENSE sb's inquisitive or inquiring sense (informal; often used in the plural) **3.** US BROADCAST = aerial [Mid-17thC. From Latin, literally 'pole supporting a sail'.] —**antennal** adj.

antenuptial contract /ánti núpsh'l-/ n. S Africa = **prenuptial agreement**

antependium /ánti péndi əm/ (plural **-a** /-di ə/) n. a decorative cloth that hangs on the front of an altar or lectern [Late 16thC. From medieval Latin, from Latin pendere 'to hang'.]

antepenult /ánti pi núlt/ n. the third from last syllable in a word ○ The antepenult is stressed in the word 'superfluous'.

antepenultimate /ánti pi núltimət/ adj. THIRD FROM LAST third from last in a series ○ the antepenultimate word in the paragraph ■ n. = **antepenult**

ante-post adj. used to describe odds offered, or betting placed, before the starting places of the competitors are known, especially in horse racing

anterior /an teéri ər/ adj. **1.** IN FRONT at or near the front of sth (formal) ○ an anterior view of the building **2.** EARLIER existing or happening before sth else (formal) **3.** ANAT NEAR FRONT OF BODY situated at or near the front of the body or of a body part **4.** BOT AWAY FROM STEM used to describe a leaf or flower part that is situated furthest away or facing away from the stem of a plant [Mid-16thC. Directly or via French from Latin, 'earlier', from ante 'before'.] —**anteriority** /an teéri órrəti/ n.

anteroom /ánti room, -room/ n. a subsidiary room that opens into a larger main room, often used as a waiting area

antetype /ánti tīp/ n. an earlier form of sth ○ 'Antiochus Ephiphanes, the biblical antetype of the Antichrist' (Rollan McCleary, The Dead Sea Scrolls in Astrology; 1997)

anteversion /ánti vúrsh'n/ n. the abnormal tilting forward of an organ, especially the uterus, without bending

anthelion /an theélian/ (plural **-a** /-ia/) n. a luminous spot appearing occasionally in the sky opposite the Sun [Late 17thC. From Greek, literally 'opposite the sun', from hēlios 'sun'.]

anthelix /ant heéliks, an theé-/ (plural **-lixes** /-heéliksiz/ or **-lices** /-li seez/), **antihelix** /ánti heéliks/ (plural **-lixes** or **-lices** /-li seez/) n. a ridge of cartilage located behind the folded edge (**helix**) of the outer ear and running more or less parallel to it

anthelminthic /ánt hel mínthik/ adj. CONTROLLING PARASITIC WORMS able to reduce or eliminate parasitic worm populations ■ *n.* **SUBSTANCE FOR CONTROLLING PARASITIC WORMS** a natural or pharmaceutical substance that reduces or eliminates parasitic worm populations

anthelmintic /ánthəl mínthik, ánthəl-/, **anthelminthic** /ant hel mínthik/ *adj.* **DESTRUCTIVE TO PARASITIC WORMS** used to describe a drug that destroys parasitic worms or flushes out intestinal parasitic worms ■ *n.* **SUBSTANCE KILLING PARASITIC WORMS** a substance that kills parasitic worms or allows the natural discharge of intestinal parasitic worms [Late 17thC. Formed from the Greek stem *helmint-* 'worm'.]

anthem /ánthəm/ *n.* **1. SONG OF ALLEGIANCE** a song praising and declaring loyalty to sth, e.g. country, cause or organization ○ *a rock anthem* **2. CHR SHORT HYMN FOR CHOIR** a short hymn with words from the Bible, sung by a choir as part of a church service **3. CHR RELIGIOUS SONG WITH PARTS** a religious song with parts for different singers or groups, especially a church hymn with parts sung by different members of the congregation, e.g. a responsal psalm [Pre-12thC. Via late Latin *antiphona* 'antiphon' from Greek *antiphōnos* 'responsive', from *phonē* 'sound' (source of English *phonetic* and *telephone*).]

Anthemion

anthemion /an theémi ən/ (*plural* **-a** /-ə/) *n.* a motif of radiating leaves resembling those of the honeysuckle or palm, found in classical Greek art and design [Mid-19thC. Via Greek, literally 'a small flower', from, ultimately, *anthos* 'flower'.]

anther /ánthər/ *n.* a male flower part, the top part of a stamen, that bears the pollen in pollen sacs. ◊ **filament** [Early 18thC. Via Latin, literally 'medicine made from (the pollen-bearing part of) flowers', from Greek *anthēra* 'flowery', from *anthos* 'flower'.]

antheridium /ánthə ríddi əm/ (*plural* **-a** /-di ə/) *n.* the male reproductive organ in algae, ferns, fungi, and mosses

anthesis /an theéssiss/ *n.* **1. BLOOMING OF FLOWER** the opening of a flower bud **2. FLOWERING PERIOD** the period of time between the opening of a flower and the formation of the fruit [Mid-19thC. Via modern Latin from Greek *anthēsis* 'bloom', from *anthein* 'to flower', from *anthos* 'flower'.]

anthill /ánt hil/ *n.* a mound of earth formed by ants during the construction of their nest

antho- *prefix.* flower ○ *anthozoan* [From Greek *anthos*]

anthocyanin /ánthō sí ənin/ *n.* a water-soluble pigment that produces blue, violet, and red colours in flowers, fruits, leaves, and other plant parts [Mid-19thC. Coined from ANTHO- + CYANINE.]

anthodium /an thódi əm/ (*plural* **-a** /-di ə/) *n.* BOT = **capitulum** [Mid-19thC. From modern Latin, from Greek *anthōdēs* 'flowerlike', from *anthos* 'flower'.]

anthologize /an thóllə jīz/ (**-gizes, -gizing, -gized**), **anthologise** (**-gises, -gising, -gised**) *v.* **1. vt. PUT WRITINGS INTO COLLECTION** to gather works from different writers or other artists, e.g. songwriters or painters, into a collection, or include sb's work in a collection **2. vi. COMPILE ANTHOLOGY** to compile or publish an anthology

anthology /an thóllə ji/ (*plural* **-gies**) *n.* **1. COLLECTION OF DIFFERENT WRITERS' WORKS** a book that consists of essays, stories, or poems by different writers **2. ANY COLLECTION** anything that brings together various things or ideas ○ *The quilt is an anthology of tributes to those who have died of Aids.* [Mid-17thC. Via medieval Latin from medieval Greek *anthologiā*, literally 'collection of flowers', from *anthos* 'flower'.] **—anthologist** *n.*

Susan B. Anthony

Anthony /ántəni/, **Susan B.** (1820–1906) US social reformer. She helped to found the National American Woman Suffrage Association (1869). Full name **Susan Brownell Anthony**

Anthony of Padua, St (1195–1231) Italian friar who joined the Franciscan order in 1227. A renowned preacher, he taught theology in Italy and France. Born **Fernando**

anthophilous /an thóffiləss/ *adj.* used to describe an insect that feeds on or lives among flowers

anthozoan /ánthə zṓ ən/ *n.* a marine invertebrate animal with a roundish hollow body. Corals and sea anemones are anthozoans. Class: Anthozoa. [Late 19thC. Formed from modern Latin *Anthozoa*, class name, from ANTHO- + Greek *zōia* 'animals'.] **—anthozoic** *adj.*

anthracene /ánthrə seen/ *n.* an aromatic crystalline solid with a faint blue glow, obtained by distilling coal tar and used to make dyes and chemicals, e.g. alizarin. Formula: $C_{14}H_{10}$. [Mid-19thC. Formed from Greek *anthrax* 'coal'.]

anthraces plural of **anthrax**

anthracite /ánthrə sīt/ *n.* a hard shiny black type of coal that is clean-burning, high in carbon content, and low in volatile matter [Early 19thC. Via Latin from Greek *anthrakitēs*, from *anthrax* 'coal'.] **—anthracitic** /ánthrə síttik/ *adj.*

anthracnose /an thráknōss/ *n.* a fungal disease of beans and vines that produces dark sunken spots on fruit, stems, and leaves [Late 19thC. From French, from Greek *anthrax* 'coal' + *nosos* 'disease'.]

anthracosis /ánthrə kṓssiss/ *n.* MED pneumoconiosis caused by long-term inhalation of coal dust [Mid-19thC. Formed from Greek *anthrax* 'coal'.]

anthraquinone /ánthrə kwínnōn/ *n.* a yellow crystalline chemical that is used in the manufacture of dyes. Formula: $C_{14}H_8O_2$. [Late 19thC. A blend of ANTHRACENE and QUINONE.]

anthrax /ánthraks/ (*plural* **-thraces** /-thrə seez/) *n.* **1. FATAL DISEASE** a highly infectious fatal bacterial disease of mammals, especially cattle and sheep, that causes skin ulcers and is transmittable to humans by inhalation and through faeces and infected meat **2. SKIN SORE CAUSED BY ANTHRAX** an open sore on the skin that results from infection with anthrax [14thC. From Greek, 'coal'. Originally in the meaning 'carbuncle' (from its resemblance to a burning coal).]

anthrop. *abbr.* **1.** anthropology **2.** anthropological

anthropo- *prefix.* human being ○ *anthropocentric* [From Greek *anthrōpos* (source of English *misanthrope* and *philanthropy*)]

anthropocentric /ánthrəpō séntrik/ *adj.* **1. TREATING HUMANS AS PREEMINENT** regarding humans as the universe's most important entity **2. FROM POINT OF VIEW OF HUMANKIND** seeing things in human terms, especially judging things according to human perceptions, values, and experiences ○ *anthropocentric responses to the condition of animals* **—anthropocentrically** *adv.* **—anthropocentrism** *n.*

anthropogenesis /ánthrəpō jénnəssiss/, **anthropogeny** /ánthrō pójjəni/ *n.* the scientific study of the origin of humankind and how it has developed

anthropogenic /ánthrəpō jénnik/, **anthropogenetic** /ánthrəpōjə néttik/ *adj.* **1. CAUSED BY HUMANS** relating to or resulting from the influence humans have on the natural world **2. RELATING TO ORIGIN OF HUMANKIND** relating to the origin and development of human beings

anthropogeny *n.* = **anthropogenesis**

anthropoid /ánthrə poyd/ *adj.* **1. ZOOL RELATING TO APES** used to describe monkeys and apes **2. LIKE HUMANS** physically resembling human beings or human parts **3. RESEMBLING AN APE** rough-mannered, clumsy, ugly, or unintelligent, as apes are sometimes characterized (*informal*) ■ *n.* **1. PRIMATE** an animal belonging to the group that includes monkeys, gibbons, great apes, and humans. Suborder: Anthropoidea. **2.** = **anthropoid ape**

anthropoidal /ánthrə póyd'l/ *adj.* = **anthropoid** *adj.* 1

anthropoid ape *n.* a tailless animal with long arms and a highly developed brain that belongs to the family that includes the gorillas, chimpanzees, orangutans, and gibbons

anthropological /ánthrəpə lójjik'l/ *adj.* relating to the study of humankind, especially the study of cultures **—anthropologically** *adv.*

anthropological linguistics *n.* a branch of linguistic research that investigates the relationship between language and culture (*takes a singular verb*)

anthropology /ánthrə póllaji/ *n.* **1. ANTHROP STUDY OF HUMANKIND** the study of humankind in all its aspects, especially human culture or human development. It differs from sociology in taking a more historical and comparative approach. **2. CHR CHRISTIAN DOCTRINE CONCERNED WITH HUMANKIND** the parts of Christian doctrine that are concerned with the nature, origin, and destiny of humankind **—anthropologist** *n.*

anthropometry /ánthrə pómmətri/ *n.* the study of human body measurements. The uses of anthropometry include the creation of ergonomic furniture designs and the examination and comparison of populations. **—anthropometric** /ánthrəpə méttrik/ *adj.* **—anthropometrically** *adv.* **—anthropometrist** /ánthrə pómmətrist/ *n.*

anthropomorphise *vt.* = **anthropomorphize**

anthropomorphism /ánthrōpō máwrfizəm/ *n.* the attribution of a human form, human characteristics, or human behaviour to nonhuman things such as gods in mythology and animals in children's stories **—anthropomorphic** *adj.* **—anthropomorphically** *adv.*

anthropomorphize /ánthrəpə máwr fīz/ (**-phizes, -phizing, -phized**), **anthropomorphise** (**-phises, -phising, -phised**) *vt.* to give a nonhuman thing a human form or human characteristics ○ *Mythology and children's stories anthropomorphize animals and inanimate objects.* **—anthropomorphization** /ánthrəpə máwr fī záysh'n/ *n.*

anthropomorphous /ánthrəpə máwrfəss/ *adj.* with the shape of the human body or a human body part

anthropopathism /ánthrə póppəthizzəm/, **anthropopathy** /ánthrə póppəthi/ *n.* the attribution of human emotions to a nonhuman thing, e.g. a god or an object of worship [Mid-19thC. Coined from ANTHROPO- + -PATHY + -ISM.]

anthropophagus /ánthrə póffəgəss/ (*plural* **-gi** /-póffəjī/) *n.* sb who eats the flesh of other human beings (*technical*) [Mid-16thC. Via Latin from Greek *anthrōpophagos*, literally 'man-eating', from *anthrōpos* (see ANTHROPO-).] **—anthropophagic** /ánthrəpə fájjik/ *adj.* **—anthropophagous** /ánthrə póffəgəss/ *adj.* **—anthropophagy** /-póffəji/ *n.*

anthroposophy /ánthrə póssəfi/ *n.* a religious philosophy developed by Rudolf Steiner from theosophy, holding that spiritual development should be humanity's foremost concern **—anthroposophical** /ánthrəpə sóffik'l/ *adj.* **—anthroposophist** /ánthrə póssəfist/ *n.*

anthurium /an thyoóri əm/ *n.* a tropical evergreen American plant cultivated for its glossy heart-shaped red or white flowers enclosing a spike of yellow florets. Genus: *Anthurium*. [Mid-19thC. From modern Latin, genus name, from Greek *anthos* 'flower' (see ANTHO-) + *oura* 'tail'.]

anti /ánti/ *adj.* **OPPOSED TO STH** expressing or holding an opposing view, particularly regarding a political issue or moral principle (*informal*) ○ *She's very anti smoking.* ■ *n.* (*plural* **-tis**) **SB WHO DISAGREES** sb who holds or expresses an opposing view, particularly regarding a political issue or principle (*informal*) ○ *Are you a pro or an anti?* [Late 18thC. From ANTI-.]

anti-, **ant-** *prefix.* against, opposite ○ *anticonvulsive* [Via Latin from, ultimately, Greek *anti* 'opposite, against']

antiabortion /ánti ə báwrsh'n/ *adj.* opposed to the practice of abortion —**antiabortionist** *n.*

antiadrenergic /ánti áddrə núrjik/ *adj.* COUNTERACTING ADRENALINE blocking or counteracting the physiological effects of adrenaline ■ *n.* ANTIADRENERGIC DRUG a drug that counteracts the effects of adrenaline

antiaircraft /ánti áir kraaft/ *adj.* designed and used to destroy enemy aircraft

antialiasing /ánti áyli əssing/ *n.* smoothing the jagged edges of diagonal lines in computer-generated images by varying the colour or shades of grey at the edges

antiapartheid /ánti ə paárt hayt, -hīt/ *adj.* expressing or working in opposition to apartheid, particularly as it was legally enforced in South Africa between 1948 and 1991

antiarrhythmic /ánti ay ríthmik/ *adj.* COUNTERACTING IRREGULAR HEART BEAT preventing or correcting irregularities in the heart's action ■ *n.* ANTIARRHYTHMIC DRUG a drug that prevents or corrects irregularities in the heart's action

anti-art *n.* EARLY 20TH-CENTURY ART MOVEMENT the rebellion against easel painting and conventional art launched by the Dada movement during World War I. The term is meant to indicate the movement's rejection of conventional artistic practices and bourgeois tastes. ■ *adj.* OPPOSED TO CONVENTIONAL ART rejecting established artistic conventions

antiatom /ánti áttəm/ *n.* an atom made up of antiparticles

antibacterial /ánti bak téeri əl/ *adj.* ACTING AGAINST GROWTH OF BACTERIA preventing, killing, or reducing the growth of bacteria ■ *n.* AGENT ACTING AGAINST BACTERIA an agent that prevents, kills, or reduces the growth of bacteria

antiballistic missile /ánti bə lístik-/ *n.* a missile used to prevent a ballistic missile from reaching its target by destroying it in flight

Antibes /on téeb/ port and resort southwest of Nice in the Alpes-Maritimes Department in the Provence-Alpes-Côte d'Azur Region of France. Population: 63,000 (1990).

antibiosis /ánti bī óssiss/ *n.* a relationship between organisms that is harmful to one of them, e.g. the production by one microorganism of chemicals that harm another [Late 19thC. Coined from ANTI-, on the model of *symbiosis.*]

antibiotic /ánti bī óttik/ *n.* AGENT THAT DESTROYS BACTERIA a substance that is able to kill or inactivate bacteria in the body. Antibiotics are derived from microorganisms, especially fungi, or are synthetically produced. They have no effect against viruses. ■ *adj.* WORKING AS AN ANTIBIOTIC able to kill bacteria or render them inactive [Mid-19thC. Coined from ANTI- + BIOTIC.] —**antibiotically** *adv.*

antibody /ánti bodi/ (*plural* **-ies**) *n.* a protein produced by B cells in the body in response to the presence of an antigen, e.g. a bacterium or virus. Antibodies are a primary form of immune response in resistance to disease and act by attaching themselves to a foreign antigen and weakening or destroying it. [Early 20thC. Translation of German *Antikörper*, a contraction of *anti-toxischer Körper* 'antitoxic body' or a similar phrase.]

antibusing /ánti bússing/ *adj.* *US* opposed to the policy or practice of transporting children by bus (**busing**) to schools outside their district in order to achieve an ethnic balance in individual schools

antic /ántik/ *n.* CLOWN an actor or performer playing a crazily comic role (*archaic*) ■ **antics** *npl.* SILLY PRANKS amusing, frivolous, or eccentric behaviour ■ *adj.* STRANGE ludicrously or amusingly strange and eccentric (*archaic*) [Early 16thC. Via Italian *antico* 'old, old-fashioned' from Latin *anticus, antiquus.*] —**antically** *adv.*

anticancer /ánti kánssər/ *adj.* preventing or arresting the development of cancer

anticatalyst /ánti kátt'list/ *n.* **1.** ENG, CHEM = **inhibitor** **2.** SUBSTANCE TO PREVENT ACTION OF CATALYST a substance that inhibits or prevents the action of a catalyst

anticathode /ánti káthōd/ *n.* the anode in a vacuum tube, e.g. an X-ray tube, towards which electrons flow

anticholinergic /ántikōli núrjik/ *adj.* BLOCKING NERVE IMPULSES blocking impulses from the part of the nervous system that controls heartbeat, blood pressure, and other responses to stress, by neutralizing the effects of acetylcholine ■ *n.* SUBSTANCE THAT BLOCKS NERVE IMPULSES an agent with an anticholinergic effect

anticholinesterase /ántikōl néstə rayz, -rayss/ *n.* a substance that blocks the activity of the enzyme cholinesterase, increasing the concentration of acetylcholine in the body

Antichrist /ánti krīst/ *n.* **1.** ANTAGONIST OF JESUS CHRIST an antagonist of Jesus Christ, expected by the early Christians to spread evil throughout the world, but then to be overcome by the second coming of Christ **2. Antichrist, antichrist** ANY OPPONENT OF JESUS CHRIST any person or power opposed to Jesus Christ [Pre-12thC. Via ecclesiastical Latin from Greek *antikhristos.*]

anticipant /an tíssipənt/ *adj.* **1.** ACTING IN ADVANCE working or taking action in advance **2.** FEELING ANTICIPATION expecting or looking forward to sth [Early 16thC. From Latin *anticipant-*, the present participle stem of *anticipare* (see ANTICIPATE).]

anticipate /an tíssi payt/ (**-pates, -pating, -pated**) *vt.* **1.** ACT BEFOREHAND TO ADDRESS STH IMMINENT to imagine or consider sth before it happens and make any necessary preparations or changes **2.** EXPECT STH to think or be fairly sure that a certain thing will happen or come **3.** LOOK FORWARD TO STH to feel excited, hopeful, or eager about sth that is going to happen **4.** PREVENT STH to imagine or consider sth that might happen and take action to prevent it **5.** START STH AHEAD OF TIME to say or do sth before it becomes fashionable or comes into widespread use (*formal*) **6.** USE STH NOT YET RECEIVED to make use of sth before it has actually been received (*formal*) [Mid-16thC. From Latin *anticipare*, literally 'to catch beforehand', from *capere.*] —**anticipatable** *adj.* —**anticipator** *n.*

WORD KEY: USAGE

Anticipating trouble If you **anticipate** trouble, it often just means that you are expecting or foreseeing trouble, whereas its proper meaning is that you are taking steps to prevent trouble, that is 'forestalling' rather than 'expecting' it.

anticipation /an tíssi páysh'n/ *n.* **1.** EXPECTANT WAITING the feeling of looking forward, usually excitedly or eagerly, to sth that is going to happen **2.** FIN PREMATURE USE OF FUNDS the seizure or use of funds before they are legally available, especially from a trust fund **3.** MUSIC NOTE PLAYED BEFORE CHORD a note related to a chord that is played just before the chord itself

anticipative /an tíssipətiv/ *adj.* expecting or looking forward to sth —**anticipatively** *adv.*

anticipatory /an tíssipətəri/ *adj.* experienced or done in the expectation of a future event

anticlerical /ánti klérrik'l/ *adj.* opposed to the involvement by the church or clergy in politics and public affairs —**anticlericalism** *n.*

anticlimax /ánti klī maks/ *n.* **1.** DISAPPOINTING END AFTER BIG BUILDUP an ordinary or unsatisfying event that follows an increasingly exciting, dramatic, or unusual series of events or a period of increasing anticipation and excitement **2.** LITERAT SUDDEN LOWERING OF TONE an unexpected change in tone or subject matter from the high-minded, serious, or compelling to the trivial, comic, or dull —**anticlimactic** /ánti klī máktik/ *adj.* —**anticlimactically** /-máktikli/ *adv.*

anticlinal /ánti klīn'l/ *adj.* **1.** OF ARCHING ROCK LAYERS relating to, or in the form of, layers of sedimentary rock pushed up into an arch shape (**anticline**) by movements in the earth's crust **2.** BOT PERPENDICULAR TO PLANT SURFACE used to describe a plant cell layer that is perpendicular to the surface of a plant part [Early 19thC. Coined from ANTI- + Greek *klinein* 'to lean', on the model of *incline.*]

anticline /ánti klīn/ *n.* an arch-shaped formation of layers of sedimentary rock folded upwards by movements in the earth's crust [Mid-19thC. Back-formation from ANTICLINAL.]

anticlockwise /ánti klók wīz/ *adj., adv.* in the opposite direction to the way the hands of a clock move. US term **counterclockwise**

anticoagulant /ánti kō ággyŏŏlənt/ *adj.* STOPPING BLOOD CLOTTING preventing the normal clotting process of blood ■ *n.* SUBSTANCE THAT STOPS BLOOD CLOTTING a natural or synthetic agent that prevents blood clots from forming

anticodon /ánti kō don/ *n.* a unit of genetic code, comprising a set of three nucleotides in transfer RNA involved in the formation of a specific protein

anticoincidence /ánti kō ínssidənss/ *adj.* used to describe an electronic circuit that produces an output pulse if one, but not both, of its input terminals receives a pulse within a specified time frame

anticompetitive /ántikəm péttətiv/ *adj.* likely or certain to discourage competition

anticonvulsant /ántikən vúlssənt/ *adj.* CONTROLLING CONVULSIONS preventing or reducing the incidence of seizures, e.g. in epilepsy ■ *n.* DRUG FOR CONTROLLING CONVULSIONS a drug for preventing or reducing the incidence of seizures, e.g. in epilepsy —**anticonvulsive** *n., adj.*

Anticosti Island /ánti kówsti-/ island in the Gulf of St. Lawrence, Quebec, Canada. Its abundant forests shelter diverse wildlife. Area: 7,941 sq. km/3,066 sq. mi.

anticrime /ánti krīm/ *adj.* designed to prevent or reduce the incidence of crime in a particular area or among particularly vulnerable groups of people

anticyclone /ánti sīklōn/ *n.* a large system of atmospheric high pressure marked by circulating winds moving clockwise from the centre in the northern hemisphere and anticlockwise in the southern hemisphere, bringing generally settled weather —**anticyclonic** /ánti sī klónnik/ *adj.*

antidemocratic /ánti demmə kráttik/ *adj.* opposed to or working in a way that undermines democratic procedures or policies, especially the political institution of representative government

antidepressant /ánti di préss'nt/ *n.* DRUG TO CONTROL DEPRESSION a drug used to prevent or reduce depression ■ *adj.* CONTROLLING DEPRESSION acting to prevent or reduce depression —**antidepressive** *adj.*

antidiarrhoeal /ánti dī ə rée əl/, **antidiarrheal** *adj.* CONTROLLING DIARRHOEA preventing or reducing diarrhoea ■ *n.* DRUG FOR CONTROLLING DIARRHOEA a drug for preventing or reducing diarrhoea

antidiuretic /ánti dīyŏŏ réttik/ *adj.* CONTROLLING URINE OUTPUT preventing the excessive output of urine ■ *n.* DRUG FOR CONTROLLING URINE OUTPUT a drug for preventing or reducing the excessive output of urine

antidiuretic hormone *n.* = **vasopressin**

antidote /ántidōt/ *n.* **1.** SUBSTANCE THAT COUNTERACTS POISON a substance that counteracts the effect of a poison or toxin **2.** WELCOME RELIEF OR REMEDY sth that will take away or reduce the bad effects of sth experienced earlier [15thC. Via Latin from Greek *antidoton*, from *antididonai*, literally 'to give against', from *didonai* 'to give' (see DOSE).] —**antidotal** /ánti dōt'l/ *adj.* —**antidotally** /-dōt'li/ *adv.*

antielectron /ánti i lék tron/ *n.* = **positron**

antiemetic /ánti i méttik/ *adj.* PREVENTING VOMITING acting to prevent vomiting ■ *n.* DRUG PREVENTING VOMITING a drug that prevents vomiting

antifebrile /ánti féeb rīl/ *adj., n.* = **antipyretic**

antifederalist /ánti féddərəlist/ *n.* **1.** SB OPPOSED TO FEDERALISM sb who disagrees with a political system or philosophy that calls for division of power between a central government and regional governments **2. antifederalist, Antifederalist** HIST HISTORICAL OPPONENT OF US CONSTITUTION sb who did not agree that the US Constitution should be formally approved and recognized at the time it was drawn up ■ *adj.* AGAINST FEDERALISM hostile to the idea or practice of federalism —**antifederalism** *n.*

antiferromagnetic /ánti férrō mag néttik/ *adj.* used to describe substances that behave like paramagnetic substances with respect to their permeability but behave like ferromagnetic substances when their temperature is changed —**antiferromagnet** /ánti férrō mágnit/ *n*. —**antiferromagnetism** /-mágnitizzəm/ *n*.

antifouling paint /ánti fówling-/ *n*. a very poisonous type of paint used to prevent barnacles and other organisms from growing on the bottoms of boats or ships

antifreeze /ánti freez/ *n*. a liquid that lowers the freezing point of another liquid. An antifreeze such as ethylene glycol is added to or substituted for the water in a vehicle's engine to stop it from freezing in winter.

antifungal /ánti fúng g'l/ *adj*. preventing or reducing the growth of fungi, or killing fungi

antigen /ántijən/ *n*. a substance, usually a protein, on the surface of a cell or bacterium that stimulates the production of an antibody [Early 20thC. Via German from French *antigène*, from *anti-* 'anti-' + Greek *-genēs* (see -GEN).] —**antigenic** /ánti jénnik/ *adj*. —**antigenically** /-jénnikli/ *adv*. —**antigenicity** /ántijə níssəti/ *n*.

Antigone /an tíggəni/ *n*. in Greek mythology, the daughter of Oedipus and Jocasta. She killed herself after being condemned to death by Creon, king of Thebes, for cremating her brother's body.

Antigonus I /an tíggənəss/ (382–301 BC) Greek general. He secured a large part of Asia Minor after the break-up of Alexander the Great's empire in 323 BC.

antigravity /ánti grávvəti/ *n*. HYPOTHETICAL FORCE CANCELLING GRAVITATIONAL FORCE a hypothetical force that would cancel the force of gravity ■ *adj*. OPPOSING GRAVITATIONAL FORCE counteracting the effects of gravity or of high acceleration

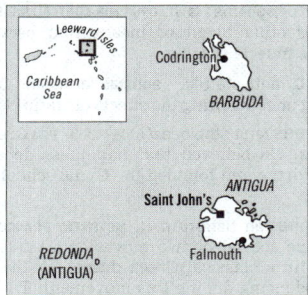

Antigua and Barbuda

Antigua and Barbuda /an teégə ənd baar boódə/ island nation in the Leeward Isles, east of Puerto Rico and north of Venezuela in the Caribbean Sea. Language: English. Currency: East Caribbean dollar. Capital: Saint John's. Population: 63,739 (1997). Area: 440 sq. km/170 sq. mi. —**Antiguan** *adj*., *n*.

antihelix *n*. = anthelix

antihero /ánti heerō/ (*plural* **-roes**) *n*. sb who is the central character in a story but who is not brave, noble, or morally good as heroes traditionally are —**antiheroic** /ánti hə rō ik/ *adj*. —**antiheroism** /ánti hérrō izzəm/ *n*.

antihistamine /ánti hístə meen/ *n*. a drug that blocks cell receptors for histamine, either to prevent allergic effects such as sneezing and itching or to reduce the rate of certain secretions in the stomach —**antihistaminic** /ánti hístə mínnik/ *adj*.

antihypertensive /ánti hĩpər ténssiv/ *adj*. CONTROLLING HIGH BLOOD PRESSURE preventing or reducing abnormally high blood pressure ■ *n*. DRUG THAT CONTROLS HYPERTENSION an agent or means used to prevent or reduce abnormally high blood pressure

anti-inflammatory (*plural* **anti-inflammatories**) *n*. a drug that acts to reduce inflammation. Aspirin and corticosteroids are anti-inflammatories. —**anti-inflammatory** *adj*.

antiknock /ánti nók/ *n*. a substance used to reduce or stop faulty fuel combustion in vehicle engines, a problem identified with a knocking sound

Anti-Lebanon Mountains mountain range running from north to south in Lebanon, parallel to the Mediterranean coast

antilepton /ánti lépton/ *n*. the antiparticle of a lepton

antilife /ánti līf/ *adj*. preventing or opposed to living life to the full or fully in tune with the natural world (*informal*)

antilock brake /ánti lók-/ *n*. an electronically controlled brake or braking system designed so that the vehicle's wheels do not lock if the driver brakes very suddenly

antilogarithm /ánti lóggərithəm/, **antilog** /ánti log/ *n*. a number for which the logarithm is a given number, so for $logarithm_a b = c$, then $antilogarithm_a c = b$

antilogy /an tílləji/ (*plural* **-ogies**) *n*. a phrase that contradicts itself or cancels itself out [Early 17thC. Via French from Greek *antilogia*, literally 'speaking against', from *-logia* (see -LOGY).]

antimacassar /ánti mə kássər/ *n*. a washable piece of fabric, usually embroidered, placed over the back of an armchair to keep it clean where heads rub against it (*dated*) [Mid-19thC. Coined from ANTI- + *Macassar*, a brand of hair oil.]

antimagnetic /ánti mag néttik/ *adj*. used to describe a material that does not become permanently magnetized in a magnetic field

antimalarial /ánti mə láiri əl/ *adj*. CONTROLLING MALARIA preventing or curing malaria ■ *n*. DRUG FOR CONTROLLING MALARIA a drug that prevents or cures malaria

antimasque /ánti maask/, **antimask** *n*. an interlude in or prelude to a 17th-century masque that contrasts with the main performance and often involves grotesque costume and dancing

antimatter /ánti mattər/ *n*. a hypothetical form of matter composed of subatomic particles (**antiparticles**) that correspond to and can annihilate other elementary particles

antimere /ánti meer/ *n*. a part of a radially symmetrical animal that is the opposite of a corresponding part of the animal —**antimeric** /ánti mérrik/ *adj*.

antimetabolite /ánti mə tábbə līt/ *n*. a substance that disrupts cell growth by taking the place of a normal nutrient metabolite with similar properties. Some antimetabolites are effective in treating certain cancers.

antimissile missile /ánti míssīl-/ *n*. a missile used to prevent another missile from reaching its target by destroying it in flight

antimitotic /ánti mĩ tóttik/ *adj*. preventing or reducing the rate of cell division (**mitosis**) —**antimitotic** *n*.

antimonial /ánti mốni əl/ *adj*. CONTAINING ANTIMONY used to describe drugs that contain antimony ■ *n*. SUBSTANCE CONTAINING ANTIMONY a drug or other substance containing antimony

antimony /ántiməni, an tímməni/ *n*. a toxic crystalline chemical element that occurs in metallic and nonmetallic forms. The metallic form is silver-white, brittle, and lustrous, and is used in alloys and electronics. Symbol **Sb** [15thC. From medieval Latin *antimonium*, of uncertain origin.]

antineoplastic /ánti nee ō plástik/ *adj*. preventing or inhibiting the growth of cancers —**antineoplastic** *n*.

antineutrino /ánti nyoo treénō/ (*plural* **-nos**) *n*. the antiparticle of a neutrino. When a neutrino and an antineutrino are brought together mutual annihilation occurs.

antineutron /ánti nyoó tron/ *n*. the antiparticle of a neutron. When a neutron and an antineutron are brought together mutual annihilation occurs.

anting /ánting/ *n*. a behavioural practice in which birds pick up ants in their beaks and rub them on their feathers to spread fluids repellent to parasites

antinode /ántinōd/ *n*. a point of maximum amplitude of a wave characteristic in a system in which the wave form is stationary in time

antinomian /ánti nốmi ən/ *n*. CHRISTIAN BELIEVING SALVATION DEPENDS ON FAITH sb who maintains that Christians are not bound by established laws, especially moral laws, but should rely on faith and divine grace for salvation ■ *adj*. **1.** OPPOSING FIXED MORAL LAWS disagreeing with the philosophy that the same fixed rules of morality and other laws should apply to

everybody **2.** HOLDING ANTINOMIAN BELIEFS holding or relating to the view that Christians are not bound by established laws, especially moral laws, but should rely on faith and divine grace for salvation [Mid-17thC. Formed from medieval Latin *Antinomi* 'Antinomians', from Latin *antinomia* (see ANTINOMY).]

antinomianism /ánti nốmi ənizzəm/ *n*. **1.** CHRISTIAN MORAL DOCTRINE the Christian philosophy that they are not bound by established laws, especially moral laws, but should rely on faith and divine grace for salvation **2.** FLEXIBLE CONCEPT OF MORALITY the belief that it is impossible to apply a universal moral code because it will have a different meaning for different people

antinomy /an tínnəmi/ (*plural* **-mies**) *n*. **1.** PHILOS PARADOXICAL RESULT two apparently correct and reasonable statements or facts that do not agree and therefore produce a contradictory and illogical conclusion **2.** LAW LEGAL DISCREPANCY a contradiction between two laws, principles, or authorities [Late 16thC. Via Latin from Greek *antinomia*, literally 'against law', from *nomos* 'law, rule'.] —**antinomic** /ánti nómmik/ *adj*.

antinovel /ánti nov'l/ *n*. a work of fiction that lacks the elements traditionally used in a novel, especially one with no coherent plot and characters, or in which the writer's perspective is deliberately inconsistent —**antinovelist** *n*.

antinuclear /ánti nyoókli ər/ *adj*. **1.** AGAINST USE OF NUCLEAR POWER opposed to nuclear weapons or power **2.** IMMUNOL DESTROYING CELLS reactive with or destructive to cell nuclei

antinucleon /ánti nyoókli on/ *n*. an antiproton or antineutron. When a nucleon and an antinucleon are brought together mutual annihilation occurs.

Antioch /ánti ok/ former name for **Antakya**

anti-oncogene *n*. a recessive gene that is thought to suppress cancers by limiting cell multiplication

antioxidant /ánti óksidənt/ *n*. any substance that inhibits the destructive effects of oxidation, e.g. in the body or in foodstuffs and plastics

antiparallel /ánti párrə lel/ *adj*. parallel but opposite in linear or rotational direction

antiparticle /ánti paartik'l/ *n*. an elementary particle with the same mass as its corresponding particle but having opposite values for other properties such as charge. When an antiparticle and its particle interact mutual annihilation occurs.

antipasto /ánti pastō/ (*plural* **-ti** /-pasti/ *or* **-tos**) *n*. any of various different foods served at the beginning of an Italian meal or as a snack, especially cooked meats and sliced sausage, marinated fish, or vegetables [Early 17thC. From Italian, literally 'before food'.]

antipathetic /ántipə théttik/ *adj*. **1.** FEELING DISLIKE FOR STH OR SB feeling or expressing anger, hostility, strong opposition, or disgust, especially towards a particular person or thing **2.** REPULSIVE stirring up or causing strongly negative feelings such as anger, hostility, or disgust [Early 17thC. From ANTIPATHY, modelled on PATHETIC.] —**antipathetically** *adv*.

antipathy /an típpəthi/ (*plural* **-thies**) *n*. **1.** STRONGLY NEGATIVE FEELING anger, hostility, fixed opposition, or disgust directed towards a particular person or thing **2.** OBJECT OF LOATHING a source of sb's anger, hostility, fixed opposition, or disgust [Late 16thC. Via French *antipathie* from, ultimately, Greek *antipathēs*, literally 'feeling the opposite', from *pathos* 'feeling' (see PATHOS).]

—— **WORD KEY: SYNONYMS** ——
See Synonyms at *dislike*.

antiperiodic /ánti peeri óddik/ *adj*. preventing the periodic recurrence of symptoms or of a disease such as malaria —**antiperiodic** *n*.

antiperistalsis /ánti perri stálsiss/ (*plural* **-ses** /-seez/) *n*. contractions of the intestine in the reverse direction to what is usual, tending to cause vomiting —**antiperistaltic** *adj*.

antipersonnel /ánti purssə nél/ *adj*. intended to injure and kill enemy personnel rather than to blow up buildings, structures, arsenals, or missiles

antiperspirant /ánti púrspərənt/ *n*. SUBSTANCE TO CONTROL SWEATING an astringent preparation applied especially under the arms to help prevent perspiration. Antiperspirants are produced in many forms, including aerosols, roll-ons, and sticks. ■ *adj.* CONTROLLING SWEATING used to reduce or prevent perspiration

antiphon /ántifən/ *n.* **1.** MUSIC SUNG IN ALTERNATING PARTS a hymn or psalm performed by two groups of singers chanting alternate sections **2.** SECTION OF FORMAL CHURCH SERVICE a short piece of biblical or devotional text that is chanted or sung before or after a psalm verse in a Roman Catholic or Anglican church service **3.** RESPONSE a response or reply (*literary*) [15thC. Via ecclesiastical Latin *antiphona* (source of English *anthem*) from Greek *antiphōnos*, literally 'sounding in response', from *phōnē* (see -PHONE).]

antiphonal /an tíffənəl/ *adj.* **1.** PERFORMED IN ALTERNATING SECTIONS sung, played, or recited by two or more groups performing alternate sections **2.** WITH RESPONSES with alternating phases or responses, as in an antiphon ■ *n.* = **antiphonary** —**antiphonally** *adv.*

antiphonary /an tíffənə ri/ (*plural* **-ies**) *n.* a book, often large and richly decorated, containing antiphons or anthems to be sung or chanted responsively

antiphony /an tíffəni/ (*plural* **-nies**) *n.* **1.** = **antiphon** *n.* 1 **2.** MUSIC PERFORMED IN ALTERNATING SECTIONS responsive chanting, recitation, or singing, e.g. of liturgical antiphons **3.** RESPONSE IN MUSIC a musical response or answering phrase [Formed from ANTIPHON]

antiphrasis /an tíffrəssiss/ *n.* the use of a word or phrase to mean the opposite of its usual or literal sense, e.g. saying on a rainy day, 'What a lovely day for a picnic!' [Mid-16thC. Via late Latin from, ultimately, Greek *antiphrazein*, literally 'to express oppositely', from *phrazein* 'to declare' (see PHRASE).]

antipodal /an típpəd'l/ *adj.* **1.** ON SPHERE'S OPPOSITE SIDE used to describe a point at the opposite end of the diameter of a sphere to another point ○ *The North and South Poles are antipodal.* **2.** DIAMETRICALLY OPPOSITE diametrically opposite or reversed ■ *n.* BOT EMBRYO CELLS IN PLANT a group of three cells in the embryo sac of a plant lying at the opposite end to the canal (**micropyle**) through which the pollen tube enters for fertilization

antipode /ántipōd/ *n.* an exact or diametrical opposite [Early 17thC. Back-formation from ANTIPODES.]

antipodean /an típpə dée ən/, **Antipodean** *adj.* coming from or relating to Australia or New Zealand

antipodes /an típpə deez/ *npl.* **1.** PLACES AT OPPOSITE SIDES OF WORLD places at opposite sides of the world to each other, or the areas at the side of the world opposite to a given place **2.** OPPOSITES two points, places, or things that are diametrically opposite each other [14thC. Via French or late Latin from Greek *antipodes*, literally 'those who have their feet opposite', from *pod-*, the stem of *pous* 'foot'.]

Antipodes /an típpə deez/ *n.* Australia and New Zealand, from the perspective of the United Kingdom or Europe (*informal*)

antipollution /ánti pə lóosh'n/ *adj.* designed to stop or reduce pollution of the environment

antipope /ántipōp/ *n.* sb who claims or is declared to be pope, even though a pope chosen by the orthodox canonical system already holds office [15thC. Via French *antipape* from medieval Latin *antipapa*, from *papa* 'pope', on the model of *antichristus* 'antichrist'.]

antiproton /ántiprō ton/ *n.* the antiparticle of a proton. When a proton and an antiproton are brought together mutual annihilation occurs.

antipruritic /ánti proor ríttik/ *adj.* CONTROLLING ITCHING preventing or reducing itching ■ *n.* AGENT FOR CONTROLLING ITCHING a drug or other agent that prevents or reduces itching

antipsychiatry /ántī sī kī́ ətri/ *n.* a way of treating people with psychiatric disorders that is derived from psychoanalysis and is opposed to the conventional medical mode, which uses medication

antipsychotic /ánti sī kóttik/ *adj.* REDUCING PSYCHOSIS counteracting or alleviating the symptoms of a psychiatric disorder such as schizophrenia ■ *n.* DRUG THAT REDUCES PSYCHOSIS a drug that counteracts or alleviates the symptoms of a psychiatric disorder such as schizophrenia

antipyretic /ánti pī réttik/ *adj.* REDUCING FEVER acting to reduce fever ■ *n.* DRUG THAT REDUCES FEVER a drug or other agent that reduces fever —**antipyresis** /ánti pī réessiss/ *n.*

antiq. *abbr.* **1.** antiquarian **2.** antiquity

antiquarian /ánti kwáiri ən/ *adj.* IN THE ANTIQUES BUSINESS dealing with or relating to antiques or antiquities, especially rare and old books ■ *n.* = **antiquary** —**antiquarianism** *n.*

antiquark /ánti kwaark/ *n.* the antiparticle of a quark. When a quark and an antiquark are brought together mutual annihilation occurs.

antiquary /ántikwəri/ (*plural* **-ies**) *n.* a collector, scholar, or seller of antiques or antiquities [Mid-16thC. From Latin *antiquarius*, from *antiquus* (see ANTIQUE).]

antiquate /ánti kwayt/ (**-quates, -quating, -quated**) *vt.* **1.** MAKE STH OLD-FASHIONED to cause sth to become out of date or old by replacing it with sth newer **2.** = **antique** [Late 16thC. Via ecclesiastical Latin *antiquare* 'to make old' from, ultimately, Latin *antiquus* (see ANTIQUE).]

antiquated /ánti kwaytid/ *adj.* quaint, extremely out of date, or badly in need of updating or replacing —**antiquatedness** *n.*

WORD KEY: SYNONYMS

See Synonyms at ***old-fashioned***.

antique /an téék/ *n.* (*plural* **-tiques**) **1.** OLD ITEM a collectable decorative or household object, often a piece of furniture, which is valued because of its age **2.** CLASSICAL ART the style, traditions, and qualities of ancient times, usually specifically the art and sculpture of ancient Greece and Rome ■ *adj.* **1.** MADE LONG AGO old and often valuable, of interest to collectors, and characteristic of a particular period and style of manufacture **2.** FROM CLASSICAL TIMES derived from a period of ancient history, especially ancient Greece or Rome, or stylistically typical of such a period (*formal*) **3.** ANCIENT very old or old-fashioned (*informal*) ■ *vt.* (**-tiquing, -tiqued**) MAKE STH APPEAR OLD to treat sth, especially a new object, so that it looks antique or worn with time [15thC. Via French from Latin *antiquus* 'old' (source of English *antic*).] —**antiquely** *adv.* —**antiqueness** *n.*

antiquity /an tíkwəti/ (*plural* **-ties**) *n.* **1.** ANCIENT HISTORY ancient history, especially the period of time during which the ancient Greek or Roman civilizations flourished **2.** OLDNESS the state of being very old or ancient ○ *a sculpture of great antiquity* **3.** OLD OBJECT an object, especially sth collectable, decorative, valuable, or interesting, that dates from a previous era **4.** PEOPLE OF ANCIENT TIME the people of ancient civilizations, especially those of ancient Greece or Rome

antiracism /ánti ráyssizzəm/ *n.* policies, views, or actions that oppose racial prejudice and discrimination and promote racial equality —**antiracist** *adj., n.*

antirejection /ánti ri jéksh'n/ *adj.* designed to prevent the immune system from rejecting a newly grafted organ or tissue

anti-roll bar *n.* a cross-mounted metal bar incorporated in the suspension system of a motor vehicle, designed to prevent the vehicle from swinging dangerously or overturning

antisatellite /ánti sátt'l īt/ *adj.* designed to destroy or incapacitate satellites

anti-Semitic *adj.* hating or discriminating against Jewish people

anti-Semitism *n.* policies, views, or actions that harm or discriminate against Jewish people —**anti-Semite** *n.* —**anti-Semitic** *adj.*

antisense /ánti sénss/ *adj.* relating to or having a strand of DNA complementary to other genetic material and used in genetic engineering to regulate the expression of a trait

antisepsis /ánti sépsiss/ *n.* **1.** ELIMINATION OF MICROORGANISMS eliminating or reducing the spread of microorganisms causing disease or decay, especially with chemicals **2.** ABSENCE OF MICROORGANISMS the condition of being free from microorganisms

antiseptic /ánti séptik/ *adj.* **1.** CONTROLLING INFECTION reducing or preventing infection, especially by the elimination or reduction of the growth of microorganisms **2.** DULL unexciting and unimaginative ■ *n.* AGENT FOR CONTROLLING INFECTION an agent that prevents or reduces infection, especially by eliminating or reducing the growth of microorganisms —**antiseptically** *adv.*

antiserum /ánti seerəm/ (*plural* **-rums** *or* **-ra** /-rə/) *n.* an animal or human blood serum containing one or more specific ready-made antibodies and used to provide immunity against a disease or to counteract venom

antisexist /ánti séksist/ *adj.* opposed to discrimination on the basis of sex, particularly discrimination against women —**antisexism** *n.*

antislavery /ánti sláyvəri/ *adj.* in favour of abolishing the slave trade or preventing people from keeping slaves

antismog /ánti smóg/ *adj.* designed to stop or reduce smog

antismoking /ánti smṓking/ *adj.* established or designed to stop people smoking, especially in public places

antisocial /ánti sṓsh'l/ *adj.* **1.** NOT CARING ABOUT OTHERS annoying, inconsiderate, or indifferent to the comfort or needs of neighbours, or to society as a whole **2.** NOT SOCIABLE preferring not to spend time with other people —**antisociality** /ánti sṓshi álləti/ *n.* —**antisocially** /ánti sṓsh'li/ *adv.*

antispasmodic /ánti spaz móddik/ *adj.* CONTROLLING SPASMS preventing or reducing the number and frequency of spasms ■ *n.* DRUG FOR CONTROLLING SPASMS a drug or other agent or means that prevents or relieves muscle spasms

antistatic /ánti státtik/, **antistat** /ánti stat/ *adj.* preventing or controlling the effects of static electricity

Antisthenes /an tísthə neez/ (444?–365? BC) Greek philosopher. He believed that happiness depends on moral virtue and founded the Cynic school of philosophy.

antistrophe /an tístrəfi/ *n.* **1.** MOVEMENT IN ANCIENT GREEK DRAMA the second of two movements made by the chorus in a classical Greek drama, or the section of an ode sung during this movement. The chorus move back in the opposite direction after the first movement (**strophe**). **2.** SECOND METRICAL FORM IN POEM the second type of metrical form in a poem that alternates two contrasting metrical forms [Mid-16thC. Via late Latin from Greek *antistrophē*, from *antistrephein*, literally 'to turn back', from *strophē* (see STROPHE).] —**antistrophic** /ánti stróffik/ *adj.* —**antistrophically** /-stróffikli/ *adv.*

antisubmarine /ánti súbmə reen/ *adj.* designed to destroy or incapacitate submarines

antitank /ánti tánk/ *adj.* designed to destroy or incapacitate military tanks

antitheft /ánti théft/ *adj.* designed to prevent sth, e.g. a motor vehicle, from being stolen

antithesis /an títhəssiss/ (*plural* **-ses** /-seez/) *n.* **1.** DIRECT OPPOSITE the complete or exact opposite of sth **2.** FIGURE OF SPEECH a use of words or phrases that contrast with each other to create a balanced effect **3.** PHILOS CONTRASTING PROPOSITION a proposition that is the opposite of another already proposed [Early 16thC. Via late Latin from, ultimately, Greek *antitithenai*, literally 'to set against', from *tithenai* 'to set' (see THESIS).]

antithetical /ánti théttik'l/, **antithetic** /ánti théttik/ *adj.* **1.** DIAMETRICALLY OPPOSED expressing or constituting the complete or exact opposite (*formal*) ○ *policies that are antithetical to the prevailing mood of the country* **2.** PHILOSOPHY CONTRASTING WITH EARLIER PROPOSITION amounting or relating to a proposition that is the opposite of another already proposed [Late 16thC. Formed from Greek *antithetikos*, from *antitithenai* (see ANTITHESIS).] —**antithetically** *adv.*

antitoxic /ánti tóksik/ *adj.* acting to counteract toxins

antitoxin /ánti tóksin/ *n.* **1.** ANTIBODY OPPOSING TOXIN an antibody produced in response to a particular toxin **2.** = **antiserum**

antitrade /ánti trayd/ *n.* a wind in the planetary wind system that is above the trade winds and blows in the opposite direction from them

antitragus /an títtrəgəss/ (*plural* **-gi** /-jī/) *n.* a bump of cartilage just below the opening of the external ear

antitrust /ánti trúst/ *adj. US* intended to oppose trusts and cartels, e.g. from using monopolistic business practices to make unfair profits

antitussive /ánti tússiv/ *adj.* CONTROLLING COUGHING preventing or alleviating coughing ■ *n.* MEDICINE FOR CONTROLLING COUGHING a drug that prevents or alleviates coughing

antitype /ánti tīp/ *n.* **1.** LATER OF ASSOCIATED BIBLICAL PAIR sb or sth seen as being foreshadowed by or having striking similarities to an earlier person or thing (**type**) in the Bible **2.** OPPOSITE TYPE an opposite or contrasting type [Early 17thC. Via late Latin from Greek *antitupos*, literally 'corresponding as an impression (to the die in which it was cast)', from *tupos* (see TYPE).] —**antitypical** /ánti típpik'l/ *adj.*

antivenin /ánti vénnin/, **antivenom** /-vénnəm/ *n.* **1.** ANTIBODY TO VENOM an antitoxin to the venom of a particular animal or insect **2.** SERUM COUNTERACTING VENOM an antiserum containing antibodies to venom [Early 20thC. Coined from ANTI- + VENOM + -IN.]

antiviral /ánti vírəl/ *adj.* FOR USE AGAINST VIRUSES capable of eliminating or inactivating viruses ■ *n.* AGENT USED AGAINST VIRUSES a drug or other agent used to eliminate or inactivate a virus

antivirus /ánti vírəss/ *adj.* **1.** MED = **antiviral** *n.* **2.** COMPUT FOR REMOVING COMPUTER VIRUSES used to describe a utility program that identifies and removes viruses in a computer's memory or on disks before damage occurs to the computer system

antivitamin /ánti víttəmin/ *n.* a substance that inhibits the effects of a vitamin

antivivisectionist /ánti vivvi séksh'nist/ *n.* sb who is opposed to scientific experiments that involve dissecting or cutting into the body of live animals (**vivisection**) —**antivivisectionism** *n.* —**antivivisectionist** *adj.*

antiwar /ánti wáwr/ *adj.* wanting to prevent a war or bring a war to an end

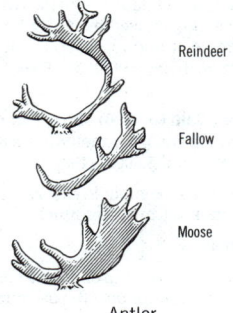

Reindeer

Fallow

Moose

Antler

antler /ántlər/ *n.* a solid bony branched horn found in pairs on the head of animals, especially males, of the deer family, including caribou and elk. Antlers are shed each year. [14thC. From an Anglo-Norman variant of Old French *antoillier*, of uncertain origin: possibly from assumed Vulgar Latin *anteoculare*, literally 'in front of the eye' from Latin *oculus* (see OCULAR).] —**antlered** *adj.*

Antlia /ántli ə/ *n.* a faint constellation of the southern hemisphere near Centaurus and Hydra

ant lion *n.* a nocturnal insect that resembles the damselfly when adult. The larvae lie buried under sand at the bottom of a cone-shaped pit and trap insects such as ants. Family: Myrmeleontidae. [Translation of Greek *murmēko-leōn*; from its usual prey and its fierce-looking jaws]

Antonello da Messina /ántə néllō daa mə seénə/ (1430?–79) Italian painter who was influenced by Flemish realism.

Antonescu /ántə nés kyoo, -nés koo/, **Ion** (1882–1946) Romanian general and politician who became prime minister of Romania in 1940. He commanded the army in Bessarabia in 1941, and was executed for war crimes.

Antoninus Pius /ántə nínəss pi əss/ (86–161) Roman emperor. He succeeded Hadrian and conducted a peaceful and prosperous reign (138–161). Full name **Titus Aurelius Fulvius Boionius Arrius Antoninus**

Antonioni /án tōni ōni/, **Michelangelo** (*b.* 1912) Italian film maker whose films include *The Adventure* (1959) and *Zabriskie Point* (1974).

antonomasia /ántənə máyziə/ *n.* **1.** USING TITLE INSTEAD OF NAME the use of a title or formal description such as 'Your Highness' or 'His Excellency' in place of sb's proper name **2.** USING PROPER NAME FOR GENERAL IDEA the use of a proper name as a common noun to refer to sb or sth with associated characteristics, e.g. in calling a handsome young man 'an adonis' [Mid-16thC. Via Latin from, ultimately, Greek *antonomazein* 'to name instead', from *anti-* 'against, instead' + *onoma* 'name' (see ONOMASTIC).]

Antony /ántəni/, **Mark** (83?–30 BC) Roman politician and general. He fought in Rome's last civil war allied with Cleopatra and was defeated by Octavian.

antonym /ántənim/ *n.* a word that means the opposite of another word. For example 'hot' is the antonym of 'cold'. [Mid-19thC. From French *antonyme*, from Greek *anti-* 'against, opposite' + *onuma* 'name'.] —**antonymic** /ántə nímmik/ *adj.* —**antonymous** /an tónnəməss/ *adj.* —**antonymy** /-mi/ *n.*

antra /ántrə/ *plural of* **antrum**

antre /ántər/ *n.* a cavern or cave (*literary*) [Early 17thC. Via French from Latin *antrum* (see ANTRUM).]

Antrim /ántrim/ **1.** historic town in County Antrim, Northern Ireland. Population: 20,878 (1991). **2.** historic county in Ulster Province, Northern Ireland. Area: 578 sq. km/223 sq. mi.

Antrim Coast and Glens Area of Outstanding Natural Beauty in Northern Ireland. Area: 706 sq. km/273 sq. mi.

antrum /ántrəm/ (*plural* **-tra** /ántrə/) *n.* a cavity within a bone, especially a sinus cavity [Early 19thC. Via Latin, 'cave', from Greek *antron*.]

antsy /ántsi/ (**-sier**, **-siest**) *adj. US* (*informal*) **1.** NERVOUS tensely nervous or apprehensive **2.** FIDGETY moving or squirming about in a restless, bored, or impatient way [Mid-20thC. Origin uncertain: probably from the expression *to have ants in your pants*.]

Antwerp /án twurp/ leading port of Belgium, situated on the Schelde river estuary 88 km/55 mi. from the sea. Population: 455,852 (1996).

ANU *abbr.* Australian National University

Anubis /ə nyoóbiss/ *n.* in Egyptian mythology, a god represented with the head of a jackal, who leads the dead to judgment

anuran /ə nyoórən/ *n.* an amphibian such as a frog or toad that does not have a tail as an adult and has long powerful hind legs. Order: Anura. [Late 19thC. Formed from modern Latin *Anura*, order name, from Greek *an-* 'without' + *oura* 'tail'.]

anuresis /ánnyoo reéssiss/ *n.* inability to pass urine (*archaic*) [Late 19thC. Coined from AN- + Greek *ourēsis* 'urination', from *ourein* 'to urinate' (see URETER).] —**anuretic** /ánnyoo réttik/ *adj.*

anuria /a nyoóri ə, ə-/ *n.* inability of the kidneys to form urine, leading to a build-up of toxic waste in the blood —**anuric** *adj.*

anurous /ánnyoórəss/ *adj.* without a tail

anus /áynəss/ *n.* ANAT, ZOOL the opening at the lower end of the alimentary canal through which faeces are released [15thC. From Latin, literally 'ring'.]

anvil /ánvil/ *n.* **1.** METALWORKER'S HAMMERING BLOCK a sturdy piece of iron onto which heated metal is placed to be beaten into the required shape, especially by a blacksmith **2.** ANAT = **incus** [Old English *anfilte*, *anfealt*. Ultimately from an Indo-European word meaning 'to beat', which is also the ancestor of English *pelt* and *felt*.]

anvil technique *n.* a prehistoric method of making chipped stone tools that involves striking a stone repeatedly against a static boulder used as an anvil

anxiety /ang zí əti/ (*plural* **-ties**) *n.* **1.** FEELING OF WORRY nervousness or agitation, often about sth that is

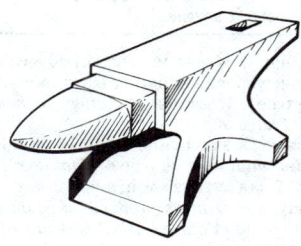

Anvil

going to happen **2.** STH THAT WORRIES SB a subject or concern that causes worry **3.** STRONG WISH TO DO STH the strong wish to do a particular thing, especially if the wish is unnecessarily or unhealthily strong **4.** PSYCHIAT EXTREME APPREHENSION a state of abnormal and intense apprehension or fear of real or imagined danger, manifested physiologically as increased heart rate, sweating, trembling, weakness, and stomach or intestinal discomfort [Early 16thC. Via French *anxiété* from, ultimately, Latin *anxius* (see ANXIOUS).]

— **WORD KEY: SYNONYMS** —
See Synonyms at **worry**.

anxiety disorder *n.* a psychiatric disorder causing feelings of persistent anxiety, e.g. panic disorder or post-traumatic stress disorder

anxiety neurosis (*plural* **anxiety neuroses**) *n.* a persistent panic disorder characterized by emotional distress, constant worry, a strong tendency to avoid specific situations, and overaction of the sympathetic nervous system

anxiolytic /ángzi ə líttik/ *adj.* RELIEVING ANXIETY with the effect of relieving anxiety ■ *n.* DRUG FOR RELIEVING ANXIETY a drug that relieves anxiety [Mid-20thC. Coined from ANXIETY + -LYTIC.]

anxious /ánkshəss/ *adj.* **1.** FEELING NERVOUS worried or afraid, especially about sth that is going to happen or might happen **2.** EAGER wanting very much, or in a desperate or nervous way, to do or receive sth **3.** PRODUCING ANXIETY producing feelings of fear, uncertainty, or nervousness [Early 17thC. From Latin *anxius*, from *anx-*, the past participle stem of *angere* 'to torment', literally 'to strangle'.] —**anxiously** *adv.* —**anxiousness** *n.*

any /énni/ CORE MEANING: a grammatical word used to indicate one, some, or several, when the quality, type, or number is not important ○ (*det*) *Do you have any German beer?* ○ (*pron*) *for any who wish to enter*
   1. *det., pron.* EVEN ONE OR A LITTLE even one or even the least amount (*used in negative statements*) ○ *I don't want any dessert.* ○ *I didn't see any.* ○ *This isn't any of your business.* **2.** *det., pron.* EVERY every person or thing stated, no matter who or what ○ *Any financial advisor would agree.* **3.** *det.* WITHOUT LIMIT an unlimited or indefinite amount or number of ○ *any number of foods including soups, stews, and salads* **4.** *adv.* AT ALL to even the smallest extent or degree ○ *Is it getting any louder?* [Old English *ǣnig*. Ultimately from an Indo-European word meaning 'one of a kind', which is also the ancestor of English *unique* and *inch*.]

— **WORD KEY: USAGE** —
American **any** The use of **any** as an adverb meaning 'at all' is a distinctly American idiom that is not yet a part of British English: *Her manners haven't improved any.*

— **WORD KEY: USAGE** —
Singular or plural? **Any** used as a pronoun is followed by a singular or plural verb depending on the sense: *Any of these suggestions is acceptable. Are any of the children coming?* (*Is any of the children coming?* implies that one is expected, with uncertainty as to which).

anybody /énni bodi, -bədi/ *pron.* **1.** = **anyone 2.** FAMOUS OR IMPORTANT PERSON sb considered to be of particular importance or influence ○ *Nobody who was anybody missed the opening night.*

——— WORD KEY: USAGE ———

See Usage note at **anyone**.

anyhow /énni how/ CORE MEANING: an adverb meaning no matter what the situation is or no matter what may be true ○ *What does it matter, anyhow?* ○ *and anyhow I have to go*
adv. **1. IN ANY CASE** no matter what the situation is or no matter what may be true ○ *What does it matter, anyhow?* **2. IN A CARELESS WAY** in a haphazard, careless, or untidy way ○ *ideas produced anyhow* **3. NEVERTHELESS** in spite of sth ○ *I asked him to wait, but he left anyhow.*

any more /énni máwr/, **any longer** adv. **1. STILL** at present and continuing from a point in the past (*used in negative statements or questions*) ○ *They don't make them like this any more!* **2. FROM NOW ON** from the present and ongoing (*used in negative statements or questions*) ○ *I'm not tolerating this any more.* **3. US NOWADAYS** these days (*regional nonstandard informal; used in positive sentences*) ○ *We always use a taxi anymore.*

——— WORD KEY: USAGE ———

anymore or **any more**? In British English, **any more** used as an adverbial phrase after a negative or a question is normally written as two words: *She doesn't live here any more.* In American English and in some other varieties (for example South African English) it is also, though not exclusively, written as one word, **anymore**, and there are signs that this is occurring in British contexts too, although this is not yet standard.

anyone /énni wun/ CORE MEANING: an indefinite pronoun used to mean one or more people, when exactly which person or which people is not known or not important ○ *Can I get anyone more coffee?* ○ *Did anyone show up?* ○ *There isn't anyone home.*
pron. **1. EVERY PERSON** any or every particular person who could be named or thought of ○ *more qualified than anyone in the business* **2. EVEN ONE PERSON** used to emphasize the unlikelihood of finding even one person to match the stated description or criteria ○ *Why would anyone want to hurt me?* **3. UNIMPORTANT PERSON** an unimportant and unknown person ○ *It's not just anyone, it's your sister!*

——— WORD KEY: USAGE ———

anyone or **any one**? **Anyone** is rather more common than **anybody** (which has the same meaning), and is used only of a person: *Has anyone seen my pen?* The words **any** and **one** are written separately when they are meant to retain their distinct meanings, and in this case **any one** can be used of a person or thing: *Any one of them could have started the fire. The tables are all free, so you can sit at any one you like.*

anyplace /énni playss/ adv. US, Can at, in, or to any place (*informal*)

——— WORD KEY: USAGE ———

American **anyplace** and **anytime** In British English, **any place** and **any time** are not yet regarded as a unit and are usually spelt as two words in each case, whereas in American English they are more often spelt as single words and are entered that way in dictionaries: *I don't recall seeing him anyplace. You can come anytime you like.*

anyroad /énni rōd/ adv. N England anyway

anyroads /énni rōdz/ adv. N England in any case or no matter what (*informal*) ○ *Anyroads, that's what I heard.*

anything /énni thing/ pron. STH UNSPECIFIED OR UNKNOWN any object, event, action, situation, or fact ○ *Is there anything I need to know?* ■ adv. AT ALL in any way (*used in negative statements or questions*) ○ *He isn't anything like his brother.* ◇ **anything but** used as an emphatic way of contradicting or negating a statement

anytime /énni tīm/ adv. US, Can at some undecided time, whenever you like, or whenever seems appropriate (*informal*)

——— WORD KEY: USAGE ———

See Usage note at **anyplace**.

anyway /énni way/ CORE MEANING: an adverb meaning no matter what the situation is ○ *Anyway, we have to pay whether it was accidental or not.* ○ *Recycling, according to some anyway, is like a new religion.*
adv. **1. IN ANY CASE** no matter what **2. REGARDLESS OF STH** in spite of the situation already stated ○ *I knew it would be a sad movie but I went anyway.* **3. IN A CARELESS WAY** in a careless, haphazard, or lazy way ○ *According to my mother, packing is a skilled operation, not throwing your clothes into a case just anyway.* **4. any way, any way BY ANY MEANS** in any manner or way (*informal*) ○ *We have to teach our children moral values anyway we can.*

anyways /énni wayz/ adv. US, Can anyway (*regional*)

anywear /énni wair/ n. clothing that can be worn for both casual and more formal occasions (*informal*)

anywhere /énni wair/ CORE MEANING: an indefinite pronoun and adverb referring to one or many places unknown or unspecified ○ (pron-indef) *Is there anywhere you prefer?* ○ (pron-indef) *Anywhere we live now will seem warm.* ○ (adv) *She can sleep anywhere.*
1. pron. SOME UNIDENTIFIED PLACE one or many places unknown or unspecified **2.** adv. TO ANY PLACE to one or many places unknown or unspecified ○ *I'll follow you anywhere!* **3.** adv. AT OR IN ANY PLACE at or in any place there is, or any place with the stated description ○ *We couldn't find her anywhere.* ○ *will live anywhere with a beach* ◇ **anywhere from...to** used to state an approximate measurement of sth by stating the smallest and largest possible measurements ○ *weighing anywhere from six to ten pounds*

anywise /énni wīz/ adv. US in any way or in any case (*regional; usually used in negative statements*) ○ *With or without them, I wouldn't go anywise.*

Anzac /án zak/ n. **1.** ANZ WORLD WAR I SOLDIER a soldier who served in the Australian and New Zealand Army Corps in World War I **2.** Aus AUSTRALIAN SOLDIER an Australian soldier **3.** Aus TYPICAL AUSTRALIAN MALE a typical Australian male seen as having the courage and spirit shown by the Anzacs at Gallipoli in World War I

Anzac biscuit, **anzac biscuit** n. Aus a biscuit made from wheat flour, oats, coconut, and syrup [From its use by Anzac soldiers in World War I]

Anzac Day April 25, the anniversary of the landing of the Australian and New Zealand Army Corps at Gallipoli in 1915 and a public holiday in Australia and New Zealand. The day commemorates those who fought at Gallipoli and those who have fought for Australia in the two world wars, the Korean War, and in Vietnam.

Anzio /ánzi ō/ port and resort on the western coast of Italy 60 km/37 mi. south of Rome. Heavy fighting occurred there during World War II when Allied forces secured a beachhead in January 1944. Population: 32,383 (1991).

AO abbr. Aus Officer of the Order of Australia

a/o, **A/O** abbr. account of

AOAI abbr. Area of Archaeological Importance

AOB abbr. any other business

AOC abbr. appellation d'origine contrôlée

A-OK, **A-okay** adj. in excellent condition or working order (*informal*) [Mid-20thC. From *all (systems) OK*.]

AONB n. an area of countryside officially designated for the purposes of town and country planning as being special and deserving of protection. Full form **Area of Oustanding Natural Beauty**

AOR abbr. adult-oriented rock

aorist /áyərist, áirist/ n. a verb tense used to express a past action in an unqualified way, without specifying whether that action was repeated, continuing, or completed or how long it lasted, found especially in classical Greek [Late 16thC. From Greek *aoristos* 'indefinite', from *a-* 'not' + *horistos* 'delimited', from *horizein* 'to delimit' (see HORIZON).] —**aoristic** /áyə rístik, air-/ adj. —**aoristically** /-rístikli/ adv.

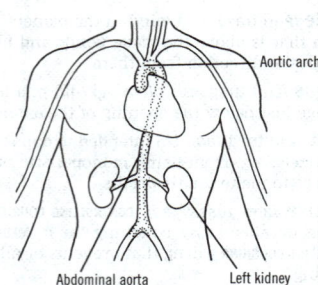

Aorta

aorta /ay áwrtə/ (*plural* **-tas** or **-tae** /-tee/) n. the main artery in mammals that carries blood from the left ventricle of the heart to all the branch arteries in the body except those in the lungs [Mid-16thC. Via modern Latin from Greek *aortē*, from *aeirein* 'to raise'; perhaps from the notion that the heart was held up by the aorta.] —**aortal** adj. —**aortic** adj.

aortic arch n. **1.** CURVED SECTION OF MAIN ARTERY the section of the largest artery (**aorta**) in the body that forms the curve between the ascending and descending parts. As it leaves the heart, the aorta goes upwards and then bends back on itself to form the arch. **2.** SET OF PAIRED ARTERIES a set of paired curved arteries, one of several in the vertebrate embryo that begin in the aorta, rise through the pharynx, and join with the dorsal arterial system

aortic valve n. the valve in the largest artery (**aorta**) in the body at the point where it leaves the heart. It allows the blood to flow out but not back into the heart.

aortography /áy awr tóggrəfi/ n. the X-ray examination of the largest artery (**aorta**) in the body after a substance that will be shown up by the X-rays has been injected into the bloodstream —**aortographic** /áy awrtə gráffik/ adj.

Aotearoa /áa ō tee ə rō ə/ n. NZ the preferred Maori name for New Zealand (*often used in combination*) ○ *Aotearoa-New Zealand*

aoudad /ów dad, áʹa oo dad/ n. a wild North African sheep that has long curved horns and a long fringe of hair on the neck and forelegs. Latin name: *Ammotragus lervia*. [Early 19thC. Via French from Berber *udād*.]

Aouita /ow éetə/, **Said** (b. 1960) Moroccan runner who held many world records, including 2,000m (1987), 1,500m (1987–93), and 5,000m (1987–94).

AP abbr. **1.** PUBL Associated Press **2.** Air Police **3.** American plan **4.** MIL antipersonnel

ap. abbr. apothecary

a.p. abbr. **1.** FIN additional premium **2.** PHARM before a meal (*used in prescriptions*) **3.** PUBL author's proof

ap-[1] prefix. = ad- (*used before p*)

ap-[2] prefix. = apo- (*used before vowels and h*)

apace /ə páyss/ adv. **1.** QUICKLY at a good or fast pace **2.** US ABREAST at a sufficient rate to keep up with or be alongside sb or sth [14thC. From Old French *a pas*, literally 'on step'.]

Apache /ə páchi/ (*plural* **-e** or **-es**) n. **1.** PEOPLES MEMBER OF NOMADIC NATIVE AMERICAN PEOPLE a member of one of six nomadic Native American peoples who used to live in the southwestern United States and northern Mexico. A number of Apache peoples live in Arizona, Oklahoma, and New Mexico. **2.** LANG ATHABASKAN LANGUAGE a Native American language spoken in parts of New Mexico, Oklahoma, and Arizona, belonging to the Athabaskan group. Apache is spoken by about 50,000 people. [Mid-18thC. From American Spanish, of uncertain origin: perhaps ultimately from Zuñi *Ápachu*, literally 'enemy'.] —**Apache** adj.

Apachean /ə páchi ən/ adj. **1.** PEOPLES OF APACHE PEOPLE relating to or typical of the Apache people or their culture **2.** LANG OF APACHE AND RELATED LANGUAGES relating to a subgroup of Athabaskan languages that includes Apache and Navajo

apanage *n.* = **appanage**

aparejo /àppə ráy ō/ (*plural* **-jos**) *n.* *Southwest US* a padded leather saddle used for carrying goods on a horse or mule [Mid-19thC. Via American Spanish, literally 'equipment', from, ultimately, Latin *apparare* 'to prepare' (see APPARATUS).]

apart /ə paárt/ CORE MEANING: a grammatical word meaning separated in space or time ○ (adv) *scheduled appointments a month apart* ○ (adv) *living apart* ○ (adj) *hard to be apart* ○ (adj) *sitting with legs apart*
1. *adv.* NOT TOGETHER separated in space or time ○ *She placed the chairs some distance apart.* **2.** *adv.* INTO PIECES into separate parts or sections ○ *take the machine apart* **3.** *adv.* MOVING AWAY AFTER BEING TOGETHER away from sb or sth after previously being together ○ *We've drifted apart over the years.* **4.** *adv.* REMOVED FROM CONSIDERATION set aside or excluded from consideration, or taken as an exception ○ *The orange flowered tie apart, it was a rather smart outfit.* **5.** *adv.* INTO DIFFICULTY into a poor or difficult condition **6.** *adv.* OF A SEPARATE KIND different and consequently separate from others ○ *a world apart* **7.** *adj.* SEPARATED away from each other in position or location ○ *with legs apart* ○ *think of her all the time we're apart* [14thC. From Old French *a part*, literally 'to the side'.] ◇ **apart from 1.** with the exception of sb or sth **2.** in addition to sth, or besides sth

apartheid /ə paárt hayt, -hīt/ *n.* a political system in South Africa from 1948 to the early 1990s that separated the different peoples living there and gave particular privileges to those of European origin [Mid-20thC. From Afrikaans, literally 'separateness', from Dutch *apart* 'separate', from French.]

a-particle *n.* = **alpha particle**

apartment /ə paártmənt/ *n.* **1.** *US* = **flat 2. apartment, apartment building, apartment block, apartment house** *US* BLOCK OF FLATS a block of flats **3.** ROOM a single room in a residential building (*formal*) ■ **apartments** *npl.* SPECIAL ROOMS IN BIG BUILDING a suite of adjoining rooms used for a particular purpose, e.g. as an office, entertainment suite, or place to live (*formal*) [Mid-17thC. Via French *appartement* from, ultimately, Italian *a parte* 'apart', literally 'to the side'; the underlying sense is 'separate place'.]

apatetic /àppə téttik/ *adj.* used to describe protective camouflage colouring [Late 19thC. Via Greek *apatētikos* 'deceptive' from, ultimately, *apatē* 'deceit', of unknown origin.]

apathetic /àppə théttik/ *adj.* not taking any interest in anything, or not bothering to do anything [Mid-18thC. Formed from APATHY, on the model of *pathetic*.] — **apathetically** *adv.*

WORD KEY: SYNONYMS

See Synonyms at ***impassive***.

apathy /áppəthi/ *n.* **1.** LACK OF ENTHUSIASM OR ENERGY lack of interest in anything, or the absence of any wish to do anything **2.** EMOTIONAL EMPTINESS inability to feel normal or passionate human feelings or to respond emotionally [Early 17thC. Via French *apathie* from, ultimately, Greek *apathēs*, literally 'without feeling', from *pathos* 'feeling' (see PATHOS).]

apatite /áppə tīt/ *n.* a glassy calcium-phosphate mineral, belonging to a group that ranges from colourless to purple, green, or brown in colour, used in making fertilizers and as a source of phosphorus [Early 19thC. Formed from Greek *apatē* 'deceit'; from its diversity of form and colour.]

APB *abbr.* all-points bulletin

ape /ayp/ *n.* **1.** TAILLESS PRIMATE any tailless primate such as a chimpanzee, gorilla, or orangutan. Family: Pongidae. **2.** PRIMATE any primate (*informal*) **3.** = **monkey 4.** IMITATOR an imitator or mimic of sb or sth **5.** *US* CLUMSY PERSON a clumsy or unintelligent person (*informal*) ■ *vt.* (**apes, aping, aped**) IMITATE SB OR STH to copy sb or sth in an absurd or mindless way [Old English *apa*] ◇ **go ape** to lose self-control, because of either anger or excitement (*slang*)

WORD KEY: SYNONYMS

See Synonyms at ***imitate***.

apeak /ə peék/ *adj., adv.* NAUT in a vertical position or direction [Late 16thC. From French *à pic*, literally 'at the peak'.]

APEC /áy pek/ *abbr.* Asia-Pacific Economic Co-operation

apeman /áyp man/ (*plural* **-men** /-men/) *n.* a non-technical name for any of various extinct primates believed to be ancestors of modern humans. ◊ **hominid**

Apennines /áppə nīnz/ mountain range that forms the backbone of peninsular Italy. It extends about 1,290 km/800 mi. from the area north of Genoa to the toe of Italy. The highest peak is Monte Corno 2,912 m/9,554 ft.

aperçu /-syóo/ *n.* (*formal*) **1.** INSIGHT a revealing glimpse or insight **2.** SUMMARY a concise outline or summary [Early 19thC. From French, literally 'sth perceived'.]

aperient /ə peéri ənt/ *adj.* WITH A LAXATIVE EFFECT mildly stimulating the opening and emptying of the bowels ■ *n.* LAXATIVE SUBSTANCE a mild laxative [Early 17thC. From Latin *aperient-*, the present participle stem of *aperire* (see APERTURE).]

aperiodic /áy peeri óddik/ *adj.* **1.** IRREGULAR happening at irregular intervals ○ *aperiodic floods* **2.** PHYS NOT EXHIBITING RESONANCE used to describe a mechanical or electrical system that does not exhibit resonance when a periodic disturbance is applied —**aperiodically** *adv.* —**aperiodicity** /áy peeri ə díssəti/ *n.*

apéritif /ə pérrə teéf/ *n.* an alcoholic beverage to be drunk before a meal [Late 19thC. Via French from, ultimately, Latin *apertus*, the past participle of *aperire* (see APERTURE).]

aperture /áppər tyoor/ *n.* **1.** NARROW OPENING a small narrow opening **2.** OPENING THROUGH LENS OR MIRROR a fixed or adjustable opening in a device, e.g. a camera or microscope, that lets light pass through a lens or mirror **3.** DIAMETER OF APERTURE the diameter of an aperture, e.g. in a camera [Mid-17thC. Formed from Latin *apert-*, the past participle stem of *aperire* 'to open' (source of English *overt*).] —**apertural** *adj.*

WORD KEY: SYNONYMS

See Synonyms at ***opening***.

aperture priority *n.* the system in a semi-automatic camera in which the user sets the lens aperture and the camera then selects the appropriate shutter speed automatically

aperture stop *n.* = **f-stop**

apex /áy peks/ (*plural* **apexes** *or* **apices** /áypi seez, áp-/) *n.* **1.** HIGHEST POINT the highest point of sth **2.** HIGHEST POINT OF SB'S CAREER the most successful part of sth, especially sb's career or life **3.** TIP OF STH the tip or top of sth, especially sth that is pointed, e.g. a triangle [Early 17thC. From Latin.]

Apex, APEX *n.* a system whereby air or rail tickets are available at a reduced price when bought a certain period of time in advance [Abbreviation of 'advance-purchase excursion']

Apgar score /áp gaar-/ *n.* a score that is given after assessing the condition of a newborn baby in the five areas of heart rate, breathing, skin colour, muscle tone, and reflex response. Each area has a maximum of two points. [Named after the US physician Virginia *Apgar* (1909–74), who developed it]

aphaeresis /a feérəssis, ə-/, **apheresis** *n.* the loss of a syllable from the beginning of a word, e.g. in 'coon' for 'raccoon' [Mid-16thC. Via late Latin from Greek *aphairesis*, from *aphairein* 'to take away', from *hairein* 'to take' (source of English *heresy*).] —**aphaeretic** /àffə réttik/ *adj.*

aphagia /ə fáyji ə/ *n.* the inability or refusal to swallow

aphakia /ə fáyki ə/ *n.* a medical condition in which the internal crystalline lens of the eye is absent [Mid-19thC. Formed from Greek *phakos* 'lentil', because of its shape.]

aphanite /áffə nīt/ *n.* an igneous rock with mineral components that are too fine to be seen by the naked eye [Early 19thC. Formed from Greek *aphanēs* 'unseen', from *phan-*, the stem of *phainesthai* 'to appear' (see PHENOMENON).] —**aphanitic** /àffə níttik/ *adj.*

aphasia /ə fáyzi ə, -zhə/ *n.* the partial or total loss of the normal ability to produce and understand speech as a result of brain damage caused by injury or disease [Mid-19thC. From Greek, from *aphatos* 'speechless', from *phanai* 'to speak'.] —**aphasic** /ə fáyzik/ *adj.*

aphelandra /àffə lándrə/ *n.* an evergreen shrub, native to tropical America, that has shiny leaves and brightly coloured flowers. It is often grown as a house plant. Genus: *Aphelandra*.

aphelion /a feéli ən, ap heéli ən/ (*plural* **-a** /-li ə/) *n.* the point in the orbit of a planet, comet, or other celestial body that is farthest from the Sun [Mid-17thC. From modern Latin *aphelium*, from Greek *apo-* 'away' + *hēlios* 'sun' (see HELIO-).] —**aphelian** *adj.*

apheresis /àffə reéssiss/ *n.* **1.** MED RETRANSFUSION OF TREATED BLOOD the retransfusion of a donor's or patient's own blood from which certain constituents have been removed **2.** LING = **aphaeresis**

aphesis /áffississ/ *n.* the loss of an unstressed vowel at the beginning of a word, e.g. in 'round' for 'around' [Late 19thC. From Greek, literally 'letting go', from *aphienai*, literally 'to send away', from *hienai* 'to send' (see CATHETER).] —**aphetic** /ə féttik/ *adj.* —**aphetically** /ə féttikli/ *adv.*

aphid /áy fid/ *n.* an insect that has specially adapted mouthparts for piercing and sucking the sap from plants. Many aphids transfer viruses from plant to plant as they feed. Family: Aphididae. [Late 19thC. From modern Latin *aphid-*, the stem of *Aphis*, genus name.] —**aphidian** /ə fíddi ən/ *adj.* —**aphidious** /ə fíddi əss/ *adj.*

aphid lion *n.* a larva of a green lacewing, or of other insects belonging to the same family, that feeds on aphids and other insects

aphonia /áy fṓni ə/ *n.* the loss of the voice as a result of injury or disease of the larynx or mouth or of various psychological conditions [Late 17thC. Formed from Greek *aphōnos*, literally 'having no voice', from *phōnē* 'voice' (see -PHONE).] —**aphonic** /áy fónnik/ *adj.*

aphorism /áffərizəm/ *n.* a succinct statement expressing an opinion or a general truth [Early 16thC. Via French from, ultimately, Greek *aphorizein* 'to define', from *horizein* 'to delimit' (see HORIZON).] —**aphorist** *n.* —**aphoristic** /àffə rístik/ *adj.* —**aphoristically** /-rístikli, -kəli/ *adv.*

aphorize /áffə rīz/ (**-rizes, -rizing, -rized**), **aphorise** (**-rises, -rising, -rised**) *vi.* to speak or write using aphorisms

aphotic /ə fóttik/ *adj.* used to describe those parts of the ocean that are not reached by sunlight, or plants that grow there without photosynthesizing

aphrodisiac /àffrə dízzi ak/ *n.* STH AROUSING PHYSICAL DESIRE sth that arouses or intensifies physical desire ■ *adj.* ABLE TO INCREASE PHYSICAL DESIRE able to arouse or intensify physical desire [Early 18thC. From Greek *aphrodisiakos* 'arousing sexual desire', from *aphrodisia* 'sexual pleasures', from *Aphroditē* (see APHRODITE).] —**aphrodisiacal** /àffrədi zī ək'l/ *adj.*

Aphrodite /àffrə dīti/ *n.* in Greek mythology, the goddess of love and beauty. She was the daughter of Zeus. Roman equivalent **Venus**

aphtha /áfthə/ (*plural* **-thae** /-thee/) *n.* a small white ulcer that appears in groups in the mouth and on the tongue as a result of the fungal condition thrush (*technical*) (*usually used in the plural*) [Mid-17thC. Via Latin from Greek.] —**aphthous** *adj.*

Apia /ə peé ə/ capital of Western Samoa, on northern Upolu Island in the South Pacific Ocean, northeast of Nuku'alofa in Tonga. Population: 34,126 (1991).

apian /áypi ən/ *adj.* relating to or resembling bees [Early 19thC. From Latin *apianus*, from *apis* 'bee', of unknown origin.]

apiarian /áypi áiri ən/ *adj.* related to bees or beekeeping

apiarist /áypi ərist/ *n.* sb who keeps bees, often for commercial purposes

apiary /áypi əri/ (*plural* **-ies**) *n.* a place where beehives are kept and bees are raised for their honey [Mid-17thC. From Latin *apiarium* 'beehive', from *apis* 'bee', of unknown origin.]

zh vision In foreign words: kh German Bach; aN French vin; aaN French blanc; ö German schön, French feu; öN French bon; ü French rue Stress marks: ´ as in secret \seék rət\; academic \àkə démmik\

apical /áppik'l, áy-/ *adj.* **1. FORMING TOP** used to describe the top of sth **2. PHON USING TOP OF TONGUE** used to classify a consonant that is pronounced with the tip of the tongue, e.g. 't' or 'd' [Early 19thC. Formed from Latin *apic-*, the stem of *apex* 'apex'.] —**apically** *adv.*

apical dominance *n.* the inhibition exerted on the growth of lateral buds by the terminal bud of a growing plant shoot

apical meristem *n.* the zone of actively dividing tissue at the tip of a shoot or root that produces new tissue, mainly to increase length

apices plural of **apex**

apiculate /ə píkyoolət, -layt/ *adj.* used to describe a leaf that has a short broad tip [Early 19thC. Formed from modern Latin *apiculus*, literally 'little apex', from *apex* 'apex'.]

apiculture /áypi kulchər/ *n.* the keeping of bees, especially for commercial purposes [Mid-19thC. Coined from Latin *apis* 'bee' + CULTURE.] —**apicultural** /áypi kúlchərəl/ *adj.* —**apiculturist** /-kúlchərist/ *n.*

apiece /ə peéss/ *adv.* to or for each one ○ *gold watches, from £150 to £550 apiece* [Mid-16thC. Formed from A + PIECE.]

apish /áypish/ *adj.* **1. BOORISH** silly, ridiculous, or boorish **2. IMITATIVE** imitating sb else or sb's style — **apishly** *adv.* —**apishness** *n.*

aplacental /áyplə sént'l/ *adj.* used to describe mammals such as marsupials that do not develop a placenta

aplanatic /ápplə náttik/ *adj.* used to describe a lens that does not have, or is corrected for, spherical aberration and so produces a clear undistorted image [Late 18thC. Formed from Greek *planasthai* 'to wander' (source of English *planet*).]

aplasia /ə pláyzi ə/ *n.* the absence or defective development of an organ, part of an organ, or tissue

aplastic /ay plástik/ *adj.* unable to develop new cells or tissue

aplastic anaemia *n.* severe anaemia in which the capacity of bone marrow cells to generate red blood cells is diminished

aplenty /ə plénti/ *adj.* in large or excessive amounts ○ *There are apples aplenty for all of you.*

aplite /á plīt/ *n.* a light-coloured, fine-grained igneous rock [Late 19thC. Via German *Aplit* from, ultimately, Greek *haplous* 'single', because of its chemical composition (see HAPLOID).] —**aplitic** /ə plíttik/ *adj.*

aplomb /ə plóm/ *n.* confidence, skill, and poise, especially in difficult or challenging circumstances [Early 19thC. From French *à plomb* 'perpendicular', literally 'according to the plumb-line'.]

apnea *n.* US = **apnoea**

apneusis /ap nyoóssiss/ *n.* an abnormal form of breathing caused by brain damage, in which each full inhalation is held for a prolonged period — **apneustic** *adj.*

apnoea /ápni ə, apní ə/ *n.* a temporary suspension or absence of breathing [Early 18thC. Via modern Latin from Greek *apnoia*, literally 'not breathing', from *pnein* 'to breathe'.]

apo-, **ap-** *prefix* away from, detached ○ *apolune* ○ *apocarp* [From Greek *apo* 'off, away'. Ultimately from an Indo-European base that is also the ancestor of English *of*, *off*, *after*, and *aft*.]

Apoc. *abbr.* **1.** Apocalypse **2.** Apocrypha

apocalypse /ə pókə lips/ *n.* **1. TOTAL DESTRUCTION** the total destruction or devastation of sth, or an instance of this **2. REVELATION OF FUTURE** a revelation made concerning the future [13thC. Via late Latin from Greek *apokalupsis* 'revelation', from *apokaluptein* 'to uncover', from *kaluptein* 'to cover'.]

—————— **WORD KEY: CULTURAL NOTE** ——————

Apocalypse Now, a film by US director Francis Ford Coppola (1979). This surreal, hallucinatory account of the Vietnam War is based loosely on Joseph Conrad's *Heart of Darkness*. It follows an American captain on his mission to assassinate a rebel officer, played by Marlon Brando, conducting his own independent war in the heart of the jungle.

Apocalypse *n.* = **Revelation**

apocalyptic /ə pókə líptik/ *adj.* **1. PREDICTING DISASTER** warning about or predicting a disastrous future or outcome ○ *an apocalyptic scenario of global warming* **2. BIBLE RELATING TO THE APOCALYPSE** relating to the events in the Book of Revelation in the Bible **3. INVOLVING DESTRUCTION** involving widespread destruction and devastation —**apocalyptically** *adv.*

apocalypticism /ə pókə líptisizzəm/ *n.* the belief that the end of the world is coming, with the resulting triumph of good over evil, as prophesied in the biblical Book of Revelation

apocalyptist /ə pókə liptist/ *n.* a believer in the prophecies in the biblical Book of Revelation or in the eventual triumph of good over evil [Mid-19thC. Formed from Greek *apokaluptein* (see APOCALYPSE).]

apocarpous /áppə kaárpəss/ *adj.* used to describe a flower that has separate carpels [Mid-19thC. Coined from APO- + Greek *karpos* 'fruit'.] —**apocarpy** /áppə kaárpi/ *n.*

apochromat /áppə krómat/ *n.* a lens that is corrected for chromatic aberration by incorporating different types of glass

apochromatic /áppəkrō máttik/ *adj.* used to describe a lens that has been corrected for chromatic aberration —**apochromatism** /áppə krómətizzəm/ *n.*

apocope /ə pókəpi/ *n.* the loss or omission of one or more syllables from the end of a word, e.g. the shortening of 'margarine' to 'marge' [Mid-16thC. Via late Latin from Greek *apokopē*, literally 'cutting off', from *koptein* 'to cut' (see COMMA).] —**apocopate** *vt.*

apocrine /áppə krīn, -krin/ *adj.* used to describe glands that secrete part of their secreting cells with the secretory products [Early 20thC. Coined from APO- + Greek *krinein* 'to separate' (see CRITIC).]

Apocrypha /ə pókrifə/ *n.* **1. BIBLICAL WRITINGS OF DISPUTED AUTHENTICITY** books of the Bible that are included in the Vulgate and Septuagint versions of the Christian Bible, but not in the Protestant Bible or the Hebrew canon (*may be singular or plural*) See table at **Bible 2. EARLY CHRISTIAN WRITINGS** a group of Christian writings dating from the early centuries AD that are not included in the New Testament [14thC. Via ecclesiastical Latin from, ultimately, Greek *apokruphos*, literally 'hidden away', from *kruptein* 'to hide' (see CRYPT).]

apocryphal /ə pókrif'l/ *adj.* **1. NOT TRUE** probably not true, but widely believed to be true **2. OF THE APOCRYPHA** relating to the Apocrypha —**apocryphally** *adv.*

apodal /áppəd'l/, **apodous** /áppədəss/ *adj.* without limbs, feet, or pelvic fins. Eels and snakes are apodal organisms. [Mid-18thC. Formed from the Greek stem *apod-* 'footless', from *pous* 'foot' (see PODIUM).]

apodictic /áppə díktik/, **apodeictic** /-dík-/ *adj.* demonstrably or indisputably true [Mid-17thC. From, ultimately, Greek *apodeiknunai* 'to demonstrate', from *deiknunai* 'to show' (see DEICTIC).] —**apodictically** *adv.*

apodosis /ə póddəssiss/ (*plural* -ses /-seez/) *n.* the main clause explaining the consequence in a conditional statement, e.g. 'we can watch the film' in 'If you come early, we can watch the film'. In logic the apodosis is the 'q' component of propositions of the form 'if p then q'. [Early 17thC. Via late Latin from, ultimately, Greek *apodidonai*, literally 'to give back' (see DOSE).]

apodous *adj.* = **apodal**

apoenzyme /áppō én zīm/ *n.* the protein component of an enzyme that determines the enzyme's specific function but has no physiological effect until it becomes attached to another compound (**coenzyme**)

apogamy /ə póggəmi/ *n.* the development of an embryo without prior fertilization. Apogamy occurs in some ferns, algae, and fungi. —**apogamic** /áppə gámmik/ *adj.*

apogee /áppə jee/ *n.* **1. CULMINATION** the best or greatest point **2. ASTRON POINT IN ORBIT FARTHEST FROM EARTH** the point when the Moon, or a satellite or other object orbiting around the Earth, is farthest from the centre of the Earth [Late 16thC. Via French from, ultimately, Greek *apogaios* 'away from the earth', from *gaia* 'earth' (source of English *geo-*).] —**apogean** /áppə jeé ən/ *adj.*

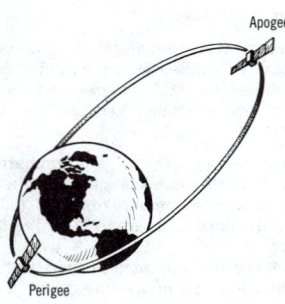

Apogee

apolitical /áypə líttik'l/ *adj.* having no interest in politics, or not concerned with politics —**apolitically** *adv.*

Apollinaire /ə pólli náir/, **Guillaume** (1880–1918) Italian-born French poet of Polish descent. His verse includes *Les alcools* (1913) and *Calligrammes* (1918). His play *Les mamelles de Tirésias* (1917) coined the word 'surrealist'.

Apollo /ə pólló/ *n.* **1. GREEK GOD OF PROPHECY** in Greek mythology, the god of prophecy, sunlight, music, and healing, also worshipped by the Romans **2. Apollo** (*plural* **-los**), **apollo** (*plural* **-los**) **HANDSOME MAN** a very handsome young man (*literary*) [Via Latin from Greek *Apollōn*]

Apollonian /áppə lóni ən/ *adj.* **1. RELATING TO APOLLO** relating to Apollo or the worship of Apollo **2. ORDERLY** calm, ordered, and balanced [Early 17thC. Formed from Latin *Apollonius*, from *Apollo* 'Apollo'.]

apologetic /ə póllə jéttik/ *adj.* **1. EXPRESSING APOLOGY** expressing apology or contrition for sth **2. DEFENSIVE** defending sth in speech or writing [Mid-17thC. Via French and Latin from, ultimately, Greek *apologeisthai* 'to speak in your own defence', from *apologia* 'defence' (see APOLOGY).] —**apologetically** *adv.*

apologetics /ə póllə jéttiks/ *n.* a branch of theology that is concerned with proving the truth of Christianity (*takes a singular verb*)

apologia /áppə lóji ə/ *n.* a formal, usually written, defence or justification of a belief, theory, or policy (*formal*) [Late 18thC. From Latin (see APOLOGY).]

apologise *vi.* = **apologize**

apologist /ə pólləjist/ *n.* sb who argues to defend or justify a particular doctrine or ideology

apologize /ə póllə jīz/ (**-gizes, -gizing, -gized**), **apologise** (**-gises, -gising, -gised**) *vi.* **1. EXPRESS REMORSE FOR STH** to say you are sorry for sth that has upset or inconvenienced sb else **2. ACKNOWLEDGE THAT STH IS NOT IDEAL** to acknowledge that sth is not as it should be, especially when you feel embarrassed or guilty about it **3. DEFEND FORMALLY** to defend sth formally in writing or speech [Late 16thC. From Greek *apologizesthai*, from *apologia* (see APOLOGY).] —**apologizer** *n.*

apologue /áppə log/ *n.* a fable that is intended to teach a moral lesson, especially one that has animals as characters [Mid-16thC. Via French or late Latin from Greek *apologos* 'story', from *logos* 'speech' (see LOGOS).]

apology /ə pólləji/ (*plural* **-gies**) *n.* **1. STATEMENT EXPRESSING REMORSE** a written or spoken statement expressing remorse for sth **2. NOTIFICATION OF NON-ATTENDANCE AT MEETING** a notification that sb cannot attend a meeting (*formal*) **3. INFERIOR EXAMPLE** an inferior or poor example of sth (*humorous*) ○ *I can't work in this apology for an office!* **4. FORMAL JUSTIFICATION** a formal defence or justification of sth [Mid-16thC. Via French *apologie* and Latin *apologia* from Greek 'speech in defence', literally 'speaking off', from *logos* 'speech' (see LOGOS).]

apolune /áppə loon/ *n.* the point in the orbit of a spacecraft circling the Moon when it is farthest from the Moon's centre [Mid-20thC. Coined from APO- + Latin *luna* 'moon' (see LUNAR), on the model of English *apogee*.]

apomictic /áppə míktik/ *adj.* used to describe an organism that reproduces asexually —**apomict** /áppə mikt/ *n.* —**apomictically** /áppə míktikli/ *adv.*

apomixis /áppə míksiss/ *n.* asexual reproduction in organisms that are also able to reproduce sexually, in which embryos are formed without fertilization or the creation of specialized reproductive cells [Early 20thC. Formed from Greek *mixis* 'mingling' (see AMPHIMIXIS).]

aponeurosis /áppō nyŏŏ rṓssiss/ (*plural* **-ses** /-seez/) *n.* a broad sheet of fibrous tissue or expanded tendon that joins muscles together or connects muscle to bone [Late 17thC. Via modern Latin from, ultimately, Greek *aponeurousthai* 'to become like a tendon', from *neuron* 'sinew' (see NEURON).] —**aponeurotic** /áppō nyŏŏ róttik/ *adj.*

apophasis /ə póffəssiss/ *n.* the rhetorical device of alluding to sth by denying that it will be mentioned, e.g. in 'I shall not bring up the question of age now that you are forty' [Mid-17thC. Via late Latin from Greek *apophasis* 'to deny', literally 'to speak off', from *phanai* 'to speak' (see -PHASIA).]

apophthegm /áppə them/, **apothegm** *n.* a terse saying that embodies an important truth, e.g. 'Haste makes waste' [Mid-16thC. From Greek *apophthegma*, formed from *apophtheggesthai* 'to speak plainly', from *phtheggesthai* 'to speak'.] —**apophthegmatic** /áppə theg máttik/ *adj.* —**apophthegmatically** *adv.*

apophyge /ə póffəji/ *n.* the outward curve at the top of an architectural column where it joins the capital, or at the bottom where it joins the base [Mid-16thC. From Greek *apophugē*, literally 'fleeing away', from *pheugein* 'to flee'. The underlying idea is of the column escaping into its base.]

apophyllite /áppə fíllīt, ə póffi līt/ *n.* a crystalline mineral that is white, pale pink, or pale green and is composed of hydrated potassium, calcium silicate, and fluorine [Early 19thC. Coined from APO- + Greek *phullon* 'leaf' (see PHYLLO-), because it peels when heated.]

apophysis /ə póffəssiss/ (*plural* **-ses** /-seez/) *n.* **1.** BIOL **NATURAL SWELLING ON ANIMAL OR PLANT** a natural swelling or outgrowth on an animal or plant, e.g. a bony protuberance on a vertebra **2.** GEOL **OFFSHOOT FROM ROCK** a small offshoot or network of veins from a large igneous mass of rock such as granite [Late 16thC. Via modern Latin from, ultimately, Greek *apophuein*, literally 'to grow out', from *phuein* 'to grow' (see PHYSICS).] —**apophysate** *adj.* —**apophysial** /ə póffə sée əl/ *adj.*

apoplectic /áppə pléktik/ *adj.* **1.** **FURIOUS** overcome with anger **2.** MED **EXHIBITING SYMPTOMS OF STROKE** having the symptoms of a stroke (*archaic*) [Early 17thC. Via French or late Latin from Greek *apoplēktikos*, from *apoplēxia* (see APOPLEXY).] —**apoplectically** *adv.*

apoplexy /áppə pleksi/ *n.* **1.** **ANGRY FIT** a fit of anger **2.** MED **STROKE CAUSED BY BRAIN HAEMORRHAGE** a cerebral stroke, usually caused by a haemorrhage in the brain (*archaic*) [14thC. Via French and Latin from Greek *apoplēxia*, from *apoplēssein*, literally 'to strike completely', from *plēssein* 'to strike' (see PLECTRUM).]

aporia /ə páwri ə/ *n.* a confusion in establishing the truth of a proposition [Mid-16thC. Via late Latin from, ultimately, Greek *aporos*, literally 'without passage', from *poros* 'passage' (see PORE[1]).] —**aporetic** /áppə réttik/ *adj.*

aport /ə páwrt/ *adv., adj.* on or towards the port or left-hand side of a ship as you face forward

aposematic /áppə se máttik/ *adj.* used to describe natural colours and bright markings on an animal that warn predators that it is poisonous ○ *aposematic coloration*

aposiopesis /áppə sī ə péessiss/ (*plural* **-ses** /-seez/) *n.* a sudden break in speaking, giving the impression that the speaker does not want to or cannot continue, e.g. in the sentence 'On Tuesday morning I came in just as I always do, and I saw—I can't go on' [Late 16thC. Via Latin from, ultimately, Greek *aposiopan* 'to stop speaking', from *siopē* 'silence'.] —**aposiopetic** /áppə sī ə péttik/ *adj.*

apospory /áppə spawri, ə póspəri/ *n.* the process of asexual reproduction without the occurrence of cell division (**meiosis**) or spore formation, in certain ferns and mosses [Late 19thC. Coined from APO- + SPORE + -Y.]

apostasy /ə póstəssi/ *n.* the renunciation of a religious or political belief or allegiance [14thC. Via French from, ultimately, Greek *apostasis*, literally 'standing away', from *histanai* 'to stand' (source of English *prostrate* and *system*).]

apostate /ə pó stayt/ *n.* sb who has renounced a religious or political belief or allegiance [14thC. Via French and Latin from Greek *apostatēs*, literally 'sb caused to stand away', from *stat-*, related to *histanai* 'to cause to stand'.]

apostatize /ə póstə tīz/ (**-tizes, -tizing, -tized**), **apostatise** (**-tises, -tising, -tised**) *vi.* to renounce a religious faith, a political party, a set of principles, or a moral allegiance (*formal*)

a posteriori /áy pos térri áw rī, àa-, -teeri-/ *adj., adv.* deriving knowledge from experience, or reasoning from observed facts or events back to their causes [From Latin, literally 'from what comes later']

apostle /ə póss'l/ *n.* **1.** **STRONG BELIEVER IN STH** sb who believes strongly in an idea or cause and tries to persuade others to share it ○ *an apostle of free trade* **2.** **PROMINENT CHRISTIAN MISSIONARY** a prominent Christian missionary, especially one who is responsible for first converting a nation **3.** **OFFICIAL IN MORMON CHURCH** a member of the 12-person administrative council of the Church of Jesus Christ of Latter-Day Saints [Pre-12thC. Via ecclesiastical Latin from Greek *apostolos*, literally 'sb sent out', from *stellein* 'to send' (source of English *epistle*).] —**apostleship** *n.*

Apostle *n.* one of the 12 followers of Jesus Christ chosen by him to preach the news about Christianity

apostlebird /ə póss'l burd/ *n.* a medium-sized Australian grey bird, usually found in small flocks. Latin name: *Struthidea cinerea.* [So called because they congregate in flocks]

Apostles' Creed *n.* a statement of Christian belief ascribed to the Apostles and dating from around AD 500. It is frequently used in services in Eastern Orthodox, Anglican, and Lutheran churches.

apostle spoon *n.* a silver spoon with the figure of an Apostle on the handle. Apostle spoons were traditionally given as presents at baptisms.

apostolate /ə póstə layt/ *n.* **1.** **WORK OF AN APOSTLE** the duties or mission of an apostle **2.** **GROUP OF PEOPLE PROPAGATING RELIGION** a group involved in converting new followers to a religion or doctrine [Mid-17thC. From ecclesiastical Latin *apostolatus*, from *apostolus* 'apostle' (see APOSTLE).]

apostolic /áppə stóllik/ *adj.* **1.** **RELATING TO POPE** relating to, given by, or on behalf of the pope **2.** **RELATING TO APOSTLES** connected with the Apostles or their teachings, or contemporary with them [Mid-16thC. Via French and ecclesiastical Latin from, ultimately, Greek *apostolos* 'apostle' (see APOSTLE).] —**apostolical** *adj.* —**apostolically** *adv.*

apostolic delegate *n.* a representative of the pope who is sent to a country that has no formal diplomatic relations with the Vatican

Apostolic Father *n.* a Christian church leader of the first or second century AD who was contemporary with or lived shortly after the Apostles

Apostolic See *n.* the area of jurisdiction (**see**) of the pope

apostolic succession *n.* the doctrine of some Christian denominations that the ordination of bishops follows in an unbroken line of succession from the Apostles, providing the basis of their spiritual authority

apostrophe[1] /ə póstrəfi/ *n.* the punctuation mark (') used to show where letters are omitted from a word, to mark the possessive, and sometimes to form the plural of numbers, letters, and symbols [Mid-16thC. Via French from, ultimately, Greek *apostrophos*, literally 'turned away', formed from *apostrephein* 'to turn away', from *strephein* 'to turn' (see STROPHE).]

apostrophe[2] /ə póstrəfi/ *n.* a speech, especially in the form of a digression, addressing an absent or imaginary person or a personification of an abstract or inanimate entity [Mid-16thC. Via Latin from, ultimately, Greek *apostrephein* (see APOSTROPHE[1]).] —**apostrophic** /áppə stróffik/ *adj.*

apostrophize /ə póstrə fīz/ (**-phizes, -phizing, -phized**), **apostrophise** (**-phises, -phising, -phised**) *vti.* to address an absent or imaginary person or a personified abstraction

apothecaries' measure *n.* a system of liquid volume measure formerly used in pharmacy and based on the minim, fluid drachm, fluid ounce, and pint

apothecaries' weight *n.* a system of weights formerly used in pharmacy and based on a troy ounce equal to 480 grains and a pound equal to 12 ounces

apothecary /ə póthəkəri/ (*plural* **-ies**) *n.* (*archaic*) **1.** **PHARMACIST** a pharmacist **2.** **PHARMACY** a pharmacy [14thC. Via Old French from, ultimately, Greek *apothēkē* 'storehouse' (source of English *boutique*), formed from *apotithenai* 'to put away', from *tithenai* 'to put'.]

apothecium /áppə théessi əm/ (*plural* **-a** /-si ə/) *n.* a disc-shaped or cup-shaped spore-bearing structure found in certain fungi, including the fungal component of most lichens [Early 19thC. Via modern Latin from Greek *apothēkē* (see APOTHECARY).] —**apothecial** /áppə théessi əl/ *adj.*

apothegm *n.* = **apophthegm**

apotheosis /ə póthi ṓssiss/ (*plural* **-ses** /-seez/) *n.* **1.** **HIGHEST LEVEL OF GLORY OR POWER** the highest point of glory, power, or importance **2.** **BEST EXAMPLE OF STH** the best or most glorious example of sth ○ *the apotheosis of romantic music* **3.** **TRANSFORMATION INTO GOD** the transformation of a human being into a god [Late 16thC. Via late Latin from, ultimately, Greek *apotheoun*, literally 'to make into a god completely', from *theos* 'god' (see THEO-).]

apotheosize /ə póthi ə sīz/ (**-sizes, -sizing, -sized**), **apotheosise** (**-sises, -sising, -sised**) *vt.* **1.** **MAKE SB INTO A GOD** to elevate sb to the status of a god **2.** **GLORIFY** to glorify or exalt sb or sth

apotropaic /áppətrə páy ik/ *adj.* intended to ward off evil or bad luck [Late 19thC. Formed from Greek *apotropaios*, from *apotrepein*, literally 'to turn away' from *trepein* 'to turn' (see -TROPOUS).] —**apotropaically** *adv.* —**apotropaism** *n.*

app /ap/ *n.* COMPUT = **application** *n.* **6** (*informal*)

app. *abbr.* **1.** apparatus **2.** PUBL appendix **3.** applied **4.** appointed **5.** apprentice **6.** approved **7.** approximate

appal /ə páwl/ (**-pals, -palling, -palled**) *vt.* to make sb feel shock, horror, or disgust [Mid-16thC. From Old French *apallir* 'to grow pale or faint', from *pale* 'PALE'.]

Appalachia /áppə láychi ə/ *n.* the region in the United States that includes the southern Appalachian Mountains, extending roughly from southwestern Pennsylvania through West Virginia and parts of Kentucky and Tennessee to northwestern Georgia

Appalachian /áppə láychi ən/ *adj.* **1.** **RELATING TO APPALACHIAN MOUNTAINS** in, from, or relating to the Appalachian Mountains **2.** **OF APPALACHIA** relating to or typical of Appalachia, or its people or culture ■ *n.* **SB FROM APPALACHIA** sb who lives in or was born or brought up in Appalachia in the United States [Late 17thC. Formed from *Apalachee*, the name of a Native American people of the southeastern United States.]

Appalachian Mountains, **Appalachians** North American mountain system, stretching from southeastern Canada to central Alabama. Major ranges include the White, Green, Catskill, Allegheny, Blue Ridge, Great Smoky, and Cumberland mountains. The highest point is Mount Mitchell 2,037 m/6,684 ft.

Appalachian Trail *n.* a long-distance footpath in the eastern United States, extending about 3,298 km/2,050 mi. from Mount Katahdin in central Maine to Springer Mountain in northern Georgia. It is one of the longest continuous mountain trails in the world.

appall *vt.* US = **appal**

appalled /ə páwld/ *adj.* feeling or appearing to be shocked by sth dreadful or awful ○ *an appalled look*

appalling /ə páwling/ *adj.* **1.** **DREADFUL AND SHOCKING** causing shock or horror **2.** **VERY BAD** very bad, or much worse than expected —**appallingly** *adv.*

Appaloosa /áppə lóossə/, **appaloosa** *n.* a saddle horse with white hair and dark patches, first bred in northwestern North America. It was much used in the past by Native Americans. [Mid-19thC. Origin uncertain; perhaps an alteration of *Palouse*, a river in the northwestern United States.]

appanage /áppənij/, **apanage** *n.* **1.** **SOURCE OF REVENUE GIVEN BY SOVEREIGN** a source of revenue e.g. land given by a sovereign for the maintenance of a member of the royal family, especially a younger son **2. NATURAL OR EXPECTED ACCOMPANIMENT TO STH** a thing that naturally or usually accompanies sth else [Early 17thC. Via French from, ultimately, medieval Latin *appanare*, literally '(to give) bread to', from *panis* 'bread' (see PANTRY).]

apparat /áppə raát/ *n.* the administrative organization or staff of the Communist Party in the former Soviet Union and other Communist states [Mid-20thC. Via Russian from German, 'apparatus'.]

apparatchik /áppə rátchik, -raát-/ *n.* **1. UNQUESTIONINGLY LOYAL SUBORDINATE** a subordinate who is unquestioningly loyal to a powerful political leader or organization **2. COMMUNIST FUNCTIONARY** a member of the administrative organization or staff (**apparat**) of the Communist Party in the former Soviet Union and other Communist states [Mid-20thC. From Russian.]

apparatus /áppə ráytəss, -raá-, -rá-/ (*plural* **-tuses** *or* **-tus**) *n.* **1. EQUIPMENT** a piece of machinery, a tool, or a device used for a particular purpose **2. SYSTEM ALLOWING STH TO FUNCTION** the system or structure in which a process occurs or an organization functions ○ *a complex bureaucratic apparatus* **3.** ANAT **SYSTEM OF ORGANS** a group or system of organs that work together to perform a particular function [Early 17thC. From Latin, literally 'sth prepared', the past participle of *apparare* 'to prepare', from *parare* (see PARE).]

WORD KEY: SYNONYMS

See Synonyms at ***implement***.

apparatus criticus /-kríttikəss/ *n.* = **critical apparatus** [Mid-19thC. From modern Latin, literally 'critical apparatus'.]

apparel /ə párrəl/ *n.* **1. CLOTHING** clothing or garments, especially outer or decorative clothing ○ *Olympics-related sports apparel* **2.** NAUT **SHIP'S EQUIPMENT** a ship's gear and equipment ■ *vt.* (**-els, -elling, -elled**) **CLOTHE** to dress sb, especially in formal clothes (*archaic*) [13thC. Via Old French *apareil* 'preparation' from, ultimately, Latin *apparare* (see APPARATUS). The sense 'clothing' evolved via 'equipment for performing a particular function'.]

apparent /ə párrənt/ *adj.* **1. CLEAR TO SB** clearly seen or understood **2. SEEMING** appearing to show particular qualities, feelings, or attributes that may not be genuine ○ *her apparent indifference* **3.** PHYS **DIRECTLY OBSERVED BUT NEGLECTING MODIFYING FACTORS** directly observed or measured but not taking into account factors or effects that should be allowed for, e.g. distortion caused by the measuring instruments themselves [14thC. Via Old French *aparant*, the present participle of *aparoir* (see APPEAR).] —**apparentness** *n.*

WORD KEY: SYNONYMS

See Synonyms at ***evident***.

apparent horizon *n.* = **horizon** *n.* 1

apparently /ə párrəntli/ *adv.* according to what seems to be the case but may not actually be so

apparent magnitude *n.* = **magnitude**

apparent wind /-wind/ *n.* a combination of the actual wind and the wind created by a ship's motion

apparition /áppə rísh'n/ *n.* **1. APPEARANCE OF STH GHOSTLY** an appearance of a ghost or sth ghostly **2. APPEARANCE OF STH UNLIKELY** an appearance of sth or sb unexpected or strange (*humorous*) [15thC. Via French from, ultimately, Latin *apparere* (see APPEAR).] —**apparitional** *adj.*

appassionato /ə pássyə naá tō/ *adj., adv.* to be performed in an impassioned way (*used as a musical direction*) [From Italian, literally 'impassioned']

appeal /ə peél/ *n.* **1. EARNEST OR URGENT REQUEST** an earnest or urgent request to sb for sth ○ *an emotional appeal for forgiveness* **2. CAMPAIGN TO RAISE MONEY** a request or campaign to raise money or resources ○ *The hospital has launched an appeal for funds.* **3. ATTRACTION** the quality that makes sb or sth attractive ○ *The film's appeal lies in its humour and charm.* **4. FORMAL REQUEST** a formal request to a higher authority requesting a change in or confirmation of a decision ○ *An appeal to the boss might solve the matter.* **5.** LAW **HEARING OF CASE BEFORE SUPERIOR COURT** the hearing of part or the whole of a previously tried case by a superior court, a request for a hearing, or the right to have such a hearing **6.** CRICKET **REQUEST FOR UMPIRE TO DISMISS BATSMAN** a verbal request to the umpire to declare a batsman out ■ *v.* (**-peals, -pealing, -pealed**) **1.** *vi.* **REQUEST MONEY** to ask for or campaign to raise money or resources ○ *The charity is appealing for books and toys.* **2.** *vi.* **EARNESTLY REQUEST STH** to make an earnest and urgent request for sth ○ *We are appealing to the public to let us know if they see anything suspicious.* **3.** *vi.* **MAKE A FORMAL REQUEST TO SUPERIOR** to make a formal request to a higher authority requesting a change in or confirmation of a decision ○ *You will have to appeal to a senior officer.* **4.** *vi.* **ATTRACT OR FASCINATE SB** to be interesting or attractive ○ *Starting up my own business really appeals to me.* **5.** *vti.* LAW **APPLY TO SUPERIOR COURT FOR HEARING** to apply to a superior court for a hearing of the whole or part of a case previously tried in a lower court **6.** *vi.* CRICKET **ASK UMPIRE TO DISMISS BATSMAN** to make a verbal request to the umpire to declare a batsman out **7.** *vi.* SPORTS **CHALLENGE UMPIRE'S DECISION** to challenge the decision of an umpire or referee [14thC. Via Old French *apeler* from, ultimately, Latin *appellare* 'to address, entreat', related to *pellere* 'to push'.] —**appealer** *n.* ◇ **on appeal** at the stage of a court case that involves reconsideration of the decision made at the original trial

WORD KEY: ORIGIN

Latin *pellere*, from which ***appeal*** is derived, is also the source of English *compel, dispel, expel, impel, propel, pulse, repeal*, and *repel*.

appealable /ə peéləb'l/ *adj.* LAW having the right to be heard before a higher court with the possibility of a changed judgment

Appeal Court *n.* = **Court of Appeal**

appealing /ə peéling/ *adj.* **1. ATTRACTIVE** attractive and pleasing or interesting **2. REQUESTING HELP OR SYMPATHY** appearing to request help or sympathy ○ *a timid, appealing glance* —**appealingly** *adv.*

appear /ə peér/ (**-pears, -pearing, -peared**) *v.* **1.** *vi.* **COME INTO VIEW** to come into view, or become visible ○ *The main menu will appear whenever you turn on the computer.* **2.** *vi.* **BEGIN TO EXIST** to come into existence ○ *When did this rash appear?* **3.** *vi.* **BECOME AVAILABLE FOR SALE** to become available, especially as a product for sale ○ *Cheaper and better printers have appeared on the market.* **4.** *vti.* **SEEM LIKELY** to seem likely or true ○ *The police appear to be looking for three men.* **5.** *vi.* **BE SEEN IN PUBLIC** to come before the public, especially to perform a duty or to act ○ *His dream was to appear on Broadway.* **6.** *vi.* LAW **BE IN LAW COURT OFFICIALLY** to be present in a court of law as a defendant, plaintiff, witness, or legal adviser ○ *due to appear in court next week* **7.** *vi.* **FORMALLY PRESENT YOURSELF TO SB** to formally present yourself to sb after receiving an official request ○ *He was ordered to appear in the district superintendent's office.* [13thC. Via Old French *aparoir* from Latin *apparere*, literally 'to show, become visible to', from *parere* 'to show'.]

appearance /ə peéranss/ *n.* **1. COMING INTO EXISTENCE** the act of emerging, arriving, or coming into existence ○ *the appearance of the first daffodils* **2. WAY SB OR STH LOOKS** the way sb or sth looks or seems to other people ○ *an attractive appearance* **3. OUTWARD ASPECT** an outward aspect of sb or sth that creates a particular impression (*often used in the plural*) ○ *The place gives the appearance of prosperity.* ○ *I know the dog looks friendly, but don't be fooled by appearances.* **4. PERFORMANCE OR EXHIBITION IN PUBLIC** a performance or exhibition before a public audience ○ *It was the band's first British appearance.* **5. ATTENDANCE IN COURT** attendance in court as a defendant, plaintiff, witness, or legal adviser ○ *The prospect of an appearance in court was daunting.* ◇ **keep up appearances** to maintain an appearance of well-being despite difficulties ◇ **put in an appearance at sth** to attend sth, often only for a short time or to fulfil an obligation

appease /ə peéz/ (**-peases, -peasing, -peased**) *vt.* **1. PACIFY** to pacify sb, especially by acceding to demands **2. SATISFY NEED** to satisfy or relieve sth, especially a physical appetite [14thC. From Old French *apaisier*, from *pais* 'peace' (see PEACE).] —**appeasable** *adj.* —**appeasably** *adv.* —**appeaser** *n.*

appeasement /ə peézmənt/ *n.* **1. PACIFICATION OF POTENTIALLY HOSTILE NATION** the political strategy of pacifying a potentially hostile nation in the hope of avoiding war, often by granting concessions **2. GRANT OF CONCESSIONS** an attempt to stop complaints or reduce difficulties by making concessions

appel /ə pél/ *n.* **1. FENCER'S WARNING STAMP OF FOOT** a stamp of the foot that signals a fencer's intention to start attacking **2. BLOW WITH FENCING BLADE** in fencing, a sharp blow with the blade made to procure an opening [From French, literally 'call']

appellant /ə péllənt/ *n.* LAW the person or group of people in a legal action who bring an appeal [Late 16thC. From Old French *apelant*, the present participle of *apeler* (see APPEAL).]

appellate /ə péllət/ *adj.* LAW having the jurisdiction to hear appeals and review the decisions of lower courts [Mid-18thC. From Latin *appellatus*, the past participle of *appellare* (see APPEAL).]

appellate court *n.* LAW a court with the power to review and reverse the decisions of lower courts

appellate jurisdiction *n.* LAW the power vested in an appellate court authorizing it to review the decisions of lower courts

appellation /áppə láysh'n/ *n.* the name or title by which sth or sb is known (*formal*) [15thC. Via French, 'naming', from, ultimately, Latin *appellare* (see APPEAL).]

appellation contrôlée /áppə lássyoN koN trṓ lay/ (*plural* **appellations contrôlées** /áppə lássyoN koN trṓ lay/) *n.* a certification for French wine that guarantees its origin and verifies that it meets production regulations [From French, literally 'controlled name']

appellative /ə péllətiv/ *n.* **1.** = **appellation** (*formal*) **2.** GRAM = **common noun** ■ *adj.* **1. RELATING TO NAME** connected with a name or title **2. USED AS COMMON NOUN** used as a common noun to describe a class of things —**appellatively** *adv.*

append /ə pénd/ (**-pends, -pending, -pended**) *vt.* **1. ADD EXTRA INFORMATION** to add extra information to sth, especially to attach extra information to a document **2. ADD AUTHORIZED SIGNATURE TO AGREEMENT** to add an authorized signature to a bill or an official agreement as one of the final parts of the ratification or agreement process (*formal*) ○ *All principals to the sale must append their signatures.* **3. ATTACH STH** to attach sth or fasten it to sth else [Mid-17thC. From Latin *appendere*, literally 'to hang upon' (source of English *penthouse*), from *pendere* 'to hang' (see PENDANT).]

appendage /ə péndij/ *n.* **1. SECONDARY ATTACHMENT** sth fastened to sth else as a small or secondary attachment ○ *feeling like an appendage of your family* **2.** ZOOL **PROJECTING BODY PART** a body part or organ e.g. a tail, wing, or fin that projects from the main part of the body

appendant /ə péndənt/ *n.* **1. ATTACHMENT** sth that is attached or added to sth larger or more important **2.** LAW **STH ADDED TO LEGAL DOCUMENT** a secondary document that is attached to the main body of a legal document, e.g. a codicil altering the terms of a will ■ *adj.* **ATTACHED** attached or added to sth larger or more important [Early 16thC. Via Old French *apendant* from, ultimately, Latin *appendere* (see APPEND).]

appendicectomy /áppəndə séktəmi/ (*plural* **-mies** /-miz/), **appendectomy** /áppən déktəmi/ (*plural* **-mies** /-miz/) *n.* a surgical operation to remove the appendix [Late 19thC. Coined from the Latin stem of *appendix* 'APPENDIX' + -ECTOMY.]

appendices plural of **appendix**

appendicitis /ə péndi sítiss/ *n.* an inflammation of the appendix, causing severe pain

appendicular /áppən díkyōōlər/ *adj.* **1. ASSOCIATED WITH LIMBS** used to describe body parts that are associated with the limbs ○ *appendicular muscles* **2. OF APPENDIX** used to describe the appendix [Mid-17thC. Formed from Latin *appendicula*.]

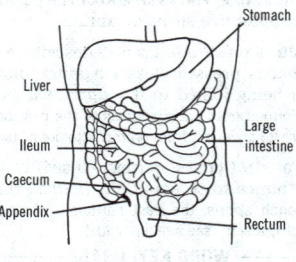

Appendix

Apple

appendix /ə péndiks/ (*plural* **-dixes** *or* **-dices** /-di seez/) *n.* **1.** ANAT SMALL OUTGROWTH FROM LARGE INTESTINE a blind-ended tube leading from the first part of the large intestine (**caecum**), near its junction with the small intestine. In humans it is small, occurs in the lower right-hand part of the abdomen, and contains cells of the immune system. **2.** ADDITIONAL INFORMATION ACCOMPANYING MAIN TEXT a collection of separate material at the end of a book or document **3.** PROJECTING PART a part that projects from sth larger [Mid-16thC. From Latin, from *appendere* (see APPEND).]

apperceive /áppər seé'v/ (**-ceives, -ceiving, -ceived**) *vt.* to comprehend or assimilate sth, e.g. a new idea, in terms of previous experiences or perceptions [Late 19thC. Back-formation from APPERCEPTION.]

apperception /áppər sépsh'n/ *n.* the comprehension or assimilation of sth, e.g. a new idea, in terms of previous experiences or perceptions [Mid-18thC. From the modern Latin stem *apperception-*, literally 'towards perception', from Latin *perceptio* 'perception' (see PERCEPTION).] —**apperceptive** *adj.*

appertain /áppər táyn/ (**-tains, -taining, -tained**) *vi.* to belong or relate to sth (*formal*) ○ *another issue that appertains to the policy under discussion* [14thC. Via Old French *apartenir* from, ultimately, late Latin *appertinere*, literally 'to belong completely to', from *pertinere* 'to belong to' (see PERTAIN).]

appestat /áppə stat/ *n.* the region of the brain that controls appetite and eating [Coined from APPETITE + -STAT]

appetence /áppətənss/, **appetency** /-tənssi/ (*plural* **-cies**) *n.* a desire or longing for sth [Early 17thC. Via French from Latin *appetentia*, from *appetent-*, the present participle stem of *appetere* (see APPETITE).]

appetiser *n.* = appetizer

appetising *adj.* = appetizing

appetite /áppi tīt/ *n.* **1.** DESIRE FOR FOOD a natural desire for food **2.** STRONG DESIRE a strong desire or craving for sth [14thC. Via French from Latin *appetitus* 'desire', from *appetere*, literally 'to seek after', from *petere* 'to seek' (see PETITION).] —**appetitive** /ə péttitiv/ *adj.*

appetizer /áppi tīzər/, **appetiser** *n.* **1.** FOOD SERVED BEFORE MAIN COURSE a small dish of food served at the beginning of a meal to stimulate the appetite **2.** STIMULATING SAMPLE a sample of sth that is meant to stimulate an interest [Mid-19thC. Formed from earlier *appetize* 'to give an appetite', a back-formation from APPETIZING.]

appetizing /áppi tīzing/, **appetising** *adj.* appealing to or stimulating the appetite [Mid-17thC. Anglicization of French *appétissant*, from *appétit* (see APPETITE).] —**appetizingly** *adv.*

appl. *abbr.* applied

applaud /ə pláwd/ (**-plauds, -plauding, -plauded**) *v.* **1.** *vti.* CLAP HANDS to clap hands as a sign of welcome, appreciation, or approval **2.** *vt.* EXPRESS APPROVAL to praise sb or sth ○ *applauded the students' achievement* [15thC. Directly and via French from Latin *applaudere*, literally 'to clap at', from *plaudere* 'to clap' (source of English *plaudit* and *explode*).] —**applaudable** *adj.* —**applauder** *n.* —**applauding** *adj.* —**applaudingly** *adv.*

applause /ə pláwz/ *n.* the clapping of hands to express welcome, enjoyment, appreciation, or approval [Late 16thC. From Latin *applausus*, from *applaus-*, the past participle stem of *applaudere* (see APPLAUD).]

apple /ápp'l/ *n.* **1.** FIRM ROUND FRUIT WITH CENTRAL CORE a firm round fruit with a central core, red or green skin, and white flesh **2.** FRUIT TREE a deciduous Eurasian tree that has white or pink flowers and produces apples. Latin name: *Malus pumila*. [Old English *æppel*] ◇ **the apple of sb's eye** sb or sth very much loved and favoured by another person

apple butter *n.* a smooth spread made of stewed apples flavoured with spices

applecart /ápp'l kaart/ *n.* in former times, a street vendor's cart or barrow from which apples were sold ◇ **upset the applecart** to spoil a plan or arrangement

apple green *n.* a bright green colour with a light tinge of yellow —**apple-green** *adj.*

Apple Isle *n. Aus* Tasmania (*informal*)

applejack /ápp'l jak/ *n.* **1.** BRANDY a brandy distilled from cider **2.** BEVERAGE an alcoholic beverage made from the liquid remaining after cider has been frozen

apple maggot *n.* the larva of a fruit fly that bores into and feeds on the fruit of apple trees. Latin name: *Rhagoletis pomonella*.

apple pie *n.* a dessert made by cooking sliced apples in a pastry case or in a dish with a pastry top

apple-pie *adj. US* characteristic of or embodying the virtues that Americans believe to be typical of US culture, e.g. neighbourliness, civic pride, and honesty (*informal*) ○ *apple-pie honesty* ◇ **in apple-pie order** neat and tidy

apple-pie bed *n.* a way of making a bed with the sheet folded up on itself so that it is impossible to lie full length in the bed [Origin uncertain: probably an alteration of French *nappe pliée* 'folded sheet']

apples and pears *npl. Cockney* stairs (*informal*) [Rhyming slang]

applesauce /ápp'l sawss/ *n.* **1.** CONDIMENT MADE FROM APPLES a sauce of sweetened stewed apples, traditionally served with roast pork **2.** *US* NONSENSE silly nonsense (*informal*)

applet /ápplit/ *n.* **1.** LIMITED COMPUTER PROGRAM a simple computer program that performs a single task and is run from within a larger application **2.** COMPUTER PROGRAM TRANSFERRABLE OVER INTERNET a small piece of computer code, often embedded within a Web page, that can be transferred over the Internet and executed by the recipient's computer

Appleton, Edward Victor (1892–1965) English physicist. He discovered the 'Appleton layer' of ionized gas in the upper atmosphere.

Appleton layer *n.* = F region [Named after Edward V. APPLETON.]

appliance /ə plí ənss/ *n.* **1.** DOMESTIC ELECTRICAL MACHINE an electrical device or machine such as a vacuum cleaner that is used for a particular purpose in the home **2.** = fire engine **3.** PUTTING STH INTO EFFECT the act of putting sth into effect

— WORD KEY: SYNONYMS —
See Synonyms at **implement**.

applicable /ə plíkəb'l, ápplikəb'l/ *adj.* affecting, connected with, or relevant to a particular person, group of people, or situation [Mid-16thC. Via French from, ultimately, Latin *applicare* 'to apply' (see APPLY).] —**applicability** /ápplikə bílləti/ *n.* —**applicably** /ápplik əbli/ *adv.*

applicant /ápplikənt/ *n.* sb who formally applies for sth, e.g. a job, a grant of money, or a place at a university [Early 19thC. From Latin *applicant-*, the present participle stem of *applicare* (see APPLY).]

— WORD KEY: SYNONYMS —
See Synonyms at **candidate**.

application /áppli káysh'n/ *n.* **1.** FORMAL REQUEST FOR STH a formal and usually written request for sth, e.g. a job, a grant of money, or a place at a university **2.** USE OF STH the use sth is put to or the process of putting it to use **3.** RELEVANCE the relevance or value that sth has, especially when it is applied to a certain field or area ○ *the industrial applications of biochemical research* **4.** SPREADING LIQUID ON SURFACE the act of spreading a liquid, such as paint or medicine on a surface **5.** HARD WORK concentration and hard work **6.** COMPUT COMPUTER SOFTWARE a computer program or piece of software designed to perform a specific task [15thC. Via French from, ultimately, Latin *applicare* (see APPLY).]

applicative /ə plíkətiv/ *adj.* capable of being applied [Mid-17thC. Formed from Latin *applicat-*, the past participle stem of *applicare* (see APPLY).] —**applicatively** *adv.*

applicator /áppli kaytər/ *n.* a device used to apply a liquid or powder to a surface [Mid-17thC. Formed from Latin *applicat-*, the past participle stem of *applicare* 'to apply' (see APPLY).]

applicatory /ə plíkətəri/ *adj.* easily or suitably applied [Mid-17thC. Formed from Latin *applicat-*, the past participle stem of *applicare* (see APPLY).]

applied /ə plíd/ *adj.* able to be put to practical use, especially as a branch of a subject that has both practical and theoretical aspects. ◊ **pure**

appliqué /ə plee kay/ *n.* FABRIC PIECES SEWN ON FABRIC shaped pieces of fabric sewn on a foundation fabric to form a design or pattern ■ *vt.* (**-qués, -quéing, -quéd**) SEW FABRIC PIECES ON FABRIC to form a design or pattern by sewing shaped pieces of fabric on a foundation fabric [Mid-18thC. From French, literally 'applied'.]

apply /ə plí/ (**-plies, -plying, -plied**) *v.* **1.** *vi.* MAKE A FORMAL REQUEST FOR STH to make a formal, usually written, request for sth ○ *How do I apply for a tax refund?* **2.** *vt.* USE STH to make use of sth to achieve a result ○ *He applied his first-aid skills to help the accident victims.* **3.** *vi.* BE RELEVANT to be relevant to sb or sth ○ *The requirement applies only if you are over 65.* **4.** *vt.* SPREAD STH to spread a liquid or other material over a surface ○ *Apply a thin layer of cream to the face and neck.* **5.** *vt.* WORK HARD to work hard or spend a significant amount of time on sth ○ *I could have done better if I'd applied myself a bit more.* [14thC. Via Old French *aplier* from Latin *applicare* 'to fold towards', from *plicare* 'to fold' (see PLY).] —**applier** *n.*

appoggiatura /ə pójjə toórə/ (*plural* **-ras** *or* **-re** /-ray/) *n.* in music, an ornamental dissonant note resolving, usually downwards by a step, into a principal note [Mid-18thC. From Italian, literally 'sth supported by another'.]

appoint /ə póynt/ (**-points, -pointing, -pointed**) *vt.* **1.** SELECT SB FOR POSITION OR JOB to select a person or a group of people for an official position or to do a particular job ○ *She's been appointed director.* **2.** AGREE UPON A TIME OR PLACE to fix or agree upon a particular time or place for sth to happen (*formal*) **3.** LAW GIVE CERTAIN POWERS TO TRUSTEE to authorize a trustee to transfer trust property to particular beneficiaries [14thC. From Old French *apointier* 'to arrange, settle', from *a point*, literally 'to a point'.]

appointed /ə póyntid/ *adj.* decorated, furnished, or equipped (*usually used in combination*) ○ *a well-appointed flat*

appointee /ə póyn teé/ *n.* **1.** SB SELECTED FOR JOB sb who is selected for an office or position or to perform a particular job **2.** LAW TRUSTEE RESPONSIBLE FOR TRUST PROPERTY a trustee with the power to transfer trust property to particular beneficiaries

appointive /ə póyntiv/ *adj.* **1.** *US* FILLED BY APPOINTMENT being or relating to a position to which sb is appointed **2.** LAW RELATING TO TRUST PROPERTY relating to trust property that is managed by a trustee with the power to transfer it to beneficiaries

appointment /ə póyntmənt/ *n.* **1. ARRANGEMENT TO MEET SB** an arrangement to have a meeting or to be somewhere at a particular time **2. CHOICE OF SB FOR JOB** the selection of sb for a position, office, or job **3. POSITION OR JOB** a position, office, or job to which sb is appointed **4. SB APPOINTED TO JOB** sb who has been appointed to a position, office, or job **5.** LAW **SELECTION OF TRUSTEE** the selection of a trustee to whom power is given to transfer trust property to beneficiaries ■ **appointments** *npl.* **FURNITURE AND FITTINGS** the furniture, fittings, and equipment belonging to a particular place

appointment book *n.* *US* = **diary**

appointment TV *n.* *US* television programmes that viewers watch regularly and are loyal to

appointor /ə póyntər/ *n.* LAW sb responsible for selecting a trustee to supervise and transfer trust property

Appomattox /àppə máttəks/ city in central Virginia. The courthouse there was the site of the 1865 Confederate surrender to the Union Army that ended the US Civil War. Population: 1,838 (1996).

apport /ə páwrt/ *n.* **1. PRODUCTION OF OBJECTS AT SÉANCE** the production of objects at a spiritualist's séance, supposedly by paranormal means **2. OBJECT PRODUCED AT SÉANCE** an object produced at a spiritualist's séance, supposedly by paranormal means [15thC. From French *aport*, literally 'bringing to', from *aporter* 'to carry to', from *porter* 'to carry' (see PORT).]

apportion /ə páwrsh'n/ (**-tions, -tioning, -tioned**) *vt.* to divide and allocate sth among different people or groups [Late 16thC. Via French from, ultimately, Latin *portio* 'portion' (see PORTION).]

apportionment /ə páwrsh'nmənt/ *n.* **1. ALLOCATION** the division and allocation of sth among people or groups **2.** *US* **DISTRIBUTION OF LEGISLATIVE SEATS** the distribution of seats in the US House of Representatives or a state legislature, based proportionally on the population of states or electoral districts

appose /ə pṓz/ (**-poses, -posing, -posed**) *vt.* to be placed near sth, or place or move sth next to sth else [Late 16thC. Formed from Latin *apponere*, on the model of English *compose* and *expose*.]

apposite /áppəzit/ *adj.* especially well suited to the circumstances [Early 17thC. From Latin *appositus*, the past participle of *apponere* 'to add to, put near', from *ponere* 'to put' (see POSITION).] —**appositely** *adv.* —**appositeness** *n.*

apposition /àppə zísh'n/ *n.* **1. JUXTAPOSITION** the relative position of two things that are next to each other **2.** GRAM **RELATIONSHIP BETWEEN NOUN PHRASES** the relationship between two usually consecutive nouns or noun phrases that refer to the same person or thing and have the same relationship to other sentence elements. In the sentence 'My son, an actor, lives with me', the phrase 'My son, an actor' is an example of apposition. **3.** BIOL **CELL GROWTH IN LAYERS** cell growth in which layers of material are deposited on already existing ones —**appositional** *adj.* —**appositionally** *adv.*

appositive /ə pózzətiv/ *adj.* used to describe words or phrases that refer to the same person or thing and have the same relationship to other sentence elements —**appositive** *n.* —**appositively** *adv.*

appraisal /ə práyz'l/ *n.* **1. EVALUATION** a judgment or opinion on sth or sb, especially one that assesses how effective or useful sth or sb is **2. VALUATION** an estimate of the value of sth

appraise /ə práyz/ (**-praises, -praising, -praised**) *vt.* **1. VALUE STH** to give an estimate of how much money sth is worth **2. ASSESS MERITS OR QUALITY** to give an opinion of sb's merits or sth's quality [15thC. Alteration of APPRIZE, on the model of PRAISE.] —**appraisable** *adj.* —**appraisement** *n.*

WORD KEY: USAGE

appraise or **apprise**? ***Appraise***, meaning 'to assess, evaluate', is used with reference to people or (more usually) the things they do or achieve. *She appraised their work at the end of each week.* **Apprise**, meaning 'inform', is a more formal word and is used with reference to people. *He apprised them of the decisions.*

appraiser /ə práyzər/ *n.* sb whose job is to make appraisals of valuables, e.g. antiques, jewels, and silver

appreciable /ə préeshəb'l/ *adj.* large or important enough to be noticed ○ *There is no appreciable difference between them.* —**appreciably** *adv.*

appreciate /ə préeshi ayt/ (**-ates, -ating, -ated**) *v.* **1.** *vt.* **FEEL GRATITUDE** to feel grateful for sth ○ *I'd appreciate it if you didn't repeat this to anyone.* **2.** *vt.* **VALUE SB OR STH HIGHLY** to recognize and like the qualities in sb or sth **3.** *vt.* **UNDERSTAND STH** to understand fully the meaning or importance of a particular situation **4.** *vi.* **GAIN IN VALUE** to increase in value, especially over time [Mid-17thC. From late Latin *appretiare* 'to value, estimate, rate, appraise', from *pretium* 'money spent, worth, value' (source of English *price*).]

WORD KEY: USAGE

Proper contexts. Language critics' opinions on **appreciate** vary widely. Some critics, explaining that the word's etymology has to do with accurate valuation, say proper use requires it to be used only in neutral contexts (*I appreciate your position*). Others, pointing out that *appreciation* is admiration or gratitude, say it should be used only in favorable contexts (*I appreciate your honesty*). Still others argue that the verb's object should always be a noun (*I appreciate your annoyance*), not a clause (*I appreciate how angry you are*). Certainly it is worth remembering the verb's continuing ties to the ideas of valuation and gratitude, and worth remembering, too, that no one objects to *recognize* or *realize* or *understand* in negative contexts or before clauses.

appreciation /ə préeshi áysh'n/ *n.* **1. GRATEFULNESS** a feeling or expression of gratitude ○ *a token of my appreciation* **2. POSITIVE OPINION** a favourable opinion of sth **3. VALUING STH HIGHLY** recognition and liking of sth's qualities **4. FULL UNDERSTANDING** a full understanding of the meaning and importance of sth **5. GROWTH IN VALUE** an increase in value, especially over time

appreciative /ə préeshi ətiv, -shətiv/ *adj.* expressing or feeling gratitude or approval —**appreciatively** *adv.* —**appreciativeness** *n.*

apprehend /àppri hénd/ (**-hends, -hending, -hended**) *vt.* **1. ARREST SB** to put sb suspected of wrongdoing into legal custody **2. UNDERSTAND STH** to grasp the importance, significance, or meaning of sth **3. BECOME AWARE OF STH** to become aware of sth by use of the senses (*formal*) **4. BE FEARFUL OF STH** to await an impending disaster or other calamity with fear or dread (*formal*) [14thC. Directly or via Old French from Latin *apprehendere* 'to take hold of', from *prehendere* 'to seize' (see PREHENSILE).]

apprehensible /àppri hénssəb'l/ *adj.* capable of being understood

apprehension /àppri hénsh'n/ *n.* **1. DREAD** a feeling of anxiety or fear that sth bad or unpleasant will happen **2. IDEA** an idea formed by observation or experience **3. ARREST** the taking of a criminal suspect into custody (*formal*) **4. ABILITY TO UNDERSTAND** the power or ability to grasp the importance, significance, or meaning of sth (*formal*) [14thC. Directly or via Old French from the late Latin stem *apprehension-*, from *apprehens-*, the past participle stem of Latin *apprehendere* (see APPREHEND).]

apprehensive /àppri hénssiv/ *adj.* **1. FEARFUL** worried that sth bad will happen **2. AWARE** aware or cognizant of sth nonphysical, e.g. implications or results (*formal*) —**apprehensively** *adv.* —**apprehensiveness** *n.*

apprentice /ə préntiss/ *n.* **1. TRAINEE** sb who works under a skilled professional in order to learn an art, craft, or trade and become qualified in it **2. INEXPERIENCED PERSON** a novice or amateur ■ *vt.* (**-tices, -ticing, -ticed**) **MAKE SB APPRENTICE** to give sb work as an apprentice to a skilled professional ○ *He was apprenticed to a master sailmaker for five years.* [14thC. From Old French *aprentis*, from *aprendre* 'to learn', from Latin *apprehendere* (see APPREHEND).]

WORD KEY: SYNONYMS

See Synonyms at ***beginner***.

apprenticeship /ə préntiss ship/ *n.* **1. STATUS OF APPRENTICE** an apprentice's status or conditions of employment **2. TIME SPENT AS APPRENTICE** the period of time that an apprentice spends training

appressed /ə prést/ *adj.* used to describe a part of a plant that is pressed closely against another part without being joined to it ○ *appressed leaves* [Late 18thC. Formed from Latin *appressus*, the past participle of *apprimere* 'to press to', from *premere* 'to press' (see PRESS).]

apprise /ə prīz/ (**-prises, -prising, -prised**) *vt.* to inform or give notice to sb about sth (*formal*) [Late 17thC. From French *appris*, the past participle of *apprendre* 'to make learn, teach' (see APPRENTICE).]

WORD KEY: USAGE

See Usage note at ***appraise***.

apprize /ə prīz/ (**-prizes, -prizing, -prized**) *vt.* to value sth very highly, e.g. because of its monetary worth (*formal*) [15thC. Via Old French *aprisier* from Latin *appretiare* (see APPRECIATE).]

approach /ə prṓch/ *v.* (**-proaches, -proaching, -proached**) **1.** *vti.* **MOVE CLOSER** to move closer to sb or sth ○ *He motioned to us to approach.* **2.** *vt.* **ASK SB** to speak to sb with a view to asking for sth **3.** *vt.* **TREAT STH IN PARTICULAR WAY** to deal with sth in a particular way ○ *Try approaching the article from a fresh angle.* **4.** *vt.* **BORDER ON STH** to be almost at a particular level or state **5.** *vti.* **COME CLOSER IN TIME** to come nearer in time to sth ○ *As spring approaches I notice people smiling more.* **6.** *vi.* GOLF **HIT BALL FROM FAIRWAY TO GREEN** to make a golf shot from the fairway towards a green ■ *n.* **1. COMING** a coming nearer in space or time **2. METHOD** a way of doing or solving sth **3. MAKING OF CONTACT** an informal request, offer, suggestion, or proposal made to sb (*often used in the plural*) **4. SIMILAR THING** one thing that is very similar in its nature or qualities to another **5. ACCESS** a way of reaching or gaining access to a building or place **6. AIRCRAFT'S COURSE TO LANDING SITE** the path that an aircraft follows as it prepares to land **7.** BOWLING **PLAYER'S PREPARATION TO RELEASE BOWLING BALL** the steps sb takes before releasing the ball in ten-pin bowling, or the part of the bowling lane used for doing this **8.** GOLF **SHOT FROM FAIRWAY TO GREEN** a golf shot made from the fairway towards the green [14thC. Via Old French *aproch(i)er* from late Latin *appropiare* 'to go nearer to', from *propius* 'nearer' (see PROPINQUITY).]

approachable /ə prṓchəb'l/ *adj.* **1. INVITINGLY FRIENDLY** friendly and easy to talk to **2. EASILY ACCESSIBLE** able to be reached with ease, especially in terms of transportation **3. USER-FRIENDLY** easy for nonspecialists to understand —**approachability** /ə prṓchə bíllətì/ *n.* —**approachableness** /ə prṓchəb'lnəss/ *n.*

approaching /ə prṓching/ *adj.* coming near in space or time

approach shot *n.* **1.** TENNIS **SHOT HIT DEEP INTO OPPONENT'S COURT** a tennis shot hit deep into the opponent's court, designed to give the player time to approach the net for the next shot **2.** GOLF = **approach** *n.* **8**

approbation /àpprə báysh'n/ *n.* **1. EXPRESSION OF APPROVAL** approval, consent, or appreciation **2. OFFICIAL SANCTION** the official approving, authorizing, or sanctioning of sth —**approbative** /àpprə baytiv/ *adj.* —**approbatory** /-báytəri/ *adj.*

appropriable /ə prṓpri əb'l/ *adj.* able or likely to be appropriated

appropriate *adj.* /ə prṓpri ət/ **FITTING** suitable for the occasion or circumstances ■ *vt.* /ə prṓpri ayt/ (**-ates, -ating, -ated**) **1. TAKE STH FOR OWN USE** to take or use sth forcefully or without permission ○ *They should act before rival parties appropriate the moral high ground.* **2. USE MONEY FOR PARTICULAR PURPOSE** to set aside an amount of money for a particular use [15thC. From late Latin *appropriatus*, the past participle of Latin *appropriare* 'to make your own', from *propius* 'own' (source of English *proper*).] —**appropriately** /ə prṓpri ətli/ *adv.* —**appropriateness** /-ətnəss/ *n.* —**appropriative** /-aytiv/ *adj.* —**appropriator** /-aytor/ *n.*

appropriation /əprṓpri áysh'n/ *n.* **1. TAKING STH FOR OWN USE** the taking or using of sth forcefully or without permission **2. MONEY FOR PARTICULAR PURPOSE** a sum of money that has been set aside from a budget, especially a government budget, for a particular purpose (*often used in the plural*)

approval /ə pro͞ov'l/ *n.* **1.** GOOD OPINION a favourable opinion or feeling about sth **2.** OFFICIAL SANCTION formal or official agreement or permission ◇ **on approval** with the opportunity to try sth before deciding whether you really want to buy it

approve /ə pro͞ov/ (**-proves, -proving, -proved**) *v.* **1.** *vi.* LIKE SB OR STH to have a favourable opinion of sb or sth **2.** *vt.* GIVE STH OFFICIAL AGREEMENT OR ACCEPTANCE to agree officially to sth, or accept that sth has reached a required standard **3.** *vt.* PROVE STH to prove sth by trial or testing (*archaic*) [14thC. Via Old French from Latin *approbare* 'to assent to as good', from *probus* 'good' (source of English *probity*).] —**approvable** *adj.*

approved /ə pro͞ovd/ *adj.* **1.** GENERALLY ACCEPTED accepted by most people as appropriate or correct **2.** OFFICIALLY SANCTIONED officially accepted or permitted

approved school *n.* a reform school or detention centre for young offenders (*dated*)

approx. *abbr.* **1.** approximate **2.** approximately

approximal /ə próksim'l/ *adj.* used to describe, or relating to, teeth that are side by side or set close together

approximate *adj.* /ə próksi mət/ **1.** NEARLY EXACT not quite exact, but only slightly more or less in number or quantity **2.** SIMILAR similar in nature, appearance, or characteristics to sth else ■ *v.* /ə próksi mayt/ (**-mates, -mating, -mated**) **1.** *vti.* BE SIMILAR TO STH to be or become similar to sth in nature, size, or extent ○ *There was nothing in the terms of the treaty that even approximated to the negotiators' original thinking.* **2.** *vt.* ESTIMATE STH to make or provide an estimate, usually a rough estimate, of sth **3.** *vti.* COME OR BRING CLOSE to come or bring sth close to sth else [15thC. From late Latin *approximatus*, the past participle of *approximare* 'to draw near to', from Latin *proximus* 'near' (source of English *proximity*).] —**approximateness** /-mətnəss/ *n.* —**approximative** /-mətiv/ *adj.*

approximately /ə próksimətli/ *adv.* not exactly, but nearly or roughly

approximation /ə próksi máysh'n/ *n.* **1.** ROUGH CALCULATION a figure that is not exact, but is only slightly higher or lower than a given amount **2.** SIMILAR THING sth that is very similar to sth else **3.** ESTIMATION the guessing or estimating of an amount or number ○ *figures arrived at by approximation*

appt *abbr.* appointment

appulse /ə púlss/ *n.* a near approach of two celestial bodies that does not result in a partial concealment or an eclipse [Early 17thC. From Latin *appulsus*, the past participle of *appellere* 'to drive to, force towards', from *pellere* 'to drive'.]

appurtenance /ə púrtinənsz/ *n.* **1.** ACCESSORY an accompanying part or feature of sth (*formal*) (*often used in the plural*) ○ *an athletic club with all the usual appurtenances* **2.** LAW MINOR RIGHT a legal right or privilege attached to a property and inherited with it ■ **appurtenances** *npl.* EQUIPMENT the equipment needed for a particular activity (*formal*) [14thC. Via Anglo-French from, ultimately, late Latin *appertinere* (see APPERTAIN).] —**appurtenant** *adj.*

APR *abbr.* **1.** annual percentage rate **2.** annual purchase rate (*used to show repayment rates in hire-purchase schemes*)

Apr. *abbr.* April

apraxia /ay práksi ə, ə-/ *n.* loss of the ability to perform complex movements, often as a result of brain damage, e.g. following a stroke [Late 19thC. Via German from Greek, 'inaction'.] —**apraxic** /ay práksik, ə-/ *adj.*

après-ski /áppray skee/ *n.* SOCIALIZING AFTER SKIING social activities taking place after skiing ■ *adj.* AFTER SKIING taking place during or appropriate to the period of time after skiing [Mid-20thC. From French, literally 'after skiing'.]

apricot /áypri kot/ *n.* **1.** FRUIT a small round fruit with a soft furry yellowish-orange skin and a single stone **2.** FRUIT TREE a tree widely cultivated in temperate climates for its small yellowish-orange fruits. Latin name: *Prunus armeniaca.* **3.** YELLOWISH-ORANGE COLOUR a pale yellowish-orange colour, like that of an apricot ■ *adj.* YELLOWISH-ORANGE of a pale yellowish-orange colour, like an apricot [Mid-16thC. Via obsolete Catalan *abrecoc* from Arabic *al-barqūq*, literally 'the apricot'.]

Apricot

WORD KEY: ORIGIN

The ***apricot*** got its name because the Romans regarded it as a type of early-ripening peach. They therefore applied to it the epithet *praecocus* (a variant of *praecox*, from which English gets *precocious*). This passed via Byzantine Greek *berikokkia* into Arabic where, with the definite article *al*, it became *al-birqūq* or *al-barqūq*. Catalan adopted this as *abrecoc*, which is how English acquired the word (the earliest recorded English spelling is *abrecock*). The final *-t* came soon after, from French.

April /áyprəl/ *n.* in the Gregorian calendar, the fourth month of the year, made up of 30 days [14thC. From Latin *Aprilis*, from Etruscan *apru*, from Greek *Aphrō*, a shortening of *Aphroditē* (see APHRODITE).]

April fool *n.* **1.** TARGET OF JOKE sb who is the victim of a practical joke on April Fools' Day **2.** JOKE PLAYED ON SB a practical joke played on sb on April Fools' Day ■ *interj.* ANNOUNCING THAT JOKE HAS BEEN PLAYED used to tell sb that he or she has been the victim of an April Fools' Day joke

April Fools' Day *n.* April 1, traditionally a day on which practical jokes are played on other people

a priori /áy prī áwrī, àa pri áwri/ *adj.* **1.** BASED ON STH KNOWN working from sth that is already known or self-evident to arrive at a conclusion **2.** ASSUMED known or assumed without reference to experience **3.** MADE BEFOREHAND conceived or formulated before investigation or experience [Mid-17thC. From Latin, literally 'from the previous (one, cause, hypothesis)'.] —**a priori** *adv.* —**apriority** /áyprī órrəti/ *n.*

apron /áyprən/ *n.* **1.** PROTECTIVE GARMENT TIED OVER CLOTHES a garment worn over the front of clothes to keep them clean during working, especially cooking. An apron is usually tied around the waist and often has a bib to cover the chest. **2.** TECH PROTECTIVE PART a shield or plate fitted to a machine that protects the user from flying debris **3.** PROJECTING EDGE the projecting edge of a platform, e.g. a theatre stage, dock, or loading bay **4.** AIR PARKING AREA FOR PLANES the hard-surfaced area immediately in front of airport buildings, on which aircraft are loaded and unloaded **5.** GOLF BORDER AROUND GREEN the outer edge of a green on a golf course **6.** BOXING AREA OUTSIDE BOXING RING ROPES the part of the floor of a boxing ring that is outside the ropes **7.** GEOG LOW-ANGLED SURFACE a gently sloping surface of sand, gravel, or bare rock, usually in front of a mountain range **8.** INDUST CONVEYOR BELT MADE OF SLATS a conveyor belt made of slats loosely attached to each other in a way that allows the belt to go around curves **9.** TRANSP = **skirt** *n.* 4 [14thC. From Old French *naperon*, literally 'small cloth', from *nape* 'tablecloth', from Latin *mappa* 'napkin' (source of English *napkin*). The original phrase 'a napron' was later construed as 'an apron'.]

apron stage *n.* a stage that juts out into the auditorium

apropos /àpprə pṓ/ *prep.* IN REGARD TO on the subject of (*formal*) ○ *We've had further correspondence from them apropos our application for funds.* ■ *adj.* JUST RIGHT appropriate in a particular situation (*formal*) ■ *adv.* INCIDENTALLY by the way (*formal*) ○ *Apropos, do you think we should delay the announcement?* [Mid-17thC. From French *à propos*, literally 'to the purpose', a translation of Latin *ad propositum*.]

aprotic /ay prṓtik/ *adj.* used to describe a solvent that is unable to donate protons [Mid-20thC. Coined from A- + PROTON + -IC.]

apse /aps/ *n.* **1.** ARCHIT ROUNDED PROJECTION ON BUILDING a semicircular projecting part of a building, especially the east end of a church that contains the altar **2.** ASTRON = **apsis** [Early 19thC. From Latin *apsis* (see APSIS).] —**apsidal** /ap sīd'l, ápsid'l/ *adj.*

apsis /ápsiss/ (*plural* **-sides** /-deez/) *n.* **1.** ASTRON NEAREST OR FARTHEST POINT IN ORBIT either of the two points in an orbit that are nearest to and farthest from the centre of gravitational attraction **2.** ARCHIT = **apse** [Late 16thC. Via Latin from Greek *(h)apsis* 'rim of a wheel, wheel, arch, vault', perhaps from *haptein* 'to fasten'.] —**apsidal** /ápsid'l, apsīd'l/ *adj.*

apt /apt/ *adj.* **1.** VERY APPROPRIATE especially suited to the circumstances **2.** LIKELY often doing sth and likely to do it again ○ *He is apt to get angry when people question him.* **3.** QUICK TO LEARN enthusiastic and quick to learn new things [14thC. Directly or via Old French from Latin *aptus*, past participle of *apere* 'to fit, fasten, join'.] —**aptly** *adv.* —**aptness** *n.*

WORD KEY: USAGE

See Usage note at ***likely.***

WORD KEY: ORIGIN

The Latin word *apere* from which ***apt*** is derived is also the source of English *adapt, adept, attitude, copulate, couple,* and *inept.*

APT *abbr.* advanced passenger train

apt. *abbr.* apartment

apteral /áptərəl/ *adj.* **1.** WITHOUT COLUMNS used to describe a classical temple that has no columns along its sides **2.** WITHOUT AISLES used to describe a church that has no aisles [Mid-19thC. Formed from Greek *apteros* 'wingless', from *pteron* 'wing, feather' (source of English *pterodactyl*).]

apterous /áptərəss/ *adj.* used to describe an insect that has no wings [Late 18thC. Formed from Greek *apteros* (see APTERAL).]

apteryx /áptəriks/ *n.* = **kiwi** [Early 19thC. From modern Latin, coined from Greek *a-* 'without' + *pterux* 'wing'.]

aptitude /ápti tyood/ *n.* **1.** POTENTIAL TO ACQUIRE SKILL a natural talent or ability for sth, especially one that is not yet fully developed ○ *pupils of varying aptitudes* **2.** QUICKNESS IN LEARNING quickness and ease in learning

WORD KEY: SYNONYMS

See Synonyms at ***ability*** and ***talent.***

aptitude test *n.* a test to determine how readily sb is likely to be able to develop certain skills, especially in order to do a particular kind of work

Apus /áypəss/ *n.* a faint constellation lying near the south celestial pole

apyrase /áppə rayz, -rays/ *n.* an enzyme that aids the breakdown of ATP, yielding phosphate and energy [Mid-20thC. Contraction of ADENYL PYROPHOSPHATASE, its chemical name.]

apyrexia /áypī réksi ə, àppī-/ *n.* absence of fever, or a period during which a patient experiences no fever [Mid-17thC. Via modern Latin from Greek *apurexia.*] —**apyretic** /-réttik, -/ *adj.* —**apyrexial** *adj.*

AQ *abbr.* EDUC achievement quotient

aq. *abbr.* **1.** aqua **2.** GEOL aqueous

Aqaba, Gulf of /ákəbə/ northeastern arm of the Red Sea, bordered by Egypt's Sinai Peninsula on the east, Israel on the north, and Saudi Arabia on the west. It is of great strategic importance in the Middle East, as it provides Israel with its only access to the Red Sea. Length: 160 km/100 mi.

Aqmola /aak móllə/ former name for **Astana**

aqua /ákwə/ *n.* (*plural* **aquae** /-wee, -wī/ *or* **aquas**) **1.** WATER water, especially when used as a solvent (*technical*) **2.** = **aquamarine** ■ *adj.* = **aquamarine** [14thC. From Latin. Ultimately from an Indo-European base that is also the source of the 'i' in *island.*]

aqua- *prefix.* water ○ *aquanaut* [From Latin *aqua* (see AQUA)]

aquacrop /ákwə krop/ *n.* a crop produced by deliberate cultivation of organisms that live in the sea or fresh water, e.g. fish produced by fish-farming [Late 20thC. Coined from AQUACULTURE + CROP.]

aquaculture /ákwə kulchər/, **aquiculture** /ákwi-/ *n.* 1. FARMING FISH AND AQUATIC PLANTS the farming of marine and freshwater plants and animals for human consumption 2. = hydroponics [Mid-19thC. Modelled on AGRICULTURE.] —**aquacultural** /ákwə kúlchərəl/ *adj.* —**aquaculturist** *n.*

aquadynamic /ákwə dī námmik/ *adj.* having a smooth or streamlined surface in order to reduce drag when passing through water [Late 20thC. Modelled on AERODYNAMIC.]

aquae plural of aqua

aquaerobics *n.* = aquarobics

aqua fortis /-fáwrtiss/ *n.* nitric acid (*archaic*) [15thC. From Latin, literally 'strong water'.]

aqualung /ákwə lung/ *n.* an underwater breathing apparatus that is used by divers

aquamarine /ákwə mə reén/ *n.* 1. GREENISH-BLUE GEMSTONE a greenish-blue variety of the mineral beryl, used as a gemstone 2. GREENISH BLUE a greenish-blue colour ■ *adj.* GREENISH-BLUE of a greenish-blue colour [Late 16thC. From Latin *aqua marina* 'sea water' (the colour of the stone).]

aquanaut /ákwə nawt/ *n.* sb with training and equipment to spend long periods working or swimming underwater [Late 19thC. Coined from AQUA- + Greek *nautēs* 'sailor', on the model of ARGONAUT.]

aquaphobia /ákwə fóbi ə/ *n.* an abnormal fear of water

aquaplane /ákwə playn/ *n.* WATER-SKIING BOARD a water-skiing board on which sb stands while being towed by a motorboat ■ *vi.* (-planes, -planing, -planed) 1. RIDE ON AN AQUAPLANE to ride on an aquaplane 2. LOSE CONTROL IN WET CONDITIONS to skid out of control at high speed on a surface that is so wet that it causes the vehicle's tyres to lose contact with the road. US term **hydroplane**

aqua regia /-reéji ə/ *n.* a fuming, highly corrosive mixture of nitric and hydrochloric acid that is used to dissolve metals, including gold [Early 17thC. From Latin, literally 'royal water', so called because it can dissolve gold and other 'noble' metals.]

aquarelle /ákwə rél/ *n.* 1. WATERCOLOUR PAINTING TECHNIQUE a painting technique that uses transparent washes of watercolour 2. PAINTED PICTURE a painting produced using the aquarelle technique [Mid-19thC. Via French from obsolete Italian *acquarella* 'watercolour', from *acqua* 'water'.] —**aquarellist** *n.*

aquaria plural of aquarium

Aquarian /ə kwáiri ən/ *n.* = Aquarius *n.* 3 —**Aquarian** *adj.*

aquarist /ákwərist/ *n.* sb who looks after an aquarium as a hobby or a profession

aquarium /ə kwáiri əm/ *n.* (plural -ums or -a /-ri ə/) *n.* 1. CONTAINER FOR FISH a water-filled transparent container, often box-shaped, in which fish and other aquatic animals and plants are kept 2. AQUATIC ZOO a building in which fish and other aquatic animals are kept and shown to the public [Mid-19thC. Formed from Latin *aquarius* (see AQUARIUS) on the model of VIVARIUM.]

Aquarius /ə kwáiri əss/ *n.* 1. ASTRON CONSTELLATION IN SOUTHERN HEMISPHERE a constellation in the sky of the southern hemisphere between Pisces and Capricornus 2. ZODIAC 11TH SIGN OF ZODIAC the 11th sign of the zodiac, represented by a man pouring water, and lasting from approximately 20 January to 18 February. Aquarius is classified as an air sign and its ruling planets are Saturn and Uranus. 3. ZODIAC SB BORN UNDER AQUARIUS sb whose birthday falls between 20 January and 18 February [14thC. From Latin, 'water carrier', a noun use of *aquarius* 'of water', from *aqua* (see AQUA).] —**Aquarius** *adj.*

aquarobics /ákwə róbiks/, **aquaerobics** *n.* aerobic exercises done to music in a swimming pool (*takes a singular or plural verb*) [Late 20thC. Blend of AQUA- and AEROBICS.]

aquatic /ə kwáttik/ *adj.* 1. OF WATER connected with, consisting of, or dependent upon water 2. LIVING IN WATER living or growing in water 3. DONE IN WATER played or performed in or on water ■ *n.* WATER PLANT

OR ANIMAL a plant or animal that lives or grows in water —**aquatically** *adv.*

aquatics /ə kwáttiks/ *n.* sports played in or on water (*takes a singular or plural verb*)

aquatint /ákwə tint/ *n.* 1. ETCHING METHOD a method of etching a copper plate in which the prints produced from it show areas similar to watercolours. This effect is produced by varying the etching times used for different areas of the plate. 2. ETCHED PICTURE an etching produced by the aquatint process [Late 18thC. Via French *aquatinte* from Italian *acquatinta*, literally 'tinted water'.] —**aquatinter** *n.* —**aquatintist** *n.*

aquavit /ákwəvit/ *n.* a potato- or grain-based spirit flavoured with caraway seeds, produced in Scandinavia [Late 19thC. Via Danish, Norwegian, Swedish *aquavit* from Latin *aqua vitae* (see AQUA VITAE).]

aqua vitae /ákwə vī tee, -vee tī/ *n.* a strong spirit, especially brandy [14thC. From Latin, literally 'water of life'.]

Aqueduct: Ancient Roman aqueduct in Tarragona, Spain

aqueduct /ákwi dukt/ *n.* 1. STRUCTURE CARRYING CANAL a structure in the form of a bridge that carries a canal across a valley or river 2. CHANNEL FOR WATER a pipe or channel for moving water to a lower level, often across a great distance 3. ANAT CHANNEL CARRYING FLUID IN BODY a channel in an organ or body part through which fluid passes [Mid-16thC. Via medieval Latin *aqueductus*, from Latin *aquae ductus* 'water conveyance'.]

aqueous /áykwi əss, ákwi-/ *adj.* 1. WATERY containing, dissolved in, or consisting mostly of water 2. GEOL FORMED FROM MATERIAL CARRIED BY WATER used to describe rocks or deposits that are formed from material carried by water [Mid-17thC. From medieval Latin *aqueus*, from Latin *aqua* (see AQUA).]

aqueous humour *n.* the transparent fluid that circulates in the eye chamber between the back of the cornea and the front of the iris and pupil. It also permeates the vitreous humour behind the lens.

aqui- *prefix.* water ○ *aquifer* [From Latin *aqua* (see AQUA)]

aquiculture *n.* = aquaculture

aquifer /ákwifər/ *n.* a layer of permeable rock, sand, or gravel through which groundwater flows, containing enough water to supply wells and springs

Aquila /ákwilə, ə kwíllə/ *n.* a constellation on the celestial equator near Aquarius lying across the Milky Way. It contains the bright star Altair.

aquilegia /ákwi leéji ə/ *n.* (plural -as or -a) a perennial plant with drooping purple, pink, blue, or red flowers on tall stalks and leaves with five rounded lobes. Genus: *Aquilegia*. [Late 16thC. From medieval Latin, of uncertain origin: probably formed from Latin *aquilegus* 'water-collecting'.]

aquiline /ákwi līn/ *adj.* 1. THIN AND CURVED thin, curved, and pointed like an eagle's beak 2. OF EAGLES resembling or connected with eagles [Mid-17thC. From Latin *aquilinus*, from *aquila* 'eagle'.] —**aquilinity** /ákwi línnəti/ *n.*

Aquinas /ə kwínəss/, **Thomas, St** (1225–74) Italian philosopher and theologian who sought to reconcile the philosophy of Aristotle with the theology of St Augustine.

Aquino /ə kee nō/, **Corazón** (b. 1933) Filipino government leader. She was president of the Philippines (1986–92) after the uprising against Ferdinand Marcos.

Aquitaine /ákwi tayn/ *n.* region of France, situated in the southwest. It includes the departments of Dordogne, Gironde, Landes, Lot-et-Garonne, and Pyrénées-Atlantiques. It corresponds roughly to the same as the Roman administrative region of Aquitania. Capital: Bordeaux. Population: 2,795,800 (1990). Area: 41,308 sq. km/15,949 sq. mi.

aquiver /ə kwívvər/ *adj.* quivering, especially from excitement or agitation

Ar *symbol.* argon

AR *abbr.* 1. A/R account receivable 2. Arkansas

ar. *abbr.* 1. arrival 2. arrive

Ar. *abbr.* Arabia ■ *abbr.* 1. Arabian 2. Arabic

a.r. *abbr.* anno regni [From Latin, 'in the year of the reign']

-ar *suffix.* of, relating to, or resembling ○ *nebular* [Via Old French *-ar* from Latin *-aris*, an alternative for *-alis*]

Ara /áarə/ *n.* a faint constellation of the southern hemisphere lying in the Milky Way near Scorpius

ARA *abbr.* Associate of the Royal Academy

Arab /árrəb/ *n.* MEMBER OF SEMITIC PEOPLE a member of a Semitic Arabic-speaking people who live throughout North Africa and the Middle East ■ *adj.* = Arabian [14thC. Via Old French and Latin from the Greek stem *Arab-* from Arabic *arab.*]

——— **WORD KEY: USAGE** ———

Arab, Arabic, Arabian: *Arab* denotes a person, and is also used attributively (i.e. before a noun) as a kind of adjective (*the Arab people, Arab fears*). *Arabian* is an adjective referring to **Arabia** in geographical terms (*the Arabian peninsula, an Arabian camel*); and **Arabic** is a noun and adjective meaning the language (*She speaks Arabic and knows Arabic literature*). **Arabic** is written with a capital initial letter in **Arabic** numerals (1, 2, 3, etc.), and with a small initial letter in the term **gum arabic**, a substance obtained from African acacia trees.

Arab. *abbr.* Arabia ■ *abbr.* 1. Arabian 2. Arabic

arabesque /árrə bésk/ *n.* 1. ARTS ORNATE DESIGN an intricate and often symmetrical design, or style of design, incorporating curves, geometric patterns, leaves, flowers, and animal shapes 2. DANCE BALLET POSTURE a ballet position in which the dancer stands on one leg with the other extended back and both arms stretched out, usually one forward and the other backward 3. MUSIC MUSIC WITH ORNATE MELODY a piece of classical music characterized by decorative melody. The term is often applied to 19th-century compositions for solo piano. [Early 17thC. Via French from Italian *arabesco* 'in the Arabian style'.]

Arabia /ə ráybi ə/ *n.* peninsula of southwestern Asia, bordering the Persian Gulf, the Arabian Sea, and the Red Sea. Area: 3,000,000 sq. km/1,160,000 sq. mi.

Arabian /ə ráybi ən/ *adj.* OF ARABIA relating to or typical of Arabia, or its peoples or cultures ■ *n.* 1. SB FROM ARABIA sb who was born or brought up in one of the countries of the Arabian Peninsula 2. = Arabian horse

——— **WORD KEY: USAGE** ———

See Usage note at *Arab.*

Arabian camel *n.* = dromedary

Arabian horse *n.* a horse belonging to a breed native to Arabia and known for its intelligence, graceful build, and speed

Arabian Peninsula = Arabia

Arabian Sea part of the Indian Ocean, extending from the Arabian Peninsula to the Indian subcontinent

Arabic /árrəbik/ *n.* SEMITIC LANGUAGE OF MIDDLE EAST a Semitic language that is the official language of several countries of North Africa and the Middle East. It is spoken by about 150 million people, with around a further 175 million using it as a second language. ■ *adj.* 1. OF ARABIA relating to or typical of Arabia, or its people or culture 2. OF ARABIC relating or belonging to the Arabic language

——— **WORD KEY: USAGE** ———

See Usage note at *Arab.*

arabica /ə rábbikə/ *n.* 1. PLANTS COFFEE SPECIES a widely grown species of coffee bush producing high-quality

coffee. Latin name: *Coffea arabica*. **2.** KIND OF STRONG
FLAVOURED COFFEE coffee made with arabica coffee
beans [Early 20thC. From modern Latin, species name,
'Arabic'.]

Arabicize /ə rábbi sīz/ (**-cizes, -cizing, -cized**), **Arabicise**
(**-cises, -cising, -cised**) v. **1.** ADAPT WORD TO ARABIC to
adapt a word or other language feature for use in
Arabic **2.** vti. = **Arabize** —**Arabicization** /ə rábbi sī
záysh'n/ n.

Arabic numeral n. any of the symbols 0, 1, 2, 3, 4, 5,
6, 7, 8, and 9 that are used to represent numbers

arabinose /ə rábbinōz, -noss/ n. a sugar (**aldose**)
derived from various plant gums and used in culturing. Formula: $C_5H_{10}O_5$. [Late 19thC. Coined from GUM
ARABIC + -IN + -OSE.]

Arabist /árrəbist/ n. **1.** EXPERT ON ARABS a student of or
expert on the Arabs, their language, or their culture
2. SUPPORTER OF ARABS sb who favours Arab causes or
political positions

Arabize /árrə bīz/ (**-izes, -izing, -ized**), **Arabise** (**-ises,
-ising, -ised**) vti. to conform, or make sth conform,
to Arab customs or culture —**Arabization** /árrə bī
záysh'n/ n.

arable /árrəb'l/ adj. **1.** SUITABLE FOR GROWING CROPS capable
of being cultivated for growing crops **2.** RELATING TO
LARGE-SCALE CULTIVATION relating to, involving, or produced by the large-scale cultivation of field crops
such as cereals and potatoes ■ n. LAND SUITABLE FOR
CULTIVATION land that is fit for planting crops [15thC.
Via Old French from Latin *arabilis*, from *arare* 'to plough'.] —
arability /árrə bílləti/ n.

Arab League n. a political and economic association
of Arab states, formed in 1945

Araby /árrəbi/ n. Arabia (*archaic or literary*) [12thC. Via
Old French *ar(r)abi* 'Arabian', probably from, ultimately,
Arabic *arab* 'Arab'.]

arachidonic acid /árrəkə dónnik-/ n. an unsaturated
fatty acid found in most animal fats and considered
essential in human nutrition. Formula: $C_{20}H_{32}O_2$.
[Early 20thC. 'Arachidonic' coined from the modern Latin
stem *arachid-* 'peanut' (from Greek *arakhos* 'type of leguminous plant') + -ONE + -IC.]

arachnid /ə ráknid/ n. a member of a large class of
animals that includes spiders, scorpions, and mites.
Arachnids have four pairs of legs and a body with
two segments. Class: Arachnida. [Mid-19thC. From
modern Latin *Arachnida*, class name, from Greek *arakhnē*
'spider'.] —**arachnidan** adj.

arachnoid /ə rák noyd/ n. **1.** ANAT MEMBRANE IN SPINAL CORD
the middle of the three membranes that envelop the
brain and spinal cord **2.** ZOOL = **arachnid** ■ adj. ZOOL
LIKE AN ARACHNID resembling or related to an arachnid [Mid-18thC. Via modern Latin from Greek *arakhnoeidēs*
'cobweb-like', from *arakhnē* (see ARACHNID).]

arachnology /árrak nólləji/ n. the branch of zoology
concerned with the study of spiders and other
arachnids [Mid-19thC. Coined from Greek *arakhnē* 'spider'
+ -LOGY.] —**arachnologist** n.

arachnophobia /ə ráknə fōbi ə/ n. an abnormally
strong fear of spiders [Early 20thC. Coined from Greek
arakhnē 'spider' + -PHOBIA.] —**arachnophobe** /ə ráknəfōb/
n. —**arachnophobic** /ə ráknə fōbik/ adj.

Yasir Arafat

Arafat /árrə fat/, **Yasir** (b. 1929) Palestinian leader.
He became chairman of the Palestine Liberation
Organization (1968) and shared the 1994 Nobel Peace
Prize with Itzhak Rabin.

Arafura Sea /árrə fóorə-/ area of the Pacific Ocean
between the northern coast of Australia, New
Guinea, and eastern Indonesia

Aragon /árrə gon/, **Louis** (1897–1982) French writer
who wrote surrealist texts and cofounded the magazine *Littérature* with André Breton. He also wrote
social realistic novels (1933–51).

aragonite /ə rággə nīt/ n. a colourless, blue to violet,
or yellow mineral consisting of calcium carbonate.
Formula: $CaCO_3$. [Late 18thC. Named after *Aragon*, the
region in northeastern Spain where it was first found.]

Araldite /árrəl dīt/ tdmk. a trademark for a type of
glue

Aral Sea /árrəl-/ inland sea straddling the Kaz-
akhstan-Uzbekistan border in western Asia, east of
the Caspian Sea. Area: 66,458 sq. km/25,660 sq. mi.
Depth: maximum 68 m/223 ft.

Aram /áirəm/, **Eugene** (1704–59) English scholar who
explored possible links between Celtic and Indo-
European languages. He was hanged for murder
(1759).

Aramaic /árrə máy ik/ n. a major language of the
ancient Near East, dating from about 300 BC and
still spoken in parts of Syria, Iraq, Iran, and other
countries. It belongs to the Semitic group of languages and is spoken by between 50,000 and 100,000
people. [Mid-19thC. Formed from Greek *Aramaios* 'of Aram'
(the Biblical name for ancient Syria).] —**Aramaic** adj.

Aran /áirən/ adj. relating to, used for, or characteristic
of a traditional style of heavy knitted garments
made from thick unbleached wool with complex
cable patterns [Mid-20thC. Named after the ARAN
ISLANDS.]

Aranda /árrəndə, ə rándə/ (*plural* **-da** *or* **-das**) n. **1.** LANG
ABORIGINAL LANGUAGE an Aboriginal language spoken in
parts of Australia's Northern Territory. Aranda
belongs to the Pama-Nyungan family and is spoken
by about 2,000 people. **2.** PEOPLES MEMBER OF ABORIGINAL
PEOPLE a member of an Aboriginal people who live
in southern central Australia [Late 19thC. From
Aranda.] —**Aranda** adj.

Aran Islands /árrən-/ group of three islands, In-
ishmoor, Inishmaan, and Inisheer, situated at the
mouth of Galway Bay in western Ireland. Population: 803 (1981). Area: 47 sq. km/18 sq. mi.

Arapaho /ə ráppəhō/ (*plural* **-ho** *or* **-hos**) n. **1.** PEOPLES
MEMBER OF NATIVE AMERICAN PEOPLE a member of a North
American people who originally lived by hunting
buffalo on the Great Plains, and who now live
mainly in Colorado, Wyoming, and Montana **2.** LANG
ALGONQUIAN LANGUAGE a North American language of
the Algonquian family of languages. Arapaho is
spoken by about 1,500 people. [Early 19thC. From Crow
alappahó, literally 'many tattoo marks'.] —**Arapaho** adj.

Ararat, Mount /árrə rat/ mountain in eastern Turkey,
which rises in two peaks, Great Ararat 5,137
m/16,854 ft and Little Ararat 3,914 m/12,840 ft. According to the Bible, it is the landing place of Noah's
Ark.

Araucanian /árraw káyni ən/ n. **1.** PEOPLES MEMBER OF
NATIVE AMERICAN PEOPLE a member of a South American
people who live in central Chile and areas of
western Argentina **2.** LANG SOUTH AMERICAN LANGUAGE a
South American language spoken in parts of Chile
and western Argentina. Araucanian is spoken by
about 300,000 people. [Early 19thC. Formed from Spanish
Araucanía, a region of Chile.] —**Araucanian** adj.

araucaria /árraw káiri ə/ (*plural* **-as** *or* **-a**) n. a coniferous tree that is native to the southern hemisphere
but widely grown elsewhere. Norfolk Island pine
and monkey puzzle are types of araucaria. Genus:
Araucaria. [Mid-19thC. From modern Latin, genus name,
coined from *Arauco*, a province in central Chile.]

Arawak /árrə wak/ (*plural* **-wak** *or* **-waks**) n. **1.** PEOPLES
MEMBER OF SOUTH AMERICAN PEOPLE a member of a South
American people who live mainly on the coast of
Guyana, but also in parts of Surinam and French
Guiana **2.** LANG ARAWAKAN LANGUAGE a South American
language of the Arawakan family, spoken in
Guyana and neighbouring countries [Mid-18thC.
From Carib *aruac*.]

Arawakan /árrə wákən/ n. LANG a family of languages
that includes Guajiro, spoken by widely scattered
communities in Central and South America. About
300,000 people speak an Arawakan language. —
Arawakan adj.

arb /aarb/ n. = **arbitrageur** (*slang*) [Late 20thC. Shortening.]

arbalest /áarbəlist/, **arbalist** n. a large medieval crossbow used to propel stones, arrows, and other missiles by mechanical power [Pre-12thC. Via Old
French *arbaleste* from late Latin *arcuballista*, from *arcus*
'bow' + *ballista* (see BALLISTA).] —**arbalester** n.

arbiter /áabitər/ n. **1.** SB MAKING JUDGMENT sb who has the
power and authority to settle a dispute or decide
an issue **2.** INFLUENTIAL PERSON OR THING sb or sth with
great influence over what people say, think, or do
3. LAW SCOTTISH JUDGE OF DISPUTE in the Scottish legal
system, sb designated to hear both sides of a dispute
and make a judgment [14thC. Directly or via Old French
arbitre from Latin *arbiter* 'judge, umpire'.]

arbitrable /áabitrab'l/ adj. able to be settled, or likely
to be best settled, by arbitration

arbitrage /áarbitrij, -traazh/ n. SIMULTANEOUS BUYING AND
SELLING the simultaneous buying and selling of the
same negotiables or commodities in different
markets in order to make an immediate riskless
profit ■ vi. (**-trages, -traging, -traged**) ENGAGE IN ARBITRAGE
to participate in arbitrage [Mid-19thC. From French,
formed from *arbitrer* 'to judge', from Latin *arbitrari* (see
ARBITRATE).]

arbitrageur /áarbi traa zhúr/ n. sb who engages in
arbitrage [Mid-19thC. From French.]

arbitral /áarbitrəl/ adj. relating to arbiters or arbitration, or arising from the intervention of an
arbitrator

arbitrary /áarbitrəri/ adj. **1.** BASED ON PERSONAL WHIM based
solely on personal wishes, feelings, or perceptions,
rather than on objective facts, reasons, or principles
2. RANDOMLY CHOSEN chosen or determined at random
3. LAW NOT ACCORDING TO RULE based on the decision of a
particular judge or court rather than accordance
with any rule or law **4.** AUTHORITARIAN with unlimited
power **5.** MATH ASSIGNED NO SPECIFIC VALUE used to describe
a constant that is not assigned a specific
value [15thC. From Latin *arbitrarius* 'uncertain, depending
on the judgment of an arbiter' (a term in Roman law), from
arbiter 'judge' (source of English *arbiter*).] —**arbitrarily**
/áabitrərəli, áabitrérrəli/ adv. —**arbitrariness** /-trəri
nəss/ n.

arbitrate /áarbi trayt/ (**-trates, -trating, -trated**) v. **1.** vti.
SETTLE DISPUTE BETWEEN OTHERS to act as a judge in a
dispute between others **2.** vt. ASK SB TO SETTLE DISPUTE to
submit a dispute to be decided by a third party [Late
16thC. From Latin *arbitrat-*, the past participle stem of
arbitrari 'to judge, decide', from *arbiter* 'judge' (source of
English *arbiter*).]

arbitration /áarbi tráysh'n/ n. the process of resolving
disputes between people or groups by referring
them to a third party, either agreed by them or
provided by law, who makes a judgment —**ar-
bitrational** adj.

arbitrator /áarbi traytər/ n. sb designated to hear both
sides of a dispute and make a judgment

arbor[1] n. US = **arbour**

arbor[2] /áabə/ n. **1.** AXLE ON MACHINE OR POWER TOOL a shaft,
axle, or spindle on a machine or a power tool, e.g.
a lathe **2.** SUPPORTING PIECE a machine part that holds
an object being worked on, or the tools being used
to work on the object **3.** INDUST REINFORCING PART OF MOULD
a part that reinforces the core of a mould used to
cast metal [Mid-17thC. Via Old French *arbre* from Latin
arbor 'tree, mast, lever, shaft'.]

arboreal /aar báwri əl/ adj. **1.** OF TREES relating to,
resembling, or consisting of trees **2.** LIVING IN TREES
used to describe a species that lives in trees —
arboreally adv.

arboreous /aar báwri əss/ adj. covered with trees

arborescent /áarbə réss'nt/ adj. resembling a tree,
especially in developing branches or similar
parts [Mid-17thC. From Latin *arborescent-*, the present
participle stem of *arborescere* 'to grow into a tree', from
arbor 'tree'.] —**arborescence** n.

arboretum /a'arbə re'etəm/ (*plural* **-tums** *or* **-ta** /-tə/) *n.* an area planted with many types of trees for study, display, and preservation [Mid-19thC. From Latin, 'place grown with trees, plantation of trees', from *arbor* 'tree'.]

arboriculture /a'arbəri kulchər, aar báwri-/ *n.* the cultivation of trees and shrubs for study, ornamentation, or profit [Mid-19thC. Blend of ARBOR and AGRICULTURE.] —**arboricultural** *adj.* —**arboriculturist** *n.*

arborio /aar báwri ó/ (*plural* **-os**), **arborio rice** *n.* a short-grained rice, used to make risotto and other Italian dishes [Late 20thC. From Italian.]

arborist /a'abərist/ *n.* an expert in the cultivation and care of trees

arborize /a'arbə rīz/ (**-rizes, -rizing, -rized**), **arborise** (**-rises, -rising, -rised**) *vi.* to develop many branching parts or formations —**arborization** /aarbə rī záysh'n/ *n.*

arbor vitae /a'arbər vītee, -vee'tī/ (*plural* **arbor vitaes**), **arborvitae** (*plural* **-taes**) *n.* a coniferous tree of the cypress family with flat closely fitted leaves resembling scales. It is native to Asia and North America and is widely grown as an ornamental. Genus: *Thuja*. [Mid-17thC. From Latin, literally 'tree of life'.]

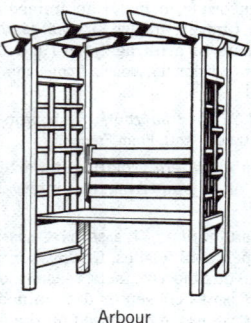
Arbour

arbour /a'arbər/ *n.* **1.** SHADY PLACE a shaded place formed by the leaves and branches of trees and plants that interweave naturally or are trained to grow around a trellis **2.** GARDENING a trellis or other structure used to support plants that form an arbour [14thC. Via Old French *(h)erb(i)er* from Latin *herbarium* (see HERBARIUM).]

arbovirus /a'arbə vīrəss/ *n.* a virus transmitted by bloodsucking arthropods, e.g. ticks and fleas. The viruses that cause encephalitis, yellow fever, and dengue are arboviruses. [Mid-20thC. Contraction of ARTHROPOD-BORNE VIRUS.] —**arboviral** /a'arbə vīrəl/ *adj.*

Arbus /a'arbəss/, **Diane** (1923–71) US photographer, known for her unconventional and occasionally morbid portraits of unusual characters.

arbutus /aar byóotəss/ (*plural* **-tuses** *or* **-tus**) *n.* **1.** EUROPEAN SHRUB a southern European shrub or tree cultivated for its white or pink flowers and reddish fruits. Genus: *Arbutus*. **2.** = **trailing arbutus** [Mid-16thC. From Latin, 'wild strawberry', from the shape of the leaves.]

arc /aark/ *n.* **1.** CURVE a curved or semicircular line, direction of movement, or arrangement of items ○ *The ball curved in a high arc.* ○ *an arc of children around their teacher* **2.** GEOM SECTION OF CIRCLE a section of a circle, ellipse, or other curved figure **3.** ASTRON VISIBLE PART OF CELESTIAL BODY'S PATH a section of the path that a planet or other celestial body appears to follow, especially that between rising above the horizon and disappearing below it **4.** ELEC ENG ELECTRIC DISCHARGE a luminous discharge caused by an electric current flowing across a gap in an electrical circuit **5.** GEOL = **island arc** ■ *vi.* (**arcs, arcing** *or* **arcking, arced** *or* **arcked**) **1.** FORM OR MOVE IN ARC to form a curve or move along a curved path **2.** ELEC ENG SPARK ACROSS GAP to produce a luminous discharge across a gap in an electrical circuit [14thC. Via Old French from Latin *arcus* 'bow, curve' (source of English *arch*).]

ARC *abbr.* Aids-related complex

arcade /aar káyd/ *n.* **1.** SERIES OF ARCHES a series of arches and the columns supporting them **2.** PASSAGEWAY WITH ARCHES a passageway or building with a series of arches and supporting columns **3.** AVENUE OF SHOPS a covered passage with shops on both sides **4.** ENCLOSED AREA WITH GAMES MACHINES an enclosed area where people can play on coin-operated games machines such as pinball machines, video games, or one-armed bandits [Mid-18thC. Via French from Italian *arcata*, from, ultimately, Latin *arcus* 'bow, curve, arch' (source of English *arch*).] —**arcaded** *adj.*

Arcadia[1] /aar káydi ə/ *n.* **1.** RURAL PARADISE IN CLASSICAL LITERATURE the imagined rural paradise used as the setting for much Greek and Roman poetry and some Renaissance literature **2.** **Arcadia, arcadia** IMAGINED PLACE OF RURAL BLISS a place in which people are imagined or believed to enjoy a perfect life of rustic simplicity [Late 19thC. Via Latin from Greek *Arkadia*, a mountainous district in the Peloponnese.] —**Arcadian** *adj.*

Arcadia[2] /aar káydi ə/ mountainous region of the central Peloponnese in Greece —**Arcadian** *adj.*, *n.*

arcana /aar káynə/ *n.* TAROT DIVISION either of two divisions of a pack of tarot cards ■ *npl.* plural of **arcanum**

arcane /aa káyn/ *adj.* **1.** MYSTERIOUSLY OBSCURE requiring secret knowledge to be understood **2.** HARD TO FATHOM difficult or impossible to understand [Early 16thC. From Latin *arcanus* (see ARCANUM).] —**arcanely** *adv.* —**arcaneness** *n.*

—— **WORD KEY: SYNONYMS** ——
See Synonyms at **obscure**.

arcanum /aar káynəm/ (*plural* **-na** /-nə/) *n.* (*usually used in the plural*) **1.** SECRET KNOWN TO FEW a secret known only to the members of a small select group **2.** SECRET OF NATURE a secret of nature, of the kind that was sought by alchemists [Late 16thC. From Latin, a noun use of the neuter form of *arcanus* 'closed, secret', from *arca* 'box' (source of English *ark*).]

Arc de Triomphe, Paris, France
AKG London

Arc de Triomphe /a'ark də treé ómf/ *n.* a triumphal arch at the end of the Avenue des Champs Elysées in Paris, completed in 1835. It was commissioned by Napoleon to commemorate military victories, and is now used as a war memorial.

arc furnace *n.* a furnace in which an electric arc supplies the heat

arch[1] /aarch/ *n.* **1.** CURVED STRUCTURE a curved structure that forms the upper edge of an open space, e.g. a window, a doorway, or the space between a bridge's supports **2.** PASSAGE UNDER ARCH an entrance or passageway under an arch **3.** ARCH SHAPE the shape of an arch, resembling an inverted U, or an object with such a shape ○ *the arch of his eyebrows* **4.** ANAT CURVED BODY PART a body part with the shape of an arch, especially the bony structure in the foot **5.** GEOG CURVED ROCK FORMATION a naturally occurring arch-shaped span of rock found in arid, especially desert, regions ■ *v.* (**arches, arching, arched**) **1.** *vt.* FORM STH INTO CURVED SHAPE to form sth into the shape of an arch **2.** *vi.* MOVE IN CURVING LINE to follow a trajectory in the shape of an arch **3.** *vt.* CROSS to extend across sth **4.** *vt.* BUILD STH IN ARCH SHAPE to build sth in the shape of an arch or with arch-shaped supports [13thC. Via Old French *arche*, from, ultimately, Latin *arcus* 'bow, curve, arch' (source also of English *arc*).]

arch[2] /aarch/ *adj.* **1.** MOST EXTREME greatest, especially most hostile **2.** KNOWINGLY PLAYFUL OR MISCHIEVOUS expressing playfulness, mischief, or shared humour in a knowing way [Mid-16thC. From ARCH-. The sense 'mischievous' developed from its use in such phrases as 'arch knave' and 'arch wag'.] —**archly** *adv.* —**archness** *n.*

arch. *abbr.* **1.** archaic **2.** archaism **3.** archery **4.** archipelago **5.** architect **6.** architecture

arch- *prefix.* **1.** chief, most important ○ *archrival* **2.** extreme ○ *archconservative* [Via Old English *ærce-* and Old French *arche* from, ultimately, Greek *arkhi-* 'first, chief' (see ARCHI-)]

-arch *suffix.* leader, ruler ○ *matriarch* [Via Old French and late Latin from, ultimately, Greek *arkhos*, from *arkhein* 'to rule')] —**-archic** *suffix.* —**-archy** *suffix.*

Archaean /aar ke'e ən/, **Archean** *adj.* **1.** OF OLDEST ROCK used to describe the oldest known kinds of rock. They are mostly igneous. **2.** OF EARLIEST GEOLOGICAL PERIOD used to describe the earliest geological period of time, dating from about four billion years ago ■ *n.* **ARCHAEAN ERA** the Archaean era [Late 19thC. Coined from Greek *arkhaios* 'old, ancient' + -AN.]

archaebacteria /a'arki bak teéri ə/ *npl.* members of one of two distinct lines of the most primitive living single-celled organisms —**archaebacterial** *adj.*

archaeo-, archae-, archeo- *prefix.* ancient ○ *archaeoastronomy* [Via modern Latin from Greek *arkhaios*]

archaeoastronomy /a'arki ō ə strónnəmi/, **archeoastronomy** *n.* the study of the astronomical beliefs, practices, and discoveries of prehistoric and ancient cultures —**archaeoastronomer** *n.* —**archaeoastronomical** /a'ark iō astrə nómmik'l/ *adj.*

archaeobotany /a'arki ō bóttəni/, **archeobotany** *n.* the scientific study of excavated plant remains from ancient times —**archaeobotanist** *n.*

archaeological /a'arki ə lójjik'l/, **archeological, archaeologic** /-lójjik/, **archeologic** *adj.* relating to archaeology, or carried out for the purposes of archaeology —**archaeologically** *adv.*

archaeology /a'arki óllǝji/, **archeology** *n.* the scientific study of ancient cultures through the examination of their material remains, e.g. buildings, graves, tools, and other artefacts usually dug up from the ground —**archaeologist** *n.*

archaeomagnetism /a'arki ō mágnǝtizzəm/, **archeomagnetism** *n.* a method of dating excavated artefacts by measuring the degree of their magnetization

archaeometry /aarki ómmǝtri/, **archeometry** *n.* the systematic dating of archaeological objects —**archaeometrical** /a'arki ə méttrik'l/ *adj.* —**archaeometrically** /-méttrikli/ *adv.* —**archaeometrist** /-ómmǝtrist/ *n.*

Archaeopteryx

archaeopteryx /a'arki óptəriks/ *n.* an extinct bird of the Jurassic period that had the feathers of modern birds but the jaw and sharp teeth of reptiles. It has been considered an evolutionary link between reptiles and birds. Latin name: *Archaeopteryx lithographica*. [Mid-19thC. Coined from ARCHAEO- + Greek *pterux* 'wing'.]

archaic /aar káyik/ *adj.* **1.** ANCIENT belonging or relating to a much earlier period **2.** NO LONGER IN ORDINARY LANGUAGE used to describe a word or phrase that is no longer in general use but is still encountered in older literature and still sometimes used for special effect **3.** OLD-FASHIONED too old to be useful or efficient [Mid-19thC. Via French from Greek *arkhaikos*, from *arkhaios* 'old, ancient', from *arkhē* 'beginning'.] —**archaically** *adv.*

—— **WORD KEY: SYNONYMS** ——
See Synonyms at **old-fashioned**.

archaic smile *n.* a facial expression typical of ancient Greek sculpture, in which the edges of the mouth are upturned but the rest of the face is fairly blank

archaism /áar kay izzəm, -ki-/ *n.* **1. OLD FORM** a word, expression, practice, or method from an earlier time that is no longer used **2. USE OF OLD THINGS** the use of expressions, techniques, and fashions from an earlier period [Mid-17thC. Via modern Latin from Greek *arkhaismos*, from *arkhaizein* 'to copy the ancients, give an archaic air to', from *arkhaios* (see ARCHAIC).] —**archaist** *n.* —**archaistic** /áar kay ístik, -ki-/ *adj.*

archaize /áark ay īz/ (**-izes, -izing, -ized**), **archaise** (**-ises, -ising, -ised**) *vt.* to cause sth to seem much older than it is by using old forms or styles —**archaizer** *n.*

archangel /áark aynjəl/ *n.* **1. PRINCIPAL ANGEL** a chief or principal angel **2. RANK ABOVE ANGEL IN MEDIEVAL CLASSIFICATION** a member of the second-lowest rank in the medieval order of celestial beings, ranking above angels and below principalities **3.** = **angelica** [Pre-12thC. Via Anglo-Norman from, ultimately, ecclesiastical Greek *arkhaggelos*, from Greek *arkhi-* 'chief' (see ARCH-) + *aggelos* (see ANGEL).] —**archangelic** /áark an jéllik/ *adj.*

archbishop /aarch bíshəp/ *n.* a bishop of the highest rank, who heads an archdiocese or an ecclesiastical province

archbishopric /aarch bíshəprik/ *n.* **1. AREA ARCHBISHOP IS RESPONSIBLE FOR** the area of an archbishop's jurisdiction **2. ARCHBISHOP'S STATUS** the status or term of office of an archbishop [Pre-12thC. From ARCHBISHOP + Old English *rice* 'realm'.]

archbp *abbr.* archbishop

archd. *abbr.* **1.** archdeacon **2.** archduke

archdeacon /aarch deékən/ *n.* a member of the clergy who ranks just below a bishop and assists the bishop with ceremonial and administrative duties —**archdeaconate** *n.* —**archdeaconship** /-ship/ *n.*

archdeaconry /aarch deékənri/ (*plural* **-ries**) *n.* **1. ARCHDEACON'S STATUS** the status or term of office of an archdeacon **2. ARCHDEACON'S HOME** the residence of an archdeacon

archdiocese /aarch dī əssiss/ *n.* the area for which an archbishop has ecclesiastical responsibility —**archdiocesan** /aarch dī óssəss'n/ *adj.*

archducal /aarch dyoók'l/ *adj.* relating or belonging to archdukes, archduchesses, or archduchies

archduchess /aarch dúchiss/ *n.* **1. ARCHDUKE'S WIFE** an archduke's wife or widow **2. AUSTRIAN PRINCESS** a princess of the former Austrian imperial family

archduchy /aarch dúchi/ (*plural* **-ies**) *n.* the land ruled by an archduke or archduchess

archduke /aarch dyoók/ *n.* a senior duke in some countries. The title was used especially in Austria and granted to the eldest son of the emperor. [Early 16thC. Via Old French *archeduc* from late Latin *archidux*, from *archi-* 'chief, first' + *dux* 'leader' (source of English *duke*).]

Archean *adj., n.* = **Archaean**

arched /aarcht/ *adj.* **1. CURVED** with a curved top in the shape of an arch **2. WITH AN ARCH ATTACHED** having or including an arch, e.g. as a support

archegonia *plural of* **archegonium**

archegoniate /áarki góni ət/ *adj.* **WITH ARCHEGONIA** bearing archegonia ■ *n.* **PLANT WITH ARCHEGONIA** a plant that bears archegonia

archegonium /áarki góni əm/ (*plural* **-a** /-ə/) *n.* the female reproductive organ of mosses, ferns, liverworts, and most gymnosperms. It contains a single egg cell. [Mid-19thC. Via modern Latin from Greek *arkhegonos*, from *arkhe-* 'chief, first' + *gonos* 'people' (source of English *gonad*).] —**archegonial** *adj.*

archenemy /áarch énnəmi/ (*plural* **-mies**) *n.* **1. WORST ENEMY** sb's main or worst enemy **2. archenemy, Archenemy SATAN** the Devil

archenteron /aar kéntə ron, -tərən/ *n.* a digestive cavity in animal embryos that develops into the gut [Late 19thC. Coined from Greek *arkhē* 'beginning'+ *enteron* 'intestine'.] —**archenteric** *adj.*

archeo- *prefix.* = **archaeo-**

archeological *adj.* = **archaeological**

archeology *n.* = **archaeology**

archer /áarchər/ *n.* sb who has been trained to use a bow and arrow [13thC. Via Anglo-Norman from Old French *archier*, from, ultimately, Latin *arcus* 'bow, curve' (source of English *arch, arcade,* and *arc*).]

Archer *n.* ZODIAC = **Sagittarius**

Archer /áarchər/, **Frederick Scott** (1813–57) British photographer. He invented the collodion, or wet plate, process for reproducing photographs (1851).

Archer, Jeffrey, Baron Archer of Weston Super Mare (*b.* 1940) British politician and writer. He was elected MP for Louth (1969) but resigned because of bankruptcy. He recouped his fortunes by writing thrillers and became a life peer in 1992. Full name **Jeffrey Howard Archer**

Archer, Robyn (*b.* 1948) Australian singer and actor. She was noted for her performances of the works of Brecht and her one-woman show *A Star is Torn* (1982).

Archer, William (1856–1924) British drama critic who translated the plays of Henrik Ibsen and encouraged George Bernard Shaw early in his career.

archerfish /áarchər fish/ (*plural* **-fish** *or* **-fishes**) *n.* a freshwater fish of Australia and Southeast Asia that hunts insects by spitting water at them. Family: Toxotidae.

archery /áarchəri/ *n.* **1. SHOOTING WITH BOW AND ARROW** the activity of shooting with a bow and arrow **2. TROOP OF ARCHERS** a troop of soldiers armed with bows and arrows **3. ARCHERS' WEAPONS** the bows and arrows used by archers

archesporium /áarki spáwri əm/ (*plural* **-a** /-ə/), **archespore** /áarki spawr/ *n.* the tissue that gives rise to spore-producing cells in a sporangium in fungi [Late 19thC. Coined from *arche-*, an alteration of ARCHI- + SPORE + -IUM.]

archetypal /áarki típ'l, -típ'l/ *adj.* **1. TYPICAL** typical of its kind, or providing a perfect example or model of sth ○ *the archetypal bachelor* **2. RELATING TO ARCHETYPES** relating to archetypes —**archetypally** *adv.*

archetype /áarki tīp/ *n.* **1. ORIGINAL MODEL** sth that served as the model or pattern for other things of the same type ○ *The film was one of the archetypes of the American Western.* **2. TYPICAL SPECIMEN** a typical, ideal, or classic example of sth ○ *It was described as an archetype of the interior design of the period.* **3.** PSYCHOL **IMAGE FROM COLLECTIVE UNCONSCIOUS** in Jungian psychology, an inherited memory represented in the mind by a universal symbol and observed in dreams and myths **4.** ARTS **RECURRING SYMBOL** an image or symbol that is used repeatedly in art or literature [Mid-16thC. Via Latin *archetypum* from Greek *arkhetupon* 'first moulded as a model', from *arkhe-* 'first, chief' + *tupon* 'mould, model'.] —**archetypic** /áarki típpik/ *adj.* —**archetypical** /-típpik'l/ *adj.* —**archetypically** /-típpikli/ *adv.*

archfiend /áarch feénd/ *n.* **1. EXTREMELY WICKED CREATURE** a supremely wicked person or creature **2. archfiend, Archfiend SATAN** the Devil

archi- *prefix.* **1.** chief, most important ○ *archimage* **2.** primitive, primary ○ *archenteron* [Via French *archi-* from, ultimately, Greek *arkhi-*, from *arkhein* 'to be first, rule']

Archibald /áarchi bawld/, **Jules François** (1856–1919) Australian journalist. He was co-founder of the journal *The Bulletin* (1880) and creator of the the Archibald Prize for portrait painting.

Archibald Prize *n.* an annual prize awarded for portrait painting in Australia. It was first awarded in 1921.

archidiaconal /áarki dī ákənəl/ *adj.* relating to the work or position of an archdeacon [15thC. Formed from Latin *archidiaconus* (see ARCHDEACON).]

archidiaconate /áarki dī ákənət/ *n.* an archdeacon's position, area of jurisdiction, or term of office [Mid-18thC. Ultimately from Latin *archidiaconus* (see ARCHDEACON).]

Archie /áarchi/ *n.* a database that Internet users can access in order to search for files and programs that they can download using File Transfer Protocol [Late 20thC. Coined from ARCHIVE + -IE, on the model of the male name *Archie*.]

archiepiscopal /áarki ə pískəp'l/ *adj.* relating to archbishops or archdioceses [Early 17thC. Formed from ecclesiastical Latin *archiepiscopus* 'archbishop', from ecclesiastical Greek *arkhiepiskopos*.] —**archiepiscopality** /áarki ə pískə pálləti/ *n.* —**archiepiscopally** /-p'li/ *adv.* —**archiepiscopate** /-pískəpət, -payt/ *n.*

archimage /áarki mayj/ *n.* a powerful magician [Late 16thC. From Greek *arkhimagos* 'chief of the magi', from *arkhe-* 'first, chief' + *magos* 'sorcerer' (see MAGI).]

archimandrite /áarki mán drīt/ *n.* in the Eastern Orthodox Church, a senior priest who heads a monastery or group of monasteries [Mid-17thC. Directly or via French from ecclesiastical Latin *archimandrita*, from ecclesiastical Greek *arkhimandritēs*, from *arkhi-* 'first, chief' + *mandra* 'enclosure, monastery'.]

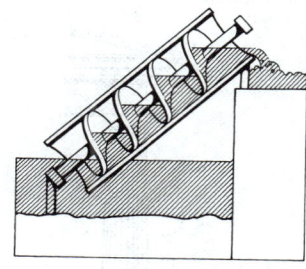

Archimedean screw

Archimedean screw /áarkə meé dee ən-/ *n.* an ancient method of raising water using either a large screw inside a sloping tube or a spiral tube curling around a sloping axis. Water is carried upwards when the screw or tube is turned. [Named after ARCHIMEDES, who invented it]

Archimedes /áarkə meé deez/ (287–212 BC) Greek mathematician. He wrote on geometry, arithmetic, and mechanics.

Archimedes' principle *n.* the principle stating that an object immersed in a liquid experiences an upward thrust equal to the weight of liquid it displaces. Light objects float because they displace more than their own weight in water, whereas heavy objects sink because they displace less.

Archimedes' screw *n.* = **Archimedean screw**

archine /aar sheén/ *n.* a unit of length equal to about 71 cm/28 in, used formerly in Russia and Turkey [Mid-18thC. From Russian.]

archipelago /áarki péllə gō/ (*plural* **-gos** *or* **-goes**) *n.* **1. ISLANDS** a group or chain of islands (*often used in place names*) **2. SEA WITH ISLANDS** an area of sea with many islands [Early 16thC. From Italian *arcipelago*, from Greek *arkhi-* 'chief, main' + *pelagos* 'sea'. First applied to the Aegean Sea.] —**archipelagic** /áarkipə lájjik/ *adj.*

archit. *abbr.* architecture

architect /áarki tekt/ *n.* **1.** ARCHIT **BUILDING DESIGNER** sb whose job is to design buildings and advise on their construction **2. CREATOR** the person who created or invented sth ○ *the architect of her own fortune* [Mid-16thC. Directly or via French and Italian from Latin *architectus*, from Greek *arkhitektōn* 'chief builder', from *tektōn* 'builder' (source of English *tectonics*).]

architectonic /áarki tek tónnik/ *adj.* **1.** ARCHIT **OF ARCHITECTURE OR ARCHITECTURAL QUALITIES** relating to architecture or the qualities, e.g. design and structure, that architecture requires **2.** PHILOS **OF CLASSIFICATION OF KNOWLEDGE** relating to the classification of knowledge used in metaphysics [Mid-17thC. Via Latin from Greek *arkhitektonikos*, from *arkhitektōn* (see ARCHITECT).] —**architectonically** *adv.*

architectonics /aárki tek tónniks/ *n.* (takes a singular verb) **1.** ARCHIT SCIENCE OF ARCHITECTURE the science of architecture **2.** STRUCTURAL DESIGN OF COMPLEX THING the way in which the parts of a complex object or system fit together ○ *the architectonics of a good novel* **3.** PHILOS CLASSIFICATION OF KNOWLEDGE in metaphysics, the classification of knowledge

architectural /aárki tékchərəl/ *adj.* **1.** ARCHIT RELATING TO BUILDING DESIGN relating to the style of buildings or the job of designing them ○ *the architectural merits of the building* **2.** COMPUT OF COMPUTER SYSTEM DESIGN relating to the architecture of a computer

architecturally /aárki tékchərəli/ *adv.* with regard to architecture as a science or an art, or in a way that involves architecture or its principles ○ *Architecturally, the city is unique.*

architecture /aárki tekchər/ *n.* **1.** BUILDING DESIGN the art and science of designing and constructing buildings **2.** BUILDING STYLE a particular style or fashion of building, especially one that is typical of a period of history or of a particular place **3.** COMPUT STRUCTURE OF COMPUTER SYSTEM the design, structure, and behaviour of a computer system, microprocessor, or system program, including the characteristics of individual components and how they interact ○ *network architecture*

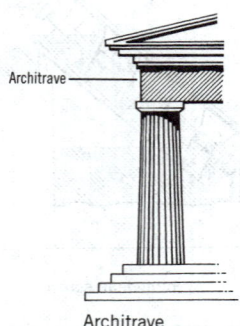
Architrave

architrave /aárki trayv/ *n.* **1.** SLAB ON COLUMNS in classical architecture, the lowest section of an entablature, which comes into contact with the top of the columns **2.** DOOR OR WINDOW SURROUND a decorative strip of wood or plaster forming a frame around a door or window [Mid-16thC. Via French from Italian, 'main beam', from *trave* 'beam', from the Latin stem *trab-*.]

archival /aar kív'l/ *adj.* kept in an archive, or relating to the storage of records in an archive

archive /aár kīv/ *n.* **1.** COLLECTION OF DOCUMENTS a collection of documents such as letters, official papers, photographs, or recorded material, kept for their historical interest (*often used in the plural*) ○ *archive material* ○ *We'll have to check the archives.* **2.** PLACE WHERE ARCHIVES ARE HELD the building or room that houses archives ○ *Duke University houses the Duke Papyrus Archive.* ○ *the Harvard Economics Symposium Archive* **3.** COMPUT BACKUP COMPUTER FILE a copy of computer files kept, often in compressed form, on tape or disk for long-term storage **4.** COMPUT COMPUTER FILE OF COMPRESSED FILES a computer file that contains other files in compressed form **5.** COMPUT DIRECTORY ACCESSED USING FILE TRANSFER PROTOCOL a directory of files that Internet users can access using anonymous File Transfer Protocol ○ *The report was filed in an archive for distribution on the Internet.* ■ *vt.* (-chiving, -chived, -chives, -chived) **1.** PUT DOCUMENT IN ARCHIVE to store a document in an archive **2.** COMPUT STORE DATA OUTSIDE HARD DISK to transfer data from a computer's hard disk to a tape or disk for long-term storage **3.** COMPUT COMBINE AND COMPRESS COMPUTER FILES to store copies of multiple computer files in compressed form in a single disk file [Early 17thC. Via French from Latin *archiva*, from Greek *arkheia* 'things kept at the public office', plural of *arkheion* 'ruler's house, public office', from *arkhē* 'beginning, government'.]

archivist /aárkivist/ *n.* sb employed to collect, catalogue, and look after the items in an archive

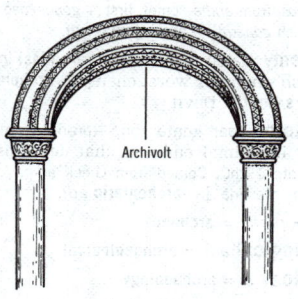
Archivolt

archivolt /aárki vōlt/ *n.* **1.** MOULDING AROUND ARCH a decorative moulding or band on the face of an arch **2.** UNDERSIDE OF ARCH the underside of an arch [Mid-17thC. Directly or via French *archivolte* from Italian *archivolto*, from, ultimately, Latin *arcus* 'arch' + *volta* 'vault'.]

archon /aárkən, -kon/ *n.* one of the nine chief magistrates in ancient Athens [Late 16thC. From Greek *arkhōn*, from *arkhein* 'to rule'.] —**archonship** *n.*

archpriest /aárch preést/ *n.* **1.** HIGH-RANKING EASTERN ORTHODOX PRIEST in the Eastern Orthodox Church, a priest with the highest rank that a married priest can have **2.** SPECIAL ROMAN CATHOLIC TITLE in the Roman Catholic Church, a title given to a priest who has a specific important duty or function **3.** BISHOP'S SENIOR ASSISTANT a title formerly given to the most senior Roman Catholic priest belonging to a cathedral chapter, who acted as the bishop's principal assistant [14thC. Via Old French *archeprestre* from late Latin *archipresbyter* 'chief priest'. The modern spelling is based on ARCH- and PRIEST.]

archrival /aárch rív'l/ *n.* sb's main or most dangerous rival

archt *abbr.* architect

archway /aárch way/ *n.* an entrance or passage under one or more arches, or an arch that forms an entrance

Archytas /aar kítəss/ (*fl.* early 4thC BC) Greek mathematician. He calculated the mathematical relationships of musical notes and scales.

Arcimboldo /aárchim bóldō/, **Giuseppe** (1530?–93) Italian painter and designer. He produced pictures of fantastic heads composed of items such as vegetables and animals.

arc light, arc lamp *n.* an intensely bright electric light with numerous uses, e.g. in floodlights and spotlights on film sets. The light is generated by passing electric current through ionized gas.

arco /aárkō/ *adv.* played using the bow of a stringed instrument, usually after a passage played by plucking the strings (**pizzicato**) (*used as a musical direction*) [Mid-18thC. From Italian, 'bow'.] —**arco** *adj.*

arctic /aárktik/ *adj.* VERY COLD extremely cold (*informal*) ■ *n.* US OVERSHOE a high waterproof overshoe with a warm lining [14thC. Via Old French *artique* from, ultimately, Greek *arktikos*, from *arktos* 'bear', also 'the constellation Ursa Major (the Great Bear)', which points to the northern Pole Star.]

Arctic /aárktik/ *n.* the region that lies around the North Pole, including the Arctic Ocean and its islands and parts of North America, Asia, and Europe. The area is extremely cold, and its border is generally considered to be the Arctic Circle. ◊ **Antarctic** —**Arctic** *adj.*

arctic char *n.* a fish of the salmon family, similar to a trout, that is found in the lakes and streams of the northern hemisphere. Latin name: *Salvelinus alpinus.*

Arctic Circle the line of latitude at 66°30'N that marks the boundary of the Arctic. North of this latitude there are periods of continuous night in the winter and day in the summer.

arctic fox *n.* a small fox found in Arctic regions. It has thick fur that is brownish-grey in summer and white or blue in winter. Latin name: *Alopex lagopus.*

Arctic Circle

arctic hare (*plural* **arctic hares** *or* **arctic hare**) *n.* **1.** N AMERICAN HARE a large hare of Arctic North America and Greenland with white fur that in southern regions turns brown in the summer. Latin name: *Lepus arcticus.* **2.** BRITISH HARE a hare found in northern Britain. Its coat is brown in summer and white in winter. Latin name: *Lepus timidus.*

Arctic Ocean the world's smallest ocean, mostly ice-covered, situated north of the Arctic Circle and surrounding the North Pole. Area: 14,055,930 sq. km/5,427,000 sq.mi. Depth: 5,500 m/17,880 ft.

arctic tern (*plural* **arctic terns** *or* **arctic tern**) *n.* a black-headed seabird that breeds in Arctic regions and migrates to southern Africa, South America, and the Antarctic. Latin name: *Sterna paradisaea.*

arctiid /aárkti id/ (*plural* **-ids** *or* **-id**) *n.* a small to medium-sized moth. There are 8,000 species of arctiid, including the tiger moth. Family: Arctiidae. [From modern Latin *arctiidae*, genus name, from Greek *arktos* 'bear']

arctophile /aárktō fīl/ *n.* sb who collects or likes teddy bears [Late 20thC. Coined from Greek *arktos* 'bear' + -PHILE.]

Arcturus /aark tyŏórəss/ *n.* the brightest star in the constellation Boötes and the fourth brightest star in the sky

arcuate /aárkyoo ət/ *adj.* in the shape of an arc or a bow [15thC. From Latin *arcuatus*, from *arcus* 'bow, arch' (source of English *arch*).] —**arcuately** *adv.*

arcus senilis /aárkŏóss se neéliss/ *n.* an opaque circle around the cornea of the eye that can develop in old age

arc welding *n.* the joining of metal components by fusing them with heat from an electric arc struck between two electrodes

ARD *abbr.* acute respiratory disease

-ard, -art *suffix.* sb who characteristically has a given quality ○ *dullard* [From Old French; of Germanic origin]

Arden /aárd'n/, **John** (*b.* 1930) British playwright. He used experimental techniques and forms in plays such as *Serjeant Musgrave's Dance* (1959) and *The Ballygombeen Bequest* (1972).

Ardennes /aar dén/ forested and thinly populated plateau in southeastern Belgium, extending into Luxembourg and northeastern France. The Battle of the Bulge took place in the Ardennes in 1944. The highest peak is Botrange, near Belgium's border with Germany 694 m/2,277 ft.

ardent /aárd'nt/ *adj.* **1.** PASSIONATE feeling passion, or felt passionately **2.** ENTHUSIASTIC feeling or showing great enthusiasm or eagerness ○ *one of his most ardent supporters* **3.** GLOWING shining or glowing brightly, with a fiery quality (*literary*) ○ *her ardent gaze* [14thC. Via Old French *ardant* from Latin *ardent-*, the present participle stem of *ardere* 'to burn' (source of English *arson*).] —**ardently** *adv.*

ardent spirits *npl.* distilled alcoholic beverages, e.g. whisky and rum

ardor *n.* US = ardour

ardour /aárdər/ *n.* fierce intensity of feelings ○ *repeated attempts to dampen their revolutionary ardour* [14thC. Via Old French from Latin *ardor*, from *ardere* 'to burn' (see ARDENT).]

Ards /aárdz/ local government region in Northern Ireland, covering the Ards Peninsula. The administrative headquarters are in Newtownards. Population: 64,764 (1991). Area: 381 sq. km/147 sq. mi.

arduous /aárdyoo əss/ adj. **1.** DIFFICULT AND TIRING requiring hard work or continuous strenuous effort **2.** STEEP OR DEMANDING very difficult to traverse, endure, or overcome [Mid-16thC. From Latin arduus 'steep, difficult', the sense 'difficult' developing from the fact that anything steep is difficult and tiring to climb.] —**arduously** adv. —**arduousness** n.

WORD KEY: SYNONYMS

See Synonyms at **hard**.

are[1] (stressed) /aar/; (unstressed) /ər/ the plural and second person singular present tense of the verb 'be' [Old English earon. Of prehistoric Germanic origin.]

are[2] /aar/ n. a metric unit of area, equal to 100 sq. m. There are one hundred ares in a hectare. [Late 18thC. Via French from Latin area (see AREA).]

area /áiri ə/ n. **1.** MEASUREMENT OF SURFACE the extent of part of a surface enclosed within a boundary, or the extent of the surface of all or part of a solid. The area of a square or rectangle can be calculated by multiplying together the lengths of two adjacent sides. **2.** PART OF SURFACE a distinct part of the surface of sth, especially a piece of land ○ The storms resulted in flooding over a large area. **3.** SPACE OR PART FOR SPECIFIC FUNCTION a space, part, or surface of sth, especially when intended for a specific use ○ an area of the brain used for memory **4.** REGION OR DISTRICT a region or district, either a distinct political or administrative division or a place that has particular qualities or features **5.** SUBJECT a particular subject, field of knowledge, or sphere of activity ○ in the area of genetic research **6.** SOCCER = **penalty area** [Mid-16thC. From Latin, 'flat piece of unoccupied land', of unknown origin.]

area bombing n. = carpet bombing

area code n. digits indicating a particular area of a country that are dialled before the local number in calls from outside that area

Area of Archaeological Importance (plural **Areas of Archaeological Importance**) n. an area of land, usually an urban one, designated and protected by law because there are known to be concentrations of archaeological remains

areca /ə reékə, árri-/ n. a tall Southeast Asian palm tree with white flowers. Genus: Areca. [Late 16thC. Via Portuguese from Malayalam aṭekka.]

areg plural of **erg**[2]

ARELS /árrəlz/ abbr. Association of Recognized English Language Schools

arena /ə reé nə/ n. **1.** STADIUM an indoor or outdoor area, surrounded by seating for spectators, where shows or sports events take place **2.** SCENE OF ACTIVITY a place or situation where there is conflict or intense activity ○ A new contestant has entered the political arena. **3.** CENTRE OF ROMAN AMPHITHEATRE the open area inside a Roman amphitheatre, in which gladiatorial contests and other entertainments were staged [Early 17thC. From Latin (h)arena 'sand, sand-strewn place'.]

arenaceous /árri náyshəss/ adj. **1.** SANDY used to describe rocks or deposits that are composed of sand grains or have a sandy texture **2.** SUITED TO SANDY SOIL used to describe plants that grow best in sandy soil [Mid-17thC. Formed from Latin arenaceus 'of sand', from arena (see ARENA).]

arena theatre n. = theatre-in-the-round

arenicolous /árri níkələss/ adj. living, burrowing, or thriving in sand [Mid-18thC. Coined from Latin arena 'sand' + -cola 'inhabiting' + -OUS.]

aren't /aarnt/ contr. (informal) **1.** ARE NOT short form of 'are not' ○ They aren't coming. **2.** AM NOT short form of 'am not', which can only be used in questions ○ I'm allowed to go too, aren't I?

WORD KEY: USAGE

Use of **aren't.** English is deficient in not having a convenient contracted form of am I not? (The logically expected form **amn't I** is used in some parts of Scotland and Ireland but has never been part of standard English.) The usual form used is **aren't I,** borrowing are from other

---

parts of the verb be, whereas in American English **ain't** I is used, though only informally. There is no contraction for the type I am not that corresponds to **I don't** and **I haven't** (as distinct from **I'm not,** which places greater emphasis on the not), and this is why the nonstandard form **ain't** tends to be used for want of anything better, although it is extremely informal. (See the Usage note at **ain't.**)

---

areola /ə reé ələ/ (plural **-lae** /-lee/ or **-las**) n. **1.** ANAT DARK AREA AROUND NIPPLE the small circular dark area around the nipple in humans **2.** MED CIRCULAR AREA a small circular area, e.g. an inflamed ring around a spot [Mid-17thC. From Latin, literally 'little area'.] —**areolar** adj. —**areolate** /ə reé ələt/ adj. —**areolation** /-láysh'n/ n.

areole /árri ōl/ n. **1.** BIOL SMALL CLEARLY DEFINED SPACE a small clearly defined space, e.g. that between veins on a leaf **2.** BOT PIT ON SURFACE OF CACTUS a depression on the surface of a cactus that the spines, hairs, or flowers grow from [Mid-19thC. Via French from Latin areola (see AREOLA).]

Arequipa /árri keépə/ city in southern Peru in the Andes. It is an important commercial centre. Population: 620,471 (1993).

Ares /aá reez/ n. in Greek mythology, the god of war and the son of Zeus and Hera. Roman equivalent **Mars**

arête /ə ráyt, -rét/ n. a narrow ridge of bare rock situated between two or more deep smooth-sided semicircular areas (**cirques**), found in a mountainous area that has been glaciated [Early 19thC. Via French from Latin arista 'ear of corn, fish bone, spine', from its shape.]

arethusa /árri thyoózə/ n. = swamp pink [Named after the mythical Greek nymph Arethusa, who changed into a spring when pursued by the river god Alpheus]

Aretino /árrə teé nō/, Pietro (1492–1556) Italian poet. He served under various nobles including Giovanni di Medici, who became Pope Leo X and withdrew his sponsorship after Aretino wrote his Lewd Sonnets (1524).

argal n. = argol

argali /aárgəli/ (plural **-li**) n. a large wild sheep found in the dry mountainous areas of central and northern Asia. Latin name: Ovis ammon. [Late 18thC. From Mongolian.]

argent /aárjənt/ n. **1.** SILVER the metal or the colour silver (archaic or literary) **2.** HERALDRY COLOUR ON COAT OF ARMS the colour white or silver on a coat of arms [14thC. Via French from Latin argentum 'silver'. Ultimately from an Indo-European word meaning 'shining, white', which is also the ancestor of English argil and argue.] —**argent** adj.

argentic /aar jéntik/ adj. containing silver with a valency of 2

argentiferous /aárjən tíffərəss/ adj. used to describe rocks or deposits containing silver

Argentina

Argentina /aárjən teé nə/ republic that occupies most of the southern tip of South America. It was settled by the Spanish in the 16th century and became independent in 1816. Language: Spanish. Currency: austral. Capital: Buenos Aires. Population: 35,797,981 (1997). Area: 2,780,400 sq. km/1,073,518 sq. mi. Official name **Argentine Republic**

---

argentine /aárjən tīn/ adj. SILVERY silvery in colour (archaic or literary) ■ n. SILVER the metal silver, or any material that looks like silver

Argentine /aárjən teen/ n. **1.** = **Argentina 2.** = **Argentinian** adj. ■ adj. = **Argentinian** n.

Argentinian /aárjən tínni ən/ n. SB FROM ARGENTINA sb who was born in or is a citizen of Argentina ■ adj. OF ARGENTINA relating to or typical of Argentina, or its people or culture

argentite /aárjən tīt/ n. a grey to black mineral consisting of silver sulphide crystallized in cubic form. Formula: Ag₂S. [Mid-19thC. Coined from Latin argentum 'silver' + -ITE.]

argie-bargie n. = argy-bargy

argil /aárjil/ n. clay, especially potter's clay [14thC. Via Old French argille from Greek argillos 'clay'. Ultimately from an Indo-European word meaning 'shining, white'.]

argillaceous /aárji láyshəss/ adj. used to describe sedimentary rock that is made up of fine silt or clay particles

argillite /aárji līt/ n. rock that is made up of clay or silt particles, especially a hardened mudstone

arginase /aárji nayz, -nayss/ n. an enzyme in the liver that aids the breakdown of the amino acid arginine, producing urea for excretion

arginine /aárji neen, -nīn/ n. an amino acid, obtained by animals from their diet, that is one of the constituents of protein. It is derived from guanidine in plant and animal tissue. Formula: C₆H₁₄N₄O₂. [Late 19thC. From German, perhaps formed from Greek arginoeis 'bright-shining, white'.]

Argive /aár gīv, -jīv/ adj. **1.** GREEK relating to or typical of ancient Greece, especially the city of Argos **2.** OF ARGOS relating to the city of Argos ■ n. **1.** ANCIENT GREEK from ancient Greece (literary) **2.** CITIZEN OF ARGOS sb from the city of Argos [Mid-16thC. From Latin Argivus 'of Argos'.]

Argo /aárgō/ n. a large constellation in the southern hemisphere, now usually regarded as consisting of the smaller constellations of Puppis, Vela, Carina, and Pyxis

argol /aár gol/, **argal** /aárg'l/ n. a deposit of potassium hydrogen tartrate, formed in wine casks and sometimes used to manufacture cream of tartar [14thC. From Anglo-Norman argoile, of unknown origin.]

argon /aár gon/ n. a chemical element in the form of an inert gas that makes up about one per cent of the Earth's atmosphere. Argon is used in electric lights and as a gas shield in welding. Symbol **Ar** [Late 19thC. From Greek, from argos 'inactive, idle', from a- 'without' + ergon 'work' (source of English ergonomics and allergy).]

argonaut /aárgə nawt/ n. ZOOL = **paper nautilus** [Mid-19thC. From modern Latin Argonauta, its genus name. From the fact that it drifts through the oceans (like Jason's ARGONAUTS).]

Argonaut n. **1.** GREEK HERO one of the heroes in Greek mythology who sailed with Jason to find the Golden Fleece **2.** **Argonaut, argonaut** ADVENTURER an adventurer, especially sb who took part in the Californian gold rush of 1849 [Late 16thC. Via Latin argonauta from Greek argonautēs 'sailor in the ship Argo'.]

Argonne /aar gón, aár gòn/ wooded highland region in northeastern France, forming a natural barrier between Champagne and Lorraine

argosy /aárgəssi/ (plural **-sies**) n. **1.** LADEN MERCHANT SHIP a large richly laden merchant ship, or a fleet of richly laden ships (literary) **2.** RICH STORE a rich plentiful store or supply of sth (archaic or literary) [Late 16thC. Probably from Italian Ragusea '(ship) from Ragusa' (now Dubrovnik in Croatia), which was an important port at the time.]

argot /aárgō, -gət/ n. jargon used by a particular group [Mid-19thC. From French, originally meaning the jargon of criminals, of unknown origin.] —**argotic** /aar góttik/ adj.

arguable /aárgyoo əb'l/ adj. **1.** PLAUSIBLE OR POSSIBLE able to be supported or proved with evidence or arguments ○ an arguable case for global warming **2.** OPEN TO DISPUTE not obviously true or accurate, and therefore likely to be questioned or argued about

○ *It's arguable whether he really is the world's best guitarist.*

arguably /aárgyoo əbli/ *adv.* used to mean that a statement is open to dispute but could be defended in an argument ○ *They are arguably the best team to come out of Europe this decade.*

WORD KEY: USAGE

arguably, debatably, disputably *Arguably*, which is the most common of the three words, tends to emphasize the affirmative position and suggests that the speaker is asserting that which is arguable: *arguably the most influential legislator in the county. Debatably* is the most nearly neutral of the three: *It was a debatably rude thing to do. Disputably*, the least common word, tends to emphasize the potential for disagreement: *The cause was disputably his work habits, although some say it was his temper that got him into trouble.*

argue /aárgyoo/ (**-gues, -guing, -gued**) *v.* 1. *vi.* EXPRESS DISAGREEMENT to express disagreement with sb, especially continuously or angrily 2. *vti.* GIVE REASONS FOR STH to give reasons for an opinion in order to support it ○ *You could argue that this calls for greater freedom, not less.* 3. *vti.* DISCUSS STH to discuss sth in all its aspects 4. *vt.* PERSUADE SB to persuade sb to do sth by giving reasons ○ *argued her out of leaving* 5. *vti.* PROVIDE EVIDENCE FOR STH to be evidence or a sign of sth [14thC. Via French *arguer* from Latin *argutari* 'to assert repeatedly', from *arguere* 'to make clear, assert'.] —**arguer** *n.*

WORD KEY: SYNONYMS

See Synonyms at *disagree*.

argufy /aárgyoo fī/ (**-fies, -fying, -fied**) *vi.* to argue about sth that is unimportant (*informal*)

argument /aárgyooˈmənt/ *n.* 1. QUARREL a disagreement in which different views are expressed, often angrily 2. REASON a reason put forward in support of a point of view ○ *the arguments for and against the planned development* 3. STATED POINT OF VIEW the main point of view expressed in a book, report, or speech 4. DISCUSSION debate or discussion about whether sth is correct 5. LING NOUN ELEMENT IN CLAUSE any of the noun elements in a clause that relate directly to the verb, such as the subject or object 6. PHILOS LOGICAL STATEMENTS WITH CONCLUSION a unit of reasoning moving from premises that provide evidence to a conclusion 7. MATH VARIABLE ELEMENT an independent variable whose value determines the value of a mathematical expression 8. COMPUT FEATURE CONTROLLING COMPUTER PROGRAM a value that modifies how a command or function operates in a computer program

argumenta plural of **argumentum**

argumentation /aárgyooˈmən táyshˈn/ *n.* 1. DEBATE a process of debating or discussing sth 2. LOGICAL REASONING reasoning that proceeds methodically from a statement to a conclusion

argumentative /aárgyoo méntətiv/ *adj.* 1. INCLINED TO DISAGREE tending to disagree and argue 2. CHARACTERIZED BY DISAGREEMENT characterized by disagreement or argument —**argumentatively** *adv.* —**argumentativeness** *n.*

argumentum /aárgyoo méntəm/ (*plural* **-ta** /-tə/) *n.* a series of statements or a demonstration that leads to a logical conclusion (*formal*) [Mid-17thC. From Latin, 'argument, rationale', from *arguere* (see ARGUE).]

argumentum ad hominem /-ad hómminem/ *n.* criticism of an opponent's character or motives, rather than of the person's argument, opinion, or beliefs (*formal*) [From Latin, literally 'argument to the person']

Argus /aárgəss/ *n.* 1. HUNDRED-EYED GIANT in Greek mythology, a giant with a hundred eyes. He was sent by the jealous Hera to watch over her husband's mistress, Io, but was later lulled to sleep and killed by Hermes. 2. WATCHFUL PERSON sb who is very alert and watchful (*literary*)

Argus-eyed *adj.* always on the alert and seeing everything (*literary*)

argus pheasant (*plural* **argus pheasants** *or* **argus pheasant**) *n.* a large pheasant found in southeast Asia and Indonesia. The male has a long tail like a peacock's. Latin name: *Argusianus argus.* [From its tail-spots, reminiscent of Argus's eyes]

argy-bargy /aárji baárji/ (*plural* **argy-bargies**), **argie-bargie** *n.* an animated or heated quarrel, or this kind of quarrelling (*informal*) [Late 19thC. A playful development of ARGUMENT.]

Argyle

argyle /aar gīl/ *adj.* WITH DIAMOND PATTERN knitted with a pattern of coloured diamonds ■ *n.* SOCK OR SWEATER WITH DIAMOND PATTERN a sock or sweater made in an argyle design [Mid-20thC. From its being based on the tartan of the branch of the Campbell clan who lived in Argyll in Scotland.]

Argyle, Lake /aar gīl/ large reservoir in northwestern Australia, created in 1972 by damming the River Ord. Area: 2,400 sq. km/927 sq. mi.

Argyll and Bute /aar gīl ənd byoot/ administrative area in Scotland created in 1996, formerly part of Strathclyde Region. It includes the historic county of Argyllshire. The administrative headquarters are in Lochgilphead.

arhat /aárhət/ *n.* a Buddhist who has reached the highest state of peace and enlightenment. ◊ **arahat** [Late 19thC. Via Pali from Sanskrit, 'deserving, meritorious'.] —**arhatship** *n.*

aria /aári ə/ *n.* a melody sung solo or as a duet in an opera, oratorio, or cantata [Early 18thC. Via Italian from Latin *aer* 'air' (see AIR).]

Ariadne /árri ádni/ *n.* in Greek mythology, the daughter of King Minos of Crete. She gave Theseus the ball of thread which he used to find his way out of the labyrinth after killing the Minotaur.

Arian[1] /áiri ən/ *n.* = **Aries** *n.* 2 —**Arian** *adj.*

Arian[2] /áiri ən/ *n.* a follower of the ancient Greek Christian theologian Arius, who argued that Jesus Christ was the highest created being, but was not divine. This doctrine was pronounced heretical in the 4th century AD. —**Arianism** *n.*

ariboflavinosis /ay ríbō fláyvi nṓssiss/ *n.* a condition caused by a dietary deficiency of vitamin B_2 (**riboflavin**). The symptoms are mouth lesions and excessive oiliness of the skin and hair. [Mid-20thC. Coined with A- + RIBOFLAVIN + -OSIS.]

arid /árrid/ *adj.* 1. WITH LOW RAINFALL used to describe a region in which annual rainfall is less than 25 cm/10 in 2. DULL completely lacking in interest or excitement [Mid-17thC. Directly or via French from Latin *aridus*, from *arere* 'to be dry'.] —**aridity** /ə ríddəti/ *n.* —**aridness** /árridnəss/ *n.*

WORD KEY: SYNONYMS

See Synonyms at *dry*.

arid zone *n.* either of two zones of latitude that are between 15° and 30° north and south of the equator, consisting mostly of desert or semidesert

Ariel /áiri əl/ *n.* a natural satellite of Uranus having a radius of 580 km, discovered in 1851

Aries /áireez/ *n.* 1. ZODIAC FIRST SIGN OF THE ZODIAC the first sign of the zodiac, represented by a ram and lasting from approximately 21 March to 19 April. Aries is classified as a fire sign and its ruling planet is Mars. 2. ZODIAC SB BORN UNDER ARIES sb whose birthday falls between 21 March and 19 April 3. ASTRON CONSTELLATION a zodiacal constellation of the northern hemisphere lying between Pisces and Taurus [Pre-12thC. From Latin *aries* 'ram'.] —**Aries** *adj.*

arietta /árri éttə/ *n.* a short simple aria in an opera, oratorio, or cantata [Early 18thC. From Italian, literally 'little aria'.]

aright /ə rīt/ *adv.* well, or in the correct or proper way (*archaic*)

aril /árril/ *n.* a fleshy, often brightly coloured seed covering in some plants. It draws attention to the seed and aids dispersal by birds. [Mid-18thC. Via modern Latin *arillus* from medieval Latin *arilli* 'dried grape pips', of unknown origin.] —**ariled** *adj.* —**arillate** /árri layt/ *adj.*

arioso /aári ṓzō, árri ṓssō/ *adj., adv.* SONGLIKE with intense lyricism or feeling ■ *n.* (*plural* **-sos**) SHORT LYRICAL PIECE a short lyrical aria or instrumental work [Early 18thC. From Italian, literally 'like an aria'.]

Ariosto /aári óstō/, **Ludovico** (1474–1533) Italian poet. His best-known work is the epic poem *Orlando Furioso* (1532).

arise /ə rīz/ (**arises, arising, arose** /ə rōz/, **arisen** /ə rízzn/) *vi.* 1. OCCUR to happen or come into existence, or be noticed or heard ○ *When did the problem arise?* 2. BE CAUSED BY STH to happen or exist as a result of sth 3. BECOME ACTIVE OR VOCAL to rise from a quiet, inactive, or subjugated state to become active, vocal, or rebellious (*literary*) 4. GO UP to move upwards to a higher place or level (*archaic or literary*) 5. STAND UP to stand up from a sitting, lying, or kneeling position (*archaic or literary*) 6. GET OUT OF BED to get out of bed (*archaic or literary*) [Old English *arisan* 'to rise up', from the same prehistoric Germanic ancestor as English *rise*]

arista /ə rístə/ (*plural* **-tae** /-tay, -tee/) *n.* 1. BOT = **awn** (*technical*) 2. INSECTS BRISTLE a bristly part of the antennae of some flies [Late 17thC. From Latin, 'ear of grain', of unknown origin.]

Aristarchus of Samos /árri staárkəss-/ (310?–250? BC) Greek astronomer. He proposed that the Earth rotates on its axis and orbits the Sun.

Aristide /árri steéd/, **Jean-Bertrand** (*b.* 1953) Haitian political leader. He was elected president of the independent republic of Haiti (1991–96) in Haiti's first free elections since 1804.

Aristides the Just /árri stī deez-/ (530–468 BC) Greek soldier-statesman. He commanded the Athenian land forces at Salamis against the Persians.

Aristippus /árri stíppəss/ (435?–360? BC) Greek philosopher. A student of Socrates, he founded the Cyrenaic school of hedonism, believing that pleasure is the highest good.

aristocracy /árris tókrəssi/ (*plural* **-cies**) *n.* 1. PEOPLE OF HIGHEST CLASS people of noble families or the highest social class 2. SUPERIOR GROUP a group acknowledged to be superior to all others of the same kind 3. GOVERNMENT BY ELITE government of a country by a small group of people, especially a hereditary nobility 4. STATE GOVERNED BY ARISTOCRACY a state governed by an aristocracy [15thC. Via French *aristocratie* from Greek *aristokratia* 'rule by the best', from *aristos* 'best' + *kratos* 'power, rule' (see -CRACY). The connotations of social class developed in the mid-17thC.]

aristocrat /árristə krat/ *n.* 1. MEMBER OF NOBILITY a member of the highest social class in a country 2. SUPPORTER OF ARISTOCRATIC RULE a member of a governing aristocracy, or sb who supports government by aristocracy 3. SUPERIOR PERSON a person, thing, or group believed to be superior to all others of the same kind

aristocratic /árristə kráttik/ *adj.* 1. OF CLASS OF NOBLES belonging or relating to the highest social class, especially the nobility 2. TYPICAL OF NOBILITY typical of people belonging to noble families, e.g. in having a grand lifestyle or elegant manners —**aristocratically** *adv.*

Aristophanes /árri stóffə neez/ (448?–385 BC) Greek dramatist. He satirized social and intellectual pretensions in plays such as *The Birds* (414 BC) and *The Clouds* (423 BC).

Aristotelian /árristə teéli ən/ *adj.* RELATING TO ARISTOTLE expressing or relating to the ideas of the Greek philosopher Aristotle ■ *n.* FOLLOWER OF ARISTOTLE a follower of Aristotle's philosophy

Aristotelian logic *n.* the system of logic developed by Aristotle, based on the kind of reasoning (**syllogism**) that reaches a conclusion from two independent statements with a common factor

Aristotle /árri stótt'l/ (384–322 BC) Greek philosopher and scientist. He was among the most influential of philosophers in Western history.

arithmetic n. /ə ríthmə tik/ **1. BASIC MATHS** the branch of mathematics that deals with addition, subtraction, multiplication, and division **2. CALCULATION USING BASIC MATHEMATICS** one or more calculations using basic mathematics **3. USE OF NUMBERS** the use of numbers in calculation, or educational exercises involving this **4. ABILITY TO DO ARITHMETIC** sb's ability to add, subtract, multiply, and divide (*informal*) ■ *adj*. /árrith méttik/ **RELATING TO ARITHMETIC** using, involving, or based on arithmetic [13thC. Via Old French *arismetique* from, ultimately, Greek *arithmētikē* (*tekhnē*) 'counting (art)', from *arithmein* 'to reckon', from *arithmos* 'number'.] —**arithmetical** /árrith méttik'l/ *adj.* —**arithmetically** /-méttikli/ *adv.* —**arithmetician** /ə ríthmə tísh'n/ *n.*

arithmetic logic unit n. the circuit in a computer's central processing unit that makes decisions based on the results of calculations

arithmetic mean n. the average of a set of numbers, calculated by adding them together and then dividing their sum by the number of terms

arithmetic progression n. a sequence of numbers in which a constant figure (**common difference**) is added to each term to give the next. For example, 3, 8, 13, 18 is an arithmetic progression in which the common difference is 5.

-arium *suffix.* a place or device connected with sth ○ *herbarium* [From Latin, neuter of *-arius*]

Ariz. *abbr.* Arizona

Arizona

Arizona /árri zṓnə/ state in the southwestern United States, bounded by New Mexico, Mexico, California, Nevada, and Utah. Capital: Phoenix. Population: 4,554,966 (1997). Area: 295,274 sq. km/114,000 sq. mi. —**Arizonan** *adj., n.* —**Arizonian** *adj., n.*

Arjuna /áarjoonə/ n. major character in the *Mahabharata*. Serving as his charioteer, Krishna explains Hindu doctrine to him.

ark /aark/ n. **1. NOAH'S SHIP** the ship that, according to biblical accounts, Noah was instructed to build by God to save his family and the animals from the Flood **2. SANCTUARY** a place providing refuge **3. ark, Ark** = Ark of the Covenant **4. ark, Ark CABINET CONTAINING TORAH SCROLLS** a cupboard in a synagogue in which the scrolls of the Torah are kept [Old English *ærc*, via prehistoric Germanic from Latin *arca* 'chest, box'] ◇ **out of the ark** extremely old or old-fashioned (*informal*)

—————— **WORD KEY: CULTURAL NOTE** ——————

Schindler's Ark, a novel by Thomas Kenneally (1982). It tells the true story of a German industrialist, Oskar Schindler, who helped thousands of Jews avoid the Nazi death camps by employing them in his factories. It was made into a film called *Schindler's List* by Steven Spielberg in 1993.

Ark. *abbr.* Arkansas

Arkansas /áarkən saw/ **1.** southern US state, bordered by Missouri, the Mississippi River, Louisiana, Texas, and Oklahoma. Capital: Little Rock. Population: 2,522,819 (1996). Area: 137,741 sq. km/53,182 sq. mi. **2.** major river of the central United States, rising in central Colorado and flowing south and eastwards to join the Mississippi River in southeastern Arkansas. The main cities along its course are Tulsa, Oklahoma, and Little Rock, Arkansas. Length: 2,350 km/1,460 mi.

Arkansas

Ark of the Covenant, Ark of the Testimony n. the chest in which, according to biblical accounts, Moses placed the two stone tablets containing the Ten Commandments. The Hebrews treasured it as the most sacred sign of God's presence among them.

arkose /áarkōss, -ōz/ n. a coarse-grained sedimentary rock rich in feldspar and quartz [Mid-19thC. From French, probably coined from Greek *arkhaios* 'ancient' (source of English *archaic*).]

Arkwright /áark rīt/, **Sir Richard** (1732–92) British industrialist. He invented the cotton spinning frame (1768) and introduced steam power into his Nottingham works (1790).

ARL *abbr.* Australian Rugby League

Arles /aarl/ city in the Bouches-du-Rhône Department in the Provence-Alpes-Côte-d'Azur Region in France, situated northwest of Marseilles. It was a major Roman city, and after the 10th century was the capital of a kingdom of the same name. Population: 52,593 (1990).

arm[1] /aarm/ n. **1. UPPER LIMB** a limb attached to the shoulder of the human body **2. PART OF GARMENT** the part of a piece of clothing that covers the arm **3. PART OF CHAIR** a side piece of a seat designed to support the arms **4. ANIMAL'S LIMB** a part of an animal's body that is similar to the human arm, or a flexible limb in an invertebrate such as an octopus **5. LONG PROJECTING PART OF STH** a part of sth that is similar to a human arm in function or appearance ○ *an arm of the sea* **6. DIVISION OF LARGER GROUP** a branch of an organization, especially a section of the armed forces [Old English *arm, earm*. Ultimately from an Indo-European word meaning 'fit, join'.] ◇ **an arm and a leg** a lot of money (*informal*) ○ *It would cost an arm and a leg to repair.* ◇ **arm in arm** holding each other affectionately by linking arms ◇ **at arm's length** in a position or situation that avoids involvement or familiarity ◇ **chance your arm** to make an attempt at sth, however unlikely you are to succeed (*informal*) ◇ **put the arm on sb 1.** *US* to try to force sb to do sth (*informal*) **2.** *US* to borrow money from sb (*informal*) ◇ **the long arm of the law** the far-reaching power of the police (*humorous*) ◇ **twist sb's arm** to try to persuade sb to do sth against his or her will ◇ **with open arms** in a friendly and welcoming way ◇ **would give your right arm for sth** would be willing to do or give almost anything to get sth that you want (*informal*)

arm[2] /aarm/ v. (**arms, arming, armed**) **1.** *vti.* **EQUIP WITH WEAPONS** to equip sb or a country with weapons **2.** *vt.* **ACTIVATE** to prepare a weapon so that it is ready to use **3.** *vt.* **PROVIDE WITH TOOLS** to provide sb with the information or equipment needed to do sth ○ *armed myself with statistics before the meeting* ■ *n.* **WEAPON** a weapon, especially one used in warfare (*often used in the plural*) ■ **arms** *npl.* **1. WARFARE** fighting and military activity **2.** = **coat of arms** [12thC. Via Old French *armer* from Latin *armare*, from *arma* (plural) 'weapons'.] ◇ **be up in arms** to protest or complain angrily ◇ **lay down your arms** to stop fighting ◇ **take up arms** to enter, or prepare to enter, a battle

ARM *abbr.* adjustable rate mortgage

armada /aar maadə/ n. a large fleet of ships [Mid-16thC. Via Spanish from, ultimately, medieval Latin *armata* (see ARMY).]

Armadillo

armadillo /áarmə díllō/ (*plural* **-los** *or* **-lo**) n. a burrowing mammal with a hard-plated body, found in temperate and tropical regions of the Americas. Armadillos are related to anteaters and sloths. Family: Dasypodidae. [Late 16thC. From Spanish, literally 'little armed man', from, ultimately, Latin *armare* 'to arm' (see ARM[2]).]

Armageddon /áarmə gédd'n/ n. **1. BIBLICAL BATTLE BETWEEN GOOD AND EVIL** in the Bible, the battle between the forces of good and evil that is predicted to mark the end of the world and precede the Day of Judgment. (Revelation 16:16). **2. ALL-DESTROYING WAR** any final and decisive war or conflict, e.g. a worldwide nuclear war [Early 19thC. Via late Latin from, ultimately, Hebrew *har megiddōn* 'hill of Megiddo'.]

Armagh /aar maa/ town in the province of Ulster, southern Northern Ireland. Population: 14,640 (1991). ■ historic county of Northern Ireland, in the province of Ulster. Area: 667 sq. km/258 sq. mi.

armament /áarməmənt/ n. **1. MILITARY WEAPONS** the guns and other weapons on a military aircraft, vehicle, or ship (*often used in the plural*) **2. PROCESS OF ARMING** the provision of weapons and equipment in preparation for war **3. FORCE EQUIPPED FOR WAR** a military force equipped for war (*archaic*) [Late 17thC. From Latin *armamentum*, from *armare* (see ARM[2]).]

armamentarium /áarmə men táiri əm/ (*plural* **-ums** *or* **-a** /-ri ə/) n. the complete range of equipment, medications, and techniques that a medical practitioner has at his or her disposal [Late 19thC. From Latin, 'arsenal, armoury', formed from *armare* (see ARM[2]).]

Armani /aar maani/, **Giorgio** (b. 1934) Italian fashion designer. He founded the Giorgio Armani fashion design company in 1975.

armature /áarməchər/ n. **1. ELEC ENG MOVING PART IN ELECTROMAGNETIC DEVICE** the moving part in an electromagnetic device, wound with coils that carry a current. In a dynamo, an electric current is induced in the coils when they revolve through a magnetic field. **2. KEEPER FOR MAGNET** a bar of soft iron or steel placed across the poles of a magnet to maintain its strength **3. BIOL PROTECTIVE PART** a protective outer covering or structure, e.g. quills on a porcupine or spines on a plant **4. SCULPTURE FRAMEWORK FOR A SCULPTURE** a framework that supports a sculpture while it is being modelled [15thC. Via French from Latin *armatura* (source also of English *armour*), from *armat-*, the past participle stem of *armare* (see ARM[2]). The original meaning was 'armour'.]

armband /áarm band/ n. a band of fabric worn around the upper arm

arm candy n. *US* a good-looking woman with whom a man does not have a relationship who accompanies him to a social event by prior arrangement, often for a fee (*slang humorous*)

armchair /áarm chair/ n. **CHAIR WITH ARMRESTS** a chair with arms, especially a comfortable upholstered chair ■ *adj.* **WITH NO FIRST-HAND EXPERIENCE** with no direct experience, only theoretical knowledge ○ *an armchair tourist*

armed /aarmd/ *adj.* **1. EQUIPPED WITH WEAPONS** equipped with one or more weapons ○ *armed robbers* **2. USING WEAPONS** involving the use of weapons ○ *armed conflict* **3. WITH EXPLODING MECHANISM ACTIVE** prepared and ready for use as a weapon, especially with a fuse or detonator activated **4. PROVIDED WITH NECESSARY THINGS**

equipped with the information or tools needed to achieve sth ○ *armed with the latest statistics*

armed forces *npl.* the combined bodies of troops of a country who fight on land, at sea, or in the air

Armenia

Armenia /aar meeénia/ country in southwestern Asia between the Black and the Caspian seas, surrounded by Azerbaijan, Azerbaijan-Nakcivan enclave, Iran, Turkey, and Georgia. Language: Armenian. Currency: dram. Capital: Yerevan. Population: 3,433,629 (1997). Area: 29,800 sq. km/11,506 sq. mi.

Armenian /aár meéeni ən/ *n.* **1.** PEOPLES SB FROM ARMENIA sb who was born or brought up in Armenia, or who is a citizen of Armenia **2.** LANG LANGUAGE OF ARMENIA the national language of Armenia, also spoken in Turkey and in many other parts of the world. It forms a distinct branch of Indo-European and is spoken by about six million people. —**Armenian** *adj.*

armful /aármfŏŏl/ *n.* the amount of sth that can be carried with one or both arms

armhole /aárm hōl/ *n.* either of the holes at the top of a garment for the wearer's arms to go through

Armidale /aármi dayl/ *n.* town in eastern New South Wales, Australia, home to the University of New England. Population: 21,330 (1996).

armiger /aármijər/ *n.* **1.** HERALDRY SB WITH COAT OF ARMS sb entitled to have a coat of arms (*archaic*) **2.** MIL MEDIEVAL SQUIRE a squire who carried a medieval knight's armour [Mid-16thC. From Latin, 'bearing weapons', formed from *arma* 'weapons' (see ARM[2]).]

Armillary sphere

armillary sphere /aar míləri-, aármiləri-/ *n.* a spherical model of the universe, first used by early Greek astronomers, in which the relative positions of the Earth and other celestial bodies are represented by intersecting metal rings ['Armillary' from modern Latin *armillaris*, from Latin *armilla* 'arm bracelet', literally 'little shoulder', from *armus* 'shoulder']

Arminian /aar mínni ən/ *adj.* OPPOSING CALVINISM relating to or following the Protestant theologian Arminius or his doctrines, which rejected the Calvinist view of absolute predestination ■ *n.* FOLLOWER OF ARMINIANISM a follower of Arminius or his doctrines [Early 17thC. Formed from *Arminius*, Latinized surname of Jakob Hermandszoon (1560–1609).] —**Arminianism** *n.*

armistice /aármistiss/ *n.* a truce in a war to discuss terms for peace [Early 18thC. Directly or via French from modern Latin *armistitium*, literally 'stoppage of weapons', coined from Latin *arma* 'weapons'.]

Armistice Day *n.* the former annual celebration of the armistice that ended World War I on 11 No-

vember 1918, now incorporated into the observance of Remembrance Sunday

armlet /aármlət/ *n.* **1.** BAND WORN ON ARM a band worn on the upper arm **2.** GEOG NARROW STRIP OF WATER a short narrow arm of a lake or the sea

armload /aárm lōd/ *n.* an amount of sth that can be carried with one or both arms

armlock /aárm lok/ *n.* a tight immobilizing grip around one or both of sb's upper arms, e.g. in wrestling or judo

armoire /aar mwaár/ *n.* a tall cupboard or wardrobe, often ornately decorated. Originally, an armoire was used for storing weapons. [Late 16thC. Via French from, ultimately, Latin *armarium* 'chest', from *arma* (plural) 'weapons, tools'.]

armor *n. US* = armour

armorial /aar máwri əl/ *adj.* relating to coats of arms or decorated with a coat of arms ○ *armorial bearings* [Late 16thC. Formed from obsolete *armory* 'heraldry', from Old French *armoi(e)rie*, from *armoier* 'to blazon', from *armes* (plural) 'weapons' (see ARM[2]).]

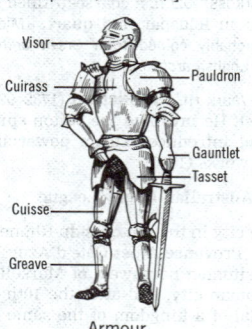
Armour

armour /aármər/ *n.* **1.** MIL PROTECTION FOR SOLDIERS protective clothing of metal or leather worn in battle by soldiers in former times **2.** MIL PROTECTION FOR MILITARY VEHICLES the protective layer of metal covering military vehicles, ships, and aircraft **3.** BIOL COVERING ON PLANTS OR ANIMALS a protective layer covering an animal or plant **4.** PROTECTION anything that gives protection or acts as a safeguard **5.** GEOG GRAVEL ON RIVER BED a surface layer of gravel in a river bed preventing erosion of the material below **6.** HERALDRY COATS OF ARMS coats of arms or the symbols and designs used on them [13thC. From French *armure* from Latin *armatura* (see ARMATURE).]

armoured /aármərd/ *adj.* **1.** WITH PROTECTIVE METAL COVERING with a protective metal covering to protect from bullets or missiles **2.** WITH ARMOURED VEHICLES using armoured vehicles **3.** WITH PROTECTIVE COVERING with a natural protective covering, e.g. a shell

armoured car *n.* **1.** LIGHT MILITARY VEHICLE a lightweight military vehicle that is lightly armoured and used mainly for reconnaissance **2.** CIVILIAN VEHICLE PROTECTED BY ARMOUR any vehicle, e.g. a security van, with an extra layer of thick metal to protect the occupants from bullets or other weapons

armourer /aármərər/ *n.* **1.** MAKER OF WEAPONS AND ARMOUR sb who makes and repairs armour and weapons **2.** SOLDIER MAINTAINING SMALL ARMS a soldier who repairs and maintains small arms

armour plate *n.* strong metal sheets used for protecting military vehicles, aircraft, and ships — **armour-plated** *adj.*

armoury /aárməri/ *n.* (*plural* -ies) *n.* **1.** STORE FOR WEAPONS a building in which weapons are stored **2.** COLLECTION OF WEAPONS a store or collection of weapons **3.** BUILDING FOR MILITARY TRAINING a building used for drilling and training militia **4.** RESOURCES OF ANY KIND a range of equipment and skills available to sb, used especially in dealing with opponents [14thC. From Old French *armoi(e)rie* 'weaponry' (see ARMORIAL), with the spelling changed on the model of ARMOUR.]

armpit /aárm pit/ *n.* **1.** HOLLOW UNDER ARM the hollow area under the arm where it joins the body **2.** US WORST PLACE a place that is the worst of its kind (*slang*)

armrest /aárm rest/ *n.* a projecting part, e.g. on a

chair, designed to support the arm of sb sitting down

arm's-length *adj.* without close contact or an intimate relationship ○ *the companies' arm's-length trading arrangement*

arms race *n.* the competition between countries for superiority in the number and power of weapons held

Armstrong, **Gillian** (*b.* 1950) Australian film-maker. She directed *My Brilliant Career* (1979) and *Oscar and Lucinda* (1997). Full name **Gillian May Armstrong**

Louis Armstrong

Armstrong, **Louis** (1900–71) US jazz musician. He was known for his trumpet playing and gravelly singing voice. Full name **Daniel Louis Armstrong**. Known as **Satchmo**

Neil Armstrong

Armstrong, **Neil** (*b.* 1930) US astronaut. He was the first person to set foot on the Moon (1969).

Armstrong, **William** (1810–1900) British engineer and industrialist. He became a major figure in the arms and shipbuilding industries and helped found the Vickers Armstrong company.

arm-twisting *n.* heavy-handed or unfair pressure on sb to do sth

arm wrestling *n.* a contest of strength between two people in which they sit opposite each other with one elbow each on a table, clasp hands, and try to force the opponent's hand onto the table

army /aármi/ (*plural* -mies) *n.* **1.** BRANCH OF ARMED FORCES the branch of a country's armed forces trained to fight on land **2.** LARGE ARMED GROUP any trained or armed fighting force **3.** LARGE ORGANIZED GROUP a large group that has been organized to do a particular task ○ *an army of volunteers* **4.** LARGE NUMBER OF THINGS a very large number of things [14thC. Via French *armée* from medieval Latin *armata* (source of English *armada*), from the past participle of Latin *armare* 'to arm' (see ARM[2]).]

army ant *n.* any nomadic tropical ant that forages in large groups

Army List *n.* an official list of all serving commissioned officers and reserve officers in the army

armyworm /aármi wurm/ *n.* the larva of any insect that travels in large migratory groups destroying vegetation and crops

Arne /aarn/, **Thomas** (1710–78) British composer. He composed operas, composed songs for the theatre (1760s), and wrote *Rule Britannia* (1740). Full name **Thomas Augustine Arne**

Arnhem /aárnəm/ city in the eastern Netherlands. It was the scene of a major battle in World War II, when Allied airborne troops fought unsuccessfully to secure Rhine bridges in September 1944. Population: 133,670 (1994).

Arnhem Land region in northern Australia, situated between the Roper and South Alligator rivers in the Northern Territory, and the site of one of Australia's largest Aboriginal reserves

arnica /aárnikə/ (plural -cas or -ca) n. 1. PLANT WITH YELLOW FLOWERS a perennial plant found in northern Europe, usually with yellow flowers like daisies. Genus: *Arnica*. 2. TREATMENT FOR BRUISES a liquid preparation made from the dried flower heads of arnica, used in alternative medicine for treating bruises and sprains [Mid-18thC. From modern Latin, of unknown origin.]

Arno /aárnō/ chief river of the Tuscany region in central Italy. It rises in the Tuscan Apennines and flows through of Florence and Pisa. Length: 240 km/about 150 mi.

Arnold, Sir Malcolm (b. 1921) British composer. He worked on film scores, including that for *Bridge Over the River Kwai* (1959), and also wrote symphonies, concertos, operas, and ballets.

Arnold, Matthew (1822–88) British poet and critic. He was professor of poetry at Oxford (1857), and in addition to poetry wrote critical and religious works.

Arnold, Thomas (1795–1842) British educator. He was the father of Matthew Arnold, and the influential reforming headmaster of Rugby school (1828–42).

Arnside and Silverdale /aárn sīd-sílvər dàyl/ Area of Outstanding Natural Beauty on the coast of Cumbria, England. Area: 75 sq. km/29 sq. mi.

A-road n. in the UK road network, a primary route other than a motorway, having the prefix 'A' in the national road numbering and classification system. An A-road is not necessarily any bigger than a B-road or other minor road, but it is more important.

aroha /aáróhə/ n. NZ love and compassion for others [From Maori, related to Hawaiian *aloha*]

aroid /árroyd/ adj. belonging to the arum family of perennial plants [Late 19thC. Coined from ARUM + -OID.]

aroma /ə rṓmə/ n. 1. SMELL a smell, especially a pleasant smell 2. QUALITY a subtle impression or quality [12thC. Via Latin from Greek, 'spice'.]

───── **WORD KEY: SYNONYMS** ─────
See Synonyms at *smell*.

aromatherapy /ə rṓmə thérrəpi/ n. the use of oils extracted from plants to alleviate physical and psychological disorders, usually through massage or inhalation [Mid-20thC. From French *aromathérapie*.] —**aromatherapist** n.

aromatic /árrə máttik/ adj. 1. WITH PLEASANT SMELL with a distinctive and pleasant smell 2. CHEM OF CLASS OF CHEMICAL COMPOUNDS used to describe a class of organic chemical compounds that contain one or more rings of carbon atoms and undergo chemical reactions that are characteristic of benzene. About half of all organic compounds are aromatic. ◊ aliphatic ■ n. FRAGRANT SUBSTANCE OR PLANT an aromatic substance or plant [14thC. Via French *aromatique* from, ultimately, Greek *arōma* 'spice'.] —**aromatically** adv.

aromatize /ə rṓmə tīz/ (-tizes, -tizing, -tized), **aromatise** (-tises, -tising, -tised) vt. 1. MAKE FRAGRANT to make sth fragrant, or release the fragrance of sth 2. CHEM CONVERT TO AROMATIC COMPOUND to convert a nonaromatic (**aliphatic**) compound to an aromatic compound —**aromatization** /ə rṓmə tī záysh'n/ n.

arose past tense of **arise**

around /ə rṓwnd/ CORE MEANING: a grammatical word used to indicate that sth surrounds a place or object or is situated on or moves around all sides of it ○ (prep) *She came in and looked at the mess all around her.* ○ (prep) *A crumbling wall still stood around the old town.* ○ (adv) *From this spot you could see the countryside for miles around.*
1. prep. TO THE OTHER SIDE OF moving or looking to the other side of ○ *around the corner* **2.** adv. IN OPPOSITE DIRECTION in the opposite direction ○ *turned around*

and walked away **3.** adv. PRESENT present or existing ○ *since computers have been around* **4.** adv., prep. FROM PLACE TO PLACE from place to place, in every or most parts ○ *rushing around* **5.** adv., prep. IN THE VICINITY in the vicinity, especially with no particular purpose or intent ○ *hanging around* **6.** adv., prep. HERE AND THERE in various unspecified parts of a place or area ○ *travelled around the country* **7.** adv., prep. APPROXIMATELY approximately ○ *around £600 a month* [13thC. Formed from A- 'on' + ROUND, probably on the model of Old French *a la reond* 'in the round, roundabout'.] ◇ **have been around** to have had enough experience of life and the ways of the world not to be easily deceived (*informal*)

around-the-clock adj. happening constantly with no breaks, for 24 hours a day

arousal /ə rṓwz'l/ n. 1. AROUSING OF EMOTION OR ACTIVITY the arousing of a feeling, response, or desire ○ *the arousal of feelings of jealousy* 2. SEXUAL DESIRE feelings of sexual desire 3. WAKING UP waking up from sleep, unconsciousness, or a similar state

arouse /ə rṓwz/ (**arouses, arousing, aroused**) v. 1. vt. STIMULATE to evoke a feeling, response, or desire 2. vt. STIMULATE SEXUAL DESIRE IN SB to cause feelings of sexual desire in sb 3. vt. ANGER to make sb angry 4. vti. WAKE UP to wake up, or wake sb up from sleep or unconsciousness (*formal*) [Late 16thC. Formed from ROUSE.]

Jean Arp

Arp /aarp/, **Jean** (1887–1966) French sculptor. A co-founder of the Dada movement (1916), he produced organic abstract sculpture based on natural forms. Also known as **Hans Arp**

arpeggio /aar péjji ō/ (plural -os) n. a sounding of the notes of a chord one after the other in rapid succession, rather than simultaneously [Early 18thC. From Italian, formed from *arpeggiare* 'to play on the harp', from *arpa* 'harp'.]

arquebus n. = **harquebus**

ARR abbr. accounting rate of return

arr. abbr. 1. MUSIC arranged 2. arrives 3. arrived 4. arrival

Arrabal /aárə bál/, **Fernando** (b. 1932) Moroccan-born Spanish dramatist and novelist. His plays, including *And They Put Handcuffs on the Flowers* (1971), were banned in France and Sweden for their deliberately shocking imagery.

arraign /ə ráyn/ (-raigns, -raigning, -raigned) vt. 1. LAW CHARGE SB IN COURT to bring sb to court to answer a charge (*usually passive*) 2. ACCUSE SB to call sb to account for a fault or mistake [14thC. Via Anglo-Norman *arainer* from assumed Vulgar Latin *adrationare* 'to call to account', literally 'to reason to', from Latin *ratio* 'reason' (source of English *reason*). The 'g' was probably introduced to give an appearance of Latin origin.] —**arraigner** n.

arraignment /ə ráynmənt/ n. LAW the legal process involved in bringing sb before a court of law to answer a charge

Arran /árrən/ island in the Firth of Clyde in western Scotland. It is noted for its mountain scenery. Area: 433 sq.km/169 sq.mi.

arrange /ə ráynj/ (-ranges, -ranging, -ranged) v. 1. vt. PREPARE FOR STH to do what is necessary to make sth happen in the future ○ *arrange a meeting* 2. vt. MAKE AGREEMENT FOR STH TO HAPPEN to make an agreement so that sth can happen or sb can have sth 3. vt. PUT SB

OR STH IN ORDER to put people or things in a position or order 4. vti. MUSIC ADAPT MUSIC to adapt a piece of music for playing or singing in a different manner (*often passive*) [Mid-18thC. From Old French *arangier*, literally 'to put in a line to', from *rangier* 'to put in a line' (see RANGE).] —**arrangeable** adj. —**arranger** n.

arranged /ə ráynjd/ adj. brought about by agreement or planning ○ *an arranged marriage*

arrangement /ə ráynjmənt/ n. 1. PREPARATION sth that has to be done so that sth else can happen in the future, or the making of such preparations (*often used in the plural*) 2. AGREEMENT an agreement made with sb to do sth, or the making of such an agreement 3. PLEASING DISPLAY a group of things organized in a way that is meant to be attractive, or the arranging of such a group 4. ORGANIZATION the way in which sth is organized 5. MUSIC MUSICAL ADAPTATION a version of a piece of music adapted for playing or singing in a different manner, or the scoring of such a version

arrant /árrənt/ adj. used to emphasize that sb or sth is an extreme example of sth disapproved of [Mid-16thC. Alteration of ERRANT 'wandering'; from its frequent application to roving vagabonds.] —**arrantly** adv.

arras /árrəss/ n. a tapestry used as a wall-hanging or hanging screen [15thC. From Anglo-Norman *draps d'Arras* 'cloth of Arras', named after *Arras*, a town in the Pas-de-Calais, northern France, which was famous for the manufacture of woollens and tapestry.]

array /ə ráy/ n. 1. COLLECTION a large number or wide range of people or things ○ *a dazzling array of talent* 2. STRIKING ARRANGEMENT a group of things arranged in an impressive or structured way ○ *an array of Greek sculptures* 3. FINE CLOTHES fine, expensive, or impressive clothes (*literary*) 4. MATH SET OF NUMBERS ARRANGED IN ORDER a set of numbers or symbols, e.g. experimental data, usually arranged in a particular order 5. TELECOM GROUP OF AERIALS a group of aerials arranged to increase their effectiveness 6. LAW JURORS a panel of jurors, or the group of people from whom a jury is selected 7. COMPUT DATA STRUCTURE an arrangement of items of computerized data in tabular form for easy reference. A computer program references an item by naming the array and the item's position in it. ■ vt. (-rays, -raying, -rayed) 1. ARRANGE STH to arrange sth for display or in readiness for use (*formal*) (*usually passive*) 2. DEPLOY TROOPS to arrange troops for battle (*literary*) (*usually passive*) 3. DRESS SB to dress sb in particular clothes (*literary; often passive*) [14thC. Via Anglo-Norman from Old French *arei*, from *areer* 'to array', from assumed Vulgar Latin *arredare* 'to arrange', from Latin *ad* 'to' + a prehistoric Germanic word meaning 'to prepare'.]

arrears /ə reérz/ npl. unpaid debts, especially debts accumulating as a result of the debtor's failure to make regular payments [15thC. From the obsolete adverb *arrear* 'to the rear, overdue', which came via Old French from medieval Latin *adretro*, from Latin *ad* 'to' + *retro* 'backward, behind' (source of English *retro*).] ◇ **in arrears 1.** behind in making regular payments of money owed **2.** be paid only after some work has been done or a period of time has elapsed

arrest /ə rést/ vt. (-rests, -resting, -rested) 1. TAKE SB INTO CUSTODY to take sb into custody on suspicion of having committed a crime 2. STOP OR SLOW STH to stop or slow a process (*formal*) ○ *a mechanism that arrests the motion of the flywheel* 3. TAKE HOLD OF STH to capture suddenly and hold sth, especially sb's attention (*formal*) 4. SEIZE STH LEGALLY to seize sth by legal authority (*formal*) ■ n. 1. TAKING OF SB INTO CUSTODY the taking of sb into custody on suspicion of having committed a crime ○ *a case of wrongful arrest* 2. CUSTODY the state of being held in custody on suspicion of having committed a crime ○ *You're under arrest!* 3. SUDDEN STOP a sudden stopping of the movement or operation of sth 4. LEGAL SEIZURE the legal seizure or detention of sth (*formal*) [14thC. Via Old French from assumed Vulgar Latin *arrestare* 'to cause to stop', literally 'to stop to', from Latin *restare* 'to stop, stay behind' (see REST).] —**arrestment** n.

arrestee /ə res teé/ n. sb who is under arrest

arrester /ə réstər/, **arrestor** /ə réstər, -awr/ n. 1. NAVY DEVICE TO STOP LANDING AIRCRAFT one of a set of cables on an aircraft carrier used to slow and stop landing aircraft **2.** LAW **ARRESTING OFFICER** sb who takes a suspect into legal custody

arresting /ə résting/ *adj.* looking so attractive or unusual that people's attention is immediately caught —**arrestingly** *adv.*

arresting cable *n.* one of a set of cables strung across the deck of an aircraft carrier to catch the tailhook of a landing aircraft and bring it to a halt (*usually used in the plural*)

arrest of judgment *n.* a delay in acting on the verdict of a court on the grounds of possible error

arrestor *n.* = **arrester**

arrhythmia /ə ríthmi ə, ay-/ *n.* an irregularity in the normal rhythm or force of a rhythmical action such as heartbeat or breathing [Late 19thC. From Greek, formed from *arruthmos*, literally 'without measure', from *rhuthmos* 'measure' (see RHYTHM).]

arrhythmic /ə ríthmik, ay-/ *adj.* **1. IRREGULAR** used to describe a rhythmical action such as heartbeart or breathing that is irregular **2. LACKING RHYTHM** without a regular or recognizable rhythm —**arrhythmically** *adv.*

arrière-pensée /árri air póN say/ *n.* (*formal*) **1. RESERVATION** a mental reservation **2. INTENTION** an unspoken intention [Early 19thC. From French, literally 'behind-thought', from the concealing of the thought.]

arris /árris/ (*plural* **-ris** *or* **-rises**) *n.* a sharp edge or ridge made by the meeting of two surfaces on an architectural column or moulding [Late 17thC. Via early modern French *areste* 'sharp edge' from Latin *arista* (see ARETE).]

arrival /ə rív'l/ *n.* **1. ARRIVING** the reaching of a place after coming from another place ○ *Her arrival caused a buzz of comment.* **2. NEWCOMER** sb or sth recently arriving at a place or joining a group ○ *a late arrival* **3. PASSENGER VEHICLE ARRIVING SOMEWHERE** an aircraft, train, or bus arriving at an airport or station **4. TIME OF ARRIVING** the time when sb or sth reaches a place after coming from another place ○ *date of arrival* **5. BEGINNING** the moment when sth begins or becomes important ○ *The arrival of television changed the world.* **6. BIRTH** the birth of a baby **7. REACHING OF STH** the achieving or reaching of sth after much work or effort ○ *Their arrival at a decision seems unlikely.*

arrive /ə rív/ (**-rives, -riving, -rived**) *vi.* **1. GET TO PLACE** to reach a place after coming from another place **2. BE DELIVERED** to be delivered or brought to sb or sth **3. BECOME AVAILABLE OR COMMON** to become available or common **4. BEGIN** to begin or happen after a period of time or waiting **5. BE BORN** to be born **6. WORK OUT SOLUTION** to reach a decision after thinking about or discussing a problem ○ *How did you arrive at the idea of using strings?* **7. SUCCEED** to become successful or famous (*informal*) ○ *You haven't arrived until you've eaten in this restaurant.* [12thC. Via Old French from assumed Vulgar Latin *arripare*, literally 'to come to shore', from Latin *ripa* 'shore' (source of English *river*).] —**arriver** *n.*

arrivederci /ə reevə dúrchi/ *interj.* goodbye for now [Late 20thC. From Italian *a rivederci*, literally 'until we see each other again', from *rivedere* 'to see again'.]

arriviste /árri veést/ *n.* sb who has recently become influential or socially prominent, especially sb suspected of self-serving or unscrupulous motives (*disapproving*) [Early 20thC. From French, literally 'sb who arrives'.]

arrogance /árrəgənss/ *n.* a strong feeling of proud self-importance that is expressed by treating other people with contempt

arrogant /árrəgənt/ *adj.* feeling or showing proud self-importance and contempt for others [14thC. Via French from Latin *arrogant-*, the present participle stem of *arrogare* 'to claim for yourself', literally 'to ask to', from *rogare* 'to ask' (see ROGATION).] —**arrogantly** *adv.*

WORD KEY: SYNONYMS

See Synonyms at ***proud***.

arrogate /árrə gayt/ (**-gates, -gating, -gated**) *vt.* (*formal*) **1. CLAIM STH WITHOUT RIGHT** to take or claim sth for yourself without the right to do so **2. ASSIGN STH TO ANOTHER** to assign or attribute sth to another in a way that is not warranted [Mid-16thC. From Latin *arrogat-*, the past participle stem of *arrogare* (see ARROGANT).] —**arrogation** /árrə gáysh'n/ *n.* —**arrogator** /-gaytər/ *n.*

arrondissement /a róN deess móN/ (*plural* **-ments** /-móN/) *n.* **1. SUBDIVISION OF FRENCH DEPARTMENT** an administrative area in France that is the largest subdivision of a department **2. AREA OF FRENCH CITY** an administrative area in some large cities in France, including Paris [Early 19thC. From French, formed from *arrondiss-*, a stem of *arrondir* 'to make round'.]

arrow /árrō/ *n.* **1. MISSILE SHOT FROM BOW** a long thin missile pointed at one end and usually with feathers at the other, fired from a bow **2. DIRECTION SIGN** a direction sign consisting of a horizontal stroke finishing in the middle of a V shape ■ *vi.* **DART** to move quickly like an arrow shot from a bow [Old English *arwe*. From the Old Norse stem *ǫrv-*. Ultimately from an Indo-European word that also produced English *arc* and *archer*. The original meaning may have been 'bow', and by extension 'thing belonging to the bow'.]

arrowhead /árrō hed/ *n.* **1. POINT OF ARROW** a sharp pointed tip fixed to an arrow **2. AQUATIC PLANT** an aquatic plant with arrow-shaped leaves and clusters of white flowers, native to Asia and North America. Genus: *Sagittaria*.

arrowroot /árrō root/ (*plural* **-root** *or* **-roots**) *n.* **1.** PLANTS **WEST INDIAN PLANT** a West Indian plant with white flowers and rhizomes that yield an edible starch. Latin name: *Maranta arundinacea*. **2.** FOOD **EDIBLE RHIZOME** the edible rhizome of the arrowroot plant **3. STARCH** starch from the rhizomes of the arrowroot plant, used as a thickener for clear sauces [Late 17thC. By folk etymology from Arawak *aru-aru*, literally 'meal of meals', from the use of the tubers to absorb poison from arrow wounds.]

arrow-wood (*plural* **arrow-woods** *or* **arrow-wood**) *n.* a shrub with tough, straight stems that were previously used by Native Americans to make arrows. Genus: *Viburnum*.

arrow worm *n.* a marine invertebrate animal that has an arrow-shaped body and spines on its head for catching prey. Phylum: Chaetognatha. [From the shape of the head with its curved bristles on either side, suggesting an arrow]

arse /aarss/ *n.* (*taboo offensive*) **1. HUMAN BOTTOM** a person's buttocks or anus. US term **ass**[2] **2. OFFENSIVE TERM** an offensive term for an unintelligent or contemptible person [Old English *ærs, ears*. Ultimately from an Indo-European word meaning 'buttocks' that is also the ancestor of *anuran* and *squirrel*.] ◇ **move** *or* **shift your arse** to hurry up (*taboo offensive*) ◇ **not know your arse from your elbow** to know very little (*taboo offensive*) **arse about, arse around** *vi.* to waste time behaving in a silly irritating way (*taboo offensive*)

arsehole /áars hōl/ *n.* **1. STUPID PERSON** a contemptible person (*taboo insult*) **2. ANUS** the anus (*taboo offensive*) = **arsehole**

arse licker *n.* sb who flatters or slavishly carries out the orders of a superior in order to gain favour (*taboo offensive*) —**arse-licking** *n.*

arsenal /áarss'nəl/ *n.* **1. ARMAMENTS** a stockpile of weapons and military equipment **2. STORE FOR WEAPONS** a building where weapons and military equipment are stored **3. RESOURCES** a supply of methods or resources ○ *arsenal of teaching strategies* [Early 16thC. Directly or via French from Italian *arzanale*, from Venetian Italian *arzanà*, from, ultimately, Arabic *dār-(aṣ-)ṣinā'a* 'workshop, factory', literally 'house of the manufacture'.]

WORD KEY: ORIGIN

Arsenal is derived from an Arabic word *dār-(aṣ-)ṣinā'a*, meaning 'workshop' or 'factory'. When the original Arabic word was borrowed into Venetian Italian, the initial *d* was lost, possibly because it was misinterpreted as the Italian preposition *de* 'of'. The word came to mean 'dock possessing naval stores', and the dockyard in Venice, which in the 15th century was the leading naval power in the Mediterranean, is known to this day as the *Arzenale*. The Romance languages retain this meaning in words from the same ancestor that still show the Arabic *d*, in Italian *darsena* 'dock', for example; in English too, 'dockyard' was the original sense, giving way in the late 16th century to 'military storehouse'.

arsenate /áarssə nayt, -nit/ *n.* any salt of arsenic acid [Early 19thC. Coined from ARSENIC + -ATE.]

arsenic /áarssnik/ *n.* **1. POISONOUS ELEMENT** a steel-grey poisonous solid chemical element that is a brittle crystalline metalloid used in alloys. Symbol **As 2.** = **arsenic trioxide** ■ *adj.* **CONTAINING ARSENIC** relating to or containing arsenic with a valency of 5 [14thC. Via French from, ultimately, Greek *arsenikon* 'yellow orpiment', from Arabic *az-zarnīk*, literally 'the orpiment', from, ultimately, Persian *zar* 'gold'.]

WORD KEY: ORIGIN

The term ***arsenic*** was originally applied to the lemon-yellow mineral arsenic trisulphide, hence its origin in *zar*, the Persian word for gold. The Arabic derivative of this word was misinterpreted by foreign listeners as including the definite article *al*, and in Greek the supposed beneficial effects on virility led the term to be associated by folk etymology with the similar-sounding words *arsenikos*, 'masculine', and *arsēn*, 'manly'. In English the word still referred to the mineral at first (for which *orpiment* was the other current name), and it is not until the early 17th century that it becomes used for white arsenic or arsenic trioxide. The element arsenic itself was isolated and so named at the start of the 19th century.

arsenic acid /aar sénnik-/ *n.* a white crystalline solid that contains arsenic. It is poisonous and is used to make arsenates and insecticides. Formula: H_3AsO_4.

arsenical /aar sénnik'l/ *adj.* **RELATING TO ARSENIC** relating to or containing arsenic ■ *n.* **SUBSTANCE CONTAINING ARSENIC** a substance, e.g. a drug or insecticide, that contains arsenic

arsenic trioxide /áarssnik trī óksīd, aar sénnik trī óksīd/ *n.* a white solid that contains arsenic. It is poisonous and is used as an insecticide, rat poison, and weed killer, and in making glass and pigments. Formula: AS_2O_3.

arsenide /áarssə nīd/ *n.* a chemical compound of arsenic and a metal [Mid-19thC. Coined from ARSENIC + -IDE.]

arsenious /aar seéni əss/ *adj.* relating to or containing arsenic with a valency of 3 [Early 19thC. Coined from ARSENIC + -IOUS.]

arsenopyrite /áarssinō pír īt, aar sénnə-/ *n.* a grey to white mineral with metallic lustre consisting of a sulphide of iron and arsenic. Formula: FeAsS. [Mid-19thC. Coined from ARSENIC + PYRITE.]

arsine /áar seen/ *n.* a colourless poisonous gas with an odour like garlic, used to make organic compounds and transistors and as a chemical weapon. Formula: AsH_3. [Late 19thC. Coined from ARSENIC + -INE.]

arsis /áarssiss/ (*plural* **-ses** /-seez/) *n.* **1. SHORT SYLLABLE** in classical Greek and Roman verse, the short syllable or syllables in a metrical foot. ◊ **thesis** *n.* 6 **2. ACCENTED SYLLABLE** in modern accentual verse, the accented syllable in a metrical foot. ◊ **thesis** *n.* 7 [14thC. Via late Latin, 'raising of the voice to greater force, accented part of the metrical foot', from Greek *arsis* 'raising (of the foot in beating time)'.]

arson /áarss'n/ *n.* the burning of a building or other property for a criminal or malicious reason [Late 17thC. Via legal Anglo-Norman *arsoun* from, ultimately, Latin *arsus*, the past participle of *ardere* 'to burn' (source of English *ardent* and *ardour*). Ultimately from an Indo-European word meaning 'to burn', which is also the ancestor of English *ash* and *arid*.]

arsonist /áars'nist/ *n.* sb who sets fire to a building or other property for a criminal or malicious reason

arsy-versy /áarsi vúrsi/ *adv.* backwards or upside down (*dated informal*) [Mid-16thC. From ARSE + Latin *versus* 'turned' (see VERSUS), with -y added to both elements to make a jingle, perhaps on the model of VICE VERSA.]

art[1] /aart/ *n.* **1. CREATION OF BEAUTIFUL THINGS** the creation of beautiful or thought-provoking works, e.g. in painting, music, or writing **2. BEAUTIFUL OBJECTS** beautiful or thought-provoking works produced through creative activity **3. BRANCH OF ART** a branch or category of art, especially one of the visual arts **4. ARTISTIC SKILL** the skill and technique involved in producing visual representations **5. STUDY OF ART** the study of a branch of the visual arts **6. CREATION BY HUMANS** creation by human endeavour rather than by nature

7. TECHNIQUES OR CRAFT the techniques used by sb in a particular field, or the use of those techniques ○ *the art of the typographer* **8. ABILITY** the skill or ability to do sth well **9. CUNNING** the ability to achieve things by deceitful or cunning methods (*literary*) ■ **arts** *npl*. **1. FORMS OF CREATIVE BEAUTY** the activities enjoyed for the beauty they create or the way they present ideas, e.g. painting, music, and literature **2. NON-SCIENTIFIC SUBJECTS** nonscientific and nontechnical subjects at school or university [13thC. Via French from the Latin stem *art-* 'skill' (source of English *artisan* and *artificial*). Ultimately from an Indo-European word meaning 'to fit together'.] ◇ **have sth down to a fine art** to be able to do sth very skilfully

─────── **WORD KEY: ORIGIN** ───────
The Latin stem *art-* is also the source of the English words *artificial*, *artisan*, and *inert*.
─────────────────────────────

art² /aart/ 2nd person present singular of **be** (*archaic or literary*)

art. *abbr*. **1.** article **2.** artificial **3.** artillery **4.** artist

-art *suffix.* = **-ard**

artal plural of **rotl**

Art deco: Chrysler Building, New York City (1930), designed by William van Alen

art deco /-dékō/, **Art Deco** *n*. a style of architecture, interior design, and jewellery most popular in the 1930s that used geometrical designs and bold colours and outlines [Mid-20thC. From French, shortening of *Arts Décoratifs*, literally 'decorative arts', from *Exposition Internationale des Arts Décoratifs et Industriels Modernes* 'International Exposition of Modern Decorative and Industrial Arts', held in Paris, France, in 1925.]

art director *n*. the person in charge of the sets and costumes when sth is being filmed or photographed

artefact, **artifact** *n*. **1. OBJECT MADE BY HUMAN** an object made by a human being, especially one that has archaeological or cultural interest **2. FOREIGN SUBSTANCE** sth in a biological specimen that is not present naturally but has been introduced or produced during some procedure [Early 19thC. From Latin *arte*, a form of *ars* 'skill' (see ART) + *factum* 'thing made' (see FACT).]

artel /aar tél/ *n*. a workers' or producers' cooperative in pre-Revolutionary Russia or the Soviet Union [Late 19thC. From Russian *artel*, of uncertain origin.]

Artemis /aártəmiss/ *n*. in Greek mythology, the goddess of hunting and the moon, and of childbirth. She was the daughter of Zeus and the sister of Apollo. Roman equivalent **Diana**

artemisia /aárti meézi ə, -mízzi ə/ (*plural* **-as** *or* **-a**) *n*. an aromatic plant found in the northern hemisphere that has greyish-green leaves and many small flower heads. Genus: *Artemisia*. [14thC. Via Latin from Greek, 'wormwood', literally 'plant sacred to *Artemis*', goddess of childbirth and fertility. Perhaps from the medicinal use of the herb for diseases of the womb.]

arterial /aar teéri əl/ *adj*. **1. OF ARTERIES** relating to, affecting, or used in arteries **2. OXYGENATED** used to describe the bright red blood in the arteries that has absorbed oxygen **3. MAIN** constituting a main route in a road, rail, or river system —**arterially** *adv*.

arterialize /aar teéri ə līz/ (**-izes**, **-izing**, **-ized**), **arterialise** (**-ises**, **-ising**, **-ised**) *vt*. to convert venous blood into arterial blood by replenishing its oxygen —**arterialization** /aar teéri ə līzáysh'n/ *n*.

arterio- *prefix.* artery, arterial ○ *arteriovenous* [From Greek *artēria* (see ARTERY)]

arteriogram /aar teéri ə gram/ *n*. an X-ray of the arteries made after a substance that shows up on an X-ray has been injected into the bloodstream

arteriography /aar teéri óggrəfi/ *n*. examination of the arteries by X-raying them after injecting into the bloodstream a substance that shows up on an X-ray —**arteriographic** /aar teéri ə gráffik/ *adj*.

arteriole /aar teéri ōl/ *n*. a blood vessel that branches off from an artery [Mid-19thC. From French *artériole*, literally 'little artery', from *artère* 'artery', from Latin *arteria* (see ARTERY).] —**arteriolar** /aar teéri ōlər/ *adj*.

arteriosclerosis /aar teéri ō sklə róssiss/ *n*. the arterial disease atherosclerosis (*dated*) —**arteriosclerotic** /-sklə róttik/ *adj*.

arteriovenous /aar teéri ō veénəss/ *adj*. involving both a vein and an artery

arteritis /aártə rítiss/ *n*. inflammation of the walls of an artery

artery /aártəri/ (*plural* **-ies**) *n*. **1. TYPE OF BLOOD VESSEL** a blood vessel that is part of the system carrying blood under pressure from the heart to the rest of the body **2. MAIN ROUTE** a main route in a road, rail, or river system [14thC. Via Latin from Greek *artēria* 'windpipe', of uncertain origin. The Greeks called arteries 'windpipes' because they regarded them as air ducts branching from the trachea; since arteries do not contain blood after death, it was supposed that their function was conveying air.]

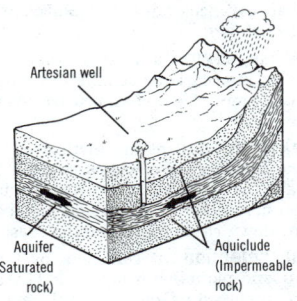
Artesian well

artesian well /aar teézi ən-/ *n*. a well drilled through impermeable rocks into strata where water is under enough pressure to force it to the surface without pumping [Mid-19thC. 'Artesian' from French *artésien*, literally 'of Artois' (*Arteis* in Old French), a region in northeastern France where such wells were first drilled in the 18thC.]

art film *n*. a film that is made as a work of art rather than for mass entertainment

art form *n*. **1. ARTISTIC MEDIUM** a creative activity or type of artistic expression that is intended to be beautiful or thought-provoking **2. STH DONE ARTISTICALLY** sth that is done in such a sophisticated or skilful way that it can be seen as artistic

artful /aártf'l/ *adj*. **1. CUNNING** using subtle and clever means to achieve things **2. PERFORMED WITH CLEVERNESS** performed with cleverness and subtlety **3. SKILFUL** done skilfully or with taste —**artfully** *adv*. —**artfulness** /-nəss/ *n*.

art gallery (*plural* **art galleries**) *n*. **1. MUSEUM OF ART** a building where works of art are displayed **2. PLACE SELLING ART** an establishment that displays and sells works of art

art house (*plural* **art houses**) *n*. a cinema where art films are shown

arthr- *prefix.* = **arthro-** (*used before vowels*)

arthralgia /aar thráljə/ *n*. pain in a joint —**arthralgic** *adj*.

arthrectomy /aar thréktəmi/ (*plural* **-mies**) *n*. the surgical removal of a joint

arthritic /aar thríttik/ *adj*. **WITH ARTHRITIS** affected by arthritis ■ *n*. **SB WITH ARTHRITIS** sb who has arthritis —**arthritically** *adv*.

arthritis /aar thrítiss/ *n*. a medical condition affecting a joint or joints, causing pain, swelling, and stiffness [Mid-16thC. Via Latin from Greek *arthritis* 'joint disease', from *arthron* 'joint'. Ultimately from an Indo-European word meaning 'to fit together', which is also the ancestor of English *read* and *logarithm*.]

arthro-, **arthr-** *prefix.* joint ○ *arthroscopic* [From Greek *arthron*. Ultimately from an Indo-European base meaning 'to fit together', which is also the ancestor of English *arm*, *article*, and *art*.]

arthrogram /aárthrə gram/ *n*. an X-ray of the inside of a damaged joint made after a substance that shows up on an X-ray has been injected into the joint

arthrography /aar thróggrəfi/ *n*. examination of the inside of a damaged joint by X-raying it after injecting a substance that shows up on an X-ray

arthropathy /aar thróppəthi/ *n*. an abnormality or disease of a joint

arthroplasty /aárthrə plasti/ (*plural* **-ties**) *n*. surgical repair of a joint or replacement of a joint or part of one by metal or plastic parts. The most common operations are hip and knee replacements.

arthropod /aárthrə pod/ *n*. an invertebrate animal that has jointed limbs, a segmented body, and an exoskeleton made of chitin. Insects, arachnids, centipedes, and crustaceans are arthropods. Phylum: Arthropoda. [Late 19thC. From modern Latin *Arthropoda*, phylum name, from Greek *arthron* 'joint' (see ARTHRITIS) + the stem *pod-* 'foot' (see -POD).] —**arthropod** *adj*. —**arthropodal** /aar thróppəd'l/ *adj*. —**arthropodous** /-əss/ *adj*.

arthroscopy /aar thróskəpi/ (*plural* **-pies**) *n*. inspection of the inside of a joint of the body using an endoscope —**arthroscope** /aárthrəskōp/ *n*. —**arthroscopic** /aárthrə skóppik/ *adj*. —**arthroscopically** /-skóppikli/ *adv*.

arthrosis /aar thróssiss/ (*plural* **-ses** /-seez/) *n*. **1. JOINT BETWEEN BONES** a joint between two bones (*technical*) **2. JOINT DISEASE** a degenerative disease of a joint [Mid-17thC. Via Latin from Greek *arthrōsis*, from *arthroun* 'to articulate', from *arthron* 'joint' (see ARTHRITIS). The sense 'joint disease' is modelled on other disease names ending in -OSIS.]

arthrotomy /aar thróttəmi/ (*plural* **-mies**) *n*. a surgical operation that involves cutting into a joint of the body

Arthur /aárthər/, **Chester A.** (1829–86) US statesman and 21st president of the United States. A Republican president (1881–85), he enacted sweeping civil service reforms (1883) that lost him the support of his party. Full name **Chester Alan Arthur**

Arthur I *n*. in medieval legend, a king of the Britons whose court was based at Camelot. He was the leader of the Knights of the Round Table. —**Arthurian** /aar thyoóri ən/ *adj*.

Arthurs Pass National Park national park in the South Island of New Zealand. It was established in 1929. Area: 980 sq. km/380 sq. mi.

artic /aar tík/ *n*. an articulated lorry (*informal*) [Mid-20thC. Shortening.]

Artichoke

artichoke /aártichōk/ (*plural* **-chokes** *or* **-choke**) *n*. **1. PLANT WITH EDIBLE FLOWER BUDS** a plant native to Europe and Asia that has flowers that resemble thistles. Latin name: *Cynara scolymus*. **2. FLOWER BUD EATEN AS VEGETABLE** the flower bud of an artichoke plant, parts of which can be eaten after cooking **3.** = **Jerusalem**

artichoke [Mid-16thC. From Northern Italian *articiocco, arciciocco*, from Italian *arcicioffo*, from Spanish *alcarchofa*, from Arabic *al-karšūf(a)*, literally 'the artichoke'.]

article /áartik'l/ *n.* **1. NEWSPAPER OR REFERENCE PIECE** a piece of nonfiction writing in a newspaper, magazine, or reference book ○ *an article on ecology* **2. ITEM** an object or item, especially one that is part of a group ○ *articles of clothing* **3.** LAW **LEGAL PARAGRAPH** a section of a legal document that deals with a particular point **4.** GRAM **WORD BEFORE NOUN** a word used with a noun that specifies whether the noun is definite or indefinite. In English the indefinite articles are 'a' and 'an', and the definite article is 'the'. ■ *vt.* **(-cles, -cling, -cled)** LAW **BIND SB BY CONTRACT** to bind sb by the articles of a contract, especially sb training in the legal profession [12thC. Via French from Latin *articulus* 'joint, section', literally 'little joint', from *artus* 'joint, limb'. The sense 'section of a text' came from the idea of a joint as a section of a limb. The meaning 'item' is a 19thC development.]

articled clerk *n.* a former title of a person being trained as a solicitor while working in a solicitor's office (*dated*)

article of faith *n.* **1. BASIC RELIGIOUS BELIEF** any one of the items that must be believed as part of a creed or statement of faith **2. DEEPLY HELD BELIEF** sth that sb believes completely

articles of association *npl.* the regulations and constitution that a registered company is legally required to have by the British Companies Acts

articulable /aar tíkyŏŏləb'l/ *adj.* able to be expressed clearly in words

articular /aar tíkyŏŏlər/ *adj.* relating to or involving a joint of the body [15thC. From Latin *articularis*, from *articulus* 'joint' (see ARTICLE).] —**articularly** *adv.*

articulate *adj.* /aar tíkyŏŏlət/ **1. ELOQUENT** able to express thoughts, ideas, and feelings coherently **2. COHERENT** spoken or expressed clearly **3. ABLE TO SPEAK** possessing the power of speech **4.** ANAT **JOINTED** with joints or jointed segments, as in the bodies of higher vertebrates and arthropods (*technical*) ■ *v.* /aar tíkyŏŏ layt/ **(-lates, -lating, -lated) 1.** *vt.* **COMMUNICATE STH** to express thoughts, ideas, or feelings coherently ○ *unable to articulate his grief* **2.** *vti.* **SPEAK DISTINCTLY** to pronounce sth or speak clearly **3.** *vti.* **JOIN TO ALLOW MOVEMENT** to form the kind of joint that allows movement **4.** *vi.* **SPEAK INTELLIGIBLY** to utter intelligible speech [Mid-16thC. From Latin *articulatus*, the past participle of *articulare* 'to divide into joints, speak distinctly', from *articulus* 'joint' (see ARTICLE).] —**articulacy** /aar tíkyŏŏlǝssi/ *n.* —**articulately** /-lǝtli/ *adv.* —**articulateness** /-lǝtnǝss/ *n.*

articulated /aar tíkyŏŏ laytid/ *adj.* made up of two or more sections connected by a joint that can pivot

articulated lorry (*plural* **articulated lorries**) *n.* a lorry made up of two parts, tractor and trailer, connected by a joint that can pivot

articulation /aar tíkyŏŏ láysh'n/ *n.* **1. SPEECH** the pronouncing of words, or the manner in which they are pronounced **2. COMMUNICATION** the coherent expression of thoughts, ideas, or feelings **3. JOINTING** the connection of the different parts of sth by joints, or the way the parts fit together **4.** ANAT **ANIMAL'S JOINT** a joint in an animal (*technical*) **5.** BOT **PLANT NODE** a node of a plant, or the space on a stem between two nodes (*technical*) —**articulative** /aar tíkyŏŏlǝtiv/ *adj.* —**articulatory** /-lǝtǝri, -tíkyŏŏ láytǝri/ *adj.*

articulator /aar tíkyŏŏ laytǝr/ *n.* **1. COMMUNICATOR** sb who speaks or expresses things clearly **2.** PHON **VOCAL ORGANS** a part of the vocal organs that helps form speech sounds

articulatory phonetics *n.* the branch of phonetics that deals with how speech sounds are made

artifact /áarti fakt/ *n.* = **artefact**

artifice /áartifiss/ *n.* (*formal*) **1. CLEVER TRICK** a clever trick or stratagem **2. CLEVERNESS** the use of clever stratagems or tricks **3. INSINCERE BEHAVIOUR** the deceiving of people in a clever or subtle way [Early 17thC. Via French from, ultimately, Latin *artificium* 'craft, art, cunning', from the stem *artific-* 'artisan, contriver', from the stem *art-* 'skill' (see ART) + *facere* 'to make' (see FACT).]

artificer /aar tíffissǝr/ *n.* (*dated*) **1. SKILLED WORKER** sb whose work requires manual skill **2. INVENTOR** sb who invents or devises things [14thC. Via Anglo-Norman (with influence from medieval Latin *artificiarius*) from, probably, Old French *artificien*, from, ultimately, Latin *artificium* 'craft, cunning'.]

artificial /áarti físh'l/ *adj.* **1. MADE BY HUMANS** made by human beings rather than occurring naturally **2. SYNTHETIC** made in imitation of sth natural **3. INSINCERE** without sincerity or spontaneity (*disapproving*) ○ *an artificial smile* **4. NOT SPONTANEOUS** produced as a result of human action rather than arising spontaneously ○ *an artificial barrier to social advancement* [14thC. Directly or via Old French from Latin *artificialis*, from *artificium* 'craft, cunning' (see ARTIFICE).] —**artificiality** /áartifishi állǝti/ *n.* —**artificially** /áarti físh'li/ *adv.*

artificial horizon *n.* an instrument that displays, usually pictorially, the amount of pitch or bank of an aircraft relative to the horizon

artificial insemination *n.* a method of inducing pregnancy in a female mammal by injecting sperm into the womb. The technique is used in agriculture to improve the breeding of livestock.

artificial intelligence *n.* **1. DEVELOPMENT OF INTELLIGENT MACHINES** a branch of computer science devoted to the development of computer programs that will allow machines to perform functions normally requiring human intelligence **2. COMPUTER INTELLIGENCE** the ability of computers to perform functions that normally require human intelligence

artificialize /áarti físhǝ līz/ **(-izes, -izing, -ized)**, **artificialise (-ises, -ising, -ised)** *vt.* to give sth an artificial appearance or quality —**artificialization** /áarti físhǝ lī záysh'n/ *n.*

artificial language *n.* a language that has been invented for international communication or for use with computers. The best known artificial language is Esperanto.

artificial respiration *n.* any method of forcing air into the lungs of sb who has stopped breathing, especially the method that involves blowing air into the mouth. Another formerly used method involved pushing down rhythmically on the chest.

artificial selection *n.* selection by humans of animals and plants with desirable characteristics for use in breeding over several generations. ◊ **natural selection**

artificial sweetener *n.* a synthetic sugar substitute used as an ingredient in low-calorie drinks or food or added to drinks such as coffee or tea by slimmers or people with diabetes

artillery /aar tíllǝri/ *n.* **1. POWERFUL GUNS** heavy-calibre firearms, e.g. cannons, howitzers, missile-launchers, and mortars **2. SOLDIERS USING POWERFUL GUNS** soldiers who specialize in operating large, powerful firearms, regarded as a group or unit [14thC. From French *artillerie*, from *artiller* 'to equip, arm', from (with influence by folk etymology from *art* 'skill') *atillier* 'to equip, arm', of uncertain origin.]

artilleryman /aar tíllǝrimǝn/ (*plural* **-men** /-mǝn/) *n.* a soldier in an artillery unit

artillery plant *n.* a tropical American plant with fleshy leaves and stamens that discharge their pollen by exploding. Latin name: *Pilea microphylla*.

artiodactyl /áarti ō dáktil/ *n.* any herbivorous, hooved mammal with an even number of toes on each foot. Cows, sheep, and deer are artiodactyls. Order: Artiodactyla. [Mid-19thC. From modern Latin *Artiodactyla*, order name, literally 'even-toed ones', which was coined from Greek *artios* 'even, fitting' + *dactylos* 'finger, toe'.] —**artiodactylous** *adj.*

artisan /áarti zan, -zán/ *n.* sb who is skilled at a craft [Mid-16thC. Via French from Italian *artigiano*, from, ultimately, Latin *artit-*, the past participle stem of *artire* 'to instruct in the arts', from the stem *art-* 'work of art, skill' (see ART).] —**artisanship** /áartiz'n ship/ *n.*

artist /áartist/ *n.* **1. CREATOR OF ART** sb who creates art, especially paintings, drawings, or sculptures **2. PERFORMER** a professional entertainer **3. SKILLED PERSON** sb who does sth with great skill and creativity **4. PERSON GOOD AT STH** sb who is very good at doing sth (*slang*) [Late 16thC. Via French *artiste* from Italian *artista*, from *arte* 'art' (see ART).]

artiste /aar téest/ *n.* **1. PERFORMER** a professional entertainer, especially a singer or dancer **2. ARTISTIC PRETENDER** sb who would like to be regarded as artistic (*ironic*) [Early 19thC. From French, 'artist' (see ARTIST).]

artistic /aar tístik/ *adj.* **1. GOOD AT ART** good at a form of creative expression **2. OF ART** involving or typical of art or artists **3. TASTEFUL** showing taste, skill, and imagination **4. APPRECIATIVE OF ART** able to appreciate the beauty and worth of art —**artistically** *adv.*

artistry /áartistri/ *n.* **1. ARTISTIC ABILITY** the creative ability and skill of an artist, or the expression of this **2. GREAT SKILL** great ability and skill in doing sth

artless /áartlǝss/ *adj.* **1. WITHOUT DECEPTION** without guile or deception **2. TOTALLY NATURAL** completely natural and unforced **3. INELEGANT** lacking skill, knowledge, or elegance —**artlessly** *adv.* —**artlessness** *n.*

WORD KEY: SYNONYMS

See Synonyms at ***naive***.

---

art music *n.* music composed in the classical tradition rather than in a folk or pop style

art nouveau /áart noo vṓ, aár-/, **Art Nouveau** *n.* a style of art, architecture, and decoration popular in the 1890s that used stylized natural forms and flowing lines [Early 20thC. From French, literally 'new art'.]

art paper *n.* a high-quality paper coated with china clay or sth similar to give it a smooth, shiny surface

arts and crafts *n.* the art of decorative design applied to everyday objects (*takes a singular or plural verb*)

Arts and Crafts *n.* a movement in the late 19th and early 20th centuries in Britain and the United States that stressed the value of artisanship

art song *n.* a lyric song composed in the classical tradition

artsy-fartsy /áartsi faártsi/ *adj. US* = **arty-farty**

artwear /áart wair/ *n.* jewellery or clothing designed and made by an artist

artwork /áart wurk/ *n.* **1. WORK OF ART** a work or works of art **2. ILLUSTRATION FOR PRINTING** the illustrations that are to be printed in a publication

arty[1] /áarti/ **(-ier, -iest)** *adj.* self-consciously and pretentiously artistic (*informal disapproving*)

arty[2] *abbr.* artillery

arty-crafty *adj.* **1. OVER-DECORATIVE** used to describe artwork that is overdecorative (*informal disapproving*) **2. ARTY IN RUSTIC WAY** self-consciously artistic, especially seeking to produce an impression of rural craft (*informal*) [Early 20thC. Formed from the phrase ARTS AND CRAFTS.]

arty-farty *adj.* representing an elitist or self-indulgent side of the arts (*informal disapproving*)

Aruba /ǝ róobǝ/ island off the Venezuelan coast, formerly a Dutch dependency and since 1986 a self-governing part of the Netherlands. Language: Dutch, Papamiento. Capital: Orangestad. Population: 67,794 (1996). Area: 193 sq. km/75 sq. mi.

arugula /ǝ róogyǝlǝ/ (*plural* **-las** *or* **-la**) *n.* = **rocket**[2] *n.* 1 [Mid-20thC. Origin uncertain: probably from dialectal Italian.]

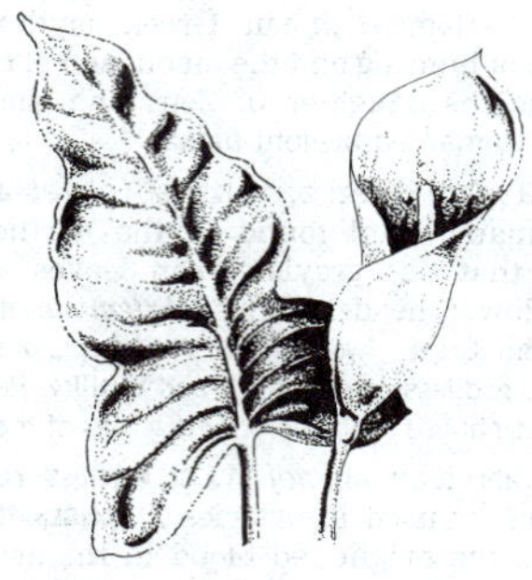

Arum

arum /áirǝm/ (*plural* **-ums** *or* **-um**) *n.* a European perennial plant that grows from tubers and has arrow-shaped leaves. Genus: *Arum*. [14thC. Via Latin from Greek *aron*, of unknown origin.]

arum lily (*plural* **arum lilies** *or* **arum lily**) *n.* an ornamental lily, originally from southern Africa, that has a white funnel-shaped cone around a long yellow spike bearing the actual flowers. Latin name: *Zantedeschia aethiopica*. US term **calla lily**

Arunachal Pradesh /àarə naak'l prə désh/, **Arunāchal Pradesh** union state of India. Situated in northeastern India, it has borders with Tibet and Myanmar. Capital: Itanagar. Population: 965,000 (1994). Area: 83,743 sq. km/32,333 sq. mi.

Arup /áwrəp/, **Sir Ove** (1895–1988) Danish-born British civil engineer who was involved in the rebuilding of Coventry Cathedral (1956–62).

aruspex *n.* = **haruspex**

arvo /áarvō/ (*plural* **arvos**) *n.* *Aus* afternoon (*informal*) [Mid-20thC. Formed from 'arv-' (representing an Australian pronunciation of the first syllable of *afternoon*) + -O.]

-ary *suffix.* of or relating to ○ *functionary* [Via Old French *-arie* from Latin *-arius*]

Aryan /áiri ən, árri-/ *n.* **1.** LANG **INDO-EUROPEAN LANGUAGE** the hypothetical parent language of the Indo-European languages (*dated*) **2.** LANG **INDO-EUROPEAN ANCESTOR** sb who spoke the hypothetical parent language of the Indo-European languages (*dated*) **3.** ETHNOL **INDO-EUROPEAN DESCENDANT** sb belonging to a people thought to be descended from the Indo-Europeans, especially a speaker of an Iranian or Indic language (*dated*) **4.** POL **NAZI IDEAL** in Nazi ideology, a person of non-Semitic descent regarded as racially superior ■ *adj.* **1.** LANG **OF INDO-EUROPEAN** belonging to or typical of any of the Indo-European languages or their hypothetical parent language (*dated*) **2.** POL **REFERRING TO NAZI IDEAL** in Nazi ideology, belonging to or characteristic of the supposed Aryan race [Mid-19thC. Formed from Sanskrit *ārya* 'noble, of good family', originally a national name denoting the worshippers of the gods of the Brahmans. Ultimately from an Indo-European word meaning 'lord, ruler', which is also the ancestor of English *else*.]

aryl /árril/ *adj.* used to describe a chemical group derived from benzene or another aromatic hydrocarbon

arytenoid /árri teén oyd/ *adj.* **arytenoid, arytenoidal 1.** **RELATING TO LARYNX CARTILAGE** used to describe either of the two small cartilages of the larynx to which the vocal cords are attached **2.** **RELATING TO LARYNX MUSCLE** used to describe any of the small muscles of the larynx ■ *n.* **ARYTENOID CARTILAGE OR MUSCLE** an arytenoid cartilage or muscle [Early 18thC. Via modern Latin from Greek *arutainoeidēs*, literally 'ladle-shaped', from *arutaina* 'ladle, funnel', from *aruein* 'to draw water'.]

as (*stressed*) /az/; (*unstressed*) /əz/ CORE MEANING: a grammatical word indicating simultaneity, causality, comparison, or the identity or function of sb or sth ○ (conj) *Once again, as I started my interview, the telephone rang.* ○ (conj) *I'll drop the book in, as I'll be passing your house anyway.* ○ (conj coord) *Here, take this pencil as it's sharper than yours.* ○ (prep) *Data is stored on the disk as magnetic patterns, much as music is stored on an audio tape or cassette.*

1. *conj.* **AT THE TIME THAT** used to indicate that sth happens at the same time as sth else ○ *A woman stands near the water's edge as two large golden retrievers frolic in the river.* **2.** *conj.* **WHAT** that which ○ *Do as you like!* **3.** *conj.* **BECAUSE** seeing that ○ *I'm not sure where we are in mathematics, as I've been absent for the last week.* **4.** *conj.* **USED FOR COMPARISON** used to compare things, people, or situations ○ (conj-coord) *Marvin's eyes are as big as saucers.* ○ (conj-subord) *The little Honda races toward its destination as fast as its little engine will take it.* **5.** *conj.* **EMPHASIZES AMOUNTS** used to indicate that an amount is small or large **6.** *conj.* **INTRODUCES CLAUSE** used to introduce a short clause referring to a previous or subsequent statement ○ *As you know, I have been in this job for a long time.* **7.** *conj.* **IN THE WAY THAT** used to indicate the way that sth happens or exists ○ *Did everything go as planned?* **8.** *conj.* **IN THE SAME WAY THAT** used to indicate that sth happens or exists in the same way as sth else ○ *Her attitude to life was very practical, as her mother's had been.* **9.** *conj.* **DESPITE** in spite of ○ *Hard-working as she is, she can't compete with the others* **10.** *prep.* **TIME WHEN** used to indicate a stage in sb's life ○ *As a teenager I was quite overweight.* [12thC. From Old English *ealswā* 'exactly so' (see ALSO).] ◇ **as against** used to indicate comparison or contrast between two facts or amounts ◇ **as ever** used to indicate that a situation is the same as usual ◇ **as far as** to the extent to which a situation holds or is relevant ◇ **as for, as to** used to introduce a topic related to what has been mentioned before ◇ **as from, as of** on and after a given date or time (*formal*) ◇ **as if, as though 1.** in a way that suggests sth ○ *He looked as though he'd been crying.* **2.** used to indicate that the speaker is saying sth ridiculous ○ *As if I'd say a thing like that!* ◇ **as is** in the present condition, with whatever faults there may be ◇ **as it were** used to indicate qualification, uncertainty, or lack of definiteness in a statement (*formal*) ◇ **as such 1.** used to indicate that a word or phrase does not apply exactly to a situation (*often used with a negative*) ○ *I have no qualifications as such, but I feel I could do the job.* **2.** used to indicate that sth is being considered separately ○ *After the earthquake, the village as such virtually ceased to exist.* ◇ **as regards** on the topic of ◇ **as to** with reference to ◇ **as yet** used to indicate that a situation has lasted up to the present time ○ *She has never once mentioned the terrible accusation nor has she, as yet, said that she is sorry for all the pain it inflicted.* ◇ **as you were** a military command to return to the same position as before ◇ **as how** used to mean 'that' in the phrases 'seeing as how' and 'allowed as how' (*informal*) ○ *Seeing as how they were almost finished, I waited.* ○ *She allowed as how I had helped her more than anybody.* ◇ **as long as 1.** provided that ○ *You can go, as long as you're home by midnight.* **2.** because or seeing that ○ *As long as we're here we may as well look round.* ◇ **as much again** twice as much ◇ **as per** in accordance with

WORD KEY: USAGE

See Usage note at ***because***.

WORD KEY: USAGE

As meaning 'in the capacity of' In this use, the preposition ***as*** is used to show the capacity in which sb or sth exists or acts: *She has a job as a copywriter. As a doctor I understand these problems.* Care has to be taken to avoid false links with the ***as*** clause, when these result in ambiguity or apparent absurdity: *As a journalist, you know I do not like being asked such questions.* (Which is the journalist?) There is less of a problem with the type *As students their rent was reduced,* since despite the logical connection no one is going to be fooled into thinking that the students and the rent are the same; but the style is poor and the sentence would be better rephrased as (for example) *Because they were students their rent was reduced.*

As *symbol.* arsenic

AS *abbr.* **1.** BANKING after sight **2. AS, A.S.** Anglo-Saxon **3.** antisubmarine

As. *abbr.* **1.** Asia **2.** Asian

ASA *adj.* **OF FILM SPEED** used to indicate the speed of photographic film ■ *abbr.* Advertising Standards Authority

Asadha /áasədə/ *n.* INDIAN RELIG in the Hindu calendar, the fourth month of the year, made up of 29 or 30 days and falling in approximately June to July. It is followed in certain leap years by an extra month (**Dvitiya Asadha**).

asafoetida /àssə féttidə, -feé-/, **asafetida** *n.* a bitter, brownish, acrid-smelling plant extract, used in Indian cooking

asana /áassənə/ *n.* a posture used in yoga [Mid-20thC. From Sanskrit *āsana* 'manner of sitting', from *āste* 'he sits'.]

a.s.a.p. *abbr.* as soon as possible

ASAT, Asat *abbr.* MIL anti-satellite

asbestos /ass béss toss, az béstəss/ *n.* a fibrous silicate mineral widely used for its chemical inertness and heat-resistant properties until discovered to be a cause of certain cancers [Early 17thC. From Greek *asbestos* 'unslaked lime', literally 'inextinguishable', from *sbestos* 'extinguished', from *sbennunai* 'to extinguish'.] — **asbestine** /as béss teen, -béstin/ *adj.*

asbestosis /àss bess tṓssiss, ás-/ *n.* inflammation of the lungs caused by prolonged inhalation of asbestos fibres [Early 20thC. Coined from ASBESTOS + -OSIS.]

ASCAP *abbr.* American Society of Composers, Authors, and Publishers

ascariasis /àskə rī́ əssiss/ *n.* infestation of the intestines by common roundworms or related nematode worms (**ascarids**) [Late 19thC. Coined from ASCARID + -IASIS.]

ascarid /áskərid/ *n.* a parasitic nematode worm such as the common roundworms. Family: Ascaridae. [Late 17thC. Back-formation from *ascarides*, the plural of modern Latin *ascaris*, from Greek *askaris* 'intestinal worm', from *askarizein* 'to jump', an alteration of *skarizein* 'to jump, throb'. From the worms' squirming.]

ascend /ə sénd/ (**-cends, -cending, -cended**) *v.* **1.** *vi.* **MOVE UPWARDS** to go upwards, usually vertically or into the air **2.** *vti.* **CLIMB** to climb up sth, e.g. a hill or staircase **3.** *vi.* **LEAD UPWARDS** to rise or lead to a higher level **4.** *vt.* **TAKE UP POSITION** to succeed to an important position, especially as a monarch (*formal*) **5.** *vti.* **RISE THROUGH IN CAREER** to rise through the ranks to a higher status [14thC. From Latin *ascendere*, literally 'to climb to', from *scandere* 'to climb' (see SCAN).] — **ascendable** *adj.*

ascendance /ə séndənss/, **ascendence** *n.* **1. COMING INTO POWER** succeeding or rising to a powerful position **2.** = **ascendancy**

ascendancy /ə séndənssi/, **ascendency** *n.* a position of power or domination over others

ascendant /ə séndənt/, **ascendent** *adj.* **1. MOVING UPWARDS** moving upwards (*literary*) **2. DOMINANT** having a position of power or domination over others (*formal*) **3.** BOT = **ascending** *adj.* 2 ■ *n.* ASTROL **POINT ON ECLIPTIC** in astrology, the point on the ecliptic or the sign of the zodiac that is rising in the east at a particular time —**ascendence** *n.* —**ascendency** *n.*

ascender /ə séndər/ *n.* **1. SB OR STH THAT ASCENDS** sb or sth that ascends sth **2.** PRINTING **LETTER PART EXTENDING UPWARDS** the part of a lower-case letter, e.g. h, d, or b, that projects above the body of the letter **3.** PRINTING **LETTER WITH ASCENDER** a letter with an ascender —**ascendent** *n., adj.*

ascendeur /àssoN dúr/ *n.* a metal grip on a rope that can be loosened, moved up, and tightened to help a climber ascend the rope [Late 20thC. From French, literally 'ascender'.]

ascending /ə sénding/ *adj.* **1. MOVING UP** moving upwards, especially on a scale **2. ascending, ascendant** BOT **GROWING UPWARDS** used to describe a plant part that grows upwards

ascension /ə sénsh'n/ *n.* an act of ascending sth (*formal*) [14thC. Via French from the Latin stem *ascension-*, from *ascens-*, the present participle stem of *ascendere* (see ASCEND).] —**ascensional** *adj.*

Ascension *n.* according to Christianity, the rising of Jesus Christ from earth to heaven after the Resurrection

Ascension Day *n.* the Thursday, forty days after Easter, when Christians celebrate the rising of Jesus Christ from earth to heaven after the Resurrection

Ascension Island island in the South Atlantic Ocean to the northwest of Saint Helena, by which it is administered as a British dependency. Population: 1,007 (1988). Area: 88 sq. km/34 sq. mi.

ascent /ə sént/ *n.* **1. CLIMB** an act of climbing a mountain or hill ○ *the ascent of Everest* **2. UPWARD MOVEMENT** an upward vertical movement **3. UPWARD SLOPE** an upward slope **4. WAY UP MOUNTAIN** a climbers' route up a mountain or hill **5. RISE TO IMPORTANCE** the process by which sb becomes more important, successful, or powerful [Late 16thC. Formed from ASCEND, on the model of DESCEND, DESCENT.]

ascertain /àssər táyn/ (**-tains, -taining, -tained**) *vti.* to find out sth with certainty (*formal*) [Late 16thC. From Old French *acertain-*, a stem of *acertener*, from *certain* CERTAIN.] —**ascertainable** *adj.* —**ascertainably** *adv.* —**ascertainment** *n.*

ascetic /ə séttik/ *n.* **SB WHO LEADS AUSTERE LIFE** sb who chooses an austere life of self-denial ■ *adj.* **1. AUSTERE** choosing or reflecting austerity and self-denial **2. RELATING TO ASCETICISM** relating to asceticism as a way of life [Mid-17thC. Directly or via medieval Latin from

Greek *askētikos*, from *askētēs* 'monk, hermit', from *askein* 'to exercise'.] —**ascetically** *adv.*

asceticism /ə séttisizzəm/ *n.* austerity and self-denial, especially as a principled way of life

Ascham /áskəm/, **Roger** (1515–68) English humanist and scholar. Tutor to Princess Elizabeth (1548–50), his works include the treatise *The Scholemaster* (1570).

asci plural of **ascus**

ascidia plural of **ascidium**

ascidian /ə síddi ən/ (*plural* **-ans** or **-an**) *n.* a marine invertebrate animal that has a body with openings through which water passes. Sea squirts are ascidians. Class: Ascidiacea. [Mid-19thC. Formed from modern Latin *Ascidia*, genus name, from Greek *askidion*, literally 'little wineskin', from *askos* 'wineskin, leather bag', of unknown origin.]

ascidium /ə síddi əm/ (*plural* **-a** /-ə/) *n.* a part of a plant or fungus shaped like a pitcher [Mid-18thC. Via modern Latin from Greek *askidion* (see ASCIDIAN).]

ASCII /áski/ *n.* a standard that identifies the letters of the alphabet, numbers, and various symbols by code numbers for exchanging data between different computer systems. Full form **American Standard Code for Information Interchange**

ASCII art *n.* illustrations using only ASCII characters, often used to decorate or enliven e-mail

ASCII file *n.* a computer file that contains text or data consisting only of ASCII characters. ◊ **binary file**

ascites /ə sít eez/ *n.* an abnormal accumulation of fluid (**serous fluid**) in the peritoneal cavity, causing abdominal swelling [14thC. Via late Latin from Greek *askītēs* 'dropsy', from *askos* 'wineskin, leather bag', of unknown origin.] —**ascitic** /ə síttik/ *adj.*

asco- *prefix.* ascus ○ *ascocarp* [Via modern Latin from Greek *askos* 'wineskin, leather bag', of unknown origin]

ascocarp /áskə kaarp/ *n.* a fleshy structure in certain fungi (**ascomycetes**) containing sexually produced spores (**ascospores**) in a membranous spore case (**ascus**)

ascogonium /áskə gṓni əm/ (*plural* **-a** /-ni ə/) *n.* a female reproductive part in certain fungi (**ascomycetes**)

ascoma /ə skṓmə/ (*plural* **-mata** /-mətə/) *n.* = **ascocarp**

ascomycete /áskəmī seét/ *n.* a fungus that produces spores sexually inside a membranous, often cylindrical, spore case (**ascus**). Yeasts and truffles are ascomycetes. Class: Ascomycetes. —**ascomycetous** /áskə mī seétəs, ás kō mī seétəs/ *adj.*

ascorbate /ə skáwr bayt, -bət/ *n.* any salt of ascorbic acid

ascorbic acid /ə skáwrbik-/ *n.* = **vitamin C** [Mid-20thC. *Ascorbic*, literally 'not scorbutic', coined from A- + SCORBUTIC.]

ascospore /áskə spawr/ *n.* a fungal spore produced sexually in a membranous spore case (**ascus**) —**ascosporic** /áskə spáwrik/ *adj.* —**ascosporous** /-spáwrəss/ *adj.*

ascot /áskət/ *n.* a broad cravat with square ends, often held in place with an ornamental stud [Early 20thC. Named after ASCOT.]

Ascot /áskət/ town in Berkshire, where race meetings are held. Population: 13,500.

ascribe /ə skríb/ (**-cribes, -cribing, -cribed**) *vt.* (*formal*) **1.** GIVE STH AS CAUSE to believe or say that sth was caused by sth else that is named ○ *His rivals could only ascribe his success to sheer good luck.* **2.** GIVE SB AS AUTHOR to believe or say that sth was originally written or said by sb who is named ○ *The researcher was confident enough to ascribe the newly discovered poems to Burns.* **3.** GIVE STH AS CHARACTERISTIC to believe that sth that is named belongs to or is typical of a person or group ○ *to ascribe contentment to the unambitious* [15thC. From Latin *ascribere* 'to add to in writing', literally 'to write to', from *scribere* 'to write'.] —**ascribable** *adj.*

ascribed status *n.* the status that an individual possesses by reason of age, sex, ethnic background, family background, or another factor outside the control of the individual

ascription /ə skrípsh'n/ *n.* **1.** ATTRIBUTION the attributing of a relationship between sth and sb or sth else (*formal*) **2.** STATEMENT OF ATTRIBUTION a statement that assigns or attributes sth to sb or sth else (*formal*) **3.** SOCIOL SOCIAL STATUS BY BIRTH the social status derived from the circumstances into which sb is born [Late 16thC. From the Latin stem *ascription-*, from *ascript-*, the past participle stem of *ascribere* (see ASCRIBE).]

ascus /áskəss/ (*plural* **-ci** /-sī, -s kī/) *n.* a membranous spore case formed by certain fungi (**ascomycetes**) that contains eight sexually produced spores (**ascospores**) [Mid-19thC. Via modern Latin from Greek *askos* 'wineskin, leather bag', of unknown origin.]

ASDE *abbr.* Airport Surface Detection Equipment

asdic /ázdik/ *n.* an early version of sonar [Early 20thC. Acronym formed from *Anti-Submarine Detection Investigation Committee.*]

-ase *suffix.* enzyme ○ *polymerase* [From DIASTASE]

ASEAN /ássi an/ *abbr.* Association of Southeast Asian Nations

aseismic /ay sízmik/ *adj.* **1.** NOT HAVING EARTHQUAKES not subject to earthquakes **2.** ABLE TO WITHSTAND EARTHQUAKES built to withstand earthquakes

aseismic creep *n.* movement of tectonic plates below the Earth's crust that is not caused by earthquakes or other seismic disturbance

asepsis /ay sépsiss, ə-/ *n.* **1.** GERM-FREE CONDITION a condition in which no living disease-causing microorganisms are present **2.** ELIMINATION OF GERMS the process or methods of bringing about a condition in which no disease-causing microorganisms are present

aseptic /ay séptik, ə-/ *adj.* **1.** WITHOUT DISEASE-CAUSING MICROORGANISMS free of disease-causing microorganisms **2.** PREVENTING INFECTION designed to prevent infection from pathogenic microorganisms —**aseptically** *adv.* —**asepticism** *n.*

asexual /ay sékshoo əl/ *adj.* **1.** BIOL WITHOUT SEX-LINKED FEATURES lacking any apparent sex or sex organs **2.** BIOL WITHOUT SEXUAL FUSION used to describe reproduction in which there is no fusion of male and female sex cells (**gametes**), e.g. vegetative reproduction or budding **3.** SEXUALLY INACTIVE without sexual desire or activity —**asexuality** /áy sekshoo álləti/ *n.* —**asexually** /ay sekshoo əli/ *adv.*

Asgard /áss gaard/ *n.* in Norse mythology, the home of the gods and of heroes killed in battle

ash[1] /ash/ *n.* **1.** REMAINS OF FIRE the powdery substance that is left when sth has been burnt (*often used in the plural*) **2.** GEOL VOLCANIC DUST fine-grained lava that erupts from a volcano in a gas cloud before settling on the ground, or that flows out ■ **ashes** *npl.* BURNT REMAINS OF BODY the remains of sb's body after it has been cremated ■ *adj.* SILVERY GREY of a silvery grey colour [Old English *æsce*. Ultimately from an Indo-European word meaning 'to burn, be dry', which is also the ancestor of English *arid*, *ardent*, and *azalea*.] ◊ **rise (like a phoenix) from the ashes** to come into existence or popularity again, seemingly from a state of ruin or destruction

Ash

ash[2] /ash/ (*plural* **ashes** or **ash**) *n.* **1.** DECIDUOUS TREE a deciduous tree that has compound leaves with paired leaflets, winged fruits, and clusters of small flowers. It is found widely in temperate regions.

Genus: *Fraxinus.* **2.** HARD WOOD OF ASH the hard durable wood of the ash tree, used to make furniture and tool handles **3.** LING SYMBOL FOR VOWEL SOUND the character 'æ' representing the vowel sound of the modern English word 'pad', used in Old English and the International Phonetic Alphabet **4.** *Aus* AUSTRALIAN TREE RESEMBLING EUROPEAN ASH any Australian tree that resembles a European ash [Old English *æsc* (related to German *Esche* and Old Norse *askr*)]

ASH /ash/ *abbr.* Action on Smoking and Health

ashamed /ə sháymd/ *adj.* **1.** FULL OF SHAME feeling full of shame **2.** EMBARRASSED embarrassed or regretful ○ *I'm ashamed to say I didn't acknowledge their invitation.* [Old English *āscamod*, from *sceamu* 'shame' (source of English *shame*)]

Ashanti /ə shánti/ (*plural* **-ti** or **-tis**), **Ashante** (*plural* **-te** or **-tes**) *n.* **1.** AREA IN GHANA a former kingdom and present-day administrative area in central Ghana **2.** PEOPLES MEMBER OF GHANAIAN PEOPLE a member of a Ghanaian people who live mainly in Ashanti **3.** LANG AFRICAN LANGUAGE a language spoken in central Ghana, now often regarded as a form of Akan [Early 18thC. From Twi *Asante.*] —**Ashanti** *adj.*

A share *n.* a share in a company that does not entitle the holder to voting rights and that may carry other restrictions

ash blonde, **ash blond** *adj.* LIGHT BLONDE light or whiteish blonde in colour (*hyphenated when used before a noun*) ■ *n.* FAIR-HAIRED PERSON sb with ash blonde hair

Ashburton[1] /ásh burt'n/ river in northwestern Western Australia. Length: 650 km/404 mi.

Ashburton[2] large reservoir in northwestern Australia, created between 1970 and 1972 by damming the River Ord. Length: 650 km/404 mi.

ashcan /ásh kan/ *n.* US **1.** = dustbin **2.** MIL DEPTH CHARGE a depth charge (*slang*)

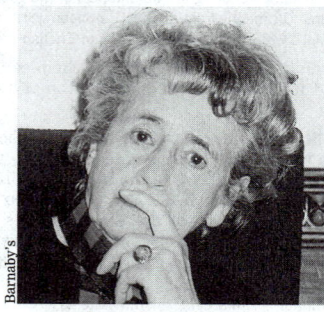

Barnaby's

Dame Peggy Ashcroft

Ashcroft, Dame Peggy (1907–91) British actress who played leading theatrical roles from the 1930s to the 1950s. Her films include *A Passage to India* (1984). Real name **Edith Margaret Emily Ashcroft**

Ashdown /ásh down/, **Paddy** (*b.* 1941) British politician. A former Royal Marine, he became an MP (1983) and leader of the Liberal Democrat Party (1988–99).

Ashe /ash/, **Arthur** (1943–93) US tennis player who was the first African American men's tennis champion. Full name **Arthur Robert Ashe, Jr.**

ashen[1] /ásh'n/ *adj.* **1.** VERY PALE extremely pale in appearance **2.** LIKE ASHES resembling or consisting of ashes

ashen[2] /ásh'n/ *adj.* relating to the ash tree, or made from its wood (*literary*)

Ashes /áshiz/ *n.* in cricket, the trophy awarded to the winner of a series of test matches between England and Australia [Late 19thC. From a mock obituary for English cricket after a defeat, and the subsequent presentation to the English of an urn containing ashes, which became the trophy.]

ashet /áshit/ *n. Scotland, N England, NZ* a large plate or shallow dish, usually oval in shape, used for serving food [Mid-19thC. From French *assiette* 'place at table, plate', from *asseoir* 'to seat' (see ASSIZE).]

Ashkenazi /áshkə naázi/ (*plural* **-im** /-im/) *n.* a member of a Jewish community originating in Germany and northern Europe, as distinguished from a Jewish person of Spanish or Portuguese origin (**Sephardi**) [Mid-19thC. From modern Hebrew, formed from medieval Hebrew *Ashkenaz* 'Germany', from Hebrew *Ashkēnāz*, name of a grandson of Noah.] —**Ashkenazi** *adj.* —**Ashkenazic** *adj.*

Ashkhabad /áshkə bad/ capital of Turkmenistan, located in the southern part of the country near the Turkmenistan-Iran border and the Kara Kum desert. Population: 517,200 (1993).

ashlar /áshlər/, **ashler** *n.* **1.** STONE SLAB USED FOR FACING a thin slab of squared stone, used for facing walls or building **2.** MASONRY USING THIN SLABS OF STONE masonry using thin slabs of squared stone as facing material [14thC. Via Old French *aisselier* 'plank' from, ultimately, medieval Latin *axicellus*, from Latin *axis* 'plank, axletree' (source of English *axis* and *axle*).]

Ashley /áshli/, **Laura** (1925–85) British fashion designer who created a chain of shops selling clothes, fabrics, and wallpapers based on 19th-century designs. Born **Laura Mountney**

Ashmore and Cartier Islands /ásh mawr ənd ka'ati ay-/ external territory lying 500 km/323 mi. off the northwest coast of Australia. It comprises the Ashmore Reef and the Cartier Islands. Area: 5 sq. km/2 sq. mi.

Ashora /ə sháwrə/ *n.* an Islamic festival celebrated on the tenth day of Muharran

ashore /ə sháwr/ *adv.* to the land from the water, or on land as opposed to a ship or boat ○ *All but the captain went ashore.*

ashram /áshrəm, aash-/ *n.* **1.** HINDU RETREAT a retreat for the practice of yoga or other Hindu disciplines **2.** SPIRITUAL COMMUNITY a commune or communal house whose members share spiritual goals and practices [Early 20thC. From Sanskrit *āśramah* 'hermitage'.]

Ashton /áshtən/, **Sir Frederick** (1904–88) British dancer and choreographer. He helped found the Ballet Rambert and Sadlers Wells, which became the Royal Ballet. Full name **Sir Frederick William Mallandaine Ashton**

Ashton-under-Lyne /-līn/ engineering town in Lancashire, England. Population: 43,906 (1991).

Ashton-Warner /-wáwrnər/, **Sylvia** (1908–84) New Zealand novelist and teacher, author of *Spinster* (1958).

Ashtoreth /áshtə reth/ *n.* MYTHOL ♦ **Ishtar**

ashtray /ásh tray/ *n.* an open receptacle for the ash from a cigarette, cigar, or pipe and for cigarette ends

Ash Wednesday *n.* a Christian religious holiday that marks the first day of Lent, the period preceding Easter [So called because of the Roman Catholic custom of marking the heads of penitents with ashes on this day]

ashy /áshi/ (**-ier**, **-iest**) *adj.* **1.** EXTREMELY PALE extremely pale or greyish in appearance (*literary*) **2.** LIKE ASH resembling or covered in ash

Asia /áyshə, áyzhə/ the world's largest continent, bordered by the Ural and Caucasus mountains and the Arctic, Pacific, and Indian oceans. Area: 44,936,000 sq. km/17,350,000 sq. mi.

Asiadollar /áyshə dollər, áyzhə-/ *n.* a United States dollar used in Asian banks and currency markets

Asia Minor peninsula in the extreme west of Asia, roughly corresponding to Asian Turkey

Asian /áysh'n, áyzh'n/ *adj.* OF ASIA relating to or typical of any of the countries of Asia, or their peoples or cultures ■ *n.* **1.** SB FROM ASIA sb who was born in or is a citizen of any of the countries that form the continent of Asia **2.** SB FROM THE INDIAN SUBCONTINENT sb who is an immigrant from, or is descended from immigrants from, the Indian subcontinent [Via Latin from Greek *Asianos*, from *Asia* 'Asia']

— WORD KEY: USAGE —
Sensitivity trap **Asian** has largely replaced **Asiatic**, both as a noun and as an adjective, when the reference is to people. **Asiatic** is now regarded as derogatory and should be strictly avoided. In British English, **Asian** is also used to refer to people from the Indian subcontinent, or their descendants, now living in Britain.

Asian-American *n.* sb who was born in Asia and is a citizen of the United States, or whose ancestors came from any of the countries that form the continent of Asia —**Asian-American** *adj.*

Asian cockroach *n.* a pale brown cockroach of medium size commonly found around dwellings in warm and temperate climates. Latin name: *Blattella asahinai.*

Asian flu *n.* influenza that occurs in sporadic worldwide epidemics, caused by a virus strain thought to have originated in China in the mid-1950s, and related strains

Asian pear *n.* **1.** TYPE OF PEAR TREE a pear tree yielding edible fruit, grown from Manchuria to New Zealand. Genus: *Pyrus*. US term **sand pear 2.** FRUIT the fruit of an Asian pear tree, which resembles a yellow apple and has crisp juicy flesh

Asia-Pacific *n.* a commercial region encompassing the countries of Asia and the Pacific Rim

Asiatic /áyshi áttik, áyzi-/ *adj.* used to describe things Asian, e.g. flora, fauna, or climatic conditions ○ *Asiatic plants and animals* ○ *parts of the Asiatic steppes* [Early 17thC. Via Latin from Greek *Asiatikos*, from *Asia* 'Asia'.]

— WORD KEY: USAGE —
See Usage note at *Asian.*

Asiatic buffalo (*plural* **Asiatic buffalo** or **Asiatic buffaloes** or **Asiatic buffalos**) *n.* an ox of Southeast Asia, with large upturned horns, now widely domesticated and rare in the wild. Latin name: *Bubalus bubalis.*

Asiatic cholera *n.* = **cholera**

Asiatic cockroach *n.* = **Asian cockroach**

aside /ə síd/ *adv.* **1.** AWAY OR TO ONE SIDE away from sb or sth, or to one side ○ *Stand aside and let the people through.* **2.** OUT OF THE WAY out of the way, or away from the area of main concern ○ *brush aside all criticism* **3.** IGNORED ignored for the sake of argument ○ *Budget constraints aside, is the deadline feasible?* **4.** FOR FUTURE USE for special or future use ○ *put aside some money each week* ■ *n.* **1.** THEATRE ACTOR'S COMMENT a remark made by an actor, usually to the audience, that the other characters on stage supposedly cannot hear **2.** CONFIDENTIAL COMMENT IN UNDERTONE a spoken remark not directed to all listeners and usually made in a quiet voice **3.** DIGRESSION a digression from a main point

A-side *n.* the side of a pop, rock, or jazz single that contains the more important recording, usually the title track (*dated*)

aside from *prep.* US **1.** IN ADDITION TO in addition to or besides sb or sth ○ *Aside from his medical practice he is also a lawyer.* **2.** OTHER THAN except for or not considering the stated thing ○ *Aside from the cold weather, I love it here.*

Asimov /ázzi mof/, **Isaac** (1920–92) Russian-born US scientist and writer, author of around 500 books for young people, including textbooks and science fiction.

asinine /ássi nīn/ *adj.* **1.** RIDICULOUS utterly ridiculous or lacking sense **2.** LIKE AN ASS relating to or resembling an ass [15thC. From Latin *asininus*, from *asinus* 'ass'.] —**asininely** *adv.* —**asininity** /ássi nínnəti/ *n.*

ASIO /áyzi ō/ *abbr.* Australian Security Intelligence Organization

ASIS /ássiss/ *abbr.* Australian Secret Intelligence Service

ask /aask/ (**asks**, **asking**, **asked**) *v.* **1.** *vti.* QUESTION SB to put a question to sb ○ *Ask them how long it will take.* **2.** *vti.* MAKE REQUEST to make a request for sth ○ *They asked me for my opinion.* **3.** *vt.* INVITE SB to invite sb to a social event ○ *Only close friends were asked to the wedding.* **4.** *vt.* REQUIRE to require sb to give or contribute sth ○ *The job asks a lot more of me than I expected.* **5.** *vt.* NAME AS PRICE to name an amount as an acceptable price ○ *They're asking £100,000 for the house.* [Old English *āscian.* Ultimately from an Indo-European word meaning 'to wish'.] ◇ **for the asking** available at no cost

ask after *vt.* to inquire about sb's welfare ○ *She asks after the children whenever we meet.*

ask for *v.* **1.** *vti.* REQUEST STH to request that sth be provided ○ *I asked for a cup of coffee.* **2.** *vt.* REQUEST SB'S APPEARANCE to request sb's appearance, especially to speak to **3.** *vt.* REQUEST TELEPHONE CONVERSATION WITH SB to request that sb be called to the telephone ○ *A man on the phone is asking for the manager.* **4.** *vt.* INVITE STH UNPLEASANT to behave in a way that deserves sth unpleasant ○ *You're asking for a lot of problems if you do that.*

ask in *vt.* to invite sb to come in

ask out *vt.* to invite sb to go on a date

askance /ə skánss, ə ska'anss/ *adv.* **1.** SUSPICIOUSLY with doubt or suspicion ○ *'They surveyed each other askance, feeling that they were rivals, and mentally calculating each other's chances'.* (Horatio Alger, Jr., *Ragged Dick*; 1868) **2.** OBLIQUELY sideways, or out of the side of the eye (*archaic*) [15thC. Origin unknown.]

askari /a ska'ari/, **askar** /áss kaar/ *n.* a soldier or police officer in various Arab or Muslim countries of eastern Africa [Late 19thC. From Arabic *askarī* 'soldier'.]

askew /ə skyoó/ *adj.*, *adv.* at an angle ○ *with his hat askew*

asking price *n.* the price set by a seller before any negotiation

aslant /ə slaánt/ *adv.* sloping or at an angle ○ *books all aslant on the shelves*

asleep /ə sleép/ *adj.* **1.** NOT AWAKE in or into a state of sleep **2.** NOT ALERT not alert enough to function or operate properly ○ *asleep on the job* **3.** NUMB numb for lack of proper blood circulation

ASLEF /ázz lef/, **Aslef** *abbr.* Associated Society of Locomotive Engineers and Firemen

A/S level *n.* in England and Wales, a school examination taken at an advanced level in a particular subject but involving less coursework than an A level (*hyphenated when used before a noun*) ○ *A/S-level biology.* Full form **Advanced Supplementary level**

aslope /ə slóp/ *adj.*, *adv.* at a sloping angle

ASM *abbr.* air-to-surface missile

Asmara /ass maárə/ capital and largest city of Eritrea. It is also the name of one of the ten provinces within Eritrea. Population: 367,300 (1991).

asocial /ay sósh'l/ *adj.* **1.** UNWILLING TO MIX SOCIALLY disinclined or averse to human social interaction **2.** NOT INTERACTING SOCIALLY lacking a need or capacity for social interaction **3.** UNSUITED TO SOCIETY not acceptable in normal society, or showing a lack of consideration for others

asp[1] /asp/ *n.* **1.** SNAKE THAT KILLED CLEOPATRA a small poisonous snake that caused the death of Cleopatra. It is thought to have been a member of the cobra family found in Africa, Asia, and Europe. Latin name: *Naja haje.* **2.** S EUROPEAN VIPER a snake of the viper family, resembling a small adder, found in southern Europe **3.** = **horned viper** [Directly or via Old French *aspe* from Latin *aspis*, from Greek, of unknown origin]

asp[2] /asp/ *n.* an aspen tree (*archaic*) [Old English *æspe* (see ASPEN)]

asparaginase /ə spárrəji nayz, -nayss/ *n.* an enzyme that aids the breakdown of the amino acid asparagine, producing aspartic acid and ammonia

asparagine /ə spárrə jeen, -jin/ *n.* an amino acid found in many plant seeds that can also be produced by humans and animals. Formula: $C_4H_8N_2O_3$. [Early 19thC. Formed from ASPARAGUS, from which it was first obtained.]

asparagus /ə spárrəgəss/ (*plural* **-gus**) *n.* **1.** PLANT CUL-

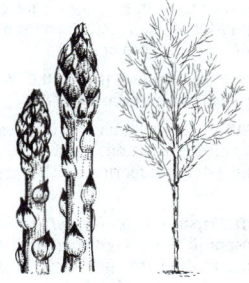

Asparagus

TIVATED FOR EDIBLE SHOOTS a perennial plant that is widely cultivated for its edible young shoots. Latin name: *Asparagus officinalis*. **2.** SUCCULENT VEGETABLE the spear-shaped young shoots of the asparagus plant, cooked and served as a vegetable [Pre-12thC. Via Latin from Greek *asparagos*, of unknown origin.]

asparagus fern *n.* a South African plant with feathery leaves, small white flowers, and purplish black berries that is grown as a houseplant. Its foliage is used in bouquets. Latin name: *Asparagus setaceus*.

aspartame /ə spaár taym/ *n.* a synthetic sweetener, many times sweeter to the taste than sugar, that is a protein produced from aspartic acid [Late 20thC. Coined from ASPARTIC ACID + *-ame*, of uncertain origin.]

aspartate /ə spaár tayt/ *n.* a salt or ester of aspartic acid

aspartic acid /ə spaártik-/ *n.* an amino acid occurring in many plant proteins that can also be produced by humans and animals. Formula: $C_4H_7NO_4$. [Mid-19thC. From French *aspartique*, from Latin *asparagus* 'asparagus', (see ASPARAGUS).]

aspect /áspekt/ *n.* **1.** ONE SIDE OR PART a facet, phase, or part of a whole ○ *consider the various aspects of the problem* **2.** APPEARANCE the appearance of sth to the mind or eye ○ *The stone has a greenish aspect in this light.* **3.** VIEWPOINT a particular view or point of view ○ *seeing life from a new aspect* ○ *the aspect of the mountain from the river* **4.** EXPOSURE exposure to a particular direction, weather, or other influence ○ *This plant requires a sunny aspect.* **5.** ASTRON ANGLE BETWEEN TWO CELESTIAL BODIES the apparent angular separation of two celestial bodies, especially as observed from the Earth **6.** ASTROL POSITIONS OF PLANETS IN ASTROLOGY the relative positions of the stars and planets, believed to influence human affairs **7.** GRAM GRAMMATICAL CATEGORY a grammatical category of verbs that considers qualities of action independent of tense. In English, the progressive or continuous and perfect aspects are recognized. **8.** LOOK a look or gaze (*archaic*) [14thC. From Latin *aspectus*, the past participle of *aspicere*, literally 'to look at', from *specere* (see SPECTACLE).]

aspect ratio *n.* **1.** SCREEN IMAGE WIDTH-HEIGHT RATIO in television and the cinema, the ratio of the width of the picture on the screen to its height. This ratio was 4:3 until the 1950s, when it increased in the cinema to 1.85:1 in the United States and 5:3 in Europe. **2.** AEROSP RATIO OF WING LENGTH TO BREADTH the ratio of the length of an aircraft's wing to the mean distance between the front and back edge of the wing. Aircraft operating at low speeds, such as gliders, need a high aspect ratio and have long narrow wings while for supersonic flight a low aspect ratio is created by swinging the wings back.

aspectual /ə spéktyoo əl/ *adj.* relating to the aspects of a verb

aspen /áspən/ (*plural* **-pens** *or* **-pen**) *n.* a tree of the poplar family, common in Europe and the northern United States, with leaves that rustle and flutter in the breeze [14thC. Formed from Old English *æspe*. The word was originally an adjective meaning 'made of aspen wood'.]

asper /áspər/ *n.* a minor unit of currency in Turkey, 120 of which are worth a piastre [Via French *aspre* from, ultimately, Greek *aspros* 'newly minted', from Latin *asper* 'rough' (source of English *asperity*)]

asperges /ə spúr jeez/ *n.* a religious ceremony of the Roman Catholic Church in which holy water is sprinkled over the altar, clergy, and congregation before High Mass [Late 16thC. From Latin, literally 'thou shalt sprinkle', the first word of the rite.]

aspergill *n.* = **aspergillum** [Mid-19thC. Anglicization of Latin *aspergillum* (see ASPERGILLUM).]

aspergillosis /ə spúrji lốssiss/ *n.* a disease affecting mucous membranes, lungs, and sometimes bones that is caused by infection with the fungus *Aspergillus*

aspergillum /áspər jílləm/ (*plural* **-la** /-ə/ *or* **-lums**), **aspergill** /áspər jil/ (*plural* **-gilla** *or* **-gills**) *n.* a brush or perforated container for sprinkling holy water [Mid-17thC. From modern Latin, literally 'little sprinkler', formed from Latin *aspergere* 'to sprinkle'.]

Aspergillum

asperity /a spérrəti/ (*plural* **-ties**) *n.* **1.** HARSHNESS OR SEVERITY harshness or severity of manner or tone (*formal*) **2.** ROUGHNESS the roughness of a surface (*literary*) **3.** HARDSHIP sth that is hard to bear because of its harshness or severity **4.** PHYS AREA WHERE TWO LOAD-BEARING SURFACES TOUCH a region of contact between two load-bearing flat surfaces [13thC. Via French *asperité* from, ultimately, Latin *asper* 'rough', of unknown origin.]

aspermia /ə spúrmi ə/ *n.* a medical condition in which no spermatozoa are present in the seminal fluid [Mid-19thC. Coined from A- + Greek *sperma* 'seed' + -IA.] —**aspermic** *adj.*

asperse /ə spúrss/ (**-perses**, **-persing**, **-persed**) *vt.* to malign sb by spreading harmful information or making false accusations (*formal*) [15thC. From Latin *aspers-*, the past participle stem of *aspergere*, literally 'to spatter on', from *spargere* (see SPARGE). The underlying meaning is 'to sling mud'.] —**asperser** *n.* —**aspersive** *adj.* —**aspersively** *adv.*

aspersion /ə spúrsh'n/ *n.* **1.** SLANDEROUS REMARK a statement that attacks sb's character or reputation (*often used in the plural*) **2.** MAKING OF SLANDEROUS REMARKS the making of defamatory remarks

aspersorium /áspər sáwri əm/ (*plural* **-ria** /-ri ə/) *n.* RELIG = **aspergillum** [Mid-19thC. From medieval Latin, formed from Latin *aspers-*, the past participle stem of *aspergere* (see ASPERSE).]

asphalt /ás falt, -fawlt/ *n.* **1.** SEMISOLID BITUMINOUS SUBSTANCE a brownish-black solid or semisolid substance used for surfacing roads and paths, waterproofing, and fungicides. It occurs naturally in some oil-bearing rocks and can be obtained as a by-product of petroleum distillation. **2.** MATERIAL USED FOR SURFACING ROADS surfacing material composed mainly of asphalt and gravel or crushed rock that hardens on cooling and is used for making roads and paths ■ *vt.* (**-phalts**, **-phalting**, **-phalted**) COVER STH WITH ASPHALT to surface a roadway, pavement, or other area with asphalt [14thC. Via late Latin from Greek *asphaltos*, of uncertain origin.] —**asphaltic** /ass fáltik/ *adj.*

asphaltite /ass fál tīt, áss-/ *n.* solid asphalt containing little inorganic material and occurring naturally in veins and beds below the surface of the ground

asphalt jungle *n.* a big city or urban area with little natural landscape

aspheric /ay sférrik/, **aspherical** /ay sférrik'l/ *adj.* not perfectly spherical

asphodel /ásfə del/ (*plural* **-dels** *or* **-del**) *n.* **1.** FLOWERING PLANT a perennial plant of the lily family, native to southern Europe, that has long clusters of white, pink, or yellow flowers. Genera: *Asphodelus* and *Asphodeline*. **2.** PLANT RESEMBLING TRUE ASPHODEL a plant similar to asphodel proper, e.g. bog asphodel **3.** MYTHOL FLOWER OF HADES in Greek mythology, the flower of Hades that was sacred to Persephone [Middle English. Via Latin *asphodilus* (source of English *daffodil*) from Greek *asphodelos*, of unknown origin.]

asphyxia /ass fíksi ə, əss-/ *n.* suffocation as a result of physical blockage of the airway or inhalation of toxic gases, causing a lack of oxygen and unconsciousness [Early 18thC. Via modern Latin from Greek *asphuxia*, literally 'lack of pulse', from *sphuxis* 'heartbeat', from *sphuzein* 'to throb'.]

asphyxiant /ass fíksi ənt, əss-/ *adj.* SUFFOCATING causing oxygen deficiency and suffocation ■ *n.* CAUSE OF

SUFFOCATION an agent that causes asphyxia, e.g. a toxic gas

asphyxiate /ass fíksi ayt, əss-/ (**-ates**, **-ating**, **-ated**) *vti.* to deprive a person or animal of oxygen, or be deprived of oxygen, usually leading to unconsciousness or death —**asphyxiation** /ass fíksi áysh'n, əss-/ —**asphyxiator** /ass fíksi aytər, əss-/ *n.*

aspic /áspik/ *n.* a cold jelly often used as a mould for fish, meat, eggs, or vegetables [Late 18thC. From French, literally 'asp', an alteration of Old French *aspe* (see ASP[1]). Possibly so called because the colours in the jelly were thought to resemble the snake's.]

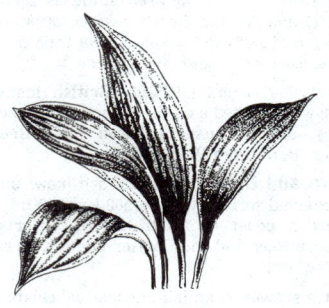
Aspidistra

aspidistra /áspi dístrə/ *n.* an Asian plant of the lily family that has large glossy leaves and small brownish flowers and is commonly grown as a houseplant. Genus: *Aspidistra*. [Early 19thC. Via modern Latin, genus name, from Greek *aspid-*, the stem of *aspis* 'shield', because of the shape of the plant's leaves.]

—— WORD KEY: CULTURAL NOTE ——

Keep the Aspidistra Flying, a novel by George Orwell (1936). The story of a young writer struggling to cope with poverty, it celebrates traditional English values of stoicism and community, symbolized by the hardy aspidistra plant.

aspirant /áspirənt, ə spírənt/ *n.* ASPIRING PERSON sb who seeks or hopes to attain sth ○ *an aspirant to the presidency* ■ *adj.* ASPIRING seeking or hoping to attain sth

—— WORD KEY: SYNONYMS ——

See Synonyms at *candidate*.

aspirate *vt.* /áspi rayt/ (**-rates**, **-rating**, **-rated**) **1.** PRONOUNCE WHILE BREATHING OUT to pronounce a sound or word while breathing out, e.g. the letter h at the beginning of such words as 'house' and 'hat' in standard English **2.** REMOVE LIQUID to remove liquid or gas by suction, especially from a body cavity ○ *using a syringe to aspirate the fluid from the cyst* **3.** INHALE STH to inhale sth, especially a liquid, into the lungs ■ *n.* /áspərət/ BREATHY LETTER a sound pronounced while breathing out, e.g. the sound of the letter h at the beginning of many English words ■ *adj.* /áspərət/ BREATHY SOUNDING pronounced while breathing out [Late 17thC. From Latin *aspirat-*, the past participle stem of *aspirare*, literally 'to breathe towards', from *spirare* (see SPIRIT).]

aspiration /áspi ráysh'n/ *n.* **1.** AMBITION a desire or ambition to achieve sth **2.** BREATHY PRONUNCIATION pronunciation accompanied by breathing out **3.** SUCTION the withdrawal of fluids or gases from the body or a body cavity **4.** INHALATION drawing matter into the lungs along with the breath —**aspiratory** /ə spírətəri, áspirətəri/ *adj.*

aspirational /áspi ráysh'nəl/ *adj.* showing a desire or ambition to achieve sth, especially self-improvement or material success ○ *the aspirational working class*

aspirator /áspi raytər/ *n.* an apparatus for drawing out fluids or gases by suction

aspire /ə spír/ (**-pires**, **-piring**, **-pired**) *vi.* **1.** HAVE PARTICULAR AMBITION to seek to attain a particular goal ○ *aspire to the priesthood* **2.** FLY HIGH to soar to a great height (*literary*) [14thC. From Latin *aspirare* 'to breathe towards'. The underlying metaphor is of projecting or breathing your desires towards sth.] —**aspirer** *n.* —**aspiring** *adj.*

aspirin /ásprin/ (*plural* **-rins** *or* **-rin**) *n.* **1.** PAIN RELIEVER a drug derived from salicylic acid that is used to relieve pain and inflammation, to lower fever, and to reduce the risk of blood clotting within an artery. Formula: $C_9H_8O_4$. **2.** TABLET CONTAINING ASPIRIN a tablet containing aspirin [Late 19thC. From German, formed from a contraction of *acetylierte Spirsäure* 'acetylated spiraeic acid' (the former name of salicylic acid).]

Aspiring, Mount /ə spíring/ mountain in southwestern South Island, New Zealand. Height: 3,035 m/9,957 ft.

asp viper *n.* = asp[1] *n.* 2

asquint /ə skwínt/ *adv.* from the corner of the eye, as if suspiciously

Asquith /áskwith/, **Herbert Henry** (1852–1928) British statesman and Liberal prime minister (1908–16). His government introduced old-age pensions and national insurance.

ASR *abbr.* airport surveillance radar

Ass

ass[1] /ass/ *n.* **1.** ANIMAL LIKE HORSE WITH LONG EARS an animal resembling a small horse with long ears, sometimes used as a beast of burden. The donkey is a domesticated descendant of the wild ass. Genus: *Equus*. **2.** OFFENSIVE TERM an offensive term for an unintelligent, thoughtless, or ridiculous person (*slang insult*) [Old English *assa*, via an unknown Celtic source from Latin *asinus* (source of English *asinine* and *easel*)]

ass[2] /ass/ *n.* US (*taboo offensive*) **1.** = arse **2.** OFFENSIVE TERM an offensive term for sexual intercourse [Euphemistic respelling of ARSE] ◇ **cover your ass** US to behave in a way that ensures you will not be blamed for sth later (*taboo offensive*) ◇ **haul ass** US to move or start to move quickly (*taboo offensive*) ◇ **have your ass in a sling** *or* **bind** US to be in trouble (*taboo offensive*) ◇ **kick (some) ass** US to behave aggressively or violently in order to get what you want (*taboo offensive*) ◇ **kiss ass** US to be very polite or obsequious to sb in authority (*taboo offensive*)

Assad /ə sád/, **Hafez al-** (*b.* 1928) Syrian government leader. He seized power in 1970 and was elected president of Syria in 1971.

assagai *n.* = assegai

assail /ə sáyl/ (**-sails, -sailing, -sailed**) *vt.* **1.** ATTACK SB to attack sb vigorously with words or actions ○ *assailed by an angry mob* **2.** TROUBLE OR BESET SB to overwhelm the mind or senses of sb ○ *'Low growls and angry snarls assailed our ears on every side'.* (Edgar Rice Burroughs, *The Gods of Mars*; 1913) [13thC. Via Old French *assaill-*, the stem of *asalir*, from assumed Vulgar Latin *assalire*, literally 'to leap at', from Latin *salire* 'to leap'.] —**assailable** *adj.* —**assailer** *n.* —**assailment** *n.*

assailant /ə sáylənt/ *n.* sb who violently attacks sb else, usually causing physical injury

Assam /ə sám/ union state of India, situated in the northeastern part of the country. Capital: Dispur. Population: 24,200,000 (1994). Area: 78,438 sq. km/30,285 sq. mi.

Assamese /ássə meéz/ (*plural* **-ese**) *n.* **1.** PEOPLES SB FROM ASSAM sb who was born in or lives in the state of Assam in northeastern India **2.** LANG INDIC LANGUAGE a language spoken in the state of Assam in northeastern India and in Bangladesh. It belongs to the Indic group of Indo-European languages and is

written in Bengali script. Assamese is spoken by about 11 million people. —**Assamese** *adj.*

assassin /ə sássin/ *n.* a killer, especially of a political leader or other public figure [Mid-16thC. Via French from, ultimately, Arabic *ḥašāšīn*, literally 'hashish users', denoting a group of 11th-century Ismaili Muslims who murdered Christian leaders.]

assassinate /ə sássi nayt/ (**-nates, -nating, -nated**) *vt.* **1.** MURDER SB to kill sb, especially a political leader or other public figure, by a sudden violent attack **2.** RUIN STH to harm or destroy sth such as sb's reputation maliciously or treacherously —**assassinator** *n.*

— WORD KEY: SYNONYMS —
See Synonyms at *kill*.

assassination /ə sássi náysh'n/ *n.* **1.** MURDER the killing of a political leader or other public figure by a sudden violent attack ○ *an assassination attempt* **2.** DESTRUCTION OF STH the destruction of sth such as sb's reputation by malicious or treacherous means

assassin bug *n.* a large long-legged insect with powerful mouthparts that kills and sucks the blood of other animals. Family: Reduviidae.

assault /ə sáwlt/ *n.* **1.** PHYSICAL OR VERBAL ATTACK a violent physical or verbal attack **2.** LAW ATTACK OR FEAR OF BODILY HARM an unlawful threat of bodily violence or harm to sb else, or an attempt to do such violence or harm **3.** LAW = sexual assault **4.** ATTEMPT TO DESTROY STH a campaign or series of actions that aims to challenge or destroy sth ○ *The proposals are under assault by various special interest groups.* ■ *vt.* (**-saults, -saulting, -saulted**) **1.** LAW ATTACK SB to attack sb physically or verbally in a violent way **2.** MIL MAKE MILITARY ATTACK ON PLACE to attack a place with a military force [Via Old French *assaut* from assumed Vulgar Latin *assaltus*, the past participle of *assalire* (see ASSAIL)] —**assaulter** *n.*

assault and battery *n.* the crime of making physical contact with and doing bodily harm to sb, e.g. knocking the victim down or burning his or her clothing

assault course *n.* an area of land on which there are various obstacles to be climbed over, crawled under, and run through, used by soldiers for training and keeping fit. US term **obstacle course**

assaultive /ə sáwltiv/ *adj.* extremely aggressive or disposed to attack

assay /ə sáy, ássay/ *n.* **1.** ANALYSIS OF STH an examination and analysis of sth **2.** CHEM CHEMICAL ANALYSIS chemical testing carried out to determine the composition of a substance or the concentration of various components in a substance **3.** SAMPLE OF MATERIAL a sample of material for analysis **4.** ATTEMPT AT STH an attempt to do sth (*archaic*) ■ *vt.* (**-says, -saying, -sayed**) **1.** EXAMINE STH to examine or test sth with a view to evaluating it **2.** CHEM ANALYSE to analyse a substance such as a metal or ore in order to discover its components **3.** ATTEMPT TO DO STH to attempt to do sth (*literary*) [The noun is from Old French *assai* 'test'; the verb from Old French *assaier* 'to test', variant of *essaier* (see ESSAY).] —**assayable** *adj.* —**assayer** /ə sáyər/ *n.*

assegai /ássə gī/, **assagai** *n.* a slender hardwood spear with an iron tip, used especially by the Zulu peoples of southern Africa [Early 17thC. Via obsolete French *azagaie* from, ultimately, Berber *zaġáya* 'spear'.]

assemblage /ə sémblij/ *n.* **1.** GATHERING TOGETHER a gathering of things or people at one point ○ *a law to forbid the assemblage of unruly mobs* **2.** COLLECTION a collection of people or things ○ *an assemblage of ideas* **3.** SCULPTURE ARTISTIC ARRANGEMENT OF MISCELLANEOUS ITEMS a work of art made from a collection of different objects

assemble /ə sémb'l/ (**-bles, -bling, -bled**) *v.* **1.** *vti.* COLLECT TOGETHER to bring people or things together or gather together in one place ○ *A crowd began to assemble.* **2.** *vt.* PUT COMPONENTS TOGETHER to fit the parts of sth together to make a finished whole ○ *assembled a model* [Via French *assembler*, from assumed Vulgar Latin *assimulare*, literally 'to put together', from Latin *simul* 'together'] —**assembled** *adj.*

— WORD KEY: SYNONYMS —
See Synonyms at *build* and *collect*.

assembler /ə sémblər/ *n.* **1.** INDUST FITTER OF PARTS a person, machine, or company that puts together the parts of a machine or piece of equipment when it is being built **2.** COMPUT COMPUTER PROGRAM a computer program that converts assembly language into machine language **3.** COMPUT = assembly language

assembly /ə sémbli/ (*plural* **-blies**) *n.* **1.** GATHERING the coming together of people for a common purpose ○ *freedom of assembly* **2.** EDUC SCHOOL MEETING a regular formal gathering of all the students in a school **3.** assembly, **Assembly** LEGISLATIVE MEETING a group of people meeting as a deliberative or law-making body **4.** FITTING COMPONENTS TOGETHER the putting together of parts to make a finished product **5.** COMPONENTS a set of components before they are put together to make a finished product **6.** MILITARY GATHERING the gathering together of a military unit prior to an event or operation **7.** MILITARY SIGNAL a signal for soldiers or other personnel to gather **8.** COMPUT TRANSLATION OF COMPUTER LANGUAGE the translation of assembly language into machine language [14thC. From French *assemblée*, the feminine past participle of *assembler* (see ASSEMBLE).]

— WORD KEY: SYNONYMS —
See Synonyms at *meeting*.

assembly language *n.* a low-level computer language that consists of mnemonic codes and symbolic addresses corresponding to machine-language instructions

assembly line *n.* a series of work stations at which individual steps in the assembly of a product are carried out by workers or machines as the product is moved along

assemblyman /ə sémblimən/ (*plural* **-men** /-mən/) *n.* a member of a legislative assembly

assemblywoman /ə sémbli woomən/ (*plural* **-en** /-wimin/) *n.* a woman member of a legislative assembly

assent /ə sént/ *vi.* (**-sents, -senting, -sented**) AGREE TO STH to agree to sth or express agreement ○ *She will never assent to their marriage.* ■ *n.* EXPRESSION OF AGREEMENT an expression of agreement or acceptance [13thC. Via Old French *assenter* from, ultimately, Latin *assentire*, literally 'to feel towards'.] —**assenter** *n.* —**assentingly** *adv.*

— WORD KEY: SYNONYMS —
See Synonyms at *agree*.

assentation /ass en táysh'n/ *n.* agreement, especially in an insincere manner (*literary*)

assentient /ə sénshi ənt/ *adj.* AGREEING agreeing or accepting (*formal*) ■ *n.* SB WHO AGREES a person or party that agrees (*formal*) [Mid-19thC. From Latin *assentient-*, the present participle stem of *assentire* (see ASSENT).]

assert /ə súrt/ (**-serts, -serting, -serted**) *v.* **1.** *vt.* CLAIM to state sth as being true ○ *She asserted that she had never seen the man before.* **2.** *vt.* INSIST ON RIGHTS to insist on or exercise your rights ○ *He asserted his right to remain silent and refused to testify.* **3.** *vr.* BEHAVE FORCEFULLY to exercise and reveal your power, influence, and prerogatives ○ *New management quickly began to assert itself two days after the takeover.* **4.** *vr.* BECOME KNOWN OR EFFECTIVE to start to have an effect or become noticeable ○ *Their relationship went well until the age difference began to assert itself.* [Early 17thC. From Latin *assert-*, the past participle stem of *asserere*, literally 'to join to', from *serere* (see SERIES).] —**assertable** *adj.* —**asserter** *n.*

assertion /ə súrsh'n/ *n.* **1.** EMPHATIC STATEMENT a strong statement that sth is true **2.** ACT OF STATING STH EMPHATICALLY stating emphatically that sth is true ○ *denied them the assertion of their rights*

assertive /ə súrtiv/ *adj.* confident in stating your position or claim ○ *Modern education encourages the assertive student.* —**assertively** *adv.*

assertiveness /ə súrtivnəss/ *n.* willingness to be forceful if a situation requires it

assertiveness training *n.* teaching people how to overcome shyness and assert themselves

assess /ə séss/ (**-sesses, -sessing, -sessed**) *vt.* **1. JUDGE** to examine sth in order to judge or evaluate it ○ *not enough information to assess whether the event occurred* **2. DETERMINE AMOUNT** to calculate a value based on various factors ○ *Loss adjustors are assessing the damage.* **3.** FIN **CALCULATE VALUE FOR TAX** to calculate the value of sth in order to establish how much tax must be paid ○ *property assessed at £300,000* [Via Old French *assesser* from Latin *assess-*, the past participle stem of *assidere*, literally 'to sit beside', from *sedere* 'to sit' (see SEDENTARY)] —**assessable** *adj.*

assessment /ə séssmənt/ *n.* **1. EVALUATION** a judgment about sth based on an understanding of the situation ○ *a fair assessment of the project* **2. PROPERTY VALUATION** a calculation of the value of sth in order to know how much tax must be paid **3. AMOUNT CALCULATED** an amount assessed, e.g. on a property **4. EDUCATIONAL EVALUATION** a method of evaluating student performance and attainment

assessor /ə séssər/ *n.* **1. SB WHO CALCULATES** sb who calculates amounts to be paid or assessed for tax or insurance purposes **2. SB WHO EVALUATES** sb who evaluates the work of a student or worker **3.** LAW **JUDGE'S ADVISOR** a specialist in a particular subject who advises a judge or committee of inquiry

asset /ásset/ *n.* **1. SB OR STH USEFUL** sb or sth that is useful and contributes to the success of sth **2. VALUABLE THING** a property to which a value can be assigned ■ **assets** *npl.* **1. OWNED ITEMS** the property that is owned by a particular person or organization **2.** LAW **SEIZABLE PROPERTY** the property of a person that can be taken by law for the settlement of debts or that forms part of a dead person's estate **3.** FIN **BALANCE SHEET ITEMS** the items on a balance sheet that constitute the total value of an organization [Mid-16thC. Via Anglo-Norman *assetz* 'sufficient goods' (to settle an estate) from, ultimately, Latin *ad satis*, literally 'to sufficiency'.]

asset-stripping *n.* the practice of buying a company cheaply and making a profit by selling all its assets individually —**asset-stripper** *n.*

asseverate /ə sévvə rayt/ (**-ates, -ating, -ated**) *vt.* to state sth earnestly or solemnly (*formal*) [Mid-16thC. From Latin *asseverat-*, the past participle stem of *asseverare*, from *severus* (see SEVERE).] —**asseveration** /ə sévvə ráysh'n/ *n.*

asshole /áss hōl/ *n.* US = **arsehole** (*taboo offensive*)

assibilate /ə síbbi layt/ (**-lates, -lating, -lated**) *v.* **1.** *vt.* **UTTER STH WITH HISS** to utter sth with a hissing sound like that of the letter s or z **2.** *vi.* **CHANGE INTO HISSING SOUND** to be transformed into a hissing sound (**sibilant**) [Mid-19thC. From Latin *assibilat-*, the past participle stem of *assibilare*, literally 'to hiss at', from *sibilare* (see SIBILANT).] —**assibilation** /ə síbbi láysh'n/ *n.*

assiduity /ássi dyoó əti/ *n.* **GREAT CARE** great care and attention in doing sth ■ **assiduities** *npl.* **ATTENTIVE BEHAVIOUR** constant attentiveness shown towards sb

assiduous /ə síddyoo əss/ *adj.* undeviating in effort and care [Mid-16thC. Formed from Latin *assiduus*, from *assidere* (see ASSESS), in a late sense 'to apply oneself'.] —**assiduously** *adv.* —**assiduousness** *n.*

WORD KEY: SYNONYMS

See Synonyms at ***careful***.

assign /ə sīn/ *vt.* (**-signs, -signing, -signed**) **1. GIVE SB TASK OR DUTY** to give sb a particular job to do ○ *assign extra duties to the latecomers* **2. SEND SB TO DO STH** to send sb to work in a particular place or with a particular group of people ○ *I assigned him to the post room.* **3.** MIL **ORDER A SOLDIER** to put a soldier or military unit under a particular command **4.** LAW **TRANSFER PROPERTY** to transfer property or rights to another by an official act **5. SET STH ASIDE FOR STH** to designate sth for a particular use ○ *The new radio station has been assigned a frequency by the authorities.* **6.** COMPUT **PLACE A VALUE** to designate a value for a computer memory location corresponding to a named variable ■ *n.* LAW = **assignee** *n.* 1 [14thC. Via French *assigner* from Latin *assignare*, from *signare* 'to mark out, designate', from *signum* (see SIGN).] —**assignability** /ə sīnə bílləti/ *n.* —**assignable** /ə sīnəb'l/ *adj.* —**assignably** /ə sīnəbli/ *adv.* —**assigner** *n.*

assignation /ássig náysh'n/ *n.* **1. LOVERS' MEETING** an appointment to meet a lover, especially secretly **2. ASSIGNING SB OR STH** the act of giving sb a particular job or designating sth for a particular use **3.** LAW = **assignment** *n.* 4 [Via French from the Latin stem *assignation-*, from *assignare* (see ASSIGN)]

assignee /ássī neé/ *n.* **1. SB RECEIVING RIGHT OVER PROPERTY** sb to whom a right over property is given or transferred **2. PROXY** a person appointed to act for another **3.** *Aus* HIST **CONVICT** in colonial Australia, a convict assigned to work for a free settler

assignment /ə sīnmənt/ *n.* **1. TASK** a specific task assigned or undertaken ○ *All team members have received their assignments.* **2. APPOINTMENT** a position, duty, or job for which sb is chosen ○ *an assignment in Japan* **3.** LAW **LEGAL TRANSFER DOCUMENT** a document, e.g. a deed, that effects a legal transfer of rights **4.** LAW **LEGAL TRANSFER** the transfer of a right in or over property to another **5.** *Aus* HIST **CHEAP LABOUR** the system by which convicts were assigned to work for free settlers as fulfilment of their sentences in colonial Australia

assignment worker *n.* a part-time, freelance, or temporary employee

assignor /ə sīnər/ *n.* sb who transfers rights in or over property to another

assimilable /ə símmiləb'l/ *adj.* capable of being integrated or assimilated —**assimilability** /ə símmilə bílləti/ *n.*

assimilate /ə símmi layt/ (**-lates, -lating, -lated**) *v.* **1.** *vti.* SOC SCI **INTEGRATE** to integrate sb into a larger group, so that differences are minimized or eliminated, or become integrated in this way **2.** *vt.* **ABSORB INFORMATION** to integrate knowledge or information with what is already known **3.** *vt.* PHYSIOL **ABSORB NUTRIENTS** to incorporate digested food materials into the cells and tissues of the body ○ *assimilate protein* **4.** *vti.* PHON **SOUND LIKE ADJACENT SOUND** to make a speech sound similar to an adjacent sound or to become similar to an adjacent sound [15thC. From Latin *assimilat-*, the past participle stem of *assimilare*, literally 'to make the same', from *similis* 'like'.] —**assimilator** *n.*

assimilation /ə símmi láysh'n/ *n.* **1. ACT OF BECOMING PART OF STH** the process of becoming part of or more like sth greater **2.** SOC SCI **INTEGRATION INTO GROUP** the process in which one group takes on the cultural and other traits of a larger group **3. LEARNING PROCESS** the integration of new knowledge or information with what is already known **4.** PHYSIOL **NUTRIENT CONVERSION** incorporation of nutrients into the cells and tissues of plants and animals involving digestion, photosynthesis, and root absorption **5.** PHON **SPEECH SOUND CHANGE** the changing of a speech sound under the influence of an adjacent sound

assimilationism /ə símmi láysh'nizzəm/ *n.* a policy of assimilating differing ethnic or cultural groups —**assimilationist** *n., adj.*

assimilatory /ə símmilətəri, -láytəri/, **assimilative** /ə símmilətiv, -laytiv/ *adj.* connected with or capable of assimilation

Assiniboin /ə sínnə boyn/ (*plural* **-boin** *or* **-boins**), **Assiniboine** (*plural* **-boine** *or* **-boines**) *n.* **1.** PEOPLES **MEMBER OF NATIVE N AMERICAN PEOPLE** a member of an Aboriginal people of North America who originally occupied lands in northern parts of the Great Plains, and whose members now live mainly in Saskatchewan, Alberta, and Montana **2. NATIVE N AMERICAN LANGUAGE** a language spoken in parts of southern and western Canada and Montana by the Assiniboin people. It belongs to the Siouan language family. [Late 17thC. Via Canadian French from Ojibwa *assini:-pwa:n*, literally 'stone Sioux'.] —**Assiniboin** *adj.*

Assisi /ə seé si/ town in central Italy, famous as the birthplace of St Francis in 1182. The Basilica of St Francis suffered considerable earthquake damage in 1997. Population: 24,700 (1990).

Assisi embroidery *n.* a type of embroidery in which designs are outlined, some design areas are left open, and the background is filled in with cross stitch

assist /ə síst/ *v.* (**-sists, -sisting, -sisted**) **1.** *vti.* **HELP SB** to help sb to do or accomplish sth ○ *a programme to assist new parents* **2.** *vi.* **ATTEND STH** to attend sth or be present (*archaic*) ■ *n.* **1.** SPORTS **TEAM PLAYER HELP** an act by a player in a sport that enables another member of the team to score or achieve a successful defensive move **2.** *US* **ACT OF HELPING** an act or series of actions helping another [15thC. Via French *assister* from Latin *assistere*, literally 'to stand beside', from *sistere* 'to stand', from *stare* (see STATION).] —**assister** *n.*

assistance /ə sístənss/ *n.* help given or made available to another ○ *technical assistance*

assistant /ə sístənt/ *n.* **1. HELPER** sb, especially a subordinate, who helps sb else to do sth **2. SHOP EMPLOYEE** sb who serves customers in a shop ■ *adj.* **1. HELPING** subordinate to or helping another ○ *an assistant teacher* **2. HELPFUL** serving to help or be useful

WORD KEY: SYNONYMS

assistant, helper, deputy, aide, right-hand man or woman

CORE MEANING: sb who helps another person in carrying out a task

assistant sb who works to sb else's instructions, often in a paid capacity; **helper** a more informal term than *assistant*, usually implying unpaid voluntary help; **deputy** an officially designated chief assistant authorized to act on a superior's behalf; **aide** an assistant in a military context, now extended to cover an executive assistant in political or commercial contexts; **right-hand man** *or* **woman** a trusted deputy who a superior relies on particularly for support and advice.

assisted conception *n.* = **assisted reproduction**

assisted place *n.* a place at a fee-paying school or university for which funding is granted by an official body

assisted reproduction *n.* the use of a technique, e.g. in vitro fertilization, to aid human reproduction in cases where this is problematic

assisted suicide *n.* the suicide of a patient, usually sb who is terminally ill, that is aided by a carer or especially a doctor, by the express wish and consent of the patient

assize /ə síz/ *n.* US **INQUEST** a judicial inquest, or the verdict of the jurors involved ■ **assizes** *npl.* **PERIODIC COURTS** periodic judicial proceedings that were held formerly in the counties of England and Wales and presided over by itinerant judges. They were replaced by the Crown Courts in 1971. [Middle English. Via Old French *assise*, the past participle of *asseoir* 'to settle', from Latin *assidere* (see ASSESS).]

ass kisser *n.* US = **arse licker** (*taboo offensive*)

assn, **assoc.** *abbr.* association

associable /ə sṓshi əb'l, ə sṓshəb'l, ə sṓssi-/ *adj.* capable of being linked or associated —**associability** /ə sṓshi ə bílləti, ə sṓssi-/ *n.*

associate *v.* /ə sṓshi ayt, ə sṓs i-/ (**-ates, -ating, -ated**) **1.** *vt.* **CONNECT THINGS IN MIND** to connect one thing with another in the mind **2.** *vi.* **SPEND TIME WITH SB** to spend time together with sb ○ *Before the race she associated only with other skiers.* **3.** *vr.* **JOIN AS PARTNER** to join other people in a professional or social relationship ○ *Two artists were associated with the design firm.* **4.** *vi.* **FORM AN ASSOCIATION** to form an association ■ *n.* /ə sṓshi ət, -ayt, ə sṓssi ət, -ayt/ **1. PARTNER** a partner in business or other undertaking ○ *my associates in the firm* **2. CONNECTED PERSON** sb who is seen with or known to spend time with another ○ *I couldn't identify any of his associates.* **3. MEMBER** a member who does not have full status, rights, or privileges ■ *adj.* /ə sṓshi ət, -ayt, ə sṓssi ət, -ayt/ **1. ALLIED** joined with others in purpose on an equal or nearly equal basis **2. SECONDARY** with subordinate status or less than full membership in an organization ○ *an associate member* [14thC. From Latin *associat-*, the past participle stem of *associare*, from *socius* 'ally, companion' (see SOCIAL).] —**associateship** /ə sṓshi ət ship, ə sṓssi-/ *n.* —**associator** /-aytər/ *n.*

associate degree *n.* in the United States, a degree earned on completion of a two-year course at a community college, junior college, technical school, or other institution of higher education

associated statehood *n.* the status of several former British colonies, mostly in the Caribbean, after dissolution of direct rule from Britain but before full independence

association /ə sṓsi áysh'n, ə sṓshi-/ n. **1.** GROUP a group of people or organizations joined together for a purpose ○ *form an association to represent dairy farmers* **2.** CONNECTION a linking or joining of people or things ○ *She hasn't profited from her association with him.* **3.** COMING TOGETHER coming together and social interaction between people ○ *freedom of association* **4.** PSYCHOL PSYCHOLOGICAL CONNECTION a connection of ideas, memories, or feelings with each other, or with events. ◊ **free association 5.** LINKED IDEA a thought, idea, or feeling that is linked with an event **6.** CHEM GROUPING OF MOLECULES the formation of groups of loosely bound molecules **7.** ECOL GROUPING OF ORGANISMS a major ecological community dominated by one or more species, e.g. oak in a deciduous forest —**associational** adj.

association football n. football played according to the rules of the Football Association (*formal*)

associationism /ə sṓssi áysh'nizzəm, ə sṓshi-/ n. a psychological theory that explains complex thought and feelings in terms of associations with simpler elements —**associationist** n. —**associationistic** /ə sṓssi áyshə nístik, ə sṓshi-/ adj.

associative /ə sṓshi ətiv, ə sṓssi-/ adj. **1.** OF PSYCHOLOGICAL CONNECTIONS connected with the association of ideas, or of ideas with events and experiences **2.** MATH, LOGIC GIVING SAME RESULT IN ANY ORDER giving the same result irrespective of the order taken, thus since a + (b + c) = (a + b) + c, addition is associative. Multiplication is also associative but subtraction and division are not. —**associatively** adv.

associative learning n. a learning process in which separate ideas and beliefs are linked in order to increase learning effectiveness

associative memory n. computer memory organization in which stored information is accessed by its content rather than by memory address

assoil /ə sóyl/ (**-soils, -soiling, -soiled**) vt. (*archaic*) **1.** ABSOLVE SB to absolve sb **2.** ATONE to atone for sth [13thC. Via Anglo-Norman *assoilier* from, ultimately, Latin *absolvere* (see ABSOLVE).]

assonance /ássənənss/ n. the similarity of two or more vowel sounds, or the repetition of two or more consonant sounds, especially in words that are close together in a poem [Early 18thC. Via French from Latin *assonare*, literally 'to respond to', from *sonare* 'to sound'.] —**assonant** adj.

assort /ə sáwrt/ (**-sorts, -sorting, -sorted**) v. **1.** vt. SORT to sort things by type or category **2.** vi. FIT INTO GROUP to fit into a particular group [15thC. From Old French *assorter*, from *sorte* 'a sort' (see SORT).] —**assorter** n.

assorted /ə sáwrtid/ adj. **1.** VARIOUS consisting of various kinds ○ *arrived with assorted excuses* **2.** ARRANGED arranged in groups

assortment /ə sáwrtmənt/ n. a collection of various kinds ○ *an assortment of drawings*

ASSR abbr. Autonomous Soviet Socialist Republic

asst abbr. assistant

asstd abbr. **1.** assisted **2.** assorted

assuage /ə swáyj/ (**-suages, -suaging, -suaged**) vt. to provide relief from sth distressing or painful ○ *Constant reassurance could not assuage their fears.* [13thC. Via Old French *assuagier* from assumed Vulgar Latin *assuaviare*, literally 'to sweeten', from Latin *suavis* 'sweet' (see SUAVE).] —**assuagement** n. —**assuager** n. —**assuasive** /ə swáyssiv, -ziv/ adj.

assumable /ə syōoməb'l/ adj. **1.** FIN TRANSFERABLE used to describe a financial obligation that can be taken over by sb else **2.** ABLE TO BE ASSUMED that can be supposed or taken for granted —**assumably** adv.

assume /ə syōom/ (**-sumes, -suming, -sumed**) vt. **1.** SUPPOSE to think that sth is true even though you have no evidence for it ○ *Don't assume that all has been revealed.* **2.** TAKE RESPONSIBILITY FOR STH to start being responsible for sth ○ *She assumed all of her brother's debts when he died.* **3.** ADOPT STH to adopt or take on sth ○ *spirits that assume the form of animals* **4.** TAKE ON ROLE to take on a particular role or function ○ *assumed the office of mayor* **5.** PRETEND STH to put on a pretence of sth, usually in order to hide your true feelings ○ *He assumed an air of indifference.* [From

Latin *assumere*, literally 'to take up', from *sumere* (see SUMPTUOUS)] —**assumer** n.

━━━━ **WORD KEY: SYNONYMS** ━━━━
See Synonyms at **deduce**.

assumed /ə syōomd/ adj. **1.** EXPECTED taken for granted ○ *an assumed increase in expenditure* **2.** ARTIFICIAL not genuine or true ○ *Better to express your feelings than sit there with an assumed smile.* —**assumedly** /ə syōomidli/ adv.

assumed name n. a false name, especially one used by sb doing sth illegal

assuming /ə syōoming/ adj. EXPECTING TOO MUCH expecting too much of other people ■ conj. ON THE ASSUMPTION THAT if it is assumed that —**assumingly** adv.

assumpsit /ə súmpsit/ n. **1.** CONTRACT OFF THE RECORD an oral or written agreement, contract, or promise that exists without being on the record or under seal **2.** LEGAL ACTION an attempt to recover damages from a breached assumpsit [Late 16thC. From Latin, literally 'he has undertaken'.]

assumption /ə súmpsh'n/ n. **1.** STH TAKEN FOR GRANTED sth that is believed to be true without proof ○ *Make no assumptions before looking at the evidence.* ○ *'Cruelty will be slyly advocated by the assumption that its only opposite is sentimentality'.* (C. S. Lewis, *Reflections on the Psalms*; 1961) **2.** TAKING STH FOR GRANTED believing sth to be true without proof **3.** ADOPTING STH taking sth upon yourself ○ *With the assumption of power comes responsibility.* **4.** TAKING RESPONSIBILITY FOR STH taking over responsibility for sth **5.** INCLINATION TO HIGH EXPECTATIONS the tendency to expect too much **6.** LOGIC UNPROVED STARTING POINT sth taken as a starting point of a logical proof rather than given as a premise [From the Latin stem *assumption-*, from *assumpt-*, the past participle stem of *assumere* (see ASSUME)]

Assumption (1649–50) by Nicolas Poussin

Assumption, Assumption of the Virgin Mary n. **1.** MARY'S JOURNEY TO HEAVEN the ascent of the Virgin Mary to heaven at her death, as believed by some Christians **2.** CHRISTIAN FEAST a Christian feast that celebrates the Assumption, commemorated on 15 August

assumptive /ə súmptiv/ adj. predicated on an assumption or a set of assumptions

assurance /ə sháwrənss, ə shōorənss/ n. **1.** PLEDGE OR PROMISE a declaration that inspires or is intended to inspire confidence ○ *They gave us every assurance it would arrive on time.* **2.** CONFIDENCE confidence in your ability or status ○ *He steered the ungainly machine with smooth assurance.* **3.** CERTAINTY freedom from uncertainty ○ *took heart in the assurance that the problem was solved* **4.** MAKING STH CERTAIN making sth certain or overcoming doubt **5.** INSUR INSURANCE AGAINST CERTAINTY insurance against sth that is certain to happen, e.g. death, rather than sth that might happen, e.g. loss of or damage to property ○ *life assurance*

assure /ə sháwr, ə shōor/ (**-sures, -suring, -sured**) vt. **1.** MAKE SB CONFIDENT to overcome sb's doubt or disbelief about sth ○ *I can assure you that every word is true.* **2.** CONVINCE SB to convince sb of sth ○ *assured us of her sincerity* **3.** MAKE STH CERTAIN to make sth certain ○ *Proper planning assures that the job will be done right.* **4.** INSUR INSURE AGAINST CERTAINTY to insure sb against sth that is certain to happen, e.g. death, rather than sth that might happen, e.g. loss of or damage to property [14thC. Via French *assurer* from assumed Vulgar Latin *assecurare*, literally 'to make secure',

from Latin *securus* (see SECURE).] —**assurable** adj. —**assurer** n.

━━━━ **WORD KEY: USAGE** ━━━━
assure, ensure, or **insure**? You use **assure** when you are referring to sb being made sure about sth, and **ensure** when you are referring to sth that you want to be sure of. *I assure you it doesn't hurt. She wanted to ensure that it wouldn't hurt.* **Insure** is used in connection with insurance (ie financial protection), and is also a variant spelling of **ensure** in American English.

assured /ə sháwrd, ə shōord/ adj. **1.** GUARANTEED certain to happen ○ *an assured victory* **2.** SELF-CONFIDENT confident about your abilities or other qualities ○ *the most assured conductor the orchestra had ever seen* **3.** INSUR WITH LIFE ASSURANCE covered by a life assurance policy ■ n. INSUR **1.** (*plural* **assured**) PERSON WITH LIFE ASSURANCE the person whose life is covered by assurance **2.** SB RECEIVING ASSURANCE MONEY the person named as the beneficiary in a life assurance policy —**assuredly** /ə sháwridli, ə shōor-/ adv. —**assuredness** /ə sháwridnəss, ə shōor-/ n.

assy abbr. assembly

Assyria /ə sírri ə/ ancient Mesopotamian kingdom with a large empire extending southwards and eastwards, at its height from the ninth to the seventh centuries BC

Assyrian /ə sírri ən/ n. **1.** LANG AKKADIAN DIALECT the Akkadian language, particularly in the form that is recorded in cuneiform tablets from Assyria **2.** PEOPLES SB FROM ASSYRIA sb who lived in Assyria —**Assyrian** adj.

AST /ast/ abbr. Atlantic Standard Time

astable /ay stáyb'l/ adj. **1.** UNSTABLE lacking stability **2.** ELEC OSCILLATING BETWEEN STATES oscillating between two unstable states

Fred Astaire

Astaire /ə stáir/, **Fred** (1899–1987) US dancer and actor who was known for his performances in Broadway musicals and films. He famously partnered Ginger Rogers. Real name **Fred Austerlitz**

Astana /ə stáanə/ capital of Kazakhstan. It is situated in the northern part of the country, on the River Ishim. Population: 281,000 (1990). Former name **Aqmola** (until 1998)

Astarte /ə stáarti/ n. MYTHOL ◊ **Ishtar**

astasia /ə stáyzi ə/ n. inability to stand caused by a lack of muscle coordination [Late 19thC. From Greek, 'unsteadiness', from *astatos*, literally 'not standing', from *statos* 'standing'.]

astatic /ay státtik/ adj. unsteady because of poor muscle coordination [Early 19thC. Formed from Greek *astatos* 'unstable', from *statos* 'standing'.] —**astatically** adv. —**astaticism** /ay státtissizzəm/ n.

astatic galvanometer n. an instrument for measuring electric current (**galvanometer**) that is not significantly affected by the Earth's magnetic field

astatine /ásstə teen/ n. a highly unstable radioactive element, the heaviest in the halogen series, found naturally in trace amounts. It is produced artificially and used in medicine as a radioactive tracer. Symbol **At** [Mid-20thC. Formed from Greek *astatos* (see ASTATIC).]

aster /ástər/ n. **1.** PLANTS GARDEN PLANT WITH DAISY-LIKE FLOWERS an annual plant of the daisy family, grown for its white, pink, or violet flowers **2.** CELL BIOL STAR-SHAPED STRUCTURE IN CELL a star-shaped structure seen

━━━━

during cell division (mitosis) [Early 18thC. Via Latin from Greek *astēr* 'star' (source of English *asterisk* and *disaster*). Ultimately from an Indo-European word that is also the ancestor of English *star*.]

-aster *suffix.* one that is inferior ○ *criticaster* [From Latin]

asteriated /a ste'eri aytid/ *adj.* used to describe a crystal that reflects light in a star shape [Early 19thC. Formed from Greek *asterios* 'starry'.]

asterisk /ástərisk/ *n.* **1.** PRINTING **STAR-SHAPED SYMBOL** (*) a star-shaped symbol (*) used in printing **2.** LING **ASTERISK AS LINGUISTIC SYMBOL** an asterisk used to mark a sound, form, or structure that is believed to have existed but is unrecorded, or that is wrong or ungrammatical ■ *vt.* **(-isks, -isking, -isked)** MARK STH WITH ASTERISK to mark a printed or written item with an asterisk [14thC. Via late Latin from Greek *asteriskos*, literally 'little star', from *astēr* 'star' (see ASTER).]

asterism /ástərizzm/ *n.* **1.** PRINTING **PRINTER'S MARK OF THREE ASTERISKS** a triangle formed of three asterisks to call the reader's attention to a following passage **2.** ASTRON **STAR CLUSTER** a cluster of stars that is smaller than a constellation **3.** CRYSTALS **STAR-SHAPED REFLECTION IN CRYSTALS** an optical effect appearing as a star in the light reflected from certain crystals [Late 16thC. From Greek *asterismos* 'constellation', from *astēr* 'star' (see ASTER).]

astern /ə stúrn/ *adv.* **1.** IN OR TO THE STERN in, on, to, or towards the stern of a ship or boat ○ *The deckhand walked astern.* **2.** WITH STERN FOREMOST into a position with the stern pointing in the direction of motion ○ *Bring the captain's gig astern.* ■ *adj.* BEHIND BOAT positioned behind a boat ○ *The astern line has been cut.*

asteroid /ástə royd/ *n.* **1.** ASTRON **ROCKY OBJECT ORBITING SUN** an irregularly shaped rock that orbits the Sun, mostly in a band **(asteroid belt)** between the orbits of Mars and Jupiter. Asteroids range in size from the largest, Ceres, with a diameter of 930 km/580 mi. down to dust particles. **2.** ZOOL **STARFISH** a starfish *(technical)* [Early 19thC. From Greek *asteroeidēs* 'starlike', from *astēr* 'star' (see ASTER).] —**asteroidal** /ástə róyd'l/ *adj.*

asthenia /ass the'eni ə/ *n.* a condition marked by loss of strength in the body [Late 18thC. Via modern Latin from, ultimately, Greek *asthenēs* (see ASTHENIC).]

asthenic /ass thénnik/ *adj.* **1.** PHYSICALLY WEAK showing abnormal physical weakness **2.** OF SLENDER BUILD having a slender and lightly muscled build [Late 18thC. From Greek *asthenikos*, from *asthenēs*, literally 'without strength', from *sthenos* 'strength', of unknown origin.]

asthenosphere /ass thénnə sfeer/ *n.* a weak zone in the upper part of the Earth's mantle where rock can be deformed in response to stress, resulting in movement of the overlying crust [Early 20thC. Coined from Greek *asthenēs* (see ASTHENIC) + -SPHERE.]

asthma /ásmə/ *n.* a chronic disease of the respiratory system, sometimes caused by allergies, with symptoms including coughing, sudden difficulty in breathing, and a tight feeling in the chest [14thC. Via medieval Latin from Greek, from *azein* 'to breathe hard'.]

asthmatic /ass máttik/ *adj.* **1.** WITH ASTHMA affected with or prone to attacks of asthma **2.** OF ASTHMA relating to the respiratory difficulties associated with asthma ■ *n.* SB WITH ASTHMA sb who is affected with or prone to attacks of asthma [Early 16thC. Via Latin *asthmaticus* from Greek *asthmatikos*, which was formed from, ultimately, *azein* (see ASTHMA).] —**asthmatically** *adv.*

astigmatism /ə stígmətizzəm/ *n.* **1.** VISUAL DEFECT a visual defect caused by the unequal curving of one or more of the refractive surfaces of the eye, usually the cornea. It prevents light rays lying in certain planes from coming to a focus on the retina, thus producing blurred vision. **2.** OPTICAL LENS DEFECT a defect in a lens or mirror that prevents light rays from meeting at a single point, producing an imperfect image [Mid-19thC. Formed from the Greek stem *stigmat-* 'point'.] —**astigmatic** /ástig máttik/ *adj.* —**astigmatically** /-máttikli/ *adv.*

astilbe /ə stílbi/ (*plural* **-bes** *or* **-be**) *n.* a perennial plant with attractive plume-shaped flowers. It was originally found in eastern Asia but now is widely

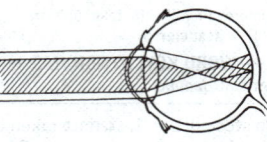

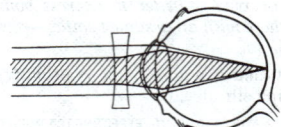

Astigmatism: Visual defect in the eye causing blurred vision (top) and corrected with concave lens (bottom)

cultivated in shady damp gardens. Genus: *Astilbe*. [Mid-19thC. From modern Latin, genus name, literally 'not glittering', from Greek *a-* 'not' + *stilbos* 'glittering'.]

astir /ə stúr/ *adj.* **1.** UP AND ABOUT awake and moving around, especially out of bed ○ *The children were astir early as usual.* **2.** MOVING moving around ○ *leaves astir in the breeze*

Asti spumante /ásti spyoo mánti/ *n.* sparkling white wine from Asti in northwestern Italy

Astley /ástli/, **Thea** (*b.* 1925) Australian novelist, author of *The Slow Natives* (1965). Full name **Thea Beatrice May Astley**

astonish /ə stónnish/ (**-ishes, -ishing, -ished**) *vt.* to amaze sb to a great degree [Early 16thC. Formed from a variant of earlier *astone* (see ASTOUND).] —**astonishing** *adj.* —**astonishingly** *adv.*

astonishment /ə stónnishmənt/ *n.* great amazement, often eliciting shock ○ *He was on time, to my astonishment.*

Astor, John Jacob (1763–1848) German-born US fur trader, property millionaire, and founder of the Astor family and fortune. He endowed the Astor Library, now part of the New York Public Library.

Astor, Nancy, Viscountess (1879–1964) American-born British politician. She was the first woman member of Parliament (elected 1919).

Astoria /ə stóri ə/ city and port in northwest Oregon. The Lewis and Clark Expedition ended here in 1806. Population: 9,844 (1996).

astound /ə stównd/ (**astounds, astounding, astounded**) *vt.* to overwhelm and stun sb with sudden surprise ○ *astounded by the viciousness of the attacks* [14thC. Alteration of earlier *astoned*, past participle of *astone* 'to stun', via Old French *estoner* (source of English *stun*) from assumed Vulgar Latin *extonare*, literally 'to thunder out'.] —**astounding** *adj.* —**astoundingly** *adv.*

astr- *prefix.* = **astro-** (used before vowels)

astraddle /ə strádd'l/ *prep., adv.* with one leg or part on either side of sth

astragal /ástrəg'l/ *n.* **1.** TYPE OF DECORATIVE MOULDING a narrow convex moulding, often taking the form of beads **2.** *Scotland* BUILDING GLAZING BAR any of the bars framing the individual panes that make up a window [Mid-17thC. Via French from Greek *astragalos* (see ASTRAGALUS).]

astragalus /ə strággələss/ (*plural* **-li** /-lee/) *n.* ANAT = **talus**[2] *n.* [Mid-16thC. Via Latin from Greek *astragalos*. Ultimately from an Indo-European word meaning 'bone', which is also the ancestor of English *osteo-*, *oyster*, and *ostracize*.]

astrakhan /ástrə kán, -káan/ *n.* fur fabric originally made from the expensive curly black or grey fleece of lambs from Astrakhan, southern Russia, now usually made from acrylic fibres. It is used for hats and trimming coats.

astral /ástrəl/ *adj.* **1.** ABOVE MATERIAL WORLD in theosophical belief, belonging to the ethereal region that is believed to exist throughout and at a higher level than the material world, in which personal auras are said to be perceived **2.** EXALTED likened to stars, e.g. in height or distance from ordinary places or people ○ *the astral position of king or president* **3.** RELATING TO STARS relating to, characteristic of, or consisting of stars [Early 17thC. Via late Latin *astralis*

from, ultimately, Greek *astron* 'star', from *astēr* (see ASTER).] —**astrally** *adv.*

astral body (*plural* **astral bodies**) *n.* in theosophical belief, a second body, not directly perceivable by the human senses, believed to coexist with and survive the death of the physical body

astral plane *n.* in theosophical belief, a level of existence where the spirit goes between death and entry into the spirit world

astral projection *n.* in theosophical belief, the ability to send the astral body outside of the physical body, while both remain connected

astray /ə stráy/ *adv.* **1.** OFF RIGHT PATH away from the right path ○ *went astray and ended up lost* **2.** INTO ERROR OR SIN in or into an evil or undesirable course of life ○ *a young man who was led astray* ■ *adj.* *Ireland* UPSET deeply upset and disturbed [13thC. From Old French *estraie*, past participle of *estraier* 'to stray' (see STRAY).] ◇ **go astray** to be mislaid or missing

astride /ə stríd/ *prep.* **1.** WITH LEGS AROUND on top of and with a leg on each side of sth ○ *astride a horse* **2.** EXTENDING ACROSS extending across in terms of influence or power ○ *a military colossus astride the world* ■ *adv.* WITH LEGS APART with legs spread wide apart ○ *He stood menacingly at the exit, arms folded and legs astride*

astringent /ə strínjənt/ *n.* PORE-CLOSING SUBSTANCE a substance used on the skin to draw tissue together ■ *adj.* SHARP AND ACIDIC IN TONE speaking or writing in a manner that is critical and hurtful in tone and content [Mid-16thC. From Latin *astringent-*, the present participle stem of *astringere*, literally 'to bind to', from *stringere* 'to bind'.] —**astringency** *n.* —**astringently** *adv.*

astro-, astr- *prefix.* **1.** star, the stars, outer space ○ *astrobiology* **2.** aster of a cell ○ *astrosphere* [From Greek, from *astron* 'star', from *astēr* (see ASTER)]

astrobleme /ástrə bleem/ *n.* a depression, usually circular, on the surface of the Earth that is caused by the impact of a meteorite [Mid-20thC. Coined from ASTRO- + Greek *blēma* 'wound from a missile'.]

astrochemistry /ástrō kémmistri/ *n.* the application of the principles of chemistry to celestial bodies and interstellar space —**astrochemist** *n.*

astrocompass /ástrō kumpəss/ *n.* a nonmagnetic navigational instrument used to determine the position of true north relative to a celestial body

astrocyte /ástrə sīt/ *n.* a star-shaped cell in the central nervous system's supportive tissue **(glia)**

astrocytoma /ástrə sī tóma/ (*plural* **-mas** *or* **-mata** /-mətə/) *n.* a commonly occurring malignant brain tumour made up of star-shaped cells **(astrocytes)**

astrodome /ástrədōm/ *n.* a transparent dome on an aircraft or spacecraft through which celestial observations are made in order to navigate

astrodynamics /ástrō dī námmiks/ *n.* the study of the effects of gravitational and other forces on the motion of natural and artificial bodies in outer space (*takes a singular verb*) —**astrodynamic** *adj.*

astrogeology /ástrō ji ólləji/ *n.* the study of the origin, history, and structure of cosmic bodies other than the Earth —**astrogeologist** *n.*

astrol. *abbr.* **1.** astrologer **2.** astrological **3.** astrology

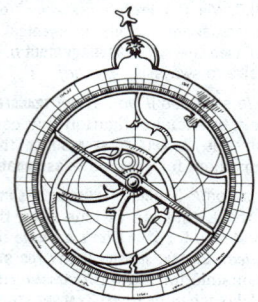

Astrolabe

astrolabe /ástrə layb/ *n.* an early instrument used to observe the position and determine the altitude of the Sun or other celestial body. The astrolabe was used for navigation from the Middle Ages until the 18th century when it was replaced by the sextant. [14thC. Via Old French and medieval Latin from Greek *astrolabon*, literally 'to take a star'.]

Aries 21 March- 20 April	Taurus 21 April- 21 May
Gemini 22 May- 21 June	Cancer 22 June- 22 July
Leo 23 July- 23 August	Virgo 24 August- 23 September
Libra 24 September- 23 October	Scorpio 24 October- 22 November
Sagittarius 23 November- 21 December	Capricorn 22 December- 20 January
Aquarius 21 January- 18 February	Pisces 19 February- 20 March
Rat 1936-1948-1960 1972-1984	Ox 1937-1949-1961 1973-1985
Tiger 1938-1950-1962 1974-1986	Rabbit 1936-1951-1963 1975-1987
Dragon 1940-1952-1964 1976-1988	Snake 1941-1953-1965 1977-1989
Horse 1942-1954-1966 1978-1990	Sheep 1943-1955-1967 1979-1991
Monkey 1944-1956-1968 1980-1994	Rooster 1945-1957-1969 1981-1993
Dog 1946-1958-1970 1982-1994	Wild Boar 1947-1959-1971 1983-1995

Astrological signs

astrology /ə strólləji/ *n.* the study of the positions of the Moon, Sun, and other planets in the belief that their motions affect human beings [14thC. Via French from, ultimately, Greek *astrologia*, literally 'account of the stars', which was coined from *astro-* 'ASTRO-' + *-logia* (see -LOGY). Used scientifically for 'observation of the stars'.] —**astrologer** /ə strólləjər/ *n.* —**astrological** /ástrə lójjik'l/ *adj.* —**astrologically** /-lójjikli/ *adv.* —**astrologist** /ə strólləjist/ *n.*

astrometry /ə strómmətri/ *n.* the measurement of the real and apparent motions and the positions of celestial bodies —**astrometrical** /ástrə méttrik'l/ *adj.*

astron. *abbr.* 1. astronomer 2. astronomical 3. astronomy

astronaut /ástrə nawt/ *n.* 1. SPACE TRAVELLER sb trained to travel and perform tasks in space 2. Can CANADIAN

IMMIGRANT WORKING IN ASIA a Canadian immigrant, usually Asian, whose family is settled in Canada but who frequently travels to Asia to work (*informal*) [Early 20thC. Coined from ASTRO-, on the model of *aeronaut*.]

astronautics /ástrə náwtiks/ *n.* 1. SCIENCE OF SPACECRAFT DESIGN the science and technology of designing and building spacecraft (*takes a singular verb*) 2. SPACECRAFT OPERATION the skills and activities associated with the operation of a spacecraft (*takes a plural verb*) [Early 20thC. Coined from ASTRO-, on the model of *aeronautics*.] —**astronautic** *adj.* —**astronautically** *adv.*

astronavigation /ástrō navi gáysh'n/ *n.* 1. = **celestial navigation** 2. NAVIGATION IN SPACE the navigation of a spacecraft among celestial bodies, especially stars —**astronavigator** /-gaytər/ *n.*

astronomer /ə strónnəmər/ *n.* sb who specializes in studying celestial bodies

astronomical /ástrə nómmik'l/ *adj.* 1. IMMEASURABLY GREAT immeasurably numerous, high, or great (*informal*) ○ *reached astronomical proportions* 2. RELATING TO ASTRONOMY relating to the science of astronomy —**astronomically** *adv.*

astronomical clock *n.* a clock that shows astronomical information such as the phases of the Moon

astronomical telescope *n.* a telescope used to view celestial objects

astronomical twilight *n.* the period of time during which the Sun is at 18° below the horizon

astronomical unit *n.* a unit of astronomical distances especially within the solar system, equal to the mean distance between the Earth and the Sun, about 150 million km/93 million mi

astronomical year *n.* = **solar year**

astronomy /ə strónnəmi/ *n.* the scientific study of the universe, especially of the motions, positions, sizes, composition, and behaviour of celestial objects. These objects are studied and interpreted from the radiation they emit and from data gathered by interplanetary probes. [13thC. Via Old French and Latin from Greek *astronomia*, literally 'star-arranging', from *astro-* 'ASTRO-' + *-nomia* (see -NOMY).]

astrophysics /ástrō fízziks/ *n.* the study of the physical properties, origin, and development of celestial objects and events (*takes a singular verb*) —**astrophysical** *adj.* —**astrophysically** *adv.* —**astrophysicist** *n.*

AstroTurf *tdmk.* a trademark for synthetic turf resembling grass

astute /ə styoot/ *adj.* shrewd and discerning, especially where personal benefit is to be derived ○ *an astute investor* [Early 17thC. From Latin *astutus*, from *astus* 'cleverness, skill'.] —**astutely** *adv.* —**astuteness** *n.*

astylar /ay stílər/ *adj.* used to describe a classical building that has no columns [Mid-19thC. Formed from Greek *astulos* 'without pillars', from *stulos* 'pillar'.]

ASU *abbr.* Australian Services Union

Asuncion /a sōónssi ón/ capital of Paraguay and of the Asuncion and Central departments and the largest city in Paraguay, located on the River Paraguay. Population: 502,426 (1992).

asunder /ə súndər/ *adv.* into separate parts, pieces, or places (*formal*) [Old English *onsundran*, literally 'into parts', from *on* 'into' + *sundran* 'parts', from a prehistoric Germanic base that is also the ancestor of English *sundry*]

asura /ússoorə/ *n.* in Hindu myth, a member of a class of nonhuman beings who are enemies of heavenly beings [From Sanskrit, 'demon', originally 'mighty Lord']

Asvina /ásh vin/ *n.* in the Hindu calendar, the seventh month of the year, falling in approximately the same time as September to October

Aswān /ə swaan/ city on the River Nile in southern Egypt. The Aswan High Dam, south of the city, holds back Lake Nasser. Population: 220,000 (1992 est.).

aswarm /ə swáwrm/ *adj.* full of moving living beings (*literary*)

aswirl /ə swúrl/ *adj.* moving with a swirling or twirling motion (*literary*)

aswoon /ə swoón/ *adj.* experiencing a swoon or faint (*literary*)

ASX *abbr.* Australian Stock Exchange

asyllabic /áy si lábbik/ *adj.* used to describe a speech sound that does not constitute a syllable

asylum /ə síləm/ *n.* 1. SHELTER AND PROTECTION protection or safety from danger or imminent harm provided by a sheltered place ○ *They sought asylum in a neutral country.* 2. PROTECTION FROM EXTRADITION protection and immunity from extradition 3. PSYCHIATRIC HOSPITAL an institution for people with psychiatric disorders (*dated offensive*) 4. HIST PLACE OF SANCTUARY a place that once offered shelter to criminals and debtors, especially a church [15thC. Via Latin from Greek *asulon* 'refuge', from *asulos*, literally 'without right of seizure', from *sulon* 'right of seizure'.]

asymmetric /ássi méttrik, áy si-/, **asymmetrical** /-méttrik'l/ *adj.* 1. NOT SYMMETRIC not arranged in a symmetrical way ○ *an asymmetric flower arrangement* 2. CHEM WITH PARTICULAR SPATIAL ARRANGEMENT OF ATOMS used to describe a carbon atom with four different atoms or radicals attached. This results in molecules with the same structure but a different spatial arrangement of their atoms (**stereoisomerism**). 3. ELEC ENG WITH VARYING CONDUCTIVITY used to describe a substance or a device that exhibits varying or different conductivities for currents flowing through it in different directions 4. AEROSP WITH UNEQUAL THRUST FROM ENGINES unbalanced because of unequal thrust from two or more sources, e.g. when one engine of a pair is not functioning properly 5. LOGIC, MATH NOT INTERCHANGEABLE used to describe a relation between two things where the first has a relation to the second, but the second cannot have the same relation to the first —**asymmetrically** *adv.*

asymmetry /a símmətri, ay-/ *n.* 1. BEING ASYMMETRIC the condition of being asymmetric in arrangement ○ *some asymmetry in the design* 2. LOGIC, MATH UNRECIPROCAL RELATION BETWEEN TWO THINGS a relation between two things where the first has a relation to the second, but the second cannot have the same relation to the first. Asymmetry is illustrated in the statement 'A is the father of B', since B cannot be the father of A.

asymptomatic /áyssimptə máttik/ *adj.* not showing or producing indications of a disease or other medical condition ○ *Although the blood tests were positive, she remained asymptomatic for some time.* —**asymptomatically** *adv.*

asymptote /ássimptōt/ *n.* a line that draws increasingly nearer to a curve without ever meeting it [Mid-17thC. Via modern Latin from Greek *asumptōtos*, literally 'not adapted to fall together', from *sun-* 'together' + *ptōtos* 'adapted to fall', literally 'to fall together' (see SYMPTOM).] —**asymptotic** /ássimp tóttik/ *adj.* —**asymptotically** /-tóttikli/ *adv.*

asynapsis /áy si nápsiss/ *n.* the failure of chromosomes that are alike (**homologous**) to pair during cell division (**meiosis**)

asynchronism /ay síngkrənizzəm/, **asynchrony** /ay sínkrəni/ *n.* the occurrence of two or more processes at different times —**asynchronous** *adj.* —**asynchronously** *adv.*

asyndeton /a síndtən, ə-/ (*plural* **-ta** /-tə/) *n.* the leaving out of conjunctions in sentence constructions in which they would usually be used. ◊ **parataxis** [Mid-16thC. Via late Latin from, ultimately, Greek *asundetos*, literally 'not bound together', from *sundein* 'to bind together' (source of English *syndetic*).] —**asyndetic** /ássin déttik/ *adj.* —**asyndetically** /-déttikli/ *adv.*

asynergy /ay sínnərji/, **asynergia** /áy si núrji ə/ *n.* a failure of coordination between different muscle groups so that delicate, skilled, or rapid movements become impossible [Mid-19thC. Formed from Greek *sunergia* (see SYNERGY).] —**asynergic** /áy si núrjik/ *adj.*

asystole /ay sístəli/ *n.* the absence of any heartbeat —**asystolic** /áy si stóllik/ *adj.*

at[1] (*stressed*) /at/; (*unstressed*) /ət/ CORE MEANING: a preposition used to indicate general position or location. In order to be more precise about exact physical location, other prepositions such as 'on', 'over', 'under', and 'by' are used instead. ○ *a con-*

ference at the school ○ Someone's at the door. ○ I work at home.

prep. 1. ATTENDING attending regularly ○ *not at school yet* **2.** FROM AN INTERVAL OF used to describe the position of sth by indicating its distance or angle ○ *She followed them at a distance.* **3.** INDICATES WHEN STH HAPPENS used to indicate the time or age when sth happens ○ *Lunch is at noon.* **4.** DURING AN EVENT while present during an event ○ *had a good time at the carnival* **5.** INDICATES RATE OR FREQUENCY used to indicate the rate, frequency, level, or price of sth ○ *driving at 65 miles per hour* **6.** TOWARDS to or in the direction of sb or sth ○ *He glanced over at her.* **7.** AS A REACTION TO used to indicate what sb is reacting to ○ *amazed at what had happened* **8.** IN THE STATED ACTIVITY used to indicate an activity or subject that a judgment about sb relates to ○ *an expert at windsurfing* **9.** IN A CONDITION OR STATE indicating the state or condition that sb or sth is in ○ *at risk of infection* **10.** DOING engaged or occupied in ○ *hard at work* **11.** IN THE MANNER INDICATED used to indicate how sth is done ○ *set off at a run* **12.** INDICATES REPEATED ACTIONS used to indicate the object of a repeated action ○ *She just picks at her food.* **13.** ACCORDING TO SB'S WISHES in response to or based on sb's wish or decision ○ *Spend this money at your discretion.* [Old English *æt*. Ultimately from an Indo-European word that is also the ancestor of Latin *ad* 'to, towards' (source of English *aid*).] ◇ **where it's** *or* **sth is at** where all the action and excitement is happening (*informal*) ◇ **at all 1.** in any way, to any extent, or under any conditions ○ *don't like it at all* **2.** in any way

at² /at/ (*plural* **at**) *n.* **1.** see table at **currency 2.** COIN WORTH AN AT a coin worth one at [Mid-20thC. From Thai.]

At *symbol*. astatine

AT *abbr.* **1.** antitank **2.** EDUC attainment target **3.** Atlantic Time

at. *abbr.* **1.** atomic **2.** PHYS, MEASURE atmosphere

at-¹ = **ad-** [From Latin *ad-*]

at-² *prefix*. = **ad-** (*used before t-*)

Atacama Desert /áttə kaámə-/ barren, arid, sparsely populated plateau in northern Chile known for its once enormously abundant nitrate and copper resources. Area: 363,000 sq. km/140,000 sq. mi.

ataghan *n.* = **yataghan**

ataman /áttəmən, -man/ *n.* a Cossack chieftain [Mid-19thC. Via Russian from Turkic, literally 'great father'.]

atar *n.* = **attar**

ataractic /áttə ráktik/, **ataraxic** /-ráksik/ *adj.* TRANQUILLIZING used to describe a drug or other agent that produces calm and peace of mind ■ *n.* TRANQUILLIZER a tranquillizer (*technical*) [Mid-20thC. Formed from Greek *ataraktos*, literally 'not disturbed', from *tarassein* 'to disturb'.]

ataraxia /áttə ráksi ə/ *n.* freedom from worry or any other preoccupation [Mid-19thC. From Greek, from *ataraktos* (see ATARACTIC).]

ataraxic *adj., n.* = **ataractic**

Mustafa Kemal Atatürk

Atatürk /áttə turk/, **Mustafa Kemal** (1881–1938) Turkish statesman. He was the founder and the first president of the republic of Turkey (1923–38).

atavism /áttəvizzəm/ *n.* **1.** REAPPEARANCE OF GENETIC FEATURE the recurrence of a genetically controlled feature in an organism after it has been absent for several generations, usually because of an accidental recombination of genes **2.** SB WITH ATAVISM an individual

showing atavism [Mid-19thC. Via French from Latin *atavus*, literally 'beyond a grandfather', from *avus* 'grandfather'.]

atavistic /áttə vístik/ *adj.* **1.** RELATING TO GENETIC REAPPEARANCE relating to or displaying the recurrence of a genetic feature that has been absent for several generations **2.** PRIMITIVE relating to or displaying the kind of behaviour that seems to be a product of primitive impulses long since suppressed by society's rules —**atavistically** *adv.*

ataxia /ə táksi ə/, **ataxy** /ə táksi/ *n.* loss of the ability to coordinate the movements of muscles [Late 19thC. Via modern Latin from Greek, literally 'without order', from *taxis* 'order' (see TAXIS).] —**ataxic** *adj.*

ATB *abbr.* all terrain bike

ATC *abbr.* **1.** air-traffic control **2.** Air Training Corps

ate past tense of **eat**

-ate *suffix*. **1.** having, characterized by ○ *lobate* **2.** office, rank ○ *archdeaconate* **3.** to act on in a particular way ○ *fluoridate* **4.** a chemical compound derived from a particular element or compound ○ *borate* [From Latin *-atus*, past participle ending of verbs in '-are']

A-team *n.* a group of people who are the very best of their type [From A 'first one in a series', modelled on 'A-detachment']

Atebrin *tdmk.* a trademark for the antimalarial drug quinacrine

atelectasis /áttə léktəssiss/ *n.* **1.** COLLAPSE OF A LUNG partial or total collapse of a lung **2.** NONEXPANSION OF LUNGS AT BIRTH a condition in which the lungs fail to expand completely at birth [Mid-19thC. Coined from Greek *ateles* 'incomplete' + *ektasis* 'extension'.]

atelier /ə télli ay/ *n.* a studio or workshop where an artist works [Late 17thC. Via French, literally 'carpenter's workshop', from, ultimately, late Latin *astella* 'board'.]

a tempo /aa témpō/ *adv., adj.* in or back into a previous musical tempo (*used as a musical direction*) [From Italian, literally 'in time']

atenolol /ə ténnə lol/ *n.* a medication that is used to treat high blood pressure and angina

Athabasca /átha báska/ river flowing northeast from the Rocky Mountains in Alberta, Canada, into Lake Athabasca. Length: 1,231 km/765 mi.

Athabasca, Lake fourth largest lake in Canada, bridging the border of Alberta and Saskatchewan. Area: 7,936 sq. km/3,064 sq. mi.

Athabaskan /átha báskən/, **Athapaskan** /-páskən/ *n.* **1.** LANG GROUP OF NORTH AMERICAN LANGUAGES a group of languages spoken in northwestern Canada and parts of Alaska, Oregon, and California. It includes Apache and Navajo and is a branch of the Na-Dene family. About 180,000 people speak an Athabaskan language. **2.** PEOPLES SPEAKER OF AN ATHABASKAN LANGUAGE a member of one of the Athabaskan-speaking peoples [Mid-19thC. Named after Lake ATHABASCA.] —**Athabaskan** *adj.*

Athanasian Creed /átha náyzh'n-, -náysh'n-/ *n.* a 5th-century Christian statement of belief of unknown authorship, formerly attributed to St Athanasius, Greek patriarch of Alexandria

Athanasius /átha náyshəss/, **St** (293?–373?) Greek theologian, prelate, Patriarch of Alexandria and Primate of Egypt. He wrote on the three-fold nature of God.

Athapaskan *n., adj.* = **Athabaskan**

atheism /áythi izzəm/ *n.* disbelief in the existence of a God or gods [Late 16thC. Via French from, ultimately, Greek *atheos* 'godless', from *theos* (see THEO-).]

atheist /áythi ist/ *n.* sb who does not believe in a God or gods

atheistic /áythi ístik/, **atheistical** /-ístik'l/ *adj.* relating to or characteristic of atheists or atheism —**atheistically** *adv.*

atheling /áthəling/ *n.* an Anglo-Saxon nobleman or prince, usually the heir to a throne [Old English *æpeling*. Ultimately from a prehistoric Germanic word meaning 'noble', which is also the ancestor of English *edelweiss*.]

Athelstan /áthəlstən/, **King of Wessex and Mercia** (895?–939). The grandson of Alfred the Great, he was the first monarch to claim the title, 'King of all Britain' (926?). He defeated an alliance of Scots, Welsh, and Vikings at the battle of Brunanburh (937).

athematic /áthi máttik/ *adj.* used to describe music that is not based on themes or tunes

Athena /ə theénə/, **Athene** /ə theéni/ *n.* in Greek mythology, the goddess of wisdom and warfare, and the patron goddess of Athens. She was born from Zeus's head. Roman equivalent **Minerva**

athenaeum /áthi neé əm/ *n.* **1.** INSTITUTION ADVOCATING LEARNING an institution that encourages learning, e.g. an academy of science **2.** READING ROOM OR LIBRARY any institution where reading materials are made available to the public, e.g. a library [Mid-18thC. Via Latin from Greek *Athēnaion*, the temple of Athena in Athens, which was used for teaching.]

Athenagoras I /ə theénə gáwrəss/ (1886–1972) Turkish religious leader. He was patriarch of the Orthodox Church (1948–72).

atheneum *n.* US = **athenaeum**

Athenian /ə theéni ən/ *n.* SB FROM ATHENS sb from the ancient or modern city of Athens in Greece ■ *adj.* OF ATHENS relating to or typical of the ancient or modern city of Athens in Greece, or its people or culture

Athens /áthənz/ capital and largest city of Greece, situated in the southeastern part of the country. Population: 3,096,775 (1991).

atheoretical /áytheər réttik'l/ *adj.* without a theoretical basis

athermancy /ə thúrmənssi/ *n.* the inability of a substance to transmit infrared radiation or radiant heat [Mid-19thC. Formed from Greek *athermantos*, literally 'not heated', from *thermainein* 'to heat'.]

atherogenesis /áthərō jénnəssiss/ *n.* the origination and formation of fatty deposits (**atheromas**) in arteries [Mid-20thC. Coined from ATHEROMA + -GENESIS.] —**atherogenic** *adj.* —**atherogenicity** /áthərōjə níssəti/ *n.*

atheroma /átha rōmə/ *n.* (*plural* **-mas** *or* **-mata** /-mətə/) *n.* an accumulation in the inner lining of an artery of a plaque of cholesterol and other constituents (**atheromatous plaque**) [Late 16thC. Via Latin from, ultimately, Greek *athērē* 'porridge', from its texture.] —**atheromatosis** /átha rōmə tóssiss/ *n.* —**atheromatous** /átha rómmətəss, -rōmətəss/ *adj.*

atherosclerosis /áthərōsklə róssiss/ *n.* a common arterial disease in which raised areas of degeneration and cholesterol deposits (**plaques**) form on the inner surfaces of the arteries. These tend to obstruct blood flow when the blood clots on the roughened plaques. [Early 20thC. Coined from ATHEROMA + SCLEROSIS.] —**atherosclerotic** /-sklə róttik/ *adj.* —**atherosclerotically** /-sklə róttikli/ *adv.*

Atherton /áthərtən/, **Mike** (*b.* 1968) British cricketer and captain of the England cricket team (1993–98). Full name **Michael Andrew Atherton**

athetosis /átha tóssiss/ *n.* a condition characterized by involuntary slow movements of the fingers, toes, hands, and feet and usually caused by a brain lesion [Late 19thC. Formed from Greek *athetos*, literally 'without a place', from *tithenai* 'to place' (see THESIS).]

athirst /ə thúrst/ *adj.* **1.** EAGER eager or longing for sth (*literary*) **2.** THIRSTY thirsty (*archaic*) [Old English *ofpyrst*, formed from the past participle of *of þyrstan* 'to thirst greatly', from *þurst* (see THIRST)]

athlete /áth leet/ *n.* **1.** SB WITH ATHLETIC ABILITY sb who has the necessary abilities to participate in physical exercise, especially in competitive situations such as games, races, and matches **2.** TRACK-AND-FIELD COMPETITOR sb who competes in track or field events [15thC. Via Latin from Greek *athlētēs*, from *athlein* 'to contend for a prize'. Originally used in English for 'wrestler'.]

athlete's foot *n.* a contagious fungal infection affecting the feet [From the fact that it flourishes in the heat and dampness of athletes' shoes]

athletic /ath léttik/ *adj.* **1.** OF ATHLETES OR ATHLETICS relating to athletes, athletics, or other sports activities ○ *athletic uniforms* **2.** MUSCULAR AND STRONG possessing a large skeletal structure and having strong muscles ○ *an athletic build* [Early 17thC. Via French and Latin from Greek *athlētikos*, from *athlētēs* (see ATHLETE).] —**athletically** *adv.* —**athleticism** *n.*

athletics /ath léttiks/ *n.* **1.** TRACK-AND-FIELD EVENTS sports activities carried out on a field, e.g. discus, high jump, and long jump, or on a track, e.g. running (*takes a singular or plural verb*) US term **track and field** **2.** *US* SPORTS ACTIVITIES activities such as sports and exercises that require physical skill and strength (*takes a singular or plural verb*) **3.** METHODS OF ATHLETIC TRAINING the methods, systems, or principles of training and practice for activities involving athletics (*takes a plural verb*)

athletic shoe *n. US* a shoe designed to be worn during athletic activities or exercising

athletic support *n.* = jockstrap

athodyd /áthədid/ *n.* a simple tubular jet engine [Mid-20thC. Contraction of *aero-thermodynamic duct*.]

at-home *n.* an informal social gathering in sb's own home

athwart /ə thwáwrt/ *prep.* **1.** ACROSS so as to be across or positioned crosswise over sth **2.** OPPOSING so as to oppose or obstruct sth

athwartships /ə thwáwrtships/ *adv.* from one side of a ship to the other

atilt /ə tílt/ *adv., adj.* in or into a slanting position ○ *Her hat was atilt on her head.*

atingle /ə tíng g'l/ *adj.* feeling a tingling sensation, often associated with excitement (*literary*) ○ *atingle with anticipation*

-ation *suffix.* an action or process, or the result of it ○ *alienation* [Via French from the Latin stem *-ation-*, a suffix forming nouns from verbs in *-are*]

-ative *suffix.* ◊ -ate

Atkinson /átkins'n/, **Sir Harry** (1831–92) English-born New Zealand statesman and premier of New Zealand (1876–77, 1883–84, 1887–91). As Treasurer, he introduced a national insurance scheme in 1882. Full name **Sir Harold Albert Atkinson**

Atlanta /at lántə/ capital of Georgia, and its largest city. It was an important Civil War battle site. Population: 401,907 (1996).

atlantes /at lán teez/ plural of **atlas** *n.* 3

Atlantic /ət lántik/ *adj.* OF THE ATLANTIC OCEAN relating to or situated in or near the Atlantic Ocean ■ *n.* **1.** = **Atlantic Ocean 2.** WEST AFRICAN LANGUAGE GROUP a group of languages of West Africa, considered by many linguists to be related to one another and to belong to the Niger-Congo language family [15thC. Via Latin from Greek *Atlantikos*, from *Atlas* (see ATLAS).]

Atlantic City city in southeastern New Jersey, on the Atlantic Ocean, noted for its beaches and casinos. Population: 38,361 (1996).

Atlantic Intracoastal Waterway system of protected inland waterways along the US Atlantic Ocean coast, stretching from Cape Cod, Massachusetts, to southern Florida. It is mostly used by pleasure boats.

Atlanticism /ət lántissəm/ *n.* a doctrine assuming that both western Europe and the United States can benefit politically and economically from co-operation, especially in military matters —**Atlanticist** *n.*

Atlantic Ocean, **Atlantic** the world's second largest ocean, which separates Europe and Africa from North and South America. Area: about 82,362,000 sq. km/31,800,000 sq. mi.

Atlantic Provinces Canadian provinces of New Brunswick, Nova Scotia, Prince Edward Island, and Newfoundland

Atlantic Rim *n.* those regions that have shores on the Atlantic Ocean, especially the north Atlantic

Atlantic salmon (*plural* **Atlantic salmon** or **Atlantic salmons**) *n.* a species of salmon that lives in northern Atlantic waters, swims up rivers in North America and Europe to spawn, and is valued as food. Latin name: *Salmo salar.*

Atlantic Standard Time, **Atlantic Time** *n.* the standard time in the fourth time zone west of Greenwich,

reckoned at 60° West. It is used, e.g. in Puerto Rico and the Canadian Maritime Provinces.

Atlantis /at lántiss, ət-/ *n.* in ancient mythology, an idyllic island that sank in an earthquake

atlas /átləss/ *n.* **1.** MAP BOOK a book containing maps and vital statistics relating to geographical regions **2.** ANAT TOP BONE IN THE NECK the vertebra that is at the top of the spinal column and supports the skull **3.** (*plural* **-lantes**) ARCHIT FIGURE OF MAN USED AS SUPPORT a figure of a man, either standing or kneeling, used as a support for the upper part of a classical building [Late 16thC. From Greek.]

Atlas[1] /átləss/ *n.* in Greek mythology, a Titan who was forced by Zeus to support the heavens on his shoulders as a punishment

Atlas[2] /átləss/ *n.* a small natural satellite of Saturn, discovered in 1980

Atlas cedar *n.* an evergreen tree from northern Africa, widely grown as an ornamental for its green to silvery-blue foliage. Latin name: *Cedrus atlantica.* [Named after the ATLAS MOUNTAINS where it grows]

atlas moth *n.* a large moth of tropical Asia and Australia, with a wingspan of 25 cm/10 in or more and strongly hooked and boldly patterned wings. Latin name: *Attacus atlas.*

Atlas Mountains /átləss-/ system of mountain ranges that extends through Morocco, Algeria, and Tunisia. The highest peak is Jebel Toubkal in Morocco. Height: 4,165 m/13,665 ft.

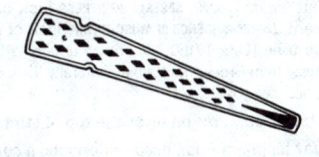

Atlatl

atlatl /át latt'l/ *n.* a spear-throwing device, usually a stick fitted with a thong or socket, used to steady the butt of the spear during the throwing motion [Late 19thC. From Nahuatl *ahtlatl*.]

ATM *n.* an electronic machine, usually situated outside a bank, that enables customers to withdraw paper money or carry out other banking procedures on insertion of an encoded plastic card. Full form **automated teller machine**

atm. *abbr.* **1.** atmosphere **2.** atmospheric

atman /áatmən/ *n.* in Hinduism, the essence of an individual [Late 18thC. From Sanskrit *ātman* 'breath, spirit' (source of English *mahatma*).]

Atman /áatmən/ *n.* in Hinduism, Brahman regarded as the Universal Soul

atmo- *prefix.* gas, vapour ○ *atmolysis* [From Greek *atmos* 'breath, vapour'. Ultimately from an Indo-European word meaning 'to blow', which is also the ancestor of English *fan*.]

atmosphere /átməss feer/ *n.* **1.** GAS AROUND CELESTIAL BODY the mixture of gases that surrounds a celestial body such as the Earth **2.** AIR OR CLIMATE the air or climate in a given place **3.** MOOD OR TONE a prevailing emotional tone or attitude, especially one associated with a specific place or time ○ *'The atmosphere of the place was heavy and mouldy, being rendered additionally oppressive by the closing of the door which led into the church'.* (Wilkie Collins, *The Woman in White*; 1860) **4.** MOOD OR TONE OF ARTWORK the prevailing tone or mood of a work of art **5.** INTERESTING MOOD OF PLACE an interesting or exciting mood existing in a particular place ○ *a jazz club with lots of atmosphere* **6.** PHYS UNIT OF PRESSURE a unit of pressure defined as the pressure that will support a 760 mm column of mercury at 0°C at sea level, equal to 1.01325×10^5 newtons per square metre [Mid-17thC. From modern Latin *atmosphaera*, literally 'sphere of vapour', from Greek *atmos* (see ATMO-) + Latin *sphaera* (see SPHERE).]

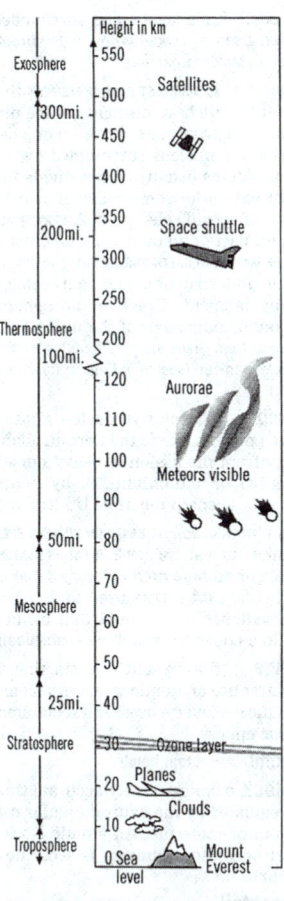

Atmosphere: Divisions of the Earth's atmosphere

atmospheric /átməss férrik/, **atmospherical** /-férrik'l/ *adj.* **1.** RELATING TO ATMOSPHERE relating to the atmosphere of a celestial body or of a particular place ○ *atmospheric pollution* **2.** ELICITING TONE OR AESTHETIC QUALITY evoking or producing an emotional tone or aesthetic quality ○ *a mural with a misty atmospheric effect* —**atmospherically** *adv.*

atmospheric pressure *n.* the downward pressure exerted by the weight of the overlying atmosphere. It has a mean value of one atmosphere at sea level but decreases as elevation increases.

atmospherics /átməss férriks/ *n.* STUDY OF ATMOSPHERIC INTERFERENCE the study of electromagnetic radiation emanating from natural sources in the atmosphere (*takes a singular verb*) ■ *npl.* (*takes a plural verb*) **1.** ATMOSPHERIC INTERFERENCE WITH ELECTRONIC SIGNALS static on a radio or flickering white spots (**snow**) on a television screen caused by electromagnetic radiation from natural sources in the atmosphere **2.** PREVAILING MOOD the mood or atmosphere suffusing a situation, group, or place

at. no. *abbr.* atomic number

ATOL *abbr.* Air Travel Organizers' Licence

atoll /áttol, ə tól/ *n.* a ring-shaped coral reef and small

Atoll

island, enclosing a lagoon and surrounded by open sea (*often used in placenames*) ○ *Bikini Atoll* [Early 17thC. From Maldivian *atolu*.]

atom /áttəm/ *n.* **1.** SMALLEST PART OF ELEMENT the smallest portion into which an element can be divided and still retain its properties, made up of a dense, positively charged nucleus surrounded by a system of electrons. Atoms usually do not divide in chemical reactions except for some removal, transfer, or the exchange of specific electrons. **2.** VERY SMALL AMOUNT a very small part or amount ○ *not an atom of truth* **3.** PARTICLE OF MATTER IN GREEK PHILOSOPHY the basic particle of matter, indestructible and indivisible, first proposed by ancient Greek philosophers as the fundamental component of the universe [16thC. Via Latin *atomus* from Greek *atomos*, literally 'unable to be cut', from *temnein* 'to cut' (source of English *tome, anatomy,* and *epitome*).]

atom bomb *n.* an explosive device whose great destructive power is due to the uncontrollable release of energy from the fission of heavy nuclei, such as uranium-235 or plutonium-239, by neutrons sustaining a rapid chain reaction. US term **atomic bomb**

atomic /ə tómmik/ *adj.* **1.** BASED ON NUCLEAR ENERGY based on or using nuclear energy **2.** RELATING TO ATOM relating to an atom or atoms ○ *atomic theory* **3.** TINY extremely small **4.** LOGIC UNANALYSABLE used to describe a proposition, sentence, or formula that cannot be analysed into a coherent structure —**atomically** *adv.*

Atomic Age *n.* the present era, starting with 1945 and the first use of atomic weaponry, considered in terms of the discovery, uses, and social implications of nuclear energy

atomic bomb *n.* = **atom bomb**

atomic clock *n.* an extremely accurate timekeeping device regulated by the natural regular oscillations of an atom or molecule. An atomic clock powered by a hydrogen atom **(maser)** is accurate to 1 part in 2 quadrillion.

atomic cocktail *n.* a radioactive substance in liquid form, used to diagnose or treat cancer (*informal*)

atomic energy *n.* = **nuclear energy**

atomic heat *n.* a value obtained by multiplying the specific heat of an element by its atomic weight

atomicity /áttə míssəti/ *n.* **1.** ATOMIC COMPOSITION the number of atoms in a molecule of a chemical element **2.** ATOMIC NATURE the state of being composed of atoms **3.** = **valency** *n.* 1

atomic mass *n.* = **relative atomic mass**

atomic mass unit *n.* a unit of mass defined as one twelfth of the mass of a carbon-12 atom, equal to 1.66×10^{-27} kg. It is useful for expressing the masses of atoms and molecules.

atomic number *n.* the number of protons in the nucleus of an atom of an element. The atomic number of all the isotopes of an element is the same and determines that element's position in the periodic table. ○ *The atomic number of carbon is 6.* Symbol **Z**

atomic theory *n.* any theory proposing that matter is composed of atoms

atomic weight *n.* relative atomic mass (*dated*)

atomise *vti.* = **atomize**

atomism /áttəmizəm/ *n.* **1.** IDEA THAT ATOMS MAKE UP EVERYTHING the theory that all matter in the universe is made up of small, individual, finite, and indivisible particles **2.** PSYCHOLOGICAL THEORY a theory of psychological states that attempts to reduce them to simple elements —**atomist** *n.* —**atomistic** /áttə místik/ *adj.* —**atomistically** /-místikli/ *adv.*

atomize /áttə mīz/ (**-izes, -izing, -ized**), **atomise** (**-ises, -ising, -ised**) *v.* **1.** *vt.* SEPARATE STH INTO ATOMS to reduce sth to atoms or separate sth into free atoms **2.** *vti.* MAKE INTO SPRAY to convert a liquid into fine particles or to spray particles converted in this way **3.** *vt.* DESTROY STH to destroy sth with atomic weapons —**atomization** /áttə mī záysh'n/ *n.*

atomizer /áttə mīzər/, **atomiser** *n.* a device that converts a liquid into a fine spray

atom smasher *n.* a device that speeds up subatomic particles (*informal*) [From the fact that it creates collisions between atomic nuclei in order to break them down into subatomic particles]

atomy /áttəmi/ (*plural* **-mies**) *n.* a skeleton (*archaic*) [Late 16thC. From ANATOMY, understood as 'an atomy', in phrases such as 'to study anatomy'.]

atonal /ay tṓn'l/ *adj.* used to describe music in which the notes are not related by any mode or key. ◊ **tonal** —**atonally** *adv.*

atonalism /ay tṓn'lizzəm/ *n.* the process of composing music in an atonal style or using atonality —**atonalist** *n., adj.*

atonality /áy tō nálləti/ *n.* in music, the fact of consisting of notes that are not related by any mode or key. ◊ **tonality**

atone /ə tṓn/ (**atones, atoning, atoned**) *vi.* to make reparation for a sin or a mistake (*formal*) [Mid-16thC. From *at one* 'in agreement', as in the phrase *(to set) at one* 'to reconcile'.] —**atonable** *adj.* —**atoner** *n.*

atonement /ə tṓnmənt/ *n.* **1.** MAKING OF AMENDS the making of reparation for a sin or a mistake **2.** **atonement, Atonement** RECONCILIATION BETWEEN GOD AND HUMANS in Christian belief, the reconciliation between God and human beings brought about by the death of Jesus Christ [Early 16thC. Formed from ATONE, partly modelled on medieval Latin *adunamentum*, from *adunare* 'to unite', and partly on earlier English *onement* 'unification'.]

atonic /ay tónnik/ *adj.* **1.** LING UNSTRESSED used to describe a syllable or sound that is not accented or stressed **2.** MED LACKING MUSCLE TONE connected with, caused by, or showing a lack of muscle tone [Mid-18thC. Formed from TONIC and ATONY.] —**atonicity** /áytə níssəti/ *n.*

atony /átt'ni/ *n.* **1.** LING ABSENCE OF STRESS lack of stress or accent **2.** MED ABSENCE OF MUSCLE TONE lack of normal muscle tone [Late 17thC. Via French or late Latin *atonia* 'weakness' from Greek, from *atonos*, literally 'lacking tone', from *tonos* (see TONE).]

atop /ə tóp/ *prep., adv.* on or at the top of sth (*literary*)

atopic /ay tóppik, ə-/ *adj.* used to describe a condition that is caused by a hereditary tendency to react to certain allergens, such as occurs in hay fever, some skin irritations, and asthma [Early 20thC. Formed from Greek *atopia* 'unusualness', from *atopos*, literally 'out of place', which itself was formed from *topos* 'place' (see TOPIC).] —**atopy** /áttəpi/ *n.*

-ator *suffix.* sth or sb that acts in a given way ○ *demonstrator* —**-atory** *suffix.*

ATP *n.* ORGANIC CHEMICAL COMPOUND a chemical compound **(nucleotide)** occurring in living organisms that provides most of the energy required by cells during its conversion to another nucleotide **(ADP)**. Full form **adenosine triphosphate** ■ *abbr.* Association of Tennis Professionals

ATPase /áy tee peé ayz, -ayss/ *abbr.* adenosine triphosphatase

atrabilious /áttrə bílli əss/ *adj.* (*literary*) **1.** GLOOMY tending to feel very sad **2.** PEEVISH inclined to peevishness and irritability [Mid-17thC. Formed from Latin *atra bilis*, literally 'black bile' (a translation of Greek *melankholia*), the bodily fluid thought to cause sadness and irritability.] —**atrabiliousness** *n.*

atrazine /áttrə zeen/ *n.* a herbicide used to kill weeds, especially in agricultural crops. Formula: $C_8H_{14}N_5Cl$. [Mid-20thC. Coined from the Latin stem *atr-* 'black' (because it prevents photosynthesis) + TRIAZINE.]

atremble /ə trémb'l/ *adj.* shaking or trembling from a strong emotion such as fear or excitement (*literary*)

atresia /ə treézi ə, -zhə/ *n.* the abnormal and usually congenital absence of a body opening such as the anus, ear canal, or intestine [Early 19thC. Formed from Greek *trēsis* 'perforation'. Ultimately from an Indo-European base meaning 'to twist, drill', which is also the ancestor of English *drill*.]

Atreus /áytri əss/ *n.* in Greek mythology, king of Mycenae and father of Agamemnon and Menelaus

atria plural of **atrium**

atrioventricular /áytri ō ven tríkyŏŏlər/ *adj.* relating to the upper and lower chambers, atria, and ventricles of the heart [Mid-19thC. Coined from ATRIUM + VENTRICULAR.]

atrip /ə tríp/ *adj.* used to describe an anchor that has just been raised clear of the sea bottom

at-risk *adj.* exposed to danger or harm of some kind, e.g. abuse or violence

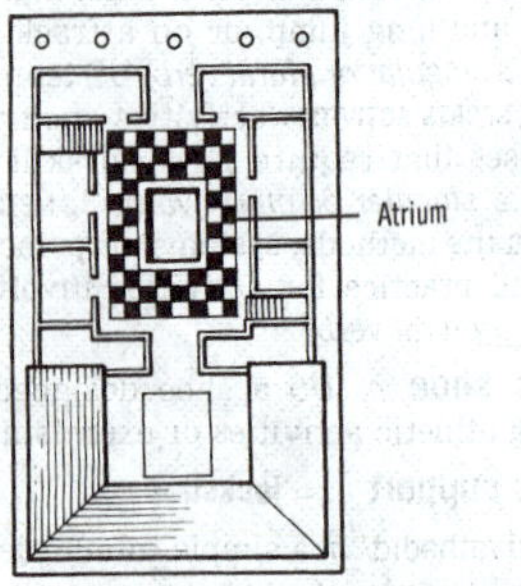

Atrium

atrium /áytri əm/ (*plural* **-ums** or **-a** /-ə/) *n.* **1.** ARCHIT CENTRAL HALL WITH SKYLIGHT a central hall usually with a glass roof or skylight and extending the full height or several storeys of a building **2.** ARCHIT, HIST ROMAN COURTYARD the open central courtyard of an ancient Roman house **3.** ANAT BODY CHAMBER OR CAVITY a cavity or chamber of the body, especially one of the upper chambers of the heart that takes blood from the veins and pumps it into a ventricle [Late 16thC. From Latin.]

atrocious /ə trṓshəss/ *adj.* **1.** VERY BAD appallingly bad ○ *atrocious manners* **2.** VERY CRUEL extremely evil or cruel ○ *atrocious treatment of prisoners* [Mid-17thC. Formed from the Latin stem *atroc-*, from *atrox*, literally 'dark in appearance', from *ater* 'dark'. Originally in English, 'wantonly cruel'.] —**atrociously** *adv.* —**atrociousness** *n.*

atrocity /ə tróssəti/ (*plural* **-ties**) *n.* **1.** SHOCKINGLY CRUEL ACT a shockingly cruel act, especially an act of wanton violence against an enemy in wartime ○ *to deplore the atrocities of war* **2.** EXTREME CRUELTY extreme evil or cruelty ○ *an act of atrocity* **3.** STH VERY BAD sth repellent or extremely bad of its kind [Mid-16thC. Directly or via French from Latin *atrocitas*, from *atrox* (see ATROCIOUS).]

atrophy /átrəfi/ *n.* **1.** WASTING AWAY the shrinking in size of some part or organ of the body, usually caused by injury, disease, or lack of use **2.** LESSENING OF ABILITY weakening or lessening of some ability ■ *vi.* (**-phies, -phying, -phied**) WEAKEN to weaken or waste away through disuse or the effects of disease [Early 17thC. Via late Latin *atrophia* from Greek, literally 'lack of food', from *trophē* 'food' (see -TROPHY).] —**atrophic** /ə tróffik/ *adj.*

atropine /áttrə peen, -pin/, **atropin** /-pin/ *n.* a poisonous alkaloid obtained from belladonna or related plants, used medically to dilate the pupils of the eyes and to stop spasms. It is also used by the armed forces as an antidote for nerve-gas poisoning. Formula: $C_{17}H_{23}NO_3$. [Mid-19thC. Formed from modern Latin *Atropa*, genus name of the belladonna plant.]

Atropos /áttrə poss/ *n.* in Greek mythology, one of the Fates, who were three goddesses who influenced human destiny. Atropos was known as the Inexorable, and carried the shears that cut the thread of life. ◊ **Clotho, Lachesis**

ATS *abbr.* Applications Technology Satellite

att. *abbr.* **1.** attached **2.** attention **3.** attorney

attaboy /áttə boy/ *interj.* US used to express enthusiastic encouragement or approval to a man or boy (*slang*) [Early 20thC. Alteration of 'That's the boy!'.]

attach /ə tách/ (**-taches, -taching, -tached**) *v.* **1.** *vt.* SECURE STH TO STH ELSE to secure one thing to another ○ *attached the door to the frame* **2.** *vt.* ADD STH TO STH ELSE to append one thing to another as a separate piece, the two being held together ○ *attached copies of the contracts* **3.** *vt.* ASCRIBE STH to assign a certain character or quality to sth under consideration ○ *I attach no importance whatsoever to their claims.* **4.** *vi.* BE ASSOCIATED WITH STH to have a close inherent relationship to sth ○ *little prestige attached to this post* **5.** *vr.* JOIN IN WITH SB OR STH to join and go along with sb or sth, often without an invitation **6.** *vt.* MIL PLACE SB ON TEMPORARY DUTY to assign military personnel to a military group on a temporary basis **7.** *vt.* LAW **SEIZE STH LEGALLY** to seize people or property by legal writ ○ *They've attached her salary for nonpayment of taxes.* **8.** *vt.* **BIND EMOTIONALLY** to bind sb emotionally to sb else or to sth (*usually passive*) [14thC. From Old French *atachier*, alteration of *estachier* 'to fasten with a stake', of Germanic origin. Originally in English, 'to arrest', the modern sense was reborrowed later from French.] —**attachable** *adj.* —**attacher** *n.*

attaché /ə tásh ay/ *n.* sb on the staff of a diplomatic mission who has responsibilities in a specific area [Early 19thC. From French, the past participle of *attacher* 'to attach'.]

attaché case *n.* a hard flat rectangular briefcase used for carrying business documents [From the fact that diplomats customarily use one to carry documents]

attached /ə tácht/ *adj.* **1. ENCLOSED** fastened to or enclosed with sth else ○ *Please see the attached documents and call if you have any questions.* **2. DEVOTED** devoted to or fond of sb or sth **3. COMMITTED EMOTIONALLY TO SB** committed to an emotional relationship with sb else (*informal*) **4.** ARCHIT **TOUCHING ANOTHER STRUCTURE** sharing a wall with another building, and thus not standing alone **5.** *Malaysia, Singapore* **EMPLOYED** having a permanent job with a person or organization ○ *My brother is attached to the Ministry.*

attachment /ə táchmənt/ *n.* **1. PART ATTACHED** an accessory attached or to be attached to a machine **2. MEANS OF ATTACHING STH** a means by which sth is attached to sth else **3. EMOTIONAL BOND** an emotional bond or tie to sb or sth. ◊ **bonding 4. ATTACHED TEXT** a document or file attached to another or to an e-mail message **5. ACT OF ATTACHING** the action of attaching one thing to another **6.** LAW **LEGAL SEIZURE** the legal seizure of people or property, especially to acquire jurisdiction over them or it

attachment of earnings *n.* a court order directing a third party, usually an employer, to withhold sb's wages in order to satisfy unpaid debts or to pay maintenance to the person's former spouse

attack /ə ták/ *v.* (**-tacks, -tacking, -tacked**) **1.** *vti.* **HARM** to try to harm sb by using violence or try to defeat an enemy or capture an enemy position **2.** *vt.* **CRITICIZE SB OR STH** to subject sb or sth to strong or vehement criticism ○ *The press has repeatedly attacked his plan.* **3.** *vti.* **INFECT SB OR DAMAGE STH** to cause an infection, illness, or damage in sb or sth ○ *The disease can attack at any age.* **4.** *vt.* **MAKE A VIGOROUS START ON STH** to begin sth such as work with enthusiasm or determination and deal vigorously with it **5.** *vti.* SPORTS, GAMES **TRY TO WIN** to attempt to defeat, or score against, an opponent or an opposing team in a competitive game or team sport ○ *The chess game began sluggishly, with both sides slow to attack.* ■ *n.* **1. ACTION OF ATTACKING** the process or an instance of attacking **2. BOUT OF ILLNESS** an occurrence of sth such as a medical disorder that is temporarily debilitating ○ *an attack of asthma* **3. ATTACKING MEMBERS OF TEAM** the attacking members of a team, especially the forwards in a football team (*takes a singular or plural verb*) **4.** MUSIC **ENERGETIC WAY OF PLAYING** the decisive or energetic way in which a musician begins to play a piece or passage [Early 17thC. Via French *attaquer* from Italian *attacare battaglia* 'to join battle'. Ultimately from a prehistoric Germanic word meaning 'to join', which is also the ancestor of English *attach*.]

attacker /ə tákər/ *n.* **1. SB WHO ASSAULTS** sb who commits an assault on sb else **2. CRITIC** sb who criticizes sb or sth **3.** SPORTS **PLAYER WITH SCORING ROLE** a player whose role is to score or create scoring opportunities

attain /ə táyn/ (**-tains, -taining, -tained**) *vt.* **1. ACCOMPLISH STH** to achieve a goal or desired state, usually with effort **2. REACH SPECIFIED STATE** to reach a specified age, speed, or size [13thC. Via Old French *ataindre* from Latin *attingere*, literally 'to reach to', from *tangere* 'to touch' (see TANGENT).] —**attainability** /ə táynə bílləti/ *n.* —**attainable** /-əb'l/ *adj.* —**attainableness** /-nəss/ *n.*

WORD KEY: SYNONYMS

See Synonyms at ***accomplish***.

attainder /ə táyndər/ *n.* in former times, the removal of the rights or the confiscation of the property of sb outlawed or sentenced to death for a serious crime, often treason [15thC. From Anglo-Norman, a variant of Old French *ataindre* 'to affect, dishonour' (see ATTAIN).]

attainment /ə táynmənt/ *n.* **1. ACCOMPLISHMENT OF STH** the achievement of the goals that sb has set **2. TALENT OR ABILITY** a skill, accomplishment, or distinction, especially one achieved through effort (*often used in the plural*)

attainment target *n.* in Britain, the required level of ability that schoolchildren should demonstrate in any subject at certain key stages in the National Curriculum

attaint /ə táynt/ *vt.* (**-taints, -tainting, -tainted**) **DEPRIVE SB OF RIGHTS** in former times, to take away the civil rights of sb outlawed or sentenced to death for committing a serious crime, often treason (*archaic; often passive*) ■ *n.* **LOSS OF REPUTATION** loss of honour or good reputation (*archaic*) [14thC. From Old French *atainte*, the feminine past participle of *ataindre* 'to affect' (see ATTAIN).]

attar /áttər, á taar/, **atar** *n.* essential oil extracted from flowers, especially the oil extracted from rose petals [Mid-17thC. From Arabic dialect *atar*.]

attempt /ə témpt/ *vti.* (**-tempts, -tempting, -tempted**) **TRY TO DO STH** to try to do sth, especially without much expectation of success ■ *n.* **1. EFFORT TO DO STH** an act of trying to do sth ○ *a successful attempt at cooking* **2. ATTACK** an attack or assault ○ *an attempt on his life* [14thC. Via Old French from Latin *attemptare*, literally 'to try for', from *temptare* (see TEMPT).] —**attemptable** *adj.* —**attempter** *n.*

WORD KEY: SYNONYMS

See Synonyms at ***try***.

attempted /ə témptid/ *adj.* used to describe sth at which a failed attempt has been made, especially a crime or offence ○ *an attempted robbery*

Attenborough /átt'nbərə/, **Sir David** (*b.* 1926) British naturalist and broadcaster who created documentary series such as *Life on Earth* (1979) and *The Living Planet* (1984). Full name **Sir David Frederick Attenborough**

Attenborough, Sir Richard, Baron Attenborough of Richmond-upon-Thames (*b.* 1923) British actor and director. He acted in films such as *Brighton Rock* (1947) and went on to produce and direct films including *Gandhi* (1982). Full name **Sir Richard Samuel Attenborough**

attend /ə ténd/ (**-tends, -tending, -tended**) *v.* **1.** *vti.* **GO TO EVENT** to go to or be present at an event ○ *Hundreds attended the wedding.* **2.** *vti.* **REGULARLY GO TO SPECIFIC ESTABLISHMENT** to go regularly to an institution such as a school, church, or hospital for instruction, worship, or treatment **3.** *vi.* **LISTEN OR WATCH CAREFULLY** to listen or play close attention to sb or sth **4.** *vt.* **OCCUR ALONG WITH STH** to accompany sth or be associated with it (*usually passive*) **5.** *vt.* **BE SB'S ATTENDANT** to escort sb or act as an attendant to sb (*usually passive*) **6.** *vi.* **RESULT FROM STH** to be the consequence of sth (*literary*) [14thC. Via Old French *atendre* from Latin *attendere*, literally 'to reach towards', from *tendere* 'to stretch' (see TEND).] —**attender** *n.*

attend to *vti.* to deal with or look after sb or sth ○ *patients to attend to* ○ *attend to business*

attendance /ə téndənss/ *n.* **1. PRESENCE AT EVENT OR INSTITUTION** an instance of being at an event or regularly going to a school, church, or other institution **2. NUMBER ATTENDING** the number of people who are present at an event or institution ◇ **dance attendance on sb** to be ready to carry out all sb's wishes

attendance allowance *n.* a tax-free state benefit paid to people with severe disabilities, to cover the cost of constant care or supervision

attendance centre *n.* a centre to which young offenders are required by the court to report regularly, as an alternative to a custodial sentence

attendant /ə téndənt/ *n.* **1. SB SERVING IN A PUBLIC PLACE** sb employed to serve or help members of the public in a public institution or place ○ *a museum attendant* **2. ESCORT** sb who escorts or serves another, especially bridesmaids or pageboys escorting a bride ■ *adj.* **OCCURRING ALONG WITH STH** associated with sth, or resulting or following from it ○ *parenthood and its attendant anxieties*

attendee /ə tén dée, á ten-/ *n.* any of the people attending sth, especially a conference, course, or seminar

attending /ə ténding/ *n.* *US* a physician who serves on the staff of a teaching hospital ○ *The orders for these medications were written by two attendings.*

attention /ə ténsh'n/ *n.* **1. CONCENTRATION** mental focus, serious consideration, or concentration **2. INTEREST** notice or interest ○ *media attention* ○ *A letter for the attention of Mr Brown.* **3. APPROPRIATE TREATMENT** care, tending, or appropriate treatment **4. AFFECTIONATE ACT** a polite, considerate, or affectionate act (*formal; often used in the plural*) **5.** MIL **FORMAL MILITARY POSTURE** a formal standing attitude assumed by members of the armed forces in drill and often when receiving orders, with feet together, eyes forward, and arms at the sides ■ *interj.* MIL **MILITARY ORDER** a shouted military order to assume posture of attention [14thC. From Latin *attention-*, from the stem of *attendere* (see ATTEND).]

attention deficit disorder, attention deficit hyperactivity disorder *n.* a condition, occurring mainly in children, characterized by hyperactivity, inability to concentrate, and impulsive or inappropriate behaviour

attention line *n.* a line in a formally addressed letter indicating for whom, especially for which employee or member of staff, the letter is intended

attention span *n.* the length of time that sb can concentrate effectively on a particular task or activity

attentive /ə téntiv/ *adj.* **1. CONSIDERATE OR RESPONSIVE** behaving towards sb in a way that shows special regard or affection **2. PAYING ATTENTION** listening or watching carefully and with concentration [14thC. From French *attentif*, from *atendre* (see ATTEND).] —**attentively** *adv.* —**attentiveness** *n.*

attenuate /ə ténnyoo ayt/ (**-ates, -ating, -ated**) *v.* **1.** *vti.* **MAKE OR BECOME WEAKER** to reduce the size, strength, or density of sth, or to become thinner, weaker, or less dense **2.** *vt.* BIOL **MAKE PATHOGEN LESS VIRULENT** to reduce the virulence of a bacterium or virus, e.g. by exposing it to heat or producing a culture of it in a special medium. Attenuated bacteria or viruses are used in some vaccines. [Mid-16thC. From Latin *attenuat-*, the past participle stem of *attenuare*, literally 'to make thin', from *tenuis* 'thin' (see TENUOUS).] —**attenuation** /ə ténnyoo áysh'n/ *n.*

attenuated /ə ténnyoo aytid/ *adj.* long, narrow, and sometimes tapering

attenuator /ə ténnyoo aytər/ *n.* a device for reducing the strength of a wave, especially an electrical signal

attest /ə tést/ (**-tests, -testing, -tested**) *vti.* **1. BE EVIDENCE OF STH** to show that sth exists or is true or valid **2. CONFIRM STH** to state that sth is true, especially in a formal written statement [15thC. Via French *attester* from Latin *attestari*, literally 'to witness to', from *testis* 'witness' (see TESTAMENT).] —**attestant** *n.* —**attestation** /á te stáysh'n/ *n.* —**attestor** /ə téstər/ *n.*

Att. Gen. *abbr.* Attorney General

attic /áttik/ *n.* a room or the area that occupies the space under a pitched roof [Late 17thC. Via French *attique* 'Attic' from Latin *Atticus* (see ATTIC). The word originally described a decorative structure (in the Attic style) above the main façade of a building.]

Attic /áttik/ *adj.* **1. OF ATTICA** relating to or typical of the ancient Greek territory of Attica or of the modern Greek department of Attica **2. ELEGANTLY WITTY** elegantly succinct or drily witty ■ *n.* **EXTINCT DIALECT OF ATTICA** a dialect of ancient Greek that was spoken in Athens and surrounding areas. Most of the literature of Classical Greece is written in Attic. [Late 16thC. Via Latin from Greek *Attikos*, from *Attikē* 'Attica'.]

Attica /áttikə/ **1.** department of east-central Greece. Capital: Athens. Area: 14,257 sq. km/5,466 sq. mi. **2.** peninsula region of ancient Greece that was divided into 12 states

Atticism /áttisizzəm/ *n.* a witty or elegantly simple and concise turn of phrase [Late 16thC. From Greek *Attikismos*, from *Attikos* (see ATTIC).]

Attila /ə tíllə/ (406?–453?) Hunnish warrior king who led an army of Mongolian nomads and subdued lands from the Rhine to the frontiers of China.

attire /ə tír/ *n.* CLOTHING clothing, especially a garment or combination of garments, worn on a particular occasion (*formal*) ■ *vt.* (**-tires, -tiring, -tired**) DRESS to dress yourself or sb else, especially in clothes of a particular type (*formal*) [13thC. From Old French *atirier* 'to array', literally 'to put in order', from *tire* 'order' (see TIER).]

attitude /átti tyood/ *n.* **1.** PERSONAL VIEW OF STH an opinion or general feeling about sth ○ *a positive attitude to change* **2.** BODILY POSTURE a physical posture, either conscious or unconscious, especially while interacting with others **3.** CONSCIOUS ASSERTIVENESS an arrogant or assertive manner or stance assumed as a challenge or for effect (*informal*) ○ *a streetwise teenager with attitude* **4.** AEROSP ORIENTATION OF AIRCRAFT'S AXES the angle of an aircraft in relation to the direction of the airflow or to the horizontal plane **5.** SPACE TECH ORIENTATION OF SPACECRAFT the angle of a spacecraft in relation to its direction of movement [Late 17thC. Via French from, ultimately, late Latin *aptitudo* 'disposition'.]

attitudinal /átti tyoódinəl/ *adj.* US insisting strongly on your rights [Late 20thC. From ATTITUDE in the sense 'contentiousness'.]

attitudinize /átti tyoodi nīz/ (**-nizes, -nizing, -nized**), **attitudinise** (**-nises, -nising, -nised**) *vi.* to strike exaggerated or unspontaneous poses, or adopt extreme opinions, for effect

Attlee /átli/, **Clement, 1st Earl Attlee** (1883–1967) British politician who was Labour prime minister (1945–51) and deputy prime minister in Churchill's wartime coalition government. His post-war government introduced the welfare state and granted independence to India.

attn *abbr.* attention

attorney /ə túrni/ (*plural* **-neys**) *n.* **1.** SB GIVEN LEGAL POWER sb legally empowered by a document (**power of attorney**) to make decisions and act on behalf of sb else **2.** US LAWYER a qualified lawyer, especially one who represents clients in court proceedings [14thC. From Old French *atorne*, the past participle of *atorner* 'to appoint', literally 'to turn over', from *torner* (see TURN).] — **attorneyship** *n.*

WORD KEY: SYNONYMS
See Synonyms at *lawyer*.

attorney at law (*plural* **attorneys at law**) *n.* a solicitor (*archaic*)

attorney general (*plural* **attorney generals** *or* **attorneys general**) *n.* **1.** COUNTRY'S CHIEF LEGAL OFFICER a country's chief legal officer, and its government's chief legal adviser. In the United Kingdom, the attorney general is a government minister giving advice on English law. **2.** US CHIEF LEGAL OFFICER OF US STATE in the United States, the chief law officer of a state, and its government's chief legal adviser **3.** CHIEF LAW OFFICER OF AUSTRALIA the chief law officer of the Australian Commonwealth or one of its states or territories

attract /ə trákt/ (**-tracts, -tracting, -tracted**) *v.* **1.** *vt.* DRAW CLOSER to draw objects nearer, e.g. as a magnet draws iron objects towards it **2.** *vt.* ENTICE to be appealing enough to make people visit a place or spend their money **3.** *vt.* GET A RESPONSE to win or elicit a response from people, especially support or encouragement **4.** *vt.* DRAW SB'S ATTENTION to draw or secure sb's attention, or become the focus of sb's attention ○ *'It takes a big idea to attract the attention of consumers and get them to buy your product'.* (David Ogilvy, *Ogilvy on Advertising*; 1985) **5.** *vt.* HAVE APPEAL to appeal to people or awaken a response in them **6.** *vti.* AROUSE SEXUAL FEELINGS to rouse or fascinate sb sexually [15thC. From Latin *attract-*, the past participle stem of *attrahere*, literally 'to draw towards', from *trahere* 'to draw' (see TRACTION).] — **attractable** *adj.* — **attracter** *n.*

attraction /ə tráksh'n/ *n.* **1.** POWER OF ATTRACTING the power of attracting or the feeling of being attracted ○ *'Our mutual attraction was immediate, and we enjoyed one another's company'.* (Peter Ustinov, *Dear Me*; 1977) **2.** APPEALING QUALITY OR FEATURE a quality or feature that attracts sb ○ *The idea has its attractions.* **3.** THING OR PLACE THAT DRAWS TOURISTS sth, e.g. a historical

site or building, that people, especially tourists, like to see or visit

attractive /ə tráktiv/ *adj.* **1.** AGREEABLE pleasing in appearance or manner **2.** GOOD-LOOKING good-looking or sexually desirable **3.** INTERESTING interesting or appealing because of the probable advantages ○ *an attractive proposition* — **attractiveness** *n.*

WORD KEY: SYNONYMS
See Synonyms at *good-looking*.

attractively /ə tráktivli/ *adv.* in a pleasing, appealing, or sexually interesting way ○ *attractively priced furnishings* ○ *attractively situated a few minutes from the beach*

attractor /ə tráktər/ *n.* a fixed point or state of equilibrium that the behaviour of a system is attracted to and tends to imitate

attrib. *abbr.* attributive

attributable /ə tríbbyōōtəb'l/ *adj.* caused or explained by sth

attribute *vt.* /ə tríbbyoot/ (**-utes, -uting, -uted**) **1.** ASCRIBE A FEATURE to think of sth as caused by a particular circumstance ○ *To what do you attribute your success?* **2.** GIVE CREDIT to give credit for a certain thing, such as a work of art or literature, or a saying, to a particular person, often wrongly ○ *It's a bon mot that is often wrongly attributed to Saki.* **3.** ASSIGN QUALITIES to regard sb or sth as having particular qualities ○ *the pigheadedness you attribute to your computer on bad days* ■ *n.* /áttri byoot/ QUALITY OR PROPERTY a quality, property, or characteristic of sb or sth [14thC. Directly or via French from Latin *attribut-*, the past participle stem of *attribuere*, literally 'to allot to', from *tribuere* (see TRIBUTE).] — **attributer** /ə tríbbyōōtər/ *n.*

attribution /áttri byoosh'n/ *n.* the ascribing of sth to sb or sth, e.g. a work of art to a certain artist or circumstances to a particular cause

attributive /ə tríbbyōōtiv/ *adj.* forming part of a noun phrase and typically preceding the noun. For example, the adjective 'tiny' in the noun phrase 'one tiny problem' is in the attributive position. — **attributively** *adv.* — **attributiveness** *n.*

attrit /ə trít/ (**-trits, -tritting, -tritted**) *vt.* US to wear sth down little by little, especially enemy forces by constant attacks (*informal*) [Mid-20thC. Back-formation from ATTRITION.]

attrition /ə trísh'n/ *n.* **1.** WEARING AWAY OF SURFACE the wearing away of a surface, typically by friction or abrasion **2.** WEAKENING BY PERSISTENT ATTACK the gradual wearing away of morale and the powers of resistance by persistent attacks **3.** LOSS OF STAFF the gradual reduction of the size of a workforce by not replacing staff lost through retirement or resignation **4.** SORROW FOR SIN remorse for sin typically engendered by the fear of damnation [15thC. Via French from, ultimately, Latin *attrit-*, the past participle stem of *atterere*, literally 'to rub away', from *terere* 'to rub' (see TRITE).]

attune /ə tyoon/ (**-tunes, -tuning, -tuned**) *vt.* to adjust or accustom sth to become receptive or responsive to sth else

Atty. Gen. *abbr.* attorney general

ATV *abbr.* all-terrain vehicle

atwitter /ə twíttər/ *adj.* full of excited chatter about sth

Atwood /át wood/, **Margaret** (*b.* 1939) Canadian writer

Margaret Atwood

whose works include poems and novels such as '*The Handmaid's Tale*' (1986).

at. wt. *abbr.* atomic weight

atypical /ay típpik'l/ *adj.* not conforming to the usual type or expected pattern

Au *symbol.* gold [From Latin *aurum* (see GOLD)]

AU, **a.u.** *abbr.* **1.** angstrom unit **2.** astronomical unit

aubade /ō baád/ *n.* a song, poem, or piece of instrumental music celebrating or greeting the dawn (*literary*) [Late 17thC. Via French from Provençal *albada*, from *alba* 'dawn', from Latin *albus* 'white' (see ALB).]

aubergine /ṓbər zheen/ *n.* ◊ **eggplant 1.** VEGETABLE a large vegetable with shiny purple skin, eaten cooked **2.** AUBERGINE PLANT the bushy perennial plant that aubergines grow on. It belongs to the potato family. Latin name: *Solanum melongena.* ■ *adj.* DARK PURPLE dark reddish-purple in colour [Late 18thC. Via French, Catalan, and Arabic from Persian *bādingān*.]

Aubrey /áwbri/, **John** (1626–97) English antiquary whose biographical anecdotes were collected as *Brief Lives* (1813, definitive ed. 1898).

auburn /áwbən, áw burn/ *adj.* dark coppery red or reddish-brown in colour ○ *auburn hair* [15thC. From Old French (influenced in sense by the similarity of the variant spelling *abrun* to *brun* 'brown'), from medieval Latin *alburnus* 'whitish', from Latin *albus* 'white'.] — **auburn** *n.*

AUC *abbr.* **1.** ab urbe condita (*used by Roman classical writers to specify the dates of events in terms of the number of years since Rome's foundation in 753 BC*) **2.** Australian Universities Commission

Auckland /áwklənd/ **1.** administrative region of New Zealand, located in northwestern North Island and including the city of Auckland. Population: 1,077,205 (1996). Area: 16,282 sq. km/6,287 sq. mi. **2.** the largest city in New Zealand, located in northwestern North Island. Founded in 1840, it is a commercial and industrial centre and port. Population: 997,940 (1996).

Auckland Islands group of uninhabited islands in the southern Pacific Ocean, 467 km/290 mi. south of New Zealand. The islands are part of New Zealand. Area: 606 sq. km/234 sq. mi.

au contraire /ṓ kon traír/ *adv.* indeed, the opposite is really the case [From French, literally 'to the contrary']

au courant /ṓ koo róN/ *adj.* abreast of the latest developments [From French, literally 'in the current']

auction /áwksh'n/ *n.* **1.** SALE BY BIDDING a sale of goods or property at which intending buyers bid against one another for individual items. Each item is sold to the bidder offering the highest price. **2.** BRIDGE BIDDING IN GAME OF BRIDGE the bidding phase in a game of bridge, during which players contract to win a certain number of tricks if a certain suit is trumps ■ *vti.* (**-tions, -tioning, -tioned**) SELL AT AUCTION to sell goods by auction [Late 16thC. From the Latin stem *auction-*, literally 'increase', from *augere* (see AUGMENT).] — **auctionable** *adj.*

auction bridge *n.* a form of bridge in which all tricks won count towards the score, as distinct from contract bridge, in which only those tricks contracted to win count

auctioneer /áwkshə neér/ *n.* sb who is in charge of and announces the bids at an auction — **auctioneering** *n.*

AUD *abbr.* Australian dollar

aud. *abbr.* **1.** audit **2.** auditor

audacious /aw dáyshəss/ *adj.* bold, daring, or fearless, especially in challenging assumptions or conventions [Mid-16thC. Formed from Latin *audac-*, the stem of *audax* 'bold', from *audere* 'to dare', from *avidus* (see AVIDITY).] — **audaciousness** *n.*

WORD KEY: SYNONYMS
See Synonyms at *bold*.

audaciously /aw dáyshəssli/ *adv.* in a bold way that challenges assumptions or conventions

audacity /aw dássəti/ *n.* **1.** BOLDNESS OR DARING daring or willingness to challenge assumptions or conventions or tackle sth difficult or dangerous **2.** IMPUDENCE lack of respect in sb's behaviour towards another

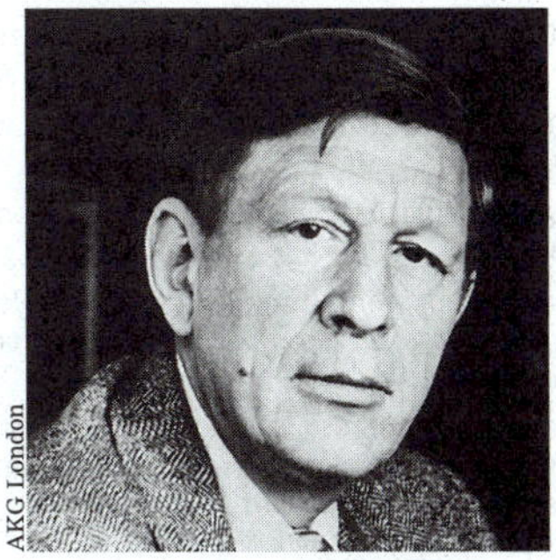
AKG London

W. H. Auden

Auden /áwd'n/, **W. H.** (1907–73) British-born US poet and dramatist. One of the most influential poets of his generation, he wrote numerous works including *'September 1939'* and *'Lullaby'*, and won the Pulitzer Prize for *The Age of Anxiety* (1947). Full name **Wystan Hugh Auden**

audi- *prefix.* = **audio-**

audial /áwdi əl/ *adj.* relating to hearing or sounds [Mid-20thC. Formed from AUDIO.]

audible /áwdəb'l/ *adj.* loud or clear enough to be heard ○ *an audible gasp from the crowd* [15thC. From late Latin *audibilis*, from Latin *audire* 'to hear'. Ultimately from an Indo-European word meaning 'to perceive', which is also the ancestor of English *audience*, *obey*, and *aesthetic*.] —**audibility** /áwdə bíllәti/ *n.* —**audibleness** /áwdəb'lnəss/ *n.*

audibly /áwdəbli/ *adv.* loudly enough to allow others to hear ○ *a man in the back row sobbing audibly*

audience /áwdi ənss/ *n.* **1. PEOPLE WATCHING LIVE PERFORMANCE** a group of people who are watching and listening to a show, concert, or other live performance **2. PEOPLE WATCHING OR LISTENING TO BROADCAST** the viewers of a film or a television programme, or the listeners to a radio programme, **3. AUTHOR'S READERSHIP** the people who read a particular writer's books **4. FORMAL INTERVIEW** a formal, usually prearranged, interview with sb important [14thC. Via French from Latin *audientia*, literally 'a hearing', from *audire* 'to hear' (see AUDIBLE).]

audile /áw dīl/ *adj.* = **auditory** [Late 19thC. Formed from Latin *audire* 'to hear' (see AUDIBLE).]

audio /áwdi ō/ *n.* the recording and reproduction of sound [Early 20thC. The prefix AUDIO-, used as a word.]

audio-, **audi-** *prefix.* sound, hearing ○ *audiogram* [From Latin *audire* 'to hear' (see AUDIBLE)]

audio book *n.* a commercial recording, usually on a cassette tape, of sb reading the text of a well-known book

audiocassette /áwdi ō kə sét/ *n.* a cassette containing an audiotape, for use in a tape recorder

audio clip *n.* an extract from a longer sound recording, e.g. from a film soundtrack, that can be listened to on a personal computer

audio console *n.* a cabinet for vertically stacked pieces of audio equipment, typically a radio, record-player, cassette recorder, and compact-disc player

audio frequency *n.* a frequency that is audible to the human ear, between 20 and 20,000 hertz in people with normal hearing

audiogram /áwdi ō gram/ *n.* a tracing produced by an audiometer, recording the sharpness of sb's hearing

audiology /áwdi óllәji/ *n.* the scientific study of hearing, especially for diagnosing and treating hearing defects —**audiological** /áwdi ə lójjik'l/ *adj.* —**audiologist** /-óllәjist/ *n.*

audiometer /áwdi ómmitər/ *n.* an instrument for testing the ability of a human ear to detect sounds over a range of frequencies and intensities —**audiometric** /áwdi ō méttrik/ *adj.* —**audiometry** /-ómmətri/ *n.*

audiophile /áwdi ō fīl/ *n.* sb who has an enthusiasm for sound reproduction, especially high-fidelity recordings or broadcasts of music

audiotape /áwdi ō tayp/ *n.* **1. SOUND-RECORDING TAPE** magnetic tape for recording sound, or a length of this, typically in a cassette **2. SOUND RECORDING ON TAPE** a sound recording on magnetic tape, especially an audiocassette for use in a tape recorder

audiotyping /áwdi ō tīping/ *n.* the skill or activity of typing up recorded dictation as you are listening to it —**audiotypist** *n.*

audiovisual /áwdi ō vízhoo əl/ *adj.* **1. OF SOUND AND VISION** relating to sound and vision, especially when combined, e.g. in a presentation using both film and sound recordings **2. OF HEARING AND SIGHT** relating to the faculties of hearing and seeing ■ *n. US* = **audiovisual aid**

audiovisual aid *n.* any aid to teaching or lecturing that combines sound and vision, for instance in the form of video equipment, or software programs, or slides accompanied by sound recordings. US term **audiovisual**

audit /áwdit/ *n.* **1. CHECK OF ACCOUNTS** a formal examination, correction, and official endorsing of financial accounts, especially those of a business, undertaken annually by an accountant **2. EFFICIENCY CHECK** a systematic check or assessment, especially of the efficiency or effectiveness of an organization or department, typically carried out by an independent assessor ■ *vt.* (**-dits, -diting, -dited**) **1. CARRY OUT AUDIT** to carry out an audit of the financial accounts of a firm, department, or organization to establish accuracy or efficiency **2.** *US* **SIT IN ON CLASS** to attend a class without asking for or receiving graduation credit for it, usually attending all the sessions but not doing the assignments [15thC. From Latin *auditus* 'hearing', from *audit-*, the past participle stem of *audire* 'to hear' (see AUDIBLE); so called because originally the accounts were read aloud.] —**auditable** *adj.*

auditee /áwdi tée/ *n.* a person or organization that is being audited

audition /aw dísh'n/ *n.* **1. TEST PERFORMANCE BY CANDIDATE** a test in the form of a short performance, taken, e.g., by an actor applying for a role in a film or play **2.** PHYSIOL **HEARING** the sense, faculty, or process of hearing ■ *vti.* (**-tions, -tioning, -tioned**) **DO OR GIVE AN AUDITION** to do an audition or give sb an audition for a role [Late 16thC. From the Latin stem *audition-*, literally 'hearing', from *audire* (see AUDIBLE).]

auditive /áwditiv/ *adj.* = **auditory** [Early 17thC. Via French from, ultimately, Latin *audire* 'to hear' (see AUDIBLE).]

auditor /áwditər/ *n.* **1.** BUSINESS **SB CHECKING ACCOUNTS OR SYSTEMS** sb who is qualified to audit accounts or to conduct an audit of a department or organization **2.** *US* **STUDENT SITTING IN ON CLASS** a student who attends a class without asking for or receiving graduation credit **3. HEARER** a hearer or listener, e.g. a member of an audience or sb listening to sb who is talking (*formal*) [14thC. Via Anglo-Norman from Latin *auditor* 'hearer', from *audire* (see AUDIBLE).]

auditor-general (*plural* **auditor-generals** *or* **auditors-general**) *n.* an officer of the Australian government who monitors government expenditure and ensures that it is authorized by Act or regulation

auditorium /áwdi táwri əm/ (*plural* **-ums** *or* **-a** /-ri ə/) *n.* **1. PART OF THEATRE WHERE AUDIENCE SITS** the area of a theatre or concert hall where the audience sits **2. HALL OR LECTURE ROOM** a lecture theatre or a hall that is used for lectures, concerts, and other events [Early 17thC. From Latin, literally 'a place for hearing', formed from *audire* (see AUDIBLE).]

auditory /áwditəri/ *adj.* relating to the faculty, organs, or process of hearing [Late 16thC. From late Latin *auditorius*, from Latin *audire* (see AUDIBLE).]

audit trail *n.* a record kept, e.g. by a computer, of a sequence of events or transactions

Auerbach /ówər bak/, **Frank** (*b.* 1931) German-born British painter. He is noted for landscapes and portraits characterized by thickly applied oil paint.

au fait /ō fáy/ *adj.* abreast of the latest developments in sth, or supplied with the most recent facts about sth [From French, literally 'to the fact']

aug. *abbr.* GRAM augmentative

Aug. *abbr.* August

Augean /aw jée ən/ *adj.* **1. FILTHY** disgustingly dirty, like the Augean stables **2. DIFFICULT** extremely difficult and unpleasant

Augean stables *n.* in Greek mythology, the stables owned by King Augeas that had not been cleaned in 30 years. One of Hercules' tasks was to clean them in one day, which he achieved by diverting two rivers through them. ◇ **cleanse the Augean stables** to put sth that is extremely untidy and disorganized into a state of order and tidiness

auger /áwgər/ *n.* a hand tool with a corkscrew-shaped bit for boring holes, or a larger tool, using the same principle, for boring holes in the ground [Old English *nafogār*, formed from NAVE[2] and *gār* 'spear' (see GORE[1]). The initial 'n' was lost in the 16thC by false division of 'a nauger' as 'an auger'.]

aught /awt/ *pron.* anything whatever (*archaic literary*) [Old English *āwiht*, literally 'ever a thing'. Ultimately from a prehistoric Germanic word that was formed from the ancestors of English *aye*[2] and *wight*.]

augite /áw gīt/ *n.* a dark green mineral of the pyroxene group, containing aluminium, calcium, iron, and magnesium. It is found in igneous rock. [Early 19thC. Via Latin *augites*, a precious stone (possibly turquoise), from Greek *augitēs*, from *augē* 'lustre'.]

augment /awg mént/ *v.* (**-ments, -menting, -mented**) **1.** *vti.* **INCREASE** to grow, or to increase sth in number, amount, size, strength, or intensity (*formal*) **2.** *vt.* MUSIC **ENLARGE INTERVAL BY SEMITONE** in music, to enlarge a perfect or major interval by a semitone ■ *n.* GRAM **PREFIXED VOWEL** in Greek or Sanskrit grammar, a vowel prefixed to a verb, or added to its initial vowel so as to lengthen it into a diphthong, to form a past tense [14thC.Via French from, ultimately, Latin *augere* 'to increase' (source also of English *auction*). Ultimately from an Indo-European word that is also the ancestor of English *wax*, *eke*, and *august*.] —**augmenter** *n.*

WORD KEY: SYNONYMS

See Synonyms at ***increase***.

augmentation /áwg men táysh'n, -mən-/ *n.* **1. INCREASE** the increasing, or growth, of sth in number, amount, size, strength, or intensity, or the amount by which sth grows or is added to ○ *augmentation in costs* ○ *breast augmentation* **2.** MUSIC **INCREASING NOTE VALUES** the technique of varying a theme by increasing its note values proportionally

augmentative /awg méntətiv/ *adj.* **1. CAUSING AN INCREASE** tending to add to or increase sth or to enable sth to grow or increase (*formal*) **2.** GRAM **DENOTING GREAT SIZE OR IMPORTANCE** used to describe an affix, such as Spanish '-ote' or Italian '-one', that signifies great size or importance, or a word to which an affix of this kind has been added ■ *n.* GRAM **AUGMENTATIVE AFFIX OR WORD** an affix signifying great size or importance, or a word to which an affix of this kind has been added

augmented /awg méntid/ *adj.* in music, used to describe a perfect or major interval that has been enlarged by a semitone

au gratin /ō gráttaN/ *adj.* sprinkled with breadcrumbs, sometimes mixed with grated cheese, and browned before serving [From French, literally 'with a gratin crust']

Augsburg /ówks burg/ city in Bavaria in southern Germany, situated to the northwest of Munich. Population: 263,800 (1994).

augur /áwgər/ *n.* **1. INTERPRETER OF MESSAGES FROM ROMAN GODS** a religious official in ancient Rome who interpreted natural phenomena, such as the flight of birds, as signs that the gods favoured or disapproved of actions proposed by the city **2. SOOTHSAYER OR PROPHET** any soothsayer, prophet, or diviner ■ *vt.* (**-gurs, -guring, -gured**) **INDICATE WHAT WILL HAPPEN** to suggest or indicate what will happen in the future [14thC. From Latin (source also of English inaugurate). Probably ultimately from an Indo-European word meaning 'to increase', which in Latin developed the sense 'divine favour' (see AUGMENT).] —**augural** /áwgyŏŏrəl/ *adj.*

augury /áwgyŏŏri/ (*plural* **-ries**) *n.* **1. DIVINATION** the art, activity, prophecies, or pronouncements of an augur, soothsayer, or diviner **2. PORTENT OR OMEN** an indication of what will happen in the future

august /aw gúst/ *adj.* full of solemn splendour and dignity (*formal*) [Mid-17thC. Directly or via French from Latin *augustus*. Ultimately from an Indo-European word meaning 'to increase', which is also the ancestor of English *wax*, *eke*, and *augment*.]

August /áwgəst/ *n.* the eighth month of the year in the Gregorian calendar. It has 31 days. [Pre-12thC. From Latin *augustus*, named after the Roman emperor *Augustus* Caesar.]

Augustan /aw gústən/ *adj.* **1.** OF AUGUSTUS CAESAR OR HIS TIME relating to the Roman emperor Augustus Caesar, to his reign, or to the classical writers, including Virgil, Ovid, and Horace, who flourished during this period **2.** CHARACTERIZED BY CLASSICAL WRITING relating to any period or the writers or works of a period during which writing in the classical style flourished, especially during 17th-century France and 18th-century England ■ *n.* AUGUSTAN WRITER OR STUDENT a writer from an Augustan period, or sb who studies Augustan literature

Augustine /aw gústin/, **St** (354–430) Roman priest and theologian. His masterpiece, *De Civitate Dei* (*The City of God*), greatly influenced the development of Christianity. He was bishop of Hippo, North Africa, from 396 until his death.

Augustine, St (*d.* 604) Roman priest. Sent by Pope Gregory I to convert the Anglo-Saxons, he became the first Archbishop of Canterbury (597–604).

Augustinian /áwgə stínni ən/ *adj.* OF ST AUGUSTINE relating to St Augustine of Hippo, or to his teachings, or to any of the Christian religious orders living according to his rule or system of monastic life ■ *n.* FOLLOWER OF AUGUSTINE OR HIS RULE a follower of St Augustine, especially a member of one of the religious orders living according to his rule

Augustus /aw gústəss/ (63 BC–AD 14) Roman emperor. The founder of the Roman Empire, he was the adopted son of Julius Caesar. He succeeded his adoptive father as absolute ruler in 27 BC after a period of civil war.

Auk

auk /áwk/ *n.* a small black-and-white heavy-bodied sea bird that belongs to the puffin family. Auks are found in cool northern seas and are skilled divers for fish. Family: Alcidae. [Late 17thC. Via Norwegian *alk* from Old Norse *álka*.]

auklet /áwklət/ *n.* a small auk found in the North Pacific that nests in burrows or rock slides. Family: Alcidae.

auld lang syne /áwld lang zín/ *n. Scotland* old times or times long gone (*archaic*) [Literally 'old long since', 'old long ago']

au naturel /ō náttyoō rél/ *adv., adj.* **1.** SIMPLY OR UNCOOKED served simply and plainly, e.g. uncooked or without seasoning or salt **2.** NAKED wearing no clothes (*humorous*) [From French, literally 'in the natural state']

Aung San Suu Kyi /áwng san soo kée, **Daw** (*b.* 1945)

Aung San Suu Kyi

Burmese human rights activist who won the Nobel Peace Prize (1991) for establishing Burma's National League for Democracy (NLD) party.

aunt /aant/ *n.* sb's mother's or father's sister, or sb's uncle's wife, used before her forename as a title or form of address, now rather formal [13thC. Via Anglo-Norman from Latin *amita* 'father's sister'.] —**aunthood** *n.*

auntie /aánti/, **aunty** (*plural* **-ies**) *n.* an aunt or close woman friend of a child's parents (*informal*)

Auntie, Aunty *n.* (*informal*) **1.** BBC a nickname for the British Broadcasting Corporation, or BBC, in reference to its image as a kindly and well-intentioned, if old-fashioned, guardian of standards **2.** *Aus* AUSTRALIAN BROADCASTING CORPORATION a nickname for the Australian Broadcasting Corporation **3.** *Malaysia, Singapore* FORM OF ADDRESS TO WOMAN used as a form of address to an older woman, e.g. one who is not a relative of the speaker and whose name is not known ○ *Hey, Auntie, do you want to buy some?*

Aunt Sally /-sálli/ (*plural* **Aunt Sallies**) *n.* **1.** FAIRGROUND TARGET a traditional target used in throwing-games in fairgrounds, in the shape of an old woman's head, typically with a clay pipe in her mouth, that throwers try to break **2.** BUTT OF CRITICISM a person or organization that is the constant target of criticism and abusive comment **3.** ARGUMENT TO BE DEMOLISHED in formal discussion, an argument put forward so that it can be demolished and dismissed

aunty /aánti/ (*plural* **-ies**) *n.* **1.** *S Asia* WOMAN used as a form of address for an older woman, not necessarily a relative of the speaker **2.** = **auntie**

au pair /ō paír/ *n.* a young person from abroad living with a family to learn the language, and helping with childcare and domestic work in return for board and accommodation [From French, literally 'on equal terms']

aura /áwrə/ (*plural* **-ras** *or* **-rae** /-ree/) *n.* **1.** DISTINCTIVE QUALITY a characteristic or distinctive impression created by sb or sth ○ *an aura of mystery* **2.** PARANORMAL FORCE EMANATING FROM SB OR STH a force that is said to surround all people and objects, discernible, often as a bright glow, only to people of unusual psychic sensitivity **3.** MED WARNING SENSATION BEFORE EPILEPTIC SEIZURE a distinctive sensation or visual disturbance that may signal the beginning of an epileptic seizure or a migraine [Mid-18thC. Via Latin, 'gentle breeze', from Greek.]

aural /áwrəl/ *adj.* relating to the ear, hearing, or to receptiveness and response to speech or other sounds [Mid-19thC. Formed from Latin *auris* 'ear'. Ultimately from an Indo-European word meaning 'ear', which is also the ancestor of English *ear* and *scout*.] —**aurally** *adv.*

--- WORD KEY: USAGE ---

aural or **oral**? These two words are often confused because they are pronounced in a similar way and have meanings that are close. Essentially *aural* is to do with hearing whereas *oral* is to do with speaking. An *aural* test is a medical examination of the ears, whereas an *oral test* is any kind of test in which the answers are spoken rather than written.

aurar plural of **eyrir**

aureate /áwri ayt, -ət/ *adj.* **1.** GOLDEN gold, gilded, golden, or gold-coloured **2.** ELABORATELY WORDED expressed or written in a highly or excessively ornamented, florid, or elaborate style [15thC. From Latin *aureatus*, from *aureus* 'golden', from *aurum* 'gold'.]

aurei plural of **aureus**

Aurelian /aw reéli ən/ (215?–275) Roman soldier and emperor. Elected emperor by the army (270–75), he recovered Gaul and made the Danube the empire's frontier.

aureole /áw ri ōl/, **aureola** /aw reé ələ, áw ri ólə/ *n.* **1.** HALO a painted or carved representation of a circle of light around the head of a divine being or a saint **2.** METEOROL = **corona** *n.* 2 [Mid-19thC. Via French from late Latin *corona aureola*, literally 'golden crown'.]

aureus /áwri əss/ (*plural* **-i** /-ī/) *n.* a gold coin that was a unit of currency in the Roman Empire between 30 BC and AD 310 [Early 17thC. From Latin, noun use of *aureus* 'golden' (see AUREATE).]

au revoir /ō rə vwaár/ *interj.* goodbye till we see each other again [From French, literally 'until seeing again']

auri-[1] *prefix.* ear, hearing ○ *auriform* [from Latin *auris* (see AURAL)]

auri-[2] *prefix.* gold ○ *auriferous* [From Latin *aurum* (see AURUM)]

auric /áwrik/ *adj.* containing gold with a valency of three ○ *auric oxide* [Early 19thC. Formed from Latin *aurum* 'gold'.]

Auric /aw reék/, **Georges** (1899–1983) French composer who produced orchestral works, ballets, and film scores. He was director of the Paris Opera and the Opéra Comique (1962–68).

auricle /áwrik'l/ *n.* **1.** VISIBLE PART OF EAR the part of the external ear that projects outwards from the head **2.** PART OF HEART CHAMBER an ear-shaped muscular part that sticks out from the surface of each upper chamber (**atrium**) of the heart **3.** ATRIUM an atrium of the heart (*dated*) [Mid-17thC. From Latin *auricula*, literally 'little ear', from *auris* 'ear' (see AURAL).] —**auricled** *adj.*

auricula /aw ríkyoōlə/ (*plural* **-las** *or* **-lae** /-lee/) *n.* a yellow-flowered alpine primrose with leaves shaped like a bear's ear. Latin name: *Primula auricula*. [Mid-17thC. From Latin (see AURICLE).]

auricular /aw ríkyoōlər/ *adj.* **1.** EAR-SHAPED shaped like an ear **2.** RELATING TO HEARING ORGANS relating to the ear or to the sense of hearing **3.** RELATING TO HEART CHAMBERS relating to the ear-shaped muscular part (**auricle**) on the surface of each upper chamber (**atrium**) of the heart

auriculate /aw ríkyoō layt/ *adj.* **1.** WITH EAR-SHAPED LEAF ATTACHMENT used to describe leaves that have an attachment at the base that is shaped like an ear **2.** WITH EARS relating to an animal that has ears, auricles, or extensions that resemble earlobes

auriferous /aw rífərəss/ *adj.* used to describe rock or minerals that contain gold

Auriga /aw rígə/ *n.* a large and prominent constellation of the northern hemisphere lying on the Milky Way between Gemini and Perseus. It contains the bright star Capella.

Aurignacian /áwrig náysh'n/ *adj.* belonging to a prehistoric culture associated with Cro-Magnon people in Europe around the period 30,000 to 22,000 BC [Early 20thC. Named after the village of *Aurignac* in southern France, where the first evidence of such a culture was discovered.]

Auriol /áwri ol/, **Vincent** (1884–1966) French statesman who fought in the Resistance in World War II and became first President of the Fourth Republic (1947–53).

aurochs /áwroks/ (*plural* **-rochs**) *n.* a long-horned wild ox, now extinct but thought to be an ancestor of modern domestic cattle. The aurochs once inhabited the forests of North Africa, Europe, and Southwest Asia. [Late 18thC. From German, variant of *Auerochs*, literally 'original ox'.]

aurora /ə ráwrə/ (*plural* **-ras** *or* **-rae** /-ree/) *n.* **1.** NORTHERN OR SOUTHERN LIGHTS a phenomenon occurring in the night sky around the polar regions, caused by atmospheric gases interacting with solar particles to create streamers, folds, or arches of coloured light **2. aurora, Aurora** DAWN the dawn, usually personified or regarded, as in classical literature, as a goddess [15thC. From Latin, 'dawn'. Ultimately from an Indo-European word meaning 'to shine', which is also the ancestor of English *east* and *Easter*.] —**auroral** *adj.*

aurora australis /-o stráyliss/ *n.* the coloured lights seen in the skies around the South Pole [From modern Latin, literally 'southern aurora']

aurora borealis /-bawri áyliss/ *n.* the coloured lights seen in the skies around the North Pole [From modern Latin, literally 'northern aurora']

aurora trout (*plural* **aurora trout** *or* **aurora trouts**) *n.* a rare, brilliantly coloured, unspotted brook trout found in northern Ontario. Latin name: *Salvelinus fontinalis*.

AUS *abbr.* Australian Union of Students

Aus. *abbr.* Australia ■ *abbr.* Australian ■ *abbr.* Austria ■ *abbr.* Austrian

Auschwitz /ów shvits/ site of the largest Nazi concentration camp, where between 1.5 and 4 million people were murdered between 1941 and 1945. Situated in southern Poland, southeast of Katowice, it is now a museum and archive.

Auschwitz Lie *n.* denial that the attempted extermination of the Jews by the Nazis ever took place

auscultate /áwsk'l tayt/ (**-tates, -tating, -tated**) *vt.* to listen to various sounds made by a patient's internal organs, usually with the help of a stethoscope, in order to make a diagnosis [Mid-19thC. Back-formation from AUSCULTATION.] —**auscultative** /aw skúltətiv/ *adj.* —**auscultatory** /-skúltə təri/ *adj.*

auscultation /áwsk'l táysh'n/ *n.* listening to the sounds made by a patient's internal organs, especially the heart, lungs, and abdominal organs, usually with a stethoscope, in order to make a diagnosis [Mid-17thC. From the Latin stem *auscultation-*, from *auscultare* 'to listen to'.]

auslese /ówss layzə/ *n.* a middle grade of high-quality German table wine, made from selected late-picked grapes and typically medium sweet to sweet [Mid-19thC. From German, literally 'selection'.]

auspice /áwspiss/ *n.* (*plural* **-pices** /-iz/) OMEN a sign or token for the future, especially a happy or promising one ■ **auspices** *npl.* SUPPORT the help or support of a person or organization ○ *a study conducted under the auspices of the United Nations* [Mid-17thC. Via French from Latin *auspicium* 'taking omens', from *auspex* 'soothsayer', originally literally 'sb who foretells the future by studying the flight pattern of birds', from *avis* 'bird' + a stem of *specere* 'to look'.]

auspicious /aw spíshəss/ *adj.* marked by lucky signs or good omens, and therefore by the promise of success or happiness —**auspiciously** *adv.* —**auspiciousness** *n.*

Aussie /ózzi/ *adj.* AUSTRALIAN Australian (*informal*) ■ *n.* AN AUSTRALIAN sb who is Australian (*informal*) [Early 20thC. Shortening.]

Aust. *abbr.* Australia ■ *abbr.* Australian ■ *abbr.* Austria ■ *abbr.* Austrian

AUSTEL /ó tel/ *abbr.* Australian Telecommunications Authority

AKG London

Jane Austen

Austen /óstin/, **Jane** (1775–1817) British novelist, writer of elegant, satirical fiction, including *Pride and Prejudice* (1813).

austenite /áwstə n īt, óstə-/ *n.* a solid solution of carbon in iron that occurs as a component of steel at a certain stage of manufacture [Early 20thC. Named after the English metallurgist Sir William Roberts- *Austen* (1843–1902).] —**austenitic** /áwstə níttik/ *adj.*

austere /aw steer, o-/ *adj.* **1.** SUGGESTING PHYSICAL HARDSHIP imposing or suggesting physical hardship **2.** UNSMILING grimly unsmiling, humourless, or suggesting strict self-denial **3.** PLAIN AND WITHOUT LUXURY plain and simple, without luxury or self-indulgence **4.** PLAIN IN STYLE OR DESIGN severely plain in design or lines, without distractions or decoration [14thC. Via French and Latin from Greek *austēros*. Ultimately from an Indo-European word meaning 'dry, harsh', which is also the ancestor of English *sere* and *sear*.] —**austerely** *adv.* —**austereness** *n.*

austerity /aw stérrəti, o-/ *n.* (*plural* **-ties**) **1.** SEVERITY OR PLAINNESS severity of discipline, regime, expression, or design **2.** ECONOMY MEASURE a saving, economy, or act of self-denial, especially in respect of sth re-

garded as a luxury **3.** ECON ENFORCED THRIFT thrift imposed as government policy, with restricted access to or availability of consumer goods

Austerlitz /ówsterlitz/ site of a major battle in 1805 in what is now the eastern Czech Republic, when Napoleon defeated Russian and Austrian forces

Austin /áwstən/ capital of Texas and university town in the south of the state, on the Colorado River. Population: 541,278 (1996).

austral[1] /áwstrəl/ *adj.* relating to, belonging to, or coming from the south [15thC. From Latin *australis*, from *auster* 'south', of unknown origin.]

austral[2] /ówstrəl/ (*plural* **-trals** *or* **-trales**) *n.* **1.** UNIT OF CURRENCY IN ARGENTINA a subunit of currency in Argentina. See table at **currency 2.** COIN WORTH AN AUSTRAL a coin worth an austral [Late 20thC. Via Spanish from Latin *australis* (see AUSTRAL[1].]

Austral. *abbr.* **1.** Australasia **2.** Australia ■ *abbr.* Australian

Australasia /áwstrə láyzhə/ region consisting of Australia, New Zealand, New Guinea, and neighbouring islands of the South Pacific —**Australasian** *adj., n.*

Australia /o stráyli ə/ country occupying the continent of Australia. Australia was founded in 1901. Language: English. Currency: Australian dollar. Capital: Canberra. Population: 18,311,000 (1996). Area: 7,682,300 sq. km/2,966,200 sq. mi.

Australia Day *n.* a public holiday in Australia, held on the first Monday after 26 January to commemorate the landing of the British First Fleet at Port Jackson, now Sydney Harbour, in 1788

Australian /o stráyli ən/ *adj.* **1.** OF AUSTRALIA relating to or typical of Australia, or its people or culture **2.** OF ABORIGINAL LANGUAGES OF AUSTRALIA relating to the family of languages spoken in Australia before European settlement. Most Australian languages are now extinct or approaching extinction. ■ *n.* **1.** SB FROM AUSTRALIA sb who was born in or who is a citizen of Australia **2.** AUSTRALIAN ENGLISH the form of English that is spoken in Australia

Australian Alps mountain chain in southeastern Australia

Australian Antarctic Territory uninhabited region incorporating part of the continent of Antarctica and a number of adjacent islands. Area: 6,119,818 sq. km/2,362,862 sq. mi.

Australian ballot *n. US* = secret ballot

Australian Capital Territory internal federal territory in southeastern Australia, which incorporates Canberra, the national capital. Capital: Canberra. Population: 308,000 (1996). Area: 2432 sq. km/939 sq. mi.

Australian English the form of English spoken in Australians as distinct from other forms of English such as American English or British English

―――**WORD KEY: WORLD ENGLISH**―――

Australian English is the English language as used in the Commonwealth of Australia, population 15 million, which is, with Canada, third in size and distinctness among the primary English-speaking countries. English has been used in Australia for about 200 years. Australian English, after the United States and the United Kingdom, is markedly homogeneous, with three kinds of accent: (1) *Cultivated Australian*, similar to Received Pronunciation in the United Kingdom, and formerly highly regarded; (2) *Broad Australian*, often compared with Cockney; and (3) *General Australian*, the majority variety, occupying the social middle ground. Australian English is 'non-rhotic' (that is, *r* is not pronounced in words such as *art*, *door*, and *worker*), the vowel in *can't dance* is closer to that in 'kent dense' than in 'cahnt dahnce' or 'kaynt daynce', and the Broad version of *I'm going there today* sounds to some ears like 'I'm going there to die'. Australian English and British English spelling are generally identical (with some ambivalence in the *-or/our* endings, most notably in US-style *Labor*, the name of a political party). Grammar is comparable to general usage in both Britain and the United States, but Australian English has a large and distinctive home-grown vocabulary that includes: (1) Adoptions from Aboriginal languages, with a penchant for spelling with double letters (as in *corroboree* and *kookaburra*) and

Australia

mainly relating to animals, plants, objects, and localities, for example, *billabong*, *boomerang*, *didgeridoo*, *dingo*, *koala*, *Murrumbidgee*, *Woomera*) a process similar to American English's adoption from Native American languages; (2) Extensions in meaning of everyday words, for example, *to feel crook* 'to feel ill', *to farewell someone* 'to give someone a farewell party', *mob* 'a flock or group (of sheep, kangaroos, etc.)', *station* 'a ranch', as in *sheep station*; (3) Extensions or shifts in the meaning of British dialect words, such as *cobber* (a friend, mate), *dinkum* 'reliable, genuine', *dunny* 'a lavatory', *wowser* 'a spoilsport, prude'; (4) Distinctive informal word endings, e.g., *-o* in abbreviations such as *arvo* 'afternoon' and *journo* 'journalist', and *-ie* in names for workers, such as *truckie* 'truck-driver' and *wharfie* 'stevedore'. See **New Zealand English**.

Australianism /o stráyli ənizzəm/ *n.* a word or expression that originated in, or is used mainly in, Australia

Australian Museum *n.* a museum in Sydney that contains the Australian national collections of natural history and anthropology. It was founded in 1836.

Australian Rules *n.* an Australian game resembling rugby, played on an oval pitch with 18 to a team and a large oval ball that can be punched, kicked, or carried (*takes a singular verb*)

Australian terrier *n.* a short stocky terrier with erect ears and a straight, wiry coat that is normally blue- or silver-grey with brown patches on the muzzle and feet

Australoid /óstrə loyd/ *adj.* **ABORIGINAL** belonging or relating to the ethnic group that includes the Australian Aborigines and certain other southern Asian and Pacific peoples ■ *n.* **AUSTRALOID PERSON** a member of one of the Australoid peoples

australopithecine /óstrələ píthə seen/ *adj.* **OF PREHISTORIC AFRICAN PRIMATE** relating to a prehistoric primate whose fossilized remains, resembling those of humans, have been found in southern and eastern Africa ■ *n.* **PREHISTORIC PRIMATE** an australopithecine primate. Genus: *Australopithecus*. [Mid-20thC. Formed from modern Latin *Australopithecus*, from Latin *australis* 'southern' + Greek *pithēkos* 'ape'.]

Austrasia /aw stráyzhə/ eastern part of the medieval kingdom of the Franks, consisting of what are now parts of France, Germany, and the Netherlands

Austria

Austria /óstri ə/ democratic federal republic in central Europe. Language: German. Currency: Schilling. Capital: Vienna. Population: 8,054,000 (1995). Area: 83,858 sq. km/32,378 sq. mi. —**Austrian** *adj., n.*

Austrian blind *n.* a type of fabric window blind that consists of parallel panels that can be gathered up vertically into loose billowing folds

Austro- *prefix.* southern ○ *Austroasiatic* [From Latin *auster*]

Austro-Asiatic /óstrō-, -ayzi-/ *n.* a family of over 100 languages spoken in Southeast Asia and in central India by about 70 million people. Its three main branches are Mon-Khmer, Munda, and Nicobarese.

Austronesia /óstrō néezhə, -néeshə/ region consisting of Indonesia, Melanesia, Micronesia, Polynesia, and neighbouring islands in the Pacific Ocean

Austronesian /óstrō néezh'n, -néesh'n/ *adj.* **OF AUSTRONESIA** relating to or typical of the countries of Austronesia, or its peoples, culture, or languages ■ *n.* **LANG LANGUAGE FAMILY OF ASIA** a family of languages spoken in Taiwan, parts of Southeast Asia, the Philippines, the Malay Archipelago, the Pacific Islands, New Zealand, and Madagascar. About 250 million people speak an Austronesian language. Malay, Javanese, and Tagalog are major languages of the family.

AUT *abbr.* Association of University Teachers

aut- *prefix.* = auto (*used before vowels*)

autarchy /áw taarki/ (*plural* **-chies**) *n.* **1.** **UNLIMITED POLITICAL POWER** absolute power, especially such power wielded by a despotic ruler **2.** **SELF-GOVERNMENT** self-government of a country by representatives drawn from among its own citizens **3.** **COUNTRY WITH DESPOTIC RULER** a country governed by a ruler who has absolute power **4.** **SELF-GOVERNING COUNTRY** an independent country with its own government, as distinct from a colony or dependency [Mid-17thC. Formed from Greek *autarkhos*, literally 'self-governing', from *arkhein* 'to rule'.] —**autarchic** /aw taárkik/ *adj.* —**autarchical** /-kik'l/ *adj.* —**autarchist** /áw taarkist/ *n.*

autarky /áw taarki/ (*plural* **-kies**) *n.* **1.** **ECONOMIC SELF-SUFFICIENCY** an economic policy or situation in which a nation is independent of international trade and not reliant upon imported goods **2.** **SELF-SUFFICIENT COUNTRY** a nation that is economically self-sufficient [Early 17thC. From Greek *autarkeia* 'self-sufficiency', from *autarkēs* 'self-sufficient', from *autos* 'self' + *arkein* 'to be sufficient'.] —**autarkic** /aw taárkik/ *adj.* —**autarkical** /-kik'l/ *adj.*

autecology /áwti kólləji/ *n.* the study of individuals or populations of a single species and their relationship to their environment —**autecological** /áwtikə lójjik'l/ *adj.*

auteur /aw túr/ *n.* a film director whose films are so distinctive that he or she is perceived as a film's creator [Mid-20thC. From French, 'author'.]

auteurism /aw túriz əm/ *n.* = auteur theory —**auteurist** *adj.*

auteur theory /aw túr theeri/ *n.* a type of film criticism that considers the director of a film to be its primary creator

auth. *abbr.* **1.** authentic **2.** author **3.** authority **4.** authorized

authentic /aw théntik/ *adj.* **1.** **NOT FALSE OR COPIED** genuine and original, as opposed to sth that is a fake or reproduction **2.** **TRUSTWORTHY** shown to be true and trustworthy **3.** **LAW** **VALID** legally valid because all necessary procedures have been followed correctly **4.** **MUSIC** **IN STYLE OF ORIGINAL PERIOD** performed in the style current at the time of composition, and on instruments similar to those of the time **5.** **MUSIC** **WITH UPWARD RANGE FROM MAIN NOTE** used to describe church music, such as Gregorian chant, that has an upward range from the keynote of the scale [14thC. Via Old French from, ultimately, Greek *authentikos* 'genuine', from *authentes* 'master, doer', from *autos* 'self'.] —**authentically** *adv.*

——— **WORD KEY: USAGE** ———
See Usage note at **genuine**.

authenticate /aw thénti kayt/ (**-cates, -cating, -cated**) *vt.* **1.** **CONFIRM GENUINENESS OR TRUTH OF STH** to establish that sth is genuine or that an account is true **2.** **LAW** **ESTABLISH AS VALID** to establish sth such as a deed or document as legally valid —**authentication** /aw thénti káysh'n/ *n.* —**authenticator** /aw thénti kaytər/ *n.*

authenticity /áw then tíssəti, áwthən-/ *n.* **1.** **GENUINENESS** the genuineness or truth of sth **2.** **LAW** **CORRECTNESS** the legal validity or correctness of a legal document

author /áwthər/ *n.* **1.** **WRITER** sb who writes a book or other text, e.g. a literary work or a report **2.** **PROFESSIONAL WRITER** sb who writes books as a profession **3.** **CREATOR OR SOURCE** sb who causes or creates sth ■ *vt.* (**-thors, -thoring, -thored**) **1.** **WRITE STH** to write or be responsible for the final form of a book, report, or other text **2.** **CAUSE STH** to be the cause, creator, or originator of sth [14thC. Via Old French from Latin *auctor* 'creator, originator', from, ultimately, *augere* 'to originate,

increase' (source of English *augment*).] —**authorial** /aw tháwri əl/ *adj.*

authoress /áwthərəss, -réss/ *n.* a woman who writes books (*dated or disapproving*)

authoring /áwthəring/ *n.* the creation of multimedia documents, e.g. training packages or sales presentations, using special software geared to a non-programmer

authoring language *n.* a software development system that lets users develop applications such as databases and multimedia educational materials without having to learn a formal programming language

authorisation *n.* = authorization

authorise *vt.* = authorize

authoritarian /aw thórri táiri ən/ *adj.* **1.** **STRICT AND DEMANDING OBEDIENCE** favouring strict rules and established authority **2.** **POL** **DEMANDING POLITICAL OBEDIENCE** belonging to or believing in a political system in which obedience to the ruling person or group is strongly enforced ■ *n.* **1.** **SB WHO DEMANDS OBEDIENCE** sb who favours or maintains strict rules and obedience to authority **2.** **POL** **SB WHO UPHOLDS RULES AND AUTHORITY** sb who favours or belongs to a political system in which obedience to authority is strongly enforced —**authoritarianism** *n.*

authoritative /aw thórritətiv/ *adj.* **1.** **RELIABLE** convincing, reliable, backed by evidence, and showing deep knowledge **2.** **BACKED BY AUTHORITY** backed by an established and accepted authority **3.** **SHOWING AUTHORITY** showing that the person is used to being obeyed or expects to be obeyed —**authoritatively** *adv.* —**authoritativeness** *n.*

authority /aw thórriti/ (*plural* **-ties**) *n.* **1.** **RIGHT TO COMMAND** the right or power to enforce rules or give orders **2.** **HOLDER OF POWER** sb or sth with official power **3.** **POWER GIVEN TO SB** power to act on behalf of sb else or official permission to do sth **4.** **SOURCE OF RELIABLE INFORMATION** sb who is accepted as a source of reliable information on a subject, or a book in which such information is given **5.** **PUBLIC ADMIN** **ADMINISTRATIVE BODY** an official body that is set up by a government to administer an area of activity (*often used in the plural*) **6.** **JUSTIFICATION** a statement that makes sb believe sth is true **7.** **QUALITY THAT IS RESPECTED** the ability to gain the respect of other people and to influence or control what they do **8.** **OBVIOUS KNOWLEDGE AND EXPERIENCE** knowledge, skill, or experience worthy of respect **9.** **LAW** **SOURCE OF PRECEDENT OR PRINCIPLE** a law or legal decision that is cited as establishing a precedent or a principle **10.** **SOC SCI** **LEGITIMATE POWER** a form of rule that is seen as legitimate [13thC. Via French from Latin *auctoritas*, from *auctor* (see AUTHOR).]

authority figure *n.* sb who is, or appears to be, strong and powerful and able to command and influence others

authorization /áwthə rī záysh'n/, **authorisation** *n.* **1.** **PERMISSION** official power or permission to do sth **2.** **DOCUMENT GIVING PERMISSION** a letter or document that confirms that sb has permission to do sth or be somewhere

authorize /áwthə rīz/ (**-izes, -izing, -ized**), **authorise** (**-rises, -rising, -rised**) *vt.* to give sb or sth power or permission to do sth or be somewhere [14thC. Via French from medieval Latin *auctorizare*, from Latin *auctor* (see AUTHOR).] —**authorized** *adj.* —**authorizer** *n.*

Authorized Version, Authorised Version *n.* a version of the Bible published in England in 1611 and authorized by James I for use in the Church of England. US term **King James Bible**

authorship /áwthərship/ *n.* **1.** **WRITING AS OCCUPATION** the practice or profession of writing books or other works **2.** **ORIGIN OF STH** the origin or source of sth, especially the person who wrote a particular literary work

autism /áwtizzəm/ *n.* a disturbance in psychological development in which use of language, reaction to stimuli, interpretation of the world, and the formation of relationships are not fully established and follow unusual patterns [Early 20thC. Coined from Greek *autos* 'self' + -ISM.]

autistic /aw tístik/ *adj.* showing evidence of autism, e.g. failure to use language and perceive surroundings normally —**autistically** *adv.*

auto /áwtō/ (*plural* **-tos**) *n.* US a motor car (*informal*) [Late 19thC. Shortening of AUTOMOBILE.]

auto. *abbr.* **1.** automatic **2.** automotive

auto-, aut- *prefix.* **1.** self ○ *autograft* **2.** automatic ○ *autorotation* [From Greek *autos* 'self', of unknown origin]

autoantibody /áwtō ánti bodi/ (*plural* **-ies**) *n.* : an antibody that reacts against normal substances present in the organism producing it, and is present in certain diseases (**autoimmune diseases**)

autobahn /áwtō baan, ówtō-/ *n.* a motorway in a German-speaking country or region [Mid-20thC. From German, literally 'automobile track'.]

autobiographical /áwtō bī ō gráffik'l/ *adj.* told or written by a writer about him- or herself —**autobiographically** *adv.*

autobiography /áwtō bī óggrəfi/ (*plural* **-phies**) *n.* an account of sb's life written by that person —**autobiographer** *n.*

autobus /áwtō buss/ *n.* US a bus or motor coach

autocatalysis /áwtō kə tállississ/ *n.* the speeding up of a chemical reaction by a catalyst that is a product of the reaction —**autocatalytic** /áwtō káttə líttik/ *adj.* —**autocatalytically** /-líttikli/ *adv.*

autocephalous /áwtō séffələss/, **autocephalic** /áwtō si fállik/ *adj.* used to describe an Eastern Orthodox church that is governed by its own elected bishop or patriarch [Mid-19thC. Formed from AUTO- + Greek *kephalē* 'head'.]

autochthon /aw tókthən, -thon/ (*plural* **-thons** *or* **-thones** /-thə neez/) *n.* **1.** BIOL **NATIVE PLANT OR ANIMAL** a plant or animal that originated in the country where it is found **2.** SOC SCI **ABORIGINAL PERSON** sb who is descended from the earliest inhabitants of a region **3.** GEOL **GEOLOGICAL DEPOSIT ORIGINATING WHERE FOUND** a rock formation, mineral deposit, or geological feature that was formed in the area where it is now found [Early 19thC. From Greek *autokhthōn* 'indigenous', from *khthōn* 'earth, soil'.]

autochthonous /aw tókthənəss/ *adj.* **1.** GEOL **FORMED WHERE FOUND** used to describe a rock, mineral deposit, or geological feature that was formed in the area where it is found **2.** BIOL **PRESENT FROM EARLIEST TIMES** descended from the original flora, fauna, or inhabitants of the region in which it is found **3.** PHYSIOL **PRODUCED WHERE SITUATED** produced or originating as a physical function or disorder in the place where it is found —**autochthonism** *n.* —**autochthonously** *adv.* —**autochthony** *n.*

WORD KEY: SYNONYMS

See Synonyms at ***native***.

autocidal /áwtō sīd'l/ *adj.* used to describe a method of pest control in which sterile or genetically altered insects are released to reduce the breeding success of the local insect population

autoclave /áwtə-/ *n.* **1.** SCI **STERILIZATION EQUIPMENT** a strong steel vessel that is used for the steam sterilization of equipment or materials, or for chemical reactions, at high temperature and under pressure **2.** CIV ENG **STEAMER FOR CONCRETE** an apparatus with which newly cast concrete is cured by steam under pressure ■ *vt.* (**-claves, -claving, -claved**) **USE AUTOCLAVE** to use an autoclave to steam sth [Late 19thC. From French, from, ultimately, Greek *autos* 'self' + Latin *clavus* 'nail' or *clavis* 'key'; so called because it is self-fastening.]

autocorrelation /áwtō kórri láysh'n/ *n.* a property displayed by some sequences of adjacent items not being independent of each other

autocracy /aw tókrəssi/ (*plural* **-cies**) *n.* **1. RULE BY ONE PERSON** a government in which sb holds unlimited power **2. RULER'S ABSOLUTE POWER** the unlimited political power of a single ruler **3. PLACE RULED BY ONE PERSON** a country governed by a single ruler who has unlimited power [Mid-17thC. From Greek *autokrateia*, from *autokratēs* (see AUTOCRAT).]

autocrat /áwtə krat/ *n.* **1. RULER WITH ABSOLUTE AUTHORITY** a ruler who holds unlimited power and is answerable to no other person **2. BOSSY PERSON** sb who dominates other people [Early 19thC. Via French *autocrate* from Greek *autokratēs* 'independent authority', from *kratos* 'power'.] —**autocratic** /-ik/ *adj.* —**autocratically** *adv.*

autocross /s/ *n.* timed motor racing across rough ground [Mid-20thC. Contraction of AUTOMOBILE + CROSS-COUNTRY.]

Autocue *tdmk.* a trademark for a device that displays an enlarged line-by-line text on a television screen to a speaker while remaining unseen to the audience

auto-da-fé /áwtō də fáy/ (*plural* **autos-da-fé** /áwtō də fáy/) *n.* a sentence of death pronounced on a heretic by a court of the Spanish Inquisition and carried out by the civil authorities. The condemned person was burned at the stake. [Early 18thC. From Portuguese, literally 'act of the faith'.]

autodeconstruction /áwtō deekən strúksh'n/ *n.* critical analysis of artistic works that is done by the artists themselves rather than critics

autodestruct /áwtō di strúkt/ *vi.* (**-structs, -structing, -structed**) MIL **SELF-DESTRUCT** to undergo self-destruction (*technical*) ○ *The missile auto-destructed after an aborted launch.* ■ *adj.* **ENABLING SELF-DESTRUCTION** allowing or causing sth to destroy itself

autodial /áwtō dī əl/ *n.* a device that automatically dials a prerecorded number in response to an input signal, e.g. pressing a button [Late 20thC. Contraction.] —**autodialler** *n.*

autodidact /áwtō dī dakt/ *n.* sb who has acquired a great deal of knowledge despite little or no formal education [Mid-18thC. From Greek, formed from *didaskein* 'to teach' (source of English *didactic*).] —**autodidactic** /áwtō dī dáktik, -di-/ *adj.*

autodyne /áwtō dīn/ *n.* **TYPE OF ELECTRONIC CIRCUIT** an electronic circuit containing an element such as a transistor that acts simultaneously as a detector and oscillator ■ *adj.* **WITH AUTODYNE** used to describe a radio device containing an element, such as a transistor, that acts simultaneously as a detector and oscillator [Early 20thC. Coined from AUTO- + Greek *dunamis* 'force, power' (source of English *dynamic*).]

autoecious /aw teeshəss/ *adj.* living as a pest or parasite on a single host species [Late 19thC. Coined from AUTO- + Greek *oikia* 'house' + -IOUS.] —**autoecism** *n.*

autoeroticism /áwtō i rótti sizzəm/, **autoerotism** /áwtō érrətizzəm/ *n.* sexual arousal and gratification that sb gets from self-stimulation —**autoerotic** /áwtō i róttik/ *adj.*

autofocus /áwtō fōkəss/ *n.* a device that automatically adjusts the focus of a camera

autogamy /aw tóggəmi/ *n.* **1.** BOT **SELF-POLLINATION** the process by which some flowering plants fertilize themselves **2.** BIOL **TYPE OF REPRODUCTIVE PROCESS** the division and subsequent reunification of a single cell in the reproductive processes of certain simple one-celled animals and algae [Late 19thC. Coined from AUTO- + -GAMY.] —**autogamic** /áwtə gámmik/ *adj.* —**autogamous** /aw tóggəməss/ *adj.*

autogenesis /áwtō jénnississ/ *n.* BIOL = **abiogenesis** —**autogenetic** /áwtō ji néttik/ *adj.* —**autogenetically** /-néttikli/ *adv.*

autogenic *adj.* = **autogenous** [Late 19thC. Coined from AUTO- + -GENIC.] —**autogenically** *adv.*

autogenics /áwtō jénniks/ *n.* = **autogenic training**

autogenic training *n.* a method of relieving stress by using meditation and other mental exercises to produce physical relaxation

autogenocide /áwtō jénnə sīd/ *n.* the extermination of people by their fellow citizens to achieve an alleged social goal [Late 20thC]

autogenous /aw tójjənəss/, **autogenic** *adj.* **1. PRODUCED INSIDE STH** produced or created within sth itself, without external help or influence **2.** MED **PRODUCED FROM STH FROM RECIPIENT'S BODY** produced in, or with tissue from, the body of the person to whom it will be given **3.** INSECTS **NOT NEEDING BLOOD** used to describe insects that do not require a meal of blood in order to produce viable eggs [Mid-19thC. Formed from Greek *autogenēs*, from, ultimately, *gignesthai* 'to be born'.] —**autogenously** *adv.*

autogiro /áwtō jīrō/ (*plural* **-ros**) *n.* an aircraft that uses a propeller for forward motion and an unpowered horizontal rotor for lift and stability. ◊ **gyroplane** [Early 20thC. From Spanish, literally 'self-turning', formed from *giro* 'gyration'.]

autograft /áwtə graaft/ *n.* a graft of skin or other tissue obtained from the patient's own body

autograph /áwtə graaf, -graf/ *n.* **1. SB'S SIGNATURE** a signature, especially the signature of a famous person **2. HANDWRITTEN TEXT** a copy of a document or text handwritten by its creator (*formal*) ■ *vt.* (**-graphs, -graphing, -graphed**) **SIGN WITH NAME** to write your signature on sth such as a book or photograph [Early 17thC. Via French or late Latin from Greek *autographon*, literally 'written with your own hand', from *graphein* (see GRAPHIC).]

autograph hunter *n.* sb who collects the signatures of famous people (*informal*)

autography /aw tóggrəfi/ *n.* the writing of sth in your own hand

autoharp /áwtō haarp/ *n.* an instrument with many strings on which chords are played by strumming, strings not to be sounded being held down by a button-controlled damper

autohypnosis /áwtō hip nṓsiss/ *n.* a process by which sb hypnotizes himself or herself —**autohypnotic** /áwtō hip nóttik/ *adj.*

autoimmune /áwtō i myoón/ *adj.* caused by the reaction of an antibody to substances that occur naturally in the body —**autoimmunity** *n.* —**autoimmunization** /áwtō ímyoo nī záysh'n/ *n.*

autoimmune disease *n.* a disease caused by the reaction of antibodies to substances occurring naturally in the body. Three common autoimmune diseases are lupus erythematosus, Addison's disease, and rheumatoid arthritis.

autoinfection /áwtō in féksh'n/ *n.* infection caused by an organism already present in another part of the body or by the larval reproduction of a parasite already present in the body

autoinoculation /áwtō i nókyoo láysh'n/ *n.* a disease that occurs when an infection spreads from one part of the body to another —**autoinoculable** /áwtō i nókyooləb'l/ *adj.*

autointoxication /áwtō in tóksi káysh'n/ *n.* poisoning by sth that has been produced within the body of the person who is poisoned

autojumble /áwtō júmb'l/ *n.* obsolete car and vehicle components and spares, often found on sale at classic car and commercial vehicle rallies, country shows, or car boot sales (*informal*)

autoload /áwtō lōd/ *adj.* US ARMS = **semiautomatic** —**autoloader** *n.*

autologous /aw tólləgəss/ *adj.* derived from the patient's own body [Early 20thC. Coined from AUTO- + *-logous*, from -LOGY.]

autolysate /aw tóllə sayt, -zayt/ *n.* a product of the process (**autolysis**) by which cells are broken down by enzymes produced in the cells themselves

autolysin /aw tóllissin, áwtə līssin/ *n.* an enzyme that can break down the cell in which it is produced

autolysis /aw tóllississ/ *n.* the breaking down of cells by an enzyme that is produced within them —**autolytic** /áwtə líttik/ *adj.*

automata plural of **automaton**

automate /áwtə mayt/ (**-mates, -mating, -mated**) *vti.* to convert a process or workplace to automation [Mid-20thC. Back-formation from AUTOMATION.]

automated teller machine *n.* full form of **ATM**

automatic /áwtə máttik/ *adj.* **1. STARTING OR FUNCTIONING BY ITSELF** started, operated, or regulated by a process or mechanism without human intervention **2. DONE BY PRIOR ARRANGEMENT** beginning when certain conditions are fulfilled, without the need for a decision or action **3.** PHYSIOL **INDEPENDENT OF SB'S WILL** done without thought or intention, especially as the result of a reflex **4. DONE WITHOUT THOUGHT** performed without conscious thought as the result of habit or custom ■ *n.* **1. MACHINE OPERATING WITHOUT HUMAN INTERVENTION** a machine, e.g. a washing machine, that controls its own operating process **2.** AUTOMOT **MOTOR VEHICLE NOT REQUIRING MANUAL GEAR** a motor vehicle that has a built-in mechanism (**automatic transmission**) for changing gears without requiring the driver to do it **3.** ARMS **GUN THAT FIRES CONTINUOUSLY** a gun that continues to fire for as long as the trigger is pressed, automatically ejecting used cartridges and reloading [18thC. Formed from Greek *automatos* (see AUTOMATON).] —**automatically** *adv.*

automatic exposure *n.* a control system in a camera that sets the lens aperture and shutter speed according to the amount of light that is present

automatic frequency control *n.* a control system in a radio or television receiver that keeps it tuned to a signal in spite of minor variations in the signal's frequency

automatic gain control *n.* a radio receiver control system by which the amplifier is adjusted to compensate for variations in the volume of the signal, so that the volume of the output is constant

automatic pilot *n.* **1.** AEROSP, NAUT **AUTOMATIC STEERING SYSTEM** a control in the steering system of a ship, aircraft, or spacecraft that can be set to put or keep it on a steady course **2.** PHYSIOL, PSYCHOL **PRESET OR INSTINCTIVE BEHAVIOUR** a condition in which sb is not fully aware of what he or she is doing but is acting in a habitual and unthinking way, e.g. because of stress

automatic transmission *n.* a transmission system for motor vehicles in which changes of gear are made automatically in response to the speed of the vehicle

automatic writing *n.* the production of writing while in a trance or similar state as an attempt to make contact with the writer's unconscious or telepathically with a spirit

automation /áwtə máysh'n/ *n.* the conversion of a workplace to one that replaces or minimizes human labour with mechanical or electronic machines or processes [Mid-20thC. Formed from AUTOMATIC.]

automatise *vt.* = automatize

automatism /aw tómmətizzəm/ *n.* **1.** PHYSIOL, PSYCHOL **INVOLUNTARY ORGANIC FUNCTION** a physical reflex or involuntary activity of the body **2.** PHILOSOPHY, LAW **THEORY THAT ACTIONS ARE PERFORMED AUTOMATICALLY** the philosophical theory that all bodily actions have involuntary physical or physiological causes, or the legal defence that an action had such a cause **3.** PSYCHOL **ACTIVITY NOT CONSCIOUSLY CAUSED** behaviour that is not consciously motivated, e.g. sleepwalking or involuntary repetitive actions **4.** PAINTING, LITERAT **ARTISTIC METHOD** an artistic approach, associated with the surrealists, in which the painter or writer empties the mind and allows the unconscious to direct the work —**automatist** *n.*

automatize /aw tómmə tīz/ (**-tizes, -tizing, -tized**), **automatise** (**-tises, -tising, -tised**) *vt.* to make a process or workplace operate automatically using electronic or mechanical devices —**automatization** /aw tómmə tī záysh'n/ *n.*

automaton /aw tómmətən, -ton/ (*plural* **-tons** *or* **-ta** /-mətə/) *n.* **1.** ENG **INDEPENDENT AND COMPLEX MACHINE** a machine that contains its own power source and can perform a complicated series of actions, including responses to external stimuli, without human intervention **2.** SB **WHO ACTS LIKE MACHINE** sb who resembles a machine by obeying instructions automatically, performing repetitive actions, or showing no emotion [Early 17thC. Via Latin from Greek, neuter of *automatos* 'acting by itself' (source of English *automatic*).] —**automatous** *adj.*

automobile /áwtə mə beel/ *n.* a road vehicle, usually with four wheels and powered by an internal-combustion engine, designed to carry a small number of passengers [Late 19thC. From French, literally 'self-mobile'.]

automobilia /áwtə mə beeli ə/ *npl.* things to do with cars or motoring that appeal to collectors and enthusiasts [Late 20thC. Coined from AUTOMOBILE, on the model of MEMORABILIA.]

automotive /áwtə mótiv/ *adj.* **1.** **OF MOTOR VEHICLES** relating to or involving motor vehicles **2.** **SELF-PROPELLED** propelled by its own motor or engine

autonomic /áwtə nómmik/ *adj.* **1.** PHYSIOL **CONTROLLED BY AUTOMATIC RESPONSES** used to describe functions of the nervous system not under the voluntary control of

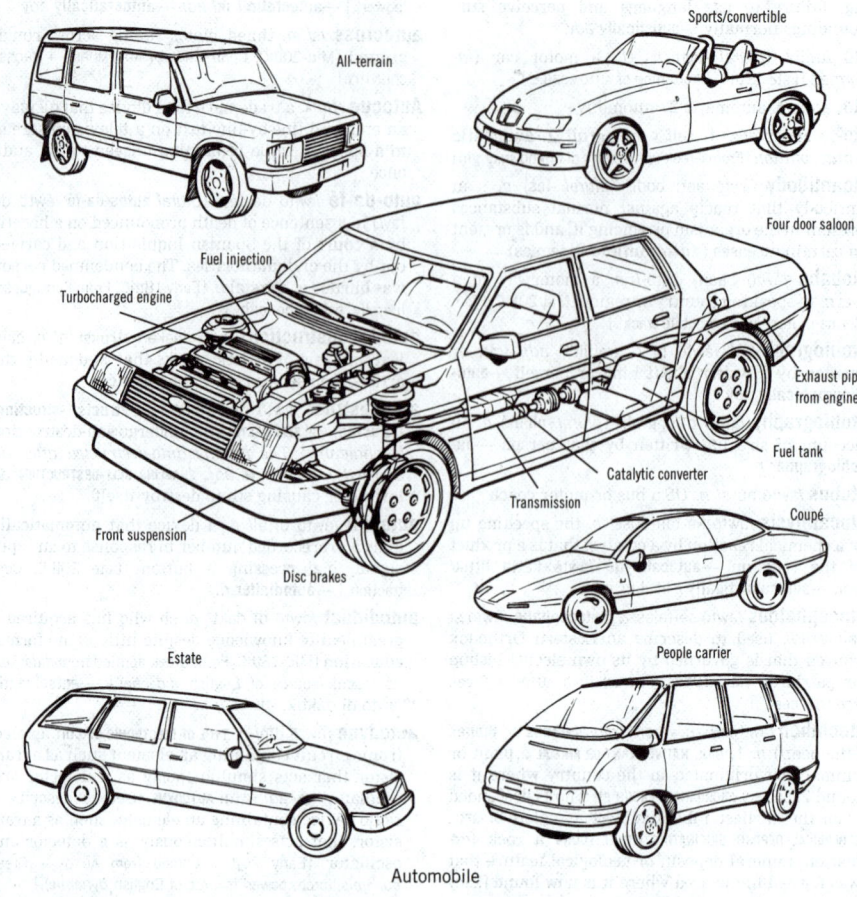

All-terrain

Sports/convertible

Four door saloon

Fuel injection

Turbocharged engine

Exhaust pipe from engine

Fuel tank

Catalytic converter

Transmission

Coupé

Front suspension

Disc brakes

Estate

People carrier

Automobile

the individual, e.g. the regulation of heartbeat or gland secretions **2.** PHYSIOL **WITHOUT THOUGHT** used to describe an action or response that occurs without conscious control **3.** BIOL **FROM INTERNAL STIMULI** produced or caused by internal stimuli —**autonomically** *adv.*

autonomic nervous system *n.* the part of the nervous system in humans and other vertebrates that controls involuntary activity, e.g. the action of the heart and glands, breathing, digestive processes, and reflex actions. ◊ **somatic nervous system**

autonomous /aw tónnəməss/ *adj.* **1.** **SELF-GOVERNING** politically independent and self-governing **2.** **ABLE TO CHOOSE** able to make decisions and act on them as a free and independent moral agent **3.** **SELF-SUFFICIENT** existing, reacting, or developing as an independent, self-regulating organism —**autonomously** *adv.*

autonomy /aw tónnəmi/ *n.* **1.** POL **SELF-GOVERNMENT** political independence and self-government **2.** PHILOSOPHY **EXISTENCE AS INDEPENDENT MORAL AGENT** personal independence and the capacity to make moral decisions and act on them **3.** LITERAT **INDEPENDENCE OF A TEXT** the status of a text as an aesthetic object not to be judged or commented on in the light of external knowledge, e.g. of the biography of the author [Early 17thC. From Greek *autonomia*, from *autonomos* 'having its own laws', from *nomos* 'law'.] —**autonomist** *n.*

autopilot /áwtō pīlət/ *n.* AEROSP, NAUT = **automatic pilot** *n.* **1** ◊ **on autopilot** without guidance, control, or proper attention (*informal*) ○ *The business has been on autopilot since she resigned.*

autopista /áwtō peéstə/ *n.* a motorway in a Spanish-speaking country or region [Mid-20thC. From Spanish, literally 'automobile track'.]

autoplasty /áwtə plasti/ (*plural* **-ties**) *n.* the repair of a patient's body using tissue, e.g. skin, taken from another part of the patient's body —**autoplastic** /áwtə plástik/ *adj.* —**autoplastically** /-plástikli/ *adv.*

autopsy /áwt opsi/ (*plural* **-sies**) *n.* **1.** MED **EXAMINATION TO FIND CAUSE OF DEATH** the medical examination of a dead body in order to establish the cause and cir-

cumstances of death **2.** **EXHAUSTIVE EXAMINATION** an exhaustive critical examination of sth [Mid-17thC. Via French or modern Latin from Greek *autopsia* 'seeing with your own eyes', from *autoptēs* 'eye witness'.]

auto racing *n.* *US* = **motor racing**

autoradiograph /áwtō ráydi ə graaf, -graf/, **autoradiogram** /-gram/ *n.* a photograph that reveals how radioactivity is distributed in a specimen or sample, made by exposing a photographic plate to the radiation —**autoradiographic** /áwtō ráydi ə gráffik/ *adj.* —**autoradiography** /-ráydi óggrəfi/ *n.*

autorickshaw /áwtō rík shaw/ *n.* a vehicle with three wheels, like a covered motor scooter with a back seat for passengers, that is used as a taxi in the Indian subcontinent

autoroute /áwtō root/ *n.* a motorway in a French-speaking country or region [Mid-20thC. From French, literally 'automobile route'.]

autosave /áwtō sayv/ *n.* a computer program feature in which data in an open file is saved automatically at intervals usually determinable by the user. This feature can minimize data loss in the event of a crash.

autosome /áwtə sōm/ *n.* a chromosome other than one that determines sex [Early 20thC. Coined from AUTO- + -SOME, on the model of CHROMOSOME.] —**autosomal** /áwtə sṓm'l/ *adj.* —**autosomally** /-sṓməli/ *adv.*

autostrada /áwtō straadə/ *n.* a motorway in an Italian-speaking country or region [Early 20thC. From Italian, literally 'automobile road'.]

autosuggestion /áwtō sə jéschən/ *n.* the process by which sb's perceptions, behaviour, or physical condition may be altered by means of his or her power of suggestion —**autosuggest** *vt.* —**autosuggestibility** /áwtō sə jéstə bílləti/ *n.* —**autosuggestible** /-jéstəb'l/ *adj.* —**autosuggestive** /-jéstiv/ *adj.*

autotelic /áwtō téllik, -teélik/ *adj.* **1.** PHILOSOPHY **POSSESSING INTERNAL PURPOSE** concerning an entity or event that has within itself the purpose of its existence or occurrence **2.** LEISURE **DONE FOR ITS OWN SAKE** done for its own sake rather than to gain a material reward or avoid a punishment [Early 20thC. Formed from Greek *autotelēs*, from *autos* 'self' + *telos* 'end'.] —**autotelism** *n.*

autotimer /áwtō tīmər/ *n.* an automatic timing device, e.g. on a cooker

autotomize /aw tóttə mīz/ (**-mizes, -mizing, -mized**), **autotomise** (**-mises, -mising, -mised**) *vti.* to cast off a part of the body such as the tail or a leg in order to escape from an attacker or because it has become trapped. This is done, e.g., by lizards, snakes, worms, and crustaceans.

autotomy /aw tóttəmi/ *n.* the casting off of part of the body by an animal such as a lizard, snake, worm, or crustacean when it is caught or attacked by a predator [Late 19thC. Coined from AUTO- + -TOMY.] —**autotomic** /áwtə tómmik/ *adj.*

autotoxaemia /áwtō tok seémi ə/ *n.* = **autointoxication**

autotoxin /áwtə tóksin/ *n.* a substance that poisons the system within which it is formed

autotransformer /áwtō transs fáwrmər/ *n.* a transformer in which the primary and secondary coils share all or some windings

autotransfusion /áwtō transs fyoózh'n/ *n.* a blood transfusion using the patient's own blood

autotrophic /áwtə tróffik/ *adj.* used to describe organisms, especially green plants, that are capable of making nutrients from inorganic materials [Late 19thC. Coined from AUTO- + -TROPHIC.] —**autotroph** /-trōf/ *n.* —**autotrophically** /-tróffikli/ *adv.* —**autotrophy** /aw tóttrəfi/ *n.*

autowinder /áwtō wīndər/ *n.* a device that automatically winds the film in a camera forward after a photograph is taken

autoxidation /aw tóksi dáysh'n/ *n.* **1.** OXIDATION IN AIR the oxidation of certain substances that occurs at normal temperatures as a result of contact with air **2.** OXIDATION OF TWO SUBSTANCES oxidation that occurs only when there is another substance present that also undergoes oxidation

autumn /áwtəm/ *n.* **1.** SEASON AFTER SUMMER AND BEFORE WINTER the season occurring between summer and winter. In the northern hemisphere it is the time when weather begins to become colder, many fruits ripen, and leaves change colour and drop. Autumn traditionally lasts from 22 September to 21 December in the northern hemisphere, and from 21 March to 21 June in the southern hemisphere. **2.** TIME OF LATE MATURITY a time in the development of sth that follows its most vigorous and successful phase, before its decline ○ *in the autumn of his career as a cellist* [14thC. From Latin *autumnus*, of uncertain origin. The word replaced HARVEST as the term for this time of year.]

autumnal /aw túmn'l/ *adj.* occurring in or typical of autumn

autumnal equinox *n.* **1.** CALENDAR TIME WHEN SUN CROSSES EQUATORIAL PLANE the first day of autumn, when the sun crosses the plane of the Earth's equator and makes day and night approximately of equal length. The day occurs about 22 September in the northern hemisphere and 21 March in the southern hemisphere. **2.** ASTRON SUN'S PATH CROSSING CELESTIAL EQUATOR the position of the sun during the autumnal equinox

autumn crocus (*plural* **autumn crocuses** *or* **autumn croci**) *n.* an autumn-flowering plant that has crocus-shaped purple or pink flowers growing directly from the ground after the leaves have died down. Latin name: *Colchicum autumnale*.

autunite /áwtə nīt/ *n.* a yellow radioactive fluorescent mineral consisting of hydrated calcium uranium phosphate [Mid-19thC. Named after the town of *Autun* in eastern France, near where the mineral was first discovered.]

aux. *abbr.* auxiliary

auxesis /awg zeéssiss, -seéssiss/ *n.* growth in animals or plants caused by an increase in the size of cells, not by cellular division [Mid-19thC. Via late Latin from Greek.] —**auxetic** /awk séttik/ *adj.* —**auxetically** /-séttikli/ *adv.*

auxiliary /awg zíllyəri, -zílləri/ *adj.* **1.** GIVING SUPPORT acting to support or supplement a group of people **2.** HELD IN RESERVE available as backup for a system, process, or piece of equipment **3.** SECONDARY secondary to sth larger **4.** NAUT WITH MOTOR AND SAILS used to describe a boat with an engine to supplement or

replace the sails ■ *n.* (*plural* **-ries**) **1.** HR SUPPORTING PERSON OR THING sb who or sth that acts in a supporting, backup, or supplementary role **2.** GRAM = **auxiliary verb 3.** NAUT SAILING SHIP WITH ENGINE a sailing ship equipped with an engine **4.** NAVY NAVAL SUPPORT VESSEL a naval vessel, e.g. a tug or transport ship, that does not engage in combat **5.** MIL MEMBER OF SUPPORTING TROOPS a member of a foreign troop that fights with an army as allies or mercenaries and has its own command structure (*often used in the plural*) [Early 17thC. From Latin *auxiliarius*, from *auxilium* 'help, assistance'.]

auxiliary language *n.* a language, e.g. English, Esperanto, or Kiswahili, that is used by speakers of other languages in order to communicate

auxiliary note *n.* MUSIC a note that falls between two adjacent notes of the same pitch and is not an overtone

auxiliary rotor *n.* the tail rotor of a helicopter

auxiliary verb *n.* a verb that is used with another verb to indicate person, number, mood, tense, or aspect. Some auxiliary verbs in English are 'be', 'have', 'will', and 'do'.

———— **WORD KEY: USAGE** ————

Auxiliary verb: The auxiliary verbs are *be*, *do*, and *have*, which together with the so-called modal (or modal auxiliary) verbs *can*, *may*, *shall*, *should*, *will*, and *would* are used with other verbs to form past and future tenses, negatives, questions, the passive voice, and other special functions. Most ordinary verbs cannot fulfil these functions by themselves; for example you have to use the auxiliary verb *do* to form negatives and questions (*They don't like it. Do you want to leave?*), the auxiliary verbs *be* and *have* to form past tenses (*We were leaving. They haven't decided.*), and the modal verbs *shall* and *will* to form future tenses (*He will drive you to the station. Shall we go now?*). Sometimes more than one auxiliary verb is used to form a tense, as in *We will be going* and *They have been paid*. The verb *be* is used to form the passive voice: *The letter was posted last night*. See also the note at *modal*.

auxin /áwksin/ *n.* a natural plant hormone or synthetic substance that affects growth and the development of shoots, roots, fruit, and flowers [Mid-20thC. Coined from Greek *auxein* 'to increase' + -IN.] —**auxinic** /awk sínnik/ *adj.* —**auxinically** /-sínnikli/ *adv.*

auxotonic /áwksə tónnik/ *adj.* occurring against increasing force as part of a muscle contraction [Coined from Greek *auxein* 'to increase' + TONIC]

auxotroph /áwksə trōf/ *n.* a mutant strain of an organism, e.g. a bacterium, that has lost the ability to synthesize a particular nutrient (**growth factor**) and must obtain it from its environment to survive. ◊ **prototroph** [Mid-20thC. Back-formation from AUXOTROPHIC.]

auxotrophic /áwksə trófik/ *adj.* used to describe a mutant strain of an organism, e.g. a bacterium, that has lost the ability to synthesize a particular nutrient (**growth factor**) and must obtain it from its environment to survive [Mid-20thC. Coined from Greek *auxein* 'to increase' + -TROPHIC.]

Av /av, awv, aab/ *n.* = **Ab**

AV *abbr.* **1.** COMMUNICATION audiovisual **2.** BIBLE Authorized Version

av. *abbr.* **1.** av., Av. avenue **2.** average **3.** MEASURE avoirdupois

A/V, a/v, a.v. *abbr.* FIN ad valorem

avadavat /ávvədə vát/ *n.* an Asian waxbill often kept as a cagebird. The male of one species is green and the male of the other species is red. Genus: *Estrilda*. [Late 17thC. Alteration of *Ahmadabad*, a city in western India where these birds were sold.]

avail /ə váyl/ *v.* (**avails, availing, availed**) **1.** *vr.* USE STH to make use of sth useful or helpful while you have the opportunity **2.** *vti.* HELP to be helpful or useful to sb or to help sb succeed ■ *n.* HELP OR ADVANTAGE help, advantage, or success in achieving sth (*used in negative statements*) ○ *His defence was to no avail, a conviction was secured.* ■ **avails** *npl.* BUSINESS PROFITS profits or proceeds from sth (*archaic*) [14thC. Formed from Old French *vail-*, the stem of *valoir* 'to be worth' (source of English *valour* and *value*), from Latin *valere* 'to be strong'.]

available /ə váylǝb'l/ *adj.* **1.** ABLE TO BE GOT able to be used or obtained, or spoken to or consulted **2.** US POL ELIGIBLE FOR OFFICE eligible and willing to undertake a public office or stand for election **3.** UNATTACHED not currently involved in a romantic or sexual relationship but ready to engage in one (*informal*) [15thC. Originally, the word meant 'effective, useful'; the underlying sense is 'possible or suitable to avail yourself of'.] —**availability** /ə váylə bílliti/ *n.* —**availably** /ə váyləbli/ *adv.*

avalanche /ávvə laanch/ *n.* **1.** DOWNHILL FALL OF SNOW a rapid downhill flow of a large mass of snow or ice dislodged from a mountainside or the top of a precipice, or a similar fall of rocks and earth **2.** OVERWHELMING QUANTITY a sudden overwhelming quantity of sth **3.** PHYS INCREASE IN NUMBER OF IONS an increase in the number of ions or electrons, usually within a medium exposed to an applied electromagnetic field, caused by collisions of the ions or electrons with the medium ■ *vti.* (**-lanches, -lanching, -lanched**) FLOW DOWN IN LARGE QUANTITY to descend in a large mass on sth or sb [Late 18thC. Via French from Romansh *avalantze*, from, ultimately, assumed Vulgar Latin *labanca*, of unknown origin.]

Avalon /ávvə lon/ *n.* in Celtic mythology, an island paradise in the West. In the legend of King Arthur, he is said to have been taken to Avalon after being apparently mortally wounded.

avant-garde /ávong gaárd/ *n.* ARTISTS WITH NEW IDEAS AND METHODS writers, artists, film makers, or musicians whose work is innovative, experimental, or unconventional (*takes a singular or plural verb*) ■ *adj.* **1.** ARTISTICALLY NEW artistically new, experimental, or unconventional **2.** OF THE AVANT-GARDE belonging to the artistically innovative [Early 20thC. From French, literally 'before the guard' (see VANGUARD).] —**avant-gardism** *n.* —**avant-gardist** *n.*

Avar /aá vaar, áv-/ *n.* a language of the Caucasian family spoken in the Dagestan republic of Russia —**Avar** *adj.*

avarice /ávvəriss/ *n.* an unreasonably strong desire to obtain and keep money [13thC. Via French from Latin *avaritia*, from *avarus* 'greedy', from *avere* 'to desire' (source of English *avid*).]

avaricious /ávvə ríshəss/ *adj.* showing an unreasonably strong desire for money —**avariciously** *adv.* —**avariciousness** *n.*

avascular /ə váskyŏŏlər/ *adj.* lacking blood vessels in body tissue —**avascularity** /ə váskyŏŏ lárrəti/ *n.*

avast /ə vaást/ *interj.* used by sailors as a command to stop doing sth or to ignore a previous order [Early 17thC. Alteration of Dutch *hou'vast*, shortening of *houd vast*, literally 'hold fast'.]

avatar /ávvə taar/ *n.* **1.** INCARNATION OF HINDU GOD an incarnation of a Hindu god in human or animal form, especially one of the incarnations of Vishnu such as Rama and Krishna **2.** EMBODIMENT OF STH sb who embodies, personifies, or is the manifestation of an idea or concept **3.** COMPUT IMAGE OF PERSON IN VIRTUAL REALITY a movable three-dimensional image that can be used to represent sb in cyberspace, e.g. an Internet user [Late 18thC. From Sanskrit *avatāra* 'descent', referring to the descent of a god to earth.]

avaunt /ə váwnt/ *interj.* used as a command to go away, especially to an evil spirit (*archaic*) [14thC. From French *avant* 'forward', from Latin *ante* 'before'.]

AVC *abbr.* PENSIONS additional voluntary contribution

avdp. *abbr.* avoirdupois

ave /aá vay, aávi/, **Ave** *interj., n.* = **Hail Mary** ■ *interj.* GREETING OR FAREWELL used as a greeting or farewell (*archaic*) ■ *n.* **1.** TIME FOR PRAYER the time when the Hail Mary is to be said, marked by the ringing of a bell **2.** ROSARY BEAD a small bead on a rosary, used for keeping track of how many times the Hail Mary has been said [13thC. From Latin, imperative of *avere* 'to be or fare well'.]

Ave., ave. *abbr.* avenue

Avebury /áyvbəri/ village in Wiltshire, England, site of the largest ancient stone circle in the country

Ave Maria, ave, Ave *n.* = **Hail Mary** [13thC. From the Latin original of the HAIL MARY.]

———

avenge /ə vénj/ **(avenges, avenging, avenged)** *vt.* to inflict punishment on sb for a wrong done, or retaliate on behalf of sb else [14thC. From Old French *avengier*, from *vengier* (see VENGEANCE).] —**avenger** *n.* —**avenging** *adj.* —**avengingly** *adv.*

WORD KEY: USAGE

avenge or **revenge**? Both words are about repaying a wrong, and the differences between them have more to do with grammar than meaning. ***Avenge*** is a verb only whereas **revenge** is a verb and (more usually, in fact) a noun. But as a verb ***avenge*** is more versatile than **revenge**: you can ***avenge*** a person (including yourself but more usually sb else) or an act but you can only **revenge** an act or yourself (in an awkward construction with *on*). The possibilities therefore are: *They took revenge on their enemies. We revenged ourselves on our enemies. We will revenge the wrong done to us. They avenged the wrong done to them. He avenged his murdered brother.*

avens /ávvinz, áyvənz/ (*plural* **-ens**) *n.* = **mountain avens** [12thC. From Old French *avence*, of unknown origin.]

aventurine /ə véntyŏŏrin, -reen/, **aventurin** /-rin/ *n.* **1.** CRAFT **GLASS CONTAINING SHINY PARTICLES** dark brown or green glass that contains sparkling mineral particles **2.** MINERALS **MINERAL CONTAINING SHINY PARTICLES** feldspar or quartz containing minute particles of iron compounds or, in some of the quartz types, mica [Early 18thC. Via French from Italian *avventurino* 'chance' (because it was discovered accidentally).]

avenue /ávvə nyoo/ *n.* **1.** TRANSP **WIDE STREET** a wide street or road in a town **2.** **MEANS OF APPROACH** a course of action to be taken in order to approach, attain, or gain access to sb or sth ○ *need to explore all avenues* **3.** **TREE-LINED ROAD** a road lined with trees, especially a tree-lined path leading through grounds to a country residence [Early 17thC. From French, literally 'approach', feminine past participle of *avenir* 'to arrive', from Latin *advenire* (see ADVENT).]

aver /ə vúr/ **(avers, averring, averred)** *vt.* **1.** **ASSERT CONFIDENTLY** to assert or allege sth confidently (*formal*) **2.** LAW **ALLEGE** to state or allege that sth is true [14thC. Via French *avérer* from, ultimately, Latin *verus* 'true' (source of English *veracity, verify,* and *very*).] —**averment** *n.* —**averrable** *adj.*

average /ávvərij/ *n.* **1.** **TYPICAL AMOUNT** the level, amount, or degree of sth that is typical of a group or class of people or things **2.** MATH **NUMBER CONSIDERED TYPICAL OF NUMBER GROUP** a number that can be regarded as typical of a group of numbers, calculated by adding the numbers together, then dividing the total by the amount of numbers **3.** SPORTS **MEASURE OF PLAYING PERFORMANCE** a measure of a player's or team's achievement, reached by dividing the number of opportunities for successful performances by how many times a successful performance was achieved **4.** LAW **LOSS AT SEA** in maritime law, the loss or damage of a ship and its cargo, or the division of the costs of this loss or damage among the owner or partners involved **5.** STOCK EXCH **INTERMEDIATE PRICE** a measure of stock exchange performance, based on the total of prices for a group or class of securities, divided by the number of securities ■ *adj.* **1.** **TYPICAL** without any extraordinary, untypical, or exceptional characteristic ○ *just an average guy* **2.** MATH **CALCULATED AS TOTAL DIVIDED BY MEMBERS** obtained by adding the numerical value for each member or part of a group or class and dividing the total by the number of members **3.** **NOT VERY GOOD** not terrible but not very good either ○ *The performance was no better than average.* ■ *vt.* **(-ages, -aging, -aged) 1.** MATH **CALCULATE NUMERICAL AVERAGE** to calculate a numerical average of sth, by finding the total amount and dividing it by the number of members in the group **2.** **HAVE AS AVERAGE** to have or show as an average **3.** **ACHIEVE OR GET AS AVERAGE** to do, produce, or receive a particular amount of sth as an average ○ *She averages one trip to Asia each year.* [15thC. Alteration, modelled on DAMAGE, of French *avarie*, from, ultimately, Arabic *'awār* 'damage to goods'.] —**averagely** *adv.* —**averageness** *n.*

average down *vi.* to purchase more shares of a security when its price is falling, in the hope of reducing costs and increasing profits

average out *v.* **1.** *vi.* **HAVE AS AVERAGE** to have or show as an average **2.** *vt.* MATH **CALCULATE AVERAGE** to calculate the numerical average of sth

average up *vi.* to purchase more shares of a security when its price is rising, in the hope of increasing profits

average deviation *n.* STATS = **mean deviation**

averse /ə vúrss/ *adj.* **1.** **OPPOSED TO STH** strongly opposed to or disliking sth (*formal*) ○ *The board is not averse to the idea of further talks.* ○ *risk-averse* **2.** BOT **TURNED AWAY FROM STEM** used to describe a leaf or flower that is turned away from the main stem or axis [Late 16thC. From Latin *aversus*, literally 'turned away', past participle of *avertere* (see AVERT).] —**averseness** *n.*

WORD KEY: USAGE

See Usage note at ***adverse***.

WORD KEY: SYNONYMS

See Synonyms at ***unwilling***.

aversion /ə vúrsh'n/ *n.* **1.** **STRONG DISLIKE** a strong feeling of dislike or hatred of sb or sth **2.** **SB OR STH DISLIKED** sb or sth strongly disliked

WORD KEY: SYNONYMS

See Synonyms at ***dislike***.

aversion therapy *n.* **1.** **THERAPY GIVING CERTAIN BEHAVIOUR UNPLEASANT CONSEQUENCES** a method of therapy that attempts to eliminate undesired behaviour by associating it repeatedly with painful or unpleasant effects **2.** **THERAPY TO OVERCOME FEARS OR DISLIKES** therapy aimed at eliminating an irrational fear or dislike by making sb experience the thing feared or disliked in remote or indirect ways that gradually become closer and more direct

aversive /ə vúrssiv/ *adj.* inducing dislike or loathing of sth —**aversively** *adv.* —**aversiveness** *n.*

avert /ə vúrt/ **(averts, averting, averted)** *vt.* **1.** **PREVENT STH FROM HAPPENING** to prevent sth from occurring, especially sth harmful **2.** **LOOK AWAY** to turn your eyes away from sth [14thC. Via Old French from Latin *avertere* 'to turn away', from *vertere* 'to turn' (see VERSE), evolving from 'to turn someone away'.] —**avertible** *adj.*

Avesta /ə véstə/ *n.* the sacred book of the Zoroastrian religion [Early 16thC. From Middle Persian *Avastāk*, literally 'original text'.]

Avestan /ə véstən/, **Avestic** /ə véstik/ *n.* an ancient language once spoken in various parts of the Middle East. It belongs to the Iranian group of languages. The sacred writings of the Zoroastrians are written in Avestan. [Mid-19thC. Formed from AVESTA.] —**Avestan** *adj.*

avg. *abbr.* average

avian /áyvi ən/ *adj.* belonging to, relating to, or characteristic of birds [Late 19thC. Formed from Latin *avis* 'bird' (source of English *augur* and *inaugurate*).]

aviary /áyvi əri/ (*plural* **-ies**) *n.* an enclosure or large cage where birds are kept [Late 16thC. From Latin *aviarium*, from *avis* (see AVIAN).]

aviate /áyvi ayt/ **(-ates, -ating, -ated)** *vi.* to pilot or fly in an aircraft (*formal*) [Late 19thC. Back-formation from AVIATION.]

aviation /áyvi áysh'n/ *n.* the design, manufacture, use, or operation of aircraft [Mid-19thC. From French, formed from Latin *avis* 'bird' (see AVIAN).]

aviation medicine *n.* the branch of medicine concerned with the physical and psychological effects of flying in aircraft

aviator /áyvi aytər/ *n.* the pilot of an aircraft

aviator glasses *npl. US* spectacles with oval tinted lenses and a metal frame

aviculture /áyvi kulchər, ávvi-/ *n.* the care and rearing of birds in cages, aviaries, or enclosures [Late 19thC. Coined from Latin *avis* 'bird' + CULTURE.] —**aviculturist** *n.*

avid /ávvid/ *adj.* eager for, dedicated to, or enthusiastic about sth [Mid-18thC. Back-formation from AVIDITY.] —**avidly** *adv.*

avidin /ávvidin/ *n.* a protein found in egg white that inactivates the vitamin biotin by binding with it but that loses its ability to bind when subjected to heat [Mid-20thC. Formed from AVID, because of its 'avidity' for BIOTIN.]

avidity /ə víddəti/ *n.* **1.** **EAGERNESS OR GREED** great eagerness or greed for sth **2.** CHEM = **affinity 3.** BIOL **STRENGTH OF ANTIGEN-ANTIBODY BINDING** a measure of the strength with which an antibody binds to an antigen [15thC. Via French from Latin *avidus*, from *avere* 'to desire' (source of English *avarice*).]

Aviemore /ávvi mawr/ village in northeastern Scotland. It is a holiday resort and winter skiing area. Population: 2,214 (1991).

avifauna /áyvi fáwnə, ávvi-/ (*plural* **avifaunas** *or* **avifaunae** /-fáwnee/) *n.* all the birds present in a region, environment, or period of time [Late 19thC. Coined from Latin *avis* 'bird' + FAUNA.] —**avifaunal** *adj.*

Avignon /ávvee nyoN/ capital of the Vaucluse Department in the Provence-Alpes-Côte d'Azur Region in southeastern France. Population: 89,440 (1990).

avionics /áyvi ónniks/ *n.* **TECHNOLOGY APPLIED TO AIRCRAFT AND SPACECRAFT** the development and use of electric and electronic equipment for aircraft and spacecraft (*takes a singular verb*) ■ *npl.* **PLANE OR SPACECRAFT TECHNOLOGICAL DEVICES** the electrical and electronic equipment of an aircraft or spacecraft (*takes a plural verb*) [Mid-20thC. A blend of AVIATION and ELECTRONICS.] —**avionic** *adj.*

avirulent /ay vírrŏŏlənt, -ryŏŏ-/ *adj.* used to describe microorganisms that are not likely to cause disease in another organism —**avirulence** *n.*

avitaminosis /áy víttəmin óssiss/ (*plural* **-ses** /-seez/) *n.* a disease caused by deficiency of a particular vitamin —**avitaminotic** /-nóttik/ *adj.*

Aviv /ə veev/ *n.* JUDAISM = **Nisan**

AVM (*plural* **AVMs**) *abbr.* Air Vice-Marshal

avn *abbr.* aviation

avo /ávvoo/ (*plural* **avos**) *n.* a subunit of currency in Macao. See table at **currency** [Early 20thC. From Portuguese, shortened from *oitavo* 'eighth', from Latin *octavus* (source of English *octave*), from *octo* 'eight'.]

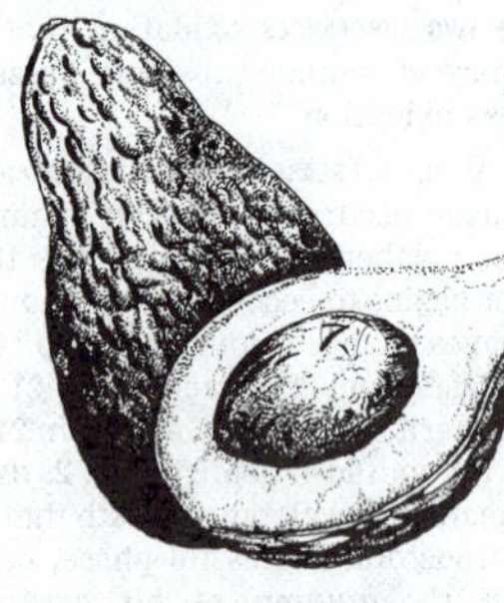

Avocado

avocado /ávvə kaádō/ *n.* (*plural* **-dos**) **1.** **avocado, avocado pear** **GREEN-FLESHED EDIBLE FRUIT** a fruit with a leathery dark green or blackish skin with a soft, smooth-tasting, pale green flesh and a large stony seed, eaten raw in salads or dips **2.** **TREE ON WHICH AVOCADOS GROW** a tropical tree that bears avocados. Latin name: *Persea americana*. **3.** **CREAMY GREEN** a dull creamy green colour, like that of the flesh of an avocado ■ *adj.* **OF CREAMY GREEN COLOUR** of a dull creamy green colour, like the flesh of an avocado [Mid-17thC. From Spanish, an alteration (influenced by *avocado* 'lawyer') of *aguacate*, from Nahuatl *ahuacatl*, literally 'testicle' (because of the shape of the fruit).]

avocation /ávvə káysh'n/ *n.* **1.** **OCCUPATION** a calling or occupation (*formal*) **2.** **HOBBY** a hobby or pastime (*formal*) **3.** **DISTRACTION** sth that distracts or diverts sb from what he or she is doing (*archaic*) [Early 17thC. From Latin, 'distraction', from, ultimately *vocare* 'to call' (see VOCATION).] —**avocational** *adj.* —**avocationally** *adv.*

avocet /ávvə set/ *n.* a shore bird with black and white plumage, long legs, and a long slender upward-curving beak. Genus: *Recurvirostra*. [Late 17thC. Via French *avocette* from Italian *avosetta*.]

Avogadro /ávvə gaá drō/, **Amedeo, Conte di Quaregna e Ceretto** (1776–1856) Italian physicist and chemist who formulated Avogadro's law. Full name **Lorenzo Romano Amedeo Carlo Avogadro**

Avogadro's law *n.* a principle in physics stating that equal volumes of different gases at the same temperature and pressure contain the same number of molecules [Late 19thC. Named after Amedeo AVOGADRO.]

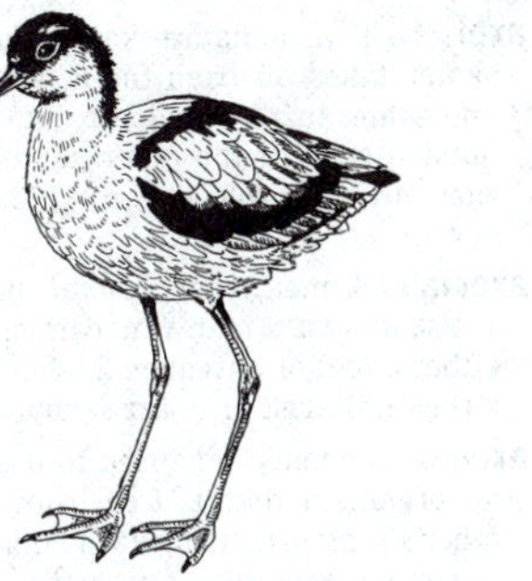

Avocet

Avogadro's number, **Avogadro's constant** *n.* the number of atoms or molecules, 6.023 x 10^{23}, contained in one mole of a substance. Symbol N_A [Late 19thC. Named after Amedeo AVOGADRO.]

avoid /ə vóyd/ (**avoids, avoiding, avoided**) *v.* **1.** *vt.* **NOT GO NEAR** to keep away from sb or sth ○ *a place to be avoided* **2.** *vti.* **NOT DO STH OR PREVENT STH** to manage not to do sth or to stop sth happening ○ *I narrowly avoided colliding with it.* **3.** *vt.* LAW **STATE STH IS NOT VALID** to say that sth is void or invalid [14thC. Via Anglo-Norman from, ultimately, Old French *vuide* 'empty' (see VOID).] —**avoidable** *adj.* —**avoidably** *adv.* —**avoider** *n.*

WORD KEY: USAGE

avoid, evade, or **elude**? All three words involve keeping away from sb or sth or keeping sb or sth away from you. The main difference between ***avoid*** and **evade** is that ***avoid*** is neutral in tone whereas **evade** implies dishonesty or deception, or at least some sort of ulterior motive. If you avoid a responsibility, you take measures to prevent it being necessary, whereas if you evade a responsibility you get out of it in an underhand or deceitful way when the necessity is still there. ***Avoid*** can be followed by a verbal noun in *-ing*, whereas **evade** must be followed by an ordinary noun: *We avoided having to pay. We evaded payment.* **Elude** implies clever or ingenious avoidance without it being devious or wrong. It also has the special meaning 'escape', as in *Her name eludes me.*

WORD KEY: SYNONYMS

See Synonyms at ***escape***.

avoidance /ə vóydənss/ *n.* **1.** **ACT OF KEEPING AWAY** the act of staying away from sb or sth **2.** **ACT OF NOT DOING STH** the act of refraining from doing sth or preventing sth from happening or applying **3.** LAW **ACT OF MAKING STH INVALID** the act of making sth void or invalid

WORD KEY: USAGE

avoidance or **evasion**? The difference corresponds to the difference between **avoid** and **evade**. In particular, ***tax avoidance*** means a legal method, whereas **tax evasion** means an illegal method, of reducing a liability to pay tax.

avoirdupois /ávv waar dyoo pwaá, ávvərdə poyz/ *n.* **1.** MEASURE = **avoirdupois weight 2. SB'S WEIGHT** the amount that sb weighs (*humorous*) [14thC. From Old French *aveir de peis*, literally 'goods of weight'. The word originally denoted merchandise sold by weight, hence the system used to weigh them.]

avoirdupois weight, **avoirdupois** *n.* a system for measuring weights based on the pound

Avon /ayvən/ **1.** former county (1974–98) in the west of England. The name is retained in postal addresses. **2.** river in central England, rising in Northamptonshire and flowing through Stratford to join the River Severn. Length: 154 km/96 mi. ■ **1.** river in southwestern England, rising in Gloucestershire and flowing through Bristol to the Bristol Channel. Length: 120 km/75 mi. **2.** river in southern England, rising in Wiltshire and flowing through Salisbury to the English Channel. Length: 96 km/60 mi.

avouch /ə vówch/ (**avouches, avouching, avouched**) *vt.* to acknowledge, guarantee, or confirm that sth is true (*archaic*) [15thC. Via Old French *avochier* from Latin *advocare* (see AVOW).]

avow /ə vów/ (**avows, avowing, avowed**) *vt.* to state or affirm that sth is a fact (*formal*) [13thC. Via Old French *avouer* 'to acknowledge' from Latin *advocare* 'to summon' (see ADVOCATE).] —**avowable** *adj.* —**avowably** *adv.* —**avowedly** /ə vówidli/ *adv.*

avowal /ə vów əl/ *n.* a frank statement or admission (*formal*)

avulsion /ə vúlsh'n/ *n.* **1.** MED **SEPARATION OF BODY PART** the tearing away or separation of part of the body, resulting from an accident or performed during surgery **2.** LAW **REMOVAL OF SOIL** the removal of soil from one person's land to another's, especially by a flood [Early 17thC. Directly or via French from the Latin stem *avulsion-*, from, ultimately, *vellere* 'to pull' (source of English *convulse* and *svelte*).]

avuncular /ə vúngkyŏŏlər/ *adj.* **1.** **LIKE AN UNCLE** resembling an uncle, especially one who is friendly, helpful, or good-humoured **2.** **OF AN UNCLE** relating to or deriving from an uncle (*formal or humorous*) [Mid-19thC. Formed from Latin *avunculus* 'maternal uncle', literally 'little uncle' (see UNCLE).] —**avuncularity** /ə vúngkyŏŏ lárrəti/ *n.* —**avuncularly** /ə vúngkyŏŏlərli/ *adv.*

avunculate /ə vúngkyŏŏlət/ *n.* in some patrilineal societies, a special relationship similar to that of father and son that exists between a man and his sister's sons —**avunculate** *adj.*

aw /aw/ *interj. US, Scotland* used to express surprise, disappointment, or pity (*informal*) [Mid-19thC. Natural exclamation.]

a.w. *abbr.* **1. a.w., A/W** MEASURE actual weight **2.** MEASURE, PHYS atomic weight **3.** NAUT all water

AWACS /áy waks/ *n.* a radar and computer system carried in an aircraft to track large numbers of low-flying aircraft [Acronym formed from *airborne warning and control system*]

await /ə wáyt/ (**awaits, awaiting, awaited**) *v.* **1.** *vti.* **WAIT FOR STH** to expect or be looking for sb or sth **2.** *vt.* **BE WAITING FOR SB** to be going to happen or be given to sb ○ *'Where we find a difficulty we may always expect that a discovery awaits us'.* (C. S. Lewis, *Reflections on the Psalms*; 1961) [13thC. Via Anglo-Norman *awaitier*, from, ultimately, Old French *guaitier*, from a prehistoric Germanic base that is also the ancestor of English *wake*.]

awake /ə wáyk/ *adj.* **1.** **NOT ASLEEP** fully conscious and not asleep **2.** **ALERT** alert and vigilant about what is going on all around ○ *'The colour had come back to his face, and his eyes were clear, and fully awake and aware'.* (J. R. R. Tolkien, *The Fellowship of the Ring*; 1954) **3.** **AWARE OF STH** fully aware of sth or alert to it ■ *vti.* (**awakes, awaking, awoke** /ə wṓk/ *or* **awaked, awoken** /ə wṓkən/ *or* **awaked**) **1.** **EMERGE FROM SLEEP** to rouse sb or be roused from sleep **2.** **BECOME OR MAKE SB AWARE** to become or make sb become alert to sth **3.** **AROUSE SB** to arouse yourself or sb else from a dazed or dreamlike state **4.** **AROUSE FEELINGS** to arouse feelings or memories [Old English *āwæcnan*, from two Old English verbs, *wacian* 'to be awake' and assumed *wacen* 'to wake up', both ancestors of English *wake*[1]]

WORD KEY: USAGE

awake or **awaken** or **wake** or **waken**? Although all four verbs are interchangeable in both the transitive and the intransitive meanings, in practice **awake** and **awaken** are preferred in figurative meanings: *At last we awoke to the dangers that faced us.* When used in literal meanings **awake** and **awaken** are normally used intransitively or in the passive: *He awoke at four in the morning. I was awoken by shouts in the street. Will you wake us at four?* **Wake** is the only one of these verbs that can be followed by *up*.

awaken /ə wáykən/ (**-ens, -ening, -ened**) *vti.* to wake up from a state of sleep or a state likened to sleep [Old English *āwæcnian*, from *wæcnan* 'to waken'] —**awakener** *n.*

awakening /ə wáykəning/ *adj.* **JUST BEGINNING** just beginning or growing ■ *n.* **1.** **AROUSAL FROM SLEEP** the act or process of waking from sleep **2.** **RENEWED ATTENTION TO STH** a revival or renewal of interest in sth, especially religion **3.** **SUDDEN AWARENESS** a sudden recognition or realization of sth

award /ə wáwrd/ *n.* **1.** **STH GIVEN FOR ACHIEVEMENT** sth, e.g. a prize, that is given in recognition of sb's merit or an achievement **2.** LAW **STH GRANTED BY LAW COURT** sth bestowed, granted, or assigned to sb by a court of law or by arbitration **3.** *ANZ* BUSINESS = **award wage** ■ *vt.* (**awards, awarding, awarded**) **1.** **GIVE STH FOR MERIT** to give sb sth in recognition of merit **2.** LAW **BESTOW AS RESULT OF COURT'S DECISION** to bestow or grant sth by a judicial decision or by arbitration [14thC. Via Anglo-Norman, 'to decide a legal case', from, ultimately, Old French *warder* 'to judge', from a prehistoric Germanic base that is also the ancestor of English *warden*.] —**awardable** *adj.* —**awarder** *n.*

awardee /ə wáwr deé/ *n.* sb who receives an award by a judicial decision or by arbitration

award wage, **award rate** *n. ANZ* a statutory minimum wage paid for a specified type of work, as set by an industrial court

aware /ə wáir/ *adj.* **1.** **KNOWING STH** having knowledge of sth because you have observed it or sb has told you about it ○ *We are already aware of the problem, and we are dealing with it.* **2.** **NOTICING OR REALIZING STH** mindful that sth exists because you notice it or realize that it is happening ○ *He became aware of a pain in his left side.* **3.** **KNOWLEDGEABLE** well-informed about what is going on in the world or about the latest developments in a particular sphere of activity ○ *More financially aware investors were starting to sell their stock.* [Old English *gewær*, literally 'very watchful', from *wær* 'watchful' (source of English *wary* and *beware*)] —**awareness** *n.*

WORD KEY: SYNONYMS

aware, conscious, mindful, cognizant, sensible

CORE MEANING: having knowledge of the existence of sth

aware the most wide-ranging term, indicating that sb knows sth either intellectually or intuitively; **conscious** having sth in the forefront of the mind, often in a slightly troubling way; **mindful** actively attentive, or deliberately keeping sth in mind; **cognizant** a formal term indicating that sb has a special knowledge about sth, sometimes because of having made a deliberate effort to find out; **sensible** a formal or literary term for *aware*.

awash /ə wósh/ *adj.* **1.** **COVERED IN WATER** covered in water or some other liquid **2.** **OVERSUPPLIED** having more of sth than is desirable or manageable ○ *an office awash with letters of complaint* **3.** SHIPPING **WITH WATER RUNNING OVER THE SIDES** sunk so low that water is able to come in over the sides of the vessel

away /ə wáy/ CORE MEANING: an adverb used to indicate that sth or sb moves so as to leave a particular place ○ *I really need to go away for a while.* ○ *The truck drove away leaving us stranded.* ○ *The cat has run away.*

1. *adv.* **UNINVOLVED** separated or far from sb or sth ○ *I try to stay away from trouble.* **2.** *adv.* **IN A DIFFERENT DIRECTION** in a different direction from the one sb was originally facing or looking in ○ *He turned his face away.* **3.** *adv.* **INTO THE DISTANCE** towards the distance ○ *olive groves stretching away towards the sea* **4.** *adv.* **IN THE FUTURE** at a particular time in the future (*follows a span of time*) ○ *Christmas is only a week away.* **5.** *adv.* **INTO STORAGE OR SAFEKEEPING** into the place where sth is normally stored, or into a safe place ○ *We put the cutlery away.* **6.** *adv.* **OFF STH** so as to remove or separate sth, or so as to be removed or separated (*follows a verb*) ○ *a tool to chip away the old paint* **7.** *adv.* **TO OR FROM SB** into or out of the possession of sb or sth (*follows the verb or object of the verb*) ○ *decided to give the old car away* **8.** *adv.* **UNTIL STH IS USED UP** so as to make sth disappear or be expended (*follows a verb and precedes the object*) **9.** *adv.* **GRADUALLY** gradually until it ceases or is no longer noticed ○ *The music gradually died away.* **10.** *adv.* **SO AS TO SHOW A CHANGE** so that a perceptible change from one thing to another occurs ○ *a shift away from heavier taxation* **11.** *adv.* **WITHOUT STOPPING** continuously and usually energetically over a period of time ○ *hammering away in the garage* **12.** *adv.* **SO AS TO SET OUT** so as to be on a journey ○ *hope to get away after breakfast* **13.** *adv., adj.* **IN ANOTHER PLACE** not in the particular place or the place where sb usually is, especially at home or at work ○ *I'll be away until Thursday.* ○ *She works away from the office.* **14.** *adv., adj.* **IN DISTANCE OR TIME** as measured in distance or time from here (*follows a measure or indication of distance or time*) ○ *He works about 10 minutes away.* ○ *The mountains are not far away.* **15.** *adv., adj.* SPORTS **ON OPPOSING TEAM'S FIELD OR TURF** played on an opponent's ground ○ *Their next three games will be played away.* ○ *Their away record has been very poor this season.* **16.** *adj.* GOLF **FURTHEST FROM THE HOLE** placed furthest from the hole in a game of golf [Old English *aweg*, from *on weg* 'on (your) way'. The meaning evolved from 'on' (as in 'move on') to 'from this (or that) place'.]

awe /aw/ *n.* **1. MIXTURE OF WONDER AND DREAD** a feeling of amazement and respect mixed with fear that is often coupled with a feeling of personal insignificance or powerlessness ○ *Filled with awe, they gazed at the ruins of the massive temple.* **2. ABILITY TO INSPIRE DREAD** the ability to inspire dread or reverence (*archaic*) ■ *vt.* (**awes, awing, awed**) **CAUSE AWE IN SB** to make sb feel awe (*usually passive*) ○ *The visiting ambassadors were awed by this display of military might.* [13thC. From Old Norse *agi*. Ultimately from an Indo-European word meaning 'to be afraid', which is also the source of English *ail*.]

aweary /ə wéeri/ *adj.* weary or tired (*archaic or literary*) ○ *'By my troth, Nerissa, my little body is aweary of this great world!'* (Shakespeare *The Merchant of Venice*)

aweather /ə wéthər/ *adv.* SAILING towards the windward side

aweigh /ə wáy/ *adj.* SAILING hanging clear of the bottom of a body of water ○ *Anchors aweigh!*

awe-inspiring *adj.* so impressive as to make a person feel humble or slightly afraid

awesome /áwsəm/ *adj.* **1. IMPRESSIVE AND FRIGHTENING** so impressive or overwhelming as to inspire a strong feeling of admiration or fear ○ *the awesome destructive power of a tornado* **2. EXCELLENT** used as a general term of enthusiastic approval (*slang*) ○ *The second track on this CD is totally awesome.* ○ *That's awesome skateboarding!* —**awesomely** *adv.* —**awesomeness** *n.*

awestruck /áw struk/, **awestricken** /-strikən/ *adj.* filled with a feeling of awe

awful /áwf'l/ *adj.* **1. EXTREMELY BAD** very bad or unpleasant ○ *an awful smell* **2. CAUSING SHOCK OR SADNESS** extremely shocking, saddening, or unpleasant ○ *an awful accident* **3. NOT VERY WELL** in very poor health ○ *I feel awful this morning.* **4. VERY GREAT** enormous in size, amount, number, or extent (*informal*) ○ *We spent an awful lot of money on furniture.* **5. AWE-INSPIRING** so impressive as to inspire awe (*literary*) ■ *adv.* **EXTREMELY** to an extreme degree or extent (*informal*) ○ *It's awful hot this morning.* [13thC. The original meaning was 'awe-inspiring'.] —**awfulness** *n.*

WORD KEY: USAGE

The weather has been **awful**. The most common use of ***awful*** in current English has nothing to do with inspiring awe but has the generalized meaning 'bad, poor', as in the example given and in certain common phrases, for example *an awful shame* and *an awful cheat*, in which ***awful*** is reduced further in meaning and draws all its meaning from the word it accompanies (here, *shame* and *cheat*). This use of ***awful*** is deep-rooted in idiomatic English and is normally unexceptionable, but it is often better to avoid it in more formal contexts.

awfully /áwfli, -fəli/ *adv.* **1. VERY** to an extremely great degree ○ *I'm awfully grateful to you for helping me out.* **2. BADLY OR UNPLEASANTLY** in a very bad or unpleasant way ○ *treated them awfully*

awhile /ə wíl/ *adv.* for a short time (*literary*)

WORD KEY: USAGE

awhile or a while? Both expressions are derived from the word **while**, but they have a different role in the sentence. ***Awhile*** is an adverb (*Let us wait awhile*), whereas **a while** written as two words is a noun phrase (and is normally preceded by *for*): *I'm going to be away for a while.* Sometimes, however, the word *for* is left out, making **a while** look more like an adverbial phrase, although it is still strictly a noun phrase: *We had to wait quite a while.* This use is fairly easy to identify because **while** is qualified in some way, for example *quite a while* or *a long while*.

awhirl /ə wúrl/ *adj.* **1. IN A DIZZY STATE** in a dizzy state of excitement or confusion ○ *Her mind was awhirl with new ideas.* **2. AROUND AND AROUND** moving round and round (*literary*) ○ *red and golden leaves awhirl in the autumn breeze*

awkward /áwkwərd/ *adj.* **1. EMBARRASSING** embarrassing and requiring great tact or skill to resolve ○ *I find myself in an awkward situation.* **2. DIFFICULT OR UNCOMFORTABLE TO USE** difficult to use because you have to move your body into an uncomfortable position **3. PERFORMED GRACELESSLY** performed in a way that lacks grace and looks uncomfortable **4. WITHOUT GRACEFUL COORDINATION** lacking physical coordination and grace ○ *an awkward, gangling adolescent* **5. SHYLY UNCOMFORTABLE** shy, uncomfortable, and embarrassed ○ *He was always awkward around kids.* **6. UNCOOPERATIVE** showing no willingness to cooperate or be reasonable ○ *I think she's being deliberately awkward.* [Mid-16thC. Formed from obsolete *awke* 'turned the wrong way' (from Old Norse *afugr* 'turned backwards') + -WARD.] —**awkwardly** *adv.* —**awkwardness** *n.*

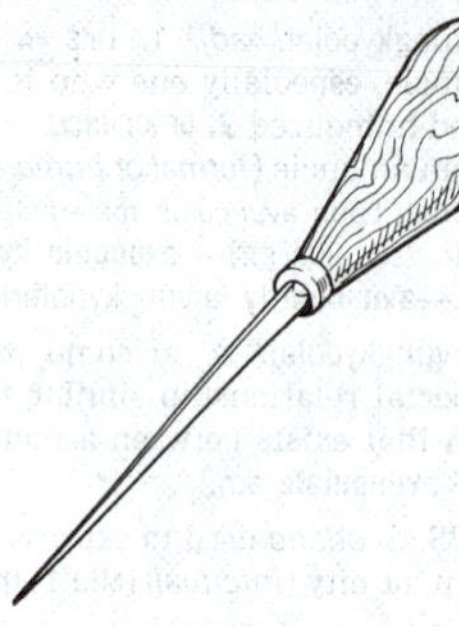

Awl

awl /awl/ *n.* a tool consisting of a handle and a slim metal shaft with a sharp point, used for boring small holes in leather or wood [Old English *æl*, of uncertain origin: perhaps from a non-Indo-European language in Anatolia (Asia Minor)]

awn /awn/ *n.* a stiff bristle projecting from the tip of a plant organ, e.g. from the sheath surrounding a cereal or grass seed [12thC. From the Old Norse stem *agn-* 'chaff'.] —**awned** *adj.* —**awnless** *adj.*

awning /áwning/ *n.* a plastic, canvas, or metal roof supported by a frame and often foldable, that is placed over a shopfront, doorway, window, or side of a caravan [Early 17thC. Origin uncertain.]

awoke past tense of **awake**

awoken past participle of **awake**

AWOL /áy wol/ *adj.* absent from a post, especially a military post, without official permission [From *a(bsent) w(ith)o(ut) l(eave)*]

Awolowo /ə wólləwə/, **Obafemi** (1909–87) Nigerian Yoruba chief and political leader. He became leader of the opposition in the federal parliament (1960–62) and was imprisoned until the coup of 1966.

awry /ə rí/ *adj.* **1. CROOKED** not in the proper position but turned or twisted to one side ○ *The cushions were awry and there was mud on the carpet.* **2. AMISS** not in keeping with plans or expectations ○ *Our plans have gone awry.* [14thC. From the phrase *on wry*, literally 'in a twist'.]

ax *n.*, *vt.* US = **axe**

ax. *abbr.* axiom

axe *n.* **1. TOOL FOR CUTTING** a tool consisting of a flat heavy metal head with a sharpened edge attached to a long handle, used to chop wood or fell trees **2. JOB LOSS** dismissal from a job (*slang*) ○ *Her secretary got the axe yesterday.* **3. IMMEDIATE CLOSURE** the immediate closure of an institution or the sudden discontinuation of a project or funding (*slang*) ○ *schemes facing the axe* **4.** MUSIC **MUSICAL INSTRUMENT** a musical instrument, specifically a rock guitar or a jazz saxophone (*slang*) ■ *vt.* (**axes, axing, axed**) **1. TERMINATE STH** to end sth, e.g. a job, a service, or a television programme usually without prior warning or discussion (*informal*) (*usually passive*) ○ *In July, the show was axed.* **2. FIRE SB** to dismiss sb from a job, especially abruptly (*informal*) **3. REDUCE STH DRASTICALLY** to cut sth, e.g. expenditures or services, drastically ○ *Most of the welfare provisions were axed from the budget.* [Old English *æcs*. Ultimately from an Indo-European word denoting a cutting or hewing tool.] ◇ **have an axe to grind** to be motivated by some personal consideration, usually a negative one ○ *It was clear from their hostile questioning that certain reporters had an axe to grind on this issue.*

axel /áks'l/ *n.* a figure-skating jump in which the skater takes off from the forward outside edge of one skate, turns in midair, and lands on the rear outside edge of the other skate [Mid-20thC. Named after *Axel* Rudolph Paulser (1885–1938), Norwegian skater.]

axeman /áksmən, -man/ (*plural* **-men** /-mən, -men/) *n.* **1. MAN WITH AXE** a man who carries or uses an axe as either a tool or a weapon **2.** MUSIC **ROCK OR JAZZ MUSICIAN** a rock guitarist or a jazz saxophone player (*slang*)

axenic /ay zéenik/ *adj.* used to describe a culture of an organism that is free from contamination by other living organisms [Mid-20thC. Coined from Greek *a-* 'not' + *xenikos* 'alien, strange'.]

axes plural of **axis**[1]

axial /áksi əl/ *adj.* **1.** GEOM **OF AXIS** relating to or forming an axis **2.** CRYSTALS **LOCATED ALONG PLANE OF AXIS** located on or in the plane of an axis of a crystal **3.** ANAT **OF AXIS OF ORGANISM** located in or relating to the axis of an organism —**axially** *adv.*

axial skeleton *n.* the bones that make up the vertebral column and skull

axil /áksil/ *n.* the space between a leaf or branch and the stem to which it is attached [Late 18thC. From Latin *axilla* (see AXILLA).]

axile /áksil, -sīl/ *adj.* used to describe a plant structure that grows along an axis

axilla /ak síllə/ (*plural* **-lae** /-síllee/) *n.* **1.** ANAT = **armpit** (*technical*) **2.** ZOOL **HOLLOW UNDER BIRD'S WING** the hollow underneath the wing of a bird [Early 17thC. From Latin, literally 'little wing', from *ala* 'wing, upper arm'.]

axillar /ak síllər/ *n.* ZOOL a feather growing from the hollow (**axilla**) under a bird's wing

axillary /ak sílləri/ *adj.* **1.** ANAT **OF ARMPIT** relating to or near the armpit **2.** BOT **BETWEEN LEAF OR BRANCH AND STEM** relating to or growing in the space (**axil**) between a leaf or branch and the stem ■ *n.* (*plural* **-ies**) ZOOL = **axillar**

axinite /áksi nīt/ *n.* a brilliant brown mineral consisting of wedge-shaped crystals of calcium and aluminium borosilicate with some iron and manganese [Early 19thC. Coined from Greek *axinē* 'axe' + -ITE.]

axiology /áksi óllәji/ *n.* the study of the nature, types, and governing criteria of values and value judgments [Early 20thC. From French *axiologie*, from Greek *axia* 'value' (see AXIOM).] —**axiological** /áksi ə lójjik'l/ *adj.* —**axiologically**/-lójjikli/ *adv.* —**axiologist** /-ólləjist/ *n.*

axiom /áksi əm/ *n.* **1. GENERALLY ACCEPTED TRUTH** a statement or idea that people accept as self-evidently true **2.** MATH, LOGIC **BASIC PROPOSITION ASSUMED TO BE TRUE** a basic proposition of a system that, although unproven, is used to prove the other propositions in the system [15thC. Directly or via French from Latin *axioma*, from Greek *axiōma*, literally 'sth worthy', from, ultimately, *axios* 'weighty, worthy'.]

axiomatic /áksi ə máttik/ *adj.* **1. SELF-EVIDENT** self-evidently true, or universally accepted as being true **2.** MATH, LOGIC **BASED ON AXIOMS** consisting of or based on axioms [Late 18thC. From Greek *axiōmatikos*, from the stem of *axiōma* (see AXIOM).]

axis[1] /áksiss/ (*plural* **-es** /ák seez/) *n.* **1.** SCI **LINE AROUND WHICH OBJECT ROTATES** an imaginary straight line around which an object, such as the earth, rotates **2.** GEOM **LINE AROUND WHICH SHAPE IS SYMMETRICAL** a straight line around which a geometric figure or three-dimensional object is symmetrical **3.** GEOM one of two or more lines on which coordinates are measured. Often on a graph two axes form its left and lower margins. **4. ALLIANCE** an alliance or association between two or more people, organizations, or countries that is thought of as forming a centre of power or influence ○ *the Paris-Bonn axis* **5.** AIR **LINE DEFINING DIRECTION OF AIRCRAFT** any one of the three mutually perpendicular lines in an aircraft that define its orientation **6.** ANAT **SECOND VERTEBRA IN NECK** the second vertebra in the neck, which acts as the pivot on which the head and first vertebra turn **7.** BOT **CENTRAL PART OF PLANT** the main part of a plant, usually the stem and the root, from which all subsidiary parts develop **8.** OPTICS **LINE PERPENDICULAR TO LENS OR MIRROR** the axis of symmetry of an optical system, especially a line perpendicular to the surface of a lens or mirror

9. GEOL LINE AT MAXIMUM CURVATURE an imaginary line along the crest of an anticline or the trough of a syncline at the point of maximum curvature **10.** CRYSTALS LINE PASSING THROUGH CRYSTAL an imaginary line, one of three or four that pass through the centre of a crystal and are used to define its symmetry and the arrangement of its atoms [14thC. From Latin, 'axle, pivot'. Ultimately from an Indo-European word meaning 'axis', which is also the ancestor of English *axle*.]

axis² *n.* = **axis deer** [Early 17thC. From Latin *axis*, an unidentified wild animal in India, of unknown origin.]

Axis *n.* the military and political alliance of Germany, Italy, and, later, Japan that fought the Allies in World War II [Mid-20thC. From Mussolini's idea of 'an axis round which all European states animated by the will to collaboration and peace can also assemble'.]

axis deer (*plural* **axis deer**), **axis** *n.* a deer with a reddish-brown, white-spotted coat that lives in India and central Asia. Latin name: *Axis axis*.

axisymmetric /áksi si méttrik/, **axisymmetrical** /-méttrik'l/ *adj.* symmetrical with respect to an axis —**axisymmetrically** *adv.*

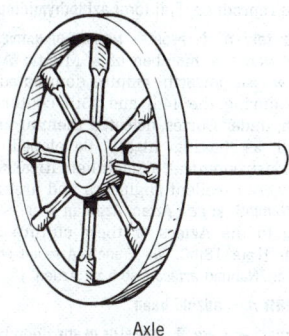

Axle

axle /áks'l/ *n.* **1.** SHAFT ON WHICH WHEEL TURNS a shaft on which a wheel or set of wheels revolves, especially a shaft under the body of a vehicle that connects a pair of wheels **2.** SPINDLE ON WHICH WHEEL TURNS the spindle on which one or more wheels revolve [Late 16thC. Shortening of AXLETREE.]

axletree /áks'l tree/ *n.* a shaft that runs underneath the body of a vehicle such as a cart or carriage and connects a pair of wheels [13thC. From Old Norse *öxultré*, from *öxull* 'axle' + *tré* 'tree, beam'.]

Axminster /áksminstər/ *n.* a high-quality carpet with a cut pile that is usually woven into a colourful pattern [Early 19thC. Named after *Axminster*, a town in Devon, southwestern England, where they were originally made.]

axolemma /áksə lémmə/ *n.* the membranous sheath that encloses the long thin extension of a nerve cell (**axon**) [Late 19thC. Coined from Greek *axōn* 'axis' + *lemma* 'skin, husk'.]

Axolotl

axolotl /áksə lott'l/ (*plural* **-lotls** *or* **-lotl**) *n.* an aquatic salamander native to Mexico and the western United States that often retains its external gills as an adult. Genus: *Ambystoma*. [Late 18thC. From Nahuatl, from *atl* 'water' + *xolotl* 'servant'.]

axon /ák son/, **axone** /áksōn/ *n.* an extension of a nerve cell, similar in shape to a thread, that transmits impulses outwards from the cell body [Late 19thC. From Greek *axōn* 'axis'.]

axoneme /áksə neem/ *n.* BIOL a bundle of fibrils that form the central core of a cilium or flagellum. It consists of nine pairs of microtubules surrounding a central pair. [Early 20thC. Coined from Greek *axōn* 'axis' + *nēma* 'thread'.]

axonometric /áksōnō méttrik/ *adj.* used to describe a method of drawing a three-dimensional object so that the vertical and horizontal axes are drawn to scale but the curves and diagonals appear distorted

axoplasm /áksə plazəm/ *n.* the cytoplasm of a nerve cell extension (**axon**) —**axoplasmic** /áksə plázmik/ *adj.*

ay¹ *interj., n.* = **aye¹**

ay² *adv.* = **aye²**

Ayacucho /íə koóchō/ city in southern Peru. It is an important centre for agriculture and manufacturing. Population: 114,809 (1993). Former name **Huamanga** (until 1825)

ayah /í yə/ *n.* S Asia a maid whose duties include the care of children [Late 18thC. Via Portuguese *aia* 'female tutor' from Latin *avia* 'grandmother'.]

ayatollah /í ə tóllə/ *n.* a Shiite religious leader in Iran, often one who takes an important political as well as religious role [Mid-20thC. Via Persian from Arabic *'āyatu-llāh* 'miraculous sign of God', from *'āya* 'sign, miracle' + *allāh* 'God'.]

Ayckbourn /áyk bawrn/, **Alan** (*b.* 1939) British dramatist. His plays include *Relatively Speaking* (1967), *Absurd Person Singular* (1973), and *The Norman Conquests* (1974).

aye¹ /ī/, **ay** /ay/ *interj.* YES used to say yes (*regional*) ■ *n.* (*plural* **ayes**) VOTE OR VOTER IN FAVOUR a vote in favour of a motion, or sb who casts a vote in favour [Late 16thC. Origin uncertain: perhaps from the pronoun I (at first it was always written as I), or perhaps from AYE².]

aye² /ī/, **ay** *adv.* always or forever (*archaic or regional*) [13thC. From Old Norse *ei, ey*; probably related to English *ever*.]

Aye-aye

aye-aye /í ī/ *n.* a small nocturnal primate that lives in trees and is found in Madagascar, and has a long bushy tail, long bony fingers, and teeth resembling those of a rodent. Latin name: *Daubentonia madagascariensis*. [Late 18thC. Via French from Malagasy *aiay*; probably an imitation of its cry.]

Ayer /air/, **A.J., Sir** (1910–89) British philosopher. He was a logical positivist whose works include *Language, Truth, and Logic* (1936). Full name **Alfred Jules Ayer**

Ayers Rock /áirz rók/ former name for **Uluru**

ayin /áa yin/ *n.* the 16th letter of the Hebrew alphabet, written as an apostrophe and pronounced approximately like an 'o'. See table at **alphabet** [Early 19thC. From Hebrew *'ayin*, literally 'eye'.]

Aylesbury /áylzbəri/ historic town in Buckinghamshire, England. Population: 58,058 (1991).

Aylesbury Vale local government district in central Buckinghamshire, England. Population: 153,600 (1995).

Aymara /ímə raá/ (*plural* **-ra** *or* **-ras**) *n.* **1.** PEOPLES MEMBER OF NATIVE AMERICAN PEOPLE a member of a South American people who live around Lake Titicaca in Bolivia and Peru. The great ruins at Tiahuanaco are believed to have been built by the Aymara around AD 500. **2.** LANG S AMERICAN LANGUAGE a language of Bolivia and Peru, related to or strongly influenced by

Quechua. About two million people speak Aymara. [Mid-19thC. From Bolivian Spanish.] —**Aymaran** /íma raán/ *adj.*

Aymé /e máy/, **Marcel** (1902–67) French writer. He satirized contemporary corruption in novels, stories, and plays.

Ayr /air/ historic city in the district of South Ayrshire, Scotland. Population: 47,962 (1991).

Ayrshire /áirshər/ formerly, until 1953, a county of southwestern Scotland, now divided into North Ayrshire, East Ayrshire, and South Ayrshire

ayu /aá yoo/ (*plural* **ayus** *or* **ayu**) *n.* a marine salmon of Japan that migrates up rivers to spawn and is a valuable food fish. Latin name: *Plecoglossus altivelis*. [From Japanese]

Ayub Khan /aí yoob kaán/, **Muhammad** (1907–74) Pakistani soldier and politician. He became president of Pakistan (1958–69) but resigned after an unsuccessful war with India and charges of corruption.

Ayurveda /áa yoor vaydə, -veedə/ *n.* an ancient Hindu treatise on the art of healing and prolonging life [Early 20thC. From Sanskrit *āyur-veda* 'medicine', literally 'science of life', from *āyur-* 'life, vital power' + *veda* 'knowledge'.] —**Ayurvedic** *adj.*

Ayurvedic medicine *n.* an ancient Indian system of healing that assesses an individual's constitution and lifestyle, and recommends treatment based on herbal preparations, diet, yoga, and detoxification

AZ *abbr.* Arizona

az. *abbr.* **1.** ASTRON azimuth **2.** HERALDRY azure

Azalea

azalea /ə záyli əl/ (*plural* **-eas** *or* **-ea**) *n.* a flowering shrub that is widely grown for its large pink, purple, white, or yellow flowers. Some azaleas lose their leaves, while the small varieties of Japanese origin are evergreen. Genus: *Rhododendron*. [Mid-18thC. Via modern Latin from Greek, from *azaleos* 'dry' (related to English *ardent*, *arid*, and *ash*). From the dry soil in which it flourishes, or from its dry brittle wood.]

azan /aa zaán/ *n.* the Islamic call to prayer that the muezzin repeats five times a day from the minaret of a mosque [Mid-19thC. From Arabic *aḏān* 'announcement'.]

Azania /ə záyni əl/ *n.* S African a name for South Africa used by resistance movements in the apartheid era

Azapo /ə záppō/ *n.* a Socialist political movement in South Africa [Late 20thC. Acronym formed from *Azanian People's Organization*.]

azathioprine /ázzə thí ō preen/ *n.* a synthetic drug that suppresses the body's immune responses and is widely used during and after transplant surgery to prevent rejection of the transplanted organ [Mid-20thC. Coined from AZA- + THI- + PURINE.]

azeotrope /ə zeé ə trōp/ *n.* a mixture of liquids that has a different boiling point from any of its components and retains its composition when it is a vapour [Early 20thC. Coined from A- 'not' + Greek *zeo-*, the combining form of *zein* 'to boil' (source of English *eczema*)+ Greek *-tropos* 'turning, changing'.] —**azeotropic** /áyzi ə tróppik/ *adj.* —**azeotropy** /-óttrəpi/ *n.*

Azerbaijan

Azerbaijan /ázzər bī jaán/ country of southwestern Asia bisected by Armenia. It is surrounded by the Caspian Sea, Russia, Georgia, and Iran. Language: Azeri. Currency: manat. Capital: Baku. Population: 7,797,476 (1997). Area: 86,600 sq. km/33,436 sq. mi. — **Azerbaijani** /ázzər bī jaáni/ *n., adj.*

Azeri /ə záiri/ *n., adj.* LANG the official language of independent Azerbaijan, also spoken in the province of Azerbaijan in northwestern Iran. A Turkic language from the Altaic family, it is spoken by about 14 million people.

azerty /ə zúrti/, **AZERTY** *adj.* using the commonest type of computer or typewriter keyboard layout in continental Europe, where the top row of letters, beginning from the left, runs A, Z, E, R, T, Y. ◊ **qwerty**

azide /áy zīd/ *n.* any chemical compound containing a group of three adjacent nitrogen atoms. Formula: N_3. [Early 20thC. Coined from AZO- + -IDE.]

azidothymidine /ə zíddō thímə deen/ *n.* full form of **AZT**

Azikiwe /áə zee keé way/, **Nnamdi** (1904–96) Nigerian statesman. He became Nigeria's first president (1963) and was overthrown by a military coup (1966).

Azilian /ə zílli ən/ *n.* a prehistoric culture that existed in Spain and southwestern France from around 10,000 to 8,000 BC. The distinctive artefacts produced by this culture include flat bone harpoons and painted pebbles. [Late 19thC. Named after Mas d' *Azil* in the French Pyrenees, where a cave containing bone and flint implements was found.]

azimuth /ázziməth/ *n.* **1.** ASTRON EASTWARD ANGLE TO OBJECT FROM NORTH the angle measured from north, eastwards along the horizon to the point where a vertical circle through a celestial object intersects the horizon **2.** NAVIG HORIZONTAL ANGLE OF BEARING the angular distance along the horizon between a point of reference,

usually the observer's bearing, and another object [Early 17thC. Via French *azimut* from Arabic *as-samūt*, plural of *as-samt*, literally 'the way', from *samt* 'way, direction' (see ZENITH).] —**azimuthal** /ázzi múth'l/ *adj.* — **azimuthally** /-múth'li/ *adv.*

azimuthal equidistant projection *n.* a method of map projection in which a straight line from the centre to any given point represents the shortest distance to that point and can be measured to scale

azine /áyzin/ *n.* an organic chemical compound with a six-sided ring structure containing one or more atoms of nitrogen [Late 19thC. Coined from AZO- + -INE.]

azo /áyzō, ázzō/ *adj.* relating to or containing two adjacent nitrogen atoms. Formula: -N=N-. ◊ **diazo** [Late 19thC. From AZO-.]

azo- *prefix.* containing a nitrogen group ○ *azole* [From French *azote* 'nitrogen', from Greek *a-* 'not' + *zōē* 'life', so called because living creatures cannot breathe it]

azobenzene /áyzō bén zeen/ *n.* a yellow or orange crystalline solid that is used mainly for making dyes. Formula: $C_6H_5N=NC_6H_5$.

azo compound *n.* any compound containing two adjacent nitrogen atoms attached to aromatic groups

azo dye *n.* an artificial dye containing an azo group. Azo dyes, usually orange, yellow, or brown, are derived from amines.

azoic /ə zō ik/ *adj.* **1.** GEOL, PALAEONT BEFORE THERE WAS LIFE ON EARTH belonging to a geological period before the appearance of living organisms on Earth **2.** GEOL WITHOUT ANY LIFE without any trace of life or organic remains [Mid-19thC. Formed from Greek *azōos*, literally 'without life', from *zōē* 'life'.]

azole /áyzōl, ə zṓl/ *n.* an organic chemical compound with a ring structure comprising five linked atoms, of which at least one is nitrogen [Late 19thC. Coined from AZO- + -OLE.]

azonal /ay zṓn'l/ *adj.* **1.** WITH NO ZONES not divided into zones **2.** NOT RESTRICTED TO AN AREA not restricted to a specific zone or geographical area

azonal soil *n.* a soil with characteristics that are not determined by the climate and vegetation of the area in which it is found, e.g. glacial or volcanic soil

azonic /ay zṓnik/ *adj.* = **azonal** *adj.* 2

azoospermia /ay zṓ ə spúrmi ə/ *n.* = **aspermia**

Azores /ə záwrz/ archipelago in the North Atlantic Ocean, west of Portugal, of which it is an autonomous region. There are nine main islands. Capital: Ponta Delgada. Population: 239,900 (1992). Area: 2,247 sq. km/868 sq. mi.

Azorín /ázzə reén/ (1873–1967) Spanish writer. A member of a group of writers that rejected traditional literary forms, he wrote the novel *Don Juan* (1922). Real name **José Martínez Ruiz**

azotaemia /ázzə teémi ə/ *n.* = **uraemia** [Early 20thC. Coined from obsolete *azote* 'nitrogen' (see AZO-) + -EMIA.] — **azotaemic** *adj.*

azotic /ay zóttik/ *adj.* relating to or containing nitrogen [Late 18thC. Formed from obsolete *azote* 'nitrogen' (see AZO-).]

azotobacter /ə zṓtō baktər/ *n.* a rod-shaped or spherical bacterium found in soil and water that fixes atmospheric nitrogen. Family: Azotobacter. [Early 20thC. From modern Latin, family name, coined from French *azote* 'nitrogen' (see AZO-) + *bacterium*.]

Azov, Sea of /ázzov, áy zov/ shallow inland sea in southern Russia, linked with the Black Sea by the Kerchenskiy Strait. Area: 37,555 sq. km/14,500 sq. mi.

AZT *n.* an antiviral drug used in the treatment of Aids. It works by inhibiting the enzyme reverse transcriptase, which the Aids virus requires in order to reproduce. Full form **azidothymidine**

Aztec /áz tek/ *n.* **1.** PEOPLES MEMBER OF NATIVE AMERICAN PEOPLES OF MEXICO a member of a Middle American people whose powerful empire dominated central Mexico during the 14th and 15th centuries. The Spanish, under Cortés, defeated them around 1520. As well as having highly developed artistic, musical, astronomical, and mathematical skills, the Aztecs were excellent engineers and architects. **2.** LANG = **Nahuatl** ■ *adj.* **Aztec, Aztecan** PEOPLES OF AZTECS relating to the Aztecs or their culture and civilisation [Late 18thC. Via French *Aztèque* or Spanish *Azteca* from Nahuatl *aztecatl* 'sb from Aztlan'.]

azuki bean *n.* = **adzuki bean**

azure /ázhər, áy-/ *adj.* **1.** DEEP BLUE IN HUE deep blue, like the colour of a clear sky on a warm day (*literary*) ○ *the azure depths of the ocean* **2.** HERALDRY BLUE coloured blue on a coat of arms ■ *n.* (*literary*) **1.** BLUE SKY a clear blue sky **2.** DEEP BLUE HUE a deep blue colour, like that of a clear sky in a warm country ○ *the azure of her eyes* [13thC. Via Old French *azur* from medieval Latin *azzurum*, from Arabic *al-lāzaward*, literally 'the lapis lazuli', from Persian *lāžward* 'lapis lazuli' (source of 'lazuli' in English *lapis lazuli*).]

azurite /ázhōō rīt/ *n.* a deep blue mineral consisting of a hydrated carbonate of copper. It is a source of copper, and some forms are used as gemstones.

azygous /ázzigəss/ *adj.* occurring as a single muscle or vein rather than as a pair [Mid-17thC. Formed from Greek *azugos*, literally 'without yoke', from *zugon* 'yoke' (see ZYGOTE).]

Bb

b[1] /bee/ (*plural* **b's** /beez/), **B** (*plural* **B's** *or* **Bs**) *n.* **1. 2ND LETTER IN ENGLISH ALPHABET** the second letter and first consonant in the alphabet in modern English, and in other languages that also use the Latin alphabet **2. SOUND OF 'B'** the speech sound represented by the letter 'b' **3. LETTER 'B' WRITTEN** a written representation of the letter 'b'

b[2] *abbr.* PHYS **1.** barn **2.** b, B bel

B[1] *n.* **1.** MUSIC **7TH NOTE OF SCALE IN C** the seventh note of a scale in C major **2.** MUSIC **STH THAT PRODUCES A B** a string, key, or pipe tuned to produce the note B **3.** MUSIC **SCALE BEGINNING ON B** a scale or key that starts on the note B **4.** MUSIC **WRITTEN SYMBOL OF B** a graphic representation of the note B **5.** EDUC **SECOND HIGHEST GRADE** the second highest grade in a series, e.g. an above-average grade for academic work **6.** ANAT **BLOOD TYPE** a type of human blood in the ABO group

B[2] *symbol.* **1.** boron **2.** black (*used on pencils to indicate that the lead is soft*) **3.** TRANSP a secondary road **4.** eleven (*used in hexadecimal notation*) **5.** PHYS magnetic flux density **6.** CHESS the second row from the left on a chessboard **7.** PHYS baryon number

B[3] *abbr.* **1.** bachelor (*used in degree titles*) **2.** MEASURE Baumé scale **3.** bishop

b. *abbr.* **1.** b., B. MUSIC bass[1] **2.** b., B. MUSIC basso **3.** billion **4.** b., B. book **5.** born **6.** CRICKET bowled **7.** b., B. breadth **8.** CRICKET bye

B. *abbr.* **1.** GEOG Bay (*used on maps*) **2.** MUSIC basso **3.** Bible **4.** B. billion

Ba *symbol.* barium

BA *abbr.* **1.** EDUC Bachelor of Arts **2.** British Academy **3.** British Airways **4.** British Association (for the Advancement of Science)

baa /baa/ *vi.* (**baas, baaing, baaed**) BLEAT LIKE SHEEP to make the long wavering cry characteristic of a sheep or lamb ■ *n.* (*plural* **baas**) **1.** CRY OF SHEEP the long wavering cry characteristic of a sheep or lamb **2.** N England, Ireland CHILD a child, especially a youngest child (*informal*) ○ *Where's the baa? Is he sleeping?* [Early 16thC. An imitation of the sound.]

BAA, B.A.A. *abbr.* Bachelor of Applied Arts

Baal /baal, báyəl/ (*plural* **-alim** /baálim, báyəlim/ *or* **-als**) *n.* **1.** ANCIENT SEMITIC GOD any of the fertility or nature gods worshipped by the Canaanites and the Phoenicians, and considered false idols by the ancient Hebrews **2.** Baal, baal FALSE GOD an idol or false god

Baalbek /báal bek/ town in eastern Lebanon between the Litani and Asi rivers. It is the site of the ancient ruins of Heliopolis. Population: 15,600 (1995).

baal teshuvah (*plural* **baalei teshuvah**), **baal tshuva** (*plural* **baalei tshuva**) *n.* sb who returns to Orthodox Jewish practice after having previously abandoned it [From Hebrew, literally 'master of return']

baas /baass/ *n.* S Africa a form of address used mainly under apartheid by Africans and Coloureds to show respect when addressing a European male, especially an employer [Late 18thC. Via Afrikaans, from Dutch, literally 'master' (source of English boss).]

baaskap /báass kap/ *n.* S Africa the principle of the supremacy of whites over non-whites or the system that ensured it, which prevailed in South Africa under Nationalist rule until the elections in 1994 [Mid-20thC. Via Afrikaans, 'domination, mastership', from Dutch baasschap, from baas 'master'.]

Bab /baab/ *n.* the title of a Persian religious leader, Mirza Ali Muhammad (1819–50), who founded Babism and was executed as a heretic to Islam [Mid-19thC. Via Persian, from Arabic *bāb* 'intermediary', literally 'gate'.]

baba /baá baa, -bə/ (*plural* **-bas**) *n.* a dessert made of leavened dough soaked in a rum-flavoured syrup and baked in a tin [Early 19thC. Via French, from Polish, literally 'married (peasant) woman, old woman'.]

Babangida /bə báng geedə/, **Ibrahim** (*b.* 1941) Nigerian soldier and politician. He was president of Nigeria from 1985 to 1993.

babassu /baá bə soó/ (*plural* **-sus** *or* **-su**) *n.* a tall Brazilian palm tree that produces nuts whose oil is used in the manufacture of soap, margarine, cosmetics, and cooking oil. Genus: *Orbignya.* [Early 20thC. From Brazilian Portuguese babaçu, from Tupi ybá 'fruit' + guasu 'large'.]

Babbage /bábbij/, **Charles** (1792–1871) British mathematician and inventor. He designed and attempted to build mechanical calculating machines now regarded as forerunners of the computer.

babbitt /bábbit/ *n.* BEARING a bearing made of babbitt metal ■ *vt.* (**-bitts, -bitting, -bitted**) COVER SURFACE WITH BABBITT METAL to cover or line a surface with babbitt metal or a similar alloy [Late 19thC. Named after Isaac Babbitt (1799–1862), US inventor of the alloy.]

Babbitt /bábbit/ *n.* US a self-satisfied narrow-minded man who cannot see beyond his own business and social interests ○ *'His name was … Babbitt, and … he was nimble in the calling of selling houses for more than people could afford to pay'* (Sinclair Lewis, Babbitt; 1922) [Early 20thC. Named after George F. Babbitt, the main character in the satirical novel *Babbitt* (1922) by Sinclair Lewis.] —**Babbittry** *n.*

Babbitt /bábbit/, **Milton** (*b.* 1916) US composer. He was a leader in the development of serialism and electronic music. Full name **Milton Byron Babbitt**

babbitt metal *n.* a soft alloy used especially in the manufacture of antifriction bearings. It originally consisted of tin, copper, and antimony, but now often contains lead. [Named after its US inventor, Isaac Babbitt (1799–1862)]

babble /bább'l/ *v.* (**-bles, -bling, -bled**) **1.** *vti.* SPEAK INCOHERENTLY to say sth rapidly and incoherently without pausing, usually because of excitement or fear ○ *He babbled something about leaving a deposit and then dashed out.* **2.** *vi.* SPEAK IN AN IRRELEVANT WAY to talk rapidly or at length in a way people find irrelevant ○ *He babbled on about the importance of some new gadget.* **3.** *vi.* MURMUR to make a continuous low murmuring or bubbling sound ○ *a brook babbling through the pasture* **4.** *vti.* BLURT STH OUT to reveal sth thoughtlessly or impulsively that is supposed to be secret or confidential ○ *immediately babbled the whole story to the neighbours* ■ *n.* **1.** SOUND OF LOUD UNINTELLIGIBLE VOICES the sound of voices speaking too excitedly and rapidly to be heard properly ○ *the babble of guests in the hallway* **2.** FOOLISH TALK irrelevant chatter **3.** SOUND OF RUNNING WATER the low continuous murmuring or bubbling sound made by water as it flows along. **4.** TELECOM BACKGROUND INTERFERENCE ON PHONE LINES background noise on a telephone line caused by interference from other conversations [13thC. Origin uncertain; probably from Middle Low German or Middle Dutch babbelen, an imitation of the sound, or from a similar formation in English.] —**babblement** *n.*

babbler /bábblər/ *n.* **1.** SB WHO BABBLES sb who babbles, especially sb who is inclined to give away secrets **2.** BIRDS SMALL BIRD OF FORESTS a small bird that lives in forests and bush throughout Europe, Asia, and Africa. The family includes the laughing thrush, a popular cage bird. Family: Timaliidae.

babe /bayb/ *n.* **1.** LOVER used as an affectionate term of address to a lover or sb you love (*slang*) **2.** YOUNG WOMAN CONSIDERED GOOD-LOOKING an young woman who is considered good-looking (*slang*) **3.** BABY a baby or small child (*literary or archaic*) **4.** US HANDSOME YOUTH an attractive young man (*slang*) [14thC. Origin uncertain, probably from obsolete baban 'baby', ultimately an imitation of childish utterances.] ◇ **a babe in arms** sb who is innocent and inexperienced ◇ **a babe in the woods** sb who is naive and trusts other people too easily

babel /báyb'l/ *n.* (*literary*) **1.** CONFUSED NOISE a confused noise, especially the noise of loud unintelligible voices all talking at once **2.** NOISY PLACE a scene or place of noisy confusion [Early 16thC. From the TOWER OF BABEL.]

Babel /báyb'l/ ♦ Tower of Babel

Babi /baá bi/ (*plural* **-bis**) *n.* EASTERN RELIG a follower of the Bab or of Babism [Mid-19thC. Via Persian, from Arabic, formed from *bāb* (see BAB).]

Babington /bábbingtən/, **Antony** (1561–86) English conspirator. He planned to murder Elizabeth I and release Mary, Queen of Scots. He and his fellow conspirators were captured and executed.

Babinski reflex /bə bínski reé fleks/, **Babinski's reflex** /bə bínskiz-/ *n.* a curling upwards of the big toe when the sole of the foot is stroked, which is a normal reflex in children up to two years old but indicates disease of the brain or spinal cord in older people [Early 20thC. Named after J. F. F. Babinski (1857–1932), French neurologist.]

babirusa /baá bi roóssə/ (*plural* **-sas** *or* **-sa**), **babirussa** (*plural* **-sas** *or* **-sa**), **babirousa** (*plural* **-sas** *or* **-sa**) *n.* a wild pig living in the forests of Indonesia and Malaysia that has almost hairless skin and very large curved tusks. Latin name: *Babyrousa babyrussa.* [Late 17thC. From Malay, from babi 'pig' + rusa 'deer', from its horns, which suggest a deer's antlers.]

Babism /baá bizzəm/ *n.* a pantheistic religion founded in Persia by the Bab, Mirza Ali Muhammad (1819–50), that forbade polygamy, begging, slave-trading, and the use of alcohol or drugs

babka /bábkə/ *n.* a sweet cake made with candied citrus peel, raisins, almonds, and sometimes rum [Late 20thC. From Polish, literally 'little old woman', formed from baba (see BABA).]

baboo *n.* = babu

baboon /bə boón/ *n.* **1.** LARGE MONKEY a large ground-dwelling monkey native to Africa and Asia with a prominent snout resembling a dog's muzzle, large teeth, and bare pink patches on the buttocks. Genus: *Papio.* **2.** RUDE CLUMSY PERSON sb who is thought of as rude or oafishly clumsy (*insult*) [15thC. From French babuin 'gaping figure, baboon' or medieval Latin babewynus, both of uncertain origin: possibly from French baboue 'muzzle, grimace'.]

zh vision In foreign words: kh German Bach; aN French vin; əəN French blanc; ö German schön, French feu; oN French bon; öN French un; ü French rue   Stress marks: ´ as in secret \séek rət\; academic \ákə démmik\

Baboon

babu /baʹa booʹ/, **baboo** n. **1.** HINDI COURTESY TITLE a courtesy title or form of address in Hindi equivalent to 'Mr' **2.** OFFENSIVE TERM in the former colonial period of the 19th and 20th centuries, an Indian, especially a clerk or official, who had only a superficial knowledge of the English language and culture (*offensive*) [Late 18thC. From Hindi *bābū*, literally 'father'.]

babul /baa boolʹ, baʹa boolʹ/ (*plural* **-buls** or **-bul**) n. an acacia tree found in North Africa and India that is a source of gum arabic, tannin, and hardwood. Latin name: *Acacia nilotica*. [Early 19thC. Via Hindi *babūl*, Bengali *bābul* from Sanskrit *babbūla*.]

babushka /bə booʹshkə/ n. **1.** SCARF a headscarf folded and tied under the chin in the style of Russian peasant women **2.** RUSSIAN GRANDMOTHER a traditional Russian grandmother figure [Mid-20thC. From Russian, 'grandmother', literally 'little old woman', formed from *baba* (see BABA).]

baby /báybi/ n. (*plural* **-bies**) **1.** VERY YOUNG CHILD a very young child who is not yet able to walk or talk **2.** UNBORN CHILD a child that is still in the womb **3.** CHILDISH PERSON sb who behaves childishly or is overly dependent on others ○ *told him not to be such a baby* **4.** YOUNGEST MEMBER the youngest member of a family or group ○ *the baby of the team* **5.** IMMATURE ANIMAL a very young animal **6.** TERM OF ENDEARMENT an affectionate term of endearment, especially for a woman (*slang*) ■ adj. SMALLER AND YOUNGER smaller and younger than usual, as are certain vegetables served as delicacies ■ vt. (**-bies, -bying, -bied**) TREAT SB WITH GREAT CARE to show a great or inordinate amount of care to sth or sb [14thC. Pet form of BABE.] ◇ **be left holding the baby** to be left in a situation of being solely responsible for sth because other people have abdicated their own responsibility ◇ **throw out the baby with the bathwater** to reject sth in its entirety without discriminating between what is bad and what is good or would be useful to retain

—— **WORD KEY: ORIGIN** ——
In Old English, the term for what we would now call a *baby* was *child*, and it seems only to have been from about the 11th century that *child* began to extend its range to the slightly more mature age that it now covers. Then when the word *baby* came into the language in the 14th century, it was also used in this developed sense of 'child', and only gradually came to refer to infants not yet capable of speech or walking.

baby blue n. a pale pastel blue colour [Origin uncertain, perhaps from the lightness of the colour] —**baby-blue** adj.

baby-blue-eyes (*plural* **baby-blue-eyes**) n. a spreading annual plant that has serrated grey-green leaves and small bowl-shaped blue flowers with white centres. Latin name: *Nemophila menziesii*. (*takes a singular or plural verb*) [From the fancied resemblance of its spots to eyes]

baby blues npl. the depression experienced by some women after giving birth (*informal*) (*used with a singular or plural verb*)

baby boom n. a sudden large increase in the birthrate over a particular period, especially the 15 years after World War II

baby boomer n. sb born during a baby boom, especially the one following the end of World War II

baby bouncer n. a type of harness with elastic straps that allows a baby to be seated within it and sus-pended from a doorway, letting the infant bounce up and down

baby buggy n. US a baby's or young child's stroller (*regional*)

baby carriage n. US = pram

baby-dolls npl. women's nightwear consisting of a loose top and loose shorts, popularized by the short pyjamas worn in the film *Baby Doll* in 1956

baby face n. **1.** FACE LIKE A BABY'S a smooth round face that gives sb a childlike innocent look **2.** SB WITH CHILDLIKE FACE sb who has a baby face

baby grand n. a small grand piano about 1.5 m/5 ft long

Babygro /báybigrō/ tdmk. a trademark for a baby's all-in-one suit made from stretch fabric

babyhood /báybihood/ n. the period during which a child is considered to be a baby, usually from birth to two or three years

babyish /báybi ish/ adj. **1.** LIKE A BABY like a baby in appearance or behaviour ○ *She has a really babyish voice* **2.** SUITABLE FOR A BABY suitable for a baby or for a younger child ○ *Clothes like these are too babyish for a child his age.*

Babylon[1] /bábbilən, -lon/ the capital of ancient Babylonia, sited on the Euphrates in modern Iraq. It was known for its opulence, and the Hanging Gardens there were one of the Seven Wonders of the World.

Babylon[2] /bábbilən/ n. **1.** PLACE OF IMMORALITY a place of great luxury or immorality (*disapproving*) **2.** PLACE OF EXILE a place of exile or captivity

Babylonia /bábbi lṓni ə/ n. an empire in Mesopotamia that flourished from the first half of the second millennium BC until its conquest by Persia in 539 BC

Babylonian /bábbi lṓni ən/ n. **1.** HIST, PEOPLES SB FROM BABYLON sb who lived in ancient Babylon or Babylonia **2.** LANG DIALECT OF AKKADIAN the Akkadian language, particularly the form of it that is recorded in cuneiform texts from Babylonia —**Babylonian** adj.

Babylonian captivity n. the period of time that the Jews spent in exile in Babylonia in the sixth century BC

baby minder n. sb whose job is to look after other people's babies or very young children while their parents are at work or otherwise away

baby's breath (*plural* **baby's breath** or **baby's breaths**) n. **1.** PLANT WITH SPRAYS OF SMALL FLOWERS a flowering plant that has a mass of delicate branched stems bearing small fragrant white or pink flowers, often used in bouquets and floral arrangements. Latin name: *Gypsophila paniculata*. **2.** BEDSTRAW PLANT a perennial plant that has many flowers on the end of delicate stems, especially a bedstraw [From its delicate scent]

babysit /báybisit/ (**-sits, -sitting, -sat**) v. **1.** vti. LOOK AFTER CHILD to look after a child or children in the child's home while the parents are out **2.** vt. TAKE CARE OF SB OR STH to look after sb or sth unable to be left unsupervised or needing constant attention (*informal*) ○ *Would you babysit my plants next week?* [Mid-20thC. Back-formation from BABYSITTER.]

babysitter /báybisitər/ n. sb who looks after children in their own home while their parents are out

baby snatcher n. **1.** KIDNAPPER sb who steals a baby (*slang*) **2.** = **cradle snatcher** (*informal humorous*)

baby's tears (*plural* **baby's tears**) n. an evergreen plant that has many small roundish leaves and tiny flowers. It is native to Corsica and Sardinia. Latin name: *Soleirolia soleirolii*. (*takes a singular or plural verb*) [From the small size of the flowers]

baby talk, **babytalk** n. the simplified or specially modified language and exaggerated intonation that adults use to show affection when talking to very small children

baby tooth n. = **milk tooth**

baby walker n. a frame mounted on wheels that helps keep babies upright when they are learning to walk. US term **walker**

Bacall /bə káwl/, **Lauren** (*b.* 1924) US actor. She starred in musicals and films including *To Have and Have Not* (1944) and *The Big Sleep* (1946). Her first husband was Humphrey Bogart. Real name **Betty Joan Perske**

Bacău /bə kówʹ/ city in eastern Romania. It is the capital of Bacău County, and a major rail junction. Population: 204,495 (1992).

baccalaureate /bákə láwri ət/ n. **1.** SCHOOL-LEAVING EXAM IN FRANCE an examination taken at the conclusion of a student's secondary school studies, especially in France, that enables successful candidates to enter university **2.** BACHELOR'S DEGREE a bachelor's degree (*formal*) [Mid-17thC. Directly or via French, from medieval Latin *baccalaureatus*, from *baccalaureus* 'bachelor'.]

baccarat /bákə raa, -ráa/ n. a card game, similar to chemin de fer, in which three hands are dealt and players bet against the banker. The winning hand is the one that totals nine points or is closest to nine points without exceeding it. [Mid-19thC. From French *baccara*, of unknown origin.]

baccate /bák ayt/ adj. similar to a berry in shape or texture [Early 19thC. From Latin *baccatus*, from *bacca* 'berry', of uncertain origin.]

Bacchae /bákee/ npl. in Greek and Roman mythology, the priestesses and women who participated in the orgiastic rites of Bacchus [Early 20thC. Via Latin, from Greek *Bakkhai*, plural of *Bakkhē* 'priest of Bacchus', from *Bakkhos* 'Bacchus'.]

bacchanal /bákə nálʹ/ n. **1.** PARTICIPANT IN ORGIASTIC RITES sb who took part in the orgiastic rites of the god Bacchus **2.** LOUD DRUNK a riotous drunken reveller (*literary*) **3.** DRUNKEN PARTY a noisy drunken celebration or spree (*literary*) ■ adj. RELATING TO BACCHUS relating to Bacchus or the worship of Bacchus [Mid-16thC. From Latin *bacchanalis* 'of Bacchus', from *Bacchus* 'Bacchus'.]

bacchanalia /bákə náyli ə/ npl. **1.** bacchanalia, Bacchanalia ANCIENT ROMAN FESTIVITIES ancient Roman festivities in honour of Bacchus that involved orgiastic rites **2.** DRUNKEN REVELRY riotous drunken revels (*literary*) [Late 16thC. From Latin *bacchanalia*, plural of *bacchanalis* (see BACCHANAL).] —**bacchanalian** adj.

bacchant /bákənt/ n. a priest, priestess, or other devotee of Bacchus [Late 16thC. Via French *bacchante* from Latin *baccant-*, the present participle stem of *bacchari* 'to celebrate the feast of Bacchus', from *Bacchus* 'Bacchus'.]

bacchante /bə kántiʹ/ n. a priestess or female devotee of Bacchus [Late 18thC. From French *bacchante* (see BACCHANT).]

bacchantic /bə kántik/ adj. relating to the worship of Bacchus and the orgiastic rites associated with it

Bacchic /bákik/ adj. **1.** MYTHOL OF BACCHUS relating to Bacchus **2.** Bacchic, bacchic RIOTOUSLY DRUNK characterized by riotous drunkenness (*literary*)

bacchius /bə kíʹ əss/ (*plural* **-chii** /bə kíʹ ī/) n. a metrical foot consisting of one short syllable followed by two long ones [Late 16thC. Via Latin, from Greek *bakkheios (pous)*, literally 'Bacchic (foot)', from *Bakkhos* 'Bacchus'.]

Bacchus /bákəss/ n. in classical mythology, the god of wine, identified with the Greek god Dionysus and the Roman god Liber. He was worshipped with orgiastic and ecstatic rites. [Via Latin, from Greek *Bakkhos*]

Bacchus Marsh /bákəss-/ town in Victoria, south-eastern Australia. Population: 7,640 (1986).

bacciferous /bak sífferəss/ adj. used to describe plants that produce berries [Mid-17thC. Formed from Latin *baccifer*, literally 'bearing berries', ultimately from *bacca* 'berry'.]

baccy /báki/ n. tobacco (*dated informal*) [Early 19thC. Shortening and alteration.]

bach[1] /bach/ vi. US, ANZ TO KEEP HOUSE FOR YOURSELF to live alone as a single man and keep house for yourself (*informal*) ■ n. ANZ COTTAGE a cottage or holiday home (*informal*) [Mid-19thC. Shortening of BACHELOR.]

bach[2] /baakh, baak/ n. Wales an affectionate form of address, used alone or after sb's name ○ *Alan bach, how are you?* [Late 19thC. From Welsh, literally 'little'.]

—— **WORD KEY: REGIONAL NOTE** ——
Terms of endearment are often carried over into English by speakers of other mother tongues. We see it with

Welsh *bach* and *fach*, literally 'small' and implying 'loved one', and with Irish *alannah*, literally 'child' but suggesting 'darling'. ***Bach*** is often replaced by *boy*, as in *There's nice for you, boy.*

Bach /baak, baakh/, **C.P.E.** (1714–88) German composer. The son of Johann Sebastian Bach, he composed numerous concertos and sonatas as well as chamber and church music. He also wrote *The True Art of Clavier Playing* (1753). Full name **Carl Philipp Emanuel Bach**. Known as **Berlin Bach, Hamburg Bach**

Bach, J.C. (1735–82) German composer. The youngest son of Johann Sebastian Bach and a composer of church music and operas, he settled in London (1762) and was musician to Queen Charlotte. Full name **Johann Christian Bach**. Known as **London Bach, English Bach**

Johann Sebastian Bach

Bach, Johann Sebastian (1685–1750) German composer and organist. Known as a supreme master of counterpoint, he wrote many organ works, chamber and keyboard works, and oratorios, and over 295 cantatas. His works include the *'Brandenburg' Concertos* (1721) and *St Matthew Passion* (1727).

Bach, W.F. (1710–84) German composer. He led a dissolute life despite being a gifted organist and composer. He was the eldest son of Johann Sebastian Bach. Full name **Wilhelm Friedemann Bach**. Known as **Halle Bach**

bachelor /báchələr/ *n.* **1. UNMARRIED MAN** a man who is not married, or one who has never been married **2. YOUNG KNIGHT** a young knight in feudal times who served under the banner of another knight or a great lord **3. UNMATED YOUNG MALE SEAL** a young male seal, especially a fur seal, that older male seals keep from having access to breeding grounds **4.** *Can* = **bachelor apartment** [13thC. Via Old French *bacheler* 'young man aspiring to knighthood' from assumed Vulgar Latin *baccalaris*, of uncertain origin.] —**bachelordom** *n.* —**bachelorhood** *n.* —**bachelorship** *n.*

bachelor apartment *n. Can* an flat consisting of a large single room, a small kitchen, and a bathroom

bachelor girl *n.* a young unmarried woman, usually one who is self-supporting (*dated*)

Bachelor of Arts *n.* a college or university degree awarded to sb who has successfully completed an undergraduate course in an aspect of the arts or humanities

Bachelor of Science *n.* a college or university degree awarded to sb who has successfully completed an undergraduate course in an aspect of the sciences or technology

bachelor's degree *n.* a degree awarded on the successful completion of an undergraduate course at a college or university and, at some universities, on completion of a usually short postgraduate course

Bach flower remedy /bách-/ (*plural* **Bach flower remedies**) *n.* a healing method using extracts of 38 flowers, each treating a different emotional disorder, based on the theory that improvement of sb's emotional state will promote physical healing of disease [Late 20thC. Named after its inventor Edward *Bach* (1886–1936), British physician.]

Bach trumpet /baák-, baákh-/ *n.* a modern valve trumpet, smaller than an ordinary trumpet, specially designed for playing the high-pitched trumpet parts in music byJ.S. Bach and other baroque composers

bacillary /bə síllərі/ *adj.* **1. OF BACILLI** relating to or caused by rod-shaped bacteria (**bacilli**) **2. ROD-SHAPED** shaped like a small rod or consisting of small rod-shaped parts

bacillus /bə sílləss/ (*plural* **-li** /-seé lī/) *n.* **1. ROD-SHAPED BACTERIUM** an aerobic, rod-shaped, spore-producing bacterium. Bacilli occur mainly in chains and include many saprophytes, some parasites, and the bacterium that causes anthrax. Genus: *Bacillus.* **2. ROD-SHAPED BACTERIUM** a rod-shaped bacterium [Late 19thC. From late Latin, literally 'little rod', formed from *baculus* 'rod, stick' (source of English *baguette* and *imbecile*).]

bacitracin /bássi tráyssin/ *n.* an antibiotic that is used mainly in the treatment of skin infections caused by gram-positive bacteria [Mid-20thC. Coined from BACILLUS + Margaret *Tracy*, name of a US child in whom the substance was discovered in a wound + -IN.]

back /bak/ *n.* **1.** ANAT **REAR PART OF BODY** the rear part of the human body between the neck and the pelvis **2.** ANAT **SPINE** the spinal column **3.** ZOOL **BACK OF AN ANIMAL** the area of a vertebrate animal's body on either side of the backbone **4.** CLOTHES **PART OF GARMENT** the part of a garment designed to cover the wearer's back **5. PART AT THE REAR** the part that is at the rear of sth or is furthest from the front ○ *Someone at the back of the crowd called out.* **6. SIDE NOT USUALLY SEEN** the side of sth such as a sheet of paper or a photo that carries less information or is away from the viewer **7.** FURNITURE **PART OF PIECE OF FURNITURE** the part of a seat designed to support sb's spine **8.** SPORTS **DEFENSIVE PLAYER** a player in games such as soccer or hockey whose role is mainly to prevent the other team scoring **9.** PUBL **PART OF BOOK OR PERIODICAL** the part of a book, magazine, or newspaper that is located towards the last page ○ *the index at the back of the book* **10.** PRINTING **PART TO WHICH PAGES ARE FIXED** the part of the book where the pages are glued or stitched to the binding ■ *adv.* **1. IN A REVERSE DIRECTION** in the opposite direction to the one sb or sth was previously facing or moving ○ *He looked back at us over his shoulder.* **2. AT A DISTANCE** at a distance from where sth is situated or taking place ○ *Stay back; the dog might bite you.* **3. IN RESERVE** as a reserve or supply kept for future use ○ *I kept back part of the proceeds.* **4. SO AS TO UNCOVER STH** away from sth so as to leave sth else uncovered or revealed ○ *roll back the carpet* **5. SO AS TO RECLINE** in or into a reclining position ○ *Sit back and relax.* **6. IN OR INTO THE PAST** used to indicate a time in the past ○ *Back then, people grew their own food.* ○ *It happened about three weeks back.* ◊ **ago 7. TO THE ORIGINAL OWNER** to or into the keeping of the original or former owner or possessor ○ *You can have it back now, because I've finished with it.* **8. IN RETURN** as a reaction or response to sth ○ *She called me while I was out, so I called her back.* **9. INDICATES DIRECTION AND DISTANCE** in the distance behind sth, especially sb's present position ○ *We passed it about two miles back.* **10. RETURNED TO CONDITION OR TOPIC** used to indicate a return to a state, situation, or subject of discussion ○ *to get back to your point* **11. POPULAR AGAIN** into fashion or popularity again ○ *The 70s are back.* ○ *Do you think Depression glass will ever come back?* ■ *adj.* **1. LOCATED AT THE REAR** located at the rear of sth or at the part furthest from the front ○ *Use the back entrance.* **2.** PUBL **ISSUED EARLIER** published or issued at an earlier date ○ *a back issue* **3. DUE EARLIER** due at or owed from an earlier date ○ *paid the back taxes in full* **4. LOCATED AWAY FROM MAIN ROADS** located away from the main roads or the centre of a town ○ *a quiet back street* **5. REMOTE** situated away from the main centres of population or activity ○ *explored the back areas of the huge canyon* **6. REVERSE** moving in an opposite direction to the usual one **7.** LING **FORMED AT REAR OF MOUTH** formed at or towards the rear of the mouth, as the vowel in 'ball' is ○ *a back vowel* ■ *v.* (**backs, backing, backed**) **1.** *vti.* **MOVE BACKWARDS** to move backwards, or make sb or sth move backwards ○ *The vehicle in front backed into me.* **2.** *vt.* **SUPPORT PERSON OR CAUSE** to give a person or cause financial, political, or moral support **3.** *vt.* GAMBLING **BET ON OUTCOME OF RACE** to bet money on the person, team, or horse thought likely to win a race or competition **4.** *vt.* **PROVIDE PROOF TO SUPPORT STH** to provide evidence or proof in support a statement ○ *But can they back their allegations?* **5.** *vt.* **REINFORCE STH** to reinforce sth by adding a support or backing ○ *coloured paper backed with cardboard* **6.** *vt.* **BE BEHIND STH** to be situated behind sth (*usually passive*) ○ *a lake backed by a range of mountains* **7.** *vt.* MUSIC **PROVIDE MUSICAL ACCOMPANIMENT FOR SB** to provide an instrumental or vocal accompaniment to sb or sth **8.** *vi.* SAILING **CHANGE DIRECTION** to change direction, moving in an anticlockwise direction (*refers to wind*) [Old English *bæc*, from prehistoric Germanic] ◇ **back and fill 1.** to dither or vacillate in actions or decision-making **2.** SAILING to adjust the sails of a vessel in order to allow the wind to move in and out of them in an alternating manner as the boat is manoeuvred in a narrow channel ◇ **back of** *US, Can* at the back of or behind sth (*informal*) ◇ **behind sb's back** when sb is not present ◇ **be** *or* **get on sb's back** to criticize or pressurize sb (*slang*) ◇ **get off sb's back 1.** to stop criticizing or pressurizing sb (*slang*) **2.** to make sb feel annoyed or defensive ◇ **have your back to the wall** to be in a very difficult situation, with little chance of getting out of it ◇ **in back of** *US, Can* behind sth ◇ **put your back intosth** to put effort and especially physical strength into doing sth ◇ **the back of (the) beyond** a remote inaccessible place that has few amenities ○ *They bought a small cottage in the back of beyond, just to get away from it all.* ◇ **turn your back on sb** *or* **sth** to ignore or reject sb or sth ◇ **you scratch my back I'll scratch yours** if you help me, I will help you in return (*often refers to unofficial or dishonest business dealings*)

WORD KEY: USAGE

Movement in time: ***back*** as it applies to the past refers to a change to an earlier time. *They have moved the estimate of its date of origin back a hundred years* would mean a change from, say, AD 1000 to AD 900. As the word applies to the future, however, it usually signifies a change to a later time: *The forecast is for rain, so let's move the picnic back a week.* What the two uses have in common is movement in time away from the present. *Up* is the opposite of ***back*** in this sense: *Let's move the date up* means moving the date closer to the present, and thus in future contexts changing it to an earlier one. *Forward* in future contexts is used less consistently than either ***back*** or *up*; it is best avoided. All these words become particularly confusing when the subject is, e.g., a decision, now in the past, about what was at the time the future: *Last month she told me she wanted to move my appointment back.* In a context like this, *make earlier* or *make later* is clearer.

WORD KEY: USAGE

back of and **in back of** The phrase ***back of*** is standard in American English and ***in back of*** is its informal variant. They would not be normally used elsewhere except as consciously adopted Americanisms. Both mean 'behind', and ***in back of*** is formed on the direct analogy of ***in front of***, which is standard in both varieties of English: *There was a swimming pool (in) back of the house.*

back away *vi.* **1. MOVE AWAY BACKWARDS** to walk backwards away from sb or sth, usually because of fear **2. RETREAT FROM A SITUATION** to withdraw from a situation or previous position ○ *We think they'll back away from any direct confrontation over sanctions.*

back down *vi.* to abandon a claim, opinion, or commitment because of the degree of opposition it arouses

back off *vi.* **1. MOVE BACK** to move away backwards **2. EASE PRESSURE ON SB** to stop putting pressure on sb to do sth

back out *v.* **1.** *vi.* **WITHDRAW** to withdraw from a previous commitment ○ *The buyer backed out before the papers were signed.* **2.** *vti.* **GO BACKWARDS** to move out backwards, or cause sth to move out backwards

back up *v.* **1.** *vt.* **TO SUPPORT SB** to provide support for a person or idea ○ *I'm sure you'll back me up on this.* **2.** *vt.* COMPUT **COPY COMPUTER FILES** to make a copy or copies of computer data to keep in case anything goes wrong with the original **3.** *vti.* **GO BACKWARDS** to go or move sth backwards **4.** *vt.* **PRINT OTHER SIDE OF SHEET** to print the other side of a sheet that has already been printed on one side **5.** *vti.* **ACCUMULATE** to build up, or cause sth to build up, especially because normal flow is obstructed ○ *Traffic was backed up three miles from the accident.* **6.** *vi.* CRICKET **START TO RUN EARLY** to begin moving down the wicket towards the receiving batsman in anticipation of a run before the ball is bowled **7.** *vt.* **PROVE STATEMENT** to supply proof that a statement is true ○ *Evidence of growth is backed up by recent economic statistics.*

backache /bák ayk/ *n.* an ache or pain affecting the back, most commonly the lower back

back bacon *n.* a cut of bacon that provides very lean rashers for frying. It comes from the back of the pigin front of the rear haunches.

backbeat /bák beet/ *n.* **MUSIC** a loud rhythmic beat occurring on the offbeats of the bar, used especially in rock music

backbench /bák bénch/ *n.* **UK, Can, ANZ AREA FOR MPS NOT IN GOVERNMENT** a bench in a legislative assembly reserved for Members of Parliament who do not hold office or are not official spokespersons for the Opposition (*usually plural*) ○ *on the back benches* ■ *adj.* **RELATING TO MPS NOT IN GOVERNMENT** relating to Members of Parliament who are not members of the government or official spokespersons for the Opposition

backbencher /bák benchər/ *n.* **1.** **UK, Can, ANZ MP NOT IN GOVERNMENT** a member of the lower house of a legislative assembly who is not a government minister or an official Opposition spokesperson **2.** *US* **NEW MEMBER OF CONGRESS** a new member of Congress, or one who has low seniority

backbend /bák bend/ *n.* an exercise in gymnastics in which sb bends over backwards from a standing position until the hands touch the floor

backbite /bák bīt/ (**-bites, -biting, -bit** /-bit/, **-bitten** /-bitt'n/ *or* **-bit**) *vti.* to make spiteful or slanderous comments about sb who is not present [12thC. From the idea of an animal biting another (usually of the same species) on the back, often in play.]—**backbiter** *n.*

backboard /bák bawrd/ *n.* **1.** **BOARD FORMING BACK OF STH** a board that forms the back of sth, e.g. a cart or boat **2.** **BASKETBALL BOARD BEHIND THE BASKET** the board situated behind the basket that serves to rebound the ball onto the court

back boiler *n.* a water tank or set of pipes placed behind a fireplace so that a domestic fire will also heat water

backbone /bák bōn/ *n.* **1.** = **spinal column 2. STH SIMILAR TO SPINAL COLUMN** sth that is similar in shape or position to a spinal column ○ *the Pennines, the backbone of England* **3.** **CENTRAL SUPPORTING PART** the part of an organization or system that is its strongest unifying factor and main support ○ *The middle classes are the backbone of this nation.* **4.** **FORTITUDE** strength of character and determination ○ *He doesn't have the backbone to stand up to his critics.* **5.** **COMPUT HIGH-SPEED RELAY** a high-speed relay, e.g. over fibre-optic cables or satellites, that feeds smaller channels in corporate networks and the Internet

back boundary line *n.* either of two lines parallel to the net that mark the rear limit of the playing area on a badminton court

backbreaker /bák braykər/ *n.* **1.** **WRESTLING HOLD** a wrestling hold in which sb's back is bent backwards over the opponent's knee or shoulder **2.** **BACKBREAKING TASK** an exhausting task, or one that demands a tremendous physical effort (*informal*)

backbreaking /bák brayking/ *adj.* involving enormous physical effort

backburn /bák burn/ (**backburns, backburning, backburned, backburnt**) /-burnt/ *vt.* **1.** **ANZ CREATE FIREBREAK IN PATH OF BUSHFIRE** to prevent a bushfire from spreading by lighting another fire in its path **2.** **CLEAR BUSHLAND WITH FIRE** to clear an area of bush or grassland by setting fire to it

back burner ◇ **put sth on the back burner** to assign sth a lower priority or give sth less prominence ○ *The project has been put on the back burner.*

back channel *n.* a covert way of exchanging sensitive information in politics or diplomacy that circumvents the usual procedures

backchat /bák chat/ *n.* rude or impertinent answers or comments (*informal*) ○ *I don't want any backchat if he asks you whether you like school.* US term **back talk**

backcheck /bák chek/ (**-checks, -checking, -checked**) *vti.* to skate back towards your own goal in ice hockey while trying to block an opponent with the body or stick —**backchecker** *n.*

backcloth /bák kloth/ (*plural* **-cloths**) *n.* **THEATRE** = **backdrop** *n.* **1**

backcomb /bák kōm/ (**-combs, -combing, -combed**) *vt.* to comb hair with quick short movements towards the roots so that it stands up away from the head and can be brushed into a bouffant hairstyle. US term **tease**

back country *n.* *US, Can, ANZ* a remote, sparsely populated rural area, often used for various forms of outdoor recreation, including backpacking and camping ○ *backpacking in rugged back country*

backcourt /bák kawrt/ *n.* **1.** **RACKET GAMES REAR OF COURT** the area between the baseline and the service line on a tennis court or the area of the court nearest the back boundary line or back wall in similar games **2.** **BASKETBALL DEFENDED HALF OF BASKETBALL COURT** the half of the court where the basket being defended is located **3.** **BASKETBALL DEFENSIVE PLAYERS** the players who defend the backcourt

back crawl *n.* = **backstroke**

backcross /bák kross/ *vt.* (**-crosses, -crossing, -crossed**) **CROSS HYBRID WITH PARENT** to cross an organism, especially a hybrid, with one of its parents or an individual genetically identical to that parent ■ *n.* **1.** **HYBRID OBTAINED BY BACKCROSSING** a hybrid obtained by backcrossing **2.** **ACT OF BACKCROSSING** the act or the process of backcrossing organisms

backdate /bák dayt/ (**-dates, -dating, -dated**) *vt.* **1.** **PUT EARLIER DATE ON STH** to put a date on a document that is earlier than the actual date of its writing or signing **2.** **MAKE AGREEMENT EFFECTIVE FROM EARLIER DATE** to make an agreement or document valid from an earlier date than the present date

back dive *n.* a dive made when the diver's back is facing the water

back door *n.* **1.** **REAR DOOR** a door or entrance at the rear of a building **2.** **backdoor, back door DISHONEST ADVANTAGE** an underhand or indirect way that gives sb an unfair advantage

backdoor /bák dawr/ *adj.* carried out in secrecy or in a surreptitious way ○ *There's been a lot of backdoor pressure on her to step down.*

backdown /bák down/ *n.* the abandonment of a course of action or an opinion in the face of opposition from other people

backdrop /bák drop/ *n.* **1.** **THEATRE PAINTED CLOTH AT BACK OF STAGE** a large painted cloth hung at the back of the stage that usually depicts the setting in which the action of a scene takes place **2.** **SETTING FOR STH** the setting for sth, e.g. the scenery or colours behind it ○ *The ski-jumping took place against a backdrop of jagged mountain peaks.*

back emf /-émf/ *n.* an electromagnetic force that opposes any change of current in an inductive circuit ['Emf' shortening of *electromagnetic force*]

back emission *n.* the production of electrons from the anode of a vacuum tube

back end load *n.* a mutual fund sales charge paid when shares are sold

backer /bákər/ *n.* **1.** **SUPPORTER** sb who gives moral or financial support to sb or sth **2.** **GAMBLER** sb who bets on sb or sth

—————————— **WORD KEY: SYNONYMS** ——————————
backer, angel, guarantor, patron, sponsor
CORE MEANING: sb who provides financial support
backer the most general term of the group, indicating support of either a financial or non-financial nature; **angel** a person who provides financial support for an enterprise, for example a theatrical venture; **guarantor** sb who gives a legal undertaking to make good any financial losses incurred in a venture; **patron** a person who provides an artist or writer with the financial means to pursue his or her art, or who contributes money to an institution, such as a theatre or art gallery, or cause; **sponsor** a person who contributes money to sb participating in some kind of fundraising event, such as a marathon race, or a company that provides financial support for an activity such as a sporting or musical

event, usually in return for publicity for the company and its products.

backfield /bák feeld/ *n.* **AMERICAN FOOTBALL 1.** **AREA OF FIELD** in American football, the area of the playing field behind the line of scrimmage **2.** **PLAYERS** the players who line up behind the line of scrimmage **3.** **POSITIONS** the positions of the players who line up behind the line of scrimmage

backfile /bák fīl/ *n.* an archive consisting of previous issues of a newspaper or magazine

backfill /bákfil/ *vt.* (**-fills, -filling, -filled**) **REFILL A TRENCH** to refill a trench or other excavation with the soil dug out of it ■ *n.* **SOIL** the soil used to refill a trench

backfire /bák fīr/ *vi.* (**-fires, -firing, -fired**) **1.** **HAVE OPPOSITE EFFECT** to have an effect opposite to the one intended ○ *The policy of mandatory testing may well backfire and do more harm than good.* **2.** **AUTOMOT MAKE EXPLOSION IN EXHAUST PIPE** to produce an explosion of prematurely ignited fuel in an internal-combustion engine or of unburnt exhaust gases in the exhaust pipe **3.** **FORESTRY START FIRE TO CREATE FIREBREAK** to start a fire in the path of an advancing wildfire in order to halt its advance ■ *n.* **1.** **AUTOMOT EXPLOSION IN CAR EXHAUST** an explosion of prematurely ignited fuel in an internal-combustion engine or of unburnt exhaust gases in the exhaust pipe **2.** **FORESTRY FIRE STARTED TO CREATE FIREBREAK** a fire deliberately started in order to clear the ground in front of an advancing wildfire so as to halt it

backflow /bák flō/ *n.* the flowing back of sth towards the source

back-formation *n.* **1.** **PROCESS OF WORD FORMATION** a process of word formation in which a new word is coined by removing a real or imagined affix from an existing word **2.** **NEW WORD FORMED BY AFFIX REMOVAL** a word formed by back-formation, e.g. 'greed' from 'greedy', or 'televise' from 'television'

back four *n.* a defensive formation in football that consists of two wing backs and two centre backs deployed in a straight line across the field

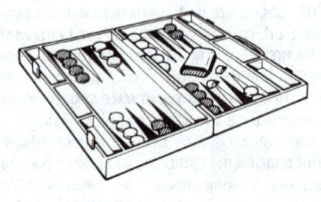

Backgammon

backgammon /bák gamən/ *n.* **1.** **BOARD GAME INVOLVING DICE** a board game for two players who each move their 15 pieces round the board according to the throw of a pair of dice. The object of the game is to be the first to gather all your pieces in one corner and remove them from the board. **2.** **COMPLETE VICTORY IN BACKGAMMON** the most complete form of victory in backgammon, when a player succeeds in removing all 15 pieces while the other still has a piece furthest from the point at which he or she can remove pieces from the board [Mid-17thC. From BACK + obsolete *gamen*, an early form of GAME; probably from the pieces sometimes being put 'back' on the table.]

back green *n.* *Scotland* a garden or area of grass behind a house or tenement building

background /bák grownd/ *n.* **1.** **PERSONAL CIRCUMSTANCES AND EXPERIENCES** the personal circumstances and experiences that shape sb's life, e.g. ethnic and social origins, upbringing, education, and work experience ○ *a group of people from very different backgrounds* **2.** **CAUSES OF AN EVENT** the circumstances leading up to an event that explain its cause ○ *The meeting takes place against a background of rising tension.* **3.** **SCENERY BEHIND STH** the setting for a scene, e.g. the scenery behind it ○ *A silvery lake shone against a background of tall dark firs.* **4.** **ARTS PART OF PICTURE** the part of a picture or pattern that appears to be in the distance or behind the most important part **5.** INFORMATION information that helps to explain what sth or sth is like or why sth is happening **6.** INCONSPICUOUS POSITION a position of relative inconspicuousness or unimportance ○ *working tirelessly in the background* **7.** NUCLEAR PHYS = **background radiation 8.** ELECTRON ENG, PHYS SIGNAL CAUSING DISTORTION OR INTERFERENCE an extraneous signal, often in the form of electronic or acoustic noise, that can cause distortion or affect an instrument reading (*often used before a noun*) ○ *background interference* **9.** COMPUT LOW-PRIORITY ENVIRONMENT IN COMPUTERS the low-priority environment in computers that can perform more than one task at a time ■ *adj.* **1.** AS PART OF THE BACKGROUND situated or depicted in, or forming part of, the background to sth **2.** ACCOMPANYING functioning or suitable as an accompaniment to sth else

background music *n.* music used as a suitable accompaniment to action or dialogue in a film, or to create a pleasant atmosphere for an activity or in a public place

background processing *n.* COMPUT execution of computer programs and tasks either while the user works with an interactive application in the foreground or during pauses in the execution of a foreground program or task. Once started, background tasks such as printing or copying data execute without user input.

background radiation *n.* low-level radiation occurring naturally as a result of radioactivity present in the air, soil, and buildings and other structures

backhand /bák hand/ *n.* **1.** RACKET GAMES BACKHANDED STROKE in tennis and similar games, a stroke made with the back of the hand turned towards the ball as the arm moves outwards from a position across the body **2.** RACKET GAMES BACKHAND SIDE the side of a tennis court, or of the body, on which a player would naturally play a backhand stroke. It is the left-hand side for a right-handed player. **3.** HANDWRITING SLOPING LEFTWARDS a style of handwriting in which the letters slope to the left ■ *adj.* WITH BACK OF HAND TOWARDS BALL carried out with the back of the hand facing in the direction in which the stroke, movement, or blow is made ■ *adv.* BACKHANDEDLY with a backhand stroke ■ *vt.* (**-hands, -handing, -handed**) **1.** CONTACT BALL WITH BACKHAND to strike a ball with a backhand stroke ○ *She backhanded the ball just over the net.* **2.** HIT SB WITH BACK OF HAND to hit sb or sth with the back of the hand ○ *accidentally backhanded an opponent*

backhanded /bák hándid/ *adj.* **1.** PLAYED BACKHAND carried out with the back of the hand facing in the direction in which the stroke, movement, or blow is made ○ *a backhanded return* **2.** WITH DOUBLE MEANING with a doubtful or double meaning, especially one that can be understood equally as a compliment or as an insult ○ *a backhanded compliment* **3.** WRITTEN WITH LETTERS SLOPING LEFTWARDS written in a style of handwriting in which the letters slope to the left ■ *adv.* WITH BACKHANDED STROKE with the back of the hand facing in the direction in which a stroke, movement, or blow is made —**backhandedly** *adv.* —**backhandedness** *n.*

backhander /bák hándər/ *n.* **1.** BACKHANDED BLOW a blow struck with the back of the hand ○ *caught the opposing team member with a terrific backhander across the face during hard play* **2.** BACKHAND STROKE a backhand stroke **3.** BRIBE an illicit payment made as a bribe (*informal*) **4.** BACKHANDED COMPLIMENT a backhanded compliment or similar veiled verbal attack on sb (*informal*)

backhoe /bák hō/ *n.* a digging machine or attachment consisting of a hinged scoop attached to a jointed mechanical arm that drags the scoop back towards the tractor from which it is operated

backing /báking/ *n.* **1.** SUPPORT OR HELP active approval, support, or help, often in financial form, given to an individual, organization, or cause **2.** SUPPORTERS the people or organizations giving support to a person or cause **3.** REAR SURFACE material forming or covering the back of sth, especially to strengthen, stiffen, or protect it **4.** MUSIC MUSICAL ACCOMPANIMENT the music or singing that accompanies the playing or

singing of the main performer of a piece of popular music or jazz

backing track *n.* a recorded musical accompaniment for use by a solo performer

back issue *n.* US PUBL = **back number**

back judge *n.* US in American football, a referee stationed behind the line of scrimmage who keeps the time in a game and determines players eligible to receive a pass [From the fact that this referee is responsible for calls in the backfield]

back kitchen *n.* a pantry or other small room off a kitchen (*informal*)

backlash /bák lash/ (*plural* **-lashes**) *n.* **1.** STRONG REACTION a strong adverse reaction among a group of people to an event, development, or trend, especially one that benefits another group **2.** VIOLENT BACKWARD MOVEMENT a sudden violent backward jerking movement, e.g. when a cable breaks under strain **3.** MECH ENG RECOIL BETWEEN MACHINE PARTS a jarring recoil that sometimes occurs when worn or badly fitting parts of a mechanism come together **4.** MECH ENG PLAY BETWEEN MACHINE PARTS excessive play between adjacent parts in a mechanism such as a set of gears, usually as a result of the parts being worn or badly fitted **5.** ANGLING FISHING LINE TANGLE a tangle in the part of a fishing line that is wound on the reel

backless /báklǝss/ *adj.* with the back cut very low ○ *a backless dress*

backlight /bák līt/ *n.* LIGHT FROM BEHIND light that illuminates the subject of a photograph or painting from behind ■ *vt.* (**-lights, -lighting, -lighted** *or* **-lit** /-lit/, **-lighted** *or* **-lit**) ILLUMINATE FROM BEHIND to illuminate a subject from behind —**backlighting** *n.*

backlist /bák list/ *n.* PUBL the range of books already published by a publisher that are still in print ○ *The departing editor had built up a highly respectable backlist.*

backlit past tense, past participle of **backlight**

backlog /bák log/ *n.* **1.** THINGS STILL TO BE DONE a quantity of unfinished business or work that has built up over a period of time and must be dealt with before progress can be made ○ *She faced a backlog of work when she came back from the Bahamas.* **2.** LARGE LOG ON A FIRE a large log placed at the back of an open fire

back matter *n.* PUBL the parts of a book that appear after the main text, e.g. the index or an appendix

backmost /bák mōst/ *adj.* furthest back from a given point ○ *Spectators in the backmost seats couldn't hear a thing.*

back mutation *n.* the reversion of a mutated gene to its original form

back number *n.* **1.** PUBL OLD ISSUE OF A PUBLICATION a previous issue of a magazine or newspaper **2.** OLD-FASHIONED SB OR STH a person or thing considered to be out of date (*informal*)

Backpack

backpack /bák pak/ *n.* **1.** LEISURE RUCKSACK a large straight-sided canvas bag, often attached to a metal frame, worn strapped to the back and used by walkers and travellers for carrying their belongings, equipment, and supplies **2.** EQUIPMENT CARRIED ON THE BACK a pack or carrier for a piece of equipment, such as an astronaut's personal life-support system, that is designed to be strapped on the user's back ■ *v.* (**-packs, -packing, -packed**) **1.** *vi.* LEISURE HIKE WITH BACKPACK to travel, especially hike, carrying be-

longings or supplies in a backpack ○ *She spent a month backpacking in the Rockies.* **2.** *vt.* CARRY STH ON THE BACK to transport sth, usually equipment or supplies, in a pack on the back ○ *astronauts backpacking oxygen during a spacewalk* —**backpacker** *n.*

back pass *n.* SOCCER a pass from an outfield player back to the goalkeeper, in football. Goalkeepers are forbidden to handle back passes with their hands.

back passage *n.* the anal canal (*informal*)

back pay *n.* pay that is owed to an employee for work done before the current payment period and is either overdue or results from a backdated pay increase

backpedal /bák pedd'l/ (**-als, -alling, -alled**) *v.* **1.** *vti.* CYCLING PEDAL BACKWARDS to turn the pedals of a bicycle backwards, e.g. in order to operate a brake **2.** *vi.* SPORTS MOVE BACKWARDS to move quickly backwards, e.g. in order to get away from an opponent or to catch a ball **3.** *vi.* RETREAT to try to escape the consequences of a statement or action by retracting it, modifying it, or toning it down

backplate /bák playt/ *n.* a piece of armour protecting the back

back pressure *n.* **1.** ENG RESISTANT PRESSURE resistant pressure exerted by any solid, liquid, or gas to the forward motion of a system, especially the pressure opposing the exhaust stroke of a piston in an internal-combustion engine **2.** INDUST OIL OR GAS PRESSURE the pressure exerted by fluids in the bore of an oil well on the oil and gas in the reservoir. Careful control of this pressure ensures an even supply of oil. **3.** MED PRESSURE DUE TO OBSTRUCTION pressure within a blood vessel or the urinary system that builds up when there is an obstruction to the flow of fluid

back projection *n.* the cinematic technique of projecting a film onto a translucent screen from behind, usually to provide a moving background against which other action can be filmed

backrest /bák rest/ *n.* a part of a seat designed to support the user's back

backroom /bák room, -rōom/, **back room** *n.* **back room** SITE OF SECRET RESEARCH OR PLANNING a place away from the centre of activities where important and usually secret research or planning is supposed to be carried out ■ *adj.* **backroom, back-room** UNOBTRUSIVE OR CLANDESTINE taking place away from the centre of activity or attention, but usually important or influential nonetheless

back row *n.* RUGBY the players forming the third row on either side of a rugby scrum, traditionally the two wing forwards and the number eight

backsaw /bák saw/ *n.* a small saw stiffened and strengthened by a strip of metal on its noncutting edge

backscatter /bák skatər/ *n.* **1.** DEFLECTION OF RADIATION OR PARTICLES the deflection of radiation or particles through angles of greater than 90 degrees measured with respect to the original direction of travel through a medium **2.** DEFLECTED RADIATION OR PARTICLES radiation or particles deflected more than 90 degrees while passing through a medium

backscratcher /bák skrachǝr/ *n.* **1.** TOOL FOR SCRATCHING THE BACK a long-handled implement, often ending in a claw or hand shape, for scratching your own back **2.** SB WHO EXCHANGES FAVOURS sb who does favours for others in order to receive similar favours from them (*informal*)

backscratching /bák scraching/ *n.* the doing of favours for other people in return for similar favours from them (*informal*) —**backscratch** *vi.*

back seat *n.* **1.** SEAT IN THE BACK a seat at the back of a vehicle **2.** LESS IMPORTANT ROLE a less important or active role ◇ **take a back seat (to sb)** to allow sb else to direct or control sth while taking on a relatively less important role yourself

back-seat driver *n.* (*informal*) **1.** PASSENGER WHO PESTERS A DRIVER a passenger in a vehicle who continually pesters the driver with unwanted advice or criticism **2.** SB GIVING UNWANTED ADVICE sb who gives unwanted advice or criticism while sb else carries out a task, or who attempts to control sth for which he or she has no responsibility

backset /bák set/ *n.* an eddy or a current flowing against the direction of the main current in a body of water

back shift *n.* US term **swing shift 1.** INDUST **SHIFT BETWEEN DAY AND NIGHT SHIFTS** a period of work beginning in the afternoon and ending at night. It overlaps between the day shift and the night shift. **2. WORKERS ON BACK SHIFT** a group of employees working on a back shift

backshore /bák shawr/ *n.* the area of the shore that is above the high-water mark except in very severe weather [Early 20thC. Coined from SHORE, on the model of *foreshore*.]

backside /bák sīd, bák sīd/ *n.* a person's buttocks (*informal*)

backsight /bák sīt/ *n.* **1.** ARMS **REAR SIGHT ON GUN** a sight on the part of a firearm nearest to the aimer's eye **2.** CIV ENG **SURVEYING SIGHT TAKEN BACKWARDS** a sight or reading taken by a surveyor back towards a position from which a previous sight has been made

back slang *n.* a type of slang in which words are disguised by being pronounced as if spelt backwards

backslap /bák slap/ (**-slaps, -slapping, -slapped**) *vti.* to treat sb, or treat each other, in a hearty, jovial, and enthusiastically complimentary way, with or without physical slaps on the back ○ *a political candidate who backslapped his way around the country* —**backslapper** *n.*

backslash /bák slash/ (*plural* **-slashes**) *n.* a keyboard character (\) with various uses in computing and programming

backslide /bák slīd/ (**-slides, -sliding, -slid** /-slid/, **-slid** *or* **-slidden** /-slidd'n/) *vi.* to fall back into wrongdoing after attempting to live morally, or to lose faith in a religion after being a believer —**backslider** *n.*

backspace /bák spayss/ *vi.* (**-spaces, -spacing, -spaced**) **MOVE BACK ONE SPACE** to move the cursor of a computer or the carriage of a typewriter back one or more spaces using the key designed for this purpose ■ *n.* **KEY FOR MOVING BACK ONE SPACE** a key on a computer or typewriter keyboard that moves the cursor or carriage back one space at a time

backspin /bák spin/ *n.* spin that makes a ball rotate in the opposite direction to its line of movement so that when it lands or strikes sth its forward momentum will be reduced

backstab /bák stab/ (**-stabs, -stabbing, -stabbed**) *vt.* to do or say sth harmful to sb after pretending to be a friend [Early 20thC. From the expression *to stab sb in the back.*] —**backstabber** *n.* —**backstabbing** *n.*

backstage /bák stáyj/ *adv.* **1.** THEATRE **BEHIND THE SCENES** behind the area of a theatre stage that is visible to an audience, e.g. in the areas where stage technicians work or in the dressing rooms ○ *Journalists were allowed backstage to interview the star.* **2. IN PRIVATE** in private or out of the view of the general public ■ *adj.* **1.** THEATRE **SITUATED OR WORKING BEHIND THE SCENES** situated or working in the area of a stage not visible to an audience **2. NOT VISIBLE TO PUBLIC** taking place in private or out of the view of the general public

backstairs /bák stairz/ *npl.* **PRIVATE STAIRS** a set of stairs in a private part of a house, often originally for the use of servants ■ *adj.* **SECRET** carried on secretly or furtively [Mid-17thC. The sense 'secret' derives from the backstairs in royal palaces, which were inaccessible to state visitors.]

backstay /bák stay/ *n.* **1.** SAILING **SUPPORTING ROPE** a rope leading backwards from the top of a mast to the side or stern and giving support to the mast **2. BACK SUPPORT** a thing that supports or strengthens the back of sth else, e.g. a piece of leather covering the back seam of a shoe

backstitch /bák stich/ *n.* **REINFORCED STITCH** a method of stitching in which each new stitch starts from the middle of the previous stitch ■ *vti.* (**-stitches, -stitching, -stitched**) **STITCH STRONGLY** to sew fabric using backstitches

backstop /bák stop/ (**-stops, -stopping, -stopped**) *n.* **1.** SPORTS **SCREEN TO STOP A BALL** a screen or barrier to stop the ball travelling out of the playing area **2.** BASEBALL = **catcher** *n.* 1 **3.** MECH ENG **CATCH STOPPING BACKWARD MOVEMENT** a catch on a mechanism designed to prevent it from moving back too far **4. ADDITIONAL SUPPORT** sb or sth providing additional support or protection in case sb or sth else fails

back-story (*plural* **back-stories**) *n.* **1. BACKGROUND TO STORY** the events that are supposed to have taken place before the action of a film, television programme, or novel begins (*informal*) **2.** = **prequel**

back straight *n.* the straight section of a racing circuit opposite the home straight. US term **back stretch**

backstreet /bák street/ *n.* **backstreet, back street MINOR STREET** a small unimportant street off the main roads in a city or town ■ *adj.* **1. backstreet, back-street IN A BACKSTREET** situated or taking place in a backstreet **2. back-street ILLICIT** carried out furtively or illicitly in a place where it is unlikely to attract public attention

back stretch *n.* US = **back straight**

backstroke /bák strōk/ *n.* **1.** SWIMMING **SWIMMING ON THE BACK** a method of swimming on the back in which the swimmer makes circular backward movements with each arm alternately while kicking the legs rhythmically up and down **2. RETURN STROKE** a stroke or movement in the opposite direction to that of the original or forward one **3.** US SPORTS **BACKHAND STROKE** a backhand stroke ■ *vi.* (**-strokes, -stroking, -stroked**) SWIMMING **SWIM BACKSTROKE** to swim using the backstroke —**backstroker** *n.*

backswept /bák swept/ *adj.* angled, slanting, or brushed backwards ○ *a backswept hairstyle*

backswimmer /bák swimmər/ *n.* a North American water bug that swims lying on its back and propelled by its broad hindlegs. Family: Notonectidae.

backswing /bák swing/ *n.* SPORTS the backward movement of a player's club, bat, or racket away from the eventual point of contact with the ball in preparation for playing the actual stroke

backsword /bák sawrd/ *n.* **1.** ARMS **ONE-EDGED SWORD** a sword with a cutting edge on one side of the blade only **2.** FENCING **FENCING STICK** a stick with a basket-shaped hilt used in fencing practice

back talk *n.* US = **backchat**

back to back *adv.* **1. WITH BACKS TO EACH OTHER** with backs turned towards, and sometimes touching, each other ○ *The palace guards stood back to back, getting ready to begin pacing.* **2. CONSECUTIVELY** one immediately after the other ○ *We've all worked two shifts back to back.*

back-to-back *adj.* **1. WITH BACKS TO EACH OTHER** standing or sitting with backs turned to, and sometimes touching, one another **2. BUILT CLOSE TOGETHER** used to describe houses that are built so that their backs join or are only narrowly separated ○ *street after street of back-to-back houses* **3. CONSECUTIVE** following immediately one after the other ○ *We had back-to-back meetings prior to the new-product launch.* ■ *n.* **HOUSE BUILT BACK TO BACK** a house built with its back touching the back of another house or only narrowly separated from it —**back-to-back** *adv.*

back to front *adv.* with the back part at the front, or in reverse order ○ *I hadn't noticed I'd put my sweater on back to front.*

backtrack /bák trak/ (**-tracks, -tracking, -tracked**) *vi.* **1. GO BACK** to go back in the direction from which you have come **2. CHANGE YOUR MIND** to change, or distance yourself from, a previous action, opinion, statement, or policy, especially as a result of other people's opposition to it ○ *After a lot of public outrage, the government backtracked on its proposed ban.*

backup /bák up/ *n.* **1. SUPPORT** support or assistance from other people, e.g. from the supplier of a product when it breaks down **2. REINFORCEMENTS** reinforcements to help personnel already committed, especially police officers ○ *The officers at the scene are calling for backup from another force.* **3. SUBSTITUTE OR RESERVE** a substitute or reserve that can be used if the thing normally used fails **4.** COMPUT **SECURITY COPY** a separate copy of data with which sb is working that is stored, e.g., on a floppy disk **5.** COMPUT **COPYING** the procedure for making a separate copy or copies of data with which sb is working ○ *The backup is done automatically every morning.* **6. OVERFLOW** an overflow from a pipe caused by a blockage ○ *a backup of water* ■ *adj.* **1. SUPPORTING** acting as a support, reserve, or reinforcement ○ *The field commander radioed for backup troops.* **2.** COMPUT **COPIED** made or kept in case sth goes wrong with the original ○ *Check the condition of your backup disk.* [Mid-20thC. From the phrase *back up.*]

backup light *n.* US = **reversing light**

backward /bákwərd/ *adj.* **1. TO THE REAR** in the opposite direction to the one in which sb or sth is facing **2. REVERSED** positioned the opposite way round, arranged in the opposite order, or proceeding in the opposite direction to the normal one **3. NOT ACHIEVING USUAL OR EXPECTED STANDARD** lagging behind the progress and development of others of comparable status ○ *a backward economy* **4. RETROGRADE** causing or representing a return to a previous or less advanced, and usually less satisfactory, state ○ *a backward step developmentally* **5. TOWARDS THE PAST** directed towards the past ○ *a backward look over the city's progress during the last century* **6. SHY** shy or lacking in self-confidence ■ *adv.* US = **backwards** —**backwardness** *n.* ◇ **not be backward in coming forward** to be quick and eager to present yourself for sth, especially to claim sth that could benefit you

WORD KEY: USAGE

backward or **backwards**? ***Backward*** is the only form available for the adjective: *A backward glance.* In British, Canadian, Australian, and New Zealand English, ***backwards*** is commonly used as well as ***backward*** for the adverb, but in American English ***backward*** is more common for both parts of speech. *The vehicle moved slowly backwards/backward.*

backwardation /bákwər dáysh'n/ *n.* **1.** COMM **PRICE DIFFERENCE ACCORDING TO DELIVERY DATE** the amount by which the price of goods for immediate delivery differs from the price of goods for delivery at a future time **2.** STOCK EXCH **DELAYING DELIVERY OF PURCHASED SECURITIES** on the London Stock Exchange, the right to delay delivery of securities purchased by sb until the next settlement period, or the percentage paid by the seller for this right (*dated*)

backward-looking *adj.* more concerned with or relevant to a past state of affairs than the present

backwards *adv.* US term **backward 1. BACK FIRST** with your back or the back of an object facing in the direction in which you move or it moves ○ *She walked backwards out of the room.* **2. TOWARDS THE REAR** behind you or in a direction away from the front of sth **3. WRONG WAY ROUND** the opposite way round, or in the reverse order or direction to the usual ○ *The kids are trying to say the alphabet backwards.* **4. TOWARDS THE PAST** towards or into the past ○ *to travel backwards in time* **5. INTO A WORSE CONDITION** into a state that is worse or less advanced than the previous or original one ○ *Everything's gone backwards since the new committee took over.* ◇ **backwards and forwards** in one direction and then in the other ○ *travelling backwards and forwards between London and New York* ◇ **bend or lean over backwards** to make an exceptional effort to do sth, especially to help sb ◇ **know sth backwards** know sth very well

backwash /bák wosh/ *n.* **1. RETREATING WAVE** the movement of water back down a beach after a wave has broken **2.** NAUT **WATER PUSHED BACKWARDS** a backward movement or flow in water produced by a ship's propeller or by oars **3.** AIR **AIR PUSHED BACKWARDS** a backward rush of air produced by an aircraft propeller or jet engine **4. CONSEQUENCES** the consequential effects of an event or action, especially unpleasant or unsettling ones

backwater /bák wawtər/ *n.* **1. SMALL STAGNANT BRANCH OF RIVER** a still body of water connected to a river but not affected by its current **2. STILL WATER** a still body of water held back by a dam, obstruction, or prevailing countercurrent **3. DULL PLACE** a place or situation regarded as cut off from the mainstream of activity or development and consequently seen as quiet and uneventful or unimportant and dull

backwoods /bák wŏŏdz/ *npl.* **1. REMOTE WOODED AREAS** a sparsely inhabited forested area distant from the main centres of population **2. UNSOPHISTICATED AREA** an area regarded as remote, rustic, and culturally unsophisticated ■ *adj.* **1. IN OR FROM REMOTE AREA** situated in, coming from, or typical of a sparsely settled area **2. UNSOPHISTICATED** rustic, uncouth, or culturally unsophisticated

backwoodsman /bák wŏŏdzmən/ (*plural* **-men** /-mən/) *n.* **1. BACKWOODS INHABITANT** sb who lives in the backwoods **2. SELDOM-ATTENDING PEER** a member of the House of Lords who does not often attend (*informal*)

backword /bák wurd/ *n.* **BROKEN PROMISE** failure to keep a promise or honour a commitment (*regional*) ■ *v.* (**-words, -wording, -worded**) **BREAK PROMISE** to break a promise or commitment to sb (*regional*)

back yard (*plural* **back yards** *or* **backyards**) *n.* **1. YARD BEHIND A HOUSE** a yard or, in the United States, a garden behind a house **2.** *US, Can* **GARDEN** a back garden **3. SB'S NEIGHBOURHOOD** sb's immediate neighbourhood or the area considered as sb's home ground ○ *The gangs know better than to cause trouble in each other's back yard.*

backyard /bák yaard/ *adj.* situated or happening in a back yard

bacon /báykən/ *n.* meat from the back and sides of a pig that has been salted, dried, and often smoked [14thC. Via Old French, from a prehistoric Germanic word meaning literally 'back meat', which is also the ancestor of English *back*.] ◇ **bring home the bacon** to earn the money on which a family lives (*informal*) ◇ **save sb's bacon** to save sb from serious trouble, punishment, injury, or danger (*informal*)

Bacon /báykən/, **Sir Francis, 1st Baron Verulam and Viscount St Albans** (1561–1626) English philosopher, lawyer, and statesman. A pioneer of modern scientific thought, he wrote *The Advancement of Learning* (1605) and *Essayes* (1597–1625). He was Lord Chancellor (1618–21), but was dismissed for bribery.

Bacon, Francis (1909–92) Irish-born British painter. A major late-20th century painter, he often used gory and shocking imagery, as in *Head Surrounded by Sides of Beef (Study After Velázquez)* (1954).

Bacon, Roger (1214?–94) English philosopher and scientist. A Franciscan monk, he published works on mathematics, philosophy, and logic, including his *Great Work* (1266–67). He was imprisoned by his order for his 'novelties'. Known as **Doctor Mirabilis 'Wonderful Doctor'**

bacon-and-eggs *n.* **BOT** = **bird's-foot trefoil** [From its yellow flowers streaked with red]

baconer /báykənər/ *n.* a pig reared to produce bacon

Baconian /bay kṓni ən/ *adj.* **OF WORKS OF SIR FRANCIS BACON** typical of or similar to the philosophy of Sir Francis Bacon, particularly his method of inductive reasoning in which the emphasis is placed on collecting instances rather than testing theories ■ *n.* **1.** **PHILOS FOLLOWER OF SIR FRANCIS BACON** sb who studies the philosophy of Sir Francis Bacon or whose own philosophy or philosophical method is strongly influenced by him **2.** **LITERAT BELIEVER IN BACON AS AUTHOR OF SHAKESPEARE'S PLAYS** sb who believes that the plays usually attributed to Shakespeare were actually written by Sir Francis Bacon

bact. *abbr.* **1.** bacteria **2.** bacteriology

bacteraemia /báktə rė̇́emi ə/ *n.* the presence of bacteria in the blood —**bacteraemic** *adj.* —**bacteraemically** *adv.*

bacteremia *n.* US = **bacteraemia**

bacteri- *prefix.* = **bacterio-**

bacteria plural of **bacterium**

bacterial /bak tė́eri əl/ *adj.* consisting of, caused by, or connected with bacteria —**bacterially** *adv.*

bactericide /bak tė́eri sīd/ *n.* a substance or agent that destroys bacteria —**bactericidal** *adj.*

bacterio- *prefix.* **1.** bacteria, bacterial ○ *bacteriostat* **2.** pressure, weight ○ *barometer* [From modern Latin *bacterium* 'BACTERIUM']

bacteriol. *abbr.* **1.** bacteriological **2.** bacteriology

bacteriology /bak tė́eri ólləji/ *n.* the scientific study of bacteria, especially in relation to medicine and agriculture —**bacteriological** /bak tė́eri ə lójjik'l/ *adj.* —**bacteriologically** /-lójjikli/ *adv.* —**bacteriologist** /bak tė́eri ólləjist/ *n.*

bacteriolysis /bak tė́eri óllississ/ (*plural* **-ses** /-seez/) *n.* the dissolution or destruction of a bacterial cell, e.g. as a result of the use of a bactericidal agent during disinfection —**bacteriolytic** /bak tė́eri ə líttik/ *adj.*

bacteriophage /bak tė́eri ə fayj/ *n.* a virus that infects bacteria and may integrate into the genetic material of its host cell. Bacteriophages are used as vectors in gene cloning and have other biotechnological uses. —**bacteriophagic** /bak tė́eri ə fájjik/ *adj.* —**bacteriophagous** /-óffəgəss/ *adj.* —**bacteriophagy** /-óffə ji/ *n.*

bacteriostasis /bak tė́eri ō stáyssiss/ *n.* inhibition of bacterial growth and multiplication by a chemical agent

bacteriostat /bak tė́eri ə stat/ *n.* a substance that restricts the growth and activity of bacteria without killing them —**bacteriostatic** /bak tė́eri ō státtik/ *adj.* —**bacteriostatically** /-státtikli/ *adv.*

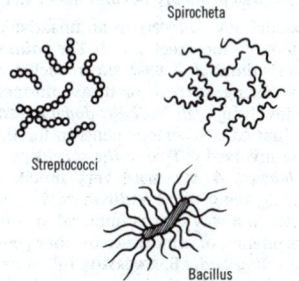

Streptococci   Spirocheta

Bacillus

Bacteria

bacterium /bak tė́eri əm/ (*plural* **-a** /-ri ə/) *n.* a single-celled, often parasitic microorganism without distinct nuclei or organized cell structures. Various species are responsible for decay, fermentation, nitrogen fixation, and many plant and animal diseases. Kingdom: *Eubacteria*. [Mid-19thC. From, ultimately, Greek *baktērion* 'little rod' (because the first ones discovered were rod-shaped), from *baktron* 'rod'.]

bacteriuria /bak tė́eri yoóri ə/ *n.* the presence of bacteria in urine

bacteroid /báktə royd/ *n.* **BACTERIUM IN HUMAN MOUTH AND GUT** a bacterium that can grow only in the absence of air, found in the human mouth and intestinal tract, in the rumen of ruminant animals, and in sewage. Genus: *Bacteroides*. ■ *adj.* **RESEMBLING A BACTERIUM** resembling a bacterium in structure or behaviour

Bactrian camel

Bactrian camel /báktri ən-/ *n.* a two-humped camel, originally from central Asia but now found only in the Gobi Desert. Latin name: *Camelus bactrianus*. [Early 17thC. *Bactrian* from, ultimately, Latin *Bactrianus*, from *Bactria*, an ancient country in central Asia.]

baculiform /bə kyoóli fawrm/ *adj.* shaped like a rod [Coined from Latin *baculum* 'rod' (see BACULUM) + -FORM]

baculum /bákyoŏləm/ (*plural* **-ula** /-lə/ *or* **-ulums**) *n.* a small bone found in the penis of many mammals, especially carnivores, but also in primates, rodents, bats, and insectivores [Mid-20thC. From Latin, 'rod' (source of English *bacillus*, *baguette*, and *debacle*). Ultimately from an Indo-European word meaning 'stick', which is also the ancestor of English *bacterium*.]

bad /bad/ *adj.* (**worse** /wurss/, **worst** /wurst/) **1. OF POOR QUALITY** below an acceptable standard in quality or performance ○ *bad driving* **2. UNSKILFUL** lacking the skill or competence to perform a task adequately ○ *I've always been bad at remembering dates.* **3. NOT FUNCTIONING PROPERLY** not functioning properly because of a fault ○ *bad TV reception* **4. INCORRECT** incorrect according to the normal rules, especially those governing the use of language ○ *used bad grammar in the essay* **5. WICKED** morally evil, blameworthy, or unacceptable ○ *It's how you tell the good guys from the bad guys.* **6. MISBEHAVING AND DISOBEDIENT** troublesome or annoying to other, especially older, people, usually through rudeness, disobedience, or mischievousness ○ *Go to your room, you bad child!* **7. ANGRY AND UNPLEASANT TOWARDS OTHERS** characterized by anger and unpleasantness towards other people ○ *in a bad mood* **8. OFFENSIVE** likely to cause offence to other people because it deals with a taboo subject or expresses violent feelings ○ *swearing and other bad language* **9. HARMFUL** liable to damage health or cause injury ○ *Reading in a dim light is bad for the eyes.* **10. ROTTEN** rotted or deteriorated in quality to the point of being unfit to eat or drink ○ *This milk is bad.* **11. INJURED OR DISEASED** affected by an injury or disease, or not functioning properly, and often causing pain ○ *She's got a bad tooth.* **12. UNWELL** unwell or in pain ○ *I've been feeling bad for a couple of days.* **13. UNEASY** uneasy or regretful about sth, or causing sb to feel this way ○ *I feel really bad about having had to reprimand you.* **14. MORE UNPLEASANT THAN USUAL** possessing an unpleasant, painful, or troublesome quality to a higher degree than usual ○ *Was the pain very bad?* **15. DISTRESSING** likely to cause unhappiness or disappointment ○ *I'm afraid the news is bad.* **16. UNFAVOURABLE** containing or indicating an unfavourable assessment of sb's performance, work, or character ○ *received a bad job evaluation* **17.** (*comparative* **badder**, *superlative* **baddest**) **VERY GOOD** extremely good (*slang*) ○ *the baddest outfit at the party* ■ *n.* **1. EVIL** wrong or immoral behaviour ○ *You're old enough to know good from bad.* **2. UNSATISFACTORY OR UNPLEASANT THINGS** things or events that are unsatisfactory or unpleasant ○ *You've got to take the good with the bad.* ■ *adv.* (*informal*) **1. BADLY** in an unsatisfactory manner ○ *We didn't do too bad.* **2. VERY MUCH** to an intense or extreme degree ○ *He's got it bad!* [13thC. Origin uncertain, possibly from Old English *bǣddel* 'effeminate man'.] —**baddish** *adj.* —**badness** *n.* ◇ **go bad** to become rotten or unfit to eat ◇ **go from bad to worse** to become even more unpleasant, unsatisfactory, or morally unacceptable than before ◇ **go to the bad** to adopt or fall into a way of life that other people consider morally or socially debased and unacceptable (*dated*) ◇ **not bad** fairly good or of a standard that is admitted to be satisfactory, sometimes grudgingly or cautiously, but often in a positive or definitely approving way ○ *That's not bad for a first attempt.*

── WORD KEY: SYNONYMS ──

bad, criminal, delinquent, mischievous, naughty
CORE MEANING: indicating wrongdoing
bad the most general and widely used term, applying to a whole range of wrongdoing from the most trivial to the most immoral or evil; **criminal** specifically used in connection with wrongdoing that constitutes a criminal offence, but also used informally to indicate strong disapproval; **delinquent** a formal word, literally meaning neglectful of duty, for wrongdoing of a criminal or socially unacceptable nature; **mischievous** applied to children or their actions to suggest wrongdoing of a minor and often playful kind, but, when used of adults, suggesting more harmful wrongdoing designed to cause trouble; **naughty** used of children or their actions to describe both relatively trivial misdeeds and more major ones; sometimes used of adults in a rather arch or humorous way.

──── WORD KEY: REGIONAL NOTE ────

In many Caribbean pidgins and creoles (forms of language that develop when speakers of different languages have to communicate with each other) *bad* means 'very much, very good', as in: *A laikam bad.* (I like it very much indeed.). This usage has been popularized in Britain by young people of Afro-Caribbean ancestry: *It's bad, man.* (It's really good.). This *bad* is distinguished from traditional *bad* by intonation and often by a lengthening of the vowel. Other words that have undergone a similar transformation are *wicked* and *crucial*.

bad apple *n.* sb who is thought to be the source of a bad influence on others, especially a source of moral corruption (*informal*) [From the idea that one bad apple can spoil a whole bunch]

bad blood *n.* an intense and usually long-lasting feeling of hatred, anger, or resentment [From blood in the sense of 'feelings, emotions']

bad breath *n.* unpleasant-smelling breath

bad cheque *n.* a cheque that is invalid because there are insufficient funds in the account to cover it

bad debt *n.* a sum of money owed that is unlikely to be repaid

baddie /báddi/, **baddy** (*plural* **-dies**) *n.* sb, especially a character in a film or a novel, who does evil or criminal things (*informal*)

bade past tense of **bid**

Baden-Baden /báad'n báad'n/ resort and spa town in the Black Forest in Baden Württemberg State, southwestern Germany. Population: 52,800 (1992).

Baden-Powell /báyd'n pó əl, -pówəl/, **Agnes** (1858–1945) British founder of the Girl Guides Association. Together with her brother Robert, she set up the Girl Guides (1910) as the companion organization to the Boy Scouts.

Baden-Powell, Robert, 1st Baron Baden-Powell of Gilwell (1857–1941) British soldier and founder of the Boy Scout movement. He is famed for defending Mafeking during the Boer War (1899–1900). Full name **Robert Stephenson Smyth Baden-Powell**

Baden-Württemberg /báad'n vúrtəm burg/ state in southwestern Germany. It is bordered to the west by France and to the south by Switzerland. Capital: Stuttgart. Population: 10,272,000 (1994). Area: 35,752 sq. km/13,804 sq. mi.

Bader /báadər/, **Sir Douglas** (1910–82) British fighter pilot. He lost both legs in a flying accident (1931), but still commanded an RAF squadron in World War II. He was knighted (1976) for his work with the disabled. Full name **Sir Douglas Robert Stuart Bader**

bad faith *n.* insincerity, especially as evidenced by actions that do not accord with sb's stated intentions

badge /baj/ *n.* 1. EMBLEM a small distinctively shaped or marked piece of fabric, metal, or plastic worn on clothing as a sign of rank, membership, achievement, or personal enthusiasm and support for sth 2. IDENTIFYING FEATURE a characteristic or identifying mark of a particular quality or of a particular type of person ■ *vt.* (**badges, badging, badged**) 1. PUT IDENTIFYING MARK ON STH to put a badge or a distinctive identifying mark on sth 2. SELL WITH BADGE ON to market a product under different badges or brand names [14thC. From Old French *bage*, of unknown origin.]

Badger

badger /bájjər/ *n.* BURROWING MAMMAL a medium-sized burrowing animal that is related to the weasel and has short legs, strong claws, and a thick coat. It usually has black and white stripes on the sides of its head. Subfamily: Melinae. ■ *vt.* (**-ers, -ering, -ered**) PESTER SB to pester or annoy sb continually ○ *kept badgering me to go shopping* [Early 16thC. Origin uncertain, perhaps from BADGE, because of the markings on its head.]

bad hair day *n.* a day during which sb feels bad, looks bad, and experiences a series of difficulties or annoyances (*slang*)

badinage /báddi naazh, -naaj, báddi naazh/ *n.* the exchange of playful or joking remarks between people in conversation [Mid-17thC. From French, via *badin* 'fool, joker' from, ultimately, assumed Vulgar Latin *badare* 'to yawn, gape' (source of English *bay* and *abash*).]

badlands /bád landz/ *npl.* a barren area of gullies and bare mountain peaks or mesas formed by erosion

bad lot *n.* sb whose character and behaviour is strongly disapproved of and who is considered to be immoral or pernicious ○ *I knew he was a bad lot the moment I set eyes on him.*

bad luck *n.* 1. THINGS GOING WRONG an unpleasant experience, disappointment, or failure that seems to happen to sb by chance or undeservedly ■ *interj.* SYMPATHETIC STATEMENT used to show sympathy for sb when sth has gone wrong and to suggest that what happened was probably beyond his or her control

badly /báddli/ *adv.* 1. POORLY in an unsatisfactory, incompetent, or incorrect way ○ *The paintwork had been badly finished.* 2. UNHAPPILY in such a way as to cause suffering, sorrow, or disappointment to the people involved ○ *felt badly let down* 3. SEVERELY to a degree that causes serious concern for the person or thing involved ○ *Two of the survivors were very badly burned.* 4. VERY MUCH very much, or to an extreme degree ○ *We're badly in need of new ideas.* 5. WICKEDLY in a way that is immoral, or that causes trouble, offence, or annoyance to other people ○ *had been behaving badly* 6. REMORSEFUL full of remorse or regret ○ *feel badly about it* ■ *adj.* N England ILL unwell or ill ○ *She's still badly after that accident.*

badly off (**worse off, worst off**) *adj.* 1. POOR poor or short of money, or comparatively so (*hyphenated when used before a noun*) ○ *badly-off families* 2. LACKING IN poorly or inadequately supplied with sth ○ *We're badly off for good singers at the moment.*

badminton /bádmintən/ *n.* 1. SPORTS GAME WITH A NET AND RACKETS a game similar to tennis, played usually on an indoor court, using rackets to strike a shuttlecock back and forth across a high net 2. BEVERAGES CLARET COCKTAIL a long drink based on claret, with sugar and soda water added [Mid-19thC. Named after BADMINTON.]

Badminton /bádmintən/ village in southwestern England, known for the country house of the Duke of Beaufort, Badminton House, where horse trials are held annually

badmouth /bád mowth, -mowth/ (**-mouths, -mouthing, -mouthed**) *vt.* to make sharply critical or disparaging remarks about sb to other people (*slang*)

bad news *n.* sb or sth that is likely to cause trouble and should be avoided (*slang*) ○ *Something tells me this guy's bad news.*

bad-tempered *adj.* characterized by anger and unpleasantness towards other people —**bad-temperedly** *adv.*

Baedeker /báydikər/, **baedeker** *n.* any guidebook for travellers [Mid-19thC. From Karl BAEDEKER.]

Baedeker /báydikər/, **Karl** (1801–59) German publisher. His *Rhine Handbook* (1839) was the first of the famous guidebooks that still bear his name.

Baedeker raid *n.* any of the air raids carried out by the Luftwaffe in 1942 on cities in England, e.g. Canterbury and Bath, of cultural rather than military or economic importance (*dated*) [Because the targets were places that appeared in tourist guidebooks]

bael /báy əl/ *n.* a pear-shaped thick-shelled edible fruit similar to a quince, used in India as food and as a medicine for dysentery [Early 17thC. Via Hindi *bel* from, ultimately, Tamil *viḷavu*.]

Baeyer /bī ər/, **Johann** (1835–1917) German chemist. He explained the mechanism of photosynthesis and synthesized indigo dye. He received the Nobel Prize in chemistry in 1905. Full name **Johann Friedrich Wilhelm Adolf von Baeyer**

Baez /bī ez, bī éz, bīz/, **Joan** (b. 1941) US folksinger and activist. From the 1960s, she was widely known for her folk and protest songs and for her human rights campaigning.

Baffin /báffin/, **William** (1584–1622) English navigator. While trying to find the Northwest Passage (1612–16), he explored the Hudson Strait and Baffin Island.

Baffin Island Canada's largest island, located in the northeast of the country, forming part of Nunavut. Area: 476,070 sq. km/183,810 sq. mi.

baffle /báff'l/ *vt.* (**-fles, -fling, -fled**) 1. PUZZLE SB to prove too difficult or complicated for sb to understand, solve, or deal with, and cause a feeling of confusion or helplessness 2. FRUSTRATE STH to hinder or thwart an action or intention (*formal*) 3. TECH CONTROL STH to impede or control the movement of a fluid or gas or the emission of sound or light waves ■ *n.* 1. TECH RESTRAINING DEVICE a device used to control or impede the flow or emission of sth and reduce its force 2. ACOUSTICS PARTITION IN LOUDSPEAKER a partition in a loudspeaker or microphone intended to prevent sound waves of different frequencies from interfering with one another [Mid-16thC. Perhaps a blend of French *bafouer* 'to ridicule' and Scots *bauchle* 'to revile', both of unknown origin. Its earliest meaning was 'to disgrace publicly'.] —**bafflement** *n.*

baffling /báffling/ *adj.* impossible for the mind to understand, and causing a feeling of confusion or helplessness ○ *I find the new technology baffling.*

baffy /báffi/ (*plural* **-fies**) *n.* GOLF a hickory-shafted golf club similar to a modern number 4 or 5 wood (*dated*) [Late 19thC. Formed from Scots *baff* 'blow with sth soft or flat'.]

Bafta /báftə/ *n.* an award given for films and television programmes in Britain ○ *The film won two Baftas.*

BAFTA /báftə/ *abbr.* British Academy of Film and Television Arts

bag /bag/ *n.* 1. FLEXIBLE CONTAINER a nonrigid portable container made of fabric, leather, paper, or plastic in a wide variety of sizes, opening at one end and used mainly for packaging or carrying goods 2. AMOUNT IN FLEXIBLE CONTAINER the amount that can be contained in a bag, often used as a measure ○ *eating a bag of crisps* 3. PORTABLE CONTAINER FOR EQUIPMENT OR BELONGINGS a portable container made of strong flexible material for carrying sb's belongings or equipment ○ *I threw everything into a bag and rushed out.* 4. ITEM OF BAGGAGE an item of traveller's baggage, e.g. a suitcase, that can be carried by hand (*often used in the plural*) ○ *Our bags went missing at the airport.* 5. HANDBAG a handbag 6. HUNT NUMBER OF ANIMALS SHOT the number of animals shot or captured by an individual hunter or party 7. OFFENSIVE TERM an offensive term deliberately insulting a woman's age and appearance (*slang insult*) 8. SB'S SPECIALITY sth that sb is particularly interested in or good at (*slang dated*) 9. BASEBALL = base[1] n. 21 10. DRUGS SMALL QUANTITY OF ILLEGAL DRUG a small quantity of an illegal drug, e.g. heroin or marijuana, in a piece of folded paper, a plastic bag, or a similar container (*slang*) ■ *v.* (**bags, bagging, bagged**) 1. *vt.* CLAIM STH FOR YOURSELF to claim or get possession of sth for yourself before anyone else can claim it (*informal*) ○ *She quickly bagged the window seat.* 2. *vt.* PUT INTO BAG to put sth into a bag 3. *vti.* BULGE to bulge or become baggy, or cause sth to do this 4. *vt.* HUNT SHOOT OR CAPTURE ANIMAL to shoot or capture a game animal or bird ○ *He bagged a six-point buck.* 5. *vt.* OBTAIN STH to take, catch, seize, or steal sth, usually in an opportunistic way (*informal*) ○ *They've got hold of our address list and are using it to try and bag some of our customers.* 6. *vt.* SPOT STH to do, acquire, or see sth that is of particular interest or value to you and counts as an achievement in terms of one of your regular hobbies or pursuits (*informal*) 7. *vt.* Aus CRITICIZE STH to make disapproving comments about sth (*slang*) ■ *interj.* **bags** I WANT used to indicate that the speaker wants to claim the right to have or do sth, or demands that a particular thing should happen (*informal*) (*usually used by children*) ○ *Bags I go first!* [13thC. From Old Norse *baggi*.] —**bagger** *n.* ◇ **bag and baggage** with all your belongings ◇ **bag of tricks** 1. everything, especially all the equipment necessary to do sth (*informal*) ○ *They picked up the whole bag of tricks and slung it onto the back of a truck.* 2. a magician's collection of equipment and props ◇ **bags of** a huge amount or number of sth (*informal*) ◇ **in the bag** certain to be achieved or obtained (*informal*)

Baganda /bə gándə/ *npl.* an ethnic group living in East Africa, mainly in Uganda, and representing about 30 per cent of the population [Late 19thC. From Bantu.]

bagasse /bə gáss/ *n.* **1.** AGRIC PULP the pulp or dry refuse left after the juice has been extracted from sugar cane, and used as fuel, in making paper, and as cattle feed **2.** PAPER PAPER paper made from bagasse [Early 19thC. Via French, from Spanish *bagazo* 'dregs', from Latin *baca* 'berry'.]

bagatelle /bággə tél/ *n.* **1.** STH UNIMPORTANT a thing of little importance (*formal*) ○ *a mere bagatelle* **2.** GAME BOARD GAME a game played on a board or table, in which balls have to be propelled by a cue or spring-loaded launcher past obstacles and into numbered holes **3.** MUSIC SHORT PLAYFUL PIECE OF MUSIC a short piece of classical music, usually for piano, written in a playful style [Mid-17thC. Via French, from Italian *bagatella*, of unknown origin.]

Bagehot /bájjət/, **Walter** (1826–77) British economist and journalist. Editor of *The Economist* from 1860 until his death, he also wrote *The English Constitution* (1867), still a standard text.

bagel /báyg'l/ *n.* a glazed ring-shaped bread roll made from dough that is dropped in boiling water and then baked, which gives a slightly chewy texture to the crust [Early 20thC. Via Yiddish *beygl* from, ultimately, Old High German *boug* 'ring'.]

bagful /bágfŏŏl/ *n.* the amount a bag holds

baggage /bággij/ *n.* **1.** PACKED SUITCASES AND BAGS suitcases and other containers holding the belongings of people who are travelling **2.** MIL PORTABLE EQUIPMENT the equipment and supplies that a military force carries with it on campaign **3.** PRECONCEIVED IDEAS ideas, beliefs, or practices retained from sb's previous life experiences, especially insofar as they affect a new situation where they may be no longer relevant or appropriate (*informal*) ○ *emotional baggage* **4.** IMPUDENT GIRL OR WOMAN a girl or woman who is thought of as impudent or obstinate (*insult dated*) **5.** PROSTITUTE an immoral woman, especially a prostitute (*insult dated*) [15thC. Via French, from Old French *bague* 'bundle', of uncertain origin: probably from Germanic.]

baggage check *n.* US = left-luggage office

baggage handler *n.* sb whose job it is to load and unload baggage onto and off aeroplanes

baggies /bággiz/ *npl.* US clothing that is cut extra large for the size of the wearer and hangs loosely on the body (*informal*)

bagging /bágging/ *n.* **1.** CLOTH FOR BAGS coarse material used for making bags **2.** *ANZ* SEVERE CRITICISM a verbal attack or critically hostile response or reception

baggy /bággi/ (**-gier**, **-giest**) *adj.* hanging loosely, puffed out, or bulging, either as a deliberate style or as a result of being too big for the wearer or having stretched while being worn —**baggily** *adv.* —**bagginess** *n.*

bagh /baag/ *n. S Asia* a garden

Baghdad /bág dád/, **Bagdad, Baghdād** capital of Iraq in the eastern part of the country, on the River Tigris, northwest of Basra. Population: 4,478,000 (1995).

bag lady *n.* a homeless woman who carries her possessions in shopping bags (*informal*)

bagman /bágmən/ (*plural* **-men** /-mən/) *n.* **1.** COMM TRAVELLING SALESMAN a travelling salesman (*dated informal*) **2.** *Aus* TRAMP a tramp or vagrant worker (*informal*)

bagnio /bánnyŏ, baan-/ (*plural* **-gnios**) *n.* **1.** BROTHEL a house of prostitution (*literary*) **2.** PRISON a prison, especially a prison in Asia (*archaic*) **3.** BATHHOUSE a bathhouse in Italy or Turkey (*archaic*) [Late 16thC. Via Italian *bagno* 'bath' from Latin *balneus*, because public baths were often the site of illicit encounters and prostitution.]

Bagnold /bág nŏld/, **Enid** (1889–1981) British author and playwright. She is best known as the author of *National Velvet* (1935).

bag people *npl.* homeless people as a group (*informal*) [From the fact that they often keep their possessions in shopping bags]

bag person *n.* a homeless person who carries his or her possessions in shopping bags (*informal*)

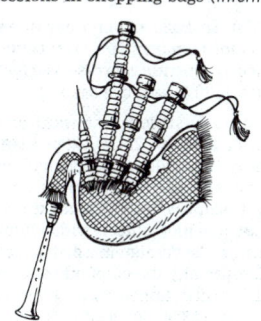
Bagpipe

bagpipes /bág pīps/ *npl.* a wind instrument consisting of an inflatable bag with an inlet pipe and one or more outlet pipes that produce either a fixed or a variable note. The player squeezes the inflated bag under his or her arm, forcing the air out through the speaking pipes and using finger holes to control the pitch of the note. (*sometimes singular*) —**bagpiper** *n.*

bags /bagz/ *npl.* **1.** LOOSE SKIN UNDER THE EYES prominent folds of skin beneath the eyes, often caused by fatigue **2.** TROUSERS a pair of trousers (*dated informal*)

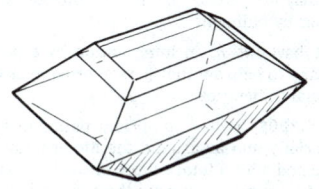
Baguette

baguette /ba gét/ *n.* **1.** FOOD STICK-SHAPED LOAF a long thin loaf of French bread **2.** RECTANGULAR GEM a gem cut into a long rectangular shape **3.** SHAPE OF BAGUETTE GEM the long narrow rectangular shape that a baguette gem is cut into **4.** ARCHIT CONVEX MOULDING a small narrow rounded convex moulding on a wall or column [Early 18thC. Via French from, ultimately, Latin *baculum* 'stick' (see BACULUM).]

Baguio /bággi ŏ/ city in Benguet Province on Luzon Island, the Philippines. It is the country's summer capital. Population: 183,000 (1990).

bagwash /bág wosh/ (*plural* **-washes**) *n.* (*archaic*) **1.** WASHING BUT NOT DRYING OR PRESSING the process or business of washing clothes but not drying or pressing them, or an amount of washing to be dealt with in this way **2.** LAUNDRY a laundry where clothes were washed but not dried or pressed [Bag because the bagwash is finished when the clothes are in the bag]

bagwig /bág wig/ *n.* an 18th-century wig with the back hair gathered in a decorative bag

bah /baa/ *interj.* used to express scornful irritation, disgust, or contempt

bahadur /bə háadər/ *n. S Asia* a title of respect used before an Indian surname in British India, originally applied to officers [Late 18thC. Via Urdu and Persian *bahādur* from Mongolian.]

Baha'i /bə hí, baa-, bə háa i, -hí i/ *n.* (*plural* **-ha'is**) **1.** RELIGION EMPHASIZING SPIRITUAL UNITY OF HUMANKIND a religion founded in Iran in 1863 that maintains that the teachings of all religions are of value and humankind is spiritually one, and advocates world peace **2.** BELIEVER IN BAHA'I sb who believes in and follows the teachings of Baha'i ■ *adj.* CONNECTED WITH BAHA'I connected with or characteristic of Baha'i [Late 19thC. Via Persian *bahā'ī* from Arabic *bahā* 'splendour'.] —**Baha'ism** *n.* —**Baha'ist** *n.*

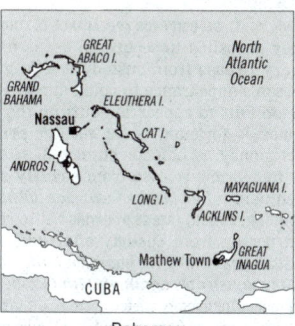
Bahamas

Bahamas /bə háaməz/ nation consisting of hundreds of islands, islets, and keys in the Atlantic Ocean southeast of Florida and north of Cuba. It was settled by the British in the 17th century and became independent in 1973. Language: English. Currency: Bahamian dollar. Capital: Nassau. Population: 259,367 (1996). Area: 13,940 sq. km/5,380 sq. mi. —**Bahamian** /bə háymi ən/ *n., adj.*

Bahasa Indonesia /baa háassə-/ *n.* the form of Malay that is the official language of Indonesia [From Malay, 'language of Indonesia']

Bahasa Malaysia /baa háassə-/ *n.* the form of Malay that is the official language of Malaysia [From Malay, 'language of Malaysia']

Bahawalpur /báhə wólpər/ city, district, and division of Punjab Province, Pakistan, situated on the River Sutlej. Population: 180,263 (1981).

Bahia /bə heé ə, -eé ə/ former name for **Salvador**

Bahía Blanca /bə heé ə blángkə, baa eé ə-/ city and port in the province of Buenos Aires, eastern Argentina. It is an important transport and commercial centre. Population: 244,145 (1991).

Bahia grass /bə heé ə-/ *n.* a perennial tropical American grass, grown in the southern United States for lawns, to stabilize soil, and as forage. Latin name: *Paspalum notatum.* [Early 20thC. Named for BAHIA.]

bahookie /bə hŏóki/ *n. Scotland* the buttocks (*humorous*)

Bahrain

Bahrain /baa ráyn/, **Bahrein** independent island state on the Persian Gulf off the coast of Saudi Arabia, northwest of Qatar. Language: Arabic, English, Farsi, Urdu. Currency: Bahraini dinar. Capital: Manama. Population: 603,318 (1997). Area: 707 sq. km/273 sq. mi. —**Bahraini** (*plural* **-is**) *n., adj.*

baht /baat/ (*plural* **bahts** *or* **baht**) *n.* **1.** see table at currency **2.** STH WORTH A BAHT a note or coin worth one baht [Early 19thC. From Thai *bāt*.]

bahuvrihi /báa hoo vreé hee/ (*plural* **-his**) *n.* a compound word in which the first part describes the second or governs it grammatically, and the second element cannot be substituted for the whole, e.g. 'yellowhammer' or 'afternoon' [Mid-19thC. From Sanskrit *bahuvrīhi* 'possessing much rice', a typical example of this class.]

baigan *n. Carib* = **bhaigan**

Baikal, Lake /bī ka͞al/ the world's deepest lake and the largest freshwater lake on the Eurasian continent, in southern Siberia, Russia. Area: 31,500 sq. km/12,200 sq. mi. Depth: 1,637 m/5,371 ft.

bail[1] /bayl/ *n.* **1. SECURITY FOR APPEARANCE IN COURT** a sum of money deposited to secure an accused person's temporary release from custody and to guarantee that person's appearance in court at a later date. If the person fails to appear in court on the date set, the money is forfeited. **2. SB WHO PAYS BAIL** sb who deposits money as bail for sb else **3. RELEASE UNDER SECURITY** temporary release from custody after bail has been paid ○ *Her brother was out on bail.* ■ *vt.* **(bails, bailing, bailed) FREE SB BY PAYING BAIL** to release an accused person from custody after bail has been paid (*usually passive*) ○ *He has been bailed to appear before the magistrates again on 11th October.* [14thC. Via Old French, 'temporary custody', from, ultimately, Latin *bajulus* 'sb who carries (responsibility)', of unknown origin.] ◇ **jump** *or* **skip bail** to fail to appear in court as promised at the end of a bail period (*informal*)

bail out *vt.* to secure sb's release from legal custody by paying bail, or posting bond

bail[2] /bayl/ **(bails, bailing, bailed), bale (bales, baling, baled)** *vti.* to empty water out of a boat, using a bucket or similar container ○ *We bailed the sinking boat for an hour.* [Early 17thC. From earlier *baille* 'bucket', via Old French, from an assumed Vulgar Latin *bajula* 'water carrier'.] —**bailer** *n.*

bail out, bale out *v.* **1.** *vti.* **EMPTY WATER OUT OF BOAT** to empty water out of a boat, using a bucket or similar container ○ *bailing water out as the boat slowly sank* **2.** *vi.* **PARACHUTE FROM PLANE** to escape from a plane that is in danger of crashing by making a parachute jump **3.** *vi.* **ESCAPE FROM DIFFICULT SITUATION** to abandon hurriedly and unceremoniously a situation that is dangerous or difficult ○ *When the company hit the skids, she was the first to bail out.* **4.** *vt.* **HELP SB OUT OF TROUBLE** to help sb out of a difficult situation

bail[3] /bayl/ *n.* **1. CROSSPIECE OF WICKET** in cricket, either of the two short pieces of wood laid on top of the stumps to make the wicket **2. PARTITION** a pole or framework used to separate horses in a barn or stable [Mid-18thC. Origin uncertain, possibly via Old French from, ultimately, Latin *baculum* 'stick' (see BACULUM). Originally 'outer wall of a castle'.]

bail up *vt. Aus* to stop sb in order to speak to him or her, often in a situation where that person does not want to be stopped or spoken to (*informal*) ○ *I was hoping I wouldn't have to speak to him, but he bailed me up as I was leaving.* [From BAIL[3]]

bail[4] /bayl/, **bale** *n.* **1. HINGED BAR** a hinged bar on a typewriter or printer that holds the paper against the platen **2. SEMICIRCULAR HANDLE** a semicircular handle, e.g. on a bucket **3. SEMICIRCULAR SUPPORT** a semicircular support, e.g. to hold up the canopy on a covered wagon [15thC. Origin uncertain, probably from assumed Old English *bēgel* or a Scandinavian word meaning 'ring'.]

Bail /bayl/, **Murray** (*b.* 1941) Australian writer, best known for his novels *Homesickness* (1980) and *Eucalyptus* (1998).

bailable /bayləb'l/ *adj.* **1. ELIGIBLE FOR BAIL** eligible to be released on bail ○ *a bailable prisoner* **2. ALLOWING BAIL** for which bail is allowable ○ *a bailable offence*

bail bar *n.* = **bail**[4] *n.* 1

bail bond *n.* a document in which the prisoner released on bail and the person who pays the bail money promise that the prisoner will appear in court at a set time

bail bondsman (*plural* **bail bondsmen**) *n. US* sb engaged in the business of providing bail money, or acting as surety, for an accused person

bailee /bay leé/ *n.* sb to whom goods are temporarily entrusted by bailment

bailey /báyli/ (*plural* **-leys**) *n.* **1. OUTER WALL OF A CASTLE** the outermost wall surrounding a castle **2. COURT INSIDE A CASTLE WALL** a courtyard inside the walls, especially the outermost walls, of a castle [13thC. Origin uncertain, probably an alteration of BAIL[3], under the influence of medieval Latin *ballium*.]

Bailey /báyli/, **David** (*b.* 1938) British photographer. He is best known for his fashion and portrait photography of the 1960s and 70s. Full name **David Royston Bailey**

Bailey bridge *n.* a temporary steel bridge made of prefabricated parts and designed for quick construction [Mid-20thC. Named after the English engineer Sir D. Coleman *Bailey* (1901–85), who designed it.]

bailie /báyli/ *n. Scotland* an honorary title sometimes given to senior members of a local council in Scotland. Formerly, the title was reserved for municipal magistrates. [13thC. Variant of BAILIFF.]

bailiff /báylif/ *n.* **1. STEWARD** a steward or agent of a landowner or landlord **2.** LAW **SHERIFF'S OFFICER** a legal officer who serves under a sheriff and is empowered to take possession of a debtor's property, forcibly if necessary, to serve writs, and to make arrests **3.** HIST **SENIOR OFFICIAL** a senior officer with judicial powers representing the sovereign in a district, e.g. a mayor or sheriff, especially the chief officer of a hundred. The word is still retained as an honorary title in some districts. [13thC. Via the Old French stem *baillif-* 'overseer' from assumed medieval Latin *bajulivus*, from Latin *bajulus* (see BAIL[1]).]

bailiwick /báyliwik/ *n.* an area of activity in which sb has particular responsibility, or in which he or she has specialized knowledge or ability ○ *Export permits are her bailiwick.* [15thC. From BAILIFF + *wik* 'town' (via Old English *wīc* from Latin *vicus*; see VICINITY).]

Baillie, Dame Isobel (1895–1983) British soprano. She regularly performed with Sir Thomas Beecham and Arturo Toscanini, and gave over 1,000 performances of Handel's *Messiah*.

bailment /báylmənt/ *n.* **1. ENTRUSTMENT OF GOODS** the temporary entrustment, subject to a contract, of goods to sb for a particular purpose **2. GRANTING BAIL** the granting of bail to sb in custody

bailor /báy láwr, báylər/ *n.* sb who entrusts goods to another by bailment

bailout /báyl owt/ *n.* an intervention by a person or company to help another person or company out of financial difficulties

Baily's beads /báyliz-/ *npl.* bright points of sunlight that briefly appear around the Moon immediately before and after a total eclipse of the Sun. They are caused by sunlight shining through valleys on the Moon. [Mid-19thC. Named after the English astronomer Francis *Baily* (1774–1844).]

báinín /báw neen/, **bawneen** *n. Ireland* **1. WOOLLEN JACKET** a collarless jacket for men, made of white wool **2. WHITE WOOL** a type of white wool prepared with some of the natural oil retained, used for jackets and skirts [Early 20thC. From Irish, from *bán* 'white'. Ultimately from an Indo-European base meaning 'to shine', which is also the ancestor of English *beacon*.]

Bain-marie

bain-marie /báN mə reé/ (*plural* **bain-maries**) *n.* a cooking utensil containing heated water into which another container is placed to be kept warm or cooked gently [Early 19thC. From French, translation of medieval Latin *balneum Mariae*, translation of Greek *kaminos Marias* 'alchemist's apparatus', literally 'furnace of Maria', alchemist and sister of Moses.]

Bairam /bī raám/ *n.* either of two Islamic festivals, the Lesser Bairam celebrated at the end of Ramadan or the Greater Bairam seventy days later, at the end of the Islamic year [Late 16thC. Via Turkish *bayram* from, ultimately, Persian *bazrām*.]

Baird /baird/, **John Logie** (1888–1946) British inventor. He demonstrated the first television system in 1926. He also researched into radar.

Bairiki /bī reéki/ administrative centre of Kiribati, situated on Tarawa atoll in the western Pacific Ocean. Population: 1,956.

bairn /bairn/ *n. Scotland, N England* a young child [Old English *bearn*. Ultimately from an Indo-European word meaning 'to carry, bear children', which is also the ancestor of English *bear, bring, suffer*, and *metaphor*.]

Bairnsdale /báirnz dayl/ town in southeastern Victoria, Australia, situated on the Mitchell River near Lake King. Population: 10,890 (1996).

Baisakhi /bī sáki/ *n.* the Sikh New Year festival, usually celebrated on 13 April. It commemorates the founding in 1699 of the Khalsa order by Gobind Singh.

bait[1] /bayt/ *n.* **1.** ANGLING, HUNT **FOOD FOR ATTRACTING ANIMALS** a piece of food attached to the end of a hook or thrown into water to entice a fish into biting it, or placed in a trap to lure an animal in ○ *fishing with live bait* **2. ENTICEMENT** sth used to attract sb or sth else into being caught, or used to tempt sb to do sth ■ *vt.* **(baits, baiting, baited) 1.** ANGLING, HUNT **PUT FOOD ON HOOK** to put a food attractant on a hook or in a trap ○ *This line's baited with a minnow.* **2. HARASS SB** to persecute, tease, or harass sb ○ *Stop baiting your little brother!* **3. ATTACK ANIMAL WITH DOGS** to set dogs onto a tethered animal, usually a bear or bull, for sport [13thC. Noun: from Old Norse *beit* 'food'; verb: from *beita* 'to hunt with dogs', from *bíta* 'to bite'.] —**baiter** *n.* ◇ **rise to the bait** to react to sth, especially to temptation or provocation, in precisely the way that sb wants you to, e.g. by getting angry when sb teases you

bait[2] /bayt/ *vi.* = **bate**[2]

bait box (*plural* **bait boxes**) *n.* a container with water in it for keeping bait alive during fishing

bait casting, bait cast *n.* a fishing rod used to present live or dead bait in order to catch fish

baiza /bízə/ (*plural* **-zas** *or* **-za**) *n.* see table at **currency** [Late 20thC. Via Arabic from Hindi *paisā*.]

baize /bayz/ *n.* a green woollen cloth, similar to felt, used chiefly for covering the tops of billiard and snooker tables or card tables [Late 16thC. From French *baies*, the plural of *bai* 'bay-coloured' (see BAY[4]), probably because of its original colour.]

Baja California /baá haa-/ peninsula in northwestern Mexico between the Gulf of California and the Pacific Ocean, divided into the states of Baja California and Baja California Sur. Length: 1,220 km/760 mi.

Bajan /báyjən/ *n., adj. Carib* Barbadian (*informal*) [Mid-20thC. Shortening and alteration of *Barbadian*.]

bajee *n.* FOOD = **bhaji**

bake /bayk/ *v.* **(bakes, baking, baked) 1.** *vti.* **COOK FOOD IN OVEN** to cook sth such as bread, a cake, or a pie in an oven by dry heat, or be cooked in this way **2.** *vti.* **HARDEN BY HEAT** to become hardened, or harden sth, by exposing it to dry heat **3.** *vi.* **BE VERY HOT** to be or feel very hot (*informal*) ○ *You must be baking in that heavy coat.* ■ *n.* **1. AMOUNT BAKED** a number of things baked at the same time **2.** *Scotland* **TYPE OF BISCUIT** a type of biscuit **3. OVEN-COOKED DISH** a dish of food that is cooked in the oven ○ *a cheese and vegetable bake* [Old English *bacan* (source of English *batch*). Ultimately from an Indo-European base meaning 'to warm', which is also the ancestor of English *bath*.]

baked Alaska *n.* a dessert consisting of a cooked cake base that is cooled, topped with ice cream, covered with meringue, and then quickly browned in a very hot oven

baked beans *npl.* baked haricot beans in a tomato sauce, usually bought in tins

bakehouse /báyk howss/ *n.* = **bakery**

Bakelite /báykə līt/ *tdmk.* a trademark for any of various synthetic resins used in many manufacturing applications

baker /báykər/ *n.* **1. SB WHO MAKES BREAD AND CAKES** sb who makes bread, cakes, and other baked foods, especially sb who makes them for sale **2. PORTABLE OVEN** a portable oven

Baker /báykər/, **Dame Janet** (*b.* 1933) British mezzo-soprano. After performing as a soloist for Sir John Barbirolli in the 1960s, she moved on to opera, and is especially associated with English music. Born **Janet Abbott**

AKG London

Josephine Baker

Baker, Josephine (1906–75) US-born French dancer and entertainer. She performed as a singer and dancer in New York before settling in Paris in 1925. Highly popular in Europe, she campaigned for racial equality in the United States in the 1950s and 1960s. Born **Freda Josephine McDonald**

Baker, Sir Samuel (1821–93) British explorer. He searched for the sources of the Nile and reached present-day Lake Mobutu Sese Seko, which he called Lake Albert (1864). Full name **Sir Samuel White Baker**

baker's dozen *n.* a set of thirteen items [From the fact that retailers of bread formerly received an extra loaf with each dozen from the baker, which they were entitled to keep as profit]

bakery /báykəri/ (*plural* **-ies**) *n.* **1.** PLACE WHERE THINGS ARE BAKED a building or part of a building where items of food, especially bread and cakes, are baked **2.** SHOP SELLING BAKED FOOD a shop or part of a store where items of baked food, especially bread and cakes, are sold [Mid-19thC. Its earliest meaning was 'the work of a baker'.]

Bakewell /báyk wel/, **Robert** (1725–95) British agriculturalist. He used selective breeding to improve farm livestock and established the Leicester breed of sheep.

Bakewell tart *n.* a tart with a pastry base covered with jam and topped with almond-flavoured sponge [Named after the town of Bakewell in Derbyshire]

Bakhtaran /báktə raàn/, **Bākhtarān** city in western Iran and capital of Bakhtaran Province, situated on the Hamadan-Baghdad trading route. Population: 624,084 (1991).

baking /báyking/ *n.* **1.** COOKING OF BREAD AND CAKES the cooking of bread, cakes, and other foods by dry heat in an oven ○ *did the baking early in the morning* **2.** AMOUNT BAKED AT ONE TIME a quantity of items baked at one time ○ *a baking of 46 rolls* ■ *adj.* VERY HOT very hot and dry ○ *a baking sun*

baking powder *n.* a mixture containing sodium bicarbonate, starch, and acids, used to make cakes and some light doughs rise. The acids react with bicarbonate of soda when liquid is added, releasing carbon dioxide that aerates the mixture.

baking sheet *n.* US = baking tray

baking soda *n.* = bicarbonate of soda

baking tray *n.* a flat metal tray used for cooking, especially baking, food in an oven

bakkie /báki/ *n. S Africa* **1.** PICK-UP TRUCK a pick-up truck with an open back **2.** BOWL a bowl or basin

baklava /baàklə vaa, bákləvə/ *n.* a dessert, originally from Turkey, made of filo pastry brushed with butter, layered with nuts and baked, with syrup or honey poured over it after cooking [Mid-17thC. From Turkish.]

bakra /bákrə/ *n. Carib* a white person, particularly one from Britain [Mid-18thC. From Ibibio and Efik *(m)bakara* 'European, master'.]

baksheesh /bák sheesh, bák sheesh/ *n.* in the Middle East, money given as a tip or bribe, or as charity [Mid-18thC. From Persian *bakšīš*. Ultimately from an Indo-European word meaning 'to share out', which is also the ancestor of English *pagoda* and *nebbish*.]

Baku /baa koó/ capital of Azerbaijan, on the shores of the Caspian Sea, in the centre of an oil-producing region in the eastern part of the country. Population: 1,780,000 (1990).

Bakunin /bə koónin/, **Mikhail** (1814–76) Russian-born anarchist. Born an aristocrat, he was sent in exile to Siberia in 1857, but escaped to England in 1861 to become Europe's leading anarchist. Full name **Mikhail Aleksandrovich Bakunin**

BAL *n.* = dimercaprol [An acronym of *British anti-lewisite*]

bal. *abbr.* balance

Bala, Lake /bállə/ lake in Gwynedd, Wales, the chief source of the River Dee. Area: 10 sq. km/4 sq. mi.

Balaam /báyləm, báy lam/ *n.* in the Bible, a Mesopotamian seer who, when called on to curse the Israelites, instead praised them after being reproached by his ass (Numbers 22–24)

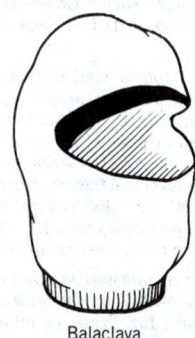

Balaclava

balaclava /bállə klaàvə/, **balaclava helmet** *n.* a close-fitting knitted covering for the head and neck, leaving only the face, or parts of it, exposed [Late 19thC. Named after the village of *Balaklava* in the Crimea, probably because the cap was worn by infantry involved in the campaign there.]

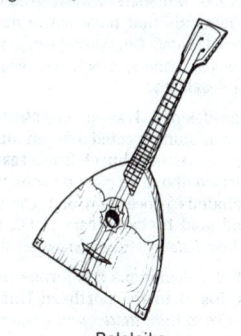

Balalaika

balalaika /bállə lĩkə/ *n.* a Russian musical instrument with a triangular sound box and three strings that produces sounds similar to a mandolin when plucked or strummed [Late 18thC. From Russian, of Turkic origin.]

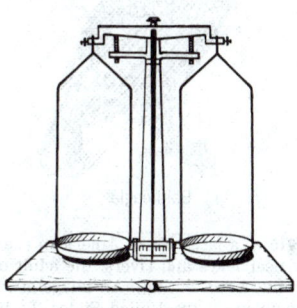

Balance

balance /bálənss/ *n.* **1.** STEADY STATE ON A NARROW BASE a state in which a body or object remains reasonably steady in a particular position while resting on a base that is narrow or small relative to its other dimensions. For human beings, this most commonly involves remaining upright and steady on

the feet. ○ *He lost his balance and fell from the beam.* **2.** OPPOSITION OF EQUAL FORCES a state in which two opposing forces or factors are of equal strength or importance so that they effectively cancel each other out and stability is maintained **3.** HARMONY a state in which various elements form a satisfying and harmonious whole and nothing is out of proportion or unduly emphasized at the expense of the rest **4.** EMOTIONAL STABILITY a state of emotional and mental stability in which sb is calm and able to make rational decisions and judgments **5.** TECH WEIGHING MACHINE a simple mechanical device for weighing objects or samples, often consisting of a pivoted horizontal beam with a pan suspended from each end. Material to be weighed is put in one pan and weights of a fixed value are gradually added to the other until the beam returns to the horizontal. **6.** COUNTERWEIGHT sth that offsets or counters the weight or influence of another element ○ *a system of checks and balances* **7.** GREATER PART the greater, more significant, or more influential part of sth, such as evidence or opinion that is likely to sway a decision **8.** REMAINDER a remaining or outstanding amount, e.g. the amount remaining in a bank account after a withdrawal or the amount still to be paid to settle a bill **9.** ACCT EQUAL DEBIT AND CREDIT a position where the amounts on the debit and credit sides of an account are equal and cancel each other out **10.** ACCT DIFFERENCE BETWEEN DEBIT AND CREDIT the amount by which the debit and credit sides of an account differ **11.** CHEM EQUALITY OF ELEMENTS IN AN EQUATION a state of a chemical equation where the number of the atoms of each chemical element are equal on both sides of the equation ■ *v.* (**-ances, -ancing, -anced**) **1.** *vti.* REMAIN IN OR GIVE STH EQUILIBRIUM to achieve or maintain, or cause sb or sth to achieve or maintain, a position of steadiness while resting on a narrow base ○ *balanced precariously on a branch* **2.** *vti.* PLACE IN PRECARIOUS POSITION to place an object in a position where it is or seems to be in imminent danger of falling over or of falling off sth (*often passive*) **3.** *vt.* ASSESS STH to assess and compare the relative importance of different factors or alternatives before making a choice or decision ○ *balanced the pros and cons of the plan before moving ahead with it* **4.** *vt.* WEIGH IN BALANCE to weigh sth in a balance or by an action or method that resembles the working of a balance **5.** *vti.* EQUAL OR CANCEL OUT to be equal to sth in force, weight, or importance, or cancel it out **6.** *vt.* ARTS BRING ELEMENTS INTO HARMONY to arrange the different elements of sth so that they form a harmonious and well-proportioned whole **7.** *vt.* MATH, CHEM BRING EQUATION INTO EQUALITY to bring the elements of a chemical or mathematical equation into a state of equality **8.** *vt.* ACCT ASSESS ACCOUNT to assess the relative positions of the debit and credit sides of an account **9.** *vt.* ACCT EQUALIZE ACCOUNT to make the debit and credit sides of an account equal [13thC. Via Old French from, ultimately, Latin (*libra*) *bilanx*, literally '(scales) with two pans', from *lanx* 'plate, pan'.] —**balanceable** *adj.* ◇ **balance the books** to ensure that the debit and credit or income and expenditure sides of an account show the same total, usually by making additional entries ◇ **hang in the balance** to be in a dramatic and tense situation where two diametrically opposed outcomes are possible and the possibility of an unfavourable one is real and greatly feared ◇ **hold the balance 1.** to have the power to decide in which way a situation will develop or which of two opposing sides will prevail **2.** to control the key to maintaining an existing state of equilibrium between two opposing forces ◇ **on (the) balance** having taken all the relevant factors into consideration and assessed their relative significance ○ *The situation, on balance, is relatively hopeful.* ◇ **redress the balance** to make the situation more fair or equal, usually by giving sth to or assisting sb who was previously at a disadvantage ◇ **strike a balance** to reach a compromise between two extremes ◇ **throw sb off balance** to surprise or confuse sb

---

——— WORD KEY: USAGE ———

Balance meaning 'remainder'. This use of *balance* in unquantified contexts meaning 'remainder, the rest', as in *The balance of the work must be finished tomorrow*, is used informally but thought to be in poor style where simpler and more suitable words are available, e.g. *The*

rest of the work must be finished tomorrow is greatly preferable. In American English the use has been standard for the past two hundred years.

balance out *v.* **1.** *vti.* CANCEL STH OUT to act as an equal and opposing weight, force, or value to sth and either neutralize or complement its effect ○ *This gain balances out last month's losses.* **2.** *vi.* WORK OUT EVENLY to arrive at a state of equality or harmony, usually through one thing offsetting the other over a period of time ○ *These things tend to balance out in the end.*

Balance *n.* ZODIAC = **Libra**

balance beam *n.* = **beam**

balanced /bállənst/ *adj.* **1.** EVEN-HANDED taking account of all sides on their merits without prejudice or favouritism ○ *a balanced assessment* **2.** HEALTHY containing different elements in suitable quantities or suitably arranged to produce a satisfying and effective whole ○ *a balanced diet* **3.** MENTALLY STABLE in a state of mental and emotional stability and able to make rational judgments

balance of payments *n.* the difference between the amount paid by a national government to other countries and the amount it receives from them

balance of power *n.* **1.** EQUILIBRIUM OF POWER BETWEEN NATIONS the distribution of power among two or more states, where the pattern of force and dominance among them is balanced such that no single state has dominance over the others **2.** POWER TO AFFECT SITUATION DECISIVELY the power of a single country, group, or individual to affect a situation decisively by supporting either of two opposing sides whose powers are equally balanced

balance of terror *n.* a situation in which two potentially hostile states or groups have the military capability to inflict roughly equal destruction on each other and war is thus prevented

balance of trade *n.* the difference between the value of the total imports and total exports of a country as assessed over a fixed period

balance pipe *n.* a pipe that ensures that the pressure remains equal in both parts of a system

balance sheet *n.* a statement showing the assets and liabilities of a company or institution at a particular time

balance weight *n.* a weight used to counterbalance a moving part in a machine

balance wheel *n.* a wheel in a machine, especially in a clock, that regulates the rate of movement of the main mechanism

Balanchine /bállən cheen, bállən cheén/, **George** (1904–83) Russian-born US dancer and choreographer. Cofounder of the New York City Ballet (1948), he revolutionized classical ballet with his innovative choreography. Born **Georgy Melitonovich Balanchivadze**

balancing act *n.* **1.** ATTEMPT TO DEAL WITH MANY THINGS a skilful or precarious attempt to deal with or survive a situation where you have to conciliate opposing groups, reconcile opposing views, or perform a large variety of tasks (*informal*) **2.** ARTS PERFORMANCE OF BALANCING THINGS an entertainment in which the performer keeps objects balanced in precarious positions, or balances himself or herself on an unstable object, such as an upended chair

balanitis /bállə nítiss/ *n.* inflammation of the head of the penis, usually caused by an infection [Mid-19thC. Formed from Greek *balanos* 'acorn, glans penis'.]

balas /bálləss, báyləss/, **balas ruby** *n.* a red form of the mineral spinel, used as a gemstone [15thC. Via Old French *balais* and Spanish *balax* from, ultimately, Arabic *balakš*, from Persian *Badakšān*, the region of Afghanistan where it is found.]

balata /bállətə/ *n.* **1.** MATERIAL SIMILAR TO RUBBER a gum resembling and used as a substitute for rubber, made from the sap of a tropical tree. It is used for making gaskets and chewing gum, and as a substitute for gutta percha. **2.** TREE YIELDING GUM SIMILAR TO RUBBER a tropical American tree that yields a sap from which balata is made. Latin name: *Manilkara bidentata.* US term **bully tree** [Early 17thC. From Carib *balatá.*]

Balaton, Lake /bálə ton/ the largest lake in central Europe and resort area in west-central Hungary. Area: 601 sq. km/232 sq. mi.

balboa /bal bô ə/ *n.* **1.** UNIT OF CURRENCY IN PANAMA the main unit of currency in Panama, with 100 centesimos. See table at **currency 2.** STH WORTH A BALBOA a coin worth one balboa [Early 20thC. Named after Vasco Núñez de BALBOA.]

Balboa /bal bô ə/, **Vasco Núñez de** (1475?–1519) Spanish explorer. He was the first European to reach the Pacific Ocean (1513).

balbriggan /bal bríggən/ *n.* a knitted unbleached cotton fabric, used especially for making underwear [Late 19thC. Named after the town of *Balbriggan* in Ireland, where it was first made.]

Balcon /báwlkən/, **Sir Michael** (1896–1977) British film producer. He worked for Ealing Films (1938–59). His films include *Whisky Galore* (1948) and *The Lavender Hill Mob* (1951). Full name **Sir Michael Elias Balcon**

balcony /bálkəni/ (*plural* **-nies**) *n.* **1.** ARCHIT PLATFORM ON WALL OF BUILDING a platform projecting from the interior or exterior wall of a building, usually enclosed by a rail or parapet **2.** THEATRE THEATRE GALLERY one of the separate areas of seating raised entirely above the floor level in a theatre, cinema, or concert hall [Early 17thC. Via Italian *balcone* from Old Italian, 'scaffold', from a prehistoric Germanic word that is also the ancestor of English *balk* 'wooden beam'.] —**balconied** *adj.*

bald /bawld/ *adj.* **1.** WITH HAIRLESS HEAD having little or no hair on the head **2.** WITHOUT NATURAL COVERING with little or no hair, fur, grass, or other natural covering, and with the bare skin or surface showing ○ *a bald patch on the grass* **3.** AUTOMOT WORN having a very worn-down tread ○ *Bald tyres are dangerous on wet roads.* **4.** PLAIN plain and direct, with no attempt to elaborate or explain ○ *a bald statement of the facts* **5.** UNORNAMENTED plain, bare, and without ornamentation, often to the point of seeming dull or prosaic **6.** ZOOL WITH WHITE MARKINGS used to describe birds and mammals that have white markings on the face or head [14thC. Origin uncertain, possibly formed from an earlier *bal* 'white spot or streak, especially on a horse's face'.] —**baldness** *n.*

baldachin /báwldəkin/ *n.* **1.** ARCHIT, CHR CANOPY a canopy made of cloth or stone erected over an altar, shrine, or throne in a Christian church **2.** CHR PORTABLE CANOPY a canopy carried above a priest or venerated object during a religious procession **3.** TEXTILES BROCADE a rich silk and gold brocade [Late 16thC. From Italian *baldacchino*, from *Baldacco* 'Baghdad', where it was made.]

bald cypress *n.* a deciduous coniferous tree, related to sequoias, found in the northern United States. Latin name: *Taxodium distichum.* [*Bald* from the fact that it sheds its needles, unlike most members of its family]

Bald eagle

bald eagle *n.* a large North American eagle found mainly near lakes and rivers, the adult of which has a white head and tail. An image of it is used as an emblem of the United States. Latin name: *Haliaeetus leucocephalus.*

Balder /báwldər/ *n.* in Norse mythology, one of Odin's sons, who was god of the summer sun. He was vulnerable only to mistletoe, by which he was killed.

balderdash /báwldər dash/ *n.* senseless or pointless talk or writing [Late 16thC. Origin unknown.]

bald-faced *adj.* US = **barefaced** *adj.* 1

baldhead /báwld hed/ *n.* sb with a bald head (*informal offensive*)

baldheaded /báwld héddid/ *adj.* BALD with a bald head ■ *adv.* IMPETUOUSLY impetuously or without restraint (*informal*) —**baldheadedness** *n.*

baldie /báwldi/ *n.* = **baldy**

balding /báwlding/ *adj.* partly bald, or in the process of losing the hair on the head

baldly /báwldli/ *adv.* in a simple and blunt way ○ *To put it baldly, she did a lousy job.*

baldpate /báwld payt/ *n.* = **wigeon**

baldric /báwldrik/ *n.* a sash or belt worn from one shoulder to the opposite hip, used to support a sword [13thC. Directly and via Old French *baudre* from Middle High German *balderich*, of unknown origin.]

Bob Adelman

James Baldwin

Baldwin /báldwin/, **James** (1924–87) US writer. His novels and essays addressed racism in the United States, and include *Go Tell It on the Mountain* (1953) and *Notes of a Native Son* (1955). Full name **James Arthur Baldwin**

Baldwin, Stanley, 1st Earl Baldwin of Bewdley (1867–1947) British statesman. Conservative party leader and prime minister (1923–24, 1924–29, 1935–37), he retired from politics in 1937 amid criticism that he had ignored Germany's preparations for World War II.

baldy /báwldi/ (*plural* **baldies**), **baldie** *n.* sb who is bald or balding (*informal offensive*)

bale[1] /bayl/ *n.* LARGE BUNDLE OR PACKAGE a large bundle or package of hay or a raw material such as cotton, tightly bound with string or wire to keep it in shape during transportation or storage ■ *vti.* (**bales, baling, baled**) MAKE INTO BUNDLES to gather and fasten material or goods into bales ○ *baling hay* [14thC. From Old French, from a prehistoric Germanic word that is also the ancestor of English *ball* and *balloon*. The underlying meaning is 'rolled-up bundle'.] —**baler** *n.*

bale[2] /bayl/ *n.* evil or suffering (*archaic or literary*) [Old English *bealu*]

bale[3] /bayl/ *vti.* = **bail**[2]

Balearic /bálli árrik/ *adj.* belonging to or typical of the Balearic Islands

Balearic Islands

Balearic Islands /bálli árrik-/ island group in the western Mediterranean that includes Mallorca, Menorca, and Ibiza. It is a province and autonomous region of Spain. Population: 736,865 (1991). Area: 5,012 sq. km/1,935 sq. mi.

baleen /bə leén/ *n.* a horny substance that grows as fringed plates from the upper jaws of certain whales, acting to strain food, especially small crustaceans, from the water [14thC. Via Old French *balaine* from Latin *balaena* 'whale', from Greek *phalaina*.]

baleen whale *n.* a large whale that has two blowholes and a set of horny fringed plates (**baleen**) instead of teeth. Right, grey, and blue whales are baleen whales. Suborder: Mysticeti.

baleful /báylf'l/ *adj.* **1.** THREATENING threatening, or seeming to threaten, harm, or misfortune ○ *a baleful stare* **2.** HARMFUL causing or threatening to cause harm —**balefully** *adv.* —**balefulness** *n.*

━━━━ WORD KEY: USAGE ━━━━

baleful or **baneful**? *Baleful*, meaning 'harmful', is a much more common term than *baneful*, meaning 'destructive', which is largely confined to literary use.

Balfour /bálfər, -fawr/, **Arthur James, 1st Earl of Balfour** (1848–1930) British statesman. He was Conservative prime minister (1902–05) and author of the Balfour Declaration (1917), supporting a Jewish homeland in Palestine.

Bali /baáli/ mountainous island east of Java, Indonesia, that is a popular holiday destination. Capital: Denpasar. Population: 2,895,600 (1995). Area: 5,623 sq. km/2,171 sq. mi.

balibuntal /bálli búnt'l/ *n.* **1.** WOVEN STRAW fine straw woven into material, used especially for making hats in the Philippines **2.** STRAW HAT a hat made from balibuntal [Early 20thC. From *Baliuag* in the Philippines, where it was made, + Tagalog *buntal* 'straw from the talipot palm tree'.]

Balikpapan /baálik paá paan/ city and port in Indonesia, situated on the island of Borneo, on the Makassar Strait. Population: 368,729 (1990).

Balinese /baáli neéz/ (*plural* **-nese**) *n.* **1.** SB FROM BALI sb who was born or brought up on the Indonesian island of Bali **2.** AUSTRONESIAN LANGUAGE a language spoken on Bali that is a member of the Austronesian language family. Balinese is spoken by between two and three million people. [Early 19thC. From Dutch *Balinees*, from *Bali* (see BALI).] —**Balinese** *adj.*

Balinese cat *n.* a domestic cat belonging to a breed resembling Siamese cats but with long hair

balisier /ba líz yay/ *n.* a small bushy shrub bearing a distinctive flower ranging in colour from yellow to bright red. The flower is the symbol of the People's National Movement, one of the major political parties of Trinidad. Family: Heliconia.

balk *v., n.* = baulk

Balkan /báwlkən, bólk-/ *adj.* relating to the states of the Balkan Peninsula, or their peoples or cultures [Mid-19thC. From Turkish, name of a mountain chain.]

Balkanization /báwlkə nī záysh'n, bólkə-/, **balkanization, Balkanisation** *n.* division of an area, region, or group into smaller and often mutually hostile units [Early 20thC. From the political fragmentation of the Balkan states between the Treaty of Berlin (1878) and the Balkan Wars (1912–13).] —**Balkanize** *vt.*

Balkan Mountains extension of the Alpine mountain system, running across central Bulgaria. The highest point is Botev Peak 2,376 m/7,795 ft.

Balkan Peninsula mountainous peninsula in southeastern Europe between the Adriatic and Ionian seas in the west and the Aegean and Black seas in the east. It includes Albania, Bosnia and Herzegovina, Bulgaria, mainland Greece, Macedonia, European Turkey, and parts of Croatia, Slovenia, and Yugoslavia. The Sava and Danube are considered to be the northern borders.

Balkans = Balkan States

Balkan States, **Balkans** the countries in the Balkan Peninsula, including Albania, Bosnia-Herzegovina, Bulgaria, Croatia, Greece, Macedonia, the European part of Turkey, and the Federal Republic of Yugoslavia

balky /báwki, báwlki/ (**balkier, balkiest**), **balky** (**baulkier, baulkiest**) *adj.* US difficult and uncooperative ○ *a balky mule that stopped dead in its tracks* —**balkily** *adv.* —**balkiness** *n.*

ball[1] /bawl/ *n.* **1.** ROUND OBJECT PLAYED WITH an object, usually round in shape and often hollow and flexible, central to many games and sports in which it is thrown, struck, or kicked **2.** ROUND OR ROUNDISH THING sth spherical or almost spherical, especially a spherical mass or arrangement of material ○ *a ball of wool* **3.** A GAME WITH BALL a game, especially one played by children, in which a ball is used and, e.g., is thrown from one player to another ○ *Who's coming out to play ball?* **4.** SPORTS BALL PLAYED IN A PARTICULAR WAY a particular use, movement, or way of transferring the ball to another player in the course of a game ○ *a long ball into the penalty area* **5.** CRICKET DELIVERY BY BOWLER a single instance of a bowler bowling the ball to a batsman in cricket ○ *The last ball of the over.* **6.** BASEBALL PITCH THAT IS NOT A STRIKE in baseball, any single pitch of the ball that does not pass through the strike zone and at which the batter does not swing **7.** RUGBY POSSESSION AFTER SET PIECE useful possession, usually with an opportunity to develop an attacking movement, arising from skilful delivery of the ball by another player **8.** ARMS SOLID PROJECTILE a solid non-exploding and usually round projectile shot from an old-fashioned pistol, musket, or cannon **9.** ARMS SOLID PROJECTILES COLLECTIVELY a collective term for the solid projectiles fired from old-fashioned guns ○ *The gunners were ordered to change from ball to case-shot.* **10.** ROUNDED BODY PART a rounded part of the body, at the base of the thumb or just behind the toes ○ *the ball of the foot* **11.** ANAT TESTICLE a testicle (*slang offensive*) ■ *vti.* (**balls, balling, balled**) **1.** MAKE INTO OR FORM BALL to mould, gather, or wind sth into a ball, or become a ball-shaped mass ○ *She balled her fists.* **2.** OFFENSIVE TERM an offensive term meaning to have sexual intercourse (*taboo offensive*) [13thC. From Old Norse *böllr* or assumed Old English *beall*, from a prehistoric Germanic word that is also the ancestor of English *balloon*, *bale*[1], and *ballot*.] ◇ **get** or **set** or **start the ball rolling** to start sth off, especially a conversation or project ◇ **on the ball** aware of what is going on and quick to respond and take action (*informal*) ◇ **play ball (with sb)** to cooperate together or with sb (*slang*) ◇ **the ball is in sb's court** used to say that it is sb's turn to take action (*slang*) **balls up** *vt.* to make a complete mess of sth by mistake or through lack of skill (*slang*) US term **ball up** [From *balls* 'muddle', from the sense of 'testicles'] **ball up** *vt.* US = **balls up** (*slang offensive*) [From BALL 'to become clogged' (as if with a ball)]

ball[2] /bawl/ *n.* a large-scale formal social event at which the main activity is dancing [Early 17thC. Via French *bal* from, ultimately, late Latin *ballare* 'to dance', from Greek *ballizein*.] ◇ **have a ball** to enjoy yourself very much (*dated slang*) ○ *It was a great party; we really had a ball!*

Ball /bawl/, **John** (1338?–81) English rebel. An excommunicated priest, he was one of the leaders, with Wat Tyler, of the Peasants' Revolt (1381). He was executed for his part in the rebellion.

Ball, Lucille (1911–89) US actor. A gifted comedian, she appeared with her husband Desi Arnaz in the television comedy *I Love Lucy* (1951–57), the first of several popular series. She was also a successful television producer. Full name **Lucille Désirée Ball**

Ball, Murray Hone (*b.* 1939) New Zealand cartoonist. He created cartoon strips, including *Footrot Flats*.

Balla /bállə/, **Giacomo** (1871–1958) Italian painter, known for using cubist techniques to suggest motion.

ballad /bálləd/ *n.* **1.** MUSIC, LITERAT NARRATIVE SONG a song or poem, especially a traditional one or one in a traditional style, telling a story in a number of short regular stanzas, often with a refrain ○ *the Ballad of Bonnie and Clyde* **2.** MUSIC SLOW ROMANTIC SONG a slow romantic popular song ○ *two up-tempo numbers followed by a ballad* [Late 15thC. Via French *ballade* from, ultimately, late Latin *ballare* (see BALL[2]).] —**balladic** /bə láddik/ *adj.* —**balladist** /bállədist/ *n.*

ballade /ba laád, bə-/ *n.* **1.** LITERAT POEM WITH REFRAIN a poem consisting of three stanzas of eight or ten lines and a short concluding explanatory stanza (**envoy**), all of which end with the same refrain **2.** INSTRUMENTAL PIECE SUGGESTING A STORY an instrumental piece, usually for piano, intended to suggest the telling of a story as in a ballad. The best-known

ballades in the classical repertoire are by Chopin and Brahms. [14thC. Variant of BALLAD.]

balladeer /bállə deér/ *n.* sb who sings ballads

ballad opera *n.* a form of opera with spoken dialogue and popular tunes made into songs. The most famous example is John Gay's *The Beggar's Opera*.

balladry /bállədri/ *n.* **1.** BALLADS COLLECTIVELY ballads considered collectively **2.** WRITING OR PERFORMING BALLADS the composing or performing of ballads

ballad stanza *n.* a stanza form frequently used in ballads that has four lines, the first and third with four stresses and unrhymed, the second and fourth with three stresses and rhyming

Balladur /bállə door/, **Édouard** (*b.* 1929) French politician and business leader. He was prime minister of France (1993–95).

Ballance /bállənss/, **John** (1839–93) British-born New Zealand statesman. A Liberal politician and premier of New Zealand (1890–93), he was noted for his progressive legislation.

ball and chain *n.* **1.** IRON BALL ON A CHAIN a type of restraint formerly used for prisoners consisting of an iron ball on a chain that is attached at its other end to the prisoner's ankle **2.** GREAT HINDRANCE sth considered to be a great hindrance or restraint ○ *Censorship is the ball and chain fettering artistic freedom of expression.* **3.** OFFENSIVE TERM an offensive term deliberately insulting a man's wife (*dated slang insult*)

ball-and-claw *adj.* having a foot or another part modelled in the shape of an animal's claw holding a ball ○ *a ball-and-claw bathtub*

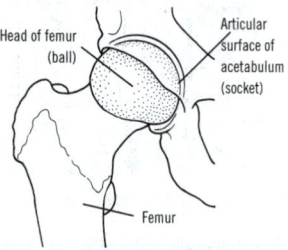

Head of femur (ball)

Articular surface of acetabulum (socket)

Femur

Ball and socket joint

ball and socket joint, **ball joint** *n.* **1.** ANAT JOINT LIKE HIP JOINT a joint such as the hip joint, in which a bone with a rounded end fits into a concave area of the adjoining bone, allowing a wide range of movement **2.** MECH ENG JUNCTION BETWEEN MOVING PARTS a junction between two moving parts of a mechanism in which the rounded end of one part fits into a cup-shaped socket on the other

Ballarat /bállə rat/ city in southern Victoria, Australia. It was a major gold-mining town in the mid-19th century and is now an industrial centre. Population: 64,980 (1991).

ballast /bálləst/ *n.* **1.** NAUT STABILIZING HEAVY WEIGHTS heavy material carried in the hold of a ship, especially one that has no cargo, or in the gondola of a balloon, to give the craft increased stability **2.** STH THAT GIVES BULK OR STABILITY anything that serves no particular purpose except to give bulk or weight to sth or that provides additional stability **3.** TRANSP FOUNDATION MATERIAL stones or gravel used as a foundation for a road or a railway track **4.** BUILDING GRAVEL USED IN MAKING CONCRETE gravel used in making concrete and in earthworks ■ *vt.* (**-lasts, -lasting, -lasted**) **1.** LOAD STH WITH BALLAST to load ballast onto sth **2.** STABILIZE STH to give stability to sth [Mid-16thC. Origin uncertain, probably from Old Danish, literally 'mere weight', from *bar* 'bare, mere' + *last* 'load'.]

ball bearing *n.* **1.** FRICTION-REDUCING METAL BALL a metal ball used to reduce friction between moving parts **2.** TYPE OF BEARING a bearing containing a number of metal balls that rotate freely to reduce friction between moving parts

ball boy *n.* **1.** TENNIS COLLECTOR OF TENNIS BALLS a boy who retrieves balls during a tennis match at the end of

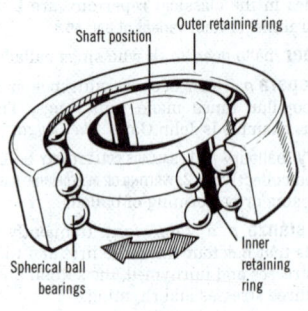

Ball bearing

each point and delivers them to the server when required **2. BASEBALL KEEPER OF BASEBALLS** a boy who takes care of the balls that are out of play during a baseball game or practice

ballbreaker /báwl braykər/ *n. US* a deliberately offensive term for a woman who is regarded as aggressive towards men (*slang taboo*)

ballbuster /báwl bustər/ *n. US* (*slang taboo*) **1. DIFFICULT JOB** a difficult and unpleasant job **2. = ballbreaker**

ball clay *n.* a sedimentary clay containing kaolin, mica, other minerals, and organic matter, used in ceramics [*Ball* from an obsolete mining process in which clay was handled as rounded cubes (balls)]

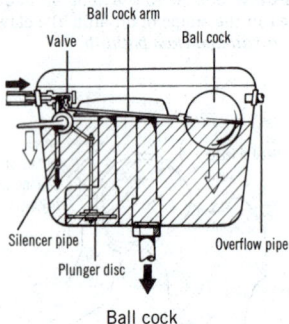

Ball cock

ball cock *n.* a floating ball on the end of an arm that is connected to a valve controlling the water level in a cistern or tank. The valve opens as the ball falls and closes as it rises.

ballerina /bállə reénə/ *n.* **1. WOMAN DANCER** a woman ballet dancer **2.** *US* **PRINCIPAL WOMAN BALLET DANCER** a woman dancer in a ballet company who is regularly given principal parts [Late 18thC. From the feminine form of Italian *ballerino* 'dancing master' from *ballare* 'to dance', ultimately from the same Greek source as BALL[2].]

Ballesteros /bállə steér oss/, **Severiano** (b. 1957) Spanish golfer. The youngest golfer to win the Open (1979), he won that tournament twice more as well as the US Masters and the World Matchplay.

Ballet: Darcy Bussell performing in the Royal Ballet's *Laurencia* (1990)

ballet /bállay/ *n.* **1. FORM OF DANCE** a form of dance characterized by conventional steps, poses, and graceful movements including leaps and spins. Women ballet dancers often wear pointe shoes to perform steps balancing on the tips of their toes. **2. STORY PERFORMED BY DANCERS** a choreographed pre-

sentation of a story or theme performed to music by ballet dancers, or the musical score written for this **3. GROUP OF DANCERS** a company of ballet dancers who perform together [Mid-17thC. Via French, from Italian *ballo* (see BALL[2].)]

balletic /ba léttik/ *adj.* with the grace of sb dancing in a ballet

balletomane /bálletō mayn/ *n.* sb who passionately loves ballet [Mid-20thC. Coined from BALLET + -MANE.] — **balletomania** /bálletō máyni ə/ *n.*

ballet shoe *n.* **1. BALLET DANCER'S SHOE** a flat light flexible slipper made of silk or leather, worn by ballet dancers for performing and practice **2. = toe shoe 3. LIGHT FLAT SHOE** a flat shoe resembling one worn by a ballet dancer

ball game *n.* **1. GAME PLAYED WITH BALL** any game played with a ball **2.** *US* **BASEBALL** a game of baseball ◇ **a whole new ball game** a completely new or different set of circumstances (*slang*)

ball girl *n.* TENNIS a girl who retrieves balls during a tennis match at the end of each point and delivers them to the server when required

ballgown /báwl gown/ *n.* a full-length formal dress suitable for wearing to a ball

Ballina /bállinə/ coastal town in northeastern New South Wales, Australia, situated at the mouth of the Richmond River. Population: 16,056 (1996).

Balliol /báyli əl/, **John, King of Scots** (1250?–1314). He rebelled against English rule, but was defeated by Edward I at Dunbar (1296) and deposed.

ballista /bə lístə/ (*plural* **-tae** /-tee/) *n.* a piece of military equipment that was used in ancient times to hurl stones and other missiles over a distance [Early 16thC. Via Latin, from, ultimately, Greek *ballein* 'to throw'.]

ballistic /bə lístik/ *adj.* relating to the movements of objects propelled through the air [Mid-18thC. Formed from BALLISTA.] —**ballistically** *adv.* ◇ **go ballistic** to become extremely angry (*slang*)

ballistic missile *n.* a missile that maintains a course determined by its initial orientation and engine thrust, rather than one calculated by guidance systems during flight

ballistics /bə lístiks/ *n.* **1. STUDY OF PROJECTILES** the study of the movements and forces involved in the propulsion of objects through the air (*takes a singular verb*) **2. STUDY OF FIREARMS** the study of firearms and ammunition (*takes a singular verb*) **3. FIRING CHARACTERISTICS OF WEAPON** the characteristics of a firearm that affect the way missiles are fired (*takes a singular or plural verb*)

ball joint *n.* = ball and socket joint *n.* 2

ball lightning *n.* a rare form of lightning that takes the shape of a moving glowing ball, typically disappearing without explosion

ballocks /bólləks/ *interj.*, *npl.* = **bollocks** (*slang offensive*) [Old English *bealluc*. Ultimately from a prehistoric Germanic word meaning 'little ball', which was also the ancestor of English *ball*.]

ball of fire *n.* an extremely energetic and dynamic person (*informal*)

balloon /bə loón/ *n.* **1. GAS-FILLED BAG USED AS TOY** a small coloured bag made of thin rubber or plastic that is inflated with air or helium and used as a toy or decoration **2. AIR GAS-FILLED BAG USED IN AIR TRANSPORT** an extremely large bag filled with a lighter-than-air gas and used as a form of air transport, carrying passengers or equipment in a suspended basket or gondola **3. SPEECH CIRCLE IN CARTOON** a rounded outline with a point directed towards a character in a cartoon that encloses the text of the character's speech or thought **4. BRANDY GLASS** a glass with a large rounded bowl, used for drinking brandy ■ *vi.* **(-loons, -looning, -looned) 1. SWELL** to form a large round swollen shape **2. INCREASE IN AMOUNT** to increase in amount suddenly and rapidly [Late 16thC. Via French *ballon* or Italian *ballone* 'large ball' (see BALL[1].)] ◇ **go over** or **down like a lead balloon** to be completely unsuccessful (*slang*) ◇ **if** or **when the balloon goes up** if or when the expected or likely trouble or excitement starts (*slang*)

balloon angioplasty *n.* the use of a balloon catheter to widen a narrowed artery

balloon catheter *n.* a tube that can be inserted into a blood vessel or other body part and inflated while inside, e.g. to widen a narrowed artery

ballooning /bə loóning/ *n.* the sport of riding in or piloting a balloon

balloonist /bə loónist/ *n.* sb who pilots a balloon for sport

balloon loan *n.* a loan that is repaid with a series of regular payments and one much larger payment at the end

balloon mortgage *n.* a mortgage that is paid back in a series of regular payments with one much larger payment at the end

balloon tyre *n.* a pneumatic tyre with a wide tread inflated to a low pressure, used to drive on soft surfaces such as deep sand

balloon vine *n.* a tropical vine with small flowers and ornamental pods shaped like balloons. Latin name: *Cardiospermum halicacabum.*

balloon whisk *n.* a hand-held whisk made of stiff wires that form a loop at one end and are gathered into a covered handle at the other

ballot /bállət/ *n.* **1. VOTING SYSTEM** a system in which eligible people vote, usually in secret, to determine the outcome of an election or make some other collective decision **2. SECRET VOTE** a secret vote held to determine the outcome of an election or some other decision **3. = ballot paper 4. TOTAL VOTES** the total number of votes that have been cast in an election ■ *v.* **(-lots, -loting, -loted) 1.** *vt.* **ASK PEOPLE TO VOTE** to carry out a ballot on members of an organization or an electorate **2.** *vi.* **VOTE** to vote in a ballot [Mid-16thC. From Italian *ballotta* 'little ball', from *balla* 'ball' (see BALL[1]). From the small balls that were used for casting votes.] —**balloter** *n.*

ballot box *n.* **1. BOX FOR VOTES** a box in which voters put their ballot papers after marking them **2. ELECTION BY BALLOT** the system in which leaders are elected or decisions are made using a ballot ○ *The people will decide at the ballot box.*

ballot paper *n.* a piece of paper or card on which sb can record a vote

ballot rigging *n.* the use of dishonest or illegal methods of voting to ensure victory for a particular candidate or party in an election

ballpark /báwl paark/ *n. US, Can* **1.** SPORT **PARK FOR PLAYING BALL GAMES** a stadium or area of land for playing ball games, especially baseball **2.** AEROSP **TOUCHDOWN AREA FOR SPACECRAFT** the approximate area within which a spacecraft is intended to touch down ■ *adj. US* **APPROXIMATE** rough or approximate (*informal*) ○ *a ballpark figure* ◇ **in the right ballpark** within the right general range or scope (*slang*)

ballpoint /báwl poynt/, **ballpoint pen** *n.* a pen with a small rotating ball at its tip that transfers the ink from an inner tube onto the writing surface

ballroom /báwl room, -roóm/ *n.* a very large room with a smooth floor and a high ceiling, used for formal dances

ballroom dancing *n.* formal dancing with a partner in dances that use a set pattern of steps, e.g. the foxtrot, quickstep, and waltz (*formal*)

balls-up *n.* a complete mistake or totally unsuccessful attempt at sth (*slang*)

ballsy /báwlzi/ **(-ier, -iest)** *adj. US* unusually tough, courageous, or determined (*slang taboo*) [Mid-20thC. From BALL[1].]

ball valve *n.* a nonreturn valve in which a ball moves in and out of an aperture in response to changes in fluid or mechanical pressure

bally /bálli/ *adj.*, *adv.* used to express anger or frustration, or to add emphasis (*dated informal*) [Late 19thC. An alteration of BLOODY, perhaps influenced by the written form 'bl-y'.]

ballyhoo /bálli hoó/ *n.* (*plural* **-hoos**) **1. UPROAR** a noisy argument or disturbance **2. SENSATIONAL ADVERTISING** sensational, loud, or sustained advertising ■ *vt.* **(-hoos, -hooing, -hooed) ADVERTISE STH LOUDLY** to advertise or publicize sth loudly and insistently [Mid-19thC. Origin unknown.]

Ballymena /bálli meéenə/ town in County Antrim, Northern Ireland, the administrative headquarters of the district of Ballymena. Population: 28,717 (1991).

Ballymoney /bálli múnni/ district in County Antrim, Northern Ireland. The administrative headquarters are in Ballymoney town. Population: 24,600 (1995). Area: 417 sq.km/161 sq. mi.

ballyrag *vt.* = bullyrag [Late 18thC. Origin unknown.]

balm /baam/ *n.* **1. SOOTHING OIL** a fragrant oily substance obtained as a resin from various plants such as evergreen trees, used in soothing ointments or other preparations **2. PLEASANT SCENT** a pleasant scent (*literary*) **3. STH THAT SOOTHES** sth that has the effect of calming, soothing, or comforting ○ *balm to his wounded ego* **4.** BOT = **lemon balm** [13thC. Via French *bame* from Latin *balsamum* (SEE BALSAM). The 'l' found its way into the English spelling from the Latin form.]

Balmain /bál maN/, **Pierre** (1914–86) French couturier, known for his simple and elegant designs. Full name **Pierre Alexandre Claudius Balmain**

Balmer series /bálmər-/ *n.* a series of lines in the visible part of the atomic spectrum of hydrogen [Early 20thC. Named after the Swiss physicist J. J. *Balmer* (1825–98), who discovered it.]

balm of Gilead /-gílli ad/ *n.* **1.** = **balsam fir 2. POPLAR TREE** a hybrid poplar tree that has heart-shaped leaves and resinous buds. Genus: *Populus.* **3. FRAGRANT RESIN** the fragrant resin produced by the balm of Gilead tree [Mid-18thC. Named after the *balm of Gilead* in Coverdale's Bible.]

Balmoral /bal mórrəl/, **balmoral** *n.* **1. LACED WALKING SHOE** a strong walking shoe that is fastened with laces **2. WOOLLEN CAP** a traditional Scottish flat woollen cap [Mid-19thC. Named after the royal estate of *Balmoral* in Scotland. Because of Queen Victoria's fondness for this estate, Scottish items became fashionable during her reign.]

balmy /baámi/ (**-ier, -iest**) *adj.* **1. PLEASANTLY MILD** used to describe weather that is pleasantly mild ○ *a balmy summer's evening* **2.** = **barmy** (*informal*) —**balmily** *adv.* —**balminess** *n.*

balneology /bálni ólləji/ *n.* a branch of medicine concerned with therapeutic bathing, especially in natural mineral spring water —**balneological** /-ə lój jik'l/ *adj.* —**balneologist** /-ólləjist/ *n.*

balneotherapy /bálni ə thérrəpi/ *n.* the medical practice of treatment by immersion in baths, especially those in spas containing water with a high mineral content [Late 19thC. Coined from Latin *balneum* 'bath' + THERAPY.]

Balochi *n., adj.* = **Baluchi**

baloney /bə lóni/ *n.* any silly or stupid talk (*informal*) ○ *Don't talk baloney.* [Early 20thC. Origin uncertain: perhaps an alteration of *Bologna* in BOLOGNA SAUSAGE.]

Balqash, Lake /bal kásh/ shallow lake in southeastern Kazakhstan into which the River Ili flows. Area: 18,200 sq. km/7,030 sq. mi.

balsa /báwlssə/ (*plural* -**sas** *or* -**sa**) *n.* **1. TREE WITH LIGHTWEIGHT WOOD** a South American tree that yields a lightweight softwood. Genus: *Ochroma.* **2. balsa, balsa wood LIGHTWEIGHT WOOD** a lightweight wood obtained from the balsa tree, used in making rafts and toy models and as insulation [Early 17thC. From Spanish, 'raft', because the tree was useful for making rafts.]

balsam /báwlssəm/ *n.* **1. OILY RESINOUS PLANT SUBSTANCE** an oily resinous substance (**oleoresin**) obtained from plants, especially one containing benzoic acid or cinnamic acid, that is used in making perfume and medicine **2. PREPARATION CONTAINING BALSAM** a preparation containing or resembling balsam **3. FLOWERING PLANT** a plant of the family that includes busy lizzie. Family: Balsaminaceae. [Pre-12thC. Via Latin, from Greek *balsamon*, of uncertain origin: perhaps from Hebrew *bāsām* 'spice'.] —**balsamic** /bawl sámmik/ *adj.*

balsam fir (*plural* **balsam firs** *or* **balsam fir**) *n.* a pyramid-shaped North American fir tree, used for pulpwood and popular as a Christmas tree. It is the source of Canada balsam. Latin name: *Abies balsamea.*

balsamic vinegar /bawl sámmik-/ *n.* an expensive Italian vinegar made from the juice of white grapes. It is matured in wood for 10 to 50 years, giving it a characteristic dark colour and rich sweet-sour taste.

balsam poplar *n.* a North American poplar tree with broad leaves and sticky resinous buds. Latin name: *Populus balsamifera.*

Balt /bawlt/ *n.* **1. SB FROM ONE OF BALTIC STATES** sb who lives in or was born or brought up in Lithuania, Latvia, or Estonia **2. SPEAKER OF BALTIC STATES LANGUAGE** sb whose native language is Lithuanian, Latvian, or Estonian [Late 19thC. From late Latin *balthae*.] —**Balt** *adj.*

Balthazar[1] /bal tházzə, bálthə zaar/ *n.* a bottle that contains 12 litres of wine, the equivalent of 16 bottles [Mid-20thC. Named after *Balshazzar*, King of Babylon, who, according to the book of Daniel in the Bible, 'made a great feast . . . and drank wine before the thousand'.]

Balthazar[2], **Balthasar** *n.* one of the three wise men who, according to the Bible, brought gifts to Bethlehem to honour the birth of Jesus (Matthew 2:1–12)

balti /báwlti, bál-/ *n.* a spicy dish originally from Pakistan that is traditionally served in the bowl-shaped pan it is cooked in

Balti /báwlti, bál-/ *n.* a language spoken in northern Kashmir that may be counted as a dialect of Tibetan [Early 20thC. From a Ladakhi dialect name.] —**Balti** *adj.*

Baltic[1] /báwltik/ *n.* a group of northeastern European languages that includes Latvian, Lithuanian, and the extinct Old Prussian. It is a branch of the Indo-European family, closely linked with the Slavonic group. About five million people speak a Baltic language. [Late 16thC. From late Latin *Balticus*.] —**Baltic** *adj.*

Baltic[2] *n.* **1.** = **Baltic Sea 2.** = **Baltic States** —**Baltic** *adj.*

Baltic Exchange *n.* a commodity market in the City of London that deals in international trade, especially international bulk shipping

Baltic Sea, **Baltic** sea in northwestern Europe. Nearly landlocked, it borders Sweden, Finland, Russia, Estonia, Latvia, Lithuania, Poland, Germany, and Denmark. Area: 414,000 sq. km/160,000 sq. mi.

Baltic States, **Baltic** the nations of Estonia, Latvia, and Lithuania, considered as a group

Baltimore /báwltəmor/ the largest city in Maryland, near the Chesapeake Bay. This port town is home to the Johns Hopkins University. Population: 702,979 (1994).

Balto-Slavonic /báwl tō-/, **Balto-Slavic** *n.* the Baltic and Slavonic branches of the Indo-European language family, sometimes considered to form a unified grouping —**Balto-Slavonic** *adj.*

Baluchi /bə loóchi/ (*plural* -**chis** *or* -**chi**), **Balochi** /bə lôchi/ (*plural* -**chis** *or* -**chi**) *n.* **1. SB FROM BALUCHISTAN** sb who lives in or was born or brought up in the region of Baluchistan **2. IRANIAN LANGUAGE** a language spoken in Baluchistan belonging to the Eastern Iranian group of languages. Baluchi is spoken by about five million people. [Early 17thC. From Persian *Baluči*.] —**Baluchi** *adj.*

Baluchistan /bə loôchi staán/ mountainous desert region in southwestern Pakistan and southeastern Iran

balun /bállən/ *n.* a transformer used to couple balanced and unbalanced transmission lines [Contraction of BALANCED + UNBALANCED]

baluster /bálləstər/ *n.* **1. POST SUPPORTING HANDRAIL** an upright post supporting a handrail, e.g. in the banister of a staircase **2. VASE-SHAPED LEG OR STEM** a support, e.g. a chair leg or the stem of a glass, that is shaped like a long narrow vase [Early 17thC. Via French *balustre* from Italian *balaustro*, from, ultimately, Greek *balaustion* 'blossom of the wild pomegranate', because early balusters resembled its shape.]

Balustrade

balustrade /bállə stráyd/ *n.* a decorative railing together with its supporting balusters, often used at the front of a parapet or gallery [Mid-17thC. Via French from either Spanish *balastrada* or Italian *balaustrata* from *balaustro* (SEE BALUSTER).]

Balzac /bál zak/, **Honoré de** (1799–1850) French novelist. He wrote 90 novels that provide a panoramic social history of France from 1789 to 1830, and arranged them under the collective title *The Human Comedy.* —**Balzacian** /bal záki ən/ *adj.*

Bamako /bámməkō/ capital and largest city of Mali, situated on the River Niger. Population: 800,000 (1993).

Bambara /bám baára, baám-/ (*plural* -**ra** *or* -**ras**) *n.* **1. MEMBER OF W AFRICAN PEOPLE** a member of an African people living mainly in Mali, western Africa **2. MANDE LANGUAGE** a language spoken in Mali, Senegal, Burkina Faso, and Côte d'Ivoire. It belongs to the Mande group of Niger-Congo languages and is spoken by between one and two million people. [Late 19thC. From Bambara.] —**Bambara** *adj.*

Bamberg /baám burg/ city and river port north of Nuremberg in Bavaria, Germany. Population: 70,700 (1992).

bambino /bam beénō/ (*plural* -**nos** *or* -**ni** /-ni/) *n.* **1. BABY** a baby or young child (*informal*) **2. IMAGE OF INFANT JESUS CHRIST** a representation of Jesus Christ as a baby [Early 18thC. From Italian, 'baby', literally 'silly little one', formed from *bambo* 'silly'.]

bamboo /bam boó/ (*plural* -**boos**) *n.* **1. TALL STIFF-STEMMED PLANT** a plant with long woody, often hollow, stems that grows in dense clumps in tropical and semi-tropical regions. Family: Bambusaceae. **2. BAMBOO STEM** the strong hollow stems of bamboo plants, used to make furniture, for building, and as canes and fishing rods [Late 16thC. Via Dutch *bamboes* from modern Latin *bambusa* from, ultimately, Malay *mambu*. The 's' of the Dutch form was later assumed to be a plural and dropped.]

bamboo curtain *n.* the political, military, and ideological barrier that effectively isolated China from Western countries from the Communist revolution of 1949 until China's relaxation of trade barriers in 1979 [Coined on the model of IRON CURTAIN]

bamboo shoot *n.* an edible young shoot of the bamboo plant that is eaten sliced and cooked in Asian dishes

bamboozle /bam boôz'l/ (-**zles, -zling, -zled**) *vt.* (*informal*) **1. CHEAT SB** to trick or deceive sb through misleading statements or falsehoods **2. PERPLEX SB** to make sb confused [Early 18thC. Of obscure origin.] —**bamboozler** *n.*

ban[1] /ban/ *vt.* (**bans, banning, banned**) **1. FORBID STH** to forbid sth officially or legally so that it cannot be done, used, seen, or read **2. STOP SB DOING STH** to forbid sb to do sth or go somewhere **3. HIST RESTRICT RIGHTS IN SOUTH AFRICA** during the apartheid era in South Africa, to punish sb suspected of breaking the apartheid laws by preventing the person from moving around freely and having contact with other people ■ *n.* **1. ORDER FORBIDDING STH** an order officially or legally forbidding sth so that it cannot be done, used, seen, or read **2. PUBLIC REVILEMENT** public condemnation of sb or sth (*archaic*) **3. CURSE** a powerful curse on sb (*archaic*) [Old English *bannan* 'to summon, proclaim'; the noun came via Old French *ban* 'summons for military duty, proclamation']

ban[2] /ban/ (plural **bani** /baánni/) n. SUBUNIT OF ROMANIAN CURRENCY a subunit of currency in Romania, 100 of which are worth one leu. See table at **currency** [Late 19thC. Via Romanian, from Serbo-Croat *bān* 'lord', from Turkic *bayan* 'very rich person', formed from *bay* 'rich gentleman'.]

Banaba /bə naába/ one of the 33 islands of Kiribati in the western Pacific Ocean. Population: 284 (1990). Area: 5 sq. km/2 sq. mi. Former name **Ocean Island**

banal /bə naál/ adj. boringly ordinary and lacking in originality [Mid-19thC. From French, from *ban* (see BAN[1]), which developed in French from 'compulsory military service' via '(sth) common to all' to 'commonplace'.] —**banally** adv.

banality /bə nálləti/ (plural **-ties**) n. **1.** BORING ORDINARINESS conventional or dull ordinariness **2.** UNREMARKABLE COMMENT OR FEATURE an ordinary remark or feature that lacks originality

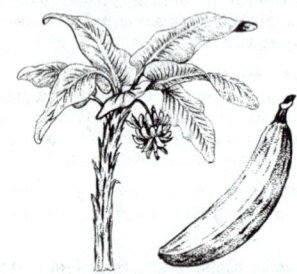
Banana

banana /bə naánə/ (plural **-as** or **-a**) n. **1.** LONG CURVED YELLOW FRUIT a long and slightly curved fruit with a skin that turns from green to yellow when ripe. The edible part inside has a creamy colour and soft texture. ◊ **plantain 2.** PLANT ON WHICH BANANAS GROW a tropical plant with large leaves and hanging clusters of long curved fruits. Genus: *Musa*. [Late 16thC. Via Spanish and Portuguese, from Mande.] ◊ **go bananas** to become uncontrollably or unreasonably angry or excited (*informal*)

Banana bender n. *Aus* sb who comes from or lives in Queensland (*informal insult*) [Either from the fact that the 'job' is useless, or that it requires no intelligence]

banana plug n. a single conductor plug with a spring metal tip shaped like a banana

banana republic n. a small country with an unstable government, typically a military dictatorship, and an economy dependent on the export of a single product or on outside financial help (*disapproving*)

banana split n. a dessert made from a peeled banana cut in half lengthways, filled with scoops of ice cream, sweet sauce, whipped cream, and chopped nuts

banausic /bə náwzik/ adj. **1.** UNCREATIVE with no art, creativity, or imagination **2.** PRACTICAL OR MATERIALISTIC practical or materialistic rather than uplifting or inspiring [Mid-19thC. Formed from Greek *banausikos* 'of or for artisans'.]

Banbridge /bán brij/ district council in County Down, Northern Ireland. The administrative headquarters are in Banbridge town. Population: 37,300 (1995).

Banbury cake /bánbəri-/ n. a cake consisting of pastry filled with dried fruit and candied peel mixed with butter and spices [Named after the town of *Banbury* in Oxfordshire where they were first made]

banco /bángkō/ interj. USED FOR BETTING AGAINST THE BANK used in baccarat and chemin de fer to declare that a player wishes to place a bet equivalent to the total worth of the bank ■ n. BET AGAINST THE BANK in baccarat and chemin de fer, a bet placed equivalent to to the total worth of the bank [Late 18thC. Via French, from Italian (see BANK[1]).]

band[1] /band/ n. **1.** MUSIC MUSICIANS PLAYING TOGETHER a group of musicians who play together, particularly a group playing popular or rock music. ◊ **pop group 2.** MUSIC, HIST INSTRUMENTAL ENSEMBLE in pre-18th-century Europe, an instrumental ensemble (*archaic*) **3.** GROUP WITH SAME BELIEFS OR PURPOSE a group of people who have the same ideas or beliefs or who are pursuing

the same activity together ○ *a growing band of supporters* **4.** ANTHROP SMALL SIMPLY-STRUCTURED GROUP a small group of people with a relatively simple social structure [15thC. From French *bande*, of uncertain origin: probably from the same prehistoric Germanic ancestor as English *banner*.] ◊ **to beat the band** to a very great extent or degree (*dated*)

band together vi. to form a group in order to achieve a goal

band[2] /band/ n. **1.** STRIP OR LOOP OF MATERIAL a strip of fabric, metal, elastic, or other material placed around sth to strengthen it or around several things to hold them together **2.** CONTRASTING STRIPE a long narrow area that is different in material, colour, or texture from the adjacent parts **3.** CLOTHES STRIP OR CIRCLE OF MATERIAL a strip or circle of fabric or elastic used for such purposes as decoration, identification, strengthening parts of clothing, or absorbing sweat on the forehead or hands **4.** ACCESSORIES RING a plain ring worn on a finger ○ *a wedding band* **5.** MECH ENG MOVING BELT a moving belt in a piece of machinery **6.** RANGE OF VALUES WITHIN LARGER RANGE a range of values relating to people, e.g. age or amount of tax paid, within the overall range of all people ○ *the highest tax band* **7.** RADIO RANGE OF RADIO FREQUENCIES a range of frequencies or wavelengths assigned to a radio station or radio broadcaster **8.** EDUC GROUP OF PUPILS TAUGHT TOGETHER a group of pupils from the same school year, taught together because they are at the same level of ability **9.** PHYS RANGE OF ENERGIES the range of energies possessed by electrons in a solid **10.** GEOL ORE OR MINERAL LAYER a layer of rock with a different composition or texture from the adjacent layers ■ vt. (**bands, banding, banded**) **1.** PUT BAND ON OR ROUND STH to put a strip on or round sth to decorate or identify it or to hold a number of things together **2.** CATEGORIZE THINGS to divide things into ranges of value **3.** EDUC DIVIDE PUPILS INTO GROUPS to divide pupils from one school year into groups to be taught together because they are at the same ability level [13thC. From Old Norse, later reinforced by French *bande*, both, ultimately, from a prehistoric Germanic ancestor that was also the source of English *bind*, *bend*, and *bond*.]

Banda /bándə/, **Hastings, Dr** (1906?–97) Malawi statesman. He was prime minister (1964–66), then president (1966–94), of Malawi. Full name **Hastings Kamuzu Banda**

bandage /bándij/ n. CLOTH STRIP FOR COVERING INJURY a long narrow strip of thin or elasticated fabric that can be wrapped and fastened around a wound or injured part of the body to protect or support it ■ vt. (**-ages, -aging, -aged**) APPLY BANDAGE to protect a wound or support an injured body part by applying a bandage [Late 16thC. From French, from *bande* (see BAND[2]).] —**bandager** n.

Band-Aid tdmk. a trademark for a sticking plaster with a central gauze pad

bandanna /ban dánnə/, **bandana** n. a large square of brightly coloured cotton or silk cloth worn over the hair or around the neck [Mid-18thC. Probably via Portuguese, from Hindi *bāndhnū*, the name of a method of tie-dyeing, from *bāndhnā* 'to tie'.]

Bandaranaike /bándərə nīˈəkə/, **Chandrika** (b. 1945) Sri Lankan politician. The daughter of S.W.R.D. Bandaranaike, she was elected president of Sri Lanka in 1994 and appointed her mother, Sirimavo Bandaranaike, prime minister. Full name **Chandrika Bandaranaike Kumaratunga**

Bandaranaike, Sirimavo (b. 1916) Sri Lankan politician. The succeeded her husband S.W.R.D. Bandaranaike to become the world's first woman prime minister (1960–65, 1970–77, 1994 -). She nationalized schools and foreign-owned plantations in Sri Lanka. Born **Sirimavo Ratwatte**

Bandaranaike, S.W.R.D. (1899–1959) Sri Lankan statesman. Prime minister of Sri Lanka (1956–59), he was assassinated by a Buddhist monk. Full name **Solomon West Ridgeway Dias Bandaranaike**

Bandar Seri Begawan /bán daar sérri bə gaáwən/ capital of Brunei, in the northern part of the country, on Brunei Bay. Population: 50,000 (1995).

Banda Sea /bándə-/ sea in the Pacific Ocean in eastern Indonesia, north of the island of Timor

and southeast of Celebes Island. Area: 738,150 sq. km/285,000 sq. mi.

B & B abbr. bed and breakfast (*informal*)

bandbox /bánd boks/ n. a round lightweight box for carrying accessories such as hats [Mid-17thC. Formed from BAND[2] + BOX, so called because they were originally used to carry neckbands.]

bandeau /bándō/ (plural **-deaux** /-dōz/) n. *US* a ribbon or band of material worn around the head to keep the hair in place [Early 18thC. From French, from Old French *bandel* 'little band', from *bande* (see BAND[2]).]

banded /bándid/ adj. marked with bands of different or contrasting colours ○ *banded agate*

banderilla /bándə reē ə, -reē yə/ n. in a bullfight, a long decorated barbed dart that is thrust into the neck or shoulder of a bull by a bullfighter's assistant [Late 18thC. From Spanish 'a little banner', from *bandera* 'banner'.]

banderillero /bándə reē áirrō, -lyáirō/ (plural **-ros**) n. a bullfighter's assistant who sticks a banderilla into the bull during a bullfight [Late 18thC. From Spanish, from *banderilla* (see BANDERILLA).]

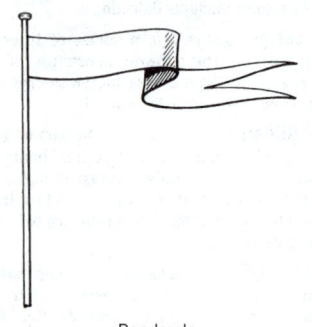
Banderole

banderole /bándə rōl/, **banderol, bannerol** /bánnə rōl/ n. **1.** NAUT FLAG ON MASTHEAD a long narrow flag with a divided end that is flown on a ship's masthead **2.** FLAG AT FUNERAL a flag that is carried at a funeral or used to cover a tomb **3.** ARCHIT INSCRIBED BAND a sculpted scroll or band bearing an inscription **4.** HIST RIBBON ON KNIGHT'S LANCE a ribbon or streamer hanging from a knight's lance [Mid-16thC. Via French, from Italian *banderuola* 'small banner', from *bandiera* 'banner'. Ultimately from the same prehistoric Germanic ancestor as English *band*[2].]

bandh /bund/, **bundh** n. *South Asia* a short general strike called in a city or district [From Hindi, literally 'a tying up']

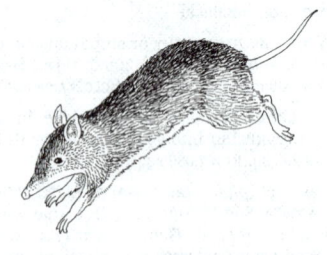
Bandicoot

bandicoot /bándi koot/ n. a marsupial with a long nose, strong hind legs, and a long tail. Bandicoots eat mainly insects and plants and are found in Australia, Tasmania, and New Guinea. Family: Peramelidae. [Late 18thC. From Telugu *pandikokku*, literally 'pig-rat'.]

bandicoot rat n. a large rodent found in southern Asia that is a serious pest to farmers. Latin name: *Bandicota indica*.

banding /bánding/ n. the grouping of pupils from the same school year into bands, usually of the same ability level, to be taught together. Banding is sometimes done to make the school timetable easier to administer. US term **tracking**

bandit /bándit/ (*plural* **-dits** *or* **-ditti** /ban dítti/) *n*. **1.** ARMED ROBBER an armed robber who steals from travellers and other people, usually at gunpoint **2.** GANGSTER a member of a gang of violent criminals **3.** *US* EXPLOITATIVE PERSON sb who cheats or swindles other people **4.** AIR FORCE ENEMY AIRCRAFT an enemy aircraft sighted by a crew while flying (*informal*) ◦ *Bandits at twelve o'clock high!* [Late 16thC. From Italian *bandito*, from *bandire* 'to ban'. Ultimately from the same prehistoric Germanic ancestor as English *ban*[1].] ◇ **make out like a bandit** *or* **bandits** *US* to be extremely successful, especially by making a lot of money in a short period of time (*informal*)

banditry /bánditri/ *n*. the occurrence or prevalence of armed robbery and violent crime

banditti plural of **bandit**

bandleader /bánd leedər/ *n*. the conductor of a band, especially of a dance band

Bandler /bándlər/, **Faith** (b. 1918) Australian writer and activist. She was co-founder of the Aboriginal Australian Fellowship (1956). Full name **Ida Lessing Faith Bandler**

bandmaster /bánd maastər/ *n*. the conductor of a band, especially of a brass band or a military band

bandog /bán dog/ *n*. an aggressive dog produced by cross-breeding a pit bull terrier with a mastiff, rottweiler, or Rhodesian ridgeback [15thC. A blend of BAND[2] and DOG, because it originally referred to a dog that was chained up or bound.]

bandoleer /bándə leër/, **bandolier** *n*. a soldier's belt with loops or small pockets for storing cartridges, worn over the shoulder and across the chest [Late 16thC. From French, perhaps from Spanish *bandolera*, from *banda* 'sash', or from Catalan *bandolera*, from *bandoler* 'bandit'.]

bandoneon /ban dóni ən/ *n*. a square concertina, used especially in Argentina [Early 20thC. Via Spanish *bandonéon* from German *Bandonion*, which was named after its 19thC German inventor Heinrich *Band*.] —**bandoneonist** *n*.

bandore /ban dáwr, bán dawr/ *n*. a musical instrument similar to a large guitar or lute that was played in the 16th and 17th centuries [Mid-16thC. Of uncertain origin. Forms of the word are found in many European languages and appear to go back to Latin *pandura*, from Greek *pandoura* 'three-stringed lute'.]

band-pass filter *n*. **1.** FREQUENCY FILTER an electronic filter that passes only those frequencies within a specified range **2.** DEVICE TRANSMITTING LIGHT OF PARTICULAR WAVELENGTHS a device transmitting electromagnetic radiation, especially visible light, within a restricted wavelength range

band saw *n*. a stationary power saw with a continuous vertically mounted blade

B and S Ball *n*. a social event for young people held in the Australian outback, typically comprising a weekend of music, dancing, and drinking. Guests normally wear formal evening attire, but sleep in tents or in their vehicles. [Shortening of *Bachelor and Spinsters Ball*]

band shell *n*. a bandstand with a curved wall at the back that is designed to reflect the sound towards the audience

bandsman /bándzmən/ (*plural* **-men** /-mən/) *n*. a player in a brass band or military band

bandspreading /bánd spredding/ *n*. a function of some radios that allows the user to select a narrow band of frequencies and space them further apart, to make tuning into a specific frequency easier

bandstand /bánd stand/ *n*. a platform for a band or small orchestra to perform on, especially outdoors

band theory *n*. a theory that explains the electrical conductivity of solids in terms of energy bands containing electrons

Bandung /bán doong/ *n*. city in southern Indonesia, on western Java Island, southeast of Jakarta. Population: 2,056,915 (1990).

B & W, **b & w** *abbr*. PHOTOGRAPHY black-and-white

bandwagon /bánd wagən/ *n*. **1.** INCREASINGLY POPULAR MOVEMENT a cause or movement that is gaining popularity and support **2.** *US* WAGON FOR MUSICIANS an ornately decorated wagon that musicians perform on during a parade ◇ **jump** *or* **climb on the bandwagon** to join in sth only because it is fashionable or likely to be profitable

bandwidth /bánd width/ *n*. **1.** RADIO, TELECOM RANGE OF RADIO FREQUENCIES a range of radio frequencies used in radio or telecommunications transmission and reception **2.** COMPUT COMMUNICATION CAPACITY the capacity of a communication channel, e.g. a connection to the Internet, often measured in bits per second

bandy /bándi/ *vt*. (**-dies**, **-dying**, **-died**) CASUALLY EXCHANGE WORDS to toss words back and forth casually, often without caring whether they are true or what effect they may have ◦ *I've heard the name being bandied about.* ■ *adj*. (**-dier**, **-diest**) CURVED SO KNEES CANNOT MEET used to describe legs that curve outward so that the knees cannot meet [Late 16thC. Origin uncertain, perhaps from French *bander* 'to take sides at tennis', which probably goes back to the same ancestor as BAND[1].] ◇ **bandy words with sb** to have an argument or discussion with sb, often one that is unnecessary or a waste of time

bandy-bandy (*plural* **bandy-bandies**) *n*. ANZ a small, mildly venomous Australian snake marked with black-and-white bands. Latin name: *Vermicella annulata*. [Early 20thC. From an Aboriginal language.]

bandy-legged *adj*. having legs that curve outward, so that the knees do not touch

bane /bayn/ *n*. **1.** STH THAT CAUSES MISERY sth that continually causes problems or misery ◦ *It's the bane of my life.* **2.** STH THAT CAUSES RUIN sth that causes death, destruction, or ruin (*literary or archaic*) **3.** DEADLY POISON a fatal poison (*often used in combination in the names of poisonous plants*) [Old English *bana*, ultimately from a prehistoric Germanic word] ◇ **the bane of sb's life** sb or sth that is a constant source of trouble or annoyance

baneful /báynf'l/ *adj*. causing ruin or destruction (literary) —**banefully** *adv*. —**banefulness** *n*.

─────── **WORD KEY: USAGE** ───────
See Usage note at *baleful*.

Banff /bamf/ market town and seaport in Aberdeenshire, Scotland. Population: 6,230 (1991).

Banffshire /bámfshər/ former county in northeastern Scotland, now part of Aberdeenshire

bang[1] /bang/ *n*. **1.** SUDDEN LOUD NOISE a sudden loud noise, e.g. the sound of a gun firing or a door slamming shut **2.** SHARP HIT a sharp blow or hit ◦ *a nasty bang on the head* **3.** ENERGY BURST a burst of energy or activity (*informal*) ◦ *The party started with a bang.* **4.** SEX ACT the act of having sexual intercourse (*slang offensive*) **5.** DRUGS INJECTION OF DRUG an injection of an illegal drug such as heroin (*slang*) **6.** *US* COMPUT CHARACTER IN TYPESETTING the character (!) in typesetting ■ **bangs** *npl*. *US* FRINGE OF HAIR ACROSS FOREHEAD the hair falling over the forehead when it is cut square above the eyes ■ *v*. (**bangs**, **banging**, **banged**) **1.** *vti*. HIT to hit sth hard, or slam sth against a surface ◦ *He banged his fist on the table.* **2.** *vti*. HIT ACCIDENTALLY to hit sth unintentionally ◦ *She banged her knee.* **3.** *vti*. CLOSE HARD AND NOISILY to close suddenly and loudly, or make sth close, with a sudden loud noise ◦ *The door banged shut.* **4.** *vi*. MAKE LOUD NOISE to make a sudden loud noise ◦ *children banging on pots and pans* **5.** *vi*. MOVE AROUND NOISILY to move around making a lot of noise ◦ *I could hear her banging about in the kitchen.* ◦ *bang sulkily about the house* **6.** *vti*. OFFENSIVE TERM an offensive term meaning to have sexual intercourse with sb (*slang offensive*) **7.** *vt*. STOCK EXCH MAKE SHARE PRICES FALL to cause share prices to fall **8.** *vi*. DRUGS INJECT A DRUG to inject an illegal drug such as heroin (*slang*) ■ *adv*. **1.** exactly or precisely ◦ *Our hotel is bang in the centre of the town.* **2.** SUDDENLY suddenly and unexpectedly ◦ *I turned round and bang, there he was!* ■ *interj*. IMITATING EXPLOSIVE SOUND used especially by children to imitate the sound of a gun firing (*informal*) ◦ *Bang! You're dead!* [Mid-16thC. An imitation of the sound.] ◇ **bang for your buck** value for money spent or effort expended (*slang*) ◇ **bang goes sth!** used as a rueful acknowledgment that sth is no longer available or likely to happen (*informal*) ◇ **bang on** *UK*, *Can* exactly right ◇ **go out with a bang** to end or finish

sth in a dramatic way (*informal*) ◇ **go with a bang** to be very successful

bang away *vi*. to keep doing sth persistently and determinedly

bang on to keep on talking about the same topic (*informal*)

bang out *vt*. (*informal*) **1.** PRODUCE STH QUICKLY to produce sth speedily ◦ *bang out an essay overnight* **2.** PLAY A TUNE LOUDLY to play a tune on a musical instrument loudly and without sensitivity to the music

bang up to lock a prisoner in a cell (*informal*)

bang[2] /bang/ *n*. = **bhang**

Bangalore /bángg ə láwr/ capital of Karnataka State in south-central India. Population: 2,651,000 (1991).

bangalore torpedo (*plural* **bangalore torpedoes**) *n*. an explosive device in a metal tube, used to blow holes in barbed-wire fences or to detonate land mines [Early 20thC. Named after BANGALORE where it was invented.]

bangalow /báng gəlō/ *n*. an Australian palm tree found in New South Wales and Queensland. Latin name: *Archontophoenix cunninghamiana*. [Early 19thC. From an Aboriginal name.]

Bangasi = **Banghazi**

banger /bángər/ *n*. **1.** SAUSAGE a fried or grilled sausage (*informal*) **2.** OLD CAR an old car that is not in very good condition (*informal*) **3.** LOUD FIREWORK a firework that explodes very noisily

Bangka /bángkə/, **Banka** island in western Indonesia forming part of the Malay Archipelago. Pangkalpinang is the largest town. Area: 11,937 sq. km/4,609 sq. mi.

Bangkok /báng kók, báng kok/ capital city and port on the River Chao Phraya, just north of the Gulf of Thailand, southern Thailand. Population: 5,562,141 (1992).

Bangla /báng glə/ *n*. LANG = **Bengali**

Bangladesh

Bangladesh /bán glə désh/ republic in south-central Asia, formerly part of India and then, from 1947 to 1971, Pakistan. It became a separate nation following a civil war in 1971. Language: Bengali. Currency: taka. Capital: Dhaka. Population: 125,340,261 (1997). Area: 147,570 sq. km/56,977 sq. mi. Official name **People's Republic of Bangladesh** —**Bangladeshi** *n*., *adj*.

bangle /báng g'l/ *n*. **1.** RIGID BRACELET a stiff metal, plastic, or wooden bracelet that is worn around the arm, wrist, or ankle **2.** DISC ATTACHED TO BRACELET a decorative disc, charm, or other ornament that hangs from a bracelet [Late 18thC. From Hindi *bangri* 'coloured glass bracelet'.]

Bangor /báng gər/ coastal resort and fishing port in County Down, Northern Ireland. Population: 52,437 (1991). ■ university city in Gwynedd, northern Wales, on the Menai Strait. Population: 12,330 (1991).

Bang's disease /bángz-/ *n*. brucellosis in animals, especially in cattle [Early 20thC. Named after the Danish veterinary surgeon Bernhard L. F. *Bang* (d. 1932).]

bangtail /báng tayl/ *n*. *US* an envelope with a detachable section that can be used as an order form or to provide marketing information

Bangui /baang gée/ capital city and major port of the River Ubangi, southern Central African Republic. Population: 451,690 (1988).

─────────────────
zh vision   In foreign words: kh German Bach; aN French vin; aaN French blanc; ö German schön, French feu; oN French bon; öN French un; ü French rue   Stress marks: ´ as in secret \séek rət\; academic \ákə démmik\

bani plural of ban[2]

banish /bánnish/ (**-ishes, -ishing, -ished**) *vt.* **1. SEND SB AWAY** to exile sb from a place, or send sb to another place officially as a punishment **2. GET RID OF STH** to forbid or expel sth, or put it out of your mind ○ *Let us banish from our minds all dark thoughts.* [14thC. From French *baniss-*, the stem of *banir* 'to proclaim', from assumed Vulgar Latin *bannire.* Ultimately from a prehistoric Germanic word, the ancestor of English *ban*[1] and *bandit.*] —**banisher** *n.*

banishment /bánnishmənt/ *n.* **1. EXPULSION** the forcible expulsion or exile of sb or sth **2. PERIOD OF EXILE** a period of time spent in exile

banister /bánnistər/, **bannister** *n.* **1. HANDRAIL ON STAIRCASE** a handrail supported by posts running up the outside edge of a staircase (*often used in the plural*) **2. POST SUPPORTING HANDRAIL** any one of the posts supporting a handrail on a staircase [Mid-17thC. Alteration of BALUSTER.]

Banja Luka /bánnyə lóokə/ city on the River Vrbas in northern Bosnia-Herzegovina. Population: 142,644 (1991).

Banjarmasin /bánjə maá sin/, **Bandjarmasin** city in southeastern Borneo, Indonesia. It is the capital of South Kalimantan Province. Population: 480,737 (1990).

banjax /bán jaks/ (**-jaxes, -jaxing, -jaxed**) *Ireland* to damage or smash sth (*informal*) [Mid-20thC. Origin unknown.]

banjo /bán jō/ (*plural* **-jos** *or* **-joes**) *n.* a musical instrument that has a round sound box covered with parchment, five strings, and a long neck. Plucked or strummed, it is popular in North American folk music. [Mid-18thC. Related to Jamaican English *banja* 'fiddle', of uncertain origin, probably from an African language, and related to Kimbundu *mbanza* 'stringed musical instrument'.]

Banjul /ban jóol/ capital and largest city of the Gambia. It is situated at the mouth of the River Gambia. Population: 42,407 (1993).

bank[1] /bangk/ *n.* **1. BUSINESS OFFERING FINANCIAL SERVICES** a business that keeps money for individuals or companies, exchanges currencies, makes loans, and offers other financial services **2. BANK'S LOCAL OFFICE** a local office of a bank **3.** GAMBLING **FUND OF MONEY OR TOKENS** the fund of money, tokens, chips, or other pieces that players can draw out in certain games, or the player who holds the fund **4. STORE OF STH** a supply of sth stored, ready for immediate use, e.g. data, food, or blood ■ *v.* (**banks, banking, banked**) **1.** *vt.* **DEPOSIT MONEY IN BANK** to pay money into a bank ○ *banked the cheque immediately* **2.** *vi.* **HAVE ACCOUNT WITH FINANCIAL INSTITUTION** to have an account with or use a particular bank ○ *bank with a local institution* [15thC. Directly or via French *banque* from Italian *banca* 'bank, bench, table'. The sense bank developed in the source language from the table on which banking was transacted.] ◇ **break the bank 1.** *US* GAMBLING to win more money than is available **2.** to leave sb very short of or without money (*informal*)

bank on *vt.* to count on sth happening ○ *We're banking on your support.*

bank[2] /bangk/ *n.* **1. SIDE OF WATERWAY** the steep side of a river, stream, lake, or canal **2. RAISED AREA OF LAND BELOW WATER** a ridge of sand or other sedimentary deposit in a river or coastal sea that decreases the depth of the water above it and may become visible at low tide **3. EARTH OR SNOW WITH SLOPING SIDE** a pile of earth, snow, or sand, or a raised area of ground with a sloping side **4.** METEOROL **MASS OF CLOUD** a large dense area of cloud or fog **5.** RAIL **LONG TRACK GRADIENT** a long gradient or slope on a railway **6.** MOTOR SPORTS **SLOPE AT BEND IN RACETRACK** an upward slope at a bend in a road or racetrack, designed to reduce the likelihood of drivers going off the road or track when travelling around the bend at speed **7.** AIR **TURNING ANGLE OF AIRCRAFT** the angle made by an aeroplane as it turns **8.** CUE GAMES **CUSHION OF BILLIARD TABLE** the cushion of a billiard or pool table **9.** MINING **MOUTH OF MINE SHAFT** the area around the mouth of a mine shaft ■ *v.* **1.** *vti.* **FORM INTO PILE** to make sth into a pile or a large heap or form a pile or heap ○ *snow banked against the fence* **2.** *vt.* **MAKE RAISED SLOPE** to make a raised slope as an edge or border to sth ○ *bank earth along the river* **3.** *vt.* **COVER FIRE** to cover a fire with ashes or fuel so that it will continue to burn slowly for a long time **4.** *vti.* AIR **TILT WHILE TURNING PLANE** to tilt an airplane with one wing higher than the other while turning, or turn an aeroplane so that it tilts **5.** *vti.* MOTOR SPORTS **TILT WHILE DRIVING** to tilt a vehicle, especially a motorcycle while travelling around a bend at speed, or travel around a bend like this **6.** *vt.* MOTOR SPORTS **BUILD SLOPE INTO ROAD OR RACETRACK** to build a slope into a road or racetrack at a bend **7.** *vt.* CUE GAMES **HIT BILLIARD BALL INTO CUSHION** to hit a billiard ball into the cushion [12thC. From assumed Old Norse *banki* 'ridge, bank'. Ultimately from a prehistoric Germanic ancestor that is also the ancestor of English *bench* and *bank*[1].]

bank[3] /bangk/ *n.* **1. ROW OF SIMILAR THINGS** a row or several rows of things of one type ○ *a bank of switches* **2.** NAUT **GALLEY ROWERS' BENCH** a bench for rowers in a galley **3.** NAUT **GALLEY OARS** a row of oars in a galley ■ *vt.* (**banks, banking, banked**) **PUT THINGS INTO ROWS** to arrange things in rows or tiers [13thC. From French *banc* 'bench'. Ultimately from a prehistoric Germanic word that is also the ancestor of English *bank*[2] and *bench.*]

bankable /bángkəb'l/ *adj.* **1. LIKELY TO BRING IN MONEY** likely to become financially profitable ○ *a bankable movie star* **2. ACCEPTABLE TO A BANK** readily and legally acceptable to a bank —**bankability** /bángkə bíllәti/ *n.*

bank account *n.* an arrangement according to which a bank accepts deposits of money and keeps that money available for withdrawal by the named account holder or holders

bank annuities *npl.* = **consols**

bank balance *n.* the amount of money in a bank account at any given time

bank barn *n.* in the United States or Canada, a two-storey barn built into a hillside that has an entrance to the first storey at the front and an entrance to the second storey at the back

bank bill *n.* = **bank draft**

bankbook /bángk bóok/ *n.* = **passbook**

bank card *n. UK* = **cheque card**

bank discount *n.* the interest on a loan that is deducted from the amount borrowed at the time the loan is taken out

bank draft *n.* a bill of exchange drawn by one bank on another

banker /bángkər/ *n.* **1. SB SENIOR IN BANKING** sb who owns or works at a senior level in a bank **2.** GAMBLING **PLAYER IN CHARGE OF BANK** the player in charge of the bank in a gambling game [Mid-16thC. From BANK[1].] —**bankerly** *adj.*

banker's draft *n.* an order for the payment of money from one bank to another bank's own funds

banker's order *n.* = **standing order**

banket /bángkit/ *n.* a type of rock with gold in it found in South Africa [Late 19thC. From Afrikaans, literally 'almond toffee'. From the appearance of the rock.]

Bankhead /bángk hed/, **Tallulah** (1902–68) US actor. She was famous for the husky voice and extravagant acting style on stage in such plays as Lillian Hellman's *The Little Foxes* (1939) and in films including *Lifeboat* (1944). Born **Tallulah Brockman**

bank holiday *n.* a weekday regarded as a legal holiday on which banks, shops, and many businesses are closed

banking /bángking/ *n.* the work carried out by banks or bankers

bank manager *n.* sb who is in charge of a branch of a bank

banknote /bángk nōt/ *n.* a piece of paper money issued by a bank that may be freely exchanged for goods or services

Bank of Canada *n.* the federal central bank of Canada

Bank of England *n.* the central bank of England and Wales

bank rate *n.* the annual rate of interest set by a country's central bank. = **base rate**

bankroll /bángk rōl/ *n.* **1. FUND OF MONEY** a fund of money used to finance a project **2.** *US* **ROLL OF PAPER MONEY** a roll of banknotes ■ *vt.* (**-rolls, -rolling, -rolled**) **FINANCE STH** to provide the money needed to finance a project on a continuing basis (*informal*) —**bankroller** *n.*

bankrupt /bángk rupt/ *adj.* **1. UNABLE TO PAY DEBTS** judged legally to be unable to pay off personal debts **2. WITHOUT RESOURCES** completely lacking in a particular quality, especially in good or ethical qualities ○ *morally bankrupt* ■ *n.* **1. SB WHO CANNOT PAY DEBTS** sb who has been declared legally unable to pay his or her outstanding debts **2. SB WITHOUT RESOURCES** sb who is completely lacking a particular quality, especially good or ethical qualities ■ *vt.* (**-rupts, -rupting, -rupted**) **DEPLETE SB'S FUNDS** to cost so much that a person or business will have hardly any money left or will be declared bankrupt [Mid-16thC. From Italian *banca rotta*, literally 'broken table', from *banca* (see BANK[1]) + *rotto*, from Latin *ruptus* 'broken'. Formerly a symbol for a bankrupt moneylender.]

bankruptcy /bángk ruptsi/ (*plural* **-cies**) *n.* **1. LEGAL INABILITY TO PAY DEBTS** the state of having been legally declared bankrupt **2. LACK OF RESOURCES** the complete lack of a particular quality, especially good or ethical qualities ○ *moral bankruptcy*

Banks /bangks/, **Sir Joseph** (1743–1820) British naturalist. A member of Captain Cook's expedition round the world (1768–71), he helped to establish botany as a science and was instrumental in developing Kew Gardens in London.

banksia /bángksi ə/ (*plural* **-as** *or* **-a**) *n.* a small Australian evergreen tree or shrub with leathery narrow leaves and cylindrical flowers. Family: Proteaceae. [Early 19thC. Modern Latin, named after Joseph BANKS.]

Banks Island /bángks-/ island in the Inuvik Region, Northwest Territories, Canada. It has a predominantly Inuit population. Area: 70,028 sq. km/27,038 sq. mi.

Banks Peninsula peninsula on the eastern coast of South Island, New Zealand, near Christchurch. Length: 48 km/30 mi.

bank statement *n.* a document showing all the transactions in a bank account over a specific period of time

banner /bánnər/ (**-ners, -nering**) *n.* **1. CLOTH SUSPENDED BETWEEN TWO POLES** a long piece of cloth, often bearing a symbol or slogan, and attached at each end to a pole or hanging from the top of a pole **2. GUIDING PRINCIPLE** a guiding principle, cause, or philosophy ○ *under the banner of the trade union movement* **3. NATION'S OR ARMY'S FLAG** the flag of a country or army **4.** HIST **FLAG OF KING, EMPEROR, OR KNIGHT** a flag used by a king, emperor, or knight when going into battle **5.** PRESS = **banner headline** **6.** COMPUT **WEB SITE ADVERT** an advertisement in the form of a rectangular logo or headline spread across the width of a Web page [13thC. Via Anglo-Norman *banere* from Old French *banière* from, ultimately, medieval Latin *bandum* 'standard'. Ultimately from the same prehistoric Germanic word that is also the ancestor of English *band*[1].]

WORD KEY: CULTURAL NOTE

The Star-Spangled Banner, a patriotic song with lyrics by US writer Francis Scott Key set to music by English composer John Stafford Smith (1814). Penned by Key after he had witnessed the successful defence of the city of Baltimore by US troops against a British attack in 1814, it soon became a popular patriotic song. It was adopted as the national anthem of the United States on March 3, 1931.

banneret /bánnərət, -ret/ *n.* **1. KNIGHT WITH OWN ARMY** a knight who was entitled to lead his own men into battle and was thus of a higher rank than other knights **2. HISTORICAL TITLE FOR BRAVERY** in former times, a title given by a king or queen for bravery in battle [13thC. From Old French *baneret*, literally 'bannered', from *banière* (see BANNER).]

banner headline *n.* a headline in large letters that runs across an entire page of a newspaper

bannerol *n.* = **banderole**

bannister *n.* = **banister**

Bannister /bánnistər/, **Sir Roger** (*b.* 1929) British athlete. He was the first man to run the mile in under four minutes (1954). Full name **Sir Roger Gilbert Bannister**

bannock /bánnək/ *n.* a traditional Scottish bread in the shape of a round flat savoury cake cooked on a griddle [Old English *bannuc*, from an earlier word meaning 'drop']

Bannockburn /bánnək burn/ town in central Scotland, where the Scots, led by Robert the Bruce, defeated Edward II of England in 1314. Population: 2,675 (1991).

banns /banz/ *npl.* an announcement of a forthcoming marriage, proclaimed in the parish churches of the engaged couple on three successive Sundays [14thC. From BAN[1].]

banoffee /bə nóffi/, **banoffi** *n.* a creamy filling made from bananas and toffee, eaten in a pastry or biscuit base ○ *banoffee pie* [Late 20thC. Blend of BANANA and TOFFEE.]

banquet /bángkwit/ *n.* **1.** CEREMONIAL MEAL an elaborate formal meal attended by many guests, often held in honour of a particular person or occasion and followed by speeches **2.** BIG MEAL an elaborate or lavish meal of many courses ■ *vi.* (**-quets, -queting, -queted**) EXPERIENCE A BANQUET to eat or drink as a guest at a banquet [15thC. From French, literally 'little bank' (see BANK[3]). Originally, this referred to a small snack eaten while seated on a bench, not at a table.] —**banqueter** *n.*

banqueting hall *n.* a room large enough to accommodate a banquet, usually in a palace, castle, or stately home

banqueting room *n.* a room large enough to accommodate a banquet in a hotel or restaurant

banquette /báng két/ *n.* **1.** UPHOLSTERED BENCH an upholstered bench along a wall, especially in a restaurant **2.** RAISED STEP FOR GUNNER a raised step in a trench or behind a parapet on which a soldier may stand to fire or a gun may be mounted [Early 17thC. Via French, from Italian *banchetta* 'little bench', formed from *banca* 'bench, shelf' (see BANK[1]).]

bansela *n.* = **bonsela**

banshee /bán shee/ *n.* **1.** SPIRIT WHO WARNS OF DEATH in Gaelic folklore, a spirit of a woman who appears, wailing, to signal that sb in the household is going to die **2.** *Ireland* FEMALE FAIRY a female fairy [Late 17thC. Via Irish *bean sidhe* from Old Irish *ben* 'woman' + *side* 'of the fairy world'.]

WORD KEY: REGIONAL NOTE

Old Irish *ben side* meant 'fairy woman'. The term is used of a supernatural being in both Ireland and the Scottish Highlands. The ***banshee*** wails near a house as a warning that a member of the household is about to die. Not every family has the dubious privilege of a forewarning from a ***banshee***. Some clans are visited by a bird, while others are warned by breaking mirrors, falling pictures, and fires that refuse to burn properly.

Banstead /bán sted/ suburban town in northeastern Surrey, England. Population: 37,245 (1991).

bantam /bántəm/ *n.* **1.** SMALL DOMESTIC FOWL a bird belonging to a breed of small domestic fowl **2.** = **bantamweight** ■ *adj. US* OVERCONFIDENT overconfident and slightly aggressive [Mid-18thC. Named after the town of *Bantam* in Java from where the birds are supposed to have been imported, although they are not native there.]

bantamweight /bántəm wayt/ *n.* **1.** BOXER WEIGHING LESS THAN FEATHERWEIGHT a professional boxer weighing 51–53.5 kg/112–118 lb, or an amateur weighing 51–54 kg/112–119 lb **2.** LIGHTWEIGHT WRESTLER a wrestler weighing 52–57 kg/115–126 lb

banter /bántər/ *n.* LIGHT TEASING REMARKS lighthearted teasing or amusing remarks that are exchanged between people ■ *vi.* (**-ters, -tering, -tered**) EXCHANGE TEASING REMARKS to exchange lighthearted teasing remarks [Late 17thC. Origin unknown.] —**banterer** *n.*

Banting /bánting/, **Sir Frederick Grant** (1891–1941) Canadian physician. He co-discovered insulin with Charles Best (1922), for which he shared the Nobel Prize in physiology or medicine (1923).

Bantu /bán tóo/ (*plural* **-tu** *or* **-tus**) *n.* **1.** LANG AFRICAN LANGUAGE GROUP a group of over 500 languages, including Kiswahili, Xhosa, and Zulu, spoken in central, eastern, and southern Africa. It belongs to the Benue-Congo subfamily of Niger-Congo languages and has over 150 million speakers. **2.** PEOPLES MEMBER OF AFRICAN PEOPLE a member of a large group of peoples living in equatorial and southern Africa [Mid-19thC. In some Bantu languages the plural of *-ntu* 'person'.] —**Bantu** *adj.*

WORD KEY: USAGE

Sensitivity trap: In post-apartheid South Africa, ***Bantu*** is considered highly offensive when used with reference to Black people, especially in the singular to refer to one person, and ***Black*** or ***African*** are the normally accepted terms. In technical contexts outside South Africa, for example academic discussions of anthropology and language, the term continues in use.

bantustan /bán too staan, bán too stáan/, **Bantustan** *n.* formerly, during the apartheid era from the 1950s until 1994, an area in South Africa where Black people lived with limited self-government. Bantustans are no longer in existence. (*sometimes used derogatorily*) [Mid-20thC. Formed from BANTU on the model of such names as HINDUSTAN.]

Banville /báaN veel/, **Théodore de** (1823–91) French poet and playwright. He was famed for his facility with difficult verse forms. Full name **Etienne Claude Jean Baptiste Théodore Faullain de Banville**

Banyan

banyan /bánnyən, -yan/ *n.* **1.** TROPICAL TREE WITH AERIAL ROOTS a tree grown in the Indian subcontinent and East Indies for shade or ornament. The roots grow down from the branches into the ground to form new secondary trunks. Latin name: *Ficus benghalensis.* **2.** MAN'S LOOSE GARMENT a loose jacket, shirt, or gown, worn by men in parts of the Indian subcontinent [Late 16thC. Via Portuguese, from Gujarati *vāṇiyo* 'man of the trading class', from Sanskrit *vāṇija* 'merchant'. Applied to a tree under which some traders had built a pagoda.]

banzai /ban zí, baan-/ *interj.* PATRIOTIC JAPANESE SHOUT a patriotic Japanese battle cry or shout ■ *adj.* RECKLESS AND FEROCIOUS IN BATTLE reckless and utterly ferocious in a military attack [Late 19thC. From Japanese, literally '(may you live) ten thousand years'.]

baobab /báy ō bab/ *n.* a tropical tree native to southern Africa and northwestern Australia that has a very thick trunk, and bears fruit with a hard rind and edible pulp. Latin name: *Adansonia digitata.* [Mid-17thC. Origin uncertain: perhaps from North African Arabic *bū ḥibab* 'fruit of many seeds'.]

Baotou /bów tó/ city on the Yellow River west of Hohhot in Inner Mongolia, northern China. Population: 1,200,000 (1991).

bap /bap/ *n.* a large soft flattish bread roll [Late 16thC. Origin unknown.]

baptise = **baptize**

baptism /báptizzəm/ *n.* **1.** RITE OF PURIFICATION a religious ceremony in which sb is sprinkled with or immersed in water to symbolize purification. In Christian baptisms, the person is often named and accepted into the Christian faith. **2.** INITIATION OR NAMING CEREMONY a ceremony that serves as an initiation or naming ritual —**baptismal** /bap tízm'l/ *adj.* —**baptismally** *adv.*

baptism of fire *n.* **1.** INITIAL ORDEAL a difficult or dangerous first experience in a new situation **2.** SOLDIER'S FIRST BATTLE a soldier's first experience of battle

Baptist /báptist/ *n.* a member of a Protestant denomination that baptizes people by total immersion when they are old enough to understand and declare their faith —**Baptist** *adj.*

baptistery /báptistri/ (*plural* **-ies**), **baptistry** (*plural* **-tries**) *n.* **1.** PART OF CHRISTIAN CHURCH a part of a Christian church used for baptisms **2.** POOL IN CHURCH FOR BAPTISMS a tank or pool in a Baptist church used for baptisms by total immersion

baptize /bap tíz/ (**-tizes, -tizing, -tized**), **baptise** (**-tises, -tising, -tised**) *v.* **1.** *vti.* PERFORM CEREMONY OF BAPTISM to sprinkle sb with or immerse sb in water as a sign that the person has been accepted into the Christian faith **2.** *vt.* NAME SB IN BAPTISM to give a personal name to sb during the Christian ceremony of baptism [13thC. Via French *baptiser* and ecclesiastical Latin *baptisare* from Greek *baptizein* 'to baptize', from *baptein* 'to dip'.] —**baptizer** *n.*

bar[1] /baar/ *n.* **1.** LENGTH OF SOLID MATERIAL a length of metal, wood, or other solid material used as a barrier, or as part of a structure **2.** SMALL BLOCK a small, solid, usually rectangular, block of some substance ○ *a bar of soap* **3.** BARRIER sth that blocks or hinders progress ○ *Aloofness is a bar to making friends easily.* **4.** PLACE FOR DRINKING a place where alcoholic drinks can be bought and drunk **5.** DRINKS COUNTER a counter where alcoholic drinks are served **6.** PLACE PROVIDING PRODUCT OR SERVICE a commercial establishment, or a counter inside one, where a product or service is provided ○ *a juice bar* **7.** NARROW BAND a narrow stripe or band of colour or light **8.** STH USED AS A STANDARD sth referred to as an authority or standard ○ *We need to raise the bar of academic courses for all our students.* **9.** LAW PART OF LAW COURT the railing in a law court that separates the judge, jury, and Queen's Counsel from solicitors, junior barristers, and the public **10.** LAW PLACE FOR DEFENDANT IN COURT the place in a law court where sb on trial stands or sits **11.** LAW TRIBUNAL a tribunal or court of law **12.** LAW DEFEAT OF LEGAL ACTION the defeat, prevention, or nullification of an action or claim, or the process by which this is achieved **13.** POL PLACE IN BRITISH PARLIAMENT the place in the House of Commons or House of Lords where nonmembers must stand to address either House **14.** MUSIC UNIT OF TIME IN MUSIC a fundamental unit of time into which all music is divided, according to the number of beats **15.** MUSIC VERTICAL LINE SEPARATING MUSICAL UNITS any one of the vertical lines on a sheet of music that separates each unit of musical time **16.** MIL INSIGNIA an insignia added to a decoration to show that an award has been won twice **17.** SPORTS = **crossbar 18.** GYMNASTICS = **horizontal bar 19.** BALLET = **barre 20.** HERALDRY LINE ACROSS SHIELD a horizontal line on a shield, usually one of two or three parallel lines **21.** GEOG RIDGE OF SAND a low ridge of sand or shingle in the shallow part of the bed of a body of water **22.** GEOG RIVER'S CRESCENT-SHAPED SAND DEPOSIT a crescent-shaped area of alluvium deposited on the convex bend of a river bed **23.** BACKGAMMON STRIP IN BACKGAMMON BOARD the central dividing strip on a backgammon board ■ *vt.* (**bars, barring, barred**) **1.** FASTEN WITH BAR to fasten sth with a bar ○ *barred the door* **2.** BLOCK STH to block sth by means of bars or barriers **3.** NOT ALLOW SB ENTRY to refuse sb entry to a place ○ *He was barred from the club.* **4.** NOT ALLOW SB TO DO STH to prevent sb or forbid sb to do sth **5.** MARK STH WITH BARS to mark sth with stripes or bands of colour (*usually passive*) **6.** LAW HALT COURT CASE to prevent a court case from going ahead by making a legal objection to it ■ *prep.* EXCLUDING except for ○ *The fight was all over, bar the shouting.* [12thC. Via Old French *barre* from Vulgar Latin *barra*, of unknown origin.] ◇ **behind bars** in prison ○ *a convicted felon who spent 20 years behind bars*

bar[2] /baar/ *n.* a cgs unit of pressure that can be used in combination with SI units and prefixes, equal to 10^5 newtons per square metre [Early 20thC. From Greek *baros* 'weight'.]

Bar *n.* LAW **1.** BARRISTERS OR THEIR PROFESSION barristers considered collectively, or the profession of a barrister **2.** LAWYERS OR THEIR PROFESSION in the United States, lawyers considered collectively, or the profession of a lawyer ○ *the federal and state Bars*

BAR *abbr.* Browning automatic rifle

bar. *abbr.* **1.** barometer **2.** barometric **3.** barrel

Bar. *abbr.* **1.** barrister **2.** BIBLE Baruch

Barabbas /bə rábbəss/ *n.* in the Bible, a condemned thief who was freed by Pilate on Passover instead of Jesus Christ (Matthew 27)

bara brith /bárrə bríth/ *n.* *Wales* traditional fruit cake made with tea

Baranof Island /bárrənəf-/ island off southeastern Alaska, part of the Alexander Archipelago. It is named after the first governor of the Russian colony of Alaska, Aleksandr Baranov (1746–1819). Area: 4,162 sq. km/1,607 sq. mi.

barasingha /bárrə síng gə/ (*plural* **-ha**) *n.* = **swamp deer** [Mid-19thC. From Hindi *barah-singā*, literally 'twelve-tined'.]

Barassi /bə rássi/, **Ron** (*b.* 1936) Australian footballer and coach. He coached Carlton (1968, 1970) and North Melbourne (1975, 1977) to Australian Rules Grand Final championships. Full name **Ronald Dale Barassi**

barathea /bárrə thée ə/ *n.* a type of fabric made from a combination of silk, cotton, wool, or synthetic material, often used for making coats [Mid-19thC. Origin unknown.]

baraza /bə ráazə/ *n.* a public meeting or a place where meetings are held in East Africa [Late 19thC. From Kiswahili.]

Barb

barb[1] /baarb/ *n.* **1.** REVERSE POINT OF ARROW a sharp point facing away from the head of an arrow, fishhook, or harpoon, designed to make it difficult to remove **2.** WOUNDING REMARK a pointed or wounding remark **3.** (*plural* **barbs** *or* **barb**) ZOOL AQUARIUM FISH a small fish often kept in aquariums. Genera: *Barbus* and *Puntius*. **4.** CLOTHES MEDIEVAL HEADDRESS a white cloth headdress covering the chin and throat, worn by women in the Middle Ages **5.** ZOOL PART OF FEATHER a stiff filament that forms the framework of a feather. The barbs stick out on each side of the main shaft. **6.** ZOOL WHISKER ON ANIMAL'S HEAD a growth on an animal's head like a beard or whisker **7.** BOT BRISTLE OF A PLANT a hooked projection on some plants and fruits ■ *vt.* (**barbs, barbing, barbed**) FIT WITH BARB to provide sth with a barb or barbs [14thC. Via Old French *barbe* 'beard', appendage like a beard', from Latin *barba* 'beard'.]

barb[2] /baarb/ (*plural* **barbs** *or* **barb**) *n.* a horse belonging to a breed originally from North Africa, noted for speed and stamina [Mid-17thC. Via French *barbe* from Italian *barbero* 'of Barbary'.]

barb[3] /baarb/ *n.* a barbiturate (*slang*) [Mid-20thC. Shortening.]

BARB /baarb/ *abbr.* Broadcasters' Audience Research Board

Barbados /baar báy doss/ island nation in the West

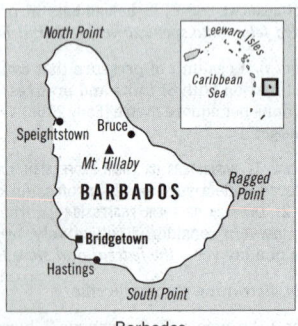

Barbados

Indies off northeastern South America. Settled by the British in the 17th century, it has been an independent state within the Commonwealth since 1966. Language: English. Currency: Barbados dollar. Capital: Bridgetown. Population: 258,756 (1997). Area: 430 sq. km/166 sq. mi. —**Barbadian** /baar báydi ən/ *n.*, *adj.*

Barbados almond *n.* = **Indian almond**

barbarian /baar báiri ən/ *n.* **1.** PERSON FROM PRIMITIVE CULTURE especially in ancient times, a member of a people whose culture and behaviour was considered primitive and uncivilized **2.** UNCULTURED PERSON sb who is considered to have no interest in culture **3.** AGGRESSIVE PERSON an extremely aggressive or violent person [14thC. From Old French *barbarien* or Latin *barbarianus*, from *barbarus* (see BARBAROUS).] —**barbarianism** *n.*

barbaric /baar bárrik/ *adj.* **1.** CRUEL cruel or extremely brutal **2.** OF PRIMITIVE CULTURES typical of peoples and cultures seen as primitive and unsophisticated [14thC. Directly or via Old French *barbarique* from Latin *barbaricus*, from Greek *barbarikos*, from *barbaros* (see BARBAROUS).] —**barbarically** *adv.*

barbarise = **barbarize**

barbarism /báarbərizzəm/ *n.* **1.** CRUEL ACT a cruel or brutal act **2.** PRIMITIVE QUALITY the primitive nature of a culture or civilization **3.** GRAM UNGRAMMATICAL WORD a word or expression considered to be grammatically incorrect **4.** UNCONVENTIONAL OR UNACCEPTABLE THING sth that breaks rules of convention or good taste [15thC. Via French *barbarisme* from Latin *barbarismus*, from Greek *barbarismos*, from *barbarizein* (see BARBARIZE).]

barbarity /baar bárrəti/ (*plural* **-ties**) *n.* **1.** CRUEL ACT a cruel act **2.** PRIMITIVE STATE a primitive or uncivilized state [Mid-16thC. From Latin *barbarus* (see BARBAROUS).]

barbarize /báarbə ríz/ (**-rizes, -rizing, -rized**), **barbarise** (**-rises, -rising, -rised**) *vti.* **1.** MAKE OR BECOME CRUEL to become, or make sb, cruel or brutal **2.** MAKE OR BECOME MORE PRIMITIVE to become more primitive, or less cultured, or reduce sth to this state [15thC. From Greek *barbarizein* 'to act or speak like a foreigner, to speak gibberish', from *barbaros* (see BARBAROUS).] —**barbarization** /báarbə rí záysh'n/ *n.*

Barbarossa /báarbə róssə/ (1483?–1546) Greek-born Ottoman admiral and pirate. Admiral of the Ottoman fleet after 1533, he was feared as a pirate on the Barbary coast. He defeated Holy Roman Emperor Charles V (1538) and sacked Gibraltar (1540). Born **Khair ad-Din**

barbarous /báarbərəss/ *adj.* **1.** EXTREMELY CRUEL showing extreme cruelty **2.** PRIMITIVE OR UNCIVILIZED characterized by a primitive or uncivilized culture **3.** NOT SOPHISTICATED lacking sophistication or refinement **4.** GRAM UNGRAMMATICAL using ungrammatical language [15thC. Via Latin *barbarus* from Greek *barbaros* 'non-Greek, foreign, ignorant, uncivilized'.] —**barbarously** *adv.* —**barbarousness** *n.*

Barbary /báarbəri/ former region of North Africa stretching from the Atlantic coast to western Egypt. It included the Barbary States of Morocco, Algeria, Tripolitania, Tunisia, and Moorish Spain.

Barbary ape *n.* a tailless monkey that lives in caves and cliffs on Gibraltar and in northwestern Africa. Latin name: *Macaca sylvana*.

Barbary Coast formerly, the Mediterranean coast of North Africa. It was an important base for pirates between the 16th and 19th centuries.

barbastelle /báarbə stél/ *n.* an insect-eating bat with large ears and a wrinkly face, native to Europe and Asia. Latin name: *Barbastella barbastellus*. [Late 18thC. Via French, from Italian *barbastello*, from Latin *vespertilio* 'bat' (source of English *pipistrelle*).]

barbecue /báarbi kyoo/, **barbeque** *n.* **1.** EQUIPMENT FOR COOKING OUTDOORS an apparatus, including a grill and fuel, used for cooking food outdoors **2.** OUTDOOR PARTY WITH FOOD COOKED OUTDOORS an outdoor party where people eat food cooked on a barbecue ■ *vt.* (**-cues, -cuing, -cued**) COOK FOOD ON BARBECUE to cook food on a grill outdoors [Mid-17thC. From American Spanish *barbacoa*, of uncertain origin, probably from Arawak *barbakoa* 'frame of sticks'. Current senses evolved from the practice of drying or smoking meat on a wooden frame.]

barbecue sauce *n.* a sweet-sour and spicy sauce, sometimes with chilli, used to marinate meat or served as an accompaniment to meat

barbed /baarbd/ *adj.* **1.** WITH BARBS with one or more backward-facing points **2.** SPITEFUL critical or biting ○ *a barbed comment*

barbed wire *n.* strong wire with pointed projections along its length, used to make fences and barriers

barbel /báarb'l/ *n.* **1.** FEELER ON MOUTH OF FISH a slender feeler resembling a whisker on the lips or jaws of some fishes **2.** FISH WITH BARBELS a toothless European fish with barbels that resembles the carp. Genus: *Barbus*. [From Latin *barba* 'beard']

barbell /báar bel/ *n.* a metal bar with removable weights at either end, used in weightlifting [Late 19thC. Blend of BAR[1] and DUMBELL.] —**barbeller** *n.*

barbellate /báarbi layt, baar béllət, baar béllayt/ *adj.* with short hooked barbs or bristles [Mid-19thC. From modern Latin *barbella* 'very small beard', from Latin *barbula* (see BARBULE).]

barbeque *n.* = **barbecue**

barber /báarbər/ *n.* SB WHO CUTS HAIR sb whose profession it is to cut men's hair and shave their beards ■ *v.* (**-bers, -bering, -bered**) **1.** *vt.* CUT SB'S HAIR to cut or shave sb's hair, especially a man's **2.** *vi.* WORK AS BARBER to work as a barber [13thC. From Anglo-Norman *barbour*, which was formed from French *barbe* (see BARB[1]).]

――――― **WORD KEY: CULTURAL NOTE** ―――――
The Barber of Seville, an opera by Italian composer Gioacchino Antonio Rossini (1816). A comedy based on a play by Beaumarchais (1775), it tells of the attempts of Count Almaviva, disguised as a poor student called Lindoro, to woo Rosina, ward of Doctor Bartolo. Almaviva is assisted in his eventful courtship by the wily local barber, Figaro.

Barber /báarbər/, **Samuel** (1910–81) US composer. His neo-Romantic works, which include *Adagio for Strings* (1936), won two Pulitzer Prizes.

barberry /báarbəri/ (*plural* **-ries**) *n.* a thorny flowering shrub native to Asia but widely grown as a garden or hedge plant, especially a yellow-flowered variety that has orange or red berries. Genus: *Berberis*. [14thC. From Old French *berberis* (see BERBERIS), influenced by BERRY.]

barbershop /báarbər shop/ *n.* MUSIC a style of popular music for unaccompanied single-sex voices in close harmony, originally for four male voices. There are now many female barbershop groups and larger barbershop choirs.

barber's itch *n.* any rash or skin eruption on the face and neck, especially around the beard, caused by a fungal infection

barber's pole *n.* a short pole with red and white stripes found outside a barber's shop

barber's rash *n.* = **barber's itch**

barbet /báarbit/ *n.* a small brightly coloured tropical bird related to the toucan, with a large head, a thick hairy bill, short rounded wings, and a short tail. Family: Capitonidae. [Late 16thC. From French, literally 'small beard', formed from *barbe* (see BARB[1]).]

barbette /baar bét/ *n.* **1.** WARSHIP ARMOUR a metal cylinder giving armoured protection to a gun turret on a warship **2.** GUN PLATFORM a mound of earth inside a fortress used as a platform for cannons [Late 18thC. From French, literally 'small beard' (perhaps from the idea of cannon sticking over the parapet like a line of bristles), formed from *barbe* (see BARB[1]).]

barbican /báarbikən/ *n.* a strong defensive tower at the entrance to a town or fortress [13thC. Via Old French *barbacane* from, ultimately, Persian *barbarkhana* 'guard house'.]

Barbican /báarbikən/ *n.* a major arts centre in the City of London, completed in 1982

barbicel /báarbi sel/ *n.* a tiny projection on the filaments (**barbules**) of feathers, linking them together [Mid-19thC. From Italian or modern Latin *barbicella* 'small beard', formed from Latin *barba* 'beard'.]

barbie /báarbi/ *n.* *Aus* a barbecue (*informal*) [Late 20thC. Shortening.]

Barbican

Barbie /baÃ¡rbi/, **Klaus** (1913–91) German SS officer. In occupied France during World War II, he deported thousands of Jews to Auschwitz and killed French Resistance workers. He was tried in France after extradition from Bolivia (1983) and imprisoned for life. Known as the **Butcher of Lyons**

bar billiards *n.* a billiards-style game, once popular in British pubs, played on a small table with holes instead of pockets and peg-like obstacles

Barbirolli /baÃ¡rbÉ™ rÃ³lli/, **Sir John** (1899–1970) British conductor. He was long associated with the HallÃ© Orchestra (1943–68). Born **Giovanni Battista Barbirolli**

barbiturate /baar bÃchÃ³Ã³rÉ™t/ *n.* one of a class of barbituric acid derivatives with sedative and hypnotic properties [Late 19thC. From BARBITURIC ACID.]

barbituric acid /baÃ¡rbi tyÃ³Ã³rik-/ *n.* a white crystalline solid used for making barbiturates. Formula: $C_4H_4N_2O$. [*Barbituric* from French *acide barbiturique*, used to translate German *BarbitursÃ¤ure*, coined in 1863 by Adolf von Baeyer, a German chemist, from the name Barbara]

Barbizon School /baÃ¡rbizon-/ *n.* a group of mid-19th-century French painters, which included Corot, Millet, Daubigny, and Rousseau, noted for their realistic depictions of landscapes [Late 19thC. Named after the village of *Barbizon* in France, where the artists met.]

Barbour /baÃ¡rbÉ™r/ *tdmk.* a trademark for a waxed waterproof jacket regarded as typically worn by people who enjoy country pursuits

Barbuda /baar bÃ³Ã³dÉ™/ coral island of the independent state of Antigua and Barbuda, in the Caribbean Sea. Population: 1,280 (1995). Area: 161 sq. km/62 sq. mi. ♦ **Antigua and Barbuda** —**Barbudan** *n.*, *adj.*

barbule /baÃ¡rbyool/ *n.* a slender filament attached to the thicker spines (**barbs**) on a feather's central shaft that interlocks with others [Mid-19thC. From Latin *barbula* 'little beard', from *barba* 'beard'.]

barcarole /baÃ¡rkÉ™ rÅl/, **barcarolle** *n.* **1.** GONDOLIERS' SONG a song traditionally sung by Venetian gondoliers **2.** INSTRUMENTAL PIECE IMITATING BARCAROLE a piece of instrumental music that imitates a barcarole, made popular especially by Chopin and Mendelssohn [Early 17thC. Via French, from Venetian Italian *barcaruola*, from *barcarolo* 'gondolier',from late Latin *barca* 'bark'.]

Barcelona /baÃ¡rssÉ™ lÅnÉ™/ second largest city of Spain and a major seaport on the northern Mediterranean coast. It is capital of Barcelona Province and the autonomous region of Catalonia. Population: 1,630,867 (1994).

barchan /baar kaÃ¡n/ *n.* a crescent-shaped sand dune in which the tips of the crescent point in the direction of dune movement [Late 19thC. From Turkic *barkhan*.]

bar chart *n.* = bar graph

bar code *n.* a sequence of numbers and vertical lines identifying an item and often its price when interpreted by an optical scanner

bar code reader *n.* an optical scanner used to read bar codes

Barcoo /baar kÃ³Ã³/ river in central Queensland, Australia, that rises in the Warrego Ranges and joins the Thomson River upstream of Cooper Creek. Length: 480 km/298 mi.

bard[1] /baard/ *n.* **1.** ANCIENT CELTIC POET in ancient Celtic culture, a poet who composed and recited epic poems describing important events **2.** POET WINNING EISTEDDFOD PRIZE a poet who has won a prize at a modern Welsh eisteddfod **3.** POET a poet, especially one of national importance (*literary or humorous*) [15thC. Via Gaelic *bÃ rd* from Celtic. Originally a Scottish term for an itinerant minstrel-poet; the elevated sense of 'poet' dates from the 17thC.] —**bardic** *adj.*

bard[2] /baard/ *n.* ARMOUR FOR HORSE a piece of armour for a horse ■ *vt.* (**bards, barding, barded**) **1.** DECORATE HORSE WITH BARD to put a bard on a horse **2.** COOK COVER MEAT WITH FAT to cover meat with fat before roasting it to prevent it from drying out [15thC. Via French *barde* from, ultimately, Arabic *barda'a* 'saddle cloth, padded saddle'.]

bar diagram *n.* = bar graph

bardolatry /baar dÃ³llÉ™tri/ *n.* the idolizing of a poet, especially Shakespeare, who is sometimes referred to as the Bard of Avon (*disapproving*)

Bardot /baar dÅ/, **Brigitte** (*b.* 1934) French actor and activist. She became an international symbol for films including *And God Created Woman* (1956). She retired from films in 1973 to devote herself to campaigning for animal welfare. Real name **Camille Javal**

bare /bair/ *adj.* (**barer, barest**) **1.** NOT COVERED not covered by clothing ○ *bare legs* **2.** WITHOUT DECORATION without the usual furnishings or decorations ○ *the room was bare except for an iron bedstead* **3.** WITHOUT PLANTS without vegetation ○ *a bare hillside* **4.** BASIC simple or essential ○ *the bare facts* **5.** EMPHASIZING SMALLNESS used to emphasize how small sth is ○ *the bare minimum of supplies* **6.** MINIMUM only just sufficient ○ *the bare essentials* ■ *vt.* (**bares, baring, bared**) EXPOSE STH to reveal or expose sth ○ *The dog bared its teeth.* ○ *an investigative report that bared the details of the conspiracy* [Old English *baer*, ultimately from a prehistoric Germanic word] —**bareness** *n.*

— **WORD KEY: SYNONYMS** —
See Synonyms at **naked**.

bareback /bÃ¡ir bak/, **barebacked** /-bakt/ *adv.*, *adj.* on the bare back of a horse that is usually saddled

bare bones *npl.* the essential elements or structure of sth, without any elaboration (*informal*)

barebones /bÃ¡ir bÅnz/ *adj.* containing only the basic elements or components ○ *the cost of a barebones computing system*

barefaced /bÃ¡ir fÃ¡yst/ *adj.* **1.** UNDISGUISED shamelessly undisguised ○ *a barefaced lie.* US term **bald-faced 2.** WITH BARE FACE with an uncovered or clean-shaven face —**barefacedly** /bÃ¡ir fÃ¡ystli, -fÃ¡ysidli/ *adv.* —**barefacedness** /-fÃ¡ystnÉ™ss, -fÃ¡ysidnÉ™ss/ *n.*

barefoot /bÃ¡ir fÃ³Ã³t/, **barefooted** /-fÃ³Ã³tid/ *adj.*, *adv.* wearing nothing on the feet

barefoot doctor *n.* an auxiliary healthcare worker who is trained to carry out various activities, e.g. dispensing of medications, first aid, and midwifery, especially one working in rural areas of China

barehanded /bÃ¡ir hÃ¡ndid/ *adj.*, *adv.* without weapons, or with ungloved hands —**barehandedness** *n.*

bareheaded /bÃ¡ir hÃ©ddid/ *adj.*, *adv.* wearing nothing on the head —**bareheadedness** *n.*

Bareilly /bÉ™ rÃ¡yli/ city in the state of Uttar Pradesh in northern India. Population: 583,473 (1991).

bareknuckle /bÃ¡ir nuk'l/, **bareknuckled** /-nuk'ld/ *adv.* BOXING WITHOUT BOXING GLOVES not wearing boxing gloves ■ *adj.* **1.** BOXING USING BARE HANDS using ungloved hands ○ *He was a great bareknuckle champion in his time.* **2.** AGGRESSIVE AND COMPETITIVE characterized by open aggression or competitiveness ○ *a bareknuckle exchange in the House*

barelegged /bÃ¡ir lÃ©gd, -lÃ©ggid/ *adj.*, *adv.* with nothing covering the legs —**bareleggedness** /bair lÃ©ggid nÉ™ss/ *n.*

barely /bÃ¡irli/ *adv.* **1.** TO A VERY LIMITED EXTENT almost not, or for a very inadequate amount of time ○ *They had barely enough money to pay the rent.* ○ *She had barely sat down when the phone rang.* ◊ **scarcely** *adv.* **2.** SIMPLY AND WITHOUT DECORATION sparsely or simply, with no adornments ○ *a barely furnished office*

See Usage note at **hardly**.

Barenboim /bÃ¡rrÉ™n boym/, **Daniel** (*b.* 1942) Argentinian-born Israeli pianist and conductor. A noted performer of the classical repertoire, he was musical director and conductor of orchestras including the English Chamber Orchestra, the Orchestre de Paris, and the Chicago Symphony Orchestra.

Barents /bÃ¡rrÉ™nts/, **Barentz, Willem** (1550?–97) Dutch explorer. In his search for a Northeast Passage to Asia, he discovered Spitsbergen. Barents Sea is named after him.

Barents Sea /bÃ¡rrÉ™nts-/ shallow part of the Arctic Ocean, north of Norway, Finland, and Russia and south of Franz Josef Land. Area: 1,370,100 sq. km/529,000 sq. mi.

barf /baarf/ *vti.* (**barfs, barfing, barfed**) US VOMIT to vomit (*informal*) ■ *n.* US (*informal*) **1.** ACT OF VOMITING an act of vomiting **2.** STH VOMITED vomited food [Mid-20thC. Probably an imitation of the sound.] —**barfy** *adj.*

bargain /baÃ¡rgin/ *n.* **1.** CHEAP PURCHASE sth offered or bought at less than the normal price **2.** MUTUAL PACT an agreement between two people or parties in which each side promises to carry out an obligation **3.** PRICE AGREEMENT a commercial agreement between two parties that fixes the price of sth **4.** THINGS RECEIVED BY AGREEMENT goods or services obtained by a commercial agreement ■ *v.* (**-gains, -gaining, -gained**) **1.** *vi.* NEGOTIATE WITH SB to negotiate the terms of an agreement with sb **2.** *vt.* EXCHANGE STH to exchange one thing for another [14thC. From Old French *bargaignier* 'to trade, negotiate, dispute', of uncertain origin, probably ultimately from a prehistoric Germanic word.] —**bargainer** *n.* ◊ **into the bargain** as well ○ *hardworking and very intelligent into the bargain*

bargain away *vt.* to lose sth by giving it away as part of an agreement that is ultimately disadvantageous

bargain for *vt.* to expect or believe sth to be of a certain nature, and prepare for it ○ *The bill was a lot more than we'd bargained for.*

bargain on *vt.* expect or believe sth will happen, and prepare for it ○ *We hadn't bargained on the train arriving early.*

bargain basement *n.* PART OF SHOP SELLING CHEAP GOODS an area of a shop, often in the basement, selling goods cheaply ■ *adj.* **bargain-basement** lower than normal ○ *at bargain-basement prices*

bargain hunter *n.* sb who enjoys seeking out bargains —**bargain hunting** *n.*

bargaining /baÃ¡rgining/ *n.* negotiations to reach an agreement, especially between employers and employees

bargaining chip, **bargaining counter** *n.* sth that can be used as leverage in negotiations

barge /baarj/ *n.* **1.** FREIGHT BOAT a long narrow flat-bottomed boat used for transporting freight on rivers or canals **2.** OPEN BOAT USED CEREMONIALLY a large open boat used during ceremonies **3.** SMALL NAVAL BOAT a motor launch used by a high-ranking naval officer for ceremonial occasions ○ *an admiral's barge* ■ *v.* (**barges, barging, barged**) **1.** *vti.* MOVE ROUGHLY to move roughly, colliding with other people **2.** *vti.* PUSH to push sb or sth roughly **3.** *vt.* TRANSPORT BY BARGE to transport freight by barge [13thC. From Old French *barge* or medieval Latin *bargia*, of uncertain origin, perhaps from late Latin *barca* (source of English *bark*[3]), or from Greek *baris* 'Nile boat'.]

barge in *vi.* to enter or intrude suddenly or rudely ○ *Don't just barge in without knocking.*

barge in on *vt.* to interrupt sb in a clumsy or rude manner ○ *Don't barge in on them; they are having a private meeting.*

bargeboard /baÃ¡rj bawrd/ *n.* an ornamental board along the gable end of a roof [Mid-19thC. *Barge* from medieval Latin *bargus*, a kind of gallows.]

barge course *n.* **1.** ROOF'S OVERHANG the overhang of a roof at its gable end **2.** WALL'S TOP LAYER OF BRICKS bricks laid on their edge as the top layer of a brick wall [*Barge* from medieval Latin *bargus*, a kind of gallows]

bargee /baar jÃ©e/ *n.* a captain or crew member who

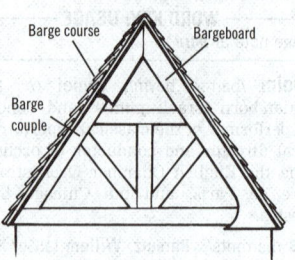

Barge course   Bargeboard

Barge couple

Bargeboard

works on a freight-carrying barge. US term **bargeman**

bargello /baar jéllō/ (plural **-los**) n. a straight needlepoint stitch that is worked in zigzag waves across the canvas to create chevron or scallop patterns [Mid-20thC. Named after the *Bargello* Palace in Florence, where there are several examples.]

bargeman /baárjmən/ (plural **-men** /-mən/) n. US = **bargee**

bargepole /baárj pōl/ n. a long pole used to propel barges ◇ **not touch sb** or **sth with a bargepole** to not want any involvement with sb or sth

barghest /baár gest, -gəyst/, **barguest** n. a spirit that takes the form of a black dog or other animal, believed to portend death or tragedy to anyone who sees it [Mid-18thC. From *bar* of uncertain origin (possibly from BARROW²) + ghest, a dialectal variant of GHOST.]

bar graph n. a graph consisting of a series of vertical or horizontal bars representing statistical data. Also called **bar diagram**

barguest n. = **barghest**

Bari /baári/ city and port on the southeastern coast of Italy. It is the capital of the Apulia Region. Population: 342,309 (1991).

bariatrics /bárri áttriks/ n. the branch of medicine concerned with the treatment of obesity (*takes a singular verb*) [Mid-20thC. Coined from BARO- + -IATRICS.] —**bariatric** adj.

baric /baírik/ adj. **1.** OF BARIUM relating to or containing barium **2.** OF BAROMETRIC PRESSURE relating to barometric pressure

barilla /bə rílla/ n. **1.** PLANT BURNED FOR SODIUM CARBONATE a European plant once burned to produce a form of sodium carbonate. Latin name: *Salsola kali* and *Salsola soda.* **2.** ASH FROM BARILLA PLANT a sodium carbonate and sodium sulphate alkali ash obtained from burning the barilla plant, formerly used in making soap [Early 17thC. From Spanish *barilla* 'small bar', from *barra* 'bar'.]

barit. abbr. baritone

barite /baír īt/ n. US = **barytes** [Mid-19thC. From BARIUM and -ITE.]

baritone /bárritōn/, **barytone** n. **1.** MALE SINGER OR VOICE a male singing voice with a range lower than a tenor and higher than a bass, or a singer with this voice **2.** WIND INSTRUMENT a wind instrument with the second lowest range in its family [Early 17thC. Via Italian *baritono* from Greek *barutonos*, 'deep-sounding, baritone'.]

barium /baíri əm/ n. a soft silver-white toxic chemical element used in alloys. Symbol **Ba** [Early 19thC. From BARYTA + -IUM.]

barium enema (plural **barium enemas** or **barium enemata**) n. the introduction of a barium salt suspension into the rectum and colon before an X-ray is taken

barium meal n. a barium salt suspension, given by mouth before X-raying the oesophagus, stomach, and upper intestine

barium sulphate n. a white or yellowish odourless powder, useful in medicine because it cannot be penetrated by X-rays. Formula: BaSO₄.

bark¹ /baark/ n. **1.** DOG'S NOISE the natural loud abrupt sound made by a dog or fox **2.** SOUND RESEMBLING DOG'S NOISE a sound similar to the bark of a dog ◇ *the bark of guns in the distance* ■ v. (**barks, barking, barked**)

1. vi. MAKE DOG'S SOUND to make the loud abrupt sound of a dog or fox **2.** vi. MAKE SOUND SIMILAR TO DOG'S to make a sound similar to a dog's bark **3.** vti. SPEAK AGGRESSIVELY to say sth in a loud or aggressive manner ◇ *He barked out an order.*

bark² /baark/ n. OUTER LAYER OF TREE the rough outer covering of the woody stems of trees or other plants ■ vt. (**barks, barking, barked**) **1.** GRAZE SKIN to have the skin rubbed off a part of the body through abrasive contact with another object ◇ *I barked my shins climbing the fence.* **2.** STRIP BARK FROM TREE to remove the bark from a tree or log **3.** MANUF TAN LEATHER USING BARK to tan leather using tannins derived from some kinds of bark [13thC. From Old Norse *börkr.*] —**barky** adj.

bark³ n. = **barque**

bark beetle n. a beetle that burrows under the bark of trees. Family: Scolytidae.

barker¹ /baárkər/ n. **1.** ADVERTISER OF FAIRGROUND ATTRACTIONS sb who stands outside the entrance to a fair, carnival, or other place of entertainment and shouts out its attractions **2.** BARKING DOG a dog that barks, especially one that barks a lot

barker² /baárkər/ n. a person or machine that strips bark off trees and logs or prepares bark for tanning

barking /baárking/ adj. extremely irrational (*informal*) [Mid-20thC. Probably analogous to HOWLING.]

barking deer (plural **barking deer**) n. = **muntjac**

Barkly Tableland /baárkli táyb'l land/ plateau region situated on the Northern Territory-Queensland border in Australia. Area: 130,000 sq. km/50,200 sq. mi.

bark mantis (plural **bark mantises** or **bark mantes**) n. an insect whose shape and colour blends in well with tree bark. Latin name: *Gonatista grisea.*

Barlee, Lake /baárli/ lake in southwestern Western Australia, between lakes Moore and Ballard

barley /baárli/ n. **1.** GRAIN CROP a cereal plant with a long head of whiskered grains, widely grown for food, malt production, and livestock feed. Latin name: *Hordeum vulgare.* **2.** GRAIN the grain from a barley plant [Old English *bærlic* 'barley-like', formed from *bære, bere* 'barley', (source of English *barn*). Ultimately from an Indo-European base that is also the ancestor of English *farina* and *farrago.*]

barley-bree /baárli bree/ n. Scotland whisky or beer (*archaic*) [*Bree* from Old English *brīw* 'thick soup', later 'broth', ultimately from a prehistoric Germanic word]

barleycorn /baárli kawrn/ n. **1.** GRAIN OF BARLEY a single grain of barley (*archaic*) **2.** BARLEY GRAINS barley grain, especially used for malt

barley sugar n. a clear hard sweet made from boiled-down sugar,

barley water n. a sweet cordial made from water, barley extract, and sugar

barley wine n. a type of very strong, slightly sweet beer

bar line n. MUSIC = **bar¹**

Barlow knife /baárlō-/ (plural **Barlow knives**) n. a penknife with one blade for cutting and another for poking or gouging [Late 18thC. Named after the original makers, the *Barlow* family, cutlers in Sheffield.]

barm /baarm/ n. the foam that rises to the surface during the fermentation of malt liquor [Old English *beorma.* Ultimately from a prehistoric Germanic word that is also the ancestor of English *brew, bread,* and *broth.*]

barmaid /baár mayd/ n. a woman who serves in a pub or bar

barman /baármən/ (plural **-men** /-mən/) n. a man who serves in a pub or a bar

barmbrack /baárm brak/ n. Ireland rich sweet bread with currants in it, usually served with tea [Mid-19thC. From Irish *bairin breac* 'speckled cake'.]

Barmecidal /baármi síd'l/, **Barmecide** /-sīd/ adj. abundant or lavish only in appearance and not in reality (*literary*) [Mid-18thC. From *Barmecide,* a prince in *The Arabian Nights' Entertainments* who served a series of empty dishes to a hungry beggar to test his sense of humour.]

bar mitzvah /baar mítsvə/ n. **1.** JEWISH RITE OF PASSAGE the ritual ceremony that marks the 13th birthday of a

Jewish boy, after which he takes full responsibility for his moral and spiritual conduct **2.** JEWISH BOY REACHING 13 a Jewish boy who has reached the age of 13, the age of religious responsibility [Early 19thC. From Hebrew *bar miṣwāh,* literally 'son of the commandment'.]

barmpot /baárm pot/ n. N England a foolish or stupid person (*informal*)

barmy /baármi/ (**-ier, -iest**), **balmy** (**-ier, -iest**) adj. (*informal*) **1.** SLIGHTLY IRRATIONAL unconventional or slightly irrational in behaviour **2.** NONSENSICAL completely lacking in good sense or reason ◇ *That's a barmy idea and you know it.* [15thC. Literally 'frothy', formed from BARM.]

barn /baarn/ n. **1.** LARGE FARM OUTBUILDING a large outbuilding on a farm used to store grain or shelter livestock **2.** LARGE BUILDING any large building, especially one that is plain and functional [Old English *ber(e)n* 'barley house', from *bere* 'barley' (see BARLEY) + *ærn* 'house, place']

Barnabas /baárnəbəss/, St (fl. 1st century AD) Cypriot missionary. He was a companion of St Paul during Paul's early ministry, and is traditionally thought to have founded the Cypriot church. Born **Joseph**

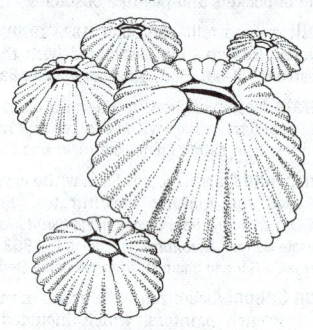

Barnacle

barnacle /baárnək'l/ n. **1.** MARINE BIOL CLINGING MARINE ORGANISM a small marine organism with a shell that clings to rocks and ships and draws food by using slender hairs (**cirri**). Subclass: Cirripedia. **2.** ZOOL = **barnacle goose**. **3.** SB WHO CLINGS a clinging or dependent person or thing [12thC. From medieval Latin *berneca,* of unknown origin.]

barnacle goose (plural **barnacle geese**) n. a wild goose found in northern Europe and Greenland that has grey wings and a black-and-white head and body. Latin name: *Branta leucopsis.*

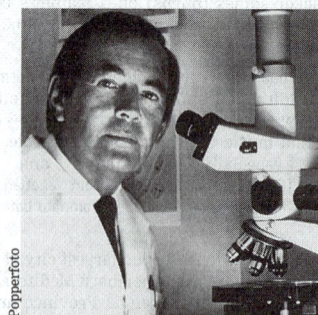

Christiaan Barnard

Barnard /baár naard/, **Christiaan** (b. 1922) South African surgeon. He performed the world's first successful human heart transplant operation in 1967. Full name **Christiaan Neethling Barnard**

Barnardo /bər naárdō/, **Thomas** (1845–1905) Irish-born British physician and philanthropist. He founded the East End Mission for destitute children in London (1867). His establishments came to be known as Doctor Barnardo's Homes. Full name **Thomas John Barnardo**

Barnard's star /baárnərdz-, baár naardz-/ n. a red dwarf star in the constellation Ophiuchus [Early 20thC. Named after Edward Emerson *Barnard.*]

Barnaul /baárnə oól/ capital city of Attay Territory,

southwestern Siberia, Russia. Population: 606,200 (1992).

barnbrack /ba̱arn brak/ n. = **barmbrack**

barn dance n. **1.** PARTY WITH COUNTRY DANCING a party, originally held in a barn, with country dancing **2.** ANY COUNTRY DANCE a name for various kinds of country dance

barn door n. **1.** DOOR OF BARN either of the huge doors that close the entrance to a traditional wooden barn **2.** ADJUSTABLE FLAP ON LARGE LIGHT any of the four rectangular adjustable flaps on the front of a large industrial light used, e.g., on film sets and in the theatre

barney /ba̱arni/ (plural **-neys**) n. a noisy argument (informal) [Mid-19thC. Origin uncertain; perhaps from *Barney* as a typical Irish name.]

barn owl n. an owl with white and pale brown feathers that often nests in barns

Barnsley /ba̱arnzli/ industrial town in Yorkshire, northern England. Population: 217,300 (1991).

barnstorm /ba̱arn stawrm/ (**-storms**, **-storming**, **-stormed**) v. **1.** vti. MAKE PERFORMING TOUR OF RURAL AREAS to travel from place to place giving performances **2.** vi. DO FLYING STUNTS to perform exhibitions of aerial acrobatics at shows and fairs —**barnstormer** n. —**barnstorming** adj.

barn swallow n. a common swallow, that has long pointed wings, a forked tail, a navy blue back, and light brown underparts. Latin name: *Hirundo rustica*.

Barnum /ba̱arnəm/, **P. T.** (1810–91) US showman, known for his spectacular circuses, including 'The Greatest Show on Earth' (1871). With James Bailey (1847–1906) he originated the Barnum and Bailey Circus (1881). Full name **Phineas Taylor Barnum**

barnyard /ba̱arn yaard/ n. AREA OF FARM AROUND BARN the area around a barn, where small farm animals roam ■ adj. CRUDE crude or vulgar (informal) ○ *barnyard humour*

barnyard grass n. a coarse weedy grass with spiky clusters of flowers, sometimes grown as forage. Latin name: *Echinochloa crusgalli*.

baroceptor /ba̱rrə septər/ = **baroreceptor**

Baroda /bə ro̱də/ former name for **Vadodara** (until 1976)

barogram /ba̱rrə gram/ n. a record of atmospheric pressure produced by a barograph or other meteorological instrument

barograph /ba̱rrə graaf, -graf/ n. a barometer that gives a continuous printed record of variations in atmospheric pressure —**barographic** /ba̱rrə gra̱ffik/ adj.

Barolo /bə ro̱llō/ n. a full-bodied red wine made in the area around Barolo in northwestern Italy

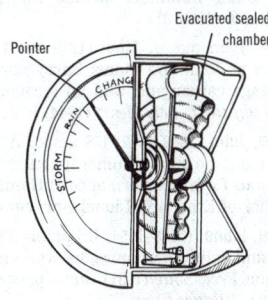

Barometer

barometer /bə ro̱mmitər/ n. **1.** INSTRUMENT MEASURING ATMOSPHERIC PRESSURE an instrument measuring changes in atmospheric pressure, used in weather forecasting **2.** INDICATOR OF MOOD sth that indicates an atmosphere or mood ○ *the barometer of public opinion* —**barometric** /ba̱rrə me̱ttrik/ adj. —**barometrical** /-me̱ttrik'l/ adj. —**barometrically** /-me̱ttrikli/ adv. —**barometry** /bə ro̱mmitri/ n.

barometric pressure n. atmospheric pressure as recorded by a barometer

baron /ba̱rrən/ n. **1.** NOBLEMAN a male member of the lowest rank of British or Japanese nobility, or a nobleman of various ranks in some European countries **2.** POWERFUL PERSON sb who has power or influence ○ *an oil baron* **3.** MEDIEVAL NOBLEMAN a nobleman in the Middle Ages who was given land in return for loyal service [12thC. Via Anglo-Norman *barun* and Old French *baron* from medieval Latin *baron-* 'man, warrior'. Probably ultimately from a prehistoric Germanic word that is also the ancestor of English *bairn*.]

baronage /ba̱rrənij/ n. **1.** BARONS AS A GROUP barons considered collectively **2.** RANK OF BARON a baron's rank or position

baroness /ba̱rrənəss/ n. **1.** MINOR NOBLEWOMAN a woman who belongs to the lowest rank of British or Japanese nobility, or to any of various ranks of the nobility in some European countries **2.** BARON'S WIFE OR WIDOW a baron's wife or widow

baronet /ba̱rrənət/ n. a British man who holds the lowest hereditary rank of honour

baronetage /ba̱rrənitəj/ n. **1.** BARONETS AS A GROUP baronets collectively **2.** = **baronetcy**

baronetcy /ba̱rrənətsi/ n. a baronet's rank or position

barong /ba róng/ n. a large knife with a broad blade, used by the Moro people of the Philippines [Late 19thC. From Malayo-Polynesian.]

baronial /bə ro̱ni əl/ adj. **1.** RELATING TO BARONS relating to or associated with barons **2.** LARGE AND IMPRESSIVE large, imposing, or sumptuous ○ *a baronial fireplace* **3.** *Scot* LARGE AND WITH TURRETS used to describe a large solid-looking country house with turrets

baron of beef n. a cut of beef consisting of a double sirloin, joined at the backbone [Mid-18thC. A humorous exaggeration due to the popular etymology for SIRLOIN.]

barony /ba̱rrəni/ (plural **-nies**) n. **1.** BARON'S RANK OR LAND a baron's rank or position, or the land held by a baron **2.** INFLUENTIAL PERSON'S TERRITORY a powerful businessperson's area of influence ○ *a newspaper tycoon zealously guarding his barony*

barophilic /ba̱rrə fi̱llik/ adj. used to describe an organism that can tolerate high atmospheric pressure —**barophile** /ba̱rrə fīl/ n.

baroque /bə ró̱k/ adj. **1.** IN 17THC STYLE in the Baroque style of art or architecture **2.** IN VERY ORNAMENTAL STYLE bizarre or highly exaggerated in style [Mid-18thC. Via French, applied to ornate architecture, from Italian *barocco* and Portuguese *barroco* 'irregularly shaped pearl', of unknown origin.] —**baroquely** adv.

Baroque: Statue of Louis XIV (17th century) by Gianlorenzo Bernini at Versailles, France

Baroque n. **1.** FLAMBOYANT STYLE OF ARCHITECTURE AND ART a highly ornamental style of European architecture and art that lasted from the mid-16th to the early 18th centuries, or this period in European history **2.** 17THC CLASSICAL MUSIC classical music of the 17th century, the period of such composers as Purcell, Vivaldi, and Telemann —**Baroque** adj.

baroreceptor /ba̱rrō ri septər/ n. a nerve ending that is sensitive to blood pressure changes

Barossa Valley /bə ró̱ssə-/ major grape-growing region north of Adelaide in South Australia, Australia

barothermograph /ba̱rrə thúrmə graaf, -graf/ n. an instrument that records atmospheric pressure and temperature simultaneously

barotitis n. pain in the ear caused by pressure differences, e.g. during air travel (informal)

barotrauma /ba̱rrō trawmə/ n. MED pain in and possible damage to an organ occurring as a result of changes in atmospheric pressure

barouche /bə ro̱osh/ n. a four-wheeled horse-drawn carriage, widely used in the 19th century, with two facing double seats, a retractable hood, and a box seat at the front for the driver [Early 19thC. Via German dialect *Barutsche* from Italian *baroccio* 'two-wheeled', from, ultimately, Latin *birotus*, from *rota* 'wheel'.]

barperson /ba̱ar purss'n/ (plural **-people** /-peep'l/) n. sb who serves in a pub or bar

bar point n. the seventh point on a large backgammon board, near the bar

barque /baark/, **bark** n. **1.** SMALL SHIP WITH SAILS RUNNING BREADTHWAYS a small sailing ship with masts whose sails are fixed breadthways (**square**) except for the last mast, which has its sail running lengthwise (**fore-and-aft**) **2.** SMALL BOAT any small sailing ship or boat [15thC. Via French *barque* from, ultimately, late Latin *barca*.]

barra /ba̱rrə/ (plural **-ras** or **-ra**) n. = **barramundi**.

Barra /ba̱rrə/ island at the southern end of the Outer Hebrides, Scotland. Population: 1,200. Area: 90 sq. km/35 sq. mi.

barrack[1] /ba̱rrək/ n. = **barracks** ■ vt. (**-racks**, **-racking**, **-racked**) **1.** PUT SOLDIERS IN BARRACKS to house soldiers in a barracks **2.** PUT SB IN TEMPORARY ACCOMMODATION to house people in any kind of temporary accommodation (often passive) [Late 17thC. From BARRACKS.]

barrack[2] /ba̱rrək/ (**-racks**, **-racking**, **-racked**) vti. (informal) **1.** SHOUT AT SB IN PROTEST to shout at sb in criticism or protest **2.** Aus SHOUT IN SUPPORT OF SB to shout support for sb, especially a player or team [Late 19thC. Origin uncertain, possibly from Northern Irish dialect *barrack* 'brag'. Originally Australian.] —**barracker** n.

barrack-room lawyer n. sb who thrusts unwanted advice or opinions on people, or who aggressively questions everything

barracks /ba̱rrəks/ n. (takes a singular or plural verb) **1.** SOLDIERS' QUARTERS a building used to accommodate military personnel **2.** TEMPORARY ACCOMMODATION any temporary accommodation [Late 17thC. Via French *baraque* from Italian *baracca* or Spanish *barraca* 'soldier's tent', also called 'barrack', of unknown origin.]

barracoon /ba̱rrə ko̱on/ n., in former times, a large building used to confine slaves or convicts in temporarily [Mid-19thC. From Spanish *barracon* 'large barracks', from *barraca* 'barracks'.]

barracouta /ba̱rrə ko̱otə/ (plural **-tas** or **-ta**) n. **1.** PREDATORY PACIFIC FISH a large predatory sea fish with strong teeth and a projecting lower jaw, found only in the Pacific Ocean. It has teeth like a barracuda, but is not related to it. Family: Gempylidae. **2.** NZ LOAF OF BREAD a long bread loaf [Late 17thC. Alteration of BARRACUDA.]

Barracuda

barracuda /ba̱rrə kyo̱odə/ (plural **-das** or **-da**) n. a predatory sea fish with a long body and protruding jaws and teeth, found in tropical seas. Genus: *Sphyraena*. [Late 17thC. Via American Spanish, from Spanish dialect *barraco* 'overlapping tooth', of unknown origin.]

barrage /ba̱rraazh, ba̱rraaj/ n. **1.** MILITARY BOMBARDMENT a long continuous burst of gunfire **2.** ATTACKING FLOW OF STH a rapid attacking outpouring of sth ○ *a barrage* *of criticism* **3.** RIVER BARRIER an artificial barrier built across a river or canal to provide water or prevent flooding ■ *vt.* (**-rages, -raging, -raged**) **1.** FIRE CONTINUOUSLY ON ENEMY to attack an enemy with rapid and continuous gunfire **2.** ATTACK SB CONTINUOUSLY to subject sb to a relentless onslaught ○ *Those two have been barraging me with questions all morning.* [Mid-19thC. From French, 'barrier', from *barrer* 'to block', from *barre* 'bar' (see BAR[1]).]

barrage balloon *n.* any one of a set of large balloons anchored to the ground in wartime to deter enemy aircraft

barramundi /bárrə múndi/, **barramunda** /-múndə/ *n.* (*plural* **-dis** *or* **-dies** *or* **-di**; *plural* **-das** *or* **-da**) EDIBLE AUSTRALIAN FISH an edible Australian fish of the perch family. Latin name: *Lates calcarifer.* ■ TROPICAL FRESHWATER FISH a tropical freshwater fish with a long robust body and a single dorsal fin near the rounded tailfin, belonging to a group of six species. Family: Osteoglossidae. [Late 19thC. Origin uncertain, probably from a Queensland Aboriginal word.]

Barranquilla /bárran kée yə/ river port and capital of Atlántico Department, northern Colombia. It is situated on the Magdalena River, about 13 km/8 mi. inland from the Caribbean Sea. Population: 1,064,255 (1995).

barratry /bárrətri/, **barretry** *n.* **1.** LAW BRINGING OF UNREASONABLE LAWSUITS the illegal action of persistently bringing lawsuits for little or no reason **2.** ILLEGAL SHIPPING PRACTICE any unlawful practice committed by a ship's master or crew that harms its owner or charterer **3.** BUYING OF CHURCH OR GOVERNMENT POSITION the sale or purchase of a position in government or the church [15thC. From French *baraterie* 'combat, deceit', from *barater* 'to fight, cheat', ultimately from Greek *prattein* 'to do' (source of English *practise*).] —**barrator** *n.* —**barratrous** *adj.* —**barratrously** *adv.*

Barrault /ba ró/, **Jean-Louis** (1910–94) French actor and producer. He directed the Théâtre de France (1959–68). His films include *Les Enfants du Paradis* (1944).

Barr body /baár-/ (*plural* **Barr bodies**) *n.* an inactive X chromosome present in the cells of females, used in a test to determine sex [Mid-20thC. Named after the Canadian anatomist Murray L. *Barr*, born 1908, who first reported its existence.]

barre /baar/ *n.* a rail fixed to a wall, at about hip height, used by ballet dancers when exercising [Mid-20thC. From French (see BAR[1]).]

barré /bárray/ *n.* **1.** USING FINGER TO RAISE GUITAR'S PITCH the placing of the index finger over all the strings of a guitar or similar string instrument to raise the pitch of each string simultaneously **2.** CHORD PLAYED IN BARRÉ FASHION a chord played on a guitar or similar string instrument in a barré fashion [Late 19thC. From French *barre*, past participle of *barrer* (see BARRAGE).]

barred /baard/ *adj.* **1.** WITH STRIPES having strips of colour **2.** WITH BARS FITTED fitted with or made of bars

barred owl *n.* a large North American owl with dark eyes, broad brownish stripes across its breast, and streaked underparts. Latin name: *Strix varia.*

barred spiral galaxy (*plural* **barred spiral galaxies**) *n.* a galaxy in which the stars form a spiral with a bright bar across the centre

barrel /bárrəl/ *n.* **1.** LARGE CASK a cylindrical container with a flat top and bottom, used to store liquids **2.** AMOUNT HELD BY BARREL the amount held by a barrel **3.** UNIT OF VOLUME IN OIL INDUSTRY a unit of liquid volume used in the oil industry, usually taken to be 35 imperial gallons or 42 US gallons (approximately 159 litres) **4.** UNIT OF VOLUME IN BREWING INDUSTRY a unit of liquid volume used in the brewing industry, equal to 36 imperial gallons or 31 US gallons (approximately 164 litres) **5.** TUBE-LIKE PART OF A GUN the tube-shaped part of gun through which bullets are fired **6.** CYLINDRICAL PART any one of various hollow cylindrical devices that form part of a mechanism, e.g. in clocks and watches ■ *vti.* (**-rels, -relling, -relled**) *US* TRAVEL FAST to move somewhere at high speed (*informal*) [13thC. Via Old French *barril* from medieval Latin *barriclus* 'small cask'.] ◇ **scrape the bottom of the barrel** to use sb or sth of very poor quality because nothing or no one else is available ◇ **over a barrel** having little room to manoeuvre ◇ **not be a barrel of laughs** to be far from being interesting or amusing

barrel cactus *n.* a cactus with unbranched spiny stems, native to Mexico and the southwestern United States. Genera: *Ferocactus* and *Echinocactus.*

barrel-chested *adj.* with a large rounded chest

barrelful /bárrəl fòol/ *n.* = **barrel** *n.* 2

barrelhead /bárrəl hed/ *n.* the flat circular top of a barrel

barrelhouse /bárrəl howss/ (*plural* **-houses** /-howziz/) *n.* **1.** *US* SEEDY BAR a cheap disreputable bar, especially one where there is music and dancing (*dated*) **2.** STYLE OF JAZZ a loud rough style of jazz characterized by a heavy two-beat rhythm [Late 19thC. So called from the barrels of liquor along the walls.]

barrel organ *n.* a mechanical musical instrument consisting of a cylinder turned with a handle, which allows air to pass through a set of pipes [So called from the internal cylinder or *barrel*]

barrel roll *n.* FLIGHT MANOEUVRE a flight manoeuvre in which an aircraft makes one complete sideways revolution ■ *vi.* (**barrel rolls, barrel rolling, barrel rolled**) DO BARREL ROLL to carry out a barrel roll

barrel vault *n.* a ceiling in the shape of a half cylinder

barren /bárrən/ *adj.* **1.** BARE OF VEGETATION with no trees or other plants growing **2.** NOT FRUITING producing no fruit or seed **3.** UNABLE TO HAVE CHILDREN not able to bear children (*archaic or literary*) **4.** WITH NO USEFUL RESULT not producing valuable results or interesting effects ○ *It was a barren period in her career.* **5.** LACKING IN STH lacking in a particular thing (*literary*) ○ *Our writers seem somewhat barren of new ideas.* [12thC. From Old French *baraigne*, of unknown origin.] —**barrenly** *adv.* —**barrenness** *n.*

barret /bárrət/ *n.* a flat cap similar in shape to the biretta worn by Roman Catholic clergy [Early 19thC. Via French *barrette* from Italian *berretta* 'biretta' (see BIRETTA).]

barretry *n.* = **barratry**

barrette /bə rét/ *n.* a metal or plastic clasp used by women and girls to keep their hair in place [Early 20thC. From French, literally 'small bar', formed from *barre* 'bar' (see BAR[1]).]

barricade /bárri káyd, -kayd/ *n.* DEFENSIVE BARRIER a barrier that protects defenders or blocks a route ■ *vt.* (**-cades, -cading, -caded**) OBSTRUCT STH WITH BARRICADES to obstruct or protect sth, or protect yourself, using barricades [Late 16thC. From French, formed from *barrique* 'barrel'. So called because the earliest barricades were made of barrels filled with earth, rock, and debris.]

Barrie /bárri/, **Sir J. M.** (1860–1937) British author. He wrote *Peter Pan* (1904) and numerous other plays including *The Admirable Crichton* (1902). Full name **Sir James Matthew Barrie**

barrier /bárri ər/ *n.* **1.** STRUCTURE BLOCKING ACCESS a structure, e.g. a fence, intended to stop access or keep one place separate from another **2.** THING THAT OBSTRUCTS sth that obstructs or separates, often by emphasizing differences **3.** LIMIT OR STANDARD sth considered as a limit, standard, or boundary **4.** GEOG ICE SHELF the part of the Antarctic ice shelf that extends over the sea and partly rests on the ocean floor [14thC. Via Old French *barriere* from, ultimately, Vulgar Latin *barra* 'bar' (see BAR[1]).]

barrier cream *n.* any cream that protects the skin against dirt, harmful moisture, or infection

barrier island *n.* a long sandy island that runs parallel to a coastline and serves to protect the shore from erosion

barrier method *n.* a method of contraception in which the access of sperm to the womb is blocked, e.g. by use of a condom or diaphragm

barrier nursing *n.* the nursing of patients with infectious diseases in isolation, to prevent the spread of infection —**barrier-nurse** *vt.*

barrier reef *n.* a narrow ridge of coral lying parallel and close to a coastline and separated from it by a wide deep lagoon

barring /baáring/ *prep.* except for sth, or unless sth happens ○ *Barring delays, we'll arrive this afternoon.* [15thC. Present participle of BAR[1].]

Barrington /bárringtən/, **Jonah** (*b.* 1940) British squash player. He popularized the sport in the United Kingdom, winning the Open Championships six times between 1966 and 1972.

barrio /bárri ō/ (*plural* **-os**) *n.* **1.** DISTRICT OF SPANISH TOWN an area of a town in a Spanish-speaking country **2.** *US* SPANISH-SPEAKING PART OF US CITY a Spanish-speaking quarter in a city or town in the United States [Mid-19thC. Via Spanish from, ultimately, Arabic *barr* 'open area'.]

barrister /bárristər/ *n.* **1.** LAWYER IN HIGHER COURT a lawyer who is qualified to represent clients in the higher law courts in England and Wales **2.** *Can* LAWYER IN CANADIAN COURT a lawyer who represents clients in any law court in Canada [15thC. From BAR[1], perhaps modelled on words such as *minister* and *chorister.*]

WORD KEY: SYNONYMS

See Synonyms at ***lawyer.***

barrow[1] /bárrō/ *n.* **1.** HAND CART a two-wheeled cart used by street vendors to sell their wares. US term **pushcart** **2.** = **wheelbarrow** [Old English *bearwe* 'stretcher, bier'. Ultimately from a prehistoric Germanic word meaning 'to bear', which is also the ancestor of English *bear* and *bier.*]

barrow[2] /bárrō/ *n.* a large mound of earth above a prehistoric tomb [Old English *beorg* 'hill, tumulus', from a prehistoric Germanic word meaning 'to hide or protect', which is also the ancestor of English *borough* and *belfry*]

barrow[3] /bárrō/ *n.* a pig that has been castrated before sexual maturity [Old English *b(e)arg*, from prehistoric Germanic]

Barrow /bárrō/ village in northwestern Alaska with a predominantly Inuit population. It is southwest of Point Barrow, the northernmost point of the United States. Population: 4,080 (1996).

Barrow, Clyde (1909–34) US outlaw. He and Bonnie Parker robbed banks and killed 12 people (1932–34) before being killed by Louisiana police.

barrow boy *n.* a man who sells wares from a barrow

Barrow-in-Furness /-fúrniss/ industrial town on the Furness Peninsula, southern Cumbria, England. Population: 48,947 (1991).

Barrow Island island off the northwestern coast of Western Australia. It is a nature reserve and the site of an important oilfield. Area: 202 sq. km/78 sq. mi.

barrowload /bárrō lōd/ *n.* the amount contained by a barrow

Barry /bárri/ industrial city, seaport, and coastal resort in the Vale of Glamorgan on the Bristol Channel, Wales. Population: 49,887 (1991).

Barry, Sir Charles (1795–1860) British architect. Influenced by the Italian Renaissance, he helped to design the Houses of Parliament in London (1840–70). His other buildings include the Travellers' Club, London (1829–31).

Barrymore /bárri mawr/, **Ethel** (1879–1959) US actor. The sister of John and Lionel Barrymore, she had a long stage career and won an Academy Award for *None but the Lonely Heart* (1944).

Barrymore, John (1882–1942) US actor. A handsome leading man, he made numerous films, but was most famous for his performance of Hamlet. He was the brother of Ethel and Lionel Barrymore.

Barrymore, Lionel (1878–1954) US actor. The brother of Ethel and John Barrymore, he won an Academy Award for *Free Soul* (1931) and appeared in the original *Dr Kildare* films.

Barsac /baár sak/ *n.* a sweet white Bordeaux wine from the area around the town of Barsac, France

bar sinister (*plural* **bars sinister**) *n.* **1.** HERALDRY = **bend sinister** **2.** EVIDENCE OF SB'S ILLEGITIMACY evidence suggesting that sb is of illegitimate birth

Bart. *abbr.* baronet

bar tack *n.* a straight stitch that crosses a piece of cloth at a right angle to a slit, e.g. at the end of a buttonhole

bartender /baár tendər/ *n.* sb who serves in a pub or bar

barter /baártər/ v. (-ters, -tering, -tered) 1. *vti.* **EXCHANGE GOODS OR SERVICES** to exchange goods or services in return for other goods or services 2. *vi.* **NEGOTIATE TERMS OF AGREEMENT** to negotiate or argue over the terms of a transaction ■ *n.* 1. **BARTERING** the practice or system of bartering 2. **THINGS BARTERED** goods or services that are bartered [15thC. Origin uncertain, probably from Old French *barater* (see BARRATRY).] —**barterer** *n.*

Barth /baarth, baart/, **Karl** (1886–1968) Swiss theologian. He was a leading theorist of Reformed theology. His numerous writings include *The Epistle to the Romans* (1919) and the monumental *Church Dogmatics* (1932–62).

Barthes /baart/, **Roland** (1915–80) French philosopher and writer. He was a leading proponent of structuralism and author of the seminal critical work *Writing Degree Zero* (1953). He formulated the literary theory that the 'meaning' of a text lies not in its author's intentions but in its underlying semiotic structure. Full name **Roland Gérard Barthes**

Bartholin's gland /baárthəlinz-/ *n.* either of two small glands on either side of the lower vagina that secrete a lubricating mucus during sexual stimulation. ◊ **Cowper's gland** [Early 20thC. Named after Kaspar Bartholin (1655–1738), the Danish anatomist who described them.]

Bartizan

bartizan /baártiz'n, baárti zán/ *n.* a small turret that projects from a tower or wall of a fortress or castle, used as a lookout or a defensive position [Mid-16thC. From *bartisane*, a Scots variant of *bratticing* 'timberwork', from BRATTICE.] —**bartizaned** *adj.*

Bartle Frere /baárt'l freer/ mountain near the city of Cairns in northeastern Queensland, Australia. It is the highest mountain in Queensland. Height: 1,612 m/5,287 ft.

Bartók /baár tok/, **Béla** (1881–1945) Hungarian composer. Influenced by Hungarian folk music, he wrote piano concertos, string quartets, and the opera *Duke Bluebeard's Castle* (1911).

barton /baárt'n/ *n.* a farmyard (*archaic*) [Old English *beretun* 'threshing floor', from *bere* BARLEY + *tun* 'place, farm, town' (see TOWN)]

Barton /baárt'n/, **Sir Edmund** (1849–1920) Australian statesman. He was the first prime minister of Australia (1901–03).

Baruch /bə rook/ *n.* a book in the Roman Catholic Old Testament and the Protestant Apocrypha traditionally ascribed to Baruch, a disciple of the prophet Jeremiah. See table at **Bible**

Barwick /bárrik/, **Sir Garfield** (1903–97) Australian judge and politician. He was federal attorney-general (1958–64) and chief justice of the High Court of Australia (1964–81). Full name **Sir Garfield Edward John Barwick**

barycentre /bárri sentər/ *n.* the centre of the mass of a system, especially a system of celestial bodies [Late 19thC. From Greek *barus* 'heavy' + CENTRE.] —**barycentric** /bárri séntrik/ *adj.*

baryon /bárri on/ *n.* a subatomic particle belonging to a group that undergo strong interactions, have a mass greater than or equal to that of the proton, and consist of three quarks [Mid-20thC. From Greek *barus* 'heavy' + -ON.] —**baryonic** /bárri ónnik/ *adj.*

Mikhail Baryshnikov

Baryshnikov /bə ríshnikof/, **Mikhail** (b. 1948) Russian-born US dancer and choreographer. He defected from the Soviet Union (1974) and danced for and directed (1980–89) the American Ballet Theatre. Full name **Mikhail Nikolayevich Baryshnikov**

barysphere /bárri sfeer/ *n.* the Earth's core (*dated*) [Early 20thC. From Greek *barus* 'heavy' + SPHERE.]

baryta /bə rítə/ *n.* any one of various barium compounds [Early 19thC. From BARYTES with remodelling *-a* from SODA.] —**barytic** /bə ríttik/ *adj.*

barytes /bə rí teez/ *n.* barium sulphate in the form of a yellow, white, or colourless mineral, the main ore from which barium is obtained. Formula: BaSO₄. US term **barite** [Late 18thC. From Greek *barutēs* 'weight'.]

barytone *n.* = baritone

basal /báyss'l/ *adj.* 1. **AT THE BASE OR BOTTOM** at or forming the bottom of sth 2. **BASIC** basic or fundamental —**basally** *adv.*

basal body *n.* a structure found near the base of cells that have projecting threads (**cilia**)

basal cell *n.* a cell forming the deepest layer of the skin

basal cell carcinoma *n.* a slow-growing malignant tumour that typically affects the facial skin of older persons. It rarely spreads to other parts, and is generally curable by surgery or radiotherapy.

basal ganglion *n.* a mass of grey matter that lies in the white matter near the base of each cerebral hemisphere of the brain. The basal ganglia help to regulate the body's voluntary movements.

basal metabolic rate *n.* the rate at which an organism consumes oxygen while awake but at rest, measured in kilocalories per square metre of body surface per hour

basal metabolism *n.* the amount of energy consumed by a resting organism simply in maintaining its basic functions

basalt /bássawlt/ *n.* 1. **BLACK SHINY VOLCANIC ROCK** a hard black, often glassy, volcanic rock. It covers more than half the Earth's surface and was produced by the partial melting of the Earth's mantle. 2. **BLACK UNGLAZED POTTERY** a hard black unglazed pottery [Early 17thC. Via Latin *basaltes*, a variant of *basanites*, from Greek *basanitēs* 'very hard stone, touchstone', from Egyptian *bakhan* 'slate'.] —**basaltic** /bə sáwltik/ *adj.*

basaltware /bássawlt wair/ *n.* a hard black stoneware pottery made in England and parts of continental Europe in the 18th century

basanite /bássə nīt/ *n.* volcanic basaltic rock containing olivine and additional alkaline minerals [Mid-18thC. From Latin *basanites* (see BASALT).]

bascule /báss kyool/ *n.* 1. **PIVOTING DEVICE** a counterbalanced device that pivots on a central axis so that the unweighted end rises as the weighted end is allowed to fall 2. **bascule, bascule bridge** **BRIDGE WITH LIFTING ROADWAY** a bridge with a roadway that can be raised to allow tall boats and ships to pass through [Late 17thC. From French, 'see-saw', ultimately from *battre* 'to batter' (see BATTER) + *cul* 'buttocks'.]

base¹ /bayss/ *n.* 1. **LOWEST PART** the lowest, bottom, or supporting part or layer of sth 2. **LOWER PART OF BUILT STRUCTURE** the lower part of a built structure, e.g. a wall, pillar, or column, regarded as a separate

feature 3. **MAIN SUPPORTING ELEMENT** the main source of an important component in an economy or sphere of influence ○ *improve our customer base* 4. **FUNDAMENTAL PRINCIPLE** the main principle or starting point of a system or theory 5. **CENTRE FROM WHICH ACTIVITIES START** a centre from which activities start or are coordinated 6. **MILITARY CENTRE** a coordinating or supply centre for military operations 7. **MAIN INGREDIENT** a main ingredient to which others are added 8. **SOLVENT** a medium in which ingredients or constituents may be dissolved or carried 9. **ATTACHING PART OF ORGAN** the part of an organ or body part by which it is attached to a more central structure of an organism 10. **LOWER PART OF HERALDIC SHIELD** the lower part of a heraldic shield 11. **GRAM STEM OF WORD** in morphology, any part of a word regarded as a unit to which affixes or other bases may be added to form a derived word. For example 'paint' is the base of 'painter' and 'repaint'. 12. **MATH REFERENCE NUMBER** the number that is the basis for a system of calculation, represented by the total countable digits in the system. The base 10 system contains the ten digits 0–9. 13. **MATH LOGARITHM REFERENCE** a number raised to a power denoted by a superscript. In the equation $10^2 = 100$, 10 is the base. Natural logarithms have a base e (= 2.718). 14. **GEOM LOWER SIDE OF FIGURE** the lower side or face of a geometric figure 15. **MEASURE** = **baseline** *n.* 1 16. **LOWEST STOCK PRICE** the lowest recorded price level of a tradable commodity or security 17. **CHEM CHEMICAL COMPOUND** a chemical compound having a pH value between 8 and 14 that reacts with acids to form salts 18. **CHEM CHEMICAL COMPOUND FORMING COVALENT BOND** a chemical compound that can accept a proton or donate a pair of electrons to form a covalent bond with an acid 19. **PHOTOGRAPHY FILM FOUNDATION** an inert medium supporting the photographic emulsion of films 20. **ELEC ENG MIDDLE REGION OF TRANSISTOR** the middle region of a transistor between the emitter and the collector 21. **BASEBALL FIELD MARKER** in baseball any one of the four corners of the diamond-shaped infield that a batter must touch in order to score a run ■ *vt.* (**bases, basing, based**) 1. **MAKE A BASE** to create or provide a base for sth 2. **ASSIGN SB TO BASE** to station, post, or assign sb to a base 3. **USE STH AS A BASIS** to use sth as a base or basis for sth else [14thC. Directly or via Old French from Latin *basis*, from Greek *basis* (see BASIS).] —**baseness** *n.* ◊ **off base** US wrong or inexact ○ *Your calculations are all off base*

— **WORD KEY: SYNONYMS** —
See Synonyms at **mean**.

base² /bayss/ *adj.* 1. **LACKING MORALS** lacking proper social values or moral principles 2. **OF POOR QUALITY** inferior in value or quality 3. **COUNTERFEIT** containing a higher proportion of base metals than usual 4. **ILLEGITIMATE** of humble or illegitimate birth (*archaic*) 5. **HIST RELATING TO PEASANT** relating to a peasant (**villein**) renting land from a feudal lord (*archaic*) [14thC. Via French *bas* from medieval Latin *bassus* 'short, low', which is found in classical Latin only as part of sb's name.] —**basely** *adv.* —**baseness** *n.*

Baseball: A batter swings at the ball

baseball /báyss bawl/ *n.* 1. **BAT AND BALL GAME** a game played with a bat and ball by two teams of nine players, on a field that has four bases arranged in a diamond pattern to mark the course a batter must take to score a run. Each team fields and bats alternately, and the aim is to score the most runs. 2. **BALL USED IN BASEBALL** a hard leather-covered ball, about 23 cm/9 in in circumference, used in the game of baseball

baseball cap *n.* a close-fitting cap with a long peak, originally worn by baseball players

baseband /báyss band/ *n.* the frequency band of a transmitted message

baseboard /báyss bawrd/ *n.* **1.** BOARD SERVING AS BASE a board that serves as the base of sth **2.** *US* = **skirting board**

baseborn /báyss bawrn/ *adj.* (*archaic*) **1.** OF HUMBLE BIRTH born of poor or disgraced parents **2.** ILLEGITIMATE born of unmarried parents **3.** IGNOBLE dishonourable or unworthy

base coin *n.* a counterfeit coin made of cheap metal

Basedow's disease /bázzidōz-/ *n.* = **Graves' disease** [Late 19thC. Named after Karl Adolph von *Basedow* (1799–1854), German physician.]

base hospital *n. Aus* a central hospital that serves an extensive rural area

Basel /báaz'l/, **Basle** /baal/ city in northwestern Switzerland, situated on the highest navigation point of the Rhine. It is the capital of the half canton of Basel-Stadt. Population: 179,639 (1994).

baseless /báyssləss/ *adj.* **1.** UNTRUE without grounds or a factual basis **2.** LACKING SUPPORTING PART lacking a base or foundation —**baselessly** *adv.* —**baselessness** *n.*

base level *n.* the lowest level to which moving water can erode a land surface, e.g. the bed of a stream, lake, or sea

baseline /báysslīn/ *n.* **1.** MEASURE MEASURING LINE a line used as a basis for measurement, calculation, or location, e.g. in surveying or navigation **2.** STANDARD OF VALUE a standard of value to which other similar things are compared **3.** REFERENCE DATA the data used as a reference with which to compare future observations or results **4.** SPORTS BOUNDARY LINE AT END OF COURT a boundary line at each end of a court that marks the limit of play in tennis, badminton, or basketball

baseliner /báysslīnər/ *n.* a tennis player who prefers to play on or near the baseline, and who only occasionally moves to the net

base load *n.* the average demand placed on an electrical power supply system

baseman /báyssmən/ (*plural* -**men** /-mən/) *n.* BASEBALL any of the three baseball fielders positioned near first, second, and third base

basement /báyssmənt/ *n.* **1.** UNDERGROUND STOREY OF BUILDING a storey of a building that is wholly or partly below ground level **2.** ARCHIT LOWEST PART OF WALL OR BUILDING the foundation, substructure, or lowest part of a wall or building **3.** GEOL PART OF EARTH'S CRUST the highly folded igneous or metamorphic layer of rocks that lies beneath more recent, softer sedimentary rocks [Mid-18thC. Origin uncertain: possibly via obsolete Dutch *basement* from Italian *basamento* 'base of a column', from *basare* 'to base'.]

base metal *n.* a common inexpensive metal, e.g. copper, iron, lead, tin, or zinc, as distinguished from the precious metals of gold, silver, and platinum

basenji /bə sénji/ *n.* a dog belonging to a small curly-tailed African breed that rarely barks and has a short smooth coat varying from black to chestnut [Mid-20thC. From Bantu.]

base pair *n.* a chemical unit that forms the bridge linking the complementary strands of DNA or RNA. It consists of a purine linked to a pyrimidine by hydrogen bonds.

base pairing *n.* the hydrogen bonding between complementary purine and pyrimidine bases, specifically adenine with thymine, and guanine with cytosine, that forms the double-stranded structure of DNA, RNA, and DNA/RNA hybrid molecules

base rate *n.* the rate of interest used by UK clearing banks as a basis for calculating their lending rates

bases plural of **basis**

base unit *n.* a fundamental unit within a system of measurement from which other units in the system are derived

bash /bash/ *v.* (**bashes, bashing, bashed**) **1.** *vt.* STRIKE WITH HEAVY BLOW to strike sth or sb with a heavy blow (*informal*) **2.** *vt.* SMASH to smash or strike sth violently

or damagingly (*informal*) **3.** *vt.* MAKE DENT to make a dent in sth (*informal*) **4.** *vi.* COLLIDE WITH to crash into or collide with sth (*informal*) **5.** *vt.* CRITICIZE to criticize harshly (*informal*) **6.** *vt.* BATTER to beat sb severely (*dated informal*) ■ *n.* **1.** BLOW a strong blow (*informal*) **2.** DENT a dent (*informal*) **3.** CELEBRATION a party or celebration **4.** soliciting as a prostitute (*slang*) [Mid-17thC. Probably an imitation of the sound of hitting; perhaps a blend of BANG¹ and either SMASH or DASH.] ◇ **have a bash (at sth)** to make an attempt to do sth (*informal*) **bash up** *vt.* to attack and injure sb (*informal*)

bashaw /bə sháw/ *n.* a pompous or haughty person (*archaic*) [Variant of PASHA]

bashful /báshf'l/ *adj.* shy, self-conscious, or modest [15thC. Formed from a shortened form of ABASH.] —**bashfully** *adv.* —**bashfulness** *n.*

bashibazouk /báshibə zoók/ *n.* a 19thC Turkish irregular mercenary soldier, notorious for brutality [Mid-19thC. From Turkish *başi bozuk* literally 'wrong-headed', from *başi* 'head' + *bozuk* 'out of order'.]

Bashkir /bash keér/ (*plural* -**kirs** *or* -**kir**) *n.* **1.** MEMBER OF RUSSIAN MUSLIM PEOPLE a member of a Turkic-speaking Muslim people who live in east-central Russia **2.** TURKIC LANGUAGE a language spoken in an area west of the Ural Mountains in central Russia. It belongs to the Turkic group of languages and is spoken by about one million people. [Early 19thC. Via Russian from Turkic *Başkurt*.] —**Bashkir** *adj.*

Bashkortostan /bash káwrtə staan/ autonomous republic in central Russia, west of the Urals, bordering the republic of Tatarstan to the northwest and the republic of Udmurtia to the north. Capital: Ufa. Population: 4,055,300 (1994). Area: 143,600 sq. km/55,444 sq. mi. Former name **Bashkiria** (until 1992)

basho /báshō/ (*plural* -**os**) *n.* a sumo wrestling tournament [Late 20thC. From Japanese.]

basi- *prefix.* = **baso-**

basic /báyssik/ *adj.* **1.** MOST IMPORTANT most important or essential ○ *a few basic guidelines* **2.** ELEMENTARY serving as a starting point or minimum **3.** WITHOUT EXTRA without anything extra ○ *a basic salary* **4.** PLAIN plain and utilitarian rather than luxurious or fancy (*informal*) **5.** CHEM RELATING TO CHEMICAL BASE containing, relating to, or being a chemical base **6.** CHEM ALKALINE having an alkaline reaction **7.** CHEM CONTAINING HYDROXIDE OR OXIDE GROUPS used to describe a salt that contains hydroxide or oxide groups in addition to other anions, e.g. the carbonate ion **8.** GEOL LOW IN SILICA used to describe rock that contains 45–53 percent total silica by weight, e.g. basalt **9.** METALL USING A BASE IN STEELMAKING used to describe a steelmaking process in which the furnace is lined with a base that combines with acidic impurities in the ore to produce basic slag ■ **basics** *npl.* MOST IMPORTANT THINGS the most important or fundamental elements of sth —**basicity** /bay síssiti/ *n.*

BASIC /báyssik/, **Basic** *n.* a high-level computer programming language that uses a combination of common English terms and algebra [Acronym for Beginners All-purpose Symbolic Instruction Code]

basically /báyssikli/ *adv.* **1.** ESSENTIALLY used to emphasize the most important aspect of sth, or to give a simplified account of sth more complicated **2.** IN GENERAL generally or in most respects **3.** SIMPLY in a simple way, using only essentials

━━━━ **WORD KEY: USAGE** ━━━━

Basically as a sentence adverb: This use, in which *basically* is reduced to adding emphasis, is common in informal conversation but should be avoided otherwise. So too should the meaning 'to speak generally rather than in detail', as in *It is basically the case that fats can cause heart disease.*

Basic Curriculum *n.* in schools in England and Wales, the National Curriculum plus religious education

Basic English *n.* a simplified form of English intended as an introductory version of the language for non-native speakers and for use as an auxiliary international language. It consists of a vocabulary of 850 words for general needs, plus additional international and scientific words.

basic rate *n.* **1.** COMM UNMODIFIED RATE the standard cost or rate of pay excluding any discounts or additions **2.** FIN STANDARD TAX the standard rate of income tax

basic slag *n.* the slag from steelmaking using a basic process. It is rich in phosphates and is used as a fertilizer.

basic training *n.* the initial training of a military recruit

basidiomycete /bə síddi ō mī seét/ *n.* a fungus that produces spores in a specialized structure (**basidium**). Mushrooms, puffballs, rusts, shelf fungi, and smuts are basidiomycetes. Class: Basidiomycetes. [Late 19thC. From modern Latin *Basidiomycetes*, class name, from *basidium* 'basidium' (see BASIDIUM) + Greek *mukētes* 'fungi'.] —**basidiomycetous** *adj.*

basidium /bə síddi əm/ (*plural* -**a** /-ə/) *n.* a cell or organ found in certain fungi from which external sexual spores are produced [Mid-19thC. From modern Latin, literally 'small base', from Greek *basis* 'step, base'.] —**basidial** *adj.*

Basie /báyzi/, **Count** (1904–84) US composer and bandleader. He was one of the most enduring popular American musicians as the leader of his own big-band swing ensembles from 1935 until his death, and composed numbers including 'One O'Clock Jump'. Real name **William Basie**

basify /báyssifī/ (-**fies, -fying, -fied**) *vt.* CHEM **1.** MAKE INTO BASE to change a chemical into a base **2.** MAKE ALKALINE to make sth alkaline —**basification** /báyssifi káysh'n/ *n.*

basil /bázz'l/ *n.* a herb with aromatic leaves used for seasoning, especially sweet basil. Latin name: *Ocimum basilicum*. [15thC. Via Old French *basile* from Latin *basilicum*, from Greek *basilikon (phuton)* 'royal (herb)', from its usefulness in cooking and medicine.]

Basil /bázz'l/, **St** (329?–379 AD) Greek prelate and scholar. He studied at Byzantium and Athens, became Bishop of Caesarea (370), and defended Christian philosophy against heresies such as Arianism. Known as **Basil the Great**

Basilan /bássi laán/ former name for **Isabela**

basilar /bássilər/ *adj.* relating to or situated at the base of sth, for examplethe skull [Mid-16thC. From modern Latin *basilaris*, from Latin *basis* (see BASIS).]

Basildon /bázz'ldən/ town in southeastern Essex, England. It was designated a new town in 1949. Population: 162,800 (1995).

basilica /bə zíllikə, -síllikə/ *n.* **1.** PRIVILEGED ROMAN CATHOLIC CHURCH a Roman Catholic church or cathedral given ceremonial privileges by the Pope **2.** ARCHIT ANCIENT ROMAN BUILDING a type of ancient Roman building that had a central nave with an aisle on each side formed by two rows of columns, and typically a terminal semicircular apse. It was used as a court of justice, an assembly hall, or an exchange. **3.** LARGE CHRISTIAN CHURCH a Christian church building formed out of a Roman basilica or built to a similar design [Mid-16thC. Via Latin, 'royal palace' from Greek *basilikē*, from *basilikos* 'royal', from *basileus* 'king' (source of English basil and basilisk).] —**basilican** *adj.*

Basilisk

basilisk /bázzə lisk/ *n.* **1.** MYTHOL LEGENDARY REPTILE a legendary reptile whose look or breath was supposed to be fatal. It was said to have been hatched by a serpent from a cock's egg. **2.** ZOOL LIZARD RELATED TO IGUANA a tropical American lizard, related to the iguana, that is able to run upright on its long hind legs. The males have an inflatable crest at the back of the head. Genus: *Basiliscus*. [14thC. Via Latin from Greek *basilikos*, literally 'kinglet', also 'kind of serpent', formed from *basileus* 'king' (source of English *basil* and *basilica*).]

basin /báyss'n/ *n*. **1.** OPEN CONTAINER FOR WASHING an open metal, ceramic, or plastic container with sloping sides, typically used for holding water or washing **2.** COOK BOWL FOR PREPARING FOOD a deep bowl, especially a round one, used for storing, mixing, or cooking food **3.** BASIN CONTENTS the contents of or amount contained in a basin **4.** DOCK NEAR SEA a dock built in a harbour or river that opens to the sea **5.** DEPRESSION IN LAND FILLED WITH WATER any depression in the Earth's surface that contains water **6.** GEOG LAND DRAINING INTO RIVER OR LAKE a broad area of land drained by a single river and its tributaries, or draining into a lake **7.** GEOL BOWL-SHAPED DEPRESSION a bowl-shaped depression on land or on the ocean floor in which sediments may be deposited **8.** GEOL CIRCULAR FORMATION OF SLOPING ROCK STRATA a large circular outcrop of rock in which strata dip inwards towards the centre [13thC. Via Old French from medieval Latin *ba(s)cinus*, from *bacca* 'water container', a word probably borrowed from Gaulish.]

basinet /bássinət/ *n*. a lightweight steel helmet, sometimes with a visor, worn in medieval times [14thC. From Old French *bacinet*, literally 'little basin', from its shape.]

basinful /báyss'nfool/ *n*. the quantity that a basin holds

Basingstoke /báyzing stōk/ town in Hampshire, southern England. Population: 77,837 (1991).

Basingstoke and Deane /-deen/ a local government district in Hampshire, southern England. Population: 147,400 (1991).

basipetal /bay síppit'l/ *adj*. developing from the top of a stem towards the base so that the oldest leaves or flowers are at the top —**basipetally** *adv*.

basis /báyssiss/ (*plural* **-ses** /-seez/) *n*. **1.** FOUNDATION sth that acts as a support or foundation, especially of an idea or argument **2.** STARTING POINT the point from which sth, e.g. a discussion, starts or is developed **3.** WAY OF PROCEEDING the basic method or system according to which sth is done or organized ○ *work on a part-time basis* **4.** MAIN COMPONENT the main component or ingredient of sth **5.** MATH SET OF VECTORS in a vector space, the minimal set of vectors necessary to define all other vectors in the space [Late 16thC. Via Latin *basis* (source of English *base*) from Greek *basis* ''step, base',from *bainen* 'to go'.]

──── **WORD KEY: USAGE** ────

Basis does a number of jobs that other words can do better or that need not be done at all. Expressions such as *on a continuing basis*, *on a daily basis*, and *on a regular basis*, are only wordier ways of saying *continually, daily*, and *regularly*. By the same token, *providing expert resources on a global basis* means providing them anywhere; and *we can help develop your basis for facilities design* means, essentially, *we can help you plan*. Careful writers should avoid the unnecessary use of *basis*.

bask /baask/ (**basks, basking, basked**) *vi*. **1.** EXPOSE YOURSELF TO WARMTH to lie in or expose yourself to enjoyable warmth, especially from the sun **2.** GET PLEASURE FROM STH to derive great satisfaction or pleasure from sth [14thC. Origin uncertain: probably from Old Norse *bathask* 'to bathe oneself', ultimately from the same prehistoric Germanic source as English *bath*.]

Baskerville /báskər vil/ *n*. a typeface characterized by serifs [Early 19thC. Named after John BASKERVILLE.]

Baskerville /báskər vil/, **John** (1706–75) British printer. The printer to Cambridge University, he produced several typefaces, including the one that now bears his name.

basket /báaskit/ *n*. **1.** WOVEN CONTAINER a container made of woven strips of material such as cane, wire, wood, or plastic, often with a handle or handles **2.** BASKET CONTENTS the contents of, or amount contained in a basket **3.** STH LIKE A BASKET sth that looks like or is used like a basket, e.g. the open gondola attached to a hot-air balloon **4.** BASKETBALL BASKETBALL GOAL a mounted horizontal metal hoop with a hanging open net, through which a basketball player must

throw the ball in order to score **5.** BASKETBALL GOAL SCORED a goal scored in basketball by throwing the ball through the basket. It is worth 1, 2, or 3 points depending on circumstances. **6.** GROUP OF RELATED ITEMS a group or collection of similar or related things or ideas **7.** BASTARD used as a euphemism for bastard (*informal insult*) [14thC. Origin unknown, found earlier in Old French.]

Basketball: Two players attempt to block a pass

basketball /báaskit bawl/ *n*. **1.** BALL GAME PLAYED ON COURT a game played by two teams of five players, who score points by throwing a ball through a basket mounted at the opponent's end of a rectangular court **2.** BALL USED IN BASKETBALL a ball of the type used in the game of basketball

basket case *n*. **1.** OFFENSIVE TERM an offensive term for sb who is suffering from severe nervous strain (*offensive*) **2.** SB INCAPACITATED sb who is completely incapacitated or ineffective (*informal*)

basket chair *n*. a deep chair made of wickerwork or cane

basketful /báaskitfool/ *n*. the quantity that a basket holds

basket hilt *n*. a sword hilt with a guard made of interwoven strips —**basket-hilted** *adj*.

basket of currencies *n*. a group of currencies of which the average value is used as a basis for comparison with another currency

basket-of-gold *n*. US = alyssum

basketry /báaskitri/ *n*. **1.** CRAFT BASKETMAKING the art or craft of making baskets **2.** BASKETS baskets collectively

basket weave *n*. a textile weave that resembles the chequered pattern of a woven basket

basketwork /báaskit wurk/ *n*. CRAFT = basketry *n*. 1

basking shark *n*. a large plankton-eating shark measuring up to 12 m/40 ft that often floats on the surface of the sea. Latin name: *Cetorhinus maximus*.

basmati /baz maáti/ *n*. a long-grained aromatic brown or white rice originally grown in North India and Pakistan [Mid-19thC. From Hindi *bāsamatī* 'fragrant'.]

bas mitzvah /baass mítsvə/, **Bas Mizvah** *n*. = bat mitzvah

baso- *prefix*. bottom, base ○ *basipetal* ■ chemical base ○ *basophil* [From Latin *basis* (see BASE)]

basophil /bássə fil/, **basophile** /-fīl/ *n*. a white blood cell with granules that are readily stained by basic dyes, occurring in some blood diseases

basophilia /báyssə fílli ə/, **basiphilia** *n*. **1.** BIOL AFFINITY FOR BASIC DYES the property of microorganisms and white blood cells of being stained with basic dyes **2.** MED INCREASE IN STAINED CELLS an abnormal increase in the blood of the type of cells that stain with basic dyes, occurring in a variety of blood diseases

basophilic /báyssə fíllik/, **basophilous** /bə sóffələss/ *adj*. used to describe cells or cell components that are readily stained by basic dyes

Basotho /bə soó too/ *npl*. an African Sotho people who live in Lesotho [Mid-19thC. From Sesotho.]

basque /bask, baask/ *n*. **1.** LONG CORSET a woman's tight-fitting corset that covers the area from the breasts to the top of the thighs **2.** JACKET EXTENSION a part of the bodice of a woman's jacket that extends below the waist [Mid-19thC. Origin uncertain: perhaps from some perceived similarity to the Basque national costume.]

Basque /bask, baask/ *n*. **1.** PEOPLES MEMBER OF EUROPEAN PEOPLE a member of a people of unknown origin living in the western Pyrenees, in northeastern Spain and southwestern France **2.** LANG LANGUAGE OF BASQUES the language spoken by the Basque people. It has no known relationship with any other languages and is spoken by about 700,000 people. [Early 19thC. Via French from Latin *Vasco*, the Romans' name for these people, which also developed into *Gascon*.] —**Basque** *adj*.

Basque Country autonomous region of northern Spain, consisting of the provinces of Álava, Guipúzcoa, and Vizcaya. The regional capital is Vitoria. Population: 2,130,783 (1995). Area: 7,261 sq. km/2,803 sq. mi. Spanish **País Vasco**. Basque **Euskadi**

Basra /bázzra/ city and port in southeastern Iraq, at the northern end of the Shatt al Arab waterway. Population: 872,176 (1987).

bas-relief /báa-/ *n*. **1.** FLAT SCULPTURE a type of sculpture in which the design projects slightly from a flat background, but without any part being totally detached from the background. ◊ **high relief 2.** PIECE OF BAS-RELIEF an example or piece of bas-relief sculpture [Early 17thC. From the earlier BASSO RILIEVO, altered to match the French form of the word.]

bass¹ /bayss/ *n*. **1.** MUSIC LOWEST SINGING VOICE a voice of the lowest range, or sb with that voice **2.** MUSIC LOWEST PITCHES the lower half of the total range of pitches produced by a voice or an instrument **3.** MUSIC LOWEST MUSICAL PART the lowest part in instrumental or vocal part music **4.** MUSIC LOWEST INSTRUMENT IN FAMILY the instrument that has the lowest range in a family of musical instruments **5.** MUSIC LOW FREQUENCY IN AUDIO REPRODUCTION the low-frequency part of the sound output from an electric amplifier **6.** BASS CONTROL a knob on a record player, CD player, or cassette player that controls the low-frequency part of its sound output ■ *adj*. **1.** DEEP IN TONE deep or grave in tone **2.** LOW IN PITCH low in pitch **3.** RELATING TO BASS relating to a bass [15thC. Via French *bas* from medieval Latin *bassus*, influenced by Italian *basso* 'basso' (see BASSO).]

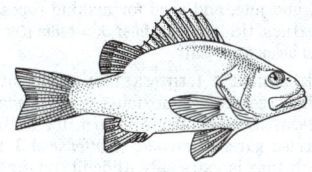
Bass

bass² /bass/ (*plural* **bass** *or* **basses**) *n*. a spiny-finned fish found in rivers, lakes, and seas that is caught for food. Families: Centrarchidae and Percichthyidae and Serranidae. [15thC. Alteration of Old English *bærs*, bears, of prehistoric Germanic origin.]

bass³ /bass/ *n*. **1.** = bast **2.** INDUST = basswood *n*. 1 [Late 17thC. Alteration of BAST.]

bass clef *n*. a symbol on a musical staff indicating that a note on the fourth line from the bottom represents the F fifth below middle C

bass drum *n*. a large drum that has a cylindrical body, two drumheads, and a low indefinite pitch

Bassein /ba sáyn/ city in southern Myanmar (Burma), about 137 km/85 mi. west of the capital, Yangon. Population: 144,092 (1983).

basset *n*. = basset hound

Basseterre /bass táir/ capital of St Kitts and Nevis, in the Leeward Islands. It is situated on the southwestern coast of St Kitts island. Population: 12,600 (1994).

basset horn /bássit-/ *n*. an alto clarinet in F, used in classical music [Mid-19thC. From German, itself a translation of French *cor de basset*, from Italian *corno di* *bassetto*, literally "cello-horn", from its sharing the cello's range.]

basset hound *n.* a dog of a breed with short legs, long ears, and a short-haired, white, black, and tan coat, originally bred for hunting [Early 17thC. From French, formed from *bas* 'low', from its short legs.]

bass guitar *n.* a four-string guitar, usually electric, that has the same pitch and tuning as a double bass

bassinet /bássi nét/ *n.* a baby's bed or pram in the shape of a basket, often with a hood over one end and commonly made of wood or wickerwork [Mid-19thC. From French, literally 'little basin' from *bassin* (see BASIN).]

bassist /báyssist/ *n.* a player of a bass guitar or a double bass

basso /bássō/ (*plural* **-sos** *or* **-si** /-see/) *n.* a bass singer, especially of opera [Early 18thC. Via Italian from medieval Latin *bassus* (see BASE[2]).]

basso continuo *n.* = continuo

bassoon /bə soón/ *n.* a low-pitched double-reed instrument of the oboe family. Its wooden body is a long U-shaped tube, attached to the mouthpiece by means of a thin metal pipe. [Early 18thC. Via French from Italian *bassone*, literally 'large bass', from *basso* 'basso' (see BASSO).]

basso profundo /-prō fúndō/ (*plural* **basso profundos**) *n.* a bass singer with an exceptionally low range [Mid-19thC. From Italian, literally 'deep bass'.]

Bass Rock /báss-/ tiny steep-sided islet with a lighthouse in the Firth of Forth, Scotland

Bass Strait /báss-/ area of ocean situated between mainland Australia and the island of Tasmania. It is approximately 225 km/140 mi. wide.

bass viol *n.* **1.** = viola da gamba **2.** *US* = double bass

basswood /básswŏod/ *n.* **1.** TREES **N AMERICAN LIME TREE** a North American lime tree, commonly used as a shade tree. Latin name: *Tilia americana*. **2.** INDUST **WOOD OF BASSWOOD TREE** the soft light-coloured wood of the basswood tree, used for making boxes and crates and for carving [From BASS[3]]

bast /bast/ *n.* **1.** BOT = phloem **2.** INDUST **FIBROUS MATERIAL FROM PLANTS** a strong woody fibrous material obtained chiefly from the phloem of plants such as flax, hemp, and jute, and used for making ropes, mats, and textiles. US term **bast fiber 3.** = raffia [Old English *bæst*, of unknown origin]

bastard /báastərd/ *n.* **1.** OFFENSIVE TERM an offensive term for a disagreeable or obnoxious person (*slang insult*) **2.** OFFENSIVE TERM an offensive term for sb born to unmarried parents (*archaic or offensive*) **3.** DIFFICULT THING sth that is extremely difficult, trying, or unpleasant (*slang*) **4.** ABNORMAL THING sth that is abnormal, inferior, or of questionable or mixed origin **5.** PERSON used to refer to sb, especially a man, sometimes affectionately or humorously (*informal*) ■ *adj.* **1.** NOT GENUINE not the real thing **2.** OF INFERIOR OR MIXED ORIGIN of an inferior, ill-conceived, or mixed origin **3.** ZOOL SIMILAR used to describe plants and animals that are similar but not identical to, and usually slightly inferior to, a particular kind or species **4.** ABNORMAL abnormal or irregular in shape, size, or appearance [14thC. Via Old French *bastart* from medieval Latin *bastardus*, probably from *bastum* 'pack saddle', the idea probably being of a child produced from a relationship with a traveller.] —**bastardly** *adj.*

bastardize /báastər dīz/ (**-izes, -izing, -ized**), **bastardise** (**-ises, -ising, -ised**) *vt.* **1.** DEBASE to lower the value or quality of sth **2.** DECLARE SB ILLEGITIMATE to prove or declare sb to be illegitimate (*archaic*) —**bastardization** /báastər dī záysh'n/ *n.*

bastardry /báastərdri/ *n. Aus* mean-spirited, treacherous, or obnoxious behaviour (*informal*)

bastard title *n.* PUBL = half title

bastard wing *n.* the part of a bird's wing that corresponds to a thumb and contains a few short feathers

bastardy /báastərdi/ *n.* the state of being a child with unmarried parents (*archaic*)

baste[1] /bayst/ (**bastes, basting, basted**) *vt.* COOK to moisten meat or fish at intervals during cooking with a liquid such as melted fat or cooking

juices [14thC. Via Old French *bastir* from, ultimately, a prehistoric Germanic word meaning 'to join together with bast'.]

baste[2] /bayst/ (**bastes, basting, basted**) *vt.* to beat sb severely [15thC. Origin unknown.]

baste[3] /bayst/ (**bastes, basting, basted**) *vt.* **1.** SEW SEW LOOSELY to sew fabric with long loose stitches in order to hold pieces of material together temporarily **2.** SEW DIAGONALLY to sew fabric with rows of long diagonal stitches [Mid-16thC. Origin uncertain: perhaps from BASTE[2].]

basti /bústi/ *n. S Asia* a slum [Late 19thC. From Hindi *bastī*.]

Bastia /ba stee ə/ city and capital of Haute-Corse Department on the northeastern coast of the island of Corsica, France. Population: 38,728 (1990).

Bastille Day /ba steel-/ *n.* a French national holiday observed on July 14, commemorating the storming of the Bastille in 1789 at the beginning of the French Revolution

bastinado /básti náydō/ *n.* (*plural* **-does**) **1.** PUNISHMENT BY BEATING FEET a punishment or torture in which the soles of the victim's feet are beaten with a stick **2.** THRASHING a beating or a blow with a club **3.** CLUB a stick or club ■ *vt.* (**-does, -doing, -doed**) BEAT WITH STICK to beat sb with a stick, especially on the soles of the feet [Late 16thC. From Spanish *bastonada*, from *bastón* 'cudgel'.]

basting /báysting/ *n.* SEW loose or temporary stitches

bastion /básti ən/ *n.* **1.** PROJECTING PART a projecting part of a wall, rampart, or other fortification **2.** FORTIFICATION a fortified place **3.** STRONG SUPPORTER sb or sth regarded as providing strong defence or support, especially for a belief or cause [Mid-16thC. Via French from Italian *bastione*, from *bastire* 'to build'.]

bastnaesite /bástnə sīt/, **bastnasite** *n.* a rare yellow to reddish-brown mineral, a fluorocarbonate of lanthanum and cerium, that is a source of rare-earth elements [Late 19thC. Named after *Bastnäs* in Sweden, where it was found.]

BASW *abbr.* British Association of Social Workers

bat[1] /bat/ *n.* **1.** SPORTS **CLUB USED IN SPORTS** a club used to strike the ball in sports such as cricket, table tennis, and baseball, usually wooden but sometimes made of metal or plastic **2.** AIR **DEVICE FOR GUIDING AIRCRAFT** either of a pair of hand-held devices that look like table-tennis bats and are used by sb on the ground to guide taxi-ing or landing aircraft. US term **paddle 3.** HEAVY STICK OR CLUB a heavy stick or wooden club **4.** BLOW FROM STICK a blow from a stout stick or club **5.** CRICKET **CRICKET BATSMAN** a batsman in cricket **6.** PACE rate, pace, or speed (*informal*) ■ *v.* (**bats, batting, batted**) **1.** *vt.* STRIKE WITH BAT to strike sb or sth with a bat **2.** *vi.* SPORTS HAVE TURN AT BATTING to take a turn at batting in sports such as cricket or baseball [Old English *batt*, of uncertain origin, possibly influenced by Old French *batte*] ◇ **off your own bat** on your own initiative and without instructions or help from anyone (*informal*)

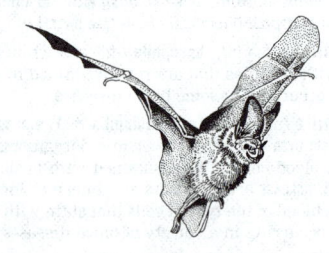

Bat

bat[2] /bat/ *n.* ZOOL a small nocturnal flying mammal with leathery wings stretching from the forelimbs to the rear legs and tail. Bats eat fruit or insects, usually hang upside down when resting, and often use echolocation to detect prey and to navigate. Order: Chiroptera. [Late 16thC. Alteration of Middle English *backe*, from a Scandinavian word such as Old Swedish *natbakka* 'night bat' or Old Norse *leðerblaka* 'leather

flapper'.] ◇ **have bats in the belfry** to be slightly but harmlessly eccentric (*informal*)

─── **WORD KEY: REGIONAL NOTE** ───
Changes to farming methods have caused **bats** to become quite rare in Britain. Once, they were found in the eaves of thousands of barns and had different names in different regions. The commonest were *bat-mouse, batty-mouse, billy-bat, blind bat, ekkymowl, flitterbat, flittermouse, hairy bat, inkmouse, leather bat,* and *mouse bat*.

bat[3] /bat/ (**bats, batting, batted**) *vt.* to wink or flutter sth, especially the eyes or eyelids [Early 19thC. Variant of BATE[2].]

bat. *abbr.* **1.** battalion **2.** COMPUT batch

Bataan /bə tán, -taán/ peninsula of Luzon Island in the Philippines, the scene of intense Japanese-American World War II combat. Area: 1,373 sq. km/530 sq. mi.

Batak /báttək/ *n.* a group of Austronesian languages spoken by about three million people in Sumatra, Indonesia. Toba Batak is the best known of the Batak languages. [Early 19thC. From Batak.] —**Batak** *adj.*

Batangas /bə táng gass/ city and port on Luzon Island in the Philippines. It is the capital of Batangas Province. Population: 185,000 (1990).

Batavia /bə táyvi ə/ former name for Jakarta

batch[1] /bach/ *n.* **1.** QUANTITY REGARDED AS GROUP a quantity of people or things treated or regarded as a group, especially when subdivided from a larger group **2.** COOK AMOUNT BAKED the amount of sth baked at one time or produced at one baking **3.** AMOUNT FOR ONE OPERATION the amount of material prepared or needed for, or produced in, one operation **4.** COMPUT PROGRAMS PROCESSED TOGETHER a set of programs or jobs submitted for processing on a computer at one time ■ *vt.* (**batches, batching, batched**) PROCESS ITEMS AS BATCH to process or assemble items as a batch or in batches [15thC. From assumed Old English *bæcce* 'sth baked', from *bacan* 'to bake' (see BAKE).]

batch[2] /bach/ *vi.* = bach

bat chayil /baat khaáyil/, **bat hayill** *n.* = bat mitzvah **2** [Late 20thC. From Hebrew, literally 'daughter of valour'.]

batch file *n.* a computer file containing a series of commands to be processed by a computer, as if they were entered from the keyboard consecutively. Most personal computers execute a batch file called AUTOEXEC.BAT at the start of each operating session to prepare the system for use.

batch processing *n.* a mode of computer operation in which programs are executed without the user being able to influence processing while it is in progress

bate[1] /bayt/ (**bates, bating, bated**) *vt.* (*archaic*) **1.** HOLD STH BACK to hold back or moderate sth **2.** SUBTRACT to subtract sth, or take sth away [14thC. Shortened form of ABATE.]

bate[2] /bayt/ (**bates, bating, bated**), **bait** (**baits, baiting, baited**) *vi.* to beat the wings wildly or impatiently in an attempt to fly off sth, e.g. a perch or a falconer's fist, when still attached by a leash (*refers to a falcon or other hunting bird*) [13thC. From Old French *batre* (see BATTER[1]).]

bate[3] /bayt/ *n.* a fit of anger (*dated informal*)

Batei Din *n.* plural of Beth Din

bateleur /báttə lur/, **bateleur eagle** *n.* a crested African eagle that has a short tail and long broad wings. It feeds mainly on carrion. Latin name: *Terathopius ecaudatus*. [Mid-19thC. From French, literally 'juggler, rogue'.]

Bates /bayts/, **Daisy May** (1863–1951) Irish-born Australian journalist and anthropologist. She was the author of *The Passing of the Aborigine* (1938), an account of the many years she spent among the Aborigines of central Australia. Born **Daisy May O'Dwyer**

Bates, H.W. (1825–92) British naturalist. He explored Amazonia (1848–59), returning with 14,700 specimens, including 8,000 unknown insect species. Full name **Henry Walter Bates**

Batesian mimicry /báytsi ən-/ *n.* a type of mimicry in which a harmless species is protected from predators by its resemblance to a species that is harmful or unpalatable to them [Late 19thC. Named after H.W. BATES.]

batfish /bátfish/ (*plural* **-fish** *or* **-fishes**) *n.* a marine angler fish that has a flattened head and body and waddles on the sea bottom using pectoral and pelvic fins. Family: Ogcocephalidae.

bath /baath/ *n.* (*plural* **baths** /baathz/) **1.** LARGE CONTAINER FOR WASHING BODY IN a large container, usually oblong in shape and made of plastic or enamelled metal, that people sit in to wash their bodies. US term **bathtub 2.** IMMERSION OF BODY the act of immersing all or part of the body in a bath in order to wash it **3.** BODY TREATMENT the act of immersing all or part of the body in an enveloping substance, e.g. mud, usually for therapeutic reasons **4.** WATER IN BATH water used for bathing **5.** CHEM LIQUID a liquid, or a liquid and its container, used for a particular purpose such as developing photographs or maintaining sth at a constant temperature ■ *n.* npl. **1.** BATHHOUSE a building with facilities for people to have baths **2.** SWIMMING POOL a swimming pool for public use ■ *vi.* (baths, bathing, bathed) WASH IN BATH to wash yourself or sb else in a bath. US term **bathe** [Old English *bæþ*, from prehistoric Germanic] ◇ **take a bath** *US* to suffer a severe financial setback (*slang*)

─── **WORD KEY: USAGE** ───

bath or **bathe**? There are major differences between the United States and other parts of the English-speaking world in the use of these words. In British, Canadian, Australian, and New Zealand English, **bath** is used as a verb and **bathe** is used as a noun, whereas in US English they are not. *Shall I bath the baby?* and *I'm going for a bathe* are non-American uses, in which the difference between the two words is that the first refers to washing and the second to swimming in the sea. In most varieties of English, **bathe** is also used of immersing things in water to clean or moisten them. In the United States, **bathe** means 'to take a bath, or give a bath to sb': *I'm going to bathe. I'm going to bathe the baby.*

Bath /baath/ city on the River Avon in Somerset, England. It is the site of the only natural hot springs in England and has been a spa since Roman times. Population: 85,202 (1991).

Bath bun *n.* a sweet sticky spiced bun containing dried fruit [From its originally being made in BATH]

bath chair *n.* an old-fashioned type of wheelchair, often with a hood [From its being first used in BATH]

bath cube *n.* a cube of soluble material used to perfume and soften bathwater

bathe /bayth/ *v.* (bathes, bathing, bathed) **1.** *vi.* SWIM OR PADDLE IN OPEN WATER to swim or paddle, especially for pleasure, in an area of open water such as the sea or a river **2.** *vt.* CLEANSE WOUND to apply water or another liquid to a wound or part of the body in order to cleanse, heal, or soothe it **3.** *vt.* DIP STH IN LIQUID to immerse sth in liquid **4.** *vt.* COVER STH to cover or surround sth with light, colour, or a substance ◦ *bathed in a golden glow* **5.** *vt.* FLOW ALONG EDGE OF STH to flow along the edge of sth **6.** *vti.* *US* = **bath** ■ *n.* ACT OF SWIMMING OR BATHING an act of swimming or bathing, especially in an area of open water (*dated*) [Old English *bæþ*, from prehistoric Germanic]

bather /báythər/ *n.* sb who is swimming

bathers /báythərz/ *npl.* a swimming costume (*informal*)

bathetic /bə théttik/ *adj.* **1.** SHOWING BATHOS showing or characterized by bathos **2.** TRITE trite, commonplace, or absurdly sentimental [Late 18thC. Formed from BATHOS, on the model of *pathos*, *pathetic*.] —**bathetically** *adv.*

bathhouse /báath howss/ (*plural* **-houses** /-howziz/) *n.* a building equipped with baths, especially for public use

Bathinette /báthə nét, baáthə-/ *tdmk. US* a trademark for a portable device for bathing babies

bathing /báything/ *n.* the activity of swimming in an area of open water, e.g. the sea or a river (*dated*)

bathing cap *n.* a tight-fitting rubber cap that swimmers wear to keep their hair dry (*dated*)

bathing costume *n.* a swimming costume (*dated*)

bathing machine *n.* a small hut on wheels that bathers changed in, in the 18th and 19th centuries. It was pulled to the sea's edge, allowing them to slip into the water modestly.

bathing trunks *npl.* a pair of swimming trunks (*dated*)

bathing waters *npl.* bodies of seawater or fresh water that are used for public bathing, and to which particular water quality standards apply under EU and UK law

bathmat /baáth mat/ *n.* **1.** MAT BESIDE BATH a mat that is placed beside a bath or shower for sb to step out onto **2.** MAT INSIDE BATH a mat, often made of rubber, that is placed in a bath or shower to prevent sb from slipping

batho- deep, depth ◦ *bathometer* [From Greek *bathos* 'depth']

bathochromic /báthə krŏmik/ *adj.* used to describe a move to a longer wavelength in a compound's absorption spectrum

bath oil *n.* a scented oil used to add fragrance to bathwater

batholith /báthəlith/, **batholite** /-līt/ *n.* a large mass of igneous rock, composed of granite or gabbro, formed deep in the Earth's crust and intruded in a molten state —**batholithic** /báthə líthik/ *adj.*

Bath Oliver *n.* a thin dry unsweetened biscuit, usually eaten with cheese [Named after its creator, Dr William *Oliver* (1695–1764) of BATH]

bathometer /bə thómmitər/ *n.* an instrument for measuring the depth of a body of water —**bathometric** /báthə méttrik/ *adj.* —**bathometry** /bə thómmətri/ *n.*

bathophilous /bə thóffiləss/ *adj.* used to describe organisms that are adapted to living in very deep water

bathos /báy thoss/ *n.* **1.** ABRUPT CHANGE TO ORDINARY STYLE in writing or speech, a sudden descent in style or manner from the elevated or sublime to the commonplace, producing a ludicrous effect **2.** EXCESSIVE PATHOS insincere and excessively sentimental pathos **3.** = **anticlimax** [Early 18thC. From Greek, 'depth', from *bathus* 'deep' (source of English *bathy-*). The English meaning seems to have been coined by the English poet Alexander POPE (1688–1744).]

bathrobe /baáth rŏb/ *n.* **1.** LOOSE GARMENT a loose-fitting garment with a belt usually made of towelling, worn before or after bathing **2.** *US* = **dressing gown**

bathroom /baáth room, -rŏŏm/ *n.* **1.** ROOM CONTAINING BATH a room containing a bath or shower and, usually, a washbasin and a toilet **2.** TOILET a room with a toilet

bathroom scales *npl.* a step-on device for people to weigh themselves on at home, usually kept in a bathroom

bath salts *npl.* soluble mineral salts used to perfume and soften bathwater

Bathsheba /bath shéeba, báthshibə/ in the Bible, the wife of Uriah and later of David, by whom she became the mother of Solomon (II Samuel 11–12)

Bath stone *n.* a white limestone used for building, quarried near Bath

bath towel *n.* a large towel used to dry the body after a bath or shower

bathtub /baáth tub/ *n.* = **bath**

Bathurst[1] /báth urst/ *n.* former name for **Banjul**

Bathurst[2] /báth urst/ **1.** city and summer holiday resort in northeastern New Brunswick, Canada. Population: 13,815 (1996). **2.** city in central New South Wales, Australia. Founded in 1815, it is Australia's oldest inland town and was the site of the first Australian gold rush. Population: 26,029 (1996).

Bathurst Island island in the Timor Sea off the northern coast of the Northern Territory, Australia. Population: 1,000 (1996). Area: 2,600 sq. km/1,000 sq. mi.

bathwater /baáth wawtər/ *n.* the water used for a bath

bathy- deep, depth ◦ *bathysphere* [From Greek *bathus* 'deep']

bathyal /báthi əl/ *adj.* relating to or living in ocean depths between 200 and 2,000 m/650 and 6,550 ft

bathylimnetic /báthəlim néttik/ *adj.* used to describe organisms that live deep in lakes and marshes [Early 20thC. Coined from BATHY- + Greek *limnon* 'pool' + -ETIC.]

bathymetry /bə thímmətri/ *n.* **1.** MEASUREMENT OF WATER DEPTH the measurement of the depth of large bodies of water, e.g. lakes, oceans, and seas **2.** DEPTH MEASUREMENTS the data obtained by the use of bathymetry —**bathymetric** /báthi méttrik/ *adj.* —**bathymetrically** /-méttrikli/ *adv.*

bathypelagic /báthipə lájjik/ *adj.* relating to or living in the depths of the ocean, especially between 600 and 3600 m/2000 and 12,000 ft

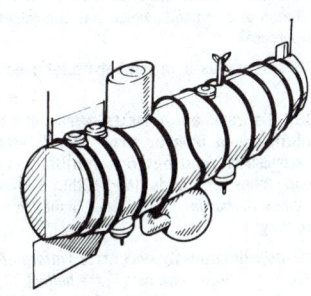

Bathyscaphe

bathyscaphe /báthi skayf/, **bathyscaph** *n.* a deep-sea research vessel that has a large flotation hull and an observation cabin attached to its underside, and can dive to depths over 10,000 m/6.2 mi [Mid-20thC. Coined from BATHY- + Greek *skaphos* 'ship'.]

bathysphere /báthi sfeer/ *n.* a strong steel diving sphere that can be lowered by cable to depths of 900 m/3,000 ft

batik /báttik, bə teék/, **battik** /báttik/ *n.* **1.** FABRIC PRINTING TECHNIQUE a method of hand-printing a fabric by covering with removable wax the parts that will not be dyed **2.** HAND-DYED FABRIC fabric that has been hand-dyed by the batik method [Late 19thC. From Javanese, literally 'painted'.]

Batista y Zaldívar /ba téesta ee zal deé vaar/, **Fulgencio** (1901–73) Cuban soldier and political leader. His presidency of Cuba (1940–44, 1952–59) was ended by Fidel Castro's revolution (1959).

batiste /ba teést/ *n.* a fine soft plain-woven fabric made of cotton or linen, used especially for clothing [Early 19thC. From French, possibly from the name of *Baptiste* of Cambrai, a 13th-century cloth maker.]

Batley /báttli/ town in West Yorkshire, northern England. Population: 48,030 (1991).

batman /bátmən/ (*plural* **-men** /-mən/) *n.* a British military officer's personal servant [Mid-18thC. Via Old French from medieval Latin *bastum* 'pack saddle' (probable source of English *bastard*). A batman was originally in charge of the packhorse carrying an officer's belongings.]

Batman /bát man/, **John** (1801–39) Australian pioneer. He was the first European to explore and recognize the potential of the site of present-day Melbourne.

bat mitzvah /baat mítsvə/, **bath mitzvah, bas mitzvah** /baass-/ *n.* **1.** JEWISH RITE OF PASSAGE the ritual that marks the 13th birthday of a Jewish girl, after which she takes full responsibility for her moral and spiritual conduct **2.** JEWISH GIRL REACHING 13 a Jewish girl who has reached the age of about 13, the age of religious responsibility [From Hebrew *baṭ miṣwāh* 'daughter of commandment']

BATNEEC /bát neek/ a principle that is applied to the control of emissions to air, land, and water from polluting processes, minimizing pollution without requiring technology or methods which are not yet available or unreasonably expensive. Abbr of **best available technology not entailing excessive cost**

baton /bátton, bátt'n/ *n.* **1.** MUSIC CONDUCTING STICK a short thin stick used by a conductor to direct musical performers **2.** PUBLIC ADMIN POLICE STICK a short thick stick used as a weapon, e.g. by police **3.** SPORTS RELAY TEAM STICK a short stick or hollow cylinder passed by each runner in a relay team to the next runner **4.**

OFFICIAL STAFF a staff carried by an official, e.g. a field marshal, as a symbol of office **5.** DRUM MAJOR'S STICK a long stick with a knob at one or both ends, carried and twirled by a drum major or majorette **6.** HERALDRY DIAGONAL LINE ON COAT OF ARMS a shortened narrow diagonal line on a coat of arms, especially one signifying bastardy [Early 16thC. Via French from, ultimately, late Latin *bastum* 'stick'.]

baton charge *n.* a charge made by people armed with batons, especially police officers

bâton de commandement /báttoN də kə maáNd maaN/ (*plural* **bâtons de commandement** /báttoN də kə maáNd maaN/) *n.* an antler fragment from prehistoric times, often marked with carving and thought to have been used as a tool [From French, literally 'baton of command', which was originally thought to be its purpose]

baton round *n.* a plastic or rubber bullet used in riot control

batrachian /bə tráyki ən/ *n.* TAILLESS AMPHIBIAN a tailless amphibian, e.g. a frog or toad ■ *adj.* RELATING TO TAILLESS AMPHIBIANS relating to amphibians without tails, e.g. frogs or toads [Mid-19thC. Formed from modern Latin *Batrachia*, former order name, from Greek *batrakhos* 'frog'.]

bats /bats/ *adj.* harmlessly eccentric (*informal*) [Early 20thC. From the phrase *have bats in the belfry.*]

batsman /bátsmən/ (*plural* **-men** /-mən/) *n.* **1.** PLAYER WHO BATS OR IS BATTING a cricket player who bats or is batting **2.** PLAYER WHO SPECIALIZES IN BATTING a cricket player who specializes in batting, rather than bowling or fielding **3.** GROUND OFFICIAL WHO GUIDES AIRCRAFT a ground official who uses a pair of bats to guide landing and taxiing aircraft

batt /bat/ *n.* TEXTILES = **batting**[2] [Late 19thC. shortening.]

batt. *abbr.* battalion

battalion /bə tályən/ *n.* **1.** LARGE BODY OF SOLDIERS a large body of soldiers organized to act together **2.** MILITARY UNIT a military unit typically consisting of a headquarters and three or more companies, batteries, or other subunits of similar size **3.** LARGE NUMBER a large group or number (*often used in the plural*) [Late 16thC. Via French from Italian *bataglione*, literally 'great battle', ultimately from late Latin *bat(t)uere* 'to beat' (source of English *batter* and *battle*).]

battels /bátt'lz/ *npl.* at Oxford University, the bill or account of a member of a college for accommodation, food, and other expenses [Late 16thC. Origin uncertain: perhaps from BATTLE 'to fortify, build battlements', with the idea of fortifying oneself with food.]

battement /bát maaN/ *n.* a ballet movement in which one leg is extended, either once or repeatedly, to the front, side, or back, and then beaten against the supporting foot [Mid-19thC. From French, literally 'beating'.]

batten /bátt'n/ *n.* **1.** BUILDING BUILDING SUPPORT a thin strip of wood used in building, e.g. to seal or reinforce a joint or to support laths, slates, or tiles **2.** NARROW PIECE OF WOOD a long narrow piece of wood used especially for flooring **3.** NAUT STRIP FOR KEEPING SAILS IN SHAPE a thin flexible strip of wood or plastic inserted in pockets at the edge of a sail to keep it taut and flat **4.** NAUT SLAT FOR FASTENING DOWN TARPAULIN a narrow metal or wooden slat used to fasten down the edges of a tarpaulin covering a ship's raised hatch in poor weather **5.** THEATRE LIGHTS IN THEATRE a row of lights in a theatre, or the strip or bar that holds it ■ *vt.* (**-tens, -tening, -tened**) PROVIDE WITH BATTENS to provide, strengthen, or secure sth with battens [Late 16thC. From Old Norse *batna* 'to improve, get better', ultimately from the same prehistoric Germanic source as English *better* and *best.*]

Batten /bátt'n/, **Jean** (1909–82) New Zealand aviator. She broke Amy Johnson's record for a solo flight from England to Australia and became the first woman to complete the return trip (1934–35). She wrote *Alone in the Sky* (1939). Full name **Jean Gardner Batten**

Battenberg /bátt'n burg/ *n.* an oblong cake coated with marzipan and made of squares of yellow and pink sponge, so that a slice of it has two yellow and two pink squares [Early 20thC. Named after Prince Louis of *Battenberg*, in honour of his marriage to Princess Victoria of Hesse-Darmstadt in 1884.]

batter[1] /báttər/ *vt.* (**-ters, -tering, -tered**) **1.** HIT REPEATEDLY to hit or beat sth repeatedly using heavy blows in order to break, bruise, or damage it **2.** SUBJECT TO ATTACK to subject sb to persistent attack or violence **3.** DAMAGE BY HEAVY BLOWS OR WEAR to damage or injure sth by hard blows or heavy wear (*often passive*) ■ *n.* PRINTING **1.** DAMAGED TYPE a damaged or worn printing type or plate **2.** FAULTY IMPRESSION a defective impression resulting from a printing batter [14thC. Via Old French *batre* from, ultimately, late Latin *bat(t)uere* 'to beat' (source of English *batten* and *battle*).] —**batterer** *n.*

batter[2] /báttər/ *n.* COOK MIXTURE OF FLOUR, MILK, AND EGGS a liquid mixture of flour, milk, and eggs used in making cakes and pancakes, and for coating foods before frying ■ *vt.* (**-ters, -tering, -tered**) COOK COAT FOOD IN BATTER to cover food with batter before frying [Mid-16thC. Origin unknown.]

batter[3] /báttər/ *vt.* (**-ters, -tering, -tered**) BUILD IN RECEDING SLOPE to build sth, e.g. a wall or similar structure, in a way that forms an upwardly receding slope ■ *n.* RECEDING UPWARDS SLOPE a receding upwards slope of the outer face of a wall, hedge, or similar structure [14thC. From Old French *bateüre* 'act of beating', from *batre* (see BATTER[1]); from the idea of beating the mixture.]

batter[4] /báttər/ *n.* SPORTS a player who bats, especially in baseball

battered /báttərd/ *adj.* **1.** MALTREATED subjected to persistent physical assault, especially by a spouse, partner, or caregiver **2.** SHOWING SIGNS OF WEAR marked by dents, scratches, and other signs of heavy wear

batterie /báttəri, ba treé/ *n.* a ballet movement in which the dancer beats the feet or calves together during a leap [Early 18thC. From French, literally 'battery'.]

batterie de cuisine /ba treé də kwi zeén/ (*plural* **batteries de cuisine** /ba treé də kwi zeén/) *n.* a set of cooking utensils, pots, and pans [Late 18thC. From French, literally 'set (of implements) for cooking'.]

battering ram *n.* **1.** HEAVY BEAM a large heavy beam used in ancient times to break down the walls and doors of a fortification under siege **2.** DOOR BREAKER a heavy metal bar used by police officers and firefighters to break down doors

Battersea /báttərssi/ district of Wandsworth, on the southern bank of the River Thames, London

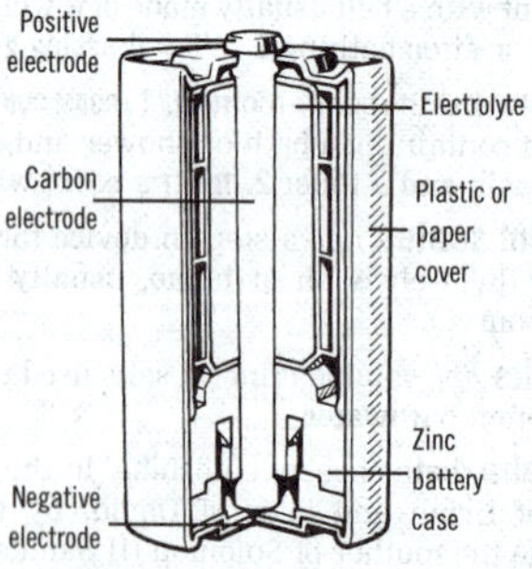

Battery: Cutaway view of a simple battery

battery /báttəri/ (*plural* **-ies**) *n.* **1.** ELEC POWER SOURCE a number of connected electric cells that produce a direct current through the conversion of chemical energy into electrical energy **2.** ACT OF BATTERING the act of battering, beating, or pounding sth **3.** LAW UNLAWFUL USE OF FORCE ON SB the unlawful use of any physical force on another person, including beating or offensive touching without the person's consent **4.** MIL GROUPING OF ARTILLERY a grouping of similar artillery pieces, e.g. guns or missile launchers, that function as a single tactical unit **5.** MIL ARMY ARTILLERY UNIT an army artillery unit corresponding to a company in an infantry regiment **6.** MIL GUN EMPLACEMENT a prepared position for artillery **7.** AGRIC SYSTEM OF CAGES FOR REARING ANIMALS a series of cages used for the intensive rearing of livestock, especially poultry **8.** GROUPING OF SIMILAR THINGS USED TOGETHER an array or grouping of similar things intended to be used together **9.** SIMILAR THINGS TOGETHER a cluster of similar things or ideas taken, used, or considered together **10.** MUSIC PERCUSSION SECTION the percussion section of an orchestra [Mid-16thC. Via Old French *baterie* from, ultimately, late Latin *bat(t)uere* 'to hit' (source of English *battle*). 'Group of guns' comes from the idea of 'beating' a target down.]

battery charger *n.* a device for restoring power to electrical batteries

battik *n.* = **batik**

batting[1] /bátting/ *n.* SPORTS the action or ability of a player or team that hits with a bat, especially in cricket or baseball

batting[2] /bátting/ *n.* TEXTILES bulky material made from fabric or other fibres, used for padding and stuffing [Early 19thC. Formed from BAT[1] 'to hit', from the beating out of impurities from cotton.]

batting average *n.* **1.** *US* SPORTS BATTER'S PERFORMANCE MEASURE a measure of a baseball batter's performance, calculated by dividing the total of base hits gained in a given period by the number of times at bat **2.** CRICKET MEASURE OF CRICKET BATSMAN'S PERFORMANCE a measure of a cricket batsman's performance, calculated by dividing the total number of runs scored in a given period by the number of innings or matches played

batting crease *n.* CRICKET = **popping crease**

battle /bátt'l/ *n.* **1.** MIL ARMED FIGHT a large-scale fight between armed forces involving combat between armies, warships, or aircraft **2.** STRUGGLE a drawn-out conflict between adversaries, or against powerful forces ○ *the battle against malaria* ■ *v.* (**-tles, -tling, -tled**) **1.** *vti.* FIGHT to fight in a battle **2.** *vi.* STRIVE to strive or contend in order to overcome or achieve sth [13thC. Via French *bataille* from, ultimately, late Latin *battualia* 'military or gladatorial exercises', from *bat(t)uere* 'to beat' (source of English *battery* and *batten*).] ◇ **fight a losing battle** to try hard with no prospect of success ◇ **be half the battle** to be an important first part of a difficult task ○ *Shipping the books on time is only half the battle; we have to sell them too* ◇ **do battle with sb or sth** to fight or struggle against sb or sth

WORD KEY: USAGE

The people of South Carolina have been battling a hurricane. This transitive use of ***battle*** (with a direct object, instead of *battle against* or *battle with*) is a feature of American usage that has begun to enter other Englishes also. This is partly a revival of an older use that died out in the 19th century.

WORD KEY: SYNONYMS

See Synonyms at ***fight***.

WORD KEY: ORIGIN

The Latin word *bat(t)uere* from which ***battle*** is derived is also the source of English *abate, battalion, battery, battlements, combat, debate,* and *rebate.*

Battle /bátt'l/ town in East Sussex, southeastern England, the site of the Battle of Hastings in 1066. Population: 5,235 (1991).

Battle, Kathleen (*b.* 1948) US soprano. An internationally renowned concert and opera singer, she sang with the Metropolitan Opera Company in New York City (1977–94).

battleaxe /bátt'l aks/ *n.* **1.** BROAD-HEADED AXE a large heavy broad-headed axe used as a weapon **2.** FEROCIOUS WOMAN a domineering and fearsome woman (*insult*)

battle cruiser *n.* a heavily armed warship but with lighter armour, fewer guns, greater manoeuvrability, and a faster speed than a battleship

battle cry *n.* **1.** SOLDIERS' SHOUT a rallying or encouraging shout that soldiers make when going into battle **2.** SUPPORTERS' SLOGAN a slogan used by supporters of a cause to rally fellow supporters

battledore /bátt'l dawr/ *n.* **1.** EARLY RACKET GAME an early racket game played by two people with flat wooden rackets and a shuttlecock **2.** LIGHT RACKET USED IN BATTLEDORE a light racket, smaller than a tennis racket, used for hitting the shuttlecock in battledore **3.** WOODEN BAT a wooden bat used in the past to beat clothes when washing them [15thC. Origin uncertain: probably from Provençal *batedor* 'beater', from *battre* 'to beat', from late Latin *bat(t)uere* (see BATTLE).]

battledress /bátt'l dress/ *n.* the ordinary uniform worn by a soldier

battle fatigue *n.* = **combat fatigue**

battlefield /bátt'l feeld/ *n.* **1. PLACE OF BATTLE** the place where a battle is fought **2. AREA OF CONFLICT** an area of conflict or contention

battleground *n.* = **battlefield**

battle line *n.* a position along which a battle takes place

battlements /bátt'lmənts/ *npl.* a defensive or decorative parapet with indentations [14thC. Formed from French *bateiller* 'to fortify'.]

Battle of Britain *n.* the aerial battle fought early in World War II between the German Luftwaffe, which carried out extensive bombing in Britain, and the Royal Air Force, which offered successful resistance

Battle of the Atlantic *n.* the struggle during World War II for control of the routes used to bring supplies to Britain across the Atlantic

battle plan *n.* **1. FIGHTING STRATEGY** a strategy for fighting a battle **2. OPERATION STRATEGY** a strategy for any operation or contest

battler /bátt'lər/ *n.* **1. FIGHTER** sb who fights, especially in a courageous or indomitable way **2.** *ANZ* **SB WHO STRUGGLES** sb who struggles continuously or energetically **3.** *ANZ* **LOW EARNER** sb who works hard for a low wage **4.** *ANZ* **PROSTITUTE** a prostitute (*informal*)

battle royal (*plural* **battles royal** *or* **battle royals**) *n.* **1. BATTLE INVOLVING MANY COMBATANTS** a battle involving many combatants, especially a fight to the finish **2. GREAT CONFLICT** a passionate conflict, especially one that unfolds in public

battleship /bátt'l ship/ *n.* the largest type of warship that carries the heaviest armour

battleship grey *adj.* of a medium grey colour tinged with blue, like the colour in which battleships are commonly painted —**battleship grey** *n.*

battue /ba tóo/ *n.* **1. DRIVING OF GAME IN HUNT** the beating of woodland or cover in order to drive game towards hunters **2. HUNT USING BATTUE** a hunt in which battue is used **3. SLAUGHTER** a wholesale massacre or indiscriminate slaughter [Early 19thC. From French, literally 'beaten', from the past participle of *battre* (see BATTER[1]).]

batty /bátti/ (**-tier, -tiest**) *adj.* slightly eccentric (*informal*) [Early 20thC. From the phrase *have bats in the belfry.*] —**battiness** *n.*

Batumi /baa tóomi/, **Batum** /-tóom/ city and port in southwestern Georgia on the Black Sea, and the capital of Ajaria autonomous region. Population: 137,500 (1991).

batwing sleeve /bátwing-/ *n.* a sleeve that is wide at the armhole and tight at the wrist

bauble /báwb'l/ *n.* **1. TRINKET** sth that is small and decorative but of little real value **2. MOCK SCEPTRE** a mock sceptre of office carried by a court jester (*archaic*) [14thC. From Old French, 'plaything', of unknown origin.]

baud /bawd/ *n.* a unit for measuring data transmission speed, equal to one unit element per second [Mid-20thC. Named after the French engineer J M E *Baudot* (1845–1903), who invented a method of transmitting information using binary digits.]

Baudelaire /bōd lair/, **Charles** (1821–67) French critic and poet. His symbolist verse, notably *Les fleurs du mal* (1857), explored his sense of melancholy, isolation, and the attractions of evil and vice. Full name **Charles Pierre Baudelaire**

Baudouin I /bṓ dwaN/, **King of the Belgians** (1930–93). He spent five years in voluntary exile in Switzerland before ascending the throne on the abdication of his father, Leopold III, in 1951. Full name **Baudouin Albert Charles Leopold Axel Marie Gustave**

Bauhaus /bów howss/ *n.* an influential German school of architecture and design, founded in 1919 by Walter Gropius. It attempted to synthesize technology, craftsmanship, design, and art, and was noted for a style of functional architecture. [Early 20thC. From German, coined by Gropius from *Bau* 'building' + *Haus* 'house'.]

baulk /bawk, bawlk/, **balk** *v.* (**baulks, baulking, baulked; balks, balking, balked**) **1.** *vi.* **STOP SHORT** to stop suddenly and refuse to go on, especially when faced with an obstacle ○ *The horse balked and refused the jump.* **2.** *vi.* **TURN AWAY** to hesitate or be unwilling to do sth, usually because of a natural revulsion or moral scruples ○ *I baulked at getting down on my hands and knees to wipe the floor.* **3.** *vti.* **REFUSE TO TACKLE STH** to refuse to tackle sth that presents a difficulty **4.** *vt.* **FOIL SB** to prevent sb from carrying out a plan or intention (*often passive*) ○ *acted like a lion baulked of its prey* **5.** *vi.* BASEBALL **MAKE ILLEGAL PITCHING MOTION** to make an illegal motion in baseball, by pretending to pitch but not actually pitching ■ *n.* **1.** BUILDING **LARGE PIECE OF WOOD** a large squared piece of wood **2.** BUILDING **WOODEN BEAM IN HOUSE ROOF** a wooden tie beam in the roof of a house **3.** AGRIC **UNPLOUGHED RIDGE** a ridge of land left unploughed to serve as a boundary or to counter erosion **4. OBSTACLE** sth that hinders or frustrates ○ *a baulk to further progress in the peace negotiations* **5.** BASEBALL **ILLEGAL PITCHING MOVE** an illegal motion by the pitcher when there are runners on base, in which the pitcher pretends to throw the ball towards the plate or to a base but does not release it **6.** *US* **AREA BEHIND BAULK LINE** the area between the baulk line and the bottom cushion on a billiard table, or in baulk-line billiards between any baulk line and the cushion **7. BILLIARDS SHOT** a shot from behind the baulk line on a billiards table [From Old English *balca* 'ridge' and Old Norse *bálkr* 'beam, bar', both ultimately from an Indo-European word meaning 'beam', which is also the ancestor of English *balcony, fulcrum*, and *debauch*] —**balker** *n.*

baulk line, **line** *n.* **1. LINE ON BILLIARD TABLE** a straight line parallel to the end of a billiard table, from behind which opening shots with the cue ball are made **2. DIVIDING LINE ON BILLIARD TABLE** one of four lines parallel to the edges of a billiard table that divide it into the central area and eight smaller compartments that are used in a particular variety of billiards **3. VARIETY OF BILLIARDS** the variety of billiards in which baulk lines are used —**baulk-line** *adj.*

baulky /báwki, báwlki/ *adj.* = **balky**

Baumé scale /bō máy-, bṓ may-/ *n.* a scale for calibrating hydrometers that are used to ascertain the relative density of liquids [Mid-19thC. Named after its inventor, the French chemist Antoine *Baumé* (1728–1804).]

Baur /bowr/, **Ferdinand Christian** (1792–1860) German theologian. He studied early Christianity using stringent historical research methods.

Bausch /bowsh/, **Pina** (*b.* 1940) German dancer and choreographer. One of the foremost modern dance choreographers, she created expressionist works, and founded the Wuppertal Dance Theatre (1973). Full name **Philippine Bausch**

bauxite /báwk sīt/ *n.* an impure amorphous mixture of aluminium hydroxides that is the principal ore of aluminium [Mid-19thC. Named after the southern French village of Les *Baux*, where the first sample described in the scientific press came from.]

Bavaria /bə váiri ə/ the largest state of Germany. It is situated in the southeast and has borders with Baden-Württemberg, Hessen, Thüringen and Saxony states, and the Czech Republic and Austria. Capital: Munich. Population: 11,922,000 (1994). Area: 70,546 sq. km/27,238 sq. mi.

Bavarian /bə váiri ən/ *n.* **1. SB FROM BAVARIA** sb who lives in or was born or brought up in the German state of Bavaria **2. GERMAN DIALECT** a group of High German dialects spoken in Bavaria and parts of Austria —**Bavarian** *adj.*

Bavarian cream *n.* = **bavarois**

bavarois /bávvər waá/ *n.* a dessert of flavoured rich set custard, eaten cold [Mid-19thC. From French, literally 'Bavarian'.]

bawbee /baw bée, báw bee/ *n.* **OLD SCOTTISH COIN** an obsolete Scottish silver coin worth three Scots pennies ■ **bawbees** *npl.* *Scotland* **MONEY** money, especially scarce or hard-earned money (*informal*) [Mid-16thC. From *Sillebawby*, whose laird, Alexander Orok, was Scottish mintmaster.]

bawd /bawd/ *n.* a woman who runs a brothel [14thC. Origin uncertain: probably from Old French *baude* 'bold, lively', of prehistoric Germanic origin.]

bawdry /báwdri/ *n.* **1. LEWD LANGUAGE** vulgar and lewd language (*archaic literary*) **2. PROCURING OF PROSTITUTES** the supplying of prostitutes for men (*archaic*)

bawdy /báwdi/ (**-ier, -iest**) *adj.* ribald in a frank, humorous, and often crude way —**bawdily** *adv.* —**bawdiness** *n.*

bawdyhouse /báwdi howss/ (*plural* **-houses** /-howziz/) *n.* a house of prostitution (*archaic*)

bawl /báwl/ *vti.* (**bawls, bawling, bawled**) **1. SHOUT** to shout sth in a loud and usually aggressive voice **2. CRY NOISILY** to cry very loudly and energetically (*informal*) ■ *n.* **LOUD SHOUT** a loud cry or shout [15thC. Origin uncertain: perhaps from Old Norse *baula* 'to low', but ultimately an imitation of the sound.] —**bawler** *n.*

bawl out *vt.* to tell sb off loudly and angrily (*informal*)

Baxter /bákstər/, **James K** (1926–72) New Zealand poet. Author of several verse collections, including *Autumn Testament* (1972), he founded a religious community on the Wanganui River (1969). Full name **James Keir Baxter**

bay[1] /bay/ *n.* **1. CURVED INLET OF SEA** an area of sea enclosed by a wide inward-curving stretch of coastline **2. LAND WITH CURVING HILLS AROUND** a lowland area with curving hills partly surrounding it [14thC. Via French *baie* from Spanish *bahía*, of Iberian origin.]

bay[2] /bay/ *n.* **1. SPECIAL AREA OR COMPARTMENT** an area, e.g. in a building, bus station, or aircraft, that is divided off and used for a particular purpose **2. SPACE BETWEEN TWO PILLARS** a section of a wall or building between two vertical structures such as pillars or buttresses **3. RECESS** a recess or alcove in a wall **4.** = **bay window** *n.* [14thC. From French *baie* 'opening', from *bayer* 'to gape, stand open', from assumed Vulgar Latin *batare* 'to yawn, gape'.]

bay[3] /bay/ *n.* **1. TREE WITH AROMATIC LEAVES** a small evergreen Mediterranean tree of the laurel family with stiff dark green aromatic leaves that are used dried as a flavouring in cooking. Latin name: *Laurus nobilis.* **2.** = **laurel** *n.* 2 **3. TREE LIKE THE LAUREL** a shrub or tree resembling the laurel ■ **bays** *npl.* **WREATH FOR POET OR VICTOR** a wreath woven out of laurel leaves, classically presented to poets and victors, or the honour conferred by this (*literary*) [14thC. Via Old French *baie* from Latin *baca* 'berry'.]

bay[4] /bay/ *n.* **1. BROWN-COLOURED ANIMAL** an animal with a reddish-brown coat, especially a horse **2. REDDISH-BROWN** a reddish-brown colour ■ *adj.* **BAY-COLOURED** of a reddish-brown colour (*refers to horses*) ○ *a bay mare* [14thC. Via Old French *bai* from Latin *badius* 'chestnut-coloured' (used only of horses).]

bay[5] /bay/ *v.* (**bays, baying, bayed**) **1.** *vi.* **HOWL** to make the howling sound of a hunting dog on the trail of an animal **2.** *vi.* **MAKE LOUD OUTCRY FOR STH** to call noisily and aggressively for sth bad to happen to sb **3.** *vt.* **CORNER HUNTED ANIMAL** to corner or exhaust a hunted animal so that it must turn and face its hunters ■ *n.* **POSITION OF NO ESCAPE** the position in which a hunted animal or a person being pursued has to face the hunters or pursuers [13thC. Via Old French *(a)baier* from assumed Vulgar Latin *abbaiare*; ultimately an imitation of the sound.] ◇ **keep sb** *or* **sth at bay** to keep sb or sth unpleasant at a distance to avoid difficulty or harm ○ *Take these drops twice a day and you'll keep colds and flu at bay.*

bayadere /bī ə déer/ *n.* fabric with horizontal stripes of bold contrasting colours [Mid-19thC. Via French from Portuguese *bailladeira* 'woman dancer', from *bailar* 'to dance'; from the fabric of the dancers' costumes.]

Bayamón /bī ə món/ city in northeastern Puerto Rico, west of the River Bayamón, and west of San Juan. Population: 231,845 (1996).

Bayazid II /bī əzid/, **Sultan of the Ottoman Empire** (1448–1512). He ruled from 1481 to 1512, and constructed the Mosque of Bayazid in Constantinople (1505).

Baybars I /bī baárss/, **Sultan of Egypt and Syria** (1233?–77). During his reign (1260–77) he extended his control into Armenia, Asia Minor, Nubia, and Arabia.

bayberry /báybəri/ (*plural* **-ries**) *n.* **1. N AMERICAN SHRUB** a shrub of the eastern coast of North America that has aromatic leaves and fruits covered with a waxy substance used in making candles. Genus: *Myrica.*

2. = **bay rum tree** 3. FRUIT OF BAYBERRY SHRUB the fruit of the North American bayberry shrub

Bayes' theorem /báyz-/ *n.* a theorem of conditional probability that allows estimates of probability to be continually revised based on observations of occurrences of events [Mid-19thC. Named after *Thomas Bayes* (1702–61), British mathematician.]

Bayeux /bī yúr/ town in Calvados Department, northern France. The Bayeux Tapestry, and 11th-century embroidery depicting the Norman conquest of 1066, is housed in the town's museum. Population: 15,106 (1990).

Bayeux tapestry *n.* a linen embroidery from the 11th century that hangs in Bayeux, France, and depicts the Norman conquest of England

bay laurel *n.* = **bay**³ *n.* 1

Bayle /bayl, bel/, **Pierre** (1647–1706) French philosopher. His *Dictionary* (1696) and his controversial proposition that morality is independent of religion were major influences on the 18th-century European Enlightenment.

bay leaf *n.* the aromatic leaf of the Mediterranean bay tree, used for flavouring in cooking

Bay of Islands bay on the northeastern coast of the North Island, New Zealand. About 18 km/11 mi. wide, the bay contains about 149 islands and is a popular tourist destination.

Bay of Pigs bay on the southwestern coast of Cuba that was the site of an abortive attempt by US-backed Cuban exiles to overthrow the government of Fidel Castro in 1961

Bay of Plenty region in northeastern North Island, New Zealand, around the bay of the same name that extends from the Coromandel Peninsula in the west to Cape Runaway in the east. Population: 230,465 (1996). Area: 21,576 sq. km/8,330 sq. mi.

Bayonet

bayonet /báyənit/ *n.* 1. BLADE FITTED TO RIFLE a blade that can be attached to the end of a rifle and used for stabbing 2. FITTING WITH PROJECTING PINS a type of fitting with projecting pins that are pushed into a socket and then twisted into slots, used, e.g., on electric light bulbs ■ *vt.* (-nets, -neting, -neted) STAB WITH BAYONET to stab or kill sb with a bayonet [Early 17thC. From French *baïonnette*, named after BAYONNE where it was first made.]

Bayonne /bī ón/ city in the Pyrénées-Atlantiques Department of the Aquitaine Region, southwestern France. Population: 41,846 (1990).

bayou /bí yoo/ (*plural* **-ous**) *n.* in the southern United States, an area of slow-moving water, often overgrown with reeds, leading from a river or lake [Mid-18thC. Via Louisiana French from Choctaw *bayuk* 'small river forming part of a delta'.]

bay platform *n.* a railway platform at which a line ends in a station where other lines continue, often where a branch line ends in a main-line station

Bayreuth /bī róyt/ city in Bavaria, southern Germany, northeast of Nuremberg. It is the site of an annual Wagner opera festival. Population: 73,100 (1992).

bay rum *n.* a liquid used in men's cosmetics made by dissolving the oil of the leaves of the bay rum tree and other fragrant oils in alcohol and water. It was originally made by distilling the oil with rum

bay rum tree *n.* a tropical American tree whose leaves produce an oil used to make bay rum and in

perfumes and soaps. Latin name: *Pimenta racemosa.*

Bay Street *n.* the controlling financial interests of Toronto, Canada

bay window *n.* a rounded or three-sided window that sticks out from an outside wall and forms a recess on the inside

baywood /báy woŏd/ *n.* a light variety of mahogany from southern Mexico [Named after the *Bay* of Campeche, Mexico]

bazaar /bə zaár/ *n.* 1. CHARITABLE SALE a sale of goods to raise money for charity 2. SHOP SELLING MISCELLANEOUS ITEMS a retail store that sells a wide variety of items (*dated*) 3. MIDDLE EASTERN MARKET a street market in Middle Eastern countries [Late 16thC. Via Italian and Turkish from Persian *bāzār* 'market'.]

bazodee /bə zó dee/ *adj.* Carib unable to think clearly, either because of psychological turmoil or because of some physical condition or effect (*slang*) [Via French Creole from French *abasourdi* 'stunned, bewildered']

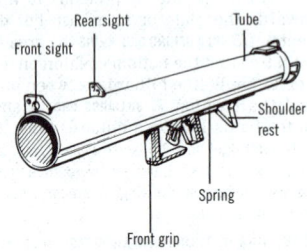

Bazooka

bazooka /bə zooka/ *n.* a tube-shaped weapon, fired from the shoulder, that launches a missile that can disable a tank [Mid-20thC. Origin uncertain: originally applied to a crude musical instrument similar to a trombone, and perhaps coined from earlier US slang *bazoo* 'kazoo', of unknown origin.]

BB *abbr.* Boys' Brigade ■ *symbol.* double black (*used to describe pencils with very soft leads*)

BBA *abbr.* Bachelor of Business Administration

BBBC *abbr.* British Boxing Board of Control

BBC *abbr.* British Broadcasting Corporation

BBFC *abbr.* British Board of Film Classification

bbl, bbl. *abbr.* barrel

BBQ *abbr.* barbecue

BBS *abbr.* COMPUT Bulletin Board System

BC, BC *adv.* used to indicate a date that is a specified number of years before the birth of Jesus Christ (*used after a date*) Full form **before Christ**

B.C. *abbr.* British Columbia

bcc, b.c.c. *abbr.* blind carbon copy

BCC *abbr.* British Coal Corporation

BCD *abbr.* binary coded decimal

BCE, BCE *abbr.* Before the Common Era

B cell *n.* a type of white blood cell (**lymphocyte**), formed in bone marrow in mammals and present in blood and lymph, that creates antibodies in response to a specific antigen

BCF *abbr.* bromochlorodifluoromethane (*formerly used in fire extinguishers*)

BCG *n.* an anti-tuberculosis vaccine made from a weakened strain of the tubercle bacillus. Full form **bacillus Calmette-Guérin (vaccine)**

BCh *abbr.* Bachelor of Surgery [From Latin *Baccalaureus Chirurgiae*]

BCL *abbr.* Bachelor of Civil Law

BCNZ *abbr.* Broadcasting Corporation of New Zealand

B complex *n.* = **vitamin B complex**

BC soil *n.* soil made up of two distinct layers

bd *abbr.* 1. board 2. bond 3. bundle 4. PUBL bound 5. MED bis in die ♦ **b.i.d.**

BD *abbr.* 1. Bachelor of Divinity 2. bills discounted 3. Bangladesh (*international vehicle registration*)

b/d *abbr.* ACCT brought down

B/D, b/d *abbr.* 1. bank draft 2. bills discounted 3. ACCT brought down

BDA *abbr.* British Dental Association

Bde, bde *abbr.* brigade

bdellium /délli əm/ *n.* 1. RESINOUS TREE a tropical tree of Africa and western Asia that produces a resin similar to myrrh. Genus: *Commiphora.* 2. VALUABLE RESIN the transparent yellowish resin of the bdellium tree, valued for its perfume [14thC. Via Latin and Greek from, ultimately, a Semitic language.]

bd ft *abbr.* board foot

bdl *abbr.* bundle

Bdr *abbr.* Bombardier

bdrm *abbr.* bedroom

bds *abbr.* 1. PUBL bound in boards 2. bundles

BDS *abbr.* 1. Bachelor of Dental Surgery 2. Barbados (*international vehicle registration*)

be (*stressed*) /bee/; (*unstressed*) /bi/ (*1st person present singular* **am**, *2nd person present singular* **are**, *3rd person present singular* **is**, *1st person present plural* **are**, *2nd person present plural* **are**, *present subjunctive* **be**, *1st person singular past indicative* **was**, *2nd person singular past indicative* **were**, *3rd person singular past indicative* **was**, *1st person plural past indicative* **were**, *2nd person plural past indicative* **were**, *3rd person plural past indicative* **were**, *past subjunctive* **were**, *past participle* **been**) CORE MEANING: a verb used most commonly to link the subject of a clause to a complement in order to give more information about the subject, e.g. its identity, nature, attributes, position, or value ○ *This is my colleague.* ○ *He's a very sweet person.* ○ *Her new car is blue.* ○ *The supermarket is on the left.* ○ *The clock was worth £3,000.*

vi. 1. GIVING A DESCRIPTION used after 'it' as the subject of the clause, to give a description or judgment of sth ○ *It was a good thing they didn't go after all.* ○ *It is up to you to make a success of the business.* 2. EXIST OR BE TRUE used after 'there' to indicate that sth exists or is true ○ *There was nothing in the news today about the resignation.* ○ *There are too many people in here.* 3. EXIST to exist, have presence, or live ○ *I think, therefore I am.* ○ *Our cat has ceased to be.* 4. HAPPEN to happen or take place ○ *The meeting will be at 2 o'clock in the conference room.* 5. STAY to stay or visit ○ *He wanted nothing but to be with the family.* ○ *Have you ever been to Italy?* 6. HAVE PARTICULAR QUALITY to have a particular quality or attribute ○ *To be really precise, you must state the exact time at which the accident happened.* 7. REMAIN used to indicate that a certain situation remains ○ *The fact of the matter is, I just don't want to stay here any more.* 8. EXPRESSING CONTINUATION used with the present participle of verbs to express continuation ○ *The firm will be instituting more training programs next year.* 9. FORMING THE PASSIVE used with the past participle of transitive verbs to form the passive voice ○ *She was sent on the mission.* 10. FORMING PERFECT TENSE used with the past participle of some intransitive verbs to form a perfect tense (*archaic*) ○ *She is gone.* 11. EXPRESSING THE FUTURE used to indicate that sth is planned, expected, intended, or supposed to happen in the future (*used with an infinitive*) ○ *The meeting is to take place tomorrow.* ○ *What am I to do?* 12. EXPRESSING UNPLANNED ACTION IN THE PAST used when reporting past events to indicate that sth happened later than the time reported and was unplanned or uncertain at the time (*used with an infinitive*) ○ *He kissed her goodbye; it was to be the last time he ever saw her.* [Old English *bēon*, via a prehistoric Germanic base meaning 'exist, dwell' from an Indo-European base meaning 'exist, grow'] ◇ **be that as it may** even if that is the case ○ *'I don't even like camping holidays' –* '*Be that as it may, you're still coming with us'.* ◇ **be off** go away ○ *It's already seven o'clock; I'm off.*

─── **WORD KEY: ORIGIN** ───

The prehistoric Germanic word that is the ancestor of the verb *be* is also the source of English *boor, booth, bower, build, byelaw, husband,* and *neighbour.*

Be *symbol.* beryllium

BE *abbr.* bill of exchange

be- *prefix.* **1.** thoroughly, excessively ○ *bedazzle* ○ *bespatter* **2.** on, over, about ○ *bewail* **3.** to surround or cover with ○ *befog* ○ *bedew* **4.** to furnish with ○ *befriend* **5.** to make ○ *belittle* [ETYMOLOGY: Old English *be-*, *bi-*. Ultimately from an Indo-European base meaning 'around', which is also the ancestor of English *ambi-*, *amphi-*, and *by*.]

BEAB *abbr.* British Electrical Approvals Board

beach /beech/ *n.* **COASTAL SAND** a strip of sand or pebbles at the point where land meets the sea or a lake ■ *vti.* **(beaches, beaching, beached) HAUL BOAT ASHORE** to pull or run a boat onto a beach, or be pulled onto a beach [Mid-16thC. Origin uncertain: perhaps from Old English *bæce* 'brook'. Originally in the meaning of 'shingle'.]

beach ball *n.* a large light easily inflated ball, often brightly coloured, for playing with on a beach

beach buggy *n.* a motorized beach vehicle, usually with no top and having oversized tyres to prevent it from getting mired in sand

beachcomber /beéch kōmər/ *n.* **1. SB SALVAGING THINGS FROM BEACH** sb who wanders along beaches looking through debris for useful or valuable things **2. BIG WAVE HITTING BEACH** a long high wave that crashes onto a beach. US term **comber**

beached /beecht/ *adj.* stranded on a beach or out of the water

beach flea *n.* = **sand hopper**

beachhead /beéch hed/ *n.* a part of an enemy shoreline that troops have captured and are using as a base for launching an attack [Modelled on BRIDGEHEAD]

Beach-la-Mar /beéch lə maár/ *n.* a pidgin based on English that originally developed in Vanuatu, Fiji, and other nearby islands as a trading lingua franca. The modern form that is the national language of Vanuatu is known as Bislama. [Early 19thC. By folk etymology from Portuguese *bicho do mar* 'sea cucumber', literally 'sea worm', by association with BEACH.]

beach pea *n.* *US* = **sea pea**

beach plum *n.* **1. N AMERICAN SHRUBBY PLUM TREE** a small shrubby plum tree that has large white flowers and grows in coastal regions of northeastern North America. Latin name: *Prunus maritima.* **2. EDIBLE PURPLE FRUIT** the dark purple edible fruit of the beach plum tree

beachscape /beéch skayp/ *n.* a view of a beach, either in reality or in a painting or photograph

beachwear /beéch wair/ *n.* casual clothing designed to be worn on a beach

Beachy Head /beéchi-/ chalk headland on the English Channel near Eastbourne, East Sussex, southern England. Height: 171 m/570 ft.

beacon /beékən/ **(-cons, -coning, -coned)** *n.* **1.** SHIPPING **FLASHING LIGHT FOR SHIPS** a lighthouse or signalling buoy that produces a flashing light to warn or guide ships **2.** NAVIG **RADIO TRANSMITTER PRODUCING NAVIGATION SIGNAL** a radio transmitter that continuously broadcasts a signal that aircraft use for guidance **3. SIGNALLING FIRE ON HILL** a fire lit on a hilltop or tower in former times as a signal, e.g. to warn of invasion **4. HILL SUITABLE FOR SIGNALLING FIRES** a prominent hill on which fires were formerly lit as a signal (*often used in placenames*) **5.** TRANSP = **Belisha beacon 6. SOURCE OF INSPIRATION** sb or sth that inspires or guides others (*literary*) [Old English *bēacen* 'signal, sign'. Ultimately from a prehistoric Germanic word that also produced English *beckon*.]

bead /beed/ *n.* **1. BALL FOR A NECKLACE** a small gemstone or sphere of glass, plastic, or wood, pierced for stringing on a necklace or for sewing onto fabric **2. DROP OF MOISTURE** a drop of moisture, especially of sweat **3.** ARCHIT, FURNITURE **BUILDING OR FURNITURE TRIM** an edge or rim that sticks out on a building or a piece of furniture, traditionally with a pattern of rounded knobs **4.** ARMS **GUN SIGHT** a knob sticking up on the end of the barrel of a gun, forming the front part of the gun's sight **5.** AUTOMOT **SEAL ON A TYRE** a projecting lip on the tyre of a motor vehicle that seals to the wheel rim **6.** METALL **DEPOSIT OF METAL** a deposit of metal used in welding ■ **beads** *npl.* **1.** RELIG **ROSARY** a rosary **2. NECKLACE** a necklace made of beads ■ *v.* **(beads, beading, beaded) 1.** *vt.* **DECORATE WITH BEADS** to trim or ornament sth with beads **2.** *vi.* **FORM INTO BEADS** to form drops of moisture [Old English *gebed* 'prayer'. The meaning 'small ball' evolved in the 14thC via 'prayer said on a rosary' and 'rosary bead'.] ◇ **draw a bead on sb** *or* **sth** to take careful aim at sb or sth ◇ **tell** *or* **say** *or* **count your beads** to say prayers recited in sequence and counted using a rosary

beading /beéding/ *n.* an edge or rim that sticks out on a building or a piece of furniture, traditionally with a pattern of rounded knobs

beadle /beéd'l/ *n.* **1.** CHR **MINOR CHURCH OFFICIAL** a minor parish official once employed in the Church of England to usher and keep order **2.** JUDAISM **CARETAKER OF A SYNAGOGUE** an official who acts as caretaker of a synagogue and oversees the running of the service [13thC. From Old French *bedel*, literally 'proclaimer, messenger', from a prehistoric Germanic word that is also the ancestor of English *bid*.]

beadsman /beédzmən/ (*plural* **-men** /-mən/) *n.* a man paid, or given food, in return for praying for the souls of others (*archaic*)

beady /beédi/ **(-ier, -iest)** *adj.* **1. LIKE BEADS** small, round, and shiny like glass beads **2. COVERED WITH BEADS** covered or ornamented with beads **3. WATCHFUL** carefully attentive (*informal*) ○ *a beady eye* —**beadily** *adv.* —**beadiness** *n.* ◇ **keep a** *or* **your beady eye on sb** *or* **sth** to watch sb or sth very carefully (*informal*)

beagle /beég'l/ *n.* a small smooth-haired dog belonging to a breed with a white, tan, and black coat and long drooping ears, often used for hunting [15thC. Origin uncertain: perhaps from Old French *beegueule* 'noisy person', from *beer*, 'to gape' (source of English *bay*[2]) + *gueule* 'throat' (see GULLET).]

Beagle Channel /beég'l-/ strait in the Tierra del Fuego archipelago, at the southernmost tip of South America. Length: 240 km/150 mi.

beagler /beéglər/ *n.* sb who hunts, especially for rabbits or hares, using beagles

beagling /beégling/ *n.* hunting, especially for rabbits or hares, using beagles

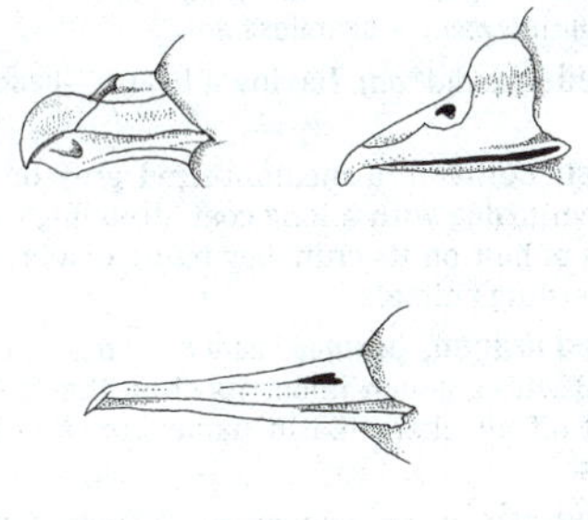

Beak

beak /beek/ *n.* **1.** BIRDS **BIRD'S MOUTH** the strong horny outer parts of a bird's mouth that stick out from its head. Beaks take many different shapes adapted to the eating habits of individual bird species. **2.** ZOOL **PROTRUDING PART OF ANIMAL'S MOUTH** a projecting part of the mouth or jaw of animals other than birds, e.g. the sucking mouthpart of an insect or the bony jaw projection of a fish **3.** ZOOL **PART OF MOLLUSC'S SHELL** the oldest part of the shell of a mollusc with a hinged shell, found nearest the hinge **4. SB'S NOSE** sb's nose, especially when it is long or hooked (*slang*) **5. PROJECTING PART** a part that sticks out, e.g. the lip of a container **6.** ARCHIT **CURVED CORNICE OR MOULDING** a cornice or moulding with a downward-curving edge **7.** LAW **MAGISTRATE** a court judge or a magistrate (*dated slang*) **8.** EDUC **TEACHER** a headmaster or schoolmaster (*dated slang*) [13thC. Via Old French *bec* from Latin *beccus*, of Gaulish origin.] —**beakless** *adj.* —**beaklike** *adj.*

beaked /beekt/ *adj.* having a beak or some part resembling a beak

beaked whale *n.* a widely found, medium-sized, toothed whale with a long snout. Family: Ziphiidae.

beaker /beékər/ *n.* **1. WIDE CUP** a wide-mouthed cup, especially a plastic one without a handle **2. LABORATORY CONTAINER** a flat-bottomed glass container used in laboratories [14thC. Via Old Norse *bikarr* from assumed Vulgar Latin *bicarium*, perhaps ultimately from Greek *bikos* 'wine jar, earthen vessel'.]

Beaker folk /beékər/ *npl.* a prehistoric people who lived throughout central Europe during the period 2000 to 1000 BC. The remains of pottery beakers are often found in areas where they are known to have lived.

beaky /beéki/ **(-ier, -iest)** *adj.* having a large, long, or hooked nose (*informal*)

beal /beel/ **(beals, bealing, bealed)** *vi.* *Scotland* **1. FESTER** to fester or suppurate **2. SEETHE WITH ANGER** to display barely contained rage [14thC. Origin uncertain: probably an alteration of BOIL.]

Beale /beel/, **Dorothea** (1831–1906) British educator and suffragette. She founded the first women's teacher training college (1885) and sponsored St Hilda's Hall, Oxford, for women teachers (1893).

be-all ◇ **the be-all and end-all** the thing that is most important

beam /beem/ *n.* **1.** CONSTR **HORIZONTAL STRUCTURAL SUPPORT** a horizontal structural member that carries the load by bending, e.g. a long piece of timber, metal, or concrete spanning a room and supporting the storey or roof above **2. LINE OF LIGHT** a narrow line of light, e.g. from a flashlight **3.** NAUT **STRUCTURAL CROSS-PIECE IN SHIP** a structural member of a ship or boat that joins the sides and supports the deck **4.** NAUT **SHIP'S BREADTH** the full breadth of a ship **5.** NAUT **SIDE OF SHIP** either of the sides of a ship **6.** PHYS **FLOW OF RADIATION** a narrow stream of radiation or particles flowing in one direction **7.** NAVIG **GUIDING SIGNAL** a radio or radar signal intended to guide a ship or aircraft, or the direction indicated by this **8. BROAD SMILE** a broad smile of happiness or satisfaction **9. HORIZONTAL PART OF BALANCE** the pivoted horizontal bar of a balance on which the two scales hang **10. MAIN SUPPORTING SHAFT** a main bar or shaft, e.g. either of the main stems of a deer's antlers or the central shaft of a plough **11.** MECH ENG **CONNECTING LEVER IN ENGINE** a lever connecting the piston rod and crankshaft in an engine **12.** MANUF **ROLLER IN LOOM** a cylinder in a loom on which either the warp or the cloth is wound ■ *v.* **(beams, beaming, beamed) 1.** *vti.* **SMILE BROADLY** to smile broadly with happiness or satisfaction, or express feelings by smiling broadly **2.** *vt.* BROADCAST **SEND AS RADIO OR TV SIGNAL** to send or transmit a programme to a distant place in the form of a radio or television signal **3.** *vti.* **SHINE** to shine in a particular direction **4.** *vti.* **CHANGE CIRCUMSTANCES SUDDENLY** to move between completely different places or situations in a sudden and disorienting way (*slang*) (*used with 'up' or 'down'*) [Old English *bēam* 'tree, piece of timber, column, ray', from a prehistoric Germanic word that is also the ancestor of English *boom*] ◇ **broad** *or* **wide across** *or* **in the beam** having wide hips (*informal humorous*) ◇ **off beam, off the beam** missing the point or relevancy ◇ **on the beam 1.** using a beam for guidance **2.** on track or working effectively

beam aerial *n.* a radio or television aerial designed to transmit or receive signals in or from a particular direction

beam compass *n.* a tool for drawing very large circles or arcs, consisting of a horizontal bar with sliding legs

beam-ends *npl.* the ends of the beams supporting the deck of a vessel ◇ **on her** *or* **its beam-ends** used to describe a ship leaning so far to one side that its deck is vertical ◇ **on your beam-ends** having very little money to live on (*informal*)

beam engine *n.* an early type of steam engine with a piston that pushes a pivoted horizontal beam up and down in a see-saw motion

Beamer /beémər/ *n.* a BMW™ motor car (*informal*) [Late 20thC. Alteration of BMW™, the name of the manufacturer.]

Beamon /beémən/, **Bob** (*b.* 1946) US athlete. He set a world long jump record of 8.9 m/29 ft 2.5 in at the 1968 Olympic Games in Mexico City; it lasted for 23 years. Full name **Robert Beamon**

beam splitter *n.* a device used in holography to divide a laser light into two beams by means of a prism and mirror to produce a three-dimensional image

beamy /beémi/ (**-ier, -iest**) *adj.* **1.** SHINING BRIGHTLY sending out beams of light (*literary*) **2.** WITH BROAD BEAM having a broad beam, or broad in the beam (*refers to a ship*)

bean /been/ *n.* **1.** PLANT WITH EDIBLE PODS AND SEEDS a climbing or short bushy plant that is cultivated for its edible, usually green, pods and seeds. Genus: *Phaseolus.* ◊ **French bean, runner bean 2.** EDIBLE GREEN POD a long thin usually green seed pod of a bean plant eaten cooked as a vegetable **3.** SMALL ROUND VEGETABLE a small round or kidney-shaped seed of various colours that is eaten as a vegetable and can be dried to preserve it **4.** *US* = **soybean 5.** = **broad bean 6.** SEED USED IN FOOD OR DRINK a coffee, cocoa, or carob seed that is processed and used in food or drink ■ **beans** *npl. US* NOTHING nothing at all (*informal*) ■ *vt.* (**beans, beaning, beaned**) *Can, US* HIT ON HEAD to hit sb on the head (*slang*) [Old English *bēan*, from prehistoric Germanic] ◊ **full of beans** bright and energetic (*informal*) ◊ **not have a bean** to have no money (*informal*) ◊ **not know beans about sth** *US* to have no knowledge or understanding of sth (*informal*) ◊ **spill the beans** to reveal secret information (*informal*)

Bean /been/, **Charles Edwin Woodrow** (1879–1968) Australian writer. He was the general editor and author of six volumes of the *Official History of Australia in the War of 1914–18* (1921–42).

beanbag /beén bag/ *n.* **1.** GAME BEAN-FILLED BAG USED IN GAMES a small cloth bag filled with dried beans or sth similar, thrown or otherwise used in children's games **2.** FURNITURE LARGE CUSHION USED AS SEAT an over-sized cushion filled with tiny polystyrene balls, laid on the floor and used as a chair

bean beetle *n.* = **Mexican bean beetle**

bean curd *n.* tofu, especially as used in Chinese cookery

beanery /beénəri/ (*plural* **-ies**) *n. US* a cheap restaurant (*informal*)

beanfeast /beén feest/ *n.* (*dated informal*) **1.** CELEBRATION a party or social gathering **2.** ANNUAL DINNER an annual dinner given to employees

beanie /beéni/ *n. US* a round tight-fitting hat like a skullcap [Formed from BEAN in the sense of 'head']

beano /beénō/ *n.* a noisy or enjoyable party or celebration (*dated informal*)

beanpole /beén pōl/ *n.* **1.** STICK SUPPORTING BEAN PLANT a stick or pole for supporting a climbing bean plant **2.** TALL THIN PERSON sb who is very tall and thin (*informal*)

bean sprouts *npl.* long pale shoots of sprouted bean seeds, particularly of mung bean, harvested while crisp and used raw or very lightly cooked

bear[1] /bair/ *n.* **1.** ZOOL LARGE FURRY ANIMAL a large strong omnivorous four-legged mammal that has thick shaggy fur and sharp claws and walks on the flat of its paws. Family: Ursidae. **2.** ZOOL MEDIUM-SIZED FURRY ANIMAL an animal that resembles but is unrelated to the true bear, e.g. the koala **3.** = **teddy bear 4.** BAD-TEMPERED PERSON sb who is surly or ill-tempered (*informal*) **5.** STOCK EXCH SB WHO ANTICIPATES FALLING PRICES sb who sells stocks or commodities in anticipation of falling prices. ◊ **bull**[1] *n.* **5** [Old English *bera*, from a prehistoric Germanic word meaning 'the brown one'. In the financial sense, probably from the expression 'to sell the bear's skin before you have caught the bear'.]

bear[2] /bair/ (**bears, bearing, bore** /bawr/, **borne** /bawrn/) *v.* **1.** *vti.* TOLERATE to be able to endure sth without great distress or annoyance (*used with a negative*) ○ *couldn't bear to see them unhappy* **2.** *vt.* SUPPORT STH to hold or support a weight or sth heavy **3.** *vti.* BE FIT FOR STH to withstand being subjected to a particular action ○ *Will her theories bear scrutiny?* **4.** *vt.* MERIT STH to be worthy of an action ○ *These allegations bear further investigation.* **5.** *vt.* ACCEPT AS RESPONSIBILITY to accept sth as a duty or responsibility **6.** *vt.* BE CHARACTERIZED BY STH to have sth as a quality, characteristic, or permanent attribute ○ *The description bore no relation to reality.* **7.** *vt.* BE MARKED BY STH to show physical signs of sth **8.** *vt.* CARRY to hold or support and transport sb or sth **9.** *vt.* PRODUCE STH to yield sth by a natural process, or produce sth desirable or valuable ○ *the tree bore fruit* **10.** *vt.* GIVE BIRTH to give birth to a child or young. ◊ **born 11.** *vt.* THINK STH to hold a particular thought, feeling, or idea in the mind ○ *I bore him no ill will.* **12.** *vt.*

TRANSMIT to hold sth in mind and communicate it to others (*formal*) **13.** *vi.* HEAD IN A CERTAIN DIRECTION to move or turn in a particular direction ○ *Bear right when the road divides.* **14.** *vt.* BEHAVE IN A CERTAIN WAY to conduct or carry yourself in a particular way [Old English *beran*] ◊ **bring sth to bear (on sth)** to use sth to force a desired outcome

bear down *vi.* to push with the vaginal muscles during childbirth

bear down on *vt.* **1.** APPROACH to move quickly and menacingly towards sb or sth **2.** PRESS DOWN to exert downward pressure on sth

bear on, bear upon *vt.* **1.** BE RELEVANT to relate to or affect sth **2.** CAUSE DIFFICULTY to be a problem for, or a burden to, sb or sth

bear out *vt.* to prove sth or sb to be true or justified ○ *This bears out my theory.*

bear up *vi.* **1.** STAY CHEERFUL IN DIFFICULTIES to remain cheerful and determined in spite of problems **2.** WITHSTAND EXAMINATION to remain true or undamaged after being examined or criticized

bear upon *vt.* = **bear on**

bear with *vt.* to be patient with sb trying to do sth

─── **WORD KEY: ORIGIN** ───

The prehistoric Germanic word from which *bear* is derived is also the ancestor of English *amphora, barrow, berth, bier, birth, born, burden, fertile, paraphernalia,* and *suffer.*

─────────

bearable /báirəb'l/ *adj.* not too unpleasant to put up with or accept

bearbaiting /báir bayting/ *n.* the setting of fierce dogs onto a chained bear, once a popular form of public entertainment

bearcat /báir kat/ *n.* = **red panda**

beard /beerd/ *n.* **1.** HAIR GROWING ON MAN'S CHIN the hair on a man's chin and, often, his neck and cheeks **2.** ZOOL TUFTS GROWING ON PLANTS AND ANIMALS a growth of longer hair on an animal, e.g. on a goat's chin, or a long slender growth on plants, e.g. on barley and wheat heads ■ *vt.* (**beards, bearding, bearded**) STAND UP TO SB OPENLY to oppose or confront sth or sb confidently or disrespectfully [Old English. Ultimately from an Indo-European word meaning 'beard', which is also the ancestor of English *barber*.] —**beardless** *adj.*

bearded /beérdid/ *adj.* having a beard —**beardedness** *n.*

bearded collie *n.* a medium-sized grey or brown-and-white dog with a long coat, drooping ears, and a tuft of hair on its chin, belonging to a breed used for herding animals

bearded dragon, bearded lizard *n.* a large Australian lizard with a pouch under its chin, that inflates to ward off attackers. Latin name: *Amphibolus barbatus.*

bearded iris *n.* an iris growing from a rhizome that has numerous hairs, often coloured, along the centre of each drooping lower petal

bearded lizard *n.* = **bearded dragon**

bearded tit *n.* = **reedling**

bearded vulture *n.* = **lammergeier**

Beardsley /beérdzli/, **Aubrey** (1872–98) British artist and illustrator. One of the 'Decadents' in the 1890s, he produced art nouveau illustrations in a distinctive black-and-white style, including series for *Morte d'Arthur* (1893) and *Salomé* (1894). Full name **Aubrey Vincent Beardsley**

bearer /báirər/ *n.* **1.** BRINGER sb who brings or carries sth **2.** FIN HOLDER OF REDEEMABLE NOTE sb possessing a document redeemable for payment **3.** = **pallbearer 4.** PORTER a local person employed to carry equipment on an expedition

bearer bond *n.* a bond payable only to the person who presents it

bear garden *n.* **1.** ROWDY PLACE a noisy or unruly place or occasion **2.** PLACE SHOWING LIVE BEARS in former times, a place where live bears were on public display and where bearbaiting took place

bear hug *n.* **1.** TIGHT EMBRACE an enthusiastic or energetic embrace **2.** WRESTLING SQUEEZING HOLD IN WRESTLING in wrestling, a tight, squeezing hold around an opponent's chest and arms **3.** COMM WARNING OF INTENDED

TAKEOVER one company's warning to another of its intention to assume control

bearing /báiring/ *n.* **1.** RELEVANCE an effect on sth, or a connection with it ○ *This has no bearing on the matter under discussion.* **2.** WAY OF MOVING OR STANDING sb's way of moving, standing, or behaving generally ○ *her dignified bearing* **3.** NAVIG CALCULATION OF DIRECTION OR GEOGRAPHIC POSITION sb's location or direction of movement calculated using a map or compass **4.** MECH ENG HOUSING FOR A MOVING PART the part of a machine that supports a sliding or rotating part **5.** BUILDING SUPPORT FOR BEAM a support for a beam or girder **6.** HERALDRY HERALDIC DEVICE a heraldic device or charge ◊ **find** *or* **get your bearings 1.** to learn exactly where you are and in which direction you should proceed **2.** to become familiar with a new environment ◊ **lose your bearings 1.** to become uncertain about where you are and in which direction you should proceed **2.** to become unable to react in a normal manner

bearing pile *n.* a column of concrete, steel, or timber driven vertically into the ground to transfer the weight of a structure built above onto firm soil below

bearing rein *n.* a short rein joining a horse's bit to a hook on the saddle, used to keep the horse's head up. US term **checkrein**

bearish /báirish/ *adj.* **1.** BAD-TEMPERED surly or ill-tempered towards people **2.** CLUMSY moving or behaving roughly or clumsily **3.** STOCK EXCH ANTICIPATING FALLING PRICES conducive to or characterized by selling rather than buying stocks or commodities in anticipation of falling prices

bear market *n.* STOCK EXCH a situation in a stock or commodity market in which shareholders are selling in anticipation of falling prices

béarnaise sauce /báyər nayz-/ *n.* a savoury sauce served with steak, chicken, or fish, made from egg yolks, butter, shallots, tarragon, and sometimes other herbs, and vinegar or lemon juice [Late 19thC. *Béarnaise* from French, formed from *Béarn*, name of a district in southwestern France.]

bear raid *n.* STOCK EXCH an attempt to lower a stock or commodity price by selling large numbers of shares, usually in order to buy them back at a lowered price

bear's breech *n.* a large garden plant with spiky leaves and whitish purple-streaked flowers. Latin name: *Acanthus mollis.*

Bearskin: Two Guardsmen wearing bearskins

bearskin /báir skin/ *n.* **1.** BEAR'S PELT a bear's skin with the fur still attached, stripped from the animal **2.** TEXTILES SHAGGY WOOLLEN CLOTH coarse woollen fabric, often used to make overcoats **3.** MIL SOLDIER'S TALL FUR HAT a tall fur hat worn as part of the ceremonial uniform of soldiers in the Guards regiments

beast /beest/ *n.* **1.** LARGE ANIMAL an animal, especially a large four-footed mammal **2.** IRRATIONAL SIDE OF SB'S PERSONALITY the instinctive, irrational, or aggressive part of sb's personality **3.** BRUTAL PERSON a cruel or aggressive person **4.** STH UNPLEASANT a thing or situation that is difficult or unpleasant (*informal*) ○ *This is truly a beast of a job!* [12thC. Via Old French *beste* from Latin *bestia*, of unknown origin.] —**beastlike** *adj.*

beast fable *n.* a story that teaches a moral lesson using the exploits of animals that speak and act like human beings

beastie /beésti/ *n. US, Scotland* a small animal, especially an insect or small crawling creature (*informal*)

beastly /beéstli/ *adj.* **NASTY** thoroughly unpleasant or objectionable (*dated informal*) ■ *adv.* **VERY** exceedingly (*dated informal*) —**beastliness** *n.*

beast of burden *n.* an animal, e.g. a donkey or an ox, used to carry or pull things or do other heavy work

beast of prey *n.* a mammal that hunts other animals for food

beat /beet/ *v.* (**beats, beating, beat, beaten** /beét'n/) **1.** *vt.* **DEFEAT** to defeat sb in a contest ○ *She was beaten in the semifinal.* **2.** *vt.* **HIT REPEATEDLY** to hit sb or sth with repeated heavy blows ○ *beaten nearly to death.* **3.** *vi.* **KNOCK AGAINST REPEATEDLY** to knock or strike against sth repeatedly ○ *waves beating against the rocks* **4.** *vt.* **FLOG** to inflict physical punishment or injury on sb using an instrument such as a whip, stick, or belt ○ *He was beaten with a strap.* **5.** *vi.* **PULSATE** to make natural short rhythmical movements (*refers to the heart or pulse*) **6.** *vti.* MUSIC **HIT DRUM** to hit a drum repeatedly to produce a musical rhythm or a signal **7.** *vt.* MUSIC **SET MUSICAL RHYTHM** to show or establish a musical rhythm, e.g. with a conductor's baton or by clapping hands **8.** *vt.* COOK **STIR VIGOROUSLY** to mix moist ingredients vigorously to combine them, make them smooth, or incorporate air into them ○ *Now, beat the eggs.* **9.** *vt.* **OVERCOME OBSTACLES IN STH** to overcome the difficulties or obstacles created by sth ○ *You can't beat the system.* **10.** *vt.* **ARRIVE AHEAD OF SB** to arrive or finish sth sooner than sb else or than a time limit ○ *She beat me to the office.* **11.** *vt.* **AVOID LATER DELAYS** to take early action to avoid being prevented or delayed by sth ○ *Order now and beat the rush!* **12.** *vt.* **SURPASS** to surpass a previous best performance ○ *beat the long jump record* **13.** *vti.* **BE BETTER** to be or do better than a particular thing, activity, or quality (*informal*) ○ *Sitting by the pool certainly beats working.* **14.** *vt.* **MAKE BY BLOWS** to shape or make sth by pounding or trampling ○ *beat silver into jewellery* **15.** *vti.* BIRDS **FLAP WINGS** to move the wings up and down in flight or an attempt at flight, or be moved in this way ○ *The vulture beat its wings.* **16.** *vt.* **FORCE TO WITHDRAW** to force sb to retreat or accept a weaker position ○ *they beat back the enemy* **17.** *vti.* HUNT **DRIVE GAME FROM BRUSH** to move through or disturb cover in order to frighten animals and birds for hunting **18.** *vi.* NAUT **SAIL INTO WIND** to sail a boat or ship as nearly as possible in the direction from which the wind is blowing ■ *n.* **1. STEADY THROBBING** a rhythmical sound or movement made by sth throbbing or pulsating (*often used in combination*) ○ *a fast heartbeat* **2. STROKE** an act of striking one thing against another, or the sound of one thing striking against another, especially repeatedly and rhythmically ○ *a drum beat* **3.** MUSIC **SET RHYTHM** a single element of measured time in a musical piece or poem. Beats occur at regular intervals and are the rhythmic and metrical foundations of music. **4.** MUSIC **CONDUCTOR'S SIGNAL** a movement made by a conductor's baton or hand to indicate a musical beat **5.** MUSIC **DOMINANT RHYTHM** the dominant rhythm in a piece of music, especially a strong rhythm in rock music **6. USUAL ROUTE** a regular route followed or area covered while working, e.g. by a police officer ○ *the local police officer on the beat* **7. AREA SB USUALLY GOES TO** the places sb usually frequents, especially sb's usual hunting or fishing area ■ *adj.* **1. TIRED OUT** completely exhausted (*informal*) **2. PUZZLED** unable to understand or think how to proceed (*informal*) ○ *It has me beat.* **3. beat, Beat OF THE BEAT GENERATION** typical of or produced by members of the Beat Generation [Old English *bēatan*. Via a prehistoric Germanic base that also produced (via French) English *button* and *buttress*, from an Indo-European base meaning 'strike', which also produced English *confute* and *refute*.] ◇ **beat it!** *US* used to tell sb to go away (*informal*) ◇ **beat sb to it** *or* **sth** to succeed in doing sth before sb else can do it (*informal*) ◇ **it beats me** used to indicate you have no answer (*informal*) ◇ **not miss a beat** to show no sign of surprise or upset

WORD KEY: SYNONYMS

See Synonyms at ***defeat.***

beat down *v.* **1.** *vi.* **COME DOWN STRONGLY** to shine intensely or fall heavily from the sky (*refers to sun or rain*) **2.** *vt.* **PERSUADE SB TO SELL FOR LESS** to persuade sb to charge less than the intended selling price (*informal*)

beat off *v.* **1.** *vt.* **REPEL ATTACK** to stop an attack or challenge by vigorous action **2.** *vi. US* **MASTURBATE** to masturbate (*slang taboo*)

beat up *vt.* to injure sb badly by repeated punches or kicks (*informal*)

beat upon *v. US* = **beat up**

beatbox /beét bòks/ *n. US* MUSIC an electronic drum used mainly in hip-hop and rap music to provide accompanying rhythm and sounds (*informal*)

beaten past participle of **beat**

beater /beétər/ *n.* **1. TOOL FOR BEATING** a tool for beating sth, e.g. a shaped stick for beating the dust out of carpets, or an electric food mixer attachment for beating eggs (*often used in combination*) **2.** HUNT **HUNTER'S ASSISTANT FOR DRIVING BIRDS OUT** sb who scares game from hiding, usually by hitting trees and bushes with a stick, so that hunters can shoot them **3. SB WHO BEATS METAL** sb who beats or hammers metal

Beat Generation *n.* **1. YOUTH MOVEMENT IN 1950S AMERICA** young people in the 1950s who rejected the traditional values, customs, and dress of Western society and experimented with Eastern philosophies, communal living, and illegal drugs **2. 1950S WRITERS** a group of writers associated with the attitudes of the Beat Generation, including Jack Kerouac, Allen Ginsberg, and Laurence Ferlinghetti

beatific /beé ə tíffik/ *adj.* (*literary*) **1. BLISSFUL** expressing or radiating great happiness and serenity **2. OF HEAVENLY HAPPINESS** bringing or expressing the perfect happiness and inner peace supposed to be enjoyed by the soul in heaven [Mid-17thC. Directly or via French *béatifique* from Latin *beatificus*, from *beatus* 'blessed'.] —**beatifically** *adv.*

beatify /bi áttifī/ (**-fies, -fying, -fied**) *vt.* **1.** CHR **DECLARE SB TO BE HOLY** in the Roman Catholic Church, to state officially that a dead person lived a holy life, usually as the first step towards sainthood **2. MAKE SB HAPPY** to make sb extremely happy (*literary*) [Mid-16thC. Directly or via French *béatifier* from ecclesiastical Latin *beatificare*, from Latin *beatificus* (see BEATIFIC).] —**beatification** /bi áttifi káysh'n/ *n.*

beating /beéting/ *n.* **1. REPEATED HITTING** an attack or punishment in which sb is repeatedly hit **2. DEFEAT** a severe defeat or setback, e.g. in a competition or in business ◇ **take some beating** to be difficult to improve on because of its excellence ○ *Her speech will take some beating.*

beating reed *n.* a reed in woodwind instruments that vibrates as air passes over it

beatitude /bi átti tyood/ *n.* (*literary*) **1. HEAVENLY HAPPINESS** the perfect happiness and inner peace supposed to be enjoyed by the soul in heaven **2. BLISS** extreme happiness and serenity [15thC. Directly or via French from the Latin stem *beatitud-*, from *beatus* 'blessed'.]

Beatitude *n.* **1.** BIBLE **STATEMENT OF THOSE WHO ARE BLESSED** each of the sayings of Jesus Christ in the Sermon on the Mount about the eight groups of people who will receive blessing in heaven (Matthew 5:3–11) **2.** CHR **TITLE OF NON-ORTHODOX BISHOP** a title given to a senior bishop in non-Orthodox churches of the eastern Mediterranean

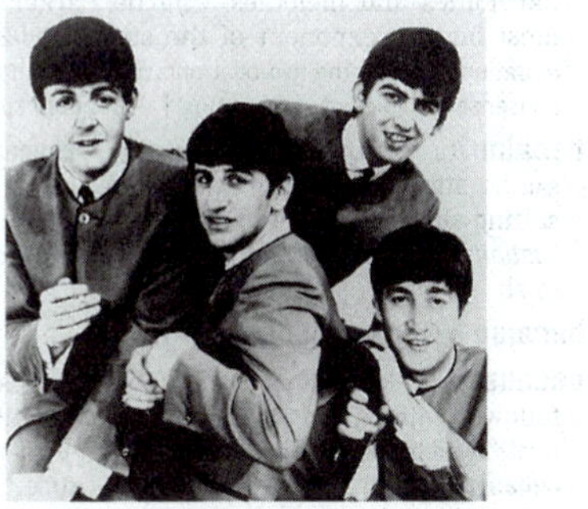

The Beatles

Beatles /beét'lz/ (1959–70) British pop music group. This group of musicians from Liverpool, Paul McCartney, John Lennon, George Harrison, and Ringo Starr, revolutionized popular music in the 1960s.

beatnik /beétnik/ *n.* a member of the Beat Generation of the 1950s

Beaton /beét'n/, **Sir Cecil** (1904–80) British photographer and designer. He was a fashion and high-society photographer. He also designed scenery and costumes for *My Fair Lady*, *Gigi*, and other productions. Full name **Sir Cecil Walter Hardy Beaton**

Beatrix /beé ətriks/, **Queen of the Netherlands.** (*b.* 1938). She acceded to the throne on the abdication of her mother, Queen Juliana, in 1980. Full name **Beatrix Wilhelmina Armgard**

Beatty /beéti/, **David, 1st Earl** (1871–1936) British admiral. He was appointed commander of the grand fleet after serving at the Battle of Jutland in 1916. He was First Sea Lord of the Admiralty (1919–27).

beat-up *adj.* **DILAPIDATED** in bad condition because of overuse (*informal*) ■ *n. ANZ* **SENSATIONALIZED JOURNALISM** a media report that has been sensationalized and made to seem more significant than it really is

beau /bō/ (*plural* **beaus** *or* **beaux** /bō, bōz/) *n.* **1. BOYFRIEND** a boyfriend or male admirer (*dated*) **2. FASHIONABLY DRESSED MAN** a man who is always smartly dressed in the most fashionable clothes (*archaic*) [Late 17thC. From French, from *beau* 'beautiful', from Latin *bellus* (see BEAUTY).]

Beaufort /bṓfərt/, **Henry, Cardinal** (1377–1447) English prelate and statesman. He became a cardinal in 1426 and in the 1430s was the real power behind the government of the young King Henry VI.

Beaufort scale /bṓfərt-/ *n.* an international scale of wind speeds indicated by numbers ranging from 0 for calm to 12 for hurricane. Each force is recognized by its effects on things such as flags and trees and on people and the surface of the sea. [Mid-19thC. Named after Sir Francis *Beaufort* (1774–1857), British admiral who devised the scale.]

Beaufort Sea section of the Arctic Ocean northwest of Canada and north of Alaska. Area: 450,000 sq.km/170,000 sq. mi. Depth: 4,682 m/15,360 ft.

beau geste /bō zhést/ (*plural* **beaux gestes** /bṓ zhést/) *n.* a kind or magnanimous act (*literary*) [Early 20thC. From French, literally 'fine gesture'.]

Beauharnais /bṓ aar náy/, **Alexandre, vicomte de** (1760–94) French soldier and politician. He embraced the French Revolution and became president of the Constituent Assembly (1791), but was later guillotined.

beau ideal /bṓ ee day áal/ *n.* sb's idea of perfection or beauty, or a perfect example of sth (*literary*) [Early 19thC. From French, literally 'ideal beauty' (but usually taken as meaning 'beautiful ideal').]

Beaujolais /bṓzhə lay/ (*plural* **-lais** /bṓzhə lay/) *n.* a fruity fairly light red or white wine produced in the Beaujolais district of the Burgundy region in central France

Beaujolais nouveau /-noo vṓ/ *n.* Beaujolais sold from November in the year of its production

Beaulieu /byóoli/ village in Hampshire, southern England, the site of the Montagu Motor Museum and the ruins of Beaulieu Abbey. Population: 1,200.

Beaumarchais /bṓ maar shay/, **Pierre Augustin Caron de** (1732–99) French dramatist. He wrote the comedies *The Barber of Seville* (1775) and *The Marriage of Figaro* (1784). These were made into operas by Rossini and Mozart, respectively. Born **Pierre Augustin Caron**

Beaumes-de-Venise /bṓm də və neéz/ *n.* a sweet fortified white wine made from the muscat grape in the area around Beaumes-de-Venise in the southern Rhône valley, France

beau monde /bṓ mónd/ *n.* the part of society made up of the richest and most fashionable people [Late 17thC. From French, literally 'beautiful world'.]

Beaumont /bṓ mont/, **Francis** (1584–1616) English dramatist. He co-wrote plays with John Fletcher, including *Philaster* (1610?) and *A King and No King* (1611).

Beaumont, William (1785–1853) US physician. His principal work was a study of the digestive system (1833).

beaut /byoot/ *n. ANZ, US* STH OUTSTANDING a fine or impressive thing (*informal*) ■ *adj., interj. ANZ* EXCELLENT outstanding or first-rate (*informal*) [Mid-19thC. Shortening of BEAUTY or BEAUTIFUL.]

beauteous /byoóti əss/ *adj.* beautiful to look at (*literary*) —**beauteously** *adv.* —**beauteousness** *n.*

beautician /byoo tísh'n/ *n. US* sb trained to give beauty treatments, e.g. application of makeup and facial treatments

beautiful /byoótəf'l/ *adj.* **1.** PLEASING TO THE SENSES very pleasing and impressive to listen to, touch, or especially to look at **2.** EXCELLENT very good or enjoyable —**beautifully** *adv.* —**beautifulness** *n.*

--- **WORD KEY: SYNONYMS** ---
See Synonyms at *good-looking*.

beautiful people *npl.* **1.** HIGH SOCIETY rich fashionable people **2.** PEOPLE PARADING THEIR ATTRACTIVENESS attractive people who like to show off their good looks **3.** in the 1960s, hippies collectively

beautify /byoóti fī/ (**-fies, -fying, -fied**) *vt.* to make sth pleasing and impressive to look at —**beautification** /byoótifi káysh'n/ *n.* —**beautifier** /byoóti fī ər/ *n.*

beauty /byoóti/ (*plural* **-ties**) *n.* **1.** PLEASING AND IMPRESSIVE QUALITIES the combination of qualities that make sth pleasing and impressive to listen to or touch, or especially to look at **2.** PLEASING PERSONAL APPEARANCE personal physical attractiveness, especially with regard to the use of cosmetics and other methods of enhancing it **3.** BEAUTIFUL WOMAN a beautiful woman or girl ○ *her reputation as a great beauty* **4.** FINE EXAMPLE very good, attractive, or impressive of its kind **5.** EXCELLENT ASPECT an attractive, useful, or satisfying feature ○ *Great fuel economy is one of the beauties of this vehicle.* [13thC. Via Old French *bealte* from the Vulgar Latin stem *bellitat-*, from Latin *bellus* 'handsome, fine', from *bonus* 'good'.]

--- **WORD KEY: CULTURAL NOTE** ---
Sleeping Beauty, a ballet by Russian composer Peter Ilich Tchaikovsky (1889). Based on Charles Perrault's fairy tale *La belle au bois dormant*, it tells the story of Princess Aurora, who is condemned to death by the wicked fairy Carabosse. Her sentence is commuted to a hundred years' sleep, from which she is eventually awakened by the handsome Prince Florimund.

beautybush /byoóti boosh/ *n.* a Chinese shrub of the honeysuckle family, grown for its pink flowers and fruit with hairy knobbly skin. Latin name: *Kolkwitzia amabilis*.

beauty mark *n. US* = beauty spot *n.* 2

beauty parlour *n.* = beauty salon

beauty quark *n.* = bottom quark

beauty queen *n.* a woman judged to be the most beautiful of all the candidates in a competition

beauty salon *n.* a business establishment where beauty treatments are provided, e.g. hair styling, facials, and manicures

beauty sleep *n.* deep restful sleep, especially before midnight, supposed to preserve youthful good looks (*informal*)

beauty spot *n.* **1.** POPULAR SCENIC PLACE a place that people often visit because of its attractive scenery **2.** SMALL NATURAL MARK ON FACE a mole or other small round blemish on sb's face **3.** DOT WORN ON THE FACE a small black or brown dot of silk or makeup on sb's face used to emphasize the skin's paleness or hide a blemish. Beauty spots were especially popular among aristocratic women in 18th-century Europe.

Beauvoir /bó vwaar/, **Simone de** (1908–86) French writer. She wrote the feminist classic *The Second Sex* (1949) and the novel *The Mandarins* (1954). She was the lifelong companion of Jean-Paul Sartre.

beaux plural of **beau**

beaver[1] /beévər/ *n.* **1.** (*plural* **-vers** *or* **-ver**) ZOOL FURRY FLAT-TAILED WATER ANIMAL a semiaquatic rodent that lives in North America, Europe, and Asia and has a broad flat tail and webbed hind feet. Beavers are noted for felling trees to build dams and partially

Simone de Beauvoir

Beaver

submerged dens called lodges. Genus: *Castor*. **2.** INDUST FUR FROM BEAVER the valuable fur of the beaver **3.** CLOTHES MAN'S FUR HAT a man's hat made of beaver fur, felt, or a fabric imitating beaver fur **4.** TEXTILES THICK FABRIC thick woollen or cotton fabric **5.** OFFENSIVE TERM a woman's outer sex organs and pubic hair (*slang taboo*) ■ *vi.* (**-vers, -vering, -vered**) WORK HARD AND CONTINUOUSLY to work hard with unflagging energy and attention (*informal*) [Old English *beofor*. Ultimately from an Indo-European word meaning 'brown animal'.]

beaver[2] /beévər/ *n.* the guard for the lower part of the face on a medieval helmet [15thC. From French *baviere*, originally 'child's bib', from *baver* 'to slaver'.]

Beaver /beévər/, **Beaver Scout** *n.* a member of the most junior branch of the Scout Association, for boys and girls aged between six and eight

beaverboard /beévər bawrd/ *n.* a thick board made of compressed wood fibres, used to make the ceilings and inner walls of buildings

Beaverbrook /beévər brook/, **Max Aitken, 1st Baron** (1879–1964) Canadian-born British newspaper owner and politician. His news empire included the *Daily Express*, the *Sunday Express*, and the *Evening Standard*. Full name **William Maxwell Aitken**

Beazley /beézli/, **Kim** (*b.* 1948) Australian politician. He became leader of the Australian Labor Party in 1996. Full name **Kim Christian Beazley**

Bebel /báyb'l/, **August** (1840–1913) German politician. He helped to found the German social democratic movement (1868) and wrote on socialism and the status of women. Full name **Ferdinand August Bebel**

bebop /beé bop/ *n.* fast jazz music with complex harmonies and melodies. Charlie Parker was the most famous exponent of the style. [Mid-20thC. An imitation of either the two-beat phrase of such music or the nonsense syllables of scat singing.] —**bebopper** *n.*

becalm /bi kaám/ (**-calms, -calming, -calmed**) *vt.* **1.** SAILING STOP A SAILING BOAT to cause a sailing boat or sailing ship to stop moving because of lack of wind (*usually passive*) **2.** SOOTHE SB to bring peace and quiet to sb

became past tense of **become**

because /bi kóz, -kəz/ *conj.* for the reason that follows [14thC. From the phrase *by cause* 'for the reason (that)', which was modelled on Old French *par chance*.] ◇ **because of** indicating the reason or cause

--- **WORD KEY: USAGE** ---
because, as, for, or **since**? *As* and *since* are used more often at the beginning of a sentence than *because*, and tend to be used when the reason is already well known

or when the reason is considered not as important as the main statement: *As you're only staying a little while, we'd better eat now. He refrained from comment, since he knew it might annoy his companions.* **Because** puts a greater emphasis on the cause: *He liked her because she was witty and lively.* **Because** and *for* are both used to introduce reasons that justify a statement as distinct from giving a reason for it: *You must have forgotten to invite them, because/for they didn't turn up.* **For** is never used at the beginning of a sentence. *As* can sometimes be understood to mean 'while' as well as 'because': *As Luisa went back to work, Tony stayed behind to look after the baby.* In these cases, it is better to avoid ambiguity and use either **because** or **while** as appropriate.

beccafico /békə feékō/ (*plural* **-cos**) *n.* = Orphean warbler [Mid-17thC. From Italian, literally 'fig-pecker', from *beccare* 'to peck' (from, ultimately, late Latin *beccus* 'beak', source of English *beak*) + *fico* 'fig'.]

béchamel sauce /báyshə mel-/ *n.* a sauce made from milk thickened and made rich with butter and flour, flavoured with onion, bay, and mace, and served hot with meat or fish [Late 18thC. Named after its inventor, Louis, Marquis de *Béchamel* (1630–1703), steward to Louis XIV of France.]

bêche-de-mer /bésh də máir/ (*plural* **bêches-de-mer** /bésh də máir/ *or* **bêche-de-mer**) *n.* ZOOL = trepang [Early 19thC. A pseudo-French word based on Portuguese *bicho do mar* (see BEACH-LA-MAR).]

Bechuanaland /béchoo aánə land/ former name for **Botswana** (until 1966)

beck[1] /bek/ *n. N England* a stream, especially a mountain stream [13thC. From Old Norse *bekkr*.]

beck[2] /bek/ *n.* a nod, wave, or similar gesture to attract attention (*literary*) [14thC. From the obsolete verb *beck* 'to beckon, bow', a shortening of BECKON.] ◇ **at sb's beck and call** always available and ready to carry out sb's wishes

Beckenbauer /békən bowər/, **Franz** (*b.* 1945) German footballer. An outstanding midfielder, he captained the West German World Cup championship team in 1974, and coached the national team to another World Cup win in 1990.

Becker /békər/, **Boris** (*b.* 1967) German tennis player. The youngest ever men's singles champion at Wimbledon (1985), he won again in 1986 and 1989.

becket /békit/ *n.* a rope with a knot at one end and a small loop or hook at the other, used for tying down loose equipment on a ship or boat [Mid-18thC. Origin unknown.]

Becket /békit/, **Thomas à, St** (1118?–70) English saint and martyr. He became Archbishop of Canterbury in 1162 and was assassinated by knights of Henry II. In 1155 he became the first Englishman to hold the office of Chancellor since the Norman Conquest. His strong views on religious prerogative brought him into conflict with Henry II.

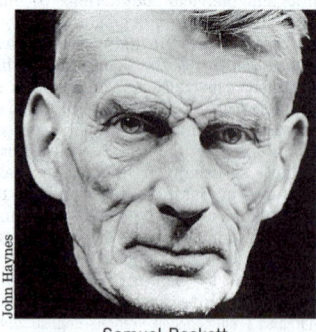
Samuel Beckett

Beckett, Samuel (1906–89) Irish writer. His bleak dramas of the absurd include *Waiting for Godot* (1954) and *Not I* (1973). He won a Nobel Prize in literature (1969). Beckett settled in Paris in 1937, and produced novels, plays, and poems in both English and French. Full name **Samuel Barclay Beckett**

Beckford /békfərd/, **William** (1760–1844) English writer and art collector. Best known for his Gothic novel, *Vathek: An Arabian Tale* (1787), he built a celebrated Gothic mansion at Fonthill Abbey (1816).

Beckmann /bék man/, **Max** (1884–1950) German painter. His expressionistic works captured the emotional climate of Germany after 1918.

beckon /békən/ (**-ons, -oning, -oned**) *vti.* **1. GESTURE TO SB TO COME** to signal to sb to approach with a movement of the hand or head **2. ATTRACT OR TEMPT** to be an attraction or temptation to sb (*literary*) [Old English *bēcnan*. Ultimately from the same prehistoric Germanic base as *beacon*.] —**beckoner** *n.* —**beckoningly** *adv.*

becloud /bi klówd/ (**-clouds, -clouding, -clouded**) *vt.* (*literary*) **1. COVER WITH CLOUD** to cover or conceal sth with cloud or mist **2. CONFUSE OR OBSCURE** to make sth confused or difficult to understand

become /bi kúm/ (**-comes, -coming, -came** /-káym/, **-come**) *v.* **1.** *vi.* **COME TO BE STH** to change or develop into sth ○ *The caterpillar will soon become a moth.* **2.** *vt.* **SUIT** to suit the appearance or personality of sb ○ *That colour really becomes you.* **3.** *vt.* **BE APPROPRIATE** to be an appropriate or socially acceptable thing for sb to do or say (*formal*) [Old English *becuman*]
become of *vt.* to happen to sb or sth

becoming /bi kúmming/ *adj.* **1. SHOWING SB TO ADVANTAGE** attractively suitable for sb's appearance **2. BEFITTING** appropriate or fitting for sb —**becomingly** *adv.* —**becomingness** *n.*

becquerel /békə rel/ *n.* the SI unit for measuring radioactivity, equal to the activity resulting from the decay of one nucleus of radioactive matter in one second. Symbol **Bq** [Late 19thC. Named after Alexandre Edmond *Becquerel* (1852–1908), French physicist.]

BECTU /bék too/ *abbr.* Broadcasting, Entertainment, and Cinematograph Technicians Union

bed /bed/ *n.* **1. FURNITURE ON WHICH TO SLEEP** a piece of furniture on which to sleep, usually consisting of a rectangular frame with a mattress on top **2. MATTRESS** a mattress, especially with its coverings **3. SLEEP** sleep or rest in bed, or the time for this **4. PLACE FOR SLEEPING** a place in which to sleep, or an object on which to sleep ○ *looking for a bed for the night* **5. ACCOMMODATION FOR GUEST OR PATIENT** a place for one person to stay or sleep as a guest in a hotel or a patient in a hospital **6.** GARDENING **PATCH OF SOIL** an area of soil prepared for plants, especially flowers, or an area where particular plants are growing ○ *a rose bed* **7.** GEOG **GROUND UNDER WATER** the ground at the bottom of the sea, a river, or a lake **8. STATE OF INTIMACY** the state of sexual intimacy associated with being in bed with sb ○ *the marriage bed* **9. SURFACE ON WHICH TO BUILD** a prepared surface on which sth is built or laid, e.g. the foundation of a road or a railway **10.** COOK **LAYER OF FOOD** a layer of food on which another item of food is placed for serving **11. AREA OF SEA WITH SHELLFISH** an area of the sea, a river, or a lake, where a particular kind of shellfish is found or cultivated ○ *oyster beds* **12.** GEOL **LAYER OF ROCK** a layer of rock, normally sedimentary, that is generally homogeneous and was deposited more or less continuously without erosion ■ *v.* (**beds, bedding, bedded**) **1.** *vt.* **FIX INTO SURROUNDING SURFACE** to embed sth firmly in a surrounding mass of a substance such as rock or concrete **2.** *vt.* **HAVE SEXUAL INTERCOURSE WITH SB** to have sexual intercourse with sb (*informal*) **3.** *vti.* **FORM LAYER** to arrange sth, or be arranged, in a layer or stratum [Old English *bedd*, from a prehistoric Germanic word meaning 'dig'] ◇ **a bed of nails** an extremely difficult situation or existence ◇ **go to bed with sb** to have sexual intercourse with sb ◇ **put sth to bed** to finish work on a newspaper or magazine so it is ready to go to press ◇ **get out of bed on the wrong side** to be in an irritable or angry mood right from the start of the day

WORD KEY: ORIGIN

Bed meant both 'sleeping place' and 'garden plot' in Old English, and if the latter is the original sense, it could mean that the word comes ultimately from a prehistoric Germanic ancestor meaning 'dig' (which is also the ancestor of English *fossil*), and that the underlying notion of a **bed** was originally of a sleeping place dug or scraped in the ground, like an animal's lair.

bed down *v.* **1.** *vi.* **GO TO BED** to settle down somewhere, not usually in a proper bed, ready for sleep **2.** *vt.* **PUT TO BED** to put a person to bed or an animal in a place with bedding for the night **3.** *vi.* **SETTLE INTO POSITION** to sink and settle into position or become flatter and denser
bed in *vti.* to fit sth firmly into place, or fit firmly into place
bed out *vt.* to put young plants raised indoors into their final growing position outside

BEd /bee ed/ *abbr.* Bachelor of Education

bed and board *n.* accommodation and meals provided for sb

bed and breakfast *n.* **1. ROOM AND BREAKFAST** overnight accommodation and breakfast provided for paying guests **2. GUESTHOUSE** a small hotel or, more often, a private home that offers overnight accommodation and breakfast for paying guests ■ *adj.* STOCK EXCH **INVOLVING SELLING THEN QUICK REACQUISITION** used to describe transactions involving selling shares late one day and buying them back for less the next morning, to create an apparent financial loss for tax purposes (*informal*)

bedaub /bi dáwb/ (**-daubs, -daubing, -daubed**) *vt.* to smear a surface thickly or carelessly with sth that spoils it or makes it dirty (*literary*)

bedazzle /bi dázz'l/ (**-zles, -zling, -zled**) *vt.* (*literary*) **1. IMPRESS SB GREATLY** to astonish sb by being immediately impressive (*usually passive*) **2. BLIND WITH LIGHT** to make sb temporarily unable to see by shining a bright light

bed bath *n.* an all-over wash for sb confined to bed. US term **sponge bath**

bedbug /béd bug/ *n.* a small wingless bloodsucking insect that infests the bedding and furnishings of dirty houses and the nests of mammals. Family: Cimicidae.

bedclothes /béd klōthz, -klōz/ *npl.* the sheets, blankets, duvet, and any other similar coverings on a bed

beddable /béddəb'l/ *adj.* considered attractive enough to make a good sexual partner (*informal*)

bedder /béddər/ *n.* **1.** EDUC **COLLEGE CLEANER** sb who is employed to clean students' rooms in the colleges of Cambridge University **2.** GARDENING = **bedding plant**

bedding /bédding/ *n.* **1. BED COVERINGS** the coverings, e.g. sheets, quilts, and blankets, and the mattress and pillows used to prepare a bed **2. STH USED AS BED** sth used to make a bed **3. BED FOR ANIMALS** material such as straw put down for animals to lie on **4.** BUILDING **UNDER LAYER** a layer of material put down under sth else, especially to serve as a foundation **5.** GEOL **ARRANGEMENT OF ROCK STRATA** the arrangement of a group of rock strata, or beds, in a particular area or outcrop

bedding plant *n.* a plant suitable for planting in a flower bed for one season's display

Bede /beed/, **Baeda** /beedə/, **St** (673?–735) English theologian and historian. He wrote many grammatical and historical works, including his *Ecclesiastical History of the English People* (completed in 731). Known as the **Venerable Bede**

bedeck /bi dék/ (**-decks, -decking, -decked**) *vt.* to make sth look pretty or festive, especially by decorating it with colourful flags, ribbons, or streamers (*literary*)

bedevil /bi dévv'l/ (**-ils, -illing, -illed**) *vt.* to be a continual source of problems or irritation to sth or sb —**bedevilment** *n.*

bedew /bi dyoō/ (**-dews, -dewing, -dewed**) *vt.* to wet or cover sth with dew or drops of liquid (*literary*)

bedfellow /béd felō/ *n.* **1. ASSOCIATE** sb who or sth that becomes paired or allied with sb or sth else **2. SB WHO SHARES BED** sb who sleeps in the same bed as sb else (*archaic*)

Bedford /bédfərd/ market town on the River Ouse in Bedfordshire, south-central England. Population: 73,917 (1991).

Bedford cord *n.* a heavy ribbed fabric resembling corduroy

Bedfordshire /bédfərdshər/ county in central England that contains the unitary authority of Luton. Population: 543,100 (1994). Area: 1,235 sq. km/477 sq. mi.

bedhead /béd hed/ *n.* the upper end of a bed, often with a headboard or rail

bed-hopping *n.* casual sex with successive partners (*informal*)

bedim /bi dím/ (**-dims, -dimming, -dimmed**) *vt.* (*literary*) **1. MAKE LESS PERCEPTIVE** to make the eyes or mind less able to perceive things clearly **2. MAKE INDISTINCT** to make sth appear less bright or distinct

bed jacket *n.* a woman's short light jacket worn over a nightdress when sitting up in bed

bedlam /bédləm/ *n.* **1. CHAOS** a place or situation full of noise, frenzied activity, and confusion **2. PSYCHIATRIC HOSPITAL** a psychiatric hospital (*archaic*) [15thC. Alteration of BETHLEHEM.]

bed linen *n.* the sheets, pillowcases, and other fabric coverings that go on a bed

Bedlington terrier /bédlingtən-/, **Bedlington** *n.* a dog belonging to a breed of English terriers that have a tapering head and fleecy coat that makes them look similar to lambs [Mid-19thC. Named after the Northern English town of *Bedlington*, where this breed was developed in the early 19thC.]

bed moulding *n.* in classical architecture, the lowest section of a cornice, protruding less than the topmost part

Bedouin /béddoo in/ (*plural* **-ins** *or* **-in**), **Beduin** (*plural* **-ins** *or* **-in**) *n.* a nomadic Arab of the desert regions of Arabia and North Africa [15thC. Via Old French *beduin* from, ultimately, Arabic *badw* 'desert, nomadic desert people'.] —**Bedouin** *adj.*

bedpan /béd pan/ *n.* a shallow container into which a sick or frail person can urinate or defecate while lying in bed

bedplate /béd playt/ *n.* a heavy metal base or platform to which the frame of an engine or machine is attached

bedpost /béd pōst/ *n.* one of the posts at the corners of a bed, especially a four-poster bed

bedraggled /bi drágg'ld/ *adj.* wet, dirty, and unkempt, or with hair or clothes in this state

bedrail /béd rayl/ *n.* a rail at the head, foot, or side of a bed

bed rest *n.* staying in bed to rest and recover when not well

bedridden /béd rid'n/ *adj.* forced to remain in bed because of illness, weakness, or injury [Old English *bedrida*, literally 'bed-rider', hence 'sb who is carried about in a bed']

bedrock /béd rok/ *n.* **1.** GEOL **UNDERLYING ROCK** the solid rock beneath a layer of soil, rock fragments, or gravel **2. UNDERLYING FACTS OR PRINCIPLES** the facts or principles on which sth is based

bedroll /béd rōl/ *n.* a roll of bedding carried by sb who is hiking or camping

bedroom /béd room, -rŏom/ *n.* **ROOM FOR SLEEPING** a room that has a bed in it and is used mainly for sleeping ■ *adj.* **FEATURING SEX** involving, depicting, or suggesting sexual activity ○ *a bedroom comedy*

beds *abbr.* bedrooms (*used in advertisements*)

Beds. /bedz/ *abbr.* Bedfordshire

bedside /béd sīd/ *n.* the side of a bed, or the space next to it —**bedside** *adj.*

bedside manner *n.* a doctor's way of talking to and dealing with patients

bedsitter /béd sitər, -síttər/, **bedsit** /béd sit/ *n.* a combined bedroom and living room, especially one that is rented and serves as sb's residence [*Sitter* formed from SITTING ROOM + -ER]

bedsock /béd sok/ *n.* either of a pair of socks that are worn to keep the feet warm in bed

bedsore /béd sawr/ *n.* an ulcer on the skin caused by pressure and friction from bedding when sb is confined to bed for a long time

bedspread /béd spred/ *n.* a decorative covering placed on top of bedclothes

bedstead /béd sted/ *n.* the structural framework of a bed, excluding the mattress and coverings [*Stead* because it originally denoted the place where the bed stood]

bedtime /béd tīm/ *n.* the time when sb normally goes to bed

Beduin *n., adj.* = Bedouin

bedwarmer /béd wawrmər/ *n.* a covered metal container for hot coals, formerly used to warm a bed

bed-wetting *n.* accidental urination in bed during sleep (*especially of children*) —**bedwetter** *n.*

Bee (life size ×2)

bee /bee/ *n.* **1.** HONEY-MAKING INSECT a flying insect with a furry body that makes a buzzing sound as it flies. Some species of bees have stings, and some live in hives and produce honey. Superfamily: Apoidea. ◊ **bumblebee, honeybee 2.** US GATHERING FOR ACTIVITY AND SOCIALIZING a gathering at which people combine working together at a particular activity or having a friendly competition with socializing ○ *a sewing bee* ○ *a quilting bee* [Old English *bēo* from a prehistoric Germanic word]

Beeb /beeb/ *n.* the BBC (*informal humorous*) [Mid-20thC. Representing the first three sounds.]

bee balm *n.* = bergamot

beebread /bee bred/ *n.* a yellow-brown pollen stored by bees and mixed with honey as food for their larvae

beech /beech/ *n.* **1.** TREES DECIDUOUS TREE a tall tree found in temperate regions that has smooth grey bark, glossy leaves, and nuts enclosed in spiny cases. Genus: *Fagus*. **2.** INDUST BEECH WOOD the wood of the beech tree, used especially for furniture [Old English *bēce* from a prehistoric Germanic word]

Beecham /beechəm/, **Sir Thomas** (1879–1961) British conductor and impresario. He founded the London Philharmonic Orchestra (1932) and the Royal Philharmonic Orchestra (1946), and was musical director of Covent Garden (1932–39).

beech marten *n.* = stone marten

beech mast *n.* the fruits and seeds of beech trees

beechnut /beech nut/ *n.* the small triangular hard edible fruit of the beech tree

beeda /beedə/ *n.* a combination of betel leaf and areca nuts, eaten in India after a meal [Mid-20thC. From Hindi.]

bee-eater *n.* a small brightly coloured bird found in Europe and Asia that preys on insects. Family: Meropidae.

beef /beef/ *n.* **1.** FOOD MEAT FROM CATTLE meat from a cow, heifer, bull, or bullock **2.** (*plural* **beeves**) AGRIC ANIMAL GIVING BEEF a cow, heifer, bull, or bullock being reared for meat **3.** STRENGTH muscular strength or effort (*informal*) **4.** COMPLAINT a complaint (*slang*) ■ *vi.* (**beefs, beefing, beefed**) COMPLAIN to complain about sth (*slang*) [12thC. Via Anglo-Norman *boef* from the stem of Latin *bos* 'ox' (source of English *bovine*).]
beef up *vt.* to make sth stronger or more effective (*informal*) [From the idea of adding muscle in the same way as fattening up cattle for meat] —**beefed-up** *adj.*

beefalo /beefə lō/ (*plural* **-lo** or **-loes**) *n.* a cross between the North American bison and domestic cattle that is raised for its resistance to disease and its lean meat [Late 20thC. Blend of BEEF and BUFFALO.]

beef bourguignon /-báwr geen yoN/ *n.* a rich French stew consisting of chunks of beef braised in red wine, with carrots, onions, mushrooms, and sometimes bacon [*Bourguignon* from French, 'of Burgundy']

beefburger /beef burgər/ *n.* = hamburger

beefcake /beef kayk/ *n.* muscular men or pictures of them, considered from the point of view of their physical appearance (*informal*) [Modelled on CHEESECAKE]

Beefeater: A Yeoman of the Guard at the Tower of London, with Tower Bridge in the background

beefeater /beef eetər/ *n.* one of the Yeomen of the Guard, a group who act as warders of the Tower of London wearing a uniform of Tudor dress

bee fly *n.* a fly that resembles a bee, eats pollen and nectar, and whose larvae develop as parasites on insect larvae. Family: Bombyliidae.

beefsteak fungus /beef stayk-/, **beefsteak mushroom** *n.* an edible bracket fungus with a large reddish cap that grows especially on oak and ash trees. Latin name: *Fistulina hepatica*. [Because its cap resembles a beef steak]

beefsteak tomato *n.* US = beef tomato [From its colour and density]

beef stroganoff /beef stróggə nof/ *n.* a dish consisting of thin strips of sautéed beef cooked with onions and mushrooms in a sour cream sauce [Named in honour of Count Paul *Stroganoff*, a 19thC Russian diplomat]

beef tea *n.* a drink made by boiling beef to extract the juices, formerly given to invalids as a digestible form of nourishment

beef tomato *n.* a large firm-fleshed tomato. US term **beefsteak tomato**

beef Wellington *n.* a dish consisting of a fillet of beef, covered in pâté de foie gras, wrapped in pastry, and baked

beefwood /beef wood/ *n.* **1.** INDUST HARD REDDISH WOOD a hard red-coloured wood used in construction and cabinet-making **2.** TREES AUSTRALIAN EVERGREEN TREE an Australian tree that produces beefwood. Genus: *Casuarina*.

beefy /beefi/ (**-ier, -iest**) *adj.* **1.** MUSCULAR strong and muscular **2.** POWERFUL having strength, power, or substance (*informal*) ○ *a novel with a really beefy plot* **3.** LIKE BEEF containing, produced by, or resembling beef —**beefily** *adv.* —**beefiness** *n.*

bee glue *n.* = propolis

beehive /bee hīv/ *n.* **1.** HIVE FOR BEES a structure housing a colony of bees **2.** TALL HAIRSTYLE a hairstyle for women, popular around 1960, in which the hair is arranged in a high rounded shape on top of the head ■ *adj.* BEEHIVE-SHAPED shaped like a beehive, with a round base rising in a cone to a domed top

Beehive /bee hīv/ *n.* NZ the dome-shaped Parliament building in Wellington, New Zealand

beehive house *n.* a type of round prehistoric house with a domed roof

beekeeper /bee keepər/ *n.* sb who keeps bees in hives for the purpose of producing honey or pollinating crops —**beekeeping** *n.*

bee killer *n.* = robber fly

beeline /bee līn/ *n.* a very direct line, path, or other course from one point to another [From the belief that bees return to their hives in a straight line]

Beelzebub /bi élzi bub/ *n.* the Devil, or one of the chief devils in hell [Pre-12thC. Via Latin from Hebrew *ba'al zebub*, literally 'Lord of Flies', a Philistine god.]

been past participle of **be** ◊ **been there, done that (bought the T-shirt)** used to indicate sb's blasé attitude (*informal humorous*)

Beenleigh /beenli/ town in southeastern Queensland, Australia, directly south of Brisbane. Population: 16,387 (1991).

bee orchid *n.* a European orchid with a flower that looks like a bee. Latin name: *Ophrys apifera*.

beep /beep/ *n.* SHORT HIGH NOISE a short high-pitched noise emitted as a signal by a piece of electronic equipment or the horn of a vehicle ■ *v.* **1.** *vti.* MAKE BEEP to make a beep, or cause a vehicle horn or other device to make a beep **2.** *vt.* SIGNAL WITH CAR HORN to signal to sb by using the horn of a vehicle [Early 20thC. An imitation of the sound.]

beeper /beepər/ *n.* = pager (*informal*)

bee plant *n.* any plant that is particularly attractive to bees

beer /beer/ *n.* **1.** DRINK BREWED FROM MALT a typically bitter-tasting alcoholic drink brewed by fermenting malt with sugar and yeast and flavouring it with hops **2.** DRINK OF BEER a drink or glass of beer **3.** HERBAL DRINK a fizzy or slightly fermented drink made from, or flavoured with, the roots, leaves, or seeds of a plant [Old English *bēor*. Ultimately from late Latin *biber* 'drink', from *bibere* 'to drink' (source of English *imbibe* and *beverage*).]

beer and skittles *n.* pleasure and amusement (*informal*)

beer belly *n.* an extended stomach often associated with having drunk too much beer (*slang*)

Beerbohm /beer bōm/, **Sir Max** (1872–1956) British writer and caricaturist. He wrote *Zuleika Dobson* (1911), a satire on Oxford undergraduate life, and much drama criticism. He also drew witty caricatures of leading literary and political figures. Full name **Sir Henry Maximilian Beerbohm**. Known as the **Incomparable Max**

beer garden *n.* an open space or garden, often attached to a pub or similar establishment, where beer and other alcoholic drinks can be purchased and drunk in the open air

beer gut *n.* = beer belly (*slang*)

Beersheba /beer sheebə/ city on the edge of the Negev Desert, southwest of Jerusalem, Israel. In biblical times it was in the extreme southern part of Palestine. Population: 156,500 (1997).

beery /beeri/ (**-ier, -iest**) *adj.* **1.** SLIGHTLY INEBRIATED typical of sb who is slightly inebriated from having drunk too much beer **2.** LIKE BEER smelling or tasting of beer —**beerily** *adv.* —**beeriness** *n.*

bee's knees *npl.* sb or sth considered outstanding and wonderful (*dated informal*) [Modelled on CAT'S WHISKERS]

beestings /beestingz/ *n.* the first milk secreted by a mammal, especially a cow or goat, after it has given birth [Old English *bȳsting*. Ultimately from a prehistoric Germanic word of unknown origin.]

bee-stung *adj.* full and rounded, as if stung by a bee ○ *bee-stung lips*

beeswax /beez waks/ *n.* **1.** WAX MADE BY BEES the dark yellow substance secreted by honeybees and used for building honeycombs **2.** COMMERCIALLY PROCESSED BEESWAX wax produced by bees that has been commercially processed for use in furniture polishes,

Beet

candles, and crayons ■ *vt.* (**-waxes, -waxing, -waxed**) **POLISH WITH BEESWAX** to polish sth with beeswax

beeswing /béez wing/ *n.* a thin shiny sediment that forms in port and some other wines when they are kept for a long time after bottling

beet /beet/ *n.* **1. PLANT WITH SWOLLEN ROOT** a plant with a large swollen root. Some types are eaten cooked, others are fed to animals, and one type yields sugar. Genus: *Beta.* ◊ **beetroot, spinach beet, sugar beet, mangelwurzel 2.** *US* = **beetroot** [Old English *bēte*, related to German *Bete*. Ultimately from Latin *beta*, perhaps of Celtic origin.]

Ludwig van Beethoven

Beethoven /báyt hōvan/, **Ludwig van** (1770–1827) German composer. His symphonies and chamber pieces reached new levels of expressivity, inspiring the romantics. He composed nine symphonies, 32 piano sonatas, and 16 string quartets, among many other works.

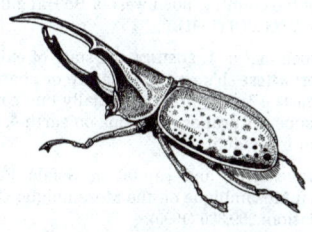

Beetle

beetle[1] /béet'l/ *n.* **1. INSECTS HARD-BACKED INSECT** an insect belonging to a large order characterized by a modified outer pair of wings that form a hard covering for the inner pair. Order: Coleoptera. **2.** **GAME DICE GAME** a game in which players attempt to draw or assemble a complete beetle-shape by throwing a dice and drawing in or collecting the part corresponding to the number thrown ■ *vi.* (**-tles, -tling, -tled**) **GO QUICKLY** to go somewhere quickly (*informal*) [Old English *bitula, bitela,* from *bītan* 'to bite', from its biting mouthparts]

beetle[2] /béet'l/ *n.* **1. BUILDING LARGE MALLET** a large tool with a long handle and a heavy wooden head, used for driving in stakes, ramming, and pounding **2.** **TEXTILES TEXTILE-FINISHING MACHINE** a machine that beats cloth to give it a smooth finish ■ *vt.* (**-tles, -tling, -tled**) **TEXTILES FINISH CLOTH** to give a finishing treatment to cloth with a beetle [Old English *bētel, bīetel.* Ultimately from a prehistoric Germanic word.]

beetle[3] /béet'l/ *vi.* (**-tles, -tling, -tled**) **OVERHANG** to overhang or jut out (*literary*) ■ *adj.* **JUTTING OUT** jutting out and shaggy (*literary*) ○ *beetle brows* [14thC. Of unknown origin: perhaps from the resemblance of a beetle's antennae to eyebrows.] —**beetling** *adj.*

beetle-browed *adj.* having eyebrows that are thick and bushy, or that jut out over the eyes

beetle-crushers *npl.* heavy boots, or shoes with thick soles (*informal*)

beetle drive *n.* a social gathering to play the game of beetle

Beeton /béet'n/, **Isabella Mary** (1836–65) British cookery writer. Her *Book of Household Management*

(1859–60) is one of the most influential cookery books ever written. Born **Isabella Mary Mayson.** Known as **Mrs Beeton**

beetroot /beet root/ *n.* **1. PLANT WITH EDIBLE RED ROOT** a beet plant with a round dark-red edible root. Latin name: *Beta vulgaris.* US term **beet** *n.* **2** **2. RED VEGETABLE** the root of the beetroot plant cooked and usually eaten cold as a salad vegetable or pickled. US term **beet**

beet sugar *n.* sugar that has been extracted from sugar beet

beeves plural of **beef** *n.* **2**

BEF the British Army that served overseas during World War I and World War II. Abbr of **British Expeditionary Force**

befall /bi fáwl/ (**-falls, -falling, -fell** /bi fél/, **-fallen** /bi fáwlən/) *vti.* to happen, or happen to sb, especially through the unexpected workings of chance or fate (*archaic or literary*)

befit /bi fít/ (**-fits, -fitting, -fitted**) *vt.* to be suitable or appropriate for sb or sth —**befitting** *adj.* —**befittingly** *adv.*

befog /bi fóg/ (**-fogs, -fogging, -fogged**) *vt.* (*literary*) **1.** **CONFUSE** to make sb or sth vague or confused **2.** **COVER WITH FOG** to make sth difficult to see or see through because it is covered in fog

before /bi fáwr/ **CORE MEANING**: a grammatical word indicating that a point in time, event, or situation precedes another in a sequence ○ (prep) *We try all of the products before deciding to stock them.* ○ (conj) *We lost a lot of manufacturing jobs in the 12 years before I became president.* ○ (conj) *She died at the hospital before her parents could reach her side.* ○ (adv) *He has had this nightmare before.* **1.** *prep.* **IN THE PRESENCE OF** in the presence of a person or body of people ○ *spoke before a huge crowd* **2.** *prep.* **WITH MORE IMPORTANCE THAN** indicating that one thing is preferable to or more important than another ○ *Their needs come before yours.* **3.** *prep.* **INDICATES LOCATION** located close to sth but just ahead of it **4.** *prep.* **AHEAD OF** stretching ahead of sb **5.** *prep., conj., adv.* **EARLIER** earlier than a particular date, time, or event **6.** *prep., conj.* **INDICATES SEQUENCE** used to indicate a sequence of actions, one preceding the other and closely connected with it **7.** *adv.* **PREVIOUSLY** on a previous occasion **8.** *conj.* **RATHER THAN** used to indicate that sb would prefer to do one thing rather than what they consider to be a worse thing ○ *I'll die before I tell you anything about it.* [Old English *beforan.* Ultimately from a prehistoric Germanic word that is also the ancestor of English *for,* which originally meant 'before'.]

beforehand /bi fáwr hand/ *adv.* used to indicate that a situation, action, or event happens ahead of time or in advance of sth

beforementioned /bi fáwr mensh'nd/ *adj.* that has been mentioned before (*formal*)

befoul /bi fówl/ (**-fouls, -fouling, -fouled**) *vt.* to make sth dirty or impure, or diminish sb or sth's moral purity or reputation (*archaic or literary*) —**befoulment** *n.*

befriend /bi frénd/ (**-friends, -friending, -friended**) *vt.* to be friendly to sb, especially to sb who has no friends and needs help —**befriender** *n.*

befuddle /bi fúdd'l/ (**-dles, -dling, -dled**) *vt.* to make sb confused or perplexed —**befuddled** *adj.* —**befuddlement** *n.*

beg /beg/ (**begs, begging, begged**) *v.* **1.** *vti.* **ASK WITH EMOTION** to ask sb for sth in a very intense, humble, or even humiliating way **2.** *vti.* **ASK FOR CHARITY** to ask people for gifts of money or food, especially in the street **3.** *vi.* **SIT UP AND ASK FOR FOOD** to ask for food by performing an action that has been previously taught, especially, for a dog, by sitting up and holding out the front legs **4.** *vt.* **EVADE** to avoid answering or dealing with a point, especially by assuming that it has already been dealt with ○ *beg the question* [Probably from Old English *bedecian,* ultimately from a prehistoric Germanic base that is also the ancestor of English *bid*]

― **WORD KEY: USAGE** ―

Begging the question To *beg the question* is often used to mean 'to raise the question' or 'to avoid a direct answer', since both meanings are consistent with the form of the

idiom. But the original and more correct meaning of this idiom relates to the validity of a proposition that is used as a basis of argument. For example, in an argument about the effect on the environment of gas emissions from road traffic, the proposition that a higher tax on vehicles would contribute to cleaner air begs the question, because it needs to be proved that raising taxes would result in fewer road users. The fallacy implied by the notion of begging the question usually involves the omission of one stage in an argument, or a questionable assumption of its validity.

beg off *vi.* to ask to be excused from doing sth

begad /bi gád/ *interj.* used to add emphasis to sth that is said (*archaic*) [Late 16thC. Alteration of 'by God' to avoid offence.]

began past tense of **begin**

beget /bi gét/ (**-gets, -getting, -got** /-gót/ *or* **-gat** /-gát/, **-gotten** /-gótt'n/ *or* **-got**) *vt.* **1.** **FATHER** to be the father of a child (*archaic*) **2.** **CAUSE** to be the cause of sth [Old English *begietan* 'to get'] —**begetter** *n.*

beggar /béggər/ *n.* **1.** **SB WHO BEGS** sb who begs for money or food from strangers **2.** **VERY POOR PERSON** sb who is very poor **3.** **PERSON** a person (*informal*) ○ *You lucky beggar!* ■ *vt.* (**-gars, -garing, -gared**) **1.** **MAKE POOR** to make sb poor (*literary*) **2.** **BE BEYOND SCOPE OF** to be so extraordinary as to make description or belief impossible

― **WORD KEY: CULTURAL NOTE** ―

The Beggar's Opera, a ballad-opera by John Gay with music selected and arranged by John Christopher Pepus (1728). Set to traditional melodies, it tells of the relationship between highwayman Macheath and Polly Peachum, daughter of a gang leader. The work is at once a vivid depiction of London lowlife, a satire on political corruption, and a parody of fashionable Italian operas.

beggarly /béggərli/ *adj.* insufficient and showing meanness —**beggarliness** *n.*

beggar-my-neighbour *n.* **CARD GAME FOR TWO** a simple card game for two players in which cards are won and lost until one person holds them all ■ *adj.* **RUTHLESSLY ACQUISITIVE** involving a ruthless attitude towards another person, organization, or country, especially as regards taking over resources

beggary /béggəri/ *n.* a state of extreme poverty

begging bowl *n.* a bowl carried by sb who begs to collect gifts of food or money

begging letter *n.* a letter written to sb who is rich or famous, asking for money or help

begin /bi gín/ (**-gins, -ginning, -gan** /-gán/, **-gun** /-gún/) *v.* **1.** *vti.* **START** to do sth that was not being done before ○ *People began to leave.* **2.** *vti.* **HAVE AS ITS STARTING POINT** to have as its starting point, first action, or first part, or be the starting point or first part of sth ○ *The story begins with a birthday party.* **3.** *vti.* **COME OR BRING INTO BEING** to come into existence, or cause sth to come into existence or take place ○ *The business began as a two-person operation.* **4.** *vt.* **UNDERTAKE FOR FIRST TIME** to undertake, use, or give attention to sth for the first time **5.** *vti.* **START TO SPEAK** to start to say sth, or start by saying sth **6.** *vt.* **BE CAPABLE OF** to be able to succeed in accomplishing a particular task (*used in negative statements*) ○ *The salary doesn't even begin to meet her expectations* ○ *I couldn't begin to explain how awful it was* [Old English *beginnan.* Ultimately from a prehistoric Germanic word that is also the ancestor of German and Dutch *beginnen*.]

Begin /báygin/, **Menachem** (1913–92) Russian-born Israeli statesman. As prime minister of Israel (1977–83), he shared the 1978 Nobel Peace Prize with Egyptian president Anwar al-Sadat and signed the first-ever Israeli treaty with an Arab state (1979). Full name **Menachem Wolfovitch Begin**

beginner /bi gínnər/ *n.* sb who has just started to do or learn sth

― **WORD KEY: SYNONYMS** ―

beginner, apprentice, greenhorn, novice, trainee, tyro **CORE MEANING**: a person who has not acquired the necessary experience or skills to do sth

beginner the most general term and one of the most informal, without the negative connotations of some of the other terms; **apprentice** a somewhat technical term, usually without negative connotations, indicating sb who is being taught the skills of a trade by sb fully trained; **greenhorn** a derogatory term used to emphasize the lack of experience and gullibility of sb who has just started sth; **novice** a derogatory term that emphasizes the general ineptness of sb who has just started sth; **trainee** a more general term than *apprentice* but one that also suggests that sb has started on a training programme of some kind to learn the skills of a job; **tyro** a more derogatory word than *beginner*, used to emphasize the rawness and inexperience of sb.

beginner's luck *n.* early success that seems inconsistent with sb's lack of experience

beginning /bi gínning/ *n.* **1. FIRST PART** the first part or early stages of sth **2. START** the point in time or space at which sth starts, comes into existence, or is first encountered ■ **beginnings** *npl.* **EARLY CONDITIONS** the conditions in which sth or sb starts

begone /bi gón/ *interj.* used to tell sb to go away (*archaic*)

begonia /bi gṓni ə/ *n.* a widely grown houseplant and garden plant that has round brightly coloured flowers and ragged-edged leaves. Genus: *Begonia.* [Mid-18thC. From Modern Latin, named after Michel *Bégon*, (1638–1710), Governor of French Canada and patron of botany.]

begorra /bi górrə/ *interj. Ireland* used as an exclamation or a mild oath (*archaic*) [Mid-19thC. Alteration of 'by God' to avoid offence.]

begot past tense, past participle of **beget**

begotten past participle of **beget**

begrime /bi grīm/ (**-grimes, -griming, -grimed**) *vt.* to cover sth with grime (*literary*)

begrudge /bi grúj/ (**-grudges, -grudging, -grudged**) *vt.* **1. RESENT STH SB HAS** to resent the fact that sb has sth ○ *begrudged me my success* **2. NOT WANT TO GIVE** to be unwilling to give or pay sth

begrudging /bi grújjing/ *adj.* showing unwillingness to give sb sth or to let sb be admired or praised —**begrudgingly** *adv.*

beguile /bi gīl/ (**-guiles, -guiling, -guiled**) *vt.* **1. CHARM** to win and hold sb's attention, interest, or devotion **2. DECEIVE** to mislead or deceive sb (*literary*) **3. CHEAT** to rob sb of sth (*literary*) **4. PASS** to pass time in a pleasant way (*literary*) [13thC. *guile* in the obsolete sense 'to trick'.] —**beguilement** *n.* —**beguiler** *n.*

beguiling /bi gīling/ *adj.* having the power to gain people's interest or devotion —**beguilingly** *adv.*

beguine /bi géen/ *n.* a ballroom dance similar to the rumba, originating in the West Indies [Early 20thC. Via French *béguine* from *béguin* 'flirtation', originally 'hood', from *beguine* 'lay sister in the Netherlands', from, ultimately, Middle Dutch *beggaert*, literally 'sb who rattles off prayers'.]

begum /báygəm, bée-/ *n.* **1. WOMAN'S TITLE** a title of respect for a woman in some Islamic communities **2. IMPORTANT WOMAN** a woman of high rank in some Islamic communities [Mid-17thC. Via Urdu from East Turkic, literally 'my mistress'.]

begun past participle of **begin**

behalf /bi haáf/ *n.* ◇ **in sb's behalf** *US* on sb's behalf ◇ **on sb's behalf** for sb's benefit or support, or in sb's best interests. ○ *We chose James to speak on our behalf.*

Behan /bée ən/, **Brendan** (1923–64) Irish playwright and author He wrote *The Quare Fellow* (1954), *The Hostage* (1958), and the autobiographical novel *Borstal Boy* (1958). His alcoholism led to his premature death. Full name **Brendan Francis Behan**

behave /bi háyv/ (**-haves, -having, -haved**) *vi.* **1. ACT** to act in a particular way that expresses general character, state of mind, or response to a situation or other people ○ *He's been behaving oddly.* **2. BEHAVE WELL** to act in an acceptable way, especially by being polite, good-tempered, and self-controlled **3. PERFORM** to perform in or react to particular conditions, or operate in accordance with natural laws [15thC. Formed from HAVE in the obsolete sense 'to hold, comport'.]

behavior *n.* US = **behaviour**

behaviour /bi háyvyər/ *n.* **1. THE WAY SB BEHAVES** the way in which sb behaves **2.** PSYCHOL **RESPONSE** the way in which a person, organism, or group responds to a certain set of conditions **3. WHAT STH DOES** the way that a machine operates or a substance reacts under a certain set of conditions [15thC. Modelled on earlier *haviour* 'possession', from, ultimately, Old French *aveir* 'to have'.] —**behavioural** *adj.* —**behaviourally** *adv.*

behavioural contagion *n.* the spread of a type of behaviour first exhibited by a few people in a group to the group as a whole

behavioural psychology *n.* a branch of psychology based on the observation and modification of the way that people behave

behavioural science *n.* **1. SCIENCE STUDYING BEHAVIOUR** a science such as sociology, psychology, or anthropology that is concerned with the ways in which people or animals behave **2. STUDY OF BEHAVIOUR** the use of scientific methods to study the behaviour of living creatures —**behavioural scientist** *n.*

behavioural therapy *n.* = **behaviour therapy**

behaviourism /bi háyvyərizzəm/ *n.* **1.** PSYCHOL **NON-ANALYTICAL PSYCHOLOGY** an approach to the study of psychology that concentrates exclusively on observing, measuring, and modifying behaviour **2.** PHILOS **MATERIALIST PHILOSOPHICAL THEORY** the theory that statements about the mind and mental states are really about actual or potential behaviour —**behaviourist** *adj., n.* —**behaviouristic** /-rístik/ *adj.*

behaviour modification *n.* psychological treatment that attempts to change sb's behaviour by rewarding new and desirable responses and making accustomed undesirable ones less attractive

behaviour therapy *n.* a form of psychotherapy, the goal of which is observable changes in problem behaviours rather than changes in mental state

behead /bi héd/ (**-heads, -heading, -headed**) *vt.* to cut the head off sb or sth, especially as a form of execution

beheld past tense, past participle of **behold**

behemoth /bi hée moth, -m əth/ *n.* **1. behemoth, Behemoth** BIBLE **HUGE ANIMAL** a huge beast referred to in the Bible, usually thought to be a hippopotamus (Job 40:15) **2. STH HUGE** sth that is enormously big or powerful [14thC. From Hebrew *bəhēmōt*, from *bəhēmāh* 'beast'.]

behest /bi hést/ *n.* an order or request (*formal*) ○ *arrived at the conference only at her behest* [Alteration of Old English *behǣs*. Ultimately from a prehistoric Germanic base meaning 'to bid, call'.]

behind /bi hīnd/ CORE MEANING: a grammatical word indicating that sb or sth is in or is going towards a position at the back or rear of sth ○ (prep) *From behind the door we heard country music.* ○ (prep) *She was behind the wheel, and I was in the back .* ○ (adv) *their car was hit from behind* ○ (adv) *She had to go back because she'd left her money behind.*

1. *prep., adv.* **AT THE BACK OF** in or towards a position further back or at the rear of sth **2.** *prep., adv.* **FOLLOWING** following sb or sth **3.** *adv.* **IN DEBT** in debt or in arrears on a payment ○ *months behind on the payments* **4.** *adv.* **REMAINING** used to indicate that sb or sth is left after another's departure **5.** *prep.* **IN THE PAST** indicates that an achievement or experience happened in the past ○ *My best days are behind me.* **6.** *prep.* **LATE** indicates that sth is not as far advanced as it should be ○ *seven weeks behind schedule* **7.** *prep.* **CAUSING STH** causing or being responsible for sth ○ *the reason behind it* **8.** *prep.* **SUPPORTING SB** backing or supporting sb ○ *I'm behind you all the way on this issue.* **9.** *prep.* **UNDERNEATH** underneath the external appearance of sb or sth ○ *Behind his calm exterior, he was very confused* **10.** *n.* **BUTTOCKS** sb's buttocks (*informal*) [Old English *behindan*, literally 'by from behind', from *hindan* 'from behind', of prehistoric Germanic origin]

behindhand /bi hīnd hand/ *adj.* **1. BEHIND SCHEDULE** behind schedule **2. LAGGING BEHIND** behind in development or achievement **3.** FIN **IN ARREARS** in arrears for payment of a debt [Mid-16thC. Modelled on BEFOREHAND.]

behind-the-scenes *adj.* carried out privately or secretly ○ *a lot of frantic behind-the-scenes negotiation*

Behn /ben/, **Aphra** (1640–89) English writer. The first professional woman writer in England, she wrote poems, plays, and the early novel *Oroonoko* (1688). Born **Aphra Amis**

behold /bi hṓld/ (**-holds, -holding, -held** /bi héld/, **-held**) *v.* **1.** *vt.* **SEE** to see sth or sb (*archaic or literary*) **2.** *vi.* **TAKE NOTE** used to tell sb to look at sth or listen to sth, especially sth amazing or unexpected (*humorous*) (*used as a command*) ○ *Behold the fellow who didn't listen to his lawyer; he's now in jail.* [Old English *bihaldan*. Ultimately from a prehistoric Germanic word meaning 'to watch, guard'.] —**beholder** *n.*

beholden /bi hṓld'n/ *adj.* under an obligation to sb because of sth helpful that person has done [14thC. Originally the past participle of BEHOLD, in the obsolete sense 'to hold under obligation'.]

behove /bi hṓv/ (**-hoves, -hoving, -hoved**) *vt.* to be right and proper or appropriate for sb (*formal*) ○ *It ill behoves him to complain.* [Old English *behōfian* 'to need']

Behrens /báirənz/, **Peter** (1868–1940) German architect and designer. He applied the principles of industrial design to all aspects of his work, and influenced Le Corbusier and Walter Gropius.

Behring /báiring/, **Emil von** (1854–1917) German bacteriologist. He developed serum therapy against tetanus and diphtheria (1890) and won the first Nobel Prize in physiology or medicine (1901). Full name **Emil Adolph von Behring**

Beiderbecke /bīdər bek/, **Bix** (1903–31) US musician. He was one of the major jazz musicians of his generation. Real name **Leon Bismarke Beiderbecke**

beige /bayzh/ *adj.* COLOURS **VERY PALE BROWN** of a very pale brown colour with a tinge of yellow or pink ■ *n.* **1.** COLOURS **PALE BROWN** a very pale brown hue with a tinge of yellow or pink **2.** TEXTILES **UNDYED WOOLLEN CLOTH** cloth made of wool that has not been dyed or bleached [Mid-19thC. Via French, perhaps from, ultimately, late Latin *bombax* 'cotton' (source of English *bombastic*).]

Beijing /bay jíng/, **Peking** /pee kíng/ national capital of China as well as a cultural, administrative, and educational centre. It is situated in the northeastern part of the country, northwest of Bo Hai gulf. Population: 7,000,000 (1991).

being /bée ing/ *n.* **1. EXISTENCE** the state of existing **2. ESSENTIAL NATURE** sb's essential nature or character **3. LIVING THING** a living thing, especially one conceived of as supernatural or not living on earth **4. PERSON** a human individual

Beira /bīrə/ port and capital of Sofala Province, eastern Mozambique on the Mozambique Channel. Population: 299,300 (1990).

Beirut /bay róot/ capital, port, and largest city in Lebanon, situated on the Mediterranean Sea. Population: 1,500,000 (1998).

bejabers /bi jáybərz/ *interj., n. Ireland* = **bejasus** [Early 19thC. Alteration of 'by Jesus' to avoid offence.]

Béjart /báy zhaar/, **Maurice** (*b.* 1928) French dancer and choreographer. He founded the Ballet of the 20th Century and was known for his expressionist fusion of modern dance, ballet, and acrobatics. Real name **Maurice Jean de Berger**

bejasus /bi jáyzəss/, **bejesus** /bi jéezəss, bi jáyzəss/ *n. Ireland* **USED AS AN EMPHASIZING EXPRESSION** used to emphasize a statement or question ■ *interj. Ireland* **USED AS OATH** used as an exclamation or a mild oath [Early 20thC. Alteration of 'by Jesus' to avoid offence.]

bejewel /bi jóo əl/ (**-els, -elling, -elled**) *vt.* to decorate sth lavishly with jewels or colourful decorative objects (*literary*) —**bejewelled** *adj.*

Bekaa Valley /bi kaá/, **Bekáa Valley** valley in Lebanon, east of Beirut, running down the centre of the country between the Lebanon and Anti-Lebanon Mountains. Length: 120 km/75 mi.

bel /bel/ *n.* a logarithmic unit for comparing the loudness or strength of signals, equal to an intensity ratio of 10 to 1 [Early 20thC. Named after the Scottish-born scientist Alexander Graham *Bell* (1847–1922), the inventor of the telephone.]

belabor *vt.* US = **belabour**

belabour /bi láybər/ (**-bours, -bouring, -boured**) *vt.* **1. HARP ON** to repeat sth unnecessarily, or discuss it at too great a length or in too much detail **2. CRITICIZE** to subject sb to a sustained verbal or literary attack (*literary*) **3. BEAT** to hit sb hard and repeatedly with sth (*literary or humorous*)

Belarus

Belarus /béllə ro͞oss, byéllə-/ republic in eastern Europe. It became an independent nation after the dissolution of the former Soviet Union in 1991. Language: Belarusian, Russian. Currency: Belarusian rouble. Capital: Minsk. Population: 10,412,219 (1997). Area: 207,595 sq. km/80,153 sq. mi. Official name **Republic of Belarus**

Belarusian /béllə ru͞sh'n/ n. **1.** PEOPLES SB FROM BELARUS sb who was born or brought up in Belarus, or who is a citizen of Belarus **2.** LANG SLAVONIC LANGUAGE the official language of the Republic of Belarus, belonging to the East Slavonic group of Indo-European languages. Belarusian is spoken by about 11 million people. —**Belarusian** adj.

belated /bi láytid/ adj. occurring after the appropriate or expected time, especially too late to be effective or useful [Early 17thC. Formed from earlier belate 'to make late, delay'.] —**belatedly** adv. —**belatedness** n.

Belau = **Palau**

belay /bi láy/ vti. (-lays, -laying, -layed) **1.** NAUT FASTEN LINE ON SHIP to fasten a rope or line to a securing point on a ship or boat **2.** CLIMBING SECURE ROPE to fasten or control the rope to which a climber is attached by wrapping it round a metal device or another person **3.** NAUT STOP to tell sb to stop doing sth or to cancel an earlier instruction (used as a command) ■ n. CLIMBING **1.** SECURING OF CLIMBER'S ROPE the fastening or controlling of a climber's rope by wrapping it around a metal device or another person, or the method by which this is done **2.** FASTENING POINT the point to which a climber's rope is fastened [Old English belecgan 'to surround'. Ultimately from a prehistoric Germanic word that is also the ancestor of Dutch beleggen. Re-introduced from Dutch in the 16thC in nautical senses.]

belaying pin n. a large wooden or metal pin that fits into a hole in a rail on a ship or boat and to which a rope can be fastened

bel canto /bel kántō/ n. **1.** STYLE OF SINGING a style of operatic singing that concentrates on producing a pure and even tone. It was developed in Italy in the 17th and 18th centuries. **2.** INSTRUMENTAL STYLE a style of expressive melodic instrumental playing that uses the principles of bel canto singing [Late 19thC. From Italian, literally 'fine song'.]

belch /belch/ vti. (**belches, belching, belched**) **1.** RELEASE GAS FROM MOUTH NOISILY to let gas from the stomach out through the mouth, making a loud noise in the throat **2.** SEND OR COME OUT VISIBLY to send out large amounts of steam, smoke, or gas, or come out of sth in a thick cloud ■ n. BURPING an act or the noise of burping [Old English bealcettan, bælcan. Perhaps ultimately from a prehistoric Germanic word that is also the ancestor of German bölken 'to bleat, belch'.]

beleaguer /bi léegər/ vt. (**-guers, -guering, -guered**) (usually passive) **1.** ANNOY to make sb feel harassed, hemmed in, or under severe pressure **2.** BESIEGE to surround sb or sth with an army [Late 16thC. From Dutch belegeren, literally 'to camp around', hence 'to besiege'.] —**beleaguerment** n.

Belém /bə lém/ port and capital of Pará State on the Pará River in northern Brazil. Population: 1,244,690 (1992).

belemnite /bélləm nīt/ n. any of the fossilized cylinder-shaped internal shells of an extinct order of cephalopods that were common in the Mesozoic era [Early 17thC. From Modern Latin belemnon, from Greek belemnon 'a dart', from its shape.]

bel esprit /bél ess prée/ (plural **beaux esprits** /bōz es prée/) n. a witty, intelligent, and cultured person [Mid-17thC. From French, literally 'fine mind'.]

Belfast /bél faast, bel faást/ port and capital of Northern Ireland, located at the head of Belfast Lough on the Lagan River. Population: 296,700 (1995).

Belfast roof n. a wooden bow-string girder that is made of short lengths of timber but is able to span a length of up to 30 m/100 ft

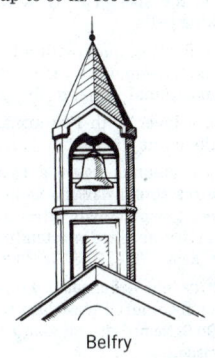
Belfry

belfry /bélfri/ (plural **-fries**) n. **1.** SPACE FOR BELLS the part of a church steeple or a tower in which bells are hung **2.** BELL TOWER a tower on a building, in which a bell or bells are hung [13thC. By folk etymology from Old French berfrei 'movable siege-tower' (from assumed Frankish, literally 'to protect peace'), by association with BELL.] —**belfried** adj.

Belgae /bél zhi, bél gī/ n. an ancient Celtic people who lived in northern Gaul and parts of southern England

Belgaum /bel gówm/ city in northern Karnataka State, southwestern India. It was the capital of the Ralta dynasty in the 13th century. Population: 401,619 (1991).

Belgian /béljən/ n. SB FROM BELGIUM sb who was born or brought up in Belgium, or who is a citizen of Belgium ■ adj. **1.** OF BELGIUM relating to or typical of Belgium, or its people or culture **2.** OF FLEMISH OR WALLOON relating to the Flemish or Walloon French languages

Belgian hare n. a breed of slender reddish-brown domestic rabbit with long legs and ears, or any member of the breed

Belgium

Belgium /béljəm/ kingdom in northwestern Europe that became independent in 1830. Language: Flemish, French, German. Currency: Belgian franc. Capital: Brussels. Population: 10,165,059 (1997). Area: 30,528 sq. km/11,787 sq. mi. Official name **Kingdom of Belgium**

Belgrade /bél grayd/ capital of Yugoslavia and the Republic of Serbia that forms part of Yugoslavia. It is situated at the junction of the Danube and Sava rivers. Population: 1,136,786 (1991).

Belgrano /bel graánō/, **Manuel** (1770–1820) Argentine general and statesman. He led Argentine troops in revolt against Spanish rule, winning major battles (1812 and 1813) and was later a diplomat.

Belial /beéli əl/ n. a personification of wickedness or worthlessness, mentioned in the Bible and often thought of as a devil or demon [13thC. From Hebrew bĕliyya'al 'worthlessness'.]

belie /bi líˊ/ (-lies, -lying, -lied) vt. **1.** GIVE FALSE IMPRESSION to disguise the true nature of sth **2.** SHOW TO BE FALSE to show that sth is not true or real ○ The evidence belies the testimony of the witness [Old English belēogan. Ultimately from a prehistoric Germanic word that is also the ancestor of German belügen.]

belief /bi leéf/ n. **1.** ACCEPTANCE OF TRUTH OF STH acceptance by the mind that sth is true or real, often underpinned by an emotional or spiritual sense of certainty ○ belief in an afterlife **2.** TRUST confidence that sb or sth is good or will be effective ○ belief in democracy **3.** STH THAT SB BELIEVES IN a statement, principle, or doctrine that a person or group accepts as true **4.** OPINION an opinion, especially a firm and considered one **5.** RELIG RELIGIOUS FAITH religious faith [12thC. Alteration of Old English gelēafa on the model of BELIEVE.]

belief system n. **1.** SET OF BELIEFS a set of beliefs, e.g. in religion or politics, that form a unified system **2.** ORGANIZED SOCIETAL BELIEFS a collection and organization of beliefs prevalent in a community or society

believable /bi leévəb'l/ adj. seeming to be true or authentic, and capable of being believed or believed in —**believability** /bi leévə billəti/ n. —**believably** /-bli/ adv.

believe /bi leév/ v. (-lieves, -lieving, -lieved) v. **1.** vt. ACCEPT AS TRUE to accept that sth is true or real ○ I don't know which story to believe. **2.** vt. ACCEPT AS TRUTHFUL to accept that sb is telling the truth ○ Nobody will believe you! **3.** vt. CREDIT WITH STH to accept that sb or sth has a particular quality or ability ○ No one believed her capable of such a malicious remark. **4.** vi. THINK THAT STH EXISTS to be of the opinion that sth exists or is a reality, especially when there is no absolute proof of its existence or reality ○ believe in reincarnation **5.** vi. TRUST to be confident that sb or sth is good, or will be effective ○ We all believe in you. **6.** vi. THINK STH IS GOOD to be of the opinion that sth is right or beneficial, and, usually, to act in accordance with that belief ○ believe strongly in freedom of expression **7.** vi. RELIG HAVE RELIGIOUS FAITH to have a religious belief [Old English belyfan, an alteration of earlier gelēfan. Ultimately from a prehistoric Germanic word meaning 'to love, trust'.]

believer /bi leévər/ n. **1.** SB WITH RELIGIOUS FAITH sb who believes in God and in the teachings of a particular religious faith **2.** SUPPORTER OF AN IDEA sb who holds a belief and usually acts in accordance with it ○ a great believer in discipline

belike /bi líˊk/ adv. probably (archaic) [Mid-16thC. From an earlier form of BY + LIKE.]

Belinda /bə líndə/ n. a small natural satellite of Uranus, discovered in 1986 by the Voyager 2 planetary probe

Belisha beacon /bə leéshə-/ n. UK a sign at each end of a zebra crossing consisting of an amber ball with a flashing light inside it on top of a black-and-white-striped pole [Mid-20thC. Named after Leslie Hore-Belisha (1895–1957) the British Minister of Transport who introduced it.]

belittle /bi líttˈl/ (-tles, -tling, -tled) vt. to make sth seem less good or important than it is —**belittlement** n. —**belittler** n.

Belize

Belize /be leéz, bə-/ country in Central America on the Caribbean Sea, bordered to the west by Mexico and Guatemala. It became a British crown colony in 1862 and became an independent Commonwealth state in 1981. Language: English, Spanish. Currency: Belizean dollar. Capital: Belmopan. Population: 224,663 (1997). Area: 22,965 sq. km/8,867 sq. mi. Former name **British Honduras** —**Belizean** /be leĕzh'n, bə-/ n., adj.

Belize City city and the main port of Belize on the Caribbean Sea. It was the capital of British Honduras between 1884 and 1972. Population: 50,000 (1990).

bell[1] /bel/ n. **1.** OBJECT WITH RINGING SOUND a hollow open-ended metal instrument with a rounded top that produces a ringing sound when struck. Bells are traditionally used as summonses and signals. **2.** ELECTRICAL DEVICE PRODUCING SOUND a device activated by electricity that produces a ringing or buzzing signal **3.** STH BELL-SHAPED sth with the curved and open-ended shape of a bell, especially a flower **4.** MUSIC FLARED END OF WIND INSTRUMENT the flared end of a wind instrument, from which the sound emerges **5.** NAUT DURATION OF SHIP'S WATCH the time during a watch on a ship, indicated by rings on a bell, one ring for each half hour that has passed ∎ **bells** npl. MUSIC PERCUSSION INSTRUMENT a percussion instrument consisting of metal tubes or bars hung from a frame that give out a ringing sound when struck ∎ vti. (**bells, belling, belled**) BECOME OR MAKE WIDER to open out, or open sth out, into a curved or flared shape similar to that of a bell [Old English belle, from prehistoric Germanic] ◇ **give sb a bell** to telephone sb (informal) ◇ **ring a bell** to evoke a vague memory of sth or sb ∘ Her name doesn't ring a bell

───── **WORD KEY: CULTURAL NOTE** ─────
Five Bells, a long poem by Australian poet Kenneth Slessor (1939). This verse sequence is a meditation on time and the fragility of human existence cast as an elegy for Joe Lynch, a friend of the author who drowned in Sydney Harbour.

───── **WORD KEY: CULTURAL NOTE** ─────
For Whom the Bell Tolls, a novel by US writer Ernest Hemingway (1940). Widely viewed as Hemingway's most ambitious work, it is set during the Spanish Civil War and tells the story of Robert Jordan, a US volunteer fighting for the Republicans, who falls in love with a fellow volunteer called Maria. It was made into a film by Sam Woods in 1943.

bell[2] /bel/ n. BELLOW a bellowing sound made by a rutting stag or by a hunting dog during the chase ∎ vi. (**bells, belling, belled**) BELLOW to make a bellowing sound [Old English bellan, from prehistoric Germanic]

Bell /bel/, **Alexander Graham** (1847–1922) Scottish-born US inventor and educator. He made the first intelligible telephonic transmission (1876), patented the telephone (1876), and founded Bell Telephone Company (1877). Among his numerous other inventions were wax cylinder recordings (1886) and the hydrofoil (1917).

Bell, Sir Francis Henry Dillon (1851–1936) New Zealand statesman. He was a Reform Party politician and was briefly prime minister of New Zealand (1925).

Bell, Gertrude (1868–1926) British archaeologist and traveller. She travelled extensively in the Middle East and left money to found the British Institute of Archaeology in Iraq. Full name **Gertrude Margaret Lowthian Bell**

Bell, Vanessa (1879–1961) British painter. A member of the London Group of artists, she painted many portraits in the Fauvist style. She was the sister of Virginia Woolf. Born **Vanessa Stephen**

belladonna /bélla dónnə/ n. **1.** PLANTS = **deadly nightshade 2.** PHARM DRUG FROM BELLADONNA a drug, e.g. atropine or hyoscyamine, that is made from belladonna [Mid-18thC. Via Modern Latin from Italian, literally 'beautiful lady', from the use of belladonna to dilate the pupils, making the eyes look larger and brighter.]

belladonna lily n. = **amaryllis**

bellarmine /béll aar meen/ n. a large earthenware or stoneware jug decorated with a bearded face [Mid-17thC. Named after St Robert Bellarmin, 1542–1621, Jesuit cardinal lampooned by the original jugs.]

Bell Bay bay on the northern coast of Tasmania, Australia, beside George Town

bellbird /bél burd/ n. a tropical American or Australasian bird with a call that sounds like a bell. The members of the cotinga and honey-eater families are bellbirds.

bell-bottom trousers, **bell-bottoms** npl. trousers that widen below the knees into a bell shape

bellboy /bél boy/ n. a male employee in a hotel, acting as a porter or page. US term **bellhop**

bell bronze n. the special alloy of copper and tin used in making bells

bell buoy n. a floating buoy with a bell on top that is rung by the movement of the waves and gives a warning or positional signal to shipping

bell crank n. a lever with two arms that share a fulcrum at the point where they join

belle /bel/ n. **1.** BEAUTIFUL WOMAN a beautiful girl or woman **2.** MOST BEAUTIFUL WOMAN a woman considered to be the most conspicuously attractive of all those living in a particular place or attending a particular social event [Early 17thC. From French 'beautiful'.]

Belleek ware /bə léek-/, **Belleek** n. a type of very thin, typically cream-coloured porcelain with a lustrous glaze [Mid-19thC. Named after the town in Northern Ireland where it was made.]

belle époque /bél ay pók/ n. an era of cultural refinement, social elegance, and general prosperity and security, especially the last decades of the 19th century and the early years of the 20th prior to World War I [Mid-20thC. French, literally 'fine period'.]

Bellerophon /bə lérrəfən/ n. in Greek mythology, a hero who tamed the winged horse Pegasus and slew the fire-breathing monster Chimera

belles-lettres /bél léttrə/ n. writings that are valued for their elegance and aesthetic qualities rather than for any human interest or moral or instructive content (takes a singular or plural verb) [Mid-17thC. French, literally 'fine letters'.] —**belletrism** /bél léttrizzəm/ n. —**belletrist** n.

bellflower /bél flowər/ n. = **campanula**

bellfoundry /bél fowndri/ n. (plural **-ries**) a foundry that specializes in making bells

bell glass n. = **bell jar** n. 2

bell heather n. a heather with deep reddish-purple flowers. Latin name: Erica cineria.

bellhop /bél hop/ n. US, Can = **bellboy**

bellicose /béllikôss/ adj. ready or inclined to quarrel, fight, or go to war [15thC. From Latin bellicosus, from bellum 'war' (source of English rebel).] —**bellicosely** adv. —**bellicoseness** n. —**bellicosity** /bélli kóssəti/ n.

belligerence /bə líjjərənss/ n. the quality of being hostile, ready to start a fight, or ready to go to war

belligerency /bə líjjərənssi/ n. **1.** = **belligerence 2.** STATE OF WAR the state of being at war

belligerent /bə líjjərənt/ adj. **1.** HOSTILE OR AGGRESSIVE hostile, ready to start a fight, or ready to go to war **2.** ENGAGED IN WAR taking part in warfare, especially in a war recognized by the law of nations **3.** RELATING TO BELLIGERENT NATION relating to or characteristic of a participant in war or a fight ∎ n. PARTICIPANT IN WAR a participant in a war or fight, especially a nation engaged in a war recognized by the law of nations [Late 16thC. From Latin belligerare 'to wage war', from belliger, literally 'carrying on war', from bellum 'war' + gerere 'to carry on'.] —**belligerently** adv.

Bellingshausen Sea /béllingz howz'n-/ predominantly ice-covered sea constituting part of the southern Pacific Ocean, off the coast of Antarctica

Bellini /be leĕni/, **Giovanni** (1430?–1516) Italian painter. The son of Jacopo Bellini, he produced calm yet sensuous religious pictures, combining figures and landscape in naturalistic light.

Bellini, Jacopo (1400?–70?) Italian painter. He produced stylized paintings and drawings with strong architectural elements.

bell jar n. **1.** GLASS COVER FOR DISPLAYED OBJECTS a glass cover, shaped like a bell, used to protect and display delicate items **2.** CHEM GLASS COVER FOR EXPERIMENTS a glass cover shaped like a bell used in laboratories to enclose equipment in experiments, especially to prevent gases from escaping or entering

bell magpie n. = **currawong** [From its bell-like call]

bellman /bélmən/ (plural **-men** /-mən, -men/) n. **1.** MAN WHO RINGS BELL a man who rings a bell, especially a town crier (archaic) **2.** US = **bellboy**

bell metal n. an alloy of copper with 20 to 25 percent tin, used to cast bells and plain bearings

Belloc /béllòk/, **Hilaire** (1870–1953) French-born British writer. He wrote Cautionary Tales for Children (1907) and biographies of historical figures including Napoleon (1932). He was a leading Roman Catholic and Liberal Member of Parliament (1906–10). Full name **Joseph Hilaire Pierre Belloc**

bellow /béllō/ v. (**-lows, -lowing, -lowed**) **1.** vi. UTTER ROAR LIKE BULL to give a bull's loud deep roar or a roar like that of a bull **2.** vti. SHOUT LOUDLY to shout sth in a loud deep voice ∎ n. **1.** ROAR LIKE BULL'S a bull's loud deep roar, or a roar like that of a bull **2.** LOUD SHOUT a loud deep shout or cry [Origin uncertain: perhaps from Old English bylgan, or from belgan 'to be enraged'] —**bellower** n.

Bellow /béllō/, **Saul** (b. 1915) Canadian-born US writer. He won the Nobel Prize in literature (1976). His novels include the Pulitzer prize-winning Humboldt's Gift (1975).

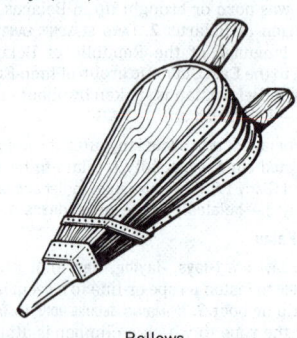
Bellows

bellows /béllōz/ (plural **-lows**) n. (takes a singular or plural verb) **1.** COMPRESSIBLE CHAMBER FOR PUMPING AIR a device or piece of equipment with a chamber with flexible sides that can be expanded to draw air in and compressed to force the air out **2.** PLEATED EXPANDABLE PART sth constructed of a pleated material and, like a bellows, able to be expanded and contracted, e.g. the part enclosing the lenses on some cameras or photographic enlargers [12thC. Origin uncertain: probably from Old English belga, a shortening of blæstbelig, literally 'blowing bag', from blæst 'blowing' (source of blast) + belig 'bag' (source of belly).]

bell pepper n. US = **sweet pepper** [From its shape]

bell pull n. a handle or cord that when pulled makes a bell ring

bell push n. a button that when pressed causes an electric bell to ring

bell-ringer n. **1.** SB RINGING CHURCH BELLS sb who rings church bells, whether as an ecclesiastical function or as a hobby **2.** SB PLAYING HANDBELLS a musician who plays handbells —**bell-ringing** n.

bells and whistles npl. special features that are not necessary but are incorporated in a product to make it appear more desirable or useful (informal)

bells of Ireland n. an annual plant with small flowers surrounded by green cup-shaped sepals. Latin name: Moluccella laevis.

Bell's palsy /bélz-/ n. paralysis of the muscles on one side of the face, causing a distorted facial expression. It results from injury to the facial nerve and is usually temporary. [Mid-19thC. Named after the Scottish anatomist Sir Charles Bell, 1774–1842, who described it.]

bell tent n. a tent shaped like a bell or a cone, held up by a central pole

bell tower n. a tower with a bell or bells housed in it

bellwether /bél wethər/ n. **1.** SHEEP LEADING FLOCK a sheep that leads the rest of the flock, usually wearing a bell around its neck **2.** LEADER sb who takes the initiative or leads others **3.** INDICATOR OF FUTURE DE-

VELOPMENTS sb who or sth that acts as an indicator of future developments or trends

belly /bélli/ *n.* (*plural* **-lies**) **1. MIDDLE PART OF BODY** the part of the body of a vertebrate that contains the stomach, intestines, and other organs **2. FRONT OF BODY AROUND STOMACH** the surface of the body of a vertebrate around the stomach **3. STOMACH** the stomach (*informal*) **4. APPETITE** the desire or need for food and drink **5. DESIRE OR PERSISTENCE** the courage or desire to have or do sth ○ *They have no belly for a fight.* **6. BULGING PART** a part of sth that bulges out, e.g. a sail **7. INTERIOR CAVITY** the interior cavity of a structure, especially a ship **8.** MUSIC **UPPER SURFACE OF STRINGED INSTRUMENT** the top or front surface of the body of a stringed instrument, over which the strings are stretched ■ *vti.* (**-lies, -lying, -lied**) **BULGE** to bulge or make sth bulge ○ *The wind bellied out the sail.* [Old English *belig* 'bag'. Ultimately from an Indo-European word meaning 'to swell' that is also the ancestor of English *billow* and *bolster.*] ◇ **go** *or* **turn belly up** to go bankrupt, fail, or fall through

bellyache /bélli ayk/ *n.* **STOMACH ACHE** a painful or upset stomach (*informal*) ■ *vi.* (**-aches, -aching, -ached**) **COMPLAIN** to complain in a whining manner (*informal*) —**bellyacher** *n.*

bellyband /bélli band/ *n.* a strap passed around the belly of a draught animal and attached to the shafts of the vehicle it is pulling

bellybutton /bélli butt'n/ *n.* the human navel (*informal*)

belly dance *n.* a dance for women, originally from the Middle East, in which rhythmic movement of the hips and abdomen is emphasized —**belly dancer** *n.* —**belly dancing** *n.*

belly flop *n.* **1.** SWIMMING **DIVE IN WHICH STOMACH SMACKS WATER** an almost horizontal dive where the front of the diver's body hits the water first **2.** AIR = **belly landing** —**belly-flop** *vi.*

bellyful /béllifŏŏl/ *n.* (*informal*) **1. ALL SB CAN EAT** all the food that sb wants or is able to eat **2. EXCESS** an undesirable or excessive amount of sth

belly landing *n.* an emergency landing of an aircraft with the wheels not extended —**belly-land** *vti.*

belly laugh *n.* a deep and unrestrained laugh

belly pork *n.* a streaky cut of pork from a pig's belly

Belmopan /bélmə pán/ capital of Belize, located on the Belize River in the eastern part of the country. Population: 6,500 (1996).

Belo Horizonte /béllō horri zóntay/ city and capital of Minas Gerais State in eastern Brazil. Population: 2,091,770 (1996).

belong /bi lóng/ (**-longs, -longing, -longed**) *vi.* **1. BE SB'S PROPERTY** to be the property of a person or organization ○ *Who does this coat belong to?* **2. BE PERSONALLY LINKED** to be linked to a particular place or person by a relationship such as birth, affection, or membership **3. BE CLASSIFIED** to be part of a class or group ○ *Tulips belong to the lily family.* **4. BE PART OF** to be a part or component of sth else **5. BE IN RIGHT PLACE** to be in an appropriate or usual place ○ *He belongs in jail.* **6. BE ACCEPTED** to be accepted or made welcome in a place or group ○ *feeling that I didn't belong* [14th C. Formed from obsolete English *long* 'to relate to', with the literal sense of 'to relate to thoroughly'.]

Belonger /bi lóngər/ *n. Carib* sb of African descent who was born and lives on a Caribbean island

belonging /bi lónging/ *n.* **FEELING AT HOME** the state of being comfortable and accepted in a place or community ■ **belongings** *npl.* **PERSONAL POSSESSIONS** the things sb owns or has with him or her

Belorussia /béllō rúshə/ = **Belarus**

Belorussian /béllō rúsh'n/ *adj., n.* Belarusian (*dated*)

beloved /bi lúvvid/; (*predicatively*) /-lúvd/ *adj.* **ADORED** very much loved ■ *n.* **LOVED PERSON** sb who is very much loved

below /bi lṓ/ CORE MEANING: a grammatical word indicating sth situated or placed beneath sth else or lower than sth else ○ (prep) *a river below the town* ○ (adv) *on the shelf below*

1. *prep., adv.* **IN LOWER GRADE** at or to a level, standard, or grade that is lower than that specified or understood ○ *animals ranked below humans* ○ *below average* ○ *30 degrees below* **2.** *adv.* **FURTHER DOWN** lower down or later on in a text, especially on the same page ○ *see below* ○ *on page 29 below* **3.** *adv.* NAUT **LOWER THAN THE DECK** on or to a level of a ship or boat that is lower than the deck **4.** *adv.* RELIG **ON EARTH** on earth or in hell, as opposed to in heaven (*archaic*) [14thC. Formed from an earlier form of *by* + LOW, possibly modelled on *beneath.*]

belowground /bi lṓ grownd, -grównd/ *adj.* **UNDERGROUND** situated under the ground ■ *adv.* **UNDER THE GROUND** into or under the ground

Belsen /béss'n/ village in northwestern Germany, about 16 km/10 mi. north of Celle. It is the site of the Bergen-Belsen Nazi concentration camp (1943–45).

Belshazzar /bel shăzzər/ *n.* a king of Babylon in the sixth century BC. The Bible tells of the foretelling of his death in an inscription that mysteriously appears on the wall of his palace during a feast (Daniel 5).

belt /belt/ *n.* **1.** ACCESSORIES **STRIP OF MATERIAL ROUND WAIST** a strip of material worn round the waist, used to hold up clothing for the lower body, as decoration, or to carry tools or weapons **2. STRIP OF STH DIFFERENT** a band or stripe of a different colour, texture, or substance from what it encircles or crosses **3. SPECIFIC AREA** an area or region where a particular item or quality is characteristic ○ *a wheat belt* ○ *the stockbroker belt* **4.** SPORTS **BELT GIVEN FOR ACHIEVEMENT** a belt awarded to a sports competitor, especially in boxing or the martial arts, as a trophy or a sign of having attained a particular grade **5.** SPORTS **SB HOLDING BELT FOR ACHIEVEMENT** sb awarded a particular belt for a achievement, usually in boxing or one of the martial arts **6. BELT AS SIGN OF RANK** a belt worn as a sign of a particular rank, e.g. by a knight or an earl **7.** TRANSP = **seat belt** **8.** INDUST **BAND AS PART OF MACHINE** a band of strong flexible material used in machinery to transmit motion or power or to move articles **9. BLOW** a hard blow (*informal*) **10.** *US* **DRINK** a drink of spirits (*slang*) **11.** EDUC, HISTORY **STRAP USED TO PUNISH** a leather strap, usually split into several thongs at one end, formerly used in schools for corporal punishment ■ *v.* (**belts, belting, belted**) **1.** *vt.* **FASTEN WITH BELT** to fasten or attach sth with a belt **2.** *vt.* **HIT WITH BELT** to strike sb with a belt **3.** *vt.* **HIT HARD** to strike sb or sth with a hard blow (*informal*) **4.** *vi.* **MOVE FAST** to move or travel very quickly (*informal*) [Old English. Ultimately from Latin *balteus* 'girdle', of, perhaps, Etruscan origin.] ◇ **below the belt** unfair and often hurtful ◇ **have sth under your belt** to have done or acquired sth that will be of benefit to you in the future ○ *She has 12 computer science courses under her belt.* ◇ **tighten your belt** to reduce your expenditure

belt out *vt.* to sing or play sth loudly and enthusiastically (*informal*)

belt up *v.* **1.** *vi.* **SHUT UP** to be quiet or stop talking (*slang*) (*usually used as a command*) **2.** *vti.* **PUT ON SAFETY BELT** to fasten a safety belt, or secure sb with a safety belt

Beltane /bél tayn/ *n.* an ancient Celtic festival at the beginning of May, marked by the lighting of bonfires [15thC. Via Gaelic *bealltainn* from Old Irish.]

beltcourse /bélt kawrss/ *n.* ARCHIT = **string course**

belt drive *n.* a system for transmitting power from one shaft to another by means of an endless flexible belt looped over pulleys mounted on the shafts

belted Galloway *n.* a breed of hornless beef cattle with a white belt round a black body, originating in Galloway

belter /béltər/ *n.* (*informal*) **1. SB OR STH EXCELLENT** sb or sth considered remarkable or outstanding **2. SONG SUITABLE FOR BELTING OUT** a popular song that lends itself to a loud and rousing performance

belting /bélting/ *n.* **1. MATERIAL FOR BELTS** material used for making belts **2. BELTS COLLECTIVELY** belts considered collectively

belt sander *n.* a sander that uses a continuous belt coated with an abrasive

beltway /bélt way/ *n. US* = **ring road**

beluga /bə lóogə/ (*plural* **-gas** *or* **-ga**) *n.* **1. RUSSIAN STURGEON** a large white sturgeon found in the Black Sea and the Caspian Sea. Its eggs are used in caviar, and isinglass was traditionally made from its air bladders. Latin name: *Huso huso* and *Acipenser huso.* **2. beluga, beluga caviar CAVIAR** caviar made from the eggs of the beluga sturgeon **3.** = **white whale** [Late 16thC. From Russian, literally 'large white', from *belyĭ* 'white'.]

belvedere /bélvə deer/ *n.* a building or part of a building positioned to offer a fine view of the surrounding area [Late 16thC. From Italian, literally 'beautiful to see'.]

bema /beémə/ *n.* **1. bema, bima, bimah** JUDAISM **PLATFORM FOR SCRIPTURE READINGS** in a synagogue, the raised platform where the scriptures are read **2.** CHR **PLATFORM THAT ALTAR IS ON** in an Orthodox church, the raised area where the altar is located [Late 17thC. From Greek *bēma* 'step, platform'.]

Bemba /bémbə/ (*plural* **-ba** *or* **-bas**) *n.* **1.** PEOPLES **MEMBER OF AFRICAN PEOPLE** a member of an African people chiefly located in Zambia **2.** LANG **AFRICAN LANGUAGE** a Bantu language spoken in east-central Africa and belonging to the Benue-Congo group of languages. Bemba is spoken by more than two million people. [Mid-20thC. From Bantu.] —**Bemba** *adj.*

bemire /bi mí r/ (**-mires, -miring, -mired**) *vt.* **1. SOIL** to soil sth or sb with mud or dirt (*archaic*) **2. CAUSE TO STICK IN MUD** to cause sb or sth to become stuck in mud (*archaic or literary*) (*usually passive*)

bemoan /bi mṓn/ (**-moans, -moaning, -moaned**) *vt.* to express grief or disappointment about sth

bemuse /bi myóoz/ (**-muses, -musing, -mused**) *vt.* to cause sb to be confused or puzzled —**bemusement** *n.*

bemused /bi myóozd/ *adj.* confused, puzzled, and unable to understand or think clearly —**bemusedly** /bi myóozidli/ *adv.*

ben[1] /ben/ *n. Scotland, Ireland* a mountain ○ *Ben Nevis* [Late 18thC. From Scottish Gaelic and Irish *beann.*]

ben[2] /ben/ *n. Scotland* the inner room of a house, especially of an old-fashioned rural cottage with two rooms. ◊ **but and pen** [14thC. Variant of an earlier dialect word meaning 'within', from Old English *binnan.*]

Ben Ali /ben aáli/, **Zine al-Abidine** (*b.* 1936) Tunisian politician. He forced the retirement of President Habid Bourgiba (1987) and began reforms as the new president of Tunisia.

Benares /bi náariz/ former name for **Varanasi**

Benaud /bénnō/, **Richie** (*b.* 1930) Australian cricketer and broadcaster. He was the first Australian, and only the second cricketer, to score 2,000 runs and take 200 wickets in international matches. Full name **Richard Benaud**

Ben Bella /bén béllə/, **Ahmed** (*b.* 1919) Algerian political leader. A leading figure in Algeria's war of independence, he was the country's first prime minister (1962–3) and president (1963–5). Imprisoned from 1965–80, he was exiled in 1990. Full name **Mohammed Ahmed Ben Bella**

Benbow /bénbō/, **John** (1653–1702) English naval commander. He commanded the English fleet in the West Indies, where he died from his wounds after a sea battle against a French force.

bench /bench/ *n.* **1.** FURNITURE **LONG BACKLESS SEAT** a long seat for two or more people, usually made without a back or arms **2.** NAUT **SEAT IN BOAT** a seat for a rower in a boat **3. WORK TABLE** a long strong work table **4.** LAW **JUDGE'S SEAT** the seat where a judge sits in a court **5.** LAW **JUDGE** a judge or magistrate presiding over a court **6.** LAW **JUDGES** the judges of a court system **7.** LAW **JUDGESHIP** the office or position of a judge **8.** SPORTS **SEAT FOR NONPLAYING ATHLETES** in team sports, the seat for officials and for players not on the field or court during play **9.** SPORTS **PEOPLE WHO OCCUPY BENCH** the people who sit on the bench in a team sports event **10.** GEOL **LEDGE OF LAND** a narrow flat ledge of land, often the remnant of a former shoreline **11.** MINING **LEDGE IN MINE** a ledge formed by excavation in a mine **12. PLATFORM FOR SHOWING ANIMALS** a platform used for displaying dogs, cats, or other animals at a show ■ *vt.* (**benches, benching, benched**) **1. PROVIDE WITH BENCHES** to provide sth with benches **2. DISPLAY ANIMAL AT SHOW** to display a dog, cat, or other animal at a show on a bench **3.** SPORTS **PUT ON NONPLAYERS' BENCH** to exclude or remove a member of a sports team from play [Old

English *benc*. Ultimately from a prehistoric Germanic word that was also the ancestor of German *Bank* and English *bank* 'riverbank', the underlying idea being of a 'raised ridge'.]

bencher /bénchər/ n. a member of the governing body of an Inn of Court

benchmark /bénch maark/ n. 1. STANDARD a standard against which sth can be measured or assessed 2. COMPUT TEST OF COMPUTER PERFORMANCE a test or set of tests used to measure the performance of computer hardware or software ■ adj. USED AS STANDARD used as a standard for measuring or assessing sth ■ vt. (-marks, -marking, -marked) 1. PROVIDE STANDARD to provide a standard against which sth can be measured or assessed 2. COMPUT TEST COMPUTER PERFORMANCE to test the performance of computer hardware or software for the purpose of comparison with similar products

bench mark n. a mark made by a surveyor on a permanent object that shows an established position and elevation and is used as a reference point

bench press n. in weightlifting, a lift where sb lies on a bench with the feet on the floor and raises a weight from chest level to arm's length —**bench-press** vti.

bench seat n. in a motor vehicle, a seat that extends across the full width of the vehicle

bench test n. a trial of a machine or part in the laboratory or workshop to confirm that it works properly before it is installed —**bench-test** vti.

bend[1] /bend/ v. (bends, bending, bent /bent/) 1. vti. BECOME OR MAKE CURVED to take on or cause sth to take on a curved or angled shape ○ *The wooden struts bent under pressure.* 2. vti. STOOP to make or cause sb to make a stooping or inclined movement ○ *I bent to pick up the ball.* 3. vti. YIELD OR FORCE TO YIELD to yield in response to a strong will or force, or force sb or sth to yield 4. vti. CHANGE OR CAUSE TO CHANGE DIRECTION to change or cause sth to change direction or course ○ *The path bends to the right.* 5. vti. CONCENTRATE ON DOING STH to concentrate on doing sth ○ *bent her mind to the task in hand* 6. vt. DISTORT FOR SB'S BENEFIT to adapt or interpret sth in a way that was not originally intended, especially for personal benefit or to help sb else ○ *bend the rules* 7. vt. NAUT ATTACH to attach or fasten sth, especially a pair of lines or ropes ■ n. 1. CURVE a curved part of sth, especially a sharp curve in a road 2. ACT OF BENDING an act of bending 3. NAUT KNOT JOINING TWO ROPES a knot that joins one line to another [Old English *bendan* 'to tie, curve' (because if you tie sth it becomes curved). Ultimately from a prehistoric Germanic word that was also the ancestor of English *bind*, *bond*, and *bundle*.] —**bendability** /béndə bílləti/ n. —**bendable** adj. —**bendy** adj. ◇ **round the bend** wild or distracted (slang)

— **WORD KEY: ORIGIN** —
The prehistoric Germanic word from which *bend* comes is also the ancestor of English *band*, *bind*, *bond*, and *bundle*.

bend[2] /bend/ n. HERALDRY a band that crosses a heraldic shield diagonally from top right to bottom left [Old English, 'band', originally a sense of BEND[1] and, later, from Old French *bende*]

benday /bén dáy/, **Ben Day** adj. used to describe a printing process of adding tone to an image by overlaying a transparent sheet patterned with dots before the image is reproduced to make a plate [Early 20thC. Named after the US printer *Benjamin Day* Jr (1838–1916), who invented the process.]

bended /béndid/ adj. in a position so as to be curved or bent (archaic) ○ *on bended knee*

bender /béndər/ n. 1. DRINKING SPREE a prolonged bout of drinking (slang) 2. OFFENSIVE TERM an offensive term for a gay man (slang offensive) 3. TEMPORARY SHELTER a usually dome-shaped temporary shelter made by bending and interweaving branches and covering them with plastic sheeting or tarpaulin (informal)

Bendigo /béndigō/ former gold-mining town in central Victoria, Australia, now an important industrial, commercial, and agricultural centre. Population: 59,936 (1996).

bendrofluazide /béndrō floo ə zīd/ n. a diuretic drug used in the treatment of oedema and hypertension.

It acts on a part of the kidney to promote the excretion of salt and water. US term **bendroflumethiazide**

bendroflumethiazide n. US = bendrofluazide

bends /bendz/ n. decompression sickness, especially in divers (informal) (takes a singular or plural verb)

bend sinister (plural **bends sinister**) n. a band that crosses a heraldic shield diagonally from top left to bottom right, used to indicate a bastard line of descent [From SINISTER 'on the left']

beneath /bi néeth/ CORE MEANING: a grammatical word indicating a position underneath or lower than sth 1. prep., adv. UNDERNEATH in, at, or to a lower position or less superficial level than that specified or understood (formal) ○ *kept in a box beneath the bed* ○ *a door giving access to the cellar beneath* ○ *Beneath his veneer of politeness lay hostility.* 2. prep., adv. LOWER in, at, or to a lower level, grade, or standard than that specified or understood (formal) ○ *She always supported those beneath her.* 3. prep. TOO LOW FOR too low in status or character for ○ *beneath contempt* ○ *Telling tales should be beneath you.* [Old English *binithan*, *bineothan*, literally 'by or from below'. Ultimately from a prehistoric Germanic word that is also the ancestor of English *nether*.]

benedicite /bénnə díssəti/ n. a blessing or grace used in some Christian religious communities [13thC. From Latin, 'bless you'!, a form of *benedicere*, literally 'to say well to', from *bene* 'well' + *dicere* 'to say'.]

Benedicite n. a Latin hymn beginning 'Benedicite omnia opera Domini Domino', traditionally translated as 'O all ye works of the Lord, bless ye the Lord'

Benedict XV /bénnidikt/, **Pope** (1854–1922). As pope (1914–22) he was active in organizing war relief during World War I. Born **Giacomo della Chiesa**

Benedictine /bénni díktin/ n. MONK OR NUN a monk or nun belonging to a religious order founded by St Benedict or following his rule ■ adj. OF ST BENEDICT relating to or characteristic of St Benedict, his rule, or the monastic order that he founded

benediction /bénni díksh'n/ n. 1. EXPRESSION OF APPROVAL an expression of approval or good wishes 2. PRAYER ASKING FOR GOD'S BLESSING a prayer asking for God's blessing, usually at the end of a Christian service 3. **Benediction, benediction** CATHOLIC DEVOTIONAL SERVICE in the Roman Catholic Church, a devotional service during which the congregation is blessed with the Host 4. BLESSEDNESS the state of being blessed [15thC. Directly or via French *bénédiction* from the Latin stem *benediction-* from, ultimately, *benedicere*, literally 'to say well to', from *bene* 'well' + *dicere* 'to say'.] —**benedictive** adj. —**benedictory** adj.

Benedict's solution /bénnidikts-/, **Benedict's reagent** n. a solution of copper sulphate, sodium citrate, and sodium carbonate that turns red in the presence of glucose and other sugars that are reducing agents. It is used in urine tests for diabetes. [Early 20thC. Named after the US chemist Stanley Rossiter *Benedict*, 1884–1936.]

Benedictus /bénni díktəss/ n. 1. LATIN HYMN FROM LUKE a Latin hymn from Luke, beginning 'Benedictus qui venit in nomine Domini' ('Blessed is he that cometh in the name of the Lord') 2. LATIN HYMN FROM MATTHEW a Latin hymn from Matthew, beginning 'Benedictus Dominus Deus Israel' ('Blessed be the Lord God of Israel') [Mid-16thC. From Latin *benedicere* (see BENEDICTION).]

benefaction /bénni fáksh'n/ n. 1. DOING GOOD an act of doing good 2. GOOD DEED a good deed, especially an act of charity 3. DONATION a donation given to a charity [Mid-17thC. From Late Latin *benefaction-*, formed from *bene facere*, literally 'to do well to', from *bene* 'well' + *fact-*, the past participle stem of *facere* 'to do'.]

benefactor /bénni faktər/ n. sb who aids a cause, institution, or individual, especially with a gift of money

benefactress /bénni faktrəss/ n. a woman who aids a cause, institution, or individual, especially with a gift of money

benefic /bə néffik/ adj. doing good or charitable acts (literary) [Early 17thC. From Latin *beneficus*, from *bene facere* (see BENEFACTION).]

benefice /bénnifiss/ n. 1. CHR ENDOWED CHURCH LIVING a church office that provides a living for its holder through an endowment attached to it 2. CHR REVENUE FOR CHURCH LIVING the revenue or property that provides the living of the holder of a church benefice 3. HIST FORM OF FEUDAL TENURE a form of feudal tenure in which a vassal held land from a superior, especially in return for military service ■ vt. (-fices, -ficing, -ficed) CHR PROVIDE WITH BENEFICE to provide a member of the clergy with a church office that will yield a living [14thC. Via Old French from Latin *beneficium*, literally 'doing well', from *bene* 'well' + *fic-*, a variant of the stem of *facere* 'to do'.]

beneficence /bə néffissənss/ n. 1. GENEROSITY generosity or charity 2. GENEROUS GIFT a good or charitable act, especially a generous gift 3. BENEFICIAL EFFECT the beneficial nature or effect that sth has

beneficent /bə néffissənt/ adj. 1. DOING GOOD doing good or charitable acts 2. PRODUCING BENEFIT producing benefits or advantages [Early 17thC. From Latin *beneficent-*, the stem of *beneficentior*, literally 'more beneficent', from *beneficus*, from *bene facere* (see BENEFACTION).] —**beneficently** adv.

beneficial /bénni físh'l/ adj. 1. HAVING GOOD EFFECT producing a good or advantageous effect ○ *The exercise should prove beneficial to his health.* 2. LAW PROFITABLE entitling sb to or entitled to profits or property [15thC. Directly or via French *bénéficial* from Late Latin *beneficialis*, from Latin *beneficium* (see BENEFICE).] —**beneficially** adv. —**beneficialness** n.

beneficiary /bénni físhəri/ n. (plural -ies) 1. SB BENEFITING sb who receives a benefit from sth 2. LAW LEGAL RECIPIENT OF MONEY sb who is entitled under a will, trust, or insurance policy to receive money or property 3. CHR HOLDER OF BENEFICE a member of the clergy who holds an office that provides a living (**benefice**) 4. NZ SOC WELFARE SB RECEIVING GOVERNMENT ASSISTANCE sb who receives a state welfare benefit, e.g. unemployment benefit or sickness benefit ■ adj. CHR RELATING TO BENEFICE relating to a church office that provides a living (**benefice**) or the member of the clergy who holds it [Early 17thC. From Latin *beneficarius*, from *beneficium* (see BENEFICE).]

benefit /bénnifit/ n. 1. ADVANTAGE sth that has a good effect or promotes wellbeing ○ *They eventually reaped the benefits of all their hard work.* 2. SOC WELFARE GOVERNMENT PAYMENT TO SB NEEDING ASSISTANCE a regular payment made by the government under the national insurance scheme or social security to sb qualified to receive it or in need of financial assistance (often used in the plural) 3. MONEY PAID TO CLAIMANT a payment made to a claimant or entitled person by an employer, insurance company, or other institution 4. PERFORMANCE FOR CHARITY a performance by entertainers, athletes, or others to raise money for sb or sth, especially a charity ■ vti. (-fits, -fiting or -fitting, -fited or -fitted) GIVE OR RECEIVE BENEFIT to give or receive help, an advantage, or another benefit [14thC. Via Anglo-Norman *benfet* and Old French *bienfait* from, ultimately, Latin *benefactum* 'good deed', from *bene facere* (see BENEFACTION).] ◇ **give sb the benefit of the doubt** to assume that sb is telling the truth about sth or is innocent of sth because there is not enough evidence that the person is lying or guilty

benefit of clergy n. 1. CHR CHURCH BLESSING the official approval or ministration of the church ○ *married without benefit of clergy* 2. LAW, HISTORY CLERICAL EXEMPTION FROM CIVIL TRIAL the privilege held by the clergy in the Middle Ages that entitled them to trial by an ecclesiastical court and exemption from trial by secular authorities

Benelux /bénni luks/ n. the countries of Belgium the Netherlands and Luxembourg as a group. The three countries formed a customs union in 1948 that was replaced by the Benelux Economic Union in 1960. [Mid-20thC. Acronym of 'Belgium', 'Netherlands', and 'Luxembourg'.]

Beneš /bénnesh/, **Eduard** (1884–1948) Czech statesman. As president of Czechoskovakia (1935–48) he led the Czech government-in-exile during World War II. He resigned after the Communist takeover of his country in 1948.

Benét /bə náy/, **Stephen Vincent** (1898–1943) US author and poet. He wrote *John Brown's Body* (1928), which won a Pulitzer Prize.

Benét, **William Rose** (1886–1950) US poet, critic, and editor. The brother of Stephen Vincent Benét, he cofounded the US magazine *The Saturday Review of Literature* in 1924.

benevolence /bə névvələnss/ *n.* **1.** TENDENCY TO BE KIND an inclination to be kind and helpful or generous **2.** GENEROUS ACT sth done or given out of kindness **3.** HIST FORCED LOAN IMPOSED BY ENGLISH KING a compulsory loan or gift of money imposed by English kings of the late Middle Ages on their subjects [15thC. Via French *bénévolence* from Latin *benevolentia*, from *benevolent-* (see BENEVOLENT).]

benevolent /bə névvələnt/ *adj.* **1.** KIND showing kindness or goodwill **2.** CHARITABLE performing good or charitable acts and not seeking to make a profit [15thC. Via Old French *benivolent* from Latin *benevolent-*, the present participle stem of *bene velle* 'to wish well'.] —**benevolently** *adv.*

Bengal /ben gáwl, beng-/ former province of northeastern India. In 1947 it was divided into the Indian state of West Bengal and East Bengal, now Bangladesh. Area: 224,500 sq. km/87,700 sq. mi. —**Bengalese** *n.*

Bengal, Bay of northeastern section of the Indian Ocean bordered by India, Bangladesh, and Myanmar (Burma). Area: 2,172,000 sq. km/839,000 sq. mi.

Bengali /ben gáwli, beng gáwli/ *n.* **1.** PEOPLES SB FROM BANGLADESH OR WEST BENGAL sb who lives in or was born or brought up in Bangladesh or the state of West Bengal in India **2.** LANG INDIC LANGUAGE the national language of Bangladesh and state language of West Bengal, India. It is an Indic language of the Indo-European family. There are Bengali-speaking communities in many parts of the world, and the language is spoken by at least 170 million people. [Late 18thC. Formed from Hindi *baṅgālī*.] —**Bengali** *adj.*

bengaline /béngəlin, -ə leèn/ *n.* a heavyweight corded fabric, usually of cotton and silk or wool [Late 19thC. From French, because of its similarity to cloth made in Bengal.]

Benghazi /ben gáazi, beng-/, **Bengasi, Banghāzī** city and port in northeastern Libya on the gulf of Sidra. It is near the site of the ancient Greek colony of Euhesperides. Population: 446,250 (1988).

Benguela /ben gwéllə/ city and capital of Benguela District on the Atlantic coast of western Angola. Population: 155,000 (1984).

David Ben-Gurion

Ben-Gurion /ben góori ən/, **David** (1886–1973) Polish-born Israeli statesman. He was the first prime minister of Israel (1948–53, 1955–63). Born **David Gruen**

benighted /bi nítid/ *adj.* **1.** UNENLIGHTENED unenlightened intellectually, socially, or morally **2.** OVERTAKEN BY NIGHT overtaken by night or the dark —**benightedly** *adv.* —**benightedness** *n.*

benign /bi nín/ *adj.* **1.** KINDLY having a kind and gentle disposition or appearance **2.** FAVOURABLE mild or favourable in effect ○ *a benign climate* **3.** HARMLESS neutral or harmless in its effect or influence **4.** MED NOT LIFE-THREATENING not a threat to life or long-term health, especially by being noncancerous [14thC. Via French *bénigne* from Latin *benignus* of uncertain origin: probably from, ultimately, *bene genus*, literally 'well born', from *bene* 'well' + *-genus* 'born'.] —**benignly** *adv.*

benignant /bə nígnənt/ *adj.* kind and gracious in behaviour or appearance, especially towards social inferiors —**benignancy** *n.*

benignity /bə nígnəti/ (*plural* **-ties**) *n.* **1.** KINDLINESS kindness and gentleness of disposition or appearance **2.** KIND ACT a kind or gracious act

Benin

Benin /bə neén/ republic in western Africa between Togo and Nigeria, with a short coastline on the Bight of Benin. It became independent from France in 1960. Language: French. Currency: CFA franc. Capital: Porto-Novo. Population: 5,902,178 (1997). Area: 112,622 sq. km/43,484 sq. mi. Official name **Republic of Benin**. Former name **Dahomey** (until 1975) —**Beninese** /bénni néez/ *adj.*, *n.*

Benin, Bight of wide bay in West Africa, the western section of the Gulf of Guinea. It stretches from the mouth of the River Volta to the mouth of the River Niger, with Lagos as one of its principal ports. Length: approximately 720 km/450 mi.

Benin City capital of Edo State in southern Nigeria. It was the capital of the Kingdom of Benin that flourished in the 15th and 16th centuries, producing magnificent brass, bronze, and ivory sculptures. Population: 223,900 (1995).

benison /bénnizən, -ssən/ *n.* a blessing or benediction (*archaic*) [12thC. Via Old French *benisson* from the Latin stem *benediction-* (see BENEDICTION).]

benjamin /bénjəmin/ *n.* = **benzoin** [Mid-16thC. Alteration of an earlier form of BENZOIN by association with the male forename 'Benjamin'.]

Benjamin /bénjəmin/ *n.* in the Bible, the youngest son of Jacob and Rachel and father of the smallest tribe of Israel

Benjamin /bénjəmin/, **Walter** (1892–1940) German literary critic. He became a Marxist in the 1920s after meeting Bertolt Brecht. His essays include *The Work of Art in an Age of Mechanical Reproduction* (1936).

Ben Lomond /ben lómənd/ mountain in western Scotland, on the eastern side of Loch Lomond. Height: 973 m/3,192 ft.

Benn /ben/, **Tony** (b. 1925) British politician. He was first elected as a Labour MP in 1950, and first became a minister in 1966. The son of Lord Stansgate, he renounced his title in 1963 to stay in the House of Commons. Full name **Anthony Neil Wedgwood Benn**

benne /bénni/, **benni** *n.* = **sesame** *n.* **2** [Mid-18thC. From Mande.]

Bennelong /bénnə long/ (1764?–1813) Australian Aborigine, who was abducted by Governor Phillip in 1789 and taken to England. On his return he was shunned by both the Aboriginal and European communities.

bennet /bénnit/ *n.* = **herb bennet** [15thC. Via French *herbe benéite* from Medieval Latin *herba benedicta* 'blessed plant', because it was said to frighten off the Devil.]

Bennett /bénnit/, **Alan** (b. 1934) British playwright and actor. His many stage and television dramas include *An Englishman Abroad* (1983) and *The Madness of George III* (1991).

Bennett, Arnold (1867–1931) British novelist. He wrote *The Old Wives' Tale* (1908) and the *Clayhanger* series. Full name **Enoch Arnold Bennett**

Bennett, James Gordon (1841–1918) US newspaper owner and editor. As editor of the *New York Herald*, he financed H.M. Stanley's African expeditions.

Bennett, Richard Bedford, 1st Viscount (1870–1947) Canadian statesman and business executive. He was Conservative prime minister of Canada (1930–35). Known as **Iron Heel Bennett**

Bennett, Richard Rodney (b. 1936) British composer. His work incorporates the 12-tone scale and jazz influences, and includes the score for the film *Murder on the Orient Express* (1973).

Ben Nevis /ben névviss/ the highest mountain in the British Isles. It is in western Scotland, in the Grampian Mountains, overlooking the Great Glen. Height: 1,343 m/4,406 ft.

benny /bénni/ (*plural* **-nies**) *n.* an amphetamine tablet, especially Benzedrine™ (*dated slang*) [Mid-20thC. Shortening of BENZEDRINE™.]

Benny /bénni/, **Jack** (1894–1974) US comedian. He is known for his miserly self-caricature in the *Jack Benny Show* on US radio and television (1932–65). Real name **Benjamin Kubelsky**

Benoni /bi nóni/ city in Gauteng Province, northeastern South Africa. Situated about 29 km/18 mi. east of Johannesburg, it is a major industrial city in an important gold-mining region. Population: 113,501 (1991).

bensh /bench/ (**benshes, benshing, benshed**), **bentsh** (**bentshes, bentshing, bentshed**) *vi.* to say a Jewish benediction after eating a meal [Via Yiddish *bentshen* from Latin *benedicere* 'to bless']

bent[1] past tense, past participle of **bend**[1]

bent[2] /bent/ *adj.* **1.** CURVED having a curved, twisted, or angled shape **2.** DETERMINED having a fixed desire to do or accomplish sth ○ *bent on making a name for herself* **3.** OFFENSIVE TERM an offensive term for homosexual (*slang offensive*) **4.** CORRUPT dishonest or corrupt in behaviour (*slang*) ○ *a bent cop* **5.** STOLEN dishonestly acquired or made (*slang*) **6.** SUFFERING FROM THE BENDS suffering from decompression sickness (*informal*) ■ *n.* **1.** NATURAL INCLINATION a strong natural inclination or talent for sth **2.** CIV ENG CROSSWISE SUPPORT a crosswise framework or member used to strengthen a structure

— **WORD KEY: SYNONYMS** —
See Synonyms at *talent*.

bent[3] /bent/ *n.* **1.** GRASS OF TEMPERATE REGIONS a perennial grass of temperate regions, grown for hay and planted for lawns or putting greens. Genus: *Agrostis*. **2.** REEDY GRASS a stiff reedy grass (*archaic*) **3.** GRASS STALK a flower stalk of a stiff grass (*archaic*) **4.** HEATH an area of open moor or grassland (*archaic*) [Old English *beonet*. Ultimately from a prehistoric Germanic word that is also the ancestor of German *Binse*.]

Bentham /bénthəm/, **Jeremy** (1748–1832) British philosopher, jurist, and social reformer. The chief proponent of utilitarianism, he wrote *Introduction to the Principles of Morals and Legislation* (1789). He helped found University College London.

Benthamism /bénthəmizzəm/ *n.* the utilitarian philosophy of Jeremy Bentham, which argues that the highest good is the happiness of the greatest number. ◊ **consequentialism, deontology** —**Benthamite** /bénthə mīt/ *n.*, *adj.*

benthic /bénthik/, **benthonic** /ben thónnik/ *adj.* relating to or characteristic of the bottom of a sea, lake, or deep river, or the animals and plants that live there

benthos /bénthoss/ *n.* the animals and plants that live on or in the sediment at the bottom of a sea, lake, or deep river [Late 19thC. From Greek, 'depth of the sea'.]

Bentley /béntli/, **E. C.** (1875–1956) British writer. He invented the witty four-line verse form known as the 'clerihew'. His writings include the detective novel *Trent's Last Case* (1913). Full name **Edmund Clerihew Bentley**

bento /béntō/ (*plural* **-tos**) *n.* FOOD = **obento**

bentonite /béntə nīt/ *n.* a light-coloured valuable clay that expands with the addition of water and is used as oil-well drilling mud and as a filler in the building, paper, soap, and pharmaceutical industries [Late 19thC. Named after Fort *Benton*, Montana, USA, where it was first identified.] —**bentonitic** /béntə níttik/ *adj.*

bentsh *vi.* = **bensh**

bent-wing moth *n.* a large Australian ghost moth whose larvae, up to 15 cm/6 in long, bore into and are harmful to eucalyptus trees. Latin name: *Leto staceyi*.

bentwood /bént wŏŏd/ *n.* wood that has been bent into a curved shape by being steamed and then put into a mould. It is used to make furniture.

Benue /bénnoo ay/ the longest tributary of the River Niger in Africa. It rises in northern Cameroon and flows northwards and then westwards across central Nigeria. Length: 1,400 km/870 mi.

Benue-Congo *n.* a group of about 700 languages spoken across central and southern Africa and belonging to the Niger-Congo family of languages. Bantu languages form the largest subgroup of Benue-Congo. —**Benue-Congo** *adj.*

benumb /bi núm/ (**-numbs**, **-numbing**, **-numbed**) *vt.* **1.** **MAKE UNABLE TO FEEL** to remove the sense of feeling from a faculty or part of the body, especially by exposure to extreme cold **2.** **MAKE INACTIVE** to make sb incapable of activity or thought (*usually passive*) —**benumbment** *n.*

Benz /benz/, **Karl** (1844–1929) German engineer and automobile manufacturer. He built one of the first petrol-driven automobiles. His company merged with Daimler (1927) to form Daimler-Benz and Co. Full name **Karl Friedrich Benz**

benz- /benz, bents/ *prefix.* = **benzo-** (*used before vowels*)

benzaldehyde /ben záldi hīd/ *n.* a colourless volatile liquid with the odour of, and occurring naturally in, almonds. It is used in the manufacture of dyes, flavourings, and perfumes. Formula: C_6H_5CHO.

Benzedrine /bénzə dreen/ *tdmk.* a trademark for a preparation of amphetamine, a medical stimulant

benzene /bén zeen/ *n.* a colourless volatile toxic liquid with a distinctive odour, obtained from petroleum and used in the manufacture of dyes, polymers, and industrial chemicals such as phenol. Formula: C_6H_6. Former name **benzol** [Mid-19thC. Formed from BENZOIC.]

benzene ring *n.* a molecular structure common to benzene and its derivatives in which six carbon atoms are bonded in a hexagon by alternating single and double bonds

benzine /bén zeen/, **benzin** /-zin/ *n.* a liquid that is obtained from crude oil and has a carefully selected boiling point range. It is used widely as an industrial solvent, e.g. to extract oils from seeds. [Mid-19thC. Formed from BENZOIC.]

benzo- *prefix.* benzene, benzoic acid ○ *benzopyrene* [From BENZOIN]

benzodiazepine /bénzō dī áyzə peen/ *n.* a compound belonging to a group used as minor tranquillizers and as a short-term treatment for sleeping difficulties

benzoic acid /ben zṓik-/ *n.* a colourless crystalline solid found in some natural resins and manufactured synthetically. It is used as a food preservative and in the manufacture of pharmaceuticals and cosmetics. Formula: C_6H_5COOH.

benzoin /bénzō in/ *n.* a toxic white crystalline solid occurring in natural resins or manufactured synthetically. It is used in medications, perfumes, and incense. Formula: $C_{14}H_{12}O_2$. [Mid-16thC. Via French *benjoin* from, ultimately Arabic *lubānjāwī* 'incense from Sumatra'.]

benzol /bén zol/, **benzole** *n.* = **benzene** [Mid-19thC. Formed from *benzoic*.]

benzopyrene /bénzō pīrin/ *n.* a yellow carcinogenic crystalline solid that is one of the most harmful constituents of cigarette smoke. Formula: $C_{20}H_{12}$.

benzoquinone /bénzō kweenōn/ *n.* a yellow crystalline solid with an unpleasant odour. It is used in the manufacture of dyes, antioxidants, and as a photographic developer. Formula: $C_6H_4O_2$.

benzoyl /bénzōil/ *adj.* relating to or containing a particular group of carbon and hydrogen atoms. Formula: $C_6H_5CO–$. [Mid-19thC. From German, from *Benzoësäure* 'benzoic acid' + Greek *hylē* 'wood, matter'.]

benzpyrene *n.* = **benzopyrene**

benzyl /bénzil/ *adj.* relating to or containing a particular group of carbon and hydrogen atoms. Formula: $C_6H_5CH_2–$.

Beowulf /báyō wŏŏlf/ *n.* an anonymous Old English epic poem of the eighth century AD describing the exploits of the hero Beowulf, in particular his slaying of the monster Grendel and its mother

bequeath /bi kweeth, -kweeth/ (**-queaths**, **-queathing**, **-queathed**) *vt.* **1.** **LEAVE SB STH IN WILL** to leave personal or other property to sb after death by means of a will **2.** **HAND DOWN TO POSTERITY** to hand sth, e.g. knowledge or a practice, down to future generations [Old English *becweðan*, literally 'to speak about', from *cweðan* 'to speak'. The underlying idea is of expressing your will.] —**bequeathal** /bi kweeth'l/ *n.* —**bequeather** /bi kweethər/ *n.* —**bequeathment** /bi kweethmənt/ *n.*

bequest /bi kwést/ *n.* **1.** **ACT OF BEQUEATHING** an act of bequeathing sth **2.** **STH LEFT IN WILL** sth disposed of in a will **3.** **STH HANDED DOWN TO POSTERITY** sth passed down to future generations [14thC. Formed from BEQUEATH.]

Béranger /báy raaN zhay/, **Pierre Jean de** (1780–1857) French poet. His witty political poems were very popular, though they earned him several spells in jail.

berate /bi ráyt/ (**-rates**, **-rating**, **-rated**) *vt.* to scold sb vigorously and lengthily [Mid-16thC. Formed from RATE 'to berate'.]

Berber /búrbər/ (*plural* **-bers** *or* **-ber**) *n.* **1.** **PEOPLES MEMBER OF N AFRICAN PEOPLE** a member of a people living in North Africa **2.** **LANG GROUP OF AFRO-ASIATIC LANGUAGES** a group of about twenty languages spoken across North Africa, especially in Algeria and Morocco, and constituting a branch of the Afro-Asiatic languages. Berber is sometimes regarded as a single language with very divergent dialects. About 12 million people speak a Berber language. [Mid-18thC. From Arabic *barbar* (source also of English *barbary*).] —**Berber** *adj.*

Berbera /búrbərə/ port situated on the Gulf of Aden in northwestern Somalia. Population: 65,000 (1987).

berberine /búrbərin/, **berberin** *n.* a pale yellow toxic crystalline solid obtained from the roots of barberry and other plants, used formerly as an amoebicide and in the treatment of cholera. Formula: $C_{20}H_{19}NO_5$. [Mid-19thC. Formed from BERBERIS.]

berberis /búrbəriss/ *n.* BOT = **barberry** [Late 16thC. Via Modern Latin or Old French from Medieval Latin *barbaris* (source of English *barberry*).]

berceuse /bair súrz/ *n.* **1.** **LULLABY** a lullaby or cradlesong **2.** **MUSIC PIECE OF MUSIC RESEMBLING LULLABY** an instrumental piece of music, usually in six-eight time, meant to sound like a lullaby [Late 19thC. From French, from *bercer* 'to rock'.]

Berchtesgaden /báirktəss gaad'n, báirkhtəss-/ town in southeastern Bavaria, Germany, a popular ski resort. Adolf Hitler's fortified retreat, the Berghof was nearby. Population: 7,979 (1991).

bereave /bi reev/ (**-reaves**, **-reaving**, **-reaved**) *vt.* to deprive sb of a beloved person or a treasured thing, especially through death (*often passive*) [Old English *bereafian* 'to deprive, rob'. Ultimately from a prehistoric Germanic word that is also the ancestor of Dutch *beroven*, German *berauben* and English *rob*.] —**bereavement** *n.* —**bereaver** *n.*

bereaved /bi reevd/ *adj.* DEPRIVED OF LOVED ONE BY DEATH having lost a loved one through death ■ *n.* (*plural* **-reaved**) SB BEREAVED sb who has suffered the loss by death of a loved one

bereft /bi réft/ *adj.* **1.** DEPRIVED deprived of sb or sth loved or valued ○ '*Lively as the Tabloid Decade* (the 1990s) *has been, it wouldn't be the worst thing if it uncharacteristically just dribbled out, bereft of new material*' (David Kamp, *Vanity Fair*; February 1999) **3.** FEELING SENSE OF LOSS filled with a sense of loss [Late 16thC. Old past participle of BEREAVE.]

Berenice's Hair /bérrə níssiz-/ *n.* = **Coma Berenices** [Mid-16thC. Named after a third century BC Egyptian queen whose hair, cut off and dedicated as an offering for her husband's safe return from war, is said to have been placed in the stars.]

Beresford /bérrisfərd/, **Bruce** (*b.* 1940) Australian film director. He directed *Breaker Morant* (1980) and the Academy Award-winning *Driving Miss Daisy* (1989).

beret /bérray/ *n.* a flat round soft hat, usually woollen, with a tight-fitting headband [Early 19thC. Via French from, ultimately, late Latin *birrus* 'hooded cloak' (source also of English *biretta*), possibly of Celtic origin.]

beretta *n.* CHR = **biretta**

berg[1] /burg/ *n.* an iceberg [Early 19thC. Shortening.]

berg[2] /burg/ *n.* S Africa a mountain [Early 19thC. Via Afrikaans from Dutch *bergh* 'mountain'.]

Berg /burg/, **Alban** (1885–1935) Austrian composer. He mixed modern and traditional styles. He wrote the opera *Wozzeck* (1925).

Bergamot

bergamot /búrgə mot/ (*plural* **-mots** *or* **-mot**) *n.* **1.** **bergamot, bergamot orange** SPINY ASIAN CITRUS TREE a spiny Asian citrus tree that bears sour pear-shaped fruit. Latin name: *Citrus bergamia*. **2.** **bergamot, bergamot oil** OIL FROM FRUIT OF BERGAMOT TREE a fragrant yellow-green essential oil extracted from the rind of the fruits of bergamot trees, used in making perfumes and as the flavouring in Earl Grey tea **3.** MEDITERRANEAN MINT PLANT a Mediterranean mint plant that is the source of a fragrant oil similar to bergamot oil. Latin name: *Mentha citrata*. **4.** N AMERICAN MINT PLANT a North American mint plant with showy scarlet flowers. The flowers of garden varieties may be white, pink, red, or purple. Latin name: *Monarda didyma*. US term **bee balm 5.** = **wild bergamot** [Late 17thC. Named after BERGAMO.]

Bergen /búrgən/ city and port in southwestern Norway and the administrative capital of Hordaland County. Population: 221,717 (1995).

Bergen-Belsen ♦ **Belsen**

bergenia /bə géeni ə/ (*plural* **-ias** *or* **-ia**) *n.* a perennial plant with large leathery leaves, grown in gardens for its early, usually red, purple, or pink, flowers. Genus: *Bergenia*. [Mid-19thC. Named after the German botanist and physician Karl August von *Bergen*, 1704–60.]

bergère /bər zháir/ (*plural* **-gères**) *n.* a type of chair or sofa with sides and back made of woven cane [Mid-18thC. From French, literally 'shepherdess'.]

Bergman /búrgmən/, **Ingmar** (*b.* 1918) Swedish film director. His many films include dark, brooding cinema classics such as *Wild Strawberries* (1957) and *The Seventh Seal* (1957). Full name **Ernst Ingmar Bergman**

Bergman, Ingrid (1915–82) Swedish-born US film actor. Best known for her role in the film *Casablanca* (1942), she acted in numerous US and European films, and won two Academy Awards.

bergschrund /búrk shrŏŏnt/ (*plural* **-schrunds** *or* **-schrunde** /-shrŏŏndə/) *n.* a crevasse formed at the head of a glacier [Mid-19thC. From German, literally 'mountain cleft'.]

Bergson /búrgss'n/, **Henri** (1859–1941) French philosopher. One of his most influential ideas was the central role that creative energy plays in human development. He won the Nobel Prize in literature in 1927. Full name **Henri Louis Bergson** —**Bergsonian** *n., adj.*

Bergsonism /búrgss'nizzəm/ *n.* the philosophy of Henri Bergson, which posits the existence of a universal life-giving force (**élan vital**)

berg wind *n. S Africa* a hot dry wind blowing from the South African interior to the coast [From BERG[2], because it comes from the mountains]

beriberi /bérri bérri/ *n.* a degenerative disease of the nerves caused by a deficiency of the vitamin thiamine and marked by pain, paralysis, and swelling [Early 18thC. From Sinhalese, 'weakness'.]

Bering /báiring/, **Vitus** (1681–1741) Danish-born Russian explorer. He investigated the theory that Asia and North America were once connected. The Bering Sea and Bering Strait are named after him. Full name **Vitus Jonassen Bering**

Bering land bridge *n.* a link between Alaska and Siberia that was above sea level during the Ice Age between 13,000 and 10,000 years ago and provided a route for prehistoric man and animals into the Americas

Bering Sea part of the North Pacific Ocean surrounded by the Aleutian Islands, Siberia, and Alaska. Area: 2,261,000 sq. km/873,000 sq. mi. Depth: 4,773 m/15,659 ft.

Bering Strait narrow stretch of sea connecting the Bering Sea to the Arctic Ocean, and separating Russia from Alaska. At its narrowest point it is 82 km/51 mi. wide.

Berio /bérri ō/, **Luciano** (*b.* 1925) Italian-born composer. His experimental compositions combined prerecorded and electronic sounds, and spoken words.

Berisha /bə réeshə/, **Sali** (*b.* 1944) Albanian statesman. One of the leaders of post-communist reform in Albania, he was elected as the country's first non-communist president (1992–7).

berk /burk/, **burk** *n.* sb stupid or foolish (*slang insult*) [Mid-20thC. From rhyming slang *Berkeley Hunt* 'cunt'.]

Berkeleianism /baárkli ə nizzəm/ *n.* the philosophy of George Berkeley, particularly his view that the material world is an idea in God's mind and that an object's existence consists in its being perceived [Early 19thC. Named after Bishop BERKELEY.] — **Berkeleian** *adj.*, *n.*

Berkeley /búrkli/ city in western California on San Francisco Bay, home to the University of California. Population: 103,243 (1996).

Berkeley /baárkli/, **Busby** (1895–1976) US film director and choreographer. He is famous for his work in Broadway and Hollywood musicals including *42nd Street* (1933). Real name **William Berkeley Enos**

Berkeley, George (1685–1753) Irish Anglican bishop and philosopher. He propounded idealist philosophy in *A Treatise Concerning the Principles of Human Knowledge* (1710) and other works.

Berkeley, Sir William (1606–77) English-born US administrator of the colony of Virginia (1641–51, 1660–76).

berkelium /bur keéli əm/ *n.* a synthetic radioactive element produced by bombarding the element americium-241 with helium ions. Symbol **Bk** [Mid-20thC. Named after BERKELEY, California, where it was first made.]

Berkoff /búrk of/, **Steven** (*b.* 1937) British actor, director, and dramatist. He founded the London Theatre Group and became known for his controversial adaptations of classical drama.

Berks. /baarks/ *abbr.* Berkshire

Berkshire /baárkshə/ county in south-central England. Since 1998 it has had only ceremonial functions and has been divided into six unitary authorities. Population: 783,200 (1995). Area: 1,259 sq. km/486 sq. mi.

berley /búrli/, **burley** *n. Aus* **1.** BAIT SCATTERED TO ATTRACT FISH bait scattered into the water to attract fish **2.** NONSENSE nonsensical thinking or talk (*slang*) ■ *vt.* (**-leys, -leying, -leyed**) *Aus* **1.** SCATTER BAIT OVER WATER to scatter bait over water to attract fish **2.** HURRY SB UP to cause sb to hurry [Late 19thC. Origin unknown.]

berlin /bur lín/ *n.* **berlin, berline** **1.** FOUR-WHEELED COVERED CARRIAGE a four-wheeled covered carriage popular in the 18th century **2.** LIMOUSINE a large and luxurious car with a glass partition between the driver and the passengers [Late 17thC. Named after the city of *Berlin*.]

Berlin /bur lín/ capital and the largest city of Germany. At the end of World War II (1945), the city was divided into East and West Berlin. It became the national capital again following the reunification of East and West Germany in 1990. Population: 3,472,000 (1997). ◆ **Berlin Wall** —**Berliner** *n.*

Irving Berlin

Berlin, Irving (1888–1989) Russian-born US songwriter. One of the all-time great writers of American popular songs, including *White Christmas*, he also wrote numerous musicals, including *Annie Get Your Gun* (1946). Born **Israel Baline**

Berlin, Sir Isaiah (1909–97) Latvian-born British philosopher and historian. He espoused liberal humanism in works such as *Two Concepts of Liberty* (1959), *Vico and Herder* (1976), and *The Crooked Timber of Humanity* (1990).

berline *n.* = **berlin** *n.* **1, berlin** *n.* **2** [Mid-18thC. French form of BERLIN.]

Berlin Wall *n.* a fortified wall surrounding West Berlin, built in 1961 to prevent East German citizens travelling to the West. Its demolition in 1989 marked the end of the Cold War.

Berlin wool *n.* a fine wool yarn used for making clothes and in tapestry

Berlin woolwork *n.* needlepoint embroidery stitched with Berlin wools from handpainted coloured charts, popular especially in the second half of the 19th century

Berlioz /báirli ōz/, **Hector** (1803–69) French composer. He was a seminal figure in 19th-century romanticism. Major works among his symphonies, operas, and masses include *Symphonie Fantastique* (1831) and the opera *The Trojans* (1856–58). Full name **Louis Hector Berlioz**

berm /burm/, **berme** *n.* **1.** NARROW PATH a ledge or narrow path along the top or bottom of a slope, at the edge of a road, or along a canal **2.** RIDGE ABOVE HIGH TIDE MARK a natural ridge or flat platform formed at the rear of a beach, above the high tide mark **3.** MIL RIDGE OF SAND FOR ANTITANK DEFENCE a ridge of sand or soil erected as a defence against tanks, which in crossing it expose their vulnerable undersides to attack **4.** MIL LEDGE BETWEEN MOAT AND RAMPART a ledge or narrow path between a moat or ditch and a rampart **5.** MINING ROADWAY IN OPEN-CAST MINE a narrow roadway cut in the slope of an open-cast mine **6.** *NZ* GRASS VERGE OF SUBURBAN STREET the grass verge of a suburban street, usually kept mown [Early 18thC. Via French from Dutch, of uncertain origin.]

Bermuda /bər myoódə/ self-governing British dependency in the western North Atlantic Ocean. It contains more than 150 islands, 20 of which are inhabited. Language: English. Currency: Bermuda dollar. Capital: Hamilton. Population: 61,600 (1995). Area: 53 sq. km/21 sq. mi. —**Bermudan** *adj.*

Bermuda bag *n.* an oval-shaped handbag with wooden handles and removable covers

Bermuda grass *n.* a creeping grass with wiry roots, native to southern Europe but now widely spread.

It is used for lawns and pastures and to stabilize sand dunes. Latin name: *Cynodon dactylon.*

Bermuda rig *n.* a fore-and-aft arrangement of a boat's mast and sails that has a tall pointed mainsail on a sharply raked mast

Bermuda shorts, **Bermudas** *npl.* tailored shorts whose legs extend almost to the knee

Bermuda Triangle *n.* an area in the western Atlantic Ocean, between Bermuda, Florida, and Puerto Rico, where many ships and aircraft are believed to have disappeared in mysterious circumstances

Bern /burn/, **Berne** capital of Switzerland since 1848. Situated on the Aar River in western Switzerland, it is also capital of Bern Canton. Population: 134,129 (1994).

Bernadette of Lourdes /búrnə dét əv loórd, -loórdz/, **St** (1844–79) French nun and visionary. She claimed (1858) to have received apparitions of the Virgin Mary near her birthplace, Lourdes, which became a popular place of Roman Catholic pilgrimage. Born **Marie Bernarde Soubirous**

Bernadotte /búrnə dot/, **Folke, Count** (1895–1948) Swedish diplomat. He was assassinated by Jewish terrorists while serving as a UN mediator in Palestine prior to the creation of Israel.

Bernanos /báirnə nóss/, **Georges** (1888–1948) French novelist. He wrote *Diary of a Country Priest* (1936).

Bernard /búrnərd/, **Claude** (1813–78) French physiologist. He made important discoveries on the role of the pancreas and liver.

Bernardine /búrnədin/ *n.* **1.** CISTERCIAN MONK a monk belonging to a stricter branch of the Cistercian order **2.** NUN a nun belonging to a non-Cistercian order that follows a rule based on the original Cistercian rule ■ *adj.* **1.** OF THE BERNARDINES relating to or characteristic of a Bernardine **2.** OF ST BERNARD relating to or characteristic of St Bernard of Clairvaux or his monastic reforms

Bernard of Clairvaux /búrnərd əv klair vố/, **St** (1090–1153) French theologian. He joined the Cistercian order (1113) and founded over 70 monasteries.

Berne = **Bern**

Bernese Alps /búr neez-/ mountain range in southwestern Switzerland, south of Bern. The highest peaks are the Finsteraarhorn, 4,274 m/14,022 ft and the Jungfrau, 4,158 m/13,642 ft. The region is a major tourist area with many mountain resorts.

Sarah Bernhardt

Bernhardt /búrn haart/, **Sarah** (1844–1923) French actor. Known for her passionate performances in tragedy, she founded her own theatre company in 1899. Among her famous roles were Cordelia, Phèdre, and Hamlet. Real name **Henriette Rosine Bernard**

Bernini /bur néeni/, **Gianlorenzo** (1598–1680) Italian sculptor and architect. The foremost Italian artist of the Baroque period, he produced bronze and marble sculptures and designed many of the most impressive elements of St Peter's Cathedral in Rome. Full name **Giovanni Lorenzo Bernini**

Bernoulli /bur nóoli/, **Daniel** (1700–82) Dutch-born Swiss mathematician and physicist. The son of Johann Bernoulli, he formulated Bernoulli's principle governing the conservation of energy in fluid dynamics.

Bernoulli, Jacques (1654–1705) Swiss mathematician. The brother of Johann Bernoulli, he wrote *Ars conjectandi* (1713) on the theory of probability and made theoretical advances in geometry and calculus.

Bernoulli, Johann or **Jean** (1667–1748) Swiss mathematician. He helped write the first textbook on differential calculus. He was the brother of Jacques Bernoulli and the father of Daniel Bernoulli.

Bernoulli distribution *n.* = binomial distribution [Mid-20thC. Named after Jacques BERNOULLI.]

Bernoulli's law *n.* = law of large numbers [Named after Jacques BERNOULLI]

Bernoulli's theorem *n.* the sum of the pressure and the product of one half of the density times the velocity squared is constant along a streamline for steady flow in an incompressible non-viscous fluid at constant height

Leonard Bernstein

Bernstein /búrn stīn/, **Leonard** (1918–90) US conductor, composer, and pianist. He composed classical works and the musicals *Candide* (1956) and *West Side Story* (1957).

Berri /bérri/ town in southeastern South Australia, Australia, on the Murray River. Population: 3,502 (1986).

berry /bérri/ *n.* (*plural* -ries) 1. BOT SMALL JUICY FRUIT any small juicy or fleshy fruit. Berries are usually round and may be edible or inedible. 2. BOT FLESHY SEED-CONTAINING FRUIT a soft fleshy fruit that contains many seeds. Tomato, grape, and banana fruits are berries. (*technical*) 3. BOT KERNEL a seed or kernel, e.g. a coffee bean 4. ZOOL LOBSTER EGG an egg of a lobster or other egg-carrying crustacean ■ *vi.* (-ries, -rying, -ried) 1. BEAR BERRIES to produce berries (*refers to bushes*) 2. SEARCH FOR EDIBLE BERRIES to gather or hunt for berries to eat [Old English beri(g)e. Ultimately from a prehistoric Germanic word that is also the ancestor of Dutch *bes* and German *Beere*.] —**berried** *adj.*

bersagliere /búrss'l yáiri/ (*plural* -ri) *n.* a soldier in a rifle unit of the Italian army [Mid-19thC. From Italian, from *bersaglio* 'target', because they were originally sharpshooters.]

berseem /bər seém/ *n.* a Mediterranean clover grown for forage for grazing livestock and to improve soil quality, especially in the southern United States and the Nile Valley. Latin name: *Trifolium alexandrinum*. [Early 20thC. Via Arabic *birsīm* from Coptic *bersīm*.]

berserk /bə zúrk/ *adj.* AGGRESSIVE OR ANGRY extremely aggressive or angry ○ *go berserk* ■ *n.* 1. SB RECKLESS sb who behaves violently or with a reckless lack of restraint 2. = **berserker** [Early 19thC. From Old Norse *berserk* 'wild warrior', probably from the stem of *bjorn* 'bear' + *serkr* 'shirt', because either they wore bearskins or were fierce like bears.] —**berserkly** *adv.*

berserker /bər zúrkər/ *n.* a member of a group of Norse warriors who fought with wild unrestrained aggression

berth /burth/ *n.* 1. BED ON SHIP OR TRAIN a bed, usually built-in, on a ship or a train 2. NAUT DOCK FOR SHIP a place, usually alongside a quay or dock, where a ship ties up or anchors 3. NAUT ROOM TO MANOEUVRE AT SEA sufficient room between a ship and the shore or between a ship and another vessel or object to allow the ship to manoeuvre safely 4. PARKING PLACE a place for a motor vehicle to park or be loaded or unloaded 5. NAUT JOB ON SHIP a post as part of a ship's crew 6.

JOB a job or position of employment (*informal*) ■ *v.* (**berths, berthing, berthed**) 1. *vti.* NAUT DOCK A SHIP to dock or moor a vessel, or be docked or moored 2. *vt.* NAUT ASSIGN MOORING TO VESSEL to assign a vessel a place to dock or moor 3. *vt.* ASSIGN BERTH TO SB to assign sb a berth on a ship or train [Early 17thC. Formed from BEAR 'to carry'. Originally in the sense 'enough room to steer in', probably influenced by BEAR in the sense 'to steer in a particular direction'.] ◇ **give sb** or **sth a wide berth** to keep well away from sb or sth

bertha /búrthə/ *n.* a wide long collar around the shoulders of a woman's low-necked dress [Mid-19thC. From French *berthe*, named after the Carolingian Queen *Bertha*, died A.D. 783, wife of Pepin the Short.]

Bertillon system /búrtilən-/ *n.* a former method of identifying people, especially criminals, on the basis of detailed records of their physical measurements and characteristics [Late 19thC. Named after the French criminologist Alphonse *Bertillon*, 1853–1914, who invented it.]

Berwickshire /bérrikshər/ former county in southeastern Scotland that is now part of the Scottish Boarders Council area

Berwick-upon-Tweed /bérrik ə pón tweéd/ walled town in Northumberland, northern England. Situated on the mouth of the River Tweed, it was ceded to England from Scotland in 1482. Population: 13,544 (1991).

beryl /bérrəl/ *n.* a hard mineral, beryllium aluminium silicate, that occurs in white, yellow, pink, green, or blue forms. The green form is emerald, the blue is aquamarine, and the other forms are also valued as gems. Formula: $Be_3Al_2Si_6O_{18}$. [12thC. Via French and Latin *beryllus* from Greek *bērullos*, probably from, ultimately, Pali *veluriya*, perhaps meaning 'white, pale'.] —**berylline** *adj.*

beryllium /bə rílli əm/ *n.* a metallic grey-white chemical element that is light, hard, brittle, and resists corrosion. It is used in alloys, as a lightweight construction material, and in windows in X-ray tubes. Symbol **Be** [Mid-19thC. Formed from BERYL, which is a major source.]

Berzelius /bər zeéli əss/, **Jöns Jakob, Baron** (1799–1848) Swedish chemist. He drew up the table of atomic weights and discovered the elements selenium, thorium, and cerium.

Besançon /bə zón soN/ city and capital of Doubs Department, in the Franche-Comté Region, eastern France. Population: 119,194 (1990).

Besant /bézz'nt/, **Annie** (1847–1933) British theosophist and politician. She introduced theosophy in India, and was the first woman elected president of the Indian National Congress (1917). Born **Annie Wood**

Besant /bə zánt/, **Sir Walter** (1836–1901) British reformer and novelist. His novels advocated social reform and included *The Children of Gideon* (1881).

beseech /bi seéch/ *vt.* (-seeches, -seeching, -sought /bi sáwt/ or -seeched) *vt.* (*literary*) 1. BEG SB to ask earnestly or beg sb to do sth 2. BEG FOR STH to ask urgently for sth [12thC. Formed from SEEK.] —**beseecher** *n.* —**beseechingly** *adv.*

beset /bi sét/ *vt.* (-sets, -setting, -set) *vt.* (*usually passive*) 1. HARASS to harass or trouble sb or sth continually (*formal*) 2. SURROUND to attack sb or sth on all sides (*formal*) 3. SET WITH JEWELS to surround or set sth with jewels or other ornaments (*literary*) [Old English *besettan*, literally 'to set about'] —**besetment** *n.* —**besetter** *n.*

besetting /bi sétting/ *adj.* harassing or troubling sb continually

beshrew /bi shroó/ *vt.* (-shrews, -shrewing, -shrewed) *vt.* to curse or wish evil upon sb (*archaic*) (*usually used in mild oaths*) [13thC. Formed from SHREW in its obsolete sense 'to nag'.]

beside /bi síd/ *prep.* 1. AT THE SIDE OF in a position next to or alongside ○ *Sit beside me.* ○ *beside the seaside* 2. COMPARED WITH in comparison with ○ *handsome beside his brother* 3. AS WELL AS in addition to ○ *in another dictionary beside this one* [Old English *be sīdan*, literally 'by the side of'] ◇ **beside yourself** in a very excited or agitated state

beside or **besides**? *Beside* is used with reference to physical position: *Come and sit beside me.* It is also used in the idiomatic expression **to be beside yourself**: *They were beside themselves with worry.* **Besides** is an adverb meaning 'moreover': *it's late and besides, the weather's too cold,* and a preposition meaning 'in addition to': *They've already paid a lot for the house besides what they'll need for improvements.* Note that **besides** is inclusive, whereas **except** is exclusive, so that *they are all friends of mine besides Larry* means that Larry is also a friend whereas *they are all friends of mine except Larry* means that Larry is not a friend.

besides /bi sídz/ *prep., adv.* AS WELL in addition to sth or sth specified or understood ○ *Besides fruit, we will also need cheese, and crackers.* ■ *adv.* MOREOVER what is more ○ *He's my cousin. Besides, he's good company.*

besiege /bi seéj/ (-sieges, -sieging, -sieged) *vt.* 1. SURROUND WITH ARMY to surround a city or strongpoint with armed forces in order to bring about its surrender or capture 2. CROWD AROUND SB to crowd around sb in an oppressive way (*usually passive*) ○ *the newlyweds were besieged by reporters outside their hotel* 3. HARASS to harass a person or organization with insistent demands or complaints (*usually passive*) ○ *The box office was besieged by fans wanting tickets.* [13thC. Formed from earlier *assiege*, via Old French *asegier* from, ultimately, Latin *sedere* (see SIEGE).] —**besiegement** *n.* —**besieger** *n.*

besmear /bi smeér/ (-smears, -smearing, -smeared) *vt.* 1. SMEAR WITH SUBSTANCE to smear sb or sth with mud, dirt, or some greasy or sticky substance 2. SULLY to bring shame or disgrace on sb or sth

besmirch /bi smúrch/ (-smirches, -smirching, -smirched) *vt.* 1. SULLY to bring shame or disgrace on sb's reputation 2. MAKE DIRTY to make sth dirty (*literary*) —**besmircher** *n.* —**besmirchment** *n.*

besom /beézəm/ *n.* 1. BROOM MADE FROM TWIGS a broom, especially one made with a bundle of twigs 2. SPORTS BROOM USED IN CURLING a broom used in curling to sweep the ice in front of a moving stone in order to help it slide 3. WOMAN OR GIRL a mildly derogatory term for a woman or girl (*regional insult*) ■ *vt.* (-soms, -soming, -somed) SWEEP WITH BROOM to sweep sth with a broom [Old English *bes(e)ma*. Ultimately from a prehistoric Germanic word that is also the ancestor of Dutch *bezem* and German *Besen*.]

besotted /bi sóttid/ *adj.* 1. INFATUATED made confused through affection for or attraction to sb 2. MUDDLED in a confused mental state, especially through having drunk too much alcohol (*archaic*) [Late 16thC. Formed from earlier *sot* 'to stupefy', from Old French, 'fool'.]

besought past tense, past participle of **beseech**

bespangle /bi spáng g'l/ (-gles, -gling, -gled) *vt.* to ornament sth with sth bright, especially spangles

bespatter /bi spáttər/ (-ters, -tering, -tered) *vt.* to splash sth with mud, paint, or some other substance

bespeak /bi speék/ (-speaks, -speaking, -spoke /-spók/, -spoken /-spókən/) *vt.* 1. SIGNIFY to be a sign or indication of sth 2. ORDER IN ADVANCE to reserve or order sth in advance 3. ASK FOR POLITELY to ask politely for sth, e.g. a favour (*formal*) 4. ADDRESS SB to speak to sb (*literary*) 5. PORTEND to foretell sth (*archaic*) [Old English *bisprecan*, literally 'to speak about', from *sprecan* 'to speak' (see SPEAK)]

bespectacled /bi spéktək'ld/ *adj.* wearing spectacles

bespoke past tense of **bespeak** ■ *adj.* 1. MADE TO ORDER made to a customer's specifications 2. MAKING CLOTHES OR SHOES TO ORDER making clothes or shoes to customers' specifications ○ *a bespoke tailor*

bespoken past participle of **bespeak**

besprinkle /bi spríngk'l/ (-kles, -kling, -kled) *vt.* to sprinkle small quantities of liquid or sth light over the surface of sth (*often passive*)

Bessarabia /béssə ráybi ə/ Historic region in southeastern Europe, between the Prut and Dniester Rivers, corresponding roughly to present-day Moldova and part of Ukraine. A much-contested area, it was a province of Romania between 1918 and 1940.

Bessel /béss'l/, **Friedrich Wilhelm** (1784–1846) German mathematician and astronomer. He identified and determined the distance of the nearest stars, and predicted the existence of a planet beyond Uranus.

Bessemer /béssəmər/, **Sir Henry** (1813–98) British metallurgist. He invented the 'Bessemer process' for transforming molten pig iron into steel.

Bessemer process *n.* a largely obsolete method for making steel from impure iron by forcing air through the molten metal in a specialized furnace (**Bessemer converter**) [Late 19thC. Named after Sir Henry *Bessemer*, who patented it.]

best /best/ CORE MEANING: better than anybody or anything else

1. *adj.* BETTER THAN ALL OTHERS of the highest quality or standard or the most excellent type ○ *the best days of your life* ○ *wearing her best dress* ○ *the best sprinter this decade* **2.** *adj.* MOST LIKELY TO SUCCEED most likely to have or come near to the desired outcome ○ *the best thing to do in the circumstances* **3.** *adj.* MOST INTIMATE liked, trusted, and confided in more than anybody else ○ *my best friends* **4.** *adv.* MORE THAN ALL OTHERS in the highest degree or to the greatest extent ○ *likes me best* **5.** *adv.* MOST SUCCESSFULLY in a way that is most likely to have or come near to the desired outcome ○ *It works best if you warm it up first.* **6.** *adv.* TO THE HIGHEST STANDARD to a higher standard than anybody or anything else ○ *the best trained horse in the competition* **7.** *n.* WHAT IS BEST the best possible things or circumstances ○ *want the best for their family* ○ *will only buy the best* **8.** *n.* SB OR STH BETTER THAN OTHERS sb or sth of the highest quality or standard ○ *is the best at hockey* **9.** *n.* TOP QUALITY the highest quality or standard that sb or sth is capable of ○ *do your best* ○ *past its best* **10.** *n.* SPORTS TOP ACHIEVEMENT the best time or score that sb has achieved in a sport or game ○ *trying to beat her personal best in the marathon* **11.** *n.* ENDORSEMENT used as an enthusiastic endorsement of sth (*slang*) ○ *How is your hotel? – It's the best!* [Old English *betest*; superlative of GOOD and WELL. Ultimately from a prehistoric Germanic word that is also the ancestor of German and Dutch *best*.] ◇ **at best** according to the most favourable interpretation ◇ **at the best of times** even when circumstances are at their most favourable ◇ **at your** *or* **its best** performing at the peak of ability or effectiveness ◇ **make the best of sth** to do what is required to deal with an unfavourable situation

Best /best/, **Elsdon** (1856–1931) New Zealand ethnologist, author of pioneering studies of the Tuhoe people of the Urewera Region of New Zealand. His works include *The Maori As He Was* (1924).

Best, George (*b.* 1946) Northern Irish footballer. He scored 177 goals playing for Manchester United (1967–68) and played 37 times for Northern Ireland.

best-ball *adj.* using a scoring method in which a golfer competes against a team of two or three other golfers, with the team recording only the best individual score for each hole

best boy *n.* the chief assistant to the electrician in charge of lighting on a film or television set

best end *n.* meat cut from the end of the neck nearest to the shoulder of a butchered animal

bestial /bésti əl/ *adj.* **1.** INHUMAN lacking normal human feelings of pity or remorse ○ *bestial cruelty* **2.** SEXUALLY DEPRAVED sexual in a depraved or purely physical manner **3.** BRUTISH lacking intellect, reason, or culture **4.** RELATING TO BEASTS relating to or characteristic of a beast [14thC. Via Old French from, ultimately, Latin *bestia* (see BEAST).] —**bestially** *adv.*

bestialise *vt.* = **bestialize**

bestiality /bésti álləti/ *n.* **1.** SEX WITH ANIMAL sexual intercourse or other sexual activity between a human being and an animal **2.** INHUMAN BEHAVIOUR an act, behaviour, or condition more appropriate for an animal than a human being

bestialize /bésti ə līz/ (**-izes, -izing, -ized**), **bestialise** (**-ises, -ising, -ised**) *vt.* **1.** REDUCE TO LEVEL OF ANIMAL to make sb behave or live like an animal **2.** MAKE INHUMAN to make sb inhuman or savage

bestiary /bésti əri/ (*plural* **-ies**) *n.* a medieval book containing pictures and moralizing stories about real and imaginary animals [Mid-19thC. From medieval Latin *bestiarium*, from Latin *bestia* 'beast'.]

bestir /bi stúr/ (**-stirs, -stirring, -stirred**) *vr.* to begin to do sth after a period of inactivity (*formal*) ○ *After a long afternoon nap, they finally bestirred themselves to start the supper preparations.* [14thC. Coined from BE- 'all over, thoroughly' + STIR.]

best maid *n. Scotland* the chief bridesmaid at a wedding, the counterpart of the best man

best man (*plural* **best men**) *n.* a male attendant of a bridegroom, who carries out important duties during the wedding celebrations

bestow /bi stṓ/ (**-stows, -stowing, -stowed**) *vt.* **1.** GIVE OR PRESENT STH to present sth to sb (*formal*) **2.** PUT SOMEWHERE to put sth somewhere (*archaic*) ○ *'Alonso hence, and bestow your luggage where you found it'.* (William Shakespeare, *The Tempest*; 1611) — **bestowment** *n.* —**bestowal** *n.*

WORD KEY: SYNONYMS

See Synonyms at ***give***.

bestrew /bi stróo/ (**-strews, -strewing, -strewed, -strewn** /bi stróon/ *or* **-strewed**) *vt.* (*literary*) **1.** SCATTER THINGS to scatter things over sth ○ *a church aisle bestrewn with flowers* **2.** BE SCATTERED OVER STH to be scattered over sth ○ *the confetti that bestrewed the church steps after the wedding*

bestride /bi strīd/ (**-strides, -striding, -strode** /-strṓd/ *or* **-strid, -stridden** /-strídd'n/ *or* **-strid** *archaic* /-stríd/) *vt.* to sit or stand with one leg on each side of sth ○ *He bestrode the hearthrug, holding forth on the merits of the case* .

bestseller /bést séllər/ *n.* **1.** POPULAR PRODUCT sth, especially a book, that is commercially very successful **2.** AUTHOR OF POPULAR BOOKS an author who writes bestsellers

bestselling /bést sélling/ *adj.* far more popular and successful than other products on sale at the same time ○ *his bestselling account of life in Provence*

bet /bet/ *vti.* (**bets, betting, bet** *or* **betted**) **1.** RISK STH OF VALUE to agree with sb that sth specified, usually money, will be forfeited by the person who incorrectly predicts the outcome of a future event to the other **2.** THINK STH IS TRUE to express certainty that sth will happen, has happened, or is true (*informal*) ○ *I bet he's forgotten to bring the keys.* ■ *n.* **1.** ACT OF BETTING an agreement that the person who incorrectly predicts the outcome of a future event will forfeit sth, usually money, to another **2.** AMOUNT WAGERED the amount of money that sb agrees to pay as a bet ○ *She placed a bet of £5, and won £500.* **3.** WHAT SB EXPECTS OR THINKS what sb expects to happen or thinks is true ○ *My bet is they'll decide to overlook the whole thing.* **4.** SB OR STH LIKELY TO WIN sb or sth likely to be successful ○ *She's a good bet for a vice-presidency.* [Late 16thC. Origin uncertain: perhaps a shortening of ABET; the underlying idea would be of support for what you think may happen.] ◇ **your best** *or* **safest bet** the course of action most likely to be productive ◇ **you bet!** used to show emphatic agreement (*informal*)

beta /beétə/ *n.* **1.** 2ND LETTER OF GREEK ALPHABET the second letter of the Greek alphabet, represented in English as 'b'. See table at **alphabet** **2.** EDUC ACADEMIC GRADE a letter such as 'B' used as a grade for good, but not excellent, academic work **3.** FIN MEASURE OF PRICE SENSITIVITY a measure of the relative price sensitivity of a security to that of the overall market **4.** COMPUT TEST a beta test (*informal*) ■ *adj.* **1.** NUCLEAR PHYS RELATING TO ELECTRONS PRODUCED BY RADIOACTIVITY used to describe electrons, especially those formed by the splitting of a neutron into a proton and an electron **2.** CHEM SECOND NEAREST TO DESIGNATED ATOM used to describe the second nearest atom to a designated atom or group of atoms in an organic molecule **3.** DESCRIBING MINOR FORM OF ELEMENT used to describe a minor form of a chemical element with more than one form (**allotrope**) [14thC. Via Latin and Greek from Canaanite *bet* 'house' (see BETH).]

Beta /beétə/ *n.* the second brightest star in a constellation (*followed by the Latin genitive*) ○ *Beta Centauri*

beta-blocker *n.* a drug belonging to a group used to regulate the activity of the heart, especially in the treatment of high blood pressure, by suppressing the activity of beta-receptors

beta-carotene *n.* = **carotene**

beta decay *n.* the radioactive transformation of an atomic nucleus during which an electron or positron is produced, although the mass number remains unchanged

betaine /beétə een, -in, bi táy-/ *n.* a sweet-tasting organic compound that occurs naturally in plants and animals, especially in sugar beet. It has been used as a treatment for muscular degeneration. Formula: $C_5H_{11}NO_2$. [Mid-19thC. Formed from Latin *beta* 'beet' (see BEET.)]

betake /bi táyk/ (**-takes, -taking, -took** /-tóok/, **-taken** /-táykən/) *vr.* to go somewhere (*archaic or literary*)

beta-oxidation *n.* BIOCHEM the breakdown of fatty acids that occurs during cellular metabolism, characterized by the successive removal from one end of the molecule of segments that contain two carbon atoms

beta particle *n.* a high-speed electron emitted from the nucleus of an atom during radioactive decay and created by the splitting of a neutron into a proton and an electron

beta process *n.* = **beta decay**

beta ray *n.* a stream of beta particles

beta-receptor *n.* a site on cells in the autonomic nervous system that responds to hormones such as adrenalin and operates to control blood pressure, regulate the heartbeat, and contract muscles

beta rhythm *n.* a pattern of electrical waves in the brain of sb who is awake and active (**beta waves**), registering on an electroencephalograph at a reading between 18 and 30 hertz

beta test *vt.* (**beta tests, beta testing, beta tested**) GIVE TO USERS TO TRY to test a product, especially computer software, by giving it to customers to try out before the final version is put on sale ■ *n.* TEST BY CUSTOMERS a test of a product, especially computer software, by giving it to a few customers to try out, before the final version is put on sale

beta transformation *n.* = **beta decay**

betatron /beétə tron/ *n.* a device that accelerates electrons in a circular orbit by means of a rapidly alternating magnetic field. In this way, electrons can reach energies of 340 MeV and may be used to strike a metal target to produce a continuous stream of gamma rays. [Mid-20thC. Coined from BETA+ -TRON.]

betaware /beétə wair/ *n.* a version of computer software that is to be tested by giving it to customers before the final version is put on sale

beta wave *n.* a high-frequency electrical wave produced in the human brain and associated with normal wakefulness. ◊ **beta rhythm**

betcha /béchə/ *contr.* a form of 'bet you' used mainly in conversation (*nonstandard*) ○ *Betcha the Lions win by 20 points.*

betel /beét'l/ (*plural* **-tels** *or* **-tel**) *n.* an evergreen Asian climbing plant with wide leaves that people in Asia chew as a mild stimulant and digestive aid. Latin name: *Piper betle.* [Mid-16thC. Via Portuguese from Malayalam *verrila*, from Tamil *vrrilai*.]

Betelgeuse /beét'l júrz, beét'l jurz, beét'l jooz/ *n.* a bright red variable supergiant star that is the second brightest star in the constellation Orion and the twelfth brightest in the night sky

betel nut *n.* one of the dark red seeds of the betel palm that is wrapped in betel leaves with lime and chewed by people in Asia as a mild stimulant

betel palm *n.* a tropical Asian palm tree that has orange fruit and dark red seeds. Latin name: *Areca catechu.*

bete noire /bét nwaár/ (*plural* **betes noires** /bét nwaár/) *n.* sb or sth you particularly dislike (*literary*) [Mid-19thC. From French, literally 'black beast'.]

beth /beth/ *n.* the second letter of the Hebrew alphabet, represented as 'b' in English. See table at **alphabet** [Early 19thC. From Hebrew, from *bayith* 'house'.]

Bethany /béthəni/ village at the foot of the Mount of Olives near Jerusalem in ancient Palestine. According to the New Testament it is where Lazarus arose from the dead.

Beth Din /bét dín, béth-/ (*plural* **Batei Din** /baá tay dín/) *n.* a Jewish religious court regulating matters of Jewish law such as dietary laws, divorce, and conversion [Late 18thC. From Hebrew *bēṭ dīn* 'house of judgment'.]

bethink /bi thíngk/ (**-thinks**, **-thinking**, **-thought** /-tháwt/, **-thought**) *vr.* to think of or remember sth (*archaic*)

Bethlehem /béthli hem/ town in the West Bank near Jerusalem. Part of Israel since 1967, it has been administered by the Palestinian Authority since 1995. Thought to be the birthplace of King David and Jesus, it is regarded as a holy city by Christians. Population: 34,100 (1987).

bethought past tense, past participle of **bethink**

Corbis/Library of Congress

Mary McLeod Bethune

Bethune /be thyo͞on/, **Mary McLeod** (1875–1955) US educator and activist. The child of slaves, she founded and was president of what became Bethune-Cookman College, Daytona Beach, Florida. She promoted education for African Americans and founded the National Council of Negro Women (1935).

betide /bi tíd/ (**-tides**) *vti.* to happen, or happen to sb (*archaic*) ○ *Whether good or ill betide you, trust in God.*

betimes /bi tímz/ *adv.* (*archaic*) **1.** EARLY early, or in good time **2.** SOON in a short time [13thC. From BY + TIME.]

bêtise /be teéz/ (*plural* **-tises** /be teéz/) *n.* mildly ridiculous action or remark (*literary*) [Early 19thC. From French, from *bête* 'foolish', from Old French *beste* 'beast'.]

Betjeman /béchəmən/, **Sir John** (1906–84) British poet He was poet laureate (1972–84). His books, largely poetical celebrations of rural England, include *A Few Late Chrysanthemums* (1954).

betoken /bi tókən/ (**-kens**, **-kening**, **-kened**) *vt.* to be a sign that sth exists or will happen (*literary*)

betony /béttəni/ (*plural* **-nies**) *n.* **1.** PLANT WITH PURPLISH FLOWERS a plant of the mint family that grows in Europe and Asia and has purplish flowers, formerly used in medicine. Latin name: *Stachys officinalis.* **2.** PLANT LIKE TRUE BETONY any plant resembling betony proper [14thC. From, ultimately, Latin *betonica*, variant of *Vettonica*, of uncertain origin: perhaps formed from *Vettones* (plural), an Iberian people.]

betook past tense of **betake**

betray /bi tráy/ (**-trays**, **-traying**, **-trayed**) *vt.* **1.** HELP AN ENEMY to harm or be disloyal to your own country or another person by helping or giving information to an enemy **2.** SURRENDER SB OR STH TREACHEROUSLY to deliver sb or sth to an enemy ○ *He betrayed his own brother to the secret police.* **3.** GO AGAINST A PROMISE to act in a way that is contrary to a promise made ○ *'If an intelligent person is betrayed repeatedly, and humiliated publicly, yet chooses to remain in that situation, one must ask: what are the rewards?'* (Gail Sheehy, *Vanity Fair*; February 1999) **4.** REVEAL STH to show sth, often unintentionally ○ *She said nothing, but her bright eyes betrayed her excitement.* **5.** DECEIVE SB to deceive sb, or lead sb into doing sth wrong (*dated*) [13thC. Formed from Old French *trair*, from Latin *tradere* 'to hand over'.] —**betrayer** *n.*

betrayal /bi tráy əl/ *n.* the act or an instance of betraying sb or sth

betroth /bi trôth/ (**-troths**, **-trothing**, **-trothed**) *vt.* to promise to marry sb, or promise that sb will marry sb (*formal*) [14thC. Coined from BE- + TRUTH.]

betrothal /bi trôthəl/ *n.* the act of becoming engaged to marry sb, or the state of being engaged to sb (*formal*)

betrothed /bi trôthd/ (*plural* **-trotheds** or **-trothed**) *n.* the person to whom sb is engaged to be married (*formal*) —**betrothed** *adj.*

better[1] /béttər/ (**-ters**, **-tering**, **-tered**) CORE MEANING: indicating that a thing or an action is superior in some way to sth else or is an improvement upon a situation ○ (adj) *Concentrated laundry detergent is better because it requires a smaller box or bottle.* ○ (adj) *She is gradually getting better, albeit slowly.* ○ (adv) *Treatment programmes may get the job done better.*

1. *adj.* MORE LIKABLE more attractive or likable than sth else ○ *That hairstyle is far better than the one you had before.* **2.** *adj.* OF GREATER QUALITY of greater quality, usefulness, or suitability than sth else ○ *Economic security helps ensure a better future for our children.* ○ *It is better to light a candle than to curse the darkness.* **3.** *adj.* IMPROVED IN HEALTH in an improved state of health, after not being well ○ *I'm feeling much better today, thank you.* **4.** *adv.* MORE OR TO A HIGHER STANDARD more, or in a more skilful or effective way ○ *He plays tennis much better than I do.* ○ *I liked her much better after I got to know her.* **5.** *adv.* PREFERABLY in a way that is preferable or more advantageous ○ *Such things are better left unsaid.* **6.** *adv.* OUGHT TO OR MUST DO STH indicates that it would be more advantageous for sb to act in a particular way (*nonstandard*) ○ *You better listen to me!* **7.** *vt.* SURPASS STH to improve on sth ○ *She hopes to better the record that she set at the Commonwealth Games.* ○ *He summed the whole thing up in a way that I couldn't possibly better.* **8.** *vt.* IMPROVE SELF OR THING to improve yourself or sth (*formal*) ○ *They tried to better themselves by attaining a good education.* ○ *attempts to better the lot of the refugees* **9.** *n.* SUPERIOR PERSON a person who is superior to another in some way (*often used in the plural*) ○ *You should listen to the advice of your elders and betters.* [13thC. From Old English *bettra*, from the comparative of a prehistoric Germanic word meaning 'advantageous', which is also the ancestor of English *best* and *boot* 'remedy'.] ◇ **for better or worse** whatever the outcome may be ◇ **get the better of sb 1.** to defeat sb in some way **2.** to be too strong for sb to control ◇ **go one better** to do sth that has been done before but in a superior or preferable way ◇ **had better do sth** ought to or must do sth ○ *You'd better tell them soon.* ◇ **think better of sth** to change your mind and decide not to do sth ○ *After seeing the ice on the streets we thought better of making the trip.*

better[2] /béttər/ *n.* GAMBLING = **bettor**

better half (*plural* **better halves**) *n.* sb's wife or husband (*informal*)

betterment /béttərmənt/ *n.* **1.** CHANGE FOR BETTER a change that improves sth, especially sb's financial or social condition (*formal*) **2.** PROPERTY IMPROVEMENT improvement of a building or land that increases its value

Betti /bétti/, **Ugo** (1892–1953) Italian dramatist and poet. His books include *Corruption in the Palace of Justice* (1944) and the verse collection *The Thoughtful King* (1922).

betting /bétting/ *n.* the activity of placing bets

bettong /be tóng/ *n.* a small nocturnal member of the kangaroo family of Australia, with small rounded ears and a bushy tail. Genus: *Bettongia.* [Early 19thC. From an Aboriginal language.]

between /bi tween/ CORE MEANING: a grammatical word indicating an intermediate point between two places or times ○ (prep) *I was standing between two other women.* ○ (prep) *I intend to pay off my mortgage between now and 2010.* ○ (adv) *He worked two shifts, with an hour off between.*

prep. **1.** TO AND FROM from one place to another ○ *She travels between Oxford and Birmingham most days.* **2.** TOGETHER together or in combination with ○ *Between us we should have enough money to pay for the trip.* **3.** INDICATES COMPARISON indicates a com-

parison, discussion, or relationship involving two people or groups ○ *Reconciliation was hampered by personality conflicts between company executives.* **4.** INDICATES CHOICES indicates two or more possible courses of action ○ *Police offer them a choice between school, a stiff fine, or community service.* [13thC. From Old English *betwēonum*, literally 'by two each', from *twēonum* 'two each' (related to *twā* 'two' (see TWO).] ◇ **(just) between you and me (and the gatepost or bedpost)** used to indicate that sth is very confidential

betweentimes /bi tween tímz/ *adv.* in the intervals between doing other things

betwixt /bi twíkst/ *adv.*, *prep.* between (*archaic*) [14thC. From Old English *betweox*, from *tweox* 'for two' (see TWO). The final 't' began to be used widely in the 16thC.] ◇ **betwixt and between** between two groups or categories, without belonging to one or the other

Beuys /boyz, boyss/, **Joseph** (1921–86) German artist. His avant-garde artworks included assemblages and happenings. He helped to found Germany's Green Party.

Bevan /bévv'n/, **Nye** (1897–1960) British politician. As health minister for the postwar Labour government (1945–51) he introduced the National Health Service (1948). He edited the left-wing journal *Tribune* (1940–45). Full name **Aneurin Bevan**

bevel /bévv'l/ *n.* **1.** SLANTING EDGE a surface that joins another surface at an angle that is not a right angle **2.** ANGLE the angle at which one surface joins another, when this is not a right angle **3.** TOOL a tool with two legs that can be adjusted to make various angles, and used to measure or mark an angle on sth ■ *vt.* (**-els**, **-elling**, **-elled**) MAKE SLANTING EDGE to shape the edge of sth so that it forms an angle other than a right angle with the main surface ○ *a mirror with bevelled edges* [Late 17thC. From assumed Old French, of uncertain origin: perhaps formed from *baif* 'gaping'.]

bevel gear *n.* either of a pair of gear wheels, one conical and the other flat or conical, connecting and transmitting power between shafts that are not parallel

bevel square *n.* = **bevel** *n.* 3

beverage /bévvərij/ *n.* a drink other than water (*formal*) (*used mainly in commercial contexts*) [14thC. From Old French *bevrage*, from *bevre*, variant of *boire*, from Latin *bibere* 'to drink' (source of English *bib* and *imbibe*).]

Beveridge /bévvərij/, **William, 1st Baron Beveridge of Tuggal** (1879–1963) Indian-born British economist. His report on social insurance (the so-called 'Beveridge Report', 1942) provided the basis for the creation of the British welfare state. Full name **William Henry Beveridge**

Beverley /bévvərli/ market town in northern Yorkshire, northern England, It is noted for its ancient minster. Population: 23,632 (1991).

Beverly Hills wealthy residential and commercial city in southwestern California, Los Angeles. Population: 32,367 (1996).

Bevin /bévvin/, **Ernest** (1881–1951) British trade union leader and politician. The organizer and secretary of the Transport and General Workers' Union (1921–40), he was later minister of labour and foreign secretary.

bevvy /bévvi/ *n.* (*plural* **-vies**) A DRINK an alcoholic drink (*slang*) ○ *We went out for a few bevvies.* ■ *vi.* (**-vies**, **-vying**, **-vied**) TO DRINK to drink alcohol (*slang*) [Late 19thC. Shortening of BEVERAGE.] ◇ **on the bevvy** spending time drinking alcohol (*slang*)

bevy /bévvi/ (*plural* **-ies**) *n.* **1.** GROUP OF PEOPLE a group of people **2.** GROUP OF ANIMALS a group of animals, especially quail, larks, or roe deer [15thC. Origin uncertain: perhaps from Old French *bevee* 'drink' (hence, perhaps, 'drinking party').]

bewail /bi wáyl/ (-wails, -wailing, -wailed) vt. to express great sadness about sth (formal)

beware /bi wáir/ vti. to be on guard against sb or sth (used only as a command and in the infinitive) [13thC. From the phrase be ware 'be careful' (see AWARE).]

bewhiskered /bi wískərd/ adj. sporting whiskers or a beard ○ bewhiskered gentlemen drinking port in their club

Bewick /byóo ik/, **Thomas** (1753–1828) British wood engraver. He illustrated the History of Quadrupeds (1790) and Fables of Æsop (1818).

Bewick's swan n. a small swan belonging to the race of tundra swan that lives mainly in marshy and swampy Arctic regions of Europe and Asia. Latin name: Cygnus bewickii.

bewigged /bi wígd/ adj. wearing a wig

bewilder /bi wíldər/ (-ders, -dering, -dered) vt. to confuse or puzzle sb completely [Late 17thC. Back-formation from BEWILDERED.] —**bewilderment** n.

bewildered /bi wíldərd/ adj. extremely confused [Late 17thC. Coined from BE + archaic wilder, of uncertain origin: probably a back-formation from WILDERNESS on the model of WANDER.] —**bewilderedly** adv. —**bewilderedness** n.

bewildering /bi wíldəring/ adj. extremely confusing —**bewilderingly** adv.

bewitch /bi wích/ (-witches, -witching, -witched) vt. 1. ENCHANT SB to fascinate or be very attractive to sb (often passive) 2. CAST SPELL ON SB OR STH to affect sb or sth using a magic spell [13thC. Coined from BE- + wicchen 'to enchant', from, ultimately, an earlier form of WITCH.] —**bewitcher** n. —**bewitchment** n.

bewitching /bi wíching/ adj. fascinating, charming, or very attractive —**bewitchingly** adv.

bey /bay/ (plural **beys**) n. 1. GOVERNOR a title used for various high-ranking officials in the Ottoman Empire, especially governors of a province 2. TITLE a respectful form of address for men used in Turkey and Egypt [Late 16thC. From Turkish, from Old Turkish beg 'prince'.]

beyond /bi yónd/ CORE MEANING: a grammatical word indicating that sth is on the other side of sth else, either physically or in the abstract ○ (prep) They are expanding environmental protection programmes beyond the border area. ○ (prep) The gift of laughter is beyond price.
1. prep., adv. AFTER A STATED TIME indicates that sth continues after a particular time ○ will remain the world's leading economy in the next decade and beyond ○. 2. prep. PAST past a particular stage or situation ○ Don't attempt to live beyond your income. 3. prep. FURTHER THAN further than a particular state of mind or emotion ○ The site has proved to be popular beyond anyone's wildest dreams. 4. prep. EXCEPT indicates an exception ○ He was incapable of any emotion beyond a certain rueful irony. 5. prep. IMPOSSIBLE FOR indicates that sth is impossible for sb to do ○ I find it quite beyond me to describe what this woman was to me. 6. n. THE HEREAFTER the form of existence that some people believe the spirit reaches after death ○ Our loved ones may speak to us from the beyond. 7. n. WHAT IS OUT THERE an area that lies outside what is known ○ Humanity stands at the edge of the solar system, contemplating the beyond. [14thC. From Old English begeondan, from geond 'yonder' + -an 'from'.]

bezel /bézz'l/ n. 1. SLOPING EDGE OF TOOL the face of a cutting tool, especially a chisel, that slopes towards the cutting edge 2. GROOVE TO HOLD WATCH GLASS the groove that holds the glass of a watch, light, or instrument dial in position [Late 16thC. From Old French, of uncertain origin.]

Béziers /bézzi ay/ city in Hérault Department in the Languedoc-Roussillon Region of southern France. It is situated in an important wine-producing region. Population: 72,362 (1990).

bezique /bi zéek/ n. 1. CARD GAME a card game like whist, played with the highest 64 cards from two packs 2. HAND AT CARDS the combination of the queen of spades and the jack of diamonds, which gains a high score in the game of bezique [Mid-19thC. From French besigue, of uncertain origin: perhaps from Persian bazigar 'acrobat' or bazi 'game'.]

bezoar /bée zawr/ n. a hard mass of material such as fruit or hair found in the intestines of a ruminant animal and believed in the past to be an antidote to poison [15thC. Via French bezoard from Arabic badhizahr, from Persian padzahr, from pad 'protection (against)' + zahr 'poison'.]

bf, **b.f.**, **B/F**, **b/f** abbr. 1. bloody fool (dated informal) 2. ACCT brought forward 3. PRINTING boldface

BF symbol. Belgian franc

BFI abbr. British Film Institute

BFPO abbr. British Forces Post Office

BG/B.G. abbr. brigadier general

BH abbr. Belize (international vehicle registration)

Bhadrapada /baádrə paadə/ n. in the Hindu calendar, the sixth month of the year, made up of 29 or 30 days and falling in approximately August to September

Bhagavadgita /búggəvəd geétə/, **Bhagavad-Gita** n. a Hindu religious text in which the god Krishna teaches the importance of detachment from personal aims, fulfilment of religious duties, and devotion to God [Late 18thC. From Sanskrit Bhagavadgītā, literally 'song of the blessed one' (referring to Krishna), from bhagavant- 'blessed' + gītā 'song'.]

Bhagwan /bug waán/ n. S Asia 1. GOD God 2. GURU a teacher, or sb who is greatly revered

bhai /bī/ n. S Asia 1. BROTHER a brother 2. MAN used as a friendly form of address for a man [From Hindi bhāi related to Sanskrit bhrātr 'brother']

Bhai n. a title of respect that is used after a Sikh man's name to indicate distinction

bhajan /búijən/ n. S Asia a Sikh or Hindu hymn [Early 20thC. From Sanskrit bhajana.]

bhaji /baáji/ (plural -jis), **bhajee**, **bajee** n. an Indian dish consisting of vegetable fritters, often made with gram flour or chickpea flour

bhakti /baákti/ n. the Hindu practice of loving devotion to God as the means of salvation [Mid-19thC. From Sanskrit, 'devotion'.]

bhang /bang/, **bang** n. a drug made from the Indian hemp or cannabis plant [Late 16thC. Via Portuguese bangue from Persian and Urdu bang and Hindustani bhan, from Sanskrit bhanga.]

bhangra /báng grə/ n. a style of popular music that originated in the Asian community in Britain and mixes Punjabi folk music with western pop music [Mid-20thC. From Punjabi.]

bharal /búrrəl/ n. a wild sheep from the Himalayas with a bluish-grey coat and curved-back horns. Latin name: Pseudois nayaur. [Mid-19thC. From Hindustani.]

Bharat /búrrət/ n. S Asia the Hindi name for India —**Bharatiya** /búrrə tee yə/ adj.

Bharat Natyam /búrrət naátyəm/ n. a type of classical dance from southern India, usually performed by a solo dancer, in which the movements of the hands and arms often have a symbolic meaning

bharta /baártə/ n. a spicy vegetable dish in Indian cookery, made with broiled vegetables and yogurt

Bhatpara /baat paárə/, **Bhātpāra** city and ancient seat of Sanskrit learning in the state of West Bengal, north of Calcutta, India. Population: 304,000 (1991).

bhavan /búvv'n/ n. a large important house or official building in India, often used as part of a building's name ○ Rasthrapati Bhavan [From Hindi]

Bhavnagar /baávnəgər/, **Bhāvnagar** city on the Gulf of Khambhat in Gujarat State in western India. Founded in 1723, it is a major industrial and commercial centre. Population: 403,521 (1991).

BHC abbr. benzene hexachloride

bhelpuri /báyl poori/ n. in Indian cookery, a spicy snack made with puffed rice and onions

bhindi /bíndi/ n. S Asia = okra

Bhindranwale /bíndrən waali/, **Sant Jarnail Singh** (1947–84) Indian Sikh leader. He campaigned for a separate Sikh state in the early 1980s and was killed by security forces at the Golden Temple at Amritsar.

Bhopal /bō paál/, **Bhōpal** city and capital of Madhya Pradesh State, central India. It was the site of the world's worst industrial accident when a gas leak at a chemical plant killed more than 3,300 people in 1984. Population: 1,063,662 (1991).

bhp abbr. brake horsepower

Bhumibol Adulyadej /póomi pōn aa doón lə dayt/, **Rama IX** (b. 1927). He ascended the throne in 1946. Known as **Rama VI**

bhuna /bóona/ n. a type of curry from southern India with a thick spicy sauce

Bhutan

Bhutan /boo taán/ landlocked kingdom in the eastern Himalayas between India and the Tibet region of China. It is an absolute monarchy and one of the world's least developed countries. Language: Dzongkha. Currency: ngultrum. Capital: Thimphu. Population: 842,000 (1996). Area: 47,000 sq. km/18,100 sq. mi. Official name **Kingdom of Bhutan** —**Bhutanese** n., adj.

bhuti n. = boetie

Benazir Bhutto

Bhutto /bóotō/, **Benazir** (b. 1953) Pakistani politician. The daughter of Prime Minister Zulfikar Ali Bhutto (1928–79), she led the Pakistan People's Party and was herself elected prime minister (1988–90, 1993–96).

bi /bī/ adj. BISEXUAL bisexual (slang) ■ n. (plural **bi's**) BISEXUAL PERSON sb who is bisexual (slang)

Bi symbol. bismuth

bi- prefix. two, twice, both ○ biaxial ○ bimonthly [From Latin bi-, the stem of bis 'twice', and bini 'two by two'. Ultimately from the Indo-European root bi 'two', which is also the ancestor of English two, dual, and binary.]

Biafra /bi áffrə/ region of eastern Nigeria that was declared a secessionist state by the majority Ibo people between 1967 and 1970. Official name **Republic of Biafra** —**Biafran** n., adj.

Bianca /bi ángkə/ n. a small natural satellite of Uranus, discovered in 1986 by the Voyager 2 planetary probe

biannual /bī ánnyoo əl/ adj. happening twice in a year

— WORD KEY: USAGE —

biannual or **biennial**? Biannual means 'twice a year' whereas biennial means 'every two years'. Because many people are unsure about which is which, it is often advisable to use the more straightforward expressions **twice-yearly** and **two-yearly**: Interest is paid on a twice-yearly basis. (or, less formally, Interest is paid twice a year.) They met at a series of two-yearly conferences on the environment.

Biarritz /beer rìts/ tourist resort on the Bay of Biscay in the Pyrénées-Atlantiques Department, southwestern France. Population: 28,887 (1990).

bias /bí əss/ *n.* (*plural* **-ases** *or* **-asses**) **1. PREFERENCE** an unfair preference for or dislike of sth ○ *a bias in favour of internal candidates* **2.** TEXTILES **DIAGONAL LINE** a line that runs diagonally across the weave of a fabric ○ *a dress cut on the bias* **3.** ELECTRON ENG **VOLTAGE APPLIED** the voltage applied across an electronic device, especially a transistor or valve, to determine the conditions under which it operates **4.** BOWLS **UNBALANCED WEIGHT IN BOWL** a bulge or internal weight in one side of a bowl that makes it run in a curved path **5.** BOWLS **CURVED PATH** the curved path in which a bowl containing a bulge or internal weight runs **6.** STATS **DISTORTION OF RESULTS** the distortion of a set of statistical results by a variable not considered in the calculation, or the variable itself ■ *vt.* (**-ases** *or* **-asses, -asing** *or* **-assing, -ased** *or* **-assed**) **INFLUENCE** to influence sb or sth unfairly or in a biased way ■ *adj.* **DIAGONAL** running diagonally across the weave of a fabric ○ *a bias seam* ■ *adv.* **DIAGONALLY** diagonally across the weave of a fabric ○ *The sleeves are cut bias.* [Mid-16thC. Via French from Old Provençal *biais* 'slant', from Greek *epikarsios* 'oblique'.]

bias binding *n.* a long narrow strip of material cut on the bias and used to form the edge of a hem or to bind the edges of a garment. US term **bias tape**

biased /bí əst/, **biassed** *adj.* **1. PREJUDICED** unable or unwilling to form a fair or objective opinion about sb or sth ○ *a biased opinion* **2. UNFAIR** unfair or partial because of a preference for or dislike of sth ○ *a biased sample*

bias tape *n.* *US* = **bias binding**

bias voltage *n.* = **bias** *n.* 3

biaxial /bī áksi əl/ *adj.* having two axes —**biaxially** *adv.*

Białystok /bi álli stok/ capital of Białystok Province in northeastern Poland. It is an industrial city in a predominantly agricultural region. Population: 277,800 (1995).

bib /bib/ *n.* **1. PROTECTIVE CLOTHING** a small piece of material fastened under a child's chin to protect the clothing while eating **2. PART OF GARMENT** the front part of a pinafore, apron, or pair of dungarees that covers the chest **3.** ZOOL **FISH OF COD FAMILY** a European sea fish of the cod family. Latin name: *Trisopterus luscus.* [Late 16thC. Origin uncertain: probably from Latin *bibere* 'to drink' (source of English *imbibe*).] ◇ **sb's best bib and tucker** sb's finest clothes (*informal*)

Bib. *abbr.* **1.** Bible **2.** biblical

bibb /bib/ *n.* a part attached to the mast of a sailing ship to support the trestletrees [Late 18thC. Variant of BIB.]

bibber /bíbbər/ *n.* sb who regularly drinks alcohol (*archaic*) [Mid-16thC. Formed from *bib* 'to drink frequently' (see BIB).]

bibcock /bíb kok/ *n.* a tap with a nozzle that is bent downwards [Late 18thC. Origin uncertain: perhaps from BIB + COCK.]

bibelot /bíbblō/ *n.* a small and attractive ornament or piece of jewellery [Late 19thC. From French, a variant by doubling of *bel* 'beautiful'.]

bibl. *abbr.* **1.** bibliography **2.** bibliographical

Bible /bīb'l/ *n.* **1. CHRISTIAN HOLY BOOK** the sacred book of the Christian religion, consisting of the Old Testament, the New Testament, and, for some Christians, the Apocrypha **2.** BIBLE **JEWISH HOLY BOOK** the Hebrew scriptures, consisting of the Torah or Law, the Prophets, and the Hagiographa or Writings **3. Bible, bible RELIGION'S HOLY BOOK** the holy book of any religion **4. Bible, bible COPY OF BIBLE** a copy or edition of the Bible **5. ESSENTIAL BOOK** a book that is considered an authority on a particular subject ○ *a bible for amateur renovaters* [14thC. From, ultimately, Latin *biblia (sacra)* (plural) '(sacred) books', from Greek, plural of *biblion* 'book', from *biblos* 'papyrus, scroll'.]

Bible-basher *n.* a committed Christian whose outspoken evangelizing is regarded by some as extreme (*slang*) US term **Bible-thumper** —**Bible-bashing** *n.*

Bible belt *n.* those areas of the southern and midwestern United States that are characterized by strong Protestant beliefs and strict interpretation of the Bible

Bible paper *n.* thin strong paper often used for Bibles and reference books

Bible-thumper *n.* *US* = **Bible-basher** (*slang*) —**Bible-thumping** *n.*

biblical /bíbblik'l/, **Biblical** *adj.* **1. OF THE BIBLE** relating to the Bible, or written about in the Bible **2. LIKE THE BIBLE** like the Bible, especially in style of language —**biblically** *adv.*

Biblicist /bíbblissist/, **biblicist** *n.* **1. BIBLICAL SCHOLAR** a scholar who studies the Bible **2. STRICT CONSTRUCTIONIST OF BIBLE** sb who interprets the Bible in a strict or literal way —**Biblicism** *n.*

biblio- *prefix.* book ○ *bibliomania* [From Greek *biblion*, literally 'small book', from *biblos* 'papyrus, scroll', from *Bublos*, Phoenician city from which papyrus was imported]

bibliography /bíbbli óggrəfi/ (*plural* **-phies**) *n.* **1. BOOK SOURCES** a list of books and articles consulted, appearing at the end of a book or other text **2. BOOKS ON SUBJECT** a list of books and articles on a particular subject **3. LIST OF PUBLICATIONS** a list of the books and articles written by a particular author or issued by a particular publisher **4. BOOK HISTORY** the history of books and other publications, and the work of classifying and describing them —**bibliographer** *n.* —**bibliographic** /bíbbli ə gráffik/ *adj.* —**bibliographical** /-gráffik'l/ *adj.* —**bibliographically** /-gráffikli/ *adv.*

bibliomancy /bíbbli ə manssi/ *n.* an attempt to foretell the future or answer a question by picking a passage at random from a book, especially the Bible

bibliomania /bíbbli ə máyni ə/ *n.* an extreme fondness for books, or an obsessive urge to collect them — **bibliomaniac** *n.*

bibliophile /bíbbli ə fīl/ *n.* sb who loves or collects books

bibulous /bíbbyŏŏləss/ *adj.* tending to drink too much alcohol (*literary or humorous*) [Late 17thC. From Latin *bibulus* from *bibere* 'to drink'.] —**bibulously** *adv.* —**bibulousness** *n.*

WORD KEY: ORIGIN

The Latin word *bibere* from which ***bibulous*** is derived is also the source of English *beer*, *beverage*, and *imbibe*.

bicameral /bī kámmərəl/ *adj.* having two separate and distinct law-making assemblies, e.g. the House of Commons and House of Lords in Britain [Mid-19thC. Formed from Latin *camera* 'chamber' (see CAMERA).] —**bicameralism** *n.* —**bicameralist** *n.*

bicarb /bī káarb/ *n.* sodium bicarbonate (*informal*) [Early 20thC. Shortening of BICARBONATE.]

bicarbonate /bī káarbənət, -nayt/ *n.* = **hydrogen carbonate**

bicarbonate of soda *n.* **1.** PHARM **ANTACID** sodium bicarbonate taken medicinally to counter the effects of excess acid in the stomach **2.** COOK **RAISING AGENT** sodium bicarbonate used in cooking as a raising agent. US term **baking soda**

bice /bīss/ *n.* a dull blue or colour pigment [14thC. From French *bis* 'dark grey', of unknown origin.]

bice blue *n.* a deep sky-blue colour

bice green *n.* a bright leaf-green colour

bicentenary /bí sen téenəri, -ténn-/ *n.* (*plural* **-ries**) **200TH ANNIVERSARY** an anniversary on which sth is 200 years old. US term **bicentennial** ■ *adj.* **CELEBRATING 200 YEARS** marking or celebrating a 200th anniversary ○ *bicentenary celebrations.* US term **bicentennial**

bicentennial /bí sen ténni əl/ *n.*, *adj.* *US* = **bicentenary** ■ *adj.* *US* = **bicentenary** —**bicentennially** *adv.*

bicephalous /bī séffələss/ *adj.* having two heads, or two parts resembling heads [Early 19thC. Coined from BI- + Greek *kephalē* 'head' + -OUS.]

biceps /bí seps/ (*plural* **-ceps**) *n.* **1. ARM MUSCLE** a large muscle in the upper arm that contracts to bend the elbow **2. MUSCLE WITH TWO ATTACHMENT POINTS** a muscle that has two points of attachment at one end, especially one (**biceps brachii**) in the upper arm and one (**biceps femoris**) in the back of the thigh [Mid-17thC. Via French from Latin, 'two-headed', from *caput* 'head'.]

bicipital /bī síppit'l/ *adj.* relating to or typical of a biceps muscle [Mid-17thC. Formed from Latin *bicipit-*, stem of *biceps* (see BICEPS).]

bicker /bíkər/ (**-ers, -ering, -ered**) *vi.* to argue in a bad-tempered way about sth unimportant [13thC. Coined from Middle Dutch *bicken* 'to stab, attack' + English *-er* 'repeatedly'.]

bickering /bíkəring/ *n.* bad-tempered arguing about sth unimportant

bickie /bíki/ *n.* a biscuit (*informal*) [Early 20thC. Literally 'small biscuit', from BISCUIT.]

bicolour /bī kúllər/, **bicoloured** /bī kúllərd/ *adj.* having two colours

biconcave /bī kóng kayv/ *adj.* OPTICS used to describe a lens with two faces that are concave

biconditional /bí kən dísh'nəl/ *n.* a proposition in logic involving two statements, one of which is true if, and only if, the other is true

biconvex /bī kón veks/ *adj.* OPTICS used to describe a lens with two faces that are convex

bicultural /bī kúlchərəl/ *adj.* relating to or containing two cultures ○ *a bicultural society* —**biculturalism** *n.*

bicuspid /bī kúspid/ *adj.* BIOL **WITH TWO POINTS** with two cusps or points ○ *a bicuspid tooth* ■ *n.* **PREMOLAR TOOTH** a tooth with two points, especially one of the eight teeth (**premolars**) that come between the canines and the molars in adult humans [Mid-19thC. Coined from BI- + Latin *cuspid-*, stem of *cuspis* (see CUSP).]

bicuspid valve *n.* ANAT = **mitral valve**

bicycle /bí sik'l/ *n.* **TWO-WHEELED VEHICLE** a vehicle with two wheels and a seat that is moved by pushing pedals with the feet, and steered by handlebars at the front wheel ■ *vi.* (**-cles, -cling, -cled**) **RIDE A BICYCLE** to travel by bicycle [Mid-19thC. Coined from BI- + CYCLE on the model of TRICYCLE.] —**bicycler** *n.*

bicycle clip *n.* one of a pair of circular clips used to prevent the ends of a cyclist's trousers getting in the way of the bicycle chain

bicycle motocross *n.* full form of **BMX**

bicyclic /bī síklik, -sík-/ *adj.* **1. WITH TWO CIRCLES OR RINGS** consisting of or arranged in two circles, rings, or cycles **2.** CHEM **WITH TWO RINGS OF ATOMS** used to describe a molecule containing atoms arranged in two rings

bid /bid/ *v.* (**bids, bidding, bad** *archaic* /bad/ *or* **bade** *or* **bid, bidden** /bídd'n/ *or* **bid**) **1.** (*past and past participle* **bid**) *vti.* **OFFER MONEY AT AUCTION** to offer a particular amount of money for sth at an auction **2.** (*past and past participle* **bid**) *vi.* **OFFER PRICE FOR WORK** to offer to do a piece of work for a particular price **3.** (*past and past participle* **bid**) *vti.* CARDS **STATE NUMBER OF TRICKS** to declare the number of card tricks to be taken **4.** *vt.* **ORDER** to tell sb to do sth (*archaic*) ○ *We were bidden to sit quietly, and so we did.* **5.** *vt.* **INVITE** to invite sb somewhere (*archaic*) **6.** (*past and past participle* **bid**) *vi.* **TRY TO ACHIEVE STH** to make an attempt to achieve a particular goal ○ *He hasn't decided whether or not he'll bid for the Presidency.* ■ *n.* **1. OFFER MADE TO PAY** an offer of money for sth at an auction **2. OFFER** an offer to do a piece of work for a particular price ○ *bids were invited for the contract* **3. ATTEMPT** an attempt to do sth or get sth ○ *in a desperate bid to save the situation.* ◊ **takeover bid 4.** CARDS **STATEMENT OF TRICKS** a statement of the number of tricks that a player will take in a card game [12thC. Partly from Old English *biddan* 'to request', and partly from Old English *beodan* 'to offer'.]

WORD KEY: USAGE

Bid meaning 'attempt' The use of ***bid*** to mean 'attempt', as in *Rescue bid fails*, is common in newspaper headlines, where its shortness is particularly welcome. *England star's record bid fails.*

bid in *vt.* to bid at an auction for sth already owned, in order to increase its final selling price

bid up *vt.* to make bids that are intended to increase the price of sth, not to obtain it

b.i.d. *adv.* twice a day (*used in prescriptions*) [Abbreviation of Latin *bis in die* 'twice a day']

Bidault /bee dṓ/, **Georges** (1899–1983) French statesman. He was a resistance leader during World War

BOOKS OF THE BIBLE

There is no straightforward explanation of the origin of either the Jewish or the Christian canon of scripture. The Jewish scriptures listed represent the Hebrew Bible as it came to be fixed probably at some time in the 2nd century AD. There existed, however, an alternative version in Greek, known as the Septuagint, which contained seven books that are now found in the Roman Catholic and Eastern Orthodox canons. These are usually known collectively as the Apocrypha, though modern biblical scholars prefer the term Deuterocanonical.

The Old Testament canon was formally fixed for western Christians in the 16th century, when Protestant denominations for the most part adopted the shorter Jewish canon. Roman Catholicism formally embraced the Septuagint as the basis for its Bible at the Council of Trent in 1546. The Orthodox Churches accepted effectively the same canon as the Roman Catholic one in 1672 at the Synod of Jerusalem, though the Russian Orthodox Church remained ambivalent, and at least down to the mid-20th century tended to omit the Deuterocanonical texts from its canon.

*indicates Deuterocanonical books

Jewish Scriptures	Old Testament Roman Catholicism and Eastern Orthodoxy	Protestant Churches		Jewish Scriptures	Old Testament Roman Catholicism and Eastern Orthodoxy	Protestant Churches		New Testament
The Law Genesis	Genesis	Genesis		**Prophets** (continued)	Lamentations	Lamentations		Matthew
Exodus	Exodus	Exodus			Baruch*			Mark
Leviticus	Leviticus	Leviticus		Ezekiel	Ezekiel	Ezekiel		Luke
Numbers	Numbers	Numbers		Hosea	Daniel	Daniel		John
Deuteronomy	Deuteronomy	Deuteronomy			Hosea	Hosea		Acts of the Apostles
The Prophets Joshua	Joshua	Joshua		Joel	Joel	Joel		Romans
Judges	Judges	Judges		Amos	Amos	Amos		1 Corinthians
	Ruth	Ruth		Obadiah	Obadiah	Obadiah		2 Corinthians
1 Samuel	1 Samuel	1 Samuel		Jonah	Jonah	Jonah		Galatians
2 Samuel	2 Samuel	2 Samuel		Micah	Micah	Micah		Ephesians
1 Kings	1 Kings	1 Kings		Nahum	Nahum	Nahum		Philippians
2 Kings	2 Kings	2 Kings		Habakkuk	Habakkuk	Habakkuk		Colossians
	1 Chronicles	1 Chronicles		Zephaniah	Zephaniah	Zephaniah		1 Thessalonians
	2 Chronicles	2 Chronicles		Haggai	Haggai	Haggai		2 Thessalonians
	Ezra	Ezra		Zechariah	Zechariah	Zechariah		1 Timothy
	Nehemiah	Nehemiah		Malachi	Malachi	Malachi		2 Timothy
	Tobit*							Titus
	Judith*			**The Writings** Psalms				Philemon
	Esther	Esther		Proverbs				Hebrews
	1 Maccabees*			Job				James
	2 Maccabees*			Song of Songs				1 Peter
	Job	Job		Ruth				2 Peter
	Psalms	Psalms		Lamentations				1 John
	Proverbs	Proverbs		Ecclesiastes				2 John
	Ecclesiastes	Ecclesiastes		Esther				3 John
	Wisdom*			Daniel				Jude
	Ecclesiasticus*			Ezra				Revelation
	Song of Songs	Song of Solomon		Nehemiah				
Isaiah	Isaiah	Isaiah		1 Chronicles				
Jeremiah	Jeremiah	Jeremiah		2 Chronicles				

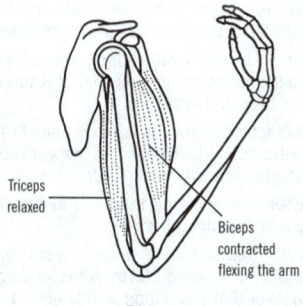

Triceps relaxed

Biceps contracted flexing the arm

Biceps

Bicycle

II, and served as French prime minister (1946, 1949–50). Full name **Georges Augustin Bidault**

biddable /bíddəb'l/ adj. likely to do as asked or ordered —**biddability** /bíddə bílləti/ n. —**biddableness** /bíddəb'lnəss/ n.

bidder /bíddər/ n. sb who makes a bid, especially at an auction

bidding /bídding/ n. **1. MAKING OF BIDS** the making of bids at an auction or in a card game **2. SB'S ORDERS** sb's orders or instructions ○ *lots of paperwork to do at the boss's bidding*

Biddle /bídd'l/, **Nicholas** (1786–1844) US financier. A lawyer and editor, he was president of the Second Bank of the United States (1822–39).

biddy /bíddi/ (plural **-dies**) n. **1. OFFENSIVE TERM** an offensive term that insults a woman's behaviour as fussing or interfering (slang insult) **2. CHICKEN** a chicken (regional) [Early 17thC. Origin unknown.]

biddy-biddy /bíddi bíddi/ (plural **biddy-biddies**), **bidi-bidi** (plural **bidi-bidis**) n. NZ a wind-pollinated New Zealand plant. Latin name: *Acaena novae-zelandiae*. [Mid-19thC. Alteration of Maori *piripiri*.]

bide /bīd/ (**bides, biding, bided** or **bode** archaic /bōd/, **bided**) v. **1.** vi. **STAY** to stay, remain, or wait (archaic) ○ *Bide here with us a while.* **2.** vt. **ENDURE** to bear or endure sth (archaic) ○ *We must bide the king's displeasure.* **3.** vi. Scotland **REMAIN** remain, stay, or reside in a place or situation [Old English *biden.* Ultimately from an Indo-European word that is also the ancestor of English *beetle, boat,* and *fission*.] ◇ **bide your time** to wait for a good opportunity to do sth

bidet /beé day/ *n.* a low bathroom plumbing fixture resembling a toilet and equipped with a spray or jet of water, used for washing the genital and anal areas [Mid-17thC. From French, literally 'pony', from *bider* 'to trot', of unknown origin.]

bidi /beédi/, **beedi, biri** /beéri/ *n. S Asia* a cheap cigarette made with coarse tobacco [From Hindi bīḍī 'betel plug, cigar']

bidi-bidi *n.* = **biddy-biddy**

bid price *n.* the price that a dealer on the stock exchange will pay for a security

Biedermeier /beédər mī ər/ *adj.* belonging to or typical of a highly conventional neoclassical style of home decoration and furnishing that was popular among the middle class in 19th-century Germany [Early 20thC. Named after the fictional poet Gottlieb *Biedermeier*, created in 1854 by Ludwig Eichrodt (1827–92).]

Bielefeld /beélə felt/ city in North Rhine-Westphalia State, western Germany, situated on the northern edge of the Teutoberg Forest. Population: 324,200 (1994).

Bien Hoa /byén hó ə/ city in southern Vietnam east of Ho Chi Minh City, on the River Dong Nai. Population: 273,953 (1989).

biennial /bī énni əl/ *adj.* **1. BIANNUAL** happening every two years **2. FLOWERING IN SECOND YEAR** used to describe a plant that lives for two years and produces flowers and fruit in the second year ■ *n.* **1. PLANT THAT LIVES TWO YEARS** a plant that lives for two years and produces fruit and flowers in the second year **2. EVENT** an event that happens every two years [Early 17thC. From, ultimately, Latin *biennium* 'two-year period'.] —**biennially** *adv.*

WORD KEY: USAGE

See Usage note at ***biannual***.

bier /beer/ *n.* **1. STAND FOR COFFIN** a table on which a coffin or a corpse is placed **2. FRAME FOR CARRYING COFFIN** a wooden frame on which a corpse or a coffin is carried to where it will be buried (*literary*) [Old English *bǣr*, from a prehistoric Germanic word that is also the ancestor of English *bear* 'to carry']

Bierce /beerss/, **Ambrose** (1842–1914?) US writer. Known for his satirical political articles and short stories, he wrote *The Devil's Dictionary* (1906). He disappeared in Mexico in 1913. Full name **Ambrose Gwinett Bierce**

bifacial /bī fáysh'l/ *adj.* **1.** BOT **WITH DIFFERENT SURFACES** used to describe leaves with upper and lower surfaces that are different from each other **2. TWO-SIDED** having two sides or surfaces

bifarious /bī fáiri əss/ *adj.* used to describe plant parts that are arranged in two rows, one on either side of an axis [Mid-17thC. Formed from Latin *bifarius*, literally 'doing twice', from *-farius* 'doing'.] —**bifariously** *adv.*

biff /bif/ (**biffs, biffing, biffed**) *vt.* to hit sb with the fist (*informal*) [Mid-19thC. An imitation of the sound caused.] —**biff** *n.*

bifid /bífid/ *adj.* BOT, ZOOL divided at one end into two equal parts [Mid-17thC. From Latin *bifidus*, literally 'twice divided', from *findere* 'to divide'.] —**bifidity** /bī fíddəti/ *n.* —**bifidly** /bífidli/ *adv.*

bifilar /bī fílər/ *adj.* used to describe a part suspended on two parallel wires or threads, especially the moving part of an electrical measuring instrument [Mid-19thC. Coined from BI- + Latin *filum* 'thread'.]

biflagellate /bī flájjilət, -layt/ *adj.* used to describe a cell that has two slender appendages (**flagella**)

bifocal /bī fók'l/ *adj.* **WITH TWO FOCAL LENGTHS** used to describe lenses with sections that have different focal lengths, especially in glasses for near and distant vision ■ **bifocals** *npl.* **GLASSES FOR NEAR AND DISTANT VISION** a pair of glasses with bifocal lenses [Late 19thC. Benjamin Franklin developed bifocals under the name 'double spectacles' 100 years before the term was coined.]

bifurcate *vti.* /bí fur kayt/ (**-cates, -cating, -cated**) **DIVIDE IN TWO** to split or branch off into two parts, or split sth into two parts ■ *adj.* /bí fur kayt, -kət/ **DIVIDING IN TWO** separating or branching off into two parts [Early 17thC. From, ultimately, Latin *bifurcare*, literally 'to fork twice', from *furca* 'fork' (see FORK).] —**bifurcation** /bí fur káysh'n/ *n.*

big /big/ *adj.* (**bigger, biggest**) **1. OF GREAT SIZE** of great size, number, or amount ○ *a big crowd* **2. OF GREAT POWER** of great power or volume ○ *A big cheer went up.* **3. SIGNIFICANT** significant or important to sb ○ *your big moment* **4. SIGNIFICANTLY GREAT** significantly or surprisingly great ○ *You're making a big mistake.* **5. OLDER** older or grown-up (*usually used by or to children*) ○ *When I'm big, I'll be rich and famous.* **6. IMPORTANT** important and powerful ○ *one of the big fashion houses* **7. ENTHUSIASTIC** enthusiastic about sth or sb (*informal*) ○ *I'm a big baseball fan.* **8. GREAT** used to make a word convey greater dislike or disapproval (*informal*) ○ *It's all a big con, really.* **9. MAGNANIMOUS** generous or noble ○ *She's a woman with a big heart.* **10. AMBITIOUS** full of boastful or unrealistic ambition ○ *She's not likely to fall for his big talk.* **11. FILLED** filled with or swollen by sth (*literary*) ○ *eyes big with tears* **12. PREGNANT** in an obvious state of pregnancy (*archaic*) ○ *She was big with child.* **13.** WINE **FULL-BODIED** full-bodied and full of flavour ○ *The best accompaniment to this dish would be a big Chianti.* ■ *adv.* **1. AMBITIOUSLY** in a way that is ambitious, and often boastful or unrealistic ○ *You have to think big if you want to get anywhere.* **2. SUCCESSFULLY** in a highly successful way (*informal*) ○ *This approach should go over big at the convention.* [14thC. Origin uncertain: perhaps from Scandinavian.] ◇ **big on** enthusiastic about sth or recognizing its importance (*informal*) ◇ **too big for your boots** overconfident (*informal*) ◇ **make it big** to be extremely successful (*informal*)

bigamist /bíggəmist/ *n.* sb who is married illegally to two people simultaneously

bigamous /bíggəməss/ *adj.* involved in or constituting an illegal marriage made when an existing marriage is still valid [Late 19thC. Formed from Latin *bigamus* (see BIGAMY).] —**bigamously** *adv.*

bigamy /bíggəmi/ *n.* the crime of marrying sb while being legally married to sb else [13thC. From, ultimately, Latin *bigamus*, literally 'marriage twice', from Greek *gamos* 'marriage'.]

Big Apple *n.* an informal name for New York City [From APPLE, used by jazz musicians to mean 'job', and the fact that New York was the most sought-after place to have a job or engagement]

big band *n.* a large jazz or dance band, especially one that was popular in the 1930s and 1940s ○ *the big band sound of Tommy Dorsey*

big bang *n.* the explosion of a single extremely dense mass of matter that started the universe according to the big bang theory

big bang theory *n.* the theory that the universe started with the explosion of a small amount of extremely dense matter. The theory is supported by evidence that the universe is still expanding.

Big Ben *n.* **1. CLOCK ABOVE PARLIAMENT BUILDING** the large clock above the Houses of Parliament in London, or the tower in which it stands **2. LARGE BELL** the large bell that chimes the hours in the clock tower of the Houses of Parliament in London [Named after Sir *Benjamin* Hall, the Chief Commissioner of Works when the bell was cast in 1856]

Big Bertha *n.* a type of long-range gun used by Germany in World War I [Early 20thC. Named after *Bertha* Krupp, daughter of the armaments manufacturer Alfred Krupp.]

Big Brother *n.* a person or group who exerts dictatorial control and maintains a constant watch over others, often while presenting a caring image [Coined by George Orwell in his novel *Nineteen Eighty-Four* (1949)] —**Big Brotherism** *n.*

big bucks *npl.* a large amount of money (*slang*)

big bud *n.* a disease of blackcurrant plants that causes the leaf buds to swell and stop developing, for which the only control is destruction of the plants. It is caused by a gall mite that may also transmit a virus.

big business *n.* the activity of large commercial organizations, or these organizations considered as a group

big cat *n.* any large carnivorous wild mammal related to the domestic cat. Lions, tigers, leopards, lynxes, and mountain lions are types of big cat. Family: Felidae.

big cheese *n.* sb who is important, especially the head of an organization (*slang dated*)

big city (*plural* **big cities**) *n.* the largest city in an area ○ *the lure of the big city*

big-city *adj.* typical of life in a large metropolitan area ○ *the fast-paced big-city lifestyle*

big daddy *n.* (*slang*) **1. SB OR STH REGARDED WITH RESPECT** sb who or sth that is respected, powerful, or well known for sth in particular ○ *the big daddy of the blues guitar* **2. PATERNALISTIC HEAD** the head of an organization, especially one who exerts paternalistic control

big deal *interj.* **IS THAT ALL?** used to counter that sth is less impressive or important than sb thinks it is (*informal*) ○ *So he's head of department. Big deal.* ■ *n.* **STH IMPORTANT** sth that is very important (*informal*) ○ *Let's not make a big deal out of a minor misunderstanding.*

big dipper *n.* = **roller coaster**

Big Dipper *n. US* = **Plough**

Big Easy *n.* an informal name for New Orleans, Louisiana ○ *a night on the town in the Big Easy* [From *The Big Easy* (1970), a novel by James Conaway]

big end *n.* the larger end of the connecting rod in an internal combustion engine

bigeneric /bí jə nérrik/ *adj.* BOT used to describe a hybrid produced from two different genera

bigeye /bíg ī/ (*plural* **-eyes** *or* **-eye**) *n.* a small tropical or subtropical sea fish with rough reddish or silvery scales and very large eyes. Family: Priacanthidae.

Bigfoot /bíg foot/, **bigfoot** *n.* a large hairy humanoid creature supposed to live in the wilderness areas of northwestern North America, and described as standing 2–3 m/7–10 ft tall [Mid-20thC. From the size of the footprints it is said to leave.]

big game *n.* large wild animals hunted for sport, especially the larger African mammals

biggie /bíggi/ *n.* (*informal*) **1. LARGE THING** sth that is big **2. STH OR SB IMPORTANT** sb or sth that is very significant, important, powerful, or successful [Mid-20thC. Formed from BIG.]

big girl's blouse *n.* a man who is considered to be insufficiently masculine or effective (*slang insult*)

big government *n.* government perceived as being excessively high-spending and attempting to control too many aspects of people's lives

Biggs /bigz/, **Ronnie** (*b.* 1929) British train robber. One of the perpetrators of the Great Train Robbery (1963), he escaped from prison (1965) and fled to Brazil. Real name **Ronald Biggs**

big gun *n.* a powerful or influential person (*informal*) [From the earlier meaning 'heavy artillery']

big hair *n.* hair that is rather long with a lot of body, often backcombed or sprayed so that it stands away from the head (*informal*)

bighead /bíg hed/ *n.* sb who is too proud of his or her own abilities, achievements, or appearance (*informal*) —**bigheaded** /bíg héddid/ *adj.*

big-hearted *adj.* showing kindness and willingness to help and support others

bighorn /bíg hawrn/ (*plural* **-horns** *or* **-horn**) *n.* a large wild sheep of western North America and northeastern Asia that has a long coarse brown coat and very large curving horns. It is well adapted for living in mountainous regions and can leap over rocky terrain with great agility and speed. Genus: *Ovis*. ◊ **mountain sheep**

bight /bīt/ *n.* **1. CURVE OF COASTLINE** a wide curving indent in a shoreline, forming a bay **2. ROPE LOOP** a loop or slack curve in a rope [Old English *byht*. Ultimately from an Indo-European word meaning 'to bend', also the ancestor of English *bow* and *bagel*.]

big league *n.* the highest level of achievement in any field, or the people who occupy the top positions in it (*informal*)

big-league *adj.* TOP-RANKING among the most successful or influential in a particular field ■ *n., adj.* OUT-AND-OUT of a wholehearted and unrestrained kind (*slang*) ○ *They're into big-league partying*

Big Man *n.* in some cultures, including prehistoric cultures, a male leader whose leadership is based on influence, not official or formally recognized authority

bigmouth /bígg mowth/ (*plural* **-mouths**) *n.* (*informal*) **1.** INDISCREET PERSON sb who cannot keep a secret **2.** BOASTFUL PERSON a noisy, vulgar, or boastful person

big name *n.* a well-known and successful person, organization, or product —**big-name** *adj.*

big noise *n.* an important or influential person (*dated informal*)

big-note (**big-notes, big-noting, big-noted**) *vi. Aus* to make yourself seem more important or successful by boasting about your achievements (*informal*)

bigot /bíggət/ *n.* sb who has very strong opinions, especially on matters of politics, religion, or ethnicity and refuses to accept different views [Late 16thC. From French, of unknown origin.]

bigoted /bíggətid/ *adj.* holding very strong opinions, especially on matters of politics, religion, or ethnicity and unwilling to accept different views —**bigotedly** *adv.* —**bigotedness** *n.*

bigotry /bíggətri/ *n.* intolerance towards people who hold different views, especially on matters of politics, religion, or ethnicity [Late 17thC. Formed from BIGOT, on the model of French *bigoterie*.]

big science *n.* any area of scientific research that needs major capital investment

big screen *n.* the cinema and films made for the cinema, as opposed to television or video

big shot *n.* a person with a great deal of power or influence, or sb who thinks they are important or powerful (*informal*)

Big Smoke *n.* a nickname for a large city, especially a capital city (*informal*)

big stick *n.* a threat of force or severe penalties [From 'speak softly and carry a big stick', an adage made popular by US President Theodore Roosevelt]

big-ticket *adj. Can, US* costing a lot of money (*informal*)

big time *n.* TOP LEVEL OF ACHIEVEMENT the highest level of achievement and success in a profession or other activity (*slang*) ■ *adv.* GREATLY on a grand scale or to a significant degree (*slang*) ○ *He had messed up his life big time.* —**big timer** *n.*

big top *n.* **1.** CIRCUS TENT a large round tent, especially the main tent, used for circus performances **2.** CIRCUS the circus, or the life of a circus performer

big wheel *n.* = Ferris wheel

bigwig /bíg wig/ *n.* an important person with a lot of power or influence (*informal*) [Early 18thC. From the fact that important people once wore full-length wigs, whereas ordinary people wore short ones.]

Bihar /bi haár/, **Bihār** state in northeastern India that is crossed by the River Ganges and shares a border with Nepal. Capital: Patna. Population: 93,080,000 (1994). Area: 173,876 sq. km/67,134 sq. mi.

Bihari /bi haári/ (*plural* **-ri** *or* **-ris**) *n.* **1.** PEOPLES MEMBER OF PEOPLE IN INDIAN SUBCONTINENT a member of a people who live mostly in the Indian state of Bihar, but also in Bangladesh and Pakistan **2.** LANG HINDI AREA LANGUAGE a language of the state of Bihar, in India, belonging to the Indic group and closely related to Hindi [Late 19thC. From Hindi *bihārī*.] —**Bihari** *adj.*

Bijapur /bi jaá poor/, **Bijapur** city in northern Karnataka State, southern India. It is known for its medieval Islamic architecture. Population: 193,038 (1991).

bijection /bī jéksh'n/ *n.* a mathematical mapping between two spaces in which every element in each space corresponds to only one element of the other

space for mapping in either direction [Mid-20thC. Formed from BI-, on the model of INJECTION.] —**bijective** *adj.*

bijou /bee zhoo, bee zhoó/ *adj.* FASHIONABLE small but fashionable and elegant (*humorous*) ○ *a bijou apartment* ■ *n.* (*plural* **-jous** /bee zhooz/ *or* **-joux** /bee zhoo/) DELICATE TRINKET a small delicate jewel or ornamental object [Mid-17thC. Via French, 'trinket', from Breton *bizou* 'jewelled ring', from *biz* 'finger', of unknown origin.]

Bikaner /beeka neer/, **Bīkāner** walled city in Rajasthan State, northwestern India. It was founded in 1488 and was formerly capital of the princely state of Bikaner. Population: 415,355 (1991).

bike[1] /bīk/ *n.* **1.** BICYCLE OR MOTORCYCLE a bicycle or a motorcycle (*informal*) **2.** OFFENSIVE TERM an offensive term for a woman who has many sexual relationships (*offensive*) ■ *vi.* (**bikes, biking, biked**) GO BY BIKE to ride somewhere on a bicycle or motorcycle (*informal*) [Late 19thC. Shortening of BICYCLE.] ◇ **on your bike** used as a mildly rude way of telling sb to go away or of dismissing sb's suggestion (*informal*)

bike[2] /bīk/, **byke** *n. Scotland* WASPS' NEST a nest of wasps or wild bees ■ *vi.* (**bikes, biking, biked; bykes, byking, byked**) *Scotland* SWARM to swarm (*refers to bees and wasps*) [13thC. Origin unknown.]

biker /bíkər/ *n.* sb who rides a motorcycle, especially sb who belongs to a gang of riders

bikeway /bík way/ *n.* = cycle path

bikie /bíki/ *n. ANZ* sb who rides a motorcycle, especially sb who belongs to a gang of riders (*informal*)

Bikila /bi keéla/, **Abebe** (1932–73) Ethiopian athlete. The first Black African Olympic gold medallist, he set a world record running barefoot in the marathon in the Rome Olympics in 1960.

bikini /bi keéni/ *n.* **1.** WOMAN'S TWO-PIECE SWIMMING COSTUME a woman's or girl's two-piece swimming costume consisting of a bra-style top and panties-style bottoms **2.** **bikini, bikinis** BRIEFS very scanty briefs for women [Mid-20thC. Named after BIKINI ATOLL, where an atom bomb was tested in 1946. The impact of the swimming costume was supposed to be similar.] —**bikinied** *adj.*

Bikini /bi keéni/ atoll consisting of 36 islets in the Marshall Islands, the western Pacific Ocean. It was used as a nuclear testing site by the United States between 1946 and 1958. Area: 5 sq. km/2 sq. mi.

bikini line *n.* the area where the top of a woman's thighs meets the lower edge of her bikini or underwear

Biko /beéko/, **Steve** (1946–77) South African political activist. He founded and led the Black Consciousness Movement. He was beaten to death in police custody. Full name **Stephen Bantu Biko**

bilabial /bī láybi əl/ *adj.* USING BOTH LIPS used to describe a consonant pronounced by closing or rounding both lips ■ *n.* CONSONANT PRONOUNCED USING BOTH LIPS a consonant pronounced by bringing both lips into contact with each other or by rounding them. In English, the bilabials are 'b', 'p', 'm', and 'w'. —**bilabially** *adv.*

bilateral /bī láttərəl/ *adj.* **1.** POL INVOLVING TWO GROUPS involving or carried out by two groups, especially the political representatives of two countries ○ *bilateral talks* **2.** ON BOTH SIDES relating to or affecting both of two sides ○ *bilateral kidney failure* —**bilateralism** *n.* —**bilaterally** *adv.*

bilateral symmetry *n.* symmetry in which an imaginary plane divides an object into right and left halves, each side being a mirror image of the other. Most animals exhibit this symmetry.

bilayer /bī́ layər/ *n.* **1.** BIOCHEM TWO-MOLECULE LAYER a membrane that consists of two layers of molecules **2.** BIOL = lipid bilayer

Bilbao /bil baá ō/ industrial city and Spain's leading port in the Basque Country, northern Spain. It is the site of the Guggenheim Museum Bilbao that was opened in 1997. Population: 370,997 (1995).

bilberry /bílbəri/ (*plural* **-ries**) *n.* **1.** BLUE-BLACK BERRY a small edible blue-black berry from a hardy shrub that grows wild in northern Europe **2.** FRUIT BUSH the shrub that produces bilberries. Genus: *Vaccinium*. [Late 16thC. Bil- of uncertain origin: probably from Scandinavian.]

bilby /bílbi/ (*plural* **-bies**) *n.* an Australasian marsupial resembling a rat with large ears, a pointed nose, and a long tail. It lives in a burrow and eats small mammals and lizards. Genus: *Macrotis*. [Late 19thC. From Yuwaalaraay *bilbi* (an Aboriginal language).]

bildungsroman /bíll dŏŏngz rō maan/ *n.* a novel about the early years of sb's life, exploring the development of his or her character and personality [Early 20thC. From German, literally 'education-novel'.]

bile /bīl/ *n.* **1.** PHYSIOL DIGESTIVE FLUID a yellowish-green fluid produced in the liver, stored in the gallbladder, and passed through ducts to the small intestine, where it plays an essential role in emulsifying fats **2.** BITTERNESS feelings of bitterness and irritability (*literary*) **3.** HIST BODILY HUMOUR according to medieval medicine, one of the four basic fluids of the body (**humours**), an excess of which was thought to make sb prone to anger [Mid-16thC. Via French from Latin *bilis*; probably ultimately of Celtic origin.]

bile duct *n.* a tube that carries bile from the liver or gallbladder to the small intestine. The (**hepatic**) and (**cystic**) ducts merge to form the common bile duct.

bi-level *adj.* **1.** TWO-LEVEL with two levels for cargo or passengers **2.** *Can, US* HAVING TWO GROUND-FLOOR LEVELS having two ground-floor levels divided by a vertical partition ■ *n. Can, US* a bi-level house

bilge /bilj/ *n.* **1.** LOWER HULL OF BOAT the part of a boat below the water where the sides curve inwards to the keel **2.** LOWER HULL'S INSIDES the area inside the bottom of a boat, beneath the lowest floorboards **3.** DIRTY WATER IN BOAT BOTTOM dirty water that collects inside the bottom of a boat **4.** BARREL'S WIDEST PART the widest part of a barrel or cask **5.** NONSENSE ridiculous silly talk or ideas (*informal*) ○ *a load of bilge* ■ *vti.* (**bilges, bilging, bilged**) SPRING A LEAK to be, or cause a boat to be, damaged in the lower part of the hull and start leaking [15thC. Origin uncertain: probably an alteration of BULGE.]

bilge keel *n.* either of two fin-shaped underwater projections on either side of a boat's hull, designed to control rolling

bilge water *n.* = bilge *n.* 3

bilharzia /bil haár zi ə/ *n.* **1.** ZOOL = schistosome **2.** MED = schistosomiasis [Mid-19thC. From modern Latin, genus name, after the German physician Theodor *Bilharz*, 1825–62, who first identified the parasite.]

bilharziasis /bíl haar zí əssiss/ *n.* = schistosomiasis

biliary /bílyəri/ *adj.* **1.** ANAT RELATING TO BILE relating to bile or the transporting of bile **2.** MED AFFECTING A BILE DUCT affecting a bile duct or the system of ducts in the liver ○ *biliary cirrhosis* [Mid-18thC. Formed from Latin *bilis* 'bile'.]

bilinear /bī línni ər/ *adj.* relating to or representing a mathematical expression with two variables, such as $x + y$, neither of which is squared, cubed, or raised to another power or exponent

bilingual /bī líng gwəl/ *adj.* **1.** SPEAKING TWO LANGUAGES able to speak two languages easily and naturally **2.** IN TWO LANGUAGES written, expressed, or conducted in two languages ○ *a bilingual dictionary* ■ *n.* BILINGUAL SPEAKER sb who speaks two languages easily and naturally [Mid-19thC. Formed from Latin *bilinguis*, from *bi-* 'two' + *lingua* 'tongue, speech'.] —**bilingually** *adv.*

bilingualism /bī líng gwə lizzəm/ *n.* **1.** FLUENCY IN TWO LANGUAGES the ability to speak two languages easily and naturally **2.** USE OF TWO LANGUAGES the regular use of two languages in everyday communication

bilious /bílli əss/ *adj.* **1.** FEELING NAUSEATED feeling as if about to vomit **2.** NAUSEATINGLY UNPLEASANT extremely unpleasant to look at ○ *The walls were painted bilious green.* **3.** SHOWING BAD MOOD bad-tempered and irritable, or indicating this ○ *a bilious stare* [Mid-16thC. From Latin *biliosus*, from *bilis* 'bile' (see BILE).] —**biliously** *adv.* —**biliousness** *n.*

bilirubin /bílli roŏbin, bíli-/ *n.* a reddish-yellow bile pigment that is an intermediate product of the breakdown of haemoglobin in the liver. Too much bilirubin in the blood causes jaundice. [Late 19thC. From German, from Latin *bilis* 'bile' + *ruber* 'red'.]

biliverdin /bílli vúrdin/ *n.* a greenish bile pigment that is an intermediate product of the breakdown of haemoglobin in the liver and that in turn can break down to produce bilirubin [Mid-19thC. From German, from Latin *bilis* 'bile' + French *vert* 'green'.]

bilk /bilk/ (**bilks, bilking, bilked**) *vt.* **1.** CHEAT to cheat sb, especially by swindling him or her out of money (*informal*) **2.** AVOID PAYING to avoid paying a debt or the person to whom money is owed (*informal*) **3.** AVOID OR EVADE to escape from sb, or manage to lose a pursuer [Mid-17thC. Origin uncertain: perhaps an alteration of BAULK.] —**bilker** *n.*

bill[1] /bil/ *n.* **1.** STATEMENT OF MONEY OWED a written statement of how much money has to be paid for items that have been bought or for services provided ○ *I'll send you the bill.* **2.** AMOUNT OWED the amount of money owed for items or services provided, as shown on a statement ○ *The bill for the meal came to £550!* **3.** POL LAW PROPOSAL a written proposal for a new law, discussed and voted upon by the members of a legislative assembly **4.** ADVERTISING NOTICE a notice, poster, or leaflet advertising sth **5.** LIST OF ITEMS a list, especially of entertainment features or acts in a show, or the programme of entertainment itself ○ *We've got a brilliant new comedian on the bill tonight.* **6.** *US, Can* = **note** *n.* 7 ■ *vt.* **1.** SEND REQUEST FOR PAYMENT to send sb a statement of how much money is owed for items bought or services provided ○ *Bill me for the cost of dry-cleaning.* **2.** ADVERTISE to advertise an event or performance, especially using posters ○ *It's billed as the biggest ice show in Britain.* **3.** DESCRIBE to describe an emerging or forthcoming thing in a particular way ○ *billed as the technological advance of the decade* [14thC. Via Anglo-Norman *bille* from, ultimately, medieval Latin *bulla* 'seal on a document'.] —**biller** *n.* ◇ **fill** *or* **fit the bill** to be suitable for a particular purpose

bill[2] /bil/ *n.* **1.** BIRDS BIRD'S BEAK the beak of a bird, consisting of two pointed jaws protected by a horny covering **2.** ZOOL MOUTHPART OF ANIMAL the mouthparts of a platypus or other animal **3.** GEOG NARROW STRIP OF LAND a narrow strip of land that juts out into the sea (*often used in placenames*) **4.** NAUT POINT OF AN ANCHOR the point at the very end of one of the arms of an anchor [Old English *bile*, of unknown origin] ◇ **bill and coo** to kiss and whisper intimately, as young lovers do, in a way thought to be reminiscent of the affectionate behaviour of doves

bill[3], **Bill** *n.* the police (*informal*) (*takes a plural verb*) ○ *Are the bill still after him for that jewellery job?* [Mid-20thC. From *Bill*, nickname for 'William'.]

billabong /bíllə bong/ *n. Aus* a pool or waterhole formed by a side-channel of a river during the wet season [Mid-19thC. From Wiradhuri (an Aboriginal language), from *bila* 'river' + *bang* 'watercourse that only runs after rain'.]

billboard[1] /bíll bawrd/ *n.* a very large board erected by the roadside or attached to a building, used for displaying advertisements

billboard[2] *n.* a ledge on the front of a boat or ship to which the anchor is secured

billet[1] /bíllət/ *n.* **1.** MIL ACCOMMODATION FOR SERVICE PEOPLE a private home or a guest house providing temporary accommodation for people in the armed forces **2.** MIL ORDER TO PROVIDE ACCOMMODATION an official order stating that a householder has to provide temporary accommodation for a member of the armed forces **3.** EMPLOYMENT POSITION a position of employment together with its tasks (*informal*) **4.** BRIEF LETTER a short letter or a note to sb (*archaic*) ■ *v.* (**-lets, -leting, -leted**) MIL **1.** *vti.* ASSIGN SOLDIER TO TEMPORARY ACCOMMODATION to arrange for a member of the armed forces have temporary accommodation in a particular house, or to have such temporary accommodation somewhere **2.** *vt.* PROVIDE TEMPORARY ACCOMMODATION FOR SOLDIER to provide temporary accommodation in your home for a member of the armed forces [15thC. From Anglo-Norman *bilette* 'written orders', literally 'small document', from Old French *bulle*.]

billet[2] /bíllət/ *n.* **1.** CHUNK OF WOOD a short thick piece of wood, especially firewood **2.** METALL METAL BAR IN SEMI-FINISHED STATE a metal bar or block with a simple shape that requires further working **3.** ARCHIT DECORATIVE MOULDING any one of a series of short, evenly spaced blocks or cylinders forming part of a decorative moulding [15thC. From Old French *billette*, literally 'small log', from *bille* 'log', from assumed Vulgar Latin *bilia*; probably ultimately of Celtic origin.]

billet-doux /bílli dóo/ (*plural* **billets-doux** /bílli dóoz/) *n.* a letter expressing affectionate and romantic thoughts (*literary*) [Late 17thC. From French, literally 'sweet note'.]

billfish /bíll fish/ (*plural* **-fish** *or* **-fishes**) *n.* a large fish with jaws resembling spears that lives near the surface of tropical and semitropical waters and is hunted for sport. Marlin, sailfish, and swordfish are billfish. Family: Xiphiidae. [Formed from BILL[2]]

billfold /bíll fōld/ *n. Can, US* a pocket-sized folding container for paper money, credit cards, stamps, and photographs, sometimes with a compartment for loose change [Formed from BILL[1]]

billhook /bíll hook/ *n.* a woodcutting tool with a wooden handle and a large broad curved blade, used especially to lop branches off trees [Formed from obsolete *bill* 'a bladed or pointed weapon']

billiard /bíllyərd/ *adj.* relating to or used in the cue game billiards ○ *a billiard table*

billiards /bíllyərdz/ *n.* an indoor game in which a felt-tipped stick (**cue**) is used to hit three coloured balls across a cloth-covered table into pockets (*takes a singular verb*) [Late 16thC. From French *billard*, from *bille* 'log' (see BILLET[2]).]

billing /bílling/ *n.* **1.** POSITION IN TERMS OF ADVERTISING the particular importance or prominence given to a performer or event in advertisements ○ *an exciting young band currently getting top billing* **2.** COMM SENDING OUT CUSTOMERS' BILLS the preparing and sending out of bills to customers **3.** *US* ADVERTISING the advertising or promoting of a performance, event, or product [Formed from BILL[1]]

billingsgate /bíllingz gayt/ *n.* rude or offensive language (*dated*) [Mid-17thC. Named after BILLINGSGATE market, where the workers were noted for their strong language.]

Billingsgate the largest wholesale fish market in London, on the north bank of the River Thames established in the 16th century, and since 1982 located in the Isle of Dogs in the East End of London

billion /bíllyən/ (*plural* **-lions** *or* **-lion**) *n.* **1.** ONE THOUSAND MILLION one thousand million, written as 1 followed by nine zeros **2.** ONE MILLION MILLION one million million, written as 1 followed by 12 zeros (*dated*) **3.** LARGE NUMBER an extremely large but unspecified number of people or things (*informal*) (*often plural*) [Late 17thC. From French, 'a million million', from *bis* 'twice' + *million* 'MILLION'.] —**billionth** *n., adj.*

WORD KEY: USAGE

A thousand million or a million million? In current use, a ***billion*** means a thousand million. In earlier use it often meant a million million, but a number as large as this is needed far less often. In its colloquial (singular or plural) use, ***billions*** (like *hundreds, thousands*, etc.) has no precise numerical meaning: *I must have called his office a billion times. That must have cost billions.* The word now used to mean a million million is *trillion*.

billionaire /bíllyə náir/ *n.* a very rich person, literally sb who has money and property worth more than a billion pounds [Late 19thC. Modelled on MILLIONAIRE.]

bill of entry *n.* a list of goods to be imported or exported, presented to officials at a customs house

bill of exchange *n.* a document setting out an instruction to pay a named person a fixed sum of money on a specified date or when the person requests payment

bill of fare *n.* **1.** MENU a menu of food available in a restaurant or served at a special function **2.** LIST OF ITEMS a list of items of any kind, especially events in a programme of entertainment (*informal*)

bill of health *n.* a certificate stating that the crew of a ship are healthy and are not affected by infectious diseases ◇ **a clean bill of health** a good report on sb's health, or a good report about the state of sth, e.g. an organization's efficiency or profitability

bill of indictment *n.* a document setting out the criminal charges against sb, formerly presented to a grand jury

bill of lading *n.* a list of goods being transported, especially by ship, together with the conditions that apply to their transportation

bill of rights *n.* a list of basic human rights as guaranteed by the laws of a country

Bill of Rights *n.* **1.** ENGLISH LAW ENSHRINING FREEDOMS an English act of law, passed in 1689, guaranteeing people, especially landowners and parliamentarians, freedom and basic rights **2.** US HUMAN RIGHTS LAW the first ten amendments to the US Constitution, which protect people's basic human rights

bill of sale *n.* a document stating that sth has been sold or transferred to the ownership of another party

billon /bíllən/ *n.* **1.** ALLOY USED FOR COINS an alloy consisting of a small amount of silver or gold mixed with a base metal such as copper, used especially for making coins **2.** SILVER-COPPER ALLOY USED FOR MEDALS an alloy of silver with copper in high proportion, used especially for making medals [Early 18thC. From French, 'ingot, bronze money', from *bille* 'log' (see BILLET[2]).]

billow /bíllō/ *v.* **1.** *vt.* SWELL WITH AIR to fill with air, or cause sth made of fabric to fill with air, and swell outwards ○ *the wind billowing their dresses* **2.** *vi.* FLOW IN CURLING MASS to flow upwards or along in a curling mass ■ *n.* FLOWING CURLING MASS a curling or rolling mass of sth, e.g. waves or clouds of smoke [Mid-16thC. From Old Norse *bylgja* 'wave'. Ultimately from an Indo-European word meaning 'to swell', which is also the ancestor of English *bellows, belly*, and *bulge*.]

billowy /bíllōwi/ *adj.* moving in a large curling or rolling mass

billposter /bíll pōstər/ *n.* sb who puts up advertising notices in public places ○ *Billposters will be prosecuted.* [Formed from BILL[1]] —**billposting** *n.*

billy[1] /bílli/ *n.* (*plural* **-lies**) CAMP COOKING POT a light metal cooking pot, used for boiling water or cooking food on a campfire ■ *adj. ANZ* COOKED IN CAMPFIRE POT cooked or prepared in a pot over a campfire [Mid-19thC. Origin uncertain: perhaps from Scottish dialect *billy-pot* 'cooking utensil', or of Australian Aboriginal origin.]

billy[2] /bílli/ (*plural* **billies**) *n.* = **billy goat**

billycan /bílli kan/ *n.* = **billy**[1] *n.*

billy goat *n.* a male goat [From *Billy*, a nickname for William]

Billy the Kid /bílli-/ (1859–81) US outlaw. A notorious robber and cattle rustler on the US Western frontier, he claimed to have killed at least 21 people. He used numerous aliases, and the facts of his life are not clearly known. Real name **Henry McCarty**

bilobate /bī lō bayt/, **bilobed** /bī lōbd/ *adj.* having or in the form of two lobes ○ *a bilobate leaf*

biltong /bíll tong/ *n. S Africa* strips of lean meat dried in the sun [Early 19thC. From Afrikaans, from Dutch *bil* 'buttock, rump' + *tong* 'tongue'. So called because the meat is usually taken from the hind quarter, and is said to taste like smoked tongue.]

Bim /bim/ *n.* sb who lives in, or comes from, Barbados (*informal*) [Mid-19thC. Origin unknown.]

BIM *n., abbr.* British Institute of Management

bima, **bimah** *n.* JUDAISM = **bema** *n.* 1

bimanual /bī mánn yoo əl/ *adj.* done with two hands, or needing the use of two hands —**bimanually** *adv.*

Bimberi Peak /bímbəri-/ mountain in the Australian Capital Territory in southeastern Australia. Height: 1,912 m./6,273 ft.

bimbo /bímm bō/ (*plural* **-bos** *or* **-boes**) *n.* (*slang insult*) **1.** OFFENSIVE TERM an offensive term that deliberately insults a woman's intelligence while implying that she is good-looking **2.** *US* OFFENSIVE TERM an offensive term for a man or woman who is regarded as being unintelligent or superficial [Early 20thC. Origin uncertain: probably from Italian, 'baby, small child'.]

bimetallic /bī me tállik/ *adj.* containing or consisting of two metals

bimetallic strip *n.* a strip composed of two metals with different coefficients of expansion fixed together that bend at different rates when heated. Bimetallic strips are used in thermostats, thermal switches, and some thermometers.

bimillenary /bī mi lénnəri/ *adj.* **RELATING TO 2,000TH ANNIVERSARY** relating to or celebrating a 2,000th anniversary ■ *n.* (*plural* **-ies**) **2,000TH ANNIVERSARY** the 2,000th anniversary of sth

bimodal /bī mṓd'l/ *adj.* STATS relating to or consisting of a set of observations with two peaks, representing two values that occur with equal frequency and more often than any other value ○ *bimodal distribution* —**bimodality** /bī mō dálləti/ *n.*

bimolecular /bī mə lékyŏolər/ *adj.* relating to, consisting of, or formed from two molecules

bimonthly /bī múnthli/ *adj.* **OCCURRING EVERY TWO MONTHS** produced or held every two months ■ *adj., adv.* **OCCURRING TWICE A MONTH** produced or held twice a month ■ *n.* (*plural* **-lies**) PUBL **PUBLICATION ISSUED BIMONTHLY** a publication, e.g. a magazine or journal, that appears every two months or twice a month

bimorphemic /bī mawr fe̅emik/ *adj.* consisting of two of the smallest units of meaning in language (**morphemes**). The word 'fallen' is bimorphemic, comprising the free morpheme 'fall' and the bound past participle morpheme '-en'.

bin /bin/ *n.* **1. RUBBISH CONTAINER** a container for rubbish or waste paper (*often used in combination*) **2. LARGE STORAGE CONTAINER** a large storage container, e.g. an industrial container for grain or coal or an open container holding goods in a shop **3.** WINE **STORAGE SHELVES FOR WINE** a set of shelves with compartments for storing bottles of wine in a cellar ■ *vt.* (**bins, binning, binned**) **1. DISPOSE OF** to throw sth away ○ *I bin all the junk mail without even looking at it.* **2. STORE IN BIN** to put sth in a storage bin [Old English *binn*, of Celtic origin]

binary /bīnəri/ *adj.* **1. IN TWO PARTS** consisting of two parts or two separate elements **2.** MATH **RELATING TO NUMBER SYSTEM BASED ON TWO** used to describe a number system, or a number belonging to it, that has 2 rather than 10 as its base **3.** CHEM **HAVING ONLY TWO CHEMICAL ELEMENTS** consisting of two different chemical elements only **4.** CHEM **HAVING TWO CHEMICALS MIXING TOXICALLY** consisting of or using two harmless components that, when combined, become extremely toxic **5.** MUSIC = **duple** ■ *n.* (*plural* **-ries**) **1.** MATH **BINARY NUMBER SYSTEM** the binary number system ○ *written in binary* **2.** MATH **BINARY DIGIT** a binary number or digit **3.** ASTRON = **binary star 4.** ARMS = **binary weapon** [15thC. From late Latin *binarius*, from Latin *bini* 'two by two'.]

binary code *n.* a computer code that uses the binary number system. Numbers and letters are translated into signals that a computer reads as sequences of ones and zeros called binary digits (**bits**).

binary coded decimal *n.* a numbering system in which each digit of a decimal is converted into a binary number

binary digit *n.* either of the digits 0 and 1, used in the binary system. ◊ **bit**

binary file *n.* a computer file that contains data in a raw or nontext state made up of characters that only a computer can read. Executable programs are stored and transmitted in binary files, as are most numeric data files. ◊ **ASCII file**

binary fission *n.* the reproduction of a cell or a one-celled organism by division into two nearly equal parts

binary form *n.* a musical form that has two complementary parts, both usually repeated

binary notation *n.* = **binary system**

binary star *n.* a pair of stars that revolve around their common centre of mass under mutual gravitational attraction

binary system *n.* the number system with 2 as its base, decimal numbers being expressed as sequences of the digits 0 and 1. For example, the number 5 breaks down as one 1, no 2s, and one 4, written as 101 read from right to left.

binary weapon *n.* a chemical weapon, e.g. a bomb or artillery shell, containing two chemicals that are harmless in isolation but combine to form a toxic compound before reaching the target

binational /bī násh'nəl/ *adj.* relating to two nations, or with two nations taking part

binaural /bī náwrəl, bi-/ *adj.* **1. INVOLVING BOTH EARS** relating to both ears, or the perception of sound by both ears **2. IN STEREO** recorded onto two separate channels using two microphones, so as to sound realistic when heard through headphones

bind /bīnd/ *v.* (**binds, binding, bound** /bownd/, **bound**) **1.** *vt.* **TIE FIRMLY TO STH** to tie sth firmly to sth else by winding a cord tightly round and round both things **2.** *vt.* **WRAP RIBBON OR BANDAGE ROUND** to wind a cord, tape, or bandage firmly round sth to protect it or hold it together ○ *You have to bind the wound firmly.* **3.** *vt.* **TIE SB'S HANDS OR FEET TOGETHER** to tie sb's hands or feet together to make it difficult to escape (*often passive*) ○ *bound hand and foot* **4.** *vt.* SEW **PROTECT EDGE OF FABRIC** to protect or decorate the edge of a piece of material by stitching over it or fixing a strip of fabric to it **5.** *vti.* **CAUSE FEELINGS OF LOYALTY OR CLOSENESS** to form a link or relationship based on loyalty, affection, or a shared experience ○ *the natural instinct that binds mother and child* **6.** *vt.* **FORCE TO DO STH** to oblige or compel sb to do sth, e.g. by invoking a law or a promise that has been made (*often passive*) ○ *priests who are bound by their vow of celibacy* **7.** *vt.* PUBL **PUT BOOK TOGETHER** to fix pages together and put them in a cover to form a book, leaflet, or other publication **8.** *vti.* **STICK TOGETHER** to stick together, or cause elements or ingredients to stick together, so as to form a solid mass ○ *The water, sand, and cement bind to form workable mortar.* **9.** *vti.* CHEM **FORM CHEMICAL BOND** to form a chemical bond **10.** *vt.* MED **MAKE FAECES FIRMER** to make the faeces firmer and more solid, especially to curb diarrhoea ○ *White rice is said to bind you.* **11.** *vi.* ENG **BECOME STIFF OR STUCK** to become stiff, stuck, or unable to move freely (*refers to mechanical parts*) ○ *The brakes are binding.* **12.** *vt.* **EMPLOY AS APPRENTICE** in former times, to employ sb as an apprentice under the terms of an agreement that obliged the apprentice to work for a fixed period, often several years ■ *n.* **1. NUISANCE** sth that is annoying or causes inconvenience ○ *I have to go to the hospital every two weeks: it's a real bind.* **2.** FENCING **FENCING MOVEMENT** a fencing movement that pushes an opponent's blade out of line **3.** CHESS **DOMINANT POSITION IN CHESS** in chess, a position of dominance in the centre of the board that restricts an opponent's moves **4.** MUSIC = **tie** *n.* **8** [Old English *bindan*. Ultimately from an Indo-European word that is also the ancestor of English *band, bend, bond,* and *bundle*.] ◇ **in a bind** in a difficult or unpleasant situation, especially a situation in which every option leads to difficulties

bind off *vti. US* KNITTING = **cast off**

bind over *vt.* to place a legal order on sb, stating that he or she must or must not behave in a particular way for a specified period of time (*often passive*) ○ *He was fined £200 and bound over to keep the peace for twelve months.*

binder /bīndər/ *n.* **1. HARD COVER FOR PAPERS** a stiff cover with clips inside for holding loose sheets of paper or magazines **2. MACHINE FOR BINDING BOOKS OR PAPERS** a machine for fixing sheets of paper together to form a book or booklet **3. BOOKBINDER** sb whose job is to make books by assembling the pages and putting on the cover **4. CORD OR TIE** a length of cord, string, or tape that is used to tie things together **5. STH THAT STICKS THINGS** a substance added to form dry ingredients into a solid mass or to maintain an even consistency throughout a liquid or semi-liquid substance **6.** AGRIC **MACHINE FOR MAKING SHEAVES** an attachment on a reaping machine for bundling cut grain into sheaves, or a reaping machine with this attachment

bindery /bīndəri/ (*plural* **-ies**) *n.* a place where the pages and covers of books are put together

bindi-eye /bindi-/ (*plural* **bindi-eyes** *or* **bindi-eye**) *n.* a small Australian flowering plant of the daisy family with fruits that are covered in small hooks or prickles. Genus: *Calotis.* [Early 20thC. Alteration of Kamilaroi and Yuwaalaraay (Aboriginal languages) *bindayaa*.]

binding /bīnding/ *n.* **1. CORD USED FOR TYING** sth that is used to tie or protect things, especially a cord or tape that is wound round and round sth **2.** PUBL **BOOK COVERING** the cover of a book, or the material used to cover books **3.** PUBL **STH HOLDING BOOK'S PAGES TOGETHER** the glue, strip of plastic, or other material that holds the pages of a book or booklet together **4.** SEW **FABRIC EDGING** a strip of fabric or tape attached to the edge of a piece of material to prevent it from fraying **5.** SKIING **SKI FASTENING** one of the fastenings on a ski that hold the ski to the boot ■ *adj.* **OBLIGING SB TO DO STH** creating a legal or moral obligation to do sth, with no possibility of withdrawal or avoidance

binding energy *n.* PHYS **1. ENERGY TO REMOVE PARTICLE FROM SYSTEM** the energy required to remove a particle from a system, e.g. an electron from an atom **2. ENERGY TO SEPARATE SYSTEM INTO COMPONENTS** the energy required to separate a system into its individual particles or components

bindweed /bīnd weed/ *n.* a plant with long twining stems, especially a wild plant with large white funnel-shaped flowers, generally regarded as a weed. Genera: *Convolvulus* and *Calystegia.*

bin end *n.* one of the last bottles remaining from a single quantity of wine, often sold at a reduced price

bing /bing/ *n. Scotland* a heap or pile of sth, especially a slag heap [Early 16thC. From Old Norse *bingr* 'heap, bolster'.]

binge /binj/ *n.* **1. HEAVY DRINKING OR EATING SESSION** a short period when sb drinks or eats far too much, especially a period of uncontrolled drinking or eating caused by a disorder such as alcoholism or bulimia **2. SPREE** a short period of time when sth enjoyable is done in an unrestrained way ○ *a shopping binge* ■ *vi.* (**binges, bingeing** *or* **binging, binged**) **1. EAT TOO MUCH** to eat far too much food very quickly, sometimes as a symptom of an eating disorder such as bulimia **2. BE SELF-INDULGENT WITH STH** to do or consume sth in an unrestrained self-indulgent way ○ *stay in all day and binge on old movies* [Early 19thC. From a dialect word meaning 'to soak', of unknown origin.] —**binger** *n.*

binge eating *n.* uncontrolled eating, especially when caused by bulimia

bingo /bíng gō/ *n.* **LOTTERY GAME WITH NUMBERED CARDS** a game played communally with numbered cards in which numbers are selected at random and the first person to cover all or specified numbered slots on his or her card wins ■ *interj.* **1. CALL IN BINGO** a shout of success, called by a player who has won a game of bingo **2. EXCLAMATION OF SUCCESS** used to express satisfaction at sudden success or achievement [Early 20thC. Origin uncertain: perhaps from *bing*, the sound of a bell ringing or a target being hit.]

binman /bín man/ (*plural* **-men** /-men/) *n.* a dustman (*informal*)

binnacle /bínnək'l/ *n.* a support or mounting for a ship's compass [15thC. Alteration of Spanish *bitácula*, from Latin *habitaculum* 'housing', from *habitare* 'to inhabit'.]

binocular /bī nókyŏolər, bi-/ *adj.* involving or using both eyes, or relating to vision using both eyes. ◊ **monocular** [Mid-18thC. Coined from Latin *bini* 'two together' + *oculus* 'eye'.] —**binocularity** /bī nókyŏo lárrəti, bi-/ *n.*

binoculars /bī nók yŏolərz, bi-/ *npl.* a device for

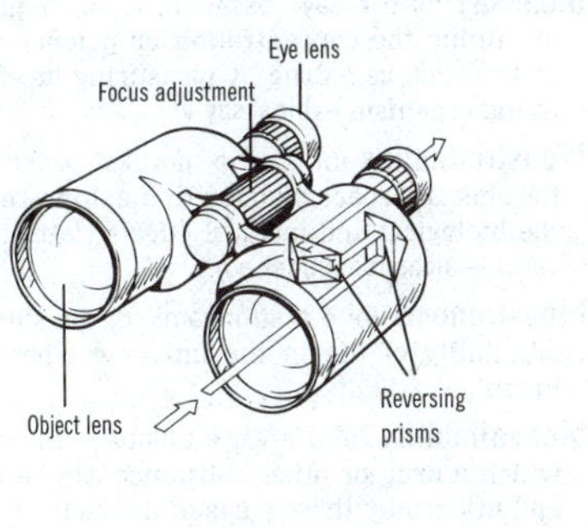
Eye lens
Focus adjustment
Object lens
Reversing prisms
Binoculars

looking at distant objects that magnifies what is seen using a lens for each eye

binomial /bĭ nṓmi əl/ n. **1.** MATH EXPRESSION WITH TWO TERMS a mathematical expression made up of two terms and a plus or minus sign **2.** BIOL ORGANISM'S TWO-PART NAME a pair of Latin or Latinized words forming a scientific name in the classification of plants, animals, and microorganisms. The first word represents the genus and the second the species. ■ adj. HAVING TWO NAMES OR TERMS relating to or consisting of two names, especially the two elements of a scientific name, or two terms, e.g. the terms of a mathematical expression [Mid-16thC. Formed from modern Latin binomius, from Latin bi- 'two' + Greek nomos 'part'.] —**binomially** adv.

binomial coefficient n. a number that multiplies the variables in a two-part mathematical expression, e.g. the numbers 3 and 4 in the expression 3x-4y

binomial distribution n. a formula that indicates the probability of achieving a given number of successful outcomes in a predetermined number of statistical trials when the probability of success is the same for each trial

binomial nomenclature n. the system of assigning two-part Latin or Latinized scientific names to plants, animals, and microorganisms, with the first word denoting the genus and the second the species

binomial theorem n. a mathematical formula used to calculate the value of a two-part mathematical expression that is squared, cubed, or raised to another power or exponent, e.g. $(x+y)^n$, without explicitly multiplying the parts themselves

bint /bint/ n. a girl or woman (slang insult) [Mid-19thC. From Arabic, 'girl, daughter'.]

binturong /bíntyoŏ rong, bin tyoŏr ong/ n. a Southeast Asian mammal resembling a cat, with a thick black coat, a long tail, and tufts on its ears. The largest of the civet family, it lives in dense forests, uses its tail for grasping branches when climbing, and can also swim to catch fish. Latin name: Arctictus binturong. [Early 19thC. From Malay.]

binucleate /bī nyoŏkli ət/, **binucleated** /-kli aytid/, **binuclear** /-kli ər/ adj. BIOL having two distinct cell nuclei

Binyon /bínnyən/, **Laurence** (1869–1943) British poet. He wrote the World War I poem 'For the Fallen' and translated Dante's Divine Comedy (1933–43). Real name **Robert Laurence Binyon**

bio /bĭ ṓ/ (plural -os) n. Can, US a biographical work (informal) ○ mostly fiction and celebrity bios [Mid-20th C. Shortening of BIOGRAPHY.]

bio- prefix. BIOL life, biology ○ bioengineering [From Greek bios 'life, way of living'. Ultimately from an Indo-European base meaning 'to live', which is also the ancestor of English quick, vital, zoo-, and hygiene.]

bioaccumulation /bĭ ə kyoŏmyoŏ láysh'n/ n. the accumulation of a harmful substance such as a radioactive element, a heavy metal, or an organochlorine in a biological organism, especially one that forms part of the food chain —**bioaccumulative** /bĭ ə kyoŏmyoŏblativ/ adj.

bioactive /bĭ ó áktiv/ adj. capable of producing an effect or reaction in living tissue

bioactivity /bĭ ó ak tívvəti/ n. the effect that a substance or agent has on living tissue or an organism

bioassay /bĭ ó ə sáy, -ássay/ n. a technique for determining the concentration or potency of a substance such as a drug by measuring its effect on a living organism —**bioassay** vt.

bioastronautics /bĭ ó astrə náwtiks/ n. the study of the effects of space flight on living things, especially the biological and medical effects (takes a singular verb) —**bioastronautical** adj.

bioastronomy /bĭ ó ə strónnəmi/ n. the study of the possibility of life in the universe other than on Earth

bioavailability /bĭ ó ə váylə bílləti/ n. the degree to which a drug or other substance can be absorbed and utilized by those parts of the body on which it is intended to have an effect

biocenosis n. ECOL = biocoenosis

biochemical /bĭ ó kémmik'l/ adj. relating to the chemical substances present in living organisms and the reactions and methods used to identify or characterize them —**biochemically** adv.

biochemical engineering n. the branch of chemical engineering that is concerned with the large-scale culture of living cells in fermentation processes

biochemical oxygen demand n. a measure of the pollution present in water, obtained by measuring the amount of oxygen absorbed from the water by the microorganisms present in it

biochemistry /bĭ ó kémmistri/ n. **1.** CHEMISTRY OF LIVING ORGANISMS the scientific study of the chemical substances, processes, and reactions that occur in living organisms **2.** CHEMICAL NATURE OF ORGANISM OR SYSTEM the chemistry or composition of a particular organism or system —**biochemist** n.

biocide /bĭ ó sīd/ n. = pesticide —**biocidal** /bĭ ó sīd'l/ adj.

bioclimatic /bĭ ó klī máttik/ adj. relating to the relationship between climate and living organisms, or to the study of bioclimatology

bioclimatology /bĭ ó klīmə tólləji/ n. the study of how climate affects living things —**bioclimatologist** n.

biocoenosis /bĭ ó sə nṓssiss/ (plural -coenoses /-seez/), **biocenosis** (plural -cenoses) n. a diverse group of species or organisms with its own distinct habitat, interacting to form an ecological community [Late 19thC. From modern Latin, from Greek bios 'life' + koinōsis 'sharing', from koinos 'common'.]

biocompatibility /bĭ ó kəm páttə bílləti/ n. the compatibility of a donated organ or artificial limb with the living tissue into which it is implanted or with which it is brought into contact. Incompatibility leads to toxic reactions or immunological rejection. —**biocompatible** /bĭ ó kəm páttəb'l/ adj.

biocomputer /bĭ ó kəm pyoŏtər/ n. a very fast computer made from biochemical substances instead of conventional materials. Its calculations are performed using biological processes instead of semiconductor technology. [Late 20thC]

biocontrol /bĭ ó kən trṓl/ n. = biological control

bioconversion /bĭ ó kən vúrsh'n/ n. the conversion of organic material into a source of energy, using biological processes or organisms

biodata /bĭ ó dáytə, -dáatə/ n. S Asia sb's curriculum vitae (takes a singular or plural noun)

biodegradable /bĭ ó di gráydəb'l/ adj. made of substances that will decay relatively quickly as a result of the action of bacteria and break down into elements such as carbon that are recycled naturally —**biodegradability** /bĭ ó di gráydə bílləti/ n.

biodegrade /bĭ ó di gráyd/ (-grades, -grading, -graded) vi. to decay naturally as the result of the action of bacteria —**biodegradation** /bĭ ó déggrə dáysh'n/ n.

biodiesel /bĭ ó deez'l/ n. a substitute for diesel fuel made wholly or partly from organic products, especially processed vegetable oils such as soya bean oil and groundnut oil

biodiversity /bĭ ó dī vúrssəti/ n. the range of organisms present in a given ecological community or system. It can be measured by the numbers and types of different species, or the genetic variations within and between species.

biodynamics /bĭ ó dī námmiks/ n. the study of how energy, motion, and other forces affect living things (takes a singular verb) —**biodynamic** adj.

bioelectricity /bĭ ó ilek tríssəti/ n. electric current generated by living tissue —**bioelectric** adj.

bioenergetics /bĭ ó énnər jéttiks/ n. (takes a singular verb) **1.** BIOL STUDY OF ENERGY IN LIVING THINGS the study of the conversion of energy in organisms and biological systems, e.g. in photosynthesis **2.** PSYCHOL REICHIAN THERAPY a therapy, devised by Wilhelm Reich in the 1940s, that uses an analysis of sb's physical posture and movements to enhance emotional well-being —**bioenergetic** adj.

bioengineering /bĭ ó énji neéring/ n. the use of engineering principles and techniques to solve

medical problems, e.g. in the design of artificial limbs or in organ replacement —**bioengineer** n.

bioethics /bĭ ó éthiks/ n. the study of the moral and ethical choices faced in medical research and in the treatment of patients, especially when the application of advanced technology is involved (takes a singular verb) —**bioethical** adj. —**bioethicist** n.

biofeedback /bĭ ó feéd bak/ n. the use of monitoring devices that display information about the operation of a bodily function, e.g. heart rate or blood pressure, that is not normally consciously controlled. This helps a patient to learn to control the function consciously.

bioflavonoid /bĭ ó fláyvə noyd/ n. a biologically active compound found in the rinds of citrus fruits and some other plants

biofuel /bĭ ó fyoo əl/ n. a renewable fuel, e.g. biodiesel, biogas, and methane, that is derived from biological matter

biog. abbr. **1.** biographer **2.** biographical **3.** biography

biogas /bĭ ó gass/ n. a mixture of carbon dioxide and methane formed by the decay of organic waste matter and used as a fuel

biogenesis /bĭ ó jénnəssiss/ n. **1.** DEVELOPMENT OF LIVING THINGS the generation of living things from other pre-existing life forms **2.** ORIGINS OF LIFE the theory that living things can arise only from other living things and cannot be spontaneously created **3.** BIOL = recapitulation n. 2 —**biogenetic** /bĭ ó jə néttik/ adj.

biogenic /bĭ ó jénnik/ adj. resulting from biological activity or from living things ○ a biogenic amine

biogeochemistry /bĭ ó jee ó kémmistri/ n. the study of the chemical relationships between organisms and their physical environment —**biogeochemical** adj.

biogeography /bĭ ó ji óggrəfi/ n. the study of the geographical distribution of plants and animals —**biogeographer** n. —**biogeographic** /bĭ ó jee ə gráffik/ adj. —**biogeographical** /-gráffik'l/ adj.

biographee /bī óggrə feé/ n. sb whose life is described in a biography

biographical /bĭ ó gráffik'l/ adj. **1.** RELATING TO SB'S LIFE STORY relating to, containing, or consisting of a description of sb's life, written by another person ○ a biographical dictionary **2.** RELATING TO WRITING OF BIOGRAPHIES relating to biography as a form of writing —**biographically** adv.

biography /bī óggrəfi/ (plural -phies) n. **1.** ACCOUNT OF SB'S LIFE an account of sb's life, e.g. in the form of a book, film, or television programme, written or produced by another person **2.** BIOGRAPHIES IN GENERAL books about people's lives, considered as a whole or as a type of literature [Late 17thC. Via French and Latin from medieval Greek biographia 'writing about lives', from Greek bios 'life' (see BIO-) + graphein 'to write' (see GRAPHIC).] —**biographer** n.

biohazard /bĭ ó hazərd/ n. a risk to human beings or their environment, especially one presented by a toxic or infectious agent —**biohazardous** /bĭ ó házzərdəss/ adj.

bioinstrumentation /bĭ ó instróomən táysh'n/ n. instruments used to record and display information about the body's functions

Bioko /bi ṓkṓ/ island in the Gulf of Guinea that forms part of Equatorial Guinea. It contains the national capital, Malabo. Population: 57,190 (1983). Area: 2,017 sq. km/779 sq. mi. Former name **Fernando Póo** (until 1973), **Macias Nguema**

biol. abbr. **1.** biological **2.** biology

biological /bĭ ó ə lójik'l/ adj. **1.** CONCERNING LIVING THINGS relating to living organisms ○ biological diversity **2.** RELATING TO BIOLOGY relating to the science of biology **3.** CONTAINING ENZYMES containing enzymes that are intended to digest stains caused by natural substances ○ biological detergent **4.** GENETICALLY RELATED related by birth rather than by adoption ○ my biological mother ■ n. MEDICATION OR VACCINE FROM LIVING ORGANISMS a drug or other compound such as an antibiotic or a vaccine that is produced by living organisms. It is often a commercially important product of genetic engineering. —**biologically** adv.

biological clock *n.* the set of mechanisms within living organisms that link physiological processes with daily, monthly, or seasonal cycles or with stages of development and ageing

biological control *n.* a method of reducing or eliminating plant pests by introducing predators or microorganisms that attack the targeted pests but spare other species in the area

biological oxygen demand *n.* = **biochemical oxygen demand**

biological shield *n.* a massive structure, usually made of concrete and steel, built around the core of a nuclear reactor to protect operating staff from radiation

biological warfare *n.* the use of microorganisms and toxic biological products to cause death or injury to plants and animals, including humans

biological weapon *n.* a missile, bomb, or other device used to deliver and disseminate biological agents that are designed to cause disease, death, or damage to the environment and to humans

biology /bī óllәji/ *n.* **1.** SCIENCE OF LIFE the science that deals with all forms of life, including their classification, physiology, chemistry, and interactions **2.** LIFE IN ONE PLACE the forms of life in a particular environment and their behaviour, development, and history ○ *the biology of desert regions* **3.** PLANT'S OR ANIMAL'S MAKEUP the physical makeup and functioning of a particular plant or animal ○ *the biology of the fruit fly* [Early 19thC. Via French *biologie* from German, from Greek *bios* 'life' (see BIO-).] —**biologist** *n.*

bioluminescence /bī ō loomi néss'nss/ *n.* the generation and emission of light by living organisms such as fireflies, some bacteria and fungi, and many marine animals —**bioluminescent** *adj.*

biomagnification /bī ō mágnfi káysh'n/ *n.* = **bioaccumulation**

biomass /bī ō mass/ *n.* **1.** MASS OF ORGANISMS IN ECOSYSTEM the mass of living organisms within a given environment, measured in terms of weight per unit of area **2.** PLANT AND ANIMAL WASTE AS FUEL plant and animal material, e.g. agricultural waste products, used as a source of fuel **3.** ORGANISM'S DRY WEIGHT the mass of material in a living organism, or in a community of organisms, usually measured in terms of dry weight

biomaterial /bī ō mә teeri әl/ *n.* material that can safely be implanted into the human body and left there without causing an adverse reaction

biomathematics /bī ō mathә máttiks/ *n.* the application of mathematical methods and formulas to medical or biological phenomena (*takes a singular verb*) —**biomathematical** *adj.* —**biomathematician** /bī ō mathәmә tísh'n/ *n.*

biome /bī ōm/ *n.* a division of the world's vegetation that corresponds to a particular climate and is characterized by certain types of plants and animals, e.g. tropical rain forest or desert. The world's lakes and oceans may also be considered biomes, although they are less susceptible to climatic influences than terrestrial biomes. [Early 20thC. Coined from BIO- and -OME.]

biomechanics /bī ō mi kánniks/ *n.* MED MOTION STUDY the study of body movements and of the forces acting on the musculoskeletal system (*takes a singular verb*) ■ *npl.* MECHANICAL FORCES ACTING ON BODY the mechanical forces at work in a particular body or organ (*takes a plural verb*) —**biomechanical** *adj.* —**biomechanically** *adv.*

biomedical engineering *n.* = **bioengineering**

biomedicine /bī ō médss'n/ *n.* **1.** BASIC SCIENCE APPLIED TO MEDICINE the employing of the principles of biology, biochemistry, physiology, and other basic sciences to solve problems in clinical medicine **2.** STUDY OF BODY IN EXTREME CONDITIONS the study of the body's ability to withstand the stresses of unusual environments, e.g. outer space —**biomedical** *adj.*

biometeorology /bī ō meéti ә rólläji/ *n.* the study of how weather conditions affect living things

biometry /bī ómmәtri/ *n.* the application of statistical techniques to biological studies —**biometrist** *n.*

biomolecule /bī ō mólli kyool/ *n.* **1.** MOLECULE THAT ORGANISMS ARE MADE OF one of the molecules from which living organisms are made **2.** MOLECULE OF BIOLOGICAL COMPOUND a molecule of a compound produced by or important to a biological organism —**biomolecular** /bī ō mә lékyŏolәr/ *adj.*

bionic /bī ónnik/ *adj.* **1.** HAVING ELECTRONICALLY POWERED ORGANS having many or most ordinary human organs or functions replaced or enhanced by electronically powered parts that give superhuman capabilities, in the realm of science fiction **2.** HAVING SUPERHUMAN QUALITIES having superhuman strength, speed, or intensity (*informal*) ○ *a bionic appetite* **3.** BIOL INVOLVING BIONICS involving or relating to bionics [Early 20thC. Coined from BIO- + ELECTRONIC.]

bionics /bī ónniks/ *n.* (*takes a singular verb*) **1.** APPLICATION OF BIOLOGICAL INFORMATION TO MACHINES the study of biological function and mechanics, and the application of them to machine design **2.** USE OF ELECTRONICALLY OPERATED REPLACEMENT ORGANS the use of electronic devices to replace damaged limbs and organs

-biont *suffix.* an organism that lives under particular conditions ○ *halobiont* [From SYMBIONT]

bioorganic /bī ō awr gánnik/ *adj.* used to describe a carbon-based (**organic**) compound produced by a living organism or of biological importance

biophysics /bī ō fízziks/ *n.* the science that applies the laws and methods of physics to the study of biological processes (*takes a singular verb*) —**biophysical** *adj.* —**biophysically** *adv.* —**biophysicist** *n.*

biopolymer /bī ō póllimәr/ *n.* a substance that is composed of molecules joined in long chains (**polymers**) and is produced in living organisms. Proteins and DNA are biopolymers.

bioprocess /bī ō prō sess/ *n.* any method for producing commercially useful biological material

biopsy /bī opsi/ (*plural* **-sies**) *n.* the removal of a sample of tissue from a living person for laboratory examination [Late 19thC. Coined from BIO- + Greek *opsis* 'a viewing', from *ōps* 'eye'; modelled on NECROPSY.] —**biopsic** /bī ópsik/ *adj.* —**bioptic** /bī óptik/ *adj.*

biopsychology /bī ō sī kólläji/ *n.* = **psychobiology**

bioreactor /bī ō ri áktәr/ *n.* **1.** MICROORGANISM USED IN INDUSTRIAL PROCESSES a microorganism that, through its biochemical reactions, can produce medically or commercially useful materials, e.g. beer from fermentation of yeast or insulin from genetically altered bacteria **2.** TANK FOR GROWING MICROORGANISMS a large tank for growing microorganisms used in industrial production

bioremediation /bī ō ri meédi áysh'n/ *n.* the use of biological means to restore or clean up contaminated land, e.g. by adding bacteria and other organisms that consume or neutralize contaminants in the soil

biorhythm /bī ō rithәm/ *n.* a cyclical change, e.g. sleeping, waking, or the reproductive cycle, that takes place within living organisms. Some people believe that biorhythms affect behaviour, mood, and sense of well-being. (*often used in the plural*) —**biorhythmic** /bī ō ríthmik/ *adj.* —**biorhythmically** *adv.*

biorhythmics /bī ō ríthmiks/ *n.* a branch of science dealing with biorhythms (*takes a singular verb*)

BIOS /bī oss/ *abbr.* COMPUT Basic Input-Output System

biosatellite /bī ō satt'l īt/ *n.* a satellite designed for living beings, including humans, to live in

bioscience /bī ō sī әnss/ *n.* a science, e.g. biology, ecology, physiology, or molecular biology that studies structures, functions, interactions, or other aspects of living organisms

bioscientist /bī ō sī әntist/ *n.* a specialist in any of the life sciences, e.g. biology, ecology, physiology, or molecular biology

biosensor /bī ō senssәr/ *n.* an apparatus for detecting chemical or physical signals that provide information about specific biological activities. Blood pressure or heart monitors and systems that use live organisms are types of biosensor.

-biosis *suffix.* a particular mode of life ○ *necrobiosis* [From Greek *biōsis* 'way of living', from *bioun* 'to live', from *bios* 'life' (see BIO-)] —**-biotic** *suffix.*

biosphere /bī ә sfeer/ *n.* the whole area of the Earth's surface, atmosphere, and sea that is inhabited by living things —**biospheric** /bī ō sférrik/ *adj.*

biosphere reserve *n.* a type of nationally or internationally protected area managed primarily to preserve natural ecological processes. Biosphere reserves are often open to tourists.

biospheric cycles *npl.* the natural recycling processes essential to life on Earth, involving the principal elements that make up the biosphere. They include the oxygen cycle, carbon cycle, nitrogen cycle, and water cycle.

biostatics /bī ō státtiks/ *n.* a branch of science dealing with the relationship between the structure and the function of an organism (*takes a singular verb*) —**biostatic** *adj.* —**biostatically** *adv.*

biostratigraphy /bī ō strә tíggrәfi/ *n.* the branch of science that uses animal and plant fossils to date and correlate sequences of sedimentary rocks

biostrome /bī ә strōm/ *n.* a thin layer in a rock formation that consists of organic material such as fossils, deposited at the site where they lived [Early 20thC. From modern Latin, formed from Greek *strōma* 'bed, covering'.]

biosynthesis /bī ō sínthәssiss/ *n.* the synthesis of chemical substances as the result of biological activity —**biosynthetic** /bī ō sin théttik/ *adj.* —**biosynthetically** /-théttikli/ *adv.*

biosystematics /bī ō sistә máttiks/ *n.* the study of the relationships among groups of species using criteria such as morphology, biochemistry, and DNA comparisons, especially to determine the evolutionary history of a species (*takes a singular verb*) —**biosystematic** *adj.*

biota /bī ōtә/ *n.* the total complement of animals and plants in a particular area ○ *The biotas of tropical forests are the richest of all.* [Early 20thC. Via modern Latin from Greek *biotē* 'life', from *bios* 'life' (see BIO-).]

biotech /bī ō tek/ *n.* = **biotechnology** [Late 20thC. Shortening.]

biotechnical /bī ō téknik'l/ *adj.* relating to or involving biotechnology

biotechnology /bī ō tek nóllәji/ *n.* PRACTICAL USE OF BIOLOGICAL PROCESSES the use of biological processes or living microorganisms in industrial production. Early examples of biotechnology include the making of cheese, wine, and beer, while later developments include vaccine and insulin production. ■ = **ergonomics** —**biotechnological** /bī ō teknә lójjik'l/ *adj.* —**biotechnologically** /-lójjikli/ *adv.* —**biotechnologist** /bī ō tek nóllәjist/ *n.*

biotelemetry /bī ō tә lémmәtri/ *n.* the remote monitoring of vital processes, e.g. by attaching a signalling device to an animal

biotic /bī óttik/ *adj.* used to describe the features of a natural system that are living [Early 17thC. Via late Latin from Greek *biōtikos* 'of life, lively', ultimately from *bios* 'life' (see BIO-). In modern use from French *biotique*.]

biotic potential *n.* the optimal ability of an organism or a species to survive and reproduce successfully

biotin /bī әtin/ *n.* a vitamin in the B complex that is found in egg yolk, cereals, milk, and liver and is used by the body in metabolizing fat and carbohydrates. Deficiency can lead to dermatitis, loss of appetite, hair loss, and anaemia. Formula: $C_{10}H_{16}N_2O_3S$. [Mid-20thC. Coined from Greek *biōtos* 'life, sustenance', from *bios* 'life' (see BIO-) + -IN.]

biotite /bī ә tīt/ *n.* a black, dark brown, or green silicate mineral found in igneous and metamorphic rocks. It is a member of the mica group of minerals and shares a similar crystal structure. [Mid-19thC. Named after the French physicist J.-B. *Biot* (1774–1862).]

biotope /bī әtōp/ *n.* a small area with a distinct set of environmental conditions that supports a particular ecological community of plants and animals [Early 20thC. From German *Biotop*, formed from Greek *topos* 'place'.]

biotroph /bī әtrōf/ *n.* a parasite that feeds on the living tissue of its host

biotype /bí ə tīp/ *n.* a naturally occurring group of individuals with the same genetic make-up (**genotype**) —**biotypic** /bí ə típpik/ *adj.*

biparental /bí pə rént'l/ *adj.* descended from two parents, male and female, as opposed to being the product of asexual reproduction

biparietal /bí pə rí ət'l/ *adj.* relating to or involving both parietal bones of the skull, particularly with respect to the measurement of the distance between their rounded projections

biparous /bíppərəss/ *adj.* ZOOL giving birth to two offspring at one time [Mid-18thC. Coined from BI- + -PAROUS.]

bipartisan /bí paarti zán, bī pa̅arti zan/ *adj.* relating to, undertaken by, or including two political parties ○ *bipartisan support* —**bipartisanism** *n.* —**bipartisanship** *n.*

bipartite /bī pa̅ar tīt/ *adj.* **1.** POL TWO-PART made or shared by two groups of people ○ *a bipartite agreement* **2.** BOT DIVIDED IN TWO used to describe leaves that are almost completely divided into two parts —**bipartitely** *adv.* —**bipartition** /bí paar tísh'n/ *n.*

biped /bí ped/ *n.* an animal, e.g. a human, with only two legs for locomotion [Mid-17thC. Directly or via French *bipède* from the Latin stem *biped-* 'two-footed', from *ped-* 'foot'.]

bipedal /bī peéd'l, -pédd'l/ *adj.* used to describe an animal that has two legs or feet [15thC. From Latin *bipedalis*, from the stem *biped-* (see BIPED).]

bipedalism /bī peéd'l izzəm, -pédd'l-/ *n.* walking upright on two feet as opposed to moving on all four limbs

biphasic /bī fáyzik/ *adj.* having two phases

biphenyl /bī fénn'l, -feén'l/ *n.* a white crystalline substance used as a fungicide, in organic synthesis, and as a heat transfer agent. Formula: $C_{12}H_{10}$.

bipinnate /bī pínnayt/ *adj.* used to describe leaves divided into leaflets that are themselves subdivided —**bipinnately** *adv.*

biplane /bí playn/ *n.* an aeroplane with two sets of wings, one above the other. The type was built and flown mainly in the early part of the 20th century.

bipod /bí pod/ *n.* a stand or support that has two legs

bipolar /bī pőlər/ *adj.* **1.** TWO-POLED with two poles **2.** HAVING TWO DIFFERENT IDEAS having two quite different opinions, attitudes, or natures **3.** GEOG RELATING TO N AND S POLES involving, found at, or relating to both the North and South Poles **4.** PSYCHIAT HAVING MANIC AND DEPRESSED PERIODS characterized by shifts between episodes of mania and depression **5.** ELECTRON ENG USING NEGATIVE AND POSITIVE CHARGE CARRIERS used to describe electronic devices, especially transistors, in which both negative and positive charge carriers are utilized —**bipolarity** /bí pō lárrəti/ *n.*

bipolar disorder *n.* a psychiatric disorder characterized by extreme mood swings, ranging between episodes of acute euphoria (**mania**) and severe depression

bipotentiality /bípə ténshi álləti/ *n.* the potential early in embryological development for a cell or organ to differentiate in one of two ways, especially for a gonad to become either an ovary or a testis

biprism /bí prizzəm/ *n.* a glass prism that produces a double image of a single object

bipropellant /bí prə péllənt/ *n.* a substance made up of two elements, usually a fuel and an oxidizer, that is used to propel a rocket

biquadratic /bí kwo dráttik/ *adj.* OF THE SQUARE OF A SQUARE relating to the fourth power of a number ○ *a biquadratic equation* ■ *n.* EQUATION INVOLVING SQUARE OF SQUARE an equation that involves the fourth power of a number

biradial /bī ráydi əl/ *adj.* MARINE BIOL with both bilateral and radial symmetry, as found in some primitive marine animals

biramous /bírrəməss, bī ráy əl/ *adj.* BIOL divided into or forming two branches ○ *a biramous appendage*

Birch

birch /burch/ *n.* **1.** TALL TREE WITH PEELING BARK a tall tree that grows in the northern hemisphere and has thin, papery, peeling bark. Genus: *Betula*. **2.** WOOD OF A BIRCH the wood that comes from the birch tree **3.** ROD FOR FLOGGING SB a birch rod or bundle of twigs, especially one formerly used to beat people as a punishment **4.** PUNISHMENT BY BEATING the action of beating sb with a birch rod as a punishment ■ *vt.* (**birches, birching, birched**) PUNISH BY BEATING to beat sb with a birch rod as a punishment [Old English *birce*, from a prehistoric Germanic word that also produced Dutch *berk* and German *Birke*. Ultimately from an Indo-European word that is also the ancestor of English *bright*.]

Bircher /búrchər/ *n.* a member of the John Birch Society, a right-wing political organization in the United States with the prime mission of fighting Communism [Mid-20thC. Named after John *Birch*, a US Baptist missionary killed in 1945 by Chinese Communists.]

bird /burd/ *n.* **1.** TWO-LEGGED WINGED ANIMAL a two-legged warm-blooded animal that has wings, a hard beak, and a body covered with feathers. Birds lay eggs from which their young hatch, and most species can fly. Class: Aves. **2.** FOWL EATEN AS FOOD a fowl, e.g. a turkey, chicken, duck, or goose, cooked and eaten as food **3.** KIND OF PERSON sb of a particular type (*informal*) ○ *he's a wise old bird* **4.** WOMAN a girl or woman (*dated offensive*) **5.** US AEROPLANE OR SPACECRAFT an aircraft, satellite, or rocket (*slang*) **6.** CRIMINOL PRISON prison, or a period in prison (*slang*) **7.** SPORTS = clay pigeon [Old English *brid* 'young bird', of unknown origin] ◇ **get the bird** to be received badly, often with booing (*informal*) ◇ **kill two birds with one stone** to achieve two aims with one action ◇ **(strictly) for the birds** worthless or unacceptable (*informal*) ◇ **the birds and the bees** the facts about sexual reproduction in humans (*informal humorous*)

birdbath /búrd baath/ (*plural* **-baths** /-baathz/) *n.* a small shallow basin containing water that is placed outside a house for birds to bathe in

birdbrain /búrd brayn/ *n.* sb who is silly or mildly unintelligent (*informal*) —**birdbrained** *adj.*

birdcage /búrd kayj/ *n.* a cage with wire or bamboo bars used to keep birds in captivity

birdcall /búrd kawl/ *n.* **1.** BIRD'S CRY the sound or cry of a bird, especially a warning cry **2.** INSTRUMENT IMITATING BIRD'S SOUND a device that imitates a bird's call, used especially in trying to hunt or catch birds

bird dog *n.* US, Can a dog used to bring back game birds after they have been shot

birder /búrdər/ *n.* US = birdwatcher

bird feeder *n.* a device containing food such as nuts that allows birds to feed at will

birdhouse /búrd howss/ (*plural* **-houses** /-howziz/) *n.* **1.** US SHELTER FOR BIRDS a small box or shelter that is specially built for birds to nest in **2.** LARGE BIRDCAGE a large cage in which birds are kept in captivity

birdie /búrdi/ *n.* **1.** GOLF GOLF SCORE a score in golf in which the ball is hit into the hole using one stroke fewer than the accepted standard number of strokes (**par**) for that hole **2.** BIRD a bird (*babytalk*) ■ *vt.* (**-ies, -ieing, -ied**) GOLF PLAY HOLE ONE STROKE UNDER PAR to play a hole in golf in one stroke less than the accepted standard number (**par**) [Late 18thC. In the sense 'golf score', perhaps from US slang *bird* 'exceptionally smart or accomplished person'.]

birdlife /búrd līf/ *n.* all the birds that live in a particular area or region

birdlime /búrd līm/ *n.* STICKY SUBSTANCE FOR TRAPPING BIRDS a sticky substance made from plants that is spread on trees to catch birds ■ *vt.* (**-limes, -liming, -limed**) TRAP BIRDS WITH STICKY SUBSTANCE to spread a sticky substance on trees in order to catch birds

bird louse (*plural* **bird lice**) *n.* a wingless insect with a flattened body that is not truly parasitic but lives on the feathers and skin debris of birds, often causing skin irritation. Suborder: Mallophaga.

bird of paradise *n.* **1.** BIRDS BIRD WITH BRIGHT FEATHERS a bird from New Guinea and Australia, the male of which has bright feathers used in spectacular mating displays. Family: Paradisaeidae. **2.** PLANTS PLANT WITH FLOWERS LIKE BIRD'S HEAD a South African or South American plant that has flowers containing erect orange-and-blue petals resembling a bird's head and crest in shape. Genus: *Strelitzia*.

bird of passage *n.* **1.** MIGRATORY BIRD a bird that migrates from one region or country to another according to the season **2.** TRANSIENT sb who travels about a lot, rarely staying in the same place for long

bird of peace *n.* a white dove as a symbol of peace

bird of prey *n.* a bird that kills other birds and animals for food and has excellent eyesight, sharp talons, and a sharp curved beak. Owls, eagles, and hawks are birds of prey.

bird pepper *n.* **1.** PLANTS PEPPER PLANT a tropical plant that has a thin hot-tasting fruit. The bird pepper is thought to be the ancestor of the sweet pepper and many hot peppers. Latin name: *Capsicum frutescens*. **2.** FOOD HOT-TASTING PEPPER the small pod-shaped hot-tasting fruit of the bird pepper plant

bird sanctuary (*plural* **bird sanctuaries**), **bird reserve** *n.* a natural area where birds are kept under protection so that they can live and breed in safety and under observation

birdseed /búrd seed/ *n.* seed or a mixture of seeds, usually used for feeding caged or wild birds

bird's-eye *n.* **1.** FABRIC PATTERN a pattern for fabric that is composed of diamond shapes with a dot in the middle of each **2.** PATTERNED FABRIC fabric with a bird's-eye pattern

bird's-eye maple *n.* timber from the sugar or rock maple that has a curled pattern in the grain reminiscent of a bird's eye

bird's-eye view *n.* **1.** VIEW FROM HIGH UP a view that is seen from somewhere very high up **2.** GENERAL IMPRESSION an overall impression or summary of sth without details

bird's-foot trefoil *n.* a creeping wild plant that has yellow flowers with red tips and seed pods in the shape of a bird's foot. Latin name: *Lotus corniculatus*.

birdshot /búrd shot/ *n.* small lead shot designed to be fired from a shotgun

bird's nest *n.* a food delicacy obtained from high cliffs in Southeast Asia, believed to be swifts' nests built with the birds' saliva. Bird's nest, usually used in soups, is believed by the Chinese to be good for the skin and lungs. (*hyphenated when used before a noun*) ○ *bird's-nest soup*

bird's-nest fern *n.* a fern with long green fronds shaped like a bird's nest that grows on the ground or on trees in parts of Australia, India, and the South Pacific islands. Latin name: *Asplenium nidus*.

birdsong /búrd song/ *n.* the sounds made by a bird to attract a mate or defend territory

bird spider *n.* a large hairy spider from tropical America that eats birds. Family: Aviculariidae.

bird strike *n.* a collision between a bird and an aircraft in flight

Birdsville /búrdz vil/ town in a remote part of south-western Queensland, Australia. It is the home of the annual Birdsville horse races. Population: 102 (1996).

bird table *n.* a small table or platform in a garden on which food is laid out for birds to eat

birdwatcher /búrd wochər/ *n.* sb who as a hobby observes birds in their natural habitats, usually from a distance using binoculars —**birdwatching** *n.*

birefringence /bī́ ri frínjənss/ *n.* = **double refraction** —**birefringent** *adj.*

bireme /bī́ reem/ *n.* an ancient warship that had two ranks of oars on each side [Late 16thC. From Latin *biremis*, literally 'two-oared', from *remus* 'oar'.]

Birendra Bir Bikram Shah Dev /bi réndrə beer bík ram sháa dév/, **Shah Dev, King of Nepal** (*b.* 1945). He acceded to the throne in 1972 and ruled as an absolute monarch before instituting democratic reforms in 1990.

biretta /bə réttə/, **beretta** *n.* a stiff hat worn by Roman Catholic clerics that has three upright sections meeting at the centre on top. Priests wear black birettas, bishops purple ones, and cardinals red ones. [Late 16thC. From Italian *berretta* or Spanish *birreta*, from late Latin *birrus*, *birrum* 'hooded cape or cloak' (source of English *beret*), perhaps ultimately of Celtic origin.]

biri *n.* = **bidi**

biriani *n.* = **biryani**

Birinus /bi rī́nəss/, **St** (*d.* 650?) Roman-born English missionary. He went to Britain on the orders of Pope St Honorius and converted the King of the West Saxons.

birk /burk/, **birken** /búrkən/ *n. N England, Scotland* a birch tree [14th C. Variant of BIRCH.]

Birkenhead /búrkən hed/ town and port in Merseyside, England, opposite Liverpool on the Wirral Peninsula. Population: 116,000 (1991).

Birkenhead, Frederick Edwin Smith, 1st Earl of (1872–1930) British lawyer and statesman. He was attorney-general (1911–19), and as lord chancellor (1919–22) was an architect of the Anglo-Irish settlement (1921) and the Law of Property Act (1922).

Birkenstock /búrkən stok/ *tdmk.* a trademark for a brand of footwear that includes sandals and clogs

birl /burl/ (**birls, birling, birled**) *v.* **1.** *vi. Scotland* to spin round **2.** *vt. US, Can* MAKE FLOATING LOG SPIN to cause a floating log to spin round in water [Early 18thC. Thought to be an imitation of the sound of sth rotating rapidly.] —**birler** *n.*

Birmingham /búrmingəm/ the second largest city in central England and a major industrial centre. Located in the west Midlands, it has three universities, two cathedrals, and the National Exhibition Centre, built in 1976. Population: 1,017,500 (1995).

Biro /bī́rō/ *tdmk.* a trademark for a pen with a small metal ball at the tip that transfers the ink contained in the pen to the paper

Biro /bī́rō/, **Lazio José** (1899–1985) Hungarian inventor. He invented the ballpoint pen in 1944.

birr[1] /bur/ *vti.* (**birrs, birring, birred**) *US, Scotland* MAKE WHIRR to make a whirring sound, or cause sth to make a whirring sound ■ *n.* **1.** *US, Scotland* WHIRR a whirring sound **2.** *Scotland, US* FORCE a forward-moving driving force [14thC. From Old Norse *byrr* 'favourable wind', of uncertain origin: perhaps literally 'thing carried', and ultimately from an Indo-European word that also produced English *burden*.]

birr[2] /bur/ *n.* **1.** ETHIOPIAN UNIT OF CURRENCY . See table at **currency** **2.** NOTE AND COIN WORTH A BIRR a note and coin worth one birr [Late 20thC. From Amharic.]

birth /burth/ *n.* **1.** EVENT OF BEING BORN the emergence of the young of a human or animal from the mother's womb into the outside world ○ *The father was present at the birth.* **2.** PROCESS OF BEING BORN the process of bringing forth young from a mother's womb ○ *the growing number of home births* **3.** TIME OR PLACE OF BIRTH the time or place of birth **4.** SB'S HERITAGE sb's social or national origins ○ *a man of noble birth* ○ *Italian by birth* **5.** ORIGIN OF STH the origin, beginning, or formation of sth ○ *the birth of jazz* **6.** SB'S CHILD the child of a particular mother born at a particular time (*archaic*) ■ *adj.* BIOLOGICALLY RELATED AS A PARENT biologically related to sb, especially as a parent, rather than related by adoption [13thC. From Old Norse *byrð*, ultimately from an Indo-European word that also produced English *bear* 'to carry'.] ◇ **give birth 1.** to produce a child or young from the womb **2.** to originate or be responsible for creating sth ○ *a revolution that gave birth to a free nation*

birth canal *n.* the passageway including the cervix and vagina through which a foetus emerges from the womb into the outside world

birth certificate *n.* an official document that states when and where sb was born and the parents' names

birth control *n.* the deliberate limiting, usually by contraceptive means, of the number of children born

birth control pill *n.* = **oral contraceptive**

birthday /búrth day, -di/ *n.* **1.** ANNIVERSARY OF DAY OF BIRTH the day in each year that is the anniversary of the day sb was born (*often used before a noun*) **2.** DAY SB IS BORN the day on which sb is born

WORD KEY: CULTURAL NOTE

The Birthday Party, a play by Harold Pinter (1958). It tells the story of a young man called Stanley whose comfortable life in a seaside boarding house is disrupted by the arrival of two mysterious intimidating strangers, Goldberg and McCann. Noted for its sinisterly formal dialogue, the play creates a disturbing atmosphere of paranoia and fear.

Birthday Honours *npl.* honorary titles given by the British sovereign on his or her official birthday to people who have in some way distinguished themselves

birthday suit *n.* a state of nakedness (*slang humorous*)

birthing /búrthing/ *n.* GIVING BIRTH the process of giving birth, especially when using natural childbirth methods ■ *adj.* FOR FACILITATING CHILDBIRTH designed to facilitate childbirth ○ *a birthing pool*

birthing chair *n.* a chair designed to support a woman and ease the process of childbirth by enabling gravity to act on the foetus as it moves through the birth canal

birthing room *n.* an area with nonclinical-looking surroundings in a hospital or other building set up for childbirth

birthmark /búrth maark/ *n.* a reddish or brown marking seen on the skin of some newborn babies that typically remains visible for life

birth pangs *npl.* a difficult or troubled period at the start of sth

birth parent *n.* sb's biological mother or father, especially in the case of an adopted child

birthplace /búrth playss/ *n.* a place where sb was born or where sth first started ○ *Shakespeare's birthplace* ○ *the birthplace of classical philosophy*

birthrate /búrth rayt/ *n.* the number of live births per 1,000 members of the population in a year ○ *a declining birthrate*

birthright /búrth rīt/ *n.* **1.** BASIC ENTITLEMENT a basic right that sb has or is thought to be entitled to from birth ○ *Freedom of speech is our birthright.* **2.** FAMILY PROPERTY SB EXPECTS TO OWN property or money that sb feels entitled to because it belongs in the family, particularly if the person is the eldest son of the family

birthroot /búrth root/ (*plural* **-roots** *or* **-root**) *n.* a North American plant whose roots were once used by Native Americans to help ease childbirth. Genus: *Trillium.* ◊ **trillium**

birthstone /búrth stōn/ *n.* a precious or semi-precious stone such as an amethyst or garnet that is popularly associated with the month in which sb was born. A birthstone is believed by some people to bring luck.

birthwort /búrth wurt/ *n.* a European climbing plant that was formerly used to help ease pain during childbirth. Latin name: *Aristolochia clematitis.*

Birtwistle /búrt wiss'l/, **Sir Harrison** (*b.* 1934) British composer. He helped form the New Manchester Group for the performance of modern music. His works include *Earth Dances* (1986).

biryani /bírri áani/, **biriani** *n.* an Indian dish containing spicy coloured rice mixed with meat, fish, or vegetables ○ *chicken biryani* [Mid-20thC. Via Hindi from Persian *biriyān*, literally 'fried, grilled'.]

bis /biss/ *adv.* TO BE REPEATED to be played or sung again (*used as a musical direction*) ■ *interj.* CALLING FOR ENCORE used by members of an audience to call for an encore [Early 17thC. Via French and Italian from Latin, 'twice', ultimately from an Indo-European word meaning 'two', which is also the ancestor of English *two*.]

Biscay, Bay of /bís kay/ arm of the North Atlantic Ocean between western France and northern Spain. Area: 223,000 sq. km/86,000 sq. mi.

biscuit /bískit/ *n.* **1.** FOOD SMALL FLAT CAKE a small flat dry cake that is usually sweet and crisp and can additionally contain fruit, nuts, or chocolate. Biscuits are often eaten with tea or coffee as a snack. US term **cookie** **2.** *US* FOOD SMALL ROUND PIECE OF BREAD a small round plain piece of bread that rises with baking powder or soda and is then baked in an oven **3.** COLOURS LIGHT BROWN a light brown colour **4.** CERAMICS UNGLAZED POTTERY pottery that has been fired but not glazed ■ *adj.* COLOURS LIGHT BROWN of a light brown colour [14thC. From Old French *bescuit*, literally 'twice-cooked', ultimately from Latin *bis* 'twice' + *coctus*, past participle of *coquere* 'to cook' (source of English *cook*).] ◇ **take the biscuit** to be the worst in a series of bad or annoying things that have already happened (*informal*)

biscuit firing *n.* the first firing of sth made of clay, at a relatively low temperature

biscuit ware *n.* pots or pottery that have been through a first firing at a relatively low temperature

bise /beez/ *n.* a sharp dry northerly wind that blows in Switzerland and neighbouring parts of Italy and France [14thC. From French, of unknown origin.]

bisect /bī sékt/ (**-sects, -secting, -sected**) *vt.* **1.** SPLIT INTO TWO to split sth into two parts ○ *The river bisects the town.* **2.** MATH HALVE to divide sth into two exactly equal parts [Mid-17thC. Coined from BI- + Latin *sect-*, the past participle stem of *secare* 'to cut' (see SECTION).] —**bisection** /bī séksh'n/ *n.* —**bisectional** *adj.* —**bisectionally** *adv.*

bisector /bī séktər/ *n.* a straight line or plane that divides an angle or another line into two exactly equal parts

bisexual /bī sékshoo əl/ *adj.* **1.** ATTRACTED TO BOTH SEXES sexually attracted to both men and women, or engaging in both heterosexual and homosexual activity **2.** BOTH MALE AND FEMALE IN CHARACTERISTICS having both male and female characteristics **3.** BIOL WITH MALE AND FEMALE REPRODUCTIVE ORGANS used to describe sth such as a flower that has both male and female reproductive organs ■ *n.* SB SEXUALLY ATTRACTED TO BOTH SEXES sb who is sexually attracted to both men and women, or who engages in both heterosexual and homosexual activity —**bisexuality** /bī sékshoo álləti/ *n.* —**bisexually** *adv.*

Bishkek /bish kék/ capital of Kyrgyzstan, in the northern part of the country, on the River Chu, just south of the border with Kazakhstan. Population: 630,000 (1994).

bishop /bíshəp/ *n.* **1.** CHR SENIOR CHRISTIAN CLERIC a senior Christian cleric, especially in the Roman Catholic, Anglican, and Orthodox churches, who is in charge of the spiritual life and administration of a particular region (**diocese**) **2.** CHESS CHESS PIECE a chess piece that can be moved diagonally across the board over any number of squares of the same colour [Pre-12thC. Via Latin *episcopus* 'bishop, overseer' from Greek *episkopos* 'overseer', from *skopos* 'watcher' (source of English *scope*).]

Bishop /bíshəp/, **Elizabeth** (1911–79) US poet. Known for her personal, reflective poetry, she won the Pulitzer Prize for her collections *North and South: A Cold Spring* (1955).

bishopbird /bíshəp burd/ *n.* an African weaverbird, the males of which have black feathers with red or yellow markings. Genus: *Euplectes.*

bishopric /bíshəp rik/ *n.* **1.** BISHOP'S DIOCESE an area that a bishop is in charge of **2.** BISHOP'S SEE a place where a bishop's cathedral is situated **3.** RANK OF BISHOP the rank or office of a bishop [Pre-12thC. Formed from BISHOP + Old English *rīce* 'realm, power'.]

bishop's cap *n.* = **mitrewort**

bishop sleeve *n.* a wide sleeve that is gathered at the wrist

bishop's mitre *n.* a European insect, the larvae of which destroy cereal grasses. Latin name: *Aelia acuminata.*

bishop's weed *n.* = **ground elder**

Biskra /biss kraa/ city and oasis on the edge of the Sahara Desert in Biskra Province, northeastern Algeria. Population: 128,280 (1987).

Bislama /bíshlə maa/ *n.* the national language of Vanuatu in the Pacific, a modern form of the English-based pidgin language known as Beach-la-Mar. Approximately 128,000 people speak Bislama. [Late 20thC. Local pronunciation and official spelling of BEACH-LA-MAR.]

Bismarck /bíz maark/, **Otto Edward Leopold von, Prince** (1815–98) German statesman. As Prussian prime minister after 1862, he embarked on the European wars that unified the German states. He was the most powerful statesman in Europe as chancellor of the new German Empire from 1871 to 1890. Known as **the Iron Chancellor**

bismuth /bízməth/ *n.* a heavy reddish-white crystalline metallic element that breaks easily and is widely used in alloys. The compounds of bismuth are used in medicines. Symbol **Bi** [Mid-17thC. From obsolete German *Bismut* and modern Latin *bisemutum* from Middle High German *wise* 'meadow' + *muth* 'claim to a mine'.]

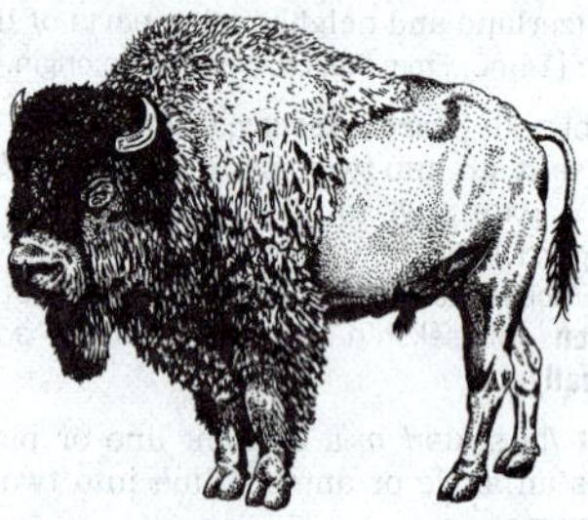

Bison

bison /bīss'n/ (*plural* **-son**) *n.* a large hairy animal resembling an ox, but with massive head and shoulders and a humped back. Bison were once common in North America and Europe, but are now mainly found only in protected areas. Genus: *Bison.* ◊ **buffalo, wisent** [Early 17thC. Directly or via French from Latin *bison*, which came from a prehistoric Germanic source that also produced English *wisent.*]

bisque[1] /bisk/ *n.* a rich soup made from shellfish ○ *lobster bisque* [Mid-17thC. From French, of unknown origin: perhaps an alteration of *Biscaye* 'Biscay'.]

bisque[2] /bisk/ *n.* **1.** CERAMICS = **biscuit** *n.* 4 **2.** COLOURS **PINKISH BROWN** a pinkish-brown colour ■ *adj.* **PINKISH-BROWN** pinkish-brown in colour [Mid-17thC. Alteration of BISCUIT, perhaps in order to seem fashionably French.]

bisque[3] /bisk/ *n.* an extra turn, stroke, or point that is given as an advantage to a weaker player in a game of tennis, golf, or croquet [Mid-17thC. From French, of unknown origin.]

Bissau /bi sów/ city on the northern shore of the Geba River estuary and capital of Guinea-Bissau since 1941. Population: 200,000 (1994).

bissextile /bi séks tīl/ *adj.* **MAKING A LEAP YEAR** having the extra day in a year that makes it a leap year ○ *bissextile month* ■ *n.* **LEAP YEAR** a leap year [Late 16thC. From late Latin *bis(s)extilus*, from Latin *bi(s)sextus (dies)*, literally 'twice-sixth (day)' (24 February, counted twice in a leap year; the sixth day before 1 March), in the ancient Roman calendar from *sextus* 'sixth'.]

Bisto /bístō/ *tdmk.* a trademark for a powder that is mixed with water or the juice of roasting meat to make gravy

bistort /bís tawrt/ *n.* a plant found in Europe and Asia with an S-shaped underground stem (**rhizome**) that was dried and used in traditional medicine. Latin name: *Polygonum bistorta.* [Early 16thC. Directly or via French from assumed medieval Latin *bistorta*, from *bis* 'twice' + *torta*, feminine past participle of *torquere* 'to twist' (see TORQUE); from its twisted roots.]

bistoury /bístəri/ (*plural* **-ries**) *n.* a thin surgical knife designed to cut from the inside outward, formerly used to cut open abscesses or enlarge fistulas [Mid-18thC. From French, of uncertain origin: perhaps from Italian dialectal *bistori* 'dagger', which evolved from *pistorino* 'of Pistoia', a city in northern Italy famous for the manufacture of knives.]

bistro /beéstrō/ (*plural* **-tros**) *n.* a small restaurant or bar [Early 20thC. From French, originally 'little restaurant', of uncertain origin, perhaps related to *bistouille* 'raw spirits', or from dialect *bistraud* 'little shepherd'.]

bisulphate /bī súl fayt/ *n.* = **hydrogen sulphate**

bisulphide /bī súl fīd/ *n.* = **disulphide**

bisulphite /bī súl fīt/ *n.* = **hydrogen sulphite**

bit[1] /bit/ *n.* **1.** **PIECE** a small piece of sth ○ *There were bits of paper everywhere.* **2.** **SMALL AMOUNT** a small part or amount of sth ○ *a bit of housework* **3.** **SHORT AMOUNT OF TIME** a very short period of time or distance ○ *I'll do it in a bit.* **4.** MONEY **SMALL COIN** a small coin of a particular value (*informal dated*) ○ *a threepenny bit* **5.** ARTS **SHORT PERFORMANCE** a short routine, joke, or skit in a performance **6.** CINEMA **SMALL ACTING PART** a small part in a film or play (*often used before a noun*) ○ *I had a bit part in one of her films.* **7.** **EVERYTHING ABOUT A ROLE** all the aspects of a particular role in life (*informal*) ○ *did the whole two-career marriage bit* [Old English *bita*, formed from *bītan* 'to bite' (see BITE). Originally 'piece bitten off, morsel'; the more general meaning 'piece' dates from the 13thC.] ◇ **a bit** somewhat (*informal*) ◇ **a bit of all right** very good-looking (*informal*) ◇ **bit by bit** gradually ◇ **bit of fluff** a young woman who is regarded as very attractive but unintelligent, often sb's girlfriend or mistress (*informal insult*) ◇ **bit of stuff** a woman or girl considered from the point of view of her sexual attractiveness (*dated informal offensive*) ◇ **bits and pieces, bits and bobs** **1.** personal belongings (*informal*) **2.** miscellaneous small objects (*informal*) ○ *I collected up my bits and pieces and left.* ◇ **do your bit** to contribute your share to work that needs to be done ◇ **every bit** in every way ○ *She is every bit as skilled as he is.* ◇ **fall to bits** to break, sometimes into small pieces ◇ **to bits** very much or to the greatest degree possible (*informal*) ○ *I just love the kids to bits!*

bit[2] /bit/ *n.* **1.** **MOUTHPIECE OF BRIDLE** a part of a bridle, that consists of a metal mouthpiece held in a horse's mouth by the reins and used to control the horse **2.** **DETACHABLE PART OF DRILL** a small metal tool that is inserted into a drill or brace and used for boring or drilling **3.** **TOOL BLADE** the part of a plane that is used for cutting **4.** **PART OF PINCERS** the gripping part of a pair of pincers **5.** **TIP OF SOLDERING IRON** the tip of a soldering iron that is made from copper ■ *vt.* (**bits, bitting, bitted**) **1.** **INSERT BRIDLE BIT** to put a bit into the mouth of a horse **2.** **RESTRAIN** to restrain sb, or hold sb back [Old English *bite*, from, ultimately, an Indo-European base that is also the ancestor of English *bitter* and *bite*. The original meaning was 'a bite'.] ◇ **champ** *or* **chafe at the bit** to be impatient for sth to happen, or impatient because no action is possible ◇ **get** *or* **take** *or* **have the bit between your teeth** to start sth and refuse stubbornly to stop

bit[3] /bit/ *n.* **1.** **DIGIT IN BINARY NOTATION** in binary notation, either of the digits 0 or 1 used to represent one of only two outcomes, e.g. on or off **2.** **UNIT OF INFORMATION IN COMPUTER** the smallest unit of information storable in a computer or a peripheral device, expressed as 0 or 1. Eight bits make a byte, the common measure of memory or storage capacity. [Mid-20thC. Blend of BINARY and DIGIT.]

bit[4] /bit/ past tense, past participle of **bite**

bitch /bich/ *n.* **1.** ZOOL **FEMALE DOG** a female dog, or the female of another related animal, e.g. the fox, or another carnivore, e.g. the ferret **2.** **OFFENSIVE TERM** an offensive term that deliberately insults a woman's temperament (*taboo insult*) **3.** **SPITEFUL CONVERSATION** a conversation that involves complaining or saying unpleasant things about sb who is not present (*informal*) **4.** *US* **COMPLAINT** a querulous nagging complaint (*slang*) **5.** **STH DIFFICULT** a difficult thing or situation (*slang*) ○ *That lock's a real bitch to open.* ■ *vi.* (**bitches, bitching, bitched**) **1.** **BE NASTY ABOUT SB** to talk about sb who is not present in an unpleasant or malicious way (*slang*) **2.** *US* **COMPLAIN CONTINUALLY** to complain or grumble about sth continually [Old English *bicce*, perhaps from an Old Norse word]

bitchin /bíchin/ *adj.* *US* **GREAT** particularly or extremely good (*slang*) ■ *adv.* *US* **VERY** extremely (*slang*) [Mid-20th C. Alteration of bitching, shortening of sonofabitching, from SON OF A BITCH.]

bitchy /bíchi/ (**-ier, -iest**) *adj.* malicious or unpleasant in speaking to, talking about, or behaving toward sb (*slang*) —**bitchily** *adv.* —**bitchiness** *n.*

bite /bīt/ *v.* (**bites, biting, bit** /bit/, **bitten** /bítt'n/) **1.** *vti.* **GRIP WITH THE TEETH** to hold sth tightly, tear sth off, or cut through sth using the teeth ○ *I bit into the fruit.* **2.** *vt.* **STING** to puncture or tear the skin of a person or animal using fangs or teeth ○ *got bitten by a wasp* **3.** *vti.* **GRIP STH FIRMLY** to make firm or secure contact with sth ○ *The wheel's not biting.* **4.** *vi.* **CORRODE STH** to eat into sth with a corrosive action ○ *The acid had bitten into the metal surface.* **5.** *vi.* **CUT INTO SB OR STH** to penetrate sb or sth sharply, as if with a honed blade **6.** *vi.* **TAKE BAIT** to attempt to take the bait that has been placed on the end of a fishing line (*refers to fish*) **7.** *vi.* **RISE TO SB ELSE'S BAIT** to respond when sb else tries to get you involved in a scheme or an argument (*informal*) ○ *Even though baited by the Opposition, she refused to bite.* **8.** *vt.* **ANNOY OR UPSET** to annoy or preoccupy sb, or put sb in a bad mood ○ *What's biting you today?* **9.** *vi.* **BE EFFECTIVE** to have an effect or influence ○ *The trade sanctions are at last beginning to bite.* **10.** *vt.* *Aus* **SCROUNGE** to ask for money or goods from sb else rather than earning or paying for sth personally (*informal*) ○ *Can I bite you for ten bucks?* ■ *n.* **1.** **SEIZURE OF STH WITH TEETH** the action of taking sth between the teeth and tearing it off **2.** **MOUTHFUL** a piece of food torn off with the teeth **3.** **INJURY FROM TEETH OR INSECT** an injury that has been caused by an animal or insect puncturing or tearing the skin with its teeth or fangs ○ *a mosquito bite* **4.** **ATTEMPT BY FISH TO TAKE BAIT** an attempt by a fish to eat the bait that has been put on the end of a fishing line **5.** **PIQUANCY** a pleasantly sharp taste **6.** **WIT AND INTELLIGENCE** a penetrating and intelligent quality **7.** **COLDNESS** a cold sharp sensation that is quite painful ○ *There's a bit of a bite in the air today.* **8.** MECH ENG **DEPTH OF MACHINE TOOL'S BLADE** the depth to which a machine tool can cut **9.** **GRIP** the grip that sth such as a tool has on sth else **10.** DENT **FIT BETWEEN TEETH** the way the upper and lower teeth meet and fit together when the jaw is closed **11.** **CORROSIVE EFFECT** the corrosive effect of acid on a surface **12.** **PERIOD WHEN FISH EAT** a time when fish usually feed ○ *The catfish bite is usually the heaviest and best in the evening.* [Old English *bītan*, from, ultimately, an Indo-European base that also produced English *beetle* and *fission*] —**bitable** *adj.* —**biter** *n.* ◇ **bite off more than you can chew** to take on more than you can deal with (*informal*) ◇ **have two bites at the cherry** to have more than one attempt at doing sth

bite back *v.* **1.** *vt.* **STOP FROM EXPRESSING** to hold back from saying sth or openly crying ○ *I bit back my tears.* **2.** *vti.* **GIVE SHARP RETORT** to retort sharply, or say sth in a very sharp manner in response to sb else

biteplate /bít playt/ *n.* a removable acrylic dental device that sticks to the roof of the mouth and is worn to encourage the back teeth to come through or to correct an overbite

bite-sized, bite-size *adj.* small enough to be eaten as a single mouthful ○ *cut the meat into bite-sized pieces*

Bithynia /bi thínni ə/ ancient country of northwestern Asia Minor, on the Black Sea in present-day Turkey

biting /bíting/ *adj.* **1.** **VERY COLD** cold enough to cause discomfort or pain ○ *a biting north wind* **2.** **CLEVERLY SARCASTIC** sarcastic and clever

biting louse (*plural* **biting lice**) *n.* a wingless insect that spends its entire life cycle as a parasite on the body of a bird or mammal and feeds on skin flakes, feathers, glandular secretions, and blood. Suborder: Mallophaga.

biting midge *n.* a fly, virtually invisible to the naked eye, that sucks the blood of animals and other insects, leaving painful itching welts. Family: Ceratopogonidae. US term **punkie**

bit map *n.* COMPUTER IMAGE REPRESENTED AS BITS a representation of a graphics image in computer memory consisting of rows and columns of dots, each corresponding to a pixel. For monochrome images one bit is sufficient to represent each dot, while colours and shades of grey require more than one bit of data for each dot. ■ *vt.* **(bit-maps, bit-mapping, bit-mapped)** REPRESENT COMPUTER IMAGE AS BITS to represent a graphics image in computer memory as a matrix of dots or to recreate the image on a computer screen from such a bit map [From BIT[3]]

BITNET /bít net/ *abbr.* Because It's Time Network

bitok /bíttok/ *n.* fried mince patties served with a sour cream sauce [Via Russian from French *bifteck (haché)*, '(minced) beef', from English *beefsteak*]

bitser /bítsər/ *n.* *Aus* a mongrel dog [Mid-20thC. Formed from *bits (and pieces)*.]

bitt /bit/ *n.* POST ON SHIP either of a pair of posts on a ship's deck for fastening cables (*often used in the plural*) ■ *vt.* **(bitts, bitting, bitted)** TIE TO A BITT to fasten sth round a bitt [15thC. Origin uncertain: perhaps from Old Norse *biti* 'beam', from, ultimately, an Indo-European base that is also the ancestor of English *bite*.]

bitten past participle of **bite**

bitter /bíttər/ *adj.* **1.** STRONG AND SHARP IN TASTE having a sharp strong unpleasant taste, e.g. like that of orange peel **2.** RESENTFUL angry and resentful ○ *a bitter smile* **3.** DIFFICULT TO ACCEPT painful or very hard to accept ○ *a bitter blow* **4.** HOSTILE expressing intense hostility ○ *bitter fighting.* **5.** VERY COLD penetratingly and unpleasantly cold ○ *a bitter wind* ■ *n.* *UK* BEVERAGES BEER beer that is made with a lot of hops and has a slightly sharp taste ○ *a pint of bitter* [Old English *biter*, from, ultimately, an Indo-European base that also produced English *bite, beetle*, and *fission*] —**bitterness** *n.*

bitter almond *n.* a type of almond tree that produces nuts containing hydrogen cyanide. When detoxified, the almond oil can be used as a flavouring.

bitter aloes *n.* = **aloes**

bitter cress *n.* a plant belonging to the mustard family that has clusters of typically white flowers and often grows in damp places. Genus: *Cardamine.*

bitter end *n.* the very end of sth, however unpleasant it is ○ *They held out to the bitter end.* [Originally 'end of a ship's cable or mooring rope secured on board the ship'; *bitter* perhaps from BITT, but now interpreted as 'painful']

bitter lemon *n.* a fizzy nonalcoholic drink that is flavoured with lemon and is a greyish-green colour

bitterling /bíttərling/ *n.* a small brightly-coloured freshwater fish from central Europe that is often kept in aquariums. Latin name: *Rhodeus sericeus.* [Late 19thC. From German, literally 'small bitter (fish)'.]

bitterly /bíttərli/ *adv.* **1.** RESENTFULLY AND ANGRILY with feelings of anger, injustice, and resentment ○ *wept bitterly* **2.** INTENSELY AND NEGATIVELY intensely or profoundly, in reaction to an unpleasant situation ○ *a bitterly fought divorce case* **3.** EXTREMELY AND PENETRATINGLY to an extreme and penetrating degree ○ *bitterly cold*

bittern[1] /bíttərn/ *n.* a wading bird of the heron family, similar to the herons but with mottled brownish plumage, shorter legs and neck, and a booming call. Family: Ardeidae. [Early 16thC. Alteration of *bitore*, probably from, ultimately, Anglo-Latin *butorius* or Old French *butor*, both ultimately from Latin *butio* 'bittern' + *taurus* 'bull', from its booming voice.]

bittern[2] /bíttərn/ *n.* the bitter liquid that is left after common salt has crystallized from sea water [Late 17thC. Formed from BITTER, but the origin of the final *-n* is not known.]

bitternut /bíttər nut/ *n.* **1.** HICKORY TREE a type of hickory tree, native to eastern North America, that bears thin-shelled nuts with a bitter kernel. Latin name: *Carya cordiformis.* **2.** THIN-SHELLED NUT the nut that grows on the bitternut tree

bitter orange *n.* = **Seville orange**

bitter pill *n.* sth unpleasant that nonetheless must be accepted ○ *Not getting the job was a bitter pill for him to swallow.*

bitterroot /bíttər root/ *n.* a western North American plant of the purslane family that has edible starchy roots and is able to grow and live in dry surroundings. Latin name: *Lewisia rediviva.*

bitters /bíttərz/ *n.* ALCOHOLIC LIQUID a slightly alcoholic liquid flavoured with plant extracts and used as a mixer with certain cocktails (*takes a singular verb*) ■ *npl.* DIGESTIVE TONIC a bitter-tasting liquid used as a digestive tonic

bittersweet /bíttər sweet/ *adj.* **1.** BOTH BITTER AND SWEET smelling or tasting both bitter and sweet at the same time **2.** BOTH HAPPY AND SAD causing feelings of happiness and sadness at the same time ■ *n.* PLANTS **1.** PLANT WITH BRIGHT CAPSULES AND SEEDS a poisonous climbing plant found in North America that has orange capsules containing bright red seeds. Genus: *Celastus.* **2.** = **woody nightshade**

bitty /bítti/ **(-tier, -tiest)** *adj.* made up of lots of different parts that do not seem to fit together ○ *A very bitty film* —**bittiness** *n.*

bitumen /bíttyoōmən/ *n.* **1.** ROAD-SURFACING MATERIAL a sticky mixture of hydrocarbons derived from petroleum and found in substances such as asphalt and tar that are used for road surfacing and roofing **2.** *Aus* TARRED ROAD a tarred road or sealed road or system of roads, as opposed to a dirt road [15thC. From Latin, 'asphalt', probably from a Celtic source.]

bituminize /bi tyoōmi nīz/ **(-nizes, -nizing, -nized)**, **bituminise (-nises, -nising, -nised)** *vt.* to cover or treat sth with bitumen or to convert sth into bitumen —**bituminization** /bi tyoōmə nī záysh'n/ *n.*

bituminous /bi tyoōminəss/ *adj.* relating to or containing bitumen

bituminous coal *n.* a type of soft coal that burns with a smoky flame

bivalence /bī váylənss/, **bivalency** /-lənssi/ *n.* the property that a proposition has in classical systems of logic of being either true or false

bivalent /bī váylənt/ *adj.* **1.** CHEM = **divalent 2.** GENETICS PAIRED used to describe structurally identical **(homologous)** chromosomes that come together during cell division **(meiosis)** ■ *n.* GENETICS PAIR OF CHROMOSOMES a pair of structurally identical **(homologous)** chromosomes that come together during cell division **(meiosis)**

bivalve /bī valv/ *n.* a marine or freshwater mollusc that has its body contained within two shells joined by a hinge. Oysters, mussels, and cockles are bivalves. —**bivalved** *adj.* —**bivalvular** /bī válvyoōlər/ *adj.*

bivariate /bī váiri ət, -ayt/ *adj.* relating to or involving two variables

bivouac /bívvoo ak/ *n.* **1.** MILITARY OR MOUNTAINEERING CAMP a very simple temporary camp that is set up and used by soldiers or mountaineers **2.** MOUNTAINEERING BRIEF OVERNIGHT STAY a short stay, usually overnight, often with minimum equipment ■ *vi.* **(-acs, -acking, -acked)** MAKE CAMP to set up and stay in a very simple temporary camp [Early 18thC. Via French from, probably, Low German *bīwake*, from *bi-* 'by' + *wake* 'watch, vigil'.]

bivvy /bívvi/ (*plural* **-vies**) *n.* ARMY a very simple shelter or tent (*slang*) [Early 20thC. Formed from BIVOUAC.]

biweekly /bī weékli/ *adj.* **1.** COMING OUT EVERY TWO WEEKS produced or appearing every two weeks **2.** COMING OUT TWICE A WEEK produced or appearing twice a week ■ *adv.* **1.** ONCE EVERY TWO WEEKS at two-week intervals **2.** TWICE A WEEK twice during a one-week period ■ *n.* (*plural* **-lies**) TWICE-WEEKLY PUBLICATION a publication that appears every two weeks

WORD KEY: USAGE

How many times is **biweekly**? Confusion is caused by the fact that ***biweekly*** and ***bimonthly*** can mean either 'once every two weeks (or months)' or 'twice a week (or month)'. If you want to avoid doubt it is better to rephrase: *The talks are held twice a week at the local school. The talks are held every two weeks at the local school.*

biyearly /bī yeérli/ *adj.* **1.** COMING OUT EVERY TWO YEARS produced or appearing every two years **2.** COMING OUT TWICE A YEAR produced or appearing twice a year ■ *adv.* **1.** ONCE EVERY TWO YEARS at two-year intervals **2.** TWICE A YEAR twice during a one-year period

biz /biz/ *n.* (*slang*) **1.** STH WONDERFUL sth that is really excellent **2.** BUSINESS a business of a particular type, typically involving fashion, entertainment, or the media [Mid-19thC. Shortened from BUSINESS.]

bizarre /bi zaár/ *adj.* amusingly or grotesquely strange or unusual [Mid-17thC. Via French, 'odd', formerly 'brave, handsome', from Spanish *bizarro* 'brave' (perhaps influenced by Basque *bizar* 'beard', taken as a symbol of vigour), from, ultimately, Italian *bizzarro* 'angry'.] —**bizarrely** *adv.* —**bizarreness** *n.*

bizarrerie /bi zaárəri/ *n.* amusing or grotesque strangeness or oddity [Mid-18thC. From French.]

Bizet /beé zay/, **Georges** (1838–75) French composer. He completed the opera *Carmen* just before his death. Born **Alexandre César Léopold Bizet**

bizonal /bī zṓn'l/ *adj.* made up of two zones

Bjelke-Petersen /byélki peétərss'n/, **Sir Johannes** (*b.* 1911) New Zealand-born Australian politician. A National Party politician, he was premier of Queensland (1968–87).

Bjørnson /byúrnss'n/, **Bjørnstjerne** (1832–1910) Norwegian writer and politician. The national poet of Norway, he won the Nobel Prize in literature (1903). His work includes the Norwegian national anthem and the novel *The Fisher Girl* (1868). Full name **Bjørnstjerne Martinius Bjørnson**

bk *abbr.* **1.** bank **2.** book

Bk *symbol.* berkelium

bkcy *abbr.* bankruptcy

bkg *abbr.* banking

bkpt *abbr.* bankrupt

bks *abbr.* **1.** barracks **2.** books

BL *abbr.* **1.** Bachelor of Law **2.** Bachelor of Letters **3.** *US* Barrister-at-Law **4.** British Library **5.** bill of lading

bl. *abbr.* **1.** black **2.** blue **3.** bale

B/L *abbr.* bill of lading

blab /blab/ *vi.* **(blabs, blabbing, blabbed)** (*informal*) **1.** TELL SECRETS to talk indiscreetly about sth that is supposed to be secret **2.** CHATTER to chatter in a mildly incoherent way ■ *n.* = **blabbermouth** [13thC. Origin uncertain, but ultimately probably from a prehistoric Germanic word imitating the sound of vacuous talking (compare Danish *blabbre* 'to gabble').]

blabber /blábbər/ *vi.* **(-bers, -bering, -bered)** CHATTER to chatter in a mildly incoherent way ■ *n.* **1.** = **blabbermouth 2.** NOISE OF CHATTER the sound made by people talking loudly and incoherently [14thC. Origin uncertain, but probably formed from BLAB.]

blabbermouth /blábbər mowth/ (*plural* **-mouths** /-mowthz/) *n.* sb who in unable to keep from talking too much or from revealing secrets (*informal*)

black /blak/ *adj.* **1.** COLOURS OF THE DARKEST COLOUR being the colour of coal or carbon **2.** DEVOID OF LIGHT completely dark, with no light **3. black, Black** DARK-SKINNED belonging to an African ethnic group, or to any other ethnic group with very dark skin **4.** FULL OF ANGER filled with anger or hostility **5.** HOPELESS so depressing as to end all hope **6.** EVIL evil, or associated with evil **7.** DIRTY covered with mud, soil, or any other dark substance **8.** BEVERAGES WITHOUT MILK served without adding milk or cream **9.** FUNNY AND MACABRE dealing with very serious things in a humorous and often macabre way **10.** MANAGEMT BOYCOTTED boycotted by trade unions, especially in support of industrial action that is being taken by other unions **11.** SERIOUSLY BAD OR UNFORTUNATE causing or associated with severely bad conditions or misfortune **12.** DISHONOURABLE extremely dishonourable and deserving the most serious criticism **13.** MIL CLANDESTINE carried out in the utmost secrecy ■ *n.* **1.** COLOURS DARKEST COLOUR a colour value that has no hue as a result of the absorption of nearly all light from all visible wavelengths **2.** COLOURS COAL-COLOURED DYE OR PIGMENT a pigment or dye that is the colour of carbon or coal **3. black, Black** PEOPLES MEMBER OF DARK SKINNED PEOPLE a member of an African ethnic group or any other ethnic group with very dark skin, e.g. Australian Aborigines **4.** BLACK MATERIAL OR CLOTHES fabric or clothing that is black in colour **5.** TOTAL DARKNESS complete darkness **6.** BOARD GAMES BLACK PIECE a black piece in a game such as chess or draughts **7.** BOARD GAMES **PLAYER WITH BLACK PIECES** a player in games such as chess or draughts who is playing with the black pieces **8.** CUE GAMES **BLACK BALL** a black ball in snooker, which is the last ball to be potted **9.** ARCHERY **BLACK RING ON ARCHERY TARGET** a black ring on a target in archery, which gives a player a score of three **10.** GAMBLING **BLACK COLOUR BETS ARE PLACED ON** one of the colours on which players can lay their bets when gambling at such games as roulette ■ *vt.* (**blacks, blacking, blacked**) **1.** MAKE BLACK to make sth black, or cover sth in black **2.** USE BLACK POLISH to cover sth, e.g. shoes or boots, with black polish **3.** BRUISE THE EYE to hit sb's eye so that it becomes very bruised and turns a purplish-black colour **4.** MANAGEMT **BOYCOTT** to organize a boycott of goods or some action, especially in support of industrial action being carried out by other trade unions [Old English *blæc*, of uncertain origin: perhaps ultimately from an Indo-European base meaning 'shine, burn', which also produced English *flame*; the underlying sense would be 'scorch' and, hence, 'make dark'] —**blackish** *adj.* —**blackness** *n.* ◇ **in the black 1.** not in debt or overdrawn **2.** having or making money or a profit

---

WORD KEY: USAGE

Sensitivity trap: The word *black* is standard in current usage for a dark-skinned person of African or Afro-Caribbean origin or descent. It is the term that Afro-Caribbeans in the UK prefer. However, many Americans of African descent prefer the more formal term *African American*, used both as noun and adjective. The term *black* is sometimes extended to include other nonwhite peoples such as those of South Asia, but this use is generally regarded as unacceptable, the preferable use being specific names such as *Indian* or *Malay*. See also the note at coloured.

Black /blak/, **Hugo** (1886–1971) US Supreme Court justice. On the US Supreme Court (1937–71), he was known for upholding a literal interpretation of the First Amendment of the Constitution. Full name **Hugo LaFayette Black**

Black, Sir James Whyte (*b.* 1924) British pharmacologist. He discovered the first beta-blocking drug, leading to new treatments for heart disease. He shared the Nobel Prize in physiology or medicine (1988).

Black, Shirley (*b.* 1927) US actor and former ambassador. She is arguably the most popular child actress starring in 'The Littlest Rebel' and 'Bright Eyes' (1934).

blackamoor /blákə moor, -mawr/ *n.* a highly offensive term used for Black person, or sb with very dark skin (*archaic offensive*) [Early 16thC. A variant of *black moor*, although the connecting -*a*- has never been satisfactorily explained.]

black-and-blue *adj.* covered with bruises, or feeling very bruised (*not hyphenated after a verb*)

Black and Tan *n.* a member of the armed force that was sent by the British to Ireland in 1921 to fight Sinn Fein. Their uniform was khaki, with a black beret and armband.

black-and-tan *n.* a drink consisting of ale mixed with stout or porter

black and white *n.* **1.** PRINTED OR WRITTEN MATTER material either handwritten or printed **2.** VISUAL MEDIUM WITHOUT COLOURED IMAGES a visual medium without colours, and in hues of black, white, and shades of grey

black-and-white *adj.* **1.** NOT IN COLOUR representing an image in which colours have been converted to black, white, and shades of grey ○ *a black-and-white photograph* **2.** REPRODUCING IMAGES NOT IN COLOUR reproducing images in which colours have been converted to black, white, and shades of grey ○ *a black-and-white television* **3.** CLEAR-CUT clear-cut and straightforward, allowing no room for compromise or doubt (*not hyphenated after a verb*) ○ *Everything is black and white as far as she's concerned.*

black arts *npl.* magic that is used for evil purposes, calling upon the help of the Devil

black-backed gull *n.* either of two species of common gull with a black back and wings and white underparts, found in North Atlantic coastal

waters. Latin name: *Larus marinus* and *Larus fuscus.*

blackball /blák bawl/ *vt.* (**-balls, -balling, -balled**) **1.** PREVENT FROM JOINING to prevent sb from becoming a member of a club by voting against the person **2.** EXCLUDE FROM GROUP to exclude sb from a group or profession ■ *n.* **1.** NEGATIVE VOTE a vote against sb, especially sb wanting to join a group **2.** VOTING TOKEN a black ball used to show a negative vote (*archaic*)

black bass (*plural* **black bass**) *n.* a large freshwater bass of North America that is popular as a game fish. Genus: *Micropterus.*

black bean *n.* **1.** PLANTS BEAN PLANT any bean plant with small black seeds that are dried and used in cooking **2.** FOOD DRIED BEAN a dried seed from a black bean plant, used in cooking, often as an accompaniment to rice **3.** TREES BEAN TREE a tree found in the rainforests of eastern Australia that has smooth bark, dark green leaves, and yellow or red flowers. It is used in furniture-making. Latin name: *Castanospermum australe.* **4.** FOOD FERMENTED SOYA BEAN a soya bean sauce fermented in oriental cookery ○ *black bean sauce*

black bear *n.* **1.** N AMERICAN BEAR a bear that lives in the forests of North America and ranges from brownish yellow to black in colour. Latin name: *Euarctos americanus.* **2.** ASIATIC BEAR a bear that lives in central and eastern Asia and has a black coat with a whitish V-shaped mark on its chest. Latin name: *Selenarctos thibetanus.*

black-bellied plover *n.* BIRDS = **grey plover**

black belt *n.* **1.** BELT SHOWING SKILL IN MARTIAL ARTS a belt that is worn by sb who has reached the highest level of skill in a martial art such as judo or karate **2.** SB WITH BLACK BELT sb who has reached the highest level of skill in a martial art such as judo or karate, and who is entitled to wear a belt that is black **3.** black belt, Black Belt FERTILE AGRICULTURAL REGION a region in the southern United States, stretching from Georgia across Alabama and Mississippi, with extremely fertile dark soil

Blackberry

blackberry /blákbəri/ (*plural* **-ries**) *n.* **1.** PLANTS THORNY BUSH WITH SMALL PURPLE FRUITS a thorny European bush of the rose family that has pink or white flowers and purple edible fruit made up of a cluster of small round sections. Latin name: *Rubus fruticosus.* **2.** FOOD FRUIT OF BLACKBERRY the fruit of the blackberry bush

blackberry lily *n.* an ornamental plant from China that has orange flowers with small red spots and clusters of blackish seeds that look like blackberries. Latin name: *Belamcanda chinensis.*

black bile *n.* one of the four humours that were once believed to be the base of sb's character, associated with a melancholy temperament. It was characterized as cold and dry. (*archaic*)

blackbird /blák burd/ *n.* **1.** COMMON BIRD WITH BLACK FEATHERS a common European bird, the male of which has black feathers and a yellow beak. The female has brown feathers. Latin name: *Turdus merula.* **2.** AMERICAN BIRD WITH BLACK FEATHERS a bird belonging to a family widespread throughout North and South America, with black feathers showing a metallic sheen or bold patterns of yellow, orange, or red. Family: Icteridae.

blackboard /blák bawrd/ *n.* a board of either a dark colour or white that is written on with contrasting

Blackbird

chalk or erasable markers, used especially in classrooms. ◊ **whiteboard**

black body (*plural* **black bodies**) *n.* PHYS an ideal object that would absorb all of the radiation incident on it without reflecting any

black book *n.* **1.** BOOK OF BLACKLISTED PEOPLE a book in which the names of people who are to be punished or blacklisted are kept **2.** BOOK OF PHONE NUMBERS a book in which sb keeps the names and telephone numbers of private friends, especially boyfriends or girlfriends (*informal*)

black box *n.* **1.** AIR = **flight recorder** **2.** COMPUT COMPONENT OF UNKNOWN CONSTRUCTION an electronic component whose constituents or circuitry are unknown or irrelevant, but whose function is understood

black bread *n.* a very dark rye bread that is particularly popular in Germany and Slavic countries

blackbuck /blák buk/ (*plural* **-bucks** *or* **-buck**) *n.* a small antelope, the male of which has a black back, white underbelly, and spiral horns. It was once abundant in India but is now rare. Latin name: *Antilope cervicapra.*

black bun *n. Scotland* a dark rich fruit cake in a pastry case, traditionally eaten at Hogmanay

Blackburn /blák burn/ industrial town in Lancashire, northwestern England. Population: 132,800 (1991).

blackbutt /blák but/ *n. Aus* a eucalyptus tree, native to eastern Australia, with a tall straight trunk, sickle-shaped leaves, and white flowers. Its wood is used for timber. Latin name: *Eucalyptus pilularis.*

blackcap /blák kap/ *n.* **1.** SMALL SONGBIRD a small brown-grey warbler of Eurasia and Africa, the male of which has a black-topped head. Latin name: *Sylvia atricapilla.* **2.** BIRD WITH BLACK CROWN any bird similar to the blackcap warbler that has a black-topped head, e.g. a chickadee **3.** LAW JUDGE'S CAP a black cap formerly worn by a judge when passing a death sentence on sb

black cherry *n.* a large wild North American cherry tree that has dark bark, white flowers, and black fruits. Latin name: *Prunus serotina.*

blackcock /blák kok/ (*plural* **-cocks** *or* **-cock**) *n.* **1.** MALE BLACK GROUSE the male of the black grouse **2.** CAUCASUS GROUSE a grouse of the Caucasus mountains that is smaller and duller than the black grouse. Latin name: *Lyrurus mlokosiewiczi.*

black cod *n.* = **sablefish**

black comedy *n.* comedy containing bitter jokes about unpleasant aspects of life

Black Country region of the West Midlands, England, so named because of its concentration of former heavy industries

blackcurrant /blák kúrrənt/ *n.* **1.** PLANTS BUSH WITH EDIBLE BLACK BERRIES a medium-sized bush grown in temperate regions for its bunches of small edible black berries. Latin name: *Ribes nigrum.* **2.** FOOD SMALL BLACK BERRY the small round black berry of the blackcurrant bush

blackdamp /blák damp/ *n.* atmospheric conditions in a mine that prevent normal breathing because insufficient oxygen remains after an explosion

Black Death *n.* the bubonic plague epidemic that killed over 50 million people throughout Asia and Europe in the 14th century [*Black* probably from the colour of the buboes]

black diamond n. **1.** = carbonado **2.** BLACK HAEMATITE the black variety of haematite, the principal ore of iron ■ **black diamonds** npl. COAL coal (informal)

Blackdown Hills /blákdown-/ designated Area of Outstanding Natural Beauty in Devon and Somerset, southwestern England

black duck n. a brownish duck of northeastern North America. Latin name: Anas rubripes.

black economy n. the part of an economy that consists of unofficial or illegal, and therefore untaxed, earnings

blacken /blákən/ (-ens, -ening, -ened) v. **1.** vti. TURN BLACK to become, or cause sth to become, darker or black **2.** vt. SLANDER to harm or damage sb's reputation

Black English n. any one of the varieties of English that have developed in Black communities worldwide, many of which share features of grammar and vocabulary. ♦ African American Vernacular English

Blacket /blákit/, **Edmund Thomas** (1817–83) British-born Australian architect. He designed many Gothic-style public buildings in Sydney, including St Andrew's Cathedral and the University of New South Wales.

Blackett, Patrick M. S. Blackett, Baron (1897–1974) British physicist. He discovered the positron (1932) and received the Nobel Prize (1948) for his work on cosmic radiation. Full name **Patrick Maynard Stuart Blackett**

black eye n. an area of bruising round sb's eye

black-eyed bean n. US term **black-eyed pea 1.** EDIBLE LEGUME a legume widely cultivated in the southern United States for forage and for its seeds. Latin name: Vigna unguiculata. **2.** SMALL BEAN WITH BLACK SPOT a small beige bean with a black spot

black-eyed pea n. US = black-eyed bean

black-eyed Susan n. **1.** FLOWER WITH DARK CENTRE a North American plant that has yellowish-orange flowers with a dark conical centre. Genus: Rudbeckia. **2.** CLIMBING PLANT WITH YELLOW FLOWERS a tropical African climbing plant that has yellow flowers with purple centres. Latin name: Thunbergia alata.

black-faced cuckoo shrike n. a medium-sized bird with sleek grey plumage and a black face, common throughout Australia. Latin name: Coracina novaehollandiae.

blackfish /blák fish/ (plural **-fish** or **-fishes**) n. **1.** SMALL ARCTIC FISH a small freshwater fish that is very abundant in Arctic North America and Siberia. Latin name: Dallia pectoralis. **2.** SALMON AFTER SPAWNING a female salmon that has spawned **3.** = pilot whale

black flag n. = Jolly Roger ■ vt. (black-flags, black-flagging, black-flagged) CALL RACING DRIVER INTO PITS to signal to a racing driver to pull into the pits by waving a black flag

black fly /blák flī/ (plural **black flies** or **black fly**) n. a small dark biting gnat that causes painful itchy welts in people and animals. Family: Simuliidae.

blackfly (plural **-flies** or **-fly**) n. a black aphid that infests many types of plant. Genus: Aphis.

Blackfoot /blák foot/ (plural **-feet** /-feet/ or **-foot**) n. **1.** PEOPLES NATIVE AMERICAN a member of a group of Native American peoples living in Alberta, Saskatchewan, and Montana **2.** LANG ALGONQUIAN LANGUAGE an Algonquian language spoken in Alberta, Canada, and in Montana, the United States. Blackfoot is spoken by about 8,000 people. [Late 18thC. Translation of Blackfoot Siksika, said to be from the blackening of the soles of their moccasins when they walked across burnt prairies.] — **Blackfoot** adj.

black-footed albatross n. a dark albatross of the Pacific that spends most of its time at sea. Latin name: Diomedea nigripes.

Black Forest wooded highland region in Baden-Württemberg State, southwestern Germany that contains the sources of the Danube and Neckar rivers. Area: 5,180 sq. km/about 2,000 sq. mi.

Black Forest cake n. US = Black Forest gateau

Black Forest gateau n. a rich chocolate cake that is topped and filled with cherries and whipped cream.

US term **Black Forest cake** [Origin uncertain, perhaps from the cake's dark colour]

Black Friar n. a member of the Dominican order of monks

black grouse (plural **black grouse**) n. a large grouse of Europe and western Asia with a lyre-shaped tail. The male is black with white patches on its wings. Latin name: Lyrurus tetrix.

black guillemot n. a small seabird of northeastern North America that belongs to the auk family and has black plumage with white wing patches in summer. Latin name: Cepphus grylle.

blackhead /blák hed/ n. **1.** DARK BLOCKED PORE a small plug of dark fatty matter blocking a follicle on the skin, especially on the face **2.** VET FOWL DISEASE an infectious disease of turkeys and related fowl resulting in darkened head skin. It is caused by a protozoan. **3.** BIRDS BIRD WITH BLACK HEAD a bird with a dark-coloured head, especially a duck or gull

Blackheath /blak heeth/ village and area of open ground in Greenwich, London, where golf was introduced to England

Black Hills mountainous region in western South Dakota and northeastern Wyoming, a mining area famous for the granite sculptures of Mount Rushmore National Memorial. The highest point is Harney Peak. Height: 2,207 m/7,242 ft. Area: 15,000 sq. km/6,000 sq. mi.

black hole n. **1.** OBJECT IN SPACE an object in space thought to contain a celestial object with such a strong gravitational pull that no matter or energy can escape from it. Black holes are believed to form when stars collapse in upon themselves. **2.** PLACE WHERE THINGS GET LOST a place or thing into which objects disappear and are not expected to be seen again (humorous)

Black Hole of Calcutta n. **1.** SUFFOCATING DUNGEON a dungeon in Calcutta in which, in 1756, 123 out of 146 prisoners were said to have died of suffocation **2.** SUFFOCATING PLACE a most uncomfortably overcrowded place (informal)

black humour n. humour that deals with unpleasant aspects of life in a bitter or ironic way — **black humourist** n.

black ice n. a thin, almost invisible, layer of ice formed when rain falls on a surface that is below freezing [Black from the typical colour of the underlying road surface]

blacking /bláking/ n. polish used, especially formerly, to make shoes and stoves black

Black Isle peninsula between the Cromarty and Moray Firths, northeastern Scotland

blackjack /blák jak/ n. **1.** CARDS = pontoon **2.** MINERALS BLACK MINERAL a black variety of the mineral sphalerite or zinc blende **3.** US ARMS SHORT CLUB a weapon in the form of a short leather-covered club **4.** S Africa PLANTS S AFRICAN WEED a weed of South Africa with barbed seeds that cling to clothing and animals. Latin name: Bidens pilosa. **5.** S Africa PLANTS CLINGING SEEDS the seeds of the blackjack ■ interj. CARDS INDICATING A WIN AT BLACKJACK used to indicate to other players that a blackjack has been dealt ■ vt. (-jacks, -jacking, -jacked) US **1.** HIT WITH CLUB to hit sb with a short club **2.** FORCE to force sb to do sth [Jack from jack 'knave in a pack of cards']

blackjack oak n. a small oak tree with blackish bark that is common in the southeastern United States. Latin name: Quercus marilandica.

black knight n. a company that makes an unwelcome attempt to take over another

black lead n. a commercial form of graphite

blackleg /blák leg/ n. **1.** VET DISEASE OF FARM ANIMALS an infectious bacterial disease of farm animals that causes swellings on the legs **2.** SB WHO WORKS DURING STRIKE a worker who is criticized and despised by striking colleagues for working during a strike (slang) US = scab **3.** BOT POTATO DISEASE a disease of potato plants caused by the bacterium Erwinia carotovora that makes the lower stems rot **4.** GAMBLING GAMBLER WHO CHEATS a cheat at cards or horseracing (informal) ■ vi. (-legs, -legging, -legged) WORK DURING

STRIKE to continue to work while colleagues are on strike (informal)

black letter n. PRINTING = Gothic

black light n. **1.** INVISIBLE LIGHT any invisible electromagnetic radiation, e.g. ultraviolet or infrared light **2.** DEVICE EMITTING BLACK LIGHT a bulb, tube, or other device that emits black light when stimulated with electrical current

blacklist /blák list/ n. LIST OF DISAPPROVED PEOPLE a list of people or groups who are under suspicion or excluded from sth ○ a credit blacklist ■ vt. (-lists, -listing, -listed) PUT ON BLACKLIST to add sb's name to a blacklist

black lung n. MED = anthracosis

blackly /blákli/ adv. **1.** ANGRILY in an angry or threatening way **2.** WITH A BLACK APPEARANCE showing or making use of the colour black

black magic n. magic that involves evil forces and spirits

blackmail /blák mayl/ n. **1.** USE OF SECRETS TO COMPEL the act of forcing sb to pay money or do sth by threatening to reveal shameful or incriminating facts about him or her. ◊ greenmail, greymail **2.** COERCION unfair threatening or incriminating of sb, as a way of achieving a result ■ vt. (-mails, -mailing, -mailed) USE SECRETS TO COMPEL SB to force sb to pay money or do sth by threatening to reveal shameful or incriminating facts about him or her [Mid-16thC. Mail from obsolete mail 'tribute, tax', from Old Norse mál 'speech, agreement'; the word originally referred to protection money extorted by Scottish border bandits.] — **blackmailer** n.

Blackman /blákmən/, **Charles Raymond** (b. 1928) Australian painter. His works include many melancholy paintings of children, in which the figures are often little more than silhouettes.

black mark n. a record of sth that sb has done that gives people a bad opinion of him or her ○ Avoiding the family reunion counted as a black mark against me.

black market n. a system of buying and selling officially controlled goods illegally — **black marketeer** n. — **black marketeering** n. — **black marketer** n.

black mass n. an imitation of a Christian Mass said to be conducted by worshippers of the Devil

black money n. money earned unofficially or illegally

Black Monk n. a member of the Benedictine order of monks, who wear black cloaks over their white habits

Blackmore /blák mawr/, **R. D.** (1825–1900) British writer. The best known of his novels is Lorna Doone (1869). Full name **Richard Doddridge Blackmore**

Black Mountains 1. mountain range in southern Wales, in eastern Dufed and western Powys. Its highest peak is Carmarthen Van, 1,802 m/2,630 ft. **2.** mountain range in southern Wales, in eastern Gwent. It's highest peak is Waunfach, 811 m/2,660 ft.

Black Muslim n. a member of the Nation of Islam, an almost exclusively Black Islamic denomination based in the United States

black mustard n. a yellow-flowered plant of Europe and Asia with strong-tasting seeds used to make mustard. Latin name: Brassica nigra.

Black nationalist n. a member of any political organization that promotes separate self-governing communities or states for Black people — **Black nationalism** n.

black nightshade n. a widely found plant of the nightshade family that has poisonous leaves, white star-shaped flowers, and black berries. Latin name: Solanum nigrum.

blackout /blák owt/ n. **1.** MED LOSS OF CONSCIOUSNESS a temporary loss of consciousness, sight, or memory **2.** BROADCAST WITHDRAWAL OF BROADCASTING a refusal to broadcast radio or television programmes, usually because of a strike, **3.** ELEC LOSS OF ELECTRIC LIGHT a failure of an electricity supply **4.** COMMUNICATION WITHHOLDING OF INFORMATION the withholding of news or information about a subject, especially by official sources **5.** RADIO **LOSS OF RADIO COMMUNICATION** a loss of radio communication between an aircraft or ship and headquarters **6.** MIL **PERIOD OF EXTINGUISHING OR HIDING LIGHTS** a period during wartime in which all lights are to be turned off or covered up at night to prevent towns being seen from enemy aircraft

Black Panther n. a member of a militant Black political organization opposed to white domination that was active in the United States especially in the late 1960s and early 1970s [*Panther* from the emblem used by certain Black Power electoral candidates in Alabama in the mid-1960s]

black pepper n. dark brown seasoning made by grinding pepper seeds that have not had their black outer covering removed

black pine n. ANZ = **matai**

blackpoll /blák pōl/, **blackpoll warbler** n. a small bird found in northern North America that has streaky plumage and is abundant in conifer forests. Latin name: *Dendroica striata*. [Poll from obsolete *poll* 'head']

Blackpool /blák pool/ seaside town and resort in Lancashire, northwestern England, famous for its Blackpool Tower, built in 1895 and modelled on the Eiffel Tower, Paris. Population: 153,600 (1995).

Black Power n. a movement formed by Black people to engender social equality and emphasize pride in their racial identity via Black cultural and political institutions and organizations

black pudding n. UK, Southern US a dark kind of sausage made from pig's blood and pork fat. US term **blood sausage**

black rat n. a common dark-brown rat that is a household pest and disease carrier. It was originally from Eurasia but was imported to coastal cities throughout the world, and is an important carrier of plague. Latin name: *Rattus rattus*.

black rot n. any plant disease that causes blackening as well as decay

Black Sash n. an organization of white South African women who campaigned against apartheid and now provide social services

Black Sea large inland sea linked to the Mediterranean by the Bosporus, the Sea of Marmara, and the Dardanelles. It is bordered by Bulgaria, Romania, Ukraine, Russia, Georgia, and Turkey. Area: 436,400 sq. km/168,500 sq. mi.

black shale n. a mudstone that contains organic carbon, e.g. an oil-bearing shale

black sheep n. sb regarded with shame or contempt by the other members of a family or group [From black sheep's wool being less valuable to the shepherd than white]

Blackshirt /blák shurt/ n. a member of any European fascist movement active before and during World War II, especially a member of the Italian Fascist Party [From the distinctive item of the party's uniform]

blacksmith /blák smith/ n. sb whose job is making and repairing iron and metal objects, including horseshoes. Blacksmiths originally worked by hand with a hammer and anvil, but now more often use electrically powered tools. [*Black* from their working with iron or black metal (as opposed to tin or white metal)]

blacksnake /blák snayk/ n. a dark-coloured poisonous snake that inhabits forests in eastern Australia. Latin name: *Pseudechis porphyriacus*.

black spot n. **1.** NOTORIOUS PLACE a place where sth bad exists or happens ◇ *an unemployment black spot* **2.** BOT **PLANT DISEASE** a plant disease that causes black patches to form on leaves, particularly on roses

black spruce n. a dark-green conifer found in boggy areas in northern North America. Latin name: *Picea mariana*.

Blackstone /blák stōn, -stən/, **Sir William** (1723–80) British jurist. He wrote the classic *Commentaries on the Laws of England* (1765–69).

Black Stone n. the sacred stone in the Kaaba in the great mosque in Mecca, said to have been given to God. It is reddish-black in colour.

blackstrap /blák strap/, **blackstrap molasses** n. molasses from which all refinable sugar has been

removed [From *blackstrap* 'strong dark port', drink made from rum and treacle]

black stump n. Aus an imaginary stump marking the farthest edge of civilization (*informal*) ◇ *I grew up beyond the black stump and didn't see a city until I was 25.* [Perhaps from the frequency with which fire-blackened tree stumps were mentioned in direction-giving in the Australian outback]

black swan n. a large swan with black plumage and a red beak found throughout Australia and in New Zealand, where it is an introduced species. Latin name: *Cygnus atratus*.

black-tailed deer n. a mule deer with a tail that is black on top, found west of the North American Continental Divide. Latin name: *Odocoileus hemionus columbianus*.

black tea n. **1.** TEA LEAVES FERMENTED BEFORE DRYING dark-coloured tea leaves that have been fermented before being dried. ◇ **green tea 2.** TEA WITHOUT MILK tea served without milk

blackthorn /blák thawrn/ n. **1.** THORNY BUSH a thorny black-stemmed bush of Europe and Asia that has white flowers and small blue-black berries. Latin name: *Prunus spinosa*. **2.** HARDWOOD WALKING STICK a walking stick made from the hard wood of the blackthorn

black tie n. **1.** BLACK BOW TIE a black bow tie worn on formal occasions **2.** FORMAL STYLE OF DRESS FOR MEN a formal style in men's dress that includes a black bow tie and a dinner jacket —**black-tie** adj.

blacktop /blák top/ n. US, Can **1.** ROAD-SURFACING MATERIAL a road-surfacing material bound together with a tarry substance such as asphalt **2.** ROAD MADE WITH BLACKTOP a road or other area with a blacktop surface ■ vti. (**-tops, -topping, -topped**) US, Can COAT SURFACE WITH BLACKTOP to cover a road or other surface with blacktop

black treacle n. = **treacle**

black velvet n. an alcoholic drink consisting of stout and champagne

black walnut n. **1.** TREES N AMERICAN WALNUT TREE a North American walnut tree with hard dark wood and edible nuts in very hard shells. Latin name: *Juglans nigra*. **2.** INDUST N AMERICAN WALNUT WOOD the hard wood of the black walnut tree, used especially for veneer and cabinets **3.** FOOD EDIBLE NUT an edible nut from the black walnut tree

Black Watch n. the Royal Highland Regiment in the British Army [Black because of its dark tartan; watch in sense 'group of guards']

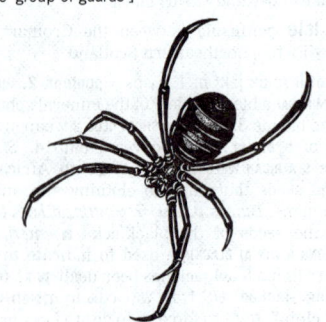

Black widow

black widow n. a highly poisonous spider of temperate North America and the Far East. The female has a black body with an hourglass-shaped red marking on the abdomen. Latin name: *Latrodectus mactans*. [Widow from the female's habit of eating her mate]

bladder /bláddər/ n. **1.** ANAT BODILY SAC FOR LIQUID OR GAS an organ or other body part for storing a liquid or gas, especially the sac that stores urine (**urinary bladder**) or the sac that stores bile (**gall bladder**) **2.** INFLATABLE INNER BAG an inflatable part of sth, especially a football, that resembles a bag **3.** BOT SAC IN PLANT a sac found in some plants, e.g. in bladder wrack to store air allowing the plant to float, or in bladderwort to trap insects **4.** MED FLUID-FILLED BLISTER a blister or small sac filled with fluid [Old English

blædre, blæddre. Ultimately from an Indo-European base that is also the ancestor of English *blow* 'to puff', *flatulent*, and *inflate*.] —**bladdery** adj.

bladder campion n. a wild European plant with a swollen calyx below the petals of its white flowers. Latin name: *Silene vulgaris*.

bladder fern n. a small delicate fern that grows in rocks and walls and has a bulbous seed pod. Latin name: *Cystopteris fragilis*.

bladder kelp n. any of various brown algae with inflated bladders from which leaflike streamers are suspended

bladdernose /bláddər nōz/ n. ZOOL = **hooded seal** [Bladder from the inflatable pouch near its nose]

bladdernut /bláddər nut/ n. **1.** TREE WITH BULBOUS SEED POD a small tree or shrub that produces clusters of small white flowers and bulbous seed pods. Genus: *Staphylea*. **2.** SEED POD the seed pod of a bladdernut tree or shrub

bladder worm n. the larva of a tapeworm, shaped like a sac and armed with six hooks. Class: Cestoda.

bladderwort /bláddər wurt/ n. an aquatic plant with floating leaves bearing small bladders that are used to trap insects. Genus: *Utricularia*.

bladder wrack n. a brown seaweed that has bulbous air bladders on its fronds, allowing them to float. It grows between the high and low water line. Latin name: *Fucus vesiculosus*.

blade /blayd/ n. **1.** CUTTING PART the flat sharp-edged cutting part of a tool or weapon **2.** LONG THIN FLAT PART a long thin flat part of some tools or machines, e.g. a propeller **3.** THIN LEAF a long thin leaf, especially of grass **4.** FLAT STRIKING PART the flat striking part of sth such as an oar or a golf club **5.** RAZOR BLADE a razor blade **6.** SPORTS PART OF ICE SKATE the metal part of an ice skate that glides on the ice **7.** PHON PART OF TONGUE the flat upper part of the tongue just behind the tip **8.** ARCHAEOL STONE FRAGMENT a parallel-sided stone flake that is at least twice as long as it is wide **9.** SWORD a sword (*literary*) ◇ *'And then dreams he of cutting foreign throats/ Of breaches, ambuscadoes, Spanish blades'* (William Shakespeare, *Romeo and Juliet*) **10.** SWORDSMAN a swordsman (*archaic*) **11.** DASHING MAN an energetic fun-loving man (*dated informal*) ■ **blades** npl. **1.** ANZ SHEEP SHEARS hand-operated shears for shearing sheep **2.** US SPORTS in-line roller skates (*informal*) ■ vi. US, Can to skate on in-line roller skates (*informal*) [Old English *blæd*. Ultimately from a prehistoric Germanic stem that is also the ancestor of English *bloom, blossom, blow* 'to blossom', and *flower*. The original meaning was 'leaf'.]

blaes /blayz/ n. Scotland chips of reddish bituminous shale, used as a surface for sports pitches (*often used before a noun*) ◇ *a blaes pitch* [Mid-17thC. Plural of *blae* from Old Norse *blár* related to blue.]

blah /blaa/ n. NONSENSE talk or writing that is inane or pretentious (*informal*) ■ vi. (**blahs, blahing, blahed**) TALK NONSENSE to talk or write pretentious nonsense (*informal; often repeated for emphasis*) [Early 20thC. An imitation of the sound of sb talking vacuously.]

Blainey /bláyni/, **Geoffrey Norman** (b. 1930) Australian historian. His works include the popular trilogy *A Vision of Australian History* (1966–80).

PopperFoto

Tony Blair

Blair /blair/, **Tony** (b. 1953) British politician. A member of Parliament from 1983, he was elected Labour Party leader in 1994, and became prime minister in 1997. Full name **Anthony Charles Lynton Blair** —**Blairite** *n., adj.*

Blake /blayk/, **Robert** (1599–1657) English admiral. He blockaded Lisbon and destroyed Prince Rupert's squadron (1650). In 1657 he destroyed the Spanish treasure fleet off Tenerife.

Blake, William (1757–1827) British poet, painter, and engraver. He wrote *Songs of Innocence* (1789), *The Marriage of Heaven and Hell* (1790–93), and *Jerusalem* (1804–20), illustrating his poetry with highly original engravings and watercolours. He championed mystical wisdom and the unfettered imagination in the face of 18th-century rationalism. —**Blakeian** *adj.*

blame /blaym/ *vt.* (**blames, blaming, blamed**) **1.** CONSIDER SB RESPONSIBLE to consider sb to be responsible for sth wrong or unfortunate that has happened ○ *She blames me for what happened.* **2.** CRITICIZE to find fault with sb (*used in negative statements and questions*) ○ *I don't blame you for wanting to know what happened.* ■ *n.* RESPONSIBILITY responsibility for sth wrong or unfortunate that has happened ○ *It's still not clear where the blame lies.* [12thC. Via Old French *bla(s)mer* from Latin *blastemare*, an alteration of *blasphemare* 'to reproach' (source of English *blaspheme*).] —**blamable** *adj.* ◇ **to blame** responsible for sth wrong or unfortunate that has happened ○ *Who's to blame for the mixup?*

blameless /bláymləss/ *adj.* **1.** NOT RESPONSIBLE not responsible for sth wrong or unfortunate that has happened ○ *No one involved is entirely blameless.* **2.** INNOCENT doing nothing bad or wrong ○ *a blameless life* —**blamelessly** *adv.* —**blamelessness** *n.*

blameworthy /bláym wurthi/ *adj.* deserving blame or criticism —**blameworthiness** *n.*

Blamey /bláymi/, **Sir Thomas Albert** (1884–1951) Australian soldier. Commander of the World War II Allied Land Forces in the southwestern Pacific (1942–45), he later became Australia's first field marshal in 1950.

Blanc, Mont /bloN/ ➧ **Mont Blanc**

blanch /blaanch/ (**blanches, blanching, blanched**), **blench** /blench/ (**blenches, blenching, blenched**) *v.* **1.** *vt.* PUT FOOD BRIEFLY IN BOILING WATER to put food in boiling water for a few seconds in order to loosen the skin or to kill enzymes **2.** *vi.* TURN PALE to become pale suddenly **3.** *vt.* WHITEN VEGETABLES BY GROWING IN DARK to grow vegetables, especially celery and chicory, in dark conditions in order to whiten the stems and improve their flavour **4.** *vti.* REMOVE OR LOSE COLOUR to lose colour, or cause sth to lose colour [14thC. From French *blanchir* 'to whiten', from *blanche*, feminine of *blanc* 'white' (source of English *blank* and *blanket*).] —**blancher** *n.*

blancmange /blə maánj, -maánzh/ *n.* a dessert similar to jelly made with milk, sugar, flavourings, and cornflour and eaten cold [14thC. From Old French *blanc mangier*, from *blanc* 'white' (see BLANCH) + *mangier* 'food', from *mangier* 'to eat' (source of English *manger*), from Latin *manducare* 'to chew'.]

bland /bland/ *adj.* **1.** INSIPID lacking flavour, character, or interest ○ *a bland diet* **2.** FREE OF STRESS free from anything annoying or upsetting **3.** UNEMOTIONAL without emotion [Mid-17thC. From Latin *blandus* 'smooth, flattering', of unknown origin.] —**blandly** *adv.* —**blandness** *n.*

blandish /blándish/ (**-dishes, -dishing, -dished**) *vti.* to persuade sb by flattery (*formal*) [14thC. Via the Old French stem *blandiss-* from, ultimately, Latin *blandus* 'smooth, flattering' (source of English *bland*).] —**blandisher** *n.*

blandishment /blándishmənt/ *n.* **1.** PIECE OF FLATTERY a piece of flattery intended to persuade sb to do sth (*formal*) (*often used in the plural*) ○ *impervious to all blandishments* **2.** FLATTERY the use of flattery and enticements to persuade sb to do sth

blank /blangk/ *adj.* **1.** NOT MARKED not written on, drawn on, or printed on ○ *a blank page* **2.** UNBROKEN plain and unvaried ○ *a blank wall* **3.** LACKING INTEREST having or showing no interest or awareness ○ *a blank expression* **4.** UNEVENTFUL OR UNPRODUCTIVE characterized by lack of useful action or result ○ *It was one of those blank periods when nothing particular was happening.* **5.** DOWNRIGHT complete or absolute ○ *She stared at me in blank amazement.* ■ *n.* **1.** SPACE IN WHICH TO WRITE a space left blank in which to write, in a form or document ○ *Fill in the blanks.* **2.** MARK INDICATING MISSING WORD a mark (-) in writing or print indicating that a word or letter is missing ○ *a word meaning solitary, spelled al- - e* **3.** EMPTINESS OF MIND a complete absence of awareness or memory ○ *I remember hearing a loud noise; the rest is a blank.* **4.** VOID a period about which nothing is known ○ *There are a lot of blanks in her account of the event.* **5.** ARMS = **blank cartridge** **6.** DOCUMENT WITH BLANK SPACES a form or document with spaces for writing in **7.** MANUF PIECE FROM WHICH ARTICLE IS MADE a piece of metal or other material that will be shaped to produce a finished article **8.** BULLSEYE the bullseye of a target ■ *v.* (**blanks, blanking, blanked**) **1.** *vt.* OBLITERATE to delete or block sth out (*often used with out*) **2.** *vi.* FORGET TEMPORARILY to forget sth suddenly and temporarily ○ *I tried to recall their names, but I just blanked.* **3.** *vt. US, Can* SPORTS PREVENT SCORING to prevent an opponent scoring **4.** *vt.* IGNORE to ignore or pretend not to see sb (*informal*) [13thC. From French *blanc* 'white' (see BLANCH). Originally in the sense 'white'.] —**blankness** *n.* ◇ **draw a blank** to be unsuccessful in a search or inquiry ◇ **fire** *or* **shoot blanks** to be unable to impregnate a woman because of a low sperm count (*slang*) ◇ **go blank, go a blank** to be unable to think of or remember sth

blank cartridge *n.* a gun cartridge that contains explosive but no bullet

blank cheque *n.* **1.** CHEQUE WITH NO AMOUNT STATED a signed cheque that has not yet had the amount payable filled in **2.** PERMISSION complete freedom to act or decide (*informal*) ○ *They gave us a blank cheque in our negotiations.*

blank endorsement *n.* an endorsement on a bill of exchange that does not name a payee and so may benefit the bearer

blanket /blángkit/ *n.* **1.** LARGE PIECE OF THICK CLOTH a piece of thick cloth used as a cover for a bed **2.** COVERING LAYER a layer of sth, covering an area completely **3.** NUCLEAR PHYS LAYER AROUND CORE OF NUCLEAR REACTOR in a nuclear reactor, a layer of material surrounding the radioactive core used to reflect neutrons or to create more fissile material ■ *adj.* APPLYING GENERALLY applying to all areas or situations ○ *We have blanket approval for our proposals.* ■ *vt.* (**-kets, -keting, -keted**) **1.** COVER WITH LAYER to cover sth with a thick layer ○ *The streets were blanketed with snow.* **2.** COVER TO SUPPRESS to cover sth, especially a fire, in order to stop it or put it out ○ *Foam from the fire extinguisher quickly blanketed the flames.* **3.** SUPPRESS to prevent sth from being heard or seen ○ *Background interference keeps blanketing out the recording.* **4.** NAUT PREVENT WIND REACHING SAILS to take the wind from the sails of another yacht or ship by sailing to windward of it [14thC. From Old Northern French *blanquet*, 'blanket', Old French *blanchet*, from *blanc* 'white' (see BLANCH). The original meaning was 'white cloth'.]

blanket bath *n.* = **bed bath**

blanket bog *n.* a peat bog covering a wide area

blanket finish *n.* a situation in which the runners in a race finish very close to each other

blanket stitch *n.* looped stitching with wide gaps between stitches, used to reinforce the edge of a piece of fabric [From its use on the edges of blankets]

blankly /blángkli/ *adv.* **1.** IN A VACANT WAY in a way that suggests a complete lack of interest, understanding, or awareness ○ *She stared at me blankly.* **2.** DOWNRIGHT completely and without exception

blank verse *n.* unrhymed poetry that has a regular rhythm and line length, especially iambic pentameter

Blantyre-Limbe /blán tīr lím bay/ the largest city in Malawi and the administrative headquarters of the Southern Region. It was combined with the neighbouring town of Limbe in 1956. Population: 446,800 (1994).

blare /blair/ *v.* (**blares, blaring, blared**) **1.** *vti.* MAKE LOUD SOUND to make a loud harsh noise **2.** *vt.* ANNOUNCE STH to proclaim sth loudly ○ *'Heiress disappears', the headlines blared.* ■ *n.* LOUD STRIDENT SOUND a loud harsh noise that is intended to be heard [14thC. Origin uncertain: possibly from assumed Old English *blæren*, Middle Dutch *bleren* 'to bleat, shout', or Middle Low German *blaren*; ultimately probably an imitation of the sound.]

blarney /blaárni/ *n.* NONSENSE unintelligent or insincere talk (*informal*) ■ *vti.* (**-neys, -neying, -neyed**) WHEEDLE to persuade sb with flattery (*informal*) [Late 18thC. Named after the BLARNEY STONE.]

Blarney /blaárni/ village in County Cork, southern Ireland. Population: 2,043 (1991).

Blarney Stone *n.* a stone in Blarney Castle, near Cork in Ireland, that is said to give the power of persuasive talk to people who kiss it

blasé /blaá zay/ *adj.* not impressed or worried by sth, usually because of having experienced it before [Early 19thC. From French, 'satiated'.]

blaspheme /blass feém, blaass-/ (**-phemes, -pheming, -phemed**) *v.* **1.** SWEAR IMPIOUSLY to swear in a way that insults religion **2.** *vt.* INSULT RELIGION to treat God or sacred things disrespectfully through words or action [14thC. Via Old French *blasfemer* from ecclesiastical Latin *blasphemare* 'to revile' (source of English *blame*), from Greek *blasphēmein*, formed from *blasphēmos* 'evil-speaking'.] —**blasphemer** *n.*

blasphemous /blássfəməss/ *adj.* expressing or involving disrespect for God or sacred things —**blasphemously** *adv.* —**blasphemousness** *n.*

blasphemy /blássfəmi/ (*plural* **-mies**) *n.* **1.** DISRESPECT FOR RELIGION disrespect for God or sacred things **2.** STH SHOWING DISRESPECT FOR RELIGION sth done or said that shows disrespect for God or sacred things

blast /blaast/ *n.* **1.** AIR OR GAS CURRENT a sudden strong current of air or wind **2.** EXPLOSION an explosion, or a sudden rush of air caused by an explosion ○ *Several homes were destroyed by the blast.* **3.** LOUD EXPLOSIVE SOUND the sound made by an explosion ○ *We were almost deafened by the blasts.* **4.** INSTRUMENT'S LOUD SOUND a short loud sound made on an instrument, whistle, or car horn **5.** OUTBURST a loud or angry outburst ○ *a blast of criticism* ■ *v.* (**blasts, blasting, blasted**) **1.** *vti.* BLOW UP WITH EXPLOSIVES to destroy or break open sth using explosives ○ *Rescuers blasted a hole in the rock.* ○ *Road crews had to blast a way through the mountains.* **2.** *vti.* MAKE A LOUD NOISE to come out with great force or volume or make sth do this (*informal*) **3.** *vt.* HIT HARD to strike sth with great force (*informal*) ○ *She blasted the ball into the net* **4.** *vt.* CRITICIZE to subject sb or sth to severe criticism (*informal*) **5.** *vt.* BOT BLIGHT to affect a plant with a withering disease (*often passive*) ■ *interj.* EXPRESSING ANNOYANCE used to express mild annoyance (*informal*) ○ *Do you have to drive so blasted slow?* [Old English *blǣst*. Ultimately from an Indo-European base that is also the ancestor of English *blaze* and *blow*.] —**blaster** *n.* ◇ **(at) full blast** at maximum volume or speed

WORD KEY: SYNONYMS

See Synonyms at ***criticize***.

blast away *vi.* to fire a gun repeatedly (*informal*)
blast off *vti.* to launch a rocket, spacecraft, or astronaut into space, or be launched into space

-blast *suffix.* embryonic cell ○ *melanoblast* [From Greek *blastos* 'bud'] —**-blastic** *suffix.*

blasted /blaástid/ *adj., adv.* used to express mild irritation (*informal*) ○ *Then the blasted handle broke.*

blastema /bla steémə/ (*plural* **-mas** *or* **-mata** /-mətə/) *n.* a group of unspecialized animal cells from which an organ or new tissue develops [Mid-19thC. From Greek, 'sprout'.] —**blastemal** *adj.* —**blastematic** /blástə máttik/ *adj.* —**blastemic** /bla steémik/ *adj.*

blast furnace *n.* a vertical shaft furnace for smelting metals. Fuel, ores, and slag-forming rock are loaded from above, and air is blown in from the bottom to raise the temperature. The molten metal is tapped periodically from the base.

blasting /blaásting/ *n.* **1.** BLOWING UP ROCK the blowing up of rock in a quarry, or mine, or road-building operation ○ *'Danger! Blasting'.* **2.** RADIO DISTORTION distortion in a radio signal caused by overloading **3.** CURSING swearing in annoyance (*informal*)

blast injection *n.* a method of fuel injection that uses air pressure to atomize the fuel as it enters into the cylinder of an internal combustion engine

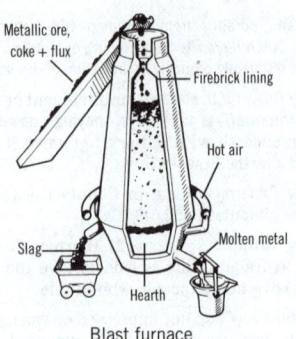

Blast furnace

blasto- *prefix.* bud, germ ○ *blastomycete* [From Greek *blastos* 'bud']

blastocoel /blástə seel/, **blastocoele** *n.* the cavity that forms within the mass of cells (**blastula**) in a developing embryo and that fills with fluid [Late 19thC. Coined from BLASTO- + Greek *koilos* 'hollow.'] —**blastocoelic** /blástə seélik/ *adj.*

blastocyst /blástəsist/ *n.* a mammalian embryo at the stage where it is implanted in the wall of the womb —**blastocystic** /blástə sístik/ *adj.*

blastoderm /blástə durm/ *n.* a layer of cells arising from the repeated division of a fertilized mammalian egg that develops into an embryo [Mid-19thC. Coined from BLASTO- + -*derm*, formed from Greek *derma* 'skin.'] —**blastodermatic** /blástə dur máttik/ *adj.* —**blastodermic** /blástə dúrmik/ *adj.*

blastoff /bláast of/ *n.* a launch of a rocket, spacecraft, or missile

blastogenesis /blástə jénnəssiss/ *n.* asexual reproduction by budding —**blastogenetic** /blástə jə néttik/ *adj.* —**blastogenic** /blástə jénnik/ *adj.*

blastopore /blástə pawr/ *n.* an opening in a young embryo that develops into the anus in some mammals —**blastoporal** *adj.* —**blastoporic** /-páwrik/ *adj.*

blastosphere /blástə sfeer/ *n.* = blastula

blastospore /blástə spawr/ *n.* a fungal spore produced by budding

blastula /blástyoŏlə/ (*plural* -las *or* -lae /-lee/) *n.* an embryo at an early stage of development, consisting of a hollow ball of cells [Late 19thC. From modern Latin, formed from Greek *blastos* 'sprout, germ.'] —**blastular** *adj.* —**blastulation** /blástyoŏ láysh'n/ *n.*

blat /blat/, **blatt** *n. US* a tabloid newspaper (*slang*) [Mid-20thC. From German *Blatt* 'leaf, sheet (of paper).']

blatant /bláyt'nt/ *adj.* **1. VERY OBVIOUS** so obvious or conspicuous as to be impossible to hide ○ *blatant falsehoods* **2. NOISY** excessively or offensively noisy (*literary*) [Late 16thC. Origin uncertain: possibly an alteration of Scottish *blatand* 'bleating', or from Latin *blatire* 'to babble.'] —**blatancy** *n.* —**blatantly** *adv.*

— WORD KEY: USAGE —

blatant or **flagrant**? Both words describe openly offensive behaviour, but there is a difference. *Blatant* emphasizes the obviousness of the offence, whereas *flagrant* emphasizes the shocking effect that the offence has. A *blatant* lie is one that is easily discerned, whereas a *flagrant* lie is one that is particularly shameless or outrageous. In youth slang, *blatantly* can be used to mean no more than 'clearly' or 'obviously': *It was blatantly time to leave.*

blate /blayt/ *adj. Scotland* lacking in self-confidence (*non-standard*) [15thC. Origin uncertain, perhaps related to Old English *blát* 'pale, ghastly.']

blather /bláthər/, **blether** /bléthər/, **blither** /blíthər/ *vi.* (-ers, -ering, -ered) **TALK INANELY** to talk in an unintelligent or inane manner, especially at length (*informal*) ■ *n.* **FOOLISH TALK** foolish and prolonged talk (*informal*) [Early 16thC. Originally a Scottish and northern English dialect word. From Old Norse *blaðra* 'to chatter, babble.'] —**blatherer** *n.*

blatherskite /bláthər skīt/, **bletherskite** /bléthər-/ *n.* (*dated informal*) **1. TALKATIVE PERSON** sb who likes to chat about silly or unimportant things **2. INANE TALK** chat about unimportant or silly things [Mid-17thC.

From BLATHER + Scottish dialect *skate* 'contemptible person'.]

blatt *n.* = blat

Blaxland /blákslənd/, **Gregory** (1778–1853) English-born Australian explorer. With William Lawson and William Wentworth, he led the first crossing by Europeans of the Blue Mountains in New South Wales (1813).

Blaxploitation /blák sploy táysh'n/ *n.* depiction of Blacks in films or other media in a way that appeals to people's popular and often inaccurate or negative notions of their experiences and qualities (*informal*) [Late 20thC. Blend of *Blacks* (plural of BLACK) and EXPLOITATION.]

blaze[1] /blayz/ *vi.* (**blazes, blazing, blazed**) **1. BURN BRIGHTLY** to burn brightly and fiercely **2. SHINE** to shine or appear to shine brightly **3. EXPERIENCE STRONG EMOTION** to be affected by a strong emotion (*informal*) ○ *blazing with indignation* **4. FIRE GUN** to fire a gun repeatedly ■ *n.* **1. BRIGHT FIRE** a bright flame or fire **2. CONSPICUOUS DISPLAY** a display that attracts attention ○ *a blaze of glory*. [Old English *blæse* 'torch, bright flame']

— WORD KEY: SYNONYMS —

See Synonyms at *fire*.

blaze[2] /blayz/ *n.* **1. WHITE MARK ON ANIMAL'S FACE** a white streak on the face of a horse or other animal **2. MARK SHOWING THE WAY** a mark indicating a path, originally a cut made in a tree trunk ■ *vt.* (**blazes, blazing, blazed**) **1. MARK PATH** to indicate a new path by making marks **2. DO STH NEW** to lead the way in doing sth new ○ *He blazed the way to the understanding of DNA's structure.* [Mid-17thC. Origin uncertain: possibly from Old Norse *blesi*, Middle High German *blasse*, or Middle Low German *bles* 'white mark'.]

blaze[3] /blayz/ *vt.* (**blazes, blazing, blazed**) to spread news or information loudly and clearly (*archaic*) [14thC. Via Middle Dutch *blāzen* 'to swell' from, ultimately, an Indo-European base that is also the ancestor of English *blow* and *blast.*]

blazer /bláyzər/ *n.* a jacket, often in the colours of, or with the badge of, a school or club [Mid-17thC. From the typically bright colour, in particular that of the red jackets once worn by members of a Cambridge University boat club.]

blazes /bláyziz/ *npl.* used to add emphasis (*informal*) (*used euphemistically*) ○ *What the blazes did you do that for?* ○ *run like blazes*

blazing /bláyzing/ *adj.* **1. INTENSE** intense and impassioned ○ *a blazing row* **2. HOT** very hot ○ *sitting in the blazing sun* ■ *adv.* **EXTREMELY** extremely or intensely ○ *blazing hot* —**blazingly** *adv.*

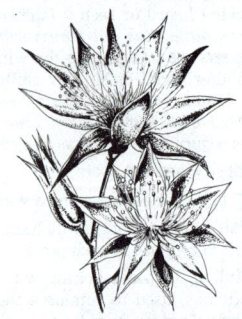

Blazing star

blazing star *n.* **1. PLANT WITH WHITE OR PURPLE FLOWERS** a North American flower of the daisy family with long heads of white or purplish flowers. Genus: *Liatris.* **2. PLANT WITH CLUSTERS OF FLOWERS** a North American plant with rough leaves and red or purple flowers. Genus: *Laevicaulis.*

blazon /bláyz'n/ *vt.* (-zons, -zoning, -zoned) **1. PROCLAIM WIDELY** to announce sth widely or ostentatiously **2. HERALDRY DEPICT COAT OF ARMS** to create or describe a coat of arms using the traditional symbols ■ *n.* **HERALDRY COAT OF ARMS** a coat of arms, or a technical description of one [13thC. From French *blason* 'shield', of unknown origin.] —**blazoner** *n.* —**blazonment** *n.*

blazonry /bláyzənri/ *n.* **1. HERALDRY MAKING OR EXPLAINING COATS OF ARMS** the art of creating or explaining coats of arms **2. HERALDRY COATS OF ARMS** coats of arms in-

dividually or collectively **3. BRILLIANT DISPLAY** a bright or showy display (*literary*)

bldg *abbr.* building

bleach /bleech/ *n.* **1. COLOUR-REMOVING SUBSTANCE** a chemical substance that removes colour and stains and is also used as a cleansing agent and disinfectant **2. APPLICATION OF BLEACH** an act of using bleach on sth ■ *v.* (**bleaches, bleaching, bleached**) **1.** *vt.* **USE BLEACH ON** to clean or whiten sth using bleach **2.** *vti.* **LIGHTEN IN COLOUR** to make sth whiter or lighter, or become lighter or whiter [Old English *blǣcan* 'to make white', from *blǣc* 'pale, shining', from a prehistoric Germanic base that is also the ancestor of English *bleak*] —**bleacher** *n.*

bleachers /bleéchərz/ *npl. US* (*sometimes used in the singular*) **1. STADIUM SEATS** seats in an uncovered area of a sports stadium **2. INDOOR SEATS IN SPORTS ARENA** retractable tiered benches for spectators in a gymnasium, at a swimming pool, or in some other indoor sports arena [Late 19thC. From the sun's bleaching of the exposed benches.]

bleaching powder *n.* a white powder, obtained from calcium hydroxide and chlorine, that is used as a disinfectant and a bleaching agent. Formula: CaCl(OCl).

bleak /bleek/ *adj.* **1. DISCOURAGING** without hope or expectation of success or improvement ○ *The company's future looks bleak.* **2. UNWELCOMING** providing little comfort or shelter ○ *a cabin on a bleak hilltop* **3. COLD AND CLOUDY** unpleasantly cold, dull, and windy ○ *bleak winter days* [14thC. From Old Norse *bleikr* 'pale, white, shining'.] —**bleakly** *adv.* —**bleakness** *n.*

blear /bleer/ (**blears, blearing, bleared**) *vt.* to make eyes misty or eyesight dim, e.g. with tears (*usually passive*) [14thC. Origin unknown.]

bleary /bleéri/ (-ier, -iest) *adj.* **1. SEEING DIMLY** not seeing clearly owing to mistiness or blurring, especially that associated with sleepiness ○ *a bleary gaze* **2. OBSCURED** obscured and not easy to see —**blearily** *adv.* —**bleariness** *n.*

bleary-eyed *adj.* seeing unclearly, especially because of sleepiness or drunkenness

Bleasdale /bleéz dayl/, **Alan** (b. 1946) British dramatist. His British television dramas include such as *The Boys from the Blackstuff* (1982).

bleat /bleet/ *v.* (**bleats, bleating, bleated**) **1.** *vi.* **MAKE SHEEP'S NOISE** to make the wavering cry of a sheep, goat, or calf **2.** *vti.* **COMPLAIN ANNOYINGLY** to complain about sth in an irritating way (*informal*) ■ *n.* **SHEEP'S SOUND** the wavering cry of a sheep, goat, or calf [Old English *blǣtan*. Ultimately from a prehistoric Germanic word that is also the ancestor of Dutch *blaten*; an imitation of the sound.] —**bleater** *n.*

bleb /bleb/ *n.* **1. MED BLISTER** a small blister on the skin **2. BUBBLE** a small bubble, e.g. in glass [Early 17thC. An alteration of BLOB.] —**blebby** *adj.*

bleed /bleed/ *v.* (**bleeds, bleeding, bled** /bled/, **bled**) **1.** *vi.* **LOSE BLOOD** to lose blood from the body, through a wound or because of illness ○ *The wound was bleeding heavily.* **2.** *vt.* **TAKE BLOOD FROM** to take blood from a person or animal, especially in order to treat a disease **3.** *vi.* **FEEL SORROW** to feel sadness or pity ○ *My heart bleeds for her in her loss.* **4.** *vi.* **EXUDE SAP** to exude sap from a plant's wound **5.** *vt.* **TAKE MONEY OR RESOURCES FROM** to use up large amounts of money or resources from an individual or organization, especially dishonestly (*informal*) ○ *bleeding public funds.* **6.** *vt.* **DRAW OFF LIQUID OR GAS** to draw liquid or gas out of a container or pressurized system ○ *bleed a radiator* **7.** *vi.* **RELEASE COLOUR** to release colour when wet or being washed (*refers to fabrics*) **8.** *vti.* **PRINTING OVERRUN PAGE** to print sth, or to be printed, so that part of sth is cut off by the edge of the page **9.** *vti.* **PRINTING MAKE COLOURS OF ILLUSTRATION RUN** to print sth, or to be printed, so that colours run into other colours or over the edge of an illustration ■ *n.* **1.** **PRINTING STH THAT OVERRUNS PRINTED PAGE** an illustration or piece of text printed in such a way that part of it is cut off the page **2. INSTANCE OF BLEEDING** an instance of losing blood [Old English *blēdan*. Ultimately from a prehistoric Germanic base that is also the ancestor of English *blood* and *bless.*]

bleeder /bleédər/ *n.* **1. PERSON** sb who is disliked (*informal offensive*) **2. MED BLEEDING BLOOD VESSEL** a blood vessel that is bleeding during surgery and requires clamping or other measures to stop it

bleeder resistor *n.* a resistor connected across the terminals of a power supply to regulate its output voltage, or to discharge capacitors

bleeding /bleéding/ *adj., adv.* used for emphasis, as a milder form of 'bloody' (*slang*)

Bleeding heart

bleeding heart *n.* **1.** PLANT WITH HEART-SHAPED FLOWERS a plant with drooping pink, red, or white heart-shaped flowers. Genus: *Dicentra*. **2.** FOOLISHLY SOFT-HEARTED PERSON sb regarded as naively kind or sympathetic (*informal*)

bleed valve *n.* a valve that can be opened to let liquid or gas out of a tank or pressurized system

bleep /bleep/ *n.* **1.** ELECTRONIC SOUND a short high-pitched electronic noise, intended as a signal and repeated intermittently **2.** = **pager** ■ *v.* (**bleeps, bleeping, bleeped**) **1.** *vi.* MAKE ELECTRONIC SOUND to make a short high-pitched electronic noise **2.** *vt.* CALL ON BLEEPER to call sb by sending a signal to a portable electronic receiver [Mid-20thC. An imitation of the sound.]

bleep out *vt.* to remove an offensive word from a broadcast, and replace it with a short high-pitched electronic sound

bleeper /bleéper/ *n.* = **pager**

bleeping /bleéping/ *adj.* used in place of a swearword to indicate mild irritation ○ *Where are the bleeping car keys?* [Mid-20thC]

blemish /blémmish/ *n.* **1.** SPOILING MARK OR FLAW a mark or imperfection that spoils the appearance of sth ○ *a cream that hides skin blemishes* **2.** SPOILING FAULT sth that spoils a person's reputation or good record ■ *vt.* (**-ishes, -ishing, -ished**) MAR to spoil the appearance or reputation of sth [14thC. From the Old French stem *ble(s)miss-* 'to make pale, injure'.] —**blemisher** *n.*

— **WORD KEY: SYNONYMS** —
See Synonyms at *flaw*.

blench[1] /blench/ (**blenches, blenching, blenched**) *vi.* to move back or away in fear [Old English *blencan* 'to deceive, cheat', of unknown origin. The modern meaning probably developed via 'to evade, dodge' and 'to move suddenly'.] —**blencher** *n.*

blench[2] *vi.* = **blanch** [Early 19thC. An alteration of BLANCH, by association with BLENCH[1].]

blend /blend/ *v.* (**blends, blending, blended**) **1.** *vti.* MIX INGREDIENTS to mix different substances together so that they do not readily separate ○ *blend the butter and sugar together* **2.** *vt.* CREATE PRODUCT BY MIXING INGREDIENTS to create food or drinks by mixing different types of ingredients (*often passive*) **3.** *vti.* INTERMINGLE to mix with other people or things without being conspicuous, or mix sth in this way ○ *blend fact and fiction* **4.** *vti.* MAKE PLEASING COMBINATION to combine things or qualities to create a pleasing effect, or be combined in this way ○ *instruments blending harmoniously* **5.** *vi.* SHADE IMPERCEPTIBLY INTO EACH OTHER to shade from one colour to another without obvious transitions and boundaries ■ *n.* **1.** MIXTURE a mixture or combination ○ *an interesting blend of traditional styles and modern materials* **2.** FOOD OR DRINK MIXTURE a food or type of drink created by mixing different types of ingredient ○ *an expensive coffee blend* **3.** WORD MADE BY JOINING TWO WORDS a new word made by joining parts of other words, as in 'telex', formed

from 'teleprinter' and 'exchange' [14thC. Probably from the Old Norse present stem *blend-* 'to mix'.]

— **WORD KEY: SYNONYMS** —
See Synonyms at *mixture*.

blend in *vi.* **1.** FIT IN to have personal qualities that suit a situation well ○ *He's a likable boy who blends in well* . **2.** BE DIFFICULT TO PICK OUT to be difficult to see or distinguish from similar things around

blende /blend/ *n.* **1.** = **sphalerite 2.** SULPHIDE ORE metallic sulphide ore that has a bright lustre [Late 17thC. From German *blenden* 'to deceive'; so called because sphalerite, despite resembling galena ore, does not yield lead.]

blender /bléndər/ *n.* **1.** APPLIANCE FOR MIXING FOOD an electrical kitchen appliance used to liquidize and blend foods **2.** SB OR STH THAT BLENDS sb or sth that blends things, especially a person or company that blends foods or drinks

Blenheim[1] /blénnim/ *n.* a dog belonging to a breed of spaniel with reddish markings [From *Blenheim* Palace in Oxfordshire, seat of the Dukes of Marlborough]

Blenheim[2] /blénnim/ **1.** wine-producing borough in the Wairau Valley in the South Island of New Zealand. Population: 25,712 (1996). **2.** site of the Battle of Blenheim (1704) when a British army, led by the 1st Duke of Marlborough, defeated French and Bavarian troops in the War of the Spanish Succession. It is near the present-day village of Blindheim, southwestern Germany.

blenny /blénni/ (*plural* **-nies** *or* **-ny**) *n.* a small scaleless long-bodied fish found in rocky coastal areas and coral reefs. Family: Blenniidae. [Mid-18thC. From Latin *blennius*, formed from Greek *blennos* 'slime' from the fish's covering of mucus.]

blephar- *prefix.* = **blepharo-**

blepharitis /bléffə rítiss/ *n.* inflammation of one or both eyelids [Formed from Greek *blepharon* 'eyelid' +-ITIS]

blepharo- *prefix.* **1.** eyelid ○ *blepharospasm* **2.** cilium, flagella ○ *blepharoplast* [From Greek *blepharon* 'eyelid', of unknown origin]

Blériot /blérri ō/, **Louis** (1872–1936) French aviator. He was the first person to fly across the English Channel (1909).

Blesbok

blesbok /bléss bok/ (*plural* **-boks** *or* **-bok**) *n.* a reddish-brown southern African antelope that has a white streak on its nose. Latin name: *Damaliscus dorcas*. [Early 19thC. From Afrikaans, from Dutch *bles* 'white facial streak' + *bok* 'buck'.]

bless /bless/ (**blesses, blessing, blessed, blest** /blest/) *vt.* **1.** RELIG MAKE HOLY to bestow holiness on sb or sth in a religious ceremony ○ *The bishop blessed the new chapel.* **2.** PROTECT to watch over sb or sth protectively ○ *We prayed for God to bless our marriage.* **3.** WISH WELL to declare approval and support for sb or sth ○ *The governor has blessed the new scheme.* **4.** CONFER PERSONAL BENEFIT ON to give sb a desirable quality or talent (*usually passive*) ○ *blessed with brains as well as good looks* **5.** THANK to express heartfelt thanks to sb (*often expressing a wish*) ○ *Bless you for speaking up for my child!* [Old English *blētsian*, from a prehistoric Germanic base that also produced English *bleed* and *blood*; the original sense seems to have been 'to mark with blood'.] —**blesser** *n.*

blessed /bléssid/ *adj.* **1.** RELIG HOLY made holy **2.** CHR BEATIFIED declared holy by the pope, usually as the first stage towards being declared a saint **3.** BESTOWING JOY bringing happiness or good luck ○ *The rain has*

brought farmers blessed relief from the long drought. ■ *adj., adv.* USED FOR EMPHASIS used to add emphasis in an expression of annoyance (*informal*) ○ *She wouldn't say a blessed thing about it.* —**blessedly** *adv.* —**blessedness** *n.*

Blessed Sacrament *n.* in various Christian churches, the bread and wine that has been blessed for use in Holy Communion

blessing /bléssing/ *n.* **1.** RELIG GOD'S HELP help from God or another deity **2.** RELIG RELIGIOUS ACT a ceremony in which an ordained person invokes or bestows divine help **3.** RELIG PRAYER BEFORE MEAL a prayer of thanks before a meal **4.** EXPRESSION OF APPROVAL approval or good wishes **5.** STH FORTUNATE sth to be glad or relieved about ○ *It's a blessing that the rescuers arrived in time to save the air crash victims*

blest past participle of **bless**

blether *vi., n. UK* = **blather**

bletherskite *n.* = **blatherskite** (*informal*)

blew 1. past tense of **blow**[1] **2.** past tense of **blow**[3]

blewits /bloó its/ (*plural* **-wits**) *n.* an edible fungus with a brown cap and a bluish stem. Genus: *Lepista*. (*takes a singular verb*) [Early 19thC. Probably formed from *blue*, reflecting the colour of its stem.]

Bligh /blī/, **William** (1754–1817) British naval officer. Cast adrift in the Pacific by mutineers of the HMS *Bounty* (1789), he navigated nearly 4,000 miles in an open boat to reach Timor. He was promoted to rear admiral in 1811 and vice admiral in 1814.

blight /blīt/ *n.* **1.** DESTRUCTIVE FORCE sth that spoils or damages things severely **2.** RUINED STATE a severely spoiled or ruined state, especially of an urban area ○ *urban blight* **3.** BOT PLANT DISEASE a plant disease, caused by bacteria, fungi, or viruses, in which symptoms range from brownish blotches on the foliage to withering of the entire plant without rotting **4.** BOT = **potato blight 5.** CAUSE OF BLIGHT IN PLANTS a bacterium, fungus, or virus that causes blight in plants ■ *vt.* **1.** RUIN to spoil or damage sth severely ○ *a football career blighted by injury* **2.** PLANTS AFFECT PLANT WITH BLIGHT to cause a plant to wither without rotting [Mid-16thC. Origin uncertain.]

blighter /blītər/ *n.* **1.** ANNOYING PERSON OR THING sb or sth that is a source of annoyance (*dated informal insult*) **2.** PERSON sb who is envied or sympathized with (*dated informal*) ○ *poor little blighter* ○ *lucky blighter*

Blighty /blīti/, **blighty** *n. UK* England or Britain (*dated humorous slang*) [Early 20thC. Anglicization of Hindi *bilāyatī*, literally 'foreign, European', originally used by British soldiers serving in India for 'home'.]

blimey /blīmi/ *interj.* used to express amazement or shock (*informal*) ○ *Blimey, that's expensive!* ◊ **cor blimey** [Late 19thC. Alteration of '*blind me!*' or '*blame me!*'.]

blimp[1] /blimp/ *n.* a nonrigid airship especially one used as a barrage balloon or for observation during World War II [Early 20thC. Origin uncertain: perhaps from 'Type B-limp', an airship without a rigid internal structure, as opposed to the 'Type A-rigid' with a rigid framework.]

blimp[2] /blimp/, **Colonel Blimp** *n.* a person, typically a middle-aged military officer, who is pompous and very conservative (*humorous*) [Mid-20thC. Named after a cartoon character invented by the cartoonist David Low (1891–1963).]

blind /blīnd/ *adj.* **1.** UNABLE TO SEE unable to see, permanently or temporarily **2.** UNABLE TO RECOGNIZE unwilling or unable to understand sth ○ *blind to the consequences* **3.** UNCONTROLLABLE so extreme and uncontrollable as to make sb behave irrationally ○ *blind rage* ○ *blind fear* **4.** UNQUESTIONING not based on fact and usually total and unquestioning ○ *blind prejudice* **5.** lacking awareness ○ *a blind stupor* **6.** NOT GIVING A CLEAR VIEW not giving a clear view and possibly dangerous ○ *a blind corner* **7.** SEW MADE ON UNDERSIDE OF FABRIC hidden from sight on the underside of a fabric **8.** WITHOUT DOORS OR WINDOWS without doors or windows, or not enclosing an open space **9.** CLOSED AT ONE END closed off at one end ○ *a blind unused tunnel* **10.** DONE WITHOUT LOOKING done without looking or while unable to see ○ *blind taste tests* **11.** DONE UNPREPARED done without preparation or the relevant information ○ *a blind presentation* **12.** WITH INFORMATION CONCEALED FOR UNPREJUDICED RESULT used to describe scientific experiments or similar evaluations in which information is withheld in order to obtain an unprejudiced result 13. BOT WITHOUT A GROWING POINT used to describe a plant in which growth stops because the growing point is damaged. It may be caused by pests, nutrient deficiency, waterlogging of the soil, or drought. ■ *adv.* 1. WITHOUT PRIOR EXAMINATION OR PREPARATION without previously thinking about or preparing for sth ○ *You shouldn't buy livestock blind.* 2. AIR USING INSTRUMENTS using information from aircraft instruments, without being able to see 3. TOTALLY totally or utterly (*informal*) ○ *an unscrupulous lawyer who robbed his clients blind* ■ *vt.* (**blinds, blinding, blinded**) 1. MAKE PERMANENTLY BLIND to make sb permanently unable to see 2. MAKE TEMPORARILY BLIND to make sb temporarily unable to see ○ *blinded by the lights* 3. MAKE UNABLE TO JUDGE PROPERLY to make sb unable to judge or act rationally ○ *blinded by rage* 4. CONFUSE to make it difficult for sb to understand sth ○ *Stop trying to blind us with statistics.* ■ *n.* 1. WINDOW COVERING a device that is pulled down to shut out the light from a window 2. COVER OR SUBTERFUGE sth that is intended to conceal the true nature of sb's activities 3. *US* HUNT = **hide** [Old English *blind.* Ultimately from an Indo-European word meaning 'confusion, obscurity', which is also the ancestor of English *blunder.* The underlying idea is of someone wandering around in darkness.] —**blindly** *adv.* —**blindness** *n.*

blind alley *n.* 1. CLOSED-OFF PASSAGE a narrow alley or passage that is closed off at one end 2. UNPRODUCTIVE UNDERTAKING sth that produces no worthwhile results

blind date *n.* 1. DATE WITH SB UNKNOWN a date arranged between people who have not seen or met each other before 2. SB MET ON BLIND DATE sb whom you meet on a blind date

blinder /blíndər/ *n.* 1. OUTSTANDING PERFORMANCE sth outstanding, especially a performance in a sport (*informal*) 2. HEAVY DRINKING BOUT a bout of excessive drinking (*slang*) ■ **blinders** *npl. US, Can* = **blinkers**

blindfold /blínd fōld/ *n.* BANDAGE TIED OVER EYES a piece of cloth tied over the eyes to prevent the wearer from seeing ■ *vt.* (**-folds, -folding, -folded**) 1. PUT BANDAGE ON EYES to prevent sb from seeing by putting a bandage or other material over the person's eyes 2. PREVENT FROM UNDERSTANDING to prevent sb from understanding clearly ■ *adj.* WEARING A BLINDFOLD wearing a blindfold ■ *adv.* 1. WHILE BLINDFOLDED wearing a blindfold or being unable to see for some other reason 2. UNPREPARED without consideration or relevant information ○ *had to field their queries blindfold* [Early 16thC. By folk etymology (from FOLD, with the idea of 'folding' sth round the eyes) from the past tense of obsolete *blindfell* 'to strike blind'.]

Blind Freddie /-fréddi/ *n. Aus* an imaginary person who epitomizes incompetence and lack of intelligence (*informal*) [Said to be named after a blind hawker in Sydney in the 1920s]

blind gut *n.* = **caecum** [From BLIND *adj.* 9 'closed at one end'.]

blinding /blínding/ *adj.* 1. IMPAIRING VISION causing blindness, especially temporarily, by being bright ○ *a blinding flash of light* 2. OUTSTANDING outstanding or extraordinary (*informal*) —**blindingly** *adv.*

blind man's buff *n.* a children's game in which one player is blindfolded and has to catch and identify other players by touch [*Buff* a shortening of BUFFET 'stroke with the hand']

blind side *n.* 1. AREA YOU CANNOT SEE the area that is out of your field of vision ○ *The cyclist came up on my blind side.* 2. SIDE CLOSER TO THE TOUCHLINE in rugby, the side of the pitch or scrum closer to the nearest touchline

blind-side, blindside *vt. US* 1. ATTACK FROM BLIND SIDE to attack sb from the blind side, especially in sports 2. ATTACK WHEN VULNERABLE to put sb at a disadvantage

blind snake *n.* a small tropical nonvenomous snake with scales over its eyes, adapted for burrowing and eating small soil invertebrates. Families: Typhlopidae and Anomalepididae.

blind spot *n.* 1. ANAT = **optic disc** 2. AREA OF IGNORANCE a subject that sb is ignorant about ○ *have a blind spot for maths* 3. DIRECTION IN WHICH VISION IS OBSCURED an area or direction, especially on a road, in which sb's vision is obscured 4. ACOUSTICS ACOUSTICALLY IMPAIRED AREA an area in an auditorium where things cannot be clearly heard 5. BROADCAST PLACE WITH POOR RADIO RECEPTION an area within the normal range of a radio transmitter where reception is poor

blind stamping *n.* PUBL = **book tooling** [From the lack of colour]

blindworm /blínd wurm/ *n.* = **slowworm** [15thC. *Blind* from the animal's small eyes.]

blini /blínni, bleéni/ (*plural* **-nis** *or* **-ni**) *n.* a small pancake made with yeast and buckwheat flour, traditional in Russia and other parts of Eastern Europe [Late 20thC. From Russian *bliný*, plural of *blin.*]

blink /blingk/ *v.* (**blinks, blinking, blinked**) 1. *vti.* CLOSE AND REOPEN EYES to close and reopen both eyes rapidly 2. *vti.* LOOK WHILE BLINKING to look at sb or sth while blinking 3. *vt.* HIDE OR REMOVE BY BLINKING to open and shut the eyes rapidly to remove sth from them ○ *He blinked away his tears.* 4. *vti.* FLASH to flash on and off, especially as a signal 5. *vi. US* WAVER to waver or lose your nerve ○ *After a ten-week strike, it was the management that finally blinked.* ■ *n.* 1. ACT OF BLINKING EYES a rapid closing and reopening of both eyes 2. *Scotland* QUICK LOOK a quick look or glance 3. METEOROL = **iceblink, snowblink** [13thC. Partly from a variant of BLENCH 'to flinch', and partly from Middle Dutch *blinken* 'to glitter', of unknown origin. The underlying idea is of 'flashing', hence 'sudden movement'.] ◇ **on the blink** not working properly (*informal*) ○ *The television's on the blink.*

blinker /blíngkər/ *n.* FLASHING LIGHT a light that flashes in order to give a message or warning, especially on a motor vehicle. Blinkers were used to send coded messages, especially between ships, to avoid interception of radio signals during World Wars I and II. ■ **blinkers** *npl.* 1. EYE COVERS FOR HORSE a pair of flaps attached to a horse's bridle, one beside each eye, to keep the horse from looking anywhere but straight ahead. US term **blinders** 2. OBSTRUCTION TO JUDGMENT a mental attitude that prevents sb from considering a situation rationally ■ *vt.* (**-ers, -ering, -ered**) 1. FIT HORSE WITH BLINKERS to put blinkers on a horse 2. HINDER SB'S JUDGMENT to prevent sb from considering a situation rationally

blinkered /blíngkərd/ *adj.* 1. NARROW-MINDED unable or unwilling to understand anything outside a very narrow range (*disapproving*) ○ *took a very blinkered attitude toward the reduction of trade barriers* 2. WEARING BLINKERS wearing blinkers

blinking /blíngking/ *adj.* used to add force to an insult or an expression of annoyance (*slang*) ○ *I don't want the blinking thing!* —**blinking** *adv.*

blip /blip/ *n.* 1. SPOT ON DISPLAY SCREEN a spot of light, often accompanied by a high-pitched sound, indicating the position of sth on a screen ○ *The submarine shows up as a series of faint blips on the screen.* 2. = **bleep** 3. SUDDEN DEVIATION a sudden temporary problem in the normal progress of sth ■ *vi.* (**blips, blipping, blipped**) MAKE A BLIP to produce a blip [Late 19thC. An imitation of the sound.]

bliss /bliss/ *n.* 1. PERFECT HAPPINESS perfect untroubled happiness ○ *It was bliss to have a day at home.* 2. SPIRITUAL JOY a state of spiritual joy [Old English *bliss*, an alteration of *blīþs*, from a prehistoric Germanic word meaning 'gentle, kind', which is also the ancestor of English *blithe*]

WORD KEY: CULTURAL NOTE

Bliss, a novel by Australian writer Peter Carey (1981). A fable about the battle between good and evil, it tells the story of advertising executive Harry Joy who, after a successful heart bypass operation, becomes convinced that he has woken up in Hell. It was made into a film by Ray Lawrence in 1985.

Bliss /bliss/, **Sir Arthur** (1891–1975) British composer. He was Master of the Queen's Musick after 1953 and wrote ballets, operas, and chamber music. Full name **Sir Arthur Edward Drummond Bliss**

blissful /blíssf'l/ *adj.* 1. PERFECTLY HAPPY characterized by perfect happiness ○ *a look of blissful contentment* 2. HAPPY BECAUSE UNAWARE serenely happy because of being unaware of sth ○ *blissful ignorance* —**blissfully** *adv.* —**blissfulness** *n.*

blister /blístər/ *n.* 1. MED PAINFUL SWELLING a painful swelling on the skin containing fluid (**serum**) 2. PLANTS PLANT DISEASE a swelling in a leaf or other plant part indicating disease 3. BUBBLE ON PAINT a bubble containing liquid or air on paintwork or rubber 4. AEROSP AIRCRAFT DOME a rounded, usually transparent dome on the fuselage of an aircraft, used for observation 5. *NZ* SHARP REBUKE a sharp and stinging rebuke (*slang*) ■ *vti.* (**-ters, -tering, -tered**) FORM BLISTERS to be raised in a blister or blisters, or to cause blisters to form [14thC. Origin uncertain: perhaps via Old French *blestre* 'swelling' from Middle Dutch *bluyster*, of unknown origin.] —**blistery** *adj.*

blister beetle *n.* a soft-bodied beetle that secretes for its own defence a substance that raises burning blisters on the skin of vertebrates. Family: Meloidae.

blistering /blístəring/ *adj.* 1. VERY HOT extremely hot 2. SCORNFUL extremely scornful or critical ○ *a blistering attack on the government's failures* —**blisteringly** *adv.*

blister pack *n.* a packet in which small items are contained in raised domes of plastic

BLit /beè lít/ *n., abbr.* Bachelor of Literature [Latin, *Baccalaureus Litterarum*]

blithe /blīth/ *adj.* 1. CHEERFUL AND CAREFREE happy, cheerful, and carefree (*literary*) 2. CASUAL casually indifferent ○ *with a blithe disregard for anyone's feelings* [Old English *blīþe*, from a prehistoric Germanic word meaning 'gentle' (see BLISS)] —**blithely** *adv.* —**blitheness** *n.*

blither *vi.* = **blather** (*informal*) [Mid-19thC. Variant of BLATHER.]

blithering /blíthəring/ *adj.* used to express annoyance and contempt for sb or sth (*informal insult*)

blithe spirit *n.* sb whose characteristic mood is one of carefree happiness (*used approvingly*)

BLitt /beè lít/ *n., abbr.* Bachelor of Literature [Latin, Baccalaureus Litterarum]

blitz /blits/ *n.* 1. MIL SUSTAINED AERIAL ATTACK a heavy air raid intended to obliterate a target 2. MIL = **blitzkrieg** 3. CONCERTED EFFORT a concentrated effort to get sth done (*informal*) 4. AMERICAN FOOTBALL CHARGE ON PASSER in American football, a direct attack on the passer, by one or more players who usually stay behind the line of scrimmage, to try to prevent a pass ■ *v.* (**blitzes, blitzing, blitzed**) 1. *vt.* MIL DESTROY BY AERIAL BOMBING to attack or destroy sth by bombardment from the air 2. *vt.* DEAL WITH ENERGETICALLY to concentrate a lot of effort on sth to get it done (*informal*) 3. *vt.* TRY TO OVERWHELM to subject sb to an overwhelming amount of sth, often in order to force him or her into agreement or submission (*informal*) ○ *blitzed with a stream of facts* 4. *vti.* AMERICAN FOOTBALL CHARGE PASSER in American football, to charge the passer in order to prevent a pass [Mid-20thC. Shortening of BLITZKRIEG.]

Blitz /blits/ *n.* the intensive bombing of British cities by the German Air Force between 1940 and 1941

blitzkrieg /blíts kreeg/ *n.* a swift military offensive using ground and air forces [Mid-20thC. From German, literally 'lightning war'.]

Blixen /blíks'n/, **Karen, Baroness** (1885–1962) Danish writer. A much-travelled author, she is best known for her semi-autobiographical *Out of Africa* (1937). Born **Karen Christence Dinesen**. Pseudonym **Isak Dinesen**

blizzard /blízzərd/ *n.* a severe snowstorm with strong winds and poor visibility [Early 19thC. Origin uncertain: perhaps coined from dialectal *blizz* 'violent rainstorm' + -ARD; or thought to suggest the sound of the wind or the falling of the snow.]

blk *abbr.* 1. block 2. bulk

BLL *abbr.* Bachelor of Laws [Latin, Baccalaureus Legum]

bloat /blōt/ *vti.* (**bloats, bloating, bloated**) 1. SWELL to become swollen or inflated, or to make sth do this 2. EXCESSIVELY EXPAND to increase excessively or to make sth do this ■ *n.* 1. *US* EXCESSIVE INCREASE an excessive amount or excessive increase in sth ○ *corporate bloat* 2. VET CATTLE DISEASE a disease affecting cattle and sheep, characterized by excessive gas in the main stomach compartment (**rumen**) [Early 17thC. Origin uncertain: probably from Old

Norse *blautr* 'soft, wet'. The modern meaning 'to swell' apparently evolved from the obsolete meaning 'flabby' via 'swollen'.]

bloated /blṓtid/ *adj.* **1.** SWOLLEN swollen with liquid, air, or gas **2.** OVERFULL AFTER OVEREATING overfull after eating too much **3.** TOO LARGE excessively large (*disapproving*) ○ *a bloated expense account* —**bloatedness** *n.*

bloater /blṓtər/ FISH CURED BY SOAKING AND SMOKING a large herring that has been soaked in brine and smoked ■ *n.* FRESHWATER FISH a common freshwater whitefish native to the Great Lakes of North America. Latin name: *Coregonus hoyi.* [Mid-19thC. From obsolete *bloat herring*, *bloat* of uncertain origin: perhaps from BLOAT, because herrings preserved by smoking are plumper than those fully dried.]

bloatware /blṓt wair/ *n.* COMPUT a computer program with many, often superfluous features that take up so much memory that the computer's performance is impaired (*informal*)

blob /blob/ *n.* **1.** SOFT MASS a soft lump or drop of sth such as paint or glue **2.** SMALL SPOT OF COLOUR a small rounded spot of colour **3.** INDISTINCT FORM an indistinct or shapeless form or object ■ *vt.* (**blobs, blobbing, blobbed**) PUT BLOBS ON STH to apply blobs of colour or a soft substance to sth [15thC. Origin uncertain: perhaps from obsolete *blober* 'bubble, bubbling'; or an imitation of the sound made by the lips in producing a bubble.]

bloc /blok/, **block** *n.* a group of countries with a shared aim ○ *former Eastern bloc countries* [Early 20thC. From French, from Old French (see BLOCK).]

Bloch /blok/, **Ernest** (1880–1959) Swiss-born US composer. He incorporated themes from Jewish music in such works as his symphony *Israel* (1912–16).

block /blok/ *n.* **1.** SOLID LUMP a large solid piece of a hard substance, usually with flat sides **2.** CONSTR BUILDING UNIT a large flat-sided piece of hard material such as stone or wood, used in building. ◊ **breeze block 3.** = **building block 4.** CHOPPING BASE a large piece of wood used for chopping things on **5.** PLACE FOR BEHEADING PEOPLE a large piece of wood or stone on which people were beheaded in former times **6.** AUCTIONEER'S PLATFORM a stand on which articles in an auction are displayed **7.** PRINTING PRINTING DEVICE a piece of wood, metal, or stone with a design engraved on it used for printing **8.** SPORTS = **starting block 9.** PAD OF PAPER a pad of writing or drawing paper **10.** LARGE BUILDING a building divided into offices or flats **11.** SPECIAL-PURPOSE BUILDING a building or part of a building designed for a particular purpose ○ *the new science block* **12.** GROUP OF BUILDINGS a group of buildings in a town or city bounded on each side by a street ○ *I'm just taking the dog for a walk round the block.* **13.** *US* DISTANCE the distance between two parallel streets ○ *They live only three blocks from here.* **14.** *US* STREET SECTION the section of a street between two parallel streets ○ *The post office is in the middle of the next block.* **15.** LAND AREA an area of land marked for division or development **16.** *ANZ* LARGE AREA OF SETTLED LAND an extensive area of land used for a particular purpose, e.g. housing or farming **17.** *NZ* AREA OF BUSH RESERVED BY HUNTER an area of bushland reserved for an individual trapper or hunter **18.** UNBROKEN EXPANSE OR AREA a uniform expanse of sth such as colour **19.** SET OF SIMILAR ITEMS a set of similar items sold as a unit ○ *a block of tickets* **20.** GROUP OF POSTAGE STAMPS a group of four or more postage stamps forming a rectangle **21.** RAIL LENGTH OF TRACK a length of railway track on which only one train is permitted at a time **22.** COMPUT UNIT OF DATA a set of contiguous data that performs some action together ○ *a block of text* **23.** POL = **bloc 24.** OBSTRUCTION sth that obstructs or prevents progress **25.** SPORTS OBSTRUCTION OF PLAY an act of deliberately preventing a ball or another player from moving forward **26.** CRICKET DEFENSIVE STROKE in cricket, a defensive stroke made by a batsman, intended only to stop the ball **27.** MED OBSTRUCTION OF PHYSIOLOGICAL FUNCTION an interruption of the normal functioning of an organ of the body **28.** DISRUPTION OF PSYCHOLOGICAL PROCESSES an inability to begin or continue a psychological process, often attributed to emotional stress **29.** = **cylinder block 30.** CRICKET BATSMAN'S MARK ON CREASE in cricket, a mark made by a batsman near the popping crease to indicate the position of his bat in relation to the wicket ■ *v.* (**blocks, blocking, blocked**) **1.** *vt.* OBSTRUCT to prevent or hinder movement through, into, or out of sth ○ *The drains are blocked with leaves.* ○ *He stood in front of me, blocking my way.* **2.** *vt.* HINDER SB'S OR STH'S MOVEMENT OR PROGRESS to prevent sth from moving or developing ○ *Her appointment was blocked by the managing director* **3.** *vt.* OBSTRUCT SIGHT OF STH to obstruct sb's line of sight **4.** *vti.* SPORTS OBSTRUCT PLAYER OR BALL to prevent a ball or another player from moving forward **5.** *vti.* MED PREVENT NORMAL FUNCTIONING to prevent the normal functioning of a physiological process ○ *a blocked tear duct* **6.** *vti.* FAIL TO REMEMBER to fail to remember sth or to have a psychological block ○ *block a memory* **7.** *vt.* MAKE INTO BLOCK to shape sth into a block **8.** *vt.* SUPPORT WITH BLOCK to support or strengthen sth using a block **9.** *vt.* SHAPE ON BLOCK to mould sth with or on a block **10.** *vt.* PRINTING STAMP USING BLOCK to stamp a surface with a title or using an engraved block **11.** *vti.* THEATRE REHEARSE BASIC MOVEMENTS FOR SCENE to plan and rehearse the basic movements and positions for the actors in a scene [14thC. Via Old French *bloc* from Middle Dutch *blok* 'tree trunk'.]
◇ **knock sb's block off** to punch sb in the head (*slang*)
◇ **on the block** *US* for sale at an auction

WORD KEY: SYNONYMS

See Synonyms at ***hinder***.

block in *vt.* **1.** PREVENT FROM MOVING to prevent sb or sth moving from a place by being, or placing sth, in the way **2.** SHADE EMPTY SPACES to fill in the blank spaces on an outline design with colour

block off *vt.* **1.** PHYSICALLY OBSTRUCT to put up or form a barrier in order to prevent anybody or anything entering ○ *Police blocked off the street.* **2.** OBSTRUCT SIGHT OF to put up or form a barrier that prevents sth from being seen

block out *vt.* **1.** PUT OUT OF MIND to prevent a disturbing thought from entering the mind **2.** DESCRIBE WITHOUT DETAIL to describe sth in a general fashion, without great detail ○ *block out a proposal* **3.** PHOTOGRAPHY COVER PART OF NEGATIVE to cover part of a negative or stencil when printing from it to prevent that part appearing

block up *vti.* to prevent movement through sth by filling all the space in, or to become completely obstructed

blockade /blo káyd/ *n.* **1.** PREVENTION OF ACCESS an organized action to prevent people or goods entering or leaving a place **2.** FORCES FORMING BLOCKADE the ships or forces used to maintain a blockade **3.** OBSTACLE OR OBSTRUCTION sth that prevents access to a place ■ *vt.* (**-ades, -ading, -aded**) **1.** SUBJECT PLACE TO BLOCKADE to impose a blockade on a place **2.** BLOCK ACCESS TO PLACE to obstruct access to a place [Late 17thC. Perhaps modelled on AMBUSCADE.] —**blockader** *n.*

blockage /blókij/ *n.* **1.** PHYSICAL OBSTRUCTION sth that obstructs movement through a pipe or channel ○ *a blockage in an artery* **2.** ACT OF BLOCKING the act of blocking sth

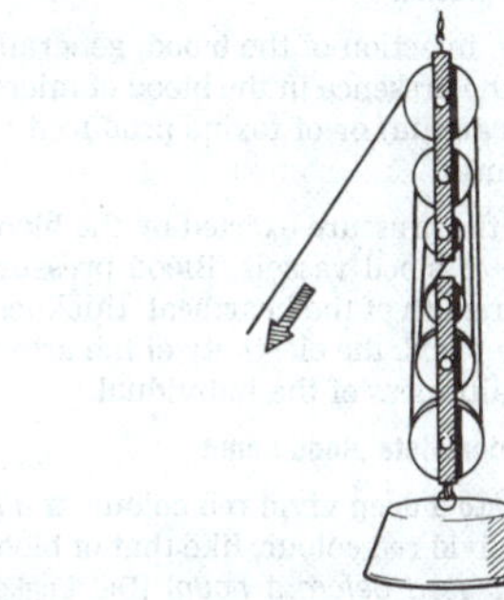

Block and tackle

block and tackle (*plural* **blocks and tackles**) *n.* a system of two pulley blocks, each with at least one pulley with rope or cable threaded through them, used for hoisting or hauling. The greater the number of pulleys, the greater the weight that can be raised by the same force on the rope or cable.

blockboard /blók bawrd/ *n.* a variety of plywood composed of soft wood squares or strips between outer layers of veneer. The direction of grain of the wood strips is perpendicular to that of the veneer.

block booking *n.* a booking of a large number of tickets for the same event or show

blockbuster /blók bustər/ *n.* **1.** POPULAR SUCCESS sth such as a book, play or film that is either very large or achieves enormous commercial success (*informal*) **2.** MIL HUGE DESTRUCTIVE BOMB a large high-explosive bomb designed to demolish buildings over a large area (*dated*) **3.** *US* BUSINESS PERSON WHO PRACTISES BLOCKBUSTING sb who attempts to persuade people to sell their houses by instilling fear of declining property values (*informal*)

blockbusting /blók busting/ *n. US* EXPLOITATION TECHNIQUE the practice of persuading homeowners to sell low for fear of declining property values (*informal*) ■ *adj.* SUCCESSFUL sensational and enormously successful commercially ○ *a blockbusting novel*

block capital *n.* a plain capital letter that is not joined to other letters ○ *Fill in the form in block capitals.*

block diagram *n.* a diagram in which the essential parts of a system or process are represented by labelled rectangles

blocker /blókər/ *n.* **1.** PHARM CHEMICAL AGENT a drug that prevents a physiological function **2.** FOOTBALL OFFENSIVE PLAYER in American football, an offensive player who tries to keep the defence from reaching the ball, kicker, or passer

block grant *n.* money from the government granted to local authorities to spend on local services

blockhead /blók hed/ *n.* a person regarded as very unintelligent (*dated insult*) [Mid-16thC. The meaning 'stupid' evolved from the wooden heads used to display hats and wigs.]

blockhouse /blók hows/ (*plural* **-houses** /-howziz/) *n.* **1.** SMALL, EASILY DEFENDED BUILDING a small military building with apertures to fire through, used as part of a defensive system or an observation post **2.** WOODEN FORT a fort of former times in America constructed from heavy wooden beams

block letter *n.* **1.** = **block capital 2.** PRINTING SANS SERIF FONT OR LETTER a compressed sans serif typeface or individual letter

block party (*plural* **block parties**) *n. US* a party for all the people who live on the same block or street

block plane *n.* a small carpenter's plane with the blade at a low pitch, used to cut across the grain of the wood

block printing *n.* printing from hand-carved or engraved blocks

block vote *n.* a single vote by a representative, typically of a trade union, on behalf of the members of his or her organization, weighted according to the number of members

Bloemfontein /bloóm fon tayn/ city and capital of Free State Province, central South Africa. Population: 126,867 (1991).

Blois /blwaa/ capital of Loir-et-Cher Department in central France, on the River Loire, north-east of Tours. It is famous for its magnificent Renaissance château. Population: 51,549 (1990).

bloke /blōk/ *n.* a man (*informal*) [Mid-19thC. From Shelta, a secret jargon used by Romany people in Britain and Ireland.]

blokeish /blṓkish/, **blokish** *adj.* typical of the character, behaviour, or interests of men, especially when they are in all-male company (*informal*) —**blokeishness** *n.*

blond /blond/, **blonde** *adj.* **1.** FAIR yellowish or golden in colour **2.** FAIR-HAIRED AND LIGHT-SKINNED with fair hair and a light-coloured skin ○ *a blond little boy* ○ *a blond little girl* **3.** LIGHT COLOURED light-coloured, ranging from light yellowish brown to greyish yellow ○ *blond wood* ■ *n.* FAIR-HAIRED PERSON a person with blond hair [15thC. Via French from, ultimately, medieval Latin *blundus* 'yellow', of uncertain origin: perhaps ultimately from a prehistoric Germanic word meaning 'clouded', which is also the ancestor of English *blend.*] —**blondness** *n.*

WORD KEY: USAGE

blond or **blonde**? When describing the colour of sb's hair, ***blond*** is normally used whether the person is male or female. *Jane has blond hair.* When used as a noun or adjective to describe sb directly, **blond** is used of a man or boy and **blonde** of a woman or girl. *He is blond. Jane is a blonde.*

Blondin /bloN dáN/, **Charles** (1824–97) French acrobat. He crossed the Niagara Falls on a tightrope (1859). Real name **Jean Francois Gravelet**

blood /blud/ *n.* **1.** PHYSIOL RED FLUID CIRCULATING IN BODY the red fluid that is pumped from the heart and circulates around the bodies of humans and other vertebrates **2.** ZOOL BODY FLUID OF INVERTEBRATES a liquid found in invertebrates, with functions similar to those of vertebrate blood **3.** BLOODSHED bloodshed or killing **4.** VITAL LIFE FORCE blood considered as a vital life force **5.** FAMILY OR KINSHIP family background or descent from a particular ancestor, especially when viewed as determining a person's character or appearance **6.** PURE BREEDING pure breeding in animals, especially horses **7.** MEMBERS OF GROUP people considered for their potential to strengthen and improve an organization (*informal*) **8.** YOUNG MAN a fashionable and wealthy young man, especially in the 18th and 19th centuries (*informal humorous*) ■ *vt.* (**bloods, blooding, blooded**) **1.** MIL INITIATE TROOPS IN BATTLE to subject troops to their first experience of battle **2.** HUNT LET DOG TASTE BLOOD to give a dog its first taste of the blood of a freshly killed animal in order to make it keen to hunt **3.** HUNT SMEAR FACE WITH BLOOD to smear sb's face with the blood of a hunted animal as an initiation into hunting [Old English *blōd*, from a prehistoric Germanic word that is also the ancestor of English *bleed*] ◇ **be out for** *or* **after sb's blood** to be intending to punish sb ◇ **blood is thicker than water** family ties and loyalties take precedence over other relationships ◇ **blood on sb's hands** responsibility for sb's death ◇ **in cold blood** deliberately, and in a way that shows a complete lack of emotion ○ *was murdered in cold blood* ◇ **make sb's blood boil** to make sb extremely angry ◇ **make sb's blood run cold** to frighten or horrify sb ◇ **sweat blood** to make a great effort

blood-and-thunder *adj.* full of melodramatic adventure and action (*informal*)

blood bank *n.* **1.** STORE FOR BLOOD a place where blood or blood plasma is stored for transfusion **2.** BLOOD SUPPLY the blood or blood plasma stored in a blood bank

bloodbath /blúd baath/ (*plural* **-baths** /-baathz/) *n.* a battle or fight characterized by mass killing

blood brother *n.* either one of two men or boys who have sworn mutual loyalty and friendship

blood clot *n.* a thick mass of coagulated blood

blood count *n.* **1.** DETERMINATION OF BLOOD CELL NUMBER a counting of the number of red and white blood cells and platelets in a given volume of blood **2.** NUMBER OF CELLS the actual number of cells and platelets found in a blood count

bloodcurdling /blúd kurd'ling/, **blood-curdling** *adj.* arousing extreme fear ○ *bloodcurdling screams*

blood donor *n.* sb who gives some of his or her own blood for use in transfusions

blood doping *n.* the practice of reinjecting an athlete with his or her own red blood cells shortly before a competition in order to enhance performance. The practice is illegal in most organized competitions.

blooded /blúddid/ *adj.* belonging to a superior breed ○ *blooded mares*

blood feud *n.* a long-lasting feud between families or clans involving murder

bloodfin /blúd fin/ *n.* a small red-finned freshwater fish native to Argentina, popular in aquariums. Latin name: *Aphyocharax rubripinnis*.

blood fluke *n.* a parasitic flatworm that is common in tropical Asia and Africa and is found in human blood. It relies on two hosts, humans and some types of snails, to complete its life cycle. Genus: *Schistosoma*.

blood group *n.* any class into which human blood is divided for transfusion purposes according to the presence or absence of genetically determined antigens that determine its immunological com-

patibility. The ABO system is the most commonly known set of blood groups.

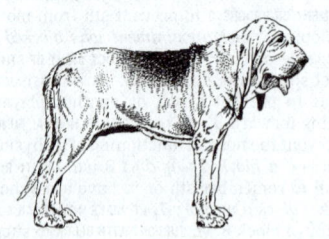

Bloodhound

bloodhound /blúd hownd/ *n.* **1.** TRACKING DOG a large powerful dog with drooping ears, sagging jowls, and a keen sense of smell, formerly used for tracking **2.** SLEUTH a detective who is relentless in pursuing people or things (*informal*) [14thC. From the dog's skill in following the scent of people and animals.]

bloodless /blúdləss/ *adj.* **1.** WITHOUT KILLING OR VIOLENCE conducted without killing or great violence ○ *a bloodless coup* **2.** PALE AND ANAEMIC pale and anaemic-looking **3.** LACKING LIVELINESS dull and lacking liveliness ○ *a bloodless performance* **4.** LACKING EMOTION cold and lacking in human emotion ○ *bloodless statistics* **5.** LACKING BLOOD lacking blood, or the expected amount of blood ○ *bloodless surgery* —**bloodlessly** *adv.* —**bloodlessness** *n.*

Bloodless Revolution *n.* = Glorious Revolution

bloodletting /blúd leting/ *n.* **1.** MED = phlebotomy **2.** BITTER QUARRELLING bitter violent fighting between rival groups **3.** *US* EJECTION AS OF PEOPLE the large-scale ejection, or laying off, of human resources in a corporation (*formal*) ○ *corporate bloodletting in which a number of senior managers were let go* —**bloodletter** *n.*

bloodline /blúd līn/ *n.* a direct line of descent from a particular human or animal ancestor, especially with respect to the common characteristics shared by that ancestor's descendants

blood lust *n.* a strong desire for killing or violence

blood money *n.* **1.** COMPENSATION PAID FOR KILLING in some cultures, compensation paid to the relatives of sb who has been killed or murdered **2.** FEE FOR HIRED KILLER the fee paid to a hired killer or to sb who reveals where the victim of a murder is to be found **3.** REWARD FOR FINDING KILLER the reward paid to sb for giving information about a criminal, especially a murderer

blood orange *n.* an orange that has deep red flesh

blood plasma *n.* = plasma

blood poisoning *n.* infection of the blood, generally caused either by the presence in the blood of micro-organisms (**septicaemia**) or of toxins produced by body cells (**toxaemia**)

blood pressure *n.* the pressure exerted by the blood against the walls of blood vessels. Blood pressure depends on the strength of the heartbeat, thickness and volume of the blood, the elasticity of the artery walls, and the healthiness of the individual.

blood profile *n.* = complete blood count

blood red *n.* BRIGHT RED a deep vivid red colour ■ *adj.* DEEP RED of a deep vivid red colour, like that of blood (hyphenated when used before a noun) [Old English *blōdrēad*]

blood relation, **blood relative** *n.* a person who is related to another person by birth rather than marriage

bloodroot /blúd root/ (*plural* **-roots** *or* **-root**) *n.* a plant of eastern North America that produces a single white flower and has poisonous, deep red sap in its roots. Latin name: *Sanguinaria canadensis*.

blood sausage *n.* *US, Can* = black pudding

bloodshed /blúd shed/ *n.* activity resulting in killings or injuries

bloodshot /blúd shot/ *adj.* inflamed and red as a result of the widening of small blood vessels in the white of the eye ○ *bloodshot eyes* [Mid-16thC. *Shot* the past participle of SHOOT.]

blood sport *n.* a sport in which animals are killed. Hunting and bullfighting are blood sports.

bloodstain /blúd stayn/ *n.* a dark stain left by dried blood —**bloodstained** *adj.*

bloodstone /blúd stōn/ *n.* a semiprecious mineral that is a deep green variety of chalcedony with small red spots or streaks of red jasper in it

bloodstream /blúd streem/ *n.* the flow of blood circulating through the blood vessels of a person or animal

bloodsucker /blúd sukər/ *n.* **1.** PARASITE THAT SUCKS BLOOD a parasite that sucks blood from its host, e.g. leeches and mosquitoes **2.** EXPLOITER sb who exploits sb else, especially by extortion or blackmail (*informal disapproving*) —**bloodsucking** *n., adj.*

blood sugar *n.* the concentration of glucose in the blood

blood test *n.* a scientific analysis of a sample of blood

bloodthirsty /blúd thurst i/ (**bloodthirstier, bloodthirstiest**) *adj.* **1.** EAGER FOR VIOLENCE eager to take part in or witness violence and bloodshed **2.** VIOLENT full of intentional violence or killing [Mid-16thC. From BLOOD + THIRSTY, modelled on German *blutdürstig*, coined by Martin Luther.] —**bloodthirstily** *adv.* —**bloodthirstiness** *n.*

blood type *n.* = blood group

blood vessel *n.* any of the arteries, veins, or capillaries through which blood flows

bloodworm /blúd wurm/ *n.* **1.** AQUATIC MIDGE LARVA the red aquatic larva of a freshwater midge. Genus: *Chironomus*. **2.** REDDISH WORM USED AS ANGLING BAIT a reddish segmented worm that is often used as angling bait. Genera: *Tubifex* and *Polycirrus*. (*regional*)

bloody /blúddi/ *adj.* (**-ier, -iest**) **1.** BLOODSTAINED covered or smeared with blood ○ *Her hands were bloody and shaking.* **2.** RELATING TO BLOOD resembling or containing blood **3.** INVOLVING MUCH BLOODSHED involving a great deal of killing and bloodshed **4.** SWEARWORD used as a swearword or to add emphasis (*slang*) ○ *a bloody nuisance* **5.** UNFAIR AND INCONSIDERATE very unfair and inconsiderate (*dated informal*) ■ *adv.* SWEARWORD used as a swearword or to add emphasis (*slang*) ○ *a bloody good job too!* ■ *vt.* (**-ies, -ying, -ied**) STAIN WITH BLOOD to stain or smear sth with blood [In the emphatic sense, perhaps originally a reference to the habits of the 'bloods', or wealthy young men, in phrases such as '*bloody drunk*', literally 'as drunk as a blood'] —**bloodily** *adv.* —**bloodiness** *n.* ◇ **bloody well** used to show anger or irritation when contradicting sth (*slang*)

bloody mary (*plural* **bloody marys**), **Bloody Mary** *n.* a cocktail consisting of vodka, tomato juice, and other spices

bloody-minded *adj.* intentionally uncooperative and obstructive (*informal*) [From earlier sense 'inclined to violence, cruel'] —**bloody-mindedly** *adv.* —**bloody-mindedness** *n.*

bloom[1] /bloom/ *n.* **1.** PLANTS FLOWER a flower, especially on a plant cultivated chiefly for its flowers **2.** PLANTS MASS OF FLOWERS the mass of flowers on a single plant **3.** PLANTS FLOWERING the state of being in flower ○ *roses in full bloom* **4.** PRIME the condition of greatest freshness or health (*literary*) ○ *in the bloom of youth* **5.** BOT HEALTHY APPEARANCE OR COMPLEXION a fresh, youthful, healthy complexion **6.** WHITE COATING ON LEAVES OR FRUIT a thin white coating on the leaves of some plants and on fruits **7.** WHITE POWDER ON COINS a fine white powder sometimes found on newly minted coins **8.** COOK COATING ON CHOCOLATE a mottled white coating on chocolate, usually caused by incorrect temperature during storage **9.** ECOL = algal bloom ■ *vi.* (**blooms, blooming, bloomed**) **1.** PLANTS TO FLOWER to open into flower ○ *The roses bloomed early this year.* **2.** PLANTS PRODUCE PLANTS to produce abundant plant life, especially unexpectedly ○ *make the desert bloom* **3.** PROSPER OR FLOURISH to reach the fullest stage of development or maturity (*literary*) **4.** APPEAR HEALTHY to appear healthy and vigorous (*literary*) **5.** *US* APPEAR SUDDENLY to appear suddenly, usually in a cloud ○ *A* *cloud of smoke bloomed under the rocket.* **6.** ECOL **BECOME COVERED WITH ALGAE** to become discoloured on the surface because of an excessive growth of algae or phytoplankton (*refers to bodies of water*) [13thC. From Old Norse *blóm*, from, ultimately, an Indo-European word that is also the ancestor of English *flower*.] —**bloomy** *adj.*

bloom² /bloom/ *n.* METALL **BAR OF SEMI-FINISHED METAL** a bar of steel or wrought iron hammered or rolled from an ingot ■ *vt.* (**blooms, blooming, bloomed**) **FLATTEN AN INGOT** to convert an ingot of iron or steel into a bloom [Pre-12thC. From Old Norse *blóm* (see BLOOM¹).]

bloomer /blóomər/ *n.* **1.** PLANTS **PLANT THAT FLOWERS** a flowering plant, especially considered with respect to the time of its flowering ○ *an early bloomer* **2.** **EMBARRASSING MISTAKE** a mildly embarrassing mistake (*informal humorous*) [Mid-18thC. 'Mistake' a shortening and alteration of *blooming error*.]

bloomers /blóomərz/ *npl.* (*dated*) **1.** **BAGGY UNDERWEAR** baggy knickers for women or girls, especially garments that reach down to just above the knee **2.** **WOMEN'S LOOSE SPORTS TROUSERS** loose trousers gathered at the knee, worn by women for cycling or swimming in the late 19th century **3.** **LONG LOOSE WOMEN'S TROUSERS** long loose trousers gathered at the ankle and formerly worn by women and girls under a shorter skirt [Mid-19thC. Named after Amelia BLOOMER.]

blooming /blóoming/ *adj.* **FLOURISHING** flourishing and in exceptionally good health or condition ■ *adj., adv.* **USED FOR EMPHASIS** used as a euphemistic alternative for 'bloody' (*dated informal*) ○ *a blooming idiot* ○ *not blooming likely*

Bloomsbury Group /blóomzbəri-/ *n.* a group of artists and writers who congregated in Bloomsbury in London after World War I. They shared political views and an experimental approach to their respective fields. [Early 20thC. Named after *Bloomsbury*.]

bloop /bloop/ *vt.* (**bloops, blooping, blooped**) BASEBALL **HIT BASEBALL** to hit a baseball just over the infield ■ *n.* BASEBALL = **blooper** *n.* 2 [Early 20thC. An imitation of the sound.]

blooper /blóopər/ *n.* **1.** *US, Can* **EMBARRASSING MISTAKE** a mildly embarrassing mistake (*informal humorous*) **2.** BASEBALL **HIT** a hit just beyond the infield **3.** BASEBALL **BASEBALL PITCH** a lobbed underhand pitch in baseball [Early 20thC. Formed from BLOOP.]

blossom /blóssəm/ *n.* **1.** **MASS OF FLOWERS ON TREE** a mass of flowers appearing on a tree or bush **2.** **SINGLE FLOWER** a single flower **3.** **FLOWERING** the state of flowering ○ *cherry trees in blossom* ■ *vi.* (**-soms, -soming, -somed**) **1.** **COME INTO FLOWER** to open into flower **2.** **DEVELOP WELL** to develop in a pleasing or promising way **3.** **blossom, blossom out** **STOP BEING SHY** to stop being shy and reserved [Old English *blōstm*. Ultimately from an Indo-European base that is related to Latin *flos* (source of English *flower*).] —**blossomy** *adj.*

blot¹ /blot/ *n.* **1.** **STAIN** a stain or spot caused by a drop of liquid **2.** **EYESORE** sth ugly that spoils the appearance of sth ○ *a blot on the landscape* **3.** **BLEMISH** sth that spoils sb or sth's good name or reputation ■ *v.* (**blots, blotting, blotted**) **1.** *vti.* **CREATE BLOT** to make a blot on paper **2.** *vt.* **BRING DISREPUTE** to bring dishonour on sb's reputation **3.** *vt.* **DRY WITH ABSORBENT MATERIAL** to soak up liquid from the surface of sth using absorbent material [14thC. Origin uncertain: probably from Scandinavian.] ◇ **blot your copybook** to damage your reputation by making a mistake

blot out *vt.* **1.** **OBSCURE** to cover sth so that it can no longer be seen **2.** **OBLITERATE FROM MEMORY** to remove sth painful from the mind

blot² /blot/ *n.* **1.** BACKGAMMON **EXPOSED PIECE** a piece placed alone on a point and therefore exposed to capture by the opposing player **2.** **WEAK POINT** a weak or exposed point (*archaic*) [Late 16thC. Origin uncertain: probably from Dutch *bloot* 'exposed, naked'.]

blotch /bloch/ *n.* **1.** **SPOT OR MARK** an irregularly shaped spot or mark **2.** **BLEMISH ON SKIN** a reddish patch on the skin ■ *vti.* (**blotches, blotching, blotched**) **MARK WITH BLOTCHES** to mark or become marked with blotches [Early 17thC. Blend of BLOT and BOTCH.] —**blotchily** *adv.* —**blotchiness** *n.* —**blotchy** *adj.*

blotter /blóttər/ *n.* **1.** **PIECE OF BLOTTING PAPER** a sheet of blotting paper that absorbs ink or water **2.** *US* **LOGBOOK** a book used for recording daily events and transactions ○ *a police blotter*

blotter acid *n.* blotting paper impregnated with LSD, designed to be a convenient form of taking single doses

blotting paper *n.* soft paper used for soaking up ink from paper

blotto /blóttō/ *adj.* extremely inebriated (*slang*) [Early 20thC. Formed obscurely from BLOT, noun or verb.]

blouse /blowz/ (**blouses, blousing, bloused,** *plural* **blouses**) *n.* **1.** **WOMAN'S SHIRT** a woman's loose-fitting shirt **2.** **PEASANT SMOCK** a loose-fitting shirt or smock, often part of peasant dress **3.** **CADET'S OR SOLDIER'S TUNIC** a tunic, sometimes loose and sometimes very snug, that is a part of some military uniforms [Early 19thC. From French, of unknown origin.]

blouson /blóo zon/ *n.* **1.** **GARMENT LIKE A SHIRT** a woman's garment resembling a shirt that is gathered at the waist **2.** **SHORT JACKET** a short jacket that fits closely at the waist and becomes looser over the upper body [Early 20thC. From French.]

blow¹ /blō/ *v.* (**blows, blowing, blew** /bloo/, **blown** /blōn/) **1.** *vi.* **BE MOVING AS AIR** to be moving as a current of air ○ *It blew all night.* **2.** *vti.* **MOVE WITH AIR CURRENT** to move sth with a current of air, especially air exhaled through the mouth ○ *I blew the dust off the shelf.* **3.** *vti.* **EXHALE** to send a stream of air out from the mouth ○ *She blew on her soup* **4.** *vt.* **MAKE BY BLOWING** to make bubbles or smoke rings by sending a stream of air out from the mouth **5.** *vt.* **CLEAR NOSE** to clear the nose by forcing air through it **6.** *vt.* CRAFT **SHAPE HOT GLASS** to give shape to molten glass by forcing air into it **7.** *vti.* MUSIC **SOUND BY BLOWING** to make a sound from a musical instrument by blowing air into it, or to emit a sound when blown **8.** *vt.* **SEND A KISS** to send sb a symbolic kiss by kissing your hand and then blowing across it **9.** *vi.* ZOOL **EXPEL MOIST AIR** to expel moist air from the lungs up through the blowhole (*refers to whales, dolphins, and other cetaceans*) **10.** *vi.* **BREATHE HARD** to breathe hard or pant through exertion **11.** *vt.* **EXHAUST HORSE** to cause a horse to breathe hard through overexertion **12.** *vti.* **DESTROY OR MOVE BY EXPLOSION** to destroy or displace sth or sb violently ○ *The blast blew the roof off.* **13.** *vt.* **OPEN BY FORCE** to break open sth that is firmly shut using explosives **14.** *vti.* CARS **PUNCTURE** to cause or experience a puncture (*informal*) **15.** *vti.* ELEC **CAUSE FUSE TO BURN OUT** to burn out and break an electrical circuit, or to cause a piece of equipment to do this ○ *The toaster blew when I plugged it in.* **16.** *vti.* **BREAK BECAUSE OF PRESSURE** to cause sth to rupture under excess pressure, or to undergo this process **17.** *vt.* **MISS AN OPPORTUNITY** to fail to take advantage of an opportunity (*slang*) **18.** *vt.* **WASTE MONEY** to spend money wastefully (*slang*) ○ *blew a bundle of dough on fast cars* **19.** *vt. US* **ENTERTAIN LAVISHLY** to treat or entertain sb lavishly (*informal*) ○ *The company blew us to a massive dinner.* **20.** *vt.* **EXPOSE** to expose sth secret (*slang*) ○ *blew his cover* **21.** *vt.* **DISREGARD** to disregard sth as trivial (*slang dated*) (*usually used as a command*) ○ *Blow the expense!* **22.** (*past participle* **blowed**) *vt.* **EXPRESSING SURPRISE** used to express surprise (*dated informal*) ○ *Blow me down, look who's here!* **23.** *vti. US* **LEAVE A PLACE SUDDENLY** to leave a place suddenly (*slang*) ○ *When the cops arrived, the thieves blew* **24.** *vti.* MUSIC **PLAY MUSIC INFORMALLY** to play music, especially informally or with other musicians (*slang*) **25.** *vt. US* **INHALE DRUG** to inhale a drug (*slang*) **26.** *vt.* **FELLATE** to fellate (*slang offensive*) **27.** *vt.* **CAPTURE PIECE IN DRAUGHTS** to capture a piece in draughts ■ *interj.* **blow, blow it** **EXPRESSING ANNOYANCE** used to express annoyance (*informal*) ■ *n.* **1.** **ACT OF BLOWING** an act of blowing **2.** **STRONG WIND** a strong wind (*informal*) **3.** **SHORT WALK** a short walk in order to get some fresh air (*informal*) ○ *We went for a blow along the cliffs.* **4.** MUSIC **JAM SESSION** a jam session (*slang*) **5.** *US, ANZ* **BOAST** an act of boasting (*informal*) **6.** **CANNABIS** cannabis (*slang*) **7.** *US* **COCAINE** the drug cocaine (*slang*) **8.** *ANZ* AGRIC **SHEAR STROKE** a stroke of the shears in sheep-shearing [Old English *blāwan*. Ultimately from an Indo-European word that is also the ancestor of English *bladder, flatulent,* and *inflate*.] ◇ **blow a fuse** *or* **gasket** to lose your temper (*informal*) ◇ **blow it** to spoil your chances of success (*slang*)

blow away *vt.* (*slang*) **1.** **KILL** to shoot sb dead **2.** *US* **DEFEAT DECISIVELY** to subject sb to an overwhelming defeat **3.** *US* **OVERWHELM** to affect sb emotionally ○ *an epic movie that just blew me away*

blow in *vi.* **1.** **ARRIVE** to arrive or enter a place in a casual way (*slang*) ○ *blew in at midnight from Toronto* **2.** **START PRODUCING** to start producing oil (*refers to oil wells*)

blow off *v.* **1.** *vti.* TECH, ENG **RELEASE GAS** to release a gas or liquid under pressure. ◊ **blow out 2.** *vi.* **FART** to noisily release stomach gases through the anus (*slang*) **3.** *vt. US* **FAIL TO MEET** to disregard an obligation to meet sb (*slang*) ○ *Lee blew me off, so I'm free for lunch.*

blow out *v.* **1.** *vti.* **EXTINGUISH** to extinguish a flame with a blast of air or wind **2.** *vr.* METEOROL **DIE DOWN** to return to a state of calm after a storm (*refers to storms and winds*) **3.** *vi.* CARS **PUNCTURE** to puncture suddenly and at speed (*refers to tyres*) **4.** *vi.* TECH, INDUST **EMIT UNCONTROLLABLY** to release oil or gas explosively (*refers to gas or oil wells*) **5.** *vi.* **OVERINDULGE** to overindulge in food or drink (*informal*) **6.** *vt.* **CANCEL MEETING** to cancel a meeting or a performance (*slang*)

blow over *vi.* **1.** **DIE DOWN** to become less violent (*refers to storms*) **2.** **BE FORGOTTEN** to no longer excite strong feelings (*informal*) ○ *It was quite a scandal but it all blew over.*

blow up *v.* **1.** *vti.* **DESTROY BY EXPLOSION** to destroy sth or kill sb by causing an explosion, or to be destroyed in this way **2.** *vti.* **INFLATE** to blow air into sth so that it becomes swollen, or to swell as a result of being filled with air **3.** *vt.* PHOTOGRAPHY **ENLARGE IMAGE** to enlarge a photograph **4.** *vi.* **BECOME ANGRY** to lose your temper suddenly (*informal*) **5.** *vi.* **BEGIN TO BLOW** to begin to develop or gather force (*refers to winds or storms*) **6.** *vi.* **ARISE OR COME ABOUT** to develop, often unexpectedly, into sth more serious **7.** *vt.* **EXAGGERATE** exaggerate the value or importance of sth (*informal*) ○ *This affair has been blown up out of all proportion.*

blow² /blō/ *n.* **1.** **HARD HIT** a hard hit with a fist or weapon ○ *a nasty blow on the head* **2.** **ACTION HELPING CAUSE** an important action that helps a cause or belief ○ *They struck an important blow for civil rights.* **3.** **SETBACK** a sudden setback ○ *a blow to his confidence* [15thC. Originally northern English and Scottish dialect *blaw*, of uncertain origin: perhaps ultimately from a prehistoric Germanic word meaning 'to strike'.]

blow³ /blō/ (**blows, blowing, blew** /bloo/, **blown** /blōn/) *vti.* to blossom or to cause sth to blossom [Old English *blōwan*. Ultimately from a prehistoric Germanic word that is also the ancestor of English *bloom*.]

Blow /blō/, **John** (1649–1708) English composer. He was organist of Westminster Abbey and a prolific composer of church music.

blowback /blṓ bak/ *n.* **1.** MECH ENG **REARWARD FLOW OF GASES** the reverse flow of gases in a system, e.g., through the carburettor of an internal-combustion engine during the compression cycle **2.** **FIREARM POWER RESIDUE** the powdery residue that is released or ejected upon firing bullets or shells from a weapon **3.** **REACTION** a reaction or effect resulting from an action or cause, usually a negative reaction (*informal*) ○ *The blowback from the press revelations was terrific.*

blow-by-blow *adj.* describing sth in great detail ○ *a blow-by-blow account* [From the idea of commenting on the sequence of punches at a boxing match]

blow-dry *vt.* **STYLE HAIR WITH HAIRDRYER** to dry and style hair using a hairdryer ■ *n.* **BLOW-DRIED HAIRSTYLE** a hairstyle produced by blow-drying

blower /blṓ ər/ *n.* **1.** **BLOWING MACHINE** a machine that produces a current of air or gas ○ *a leaf blower* **2.** **LOW-PRESSURE COMPRESSOR** an air compressor that produces air at low pressure **3.** **THE TELEPHONE** the telephone (*dated informal*)

blowfish /blṓ fish/ (*plural* **-fish** *or* **-fishes**) *n.* = **puffer**

blowfly /blṓ flī/ (*plural* **-flies**) *n.* a large fly such as a bluebottle that lays its eggs in rotting meat, in dung, or in open wounds. Family: Calliphoridae. [Early 19thC. '*Blow*' from BLOW, in the sense 'to deposit eggs'.]

blowgun /blṓ gun/ *n. US* = **blowpipe**

blowhard /blṓ haard/ *n. US* sb who boasts but is considered ineffectual [Mid-19thC. *Blow* from BLOW, in the sense 'to boast'.]

blowhole /blṓ hōl/ n. 1. MARINE BIOL NOSTRIL OF WHALE OR SIMILAR MAMMAL a nostril in the top of the head of a whale, dolphin, or similar sea mammal that allows the exchange of air from the lungs 2. MARINE BIOL BREATHING HOLE IN ICE a hole in ice where aquatic mammals come to the surface to breathe 3. CIV ENG AIR VENT a vent to permit the escape of air or gas from a tunnel or passage 4. NZ GEOL VOLCANIC VENT a vent or hole in the ground in a volcanic or thermal area through which gas or steam is forced out

blowie /blṓ i/ n. Aus a blowfly (informal) [Mid-20thC. Shortening.]

blow-in n. ANZ sb who has just arrived, especially sb who is unfamiliar or unwelcome (informal)

blow job n. the act of fellatio (slang offensive)

blowlamp n. = blowtorch

blown past participle of blow[1]

blowoff /blṓ of/, **blow-off** n. TECH, INDUST 1. DISCHARGE OF SURPLUS STEAM a discharge of surplus gas or fluid under pressure 2. VENT FOR GAS OR LIQUID a device through which surplus gas or liquid under pressure is released

blowout /blṓ owt/ n. 1. TYRE PUNCTURE a sudden puncture of a tyre 2. FAILURE OF FUSE a sudden burning of a fuse, caused by an electrical overload 3. GUSH OF OIL OR GAS a sudden rush of oil or gas from an oil well to the surface 4. = flameout 5. BIG PARTY a big party with ample food and drink (slang)

blowpipe /blṓ pīp/ n. 1. ARMS TUBE FOR SHOOTING DARTS a long narrow tube through which darts or pellets are shot by blowing. US term blowgun 2. CHEM TUBE FOR CONCENTRATING HEAT a small tube that leads a jet of air into a flame to increase its heat 3. CRAFT GLASSBLOWER'S TUBE a long narrow iron tube used in glassblowing to shape molten glass

blowsy adj. = blowzy

blowtorch /blṓ tawrch/, **blowlamp** /blṓ lamp/ n. = blowlamp

blowup /blṓ up/, **blow-up** n. 1. PHOTOGRAPHY PHOTOGRAPHIC ENLARGEMENT an enlargement of a photograph or picture 2. OUTBURST OF TEMPER a sudden outburst of temper (informal) 3. EXPLOSION an explosion caused by a bomb or similar device

blowy /blṓ i/ (-ier, -iest) adj. windy or breezy (informal)

blowzy /blṓwzi/ (-zier, -ziest), **blowsy** (-sier, -siest) adj. 1. RED-FACED with a reddish face and coarse complexion (disapproving) 2. SLOVENLY slovenly and careless in appearance [Early 17thC. Formed from obsolete blowze 'wench'.] —**blowzily** adv. —**blowziness** n.

BLT (plural BLTs or BLT's) n. a sandwich with a filling of bacon, lettuce, and tomato

blubber /blúbbər/ v. (-bers, -bering, -bered) (informal) 1. vi. SOB LOUDLY to sob in a loud and unattractive manner 2. vt. SAY WHILE SOBBING to say sth while sobbing ■ n. 1. FAT OF MARINE MAMMALS the insulating fat of whales and other large sea mammals, used as a source of oil and food 2. UNSIGHTLY FAT unsightly body fat (informal) [14thC. Origin uncertain: perhaps an imitation of the sound of bubbling water. 'Fat' may come from the sense 'fish's entrails', from their bubbling appearance when ripped open.] —**blubberer** n. —**blubbery** adj.

bludge /bluj/ v. (bludges, bludging, bludged) ANZ (informal) 1. vi. LIVE OFF OTHERS to live off sb else's earnings or on state benefits 2. vt. AVOID WORK to avoid work and shirk responsibilities 3. vti. CADGE to cadge ■ n. ANZ EASY TASK an easy task (informal) [Early 20thC. Back-formation from bludger 'one taking profit without work', earlier 'pimp', contraction of bludgeoner.] —**bludger** n.

bludgeon /blújjən/ n. SHORT CLUB a short stout club used as a weapon ■ vt. (-eons, -eoning, -eoned) 1. HIT WITH HEAVY OBJECT to hit sb repeatedly with a heavy object ○ bludgeoned to death 2. COERCE OR BULLY to coerce or bully sb into doing sth [Mid-18thC. Origin unknown.] —**bludgeoner** n.

blue /blṓ/ adj. (bluer, bluest) 1. OF THE COLOUR OF THE SKY having the colour of the sky on a cloudless day, or any similar shade 2. SLIGHTLY PURPLE IN SKIN COLOUR with the skin appearing slightly purple because of cold, bruising, or exertion 3. BIOL BLUEISH used to describe animals and plants that are blueish or blue-grey in colour ○ a blue whale ○ a blue spruce 4. DEPRESSED

depressed, or accompanied by feelings of depression (informal) ○ feeling blue ○ a blue day 5. EXPLICIT depicting or referring to sex in an explicit or offensive way (informal) 6. CONSERVATIVE holding or supporting right-wing views ■ n. 1. COLOUR OF THE SKY the colour of the sky on a cloudless day. Blue lies toward one end of the visible spectrum and is one of the three primary colours of light and pigment. 2. BLUE PIGMENT a blue dye or pigment 3. THE DISTANCE the far distance (informal) ○ disappeared off into the blue 4. blue, Blue OXBRIDGE ATHLETE sb who has represented Oxford or Cambridge University at a particular sport in a match between the two universities, thus winning the right to wear the university's colours, dark blue for Oxford and light blue for Cambridge 5. ARCHERY BLUE RING ON TARGET the blue ring on the target in archery 6. BLUE BALL IN SNOOKER the blue ball in snooker and similar games 7. blue, Blue US MEMBER OF UNION ARMY a member of the Union Army in the American Civil War. ◊ grey n. 4 8. ANZ FIGHT a fight or quarrel (slang) 9. ANZ MISTAKE a mistake or error (informal) 10. blue, Blue ANZ RED-HAIRED PERSON sb with red hair (informal) 11. ZOOL SMALL-WINGED BLUE BUTTERFLY a common blue small-winged butterfly. Subfamily: Plebeiinae. ■ v. (blues, blueing or bluing, blued) 1. vti. MAKE OR BECOME BLUE to make sth blue or to become blue 2. vt. TREAT WITH BLUING to treat sth with bluing 3. vt. SQUANDER MONEY to spend money wastefully (dated informal disapproving) [13thC. From Old French bleu. Ultimately from an Indo-European word whose meaning evolved from 'yellow' via 'white' and 'pale' to 'livid, the colour of bruised skin'. In the sense 'to squander' perhaps an alteration of BLOW.] —**blueness** n. ◊ out of the blue unexpectedly ○ The offer came out of the blue.

blue baby n. a baby born with a bluish skin colour (cyanosis) as a result of a congenital heart defect that causes the mixing of venous and arterial blood

blueback salmon /blṓ bak-/ (plural blueback salmon) n. = sockeye

blue bag n. a small bag containing bluing for use in laundering [From the colour of the bag]

bluebeard /blṓ beerd/, **Bluebeard** n. a man who marries and then kills successive wives [Early 19thC. Named after Blue Beard, a translation of French Barbe Bleue, a character in a story by Charles Perrault (1628–1703).]

Bluebell

bluebell /blṓ bel/ n. 1. EUROPEAN WOODLAND PLANT a woodland plant of the lily family that has long thin leaves and small blue bell-shaped flowers. Genus: Endymion. 2. = harebell 3. US PLANT OF EASTERN N AMERICA a plant of the borage family, native to eastern North America, that has showy blue flowers. Genus: Mertenia.

blueberry /blṓbəri/ (plural -ries) n. 1. SHRUB WITH EDIBLE BERRIES a shrub of the heath family that has tubular flowers and bears small edible bluish-black berries. Genus: Vaccinium. 2. BERRY the edible dark-blue berry of the blueberry plant, popular in pies and muffins

bluebird /blṓ burd/ n. 1. N AMERICAN SONGBIRD a North American thrush that has bright blue plumage with a bluish or reddish-brown breast. Genus: Sialia. 2. BLUE BIRD any bird with blue feathers

blue-black adj. black tinged with blue or with a blue sheen when caught by the light —**blue-black** n.

blue blood, **blueblood** n. 1. NOBLE DESCENT the quality of being royal or aristocratic by birth 2. ARISTOCRAT an aristocrat, or a noble, or a person born into a

respectable and very wealthy family —**blue-blooded** adj.

bluebonnet /blṓ bonit/ n. 1. PLANT WITH SPIKES OF BLUE FLOWERS either of two low-growing lupins, native to Texas, with spikes of light blue flowers. Latin name: Lupinus texensis and Lupinus subcarnosus. 2. = Balmoral n. 2

blue book n. 1. LIST OF ELITE a real or imaginary book listing names and details of socially prominent people (informal) 2. GOVERNMENT REPORT an official government report bound in a blue cover, especially one published by the British or Canadian government

bluebottle /blṓ bott'l/ n. 1. INSECTS LARGE BUZZING FLY a large buzzing blowfly with an iridescent blue body that lays its eggs in decaying plant and animal material. Genus: Calliphora. 2. PLANTS BLUE-FLOWERED PLANT a blue-flowered plant, especially the cornflower or grape hyacinth 3. ANZ PORTUGUESE MAN-OF-WAR a Portuguese man-of-war (informal)

blue cheese n. any whitish cheese with veins of blue mould

blue chip n. 1. STOCK EXCH VALUABLE STOCK IN RELIABLE COMPANY a stock selling for a high price because it belongs to a company that is considered to be well-established, highly successful, and reliable 2. BUSINESS VALUABLE ASSET OR COMPANY an extremely valuable asset, especially a well-established, reliable, and successful company 3. GAMBLING POKER CHIP a blue-coloured gambling chip of high value —**blue-chip** adj.

blue-chipper n. US BUSINESS a blue-chip company

blue cod (plural blue cod or blue cods) n. a sea fish, related to perches, that is a popular food in New Zealand. Latin name: Parapercis colias.

blue-collar adj. relating to, typical of, or belonging to workers who do manual or industrial work, and who often require work clothes or protective clothing. ◊ white-collar, pink-collar [Mid-20thC. From the clothing typically worn by such workers.] —**blue-collar** n.

blue devils npl. depression or low spirits (dated slang)

blue duck (plural blue ducks or blue duck) n. a grey-blue mountain duck native to New Zealand. Latin name: Hymenolaimus malacorhynchos.

Blue Ensign n. a blue flag with a Union Jack at the top inner corner, flown by auxiliary vessels of the Royal Navy and by some yacht clubs

blue-eyed boy n. sb who is the favourite of another person or group (informal) US term fair-haired boy

blue-eyed soul n. soul music written and played by white musicians (informal)

bluefish /blṓ fish/ (plural -fish or -fishes) n. 1. BLUISH SEA FISH a bluish fish with a silver underside, caught for sport and food in temperate and tropical regions of the Atlantic and Indian oceans. Latin name: Pomatomus saltatrix. 2. ANY BLUISH FISH any fish with bluish colouring

blue fox n. 1. ARCTIC FOX an Arctic fox with a tawny-brown coat that turns pale blue-grey in winter. Latin name: Alopex lagopus. 2. BLUE FOX FUR the fur of a blue fox

blue funk n. (dated informal) 1. STATE OF TERROR a state of great fear 2. US SAD MOOD a state of depression

bluegill /blṓ gil/ (plural -gills or -gill) n. a freshwater sunfish common in eastern and central North America. Latin name: Lepomis macrochirus.

bluegrass /blṓ graass/ n. 1. MUSIC STYLE OF COUNTRY MUSIC a style of country music from the southern United States, usually played on fiddle, banjo, guitar, mandolin and featuring close harmony and instrumental solos (often used before a noun) 2. BOT BLUE-GREEN GRASS a blue-green grass found in North America and Europe, used for fodder and as a lawn grass. Kentucky bluegrass is one species of bluegrass. Genus: Poa. [Mid-18thC. Originally referring to a species of grass indigenous to Kentucky and Virginia, the word came to refer to the folk-music associated with these areas.]

blue-green algae *npl.* BIOL = **cyanobacteria**

blue ground *n.* unweathered kimberlite rock lying beneath an oxidized yellow surface layer. Kimberlites occur in volcanic pipes and are the main source of diamonds.

blue gum *n.* **1.** HARD-TIMBERED AUSTRALIAN EUCALYPTUS a tall Australian eucalyptus tree, native to Tasmania, with hard timber and aromatic leaves from which a medicinal oil is extracted. Latin name: *Eucalyptus globulus.* **2.** AUSTRALIAN EUCALYPTUS an Australian eucalyptus tree that has smooth blue-grey bark. Genus: *Eucalyptus.*

blue heeler *n. Aus* **1.** AUSTRALIAN CATTLE DOG a dog with a blue-speckled coat, belonging to an Australian breed used for controlling cattle (*informal*) **2.** POLICE OFFICER a police officer (*slang*) [*Heeler* from the dog's practice of urging cattle on by biting their heels]

blueing *n.* = **bluing**

blueish *adj.* = **bluish**

blue jay *n.* a North American bird that belongs to the jay family and has blue plumage, a crested head, and a white underside. Latin name: *Cyanocitta cristata.*

blue jeans *npl. US* a pair of jeans made of blue denim

blue john *n.* a blue or purple form of the mineral fluorspar found only in Derbyshire

blue law *n.* **1.** US MORAL LAW in the United States, a law regulating moral conduct, e.g. a law prohibiting the sale of alcohol on Sundays **2.** OLD AMERICAN LAW GOVERNING MORAL CONDUCT a law intended to govern moral conduct in colonial New England [*Blue* in the US sense of 'puritanical']

blue line *n.* either of two blue lines that divide an ice hockey rink into the defensive, neutral, and offensive zones

Blue Mantle *n.* one of the four lowest-ranked heraldic officers of the British College of Arms

blue moon *n.* **1.** LONG TIME a long period of time (*informal*) ○ *once in a blue moon* **2.** 2ND FULL MOON IN A MONTH a second full moon in a calendar month. As there is a full moon every 29.5 days, a blue moon is a comparatively rare event. [From the notion of the moon appearing blue, a rare if not unheard of event. Sense 2 from the rarity of the phenomenon.]

Blue Mountains plateau region about 65 km/47 mi. west of Sydney, Australia, part of the Great Dividing Range. Its highest point is Bird Rock, 1,134 m/3,871 ft. Area: 1,400 sq. km/540 sq. mi.

blue murder *n.* a great noise of shouting (*informal*) ○ *screaming blue murder*

Blue Nile /-nīl/ river in northeastern Africa that rises in Ethiopia and supplies about 70 per cent of the water that reaches Khartoum, where it joins the White Nile to form the Nile proper. Length: 1,370 km/850 mi.

bluenose /bloo nōz/ *n.* **1.** US PURITANICAL PERSON sb who is excessively concerned with morals (*dated informal*) **2.** *Can* NOVA SCOTIAN sb from Nova Scotia (*informal*) [In the sense 'puritanical person', compare BLUE LAW]

blue note *n.* a musical note played or sung slightly lower than usual, especially in blues and jazz

blue-pencil (**blue-pencils, blue-pencilling, blue-pencilled**) *vt.* to edit a piece of writing by marking it, in order to shorten, censor, or delete it [From the use of a blue pencil in the editing process]

Blue Peter *n.* a blue flag with a white square in the middle, used by ships to signal that they are ready to sail [*Peter* from *Peter*, personal name, from the fact that the pattern on the flag represents the letter P in the International Code of Symbols]

blue-plate *adj. US* used to describe a main course offered by a restaurant at a lower price than usual ○ *We had the blue-plate special.* [Origin uncertain: probably from the fact that specially priced meals were often served on cheap, blue-patterned plates]

blue point *n.* a domestic cat, especially a Siamese, that has a bluish-cream coat and dark grey markings on its extremities (**points**). ◊ **seal point**

blueprint /bloo print/ *n.* **1.** PRINT OF PLAN a photographic print of a technical drawing with white lines printed on a blue background, usually used as a reference before and during the building process **2.** PLAN OR GUIDE a plan of action, or sth already done that can be used as a guide to doing sth in future ○ *His administration's policies became a blueprint for those that followed.* ■ *vt.* (**-prints, -printing, -printed**) **1.** MAKE BLUEPRINT OF to make a blueprint of sth, especially a technical drawing **2.** MAKE PLAN FOR to make or be a plan for sth

blue racer *n.* a blue-green subspecies of the blacksnake that is found in the United States from Michigan to Texas. Latin name: *Coluber constrictor flaviventris.*

blue riband *n.* the highest distinction or first prize in a particular field. US term **blue ribbon** —**blue-riband** *adj.*

blue ribbon *n.* **1.** BADGE MADE OF BLUE RIBBON an emblem or badge made of blue ribbon and awarded for first prize in a competition **2.** *US* = **blue riband** **3.** BADGE OF ORDER OF THE GARTER a badge made of blue ribbon, worn by members of the Order of the Garter —**blue-ribbon** *adj.*

Blue Ridge, **Blue Ridge Mountains** mountain range in the United States, extending from northern Georgia across western North Carolina and into West Virginia. It is the easternmost range of the Appalachian Mountains, with its highest point at Mount Mitchell 2,037 m/6,684 ft.

blue runner *n.* ZOOL = **runner** *n.* 16

blues[1] /blooz/ *n.* (*plural* **blues**) MUSIC PIECE OF MUSIC a song or instrumental piece of music in the style of a type of popular music that developed from Black American folk songs in the early 20th century, consisting mainly of slow sad songs often performed over a repeating harmonic pattern (*takes a singular or plural verb*) ■ *npl.* FEELING OF SADNESS a feeling of unhappiness or low spirits (*informal*) [Mid-18thC. From BLUE DEVILS.]

blues[2] /blooz/ *n. Carib* (*slang*) **1.** TRINIDAD HUNDRED DOLLAR BILL a Trinidadian hundred dollar bill, which is blue in colour **2.** PORNOGRAPHIC FILM an obscene film

Blues /blooz/ *npl.* the Royal Horse Guards

blue shark *n.* a shark that has a dark blue back and white underside and lives in tropical and temperate seas. Latin name: *Prionace glauca.*

blue sheep *n.* = **bharal**

blueshift /bloo shift/ *n.* a displacement in the wavelengths of spectral lines towards the blue end of the visible spectrum, indicating that the radiation source and observer are approaching each other. ◊ **Doppler effect, redshift**

blue-sky *adj.* (*informal*) **1.** THEORETICAL purely theoretical and having no concrete goal **2.** CREATIVE OR IMPRACTICAL idealistic or visionary and not practical —**blue-sky** *vi.*

bluesman /bloozmən/ (*plural* **-men** /-mən/) *n.* sb who plays or sings the blues

blue spruce *n.* a common North American evergreen tree of the Rocky Mountains with short sharp blue-grey needles. Latin name: *Picea pungens.*

bluestocking /bloo stoking/ *n.* a woman who is highly educated or has scholarly or literary interests (*offensive*)

───── **WORD KEY: ORIGIN** ─────

At the literary gatherings held at the houses of fashionable mid-18th-century hostesses, it became the custom to wear casual rather than full formal dress. In the case of gentlemen's stockings, this meant grey worsted (conventionally called 'blue' at that time) rather than black silk. This lack of decorum was disapproved of in some quarters, and one Admiral Boscowan dubbed the participants the 'Blue Stocking Society'. Women who attended their highbrow meetings thus became known as 'Blue Stocking Ladies' (even though it was men who had originally worn the stockings).

bluestone /bloo stōn/ *n.* **1.** BUILDING BLUE-GREY BUILDING STONE a blue-grey sandstone used in the construction industry or for paving **2.** CHEM CRYSTALLINE COPPER SUL-

PHATE the blue mineral form of copper sulphate that occurs naturally as crystals

blue streak *n.* a fast-moving person or thing (*informal humorous*) ◊ **talk a blue streak** *US* to talk very quickly and without pausing (*informal*)

bluesy /bloozi/ (**bluesier, bluesiest**) *adj.* composed or performed in or like the style of the blues (*informal*) ○ *a bluesy ballad*

bluetit /bloo tit/ (*plural* **-tits** *or* **-tit**) *n.* a small bird of the tit family that is common in Europe and has a blue cap, blue in its wings and tail, and a yellow breast. Latin name: *Parus caeruleus.*

bluetongue /bloo tung/ (*plural* **-tongues** *or* **-tongue**), **blue-tongued lizard** *n.* a Australian lizard that displays its bright blue tongue when threatened. Genus: *Tiliqua.*

bluets /bloo its/ (*plural* **-ets**) *n.* a North American plant of the madder family with small, pale blue to white, four-petalled flowers with yellow centres. Genus: *Hedyotis.* (*takes a singular or plural verb*) [Early 18thC. Plural of *bluet*, from French *bl(e)uet*, literally 'small blue', from *bleu* 'blue' (see BLUE).]

blue vitriol *n.* copper sulphate (*archaic*)

blue water *n.* the ocean far away from the shore (*literary*)

Blue whale

blue whale (*plural* **blue whales** *or* **blue whale**) *n.* a slate-blue whale with grooves along the throat that migrates between polar and equatorial seas. It is the world's largest living animal. Latin name: *Balaenoptera musculus.*

bluff[1] /bluf/ *v.* (**bluffs, bluffing, bluffed**) **1.** *vti.* PRETEND TO BE CONFIDENT to pretend to have strength, confidence, or the intention of doing sth, in order to deceive sb **2.** *vti.* CARDS DECEIVE PLAYERS ABOUT CARDS to try to deceive other players in a card game about the true value of your hand **3.** *vt. Malaysia, Singapore* DECEIVE SB IN MINOR WAY to try to mislead sb about sth relatively unimportant (*informal*) ■ *n.* FEIGNED CONFIDENCE a pretence of strength, confidence, or of the intention of doing sth [Late 17thC. From Dutch *bluffen* 'to brag' or *bluf* 'bragging'.] —**bluffable** *adj.* —**bluffer** *n.*

bluff[2] /bluf/ *n.* CLIFF WITH BROAD FACE a high steep bank, cliff, or headland, especially one with a broad face ■ *adj.* **1.** STEEP AND BROAD having a broad, flattened, or rounded steep front **2.** BLUNT BUT KIND IN MANNER cheerful and friendly but outspoken and often insensitive to others' feelings [Early 17thC. From Dutch *blaf* 'flat'.] —**bluffly** *adv.* —**bluffness** *n.*

bluing /bloo ing/, **blueing** *n.* a substance used in laundering to prevent white materials turning yellow

bluish /bloo ish/, **blueish** *adj.* of a colour that is near to blue or contains some blue

Blum /bloom/, **Léon** (1872–1950) French politician. The leader of the Socialist Party, he was prime minister of France (1936–37, 1938, 1946–47).

blunder /blúndər/ *n.* STUPID MISTAKE a serious or embarrassing mistake, usually the result of carelessness or ignorance ■ *v.* (**-ders, -dering, -dered**) **1.** *vi.* MAKE A SERIOUS MISTAKE to make a serious or embarrassing mistake as a result of carelessness or ignorance **2.** *vi.* MOVE CLUMSILY to stumble or move clumsily **3.** *vti.* ACT IN A CONFUSED WAY to act in a manner that is clumsy, ignorant, or thoughtless **4.** *vti.* SPEAK IN CLUMSY MANNER to say or write sth in a clumsy or thoughtless way [14thC. Via a Scandinavian language from, ultimately, an Indo-European base that is also the ancestor of English *blind*.] —**blunderer** *n.* —**blunderingly** *adv.*

WORD KEY: SYNONYMS

See Synonyms at **mistake**.

Blunderbuss

blunderbuss /blúndər buss/ *n.* **1.** WIDE-MOUTHED GUN a short, wide-muzzled firearm of the 17th century, used to fire shot with a scattering effect at close range **2.** BLUNDERING PERSON sb who behaves or speaks clumsily (*informal*) [Mid-17thC. Alteration of Dutch *donderbus*, from *donder* 'thunder' + *bus* 'gun'.]

blunge /blunj/ (**blunges, blunging, blunged**) *vt.* to mix clay with water and chemicals to create the material for making pottery commercially [Early 19thC. Blend of PLUNGE and other 'bl-' words such as BLOW or BLEND.]

blunger /blúnjər/ *n.* a machine for mixing clay with water and chemicals to create the material for making pottery commercially

blunt /blunt/ *adj.* **1.** NOT SHARP having a cutting edge or point that is not sharp **2.** FRANK OR HONEST WITHOUT SENSITIVITY very frank or straightforward and showing no delicacy or consideration ■ *v.* (**blunts, blunting, blunted**) **1.** *vti.* MAKE STH LESS SHARP to make the point or cutting edge of sth dull rather than sharp **2.** *vt.* LESSEN OR WEAKEN to make sth such as a sense or an emotion less effective or less intense [13thC. Origin uncertain: possibly from Old Norse *blundr* 'dozing'. Ultimately from the same Indo-European base that is the ancestor of English *blind* and *blunder*.] —**bluntly** *adv.* —**bluntness** *n.*

Blunt /blunt/, **Anthony** (1907–83) British art historian and Soviet spy. He was surveyor of the Queen's pictures (1945–72), but was stripped of his knighthood and disgraced after the public disclosure (1979) of his role as a Soviet spy in the ring that included Guy Burgess and Donald Maclean. Full name **Anthony Frederick Blunt**

blur /blur/ *n.* **1.** FUZZY OR INDISTINCT IMAGE sth that cannot be seen clearly, e.g. because it moves too quickly or because it is not distinctly remembered **2.** SMEAR OR SMEARED AREA a mark on sth that makes it unclear, or an area of sth that is unclear ■ *vti.* (**blurs, blurring, blurred**) **1.** MAKE OR BECOME VAGUE to become less clear or distinct, or to make sth such as an idea less clear or distinct **2.** MAKE OR BECOME FUZZY to become fuzzy or unclear, or to make sth such as sb's vision or an image on paper fuzzy or unclear ■ *adj.* Malaysia, Singapore CONFUSED confused or uncertain about sth (*informal*) ○ *I am very blur about linguistics.* [Mid-16thC. Probably a variant of BLEAR.] —**blurriness** *n.* —**blurry** *adj.*

blurb /blurb/ *n.* a short piece of writing that praises and promotes sth, especially a paragraph on the cover of a book (*slang*) [Early 20thC. A US slang term coined by Gelett Burgess, a US humorist.] —**blurb** *vt.*

blurt /blurt/ (**blurts, blurting, blurted**) *vti.* to say sth suddenly or impulsively, as if by accident ○ *blurted out an apology* [Late 16thC. Probably an imitation of the sound of letting out breath suddenly, modelled on BLOW and SQUIRT.]

blush /blush/ *vi.* (**blushes, blushing, blushed**) **1.** BECOME RED IN FACE to turn red in the face because of emotion, especially embarrassment, shame, modesty, or pleasure **2.** BECOME EMBARRASSED to feel embarrassed or ashamed (*formal*) **3.** TURN RED OR PINK to become red or pink (*literary*) ■ *n.* **1.** REDDENING OF FACE a reddening

of the face caused by emotion, especially embarrassment, shame, modesty, or pleasure **2.** RED OR PINK a red colour or rosy glow **3.** *US* COSMETICS = **blusher 4.** = **blush wine** [Old English *blyscan*. Ultimately from an Indo-European base that is also the ancestor of English *flame*, *blaze*, and *blue*.] —**blushful** *adj.* —**blushing** *adj.* —**blushingly** *adv.*

blusher /blúshər/ *n.* a pink or reddish powder or cream applied to the face, especially to accent the cheekbones. US term **blush**

blush wine *n.* wine with a slight pink tinge

bluster /blústər/ *v.* (**-ters, -tering, -tered**) **1.** *vti.* SPEAK OR UTTER LOUDLY OR ARROGANTLY to speak loudly, boisterously, or arrogantly, or to say sth in this way **2.** *vti.* BEHAVE IN BULLYING WAY to behave or do sth in a bullying or threatening way **3.** *vi.* BLOW LOUDLY IN GUSTS to blow in loud gusts (*refers to wind*) ■ *n.* **1.** LOUD BULLYING OR BRAGGING SPEECH loud arrogant or threatening speech or behaviour **2.** SUDDEN LOUD GUST OF WIND a loud gust of wind **3.** LOUD FUSS a loud or angry commotion [Early 15thC. From Middle Low German *blustern* 'to blow violently'.] —**blusterer** *n.* —**blusteringly** *adv.* —**blustery** *adj.*

Blu-tack *tdmk.* a trademark for a soft malleable substance that is used to stick paper temporarily to walls and other surfaces

Blvd *abbr.* Boulevard

Blyth /blīth/ industrial port in Northumberland, northern England. Population: 35,327 (1991).

Blyth, Chay (*b.* 1940) British yachtsman. He was the first person to sail single-handed around the world travelling east to west (1970–71). Real name **Charles Blyth**

Blyton /blīt'n/, **Enid** (1897–1968) British writer. She was the author of over 600 children's books, including such characters as Noddy and the Famous Five. Full name **Enid Mary Blyton**

bm *abbr.* **1.** board measure **2.** bowel movement

BM *abbr.* **1.** bench mark **2.** British Museum

BMA *abbr.* British Medical Association

BMEWS /beé myoóz/ *abbr.* ballistic missile early warning system

BMI *abbr.* body mass index

BMJ *abbr.* British Medical Journal

B movie *n.* a low-budget film that was formerly shown in addition to the main feature [*B* from its lesser importance than the main feature] —**B-movie** *adj.*

bmp, **BMP** *suffix.* used after the dot in a DOS-based computer file to show that the file is an image stored as a series of pixels

BMus /beé múz/ *abbr.* Bachelor of Music

BMX *n.* the riding of bicycles over rough terrain and open country or a racing course. Full form **bicycle motocross** [Representing an abbreviation of *bicycle motocross*]

bn *abbr.* **1.** billion **2.** Bn battalion

Bn *abbr.* **1.** baron **2.** battalion

B'nai B'rith /bə náy bə reéth, bə náy bríth/ *n.* an international Jewish social service organization founded in New York in 1843 [From Hebrew, 'Sons of the Covenant']

BO *n.* BAD SMELL FROM BODY an unpleasant smell that comes from a person because of sweat, lack of hygiene, or physical disorder (*informal*) Full form **body odour** ■ *abbr.* box office

b.o. *abbr.* **1.** branch office **2.** broker's order **3.** FIN buyer's option

B/O *abbr.* ACCT brought over

boa /bó ə/ *n.* **1.** TROPICAL SNAKE THAT SQUEEZES PREY a nonvenomous, often large, snake that kills by winding its body around its prey and crushing it. Family: Boidae. **2.** LONG FLUFFY SCARF a long fluffy scarf of feathers or fur worn by women around the neck [14thC. From Latin 'large water-snake'.]

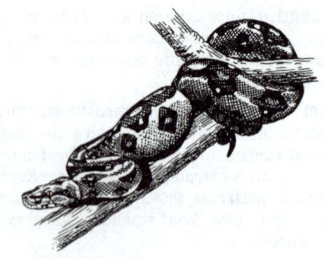

Boa constrictor

boa constrictor *n.* a large snake of the boa family that lives in tropical America and the West Indies and kills by winding its body around its prey and crushing it. Latin name: *Boa constrictor*.

Boadicea = **Boudicca**

Boar

boar /bawr/ (*plural* **boars** *or* **boar**) *n.* **1.** UNCASTRATED PIG a male pig that has not been castrated **2.** MALE MAMMAL a male mammal, e.g. a male badger, beaver, or raccoon **3.** WILD BOAR a wild boar [Old English *bār*]

board /bawrd/ *n.* **1.** FLAT PIECE OF WOOD a piece of wood cut into a flat rectangular shape, especially a long and narrow piece used for building **2.** FLAT SURFACE FOR PARTICULAR PURPOSE a flat piece of wood, plastic, or other rigid material, used for a particular purpose, e.g. chopping food **3.** BOARD GAMES FLAT SURFACE FOR GAME a flat surface on which a game is played, especially a piece of wood or cardboard marked with coloured areas for a particular game such as chess **4.** COMPOSITE MATERIAL PRESSED INTO A SHEET a rigid sheet material made by compressing layers of other materials, e.g. plywood **5.** CONTROL PANEL a panel on which the controls of a piece of electrical equipment are mounted **6.** EDUC = **blackboard 7.** NOTICE BOARD a notice board **8.** NAUT SHIP'S SIDE the side of a ship **9.** ELEC ENG CIRCUIT BOARD a printed circuit board **10.** SWIMMING = **diving board 11.** SPORTS = **surfboard 12.** SPORTS = **scoreboard 13.** SPORTS SNOWBOARD a snowboard **14.** BASKETBALL = **backboard** *n.* 2 **15.** PUBL BOOK COVER either of the pair of pieces of stiff cardboard that together form the front and back covers of a book **16.** GROUP CHOSEN TO MAKE DECISIONS a group of people chosen to make executive or managerial decisions for an organization (*takes a singular or plural verb*) **17.** DAILY MEALS daily meals provided at the place where sb lives, usually for money or in return for work **18.** TABLE WITH FOOD a table used for meals, especially one spread with food (*archaic*) **19.** SAILING DISTANCE SAILED INTO WIND the distance covered by a sailing vessel in one period of sailing as near as possible into the wind **20.** ANZ SHEEP-SHEARING FLOOR the area, sometimes raised like a platform or stage, where sheep are sheared inside a shearing shed ■ **boards** *npl.* SPORTS ICE HOCKEY RINK ENCLOSURE the wooden wall that surrounds an ice hockey rink ■ *v.* (**boards, boarding, boarded**) **1.** *vti.* GET ONTO VEHICLE AS PASSENGER to get onto a vehicle, especially a ship, train, or aircraft, as a passenger **2.** *vti.* TAKE PASSENGERS ON FOR JOURNEY to take passengers onto a ship, plane, or other vehicle ○ *This flight is now boarding.* **3.** *vt.* NAUT ATTACK OR INSPECT SHIP to come alongside a ship in order for people to go from one ship to another for the purposes of attack or inspection **4.** *vti.* COVER STH WITH BOARDS to fix boards onto sth, especially to cover any openings **5.** *vti.* BE PROVIDED WITH ROOM AND MEALS to be provided with accommodation and meals, e.g. in a school or guest house, in return for money or work, or to arrange for this to happen [Old English *bord*, from two related prehistoric Germanic words with the meanings 'board, plank' and 'border, ship's side'] ◇ **bring** *or* **get** *or* **take sb on board** to bring or accept sb, e.g. a new employee, into an existing group or project (*informal*) ◇ **go by the board** to be neglected, no longer used, cast aside, or destroyed ◇ **take sth on board** 1. to understand or realize sth fully 2. to accept or include sth, e.g. a suggestion or new idea

board bridge *n.* BOARD GAMES = **duplicate bridge**

boarder /báwrdər/ *n.* 1. SB PAYING FOR FOOD AND BED sb who pays for a room, and usually for daily meals, in a private home or a boarding house 2. PUPIL LIVING AT SCHOOL a school pupil who lives at the school during term time 3. NAUT SB TRYING TO CAPTURE SHIP sb who attempts to get onto a ship in order to capture or inspect it

board foot (*plural* **board feet**) *n.* a unit of volume for measuring timber, equal to the volume of a board that is one foot square and one inch thick

board game *n.* a game that involves moving pieces around on a board marked with coloured areas for a particular game, e.g. chess or backgammon

boarding card *n.* = **boarding pass**

boarding house *n.* a private home that provides a room and meals to paying guests who are usually long-term residents. ◊ **bed and breakfast**

boarding pass *n.* an additional ticket, or part of a ticket, that sb must have in order to be allowed onto an aircraft or ship as a passenger

boarding school *n.* a school that provides some or all pupils with a place to live and daily meals

Boardman /báwrdmən/, **Chris** (*b.* 1968) British cyclist. He won a gold medal at the Barcelona Olympics (1992) and broke several world pursuit and endurance records in 1996 and 1997. Full name **Christopher Miles Boardman**

board measure *n.* a system for measuring timber volume based on the board foot

Board of Deputies *n.* a representative body that concerns itself with the collective legal and political interests of British Jews

Board of Trade *n.* a British government department that regulates commerce and exports

boardroom /báwrd room, -rŏom/ *n.* a room where the members of a board meet

boardsailing /báwrd sayling/ *n.* = **windsurfing** —**boardsailor** *n.*

board shorts *npl. Aus* knee-length swimming shorts, often worn by surfers

boardwalk /báwrd wawk/ *n.* a raised walkway made of boards, built across marshy ground or sand

boarish /báwrish/ *adj.* brutal or crude ○ *boarish behaviour* —**boarishly** *adv.* —**boarishness** *n.*

Boas /bố az/, **Franz** (1858–1942) German-born US anthropologist. He helped establish anthropology as an academic discipline. He advocated a scientific approach to anthropological investigation and supported the theory of cultural relativism.

boast[1] /bōst/ *v.* (**boasts, boasting, boasted**) 1. *vti.* SPEAK PROUDLY ABOUT POSSESSIONS OR ACCOMPLISHMENTS to praise yourself, or speak arrogantly about things you possess or have achieved 2. *vt.* POSSESS STH DESIRABLE to possess sth, especially sth that is very desirable ○ *Our town boasts the world's biggest roller coaster.* ■ *n.* 1. EXCESSIVELY PROUD STATEMENT sth you say or write that praises yourself, or arrogantly refers to your possessions or achievements 2. DESIRABLE POSSESSION sth possessed that is very desirable [13thC. Via Anglo-Norman *bost* 'boasting' from, ultimately, the Scandinavian base that was also the source of German *böse* 'wicked'.] —**boaster** *n.* —**boastful** *adj.* —**boastfully** *adv.* —**boastfulness** *n.*

boast[2] /bōst/ (**boasts, boasting, boasted**) *vt.* SCULPTURE to shape stone roughly using a chisel [Early 19thC. Origin unknown.]

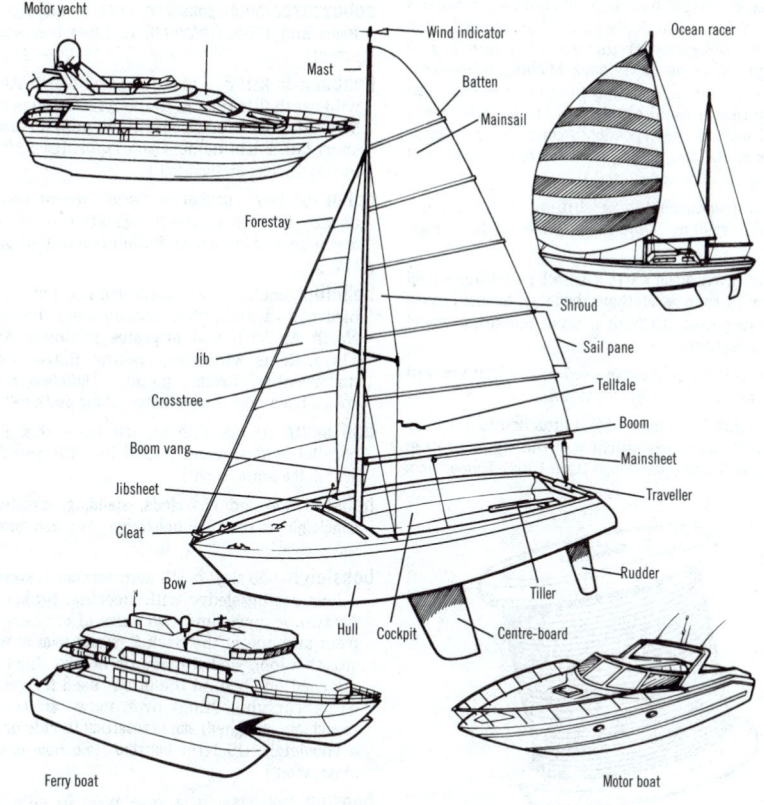

Boat

boat /bōt/ *n.* 1. SMALL VESSEL FOR TRAVELLING ON WATER a small, often open vessel for travelling on water 2. SHIP OR SUBMARINE any water vessel, including a ship or submarine 3. STH SHAPED LIKE A BOAT an open container shaped like a boat, e.g. one for holding gravy or incense ■ *v.* (**boats, boating, boated**) 1. *vi.* TRAVEL BY BOAT to travel by boat or ride in a boat for pleasure 2. *vt.* CARRY BY BOAT to move or transport sth by boat 3. *vt.* ANGLING PULL FISH TO BOAT to bring a caught fish to a boat [Old English *bāt*] ◇ **in the same boat** in the same situation or having the same problems as sb else ◇ **miss the boat** to fail to seize an opportunity ◇ **push the boat out** to spend a lot of money when celebrating sth or entertaining sb (*informal*) ◇ **rock the boat** to cause trouble, especially by questioning an accepted situation (*informal*)

boat deck *n.* a deck on a ship where the lifeboats are carried

boatel /bō tél/, **botel** *n.* 1. HOTEL FOR BOAT-OWNERS a waterside hotel where people travelling in boats can stay and moor their boats 2. SHIP USED AS HOTEL a ship that functions as a hotel [Mid-20thC. Blend of BOAT and HOTEL.]

boater /bốtər/ *n.* 1. STRAW HAT WITH FLAT TOP a straw hat with a flat brim, a flat crown, and a hat band 2. SB USING BOAT sb who travels by boat or rides in a boat for pleasure [12thC. Formed from BOAT; the hat was originally associated with boating.]

boathook /bốt hook/ *n.* a long pole with a hook on one end, used for pulling or pushing boats, rafts, or logs

boathouse /bốt howss/ (*plural* **-houses** /-howziz/) *n.* a small building beside water, in which boats are kept

boating /bốting/ *n.* riding in a boat for pleasure

boatload /bốt lōd/ *n.* 1. AMOUNT THAT FILLS BOAT an amount of sth or a number of people that fills a boat 2. LARGE AMOUNT OR NUMBER a large amount of sth or a large number of people (*informal*)

boatman /bốtmən/ (*plural* **-men** /-mən/) *n.* sb who operates or works on a boat, especially a man who takes people for rides on a boat or who rents boats out to others

boatmanship /bốtmənship/ *n.* the skill of sailing a boat

boat neck *n.* a wide shallow neckline that runs from shoulder to shoulder and is equally deep at the front and back, similar to the neckline of a traditional sailor's blouse

boat people *npl.* refugees who leave their country by boat

Boat Race *n.* 1. ANNUAL RACE BETWEEN OXFORD AND CAMBRIDGE an annual rowing race on the Thames between Oxford and Cambridge Universities, each represented by one boat with a crew of eight 2. **Boat Race, boat race** *Cockney* FACE a face (*rhyming slang*)

boatswain /bốss'n/, **bo's'n**, **bosun** *n.* a noncommissioned officer or a warrant officer on a ship in charge of the maintenance of the vessel, its boats, and other equipment [Old English *bātswegen*, from *bāt*, an earlier form of BOAT + Old Norse *sveinn* 'boy' (see SWAIN)]

boatswain's chair *n.* a board supported by ropes, slung over the side of a ship or up in the rigging so that sb can sit on it while working

boat train *n.* a train that takes people between a dockside and a town, usually timed to coincide with the arrival or departure of a ferry or liner

bob[1] /bob/ *v.* (**bobs, bobbing, bobbed**) 1. *vi.* BOUNCE to bounce up and down quickly and repeatedly, especially in and out of the water while floating 2. *vi.* MAKE CURTSY, BOW, OR NOD to make a quick movement, especially a curtsy, bow, or nod (*archaic*) 3. *vti.* TAP OR CAUSE TO TAP to tap lightly and quickly or to cause sth to tap in this way (*archaic*) ■ *n.* 1. SMALL HANGING OR BOUNCING OBJECT a small hanging or bouncing object, e.g. a curl of hair, a weight on a plumb line, or a fishing bobber 2. CURTSY, BOW, OR NOD a quick movement such as a curtsy, bow, or nod (*archaic*) [14thC. Origin uncertain: probably from earlier *bobben* 'to strike, beat', an imitation of the sound. The meaning was extended to cover a variety of short, quick movements.]

bob[2] /bob/ *n.* **1. WOMAN'S SHORT HAIRCUT** a woman's short haircut, especially a straight cut at chin length **2. STH CUT SHORT** sth that has been cut short, e.g. a horse's tail when docked, a dog's ears when clipped, or a short line of poetry at the end of a stanza **3.** = **bobsleigh** (*informal*) ■ *vt.* (**bobs, bobbing, bobbed**) **CUT HAIR SHORT** to cut a person's hair or a horse's tail short so that it is all one length [14thC. From earlier *bobbe* 'bunch, cluster', possibly from a Celtic language (compare Gaelic *bab* 'tassel, cluster') The meaning 'short haircut' arose in the early 20thC.]

bob[3] /bob/ (*plural* **bob**) *n.* a shilling in the former currency system (*informal*) [Late 18thC. Origin unknown.]

bob[4] /bob/ *n.* **POLISHING WHEEL** a small polishing wheel of felt or leather ■ *vt.* (**bobs, bobbing, bobbed**) **POLISH WITH BOB** to polish sth with a small polishing wheel of felt or leather

Bob /bob/ ◇ **Bob's your uncle** used to say that sth will be easy or simple to do (*informal*)

bobber /bóbbər/ *n.* a light object attached to a fishing line that floats on the surface of the water to keep the bait at the proper depth [Late 18thC. Formed from BOB[1].]

Bobbin

bobbin /bóbbin/ *n.* **1. CYLINDER WOUND WITH THREAD OR WIRE** a cylinder on which thread, yarn, or wire is wound, to be unwound as it is used, especially for sewing, spinning, weaving, knitting, or making lace. ◇ **spindle, reel 2. CORD USED AS TRIM** a narrow cotton cord, often braided, formerly used as a trimming or binding in dressmaking [Mid-16thC. Via French *bobine* 'sewing instrument' from Old French *balbiner*, probably an alteration of *balbier* 'to stutter', from, ultimately, Latin *balbus* 'stuttering'.]

bobbinet /bóbbi nét/ *n.* a machine-made net fabric with a hexagonal mesh

bobbin lace *n.* a lace made by winding thread by hand around bobbins or pins stuck into a pillow

bobble /bóbb'l/ *n.* **1. WOOLLEN BALL** a woollen ball used as decoration on clothing, especially on a woollen hat **2. UP-AND-DOWN MOVEMENT** a fast repeated up-and-down movement ■ *vti.* (**-bles, -bling, -bled**) **MOVE UP AND DOWN** to move, or to cause sth to move, quickly and repeatedly up and down [Early 19thC. Probably formed from BOB[1].]

bobble hat *n.* a woollen hat with a woollen ball on its crown as decoration

bobbol *n.* Carib = **bobol** (*slang*)

bobby /bóbbi/ (*plural* **-bies**) *n.* a policeman (*dated informal*) [Mid-19thC. From the diminutive of the personal name 'Robert', after Sir Robert Peel, who introduced the 1828 Police Act.]

bobby calf (*plural* **bobby calves**) *n.* a male calf of a dairy cow that is slaughtered before weaning and used for veal. Such calves, e.g. those of the Channel Island breed, are generally unsuitable for rearing as beef. [*Bobby* 'small, short', of uncertain origin: probably from BOB[2]]

bobby-dazzler *n.* an excellent thing or person, especially an attractive woman (*dated informal*) [From *bobby*, of unknown origin + DAZZLER]

bobby pin *n.* US, Can, ANZ = **hairgrip** [Probably from the use of BOB[2] to denote a hairstyle]

bobby socks, **bobby sox** *npl.* US ankle socks that fold over at the top, popular among teenage girls in the 1940s and 1950s [*Bobby* 'small, short', of uncertain origin: probably formed from BOB[2]]

bobbysoxer /bóbbi soksər/ *n.* US a teenage girl of the 1940s and 1950s (*informal*) [Because they wore BOBBY SOCKS]

bobcat /bób kat/ *n.* a medium-sized North American wild cat that is related to the lynx and has reddish-brown fur with black markings, tufted ears, and a short tail. Latin name: *Lynx rufus*. [Late 19thC. *Bob* from BOB[2], from its short tail.]

bobol /bó bol/, **bobbol** *n.* Carib corrupt behaviour, usually involving misappropriation of money, the acceptance of bribes, and other fraudulent practices (*slang*)

bobolink /bóbbə lingk/ (*plural* **-links** or **-link**) *n.* a song-bird with a distinctive bubbly song that nests in North America and migrates to South America. The male is white and yellow above and black underneath. Latin name: *Dolichonyx oryzivorus*. [Late 18thC. An imitation of the bird's call.]

bob skate *n.* US, Can an ice skate that has two parallel blades, usually used by children [Bob from BOB[2] in the sense 'short']

bobsled /bób sled/ *vi.* (**-sleds, -sledding, -sledded**) US = **bobsleigh** ■ *n.* US = **bobsleigh** [Bob from BOB[1] in the sense 'short']

bobsleigh /bób slay/ *n.* US term **bobsled 1. RACING SLEDGE** a long racing sledge with steering, brakes, a seat for two or more, and two pairs of runners, one in front and one at the back **2. SLEDGE MADE OF TWO SHORT SLEDGES** a long sledge made up of two short sledges attached one behind the other, used for recreation or for carrying things over snow ■ *vi.* (**-sleighs, -sleighing, -sleighed**) **RIDE IN BOBSLEIGH** to ride or race in a bobsleigh. US term **bobsled** [Bob from BOB[1] in the sense 'short']

bobstay /bób stay/ *n.* a rope used to hold down a ship's bowsprit [*Bob* of uncertain origin: probably from BOB[1] *v.* 1.]

bobtail /bób tayl/ *n.* **1. SHORT TAIL** an animal's tail that is naturally short or has been cut short **2. ANIMAL WITH SHORT TAIL** an animal, especially a horse or dog, that has a short or shortened tail [Mid-16thC. *Bob* of uncertain origin: probably from BOB[2].] —**bobtailed** *adj.*

bobwhite /bób wit/ (*plural* **-whites** or **-white**) *n.* a small brown mottled quail with white markings on its head. It is native to eastern and central North America and has been introduced into Europe. Latin name: *Colinus virginianus*. [Early 19thC. An imitation of the bird's call.]

Boccaccio /bo káchi ō/, **Giovanni** (1313–75) Italian writer and humanist. He wrote the *Decameron* (1348–58), a collection of 100 tales told by refugees from the Florentine plague of 1348. A classic of world literature, it profoundly influenced English writers such as Shakespeare.

bocce /bó chee/, **bocci** *n.* an Italian game similar to bowling, usually played on a long earth-floored court [Early 20thC. Via Italian *bocce*, the plural of *boccia* 'ball', from Vulgar Latin *bottia* 'boss'.]

Boccherini /bókə reéni/, **Luigi** (1743–1805) Italian composer and cellist. A prolific writer of chamber music, he composed for the Spanish and Prussian courts. Full name **Luigi Rodolfo Boccherini**

Boccioni /bo chóni/, **Umberto** (1882–1916) Italian painter and sculptor. A major theorist of the Futurist school, he worked in Paris and Rome.

Boche /bosh/, **boche** *n.* (*plural* **Boches** or **Boche**; *plural* **boches** or **boche**) **OFFENSIVE TERM** an offensive term for a German, especially a German soldier of World War I (*slang dated offensive*) ■ **Boche, boche** *npl.* **OFFENSIVE TERM FOR GERMANS** an offensive term used for the Germans collectively, especially the German soldiers of World War I (*dated slang insult*) [Early 20thC. Shortening of French *alboche*, a blend of *allemand* 'German' and *caboche* 'cabbage, blockhead'.]

Bochum /bókəm, bókhəm/ *n.* city in the German state of North Rhine-Westphalia in the industrial Ruhr district. Population: 401,100 (1994).

bod /bod/ *n.* (*slang*) **1. SB'S BODY** sb's body or figure **2. PERSON** a person [Late 18thC. Shortening.]

BOD *abbr.* biochemical oxygen demand

bodacious /bō dáyshəss/ *adj.* Southern US, Midwest (*informal humorous*) **1. IMPRESSIVE** remarkable or excellent ○ *That's one bodacious boat!* **2. BOLD** outrageously arrogant or uninhibited ○ *a bodacious lie* ■ *adv.* Southern US, Midwest VERY extremely (*informal humorous*) ○ *I'm bodacious hungry.* [Mid-19thC. Possibly an alteration of dialect *boldacious*, a blend of BOLD and AUDACIOUS.] —**bodaciously** *adv.*

bode[1] /bōd/ *vti.* (**bodes, boding, boded**) to be an indication of sth particular that is about to happen ○ *This does not bode well for the future of the organization.* [Old English *bodian* 'to announce, foretell', formed from *boda* 'messenger']

bode[2] *v.* past tense of **bide**

bodega /bō dáygə/ *n.* a wine shop or warehouse for the storage of wine in a Spanish-speaking country [Mid-19thC. Via Spanish from Latin *apotheca* 'storehouse'.]

bodge /boj/ *vti.* (**bodges, bodging, bodged**) **MAKE OR FIX STH BADLY** to make or repair sth badly (*informal*) ■ *n.* **BOTCHED PIECE OF WORK** a clumsy piece of work, or a badly done repair (*informal*) [Mid-16thC. Alteration of BOTCH.]

bodgie /bójji/ *adj.* Aus false or fake (*slang*) [Mid-20thC. Originally in the meaning 'young lout', later 'Teddy Boy'. Probably formed from BODGE.]

Bodhidharma /bóddi dáarmə/ (*fl.* 6th century) Indian monk He was the semilegendary founder of the Zen school of Buddhism.

bodhisattva /bóddi sátvə/ *n.* a god or being that has attained enlightenment worthy of nirvana but remains in the human world to help others [Early 19thC. From Sanskrit *bodhi* 'perfect knowledge' (from the stem *budh-* 'to know'; see BUDDHA) + *sattva* 'being, reality'.]

bodhrán /bów raan/ *n.* a shallow drum used in Irish and sometimes Scottish folk music, covered on one side with goat skin, held in one hand, and played with the other using a stick [Late 20thC. From Irish.]

bodice /bóddiss/ *n.* **1. UPPER PART OF DRESS** the part of a woman's dress or undergarment that covers the upper body **2. LACED-UP TOP** a close-fitting, often laced-up top worn over a blouse in the past or as part of some national costumes **3.** = **corset** [Mid-16thC. From *bodies*, plural of BODY.]

bodiless /bóddiləss/ *adj.* having no body or physical substance

bodily /bóddili/ *adj.* **PHYSICAL** relating to, involving, or typical of the body ■ *adv.* **1. PHYSICALLY** physically or in the flesh **2. USING PHYSICAL FORCE** by taking hold of sth with the hands and using physical strength ○ *bodily removed him from the building*

bodkin /bódkin/ *n.* **1. LARGE BLUNT NEEDLE** a long thick blunt needle with a large eye for pulling tape or ribbon through a hem or a series of loops **2. HOLE-PUNCHING TOOL** a small slender sharply pointed tool for making holes in cloth or leather **3. DAGGER** a small dagger (*archaic*) **4. HAIRPIN** a long ornamental hairpin (*archaic*) **5. PRINTING TYPESETTING TOOL** a long sharp tool for removing letters from set type when making a correction [14thC. Origin uncertain: probably literally 'small dagger' formed from the Celtic ancestor of Gaelic *biodag* 'dagger'.]

Bodleian /bóddli ən/ *n.* the library of Oxford University [Mid-17thC. Named after Sir Thomas Bodley, an English diplomat who refounded the library in 1603.]

Bodmin /bódmin/ historic town in southwestern Cornwall, England, near Bodmin Moor an Area of Outstanding Natural Beauty. Population: 12,553 (1991).

Bodoni /bə dóni/ *n.* a font or style of typeface [Late 19thC. Named after Giambattista *Bodoni* (1740–1813), an Italian printer.]

body /bóddi/ *n.* (*plural* **-ies**) **1. PHYSICAL FORM OF HUMAN OR ANIMAL** the complete material structure or physical form of a human being or an animal **2. DEAD HUMAN OR ANIMAL REMAINS** the physical remains of a dead person or animal. ◇ **corpse 3. TORSO** the main part of the physical structure of a human being or an animal, not including the head, arms, legs, or wings **4. SB'S FIGURE** sb's figure or build, especially with regard to shape and muscle tone ○ *a great body* **5. GROUP** an organized group of individuals, such as lawmakers, students, or soldiers ○ *a legislative body* **6. COLLECTION** a collection or amount of sth, seen as a whole ○ *a body of evidence* **7. MASS** an individual mass of sth, especially water or land ○ *a large body of water* **8. MAIN PART** the main or central part of sth, e.g. the majority of a quantity **9. ARCHIT NAVE** the nave or central part of a church **10. MAIN PART OF VEHICLE** the main part of a vehicle, e.g. the fuselage of an aircraft or the outer shell of a motor car. ◊ **bodywork 11.** MUSIC **MAIN PART OF MUSICAL INSTRUMENT** the largest part of a musical instrument, especially the sound box of a stringed instrument **12. MAIN PART OF STH WRITTEN** the main part of a piece of writing ○ *in the body of the text.* **13. FULLNESS OF FLAVOUR IN WINE** the extent to which a wine seems full when tasted. Body increases with alcohol content and density. ○ *a French red with plenty of body* **14. THICKNESS OF LIQUID** the thickness or opacity of a liquid such as paint or soup **15. FULLNESS OF TEXTURE** a fullness and bounciness in texture or appearance ○ *designed to give hair more body* **16. FIRMNESS OF FABRIC** the firmness or substantial feel of a type of cloth **17. GARMENT FOR TORSO** a tight one-piece garment that covers the torso and is fastened at the crotch. US term **body suit 18. UPPER PART OF GARMENT** the part of a garment that covers a person's torso **19. PERSON** used to refer to a person or yourself in an impersonal way (*informal*) ○ *This treatment could make a body feel unwelcome!* **20.** CERAMICS **MATERIAL FOR MAKING CERAMICS** the blend of clay and other raw materials used in a ceramic piece **21.** PHYS **PHYSICAL OBJECT** a distinguishable physical object **22.** MATH **OBJECT REPRESENTED MATHEMATICALLY** a physical object represented mathematically ■ *vt.* (-ies, -ying, -ied) **TO GIVE SHAPE** to give shape or substance to sth (*literary*) [Old English *bodig*]

body armour *n.* a protective covering for the upper part of the torso

body bag *n.* a bag designed to hold a dead body, usually made of plastic and fitted with a zip

body blow *n.* **1. SERIOUS SETBACK OR DISAPPOINTMENT** sth that causes great physical, financial, or emotional damage to sb or sth **2. BOXING BODY PUNCH** a punch that lands between the neck and the waist

body board *n.* a short polystyrene surfboard on which a surfer lies rather than stands

body building *n.* the practice of developing the muscles of the body through weightlifting and diet (*hyphenated when used before a noun*) —**body builder** *n.*

body cavity *n.* **1.** = coelom **2. OPENING INTO THE BODY** an opening into the body, e.g. the mouth, oesophagus, vagina, rectum, or ear

body cell *n.* = somatic cell

body-centred *adj.* used to describe crystals that have an atom in the middle of each unit cell as well as at the corners. ◊ **face-centred**

bodycheck /bóddi chek/ *n.* SPORTS **UNFAIR OBSTRUCTION OF OPPONENT** an illegal act of using the body to obstruct an opposing player in a game, especially ice hockey or soccer ■ *vt.* (-checks, -checking, -checked) SPORTS **UNFAIRLY OBSTRUCT OPPONENT** to use your body illegally to obstruct an opposing player in a game, especially ice hockey or soccer

body clock *n.* = biological clock

body corporate (*plural* **bodies corporate**) *n.* **1. CORPORATION** a group of people legally recognized as being able to act as one body **2. AUSTRALIAN HOUSING MANAGEMENT COMMITTEE** in Australia, a committee that manages the common property of an apartment building, e.g. the gardens or foyer. The members are usually owners of apartments within the block.

body count *n.* a count of the number of dead bodies, especially of soldiers killed after combat

body double *n.* sb whose body is filmed instead of that of an actor, especially in a scene involving nudity

body fluid *n.* **1. LIQUID PRODUCED BY THE BODY** a liquid produced by the body, including blood, saliva, semen, vaginal secretions, milk, urine, sweat, and tears **2. WATER IN BODY** the water content of the body

bodyguard /bóddi gaard/ *n.* a person or group of people paid to protect sb from physical attack

body image *n.* a person's own impression of how his or her body looks

body language *n.* bodily mannerisms, postures, and facial expressions that can be interpreted as unconsciously communicating a person's feelings or psychological state

bodyline bowling *n.* a type of fast bowling in cricket in which the bowler deliberately aims the ball at the batsman's body

body odour *n.* a rank, unpleasant smell associated with an unclean human being

body politic *n.* the people of a nation or any politically organized state, considered as a group

body popping *n.* a type of dancing, popular especially in the 1980s, involving convulsive, sinuous, or robotic movements (*slang*) —**body popper** *n.*

body search *n.* a detailed physical examination of sb suspected of hiding sth such as weapons or narcotics on his or her person

body shop *n.* a workshop where car bodies are repaired (*informal*)

body snatcher *n.* sb who steals corpses from graves, usually to sell for medical study —**body snatching** *n.*

body stocking *n.* a close-fitting, usually sheer, one-piece garment that covers the body and sometimes the arms and legs

bodysuit *n.* = body

bodysurf /bóddi surf/ (-surfs, -surfing, -surfed) *vi.* to surf without a board by lying on a wave and using the body as a surfboard —**bodysurfer** *n.*

body wall *n.* the part of an animal's body that forms its external surface, encloses the body cavity, and consists of layers of skin and muscle

bodywork /bóddi wurk/ *n.* **1. CARS CAR BODY** the outer frame of a car or other motor vehicle **2. REPAIR OF MOTOR VEHICLE BODY** the work of repairing the outer frame of a car or other motor vehicle **3. MASSAGE OR PHYSICAL MANIPULATION OF BODY** physical manipulation of the human body, including all types of massage, to improve general health or posture or to treat injuries

boehmite /búr mīt/ *n.* a mineral found in bauxite and consisting of hydrous aluminium oxide that ranges in colour from light-grey to dark reddish-brown [Early 20thC. Named after Johann Böhm, a German chemist (1895–1952).]

Boer /boor, bawr/ *n.* **1. DUTCH SOUTH AFRICAN** sb of Dutch descent who settled in South Africa **2. S Africa POLICE OFFICER** a police officer (*slang*) [Mid-19thC. From Dutch *boer* 'farmer'.] —**Boer** *adj.*

boeremusiek /bóorə myoozik/ *n.* S Africa dance music of a folk and country style popular amongst Afrikaners, usually played by a small band and including a concertina and piano accordion [Mid-20th C. From Afrikaans, from *boere* 'Afrikaner'+*musiek* 'music'.]

boerewors /bóorə vawrss/ *n.* S Africa a large spicy homemade sausage, traditionally eaten by Afrikaners [Mid-20th C. From Afrikaans, from *boere* 'Afrikaner'+ *wors* 'sausage'.]

Boer War *n.* a war fought in South Africa from 1899 to 1902 between the British and the descendants of the Dutch, ending eventually in a British victory

Boethius /bō eéthi əss/, **Anicius Manlius Severinus** (480?–524) Roman statesman and philosopher. He wrote *The Consolation of Philosophy*, works on logic, and commentaries on Aristotle. His writings influenced scholars in medieval Europe.

boetie /bóoti, bóti/ *n.* S Africa a friend

BOF *abbr.* COMPUT beginning of file

boffin /bóffin/ *n.* a scientific expert, especially one involved in research and who appears unconventional or absent-minded (*informal*) [Mid-20thC. Origin unknown.]

boffo /bóffō/ *adj.* excellent or extremely successful (*informal dated*) [Mid-20thC. Formed from *boff* 'great commercial success, especially in the theatre', of uncertain origin: perhaps from *box office*.]

Bofors gun /bófərz-/ *n.* a 40 mm anti-aircraft gun with one or two barrels, developed in Sweden and used

by British and US forces in World War II [Mid-20thC]

bog /bog/ *n.* **1. AREA OF MARSHY GROUND** an area of wet marshy ground, largely consisting of accumulated decomposing plant material. It supports vegetation such as sedges and moss and may ultimately turn into peat. **2.** UK **TOILET** a toilet (*slang*) [14thC. From Gaelic *bognach* 'marsh', formed from *bog* 'soft'.]
bog down (bogs down, bogging down, bogged down) *vt.* to slow sb's general progress (*informal*) ○ *got bogged down in unimportant details*
bog off *vi.* to go away (*slang*) (*usually used as a command*)

Humphrey Bogart

Bogart /bố gaart/, **Humphrey** (1899–1957) US film actor. The classic American 'tough-but-tender' leading man, his many films include *Casablanca* (1942) and *The African Queen* (1951). Full name **Humphrey DeForest Bogart**

bog asphodel *n.* a plant of the lily family that is common in boggy areas and has grassy leaves and clusters of small yellow flowers. Latin name: *Narthecium ossifragum.*

bogey /bógi/ *n.* **1. CAUSE OF TROUBLE** sth that troubles, annoys, or frightens sb **2. GOLF ONE OVER PAR** a golf score of one over par for a particular hole **3. NASAL MUCUS** a lump of mucus in or from sb's nose (*slang*) US term **booger** *n.* **4.** AIR FORCE **UNIDENTIFIED FLYING AIRCRAFT** an aircraft in flight that cannot be identified, especially one assumed to be hostile (*slang*) **5.** = **bogeyman** *n.* ◊ **6. POLICE OFFICER** a police officer or detective (*slang dated*) ■ *vt.* (-geys, -geying, -ged, -geyed) GOLF **SCORE ONE OVER PAR FOR HOLE** to score one over par for a particular hole in golf [Mid-19thC. Alteration of BOGLE.]

bogeyman /bógi man/ (*plural* -men /-men/), **bogyman** (*plural* -men) *n.* **1. FEAR-INDUCING PERSON** a real or imaginary person or monster that causes fear or is invoked to cause fear, especially in children **2. SB BELIEVED TO BE EVIL** sb considered to be especially hateful, evil, or frightening ○ *The press treated him as a left-wing bogeyman.*

boggle /bógg'l/ (-gles, -gling, -gled) *v.* **1.** *vti.* **BAFFLE OR BECOME BAFFLED** to astonish or confuse sb, or to become astonished or confused (*informal*) ◊ **mind-boggling 2.** *vi.* **HESITATE WITH SECOND THOUGHTS** to hesitate before doing sth, usually because of being overwhelmed, afraid, or concerned **3.** *vti.* US **MAKE A TRIVIAL MISTAKE** to make a trivial mistake or mismanage sth (*informal*) [Late 16thC. Origin uncertain: probably related to BOGLE.] —**boggler** *n.*

boggy /bóggi/ (-gier, -giest) *adj.* used to describe an area of land that is always or is usually wet or muddy

boghopper /bóg hoppər/ *n.* = bogtrotter (*slang offensive*)

bogie /bógi/ *n.* **1. FRAMEWORK WITH WHEELS** a framework mounted on a set of wheels on the undercarriage of a vehicle. Railway vehicles have one at each end and they swivel to allow the vehicle to go round a curve. **2. bogie, bogy** (*plural* -gies) **SMALL RAILWAY TRUCK** a small railway truck used for carrying heavy loads **3.** S Asia a railway compartment [Mid-19thC. Origin unknown.]

bogle /bóg'l/ *n.* = bogeyman (*regional archaic*) [Early 16thC. From earlier Scottish *bogill* 'goblin', which was probably formed from *bugge* 'terror'.]

Bognor Regis /bógnər reéjiss/ seaside resort in West Sussex, southern England. Population: 56,744 (1991).

bogong /bő gong/, **bogong moth, bugong** /bŏo gong/, **bugong moth** *n.* a large Australian nocturnal moth that is eaten by Aborigines. Latin name: *Agrotis infusa.* [Mid-19th C. From Ngayawung, an Aborginal language.]

Bogong, Mount /bő gong/ the highest mountain in the state of Victoria, Australia. It is the site of a ski resort. Height: 1,986 m./6,516 ft.

Bogor /bő gawr/ city in Indonesia, near Jakarta, on western Java island. It is known for its botanical gardens. Population: 271,711 (1990).

Bogotá /bóggə taá/ capital of Colombia situated on a plateau in the eastern Andes. It is Colombia's largest city and its commercial, cultural, and political centre. Population: 5,237,635 (1995).

bog roll *n.* toilet paper or a roll of toilet paper (*slang*)

bog spavin *n.* a chronic puffy inflammation of the soft tissue of the hock joint of horses

bog-standard *adj.* basic, ordinary, or lacking any special features (*informal*) ○ *For that price you get your bog-standard production model, without accessories.*

bogtrotter /bóg trottər/ *n.* a highly offensive term for an Irish person (*slang offensive*)

bogus /bṓgəss/ *adj.* **1.** FAKE OR DECEITFUL false, dishonest, or fraudulently imitating sth **2.** *US* BAD OR USELESS not good, pleasant, or acceptable (*slang*) [Early 19thC. After *bogus*, a machine for producing counterfeit money. The ultimate origin is uncertain.] —**bogusly** *adv.* —**bogusness** *n.*

WORD KEY: ORIGIN

The word **bogus** is first recorded in American usage in the 1820s, referring to a machine for producing counterfeit money; its modern uses seem to have developed from there. Its ultimate origins remain unclear, but one suggestion is that it comes from *tantrabogus*, a word reportedly in use in New England in the early 19th century for 'a sinister-looking object' (which itself may have been based on *bogy*, meaning 'devil'). Another theory is that it may be related to Hausa *boko*, meaning 'deceit, fraud', and have crossed the Atlantic with transported slaves.

bogy *n.* = **bogie**

bogyman *n.* = **bogeyman**

bohea /bō heé/ *n.* a low-quality black Chinese tea [Early 18thC. From Chinese dialect *Bu-yi*, a variant of *Wu-yi*, after the Wu-Yi hills in southeastern China, from where black tea first came to Britain.]

bohemia /bō heémi ə/ *n.* **1.** UNCONVENTIONAL COMMUNITY a community of artists and other people who live unconventional lives **2.** UNCONVENTIONAL LIFESTYLE the unconventional lifestyle characteristic of bohemians

Bohemia /bō heémi ə/ historic region in the western Czech Republic. A former kingdom, it was the westernmost province of Czechoslovakia from 1918 to 1939 and from 1945 to 1949, but it was then divided into several new districts. Area: 52,060 sq. km/20,100 sq. mi.

bohemian /bō heémi ən/ *n.* sb, often a writer or an artist, who does not live according to the conventions of society [Mid-19th C. From the medieval association with members of the Romany people with Bohemia.] —**bohemian** *adj.* —**bohemianism** *n.*

Bohemian /bō heémi ən/ *n.* **1.** PEOPLES SB FROM BOHEMIA sb who was born or brought up in Bohemia **2.** LANG CZECH LANGUAGE the Czech language (*dated*)

Bohemian Brethren *npl.* a Protestant Christian society founded by the Hussites in Bohemia in 1467. It became the Moravian Church in 1722.

Böhm /burm/, **Karl** (1894–1981) Austrian conductor. He was especially known for conducting Mozart operas, and premiered a number of operas of Richard Strauss.

boho /bṓhō/ *n., adj. US, UK, Can* bohemian (*slang*)

Bohr /bawr/, **Niels** (1885–1962) Danish physicist. He won the Nobel Prize in physics (1922) for his work on quantum theory. He participated in US atomic bomb development during World War II, and later worked for peaceful application of nuclear technology. Full name **Niels Henrik David Bohr**

Bohr effect *n.* the effect that carbon dioxide has on the oxygen equilibrium of haemoglobin. Increased carbon dioxide concentrations reduce haemoglobin's ability to bind to oxygen atoms. [Mid-20thC. Named after Christian *Bohr* (1855–1911), Danish physiologist.]

Bohr theory *n.* a theory of atomic structure postulating that electrons move around a nucleus in distinct orbits and a jump between orbits is accompanied by the absorption or emission of a photon. It was the earliest important attempt to apply quantum theory to atomic structure. [Named after Niels BOHR]

bohunk /bő hungk/ *n. US, Can* an offensive term for a person from central or southeastern Europe (*slang offensive*) [Early 20thC. Blend of BOHEMIAN and 'hunk', a shortening of 'Hungarian'.]

boil[1] /boyl/ *v.* (**boils, boiling, boiled**) **1.** *vti.* REACH BOILING POINT to cause a liquid to reach the temperature at which it turns to gas, when bubbles may be seen to form, or to reach this state **2.** *vti.* CONTAIN OR CAUSE TO CONTAIN BOILING LIQUID to contain liquid that has reached boiling point, or to cause the liquid in a container to boil **3.** *vti.* COOK COOK IN BOILING LIQUID to cook sth by submerging it in boiling liquid for a certain amount of time, or to be cooked in this way. ◊ **simmer 4.** *vti.* PLACE IN BOILING WATER to put sth such as clothing in boiling water, e.g. to clean or sterilize it, or to be put in boiling water for these purposes **5.** *vi.* GET VERY HOT to be or become extremely hot (*informal*) ○ *It's boiling in there!* **6.** *vi.* BUBBLE ON SURFACE to be stirred up and have bubbles breaking on the surface **7.** *vi.* GET VERY ANGRY to be or become very angry ○ *boiling with rage* ■ *n.* **1.** STATE OF BUBBLING AT HIGH TEMPERATURE the point at which a liquid bubbles because of having reached the temperature at which it turns to gas, or the state of bubbling at this temperature **2.** *Southern US* OUTDOOR PICNIC an outdoor picnic at which shellfish, such as crabs, shrimp, oysters, or crayfish, are boiled and eaten (*informal*) ○ *a Low Country crab boil* [13thC. Via Old French *boillir* from Latin *bullire* 'to bubble', from *bulla* 'a bubble'.]

boil away *vti.* to turn completely into steam, or turn all of a quantity of liquid into steam by boiling it

boil down *v.* **1.** *vti.* REDUCE LIQUID IN MIXTURE to make a liquid mixture thicker and reduce its volume by heating it rapidly until much of the liquid turns to steam, or to be made thicker in this way **2.** *vt.* SUMMARIZE to condense or summarize sth such as information or text (*informal*)

boil down to *vt.* to mean or amount to sth in essence (*informal*) ○ *It all boils down to the single question: Is he telling the truth?*

boil off *vti.* to remove sth from a mixture by heating the mixture rapidly until it turns to steam, or to be removed in this way

boil over *v.* **1.** *vti.* FROTH UP AND OVERFLOW to reach or to cause a liquid to reach boiling point and be so full of bubbles that some of it spills from the container **2.** *vi.* OVERFLOW WITH AN EMOTION to become too intense or out of control ○ *her anger boiled over*

boil[2] /boyl/ *n.* MED a painful pus-filled abscess on the skin caused by bacterial infection of a hair follicle [Old English *byl* 'inflammation']

Boileau /bwaálō/, **Nicolas** (1636–1711) French writer. He was the author of *The Art of Poetry* (1674), a statement of the principles of classical verse. Full name **Nicolas Boileau-Despréaux**

boiled sweet *n.* a hard sweet made by boiling water, sugar, and flavouring

boiler /bóylər/ *n.* **1.** WATER HEATING TANK a large tank in which water is heated and stored, either as hot water or as steam, and used for heating or generating power **2.** COOK TOUGH CHICKEN an old chicken with flesh that is so tough that it must be boiled to make it palatable

boilermaker /bóylər maykər/ *n.* **1.** SB MAKING BOILERS sb who works in heavy industry making or repairing large metal objects, especially boilers **2.** *US* WHISKY WITH BEER CHASER a drink of whisky followed by a beer

boilerplate /bóylər playt/ *n.* **1.** PLATE USED FOR MAKING BOILERS steel plate used for making boilers **2.** *US, Can* CLICHÉD WRITING writing that says nothing new, informative, or interesting **3.** *US, Can* FORMULAIC LANGUAGE stock or formulaic language, such as that used in legal forms and documents like powers of attorney and authors' contracts

boiler room *n.* an area or room that houses one or more boilers

boiler-room *adj. US* relating to or being political campaign workers who perform administrative support tasks and make polling phone calls for the candidate

boiler suit *n.* a one-piece long-sleeved garment worn over other clothes to protect them while doing manual labour or dirty jobs

boiling /bóyling/ *adj.* **1.** HOT extremely hot **2.** FURIOUS extremely angry ■ *n. Scotland* = **boiled sweet**

boiling point *n.* **1.** TEMPERATURE AT WHICH LIQUID BOILS the temperature at which a liquid turns to gas. Water turns to steam at 100°C or 212°F at sea level. **2.** CRISIS POINT the point at which people lose their tempers or a situation becomes critical

boing /boyng/ *n.* the sound made by sth that bounces [Mid-20thC. An imitation of the sound.]

boisterous /bóystərəss/ *adj.* **1.** NOISY, ENERGETIC, AND ROWDY full of noisy enthusiasm and energy, and often roughness or wildness **2.** TURBULENT wild, rough, or stormy [13thC. Alteration of earlier *boistous*, which came via Old French *boistos* 'clumsy, rough' from Latin *buxus* 'made from box-tree wood'.] —**boisterously** *adv.* —**boisterousness** *n.*

Boito /bō eétō/, **Arrigo** (1842–1918) Italian composer and librettist. He wrote the opera *Mefistofele* (1868) and the texts for Verdi's operas *Otello* (1887) and *Falstaff* (1893). Original name **Enrico Giuseppe Giovanni Boito**

Bokassa /bə kássə/, **Edine Ahmed** (1921–96) Central African president and emperor. He seized power in the Central African Republic (1966) and ruled until his overthrow in 1979, the last two years as self-declared emperor. Born **Jean Bédel Bokassa**

bok choy /bók chóy/ *n. US* = **Chinese cabbage** [Mid-20thC. From Chinese Guangdang dialect *baahk-choi*, literally 'white vegetable'.]

boke /bōk/ *vti.* (**bokes, boking, boked**) *Scotland* RETCH to retch or vomit (*informal*) ■ *n. Scotland* (*informal*) **1.** ACT OF RETCHING OR VOMITING an act or instance of retching or vomiting **2.** STH VOMITED sth that has been vomited [Mid-16thC. Dialect Variant of POKE.]

Bol. *abbr.* **1.** Bolivia **2.** Bolivian

bola /bṓlə/, **bolas** /-ləss/ *n.* a strong cord with weights attached to the ends, used for catching cows by South American cowhands (**gauchos**) who throw it to entangle the cows' legs [Early 19thC. Via Spanish, 'ball', from, ultimately, Latin *bulla* 'bubble'.]

bold /bōld/ *adj.* **1.** FEARLESS AND ADVENTUROUS willing and eager to face danger or adventure with a sense of confidence and fearlessness **2.** REQUIRING OR SHOWING A DARING PERSONALITY requiring or showing fearlessness, daring, and often originality **3.** IMPUDENT OR PRESUMPTUOUS lacking in modesty, or so assertive as to be impolite **4.** CLEAR AND CONSPICUOUS standing out and therefore easily noticed ○ *bold colours* **5.** STEEP rising abruptly and steeply from the surroundings ○ *a bold cliff* **6.** PRINTING DARKER THAN STANDARD having darker thicker lines than standard type, fonts, or lettering ■ *n.* PRINTING TYPE DARKER THAN STANDARD type, fonts, or lettering with darker thicker lines than is standard ■ *vt.* to set, print, or display text in boldface type [Old English *bald.* Ultimately from the Indo-European base that was also the source of English *fool, bull, boulder, and phallus.*] —**boldly** *adv.* —**boldness** *n.*

boldface /bṓld fayss/ *adj.* PRINTING = **bold** *adj.* 6 ■ *vt.* (**-faces, -facing, -faced**) PRINTING DARKEN LETTERS to make letters darker and thicker for emphasis

bold face *n.* = **bold** *n.*

bold-faced /bṓld fáyst/, **boldfaced** *adj.* **1.** BRAZEN showing impudence or lack of shame or modesty **2.** PRINTING = **bold** *adj.* 6

bole[1] /bōl/ *n.* the trunk of a tree [14thC. From Old Norse *bolr.*]

bole² /bōl/ n. a reddish-brown clay used as a pigment [14thC. From late Latin *bolus* 'clod of earth' (see BOLUS).]

bolection /bō léksh'n/ n. a moulding covering an architectural joint and projecting beyond it. A bolection moulding is usually S-shaped in cross section. [Mid-17thC. Origin unknown.]

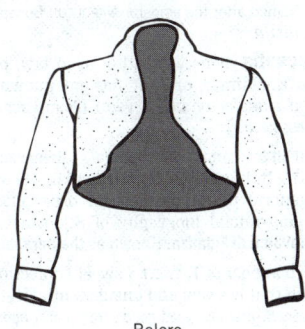

Bolero

bolero /bə láirō/ (plural **-ros**) n. **1.** SPANISH DANCE a Spanish dance in triple time that involves much foot-stamping and dramatic posing **2.** SPANISH DANCE MUSIC a piece of music for a bolero, or written in the rhythm of a bolero **3.** SHORT OPEN JACKET a short jacket, with or without sleeves, worn open over a blouse or shirt [Late 18thC. From Spanish, from *bola* 'ball' (see BOLA).]

boletus /bō leétəss/ (plural **-tuses** or **-ti** /-tī/) n. a fungus that has a rounded cap with pores rather than gills on the underside. Cep mushrooms are an edible species of boletus. Genus: *Boletus*. [Early 16thC. From Latin, of uncertain origin.]

Boleyn /boŏ lín/, **Anne, Queen of England and Ireland** (1507?–36). She was the second wife of Henry VIII (1533–36) and the mother of Elizabeth I. Henry VIII accused her of adultery and had her beheaded.

Bolger /bóljər/, **Jim** (b. 1935) New Zealand statesman. A National Party politician, he was prime minister of New Zealand (1990–97). Full name **James Brendan Bolger**

bolide /bố līd/ n. a bright meteor that explodes [Early 19thC. Via French from, ultimately, Greek *bolis* 'missile'.]

bolivar /bólli vaar/ n. **1.** see table at **currency 2.** COIN OR NOTE WORTH ONE BOLIVAR a coin or note worth one bolivar [Late 19thC. Named after Simón BOLÍVAR.]

Bolívar /bólli vaar/, **Simón** (1783–1830) South American revolutionary. He was the leader of the independence movement that drove the Spanish from Venezuela, Colombia, Ecuador, Peru, and Bolivia (1812–24). Known as **the Liberator**

Bolivia

Bolivia /bə lívvi ə/ landlocked republic in west-central South America. Part of the Inca empire, it was conquered by the Spanish in 1538 and became independent in 1825. Language: Spanish. Currency: Boliviano. Capital: Sucre. Population: 7,669,868 (1997). Area: 1,098,581 sq. km/424,164 sq. mi. —**Bolivian** n., adj.

boliviano /bə lívvi áanō/ (plural **-nos**) n. see table at **currency** [Late 19thC. From Spanish, 'Bolivian'.]

boll /bōl/ n. a rounded seed pod or capsule, especially of cotton [15thC. From Middle Dutch *bolle* 'round object'.]

Böll /bōl/, **Heinrich** (1917–85) German novelist. His novels include *The Lost Honour of Katharina Blum* (1974). He received the Nobel Prize in literature in 1972.

bollard /bóll aard/ n. **1.** NAUT POST FOR MOORING SHIPS a strong post on a quay or wharf, or on the deck of a ship, used for securing ropes **2.** TRANSP POST FOR GUIDING TRAFFIC a small post marking the edge of an area traffic must keep off **3.** MOUNTAINEERING ROCK SUITABLE FOR SECURING ROPE a spike of rock or a pillar of ice round which a rope can be secured [Mid-19thC. Origin uncertain; probably formed from BOLE¹.]

bollocking /bólləking/ n. a severe telling off (*slang offensive*) [Mid-20thC. Formed from BOLLOCKS.]

bollocks /bólləks/ (*slang offensive*) npl. TESTICLES the testicles ■ n. NONSENSE nonsense ■ interj. RUBBISH! used to say that you strongly disbelieve or disagree with sth ■ vt. (**-locks, -locksing, -locksed**) SPOIL OR CONFUSE to make a mess or muddle of sth ○ *They got my travel arrangements totally bollocksed up.* [Mid-18thC. Variant of *ballocks*, from Old English *beallucas* 'testicles'.]

boll weevil n. a weevil found in the southern United States and Mexico whose larvae infest and destroy cotton bolls. Latin name: *Anthonomus grandis*.

bollworm /bōl wurm/ n. a moth caterpillar, especially the corn earworm or pink bollworm, that feeds on and destroys cotton and other crops

Bollywood /bólli woŏd/ n. a nickname given to the Indian film industry [Mid-20th C. Blend of BOMBAY AND HOLLYWOOD.]

bolo /bốlō/ (plural **-los**) n. a machete from the Philippines with a single-edged blade [Early 20thC. From Philippine Spanish.]

Bologna /bə lṓnyə, -lṓn-/ capital of Bologna Province and Emilia-Romagna Region, in northern Italy. It was an important cultural centre in the Middle Ages and Renaissance. Population: 404,378 (1991).

bolognese /bóllə náyz/, **Bolognese** adj. used to describe an Italian sauce for pasta, made with minced meat and tomato [Early 19thC. From Italian, '(in the style) of Bologna'.]

bolometer /bō lómmitər/ n. an instrument for measuring radiant energy by determining the changes of resistance in an electrical conductor [Late 19thC. Coined from Greek *bolē* 'ray' + -METER.] —**bolometric** /bốlə méttrik/ adj. —**bolometry** /bō lómmətri/ n.

Bolshevik /bólshəvik/ n. **1.** RUSSIAN COMMUNIST a member of the radical group within the Russian Socialist party that became the Communist Party in 1918 **2.** Bolshevik, bolshevik COMMUNIST OR COMMUNIST SYMPATHIZER sb who is a Communist or is sympathetic to Communism (*informal dated*) **3.** Bolshevik, bolshevik POLITICAL RADICAL any revolutionary or radical socialist (*disapproving*) [Early 20thC. From Russian *bol'shevik*, from *bol'she* 'more'; from the fact that the radicals were in the majority.]

Bolshevism /bólshəvizzəm/, **bolshevism** n. **1.** BOLSHEVIK IDEOLOGY the ideology and policies of the Bolsheviks, especially advocacy of the forcible overthrow of capitalism **2.** COMMUNISM Communism or revolutionary socialism (*dated*) —**Bolshevist** n. —**Bolshevistic** /bólshə vístik/ adj.

bolshie /bólshi/, **bolshy** n. (plural **-shies**) BOLSHEVIK a Bolshevik (*informal dated*) ■ adj. UK, Can (*informal*) **1.** UNCOOPERATIVE tending to be argumentative or uncooperative **2.** POLITICALLY RADICAL politically radical or subversive [Early 20thC. Formed from BOLSHEVIK.]

bolster¹ /bólstər/ n. **1.** LONG CYLINDRICAL PILLOW a long firm cylindrical pillow placed under other pillows to support them **2.** MECH ENG PAD PREVENTING FRICTION a pad or cushion fitted to machinery to prevent friction or give support **3.** BUILDING HORIZONTAL SUPPORTING TIMBER a short horizontal timber positioned between the top of a post and the beam it supports, to spread the load of the post ■ vt. (**-sters, -stering, -stered**) **1.** ENCOURAGE THROUGH SUPPORT to strengthen sth through support or encouragement **2.** KEEP RAISED to prop sth up [Old English, 'cushion'. Ultimately from an Indo-European word meaning 'to swell', which is also the ancestor of English *bulge*, *billow*, *belly*, and *bellows*.] —**bolsterer** n.

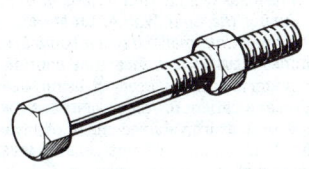

Bolt

bolster² /bólstə/ n. a chisel with a wide cutting edge, used for cutting stone [Early 20thC. Alteration of *boaster*, from *boast* 'to cut with a chisel', of unknown origin.]

bolt¹ /bōlt/ n. **1.** BAR FOR FASTENING DOOR a sliding bar that fits into a socket and secures a door or gate **2.** BUILDING SHORT SCREW a short cylindrical metal bar with a screw thread, used with a nut **3.** ARMS ARROW FOR CROSSBOW a short arrow for use with a crossbow **4.** ARMS PART OF GUN in a breech-loading firearm, a sliding rod, bar, or plate that ejects a used cartridge and closes the breech **5.** METEOROL LIGHTNING FLASH a flash of lightning **6.** TEXTILES ROLL OF FABRIC a rolled length of woven goods or wallpaper **7.** MOUNTAINEERING METAL PIN a nail-like metal shaft used to provide an anchor in rock faces ■ v. (**bolts, bolting, bolted**) **1.** vt. LOCK WITH BOLT to fasten a door by sliding a bolt into a socket **2.** vi. RUSH AWAY to move suddenly and quickly, especially out of fright **3.** vt. EXPEL FROM HIDING-PLACE to flush out a wild animal that is hidden or concealed **4.** vt. DEVOUR HURRIEDLY to swallow food hurriedly without chewing **5.** vi. BOT PREMATURELY PRODUCE SEEDS to flower and produce seeds earlier than expected or wanted **6.** vt. TEXTILES ROLL INTO BOLT to roll fabric or wallpaper into a bolt [Old English, 'crossbow bolt'] —**bolter** n. ◇ **like a bolt from the blue** very suddenly and unexpectedly ◇ **make a bolt for sth** to make a sudden rush towards sth ◇ **shoot your bolt** to use all your resources

bolt² /bōlt/ (**bolts, bolting, bolted**), **boult** (**boults, boulting, boulted**) vt. to filter a substance through a cloth or sieve, especially flour [12thC. From Old French *buleter*, of Germanic origin.]

Bolt /bōlt/, **Robert** (1924–95) British playwright. His plays include *A Man for All Seasons* (1960) and *State of Revolution* (1977). Among his screenplays are *Lawrence of Arabia* (1962) and *Dr Zhivago* (1965). Full name **Robert Oxton Bolt**

bolt-action adj. used to describe a gun with a sliding bolt that replaces the used cartridge and closes the breech

bolthole /bōlt hōl/ n. a place of escape, especially for an animal fleeing from danger ○ *The rabbit ran down a bolthole*

Bolton /bóltən/ industrial town in Lancashire, north-western England. Population: 253,300 (1991).

bolt-on /bôltən/ adj. **1.** ATTACHABLE WITH A BOLT attachable by means of a bolt **2.** ATTACHABLE AS AN EXTRA attachable as an extra without affecting or requiring change to the rest ■ n. ENG ADDITIONAL PART sth that can be added to a larger structure (*informal*)

boltrope /bōlt rōp/ n. a rope sewn along the lower edge or leading edge of a sail to strengthen it

Boltzmann constant /bóltsmən-/ n. the ratio of the universal gas constant to Avogadro's number. Symbol k [Named after the Austrian physicist Ludwig *Boltzmann* (1844–1906)]

bolus /bốləss/ n. **1.** INTRAVENOUS INJECTION OF DRUG a dose of a drug given quickly by intravenous injection **2.** LARGE PILL a very large pill **3.** ROUND MASS a soft rounded ball, especially of chewed food [Mid-16thC. Via late Latin from Greek *bōlos* 'clod of earth', of unknown origin.]

boma /bốmə/ n. **1.** ENCLOSURE in Central and East Africa, an enclosed camp or an enclosure for animals **2.** POLICE POST in Central and East Africa, a police post or magistrate's office [Late 19thC. From Kiswahili.]

bomb /bom/ *n.* **1.** ARMS **EXPLOSIVE PROJECTILE** a missile containing explosive or other destructive material **2.** ARMS **SPECIALIZED EXPLOSIVE DEVICE** a device that contains explosive material, especially one designed to explode after some time **3. bomb, Bomb** ARMS **ATOM BOMB** the atom bomb considered as the absolute weapon of mass destruction ○ *lived in dread of the Bomb during the Cold War* **4. LOT OF MONEY** a great deal of money (*informal*) ○ *it cost a bomb* **5.** MED **DEVICE FOR DIRECTING RADIATION** a device that contains radioactive material and is used to beam therapeutic radiation at a patient **6.** GEOL **SOLIDIFIED LAVA** a solidified rounded or teardrop-shaped mass of lava from a volcano **7.** *US, Can, ANZ* ARTS **ARTISTIC FAILURE** a performance that is a commercial or artistic failure (*informal*) **8.** *ANZ* **DILAPIDATED VEHICLE** a battered or dilapidated vehicle (*informal*) **9.** *US* **STH OR SB GOOD** sth or sb extremely good or exciting (*slang*) ○ *Their lead singer is the bomb.* ■ *v.* (**bombs, bombing, bombed**) **1.** *vti.* MIL **ATTACK PEOPLE AND PLACES WITH BOMBS** to drop bombs on people or places, or attack or destroy them with bombs ○ *bombing enemy territory* **2.** *vt.* ARMS **DAMAGE BUILDING WITH EXPLOSION** to destroy or damage a building by placing an explosive device there (*often used with 'out'*) ○ *the wreckage of bombed-out homes* **3.** *vi.* **MOVE VERY FAST** to move exceptionally fast, especially in a vehicle (*informal*) **4.** *vi.* **FAIL MISERABLY** to fail badly as a performance (*informal*) **5.** *vi.* COMPUT **CRASH** to fail suddenly (*informal*) [Late 17thC. Via French, Italian, and Latin from, ultimately, Greek *bombos* 'booming sound' (source of English *bombard*), ultimately an imitation of the sound.]

bomb out *vt.* (*usually passive*) **1. DESTROY BY BOMBING** to destroy a home or workplace completely by bombing it **2. FORCE OUT BY BOMBING** to drive sb out of a home or workplace by bombing

bombard /bom baàrd/ *vt.* (**-bards, -barding, -barded**) **1.** MIL **ATTACK WITH MISSILES** to attack an enemy or enemy territory intensively with sustained artillery fire or bombs **2. HIT REPEATEDLY** to attack sb persistently and vigorously **3. OVERWHELM** to overwhelm sb with sth, e.g. questions **4.** PHYS **HIT WITH HIGH-ENERGY PARTICLES** to direct high-energy particles against atoms or nuclei ■ *n.* HIST, ARMS **MEDIEVAL CANNON** a cannon used in medieval times to throw large stones [15thC. From French *bombarder*, from *bombarde* 'cannon', via medieval Latin *bombarda* from Latin *bombus*, from Greek *bombos* (see BOMB).] —**bombarder** *n.*

bombardier /bómbə deér/ *n.* **1. SB WHO RELEASES BOMBS** a member of a military aircraft crew who releases bombs **2. NON-COMMISSIONED OFFICER** in the British Royal Artillery, a non-commissioned officer below the rank of sergeant **3. ARTILLERY SOLDIER** a member of the artillery (*archaic*) [Mid-16thC. From French, from *bombarde* 'cannon' (see BOMBARD).]

bombardier beetle *n.* a beetle that squirts volatile acrid liquid when attacked. Latin name: *Brachinus crepitans.*

bombardment /bom baàrdmənt/ *n.* **1. ATTACK BY BOMBS OR ARTILLERY** an intensive and sustained attack by bombs or artillery fire **2. CONSTANT STREAM OF STH** a large number of things, e.g. questions, aggressively directed at sb or sth

bombardon /bómbərdən/ *n.* **1. BASS TUBA** a brass wind instrument of the tuba family **2. REED STOP ON ORGAN** a bass reed stop on an organ [Mid-19thC. Via Italian *bombardone* from, ultimately, medieval Latin *bombarda* 'bombard' (see BOMBARD).]

bombasine *n.* TEXTILES = **bombazine**

bombast /bóm bast/ *n.* language that is full of long or pretentious words, used to impress others [Late 16thC. Alteration of Old French *bombace* 'cotton stuffing',which came via medieval Latin *bombax* 'cotton' from Greek *bombux* 'silk, silkworm'.] —**bombastic** /bom bástik/ *adj.* —**bombastically** /bom bástikli/ *adv.*

Bombay /bom báy/ former name for **Mumbai**

Bombay duck (*plural* **Bombay ducks** *or* **Bombay duck**) *n.* **1. DRIED FISH** a fish, especially the bummalo, dried, salted, grilled, and served as a pungent accompaniment to Indian foods **2.** = **bummalo** [Mid-19thC. Marathi *bombīla* 'bummalo', by folk etymology from 'Bombay', by association with BOMBAY, from where the fish were exported.]

bombay mix *n.* a spiced mixture of fried lentils and other Asian dried foods, eaten as a snack or appetizer [Named after the city of BOMBAY]

bombazine /bómbə zeén, bómbə zeen/, **bombasine** *n.* a twilled material made from silk or cotton and worsted, usually dyed black. Black bombazine was used formerly to make mourning clothes. [Late 16thC. Via French *bombasin* from, ultimately, medieval Latin *bombycinus* 'silken', from Latin *bombyx* 'silk, silkworm', from Greek *bombux* (source of English *bombast*).]

bomb bay *n.* the compartment on board a bomber aircraft in which the bombs are carried

bomb calorimeter *n.* a device for measuring calorific values in which substances are burned inside a sealed vessel

bomb disposal *n.* the task or process of rendering bombs harmless by defusing, removing, or detonating them in a controlled explosion (*hyphenated when used before a noun*) ○ *a bomb-disposal expert*

bombe /bomb/ *n.* a dome-shaped frozen or set dessert [Late 19thC. From French, literally 'bomb', from the shape of the metal mould it is made in.]

bombé /bom báy/ *adj.* used to describe furniture with a bulging convex shape. This style is typical of French rococo furniture of the 18th century. [Early 20thC. From French, literally 'swollen'.]

bombed /bomd/ *adj.* **1. DAMAGED BY BOMBING** severely damaged or destroyed by bombing **2. INTOXICATED** drunk, or intoxicated by drugs (*slang*)

bomber /bómmər/ *n.* **1.** AIR FORCE **AIRCRAFT THAT DROPS BOMBS** an aircraft designed for carrying and dropping bombs **2.** CRIMINOL **SB WHO PLANTS BOMBS** sb who hides, places, or sets bombs

bomber jacket *n.* a short jacket, usually leather, with an elasticated waist and usually a zip at the front [From the wearing of such jackets by the crew of US bomber aircraft]

bombinate /bómbi nayt/ (**-nates, -nating, -nated**), **bombilate** /-layt/ (**-lates, -lating, -lated**) *vi.* to make a humming or buzzing noise [Late 19thC. From medieval Latin *bombinat-*, the past participle stem of *bombinare*, from Latin *bombus* 'buzzing, booming', from Greek *bombos* (see BOMB).] —**bombination** /bómbi náysh'n/ *n.*

bombing /bómming/ *n.* AIR FORCE the act or process of dropping bombs from aircraft

bomblet /bómmlət/ *n.* a small bomb or explosive device packed into a larger bomb

bombora /bom báwrə/ *n. Aus* **1. SUBMERGED REEF** a reef lying just below sea level **2. DANGEROUS SEA OVER REEF** a dangerous patch of sea where waves break over a reef [Mid-20thC. From an Australian Aboriginal language.]

bombproof /bóm proof/ *adj.* constructed to withstand the impact of bombs

bombshell /bóm shel/ *n.* **1. SURPRISING NEWS** an unexpected and shocking piece of news (*informal*) **2. STUNNING WOMAN** an exceedingly attractive and glamorous woman (*dated informal*) **3.** ARMS **ARTILLERY SHELL OR BOMB** an artillery shell or a bomb

bombsight /bóm sīt/ *n.* a device in an aircraft for aiming bombs

bomb site *n.* an area devastated by bombs

bombycid /bómbissid/ *adj.* belonging to the family of moths that includes the silkworm moths. Family: Bombycidae. [From modern Latin *Bombycidae*, family name, from Latin *bombyx* 'silkworm' (see BOMBAZINE)] —**bombycid** *n.*

Bon, Cape /bon/ peninsula in northeastern Tunisia

Bona, Mount /bṓnə/ the highest peak in the Wrangell Mountains, southern Alaska,. Height: 5,032 m/16,500 ft.

bona fide /bṓnə fīdi/ *adj.* **1. AUTHENTIC** authentic and genuine in nature ○ *a bona fide offer* **2. SINCERE AND HONEST** without any intention to deceive [From Latin, literally 'with good faith']

bona fides /-fīdeez/ *npl.* a sincere statement or evidence of good intentions

bonanza /bə nánzə/ *n.* **1. SOURCE OF WEALTH** a source that yields great riches or success **2. VALUABLE MINERAL DEPOSIT** an extremely valuable mineral deposit [Early 19thC. Via Spanish from medieval Latin *bonacia* 'calm seas', an alteration of *malacia*, 'calm seas' influenced by Latin *bonus* 'good'.]

Bonaparte ◆ **Napoleon I**

Bonapartism /bṓnə paartizzəm/ *n.* **1. NAPOLEONIC RULE** government by or on the pattern of Napoleon I **2. LOYALTY TO NAPOLEONIC TRADITION** support for Napoleon I and Napoleon III of France or their dynasty [Early 19thC. Named after the emperor NAPOLEON Bonaparte.] —**Bonapartist** *n.*

bona vacantia /bṓnə və kánti ə/ *n.* in law, property that is unclaimed or that has no known owner (*takes a singular or plural verb*) [From Latin, literally 'ownerless goods']

Bonaventure /bónnə ven tyóorə/, **Bonaventura, St** (1221?–74) Italian monk and theologian. He was minister general of the Franciscan order (1257) and wrote the official biography of St Francis (1263). Born **Giovanni di Fidanza**. Known as **the Seraphic Doctor**

bonbon /bón bon/ *n.* **1. SWEET** a sweet confection **2. STH SWEET** sth that is sweet and unsubstantial [Late 18thC. From French, literally 'good-good', from Latin *bonus* 'good' (see BONUS).]

bonbonnière /bónbə neér, -nyáir/ *n.* an ornamental bowl or box for sweets [Early 19thC. From French, from *bonbon* 'BONBON'.]

bonce /bonss/ *n.* sb's head (*dated informal*) [Mid-19thC. Origin unknown.]

bond /bond/ *n.* **1. STH THAT BINDS** an object such as a rope, band, or chain that binds sb or sth **2.** LAW **SOLEMN PROMISE** a solemn agreement promising to do sth **3.** LAW **PROMISE TO PAY** a document that legally obliges one party to pay money to another **4.** FIN **CERTIFICATE PROMISING REPAYMENT OF DEBT** a certificate issued by the government or a company promising to pay back borrowed money at a fixed rate of interest on a specified date **5. ADHESION** the way in which one surface sticks to another **6. ADHESIVE SUBSTANCE** a substance that makes objects adhere **7.** CHEM **ATTRACTIVE FORCE** a fundamental attractive force that binds atoms and ions in a molecule. There are different types of bond. **8.** CONSTR **TECHNIQUE FOR OVERLAPPING BRICKS** an overlapping pattern in which bricks or tiles can be laid **9. LINK BINDING PEOPLE TOGETHER** a link that binds people together in a relationship **10. RESTRAINT** a situation that limits sb socially, psychologically, or emotionally **11.** COMM **SECURE STORAGE** secure storage of goods before payment of duty **12.** = **bond paper 13.** *Aus* **MONEY DEPOSIT** a deposit of money, particularly one paid on rented accommodation ■ **bonds** *npl.* **IMPRISONMENT** the state of imprisonment (*archaic*) ■ *v.* (**bonds, bonding, bonded**) **1.** *vti.* **ADHERE OR MAKE ADHERE** to stick together or make two surfaces stick together **2.** *vti.* PSYCHOL **LINK EMOTIONALLY** to link together, or cause people to be linked together, emotionally or psychologically **3.** *vt.* COMM **STORE SECURELY** store goods securely until duty is paid **4.** *vti.* FIN **CONVERT INTO DEBT UNDER BOND** to convert sth or be converted into a debt with a bond as security **5.** *vt.* CHEM **LINK WITH CHEMICAL BOND** to link atoms or ions with a chemical bond **6.** *vt.* CONSTR **OVERLAP** to lay bricks or tiles so that they overlap in a pattern **7.** *vt.* SEW **FUSE TOGETHER** to fuse two fabrics together **8.** *vt. Aus* **GIVE MONEY DEPOSIT** to provide a bond against unforeseen losses [13thC. Variant of BAND[2].] —**bondable** *adj.*

Bond /bond/, **Alan** (*b.* 1938) English-born Australian business executive. He became one of Australia's richest men as chairman of the Bond Corporation (1969–90). It collapsed in 1990, and he was jailed for fraud (1997). His syndicate won the America's Cup in 1983 in the yacht *Australia II.*

Bond, Edward (*b.* 1934) British playwright and director. His plays, often controversial for their violence, include *Saved* (1965) and *Bingo* (1973).

bondage /bóndij/ *n.* **1. SLAVERY** the condition of being a slave or serf **2. CONTROL BY STH** the condition of being controlled by sth that limits freedom **3. PHYSICAL RESTRAINT** the practice of being tied up or restrained physically during sexual intercourse **4.** HIST = **villeinage** [14thC. Via Anglo-Norman from, ultimately, Old Norse *bóndi* 'husbandman', from the present participle of *búa* 'to dwell' (source of English *husband*).]

bonded /bóndid/ *adj.* **1.** COMM **STORED BEFORE TAXATION** stored securely until duty or tax is paid **2.** INDUST

MADE TO ADHERE IN LAYERS chemically attached or fused together in layers

bonded warehouse n. a warehouse that holds goods awaiting duty or tax to be paid on them

bonder /bóndər/ n. **1.** SB OR STH THAT BONDS sb who or sth that bonds **2.** CONSTR = **bondstone**

bondholder /bónd hōldər/ n. sb who owns bonds issued by a government or company

Bondi Beach /bóndī-/ coastal suburb of Sydney, Australia. It is a popular surfing and tourist centre.

bonding /bónding/ n. **1.** PSYCHOL FORMATION OF EMOTIONAL BONDS the formation of a close emotional tie between people, e.g. between a mother and her newly born infant. ◊ **attachment 2.** DENT COATING A TOOTH the process of coating a tooth with a durable resinous substance **3.** PROCESS OF BONDING STH the process by which sth is bonded

bond paper n. a strong, white, high-quality paper

bondservant /bónd survənt/ n. a slave or serf [15thC. Formed from earlier *bond* 'bound in servitude' + SERVANT.]

bondsman /bóndzmən/ (*plural* **-men** /-mən/) n. **1.** SB RESPONSIBLE FOR A LEGAL BOND sb who assumes responsibility for a legal bond **2.** HIST SERF a male slave or serf

bondstone /bónd stōn/ n. a stone that extends into the interior of a wall in order to strengthen it

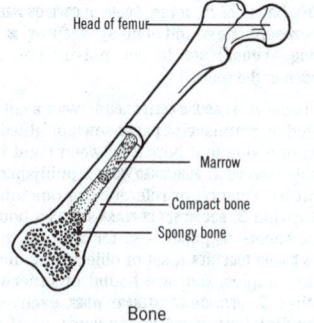

Bone

bone /bōn/ n. **1.** ANAT SECTION OF THE SKELETON any one of the hard parts forming the skeleton in vertebrate animals **2.** ANAT MATERIAL MAKING UP BONES the main material that makes up a vertebrate skeleton, formed principally from collagen fibres and calcium phosphate **3.** INDUST SUBSTANCE RESEMBLING BONE sth hard that resembles the bone of the vertebrate skeleton, e.g. whalebone or ivory **4.** COLOURS IVORY COLOUR the ivory or off-white colour of bone **5.** CLOTHES STRIP USED AS STIFFENING a flat strip of hard material, e.g. whalebone or plastic, used to stiffen a garment ■ **bones** npl. **1.** LIVING BODY sb's living body (*humorous*) ○ *I must rest my weary bones.* **2.** DEAD BODY the skeleton or corpse of a dead person or animal **3.** MUSIC PAIR OF RHYTHMICALLY CLACKING BARS a pair of bars or strips of wood, metal, or bone, that are struck together sharply to make musical rhythms **4.** STRUCTURE OF STH the structure or framework of sth **5.** DICE a pair of dice (*informal*) ■ vt. (**bones, boning, boned**) **1.** COOKING REMOVE BONES FROM to remove the bones from fish, meat, or poultry when preparing it for cooking or eating **2.** CLOTHES STIFFEN to add flat strips to stiffen a garment **3.** US OFFENSIVE TERM to have sexual intercourse (*slang offensive*) ■ adv. VERY extremely or totally ○ *bone idle* [Old English *bān*. Ultimately from a prehistoric Germanic word meaning 'long bone'.] ◊ **have a bone to pick with sb** to have cause for disagreement with sb ◊ **in your bones** without having to think or reason ◊ **make no bones about sth** to say sth openly and frankly

bone up vi. to review or study sth intensely (*informal*)

bone china n. **1.** FINE WHITE PORCELAIN a fine white porcelain made from a mixture of clay and bone ash **2.** ARTICLES MADE OF BONE CHINA articles made of bone china

bonefire /bón fīr/ n. *Ireland* a bonfire [Variant of BONFIRE]

bonefish /bón fish/ (*plural* **-fish** or **-fishes**) n. a large game fish found in warm shallow waters. Latin name: *Albula vulpes*.

bonehead /bón hed/ n. an offensive term that deliberately insults sb's intelligence (*informal*

insult) —**boneheaded** /bón héddid/ adj. —**bone-headedness** /-héddidnəss/ n.

bone marrow n. a soft reddish substance inside some bones that is involved in the production of blood cells. New white and red blood cells are formed only in the marrow of the flat bones such as the ribs, breastbone, or pelvis in adults.

bone meal n. ground animal bones, used as a fertilizer or in animal feed [*Meal* from MEAL[2]]

bone of contention n. a subject of constant argument or disagreement between people [From the fighting of dogs over possession of a bone]

boner /bónər/ n. **1.** EMBARRASSING MISTAKE an embarrassing mistake (*informal*) **2.** US ERECTION an erect penis (*slang*) **3.** DEVICE THAT BONES sth that is designed for boning sth, or sb who bones sth ○ *a fish boner*

boneset /bón set/ (*plural* **-set** or **-sets**) n. a North American plant of the daisy family believed to have healing properties. Genus: *Eupatorium.*

bonesetter /bón setər/ n. sb who sets broken or dislocated bones, especially sb not qualified as a doctor

boneshaker /bón shaykər/ n. **1.** DECREPIT CAR a decrepit or uncomfortable vehicle (*informal*) **2.** EARLY BICYCLE an early type of bicycle with solid tyres and no springs

bone spavin n. an inflammation of the bones in a horse's hock, resulting in swelling and lameness

boneyard /bón yaard/ n. a cemetery (*informal*)

bonfire /bón fīr/ n. a large fire built outside for burning rubbish or garden refuse, as part of a celebration, or as a signal [14thC. Formed from BONE + FIRE, from the original use of burnt bones as fuel.]

——— WORD KEY: CULTURAL NOTE ———

Bonfire of the Vanities, a novel by US writer Tom Wolfe (1988). Using the story of the trial of wealthy New York bond trader Sherman McCoy for the accidental killing of a young Black man, Wolfe satirizes the US media, legal system, and art world. It was made into a film by Brian de Palma in 1990.

Bonfire Night n. 5 November, the anniversary of the day on which Guy Fawkes' plot to blow up Parliament (**the Gunpowder Plot**) was discovered in 1605. In the United Kingdom and other Commonwealth countries it is celebrated with fireworks and bonfires.

bong[1] /bong/ n., interj. REVERBERATING SOUND a deep resonant sound, especially from a bell ■ vi. (**bongs, bonging, bonged**) MAKE A REVERBERATING SOUND to make a deep resonant sound [Mid-19thC. An imitation of the sound.]

bong[2] /bong/ n. **1.** DRUGS DRUG-USER'S WATER PIPE a water pipe for smoking hashish or other drugs (*slang*) **2.** MOUNTAINEERING METAL DEVICE FOR PROTECTING CLIMBERS a large metal device resembling a tube, used in providing protection for climbers [Late 20thC. Origin uncertain: probably from Thai *baung*.]

Bongaree /bóng gə rée/ tourist resort on Bribie Island, just off the coast of south-eastern Queensland, Australia. Population: 11,166 (1996).

bongo /bóng gō/ (*plural* **-gos** or **-goes** or **-go**) n. a forest-dwelling antelope found in central Africa that has a reddish coat with vertical white stripes and spiralling horns. Latin name: *Boocercus euryceros*. [Mid-19thC. From Kikongo.]

bongo drums, **bongos** npl. a set of two small deep-bodied drums that are held between the knees and beaten with the fingers [From American Spanish *bongó*]

bonham /bónnəm/ n. *Ireland* a piglet [Late 19thC. Via Irish *banbh* from Old Irish *banb*, of uncertain origin.]

Bonhoeffer /bón hurfər/, **Dietrich** (1906–45) German pastor and theologian. He was active in the German resistance during World War II, and was executed in 1945 for involvement in a plot to assassinate Hitler.

bonhomie /bónnə mee/ n. easy good-humoured friendliness [Late 18thC. From French *bonhomme*, literally 'good man'.] —**bonhomous** adj.

Boniface /bónni fayss/, St (675?–754?) Saxon missionary. Commissioned to preach to the German peoples in 718, he became a bishop in 723. He was

killed by non-Christians in Friesia. Born **Wynfrith**. Known as **the Apostle of Germany**

Boniface VIII, Pope (1234?–1303) Italian pope. As pope from 1294 to 1303, he proclaimed the supremacy of the papacy over temporal law. Born **Benedetto Caetani**

Bonington /bónningtən/, **Sir Chris** (b. 1934) British mountaineer. He led the first British team up the north face of the Eiger (1962) and led numerous other ascents of the world's highest peaks. Full name **Sir Christian John Storey Bonington**

Bonin Islands /bónin-/ volcanic island group in Japan in the Pacific Ocean. They were held under US control (1945–68). Population: 2,303 (1985). Area: 104 sq. km/40 sq. mi.

bonito /bə neetō/ (*plural* **-tos** or **-to**) n. **1.** FISH OF MACKEREL FAMILY a striped edible fish found in Atlantic and Pacific waters. Genus: *Sarda*. **2.** FISH RESEMBLING TRUE BONITO a fish such as the skipjack that resembles or is related to the bonito [Late 16thC. Origin uncertain: probably via Spanish, literally 'pretty', from Latin *bonus* 'good' (see BONUS).]

bonk /bongk/ v. (**bonks, bonking, bonked**) **1.** vt. BANG to bang or hit sth or sb (*informal*) **2.** vti. OFFENSIVE TERM to have sexual intercourse (*slang offensive*) ■ n. **1.** SHARP BLOW a sharp blow, typically on the head **2.** OFFENSIVE TERM an offensive term for sexual intercourse (*slang offensive*) [Early 20thC. An imitation of the sound.]

bonkers /bóngkərz/ adj. completely irrational (*informal*) [Mid-20thC. Origin unknown.]

bon mot /bóN mó/ (*plural* **bons mots** /bóN mó/) n. a witty comment [From French, literally 'good word']

Bonn /bon/ city on the Rhine in North Rhine-Westphalia state, west-central Germany. It was the capital of West Germany from 1949 to 1990. Population: 297,400 (1992).

Bonnard /bónnaar, bo naár/, **Pierre** (1867–1947) French painter. In his early career he was a conventional painter of decorative scenes. After 1900 his pictures, often of bathing women, were notable for their use of light and colour.

bonne /bon/ n. a French woman or girl servant (*dated*) [Late 18thC. From French, literally 'good girl'.]

bonne bouche /bón boosh/ (*plural* **bonnes bouches** /bón boosh/) n. a small piece of tasty food [From French, literally 'good mouth']

Bonner /bónnər/, **Neville Thomas** (b. 1922) Australian politician. A Liberal Party senator (1971–83), he was the first Aborigine to be elected to the Australian federal parliament.

Bonnet

bonnet /bónnit/ n. **1.** WOMAN'S HAT a hat framing the face and usually tied under the chin, worn by a woman or girl **2.** UK, Carib AUTOMOT COVER OF CAR ENGINE the hinged cover over the engine of a car or other vehicle, usually at the front. US term **hood 3.** Scotland SOFT FLAT CAP a soft flat cap, worn by men or boys **4.** NATIVE N AMERICAN HEADDRESS a ceremonial feathered headdress traditionally worn by some Native North Americans **5.** CHIMNEY COWL a wire cover fitted over a chimney pot **6.** ENG PROTECTIVE COVER a protective cap or cover fitting over a machine part **7.** SAILING EXTRA PIECE OF SAIL an extra strip of canvas laced to the base of a foresail, used to extend it when the wind is light [14thC. Via Old French from medieval Latin *abonnis* 'headgear', possibly of Germanic origin.] —**bonneted** adj.

bonnethead /bónnət hed/ (*plural* **-heads** *or* **-head**), **bonnethead shark** *n.* ZOOL = **shovelhead**

bonnet monkey *n.* a South Indian macaque that has a bonnet-like tuft of hair. Latin name: *Macaca silenus.*

Bonneville Salt Flats /bónnəvil-/ barren salt plain in northwestern Utah, the bed of a prehistoric lake. It has been used for setting world land speed records since the 1930s. Area: 260 sq. km/100 sq. mi.

bonny /bónni/ (**-nier, -niest**), **bonnie** (**-nier, -niest**) *adj. Scotland, N England* **1. ATTRACTIVE** pleasing to look at **2. SUBSTANTIAL** fairly large **3. EXCELLENT** extremely good **4. PLUMP AND HEALTHY** plump and healthy [15thC. Origin uncertain: perhaps via French *bon* 'good' from Latin *bonus*.] —**bonnily** *adv.* —**bonniness** *n.*

WORD KEY: REGIONAL NOTE

This adjective is of uncertain origin, although it has often been linked to French *bon(ne)*, meaning 'good'. It is still widely used in the north of England and Scotland to describe a young woman who is attractive both physically and in character.

Bonny /bónni/ bay in the Gulf of Guinea, western Africa, in the Atlantic Ocean. Length: 640 km/400 mi. Also known as **Biafra [Bight of]**

bonnyclabber /bónni klabər/ *n. Ireland, US* sour milk that has clotted (*regional*) [Early 17thC. From Irish *bainne clabair* 'thick milk for churning'.]

Bonsai

bonsai /bón sī/ (*plural* **-sai** *or* **-sais**) *n.* **1.** GARDENING **ART OF GROWING MINIATURE TREES** the art of growing miniaturized forms of trees and shrubs by rigorous pruning of roots and branches **2.** TREES **MINIATURIZED TREE** a tree or shrub miniaturized using bonsai techniques [Early 20thC. From Japanese, literally 'tray planting'.]

bonsela /bon séllə/, **bonsella** (*plural* **bonsellas** *or* **bonselas**) *n. S Africa* **1. GRATUITY** a tip **2. PRESENT FOR GOOD CUSTOMER** a small reward, usually of sweets, given to a good customer by a trader [Origin uncertain: perhaps from Zulu *ukubansela* 'to give thanks in tangible form' or *ibhanselo* 'gift']

bonspiel /bón speel/ *n.* SPORTS a curling match or tournament [Mid-16thC. Origin uncertain: probably from Dutch or Low German.]

bontebok /bónti buk/ (*plural* **-boks** *or* **-bok**) *n.* a southern African antelope with a reddish coat, white markings on the face and rump, and white legs. Latin name: *Damaliscus pygargus.* [Late 18thC. From Afrikaans, literally 'pied buck'.]

bon ton /bóN tóN/ *n.* (*literary*) **1. GOOD TASTE** good taste, style, or manners ○ *People thought it bon ton to be seen attending such an occasion.* **2. FASHIONABLE SOCIETY** fashionable society [From French, literally 'good tone']

bonus /bṓnəss/ *n.* **1. UNEXPECTED EXTRA** an extra unexpected advantage **2. EXTRA MONEY** an amount of money given in addition to normal pay, especially as a reward **3. PREMIUM PAID TO SB** an extra dividend or premium paid to the purchaser, holder, promoter, or vendor of a stock or insurance policy [Late 18thC. From Latin, 'good' (source of English *bounty*). Ultimately from an Indo-European base meaning 'to show favour', which is also the ancestor of English *benevolent*, *embellish*, and *beauty*.]

bonus issue *n.* an issue of free shares, distributed pro rata by a company to existing shareholders

bon vivant /bóN vee vaáN/ (*plural* **bons vivants** /bóN vee vóN/), **bon viveur** /-vee vúr/ (*plural* **bons viveurs** /bóN vee vúr/) *n.* sb who enjoys the luxuries in life, e.g. good food and wine [*Bon vivant* from French, literally 'one who lives well'; *bon viveur* formed in English on the model of *bon vivant* and French *viveur* 'living person']

bon voyage /bóN vwaa yaázh, bón voy aázh/ *interj.* used to wish sb an enjoyable and safe journey [From French, literally 'good journey']

bony /bṓni/ (**-ier, -iest**) *adj.* **1. HAVING PROMINENT BONES** extremely thin and with prominent bones **2.** FOOD **CONTAINING MANY BONES** containing a lot of bones, and often difficult to eat **3.** ANAT **OF OR LIKE BONE** consisting of or like bone **4.** ZOOL **WITH A BACKBONE** used to describe fish that have a skeleton of bone, as distinct from cartilaginous fish such as sharks. The great majority of fish are bony. Class: Osteichthyes. —**boniness** *n.*

bonze /bonz/ *n.* a Buddhist monk in Southeast Asia, China, or Japan [Late 16thC. Via French from, ultimately, Japanese *bonsō*.]

bonzer /bónzər/ *adj. ANZ* excellent, great, or superlative (*dated informal*) [Early 20thC. Origin uncertain: perhaps an alteration of BONANZA.]

boo /boo/ *interj.* **1. EXPRESSING DISAPPROVAL** used to express dissatisfaction or contempt, especially at a speaker or performer **2. USED TO STARTLE SB** used to surprise or startle sb ■ *n.* **SOUND 'BOO!'** an utterance of 'boo!' ■ *vti.* (**boos, booing, booed**) **EXPRESS DISAPPROVAL** to shout 'boo!' in order to express disapproval or contempt of sb, especially a speaker or performer [Early 19thC. Originally an imitation of a cow's lowing.] ◇ **not say boo to a goose** be extremely timid and shy (*informal*)

boob¹ /boob/, **booby** /boobi/ (*plural* **-bies**) *n.* a woman's breast (*slang*) (*considered offensive by many people; often used in the plural*) [Mid-20thC. From earlier *bubby*, of uncertain origin: perhaps from Low German.]

boob² /boob/ *n.* **1. UNFORTUNATE MISTAKE** an unfortunate and embarrassing mistake (*informal*) **2. UNINTELLIGENT PERSON** sb who is considered unintelligent or ignorant ■ *vi.* (**boobs, boobing, boobed**) *UK, Can* **MAKE AN UNFORTUNATE MISTAKE** to make an unfortunate and embarrassing mistake (*informal*) [Early 20thC. Shortening of BOOBY¹.]

boobialla /boobi állə/ (*plural* **-las** *or* **-la**) *n.* a small Australian tree with a rounded crown, long glossy leaves, and white flowers, commonly found on sand dunes and cliffs. Latin name: *Myoporum insulare.* [Mid-19thC. From an Aboriginal language.]

boo-boo *n.* a mistake or tactless remark (*informal*) [Mid-20thC. Origin uncertain.]

boobook /boobòòk/ (*plural* **-books** *or* **-book**) *n.* a small brown owl, native to Australia and New Zealand. Genus: *Ninox*. [Early 19thC. From an Australian Aboriginal language, ultimately an imitation of the bird's call.]

boob tube *n.* a short strapless stretchy top for women (*slang*) US term **tube top**

booby¹ /boobi/ (*plural* **-bies**) *n.* **1. UNINTELLIGENT PERSON** sb who is silly or unintelligent (*dated informal*) **2. POOREST PERFORMER** the poorest performer in a group, or the loser in a game (*informal*) **3.** BIRDS **LARGE TROPICAL SEABIRD** a large tropical seabird with white plumage and dark markings, often with a brightly coloured bill and feet. There are many species, including pelicans and cormorants. Family: Sulidae. [Early 17thC. Origin uncertain: probably an alteration of Spanish *bobo*, from Latin *balbus* 'stammering'.]

booby² *n.* = **boob**¹

booby hatch *n.* a cover for a small hatchway on a sailing ship [*Booby* from *booby* 'bird', because these hatches are a favourite haunt for these birds]

booby prize *n.* a prize given as a joke to the person or team coming last in a competition

booby trap *n.* **1. TRAP LAID AS JOKE** a trap set as a practical joke **2. HIDDEN EXPLOSIVE DEVICE** a bomb that is hidden or disguised and is designed to explode when touched or moved

booby-trap (**booby-traps, booby-trapping, booby-trapped**) *vt.* to place a booby trap in a place, or attach one to sth (*often passive*)

boodle /bood'l/ *n.* a large amount of money that has been acquired or used in a corrupt way (*slang*) [Early 17thC. From Dutch *boedel* 'estate, possessions'.]

boofhead /boòf hed/ *n. Aus* sb who is considered unintelligent or thoughtless (*informal*) [Mid-20thC. Origin uncertain: possibly from obsolete *bufflehead* 'simpleton'.]

boofy /boòfi/ *adj. Aus* unintelligent or thoughtless (*informal*) [Late 20th C. Back-formation from BOOFHEAD.]

booger /boòggər/ *n. US* = **bogey** (*slang*) [Mid-19thC. Origin uncertain: probably an alteration of BUGGER.]

boogie /boògi/ *vi.* (**-ies, -ieing, -ied**) **1.** DANCING **DANCE TO ROCK MUSIC** to dance to fast rock music (*informal*) **2. HAVE SEX** to have sexual intercourse (*dated slang*) ■ *n.* MUSIC = **boogie-woogie** [Mid-20thC. Of West African origin see BOOGIE-WOOGIE.]
boogie on down *vi.* to go off somewhere (*slang*)

boogie board *n.* = **body board**

boogie-woogie /boògi woògi/ *n.* a jazz piano style derived from the blues [Origin uncertain: perhaps an alteration of Black West African English *bogi-bogi* 'to dance', from Hausa *buga* 'to beat drums']

boohai /boo hī/, **booai** /boo ī/, **booay** *n. NZ* a remote rural area (*informal*) [Mid-20thC. Origin uncertain perhaps from *Puhoi*, the name of a once remote township in North Auckland, New Zealand.]

boohoo /boo hoò/ *n.*, *interj.* **SOUND OF COPIOUS WEEPING** used to represent the sound of noisy weeping ■ *vi.* (**-hoos, -hooing, -hooed**) **SOB** to cry noisily [Mid-19thC. An imitation of the sound.]

book /bòòk/ *n.* **1. BOUND COLLECTION OF PAGES** a collection of printed or manuscript pages sewn or glued together along one side and bound between rigid boards or flexible covers **2. PUBLISHED WORK** a published work of literature, science, or reference, or one intended for publication **3. BOUND SET OF BLANK SHEETS** a bound set of blank sheets of paper, e.g. for writing in **4. SET OF THINGS BOUND TOGETHER** a set of objects, e.g. matches or fabric samples, that are bound or otherwise fixed together **5. DIVISION OF LITERARY WORK** each of several major divisions of a literary work, or of the Bible **6. SCRIPT OR LIBRETTO** the script of a play, or the libretto of an opera **7. BOOKMAKER'S RECORD** a record kept by a bookmaker of the bets made and of the money paid out **8. TELEPHONE DIRECTORY** a telephone directory (*informal*) **9.** CARDS **NUMBER OF TRICKS NEEDED IN SCORING** the number of tricks that need to be won by a player or side in order to be scored **10. MAGAZINE** a magazine for reading or looking at (*informal*) **11. SET OF RULES** the body of rules or procedures relevant to a situation ○ *likes to do things by the book* **12. IMAGINARY RECORD** any imaginary record, archive, or repository of knowledge **13.** = **promptbook 14. book, Book** BIBLE the Christian Bible ■ **books** *npl.* **1.** ACCT **FINANCIAL ACCOUNTS** the financial records and accounts of an organization **2. LEARNING** academic study ■ *v.* (**books, booking, booked**) **1.** *vti.* **MAKE RESERVATION** to arrange for sb to keep a place available at a specified time, e.g. at the theatre or in a restaurant **2.** *vt.* **RESERVE A PLACE FOR** to reserve a place for sb somewhere, especially on some form of transport **3.** *vt.* **ENGAGE TO DO STH** to engage sb in advance to do sth or be somewhere, especially as a performer (*often passive*) **4.** *vt.* LAW **CHARGE WITH OFFENCE** to charge sb with a criminal offence, pending legal proceedings (*often passive*) **5.** *vt.* SPORTS **TAKE NAME OF OFFENDING PLAYER** officially to take the name of a player who has committed an offence (*often passive*) **6.** *vi. US* **LEAVE A PLACE** to leave a place (*slang*) ○ *Yo man, let's book!* [Old English *bōc* 'written document'. Ultimately from an Indo-European word meaning 'beech', which is also the ancestor of English *beech*; the early Germanic peoples carved runic inscriptions on beechwood tablets.] ◇ **a closed book** sb about whom or sth about which little if anything is known or understood ◇ **an open book** sth or sb fully comprehended ◇ **bring sb to book** to admonish sb ◇ **cook the books** to alter records, especially financial accounts, to conceal irregularities or wrongdoing (*slang*) ◇ **in sb's book** in sb's opinion ◇ **in sb's good** *or* **bad books** in *or* out of favour with sb ◇ **throw the book at sb** to charge sb with all the offences he or she may be guilty of, or punish sb with the maximum penalty
book in *v.* **1.** *vti.* **RESERVE ACCOMMODATION** to reserve ac-

commodation at a hotel or other lodgings **2.** *vi.* REPORT ARRIVAL to sign in at a hotel or other lodgings **book out** *vti.* to register that you have or sb else has completed a stay at a hotel or other accommodation **book up** *vi.* to reserve accommodation or buy a ticket for sth in advance

bookable /bŏŏkəb'l/ *adj.* **1.** ABLE TO BE RESERVED able to be applied for in advance and reserved **2.** SPORTS SERIOUS ENOUGH FOR OFFICIAL ACTION serious enough for the referee to give a warning and record it officially

bookbinder /bŏŏk bīndər/ *n.* sb who binds books, especially as a profession —**bookbindery** *n.* —**bookbinding** *n.*

bookcase /bŏŏk kayss/ *n.* a set of shelves, either fixed to a wall or free-standing, used for holding books

book club *n.* an organization that offers its members books at reduced prices

bookend /bŏŏk end/ *n.* SUPPORT FOR ROW OF BOOKS either of a pair of supports placed at each end of a row of books ■ *vt.* OCCUR EITHER SIDE OF to occur on both sides or at the beginning and end of sth (*informal*) ○ *bookend a speech with anecdotes*

Booker Prize /bŏŏkər-/ *n.* a cash prize awarded annually by the company Booker McConnell for a recently published work of fiction by a UK, Irish, or Commonwealth writer —**Booker Prizewinner** *n.*

bookie /bŏŏki/ *n.* a bookmaker (*informal*) [Late 19thC. Formed from BOOKMAKER.]

booking /bŏŏking/ *n.* **1.** ADVANCE RESERVATION an arrangement by which sth such as a theatre seat or hotel room is kept for sb's use at a specified time **2.** ARRANGEMENT TO PERFORM a contract or arrangement for an entertainer to perform somewhere

bookish /bŏŏkish/ *adj.* devoted to reading, especially to the exclusion of other things —**bookishly** *adv.* —**bookishness** *n.*

bookkeeping /bŏŏk keeping/, **book-keeping** *n.* the activity or profession of recording the money received and spent by an individual, business, or organization —**bookkeeper** *n.*

book learning *n.* knowledge obtained from books rather than from experience

booklet /bŏŏklət/ *n.* a small book with a paper cover and few pages, usually containing information about a particular subject

booklore /bŏŏk lawr/ *n.* **1.** = book learning **2.** FACTS ABOUT BOOKS information about books, especially their authors and circumstances of publication

booklouse /bŏŏk lowss/ (*plural* **-lice** /-līss/) *n.* a small wingless insect that destroys books by feeding on the paste used in the binding. Order: Psocoptera.

book lung *n.* the breathing organ in spiders and other arachnids, with membranous tissue arranged in folds that resemble the leaves of a book

bookmaker /bŏŏk maykər/ *n.* **1.** SB WHO RECEIVES BETS sb who takes bets and pays out money to people who win **2.** SB WHO MAKES BOOKS sb who designs, prints, or binds books —**bookmaking** *n.*

bookman /bŏŏkmən/ (*plural* **-men** /-mən/) *n.* sb who is interested in and knowledgable about books, especially as collector's items

bookmark /bŏŏk maark/ *n.* **1.** PLACE MARKER IN BOOK a strip of leather or other material inserted between the pages of a book to mark a place in it **2.** COMPUT PLACE MARKER IN ELECTRONIC TEXT an electronic marker inserted in a word-processed document, identifying it for later reference or retrieval **3.** COMPUT ADDRESS OF INTERNET SITE the address of a user's favourite Internet site electronically listed for easy access ■ *vt.* (**-marks, -marking, -marked**) COMPUT LIST AN INTERNET ADDRESS to list the address of an Internet site

Book of Changes *n.* = I Ching

Book of Common Prayer *n.* the official book giving the order and content of services in the Anglican Church. Since 1980 the Alternative Service Book has also been in use.

book of hours *n.* a medieval service book, used especially in monasteries, containing the offices, prayers, and services prescribed for the various canonical hours

Book of Kells /-kéllz/ *n.* an illuminated manuscript of the Christian Gospels, produced at Kells in Ireland in the 8th century and now kept in Trinity College, Dublin

Book of Life *n.* **1.** IDENTITY DOCUMENT a comprehensive personal identity document carried by South Africans. It was originally introduced for Whites only but went into general use in 1986. ◊ **dompas 2.** CHR BIBLE the Bible

Book of Mormon *n.* a book believed by Mormons to have been revealed by the prophet Mormon to Joseph Smith. It contains the history of an ancient American people to whom Jesus Christ appeared.

bookplate /bŏŏk playt/ *n.* a label for sticking into the front of a book, bearing the name of the owner and sometimes a coat of arms or personal design

bookrest /bŏŏk rest/ *n.* a support, often angled, for an open book

bookseller /bŏŏk selər/ *n.* sb who buys and sells books

bookshelf /bŏŏk shelf/ (*plural* **-shelves** /-shelvz/) *n.* a shelf designed for holding books

bookshop /bŏŏk shop/ *n.* a shop that specializes in selling books

bookstall /bŏŏk stawl/ *n.* **1.** STAND SELLING BOOKS AND NEWSPAPERS a stand in the street or at a railway or bus station where newspapers, magazines, and books are sold **2.** STALL SELLING BOOKS a stall where books are sold

bookstand /bŏŏk stand/ *n.* **1.** = bookstall **2.** SUPPORT FOR OPEN BOOK a support for an open book, often adjustable and made of wood, metal, or plastic

book token *n.* a voucher for a specified value that can be exchanged for books and is often given as a present

book value *n.* **1.** VALUE ACCORDING TO ACCOUNTING RECORDS the value of a commodity or asset according to the accounting records of the firm owning it **2.** NET VALUE OF BUSINESS ENTERPRISE the net value of a business after liabilities have been deducted from assets

bookworm /bŏŏk wurm/ *n.* **1.** INSECT EATING BOOKS any insect whose larvae eat the binding paste or paper in books **2.** ENTHUSIASTIC READER sb who reads a great deal (*informal*)

Boole /bool/, **George** (1815–64) British mathematician and logician. His system of Boolean algebra, presented in *An Investigation of the Laws of Thought* (1854), applied symbols to logical propositions. Boolean logic is important in designing and programming computers.

Boolean /bŏŏli ən/ *adj.* using or characterized by a system of symbolic logic that uses combinations of such logical operators as 'AND', 'OR', and 'NOT' to determine relationships between entities. Boolean operations are extensively used in writing computer programs and in computer searches using keywords. [Mid-19thC. Named after George BOOLE.]

Boolean algebra *n.* a form of algebra concerned with the logical functions of variables that are restricted to two values, true or false. Boolean algebra is fundamental to circuit design and to the design, function, and operation of computers.

boom[1] /boom/ *v.* (**booms, booming, boomed**) **1.** *vi.* MAKE A LOUD DEEP SOUND to make a loud deep reverberating sound **2.** *vt.* UTTER WITH DEEP SOUND to utter sth, e.g. a warning, in a loud deep voice ■ *n.* **1.** LOUD DEEP SOUND a loud deep reverberating sound **2.** ECON SIGNIFICANT INCREASE IN TRADE a significant expansion of business and investment, either across an economy or in a specific market **3.** SIGNIFICANT INCREASE a significant increase in the amount of sth, e.g. in a population level or in the public interest in sth **4.** ZOOL DEEP LOUD BIRD OR ANIMAL NOISE a deep loud cry made by some birds and animals, e.g. bitterns or grouse [15thC. Origin uncertain: possibly from Dutch *bommen* 'to hum, buzz'; ultimately an imitation of the sound.] —**boomy** *adj.*

boom[2] /boom/ *n.* **1.** SAILING BEAM HOLDING SAIL AT ANGLE a beam to which the bottom edge of a sail is attached in order to hold the sail at an advantageous angle to the wind **2.** CINEMA, TV EXTENDABLE OVERHEAD POLE an extendable pole carrying overhead equipment, such as a camera, for positioning over a television or film set **3.** MIL, INDUST FLOATING BARRIER a floating barrier used to confine or restrict sth, e.g. a barrier to protect a harbour from attack or to confine an oil spill **4.** SHIPPING POLE USED TO MOVE CARGO a long pole extending from the mast of a derrick to lift or lower cargo **5.** AIR CONNECTING SPAR FOR AIRCRAFT a spar that connects the tail and the fuselage in some aircraft [Mid-16thC. From Dutch, 'beam, pole'. Ultimately from a prehistoric Germanic word meaning 'tree', which is also the ancestor of English *beam* and *bumpkin*.]

boom and bust, **boom or bust** *n.* the alternation in an economy or market between immoderate growth and collapse and recession

boomer /boomər/ *n.* **1.** *US* = baby boomer (*informal*) **2.** *Aus* LARGE KANGAROO a very large male kangaroo (*informal*) **3.** NAVY SUBMARINE a nuclear-powered submarine armed with ballistic missiles (*slang*)

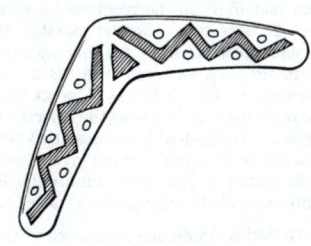

Boomerang

boomerang /boomə rang/ *n.* **1.** SOC SCI, ARMS CURVED MISSILE a flat bent or curved piece of wood used as a weapon by Australian Aborigines. It is designed to return to the person who throws it. **2.** STH HARMFUL TO INITIATOR sth that does harm to its initiator ■ *vi.* (**-angs, -anging, -anged**) BACKFIRE ON INITIATOR to backfire on an initiator of an action, causing harm [Late 18thC. From Aboriginal.]

boomkin *n.* = bumpkin[2]

boomlet /boomlət/ *n.* a short period of sudden and intense economic growth

boomslang /boom slang/ (*plural* **-slangs** *or* **-slang**) *n.* a large greenish poisonous snake, native to southern Africa, that lives in trees. Latin name: *Dispholidus typus.* [Late 18thC. From Afrikaans, literally 'tree snake'.]

boom town *n.* a town that significantly increases in size and wealth, often as the result of new and profitable industry

boon /boon/ *n.* **1.** GREAT BENEFIT sth that functions as a blessing or benefit to sb **2.** GIFT OR FAVOUR a gift or favour from sb (*archaic or literary*) [From Old Norse *bón* 'prayer, petition'. Ultimately from an Indo-European word meaning 'to speak', which is also the ancestor of English *ban*, *banish*, and *fame*.]

boon companion *n.* an intimate and inseparable friend [*Boon* via French *bon* from Latin *bonus* 'good' (see BONUS)]

boondocks /boon doks/ *npl. US, Can* anywhere far from civilization, used as an archetype of a provincial way of life and lack of sophistication (*informal*) [Mid-20thC. From Tagalog *bundok* 'mountain'.]

boong /boong/ *n. Aus* an offensive term for an Aborigine (*slang offensive*) [Mid-20thC. From Aboriginal.]

boongary /boong gari/ (*plural* **-ries** *or* **-ry**) *n.* a kangaroo, native to northern Australia, that lives in trees. Latin name: *Dendrolagus lumholtzi.* [Late 19thC. From Aboriginal.]

boonies /booniz/ *npl. US, Can* = boondocks (*informal*) [Mid-20thC. Shortening.]

boor /boor/ *n.* sb who behaves in a crass, insensitive, or ill-mannered way [Mid-16thC. From Dutch *boer* 'peasant' (source of English *Boer*). Ultimately from a prehistoric Germanic word that is also the ancestor of English *neighbour*.] —**boorish** *adj.* —**boorishly** *adv.* —**boorishness** *n.*

Boorman /báwrmən/, **John** (*b.* 1933) British film director. After a successful career making documentaries for the BBC, he directed Hollywood feature films, including *Deliverance* (1972) and *Hope and Glory* (1987).

boost /boost/ *vt.* **(boosts, boosting, boosted) 1. IMPROVE STH** to improve or strengthen sth **2. INCREASE STH** to cause sth to increase ○ *measures to boost productivity* **3.** COMM **VIGOROUSLY PROMOTE STH** to promote sth widely and intensively so that people will buy it **4.** ELEC **RAISE VOLTAGE IN STH** to increase the voltage in an electrical circuit **5. ASSIST BY PUSHING OR LIFTING** to assist sb or sth to get up or over sth by giving a push or lift from below ■ *n.* **1. ENCOURAGEMENT** sth that helps to encourage or improve sb or sth in some way **2. INCREASE IN STH** an increase in sth ○ *a boost in income* **3. ADVERTISING CAMPAIGN** a campaign advertising or promoting sth **4. PUSH OR LIFT FROM BELOW** a push from below to help sb up or over sth [Early 19thC. Origin uncertain.]

booster /bóostər/ *n.* **1.** ELECTRON ENG **RADIO-FREQUENCY AMPLIFIER** a radio-frequency amplifier that amplifies weak television or radio signals and retransmits them so that they can be received by viewers or listeners **2.** SPACE TECH = **booster rocket 3. SB OR STH THAT IMPROVES CONFIDENCE** sb or sth that encourages or improves sth such as confidence (*usually used in combination*) ○ *a morale-booster* **4. DEVICE THAT ASSISTS STH** a device used to increase the effectiveness of some piece of equipment **5.** MED **SUPPLEMENTARY DOSE OF VACCINE** a repeat dose of a vaccine given some years after the initial course to maintain the level of immunity provided by the previous dose

booster rocket *n.* an engine in a space vehicle that is used to give thrust during the launch and extra thrust during another stage of the flight

booster seat *n.* a seat that can be placed over another seat in a motor vehicle or at a table to raise a child into a higher position

boot[1] /boot/ *n.* **1. STRONG SHOE EXTENDING UP LOWER LEG** a strong item of footwear that covers part of the lower leg (*often used in combination*) ○ *an ankle boot* **2.** AUTOMOT **LUGGAGE COMPARTMENT IN A CAR** the luggage compartment of a car. US term **trunk 3. HARD KICK** the act of kicking sth hard **4. DISMISSAL FROM JOB** dismissal from employment or from a personal relationship (*informal*) **5.** EQU **COVERING FOR HORSE'S LEG** a protective covering for the lower part of a horse's leg **6.** HIST **INSTRUMENT OF TORTURE** a bootlike instrument of torture that was used to enclose and crush the victim's foot **7. OFFENSIVE TERM** an offensive term that deliberately insults a person's age and appearance (*informal*) **8.** MECH ENG **PROTECTIVE COVERING** a protective covering, e.g. a rubber sheath for protecting a coupling between two shafts **9.** *US* **DENVER BOOT** a Denver boot ■ *vt.* **(boots, booting, booted) 1. KICK SB OR STH HARD** to kick sb or sth hard **2.** *US* = **clamp** [14thC. From Old French *bote*, of unknown origin. The sense 'luggage compartment' evolved from the meaning 'outside step for attendants on a coach'.] ◇ **get too big for your boots** to start to think too highly of yourself ◇ **lick sb's boots** to be extremely obsequious to sb ◇ **put the boot in** to attack sb, often sb who is vulnerable or already hurt (*informal*)
boot out *vt.* to force sb to leave a place, group of people, or job (*informal*)

boot[2] /boot/ *n.* **COMPUTER STARTUP PROCEDURE** the process of starting or restarting a computer and loading the operating system ■ *vi.* **(boots, booting, booted, booting)** COMPUT **START UP** to start or become ready to start operating [Late 20thC. Shortening of BOOTSTRAP, from *bootstrap loader*, a simple program that enables a computer to start up and load its full operating system.]
boot up *vt.* to start or restart a computer

boot[3] /boot/ [Old English *bōt* 'remedy'. Ultimately from an Indo-European word meaning 'good', which is also the ancestor of English *better*.] ◇ **to boot** in addition

Boot /boot/, **Sir Jesse, Baron Trent** (1850–1931) British drug manufacturer. He created the largest retail pharmaceutical business in the world, beginning with a single chemist's shop in Nottingham (1877).

boot and saddle *n.* = **boots and saddles**

bootblack /bóot blak/ *n.* = **shoeblack**

booted /bóotid/ *adj.* wearing boots (*archaic or humorous*)

bootee /boó tee/, **bootie** *n.* **1. BABY'S KNITTED BOOT** a soft woollen boot for a baby **2. ANKLE BOOT** an ankle boot for a woman or child

Boötes /bō ṓ teez/ *n.* a constellation of the northern hemisphere lying between Ursa Major and Virgo. It is dominated by the bright star Arcturus.

booth /booth/ (*plural* **booths** /boothz/) *n.* **1. SMALL PARTITIONED ENCLOSURE** a partitioned enclosure or small room shaped like a box that offers privacy, e.g. when telephoning, selling tickets, or voting **2. SMALL TENT OR STALL** a tent, stall, or other light structure at a fair or exhibition, offering some form of entertainment or goods for sale **3. RESTAURANT COMPARTMENT** a small, partly enclosed area in a restaurant with a table and highbacked seats **4. SMALL ROOM USED IN BROADCASTING** a small soundproof room used for recording sound or for broadcasting [12thC. Of Scandinavian origin. Ultimately from an Indo-European base meaning 'to live, dwell', which is also the ancestor of English *bustle, husband, build*, and *neighbour*.]

Booth /booth/, **William** (1829–1912) British religious leader. He founded the Christian Mission (1865), later called the Salvation Army (1878), pursuing social reform and setting up charities in city slums.

Betty Boothroyd

Boothroyd /booth royd/, **Betty** (*b.* 1929) British politician. She became speaker of the House of Commons in 1992 and chancellor of the Open University in 1994.

bootie *n.* = **bootee**

bootjack /boót jak/ *n.* a device similar to a yoke, used for gripping the back of a boot when removing it

bootlace /boót layss/ *n.* a long shoelace, traditionally a narrow cord or a leather thong, for lacing up boots

bootleg /boót leg/ *vti.* **(-legs, -legging, -legged) DEAL IN ILLEGAL GOODS** to make, transport, or sell illegal goods, especially illegally copied or recorded material ■ *n.* **1. STH ILLEGALLY MADE** an illegally made product, especially an illegal recording **2. ILLEGAL ALCOHOL** alcohol or an alcoholic beverage that has been smuggled or illegally distilled [Early 20thC. Back-formation from BOOTLEGGER.]

bootlegger /boót legər/ *n.* sb who illegally sells smuggled or pirated goods [Late 19thC. From liquor smugglers carrying bottles in their boots.]

bootless /bóotləss/ *adj.* having little or no success [Old English *bōtlēas* 'irremediable', from BOOT[3]] —**bootlessly** *adv.* —**bootlessness** *n.*

bootlick /boót lik/ **(bootlicks, bootlicking, bootlicked)** *vti.* to flatter sb in a position of authority in order to gain an advantage (*informal disapproving*) —**bootlicker** *n.* —**bootlicking** *n., adj.*

boots /boots/ (*plural* **boots**) *n.* a servant who polishes boots and shoes, especially at a hotel (*dated*)

boot sale *n.* = **car boot sale**

boots and saddles, boot and saddle *n. US* the name of a bugle call used to give cavalry the signal to mount (*takes a singular verb*) [Alteration of French *boute-selle*, literally 'place saddles']

bootstrap /boót strap/ **(-straps, -strapping, -strapped)** *n.* a loop of leather or fabric attached to the back or side of a boot to help pull it on ◇ **pull yourself up by your (own) bootstraps** to improve your situation in life by your own efforts

boot tree *n.* **1. DEVICE FOR KEEPING BOOTS IN SHAPE** a wooden or metal device shaped like a foot and lower leg, placed inside a boot to preserve its shape **2. DEVICE FOR KEEPING BOOTS IN PLACE** a foot-shaped support for making or repairing boots

booty /bóoti/ *n.* money or valuables seized or stolen, especially by soldiers in war [15thC. Directly or via Old French *butin* from Middle Low German *būte* 'exchange'.]

booze /booz/ *vi.* **(boozes, boozing, boozed) OVERINDULGE IN ALCOHOL** to drink alcoholic beverages, especially to excess (*slang*) ■ *n.* (*slang*) **1. ALCOHOL** alcoholic drink **2. SESSION OF HEAVY DRINKING** a period of time spent overindulging in alcohol [13thC. From Middle Dutch *būsen* 'to drink to excess', of unknown origin.]

booze bus *n. ANZ* a police patrol unit that stops drivers to test their blood-alcohol levels (*informal*)

boozed up *adj.* very drunk (*informal*)

boozer /bóozər/ *n.* (*slang*) **1. PUBLIC HOUSE** a public house or bar **2. EXCESSIVE DRINKER** sb who drinks alcohol to excess

booze-up *n.* an occasion when alcohol is drunk to excess (*slang*)

boozy /bóozi/ (**-ier, -iest**) *adj.* (*slang*) **1. WITH EXCESSIVE DRINKING** featuring the drinking of alcohol to excess **2. CONTAINING ALCOHOL** containing or flavoured with alcohol **3. DRINKING EXCESSIVELY** tending to drink alcohol excessively **4. SHOWING EFFECTS OF EXCESSIVE DRINKING** showing the effects of prolonged excessive drinking —**boozily** *adv.*

bop[1] /bop/ *vi.* **(bops, bopping, bopped) DANCE** to dance to pop music, especially in a disco (*informal*) ■ *n.* **1. A SPELL OF DANCING** a session of dancing to pop music (*informal*) ○ *We had one quick bop and left.* **2. DANCE** a social event organized for the purpose of dancing to pop music (*dated informal*) **3.** MUSIC = **bebop** [Mid-20thC. Shortening of BEBOP.]

bop[2] /bop/ *vt.* **(bops, bopping, bopped) HIT** to hit sb, especially to punch sb in the face (*informal*) ■ *n.* **BLOW DELIVERED** a blow, especially a punch in the face (*informal*) [Late 19thC. An imitation of the sound.]

bopper /bóppər/ *n.* **1.** MUSIC **JAZZ MUSICIAN** a jazz musician who plays bebop **2.** *US* = **teenybopper** (*dated*)

bora /báwrə/, **Bora** *n.* a cold, dry, strong northeasterly wind that blows down the mountains of Central Europe and along the shores of the Adriatic [Mid-19thC. From a dialect variant of Italian *borea*, from Latin *boreas* 'north wind'.]

Bora-Bora /báwrə báwrə/ island and tourist resort in the southern Pacific. One of the Leeward Island of French Polynesia, it was used as a US air base in World War II. Population: 4,225 (1988). Area: 39 sq. km/15 sq. mi.

boracic /bə rássik/ *adj.* **1.** = **boric 2.** *Cockney* **PENNILESS** having no money (*slang*) [Late 18thC. Formed from medieval Latin *borac-*, stem of *borax* (see BORAX).]

borage /bórrij/ *n.* a hairy Mediterranean plant with large star-shaped blue flowers and thick oval leaves that taste of cucumber and are sometimes used in salads. It also produces oil with pharmaceutical uses. Latin name: *Borago officinalis.* [13thC. Via French *bourrache* from Latin *bor(r)ago*, of uncertain origin: perhaps from Arabic *abūhuraš*, literally 'father of roughness' (from its rough leaves).]

borane /báw rayn/ *n.* a compound containing only boron and hydrogen. Some compounds are used in the manufacture of fuels for rockets and jet engines. [Early 20thC. Coined from BORON + -ANE.]

borate /báw rayt/ *n.* a salt or ester of boric acid [Late 18thC. Coined from BORAX + -ATE.]

borax /báw raks/ *n.* a white crystalline solid that occurs in alkaline soils and salt deposits and is an ore of boron. It is used in cleaning products, as a water softener, and as a preservative. Formula: $Na_2B_4O_7.10H_2O$. [14thC. Via medieval Latin and colloquial Arabic from Pahlavi *būrak*.]

borborygmus /báwrbə rígməss/ *n.* the rumbling sounds made by the movement of gases in the stomach and intestine (*technical*) [Early 18thC. From Greek *borborugmos*, from *borboruzein* 'to have a rumbling in the bowels'.] —**borborygmic** *adj.*

Bordeaux[1] /bawr dṓ/ city on the River Garonne and capital of Gironde Department in the Aquitaine Region, southwestern France. It is an important centre for the wine trade. Population: 213,274 (1990).

Bordeaux[2] /bawr dṓ/ (*plural* **-deaux**) *n.* red or white wine produced in the region around Bordeaux, France

Bordeaux mixture *n.* a solution of copper sulphate and calcium hydroxide that is sprayed on trees and other plants as a fungicide

bordello /bawr déllō/ (*plural* **-los**) *n.* a house of prostitution (*literary*) [Late 16thC. Via Italian from French *bordel*, literally 'cabin, small hut', of uncertain origin: perhaps ultimately from Germanic.]

border /báwrdər/ *n.* **1. LINE DIVIDING TWO AREAS** the line that officially separates two countries or regions, or the land on either side of it (*often used before a noun*) ○ *across the border* ○ *border country* **2. STRIP AROUND EDGE** a band that runs along the edge of sth, e.g. a printed page or a framed painting, often decorated or itself added for decoration ○ *a handkerchief with a patterned border* **3. LAND AT EDGE** the edge of an area of land, or the ground near the edge ○ *a shy animal that rarely comes nearer than the border of the field* **4.** GARDENING **NARROW FLOWERBED** a narrow flowerbed along a wall or at the edge of a lawn or path ■ *vti.* (**-ders, -dering, -dered**) **1. FORM FRONTIER WITH PLACE** to form the frontier with another country or the boundary between two regions ○ *Italy borders Austria in the Alps.* **2. BE NEXT TO STH** to form a line along the edge of sth ○ *a field bordered by willow trees* [14thC. From Old French *bordeüre*, ultimately from a Germanic word that is also one of the ancestors of English *board*.]

border on *vt.* to be almost the same as sth ○ *an admissions policy bordering on the ridiculous*

Border /báwrdər/, **Allan** (*b.* 1955) Australian cricketer. Captain of the Australian cricket team (1984–87), in 1995 he became the highest scorer of runs in Test cricket with 10,561 runs. Full name **Allan Robert Border**

Border collie *n.* a dog with a long silky black-and-white coat, belonging to a breed often kept as sheepdogs [So called because it was originally bred in the Borders]

borderer /báwrdərər/ *n.* sb who lives in the border area between two countries or regions, especially England and Scotland

borderland /báwrdər land/ *n.* **1. AREA AT TERRITORY'S EDGE** the area near the edge of a country or region, especially a remote area **2. POINT WHERE THINGS OVERLAP** the indeterminate area between two conditions, categories, or activities that is hard to define because it contains features or qualities of both

Border Leicester *n.* a sheep with a white face and a long coat, belonging to a breed valued for its wool and meat [So called because it was bred from the Cheviot sheep (from around the Borders) and the Leicester sheep]

borderline /báwrdər līn/ *n.* **SEPARATING LINE** the notional line that separates one state or quality from another very similar one ○ *the borderline between frankness and rudeness* ■ *adj.* **1. AT CATEGORY'S EDGE** not clearly belonging to one or other of two categories ○ *Borderline candidates will take a further oral exam.* **2.** PSYCHOL **PSYCHOLOGICALLY UNSTABLE** used to describe a psychological condition characterized by emotional instability and marked by self-destructive, manipulative, and erratic behaviour **3.** MED **ALMOST DEVELOPED** used to describe a medical condition that a patient is likely to develop unless preventive steps are taken ○ *borderline hypertension*

Border terrier *n.* a small short dog belonging to a breed of terriers with rough coats that are kept as pets [So called because it was originally bred in the Borders]

Bordet /báwr day/, **Jules** (1870–1961) Belgian physiologist and bacteriologist. He discovered the immunity factor in blood serum and the whooping-cough bacterium. Full name **Jules Jean Baptiste Vincent Bordet**

Borduas /báwrdoo aa/, **Paul Émile** (1905–60) Canadian painter. His exploration of spontaneous painting (**automism**) led to abstract works such as *L'Étoile noir* (1957).

bordure /báwr dyoor/ *n.* the decorated edge running round the edge of the shield on a coat of arms, signifying that the bearer is not the chief of the family [14thC. An earlier spelling of BORDER.]

bore[1] /bawr/ *vt.* (**bores, boring, bored**) **MAKE SB UNINTERESTED** to make sb lose interest and so feel tired and annoyed ○ *He bored us stiff with a detailed explanation of his holiday itinerary.* ■ *n.* **STH THAT BORES** sb or sth regarded as wholly uninteresting or tiresome ○ *Peeling potatoes is a bore!* [Mid-18thC. Origin unknown.]

bore[2] /bawr/ *vti.* (**bores, boring, bored**) **1. MAKE HOLE IN STH** to make a deep hole in sth, such as that made by a drill, a bullet, or a boring insect **2. PENETRATE** to penetrate into the inner or hidden parts of sb or sth ○ *questioning that bores deep into their private affairs* ■ *n.* **SIZE OF PIPE** the internal diameter of a pipe, gun barrel, or any other hollow cylindrical part [Old English *borian*. Ultimately from an Indo-European word that is also the ancestor of English *perforate*.]

bore[3] /bawr/ *n.* a large powerful wave that the tide causes to move up a river or narrow estuary [Early 17thC. Origin uncertain: perhaps from Old Norse *bára* 'wave'.]

bore[4] /bawr/ *v.* past participle of **bear**[2]

boreal /báwri əl/ *adj.* used to describe a region that has a northern temperate climate, with cold winters and warm summers [15thC. Directly or via French from late Latin *borealis*, from Latin *Boreas* (see BOREAS).]

Boreas /báwri əss/ *n.* **1. GOD OF NORTH WIND** in Greek mythology, the god who personifies the north wind. ◊ **Zephyrus 2. Boreas, boreas NORTH WIND** a wind blowing from the north (*literary*) [14thC. Via Latin from Greek.]

bored /bawrd/ *adj.* feeling tired and irritable, either because of being exposed to sth uninteresting or because of having nothing to do ○ *She grew bored of living in the country.*

WORD KEY: USAGE

The usual preposition to use after the adjective ***bored*** is *with* as in *I grew bored with all their squabbling.* However nowdays the preposition *of* is sometimes seen, especially in speech or informal writing, perhaps on analogy with *tired of.* This usage is to be avoided in careful speech or writing.

boredom /báwrdəm/ *n.* the feeling of being bored ○ *I nearly died of boredom.*

borehole /báwr hōl/ *n.* a deep hole drilled into the ground to obtain samples for geological study or to release or extract water or oil

borer /báwrər/ *n.* **1.** MECH ENG **TOOL FOR BORING HOLES** a machine or hand tool used for boring holes **2.** ZOOL **ANIMAL THAT BORES** an organism, especially an insect or a mollusc, that bores into a plant or into wood or rock

Borg /bawrg/, **Björn** (*b.* 1956) Swedish tennis player. He was the Wimbledon men's singles champion from 1976 to 1980 and won the French singles title six times. Full name **Björn Rune Borg**

Borgia /báwrjə/, **Cesare, Duke of the Romagna** (1476?–1507) Italian soldier. The illegitimate son of Pope Alexander VI and the brother of Lucrezia Borgia, he conquered several central Italian city-states in an attempt to found his own kingdom.

Borgia, Lucrezia (1480–1519) Italian art patron. During her third marriage to the Duke of Este, she attracted Italy's foremost painters and writers to her court in Ferrara. She was the sister of Cesare Borgia.

boric /báwrik/ *adj.* containing or relating to boron [Mid-19thC. Coined from BORON + -IC.]

boric acid *n.* a weak acidic white crystalline solid used in the manufacture of glass and porcelain, as a fire retardant, and as an antiseptic. Formula: H_3BO_3.

boring[1] /báwring/ *adj.* stimulating no interest or enthusiasm —**boringly** *adv.* —**boringness** *n.*

WORD KEY: SYNONYMS

boring, dull, monotonous, tedious, uninteresting

CORE MEANING: causing a state of impatience and weariness

boring the most general term in this group, it can be used as a substitute for both 'dull' and 'monotonous' and simply indicates that sb or sth is lacking in interest, stimulation, or variety; **dull** uninteresting because of a lack of liveliness, humour, or variety; **monotonous** suggesting that the cause is too much uniformity and a lack of variation; **tedious** suggesting weariness to the point of physical as well mental discomfort; **uninteresting** suggesting simply that sth is not engaging sb's interest rather than it is arousing actual impatience or weariness.

boring[2] /báwring/ *adj.* used to describe animals or tools that make holes in things

Bormann /báwrmən, -man/, **Martin** (1900–45?) German Nazi politician. A close and loyal adviser of Adolf Hitler, he stayed with Hitler to the end of World War II, when he is thought to have been killed by a sniper.

born /bawrn/ *adj.* **1. BROUGHT INTO LIFE** brought into existence as a baby from a mother's womb ○ *a child born in Birmingham.* ◊ **bear**[2] **2. BEGUN** developed from a particular source or root cause ○ *a realization born of long experience* **3. NATURALLY PREDISPOSED** having the particular natural talent or innate character trait ○ *describes the young Napoleon as a born leader* **4. WITH SPECIFIED ORIGINAL STATUS** given a particular status or condition by or at birth (*often used in combination*) ○ *the Canadian-born singer-songwriter* [Old English *boren*, past participle of *beran* 'bear' (see BEAR)] ◇ **born and bred** coming from a particular place or background and usually having the qualities or character regarded as typical it

WORD KEY: USAGE

See Usage note at ***born.***

Born /bawrn/, **Max** (1882–1970) German-born British physicist. He shared the 1954 Nobel Prize for his work in quantum physics.

born-again *adj.* with all the enthusiasm of sb who has been recently converted to a cause or an idea [Originally in BORN-AGAIN CHRISTIAN]

born-again Christian *n.* sb with a new and passionately felt and expressed Christian faith [From John 3:3 'Except a man be born again, he cannot see the kingdom of God' (referring to a spiritual rebirth)]

borne past participle of **bear**[2]

WORD KEY: USAGE

born or **borne**? ***Borne*** is the primary past participle of the verb *bear*: *They had borne enough pain. The following points should be borne in mind. His account is simply not borne out by the facts.* In meanings relating to birth, ***borne*** is used when the mother is the subject of the verb, or when the verb is passive followed by the preposition 'by': *Maria had already borne six children. The twins were borne by an Italian mother.* But when the subject is the child, ***born*** is used as an adjective: *I was born on a Tuesday. A child was born to Helga that evening.*

Borneo /báwrni ō/ island of the Malay Archipelago in the Pacific Ocean, near Southeast Asia and the Philippines. Population: 12,500,000 1991. Area: 751,100 sq. km/290,000 sq. mi. —**Bornean** *n., adj.*

Bornholm /báwrn hōlm/ island and tourist area in the Baltic Sea, southeastern Denmark. Population: 45,067 (1994). Area: 588 sq. km/227 sq. mi.

Bornholm disease *n.* an acute epidemic viral infection whose symptoms include fever and pain around the base of the chest [Because the disease was first identified on BORNHOLM]

bornite /báwr nīt/ *n.* a brown mineral with a metallic sheen that is an ore of copper [Early 19thC. Named after the Austrian mineralogist Ignatius von *Born* (1742–91).]

boro-[1] *prefix.* = **boro-** (*used before vowels*)

boro-[2] *prefix.* boron ○ *borosilicate* [From BORON]

Borodin /bórrədin/, **Aleksander Porfiryevich** (1833–87) Russian composer and chemist. A professor of chemistry in St Petersburg, he wrote the opera *Prince Igor* and other orchestral works.

Borodino /bórrə deénō/ village in Russia about 110 km/70 mi. west of Moscow. It was the site in 1812 of an important Napoleon victory.

boron /báw ron/ *n.* a yellow-brown chemical element that is hard and brittle, with properties intermediate between a metal and nonmetal. It is used in alloys, glass, and ceramics, and in nuclear reactors to absorb radiation. Symbol **B** [Early 19thC. Formed from BORAX, modelled on CARBON, which it resembles in some respects.]

boronia /bə rṓni ə/ n. an aromatic evergreen Australian shrub grown for its bowl-shaped crimson, yellow, or purplish-brown flowers. Genus: *Boronia*. [Late 18thC. From modern Latin, named after the Italian botanist Francesco *Borone* (1769–94).]

borosilicate /báwrō síllikət, -sílli kayt/ n. a salt of boric and silicic acids. Borosilicates are used in the manufacture of heat- and chemical-resistant glass.

borough /búrrə/ n. 1. DISTRICT OF CITY an administrative division of a large city, responsible for running local services such as housing and education 2. ENGLISH TOWN in England a town that once had special privileges granted to it by royal charter [Old English *burg* 'fortress, fortified town', from a prehistoric Germanic word meaning 'to protect', which is also the ancestor of English *bury*, *barrow*, *belfry*, and *borrow*]

Borromini /bórrə meeni/, **Francesco** (1599–1667) Italian architect. He designed the church of San Carlo alle Quattro Fontane in Rome (1637–41). Born **Francesco Castelli**

borrow /bórrō/ v. (-rows, -rowing, -rowed) 1. vt. USE SB ELSE'S PROPERTY to get temporary possession or use of sth belonging to sb else, usually after asking permission ○ *Dad, can I borrow the car?* 2. vti. RECEIVE MONEY AS LOAN to arrange to be given money by sb or by a bank or other financial institution for a fixed period of time. The money is normally paid back in instalments, with interest. ○ *We've already borrowed heavily this year.* 3. vt. TAKE FROM LIBRARY to take out a book or other item from a library 4. vt. COPY FROM SB'S WORK to copy sth from sb else's work, especially a work of art of some kind ○ *some shots clearly borrowed from a famous director* 5. vt. LANGUAGE TAKE FROM ANOTHER LANGUAGE to adopt a word from another language 6. vi. GOLF PUTT ALLOWING FOR SLOPE to putt to the left or right of a straight line on a green to allow for the effect of the slope 7. vi. GOLF VEER LEFT OR RIGHT to veer to the left or right as a result of the slope on a green (*refers to a golf ball*) 8. vt. LEND to lend sth to sb (*nonstandard*) ■ n. GOLF EXTENT OF VEERING the degree to which a golf ball veers to the left or right as a result of the slope of a green [Old English *borgian* 'to borrow against security', from a prehistoric Germanic word meaning 'to protect'] —**borrower** n.

Borrow /bórrō/, **George** (1803–81) British writer and traveller. His works include *Lavengro* (1851) and *The Romany Rye* (1857), inspired by his travels with British Roma, and *The Bible in Spain* (1843). Full name **George Henry Borrow**

borrowing /bórrō ing/ n. 1. LOAN OF MONEY the borrowing of money or the amount of money borrowed, especially from a bank or other financial institution 2. LANGUAGE ADOPTED WORD a word that has been adopted from another language 3. COPIED IDEA an idea copied from sb else's work, especially a work of art of some kind

borrow pit n. a hole left where stones or other materials have been dug up for use in construction work elsewhere

borscht /bawrsht/ n. a Russian or Polish soup whose main ingredient is beetroot [Early 19thC. From Russian *borshch*.]

borstal /báwrst'l/ n. formerly, an institution for young offenders that combined features of prison and school. Borstals were replaced in 1953 by detention centres and youth custody centres. (*often used before a noun*) ○ *a multimillionaire and former borstal boy* [Early 20thC. Named after the village of *Borstal* in southern England, where the first one was established.]

bort /bawrt/ n. a diamond of inferior quality that is used industrially on grinding wheels and other abrasive devices [Early 17thC. Origin uncertain: perhaps from Dutch *boort*, or from Old French *bort* 'bastard'.]

borzoi /báwr zoy/ (*plural* -**zois**) n. a tall graceful domestic dog with a long silky coat, belonging to a breed formerly used in Russia to hunt wolves [Late 19thC. From Russian, formed from *borzyĭ* 'swift'.]

boscage /bóskij/ n. densely growing trees and bushes (*literary*) [14thC. From Old French, ultimately from a Germanic word that is also the ancestor of English *bush*.]

Hieronymus Bosch

Bosch /bosh/, **Hieronymus** (1450?–1516) Dutch painter. His allegorical paintings teeming with demons and monsters include *The Seven Deadly Sins* and *The Garden of Earthly Delights*. Real name **Jerome van Aken**

Bose /bōss/, **Sir Jagadis Chandra** (1858–1937) Indian physicist and botanist. He invented crescography, a means of measuring minute plant movements, and founded the Bose Research Institute, Calcutta (1917).

bosey n. = bosie

bosh /bosh/ interj. used to dismiss as nonsense what has just been said (*dated informal*) [Mid-19thC. From Turkish *boş* 'empty, worthless'.]

bosie /bṓzi/, **bosey** (*plural* -**seys**) n. Aus = **googly** [Early 20thC. Named after the English cricketer B. J. T. *Bosanquet* (1877–1936), who used it.]

bosky /bóski/ (-**ier**, -**iest**) adj. covered with small trees or bushes growing densely (*literary*) [Late 16thC. Formed from Middle English *bosk*, a variant of BUSH.]

Bosman Ruling /bózmən-/ n. the European Court ruling that made it possible for football players to leave their club at the end of a contract with no transfer fee payable [Named after the player who brought the test case to the European Court]

bo's'n n. = boatswain

Bosnia /bózni ə/ n. the northern region of Bosnia-Herzegovina —**Bosnian** adj., n.

Bosnia-Herzegovina

Bosnia-Herzegovina /bózni ə hŭrtsə gō veénə/, **Bosnia** a republic in the former Federal People's Republic of Yugoslavia that declared its independence in 1992. In 1995, following civil war between Bosnian Muslims, Serbs, and Croats, it was divided into two self-governing provinces: a Muslim-Croat Federation and a Serb Republic. Language: Serbo-Croatian. Currency: Dinar. Capital: Sarajevo. Population: 3,222,584 (1997). Area: 51,129 sq. km/19,745 sq. mi. Official name **Republic of Bosnia-Herzegovina**

bosom /bŏŏzəm/ n. 1. WOMAN'S BREASTS a woman's breasts or chest 2. CLOTHES COVERING BREASTS a part of a garment, e.g. a dress, that covers the chest 3. PROTECTIVE PLACE a familiar source of protection, security, or affection (*literary*) ○ *back in the bosom of her family* 4. SEAT OF EMOTION the place where emotions are felt (*literary*) ■ adj. CLOSE IN FRIENDSHIP used to describe a friend to whom sb is very close (*informal*) ○ *a bosom buddy* [Old English *bōsm*, of uncertain origin: perhaps ultimately from an Indo-European word that is also the ancestor of English *bough* and *bow* (of a ship)]

bosomy /bŏŏzəmi/ (-**ier**, -**iest**) adj. with large breasts

boson /bṓ zon/ n. an elementary particle that has zero or integral spin and obeys statistical rules that place no restriction on the number of identical particles that may be in the same state. Photons and alpha particles are bosons. [Mid-20thC. Named after the Indian physicist S. N. *Bose* (1894–1974), who, with Albert Einstein, stated the statistical relations that describe the behaviour of these particles.]

Bosporus /bóspərəss/, **Bosphorus** /bósfərəss/ strait linking the Black Sea and the Sea of Marmara. It separates European and Asian Turkey. Length: 32 km/20 mi.

boss[1] /boss/ n. 1. SB IN CHARGE sb who is in charge of others, especially in a work environment ○ *asked the boss for some time off* 2. DOMINANT PERSON the person who is the dominant partner in a relationship or the dominant member of a group, who tends to make decisions and give instructions (*informal; often used ironically*) 3. US POWERFUL POLITICIAN a politician who exerts a controlling influence, e.g. by applying pressure on others to vote in a particular way (*informal*) ■ vt. (**bosses, bossing, bossed**) GIVE ORDERS to give others orders in a way that seeks to demonstrate or establish authority and is often resisted or resented ○ *You find the big kids trying to boss the little kids about.* ■ adj. EXCELLENT so good as to dominate in a group (*slang*) ○ *a boss drummer* [Early 19thC. From Dutch *baas* 'master', of unknown origin.] ◇ **be your own boss 1.** to work under your own authority, e.g. with freelance or self-employed status **2.** to make decisions relating to your own life, rather than have them dictated by others

boss[2] /boss/ n. 1. KNOB a round raised part that sticks out from a surface, e.g. a stud at the centre of a shield 2. ARCHIT CEILING DECORATION a decorative knob on a vaulted ceiling at points where the ribs meet 3. BIOL SWELLING a round swelling on a plant or the horn of an animal 4. MECH ENG SHAFT PART a thicker part of a shaft at a point where another part is attached to it 5. GEOL VOLCANIC ROCK MASS a mass of volcanic rock with a roughly circular cross section and vertical sides [14thC. From Old French *boce*, of unknown origin.]

BOSS /boss/ a South African intelligence organization. Full form **Bureau of State Security**

bossa nova /bóssə nṓvə/ n. 1. DANCE a lively ballroom dance similar to the samba. It originated in Brazil in the early 1960s. 2. MUSIC FOR DANCE a piece of music for the bossa nova [Mid-20thC. From Portuguese, literally 'new trend'.]

boss cocky (*plural* **boss cockies**) n. Aus a boss who likes giving orders (*informal*) ['Cocky' is a shortening of COCKATOO in the sense of 'small farmer']

bosset /bóssit/ n. a rudimentary antler that grows on each side of a young deer's head [Mid-19thC. From French, literally 'little boss knob'.]

boss-eyed adj. with one or both eyes out of alignment (*informal*) ['Boss' of unknown origin]

bossy /bóssi/ (-**ier**, -**iest**) adj. fond of giving people orders ○ *The other children don't like it when you're bossy.* —**bossily** adv. —**bossiness** n.

boston /bóstən/ n. a version of whist in which two packs of cards are used and players bid for the right to name trumps [Early 19thC. From French, said to have been devised by French naval officers involved in the Siege of BOSTON (Massachusetts) in the American War of Independence.]

Boston /bóstən/ 1. seaport in Lincolnshire, eastern England. Population: 34,606 (1991). 2. capital and largest city of Massachusetts. Situated at the mouth of the Charles River on Boston Bay, it is home to Boston and Northeastern universities. Population: 558,394 (1996). —**Bostonian** /bo stóni ən/ n., adj.

Boston crab n. a wrestling hold in which a wrestler is grabbed by the legs, turned face down, and sat on [Named after BOSTON, Massachusetts]

Boston ivy (*plural* **Boston ivies**) n. a climbing plant with leaves having three black lobes that turn red in autumn. It is a popular garden plant. Latin name: *Parthenocissus tricuspidata*. [Named after BOSTON, Massachusetts]

Boston Tea Party *n.* a protest against British taxes made by the citizens of Boston in 1773, leading to the American Revolution. The protesters boarded three British ships and threw their cargoes of tea overboard.

bosun /bốss'n/ *n.* an officer on a ship whose job is to supervise the maintenance of the ship and its equipment [Mid-17thC. Representing a pronunciation of BOATSWAIN.]

Boswell /bóz wel, -wəl/, **James** (1740–95) Scottish lawyer and biographer. He met the writer Samuel Johnson in 1973 and after two decades of close association wrote *Life of Samuel Johnson* (1791), one of the masterpieces of English biography.

Bosworth Field /bózwərth-/ site of a decisive battle in 1485 when Henry Tudor defeated Richard III and claimed the English throne. It is near the town of Market Bosworth, central Leicestershire.

bot[1] /bot/ *n.* a larva of the botfly. It lives as a parasite inside the human body and the bodies of horses, sheep, and cattle. [Early 16thC. Origin uncertain: probably from Low Dutch.]

bot[2] /bot/ *n.* a computer program that performs routine or time-consuming tasks, e.g. searching Web sites on the Internet, automatically or semi-independently (*usually used in combination*) [Late 20thC. Shortening of ROBOT.]

BOT *abbr.* **1. BOT, BoT** Board of Trade **2.** COMPUT beginning of tape

bot. *abbr.* **1.** botanical **2.** botany

botanical /bə tánnik'l/, **botanic** /bə tánnik/ *adj.* OF PLANTS relating to plants, especially to the scientific study of plants ▪ *n.* PLANT-BASED DRUG a drug or other medicinal or cosmetic product that is made from plants (*often used in the plural*) [Mid-17thC. Directly or via French *botanique* from late Latin *botanicus*, from Greek *botanikos*, from *botanē* 'plant'.] —**botanically** *adv.*

botanical garden, **botanic garden** *n.* an area, often open to the public, in which exotic, rare, or scientifically interesting plants are grown and studied

botanise *vti.* = botanize

botanist /bótə nist/ *n.* sb with an expert scientific knowledge of, or a strong interest in, plants [Mid-17thC. From French *botaniste*, from *botanique* (see BOTANICAL.]

botanize /bótə nīz/ (**-nizes, -nizing, -nized**), **botanise** (**botanises, botanising, botanised**) *vti.* to collect or study plants (*informal*) [Mid-18thC. Via modern Latin *botanizare* from Greek *botanizein* 'to gather plants', from *botanē* 'plant'.] —**botanizer** *n.*

botany /bótəni/ (*plural* **-nies**) *n.* **1.** STUDY OF PLANTS the scientific study of plants **2.** PLANT LIFE OF SPECIFIC AREA the plant life that exists within a particular area **3.** BIOLOGICAL CHARACTERISTICS OF PLANT the biological description of a single plant or group of plants [Late 17thC. Formed from BOTANIC.]

Botany Bay /bóttəni-/ bay south of Sydney, New South Wales, Australia. It was Captain Cook's first landing site on the continent in 1770.

Botany wool *n.* a fine grade of merino wool used in the manufacture of yarns and fabrics [Named after BOTANY BAY]

botch /boch/ *vt.* (**botches, botching, botched**) DO STH BADLY to do sth very badly out of clumsiness or lack of care ○ *managed to botch a simple repair job* ▪ *n.* **botch, botch-up** BADLY DONE JOB a job or task that has been done very badly (*informal*) ○ *made a complete botch of translating the songs* [14thC. Origin unknown.] —**botcher** *n.* —**botchily** *adv.* —**botchiness** *n.* —**botchy** *adj.*

botfly /bót flī/ (*plural* **-flies**) *n.* a two-winged hairy parasitic fly that lays its eggs under the skin or in the digestive tract, sometimes causing serious illness. Botflies live as parasites on people, horses, sheep, and cattle. Families: Oestridae and Gasterophilidae.

both /bōth/ *det.* TWO relating to or being two people or things considered together ○ *For the first time I find that I like both candidates.* ○ *There are only two banks in the town, and both are shut on Saturdays.* ▪ *conj.* NOT JUST ONE used with two facts or alternatives

joined by 'and' to indicate that not just one but also the other one is included ○ *Truancy is now treated as both a policing and an educational issue.* [13thC. From Old Norse *báðir.* Ultimately from two Indo-European words meaning 'both the'.]

— **WORD KEY: USAGE** —

A flexible word, *both* has many roles, as a pronoun (*I like both*), adjective (or determiner) (*I like both boys*), and adverb (or conjunction) (*They are both pleasant and cheerful*). Its mobility in a sentence is so great that its meaning can become ambiguous. In the last example, it is not immediately clear whether *both* belongs with 'they' or with the complement of the sentence, 'pleasant and cheerful'; in speech, intonation will normally clarify the intention. However, when writing, you need to ensure that you are not leaving the reader in doubt. The principal restriction that applies to *both* is that it should refer to two people or things and no more; if three or more are meant it is necessary to use *each*, which behaves grammatically in ways quite similar to *both*. (However, *each* is regarded as singular while *both* is plural, and *both* alone allows the construction *I saw them both*.) When pairing *both* with *and*, it is important to retain a balance between the two parts of the construction, with regard to the position of *both* and the types of words linked. Examples of poor balance are *She is both charming and an intellectual* (better: *She is both charming and intelligent*) and *He is both a fine singer and likes to paint* (better: *He both sings well and likes to paint*). In terms of possession, *of + both* is preferred, as in *the parents of both*, as opposed to *both their parents* and *both their responsibility* or *both their responsibilities*.

Botha /bóortə, bố-/, **P. W.** (b. 1916) South African statesman. He was prime minister (1978–84) and first state president (1984–89) of South Africa. Full name **Pieter Willem Botha**

Botham /bóthəm/, **Ian** (b. 1955) British cricketer. One of the world's greatest cricketers, he appeared in 102 Test matches for England. Full name **Ian Terence Botham**

bother /bóthər/ *v.* (**-ers, -ering, -ered**) **1.** *vi.* MAKE EFFORT to take the time or trouble to do sth (*often used in negative statements*) ○ *He didn't even bother to get out of the car.* ○ *I shouldn't bother about a raincoat. It's clearing up.* **2.** *vti.* WORRY SB to make sb feel worried, anxious, or upset ○ *I never bother about what the neighbours think.* ○ *It bothers me to think of you all on your own.* **3.** *vt.* DISTURB SB to annoy or disturb sb, e.g. by interrupting or by making unwelcome advances ○ *Is the music bothering you?* **4.** *vt.* GIVE PAIN to make sb feel physical discomfort or pain ○ *My back is bothering me again.* ▪ *n.* **1.** EFFORT trouble or effort to do sth ○ *Don't go to all that bother for me.* **2.** SOURCE OF ANNOYANCE sb or sth that causes annoyance, e.g. by making noise ○ *I'm sorry to be a bother, but could I use your phone?* ▪ *interj.* EXPRESSING MILD ANNOYANCE used as an expression of mild annoyance ○ *Bother! I've left my glasses in the car.* [Late 17thC. Origin uncertain.]

— **WORD KEY: SYNONYMS** —

bother, annoy, bug, disturb, irk, trouble, worry
CORE MEANING: to interfere with sb's composure
bother suggesting a range of interference with composure, both mental and physical, from interrupting sb's concentration to causing discomfort or pain; **annoy** to interfere with sb's composure in such a way as to affect the nerves and cause irritation or anger; **bug** a slang word meaning much the same as *annoy*, originating in the US but becoming increasingly common in the UK; **disturb** either to interrupt sb in the process of doing sth or seriously to interfere with sb's peace of mind; **irk** a less common word meaning much the same as *annoy* but sometimes suggesting a greater degree of intolerance; **trouble** a more formal word for *disturb* in both its senses given above; **worry** to cause anxiety in sb and so interfere with his/her composure, the cause of the discomposure being often less clear-cut than in the case of *disturb* or *trouble*.

botheration /bóthə ráysh'n/ *interj.* used as an expression of mild annoyance (*dated informal*)

bothersome /bóthərsəm/ *adj.* causing annoyance and inconvenience

Bothnia, Gulf of /bóthni ə-/ northern part of the Baltic Sea, situated between Finland and Sweden. Area: 117,000 sq. km/45,200 sq. mi.

bothy /bóthi/ (*plural* **-ies**) *n. Scotland* a simple house or hut, originally a farmer's or crofter's cottage with one or two rooms only, now usually a hut providing shelter for hillwalkers or climbers [Late 18thC. Origin uncertain: probably from obsolete Scots *both* 'booth'.]

bo tree /bố tree/ *n.* an tree found in India that belongs to the fig family, regarded as sacred by Buddhists. The Buddha is said to have achieved enlightenment while sitting under a bo tree. Latin name: *Ficus religiosa*. [Mid-19thC. Partial translation of Sinhalese *bōgaha*, from *bō* (from Pali and Sanskrit *bodhi* 'perfect knowledge') + *gaha* 'tree'.]

botryoidal /bóttri óyd'l/ *adj.* used to describe minerals and plant parts shaped like a bunch of grapes [Late 18thC. Formed from Greek *botruoeidēs*, from *botrus* 'bunch of grapes'.]

bots /bots/ *n.* an intestinal disease of horses, sheep, and cattle, caused by infection with botfly larvae (*takes a singular or plural verb*)

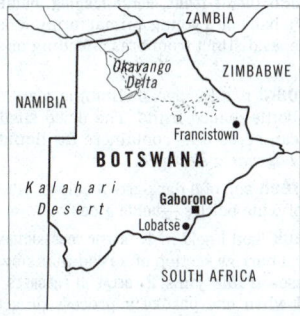

Botswana

Botswana /bot swáənə/ landlocked country in southern Africa, that shares borders with Namibia, Zambia, Zimbabwe, and South Africa. It became independent from Britain in 1966. Language: English, Setswana. Currency: Pula. Capital: Gaborone. Population: 1,431,981 (1997). Area: 581,730 sq. km/224,607 sq. mi. Official name **Republic of Botswana**. Former name **Bechuanaland** (until 1966) —**Botswanan** *n., adj.*

botte /bot/ *n.* a thrust or hit in fencing [14thC. From Old French *bot(te)* 'blow, hit'.]

Sandro Botticelli: *The Birth of Venus*
(after 1482)

Botticelli /bótti chélli/, **Sandro** (1445–1510) Italian painter. He specialized in classical themes, exemplified in paintings such as *The Birth of Venus* and *Primavera*. Real name **Alessandro di Mariano Filipepi**

bottle /bótt'l/ *n.* **1.** CONTAINER FOR LIQUIDS a container for liquids, usually made of glass or plastic, with a narrow neck and no handle **2.** AMOUNT IN BOTTLE the amount of liquid contained in a bottle **3.** CONTAINER FOR BABY'S MILK a plastic or glass container with a rubber teat used for feeding a baby, or a feed of milk given by using one of these ○ *Has he had his bottle yet?* **4.** ALCOHOL alcohol, or the habit of drinking it to excess (*informal*) **5.** COURAGE boldness or nerve (*informal*) ○ *didn't have the bottle to say it to her face* ▪ *vt.* (**-tles, -tling, -tled**) **1.** PUT IN BOTTLE to put a liquid, e.g. wine, beer, or milk, in a bottle for storage or sale **2. PRESERVE IN JARS** to store fruit or vegetables in a preserving liquid in a glass container [14thC. Via Old French *boteille* from medieval Latin *butticula* 'little cask', from late Latin *buttis* 'cask, barrel' (source of English *butt*).]

bottle out to undergo a loss of courage at a crucial moment (*informal*) ○ *He was going to tell her, then he bottled out.*

bottle up *vt.* **1. ENTRAP** to contain, hold, or entrap sth or sb, especially a group of people **2. CONTAIN FEELINGS** to conceal or repress strong feelings ○ *all the resentment she's been bottling up for years*

bottle bank *n.* a large container or group of containers in which members of the public can deposit used glass bottles and jars for recycling

bottlebrush /bótt'l brush/ *n.* an Australian shrub or small tree that has a mass of spiky red flowers with large stamens. Genera: *Callistemon* and *Melaleuca*. [From the plant's resemblance to a cylindrical brush for cleaning bottles]

bottled /bótt'ld/ *adj.* **1. IN BOTTLES** stored or sold in bottles **2. INEBRIATED** completely inebriated (*slang*)

bottle-feed (**bottle-feeds, bottle-feeding, bottle-fed**) *vt.* to feed a baby or a young animal formula milk from a bottle, as distinct from breast-feeding or suckling it

bottle gourd *n.* a European climbing plant that produces bottle-shaped fruits. The dried shells of the fruits can be used as containers for liquids. Latin name: *Lagenaria siceraria.*

bottle green *adj.* of a dark-green colour, like certain types of wine bottles —**bottle green** *n.*

bottleneck /bótt'l nek/ *n.* **1. TRAFFIC CONSTRICTION** a junction or a narrow section of a road that slows traffic or causes traffic jams **2. DELAY IN PROGRESS** a delay caused when one part of a process or activity is slower than the others and so hinders overall progress

bottle-nosed dolphin, bottlenose dolphin *n.* a dolphin with a long snout, found in warm waters. Latin name: *Tursiops truncatus.*

bottle party *n.* a party to which guests bring alcoholic drink

bottler /bótt'lər/ *n.* **1. COMPANY BOTTLING DRINKS** a company that bottles beverages as part of a manufacturing process **2.** *ANZ* **STH EXCELLENT** an excellent example of sth (*informal*) ○ *a real bottler of a film*

bottle shop *n. ANZ* a shop where bottles or cans of alcoholic beverages may be bought for consumption elsewhere

bottle store *n. ANZ, S Africa* = **off-licence**

bottle tree *n.* an Australian tree that has a swollen bottle-shaped trunk and gives off an unpleasant smell. Genus: *Brachychiton.*

bottom /bóttəm/ *n.* **1. LOWEST PART** the lowest or deepest part of sth ○ *From the bottom of the hill it seems a long way up.* **2. UNDERSIDE** the underneath side or surface of sth ○ *rust on the bottom of the boat* **3. FARTHEST POINT** the part of sth that is farthest away ○ *ponies grazing at the bottom of the field* **4. LAND UNDER WATER** the ground underneath a sea, lake, or river ○ *Can you dive down and touch the bottom?* **5. END OF LIST** the end of a list or series, especially the lowest level of excellence or achievement ○ *teams at the bottom of the league* **6. ROOT CAUSE** the fundamental, often hidden, cause or origin of sth ○ *get to the bottom of the problem* **7. LOWEST RANK** the lowest level in a hierarchy ○ *worked her way up from the bottom* **8. BUTTOCKS** sb's buttocks, or, particularly when speaking to children, any body part in this general area **9. PART COVERING LOWER BODY** the part of a two-piece garment, e.g. a tracksuit or bikini, that covers the lower body (*often used in the plural*) **10. VALLEY** a dry valley or hollow (*often used in place names*) ○ *Six Mile Bottom* ■ *adj.* **1. LOWEST** in the lower or lowest position ○ *Look on the bottom shelf.* **2. LEAST SUCCESSFUL** in the position of least excellence or achievement ○ *determined not to come bottom of the class again* ○ *the bottom five teams* ■ *v.* (**-toms, -toming, -tomed**) **1.** *vi.* **HIT SEA FLOOR** to scrape the underside against the floor of the sea or a river, because the water is too shallow (*refers to ships*) **2.** *vt.* **ELEC ENG OVERLOAD**

TRANSISTOR to overload a transistor to the point where additional input produces no additional output **3.** *vt.* **ESTABLISH NATURE OF** to discover the true nature, cause, or origin of sth (*archaic*) [Old English *botm*. Ultimately from an Indo-European word that is also the ancestor of English *found* and *fundamental*.] ◇ **at bottom** in reality, when external appearances are stripped away ◇ **bottoms up** used as a drinking toast ◇ **hit bottom** to reach the lowest point in your personal, professional, or external life

bottom out *vi.* after a decline, to stop falling any lower and stabilize at a low level ○ *After plummeting 200 points, the stock market finally bottomed out.*

bottom drawer *n.* a collection of household items, e.g. linens, that a young woman accumulates in anticipation of marriage. US term **hope chest** [Traditionally kept in the bottom drawer of her chest of drawers]

bottom feeder *n.* a fresh- or saltwater animal, especially a fish that feeds on material drifting to the bottom of a body of water

bottomless /bóttəmləss/ *adj.* **1. VERY DEEP** so deep that what is specified appears to have no bottom **2. PLENTIFUL** with unlimited or seemingly unlimited resources, especially of money ○ *a bottomless fund* **3. UNFATHOMABLE** too well hidden to be discovered or too mysterious to be understood

bottom line *n.* **1. UNAVOIDABLE FACTOR** the most important factor that must be accepted, however reluctantly ○ *The bottom line is that the sponsors want a French driver on the team.* **2. FIN PROFIT OR LOSS** the final profit or loss that a company makes at the end of a given period of time **3. FIN LOWEST ACCEPTABLE AMOUNT** the least amount of money regarded as acceptable, e.g. in a business deal

bottommost /bóttəm mōst/ *adj.* at the very lowest level ○ *the bottommost rung of the ladder*

bottoms /bóttəmz/ *n.* = **bottom** *n.* **9**

bottomset bed /bóttəmset-/ *n.* a layer of sediment deposited by a river at the base of an accumulating delta

botulin /bóttyoõlin/ *n.* a toxin produced by the bacterium *Clostridium botulinum* that causes botulism [Early 20thC. From modern Latin *botulinus* (see BOTULINUM).]

botulinum /bóttyoõ línəm/, **botulinus** /-líʹnəss/ *n.* a bacterium that causes botulism when it is present in food. It is an anaerobic bacterium, requiring the absence of free oxygen. Latin name: *Clostridium botulinum.* [Early 20thC. From modern Latin, neuter of *botulinus*, formed from Latin *botulus* 'sausage'.] —**botulinal** *adj.*

botulism /bóttyoõlizzəm/ *n.* a serious form of food poisoning caused by eating preserved food that has been contaminated with botulinum organisms [Late 19thC. From German *Botulismus*, literally 'sausage-poisoning', formed from Latin *botulus* 'sausage'.]

Bouaké /bwaʹa kay/ *city* and capital of Bouaké Department, central Côte d'Ivoire. Population: 329,850 (1988).

boubou /boõ boõ/ *n.* an African bird, a type of shrike, that is black with a white slash on each wing. It is known for singing in pairs. Genus: *Lanarius.* [Late 20thC. From an African language.]

bouchée /boõ shay, boo sháy/ *n.* a small bite-sized puff pastry case filled with a savoury mixture [Mid-19thC. From French, literally 'mouthful', formed from *bouche* 'mouth', from Latin *bucca* 'cheek'.]

Boucher /boõ shay/, **François** (1703–70) French painter. He worked at the court of Louis XV, painting mythological and pastoral scenes in the Rococo style.

bouclé /boõ klay/ *n.* a yarn with loops or bumps along its length that give a knobbly effect when knitted or woven (*often used before a noun*) [Late 19thC. From French, past participle of *boucler* 'to curl' (source of English *buckle*), ultimately from Latin *buccula* 'cheekstrap of a helmet', from *bucca* 'cheek'.]

Boudicca /boõdikə/, **Boadicea** /bṓ ədi see ə/ (d. 62 AD) English tribal queen. The queen of the Iceni, she raised a rebellion against the Romans, who had invaded her kingdom. She sacked London, Col-

chester, and St Albans, and destroyed the Ninth Legion.

boudoir /boõ dwaar/ *n.* a woman's bedroom or private sitting room [Late 18thC. From French, literally 'a place to sulk in', from *bouder* 'to pout or sulk'.]

bouffant /boõ foN/ *adj.* **BACKCOMBED INTO FULL SHAPE** used to describe a woman's hairstyle in which hair is backcombed or teased to give fullness and height ■ *n.* **HAIRSTYLE** a full, high hairstyle for women [Early 19thC. From French, present participle of *bouffer* 'to swell or puff up', ultimately an imitation of the sound.]

bouffe /boof/ *n.* = **opéra bouffe** [Via French from Italian *buffa*, feminine of *buffo* 'comic' (see BUFFOON)]

Bougainville /boõgənvil/ The largest island of the Solomon Island group in eastern Papua New Guinea, in the southwestern Pacific Ocean. Area: approximately 8,730 sq. km/3,492 sq. mi.

Bougainville /boõgənvil, boõ gaN veél/, **Louis Antoine, comte de** (1729–1811) French navigator. He made the first French circumnavigation of the world (1766–69).

bougainvillea /boõgən vílli ə/, **bougainvillaea** *n.* a climbing woody plant with insignificant flowers that have attractive red, purple, or pink surrounding leaves (**bracts**). It is native to South America and is popular in warm climates elsewhere. Genus: *Bougainvillea.* [Mid-19thC. From modern Latin, named after Louis Antoine de BOUGAINVILLE, who led the expedition on which the plant was discovered.]

bough /bow/ *n.* a large main branch of a tree, from which smaller branches grow [Old English *bōg* 'bough, shoulder'. Ultimately from an Indo-European word meaning 'arm', which is also the ancestor of English *bow* (of a ship).]

bought[1] *v.* past tense, past participle of **buy**

bought[2] /bawt/ *adj.* commercially made rather than homemade

bougie /boõ zhee, boo zheé/ *n.* a medical instrument in the form of a flexible tube, inserted into a body passage such as the rectum to open it to allow medicines or instruments to be introduced [Mid-18thC. From French, named after the town of *Bougie* (Arabic *Bijāya*) in Algeria, which traded in wax. The word originally denoted a wax candle.]

bouillabaisse /boõyə béss, -báyss/ *n.* a rich soup made with fish, shellfish, vegetables, herbs, and saffron. It originated in the south of France. [Mid-19thC. Via French from modern Provençal *bouiabaisso*.]

bouillon /boõ yoN/ *n.* a clear liquid that is traditionally made by boiling meat, bones, and vegetables together [Mid-17thC. From French, formed from *bouillir* (see BOIL).]

bouillon cube *n. US* = **stock cube**

Boulanger /boõ loN zhay/, **Nadia** (1887–1979) French composer and music teacher. She composed noble and instrumental music until 1918. During many years of teaching in Paris, her students included Elliott Carter, Aaron Copland, Walter Piston, and Virgil Thomson. Full name **Nadia Juliette Boulanger**

boulder /bṓldər/ *n.* **1. LARGE ROCK** a large round rock **2. GEOL ROCK FRAGMENT** a large fragment of rock greater than 200 mm/8 in in diameter [15thC. Shortening of *boulderstone*, a partial translation of a Scandinavian word.]

Boulder /bṓldər/ resort city in northern Colorado, northwest of Denver, southeast of Rocky Mountain National Park, original home to University of Colorado, opened in 1877. Population: 90,928 (1996).

boulder clay *n. GEOG* = **till**[4] *n.*

bouldering /bṓldəring/ *n.* rock climbing that involves climbing short and extremely difficult slopes —**boulderer** *n.*

boule /bool/ *n.* a pear-shaped imitation gemstone made in a furnace from synthetic aluminium oxide (**corundum**) [Early 20thC. From French (see BOWL[2]).]

boules /bool/ *n.* an outdoor game of French origin, similar to bowls. It is traditionally played on open dusty ground in public places with heavy metal balls that are tossed with a backhand action. (*takes a singular verb*) [Early 20thC. From French, plural of *boule* (see BOWL[2]).]

boulevard /bóol vaar, bóolə vaard/ *n.* a wide street, especially one lined with trees (*often used in place names*) [Mid-18thC. From French (originally 'rampart', later a promenade on the site of one), from Middle Low German and Middle Dutch *bolwerk* 'bulwark' (see BULWARK).]

boulevardier /bool vaárdi ay, boolə vaárdi ay/ *n.* a fashionable, sophisticated man who treats life with light-hearted cynicism (*dated*) [Late 19thC. From French, formed from *boulevard* (see BOULEVARD).]

Boulez /bóo lez/, **Pierre** (*b.* 1925) French composer and conductor. He conducted major orchestras in Europe and the United States and championed new music.

boulle /bool/ *n.* elaborate inlay work on furniture, using tortoiseshell, ivory, or brass in scroll shapes. It was popular in France in the 17th century. (*often used before a noun*) [Early 19thC. From French, named after the French cabinetmaker André Charles Boule (1642–1732), who first used it.]

Boulogne-sur-Mer /boo lóyn syoor máir/, **Boulogne** city and port on the English Channel in Pas-de-Calais Department, northwestern France. Population: 44,244 (1990).

Boumédienne /boo máydi én/, **Houari** (1932–78) Algerian nationalist and statesman. He commanded the liberation forces during Algeria's war of independence (1960) and was president of Algeria (1965–68). Real name **Muhammad Ben Brahim Boukharrouba**

bounce /bownss/ *v.* (**bounces, bouncing, bounced**) **1.** *vti.* SPRING AWAY FROM SURFACE to move away quickly after hitting a surface, or throw sth so that it hits a surface and moves away ○ *bouncing a tennis ball against a wall* ○ *Onlookers saw the car bounce off a tree.* **2.** *vi.* JUMP UP AND DOWN to jump up and down repeatedly on a soft surface ○ *children bouncing on trampolines* **3.** *vt.* LIFT REPEATEDLY ON KNEE to lift a baby or child up and down on your knee for fun **4.** *vti.* REFLECT FROM SURFACE to strike a surface, or cause sth to strike a surface, and be reflected back ○ *the use of a fixed orbiting satellite to bounce the transmission signal back to earth* **5.** *vi.* MOVE SWINGINGLY to move in an up-and-down or swinging way ○ *with her long blonde hair bouncing as she walked* **6.** *vi.* GO ENERGETICALLY to walk quickly and energetically ○ *She bounced up to the guests and breezily said hello.* **7.** *vti.* REFUSE TO PAY to refuse payment of a cheque, or be refused by a bank, because there is insufficient money in the account on which it is drawn **8.** *vt.* WRITE BAD CHEQUE to write a cheque that the bank will not honour **9.** *vt.* MENTION IN ORDER TO RECEIVE OPINIONS to put sth, especially an idea or suggestion, to sb in order to get reactions or opinions (*slang*) ○ *She bounced a couple of theories off the students* **10.** *vt.* COERCE INTO DOING STH to force sb into doing sth by restricting the alternatives (*informal*) ○ *I don't want to get bounced into making unwise investments.* **11.** *vt.* THROW OUT to eject sb from a place or expel sb from a club or other organization (*slang*) ○ *managed to get themselves bounced out of the restaurant* **12.** *vi.* COMPUT COME BACK to be returned undelivered to a sender of an electronic mail message ○ *My last e-mail to you bounced.* ■ *n.* **1.** ACT OF REBOUNDING a springing away from a surface after hitting it ○ *hit the ball before the second bounce* **2.** SPRINGINESS the capacity of a ball or other object to bounce, or of a surface to cause objects hitting it to bounce ○ *not so much bounce in the pitch* **3.** BOBBING MOVEMENT swinging or bobbing movement, or the capacity to swing or bob up and down ○ *a conditioner guaranteed to give your hair added bounce* **4.** ENERGY lively energy [13thC. Originally 'to beat, thump', of uncertain origin: perhaps it suggests the action.]

bounce back *vi.* to recover quickly and completely after a bad experience

bouncer /bównssər/ *n.* **1.** GUARD AT NIGHTCLUB a security guard who usually stands at the door of a nightclub or other place of entertainment and is responsible for preventing undesirable people from entering and for ejecting troublemakers **2.** CRICKET BALL BOUNCING HEAD HIGH in cricket, a ball that is pitched short and bounces at chest or head height to intimidate the batsman **3.** BASEBALL STRUCK BALL THAT BOUNCES a ball that bounces along the ground after being hit

bouncing /bównssing/ *adj.* used to describe a healthy active baby ○ *the proud parents of a beautiful bouncing boy*

bouncing Bet *n.* = **soapwort** [*Bet* is a pet-form of *Elizabeth*]

bouncy /bównssi/ (**-ier, -iest**) *adj.* **1.** LIVELY lively and energetic **2.** BOUNCING WELL tending to bounce or capable of bouncing well ○ *bouncy material used in making tennis balls* **3.** SPRINGY tending to bounce objects hitting it or resting on it —**bouncily** *adv.* —**bounciness** *n.*

bouncy castle *n.* a large inflatable object in the shape of a castle which children can bounce on for fun

bound[1] /bownd/ *v.* past participle, past tense of **bind**

bound[2] /bownd/ *adj.* **1.** CERTAIN TO DO STH certain to happen or do sth because custom, experience, or common sense dictates it ○ *If you play music late at night, people are bound to complain.* **2.** OBLIGED obliged to do sth or behave in a certain way, e.g. for legal or moral reasons **3.** WITH PERMANENT COVER used to describe a book or other written document that has a permanent, usually hard, cover **4.** *US* DETERMINED firmly resolved ○ *She was bound on becoming the best in the business.* [14thC. Shortening of BOUNDEN.] ◇ **bound up with sb** *or* **sth** to be closely involved with or connected to sb or sth

bound[3] /bownd/ *vi.* (**bounds, bounding, bounded**) GO ENERGETICALLY to move quickly and energetically, with large strides or jumps ○ *A puppy came bounding across the lawn.* ■ *n.* ENERGETIC LEAP an energetic long or high jump [Early 16thC. Via French *bondir* 'to resound', later 'to rebound', from, ultimately, Latin *bombire* 'to buzz', from *bombus* 'humming, booming' (source of English *bomb*), from Greek.]

bound[4] /bownd/ *adj.* **1.** ON THE WAY SOMEWHERE travelling towards a particular place (*often used in combination*) ○ *a Spanish trawler bound for the Irish Sea* ○ *homeward bound* **2.** DESTINED certain to reach or achieve sth ○ *young performers bound for international stardom* [Late 16thC. Originally *boun*, from Old Norse *búinn*, past participle of *búa* 'to prepare'; probably influenced by BOUND[1].]

bound[5] /bownd/ *vt.* (**bounds, bounding, bounded**) **1.** SURROUND to form the boundary to an area or site ○ *grounds bounded on three sides by the river* **2.** RESTRICT to impose limits on sth ○ *political views not bounded by moral convictions* ■ *n.* MATH LIMITING NUMBER a number that represents the upper or lower end of a range of possible values ■ *adj.* **1.** LING NOT ABLE TO BE USED ALONE used to describe a unit of meaning (**morpheme**) that cannot be used on its own as a word. ◊ **free** *adj.* 20 **2.** GRAM NOT ABLE TO BE USED ALONE used to describe a grammatical element such as a clause that can only be used with another element [14thC. Originally 'boundary marker', from Anglo-Norman *bounde* and Old French *bodne*, ultimately from medieval Latin *butina*, of uncertain origin: probably from Celtic.]

boundary /bówndəri/ (*plural* **-ries**) *n.* **1.** BORDER the official line that divides one area of land from another ○ *Multinational companies operate across national boundaries.* **2.** LIMIT the point at which sth ends or beyond which it becomes sth else ○ *pushing back the boundaries of human knowledge* **3.** CRICKET EDGE OF CRICKET PITCH the outer limit of the playing area of a cricket pitch **4.** CRICKET SHOT CROSSING BOUNDARY in cricket, a shot that crosses the boundary, scoring either four or six runs [Early 17thC. Alteration of *bounder*, from BOUND[4].]

Boundary Commission *n.* a public body that monitors the boundaries of parliamentary constituencies between elections and recommends changes to them based on shifts in the population

boundary condition *n.* the set of requirements that must be met in order for the solution to a set of differential equations to be found

boundary layer *n.* the region of a viscous fluid, e.g. air or water, closest to the surface of a solid that is in motion relative to the fluid

boundary rider *n. Aus* an employee on a sheep or cattle station whose job is to check that boundary fences are in good repair

bounded /bówndid/ *adj.* used to describe a mathematical set that has an upper and lower limiting number (**bound**[5])

bounden /bówndən/ *v.* past participle of **bind** (*archaic*)

bounder /bówndər/ *n.* sb, especially a man, who behaves in a dishonourable or morally unacceptable way (*dated*) (*insult*) [16thC. Formed from BOUND[2].]

bound form *n.* a linguistic unit that can only occur as part of a word and not as a separate word itself, e.g. '-ly' in 'quickly'

boundless /bówndləss/ *adj.* seeming to have no end or limit —**boundlessly** *adv.* —**boundlessness** *n.*

bounds /bowndz/ *npl.* limits, especially restrictions on what can happen or what can be done ○ *a joke that goes beyond the bounds of good taste* ◇ **know no bounds** to be very great, strong, or intense ○ *an ego that knows no bounds* ◇ **out of bounds 1.** outside the area where sb is allowed to go ○ *a basketball that is out of bounds* **2.** not open or available ○ *Discussion of the candidate's private life is out of bounds.*

bounteous /bównti əss/ *adj.* (*literary*) **1.** GENEROUS giving generously **2.** ABUNDANT given in generous measure [14thC. Alteration of Old French *bontif* (on the model of PLENTEOUS), from *bonté* (see BOUNTY).] —**bounteously** *adv.* —**bounteousness** *n.*

bountiful /bówntif'l/ *adj.* (*literary*) **1.** GENEROUS giving generously **2.** ABUNDANT in plentiful supply [Early 16thC. Formed from BOUNTY, in the sense 'goodness, generosity'.] —**bountifully** *adv.* —**bountifulness** *n.*

WORD KEY: SYNONYMS

See Synonyms at ***generous***.

bounty /bównti/ (*plural* **-ties**) *n.* **1.** REWARD a reward of money offered for finding a criminal or other wanted person, or for killing a person or a predator **2.** GENEROSITY generosity in giving (*literary*) ○ *'a trifling additional claim upon your bounty and good nature'* (Sir Walter Scott, *Waverley*; 1814) **3.** ABUNDANT SUPPLY a plentiful or generous supply (*literary*) ○ *'As a grand mansion, 'The Broadway Estate' is home to a bounty of rooms, each with a distinct personality'.* (Patti Martinhome, *Living Page, Asbury Park Press*; *1997*) [14thC. Via French *bonté* from Latin *bonitas* 'goodness', from *bonus* 'good' (source of English *bonus* and *bonanza*).]

Bounty /bównti/ *n.* the British naval ship commanded by Captain William Bligh on a scientific voyage to Tahiti in 1789. Bligh's cruelty provoked a mutiny led by Fletcher Christian.

bounty hunter *n.* **1.** SEEKER OF REWARDS sb who pursues wanted criminals or fugitives for financial reward **2.** HUNTER OF ANIMALS sb who hunts animals whose capture attracts a reward, e.g. because they are dangerous or are pests

Bounty Islands /bownti-/ group of 13 uninhabited islands in the southwestern Pacific Ocean, 668 km/415 mi. east of New Zealand. The islands are part of New Zealand. Area: 1.4 sq. km/0.5 sq. mi.

bouquet /boo káy, bō-/ *n.* **1.** BUNCH OF FLOWERS a bunch of cut flowers that have been specially chosen or arranged **2.** SCENT OF WINE a wine's characteristic scent **3.** PRAISE an expression of congratulation or praise (*literary*) [Early 18thC. From French, 'thicket', literally 'small forest', from Old French *bois* 'forest', ultimately from a Germanic word that is also the ancestor of English *bush*.]

WORD KEY: SYNONYMS

See Synonyms at ***smell***.

bouquet garni /bóo kay gaárni/ (*plural* **bouquets garnis** /bóo kay gaárni/) *n.* a bunch of mixed herbs, or an equivalent dried herb mixture in a sachet, that is used to add flavour to stews, soups, sauces, and other dishes [Mid-19thC. From French, literally 'garnished bouquet'.]

bourbon[1] /búrbən/ n. a type of whisky distilled mainly in the United States from a fermented mixture of hot water and grain (**mash**) containing at least 51% maize [Mid-19thC. Named after *Bourbon* County, Kentucky, where it was first distilled.]

bourbon[2] /boórbən/, **Bourbon** n. a rectangular chocolate-flavoured biscuit that has two layers sandwiched together with a chocolate cream filling [Mid-18thC. Named after the *Bourbon* dynasty of France.]

Bourbon /boórbən/ adj. relating to a branch of the French royal family who reigned from 1589 to 1793 and again after the French Revolution until the revolution of 1830. The Spanish royal family also belongs to this branch. [Mid-18thC. From French, named after the town of *Bourbon l'Archambault* in central France.]

bourdon /boórd'n/ n. 1. BAGPIPE PIPE OR NOTE the bass pipe on a set of bagpipes, or the bass note it produces 2. ORGAN STOP the bass stop on an organ, especially on a 16-foot pipe [Mid-19thC. From French, literally 'drone'. An imitation of the sound.]

Bourdon gauge /boórd'n-/ n. a pressure gauge with a flattened curved tube that straightens under pressure, allowing the force to be measured [Named after the French hydraulic engineer Eugène *Bourdon*, who invented it]

bourg /boorg/ a town or village, especially a medieval French market town [12thC. Via French from Latin *burgus* 'castle', later 'borough', ultimately from a Germanic word that is also the ancestor of English *borough*.]

bourgeois /boor zhwáa, boór zhwaa/ adj. 1. MIDDLE-CLASS AND CONVENTIONAL typical of affluent middle-class people, who are often characterized as conventional, conservative, or materialistic in outlook 2. POL MIDDLE-CLASS according to Marxist theory, relating to the social class that owns most of the wealth and is regarded as exploiting the working class ■ n. (*plural* **-geois**) 1. CONVENTIONAL PERSON sb with a bourgeois outlook 2. POL CAPITALIST in Marxist analysis, a member of the bourgeois social class [Mid-16thC. From French, literally 'citizen of a city or borough', ultimately from Latin *burgus* (see BOURG).]

Bourgeois /boór zhwaa/, **Léon Victor** (1851–1925) French statesman. One of the founders of the League of Nations, he received the Nobel Peace Prize in 1920. Full name **Léon Victor Auguste Bourgeois**

bourgeoisie /boór zhwaa zeé/ n. 1. EXPLOITATIVE MIDDLE CLASS the social class that, according to Marxist theory, owns the means of producing wealth and exploits the working class 2. MIDDLE-CLASS PEOPLE affluent middle-class people characterized as conventional, conservative, or materialistic in outlook [Early 18thC. From French, formed from *bourgeois* (see BOURGEOIS).]

bourgeoisify /boor zhwáazi fī/ (**-fies, -fying, -fied**) vt. to impose bourgeois values on sb or sth, or make sb or sth bourgeois in character —**bourgeoisification** /boor zhwáazifi káysh'n/ n.

Bourguiba /boor geéba/, **Habib** (b. 1903) Tunisian statesman. He led Tunisia's independence movement and was the country's first prime minister (1956–7) and president (1957–87). Full name **Habib ibn Ali Bourguiba**

bourguignonne /boór geen yón/ adj. cooked in a red wine sauce with mushrooms and small whole onions, in a style that originated in the Burgundy region of France [Early 20thC. From French, formed from *Bourgogne* 'Burgundy'.]

Bourke /burk/ town in northern New South Wales, Australia. It lies on the Darling River. Population: 2,976 (1996).

Bourke-White /búrk wít/, **Margaret** (1906–71) US photographer and writer. She was a leading photojournalist who was closely identified with *Life*. She was the magazine's staff photographer from 1936 to 1969.

bourn[1] /bawrn, boorn/ n. (archaic) 1. BOUNDARY a boundary between one place or one thing and another ○ *I'll set a bourn how far to be beloved'.* (William

Shakespeare, *Antony & Cleopatra*; 1606) 2. GOAL sth that is aimed for or aspired to [Early 16thC. From French *borne*, from Old French *bodne* (see BOUND[4].)]

bourn[2] /bawrn, boorn/, **bourne** n. a small stream that only flows in the winter months [14thC. A southern English variant of BURN.]

Bournemouth /báwrnməth/ seaside resort on the English Channel in Dorset, southern England. Population: 160,900 (1995).

bourse /boorss/, **Bourse** n. a European stock exchange, especially the one in Paris [Late 16thC. Via French from medieval Latin *bursa* 'bag, purse' from, ultimately, Greek *bursa* 'leather' (source of English *purse*).]

bouse /bowz/ (**bouses, bousing, boused**) vt. to hoist sth with a tackle [Late 16thC. Origin unknown.]

boustrophedon /boóstrə feéd'n, bówstrə-/ n. an ancient method of inscribing and writing in which lines are written alternately from right to left and from left to right [Early 17thC. From Greek, literally 'as the ox turns in ploughing', from *bous* 'ox' + *-strophos* 'turning', from *strephein* 'to turn'.] —**boustrophedonic** /boóstrə fee dónnik, bówstrə fee dónnik/ adj.

bout /bowt/ n. 1. ATTACK OF ILLNESS a temporary or short-lived attack of illness, usually a common and not very serious illness ○ *a recent bout of flu* 2. SHORT PERIOD OF ACTIVITY a short time spent doing sth, often sth considered distasteful 3. FIGHT a boxing or wrestling match [Mid-16thC. Variant of archaic *bought* 'curve', of uncertain origin: probably from Low German *bucht*. The meaning developed via 'turn of a plough' to 'turn of work'.]

boutique /boo teék/ n. 1. SMALL CLOTHES SHOP a small shop that sells fashionable clothes 2. SMALL SPECIALIST SHOP a small shop selling specialist goods or services of any kind, e.g. imported foods and wines [Mid-18thC. Via French from, ultimately, Greek *apothēkē* 'storehouse' (source of English *apothecary*).]

boutique brewery n. US = microbrewery

bouton /boó toN/ n. the knob or swelling on a nerve-cell extension (**axon**) at the point where it forms a junction (**synapse**) with a neuron [Mid-19thC. From French (see BUTTON).]

boutonniere /boó ton yáir, -tonni áir/, **boutonnière** n. = **buttonhole** (*formal*) [Late 19thC. From French, formed from *bouton* (see BUTTON).]

Boutros-Ghali /boó tross gáali/, **Boutros** (b. 1922) Egyptian diplomat. He was the sixth general secretary of the UN (1992–96).

bouvier /boóvi ay/ n. a large powerful dog with a rough fawn or black coat, originally bred in Belgium to herd cattle [Early 20thC. From French, shortened from *bouvier des Flandres*, literally 'cowherd of Flanders'.]

Bouzouki

bouzouki /boo zoóki/ (*plural* **-kis**) n. a long-necked stringed musical instrument of Greek origin. It is similar in appearance and sound to a mandolin. [Mid-20thC. From modern Greek *mpouzouki*, of uncertain origin: perhaps from Turkish *bozuk* 'spoiled' (used of roughly made instruments).]

bovid /bóvid/ adj. relating or belonging to the family of hollow-horned, hoofed, ruminant animals that includes cattle, sheep, and antelopes. Family: Bovidae. [Late 19thC. Formed from Latin *bov-* (see BOVINE).] —**bovid** n.

bovine /bố vīn/ adj. 1. OF CATTLE GENUS relating or belonging to the genus of ruminant animals that includes cattle, oxen, and buffalo. Genus: *Bos*. 2. SLOW

displaying the slowness regarded as typical of cattle and related animals (*literary*) ■ n. BOVINE ANIMAL an animal belonging to the same genus as cattle [Early 19thC. From late Latin *bovinus*, from Latin *bov-*, stem of *bos* 'ox' (source of English *beef*).]

bovine somatotrophin n. a hormone in cattle that regulates growth and milk production. It can also be produced artificially by genetic engineering and used to increase milk yields.

bovine spongiform encephalopathy n. full form of BSE

Bovril /bóvril/ *tdmk.* a trademark for a concentrated beef extract used as a stock or flavouring, or, with hot water added, as a drink

bovver /bóvvər/ n. aggressive behaviour (*dated slang*) [Mid-20thC. Representing a Cockney pronunciation of BOTHER.]

bovver boot n. UK a heavy-duty boot, often one with a steel toecap, worn by members of gangs as a fighting weapon and a symbol of toughness. In the 1960s and 1970s, such boots were a standard part of the skinhead's uniform. (*dated informal*)

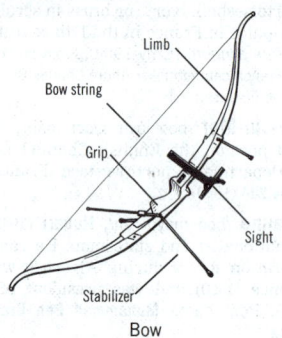

Bow

bow[1] /bō/ n. 1. LOOPED KNOT a knot in which the loops remain visible, e.g. in tied shoelaces or in ribbons used for decorating gifts or hair. ◊ **bow tie** 2. SPORTS, ARMS WEAPON FOR FIRING ARROWS a weapon used to fire arrows, consisting of a curved, flexible piece of wood and a taut string fastened to the two ends 3. MUSIC ROD FOR PLAYING STRINGED INSTRUMENTS a rod with fibres tightly stretched between the two ends, used for playing stringed instruments 4. CURVED SHAPE OR PART a rounded or semicircular shape, e.g. a part of a building or a loop in a river 5. ARCHERY, HIST = **bowman**[1] (*literary*) 6. = rainbow ■ **bows** *npl.* ARCHERY, HIST ARCHERS bowmen or archers considered as a group (*literary*) ■ v. (**bows, bowing, bowed**) 1. *vti.* BEND STH INTO BOW SHAPE to bend, or bend sth, into a rounded or bow shape 2. *vti.* MUSIC DRAW BOW ACROSS STRINGED INSTRUMENT to draw a bow across the strings of a stringed instrument 3. *vt.* MUSIC INDICATE BOWING FOR MUSIC to mark a piece of music to indicate which notes are to be played with the bow moving in one direction across the strings and which are to be played with it moving in the opposite direction [Old English *boga*. Ultimately from a prehistoric Germanic word meaning 'to bend', which is also the ancestor of English *bow*[2], *bight*, and *bagel*.]

bow[2] /bow/ v. (**bows, bowing, bowed**) 1. *vti.* BEND HEAD OR BODY FORWARD to bend the head forward, or to bend forward from the waist, as a signal of respect, greeting, consent, submission, or acknowledgment ○ *bowing her head in shame* 2. *vti.* BEND STH OR DROOP to bend sth over so that it droops, or to be bent in this way ○ *branches bowed down with fruit.* 3. *vi.* YIELD TO STH OR SB to accept sth and yield to it, often unwillingly ○ *bowed to the demands of pressure groups* ■ n. BENDING FORWARD OF UPPER BODY a bending forward of the upper part of the body to show respect, acknowledgment, subservience, courtesy, or greeting [Old English *būgan* (source also of English *buxom*). Ultimately from an Indo-European word meaning 'to bend', which is also the ancestor of English *bow*[1].] ◊ **bow and scrape** to be excessively polite or attentive in an attempt to ingratiate yourself with sb

bow[3] /bow/ n. 1. SHIPPING FRONT PART OF VESSEL the front section of a boat or other vessel 2. ROWING PERSON IN

BOW the rower closest to the front of a boat [Early 17thC. From Low German *boog* or Middle Dutch *boeg*.]

Bow /bō/, **Clara** (1905–65) US actor. She enjoyed a brief career in the late 1920s as the most popular female movie star in the country, but spent her last three decades in retirement. Known as **the It Girl**

bowdlerize /bówdlə rīz/ (**-izes, -izing, -ized**), **bowdlerise** (**-lerises, -lerising, -lerised**) *vti.* to remove parts of a work of literature that are considered indecent [Mid-19thC. Formed from the name of the English editor Thomas *Bowdler* (1754–1825), who published an edition of Shakespeare omitting scenes that he considered unsuitable.] —**bowdlerism** *n.* —**bowdlerization** /bówdlə rī záysh'n/ *n.* —**bowdlerizer** /bówdlə rīzər/ *n.*

bowel /bówəl/ *n.* **1.** INTESTINE the intestine **2.** PART OF THE INTESTINE a section or part of the intestines, especially the part of the intestine that connects to the anus ○ *empty your bowels* ■ **bowels** *npl.* DEPTHS OF STH the deepest or innermost part of sth ○ *the bowels of the ship* [13thC. Via Anglo-Norman *buel* and Old French *boël* from Latin *botellus*, literally 'small sausage' (from its shape), from *botulus* 'sausage' (source of English *botulism*).]

bowel movement *n.* **1.** EXPULSION OF FAECES the passing of faeces out of the body through the anus **2.** FAECES faeces passed through the anus

Bowen /bố in/, **Elizabeth** (1899–1973) Irish writer. Her fictional depictions of upper-middle-class life included short stories and the novels *The Death of the Heart* (1938), and *The Heat of the Day* (1949). Full name **Elizabeth Dorothea Cole Bowen**

Bowen therapy /bố in-/ *n.* a technique that balances the body and initiates healing and encourages emotional stability using gentle manipulation of muscles and connective tissues [Mid-20thC. Named after Tom *Bowen* of Victoria, Australia (1916–82), its originator.]

bower[1] /bówər/ *n.* **1.** SHADY SHELTER a shady, leafy shelter or recess, especially in a garden or wood **2.** WOMAN'S BEDROOM OR APARTMENTS a woman's bedroom or private apartments, especially in a medieval castle **3.** PICTURESQUE COTTAGE a picturesque country cottage, especially one that is used as a retreat (*literary*) [Old English *būr* 'dwelling'. Ultimately from an Indo-European base meaning 'to be, live', which is also the ancestor of English *be*.] —**bowery** *adj.*

bower[2] /bówər/ *n.* the anchor at a ship's bow

bower[3] /bówər/ *n.* the jack in euchre and other similar card games [Late 19thC. From German *Bauer* 'peasant'.]

Bowerbird

bowerbird /bówər burd/ *n.* a bird native to New Guinea and Australia that is noted for the elaborate structures that the male builds for courtship. Family: Ptilonorynchidae.

bowfin /bố fin/ (*plural* **-fins** *or* **-fin**) *n.* a freshwater fish of eastern North America, with a mottled greenish-brown body and a long dorsal fin. It is the only member of its family that survives from the Palaeocene epoch. Latin name: *Amia calva*.

bowfront /bố frunt/ *adj.* used to describe a piece of furniture with a front that curves outwards ○ *a bowfront desk*

bowhead /bố hed/ (*plural* **-heads** *or* **-head**) *n.* a baleen whale that lives in the Arctic seas and has an arched upper jaw. Latin name: *Balaena mysticetus*.

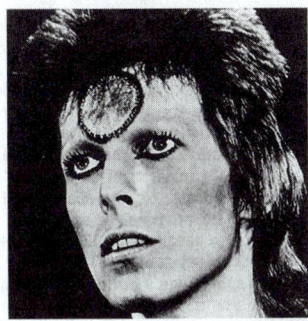

David Bowie

Bowie /bówi/, **David** (*b.* 1947) British pop singer and actor. He pioneered glam rock in the 1970s. His albums include *The Rise and Fall of Ziggy Stardust and the Spiders From Mars* (1972). Born **David Robert James**

Bowie /bố i/, **Jim** (1796?–1836) US pioneer. A colonel in the Texas army, he died at the Battle of the Alamo. Full name **James Bowie**

Bowie knife

bowie knife /bố i nīf/ (*plural* **bowie knives** /bố i nīvz/) *n.* a single-edged hunting knife, about 38 cm/15 in long and curved near the point, with a short hilt and a guard for the hand [Mid-19thC. Named after James BOWIE, who popularized it.]

bowing /bố ing/ *n.* **1.** PLAYING STRINGED INSTRUMENT WITH BOW the use of a bow to play a stringed instrument such as the violin or cello **2.** DIRECTION OF BOW the way a specific piece should be played on a stringed instrument, in respect of the direction in which the bow is moved for successive notes

bowknot /bố not/ *n.* a decorative knot in the form of a bow

bowl[1] /bōl/ *n.* **1.** ROUND CONTAINER an open container, usually round in shape and wider than it is deep, and typically used for holding food and liquids **2.** AMOUNT IN BOWL the amount a bowl can hold ○ *two bowls of cereal* **3.** PART LIKE BOWL a bowl-shaped part of sth ○ *a toilet bowl* **4.** GEOG DEPRESSION IN GROUND a round depression in the surface of the land. ◊ **dust bowl 5.** MILDLY ALCOHOLIC DRINK a mildly alcoholic beverage or the type of cup used for drinking it (*literary*) [Old English *bolla*. Ultimately from an Indo-European word meaning 'to swell, be round', which is also the ancestor of English *ball*.]
bowl out *vt.* = **bowl**[2] *v.* 3

bowl[2] /bōl/ *v.* (**bowls, bowling, bowled**) **1.** *vti.* ROLL SMOOTHLY ALONG to roll smoothly, or to make sth such as a ball, roll smoothly along the ground or some other flat surface ○ *Bowl the ball more gently this time.* **2.** *vti.* CRICKET SEND BALL TO BATSMAN OR BATSWOMAN to send a ball, usually overarm, to a batsman or batswoman **3.** *vt.* DISMISS BATSMAN OR BATSWOMAN to get a batsman or batswoman out by bowling ○ *He's been bowled!* **4.** *vi.* GO BOWLING to take part in a game of bowls or bowling **5.** *vt.* SCORE POINTS IN BOWLING to score a given number of points in bowling ○ *He bowled 250 last night.* **6.** *vi.* MOVE QUICKLY to move smoothly and quickly ○ *bowling along down the country lanes* ■ *n.* **1.** WOODEN BALL USED IN BOWLS a wooden ball used in the game of bowls, which has slightly flattened sides in order to make it roll in a curve **2.** BOWLING

BALL a bowling ball **3.** ROLL OF THE BALL one roll of the ball in bowling [15thC. Via French *boule* from Latin *bulla* 'bubble'.]
bowl over *vt.* **1.** ASTONISH SB to amaze or delight sb ○ *I was completely bowled over by their generous offer.* **2.** KNOCK STH OR SB DOWN ACCIDENTALLY to knock sth or sb down, especially accidentally during a headlong rush ○ *The dog bowled three chairs over in its excitement.*

bowlegged /bō léggid, bō légd/ *adj.* having legs that curve outwards around or below the knee area [Mid-16thC. From BOW[1].]

bow legs *n.* a condition in which the legs curve outwards around the knee area (*takes a singular verb*) —**bowleg** *n.*

bowler /bố lər/ *n.* **1.** CRICKET SB WHO THROWS BALL the player who bowls the ball in cricket **2.** PLAYER IN BOWLING sb who engages in the sport of bowling

bowler hat, **bowler** *n.* a hard felt hat with a round crown and narrow upturned brim. US term **derby** [Mid-19thC. Named after the English hatter William *Bowler*, who designed it in 1850.]

Bowles /bōlz/, **Paul** (*b.* 1910) US writer and composer. He lived in Tangier, Morocco, after 1952. He composed music for movies and opera and wrote novels about US expatriates such as *The Sheltering Sky* (1949). Full name **Paul Frederick Bowles**

bowlful /bốlfŏol/ *n.* the amount of sth that fills or would fill a bowl ○ *a bowlful of soup*

bowline /bố lin/ *n.* **1.** KNOT FORMING TIGHT LOOP a knot used to form a loop that will not slip at the end of a piece of rope **2.** SAILING LINE FOR HOLDING A SAIL STEADY a line for controlling one of the vertical edges of a square sail **3.** MOUNTAINEERING KNOT IN END OF CLIMBING ROPE a fixed knot in the end of a climbing rope [14thC. Origin uncertain: from Middle Low German *bōlīne* or Middle Dutch *boechline*, literally 'line from the ship's bow'.]

bowling /bố ling/ *n.* **1.** GAME CONSISTING OF ROLLING BALL a game played by rolling a ball so that it either hits pins, as in tenpin bowling, or moves close to another ball, as in bowls **2.** PLAYING OF BOWLING the playing of any form of bowling **3.** CRICKET THROWING BALL TO BATSMAN OR BATSWOMAN the throwing of the ball, usually overarm, to a batsman or batswoman in cricket

bowling alley *n.* **1.** BUILDING FOR TENPIN BOWLING a building for tenpin bowling **2.** SMOOTH LANE USED IN BOWLING the long, narrow, smooth expanse of floor down which a ball is rolled in tenpin bowling or skittles

bowling ball *n.* the heavy ball used in the game of bowling, especially tenpin bowling, that has holes in it for the bowler's thumb and two fingers

bowling crease *n.* in cricket, a line that a bowler must not cross before the ball has been bowled

bowling green *n.* a piece of natural grass outdoors or a piece of artificial grass indoors for playing the game of bowls

bowls /bōlz/ *n.* a game in which heavy wooden balls are rolled on a flat surface with the object of coming close to a smaller target ball (*takes a singular verb*) US term **lawn bowling**

bowman[1] /bố mən/ (*plural* **-men** /-mən/) *n.* sb who uses a bow and arrows, or a crossbow

bowman[2] /bówmən/ (*plural* **-men** /-mən/) *n.* a man or boy who rows at the bow of a boat

Bowman's capsule /bố mənz káp syool/ *n.* a cup-shaped part of the kidney that extracts waste and water from the blood and produces urine [Late 19thC. Named after the English surgeon Sir William *Bowman* (1816–92), who discovered its function.]

bowmanship /bố mənship/ *n.* the technique and skill used in archery

Bowral /bówrəl/ town in the Southern Highlands of east-central New South Wales, Australia. Population: 8,705 (1996).

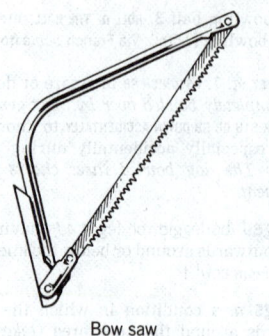

Bow saw

bow saw /bố saw/ *n.* a saw with a thin blade held in a bow-shaped frame with a narrow handle at each end, used for cutting curves

Bowser /bówzər/ *tdmk.* a trademark for a mobile tanker with a pumping apparatus, containing fuel for aircraft or military vehicles

bowshot /bố shot/ *n.* the distance that an arrow travels when it has been shot from a bow

bowsprit /bố sprit/ *n.* a spar that projects forward from the stem of a ship, to which the stays of the foremast are fastened [14thC. From Low German *bōgsprēt* or Middle Dutch *boechspriet*, literally 'pole at the bow'.]

Bow Street Runner /bố-/ *n.* one of the officers at Bow Street magistrates' court, London, from 1749 to 1829, whose duty was to pursue and arrest criminals. The Bow Street Runners were the forerunners of the modern British police force.

bowstring /bố string/ *n.* the taut string on an archer's bow, usually made of strands of hemp

bowstring hemp (*plural* **bowstring hemps** *or* **bowstring hemp**) *n.* **1.** PLANTS TROPICAL PLANT a tropical African or Asian perennial plant with thick leaves that are grouped in rosettes, cultivated for its fibres. Genus: *Sansevieria*. **2.** INDUST FIBRES OF HEMP the fibres of bowstring hemp plants, used to make bowstrings, mats, and nets

bow tie /bố tí/ *n.* a short tie, knotted in a bow at the neck

bow weight /bố-/ *n.* the amount of force needed to pull a bowstring back to its fullest extent

bow window /bố-/ *n.* a bay window that is curved

bow-wow /bów wów, bów wow/ *interj.* IMITATION OF BARKING used to imitate the bark of a dog ■ *n.* DOG a dog (*babytalk*) ■ *vi.* (**bow-wows, bow-wowing, bow-wowed**) BARK OR IMITATE BARKING to bark, or imitate the sound of barking [Late 16thC. An imitation of the sound.]

bowyangs /bố yangz/ *npl.* ANZ a pair of strings or straps secured round each trouser leg below the knee, worn in Australia and New Zealand by agricultural workers [Mid-19thC. Origin unknown.]

bowyer /bốyər/ *n.* **1.** MAKER OR SELLER OF BOWS sb who makes or sells bows for archery **2.** ARCHER an archer or bowman (*archaic*) [13thC. From BOW + -IER.]

box[1] /bóks/ *n.* **1.** CONTAINER a container for objects or dry goods, often with a removable or hinged lid, and usually square or rectangular **2.** AMOUNT BOX HOLDS the amount of sth a box holds or could hold **3.** RECTANGULAR SHAPE a square or rectangular shape printed on paper, or on a computer screen, usually containing information or requiring information to be entered in it ○ *Tick the boxes if the following items apply to you.* **4.** AREA OR STRUCTURE WITH BEST SEATS an enclosed area in a public building or at a sports venue, especially a theatre, football stadium, or racetrack, that contains the best and most luxurious seats ○ *corporate hospitality boxes* **5.** ENCLOSED AREA IN COURTROOM the enclosed area in a courtroom that is reserved for certain specified participants in a court case ○ *in the witness box* **6.** SMALL BUILDING PROVIDING SHELTER a small building that is used as a shelter, especially by military personnel (*usually used in combination*) **7.** SMALL BUILDING THAT HOUSES EQUIPMENT a small building that houses equipment and provides shelter for those who use this equipment (*always used in combination*) ○ *police box* **8.** BOX THAT HOUSES

EQUIPMENT a box, usually affixed to a wall or on a stand, that houses equipment such as a fire extinguisher, emergency telephone, or first-aid materials **9.** MAIL ANONYMOUS ADDRESS FOR MAIL an anonymous address for mail to be sent to, used either for administrative purposes or to protect the privacy of the addressee. ◊ **box number 10.** SPORTS PART OF PLAYING AREA a marked-off part of the playing area in certain sports, e.g. baseball and football, used for a specific purpose, or subject to special rules **11.** SPORTS = **penalty area 12.** SPORTS PROTECTIVE COVERING FOR SPORTSMAN'S GENITALS a protective plastic covering for a sportsman's genitals, worn especially in cricket **13.** SPORTS = **shooting box 14.** DRIVER'S SEAT IN HORSE-DRAWN COACH raised seat for the driver in a horse-drawn coach **15.** AGRIC COMPARTMENT FOR LIVESTOCK a compartment for horses or other farm animals, either in a building or in a vehicle. ◊ **loose box, horsebox 16.** = **Christmas box 17.** TELEVISION the television set (*slang*) ○ *What's on the box tonight, then?* **18.** COFFIN a casket for a corpse (*informal*) ○ *The next time he leaves that house it'll be in a box.* **19.** NZ MINING WHEELED CONTAINER FOR COAL a wheeled container, used for transporting coal in a mine **20.** Aus, US OFFENSIVE TERM an offensive term for a woman's vulva and vagina (*taboo slang*) **21.** AGRIC HOLE IN TREE TO COLLECT SAP a hole or hollow cut into the base of a tree in order to collect sap ■ *vt.* (**boxes, boxing, boxed**) **1.** PACK IN BOXES to pack individual items into boxes ○ *There are 300 pieces waiting to be boxed before shipping.* **2.** OUTLINE STH WITH BOX to enclose sth on a page or on a computer screen in a box ○ *Box the title to make it stand out more.* **3.** AGRIC CUT HOLE IN TREE FOR SAP to cut a box in the base of a tree to collect the sap **4.** ANZ MIX FLOCKS OR HERDS to mix flocks or herds of animals either accidentally or on purpose [Pre-12thC. Via late Latin *buxis* from Greek *puxis* 'wooden container', from *puxos* 'boxwood' (source of English *box*[3]).]

box in *vt.* to surround sb, or a vehicle, by or with sth, especially other people or cars, so that it is impossible to move

box up *vt.* = **box**[1] *v.* 1

box[2] /bóks/ (**boxes, boxing, boxed**) *vti.* to fight using the techniques of boxing, or fight sb in a boxing match ○ *He boxed in exhibition bouts to entertain the crowds.* [14thC. Origin unknown.] ◊ **box clever** to act in a clever and wily manner so as to defeat an opponent

box on *vi.* **1.** CONTINUE BOXING to continue with a boxing match. It is usually a command, given by the referee after a fight has been stopped, e.g., for a count. **2.** Aus PERSEVERE to continue or persevere with sth

box[3] /bóks/ (*plural* **box** *or* **boxes**) *n.* **1.** TREES EVERGREEN SHRUB a dense evergreen tree or shrub with shiny dark green oval leaves, often cultivated as a hedge. Genus: *Buxus*. **2.** INDUST = **boxwood** [Pre-12thC. Via Latin *buxus* from Greek *puxos* (source of English *box*[1]), of unknown origin.]

box[4] /bóks/ *vti.* SAILING = **boxhaul** [Mid-18thC. Origin uncertain: perhaps via Spanish *bojar* 'to sail round', from Middle Low German *bōgen* 'to bend'.]

Box and Cox /bóks ən kóks/ *npl.* two people who can share the use of sth (especially accommodation) because they need it at different times [From the title of a farce by J. M. Morton 1811–91, in which two characters unwittingly share a flat, one by day, the other by night.]

box beam *n.* = **box girder**

box bed *n.* an old-fashioned bed, enclosed on three sides and the top by a wooden structure resembling a box

boxberry /bóksbəri/ (*plural* **-ries**) *n.* = **partridgeberry, wintergreen** [Mid-19thC. From BOX[3] + BERRY.]

boxboard /bóks bawrd/ *n.* a tough cardboard made from wood and wastepaper pulp, used for making boxes

box calf *n.* black calfskin leather that has been tanned with chromium salts [Early 20thC. Named after Joseph *Box*, a 19th-century London bootmaker.]

box camera *n.* a camera shaped like a box, with a simple lens that has a fixed focus and a single shutter speed

box canyon *n.* a canyon with steep walls that can be entered readily only from the downstream direction

boxcar /bóks kaar/ *n.* US in North America, a fully enclosed railway wagon, usually with sliding doors, which is used to transport freight

box coat *n.* **1.** LOOSE COAT a coat that hangs loosely from the shoulders **2.** HEAVY COAT WORN BY COACHMEN a heavy coat, worn in the past by a coachman when sitting on the box, or by anyone riding outside a carriage

box elder (*plural* **box elders** *or* **box elder**) *n.* a fast-growing North American maple tree. Latin name: *Acer negundo*. [From BOX[3].]

boxer[1] /bóksər/ *n.* sb who fights in boxing matches

Boxer

boxer[2] /bóksər/ *n.* a medium-sized smooth-haired dog belonging to a breed developed in Germany. Its characteristics are a flat face with a black mask and a short-brownish-tan coat. [Early 20thC. Via German from English *boxer*, so called because of its wide flattened nose.]

boxer[3] /bóksər/ *n.* a person or machine whose task it is to pack things into boxes

Boxer /bóksər/ *n.* a member of a secret society in China that launched an unsuccessful rebellion in 1900 (**the Boxer Rebellion**) [Early 20thC. Translation of Mandarin *yì hé quán*, literally 'righteous harmonious fists'.]

Boxer Rebellion *n.* an unsuccessful rebellion in China in 1900, the aim of which was to drive out all foreigners, remove all foreign influence, and compel Christian Chinese people to give up that religion

boxer shorts *npl.* underpants with a gathered waistband and loose-fitting short legs [So called because they resemble the trunks worn by boxers]

boxfish /bóks fish/ (*plural* **-fish** *or* **-fishes**) *n.* = **trunkfish**

boxful /bóks fŏŏl/ *n.* the amount a box holds or can hold

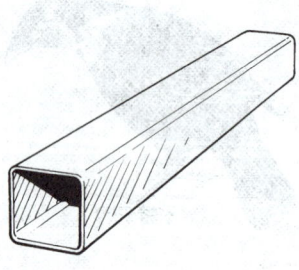

Box girder

box girder *n.* a hollow girder or beam that is square or rectangular in section

boxhaul /bóks hawl/ (**-hauls, -hauling, -hauled**) *vti.* to turn a square-rigged ship onto a new tack by back-winding the foresails and steering hard round [Mid-18thC. From BOX[1] + HAUL.]

boxing /bóksing/ *n.* the sport of fighting with the fists, with the aim of knocking out the opposing boxer, or inflicting enough punishment to cause the other boxer to retire or be judged defeated

Boxing Day *n.* 26 December, the day after Christmas Day, observed as a public holiday in England, Wales, and certain Commonwealth countries [So called because it was the day on which Christmas boxes were traditionally given to service workers]

boxing glove *n.* a thick padded glove tied at the wrist, worn by boxers for fighting

boxing ring *n.* the square raised platform with roped-in sides, used as the fighting arena in boxing matches. Each fighter has a corner diagonally opposite the other, sometimes referred to as 'the red and blue corners'.

box junction *n.* in the United Kingdom, a road junction with yellow crossed lines painted on the road surface, marking an area that traffic is not permitted to block

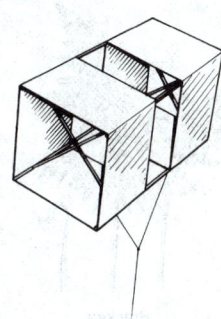

Box kite

box kite *n.* a square kite without a tail, consisting of two open-ended boxes joined by thin sticks

box lunch *n. US* = **packed lunch**

box lyre *n.* a plucked stringed instrument, formed from a hollow wooden box with strings running across the soundboard, which are attached to arms jutting out to form a crossbar. Box lyres were known in ancient Sumer in 2800 BC and were widely played in Europe until AD 1000. One type of box lyre played by professional musicians was a cithara.

box number *n.* the number assigned to an anonymous address for mail, either at a post office or as a reference for a reply to a newspaper advertisement

box office *n.* **1.** PLACE WHERE TICKETS ARE BOUGHT the place where tickets are bought for entertainments such as films, plays, or concerts (*often used before a noun*) ○ *box office takings* **2.** MONEY FROM TICKET SALES ticket sales for a piece of theatrical and cinematic entertainment, or the income from these sales (*informal*) (*often used before a noun*) **3.** AUDIENCE POPULARITY drawing power to attract an audience to a theatre (*informal*) ○ *The show makes great box office.* [So called because it was originally where a box in the theatre could be reserved]

box-on *n. Australian* a fight

Box pleat

box pleat *n.* a pleat in which fabric is folded under and then back again on both the right and left, and pressed so as to lie flat

boxroom /bóks room, -room/ *n.* a small room used for storage of household items not in regular use, or sometimes as a bedroom [Early 20thC. So called because it was used to store boxes and trunks.]

box seat *n.* **1.** THEATRE, SPORTS SEAT IN THEATRE OR STADIUM BOX a seat in a box in a theatre or a sports stadium **2.** TRANSP BOX WHERE CARRIAGE DRIVER SITS the box on a horse-drawn carriage on which the driver sits

box set *n.* **1.** THEATRE TRADITIONAL STAGE SET a stage set with a ceiling and three walls **2.** box set, boxed set SET OF SIMILAR ITEMS a set of similar items, e.g. recordings of music, that are packaged together in a box and sold as a single unit ○ *a four-CD box set*

box spanner *n.* a spanner in the form of a steel cylinder with a hexagonal end that slips over a nut. US term **box wrench**

box spring *n.* a set of coiled springs contained in a frame, which is covered with fabric and used as a base for a mattress

box stall *n. US* = **loosebox**

box step *n.* the basic step in ballroom dancing, in which the feet are moved in a pattern forming the shape of a square

boxthorn /bóks thawrn/ (*plural* **-thorns** *or* **-thorns**) *n.* = **matrimony vine** [From BOX³]

box tree *n.* = **box³** *n.* 1

boxwood /bóks wŏŏd/ (*plural* **-wood** *or* **-woods**) *n.* **1.** TREES = **box³** **2.** INDUST WOOD OF EVERGREEN BOX the hard close-grained yellow wood of the evergreen box shrub

box wrench *n. US* = **box spanner**

boxy /bóksi/ (**-ier**, **-iest**) *adj.* shaped like a cube or rectangular box, or giving the impression of squareness —**boxiness** *n.*

boy /boy/ *n.* **1.** YOUNG MALE a young male person ○ *I've had this hobby since I was a boy.* **2.** SON sb's male child ○ *I'm very proud of that boy of mine.* **3.** IMMATURE MAN a man who is regarded as immature or inexperienced, especially a young man ○ *This should separate the men from the boys.* **4.** MALE FROM CERTAIN AREA a youth or man who comes from or was brought up in a particular area **5.** WAY OF ADDRESSING MALE ANIMAL a way of addressing a male animal, especially a dog or a horse ○ *Get down, boy!* **6.** SUITABLE TOOL a tool that will do a particular job (*regional informal*) ○ *That's just the boy I need to tighten this nut.* ■ **boys** *npl.* A GROUP OF MALE FRIENDS a group of men of any age who often socialize together ○ *I'm off out with the boys.* ■ *interj.* EXCLAMATION OF SURPRISE used to express surprise, pleasure, or disgust ○ *Oh boy! Would you just take a look at that!* [13thC. Origin uncertain: perhaps from assumed Old French *embuié* 'servant', the past participle of *embuier* 'to fetter'.]

WORD KEY: REGIONAL NOTE

No one is certain of the origins of some of the commonest words in the language, including words such as *boy* and *dog*. It has been suggested that **boy** is a diminutive of *bo*, a term of address meaning 'mate'. It would thus be from *bo* + *-ie/-y*. The use of **boy** to address sb can be an insult in Africa and the United States.

boyar /bố yaar, bóyər/ *n.* from the 12th century to the early 18th century, a member of a class of the higher Russian nobility ranking below a prince [Late 16thC. From Russian *boyarin* 'grandee'.]

boy band *n.* an all-male pop band marketed for a young teenage audience

boycott /bóy kot/ *vt.* (**-cotts**, **-cotting**, **-cotted**) REFUSE TO DEAL WITH STH to cease or refuse to deal with sth such as an organization, a company, or a process, as a protest against it and to force it to become more acceptable ○ *Some called for the elections to be boycotted, insisting they were flawed.* ■ *n.* REFUSAL TO DEAL WITH STH a refusal to deal with sth such as an organization, a company, or a process, as a protest against it and to force it to become more acceptable [Late 19thC. Named after Captain Charles *Boycott* (1832–97), an estate manager in Ireland, whom workers and tradesmen stopped dealing with after he refused to reduce rents.] —**boycotter** *n.*

Boycott /bóy kot/, **Geoff** (*b.* 1940) British cricketer. During a long career he captained Yorkshire (1971–78), played 108 times for England, and scored over 150 centuries. Full name **Geoffrey Boycott**

Boyd /boyd/, **Arthur Merric** (1862–1940) New Zealand-born Australian painter. Noted for his watercolours, he was the father of Martin Boyd and grandfather of Arthur Merric Bloomfield Boyd.

Boyd, Arthur Merric Bloomfield (*b.* 1920) Australian artist. He is best known for *The Australian Scapegoat* (1987), His landscape paintings often incorporate biblical and mythological figures.

Boyd, Benjamin (1803?–51) English-born Australian pioneer and entrepreneur. He was the founder of whaling ports on Twofold Bay in southeastern New South Wales.

Boyd, Martin Beckett (1893–1972) Australian writer. Author of the novel *Lucinda Brayford* (1946), he was the uncle of Arthur Merric Bloomfield Boyd.

Boyd, Merric (1888–1959) Australian potter, the son of Arthur Merric Boyd and father of Arthur Merric Bloomfield Boyd. His works often have religious themes. Full name **William Merric Boyd**

Boyer /bóy ay/, **Charles** (1897–1978) French actor. He appeared in many romantic roles, including *Mayerling* (1936), and received a special Academy Award in 1943 for his work in promoting Franco-American cultural relations.

boyfriend /bóy frend/ *n.* a man with whom sb has a romantic or sexual relationship

boyhood /bóyhŏŏd/ *n.* the time in a male person's life when he is a boy

boyish /bóyish/ *adj.* resembling a very young man's fresh looks or youthful behaviour in a way that is pleasing or attractive —**boyishly** *adv.* —**boyishness** *n.*

boyla /bóylə/ *n. Australian* = **koradji** [Mid-19thC. From Nyungar.]

Boyle's law /bóylz-/ *n.* the principle that the volume of a confined gas at constant temperature varies inversely with its pressure [Named after the Irish-born scientist Robert *Boyle* (1627–91), who formulated it]

boy-meets-girl *adj.* based on a developing romance between a young man and a young woman, and treated in a predictable or hackneyed way in film or print ○ *It's a typical boy-meets-girl story where they live happily ever afterwards.*

Boyne /boyn/ river that rises in the Bog of Allen, county Kildare, Ireland, and empties into the Irish Sea near Drogheda. The Battle of the Boyne was fought on the banks of the river near Drogheda in 1690 when forces led by King William III of England defeated the forces of James II.

boyo /bóyō/ *n.* used as a form of address for a boy or man, or a way of referring, sometimes disparagingly, to a boy or a man, particularly one who is Welsh (*informal*) ○ *Relax, boyo.* [Late 19thC. Formed from BOY.]

boy racer *n.* a young man with a juvenile tendency to drive very fast to impress people (*informal*)

Boys' Brigade *n.* a Christian organization for boys founded in Britain in 1883 by William Alexander Smith to promote obedience, reverence, discipline, and self-respect

Boy Scout *n.* **1.** LEISURE MEMBER OF US BOYS' ORGANIZATION in the United States, a member of the Boy Scouts of America, an organization whose objectives are to develop character, physical fitness, and citizenship, often through community and outdoor activities **2.** boy scout, Boy Scout A NAIVE OR OVERZEALOUS MAN a man who is considered to be naive or overzealous (*insult*)

boysenberry /bóyz'n bari/ (*plural* **-ries**) *n.* **1.** PLANTS TYPE OF BRAMBLE a hybrid of the loganberry, blackberry, and raspberry. Genus: *Rubus.* **2.** FOOD FRUIT OF THE BOYSENBERRY the large purplish black fruit of the boysenberry, with a taste similar to a loganberry [Mid-20thC. Named after the US botanist Rudolph *Boysen* (1895–1950), who developed it.]

boys in blue *npl.* the police (*informal*)

boy toy *n. US, Can* a young woman who appears deliberately to try to attract and please men (*informal insult*)

boy wonder *n.* a talented and bright young man

bozo /bózō/ *n.* a mildly insulting term for sb who has said or done sth unwise (*informal insult*) [Early 20thC. Origin unknown.]

bp *abbr.* **1.** baptized **2.** base pair **3.** bills payable **4.** birthplace **5.** CHESS bishop **6.** bp, b.p. boiling point

BP *abbr.* **1.** BP, B/P bills payable **2.** blood pressure **3.** before the present

BPC *abbr.* British Pharmaceutical Codex

BPharm /beé faárm/ *abbr.* Bachelor of Pharmacy

BPhil /beé fíl/ *abbr.* Bachelor of Philosophy

B picture *n.* a B movie (*dated*)

bps *n.* a measurement of data transfer speed, e.g. in modems and serial ports. Abbr of **bits per second**

Bq *symbol.* becquerel

br *abbr.* bills receivable

Br *symbol.* bromine

BR *abbr.* **1.** bedroom **2.** British Rail

br. *abbr.* **1.** branch **2.** brass **3.** brief **4.** bronze **5.** brother **6.** brown **7.** bills receivable

Br. *abbr.* Britain ■ *abbr.* **1.** British **2.** Brother

bra /braa/ *n.* an undergarment designed to support and shape a woman's breasts [Mid-20thC. Shortening of *brassiere*, from French, 'bodice', from *bras* 'arm', from Latin *brachium* (see BRACHIUM).]

braaivleis /brí flayss/ *n. S African* in South Africa, a meal eaten outdoors where meat is grilled [Mid-20thC. From Afrikaans, literally 'grilled meat'.]

Brabant /brə bánt/ former duchy from 1190 to 1830 in western Europe now divided between the province of North Brabant in the Netherlands and the Belgian provinces of Flemish Brabant and Walloon Brabant

brabble /bráb'l/ *vi.* (**-bles, -bling, -bled**) QUARREL NOISILY OR SQUABBLE to quarrel or squabble noisily ■ *n.* NOISY QUARREL OR SQUABBLE a noisy quarrel or squabble [Early 16thC. Origin uncertain: possibly from Middle Dutch *brabbelen* 'to squabble'.] —**brabbler** *n.*

Brabham /brábbəm/, **Sir Jack** (*b.* 1926) Australian racing driver. He won the world championship in 1959, 1960, and 1966. Full name **Sir John Arthur Brabham**

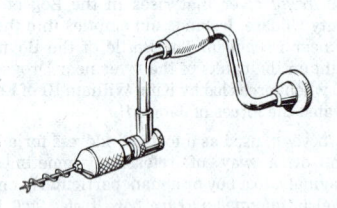

Brace

brace[1] /brayss/ *n.* **1.** MED SUPPORT FOR PART OF BODY an orthopaedic appliance that holds or supports part of the body **2.** CLAMP a device that keeps sth steady or holds two things together **3.** BUILDING A SUPPORT FOR STH CONSTRUCTED a device used in the building trade to hold a structure or part steady or upright, e.g. a beam, or wooden framework **4. brace** (*plural* **brace**) PAIR a pair of similar things, e.g. wild game, hunting dogs, or pistols ○ *two brace of pheasant* **5.** CONSTR TOOL FOR HOLDING DRILL BIT a tool with an adjustable socket at one end for holding a drill bit, and a handle like a crank at the other for turning the bit. ◊ **brace and bit 6.** PRINTING EITHER SYMBOL either of a pair of symbols, { }, used in printing or writing **7.** MUSIC ADJUSTER FOR DRUM TENSION a sliding loop on the cords of a drum, used to change its tension **8.** MUSIC BRACKET CONNECTING LINES OF MUSIC a thick line or bracket connecting a group of the staves in a piece of music, e.g. all the choral parts, or the accompaniment **9.** MATH SYMBOL OF MATHEMATICAL GROUPING either of a pair of symbols { }, for additional grouping of mathematical quantities after parentheses and square brackets have been used **10.** ARCHERY, FENCING = **bracer**[2] *n.* ■ **braces** *npl.* **1.** DENT APPLIANCE FIXED TO TEETH a dental appliance that is fixed to the teeth, and that can be tightened in order to straighten them (*sometimes used in the singular*) **2.** STRAPS FOR HOLDING UP TROUSERS a pair of elasticated straps worn to hold trousers up. They are attached to the waist of the trousers and fit over the shoulders. ■ *v.* (**braces, bracing, braced**) **1.** *vt.* SUPPORT OR STRENGTHEN STH to support or strengthen sth, especially part of a building, with a brace ○ *Anchor bolts cannot be used to brace these shelves.* **2.** *vr.* PREPARE YOURSELF FOR STH to prepare yourself for sth dangerous or unknown that is about to happen

○ *The financial markets braced themselves for a rise in interest rates.* [From Old French, literally 'two outstretched arms, fathom', from Latin *bracchia*, plural of *brachium* 'arm' (see BRACHIUM)]

brace up *vi.* to be strong and resolute in facing difficulty ○ *Brace up and face the facts.*

brace[2] /brayss/ *n.* SAILING on a square-rigged ship, a rope used to control the spar that extends a sail [Early 17thC. Origin uncertain: possibly an alteration of French *bras de vergue*, literally 'yard arm', under the influence of 'brace'.]

brace and bit *n.* a hand tool for boring holes, consisting of a crank handle at one end and a drill bit at the other. ◊ **brace**[1] *n.* 5

bracelet /bráysslət/ *n.* **1.** JEWELLERY WORN AROUND WRIST OR ARM a piece of jewellery, e.g. a chain or a bangle, that is worn around the wrist or arm **2.** METAL BAND FOR WRISTWATCH a metal band for a wristwatch ■ **bracelets** *npl.* HANDCUFFS a pair of handcuffs (*slang*) [15thC. Via French from, ultimately, Latin *bracchiale* 'armlet', from *brachium* 'arm' (see BRACHIUM).]

brace position *n.* a protective position that sb adopts before impact in a crash, protecting the head with the arms and bringing the legs up underneath the chest

bracer[1] /bráyssər/ *n.* **1.** SUPPORT sb or sth that braces **2.** BEVERAGES INVIGORATING DRINK an invigorating often alcoholic drink [Mid-16thC. Formed from BRACE[1].]

bracer[2] /bráyssər/, **brace** /brayss/ *n.* ARCHERY, FENCING a leather guard worn by fencers and archers to protect the arm [14thC. From Old French *bracière*, from *bras* 'arm', from Latin *brachium* (see BRACHIUM).]

brace root *n.* = **prop root**

brachia *n.* plural of **brachium**

brachial /bráyki əl/ *adj.* relating to or situated in the arm, foreleg, or wing [Late 16thC. From Latin *brachialis*, from *brachium* (see BRACHIUM).]

brachiate /bráyki ayt/ (**-ates, -ating, -ated**) *vi.* to move along by swinging from one hold to the next with the arms (*refers to tree-dwelling animals*) [Mid-18thC. From Latin *brachiatus*, from *brachium* (see BRACHIUM).] —**brachiation** /bráyki áysh'n/ *n.*

brachio- *prefix.* arm ○ *brachiocephalic* [From Latin *brachium* (see BRACHIUM)]

brachiocephalic /bráki ð sə fállik, bráyki ð-/ *adj.* relating to or supplying the arms and the head

brachiopod /bráki ə pod, bráyki-/ *n.* a marine invertebrate animal with hinged shells enclosing tentacles. Phylum: Brachiopoda. [Mid-19thC. From modern Latin *Brachiopoda*, phylum name, from Latin *brachium* 'arm' and -POD.] —**brachiopod** *adj.*

brachiosaurus /bráki ə sáwrəss, bráyki-/ (*plural* **-ruses** *or* **-ri** /-rī/), **brachiosaur** /bráki ə sawr/ *n.* a dinosaur with a massive sloping body up to 30 m/100 ft long. Genus: *Brachiosaurus*. [Early 20thC. From modern Latin, genus name, which was coined from BRACHIUM (from the unusual length of the animal's humerus bones) + Greek *sauros* 'lizard'.]

brachium /bráyki əm/ (*plural* **-a** /-ki ə/) *n.* **1.** ANAT ARM an arm, especially the upper arm (*technical*) **2.** ZOOL ANIMAL LIMB CORRESPONDING TO ARM a structure, e.g. a wing, that corresponds to an arm [Mid-18thC. Via Latin from Greek *brakhīon* 'upper arm', literally 'shorter' from *brakhus* 'short' (see BRACHY-).]

brachy- *prefix.* short ○ *brachyodont* [From Greek *brakhus.* Ultimately from an Indo-European word meaning 'short', which is also the ancestor of English *brief, abbreviate,* and *brace.*]

brachycephalic /bráki sə ffállik/, **brachycephalous** /bráki séffələss/ *adj.* with a short, broad, and almost spherical head —**brachycephalism** /-sséffəlizzəm/ *n.* —**brachycephaly** /-sséffəli/ *n.*

brachydactylic /bráki dak tíllik/, **brachydactylous** /bráki dáktiləss/ *adj.* with abnormally short fingers or toes —**brachydactylia** /bráki dak tílli ə/ *n.* —**brachydactyly** /bráki dáktili/ *n.*

brachylogy /bra kílləji/ *n.* **1.** BREVITY IN WORD USE brevity in speech or writing, or an instance of such brevity **2.** SHORTENED FORM OF TERM a shortened form of an expression, used in informal speech [Mid-16thC. Via

late Latin from Greek *brakhulogia*, literally 'shortness of speech'.] —**brachylogous** *adj.*

brachypterous /bra kíptərəss/ *adj.* used to describe insects and some species of diving birds with short or not fully developed wings —**brachypterism** *n.*

bracing /bráyssing/ *adj.* REFRESHINGLY INVIGORATING refreshing or invigorating ○ *a bracing cold shower* ■ *n.* BRACES SUPPORTING STH a system of braces that are used to support or strengthen a structure —**bracingly** *adv.*

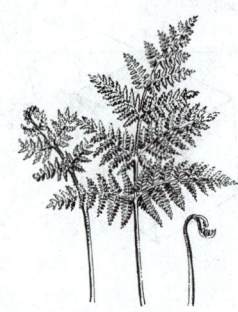

Bracken

bracken /brákən/ (*plural* **-en** *or* **-ens**) *n.* a large fern, common in most temperate and tropical regions, with extensive underground stems and large triangular fronds. Latin name: *Pteridium aquilinum.* [14thC. From assumed Old Norse *brakni.*]

bracket /brákit/ *n.* **1.** PRINTING UPRIGHT CURVED MARK IN PUNCTUATION one of a pair of shallow, curved signs, (), used to enclose an explanatory word or comment, and distinguish it from the sentence in which it occurs (*often used in plural*) US term **parenthesis 2.** US PRINTING = **square bracket 3.** L-SHAPED STRUCTURE ON WALL an L-shaped structure that is fixed to a wall to hold up sth, e.g. a shelf or speaker **4.** TYPE OF SHELF a shelf that usually has an integral part that fixes to the wall as its support and can sometimes be swivelled ○ *This TV bracket is too low.* **5.** GROUP WITHIN CERTAIN LIMITS a section of the population that falls within specific defined limits ○ *taxpayers in the £50,000 to £70,000 bracket* ■ *vt.* (**-ets, -eting, -eted**) **1.** PUT STH INSIDE BRACKETS to put sth, especially text or a mathematical equation, inside brackets **2.** SUPPORT STH WITH BRACKETS to fix brackets to sth, especially a wall, or to support sth with brackets **3.** GROUP THINGS OR PEOPLE TOGETHER to group or class things or people together, usually because they are similar in some way ○ *Rail and bus can be bracketed together under public transport.* [Late 16thC. Origin uncertain: possibly via French *braguette* 'codpiece' (because of its shape) from, ultimately, Latin *bracae* 'breeches'.] —**bracketing** *n.*

bracket clock *n.* a clock that is designed to stand on a shelf or a wall bracket

bracket creep *n.* movement into a higher tax bracket due to a slow increase in income

bracket fungus (*plural* **bracket fungi**) *n.* a fungus that forms growths that stick out like shelves. The growths generally appear on tree trunks and other wooden structures.

brackish /brákish/ *adj.* rather salty, especially from being a mixture of fresh and salt water [Mid-16thC. Formed from Dutch *brak* 'salty water', of unknown origin.] —**brackishness** *n.*

Bracknell /bráknəl/ new town in eastern Berkshire, England, designated in 1949. Population: 60,895 (1991).

bract /brakt/ *n.* BOT a modified leaf that arises from the stem at the point where the flower or flower cluster develops [Late 18thC. From Latin *bractea* 'thin metal plate, gold leaf', of uncertain origin.] —**bracteal** /brákti əl/ *adj.*

bracteate /brákti ət/ *adj.* BOT WITH BRACTS used to describe a plant that has bracts ■ *n.* ARCHAEOL DECORATED DISH a decorated dish or plate made of precious metal [Early 19thC. From Latin *bracteatus*, from *bractea* (see BRACT).]

bracteole /brákti ōl/ *n.* an organ resembling a leaf or scale that arises from a branch of a flower cluster where the flowers develop, and where the entire

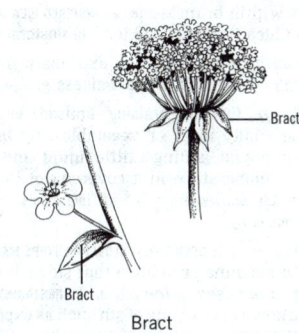

Bract

cluster itself develops above a bract [Early 19thC. From Latin *bracteola*, literally 'small bract', from *bractea* (see BRACT).] —**bracteolate** /brákti ə lət, -layt/ *adj.*

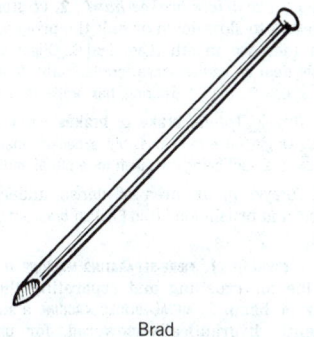

Brad

brad /brad/ *n.* a thin tapered nail with a small head that is either symmetrical or formed on one side only [13thC. From Old Norse *broddr* 'spike'.]

bradawl /brád awl/ *n.* a hand tool with a pointed tip, used for making holes in wood, leather, and other materials, to allow screws and nails to be inserted

Bradfield /brád feeld/, **John Job Crew** (1867–1943) Australian civil engineer. He created the original plan for Sydney Harbour Bridge, and supervised its construction.

Bradford /brádfərd/ industrial city in West Yorkshire, northern England. Population: 289,376 (1992).

Bradlaugh /brád law/, **Charles** (1833–91) British social reformer and free thinker. He was elected MP in 1880, but was admitted to the House of Commons only in 1886 because of his insistence on taking an affirmation rather than an oath of allegiance.

Bradley /brádli/, **A.C.** (1851–1935) British literary critic. He held professorships at the universities of Liverpool (1882–89), Glasgow (1889–1900), and Oxford (1901–06). He wrote *Shakespearean Tragedy* (1904). Full name **Andrew Cecil Bradley**

Bradley, James (1693–1762) British astronomer. The third astronomer royal (1742–62), he catalogued the positions of 60,000 stars.

Sir Don Bradman

Bradman /brádmən/, **Sir Don** (*b.* 1908) Australian cricketer. He was Australian Test captain (1936–48), and one of the highest-scoring batsmen of all time, with a Test average of 99.94 runs. Full name **Sir Donald George Bradman**

brady- /bráydi/ *prefix.* slow ○ *bradycardia* [From Greek *bradus*, of unknown origin]

bradycardia /bráddi kaárdi ə/ *n.* slowness of the heart rate, usually measured as fewer than 60 beats per minute in an adult human [Late 19thC. Coined from BRADY- + Greek *kardia* 'heart' + -IA, literally 'slow-heart condition'.] —**bradycardiac** *adj.* —**bradycardic** *adj.*

bradykinin /bráddi kínin/ *n.* a chemical (**peptide**) derived from plasma protein that forms at the site of injured tissue. It plays a role in producing inflammation, dilates blood vessels, and contracts smooth muscle. [Mid-20thC. Coined from BRADY- + Greek *kinein* 'to move' + -IN.]

brae /bray/ *n. Scotland* in Scotland, a hill or slope (*often used in placenames*) [14thC. From Old Norse *brá* 'eyelash'. The underlying meaning is 'brow of a hill'.]

brag /brag/ *vi.* (**brags, bragging, bragged**) TALK WITH TOO MUCH PRIDE to talk shamelessly or with excessive pride about achievements or possessions ○ *The police arrested him after he bragged about the bank robbery to his friends.* ■ *n.* **1.** BOASTFUL REMARK a boastful statement or display of arrogant behaviour **2.** CARDS CARD GAME a card game similar to poker [14thC. Origin unknown.] —**bragger** *n.* —**bragging** *n., adj.* —**braggingly** *adv.*

Braga /braágə/ city and capital of the mountainous district of Braga, northwestern Portugal. Population: 90,535 (1991).

Brage *n.* = **Bragi**

Bragg /brag/, **Sir Lawrence** (1890–1971) Australian-born British physicist. He collaborated with his father, Sir William Bragg, in developing an X-ray technique for examining crystals. They shared the Nobel Prize in physics in 1915. Full name **Sir William Lawrence Bragg**

Bragg, Sir William Henry (1862–1942) British physicist. With his son, Sir Lawrence Bragg, he developed an X-ray technique for examining crystals. They shared the Nobel Prize in physics in 1915.

braggadocio /brággə dóchi ō/ (*plural* -**os**) *n.* **1.** OVER-BLOWN, EMPTY BOASTING empty boasting and swaggering self-aggrandisement **2.** BRAGGART sb who makes overblown claims or empty boasts [Late 16thC. Alteration of *Braggadocchio*, the personification of boastfulness in Spenser's *Faerie Queen*.]

braggart /brággərt/ *n.* sb who talks immodestly, shamelessly, or with excessive pride about his or her achievements or possessions [Late 16thC. From French *bragard*, from *braguer* 'to brag', of uncertain origin: possibly from English *brag*.]

Bragg's law /brágz-/ *n.* a law stating the directions in which X-rays reflected from a crystal are most intense [Early 20thC. Named after Sir William Henry BRAGG and his son, Sir William Lawrence *Bragg* (1890–1971), English physicists.]

Bragi /braági/, **Brage** /-gə/ *n.* in Nordic mythology, the god of poetry, eloquence, and music

Brahe /braa, braá ə, braáhi/, **Tycho** (1546–1601) Danish astronomer. He employed extremely precise observations of stars and planets to correct inaccuracies in existing astronomical tables.

Brahma[1] /braámə/ *n.* **1.** HINDU GOD a Hindu god, the source of knowledge and understanding, regarded as the protector of the world and in later tradition called the creator **2.** = **Brahman** *n.* 1 [From Sanskrit *brāhmaṇa-*, from *brahman-* (see BRAHMIN)]

Brahma[2] /braámə/ *n.* BIRDS a large domestic fowl with heavily feathered legs and feet and a small tail and wings [Mid-19thC. Shortening of *Brahmaputra fowl*, so called because it was first imported from a town on the Brahmaputra river in India.]

Brahman /braámən/ *n.* **1.** ULTIMATE POWER UNDERLYING THE UNIVERSE in Hinduism, the ultimate impersonal reality underlying everything in the universe, from which everything comes and to which it returns **2.** = **Brahma**[1] *n.* 1 **3.** = **Brahmin** *n.* 1, **Brahmin** *n.* 2 [Late 18thC. From Sanskrit (see BRAHMIN).] —**Brahmanic** /braa mánnik/ *adj.* —**Brahmanical** /-mánnik'l/ *adj.*

Brahmana /braámənə/ *n.* a sacred Hindu text, belonging to a group of commentaries on the Vedas [From Sanskrit *brāhmaṇam*, from *brāhmaṇa-* (see BRAHMIN)]

Brahmin

Brahmani /braáməni/, **brahmani** *n.* a woman of the Brahmin caste [Late 18thC. From Sanskrit *brāhmaṇī*, feminine of *brāhmaṇa-* (see BRAHMIN).]

Brahmanism, **brahmanism** *n.* = Brahminism —**Brahmanist** *n.*

Brahmin /braámin/ (*plural* -**mins** *or* -**min**), **brahmin** (*plural* -**mins** *or* -**min**) *n.* INDIAN RELIG **1.** HIGHEST HINDU CASTE the first of the four Hindu castes, the members of which are priests and scholars of Vedic literature **2.** MEMBER OF BRAHMIN CASTE a member of the Brahmin caste [15thC. From Sanskrit *brāhmaṇa-*, from *brahman-* 'priest'. Ultimately from an Indo-European word meaning 'priest'.] —**Brahminic** /braa mínnik/ *adj.* —**Brahminical** /-mínnik'l/ *adj.*

Brahminism /braáminizzəm/, **brahminism, Brahmanism, brahmanism** *n.* the traditional social and religious system of Vedic Hinduism —**Brahminist** *n.*

Johannes Brahms

Brahms /braamz/, **Johannes** (1833–97) German composer. His works includes four symphonies, two piano concertos, and *A German Requiem* (1868).

Brahui /braa hoò i/ (*plural* -**is** *or* -**i**) *n.* **1.** DRAVIDIAN LANGUAGE a Dravidian language spoken in southwestern Pakistan. Brahui is spoken by about two million people, many of whom are bilingual in Baluchi or Sindhi. **2.** MEMBER OF ASIAN PEOPLE a member of an Asian Brahui-speaking people who live in southwestern Pakistan [Early 19thC. From Brahui.] —**Brahui** *adj.*

braid /brayd/ *n.* **1.** INDUST, CLOTHES DECORATIVE SILKY CORD decorative and often silky cord or interwoven thread, used especially to trim and bind, in decorating uniforms, and as edging for soft furnishings **2.** STH INTERWOVEN sth that is made of three or more interwoven strands ○ *wear your hair in braids* ■ *vt.* (**braids, braiding, braided**) **1.** INTERWEAVE STRANDS to interweave three or more strands of sth, especially hair **2.** MAKE STH BY BRAIDING to make sth by interweaving strands, strips, or other pieces **3.** DECORATE STH WITH BRAID to decorate uniforms or edge furnishings with braid [Old English *bregdan* 'to weave, lay hold of' (source also of English *upbraid*).]

braided /bráydid/ *adj.* **1.** INTERWOVEN interwoven from three or more strands **2.** EDGED WITH CORD decorated or edged with silky, especially gold, cord **3.** CONSISTING OF INTERCONNECTED TRACKS OR CHANNELS composed of several interconnected tracks or channels that divide and reunite ○ *a braided river*

braiding /bráyding/ *n.* **1.** INDUST SILKY THREAD OR CORD decorative silky thread or cord, used especially to decorate uniforms and furnishings **2.** SEW EMBROIDERY embroidery worked in decorative silky thread

Brăila /brə eˈelə/ city and capital of Brăila county, south-eastern Romania. Situated on the Danube, it is Romania's second largest port. Population: 235,763 (1994).

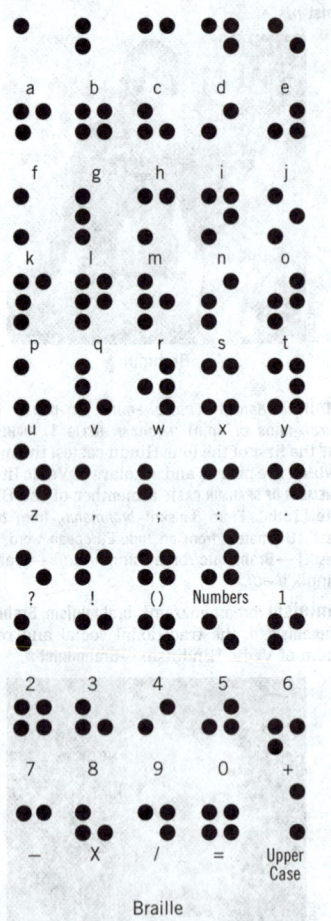

Braille

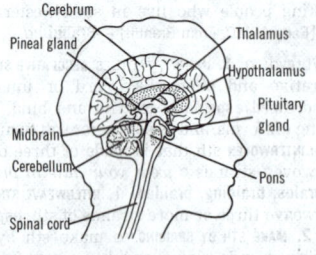

Brain: Cross-section of human brain

Braille /brayl/ n. a writing system for visually impaired or sightless people, consisting of patterns of raised dots that are read by touch [Mid-19thC. Named after Louis BRAILLE.]

Braille /brayl/, **Louis** (1809–52) French educationist. He was blind from early childhood and in 1829 he invented the Braille system of raised dots to enable visually impaired people to read and write.

Brailler /bráylər/, **Braillewriter** /bráyl rītər/ n. a machine similar to a typewriter that prints Braille

brain /brayn/ n. **1.** ANAT ORGAN OF THOUGHT AND FEELING the controlling centre of the nervous system in vertebrates, connected to the spinal cord and enclosed in the cranium. It consists of a mass of nerve tissue and nerve-supporting and nourishing tissue (**glia**), is the centre of thought and emotions, and regulates bodily activities. **2.** ZOOL CENTRE OF NERVOUS-SYSTEM IN INVERTEBRATES a nervous-system centre in some invertebrates that is functionally similar to the brain in vertebrates **3.** INTELLECT sb's intellectual abilities or intellectual centre ○ *His heart was beating vio-*

lently and his brain was in a turmoil. **4.** BRAINY PERSON a very intelligent person, especially the most intelligent person in a certain group (*informal*) ○ *Lee's the brain of the family.* ■ vt. (**brains, braining, brained**) HIT SB ON HEAD to hit sb violently on the head (*slang*) [Old English *brægen*] ◇ **have sth on the brain** to be unable to stop thinking about sth ○ *She has making money on the brain.* ◇ **pick sb's brains** to ask questions of sb, in order to learn what he or she knows about sth ○ *Let me pick your brains about how to market this new book.* ◇ **rack your brains** to try to solve a problem by thinking very hard about it ○ *I racked my brains but still could not recall her address.*

brainbox /bráyn boks/ n. sb who is very clever (*informal*) (*often used by children*)

braincase /bráyn kayss/ n. the part of the skull enclosing the brain

brainchild /bráyn chīld/ (*plural* -**children**) n. an original plan or idea attributed to a single person or to a group of people

brain coral (*plural* **brain coral** or **brain corals**) n. coral that forms rounded colonies resembling the convex folds of the human brain. Genus: *Meandrina.*

brain damage n. injury to the brain tissue that can impair normal functioning

brain dead adj. **1.** MED WITH NONFUNCTIONING BRAIN lacking functions of the brain and central nervous system as measured by brainwave activity on an electroencephalogram over a set period of time **2.** OFFENSIVE TERM an offensive term for sb considered to have extremely low intellectual ability (*slang offensive*)

brain death n. the end of all functions of the brain and central nervous system as measured by brainwave activity on an electroencephalogram over a set period of time. There are strict legal criteria for determining brain death, since its occurrence can allow cessation of life support or removal of organs for transplantation.

brain drain n. the movement of highly skilled people to a country offering better opportunities

brain fever n. a term for inflammation of the brain or its covering membranes (*archaic*)

brainless /bráynləss/ adj. lacking intelligence —**brainlessly** adv. —**brainlessness** n.

brainpan /bráyn pan/ n. = braincase

brainpower /bráyn powər/ n. sb's intellectual capability

brain scan n. **1.** IMAGE OF BRAIN SHOWING ABNORMALITIES a series of two-dimensional cross-sections of the brain produced by means of computerized imaging techniques and showing the presence of tumours or other abnormalities. Information presented in three dimensions can be derived from the combined cross-sections. **2.** PROCEDURE FOR SCANNING THE BRAIN the procedure involved in producing this image

brain stem n. the part of the brain between the spinal column and the cerebral hemispheres. It consists of the midbrain, pons, and medulla oblongata.

brainstorm /bráyn stawrm/ n. **1.** US = brain wave (*informal*) **2.** BRIEF PSYCHOLOGICAL DISTURBANCE a momentary psychological disturbance ■ vti. (-**storms,** -**storming,** -**stormed**) THINK QUICKLY AND CREATIVELY to have an intensive group discussion without allowing time for reflection, in order to generate creative ideas and usually to stimulate problem-solving —**brainstormer** n. —**brainstorming** n.

brainteaser /bráyn teezər/ n. a difficult or complex problem that requires careful thought in order to solve it, often done for amusement

brainwash /bráyn wosh/ (-**washes,** -**washing,** -**washed**) vt. **1.** IMPOSE BELIEFS ON SB to impose a set of usually political or religious beliefs on sb by the use of various coercive methods of indoctrination, including destruction of the victim's prior beliefs **2.** CONDITION SB TO BEHAVE DIFFERENTLY to induce sb to believe or do sth, e.g. to buy a new product, especially by constant repetition or advertising

brain wave n. **1.** WAVE OF VOLTAGE IN BRAIN one of the rhythmic waves of voltage arising from electrical

activity within brain tissue **2.** INSPIRED IDEA a sudden exciting idea (*informal*) US term **brainstorm** n. **1**

brainy /bráyni/ (-**ier,** -**iest**) adj. extremely intelligent (*informal*) —**brainily** adv. —**braininess** n.

braise /brayz/ (**braises, braising, braised**) vt. to cook food, especially meat or vegetables, by browning briefly in hot fat, adding a little liquid, and cooking at a low temperature in a covered pot [Mid-18thC. From French *braiser*, from *braise* 'live coals' (source of English *brazier*).]

brake[1] /brayk/ n. **1.** DEVICE THAT SLOWS OR STOPS MACHINE the part of a machine or vehicle that slows it down or stops it (*often used in the plural*) **2.** RESTRAINT ON STH a slowing down or stopping of sth such as expenditure or development, or sth that causes this ○ *The brake on investment is largely a result of political factors.* **3.** = brake van ■ v. (**brakes, braking, braked**) **1.** vti. SLOW OR STOP MACHINE to slow down or stop, or to make sth such as a vehicle or a machine go more slowly or stop ○ *The driver braked hard*. **2.** vt. SLOW OR HALT DEVELOPMENT to slow down or halt the progress of sth or an increase in sth [Late 18thC. Origin uncertain: possibly from an earlier sense 'bridle, curb', from Middle Dutch or Low German, 'nose ring, flax brake' (see BRAKE[4]).]

brake[2] /brayk/ (*plural* **brake** or **brakes**) n. = bracken [14thC. Origin uncertain: possibly a back-formation from BRACKEN, the '-en' being mistaken for a plural ending.]

brake[3] /brayk/ n. an area of dense undergrowth, shrubs, and brushwood [Old English *bracu*, of uncertain origin]

brake[4] /brayk/ n. **1.** FIBRE-SEPARATING MACHINE a tool or machine for crushing and separating the fibres of flax or hemp **2.** METAL-FOLDING MACHINE a machine, frequently hydraulically powered, for precision bending and folding of sheet metal [15thC. Origin uncertain: from Middle Low German or Middle Dutch. Ultimately from a prehistoric Germanic base meaning 'to break'.]

brake[5] /brayk/ n. a lever or handle on a pump or other machine [Early 17thC. Origin uncertain.]

brake[6] /brayk/ **break** n. an open four-wheeled horse-drawn carriage [Mid-19thC. Origin unknown.]

brake block n. a small rectangular block of rubber that is pressed against the rim of a bicycle wheel when the brake is applied

brake chute n. = brake parachute

brake drum n. the metal cylinder attached to the wheel of a vehicle that slows the rotation of the wheel when pressure is applied

brake-fade n. a decrease in braking efficiency of a motor vehicle, caused by the brakes overheating

brake fluid n. the oily liquid used in hydraulic brakes and clutches to transmit pressure

brake horsepower n. a measure of the work produced by an engine, calibrated in horsepower and determined by the force exerted on a friction brake

brake light n. a rear light on a motor vehicle that lights up when the driver brakes. US term **stoplight**

brake lining n. the renewable thin strip of material attached to a brake shoe

brakeman /bráykmən/ (*plural* -**men** /-mən/) n. a member of a train crew or other railway employee who operates, inspects, or repairs brakes

brake pad n. a renewable block of material that presses against the surface of a disc brake

brake parachute, **brake chute** n. a parachute that is attached to the back of a vehicle and acts as a brake

brake shoe n. a curved block that presses against a wheel or brake drum to slow it down

brakesman /bráyksmən/ (*plural* -**men** /-mən/) n. the person who operates the winch at a pithead

brake van n. formerly, a railway vehicle attached to a goods train from which the guard applied the brakes

braking distance n. the distance a vehicle needs to come to a complete stop when the brakes have been applied

Bramante /brə mán tay/, **Donato** (1444–1514) Italian architect and painter. He rebuilt and renovated the

Vatican and St Peter's in Rome (1505–6). Real name Donato di Pascuccio d'Antonio

bramble /brámb'l/ n. **1.** BLACKBERRY BUSH a prickly shrub that produces blackberries, especially when growing wild (often used in the plural) **2.** PRICKLY SHRUB a prickly shrub or bush similar to, or related to, the blackberry, e.g. a dog rose **3.** BLACKBERRY a blackberry ▪ vi. (**-bles, -bling, -bled**) COLLECT BERRIES FROM BRAMBLES to collect berries from brambles in hedgerows [Old English *bræmbel*. Ultimately from a prehistoric Germanic word meaning 'thorny bush', which is also the ancestor of English *broom*.]

brambling /brámbling/ n. a bird of northern Europe and Asia related to the chaffinch, with a speckled head and back and rusty-brown breast. Latin name: *Fringilla montifringilla*. [Mid-16thC. Origin uncertain: possibly formed from BRAMBLE and -LING.]

brambly /brámbli/ (**-blier, -bliest**) adj. covered in or containing prickly shrubs, especially blackberries or wild roses ○ *a brambly garden*

bran /bran/ n. the husks of cereal grain that are partly or completely removed during the milling process and used as a supplementary source of dietary fibre [13thC. From French, of unknown origin.]

Bran /bran/ n. in Celtic mythology, a giant god who ruled Britain and installed his son, Gwern, as king of Ireland

Branagh /bránnə/, **Kenneth** (b. 1960) Irish-born UK actor and director. He directed and acted in films including *Henry V* (1989). Full name **Kenneth Charles Branagh**

branch /braanch/ n. **1.** BOT PART OF TREE GROWING FROM TRUNK a woody limb of a tree that grows out from a larger limb or from the trunk **2.** BOT PART OF PLANT STEM OR ROOT a subdivision of the stem, root, or flower cluster of a plant **3.** STH LIKE TREE BRANCH sth that resembles a branch of a tree in structure **4.** LOCAL UNIT IN ORGANIZATION a shop, a bank, or another organization that is part of a larger group and is located in a different part of a geographical area from the parent organization ○ *The account is held at the bank's Oxford branch.* **5.** DISTINCT PART OF LARGE ORGANIZATION a subdivision of a large organization, usually with a specialized mission **6.** PART OF SUBJECT AREA one part of a large area of study or subject ○ *Ethics is a branch of philosophy.* **7.** FAMILY LINE one line of a family that is descended from a common ancestor ○ *the Peruvian branch of the family* **8.** MATH PART OF CURVE a distinctive part of a curve that is separated from the rest of the curve, e.g. by discontinuities or extreme points **9.** GEOG TRIBUTARY STREAM a river or stream flowing into another river ○ *a branch of the Colorado River* **10.** COMPUT ALTERNATIVE SEQUENCE OF COMPUTER INSTRUCTIONS any one of several alternative sequences of computer program instructions that are activated according to certain specific conditions, e.g. the value of a variable ▪ v. (**branches, branching, branched**) **1.** vti. DIVIDE INTO SMALLER PARTS to divide or cause sth to divide into lesser parts ○ *Part of the track branches off towards the river.* **2.** vi. BOT HAVE BRANCHES to grow branches **3.** vi. EXPAND ACTIVITIES OR INTERESTS to become involved in sth new, especially as a way of extending or expanding personal interests or business activities ○ *The company has branched into multimedia upgrade kits.* [13thC. Via French *branche* from late Latin *branca* 'paw', possibly of Celtic origin. The underlying meaning was 'limb'.]

branch out vi. to do sth different, especially if it involves an element of risk

-branch suffix. gills ○ *opisthobranch* [From Latin *branchia* 'gills' (see BRANCHIA)]

branchia /brángki ə/ (plural **-ae** /-ki ee/) n. a gill in aquatic animals or a similar structure found in the embryos of higher animals, including humans [Late 17thC. Via Latin from Greek *bragkhia*, 'gills', of unknown origin.] —**branchial** adj. —**branchiate** /bránki ət/ adj.

branchial cleft, **branchial groove** n. a gill slit (technical)

branching /braanching/ adj. HAVING TREELIKE FORM with a form, pattern, or structure that stems from one main source and divides and spreads into smaller parts, resembling the branches of a tree ▪ n. TREELIKE PATTERN, FORM, OR STRUCTURE a form, pattern, or structure that stems from one main source and divides and

spreads into smaller parts, resembling the growth of the branches of a tree

branchiopod /brángki ə pod/ n. a small, usually freshwater, crustacean with a segmented body and flat gill-bearing appendages. Subclass: Branchiopoda. [Early 19thC. From modern Latin *Branchiopoda*, subclass name, coined from Latin *branchia* 'gills' + -POD.] —**branchiopod** adj. —**branchiopodous** /brángki óppədəss/ adj.

branchlet /braanchlət/ n. a small branch, usually forming the outermost part of a larger branch

branch line n. part of a railway system that is routed to smaller towns and villages that are not served by a main line. ◊ **main line**

branch officer n. NAVY a warant officer in the Royal Navy

Brancusi /bran koózi/, **Constantin** (1876–1957) Romanian sculptor. He was a pioneer of 20th-century European sculpture and was particularly concerned with the inner form of his subject.

brand /brand/ n. **1.** COMM PRODUCT OR MANUFACTURER a name, usually a trademark, of a manufacturer or product, or the product identified by this name ○ *What brand of cosmetics does she use?* **2.** PARTICULAR TYPE OF STH a distinctive type or kind of sth ○ *Hollywood makes a certain brand of movies.* **3.** AGRIC MARK BURNED ON ANIMAL a mark burned into the hide of an animal to identify it as the property of a particular farm or owner ○ *The Triple S is the brand on all our steers.* ◊ **branding iron 4.** HIST MARK ON CRIMINAL OR SLAVE in the past, a mark made on the skin of a criminal or a slave, especially to identify the owner **5.** SIGN OR MARK OF DISGRACE a sign or mark of disgrace, infamy, or notoriety ○ *He bore the brand of disloyalty.* **6.** BURNT OR BURNING PIECE OF WOOD a piece of wood that is burnt or smouldering (archaic) **7.** TORCH a flaming torch (literary) ◊ **firebrand 8.** MAKE INDELIBLE MARK ON SB to make an indelible mark or impression on sb or sth (literary) ○ *The traditions of this sport have been branded into my heart.* [Old English, 'burning stick'. Ultimately from an Indo-European word meaning 'to be hot', which was also the ancestor of English *burn*, *brimstone*, *brandish*, and *brandy*.] —**brander** n.

branded /brándid/ adj. bearing a company name or trademark, usually considered a mark of prestige or quality

Brandeis /brán dīss/, **Louis** (1856–1941) US supreme court justice He was an important legal theoretician and a liberal member of the Supreme Court (1916–39). Full name **Louis Dembitz Brandeis**

AKG London

Brandenburg Gate, Berlin, Germany

Brandenburg Gate /brándən burg-/ n. **Brandenburg Gate** a large neoclassical stone gateway in central Berlin, completed in 1781. It has long served as a symbol of the city and a focal point for public gatherings.

brandied /brándid/ adj. cooked or preserved in brandy

branding iron n. an iron tool that is heated and pressed onto a surface, especially an animal's hide,

in order to leave a permanent identifying mark. ◊ **brand** n. 3

brandish /brándish/ (**-dishes, -dishing, -dished**) vt. to wave sth about, especially a weapon, in a menacing, theatrical, or triumphant way [14thC. From French *brandiss-*, the stem of *brandir*, from *brand* 'sword'. Ultimately of Germanic origin.] —**brandisher** n.

brand leader n. the best-selling product in a particular category

brandling /brándling/ n. a small, reddish-brown earthworm that is often used as bait by anglers. Latin name: *Eisenia foetida*. [Mid-17thC. So called because of its bright colouring, like a burning brand.]

brand loyalty (plural **brand loyalties**) n. the tendency to buy a particular brand of a product

brand name n. a trade name for a product or service produced by a particular company. It may or may not be a registered trademark. ○ *A computer with a brand name can cost 10 per cent more.*

brand-new adj. completely new and unused [From the idea of sth glowing as if newly made in a furnace]

Marlon Brando

Brando /brándō/, **Marlon** (b. 1924) US actor. He has appeared in numerous Hollywood films, including *The Wild One* (1954) and *The Godfather* (1972).

Brandt /brant/, **Bill** (1904–83) German-born British photographer. Britain's foremost social documentary photographer, he worked for the *Picture Post* and photographed the London Blitz during World War II. Full name **William Brandt**

Brandt, Willy (1913–92) German statesman. He was mayor of West Berlin (1957–66) and was elected Chancellor of the Federal Republic of Germany in 1969. His pursuit of reconciliation between East and West earned him the Nobel Peace Prize in 1971. Real name **Herbert Ernst Karl Frahm**

brandy /brándi/ (plural **-dies**) n. a spirit that is distilled from the fermented juice of grapes or other fruit [Early 17thC. Shortening of *brandy-wine*, from Dutch *brandewijn*, literally 'burnt (i.e. distilled) wine'.]

brandy Alexander n. a cocktail with a base of brandy

brandy butter n. a creamed mixture of butter, sugar, and brandy, traditionally served with Christmas pudding. US term **hard sauce**

brandy snap n. a sweet crisp biscuit with a thin lacy texture that is rolled into a cylinder and often filled with cream

brandy snifter n. = **snifter** n. 1

branks /brangks/ npl. a device consisting of a metal frame for the head and a bit to restrain the tongue, used in the past to restrain and punish quarrelsome or nagging women [Mid-16thC. Origin uncertain: perhaps from Dutch *branken* 'branches, legs', from late Latin *branca* 'paw' (source of English *branch*).]

Branson /bránss'n/, **Richard** (b. 1950) British entrepreneur. He started a chain of record shops (1971), founded an airline (1984), and launched a radio station (1993). Full name **Richard Charles Nicholas Branson**

brant /brant/ (plural **brants** or **brant**) n. US = **brent goose** [14thC. Variant of BRENT GOOSE.]

Brantôme /braaN tőm/, **Pierre de Bourdeille, seigneur de** (1540–1614) French writer and courtier. Chamberlain to Charles IX and Henry III of France, he wrote scandalous accounts of the Valois court.

bran tub *n.* a tub or barrel containing bran in which small wrapped gifts are hidden at parties or fairs, to be pulled out by people in a game of lucky dip

Braque /braak, brak/, **Georges** (1882–1963) French painter. He was one of the founders, with Picasso, of the Cubist movement.

brash[1] /brash/ *adj.* self-assertive in an aggressive or rude way [Early 19thC. Origin uncertain: perhaps an alteration of RASH.] —**brashly** *adv.* —**brashness** *n.*

brash[2] /brash/ *adj.* easily cracked or broken [Mid-16thC. Origin unknown.]

brash[3] /brash/ *n.* = **heartburn** [Early 19thC. Origin uncertain: possibly an imitation of the sound. The word originally meant 'an attack or assault'.]

brash[4] /brash/ *n.* a pile of loose rubbish, e.g. broken rock or garden refuse [Late 18thC. Origin uncertain: perhaps an alteration of French *brèche* 'breach in a wall, rubble', from Italian *breccia*.]

brashy /bráshi/ (**-ier, -iest**) *adj.* **1.** IN PIECES loosely broken or fragmented ○ *soft, brashy ice* **2.** BRITTLE easily cracked or broken

Brasília /brə zíllyə/ city and capital of Brazil. A relatively new city, laid out on an uninhabited site in 1957, it is in the Federal District, east-central Brazil. Population: 1,817,001 (1996).

Braşov /bráshov/ city and capital of Braşov county, central Romania. It is situated in a steep-sided valley in at the foot of the Transylvanian Alps. Population: 324,210 (1994).

brass /braass/ *n.* **1.** INDUST YELLOW ALLOY a hard yellow shiny metal that is an alloy of zinc and copper, frequently with the addition of other metallic elements to impart specific properties ○ *candlesticks made of brass* **2.** ITEMS MADE OF BRASS a collection of ornaments or items made of brass ○ *a collection of brass* **3.** ITEM MADE OF BRASS an individual ornament or item made of brass (*usually used in the plural*) **4.** ENGRAVED BRASS PLAQUE OR TABLET an engraved plaque or tablet made of brass, especially one set into the floor or wall of a church **5.** MUSIC BRASS MUSICAL INSTRUMENTS the musical instruments made of brass, such as the trumpet and trombone **6.** MUSIC PLAYERS OF BRASS INSTRUMENTS the players of brass instruments, especially when considered as one of the four main sections of an orchestra **7.** MIL HIGH-RANKING OFFICERS high-ranking officers, especially in the military (*informal*) **8.** *N England* MONEY money or cash (*informal*) ○ *Where there's muck, there's brass.* **9.** MECH ENG RENEWABLE BRASS LINER FOR BEARING a renewable brass or bronze liner for a bearing **10.** EXCESSIVE SELF-ASSURANCE extreme, and usually excessive, self-confidence (*informal*) ○ *He had the brass to lie about every aspect of his background.* [Old English *bræs*, of unknown origin (source of English *brazen*)]

Brassaï /bra sí/ (1899–1984) Hungarian-born French photographer. His photographs documenting Parisian nightlife in the 1930s were published as *Paris by Night* (1933). Pseudonym of **Gyula Halasz**.

brass band *n.* a band consisting of brass wind instruments and sometimes percussion instruments

brassbound /braass bownd/ *adj.* **1.** TRIMMED OR BANDED WITH BRASS trimmed or banded with brass or similar metal **2.** UNBENDING AND IRON-WILLED unreasonably inflexible in manner or character

brassed off /braast-/ *adj.* irritated and disappointed (*informal dated*)

brasserie /brássəri/ *n.* a restaurant serving a wide range of food and drinks [Mid-19thC. From French, literally 'brewery', from Old French *bracier* 'to brew', via Vulgar Latin from, ultimately, Latin *brace* 'malt', of Celtic origin.]

brass farthing *n.* any money at all (*informal*) (*usually with a negative*) ○ *didn't have a brass farthing to my name*

brassica /brássikə/ *n.* a plant of the mustard family. Cabbage, kale, broccoli, cauliflower, swede, turnip, oilseed rape, and mustard are brassicas. Genus: *Brassica*. [Early 19thC. From modern Latin, genus name from Latin, 'cabbage'.]

brassie /brássi, braássi/ *n.* a former name for a golf club (a number 2 wood), which had a brass-plated sole (*archaic*)

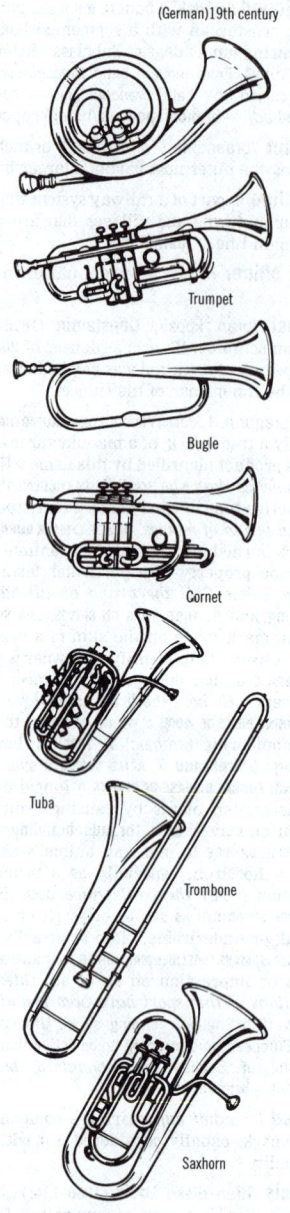

Post horn
(German)19th century

Trumpet

Bugle

Cornet

Tuba

Trombone

Saxhorn

Brass: Brass musical instruments

brassiere /brássi ər, brázzi ər/ *n.* = **bra** [Early 20thC. From French.]

brass knuckles *npl.* = **knuckle-duster**

brass-monkey weather, **brass monkeys** *n.* extremely cold weather (*informal*) [From the expression 'cold enough to freeze the balls off a brass monkey']

brass neck *n.* audacity or effrontery (*informal*)

brass rubbing *n.* **1.** COPY OF ENGRAVING a copy of an engraved plaque or tablet, especially one set into the floor or wall of a church. It is made by putting a piece of paper over the engraving and rubbing it with sth soft such as chalk or graphite. **2.** MAKING COPY OF ENGRAVING the process of making a brass rubbing

brass tacks *npl.* the most basic or fundamental parts of a situation or issue [Perhaps from their use as a medium of exchange when even iron nails were unavailable]
◇ **get down to brass tacks** to begin to deal with the most basic or important issues of a situation ○ *It's time we got down to brass tacks.*

brassware /braass wair/ *n.* items such as plates and ornaments made from brass

brassy /braássi/ (**-ier, -iest**) *adj.* **1.** FLASHY AND VULGAR brightly dressed in a cheap and showy way, and behaving too confidently or noisily (*insult*) **2.** SOUNDING LIKE BRASS INSTRUMENTS dominated by or resembling the sounds of brass musical instruments, and therefore typically short, harsh, and high-pitched ○ *a brassy mixture of reggae, funk, calypso, and jazz* **3.** BRAZENLY OVERBEARING brazen or strident in style ○ *Leadership needn't be brassy or harsh.* **4.** OF BRASS made of or containing brass **5.** OF GOLDEN-YELLOW COLOUR golden-yellow in colour or hue —**brassily** *adv.* —**brassiness** *n.*

brat /brat/ *n.* sb, either a child or an adult, who is tiresomely demanding and selfish, like a spoilt child [Mid-16thC. Origin uncertain: perhaps from an obsolete word meaning 'rag', from Old English *bratt* 'cloak', of Celtic origin.] —**bratty** *adj.* —**brattish** *adj.*

Bratby /brátbi/, **John** (1928–92) British painter. He was an exponent of 'kitchen sink' realism in the 1950s, using thick paint and heavy brush strokes.

Bratislava /brátti slaávə/ capital and largest city of Slovakia. It lies on the River Danube in the southwest of the country, about 56 km/35 mi. east of Vienna. Population: 441,453 (1994).

brat pack *n.* a group of successful or affluent young people, especially actors [Coined from BRAT, on the model of 'rat pack']

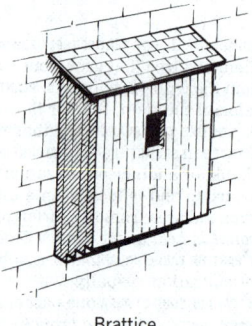

Brattice

brattice /bráttiss/ *n.* **1.** MINING PARTITION FOR MINE VENTILATION a partition used to assist ventilation in a mine **2.** MIL, HIST TEMPORARY PARAPET in medieval times, a temporary wooden parapet or gallery erected on the battlements of a fortress and used during a siege [13thC. Via Anglo-Norman and Old French *bretesche* from medieval Latin *bretescha turris* 'British tower', from Old English *brittisc* (see BRITISH).]

bratwurst /brát wurst/ *n.* a highly seasoned fresh German sausage made of pork or of pork and veal [Early 20thC. From German, literally 'frying-sausage'.]

Braun /brown/, **Wernher von** (1912–77) German-born US rocket engineer. He moved to the United States during World War II and was a major contributor to the US atomic bomb and space programmes.

brava /braá vaa/ *interj.*, *n.* a shout of approval for a woman or girl performer. ◊ *bravo* [Early 19thC. From Italian, feminine of *bravo* (see BRAVE).]

bravado /brə vaádō/ *n.* a real or pretended display of courage or boldness ○ *a breathtaking act of bravado* [Late 16thC. Alteration of Spanish *bravada*, from *bravo* (see BRAVE).]

brave /brayv/ *adj.* (**braver, bravest**) HAVING OR SHOWING COURAGE having or showing courage, especially when facing danger, difficulty, or pain ■ *n.* **1.** BRAVE PEOPLE those people who are courageous **2.** NATIVE N AMERICAN WARRIOR a Native North American warrior ■ *vt.* (**braves, braving, braved**) **1.** FACE ONSLAUGHT OF STH to face the onslaught of sth unpleasant with courage and resolution **2.** CHALLENGE STH to defy sth despite there being only a small chance of being victorious [15thC. Via French from Italian *bravo* 'bold' or Spanish *bravo* 'brave, savage', both ultimately from Latin *barbarus* (see BARBAROUS).] —**bravely** *adv.* —**braveness** *n.*

——— WORD KEY: SYNONYMS ———
See Synonyms at **bold**.

brave out *vt.* to live through sth that is difficult or unpleasant

brave new world *n.* the world of the future, usually either a technology-based utopia or a sinister to-talitarian world devoid of human values (*often used ironically*) [Mid-20th Century. From *Brave New World* (1932), a novel by Aldous HUXLEY. Huxley took the expression from Shakespeare's *The Tempest*: 'O brave new world/ That has such people in it!'.]

─────── **WORD KEY: CULTURAL NOTE** ───────

Brave New World, a novel by Aldous Huxley (1932). Written partly as a response to more utopian writers of the day, it depicts a bleak and sterile future civilization in which feelings are stimulated by drugs, and babies are bred in factories.

bravery /bráyvəri/ *n.* extreme courage in the face of danger or difficulty, or an example of extreme courage [Mid-16thC. From French *braverie* or Italian *bra-veria*, both ultimately from Italian *bravo* 'bold' (source of English *brave*).]

─────── **WORD KEY: SYNONYMS** ───────

See Synonyms at *courage*.

bravissimo /braa víssimō/ *interj.* used as a cry of great and enthusiastic approval by members of a theatre audience (*formal*) [Mid-18thC. From Italian, 'most ex-cellent', the strongest form of *bravo* (see BRAVO).]

bravo /braa vō, braa vó/ *interj.* AUDIENCE'S SHOUT OF APPROVAL used as a cry of approval by members of a theatre audience ■ *n.* (*plural* -vos) **1.** CRY OF 'BRAVO' a shout of 'bravo' to express admiration **2.** HIRED ASSASSIN a hired assassin (*archaic*) [Mid-18thC. From Italian, 'excellent' (source of English *brave*). The underlying idea is an ac-knowledgment of showmanship.]

Bravo /braávō/ *n.* the code word for the letter 'b' in the NATO phonetic alphabet, used in international radio communications

bravura /brə vyoórə/ *n.* **1.** DAZZLING ARTISTIC FLAIR great skill that is shown when sth artistic is done in an exciting or innovative way (*often used before a noun*) ○ *a bravura performance* **2.** SHOWY DISPLAY showy style or behaviour [Mid-18thC. From Italian, 'courage, spirit', from *bravo* 'bold' (source of English *brave*).]

braw /braw/ *adj. Scotland* attractive or pleasant [Late 16thC. Variant of BRAVE.]

brawl /brawl/ *n.* **1.** NOISY FIGHT a rough and noisy fight, usually in a public place and between large numbers of people **2.** LOUD NOISE a loud deep noise, especially the noise of rushing water **3.** *US, Can* LOUD PARTY a noisy boisterous party (*slang*) ■ *vi.* (**brawls, brawling, brawled**) **1.** FIGHT NOISILY to fight or wrestle noisily, especially in a public place **2.** MAKE DEEP LOUD SOUND to make a deep loud roaring sound, especially the sound of rushing water [14thC. Origin uncertain.] —**brawler** *n.* —**brawling** *n.*

brawn /brawn/ *n.* **1.** STRONG MUSCLES very strong muscles, especially on the arms and legs **2.** BODILY STRENGTH physical strength, especially as opposed to in-tellectual power **3.** FOOD COOKED MEAT FROM ANIMALS' HEADS boiled and jellied meat from the head and feet of pigs or calves. US term **headcheese** [14thC. From Anglo-Norman *braun* 'fleshy part of the leg', from, ultimately, prehistoric Germanic, and related to German *Braten* 'roast meat'.]

brawny /bráwni/ (**-ier, -iest**) *adj.* muscular and strong-looking —**brawnily** *adv.* —**brawniness** *n.*

bray[1] /bray/ *n.* **1.** DONKEY'S CRY the sound a donkey makes **2.** HARSH VOICE OR LAUGH a harsh high-pitched rasping voice or laugh ■ *v.* (**brays, braying, brayed**) **1.** *vi.* MAKE DONKEY'S SOUND to make the sound a donkey makes **2.** *vti.* SPEAK WITH HARSH VOICE to speak, laugh, or say sth in a harsh high-pitched rasping voice [13thC. From Old French *braire* 'to cry', which may, ultimately, be of Celtic origin.] —**brayer** *n.*

bray[2] /bray/ (**brays, braying, brayed**) *vt.* **1.** GRIND STH FINELY to crush sth to a fine powder or consistency **2.** PRINTING INK THINLY to spread ink in a thin layer on a surface [14thC. From Anglo-Norman *braier* and Old French *breier*, ultimately from a prehistoric Germanic word that also produced English *break*.]

Braz. *abbr.* **1.** Brazil **2.** Brazilian

braze[1] /brayz/ (**brazes, brazing, brazed**) *vt.* **1.** MAKE STH WITH BRASS to make sth out of brass or decorate sth with brass **2.** MAKE STH HARD LIKE BRASS to give sth a hardness like that of brass [Old English *brasian*. Formed from *bræs* 'brass', subsequently reinforced by the parallel GLASS and GLAZE.] —**brazer** *n.*

braze[2] /brayz/ (**brazes, brazing, brazed**) *vt.* to join two pieces of metal together with a solder that has a high melting point [Mid-16thC. From Old French *braser* 'to burn'.] —**brazer** *n.*

brazen /bráyz'n/ *adj.* **1.** BOLD AND UNASHAMED showing or expressing boldness and complete lack of shame **2.** HARSH-SOUNDING with an unpleasantly loud and res-onant sound **3.** OF OR LIKE BRASS made of brass or resembling it, especially in colour or hardness (*literary*) [Old English *bræsen* 'made of brass', from *bræs* 'brass'. The meaning 'bold' evolved from the idea of the hardness of brass.] —**brazenness** *n.*

brazen out *vt.* to face a difficult situation confidently, without showing shame or embarrassment

brazenfaced /bráyz'n fáyst/ *adj.* shameless and au-dacious

brazenly /bráyz'nli/ *adv.* in a bold or shameless way

brazier[1] /bráyzi ər/ *n.* sb who makes and repairs brass articles [14thC. Probably from BRASS + -IER, on the model of GLASS and GLAZIER.]

brazier[2] /bráyzi ər/ *n.* a metal drum with holes in it, used outdoors as a container for burning coal or charcoal, either for cooking or to keep people warm [Late 17thC. From French *brasier*, from *braise* 'hot coals' (source of English *braise*).]

brazil /brə zíl/ *n.* **1.** = brazilwood **2.** = Brazil nut [14thC. From medieval Latin *brasilium*, of uncertain origin; perhaps from French *braise* 'hot coals' (source of English *braise*), from the colour of the wood.]

Brazil

Brazil /brə zíl/ republic and the largest country in South America. Colonized by the Portuguese from 1500 onwards, it became an independent republic in 1889. Language: Portuguese. Currency: real. Capital: Brasília. Population: 167,660,687 (1997). Area: 8,547,404 sq. km/3,300,171 sq. mi. —**Brazilian** *n., adj.*

Brazil Basin basin of the Atlantic Ocean on the American side of the Mid-Atlantic Ridge. Depth: 5,000 m/16,400 ft.

Brazil nut *n.* **1.** FOOD EDIBLE SEED WITH TRIANGULAR SHELL the long thick edible seed of a tropical South American tree, with a hard shell that is nearly triangular in cross-section **2.** TREES TROPICAL SOUTH AMERICAN TREE the tropical South American evergreen tree that bears Brazil nuts in clusters inside large round capsules. Latin name: *Bertholletia excelsa*.

brazilwood /brə zíl wŏod/, **brazil** *n.* a kind of red wood obtained from various tropical and North American trees, especially one native to Brazil. It is used in the manufacture of red dyes and violin bows.

Brazzaville /brázzə vil/ capital city of the Republic of Congo and a major port on the Congo River. It was founded in 1880 by the French explorer Pierre Savorgnan de Brazza (1852–1905). Population: 937,579 (1995).

BRCS *abbr.* British Red Cross Society

breach /breech/ *v.* (**breaches, breaching, breached**) **1.** *vt.* OPENING THROUGH STH to break down an ob-struction to allow sth to pass through it **2.** *vt.* SURPASS

LIMIT to go beyond a target or limit **3.** *vt.* BREAK LAW OR PROMISE to fail to obey, keep, or preserve sth, e.g. a law or trust **4.** *vi.* LEAP OUT to leap above the surface of the water (*refers to whales*) ■ *n.* **1.** HOLE a hole in sth that is caused by sth else forcing its way through **2.** GAP a gap that results when sth or sb leaves **3.** FAILURE TO MAINTAIN STH a failure to obey, keep, or pre-serve sth, e.g. a law, a trust or a promise **4.** ES-TRANGEMENT a breakdown in friendly relations **5.** WHALE'S LEAP a leap out of the water by a whale [13thC. From Old French *breche*, ultimately from a prehistoric Ger-manic base that is also the ancestor of English *break*.]

─────── **WORD KEY: USAGE** ───────

breach or **breech**? The main uses of **breach** are as a verb meaning 'to violate a rule' and as a noun meaning 'a violation of a rule': *a breach of the peace*. **Breech** means the rear part of the body (as in **breech birth**) and the part of a gun behind the barrel.

breach of promise *n.* failure in fulfilling a promise, especially in former times the breaking of a promise to marry sb

bread /bred/ *n.* **1.** FOOD MADE FROM FLOUR AND WATER a food typically made by mixing flour, water, and yeast and allowing it to swell before baking it **2.** MEANS OF SURVIVAL food, sustenance, or a means of survival or support **3.** MONEY money to live on (*dated slang*) [Old English *brēad*, of uncertain origin: probably ultimately 'sth broken off', and related to BRITTLE.] ◇ **cast your bread upon the waters** to spend time and effort, especially to help others, without expecting any immediate advantage for yourself (*formal*) ◇ **know which side your bread is buttered (on)** to know what is to your advantage (*informal*)

bread and butter *n.* **1.** SUSTAINING INCOME a dependable source of income **2.** MAINSTAY sth that is the essential or sustaining part of sth else

bread-and-butter letter *n.* a letter or note expressing thanks for sb's hospitality

bread-and-butter pudding (*plural* **bread-and-butter puddings**) *n.* a baked pudding that is made from bread and butter layered in a dish with dried fruit and covered in a mixture of egg, sugar, milk, and spices. US term **bread pudding**

bread and circuses *npl.* sth done or given to keep people happy, especially sth provided or en-couraged by governments to win popular appeal or avert public unrest [A translation of Latin *panis et circenses* (Juvenal, *Satires*), referring to the food and entertainment provided by the authorities in ancient Rome]

breadbasket /bréd baaskit/ *n.* **1.** CEREAL-GROWING REGION a region that is an important grower of cereal crops **2.** BELLY the stomach or abdomen (*slang dated*)

bread bin *n.* a container for storing bread. US term **breadbox**

breadboard /bréd bawrd/ *n.* ELEC ENG TEST VERSION OF ELECTRICAL CIRCUIT a preliminary version of an elec-trical or electronic circuit put together for test purposes ■ *vt.* (**-boards, -boarding, -boarded**) ELEC ENG MAKE TEST VERSION OF CIRCUIT to make a preliminary version of an electrical or electronic circuit for test purposes —**breadboarding** *n.*

breadbox /bréd boks/ *n. US* = bread bin

breadcrumb /bréd krum/ *n.* a tiny piece of bread, either soft or hard (*often used in the plural*)

breadfruit /bréd froot/ (*plural* **-fruit** or **-fruits**) *n.* **1.** FOOD FRUIT WITH BREADY TEXTURE WHEN COOKED a large round seedless tropical fruit that is usually eaten baked or roasted, when it takes on the texture of bread **2.** TREES EVERGREEN PACIFIC TREE the evergreen tree that bears breadfruit. It is native to the Pacific Islands, and belongs to the fig family. Latin name: *Ar-tocarpus altilis*.

breadline /bréd līn/ *n.* **1.** LOW LIVING STANDARD a very low standard of living, with only just enough food and money to survive **2.** *US* PEOPLE WAITING FOR FOOD HANDOUTS a queue of people waiting for handouts of free food [Late 19thC. From the original sense, 'queue of needy people outside a bakery that was giving away unsold bread'.]

bread mould *n.* a fungus that grows on decaying bread and other foods, forming a dense cottony growth. Latin name: *Rhizopus nigricans*.

breadnut /bréd nut/ *n.* **1.** TREES **LARGE TROPICAL TREE** a large tree native to Central America, Mexico, and the West Indies, with yellow fruits containing edible seeds. Latin name: *Brosimum alicastrum*. **2.** FOOD **SEED FROM TROPICAL FRUIT** the edible seed of the breadnut tree, sometimes ground into flour

bread pudding *n. US* = **bread-and-butter pudding**

breadroot /bréd root/ *n.* a perennial plant of the pea family that is native to North America and has a starchy edible root. It was once an important source of food amongst the Native American population. Latin name: *Psoralea esculenta*.

bread sauce *n.* a milk-based sauce thickened with breadcrumbs and flavoured with onion, traditionally served with poultry

breadth /bredth, bretth/ *n.* **1.** **DISTANCE FROM SIDE TO SIDE** the distance or measurement of sth from one side to the other **2.** **PIECE OF FABRIC IN STANDARD WIDTH** a standardized width that sth, especially fabric, is produced or available in, or a piece of fabric in a standardized width **3.** **GREAT EXTENT** the extent of sth, especially when it is impressively great **4.** **BROAD-MINDEDNESS** an open and tolerant view of life and the world [Early 16thC. Formed from obsolete English *brede* 'breadth' (which came from the same prehistoric Germanic base as English *broad*), on the model of *length*.] —**breadthwise** *adj., adv.*

breadwinner /bréd winnər/ *n.* sb who earns money to support a family, especially sb whose earnings are the family's main income

break /brayk/ *v.* (**breaks, breaking, broke** /brōk/, **broken** /brṓkən/) **1.** *vti.* **SEPARATE STH INTO PIECES** to become damaged or damage sth so that it separates into pieces ○ *it broke in two* **2.** *vt.* MED **DAMAGE BODY** to damage a body part, e.g. a bone ○ *She broke her leg.* **3.** *vti.* **DAMAGE PART OF MACHINE** to damage a part of a tool or machine so that it stops functioning properly, or become damaged and stop functioning properly ○ *The washing machine is broken.* **4.** *vti.* **TEAR SURFACE** to become torn, or make a tear or hole in a surface or seal, allowing the possibility of a leak or spill ○ *Store in the fridge after breaking the seal on the bottle.* **5.** *vt.* **DISOBEY RULE** to disobey a rule or law ○ *He's broken the law.* **6.** *vt.* **GO BACK ON WORD** to renege on a promise or agreement **7.** *vt.* **END BAD SITUATION** to end, change, or rectify a difficult or disadvantageous situation ○ *break the deadlock between rival factions* **8.** *vt.* **END SILENCE** to end a period of silence **9.** *vti.* **FINISH RELATIONSHIP** to end an involvement with an individual or group ○ *They broke their links with the terrorists.* **10.** *vt.* **END STH** to finish sth, bring it to an end, or stop sb doing it ○ *break the coffee-drinking habit* **11.** *vt.* **INTERRUPT STH** to interrupt sth temporarily ○ *The distraction broke her train of thought.* **12.** *vt.* **RUIN SB'S LIFE** to destroy sb's career, resolve, courage, or hope of success ○ *The media can make or break her.* **13.** *vti.* **ESCAPE** to escape from a restraint ○ *break free* **14.** *vi.* **TAKE PERIOD FOR REST** to take a period of leisure ○ *break for lunch* **15.** *vt.* **STAND BETWEEN PERSON AND STH** to stand in the way of or weaken the effect of sth, e.g. a fall or blow ○ *He tried to break her fall.* **16.** *vt.* **BEAT RECORD** to beat a previous record **17.** *vt.* **EXCEED LIMIT** to exceed a limit or constraint ○ *break the speed limit* **18.** *vti.* **REVEAL OR BE REVEALED** to reveal sth personally, or to be revealed, particularly by the media ○ *She broke it to me gently.* ○ *Panic ensued when the news broke.* **19.** *vi.* **BECOME DEEPER** to settle into an adult man's register (*refers to a boy's voice*) **20.** *vi.* **STOP SPEAKING FROM EMOTION** to stop speaking and hesitate when overcome with emotion ○ *Her voice broke and tears slid down her face.* **21.** *vi.* MUSIC **CHANGE TONE WITH REGISTER** to change in tone or quality when changing register (*refers to a voice or musical instrument*) **22.** *vi.* **BECOME DAYLIGHT** to become light at sunrise **23.** *vi.* METEOROL **CHANGE WEATHER PATTERN** to change after a settled period **24.** *vi.* METEOROL **SUDDENLY START** to suddenly begin to rain, snow, or hail ○ *The storm broke.* **25.** *vi.* OCEANOG **TURN TO SURF** to start collapsing into surf when close to shore or hitting rocks or similar objects (*refers to a wave*) **26.** *vt.* **INTERPRET A CODE** to understand a code and be able to translate it accurately **27.** *vt.* **PROVE UNTRUE** to prove that sth is untrue or wrong **28.** *vt.* LAW **INVALIDATE WILL** to use legal means to declare a will invalid **29.** *vt.* **BLOW OPEN SAFE** to open a safe using explosives **30.** *vt.* EQU **TRAIN HORSE TO ACCEPT HARNESS** to train a horse to become accustomed to a saddle, bit, and rider **31.** *vt.* MONEY **SWAP NOTE FOR CHANGE** to exchange a note of money for smaller units of money, either coins or smaller notes and coins ○ *break a £20 note* **32.** *vi.* MED **FLOW OUT IN CHILDBIRTH** to flow out when the amniotic sac around an unborn baby breaks during the first stage of labour (*refers to amniotic fluid*) ○ *Her waters have broken.* **33.** *vi. US* **TURN OUT** to happen or turn out in a particular way ○ *Things are breaking well.* **34.** *vt.* **REDUCE TO POVERTY** to cause sb to be extremely poor or bankrupt **35.** *vti.* ZOOL **EMERGE OUT OF WATER** to emerge or erupt above the surface of a body of water **36.** *vt.* MIL **DEMOTE** to demote sb to a lower rank **37.** *vt.* ELEC **INTERRUPT FLOW OF ELECTRIC CURRENT** to interrupt the flow of electricity in an electrical circuit **38.** *vi.* STOCK EXCH **FALL SHARPLY** to fall in price (*refers to stock exchange quotations*) **39.** *vti.* TENNIS **WIN GAME OFF OPPONENT'S SERVICE** to win a game in tennis in which the other player is serving **40.** *vi.* BOXING, WRESTLING **SEPARATE FROM CLINCH** to separate after being in a boxing or wrestling clinch **41.** *vi.* SPORTS **SPEED UP IN RACE** to increase speed suddenly in a race **42.** *vi.* BASEBALL **CHANGE DIRECTION IN AIR** to change direction while moving through the air (*refers to a baseball*) **43.** *vi.* CRICKET **CHANGE DIRECTION ON BOUNCING** to change direction after bouncing (*refers to a cricket ball*) **44.** *vt.* CRICKET **KNOCK OVER WICKET** to hit and knock over a bail from the wicket when playing cricket **45.** *vi.* HORSERACING **START OFF IN HORSE RACE** to start off at the start of a race in horseracing **46.** *vi.* CUE GAMES **SCATTER BALLS** to scatter the balls in billiards or snooker **47.** *vi.* PHON **BECOME DIPHTHONG** to change in pronunciation, becoming a diphthong (*refers to a vowel*) ■ *n.* **1.** **PERIOD OFF FROM ACTIVITY** a period taken away from an activity for a rest, change, or meal ○ *a lunch break* **2.** **BRIEF HOLIDAY** a short holiday away from home ○ *a weekend break* **3.** **PERIOD OFF BEFORE CONTINUING** a period away from sth before continuing it again ○ *a career break* **4.** **PERIOD OFF IN SCHOOL DAY** a period in the school day when pupils can play or rest. US term **recess** **5.** **END TO RELATIONSHIP** the severance of links with a person or group or an end to a relationship ○ *He wanted to make the break with his partner.* **6.** **END** an end to sth ○ *a break with tradition* **7.** TV **PERIOD IN PROGRAMME FOR ADVERTS** a period during a television programme or between programmes when advertisements are shown **8.** SPORTS **INTERVAL IN MATCH** an interval in a sportsmatch **9.** **PAUSE IN SPEECH** a pause when speaking ○ *a break in the conversation* **10.** MED **FRACTURE** a fracture in a bone **11.** **CRACK** a crack in sth **12.** METEOROL **CHANGE IN WEATHER** a change in the weather **13.** **LUCKY OPPORTUNITY FOR SUCCESS** an unexpected opportunity that allows sb to achieve sth or become successful (*informal*) ○ *He got his first break when he was spotted playing for his college.* **14.** a piece of good luck or bad luck ○ *a lucky break* **15.** FIN **ADVANTAGEOUS FINANCIAL SITUATION** an advantageous financial situation in which sb is repaid or makes a reduced payment ○ *a tax break* **16.** **ESCAPE ATTEMPT** a sudden attempt to escape ○ *make a break for it* **17.** **DISCONTINUITY** a discontinuity in sth, by which it changes in quality or level **18.** **SUNRISE** the time when the sun first rises (*literary*) ○ *at the break of day* **19.** TENNIS **WINNING OF GAME OFF OPPONENT'S SERVICE** the winning of a game in tennis in which the other player is serving **20.** HORSERACING **START OF HORSE RACE** the start of a horse race **21.** ELEC **INTERRUPTION IN FLOW OF ELECTRICITY** an interruption in the flow of electricity in an electrical circuit **22.** MUSIC **INSTRUMENTAL PART IN SONG** an instrumental part in a piece of pop music **23.** MUSIC **IMPROVISED JAZZ SOLO** an improvised solo part in a piece of jazz music **24.** MUSIC **CHANGE IN REGISTER** a change in register in a voice or musical instrument **25.** POETRY = **caesura** **26.** STOCK EXCH **FALL IN PRICES** a sudden fall in prices, particularly in a stock market **27.** CUE GAMES **SERIES OF SUCCESSFUL SHOTS** a sequence of successful shots in one player's turn in billiards or snooker, or the points scored from them **28.** CUE GAMES **FIRST SHOT THAT SCATTERS BALLS** an opening shot in billiards or snooker, which scatters the balls **29.** BOWLS **FAILURE TO KNOCK DOWN ALL PINS** a failure to knock down all the pins in ten pin bowling after the second throw **30.** RADIO **ACCESS TO CB RADIO CHANNEL** access for a CB radio operator to a radio channel **31.** TRANSP = **brake** ■ *interj.* BOXING, WRESTLING **USED TO SEPARATE FIGHTERS** used to command boxers or wrestlers to separate from a clinch [Old English *brecan*. Ultimately from an Indo-European root that also produced Latin *frangere* 'to break' (source of English *fracture*).] ◇ **break even** to make neither a profit nor a loss from a venture ◇ **give sb a break** to stop nagging or criticizing sb or to start treating sb fairly (*informal*)

WORD KEY: SYNONYMS

See Synonyms at ***holiday***.

break away *vi.* **1.** **LEAVE OR GET AWAY** to sever relations with or detach from a person or group **2.** **DEPART FROM CUSTOM** to change or depart from established customs or procedures **3.** **PULL AWAY QUICKLY** to depart or pull away from sb or sth, usually at high speed

break down *vi.* **FAIL TO FUNCTION PROPERLY** to stop working, or to stop working properly, effectively, or usefully ■ **TEAR DOWN** to destroy sth or cause sth to fall or collapse ■ *v.* **1.** *vti.* **BECOME OR MAKE EMOTIONAL** to become upset emotionally, or to cause sb to become upset emotionally **2.** *vti.* **EXPERIENCE OR CAUSE HEALTH COLLAPSE** to experience, or cause sb to experience, a physical or psychological collapse **3.** *vti.* **STOP RESISTING** to yield or end any resistance, or to cause sb to yield or sb's resistance to end **4.** *vti.* **WEAKEN** to become or cause sb or sth to become weak and ineffective **5.** *vt.* **ANALYSE BY DIVIDING INTO PARTS** to analyse or examine sth by reducing it to its simplest terms or component parts **6.** *vi.* **BE DIVISIBLE INTO ELEMENTS** to divide into or be reducible to separate parts when analysed **7.** *vti.* **DECOMPOSE CHEMICALLY** to decompose chemically, or to cause sth to undergo chemical decomposition **8.** *vi.* ELEC ENG **EXPERIENCE ELECTRICAL INSULATION FAILURE** to experience a sudden failure of an insulating material to halt the current flow

break in **BEGIN USING SB OR STH NEW** to begin to employ sb new or use sth new, supplying the training or modifications needed for good performance ■ *vi.* **1.** **ENTER FORCIBLY** to enter a place or building forcibly and usually illegally **2.** **START TALKING** to interrupt a conversation or discussion

break into *vt.* **1.** **ENTER BUILDING FORCIBLY AND ILLEGALLY** to enter a building forcibly and usually illegally **2.** **BEGIN SPEAKING** to interrupt sth that is being said or discussed **3.** **DO STH SUDDENLY** to begin doing sth suddenly, e.g. runnning or singing **4.** **START WORK IN NEW FIELD** to begin working in a profession or field, often after having tried to do so for some time without success

break off *v.* **1.** *vt.* **TAKE OFF PIECE OF STH** to separate a piece from a solid mass or the main part of sth **2.** *vti.* **END BEING OR DOING STH TOGETHER** to discontinue a relationship or interaction with sb or a group **3.** *vi.* **STOP SPEAKING** to stop talking, usually abruptly

break out *v.* **1.** *vi.* **HAVE SKIN RASH** to develop skin blemishes or a rash, especially suddenly **2.** *vi.* **BEGIN ABRUPTLY** to happen or begin suddenly and strongly (*refers to wars and violence*) **3.** *vi.* **BECOME FREE FROM STH** to escape or emerge from sth that confines, restrains, or traps, such as a prison cell **4.** *vt.* **PREPARE STH FOR USE** to open sth or get sth ready for use or action **5.** *vt.* **CLASSIFY DATA ITEMS** to classify, summarize, outline, or separate data items in order to analyse, explain, or identify sth

break through *vti.* to burst or advance quickly and suddenly through an obstruction or opposition, e.g. from an enemy

break up *v.* **1.** *vt.* **DIVIDE OR INTERRUPT STH** to divide or separate sth into pieces or sections, or interrupt the continuity of sth **2.** *vi.* **DISPERSE** to separate, or have members separate, and go in different directions **3.** *vti.* **END** to cause a relationship, interaction, or gathering to end, or to come to an end **4.** *vti.* **CAUSE EMOTIONAL RESPONSE** to cause sb to burst into tears or laughter

break with *vt.* to separate from sb or from a tradition, rule, or trend

breakable /bráykəb'l/ *adj.* **EASILY BROKEN** likely to be broken if not handled carefully ■ *n.* **FRAGILE OBJECT** sth that is easily broken if not handled carefully (*usually used in the plural*) —**breakability** /bráykə bíllәti/ *n.* —**breakableness** /-əb'lnəss/ *n.*

breakage /bráykij/ *n.* **1.** **STH BROKEN** sth that has been broken, usually accidentally (*usually used in the plural*) ○ *All breakages must be paid for.* **2.** **BREAKING** the breaking of sth

breakaway /bráykə way/ *n*. **1.** STH BREAKING OFF sb or sth that breaks or has broken away **2.** STH MADE TO BREAK OFF sth that is designed to break away or break apart from the whole **3.** BREAKING AWAY the breaking away of sb or sth ▪ *adj*. **1.** MADE TO BREAK OFF designed to break away or apart, either as a safety mechanism or to create an illusion, e.g. a theatre prop **2.** HAVING SEVERED TIES WITH STH having broken ties or connections to sb or a group

breakbeat /brayk beet/ *n*. a drum pattern with a syncopated beat that is electronically looped, used mostly in jungle, drum and bass, and hardcore music

breakbone fever /brayk bōn-/ *n*. = **dengue** [From the pains in the joints that are one of its symptoms]

breakdancing /brayk daanssing/ *n*. a highly energetic, fast, and acrobatic style of solo dancing to rap music, typically involving spinning of the body on the ground. Breakdancing started in the United States in the 1980s. [*Break* of uncertain meaning: perhaps related to BREAKDOWN in the sense of 'fast dance'] —**breakdance** *n*., *vi*. —**breakdancer** *n*.

breakdown /brayk down/ *n*. **1.** FAILURE TO WORK a failure to operate or an interruption of the operation of a machine or vehicle **2.** FAILURE TO COMMUNICATE a disruption of the understanding and interaction between people or groups ○ *breakdown in the talks* **3.** PERSONAL HEALTH CRISIS a sudden physical or psychological collapse **4.** DATA SUMMARY OR EXPLANATION a summary, explanation, analysis, or outline of data items collected **5.** CAR OR MACHINERY FAILURE a time when a car or piece of machinery stops working **6.** DECOMPOSITION INTO PARTS a breaking down of sth into its essential components, parts, or elements **7.** ELEC ENG SUDDEN PASSAGE OF CURRENT THROUGH INSULATOR the sudden passage of electrical current through an insulator **8.** DANCE COUNTRY DANCE a fast energetic US country dance

breakdown lorry, **breakdown truck** *n*. a lorry that tows a vehicle that has broken down to a garage where it can be repaired. US term **wrecker**

breaker[1] /bráykər/ *n*. **1.** ELEC ENG = **circuit breaker 2.** LARGE WHITE-CAPPED WAVE a large, usually white-capped, wave that is cresting or breaking, especially onto the shore **3.** DANCE BREAKDANCER sb who does breakdancing (*slang*) **4.** BREAKING MACHINE sth, e.g. a machine, that is used to crush or break up rocks, fibres, or other substances **5.** HORSE TRAINER sb who trains horses so that they can be ridden ▪ *interj*. RADIO OPENING MESSAGE used by CB radio operators to announce that they are beginning to transmit on a channel

———— **WORD KEY: CULTURAL NOTE** ————

Breaker Morant, a film by Australian film-maker Bruce Beresford (1979). It is based on the true story of Australian soldier and poet, Breaker Morant, who was court-martialled and executed by the British Army in South Africa, an event which aroused strong anti-British feeling in Australia.

breaker[2] /bráykər/ *n*. a small cask for water, used especially on lifeboats [Mid-19thC. From Spanish *barrica* 'cask' (see BARRICADE).]

breakeven /brayk eev'n/, **breakeven point** *n*. the point or level of financial activity at which expenditure equals income or the value of an investment equals its cost, and the result is neither a profit nor loss

breakfast /brékfəst/ *n*. DAY'S FIRST MEAL the first meal of the day, usually eaten in the morning (*often used before a noun*) ▪ *vi*. (**-fasts**, **-fasting**, **-fasted**) HAVE BREAKFAST to eat breakfast, usually in the morning [15thC. From FAST 'period without food', from the idea of being without food while asleep.] —**breakfaster** *n*.

breakfast television *n*. informal, magazine-style television programmes broadcast in the morning

breakfront /brayk frunt/ *adj*. used to describe a piece of furniture, e.g. a cabinet or bookcase, with a central section that juts forward slightly — **breakfront** *n*.

break-in *n*. an illegal forced entry into a building or place

breaking[1] /bráyking/ *n*. LING the changing of a simple vowel into a diphthong when certain other speech

sounds come before or after it. For example the vowel in 'feet' becomes a diphthong in 'feel'.

breaking[2] /bráyking/ *n*. DANCE breakdancing (*slang*)

breaking and entering *n*. the crime of forcibly entering property, usually in order to steal from it

breaking point *n*. **1.** POINT WHEN COPING BECOMES IMPOSSIBLE the point at which sb loses the ability to deal physically, psychologically, or emotionally with a stressful situation **2.** CRITICAL MOMENT the point at which a condition or situation reaches a crisis

breakneck /brayk nek/ *adj*. so fast or quick as to be hazardous or reckless ○ *at breakneck speed*

break of day *n*. the time when the sun rises in the morning

breakoff /brayk of/ *n*. a discontinuation of sth, especially when this is abrupt ○ *the breakoff of negotiations*

breakout /brayk owt/ *n*. a forceful escape or emergence from being confined, restrained, or trapped [Early 19thC]

breakpoint /brayk poynt/ *n*. **1.** COMPUT PAUSE ALLOWING REVIEW OF COMPUTER PROGRAM a pause inserted into a computer program under development or being serviced so that the contents of registers and memory locations can be examined to correct a programming logic error **2.** POINT WHERE STOP OR CHANGE OCCURS a point where sth stops, pauses, changes, or breaks apart

break point *n*. a point in tennis which, if won, results in the player who is not serving winning the game

breakthrough /brayk throo/ *n*. **1.** IMPORTANT DISCOVERY an important new discovery, especially in science, medicine, or technology, that has a dramatic and far-reaching effect **2.** REMOVAL OF BARRIER TO PROGRESS an event that causes or marks the breaking down of a barrier to progress, e.g. in negotiations **3.** MIL PENETRATION OF ENEMY LINE an attacking army's advance through and beyond an enemy's line of defence ▪ *adj*. BRINGING PUBLIC RECOGNITION bringing public attention and fame to a performing artist

break through bleeding *n*. bleeding from the womb that occurs between menstrual periods

breakup /brayk up/ *n*. **1.** BREAKING APART OR UP a breaking into separate pieces or sections that are not connected or continuous **2.** END OF RELATIONSHIP the breaking off or discontinuation of a personal relationship **3.** SPRING THAW OF LODGED ICE the melting or breaking apart of lodged ice in rivers and harbours in the spring **4.** EMOTIONAL BREAKDOWN a loss of control over the emotions

breakwater /brayk wawtər/ *n*. an offshore barrier that protects a harbour or other coastal area from the full force of the sea

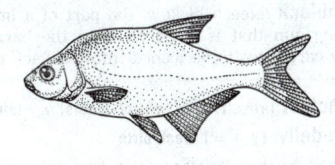

Bream

bream[1] /breem/ (*plural* **bream** *or* **breams**) *n*. **1.** EURASIAN FRESHWATER FISH a freshwater fish native to Europe and Asia that has a deep thin body and is yellowish in colour. Latin name: *Abramis brama*. **2.** FRESHWATER FISH LIKE BREAM a freshwater fish that resembles the bream, introduced into Europe and Asia from North America. Freshwater sunfishes and bluegills are bream. Genus: *Lepomis*. **3.** = **sea bream** [14thC. From Old French *bre(s)me*, ultimately of Germanic origin.]

bream[2] /breem/ (**breams**, **breaming**, **breamed**) *vt*. to clear the shells, seaweed, and mud off the bottom of a ship by heating it to soften the pitch and then scraping away the debris (*archaic*) [Early 17thC. Probably from Middle Dutch *bremme* 'broom, furze'; from the burning of broom as part of the process.]

Bream /breem/, **Julian** (b. 1933) British guitarist and lutenist. He studied under Andres Segovia. Full name **Julian Alexander Bream**

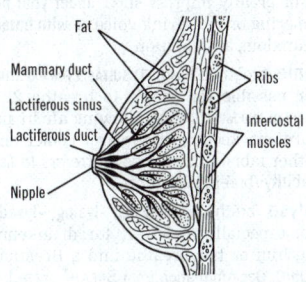

Breast: Cross-section of female breast

Fat, Mammary duct, Lactiferous sinus, Lactiferous duct, Nipple, Ribs, Intercostal muscles

breast /brest/ *n*. **1.** ANAT ORGAN ON HUMAN CHEST soft rounded organs on each side of the chest in women and men. In women the organs are more prominent and produce milk after childbirth. **2.** ZOOL ANIMAL MILK GLAND a gland in mammals corresponding to the human breast **3.** SB'S CHEST the front of the human chest **4.** CLOTHES GARMENT SECTION the part or section of clothing covering the front of the chest **5.** SEAT OF EMOTIONS the chest regarded as the place where human emotions reside (*literary*) ○ *to beat your breast* **6.** ANIMAL'S CHEST the chest of an animal, especially a mammal or bird **7.** MEAT FROM ANIMAL'S CHEST meat from the chest of an animal, especially from a chicken or other poultry **8.** FONT OF NOURISHMENT a source of sustenance or protection (*literary*) **9.** PART STICKING OUT OR UP a part that is rounded, projects, or in some way resembles a breast ▪ *vt*. (**breasts**, **breasting**, **breasted**) **1.** PUSH STH WITH CHEST to touch or push against sth with the chest ○ *managed to breast the tape ahead of her rival* **2.** REACH HILLTOP to reach the summit of a hill **3.** FACE STH BOLDLY to confront a difficulty squarely and boldly and deal with it in a determined way [Old English *brēost*. Ultimately, perhaps, from an Indo-European base denoting swelling.] ◇ **make a clean breast of sth** to confess or admit to sth, especially sth previously denied or withheld

breastbone /brést bōn/ *n*. a long bone running down the front of the chest, flat in many animals but ridged in most birds. In humans, the top seven pairs of ribs are connected to it.

breast-feed (**breast-feeds**, **breast-feeding**, **breast-fed**) *vti*. to feed a baby with milk from the breast

breastplate /brést playt/ *n*. **1.** ARMOUR COVERING CHEST a piece of armour that covers the chest **2.** JUDAISM JEWISH PRIESTLY GARMENT a garment worn over the breast by Jewish high priests in ancient times, set with twelve precious stones representing the twelve tribes of Israel

breaststroke /brést strōk/ *n*. a swimming stroke in which the arms are extended and pulled back together in a circular motion while the legs are thrust out and pulled together —**breaststroke** *vi*. —**breaststroker** *n*.

breastwork /brést wurk/ *n*. in former times, an earth wall built at chest height as a temporary barrier for defence

breath /breth/ *n*. **1.** AIR BREATHED IN AND OUT the air that a person or animal inhales and exhales **2.** AIR EXHALED the air that sb exhales, especially with reference to how it feels or smells to sb **3.** BREATHING OF AIR an inhaling or exhaling of air ○ *take a deep breath* **4.** HINT a faint hint of sth ○ *a breath of scandal* **5.** LIFE the vital force or spirit of a living person or animal **6.** SHORT PAUSE a momentary pause or respite **7.** WAFT a fleeting or slight fragrance or movement of air ○ *not a breath of wind* **8.** SOFT SOUND a sound or whispering that is soft and almost inaudible [Old English *bræþ* 'odour, especially of sth burning or cooking'. Ultimately from an Indo-European base denoting heat. The modern meaning evolved via the notion of exhalation.] ◇ **a breath of fresh air** sb or sth that is refreshingly new and exciting ◇ **catch your breath 1.** to stop breathing for an instant, e.g. from shock or physical pain **2.**

to regain a normal breathing rhythm after exertion ◇ **don't hold your breath!** used to indicate that it is extremely unlikely that sth will happen (*informal*) ◇ **in the same breath** at the same time or shortly afterwards ◇ **out of breath** breathing heavily because of physical exertion ◇ **take sb's breath away** to astonish or greatly impress sb ◇ **under your breath** in a whispering or muttering voice ◇ **with bated breath** full of anxious anticipation

breathable /bréethəb'l/ *adj.* **1.** SUITABLE FOR BREATHING suitable or possible for people to breathe **2.** TEXTILES LETTING AIR IN AND MOISTURE OUT allowing air in and body moisture out, keeping the wearer cooler and drier than other fabrics or clothes do (*refers to fabric*) —**breathability** /bréethə bíllәti/ *n.*

breathalyse /bréthə līz/ (**-lyses, -lysing, -lysed**) *vt.* to test sb, especially a driver, for drunkenness by making him or her breathe into a Breathalyser™ [Mid-20thC. Back-formation from BREATHALYZER.]

Breathalyzer /bréthə līzər/ *tdmk.* a trademark for an apparatus that measures a subject's blood alcohol concentration

breathe /breeth/ (**breathes, breathing, breathed**) *v.* **1.** *vti.* TAKE IN AIR to repeatedly and alternately take in and blow out air in order to stay alive ○ *breathe in deeply* **2.** *vti.* EXPEL SUBSTANCE WITH BREATH to expel a substance, e.g. cigarette smoke, from the mouth or nose along with the breath, or to be exhaled in this way **3.** *vt.* SMELL STH to take in the aroma of sth **4.** *vti.* TAKE IN AIR to take in air, e.g. for combustion or in order to equalize internal and external pressure (*refers to machines*) **5.** *vi.* TEXTILES ALLOW AIR THROUGH to allow air and moisture to pass through fabric or clothing **6.** *vt.* SAY STH SECRETIVELY to say sth in a soft voice or secretively **7.** *vt.* GIVE SB OR STH A QUALITY to instil a particular quality in sb or sth ○ *breathed new life into the group* **8.** *vti.* EXUDE QUALITY to suggest a particular quality in abundance, or to be suggested or displayed noticeably **9.** *vi.* LIVE to be alive **10.** *vi.* DEVELOP FLAVOUR THROUGH EXPOSURE TO AIR to be exposed to air in order to develop flavour (*refers to wine*) **11.** *vti.* PAUSE TO REST to allow a person or animal, e.g. a horse, to pause to rest or catch a breath **12.** *vi.* WAFT to blow softly or move gently [13thC. Formed from BREATH.] ◇ **breathe easy** *or* **easily** to relax and stop worrying about sth or things in general ◇ **breathe your last** to die (*literary*)

breathed /bretht, breethd/ *adj.* **1.** PHON UNVOICED pronounced without vibrating the vocal cords **2.** BREATHING with a particular type of breathing (*usually used in combination*)

breather /bréethər/ *n.* **1.** PAUSE TO REST a short rest while in the middle of doing sth (*informal*) **2.** BREATHING PERSON sb who breathes in a particular way (*used in combination*) ○ *a heavy breather* **3.** VENT a vent in an area or enclosure that is otherwise sealed [Early 20thC. From the idea of stopping for breath.]

breathing /bréething/ *n.* **1.** INHALING AND EXHALING the process of taking air into the lungs and pushing it out again **2.** PHON PRONUNCIATION OF VOWELS IN ANCIENT GREEK in ancient Greek, the pronouncing of an initial vowel with an 'h' sound before it (**rough breathing**), or without an 'h' sound (**smooth breathing**), or either of the symbols indicating these pronunciations

breathing space, **breathing room** *n.* the opportunity to relax or sort out problems without pressures, constraints, interruptions, or interference ○ *Going away should give you some breathing space to sort out any relationship problems.*

breathless /bréthləss/ *adj.* **1.** UNABLE TO BREATHE PROPERLY experiencing difficulty in breathing, or breathing faster than normal, because of physical exertion or illness **2.** WITH SHALLOW BREATHING breathing very shallowly because of intense emotion, e.g. fear or excitement **3.** EXCITING OR INTENSE capable of causing difficulties in breathing because of intense excitement, emotion, or speed **4.** HOT AND WITHOUT BREEZE lacking any air movement or breeze **5.** NOT ALIVE dead and no longer breathing (*literary*) —**breathlessly** *adv.* —**breathlessness** *n.*

breathtaking /bréth tayking/ *adj.* evoking strong emotions, especially excitement, awe, or shock [Mid-20thC] —**breathtakingly** *adv.*

breath test *n.* a test using a device that a person breathes into to determine the level of alcohol in the breath, especially one conducted by police on the driver of a road vehicle

breathy /bréthi/ (**-ier, -iest**) *adj.* **1.** WITH SOUND OF BREATHING with a discernible sound of breathing accompanying spoken words **2.** MUSIC LACKING GOOD BREATH CONTROL without proper control of the breath, which creates an uneven or weak vocal or instrumental sound —**breathily** *adv.* —**breathiness** *n.*

breccia /bréchi ə/ *n.* coarse-grained sedimentary rock made of sharp fragments of rock and stone cemented together by finer material. Breccia is produced by volcanic activity or erosion, including frost shattering. [Late 18thC. Via Italian, 'gravel', from, ultimately, an Indo-European base that also produced English *break*. The underlying sense is 'broken rock'.] —**breccial** *adj.* —**brecciate** /bréchi ayt/ *vti.* —**brecciation** /bréchi áysh'n/ *n.*

Brecht /brekht/, **Bertolt** (1898–1956) German playwright and director. One of the most influential dramatists of the 20th century, he was the author of *The Threepenny Opera* (1928) in collaboration with Kurt Weill, *Mother Courage* (1941), and *The Caucasian Chalk Circle* (1945). After 1948 he worked with the Berliner Ensemble in East Berlin. Full name **Eugene Bertolt Friedrich Brecht**

Brecon Beacons National Park /brékən beekənz/ national park in Powys, Wales, that includes the Black Mountains. The park was created in 1957 and is an important tourist area.

bred[1] /bred/ past tense, past participle of **breed**

bred[2] /bred/ *adj.* raised in a particular manner (*used in combination*) ○ *city-bred*

Breda /breedə/ city in North Brabant Province in the southern Netherlands, near Rotterdam. Population: 129,125 (1994).

brede /breed/ *n.* decorative embroidery or braiding (*archaic*) [Mid-17thC. A variant of BRAID.]

bred-in-the-bone *adj.* **1.** INGRAINED deeply instilled or firmly established **2.** HABITUAL used to describe a habit, especially a bad habit, that has become deeply ingrained over time

breech /breech/ *n.* **1.** ARMS BACK OF GUN BARREL the rear part of the barrel of a rifle or shotgun, near the stock **2.** PART OF PULLEY the lower part of a pulley block, to which the rope, cable, or chain is fixed **3.** ANAT BUTTOCKS the back lower portion of the trunk of the body [Old English *brēc*, plural of *brōc* 'garment covering the thighs and lower trunk'. The modern meanings evolved from the notion of 'lower part'.]

WORD KEY: USAGE

See Usage note at *breach*.

breech birth (*plural* **breech births**) *n.* MED the delivery of a baby with its buttocks, rather than its head, emerging first

breechblock /breech blok/ *n.* the part of a breech-loading gun that is detached from the barrel to allow cartridges to be loaded into the back of the barrel

breechcloth /breech kloth/ (*plural* **-cloths**) *n.* = **loincloth**

breech delivery *n.* = **breech birth**

breeches /bríchiz/, **britches** *npl.* **1.** KNEE-LENGTH TROUSERS trousers with legs that come down to the knee **2.** TROUSERS trousers of any kind (*informal*) [13thC. Plural of BREECH.]

breeches buoy *n.* a piece of equipment used for transferring people between moving ships, consisting of a canvas harness suspended from a pulley and line that links both ships

breeching /bríching, bree-/ *n.* **1.** EQU STRAP ON HORSE'S HARNESS the strap of a harness that passes behind the hindquarters of a horse or donkey **2.** NAVY ROPE SECURING SHIP'S GUN in former times, ropes used to secure guns to the side of a ship to control the recoil **3.** ARMS GUN'S BREECH PARTS parts of a gun that form or make up the breech

breechloader /breech lōdər/ *n.* a gun that is loaded by inserting cartridges through the back of the barrel —**breechloading** *adj.*

breed /breed/ *n.* **1.** BIOL DISTINCT ANIMAL OR PLANT a strain of an animal or plant with identifiable characteristics that distinguish it from other members of its species, especially one whose characteristics are preserved by controlled mating or propagating **2.** SB OR STH OF PARTICULAR TYPE a particular type of thing or person, especially one that can be easily distinguished from other similar things or people ○ *a new breed of managers* ■ *v.* (**breeds, breeding, bred** /bred/, **bred**) **1.** *vti.* BIOL MATE AND PRODUCE YOUNG to mate and give birth to offspring **2.** *vt.* AGRIC RAISE ANIMALS OR PLANTS to reproduce and raise animals or plants, especially for commercial purposes or for shows and competitions **3.** *vt.* GENETICS SELECT ANIMALS OR PLANTS to select animals or plants as part of a process of improving or preserving their special characteristics **4.** *vti.* PRODUCE OR BE PRODUCED to produce or create sth, or be produced or created ○ *Experience breeds confidence.* **5.** *vt.* PHYS PRODUCE NUCLEAR FUEL to make fissionable substances using a breeder reactor [Old English *brēdan* 'to produce or nurture offspring'. Ultimately from an Indo-European base denoting 'heat'; the underlying sense is 'incubation'.]

breeder /breedər/ *n.* **1.** SB WHO BREEDS ANIMALS OR PLANTS sb who raises animals or propagates and grows plants, either to maintain an existing breed or produce a new one **2.** ANIMAL OR PLANT USED FOR BREEDING an animal or plant kept to produce offspring **3.** CAUSAL FACTOR a cause or a source of sth **4.** PHYS = **breeder reactor**

breeder reactor *n.* a nuclear reactor that produces more fuel than it consumes. This kind of reactor is used mainly to produce plutonium.

breeding /breeding/ *n.* **1.** ANCESTRY sb's family or ancestry **2.** REPRODUCTION the mating and producing of young (*often used before a noun*) ○ *prime breeding stock* **3.** GENETICS DEVELOPMENT OF IMPROVED ANIMALS AND PLANTS the development of new types of plants or animals with improved characteristics **4.** UPBRINGING sb's upbringing, education, and training in manners and other social skills, especially an upbringing that produces the polished manners and self-assurance thought typical of the upper classes **5.** PHYS REACTOR'S FUEL PRODUCTION EXCEEDING CONSUMPTION production of fissionable material in a breeder reactor in quantities in excess of the fuel it consumes

breeding ground *n.* **1.** ANIMAL'S MATING AREA an area where animals mate and produce young **2.** ENVIRONMENT ENCOURAGING STH an environment or situation that is likely to produce or encourage a particular phenomenon ○ *The festival is a breeding ground for new comedy talent.*

breeks /breeks/ *npl. Scotland, N England* trousers or breeches (*informal*) [14thC. A variant of BREECHES.]

breeze /breez/ *n.* **1.** METEOROL LIGHT TO MODERATE WIND a wind ranging in strength from light to moderate, with a speed of 6 to 50 kph/4 to 31 mph **2.** STH EASY a task or object that is easily achieved (*informal*) ■ *vi.* (**breezes, breezing, breezed**) GO SOMEWHERE BRISKLY to move quickly and confidently or cheerfully [Mid-16thC. Probably from Spanish *brisa* and Portuguese *briza* 'northeast wind', of unknown origin.]

breeze through *vti.* to do sth quickly and easily

breeze block *n.* a light rectangular block made from a mixture of cement and the ashes of coal and coke, used in the building industry for lightweight walls, e.g. interior walls. US term **cinder block** [*Breeze* from French *braise* 'hot coals' (source of English *braise* and *brazier*)]

breezeway /breez way/ *n. US* a roofed passageway with open sides that connects two buildings, e.g. a house and garage

breezily /breezili/ *adv.* in a lively, cheerful, and relaxed way

breezy /breezi/ (**-ier, -iest**) *adj.* **1.** METEOROL SLIGHTLY WINDY with a light to moderate wind **2.** LIVELY AND CHEERFUL lively, cheerful, and relaxed —**breeziness** *n.*

bregma /brégmə/ (*plural* **-mata** /-mətə/) *n.* the place on the skull at the top of the forehead where the frontal bone and the two parietal bones meet, used as a reference point when measuring skulls [Late 16thC. From Greek, 'front of the head'.] —**bregmatic** /breg máttik/ *adj.*

brei /brī/ (**breis, breiing, breid**) *vi. S Africa* to make the sound of r deep in the back of the throat when speaking Afrikaans (*informal*) [Mid-20thC. Via Afrikaans *bry* from Dutch *brijen*, from *brouwen* 'to speak thickly'.]

brekky /bréki/ (*plural* **-kies**) *n.* breakfast (*informal*) [Early 20thC. Formed from *brek-*, a representation of the pronunciation of the first syllable of BREAKFAST.]

Brel /brel/, **Jacques** (1929–78) Belgian-born French singer and songwriter. His songs included 'Le Bourgeois' and 'Ne me Quitte Pas' and were widely recorded by other singers including Frank Sinatra and Ray Charles.

Bremen /brémmən/ city, major port, and capital of the state of Bremen in northwestern Germany. It is situated on the River Weser, about 69 km/43 mi. from the North Sea. Population: 551,000 (1994).

Bremerhaven /brémmə háafən/ port and city in Bremen State, northwestern Germany, on the estuary of the River Weser and is a major port. Population: 131,200 (1994).

bremsstrahlung /brémz shtraalòong/ *n.* the electromagnetic radiation that is produced by an electrically charged subatomic particle, such as an electron, when it is suddenly slowed down by the electric field of an atomic nucleus [Mid-20thC. From German, from *bremsen* 'to brake' + *Strahlung* 'radiation'.]

Brendan /bréndən/, **St.** (484–577) Irish saint and traveller. He founded the monastery of Clonfert in Co. Galway (561). Known as **the Navigator**

Bren gun /brén-/ *n.* a light machine gun used by British and Commonwealth forces in World War II. It is air-cooled and gas-operated and takes .303 calibre ammunition. [Mid-20thC. *Bren* is a blend of *Brno*, the Czech city where it was originally made, and *Enfield*, a town in southern England where it was subsequently made under licence.]

Brennan /brénnən/, **Christopher** (1870–1932) Australian poet. Noted for his symbolist style, he was the author of *Poems* (1913–14). Full name **Christopher John Brennan**

Brennan, William J., Jr. (1906–97) US Supreme Court justice. During his long Supreme Court Tenure (1956–90) he was known for his dedication to maintaining freedom of speech.

Brenner /brénnər/, **Sydney** (*b.* 1927) South African molecular biologist. He worked on molecular genetics and the DNA helix.

Brenner Pass Alpine mountain pass linking Innsbruck, Austria and Bolzano, Italy. With a maximum elevation of 1,371 m/4,497 ft, it has been an important route between Austria and Italy since antiquity.

Brentano /bren taánō/, **Clemens Maria von** (1778–1842) German writer. He produced poems, stories, and plays such as *The Foundation of Prague* (1815).

brent goose /brént-/, **brent** *n.* a small saltwater goose found along the Pacific coasts of Europe, Asia, and North America that has a dark head and dark underparts and a white band around its neck. It breeds in the Arctic and Siberia, further north than any other goose. Latin name: *Branta bernicula.* US term **brant** [Origin unknown]

Brenton /bréntən/, **Howard** (*b.* 1942) British dramatist. His plays include *Weapons of Happiness* (1976) and *Pravda* (1985, with David Hare).

Brentwood /brént wood/ town northeast of London, in Essex, southeastern England. Population: 49,463 (1991).

bresaola /bre sṓlə, bri zṓlə/ *n.* slices of salt-cured air-dried beef served with a dressing of olive oil, lemon juice, and black pepper [Late 20thC. From Italian, from *brasare* 'to cook slowly'.]

Brescia /bréshə/ city and capital of Brescia Province, Lombardy Region, northern Italy, about 40 km/25 mi. west of Milan. Population: 192,883 (1992).

Bresson /brésson/, **Robert** (*b.* 1907) French film director. His films include *Diary of a Country Priest* (1951) and *The Trial of Joan of Arc* (1962).

Brest /brést/ port and largest city in Finistère Department in the Bretagne Region, western France. Population: 153,099 (1990).

brethren /bréthrən/ plural of **brother** (*archaic*) ■ *npl.* **1.** MEMBERS OF SAME GROUP members of the same family, group, class, or community (*literary or humorous*) ○ *the weaker brethren among us* **2.** MEMBERS OF CHURCH the members, especially male members, of a particular church or other religious group, especially a Protestant Christian denomination (*archaic or literary*) [12thC. From *brōeþre, breþre*, a plural of Old English *brōþor* 'brother'. *Brethren* remained the standard plural of *brother* until the 17thC, when it was superseded by *brothers*.]

Breton /brétton, brétt'n/ *n.* **1.** SB FROM BRITTANY sb who lives in or was born or brought up in the region of Brittany in northwestern France **2.** CELTIC LANGUAGE OF BRITTANY a Celtic language spoken in mostly rural areas of Brittany, and most closely related to Cornish. It is spoken by a little over half a million people. —**Breton** *adj.*

Breton /brétton/, **André** (1896–1966) French poet and essayist. He was a Dadaist and a founder of the Surrealist movement.

breve /breev/ *n.* **1.** PHON MARK OVER SHORT VOWEL a mark ˘ placed over a vowel to show that it has a short sound **2.** POETRY MARK OVER UNSTRESSED POETIC SYLLABLE a mark ˘ that is used to show a short or unstressed syllable in poetry **3.** MUSIC LONG MUSICAL NOTE a musical note that is equal in length to two semibreves [14thC. A variant of BRIEF.]

brevet /brévit/ *n.* (*plural* **-vets**) MILITARY PROMOTION a temporary promotion of a military officer without an increase in pay ■ *vt.* (**-vets, -vetting** *or* **-veting, -vetted** *or* **-veted, -veted** *or* **-vetted**) PROMOTE IN RANK BUT NOT PAY to promote a military officer by brevet [14thC. From French, literally 'little letter', from Old French *brief* 'letter' (source of English *brief*). The modern meaning evolved from the earlier sense 'official letter'.] —**brevetcy** *n.*

breviary /breévi əri/ (*plural* **-ies**) *n.* in the Roman Catholic Church, a book that contains the hymns, psalms, and prayers prescribed for each day [15thC. From Latin *breviarium* 'summary, abridgment', from *breviare* 'to shorten' (source of English *abbreviate* and *abridge*). Originally an abridged version of the psalms.]

brevier /brə veér/ *n.* in the past, a size of printer's type that is approximately equal to modern 8-point [Late 16thC. Via Dutch or German from Latin *breviarium* (see BREVIARY). Said to be from the use of this size of type in a breviary.]

brevity /brévəti/ *n.* **1.** BRIEFNESS shortness in time **2.** USE OF FEW WORDS the economical use of words in speech or writing [15thC. Via Old French *briévete* from the Latin stem *brevitat-*, from *brevis* 'short' (source of English *brief*).]

brew /broo/ *vti.* (**brews, brewing, brewed**) **1.** MAKE BEER to make beer or similar alcoholic drinks by a process of steeping, boiling, and fermenting grain with hops, sugar, and other ingredients **2.** MAKE TEA OR COFFEE to prepare a drink of tea or coffee, or to develop the full flavour that tea or coffee should have before being ready to drink **3.** DEVELOP THREATENINGLY to form, concoct, or develop ominously or threateningly ○ *a scandal was brewing* ■ *n.* **1.** KIND OF BEER a type of beer, e.g. a lager or ale **2.** BREWED BEVERAGE a drink such as coffee or tea or a serving of such a drink (*informal*) **3.** MIXTURE a combination of ingredients or elements of any kind [Old English *breowan*] —**brewer** *n.* —**brewing** *n.*

brew up *vi.* to make tea (*regional informal*)

brewer's yeast *n.* the yeast that is used in brewing beer, also used as a dietary source of vitamins, especially vitamin B. Latin name: *Saccharomyces cerevisiae.*

brewery /broó əri/ (*plural* **-ies**) *n.* a building where beer or a similar drink is brewed, or a company that brews beers

Brewster /broóst'r/, **Sir David** (1781–1868) British physicist. He studied optics and invented the kaleidoscope (1916). Brewster's Law calculates the refraction index of a glass surface.

brewup /broó up/ *n.* a cup or pot of tea (*regional informal*)

Brezhnev /brézh nef/, **Leonid Ilyich** (1906–82) Soviet statesman. Leader of the Soviet Communist Party (1964–82), he exerted strong control over Warsaw Pact countries.

Brian Bórú /brī ən bə róo/ (926?–1014) kng of Ireland. He became king of Leinster in 984 and was acknowledged as ruler of all Ireland 1002–14. He was killed after defeating the Vikings at Clontarf. Known as **Brian Boroimhe, Boru 'Brian of the Tribute'**

Briand /breé aaN/, **Aristide** (1862–1932) French statesman. A socialist politician, he was elected Prime minister 11 times between 1909 and 1929. He shared the Nobel Peace Prize in 1929 for his contribution to the Kellogg-Briand Pact (1928) which outlawed war.

briar[1] /brī ər/ (*plural* **-ars** *or* **-ar**), **brier** (*plural* **-ers** *or* **-er**) *n.* **1.** PLANTS SHRUB OF SOUTHERN EUROPE a shrub that belongs to the heather family and is native to southern Europe. Its hard woody roots are used to make tobacco pipes. Latin name: *Erica arborea.* **2.** KIND OF TOBACCO PIPE a tobacco pipe made from the wood of the roots of the briar [Mid-19thC. From French *bruyère* 'wild heather', ultimately of Gaulish origin.]

WORD KEY: ORIGIN

English has two words *briar.* Both can also be spelt *brier*, and their meanings are similar, so they tend to get confused. One goes back to Old English, when it was applied to any prickly bush, especially the bramble; in modern usage it is applied to a type of wild rose. The other is much more recent. It means 'wild heather', and it was borrowed from French *bruyère.* At first it was spelt *bruyer* in English, but because of its similarity to ***briar*** in the 'wild rose' sense, it too came to be spelt ***briar.*** It is the root of this second type of briar that is used to make pipes.

briar[2] /brī ər/, **brier** *n.* a thorny wild plant, especially a trailing rose [Old English *brēr*, of unknown origin] —**briery** *adj.*

briard /bree áar, bree áard/ *n.* a dog belonging to an ancient French breed of strong sheepdogs with stiff and slightly wavy coats of a single colour, usually black [Mid-20thC. From French, literally 'of Brie', an area of northern France where the dog originated.]

Briareus /brī áiri əss/ *n.* in Greek mythology, a giant with fifty heads who fought alongside Zeus against the Titans

briarwood /brī ər wòod/ *n.* wood from the root of the European briar, used for making tobacco pipes

bribe /brīb/ *vti.* (**bribes, bribing, bribed**) PERSUADE SB WITH ENTICEMENT to give sb money or some other incentive to do sth, especially sth illegal or dishonest ■ *n.* INCENTIVE TO PERSUADE SB money or some other incentive that is given to persuade sb to do sth, especially sth illegal or dishonest [14thC. From Old French *briber* or *brimber* 'to beg', from *bribe* 'morsel of food given to a beggar', of unknown origin.] —**briber** *n.* —**bribable** *adj.*

bribery /brībəri/ (*plural* **-ies**) *n.* the offering of money or other incentives to persuade sb to do sth, especially sth dishonest or illegal

bric-a-brac /bríkə brak/ *n.* small, ornamental objects that are of interest or sentimental value but of little monetary value [Mid-19thC. From French, from the obsolete phrase *à bric et à brac* 'at random' (in which *brac* is a fanciful alteration of *bric* 'piece').]

brick /brik/ *n.* **1.** BUILDING HARD BLOCK USED FOR CONSTRUCTION WORK a rectangular block of clay or a similar material that is baked until it is hard and is used for building houses, walls, and other large permanent structures **2.** INDUST BRICKS OR THEIR MATERIAL bricks collectively, or the material they are made of **3.** CHILD'S BUILDING BLOCK a child's wooden or plastic block used with others to make shapes or structures **4.** BLOCK OF STH a rectangular block of sth, e.g. ice cream **5.** RELIABLE SUPPORTIVE PERSON sb who is helpful or supportive in times of difficulty (*informal dated*) ■ *vt.* (**bricks, bricking, bricked**) **1.** MAKE STH WITH BRICKS to use bricks to build sth or as a liner or paving material for sth **2.** CLOSE UP WITH BRICKS to close sth up or wall sth off with bricks and mortar ○ *the window had been bricked up* [15thC. From Middle Dutch *bricke*, later reinforced by French *brique* (perhaps borrowed from Middle Dutch). Ultimate origin uncertain: perhaps literally 'fragment'.] ◇ **hit a brick wall** to encounter an insurmountable difficulty

brickbat /brík bat/ n. **1.** CRITICISM harshly unfavourable criticism **2.** PIECE OF STH HARD a broken fragment of sth hard, e.g. a piece of a brick, used as a missile [Mid-16thC. *Bat* from *bat* 'piece (of brick)', which is probably the same word as BAT.]

brickie /bríki/ n. a bricklayer (*informal*)

bricklayer /brík layər/ n. sb trained to construct houses, walls, and other large permanent structures by cementing bricks together with mortar —**brick-laying** n.

brick-red adj. of a warm brownish-red colour similar to that of red clay bricks —**brick red** n.

brick veneer n. Aus an external wall that consists of a timber frame with a decorative facing of bricks (*hyphenated when used before a noun*)

brickwork /brík wurk/ n. **1.** STRUCTURE BUILT FROM BRICK sth, e.g. a wall, building, or walk that is made up of bricks **2.** BRICKLAYER'S TECHNIQUE the technique or skill of laying bricks

brickyard /brík yaard/ n. a place where bricks are made, stored, or sold

bricolage /bree kō laazh, bríkō-/ n. sth that is made or put together with whatever materials happen to be available [Mid-20thC. From French, from *bricoler* 'to do odd jobs', from *bricole* (see BRICOLE).]

bricole /brík'l, bri kốl/ n. **1.** CUE GAMES TYPE OF BILLIARDS SHOT in billiards, a shot where the cue ball touches the cushion after hitting the target ball and before hitting another ball **2.** ARMS ANCIENT MILITARY CATAPULT a catapult that ancient and medieval soldiers used to launch stones **3.** MIL SOLDIER'S HARNESS FOR HAULING GUNS in former times, a harness worn by soldiers for hauling guns [Early 16thC. Via French from Provençal *bricola* or Italian *briccola*, of unknown origin.]

bridal /bríd'l/ adj. for or associated with brides or weddings [By folk etymology (from BRIDE and -AL) from Old English *bryd-ealu* 'wedding festival at which much ale is drunk', literally 'bride-ale']

bridal wreath n. a shrub with arching branches that produces a mass of small white flowers in spring. Genus: *Spiraea*.

bride /brīd/ n. a woman who is about to marry or has just married [Old English *bryd*]

bridegroom /bríd groom, -groŏm/ n. a man who is about to marry or has just married [By folk etymology (from GROOM) from Old English *brýdguma*, literally 'bride-man', from *guma* 'man', which ultimately from an Indo-European word meaning 'earth', which also produced English *hominid*]

bride price n. in some societies, a payment in the form of money or property made by the groom to the bride or her family

bridesmaid /brídz mayd/ n. a girl or woman who helps the bride on her wedding day

bridewell /bríd wel/ n. a prison or other place of punishment (*literary*) [Mid-16thC. Named after *Bridewell* prison in the City of London, which stood by (St) Bride's Well.]

bridge[1] /brij/ n. **1.** CIV ENG STRUCTURE ALLOWING PASSAGE ACROSS OBSTACLE a structure that is built above and across a river, road, or other obstacle to allow people or vehicles to cross it **2.** LINK OR MEANS OF APPROACH sth that provides a link, connection, or means of coming together **3.** SHIPPING SHIP'S CONTROL ROOM OR PLATFORM the platform or room on a ship or other vessel from which the captain controls its course **4.** DENT PARTIAL FALSE TEETH a set of one or more false teeth that act as a replacement for missing natural teeth. It can be permanently anchored to natural teeth (**fixed bridge**), or set into a metal appliance and temporarily clipped on to natural teeth (**removable bridge**). **5.** ANAT TOP OF NOSE the top part of the nose between the eyes **6.** OPHTHALMOL PART OF GLASSES the part of a pair of glasses that connects the two lenses together at the front and rests on the nose **7.** MUSIC PART OF STRINGED INSTRUMENT the part of a stringed instrument that keeps the strings away from the body. It is high and curved on a violin but shallow and straight on a guitar. **8.** MUSIC CONNECTING PASSAGE a transitional or connecting section in a musical work **9.** CUE GAMES CUE REST WITH HIGH END a long-handled support for a player's cue in snooker and billiards, with a high arching end **10.** CUE GAMES HAND USED AS REST the player's hand used as a rest for the cue in billiards **11.** ELEC ENG PART OF ELECTRICAL CIRCUIT a part of an electrical circuit fitted with a device that measures electrical resistance or capacitance ■ vt. (**bridges, bridging, bridged**) **1.** CIV ENG BUILD BRIDGE ACROSS OBSTACLE to build a bridge across an obstacle to allow people or vehicles to get across it **2.** CREATE UNDERSTANDING BETWEEN PEOPLE to create a means of communication or understanding between people or a means of reconciling their differences [Old English *brycg*, perhaps literally 'structure made of logs'] —**bridge-able** adj. ◇ **build bridges** to try to make friends with sb who has previously been an enemy ◇ **burn your bridges** to do sth that makes it difficult or impossible to return to your former position ◇ **cross that bridge when you come to it** to think about or worry about sth only when it becomes a reality or a priority

bridge[2] /brij/ n. any of several card games derived from whist and played with one deck of cards divided between four players who play in two pairs. The term is generally used to refer to contract bridge, which is the most popular form of the game. [Late 19thC. Origin uncertain: perhaps from assumed Turkish *bir-ūç*, literally 'one three', since in the game of bridge one hand is exposed and three are hidden.]

bridgeboard /brij bawrd/ n. a notched board at either side of a staircase, supporting the horizontal and vertical boards that form the steps

bridgehead /brij hed/ n. **1.** END OF BRIDGE the area immediately surrounding the end of a bridge **2.** MIL DEFENSIVE MILITARY POSITION a fortified position from which troops defend the end of a bridge that is nearest to the enemy **3.** MIL ARMY'S POSITION SEIZED IN ENEMY TERRITORY a forward position seized by advancing troops in enemy territory and serving as a basis for further advances **4.** PIONEERING FOOTHOLD any position from which further advancement can be attained

bridge loan n. US = bridging loan

Bridgend /brij énd/ county in southern Wales that replaced the southern part of Mid Glamorgan in 1996. Capital: Bridgend. Population: 11,229 (1991). Area: 264 sq. km/102 sq. mi.

Bridge of Sighs n. a covered canal bridge of carved stone in Venice, Italy, built in the late 16th century between the Doge's Palace and the prison. Its name is believed to come from the sighs of prisoners crossing the bridge to be tried or executed.

bridge roll n. a small thin soft bread roll [Perhaps from its being eaten at afternoon bridge parties]

Bridges /bríjjiz/, **Robert** (1844–1930) British poet. The author of *Eros and Psyche* (1885), *The Spirit of Man* (1916), and *The Testament of Beauty* (1929), he was appointed Poet Laureate in 1913.

Bridget /bríjjit/, **St** (453?–524?) Irish abbess. She founded four monasteries for women in Ireland.

Bridgetown /brij town/ capital, main port, and tourist centre of Barbados in the West Indies. Population: 6,720 (1990).

bridgework /brij wurk/ n. **1.** WORK OF FITTING FALSE TEETH provision of false teeth to replace missing or removed natural teeth **2.** = bridge[1]

bridging loan n. money borrowed temporarily until a specific event occurs, especially a loan to finance the purchase of a property while another is being sold. US term **bridge loan**

Bridgman /bríjmən/, **P.W.** (1882–1961) US physicist. He won the Nobel Prize in physics in 1946 in recognition of his work on thermodynamics. Full name **Percy Williams Bridgman**

Bridgwater /brij wawtər/ historic town in Somerset, southwestern England. Population: 34,610 (1991).

bridie /brídi/ n. Scotland a meat pie made with a circle of puff pasty folded over a meat filling

Bridie /brídi/, **James** (1888–1951) British dramatist. The founder of the Citizens' Theatre in Glasgow, his plays include *The Anatomist* (1931) and *Dr Angelus* (1947). Real name **Henry Mavor Osborne**

bridle /bríd'l/ n. **1.** EQU HARNESS FOR HORSE'S HEAD a set of leather straps fitted to a horse's head and incorporating the bit and the reins **2.** RESTRAINING THING sth that acts as a control or restraint ■ v. (**-dles, -dling, -dled**) **1.** vt. EQU PUT BRIDLE ON HORSE to provide a horse with a bridle **2.** vi. SHOW ANGER OR INDIGNATION to react with slight anger or indignation, sometimes by rearing the head **3.** vt. EXERCISE CONTROL OR RESTRAINT to show restraint in expressing a feeling or control or in curbing sth [Old English *brídel*, ultimately from a prehistoric Germanic base meaning 'to move jerkily from side to side', which is also the ancestor of English *braid*]

bridle path, **bridleway** n. a path or trail for horse riding

Brie /bree/ n. a type of soft cow's-milk cheese with a whitish rind, originally made in Brie in north-eastern France. It is similar to Camembert, but milder in flavour.

brief /breef/ adj. **1.** NOT LENGTHY lasting for only a short time ◇ *a brief conversation* **2.** CONCISE containing only the necessary information without any extra details **3.** CLOTHES SCANTY leaving much of the wearer's body exposed **4.** CURT curt or abrupt speech or conversation ■ n. **1.** SYNOPSIS OF DOCUMENTS a digest or synopsis of a larger document or group of documents **2.** BRIEFING a briefing, or the information conveyed during one **3.** ASSIGNED DUTIES the details of what sb's job or duties involve **4.** LAW SUMMARY OF LEGAL CASE FOR BARRISTER a summary of a client's case prepared for the barrister who will deal with it in court **5.** LAW LEGAL REPRESENTATIVE a legal representative, especially a barrister (*informal*) **6.** CHR PAPAL LETTER a letter from the Pope, less formal than a papal bull ■ **briefs** npl. SNUG UNDERWEAR FOR LOWER BODY men's or women's close-fitting underwear that covers the buttocks and genital area entirely, as distinct from boxer shorts or camiknickers ■ vt. (**briefs, briefing, briefed**) **1.** GIVE INFORMATION TO PREPARE SB to give sb all the necessary information about sth in preparation for a discussion or decision. ◇ **debrief 2.** SUMMARIZE STH to make a summary of sth, especially a written summary [13thC. Via Old French from Latin *brevis* 'short' (source also of English *abbreviate*, *abridge*, and *brevity*).] —**briefer** n. —**briefly** adv. —**briefness** n.

— **WORD KEY: CULTURAL NOTE** —

Brief Encounter, a film by English director David Lean (1945). Noted for its fine central performances by Celia Johnson and Trevor Howard, it tells the story of a un-fulfilled extramarital romance between a housewife and a doctor.

Beam   Cantilever   Arch

Suspension   Portal   Muti-span beam

Bridge

Briefcase

briefcase /bréef kayss/ *n.* a small rectangular case with a handle, used for carrying books and papers

briefing /bréefing/ *n.* **1.** MEETING TO CONVEY INFORMATION a meeting held to provide information about the main facts of an issue or a situation **2.** INFORMATION FROM MEETING the information conveyed at a briefing

brier *n.* = briar¹

brig¹ /brig/ *n.* **1.** SAILING SHIP a two-masted sailing ship with square-rigged sails on both masts **2.** *US* SHIP'S PRISON a secure area in a ship of the US Navy, which can be used as a prison while the ship is at sea **3.** *US* MILITARY PRISON a building or part of a building that is used as a prison in a US military installation [Early 18thC. Shortening of BRIGANTINE.]

brig² /brig/ *n. N England, Scotland* a bridge [13thC. Alteration of BRIDGE.]

Brig. *abbr.* **1.** brigadier **2.** brigade

brigade /bri gáyd/ *n.* **1.** MILITARY UNIT a military unit consisting of two or more combat battalions or regiments and associated support units. It is smaller than a division and is commanded by a brigadier. **2.** GROUP WITH COMMON GOAL OR CHARACTERISTIC a group of people organized to achieve a particular goal, or characterized by a common trait such as attitude, background, appearance, or activities ■ *vt.* (-gades, -gading, -gaded) ORGANIZE INTO A TASK FORCE to organize a group of people in order to achieve a particular goal [Mid-17thC. Via French from Italian *brigata* 'military company', from *brigare* 'to contend, brawl', from *briga* 'strife', of unknown origin.]

─── WORD KEY: CULTURAL NOTE ───
The Charge of the Light Brigade, a poem by the English poet Lord Alfred Tennyson (1845). Based on a contemporary newspaper report, it describes a suicidal attack of the British Light Brigade the Russian army at Balaclava in the Crimea, on October 25, 1854. While acknowledging that the charge was a military blunder, Tennyson celebrates its heroism.

brigade major *n.* the chief staff officer of a brigade, not necessarily holding the rank of major

brigadier /brígga déer/ *n.* **1.** HIGH-RANKING MILITARY OFFICER an officer in the British Army or Royal Marines who ranks above a colonel and below a major general and usually commands a brigade **2.** HIST NAPOLEONIC ARMY OFFICER a noncommissioned officer in the French army at the time of Napoleon [Late 17thC. From French, formed from *brigade* (see BRIGADE).]

brigadier general (*plural* **brigadiers general**), **brigadier** (*plural* **-diers**) *n.* in the United States and Canada, an officer in the Army, Air Force, or Marines who ranks above a colonel and below a major general

brigalow /brígga lō/ (*plural* **-lows** *or* **-low**) *n.* an Australian acacia tree that grows in the semi-arid regions of northern New South Wales and Queensland. Latin name: *Acacia harpophylla*. [Mid-19thC. Origin uncertain: perhaps from Kamilaroi *burigal*.]

brigand /bríggand/ *n.* a bandit operating in wild or isolated terrain, usually as a member of a roving band (*dated*) [14thC. Via Old French from Italian *brigante*, originally 'foot-soldier', from the present participle of *brigare* (see BRIGADE).] **—brigandage** *n.* **—brigandism** *n.* **—brigandry** *n.*

brigandine /bríggan deen/ *n.* a coat of flexible medieval body armour consisting of metal links or sheets attached to fabric or leather [15thC. Directly or via Old French from Italian *brigantina*, from *brigante* (see BRIGAND).]

brigantine /bríggən teen, -tīn/ *n.* a two-masted sailing ship with square-rigged sails on the foremast and fore-and-aft sails on the mainmast [Early 16thC. Directly or via Old French *brigandine* from Italian *brigantino* 'fighting ship', from *brigante* (see BRIGAND).]

Brig. Gen. *abbr.* brigadier general

Briggs /brigz/, **Henry** (1561–1630) English mathematician. He was the first Savilian Professor of Geometry at Oxford and worked with John Napier on logarithms.

bright /brīt/ *adj.* **1.** SHOWING LIGHT reflecting or giving off strong light ○ *It was a bright moonlit night.* **2.** ILLUMINATED illuminated with strong natural or artificial light **3.** INTENSELY COLOURED intense in colour, or decorated with intense colours ○ *bright blue* **4.** INTELLIGENT showing an ability to think, learn, or respond quickly ○ *she was brighter than other children of her age.* **5.** CHEERFUL cheerful and lively ○ *he seems much brighter this morning* **6.** PROMISING SUCCESS promising a successful outcome **7.** ADMIRABLE deserving admiration and glory ○ *one of the brightest stars of the theatre* **8.** CLEAR-SOUNDING used to describe sounds with a clear crisp quality and little harmonic resonance **9.** BEAUTIFUL remarkably beautiful or handsome (*archaic*) ■ *adv.* WITH LIGHT with a great deal of light ■ **brights** *npl. US* HEADLIGHTS the headlights on a motor vehicle when set to full beam [Old English *beorht*. Ultimately from an Indo-European word meaning 'shine'.] **—brightish** *adj.*

─── WORD KEY: SYNONYMS ───
See Synonyms at *intelligent*.

─── WORD KEY: CULTURAL NOTE ───
Bright Lights, Big City, a novel by US writer Jay McInerney (1984). This is a leading example of a type of hip urban fiction that flourished in the 1980s. The hectic yuppy milieu in New York City that it describes, its inhabitants apparently having it all—glamorous careers, easy money, and easier sex—turns out to be unexpectedly fragile, however, and the novel is at heart a chronicle of loss and redemption.

Bright /brīt/, **John** (1811–89) British statesman. A leading radical, he was associated with the Anti-Corn Law League and the Reform Act of 1867.

brighten /brīt'n/ (-ens, -ening, -ened) *v.* **1.** *vi.* LOOK HAPPY to become enthusiastic, lively, or happy ○ *She brightened visibly at the suggestion.* **2.** *vt.* ADD INTEREST to add colour or interest to sth ○ *their visit brightened the day for us.* **3.** *vi.* BECOME CLEARER to become less overcast or rainy ○ *It's supposed to brighten this afternoon.* **4.** *vti.* ILLUMINATE OR GET LIGHTER to increase the amount of light emitted or reflected, or to be filled with an increasing amount of light **5.** *vti.* MAKE OR BECOME MORE PROMISING to make sth seem more promising or to appear more likely to be successful [Old English *gebeorhtnan*]

brighten up *vti.* to make sb or sth that is dark, colourless, or gloomy become brighter, or to become lighter, more colourful, or livelier

brightener /brīt'nər/ *n.* a chemical compound added to some washing powders and liquids to make white and light-coloured fabrics appear brighter by converting some of the ultraviolet radiation into visible light

bright lights *npl.* the entertainment and activities of a big city (*informal*)

brightly /brītli/ *adv.* **1.** WITH A LOT OF LIGHT in a way that reflects or gives out a great deal of light **2.** CHEERFULLY in a way that appears happy, alert, and animated ○ *'Shall we go?' said Sam brightly.* **3.** VIVIDLY in vivid and intense colours **4.** WITH A CLEAR SOUND with a clear and crisp sound quality [Old English *beorhtlice*]

bright nebula *n.* a cloud of material in space that appears bright because it is illuminated by the stars around it

brightness /brītnəss/ *n.* **1.** STRONG LIGHT the intensity of light reflected or given off by sth **2.** CLEVERNESS the ability to think, learn, or respond quickly **3.** CHEERFUL MANNER a happy or animated attitude or manner **4.** PROMISE OF SUCCESS the promise of a successful outcome **5.** CLARITY a clear crisp sound quality **6.** LIGHT EMITTED IN PARTICULAR DIRECTION the intensity of light (**luminosity**) emitted by an object in a particular direction, used

by an observer to compare the luminosity of other visible objects [Old English *beorhtnes*]

Brighton /brīt'n/ seaside resort on the English Channel in East Sussex, southern England. Population: 133,400 (1991).

Bright's disease /brīts-/ *n.* an inflammatory disease of the kidneys, such as glomerulonephritis (*dated*) [Mid-19thC. Named after the English physician Richard *Bright* (1789–1858), who first diagnosed it.]

bright spark *n.* a clever or ingenious person (*informal; used ironically*) ○ *Some bright spark had the idea of hiding my glasses.*

brightwork /brīt wurk/ *n.* fittings or trimmings of polished metal or varnished wood, e.g. on a vehicle or boat

bright young thing *n.* **1.** YOUNG CLEVER PERSON a person who is thought of as being young, clever, and likely to be successful **2.** TWENTIES SOCIALITE a member of a young and fashionable social set in the 1920s and 1930s who regarded themselves as setting new fashions in dress, music, behaviour, and style

brill¹ /bril/ (*plural* **brill** *or* **brills**) *n.* an edible European flatfish that is closely related to the turbot. Latin name: *Scophthalmus rhombus*. [15thC. Origin unknown.]

brill² /bril/ *adj., interj.* used to express satisfaction with sb or sth (*informal*) [Late 20thC. Shortening of BRILLIANT.]

Brillat-Savarin /brée yaa sávvə raN/, **Anthelme** (1755–1826) French politician and writer. His *Physiology of Taste* (1825) is a classic of gastronomic literature. Full name **Jean Anthelme Brillat-Savarin**

brilliance /bríllyənss/, **brilliancy** /-yənssi/ *n.* **1.** BRIGHTNESS dazzling brightness **2.** GREAT ABILITY OR SKILL exceptional ability, skill, or success ○ *the technical brilliance of the pianist's performance* **3.** SPLENDOUR imposing splendour

brilliant /bríllyənt/ *adj.* **1.** EXTREMELY BRIGHT OR RADIANT extremely bright or radiant ○ *brilliant sunshine* **2.** VIVID vividly coloured ○ *a brilliant shade of green* **3.** INTELLIGENT OR TALENTED showing exceptional intelligence, skill, or talent ○ *a brilliant mathematician* **4.** EXCELLENT distinguished by excellence **5.** MAGNIFICENT imposing in splendour and magnificence ■ *adj., interj.* GREAT used to express great satisfaction with sb or sth (*informal*) ■ *n.* BRILLIANT-CUT GEMSTONE a diamond or other gemstone cut with many facets to maximize brilliance [Late 17thC. From French *brillant*, the present participle of *briller* 'to shine', from Italian *brillare*, of uncertain origin: perhaps from, ultimately, Latin *berillus* 'precious stone' (source of English *beryl*).] **—brilliantly** *adv.* **—brilliantness** *n.*

brilliant-cut *adj.* used to describe a gemstone that is cut into a multifaceted shape intended to maximize brilliance while minimizing loss of weight. A brilliant-cut gemstone is shaped like two polygonal pyramids joined base to base, with the point of the upper pyramid cut off to form a large flat facet. ○ *a brilliant-cut diamond*

brilliantine /bríllyən teen/ *n.* **1.** HAIR OIL an oily hair cream used by men to keep their hair in place and make it look glossy **2.** FABRIC a lightweight fabric with a lustrous sheen, often made from cotton woven with mohair or worsted [Late 19thC. From French *brillantine*, from *brillant* (see BRILLIANT).]

brim /brim/ *n.* **1.** HAT EDGE the rim around the edge of a hat, shaped to stand out from the head **2.** TOP EDGE the top edge of a container such as a cup or bowl ■ *v.* (**brims, brimming, brimmed**) **1.** *vti.* BE FULL TO THE TOP to fill sth or to be full to the top edge ○ *The cup was brimming with hot coffee.* **2.** *vi.* BURST to have an apparently boundless supply of sth ○ *She was brimming with ideas.* **3.** *vi.* OVERFLOW to be so full as to be overflowing ○ *eyes brimming with tears* [13thC. Origin uncertain: perhaps from a prehistoric Germanic base that also produced English *bear* 'to carry'. It originally meant 'edge'; 'hat edge' first appears in Shakespeare.] **—brimless** *adj.*

brimful /brímfŏŏl/ *adj.* **1.** FULL TO THE TOP full to the top edge of sth **2.** FULLY SUPPLIED WITH with an apparently boundless supply of sth ○ *brimful of energy*

brimstone /brím stōn/ *n.* **1. SULPHUR** sulphur (*archaic*) **2. brimstone, brimstone butterfly YELLOW BUTTERFLY** a medium-sized butterfly found in gardens and woodlands in Europe and Asia. The male is bright yellow and the female is greenish-white. Latin name: *Gonepteryx rhamni.* [12thC. Literally 'burning stone', formed from Old English *byrne* 'burning', from *birnan* (see BURN).]

brimstone butterfly *n.* = **brimstone** *n.* 2 [From its yellow wings, the colour of sulphur]

Brindisi /brin deézi/ capital of Brindisi Province in the Apulia Region, southern Italy. It is a port and important ferry terminal for ships carrying tourist traffic to Greece. Population: 92,800 (1990).

brindle /brínd'l/ *adj.* = **brindled** ■ *n.* **BRINDLED COLOURING** brindled colouring [Late 17thC. Back-formation from BRINDLED.]

brindled /brínd'ld/, **brindle** /-d'l/ *adj.* tawny brown or grey marked with darker streaks or patches [Late 17thC. Alteration of earlier *brinded* (influenced by GRIZZLED or SPECKLED), of uncertain origin: probably from a Scandinavian word meaning 'marked as by burning'.]

Brindley /bríndli/, **James** (1716–72) British engineer. He built 584 km/365 mi. of canals in England, including the first canal, from Worsley to Manchester completed in 1772.

brine /brīn/ *n.* **1. SALT WATER FOR PRESERVING** water containing a significant amount of salt, used for curing, preserving, and developing flavour in food **2. SEA WATER** the salt water of the sea (*literary*) **3. STRONG SALT SOLUTION** a strong salt solution ■ *vt.* **(brines, brining, brined) TREAT STH WITH SALT WATER** to preserve, can, pickle, or soak sth in salt water [Old English *brīne*, of unknown origin] —**brinish** *adj.*

Brinell hardness /bri nél-/ *n.* the hardness of a metal or alloy, determined by pressing a steel ball into its surface under standard pressure and measuring the surface area of the resulting indentation [Early 20thC. Named after the Swedish engineer Johan *Brinell* (1849–1925), who devised the method.]

Brinell hardness number *n.* a number expressing the hardness of a metal or alloy. It is the ratio of the pressure applied to a steel ball forced into the surface of the metal to the surface area of the resulting indentation.

brine shrimp *n.* a small crustacean that lives in salt lakes and brine pools. Brine shrimp are used as food for aquarium fish. Genus: *Artemia.*

bring /bring/ **(brings, bringing, brought** /brawt/**)** *v.* **1.** *vt.* **TAKE SB OR STH ALONG** to come from one place to another with sb or sth ○ *Please bring me a glass of water.* **2.** *vt.* **ATTRACT STH** to draw sth to yourself or another person ○ *This charm is supposed to bring luck.* **3.** *vt.* **MAKE STH HAPPEN** to cause sth to take place ○ *The heavy rain brought flooding.* **4.** *vt.* **CAUSE TO BE IN A PARTICULAR STATE** to force sth or sb to arrive at a particular situation or condition ○ *The scandal brought his career to a halt.* **5.** *vt.* **CAUSE TO ENTER MIND** to cause sth to enter sb's mind ○ *Seeing you brings memories of good times.* **6.** *vr.* **MAKE YOURSELF DO STH** to persuade or force yourself to do sth (*usually with negatives or in questions*) ○ *She still can't bring herself to think about the tragedy.* **7.** *vt.* **SELL FOR PARTICULAR PRICE** to be sold for a particular price **8.** *vt.* LAW **BEGIN LEGAL ACTION** to begin a legal action **9.** *vt.* LAW **PRESENT EVIDENCE** to present evidence before a court [Old English *bringan.* Ultimately from an Indo-European word that also produced English *bier, offer,* and *paraphernalia.*] —**bringer** *n.*

bring about *vt.* to make sth happen

bring back *vt.* **1. EVOKE MEMORIES** to evoke memories of sth forgotten **2. RESTORE** to restore sth that has been discontinued ○ *widespread support for bringing back on-the-spot fines*

bring down *vt.* **1. TOPPLE STH** to cause the downfall of an authority or institution **2. KILL OR WOUND** to make a person or animal fall by wounding or killing it **3.** *Can, ANZ* POL **PRESENT A BILL** to present a bill or other piece of legislation in a parliament

bring forth *vt.* **1. GIVE BIRTH** to bear young **2. PRODUCE FRUIT** to produce fruit or flowers

bring forward *vt.* **1. BRING CLOSER IN TIME** to move sth, e.g. an appointment, to an earlier date or time **2. SUGGEST FOR DISCUSSION OR CONSIDERATION** to offer sth for discussion or consideration **3.** ACCT **CARRY AMOUNT TO NEXT PAGE** to carry a sum from one column or page to the next

bring in *vt.* **1. INTRODUCE STH** to introduce sth, e.g. a new policy or law **2. EARN OR ACQUIRE STH** to acquire money as profits, pay, or interest ○ *She barely brings in enough to live on.* **3.** LAW **PRESENT STH IN COURT** to present sth in a court of law

bring off *vt.* **1. COMPLETE STH** to succeed in doing sth difficult **2.** to cause sb to have an orgasm (*slang taboo*)

bring on *vt.* **1. CAUSE** to be the cause of sth happening or appearing ○ *exhaustion brought on by overwork* **2. ENCOURAGE DEVELOPMENT** to further the development of a quality, or of the person having it

bring out *vt.* **1. MAKE KNOWN** to make sth known **2. CALL ATTENTION TO** to emphasize a quality in sb or sth ○ *That outfit brings out the red in your hair.* **3. INTRODUCE FOR SALE** to produce or issue sth for sale to the public ○ *The company has just brought out a new version.* **4. INTRODUCE TO SOCIETY** to introduce a debutante to society

bring round, bring around *vt.* **1. ALTER OPINION** to sway sb's opinion or thinking ○ *We'll bring them round eventually* **2. REVIVE** to revive a person who has lost consciousness

bring to *vt.* **1. REVIVE** to restore sb to consciousness **2.** NAUT **TURN SHIP INTO WIND** to head a boat or ship into the wind in order to slow it down or stop it

bring up *vt.* **1. RAISE SUBJECT** to raise a subject for discussion **2. REAR A CHILD** to provide care, training, and education for a child until maturity **3. VOMIT** to cough sth up or to expel it from the stomach through the mouth **4. MAKE STH STOP SUDDENLY** to cause sb or sth to come to a standstill

bring-and-buy sale *n.* a sale, usually organized to raise funds for a school, church, or charity, in which people bring things to sell and buy things others have brought

brinjal /brínjəl/ *n. S Asia* an aubergine [Early 17thC. From Indian English, alteration of Portuguese *berinjela*, from, ultimately, Arabic *al-bāḏinjān.*]

brink /bringk/ *n.* **1. VERGE OF STH CRUCIAL** the crucial point in a situation when sth disastrous or momentous is about to happen ○ *teetering on the brink of bankruptcy* **2. EDGE OF STH** the very edge of sth, e.g. a steep drop or a river bank [13thC. From Old Norse *brekka*, literally 'slope'.]

brinkmanship /bríngkmən ship/ *n.* the practice, especially in international relations, of taking a dispute to the verge of conflict in the hope of forcing the opposition to make concessions

briny /brīni/ *adj.* **(-ier, -iest) OF SEA WATER** relating to, containing, or tasting like sea water ■ *n.* **SEA** the sea —**brininess** *n.*

brio /breé ō/ *n.* energy or vigour (*literary*) [Mid-18thC. From Italian.]

brioche /bri ósh/ *n.* a sweet French bread roll made from a dough enriched with eggs and butter [Early 19thC. From French, formed from Old French *brier* 'to knead'.]

briolette /breé ō lét/ *n.* a gem in the shape of a teardrop or oval that is cut with long triangular facets over its entire surface [Mid-19thC. From French, of uncertain origin: perhaps, in allusion to its shape, an alteration of *brignolette* 'little dried plum', named after the French city *Brignoles*, where the plums are produced.]

briquette /bri két/, **briquet** *n.* **COMPRESSED FUEL BLOCK** a small block of compressed material, e.g. charcoal, sawdust, or coal dust, that is burned as fuel for cooking or heating ■ *vt.* **(-quettes, -quetting, -quetted; -quets, -quetting, -quetted) FORM INTO BRIQUETTES** to form a material into rectangular blocks [Late 19thC. From French, literally 'little brick', formed from *brique* (see BRICK).]

bris /briss/, **brith** /brit/ *n.* the religious circumcision ceremony for Jewish males [Early 20thC. From Hebrew *bĕriṯ (mīlāh)*, literally 'covenant (of circumcision)'.]

Brisbane /brízbən/ city on the Brisbane River and the capital of Queensland, eastern Australia. Population: 1,291,117 (1996).

brisk /brisk/ *adj.* **1. QUICK** done quickly and energetically ○ *a brisk walk* **2. HURRIED** speaking or behaving in an abrupt way ○ *a brisk reply* **3. BUSY** showing or experiencing much activity ○ *business was brisk* **4. INVIGORATING** refreshingly cool ○ *brisk autumn days* ■ *vti.* **(brisks, brisking, brisked) BECOME LIVELY** to become more active or lively or to liven sth up ○ *Business brisks up in summer.* [Late 16thC. Origin uncertain: probably from French *brusque* (see BRUSQUE).] —**briskly** *adv.* —**briskness** *n.*

brisken /brískən/ **(-ens, -ening, -ened)** *vti.* to become faster or livelier or to make sth brisker ○ *She briskened her pace.*

brisket /brískit/ *n.* **1. BREAST MEAT** a cut of meat, especially of beef, taken from an animal's breast **2. BREAST OF ANIMAL** the breast of a four-legged animal [14thC. Origin uncertain: perhaps formed from Old Norse *brjósk* 'cartilage, gristle'.]

brisling /bríssling, brízz-/ (*plural* **-ling** *or* **-lings**) *n.* a small edible fish of the herring family that is smoked and canned in oil or tomato sauce. Latin name: *Clupea sprattus.* [Early 20thC. From Norwegian or Danish.]

bristle /bríss'l/ *n.* **1. STIFF HAIR** a short stiff hair on an animal or plant or a mass of short stiff hairs growing, e.g. on a pig's back or a man's face **2. HAIR ON BRUSH** the short stiff natural or synthetic hair on a brush ■ *v.* **(-tles, -tling, -tled) 1.** *vti.* **HAVE OR SET HAIR ON END** to make the hair or fur stand upright in response to fear or anger, or to show such a response **2.** *vi.* **BECOME OFFENDED BY STH** to react somewhat angrily or indignantly to sth or sb ○ *He bristled at the suggestion.* **3.** *vi.* **HAVE LARGE AMOUNT** to have an abundance of sth ○ *a mighty battleship bristling with guns* **4.** *vt.* **GIVE STH BRISTLES** to provide or cover sth with bristles [13thC. Formed from Old English *byrst* 'bristle'. Ultimately from an Indo-European word that also produced German *Borste* 'bristle'.]

bristlebird /bríss'l burd/ *n.* a small brown bird that lives in coastal scrub in eastern Australia. It is an endangered species. Latin name: *Dasyornis brachypterus.* [Early 19thC. From the bristles on its face.]

bristlecone pine /bríss'l kōn-/ *n.* a small pine tree with bristly cones, native to California. Bristlecone pines are the longest-living trees in the world. Genus: *Pinus.* [Late 19thC. From the prickles on its cones.]

bristletail /bríss'l tayl/ (*plural* **-tails** *or* **-tail**) *n.* a wingless insect that has a long segmented abdomen with two or three long bristles at the end. Order: Thysanura.

bristle worm *n.* = **polychaete** [From the bristles on its appendages]

bristling /bríssling/ *adj.* **1. WITH MANY BRISTLES** thick with stiff hairs **2. ANGRY OR INDIGNANT** reacting with anger and indignation

bristly /bríss'li/ **(-tlier, -tliest)** *adj.* **1. ROUGH WITH BRISTLES** prickly and rough with bristles **2. EASILY ANGERED** quick to anger —**bristliness** *n.*

Bristol /bríst'l/ university city and seaport on the River Avon in southwestern England. Population: 400,700 (1995).

Bristol board *n.* a type of fine smooth lightweight cardboard used in design and drawing [Early 19thC. Named for the city of *Bristol*, where it was first manufactured.]

Bristol Channel arm of the Atlantic Ocean between southern Wales and southwestern England, into which the River Severn flows. Length: 137 km/85 mi.

bristols /bríst'lz/ *n.* an offensive term for a woman's breasts (*slang offensive*) [Mid-20thC. Shortening of *Bristol Cities*, rhyming slang for 'titties', from *Bristol City*, the name of a professional football club in Bristol.]

brit /brit/ (*plural* **brits** *or* **brit**) *n.* **1. YOUNG HERRING** the young form of some fish including the herring and the sprat **2. WHALE FOOD** a mass of tiny marine organisms, especially crustaceans, that is a source of food for whalebone whales and some fish [Early 17thC. Origin unknown.]

Brit /brit/ *n.* a British person (*informal*) [Early 20thC. Shortening.]

Brit. *abbr.* Britain ■ *abbr.* British

Britain /brítt'n/ **1.** island in the Atlantic Ocean off the northwestern coast of Europe, including England,

Scotland, and Wales. Area: 94,248 sq. mi./244,101 sq. km. **2.** = **Great Britain, United Kingdom**

Britannia /bri tánnyə/ *n.* **1.** SYMBOL OF BRITAIN the personification and symbol of Britain, shown as a seated woman wearing a helmet and holding a trident **2.** SOUTHERN ANCIENT BRITAIN the name given by the Romans to the southern part of Great Britain at the time of the Roman Empire **3. Britannia, britannia** = **Britannia metal** [Pre-12thC. From Latin *Brit(t)annia*.]

Britannia coin, **Britannia** *n.* a British gold coin worth £10, £25, £50, or £100, introduced as investment coin in 1987 [From the figure depicted on the coin]

Britannia metal, **britannia metal** *n.* an alloy of tin, antimony, and copper that is similar to pewter and is used for decorative items and for bearings

Britannic /bri tánnik/ *adj.* belonging to Britain ○ *Her Britannic Majesty*

britches /brítchiz/ *npl.* = **breeches** ◇ **too big for your britches** behaving in a self-important manner

brith /brit/ *n.* JUDAISM = **bris**

Briticism /brítti sizzəm/ *n.* sth, e.g. a word or custom, that is characteristic of the British or of Britain [Mid-19thC. Formed from BRITISH, on the model of SCOTTICISM or GALLICISM.]

British /bríttish/ *n.* **1.** PEOPLE OF UNITED KINGDOM the people of the United Kingdom of Great Britain and Northern Ireland **2.** = **British English 3.** LANGUAGE OF ANCIENT BRITONS the language spoken by the ancient Celtic people who lived in southern Britain ■ *adj.* **1.** OF UNITED KINGDOM relating to or typical of the United Kingdom of Great Britain and Northern Ireland, or its peoples or cultures **2.** RELATING TO ANCIENT BRITONS relating to or typical of the ancient Britons or their culture [Pre-12thC. Originally *Brettisc*, from Bret 'ancient Briton', directly or via Latin *Britto* from a Celtic word.]

British Asian *n.* a person of Asian origin who was born in the United Kingdom

British Columbia

British Columbia westernmost province of Canada, situated on the Pacific Ocean, north of the US border, west of Alberta, and south of Yukon Territory and the Northwest Territories. Capital: Victoria. Population: 3,724,500 (1996). Area: 947,800 sq. km/365,946 sq. mi.

British Commonwealth of Nations *n.* = **Commonwealth of Nations**

British Council *n.* a London-based organization founded to promote the English language and British culture around the world. It was founded by Royal Charter in 1942.

British Empire *n.* a group of colonies, protectorates, and other territories brought under British rule after the late 16th century, and by the 19th century comprising more than one-quarter of the world's population. Most of Britain's former colonies became independent after World War II, and as sovereign states, many joined the Commonwealth.

British English *n.* the form of English used by people in Great Britain, as opposed to the form used in other English-speaking countries

───────**WORD KEY: WORLD ENGLISH**───────

British English is the English language as used in the United Kingdom of Great Britain (England, Scotland, and Wales) and Northern Ireland. With a population of over 57 million, the United Kingdom is the second largest primary English-speaking country after the

United States, and it continues to have prestige as the place of origin of the English language. The term British English is not, however, precise, being variously used to refer to: all varieties of English in the UK as a whole; all varieties in Britain as a whole; all varieties in England alone; the forms of only the standard language in the UK as a whole; those forms in Britain as a whole; those forms in England alone; and, notably, that variety of the standard language based on upper- and middle-class usage (especially at the turn of the 20th century in southeast England). See also *American English, Australian English*.

Britisher /bríttishər/ *n.* US a British subject or a person from Britain (*informal*)

British Guiana former name for **Guyana**

British Honduras former name for **Belize**

British India *n.* The part of the Indian subcontinent under British administration from 1765 to 1947, when the independent states of India and Pakistan were created

British Indian Ocean Territory a British overseas territory in the Indian Ocean, consisting of five uninhabited coral islands, the largest of which is Diego Garcia. Area: 60 sq. km/23 sq. mi.

British Isles group of islands in the northeastern Atlantic separated from mainland Europe by the North Sea and English Channel. It consists of the large islands of Great Britain and Ireland and almost 5,000 surrounding smaller islands and islets.

British Legion *n.* = **Royal British Legion** (the)

British Library *n.* the United Kingdom's national library in London that contains books, sound recordings, and manuscripts brought together from various national collections, e.g. the British Museum

British Museum *n.* the national museum of the United Kingdom, situated in London. It was founded in the 18th century and contains one of the world's finest collections of antiquities.

British Somaliland former British protectorate in East Africa from 1884 until 1960, when it united with Italian Somaliland to form the republic of Somalia

British Standards Institution *n.* an organization that issues standards for manufacturing practice and quality control, as well as for measurements and technical terms used in the United Kingdom

British Standard Time *n.* the time that was used from 1968 to 1971 in the United Kingdom, one hour ahead of Greenwich Mean Time

British Summer Time *n.* the time, one hour ahead of Greenwich Mean Time, used in the United Kingdom from the beginning of April to the end of October. It is intended to make better use of the hours of daylight in this part of the year.

British thermal unit *n.* the amount of heat needed to raise the temperature of one pound of water by one degree Fahrenheit, equal to approximately 1055 joules

British Union of Fascists *n.* a British fascist organization founded by Sir Oswald Mosley in the 1930s

British warm *n.* CLOTHES a short overcoat worn by British officers in World War I, and popular for civilian wear after the war

Briton /brítt'n/ *n.* **1.** BRITISH PERSON sb who was born or brought up in Great Britain, or who is a citizen of Great Britain **2.** INHABITANT OF ANCIENT BRITAIN a member of the ancient Celtic people who once lived in southern Britain [13thC. Via French *Breton* from the Latin stem *Britton*-, ultimately of Celtic origin.]

britska *n.* = **britzka**

Brittain /brítt'n/, **Vera** (1893–1970) British writer. Her World War I memoir *Testament of Youth* (1933) speaks for a generation of young people whose lives were forever changed by the experience of war. Full name **Vera Mary Brittain**

Brittany /brítt'ni/ peninsular region in northwestern France, between the Bay of Biscay and the English Channel. The region's capital is Rennes. Popu-

lation: 2,795,600 (1990). Area: 27,208 sq. km/10,505 sq. mi.

Britten /brítt'n/, **Benjamin** (1913–76) British composer. Regarded as one of the finest of British composers of the 20th century, he wrote major choral works including the operas *Peter Grimes* (1945) and *Billy Budd* (1951) and the *War Requiem* (1962). Full name **Edward Benjamin Britten**

brittle /brítt'l/ *adj.* **1.** HARD AND BREAKABLE hard and likely to break or crack ○ *plastic that has become brittle with age.* **2.** SHARP-SOUNDING having a sharp, unnerving quality or tone **3.** NOT LASTING lacking durability or permanence **4.** NOT FRIENDLY lacking personal warmth ○ *a brittle quality to her that I didn't like* **5.** IRRITABLE easily irritated or annoyed ■ *n.* TOFFEE-NUT SWEET a crunchy sweet made from caramel and nuts [14thC. Formed from Old English *gebryttan* 'to shatter'.] —**brittlely** *adv.* —**brittleness** *n.*

brittle-bone disease *n.* **1.** = **osteoporosis 2.** = **osteogenesis imperfecta**

brittle star *n.* a marine animal similar to a starfish but with thinner, longer, and more flexible arms that can be regenerated if broken off. Class: Ophiuroidea. [From its brittle arms]

Brittonic *adj.*, *n.* = **Brythonic** [Early 20thC. Formed from the Latin stem *Britton*- (see BRITON).]

britzka /brítskə/, **britska** *n.* a horse-drawn carriage with a rear-facing front seat and a folding top over the back seat [Early 19thC. From Polish *bryczka*.]

Brix scale /bríks-/ *n.* a scale used in a hydrometer for measuring the sugar content of a solution at a particular temperature [Late 19thC. Named after its inventor, the German scientist Adolf Brix (1798–1890).]

Brno /búrnō/ industrial city in the former region of Moravia, southeastern Czech Republic. Population: 390,000 (1993).

bro /brō/ *n.* a brother (*informal*)

bro., Bro. *abbr.* brother

broach /brōch/ *v.* (**broaches, broaching, broached**) **1.** *vt.* BRING UP DIFFICULT SUBJECT to introduce a subject for discussion, usually one that is awkward ○ *He finally broached the question of the loan* **2.** *vt.* OPEN STH to open a container for the first time ○ *broach a bottle of wine* **3.** *vt.* PIERCE CASK to make a hole in a cask to draw off liquid **4.** *vt.* BORE HOLE to make or enlarge a hole in sth **5.** *vi.* NAVY COME UP THROUGH SURFACE OF WATER to break the surface of water from below without completely emerging (*refers to a submarine*) **6.** *vi.* NAUT TURN SIDEWAYS TO THE WIND to be turned broadside to the wind, e.g. by heavy seas, with a risk of capsizing ■ *n.* **1.** TOOL FOR ENLARGING HOLES a tool for enlarging holes **2.** ROASTING SPIT a roasting spit **3.** TOOL FOR PIERCING CASKS a tool used for making holes in casks **4.** = **brooch** [14thC. From Old French *brocher* 'to stitch', from *broche* 'skewer, long needle'. The meaning 'introduce a subject' evolved from 'pierce' via 'tap a barrel'.] —**broacher** *n.*

broad /brawd/ *adj.* **1.** VERY WIDE large from one side to the other ○ *a broad forehead* **2.** LARGE AND SPACIOUS extending a great distance in all directions ○ *the broad plains of the Steppes* **3.** MEASURED ACROSS measured from side to side ○ *as broad as it is long* **4.** FULL AND CLEAR full and clear to see ○ *a broad grin* ○ *broad daylight* **5.** COVERING A WIDE RANGE comprehensive in content, knowledge, experience, ability, or application ○ *She has very broad interests.* **6.** NOT DETAILED general, rather than detailed ○ *I'll give you a broad outline of the project.* **7.** WIDESPREAD OR GENERALIZED widespread or generalized throughout a large and diverse group of people ○ *a broad feeling of disillusionment in the party* **8.** OBVIOUS meant to be easily understood ○ *dropping broad hints about their plans* **9.** UNOBSTRUCTED with nothing blocking the way **10.** TOLERANT tending to tolerate or accept rather than to condemn the ideas and conduct of other people ○ *I think I have fairly broad views on the whole.* **11.** POTENTIALLY OFFENSIVE potentially offensive to accepted standards of propriety **12.** LING STRONGLY REGIONAL used to describe a regional accent that is very strong or pronounced **13.** PHON used to describe a phonetic transcription that gives only major differences **14.** LING PRONOUNCED WITH THE TONGUE DOWN used to describe a vowel pronounced with the tongue low and flat and the mouth open wide **15.** FIN DESCRIBING MONEY IN

ANY FORM used to describe money in circulation and bank deposits ○ *broad money* ■ *n.* **1.** WIDE PART the wide part of sth ○ *He slapped Jack across the broad of his back.* **2.** GEOG RIVER COVERING LAND a river that expands to cover low-lying land **3.** *US* OFFENSIVE TERM an offensive term for a woman (*slang offensive*) ■ *adv.* COMPLETELY to the fullest extent [Old English *brād*. Ultimately from a prehistoric Germanic word that is also the ancestor of German *breit* 'broad'.] **—broadness** *n.* ◇ **in broad daylight** in open daylight for all to see

B-road *n.* a road in the UK given the prefix 'B' in the national road numbering and classification system because it is less important than an A-road

broad arrow *n.* **1.** ARROW-SHAPED GOVERNMENT IDENTIFICATION a mark in the shape of a wide arrowhead that identifies government property and was used formerly on prison clothing **2.** ARROW WITH WIDE HEAD an arrow with a wide barbed head

broadaxe /bráwd aks/ *n.* a heavy battleaxe with a wide blade

broadband /bráwd band/ *adj.* **1.** PHYS COVERING MANY FREQUENCIES using a wide range of electromagnetic frequencies **2.** COMPUT TRANSFERRING DATA FAST capable of transferring large amounts of data at high speed

broad bean *n.* **1.** BEAN PLANT a plant grown worldwide for its large flat edible seeds. Latin name: *Vicia faba.* **2.** LARGE EDIBLE BEAN SEED the large green seed of the broad bean plant, cooked and eaten as a vegetable

broadbill /bráwd bil/ (*plural* **-bills** *or* **-bill**) *n.* a tropical African or Asian bird with brightly coloured feathers and a short broad bill. Family: Eurylaemidae.

broad-brush *adj.* attempting to cover all conditions and instances ○ *a broad-brush approach*

broadcast /bráwd kaast/ *v.* (**-casts**, **-casting**, **-cast** *or* **-casted**) **1.** *vti.* TRANSMIT RADIO SIGNALS to transmit a programme or information on television or radio **2.** *vi.* BE ON TELEVISION OR RADIO to take part in a radio or television programme **3.** *vt.* MAKE STH WIDELY KNOWN to make sth widely known ○ *They broadcast the rumours all over town.* **4.** *vt.* SCATTER SEED to sow seed by scattering it ■ *n.* **1.** PROGRAMME a television or radio programme **2.** TRANSMISSION a transmission of radio or television signals **3.** SCATTERING SEED a sowing of seed by scattering it ■ *adj.* **1.** FOR BROADCASTING ON TELEVISION OR RADIO relating to, suitable for, or transmitted by radio or television **2.** SCATTERED WIDELY scattered widely ■ *adv.* WIDELY over a wide area [Mid-18thC. The meaning 'to transmit' evolved from the idea of scattering seeds widely.]

WORD KEY: SYNONYMS
See Synonyms at *scatter.*

broadcaster /bráwd kaastər/ *n.* a person who regularly takes part in television or radio programmes, especially news or chat shows

broadcasting /bráwd kaasting/ *n.* the making and transmission of television and radio programmes

broadcasting authority (*plural* **broadcasting authorities**) *n.* an organization that is responsible for maintaining standards in radio and television broadcasting

broad church *n.* a group, institution, or political party that has liberal and inclusive attitudes

Broad Church *n.* a group within the Church of England that favours a liberal interpretation of doctrine

broadcloth /bráwd kloth/ *n.* **1.** FINE WOVEN CLOTH a fine, closely woven cloth of wool, cotton, or silk with a shiny finish, used for clothing **2.** PLAIN-WEAVE WOOL FABRIC a woollen fabric with a plain weave, smooth finish, and dense texture, originally of double width [15thC. From the specification of cloth 2 yds (1.8 m) wide as 'broad cloth' in an English Act of Parliament of 1482.]

broaden /bráwd'n/ (**-ens**, **-ening**, **-ened**) *vti.* **1.** WIDEN STH to make sth wider or to become wider **2.** ENLARGE RANGE OF STH to enlarge the range or magnitude of sth, or to become more wide-ranging

broad gauge *n.* a railway track that has a distance between the tracks greater than the standard 123.2 cm/48.5 in. Broad gauge allows greater passenger comfort and carrying capacity but increases the cost of construction.

broad-gauge *adj.* **1.** FOR BROAD GAUGE relating to or designed for a railway using broad gauge **2.** WIDE-RANGING wide in application or range

broad-leaved /bráwd leevd/, **broadleaf** /-leef/ *adj.* used to describe trees that have wide leaves rather than leaves that are like pine needles. Broad-leaved plants can be evergreen, such as holly, or deciduous, such as beech.

broadloom /bráwd loom/ *adj.* WOVEN ON WIDE LOOM used to describe carpet that is woven on a wide loom ■ *n.* WIDE SEAMLESS CARPET a carpet woven on a wide loom that can be laid with few or no seams

broadly /bráwdli/ *adv.* **1.** GENERALLY in general terms, not allowing for exceptions ○ *Broadly speaking, there are two types of tourist.* **2.** MOSTLY for the most part ○ *It is broadly based on the German prototype.* **3.** WITH AN ENTHUSIASTIC SMILE with a smile that shows great enthusiasm or friendliness ○ *smiling broadly*

broad-minded *adj.* willing to tolerate a wide range of ideas and behaviour **—broad-mindedly** *adv.* **—broad-mindedness** *n.*

Broads /brawdz/ area of shallow freshwater lakes and lagoons in Norfolk and Suffolk, eastern England

broadsheet /bráwd sheet/ *n.* **1.** SERIOUS NEWSPAPER a newspaper that is printed in a large format and is associated with serious journalism as opposed to the smaller-format tabloids **2.** LARGE PAPER FOR PRINTING a large sheet of paper printed on one side. US term **broadside** *n.* 5

broadside /bráwd sīd/ *n.* **1.** NAUT SHIP'S SIDE the side of a ship above the waterline from bow to quarter **2.** NAVY SHIP'S GUNS AND GUNFIRE all the guns on one side of a ship or the simultaneous firing of them **3.** STRONG VERBAL OR WRITTEN ATTACK a strong verbal or written attack on sb ○ *a vicious broadside on the Prime Minister* **4.** LARGE FLAT SURFACE a large flat and usually vertical surface ○ *the broadside of the barn* **5.** *US* PRINTING = broadsheet ■ *adv.* **1.** FROM THE SIDE with the side facing towards sth ○ *The ship hit the rocks broadside on.* **2.** WITH NO APPARENT OBJECTIVE with no apparent objective ○ *Her proposals were attacked broadside.* ■ *vt.* (**-sides**, **-siding**, **-sided**) *US* HIT SIDE OF STH to collide with sth sideways ○ *The car was broadsided by the train.*

broad-spectrum *adj.* used to describe antibiotics and other chemicals that destroy a wide range of organisms, e.g. bacteria and agricultural pests

broadsword /bráwd sawrd/ *n.* a sword with a wide flat blade designed for cutting rather than thrusting [Old English]

broadtail /bráwd tayl/ *n.* **1.** BLACK WAVY LAMBSWOOL the black wavy fur or pelt of a prematurely born karakul lamb **2.** = karakul *n.* 1

Broadway /bráwd way/ *n.* **1.** AVENUE IN NEW YORK CITY a long avenue extending north and south through the borough of Manhattan in New York City. Part of it is the main thoroughfare of the city's theatre district. **2.** *US* THEATRE used to refer to the commercial theatre business in the United States ○ *This is not Broadway material.*

broad-winged hawk *n.* a common woodland hawk of eastern North America with broad wings that are white on the underside and a broadly banded tail. Latin name: *Buteo platypterus.*

Broadwood /bráwd wŏŏd/, **John** (1732–1812) British piano manufacturer. He founded the Broadwood Piano Company (1770) with Burkhardt Tschudi, a Swiss harpsichord-maker.

Brobdingnagian /bróbding nággi ən/ *adj.* extraordinarily large (*literary*) [Early 18thC. Formed from *Brobdingnag*, name of a fictitious land of giants in Jonathan Swift's *Gulliver's Travels* (1726).]

brocade /brō káyd, brə káyd/ *n.* FABRIC WITH RAISED DESIGN a heavy fabric of silk, cotton, or wool woven with a raised design, often using metallic threads. A true brocade is based on one or two basic colours with additional coloured threads brought from the back to the front to produce the raised design. ■ *vt.* (**-cades**, **-cading**, **-caded**) WEAVE FABRIC WITH RAISED DESIGN to weave fabric with a raised design [Late 16thC. Via Spanish or Portuguese *brocado* from Italian *broccato*, from *brocco* 'twisted thread, shoot', from, ultimately, Latin *brocchus* (see BROACH).] **—brocaded** *adj.*

brocatel /brókə tél/ *n.* a heavy fabric with raised designs, used chiefly in upholstery [Mid-17thC. Via French from Italian *broccatello* 'gold tinsel', literally 'small brocade', from *broccato* (see BROCADE).]

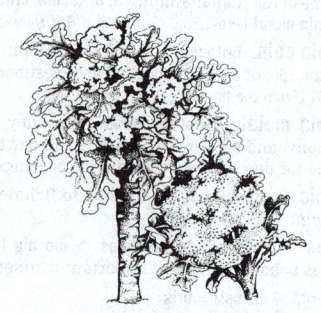
Broccoli

broccoli /brókəli/ *n.* **1.** PLANT WITH EDIBLE FLOWER HEAD a plant of the cabbage family with green, purple, or white flower heads that are cooked and eaten as a vegetable. Heading broccoli has green flower heads like cauliflowers and sprouting broccoli has multiple small purple or white flowering shoots. Latin name: *Brassica oleracea italica.* **2.** EDIBLE FLOWER HEAD the flower head of the broccoli plant, eaten as a vegetable before the flowers have opened [Mid-17thC. From Italian, the plural of *broccolo* 'cabbage sprout', from *brocco* 'shoot', from, ultimately, Latin *brocchus* (see BROACH).]

broch /brok, brokh/ (*plural* **brochs**) *n.* a prehistoric fortified dwelling in the shape of a circular stone tower, found especially on the islands and northern mainland of Scotland. They were built by the Picts, a Celtic people. [Mid-17thC. Originally a dialect form of BURGH.]

broché /brō sháy, bróshay/ *adj.* woven with a raised pattern [Late 19thC. From French, the past participle of *brocher* (see BROACH).]

brochette /bro shét/ *n.* **1.** KEBAB SKEWER a small skewer on which chunks of food are grilled or roasted **2.** SKEWERED FOOD food, e.g. meat or fish, that has been cooked on a brochette [15thC. From French, literally 'little skewer', formed from *broche* (see BROACH).]

brochure /brṓshər, bro shoor/ *n.* a booklet or pamphlet that contains descriptive information or advertising [Mid-18thC. From French, literally 'sth stitched together', formed from *brocher* (see BROACH).]

brock /brok/ (*plural* **brocks** *or* **brock**) *n.* a badger [Pre-12thC. Ultimately from a Celtic word that is also the ancestor of Welsh *broch* 'badger'.]

Brocken /brók'n/ *n.* the highest point in the Harz Mountains, central Germany. It is associated with folklore and traditional rites, including Walpurgis Night, or the Witches' Sabbath. Height: 1,141 m/3,743 ft.

broderie anglaise /brṓdəri ong gláyz/ *n.* **1.** FABRIC WITH OPEN EMBROIDERED DESIGN white or pale-coloured cotton or synthetic fabric decorated with an ornamental pattern of small holes with stitched edges (**eyelet embroidery**). It is chiefly used in thin strips as decorative edging or trimming. **2.** OPEN EMBROIDERY embroidery in the form of an ornamental pattern of small holes with stitched edges [Mid-19thC. From French, literally 'English embroidery'.]

broderie perse /-púrss/ *n.* an appliqué technique in which designs are cut from patterned fabric, e.g. chintz, and sewn onto plain fabric [From French, literally 'chintz embroidery'.]

Brodsky /bródski/, **Joseph** (1940–96) Soviet-born US poet and essayist. He won the Nobel Prize in literature (1987) and was US poet laureate (1991–92).

Broederbond /brṓodər bont/ *n.* a secret society of Afrikaner nationalists in South Africa, committed to gaining control of vital areas of government [Mid-20thC. Via Afrikaans from Dutch, literally 'league of brothers'.]

brog /brog/ (plural **brogs**) n. Scotland a bradawl [15thC. Origin unknown.]

brogan /brṓgən/ n. a heavy ankle-high work boot [Mid-19thC. From Irish or Scots Gaelic brōgan, literally 'little shoe', from brōg (see BROGUE²).]

Broglie /broy/, **Louis, 7th Duke of** (1892–1987) French physicist. He was awarded the Nobel Prize in physics (1929) for his work on electron waves and particles. Full name **Louis Victor Pierre Raymond Broglie**

brogue¹ /brōg/ n. a regional accent, especially the accent of Irish people speaking English [Early 18thC. Origin uncertain: perhaps from BROGUE², in allusion to the footwear of Irish or Scottish speakers.]

—— **WORD KEY: REGIONAL NOTE** ——
The Irish word bróg meaning 'shoe' comes ultimately from an Old Norse word meaning 'leg covering'. The use of the term for 'accent', especially an 'Irish accent', goes back to the early 18th century, but the link between the meanings is tenuous. It is possible that it was applied to the speech of people who called their shoes brogues. Certainly, Thomas Sheridan mentioned that the Irish 'brought with them each their several brogues or modes of intonation' in 1775.

brogue² /brōg/ n. **1. LEATHER SHOE WITH DECORATIVE PERFORATIONS** a rugged shoe, usually with a decorative pattern of small holes in the leather across the toe and along the sides. US term **wing tip 2. IRISH OR SCOTTISH SHOE** a simple heavy untanned shoe formerly worn in Ireland and Scotland [Late 16thC. Via Irish and Scots Gaelic brōg from Old Norse brók 'leg covering'.]

broider /brṓydər/ (-**ders, -dering, -dered**) vti. to embroider (archaic) [14thC. From Old French brosder; ultimately from a prehistoric Germanic word.]

broil¹ /broyl/ (**broils, broiling, broiled**) v. **1.** vti. **BE VERY HOT** to make sb or sth extremely hot or to be extremely hot ○ We had been broiling in the sun all morning. **2.** vt. US, Can = grill **3.** vi. US **BE VERY ANGRY** to be extremely angry [14thC. From Old French bruler, of uncertain origin: perhaps based ultimately on Latin ustulare 'to burn up', from the past participle of urere 'to burn'.]

broil² /broyl/ n. **BRAWL** a brawl (archaic) ■ vi. (**broils, broiling, broiled**) **TAKE PART IN BRAWL** to engage in a brawl (archaic) [15thC. Via Anglo-Norman broiller 'to mix up, confuse' from Old French brōoillier, from breu 'broth'.]

broiler /brṓylər/ n. **1. ROASTING CHICKEN** a young chicken for roasting **2.** US = grill, grill pan

broiler house (plural **broiler houses**) n. a building where broiler chickens are reared

broke¹ past tense of **break**

broke² /brōk/ adj. (informal) **1. HAVING NO MONEY** without any money to spend **2. BANKRUPT** totally bankrupt [Early 18thC. Alteration of BROKEN.] ◇ **go for broke** to risk everything to achieve a goal (informal)

broke³ /brōk/ vt. to broker a deal, sale, or contract [Early 20thC. Back-formation from BROKER.] — **broking** n.

broken¹ past participle of **break**

broken² /brṓkən/ adj. **1. NO LONGER WHOLE** in two or more pieces, e.g. after being dropped or struck with sth hard **2. OUT OF ORDER** no longer in working condition ○ The CD player is broken. **3. NOT KEPT** not honoured or fulfilled ○ a broken promise **4. NOT CONTINUOUS** lacking continuity **5. UNEVEN** having an uneven surface ○ We travelled over broken terrain. **6. WEAK** physically weakened ○ his health was broken **7. DESTROYED BY ADVERSITY** destroyed or badly hurt by grief or misfortune **8. SPLIT APART** split apart by divorce, separation, or desertion **9. INCOMPLETE** lacking parts necessary to be complete **10. DISORGANIZED** lacking order or harmony ○ escaping in broken ranks **11.** LANGUAGE **IMPERFECTLY SPOKEN** spoken in an imperfect or halting manner [Old English brocen]

Broken Bay /brṓkən-/ bay on the eastern coast of New South Wales, Australia. It lies at the mouth of the Hawkesbury River, north of Sydney.

broken chord n. a chord played as a quick succession of notes (**arpeggio**) rather than simultaneously

broken consort n. a musical ensemble made up of instruments of different types, used especially in music of the Renaissance

broken-down adj. **1. NOT WORKING** damaged or not working ○ a broken-down old machine **2. DILAPIDATED** in very poor condition

brokenhearted /brṓkən haártid/ adj. extremely sad, e.g. after bereavement, great disappointment, or the end of a love affair —**brokenheartedly** adv. —**brokenheartedness** n.

Broken Hill city in western New South Wales, Australia. It is an important centre for silver, lead, and zinc mining. Population: 20,963 (1996).

broken wind n. a chronic lung disorder in horses marked by difficulty in breathing and believed to be caused by dust, moulds, or other air pollutants. = **heave** npl. 2 [From the horse's irregular breathing]

broken-winded adj. used to describe a horse that is suffering from the lung disease COPD

broker /brṓkər/ n. **1. COMMERCIAL AGENT** a person who is paid to act as an agent for others, e.g. in negotiating contracts or buying and selling goods and services **2.** = stockbroker **3.** = power broker ■ vt. (-**kers, -kering, -kered**) **ARRANGE DEAL OR SALE** to act as an agent in arranging a deal, sale, or contract [14thC. From Anglo-Norman brocour 'small trader', of uncertain origin: perhaps via Portuguese alborcar 'to barter' from, ultimately, Arabic; alternatively, formed from Old French brocher (see BROACH).]

brokerage /brṓkərij/ n. **1. PAYMENT TO A BROKER** a fee paid to sb who acts as a financial agent for sb else **2. BROKER'S BUSINESS** the business of being a broker **3. STOCKBROKER'S BUSINESS** a company whose business is buying and selling stocks, shares, and bonds for its clients

brolga /brṓlgə/ (plural **-gas** or **-ga**) n. a large grey crane of northern and northeastern Australia that has a red band round its neck. It is known for its elaborate courtship dance. Latin name: Grus rubicunda. [Late 19thC. From Kamilaroi buralga.]

brolly /brṓlli/ (plural **-lies**) n. an umbrella (informal) [Late 19thC. Alteration of UMBRELLA.]

brom- prefix. bromine, bromic ○ bromate [From BROMINE and BROMIDE]

bromate /brṓ mayt/ n. **CHEMICAL COMPOUND OF BROMIC ACID** a salt, ester, or ion of bromic acid ■ vt. (-**mates, -mating, -mated**) = brominate [Mid-19thC. Coined from BROMIC + -ATE.]

bromegrass /brṓm graass/, **brome** n. a tall grass with small drooping flower spikes that grows in temperate regions. Some types of bromegrass are cultivated for hay, while others are weeds. Genus: Bromus.

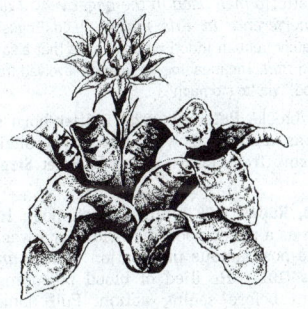

Bromeliad

bromeliad /brō meélli əd/ n. a tropical American plant with fleshy leaves forming a funnel that holds water. Many bromeliads grow on other plants for physical support. Family: Bromeliaceae. [Mid-19thC. Named after the Swedish botanist Olaf Bromel (1639–1705).]

bromic /brṓmik/ adj. relating to or containing bromine with a valency of five

bromic acid n. an unstable colourless acid that is a strong oxidizing agent and is used in the manufacture of pharmaceuticals and dyes. Formula: $HBrO_3$.

bromide /brṓ mīd/ n. **1.** CHEM **BROMINE COMPOUND** a chemical compound that contains bromine and another element or group, e.g. silver bromide **2.** CHEM **POTASSIUM BROMIDE** potassium bromide, especially when used as a sedative **3.** UNORIGINAL SAYING a saying that lacks originality or significance (dated) **4.** UNINTERESTING PERSON a tedious or uninteresting person

bromide paper n. a light-sensitive photographic paper that is coated with silver bromide emulsion

bromidic /brō míddik/ adj. without originality or interest

brominate /brṓmi nayt/ (-**nates, -nating, -nated**) vt. to treat or combine a substance with bromine or a bromine compound —**bromination** /brṓmi náysh'n/ n.

bromine /brṓ meen, -min/ n. a pungent dark red volatile liquid that is a nonmetallic chemical element of the halogen series and is used in sedatives and photographic materials. Symbol **Br** [Early 19thC. Coined from French brome (from Greek brōmos 'stench') + -INE.]

bromism /brṓmizzəm/ n. a condition caused by overuse of bromide medications and marked by memory problems, dullness, drowsiness, and loss of muscular coordination

Bromley /brṓmli/ borough of London, England. Population: 293,400 (1995).

Bromsgrove /brṓmz grōv/ town in Worcestershire, west-central England. Population: 26,366 (1991).

bronch- prefix. = broncho-

bronchi plural of **bronchus**

bronchial /brṓngki əl/ adj. relating to or affecting the tubes (**bronchi**) that carry air from the windpipe into the lungs ○ a bronchial infection —**bronchially** adv.

bronchial pneumonia n. = bronchopneumonia

bronchial tube n. a tubular passage forming part of a network of airways to and within the lungs. Two main tubes (**bronchi**) lead from the windpipe to each lung, dividing into smaller bronchi and subsequently bronchioles.

bronchiectasis /brṓngki éktəssiss/ n. chronic dilation of the airways to and within the lungs, causing coughing and excessive mucus production [Late 19thC. Coined from late Latin bronchia (see BRONCHIOLE) + Greek ektasis 'dilation'.]

bronchiole /brṓngki ōl/ n. a narrow tube inside the lungs that branches off the main air passages (**bronchi**) [Mid-19thC. From modern Latin bronchiolus, literally 'little bronchium', from late Latin bronchia, from, ultimately, Greek brogkhos (see BRONCHUS).] —**bronchiolar** /brṓngki ṓlər/ adj.

bronchitis /brong kítiss/ n. inflammation of the mucous membrane in the airways (**bronchial tubes**) of the lungs, resulting from infection or irritation and causing breathing problems and severe coughing —**bronchitic** /brong kíttik/ adj.

broncho /brṓngkō/ n. = bronco

broncho- prefix. bronchus, bronchial ○ bronchoscope [Via late Latin from, ultimately, Greek brogkhos (see BRONCHUS)]

bronchodilator /brṓngkō dī láytər/ n. a drug, often used in the treatment of asthma, that eases breathing by widening and relaxing the air passages to the lungs

bronchopneumonia /brṓngkō nyoo mṓni ə/ n. inflammation of the lungs caused by an infection in the air passages (**bronchioles**)

bronchoscope /brṓngkə skōp/ n. a thin instrument with a light on the end, used for looking inside the air passages (**bronchi**) leading to the lungs —**bronchoscopic** /brṓngkə skóppik/ adj. —**bronchoscopically** /-skóppikli/ adv. —**bronchoscopist** /brong kóskəpist/ n. —**bronchoscopy** /-kóskəpi/ n.

bronchus /brṓngkəss/ (plural **-chi** /-kī, -kee/) n. a tube leading from the windpipe to a lung, which provides for the passage of air. = **bronchial tube** [Late 17thC. Via modern Latin from, ultimately, Greek brogkhos 'windpipe'. Ultimately from an Indo-European word that is also the ancestor of English devour and gorge.]

bronco /brṓng kō/, **broncho** n. a wild or partly broken horse of the western United States, used in rodeos [Mid-19thC. From Spanish, literally 'rough, wild', of uncertain origin: perhaps from Latin *brocchus* (see BROACH).]

broncobuster /bróngkō bustər/ *n.* US a person who breaks in wild horses (*informal*)

Brontë /brónti/, **Anne** (1820–49) British novelist and poet. The sister of Charlotte Brontë and Emily Brontë, she wrote the novels *Agnes Grey* (1845) and *The Tenant of Wildfell Hall* (1847).

Charlotte Brontë

Brontë, Charlotte (1816–55) British novelist. Elder sister of Emily Brontë and Anne Brontë, she wrote novels including *Jane Eyre* (1847).

Brontë, Emily (1818–48) British poet and novelist. Sister of Charlotte Brontë and Anne Brontë, she wrote *Wuthering Heights* (1847).

brontosaurus /brónta sáwrəss/, **brontosaur** /brónta sawr/ *n.* a large vegetarian dinosaur that lived in North America during the Jurassic period and had a small head, short front legs, and a long neck and tail. Genus: *Apatosaurus*. [Late 19thC. From modern Latin *brontosaurus*, alternative genus name, which was coined from Greek *brontē* 'thunder' + *sauros* 'lizard'.]

Bronx /bronks/ the northernmost of the five boroughs of New York City, located on the mainland with the Harlem and Hudson rivers to the west, Westchester County to the north, Long Island Sound to the east, and the East River to the south. Population: 1,203,789 (1990).

Bronx cheer *n.* US = raspberry (*informal*) [Named after the BRONX]

bronze /bronz/ *n.* **1.** COPPER AND TIN ALLOY a hard yellowish-brown alloy of copper and tin, sometimes containing small amounts of other metals. Bronze is harder than copper and is often cast to make statues. **2.** COPPER-BASED ALLOY an alloy of copper with a substance other than tin, e.g. aluminium or silicon **3.** SCULPTURE BRONZE WORK OF ART an object that is made from bronze, especially a statue or other piece of cast sculpture **4.** SPORTS BRONZE MEDAL a bronze medal ○ *She was hoping for at least a bronze.* **5.** COLOURS DEEP YELLOWISH-BROWN COLOUR a deep yellowish-brown colour, like that of bronze ■ *adj.* **1.** MADE OF BRONZE made of bronze **2.** COLOURS DEEP YELLOWISH-BROWN of a deep yellowish-brown colour, like bronze ■ *v.* (**bronzes, bronzing, bronzed**) **1.** *vt.* MAKE STH LOOK LIKE BRONZE to give sth the yellowish-brown sheen or weathered patina of bronze **2.** *vti.* TAN SKIN to make sb's skin suntanned or to become suntanned (*informal*) ○ *bronzed by the sun.* [Early 18thC. Via French from Italian *bronzo*, of uncertain origin: probably from Persian *birinj* 'brass'; alternatively, named after the Italian city *Brindisi*, where in antiquity bronze mirrors were made.] —**bronzer** *n.* —**bronzy** *adj.*

Bronze Age *n.* a period of cultural history, approximately between 3500 and 1500 BC, that succeeded the Stone Age and was characterized by the use of tools made of bronze

bronzed /bronzd/ *adj.* with deeply and evenly suntanned skin

bronze medal *n.* a medal that is awarded to a person who is placed third in a competition, especially a sporting event —**bronze medallist** *n.*

Bronzino /bron dzéeno/, **il** (1503–72) Italian painter. Known as a portraitist of the Medici family, Dante, and Boccaccio, he also painted religious pictures. Real name **Agnoli Tori di Cosimo di Mariano**

bronzite /brón zīt/ *n.* an iron-containing form of orthopyroxine with a metallic sheen

brooch /brōch/, **broach** *n.* a piece of jewellery that is fastened to a garment by a hinged pin and catch. Brooches are usually worn by women, e.g. on the upper part of a dress, on the lapel of a jacket, or at the neck of a blouse. [13thC. From Old French *broche* (see BROACH).]

brood /brood/ *n.* **1.** YOUNG OF BIRDS OR ANIMALS the young of an animal, especially young birds, that are born and reared together **2.** FAMILY'S CHILDREN the children of one family (*informal humorous*) ○ *that brood of noisy brats* **3.** GROUP OF SIMILAR PEOPLE a group whose members share a common origin or background ○ *the latest brood of avant-garde artists* ■ *adj.* KEPT FOR BREEDING used to describe a female farm animal that is kept for the purpose of producing young ■ *v.* (**broods, brooding, brooded**) **1.** *vi.* BE WORRIED to be preoccupied with a troublesome or unwelcome thought **2.** *vi.* THINK UNPLEASANT THOUGHTS to think resentful, dark, or miserable thoughts **3.** *vti.* KEEP EGGS WARM to sit on or hatch eggs, or to cover young birds for warmth **4.** *vi.* BE HEAVY OR OMINOUS to loom or hang heavily and ominously (*literary*) ○ *the dark clouds brooding overhead* [Old English *brōd*. Ultimately from an Indo-European base meaning 'heat'. The underlying idea is of nursing young (or emotions) by keeping them warm.]

brooder /broodər/ *n.* **1.** HEATED PLACE FOR YOUNG ANIMAL a heated area or enclosure for rearing young animals, especially young fowl, with or without the presence of their mother. It provides an optimum environment in which heat, light, food, and water can be carefully controlled. **2.** HEN THAT BROODS EGGS a hen that sits on eggs to keep them warm before they hatch **3.** PERSON WHO WORRIES a person who worries persistently over things

brooding /brooding/ *adj.* OMINOUS seeming to contain some silent threat or danger (*literary*) ■ *n.* DEEP THOUGHT a person's private thought about sth that is causing a great deal of anxiety ○ *Her broodings were disturbed by Colette's arrival.* —**broodingly** *adv.*

brood mare *n.* a mare that is kept specially for breeding

broody /broodi/ (**-ier, -iest**) *adj.* **1.** READY TO INCUBATE EGGS used to describe a hen that is ready to sit on eggs to keep them warm before they hatch, especially a hen that is no longer able to lay eggs **2.** THOUGHTFUL OR SULLEN showing deep thought, anxiety, or resentment ○ *His long broody silences were hard to bear.* **3.** WANTING A BABY eager or anxious to have a baby (*informal*) —**broodily** *adv.* —**broodiness** *n.*

brook[1] /brook/ *n.* a small freshwater stream [Old English *brōc*. From a prehistoric Germanic word that is also the ancestor of German *Bruch* 'marsh'.]

brook[2] /brook/ (**brooks, brooking, brooked**) *vt.* to put up with sth (*formal; used in the negative*) ○ *I will brook no interference in this matter.* [Old English *brūcan*. Ultimately from an Indo-European base that also produced English *fruit*. The meaning 'to tolerate' evolved from 'to use (as food)' via 'to stomach'.]

Brook /brook/, **Peter** (*b.* 1925) British-born director. He was associated with the Royal Shakespeare Company from 1962. Full name **Peter Stephen Paul Brook**

Brooke, Rupert (1887–1915) British poet. His reputation as a major poet of World War I was secured by the posthumous publication of *1914 and Other Poems* (1915). He died of blood poisoning in the Aegean before seeing action. Full name **Rupert Chawner Brooke**

Brookeborough /brookbərə/, **Basil Stanlake Brooke, 1st Viscount** (1883–1973) British politician. A supporter of Unionist policies, he was prime minister of Northern Ireland from 1943 to 1963.

Brook Farm *n.* an experimental cooperative community established by a group of writers and scholars on a farm at West Roxbury, Massachusetts. It lasted from 1841 to 1846.

brookite /brook īt/ *n.* a translucent or reddish-brown to black mineral composed of titanium dioxide in the form of orthorhombic crystals. Formula: TiO_2. [Early 19thC. Named after the English mineralogist Henry Brook (1771–1857).]

Brooklyn /brooklin/ one of the five boroughs of New York City, located on the western tip of Long Island

with Staten Island and Manhattan to the west and Queens to the north and east. Population: 2,273,966 (1996).

Brookner /brooknər/, **Anita** (*b.* 1928) British writer. Her novels included the Booker Prize-winning *Hotel du Lac* (1984).

Brooks /brooks/, **Mel** (*b.* 1926) US film actor and director. His films include *The Producers* (1968), *Blazing Saddles* (1974), and *Spaceballs* (1987). Born **Melvin Kaminsky**

brook trout *n.* a freshwater fish of the salmon family, originally from eastern North America and introduced throughout North America and into Europe. It is a popular food and game fish. Latin name: *Salvelinus fontinalis.*

broom /broom, broom/ *n.* **1.** BRUSH FOR SWEEPING a brush with a head of twigs or bristles attached to a long thin handle, used for sweeping indoors or outdoors **2.** PLANTS PLANT WITH BRIGHT YELLOW FLOWERS a leguminous shrub that grows wild in Europe and Asia and is widely cultivated for its bright yellow flowers. Latin name: *Cytisus scoparius.* **3.** PLANTS PLANT RESEMBLING BROOM a shrub with yellow flowers that resembles broom and grows in Europe and Asia. Genera: *Genista* and *Spartium.* ■ *vt.* (**brooms, brooming, broomed**) SWEEP STH to sweep sth with a broom or brush [Old English *brōm*. From a prehistoric Germanic word that also produced English *bramble*. Originally only a plant-name, the word acquired the meaning 'brush' because brushes were made from broom twigs.]

broomcorn /broom kawrn, broom-/ *n.* a variety of sorghum with long stiff stalks that are sometimes used for making brooms. Latin name: *Sorghum bicolor.*

Broome /broom/ town on the northwestern coast of Western Australia, Australia, that used to be an important pearling centre. Population: 11,368 (1996).

broomrape /broom rayp, broom-/ *n.* a plant that has small flowers and tiny leaves resembling scales and lacking chlorophyll. It lives on the roots of other plants, including crops. Genus: *Orobanche.* [Late 16thC. 'Rape' from medieval Latin *rapum* 'tuber'.]

broomstick /broom stik, broom-/ *n.* the long handle of a broom

Broonzy /broonzi/, **Big Bill** (1893–1958) US musician. He incorporated a wide range of influences as a master composer and performer of blues. Born **William Lee Conley**

bros., Bros. *abbr.* COMM brothers

brose /brōz/ *n. Scotland* a Scottish dish like porridge, made from broth, milk, or water stirred into toasted oatmeal to form stringy dumplings [Mid-17thC. Via Old French *broez* and assumed Vulgar Latin *brodo* from, ultimately, a prehistoric Germanic word meaning 'broth'.]

broth /broth/ *n.* **1.** THIN SOUP a thin nourishing soup of poultry, meat, or vegetables, to which barley or rice is sometimes added **2.** FLAVOURFUL SOUP BASE a liquid made by cooking vegetables, meat, seafood, or poultry in water for a long time, used as a base for soups and sauces [Old English *brop*. Ultimately from an Indo-European base meaning 'heat, boil', which also produced English *brew* and *fervent*.]

brothel /bróth'l/ *n.* a place where people pay to have sexual intercourse with prostitutes [14thC. Shortening of earlier *brothel-house*, from Old English *bropen* 'ruined', which was used for 'worthless person', and came to denote a prostitute in the 15thC.]

brothel creepers *npl.* men's suede shoes with thick crepe soles, popular in the 1950s and 1960s [Perhaps from their quiet step]

brother /brúthər/ *n.* **1.** MALE SIBLING a boy or man who has the same father and mother as another person **2.** (*plural* **brothers** *or* **brethren**) FELLOW MEMBER a man who belongs to the same race, religion, profession, trade, or organization as another man **3.** (*plural* **brothers** *or* **brethren**) CHR LAY MEMBER a member of a religious order for men **4.** (*plural* **brothers** *or* **brethren**) CHR DEVOTED RELIGIOUS WORKER a man who devotes himself to the work of a men's religious order without having been professed ■ *interj.* EXPRESSING SURPRISE OR ANNOYANCE used to express surprise, annoyance, or disappointment (*informal*) ○ *Oh brother! What happened here today?* [Old English *brōpor*. Ultimately from an Indo-European word that also produced Latin *frater* 'brother' (source of English *fraternal*), Greek *phrater*, Sanskrit *bhrātṛ*, and German *Bruder*.]

brotherhood /brúther hŏŏd/ *n.* **1.** HAVING SAME PARENTS the relationship of brothers **2.** GROUP OF MEN an organization of men, e.g. a trade union, that is united for a common purpose **3.** ALL THE MEMBERS all the members of a particular profession or trade **4.** GOODWILL a feeling of fellowship and sympathy for other people

brother-in-law (plural **brothers-in-law**) *n.* **1.** SISTER'S HUSBAND the husband of sb's sister **2.** SPOUSE'S BROTHER the brother of sb's husband or wife **3.** SPOUSE'S SISTER'S HUSBAND the husband of the sister of sb's husband or wife

brotherly /brútherli/ *adj.* the showing feelings that a brother might be expected to have towards his sister or brother [Old English *brōporlic*]

brougham /broom, broó əm/ *n.* a one-horse carriage with an open seat at the front for the driver and a closed compartment at the back for passengers, used in the 19th century [Mid-19thC. Named after the English politician and educational reformer Henry Peter, Lord *Brougham* (1778–1868), who designed the original brougham.]

brought *v.* past tense, past participle of **bring**

brouhaha /broó haa haa/ *n.* a noisy commotion or uproar (formal) [Late 19thC. From French, of uncertain origin: perhaps from Hebrew *bāruḵ habbā*, literally 'blessed is the comer, welcome!'; in allusion to the loud prayers at a traditional Jewish synagogue.]

brow /brow/ *n.* **1.** FOREHEAD the area on sb's face above the eyes and below the hairline **2.** = eyebrow **3.** TOP OF HILL the top edge of a hill **4.** MINING the top of a mineshaft [Old English *brū*. Ultimately from an Indo-European word that is also the ancestor of German *Braue* 'eyebrow'. Originally in the meaning 'eyelash'.]

browallia /brə waáli ə/ (plural **-a** or **-as**) *n.* a tropical American plant of the nightshade family cultivated for its blue, white, or violet flowers. Genus: *Browallia*. [Late 18thC. From modern Latin, genus name, named after the Swedish botanist Johann *Browall* (1707–55).]

browband /brów band/ *n.* a strap that is part of a horse's bridle and goes across its forehead

browbeat /brów beet/ (-**beats, -beating, -beat, -beaten** /-beet'n/) *vt.* to bully or intimidate sb sternly ○ *His father browbeat him into joining.* [Late 16thC. Origin uncertain: perhaps the underlying idea is of intimidating sb by furrowing the brows.] —**browbeater** *n.*

brown /brown/ *n.* **1.** COLOUR BETWEEN RED AND YELLOW a colour that varies between red and yellow and ranges from light to dark, such as the colour of wood or soil **2.** BROWN CLOTHING fabric or clothing that is brown in colour ○ *We had to wear brown for school.* **3.** BROWN PIGMENT OR DYE a pigment or dye that is formed from a combination of red, yellow, and black and has or is near to the colour of wood or soil **4.** BROWN OBJECT a brown object ○ *She decided to take the brown.* ■ *adj.* **1.** BETWEEN RED AND YELLOW IN COLOUR having a colour that varies between red and yellow, and can range from light to dark, such as that of wood or soil ○ *the fruit was brown and rotten* **2.** SUNTANNED deeply suntanned or sunburnt **3.** PARTIALLY OR WHOLLY UNPROCESSED used to describe foodstuffs that are partially or wholly unprocessed so that their natural brown colour remains ■ *vti.* (**browns, browning, browned**) MAKE OR BECOME BROWN to make sth brown or to become brown, e.g. in cooking or sunbathing [Old English *brūn*. Ultimately from an Indo-European word meaning 'bright, brown', which also produced English *bear*[1], *bruin, beaver*, and *burnish*.] —**brownish** *adj.* —**brownness** /brówn nəss/ *n.*

Brown /brown/, **Capability** (1715–83) British landscape gardener. He landscaped the grounds of many English country houses, including Blenheim Palace in Oxfordshire and Chatsworth in Derbyshire, and created a naturalistic style of landscape design. Real name **Lancelot Brown**

Brown, Ford Madox (1821–93) French-born British painter. A Pre-Raphaelite and associate of William Morris, he produced dramatic historical paintings such as *The Last of England* (1855).

Brown, George Mackay (1921–96) British poet and novelist. Influenced by Orkney folklore, his work includes the poetry collection *Loaves and Fishes* (1959) and the novel *Beside the Ocean of Time* (1994).

Brown, John (1800–59) US abolitionist. Convicted of treason after a failed attempt to launch a slave rebellion, he was hanged in Virginia. The song 'John Brown's Body' commemorates his actions.

brown adipose tissue *n.* = **brown fat**

brown alga *n.* a marine alga that has chlorophyll masked by brown pigment. The kelps and wracks are brown algae. Division: *Phaeophyta*.

brown bear *n.* a bear that is mainly brown in colour, found in western North America and northern Europe and Asia. The most widely distributed of all bears, brown bears vary in size from the small Syrian variety to the giant Kodiak bear and include the North American grizzlies. Latin name: *Ursus arctos*.

Brown Bess /-bes/ (plural **Brown Besses**) *n.* a flintlock musket formerly used by the British Army [So called because of its brown walnut stock]

Brown Betty /-bétti/ (plural **Brown Betties**) *n. US* a baked apple pudding made from apples, breadcrumbs, sugar, spices, butter, and sometimes raisins

brown bread *n.* bread made using wholemeal flour

brown coal *n.* a soft, brown-black fossil fuel with visible plant remains and a high moisture content

brown dwarf *n.* a star that is smaller than a planet and has a mass equivalent to less than one-tenth of the Sun's mass

brown earth *n.* a type of soil formed in temperate humid regions under deciduous forests and characterized by a dark brown layer rich in organic material

browned-off *adj.* (dated slang) **1.** BORED OR FED UP in a state of boredom or low spirits **2.** DEPRESSED EMOTIONALLY discouraged or disheartened

brown fat *n.* a dark-coloured fatty tissue in many mammals, especially hibernating animals and human babies, that produces heat in order to control body temperature

brownfield site /brównfeeld-/ *n.* an urban development site that has been previously built on but is currently unused. ◊ **greenfield site**

brown goods *npl.* electrical consumer goods such as televisions and audio equipment that are mainly used for home entertainment, as opposed to conventionally 'white' kitchen appliances such as refrigerators and washing machines

Brownian movement /brówni ən-/, **Brownian motion** *n.* the random movement of microscopic particles suspended in a liquid or gas that occurs as a result of collisions with molecules of the surrounding medium [Named after the English botanist Robert *Brown* 1773–1858, who first described it in connection with the motions of pollen grains]

brownie /brówni/ *n.* **1.** US RICH FLAT CHOCOLATE CAKE a piece of flat rich chocolate cake baked in a square or rectangular tin and sometimes containing chopped nuts **2.** HELPFUL ELF OR GOBLIN in folklore, a small supernatural being believed to do helpful work at night [Early 16thC, with the sense 'elf'. The term was first used of a chocolate cake in late 19thC.]

Brownie[1] /brówni/, **Brownie Guide** *n.* in the UK, a member of the junior section of the Guides, aged between seven and ten years [Early 20thC. So called because of their brown uniform.]

Brownie[2] *tdmk.* a trademark for a make of box camera

Brownie Guider *n.* an adult leader of a pack of Brownie Guides, formerly known as 'Brown Owl'

brownie point, **Brownie point** *n.* a credit earned for doing sth helpful, especially in order to please (informal) [From the erroneous idea that Brownie Guides use points for advancement]

browning /brówni ng/ *n.* a substance, e.g. caramelized sugar, used to give a brown colour to soup or gravy

Browning /brówning/, **Elizabeth Barrett** (1806–61) British poet. Her works include *Sonnets from the Portuguese* (1850), *Aurora Leigh* (1856), and *Poems Before Congress* (1860). She married Robert Browning in 1846 and lived with him in Italy. Born **Elizabeth Barrett**

Browning, Robert (1812–89) British poet. His works include *Men and Women* (1855), *Dramatis Personae* (1864), and *The Ring and the Book* (1868–69). He married Elizabeth Barrett Browning in 1846.

Browning automatic rifle *n.* an air-cooled, gas-operated, magazine-fed rifle with a .30 in calibre barrel, capable of firing between 200 and 350 rounds per minute with an effective range of 600 m/2,000 ft [Named after the US arms designer John M. *Browning* 1855–1926.]

Browning machine gun *n.* an air- or water-cooled, belt-fed, automatic machine gun with either a .30 or .50 calibre barrel, capable of firing over 500 rounds per minute [Named after the US arms designer John M. *Browning* 1855–1926.]

brown lacewing *n.* an insect with brownish wings that often feeds on agricultural pests. Family: Hemerobiidae.

brownlands /brówn landz/ *npl.* land for development that has been previously developed but is currently unused. ◊ **brownfield site**

brown lung disease, **brown lung** *n.* = **byssinosis**

brown mustard *n.* **1.** PLANT OF MUSTARD FAMILY an annual plant of the mustard family with pale yellow flowers, irregularly lobed leaves, and dark reddish-brown oil-rich seeds used in cooking. Latin name: *Brassica juncea*. **2.** GROUND SEEDS USED IN COOKING the ground seeds of the brown mustard plant, used as a cooking spice

brownnose /brówn nōz/ (**-noses, -nosing, -nosed**) *vti.* to be unnaturally subservient or obsequious to sb in authority (slang; considered offensive by some speakers) ○ *He brownnosed his way to the top of the firm.* [So called with relation to its synonym: 'kiss-ass'] —**brownnose** *n.* —**brownnoser** *n.*

brownout /brówn owt/ *n.* **1.** US DIMMING OF LIGHTS a dimming or reduction in the use of electric lights in a city, town, or region, especially as an economy measure **2.** US POWER REDUCTION a temporary reduction in electrical power caused by high consumer demand or by technical malfunction **3.** LAPSE OF CONCENTRATION a temporary lapse of concentration or focus [Mid-20thC. Modelled on 'blackout'.]

brown owl *n.* = **tawny owl**

Brown Owl *n.* formerly, the adult leader of a pack of Brownies. Now called **Brownie Guider**

brown paper *n.* thick strong brown-coloured paper used for wrapping parcels

brown patch *n.* a soil-borne fungal disease of grass that produces round dead patches

brown rat *n.* an extremely destructive rat, originally from Europe and Asia, that is found worldwide in populated areas. Latin name: *Rattus norvegicus*.

brown recluse spider *n.* a pale brown poisonous spider found in the United States and South America that has a violin-shaped mark on the head area. Latin name: *Loxosceles reclusa*.

brown rice *n.* unpolished rice in which the yellowish-brown outer layer containing the bran remains intact. This type of rice retains its B vitamins, thus making it more nutritious than white rice. ◊ **white rice**

brown rot *n.* a disease of ripe tree fruits such as apples and peaches, caused by fungi. The infected fruit turns brown, and concentric yellow rings appear on the plant. Genus: *Rhizoctonia*.

brown sauce *n.* **1.** SAUCE MADE FROM MEAT STOCK a sauce made from a dark meat stock, thickened with flour that has been browned in fat **2.** SPICY SAUCE a dark-brown savoury sauce made from fruit, vinegar, sugar, and spices

brown seaweed *n.* = **brown alga**

Brown Shirt *n.* a Nazi storm-trooper [Translation of German *Braunhemd*, from the brown uniform shirts of the Nazi stormtroopers]

brown snake *n. Aus* a poisonous brown-coloured snake found in Australia. Genus: *Pseudonaja*.

brownstone /brówn stōn/ *n. US* **1.** SANDSTONE a reddish-brown sandstone used as a building material **2.** SANDSTONE BUILDING a house or building made from or faced with reddish-brown sandstone, especially houses in New York City

———— **WORD KEY: SYNONYMS** ————
See Synonyms at *house*.

brown study *n.* a state of deep thought or serious absorption (*dated*) [Origin uncertain: probably from BROWN in the sense 'gloomy']

brown sugar *n.* **1.** REFINED SUGAR WITH TREACLE a soft refined sugar that is light or dark brown in colour. It is made from refined white sugar combined with mild refined treacle and is used in cooking. **2.** UNREFINED SUGAR unrefined or partially refined sugar **3.** HEROIN the drug heroin (*slang*)

brown-tail moth (*plural* **brown-tail moths**) *n.* a white and brown moth, native to Europe and also found in the eastern United States, whose caterpillars destroy the leaves of trees and produce a poison that causes breathing problems and a rash in humans. Latin name: *Euproctis chrysorrhoea*.

brown thrasher *n.* a bird that is related to the mockingbird and has a long tail, long curving beak, reddish-brown back, and white breast with black spots. It is found in the eastern and central United States and in the rain forests of Dominica and the Lesser Antilles. Latin name: *Toxostoma rufum*.

brown trout *n.* a common freshwater fish that is brownish in colour and is caught for food or sport. It is native to Europe and also found in North America. Latin name: *Salmo trutta*.

browse /browz/ *v.* (**browses, browsing, browsed**) **1.** *vti.* READ CASUALLY to read through sth quickly or superficially **2.** *vi.* LOOK THROUGH OR OVER CASUALLY to look through or over sth, especially goods in a shop, in a leisurely manner with the hope of finding sth of interest **3.** *vti.* ZOOL FEED ON VEGETATION to feed or graze on tender vegetation such as the shoots, leaves, or twigs of shrubs or trees **4.** *vti.* COMPUT SCAN COMPUTER FILES to scan and view files in a computer database or on the Internet, especially on the World Wide Web ■ *n.* **1.** SESSION OF BROWSING a superficial read through sth, e.g. a newspaper, or a leisurely look over sth, e.g. the goods in a shop **2.** ZOOL FEEDING PERIOD a session of feeding on tender shoots or twigs of shrubs and trees **3.** TENDER VEGETATION USED AS FOOD the tender shoots, leaves, or twigs of shrubs and trees used as food by animals such as deer and cattle [Early 16thC. Via obsolete French *broust* from Old French *brost*, of Germanic origin.]

browser /brówzər/ *n.* **1.** COMPUT SOFTWARE FOR SEARCHING INTERNET a piece of computer software that allows an Internet user to search for information on the World Wide Web **2.** SB WHO BROWSES sb who reads or looks over sth, e.g. a reference book or the goods in a shop, in a leisurely or superficial manner [Mid-16thC]

Broxbourne /bróks bawrn/ largely residential town in Hertfordshire, England. Population: 82,200 (1995).

BRU *abbr.* Brunei (*international vehicle registration*)

Brubeck /bróo bek/, **Dave** (b. 1920) US pianist and composer. He is known for his progressive jazz compositions such as *Blue Rondo a la Turk* (1957). Full name **David William Brubeck**

Bruce /brooss/, **Christopher** (b. 1945) British dancer and choreographer. He worked for the Ballet Rambert and the English National Ballet. His dances include *Ancient Voices of Children* (1975).

Bruce, James (1730–94) British explorer. He traced the upper waters of the Blue Nile in 1770 and wrote *Travels to Discover the Source of the Nile* (1768–73).

Bruce, Robert, King of Scots (1274–1329). Leader of the Scottish War of Independence.

Bruce, Stanley Melbourne, 1st Viscount Bruce of Melbourne (1883–1967) Australian statesman. He was a National Party politician and prime minister of Australia (1923–29).

brucellosis /bróossə lṓssiss/ *n.* a chronic infectious disease of some domestic animals, e.g. cattle, dogs, goats, and pigs, that is caused by bacteria and may lead to spontaneous abortion. It can be transmitted to human beings through contaminated milk, causing symptoms such as fever, headache, painful joints, aches, and weakness. Genus: *Brucella*. ◊ **Bang's disease** [Mid-20thC. Coined from *Brucella* (the name of the genus of bacteria that causes the disease), from the name of Sir David *Bruce* (1855–1931), a Scottish physician.]

Bruch /brookh/, **Max** (1838–1920) German composer. His compositions include a violin concerto and the 'Kol Nidrei' variations (1880), which draw on Hebrew and Celtic folk melodies.

brucine /bróo seen/ *n.* a poisonous white crystalline alkaloid derived from the seeds of the nux vomica tree and used to render alcohol unfit for human consumption. Formula: $C_{23}H_{26}N_2O_4$. [Early 19thC. From modern Latin *Brucea*, name of a tree thought to bear the false angostura bark the substance is derived from.]

brucite /bróoss īt/ *n.* a mineral form of magnesium hydroxide that occurs in hydrothermal deposits and in metamorphized limestone [Early 19thC. Named after the US mineralogist Archibald *Bruce* (1777–1818).]

Bruckner /bróoknər/, **Anton** (1824–96) Austrian composer. He wrote nine symphonies and four masses. His music was influenced by Wagner and Schubert.

Brueghel /bróyg'l/, **Bruegel, Breughel, Jan** (1568–1625) Flemish painter. The son of Pieter Brueghel the Elder, he produced still lifes and landscape paintings.

Brueghel, Bruegel, Breughel, Pieter (1520–69) Flemish painter. He produced religious and moral allegories in contemporary landscapes, depicting peasant life in works such as *Peasant Wedding* (1568). Known as **Pieter Brueghel the Elder**

Bruges /broozh/ capital of West Flanders Province, western Belgium. It is famous for its traditional lace industries. Population: 115,815 (1996).

bruin /bróo in/, **Bruin** *n.* used as a name for a bear in folklore, fables, and children's stories [15thC. From Middle Dutch, literally 'brown'.]

bruise /brooz/ *n.* (*plural* **bruises**) **1.** SKIN DISCOLORATION CAUSED BY INJURY a tender area of skin discoloration caused by blood leaking from blood vessels damaged by pressure or impact **2.** DAMAGE TO PLANT TISSUE damage to underlying plant or fruit tissue, visible as a soft discoloured area on the unbroken surface and caused by pressure or impact **3.** EMOTIONAL INJURY an injury that is not physical, e.g. hurt feelings or damaged self-esteem ■ *v.* (**bruises, bruising, bruised**) **1.** *vti.* INJURE CAUSING SKIN DISCOLORATION to injure, or sustain an injury to, a part of the body resulting in discoloration caused by blood leaking from damaged blood vessels **2.** *vti.* DAMAGE PLANT TISSUE to damage plant tissue or to sustain damage by pressure or impact, leaving a softened and discoloured surface area **3.** *vt.* COOK CRUSH FOOD to crush or pound food, especially to extract juice from it or bring out its flavour **4.** *vt.* UPSET SB to injure sb's feelings or harm sb's self-esteem ○ *I was bruised by the criticism* [Partly from Old English *brȳsan* 'to crush', and partly from Anglo-Norman *bruser* 'to break', of prehistoric Germanic origin]

bruiser /bróozər/ *n.* a large strong man or youth, e.g. a boxer, bodyguard, or club bouncer (*informal*)

bruising /bróozing/ *n.* DISCOLORATION OF SKIN SURFACE bruises or the dark patches left on the surface of bruised skin ■ *adj.* PAINFUL causing emotional, psychological, or physical pain

bruit /broot/ *n.* **1.** MED ABNORMAL SOUND INSIDE BODY an abnormal sound heard inside the body, usually with the aid of a stethoscope, and caused by turbulent blood flow within the heart or blood vessels **2.** A RUMOUR OR REPORT a story, true or untrue, that is passed about among people (*archaic*) **3.** NOISE OR DIN loud sounds or the noise made by them (*archaic*) ■ *vt.* (**bruits, bruiting, bruited**) SPREAD STORY to circulate stories, whether true or untrue [From Old French, from the past participle of *bruire* 'to roar', from assumed Vulgar Latin *brugire*, a blend of assumed *brager* and Latin *rugire*]

Brum /brum/ *n.* = **Brummagem** (*informal*) [Mid-19thC. Shortening of *Brummagem*.]

Brumaire /brü máir/ *n.* the second month of the year in the French Revolutionary calendar, corresponding to the period from 23 October to 21 November in the Gregorian calendar [Early 19thC. From French, formed from *brume* 'brume'.]

brumby /brúmbi/ (*plural* **-bies**) *n. ANZ* a wild unbroken horse [Late 19thC. Origin unknown.]

brume /broom/ *n.* a weather condition in which fog or mist is present, or the fog or mist itself (*literary*) [Early 18thC. Via French, literally 'fog', from Latin *bruma* 'winter' (see BRUMAL).] —**brumous** *adj.*

brummagem /brúmməjəm/, **Brummagem** *n.* STH CHEAP AND SHOWY sth, especially imitation jewellery, that is cheap and gaudy ■ *adj.* CHEAPLY SHOWY cheap and shoddy [Mid-17thC. From *Brummagem*, alteration of Birmingham, England, originally referring to counterfeit coins made there.]

Brummagem /brúmməjəm/ *n.* a nickname for Birmingham, England (*informal*) [Mid-17thC. Dialectal form of *Birmingham*.]

Brummell /brúmm'l/, **Beau** (1778–1840) British dandy. A courtier and friend of George IV, he was a fashion-setter in Regency England. Real name **George Bryan Brummell**

Brummie /brúmmi/, **Brummy** *n.* (*plural* **-mies**) SB FROM BIRMINGHAM sb who was born or brought up in Birmingham (*informal*) ■ *adj.* OF BIRMINGHAM, ENGLAND relating to or typical of the English city of Birmingham (*informal*)

brunch /brunch/ (*plural* **brunches**) *n.* a meal that combines breakfast and lunch, eaten late in the morning [Late 19thC. Blend of BREAKFAST and LUNCH.]

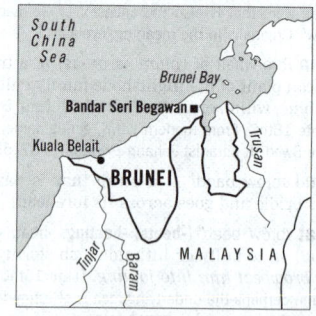

Brunei

Brunei /broo nī/ island sultanate bisected by Malaysia in northwestern Borneo, eastern Asia. Language: Malay. Currency: Brunei dollar. Capital: Bandar Seri Begawan. Population: 307,612 (1997). Area: 5,765 sq. km/2,226 sq. mi. Official name **Negara Brunei Darussalam**

Isambard Kingdom Brunel

Brunel /broo nél/, **Isambard Kingdom** (1806–59) British engineer. He designed the Clifton Suspension Bridge and constructed the *Great Western* (1837), the first steamship designed to cross the Atlantic.

Brunelleschi /broonə léski/, **Filippo** (1377–1446) Italian architect and sculptor. One of the greatest Renaissance architects, he designed the dome of the cathedral in Florence (1420–61) and built several churches in Florence. Real name **Filippo di Ser Brunellesco**

brunette /broo nét/ *n.* WOMAN WITH DARK-HAIR a girl or woman with dark brown hair ■ *adj.* **1.** DARK BROWN used to describe hair that is dark brown **2.** WITH DARK HAIR used to describe a girl or woman with dark brown hair [Early 17thC. From French, the feminine form of *brunet* 'BRUNET'.]

Brunhild /broon híld/, **Brünnhilde** /-hílde/ *n.* in medieval Germanic mythology, the queen of Iceland who promises to marry whoever can defeat her in battle. Siegfried does so on behalf of King Gunther.

Bruno /broónō/, **St** (1030?–1101) German monk in the French mountains at Chartreuse. He founded a monastery of hermit monks (1084), which later became the Carthusian contemplative order. Known as **Bruno the Carthusian**

brunt /brunt/ *n.* **1.** MAIN FORCE OF STH the main force or effect of sth, e.g. a blow or an attack **2.** GREATER BURDEN OF STH the greater part or the main burden **3.** FORCEFUL ATTACK a forceful blow or attack (*archaic*) [14thC. Origin unknown.]

Brush

brush[1] /brush/ *n.* **1.** TOOL WITH BRISTLES ATTACHED TO HANDLE an implement consisting of bristles set into a handle, used especially for grooming the hair or for painting, polishing, scrubbing, or sweeping **2.** USE OF BRUSH the use of a brush, e.g. to groom the hair or to sweep a surface **3.** LIGHT CONTACT a light stroke or momentary contact **4.** SHORT UNPLEASANT ENCOUNTER a brief unpleasant encounter ○ *a brush with evil* **5.** BUSHY TAIL OF FOX a bushy tail, especially the tail of a fox as a hunting trophy **6.** ELEC ELECTRICAL CONDUCTOR an electrical conductor that makes sliding contact between a stationary and a moving part of a generator or motor while completing a circuit and conveying a current **7.** = **brush discharge** ■ *v.* (**brushes, brushing, brushed**) **1.** *vti.* USE BRUSH ON STH to use a brush to clean, groom, paint, polish, or scrub **2.** *vt.* APPLY WITH BRUSH to apply sth such as paint or varnish to a surface using a brush **3.** *vt.* REMOVE STH WITH BRUSH remove with a brush or sweeping motion **4.** *vt.* REJECT STH to dismiss, ignore, or rebuff sth or sb in an abrupt or curt manner ○ *They brushed aside the suggestion.* **5.** *vti.* GRAZE AGAINST STH to touch sth lightly and briefly in passing **6.** *vi.* MOVE PAST STH CLOSELY AND QUICKLY to move past sth or sb very fast so as to come into brief contact [14thC. From Old French *broisse*, probably a variant of *broce* 'brushwood' (see BRUSH[2]), suggesting that cut branches were used to make brooms or brushes.] —**brusher** *n.* —**brushy** /brúshi/ *adj.*
◇ **tar sb with the same brush** to attribute unfairly the faults and deficits of sb to another
brush off *vt.* to dismiss or disregard sb or sth in an abrupt manner
brush up *vt.* to refresh or renew knowledge of or skill in sth

brush[2] /brush/ *n.* **1.** LAND COVERED WITH UNDERGROWTH land covered with a thick growth of shrubs or bushes. = **brushwood** *n.* **1 2.** TWIGS AND BRANCHES cut or broken branches and twigs **3.** BACKWOODS wild and sparsely populated woodland [14thC. Via Anglo-Norman *brousse*, a variant of Old French *broce* 'broken branches': possibly from Latin *bruscum* 'knot on a maple tree'.]

brush border *n.* a dense layer of tiny protuberances that lines certain absorbing cells, e.g. in the intestine and kidney

brush discharge, **brush** *n.* a luminous electric discharge between two conductors, consisting of a flow of ionized particles with less intensity than a spark [Late 18thC. From its brushlike appearance.]

brushed /brusht/ *adj.* **1.** FINISHED WITH SOFT AND FUZZY SURFACE used to describe a knitted or woven fabric that has a nap produced by a brushing process during manufacture **2.** NONREFLECTIVE a metallic surface with a nonreflective sheen

brush fire *n.* **1.** FIRE IN DRY BRUSH a fire in dry brush and scrub that usually spreads quickly **2.** A SMALL WAR a localized but often intensely fought war ■ *adj.* INVOLVING LOCAL MILITARY involving only small-scale and local military mobilization

brushmark /brúsh maark/ *n.* a mark or line left by the bristles of a brush on a painted or varnished surface

brushoff /brúsh of/ *n.* an abrupt dismissal, rejection, or snub (*informal*)

brushstroke /brúsh strōk/ *n.* a movement of a paintbrush that produces a particular look or mark on a painted surface, or the mark itself

brush turkey (*plural* **brush turkeys**) *n.* a heavy-bodied bird resembling a turkey, with a bare head, black plumage, and red and yellow wattles, found in the forests of northeastern Australia. It lays its eggs in mounds of rotting vegetation as a method of incubation. Latin name: *Alectura lathami*. [So called because of the wattles on its neck]

brushwood /brúsh woŏd/ *n.* **1.** THICKET a dense undergrowth of small trees and bushes **2.** LAND COVERED BY BRUSHWOOD land covered by a dense undergrowth of small trees and bushes **3.** = **brush**[2] *n.* **2**

brushwork /brúsh wurk/ *n.* **1.** ARTIST'S CHARACTERISTIC WAY OF APPLYING PAINT the characteristic manner in which an artist applies paint with a brush **2.** WORK DONE WITH BRUSH the product of an artist's use of a brush in painting

brusque /broösk/ *adj.* abrupt, blunt, or curt in manner or speech [Early 17thC. Via French from, ultimately, late Latin *bruscum* 'coarse, rough', of uncertain origin.] —**brusquely** *adv.* —**brusqueness** *n.*

brusquerie /broóskəri, broos-/ *n.* bluntness or abruptness of manner [Mid-18thC. From French, formed from *brusque* (see BRUSQUE).]

Brussels /brúss'lz/ the largest city and capital of Belgium. It is situated in the centre of Belgium and is the headquarters of the European Union and the North Atlantic Treaty Organisation (NATO). Population: 948,122 (1996).

Brussels carpet *n.* a carpet with a heavy patterned pile formed by small woollen loops attached to a linen base

Brussels griffon *n.* = **griffon** [So called because the breed originated in Belgium]

Brussels lace *n.* **1.** FINE LACE a fine lace with a floral design, made with bobbins or with needle and thread, that originated in or near Brussels **2.** MACHINE-MADE NET LACE a machine-made net lace with an appliqué design

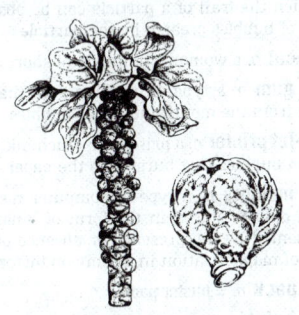

Brussels sprout

Brussels sprout *n.* **1.** PLANT PRODUCING EDIBLE GREEN BUDS a plant related to the cabbage that has a thick stalk lined with edible swollen green buds resembling small cabbages. Latin name: *Brassica oleracea*. **2.** GREEN VEGETABLE LIKE TINY CABBAGE a small green swollen bud like a tiny cabbage that is produced by the Brussels sprout plant and is eaten as a vegetable [First grown near Brussels, the capital of Belgium]

brut /broot/ *adj.* used to describe wine, especially sparkling white wine, that is extremely dry in taste [Late 19thC. Via French, 'unsweetened', literally 'rough, unrefined', from Latin *brutus* (see BRUTE).]

brutal /broot'l/ *adj.* **1.** RUTHLESS AND CRUEL extremely ruthless or cruel **2.** HARSH AND SEVERE unrelentingly harsh and severe ○ *a brutal regime* **3.** DIRECT IN MANNER direct or insensitive in manner or speech ○ *with brutal frankness* **4.** LIKE AN ANIMAL relating to or typical of beasts or lower animals (*archaic*) [15thC. Directly or via French from medieval Latin *brutalis*, from Latin *brutus* (see BRUTE).] —**brutalness** *n.*

brutalise *vt.* = **brutalize**

brutalism /broot'lizzəm/ *n.* a style of modern architecture characterized by massiveness, a lack of exterior decoration, harsh lines, and the use of structural materials such as exposed concrete and service pipes [Early 19thC. Ultimately from French *brut* 'rough (concrete)'.] —**brutalist** *n.*, *adj.*

brutality /broo tálləti/ (*plural* **-ties**) *n.* **1.** BEING CRUEL cruel, harsh, or ruthless behaviour or treatment **2.** ACT OF CRUELTY a cruel, harsh, or ruthless act

brutalize /broot'l īz/ (**-izes, -izing, -ized**), **brutalise** (**-talises, -talising, -talised**) *vt.* **1.** MAKE SB BRUTAL to make sb brutal, inhuman, or unfeeling **2.** TREAT SB CRUELLY to treat sb brutally, cruelly, or harshly —**brutalization** /broot'l ī záysh'n/ *n.*

brutally /broot'li/ *adv.* **1.** CRUELLY OR HARSHLY in a cruel or harsh manner **2.** VERY FRANKLY OR CALLOUSLY in an unpleasantly or insensitively forthright or severe manner ○ *brutally honest*

brute /broot/ *n.* **1.** SB BRUTAL sb who is very cruel, ruthless, or insensitive **2.** ANIMAL an animal other than a human being (*literary*) ■ *adj.* **1.** PURELY PHYSICAL purely physical or instinctive, rather than intellectual or reasoned **2.** CRUEL OR SAVAGE displaying extreme cruelty and savagery **3.** STARK unremittingly harsh or severe **4.** CRUDE OR BARBARIC used to describe behaviour, actions, or instincts that are considered crude, especially those prompted by physical desire and hunger **5.** OF BEASTS relating or belonging to lower animals, as opposed to human beings [15thC. Via French *brut* from Latin *brutus* 'stupid, animal-like'. Ultimately from an Indo-European word meaning 'heavy', which is also the ancestor of English *gravity*, *baritone*, and *guru*.] —**brutism** *n.*

brutish /broótish/ *adj.* **1.** RELATING TO BEASTS relating to or characteristic of lower animals **2.** CRUEL cruel, ruthless, or insensitive **3.** COARSELY UNINTELLIGENT coarse, crude, unintelligent, or lacking sensitivity **4.** CARNAL animalistically carnal or sensual —**brutishly** *adv.* —**brutishness** *n.*

Bruton /broot'n/, **John** (*b.* 1947) Irish statesman. He was prime minister of the Republic of Ireland (1994–97).

Brutus /broótəss/, **Lucius Junius** (*fl.* late 6th century BC) Roman statesman. He drove the Etruscan royal family, the Tarquins, out of Rome and founded the Roman republic. He was elected one of the first two Roman consuls.

Brutus, Marcus Junius (85?–42 BC) Roman general and politician. He sided with Pompey against Caesar during the civil war 49 BC), and was a principal conspirator in Caesar's assassination (44 BC). He was defeated by Mark Antony and Octavian at Philippi (42 BC), and committed suicide.

bruxism /broóksizzəm/ *n.* the unconscious habit of grinding or gritting the teeth that occurs during sleep or in stressful situations and can lead to excessive wear of the teeth [Mid-20thC. Formed from Greek *brukein* 'to gnash the teeth'.]

Brynhild /brínhild/ *n.* in Norse mythology, a Valkyrie who is woken from an enchanted sleep by Sigurd and later tricked into marrying his brother-in-law, Gunnar

bryo- *prefix.* moss ○ *bryophyte* [From Greek *bruon*; related to *bruein* 'to teem' (source of English *embryo*)]

bryology /brī ólləji/ *n.* the branch of botany concerned with the study of hornworts, mosses, and liverworts —**bryological** /brī ə lójjik'l/ *adj.* —**bryologist** /brī ólləjist/ *n.*

bryony /brí əni/ (plural -nies) n. a climbing plant that belongs to the marrow family, has large leaves, tendrils, and red or black berries, and is found in Europe and North Africa. Genus: *Bryonia*. [Pre-12thC. Via Latin from Greek *bruonia*, from *bruein* 'to teem' (source of English *embryo*).]

bryophyte /brí ə fīt/ n. a nonflowering plant, often growing in damp places, that has separate gamete-bearing and spore-bearing forms. Mosses are bryophytes. Division: *Bryophyta*. —**bryophytic** /brí ə fíttik/ adj.

bryophyte layer n. = moss layer

bryozoan /brí ə zṓ ən/ n. an aquatic invertebrate animal that reproduces by budding. Bryozoans often form colonies on the sea bottom or attached to seaweed. Phylum: Bryozoa. [Late 19thC. From modern Latin *Bryozoa*, which was coined from Greek *bruon* 'moss' + *zoion* 'animal'.] —**bryozoan** adj.

Brython /bríth'n/ n. sb who speaks Breton, Welsh, or Cornish [Late 19thC. From Welsh.]

Brythonic /bri thónnik/, **Brittonic** /-tónnik/ n. GROUP OF CELTIC LANGUAGES a group of languages, comprising Breton, Welsh, and Cornish, that belongs to the Celtic branch of Indo-European languages. About one million people speak a Brythonic language. ■ adj. OF BRYTHONS relating to or typical of the Brythons, or their language or culture [Late 19thC. Formed from Welsh *Brython*.]

BS abbr. 1. British Standard (used as part of the number of a British Standards Institution publication) 2. Bachelor of Surgery 3. bill of sale

b.s. abbr. 1. balance sheet 2. b.s., B/S, b/s bill of sale

BSB abbr. British Standard brass (used to identify a type of screw thread)

BSc abbr. Bachelor of Science

BSE n. a disease that affects the nervous system of cattle, believed to be caused by an abnormal transmissable protein (**prion**) and related to Creutzfeldt-Jakob disease in humans. Full form **bovine spongiform encephalopathy**

BSF abbr. British Standard fine (used to identify a type of screw thread)

bsh. abbr. bushel

BSI abbr. British Standards Institution

B-side n. the side of a pop-music or jazz single that does not contain the title track and is considered less important

BSkyB abbr. British Sky Broadcasting

BSL abbr. British Sign Language

Bs/L abbr. bills of lading

BSN abbr. Bachelor of Science in Nursing

BSP abbr. British Standard pipe (used to identify a type of screw thread)

BSS abbr. British Standards Specification

BST abbr. 1. bovine somatotrophin 2. British Summer Time

BSW abbr. British Standard Whitworth (used to identify a type of screw thread)

Bt abbr. baronet

BT abbr. British Telecom

BTEC /beé tek/ abbr. Business and Technology Education Council

BThU abbr. British thermal unit

btl. abbr. bottle

btry abbr. MIL battery

btu, Btu abbr. British thermal unit

BTU n. a unit for measuring electrical energy, equal to 1 kilowatt-hour. Abbr of **Board of Trade Unit**

BTW, **btw** abbr. by the way (used in e-mail messages)

bty abbr. MIL battery

bu. abbr. bushel

BUAV abbr. British Union for the Abolition of Vivisection

buaya /bwí ə/ n. Malaysia, Singapore a man who tends to flirt (informal) [From Malay, literally 'crocodile']

bub /bub/ n. 1. US UNNAMED MALE PERSON used as a term of address to an unnamed male person, especially one encountered and spoken to casually (slang) 2. Aus BABY a baby or toddler (informal) [Mid-19thC. Shortening and alteration of BROTHER.]

bubal /byoób'l/ (plural -bal /byoób'l/ or -bals) n. a large hartebeest of northern Africa. Latin name: *Alcephalus boselaphus*. [Late 18thC. Via French from Latin *bubalus* from Greek *boubalos* 'gazelle'.]

bubble /búbb'l/ n. 1. THIN GLOBE-SHAPED FILM a thin film of sth, usually spherical or dome-shaped and filled with air or a gas 2. STH LIKE A BUBBLE sth spherical or dome-shaped like a bubble 3. GLOBULE WITHIN LIQUID OR SOLID a globule of air or a gas within a liquid or a solid, e.g. in a fizzy drink or in glass 4. GURGLING SOUND a gurgling sound made by a boiling or effervescent liquid 5. SOUND OF MANY BUBBLES BURSTING a sound produced by bubbles forming and bursting 6. SHAPE FOR SPEECH IN CARTOON a round shape that encloses the speech or thoughts of a character in a cartoon, especially a strip cartoon 7. DOME a dome, usually made of transparent glass or plastic 8. PROTECTED AREA a protected, isolated, or exempted area 9. FALSE CONFIDENCE a false feeling of confidence or security ○ *The rocketing housing market is a bubble that will surely burst.* 10. RISKY SCHEME a risky or unreliable business enterprise or speculative scheme, especially one proving to be fraudulent or unsuccessful ■ v. (-bles, -bling, -bled) 1. vi. EFFERVESCE OR BOIL UP to form or produce spherical or dome-shaped pockets of air or gas in a liquid 2. vi. GURGLE to move or flow with a gurgling sound 3. vi. EMERGE OR APPEAR to emerge or rise to the surface 4. vi. BE ESPECIALLY LIVELY WITH EMOTION to be animated with or display an emotion such as excitement, happiness, or anger ○ *bubbling with mirth* 5. vt. EXPRESS STH ENTHUSIASTICALLY to say sth with great animation and friendly enthusiasm 6. vi. Scotland SOB to blubber or snivel 7. vt. MAKE STH BUBBLE to cause sth to form bubbles or to move in bubbles through a liquid [14thC. Origin uncertain: probably an imitation of the sound of bubbling water.]

bubble and squeak n. 1. DISH OF POTATOES AND CABBAGE a dish consisting of leftover cooked potatoes and cabbage chopped up and fried together 2. Cockney OFFENSIVE TERM an offensive term for a Greek person (slang offensive) [So called because of the sounds that come from the pan when the dish is cooking. In the sense of 'Greek person', rhyming slang.]

bubble bath n. 1. FOAM BATH PREPARATION a usually perfumed and coloured preparation in liquid or crystal form that is added to bath water in order to make it foam 2. BATH CONTAINING FOAM a bath to which a preparation has been added to make the bath water foam

bubble car n. a small two-seater car, usually three-wheeled, with a transparent, bubble-shaped dome or a single door in place of a bonnet

bubble chamber n. a chamber containing a liquid, usually liquid hydrogen just above its boiling point, in which the trail of a particle can be observed as a line of bubbles created by the particle

bubble cut n. a woman's hairstyle of short full curls

bubble gum n. a type of chewing gum that can be blown from the mouth into large bubbles

bubble-jet printer n. a printer in which ink is heated to form bubbles that burst onto the paper

bubble memory n. a type of computer memory in which data is stored in the form of binary digits represented by the presence or absence of minute areas of magnetization in a semiconductor

bubble pack n. = blister pack

bubble point n. the temperature at which vapour bubbles start to appear when a liquid mixture is heated

bubbler /búbblər/ n. 1. US, Aus DRINKING FOUNTAIN a drinking fountain, especially one that spouts water from a vertical nozzle (regional) 2. DEVICE THAT BUBBLES GAS THROUGH LIQUID a device for bubbling gas through a liquid 3. STH THAT BUBBLES sth that emits bubbles, e.g. a mountain spring [Early 18thC. when the sense was usually 'swindler']

bubble top n. a transparent glass or plastic dome used in building, e.g. one forming a roof over a swimming pool

bubblewrap /búbb'l rap/ n. a sheet of plastic material covered with air-filled bubbles, used for wrapping fragile objects in order to protect them in transit

bubbly /búbb'li/ adj. (-blier, -bliest) 1. FOAMY OR EFFERVESCENT full of or producing bubbles 2. LIKE BUBBLES resembling a bubble or bubbles 3. CHEERFULLY EXCITED feeling and exhibiting cheerful excitement ■ n. CHAMPAGNE sparkling wine, especially champagne (informal) —**bubbliness** n.

Buber /boóbər/, **Martin** (1878–1965) Austrian-born Israeli theologian and philosopher. He was an intellectual leader of German Jews before World War II and expounded his influential religious philosophy of dialogue in his best-known work, *I and Thou* (1922).

bubo /byoóbō/ (plural -boes) n. swelling and inflammation of a lymph node, especially in the area of the armpit or groin [14thC. Via Latin from Greek *boubōn* 'swelling in the groin'.]

bubonic /byoo bónnik/ adj. used to describe a swelling (**bubo**) of the lymph nodes

bubonic plague n. an infectious fatal epidemic disease caused by a bacterium transmitted by fleas that have bitten an infected host, and characterized by fever, chills, and the formation of swellings (**buboes**). In the 14th century, an extensive epidemic of it occurred known as the Black Death. In modern times, infection is limited and sporadic and can be treated successfully with antibiotics. Latin name: *Yersinia pestis*. [Formed from Latin *bubon-*, the stem of *bubo* BUBO]

buccal /búk'l/ adj. 1. OF CHEEKS relating to or forming part of the cheek ○ *the buccal surface of a tooth* 2. OF THE MOUTH relating to the mouth [Early 19thC. Formed from Latin *bucca* 'cheek' (source also of English *buckle* and *embouchure*).]

buccaneer /búkə neér/ n. 1. PIRATE a pirate, especially one who preyed on Spanish colonies and shipping in the West Indies in the 17th century 2. UNSCRUPULOUS ADVENTURER OR BUSINESSPERSON a ruthless or unscrupulous adventurer, businessperson, or politician ■ vi. (-neers, -neering, -neered) ACT LIKE BUCCANEER to be or behave like a buccaneer [Mid-17thC. From French *boucanier*, from *boucaner* 'to cook over an open fire'. The underlying meaning is 'a hunter who cooks or cures meat outdoors'.] —**buccaneering** adj., n.

buccinator /búksi naytər/ n. a flat thin muscle that compresses the cheek and is used in blowing and chewing [Late 17thC. From Latin, formed from *buccinare* 'to blow the trumpet', from *buccina*, a kind of trumpet.]

Bucephalus /byoo séffələss/ n. the favourite war horse of Alexander the Great, which he tamed when still a boy

Buchan /búkən/, **John, 1st Baron Tweedsmuir** (1875–1940) British writer and statesman. Among his many books are *Prester John* (1910) and *The Thirty-Nine Steps* (1915), famously filmed by director Alfred Hitchcock in 1935. He was appointed governor-general of Canada in 1935.

Buchanan /byoo kánnən/, **George** (1506–82) Scottish scholar and humanist. He was a tutor to Mary, Queen of Scots, and tutor to James VI of Scotland (1570–78) and wrote a monumental Latin History of Scotland (1582).

Buchanan, James (1791–1868) US statesman and 15th president of the United States. A Federalist turned Democrat, he was a US Representative (1821–23), Senator (1834–45), and secretary of state (1845–49). During his presidency (1857–61) he was unable to avert the US Civil War (1861–65).

Bucharest /boókə rést/ n. the largest city and capital of Romania. It is situated on a plain in the southeastern part of the country, north of the River Danube. Population: 2,339,156 (1994).

Buchenwald /boókh ən vald/ village near Weimar, central Germany that was the site of a World War II Nazi concentration camp (1937–45)

Buchner /búknər, boókhnər/, **Eduard** (1860–1917) German chemist. His discovery attributing the fermentation of yeast to enzyme reaction won him the Nobel Prize in Chemistry in 1907.

Büchner /byo͝okhnər/, **Georg** (1813–37) German dramatist. He was an early exponent of expressionist theatre. His plays include *Danton's Death* (1835) and *Woyzeck* (1836). Full name **Karl Georg Büchner**

Buchner funnel /búknər-/, **Büchner funnel** *n.* a cylindrical funnel, usually made of porcelain, with a flat perforated base through which liquids are drawn and filtered under reduced pressure [Named after the German chemist Eduard *Büchner* 1860–1917]

buchu /bo͞o koo/ (*plural* **-chus** *or* **-chu**), **bucku** (*plural* **-ckus** *or* **-cku**) *n.* a southern African shrub with leaves that are used as a mild diuretic and urinary antiseptic. Genus: *Agathosma.* [Mid-18thC. Via Afrikaans from Nama.]

Buchwald /búk wawld/, **Art** (*b.* 1925) US journalist. His popular column, first appearing in the *International Herald Tribune* and later widely syndicated in the United States, offered a satirical view of American life and politics. Full name **Arthur Buchwald**

buck[1] /buk/ *n.* **1.** MALE ANIMAL a male animal of some species, including antelope, deer, goat, kangaroo, and rabbit **2.** (*plural* **buck** *or* **bucks**) *S Africa* ANTELOPE OR DEER an antelope or deer of either sex **3.** VIRILE YOUNG MAN a man, especially a strong, virile, impetuous, or spirited young man (*informal dated*) **4.** DANDY OR FOP a young man who takes elaborate care to be neat and stylish (*archaic*) [Old English *buc* 'male deer' and *bucca* 'male goat']

buck up *v.* **1.** *vti.* MAKE OR BECOME MORE CHEERFUL to raise the morale or spirits of sb or to become more cheerful, confident, or encouraged (*informal*) **2.** *vt.* IMPROVE STH to make sth better or smarter (*informal*) **3.** *vi.* HURRY UP to hurry or act more quickly (*informal dated*)

buck[2] /buk/ *v.* (**bucks, bucking, bucked**) **1.** *vi.* JUMP UPWARDS to jump or rear upwards with the back arched and the legs stiff **2.** *vt.* THROW RIDER to throw a rider by rearing or jumping upwards on the hindlegs or forelegs **3.** *vi. US, Can* MAKE JOLTING MOTION to move in a jerky or erratic manner **4.** *vti.* STAND IN OPPOSITION to oppose or resist sth obstinately (*informal*) **5.** *vt.* GAMBLE AGAINST STH to take a risk against sth ○ *buck the odds* **6.** *vt.* ENCOURAGE SB to raise sb's spirits or hopes (*usually passive*) **7.** *vti. US, Can* BUTT WITH LOWERED HEAD to charge against sb or sth with the head lowered ■ *n.* ACT OF BUCKING the movement or action of bucking [Mid-19thC. From BUCK[1]. Originally, it referred to the motions of a copulating male rabbit.]

buck[3] /buk/ *n. US, Can, ANZ* (*informal*) **1.** DOLLAR a United States, Canadian, Australian, or New Zealand dollar **2.** AMOUNT OF MONEY a specified or unspecified amount of money [Mid-19thC. Shortening of BUCKSKIN, used as a unit of exchange on the American frontier.] ◇ **make a fast** *or* **quick buck** *US* to make a profit on a quick and often dishonest transaction

buck[4] /buk/ *n.* **1.** VAULTING HORSE a covered block used as a vaulting horse **2.** *US, Can* = **sawhorse** [Early 19thC. From BUCK[1].]

buck[5] /buk/ (**bucks, bucking, bucked**) *n.* a counter or marker formerly used in poker and passed from one player to another to indicate some obligation, especially sb's turn to deal [Mid-19thC. Origin uncertain.] ◇ **pass the buck** to shift responsibility to sb else (*informal*)

Buck /buk/, **Sir Peter** (1879–1951) New Zealand anthropologist and politician. An MP (1909–14) and minister for Maori affairs, he later devoted himself to anthropology. He wrote *The Coming of the Maori* (1949). Born **Te Rangi Hiroa**. Full name **Sir Peter Henry Buck**

buckaroo /búkə ro͞o/ (*plural* **-roos**), **buckeroo** (*plural* **-oos**) *n. US* a cowhand in the southwestern United States (*informal*) [Early 19thC. Alteration of Spanish *vaquero* 'cowboy', under the influence of BUCK[2].]

buckbean /búk been/ *n.* a marsh plant of the gentian family that has white, pink, or purplish flowers and is native to the northern hemisphere. Latin name: *Menyanthes trifoliata.* [Late 16thC. Translation of Flemish *boks boonen* 'goat's beans'.]

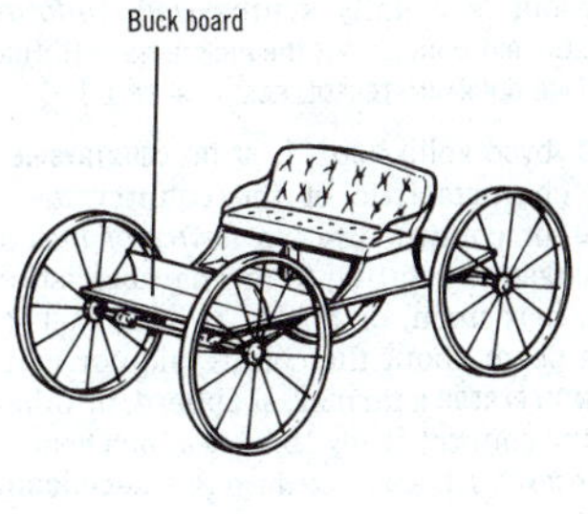

Buckboard

buckboard /búk bawrd/ *n. US, Can* an open four-wheeled horse-drawn carriage with the seat or seats mounted on a flexible board between the front and rear axles [Late 17thC. Buck from an obsolete word meaning 'belly, body (of a wagon)'.]

buckeroo *n.* = **buckaroo**

bucket /búkit/ *n.* **1.** CYLINDRICAL CONTAINER a container, usually cylindrical in shape with an open top and a semicircular handle, used for catching or holding liquids or solids **2.** BUCKETFUL the contents of a bucket or the amount that a bucket will hold **3.** LARGE QUANTITY a very large quantity or amount of sth (*informal*) (*often used in the plural*) **4.** STH LIKE A BUCKET sth resembling or suggesting a bucket in shape or function, e.g. a compartment on the outer edge of a waterwheel **5.** MACHINE PART any of various machine parts that resemble a bucket, e.g. the scoop on a mechanical shovel **6.** FOOD CONTAINER a large plastic or paper container for food, e.g. fried chicken or ice cream **7.** TRANSP = **bucket seat 8.** BASKETBALL = **basket** *n.* 4 ■ *v.* (**-ets, -eting, -eted**) **1.** *vt.* CARRY OR PUT STH IN BUCKET to carry, hold, lift, or put sth in a bucket **2.** *vi.* POUR WITH RAIN to rain very heavily (*informal*) **3.** *vi.* MOVE FAST to move or drive fast, jerkily, haphazardly, or recklessly (*informal*) ○ *We went bucketing down the motorway.* **4.** *vt.* RIDE HORSE HARD to ride a horse hard without consideration for the animal **5.** *vt. Aus* ATTACK SB VERBALLY to criticize sb severely or denigrate sb (*informal*) [13thC. From Anglo-Norman *buket*, of Germanic origin.] ◇ **kick the bucket** to die (*slang*)

bucket about *vi.* to shake or toss in an energetic manner

bucket down *vi.* to rain very heavily (*informal*)

bucket chain *n.* a line of people formed to pass buckets of water from hand to hand, especially to put out a fire

bucketful /búkitfo͝ol/ *n.* **1.** AMOUNT IN BUCKET the contents of a bucket or the amount that a bucket will hold **2.** HUGE QUANTITY a very large quantity or amount of sth (*usually plural*)

bucket ladder *n.* a continuous chain of buckets used for excavating land or dredging riverbeds (*hyphenated when used before a noun*) ○ *bucket-ladder dredger*

bucket seat *n.* an individual seat with a rounded back in a vehicle or aircraft

bucket shop *n.* **1.** DISHONEST STOCKBROKING FIRM a dishonest unregistered stockbroking firm that speculates and gambles on stocks and commodities using its client's capital **2.** COMM UNRELIABLE SMALL BUSINESS any small business that cannot be relied on by customers, especially an unlicensed travel agency that buys airline tickets in bulk and sells them cheaply [Originally referring to saloons selling small amounts of liquor in buckets]

buckeye /búk ī/ *n.* **1.** (*plural* **-eyes** *or* **-eye**) POISONOUS HORSE-CHESTNUT TREE a poisonous tree or shrub of the horse-chestnut family that is native to North America and has large shiny brown seeds encased in a prickly or smooth covering. Genus: *Aesculus.* **2.** FRUIT OR POISONOUS SEED OF BUCKEYE a prickly or smooth fruit of the buckeye tree or the large brown poisonous seed it contains [Mid-18thC. Formed from BUCK[1] + EYE, because of the seed's resemblance to a deer's eye.]

buck fever *n.* (*informal*) **1.** NERVOUS EXCITEMENT OF NOVICE HUNTER nervous excitement felt by an inexperienced hunter at the sight of game **2.** NERVOUS EXCITEMENT nervous excitement felt by sb faced with a new situation, experience, or responsibility

buckhorn /búk hawrn/ *n.* **1.** HORN OF BUCK the horn of a male deer or antelope **2.** MATERIAL FROM A BUCK'S HORN the material from the horn of a male deer or antelope, used to make handles for knives and tools **3.** (*plural* **-horns** *or* **-horn**) PLANT WITH LEAVES RESEMBLING ANIMAL'S HORN a plant of Europe and Asia with leaves shaped like the horn of a deer or antelope. Latin name: *Plantago coronopus.*

buckhound /búk hownd/ *n.* a hound used for chasing game, especially deer

buckie /búki/ *n. Scotland* **1.** SHELLFISH OR SHELL a shellfish with a spiral shell, or the shell itself **2.** OBSTINATE PERSON an obstinate person **3.** LIVELY PERSON a lively person [Early 16thC. Origin uncertain: probably an alteration of Latin *buccinum* 'whelk'.]

Buckingham /búkingəm/, **George Villiers, 2nd Duke of** (1628–1687) English statesman. He was a privy councillor to Charles II and one of the most influential political figures of the Restoration. He is remembered for his satirical comedy *The Rehearsal* (1671).

Buckingham Palace *n.* the official London residence of the British monarch. It was built in 1703 for John Sheffield, Duke of Buckingham and Normandy, and rebuilt by John Nash in the early 19th century.

Buckinghamshire /búkingamshər/ county in southern England, northwest of London, containing one unitary authority. Its administrative centre is Aylesbury. Population: 473,000 (1995). Area: 727sq. km/1,883 sq. mi.

buckjumper /búk jumpər/ *n. Aus* an untamed horse that is likely to buck [Mid-19thC. Formed from *buckjump* 'to buck', from BUCK[2] + JUMP.]

Buckland /búklənd/, **William** (1784–1856) British geologist and clergyman. An Oxford academic and cleric, he attempted to reconcile scientific discoveries about the Earth's history with the biblical version of the Creation.

buckle /búk'l/ *n.* **1.** METAL FASTENER a clasp, typically consisting of a metal frame with a hinged prong, for fastening two loose ends, especially of a belt, shoe, or strap **2.** ORNAMENT RESEMBLING BUCKLE an ornament that resembles a buckle, e.g. on a shoe or a hat **3.** A BULGE, BEND, OR KINK a bend or kink in sth, e.g. a rope, or a bulge in sth, e.g. a piece of wood ■ *v.* (**-les, -ling, -led**) **1.** *vti.* FASTEN STH WITH BUCKLE to fasten sth, e.g. a shoe or seatbelt, with a buckle, or to be fastened with such a device **2.** *vti.* BEND OR CAUSE STH TO BEND to bend out of shape, warp, or crumple, usually because of heat or pressure, or to distort sth in this way **3.** *vi.* COLLAPSE to collapse or lose strength completely, sometimes as a result of a structural defect or weakness **4.** *vi.* GIVE IN to succumb or yield to pressure, especially emotional strain or fear [14thC. Via Anglo-Norman *bucle* and Old French *bocle* from Latin *buccula* 'cheek strap of a helmet', from *bucca* 'cheek'.]

buckle down *vi.* to set out to accomplish sth with vigour or determination (*informal*)

buckle to *vi.* to make a determined or special effort

buckle under *vi.* to give in under pressure or stress

buckle up *vti.* to fasten the buckle on a seatbelt, e.g. in a motor vehicle or an aircraft

buckler /búklər/ *n.* **1.** SHIELD a small round shield either worn on the forearm or held by a short handle at arm's length **2.** MEANS OF PROTECTION a defence or means of protection (*literary*) ■ *vt.* (**-lers, -lering, -lered**) PROTECT SB OR STH to shield or defend sb or sth with a buckler (*archaic*) [13thC. From Old French *bocler*, from *bocle* 'boss of a shield' (see BUCKLE).]

buckler fern *n.* a perennial deciduous or semi-evergreen fern that grows to about 1 m/3 ft in height. There is a broad buckler fern and a narrow buckler fern. Genus: *Dryopteris.* [So called because of the kidney-shaped flap of tissue covering the receptacle in which its spores are formed]

Buckley's chance /búkliz-/, **Buckley's hope** *n. ANZ* no chance whatsoever of doing or accomplishing sth (*informal*) [Late 19thC. Origin unknown.]

buckminsterfullerene /búkminstər fo͝olə reen/ *n.* a stable form of carbon containing 60 carbon atoms that occurs naturally in certain minerals [Late 20thC. From the molecule's resemblance to the geodesic dome structure invented by the US architect R. *Buckminster Fuller* (1895–1983).]

bucko /búkō/ (*plural* **-os**) *n.* **1.** SWAGGERING BULLY a swaggering bully or bossy person (*slang*) **2.** *Ireland, US* MALE PERSON a boy or man (*informal*) [Late 19thC. Formed from BUCK[1].]

buck-passing *n.* the shifting of blame or responsibility to sb else (*informal*) [From BUCK[5]] —**buck-passer** *n.*

buckram /búkrəm/ *n.* STIFF FABRIC a coarse cotton or linen fabric that has been stiffened with starch, gum, or latex. It is used in bookbinding and for stiffening garments. ■ *adj.* LIKE BUCKRAM resembling buckram in rigidity ■ *vt.* (**-rams, -raming, -ramed**) STIFFEN STH WITH BUCKRAM to stiffen or strengthen sth with buckram [14thC. From Old French *boquerant* 'cloth from Bukhara'.]

buck rarebit *n.* Welsh rarebit topped with a poached egg

Bucks. *abbr.* Buckinghamshire

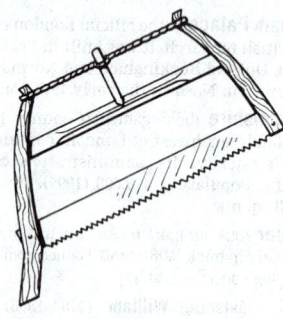

Bucksaw

bucksaw /búk saw/ *n.* a woodcutting saw in which the blade is set in an H-shaped frame [Mid-19thC. From BUCK[4].]

buck's fizz, Buck's fizz *n.* a cocktail made of champagne mixed with orange juice [Mid-20thC. Named after *Buck's Club* in London.]

buckshee /búk shee/ *adj.* (*informal*) **1.** FREE given or obtained without charge **2.** NOT ASKED FOR given without being asked for ■ *adv.* WITHOUT CHARGING free of charge (*informal*) [Early 17thC. Alteration of BAKSHEESH.]

buckshot /búk shot/ *n.* a large size of lead shot used in shotgun shells, especially for hunting game

buckskin /búk skin/ *n.* **1.** DEERSKIN the skin of a male deer **2.** SOFT LEATHER a soft pliable greyish-yellow leather, usually with a suede finish, originally made from deerskin and now usually from sheepskin ■ **buckskins** *npl. US* BUCKSKIN GARMENTS clothing made from buckskin leather, especially jackets, chaps, hats, and moccasins ■ *adj.* GREYISH-YELLOW greyish-yellow in colour

buck's party (*plural* **buck's parties**), **buck's night** *n. Aus* a stag party

buckthorn /búk thawrn/ (*plural* **-thorns** or **-thorn**) *n.* a thorny shrub or small tree with greenish flowers and black berries that were formerly used as a purgative. Genus: *Rhamnus*. [Late 16thC. Translation of modern Latin *cervi spina* 'stag's thorn'.]

bucktooth /búk tooth/ (*plural* **-teeth** /búk teeth/) *n.* a protruding upper front tooth (*informal*) —**buck-toothed** *adj.*

bucku *n.* = buchu

buckwheat /búk weet/ *n.* **1.** PLANT WITH EDIBLE SEED an Asian plant grown for its edible triangular seeds. Latin name: *Fagopyrum esculentum*. **2.** EDIBLE SEED the seed produced by the buckwheat plant. It is cooked as a cereal, ground into flour, or used as animal fodder. [Mid-16thC. Anglicization of Middle Dutch *boecweite*, literally 'beech wheat', so called because its grains resemble beech nuts.]

buckyball /búki bawl/ *n.* a ball-shaped carbon molecule found in stable forms of carbon (**fullerenes**), especially the molecule containing 60 carbon atoms

(**buckminsterfullerene**). It sometimes occurs naturally but is usually synthesized. (*informal*) [Late 20thC. Coined from *Bucky*, the nickname of R. Buckminster Fuller (see BUCKMINSTERFULLERENE) + BALL.]

bucolic /byoo kóllik/ *adj.* **1.** OF THE COUNTRYSIDE relating to or characteristic of the countryside, country people, or country life ○ *a writer of bucolic poems* **2.** OF SHEPHERDS relating to or characteristic of shepherds, herdsmen, or flocks ■ *n.* **1.** LITERAT PASTORAL POEM a poem about the countryside or country life **2.** COUNTRY PERSON a farmer, shepherd, or other person from the country [Early 16thC. Via Latin from, ultimately, Greek *boukolos*, literally 'cowherd'.] —**bucolically** *adv.*

bud[1] /bud/ *n.* **1.** OUTGROWTH ON PLANT STEM an outgrowth on a stem or branch consisting of a shortened stem and immature leaves or flowers, often enclosed by protective scales **2.** UNOPENED FLOWER a flower that has not yet opened **3.** ZOOL REPRODUCTIVE OUTGROWTH OF SIMPLE ORGANISM an asexually produced outgrowth of a simple organism, e.g. an invertebrate or a yeast, that breaks away from the parent and develops into a new individual **4.** STH RESEMBLING PLANT BUD sth shaped like a plant bud **5.** SB OR STH IMMATURE sb or sth that is small, immature, or not yet fully developed ■ *v.* (**buds, budding, budded**) **1.** *vi.* PRODUCE PLANT BUDS to produce outgrowths that develop into flowers or leaves **2.** *vi.* START TO GROW to start to develop or grow from a plant bud **3.** *vi.* BEGIN TO DEVELOP to begin to develop or grow from sth small into another, usually larger, thing ○ *Seeds of dissent are budding in the heartland.* **4.** *vi.* ZOOL REPRODUCE ASEXUALLY to reproduce asexually by producing an outgrowth that eventually develops to form a new individual, as occurs in invertebrates and yeasts **5.** *vt.* GARDENING GRAFT BUD INTO ANOTHER PLANT to insert a bud from one plant into the bark of another, usually one of a different variety, in order to propagate a plant from the bud [14thC. Origin uncertain.] —**budder** *n.* —**budless** /búddləss/ *adj.* ◇ **nip sth in the bud** to put an end to a plan or idea before it can be developed (*informal*)

bud[2] /bud/ *n. US* = buddy (*informal*) [Mid-19thC. Shortening.]

Budapest /bóodə pést/ capital and largest city of Hungary. It is situated on the River Danube in northern Hungary near the Slovak border. Population: 1,930,000 (1995).

Buddha: Daibutsu (Great Buddha), Kamakura, Japan

buddha /bóoddə/, **Buddha** *n.* **1.** SB ENLIGHTENED sb who has achieved a state of perfect enlightenment, in accord with the teachings of the Buddha **2.** IMAGE OF BUDDHA a statue, picture, or other representation of the Buddha [Late 17thC. From Sanskrit, the past participle of *budh-* 'to wake up, be enlightened'.]

Buddha /bóoddə/ (563?–483?BC) Nepalese-born Indian philosopher, he renounced his life as a prince. He attained Enlightenment about 528BC and developed and taught the doctrines of Buddhism. Born **Sidharta Gautama**. Known as **Sakyamuni**.

Buddhahood /bóoddəhood/ *n.* the state of spiritual enlightenment attained by the Buddha

Buddhism /bóoddizzəm/ *n.* a world religion or philosophy based on the teaching of the Buddha and holding that a state of enlightenment can be attained by suppressing worldly desires

Buddhist /bóoddist/ *n.* BELIEVER IN BUDDHISM sb who believes in and practises Buddhism ■ *adj.* OF BUDDHISM

relating to, associated with, or practising Buddhism —**Buddhistic** /boo dístik/ *adj.*

budding /búdding/ *adj.* PROMISING beginning to show a particular talent ○ *a budding actor* ■ *n.* **1.** BOT DEVELOPMENT OF BUDS the formation and growth of buds on a plant stem **2.** GARDENING GRAFTING A BUD artificial propagation, especially of woody plants, by grafting a bud from one variety onto the stem of another **3.** ZOOL ASEXUAL REPRODUCTION a form of asexual reproduction in which an outgrowth of the parent becomes constricted and eventually separates to form a new individual, as occurs in invertebrates and yeasts

buddle /búdd'l/ *n.* a sloping trough in which crushed ore is separated from waste by washing with water [Mid-16thC. Origin unknown.]

buddleia /búdli ə/ (*plural* **-ias** or **-ia**) *n.* a deciduous ornamental shrub or small tree that is native to warm regions and has tapering heads of small, scented, purple flowers that attract butterflies. Latin name: *Buddleja davidii*. [Late 18thC. From modern Latin, genus name, after the English botanist Adam Buddle (d. 1715).]

buddy /búddi/ *n.* (*plural* **-dies**) **1.** *US, Can* FRIEND a good friend, colleague, companion, or partner (*informal*) **2.** *US, Can* TERM OF ADDRESS FOR MALE a form of address to a man or boy (*informal*) ○ *Hey, buddy!* **3.** HELPER TO AIDS PATIENT a volunteer who gives help and support to someone who has AIDS ■ *vi.* (**-dies, -dying, -died**) ACT AS AIDS HELPER to act as a helper to someone with AIDS [Mid-19thC. Origin uncertain: possibly an alteration of BROTHER.]

buddy-buddy *adj. US* appearing to enjoy a close friendship (*informal*)

buddy movie, buddy film *n.* a style of film focusing on the adventures and friendship of two central characters of the same gender

buddy system *n. US* an arrangement by which individuals are paired for mutual safety, e.g. in mountain climbing

Buderim /búdrəm/ coastal town and resort in southern Queensland, Australia. Population: 12,458 (1996).

budge[1] /buj/ (**budges, budging, budged**) *vti.* **1.** MOVE to move, or to alter the position of sth by movement (*usually with negatives*) ○ *I tried moving the machine, but it wouldn't budge.* **2.** CHANGE OPINION to change or make sb change an attitude, decision, or opinion ○ *Once she's made up her mind, no amount of persuasion will budge her.* [Late 16thC. Via French *bouger* from assumed Vulgar Latin *bullicare*, literally 'to keep bubbling up', from Latin *bullire* (see BOIL[1]).]

budge[2] /buj/ *n.* FUR a type of fur, usually made of lambskin, worn with the wool outwards and formerly used as a trimming on academic or official gowns ■ *adj.* **1.** WITH FUR made from, trimmed with, or lined with budge **2.** FORMAL OR STIFF formal, pompous, solemn, or stiff (*archaic*) [Origin uncertain]

Budge /buj/, **Don** (b. 1915) US tennis player. One of the greatest players of his generation, he was the first tennis player ever to win a grand slam (1938). Full name **John Donald Budge**

budgerigar /bújjəri gaar/ *n.* a small bright green parrot with a yellow head, found in flocks in arid areas of central Australia. It is a popular domestic pet around the world and is bred in captivity for its bright plumage. Latin name: *Melopsittacus undulatus*. [Mid-19thC. Alteration of Yuwaalaraay *gijirigaa*.]

budget /bújjit/ *n.* **1.** SUMMARY OF INCOME AND SPENDING an often itemized estimate of income and spending, e.g. of a country or company, during a specified period. It sometimes includes systematic proposals as to how expenses will be met. **2.** PLAN FOR ALLOCATING RESOURCES a plan specifying how resources, e.g. time or money, will be spent or allocated during a particular period **3.** MONEY FOR SPECIFIC PURPOSE the total amount of money allocated or needed for a specific purpose or period of time **4.** QUANTITY OR SUPPLY a specified quantity, stock, or supply ■ *adj.* CHEAP OR ECONOMICAL suitable for people with a limited amount of money to spend ■ *v.* (**-ets, -eting, -eted**) **1.** *vti.* PLAN SPENDING to plan the allocation, expenditure, or use of resources, especially money or time **2.** *vt.* ENTER IN

BUDGET to make provision for sth or enter sth in a budget **3.** *vi.* LIVE WITHIN SPENDING LIMITS to live within a budget ○ *Having budgeted well all their lives, they can afford to retire early.* [15thC. Via Old French *bougette* 'leather pouch, purse' from, ultimately, Latin *bulga* 'leather sack' (see BULGE).]

Budget /bújjit/ *n.* a statement of the financial position of the United Kingdom for the financial year, with proposals for spending and taxation, presented in a speech by the Chancellor of the Exchequer

budget account *n.* an account with a department store or other large organization that enables a customer to pay in regular or monthly instalments for goods or services obtained on credit

budgetary /bújjitəri/ *adj.* relating to budgets

budgetary control *n.* a system for controlling the finances of a business by comparing actual income and expenditure with forecasts in order to monitor whether budgets are being maintained

budget deficit *n.* the amount of government expenditure that exceeds revenue

budgeter /bújjitər/ *n.* **1.** MAKER OF BUDGET sb who draws up a budget **2.** SB CONFINED BY BUDGET sb who is limited to a budget

budgie /bújji/ *n.* a budgerigar, especially one kept as a domestic pet (*informal*) [Early 20thC. Shortening.]

bud scale *n.* any of the scaly leaves that form a protective sheath around a plant bud and are sometimes hairy or resinous

budworm /búd wurm/ *n.* a moth larva that feeds on conifer buds and is one of the most destructive pests in North America. Latin name: *Harmolga fumiferana.*

Buenaventura /bwáynə ven tóórə, -tyóórə/ city and major port in western Colombia on the Pacific Coast. Population: 266,988 (1985).

Buenos Aires /bwáy noss íriz/ capital and largest city of Argentina, situated in the eastern part of the country. It is a port on the Río de la Plata and the nation's commercial and cultural centre. Population: 2,988,006 (1995).

BUF *abbr.* British Union of Fascists

buff[1] /buf/ *n.* **1.** COLOURS PALE YELLOWISH-BROWN a dull yellowish-beige colour **2.** INDUST SOFT LEATHER a soft thick undyed leather that is made chiefly from the skins of buffalo, elk, or oxen and has a light yellow colour **3.** POLISHING CLOTH a cloth of soft material such as leather or velvet, used for polishing, often mounted on a block **4.** ENG POLISHING DISC a revolving disc consisting of layers of cloth impregnated with abrasive powders, used for polishing metal or other hard bright surfaces **5.** CLOTHES LEATHER GARMENT a garment made of buff leather, e.g. a military uniform coat ■ *adj.* **1.** COLOURS PALE YELLOWISH-BROWN of a dull yellowish-brown colour **2.** OF BUFF LEATHER made of buff leather ■ *vt.* (**buffs, buffing, buffed**) **1.** POLISH STH to clean or polish sth with a piece of soft material **2.** MAKE SURFACE SOFT to make the surface of sth, especially of leather, soft and velvety like buff by raising a nap [Late 16thC. Alteration of French *buffle* 'buffalo', from late Latin *bufalus* (see BUFFALO).] ◇ **in the buff** naked (*informal*)

buff[2] /buf/ *n.* sb who is enthusiastic about and has a wide knowledge of a particular subject ○ *a movie buff* ○ *an opera buff* [Early 19thC. From the overcoats made of buff leather formerly worn by volunteer firemen in New York City, who were known as 'fire buffs'.]

buff[3] /buf/ *vt.* (**buffs, buffing, buffed**) DEADEN FORCE OF STH to deaden or reduce the force of sth ■ *n.* BLOW OR SLAP a blow, buffet, or slap (*archaic*) [15thC. From Old French *bufe* (see BUFFET[2]).]

buffalo /búffəlō/ *n.* (*plural* **-loes** *or* **-los** *or* **-lo**) **1.** TYPE OF HORNED CATTLE a type of horned cattle belonging to various species, including the African buffalo and domesticated breeds of the Asian water buffalo. Family: Bovidae. **2.** *US* N AMERICAN BISON the North American bison. ◊ **bison 3.** = **buffalo fish** ■ *vt.* (**-loes, -loing, -loed**) (*informal*) **1.** *US, Can* BAFFLE SB to throw sb into a state of confusion and puzzled bewilderment **2.** *Can* INTIMIDATE SB to coerce or inhibit sb aggressively [Mid-16thC. Via Portuguese or Italian from late Latin *bufalus*, from Greek *boubalos* 'gazelle'.]

Buffalo /búffəlō/ city and port in northeastern New York State beside Lake Erie and on the Niagara River. Population: 310,548 (1996).

Buffalo, Mount mountain in northern Victoria, Australia, site of a ski resort. Height: 1,723 m/5,653 ft.

buffalo berry *n.* **1.** SHRUB WITH BERRIES a North American shrub of the oleaster family with silvery foliage and edible berries. Genus: *Shepherdia.* **2.** EDIBLE BERRY the edible fruit of the buffalo berry shrub

Buffalo Bill /búffəlō bíl/ (1846–1917) US scout and statesman. He sometimes worked as an army scout in the western territories, and earned his nickname by killing thousands of buffalo to feed railway workers in the 1860s. From 1883 to 1913 he toured with his own 'Wild West Show'. Real name **William Frederick Cody**

buffalo fish *n.* a large freshwater fish of the sucker family that resembles the carp. Buffalo fish have a humped back and are found mostly in the Mississippi Valley. Genus: *Ictiobus.*

buffalo grass *n.* **1.** SHORT GREY-GREEN N AMERICAN GRASS a short grey-green grass of the plains of central North America that is used as forage and for lawns. Latin name: *Buchloë dactyloides.* **2.** *S Africa* BROAD-LEAVED S. AFRICAN GRASS a broad-leaved grass of South Africa used for lawns or as fodder. Genus: *Panicum.*

buffalo jump *n. US, Can* a cliff over which buffalo were stampeded by the Native American peoples of the North American plains in order to provide a source of food

buffalo robe *n. US, Can* the skin of the American bison, prepared with the hair left on and used as a blanket, coat, or rug

Buffalo wings *npl. US, Can* chicken wings, typically in barbecue sauce, served as an appetizer [So called because they were supposedly first served in a restaurant in or named after Buffalo, New York]

buffer[1] /búffər/ *n.* **1.** PROTECTOR AGAINST IMPACT sb or sth that reduces shock or impact or protects against other harm, usually by interception **2.** RAIL DEVICE ON TRAIN OR TRACK either of a pair of spring-loaded or hydraulic pads attached to both ends of rolling stock or at the end of a railway track. They stop the train running off the end of the track and may also absorb impact. **3.** CHEM SUBSTANCE MAINTAINING PH a substance that minimizes a change in pH of a solution by neutralizing added acids and bases, or a solution containing such a substance **4.** COMPUT MEMORY AREA a temporary storage area used for data being transmitted between two devices to compensate for differences in the rate at which each device functions or the availability of the receiving device. A buffer enables the faster device, such as a computer, to complete sending the data and begin another task without waiting for the slower device, such as a printer. ■ *vt.* (**-ers, -ering, -ered**) **1.** CUSHION STH AGAINST SHOCK to protect sth against impact or reduce the shock of an impact on sth **2.** CHEM ADD BUFFER TO SOLUTION to add to a solution a substance that will keep its pH constant [Mid-19thC. Formed from an obsolete word meaning 'to hit sth softly', possibly from French (see BUFFET[2]).]

buffer[2] /búffər/ *n.* **1.** USER OF BUFFER sb who polishes sth with a buffer **2.** = **buff**[1] *n.* 2 [Mid-19thC. Formed from BUFF[1].]

buffer[3] /búffər/ *n.* a bumbling or indecisive person, especially a man (*informal insult*) [Mid-18thC. Formed from an obsolete word meaning 'to stammer'.]

buffer state *n.* a small neutral state that lies between two potentially hostile powers and reduces the risk of conflict between them

buffer stock *n.* a stock of a basic commodity accumulated by a government, e.g. when supplies are plentiful and prices low, and held for use when supplies are short to stabilize the price

buffer zone *n.* **1.** NEUTRAL TERRITORY a neutral area that lies between hostile forces and reduces the risk of conflict between them **2.** SEPARATING AREA any area designed to form a barrier that prevents potential conflict or harmful contact

buffet[1] /bóó fay/ *n.* **1.** SELF-SERVICE MEAL a meal at which people serve themselves from various dishes set out on a table, sideboard, or counter **2.** TABLE WITH REFRESHMENTS a serving counter or table on which the meals or refreshments are displayed **3.** = **buffet car 4.** DINING-ROOM SERVING TABLE a piece of dining-room furniture with drawers for tableware, used for storing table items and for serving dishes [Early 18thC. From French, 'footstool, sideboard', of unknown origin.]

buffet[2] /búffit/ *n.* **1.** BLOW WITH HAND a blow struck with the fist or hand **2.** REPEATED BLOW a heavy or repeated blow or stroke **3.** AIR = **buffeting** ■ *v.* (**-fets, -feting, -feted**) **1.** *vt.* BATTER STH to knock or strike against sth forcefully or repeatedly **2.** *vt.* HIT STH SHARPLY to hit sth sharply, especially with the hand **3.** *vi.* STRUGGLE TO PROGRESS to proceed under difficult conditions [Pre-12thC. From Old French, literally 'small blow', from *bufe* 'blow', originally an imitation of the sound.] —**buffeter** *n.*

buffet car *n.* a railway carriage where light refreshments and beverages are served

buffeting /búffiting/ *n.* an irregular shaking of a part or the whole of an aircraft during flight, typically caused by strong winds

buffi plural of **buffo**

buffing wheel *n.* a wheel covered with a soft material such as lamb's wool, leather, or velvet and used to shine or polish sth, especially metal

bufflehead /búff'l hed/ (*plural* **-heads** *or* **-head**) *n.* a small North American diving duck, the male of which has black and white plumage and a large fluffy head, while the female is dark brown. Latin name: *Bucephala albeola.* [Mid-17thC. Formed from obsolete *buffle* 'buffalo' (from French; see BUFF[1]), so called because of its large head.]

buffo /bóófō/ *n.* (*plural* **-fi** /bóófee/ *or* **-fos**) MALE OPERA SINGER a male singer of comic roles in opera ■ *adj.* COMIC comic in a manner that is characteristic of a buffo [Mid-18thC. From Italian, formed from *buffare* 'to puff, act the clown' (source of English *buffoon*).]

buffoon /bə fóón/ *n.* **1.** CLOWN sb who amuses others by clowning, by joking, or by ridiculous behaviour **2.** BUMBLING PERSON sb who is regarded as behaving in a mildly inappropriate way [Mid-16thC. Via French *bouffon* from, ultimately, Italian *buffare* 'to clown', literally 'to puff', originally an imitation of the sound.]

buffoonery /bə fóónəri/ *n.* silly behaviour

buff-tip moth *n.* a large European moth that resembles a twig when it wraps its cream-tipped wings around its body. Latin name: *Phalera bucephala.*

buff wheel *n.* = **buffing wheel**

bug /bug/ *n.* **1.** INSECTS TYPE OF INSECT an insect with thickened forewings and mouthparts adapted for piercing and sucking. Order: Hemiptera. **2.** *US, Can* INSECTS ANY INSECT any insect or similar organism, especially one considered to be a pest, e.g. an aphid, bed bug, or cockroach **3.** GERM any unspecified germ or microorganism that causes mild illness (*informal*) **4.** AILMENT CAUSED BY GERM any mild ailment that is caused by an unspecified microorganism (*informal*) **5.** CRAZE OR OBSESSION a strong and often widespread enthusiasm for or obsession with sth (*informal*) **6.** DEVOTEE sb who is a fan or devotee of sth (*informal dated*) ○ *a classical music bug* **7.** DEFECT a defect, error, or flaw in a design, machine, or system (*informal*) **8.** COMPUT PROGRAMMING ERROR an error in a computer program (*informal*) **9.** HIDDEN LISTENING DEVICE a concealed electronic device, usually a small microphone, that is used for listening to or recording private conversations (*informal*) ■ *vt.* (**bugs, bugging, bugged**) **1.** PESTER SB to cause sb persistent trouble and annoyance (*informal*) ○ *Go away and stop bugging me!* **2.** HIDE LISTENING DEVICE IN STH to conceal an electronic listening device in sth ○ *She suspected her phone had been bugged.* **3.** LISTEN TO STH SECRETLY to listen to or eavesdrop on a conversation using an electronic surveillance device ○ *He thinks someone is bugging his phone conversations.* [14thC. Origin unknown.]

WORD KEY: SYNONYMS

See Synonyms at ***bother.***

bugaboo /búggə boo/ (*plural* **-boos**) *n.* sth that causes fear, annoyance, or trouble, especially an imagined threat or problem [Mid-18thC. Origin uncertain.]

Buganda /boŏ gándə/ kingdom in the area north of Lake Victoria, southern Uganda. It became part of Uganda in 1962 and the kingdom was dissolved in 1967.

Bugatti /boo gátti/, **Ettore** (1882–1947) Italian automobile designer and manufacturer. He is best known for the racing cars he produced in the 1930s. Full name **Ettore Arco Isidoro Bugatti**

bugbane /búg bayn/ n. a European plant whose small white flowers are reputed to repel insects. Latin name: *Cimicifuga foetida.*

bugbear /búg bair/ n. **1.** SOURCE OF FEAR a source of obsessive or groundless fear **2.** CONTINUING PROBLEM a continuing source of annoyance or difficulty **3.** GOBLIN a goblin invented to frighten children, traditionally in the form of a bear that eats those who misbehave [Late 16thC. From an obsolete word meaning 'hobgoblin' + BEAR[1].]

bug-eyed adj. (informal) **1.** WITH BULGING EYES having protruding eyes **2.** AGOG wide-eyed with amazement or fear

bugger[1] /búggər/ n. **1.** OFFENSIVE TERM an offensive term for sb who practises sodomy (slang offensive) **2.** SB OR STH UNPLEASANT a person or thing regarded as unpleasant, difficult, or contemptible (slang offensive) **3.** PERSON OF A PARTICULAR TYPE used to refer to sb with a particular characteristic or in a particular situation (slang) ○ *The jammy bugger won the prize.* ■ v. (-gers, -gering, -gered) **1.** vti. OFFENSIVE TERM to practise sodomy (taboo offensive) **2.** vt. SPOIL STH to damage, ruin, or spoil sth (slang) **3.** vt. TIRE SB UTTERLY to make sb thoroughly exhausted (slang) **4.** vt. SWEARWORD used as a swearword to express annoyance or frustration (slang) (can be used in the passive, especially to express an absolute refusal to do sth) ○ *I'm buggered if I'll agree.* ■ interj. SWEARWORD used as a swearword to express annoyance or frustration (slang) [Mid-16thC. Via French *bougre* 'heretic' from Latin *Bulgarus*, literally 'Bulgarian', from Western Christian association of heresy with sodomy.]

bugger off vi. an offensive term meaning to go away or get out, usually inopportunely (slang offensive)

bugger up vt. to spoil or ruin sth (slang offensive)

bugger[2] /búggər/ n. sb who conceals listening devices in sth, such as a room or telephone

buggery /búggəri/ n. **1.** = sodomy **2.** OFFENSIVE TERM an offensive term used as an intensifier (slang offensive) [14thC. From Middle Dutch *buggerie* (formed from *bugger*) or Old French *bougrerie*, formed from *bougre* (see BUGGER).]

buggy[1] /búggi/ (plural -gies) n. **1.** HORSE-DRAWN VEHICLE a lightweight horse-drawn carriage **2.** BATTERY-POWERED VEHICLE a small battery-powered vehicle used for a special purpose ○ *a golf buggy* **3.** US PRAM a light pram **4.** PUSHCHAIR a lightweight pushchair for young children [Mid-18thC. Origin unknown.]

buggy[2] /búggi/ (-gier, -giest) adj. infested with insects [Late 18thC. Formed from BUG.] —**bugginess** n.

bugle[1] /byoŏg'l/ n. BRASS INSTRUMENT a brass instrument like a short trumpet without valves, used for military signals ■ vi. (-gles, -gling, -gled) PLAY BUGLE to play the bugle [14thC. Via Old French from Latin *buculus*, diminutive of *bos* 'ox'. The original term was 'bugle horn', denoting the horn of an ox used as a hunting horn.] —**bugler** n.

bugle[2] /byoŏg'l/ n. a low-growing plant related to mint and with blue, pink, or white flowers, often used as ground cover in temperate gardens. Genus: *Ajuga.* [13thC. Directly or via Old French from late Latin *bugula.*]

bugle bead, **bugle** n. a tube-shaped bead made of glass or plastic used in embroidery or bead trimmings

bugloss /byoŏ gloss/ n. a hairy plant related to borage, with clusters of drooping blue flowers. Genus: *Lycopsis.* [14thC. From, ultimately, Latin *buglossus*, from Greek *buglōssos*, literally 'ox-tongued' (from the shape and roughness of the leaves).]

buhl n. = boulle [Early 19thC. Via German from French *boule* (see BOULE).]

buhrstone /búr stōn/, **burstone**, **burrstone** n. **1.** ROUGH HARD ROCK rough hard quartz rock, formerly used to make millstones and grindstones **2.** STONE FOR MILLING OR GRINDING a millstone or grindstone made from buhrstone [Mid-17thC. *Buhr* is a variant of BURR[1] (because of the stone's roughness).]

build /bild/ v. (builds, building, built /bilt/) **1.** vt. MAKE STH BY JOINING PARTS to make a structure by fitting the parts of it together ○ *to build a wall* **2.** vt. HAVE STH BUILT to have a building or other structure made ○ *The emperor built a number of these pavilions.* **3.** vti. TO FORM OR DEVELOP to form or develop an enterprise or circumstance ○ *building a solid business relationship* **4.** vt. COLLECT A SET OF PLAYING CARDS in card games, to form a set by gathering related cards **5.** vi. INCREASE to increase or mount steadily ○ *Tension is starting to build.* ■ n. **1.** BODY STRUCTURE the physical structure, shape, and size of a person ○ *the wrestler's heavy build* **2.** COMPUT STAGE OF SOFTWARE DEVELOPMENT a stage in the development of computer software in which two or more independently developed software components are linked so that they can be tested in conjunction with one another ○ *testing the first build of the software* **3.** STANDARD OF CONSTRUCTION the standard of construction of sth, e.g. a vehicle [Old English *byldan* 'to construct a house', from *bold* 'dwelling', from a prehistoric Germanic word meaning 'to dwell', which is also the source of English *bower*]

build in vt. **1.** INCORPORATE IN STRUCTURE to construct a piece of furniture so that it becomes part of the structure of a room, or to add an object so that it becomes part of another structure **2.** INCLUDE to create or add sth to a system or organization ○ *They built in the shelves.*

build into vt. to create or add sth as a permanent feature ○ *These safeguards will be built into the system.*

build up v. **1.** vti. DEVELOP to increase or develop gradually ○ *Traffic is building up on the motorway.* **2.** vt. PRAISE EXCESSIVELY to emphasize or exaggerate the good qualities of sb or sth ○ *I expected someone more impressive after the way she built him up.* **3.** vt. MAKE SB STRONGER AND HEALTHIER to make sb stronger and healthier, especially by feeding

build up to vt. to develop towards a point or climax

builder /bíldər/ n. **1.** SB WHO BUILDS a person or company engaged in building or repairing houses or other large structures **2.** DETERGENT ADDITIVE a substance added to detergents to improve their cleaning properties

——— **WORD KEY: CULTURAL NOTE** ———
The Master Builder, a play by Norwegian dramatist Henrik Ibsen (1845). Typical of Ibsen's more symbolic later works, it is the story of a successful architect, Halvard Solness, who is disturbed by his continued good fortune and fearful that he will eventually have to pay a price for it. His search for redemption eventually leads to his own death.

building /bílding/ n. **1.** WALLED ROOFED STRUCTURE a structure with walls and a roof, e.g. a house or factory **2.** MAKING LARGE STRUCTURES the business or task of constructing houses, factories, bridges, and other large structures (often used before a noun)

building block n. **1.** BRICK-SHAPED CONSTRUCTION BLOCK a large block of concrete or similar hard material, used for building houses and other large structures **2.** CHILD'S TOY BLOCK one of a set of children's wooden or plastic bricks **3.** COMPONENT an element or component regarded as contributing to the growth of an organization, plan, or system ○ *He acquired companies as building blocks for his financial empire.*

building line n. a line on a property beyond which no building is allowed

building paper n. a damp-proofing and insulating material consisting of a bitumen and fibre mix sandwiched between heavy-duty paper

building society (plural **building societies**) n. a financial organization that pays interest on savings accounts, lends money for buying and improving houses, and provides other banking services

buildup /bíld up/ n. **1.** ACCUMULATION a large amount of sth or a number of things gradually accumulated or developed ○ *prevents the buildup of plaque* **2.** IMPRESSIVE DESCRIPTION a description that emphasizes or exaggerates the good qualities of sb or sth

built past tense and past participle of **build**

built environment n. the part of the environment that consists of buildings and structures, as opposed to the countryside or the natural world

built heritage n. the part of a country's heritage that consists of buildings and structures, as opposed to natural or aesthetic assets

built-in adj. **1.** INTEGRAL designed or fitted as a fixed or permanent part **2.** NATURAL forming a natural feature or characteristic

built-in obsolescence n. = planned obsolescence

built-up adj. **1.** WITH MANY BUILDINGS used to describe an area that has many buildings **2.** MADE HIGHER OR THICKER having several layers or added thickness ○ *built-up heels*

Bujumbura /boŏjəm boŏrə/ capital and largest city of Burundi. It is situated in the western part of the country, on Lake Tanganyika. Population: 300,000 (1996).

Bukavu /boo káả voo/ capital of Sud-Kivu Region in the eastern Democratic Republic of Congo. It is situated on Lake Kivu, close to the border with Rwanda. Population: 201,569 (1994).

Bukhara /boŏ kháảrə/ city in southern Uzbekistan, in the Amu Darya valley, west of Samarkand. Population: 236,000 (1994).

Bukharin /boo káảrin, -kháảrin/, **Nicolay Ivanovich** (1888–1938) Russian revolutionary and political theorist. He was leader of the October Revolution of 1917 and edited the Communist Party newspaper *Pravda* (1917–29). He was arrested in Joseph Stalin's Great Purge, (1937), and executed.

bul. abbr. bulletin

Bulawayo /boŏllə wáyō/ industrial city on the Matsheumlope River, southwestern Zimbabwe. Population: 620,936 (1992).

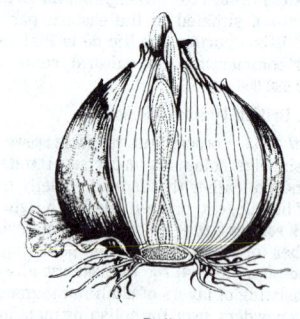

Bulb

bulb /bulb/ n. **1.** UNDERGROUND PLANT PART any underground plant storage organ, e.g. a corm, tuber, or rhizome, from which a new plant grows every year **2.** PLANT GROWING FROM BULB a plant that develops from a bulb or other underground storage organ, e.g. a tulip or crocus **3.** ROUNDED PART a rounded part of sth, e.g. the mercury reservoir of a thermometer or the squeezable rubber ball on a dropper **4.** = light bulb **5.** ROUNDED PART OF BODY ORGAN a rounded or enlarged section of a cylindrical body part [Mid-16thC. Via Latin *bulbus* from Greek *bolbos* 'bulbous root, onion'.]

bulbar /búlbər/ adj. used to describe any bulb-shaped organ of the body

bulbel n. = bulbil

bulb fly n. a fly similar to a wasp, whose larvae live in and eat bulbs. Family: Syrphidae.

bulbiferous /bul bíffərəss/ adj. used to describe plants that produce bulbs

bulbil /búl bil/, **bulbel** /búlb'l/ n. a new bulb growing like a bud on a plant or leaf stem [Mid-19thC. From modern Latin *bulbillus*, diminutive of Latin *bulbus* (see BULB).]

bulbourethral gland /búlbō reéthrəl-/ n. = Cowper's gland [*Bulbourethral* from Latin *bulbus* (see BULB) + URETHRAL]

bulbous /búlbəss/ adj. **1.** ROUNDED rounded and swollen-looking **2.** BOT GROWING FROM BULB growing from a plant bulb [Late 16thC. From Latin *bulbosus*, from bulbus (see

BULB), or directly formed from BULB.] —**bulbously** adv. —**bulbousness** n.

bulbul /boólboòl/ n. **1.** TROPICAL BIRD a greyish or brownish songbird of tropical Africa and Asia, also introduced into Australia. Family: Pycnonotidae. **2.** BIRD IN PERSIAN POETRY a songbird frequently mentioned in Persian poetry, taken to be the nightingale [Mid-17thC. From Persian, an imitation of its song.]

Bulgakov /boòl gaa kof/, **Mikhail** (1891–1940) Ukranian writer. Suppressed by the Soviet Communists, his work includes the posthumously-published modern masterpiece *The Master and Margarita* (1967). Full name **Mikhail Afanasievich Bulgakov**

Bulgar /búl gaar/ n. a member of an ancient Slavic people that settled in areas of present-day Bulgaria around the 7th century AD [Mid-18thC. From medieval Latin *Bulgarus*, from Old Church Slavonic *Blŭgary* (plural) 'Bulgars'.]

Bulgaria

Bulgaria /bul gáiri ə/ republic in southeastern Europe, on the western shores of the Black Sea. Part of the Ottoman Empire from the 14th to the late 19th centuries, it gained independence in 1908. Language: Bulgarian. Currency: Lev. Capital: Sofia. Population: 8,290,988 (1997). Area: 110,994 sq. km/42,855 sq. mi. Official name **People's Republic of Bulgaria**

Bulgarian /bul gáiri ən/ n. **1.** SB FROM BULGARIA sb who was born or brought up in, or who is a citizen of, Bulgaria **2.** SOUTH SLAVONIC LANGUAGE the official language of Bulgaria, one of the South Slavonic group of Indo-European languages. Bulgarian is spoken by about nine million people. [Mid-16thC. Formed from medieval Latin *Bulgaria*, from *Bulgar* 'Bulgar' (see BULGAR).] —**Bulgarian** adj.

bulge /bulj/ vi. (**bulges, bulging, bulged**) **1.** SWELL to expand or swell **2.** BE OVERFILLED to contain so much that the sides expand outwards (informal) ■ n. **1.** PART THAT EXPANDS OUTWARDS an area or part that curves or has expanded outwards **2.** INCREASE a sudden temporary increase ○ a bulge in the population figures **3.** BABY BOOM a baby boom (informal) [12thC. Via Old French *boulge* 'leather sack, bag', from Latin *bulga* (source of English *budget*), from Gaulish. Originally 'bag, pouch', hence 'sth rounded'.] —**bulginess** n. —**bulging** adj. —**bulgingly** adv. —**bulgy** adj.

bulgur /búlgər/, **bulghar, bulgar, bulgur wheat** n. wheat that has been parboiled, dried, and broken or cracked into small pieces. It is a common ingredient in Middle Eastern and vegetarian cooking. [Mid-20thC. Via Turkish from Persian *bulǧūr*, literally 'bruised grain'.]

bulimia /byoo límmi ə/ n. a condition in which bouts of overeating are followed by undereating, use of laxatives, or self-induced vomiting. It is associated with depression and anxiety about putting on weight. [14thC. From modern Latin, from, ultimately, Greek *boulimia*, literally 'hunger of an ox', from *bous* 'ox' + *limos* 'hunger'.] —**bulimic** adj., n.

bulk /bulk/ n. **1.** LARGE SIZE large size or mass **2.** THE GREATER PART the greater part of sth **3.** LARGE BODY a large or overweight person's body **4.** CARGO a ship's cargo **5.** PART OF SHIP the part of a ship where cargo is stored **6.** FIBRE IN FOOD the indigestible fibre that is a constituent of some food ■ adj. IN LARGE QUANTITY in or of a large quantity [15thC. Partly from Old Norse *búlki* 'heap' (ultimately from an Indo-European word meaning 'to swell', which is also the ancestor of English *bowl*); partly

from Old English *búc* 'belly'.] ◇ **bulk large** to play an important part

bulk up vti. to increase in size or volume (informal) ○ We're hoping student numbers will bulk up this year.

bulk bill (**bulk bills, bulk billing, bulk billed**) vt. Aus to claim payment for medical care directly from the insurer, Medicare, rather than charging the patient who then claims a refund —**bulk billing** n.

bulk buy n. a large amount or number of sth bought at one time, usually at a reduced rate —**bulk buying** n.

bulk carrier n. a ship that carries loose unpackaged cargo, e.g. coal or grain

bulkhead /búlk hed/ n. a partition inside a ship, aircraft, or large vehicle [15thC. *Bulk* from Old Norse *bálkr* 'partition' (source of English *baulk*).]

bulking /búlking/ n. the increase in the volume of sand, cement, and other building materials when they become damp

bulky /búlki/ (**-ier, -iest**) adj. **1.** AWKWARDLY LARGE large and awkward to carry or move **2.** BROAD heavily built, or broad and muscular —**bulkily** adv. —**bulkiness** n.

bull[1] /bool/ n. **1.** MALE OF CATTLE an uncastrated adult male of any breed of domestic cattle or other bovine animal **2.** MALE MAMMAL a sexually mature male of any of various large mammals, including whales, seals, moose, and elephants **3.** BIG MAN a hefty or aggressive man **4.** = **bullshit** (slang offensive) **5.** STOCK EXCH BUYER OF RISING SECURITIES an investor who buys securities in anticipation of rising prices, intending to resell them soon for profit. ◇ **bear**[1] n. 5 ■ n., abbr. **6.** bull's eye ■ vt. (**bulls, bulling, bulled**) STOCK EXCH RAISE PRICES WITH SPECULATIVE BUYING to attempt to raise prices in a particular commodity or market by buying large quantities and thus reducing availability and increasing demand [Pre-12thC. From Old Norse *boli* 'bull'.] ◇ **shoot the bull** US to chatter idly (slang) ◇ **take the bull by the horns** to deal with a difficult situation forcefully and decisively

bull[2] /bool/ n. a written statement formally issued by the pope and bearing an official seal [13thC. Via French *bulle* from Latin *bulla* 'bubble', later 'seal', hence 'sealed document' (source of English *boil* and *budge*).]

bull[3] /bool/ n. Ireland a glaring mistake in speech, especially a self-contradictory statement [Early 17thC. Origin unknown.]

Bull /bool/ n. ASTRON, ZODIAC = **Taurus** [Early 16thC. Translation of Latin *Taurus*.]

Bull /bool/, **John** (1563?–1628) English organist and composer. Organist to James VI and I of Scotland and England, he was the organist of Antwerp cathedral after 1613. He was an early exponent of contrapuntal keyboard music.

bull. abbr. bulletin

bulla /boóllə/ (plural **-lae** /-lee/) n. **1.** BLISTER a blister (technical) **2.** BONY PART any rounded, bony, and protruding part of the body **3.** POPE'S SEAL the pope's official seal [14thC. From, ultimately, Latin (see BULL[2]).]

Bullamakanka /boóləmə kángkə/ n. Aus an imaginary town used to represent any remote and backward place (informal) [Mid-20thC. Origin uncertain: perhaps based on pidgin English *bullamacow* 'bully beef'.]

bull ant n. = bulldog ant

bullbaiting /bool bayting/ n. the former entertainment of setting fierce dogs to attack a bull, popular in medieval times

bull bars npl. a metal framework mounted on the front of a vehicle to protect it against impact

bulldog /bool dog/ n. **1.** SMOOTH-HAIRED DOG a smooth-haired muscular dog belonging to a breed developed in England for bullbaiting **2.** PROCTOR'S ASSISTANT an assistant to a proctor at Oxford and Cambridge universities (informal) [15thC. Formed from BULL[1].]

bulldog ant n. ANZ a large Australian ant with strong jaws and a painful bite. Genus: *Myrmecia*.

Bulldog Clip tdmk. a trademark for a clip with a strong cylindrical spring, used for holding papers together or for fastening them to a board

Bulldog

bulldoze /bool dōz/ (**-dozes, -dozing, -dozed**) v. **1.** vt. DEMOLISH WITH BULLDOZERS to demolish a building or clear debris using bulldozers **2.** vti. FORCE A WAY to force way past or through an obstruction (informal) **3.** vt. FORCE ACTION to force sb to do sth or to insist on a course of action stubbornly or ruthlessly (informal) [Late 19thC. Origin uncertain; perhaps from BULL + DOSE: 'to give a "dose" (treatment) fit for a bull'.]

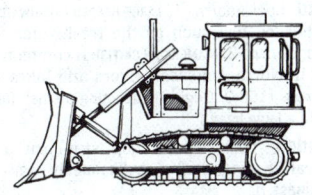
Bulldozer

bulldozer /bool dōzər/ n. a construction vehicle with tracks or large wheels and a wide blade used for moving earth or debris

bull dust n. Aus **1.** FINE DUST fine dirt or dust on roads **2.** NONSENSE talk or writing dismissed as nonsensical or inaccurate (informal)

bull dyke n. an offensive term for a lesbian who chooses masculine dress and manners (slang offensive)

Bullen /boóllən/, **Keith** (1906–76) New Zealand geophysicist and mathematician. He collaborated with Sir Harold Jeffreys, to create the Jeffreys Bullen Tables (1940), which record the speed of seismic waves as they pass through rocks of different types. Full name **Keith Edward Bullen**

Buller /boóllər/ river in the northwestern South Island, New Zealand that rises in the Southern Alps near Mount Travers and empties into the Tasman Sea near Westport. Length: 177 km/110 mi.

bullet /boóllit/ n. **1.** AMMUNITION USED IN FIREARM a projectile fire from a handgun, rifle, or other small firearm. It is usually pointed and cylindrical in shape, and usually made of metal. **2.** bullet, bullet point DOT a large printed dot used to highlight items in a printed list **3.** REPAYMENT OF LOAN the repayment of a loan, representing the initial sum borrowed excluding interest [Early 16thC. From French *boulet* 'small ball', from *boule* (see BOWL[2]).] ◇ **bite the bullet** to deal with a situation that is unpleasant but unavoidable ◇ **get** or **be given the bullet** to be dismissed (informal)

bulletin /boólletin/ n. **1.** NEWS BROADCAST a short broadcast containing a single item of news **2.** OFFICIAL NEWS an official announcement of public news **3.** NEWSLETTER a newsletter issued by an organization or institution [Mid-18thC. From Italian *bulletino*, literally 'small papal bull', from *bulla* 'papal bull', from Latin (see BULL[2]).]

bulletin board n. **1.** US, Can = notice board **2.** bulletin board, bulletin board system ON-LINE COMMUNICATION SYSTEM a computer-based forum used by an interest group to allow members to exchange e-mails, chat online, and access software

bullet loan *n.* a loan that is repaid in full in a single payment on a set date

bullet point *n.* PRINTING = **bullet** *n.* 2

bulletproof /bŏŏllit proof/ (**-proofs, -proofing, -proofed**) *adj.* **1.** ABLE TO RESIST BULLETS able to resist the penetration of bullets ◇ *bulletproof glass* **2.** INVULNERABLE TO ATTACK invulnerable to attack or criticism (*informal*) ◇ *Nobody's bulletproof in this company.*

bullet train *n.* a high-speed passenger train in Japan

bulletwood /bŏŏllit wŏŏd/ *n.* **1.** TROPICAL AMERICAN TREE a tropical American tree grown for its tough durable wood. Latin name: *Manilkara bidentata*. **2.** HARD WOOD the tough durable wood of the bulletwood tree

bullfight /bŏŏl fĭt/ *n.* a traditional public entertainment, especially in Spain and Mexico, in which a bull is baited and killed —**bullfighter** *n.* — **bullfighting** *n.*

bullfinch /bŏŏl finch/ *n.* a small Eurasian bird with a short thick beak, a black head, and a pink to red breast. Latin name: *Pyrrhula pyrrhula*. [Late 16thC. Said to be from the bird's thick 'bull-like' neck.]

bullfrog /bŏŏl frog/ *n.* a large frog of eastern North America with a deep croak. Genus: *Rana*. [Mid-18thC. So called because of its strong croak, said to sound like a bull bellowing.]

bullhead /bŏŏl hed/ *n.* **1.** LARGE-HEADED FRESHWATER FISH a large-headed fish such as the freshwater sculpin. Genus: *Cottus*. **2.** N AMERICAN CATFISH a common catfish found in North American rivers and lakes. Genus: *Ictalurus*. [15thC. Originally denoting a small freshwater fish with a large head.]

bullheaded /bŏŏl héddid/ *adj.* stubborn and uncooperative (*informal*) —**bullheadedly** *adv.* —**bullheadedness** *n.*

bullhead rail *n.* a railway rail with a narrow base and a bulbous top when viewed in cross-section

bullhorn /bŏŏl hawrn/ *n.* US, Can = **loudhailer**

bullion /bŏŏli ən/ *n.* **1.** BARS OF GOLD OR SILVER gold or silver in the form of bars or ingots **2.** MASS OF METAL any metal in the form of an unshaped mass **3.** TEXTILES GOLD OR SILVER BRAID ornamental fringing or braid made of twisted gold or silver thread and used, e.g. to edge curtains [15thC. From Anglo-Norman, literally 'mint', ultimately from Latin *bullire* 'to boil', from *bulla* (see BULL²). The underlying idea is of metal being melted.]

bullish /bŏŏllish/ *adj.* **1.** BRAWNY broad and strong **2.** EXPECTING GOOD STOCK MARKET FIGURES expecting or producing good results, especially rising stock market prices **3.** OPTIMISTIC confident and optimistic (*informal*) —**bullishly** *adv.* —**bullishness** *n.*

bull market *n.* a stock market in which prices are rising and are expected to continue rising. ◊ **bear market**

bull mastiff *n.* a dog belonging to a large muscular smooth-haired breed developed by crossing the bulldog and the mastiff

bullnecked /bŏŏl nékt/ *adj.* having a short thick neck [Middle English]

bullnose /bŏŏl nōz/ *n.* **1.** BRICK a brick with a rounded end **2.** PIG DISEASE a disease of pigs that causes the snout to swell

bullnosed /bŏŏl nōzd/ *adj.* having a rounded protruding front part

bullock /bŏŏllək/ *n.* **1.** YOUNG BULL a young domestic bull **2.** CASTRATED BULL a castrated domestic bull [Old English *bulluc* 'young bull', diminutive of *bula* 'bull']

bullock's heart *n.* = **custard apple**

bullocky /bŏŏlləki/ (*plural* **-ies**) *n.* Aus sb who drives a team of bullocks (*informal*)

bullpen /bŏŏl pen/ *n.* **1.** BASEBALL WARM-UP AREA the part of a baseball field where the relief pitchers warm up **2.** US TEMPORARY CELL a cell for prisoners waiting to be brought into court (*informal*) [Early 19thC. Originally 'pen for bulls', hence 'any enclosure'.]

bullring /bŏŏl ring/ *n.* an arena where bullfights are held

bullroarer /bŏŏl rawrər/ *n.* Aus a musical instrument used in Aboriginal music and ritual, consisting of a long thin piece of wood that is twirled round on a length of string to create a roaring sound

bull session *n.* US an informal discussion, especially between men

bull's eye *n.* **1.** SPORTS MIDDLE OF TARGET the centre of a target, which usually carries the highest score ◇ *She hit the the bull's eye perfectly.* **2.** SPORTS TOP-SCORING SHOT a shot that hits the centre of a target **3.** ROUND WINDOW a small round window, especially a disc of thick glass in a ship's deck for letting in light below deck **4.** HARD SWEET a hard round peppermint boiled sweet, usually striped **5.** THICK LENS a small thick lens for intensifying light **6.** TYPE OF LAMP a lamp fitted with a bull's-eye lens ■ *n., interj.* PRECISE ACHIEVEMENT a precise or highly effective achievement (*informal*)

bullshit /bŏŏl shit/ *n.* OFFENSIVE TERM an offensive term for talk or writing dismissed as foolish or inaccurate (*slang offensive*) ■ *vti.* (**-shits, -shitting, -shitted**) (*slang offensive*) **1.** OFFENSIVE TERM an offensive term meaning to say things that are completely untrue or very foolish **2.** OFFENSIVE TERM an offensive term meaning to try to intimidate, deceive, or persuade sb with deceitful or foolish talk —**bullshitter** *n.*

bull terrier *n.* a smooth-haired muscular dog belonging to a breed developed in England by crossing the bulldog with a breed of terrier

bullwhip /bŏŏl wip/ *n.* LARGE WHIP a long heavy whip made of plaited strips of hide, knotted at the end ■ *vt.* (**-whips, -whipping, -whipped**) BEAT to beat sb with a bullwhip

bully¹ /bŏŏlli/ *n.* (*plural* **-lies**) AGGRESSIVE PERSON an aggressive person who intimidates or mistreats weaker people ■ *vt.* (**-lies, -lying, -lied**) INTIMIDATE to intimidate or mistreat weaker people [Mid-16thC. Origin uncertain: probably from Middle Dutch *boele* 'lover'. Originally 'sweetheart', then 'fine fellow', 'blusterer'.] —**bullying** *n.* ◇ **bully for you!** used to express approval (*often used ironically*)

bully² /bŏŏlli/ *n.* (*plural* **-lies**) *n.* a small New Zealand river fish. Genera: *Gobiomorphus* and *Phylinodon*. [Mid-19thC. Origin uncertain: probably shortened from BULLHEAD.]

bully beef *n.* tinned corned or pickled beef (*dated*) [Mid-18thC. Anglicization of *bouilli* 'boiled beef', from French, past participle of *bouillir* 'to boil', from Latin *bullire*.]

bullyboy /bŏŏlli boy/ *n.* an aggressive bully or thug

bully-off *n.* the former way of starting a hockey match, in which two opposing players hit sticks over the ball before each tries to hit it first. ♦ **pushback** [Late 19thC. Of uncertain origin, perhaps from BULLY.]

bully tree *n.* US = **balata**

bulrush /bŏŏl rush/ *n.* **1.** TALL MARSH PLANT WITH BROWN HEADS a tall marsh plant with brown furry flower spikes. Genus: *Typha*. **2.** WATERSIDE PLANT a plant that grows in wet conditions, with leaves like grass and clusters of drooping brown flowers. Genus: *Scirpus*. **3.** = **papyrus** [Middle English. Origin uncertain: probably a blend of BULL and RUSH.]

bulwark /bŏŏlwərk/ *n.* **1.** DEFENSIVE WALL a wall-like structure built to keep out attackers **2.** HARBOUR WALL a wall built in the sea to shelter a harbour **3.** PROTECTION a person or thing that gives protection or support ■ **bulwarks** *npl.* SHIP'S SIDES the sides of a ship projecting above the deck ■ *vt.* (**-warks, -warking, -warked**) **1.** PROTECT WITH WALLS to fortify or protect a place by building walls round it **2.** SAFEGUARD to defend or support sb or sth strongly [15thC. From Middle Low German *bolwerk* 'rampart made of tree trunks' (source of English *boulevard*), from *bole* 'tree trunk' + *werk* 'work'.]

bum¹ /bum/ *n.* (*informal*) **1.** GOOD-FOR-NOTHING sb considered to be irresponsible or worthless **2.** US VAGRANT a homeless person living on the street **3.** DEVOTEE a person excessively devoted to a particular activity or place ◇ *a ski bum* ■ *vt.* (**bums, bumming, bummed**) CADGE to get sth by asking or begging (*informal*) ■ *adj.* USELESS useless, worthless, or of poor quality (*informal*) ◇ *gave me some pretty bum advice* [Mid-19thC. Shortening of BUMMER, in the earlier sense 'lazy, irresponsible person'.] ◇ **give sb the bum's rush** US to order or force sb abruptly to leave a place (*slang*)

bum² /bum/ *n.* the buttocks (*informal*) [14thC. Origin unknown.]

bum bag *n.* a pouch for valuables, worn on a belt. US term **fanny pack**

bumble¹ /búmb'l/ *vti.* (**-bles, -bling, -bled**) SPEAK CLUMSILY to speak in a hesitant or muddled way ■ *n., vt.* (**-bles, -bling, -bled**) MOVE CLUMSILY to move or proceed clumsily ■ *vt.* (**-bles, -bling, -bled**) = **bungle** (*informal*) [Mid-16thC. Origin uncertain: perhaps a blend of BUNGLE and STUMBLE.] —**bumbler** *n.*

bumble² /búmb'l/ (**-bles, -bling, -bled**) *vi.* to make a humming sound [14thC. An imitation of the sound.]

bumblebee /búmb'l bee/ *n.* a large hairy bee of North America and Eurasia that nests in burrows and makes a loud droning noise in flight. Genus: *Bombus*. [Mid-16thC. From the droning sound it makes when flying.]

bumbledom /búmb'ldəm/ *n.* pompous self-importance and officiousness in a minor official (*humorous*) [Mid-19thC. Named after Mr *Bumble*, an officious beadle in Dickens' novel *Oliver Twist*.]

bumble-puppy *n.* **1.** GAME WITH BALL ON A STRING a game that involves hitting a ball attached to a string on a post, so that the string winds round the post. US term **tetherball 2.** INCOMPETENT PLAYING bridge or whist played badly (*informal*) [Early 19thC. Origin unknown.]

bumbling /búmbling/ *adj.* speaking or behaving in a clumsy or confused way (*informal*)

bumboat /búm bōt/ *n.* a small boat that is used for selling goods to ships at anchor [Late 17thC. *Bum* from BUM¹. Originally 'boat collecting rubbish and filth from moored ships'.]

bumf /bumf/, **bumph** *n.* unwanted or uninteresting printed material, especially official forms and documents (*informal*) [Late 19thC. Shortening of *bum fodder* 'toilet paper'.]

bumfreezer /búm freezər/ *n.* a short jacket for men, especially one worn on formal occasions (*dated informal*)

bumkin /búmkin/ *n.* = **bumpkin²**

bummalo /búmməlō/ (*plural* **-lo**) *n.* a small bluntnosed edible fish found in brackish Indian waters. Latin name: *Harpadon nehereus*. [Late 17thC. Origin uncertain: probably an alteration of Marathi *bombīl*.]

bummed /bumd/ *adj.* US depressed as a result of an unpleasant experience (*slang*)

bummer /búmmər/ *n.* (*slang*) **1.** ANNOYING THING sth annoying or unpleasant **2.** BAD REACTION TO DRUG a bad reaction to a hallucinogenic drug [Mid-19thC. Origin uncertain: probably from German *Bummler* 'idler, layabout', from *bummeln* 'to stroll or loaf around'.]

bump /bump/ *v.* (**bumps, bumping, bumped**) **1.** *vti.* KNOCK to hit or knock sth **2.** *vti.* MOVE UNSTEADILY to move in a jolting or bouncing way ◇ *We bumped along the dirt track.* **3.** *vt.* TURN AWAY A PASSENGER to turn away an airline passenger with a reserved seat because the flight has been overbooked ■ *n.* **1.** ACCIDENTAL KNOCK a light blow or impact ◇ *that bump dented the bodywork* **2.** SWELLING ON BODY a swelling on the body caused by an impact ◇ *a bump on the elbow* **3.** LUMP ON SURFACE a raised area on a flat surface ◇ *a bump in the road* **4.** SOUND OF IMPACT the dull sound of one thing hitting another **5.** RAISED AREA ON SKULL any of numerous raised areas on the skull, formerly thought to indicate intelligence or personality type [Mid-16thC. An imitation of the sound.] ◇ **bump and grind** US to dance erotically, thrusting and rotating the pelvis (*slang*)

bump into *vt.* **1.** COLLIDE ACCIDENTALLY to knock against or hit sb or sth accidentally **2.** MEET BY CHANCE to meet sb by chance

bump off *vt.* to murder sb (*slang*)

bump up *vt.* to increase prices suddenly and sharply (*informal*)

bump up against *vt.* **1.** COME INTO CONTACT WITH to come into contact with sth, usually with a sound **2.** CONFRONT to come into conflict with sb

bumper /búmpər/ *n.* PROTECTING BAR ON VEHICLE a projecting rim or bar on the front or back of a vehicle, designed to protect it from damage ■ *adj.* LARGE unusually large ○ *a bumper crop*

bumper car *n.* a small electric car used as part of a fairground entertainment. The cars are designed to be bumped into each other in a raised enclosure.

bumper-to-bumper *adj., adv.* forming a line of close slow-moving vehicles ○ *bumper-to-bumper traffic* ○ *drive bumper-to-bumper*

bumph /bumf/ *n.* = **bumf**

bumpkin[1] /búmpkin/ *n.* a country person regarded as unsophisticated (*informal*) [Late 16thC. Origin uncertain: perhaps from Dutch *boomken* or Middle Dutch *bommekijn* 'short rotund person', literally 'little tree'.]

bumpkin[2] /búmpkin/, **bumkin** /búm-/ *n.* a pole at the back of a ship or boat to which a sail is attached by a rope [Mid-17thC. Anglicization of Dutch *boomken.*]

bump-start *n.* = **push-start**

bumptious /búmpshəss/ *adj.* stating opinions aggressively or self-importantly [Early 19thC. A playful blend of BUMP and FRACTIOUS.] —**bumptiously** *adv.* —**bumptiousness** *n.*

bumpy /búmpi/ (**-ier, -iest**) *adj.* **1.** UNEVEN having a rough or uneven surface ○ *a bumpy road* **2.** BOUNCY uncomfortably bouncy or rough ○ *a bumpy ride* —**bumpily** *adv.* —**bumpiness** *n.*

bum rap *n. US* a false or fraudulent accusation or appraisal (*slang*)

bum steer *n. US* a piece of misleading information or bad advice (*slang*)

bun /bun/ *n.* **1.** ROUND BREAD ROLL a small round bread roll, sometimes sweetened and with added fruit or spice **2.** SMALL CAKE a small round sweet cake **3.** HAIR COILED AT BACK OF HEAD hair gathered in a tight round coil on the back or top of the head ■ **buns** *npl. US* BUTTOCKS the buttocks (*slang*) [14thC. Origin unknown.] ◇ **have a bun in the oven** to be pregnant (*slang*)

Bunbury /búnbəri/ coastal town in southwestern Western Australia, a major seaport and administrative centre. Population: 24,945 (1996).

bunch /bunch/ *n.* **1.** COLLECTION OF THINGS a number of things grouped or joined together **2.** CLUSTER OF FRUITS a cluster of fruits growing on a stem **3.** GROUP OF PEOPLE a group of people, especially friends or associates (*informal*) ■ **bunches** *npl.* HAIR TIED IN TWO CLUMPS hair gathered and tied in two clumps, one at each side of the head ■ *vti.* (**bunches, bunching, bunched**) GATHER to gather things or people into a cluster or close group [14thC. Origin unknown.] —**bunchiness** *n.* —**bunchy** *adj.*

bunco /búngkō/, **bunko** *n.* (*plural* **-coes**; *plural* **-koes**) *US* SWINDLE a trick or scheme that deceives people into parting with money (*slang*) ■ *vt.* (**-cos, -coing, -coed; -kos, -koing, -koed**) *US* DEFRAUD to trick sb into giving money (*slang*) [Late 19thC. Of uncertain origin; perhaps from Spanish *banca*, a kind of card game.]

bund[1] /bund/ *n. S Asia* an embankment or dyke surrounding rice fields or acting as a breakwater to prevent flooding. ◊ **levee** [Early 19thC. From Urdu *band*, from Persian.]

bund[2] /bŏŏnd/, **Bund** *n.* a political organization, especially a socialist Jewish labour movement in Tsarist Russia or a German-American group of Nazi sympathizers in the United States in the 1930s and 1940s [Late 19thC. From German, literally 'association'.]

Bundaberg /búndə burg/ city and port on the Pacific coast in southern Queensland, Australia, an important centre for sugar and timber production. Population: 41,025 (1996).

bundle /búnd'l/ *n.* **1.** A COLLECTION OF THINGS HELD TOGETHER a number of things tied, wrapped, or held together **2.** A LOT OF MONEY a large sum of money (*slang*) **3.** BIOL BAND OF PARALLEL TISSUES a band of tissues running parallel to each other, e.g. muscle or nerve fibres, or vascular tissue in plants **4.** COMPUT SET OF COMPUTER EQUIPMENT: computer hardware and software supplied as a package at an inclusive price ■ *vt.* (**-dles, -dling, -dled**) **1.** SHOVE SB OR STH to push sb or sth roughly and hurriedly (*informal*) **2.** COMPUT SUPPLY COMPUTER EQUIPMENT to package computer hardware and software together at an inclusive price [14thC. Origin uncertain, perhaps from Old English *byndelle* 'binding' or Dutch *bundel*, both related to English *bind.*] —**bundler** *n.* ◇ **drop your bundle** *ANZ* to lose your nerve and run away (*informal*) ◇ **go a bundle on sth** to be very fond of or enthusiastic about sth (*informal*)

bundle off *vt.* to send sb away hurriedly (*informal*) ○ *We bundled the children off to school.*

bundle up *v.* **1.** *vt.* GATHER INTO BUNDLE to gather things into a bundle **2.** *vti.* DRESS WARMLY to dress in warm clothes, or to dress sb in warm clothes (*informal*) ○ *Bundle up, it's cold outside.*

bundle of nerves *n.* sb who is feeling nervous, especially before an event (*informal*)

bundu /bŏŏn doo/ *n. S Africa* any remote uninhabited area (*slang*) [Mid-20thC. Origin uncertain: probably from Shona *bundo* 'grasslands'.]

bundwall /búnd wawl/ *n.* a casing of concrete or earth around an oil storage tank

bundy /búndi/ *n.* (*plural* **bundies**) *ANZ* TIME CLOCK a time clock used to record when an employee starts and finishes work, or to regulate scheduled services ■ *vi.* (**bundies, bundying, bundied**) *ANZ* RECORD WORK PERIOD ON BUNDY to record the starting and stopping of work using a bundy [Mid-20thC. From the trade name of a factory time-clock.]

bun fight *n.* **1.** PARTY a party or large gathering, especially an official dinner (*humorous*) **2.** ARGUMENT a heated argument (*slang*)

bung /bung/ *n.* **1.** STOPPER a stopper or plug, especially one made of cork or rubber **2.** PAYOFF an illicit fee paid to a football player, manager, or agent to facilitate a player transfer (*slang*) ■ *vt.* (**bungs, bunging, bunged**) **1.** STOP STH UP to plug or seal a hole with a bung **2.** PLACE CARELESSLY to put sth somewhere roughly or hurriedly (*informal*) ○ *Bung it in the bin when you're finished.* [15thC. From Middle Dutch *bonghe*, of uncertain origin, probably from late Latin *puncta* 'puncture', from Latin *pungere* 'to prick' (source of English *pungent*).]

bung up *vt.* to block or obstruct a hole or passage (*informal*)

bungalow /búng gəlō/ *n.* **1.** SINGLE-STOREY HOUSE a single-storey house **2.** LIGHTWEIGHT TROPICAL HOUSE a simply-built one-storey house with a veranda and a wide, gently sloping roof in Southeast Asia and the South Pacific ■ *Malaysia, Singapore* DETACHED HOUSE a detached house, usually of two or more storeys [Late 17thC. From Hindi *baṅglā* 'of Bengal'.]

bungee /búnji/ *n.* a cord or rope made from elastic material [Early 20thC. Origin unknown.]

bungee jump (*unmarked inflection* **bungee jumps**) *n.* a dive from a high place using an elastic cord tied to the ankles as a restraint —**bungee jumping** *n.*

bunger /búngər/ *n. Aus* a firework that explodes with a loud noise (*informal*) [Early 20thC. Variant of BANGER.]

bunghole /búng hōl/ *n.* a hole in a barrel or vat, used for drawing off the contents and closed with a bung

bungle /búng g'l/ *vt.* (**-gles, -gling, -gled**) SPOIL STH to cause sth to fail through carelessness or incompetence (*informal*) ■ *n.* MISTAKE a careless or clumsy action or mistake (*informal*) [Mid-16thC. Thought to suggest the action.] —**bungling** *adj.* —**bunglingly** *adv.*

bungler /búng glər/ *n.* a person whose carelessness or incompetence causes failure (*informal*)

bunion /búnyən/ *n.* inflammation of the sac (**bursa**) around the first joint of the big toe, accompanied by swelling and sideways displacement of the joint [Early 18thC. Directly or via English dialect *bunny* 'lump, swelling' from Old French *buigne* 'bump on the head', probably ultimately of Germanic origin.]

bunk[1] /bungk/ *n.* **1.** SIMPLE BED a simple narrow bed built on a shelf or in a recess **2.** = **bunk bed 3.** SLEEPING PLACE any bed or place to sleep (*informal*) ■ *vi.* (**bunks, bunking, bunked**) SLEEP to sleep in a place away from home (*informal*) ○ *'You may as well bunk at the YMCA and get in on their recreation programs'.* (Garrison Keillor, *We Are Still Married*; 1989) [Mid-18thC. Origin uncertain, perhaps shortened from BUNKER.]

bunk[2] /bungk/ *n.* talk or writing dismissed as nonsensical or inaccurate (*slang*) [Early 20thC. Shortened from BUNKUM.]

bunk[3] /bungk/ (**bunks, bunking, bunked**) *vi.* to disappear or depart hurriedly [Late 19thC. Origin unknown.] ◇ **do a bunk** to leave unexpectedly and hurriedly (*informal*) ◇ **bunk off** *vt.* to sneak away, especially from school (*informal*)

bunk bed *n.* either of a pair of single beds fitted one on top of the other

bunker /búngkər/ *n.* **1.** LARGE OUTDOOR CONTAINER a large outdoor bin or chest **2.** FUEL STORAGE CONTAINER a fuel-storage container on a ship **3.** UNDERGROUND SHELTER an underground shelter, especially one built for troops, with a fortified gun position above ground **4.** SAND HAZARD a sand-filled hollow on a golf course, built as a hazard ■ *vt.* (**-kers, -kering, -kered**) **1.** PUT STH IN OUTDOOR BIN to put or store sth in a large outdoor bin or chest **2.** SEND GOLF BALL INTO BUNKER to hit a golf ball into a bunker [Mid-16thC. Origin unknown.]

bunkhouse /búngk howss/ (*plural* **-houses**) *n. US* a building providing simple sleeping facilities

bunko *n., vt.* = **bunco**

bunkum /búngkəm/ *n.* talk or writing dismissed as nonsensical or inaccurate (*informal*) [Mid-19thC. Alteration of *Buncombe* County in North Carolina, United States, whose congressman defended a dull and irrelevant speech by saying he made it to impress the people of Buncombe.]

bunny /búnni/ (*plural* **-nies**) *n.* **1.** RABBIT a child's word for a rabbit **2.** *Aus* NAIVE PERSON a gullible person or scapegoat (*informal*) [Early 17thC. From English dialect *bun* 'rabbit's tail, rabbit', from Gaelic *bun* 'stump, bottom'.]

bunny hug *n.* a lively ballroom dance popular in the United States in the early 20th century

bunny slopes *npl. US* = **nursery slopes** [Bunny of uncertain origin]

bunodont /byoōnə dont/ *adj.* having molars with separate rounded ridges (**cusps**), typical of omnivores [Late 19thC. From Greek *bounos* 'mound' + -ODONT.]

Bunraku /bŏŏn ráa koo/ *n.* traditional Japanese puppetry using large wooden puppets, each worked by several puppeteers who are visible to the audience and with a separate narrator offstage [Early 20thC. From Japanese, named after the *Bunraku-za* theatre, built in the early 19thC by the puppeteer *Bunraku-ken* Oemurea (died 1810).]

Bunsen /búnss'n/, **Robert Wilhelm** (1811–99) German chemist and physicist. One of the discoverers of spectrum analysis (1859), he also invented a galvanic battery. He popularized the laboratory gas burner that bears his name.

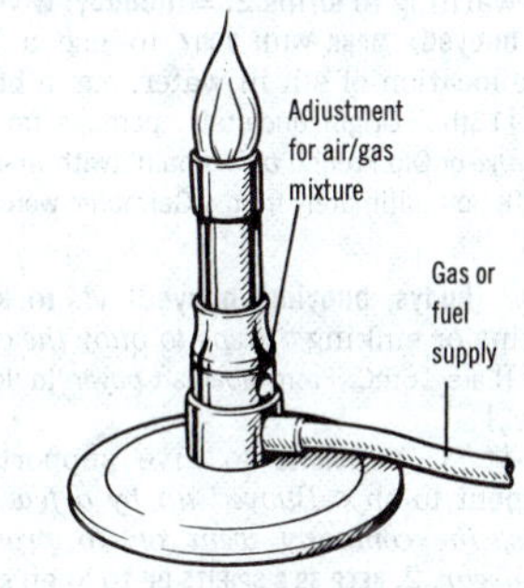
Adjustment
for air/gas
mixture
Gas or
fuel
supply

Bunsen burner

Bunsen burner *n.* a portable tube-shaped gas burner with an adjustable hole to control air intake and flame type, used in laboratories [Late 19thC. Named after Robert W. BUNSEN, who popularized it.]

bunt[1] /bunt/ *n., vt.* (**bunts, bunting, bunted**) = **butt**[1] *v.* 1 ■ *vt.* (**bunts, bunting, bunted**) HIT A BALL GENTLY in baseball, to hit a pitched ball very gently, holding the bat horizontally with both hands ■ *n.* GENTLE HIT OF BALL an instance of bunting a baseball [Mid-18thC. An imitation of the sound.] —**bunter** *n.*

bunt[2] /bunt/ *n.* the baggy pouch-like middle part of a sail [Late 16thC. Origin uncertain: perhaps ultimately from Low German *bunt* 'bundle'.]

buntal /búnt'l/ *n.* straw from the large leaves of the talipot palm tree of Southeast Asia [Early 20thC. From Tagalog.]

bunting[1] /búnting/ *n.* a small seed-eating songbird related to the finch, with a short stout bill and usually brown or grey feathers. Family: Emberizidae. [13thC. Origin unknown.]

bunting[2] /búnting/ n. strings of cloth or paper decorations for hanging outdoors [Early 18thC. Origin uncertain, perhaps from German *bunt* 'coloured'.]

buntline /búnt līn/ n. a rope attached to the bottom of a square sail, used to roll up the sail

Popperfoto
Luis Buñuel

Buñuel /boon wél/, **Luis** (1900–83) Spanish film director. One of the greatest masters of filmmaking, he incorporated uncompromising social criticisms in works such as *The Discreet Charm of the Bourgeoisie* (1972).

bunya /búnnyə/, **bunya-bunya**, **bunya pine** n. a tall Australian tree with cones containing edible seeds that are eaten raw or roasted and are ground into flour. Latin name: *Araucaria bidwillii*. [Mid-19thC. From Yagara *bunya-bunya*.]

Bunyan /búnnyən/, **John** (1628–88) English preacher and writer. A Puritan preacher, he was jailed for 12 years for his religious beliefs. He wrote the autobiographical *Grace Abounding to the Chief of Sinners* (1666) and the great spiritual allegory *Pilgrim's Progress* (1678).

bunyip /búnnyip/ n. *Aus* in Aboriginal legend, a monster said to inhabit swamps and waterholes of the Australian interior [Mid-19thC. From Wemba-Wemba *banib*.]

Buonarroti /bwónnə rótti/, **Michelangelo ▶** Michelangelo

buoy[1] /boy/ n. **1. FLOATING SIGNAL** a large anchored float, often equipped with lights or bells, that serves as a guide or warning to ships **2.** = **lifebuoy** ■ vt. (**buoys, buoying, buoyed**) **MARK WITH BUOY** to use a buoy to mark the location of sth in water, e.g. a hazard or channel [13thC. Origin uncertain: perhaps from Middle Dutch *bo(e)ye* or Old French *boie* 'chain' (with which a buoy is tethered), both ultimately from a Germanic word meaning 'signal'.]

buoy[2] /boy/ (**buoys, buoying, buoyed**) vt. to keep sth from falling or sinking ○ *steps to buoy the country's currency* [Late 16thC. From Spanish *boyar* 'to float', from *boya* 'buoy'.]

buoy up vt. **1. ENCOURAGE** to give support or encouragement to sb ○ *Buoyed up by a few wise investments, the company went on to prosper the following year.* **2. KEEP SB'S SPIRITS UP** to keep sb cheerful or optimistic in spite of difficulties ○ *The arrival of the children has buoyed us all up.*

buoyancy /bóyənssi/, **buoyance** /-ənss/ n. **1. FORCE CAUSING FLOATING** the tendency of a liquid or gas to cause less dense objects to float or rise to the surface **2. TENDENCY TO FLOAT** the tendency of an object to float **3. POWER TO RECOVER EMOTIONALLY** the ability to recover quickly from a disappointment or failure **4. CHEERFULNESS** cheerfulness or optimism

buoyant /bóyənt/ adj. **1. PUSHING UPWARDS** causing immersed objects to float or rise to the surface of a liquid, or upwards in a gas **2. ABLE TO FLOAT** tending to float or rise to the surface of a liquid, or upwards in a gas **3. QUICK TO RECOVER EMOTIONALLY** tending to recover quickly from a disappointment or failure **4. CHEERFUL** cheerful or optimistic [Late 16thC. From Old French, or from Spanish *boyante*, present participle of *boyar* 'to float', from *boya* (see BUOY).] —**buoyantly** adv.

bupivacaine /byoo pívvə kayn/ n. a powerful local anaesthetic used especially in epidural an-

aesthesia [Origin uncertain: perhaps from BUTYL + pipecoloxylidide + -vacaine (from procaine)]

buprestid /byoo préstid/ n. a metallic-coloured tropical beetle found worldwide that bores into wood during the larva stage. Family: Buprestidae. [Mid-19thC. From modern Latin *Buprestidae* (plural), family name, ultimately from Greek *bouprēstis*, literally 'ox-sweller', from *bous* 'ox'.]

bur n. = **burr**[1]

Bur. abbr. Burma ■ abbr. Burmese

Burakumin /boo rákoo min/ npl. members of the lowest Japanese caste [Mid-20thC. From Japanese, literally 'hamlet people'.]

buran /boo ra´an/ n. a strong wind in central Asia, bringing dust storms in summer and blizzards in winter [Mid-19thC. Via Russian from Turkic *boran*.]

Buraydah /boo rídə/ city in central Saudi Arabia directly north of Unayzah. Population: 69,940.

Burberry /búrbəri/ tdmk. a trademark for a brand of outerwear, especially waterproof cloth raincoats and accessories

burble /búrb'l/ v. (**-bles, -bling, -bled**) **1.** vi. **MAKE BUBBLING SOUND** to make a gentle bubbling sound, like the sound of running water **2.** vti. **SPEAK EXCITEDLY** to speak or say sth in a fast excited way (*informal*) **3.** vi. **BECOME TURBULENT** to become turbulent (*refers to the airflow around an aircraft's wing*) ■ n. **1. GENTLE SOUND** a gentle bubbling or gurgling sound **2. STREAM OF TALK** a flow of fast excited talking (*informal*) **3. BREAK IN AIRFLOW** a break in the flow of air around an aircraft's wing, which causes turbulence [14thC. An imitation of the sound.] —**burbler** n. —**burbly** adv.

burbot /búrbət/ n. (*plural* **-bot** *or* **-bots**) n. a freshwater fish of the cod family found in North America, northern Europe, and Asia. Latin name: *Lota lota*. [14thC. From Old French *borbette*, of uncertain origin: probably formed from *borbe* 'mud, slime'.]

Burckhardt /búrk haart/, **Jakob** (1818–97) Swiss art historian. Professor of history at Basel University (1843–93), he wrote works on the Italian Renaissance and Greek civilization including the classic *The Civilisation of the Renaissance in Italy* (1860). Full name **Jakob Christopher Burckhardt**

Burdekin /búrdəkən/ river in Queensland, Australia that rises in the Seaview Range west of Ingham and empties into the Pacific Ocean near Ayr. Length: 720 km/447 mi.

burden[1] /búrd'n/ n. **1. STH CARRIED** a load being carried ○ *carrying a heavy burden on his back* **2. WORRYING RESPONSIBILITY** a difficult or worrying responsibility or duty ○ *the burdens of parenthood* **3. SHIP'S CAPACITY** the maximum weight of cargo that a ship can carry ■ vt. (**-dens, -dening, -dened**) **1. GIVE RESPONSIBILITY TO SB** to give sb a task that is difficult to deal with or sth worrying to think about **2. IMPOSE BURDEN ON SB** to cause sb or sth to carry a burden [Old English *byrthen*. Ultimately from an Indo-European word meaning 'to bear', which is also the ancestor of English *birth*, *fertile*, and *suffer*.]

—————— **WORD KEY: SYNONYMS** ——————
See Synonyms at **subject**.

burden[2] /búrd'n/ n. **1. CHORUS** a chorus in a song **2. THEME** a main or recurring theme in music or literature (*literary*) [Late 16thC. Alteration of Middle English *bourdon* 'bass part underlying a melody', from French, literally 'bass, drone'.]

burden of proof n. the responsibility of proving a case or argument, especially in a court of law

burdensome /búrd'nsəm/ adj. difficult or worrying to bear or deal with

burdock /búr dok/ n. a tall biennial plant found wild in temperate areas, with a long taproot and small prickly purple flower heads. Genus: *Arctium*. [Late 16thC. From BURR + DOCK[1].]

bureau /byoo ro/ (*plural* **bureaus** *or* **bureaux** /-rōz/) n. **1. ORGANIZATION** an organization, or one of its branches **2. GOVERNMENT DEPARTMENT** a government department, or one of its branches **3. WRITING DESK** a narrow desk with a writing surface and drawers **4. US CHEST OF DRAWERS** a chest of drawers, especially a low one [Late 17thC. From French, literally 'baize' (used for desks), of

uncertain origin: probably formed from *buire* 'dark brown', from, ultimately, Greek *purros* 'red', from *pur* 'fire'.]

bureaucracy /byoor rókrəssi/ (*plural* **-cies**) n. **1. ADMINISTRATIVE SYSTEM** an administrative system, especially in a government, that divides work into specific categories carried out by special departments of nonelected officials **2. OFFICIALS COLLECTIVELY** the nonelected officials of an organization or department **3. FRUSTRATING RULES** complex rules and regulations applied rigidly **4. STATE OR ORGANIZATION** a state or organization operated by a hierarchy of paid officials [Early 19thC. From French *bureaucratie*, from *bureau* 'office' + *cracy* 'rule'.]

bureaucrat /byoor rə krat/ n. **1. ADMINISTRATIVE OFFICIAL** an administrative or government official **2. INFLEXIBLE OFFICIAL** an official who applies rules rigidly —**bureaucratism** /byoo rókrətizzəm/ n.

bureaucratic /byoor rə kráttik/ adj. **1. ADMINISTRATIVE** relating to the way administrative systems are organized ○ *the bureaucratic structure* **2. TOO RIGID** used to describe an administrative system or official that applies rules rigidly —**bureaucratically** adv.

bureaucratize /byoo rókrə tīz/ (**-tizes, -tizing, -tized**), **bureaucratise** (**-tises, -tising, -tised**) vt. **1. MAKE STH INTO BUREAUCRACY** to change a system into a bureaucracy **2. MAKE STH TOO RIGID OR COMPLEX** to make a system or procedure rigid or complex —**bureaucratization** /byoo rókrə tī záysh'n/ n.

bureau de change /byoor rō də shóNzh/ (*plural* **bureaus de change** /byoor rō-/ *or* **bureaux de change** /byoor rō-/) n. an office or part of a bank where foreign currency is exchanged [From French, literally 'office of exchange']

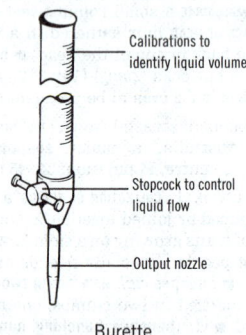
Calibrations to identify liquid volume
Stopcock to control liquid flow
Output nozzle
Burette

burette /byoo rét/ n. a glass tube with measurements marked on the side and a stopcock at the bottom, used in laboratories to release an accurately measured quantity of liquid [Mid-19thC. From French, diminutive of *buire* 'jug', probably ultimately of Germanic origin.]

burg /burg/ n. **1. ANCIENT FORTRESS** an ancient fortress or walled town **2.** *US* **TOWN** a city or town (*informal*) [Mid-18thC. *Enclosure* from late Latin *burgus* 'town', from German *Burg*; both ultimately from an ancient Germanic word that is also the ancestor of English *borough*.]

Burgas /boor gáss/ port on the Black Sea coast and capital of Burgas Province, eastern Bulgaria. Population: 199,869 (1995).

burgee /búr jee/ n. a light identification flag flown from the top of a mast [Mid-18thC. Origin uncertain: perhaps from French *bourgeois* in the sense 'master, owner', from late Latin *burgus* (see BOURG).]

burgeon /búrjən/ (**-geons, -geoning, -geoned**) vi. (*literary*) **1. PRODUCE NEW GROWTH** to produce new buds and leaves or to swell and develop into leaves and flowers **2. FLOURISH** to flourish or develop rapidly [14thC. From French *bourgeonner*, from *bourgeon* 'a shoot or bud', from, ultimately, late Latin *burra* 'wool'.]

burgeoning /búrjəning/ adj. growing or expanding rapidly ○ *burgeoning wealth*

burger /búrgər/ n. **1. MEAT SNACK** a flat round cake of cooked minced meat, usually served in a bun **2. SAVOURY SNACK** a round flat cake made of chicken, fish, vegetables, or nuts, usually served in a bun [Mid-20thC. Back-formation from HAMBURGER.]

-burger /búrgər/ suffix. Resembling minced beef or a hamburger ○ *veggieburger* [From HAMBURGER]

Burgess /búrjiss/, **Anthony** (1917–93) British writer and critic. His books include *A Clockwork Orange* (1962) and *A Dead Man in Deptford* (1993). Born **John Anthony Burgess Wilson**

Burgess, Guy (1911–63) British diplomat and spy. Recruited as a Soviet agent while a student at Cambridge in the 1930s, he worked for MI5 and the Foreign Office. After being charged with serious misconduct, he escaped to the Soviet Union in 1951 with Donald Maclean. Full name **Guy Francis de Moncy Burgess**

burgh /búrrə/ *n. Scotland* a borough

Burgh /burg/, **Hubert de, Earl of Kent** (1197–1243?) English statesman. He was chief justice of the land and was regent for Henry III from 1219 to 1227.

burgher /búrgər/ *n.* **1. MEDIEVAL MERCHANT** a merchant in a medieval European town **2. CITIZEN** a citizen, especially a prosperous or conservative member of the middle class (*humorous*) [Late 16thC. Partly formed from BURGH, partly from German or Dutch *burger*, from *burg* (see BURG).]

Burghley /búrli/, **Sir William Cecil, 1st Baron** (1520–98) English statesman. He was chief secretary of state to Elizabeth I after 1558, and formulated many of the domestic and foreign policies that made the Elizabethan Age a period of power and prosperity in England.

burglar /búrglər/ *n.* sb who enters a building illegally, usually in order to steal sth [Mid-16thC. From obsolete legal French *burgier*, from the assumed Latin stem *burg-* 'to plunder'.]

burglarize /búrglə rīz/ (**-izes, -izing, -ized**) *vt. US, Can* = **burgle** (*often passive*)

burglarproof /búrglər proof/ *adj.* secured with locks, alarms, or other devices so as to discourage or prevent unauthorized entry

burglary /búrgləri/ (*plural* **-ries**) *n.* the crime of entering a building illegally, or an instance of such a crime —**burglarious** /bur gláiri əss/ *adj.* —**burglariously** /-əssli/ *adv.*

WORD KEY: SYNONYMS

See Synonyms at ***theft***.

burgle /búrg'l/ (**-gles, -gling, -gled**) *vt.* to enter a building illegally, usually in order to steal sth (*often passive*) US term **burglarize** [Late 19thC. Back-formation from BURGLAR.]

burgomaster /búrgə maastər/ *n.* the mayor or chief magistrate in some northern European towns [Late 16thC. From Dutch *burgomeester*, literally 'town master'.]

burgoo /búr goo/ (*plural* **-goos**) *n.* **1.** *Southern US* **STEW** a spicy meat stew cooked outdoors **2.** *Southern US* **OUTDOOR PARTY** an outdoor party where burgoo is cooked and eaten **3. PORRIDGE** a kind of porridge eaten by sailors in the past (*informal*) [Late 17thC. Via Arabic *burğul* from Persian *burğūl*, variant of *burğūr*, literally 'bruised grain' (source of English *bulgur*).]

Burgos /búr goss/ capital of the Burgos Province in the autonomous region of Castile-León, northern Spain. Population: 166,732 (1995).

burgundy /búrgəndi/; **Burgundy** *n.* (*plural* **-dies**) **1. KIND OF WINE** red or white wine produced in the Burgundy region of central France **2. DEEP RED COLOUR** a deep red colour, like that of red Burgundy wine ■ *adj.* **OF DEEP RED COLOUR** of a deep red colour, like red Burgundy wine

burial /bérri əl/ *n.* the act or ceremony of putting a dead body into the ground or into the sea [Old English *byrgels*, from *byrgan* (see BURY)]

burial ground *n.* an area of land where dead bodies are buried, especially an ancient site

Buriat *n.* = **Buryat**

Buridan's ass /byoȯr rid'nz-/ *n.* a situation used to demonstrate the impracticality of making choices according to a formal system of reasoning [Named after Jean *Buridan* (1300–58), French philosopher who wrote of an ass that starves to death because it cannot choose between two identical piles of food]

burin /byoȯr rin/ *n.* **1. CHISEL** an engraver's chisel for making grooves **2. PREHISTORIC TOOL** a prehistoric chisel-like flint tool, used for cutting and engraving during the Upper Palaeolithic period [Mid-17thC. From French.]

burk /burk/ *n.* = **berk** (*slang*)

burka /búrkə/ *n.* an all-over garment with veiled eyeholes, worn by some Muslim women [Mid-19thC. Via Urdu or Persian *burka'* from Arabic *burku'*.]

burke /burk/ (**burkes, burking, burked**) *vt.* **1. KEEP STH QUIET** to prevent information from becoming known **2. KEEP SB QUIET** to prevent sb from revealing information **3. EVADE** to evade an issue or question **4. MURDER DISCREETLY** to murder sb silently and without leaving marks or wounds, especially by suffocation [Early 19thC. Named after William *Burke* (1792–1829), hanged in Edinburgh for killing people in order to sell their bodies for dissection.]

Burke /burk/, **Edmund** (1729–97) Irish-born British political philosopher and statesman. As a Whig member of Parliament (1765–94), he was one of the greatest orators of the age. He played a leading role in the impeachment of Warren Hastings (1788–95). His *Reflections on the Revolution in France* (1790) condemned the French Revolution and reached a wide European audience.

Burke, Robert O'Hara (1820–61) Irish-born Australian explorer. The leader of an ill-fated expedition across Australia from south to north, he died during the return journey.

Burke, William (1792–1829) Irish murderer and grave robber. With William Hare he procured corpses to sell to Edinburgh medical schools by murdering people or by digging up bodies. He was hanged for his crimes.

Burkina Faso

Burkina Faso /burk éenə fássō/ landlocked republic in western Africa. A former French territory, it became independent in 1960. Language: French. Currency: CFA franc. Capital: Ouagadougou. Population: 10,963,300 (1997). Area: 274,200 sq. km/105,900 sq. mi. Former name **Upper Volta** (until 1984)

Burkitt's lymphoma /búrkits-/ *n.* a rare malignant tumour attacking white blood cells, associated with a virus spread by insects. It is found mainly in children in Central Africa. [Mid-20thC. Named after the British surgeon Denis *Burkitt* (1911–93), who mapped its geographical distribution in Africa.]

burl[1] /burl/ *n.* **1. KNOT ON TREE** a knotty growth on a tree trunk **2. KNOTTY WOOD** knotty wood or a decorative veneer made from it **3. KNOT IN CLOTH** a knot in thread or cloth **4.** *Ireland, UK* **ACT OF SWINGING** an act of swinging (*regional informal*) ○ *How would you like a burl?* ■ *vt.* (**burls, burling, burled**) **1. REMOVE KNOTS FROM CLOTH** to pick knots off newly woven cloth **2.** *Ireland, UK* **MAKE SB SWING** to cause someone to swing (*regional informal*) ○ *He swung me off my feet and burled me through the air.* [15thC. Via Old French *bourle* 'tuft of wool' from, ultimately, late Latin *burra* 'wool' (source of English *burgeon*).] —**burler** *n.*

burl[2] /burl/ *n. ANZ* an attempt (*informal*) [Early 20thC. From Scots *birl*, *burl* 'to spin or toss a coin', an imitation of the sound of a coin spinning on a surface.]

burlap /búr lap/ *n.* coarse cloth woven from jute, hemp, or a similar rough thread [Late 17thC. Origin unknown.]

burlesque /bur lésk/ *n.* **1. MOCKERY BY LUDICROUS IMITATION** the mocking of a serious matter or style by imitating it in an incongruous way **2. WORK USING BURLESQUE** a literary or dramatic work that uses burlesque **3. LUDICROUS IMITATION** an incongruous imitation of sth **4.** *US* **VARIETY SHOW** a variety show of a type that often includes striptease ■ *vt.* (**burlesques, burlesquing, burlesqued**) **MOCK BY LUDICROUS IMITATION** to mock sth serious by imitating it in an incongruous way [Mid-17thC. Via French from Italian *burlesco*, from *burla* 'mockery, fun'.] —**burlesquer** *n.*

burley /búrli/ *n.* a light-coloured, thin-leaved tobacco grown mainly in Kentucky in the United States [Late 19thC. Origin uncertain, perhaps from the personal name *Burley*.]

burly /búrli/ (**-lier, -liest**) *adj.* strong and with a broad sturdy frame ○ *flanked by two burly bodyguards* [14thC. Origin uncertain: probably from assumed Old English *borlic* 'excellent', ultimately from an Indo-European word meaning 'to carry', which is also the ancestor of English *bear* 'to carry'.] —**burliness** *n.*

Burma /búrmə/ former name for **Myanmar** (until 1989)

bur marigold *n.* a wild plant with yellow flowers. It produces barbs that stick to hair, fur, and clothing. Genus: *Bidens*. US term **beggar's lice**

Burmese /búr meez/ *npl.* **PEOPLE OF MYANMAR** the people of Myanmar, formerly Burma ■ *n.* **SINO-TIBETAN LANGUAGE** the official language of Myanmar, formerly Burma, one of the Tibeto-Burman group of Sino-Tibetan languages. Burmese is spoken by between 20 and 27 million people. ■ *adj.* **OF MYANMAR** relating to or typical of Myanmar, its people, language, or culture

Burmese cat *n.* a domestic cat with a chocolate-coloured or silvery-brown coat and yellow eyes, similar in build to the Siamese cat

burn[1] /burn/ *v.* (**burns, burning, burnt** /burnt/ *or* **burned, burnt** *or* **burned**) **1.** *vti.* **BE OR SET ON FIRE** to be on fire or cause sth to be on fire **2.** *vti.* **DESTROY STH BY FIRE** to destroy sth or be destroyed by fire ○ *The house was burnt to the ground.* **3.** *vt.* **DAMAGE STH BY FIRE** to injure, damage, or affect sb or sth with fire or extreme heat ○ *I burnt my hand on the iron.* **4.** *vt.* **OVERCOOK STH** to spoil food or a cooking pan by subjecting it to too much heat **5.** *vi.* **BE OVERCOOKED** to be spoiled because of being subjected to too intense a heat or being cooked for too long **6.** *vt.* **USE STH UP** to use up or consume sth ○ *You won't burn many calories watching TV.* **7.** *vt.* **USE STH AS FUEL** to use sth as fuel ○ *burn gas* **8.** *vti.* **KILL OR DIE BY FIRE** to kill sb with fire or die by fire, usually as a form of execution **9.** *vi.* **SUFFER PAIN** to suffer pain through fire **10.** *vi.* **FEEL FEVERISH** to feel or look extremely hot or feverish because of illness or embarrassment ○ *Her cheeks were burning.* **11.** *vti.* **CAUSE OR FEEL STINGING** to feel an intense stinging or smarting sensation or cause such a sensation in a part of the body ○ *That hot coffee will burn your throat* **12.** *vi.* **IMPRESS DEEPLY** to create a deep and lasting impression on sb or sth ○ *His words were burning in my brain.* **13.** *vt.* **MAKE MARK** to cause a mark, hole, or other sign of damage to appear in sth because of intense heat or fire ○ *I burnt a hole in my shirt with the iron.* **14.** *vti.* **SUNBURN** to become sunburnt or cause a person or part of the body to become sunburnt ○ *My skin burns easily.* **15.** *vi.* **EMIT HEAT OR LIGHT** to emit heat or light ○ *A light was burning in the front room.* **16.** *vi.* **CONTAIN A FIRE** to contain a fire or operate by means of fire ○ *a fireplace burning bright* **17.** *vti. US* **ELECTROCUTE** to electrocute sb or be electrocuted (*informal*) **18.** *vt. US* **CHEAT SB** to cheat or swindle sb (*informal; usually passive*) ○ *We really got burnt on that deal.* **19.** *vi.* **FEEL STRONG EMOTION** to feel an emotion such as anger or shame very intensely ○ *burning with shame* **20.** *vi.* **YEARN** to yearn to do or acquire sth ○ *burning to succeed* **21.** *vti.* CHEM **COMBUST** to undergo combustion, thus taking in oxygen, or to cause sth to undergo combustion **22.** *vti.* CARDS **DISCARD** to exchange or discard unwanted cards (*informal*) **23.** *vi. Aus* **DRIVE FAST** to drive a motor vehicle at high speed (*informal*) ■ *n.* **1.** MED **HEAT INJURY** an injury caused by fire, heat, radiation, chemical action, electricity, or friction, resulting in redness and blistering of the skin and often causing damage to underlying tissues. ◊ **first-degree burn, second-degree burn, third-degree burn** **2. FIRE OR HEAT MARK** a mark or hole left on or in sth such as fabric, wood, or plastic as a result of burning **3.** SPACE TECH **ROCKET ENGINE ADJUSTMENT** a controlled firing of a rocket's engine for adjusting course and position **4. STINGING** a stinging sensation or feeling of intense heat ○ *the burn of the iodine on my skin* **5.** SKIN BURN sunburn or windburn **6.** FITNESS SENSATION OF BURNING a sensation of burning that occurs during strenuous exercise, and the positive psychological sensation associated with it ○ *You can feel the burn after an hour of aerobics* [Old English *birnan* 'to be on fire' and *bærnan* 'to cause to burn', from a prehistoric Germanic word that is also the ancestor of English *brand*]

burn down *vti.* to catch fire and burn until virtually nothing remains, or to burn sth such as a building in order to destroy it

burn in *vt.* **1.** PHOTOGRAPHY EXPOSE PART OF PICTURE to expose a specific part of an image on photographic paper while masking other areas so that they are not exposed any further **2.** COMPUT TEST STH BY RUNNING IT CONTINUOUSLY to operate a semiconductor-based device or piece of software for a continuous period as a test for defects or failure

burn off *v.* **1.** *vt.* GET RID OF EXCESS FAT to use up energy or get rid of unwanted fat by exercising ○ *burn off a few extra calories* **2.** *vt.* AGRIC REMOVE VEGETATION to remove vegetation by fire or with chemicals, either to clear the land or in preparation for harvesting a root crop **3.** *vt.* ENERGY GET RID OF EXCESS GAS to get rid of unwanted gas, e.g. at an oil-well head, by burning it **4.** *vti.* METEOROL DISSIPATE to dissipate fog or clouds by the heat of the sun, or to be dissipated in this way

burn out *v.* **1.** *vi.* FINISH BURNING to stop burning when reduced to nothing **2.** *vti.* WEAR OUT THROUGH HEAT to stop working or to cause sth to stop working because of too much heat or friction ○ *The car's clutch has burned out* **3.** *vti.* BECOME EXHAUSTED to become or make sb exhausted or unwell through too much hard work, stress, or reckless living (*informal*) ○ *You'll burn yourself out if you don't slow down.*

burn up *v.* **1.** *vti.* DESTROY BY FIRE to destroy sth or be destroyed by intense heat or fire **2.** *vt.* USE FUEL to use up fuel by burning **3.** *vi.* BE VERY HOT to be very hot or overheated ○ *burning up with fever* **4.** *vt.* DRIVE AT HIGH SPEED to drive at high speed on a road or track (*informal*) **5.** *vt.* DRIVE FASTER THAN SB to drive faster than sb else (*informal*) ○ *some idiot tried to burn me up on the motorway*

burn[2] /burn/ *n. Scotland* a stream or brook [Old English *burna*. Ultimately from an Indo-European word meaning 'to boil', which is also the ancestor of English *ferment*. The underlying idea is of water 'boiling' over rocks.]

Burne-Jones /búrn-/, **Sir Edward** (1833–98) British designer. A leading member of the pre-Raphaelite school, he painted classical and mythological subjects in a dreamlike style. His book illustrations and designs for stained glass and tapestries showed the strong influence of medieval art. Born **Edward Coley Jones**

burner /búrnər/ *n.* **1.** PART OF STOVE OR LAMP the part of a fuel-burning stove, lamp, or heater that produces a flame when lit **2.** RING ON COOKER one of the circular rings or plates on a gas or electric cooker that produces heat or a flame **3.** FURNACE an incinerator or furnace that burns fuel, waste products, or rubbish

burnet /búrnit/ (*plural* **-nets** *or* **-net**) *n.* a plant of the rose family with flowers of various colours. The most common variety, the salad burnet, is cultivated and used in salads and herbal teas. Genus: *Sanguisorba.* [14thC. From Old French *brunet* and *brunete*, literally 'small brown', which were formed from *brun* 'brown', from a prehistoric Germanic word that is also the ancestor of English *brown*.]

Burnet /bər nét, búrnit/, **Sir Macfarlane** (1899–1985) Australian biologist. He was joint winner of the Nobel Prize in physiology or medicine in 1960 for his work in immunology. Full name **Sir Frank Macfarlane Burnet**

Burney /búrni/, **Fanny** (1752–1840) British novelist and diarist. Her novels include *Evelina* (1778). Her diaries covering 1768–85 and published posthumously, are among the classic documents of late-18th-century British social history.

Burnham scale /búrnəm-/ *n.* a scale of salaries for teachers in English state schools [Early 20thC. Named after Viscount *Burnham* (1862–1933), first Chairman of the Burnham committee, which recommended the scale.]

Burnie-Somerset /búrni-/ city on the northern coast of Tasmania, Australia, an important port and the site of a large paper mill. Population: 19,134 (1996).

burn-in *n.* COMPUT a final stage in the manufacture of semiconductor-based devices or software in which they are operated for a prescribed period to test for defects or failures and thus improve their reliability

burning /búrning/ *adj.* **1.** VERY HOT extremely hot **2.** ON FIRE producing flames or on fire **3.** ARDENT emotionally intense or strong ○ *he spoke with a burning passion* **4.** IMPORTANT of immediate or urgent importance ○ *one of the burning issues of the day* ■ *adv.* EXTREMELY extremely ○ *a burning hot day* [Old English]

burning bush *n.* **1.** BUSHY PLANT WITH NARROW LIGHT GREEN LEAVES THAT TURN RED IN AUTUMN COLOUR a bushy annual plant with narrow light green leaves that turn red in autumn, such as kochia **2.** = **gas plant 3.** *US* SHRUB WITH RED BERRIES OR FOLIAGE a shrub that produces bright red berries or foliage. Genus: *Euonymus.* [Alludes to the burning bush of Exodus 3. In the sense of 'gas plant', from its leaves' secretion of flammable oil.]

burning glass *n.* a convex lens that can concentrate the sun's rays to produce an intense spot of heat or fire at the focus

burnish /búrnish/ *vt.* (**-nishes, -nishing, -nished**) **1.** POLISH STH to polish metal until it shines **2.** MAKE STH SHINY to produce a glossy finish on sth such as pottery or fabric by rubbing it with a smooth instrument ■ *n.* SHINY SURFACE a smooth shiny finish ○ *a bowl with a bright burnish* [14thC. From the Old French stem *burniss-* of *burnir*, variant of *brunir* 'to make bright or brown', from *brun* (see BURNET).] —**burnisher** *n.*

burnished *adj.* **1.** SHINY polished until shiny **2.** LUSTROUS brown and lustrous or smooth (*literary*) ○ *the burnished coat of the chestnut mare*

Burnley /búrnli/ town in Lancashire, north-western England, centre of coal and textile production. Population: 89,000 (1991).

burnoose /bur nóoss/, **burnous, burnouse** *n.* a long hooded cloak worn by some Arabs, or a fashionable imitation of this [Late 16thC. Via French *burnous* from Arabic *burnus*, from Greek *birros* 'hooded cloak'.]

burnout /búrn owt/ *n.* **1.** EXHAUSTION psychological exhaustion and diminished efficiency resulting from overwork or prolonged exposure to stress ○ *reported a high rate of burnout among nurses* **2.** EXTREMELY EXHAUSTED PERSON sb affected by psychological exhaustion (*informal*) **3.** MECH ENG MACHINE FAILURE THROUGH HEAT failure of a machine or part of a machine to work because of overuse or excessive heat or friction **4.** AEROSP ROCKET FAILURE failure of a rocket or jet engine to work because the fuel supply has been exhausted or cut off

Barnaby's

Robert Burns

Burns /búrnz/, **Robert** (1759–96) Scottish poet. The author of *Poems, Chiefly in the Scottish Dialect* (1786) and hundreds of songs, he is regarded as Scotland's national poet. His many songs include 'Auld Lang Syne', 'Scots Wha Hae' and the narrative poem 'Tam O'Shanter'.

burnsides /búrn sīdz/ *npl. US* heavy side whiskers and a moustache worn with a clean-shaven chin [Late 19thC. Named after Ambrose E. BURNSIDE who was known for his side whiskers.]

Burns night *n. Scotland* the anniversary of the birth of (**Robert Burns**), January 25, which is traditionally celebrated with a Burns Supper

Burns Supper *n. Scotland* ETHNOL a celebration of the birthday of (**Robert Burns**), held on or about January 25, the date of his birth, and consisting of an evening meal of haggis, mashed turnip, and mashed potato, with the drinking of whisky, the reciting and singing of Burns' works, and the giving of speeches and toasts. One of the speeches is always the 'Immortal Memory'. The toasts include a toast to the lassies, and a reply on behalf of the lassies, nowadays often given by a woman.

burnt[1] /burnt/ past tense, past participle of **burn**[1]

burnt[2] /burnt/ *adj.* **1.** AFFECTED BY BURNING affected or spoiled by burning, especially by overcooking **2.** PAINTING DARKENED BY HEAT used to describe a pigment or dye that has been darkened through a heating process ○ *burnt umber*

burnt almond *n.* sweet with an almond in the centre and a coating of burnt sugar

burnt offering *n.* **1.** SACRIFICE an animal or other offering that is burnt on an altar as a sacrifice in some religions **2.** BURNT FOOD burnt or overcooked food that is nevertheless served up (*humorous*)

burnt-out, burned-out *adj.* **1.** COMPLETELY EXHAUSTED exhausted physically or emotionally through too much hard work, stress, or reckless living **2.** DESTROYED BY FIRE destroyed on the inside by fire

burnt-out *adj.* = **burned-out**

burnt sienna *n.* **1.** PAINTING BROWN PIGMENT a reddish-brown pigment or dye originally obtained by roasting raw sienna **2.** COLOURS DARK REDDISH-BROWN a dark reddish-brown colour

burnt umber *n.* **1.** PAINTING DARK BROWN PIGMENT a dark brown pigment or dye originally obtained by roasting raw umber **2.** COLOURS DEEP BROWN a deep brown colour

Burnum /búrnəm/, **Burnum** (1936–97) Australian political activist and writer. The leader of Aboriginal protests during the Australian Bicentennial, he was the author of *Aboriginal Australia: A Traveller's Guide* (1988).

burn-up *n.* a high-speed drive in a motor vehicle (*slang*)

buroo /bə róo/ *n. Ireland, Scotland* (*dated informal*) **1.** UNEMPLOYMENT OFFICE an office where unemployed people go to seek work and sign on for state benefit **2.** UNEMPLOYMENT BENEFIT a state allowance paid to unemployed people seeking work [Mid-20thC. Alteration of BUREAU.]

burp /burp/ *n.* NOISE MADE THROUGH MOUTH a noise made through the mouth when air is suddenly forced up through the windpipe from the stomach ■ *v.* (**burps, burping, burped**) **1.** *vi.* BELCH to make a noise through the mouth when air is suddenly forced up through the windpipe from the stomach **2.** *vt.* MAKE BABY BRING UP WIND to make a baby expel air from its stomach through its windpipe after feeding by rubbing or patting its back [Mid-20thC. An imitation of the sound.]

burp gun *n. US* a lightweight submachine gun (*informal*)

burr[1] /bur/ *n.* **1.** BOT PRICKLY SEED HUSK a prickly husk covering the seeds of plants such as burdock **2. burr, bur** ENG ROUGH EDGE a rough edge on material such as metal after it has been cut or drilled **3. burr, bur** ENG TOOL FOR REMOVING BURRS a tool used for removing the rough edges from metal that has been cut or drilled **4. burr, bur** SURG DRILL FOR BONE an instrument for drilling holes in bone, especially into the skull **5. burr, bur** BOT TREE GROWTH a lumpy outgrowth of wood on a tree ■ *vt.* (**burrs, burring, burred**) **1.** CREATE ROUGH EDGE to create a rough edge on a piece of metal or other piece of work by cutting or drilling **2.** REMOVE ROUGH EDGE to remove a rough edge from a piece of metal or other workpiece [Early 17thC. A variant of BUR probably from Scandinavian, related to Danish *burre* 'burdock'.]

burr[2] /bur/ *n.* **1.** WHIRRING SOUND a whirring or buzzing sound ○ *the steady burr of the machines downstairs* **2.** ROLLED 'R' a way of speaking the letter 'r' in some regional accents of English, in which the sound is rolled or trilled ■ *v.* (**burrs, burring, burred**) **1.** *vi.* MAKE WHIRRING SOUND to make a whirring or buzzing sound ○ *The sewing machine burred away quietly* **2.** *vti.* SPEAK WITH BURR to speak with or pronounce words

a at; aa father; aw all; ay day; air hair; ə about, edible, item, common, circus; e egg; ee eel; hw when; i it, happy; ī ice; 'l apple; 'm rhythm; 'n fashion; o odd; ō open; ŏŏ good; oo pool; ow owl; oy oil; th thin; th this; u up; ur urge;

with a burr [Mid-18thC. Origin uncertain: perhaps an imitation of the sound, or from BURR¹ in the sense of a 'rough' sound.]

burr³ /bur/ n. a washer that fits around the end of a rivet [14thC. Shortening of Old English *burg* 'stronghold, fortified enclosure'; hence 'circle', later 'washer'.]

Burr /bur/, **Aaron** (1756–1836) US statesman and Vice President of the United States. He was Thomas Jefferson's first vice president (1801–05). He killed Alexander Hamilton in a duel after a long public feud (1804).

Burra /búrrə/, **Edward** (1905–76) British painter. He produced surreal watercolours of figures set in gritty urban backgrounds or in exotic settings.

Burrell Collection /búrrəl-/ n. an art collection in Glasgow that contains paintings, textiles, glass, ceramics, and many other artefacts that once belonged to the 19th-century Scottish shipping magnate, Sir William Burrell (1861–1958)

burrito /bə reetô/ (*plural* **-tos**) n. in Mexican cooking, a flour tortilla wrapped round a filling of meat, beans, or cheese [Mid-20thC. From American Spanish, literally 'small burro', from Spanish *burro* (see BURRO).]

burro /bo͞orrô/ (*plural* **-ros**) n. *US* a small donkey, especially one that is used as a pack animal [Early 19thC. From Spanish, a back-formation from *borrico* 'donkey', from late Latin *burricus* 'small horse', of uncertain origin: perhaps from Germanic.]

Burroughs /búrrōz/, **Edgar Rice** (1875–1950) US writer. He created the character Tarzan in a series of popular novels starting in 1914.

William S. Burroughs

Burroughs, **William S** (1914–97) US writer. A leading figure of the Beat Generation, he wrote *Naked Lunch* (1959) and *The Soft Machine* (1961). Full name **William Seward Burroughs**

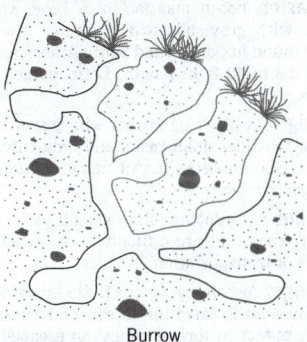

Burrow

burrow /búrrō/ n. **1.** RABBIT'S HOME a hole or tunnel dug as a living space by a small animal such as a rabbit **2.** SNUG PLACE a small snug place created by digging or hollowing ■ v. (**-rows**, **-rowing**, **-rowed**) **1.** vti. DIG HOLE OR TUNNEL to make a hole or tunnel by digging **2.** vi. SEARCH BY DIGGING to look for sth by groping or digging ○ *She burrowed in her handbag for her lipstick* **3.** vi. MOVE BY DIGGING to move through sth solid by digging or by creating a space ○ *He burrowed through the undergrowth.* **4.** vi. HIDE OR LIVE IN BURROW to hide or live in a burrow **5.** vi. LOOK INTO THOROUGHLY to research or investigate sth very thoroughly ○ *had spent years burrowing into the history of the era* [13thC. A variant of BOROUGH.] —**burrower** n.

burrowing owl n. a small owl that lives in the prairies of North and South America and nests in abandoned burrows of other animals such as prairie dogs or rabbits. Latin name: *Athene cunicularia*.

burry¹ /búri/ (**-rier**, **-riest**) adj. **1.** COVERED IN BURRS covered in burrs **2.** LIKE A BURR resembling a burr or burrs

burry² /búri/ (**-rier**, **-riest**) adj. characterized by or spoken with a burr

bursa /búrssə/ (*plural* **-sas** or **-sae** /-see/) n. ANAT a fluid-filled body sac that reduces friction around joints or between other parts that rub against one another [Early 19thC. Via modern Latin from medieval Latin, 'bag, purse', from Greek, 'wineskin' (source of English *purse*).] —**bursal** adj.

Bursa /búrssə/ city in northwestern Turkey, south of the Sea of Marmara, south of Istanbul, and west of Ankara. It was the capital of the Ottoman Empire from 1326 to 1402. Population: 996,600 (1994).

bursa of Fabricius /-fə bríshəss/ n. an organ in immature birds that produces B lymphocytes. It resembles a sac and is situated in part of the lower pelvic region (**cloaca**). [Named after Girolamo Fabrici (Latinized form *Fabricius*) (1533–1619), an Italian anatomist]

bursar /búrssər/ n. **1.** TREASURER an official who has charge of funds, particularly in a university, college, school, or monastery **2.** a student who holds a bursary [13thC. From either French *boursier* or medieval Latin *bursarius*, ultimately from *bursa* (see BURSA).] —**bursarship** n.

bursary /búrssəri/ (*plural* **-ries**) n. **1.** STUDENT'S GRANT a grant or scholarship offered to a student at a school, college, or university in some countries, e.g. Scotland and Canada **2.** BURSAR'S OFFICE the office or room where a bursar works [Late 17thC. From medieval Latin *bursaria* 'bursar's office', from *bursa* (see BURSA).] —**bursarial** /bur sáiriəl/ adj.

burse /burss/ n. **1.** CONTAINER USED IN CHURCH RITUAL in the Roman Catholic Church, a flat case that is used for carrying a special linen cloth (**corporal**) when celebrating Mass **2.** PURSE a purse (*archaic*) [13thC. Directly or via French *bourse* from medieval Latin *bursa* (see BURSA).]

bursitis /bur sítiss/ n. inflammation of a fluid-filled sac (**bursa**) of the body, particularly at the elbow, knee, or shoulder joint

burst /burst/ v. (**bursts**, **bursting**, **burst**) **1.** vi. SPLIT OR BREAK to split or break apart suddenly and violently because of excess internal pressure ○ *the suitcase had burst open* **2.** vt. MAKE STH SPLIT to cause sth to split open suddenly and disgorge its contents, e.g. by piercing it or applying external pressure **3.** vi. BE VERY FULL to be so full as to appear close to splitting open or overflowing ○ *Every hotel in town was bursting with tourists.* **4.** vt. RUPTURE to rupture an internal organ or blood vessel **5.** vt. FLOW OVER STH to overflow the normal limit of containment ○ *The river burst its banks.* **6.** vi. MOVE SUDDENLY to go, come, or move suddenly and with great energy and speed ○ *He burst into the room.* **7.** vi. BE OVERWHELMED to feel an emotion so intensely that it is almost overwhelming ○ *I thought I would burst with excitement.* **8.** vi. BECOME SUDDENLY NOTICED to appear suddenly and become noticed and prominent at a particular time and in a particular situation ○ *an exciting new product about to burst onto the market* **9.** vt. DIVIDE PAPER to separate continuous stationery, e.g. computer printout, into individual sheets ■ n. **1.** EXPLOSION OR RUPTURE a sudden and often noisy splitting or breaking open of sth ○ *There's a burst in the mains.* **2.** SHORT, INTENSE PERIOD a short, sudden, and intense period of some activity or phenomenon ○ *a burst of publicity* **3.** SUSTAINED ACTIVITY a period of sustained activity ○ *I read it in two short bursts.* ○ *a burst of speed* **4.** GUNFIRE a short, sudden, and noisy volley of gunfire [Old English *berstan*, from prehistoric Germanic] —**burster** n.

burst into vt. **1.** CHANGE STATE SUDDENLY to start to happen or appear suddenly and often dramatically ○ *The truck crashed and burst into flames.* ○ *Spring saw the landscape burst into life.* **2.** START TO EXPRESS STH to give sudden and full expression to a strong emotion such as laughter or tears

burst out v. **1.** vi. SUDDENLY START to start expressing sth

suddenly and fully ○ *burst out laughing* **2.** vt. EXCLAIM to say sth suddenly, as if a suppressed emotion or opinion had been welling up inside

bursting /búrsting/ adj. **1.** ABSOLUTELY FULL full to the point of overflowing **2.** OVERFLOWING so full of an emotion or quality that it is almost impossible to contain it **3.** EAGER wanting to do sth very much (*informal*) ○ *I was bursting to tell her the news.* **4.** WITH FULL BLADDER needing desperately to urinate (*informal*)

bursting disc n. a disc, usually made of thin metal, that is designed to protect equipment by rupturing under abnormal pressure to form a safe outlet for the process fluid

burthen /búrthən/ n. BURDEN a burden (*archaic*) ■ vt. (**-thens**, **-thening**, **-thened**) BURDEN to burden (*archaic*) [Variant of BURDEN]

burton /búrt'n/ n. a kind of light tackle with double or single blocks used for hoisting [Early 18thC. Alteration of obsolete *Breton* (tackle), of uncertain origin: probably so called because it was characteristic of Brittany.] ◇ **go for a burton** to be destroyed, ruined, or dead (*informal; usually passive*)

Burton /búrt'n/, **Richard** (1925–84) Welsh-born British actor. His films included *Look Back in Anger* (1959) and *Cleopatra* (1963).

Burton-upon-Trent /búrt'n əpon trént/ town on the River Trent in Staffordshire, England. It is a historic brewing centre. Population: 60,000 (1991).

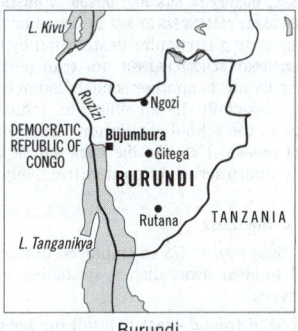

Burundi

Burundi /bo͞o ro͞ondi/ landlocked republic in east-central Africa. It is surrounded by Rwanda to the north, Tanzania to the east and south, and the Democratic Republic of the Congo to the west. Formerly part of the Belgian territory of Ruanda-Urundi, it became independent in 1962. Language: Kirundi, French. Currency: Burundi franc. Capital: Bujumbura. Population: 5,397,107 (1997). Area: 27,834 sq. km/10,747 sq. mi. Official name **Republic of Burundi**. Former name **Ruanda-Urundi** (until 1962) — **Burundian** n., adj.

bury /bérri/ (**-ies**, **-ying**, **-ied**) v. **1.** vt. PUT STH IN HOLE to dig a hole, put sth in it, and replace the soil or other material removed ○ *a dog burying its bone* **2.** vt. INTER DEAD BODY to put a dead body in a grave dug in the ground, or sometimes under water, usually as part of a religious ritual ○ *He asked to be buried at sea.* **3.** vt. LOSE SB THROUGH DEATH to lose sb, e.g. a spouse or a close relative, through death ○ *She has buried four husbands.* **4.** vt. HIDE STH BY COVERING to hide sth by covering it with a lot of things so it cannot be seen ○ *He buried the letter under a pile of books.* **5.** vt. COVER STH UP to cover sth or sb completely with sth ○ *buried alive under the rubble* **6.** vt. OBSCURE STH to make sth difficult to find or distinguish ○ *The announcement was buried at the end of the programme.* **7.** vt. SINK STH DEEPLY to sink deep into sth so that it is difficult to see or retrieve ○ *The splinter had buried itself under his nail.* **8.** vt. HIDE STH FROM SIGHT to put the face or head somewhere, usually on or under a soft and yielding surface ○ *She buried her face in her hands.* **9.** vt. CONCENTRATE INTENSELY ON STH to concentrate exclusively and intensely on sth ○ *She tended to bury herself in her work.* **10.** vt. SUPPRESS OR FORGET STH to suppress and forget sth unpleasant or undesirable ○ *their efforts to bury the past* [Old English *byrgan*, from a prehistoric Germanic base meaning 'protection, shelter' (hence 'to shelter a corpse'), which is also the ancestor of English *borough* and *burrow*]

Bury /bérri/ town in Lancashire, northwestern England, on the River Irwell. It is part of the Greater Manchester and historically a weaving centre. Population: 62,633 (1991).

Buryat /boŏri aat/, **Buriat** n. **1.** MONGOL FROM SE RUSSIA a member of a Mongoloid people living in southeastern Russia **2.** MONGOLIAN LANGUAGE a language spoken by the Buryats. It is regarded as a dialect of Mongolian and belongs to the Altaic language family. Buryat is spoken by about 300,000 people. [Mid-19thC. From Mongolian *Buriyad*.] —**Buryat** adj.

Bury St Edmunds /bérri s'nt édməndz/ market town in Suffolk, England. Its name comes from the Saxon king St Edmund who is buried there. Population: 31,237 (1991).

bus /buss/ n. (plural **buses** or **busses**) **1.** LARGE PASSENGER VEHICLE a long motor vehicle with many seats, usually divided by a central aisle and often on two decks. Buses transport fare-paying passengers along a specific route. **2.** OLD CAR OR PLANE a vehicle, especially a car or plane (informal) ○ *I can't get this old bus to start!* **3.** COMPUT DATA CHANNEL a channel or path for transferring data electronically in a computer system, particularly the path between the central processing unit and a peripheral device **4.** ARMS ROCKET WARHEAD the final stage of a multistage rocket, containing the warhead **5.** SPACE TECH SPACECRAFT COMPONENT the part of a space exploration vehicle that contains the atmospheric re-entry probes ■ v. (**buses** or **busses**, **busing** or **bussing**, **bused** or **bussed**) **1.** vti. TRAVEL OR CARRY PASSENGERS BY BUS to travel or transport passengers to a particular destination by bus **2.** vi. US TRANSPORT SCHOOLCHILDREN to transport schoolchildren by bus to another school distant from their homes, especially in an effort to achieve racial balance in the school population [Early 19thC. Shortening of OMNIBUS.] ◇ **like the back end of a bus** extremely unattractive, often unattractively large or wide

bus. abbr. business

busboy /búss boy/ n. US sb employed in a restaurant or café to clear away dishes, set tables, and assist the servers

busby /búzbi/ (plural **-bies**) n. a tall fur helmet worn by some soldiers, including some British guards regiments [Mid-18thC. Origin uncertain: perhaps from the surname *Busby*.]

Busby, **James** /búzbi/ (1800–71) British government official. He was British Resident in New Zealand (1833–40), and paved the way for the Treaty of Waitangi (1840) by persuading local Maori chiefs to accept government protection.

Busby, Sir Matt (1909–94) British footballer and manager. Injured in the air crash that killed most of the Manchester United team in 1958, he rebuilt the team, which won the European Cup in 1968. Full name **Sir Matthew Busby**

bus conductor n. an official on some buses whose job is to sell and check tickets and to signal to the driver when to stop

bush[1] /boŏsh/ n. **1.** WOODY BRANCHED PLANT a woody plant that is smaller than a tree and has many branches growing up from the lower part of the main stem **2.** THICKET a thick clump of bushes **3.** UNCULTIVATED AND UNSETTLED LAND wild, uncultivated, and sparsely populated areas of land covered with natural vegetation, especially in Africa and Australia ○ *living in the bush* **4.** DENSE MASS a dense large mass of sth, especially hair or beard ○ *a great bush of black hair* **5.** NZ NEW ZEALAND FOREST the forest of New Zealand **6.** Can = **wood lot 7.** BUSHY TAIL a bushy tail, especially of a fox **8.** VINTNER'S SIGN a bunch of ivy hung outside a tavern to show that wine is sold inside (archaic) **9.** TAVERN a tavern (archaic) ■ vi. (**bushes, bushing, bushed**) BRANCH OUT to branch out, spread, or grow thick like a bush ○ *hair bushing out round her head* [From assumed Old English *bysc* and Old Norse *buski*, from a prehistoric Germanic base that is also the ancestor of English *ambush* and *bouquet*] ◇ **beat about the bush** to discuss a subject without coming to the point

bush[2] /boŏsh/ n. a cylindrical metal sleeve used to prevent abrasion functioning as a bearing or as a guide for certain tool parts such as valve rods. US

term **bushing** [Mid-16thC. From Middle Dutch *busse* 'bush of a wheel', via prehistoric Germanic from Latin *pyxis* 'box, cap', from late Greek *puxis* 'box'.]

Bush/, **Barbara** (b. 1925) US first lady. She founded the Barbara Bush Foundation for Family Literacy (1989) to promote literacy in the United States.

George Bush

Bush, George (b. 1924) US statesman and 41st President of the United States. A Republican, he was Ronald Reagan's vice president (1981–88) before his own election to the presidency (1989–93). His presidency was notable for the passage of the Americans with Disabilities Act (1990) and, in foreign policy, the end of the Cold War and the fighting of the Gulf War (1990). Full name **George Herbert Walker Bush**

bushbaby n. a small nocturnal primate that lives in trees in Africa and has big round eyes, large ears, and a long tail. Family: Galagidae.

bush ballad n. Aus in Australian literature, a poem written in ballad form that takes as its subject some aspect of life in country areas

bushbash /boŏsh bash/ (**-bashes, -bashing, -bashed**) vi. Aus to hike through bushland by flattening the vegetation to create a path rather than following an existing trail

bush bean n. US = **dwarf bean**

bushbuck /boŏsh buk/ (plural **-bucks** or **-buck**) n. a small African antelope that has a reddish-brown coat, usually with white stripes, and twisted horns. It lives in the bush in sub-Saharan Africa. Latin name: *Tragelaphus scriptus*. [Mid-19thC. Translation of Afrikaans *bosbok*, from Dutch *bosch* 'bush' + *bok* 'buck'.]

bush clover n. a plant with three-leaved compound leaves and small flowers, typically grown for forage, erosion control, or decoration. Genus: *Lespedeza*.

bushcraft /boŏsh kraaft/ n. ANZ the skills and knowledge that enable sb to live and function successfully in the bush

bush dog n. a wild dog of South America that lives in dense undergrowth, usually near rivers. It is sometimes kept as a pet. Latin name: *Speothos venaticus*.

bushed /boŏsht/ adj. (informal) **1.** EXHAUSTED exhausted from overwork or lack of sleep **2.** ANZ BEMUSED perplexed and confused [Late 19thC. From the state typical of one who wanders in the bush.]

Bushehr /boŏ sheer/, **Bushire** /boŏ shir/ city in southwestern Iran, southwest of Shiraz, a major port on the Persian Gulf. Population: 132,824 (1991).

bushel /boŏsh'l/ n. **1.** FORMER UK UNIT OF VOLUME a unit of dry or liquid measure in the British Imperial system, equal to 8 imperial gallons (36.37 litres), formerly used for measuring items such as wheat, fruit, and liquids **2.** US UNIT OF VOLUME a unit of measure in the US Customary system used for measuring dry goods, equal to 64 US pints (35.24 litres) **3.** CONTAINER a container that has a capacity of one bushel **4.** US LARGE AMOUNT a large amount (dated informal) [15thC. From Old French *boisel*, of uncertain origin: probably formed from assumed *boisse* 'measure of grain', from assumed Gallo-Romance *bostia* 'handful', from Gaulish.]

bushfire /boŏsh fīr/ n. a fire in the bush or in a forest area that spreads quickly and easily goes out of control

bushfly /boŏsh flī/ (plural **-flies** or **-fly**) n. an Australian fly that lays its eggs in animal dung. Latin name: *Musca vetustissima*.

bush grass n. a type of grass with leaves that grow tall like reeds in the damp clay soils of Europe and Asia. Latin name: *Calamagrostis epigejos*.

bushhammer /boŏsh hamər/ n. a powered hammer with small pyramidal points cut into the working surface, used to form a rough surface on stonework [Late 19thC. Origin uncertain: probably a translation of German *Boszhammer*; *Bosz-* from *boszen* 'to beat'.]

bush honeysuckle n. a shrub of eastern North America with deciduous leaves and small clusters of yellow flowers. Genus: *Diervilla*.

bush house (plural **bush houses**) n. ANZ a hut or simple dwelling in the country or in a garden

Bushido /boo sheedō/ n. the code of honour and behaviour of the Japanese warrior class (**samurai**), emphasizing self-discipline, courage, and loyalty [Late 19thC. From Japanese, literally 'military knight's way, warrior's doctrine'.]

bushie /boŏshi/ n. ANZ a person from a remote country area, especially one regarded as unsophisticated (informal)

bushing /boŏshing/ n. **1.** INSULATION a layer of electrical insulation that allows a live conductor to pass through an earthed wall **2.** PIPE ADAPTOR an adaptor or screw-piece for connecting two different sizes of pipe **3.** = **bush**[2] [Mid-19thC. Formed from BUSH[2].]

Bushire /byoo shīr/ = **Bushehr**

bush jacket n. a lightweight cotton jacket resembling a shirt, with patch pockets and a belt

bushland /boŏsh land, boŏshlənd/ n. Aus uncultivated and undeveloped land

bush lawyer n. ANZ **1.** AUSTRALIAN BRAMBLE any Australian prickly, trailing plant **2.** UNQUALIFIED PERSON CLAIMING LEGAL KNOWLEDGE sb who offers opinions and advice on legal matters without being qualified to do so (informal)

bush line n. NZ the height on a mountain or other elevation above which the native forest does not grow

bushman /boŏshmən/ (plural **-men** /-mən/) n. ANZ sb who has long experience of living, working, or travelling in remote country areas

Bushman /boŏshmən/ (plural **-men** /-mən/) n. an offensive term for a member of the San people [Late 18thC. Modelled on Dutch *boschjesman*.]

bushman's singlet n. NZ a sleeveless black woollen top worn by lumberjacks in New Zealand

bushmaster /boŏsh maastər/ n. a large venomous snake with greyish-brown markings, the longest snake found in Central and South America, growing up to 3.6 m/12 ft in length. Latin name: *Lachesis mutus*.

bush pig n. a black or brown wild pig of southern Africa that has small tusks and long tufts of hair on the face and ears. Latin name: *Potamochoerus porcus*.

bush pilot n. a pilot who flies a small plane into and out of areas that are difficult to reach with other means of transportation

bushranger /boŏsh raynjər/ n. **1.** US BACKWOODSMAN sb who lives an isolated life in the wilderness **2.** ANZ ESCAPED CONVICT in former times, an escaped convict living on the run in the bush **3.** ANZ RURAL CRIMINAL in former times, a criminal who lived in the bush and survived by robbing passersby or local people

bush shrike n. a bird of the shrike family, typically olive-backed with a bright yellow or red breast. It chases its prey on foot in the forests of Africa. Genus: *Malaconotus*.

bush telegraph n. **1.** PRIMITIVE METHOD OF COMMUNICATION a method of communicating over distances, e.g. with drumbeats **2.** METHOD OF SPREADING GOSSIP a method of communicating information or rumours swiftly and unofficially by word of mouth or other means (informal) US term **grapevine**

bushtit /boŏsh tit/ n. a small grey North American

bird of the titmouse family, known for building hanging nests. Genus: *Psaltriparus*.

bush track *n. ANZ* a rough road in a remote area

bush tucker *n. Aus* (*informal*) **1.** SIMPLE FOOD simple food that can be cooked over a campfire in the bush **2.** WILD FOOD food consisting of items collected in the bush, e.g. native plants and fruits

bushwalk /bŏŏsh wawk/ *n. ANZ* a hike through the bush —**bushwalker** *n.* —**bushwalking** *n.*

bushwhack /bŏŏsh wak/ (**-whacks, -whacking, -whacked**) *v.* **1.** *vi. US, Can, Aus* TRAVEL THROUGH WOODS to travel through woods, forest, or the bush **2.** *vi. US, Can, Aus* CUT THROUGH WOODS to cut a way through thick woods or forest **3.** *vt. US, Can* AMBUSH SB to ambush sb (*informal*) **4.** *vi. US, Can* FIGHT AS GUERRILLA to fight as a guerrilla **5.** *vi. NZ* FORESTRY FELL TIMBER to fell timber in the native forest of New Zealand for a living [Mid-19thC. Back-formation from BUSHWHACKER.]

bushwhacker /bŏŏsh wakər/ *n.* **1.** *US, Can, Aus* SB WHO LIVES IN THE BUSH sb who travels around or lives in the bush or in wooded, isolated regions **2.** CLEARER OF BUSH sb who clears away bush or undergrowth **3.** HIST CONFEDERATE GUERRILLA IN AMERICAN CIVIL WAR a confederate guerrilla in the American Civil War **4.** *US* RURAL GUERRILLA a guerrilla who fights in remote or rural areas **5.** *NZ* FORESTRY NEW ZEALAND LUMBERJACK sb who fells timber in the bush for a living **6.** *ANZ* UNSOPHISTICATED RUSTIC an unsophisticated person from the country (*slang*) **7.** CLEARING TOOL a tool for clearing or cutting a way through bush, trees, or undergrowth [Early 19thC. From BUSH + WHACKER; possibly modelled on Dutch *boschwachter* 'forest keeper'.]

bushy /bŏŏshi/ (**-ier, -iest**) *adj.* **1.** THICK AND FULL very thick and full **2.** DENSE AND WOODY with many branches growing up together, producing a rounded shape like a bush **3.** COVERED WITH BUSHES covered or overgrown with bushes —**bushily** *adv.* —**bushiness** *n.*

busily /bízzili/ *adv.* in an active, energetic, and concentrated way ○ *busily cleaning the house*

business /bíznəss/ *n.* **1.** LINE OF WORK a particular trade or profession ○ *the retail business* **2.** COMMERCIAL ORGANIZATION a company or other organization that buys and sells goods, makes products, or provides services ○ *take over an ailing business* **3.** COMMERCIAL ACTIVITY commercial activity involving the exchange of money for goods or services ○ *a good person to do business with* **4.** LEVEL OF COMMERCE the amount of commercial activity or custom that exists at a particular time ○ *Business is poor right now.* **5.** COMMERCIAL PRACTICE commercial practice or procedure ○ *It's bad business to neglect smaller clients.* **6.** CUSTOM the commercial dealings that a person or organization has with another company or individual ○ *If this goes on, I shall take my business elsewhere!* **7.** IMPORTANT MATTERS tasks or important things that a person has to do or deal with ○ *We have important business to discuss.* **8.** PRIVATE MATTERS personal responsibilities and concerns ○ *What business is it of yours?* **9.** AFFAIR a situation or event that is characterized by difficulty, fuss, or unpleasantness ○ *that business about the tickets* **10.** UNSPECIFIED ACTIVITIES activities or things that are not clearly described or defined ○ *designing, measuring, and all that kind of business* **11.** COMPLICATED TASK an overcomplicated or irritating task or activity ○ *It's such a business even getting served in here!* **12.** THEATRE ACTOR'S SMALL ACTIONS an action or series of actions performed by an actor for dramatic or comic effect, or to fill in a pause when little is happening on stage **13.** STH EXCELLENT sth very impressive or excellent (*informal*) ○ *He thinks his new car is really the business.* ■ *adj.* OF COMMERCE relating to, belonging to, or involving commerce and the world of professional workers ○ *good business practice* [Old English *bisignis* 'anxiety, distress', from *bisig* 'anxious, busy'] ◇ **do your business** to defecate (*informal*) (*used euphemistically*) ◇ **get down to business** to deal with important matters, leaving extraneous ones behind ◇ **have no business doing sth** to have no right to do sth ◇ **like nobody's business** very hard or strongly ◇ **mean business** to have sincere and forthright intentions ◇ **mind your own business** to attend to your own affairs and not interfere in other people's concerns ◇ **not be in the business of doing sth** to consider sth inappropriate or outside the usual area of responsibility

business administration *n.* a course of study at a university, college, or other institute of higher education that teaches the basic principles of business and business practices

business card *n.* a small card printed with a person's name, job title, business address, and contact numbers

business class *n.* AIR-TRAVEL CATEGORY a superior level of service in air travel that is less expensive than first class and caters for business travellers (*hyphenated when used before a noun*) ■ *adv.* IN BUSINESS-CLASS SECTION in the business-class section of an aeroplane

business college *n.* a college of higher education where students learn basic business skills such as accounting, secretarial skills, and management

business cycle *n. US, Can* = trade cycle

business end *n.* the part of a tool or device that does the work, as opposed to the body or handle (*informal*) ○ *the business end of a gun*

business hours *npl.* **1.** HOURS OF OPERATION the hours during which business is conducted **2.** NORMAL OFFICE HOURS the normal hours that most offices and shops are open, usually between about 9 AM and 5:30 PM

businesslike /bíznəss līk/ *adj.* **1.** EFFICIENT AND PRACTICAL showing qualities or attributes that are useful and desirable in a business context, e.g. efficiency, practicality, and methodicalness ○ *a very businesslike operation* **2.** UNEMOTIONAL practical and unemotional

businessman /bíznəss man/ (*plural* -men /-mən, -men/) *n.* a man who works in business, especially at a senior level

business park *n.* an area that has been specifically designed to accommodate businesses and light industry, with large numbers of companies all grouped together, usually on the outskirts of a town or city

businessperson /bíznəss purss'n/ (*plural* -people /-peep'l/) *n.* a person who works in business, especially at a senior level

business plan *n.* a plan that sets out the future strategy and financial development of a business, usually covering a period of several years

businesswoman /bíznəss wŏŏmən/ (*plural* -en /-wimmin/) *n.* a woman who works in business, especially at a senior level

busing /bússing/, **bussing** *n. US* the transporting of children by bus to another school distant from their homes in an effort to achieve racial balance in school populations

busk[1] /busk/ (**busks, busking, busked**) *vi.* to entertain in the street or another public place in the hope of receiving money from passers-by ○ *two guys busking outside the station* [Mid-17thC. Via obsolete French *busquer* 'to seek, hunt for' from either Italian *buscare* or Spanish *buscar*, from, ultimately, prehistoric Germanic.]

busk[2] /busk/ *n.* a strip of wood, steel, or whalebone used to stiffen the front of a corset [Late 16thC. Via French *busc* from Italian *busco* 'splinter', from Germanic.]

busker /búskər/ *n.* sb who entertains in the street or a public place in the hope of receiving money from passers-by

buskin /búskin/ *n.* **1.** ATHENIAN ACTOR'S BOOT a thick-soled laced boot worn by tragic actors in ancient Greece to give them extra height **2.** GREEK DRAMA tragic drama, particularly in the ancient Greek style (*archaic*) **3.** MEDIEVAL SANDAL a calf-length laced boot worn in the Middle Ages [Early 16thC. Origin uncertain: probably via Old French *bousequin* (a variant of *brousequin*) from Middle Dutch *broseken*, of unknown origin.]

bus lane *n.* a lane on a road in some cities or towns that during certain hours of the day can only be used by buses

busload /bús lōd/ *n.* the number of passengers that a bus carries or can carry ○ *demonstrators arriving in busloads*

busman /búsmən/ (*plural* -men /-mən/) *n.* sb who drives a bus (*archaic*)

busman's holiday *n.* a holiday or leisure activity that is similar to the work sb normally engages in (*informal*) [Origin uncertain: probably from drivers of horse-

drawn buses taking a holiday being driven around on their own bus, perhaps so as to check on the treatment of their horses]

bus pass *n.* a ticket that entitles the holder to multiple rides on buses over a set period of time, either free or at a reduced rate

buss /buss/ *n.* KISS a kiss (*regional*) ■ *vti.* (**busses, bussing, bussed**) KISS SB to kiss sb or sth (*regional*) [Late 16thC. Origin uncertain: probably an alteration of obsolete *bass* 'to kiss', via French *baiser* from Latin *basiare*.]

Buss /buss/, **Frances Mary** (1827–94) British pioneer of women's education. She set up the North London Collegiate School for Ladies, was its head (1850–94), and fought for the entry of women to universities.

Busselton /búss'ltən/ city on the southern coast of Western Australia, a pastoral centre and tourist resort. Population: 10,642 (1996).

bus shelter *n.* a covered shelter at a bus stop

bussing *n. US* = busing

bus stop *n.* a designated place along a specific route where a bus stops to pick up or set down passengers

bust[1] /bust/ *n.* **1.** WOMAN'S BREASTS a woman's breasts, or the measurement around this part of her upper body **2.** SCULPTURE SCULPTURE OF HEAD AND SHOULDERS a sculpture of the head and shoulders of a person [Mid-17thC. Via French from Italian *busto*, of uncertain origin: probably from Latin *bustum* 'tomb', from, ultimately, *ambuere*, literally 'to burn around', from *urere* 'to burn'.]

bust[2] /bust/ *v.* (**busts, busting, busted** *or* **bust**) **1.** *vti.* MAKE OR BECOME USELESS to break sth mechanical or electrical, or to cease operating properly (*informal*) ○ *Your brother just busted our telly!* **2.** *vti.* BREAK OR GET BROKEN to break or damage sth by hitting it or by subjecting it to a powerful impact, or to break in this way (*informal*) ○ *I busted my leg skiing.* **3.** *vti.* BURST to burst sth or to undergo bursting **4.** *vt.* RAID PLACE OR ARREST PERSON to mount a police raid, especially in connection with illegal drugs (*slang*) **5.** *vti.* FIN MAKE OR BECOME BANKRUPT to make sb bankrupt or to become bankrupt (*informal*) **6.** *vt. US, Can* MIL DEMOTE SB to demote a member of the armed forces (*informal*) **7.** *vt. US* RIDING BREAK IN HORSE to break in a horse (*informal*) **8.** *vt. US* BREAK UP ORGANIZATION to break up an organization when it has become too powerful (*informal*) **9.** *vt. US* HIT SB to hit or punch sb (*informal*) ○ *I busted him over the head.* **10.** *vi.* CARDS GO OVER LIMIT in pontoon, to have cards totalling more than 21 points **11.** *vi.* CARDS FAIL TO COMPLETE HAND in poker, to fail to complete a flush or straight ■ *n.* **1.** POLICE RAID a police raid or arrest, especially in connection with illegal drugs (*slang*) **2.** *US* FAILURE sb or sth that fails completely (*informal*) ○ *The plan seemed perfect in theory, but it was a bust in reality.* **3.** *US* FIN BANKRUPTCY bankruptcy or financial failure (*informal*) ○ *periods of boom and bust* **4.** *US* PUNCH a punch or blow (*informal*) **5.** PARTY a disorganized party or celebration (*informal*) ■ *adj.* (*informal*) **1.** DAMAGED broken or no longer working **2.** FIN BANKRUPT bankrupt [Mid-18thC. Alteration of BURST.]

bustard /bústərd/ (*plural* -tards *or* -tard) *n.* a bird with long legs, a rotund body, and a long neck that lives on open grassy land in southern Eurasia, Africa, and Australia. Family: Otididae. [15thC. Origin uncertain: probably from assumed Anglo-Norman *bustarde*, blend of *bistarde* and *oustarde*, both from Latin *avis tarda* 'slow bird', from its slow walk.]

buster /bústər/ *n.* **1.** *US, Can* FORM OF ADDRESS used as a jocular or mildly threatening term of address, usually for a man or boy (*informal*) **2.** *US, Can* = broncobuster **3.** BREAKER sb or sth that breaks up or destroys sth (*informal*) (*usually in combination*) [Mid-19thC. Either formed from BUST[1], or an alteration of *burster*, in which sense ('person or thing that bursts') the word is first attested.]

bustier /bústi ay/ *n.* a close-fitting sleeveless and usually strapless bodice worn by women as lingerie or evening wear [Late 20thC. From French, where it was formed from *buste* (see BUST[1]).]

bustle[1] /búss'l/ *vi.* (**-tles, -tling, -tled**) GO HURRIEDLY AND SHOWILY to work or do sth in an ostentatiously hurried and energetic way ○ *He bustled about in preparation for their arrival.* ■ *n.* ENERGETIC ACTIVITY energetic, busy, and noisy activity ○ *a great bustle* *surrounding the arriving guests* [14thC. Origin uncertain: perhaps an alteration of obsolete *buskle*, from dialect *busk*, from Old Norse *búask* 'to prepare yourself'.] —**bustler** *n.*

bustle[2] /búss'l/ *n.* a pad or frame worn in the 19th century under the top of a woman's long skirt to fill it out at the back [Late 18thC. Origin uncertain; perhaps a use of the noun BUSTLE in the sense 'sth that makes a stir'.]

bustling /búss'ling/ *adj.* full of or characterized by energetic and noisy activity —**bustlingly** *adv.*

bust-up *n.* (*informal*) **1.** BREAKING UP a breaking up of sth such as a relationship or an organization **2.** FIGHT a fight or brawl ○ *There was a big bust-up in the bar last night.*

busty /bústi/ (**-ier, -iest**) *adj.* used to describe a woman with large breasts (*informal*) [Mid-20thC. Formed from BUST[1].]

busulphan /byoo súlfən/ *n.* a drug used to treat certain kinds of chronic leukaemia. Formula: $C_6H_{14}O_6S_2$. US = **busulphan** [Mid-20thC. Blend of BUTANE and SULPHONYL.]

busy /bízzi/ *adj.* (**-ier, -iest**) **1.** OCCUPIED fully occupied in a particular activity, especially work ○ *She seemed too busy even to talk to me.* ○ *He was busy writing letters all morning.* **2.** FULL OF BUSTLE full of activity, with a large number of people moving around ○ *the busy city streets* **3.** NOT FREE committed to sth that has previously been planned or arranged and so unable to undertake another activity ○ *I'm sorry but I'm busy tomorrow night.* **4.** ACTIVE engaged in or characterized by constant, and usually purposeful, activity ○ *busy people who lead busy lives* **5.** ELABORATE characterized by overcomplex detail, colours, or patterns ○ *a very busy painting* **6.** *US, Can* UTIL = **engaged** ■ *v.* (**-ies, -ying, -ied**) **1.** *vr.* OCCUPY YOURSELF to start doing sth that will keep you occupied and working for a period of time **2.** *vt.* OCCUPY SB to occupy sb ○ *The work busied him all afternoon.* [Old English *bisig* 'busy, anxious'] —**busyness** *n.*

busybody /bízzi bodi/ (*plural* **-ies**) *n.* sb who tends to meddle in other people's business (*informal*)

Busy Lizzie /bízzi lízzi/ (*plural* **Busy Lizzie** *or* **Busy Lizzies**) *n.* a cultivated species of the balsam family, popular as a house and garden plant for its low-growing, numerous colourful flowers. Latin name: *Impatiens walleriana.* US term **impatiens** [Origin uncertain: probably a rhyming phrase modelled on the plant's Latin name *impatiens* 'impatient']

busy signal *n. US* = **engaged tone**

busywork /bízzi wurk/ *n. US* activities assigned or undertaken that take up time but do not necessarily yield productive results

but[1] *stressed* /but/; *unstressed* /bət/ CORE MEANING: a grammatical word used in the middle of or at the beginning of a sentence to introduce sth that is true in spite of either being or seeming contrary to what has just been said ○ *I thought it was late, but it was only 9 o'clock.* ○ *Not one, but two offers were received.* ○ *Yes, but not now.* ○ *It's true her name is Spanish, but she's actually Greek.* ○ *I'm a blonde, but both my mother and father have dark hair.*

1. *conj.* INTRODUCING AN OPPOSING PROPOSITION used to introduce a statement that disagrees with sth just said, or that expresses an emotion such as surprise or disbelief at what was just said ○ *'I don't think you're suitable for the job'.-'But I have all the right qualifications!'* **2.** *conj.* INTRODUCING FURTHER INFORMATION used to introduce a clause or a new sentence that adds information such as background or reasoning ○ *Jeff isn't coming with us. But he doesn't like horror movies anyway.* **3.** *conj.* EXCEPT THAT used to introduce a dependent clause, e.g. a reason for doing or not doing sth ○ *I would have called, but I couldn't find a phone.* **4.** *conj.* WITHOUT STH HAPPENING used to indicate that sth does not happen without sth else happening or being the case (*formal*) (*usually used after a negative*) ○ *She never leaves home but she forgets her keys.* **5.** *conj.* THAT used to introduce a subordinate clause (*regional*) ○ *It's not so difficult, but I can't understand it.* **6.** *conj.* WHEN than or when (*informal*) **7.** *conj., prep.* EXCEPT used to indicate the exception to a statement just made ○ *He could do nothing but stand and watch her leave.* ○ *There was nothing but a lump of mouldy bread in the cupboard.* **8.** *adv.* ONLY, JUST, OR MERELY used to indicate that sth happens or is true just to the extent mentioned and not more ○ *This is but one of the breadmaking techniques used.* ○ *He arrived but a minute ago.* ○ *We can but try.* **9.** *adv. Aus* THOUGH however (*nonstandard*) **10.** *adv. US* FOR EMPHASIS used to emphasize a statement (*slang*) ○ *Man, but he's fast!* **11.** *n.* OBJECTIONS objections to sth (*informal*) ○ *Allow time to consider all the if's and but's from the children.* [Old English *būtan* 'outside, without, except, but', from a prehistoric Germanic word that is also the ancestor of English *by* and *without*] ◇ **all but** almost ○ *I was all but asleep when the phone rang.* ◇ **but for** if not for, or if it had not been for ◇ **but that 1.** except that ○ *Nothing is important but that I see you again.* **2.** used as a subordinating conjunction equivalent to 'that' following negative words such as 'doubt' and 'deny' (*archaic*) (*follows a negative*)

WORD KEY: USAGE

Can **but** begin a sentence? Some people object to the use of ***but***, like ***and***, at the beginning of a sentence, regarding it as a joining word that has to have words on either side of it. However, this is a mistaken notion that has no foundation in English structure and usage. It is, however, advisable to reserve this use for occasions when the special effect that initial position affords is needed, otherwise it can become an awkward affectation.

But is usually not followed by a comma; a comma may or may not precede ***but***, depending on the individual sentence structure and context; thus, *I wanted to leave early*[,] *but the rest of the group did not*, not *I wanted to leave early, but, the rest of the group did not.*

Avoid unnecessary redundancy in using ***but*** and other terms such as *however* together. Write *However,* [or *but*] *the Foreign Office have lodged a formal protest* not *But the Foreign Office have, however, lodged a formal protest.*

When ***but*** is used to indicate an exception, as in *No one but me* (or *I*) *has* (or *have*) *seen the document*, either wording can be used, based on your interpretation of the function of ***but***: is it a preposition, as in the first variation, or is it a conjunction, as in the second, parenthetic, variation? Though strong cases have been made for both wordings, the prepositional wording does carry slightly more weight, as you can recast the sentence to *No one has seen the document but me*, placing the ***but*** phrase at the end, where its prepositional function is quite clear.

WORD KEY: USAGE

See Usage note at ***help***.

WORD KEY: REGIONAL NOTE

But normally functions as a contrastive conjunction. In Ireland, the northeast of England, parts of Scotland, and Australia, it can occur at the end of a sentence with no contrastive implications. The following examples taken from spoken English illustrate this usage: *I didn't do it but. It's tasty but.*

but[2] /but/ *n. Scotland* OUTER ROOM OF TWO-ROOMED COTTAGE the outer room of a two-roomed cottage in Scotland, usually the living or cooking area. ◊ **but and ben** ■ *adv. Scotland* TOWARDS OUTER PART OF HOUSE in or towards the outer part of a house, cottage, or other dwelling [Early 18thC. From Old English *būtan* (see BUT[1]).]

but- *prefix.* Containing a group of four carbon atoms ○ *butene* [From BUTYRIC]

butadiene /byoòtə dí een/ *n.* a colourless flammable gas that is important in the manufacture of polymers. It is used in the production of synthetic rubber, nylon, and latex paints. Formula: $CH_2{=}CHCH{=}CH_2$. [Early 20thC. Coined from BUTANE + DI-.]

butanal /byoòtənal/ *n.* CHEM a colourless, flammable liquid that has two different molecular structures (**isomers**). It is used in the manufacture of solvents, resins, and plasticizers. Formula: C_4H_8O. [Late 20thC. Coined from BUTANOL.]

but and ben *n. Scotland* in parts of Scotland, a two-roomed cottage that consists of a living room and a bedroom

butane /byoó tayn/ *n.* a colourless, highly flammable gas that is compressed for use in lighter fluids and for household and industrial purposes. It is found in natural gas and has two different molecular structures (**isomers**). Formula: C_4H_{10}. [Late 19thC. Coined from BUTYL + -ANE.]

butanoic acid /byoòtənō ik-/ *n.* a thick colourless liquid that is the cause of the smell in rancid butter. The ester produced from it is used in flavourings and scents. Formula: C_3H_7COOH. [*Butanoic* formed from BUTANE]

butanol /byoòtə nol/ *n.* a colourless toxic liquid with four different molecular structures (**isomers**). It is used as a solvent in such items as paint remover, and also in the manufacture of other organic substances. Formula: C_4H_9OH.

butch /booch/ *adj.* **1.** MASCULINE AND STRONG used to describe a man who is extremely masculine and strong **2.** OFFENSIVE TERM an offensive term insulting a woman's appearance and sexuality (*slang offensive*) ■ *n.* **1.** OFFENSIVE TERM an offensive term that insults a woman's appearance and sexuality (*slang offensive*) **2.** *US* HAIR = **crew cut** [Mid-20thC. Origin uncertain; probably from the male nickname *Butch*.]

butcher /boòchər/ *n.* **1.** MEAT SELLER sb who cuts up, prepares, and sells meat **2.** SLAUGHTERER sb who slaughters animals in preparation for selling their meat as food **3.** BRUTAL KILLER sb who kills, or is responsible for the killing of, large numbers of people in a brutal manner **4.** BOTCHER sb who does sth badly and produces unattractive results ○ *a butcher of the sonnet form* ■ *vt.* (**-ers, -ering, -ered**) **1.** KILL ANIMAL FOR FOOD to slaughter and prepare the meat of an animal for food **2.** KILL PEOPLE BRUTALLY to kill people in a brutal way **3.** BOTCH STH to do, perform, or make sth very incompetently (*informal*) ○ *The original script had been butchered.* [13thC. Via Anglo-Norman from Old French *bo(u)chier* 'slaughterer of he-goats', from *boc* 'he-goat', of uncertain origin: probably from Celtic.] —**butcherer** *n.*

butcherbird /boòchər burd/ *n.* **1.** AUSTRALASIAN SONGBIRD an Australasian songbird of the magpie family, usually with black or black-and-white plumage. It impales insects and other prey on thorns. Genus: *Cracticus.* **2.** BIRD OF SHRIKE FAMILY a bird of the shrike family that impales its prey on thorns and barbed wire. Genus: *Lanius.*

butcher-block *adj.* made from or resembling blocks or strips of wood glued together and planed, similar to a block that a butcher chops meat on ○ *butcher-block work surfaces*

butcher knife *n.* US = **butcher's knife**

butcher's /boòchərz/ *n. Cockney* a look (*informal*) ○ *Let's have a quick butcher's at that.* [Mid-20thC. From rhyming slang *butcher's hook* 'a look'.]

butcher's broom *n.* an evergreen Mediterranean shrub with stiff stems that were formerly used for making brooms. Latin name: *Ruscus aculeatus.*

butcher's knife *n.* a large heavy-duty knife for use in the kitchen or for butchering. US term **butcher knife**

butchery /boòchəri/ (*plural* **-ies**) *n.* **1.** MASS KILLING brutal, senseless, and cruel slaughter of people, usually in large numbers ○ *an act of appalling butchery* **2.** USE OF KNIVES ON CARCASS the use of knives or other tools to remove meat from an animal's carcass ○ *'The tools are often found in association with broken animal bones, which sometimes show signs of butchery'.* (*'Ape at the Brink', Discover Magazine*; 1994) **3.** BUTCHER'S WORK OR TRADE the work or trade of a butcher **4.** BOTCHING a terrible botching of a job, performance, or activity (*informal*) ○ *the singer's butchery of the melody* **5.** SLAUGHTERHOUSE a slaughterhouse (*archaic*) **6.** *S Africa* BUTCHER'S SHOP a butcher's shop [14thC. From French *boucherie*, ultimately from Old French *bo(u)chier* (see BUTCHER).]

butch haircut *n. US* = **crew cut**

Bute /byoot/ island off the southwest coast of Scotland, in the Firth of Clyde. It is separated from the mainland by the Kyles of Bute. Area: 119 sq. km/46 sq. mi.

butene /byoó teen/ *n.* a colourless, flammable, and easily liquefiable gas with three different molecular structures (**isomers**). The butenes provide the basic molecule for manufacturing a variety of polymers. Formula: C_4H_8. [Late 19thC. Coined from BUTYL + -ENE.]

buteo /byoóti ō/ (*plural* **-os**) *n. US* = **buzzard** [Mid-20thC. Via modern Latin (genus name) from Latin '(kind of) hawk or falcon'.]

Buteshire /byoótshər/ former county in western Scotland, incorporated since 1975 into Strathclyde Region. Its main town was Rothesay.

Buthelezi /boótə láyzi/, **Mangosuthu Gatsha** (*b.* 1928) South African political leader. He was chief minister of KwaZulu, a black South African homeland (1976–94), and founded Inkatha, a Zulu nationalist organization. Known as **Chief Buthelezi**

butler /búttlər/ *n.* the male head servant in a large or important household, with responsibilities that include overseeing the other staff, taking care of the wine and silverware, and sometimes receiving guests [13thC. From Anglo-Norman *buteler* and French *bouteillier* 'cup-bearer', formed from *bouteille* 'wine vessel, bottle' (see BOTTLE).]

Butler /búttlər/, **Rab** (1902–82) British politician. He served as chancellor of the Exchequer (1951), home secretary (1957), and foreign secretary (1963–4). Full name **Richard Austen Butler**

Butler, Reg (1913–81) British sculptor. He used wrought iron and stainless steel constructions in linear forms in his early work. His later work was more realistic in style. Full name **Reginald Cotterell Butler**

Butler, Samuel (1612–80) English satirist. He wrote 'Hudibras', a poetic satire on the Puritans (1663–78).

butler's pantry /bútləri/, **butlery** *n.* a room situated between a kitchen and dining room, used for serving food and for storage

Butlin /búttlin/, **Sir Billy** (1899–1980) British holiday camp organiser. He opened his first camp at Skegness in 1936 and many more after World War II. Full name **Sir William Edmund Butlin**

Butskellism /bútskillizzəm/ *n.* the perceived consensus politics of the Labour and Conservative parties in the United Kingdom in the 1950s, when R.A. Butler and Hugh Gaitskell were the chancellors of the two parties when in power [Mid-20thC. Blend of *Butler* and *Gaitskell*.]

butt[1] /but/ *v.* (**butts, butting, butted**) **1.** *vt.* RAM SB OR STH to hit or push against sb or sth with the head or horns **2.** *vi.* STICK OUT to project or jut out ■ *n.* A PUSH a push with the head or horns [15thC. Via Anglo-Norman *buter* and Old French *bo(u)ter* from, ultimately, a prehistoric Germanic base that is also the ancestor of English *button*.] — **butter** *n.*
butt in *vi.* to interrupt and attempt to join in a conversation or activity without being invited
butt out *vi. US, ANZ* to keep out of other people's business or conversation (*slang*)

butt[2] /but/ *n.* **1.** OBJECT OF RIDICULE OR CONTEMPT sb or sth that is an object of ridicule or contempt for other people ○ *He became the butt of their satire.* **2.** GOAL a goal or aim (*archaic*) **3.** HINGE a butt hinge, or either of its two parts **4.** = **butt joint** ■ **butts** *npl.* **1.** ARCHERY, RIFLE SHOOTING MOUND BEHIND TARGET in archery and rifle shooting, a mound of earth behind the target, designed to stop any stray bullets or arrows **2.** ARCHERY TARGET RANGE a target range **3.** ARCHERY, RIFLE SHOOTING TARGET a target at a shooting or archery range ■ *vti.* (**butts, butting, butted**) ABUT to lie with one flat end against the flat end of sth else, or to place sth in such a position ○ *The beam butts against the wall.* [14thC. From French *but* 'goal', of uncertain origin: probably from prehistoric Germanic; perhaps influenced by French *butte* 'rising ground, target'.]

butt[3] /but/ *n.* **1.** THICK END the thicker or larger end of sth, such as the part of a rifle held against the shoulder **2.** CIGARETTE END the part of a cigarette that remains after the rest has been smoked **3.** *US* BUTTOCKS a person's or animal's buttocks (*informal; considered offensive by some people*) [15thC. Origin uncertain.]

butt[4] *n. NZ* = **butty**[2] *n.* 2

butt[5] /but/ *n.* a large cask for holding wine or ale [15thC. Via Anglo-Norman *but* and Old French *bot* from late Latin *buttis* (source of English *butler*).]

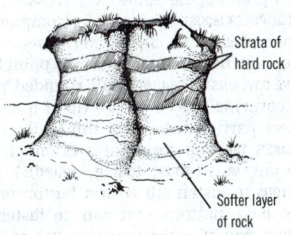

Butte

Strata of hard rock

Softer layer of rock

butte /byoot/ *n.* in the western United States and Canada, a hill that rises abruptly from a flat area of land, with steep sides and a flat top. ◊ **mesa** [Mid-19thC. From French, 'mound, hillock' (possible source of English *butt*[2]).]

butter /búttər/ *n.* **1.** SOFT CREAMY SPREAD a soft, pale yellow, fatty food made by churning cream and used for cooking or spreading on food **2.** SUBSTANCE RESEMBLING BUTTER any substance that is similar to butter in consistency or appearance ○ *apple butter* ■ *vt.* (**-ters, -tering, -tered**) PUT BUTTER ON STH to spread butter on sth or add butter to sth [Old English *butere*, via prehistoric Germanic from Latin *butyrum*, from Greek *bouturon*, of uncertain origin: perhaps originally 'cow's milk curds', formed from *bous* 'ox'.] ◇ **look as if butter wouldn't melt in your mouth** to look more innocent than you really are
butter up *vt.* to flatter sb in the hope of winning favour or cooperation (*informal*)

butter-and-eggs *n.* = **toadflax** (*used with a singular or plural verb*)

butterball /búttər bawl/ *n. US* **1.** CHUBBY PERSON sb who is chubby (*informal insult*) **2.** BIRDS = **bufflehead**

butter bean *n.* (*regional*) **1.** FLAT CREAM-COLOURED BEAN a large flat cream-coloured bean, dried before cooking **2.** *US* = **wax bean**

butterbur /búttər bur/ (*plural* **-burs** *or* **-bur**) *n.* a waterside plant that has purple flowers and large soft leaves in which butter was formerly wrapped. Genus: *Petasites.*

butter clam *n.* a large clam found off the Pacific coast of North America with a delicate flavour and a shell that was formerly used for barter by Native Americans. Genus: *Saxidomus.*

buttercup /búttər kup/ *n.* a plant with yellow cup-shaped flowers that grows in grassland in cold or temperate regions. Genus: *Ranunculus.* [Early 16thC. From the colour and shape of its flowers.]

butterfat /búttər fat/ *n.* the natural fats found in dairy products

Butterfield /búttər feeld/, **William** (1814–1900) British architect. He designed Keble College, Oxford, and churches in the Gothic Revival style.

butterfingers /búttər fingərz/ (*plural* **-gers**) *n.* sb who has a tendency to drop things accidentally out of clumsiness or poor coordination (*informal*) (*takes a singular verb*) [Early 17thC. From butter's slippery smoothness, as if the person's hands were greased with butter.] — **butterfingered** *adj.*

butterfish /búttər fish/ (*plural* **-fish** *or* **-fishes**) *n.* a small inshore fish, found worldwide, that is a popular food because of its high lipid content and fine flavour. Family: Stromateidae. [Late 17thC. From the slipperiness of its mucous coating, likened to butter.]

butterflies /búttər flīz/ *npl.* a fluttering feeling in the stomach caused by nervousness (*informal*)

butterfly /búttər flī/ *n.* (*plural* **-flies**) **1.** INSECT WITH BIG COLOURFUL WINGS an insect with two pairs of often brightly coloured wings and knobbed antennae. It develops from a caterpillar and lives for only a short time. Order: Lepidoptera. **2.** PERSON LACKING CONCENTRATION sb who is unable to concentrate on any one activity or occupation for very long **3.** = **butterfly, butterfly stroke** SWIMMING STROKE a swimming stroke in which both arms are lifted simultaneously above and over the head while both the feet are kicked up

Butterfly

and down **4.** SWIMMING COMPETITION a race in which swimmers do the butterfly stroke **5.** PIECE OF METAL FOR FASTENING EARRING a small piece of metal worn on the underside of the lobe of a pierced ear, into which the pin of an earring is fastened **6.** STOCK EXCH TYPE OF DEAL ON STOCK MARKET the buying and selling of options on the stock market on the same day but at different prices or with different expiry dates ■ *vt.* (**-flies, -flying, -flied**) COOK SPLIT FOOD to split a piece of food, such as meat or fish, along its length, separating it into halves [Old English *buttorflēoge*: *buttor*- 'butter' perhaps from the colour of some butterflies' wings or excrement, or from the belief that butterflies consume butter]

─── **WORD KEY: CULTURAL NOTE** ───

Madame Butterfly, an opera by Italian composer Giacomo Puccini (1904). Set in Nagasaki, Japan, it tells of the love of a young Japanese woman, Cio-Cio San, for a US naval officer, Pinkerton, who half-heartedly agrees to an arranged marriage with her. When Pinkerton later returns from a three-year sojourn in the United States with another wife, a heartbroken San commits suicide.

butterfly bush *n.* = **buddleia** [From the butterflies attracted to its flowers]

butterfly chair *n.* a chair made from a continuous folded metal rod with four upward-pointing corners on which a fitted canvas seat rests

butterfly diagram *n.* a graphical representation of the appearance of sunspots over an 11-year cycle [From its butterfly shape]

butterfly effect *n.* the supposed influence exerted on a dynamic system by a small change in initial conditions. ◊ **chaos theory** [Named after a 1979 paper by the US meterologist Edward N. Lorenz, (b. 1917), entitled 'Does the flap of a butterfly's wings in Brazil set off a tornado in Texas?'.]

butterfly fish *n.* a small boldly patterned tropical fish with a flattish body and a tapered snout. Family: Chaetodontidae. [From its shape or colour, likened to a butterfly]

butterfly nut *n.* = **wing nut** [From its winglike projections, likened to a butterfly's wings]

butterfly stroke *n.* = **butterfly** *n.* 3

butterfly valve *n.* **1.** VALVE IN PIPE a valve consisting of a disc that turns inside a pipe, especially one used as a throttle valve in a carburettor **2.** ONE-WAY VALVE a valve consisting of two semicircular plates that are hinged around a central spindle, used to allow flow in one direction only [From its shape, likened to a butterfly's wings]

butterfly weed *n.* a North American plant that has clusters of bright orange flowers and a root that was once used in the treatment of pleurisy. Latin name: *Asclepias tuberosa.* [From the fact that it is attractive to butterflies]

butterie /búttəri/ *n. North-Eastern Scotland* COOK a type of rich breakfast roll, eaten in the North-East of Scotland

butter knife *n.* a small knife with a broad blunt blade used for spreading butter

Buttermere /búttər meer/ lake in the Lake District, in Cumbria, northwestern England. Area: 1.6 sq. km/0.63 sq. mi. Depth: 28 m/93 ft.

buttermilk /búttər milk/ *n.* **1.** CULTURED MILK a sourtasting drink that is made by adding certain microorganisms to milk **2.** BY-PRODUCT OF CHURNING the sour-tasting liquid that is left over after milk or cream has been churned to make butter. It is used in baking.

butter muslin *n.* a type of thin loosely woven cotton fabric that was originally used for wrapping butter

butternut /búttər nut/ *n.* **1.** **N AMERICAN WALNUT TREE** a North American walnut tree that has hard light-brown wood and edible nuts enclosed in a sticky husk. Latin name: *Juglans cinerea.* **2.** **NUT OF BUTTERNUT TREE** the oily edible nut of the butternut tree, similar in appearance to a walnut and with a sweetish taste **3.** **WOOD OF BUTTERNUT TREE** the hard light-brown wood of the butternut tree, used for making furniture **4.** **BUTTERNUT BARK** the bark of the butternut tree, formerly used as a laxative **5.** **BROWN DYE** a brown dye obtained from the husks of the nuts of the butternut tree **6.** *ANZ* = **butternut pumpkin**

butternut pumpkin, **butternut** *n.* *ANZ* a pumpkin grown in Australia and New Zealand, with a rounded end shaped like a bell, dark orange rind, and edible yellow-orange flesh. Latin name: *Cucurbita moschata.*

butternut squash *n.* a beige-coloured winter squash shaped like a club with a bulbous end and with firm yellow-orange flesh

butterscotch /búttər skoch/ *n.* **1.** **BRITTLE SUGAR SWEET** a brittle brown-coloured sweet made from butter, brown sugar, corn syrup, water, and flavourings, with a taste similar to that of toffee **2.** **BUTTERSCOTCH FLAVOURING** a kind of flavouring made from the ingredients used in butterscotch **3.** COLOURS **LIGHT BROWN** a light brown colour ■ *adj.* **1.** **FLAVOURED WITH BUTTERSCOTCH** flavoured with butterscotch ○ *butterscotch ice cream* **2.** COLOURS **LIGHT-BROWN** light-brown in colour [Mid-19thC. Origin uncertain: probably formed from BUTTER + SCOTCH 'having been first made in Scotland'; or perhaps an alteration of dialect *butterscot.*]

butterweed /búttər weed/ *n.* a wild plant with yellow flowers. Family: Compositae. [Mid-19thC. *Butter* from its yellow flowers or smooth foliage, likened to butter.]

butterwort /búttər wurt/ (*plural* **-worts** *or* **-wort**) *n.* a carnivorous bog plant with violet flowers and a rosette of sticky fleshy leaves that trap and digest insects. Genus: *Pinguicula.*

buttery[1] /búttəri/ (**-ier, -iest**) *adj.* resembling, tasting like, or containing butter ○ *a smooth, buttery taste* — **butteriness** *n.*

buttery[2] /búttəri/ (*plural* **-ies**) *n.* **1.** **STOREROOM FOR FOOD OR DRINKS** a room in which food or drinks are stored **2.** **STUDENT BAR** a bar or room in certain universities where students can buy food and drinks to consume on the premises [14thC. From Anglo-Norman *boterie*, of uncertain origin: perhaps formed from *but* 'cask' (see BUTT[5]), or ultimately from Old French *botele* 'bottle' (see BOTTLE).]

butt hinge *n.* a hinge consisting of two parts, one of which is attached to a door jamb, the other to the door itself, allowing the door to swing open and shut [From BUTT[2]]

butt joint, **butt** *n.* a joint consisting of two parts of wood or other material that are placed squarely together rather than overlapping or interlocking [From BUTT[2]]

buttock /búttək/ *n.* **1.** **PART OF BOTTOM** in humans, either of the two fleshy mounds above the legs and below the hollow of the back (*often used in the plural*) **2.** **ANIMAL RUMP** the rump of an animal [Old English *buttuc* 'end ridge of land' (literally 'small butt'), from assumed *butt* 'ridge', of uncertain origin]

button /bútt'n/ *n.* **1.** **DISC FOR HOLDING CLOTHES TOGETHER** a flat and usually round piece of plastic or other material on a piece of clothing that fits into a slit or loop on another part and holds the two parts together **2.** ELEC **ELECTRICAL SWITCH** a small disc fitted in an electrical appliance or attached to a surface that activates an electrical connection when pressed **3.** **SMALL ROUND OBJECT** a small round object that resembles a button **4.** *US, Aus* **SMALL SIGN WORN ON CLOTHES** a small round flat metal or plastic object with an image or words printed on it, worn attached to clothes **5.** BIOL **ROUNDED PART** a rounded knob-shaped part or organ, such as the head of an unripe mushroom **6.** COMPUT **SMALL ACTIVATING ICON ON COMPUTER SCREEN** a small oblong image in a dialogue box of a computer-screen display, activated to perform a task by clicking with the mouse or pressing the 'Enter' key **7.** COMPUT **ACTIVATING PART OF COMPUTER MOUSE** the part of a computer mouse that when pressed or clicked performs a function, e.g. inserting the cursor at a specific point **8.** FENCING **PROTECTIVE COVERING ON FOIL** a small rounded plastic or rubber covering placed on the tip of a fencing foil to protect participants from injury **9.** ZOOL **END OF RATTLESNAKE'S TAIL** the terminal section of a rattlesnake's tail ■ *v.* (**-tons, -toning, -toned**) **1.** *vt.* **FASTEN WITH BUTTONS** to fasten sth with a button or buttons **2.** *vi.* to have buttons that can be fastened on a particular side of a garment opening or in a particular place on the garment ○ *The dress buttons at the back.* **3.** *vt.* **PUT BUTTON IN HOLE** to put a button through a slit or loop designed to receive it ○ *I never button the top button of my shirt.* **4.** *vt.* **SHUT MOUTH** to close the mouth or lips and be quiet (*informal*) ○ *Just button your mouth.* [14thC. Via French *bouton* 'bud, knob', from assumed Vulgar Latin *bottare*, from a prehistoric Germanic word that is also the ancestor of English *buttress.*] —**buttoner** *n.* ◇ **on the button 1.** exactly right (*informal*) **2.** precisely (*informal*) ○ *She was able to guess the price on the button.* ◇ **press** *or* **push all the right buttons** to do all the right or appropriate things ◇ **push sb's buttons** to provoke a reaction in sb deliberately

button up *v.* **1.** *vt.* **DO UP BUTTONS** to fasten sth with buttons **2.** *vi.* **STOP TALKING** to stop talking or refuse to talk (*informal*) **3.** *vt.* **CLOSE STH TIGHTLY** to close or seal sth tightly

buttonball /búttən bawl/ *n.* **1.** *US, Can* = **sycamore 2.** = **buttonbush** [Early 19thC. From the shape of its fruit, likened to buttons.]

buttonbush /bútt'n bo͝osh/ *n.* a North American deciduous shrub with clusters of small white flowers and leaves that grow in pairs on either side of the stem. Latin name: *Cephalanthus occidentalis.* [Mid-18thC. From its globular flower heads, likened to buttons.]

button day *n.* *Aus* a day on which badges, stickers, or buttons are sold to raise money for a particular charity

button-down *adj.* **1.** **FASTENED DOWN AT ENDS WITH BUTTONS** used to describe a collar that has a buttonhole at the end of each flap to fasten it to the front of a shirt **2.** *US* = **buttoned-down**

buttoned-down, **button-down** *adj.* *US* conservative and narrow-minded (*informal*)

buttoned-up *adj.* unwilling or unable to express feelings (*informal*)

buttonhole /búttən hōl/ *n.* **1.** **HOLE FOR BUTTON** a slit in a garment or other article of clothing through which a button is passed to fasten two pieces of material together **2.** **FLOWER WORN ON LAPEL** a flower or a small spray of flowers worn in or pinned over the buttonhole of a jacket or coat lapel. US term **boutonniere** ■ *vt.* (**-holes, -holing, -holed**) **1.** **ACCOST SB** to compel sb to listen, allowing no avenue of escape (*informal*) ○ *He buttonholed me outside my office.* **2.** **GIVE STH BUTTONHOLES** to make buttonholes in sth **3.** **SEW WITH BUTTONHOLE STITCH** to sew sth with buttonhole stitch — **buttonholer** *n.*

buttonhole stitch *n.* a tightly worked looped stitch used for reinforcing buttonholes

buttonhook /bútt'n ho͝ok/ *n.* CLOTHES a small hook formerly used for pulling small buttons through buttonholes on tight boots or gloves

buttonmould /bútt'n mōld/ *n.* a small piece of plastic, metal, or wood that forms the base of a button covered in fabric or leather

button mushroom *n.* an immature unopened mushroom [See BUTTON]

button quail *n.* a small terrestrial bird of South Eurasia, Africa, and Australia that has no hind toes. It resembles a quail, but is related to the crane. Family: Turnicidae.

buttons /bútt'nz/ *n.* a pageboy who wears a livery with rows of buttons up the jacket (*archaic informal*) (*takes a singular verb*)

button-through *adj.* fastened by a row of buttons from the top to the bottom hem

button tow *n.* a ski lift in which the occupant straddles a disc attached to a metal pole suspended from a moving cable

buttonwood /bútt'n wo͝od/ *n.* **1.** *US* = **sycamore** (*regional*) **2.** **MANGROVE TREE** a mangrove tree of the American and African tropics. Latin name: *Conocarpus erectus.*

buttress /búttrəss/ *n.* **1.** **SUPPORT FOR WALL** a solid structure, usually made of brick or stone, that is built against a wall to support it **2.** **SB OR STH THAT GIVES SUPPORT** sb or sth that acts as a source of support, help, and reinforcement ○ *The constitution is a buttress of our civil rights.* **3.** **PROJECTING ROCK** a large projecting rock mass that appears to support the rock above it **4.** **HOOF PART** the pointed horny rear part of a horse's hoof ■ *vt.* (**-tresses, -tressing, -tressed**) **1.** **SUPPORT WALL** to support a wall with a buttress **2.** **SUPPORT OR REINFORCE STH** to support or reinforce sth, especially an argument, piece of analysis, or point of view ○ *He buttressed his views with lengthy quotations from the scriptures.* [14thC. From Old French *(ars) bouterez* 'thrusting (arch)', from *bouter* 'to butt, thrust against' (see BUTT[1]).]

butt shaft *n.* a blunt-headed arrow used for archery practice [From BUTT[3]]

butt-weld (**butt-welds, butt-welding, butt-welded**) *vt.* to weld a joint in which the two pieces are placed end to end rather than overlapped —**butt weld** *n.*

butty[1] /bútti, bo͝otti/ (*plural* **-ties**) *n.* *N England* a sandwich (*informal*) [Mid-19thC. Formed from BUTTER + -Y.]

butty[2] /bútti/ (*plural* **-ties**) *n.* **1.** **FRIEND OR WORKMATE** a friend, companion, or workmate, especially in a coal mine (*regional*) **2.** *NZ* **FRIENDLY TERM OF ADDRESS FOR MAN** used as a friendly term of address for a man (*informal*) [Late 18thC. Origin uncertain; probably from the archaic phrase *play booty* 'to play sharing, unite against another player (in order to share any winnings)' (used in games).]

butut /bo͝ot oot/ *n.* **1.** **SUBUNIT OF GAMBIAN CURRENCY:** a subunit of currency in Gambia, 100 of which are worth one dalasi. See table at **currency 2.** **GAMBIAN COIN** a coin worth one butut [Late 20thC. From Wolof.]

butyl /byo͞o tīl/ *n.* a carbon and hydrogen group that can exist with any of four molecular structures (**isomers**). Formula: C_4H_9-. [Mid-19thC. Coined from BUTYRIC + -YL.]

butyl acetate *n.* = **butyl ethanoate**

butyl alcohol *n.* = **butanol**

butylate /byo͞oti layt/ (**-ates, -ating, -ated**) *vt.* to introduce a butyl group or groups into a chemical compound —**butylation** /byooti láyshən/ *n.*

butylated hydroxytoluene /byo͞oti laytəd hī dróksi tóllyoo een/ *n.* a crystalline solid that is used in petroleum products and as an antioxidant for food. Formula: $[(CH_3)_3C]_2C_6H_2OH(CH_3)$. [Mid-20thC. 'Hydroxytoluene' coined from HYDROXY- + TOLUENE.]

butylene /byo͞oti leen/ *n.* = **butene**

butyl ethanoate /-i thánnō ayt/ *n.* a colourless flammable toxic liquid with a fruity odour that has three different molecular structures (**isomers**). It is used as a solvent for lacquers. Formula: $CH_3COOC_4H_9$.

butyl rubber *n.* a synthetic rubber that is extremely resistant to abrasion, tearing, sunlight, and chemical attack. Butyl rubber is produced by a reaction between isobutylene and a small amount of isoprene. It is used in inner tubes and hosepipes, for insulation, and as seals for food jars.

butyraceous /byo͞otə ráyshəss/ *adj.* containing, resembling, or producing butter (*technical*) [Mid-17thC. Coined from BUTYRIC + -ACEOUS.]

butyraldehyde /byo͞otə ráldə hīd/ *n.* a clear colourless flammable liquid used in manufacturing solvents, resins, and plasticizers. Formula: C_4H_8O.

butyrate /byo͞otə rayt/ *n.* a chemical compound that is a salt or ester of butanoic acid [Mid-19thC. Coined from BUTYRIC + -ATE.]

butyric /byoo tírrik/ *adj.* **1.** **RELATING TO BUTYRIC ACID** relating to or containing butyric acid **2.** **RELATING TO BUTTER** relating to or containing butter (*technical*) [Early 19thC. Coined from Latin *butyrum* (see BUTTER) + -IC.]

butyric acid *n.* = **butanoic acid**

butyrin /byóotərin/ *n.* a colourless liquid or oil found in butter and formed from butanoic acid and glycerol. It can exist with any one of three molecular structures (**isomers**). [Early 19thC. From BUTYRIC + GLYCERIN.]

butyrophenone /byóotirō fēenōn/ *n.* a drug belonging a class of drugs similar to the phenothiazines, used to treat severe psychiatric disorders [Early 20thC. From BUTYRIC + PHENO-.]

buxom /búksəm/ *adj.* **1.** WITH LARGE BREASTS used to describe a woman with a full figure (*dated*) **2.** PLUMP AND HEALTHY-LOOKING used to describe a woman who is plump, attractive, and healthy-looking (*archaic*) [Assumed Old English *(ge)būhsum*, literally 'pliable' (hence 'compliant', 'lively', 'comely', 'large-breasted'), from *(ge)būgan* 'to bend' (source of English *bow*)] —**buxomly** *adv.* —**buxomness** *n.*

Buxtehude /bóokstə hóodə/, **Dietrich** (1637?–1707) Danish-born German organist and composer. A prolific composer of sacred music for the organ, he moved to Germany in 1668 and was greatly admired by J.S. Bach and Handel.

Buxton /búkstən/ spa town in the Peak District, in northwestern Derbyshire, England, with thermal and chalybeate springs. Population: 19,854 (1991).

buy /bī/ *v.* (**buys, buying, bought** /bawt/, **bought**) **1.** *vti.* ACQUIRE STH BY PAYMENT to pay money for sth in order to obtain it ○ *They bought me a bike for my birthday* ○ *People just aren't buying at the moment.* **2.** *vt.* USE MONEY TO OBTAIN STH INTANGIBLE to obtain sth intangible with money ○ *Money won't buy you happiness.* **3.** *vt.* BRIBE SB to obtain information, help, or loyalty from sb in exchange for money **4.** *vt.* OBTAIN TIME to obtain more time to reach a desired end by taking strategic action ○ *a manoeuvre that should buy us another week* **5.** *vt.* OBTAIN STH BY SACRIFICE to obtain sth by sacrificing a thing of equivalent value ○ *buy peace with land* **6.** *vi.* BE BUYER FOR COMPANY OR INDIVIDUAL to purchase goods on behalf of a company or another individual ○ *She buys for Harrods.* **7.** *vt.* BELIEVE STH to accept or believe sth proposed as true (*informal*) ○ *I don't buy the part about an international conspiracy.* ■ *n.* **1.** STH BOUGHT sth that you pay money for, considered relative to its worth ○ *a good buy* **2.** EXCHANGE OF MONEY FOR GOODS an exchange of money for goods or services [Old English *bycgan* 'to buy, pay for', from a prehistoric Germanic base] —**buyable** *adj.*

buy in *v.* **1.** *vt.* WITHDRAW ITEM FROM AUCTION to withdraw an item from sale at an auction because it has failed to reach its reserve price **2.** *vi.* BUY SHARES IN COMPANY to buy shares in a company as the controlling interest **3.** *vi.* PAY TO TAKE PART IN STH to pay in order to take part in or have a share of sth **4.** *vti.* BUY STH IN QUANTITY to buy sth in large quantities, usually in preparation for an expected period of hardship

buy into *vt.* **1.** BUY SHARES IN COMPANY to buy shares in a company **2.** PAY TO PARTICIPATE IN STH to pay money in order to take part in sth ○ *buy into a timeshare* **3.** *US* ACCEPT STH to accept or believe in a proposition or idea (*informal*) ○ *I don't buy into that 'greed is good' attitude.*

buy off *vt.* to bribe sb in order to prevent sth happening or ensure cooperation ○ *They tried to buy off the entire jury.*

buy out *vt.* **1.** COMM PURCHASE ENTIRE SHARES OF COMPANY to purchase the entire shares of or controlling financial interest in a company or business **2.** MIL RELEASE SB FROM MILITARY SERVICE to pay money to release sb from military service ○ *He bought himself out of the army and set up a business in London.* **3.** PAY SB TO RELINQUISH INTEREST to pay sb to relinquish interest in a property or other enterprise ○ *She was bought out by her partners.*

buy up *vt.* **1.** BUY ALL OF A COMMODITY to buy everything, or everything that is available, of a commodity ○ *They've been buying up property in the area.* **2.** BUY STH IN QUANTITY to buy sth in great quantity without regard to expense ○ *buying up modern paintings*

buy-back *n.* the repurchase by a company or an individual of sth, e.g. shares or goods, according to a previously made contractual agreement

buyer /bī ər/ *n.* **1.** SB BUYING STH sb who is in the process of buying sth or who intends to buy sth **2.** SB WHO BUYS GOODS FOR COMPANY a person whose job is to choose and buy goods or merchandise for a company, factory, or store

buyer's market *n.* a situation in which supply exceeds demand, prices are relatively low, and buyers therefore have an advantage. ◊ **seller's market**

buyout /bī owt/ *n.* **1.** PURCHASE OF CONTROLLING INTEREST IN COMPANY the purchase of a controlling interest in a company ○ *a management buyout* **2.** BUYING ENTIRE AMOUNT OF STH the purchase of an entire amount or quantity of sth

buzz /buz/ *n.* **1.** STEADY HUMMING SOUND a steady low humming sound like that of a bee ○ *the low buzz of insects flitting over the flowers* **2.** HUM OF TALK a low murmur of conversation made by a group of people, especially when they are excited or interested in sth ○ *a buzz of voices emerging from the living room* **3.** SOUND the sound made by a buzzer **4.** TELEPHONE CALL a telephone call (*informal*) **5.** FEELING OF EXCITEMENT a feeling of excitement or satisfaction often linked with a sense of achievement (*informal*) ○ *It gives me a tremendous buzz to hear someone saying the lines that I've written.* **6.** INTOXICATION a feeling of intoxication (*slang*) **7.** LATEST GOSSIP the latest gossip or information within a particular industry or locale (*informal*) ○ *The buzz at the festival was that he'd pick up an award for best director.* **8.** FAD a short-lived interest or enthusiasm (*informal*) **9.** publicity, or interest generated by publicity (*informal*) ■ *v.* (**buzzes, buzzing, buzzed**) **1.** *vi.* MAKE STEADY HUMMING SOUND to make a steady low humming sound like that of a bee **2.** *vi.* BE ANIMATED BY STH to be animated by the talk or activity of people ○ *The room was buzzing with excitement.* **3.** *vi.* MOVE SPEEDILY to move around speedily and busily ○ *buzzing about in small cars that dodged through traffic* **4.** *vti.* WORK BUZZER to activate a buzzer **5.** *vt.* LET SB INTO BUILDING ELECTRONICALLY to admit sb to a building by activating an electronic system that controls a door ○ *waiting for them to buzz me in* **6.** *vi.* MAKING ELECTRONIC HUMMING SOUND to make an electronic humming noise when activated ○ *When the timer buzzes, turn the oven down.* **7.** *vi.* BE EXCITED to be filled with anxious or excited thoughts ○ *My head was buzzing with all the things I'd heard that night.* **8.** *vi.* BE RINGING to be filled with a continuous ringing sound, e.g. after being exposed to loud noise ○ *My ears were buzzing after the concert.* **9.** *vt.* TELEPHONE SB to call sb on the telephone (*informal*) **10.** *vt.* FLY LOW OVER PEOPLE OR PLACE to fly an aircraft low over people or buildings, or across the path of other aircraft (*informal*) [14thC. An imitation of the sound.]

buzz off *vi.* to go away (*informal*)

buzzard /búzzərd/ (*plural* **-zards** *or* **-zard**) *n.* **1.** LARGE HAWK a large Eurasian hawk with broad wings and a broad tail. Genus: *Buteo.* US term **buteo** **2.** *US* VULTURE any North American vulture, e.g. the turkey vulture **3.** *US* BAD-TEMPERED PERSON a mean, bad-tempered, or unpleasant person (*dated*) [14thC. From Old French *busard*, of uncertain origin: probably formed from Latin *buteo(n-)* '(kind of) falcon or hawk', of unknown origin.]

buzz bomb *n.* = **V-1**

buzzer /búzzər/ *n.* an electronic device that makes a humming or buzzing sound when activated [Early 17thC. An early sense of the word is 'buzzing insect'.]

buzz saw *n. US, Can* = **circular saw**

buzzword /búz wurd/ *n.* a fashionable word or concept, often associated with a particular group of people and not understood by outsiders (*informal*) ○ *the latest media buzzword*

b.v. *abbr.* ACCT book value

B vitamin *n.* a water-soluble vitamin that acts as a coenzyme in biochemical reactions, including those concerned with the production of energy from foods. The B vitamins are B1 thiamine, B2 riboflavin, B6 pyridoxine, B12 cobalamine, B5 pantothenic acid, folic acid, and biotin.

BVM *abbr.* Blessed Virgin Mary [Latin, Beata Virgo Maria]

BW *abbr.* **1.** biological warfare **2.** bacteriological warfare **3. BW, B/W, b/w** black-and-white

bwana /bwáanə/ *n.* used as a respectful term of address for a man in East Africa [Late 19thC. From Kiswahili.]

BWB *abbr.* British Waterways Board

BWG *n.* a numerical system for specifying the diameter of metal rods. Abbr of **Birmingham Wire Gauge**

BWI *abbr.* British West Indies

BWR *abbr.* PHYS boiling-water reactor

BWV *abbr.* Bach Werke-Verzeichnis (*used before a number to indicate one of the works by J. S. Bach in the catalogue compiled by Wolfgang Schmieder*)

bx *abbr.* box

by[1] /bī/ CORE MEANING: a grammatical word expressing a spatial relationship, indicating that sb or sth is beside or close to sb or sth else ○ (prep) *standing by the window* ○ (adv) *A large crowd of shoppers stood by watching.*

1. *prep., adv.* PAST SB OR STH IN SPACE indicates movement past sb or sth, sometimes including a brief stop (*used following a verb expressing movement*) ○ *He drove by his apartment building.* ○ *The waitress came by, pouring us some more coffee.* **2.** *prep., adv.* AT THAT PLACE at the place specified or understood, usually for a short visit ○ *We stopped by Jan's place.* ○ *Drop by any time.* **3.** *prep.* THROUGH passing through sth ○ *entering by the back door* **4.** *prep.* BEFORE THAT TIME happening or required at or before the time stated ○ *reservations required by Sunday* **5.** *prep.* DURING happening during a particular time period ○ *By day he worked in a canning factory.* **6.** *prep.* IN MEASURES OF at a rate based on a particular measure, such as time, weight, or volume ○ *These vegetables are sold by weight.* **7.** *prep.* ARITH INDICATING FACTOR OR DIVISOR used in multiplication and division to indicate any number or quantity being multiplied, or to indicate the number or quantity that divides another ○ *What is 144 divided by 12?* **8.** *prep.* MEASURE INDICATES DIMENSIONS used between the measurements of the dimensions of an object, expressing area or volume **9.** *prep.* MEASURE DIFFERING IN THE AMOUNT OF used to indicate an amount, extent, or rate at which sth increases, decreases, or differs ○ *Tax rates are to be cut by 0.25%.* **10.** *prep.* MEASURE used to indicate a direction ○ *north by northwest* **11.** *prep.* IN AMOUNTS OF PARTICULAR SIZE in groups or amounts of a particular size ○ *Visitors arrived by the truckload.* **12.** *prep.* GRADUALLY used to link two identical words to indicate a progression or sequence ○ *One by one we told our stories.* ○ *You can see an improvement day by day.* **13.** *prep.* INDICATES CAUSE used to indicate the person or thing causing an action, situation, or reaction (*used following a passive verb*) ○ *He was hit by a ball.* **14.** *prep.* INDICATES CREATOR, AUTHOR, OR ARTIST used to indicate the person who wrote or created sth such as a written piece or work of art ○ *written by A.A. Milne* **15.** *prep.* USING A METHOD OR MEDIUM used to indicate the particular mode, method, or action through which sth occurs or is done ○ *travelling by ocean liner* ○ *She earns a living by playing the harp.* **16.** *prep.* INDICATING MEANS indicating the action used to achieve sth (*followed by a gerund*) ○ *The key to attracting banks back to inner cities is by attracting business.* **17.** *prep.* THROUGH A PARTICULAR MANNER with, in, or through a particular manner of doing sth ○ *used by permission of the author* **18.** *prep.* ACCORDING TO AN UNCHANGING QUALITY in terms of a particular attribute or function ○ *a teacher by profession and a learner by nature* **19.** *prep.* IN COMPLIANCE WITH in order to comply with sth, especially the law ○ *By law, patients must have access to their records.* **20.** *prep.* AT A PARTICULAR PART at a particular part of sth, such as a hand or corner ○ *held the dancer by the waist* **21.** *adv.* IN THE NAME OF STH SACRED used to indicate sth considered holy when making a solemn oath or promise ○ *By all that is sacred, I ask you to stop.* **22.** *adv.* PAST IN TIME indicates the passage of the stated amount of time (*when following a verb expressing movement*) ○ *as time goes by* **23.** *adv. Scotland* PAST over and done with **24.** *adv.* AWAY OR ASIDE in a place for safekeeping for use later ○ *I spent some of the money and put some by for hard times.* [Old English *bī*, from a prehistoric Germanic word (also the ancestor of English *be-*) of uncertain origin: ultimately probably from an Indo-European word meaning 'near'] ◇ **by and by** after a while (*literary*) ◇ **by the by, by the bye** incidentally or by the way

by[2] *n.* = **bye**[2]

by- *prefix.* **1.** secondary ○ *byroad* ○ *by-product* **2.** past ○ *bygone* [From BY]

Byatt /bĭ ət/, **A. S.** (*b.* 1936) British novelist and academic. Her novels include *The Virgin in the Garden* (1978), and the Booker Prize-winning *Possession* (1990). She is the sister of the novelist Margaret Drabble. Full name **Antonia Susan Byatt**. Born **Antonia Susan Drabble**

Byblos /bíbbləss/ an ancient Phoenician city, near modern-day Beirut, Lebanon, on the Mediterranean Sea. It was the principal city of Phoenicia in the second millennium BC, and an important source of papyrus.

by-blow *n.* a man's illegitimate child (*archaic*)

bye[1] /bĭ/ *n.* **1.** SPORTS AUTOMATIC ADVANCE TO NEXT ROUND the right to proceed to the next round of a competition without contesting the present round, often through non-appearance of an opponent **2.** GOLF INFORMAL MATCH in golf, an informal match contested over remaining holes, once the main competition is over **3.** CRICKET EXTRA RUN WITHOUT HITTING BALL in cricket, a run scored off a ball that has not been hit by a batsman, awarded to the team as a whole rather than to an individual batsman [Mid-16thC. From *by.*]

bye[2] /bĭ/ *interj.* used to say goodbye (*informal*) [Early 18thC. Shortening of GOODBYE.]

bye- *prefix.* = by-

bye-bye *interj.* GOODBYE used to say goodbye (*informal*) ■ *n.* US = **bye-byes** (*babytalk*) [Child's variation of GOODBYE]

bye-byes *n.* bed or sleep (*babytalk*) US term **bye-bye** [From a refrain used in lullabies]

by-election, **bye-election** *n.* an election held between official general or local elections to fill a vacant seat, e.g. to replace a member of parliament or local councillor who has died or resigned

Byelorussia /byéllō rúshə/ *n.* former name for **Belarus**—**Byelorussian** *n.*, *adj.*

bygone /bĭ gon/ *adj.* PAST existing or having happened a long time ago ○ *reminders of a bygone age* ■ *n.* STH FROM LONG AGO sth that happened, existed, or was manufactured a long time ago (*often used in the plural*) ◊ **let bygones be bygones** to forgive past offences or resentments

bylaw /bĭ law/ *n.* **1.** PUBLIC ADMIN LOCAL LAW a law made by a local authority that applies only in the area that the authority governs **2.** INTERNAL RULE a law or regulation that governs the internal affairs of a company or other organization **3.** LAW SECONDARY LAW a secondary law [13thC. Origin uncertain: probably from Old Norse *býlagu* 'town law' from *býr* 'town' + *lagu* 'law'.]

byline /bĭ līn/ *n.* **1.** REPORTER'S NAME the name of the author of an article in a newspaper or magazine, printed at the head of the article **2.** SOCCER = **goal line** ■ *vt.* (-lines, -lining, -lined) WRITE ARTICLE to write an article that will include a byline [Early 20thC. Because the article would be headed with the word BY, followed by the author's name.]

byname /bĭ naym/ *n.* sb's nickname [Late 16thC]

BYO *n.* ANZ a restaurant, party, or event to which guests bring their own alcoholic beverages. Full form **bring your own**

BYOB *abbr.* bring your own bottle (*used on party invitations*)

bypass /bĭ paass/ *n.* **1.** TRANSP ROAD ROUND TOWN a road built round a town or city to keep through traffic away from the centre **2.** MED OPERATION TO REROUTE BLOOD a surgical operation to redirect the blood, usually via a grafted blood vessel, carried out when the existing blood vessel has become blocked ○ *a heart bypass* **3.** MED NEW ROUTE FOR BLOOD a new route for the blood, created by a bypass operation **4.** ELEC ENG = **shunt** *n.* **4** **5.** EMERGENCY CHANNEL a channel, e.g. a pipe carrying gas or water, brought into use when the main channel is blocked ■ *vt.* (-passes, -passing, -passed) **1.** GO ROUND A PLACE to avoid a place by travelling round it **2.** TRANSP BUILD BYPASS to build a bypass round a place **3.** AVOID STH to avoid an obstacle, obstruction, or problem by using an alternative route or method **4.** AVOID STANDARD PROCEDURE to ignore or avoid a standard procedure for doing sth, or ignore sb who is usually consulted

bypath /bĭ paath/ *n.* a rarely used path, especially in the country

by-play *n.* matters of subsidiary importance or interest that take place while the main action is going on, e.g. in a stage play

byproduct /bĭ prodúkt/ *n.* **1.** INCIDENTAL PRODUCT sth produced as a secondary result of the manufacture or production of sth else, often sth useful or commercially valuable **2.** SECONDARY RESULT sth that happens as an incidental result of sth else

Byrd /burd/, **William** (1543–1623) English composer. Appointed organist for the Chapel Royal in 1572, his work includes three Latin masters (1589–91), madrigals and instrumental pieces.

byre /bĭr/ *n.* a cowshed (*regional*) [Old English *býre*. Origin uncertain: perhaps a variant of Old English *búr*, ancestor of English *bower*.]

byroad /bĭ rōd/ *n.* a side road carrying a small volume of traffic

Byron, Cape /bĭrən/ cape in northeastern New South Wales, near the town of Byron Bay. It is the most easterly point on the Australian mainland.

Lord Byron

Byron, George Gordon Noel, 6th Baron Byron (1788–1824) British poet. An influential figure of the romantic movement, his major works include 'Childe Harold's Pilgrimage' (1812–18) and the long satirical poem 'Don Juan' (1819–24). After scandalizing London with his promiscuity, Lord Byron lived abroad, largely in Italy, and died aiding the Greeks in their revolt against the Turks.

Byron Bay tourist resort in north-eastern New South Wales, Australia. Population: 6,130 (1996).

Byronic /bĭ rónnik/ *adj.* **1.** LITERAT OF BYRON relating to or characteristic of Lord Byron or his poetry **2.** MOODY used to describe a brooding and solitary man who seems capable of great passion and suffering

byssinosis /bíssi nṓssiss/ *n.* a respiratory disease caused by prolonged inhalation of dust from textile fibres, marked by coughing, wheezing, shortness of breath, and permanent lung damage [Late 19thC. Coined from Latin *byssinus* 'of fine linen', from *byssus* (see BYSSUS) + -OSIS.]

byssus /bíssəss/ (*plural* **-suses** or **-si** /-sī/) *n.* **1.** MUSSEL'S MEANS OF CLINGING a mass of strong silky threads that molluscs such as mussels use to attach themselves to rocks and other hard surfaces **2.** ARCHAEOL CLOTH FOR WRAPPING MUMMY a type of fine linen used by the ancient Egyptians to wrap mummies [14thC. Via Latin, 'fine linen', from Greek *bussos*, of, ultimately, Semitic origin.]

bystander /bĭ standər/ *n.* sb who observes an activity but is not involved in it

bystander effect *n.* the reluctance of members of a crowd to intervene in an incident they are witnessing

bystreet /bĭ street/ *n.* a side street that is not regularly used by people or traffic. = **byroad**

byte /bīt/ *n.* **1.** UNIT OF COMPUTER INFORMATION a set of adjacent bits, now commonly a group of eight, used in computing to represent a unit of data such as a number or letter **2.** COMPUTER STORAGE UNIT a unit of computer memory equal to that needed to store a single character [Mid-20thC. Origin uncertain: probably an alteration of BIT 'unit of computer information' by association with BITE 'morsel', or an acronym formed from 'binary digit eight'.]

byway /bĭ way/ *n.* **1.** SIDE ROAD a small side road not regularly used by people or traffic **2.** MINOR ASPECTS the less important aspects of a particular pursuit or field of knowledge ○ *the byways of numismatics*

byword /bĭ wurd/ *n.* **1.** WELL-KNOWN EXAMPLE sb or sth that is well known for a particular quality ○ *The magazine became a byword for cutting-edge style.* **2.** CATCHPHRASE a word or phrase that is in common use at a particular time **3.** PROVERB a proverb common to a particular place, group, or time [Old English *bīwyrde* 'proverb', a translation of Latin *proverbium* (source of English *proverb*)]

Byzantine /bĭ zán tīn, -teen, bízz'n tīn, -teen/ *adj.* **1.** HIST OF BYZANTIUM relating to or typical of the ancient city of Byzantium, or its people or culture **2.** HIST OF BYZANTINE EMPIRE relating to the Byzantine Empire, the eastern part of the late Roman Empire **3.** ARTS, ARCHIT OF BYZANTINE ART OR ARCHITECTURE relating to or typical of the colourful style of religious art or the ornate style of architecture developed under the Byzantine Empire, which was characterized by great use of marble and mosaic **4.** CHR OF ORTHODOX CHURCH relating to or typical of the Orthodox Church and its traditions **5. Byzantine, byzantine** VERY COMPLEX extremely complex or intricate **6. Byzantine, byzantine** DEVIOUS marked by deviousness or scheming ■ *n.* HIST SB FROM BYZANTIUM sb who lived in the ancient city of Byzantium or the Byzantine Empire [Late 16thC. From Latin *Byzantinus*, from *Byzantium*, from Greek *Buzantion*.]

Byzantine Church *n.* = Orthodox Church

Byzantine Empire *n.* the eastern part of the late Roman Empire, dating from AD 330, when Constantine I rebuilt Byzantium and renamed it Constantinople, to 1453, when it fell to the Ottoman Turks. It was the centre of Orthodox Christianity.

Byzantium /bĭ zánti əm, bi-, bĭ zánshi əm, bi-/ *n.* an ancient Greek city on the site of modern-day Istanbul, conquered by the Romans in AD 196, and rebuilt in AD 330 by Constantine I, who renamed it Constantinople. As the capital of the Byzantine Empire (until 1453), it was the largest city in the Christian world.

Cc

c¹ /see/ (*plural* **c's**), **C** (*plural* **C's** *or* **Cs**) *n*. **1.** 3RD LETTER IN ENGLISH ALPHABET the third letter and second consonant of the alphabet in modern English, and in other languages that also use the Latin alphabet **2.** SOUND OF any speech sound represented by the letter 'c' **3.** LETTER WRITTEN a written representation of the letter ◇ **the big C** cancer (*informal*)

c² *symbol*. PHYS speed of light in a vacuum

c³ *abbr*. **1.** cancelled **2.** ZOOL canine **3.** MEASURE carat **4.** BUSINESS carbon (paper) **5.** DOMESTIC carton **6.** LAW case **7.** SPORTS catcher **8.** SPORTS caught by **9.** FIN cedi **10.** FIN cent **11.** FIN centavo **12.** centre ■ *symbol*. **13.** MEASURE centi- ■ *abbr*. **14.** FIN centime **15.** MEASURE centimetre **16.** centum **17.** HISTORY century **18.** PUBL chapter ■ *symbol*. **19.** PHYS charm ■ *abbr*. **20.** RELIG church **21.** HIST circa **22.** ELEC circuit **23.** GEOM circumference **24.** clockwise **25.** METEOROL cloudy **26.** PHARM codex **27.** SCI coefficient **28.** MED cold **29.** ANAT colon **30.** colour **31.** MAMMAL colt ■ *symbol*. **32.** concentration ■ *abbr*. **33.** MATH constant **34.** MUSIC contralto **35.** communication copy **37.** LAW copyright **38.** MIL corps **39.** FIN cost **40.** MEASURE cubic **41.** NUCLEAR PHYS curie

C¹ (*plural* **Cs** *or* **C's**) *n*. **1.** EDUC 3RD HIGHEST GRADE the third highest grade in a series, e.g. an average grade for academic work **2.** MUSIC 1ST NOTE OF SCALE IN C the first note of a scale in C major **3.** MUSIC STH THAT PRODUCES A c a string, key, or pipe tuned to produce the note C **4.** MUSIC SCALE BEGINNING ON C a scale or key that starts on the note C **5.** MUSIC WRITTEN SYMBOL OF C a graphic representation of the tone of C **6.** COMPUT PROGRAMMING LANGUAGE a high-level computer programming language

C² *symbol*. **1.** CHEM ELEM carbon **2.** ELEC ENG capacitance **3.** 100 (*used in Roman numerals*) **4.** MEASURE Celsius **5.** MEASURE centigrade **6.** BIOCHEM cytosine **7.** heat capacity

C³ *abbr*. **1.** MAPS Cape **2.** BUILDING castle **3.** CHR Catholic ■ *symbol*. MEASURE **4.** Celsius **5.** centigrade ■ *abbr*. **6.** PHYS charm **7.** DRUGS cocaine (*slang*) **8.** POL Conservative ■ *symbol*. **9.** ELEC coulomb ■ *abbr*. **10.** College **11.** POL Chancellor **12.** POL Congress **13.** MANAGEMT chief **14.** city **15.** Companion **16.** POL congress **17.** MIL corps **18.** SPORTS court ■ **C, c 19.** ROMAN NUMERAL FOR 100 the Roman numeral for 100

C++ *n*. COMPUT an object-oriented version of the programming language C, developed in the 1980s

C1 (*plural* **C1s**) *n*. sb in a clerical or junior management position, in the market research system that classifies people according to their occupation

C2 (*plural* **C2s**) *n*. sb in a skilled manual job, in the market research system that classifies people according to their occupation

Ca *symbol*. calcium

CA *abbr*. **1.** California **2.** chronological age **3.** Central American **4.** Consumers' Association **5.** chartered accountant **6.** ACCT chief accountant **7.** RELIG consular agent

ca. *abbr*. **1.** circa (*used before dates*) **2.** ACCT chartered accountant

c/a *abbr*. BANKING current account

C/A *abbr*. **1.** FIN capital account **2.** FIN credit account **3.** BANKING current account

CAA *abbr*. Civil Aviation Authority

cab /kab/ *n*. **1.** = taxi **2.** DRIVER'S COMPARTMENT the part of a large vehicle, e.g. a lorry, a locomotive, or a large crane, where the driver or operator sits **3.** HORSE-DRAWN VEHICLE FOR HIRE a lightweight horse-drawn carriage formerly used for public hire [Early 19thC. Shortening of CABRIOLET.]

CAB *abbr*. **1.** Civil Aeronautics Board **2.** Citizens' Advice Bureau

cabal /kə bál/ *n*. **1.** GROUP OF PLOTTERS a group of conspirators or plotters, particularly one formed for political purposes **2.** SECRET PLOT a secret plot or conspiracy, especially a political one **3.** CLIQUE an exclusive group of people ■ *vi*. (**-bals, -balling, -balled**) CONSPIRE AS GROUP to form a group and plot together against sb or sth [Early 17thC. Via French *cabale* from medieval Latin *cab(b)ala* 'secret teaching' (see CABALA).]

Cabal /kə bál/ *n*. a group of ministers in the court of the English King Charles II, who governed the country between 1667–73. Their surnames were Clifford, Arlington, Buckingham, Ashley, and Lauderdale. [Mid-17thC. Acronym formed from the initials of their names, on the model of CABAL.]

cabala *n*. = kabbalah

cabaletta /kábbə léttə/ *n*. **1.** SIMPLE ARIA a short simple aria in 19th-century Italian opera, usually found in conjunction with a preceding cavatina **2.** LAST SECTION OF ARIA the final section of an aria or duet, which typically has a lively rhythm [Mid-19thC. From Italian, literally 'little stanza', ultimately from Latin *copula* 'link' (see COPULA).]

Caballé /ka bá yay, káb a yáy/, **Montserrat** (*b*. 1933) Spanish soprano, associated especially with the operas of Donizetti and Verdi.

caballero /kábbə láirō, kább'l yáirō/ (*plural* **-ros**) *n*. **1.** SPANISH KNIGHT OR GENTLEMAN a Spanish knight, cavalier, or gentleman **2.** *Southwest US* HORSEMAN a horseman, especially of Spanish-speaking regions [Mid-19thC. Via Spanish from late Latin *caballarius*, from Latin *caballus* 'horse' (source of English *cavalier* and *chivalry*).]

cabaret /kábbə ray/ *n*. **1.** FLOOR SHOW a floor show consisting of singing, dancing, and comic acts performed in a restaurant, club, or bar **2.** RESTAURANT OR BAR WITH CABARET a restaurant, club, or bar offering a cabaret [Mid-17thC. Via French from, ultimately, Old French dialect *camberet* 'little room', ultimately from Latin *camera* 'room' (see CAMERA).]

Cabbage

cabbage /kábbij/ *n*. **1.** LEAFY VEGETABLE a plant with a short stem and a roundish head of closely layered green, white, or red leaves that is eaten as a vegetable. Latin name: *Brassica oleracea* var. *capitata*. **2.** LEAVES OF CABBAGE AS FOOD the leaves or head of a cabbage prepared as food, either raw or cooked **3.** PLANT RELATED TO CABBAGE a plant related to cabbage proper, e.g. Chinese cabbage **4.** EDIBLE PALM BUD the bud of a number of species of palm, eaten as a vegetable **5.** SEVERELY BRAIN-DAMAGED PERSON sb who has no mental awareness or mental activity, usually as a result of brain injury, and who is completely dependent on other people (*offensive*) **6.** BORING PERSON a dull unimaginative person who is inactive both physically and mentally (*informal*) [15thC. From Old French *caboche* (source of BOCHE), a variant of *caboce* 'head', perhaps ultimately from Latin *caput* (see CAPITAL).] —**cabbagy** *adj*.

cabbage butterfly *n*. = cabbage white

cabbage lettuce *n*. a variety of lettuce that has a rounded head like a cabbage

cabbage palm *n*. **1.** PALM WITH EDIBLE BUDS a palm tree whose leaf buds resemble cabbages and are eaten as a vegetable. Latin name: *Roystonea oleracea*. **2.** PLANT RESEMBLING CABBAGE any palm or similar plant resembling a cabbage

cabbage palmetto *n*. a tropical palm tree native to the southeastern United States and the Bahamas, with edible leaf buds and fan-shaped leaves that are used in Christian celebrations on Palm Sunday. Latin name: *Sabal palmetto*.

cabbage root fly (*plural* **cabbage root flies**) *n*. a fly whose larvae feed on cabbages and other plants of the cabbage family such as broccoli, cauliflowers, and brussels sprouts. Latin name: *Delia radicum*.

cabbage rose *n*. a shrub of hybrid origin that is grown in gardens for its fragrant double-petalled flowers. Latin name: *Rosa centifolia*.

cabbage tree *n*. **1.** NEW ZEALAND TREE a small New Zealand tree with a palm-like top, often grown as an ornamental plant. Latin name: *Cordyline australis*. **2.** AUSTRALIAN TREE a large Australian palm tree found on and near the east coast. Latin name: *Livistona australis*.

cabbage white *n*. light-coloured butterfly whose larvae feed on the leaves of cabbages and related plants. Family: Pieridae. US term **cabbage butterfly**

cabbageworm /kábbij wurm/ *n*. a larva that feeds on cabbages and related plants, especially the larva of the cabbage white butterfly

cabby /kábbi/ (*plural* **-bies**), **cabbie** *n*. a taxi driver (*informal*)

cabdriver /káb drīvər/ *n*. a taxi driver

caber /káybər/ *n*. a long thick wooden pole used in Scottish Highland Games in an event known as 'tossing the caber', in which contestants have to throw a caber end over end [Early 16thC. From Gaelic *cabar* 'pole'.]

cabernet sauvignon /kábbər nay sóvin yon/ *n*. **1.** BLACK GRAPE USED FOR RED WINE a variety of black grape that is used to make red wine **2.** WINE DRY RED WINE dry red wine made from the cabernet sauvignon grape [From French]

cabezon /kábbi zon/ (*plural* **-zons** *or* **-zon**) *n*. a spiny striped and mottled fish found in northern Pacific waters, popular as a food fish. Latin name: *Scorpaenichthys marmoratus*.

cabin /kábbin/ *n.* **1.** BUILDING **WOODEN HUT** a small, simple house, especially one made of wood in forest or mountain areas **2.** NAUT **SMALL ROOM ON SHIP** a small room on a boat or ship, where people live or sleep **3.** NAUT **SHELTER ON SMALL BOAT** a covered compartment that houses the wheel on a small boat, used for shelter in bad weather and often as a living space **4.** TRANSP = **cab 5.** AIR **AEROPLANE INTERIOR** the part of a passenger aeroplane where the passengers sit, or the part of a cargo aeroplane where the cargo is carried **6.** SPACE TECH **CREW QUARTERS ON SPACECRAFT** the part of a spacecraft where the crew work, live, or sleep **7.** NAVY **ROOM ON SHIP** the commanding officer's room on a warship **8.** = **signal box** ■ *vti.* **(-ins, -ining, -ined) KEEP SB OR SELF CONFINED** to confine sb, or live confined, in a small enclosed space (*literary*) (*usually passive*) [14thC. Via Old French *cabane* from, ultimately, late Latin *capanna, cavanna* 'hut'.]

WORD KEY: CULTURAL NOTE

Uncle Tom's Cabin, a novel by US writer Harriet Beecher Stowe (1852). Set in the American South, it is the story of a Black slave, Uncle Tom, who is sold by his kindly owners and eventually dies at the hands of a vicious Yankee master. Such was this antislavery abolitionist novel's influence that it was described as one of the causes of the American Civil War.

cabin boy *n.* a boy who acted as a servant on board a sailing ship, waiting on officers and passengers

cabin class *n.* **INTERMEDIATE CLASS ON PASSENGER SHIPS** a class of accommodation on some passenger ships that is lower than first class and higher than tourist class ■ *adj., adv.* **IN CABIN CLASS** in cabin class on a passenger ship

cabin crew *n.* staff on a passenger aircraft whose job is to attend to passengers

cabin cruiser *n.* a large, powerful, and luxurious motor boat with generous living space

Cabinda /kə beéndə/ Angolan enclave bounded by the Republic of Congo to the north and the Democratic Republic of Congo to the south. Capital: Cabinda. Population: 152,100 (1992). Area: 7,270 sq. km/2,807 sq. mi.

cabinet /kábbinət/ *n.* **1. cabinet, Cabinet** POL **GROUP OF SENIOR MINISTERS** a group of senior government ministers chosen by a prime minister to act as the executive decision-making body of the country (*takes a singular or plural verb*) **2.** FURNITURE **PIECE OF FURNITURE** an upright piece of furniture usually made of wood and consisting of drawers, shelves, and compartments for storing or displaying objects **3. TV OR RADIO COVERING** the outer casing of a television or hi-fi system, especially the wooden casing of an old-fashioned model **4. PRIVATE ROOM** a small private room (*archaic*) ■ *adj.* **1. FOR SMALL ROOM** used to describe furniture and other items intended for a small room or a room in a private home **2. FOR DISPLAY IN CABINET** small or decorative enough to be displayed in a cabinet [Mid-16thC. From French, literally 'small room' (the original sense in English), from Old Picard *cabine* 'room for gambling'.]

cabinetmaker /kábbinət maykər/ *n.* a skilled woodworker who specializes in making furniture —**cabinetmaking** *n.*

cabinet minister *n.* a senior government minister who is in the Cabinet

cabinetry /kábbinətri/, **cabinetwork** /kábbinət wurk/ *n.* articles, especially fine furniture, made by a skilled woodworker

cabin fever *n.* an emotional condition, marked by irritability, distress, or depression, caused by prolonged isolation or confined living quarters

cable /káyb'l/ *n.* **1. STRONG ROPE OR WIRE** a strong thick rope or steel wire used for lifting, pulling, towing, or securing things **2.** ELEC **BUNDLE OF ELECTRICAL WIRES** a group of wires for transmitting electrical signals that are bound together and usually have shared or common insulation. ◊ **coaxial cable 3.** NAUT **MOORING ROPE OR CHAIN** a rope or chain attached to an anchor or used for mooring a ship **4.** TELECOM **OVERSEAS TELEGRAM** a telegram, originally sent by undersea cable, now usually by telephone, radio, or satellite **5.** TV = **cable television 6.** KNITTING = **cable stitch** ■ *v.* **(-bles, -bling, -bled) 1.** *vti.* **SEND TELEGRAM** to send sb a telegram **2.** *vt.* TELECOM **SEND STH VIA TELEGRAM** to send sth, e.g. money or information, to sb in a distant place by sending a telegram **3.** *vt.* **FASTEN OR FIT STH WITH CABLES** to fasten sth with cables, or fit cables to sth **4.** *vt.* TV **SUPPLY PLACE WITH CABLE TV** to connect a building or area to a cable television network [Pre-12thC. Via Old French dialect from late Latin *capulum* 'halter', from Latin *capere* 'to seize' (see CAPTURE).] —**cabler** *n.* —**cabling** *n.*

cable-access *adj.* *US* TV showing programmes that are made locally, often of local interest only, as opposed to commercially produced material ○ *cable-access television*

Barnaby's

Cable car

cable car *n.* **1. CABIN SUSPENDED FROM OVERHEAD CABLE** a compartment or cabin suspended from an overhead cable, used to transport passengers up and down steep hills or across valleys **2. CABLE RAILWAY CAR** a car on a cable railway

cablecast /káyb'l kaast/ *n.* a broadcast over a cable television network [Late 20thC. Coined from CABLE + '-cast' from BROADCAST.] —**cablecaster** *n.* —**cablecasting** *n.*

cablegram /káyb'l gram/ *n.* = **cable**

cable-laid *adj.* used to describe thick ropes made of three thinner ropes, each with three strands, twisted together anticlockwise

cable modem *n.* a modem that connects a computer with the cable television network for high-speed data communications

cable railway *n.* a hillside railway consisting of a track along which cars are pulled by a moving cable that is operated by a stationary engine

cable release *n.* a cable fitted with a control button and attached to a camera in order to take photographs without shaking the camera, e.g. on long exposures

cable-stayed bridge *n.* a suspension bridge with the cables that support the deck connected directly to the bridge's piers rather than to suspenders

cable stitch *n.* a knitting stitch that produces a pattern resembling twisted rope

cablet /káyblət/ *n.* a cable-laid rope that has a circumference of less than 25 cm/10 in

cable television /káyb'l télevizh'n/, **cablevision** /káyb'l vizh'n/, **cable TV** *n.* a television system in which signals are sent to a central antenna and then transmitted by cable to subscribers

cableway /káyb'l way/ *n.* any transportation system consisting of an overhead cable used for transporting suspended cars or containers

cabochon /kábbə shon/ *n.* **1. ROUND GEM** a highly polished rounded unfaceted gem **2. ROUNDED GEM-CUTTING** the gem-cutting style that results in a cabochon ■ *adj., adv.* **ROUND** in the cabochon style [Mid-16thC. From French, literally 'little head', from Old French *caboche* 'head' (source of English *cabbage*); from the size and shape of such gems.]

Caboclo /kə bókloo, -lō/, **caboclo** *n.* sb, especially a Brazilian, who is partially or entirely descended from the peoples who were the original inhabitants of Brazil [Early 19thC. Via Brazilian Portuguese from, perhaps, Tupi *Kaa-boc* 'copper-coloured one'.]

caboodle /kə bóod'l/ *n.* a lot of things, or a group of things or people (*informal*) ○ *the whole kit and caboodle* [Late 19thC. Probably an arbitrary alteration of BOODLE from Dutch *boedel* 'goods, property'.]

Caboolture /kə bóolchər/ town in southeastern Queensland, Australia, north of the city of Brisbane. It is a fruit-growing and dairy farming centre. Population: 17,571 (1996).

caboose /kə bóoss/ *n.* **1.** *US, Can* RAIL **GUARD'S VAN** the guard's van on a freight train, with eating and sleeping facilities for the train crew. Most freight trains no longer have a caboose. **2.** NAUT **SHIP'S GALLEY** the galley of a ship (*archaic*) [Mid-18thC. From Dutch *cabuyse*, of unknown origin.]

Cabot /kábbət/, **John** (1450?–99?) Italian explorer. He made the first recorded contact (1497) with North America after the Vikings. Born **Giovanni Caboto**

Cabot, Sebastian (1476?–1557) Italian-born British navigator and cartographer. He made expeditions to North and South America (1508–09, 1525–28) for Spain and England and published a world map (1544).

cabotage /kábbə taazh, -tij/ *n.* **1.** SHIPPING **NATIONAL SHIPPING** trade, shipping, or navigation that takes place in coastal waters within the boundaries of a single country **2.** AIR **INTERNAL AIR TRAFFIC** the right of a country to operate internal traffic, especially air traffic, using its own carriers and not those of other countries [Mid-19thC. From French, from *caboter* 'to coast along', from Spanish *cabo* 'cape, headland', from, ultimately, Latin *caput* 'head' (source of English *cape*).]

Cabral /kə bráal/, **Pedro Álvares** (1460?–1526?) Portuguese explorer. He was the first European to visit Bahia, Brazil, and declared it a Portuguese territory.

cabretta /kə bréttə/ *n.* a type of soft leather obtained from the skins of certain South American and African sheep and used mainly for making gloves and shoes [Early 20thC. Coined from Spanish *cabra* 'female goat' (from Latin *capra*) + Italian *-etta* 'little'.]

cabrilla /kə bríllə/ (*plural* **-las** *or* **-la**) *n.* a sea bass that lives in warm coastal waters, especially in the Mediterranean and off the Californian coast. Genera: *Epinephelus* and *Paralabrax*. [Mid-19thC. From Spanish, literally 'little female goat', from *cabra* (see CABRETTA).]

cabriole /kábbri ōl/ *n.* **1.** FURNITURE **FURNITURE LEG** a curving furniture leg tapering into a decorative foot that is often carved to look like an animal's paw, popular in the early 18th century and used in Chippendale furniture **2.** BALLET **BALLET MOVEMENT** a ballet movement in which the dancer leaps into the air with one leg outstretched sideways and the other beating against it [Late 18thC. From French 'leap', from *cabrioler*, a variant of *caprioler* 'to caper'.]

cabriolet /kábbri ə láy/ *n.* **1.** CARS **CONVERTIBLE CAR** a two-door convertible car ○ *She brought a new red cabriolet last week.* **2.** TRANSP **TWO-SEATER CARRIAGE** a two-wheeled, two-seater, horse-drawn carriage with a folding roof [Mid-18thC. From French, from *cabrioler* (see CABRIOLE), because of the bouncing motion of a horse-drawn vehicle.]

cabstand /káb stand/ *n.* *US* = **taxi stand**

cac- *prefix.* = **caco-** (*used before vowels*)

cacao /kə kków, kə káy ō, kə káa ō/ (*plural* **-os** *or* **-o**) *n.* **1. COCOA TREE** a tropical American evergreen tree with small yellowish flowers and fleshy pods containing seeds that are the source of cocoa and chocolate. Latin name: *Theobroma cacao*. **2. SEEDS OF CACAO TREE** the dried fatty seeds of the cacao tree, from which cocoa, chocolate, and other foods and products are derived **3. cacao, cacao butter** = **cocoa butter** [Mid-16thC. Via Spanish from Nahuatl *cacauatl*, from *uatl* 'tree'.]

cacao bean *n.* = **cocoa bean**

cacciatore /káchə táwri/ *adj.* cooked with mushrooms, tomatoes, and herbs (*usually used after a noun*) ○ *chicken cacciatore* [Mid-20thC. From Italian, literally 'hunter'; from its original use as a sauce for game.]

cachaca /kə sháassə/ *n.* a Brazilian rum made from sugarcane

cachalot /káshə lot/ *n.* = **sperm whale** [Mid-18thC. Via French from Spanish or Portuguese *cachalote*, perhaps from *cachola* 'big head'.]

cache /kash/ *n.* **1. HIDDEN SUPPLY** a hidden store of things, especially weapons or valuables **2. SECRET PLACE FOR HIDING THINGS** a secret place where a store of things is kept hidden **3.** COMPUT MEMORY FOR FREQUENTLY USED DATA an area of high-speed computer memory used for the temporary storage of frequently used data to allow faster access ■ *vt.* (**caches, caching, cached**) **1.** HIDE SUPPLY OF THINGS to store a hidden supply of things, especially weapons or valuables, in a secret place **2.** COMPUT HOLD DATA IN CACHE to store data in a cache [Late 18thC. From French, from *cacher* (see CACHET).]

cachectic /kə kéktik, ka-/ *adj.* MED affected by or relating to cachexia [Early 17thC. Via French *cachectique* or Latin *cachecticus* from Greek *kakhektikos* (see CACHEXIA).]

cache memory *n.* = **cache**

cachepot /kásh pō, -pot/ *n.* a decorative container for a flowerpot [Late 19thC. From French, literally 'hide pot'.]

cachet /káshay/ *n.* **1.** QUALITY THAT ATTRACTS ADMIRATION a quality of distinction and style that people admire and approve of **2.** OFFICIAL MARK an official seal or stamp on a letter or other document **3.** STAMPS COMMEMORATIVE POSTMARK a commemorative mark stamped on mail to mark a particular event **4.** STAMPS COLLECTOR'S MARK a small mark made on the back of a postage stamp by a stamp collector **5.** PHARM EDIBLE MEDICINE SACHET an edible hollow case formerly used by pharmacists to enclose unpleasant-tasting medicine in order to make it more palatable [Early 17thC. From French, 'stamp, distinguishing mark', from Old French *cacher* 'to press' (see CACHE).]

cachexia /kə kéksi ə, ka-/ *n.* a condition marked by loss of appetite, weight loss, muscle wastage, and general mental and physical debilitation, caused by chronic disease [Mid-16thC. Via French *cachexie* or late Latin *cachexia* from Greek *kakhexia*, from *kakos* 'bad' + *hexis* 'habit'.]

cachinnate /káki nayt/ (**-nates, -nating, -nated**) *vi.* to laugh convulsively and loudly (*literary*) [Early 19thC. From Latin *cacchinat-*, past participle stem of *cachinnare*, an imitation of the sound.] —**cachinnation** *n.* —**cachinnator** *n.*

cachou /ka shoo, káshoo/ *n.* **1.** BAD-BREATH SWEET a perfumed pastille or lozenge taken to sweeten the breath **2.** = **catechu** [Late 16thC. Via French from, ultimately, Malayalam *kaccu*.]

cachucha /kə choochə/ *n.* **1.** DANCE CASTANET DANCE a lively Andalusian dance for a solo dancer with castanets **2.** MUSIC MUSIC FOR CACHUCHA a piece of music that accompanies the cachucha, in 3/4 time [Mid-19thC. From Spanish.]

cacique /kə seek/ *n.* **1.** HIST NATIVE AMERICAN CHIEF a Native American chief in Latin America during colonial times **2.** POL POLITICAL LEADER a local political boss, especially in Latin America or Spain **3.** BIRDS TROPICAL AMERICAN SONGBIRD a boldly coloured tropical blackbird of Central and South America that feeds on fruit and insects. It is gregarious and nests, roosts, and feeds in colonies. Genus: *Cacicus*. [Mid-16thC. Via Spanish or French from Taino.]

cack-handed /kák hándid/ *adj.* **1.** CLUMSY clumsy (*informal*) **2.** LEFT-HANDED naturally left-handed (*regional offensive*) [Mid-19thC. Origin uncertain: perhaps from Old Norse *keikr* 'bent backwards'.] —**cack-handedness** *n.*

cackle /kák'l/ *v.* (**-les, -ling, -led**) **1.** *vi.* LAUGH HARSHLY AND SHRILLY to laugh a harsh high-pitched malicious laugh, often suggesting pleasure at others' misfortune or glee in your own good fortune **2.** *vt.* SAY STH WITH HARSH SHRILL LAUGH to say sth with a malicious high-pitched laugh **3.** *vi.* MAKE SQUAWKING NOISE to squawk shrilly, especially after laying an egg (*refers to hens*) ■ *n.* MALICIOUS LAUGH a high-pitched malicious laugh or tone of voice [12thC. From Middle Low German or Middle Dutch *kākel(e)n*, of imitative origin.] —**cackler** *n.*

caco- *prefix.* bad ○ *cacology* [From Greek *kakos* (source of English *cacophony*)]

cacodemon /kákə deemən/, **cacodaemon** *n.* an evil spirit (*archaic*) [Late 16thC. From Greek *kakodaimōn*.]

cacodyl /kákə dīl, -/ *n.* a poisonous oily flammable liquid that contains arsenic and has an unpleasant garlicky smell. Formula: $C_4H_{12}As_2$. [Mid-19thC. Coined from Greek *kakodes*, literally 'bad smelling' + -YL.] —**cacodylic** /kákə díllik/ *adj.*

cacography /kə kóggrəfi, ka-/ *n.* (*formal*) **1.** BAD HANDWRITING poor handwriting **2.** MISSPELLING incorrect spelling —**cacographic** /kákə gráffik/ *adj.* —**cacographical** /-gráffik'l/ *adj.*

cacology /kə kólləji/ *n.* poor use or choice of words when speaking (*formal*) [Late 18thC. From Greek *kakologia* 'blame', literally 'bad speech'.] —**cacological** /kákə lójjik'l/ *adj.*

cacomistle /kákə miss'l/, **cacomixle** /-miks'l/ *n.* a carnivorous mammal resembling the cat, found in the southwestern United States and Mexico, with brown fur and a long black-banded tail. It is related to but smaller than the raccoon. Latin name: *Bassariscus astutus*. [Mid-19thC. Via American Spanish *cacomixtle* from Nahuatl *tlacomiztli*, literally 'half mountain lion'.]

caconym /kákə nim/ *n.* the wrong name for sth, especially in the classification of plants or animals (*formal*) [Late 19thC. Coined from CACO- 'bad' + -ONYM 'name'.] —**caconymy** /kə kónnəmi/ *n.*

cacophonous /kə kóffənəss/ *adj.* sounding loud, jarring, and unpleasant [Late 18thC. Formed from Greek *kakophōnos* 'bad-sounding'.] —**cacophonously** *adv.*

cacophony /kə kóffəni/ (*plural* **-nies**) *n.* **1.** UNPLEASANT NOISE an unpleasant combination of loud, often jarring, sounds **2.** USE OF JARRING SOUNDS the use of harsh unpleasant sounds in language, e.g. for literary effect [Mid-17thC. Via French from Greek *kakophōnia*, from *kakophōnos* (see CACOPHONOUS).]

Cactus

cactus /káktəs/ *n.* (*plural* **-ti** /-tī/ *or* **-tuses** *or* **-tus**) SPIKY DESERT PLANT a plant belonging to a large family of spiny leafless plants with fleshy stems and branches, found in dry desert regions of the Americas. Many varieties produce brightly coloured flowers. Family: Cactaceae. ■ *adj.* (*slang*) **1.** BROKEN DOWN broken down **2.** *ANZ* DRUNK drunk [Mid-18thC. Via Latin, 'cardoon', from Greek *kaktos*, of unknown origin.] —**cactaceous** /kak táyshəss/ *adj.*

cacuminal /kə kyoomin'l, ka-/ *n.*, *adj.* = **retroflex** [Mid-19thC. Formed from Latin *cacuminare* 'to make pointed', from *cacumen* 'point, summit'.]

cad /kad/ *n.* a man who does not behave as a gentleman should, especially towards a woman (*dated*) [Mid-19thC. Shortening of CADDIE 'errand-boy'. The meaning apparently evolved from the word's use at Oxford University for 'townsperson', via 'a man of inferior social and moral stature'.] —**caddish** *adj.* —**caddishly** *adv.* —**caddishness** *n.*

CAD /kad/ *abbr.* computer-aided design

cadaster /kə dástər/, **cadastre** *n.* an official register containing information on the value, extent, and ownership of land for the purposes of taxation [Late 18thC. Via French from, ultimately, Italian *catastico*, from Greek *katastikhon* 'list', from *kata stikhan* 'line by line'.] —**cadastral** /kə dástrəl/ *adj.*

cadaver /kə dávvər, -dáy-, -daa-/ *n.* a dead body, especially one that is to be dissected [14thC. From Latin, from *cadere* 'to fall, die' (source of English *cadence* and *accident*).] —**cadaveric** *adj.*

cadaverine /kə dávvə reen/ *n.* a thick toxic colourless liquid with an extremely unpleasant smell, produced when flesh rots

cadaverous /kə dávvərəss/ *adj.* **1.** EXTREMELY THIN thin to the point of resembling a skeleton or corpse **2.** PALE deathly pale (*literary*) **3.** OF CORPSES suggesting

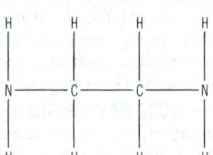

Cadaverine

death or corpses (*formal or literary*) —**cadaverously** *adv.* —**cadaverousness** *n.*

CADCAM /kád kam/ *abbr.* computer-aided design and manufacturing

caddice *n.* TEXTILES = **caddis**

caddice fly *n.* = **caddis fly**

caddice worm *n.* = **caddis worm**

caddie /káddi/, **caddy** *n.* (*plural* **-dies**) **1.** GOLFER'S ASSISTANT sb who carries a golfer's bag of clubs and assists in other ways, e.g. in judging distances and choosing clubs **2.** *Scotland* ERRAND BOY a messenger or errand boy (*archaic*) ■ *vi.* (**-dies, -dying, -died; -died**) BE GOLFER'S CADDIE to act as a caddie for a golfer [Late 18thC. Originally a Scots form of CADET. The main modern meaning 'golfer's porter' evolved from 'young member of the gentry who joins the army' via 'messenger boy'.]

caddis /káddiss/, **caddice** *n.* a type of coarse woollen fabric, braid, or yarn [Mid-16thC. Via Old French from Provençal, of unknown origin.]

caddis fly (*plural* **caddis flies** *or* **caddis fly**), **caddice fly** (*plural* **caddice flies** *or* **caddice fly**) *n.* an insect with four membranous wings, multi-jointed antennae, and larvae (**caddis worms**) that live in water. Order: Trichoptera. [*Caddis* perhaps after CADDIS 'fabric', because the larva makes a protective case from coarse silken material]

caddis worm, **caddice worm** *n.* a larva of a caddis fly. It lives in water inside a protective silken case that is covered with sand and debris. [See CADDIS FLY]

Caddo /káddō/ (*plural* **-do** *or* **-dos**) *n.* a member of a confederacy of Native Americans in central Oklahoma who formerly lived in the Red River area of Arkansas, Louisiana, and East Texas [Via American French from Caddo *kaduhdā-ču'*] —**Caddo** *adj.*

caddy[1] /káddi/ (*plural* **-dies**) *n.* a small box or tin used for storing sth, especially tea [Late 18thC. Alteration of *catty*, from Malay *kati*, a standard measure for tea set by the East India Company.]

caddy[2] *n.*, *vi.* = **caddie**

cade[1] /kayd/ *n.* a juniper tree found in Southern Europe and the Mediterranean, whose wood yields a tarry oil (**cade oil**) used to treat skin conditions. Latin name: *Juniperus oxycedrus*. [Late 16thC. Via French from medieval Latin *catanus*, perhaps ultimately from Gaulish.]

cade[2] /kayd/ *adj.* used to describe animals that have been abandoned by their mother and reared by humans [14thC. Of unknown origin.]

Cade /kayd/, **Jack** (?–1450) Irish-born English rebel leader. He led an insurrection against Henry VI and marched on London. Tricked with promises of a pardon, he was killed while fleeing.

-cade *suffix.* procession ○ *motorcade* [From CAVALCADE]

cadelle /kə dél/ *n.* a small black beetle that feeds on grain and other stored foods, found throughout the world. Latin name: *Tenebroides mauritanicus*. [Mid-19thC. Via French from, ultimately, Latin *cadellus* 'little dog'.]

cadence /káyd'nss/ *n.* **1.** RHYTHM the beat or measure of sth that follows a set rhythm, e.g. a dance or a march **2.** FALLING TONE a drop in the pitch of the voice, e.g. at the end of a sentence **3.** INTONATION the way in which the voice rises and falls in pitch when sb is speaking **4.** RHYTHM IN LANGUAGE the way in which poetry or prose flows according to a rhythm **5.** MUSIC

MUSICAL SEQUENCE a short sequence of notes that marks the end of a piece or passage of music. In tonal music, a cadence brings about a harmonic resolution. [14thC. Via Old French, 'rhythm' from Italian *cadenza*, literally 'falling away'. Ultimately from Latin *cadent-*, the present participle stem of *cadere* 'to fall' *accident*, *cadaver*, and *case*.] —**cadenced** *adj.*

------ **WORD KEY: ORIGIN** ------

The Latin word *cadere*, from which **cadence** is derived, meaning 'to fall', is also the source of English *accident*, *cadaver*, *case*, *cheat*, *coincide*, *decay*, *deciduous*, *incident*, *occasion*, and *Occident*.

cadency /káyd'nssi/ (*plural* **-cies**) *n.* **1. LINE OF DESCENT FROM YOUNGER MEMBER** a genealogical line that descends from a younger member of a family **2. CADENCE** a cadence (*archaic*)

cadent /káyd'nt/ *adj.* **1. RHYTHMIC** with a noticeable rhythm or cadence (*literary*) **2. FALLING** falling (*archaic literary*) [Early 17thC. From Latin *cadent-*; 'falling', the present participle stem of *cadere* (see CADENCE).]

cadential /kə dénsh'l/ *adj.* **1. OF RHYTHM** relating to rhythm or a rhythmical cadence **2. MUSIC OF CADENZAS** relating to cadenzas or a musical cadence

cadenza /kə dénzə/ *n.* an elaborate solo passage of virtuoso singing or playing near the end of a section or piece of music, sometimes improvised by the soloist [Mid-18thC. From Italian (see CADENCE).]

cadet /kə dét/ *n.* **1. MILITARY TRAINEE** a young man or woman who is training to become a full member of the armed forces or the police force, especially as an officer **2. YOUNG PERSON IN UNIFORMED ORGANIZATION** sb of school age who is a member of a uniformed organization offering military training **3. YOUNGER SON** a younger son or brother (*dated*) **4. ENGLISH GENTLEMAN TRAINEE** in England in former times, a gentleman, often a younger son, who entered the army without a commission, intending to work his way up to officer rank [Early 17thC. From French, originally Gascon dialect *capdet* 'younger son' (because noble Gascon families traditionally sent these into the army), literally 'chief', from, ultimately, Latin *caput* 'head' (see CAPITAL).] —**cadetship** *n.*

cadge /kaj/ (**cadges**, **cadging**, **cadged**) *vti.* to scrounge or beg sth from sb (*informal*) [Early 17thC. Back-formation from CADGER.] —**cadger** *n.*

cadger /kájjər/ *n.* sb who habitually takes or borrows things or asks for favours from people (*informal*) [15thC. Origin unknown. Originally in the sense 'itinerant peddler', the modern meaning evolved via 'beggar, opportunist'.]

cadi /káadi, káydi/, **qadi** *n.* a minor judge in a Muslim community where Islamic law is followed [Late 16thC. From Arabic *kādi*.]

Cádiz /kə diz/ capital of Cádiz Province and a major port on the autonomous region of Andalusia in southwestern Spain. Population: 154,511 (1995).

cadmium /kádmi əm/ *n.* a soft malleable toxic bluish-white metallic chemical element found in zinc, copper, and lead ores. The metal is used in alloys, in electroplating, in nuclear reactors, and in dental amalgams, and its compounds are used as pigments and in electronics. Symbol **Cd** [Early 19thC. Formed from Latin *cadmia* 'calamine, zinc ore' (source of English *calamine*), from Greek *kadm(e)ia* 'earth of Cadmus' see CADMUS, so-called because the substance came originally from Thebes.]

cadmium sulphide *n.* an orange or yellowish-brown poisonous salt used in paints as a pigment, in medicine, and in electronic parts. Formula: CdS.

Cadmus /kádməss/ *n.* in Greek mythology, a prince who slew a dragon and planted its teeth in the ground, from which armed men sprouted and fought each other. With the five survivors Cadmus founded Thebes.

cadre /kaadər, káy-/ *n.* **1. MIL MILITARY UNIT** a group of experienced professionals who are at the core of a military organization who are able to train new recruits and expand the operations of the unit **2. POL CORE OF ACTIVISTS** a core group of political activists or revolutionaries **3. CORE GROUP** a controlling or representative group at the centre of an organization **4. SMALL GROUP OF TEAM-SPIRITED PEOPLE** a tightly knit,

highly trained group of people **5. MEMBER OF CADRE** a member of a cadre [Mid-19thC. Via French, 'frame' from Italian *quadro* 'framework', from Latin *quadrum* 'square'.]

Caduceus

caduceus /kə dyoóssi əss, -dyoóshi-/ (*plural* **-i** /-I/) *n.* **1. MYTHOL HERMES' STAFF** in classical mythology, a winged staff entwined with two serpents, the symbol of Hermes or Mercury. It is also associated with the Greek god of healing, Asclepius. **2. MED MEDICAL INSIGNIA** a symbol of various medical organizations that is modelled on Hermes' caduceus. ◊ **staff of Aesculapius** [Late 16thC. Via Latin from Doric Greek *karuk(e)ion*, from *kērux* 'herald'.] —**caducean** *adj.*

caducity /kə dyoóssəti/ *n.* (*literary*) **1. INFIRMITY** the frailty or senility that sometimes characterizes old age **2. PERISHABLENESS** the quality of being perishable or impermanent [Mid-18thC. From French *caducité*, from *caduc* 'transitory', from Latin *caducus* (see CADUCOUS).]

caducous /kə dyoókəss/ *adj.* used to describe a plant or animal part that drops off or is shed in the early stages of development, as certain leaves or flower parts do [Late-18thC. Formed from Latin *caducus* 'liable to fall'(see CADUCITY).]

CAE *abbr.* computer-aided engineering

caeca plural of **caecum**

caecilian /see sílli ən/ *n.* a limbless tropical amphibian that looks like an earthworm, has small or no eyes, and burrows in the soil. Order: Gymnophiona. [Late 19thC. Formed from modern Latin *Caecilia*, genus name, from Latin *caecilia* 'slow-worm'.]

caecum /seékəm/ (*plural* **-ca**) *n.* the pouch in which the large intestine begins, which is open at one end [Early 18thC. From Latin (*intestinum*) *caecum* 'blind (gut)', from *caecus* 'blind'.] —**caecal** *adj.* —**caecally** *adv.*

Caedmon /kádmən/ (650?–680?) English monk and poet. He wrote a hymn on the Creation written down by Bede that is the earliest Christian poem in Old English.

Caelum /seéləm/ *n.* a constellation in the sky of the southern hemisphere near Columba and Eridanus [From Latin *caelum* 'chisel', from its shape]

Caen /koN/ capital of Calvados Department in the Basse-Normandie Region, in northwestern France. It was largely rebuilt after World War II. Population: 115,624 (1990).

caenogenesis, **cainogenesis** *n.* BIOL the development by an embryo, fetus, or larva of organs or body parts that are lost in adult life

Caerleon /kaar lée ən/ town in Newport county borough, southeastern Wales. It contains the remains of the Roman fortress of Isca. Population: 8,931 (1991).

Caernarvon /kər náarv'n/ walled town on the Menai Strait, in Ceredigion, Wales. Edward II, the first Prince of Wales, was born in Caernarvon Castle. Population: 9,695 (1991).

Caernarvonshire /kər náarv'nshər/ former county of Wales, abolished 1974

caerphilly /kər fílli, kair-/ *n.* a pale crumbly cheese made in Wales [Early 20thC. Named after CAERPHILLY, where it was originally made.]

Caerphilly /kər fílli, kair-/ town in the county of Mid Glamorgan in southeastern Wales, best known for the cheese that bears its name. Population: 42,736 (1986).

caeruloplasmin *n.* = ceruloplasmin

Caesar /seézər/ *n.* **1. TITLE OF ROMAN EMPERORS** the title given to a Roman emperor, especially from the reign of Augustus to that of Hadrian **2. Caesar, caesar TYRANT** sb such as a ruler or leader who acts like a dictator [Old English *casere*. From a prehistoric Germanic word (source also of German *Kaiser* and Russian *tsar*), ultimately from Latin *Caesar*, the family name of Julius Caesar, of Etruscan origin.]

Caesar /seézər/, **Gaius Julius** (100–44 BC) Roman general and statesman who emerged from civil war as dictator of Rome and was assassinated by republican conspirators. Full name **Gaius Julius Caesar**

Caesarea /seézə reé ə/ ancient seaport on the coast of Samaria, and the Roman capital of Palestine, situated approximately 35 km/22 mi. south of present-day Haifa, Israel

Caesarean /si záiri ən/, **Caesarian** *adj.* **1. OF OR LIKE CAESAR OR CAESARS** referring to or resembling Julius Caesar or the Caesars in general **2. MED OF CAESARIAN SECTION** relating to or involving a Caesarian section ■ *n.* MED = **Caesarian section**

Caesarean section *n.* an operation to deliver a baby by cutting through the mother's abdominal wall and womb. US term **cesarean section** [From the belief that Julius CAESAR was born this way]

caesar salad *n.* a salad made with lettuce, croutons, parmesan cheese, and anchovies, with an egg-based dressing [Named after *Caesar* Gardini, a restaurant proprietor in Tijuana, Mexico, who is said to have invented it]

caesium /seézi əm/ *n.* a rare silver-white chemical element of the alkali metals group that is the most reactive of the elements and is used in photoelectric cells. Symbol **Cs**

caesium clock *n.* TIME a type of clock in which caesium atoms are stimulated by an alternating magnetic field. A precise time is determined when the frequencies of atoms and the field match.

caesura /si zyoórə/ (*plural* **-ras** *or* **-rae** /-ree/), **cesura** (*plural* **-ras** *or* **-rae**) *n.* **1. POETRY PAUSE IN LINE OF VERSE** a pause in a line of poetry, especially to allow its sense to be made clear or to follow the rhythms of natural speech, often near the middle of the line **2. POETRY BREAK IN LINE OF VERSE** in classical poetry, especially Greek, a break between two words that are part of the same unit of rhythm (**foot**), usually near the middle of the line **3. PAUSE** a pause or break in speech or conversation (*formal*) **4. MUSIC MUSICAL INTERRUPTION** a brief interruption in a musical phrase [Mid-16thC. From Latin, 'cut', from *caedere* 'to cut' (source of English *concise*). The underlying idea is of cutting the line in two.] —**caesural** *adj.* —**caesuric** *adj.*

------ **WORD KEY: ORIGIN** ------

The Latin word *caedere*, meaning 'to cut', from which **caesura** is derived, is also the source of English *chisel*, *concise*, *excise*, *incise*, and *scissors*.

CAF *abbr.* cost and freight

café /káffay/ *n.* a small informal restaurant serving drinks, snacks, and often light meals [Early 19thC. Via French, 'coffee(-house)', from, ultimately, Turkish *kahveh* 'coffee' or Arabic *qahwah* 'coffee, wine' (source of English *coffee*).]

café au lait /káffay ō láy/ *n.* (*plural* **café au laits** /káffay ō láy/ *or* **cafés au lait**) **1. COFFEE WITH MILK** strong coffee with hot milk **2. COLOURS PALE BROWN COLOUR** a pale brown colour, like that of milky coffee ■ *adj.* COLOURS OF PALE BROWN COLOUR of a pale brown colour, like milky coffee [Mid-18thC. From French, literally 'coffee with milk'.]

café latte /káffay láttay/ (*plural* **café lattes** *or* **cafés latte**) *n.* = **latte**

café noir /káffay nwaár/ (*plural* **cafés noirs** /káffay nwaár/) *n.* coffee without milk or cream [From French, literally 'black coffee']

café society *n.* people such as celebrities and media people who attend fashionable events and visit fashionable restaurants, clubs, and resorts

cafeteria /káffə teéri ə/ *n.* a self-service restaurant or coffee bar, especially one in a workplace or department store [Mid-19thC. From American Spanish, formed from *café* 'coffee'.]

cafetière /káffə tyáir, -teèr/ n. a coffee pot fitted with a plunger that is used to push the floating coffee grounds to the bottom of the pot when the coffee is ready to drink. US term **French press pot** [Mid-19thC. From French, formed from *café* (see CAFÉ).]

caff /kaf/ n. a café, especially an old-fashioned British one serving tea and fried breakfasts in unstylish surroundings (*informal*) [Mid-20thC. Anglicization of French *café* (see CAFÉ).]

caffeinated /káffi naytid/ adj. containing caffeine

caffeine /káffeen, káffi een/, **caffein** n. a stimulant found in coffee, tea, the cola nuts used to make soft drinks, and cocoa. It is widely used in medicine, e.g. in tonic medicines and painkillers. [Mid-19thC. From French, formed from *café* 'coffee'.]

caffeinism /káffee nizzəm, káffi een-/ n. a condition caused by an excessive amount of caffeine in the body, resulting in symptoms of high blood pressure, diarrhoea, palpitations, accelerated breathing, and insomnia

caffè latte /káffay láttay/ n. = **latte**

caftan n. = **kaftan**

cag /kag/ n. a cagoule (*informal*) [Late 20thC. Shortening.]

cage /kayj/ n. **1.** ANIMAL ENCLOSURE an enclosure, usually made from bars or wire, in which to keep animals or birds **2.** ENCLOSING OR PROTECTING WIRE-MESH STRUCTURE a wire-mesh structure used to protect or enclose sth **3.** LIFT PLATFORM the part of a lift that people stand in, particularly one in a lift that goes down a mine shaft **4.** BASEBALL SCREEN TO STOP BALLS in baseball, a screen behind home plate that stops thrown or fouled balls **5.** BASKETBALL BASKET the basket in the game of basketball (*informal*) **6.** ICE HOCKEY HOCKEY GOAL the goal in ice hockey (*informal*) **7.** US TEMPORARY PRISON CELL a barred room or strong mesh enclosure for confining prisoners temporarily, e.g. in a police station ■ vt. (**cages, caging, caged**) PUT PERSON OR ANIMAL IN CAGE to place or keep a person or animal in a cage [12thC. Via Old French from Latin *cavea* 'enclosure, dungeon' (source also of English *jail*).] —**caged** adj. ◇ **rattle sb's cage** to annoy or upset sb deliberately ○ *'We kept after him and kept after him and finally rattled his cage a little bit, he said'.* (Cincinnati Post; 1997)

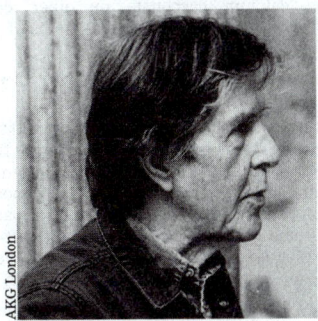
AKG London
John Cage

Cage /kayj/, **John** (1912–92) US composer. His avant-garde music includes *4'33"* (1952), in which musicians sit silently with their instruments. Full name **John Milton Cage, Jr.**

Cage, Nicholas (*b.* 1964) US actor. He frequently plays offbeat film characters such as his Academy Award-winning role in *Leaving Las Vegas* (1995).

cageling /káyj ling/ n. a bird that is kept as a pet in a cage (*archaic or literary*)

cagey /káyji/ (**-gier, -giest**), **cagy** (**-gier, -giest**) adj. cautious and secretive rather than open, honest, or direct (*informal*) [Late 19thC. Origin uncertain: perhaps formed from CAGE, the underlying idea being of keeping your intentions 'locked away' in secret.] —**cagily** adv. —**caginess** n.

cagmag /kág mag/ adj. POORLY DONE poorly done, or not properly finished (*regional*) ■ vi. (**-mags, -magging, -magged**) CHAT IDLY to chat idly (*regional*) [Mid-18thC. Origin unknown.]

James Cagney

Cagney /kágni/, **James** (1904–86) US film actor, known for both comic and tough gangster roles. Full name **James Francis Cagney**

cagoule /kə goól, ka-/ n. a lightweight hooded waterproof top that often folds up small and can be carried easily [Mid-20thC. Via French, literally 'cowl', from Latin *cucullus* 'cap, hood' (source of English *cowl*).]

cahier /kaá yay/ n. **1.** NOTEBOOK a notebook **2.** WRITTEN REPORT a written report of a meeting, e.g. of a parliamentary group [Late 18thC. Via French from Latin *quaternis* 'set of four', because it was originally used for a pamphlet made from four folded sheets of paper, from *quattuor* 'four'.]

Cahokia Mounds /kə hóki ə-/ group of prehistoric Native American mounds, including the largest prehistoric earthwork in the United States, situated 13 km/8 mi. northeast of East St Louis, Missouri

cahoots /kə hoóts/ [Early 19thC. Origin uncertain: perhaps from French *cahute* 'cabin', because partners sharing a cabin would have an opportunity to plot together.] ◇ **be in cahoots (with sb)** to have a secret agreement with sb, especially to do sth dishonest or illegal (*informal*)

CAI abbr. computer-aided instruction

Caiaphas /kí ə fass/ (*fl.* AD18–37) Jewish high priest. He presided over the trial of Jesus Christ.

Caicos Islands /káykəss-/ ▶ **Turks and Caicos Islands**

caiman /káymən/ (*plural* **-mans** *or* **-man**), **cayman** (*plural* **-mans** *or* **-man**) n. a tropical American reptile related to the alligator. It looks like a much smaller, slimmer version of the alligator with a proportionally longer tail. Genus: *Caiman*. [Late 16thC. Via Spanish *caimán* from Carib *caymán*.]

Cain /kayn/ n. in the Bible, the elder son of Adam and Eve, who killed his brother Abel (Genesis 4) ◇ **raise Cain** to cause a noisy disturbance

Caine /kayn/, **Michael** (*b.* 1933) British actor. His films include *Zulu* (1963) and *Hannah and her Sisters* (1986), for which he won an Oscar. Real name **Maurice Joseph Micklewhite**

-caine suffix. a synthetic alkaloid anaesthetic ○ *phenacaine* [From COCAINE]

cainogenesis n. = **caenogenesis**

Cainozoic adj., n. = **Cenozoic**

Caïque

caïque /kī eék, kaa-/ n. **1.** TURKISH ROWING BOAT a long narrow rowing boat used in the waters around Turkey **2.** SMALL GREEK BOAT any small rowing, sailing, or motor boat used in the Greek Islands and the eastern Mediterranean [Early 17thC. Via French from, ultimately, Turkish *kayik*.]

cairn /kairn/ n. **1.** PILE OF STONES USED AS MARKER a pile of stones set on a hill or mountain to mark a spot for walkers and climbers, or as a memorial to sb who died there **2.** = **Cairn terrier** [Mid-16thC. From Gaelic *carn* 'heap of stones'. Ultimately from an Indo-European base that is also the ancestor of English *cornet* and *horn*.] —**cairned** adj.

cairngorm /káirn gawrm/, **cairngorm stone** n. a variety of quartz, usually smoky yellow, grey, or brown in colour, found in Scotland and used in making jewellery [Late 18thC. Named after the Cairngorm Mountains, where it is found.]

Cairngorm Mountains, **Cairngorms** range of the Grampian Mountains in northeastern Scotland. Its highest peak is Ben Macdhui, 1,309 m/4,296 ft.

Cairns /kairnz/ coastal city and major tourist resort in northeastern Queensland. It is the main gateway to the northern Great Barrier Reef. Population: 92,273 (1996).

Cairn terrier n. a small terrier with a shaggy coat of rough hair, originally bred in Scotland

Cairo /kí rō/ capital of Egypt and Africa's largest city. It is situated on the River Nile, at the southern end of the Nile delta. Population: 6,800,000 (1992).

caisse populaire /késs póppyoŏ láir/ (*plural* **caisses populaires** /késs póppyoŏ láir/) n. *Quebec* in Quebec and other French-speaking parts of Canada, a financial institution resembling a credit union [From French]

caisson /káyss'n, kə soón/ n. **1.** CONSTR UNDERWATER WORK CHAMBER a bottomless watertight chamber filled with compressed air, used as a base from which construction work is carried out underwater **2.** INSUR FLOAT TO RAISE SHIPS a hollow structure attached to a sunken object, e.g. a wrecked ship, then pumped full of air until it acts as a float, raising the object to the surface **3.** CIV ENG, INSUR WATER BLOCK a floating watertight structure used to keep water from entering a dry dock, canal lock, or basin **4.** ARMS AMMUNITION BOX a large container for ammunition **5.** MIL HORSE-DRAWN VEHICLE a two-wheeled horse-drawn vehicle, formerly used to carry ammunition but now often used to carry coffins at state or military funerals **6.** BOX OF EXPLOSIVES USED AS MINE a box of explosives, formerly used as a land mine **7.** ARCHIT = **coffer** [Late 17thC. Via French from, ultimately, Italian *cassone* 'large box', from *cassa* 'box', from Latin *capsa* (source of English *case* and *capsule*).]

caisson disease n. = **decompression sickness**

Caithness /káyth ness, kayth néss/ former county of northeastern Scotland, abolished 1973. It is now part of the Highland unitary authority.

caitiff /káytif/ n. COWARD a coward (*archaic*) ■ adj. COWARDLY cowardly and despicable (*archaic*) [13thC. Via Old French *caitif* 'captive, wretched person' from Latin *captivus* (source of English *captive*) from, ultimately, *capere* 'to take'.]

cajole /kə jól/ (**-joles, -joling, -joled**) vti. to persuade sb to do sth by flattery or gentle but persistent argument [Mid-17thC. From French *cajoler*, of uncertain origin: perhaps a blend of Old French *cageoler* 'to chatter like a jay' and *gaioler* 'to lure into a cage'.] —**cajolement** n. —**cajoler** n. —**cajolery** n. —**cajolingly** adv.

Cajun /káyjən/ n. **1.** PEOPLES LOUISIANAN OF FRENCH DESCENT a native of Louisiana who is descended from the French colonists exiled from Acadia, Canada, in the 18th century **2.** LANG FRENCH DIALECT a dialect of French spoken in Louisiana that developed from the French spoken by 18th-century settlers who were expelled from Acadia, Canada **3.** MUSIC MUSIC MIXING BLUES AND FOLK the musical style, consisting of a mixture of blues and folk music, that originated among the Cajuns **4.** SB OF MIXED ANCESTRY a native of southern Alabama or southeastern Mississippi who is of mixed European, African-American, and Native American ancestry [Mid-19thC. Alteration of *Acadian* '(inhabitant) of Acadia', a former French colony in North America.] —**Cajun** adj.

cake /kayk/ n. **1.** BAKED SWEET FLOUR-BASED FOOD a baked sweet food usually made from flour, sugar, eggs, and other ingredients, baked either in a large block and served in slices, or in a size for individual servings **2.** SHAPED PORTION OF SAVOURY FOOD an individual portion of savoury food, shaped into a small round piece and cooked, often by frying or grilling **3. BLOCK OF STH** a solid block of sth, e.g. soap, ice, or chocolate **4. THICK LAYER** a thick layer of sth that has collected over a period of time **5. THING DIVIDED UP** sth, e.g. a fund of money, that is to be shared or divided up ○ *Everyone wants a slice of the cake.* ■ *v.* **(cakes, caking, caked) 1.** *vti.* **FORM CRUST ON STH** to form, or cover an object with, a thick layer of sth, especially dirt, grease, or grime ○ *My boots were caked with mud after I walked through the field.* **2.** *vi.* **FORM INTO A CAKE** to form into a solid mass [12thC. From Old Norse *kaka* 'flat round loaf'.] —**cakey** *adj.* ◇ **have your cake and eat it (too)** to try to enjoy the advantages of two things, each of which tends to make the other impossible

cakehole /káyk hōl/ *n.* sb's mouth (*slang*)

cakewalk /káyk wawk/ *n.* **1. COMPETITION BASED ON WALKING** an informal contest to music, with a cake as a prize for executing the most elaborate or amusing walking steps, popular among African Americans in the United States in the 19th century **2.** DANCE **STRUTTING DANCE** any kind of popular dancing with exaggeratedly elaborate or strutting steps **3.** MUSIC **MUSIC FOR CAKEWALK** a piece of music suitable for any kind of elaborate strutting dance **4. STH VERY EASY** sth that is very easy to do or to achieve (*informal*) ■ *vi.* **(-walks, -walking, -walked)** DANCE **DANCE WITH STRUTTING STEPS** to dance with exaggeratedly fancy strutting steps —**cakewalker** *n.*

Cal *abbr.* large calorie

CAL[1] *abbr.* **1.** TIME calendar **2.** MEASURE calibre

CAL[2] *abbr.* computer-assisted learning

Cal. *abbr.* California

Calabar bean /kállə baar-/ *n.* the dark-brown poisonous seed, used as a source of the drug physostigmine, of a tropical African climbing plant. Latin name: *Physostigma venenosum.* [Named after *Calabar*, a town and province in Nigeria]

calabash /kállə bash/ *n.* **1. TROPICAL AMERICAN EVERGREEN TREE** a tropical American evergreen tree with bell-shaped flowers and large round fruit. Latin name: *Crescentia cujete.* **2.** = **bottle gourd 3. FRUIT OF CALABASH PLANT** the large ball-shaped fruit of the calabash tree, or of the bottle gourd or some other gourd **4. GOURD USED AS CONTAINER** the hollowed-out dried shell of the calabash fruit or of the bottle gourd or some other gourd, used as a container [Mid-17thC. Via French *calabasse* from, ultimately, Persian *karbuz* 'melon'.]

Calabash /kállə bash/ *n.* a way of preparing food in the southeastern United States that involves deep-frying seafood and piling them up on serving plates [Origin uncertain: perhaps from *Calabash*, name of a town in North Carolina where the style was developed]

calabrese /kállə bráyzi, -breez/ *n.* a variety of green broccoli [Mid-20thC. From Italian, 'of Calabria', where it was developed.]

Calabria /kə lábbri ə/ region in southern Italy forming the 'toe' of the Italian peninsula. It includes the provinces of Cataranzo, Cosenza, and Reggio di Calabria. Capital: Catanzaro. Population: 2,076,128 (1995). Area: 15,080 sq. km/5,822 sq. mi.

caladium /kə láydi əm/ *n.* tropical American plant with white, green, red, or pink variegated leaves, widely grown as a pot plant. Genus: *Caladium.* [Mid-19thC. From modern Latin, formed from Malay *keladi.*]

Calais /kállay/ seaport on the English Channel in the Pas-de-Calais Department, Nord-Pas-de-Calais region, in northwestern France. The Calais-Dover route is the shortest crossing between France and the United Kingdom. Population: 101,768 (1990).

calalu /kálləloo/, **calaloo** *n. Carib* the leaves of various plants when used as salad, in soups, or cooked as greens [Mid-18thC. From American Spanish *calalú*, perhaps from, ultimately, an African source.]

calamanco /kállə máng kō/ *n.* a glossy woollen fabric with a checked pattern on one side [Late 16thC. Origin unknown.]

calamander /kállə mandər/ *n.* the hard black-and-brown striped wood of a number of Asian trees, used for making furniture [Early 19thC. From Sinhalese *kalumādirriya*, perhaps from *kalu* 'black' + English *coromandel* 'ebony'.]

calamari /kállə maári/ *npl.* squid served as food, especially in Mediterranean cuisine [Late 20thC. From Italian, plural of *calamaro* 'squid', via medieval Latin *calamarium* 'pen-case' (so called from the shape of the squid's internal shell) from Latin *calamus* 'reed pen' (see CALAMUS).]

calami plural of **calamus**

calamine /kállə mīn/ *n.* a pink powder made from zinc oxide and ferric oxide, used medicinally in lotions and creams to soothe irritated skin [Late 16thC. Via Old French from medieval Latin *calamina*, an alteration of Latin *cadmia* 'zinc ore' (see CADMIUM).]

calamint /kálləmint/ (*plural* **-mints** *or* **-mint**) *n.* a mint plant grown for its drooping white, pink, or purple flowers. Genera: *Satureja* and *Calamintha.* [14thC. Via Old French *calament* (perhaps influenced by English *mint*) from, ultimately, Greek *kalaminthē.*]

calamite /kállə mīt/ *n.* a prehistoric plant that grew in the Palaeozoic era, related to the horsetail. Genus: *Calamites.* [Mid-19thC. From modern Latin *calamites*, genus name, from Latin *calamus* (see CALAMUS).]

calamitous /kə lámmitəss/ *adj.* causing great trouble, tragedy, or disaster [Mid-16thC. Directly or via French *calamiteux* from Latin *calamitosus*, from *calamitas* (see CALAMITY).] —**calamitously** *adv.* —**calamitousness** *n.*

calamity /kə lámməti/ (*plural* **-ties**) *n.* **1. DISASTER** a disastrous situation or event (*often used ironically*) **2. DISTRESS** misery or distress resulting from a disastrous event (*archaic*) [14thC. Via Old French *calamité* from Latin *calamitas* 'disaster, defeat'. Originally used in English with the meaning 'adversity'.]

Library of Congress

Calamity Jane

Calamity Jane /kə lámməti jáyn/ (1852?–1903) US frontierswoman. She worked as a scout in the American West. Real name **Martha Jane Canary**

calamondin /kállə mundin/ *n.* **1. SMALL CITRUS TREE OF PHILIPPINES** a hybrid citrus tree native to the Philippines. Latin name: *Citrofortunella mitis.* **2. FRUIT OF CALAMONDIN** the small sour orange-yellow fruit of a calamondin tree [Early 20thC. From Tagalog *kalamunding.*]

calamus /kálləməss/ (*plural* **-mi** /-mī/) *n.* **1. ASIAN PALM** a tropical Asian palm tree, some species of which are used for rattan. Genus: *Calamus.* **2.** = **sweet flag 3. ROOT OF SWEET FLAG** the aromatic root of the sweet flag plant, the source of an aromatic oil used in perfumery **4. FEATHER SHAFT** the hollow shaft of a feather [14thC. Via Latin from Greek *kalamos* 'reed, pen'.]

calando /kə lándō/ *adv., adj.* played with gradually decreasing volume and slowing tempo (*used as a musical direction*) [Early 19thC. From Italian, literally 'slackening'.]

calandria /kə lándri ə/ *n.* the cylindrical core of a nuclear reactor with vertical holes [Early 20thC. From Spanish, formed from Greek *kylindros* 'cylinder' (source of English *cylinder*).]

calathea /kállə theé ə/ *n.* a tropical South American evergreen plant with showy variegated leaves, widely grown as a greenhouse and pot plant. Genus: *Calathea.* [From modern Latin, formed from Greek *kalathos* (see CALATHUS)]

calathus /kálləthəss/ (*plural* **-thi** /-thī/) *n.* a vase-shaped basket full of fruit that often appears in ancient Greek and Egyptian art as a symbol of fruitfulness [Mid-18thC. Via Latin from Greek *kalathos* 'basket'.]

calaverite /kə lávvə rīt, kállə váir īt/ *n.* a silvery-white or yellowish mineral that is an ore of gold [Mid-19thC. Named after *Calaveras* County, California, where it was found.]

calc. *abbr.* calculus

calc- *prefix.* = **calci-**

calcaneus /kal káyni əss/ (*plural* **-i** /-ī/) *n.* the heel bone (*technical*) [Mid-18thC. From late Latin, 'heel', from the Latin stem *calc-* 'heel' (source of English *caulk*).] —**calcaneal** *adj.*

calcar[1] /kál kaar/ (*plural* **-caria** /-káiri ə/) *n.* a spur on a plant or animal part, e.g. on a bird's leg or at the base of a petal [Early 19thC. From Latin, 'spur', from the stem *calc-* 'heel'.]

calcar[2] /kál kaar/ *n.* a furnace formerly used in glass-making for burning materials to make frit, the viscous substance from which glass is subsequently made [Mid-17thC. From Italian *calcara.*]

calcareous /kal káiri əss/ *adj.* **1. OF CALCIUM CARBONATE** containing or characteristic of calcium carbonate **2.** BOT **GROWING IN LIMESTONE CONDITIONS** growing on limestone or in earth containing limestone ○ *calcareous algae* [Late 17thC. Formed from Latin *calcarius* 'of lime', from the stem *calc-* 'lime' (source of English *chalk*).] —**calcareously** *adv.*

calcaria plural of **calcar**

calcariferous /kálkə ríffərəss/ *adj.* used to describe a plant or animal part that has a spur on it [Mid-19thC. Coined from Latin *calcar* (see CALCAR[1]) + -IFEROUS.]

calceolaria /kálssi ə láiri ə/ *n.* a tropical American plant with speckled slipper-shaped flowers. Genus: *Calceolaria.* [Late 18thC. From modern Latin, genus name, from Latin *calceolus* 'little shoe'.]

Calchas /kál kass/ *n.* in Greek mythology, a soothsayer who accompanied the Greeks during the Trojan War, advising them, amongst other things, to build the Trojan Horse

calci- *prefix.* CHEM calcium, calcium salt, lime ○ *calcific* [From Latin *calc-*, the stem of *calx* 'lime' (see CALX)]

calcic /kálssik/ *adj.* containing, derived from, or relating to calcium or lime

calciferol /kal síffə rol/ *n.* = **vitamin D_2** [Mid-20thC. Coined from CALCIFEROUS + -OL.]

calciferous /kal síffərəss/ *adj.* producing or containing calcium carbonate or other calcium salts [Late 18thC. Coined from CALCI- + -FEROUS.]

calcific /kal síffik/ *adj.* producing lime salts, or involved in their production [Mid-19thC. Coined from CALCI- + -FIC.]

calcification /kálssifi káysh'n/ *n.* **1.** CHEM **CONVERSION INTO LIME** the conversion of a substance into lime **2.** MED **ABNORMAL HARDENING** the abnormal hardening or stiffening of a body part caused by deposits of calcium salts **3.** MED **HARD BODY PART** a body part that has become hardened or stiffened by calcification **4. LACK OF CHANGE** a condition in which improvement, change, or progress ceases (*formal*)

calcifuge /kálssi fyooj/ *n.* plant that prefers an acid soil, or will not grow in chalky soil [Mid-19thC. Coined from CALCI- + -FUGE.] —**calcifugal** /kal síffyoŏg'l, kálssi fyoŏg'l/ *adj.* —**calcifugous** /kal síffyoŏgəss, kálssi fyoŏgəss/ *adj.*

calcify /kálssi fī/ (**-fies, -fying, -fied**) *vti.* **1.** CHEM **TURN INTO LIME** to convert a substance into lime, or be converted into lime **2.** MED **TURN HARD WITH CALCIUM** to become, or cause a body part to become, abnormally hard or stiff as a result of the deposit of calcium salts **3. BECOME RIGID AND UNCHANGING** to become, or cause sth to become, rigid and unchanging (*formal*)

calcimine /kálssi mīn, -min/ *n.* **COATING FOR INTERIOR WALLS** a mixture of zinc oxide, water, and glue, sometimes with a colouring added, brushed onto interior walls as a decorative and sealing finish ■ *vt.* **(-mines, -mining, -mined) COAT WALL WITH CALCIMINE** to cover a wall with calcimine [Mid-19thC. Alteration of KALSOMINE, influenced by *calci-*.]

calcine /kál sīn, -sin/ (**-cines, -cining, -cined**) *vti.* to heat a solid to a high temperature, converting it to a powdery residue by drying, decomposing, or oxidizing it, or to undergo this process [14thC. From medieval Latin *calcinare* 'to burn until like lime', from, ultimately, the Latin stem *calc-* 'lime' (see CALCIUM).] — **calcination** /kálssi náysh'n/ *n.*

calcinosis /kálssi nóssiss/ *n.* a medical condition in which nodules of calcium are deposited in soft body tissues

calcite /kál sīt/ *n.* a colourless or white crystalline mineral that is a form of calcium carbonate. It is the main constituent of limestone, marble, and chalk and is used in cement, plaster, glass, and paints. Formula: $CaCO_3$. —**calcitic** /kal síttik/ *adj.*

calcitonin /kálssi tónin/ *n.* a hormone, produced by the thyroid and parathyroid glands, that increases the deposition of calcium in bones

calcitriol[1] /kal síttri ol/ *n.* BIOCHEM the active form of Vitamin D that functions as a steroid hormone [Late 20thC. Origin uncertain; probably formed from CALCIUM + TRIOL.]

calcitriol[2] /kal síttri ol/ *n.* PHARM a drug used to control or reverse bone loss from diseases such as rickets and kidney dysfunction

calcium /kálssi əm/ *n.* a soft silver-white element that is an alkaline earth metal constituting about three per cent of the earth's crust. It is essential to the formation of bones and teeth. Symbol **Ca** [Early 19thC. Coined from Latin *calc-*, the stem of *calx* 'lime' (see CALX) + -IUM.]

calcium acetylide *n.* = **calcium carbide**

calcium antagonist *n.* a drug used to treat angina by widening the arteries and slowing the heart. The drug restricts the normal movement of calcium ions through the muscle tissue of the artery walls and heart.

calcium carbide *n.* a colourless or greyish-black powdery compound used in the generation of acetylene gas for welding. Formula: CaC_2.

calcium carbonate *n.* a white crystalline solid that is one of the most common natural substances, forming chalk, limestone, and marble, and occurs in animal shells and bones. It is a constituent of antacids for indigestion, paint, cement, and toothpaste. Formula: $CaCO_3$.

calcium channel blocker *n.* = **calcium antagonist**

calcium chloride *n.* a white salt that absorbs moisture easily and quickly, and is used for drying gases, de-icing roads, and also in pulp and paper treatment. Formula: $CaCl_2$.

calcium cyanamide *n.* a white or greyish-black crystalline compound that releases ammonia slowly in the presence of water and is used as a fertilizer. Formula: $CaCN_2$.

calcium cyanide *n.* a white or greyish-black powder that decomposes in humid conditions to give hydrogen cyanide and was formerly used as an insecticide and rodent poison and in fumigation. Formula: $Ca(CN)_2$.

calcium cyclamate *n.* a sweet-tasting salt of cyclamic acid formerly used as a sugar substitute. Formula: $Ca(C_6H_{11}NHSO_3)_2.2H_2O$.

calcium fluoride *n.* a colourless or white substance occurring naturally as fluorspar. Formula: CaF_2.

calcium gluconate *n.* a calcium salt used as a medication in cases of calcium deficiency and osteoporosis and as a mineral supplement. Formula: $CaC_{12}H_{22}O_{14}$.

calcium hydroxide *n.* a white alkaline powder derived from the action of water on calcium oxide, used to treat acid soil and in the manufacture of cement, plaster, and glass. Formula: $Ca(OH)_2$.

calcium hypochlorite *n.* a white crystalline solid, soluble in water, that is a stable chlorine carrier used as a bleaching agent, disinfectant, and bactericide. Formula: $Ca(OCl)_2$.

calcium light *n.* = **limelight**

calcium nitrate *n.* a white solid that absorbs moisture very quickly, is a strong oxidizer, and is used as a fertilizer and in some explosives. Formula: $Ca(NO_3)_2.4H_2O$.

calcium oxide *n.* a white crystalline powder used in the manufacture of steel and glass, the refining of aluminium, copper, and zinc, and sewage treatment. Formula: CaO.

calcium phosphate *n.* any of several phosphates of calcium that occur naturally in rocks and animal bones and are used, in the form of bone ash, as a fertilizer

calcrete /kál kreet/ *n.* an accumulation in the soil of a layer of calcium carbonate and other alkaline minerals just below the surface [Early 20thC. Coined from CALC- + (con)crete.]

calcspar /kálk spaar/ *n.* = **calcite** [Early 19thC. Coined from the Latin stem *calc-* 'lime' (see CALCIUM) + SPAR.]

calc-tufa /kálk-/ *n.* = **tufa** [Early 19thC. Coined from the Latin stem *calc-* 'lime' (see CALCIUM) + TUFA.]

calculable /kálkyooləb'l/ *adj.* **1.** ABLE TO BE CALCULATED able to be worked out or estimated, using mathematics **2.** PREDICTABLE likely to behave in the way that is expected —**calculability** /kálkyoolə bílləti/ *n.*

calculate /kálkyoo layt/ (**-lates, -lating, -lated**) *v.* **1.** *vti.* MATH **WORK OUT MATHEMATICALLY** to figure out or estimate a figure using mathematics **2.** *vti.* **DECIDE** to consider a situation carefully and decide what is likely to happen **3.** *vt.* **BE INTENDED TO HAVE PARTICULAR EFFECT** to be intended or designed to have a particular effect or result ○ *The attack was calculated to cause maximum loss of life.* **4.** *vi. US* **INTEND** to be planning or intending to do a particular thing (*regional*) ○ *We were calculating on going home around midnight.* [Late 16thC. From late Latin *calculat-* 'to calculate', past participle stem of *calulare* from, ultimately, Latin *calculus* 'pebble' (see CALCULUS).]

calculated /kálkyoo laytid/ *adj.* **1.** CAREFULLY CONSIDERED done or accepted after careful consideration of the possible results **2.** DELIBERATE planned or deliberate —**calculatedly** *adv.* —**calculatedness** *n.*

calculating /kálkyoo layting/ *adj.* **1.** SCHEMING determined to gain the greatest personal advantage **2.** SHOWING SB'S SCHEMING NATURE indicative of sb's scheming nature —**calculatingly** *adv.*

calculation /kálkyoo láysh'n/ *n.* **1.** MATH PROCESS OF CALCULATING STH the process, or a step in the process, of working out the answer to a mathematical problem **2.** ESTIMATE an estimate or answer obtained by calculating **3.** DELIBERATENESS consideration of sth, especially when thinking of personal advantage — **calculational** *adj.* —**calculative** /kálkyooolətiv, -laytiv/ *adj.*

Calculator

calculator /kálkyoo laytər/ *n.* a device used to carry out arithmetical operations, especially a small hand-held electronic device

calculous /kálkyoooləss/ *adj.* relating to abnormal hard formations of minerals (**calculi**) in the body

calculus /kálkyoooləss/ (*plural* **-li** /-lī/ *or* **-luses**) *n.* **1.** MATH BRANCH OF MATHEMATICS a branch of mathematics dealing with the way that relations between certain sets (**functions**) are affected by very small changes in one of their variables (**independent variable**) as they approach zero. It is used to find slopes of curves, rates of change, and volumes of curved figures. ◊ **differential calculus, integral calculus 2.** MATH, LOGIC METHOD OF CALCULATION a method or system of calculation using symbols or symbolic logic **3.** MED **STONE** a stone or concretion, especially one in the kidney, gall bladder, or urinary bladder (*technical*) **4.** DENT = **tartar** [Mid-17thC. From Latin, 'pebble', a diminutive of *calx* 'lime, limestone' (see CALX).]

Calcutta /kal kúttə/ capital of West Bengal state and one of India's largest cities. It is a major commercial and industrial city and port, situated on the River Hoogly, an arm of the Ganges about 100 km/60 mi. from its mouth at the Bay of Bengal. Population: 11,021,915 (metropolitan area) (1991).

caldarium /kal dáiri əm/ (*plural* **-a** /-ri ə/) *n.* the hot room in an ancient Roman bathhouse [Mid-18thC. Via Latin from, ultimately, *calere* 'to be warm' (source of English *calorie*).]

Alexander Young Calder

Calder /káwldər, kóld-/, **Alexander Young** (1898–1976) US painter and sculptor, known for his abstract sculptures, especially mobiles and stabiles.

caldera /kal dáirə, káwldərə/ (*plural* **-ras**) *n.* a large crater in a volcano, caused by a major eruption followed by the collapse of the volcanic pipe walls that form the volcano's cone. It may later contain a lake. [Late 17thC. Via Spanish from late Latin *caldaria* 'cooking pot', formed from Latin *caldus* 'warm'.]

Calderdale /káwldər dayl/ local government unitary authority in northern England, established 1997. Capital: Halifax is the administrative centre. Population: 193,200 (1995).

Calderón de la Barca /káldə rón də la baárkə/, **Pedro** (1600–81) Spanish dramatist and poet. He wrote comedies and religious allegories including *Life is a Dream* (1635).

Caldey Island /káwldi-/ island off the coast of Pembrokeshire, Wales, and location of a Cistercian monastery. Welsh **Ynys Pyr**

caldron *n.* = **cauldron**

Caldwell /káwld wel, kóld-/ city in southwestern Idaho, on the southern bank of the Boise River, west of Boise. Population: 21,089 (1996).

Caledonia /kállə dóni ə/ Roman name for the northern part of Britain and poetic name for Scotland

Caledonian /kálli dóni ən/ *adj.* **1.** OF SCOTLAND relating to or typical of Scotland or its people or culture (*literary*) **2.** OF PALAEOZOIC EUROPE relating to the Palaeozoic era in northwestern Europe, when many mountains were formed ■ *n.* SCOT a Scottish person (*literary*)

Caledonian Canal /kálli dóni ən-/ major waterway of Scotland. It consists of canals linking Loch Linnhe in the southwest with Loch Lochy, Loch Ness, and the Moray Firth in the northeast. Length: 60 km/97 mi.

calendar /kállindər/ *n.* **1.** SYSTEM OF CALCULATING YEAR a system of calculating the days and months of the year and when the year begins and ends **2.** CHART OF YEAR a chart showing the days and months of the year, especially a particular year **3.** TIMETABLE a timetable of events, usually covering a period of a year **4.** LIST an official list of things to be done or considered ■ *vt.* (**-dars, -daring, -dared**) SCHEDULE to enter sth in a calendar or diary [12thC. Via Anglo-Norman *calender* from Latin *calendarium* 'moneylender's account-book', from *calendae* 'first day of the month'.] —**calendrical** /kə léndrik'l/ *adj.*

calendar day *n.* the period of 24 hours from midnight to midnight

calendar month *n.* **1.** = **month** n. 1 **2.** = **month** n. 3

calendar year *n.* the period of 365 or 366 days from 1 January to 31 December

CALENDARS AND FESTIVALS

The Gregorian calendar was introduced in 1582 by Pope Gregory XIII, replacing the Julian calendar, and is based on a solar year of 365 days plus an extra day every four years (the leap year) and in centenary years evenly divisible by 400. The other calendars shown are based on lunar months. Each Hindu month is divided in two equal parts: krsna-paksa and sukla-paksa. Both the Hindu and the Jewish calendars are adjusted at intervals to the solar year. The Islamic calendar is not adjusted to the solar year so advances through the solar year on a 32.5 year cycle. The first month of each calendar is marked with a 1.

Notes

1 February has 29 days in a leap year.
2 The intercalary month Adar Sheni (29 days) is added every 3 years to adjust the Jewish calendar to the solar year.
3 The month Heshvan has 30 days in some years.
4 The month Kislev has 30 days in some years.
5 The month Dhu'l-Hijjah has 30 days in some years.

Gregorian calendar	Jewish calendar	Hindu calendar	Islamic calendar
1 January *31 days*	Tevet *29 days*	Pausa	**1** Muharram *30 days*
February *28 days* [1]	Shevat *30 days*	Magha	Safar *29 days*
March *31 days*	Adar *29 days* [2]	**1** Phalguna	Rabi I *30 days*
April *30 days*	Nisan *30 days*	Caitra	Rabi II *29 days*
May *31 days*	Iyar *29 days*	Vaisakha	Jumada I *30 days*
June *30 days*	Sivan *30 days*	Jyaistha	Jumada II *29 days*
July *31 days*	Tammuz *29 days*	Asadha	Rajab *30 days*
August *31 days*	Av *30 days*	Sravana	Shaban *29 days*
September *30 days*	**1** Elul *29 days*	Bhadrapada	Ramadan *30 days*
October *31 days*	Tishri *30 days*	Asvina	Shawwal *29 days*
November *30 days*	Heshvan *29 days* [3]	Kartika	Dhu'l-Qadah *30 days*
December *31 days*	Kislev *29 days* [4]	Margasirsa	Dhu'l-Hijjah *29 days* [5]
	Tevet	Pausa	

Christian festivals	Jewish festivals	Hindu festivals	Islamic festivals
Annunciation *25 March*	**Hanukkah** *25 Kislev for eight days*	**Dassera** *First half of Asvina*	**Ashura** *10 Muharram*
Ascension *40 days after Easter*	**Passover** *14 Nisan for seven days*	**Diwali** *Second half of Asvina*	**Id al-Adha** *10 Dhu'l-Qadah to 1 Dhu'l-Hijjah*
Christmas *25 December: Roman Catholic and Protestant churches* *6 January: Eastern Orthodox churches*	**Purim** *14 Adar*	**Ganesa caturthi** *4 sukla paksa of Bhadrapada*	**Id al-Fitr** *1 Shawwal*
	Rosh Hashanah *1 and 2 Tishri*	**Holi** *Sukla-paksa of Phalguna*	**Isra wa al-Miraj** *27 Rajab*
Easter *First Sunday after the full moon of the vernal equinox*	**Shabuoth** *6 Sivan*	**Krsna-jayanti** *8 krsna-paksa of Sravana*	**Laylat al-Baraah** *15 Shaban*
Epiphany *6 January*	**Sukkot** *15 Tishri for eight or nine days*	**Rakhi bandham** *Full moon of Sravana*	**Laylat al-Qadr** *27 Ramadan*
Pentecost *50 days after Easter*	**Yom Kippur** *10 Tishri*	**Siva-ratri** *13 krsna-paksa of Magha*	**Mawlid al-Nabi** *12 Rabi I*
Transfiguration *6 August*			**Ras al-Am** *1 Muharram*
Trinity *First Sunday after Pentecost*			**Ramadan**

---

calender /kállindər/ *n.* **ROLLERS FOR TREATING PAPER, CLOTH, ETC** a machine with rollers used to form thin sheets from paper, plastic, or other material, or to impart a desired surface finish ■ *vt.* (**-ders, -dering, -dered**) **PASS THROUGH CALENDER** to give the required thickness or surface finish to a material by pulling it through a calender [Early 16thC. Via French *calendre* from assumed Vulgar Latin *colondra*, an alteration (influenced by Latin *columna* 'column') of Latin *cylindrus* 'roller' (source of English *cylinder*).] —**calenderer** *n.*

calends /kállendz/, **kalends** *npl.* the first day of the month in the ancient Roman calendar [14thC. Via French *calendes* from Latin *calendae* 'first day of the month'.]

calendula /kə léndyoolə/ (*plural* **-las** *or* **-la**) *n.* US = **pot marigold** [Late 16thC. From modern Latin, formed from Latin *calendae* 'first day of the month' (see CALENDS). From its use in treating menstrual disorders.]

calenture /kállən tyoor, -choor/ *n.* a fever occurring in tropical regions, formerly believed to be caused by heat [Late 16thC. Via French from Spanish *calentura*, from, ultimately, Latin *calere* 'to be warm' (source of English *calorie*).]

calf[1] /kaaf/ (*plural* **calves** /kaavz/) *n.* **1.** **YOUNG COW OR BULL** a very young cow or bull of domestic cattle **2.** **YOUNG ANIMAL** the young of some other animals besides the cow, including the elephant, whale, giraffe, and buffalo **3.** = **calfskin 4.** **PIECE OF ICEBERG** a large piece of ice that has broken away from an iceberg [Old English *cælf*. Ultimately from a prehistoric Germanic word that is also the ancestor of German *Kalb* and Old Norse *kalfr*.]

calf[2] /kaaf/ (*plural* **calves** /kaavz/) *n.* the fleshy part at the back of the leg below the knee [14thC. From Old Norse *kálfi*, of uncertain origin.]

calf love *n.* = **puppy love** (*dated*)

calfskin /ka'af skin/ *n.* **1.** **LEATHER** fine leather made from the skin of calves **2.** **SKIN OF CALF** the skin of a calf

Calgary /kálgəri/ *city in southern Alberta, Canada. It is an important centre for transportation, finance, and the petroleum industry. Population: 821,628 (1996).

Cali /ka'ali/ *capital of Valle de Cauca Department and second largest city in Colombia. It is situated on the Cali River in western Colombia. Population: 1,718,871 (1995).

caliber *n.* US = **calibre**

calibrate /kálli brayt/ (**-brates, -brating, -brated**) *vt.* **1.** MEASURE **MARK SCALE ON STH** to establish and mark the units shown on a measuring instrument **2.** MEASURE **ENSURE ACCURACY OF STH** to test and adjust the accuracy of a measuring instrument or process **3.** ARMS **MEASURE BORE OF STH** to measure the internal diameter of a gun or cylinder —**calibrator** *n.*

calibration /kálli bráysh'n/ *n.* **1.** **STANDARDIZATION OF MEASURING INSTRUMENT** the checking of a measuring instrument against an accurate standard to determine any deviation and correct for errors **2.** **MARK ON SCALE**

---

a at; aa father; aw all; ay day; air hair; ə about, edible, item, common, circus; e egg; ee eel; hw when; i it, happy; ī ice; 'l apple; 'm rhythm; 'n fashion; o odd; ō open; oŏ good; oo pool; ow owl; oy oil; th thin; <u>th</u> this; u up; ur urge;

a mark showing one of the units of measurement on a measuring instrument

calibre /kállibər/ *n.* **1.** ABILITY a person's ability, intelligence, or character ○ *We don't often get candidates of her calibre.* **2.** ARMS BORE OF FIREARM the inner diameter of a pipe or cylinder, especially the barrel of a firearm **3.** ARMS SIZE OF BULLET the external diameter of a projectile, e.g. a bullet or a shell [Mid-16thC. Via French *calibre* from, ultimately, Arabic *kālib* 'mould', which is in turn ultimately from Greek *kalapous* 'shoemaker's last'.]

calices plural of **calix**

caliche /ka leéchi/ *n.* **1.** LAYER OF CLAY OR SAND a layer of clay or sand containing minerals, e.g. sodium nitrate and sodium chloride, found in arid regions of South America **2.** = **calcrete** [Mid-19thC. From American Spanish.]

calico /kállikō/ (*plural* **-coes**) *n.* **1.** WHITE COTTON CLOTH a white or unbleached cotton cloth **2.** *US* BRIGHT COTTON CLOTH a coarse cotton cloth with a bright printed pattern **3.** *US* ANIMAL WITH BLOTCHED COAT an animal with a blotched coat, usually white with black and reddish patches [Mid-16thC. Alteration of *Calicut*, former name of a city and port on the southwestern coast of India (now Kozhikode), from which such cloth was exported.]

calif *n.* = **caliph**

Calif. *abbr.* California

califate *n.* = **caliphate**

California

California /kálli fáwrnyə/ the most populous US state, bordered by the Pacific Ocean, Oregon, Nevada, Arizona, and Mexico. Capital: Sacramento. Population: 32,268,301 (1997). Area: 411,469 sq. km/158,869 sq. mi. —**Californian** *n.*, *adj.*

California, Gulf of arm of the Pacific Ocean that extends northwards between mainland Mexico and Baja California. Area: 152,810 sq. km/59,000 sq. mi. Alternate name **Sea of Cortes**

California condor *n.* a large dark grey or brown vulture of the southeastern United States, with a wingspan of about 3 m/10 ft and a naked head and neck. It is being rescued from extinction by a captive breeding programme. Latin name: *Gymnogyps californianus.*

California Current current in northern Pacific Ocean. It flows from north to south along the western coast of North America before turning west.

California poppy, Californian poppy *n.* an annual plant with bluish divided leaves, commonly cultivated for its bright red to yellow flowers. Latin name: *Eschscholzia californica.*

californium /kálli fáwrni əm/ *n.* a synthetic radioactive metallic chemical element produced by bombarding curium or americium with neutrons. It is used as a neutron source. Symbol **Cf** [Mid-20thC. The element is so named because it was first synthesized at the University of California.]

Caligula /kə líggyoōlə/ (12–AD41) Roman emperor. A despotic ruler (37–41), he bankrupted the state with his extravagance and was assassinated. Full name **Gaius Julius Caesar Germanicus**

calipash /kálli pash/, **callipash** *n.* a thick green fat obtained from beneath the upper shell of turtles [Late 17thC. Origin uncertain: perhaps an alteration of

Spanish *carapacho* 'carapace' (source of English *carapace*), or perhaps from a Caribbean language.]

calipee /kálli pee, kálli peé/ *n.* a thick yellow fat obtained from beneath the lower shells of turtles, considered to be a delicacy [Mid-17thC. Origin uncertain: perhaps from a Caribbean language.]

caliper *n.* US = **calliper**

caliph /káylif, kállif/, **calif, kalif, khalif** *n.* a title taken by Muslim rulers, e.g. the Turkish sultans, that asserts religious authority to rule derived from that of Muhammad [14thC. Via French *caliphe* from Arabic *kalīfa* 'successor, deputy', from *kalafa* 'to succeed'.]

caliphate /kálli fayt, káyli-, -fit/, **califate, kalifate, khalifate** *n.* the territory over which a caliph's rule extends, or the time for which it lasts

calix /káyliks, káll-/ (*plural* **-lices** /-li seez/) *n.* **1.** CUP a chalice or cup **2.** ANAT = **calyx** [Early 18thC. From Latin, 'cup' (see CHALICE).]

calk¹ /kawk/ (**calks, calking, calked**) *n.* a metal spike on a horseshoe to prevent slipping [Late 16thC. Origin uncertain: perhaps from Latin *calcaneum* 'heel'.]

calk² *vt.* = **caulk**

call /kawl/ *v.* (**calls, calling, called**) **1.** *vt.* NAME SB OR STH to give sb or sth a name ○ *What are you going to call the baby?* **2.** *vt.* REFER TO to use a particular term to address or refer to sb ○ *He always called his father 'Sir'.* **3.** *vt.* DESCRIBE AS STH to describe or think of sb or sth in a particular way ○ *I'd call him a fool.* **4.** *vti.* SAY LOUDLY to say sth in a loud voice ○ *'Supper's ready', he called from the kitchen.* **5.** *vt.* SUMMON to summon or alert sb or sth by means of a formal request ○ *I'll call a taxi.* **6.** *vti.* TELEPHONE to contact sb by telephone or radio **7.** *vi.* VISIT SB to visit sb, or the place where sb lives or works ○ *I called to see her yesterday.* **8.** *vi.* TRANSP STOP SOMEWHERE to stop at a particular place on a regular bus, coach, or train route ○ *Do you call at George Square?* **9.** *vti.* REQUEST STH TO HAPPEN to make an official order or request for sth, e.g. a meeting ○ *A council meeting has been called for July 15th.* **10.** *vt.* READ OUT to read names or numbers from a list **11.** *vti.* DECLARE CHOICE IN GAME to make a declaration in a game, e.g. to choose heads or tails, or choose trumps in a card game ○ *I'll toss, you call.* **12.** *vi.* CRY to give a cry (*refers to birds or animals*) **13.** *vt.* *US* PREDICT to predict what is going to happen, especially in politics ○ *It's a very hard result to call.* **14.** *vt.* SPORTS OFFICIALLY DECIDE IN GAME to make an official decision in a sporting event or a game **15.** *vti.* DANCE INSTRUCT DANCERS to give directions to people who are dancing, e.g. in a square dance **16.** *vt.* FIN DEMAND REPAYMENT OF STH to demand payment of a loan or bond issue **17.** *Aus, NZ* SPORTS ACT AS SPORTS COMMENTATOR FOR to commentate on radio or television on a sporting event, particularly a horserace ■ *n.* **1.** SHOUT a shout or cry **2.** BIRD OR ANIMAL CRY the sound made by a bird or animal **3.** SIGNAL a signal given by a sound, e.g. on a horn or whistle **4.** TELEPHONE MESSAGE a telephone conversation, or an attempt to get in touch with sb by telephone **5.** VISIT a short visit to sb at his or her house or place of work ○ *made a few calls on the way home.* **6.** REQUEST TO COME a request for sb to come ○ *The emergency services answer thousands of calls a year.* **7.** EXPRESSED WISH a demand or request for sth to be done ○ *There have been calls for him to resign.* **8.** STRONG APPEAL OF PLACE OR LIFESTYLE the feeling of strong attraction exerted by a particular place or way of life ○ *the call of the wild* **9.** FEELING OF DUTY a feeling that a particular job or way of life is a personal duty **10.** DEMAND OR OBLIGATION a demand or obligation that sb has to fulfil ○ *I'd like to help, but I have a great many calls on my time.* **11.** REMINDER a reminder, given electronically, by telephone, or in person, that sb should wake up or that sth is about to happen **12.** GAME DECLARATION IN GAME a declaration made during a game, e.g. the choice of heads or tails when a coin is tossed ○ *It's your call.* **13.** SPORTS REFEREE'S DECISION a decision made by a referee **14.** *US* PREDICTION a prediction of what is about to happen, especially in politics **15.** HUNTER'S DEVICE TO ATTRACT GAME a device that imitates the cry of a bird or other animal, used as a lure in hunting [12thC. From Old Norse *kalla*.] ◇ **be on call** to be on duty away from the workplace, available to be summoned

call back *v.* **1.** *vti.* TELEPHONE SB AGAIN to contact sb by telephone again **2.** *vi.* VISIT SB AGAIN to visit sb again **3.** *vt.* ASK TO RETURN to recall sb, e.g. for a second audition or to return to a job **4.** *vt.* ASK WORKERS BACK TO WORK to contact previously laid-off workers to ask them to return to a job site

call down *vt.* to pray or appeal for good or bad things to happen to sb

call for *vt.* **1.** REQUEST FOR STH TO HAPPEN to make a demand or request for some action to take place **2.** NEED to need or require a particular thing or quality **3.** COLLECT to collect sb

call forth *vt.* to inspire an emotion, energy, or courage

call in *v.* **1.** *vt.* ASK HELP FROM to ask sb to come and give advice or help **2.** *vi.* PAY QUICK VISIT to make a brief visit to sb **3.** *vi.* TELEPHONE PLACE OF WORK to telephone a place of work in order to collect or leave a message **4.** *vt.* ASK FOR STH TO BE REPAID to ask for a debt or loan to be repaid **5.** *vt.* ARRANGE RETURN OF STH to arrange or request for sth to be returned, e.g. outdated currency or defective goods

call off *vt.* **1.** CANCEL EVENT to cancel or stop an event **2.** STOP FROM ATTACKING to order a dog or a person to stop attacking sb

call on *vt.* **1.** ASK TO DO STH to ask or tell sb to do sth **2.** VISIT to visit sb, often in a formal manner

call out *vt.* **1.** SUMMON PEOPLE TO HELP to summon sb or an organization to come and help **2.** ORDER TO STRIKE to tell workers to stop work and go on strike **3.** CHALLENGE TO A FIGHT to challenge sb to a duel or fight

call up *vt.* **1.** RECRUIT TO FIGHT to order sb to join the armed services in time of war. US term **draft 2.** SUMMON to summon sb who or sth that is available in reserve **3.** TELEPHONE to telephone sb (*informal*) **4.** COMPUT DISPLAY ON COMPUTER SCREEN to instruct a computer to find and display a particular piece of information ○ *call up last month's sales figures* **5.** EVOKE to bring back memories of sth

call upon *vt.* **1.** ASK FORMALLY to ask sb in a formal way to do sth **2.** MAKE DEMANDS ON to make demands on sb or on sb's abilities

calla /kállə/ *n.* = **arum lily**

callable /káwləb'l/ *adj.* **1.** REPAYABLE ON DEMAND used to describe a loan that is repayable on demand **2.** CONVERTIBLE BEFORE MATURING used to describe a share or bond that is convertible before reaching maturity

Callaghan /kállə hən, -han/, **James, Baron Callaghan of Cardiff** (b. 1912) British statesman. He was Home Secretary (1967–70), Foreign Secretary (1974–76), and Labour Prime Minister (1976–79). Full name **Leonard James Callaghan**

callais /kə láyiss/ *n.* a green stone used by Stone Age and Bronze Age people in Europe to make beads and ornaments [Late 19thC. From Greek *kallais*.]

call alarm *n.* a personal alarm used for summoning help in an emergency

calla lily *n.* = **arum lily**

callant /kállənt/ *n. Scotland* a boy or young man [Early 16thC. Via Flemish *kalant* from *caland*, the Northern French dialect form of *chaland* 'customer, chap', from French *chaloir* 'to be warm' (source of English *nonchalant*), from Latin *calere*.]

Callao /kə yów/ city and chief seaport of Peru, situated on Callao Bay 13 km/8 mi. west of Lima. Population: 637,755 (1993).

Callas /kálləss, kál ass/, **Maria** (1923–77) US-born opera soprano. One of the leading opera singers of the mid-20th century, she was known for her incisive portrayals of such characters as Norma and Tosca. Born **Maria Anna Sofia Cecilia Kalogeropoulos**

callback /káwl bak/ *n.* **1.** RETURN CALL a telephone call made to sb who has recently phoned **2.** REQUEST OF SB an act of asking sb to return **3.** *US* PRODUCT RECALL the recalling of a faulty product by a manufacturer

AKG London

Maria Callas

call bird *n.* a cheap article displayed to attract customers

callboard /káwl bawrd/ *n.* a board backstage in a theatre, giving information to actors and other people involved in a production

call box *n. UK* a telephone box

callboy /káwl boy/ *n.* sb in a theatre who tells the actors when the time for them to go on stage is approaching

call centre *n.* TELECOM, BUSINESS a place that handles high-volume incoming telephone calls on behalf of a large organization

caller /káwlər/ *n.* **1.** SB PHONING OR VISITING sb who makes a telephone call or who visits sb **2.** ANNOUNCER sb who announces sth, e.g. the moves in a square dance or the numbers in a game of bingo **3.** *Aus* SPORTS SPORTS COMMENTATOR sb who provides the broadcast commentary for a sporting event, especially a horse race

caller ID *n.* an electronic device attached to a telephone that, on a small screen, shows the name and telephone number of sb who is calling or has called

call girl *n.* a prostitute who makes appointments with clients by telephone

calli- *prefix.* beautiful ◊ *calliopsis* [From Greek *kallos* 'beauty']

calligraphy /kə líggrəfi/ *n.* **1.** SKILL OF HANDWRITING the art or skill of producing beautiful handwriting **2.** HANDWRITING beautiful or artistic handwriting [Early 17thC. From Greek *kalligraphia*, literally 'beautiful writing', from *kallos* 'beauty' + *graphein* 'to write'.] —**calligrapher** *n.* —**calligraphic** /kálli gráffik/ *adj.* —**calligraphically** /-gráffikli/ *adv.* —**calligraphist** /kəlíggrəfist/ *n.*

Callil /kə líl/, **Carmen** (*b.* 1938) Australian publisher. She founded the London-based Virago publishing house (1973).

call-in *n. US* = **phone-in**

calling /káwling/ *n.* **1.** IMPULSE TO FOLLOW PARTICULAR JOB a strong urge to follow a particular career or do a particular type of work **2.** JOB a job or profession

calling card *n. US, Can* = **visiting card**

calliope /kə líf əpi/ *n. US, Can* = **steam organ** [Mid-19thC. Formed from Latin *Calliope* 'CALLIOPE'.]

Calliope /kə líf əpi/ *n.* the Muse of epic poetry, one of the nine Muses believed to inspire and nurture the arts in Greek mythology. ◊ **Muse** [Via Latin from Greek *Kalliopē*, literally 'beautiful-voiced']

calliper /kállipər/ *n.* **1.** MEASURE MEASURING INSTRUMENT an instrument used to measure the internal or external dimensions of objects and consisting of two curved hinged legs joined at one end **2.** MED LEG BRACE a leg splint consisting of metal rods and straps, that enables the hip bone, rather than the foot, to support weight when walking ■ *vt.* (-**pers, -pering, -pered**) MEASURE MEASURE WITH CALLIPERS to measure sth using a calliper [Late 16thC. Origin uncertain: perhaps an alteration of CALIBRE.]

calliper rule *n.* a graduated scale with jaws, one fixed and one sliding, set at right angles to it, used to measure the thickness of boards or the diameters of pipes or shafts

callipers /kállipəz/ *npl.* TECH a measuring instrument with two hinged legs and an attached scale that measures the distance between the tips of the legs, used particularly for measuring diameters

callipygian /kálli píjji ən/, **callipygous** /kálli pígəss/ *adj.* having well-shaped buttocks (*literary*) [Late 18thC. Formed from Greek *kallipūgos*, literally 'beautiful buttocks', a term applied to a statue of the goddess Aphrodite, from *kalli-* 'BEAUTY-' + *pūgē* 'buttocks'.]

callisthenics /kálliss thénniks/ *n.* PERFORMANCE OF CALLISTHENICS the practice of performing callisthenics (*takes a singular verb*) ■ *npl.* PHYSICAL EXERCISE ROUTINE vigorous physical exercises for improving fitness and muscle tone, including push-ups, sit-ups, and star jumps (*takes a plural verb*) [Early 19thC. Coined from the Greek stem *kalli-* 'beauty' + Greek *sthenos* 'strength' + -ICS.] —**callisthenic** *adj.*

Callisto /kə lístō/ *n.* **1.** GREEK NYMPH in Greek mythology, a nymph who was changed into a bear by Hera and later became the constellation of the Great Bear **2.** LARGE SATELLITE OF JUPITER a large satellite of Jupiter that was discovered in 1610 [Via Latin from Greek *Kallistō* from, ultimately, *kalos* 'beautiful']

call letters *npl. US, Can* = **call sign**

call loan *n.* a loan that must be repaid on demand

call mark *n.* = **call number**

call money *n.* money that has been borrowed and that is repayable on demand

call number *n.* a number that identifies a library book and its position in a library classification system

call of nature *n.* a need to urinate or defecate (*humorous*)

callose /kállōz/ *n.* an insoluble substance found in plant cell walls and formed in flowering plants in response to injury. It consists of chains of linked glucose units. [Mid-19thC. Formed from Latin *callosus* 'callous' (see CALLOUS).]

callosity /kə lóssəti/ (*plural* -**ties**) *n.* a local thickening of the outer layer of the skin caused by repeated friction or pressure

Callot /kə lót/, **Jacques** (1592–1635) French artist. His realistic and innovatory techniques distinguish such etchings as *Miseries of War* (1633).

callous /kálləss/ *adj.* showing no concern if other people are hurt or upset [14thC. Either via French *calleux* or directly from its source Latin *callosus*, from *callus* 'hard skin'.] —**callously** *adv.* —**callousness** *n.*

calloused /kálləst/ *adj.* having an area of hard thickened skin

callow /kállō/ *adj.* young or immature, and lacking the experience of life that comes with adulthood [Old English *calu*, from a prehistoric Germanic base of uncertain origin: possibly from Latin *calvus* 'bald' (source of English *Calvary*)] —**callowness** *n.*

call sign *n.* a signal, usually a group of letters and numbers, used for identification by a radio transmitting station or a unit or operator in radio communication with others. US term **call letters**

call slip *n.* a form for requesting a library book that is not kept on the shelves used by the public

call-up *n.* MIL the order to join the armed services in time of war. US term **draft**

callus /kálləss/ *n.* **1.** PATCH OF THICKENED SKIN a hard thickened area of skin, especially on the palm of the hand or the sole of the foot, caused by repeated pressure or friction **2.** MED MASS FORMED IN HEALING BONE a mass of fibrous tissue, calcium, cartilage, and bone that forms progressively during the healing of a bone fracture **3.** BOT PLANT TISSUE plant tissue that forms at the site of a wound, or that develops during tissue culture of plant parts, giving rise to new plantlets [Mid-16thC. From Latin. Ultimately from an Indo-European base meaning 'hard' that is also the ancestor of English *Excalibur*.]

calm /kaam/ *adj.* **1.** NOT ANXIOUS without anxiety or strong emotion **2.** NOT WINDY without wind or storms **3.** AT LOWEST POINT OF BEAUFORT SCALE relating to or having a wind speed of not more than 1.6 km/1 mi. per hour **4.** NOT STORMY smooth and without any large waves ◊ *smooth sailing on calm seas* ■ *n.* **1.** PEACE AND QUIET a situation of complete peace and quiet, with no noise, trouble, or anxiety **2.** ABSENCE OF WIND still weather, without wind or waves caused by wind ■ *vt.* (**calms, calming, calmed**) MAKE LESS TENSE to make sb less anxious or upset [14thC. Origin uncertain: probably via French *calme* or directly from late Latin *cauma* from Greek *kauma* 'heat of the day'.] —**calmly** *adv.* —**calmness** *n.*

calm down *vti.* to become or make sb become less excited, anxious, or upset

calmative /káəmətiv/ *adj.* CALMING having a calming or quietening effect ■ *n.* CALMING DRUG a drug or treatment that has a calming or quietening effect

calmodulin /kal móddyōolin/ *n.* a protein found in the cells of most living organisms that plays a crucial role in maintaining stable calcium concentration in the cell cytoplasm [Late 20thC. Contraction of CALCIUM + MODULATE + -IN.]

calomel /kállə mel, -məl/ *n.* a white or colourless tasteless compound used as a fungicide and insecticide and, formerly, in medicine as a purgative. Formula: Hg_2Cl_2. [Late 17thC. From modern Latin, of uncertain origin: probably formed from Greek *kalos* 'beautiful' + *melas* 'black'.]

Calor Gas /kállər/ *tdmk.* a trademark for liquid butane gas sold in cylinders for domestic use

caloric /kə lórrik, kállərik/ *adj.* relating to calories or heat transfer —**calorically** /kə lórrikli/ *adv.*

calorie /kálləri/, **calory** (*plural* -**ries** /–rīz/) *n.* **1.** UNIT OF ENERGY a unit of energy equal to 4.1855 joules, originally defined as the quantity of heat required to raise the temperature of 1 g of pure water by 1° C. It has now been superseded by the joule in scientific usage. **2.** LARGER UNIT OF ENERGY a unit of energy equal to the heat required to raise the temperature of 1 kg of pure water by 1° C **3.** UNIT OF FOOD ENERGY a unit of energy-producing potential in food, equal to one large calorie [Mid-19thC. From French, formed from Latin *calor* 'heat', from *calere* 'to be warm or hot'.]

calorific /kállə ríffik/ *adj.* relating to or generating heat or calories

calorific value *n.* the amount of heat released by the combustion of a specified mass of fuel, typically measured in joules per kilogram

calorimeter /kállə rímmitər/ *n.* an apparatus for measuring the amount of heat given out or taken in during a process such as combustion or change of state. The measurements are often made by observing the amount of solid liquefied, or liquid vaporized, under set conditions. —**calorimetric** /kálləri méttrik/ *adj.* —**calorimetrically** /-métrikli/ *adv.* —**calorimetry** /kállə rímmətri/ *n.*

calorize /kállə rīz/ (-**rizes, -rizing, -rized**), **calorise** (-**rises, -rising, -rised**) *v.* to treat the surface of steel or iron with aluminium powder and heat to 800–1,000° C to prevent or reduce rusting [Mid-20thC. Formed from Latin *calor* 'heat' (source of English *calorie*).]

calory *n.* = **calorie**

calotype /kállō tīp/ *n.* **1.** EARLY PHOTOGRAPHIC PROCESS a 19th-century photographic process producing a negative on a plate that was wetted with silver iodide **2.** EARLY PHOTOGRAPH a photograph produced by the calotype process [Mid-19thC. Coined from Greek *kalos* 'beautiful' + -TYPE.]

Caloundra /kə lówndrə/ city and beach resort in Queensland, Australia, situated 90 km/56 mi. north of Brisbane. Population: 54,000 (1996).

calque /kalk/ *n.* = **loan translation** [Mid-20thC. Via French 'copy', from, ultimately, Latin *calcare* 'to tread' (see CAULK).]

caltrop /káltrəp/ *n.* **1.** (*plural* -**trops** *or* -**trop**) SPINY PLANT a spiny European plant formally naturalized in California as a serious weed, harmful to livestock. Latin name: *Tribulus terrestris*. **2.** MIL SPIKES TO CATCH HOOVES OR TYRES a military device with four spikes arranged so that one will always point upwards, scattered on the ground to lame horses or puncture tyres **3.** = **water chestnut 4.** = **star thistle** [Pre-12thC. Variant of obsolete *calcatrippe* 'thistle', from medieval Latin *calcatrippa*, of uncertain origin: probably formed from Latin *calcare* 'to tread' (see CAULK).]

calumet /kályoo met/ *n.* a long-stemmed ceremonial pipe used by some Native American peoples [Late 17thC. Via French, 'pipe', a dialect variant of *chalumeau*, from, ultimately, Latin *calamus* 'reed'.]

calumniate /kə lúmni ayt/ (**-ates, -ating, -ated**) *vt.* to accuse sb falsely or slander sb (*formal*) [Mid-16thC. Via Latin stem *calumniat-* from, ultimately, *calumnia* 'false accusation' (see CALUMNY).] —**calumniable** /kə lúmni əb'l/ *adj.* —**calumniation** /kə lúmni áysh'n/ *n.* —**calumniator** /kə lúmni aytər/ *n.*

calumny /kállmni/ (*plural* **-nies**) *n.* (*formal*) **1.** DEFAMATION the making of false statements about sb with malicious intent **2.** DEFAMATORY STATEMENT a slanderous statement or false accusation [15thC. From Latin *calumnia* 'false accusation' (also the source of English *challenge*), from *calvi* 'to deceive'.] —**calumnious** /kə lúmni əss/ *adj.* —**calumniously** /-əssli/ *adv.*

calvados /kálvə doss/ *n.* apple brandy distilled from cider, made in the Normandy Region of France [Early 20thC. Named after *Calvados*, a department of Normandy, France, where the drink is made.]

calvarium /kal váiri əm/ (*plural* **-a** /-ə/) *n.* the upper domed portion of the skull (*technical*) [Late 19thC. Alteration of Latin *calvaria* 'skull' from, ultimately, *calvus* 'bald'.]

calvary /kálvəri/ (*plural* **-ries**) *n.* a sculpture representing Jesus Christ's crucifixion

Calvary /kálvəri/ *n.* the hill just outside the city walls of ancient Jerusalem where the crucifixion of Jesus Christ took place [Pre-12thC. Formed from Latin *calvaria* 'skull' (see CALVARIUM), a translation of Greek *golgotha*, from Aramaic *gŏgolṭā*; so called from the shape of the hill.]

Calvary cross *n.* a Christian cross mounted on three symmetrical steps

calve /kaav/ (**calves, calving, calved**) *vti.* **1.** ZOOL GIVE BIRTH TO CALF to give birth to a calf **2.** GEOG SPLIT to release a mass of ice that breaks away [Old English *calfian.* Formed from *cælf* 'calf'.]

Calvert /kálvərt, káwl-/, **Cecelius, 2nd Baron Baltimore** (1605–75) British-born US colonial administrator. He inherited Maryland (1632), settled the colony, and implemented the policies written into its charter.

Calvert, Charles, 3rd Baron Baltimore (1637–1715) British-born US colonial administrator. He governed the Maryland colony (1661–89).

Calvert, George, 1st Baron Baltimore (1580?–1632) British-born US absentee colonial administrator. He governed present-day Maryland (1632) and advocated religious tolerance.

calves plural of **calf** [1], **calf** [2]

Calvin /kálvin/, **John** (1509–64) French-born Swiss Protestant reformer. He founded a Presbyterian government in Switzerland and developed the doctrine of the Protestant Reformation in *Institutes of the Christian Religion* (1536).

Calvin cycle *n.* a series of chemical reactions, occurring in all photosynthesizing plants, by which carbon dioxide is converted to glucose [Named after Melvin *Calvin* (1911–97), US chemist who discovered it]

Calvinism /kálvinizzəm/ *n.* the religious doctrine of John Calvin, which emphasizes that salvation comes through faith in God, and also that God has already chosen those who will believe and be saved —**Calvinist** *n.*, *adj.* —**Calvinistic** /kálvi nístik/ *adj.* —**Calvinistically** /-nístikli/ *adv.*

Calvino /kal veeno/, **Italo** (1923–85) Cuban-Italian novelist. His works, including *If on a Winter's Night a Traveller* (1979), contain a unique blend of realism and fantasy.

calvities /kal víshi eez/ *n.* baldness (*technical*) [Early 17thC. From Latin, from *calvus* 'bald'.]

calx /kalks/ (*plural* **calxes** *or* **calces** /kál seez/) *n.* **1.** CHEM METAL OXIDE the powdery oxide of a metal formed when an ore or a mineral is roasted **2.** ANAT BACK OF

HEEL the rounded part at the back of the heel [15thC. From Latin, 'lime, limestone' (source of English *calcium* and *chalk*), from Greek *khalix* 'pebble'.]

calyces plural of **calyx**

calyculus /kə líkyŏŏləss/ (*plural* **-li** /-lī/), **calycle** /kállik'l/, **calicle** *n.* a small cup-shaped structure, e.g. the depression at the top of a coral skeleton [Late 19thC. From Latin, 'calyx of a flower', a diminutive of *calyx* 'husk' (see CALYX).] —**calycular** /kə líkyŏŏlər/ *adj.* —**calyculate** /kə líkyŏ layt, -lət/ *adj.*

Calydonian boar /kálli dōni ən-/ *n.* in Greek mythology, a gigantic wild boar sent by the goddess Artemis to destroy the city of Calydon, that is killed by Meleager, the son of the city's king

calypso /kə lípsō/ (*plural* **-sos**) *n.* **1.** CARIBBEAN SONG a Caribbean, especially Trinidadian, ballad with a lively dance rhythm, that deals satirically with social and political topics **2.** CARIBBEAN DANCE MUSIC Caribbean dance music that has syncopated rhythms, is usually improvised, and is often played by a steel band [Early 20thC. Origin unknown.]

Calypso[1] /kə lípsō/ *n.* in Greek mythology, a nymph who kept Odysseus on her island for seven years

Calypso[2] /kə lípsō/ *n.* a small irregularly-shaped natural satellite of Saturn, discovered in 1980

calyx /káyliks, kálliks/ (*plural* **calyxes** *or* **calyces** /-li seez/) *n.* **1.** FLOWER SEPALS the group of sepals, usually green, around the outside of a flower that encloses and protects the flower bud **2.** ANAT PART OF KIDNEY one of the funnel-shaped hollows in the pelvis of the kidney, through which urine passes to the ureter [Late 17thC. Via Latin from Greek *kalux* 'husk, shell', from *kaluptein* 'to conceal'.]

calzone /kal zṓ nay, -ni/ (*plural* **-nes** /-nis/ *or* **-ni** /-ni/) *n.* a semi-circular Italian turnover made from pizza dough with a savoury filling [Late 20thC. From Italian, literally 'trouser leg' from, ultimately, Latin *calceus* 'shoe', from *calx* 'heel'.]

cam /kam/ *n.* an irregularly-shaped projection on a rotating shaft that changes rotary motion into a reciprocating up and down motion in another machine part (**cam follower**) that touches it [Late 18thC. From Dutch *kam* 'comb'.]

CAM /kam/ *abbr.* computer-aided manufacturing

Camagüey Archipelago /kámmə gwáy-/ group of coral islands situated off east-central Cuba, including the islands of Romano, Sabinal, and Coco, and extending approximately 241 km/150 mi. from northwest to southeast

camaraderie /kámmə ráadəri, -ráddəri/ *n.* a feeling of close friendship and trust among a particular group of people [Mid-19thC. From French, formed from *camarade* 'comrade' (see COMRADE).]

Camargue /ka máarg/ delta region of marshes, lagoons, and farmland in the Bouches-du-Rhône administrative region in southern France. The sparsely populated region is known for its wild bulls, white horses, and flamingos.

camarilla /kámmə ríllə/ *n.* a group of advisers, especially a secretive group advising an important person [Mid-19thC. From Spanish, literally 'small room', formed from *camara* 'room'.]

camas /kámməss/ (*plural* **camasses** *or* **camas**), **camass** (*plural* **camasses** *or* **camass**) *n.* **1.** PLANT WITH EDIBLE BULB a North American plant with grassy leaves, a cluster of blue and white flowers, and an edible bulb. Latin name: *Camassia quamash.* **2.** = **death camas** [Early 19thC. From Chinook Jargon *qamaš.*]

Camb. *abbr.* Cambridge

camber /kámbər/ *n.* **1.** UPWARD CURVE IN ROAD a slight upward curve in a structure, especially the curve in the surface of a road **2.** SLANT OF VEHICLE'S WHEELS a slant in the steerable wheels on a vehicle that makes them slightly closer together at the bottom than at the top ■ *vti.* (**-bers, -bering, -bered**) MAKE CURVED SHAPE to form sth or be formed with a camber [Early 17thC. Via French *cambre* 'arched' from Latin *camur* 'curved inwards', of uncertain origin: perhaps from Greek *kamara* 'vault'.] —**cambered** *adj.*

Camberley /kámbərli/ town in Surrey, the site of an army staff college. Population: 46,120 (1991).

cambist /kámbist/ *n.* a dealer in foreign exchange [Early 19thC. Via French from Italian *cambista*, from medieval Latin *cambium* 'exchange' (see CAMBIUM).]

cambium /kámbi əm/ (*plural* **-biums** *or* **-bia** /-bi ə/) *n.* a cylindrical layer of cells in plant roots and stems that produces the new tissue responsible for increased girth, particularly sap-conducting tissues, xylem and phloem, and bark [Late 17thC. From medieval Latin *cambium* 'exchange', from Latin *cambire* 'to exchange' (source of English *change*).] —**cambial** *adj.*

Cambodia

Cambodia /kam bṓdi ə/ republic in southeastern Asia, in the southern part of Indochina, bordered by Thailand, Laos, Vietnam, and the Gulf of Thailand. Language: Khmer and French. Currency: riel. Capital: Phnom Penh. Population: 11,163,861 (1997). Area: 181,035 sq. km/69,898 sq. mi. Official name **Kingdom of Cambodia.** Former name **Khmer Republic, Kampuchea**

Cambodian /kam bṓdi ən/ *n.* **1.** PEOPLES SB FROM CAMBODIA sb who was born in or who lives in Cambodia **2.** LANG KHMER the Khmer language (*dated*) —**Cambodian** *adj.*

Camborne-Redruth /kám bawrn réd rooth/ district in Cornwall, southwestern England, situated 85 km/53 mi. southwest of Plymouth

Cambrai /kám bray, kaán-/ town in the Nord-Pas-de-Calais region in northern France. It is situated about 56 km/35 mi. south of Lille. Population: 34,210 (1990).

Cambrian /kámbri ən/ *adj.* **1.** RELATING TO PREHISTORIC ERA relating to the earliest part of the Palaeozoic era, in which invertebrate animal life, including trilobites, appeared, and marine algae developed **2.** WELSH relating to or from Wales [Mid-17thC. Formed from medieval Latin *Cambria* 'Wales', from Welsh *Cymry*.]

Cambrian Mountains /kámbri ən-/ mountain system of Wales, running from north to south and covering about two-thirds of the country. It includes Snowdon, the Brecon Beacons, and the Black Mountains.

cambric /káymbrik/ *n.* a thin white linen or cotton fabric [14thC. Named after *Kamerijk* 'Cambrai', where the fabric was originally made.]

Cambridge /káym brij/ **1.** university city in eastern England. It lies on the River Cam, and is the administrative headquarters of Cambridgeshire and a local government district. Population: city, 95,682 (1991); district, 114,800 (1995). **2.** city in Massachusetts. It is home to Harvard University, Radcliffe College, and the Massachusetts Institute of Technology. Population: 93,707 (1996).

Cambridge blue *adj.* COLOURS LIGHT BLUE a light bright blue. ◊ **Oxford blue** ■ *n.* SPORTS CAMBRIDGE SPORTSPERSON sb who has represented Cambridge University in a sports event and been awarded a blue. ◊ **Oxford blue**

Cambridgeshire /káym brijshər/ historic county of eastern England. Population: 693,900 (1995). Area: 3,409 sq. km/1,316 sq. mi.

Cambs. *abbr.* Cambridgeshire

Cambyses I /kam bī seez/ (*fl.* 6th century BC) Persian king. The son of Cyrus, he reigned as king of the Achaemenid dynasty around 600–559 BC.

Cambyses II /d. 523? BC) Persian king. He reigned from 529 BC to 522 BC, and conquered Egypt (525 BC) to expand the Persian Empire.

Camcorder

camcorder /kám kawrdər/ *n.* a portable video camera and recorder [Late 20thC. A blend of CAMERA + RECORDER.]

Camden /kámdən/ **1.** borough in North London, England. Population: 184,900 (1995). **2.** city and port in southwestern New Jersey, on the eastern bank of the Delaware River. Population: 84,844 (1996).

Camden, William (1551–1623) English antiquary and historian. He compiled a topographical account of the British Isles, *Britannia* (1586).

came past tense of **come**

camel /kámm'l/ *n.* **1.** (*plural* **-els** *or* **-el**) DESERT ANIMAL a ruminant animal of southern Eurasia that has either one or two humps on its back and is adapted to an arid climate. The Arabian camel or dromedary has one hump, the Bactrian camel has two. Genus: *Camelus.* **2.** = **caisson** ■ *adj.* COLOURS LIGHT BROWN a light sandy brown [Pre-12thC. Via Latin from Greek *kamēlos*, of Semitic origin.]

cameleer /kámmə leer/ *n.* sb who controls or rides a camel (*dated*)

camel hair, **camel's hair** *n.* **1.** HAIR OF CAMEL hair from the camel, used in making clothing and rugs **2.** TEXTILES FABRIC soft fabric containing camel hair or a similar fibre, often used for making coats **3.** PAINTING PAINTBRUSH a paintbrush used primarily for watercolours, normally made of squirrel hair

camelid /kámm'lid/ *n.* a member of the family that includes camels, llamas, and their relatives, all of which have feet with two toes and thick leathery soles. Family: Camelidae.

camellia /kə meéli ə/ *n.* (*plural* **-lias** *or* **-lia**) *n.* **1.** SHRUB WITH ROSE-SHAPED FLOWERS a shrub of the tea family, often grown as an ornamental for its glossy evergreen leaves and rose-shaped flowers. Latin name: *Camellia japonica.* **2.** TREE OR SHRUB RESEMBLING CAMELLIA any tree or shrub of the tea family that resembles the camellia. Genus: *Camellia.* [Mid-18thC. From modern Latin, formed from *Camellus,* the Latinized name of Joseph *Kamel* (1661–1706), Moravian Jesuit missionary and botanist who first described the plant.]

camelopard /kə méllə paard, kámmilə-/ *n.* **1.** GIRAFFE a giraffe (*archaic*) = **giraffe 2.** ASTRON = **Camelopardalis** [14thC. Formed from Latin from Greek *kamēlopardalis,* from *kamēlos* 'camel' + *pardalis* 'pard' (as the animal has a camel like head with spots like a leopard).]

Camelopardalis /kə méllə paard'liss/, **Camelopardus** /-dəss/ *n.* a large and faint constellation in the northern hemisphere, known as the Giraffe [From Latin (see CAMELOPARD)]

Camelot /kámmə lot/ *n.* the legendary city of King Arthur

WORD KEY: CULTURAL NOTE
Camelot, the 1960 musical by Alan Jay Lerner and Frederick Loewe, takes its title from the site of King Arthur's legendary sixth-century English court, and its tragic yet lavishly produced story centres on Arthur, his queen, Guinevere, and Lancelot. The word 'Camelot' soon came to be associated in the US public mind with the youthful stylishness, sophistication, and optimism of the John F. Kennedy administration (1961–63), chiefly because the musical's popularity coincided in time with the period of John and Jacqueline Kennedy's occupation of the White House. Further, the media reported that the First Couple enjoyed listening to recordings of this musical. As a result 'Camelot' eventually took on the generic meaning of 'a period, time, or place regarded

as idyllic, peaceful, idealistic, youthful, enlightened, and optimistic'.

camel's hair *n.* = **camel hair**

Camembert /kámməm bair/ *n.* a small round soft French cheese with an edible white rind that becomes more intense in flavour and softer in the centre as it ripens [Late 19thC. Named after *Camembert,* a town in Normandy, France, where the cheese was first made.]

cameo /kámmi ō/ *n.* **1.** CARVED STONE a semiprecious stone carved to give a raised design in one colour against a background of another, especially a pale head against a darker background **2.** BRIEF APPEARANCE BY FAMOUS ACTOR a single brief appearance by a distinguished actor in a film or play [15thC. From Italian, of unknown origin.]

cameo ware *n.* chinaware that has pale figures in relief on a coloured background

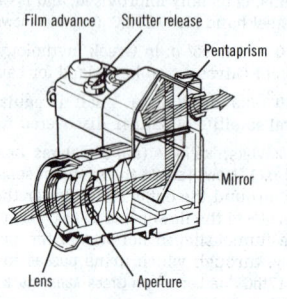

Camera

camera /kámmərə/ *n.* **1.** DEVICE FOR TAKING PHOTOGRAPHS a device for taking photographs by letting light from an image fall briefly onto sensitized film, usually by means of a lens and shutter mechanism. ◊ cine camera **2.** DEVICE FOR MAKING PICTURES a device that converts images into electrical signals for television transmission, video recording, or digital storage [Early 18thC. Via Latin, 'vault' (source of English *chamber*), from Greek *kamara.*]

camera lucida /-loossidə/ (*plural* **camera lucidas**) *n.* a box or chamber that allows images to be projected onto a surface so they can be traced [Early 18thC. From Latin, 'bright chamber'.]

cameraman /kámmrə man, -mən/ (*plural* **-men** /-men/) *n.* sb who operates a film or television camera, especially, but not always, a man

camera obscura /-ob skyoorə/ *n.* a box or small darkened room into which a moving image of what is outside is projected using a simple lens and a small hole in one of the sides of the box or room [Early 18thC. From Latin, literally 'dark chamber', because the room is darkened.]

cameraperson /kámmərə purss'n/ *n.* sb who operates a film or television camera

camera-ready *adj.* used to describe or relating to material in its final publishable format, ready to be photographed or electronically scanned for the purpose of preparing printing plates

camera-shy *adj.* with a dislike of being photographed or filmed

camerawoman /kámmərə woomən/ (*plural* **-men** /-wimin/) *n.* a woman who operates a film or television camera

camerawork /kámmərə wurk/ *n.* the ways in which cameras are used in films and television, especially their positioning and movement

camerlingo /kámmər líng gō/ (*plural* **-gos**), **camerlengo** /-léng gō/ (*plural* **-gos**) *n.* in the Roman Catholic Church, a cardinal who deals with the Pope's financial and other secular affairs [Early 17thC. Via Italian from a Frankish word that is also the source of English *chamberlain.*]

Cameron /kámmərən/, **Julia Margaret** (1815–79) British photographer, known for her sensitive portraits of eminent Victorian figures.

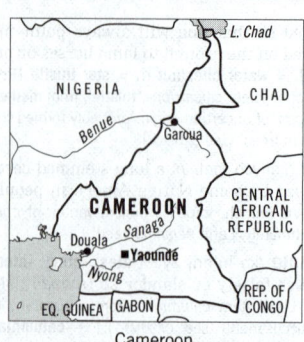

Cameroon

Cameroon[1] /kámmə róon/ country in west-central Africa. It became a German protectorate in 1884. After World War I it was divided into French and British Cameroon. French Cameroon became independent in 1960. In 1961, part of British Cameroon joined Nigeria, while the rest joined French Cameroon in a federal republic. Cameroon became a unitary state in 1972. Language: French, English. Currency: CFA franc. Capital: Yaoundé. Population: 14,611,357 (1997). Area: 475,442 sq. km/183,569 sq. mi. Official name **Republic of Cameroon**

Cameroon[2] /kámmə róon/ active volcano in southwestern Cameroon that had a major eruption in 1982. It is also the highest mountain in West Africa. Height: 4,095 m/13,435 ft.

cami /kámmi/ *n.* a camisole (*informal*) [Early 20thC. Shortening.]

camiknickers /kámmi nikərz/ *npl.* **1.** WOMAN'S UNDERGARMENT a woman's one-piece undergarment that combines a camisole with knickers **2.** LOOSE KNICKERS loose knee-length knickers for women, usually made of silky fabric and decorated with ruffles

camisado /kámmi saádō/ (*plural* **-dos**) *n.* a surprise attack at night [Mid-16thC. From Spanish *camisada,* literally 'attack in your shirt' (because attackers wore shirts over their armour in order to recognize each other), from *camisa* 'shirt'.]

camise /kə meéz/ *n.* a style of loose shirt or tunic worn in former times [Early 19thC. Via Arabic *ḳamīs* from, perhaps, late Latin *camisia* 'linen shirt, nightgown' (source of English *camisole* and *chemise*).]

camisole /kámmi sōl/ *n.* **1.** WOMAN'S UNDERGARMENT a woman's sleeveless undergarment covering the upper torso **2.** WOMAN'S TOP GARMENT a woman's sleeveless top with thin shoulder straps and a straight neckline ○ *a camisole top* [Early 19thC. Via French from, ultimately, late Latin *camisia* 'linen shirt, nightgown' (source of English *chemise*).]

Camlan /kámlən/ *n.* in Arthurian legend, the battlefield in the southwest of England where King Arthur was mortally wounded by his traitorous nephew Mordred before being carried away to Avalon

camlet /kámlət/ *n.* **1.** TEXTILES MEDIEVAL CLOTH a luxurious cloth of Asian origin used in the Middle Ages. It was a blend of goat's hair and silk, possibly originally camel hair and silk. **2.** CLOTHES GARMENT MADE FROM CAMLET a piece of clothing made from camlet [14thC. Via Old French *chamelot* from, ultimately, Arabic *kamla(t)* 'nap, pile, fibres', and popularly associated with CAMEL, hence the possibly erroneous belief that the cloth was made from camel hair.]

camo /kámmō/ *n.* camouflage clothes or material used by military personnel (*slang*) [Shortening of CAMOUFLAGE]

camogie /kə mógi/ *n.* an Irish stick and ball game that is a form of hurling played by women. Camogie was developed in 1900 by women in Dublin and the game has become increasingly popular with more than 400 clubs affiliated to the Camogie League. [Early 20thC. From Irish Gaelic *camógaíocht,* from *camóg* 'crooked stick'.]

camoodi /kə moódi/ (*plural* **-dis**) *n.* = **anaconda** [Early 19thC. From Arawak *kamudu.*]

Camorra /kə mórrə/ *n.* a secret society formed in Italy in the early 1800s that was involved in criminal and terrorist activities. The Camorra allied itself with Garibaldi and helped to eject the ruling Bourbons, then declined in the early 20th century and was suppressed in 1922 by Mussolini's Fascist government. [Mid-19thC. Via Italian from, possibly, Spanish *camorra* 'dispute'.]

camouflage /kámmə flaazh, -flaaj/ *n.* **1.** CONCEALING OF THINGS the concealing of things, especially troops and military equipment, by disguising them to look like their surroundings, e.g. by covering them with branches or leaf-clad netting **2.** CONCEALING DEVICES devices designed to conceal by imitating the colours and textures of the surrounding environment, e.g. battledress made from fabric in irregular patches of browns and greens ○ *a camouflage jacket* **3.** PROTECTIVE COLOURATION IN ANIMALS the devices that animals use to blend into their environment in order to avoid being seen by predators or prey, especially colouration **4.** DISGUISE sth that is intended to hide, disguise, or mislead ■ *vt.* (**-flages, -flaging, -flaged**) DISGUISE STH to disguise sth in order to mislead sb, often sb perceived as a threat [Early 20thC. From French, from *camoufler* 'to disguise', from Italian *camuffare* 'to disguise, deceive'.] —**camouflager** *n.*

camp[1] /kamp/ *n.* **1.** PLACE WITH REMOVABLE ACCOMMODATION a place where short-term accommodation has been temporarily erected or sited, in the form, e.g., of tents or camper vans for holidaymakers **2.** PLACE FOR TEMPORARY STAY a set of buildings where people are housed temporarily, e.g. as prisoners, refugees, or troops **3.** GROUP a group of people who share the same ideas, beliefs, or aims, or who form one of the sides in a debate ○ *the President's camp* ○ *members of the environmentalist camp* ■ *vi.* (**camps, camping, camped**) **1.** STAY TEMPORARILY to stay in temporary accommodation, especially in a tent ○ *We camped by a stream.* **2.** TAKE TEMPORARY POSITION to take up a temporary position somewhere, e.g. as a protester or in alternative accommodation ○ *We will camp on his doorstep until we get some action.* [Early 16thC. Via French from, ultimately, Latin *campus* 'level field, site for military exercises or sports' (source of English *campagna*, *campaign*, *champaign*, and *champion*).]

camp out *vi.* **1.** LIVE OUTDOORS to live or sleep outdoors, with or without a tent ○ *We would be camping out under the stars for the next three nights.* **2.** STAY SOMEWHERE TEMPORARILY to take up a temporary position somewhere, e.g. as a protester or in alternative accommodation ○ *Hordes of journalists camped out in the palace grounds.*

camp[2] /kamp/ *adj.* **1.** OVER-FEMININE exaggeratedly or affectedly feminine, especially in a man **2.** AMUSINGLY BRASH deliberately and exaggeratedly brash or vulgar in an amusing, often self-parodying way ■ *n.* **1.** EXAGGERATED FEMININITY exaggeratedly or affectedly feminine behaviour, especially in men **2.** DELIBERATE OUTRAGEOUSNESS deliberate outrageousness for humorous effect ○ *The performance is high camp.* [Early 20thC. Origin unknown, though derivation from French *camper* 'to pose' or English dialect *kemp* 'uncouth' has been suggested.] ◇ **camp it up** to behave in a deliberately outrageous way for humourous effect (*informal*)

campaign /kam páyn/ *n.* **1.** PLANNED ACTIONS a planned and organized series of actions intended to achieve a specific goal, especially fighting for or against sth or raising people's awareness of sth ○ *a national TV advertising campaign* **2.** POL VOTE-SEEKING ACTIVITIES a series of events, including rallies and speeches, that are intended to persuade voters to vote for a particular politician or party ○ *kept her campaign promises to the electorate* ○ *ran an expensive nationwide campaign* **3.** MIL MILITARY OPERATIONS a series of military or terrorist operations taking place in one area over a particular period, intended to achieve a specific objective ○ *the Falklands campaign* ■ *vi.* (**-paigns, -paigning, -paigned**) **1.** PARTICIPATE IN CAMPAIGN to take part in a campaign to achieve a specific aim ○ *parents campaigning to get the school re-opened* **2.** PARTICIPATE IN POLITICAL CAMPAIGN to take part in a political campaign ○ *We campaigned particularly strongly in the south.* [Early 17thC. Via French *campagne* 'open country' from, ultimately, Latin *campus* 'field' (source of English *camp*); the modern sense 'military operations' derives from the fighting of battles in open countryside.]

campaigner /kam páynər/ *n.* **1.** SB WHO CAMPAIGNS sb involved in a campaign for social or political change ○ *human rights campaigners* **2.** POL POLITICIAN OR POLITICAL WORKER a politician working to be elected, or a worker in an election campaign

Campanella /kámpə néllə/, **Tommaso** (1568–1639) Italian philosopher. He wrote the utopian *City of the Sun* (1623) while imprisoned by the Inquisition. Real name **Giovanni Domenico Campanella**

Campanile

campanile /kámpə neéli/ (*plural* **-les** *or* **-li** /-/) *n.* a bell tower, especially a freestanding bell tower of the kind found in Italy [Mid-17thC. From Italian *campanile*, from *campana* 'bell', from late Latin *campana* (see CAMPANOLOGY).]

campanology /kámpə nólləji/ *n.* the study or practice of bell-ringing [Mid-19thC. From modern Latin *campanologia*, from late Latin *campana* 'bell' (source of English *campanile*), from Latin *campanus* 'of Campania' (southern Italy), a former source of bronze for making bells.] — **campanologist** *n.*

campanula /kam pánnyoŏlə/ *n.* an annual or perennial plant, native to northern temperate regions, that bears bell-shaped blue, white, or pink flowers. Some species are widely grown as garden plants. Genus: *Campanula.* [Early 17thC. From modern Latin, literally 'little bell', from late Latin *campana* (see CAMPANOLOGY).]

camp bed *n.* a small narrow bed for occasional use that folds for easy storage and carriage, especially one consisting of a canvas sling supported on a sectional framework of metal tubing. US term **cot**

Campbell /kámb'l/, **Donald** (1921–67) British motor-racing driver. Son of Sir Malcolm Campbell, he set world land and water speed records and died in an attempt on the latter. Full name **Donald Malcolm Campbell**

Campbell, Sir Malcolm (1885–1948) British motor-racing driver. He was the first man to set the world land speed record above 483 kph/300 mph (1935) in 'Bluebird'.

Campbell, Mrs Patrick (1865–1940) British actor. She played Eliza in George Bernard Shaw's *Pygmalion* (1912). Born **Beatrice Stella Tanner**

Campbell, Roy (1901–57) South African-born British poet, translator, and journalist. Among his works are the satire *The Georgiad* (1931) and the autobiographical *Light on a Dark Horse* (1951).

Campbell, Thomas (1777–1844) British poet. He wrote 'The Pleasures of Hope' (1799) and patriotic lyrics such as 'Ye Mariners of England'.

Campbell-Bannerman /-bánnərmən/, **Sir Henry** (1836–1908) British statesman. He was leader of the Liberal Party (1899–1908). As British Prime Minister (1905–08) he granted self-government to the Transvaal and the Orange Free State in South Africa.

Campbell Island /kámb'l-/ uninhabited island in the southwestern Pacific Ocean, 644 km/400 mi. south of New Zealand. Area: 166 sq. km/64 sq. mi.

camper /kámpər/ *n.* **1.** SB WHO CAMPS sb who goes camping ○ *accessories for campers and hikers* **2.** RECREATIONAL VEHICLE a motor vehicle equipped as a self-contained travelling home, smaller than a motor home. It has basic facilities for cooking, washing, and sleeping. **3.** US TRAILER FOR LIVING IN a trailer equipped as a self-contained travelling home, pulled by a car

camper van *n.* = **camper** *n.* 2

Campese /kam páyzi/, **David Ian** (*b.* 1962) Australian rugby player, known for his speed and try-scoring ability.

campfire /kámp fī ə/ *n.* a wood fire built outside by campers, for cooking on or for warmth

camp follower *n.* **1.** SB UNOFFICIALLY SUPPLYING THE MILITARY a civilian who follows a military unit from place to place in order to earn money by supplying products or services, e.g. services as a prostitute **2.** UNCOMMITTED OR TEMPORARY SUPPORTER sb who supports a group or an organization but does not belong to it, often sb who becomes temporarily associated with a political party for selfish reasons

campground /kámp grownd/ *n.* US = **campsite**

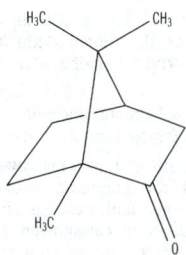

Camphor

camphor /kámfər/ *n.* a strong-smelling compound, used in medicinal creams for its mild antiseptic and anti-itching properties, and to make celluloid, plastics, and explosives [14thC. Directly or via Old French *camphore* from medieval Latin *camphora*, which came via Arabic and Malay from Sanskrit *karpūra*.] —**camphoric** /kam fórrik/ *adj.*

camphorate /kámfə rayt/ (**-ates, -ating, -ated**) *vt.* to treat or impregnate sth with camphor

camphor ice *n.* an ointment used to relieve minor skin ailments, made of camphor mixed with white wax and castor oil

camphor oil *n.* the oil that is distilled from the steamed bark and wood of the camphor tree

camphor tree *n.* an evergreen tree, native to eastern Asia, whose wood and bark are a source of camphor. Latin name: *Cinnamomum camphora.*

campimetry /kam pímmətri/ *n.* the measuring of the field of vision or the sensitivity of the retina to colour and space [Early 20thC. Coined from Latin *campus* 'field' + -METRY.]

Campinas /kam péenəss/ city in eastern São Paulo state, southeastern Brazil, situated 109 km/68 mi. northwest of the city of São Paulo. Population: 846,084 (1991).

camping /kámping/ *n.* living outdoors in a tent while on holiday or as a recreational activity ○ *a camping holiday*

campion /kámpi ən/ *n.* a flowering plant of the pink family, native to the northern hemisphere, and producing pink, red, or white flowers. Genera: *Lychnis* and *Silene.* [Mid-16thC. Origin uncertain: perhaps originally a variant of CHAMPION, from the former use of a type of campion for making garlands for athletics champions.]

Campion /kámpi ən/, **Jane** (*b.* 1954) New Zealand film

Jane Campion

director. She directed the Oscar-winning *The Piano* (1993).

Campion, St Edmund (1540–81) English priest. He worked as a Jesuit missionary in England, where he was executed on a false charge of treason.

Campion, Thomas (1567–1620) English poet. In *Observations on the Arte of English Poesie* (1602) he advocated rhymeless verse on a classical model.

campo /kámpō/ (*plural* **-pos**) *n.* a large grassy plain in South America, with scattered bushes and small stunted trees [Mid-19thC. Via either American Spanish or Portuguese, 'field', from Latin *campus* (source of English *camp* and *scamper*).]

Campo Grande /kámpō grándi/ city and capital of Mato Grosso do Sul state, southwestern Brazil. Population: 525,612 (1991).

Campos /kám poss/ city in Rio de Janeiro state, southeastern Brazil, situated 56 km/35 mi. from the mouth of the River Paraíba. Population: 275,508 (1991).

camp oven *n. ANZ* a metal pot with three short legs and a lid, used for cooking food over an open fire

campsite /kámp sīt/ *n.* **1.** AREA FOR CAMPING an outdoor area designed for camping, usually providing campers with some facilities, e.g. showers, toilets, and a shop. US term **campground 2.** *US* INDIVIDUAL CAMPING AREA a single unit of land within a campground, for a camper to pitch a tent on or park a trailer or camper on

campus /kámpəss/ *n.* **1.** UNIVERSITY SITE an area of land that contains the main buildings and grounds of a university or college, or one of the sites on which such buildings are located ○ *accommodation on campus* **2.** SITE a site on which the buildings of an organization or institution are located ○ *a dormitory for nursing students on the hospital campus* [Late 18thC. From Latin, 'level field, plain' (source of English *camp* and *champion*).]

campus novel *n.* a novel that satirizes university life. The genre appeared in Britain in the late 1970s and early 1980s.

campus university (*plural* **campus universities**) *n.* a university whose teaching, administration, and accommodation buildings are located on one main site, usually a rural site, as opposed to being spread around different sites throughout a town

campy /kámpi/ (**-ier, -iest**) *adj.* (*informal*) **1.** OVER-FEMININE exaggeratedly or affectedly feminine, especially in a man **2.** DELIBERATELY OUTRAGEOUS deliberately and humorously outrageous —**campily** *adv.* —**campiness** *n.*

campylobacter /kámpilō báktər/ *n.* a rod- or spiral-shaped bacterium that is a common cause of food poisoning in humans and of spontaneous abortion in farm animals [Late 20thC. Coined from *campylo-* (from Greek *kampulos* 'bent') + *-bacter* (from *bacterium*), literally 'bent bacterium'; so called because of the genus *Campylobacter*'s curved and spiral-shaped bacteria.]

CAMRA /kámrə/ *abbr.* Campaign for Real Ale

camshaft /kám shaaft/ *n.* a shaft that has one or more cams attached, especially one that operates the valves in a vehicle's internal combustion engine

Albert Camus

Camus /ka mo͝o/, **Albert** (1913–60) Algerian-born French novelist, essayist, and dramatist. Author of *The Outsider* (1942) and *The Plague* (1947), he was awarded the Nobel Prize in literature (1957).

cam wheel *n.* a wheel that functions as a cam

camwood /kám wo͝od/ *n.* **1.** W AFRICAN TREE a West African tree that produces hard red wood. Latin name: *Baphia nitida.* **2.** HARD RED WOOD the hard red wood of the camwood tree, formerly used in cabinetmaking and as the source of a red dye [Late 17thC. *Cam* probably from Temne *k'am.*]

can[1] /kan/ *n.* **1.** FOOD CONTAINER a sealed metal container, usually cylindrical, in which food or drink is preserved or packaged and sold **2.** METAL CONTAINER any metal container with a removable lid or cap, especially one for storing or packaging liquids, e.g. chemicals and paint **3.** CONTENTS OF CAN the contents of a metal container ○ *I drank two cans of beer.* ○ *We used up three cans of paint.* **4.** PRESSURIZED CONTAINER a metal container that holds liquid under pressure so that it can be released as a spray ○ *a can of hairspray* **5.** PRISON prison (*slang*) ○ *in the can* **6.** *US, Can* TOILET a toilet (*slang*) **7.** NAVY SHIP a ship (*slang*) **8.** *US* SHIPPING = **can buoy** ■ *vt.* (**cans, canning, canned**) **1.** PUT IN METAL CONTAINERS to package or preserve food or drink by putting it in sealed metal containers **2.** *US* STOP STH to stop sth regarded as inappropriate under the circumstances, e.g. laughter, tears, or jokes (*slang*) ○ *Just can the giggling, please.* [Old English *canne.* Either from a prehistoric Germanic word or from late Latin *canna.*] —**canful** *n.* —**canner** *n.* ◇ **carry the can** *UK, Can* to take the blame or responsibility (*informal*) ○ *An unsuspecting junior was left to carry the can.* ◇ **in the can 1.** in the final edited form ready for broadcasting or distribution (*informal*) ○ *There's a lot more to do before the film's in the can.* **2.** having been successfully completed or negotiated (*informal*) ○ *At last, after three weeks of tough negotiations, the contract was in the can.*

can[2] (*stressed*) /kan/; (*unstressed*) /kən/ CORE MEANING: a modal verb used to indicate that it is possible for sth to be done or made use of in the way mentioned ○ *Loans can be made over the phone.* *vi.* **1.** ABLE TO having the ability, knowledge, or the opportunity to do sth ○ *If you can keep a secret, so can I.* **2.** BE LIKELY be likely to be true or the case ○ *Truancy can also signal more severe, isolated problems.* **3.** BE ALLOWED to be allowed to do sth, either by legal or moral right or by permission ○ *In Britain, you can get married at 16.* **4.** BE ACCEPTABLE used to make polite requests, suggestions, and offers ○ *Can I get anybody any more coffee?* **5.** BE POSSIBLE used in questions to emphasize strong feelings about sth ○ *How can you say that?* ○ *What on earth can be the matter?* [Old English *cunnan.* Ultimately from an Indo-European base that is also the ancestor of English *know* and Latin *gnoscere* 'to know'.]

————— WORD KEY: USAGE —————

can or *may*? Purists often insist on a distinction between *can*, meaning 'be able to', and *may*, meaning 'be allowed to', but the distinction is hard to maintain in practice and the meanings often overlap. In everyday conversation *Can I go?* is as likely to be used as *May I go?*, and the context together with voice intonation usually makes it clear what is meant. In more formal situations it is wise to maintain the distinction, if only because many people expect it. Note that *may* has ambiguities of its own. *He may go* can mean either 'he is allowed to go' or 'it is possible that he will go'; again, intonation and context clarify the matter. The negative contraction *mayn't* is awkward, and for this reason *can't* is often used instead: *Can't we come too?*

can[3] *abbr.* **1.** cancelled **2.** cancellation **3.** MIL cannon **4.** MUSIC canon **5.** POETRY canto

Can. *abbr.* **1.** Canada **2.** Canadian

Canaanite /káynə nīt/ *n.* **1.** PEOPLES MEMBER OF ANCIENT SEMITIC PEOPLE a member of a Semitic people who lived in Canaan from around 3000 BC until the time of the Israelites' conquest around 1000 BC **2.** LANG EXTINCT MIDDLE EASTERN LANGUAGE an extinct language once spoken in a region between the River Jordan and the Mediterranean Sea. It belongs to the Semitic group of Afro-Asiatic languages. ■ *adj.* OF CANAAN relating to or typical of Canaan, its people, or its culture —**Canaanite** *adj.*

Canada /kánnədə/ federation occupying the northern half of North America and the second largest country in the world. Language: English, French.

Currency: Canadian dollar. Capital: Ottawa. Population: 31,000,000 (1997). Area: 9,970,610 sq. km/3,849,674 sq. mi.

Canada balsam *n.* thick resin secreted from the bark of the balsam fir. The resin is yellowish when liquid but becomes transparent when it dries. It is used for mounting specimens on microscopic slides.

Canada goose (*plural* **Canada geese**) *n.* a large North American goose with a brownish body, a black head and neck, and a white patch on its throat, also introduced into Europe. Latin name: *Branta canadensis.*

Canada jay *n.* = grey jay

Canada lily *n.* a North American lily with small orange funnel-shaped flowers. Latin name: *Lilium canadense.*

Canada thistle *n. US, Can* = creeping thistle

Canadian[1] /kə náydi ən/ *adj.* OF CANADA relating to or typical of Canada, or its people or culture ■ *n.* SB FROM CANADA sb who was born in or is a citizen of Canada

Canadian[2] /kə náydi ən/ river in the southwestern United States that flows from southern Colorado across New Mexico and Texas into Oklahoma. Length: 1,458 km/906 mi.

Canadian English *n.* the variety of English spoken in Canada

————— WORD KEY: WORLD ENGLISH —————

Canadian English is the English language as it is used in the federation of Canada, which is geographically the largest English-speaking country in the world. However, in demographic terms (with a population of over 29 million, of which over 7 million are French-speaking, mainly in the province of Quebec), it is third equal with Australia. *Canadian English* has coexisted for about 230 years with Canadian French, which predates it by a century, as the French were Canada's first main European settlers. English and French are co-official languages in a nation whose linguistic mosaic includes indigenous languages (including Cree, Inuktitut, Iroquois, and Ojibwa) and immigrant languages (including Cantonese, Italian, and Ukrainian). There are at least three regional varieties of spoken *Canadian English*: (1) the Atlantic provinces, in which the Newfoundland dialect is the most distinctive; (2) Quebec, whose English-speakers are influenced by French, and whose French-speakers, when using English, range from native-speaker fluency to varying mixtures of the two languages; (3) the rest of Canada, whose educated variety (focused on Ontario) is generally taken as the national norm. Written and printed *Canadian English* blends, to an increasing degree, the conventions of the United Kingdom (decreasingly influential) and, increasingly, those of the United States. US spelling now predominates. Official federal bilingualism often leads to hybrid formulas such as *Jeux Canada Games* (blending French *Jeux Canada* and English *Canada Games*). *Canadian English* is 'rhotic', i.e., *r* is pronounced in such words as *art*, *door*, *worker*. A feature of *Canadian English* is the use of the particle *eh* with a rising tone at the end of a sentence, as in *It's nice, eh?* Distinctively *Canadian English* vocabulary includes: (1) adoptions from indigenous languages, as in *anorak* and *kayak* (both international), *mackinaw* (a bush jacket), *muskeg* (mossy, swampy land); (2) adoptions from French, as in *anglophone* and *francophone* (both in the French style, without a capital), *caboteur* (a coastal trading vessel); (3) British English usages adapted for local purposes include *riding* (originally one of three divisions of Yorkshire, which in Canada means a political constituency), and *prime minister* (the federal first minister) contrasted with *premier* (the first minister of a provincial government).

Canadian football *n.* a form of football that is similar to American football but takes place on a larger field, has 12 players on each team, and uses three rather than four plays to advance at least ten yards or score

Canadian hemlock *n.* a coniferous evergreen tree that is native to Canada and is a valuable source of lumber and pulpwood. Latin name: *Tsuga canadensis.*

Canada

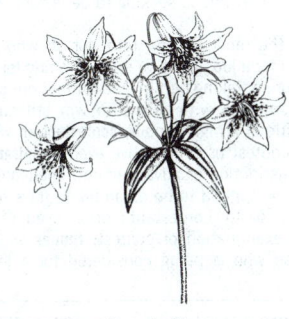

Canada lily

Canadianism /kə naydi ə nizzəm/ n. a word or other expression originating in or restricted in use to Canada

Canadianize /kə náydi ə nīz/ (**-izes, -izing, -ized**), **Canadianise** (**-ises, -ising, -ised**) vti. to make sth Canadian in form, content, or status, or become Canadian — **Canadianization** /kə náydi ə nī záysh'n/ n.

Canadian jay n. = grey jay

Canadian Shield plateau region of eastern Canada extending southwards and eastwards from Hudson Bay. Area: 4,600,000 sq. km/1,775,000 sq. mi.

Canadian whiskey n. Can blended whiskey made mainly from rye

canaille /kə nî/ n. the lowest class of people (literary disapproving) ○ 'But to think of her partaking of hospitality; all alone, too; with the canaille of Wynford!' (L. T. Meade, A Very Naughty Girl; 1907) [Late 16thC. Via French from Italian canaglia 'pack of dogs', from, ultimately, Latin canis 'dog' (source of English canine and canary).]

canal /kə nál/ n. **1. WATERWAY** an artificial waterway constructed for use by shipping, for irrigation, or for recreational use. It may take in parts of natural rivers along its course. **2. ANAT TUBE IN BODY** a tube-

shaped passage in the body, carrying air, liquids, or semi-solid material **3. ASTRON FEATURE ON SURFACE OF MARS** an apparent surface marking on Mars, formerly thought to be part of a system of water channels, a view discredited by more recent data [15thC. From French, an alteration (based on Italian canale or Latin canalis) of earlier chanel (source of English channel), from Latin canalis 'pipe, canal', from canna (see CANE).]

canal boat n. a long boat that is used on canals to carry freight or for recreational boating

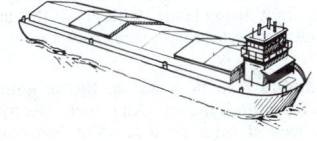

Canal boat

Canaletto /kánnə léttō/, **Antonio** (1697–1768) Italian artist, known especially for his views of Venice and London.

canaliculate /kánnə líkyoŏolət, -layt/ adj. with one or more grooves or hollows running lengthways

canaliculus /kánnə líkyoŏoləss/ (plural **-li** /-lī/) n. a minute canal or duct in the body, especially one of the four narrow tubes that carry tears from behind the eyelids to the lacrimal sac [Mid-16thC. From Latin, literally 'little pipe', from canalis (see CANAL).] —**canalicular** adj.

canalisation n. = canalization

canalise vti. = canalize

canalization /kánn'l ī záysh'n/, **canalisation** n. **1. CANAL-BUILDING** the building of canals, either from scratch or by converting existing waterways into canals **2. SYSTEM OF CANALS** a system of artificial waterways **3. DIRECTING OF STH** the directing or focussing of sth, e.g. energy, in a particular direction (formal)

canalize /kánn'l īz/ (**-lizes, -lizing, -lized**), **canalise** (**-lises, -lising, -lised**) v. **1.** vt. **BUILD CANALS** to provide an area with canals, or convert existing waterways into canals **2.** vt. **DIRECT STH** to direct or focus sth, e.g. energy or enthusiasm, in a particular direction (formal) **3.** vi. **FLOW INTO CHANNEL** to flow into or form a new channel **4.** vt. **MIL PUSH ENEMY FORCES** to drive enemy forces into a narrow space, either by firing on them or by erecting obstacles in their way

canapé /kánnə pay/ n. a bite-sized base of bread, cracker, or pastry with a topping, usually highly garnished, and served as an appetizer or to accompany drinks [Late 19thC. Via French, literally 'sofa', from medieval Latin canopeum 'mosquito net (over a bed)' (see CANOPY); the underlying idea is of a seat on which the topping sits.]

canard /kánnaard, ka naárd/ n. **1. HOAX** a deliberately false report or rumour, especially sth silly intended as a joke (literary) **2. AIRCRAFT PART LIKE WING** a small projection like a wing near the nose of an aircraft, fitted to create extra horizontal stability **3. AIRCRAFT** an aircraft fitted with a canard [Mid-19thC. From French 'duck', ultimately of imitative origin.]

canary /kə náiri/ (plural **-ies**) n. **1. BIRDS YELLOW FINCH** a small yellow finch, native to the Canaries and adjacent islands, that has been domesticated as a songbird pet and as a show bird. In the past, these birds were used to detect gas in coal mines. Latin name: Serinus canarius. **2. WINE WINE** a sweet wine from the Canary Islands, similar to Madeira **3. COLOURS** = canary yellow **4. DANCE, HIST DANCE** a lively court dance popular in the 16th century **5. WOMAN SINGER** a female singer, especially in a dance band (dated slang) **6. POLICE INFORMER** a police informer (dated slang) [Late 16thC. Via French Canarie, the chief island of the Canary Islands, from, ultimately, Latin Canaria Insula 'Isle of Dogs', from the large dogs that inhabited it in Roman times.]

canary creeper n. a climbing plant with small yellow flowers, native to Peru. Latin name: Tropaeolum peregrinum.

Canary Current /kə náiri-/ cold current of the Atlantic Ocean, flowing south from Spain down the western coast of northern Africa, joining the westward-flowing North Equatorial Current west of Mauritania-Senegal

canary grass n. an annual grass plant native to northwestern Africa and the Canary Islands, and cultivated for its seeds that are sold as birdseed. Latin name: Phalaris canariensis.

Canary Islands

Canary Islands /kə náiri-/, **Canaries** autonomous region of Spain, comprising the provinces of Las Palmas and Santa Cruz de Tenerife. Situated off the northwestern coast of Africa, they consist of seven large islands and various islets. The climate is subtropical and tourism is important, especially on the islands of Gran Canaria and Tenerife. Population: 1,631,498 (1995). Area: 7,273 sq. km/2,808 sq. mi. Spanish **Islas Canarias**

canary yellow, **canary** *adj.* of a bright yellow colour, like the plumage of certain varieties of canary —**canary yellow** *n.*

canasta /kə nástə/ *n.* **1.** VARIANT OF RUMMY a variant of the card game rummy played with two 52-card packs. Players are dealt 15 cards, the aim being to collect groups of seven similar cards. **2.** SET OF CARDS a point-scoring set of cards in canasta [Mid-20thC. Via Spanish, literally 'basket', from Latin *canistrum* (source of English *canister*), because two packs of cards (a 'basketful') are used.]

Canberra /kánbərə/ capital city of Australia, located in the Australian Capital Territory in southeastern Australia. Construction of this purpose-built capital began in 1912. Population: 322,723 (1996).

can buoy *n.* an unlighted marker buoy for shipping, cylindrical or cone-shaped above the water

canc. *abbr.* **1.** cancelled **2.** cancellation

cancan /kán kan/ *n.* a dance danced by a chorus line of women who perform high kicks to reveal their underwear. It originated in the 1840s in the music halls in Paris. [Mid-19thC. From French, possibly from *canard* 'duck', originally 'noise, uproar'.]

cancan skirt *n.* a skirt with layers of ruffles and attached knickers that is shown by cancan dancers when the skirt is lifted during the dance

cancel /kánss'l/ *v.* (**-cels, -celling, -celled**) **1.** *vti.* STOP STH HAPPENING to stop a previously arranged event from happening ○ *We had to cancel five classes because nobody showed up.* ○ *The guest speaker is ill and has had to cancel.* **2.** *vti.* END CONTRACT to withdraw officially or legally from a contract ○ *Members are free to cancel at any time.* **3.** *vt.* REVERSE INSTRUCTION to reverse an instruction to a machine, especially a computer, or bring a machine's operation to an end ○ *Cancel the download from the Internet.* **4.** *vt.* MARK AS USED to invalidate a legal or official document to show that it has been used and cannot be reused ○ *machines that cancel postage stamps* **5.** *vt.* DELETE to mark sth for deletion, usually by drawing a line through it **6.** *vti.* MATH REMOVE COMMON FACTOR to remove a common factor from the numerator and denominator of a fraction or the common terms from the two sides of an equation ○ *The twelves cancel and you end up with 8 by 6 again.* ■ *n.* **1.** PRINTING INSERTED PAGE a new page or section of a book inserted to replace a missing original or an original that contained errors **2.** PRINTING PAGE TO BE REPLACED a faulty page or section of a book replaced by another **3.** = **cancellation** [14thC. Via French *canceller* from Latin *cancellare* 'to cross out (writing)' (literally 'to make like a lattice'), from *cancelli* 'lattice' (source of English *chancel*), from *cancer* 'grating, lattice'.] —**cancellable** *adj.* —**canceller** *n.*

cancel out *vt.* to combine two opposite or equally powerful things with the result that their strengths, qualities, or effects are neutralized

cancelbot /kánss'l bot/ *n.* a computer program that finds and cancels unwanted articles sent to an Internet newsgroup by a specific user [Late 20thC. Blend of CANCEL and ROBOT.]

cancellate /kánssə layt/, **cancellated** /-laytid/ *adj.* **1.** ANAT = **cancellous 2.** BOT FORMING A MESH forming a mesh or network

cancellation /kánssə láysh'n/ *n.* **1.** CANCELLING OF STH the cancelling of sth, e.g. an appointment or order ○ *We had one cancellation for two o'clock, so we can fit you in then.* ○ *There is a cancellation charge if you withdraw your order at the last minute.* **2.** THING MADE AVAILABLE sth, e.g. a seat in a theatre, that has become available because the person who reserved it has cancelled **3.** CANCELLING MARK a mark that officially or legally invalidates sth, especially a postage stamp [Mid-16thC. Formed from Latin *cancellat-*, the past participle stem of *cancellare* (see CANCEL).]

cancellous /kánssələss/ *adj.* ANAT used to describe bone that has a mesh of hollows on the inside, as opposed to being compact or dense [Mid-19thC. Formed from Latin *cancelli* (see CANCEL).]

cancer /kánssər/ *n.* **1.** MALIGNANT TUMOUR a malignant tumour or growth caused when cells multiply uncontrollably, destroying healthy tissue. The different forms are sarcomas, carcinomas, leukaemias, and lymphomas. **2.** ILLNESS CAUSED BY TUMOUR the illness or condition that is caused by the presence of a malignant tumour **3.** FAST-SPREADING BAD PHENOMENON sth, usually sth negative, that develops or spreads quickly and usually destructively [Pre-12thC. From Latin, literally 'crab' (source of English *canker*), translated from Greek *karkinos* (source of English *carcinoma*); the sense 'tumour' evolved because of the swollen veins, thought to resemble crabs.]

Cancer /kánssər/ *n.* **1.** ASTRON CONSTELLATION BETWEEN GEMINI AND LEO a constellation in the northern hemisphere between Gemini and Leo **2.** ZODIAC 4TH SIGN OF THE ZODIAC the fourth sign of the zodiac, represented by a crab and lasting from approximately 21 June to 22 July. Cancer is classified as a water sign, and its ruling planet is the Moon. **3.** ZODIAC SB BORN UNDER CANCER SIGN sb whose birthday falls between 21 June and 22 July [Pre-12thC. From Latin (see CANCER); from the constellation's sideways movement across the sky.]

Cancerian /kan sèeri ən, -sáiri ən/ *n., adj.* = **Cancer** *n.* 3

cancerophobia /kánsərō fóbi ə/ *n.* an obsessive fear of developing cancer

cancerous /kánssərəss/ *adj.* **1.** AFFECTED BY CANCER used to describe a body part affected by cancer, or a malignant tumour ○ *cancerous cells that were detected early* **2.** CAUSING HARM developing rapidly to cause widespread harm

cancer stick *n.* a cigarette (*slang*)

cancroid /káng kroyd/ *adj.* CRABLIKE like a crab in shape, structure, or movement ■ *n.* = **squamous cell carcinoma** [Early 19thC. Formed from Latin *cancr-*, the stem of *cancer* 'crab, cancer' (see CANCER).]

Cancún /kàn kóon/ island resort on the northeastern coast of Quintana Roo state, Mexico. Population: 27,500 (1980).

candela /kan dèelə, -déllə/ *n.* the basic SI unit of luminous intensity. Symbol **cd** [Mid-20thC. From Latin, 'candle, taper' (see CANDLE).]

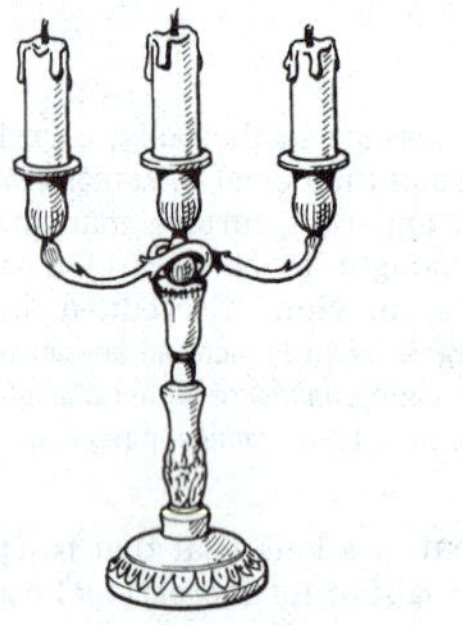

Candelabrum

candelabrum /kándə laábrəm/ (*plural* **-bra** /-laábrə/ *or* **-brums**) *n.* a large decorative candle holder with several arms or branches, or a similarly shaped electric light fitting [Early 19thC. From Latin, the plural of *candelabrum* 'candlestick', from *candela* 'candle, taper' (see CANDLE).]

candescence /kan déss'nss/ *n.* the brightness or dazzle of white light or white heat (*literary*) ○ *the candescence of snow on a cloudless morning* [Late 19thC. Formed from Latin *candescere* 'to begin to glow', from *candere* (see CANDESCENT).]

candescent /kan déss'nt/ *adj.* shining or glowing with an intense white light (*literary*) [Early 19thC. Formed from Latin *candere* 'to be white, glow' (source of English *candid*, *candle*, and *incense*).] —**candescence** *n.* —**candescently** *adv.*

C and F *abbr.* cost and freight

C and G *abbr.* City and Guilds

C & GLI *abbr.* City and Guilds of London Institute

c & i *abbr.* cost and insurance

candid /kándid/ *adj.* **1.** HONEST honest or direct in a way that people find either refreshing or distasteful ○ *a surprisingly candid admission* **2.** PHOTOGRAPHED INFORMALLY photographed or filmed without the subject knowing or having the opportunity to prepare or pose ○ *a candid documentary* **3.** UNBIASED free from prejudice or bias (*archaic*) ○ *with candid hearts and minds* **4.** KIND with innocence or purity of heart untainted by malicious thoughts and feelings (*archaic*) **5.** WHITE white, especially with the whiteness of innocence or purity (*archaic*) ○ *'kissing her candid brow, and feeling that heaven had vouchsafed him a blessing'* (George Eliot, *Middlemarch*; 1872) ■ *n. US* UNPOSED PHOTOGRAPH a photograph that is taken, unposed and informally, of a person or group ○ *hired a professional photographer to do the wedding candids* [Mid-17thC. Directly or via French *candide* 'guileless' from Latin *candidus* 'white, shining', from *candere* 'to be white, glisten'; the current sense evolved via 'pure' and 'impartial'.] —**candidly** *adv.* —**candidness** *n.*

candida /kándidə/ *n.* MED a fungus that can cause yeast infection, especially in the mouth and vagina. Latin name: *Candida albicans.* [Mid-20thC. From Latin, feminine of *candidus* 'white' (see CANDID), because of its colour.]

candidacy /kándidəssi/ *n.* sb's offering of himself or herself as a candidate ○ *She isn't expected to declare her candidacy for re-election.*

candidate /kándi dayt, -dət/ *n.* **1.** APPLICANT FOR OFFICE sb who runs for election to a political office or an official position ○ *names of candidates for the leadership of the party* **2.** APPLICANT FOR JOB sb who applies for a new job or is being considered for a new job ○ *The successful candidate will have had experience with market research.* **3.** LIKELY OR SUITABLE PERSON sb who seems suitable for sth, e.g. a surgical operation or a new treatment protocol, or who seems likely to be affected by a particular disease ○ *Men in this group are prime candidates for a heart attack.* **4.** EXAM TAKER sb sitting an examination **5.** COMPETITOR sb competing with others for a prize or award ○ *Candidates for Oscars include two Canadians and two Americans.* [Early 17thC. Directly or via French *candidat* from Latin *candidatus*, literally 'clothed in white'; from the white togas worn by candidates for election in ancient Rome.]

WORD KEY: SYNONYMS

candidate, contender, contestant, aspirant, applicant, entrant, runner

CORE MEANING: sb who is seeking to be chosen for sth or to win sth

candidate the most general term for sb who is being considered for a job, grant, or prize, running for election to a position, or taking part in an examination; **contender** sb who competes with others to win sth such as a sporting title or a high honour; **contestant** sb who takes part in a contest or competitive event; **aspirant** sb aspiring to distinction or advancement; **applicant** sb who has asked or applied to be a candidate for sth; **entrant** a term similar to 'contestant', often used of sb who enters an examination or contest; **runner** an informal term for sb who is being considered for a job or for election.

candidature /kándidəchər/ *n.* = **candidacy** [Mid-19thC. Probably modelled on French.]

candid camera *n.* the use of hidden cameras to film subjects unawares, often in stage-managed situations intended to elicit amusing responses (*hyphenated when used before a noun*)

candidiasis /kándi dī əsiss/ (*plural* **-didiases** /-sèez/) *n.* yeast infection (*technical*) [Mid-20thC. Coined from CANDIDA + -IASIS.]

Candiot /kándi ot/, **Candiote** /-ōt/ *adj.* relating to or typical of the Greek island of Crete, especially the capital, Iráklion, or its people or culture. ◊ **Cretan** —**Candiot** *n.*

candle /kánd'l/ *n.* **1.** WAX CYLINDER PROVIDING LIGHT a moulded piece of wax, tallow, or other fatty substance, usually cylindrical in shape, with a wick running through it. The encased wick burns slowly, giving light or providing decoration. **2.** CANDELA a candela (*archaic*) ■ *vt.* (**-dles, -dling, -dled**) TEST EGG to test an egg for freshness by looking at it against a bright light [Pre-12thC. From Latin *candella*, earlier *candela* (source of English *candela* and *candelabra*), from *candere* 'to be white, glisten' (source of English *candid*, *incendiary*, and *incense*).] ◇ **burn the candle at both ends** to get up very early and go to bed very late, allowing for very little rest ◇ **not hold a candle to sb** to be not nearly as good at sth as sb ○ *As a writer, he does not hold a candle to his mother.*

candleberry /kánd'lberi/ (*plural* **-ries**) *n.* any shrub or tree that has berries that can be used for making candles

candlefish /kánd'l fish/ (*plural* **-fishes** *or* **-fish**) *n.* an oily saltwater fish found in the northern Pacific Ocean. Latin name: *Thaleichthys pacificus*. [From the former use of the dried fish as a lamp by pushing a piece of bark through it as a wick]

candleholder /kánd'l hōldər/ *n.* a holder for a candle, often a decorative one. Candleholders can be of many shapes but are not necessarily tall and thin like candlesticks.

candlelight /kánd'l līt/ *n.* **1.** LIGHT FROM CANDLES the light that a burning candle provides ○ *reading by candlelight* **2.** DUSK twilight, the time when candles are lit (*literary*)

Candlemas /kánd'l mass, -məss/ *n.* **1.** CHRISTIAN FEAST DAY a Christian feast held on 2 February, commemorating the purification of the Virgin Mary and the presentation of the infant Jesus Christ in the Temple. This is also the time when church candles are blessed. **2.** SCOTTISH QUARTER DAY in Scotland, one of the four days marking the traditional three-month divisions of the year (**quarter days**), occurring on 2 February [Pre-12thC. *-Mas* from ecclesiastical Latin *missa* 'the mass' (source of English *mass*).]

candlenut /kánd'l nut/ *n.* **1.** TROPICAL TREE a tropical tree of the spurge family, native to Asia and Polynesia. Latin name: *Aleurites moluccana*. **2.** OILY NUT the seed of the candlenut tree, used as a source of oil in paints and varnishes, and, in Asia and Polynesia, threaded with a wick for use as a candle

candlepin /kánd'l pin/ *n.* a slim pin used in the bowling game candlepins [*Candle* from its shape and comparative slenderness]

candlepins /kánd'l pinz/ *n.* a bowling game using slender pins and a ball smaller than that used in tenpins (*takes a singular verb*)

candlepower /kánd'l powər/ *n.* luminous intensity measured in candelas

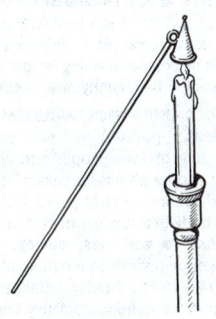
Candlesnuffer

candlesnuffer /kánd'l snufər/ *n.* a device, usually made of metal, consisting of a small cone on the end of a long thin handle, placed over the flame of a candle to put it out

candlestick /kánd'l stik/ *n.* a tall thin holder for a candle

candlewick /kánd'l wik/ *n.* **1.** COTTON FABRIC tufted cotton fabric used for bedcovers, dressing gowns, and other garments **2.** EMBROIDERY YARN soft cotton yarn used for embroidery **3.** THICK STRING thick string used for candle wicks

candlewood /kánd'l wŏŏd/ *n.* **1.** RESINOUS WOOD the resinous wood of various trees or shrubs, burnt for light and fuel **2.** RESINOUS TREE any tree or shrub that produces candlewood

can-do *adj.* keen to take on a job or challenge and confident of success (*informal*) ○ *We're only looking at can-do executives with proven track records.*

Candolle /kan dól/, **Augustin Pyrame de** (1778–1841) Swiss botanist. He was the originator of taxonomy, the science of classification of plants still in general use.

candor *n.* US = candour

candour /kándər/ *n.* **1.** CANDID QUALITY honesty or directness, whether refreshing or distasteful ○ *He spoke of their conspicuous candour and bravery.* **2.** FREEDOM FROM PREJUDICE freedom from prejudice or bias (*archaic*) **3.** KINDNESS innocence or purity of heart arising from a complete absence of malicious thoughts and feelings (*archaic*) ○ *'But the gentleness and candour of Rebecca's nature imputed no fault to Ivanhoe for sharing in the universal prejudices of his age and religion'.* (Walter Scott, *Ivanhoe*; 1819) **4.** WHITENESS whiteness, especially the whiteness of innocence or purity (*archaic*) [14thC. From Latin *candor* 'glossy whiteness, sincerity', from *cand-*, the base *candidus* 'dazzling white' (source of English *candid*) and *candere* 'to be white, glisten' (source of English *candle*).]

CANDU reactor /kán doo-/ *n.* a form of nuclear reactor designed and built in Canada that uses replaceable fuel bundles and heavy water to moderate fission and cool the reactor core [*CANDU* from the first letters of CANADA + DEUTERIUM + URANIUM]

C and W *abbr.* MUSIC country and western

candy /kándi/ *n.* (*plural* **-dies**) **1.** US, Can SMALL CONFECTION small sweet food items such as chocolate bars, mints, and toffee, usually eaten for pleasure and not as part of a meal **2.** US, Can = sweet **3.** HARD DRUGS heroin, cocaine, or any other hard drug (*slang*) ■ *v.* (**-dies, -dying, -died**) **1.** *vti.* TURN SUGAR SOLUTION INTO CRYSTALS to turn a sugar solution into crystals, especially by boiling it, or be converted into sugar crystals **2.** *vt.* STEEP IN SUGAR to dress a food by impregnating it with sugar, in order either to preserve it or to make it more pleasant to eat **3.** *vt.* COAT WITH SUGAR SYRUP to coat food with sugar or sugar syrup, or be coated with sugar or sugar syrup [13thC. Via Old French *candi* from Arabic *qandī* 'crystallized into sugar', from *qand* 'cane sugar'.]

candy apple *n.* US = toffee apple

candyfloss /kándi floss/ *n.* cooked sugar syrup, coloured and spun from a machine onto a stick in fine strands. It is eaten as a fun snack, traditionally at fairgrounds. US term **cotton candy**

candy-striped *adj.* with a pattern of narrow stripes in a single colour, usually red or pink, on a white background

candytuft /kándi tuft/ *n.* a flowering plant with thin leaves and clusters of white, red, or purple flowers. There are annual and perennial types, and the genus is native to Europe and the Mediterranean. Genus: *Iberis*. [Early 17thC. *Candy* an obsolete form of *Candia*, a former name for Crete.]

cane /kayn/ *n.* **1.** WALKING STICK a stick that people use to help them walk **2.** STICK FOR PUNISHMENT BEATINGS a long flexible stick for administering beatings, especially one formerly used to punish schoolchildren **3.** BAMBOO STEM a hollow lightweight stem of a tropical plant, especially bamboo, used in various ways in the house and garden, e.g. as a growing support for plants **4.** WOVEN STEMS the stems of various palms and grass plants, e.g. rattan, woven together to make furniture, baskets, and other household items **5.** STEM OF FRUIT PLANT the long woody stem of various fruit-bearing plants such as the raspberry or blackberry **6.** LONG-STEMMED PLANT a coarse grass or reed with long stiff stems, e.g. sugarcane or sorghum ■ *vt.* (**canes, caning, caned**) **1.** BEAT SB to beat sb, especially, formerly, a schoolchild, with a cane **2.** DEFEAT SB to subject sb to a crushing defeat (*slang*) [14thC. Via Old French *cane* and Latin *canna* from Greek *kanna* 'reed' (source also of English *canal* and *cannon*), ultimately of Semitic origin.]

cane beetle *n.* a large Australian beetle that lays its eggs in sugar cane. It is a common agricultural pest. Latin name: *Demolepida albohirtum*.

canebrake /káyn brayk/ *n.* US an area of land planted or overgrown with cane

cane grass *n.* a tall stiff-stemmed grass found in inland wetland areas of Australia. Latin name: *Eragrostis australasica*.

canephora /kə néffə rə/ (*plural* **-rae** /-rī/) *n.* an ancient Greek sculpture representing a human figure carrying a basket on its head [Early 17thC. Via Latin from Greek *kanēphoros*, literally 'basket-carrying'.]

cane piece *n.* in the Caribbean, a field of sugar cane, especially one that is isolated and belongs to a small farmer

cane rat *n.* a large rat native to sub-Saharan areas of Africa, measuring up to 60 cm/2 ft without the tail, and eaten locally as a delicacy. Genus: *Thryonomys*. [Because it eats sugarcane]

canescent /kə néss'nt/ *adj.* **1.** WHITE AND HAIRY used to describe plant parts that have a white or whitish-grey covering of fine hairs **2.** BECOMING WHITE OR GREYISH becoming white or greyish [Mid-19thC. From the present participle stem of Latin *canescere* 'to grow white', from *canus* 'white, hoary'.] —**canescence** *n.*

cane sugar *n.* sucrose obtained from sugarcane or sugar beet

Canes Venatici /káy neez və nátti sī/ *n.* a constellation of stars visible in the northern hemisphere near Ursa Major and Boötes, under the handle of the Plough [From Latin, literally 'hunting dogs']

cane toad *n.* a large South American toad introduced into Australia to control pests in sugarcane. A spectacular failure as a pest control, it has now become a major pest itself. Latin name: *Bufo marinus*.

Canetti /ka nétti/, **Elias** (1905–94) Bulgarian-born British writer. His novels include *Auto-da-Fé* (1936). He won the Nobel Prize in literature (1981).

canfield /kán feeld/ *n.* a gambling game developed from the card game patience [Early 20thC. Named after the US gambler Richard Albert *Canfield* (1855–1914), who devised the game and turned it into a form of gambling.]

cangue /kang/, **cang** *n.* a heavy wooden yoke worn on the shoulders and enclosing the neck and arms, formerly used in China for punishing petty criminals [Late 17thC. Via French from Portuguese *canga* 'yoke', from Vietnamese *gong*.]

Canicula /kə níkyŏŏlə/ *n.* = Sirius [12thC. From Latin, literally 'little dog' (see CANICULAR).]

canicular /kə níkyŏŏlər/ *adj.* relating to the star Sirius [14thC. From late Latin *canicularis*, from *canicula*, literally 'little dog' (denoting the 'dog star'), from *canis* 'dog' (source of English *canine* and *kennel*).]

canid /kánnid, káy-/ *n.* any carnivorous mammal of the dog family, which includes the foxes, wolves, jackals, dingos, coyotes, and domestic breeds [Late 19thC. From modern Latin *Canidae*, the family name, from Latin *canis* 'dog' (source of English *canine, canary*, and *kennel*).]

canine /káynīn, kánn-/ *adj.* OF DOGS relating to dogs ○ *a canine trainer* ○ *members of the canine family* ■ *n.* **1.** DENT POINTED TOOTH a pointed tooth between the incisors and the first bicuspids. Most mammals have two in each jaw. **2.** DOG a dog (*often used humorously*) [15thC. Directly or via French *canin(e)* from Latin *caninus*, from *canis* 'dog' (source of English *kennel*).]

canine distemper *n.* = distemper

canine tooth *n.* = canine *n.* 1

caning /káyning/ *n.* **1.** BEATING WITH CANE a punishment beating with a cane, especially the beatings formerly administered to schoolchildren **2.** RESOUNDING DEFEAT a resounding defeat (*informal*)

Canis Major /káyniss-/ *n.* a constellation of stars containing the star Sirius, situated southeast of Orion. Canis Major and Canis Minor represent dogs following at the heels of Orion the Hunter. ◊ **Canis Minor** [From Latin, literally 'greater dog']

Canis Minor /káyniss-/ *n.* a constellation of stars containing the star Procyon, situated east of Orion. ◊ **Canis Major** [From Latin, literally 'lesser dog']

canister /kánnistər/ *n.* **1.** PRESSURIZED CONTAINER a pressurized metal container holding a substance released as a spray **2.** SEALED CONTAINER a strong sealed metal container for hazardous chemicals **3.** FOOD CONTAINER a metal container with a lid, for storing tea, coffee, or other dry foods **4.** ARMS EXPLOSIVE a weapon used in former times consisting of a metal shell filled with gas and shot or shrapnel, designed to explode when thrown or fired from a cannon [Late 15thC. Via Latin *canistrum* (source of English *canasta*) from Greek *kanastron* 'wicker basket', from *kanna* 'reed' (source of English *cane*).]

canker /kángkər/ *n.* **1.** BOT PLANT DISEASE any disease that creates open wounds on the trunks and branches of woody plants. Cankers can be caused by bacteria, fungi, or pests. **2.** VET ANIMAL DISEASE any of several diseases of animals, e.g. a disease of horses that makes their hooves become soft and spongy, a disease that can cause ulcers in the outer ears of some animals, or a throat infection of some birds **3.** EVIL an evil or corrupting influence that spreads and is difficult to wipe out ○ *'This canker that eats up Love's tender spring'* (William Shakespeare, *Venus and Adonis*; 1593) ■ *vti.* **(-kers, -kering, -kered) 1.** BOT DEVELOP CANKER to develop canker, or cause the trunks and branches of woody plants to develop canker **2.** MAKE OR BECOME CORRUPT to become a source of spreading corruption or evil, or cause sth to decay as a result of spreading corruption or evil [14thC. Via Old Northern French *cancre* from the Latin stem *cancr-* 'crab, cancer' (see CANCER).] —**cankerous** *adj.*

canker sore *n.* an ulcer on the lips or inside the mouth

cankerworm /kángkər wurm/ *n.* the larva of either of two types of moth that destroys the leaves and fruit of trees in North America. Latin name: *Paleacrita vernata* and *Alsophila pometaria.*

canna /kánnə/ *n.* a perennial tropical plant native to the West Indies and Central America that is cultivated for its clusters of red or yellow flowers and luxuriant foliage. Genus: *Canna.* [Mid-18thC. Via modern Latin *Canna*, genus name, from Latin *canna* 'reed, cane' (see CANE).]

cannabidiol /kánnəbə dī ol, kə nábbə-/ *n.* one of the chemical constituents of cannabis. Formula: $C_{21}H_{28}(OH)_2$. [Mid-20thC. Coined from CANNABIS + DI- + -OL.]

cannabis /kánnəbiss/ *n.* **1.** DRUG a mild intoxicant and hallucinogen produced in various forms from the dried leaves and flowers of the hemp plant, smoked or chewed to induce relaxation and mild euphoria. Its recreational use is illegal in most countries. **2.** HEMP PLANT the hemp plant, especially when grown as a source of cannabis. Latin name: *Cannabis sativa.* [Early 18thC. Via Latin (source of English *canvas*) from Greek *kannabis*.]

cannabis resin *n.* the drug cannabis in the form of a greenish-black resin

Cannae /kánnee/ battlefield situated near present-day Barletta, Bari province, Puglia, southeastern Italy. It was the site of Hannibal's major defeat of the Roman army.

canned /kand/ *adj.* **1.** = **tinned 2.** PRE-RECORDED pre-recorded in a standardized form for general use, rather than recorded for a specific broadcast or performance ○ *The actors learn to leave pauses where the canned laughter is to be inserted.* **3.** UNVARYING used repeatedly with little or no variation, and therefore lacking freshness or originality ○ *gave the usual canned spiel about not wanting to raise taxes* **4.** DRUNK extremely inebriated (*slang*)

cannel /kánn'l/, **cannel coal** *n.* a bituminous coal that burns brightly and creates a lot of smoke [Mid-16thC. From northern English dialect *cannel* 'candle', from its bright flame.]

cannelloni /kánnə lṓni/ *n.* wide tubes or rolls of pasta that are stuffed with a filling, e.g. meat or cheese, topped with sauce, often tomato, then baked [Mid-20thC. From Italian, the plural of *cannellone* 'tubular noodle', from, ultimately, Latin *canna* 'cane, reed' (see CANE).]

cannelure /kánnəlyoor/ *n.* a groove around the cylindrical part of a bullet [Mid-18thC. From French, from *canneler* 'to make a groove in', from *canne* 'reed' (see CANE).]

cannery /kánnəri/ (*plural* **-ies**) *n.* a factory where food is packaged into tins

Cannes /kan, kanz/ resort and seaport on the French Riviera that is the site of an annual international film festival. It is situated in the Alpes-Maritimes Department in the Provence-Alpes-Côtes-d'Azur administrative region of southern France. Population: 335,647 (1990).

cannibal /kánnib'l/ *n.* **1.** SB WHO EATS HUMAN FLESH sb who eats human flesh, whether as food or as part of a religious ritual **2.** ANIMAL THAT EATS ITS OWN SPECIES an animal that eats the flesh of other animals of the same species [Mid-16thC. From Spanish *Canibales*, a variant (used by the explorer Columbus) of *Caribes*, the name of a cannibalistic people of Cuba and Haiti (see CARIB).]

cannibalise *vt.* = **cannibalize**

cannibalism /kánnibə lizzəm/ *n.* **1.** HUMANS EATING HUMANS the eating of human flesh by other human beings, whether for food or as a religious ritual **2.** ANIMALS EATING OWN SPECIES the eating of animal flesh by animals of the same species

cannibalistic /kánnibə lístik/ *adj.* relating to, involving, or practising cannibalism —**cannibalistically** *adv.*

cannibalize /kánnibə līz/ **(-izes, -izing, -ized), cannibalise (-ises, -ising, -ised)** *vt.* **1.** STEAL PARTS to take parts from sth, especially a machine, in order to use them elsewhere ○ *The troops, hard-pressed for spare parts, cannibalized the tracks from a wrecked tank to repair their own damaged vehicle.* **2.** EAT MEMBER OF OWN SPECIES to eat the flesh of another human being or of an animal of the same species —**cannibalization** /kánnibə lī záysh'n/ *n.*

cannikin /kánnikin/ *n.* a small can, especially one used for drinking from [Late 16thC. From Dutch *kanneken*, literally 'little can', from Middle Dutch *canne* 'can'.]

Canning /kánning/, **Charles John, 1st Earl Canning** (1812–62) British colonial administrator. He was Governor-General (1857–58) and first Viceroy (1858–62) of British India.

Canning, George (1770–1827) British statesman. As foreign secretary (1807–09, 1822–27) he encouraged independence movements in Latin America. He was briefly British prime minister (1827).

Canning Basin /kánning-/ arid lowland region in the Great Sandy Desert, northern Western Australia, extending east to the Kimberley Plateau and south to the River De Grey from Derby

Cannock /kánnək/ former mining town in Staffordshire, central England, situated 26 km/16 mi. northwest of Birmingham. Population: 77,710 (1991).

Cannock Chase area of Outstanding Natural Beauty in Staffordshire, central England, near Rugeley. Area: 6,720 hectares/16,800 acres.

cannon /kánnən/ *n.* **1.** (*plural* **-nons** *or* **-non**) FORMER WEAPON a weapon used in former times, now used only ceremonially, consisting of a simple iron tube mounted on wheels. It fires heavy iron balls and other projectiles. ○ *The cannon fired a 21-gun salute.* **2.** MODERN WEAPON a modern heavy artillery weapon large enough to need to be mounted for firing, e.g. one mounted on a warship or on a tracked vehicle **3.** AIRCRAFT GUN a rapid-firing gun mounted on an aircraft **4.** CUE GAMES BILLIARDS SHOT in cue games, a shot in which the cue ball hits one ball that then hits another ball. In billiards, this is a point-scoring shot. US term **carom 5.** BELL LOOP the loop at the top of a bell from which it is suspended ■ *v.* **(-nons, -noning, -noned) 1.** *vt.* = **cannonade 2.** *vi.* COLLIDE to collide with sth or bounce off it at great speed and with a lot of force ○ *a 35-yard shot that cannoned back off the post* ○ *The car, out of control on the icy road, cannoned into the bridge abutment and burst into flames.* **3.** *vi.* CUE GAMES MAKE A CANNON SHOT in cue games, to make a cannon shot [14thC. Via French *canon* from Italian *cannone*, literally 'large tube', from, ultimately, Latin *canna* 'reed, tube' (see CANE).]

cannonade /kánnə náyd/ *n.* **1.** MIL BOMBARDMENT a sustained bombardment with heavy artillery **2.** STH LIKE A BOMBARDMENT sth that sounds or feels like an artillery bombardment ○ *'The deep cannonade of roaring thunder belched forth its fearsome challenge'.* (Edgar Rice Burroughs, *Tarzan of the Apes*; 1914) ■ *v.* **(-ades, -ading, -aded) 1.** *vti.* BOMBARD to subject an enemy to a cannonade **2.** *vt.* ATTACK SB to subject sb to a sustained attack, e.g. with words of criticism or reproach [Mid-16thC. Via French from Italian *cannonata*, from *cannone* (see CANNON).]

cannonball /kánnən bawl/ *n.* **1.** BALL FIRED FROM CANNON a heavy metal or stone ball fired from an old-fashioned cannon **2.** JUMP INTO WATER a jump into water with the body tucked into a ball, usually with head down and knees drawn up to the chest ■ *vi.* **(-balls, -balling, -balled)** TRAVEL QUICKLY to travel at great speed (*informal*) ○ *The train cannonballed through the dark tunnel.*

cannonball tree *n.* a South American tree that produces round fruits with woody husks that are used to make containers and utensils. Latin name: *Couroupita guianensis.*

cannon bone *n.* a bone in the lower limbs of some hoofed animals, evolved from the fusing of the metatarsals or metacarpals [*Cannon* because of the bone's tubular shape]

cannoneer /kánnə néer/ *n.* in former times, a soldier who fired a cannon [Mid-16thC. Via French *canonnier* from Italian *cannoniere*, from *cannone* (see CANNON).]

cannon fodder *n.* (*informal*) **1.** LOW-RANKING MILITARY PERSONNEL members of the lowest ranks of the military, regarded as an expendable resource in wartime **2.** EXPENDABLE PERSON any person or group regarded as a resource to be exploited or sacrificed ○ *Our team ended up as cannon fodder for the opponents in the first championship game.*

cannonry /kánnənri/ (*plural* **-ries**) *n.* **1.** BURST OF ARTILLERY FIRE a burst of artillery fire **2.** ARTILLERY artillery in general

cannot /kánnot, -ət, kə nót/ *v.* an alternative way of writing 'can not'

WORD KEY: USAGE

See Usage note at ***help***.

cannula /kánnyoolə/ (*plural* **-las** *or* **-lae** /-lī/), **canula** (*plural* **-las** *or* **-lae**) *n.* a flexible tube with a sharp-pointed part at one end that is inserted into a duct, vein, or cavity in order to drain away fluid or to administer drugs [Late 17thC. From Latin, literally 'little tube', from *canna* 'reed, pipe' (see CANE).]

cannulate /kánnyoo layt/, **canulate** *vt.* **(-lates, -lating, -lated)** INSERT TUBE INTO BODY to insert a tube (**cannula**) into a vein or cavity in order to drain away fluid or to administer drugs ■ *adj.* TUBULAR tubular in shape (*technical*) —**cannulation** /kánnyoo láysh'n/ *n.*

canny /kánni/ *adj.* **(-nier, -niest) 1.** SHREWDLY KNOWING shrewd enough not to be easily deceived ○ *a canny negotiator* **2.** *N England* GOOD good, pleasant, or excellent (*informal*) **3.** *Scotland* MILD-TEMPERED docile and obedient **4.** *Scotland* PRUDENT careful and shrewd in money matters ■ *adv.* EXCEEDINGLY used to emphasize the degree or extent of sth (*regional*) ○ *We walked a canny long way.* [Late 16thC. Originally a Scots dialect form of CAN in its original meaning 'to know, come to know' (hence 'to be able').] —**cannily** *adv.* —**canniness** *n.*

canoe /kə nóo/ *n.* LIGHT NARROW POINTED BOAT a lightweight boat identically pointed at each end. It can be paddled by one or two people and sometimes can carry other people as passengers. Canoes were originally made from natural materials, but modern canoes are made of aluminium or of moulded plastic and fibreglass. ■ *vi.* **(-noes, -noeing, -noed)** TRAVEL IN CANOE to travel or paddle in a canoe, often as a sport or hobby [Mid-16thC. Alteration (influenced by French *canoë*) of Spanish *canoa* from, ultimately, Carib *canaoua*.] —**canoeable** *adj.* ◇ **paddle your own canoe** to take control of and responsibility for your own life and affairs (*informal*)

canoeing /kə nóo ing/ *n.* the sport, hobby, or activity of paddling a canoe

canoeist /kə nóo ist/ *n.* sb who canoes, especially as a hobby or a sport

can of worms *n.* a complicated situation that results from unforeseen problems, especially an issue that seems likely to create conflicts (*informal*)

canola /kə nṓlə/ *n.* = **canola oil** [Late 20thC. Coined from CANADA + -OLA (influenced by Latin *oleum* 'oil').]

canola oil *n.* a kind of rapeseed oil that has a high level of monounsaturated fatty acids, used as a cooking oil

canon[1] /kánnən/ *n.* **1.** GENERAL RULE a general rule, principle, or standard ○ *one of the fundamental canons of free-market economics* **2.** RELIGIOUS DECREE a decree issued by a religious authority, especially one ruling on religious practices **3.** BODY OF RELIGIOUS WRITINGS a set of religious writings regarded as authentic and definitive and forming a religion's body of scripture **4.** SET OF ARTISTIC WORKS a set of artistic works established as genuine and complete, e.g. the works of a particular writer, painter, or filmmaker ○ *It's not one of the best-known pictures in the Welles canon.* **5.** PART OF MASS in the Roman Catholic Mass, the prayer during which the bread and wine are consecrated **6.** MUSIC **STAGGERED SINGING OR PLAYING** a musical technique in which different instruments or voices enter one after the other, each playing or singing exactly the same sequence of notes, resulting in often complex counterpoint [Pre-12thC. Via Latin from Greek *kanōn* 'rule'.]

canon[2] /kánnən/ *n.* **1. MEMBER OF CLERGY ATTACHED TO CATHEDRAL** a member of the Christian clergy who is on the permanent staff of a cathedral and has specific duties in relation to the running of it **2.** = **canon regular** [12thC. Via Old French *canonie* from ecclesiastical Latin *canonicus* '(sb living) according to a rule', from Latin *canon* 'rule' (see CANON[1]).]

cañon *n.* = **canyon**

canoness /kánnə néss/ *n.* in the Roman Catholic Church, a woman who belongs to one of several religious orders in which members live under a rule, not a vow

canonic *adj.* = **canonical** [15thC. Directly or via French *canonique* from Latin *canonicus*, from, ultimately, Greek *kanōn* 'rule' (source also of *canon*[1]).]

canonical /kə nónnik'l/, **canonic** /kə nónnik/ *adj.* **1. OF A CANON OF WORKS** relating or belonging to the biblical canon or a canon of artistic works established as genuine and complete **2. FOLLOWING CANON LAW** conforming to or authorized by canon law **3. CONFORMING TO GENERAL PRINCIPLES** conforming to accepted principles or standard practice **4. OF CATHEDRAL OR REGULAR CANONS** relating to members of the clergy who are canons **5.** MUSIC **OF MUSICAL CANON** relating to musical canons, or sung or played in a canon [15thC. From medieval Latin *canonicalis*, from Greek *kanōn* 'rule' (source also of *canon*[1]).] —**canonically** *adv.*

canonical hour *n.* **1. PRAYER TIME** in the Roman Catholic Church, any of the daily prayer times when specific prayers are said. These times are the matins with lauds, prime, terce, sext, nones, vespers, and compline. **2. TIME FOR MARRIAGE** in the Church of England, any time between 8 am and 6 pm when marriages can be officially celebrated

canonicals /kə nónnik'lz/ *npl.* ceremonial robes worn by members of the clergy during a religious ceremony

canonicity /kánnə níssəti/ *n.* inclusion in a religious or secular canon, or status as an included item

canonise *vt.* = **canonize**

canonist /kánnənist/ *n.* = **canon lawyer** [Mid-16thC. Directly or via French *canoniste* from medieval Latin *canonista*, from, ultimately, Greek *kanōn* 'rule' (source also of *canon*[1]).] —**canonistic** /kánnə nístik/ *adj.* —**canonistical** /-nístik'l/ *adj.*

canonization /kánnən ī záysh'n/, **canonisation** *n.* **1. NOMINATION AS A SAINT** the formal process or decree by which a deceased person is declared by the Roman Catholic Church to be a saint **2. RELIGIOUS APPROVAL** the official sanctioning of sth by a religious authority **3. IDOLIZATION** the idolizing of sb, or the glorifying of sb or sth ○ *the canonization of a young president who was merely human like the rest of us* [14thC. From the medieval Latin stem *canonization-*, from *canonizare* (see CANONIZE).]

canonize /kánnə nīz/ (**-izes, -izing, -ized**), **canonise** (**-ises, -ising, -ised**) *vt.* **1. DECLARE AS SAINT** in the Roman Catholic Church, to declare a deceased person to be a saint **2. GIVE RELIGIOUS APPROVAL TO** to declare sth to be acceptable or valid according to canon law **3. GLORIFY** to idolize sb or glorify sth ○ *'And fame in time to come canonize us'* (William Shakespeare, *Troilus and Cressida*; 1601) [14thC. Via medieval Latin *canonizare*, from, ultimately, Greek *kanōn* 'rule' (source also of *canon*[1]).] —**canonizer** *n.*

canon law *n.* the body of laws that governs the affairs of the Christian church or a particular branch of it

canon lawyer *n.* a specialist in or practitioner of canon law

canon regular (*plural* **canons regular**) *n.* a member of any of several Roman Catholic orders of monks living in communities that follow Augustinian rules

canonry /kánnənri/ (*plural* **-ries**) *n.* the status or position of a religious canon

canoodle /kə nóod'l/ (**-noodles, -noodling, -noodled**) *vti.* to kiss and cuddle sb in a mildly romantic or sexual way (*informal*) ○ *couples canoodling on the back row of the dark theatre* [Mid-19thC. Origin unknown.]

can opener *n.* = **tin opener**

Canopic jar

canopic jar /kə nṓpik-/, **Canopic jar** *n.* a jar used in ancient Egypt to hold the embalmed entrails of a mummy [Late 19thC. *Canopic* from Latin *Canopicus*, from *Canopus*, port in ancient Egypt and site of ancient monuments.]

Canopus /kə nṓpəss/ *n.* the second brightest star in the sky after Sirius, 98 light-years away from Earth and situated in the Argo constellation. Because it is so bright, spacecraft often take Canopus as a reference point for orientation.

canopy /kánnəpi/ (*plural* **-pies**) *n.* **1. COVERING FOR SHELTER** a covering fixed above sth else to provide shelter or for decoration, especially a fabric covering designed to be removed or folded away **2.** BOT **TREETOPS** the uppermost layer of vegetation in a forest, consisting of the tops of trees forming a kind of ceiling **3. SKY** the sky as a covering or ceiling (*literary*) ○ *the vast canopy of stars* **4.** ARCHIT **ROOFED STRUCTURE** a roofed structure that covers an area, especially one that shelters a passageway between two buildings **5.** AIR **PART OF PARACHUTE** the part of a parachute that opens and fills with air **6.** AIR **COCKPIT COVER** the transparent cover of an aircraft's cockpit [14thC. Via medieval Latin *canopeum* 'canopy above an altar' from, ultimately, Greek *kōnōpeion* 'bed with a mosquito net', from *kōnōps* 'mosquito'.] —**canopied** *adj.*

Canova /ka nṓvə/, **Antonio, Marquis of Ischia** (1757–1822) Italian sculptor. His neoclassical works include figures of Napoleon I and George Washington.

Canso /kánsō/ town in Guysborough County, eastern Nova Scotia, Canada, situated on the Atlantic Ocean near Cape Canso. Population: 1,228 (1991).

canst *stressed form* /kanst/; *unstressed form* /kənst/ *v.* an archaic form of the verb 'can' used with 'thou'

cant[1] /kant/ *n.* **1. CLICHÉD TALK** boring talk filled with clichés and platitudes **2. HYPOCRITICAL TALK** insincere talk, especially where morals and religion are concerned **3. JARGON** the special language or vocabulary of a particular group, especially a group whom some people look down on ■ *vi.* (**cants, canting, canted**) **SPEAK CANT** to use cant, especially to speak or lecture others hypocritically on matters of religion or morals [Mid-16thC. Probably from Latin *cantare* 'to sing'; perhaps from an ironic comparison between a church choir's singing and the speech of beggars and criminals.] —**canter** *n.* —**canting** *adj.* —**cantingly** *adv.*

WORD KEY: ORIGIN

The Latin word *cantare*, meaning 'to sing', from which ***cant*** is derived, is also the source of English *accent*, *cantabile*, *cantata*, *canto*, *cantor*, and *chant*.

cant[2] /kant/ *n.* **1. SLOPE** slope, degree of slope, or a sloping surface **2. JOLT** a jolt that knocks sth out of its straight or level position ■ *vt.* (**cants, canting, canted**) **JOLT STH** to knock sth out of its straight or level position [14thC. Via Middle Low German *kante* or Middle Dutch *cant* 'edge' from assumed Vulgar Latin *canto* (source of English *decant*), from Latin *cantus* 'wheel rim, tyre', probably of Celtic origin.]

can't /kaant/ *contr.* cannot

Cant. *abbr.* **1.** BIBLE Canticle of Canticles **2.** Canterbury

Cantab /kán tab/ *adj.* of the University of Cambridge (*used after titles of academic awards*) Abbr of **Cantabrigiensis.** ◊ **Oxon.** [Shortening of Latin *Cantabrigiensis*]

cantabile /kan taá bi lay/ *adv.* **FLOWING** in a smooth, flowing, and melodious style (*used as a musical direction*) ■ *n.* **CANTABILE PIECE** a cantabile passage or piece of music [Early 18thC. Via Italian, 'that can be sung'.] —**cantabile** *adj.*

Cantabrian Mountains /kan táybri ən-/ mountain range extending about 480 km/300 mi. west from the Pyrenees across northern Spain. The highest peak is Torre Cerredo. Height: 2,678 m/8,787 ft.

Cantabrigian /kántə bríji ən/ *n.* **1. CAMBRIDGE STUDENT** a student or graduate of the University of Cambridge in England **2. SB FROM CAMBRIDGE** sb from Cambridge in England or Cambridge in Massachusetts [Mid-16thC. From Latin *Cantabrigia* 'Cambridge (England)'.] —**Cantabrigian** *adj.*

cantaloupe /kántə loop/, **cantaloup** *n.* **1. SMALL ORANGE-FLESHED MELON** a small round melon with a ridged scaly rind and aromatic orange flesh. Latin name: *Cucumis melo cantalupensis.* **2. ANY ORANGE MELON** any orange-fleshed melon [Late 18thC. Via French from Italian *Cantaluppi*, a papal villa near Rome where the melon was introduced from Armenia.]

cantankerous /kan tángkərəss/ *adj.* easily angered and difficult to get on with [Mid-18thC. Origin uncertain: probably a blend of RANCOROUS and an unknown element (or perhaps via Middle English *contekour* 'brawler' from assumed Anglo-Norman *contek* 'strife').] —**cantankerously** *adv.* —**cantankerousness** *n.*

cantata /kan taátə/ *n.* a musical composition for voices and instruments, usually on a religious theme, containing arias, choruses, and recitatives [Early 18thC. Via Italian from Latin, the feminine past participle of *cantare* 'to sing'(source of English *cant*, *chant*, and *incantation*), from *canere* 'to sing'.]

cantatrice /kaáN ta tréess/ *n.* a female singer, especially of opera [Early 19thC. Directly or via Italian from French, from Latin *cantatrix*, from *cantare* (see CANTATA).]

cant dog *n.* = **cant hook** [From CANT[2] + DOG in the sense of 'mechanical device']

canteen /kan téen/ *n.* **1. CAFETERIA** a place where food is served, especially in a school or workplace **2. SOLDIERS' SHOP** a shop selling food, toiletries, and other items on a military base **3. CUTLERY BOX** a box or chest with compartments for storing cutlery **4. PORTABLE BOWLS AND EATING UTENSILS** a portable set of cooking and eating utensils used by soldiers or campers (*dated*) **5. TEMPORARY FOOD STAND** a mobile or temporary food stand **6. RECREATION CENTRE** a recreation centre or social club, especially for soldiers or teenagers (*dated*) **7. PORTABLE DRINKING FLASK** a small container used by campers or soldiers for carrying liquids such as drinking water [Mid-18thC. Via French *cantine* from Italian *cantina* 'cellar', perhaps via *canto* 'corner (for storage)' from assumed Vulgar Latin *canthus* 'corner, edge', from Latin, 'iron tyre'.]

canter /kántər/ *n.* **1. HORSE'S MEDIUM PACE** a smooth easy gait of a horse or donkey, slower than a gallop but faster than a trot **2. HORSE RIDE AT CANTER** a horse ride at a canter ■ *v.* (**-ters, -tering, -tered**) **1.** *vi.* **MOVE AT CANTER** to move or ride at a canter **2.** *vt.* **MAKE HORSE CANTER** to make a horse go at a canter [Early 18thC. Shortening of *Canterbury gallop*, referring to the pace of medieval pilgrims who rode to the shrine of St Thomas à Becket in Canterbury in Kent.]

canterbury /kántərbəri/ (*plural* **-ies**) *n.* **1. MUSIC STAND** a stand with partitions for holding sheet music or magazines **2. CUTLERY STAND** a stand with partitions for holding cutlery and plates [Early 19thC. Probably named after Charles Manners-Sutton, first Viscount *Canterbury.*]

Canterbury /kántərbəri/ **1.** city in Kent, England. Its cathedral is the mother church of the Church of England. Population: 36,464 (1991). **2.** administrative region of New Zealand, located in eastern South Island and including the city of Christchurch. Population: 478,912 (1996). Area: 56,612 sq. km/21,858 sq. mi.

Canterbury bells *n.* a European plant cultivated for its bell-shaped flowers. Latin name: *Campanula medium.* [Perhaps from a fanciful association of the bell-shaped flowers with the bells worn by pilgrims' horses, referring to the pilgrimage destination of CANTERBURY, Kent (see CANTER)]

Canterbury Bight /kántərbəri bīt/ wide bay on the eastern coast of South Island, New Zealand, extending 135 km/84 mi. from the Banks Peninsula to Timaru

Canterbury Plains fertile lowland area in eastern South Island, New Zealand. It is the largest area of flat land in New Zealand.

cantharis /kánthəriss/ (*plural* **-tharides** /-thárri deez/) *n.* = **Spanish fly** [14thC. Via Latin from Greek *kantharis*, of unknown origin.]

canthi plural of **canthus**

cant hook *n.* a wooden pole with a pivoting metal hook at one end, used in forestry for handling logs [From CANT[2]]

canthus /kánthəss/ (*plural* **-thi** /-thī/) *n.* the corner or angle at either side of the eye [Mid-17thC. Via Latin from Greek *kanthos* (source of English *decant*).]

canticle /kántik'l/ *n.* a song or chant, especially a hymn containing words derived from the Bible, used in the Christian liturgy [13thC. From Latin *canticulum*, literally 'little song', from *canticum* 'song', from *cantus* 'song' (see CANTO).]

Canticle of Canticles /kántik'l əv kántik'lz/ *n.* = **Song of Solomon**

cantilena /kánti láynə/ *n.* a smooth-flowing melodious line in vocal or instrumental music [Mid-18thC. Directly or via Italian from Latin, 'song', from *cantus* 'song' (see CANTO).]

cantilever /kánti leevər/ *n.* **1.** CIV ENG **PROJECTION SUPPORTED AT ONE END** a projecting structure that is attached or supported at only one end **2.** BUILDING **SUPPORTING BRACKET** a bracket that supports a balcony or a cornice **3.** AEROSP **WING WITH NO EXTERNAL BRACE** an aircraft wing constructed without external braces ■ *v.* (**-vers, -vering, -vered**) **1.** *vt.* CIV ENG **ATTACH STH AT ONE END** to construct sth in such a way that it is attached or supported at only one end **2.** *vi.* **EXTEND LIKE CANTILEVER** to project outwards like a cantilever [Mid-17thC. Origin unknown.]

cantilever bridge *n.* a bridge consisting of arms projecting outwards from supporting piers and meeting in the middle of each span

cantillate /kánti layt/ (**-lates, -lating, -lated**) *vti.* to chant or intone sth, especially passages of the Hebrew Scriptures [Mid-19thC. From Latin *cantillat-*, the past participle stem of *cantillare* 'to sing low, hum', from *cantare* (see CANTATA).] —**cantillation** /kánti láysh'n/ *n.*

cantina /kan teénə/ *n.* a bar or wine shop, especially in a Spanish-speaking country [Late 19thC. Via Spanish, 'bar, wine cellar', from Italian, '(wine)cellar' (see CANTEEN).]

canting arms *npl.* a coat of arms that makes a visual reference to the bearer's name [Canting formed from CANT[1] (verb)]

cantle /kánt'l/ *n.* **1.** **BACK OF SADDLE** the raised back part of a saddle for a horse **2.** **PIECE** a corner, portion, segment, or broken-off piece of sth (*archaic*) [14thC. Via Anglo-Norman *cantel* from medieval Latin *cantellus* 'small corner', from assumed Vulgar Latin *cant(h)us* (see CANTEEN).]

canto /kánt ō/ (*plural* **-tos**) *n.* **1.** POETRY **PART OF POEM** any of the main divisions of a long poem **2.** MUSIC **SONG** a song or melody (*archaic*) **3.** MUSIC = **cantus** [Late 16thC. Via Italian from Latin *cantus* 'song' (source of English *accent* and *descant*), from *cantare* (see CANTATA).]

canton /kán ton, kan tón/ *n.* **1.** **PART OF COUNTRY** division of a country, especially one of the states into which Switzerland is divided **2.** **PART OF FRENCH ARRONDISSEMENT** a division of a French arrondissement **3.** **PART OF FLAG** a rectangular division in the top corner of a flag, next to the staff **4.** HERALDRY **PART OF SHIELD** a small square or oblong division of a shield, usually in the top left corner [Early 16thC. Via French from Italian dialect *cantone*, literally 'large corner, large part', from *canto* 'corner' (see CANTEEN).] —**cantonal** /kánt'nəl/ *adj.*

Canton /kan tón/ = **Guangzhou**

Canton crêpe, **Canton crêpe** *n.* a fine soft crinkled dress fabric of silk or rayon, slightly heavier than crêpe de Chine [Mid-19thC. Named after CANTON, where it was first made.]

Cantonese /kántə neéz/ *n.* (*plural* **-ese**) **1.** LANG **CHINESE LANGUAGE** a regional language of Guangzhou (Canton) and the province of Guangdong, China. It is a Chinese language of the Sino-Tibetan family, and the most widely spoken language in Chinese communities elsewhere in the world. It is spoken by about 70 million people. **2.** PEOPLES **SB FROM GUANGDONG** sb who was born or lives in the Chinese city of Guangzhou or the surrounding province of Guangdong ■ *adj.* **1.** **OF GUANGDONG** relating to or typical of Guangzhou, Guangdong, or their people or culture **2.** **OF A CHINESE LANGUAGE** relating to the Cantonese language **3.** COOK **TYPE OF CHINESE CUISINE** typical of or constituting the style and food of the southern Chinese city of Guangzhou and the surrounding province of Guangdong

cantonment /kan tóonmənt/ *n.* **1.** **MILITARY TRAINING CAMP** a large military training camp, especially in former times **2.** **TEMPORARY TROOP ACCOMMODATION** temporary accommodation for troops, especially the winter quarters of an army **3.** **ASSIGNMENT TO QUARTERS** the assignment of troops to temporary quarters **4.** **MILITARY CAMP IN BRITISH INDIA** a permanent military station in India during the time of British imperial rule [Mid-18thC. From French *cantonnement*, from *cantonner* 'to quarter, billet', from *canton* (see CANTON).]

Canton ware *n.* Chinese porcelain and other ceramic ware of types exported during the 18th and 19th centuries [Early 20thC. So named because, particularly during the 18th and 19th centuries, such pottery was exported from China by way of CANTON.]

cantor /kán tawr, kántər/ *n.* **1.** JUDAISM **CHIEF SINGER IN SYNAGOGUE** a Jewish religious official who is the chief singer of the liturgy in a synagogue **2.** CHR **LEAD SINGER IN CHOIR** sb who leads the singing in a church choir or congregation [Mid-16thC. From Latin, 'singer', from *cantere* (see CANTATA).]

cantorial /kan táwri əl/ *adj.* **1.** **RELATING TO CANTOR** relating to the chief singer of a synagogue or church **2.** CHR **ON NORTH SIDE OF CHOIR** used to describe the part of the choir on the north side of a cathedral or church **3.** CHR, MUSIC = **cantoris**

cantoris /kan táwriss/ *adj.* to be sung by the part of the choir on the north side of a cathedral or church [Mid-17thC. From Latin *cantoris* 'of the singer', a form of *cantor* (see CANTOR).]

cantrip /kántrip/ *n.* *Scotland* **1.** **WITCH'S SPELL** a witch's trick or spell **2.** **PRANK** a mischievous trick or prank (*often used in the plural*) ■ *adj.* *Scotland* **DONE BY MAGIC** supposedly carried out by means of magic [Late 16thC. Origin unknown, but originally a Scottish dialect word.]

cantus /kántəss/ (*plural* **-tus**) *n.* **1.** MUSIC = **cantus firmus** **2.** **HIGHEST VOCAL PART IN HARMONY** the highest vocal part of a harmony in a piece of choral music **3.** **MEDIEVAL ECCLESIASTICAL CHANT** a melody or style of singing used in the medieval church [Late 16thC. From Latin, 'song' (see CANTO).]

cantus firmus /-fúrməss/ (*plural* **cantus firmi**) *n.* a melody, often derived from chant, that forms the basis of a composition to which other melodic lines are added [From Latin, literally 'firm song, fixed song']

canty /kánti/ (**-tier, -tiest**) *adj.* *N England, Scotland* cheerful, lively, or sprightly [Early 18thC. From Scots (formerly) and northern English dialect *cant* 'bold, brisk', perhaps from Dutch *kant* 'side, edge'.] —**cantily** *adv.* —**cantiness** *n.*

Canuck /kə núk/ *n.* *US, Can* **1.** **CANADIAN** sb from Canada (*slang*) **2.** **OFFENSIVE TERM** an offensive term used to refer to a French-Canadian person (*slang offensive*) [Mid-19thC. Probably from (a Native American pronunciation of) CANADA.]

canula *n.* = **cannula**

canular *adj.* = **cannular**

canulate *v.* = **cannulate**

canvas /kánvəss/ *n.* **1.** TEXTILES **HEAVY FABRIC** a strong heavy closely woven fabric of cotton, hemp, or jute **2.** PAINTING **FABRIC FOR PAINTING ON** a piece of canvas on which a painting is done, especially in oils **3.** PAINTING **PAINTING** a painting that has been done on a canvas **4.** **BACKGROUND** the background against which events happen **5.** SEW **CLOTH FOR NEEDLEWORK** a fabric with a coarse loose weave, used for embroidery or tapestry **6.** NAUT **FABRIC FOR SAILS** any fabric used to make sails **7.** NAUT **SAIL** a vessel's sail or sails **8.** BOXING, WRESTLING **FLOOR OF RING** the floor of a boxing or wrestling ring when covered with canvas **9.** ROWING **END OF BOAT** the covered section at either end of a racing boat, sometimes used as a unit of length ■ *vt.* (**-vases** *or* **-vasses, -vasing** *or* **-vassing, -vased** *or* **-vassed**) **COVER STH WITH CANVAS** to cover or line sth with canvas [14thC. Via Old Northern French *canevas* from, ultimately, Latin *cannabis* 'cannabis, hemp' (source of English *cannabis*), canvas being originally a cloth made from hemp.] ◇ **under canvas** living in a tent

Canvasback

canvasback /kánvəss bak/ *n.* a North American wild duck, the male of which has a white back and a reddish-brown head and neck. Latin name: *Aythya valisineria.* [So called on account of the male's white back]

canvass /kánvəss/ *v.* (**-vasses, -vassing, -vassed**) **1.** *vti.* **VISIT SB TO SOLICIT STH** to travel around an area asking people for sth, e.g. sale orders, opinions, or votes **2.** *vt.* **DEBATE STH** to debate or discuss sth thoroughly **3.** *vt.* **LOOK AT STH CAREFULLY** to examine sth in detail ■ *n.* (*plural* **-vasses** *or* **-vases**) **1.** **OPINION POLL** a survey of public opinion, especially before an election **2.** **SALE OFFER TO MEMBERS OF GROUP** an offer of sth, especially sth for sale, to people in a particular area or group **3.** **CAREFUL INSPECTION** a close inspection or examination [Early 16thC. From CANVAS; possibly the original sense 'to toss in a canvas sheet (in sport or punishment)' evolved via 'to criticize roughly' into 'to debate', then 'to solicit votes'.]

canvasser /kánvəssər/ *n.* sb who canvasses, especially for a political party

canyon /kányən/, **cañon** *n.* a deep narrow valley with steep sides, often with a stream running through it [Mid-19thC. Via Mexican Spanish *cañón* from Spanish, literally 'large tube, pipe, or conduit', from *caña* 'pipe', from Latin *canna* 'reed, pipe' (see CANE).]

canzona /kan zṓnə/ *n.* **1.** MUSIC **SONGLIKE MADRIGAL** a song resembling a madrigal but simpler and less serious in form and content **2.** MUSIC **INSTRUMENTAL PIECE** an instrumental piece in the style of a canzona **3.** POETRY = **canzone** *n.* 1 [Late 19thC. From Italian, formed from *canzone* 'song' (see CANZONE).]

canzone /kan zṓ nay/ (*plural* **-ni** /-ni/) *n.* **1.** POETRY **MEDIEVAL LOVE POEM** a love poem written by the troubadours of medieval Italy and Provence **2.** MUSIC = **canzona** *n.* 1, **canzona** *n.* 2 [Late 16thC. Via Italian from, ultimately, Latin *cant-*, the past participle stem of *canere* 'to sing' (source of English *cantata* and *shanty*).]

canzonet /kánzə nét/, **canzonetta** /-néttə/ *n.* **1.** **LIGHT ENGLISH SONG** a short light English song of the 17th or 18th century, originally intended for a group of singers or for a soloist with accompaniment **2.** **SONG RESEMBLING MADRIGAL** a Renaissance song with different parts for different singers, similar to the madrigal [Late 16thC. From Italian *canzonetta*, literally 'small canzone', from *canzone* (see CANZONE).]

canzoni plural of **canzone**

cap /kap/ *n.* **1.** CLOTHES **HAT** a covering for the head, usually soft and close-fitting and often with a peak and no brim **2.** CLOTHES **UNIFORM HAT** a head covering, usually part of a uniform, worn to identify the wearer's occupation or rank **3.** CLOTHES **PROTECTIVE COVERING FOR HAIR** a head covering worn to protect the hair, usually close-fitting or elasticated around the edge **4.** SPORTS **HAT AWARDED TO PLAYER** a hat or beret awarded to a player selected for a special team **5.** SPORTS **PLAYER AWARDED HAT** a player who has been selected for a special team, e.g. a national cricket, football, or rugby team **6.** CLOTHES **HAT WORN AT GRADUATION** an academic mortarboard, worn with a gown on a ceremonial occasion **7.** COVER a removable cover or lid that closes the end of sth when it is not in use **8.** COVERING AT TIP sth that covers the top or tip of sth, especially as protection **9.** TOP PART the top part of sth, e.g. a hill or mountain **10.** UPPER LIMIT an upper limit on sth, e.g. the amount that may be spent on an item **11.** ARMS = **percussion cap 12.** EXPLOSIVE FOR TOY GUN a small quantity of explosive enclosed in paper for use in a toy gun **13.** DENT COVERING FOR TOOTH a covering to preserve or replace the crown of a tooth **14.** CONTRACEPTIVE DEVICE a contraceptive device that fits over the cervix, e.g. a Dutch cap or a diaphragm (*informal*) **15.** ARCHIT TOP OF COLUMN the upper part of a column or pedestal **16.** ARCHIT **WINDMILL ROOF** the roof of a windmill (*technical*) **17.** FUNGI TOP OF MUSHROOM the dome-shaped upper part of certain fungi, e.g. mushrooms **18.** BOT **SPORE-CAPSULE COVERING** the hood that covers the spore-bearing capsule of mosses and liverworts **19.** BIRDS **PATCH ON BIRD'S HEAD** a patch of feathers of a different colour on the top of a bird's head **20.** CELL BIOL **MOLECULE CLUSTER** an aggregation of molecules at one end of sth such as a cell or virus **21.** PAPER **PAPER SIZE** any of various sizes of paper (*dated*) **22.** MATH SET INTERSECTION SYMBOL a mathematical symbol (∩) representing the intersection of two sets **23.** HUNT COLLECTION OF MONEY a collection of money taken at a fox hunt **24.** GEOL = **cap rock** ■ *v.* (**caps, capping, capped**) **1.** *vt.* COVER STH WITH CAP to put a cap over sth **2.** *vt.* LIE ON TOP OF STH to cover the top or tip of sth **3.** *vt.* SURPASS STH to improve on sth that has already happened or been done **4.** *vt.* COMPLETE STH to add the finishing touch to sth, e.g. an effort or a process **5.** *vt.* IMPOSE LIMIT ON STH to put an upper limit on sth, e.g., the amount of money to be charged or spent **6.** *vt.* SPORTS AWARD PLAYER CAP to select a player for a special team, e.g. a national side, for which a cap is awarded **7.** *vt.* NZ, Scotland UNIV GIVE SB DEGREE to award an academic degree to sb **8.** *vt.* HUNT ASK FOR MONEY AT HUNT to take a collection of money at a fox hunt from participants who are not members of the hunt **9.** *vti.* CHEM FORM CLUSTER OF MOLECULES to form a cluster of molecules on sth [Pre-12thC. From late Latin *cappa* 'hood, hooded cloak' (source of English *cape* and Italian *cappuccino*).] ◇ **cap in hand** with a humble or apologetic attitude ◇ **if the cap fits (wear it)** if you think that a remark could apply to you, then you should take note of it ◇ **set your cap for** or **at sb** to try to attract sb, especially with a view to marriage (*dated*) ◇ **to cap it all** used to say that sth has made a bad situation as bad as it can get

cap. *abbr.* **1.** capacity **2.** capital **3.** capitalize **4.** capital letter **5.** ANAT caput

C.A.P. *abbr.* **1.** POL Common Agricultural Policy **2.** computer-aided production

capability /káypə bílləti/ (*plural* **-ties**) *n.* **1.** COMPETENCE the ability necessary to do sth **2.** TALENT THAT COULD BE DEVELOPED an ability or characteristic that has potential for development ○ *a man of immense capabilities* **3.** POTENTIAL FOR USE the potential to be used for a particular purpose or treated in a particular manner

── **WORD KEY: SYNONYMS** ──
See Synonyms at *ability*.

capable /káypəb'l/ *adj.* **1.** DOING STH WELL good at a particular task or job or at a number of different things **2.** ABLE TO DO PARTICULAR THING possessing the qualities needed to do a particular thing **3.** LIABLE TO permitting or susceptible to sth ○ *an action capable of being misinterpreted* **4.** LAW LEGALLY COMPETENT the ability or the legal power to do sth [Mid-16thC. Via French from late Latin *capabilis*, from Latin *capere* 'to take'. Originally 'able to take in'.] —**capableness** *n.*

capably /káypəbli/ *adv.* in a competent or efficient way

capacious /kə páyshəss/ *adj.* big enough to contain a large quantity [Early 17thC. From Latin *capac-*, stem of *capax* 'able to hold', from *capere* (see CAPABLE).] —**capaciously** *adv.* —**capaciousness** *n.*

capacitance /kə pássitənss/ *n.* **1.** ABILITY TO STORE ELECTRICAL CHARGE the ability of a substance to store electric charge **2.** MEASURE OF ELECTRIC CHARGE STORAGE a measure of the capacitance of a substance, equal to the surface charge divided by the electric potential. Symbol *C* **3.** PART OF ELECTRICAL CIRCUIT the part of an electrical circuit that has capacitance

capacitate /kə pássi tayt/ (**-tates, -tating, -tated**) *vt.* **1.** MAKE SB CAPABLE to make sb able, fit, or qualified to do sth (*formal*) **2.** LAW GIVE SB LEGAL POWER to make sb legally able to do sth **3.** BIOL CAUSE CHANGE IN SPERM COATING to cause the coatings on a sperm to be able to interact with proteins on the ovum

capacitation /kə pássi táysh'n/ *n.* physical changes in the coatings of a sperm to permit penetration and fertilization of an egg

capacitive /kə pássətiv/ *adj.* relating to electrical capacitance —**capacitively** *adv.*

capacitor /kə pássitər/ *n.* an electrical component, used to store a charge temporarily, consisting of two conducting surfaces separated by a nonconductor (**dielectric**)

capacity /kə pássəti/ (*plural* **-ties**) *n.* **1.** MENTAL OR PHYSICAL ABILITY the ability to do or experience sth **2.** VOLUME a measure of the amount that can be held or contained **3.** MAXIMUM VOLUME the maximum amount that can be held or taken in **4.** MAXIMUM PRODUCTIVITY the maximum amount of output or productivity **5.** OFFICIAL ROLE an official function or position that sb has **6.** ELEC MEASURE OF ELECTRICAL OUTPUT a measure of the electric output of a battery, generator, or motor **7.** COMPUT COMPUTER STORAGE SPACE the amount of data that can be stored by a specific computer device **8.** LAW LEGAL COMPETENCE the legal ability or qualification to do sth, e.g. make an arrest or a will [15thC. Via French *capacité* from, ultimately, Latin *capac-* (see CAPACIOUS).]

── **WORD KEY: SYNONYMS** ──
See Synonyms at *ability*.

cap and bells *npl.* a cap with bells attached to it, traditionally worn by a court jester, or the outfit of a court jester

cap-a-pie /káp ə pée, káp ə páy/, **cap-à-pie** *adv.* from head to foot (*archaic*) [From Old French *cap a pie* 'from head to foot']

caparison /kə párriss'n/ *n.* **1.** FANCY COVERING FOR HORSE an ornamental covering for a horse, especially a warhorse in former times **2.** HARNESS OR SADDLE DECORATIONS a decorative harness for a horse or decorations for its saddle or other fittings **3.** ELABORATE CLOTHING OR ORNAMENTS elaborate or rich clothing and ornaments ■ *vt.* (**-sons, -soning, -soned**) **1.** PUT CAPARISON ON HORSE to provide a horse with a caparison **2.** DRESS SB ELABORATELY to dress sb or yourself in finery [Early 16thC. Via obsolete French *caparasson* from, ultimately, perhaps late Latin *cappa* (see CAP).]

cape[1] /kayp/ *n.* **1.** LOOSE OUTER GARMENT a sleeveless outer garment, shorter than a cloak, that is fastened at the neck and hangs loosely from the shoulders **2.** COAT PART LIKE CAPE a piece of material like a cape that forms part of a coat or other garment **3.** BIRDS FEATHERS ON BIRD'S SHOULDER a covering of short feathers on the shoulders of certain birds, especially fowl [Mid-16thC. Via French from, ultimately, late Latin *cappa* (see CAP).]

cape[2] /kayp/ *n.* a point of land that juts out into water, especially a headland significant for navigation [14thC. Via French *cap* from, ultimately, Latin *caput* 'head'.]

Cape Canaveral /-kə návvərəl/ cape in Brevard County, Florida, situated on the eastern coast of the Canaveral peninsula. Also known as **Cape Kennedy**

Cape Coast town and capital of Central Region, Ghana. It is situated on the Gulf of Guinea, about 121 km/75 mi. southwest of Accra. Population: 57,224 (1984).

Cape Cod peninsula in southeastern part of the US state of Massachusetts

Cape Coloured (*plural* **Cape Coloureds** or **Cape Coloured**) *n.* sb of mixed ethnic descent in the Western Cape Province who speaks Afrikaans or English [*Cape* from the CAPE of Good Hope]

Cape Dutch *n.* **1.** ARCHIT 18THC ARCHITECTURAL STYLE an 18th-century style of architecture characterized by whitewashed houses with high gables **2.** FURNITURE 18THC FURNITURE STYLE a heavy style of furniture that developed in the Cape of Good Hope, South Africa in the 18th century **3.** LANG DUTCH FORERUNNER OF AFRIKAANS the form of Dutch that developed into Afrikaans ■ *adj.* IN CAPE DUTCH STYLE used to describe architecture or furniture in the style of Cape Dutch [*Cape* from the CAPE of Good Hope; *Dutch* from the early Dutch settlers or from the viewing of Afrikaans as a dialect of its parent language, Dutch]

Cape gooseberry *n.* BOT = **physalis** [*Cape* from its cultivation in the CAPE of Good Hope]

Cape Horn cape at the southern extremity of South America. Height: 424 m/1,391 ft. Spanish **Cabo de Hornos**

Cape jasmine *n.* = **gardenia**

Čapek /cháp ek/, **Karel** (1890–1938) Czech writer. His drama *R.U.R.* (Rossum's Universal Robots) (1921) satirizes mechanization.

capelin /káyp'lin/, **caplin** /káplin/ *n.* a small edible marine fish of the smelt family, found in the northern and Arctic seas. Latin name: *Mallotus villosus*. [Early 17thC. Via French from, ultimately, medieval Latin *cappellanus* 'custodian of St Martin's cloak', from late Latin *cappa* 'hooded cloak' (see CAP).]

Capella /kə péllə/ *n.* a double star that is the brightest star in the constellation Auriga, approximately 46 light-years from Earth

capellini /káppə leéni/ *n.* long and fine noodles, resembling thin spaghetti [From Italian, literally 'little hairs']

capellmeister *n.* = **kapellmeister**

Cape of Good Hope tip of the Cape Peninsula, South Africa. It is situated about 48 km/30 mi. south of Cape Town and was rounded by the Portuguese navigator Bartolomeu Dias in 1488.

Cape Peninsula peninsula that extends south of Cape Town, ending in the Cape of Good Hope, South Africa

Cape pigeon

Cape pigeon *n.* a sea bird of the petrel family with dappled black and white plumage, found in South Atlantic and Antarctic seas. Latin name: *Daption capensis*. [A common winter visitor to the Cape of Good Hope, South Africa]

Cape primrose *n.* BOT = **streptocarpus** [Origin uncertain: probably named after the CAPE of Good Hope or CAPE Province]

Cape Province /-próvvinss/ former province of South Africa that was abolished in 1994. The region is now divided into the three provinces of Eastern Cape, Northern Cape, and Western Cape.

caper[1] /káypər/ *n.* **1.** PLAYFUL JUMP a playful leap or dancing step **2.** PLAYFUL ACT OR TRICK a light-hearted adventurous act or prank **3.** QUESTIONABLE ACTIVITY a dangerous or illegal activity, especially one involving robbery (*informal*) ■ *vi.* (**-pers, -pering, -pered**) PRANCE HAPPILY to leap or dance about in a happy playful manner [Late 16thC. Shortening of CAPRIOLE.]

Caper

caper[2] /káypər/ n. 1. PICKLED FLOWER BUD an edible flower bud of a Mediterranean shrub, pickled and used as a flavouring or garnish (often used in the plural) 2. PLANT WITH EDIBLE BUDS a Mediterranean shrub with spiny trailing stems, cultivated for its edible buds. Latin name: *Capparis spinosa*. 3. PLANT RELATED TO CAPER any of various plants in the same family as the caper. Family: Capparidaceae. [14thC. Back-formation from earlier *caperis* (taken as plural), directly or via French *câpres* from Latin *capparis*, from Greek *kapparis*, of unknown origin.]

capercaillie /-káyli/, **capercailzie** /-káyli, -káylzi/ n. a large woodland bird of the grouse family, native to Europe and Asia, with dark gray plumage. Latin name: *Tetrao urogallus*. [Mid-16thC. From Gaelic *capull coille*, literally 'horse of the wood'.]

Capernaum /kə púrni əm/ city of ancient Palestine, situated on the northwestern shore of the Sea of Galilee

caper spurge n. a European plant of the spurge family that produces a milky fluid (**latex**). Latin name: *Euphorbia lathyris*. [From CAPER[2]]

capeskin /káyp skin/ n. a soft light leather made from South African sheepskin [Cape from the CAPE of Good Hope]

Cape sparrow n. a common South African sparrow. Latin name: *Passer melanurus*.

Capetian /kə péesh'n/ n. MEDIEVAL FRENCH RULER a member of the royal dynasty founded by Hugh Capet that ruled France from AD 987 to 1328 ■ adj. OF THE CAPETIANS relating to the Capetians or the period of their rule

Cape Town legislative capital of South Africa and capital of Western Cape Province. It is situated at the northern end of the Cape Peninsula at the foot of Table Mountain. Population: 854,616 (1991). Afrikaans **Kaapstad**

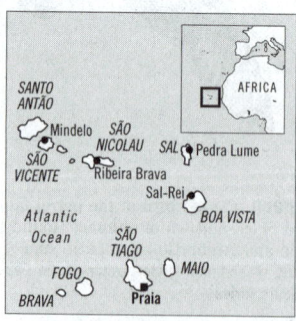
Cape Verde

Cape Verde /-vúrd/ island republic lying about 644 km/400 mi. off the coast of Senegal in West Africa. A former Portuguese colony, it became independent in 1975. Language: Portuguese. Currency: escudo. Capital: Praia. Population: 393,843 (1997). Area: 4,033 sq. km/1,557 sq. mi. Official name **Republic of Cape Verde**. Portuguese **Cabo Verde**

capework /káyp wurk/ n. the skill of a bullfighter in using a cape to control the movements of a bull

Cape Wrath extreme northwestern point of Scotland. Height: 112 m/368 ft.

Cape York Peninsula peninsula in northern Queensland, Australia, the most northerly point on the Australian mainland. Area: 127,200 sq. km/49,100 sq. mi.

capful /káp fool/ n. the amount held by the cap of a container when used to measure the contents

cap gun n. a toy gun that can be loaded with a small quantity of explosive enclosed in paper (**cap**)

capillaceous /káppi láyshəss/ adj. 1. LIKE A HAIR resembling a hair 2. BIOL WITH MANY FILAMENTS having many filaments that resemble a hair or thread [Early 18thC. Formed from Latin *capillaceus*, from *capillus* 'hair' (see CAPILLARY).]

capillarity /káppi lárrəti/ n. 1. PHYS = capillary action 2. BIOL, PHYS CAPILLARY STATE the state of being capillary [Mid-19thC. Via French *capillarité* from, ultimately, Latin *capillus* 'hair' (see CAPILLARY).]

capillary /kə pílləri/ n. (plural -ies) 1. ANAT THIN BLOOD VESSEL an extremely narrow thin-walled blood vessel that connects small arteries (**arterioles**) with small veins (**venules**) to form a network throughout the body 2. = capillary tube ■ adj. 1. PHYS RELATING TO CAPILLARY ACTION involving or relating to capillary action 2. ANAT OF BLOOD CAPILLARIES relating to the capillaries of the blood system 3. RESEMBLING HAIR as fine and slender as a hair 4. SMALL IN DIAMETER with a very small internal diameter [Mid-17thC. From Latin *capillaris*, from *capillus* 'hair' (source of English *dishevelled*); modelled on French *capillaire* 'capillary'.]

capillary action n. a phenomenon in which a liquid's surface rises, falls, or becomes distorted in shape where it is in contact with a solid. It is caused by the difference between the relative attraction of the molecules of the liquid for each other and for those of the solid.

capillary bed n. the collective mass of capillaries of the body or in any particular site

capillary tube n. a tube with a very small internal diameter, especially a glass tube with a fine bore and thick walls used in thermometers and similar pieces of equipment

capita 1. plural of **caput** 2. ◊ **per capita**

capital[1] /káppit'l/ n. 1. GEOG, POL SEAT OF GOVERNMENT a city that is the seat of government of a country, state, or province 2. CENTRE OF ACTIVITY a city that is the centre of a specified activity 3. ECON MATERIAL WEALTH material wealth in the form of money or property 4. FIN CASH FOR INVESTMENT money that can be used to produce further wealth 5. ADVANTAGE advantage derived from or useful in a particular situation ◦ *making political capital out of the dispute* 6. ECON ECONOMIC RESOURCE any resource or resources that can be used to generate economic wealth ◦ *a waste of human capital* 7. WEALTHY PEOPLE the capitalist class considered as a group ◦ *capital's influence on government policy* 8. ACCT NET WORTH the assets of a business that remain after its debts and other liabilities are paid or deducted 9. LING = capital letter (often used in the plural) ■ adj. 1. CRIMINOL RELATING TO DEATH PENALTY relating to or incurring punishment by death 2. GRAVE having extremely serious consequences ◦ *a capital blunder that sealed their fate* 3. PRINCIPAL constituting the highest category, or among those in the highest category 4. LING UPPER CASE used to describe the form of letters used at the beginning of sentences and names, e.g. A, B, and C as distinct from a, b, and c 5. GEOG, POL GOVERNMENT functioning as or relating to a seat of government 6. FIN OF FINANCIAL CAPITAL involving or relating to financial capital 7. EXCELLENT used to indicate that sb thinks sth is excellent (dated) [12thC. Via French from Latin *capitalis* 'of the head', from *caput* 'head'.]

capital[2] /káppit'l/ n. the upper part of an architectural pillar or column, on top of the shaft and supporting the entablature [Via Old French *capitel* from late Latin *capitellum*, literally 'little head' (see CAPITELLUM)]

capital account n. a statement of the value of a company's capital at a given time

capital allowance n. money spent by a company on fixed assets and deducted from its profits before taxes are calculated

capital asset n. = fixed asset

capital expenditure n. an expenditure on long-term business assets (**fixed assets**) such as buildings

capital gain n. a profit made from the sale of a financial asset such as shares or a house (often used in the plural)

capital gains tax n. a tax on profit above a fixed level made from the sale of financial assets

capital goods npl. goods that are used in the production of other goods rather than being sold to consumers. ◊ **consumer goods**

capital-intensive adj. using or requiring a proportionately large financial expenditure relative to the amount of labour involved

capitalise vt. = capitalize

capitalism /káppitəlizzəm/ n. an economic system based on the private ownership of the means of production and distribution of goods, characterized by a free competitive market and motivation by profit

capitalist /káppitəlist/ n. 1. INVESTOR sb who invests money in a business 2. BELIEVER IN CAPITALISM a supporter of capitalism or a participant in a capitalist economy 3. RICH PERSON a wealthy person, especially sb made rich by capitalism and considered to be greedy (informal) ■ adj. **capitalist**, **capitalistic** 1. OF CAPITALISM involving or relating to capitalism or capitalists 2. FAVOURING CAPITALISM practising or supporting capitalism —**capitalistically** /-lístikli/ adv.

capitalization /káppitə ÍT záysh'n/, **capitalisation** n. 1. RAISING OF CAPITAL the supplying of financial capital to a business 2. CAPITAL IN COMPANY the money that is invested in a business or the value of a company's stocks and bonds 3. ACCT TREATING STH AS CAPITAL the treatment of debt or an expenditure as capital 4. LING USE OF CAPITAL LETTERS the use of or conversion to capital letters

capitalize /káppitə ÍTz/ (-izes, -izing, -ized), **capitalise** (-ises, -ising, -ised) v. 1. vti. LING USE CAPITAL LETTERS to write or print sth with capital letters or an initial capital letter 2. vi. BENEFIT FROM STH to profit by or take advantage of sth ◦ *to capitalize on an opponent's mistake* 3. vt. USE STH AS CAPITAL to use debt or budgeted expenditure as capital for development 4. vt. AUTHORIZE ISSUE OF CAPITAL STOCK to authorize a business enterprise to issue a specified amount of capital stock 5. vt. FINANCE STH to supply capital for a business enterprise 6. vt. EXCHANGE DEBT FOR STOCK to convert a corporation's debt into shares of stock 7. vt. ACCT TREAT EXPENSES AS ASSETS to treat an expenditure as an asset in a business account instead of as an expense 8. vt. VALUE FUTURE INCOME to determine the current value of a future cash flow, earnings, or other income —**capitalizable** adj.

capital letter n. a letter of the alphabet in the form used at the beginning of sentences and names, e.g. A, B, and C as distinct from a, b, and c

capital levy n. a tax on fixed assets or property

capitally /káppit'li/ adv. in a way that arouses admiration (dated)

capital market n. a financial market involving institutions that deal with securities with a life of more than one year

capital punishment n. the punishment of death for committing a crime

capital ship n. a ship that belongs to the largest and most heavily armed class of warships

capital stock n. the face value of the share capital that a company issues. = stock

capital transfer tax n. in the United Kingdom, a tax formerly levied on the total value of gifts and bequests sb made. It was replaced by inheritance tax.

capitate /káppi tayt/ adj. 1. BOT DENSELY CLUSTERED used to describe a flower head composed of small flowers arranged in a dense cluster 2. ANAT, ZOOL ENLARGED AT END used to describe a body part that is enlarged and rounded [Mid-17thC. From Latin *capitatus* 'having a head', from *caput* 'head'.]

capitated /káppi taytid/ adj. based on the number of individuals involved, or per person ◦ *capitated payments* [Late 20thC. Formed from CAPITATION.]

capitation /káppi táysh'n/ n. 1. FIXED TAX PER PERSON a form of taxation in which each person pays the same fixed amount **2.** FIXED FEE PER PERSON a payment or fee charged at an equal amount per person **3.** COUNTING HEADS a method of assessing the number of individuals by counting heads (*formal*) [Early 17thC. Directly or via French from the late Latin stem *capitation-* 'poll tax', ultimately from the Latin stem *capit-* of *caput* 'head'.] —**capitative** /kápitətiv/ *adj.*

capitellum /kápɨ télləm/ (*plural* **-la** /-lə/) *n.* a rounded enlarged part at the end of a bone, especially that of the upper arm bone (**humerus**) that forms the elbow joint with one of the lower bones (**radius**) [Early 18thC. From Latin, literally 'little head', from *caput* 'head'.]

Capitol, Washington, D.C.

Capitol /káppit'l/ *n.* the white marble domed building in Washington, D.C. where the United States Congress meets [14thC. From Old French *capitolie*, later remodelled on its source, Latin *Capitolium*, the temple of Jupiter in Rome, from *caput* 'head' (see CAP).]

capitula plural of **capitulum**

capitular /kə píttyoõlər/ *adj.* **1.** CHR OF AN ECCLESIASTICAL CHAPTER belonging or relating to a cathedral or other ecclesiastical chapter **2.** BOT DENSELY CLUSTERED used to describe a flower head (**capitulum**) consisting of many small flowers **3.** ANAT, ZOOL ROUNDED used to describe the rounded end (**capitulum**) of a bone [Early 16thC. From late Latin *capitularis*, from *capitulum*, literally 'little head' (see CAPITULUM).] —**capitularly** *adv.*

capitulary /kə píttyoõləri/ (*plural* **-ies**) *n.* **1.** CHR MEMBER OF ECCLESIASTICAL CHAPTER sb who belongs to an ecclesiastical chapter **2.** CIVIL OR ECCLESIASTICAL DECREE a civil or ecclesiastical decree or set of decrees [Mid-17thC. From late Latin *capitularius*, from Latin *capitulum*, literally 'little head' (see CAPITULUM).]

capitulate /kə píttyoõ layt/ (**-lates, -lating, -lated**) *vi.* **1.** SURRENDER to surrender, especially under specified conditions **2.** CONSENT OR YIELD to give in to an argument, request, pressure, or sth unavoidable [Late 17thC. Directly and via French from the late Latin *capitulare* 'to come to terms' from Latin *capitulum* 'chapter' (see CAPITULUM).] —**capitulatory** /kə píttyoõlətəri/ *adj.* —**capitulant** /kə píttyoõlənt/ *n.* —**capitulator** *n.*

— **WORD KEY: SYNONYMS** —
See Synonyms at *yield*

capitulation /kə píttyoõ láysh'n/ *n.* (*formal*) **1.** GIVING UP surrender or a giving up of resistance **2.** TERMS OF SURRENDER a document that sets out the agreed terms of surrender **3.** SUMMARY an outline or summary in document form

capitulum /kə píttyoõləm/ (*plural* **-la** /-lə/) *n.* **1.** BOT TYPE OF FLOWER HEAD a flower head that looks like a large single flower but consists of numerous tiny flowers clustered together on a disc **2.** ANAT, ZOOL ROUNDED PART a rounded enlarged body part, e.g. at the end of a bone or at the tips of an insect's antennae [Early 18thC. From Latin, literally 'little head', from *caput* 'head'.]

capiz /káppiz/ *n.* **1.** MOLLUSC WITH HINGED SHELL a small mollusc with a hinged shell that is chiefly found in the Philippines. Latin name: *Placuna placenta*. **2.** capiz, capiz shell SHELL the shell of the capiz. It has a shiny translucent lining and is used in making jewellery, lampshades, and ornaments. [From a language in the Philippines]

caplet /káplət/ *n.* a small smooth oval medicinal tablet for oral use

caplin *n.* = capelin

capo¹ /káp ō, káy pō/ (*plural* **-pos**) *n.* a small movable bar fitted across all the strings of a guitar or similar instrument to raise the pitch [Mid-20thC. Shortening of *capo tasto*, from Italian, literally 'head stop'.]

capo² /káp ō, káy ō/ (*plural* **-pos**) *n.* the title of a leader in the Mafia or a similar criminal organization [Mid-20thC. Via Italian from Latin *caput* 'head'.]

capoeira /kápoo áyrə/ *n.* a martial art and dance form, originally from Brazil, that is used to promote physical fitness and grace of movement [Late 20thC. From Portuguese.]

capon /káypən, -pon/ *n.* a male chicken castrated to improve its growth and the quality of its flesh for eating [Pre-12thC. Via Anglo-Norman *capun* from, ultimately, the Latin stem *capon* 'capon'.]

caponata /kaápə náatə/ *n.* a dish made from chopped aubergine and other vegetables [Mid-20thC. Via Italian from, ultimately, the Latin stem *capon-* 'capon'.]

Al Capone

Capone /kə pōn/, **Al** (1899–1947) Italian-born US gangster and racketeer. Active in Chicago during the Prohibition era, he was imprisoned in 1931 for tax evasion. Full name **Alphonse Capone**. Known as **Scarface**

caporal /káppə raál/ *n.* a strong dark coarse tobacco [Mid-19thC. From French *tabac du caporal* 'corporal's tobacco' (being superior to *tabac du soldat* 'soldier's tobacco').]

capot /kə pót/ *n.* WINNING OF TRICKS the winning of all the tricks by one player in a game of piquet ■ *vt.* (**-pots, -poting, -poted**) WIN ALL TRICKS FROM SB to win all the tricks from an opponent in the game of piquet [Mid-17thC. Via French from, perhaps, *capoter*, a dialect variant of *chapoter* 'to castrate'.]

capote /kə pót/ *n.* a long coat or cloak, usually with a hood [Early 19thC. From French *capote*, 'little cape', from *cape* 'cape, cloak', from late Latin *cappa* (see CAP).]

Truman Capote

Capote /kə póti/, **Truman** (1924–84) US writer. He was known for technically complex novels such as *Other Voices, Other Rooms* (1948).

Capp /kap/, **Al** (1909–79) US cartoonist, known for his comic strip *L'il Abner* (1934–77). Full name **Alfred Gerald Chaplin**

cappelletti /káppi létti/ *n.* small pieces of pasta shaped like pointed hats, filled with a savoury mixture of cheese or meat (*takes a singular or plural verb*) [Mid-20thC. From Italian, literally 'little hats', from *capella* 'hat', from medieval Latin *capellus*, literally 'little hat', from Latin *cappa* (see CAP).]

capper /káppər/ *n.* **1.** CAP-FITTING MACHINE a machine that fits caps on bottles **2.** FINISHING TOUCH OR FINAL STRAW sth good or bad that is the last in a string of such events (*informal*) **3.** CAP-MAKER sb who or sth that makes caps (*archaic*) [13thC. Originally 'sb who makes caps as headwear'. The present-day meanings did not appear before the late 16thC.]

cap pistol *n.* = cap gun

cappuccino /káppoõ cheén ō/ (*plural* **-nos**) *n.* a drink made with espresso coffee and frothed hot milk, sometimes topped with powdered chocolate or cinnamon [Mid-20thC. From Italian, originally 'Capuchin (friar)', from *cappuccio* 'hood, cowl', ultimately from late Latin *cappa* (see CAP) ; from the resemblance in colour to a Capuchin friar's habit.]

Capri /kə prée/ island resort in Napoli Province, Campania Region, southern Italy. It is situated near the southern entrance to the Bay of Naples. Population: 7,400 (1990). Area: 10.4 sq. km/4 sq. mi.

capric acid /káprik-/ *n.* an acid obtained from animal fats and oils and used in the manufacture of artificial fruit flavours, perfumes, plasticizers, and resins. Formula: $C_{10}H_{20}O_2$. [*Capric* from the Latin stem *capr-* 'goat'; (see CAPRINE, because of the acid's smell]

capriccio /kə preéchi ō, -prích-/ (*plural* **-cios** or **-ci** /-chi/) *n.* **1.** MUSIC LIVELY INSTRUMENTAL WORK a piece of instrumental music with a free form, an improvisatory style, and usually a lively tempo **2.** PRANK a lighthearted act or prank **3.** WHIM a sudden idea, impulsive decision, or change of mind [Early 17thC. From Italian, literally 'head with hair standing on end' (see CAPRICE).]

capriccioso /kə preéchi óssō, -prích-/ *adv.* in a lively and fanciful manner (*used as a musical direction*) [Mid-18thC. From Italian, from *capriccio*, literally 'head with hair standing on end' (see CAPRICE).] —**capriccioso** *adj.*

caprice /kə preéss/ *n.* **1.** WHIM a sudden idea, impulsive decision, or change of mind **2.** SUDDEN CHANGE OR ACTION a sudden unexpected action or change of mind **3.** IMPULSIVE TENDENCY a tendency to sudden impulsive decisions or changes of mind **4.** MUSIC = **capriccio** [Mid-17thC. Via French from Italian *capriccio*, literally 'head with hair standing on end', from *capo* 'head' (from Latin *caput*) and *riccio* 'hedgehog' (from Latin *(h)ericius*; influenced by Italian *capra* 'goat'.]

capricious /kə príshəss/ *adj.* tending to make sudden and unpredictable changes —**capriciously** *adv.* —**capriciousness** *n.*

Capricorn /káppri kawrn/ *n.* **1.** ASTROL TENTH SIGN OF ZODIAC the tenth sign of the zodiac, represented by a goat with a fish's tail and extending from 22 December to 19 January. Capricorn is classified as an earth sign, and its ruling planet is Saturn. **2.** Capricorn, Capricornian, Capricornean ASTROL SB BORN IN CAPRICORN sb whose birthday falls between 22 December and 19 January **3.** ASTRON = Capricornus **4.** GEOG = tropic of Capricorn [Pre-12thC. From Latin *capricornus*, literally 'goat's horn', from *caper* 'goat' (source of English *caper*¹) + *cornu* 'horn' (source of English *cornet*).] —**Capricorn** *adj.*

Capricornia /káppri káwrni ə/ city in Queensland, Australia

caprifig /káppri fig/ *n.* **1.** WILD FIG TREE a wild fig tree of southern Europe and Asia Minor used in the pollination of certain edible figs. Latin name: *Ficus carica sylvestris*. **2.** FIG the fig borne by the caprifig tree [15thC. A partial translation of Latin *caprificus*.]

caprine /ká prīn/ *adj.* relating to or resembling a goat [15thC. From Latin *caprinus*, from *caper* 'goat' (source of English *cab*, *cabriole*, *caper*¹, and *capriole*).]

capriole /kápri ōl/ *n.* **1.** DRESSAGE VERTICAL LEAP BY HORSE in dressage, a vertical leap in which all four of the horse's feet leave the ground and then its hind legs are kicked out **2.** BALLET BALLET LEAP a playful leap or jump performed in ballet ■ *vi.* (**-oles, -oling, -oled**) BALLET, DRESSAGE PERFORM CAPRIOLE to perform a capriole [Late 16thC. Via French from, ultimately, Latin *capreolus*, literally 'little goat', from *caper* (see CAPRINE).]

capri pants /kə prée-/, **Capri pants, capris** /kə preéz/, **Capris** *npl.* close-fitting women's trousers that end above the ankle [Mid-20thC. Named after the island of Capri.]

Caprivi Strip /kə préevi-/ narrow extension of Namibia, running eastwards about 450 km/280 mi. from northeastern Namibia to the River Zambezi. It is bordered by Angola and Zambia to the north and Botswana to the south.

cap rock n. GEOL **1. ROCK COVERING SALT** a layer of rock that lies above a salt dome and consists of anhydrite, gypsum, or limestone **2. ROCK COVERING FOSSIL FUEL** an impermeable layer of rock that lies above a deposit of gas or oil and prevents it from percolating upwards

caproic acid /kə prő ik-/ n. a liquid fatty acid that occurs in fats and oils or is made synthetically, used in flavourings and in medicine. Formula: $C_6H_{12}O_2$. [*Caproic* from the Latin stem *capr-* 'goat' (see CAPRINE), because of the acid's smell]

caprylic acid /kə príllik-/ n. an oily fatty acid with an unpleasant taste and smell, found in animal fats and used in dyes and perfumes. Formula: $C_8H_{16}O_2$. [*Caprylic* from the Latin stem *capr-* 'goat' (see CAPRINE), because of the acid's smell]

caps. abbr. **1.** capsule **2.** capital letters

capsaicin /kap sáy issin/ n. a colourless compound obtained from hot peppers, used medicinally and as a flavouring. Formula: $C_{18}H_{27}NO_3$. [Late 19thC. An alteration of *capsicine*, from *capsicum*.]

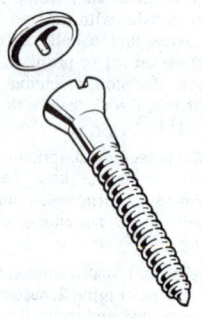

Cap screw

cap screw n. a long-threaded bolt with a head that may be square, hexagonal, slotted, or socketed

Capsian /kápsi ən/ adj. belonging to a late Palaeolithic culture of northern Africa and southern Europe, characterized by the use of geometrically shaped tools and distinctive art forms such as engraved limestone slabs [Early 20thC. From French *capsien*, from Latin *Capsa* 'Gafsa', a town in central Tunisia where Palaeolithic remains were found.]

capsicum /kápsikəm/ n. **1.** = **pepper** n. 4. ◊ **chilli 2. FRUIT** the fruit of the capsicum plant, especially a dried hot red pepper [Late 20thC. From modern Latin *capsicum*, perhaps from Latin *capsa* 'repository, box' (source of English *capsule*, *case*, and *chassis*) on account, of the podlike fruit.]

capsid /kápsid/ n. the outer coat of protein that surrounds a virus particle [Mid-20thC. Formed from Latin *capsa* 'repository, box' (source of English *capsule*, *case*, and *chassis*).]

capsize /kap síz/ (-sizes, -sizing, -sized) vti. to overturn on the surface of the water or cause a boat to overturn [Late 18thC. Of uncertain origin: perhaps, ultimately, from Spanish *capuzar* 'to sink a ship by the head'.] —**capsizal** n.

cap sleeve n. a very short sleeve that hangs over the

Cap sleeve

shoulder but does not extend beyond the armhole on the underside

caps lock n. a key on a computer keyboard or typewriter that, if pressed once, causes all subsequent letters to be typed as capital letters

capsomere /kápsə meer/ n. any of the individual protein units that make up the outer coat (**capsid**) of a virus [Mid-20thC. Coined from CAPSID + -MERE, probably modelled on French *capsomère*.]

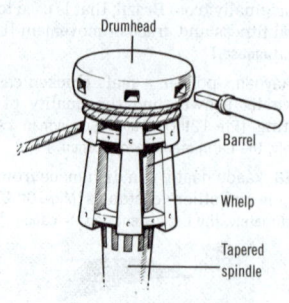

Drumhead
Barrel
Whelp
Tapered spindle

Capstan

capstan /kápstən/ n. **1.** NAUT **ROTATING CYLINDER** a device consisting of a vertical rotatable drum around which a cable is wound, used to move heavy weights or to haul in ropes on a ship **2.** HOUSEHOLD **ROTATING SHAFT IN TAPE RECORDER** a rotating shaft in a tape recorder, used to pull the magnetic tape past the head [14thC. Via Provençal *cabestan* from, ultimately, Latin *capistrum* 'halter', from *capere* 'to seize' (see CAPABLE).]

capstan bar n. NAUT a long lever used to turn a capstan by hand

capstone /káp stōn/ n. **1.** BUILDING **TOP STONE** a stone used at the top of a wall or another structure **2.** HIGH POINT sth considered the highest achievement or most important action in a series of actions

capsular /kápsyoolər/ adj. **1.** OF OR LIKE CAPSULE relating to or resembling a capsule **2.** IN OR AS CAPSULE enclosed in or in the form of a capsule

capsulate /kápsyoo layt/, **capsulated** /-laytid/ adj. enclosed in or made into a capsule (formal) —**capsulation** /kápsyoo láysh'n/ n.

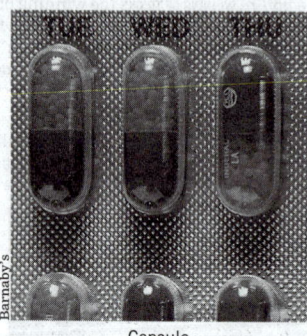

Capsule

capsule /káp syool/, **capsule** n. **1.** PHARM **PILL OR CASING** a pill consisting of a small cylindrical container made of a soluble substance such as gelatin, enclosing a dose of medicine or a nutritional supplement, or the container itself **2.** BOT **SEED CASE** a fruit containing seeds that it releases by splitting open when it is dry and mature **3.** BOT **SPORE SAC** a sac containing the spores of a moss or a liverwort **4.** MICROBIOL **GELATINOUS COVERING OF MICROORGANISM** a gelatinous covering that surrounds certain microorganisms **5.** ANAT **MEMBRANE SURROUNDING BODY PART** a membrane or sac enclosing an organ or body part **6.** ANAT **WHITE MATTER IN BRAIN** a layer of white fibres in the forebrain **7.** SPACE TECH = **space capsule 8.** AIR **EJECTABLE COCKPIT** a sealed cockpit in an aircraft that can be ejected in an emergency **9.** SEAL ON CONTAINER a protective seal such as the metal, plastic, or wax covering that protects the cork of a wine bottle **10.** SHORT SUMMARY a very brief summary ■ adj. **1.** VERY BRIEF expressed in an extremely brief or highly condensed way **2.** COMPACT very small or compact ■ vt. (**-sules, -suling, -suled**) US = **capsulize** [Mid-17thC. Via French from Latin *capsula*, literally

'little box', from *capsa* 'repository, box' (source of English *case*), from *capere* 'to take' (see CAPABLE).]

capsulize /káp syoo līz/ (-izes, -izing, -ized), **capsulise** (-ises, -ising, -ised) vt. to put sth into a capsule or into the form of a capsule

capsulotomy /kápsyoō lóttəmi/ (plural -mies) n. a surgical procedure involving cutting into the capsule surrounding a body part, e.g. that of the lens of the eye in the removal of a cataract

Capt. abbr. Captain

captain /káptin/ n. **1.** NAUT **COMMANDER OF BOAT** sb who has formal command of a boat, ship, or other vessel **2.** AEROSP **PILOT IN COMMAND** sb who has formal command of an aircraft or spacecraft **3.** NAVY **OFFICER IN NAVY** an officer in the Royal Navy or the US Navy or the Canadian navy ranking next above a commander **4.** ARMY **OFFICER IN BRITISH FORCES** an officer in the British Army or Royal Marines ranking above a lieutenant and below a major, or this rank itself **5.** MIL **OFFICER IN CANADIAN FORCES** a commissioned officer in the Canadian army or air force, ranking above a lieutenant and below a major **6.** MIL **RANK** the rank of captain **7.** SPORTS **TEAM LEADER** a leader of a team in a sport or game **8.** IMPORTANT PERSON an influential leader in a field or organization **9.** EDUC **HEAD BOY OR GIRL** a senior pupil chosen to represent a school and sometimes given certain supervisory or disciplinary responsibilities **10.** SUPERVISOR a title sometimes given to sb who supervises others ■ vt. (**-tains, -taining, -tained**) COMMAND STH to be the captain of sth [14thC. Via late Old French *capitain* from late Latin *capitaneus* 'chief', from *caput* 'head', from the captain's position as the 'head' of a team or other group.]

Captain Cooker n. NZ a wild pig (informal) [Late 19thC. Named after Captain James COOK (1728–79), the English circumnavigator who explored New Zealand and whose crew released pigs into the wild there.]

captaincy /káptənsi/ (plural -cies or -ships /-ship/) n. **1.** CAPTAIN'S RANK the position or rank that a captain holds **2.** TERM AS CAPTAIN the period or time that a captain holds that rank or position **3.** CAPTAIN'S RESPONSIBILITY an area of authority belonging to a captain **4.** CAPTAIN'S QUALITIES the ability or leadership of a captain

captain's chair n. a wooden chair with a saddle seat and a low curved back and arms supported on vertical spindles

captain's mast n. a disciplinary hearing at which a captain or commanding officer of a navy ship or force hears and acts on cases against enlisted personnel

captan /káp tan/ n. an agricultural fungicide in the form of a white powder, used on fruits, flowers, and vegetables. Formula: $C_9H_8Cl_3NO_2S$. [Mid-20thC. Shortening of MERCAPTAN.]

caption /kápsh'n/ n. **1.** COMMENT WITH ILLUSTRATION a short description or title accompanying an illustration in a printed text **2.** CINEMA **FILM OR TELEVISION SUBTITLE** a printed explanation in a film or on television, especially a translation of dialogue accompanying a scene or an explanation preceding a scene **3.** PRINTING, PUBL **HEADING OR SUBHEADING** a heading or subheading in a document or article **4.** LAW **HEADING OF LEGAL DOCUMENT** an attachment to or heading of a legal document that identifies the circumstances of its production and the sources of its authority ■ vt. (**-tions, -tioning, -tioned**) GIVE STH CAPTION to provide sth with a caption [14thC. From the Latin stem *caption-* 'act of taking', from *capt-*, the past participle stem of *capere* 'to take' (see CAPABLE); influenced by Latin *caput* 'head'.] —**captionless** adj.

captious /kápshəss/ adj. **1.** OVERLY CRITICAL tending to find fault and make trivial and excessive criticisms **2.** ENTRAPPING intended to confuse or entrap an opponent in an argument [Directly or via French *captieux* from Latin *captiosus*, from the Latin stem *caption-* 'act of taking (in)', deceptive argument' (see CAPTION)] —**captiously** adv. —**captiousness** n.

captivate /kápti vayt/ (-vates, -vating, -vated) vt. **1.** ENCHANT SB to attract and hold sb's attention by charm or other pleasing or irresistible features **2.** CAPTURE SB to take sb or sth captive (archaic) [Early 16thC. From late Latin *captivat-*, the past participle stem of *captivare* 'to

capture[1], from Latin *captivus* (see CAPTIVE).] —**captivation** /kápti váysh'n/ *n.* —**captivator** /-vaytər/ *n.*

captivating /kápti vayting/ *adj.* attracting and holding sb's attention by charm or other pleasing or irresistible features —**captivatingly** *adv.*

captive /káptiv/ *n.* **1.** PRISONER a person or animal that is forcibly confined or restrained, especially sb held prisoner **2.** SB DOMINATED BY EMOTION sb who is enslaved by a strong emotion such as love or anger ■ *adj.* **1.** UNABLE TO ESCAPE prevented from escaping **2.** FORCED TO USE OR ACCEPT STH forced by circumstances to buy, accept, or pay attention to sth, usually because there is other option or no means of escape **3.** VERY ATTRACTED irresistibly attracted to sb or sth [15thC. From Latin *captivus*, from Latin *capt-*, the past participle stem of *capere* 'to seize, take' (see CAPABLE).]

captivity /kap tívvəti/ *n.* the state of being a prisoner or a period of time that sb is held prisoner

captopril /káptəpril/ *n.* a drug used in the treatment of high blood pressure that blocks the action of a substance (**angiotensin**) that causes blood vessels to constrict. Formula: $C_9H_{15}NO_3S$. [Late 20thC. Coined from MERCAPTAN + -O- + PROLINE + -*il* (an alteration of -YL).]

captor /káptər/ *n.* a person who or animal that takes or holds another person or animal prisoner [Mid-16thC. From Latin, from the stem *capt-* (see CAPTIVE).]

capture /kápchər/ *vt.* (-tures, -turing, -tured) **1.** TAKE SB PRISONER to catch and then forcibly lock up or restrain a person or animal **2.** SEIZE PLACE to seize or gain control over a place **3.** TAKE STH IN GAME to win control or gain possession of sth in a game or contest **4.** DOMINATE SB'S THOUGHTS to enchant or dominate sb's mind, especially sb's imagination, or hold sb's attention **5.** REPRESENT STH ACCURATELY to describe or represent sth, especially sth fleeting or intangible, in a lasting medium such as painting, writing, film-making, or sculpture **6.** PHYS GAIN PARTICLE to gain an additional elementary particle **7.** COMPUT RECORD DATA ON COMPUTER to record data being processed or displayed and store it in the memory of a computer or as a file in a computer ■ *n.* **1.** BEING TAKEN OR TAKING PRISONER the act of being captured or of capturing sb or sth **2.** SB OR STH CAPTURED sb or sth that has been captured and held in captivity **3.** PHYS GAIN OF PARTICLE a process in which an atom, ion, molecule, or nucleus gains an additional elementary particle, often followed by an emission of radiation **4.** COMPUT RECORDING OF DATA the recording of data being processed or displayed and storage of it in the memory of a computer or as a file in a computer **5.** GEOG DIVERSION OF RIVER OVER TIME the diversion of the headwaters of one river into the channel of another, brought about by erosion over a long period of time [Mid-16thC. Via French from Latin *captura* 'seizure', from the stem *capt-* (see CAPTIVE).] —**capturer** *n.*

Capua /káppyoowə/ town with a medieval appearance in Caserta Province, Campania Region, in southern Italy. Population: 19,300 (1990).

capuche /kə poósh, -poóch/ *n.* a large hood on a cloak, especially the cowl worn by a Capuchin monk [Late 16thC. Via French (now *capuce*) from Italian *cappuccio* (see CAPUCHIN).]

Capuchin

capuchin /kápyoochin, -shin/ *n.* **1.** capuchin, capuchin monkey LONG-TAILED MONKEY an agile and intelligent long-tailed monkey with a tuft of hair on its head that resembles a monk's cowl, found in the forests of Central and South America. Latin name: *Cebus*

capucinus. **2.** CLOAK WITH HOOD a hooded cloak worn by women (*archaic*) [Mid-18thC. From CAPUCHIN.]

Capuchin /kápyoochin, -shin/ *n.* a member of an independent order of Franciscan friars founded in 1525 in Italy [Late 16thC. Via French from Italian *cappuccino* (see CAPPUCCINO).]

capuchin monkey *n.* ZOOL = **capuchin** *n.* 1

caput /káypət, káppət/ *n.* (*plural* -**pita** /káppitə/) *n.* ANAT **1.** HEAD the head (*technical*) **2.** PROMINENT PART the most prominent part of sth such as a bodily organ [From Latin]

Capybara

capybara /káppi baárə/ (*plural* -**ras** *or* -**ra**) *n.* the largest living rodent, resembling a large guinea pig. It lives along rivers in Central and South America and can grow to a length of more than 1.2 m/4 ft. Latin name: *Hydrochoerus hydrochaeris*. [Early 17thC. Via either Spanish *capibara* or Portuguese *capivara* from Tupi *capiuára*, from *capī* 'grass' + *uára* 'eater'.]

car /kaar/ *n.* **1.** PASSENGER-CARRYING ROAD VEHICLE a road vehicle, usually with four wheels and powered by an internal-combustion engine, designed to carry a small number of passengers **2.** RAILWAY PASSENGER VEHICLE a railway vehicle for carrying passengers rather than freight **3.** TRAVELLING COMPARTMENT FOR PEOPLE OR THINGS the part of an airship, balloon, or cable car for carrying passengers and cargo **4.** *US* VEHICLE ON RAILS a vehicle designed to run on rails, e.g. a tram or a railway carriage or wagon **5.** CHARIOT a chariot (*archaic or literary*) [14thC. Via Anglo-Norman and Old Northern French *carre* from, ultimately, Latin *carrum* (source of English *career* and *chariot*), from Celtic, the underlying meaning being 'to move swiftly'.]

car. *abbr.* carat

carabao /kárrə báyō/ (*plural* -**bao** *or* -**baos**) *n.* ZOOL = **water buffalo** [Early 20thC. Via Spanish from Visayan *karabáw*, from Malay *kêrbau*.]

carabid /kárrəbid/ *n.* a beetle that lives in the soil. Many species feed on other insects. Family: Carabidae. [Late 19thC. From modern Latin *Carabidae* (family name), from Latin *carabus* '(a kind of) seacrab', from Greek *karabos* 'horned beetle'.]

carabineer /kárribi neér/, **carabinier** *n.* a soldier armed with a lightweight short-barrelled rifle (**carbine**) [Mid-17thC. From French *carabinier*, from *carabine* 'carbine', see CARBINE.]

carabinero /kárrəbi nái rō/ (*plural* -**ros**) *n.* **1.** SPANISH POLICE OFFICER a member of the national police force of Spain **2.** FILIPINO CUSTOMS OR COAST GUARD OFFICER a customs, coast guard, or revenue officer in the Philippines [Mid-19thC. From Spanish, from *carabina* 'carbine', from French *carabine* (source of English *carbine*).]

carabinier *n.* = **carabineer**

carabiniere /kárrə binni áiri/ (*plural* **carabinieri** /-ri/) *n.* a member of the national police force of Italy [Mid-19thC. Via Italian from French *carabinier* (source of English *carabineer*).]

caracal /kárrə kal/ (*plural* -**cals** *or* -**cal**) *n.* **1.** WILDCAT OF AFRICA AND ASIA a medium-sized wildcat with long legs, a smooth reddish-brown coat, a short tail, and long tufted ears, found in the dry savannas of Africa and southern Asia. Latin name: *Lynx caracal*. **2.** CARACAL'S FUR the fur of the caracal [Mid-18thC. Via either French or Spanish from Turkish *karakulak*, literally 'black ear', from *kara* 'black' + *kulak* 'ear'.]

caracara /kárrə kaárə/ *n.* a large long-legged carrion-eating or predatory bird of the falcon family, native

Caracal

to Central, and South America. Genus: *Polyborus*. [Mid-19thC. Via Spanish or Portuguese *caracará* from Tupi-Guaraní; ultimately an imitation of the sound the bird makes.]

Caracas /kə rákəss/ city and capital of Venezuela, situated at an altitude of approximately 900 m/3,000 ft. Population: 1,964,846 (1992).

caracole /kárrəkōl/, **caracol** *n.* HALF TURN in dressage, a half turn to the left or right performed by a horse and rider ■ *vti.* (-**coles**, -**coling**, -**coled**; -**cols**, -**coling**, -**coled**) MAKE CARACOLE to perform or cause a horse to perform a caracole [Early 17thC. From French *caracoler*, from *caracol(e)* 'snail's shell, spiral'.]

Caractacus /kə ráktəkəss/ (*fl.* AD 50) British tribal ruler. He was defeated by the Romans.

caracul *n.* = **karakul**

carafe /kə ráf, kə raáf/ *n.* **1.** CONTAINER FOR SERVING DRINKS a container with a wide cylindrical base, a narrow neck, and a flared open top, usually made of glass and used to serve liquids, especially wine or water at table **2.** QUANTITY IN CARAFE the contents or capacity of a carafe [Late 18thC. Via French from Italian *caraffa*, of unknown origin.]

car alarm *n.* an electronically operated device fitted to a car, designed to make a loud noise if sb attempts to break into or tamper with the vehicle

carambola /kárrəm bōlə/ *n.* **1.** TROPICAL FRUIT TREE an evergreen tree cultivated in tropical regions, especially Southeast Asia, for its edible fruit. Latin name: *Averrhoa carambola*. **2.** STAR-SHAPED FRUIT the smooth-skinned yellow fruit of the carambola tree, with lengthways ridges that give it a star-shaped cross section. The thin skin is edible, and the juicy, slightly crisp fruit has a delicate flavour. [Late 16thC. Via Portuguese from, probably, Marathi *karambal*.]

caramel /kárrəmel, -m'l/ *n.* **1.** BURNT SUGAR sugar melted or dissolved in a small amount of water and heated until it turns golden or dark brown. It is usually used as a syrup for ice cream and other desserts. **2.** CHEWY SWEET a chewy sweet that can be soft or firm, made with butter, milk, and sugar ■ *adj.* OF YELLOWISH-BROWN COLOUR yellowish-brown in colour ■ *n.* YELLOWISH-BROWN COLOUR a yellowish-brown colour [Early 18thC. Via French from Spanish *caramelo*, an alteration of Provençal *canamel* 'sugar cane', ultimately from Latin *canna* 'cane' + *mel* 'honey'.]

caramelize /kárrəmə līz/ (-**izes**, -**izing**, -**ized**), **caramelise** (-**ises**, -**ising**, -**ised**) *vti.* to heat sugar or boil dissolved sugar until it turns dark brown, as when grilling dry sugar on top of a dessert or to undergo this process [Mid-19thC. From French *caraméliser*, from *caramel* 'burnt sugar, caramel' (see CARAMEL).] —**caramelization** /kárrəməlī záysh'n/ *n.*

carangid /kə ránjid, kə ráng gid/ *n.* any spiny-finned marine fish of a family that includes the jack and pompano. Family: Carangidae. [Late 19thC. From modern Latin *Carangidae*, family name, from *Caranx*, genus name, which came, ultimately, from Spanish *caranga* 'shad, horse mackerel', of unknown origin.]

carapace /kárrəpayss/ *n.* **1.** ZOOL ANIMAL SHELL a thick hard case or shell made of bone or chitin that covers part of the body, especially the back, of an animal such as a crab or turtle **2.** SELF-PROTECTIVENESS self-protection or a disguise that shelters sb as a shell does a turtle, e.g. shy or arrogant behaviour [Mid-19thC. Via French from Spanish *carapacho*, of unknown origin.]

carat /kárrət/ *n.* **1.** WEIGHT USED FOR GEMS a standard unit of mass used for precious stones, especially diamonds, equal to 200 milligrams **2.** UNIT FOR GOLD a unit for expressing the proportion of gold in an alloy on a scale from 1 to 24. For example, an alloy containing 50 per cent pure gold would be classified as 12-carat gold. US term **karat** [15thC. Via French from, ultimately, Greek *keration* 'fruit of the carob', from *keras* 'horn'; because carob beans were used as standard weights for small quantities.]

Caravaggio /kárrə vájji ŏ/, **Michelangelo Merisi da** (1573–1610) Italian painter. He was an exponent of the Baroque style, and his tempestuous life is reflected in his realistic and dramatically lit works.

caravan /kárrə van/ *n.* **1.** MOBILE HOME a large vehicle equipped for living in, and designed to be towed by another vehicle. US term **trailer 2.** GROUP OF DESERT MERCHANTS WITH CAMELS a group of traders, especially in Africa and Asia, crossing the desert together for safety, usually with a train of camels **3.** GROUP OF TRAVELLERS a group of people, vehicles, or supervised animals that are travelling together for security **4.** ROMANY PEOPLE'S VAN a large covered vehicle or van used as a travelling home, particularly by Romany people or circus performers ■ *vi.* (**-vans, -vanning, -vanned**) SPEND TIME IN CARAVAN to holiday or travel about in a caravan [Late 16thC. Via French *caravane* from Persian *kārvān* 'group of desert travellers' (source of English *van*).]

caravanner /kárrə vannər/ *n.* sb who stays in or travels about with a caravan

caravanning /kárrə vanning/ *n.* travelling or staying in a caravan for pleasure or a holiday

caravanserai /kárrə vánssərī/ (*plural* **-rais**), **caravansary** *n.* **1.** DESERT INN FOR TRAVELLING CARAVANS a large inn with a central courtyard, found in some eastern countries and used by caravans crossing the desert **2.** = **caravan .** n 2 [Late 16thC. From Persian *kārwānsarāī*, from *kārwān* (see CARAVAN) + *sarāī* 'inn' (see SERAI).]

caravel /kárrə vel/, **carvel** /káarv'l/ *n.* a light sailing ship with two or three masts, used in the Mediterranean from the 14th to 17th century [Early 16thC. From French *caravelle*.]

caraway /kárrə way/ *n.* **1.** ANNUAL HERB a European and Asian plant with finely divided leaves, clusters of small white or pinkish flowers, and aromatic fruits that look like seeds and are used to flavour food. Latin name: *Carum carvi*. **2.** = **caraway seed** *n.* [13thC. Directly or via Old French *carvi* from medieval Latin *carui*, of uncertain origin: probably ultimately from Greek *karon* 'cumin' (which has similar seeds).]

caraway seed *n.* the aromatic dried ripe fruit of the caraway plant, used as a spice for flavouring a variety of sweet and savoury foods

carb /kaarb/ *n.* a carburettor (*informal*) [Mid-20thC. shortening.]

carb- *prefix.* CHEM = **carbo-** (*used before vowels*)

carbamate /káarbə mayt/ *n.* any salt or ester of carbamic acid, used especially as a pesticide [Mid-19thC. Coined from CARBO- + AMIDE + -ATE.]

carbamazepine /káarbə mázzə peen/ *n.* an analgesic and anticonvulsant drug used to treat epilepsy, pain, and manic-depressive psychosis [Rearrangement of *dibenzazepinecarboxamide*, chemical name]

carbamic acid /kaar bámmik-/ *n.* an acid that exists only in the form of its salt or ester. Formula: NH_2COOH. [*Carbamic* coined from CARBO- + AMIDE + -IC.]

carbamide /káarbə mīd/ *n.* = **urea** [Mid-19thC. Coined from CARBO- + AMIDE.]

carbanion /kaar bánn ī ən/ *n.* an organic ion that has a carbon atom with a negative charge [Mid-20thC. Coined from CARB- + ANION.]

carbaryl /káarbə ril/ *n.* an insecticide used as a substitute for DDT in a broad range of applications [Mid-20thC. Blend of CARBAMATE and ARYL.]

carbene /káar been/ *n.* any molecule containing a carbon atom with only three bonds. Carbenes are highly reactive and only exist fleetingly in certain chemical reactions.

carbenicillin /káar bénni síllin/ *n.* an antibiotic derivative of penicillin, administered as a sodium or

potassium compound [Contraction of *carb(boxy)-ben(zylpen)icillin*]

carbide /káar bīd/ *n.* **1.** COMPOUND CONTAINING CARBON AND ANOTHER ELEMENT a compound containing carbon and one other element, especially a metal **2.** = **calcium carbide** [Mid-19thC. Coined from CARBON + -IDE.]

carbine /káar bīn/ *n.* a lightweight rifle with a short barrel [Early 17thC. From French *carabine*, from *carabin* 'mounted musketeer', of unknown origin.]

carbineer /káarbi neér/ *n.* = **carabineer**

carbinol /káarbi nol/ *n.* = **methanol** [Mid-19thC. Coined from CARBON + -INE + -OL.]

carbo /kaárbŏ/ (*plural* **-bos**) *n.* a carbohydrate (*slang*) ○ *pasta is a good source of carbo* [Shortening]

carbo- *prefix.* CHEM carbon, carbonic ○ *carbocyclic* [From French, from *carbone* (see CARBON).]

carbocyclic /káarbŏ síklik/ *adj.* used to describe a chemical compound containing a closed ring of carbon atoms

carbohydrase /káarbŏ hí drayz/ *n.* any enzyme that aids the breakdown of a carbohydrate. Amylase is a carbohydrase. [Early 20thC. Coined from CARBOHYDRATE + -ASE.]

carbohydrate /káarbŏ hí drayt/ *n.* **1.** ENERGY COMPONENT OF DIET an organic compound derived from carbon, hydrogen, and oxygen that is an important source of food and energy for humans and animals. Sugar, starch, and cellulose are carbohydrates. **2.** FOOD CONTAINING CARBOHYDRATES any food containing carbohydrates, e.g. bread, pasta, or potatoes [Mid-19thC. Coined from CARBO- + HYDRATE.]

carbohydrate loading *n.* a controversial practice of first starving the body of carbohydrates, then following a high-carbohydrate diet just before an athletic event in an attempt to increase performance

carbolic /kaar bóllik/ *n.* = **phenol** [Mid-19thC. Coined from CARBO- + -OL + -IC.]

carbolic acid *n.* = **phenol**

carbo-loading /káarbŏ-/ *n.* carbohydrate loading (*slang*)

car bomb *n.* an explosive device concealed inside or under a vehicle and detonated by remote control or when the engine is started

car-bomb (**car-bombs, car-bombing, car-bombed**) *vt.* to place a car bomb in or under a vehicle, or use such an explosive-laden vehicle against a target

carbon /káarbən/ *n.* **1.** CHEM ELEM NONMETALLIC CHEMICAL ELEMENT a nonmetallic chemical element that exists in two main forms, diamond and graphite. Its ability to form large numbers of organic compounds allowed living organisms to evolve. Symbol **C 2.** CARBON COPY a carbon copy of a document (*informal*) **3.** CARBON PAPER carbon paper (*informal*) **4.** ELECTRICAL COMPONENT MADE OF CARBON sth made of carbon, especially an electrode or a lamp filament [Late 18thC. Via French *carbone* from the Latin stem *carbon-* 'coal' (source of English *carbuncle*), of uncertain origin; perhaps ultimately from an Indo-European word meaning 'fire'.] — **carbonous** *adj.*

carbon 12 /káarbən twélv/ *n.* an isotope of carbon with relative atomic mass of 12. It is used as the standard in determining the relative atomic mass of other elements.

carbon 14 /káarbən fawr teén/ *n.* a naturally radioactive isotope of carbon with atomic mass of 14 and a half-life of 5780 years, used as a tracer element and in carbon dating

carbon-14 dating, **carbon-14 method** *n.* = **carbon dating**

carbonaceous /káarbə náyshəss/ *adj.* relating to, containing, or resembling carbon

carbonade /káarbə nayd, -naád/, **carbonnade** *n.* a stew made with beef and onions cooked in beer [Mid-17thC. From French, from *carbone* (see CARBON).]

carbonado[1] /káarbə náydŏ, -naádŏ/ *n.* (*plural* **-dos**) SCORED AND GRILLED MEAT OR FISH a piece of scored and grilled meat or fish (*archaic*) ■ *vt.* (**-does, -doing, -doed**) (*archaic*) SCORE AND GRILL MEAT OR FISH to prepare meat or fish by scoring and grilling it **2.** CUT OR SLASH

to cut or slash sb or sth [Late 16thC. Via Spanish *carbonada* from, ultimately, the Latin stem *carbon-* 'coal' (source of English *carbon*), because it is grilled on coals.]

carbonado[2] /káarbə náydŏ, -naádŏ/ (*plural* **-dos** or **-does**) *n.* a dark-coloured diamond or an aggregate of diamond particles that is extremely hard and is used industrially, e.g. for drilling and polishing [Mid-19thC. From Portuguese.]

carbonara /káarbə naárə/ *n.* a hot pasta dish prepared with eggs, chopped ham or bacon, and cheese ○ *spaghetti carbonara* [Mid-20thC. From Italian (*alla*) *carbonara*, literally 'on the charcoal grill', from *carbone* 'charcoal', from Latin *carbon-* (see CARBON).]

carbon arc *n.* an electric discharge between two carbon electrodes or between an electrode and a metal to be welded, characterized by bright light and intense heat

Carbonari /káarbə naári/ *npl.* members of a secret society in early 19th-century Italy that aimed to establish a unified republican government [Early 19thC. From Italian, plural of *carbonaro* 'charcoal burner', from, ultimately, Latin *carbon-* (see CARBON); from their use of symbols from the charcoal-burning trade.]

carbonate *n.* /káar bənayt, káarbənət/ **1.** SALT OR ESTER OF CARBONIC ACID any salt or ester of carbonic acid **2.** MINERAL COMPOSED OF CRYSTALLIZED CARBONATES a mineral composed of calcium, magnesium, and other carbonates in various crystal forms ■ *vt.* /káarbə nayt/ (**-ates, -ating, -ated**) **1.** CONVERT TO CARBONATE to convert a chemical compound into a carbonate **2.** MAKE LIQUID FIZZY to make a liquid fizzy by introducing carbon dioxide into it **3.** = **carbonize** —**carbonator** /káarbə naytər/ *n.*

carbonation /káarbə náysh'n/ *n.* **1.** REACTION WITH CARBON DIOXIDE permeation or reaction with carbon dioxide **2.** = **carbonization**

carbonatite /kaar bónnə tīt/ *n.* an unusual alkaline igneous rock high in carbonate materials, found in eastern Africa and thought to derive from the Earth's mantle [Early 20thC. Coined from CARBONATE + -ITE.]

carbon bisulphide *n.* = **carbon disulphide**

carbon black *n.* any form of finely divided carbon produced by partial combustion of petroleum or natural gas, used in making pigment, ink, and rubber

carbon brush *n.* a block of carbon in an engine or generator that conveys current between the moving and the stationary parts

carbon copy *n.* **1.** DUPLICATE MADE WITH CARBON PAPER a duplicate of written or drawn material that is made by using carbon paper **2.** SB OR STH IDENTICAL sb or sth that is identical to or very like sb or sth else (*informal*) ○ *This situation is a carbon copy of last year's crisis.*

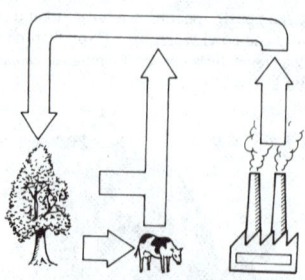

Carbon cycle

carbon cycle *n.* **1.** CARBON FLOW BETWEEN ORGANISMS AND ENVIRONMENT the series of interlinked processes, including photosynthesis and respiration, through which carbon, mainly in the form of carbon compounds, is exchanged between living organisms and the nonliving environment. Carbon dioxide is taken from the atmosphere by photosynthesizing plants and returned by the respiration of plants and animals and by the combustion of fossil fuels. **2.** SOURCE OF ENERGY IN STARS a chain reaction believed to generate significant energy in some stars, in which carbon is used as a catalyst to fuse four hydrogen nuclei into one helium nucleus

carbon dating *n.* a method of dating organic remains based on their content of carbon-14

carbon dioxide *n.* a heavy colourless odourless atmospheric gas produced during respiration and used by plants during photosynthesis. It is also formed by combustion, and increasing atmospheric levels may alter the Earth's climate. It is used in refrigeration, carbonated drinks, and fire extinguishers. Formula: CO_2.

carbon disulphide *n.* a colourless poisonous flammable liquid containing impurities that give it a rotten-egg smell. It is used in making cellophane and rayon and as a solvent and fumigant.

carbon fibre *n.* a very strong light thread manufactured from carbonized acrylic, used to reinforce resins, metal, and ceramics. Articles made with carbon fibre include turbine blades and poles for pole-vaulting.

carbon fixation *n.* the process by which plants synthesize carbon dioxide into organic compounds

carbonic /kaar bónnik/ *adj.* containing carbon

carbonic acid *n.* a weak acid formed when carbon dioxide is dissolved in water. Formula: H_2CO_3.

carbonic anhydrase /-an hídrayz, -drayss/ *n.* an enzyme in living tissue, e.g. blood cells, that contains zinc and aids the transfer of carbon dioxide from the tissues to the lungs

carboniferous /kaarbə nífferəss/ *adj.* containing or yielding coal or carbon

Carboniferous *n.* the period of geological time when true reptiles first appeared and when much of the Earth's surface was covered by forests, 362.5 million to 290 million years ago [Because numerous coal deposits were formed during this time] —**Carboniferous** *adj.*

carbonium ion /kaar bóni əm íən/ *n.* an organic ion that has a carbon atom bearing a positive charge

carbonization /kaarbən ī záysh'n/, **carbonisation** *n.* **1.** TREATMENT TO TURN STH INTO CARBON the burning, fossilization, or chemical treatment of sth that turns it into carbon **2.** COATING WITH CARBON the process of covering or coating sth with carbon **3.** = **destructive distillation**

carbonize /kaárbə nīz/ (-**izes**, -**izing**, -**ized**), **carbonise** (-**ises**, -**ising**, -**ised**) *v.* **1.** *vti.* TURN INTO CARBON to turn into carbon, or turn sth into carbon, by partial burning, by fossilization, or through chemical treatment **2.** *vt.* COVER OR COAT WITH CARBON to cover or coat the surface of sth with carbon —**carbonizer** *n.*

carbon microphone *n.* a microphone containing carbon granules that change resistance according to the vibrating pressure of sound waves, thereby modulating the frequency of the sound waves

carbon monoxide *n.* a colourless odourless toxic gas formed when carbon-containing compounds or fuels are burnt with insufficient air. Formula: CO.

carbon-nitrogen cycle *n.* = **carbon cycle** *n.* 2

carbon paper *n.* paper used for making copies, coated on one side with a waxy pigment that often contains carbon

carbon process, **carbon printing** *n.* a printing process that uses sensitized carbon tissue to produce positive prints

carbon star *n.* a star that has a lower temperature and proportionately more carbon in relation to nitrogen than other stars

carbon steel *n.* steel containing carbon with properties that vary according to the carbon content

carbon tetrachloride *n.* a colourless nonflammable toxic liquid used as a solvent, refrigerant, in fire extinguishers, and as a dry cleaning agent. Formula: CCl_4.

carbon value *n.* a measurement of the extent to which a lubricant forms carbon when in use

carbonyl /kaárbə nil, -nīl/ *adj.* relating to or containing the group of atoms found in certain organic and inorganic compounds. Formula: =C=O. ■ *n.*

METAL COMPOUND a compound that has a metal bound to a carbonyl group —**carbonylic** /kaarbə níllik/ *adj.*

carbonyl chloride *n.* = **phosgene**

car boot sale *n.* a sale of second-hand and new goods from the boots of people's cars, usually taking place on an open-air site hired for the purpose

carborundum /kaarbə rúndəm/ *n.* an abrasive composed of silicon carbide

carboxy- *prefix.* CHEM carboxyl ○ *carboxypeptidase* [From CARBOXYL]

carboxyhaemoglobin /kaar bóksi héemə glóbin/ *n.* a stable compound formed in the blood when inhaled carbon monoxide binds with haemoglobin, thus preventing it from binding with oxygen

carboxylase /kaar bóksi layz, -layss/ *n.* an enzyme that aids the absorption or release of carbon dioxide from, e.g. certain acids

carboxylate *n.* /kaar bóksi layt, -lət/ SALT OR ESTER OF CARBOXYLIC ACID any salt or ester of a carboxylic acid ■ *vt.* /kaar bóksi layt/ (-**lates**, -**lating**, -**lated**) FORM CARBOXYLIC ACID to form carboxylic acid by introducing a carboxyl group or carbon dioxide into a compound —**carboxylation** /kaar bóksi láysh'n/ *n.*

carboxylic acid /kaar bok síllik-/ *n.* any organic acid that contains the carboxyl group

carboxymethylcellulose /kaar bóksi meé thīl séllyoō lōss, -méthil-/ *n.* a derivative of cellulose used in paper production, as a stabilizer and emulsifier in foods, as an antacid, and as bulk in laxatives

carboxypeptidase /-pépti dayzs/ *n.* a protein-digesting enzyme secreted into the duodenum as a component of pancreatic juice

carboy /kaár boy/ *n.* a large container made of plastic or glass, usually protected by a wooden casing, used to hold corrosive liquids such as acids [Mid-18thC. Ultimately from Persian *karāba* 'large glass flagon'.]

carbuncle /kaár bungk'l/ *n.* **1.** MED INFLAMED SWELLING a multiple-headed boil **2.** ROUNDED RED GEMSTONE a red gemstone, especially a garnet, that is smoothly rounded and polished [13thC. Via Old French *charbu(n)cle* from Latin *carbunculus* 'red gemstone, inflamed spot' (literally 'small coal'), from *carbon-* (see CARBON).] —**carbuncled** *adj.* —**carbuncular** /kaar búng kyoōlər/ *adj.*

carburation /kaárbyoō ráysh'n/, **carburetion** /-résh'n/ *n.* the process of mixing the correct proportions of liquid fuel with air to achieve combustion [Late 19thC. Formed from CARBURET.]

carburet /kaárbyoō ret, kaárbyoō rét/ (-**rets**, -**retting**, -**retted**) *vt.* to mix a gas with hydrocarbons in order to increase fuel energy [Early 19thC. From obsolete *carburet* 'carbide'.]

carburetion *n.* = **carburation**

carburetor *n.* US = **carburettor**

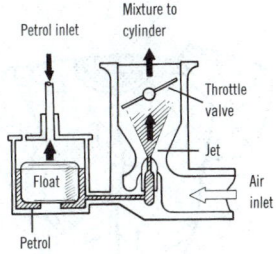

Carburettor

carburettor /kaár byoō réttər, kaárbə réttər/, **carburetter** *n.* a device in an internal combustion engine that mixes liquid fuel and air in the correct proportions, vaporizes them, and transfers the mixture to the cylinders [Mid-19thC. Formed from CARBURET.]

carburize /kaár byoō rīz, -bə-/ (-**rizes**, -**rizing**, -**rized**), **carburise** (-**rises**, -**rising**, -**rised**) *vt.* —**carbonize** [Mid-19thC. Formed from CARBURET.] —**carburization** /kaár byoō rī záysh'n, -bə-/ *n.*

carcass /kaárkəss/, **carcase** *n.* **1.** DEAD BODY OF ANIMAL the dead body of an animal, especially one slaughtered and prepared for use as meat **2.** PERSON a living person's body (*humorous*) ○ *Move your carcass!* **3.** REMAINS OF STH the remains of sth decayed or almost totally destroyed **4.** BASIC STRUCTURE the basic structure or framework of sth [14thC. From Anglo-Norman *carcois* and French *carcasse*; ultimately of unknown origin.]

Carcassonne /kaárkə són/ city and capital of Aude Department, southern France, situated on the River Aude 92 km/57 mi. southeast of Toulouse. Population: 44,991 (1990).

carcass trade *n.* the reconstruction of old worn-out pieces of furniture that are then passed off as valuable antiques (*slang*)

Carchemish /kaár kə mísh/ ancient city on the River Euphrates, northeast of Aleppo in present-day northern Syria

carcin- *prefix.* MED = **carcino-** (*used before vowels*)

carcino- *prefix.* MED cancer ○ *carcinogenic* [From Greek *karkinos* 'crab, cancer'; ultimately related to Latin *cancer* (source of English *cancer* and *canker*)]

carcinogen /kaar sínnəjən, kaárssinə jen/ *n.* a substance or agent that can cause cancer. Radiation and some chemicals and viruses are carcinogens. [Mid-19thC. Blend of CARCINOMA and -GEN.]

carcinogenesis /kaárssinō jénnəssiss/ *n.* the production of cancerous cells [Early 20thC. Blend of CARCINOMA and GENESIS.]

carcinogenic /kaárssinō jénnik/ *adj.* capable of causing cancer [Early 20thC. Blend of CARCINOMA and -GENIC.] —**carcinogenicity** /kaárssinōjə nísseti/ *n.*

carcinoid /kaárssi noyd/ *n.* a small benign or malignant tumour on the walls of the small intestine that sometimes produces physiologically active compounds such as serotonin or prostaglandins that are normally deactivated by the liver. In carcinoid syndrome excessive amounts of such compounds are released from the infected liver into the circulation and cause flushing, headache, diarrhoea, and asthma. [Early 20thC. Blend of CARCINOMA and -OID.]

carcinoma /kaárssi nómə/ *n.* **1.** MALIGNANT TUMOUR a malignant tumour that starts in the surface layer (**epithelium**) of an organ or body part and may spread to other parts of the body **2.** cancer [Early 18thC. Via Latin from Greek *karkinōma* (stem *karkinōmat-*), from *karkinos* 'crab' (source of English *cancer*); from the crablike pattern of the surrounding swollen blood vessels.] —**carcinomatoid** /kaárssi nómə toyd/ *adj.* —**carcinomatous** *adj.*

carcinomatosis /kaárssi nómə tóssiss/ *n.* a condition in which cancer has spread widely throughout the body

carcinosarcoma /kaárssinō saar kómə/ (*plural* -**mas** or -**mata** /-kómətə/) *n.* a malignant tumour containing elements of both a carcinoma and a sarcoma

carcinosis /kaárssi nóssiss/ *n.* = **carcinomatosis**

car coat *n.* an overcoat that ends at mid-thigh

card[1] /kaard/ *n.* **1.** INDUST STIFF PAPER stiff paper or thin cardboard **2.** PAPER WITH PICTURES AND GREETINGS a piece of stiff paper, usually folded in half and with designs or illustrations, used to send greetings of various kinds, especially at birthdays and holidays **3.** GAME PRINTED STIFF PAPER FOR GAMES a small piece of stiff paper, part of a set, that is printed with symbols or figures and used to play games or tell fortunes **4.** STIFF PAPER SHOWING IDENTITY a small piece of stiff paper or plastic that shows sb's identity, business position, or membership in a club or organization **5.** PLASTIC CARD HOLDING INFORMATION a small piece of plastic that holds information in a magnetic strip or microprocessor, used in financial activities such as getting cash from cash machines or making phone calls **6.** = postcard **7.** SPORTS = racecard **8.** = index card **9.** AMUSING PERSON an amusing or eccentric person (*dated informal*) **10.** COLLECTABLE STIFF PAPER WITH PICTURE a piece of stiff paper with a picture on one side, collected as part of a set of such items **11.** COMPUT PUNCH CARD a punch card. = punchedcard **12.** ELEC ENG PRINTED CIRCUIT BOARD a printed circuit board. ■ NAVIG = compass card ■ COMPUT = expansion card ■. cards GAME USING CARDS any game played using playing cards

Ace

King

Queen

Jack

Joker

Diamond

Spade

Club

Heart

Card: Playing cards

■ vt. (**cards**, **carding**, **carded**) (*informal*) **1.** *US* ASK FOR IDENTIFICATION to ask sb to show identification, usually to check that the person is of legal age to drink alcohol or be admitted somewhere **2.** GOLF RECORD A GOLF SCORE to record a score after playing a hole or round of golf [15thC. Via French *carte* from Latin *c(h)arta* 'papyrus leaf, paper', from Greek *khartēs* 'papyrus leaf' (source of English *chart* and *cartoon*), of uncertain origin: probably from Egyptian.] ◇ **have** *or* **keep a card up your sleeve** to have a secret plan or tactic ready to be used if necessary (*informal*) ◇ **a few cards short of a (full) pack** not very intelligent (*informal*) ◇ **get** *or* **be given your cards** to be dismissed from your job (*informal*) ◇ **on the cards** likely to happen (*informal*) ○ *The stock market took the collapse of the banking giant in its stride, as it had been on the cards for some time.* ◇ **play your cards right** to take the fullest possible advantage of your chances of success (*informal*) ◇ **put** *or* **lay your cards on the table** to reveal openly what your intentions and plans are (*informal*) ◇ **see how the cards stack up** to find out what are the chances of success or otherwise

card[2] /kaard/ *vt.* (**cards**, **carding**, **carded**) COMB AND CLEAN WOOL OR COTTON to comb out and clean wool, cotton, or other fibres before spinning ■ *n.* TOOL OR MACHINE FOR CARDING a tool or machine with wire teeth used to comb out or clean wool, cotton, or other fibres before spinning [14thC. Via French from late Latin *cardus* 'thistle', from Latin *carduus* 'thistle, artichoke' (source of English *chard* and *cardoon*).] —**carder** *n.*

Card. *abbr.* Cardinal

card- *prefix.* MED = **cardio-**

cardamom /kaárdəməm/, **cardamon** /-mən/, **cardamum** /-məm/ *n.* **1.** PLANTS TROPICAL PLANT a perennial tropical plant that has large hairy leaves, clusters of small white flowers, and aromatic pods and seeds. Latin name: *Elettaria cardamomum.* **2.** COOK SPICE FROM CARDAMOM PLANT the pods and seeds of the cardamom plant, used whole or crushed as a spice or flavouring [14thC. Directly or via French *cardamome* from Latin *cardamomum*, from Greek *kardamōmon*, from *kardamon* 'cress' + *amōmon* 'amomum'.]

cardan joint /kaّad'n-/ *n.* a type of universal joint that can rotate when out of alignment [Early 20thC. Named after Gerolamo *Cardano* (1501–76), Italian mathematician who invented it.]

cardan shaft /kaّard'n-/ *n.* part of the transmission system in some vehicles [See CARDAN JOINT]

cardboard /kaّard bawrd/ *n.* a stiff light material made from wastepaper pulp, often used for making containers or packaging for goods

cardboard city (*plural* **cardboard cities**) *n.* an area in a city where homeless people gather to sleep, often using large cardboard boxes as shelter (*informal*)

card-carrying *adj.* officially listed as belonging to an organization and subscribing to its beliefs [From the membership card typically held by such members; first applied to members of the Communist Party]

card catalog *n.* *US* = **card index**

carded /kaّardid/ *Can* SPORTS used to describe an amateur athlete who is being funded by a government grant to enable him or her to pursue training

card file *n.* = **card index**

cardholder /kaّard hōldər/ *n.* sb who possesses a card that carries information, especially a credit, debit, bank, or phone card

cardi- *prefix.* MED = **cardio-**

cardia /kaّardi ə/ (*plural* **-ae** /-di ee/ *or* **-as**) *n.* the opening of the oesophagus into the stomach, or the upper part of the stomach where it is connected to the oesophagus [Late 18thC. From Greek *kardia* (see CARDIAC).]

cardiac /kaّardi ak/ *adj.* **1.** HEART-RELATED relating to or affecting the heart **2.** OF THE UPPER PART OF STOMACH relating to the upper part of the stomach, where it is connected to the oesophagus [Early 17thC. Via French from Latin *cardiacus*, from Greek *kardia* 'heart, cardia'. Ultimately an Indo-European word that is also the ancestor of English *courage*, *concord*, and *heart*.]

cardiac arrest *n.* the sudden stopping of the heartbeat and therefore of the pumping action of the heart. Cardiac arrest requires immediate treatment to prevent brain damage and death.

cardiac compression, **cardiac massage** *n.* rhythmic compression of sb's heart in order to restore or maintain blood circulation after the person has had a heart attack. ◇ **CPR**

cardialgia /kaّardi álji ə, -áljə/ *n.* **1.** HEARTBURN heartburn (*technical*) **2.** HEART PAIN pain in or near the heart [Mid-17thC. Via modern Latin from Greek *kardialgia*, from *kardia* (see CARDIAC).]

cardie /kaّardi/, **cardi**, **cardy** (*plural* **-ies**) *n.* a cardigan (*informal*) [Mid-20thC. Shortening.]

Cardiff /kaّar dif/ capital and largest city of Wales. It is the home of the Welsh Assembly and is an important industrial centre. Population: 315,000 (1996). Welsh **Caerdydd**

Cardigan

cardigan /kaّardigən/ *n.* a long-sleeved knitted jacket that fastens up the front [Mid-19thC. Named after the 7th Earl of *Cardigan*, James Thomas Brudenell (1797–1868), who led the charge of the Light Brigade during the Crimean War (1854).]

Cardigan Bay /kaّardigən-/ large semicircular bay on the western coast of Wales. Tremadoc Bay forms the northern portion of it. Length: 105 km/65 mi.

Cardiganshire /kaّardigənshər/ former county of Wales, now incorporated into the county of Dyfed as the district of Ceredigion. Area: 1,797 sq. km/694 sq. mi.

Cardigan Welsh corgi *n.* a dog belonging to the larger of two breeds of corgi with a long tail [Named after CARDIGANSHIRE]

Cardin /kaّar daN/, **Pierre** (*b.* 1922) Italian-born French fashion designer. He designed costumes for Jean Cocteau's film *La Belle et la Bête* (1945).

Cardinal

cardinal /kaّardinəl, -d'nəl/ *n.* **1.** CHR ROMAN CATHOLIC DIGNITARY in the Roman Catholic Church, one of the group of clergy, next in rank to the Pope, who elect the Pope from their own number and act as his advisers **2.** COLOURS DEEP RED a deep strong red colour, the same as that of the robes worn by a cardinal **3.** BIRDS BRIGHT RED N AMERICAN BIRD a North American crested finch, the male of which has bright red plumage with a black face. Latin name: *Cardinalis cardinalis*. **4.** MATH = **cardinal number 5.** CLOTHES WOMAN'S HOODED CAPE a woman's short cape with a hood, originally scarlet in colour, that was worn in the 17th and 18th centuries ■ *adj.* **1.** IMPORTANT fundamentally important **2.** COLOURS BRIGHT RED bright red in colour [12thC. Via French from medieval Latin *cardinalis*, from the Latin stem *cardin-* 'hinge'. The underlying idea is of a hinge upon which everything hangs.] —**cardinally** *adv.*

cardinalate /kaّardinəl ayt, -d'nəl-/, **cardinalship** /-ship/ *n.* **1.** ALL CARDINALS the cardinals of the Roman Catholic Church regarded collectively **2.** TERM OF OFFICE OF CARDINAL the term of office of a Roman Catholic cardinal **3.** OFFICE OF CARDINAL the rank or office of a Roman Catholic cardinal

cardinal fish *n.* a small tropical marine fish, usually red or brown, often abundant on coral reefs. Family: Apogonidae.

cardinal flower *n.* a perennial lobelia native to central and eastern North America that has a cluster of brilliantly coloured, usually red, flowers. Latin name: *Lobelia cardinalis*.

cardinal number *n.* a number, such as 4 or 42, used to denote quantity but not order

cardinal point *n.* any of the four principal points of the compass, North, South, East, or West

cardinalship *n.* = **cardinalate**

cardinal virtue *n.* any one of the principal virtues in the classical or Christian traditions. In the classical tradition they are justice, prudence, temperance, and fortitude, and in the Christian tradition they are justice, prudence, temperance, and fortitude together with faith, hope, and charity.

cardinal vowels *npl.* a fixed set of vowel sounds, based on the position of the tongue and the shape of the mouth cavity, and spaced at approximately equal acoustic intervals. They are used in describing the vowel sounds of a language.

card index *n.* an alphabetical listing of items such as names and addresses or books in a library, with each item on a separate card. *US* term **card catalog**

cardio- *prefix.* MED heart ○ *cardiopulmonary* [From Greek *kardia* (see CARDIAC)]

cardioaccelerator /kaّardi ō ək séllə raytər/ *n.* a drug or other agent that increases the heart rate [Late 20thC.] —**cardioacceleration** /kaّardi ō ək séllə ráysh'n/ *n.*

cardiogenic /kaárdi ō jénnik/ *adj.* resulting from activity or disease of the heart

cardiogram /kaárdi ə gram/ *n.* a graphic record made by a cardiograph, especially an electrocardiogram

cardiograph /kaárdi ə graaf, -graf/ *n.* **1.** INSTRUMENT FOR RECORDING HEART ACTIVITY an instrument for recording heart activity, used in the diagnosis of heart disorders **2.** = **electrocardiograph** —**cardiographic** /kaárdi ə gráffik/ *adj.* —**cardiographical** /-gráffik'l/ *adj.* —**cardiographically** /-gráffikli/ *adv.* —**cardiography** /kaárdi óggrəfi/ *n.*

cardiographer /kaárdi óggrəfər/ *n.* a medical technician trained in using a cardiograph, especially an electrocardiograph

cardiologist /kaárdi óllәjist/ *n.* a doctor who specializes in the diagnosis and treatment of heart disorders and related conditions

cardiology /kaárdi ólləji/ *n.* a branch of medicine dealing with the diagnosis and treatment of heart disorders and related conditions —**cardiological** /kaárdi ə lójjik'l/ *adj.*

cardiomegaly /kaárdi ō méggəli/ *n.* pathological enlargement of the heart

cardiomyopathy /kaárdi ō mī óppəthi/ (*plural* **-thies**) *n.* a disease of the heart muscle, usually chronic and with an unknown or obscure cause

cardiopathy /kaárdi óppəthi/ (*plural* **-thies**) *n.* a heart disease or disorder

cardiopulmonary /kaárdi ō púlmənəri, -pŏŏl-/ *adj.* relating to both the heart and the lungs

cardiopulmonary bypass *n.* a procedure by which the blood is artificially circulated and oxygenated by a heart-lung machine so that surgery may be carried out on the heart

cardiopulmonary resuscitation *n.* an emergency technique to revive sb whose heart has stopped beating that involves clearing the person's airways and then alternating heart compression with mouth-to-mouth respiration

cardiorespiratory /kaárdi ō rə spírrətəri, -rə spīrətəri, -réspərətəri/ *adj.* relating to both the heart and the respiratory system

cardiothoracic /kaárdi ō thaw rássik/ *adj.* relating to both the heart and the chest

cardiovascular /kaárdi ō váskyŏŏlər/ *adj.* relating to both the heart and the blood vessels

carditis /kaar dītiss/ *n.* inflammation of the heart [Late 18thC. Formed from Greek *kardia* (see CARDIAC).]

-cardium *suffix.* MED part of the heart ○ *endocardium* [Via modern Latin from Greek *kardia* 'heart' (see CARDIAC)]

cardoon /kaar dóon/ (*plural* **-doon** *or* **-doons**) *n.* a large southern European perennial plant related to the artichoke that has spiny leaves and edible roots and leafstalks. Latin name: *Cynara cardunculus.* [Early 17thC. Via French *cardon* from, ultimately, Latin *carduus* 'thistle, artichoke' (see CARD[2]).]

cardphone /kaárd fōn/ *n.* a payphone operated by a phonecard

cardsharp /kaárd shaarp/, **cardsharper** /-shaarpər/ *n.* sb who regularly cheats when playing cards —**cardsharping** *n.*

card table *n.* a small table, usually folding and covered with green baize, used for playing card games

cardy *n.* = **cardie**

care /kair/ *v.* (**cares, caring, cared**) **1.** *vti.* BE CONCERNED to be interested or concerned ○ *I said I couldn't care less if he did leave.* **2.** *vi.* FEEL AFFECTION AND CONCERN to feel affection or love and concern for sb **3.** *vi.* LOOK AFTER SB OR STH to look after or supervise sb or sth **4.** *vi.* LIKE OR WANT STH to like or be in favour of sth (*formal*) ○ *Would you care for dessert, sir?* ■ *n.* **1.** UPKEEP the process of maintaining sth in good condition ○ *a skin care treatment* **2.** CAREFUL ATTENTION careful attention to avoid damage or error ○ *take care crossing the road* **3.** WORRY a worry or cause for anxiety ○ *without a care in the world* **4.** ATTENTIVE TREATMENT OF SB the providing of whatever is needed for sb's well-being, e.g. sb dependent or physically or mentally disabled ○ *responsible for the 20 children in her care* ○ *residential care* **5.** RESPONSIBILITY OF LOCAL AUTHORITY FOR CHILD the custody and maintenance of a child as the legal responsibility of a local authority after a court order ○ *She went to prison and her children were taken into care.* [Old English *caru* 'sorrow'. Ultimately from an Indo-European word that is also the ancestor of English *chary, slogan,* and *garrulous.*] ◇ **care of** into the temporary possession of an addressee who will ensure that the specified item will be delivered to the intended recipient ○ *sent the letter to her care of her parents*

WORD KEY: USAGE

could care less or **couldn't care less**? In informal English ***I could care less*** is all but synonymous with ***I couldn't care less***, except that it carries overtones of irony. However it should be pointed out that many people strongly oppose this usage.

WORD KEY: SYNONYMS

See Synonyms at ***worry.***

CARE /kair/ *abbr.* Cooperative for American Relief Everywhere

care and maintenance *n.* the condition in which a site such as a factory, shipyard, or machinery is kept when it is ready for immediate use at any time

care attendant *n.* sb employed to look after people in a variety of settings such as retirement or nursing homes

careen /kə réen/ (**-reens, -reening, -reened**) *v.* **1.** *vi.* SWAY OR SWERVE WHILE MOVING to move forwards at high speed, swaying, lurching, or swerving from one side to the other ○ *a motorcycle careening around sharp curves* **2.** *vi. US* RUSH to rush pell-mell ○ *He seemed to careen through life in a happy-go-lucky manner.* **3.** *vti.* SHIPPING TURN BOAT ON SIDE to turn over onto the side, or turn a boat over on its side, especially for repairs or cleaning **4.** *vi.* NAUT HEEL IN THE WIND to heel over to one side while sailing [Late 16thC. Via French *carène* from, ultimately, Latin *carina* 'keel', originally 'nutshell' (source of English *carina*).] —**careener** *n.*

career /kə réer/ *n.* **1.** LONG-TERM OR LIFELONG JOB a job or occupation regarded as a long-term or lifelong activity **2.** PROFESSIONAL PROGRESS sb's progress in a chosen profession or during that person's working life **3.** GENERAL PROGRESS the general path or progress taken by sb or sth ○ *a piece of legislation whose career is rich with conflicting amendments* **4.** RAPID FORWARD LURCHING MOTION a rushing onwards while lurching or swaying ■ *adj.* PROFESSIONAL FOR LIFE trained for and expecting to work in a particular occupation for an entire working life rather than briefly ○ *a career diplomat* ■ *vi.* (**-reers, -reering, -reered**) LURCH RAPIDLY ONWARDS to rush forwards while lurching or swaying [Mid-16thC. Via French *carrière* from, ultimately, Latin *carrus* 'two-wheeled wagon' (see CAR). Originally 'racecourse', then 'swift course'.]

WORD KEY: CULTURAL NOTE

My Brilliant Career, a novel by Australian writer Miles Franklin (1901). It is an account of a young girl's struggle to choose between an independent career and a comfortable life as the wife of a wealthy landowner. It was made into a film directed by Gillian Armstrong in 1979.

career counsellor *n. US* = **careers officer**

careerism /kə réerizzəm/ *n.* the behaviour of sb whose principal motivation is career advancement —**careerist** *n.*

careers master *n.* a male teacher who gives secondary school pupils advice about possible careers, usually in addition to normal teaching duties

careers mistress *n.* a female teacher who gives secondary school pupils advice about possible careers, usually in addition to normal teaching duties

careers officer *n.* sb whose job is to advise secondary pupils on possible careers and jobs as they approach school leaving age. US term **career counsellor**

career woman *n.* a woman who has a career or who takes her working life seriously

carefree /káir free/ *adj.* having no worries or responsibilities —**carefreeness** *n.*

careful /káirf'l/ *adj.* **1.** CAUTIOUS acting with caution and attention **2.** PAINSTAKING showing close attention to accuracy and detail **3.** NOT OVERSPENDING OR BEING WASTEFUL ensuring that money or resources are not spent or used wastefully or without thought **4.** WATCHFUL watchful and protective about sth **5.** ANXIOUS full of anxious cares (*archaic*)

WORD KEY: SYNONYMS

careful, conscientious, scrupulous, thorough, meticulous, painstaking, assiduous, punctilious, finicky, fussy

CORE MEANING: exercising care and attention in doing sth

careful a wide-ranging term, suggesting attention to detail and implying cautiousness in avoiding errors or inaccuracies; **conscientious** a term suggesting great care, attention, and industriousness towards work, especially as part of sb's personal ethic; **scrupulous** conscientious, particularly with respect to ethical or moral behaviour; **thorough** attentive to detail; **meticulous** a formal term suggesting a high degree of thoroughness; **painstaking** a term emphasizing that sb is expending unusual effort; **assiduous** a formal term implying that sb is working very hard or doggedly; **punctilious** a formal term suggesting a rigorous, sometimes excessive attention to fine detail, especially in the observance of rules; **finicky** an informal word suggesting an irritating and unnecessary degree of carefulness; **fussy** a disapproving term similar to 'finicky'.

carefully /káirf'li/ *adv.* **1.** PAINSTAKINGLY with painstaking attention to detail **2.** WITH CAUTION AND ATTENTION with caution and attention so as to avoid damage or potential problems

carefulness /káirf'lnəss/ *n.* **1.** CAUTION AND ATTENTION GIVEN TO STH caution and attention given to sth so as to avoid damage or potential problems **2.** ATTENTION TO DETAIL painstaking attention to detail **3.** AVOIDANCE OF OVERSPENDING a tendency to avoid spending money or using resources wastefully or unnecessarily (*informal*)

caregiver /káir givvər/ *n. US* **1.** = **carer 2.** SB ASSISTING IN MANAGEMENT OF ILLNESS a medical or other professional who assists in the management of an illness or disability —**caregiving** *n.*

care in the community *n.* a British government policy of reintegrating people with a history of psychiatric disorders into their communities by moving them from long-stay institutions to their families or community centres

care label *n.* a label, sewn onto a piece of clothing or other item, that gives cleaning instructions for the item

careless /káirləss/ *adj.* **1.** NOT GIVING CAREFUL ATTENTION not giving enough careful attention to the details of sth **2.** SHOWING NO CONCERN disregarding or showing no concern about sth **3.** NOT CAREFULLY WORKED ON not carefully worked on or practised, but done or assumed easily and naturally —**carelessly** *adv.*

carelessness /káirləssnəss/ *n.* **1.** LACK OF ATTENTION lack of careful attention to the details of sth **2.** EXAMPLE OF NEGLIGENCE an example of negligence or of a failure to take enough trouble with sth **3.** LACK OF CONCERN lack of concern about sth

carer /káirər/ *n.* the individual who has the principal responsibility of caring for a child or an elderly or dependent adult. US term **caregiver**

caress /kə réss/ *vt.* (**-resses, -ressing, -ressed**) **1.** TOUCH OR STROKE AFFECTIONATELY to touch or stroke sb or sth affectionately **2.** AFFECT IN SOOTHING WAY to touch, pass over, or affect sb in a soothing or pleasant way ■ *n.* GENTLE TOUCH a gentle affectionate touch or embrace [Mid-17thC. Via French *caresse* from, ultimately, Latin *carus* 'dear' (source of English *charity* and *cherish*).] —**caresser** *n.* —**caressive** *adj.* —**caressively** *adv.*

caressing /kə réssing/ *adj.* gentle and soothing —**caressingly** *adv.*

caret /kárrət/ *n.* a mark (ʌ) made on printed or manuscript material to show where sth such as a letter or word should be inserted [Late 17thC. From Latin *caret*, literally 'there is lacking', a form of *carere* 'to be without, lack'.]

caretaker /káir taykər/ *n.* **1.** SB WHO LOOKS AFTER BUILDING sb who looks after a property such as an office block or a school when it is empty and supervises its maintenance and cleaning. US term **janitor 2.** TEM-

PORARY OFFICE-HOLDER sb who holds an office temporarily, especially when it has fallen vacant unexpectedly **3. = carer**

caretaker government n. a government that is in power temporarily after the fall of a previous government, e.g. until an election is held

caretaking /káir tayking/ n. the occupation of looking after a property such as an office block or a school and supervising its maintenance and cleaning

Carew /kə roŏ, káiroo/, **Thomas** (1595?–1645?) English poet, diplomat, and author of witty lyrics in the Cavalier tradition, as well as the masque *Coelum Britannicum* (1634).

care worker n. sb employed to help look after people with physical or mental disabilities in residential accommodation

careworn /káir wawrn/ adj. exhausted or otherwise badly affected by anxiety or worry

Carey /káiri/, **George, Archbishop** (b. 1935) British Anglican bishop. He was Bishop of Bath and Wells (1987–91) and became Archbishop of Canterbury in 1991.

Carey, Peter Philip (b. 1943) Australian writer and author of the novels *Illywhacker* (1985) and the Booker Prize-winning *Oscar and Lucinda* (1988).

Carey Street n. a state of bankruptcy (*dated*) [Because Carey Street in London was the former location of the Bankruptcy Department of the Supreme Court]

carfax /kaár faks/ n. a place where four principal roads intersect in a town (*archaic*) [14thC. Via Anglo-Norman *carfuks* from assumed popular Latin *quadrifurcus*, literally 'four-forked', from Latin *furca* 'fork' (source of English *fork*); from the shape of the crossroads.]

carfuffle /kər fúff'l/ n. Scotland a kerfuffle (*informal*)

carful /kaár foŏl/ n. = **carload** n.

cargo /kaárgō/ (*plural* **-goes**). **1. GOODS CARRIED AS FREIGHT** goods carried as freight by sea, road, or air **2. LOAD** a load of sth [Mid-17thC. Via Spanish, from, ultimately, late Latin *car(ri)care* 'to load', from Latin *carrus* 'two-wheeled wagon' (see **CAR**).]

cargo cult n. a religion in some southwestern Pacific islands whose devotees believe that ancestral spirits will return to the island bringing modern consumer goods and wealth

cargo pocket n. a large pocket with a pleat and a flap

carhop /kaár hop/ n. **1.** US, Can **SERVER AT DRIVE-IN RESTAURANT** sb who serves food to people in parked cars at a drive-in restaurant **2.** US **SB WHO LOOKS AFTER CUSTOMERS' CARS** sb who takes care of the vehicles of guests staying at a resort or large hotel (*dated*) [Mid-20thC. From **CAR** + *hop* (from **BELLHOP**).]

cariad /kárri ad/ n. Wales used as an endearing form of address (*informal*) [From Welsh]

Carib¹ /kárrib/ (*plural* **-ibs** or **-ib**) n. **1. PEOPLES NATIVE AMERICAN** a member of a group of Native American people who inhabit part of Central America, northeastern South America, and the Lesser Antilles **2.** LANG **S AMERICAN LANGUAGE** a language of the Cariban family spoken in Venezuela and neighbouring countries. Carib is spoken by 20,000 people. [Mid-16thC. Via Spanish *caribe* from Arawak *carib* (source of English *cannibal*).] —**Carib** adj.

Carib² abbr. Caribbean

Cariban /kárribən/ (*plural* **-bans** or **-ban**) n. **1.** PEOPLES, LANG = **Carib 2.** LANG, PEOPLES **GROUP OF S AMERICAN LANGUAGES** a group of about 30 languages spoken in northern South America. About 40,000 people speak a Cariban language. —**Cariban** adj.

Caribbean /kárri beé ən/ n. **1. REGION INCLUDING THE WEST INDIES** region comprising the states and islands of the Caribbean Sea, including the West Indies **2.** SB **FROM CARIBBEAN** sb who was born in or is a citizen of any of the Caribbean islands ■ adj. **1. OF CARIBBEAN** relating to or typical of any of the countries of the Caribbean or their people or culture **2. OF THE CARIBS** relating to or typical of the Caribs or their culture

Caribbean English n. the variety of English spoken in the Caribbean islands

---

WORD KEY: WORLD ENGLISH

The English language as used in the Caribbean region, also called *West Indian English*. The islands and coasts of the Caribbean, since their discovery by Columbus in 1492, have, since that time, been claimed, disputed, settled, and governed by the Spanish, Portuguese, French, British, Dutch, Danish, and Americans with obvious, long-term, varied effects on the languages spoken there. In the second half of the 20th century, most of the territories are independent, but colonization has created a complex inheritance. In such mainland areas as Belize and Guyana, indigenous languages survive, but not on the islands, and in all territories there is a complex continuum between the standard forms of English (American and British), Dutch, French, and Spanish on the one side and their creole varieties on the other. In general terms, the creoles mix European lexical items with varying degrees of African structural features. In most Anglo-Caribbean territories, although school-based standard English is the official language it is a minority form and, in states like Belize and Guyana, English mixes with a range of other languages. Apart from Barbados and Guyana, *Caribbean English* is usually non-rhotic (i.e., r is not pronounced in such words as art, door, worker).

Caribbean Sea arm of the Atlantic Ocean, surrounded by the West Indies, northern South America, and eastern Central America. Area: 1,940,000 sq. km/750,000 sq. mi. Depth: Cayman Trench 7,535 m/24,720 ft.

caribe /kə reébi/ n. ZOOL = piranha [Mid-19thC. From Spanish (see **CARIB¹**).]

Caribou

caribou /kárri boo/ (*plural* **-bous** or **-bou**) n. a large deer that lives in large herds in northern regions and is characterized by large branched antlers present on both sexes. Reindeer are domesticated caribou. Genus: *Rangifer*. [Mid-17thC. Via Canadian French from Micmac *ɣalipu*, literally 'snow-shoveller', from the animal's removal of snow to find grass.]

Caribou Inuit n. sb belonging to any of the Inuit peoples who inhabit the Barren Grounds in northern Canada. They depend upon caribou for survival.

caricature /kárrikə choor/ n. **1. COMIC EXAGGERATION** a drawing, description, or performance that exaggerates sb's or sth's characteristics, e.g. sb's physical features, for humorous or satirical effect **2. TRAVESTY** a ridiculously inappropriate or unsuccessful version of or attempt at sth **3. OF CARICATURES** the art of creating caricatures ■ vt. (**-tures, -turing, -tured**) **REPRESENT WITH COMIC EXAGGERATION** to represent sb or sth with a caricature [Mid-18thC. From, ultimately, Italian *caricatura*, from *caricare* 'to exaggerate, load', from late Latin *carricare*, from Latin *carrus* 'wagon' (see **CAR**).] —**caricatural** /kárrikəchoŏərəl/ adj.

caricaturist /kárrikə choorist/ n. sb who creates caricatures, especially an artist

CARICOM /kárri kom/ abbr. Caribbean Community and Common Market

caries /káir eez, kaíri eez/ n. progressive decay of a tooth or, less commonly, a bone [Late 16thC. From Latin.]

CARIFTA /ka ríftə/ abbr. Caribbean Free Trade Association

carillon /kə ríllyən, kárrillyən/ n. **1. SET OF STATIONARY BELLS** a set of chromatically tuned stationary bells, usually hung in a tower and played from a keyboard

2. TUNE PLAYED ON SET OF BELLS a tune played on a keyboard connected to a set of stationary bells **3. ORGAN STOP IMITATING BELLS** an organ stop that imitates the sound of a carillon ■ vi. (**-lons, -lonning, -onned**) **PLAY STATIONARY BELLS** to play a set of stationary bells, using a keyboard [Late 18thC. From an assumed Proto-Romance word meaning 'peal of four bells'.]

carillonneur /kə ríllyə núr, kárrillyə núr/ n. sb who plays a carillon [Late 18thC. From French.]

carina /kə reénə, kə rínə/ n. **1.** ZOOL **PROJECTING PART OF BIRD'S BREASTBONE** the prominent keel-shaped projection of the breastbone of a bird to which the flight muscles are anchored **2.** BOT **BOAT-SHAPED FUSED PETALS** the boat-shaped part of a pea flower, formed by the two fused lower petals **3.** ANAT **KEEL-SHAPED BODY PART** a keel-shaped body part, e.g. the ridge at the base of the windpipe where it divides to form the bronchi [Early 18thC. From Latin, 'keel' (source of English *careen*).] —**carinate** /kárri nayt/ adj.

Carina /kə reénə, kə rínə/ n. a constellation in the sky of the southern hemisphere near the Southern Cross that contains Canopus, the second brightest star in the sky

caring /káiring/ adj. **1. SHOWING CONCERN** compassionate or showing concern for others **2. RELATING TO PROFESSION LOOKING AFTER PEOPLE** belonging or relating to a profession such as nursing or social work that involves looking after people's physical, medical, or general welfare ■ n. **PROVISION OF MEDICAL OR SIMILAR CARE** provision of medical or other types of care, either professionally or in general —**caringly** adv.

carioca /kárri ōkə/ n. **1. BRAZILIAN DANCE** a Brazilian dance similar to the samba **2. MUSIC FOR CARIOCA** a piece of music or a tune to which the carioca is danced [Mid-20thC. From Portuguese, ultimately from Tupian.]

Cariocan /kárri ōkən/, **Carioca** /-ōkə/ n. **SB FROM RIO DE JANEIRO** sb who was born in or lives in Rio de Janeiro, Brazil ■ adj. **OF RIO DE JANEIRO** relating to or typical of Rio de Janeiro or its people or culture

cariogenic /káiri ō jénnik/ adj. causing caries in the teeth [Mid-20thC. Coined from **CARIES** + **-GENIC**.]

cariole /kárri ōl/, **carriole** n. a small open carriage or covered cart, the former drawn by one horse [Mid-18thC. Via French from Italian *carriuola*, literally 'little car', from *carro* 'car', from Latin *carrus* 'wagon' (see **CAR**).]

carious /káiri əss/, **cariose** /-ōz/ adj. having caries in the teeth or bone [Mid-16thC. From Latin *cariosus*, from *caries*.] —**cariosity** /káiri óssəti, kárri-/ n. —**cariousness** /káiri əssnəss/ n.

carjacking /kaár jaking/ n. the crime of holding up a car and either stealing it, robbing the driver, or forcing the driver to drive somewhere for criminal purposes [Late 20thC. Blend of **CAR** and **HIJACKER**.] —**carjack** vti. —**carjacker** n.

cark¹ /kaark/ vi. (**carks, carking, carked**) **WORRY** to worry (*archaic*) ■ n. **ANXIETY** worry or a worry (*archaic*) [14thC. From Old Northern French *carkier*, from Old French *charkier*, from late Latin *carricare* 'to load' (see **CARICATURE**).]

cark² /kaark/ (**carks, carking, carked**) vi. Aus to fail, break down, or stop working (*slang*) [Late 20thC. Origin uncertain: perhaps an alteration of **CROAK**.]

carline /kaárlin/ (*plural* **-line** or **-lines**) n. a plant of Europe and Asia that resembles a thistle in appearance, with spiny leaves and yellow flower heads. Latin name: *Carlina vulgaris*. [Late 16thC, via French, from medieval Latin *carlina*, of uncertain origin: perhaps ultimately from Latin *carduus* 'thistle' (see **CARD²**), by folk etymology from *Carolus Magnus* (Charlemagne)]

carling /kaárling, -lin/ n. a fore-and-aft wooden beam that supports a boat's deck, especially round an opening in the deck such as a hatchway [14thC. From Old Norse.]

Carlisle /kaar líl, kaár líl/ city in Cumbria, northwestern England. It is a local government district and the administrative headquarters of Cumbria. Population: 99,800 (1991).

Carlist /kaárlist/ n. a supporter of Don Carlos or his descendants as rightful monarchs of Spain during the 19th century [Mid-19thC. From Spanish *carlista*, from the name of Don **CARLOS**.]

carload /ka'ar lōd/ n. a full complement of people able to get into and ride in a car

carload rate n. a reduced rate for shipping freight

Carlos /ka'ar loss/, **Don** (1788–1855) Spanish pretender to the throne. His claim to the Spanish throne (1833), reasserted by his descendants, led to the Carlist Wars (1834–39, 1872–76). Full name **Carlos Maria Isidro**

Carlovingian adj. = Carolingian

Carl XVI Gustaf /ka'arl goost af/, **King of Sweden** (b. 1946) Swedish monarch. He succeeded his grandfather, Gustaf VI, in 1973.

Carlyle /kaar līl/, **Thomas** (1795–1881) Scottish historian, essayist, and author of *Sartor Resartus* (1833–34), *The French Revolution* (1837), and *Oliver Cromwell* (1845).

carmagnole /ka'armən yōl, -yōl/ n. **1.** FRENCH REVOLUTIONARY TUNE AND DANCE a dance and a popular song of the French Revolution **2.** FRENCH REVOLUTIONARY'S CLOTHING the typical costume of many of the French Revolutionaries, consisting of a short jacket with a broad collar, black trousers with a tricoloured sash, and a red liberty cap [Late 18thC. From French; of uncertain origin: ultimately probably from *Carmagnola*, town in Piedmont, northwestern Italy.]

Carmarthen /kər ma'arthən/ seaport and administrative city of Carmarthenshire. Population: 13,524 (1991).

Carmarthenshire /kər ma'arthənshər/ county in southern Wales, with its headquarters in Carmarthen. Population: 169,500 (1995).

Carme /ka'armi/ n. **1.** MYTHOL GREEK NYMPH in Greek mythology, a nymph and mother of the Cretan goddess Britomaris **2.** ASTRON SATELLITE OF JUPITER a small satellite of Jupiter that was discovered in 1938

Carmel, Mount /ka'arm'l-/ mountain in northern Israel, near the Mediterranean Sea, with many biblical associations. Height: 545 m/1,789 ft.

Carmelite /ka'armə līt/ n. **1.** MEMBER OF ORDER OF FRIARS a member of an order of mendicant friars, founded around 1155 and called Our Lady of Mount Carmel **2.** MEMBER OF ORDER OF NUNS a member of the order of nuns of Our Lady of Mount Carmel, founded in 1452 and noted for the strictness of its rule ■ adj. BELONGING TO ORDER OF CARMELITES belonging or relating to either of the orders of Our Lady of Mount Carmel [15thC. Directly or via French *carmélite* from medieval Latin *Carmelita*, named after Mount CARMEL, where the order was founded.]

Carmichael /kaar mīk'l/, **Hoagy** (1899–1981) US singer and songwriter. He wrote the music to the song *Stardust* (1929). Full name **Hoagland Howard Carmichael**

carmine /ka'ar mīn, -min/ n. **1.** DEEP RED COLOUR a deep red colour tinged with purple **2.** RED PIGMENT a bright red pigment made from cochineal ■ adj. DEEP RED of a deep red tinged with purple [Early 18thC. Via French *carmin* from, ultimately, Arabic *ķirmiz* 'kermes' (source of English *crimson* and *kermes*).]

Carnaby Street /ka'arnəbi-/ a street in Soho in central London notable in the 1960s as the heart of the new youth-centred fashion trade

Prehistoric stone monuments at
Carnac, France

Carnac /ka'ar nak/ village in Morbihan Department, Bretagne Region, in western France. It is famous for its prehistoric stone monuments, which number more than 3,000.

carnage /ka'arnij/ n. widespread and indiscriminate slaughter or massacre, especially of human beings [Early 17thC. From, ultimately, medieval Latin *carnaticum* 'flesh (especially as tribute to a feudal lord)', from the Latin stem *carn-* 'flesh'.]

carnal /ka'arn'l/ adj. **1.** RELATING TO PHYSICAL NEEDS relating to sb's physical needs or appetites, especially as contrasted with spiritual or intellectual qualities (*formal*) **2.** SENSUAL sensual or sexual (*formal*) **3.** RELATING TO BODY relating to or consisting of the body (*formal*) [15thC. From Christian Latin *carnalis*, from the Latin stem *carn-* 'flesh' (source of English *carnage*, *carnival*, and *charnel*).] —**carnalist** n. —**carnality** /kaar na'lləti/ n. —**carnally** /ka'arn'li/ adv.

carnal knowledge n. sexual intercourse, especially involving penetration (*formal*)

carnallite /ka'arnə līt/ n. a white or light-coloured mineral that is a hydrous chloride of magnesium and potassium and an important source of potassium used in fertilizers [Mid-19thC. Named after Rudolf von *Carnall*, a German mining engineer (1804–74).]

carnaptious /kaar na'pshəss/ adj. Scotland quarrelsome and liable to snap at people (*informal*)

Carnarvon /kərna'arvən/ town on the western coast of Western Australia, situated at the mouth of the River Gascoyne. Population: 6,357 (1996).

Carnarvon Gorge sandstone canyon in southern Queensland, Australia

Carnarvon Range range of mountains in the Little Sandy Desert, Western Australia. The highest peak is Mount Essendon. Height: 907 m/2,975 ft.

carnassial /kaar na'ssi əl/ adj. used to describe the larger sharp cheek teeth in the upper and lower jaw of a carnivore that are adapted for cutting flesh [Mid-19thC. Via French *carnassier* 'carnivorous', from, ultimately, the Latin stem *carn-* (see CARNAL).]

Carnatic /kaar na'ttik/ linguistic region in south-central India between the Eastern Ghats and the Coromandel coast. It is now part of Madras state.

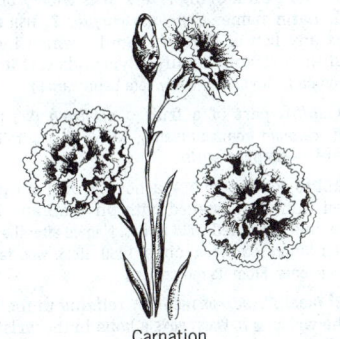

Carnation

carnation /kaar na'ysh'n/ n. **1.** PLANTS FLOWER WITH CLOVE SCENT a perennial plant of the Pink family with fringed petals, widely grown for its fragrant white, pink, or red flowers often smelling of cloves. Latin name: *Dianthus caryophyllus*. **2.** PINKISH COLOUR a pale reddish-pink colour ■ adj. of the colour carnation [Mid-16thC. Via French from the late Latin stem *carnation-* 'fleshiness', from Latin *carn-* (see CARNAL), because of its colour.]

carnauba /kaar nówbə, -náwbə/ (*plural* -ba or -bas) n. **1.** PALM TREE a fan palm native to Brazil with an edible root and leaves that yield a hard wax used, e.g., in polish and floor wax. Latin name: *Copernica prunifera*. **2.** = carnauba wax [Mid-19thC. Via Portuguese from Tupi.]

carnauba wax n. wax obtained from the young leaves of the carnauba tree and used in the manufacture of polish and candles

Carné /ka'ar nay/, **Marcel** (1909–96) French film director. His 'poetic realism' is seen at its height in *Les Enfants du Paradis* (1945).

Carnegie /kaar néggi, -náygi, -neégi, ka'arnəgi/ usually dry lake situated on the western edge of the Gibson Desert, central Western Australia. Area: 1,338 sq. km/517 sq. mi.

Carnegie /ka'arnə gi, kaar néggi/, **Andrew** (1835–1919) Scottish-born US industrialist and philanthropist who made a fortune in the steel industry. His philanthropic gifts endowed numerous public libraries in the United States.

Carnegie, Dale (1888–1955) US writer. His works on public speaking and self-esteem include *How to Win Friends and Influence People* (1936). Real name **Dale Carnegey**

carnelian /kaar neéli ən/, **cornelian** /kawr-/ n. a hard reddish translucent mineral, a form of chalcedony, used as a gemstone [Late 17thC. Alteration of *cornelian* (influenced by the Latin stem *carn-* 'flesh'), from obsolete French *corneline*, of uncertain origin: perhaps from Latin *cornu* 'horn' or *cornum* 'cornelian cherry'.]

carnet /ka'ar nay/ n. **1.** BOOK OF TRAVEL TICKETS a book of travel tickets or coupons costing less than the individual tickets purchased separately **2.** CUSTOMS DOCUMENT FOR CAR a customs document for a car that allows it to be taken across national borders without payment of duty [Early 19thC. From French.]

carnitine /ka'arni teen/ n. a chemical compound found in muscle and the liver that aids in the transport of fatty acids across cell membranes. Formula: $C_7H_{15}NO_3$. [Early 20thC. Formed from the Latin stem *carn-* (see CARNAL).]

carnival /ka'arnivəl/ n. **1.** PUBLIC CELEBRATION a public festive occasion or period, often with street processions, costumes, music, and dancing **2.** US = **fair 3.** CARNIVAL BEFORE LENT the period just before Lent begins, celebrated with a carnival in some Roman Catholic areas, e.g. Mardi Gras in New Orleans, Louisiana **4.** Aus SPORTS MEETING a sports meeting often run like a school sports day [Mid-16thC. Via Italian *carnevale* from medieval Latin *carnelevamen* 'Shrove-tide' (literally 'cessation of meat-eating'), from Latin *carn-* (see CARNAL).]

carnivore /ka'arni vawr/ n. **1.** FLESH-EATING ANIMAL an animal that eats other animals. ◊ herbivore, omnivore **2.** BOT, ZOOL a carnivorous plant **3.** SB WHO ENJOYS MEAT sb who is not a vegetarian and likes eating meat (*humorous*) [Mid-19thC. Via French from Latin *carnivorus* 'carnivorous' (see CARNIVOROUS).]

carnivorous /kaar nívvərəss/ adj. **1.** ZOOL MEAT-EATING feeding mainly on the flesh of other animals **2.** BOT ABLE TO DIGEST ANIMALS AS FOOD able to catch and digest animals such as insects and small invertebrates ◊ *a carnivorous plant* [Late 16thC. Formed from Latin *carnivorus*, literally 'meat-eating', from the stem *carn-* (see CARNAL).] —**carnivorously** adv. —**carnivorousness** n.

Carnot cycle /ka'arnō-/ n. a theoretical reversible heat-engine cycle that gives maximum efficiency

carnotite /ka'arnə tīt/ n. a yellow radioactive mineral that is a source of radium and uranium [Late 19thC. Named after Marie Adolphe *Carnot* (1839–1920), a French inspector of mines.]

Carnot principle /ka'arnō-/ n. the principle that the efficiency of a reversible heat engine depends on the maximum and minimum temperatures of the working fluid during the operating cycle

carny /ka'arni/ (-nies, -nying, -nied) vt. to try to persuade or coax sb into doing sth (*informal*) [Early 19thC. Origin unknown.]

Caro /ka'arō, kárrō/, **Qaro, Joseph ben Ephraim** (1488–1575) Spanish-born Palestinian Talmudic scholar. His *Shulhan Arukh* (1564–65), codifying religious law, is a major text of Orthodox Judaism.

carob /kárrəb/ (*plural* -obs or -ob) n. **1.** EVERGREEN TREE WITH EDIBLE PODS an evergreen tree that is native to the Mediterranean and has red flowers and edible pods. Latin name: *Ceratonia siliqua*. **2.** POD OF CAROB TREE the long dark-coloured edible pod of the carob tree that contains a sweet-tasting pulp **3.** EDIBLE POWDER LIKE CHOCOLATE an edible powder with a taste similar to that of chocolate, made from the seeds and pods of the carob tree [Mid-16thC. Via obsolete French *car(r)obe* from, ultimately, Arabic *karrūb(a)* (source of English *algarroba*).]

caroche /kə rósh/ n. a grand horse-drawn carriage used on ceremonial occasions [Late 16thC. Via obsolete French *caroche* from Italian *carraccio* 'large chariot', from, ultimately, Latin *carrum* (see CAR).]

carol /kárrəl/ *n.* **1.** JOYFUL HYMN a joyful religious song or hymn, especially a Christian song celebrating Christmas **2.** DANCE a dance in a circle, or the music accompanying it (*archaic*) ■ *v.* (**-ols, -olling, -olled**) **1.** *vi.* SING CHRISTMAS SONGS to sing hymns that celebrate Christmas, especially as a group going from house to house **2.** *vti.* SING to sing or call out sth in a joyful and lively way (*literary*) ○ *The sun shone, and the birds were carolling.* **3.** *vt.* CELEBRATE to celebrate sth, originally in song (*literary*) ○ *All the children carolled the good tidings.* [13thC. From Old French *carole*, of uncertain origin: probably via late Latin *choraula* 'choral song' from Greek *khoraulēs*, literally 'flute-player who accompanies the chorus'.] —**caroler** *n.*

WORD KEY: CULTURAL NOTE

A Christmas Carol, a novella by Charles Dickens (1843). It recounts the story of an avaricious merchant, Ebenezer Scrooge, who is visited by the ghosts of Christmas Past, Christmas Present, and Christmas Future. Confronted by the effects of his miserly behaviour on others, Scrooge resolves to become a more generous and charitable person. Over time, the name *Scrooge* has come to mean a petty malicious miser.

Carol II /kárrəl/, **King of Romania** (1893–1953) Romanian monarch who usurped the crown of his son, King Michael, in 1930 but in 1940 was himself dethroned.

Carolean /kárrə leé ən/ *adj.* = **Caroline**

caroli plural of **carolus**

Carolina /kár ə líː nə/ city in northeastern Puerto Rico, southeast of San Juan. Population: 188,427 (1996).

Carolina allspice *n.* a deciduous shrub of the southeastern United States, with large fragrant flowers. Latin name: *Calycanthus floridus.* [Named after the former British colony of *Carolina* (now the US states North Carolina and South Carolina)]

Caroline /kárrə līn/ *adj.* **1.** OF CHARLES I AND II relating to the English kings Charles I and Charles II or their reigns **2.** OF MONARCH NAMED CHARLES relating to any king or emperor called Charles [Early 17thC. From medieval Latin *Carolinus*, from *Carolus* 'Charles'.]

Caroline Islands /kárrə līn-, -lin-/ archipelago consisting of more than 600 islands, north of New Guinea in the western Pacific Ocean. Area: 1,165 sq. km/450 sq. mi.

Caroline of Brunswick /kárrə līn əv brúnzwik/, **Queen of England** (1768–1821) German-born British titular Queen Consort. She was the estranged wife of George IV, whose attempt to divorce her (1820) provoked civil disorder.

Carolingian /kárrə línji ən/ *adj.* RELATING TO EARLY EUROPEAN KINGS relating to the dynasty of Frankish kings descended from the emperor Charlemagne that ruled France and Germany from the 8th to the 10th century ■ *n.* FRANKISH KING any of the Frankish kings who ruled France and Germany from the 8th to the 10th century

Carolinian /kárrə línni ən/ *adj.* **1.** HIST = **Caroline 2.** HIST = **Carolingian 3.** OF NORTH, OR SOUTH CAROLINA relating to or typical of North or South Carolina, or their inhabitants or culture

carolus /kárrələss/ (*plural* **caroluses** *or* **caroli** /-lī/) *n.* a gold coin named after any of the kings or emperors called Charles who issued it, especially one issued by Charles I of England [Early 16thC. From medieval Latin *Carolus* 'Charles'.]

carom /kárrəm/ *n. US, Can* CUE GAMES = **cannon** ■ *vi.* (**-oms, -oming, -omed**) *US, Can* = **cannon** [Late 18thC. Shortening of CARAMBOLE.]

carotene /kárrə teen/, **carotin** /-tin/ *n.* an organic chemical compound occurring in several forms in plants and producing an orange or red colour. Carotene is a source of vitamin A. [Mid-19thC. Formed from Latin *carota* (see CARROT).]

carotenoid /kə rótti noyd/, **carotinoid** *n.* an organic chemical compound belonging to a group including the carotenes that gives a yellow, orange, or red colour to plants

carotid /kə róttid/, **carotid artery** *n.* a large artery on either side of the neck that supplies blood to the head. Each carotid branches into an internal and an external carotid. [Early 17thC. Via French *carotide* or modern Latin *carotides* from Greek *karōtides*, from, ultimately, *karoun* 'to stupefy'. From the belief that pressure on the arteries causes stupor.]

carotid body (*plural* **carotid bodies**) *n.* a cluster of cells and nerve fibres in each carotid artery that is sensitive to oxygen and acidity levels in the blood and is part of the system that regulates them

carotid sinus *n.* a slight bulge in each carotid artery that contains pressure-sensitive nerve endings and forms part of the system that monitors and controls blood pressure

carotin *n.* = **carotene**

carotinoid *n.* = **carotenoid**

carousal /kə rówz'l/ *n.* a noisy and boisterous drinking party (*literary*)

carouse /kə rówz/ *vi.* (**-rouses, -rousing, -roused**) DRINK AND BECOME NOISY to drink and become noisy, especially in a group (*literary*) ■ *n.* NOISY PARTY a noisy and boisterous drinking party (*archaic*) [Mid-16thC. From German *gar aus (trinken)*, literally '(to drink) right up'.] —**carouser** *n.*

carousel /kárrə sél, -zél/ *n.* **1.** CONVEYOR BELT a circular conveyor belt, especially one at an airport displaying luggage for arriving passengers to collect **2.** *US* = **merry-go-round** *n.* 1 **3.** HOLDER FOR PHOTOGRAPHIC SLIDES a circular rotating holder that loads photographic slides into a projector one at a time [Mid-17thC. Via French *carrousel* from Italian *carosello* 'tilting match'.]

carp[1] /kaarp/ (**carps, carping, carped**) *vi.* to keep complaining or finding fault ○ *I wish you'd stop carping, I'm doing my best.* [13thC. From Old Norse *karpa* 'to brag'. The current meaning evolved from 'to talk' under the influence of Latin *carpere* 'to pluck', also 'to slander' (source of English *carpet*).] —**carper** *n.*

WORD KEY: SYNONYMS

See Synonyms at ***complain***.

carp[2] /kaarp/ (*plural* **carp** *or* **carps**) *n.* **1.** LARGE FRESHWATER FISH a large fish with a single fin on its back, originally from Asia and now found worldwide in lakes and slow-moving rivers. It is widely bred for food. Latin name: *Cyprinus carpio.* **2.** FISH OF CARP FAMILY any fish of the carp family, which includes goldfish and koi. Family: Cyprinidae. [14thC. Via French *carpe* from, ultimately, late Latin *carpa*.]

-carp *suffix.* part of a fruit ○ *pericarp* [Via modern Latin *-carpium* from, ultimately, Greek *karpos* 'fruit' (see CARPO-] —**-carpous** *suffix.*

carpaccio /kaar páchi ō, -páchō/ *n.* a dish of raw beef sliced thinly, moistened with olive oil and lemon juice, and seasoned [Mid-20thC. Named after the Italian painter Vittore *Carpaccio* circa 1460–1525, who favoured red pigments. From its red colour.]

carpal /kaárp'l/ *adj.* OF THE WRIST relating to the bones in the wrist ■ *n.* WRIST BONE a bone in the wrist [Mid-18thC. Formed from CARPUS.]

carpal tunnel syndrome *n.* a condition of pain and weakness in the hand caused by repetitive compression of a nerve that passes through the wrist into the hand

car park *n.* an enclosure or building where cars can be parked temporarily

Carpathian Mountains /kaar páythi ən-/ mountain system in eastern Europe, situated along the border between Slovakia and Poland and extending southwards through the Ukraine and eastern Romania. Its highest peak is Gerlachovka 2,655 m/8,711 ft.

carpe diem /kaár pay deé em/ *interj.* used as an invocation to enjoy the present and not worry about the future [From Latin, literally 'seize the day']

carpel /kaárp'l/ *n.* a female reproductive organ in a flower, enclosing the fertilized ovules that are developing into seeds. It consists of the stigma and usually a style. [Mid-19thC. From French *carpelle* or modern Latin *carpellum*, literally 'little fruit', both formed from Greek *karpos* 'fruit'.] —**carpellary** /kaárpələri/ *adj.*

carpellate /kaárpi layt/ *adj.* used to describe a flower or plant that has carpels

Carpentaria, Gulf of /kaárpən táiri ə/ large gulf on the northern coast of Australia, lying between Arnhem Land in the west and the Cape York Peninsula in the east. Area: 310,000 sq. km/120,000 sq. mi.

carpenter /kaárpintər/ *n.* BUILDER OF WOODEN STRUCTURES OR OBJECTS sb who builds and repairs wooden structures, e.g. houses and boats, or the wooden parts of them ■ *v.* (**-ters, -tering, -tered**) **1.** *vi.* BUILD WOODEN STRUCTURES to build and repair wooden structures, or the wooden parts of them (*technical*) **2.** *vt.* MAKE STH WOODEN to make sth by cutting and joining pieces of wood ○ *He had carpentered a series of perfectly fitting dovetail joints.* **3.** *vt.* MAKE STH IN EFFICIENT WAY to make or devise sth efficiently and systematically ○ *They met every day, in the vain attempt to carpenter an agreement that would be acceptable to both sides.* [12thC. Via Anglo-Norman and Old French *carpentier* from late Latin *carpentarius (artifex)* 'carriage(-maker)', from *carpentum* 'two-wheeled carriage'.]

carpenter ant *n.* a large ant that bores into wood to make its nest. It usually bores into old or rotten wood, but it can also attack wood in homes and cause much damage. Genus: *Camponotus.*

carpenter bee *n.* a bee that bores tunnels into wood to lay its eggs. Families: Xylocopidae and Ceratinidae.

Carpentier /kaar páNti ay/, **Georges** (1894–1975) French boxer. Known as 'Gorgeous George', he was World Light-heavyweight Champion (1920–22).

carpentry /kaárpəntri/ *n.* **1.** THE BUILDING OF WOODEN STRUCTURES the work or occupation of building and repairing things made of wood, e.g. houses and boats, or the wooden parts of them ○ *a career in carpentry* **2.** THINGS MADE OUT OF WOOD the work or objects produced by a carpenter ○ *fine carpentry for sale*

carpet /kaárpit/ *n.* **1.** FLOOR COVERING thick fabric for covering a floor **2.** PIECE OF FLOOR COVERING a piece of thick, heavy fabric covering the floor of a room or area **3.** LAYER OR COVERING a layer or covering (*literary*) ○ *a carpet of snow* ■ *vt.* (**-pets, -peting, -peted**) **1.** COVER FLOOR WITH CARPET to cover a floor, or the floor of a room, with a carpet ○ *We could carpet every room in the house with the money she spent on that rug.* **2.** COVER to cover sth in a layer (*literary*) ○ *The valley was carpeted with flowers.* **3.** REPRIMAND to reprimand sb severely (*informal*) [14thC. Via Old French *carpite* or medieval Latin *carpita* from, ultimately, Latin *carpere* 'to pluck'. The underlying idea is of a cloth made from plucked or unravelled fabric.] ◇ **roll out the red carpet** to give a special welcome to a distinguished visitor ◇ **sweep sth under the carpet** to conceal or ignore sth that needs attention

carpetbag /kaárpit bag/ *n.* a medium-sized travelling bag originally made of a thick fabric such as carpet

carpetbagger /kaárpit baggər/ *n.* **1.** POST-CIVIL WAR OPPORTUNIST an opportunistic Northerner who moved to the southern United States after the American Civil War, especially one seeking political or commercial advantage **2.** POL OUTSIDER SEEKING LOCAL VOTE an outsider whose only interest in coming to a place is to win it as a political seat **3.** FIN OPPORTUNIST MEMBER OF BUILDING SOCIETY a member of a building society who campaigns to force it to demutualize, usually for short-term financial gain —**carpetbaggery** *n.*

carpetbag steak *n.* an Australian dish of a thick beef steak slit horizontally, stuffed with oysters, and grilled

carpet beetle *n.* a small beetle whose larvae feed on fabric, furs, or animal remains. Genera: *Anthrenus* and *Attagenus.*

carpet-bomb *vt.* (**carpet-bombs, carpet-bombing, carpet-bombed**) DESTROY AREA WITH INTENSIVE BOMBING to bomb an area intensively ■ *n. US* CAMPAIGN TO INFLUENCE PUBLIC OPINION to conduct an intensive campaign, especially in the media, to sway public opinion or to destroy sb's reputation [*Carpet* from the idea that the bombing covers an area as completely as a carpet covers a floor]

carpet grass *n.* a coarse grass that forms a tight matted growth and is widely used in warm humid areas for turf and pasture. Genus: *Axonopus.*

carpeting /kaárpiting/ *n.* **1.** FABRIC FOR FLOORS thick fabric used for covering floors **2.** CARPETS carpets regarded collectively ○ *How much do you want to spend on carpeting?*

carpet knight *n.* a lazy or cowardly person, especially a soldier who avoids battle and enjoys social and amorous activity (*archaic*) [Originally from the notion that the knight's achievements were those of luxurious carpeted chambers, or boudoirs, rather than of the battlefield]

carpet moth *n.* a large moth belonging to a group with mottled wings resembling the pattern of a carpet. Family: Larentidae.

carpet shark *n.* a shark with a mottled back resembling the pattern of a carpet. Family: Larentidae.

carpet slipper *n.* a slipper with an upper side made of a thick fabric that resembles carpet

carpet snake *n.* a large python found throughout southern Australia with a pattern of scales on its back resembling a traditional carpet. Latin name: *Morelia variegata*.

carpet sweeper *n.* a device for lifting dirt off carpets, with a long handle and revolving brushes in a wheeled casing

carpet tile *n.* a square of carpeting laid together with others to cover a floor

carpetweed /káarpit weed/ *n.* a low, close-growing North American weed with tiny greenish-white flowers. Latin name: *Mollugo verticillata*.

car phone *n.* a mobile phone designed for use in a car

carpi plural of **carpus**

carping /káarping/ *adj.* complaining or finding fault, or tending to ○ *his usual carping comments* —**carpingly** *adv.*

carpo- *prefix.* fruit ○ *carpophagous* [From Greek *karpos*. Ultimately from an Indo-European base meaning 'to gather, pick', which is also the ancestor of English *harvest* and *excerpt*.]

carpology /kaar póllǝji/ *n.* the branch of botany that deals with the study of fruits and seeds [Early 19thC] —**carpological** /káarpǝ lójjik'l/ *adj.* —**carpologist** /kaar póllǝjist/ *n.*

car pool *n.* **1.** GROUP USING OWN CARS IN TURN a group of associated people sharing the use of their cars, each in turn driving the others **2.** VEHICLES KEPT BY ORGANIZATION FOR STAFF a number of motor vehicles kept by an organization for use as needed by its personnel. US term **motor pool**

car-pool (car-pools, car-pooling, car-pooled) *vi.* to drive or be driven regularly from one place to another as a small group, with each member sharing driving responsibilities

carpophagous /kaar póffǝgǝss/ *adj.* ZOOL = **frugivorous**

carpophore /káarpō fawr/ *n.* **1.** STAMEN-BEARING PART OF FLOWER the part of a flower that bears the carpels and stamens **2.** SPORE-BEARING PART OF FUNGUS the part of some fungi that contains the spores or supports the part that contains them

carport /káar pawrt/ *n.* an open-sided shelter for a parked car, attached to a house or other building

carpospore /káarpō spawr/ *n.* a spore that forms in some red algae after fertilization

carpus /káarpǝss/ (*plural* **-pi** /-pī/) *n.* **1.** BONE IN WRIST JOINT any bone in the set of eight that form the wrist joint **2.** BONE IN ANIMAL'S FRONT LEG JOINT any bone in the set that form the joint between the forelimb of a vertebrate animal and its foot or paw, corresponding to the wrist [Late 17thC. Via modern Latin from Greek *karpos*.]

carr /kaar/ *n.* an area of marshy land with clumps of willows or other trees [14thC. From Old Norse *kjarr* 'brushwood'.]

Carraci /kǝ ráachi/, **Agostino** (1557–1602) Italian painter and engraver. He co-founded an influential academy in Bologna in 1585 with his brother Annibale and cousin Lodovico.

Carraci, **Annibale** (1560–1609) Italian painter. Co-founder of an academy in Bologna with his brother Agostino and cousin Lodovico, he painted frescoes in the Villa Farnese, Rome.

Carraci, **Lodovico** (1555–1619) Italian painter. He co-founded an influential academy in Bologna in 1585 with his cousins Agostino and Annibale.

carrack /kárrǝk/, **carack** *n.* a large Mediterranean trading ship of the 14th, 15th, and 16th centuries [14thC. From French *caraque*, of uncertain origin: probably via Spanish *carraca* from, ultimately, Arabic *ḳurḳūra* 'large merchant ship'.]

carrageen /kárrǝ geen, kárrǝ géen/, **carragheen** *n.* **1.** = **Irish moss 2.** FOOD TECH = **carrageenan** [Early 19thC. From Irish *carraigín*.]

carrageenan /kárrǝ geenǝn, kárrǝ géenǝn/, **carrageenin** *n.* a complex carbohydrate obtained from edible red seaweeds, especially the seaweed Irish moss, used in the commercial preparation of several kinds of food and drink [Late 19thC. From CARRAGEEN.]

carragheen *n.* = **carrageen**

Carrara /kǝ ráarǝ/ city in Massa-Carrara Province, Tuscany Region, in north-central Italy. It is famous for its quarry, which produces some of the world's finest marble. Population: 68,480 (1991).

carrel /kárrǝl/, **carrell** *n.* a bay, cubicle, or small room where one person can study in private, e.g. in a library [Late 16thC. Alteration of CAROL (from its earlier use for 'circle').]

Carrel /kǝ rél, kárrǝl/, **Alexis** (1873–1944) French biologist and surgeon. He won the Nobel Prize in medicine in 1912 for developing the vascular surgical technique that led to organ transplants.

Carreras /kǝ rérrǝz/, **José** (b. 1946) Spanish singer. An operatic tenor, he became an international star in the 1970s.

carriage /kárrij/ *n.* **1.** HORSE-DRAWN VEHICLE a four-wheeled horse-drawn private passenger vehicle, especially one that is large and comfortable **2.** RAILWAY COACH a railway passenger coach **3.** WHEELED PLATFORM a wheeled platform on which sth is carried or supported **4.** WAY OF HOLDING THE BODY the way sb holds his or her head and body when walking (*formal*) ○ *She was a tall woman with a beautiful upright carriage.* **5.** TAKING AND DELIVERING GOODS the transporting and delivering of goods **6.** CHARGE FOR TAKING AND DELIVERING GOODS a charge made for transporting and delivering goods **7.** MOVING PART OF MACHINE a part of a machine that holds and moves another part, e.g. the rotating and sliding paper-holder on a typewriter

carriage bolt *n.* US = **coach bolt**

carriage clock *n.* a small clock set in a case with a handle on top, originally used as travel clocks but now ornamental

carriage dog *n.* a dalmatian (*archaic*) [So called because it was trained to run behind a carriage as an ornamental guard dog]

carriage horse *n.* a horse used to pull carriages

carriage return *n.* the key or lever on a typewriter that sends the paper-holding carriage back and rotates it to move the paper upward, ready to begin a new line

carriage trade *n.* the most wealthy and prestigious of possible customers ○ *They carry only the highest quality goods, catering to the carriage trade.*

carriageway /kárrij way/ *n.* the part of a main road used for vehicles, especially one side of a major two-way road, carrying traffic in one direction only

carrick bend /kárrik-/ *n.* an intertwining knot similar to a granny knot, used for tying ropes together [*Carrick* probably an earlier variant of CARRACK]

carrick bitt /kárrik-/ *n.* one of the two posts that support a ship's windlass [See CARRICK BEND]

Carrickfergus /kárrik f/ town and county seat of Carrickfergus district, northeastern Northern Ireland, situated on the northern shore of Belfast Lough, 15 km/9.5 mi. northeast of Belfast. Population: 31,000 (1990).

carrier /kárri ǝr/ *n.* **1.** TRANSP TRANSPORTER OF PEOPLE OR GOODS a person or company whose function or business is to transport things or people from one place to another ○ *These airlines are among the world's most popular carriers.* **2.** MED TRANSMITTER OF DISEASE a living creature that is infected with a disease and can pass it to others but does not itself display any of the symptoms **3.** GENETICS TRANSMITTER OF GENETIC DEFECT an individual carrying a gene for a particular genetic trait or disorder without being affected by it, because two copies of the gene, one from each parent, are usually necessary for the disorder to show itself **4.** ENG PART OF MACHINE CONVEYING MOTION a part of a machine that carries and moves sth or transmits motion to another part **5.** LUGGAGE RACK a metal frame on which luggage can be tied to a road vehicle or bicycle **6.** NAVY AIRCRAFT CARRIER an aircraft carrier **7.** CHEM MEANS OF TRANSMITTING ACTIVE SUBSTANCE a neutral substance to which an active ingredient or agent is added as a way of applying or transferring the ingredient or agent ○ *Mix the dye and the carrier in equal proportions.* **8.** PHYS BEARER OF ELECTRIC CHARGE sth that carries electric current, e.g. an electron or ion **9.** TELECOM RADIO WAVE CARRYING INFORMATION an electromagnetic wave that is modulated to carry a signal in radio or television transmission **10.** PLASTIC BAG alternative for carrier bag

carrier air wing *n.* a squadron of aircraft operating from an aircraft carrier

carrier bag *n.* a large plastic or paper shopping bag with handles, especially one supplied by a shop

carrier pigeon *n.* **1.** PIGEON TAKING MESSAGES a domestic pigeon trained to deliver messages and return home **2.** SHOW PIGEON a large domestic pigeon bred for showing

carrier wave *n.* TELECOM = **carrier** *n.* 9

Carrington /kárringtǝn/, **Peter, 6th Baron Carrington** (b. 1919) British politician. He was British foreign secretary (1979–82) and secretary general of NATO (1984–88). Full name **Peter Alexander Rupert Carrington**

carriole *n.* = **cariole**

carrion /kárri ǝn/ *n.* **1.** ROTTING ANIMAL FLESH the rotting flesh of a dead animal **2.** STH DECAYING sth that is decaying or disgusting (*literary*) [13thC. Via Anglo-Norman and Old Northern French *caroi(g)ne* from, ultimately, Latin *caro* 'flesh' (source of English *carnal*).]

carrion crow *n.* a medium-sized European crow, similar to the rook but with a greenish tinge to its black plumage. Latin name: *Corvus corone*.

carrion flower *n.* **1.** CLIMBING PLANT WITH FOUL-SMELLING FLOWERS a North American climbing plant with small greenish flowers that smell like rotting flesh. Genus: *Smilax*. **2.** TROPICAL PLANT WITH FOUL-SMELLING FLOWERS a tropical succulent plant with foul-smelling star-shaped flowers. Genus: *Stapelia*.

Carroll /kárrǝl/, **Lewis** (1832–98) British writer. Author of *Alice's Adventures in Wonderland* (1865) and other children's books. Under his real name, he was also a distinguished geometrician and photographer. Pseudonym of **Charles Lutwidge Dodgson**

carronade /kárrǝ nayd/ *n.* a lightweight iron cannon formerly used on ships [Late 18thC. Named after *Carron*, a district in Falkirk, Scotland, where they were made.]

carron oil /kárrǝn-/ *n.* a mixture of limewater and linseed oil formerly used to soothe burns [Named after *Carron* (see CARRONADE). From its use at the ironworks there.]

carrot /kárrǝt/ *n.* **1.** FOOD THIN ORANGE ROOT VEGETABLE the thin, tapering orange-coloured root of the carrot plant that is eaten raw or cooked as a vegetable **2.** PLANTS PLANT WITH EDIBLE ORANGE-COLOURED ROOT a biennial plant of the parsley family with delicate green feathery leaves that is grown for its edible orange roots. Latin name: *Daucus carota*. **3.** INCENTIVE sth tempting, offered in order to persuade sb to do sth ○ *They offered us the carrot of a year's free petrol if we'd buy the sports car right then.* [15thC. Via French *carotte* and Latin *carota* from Greek *karōton*.]

carrot cake *n.* a cake made with finely grated carrots that give it a moist texture and delicate flavour

carrot fly (*plural* **carrot flies** or **carrot fly**) *n.* a low-flying insect whose larvae bore into the edible roots of the carrot plant. Latin name: *Psila rosae*.

carroty /kárrǝti/ *adj.* **1.** TASTING LIKE CARROTS like carrots in taste **2.** RED used to describe hair that is red or auburn **3.** OF BRIGHT ORANGE COLOUR of a bright reddish-orange colour

carry /kárri/ *v.* (**-ries, -rying, -ried**) **1.** *vt.* HOLD AND TRANSPORT SB OR STH to take sb or sth that you are holding or supporting to another place ○ *The case was too heavy for her to carry.* **2.** *vt.* BE CHANNEL OR ROUTE FOR STH to be the means by which sth passes or is transmitted from one place to another ○ *The pipeline will carry oil to the coast.* **3.** *vt.* **TELL OR CONTAIN** to communicate or convey information, an idea, or a feeling by way of content or in an indirect manner ○ *The article carries wider implications than you may think.* **4.** *vt.* **TAKE TO ANOTHER PLACE** to take sb or sth to another place ○ *a lorry carrying farm produce* **5.** *vt.* **MOVE SB, STH ALONG** to take and move sb or sth by a flow or impetus ○ *The current carried them swiftly downstream.* ○ *She could hear children's voices, carried on the light breeze.* **6.** *vt.* **HAVE TRANSMISSIBLE DISEASE** to be infected with a disease and capable of infecting others ○ *You may be carrying a virus without knowing it.* **7.** *vt.* **HAVE STH WITH YOU** to have sth with you, e.g. in your pocket or in a handbag ○ *Staff should carry identification at all times.* **8.** *vt.* **HOLD UP UNDER VEHICULAR TRAFFIC** to be able to withstand a particular degree or amount of vehicular traffic ○ *a motorway that can carry hundreds of thousands of vehicles a day* **9.** *vt.* **YIELD ENOUGH FORAGE** to yield enough forage or grazing crops for animals to survive ○ *fields that can carry llamas as well as cattle* **10.** *vt.* **BE RESPONSIBLE FOR** to bear the responsibility for sth ○ *The Prime Minister carries heavy duties.* **11.** *vt.* **MAKE SB SUCCEED OR ENDURE** to give sb the incentive, impetus, or encouragement to achieve or deal with sth ○ *Their exhilaration at this success may carry them further up the league table.* ○ *The audience cheered, carried along on a wave of enthusiasm.* **12.** *vt.* **PUBLISH, BROADCAST, OR DISPLAY** to feature or include an article, picture, item of news, or piece of information ○ *That evening, all the major networks carried the story.* ○ *Every packet carries a government health warning.* **13.** *vt.* **INCLUDE OR RESULT IN STH** to have sth as a quality, feature, or consequence ○ *Reckless driving carries a heavy penalty.* **14.** *vti.* **BE PREGNANT** to be pregnant with a child ○ *She carried the child to term, and it was born on Saturday.* **15.** *vt.* **DEVELOP AN IDEA** to develop an idea in discussion or action ○ *If you carry that argument to its logical conclusion, no one should get married at all.* **16.** *vt.* **MOVE OR BEHAVE** to move or behave in a particular way, especially with confidence or dignity ○ *He was a handsome man who carried himself with dignity.* ○ *She carried her head high, and looked her accusers in the eye.* **17.** *vt.* COMM **KEEP STH FOR SALE** to keep sth as stock in a shop ○ *We don't carry household goods.* **18.** *vi.* **BE HEARD AT A DISTANCE** to be audible at a distance ○ *Sound carries a long way over water.* **19.** *vt.* **SUPPORT WEAKER ELEMENT** to support or compensate for a weaker element or participant ○ *The rest of the department has to carry him.* **20.** *vti.* **VOTE FOR STH** to accept a proposal by voting for it ○ *The nomination was carried, 40–29.* **21.** *vt.* **GAIN SB'S SUPPORT** to win the support or sympathy of a person or group, especially by making a speech or appeal ○ *It looked for a moment as if he would carry the crowd.* **22.** *vt.* *US* POL **WIN VOTES OF AREA** to win support from sb ○ *Because the incumbent senator carried all the cities in her district, she won the election.* **23.** *vt.* MIL **CAPTURE A PLACE** to capture a place in battle ○ *Their charge carried the hill.* **24.** *vt.* MUSIC **STAY IN TUNE WHEN SINGING** to be able to sing and stay in tune ○ *Can you carry a tune?* **25.** *vt.* ACCT **TRANSFER ITEM IN ACCOUNT OR CALCULATION** to transfer a figure from one group or column to another in accounts or in a calculation **26.** *vi.* SPORTS **BE HIT A CERTAIN DISTANCE** to reach a certain distance after being struck ○ *Her approach shot didn't carry to the green.* **27.** *vt.* SPORTS **MOVE WITH BALL IN SPORT** to bring a ball forward a certain distance in a sport such as American football ○ *Their first rush carried the ball well into the defenders' half.* **28.** *vt.* ARMS **HAVE FIREPOWER RANGE** to have a particular range of fire ○ *an artillery shell that carried for miles* **29.** *vt.* **SUSTAIN EFFECTS OF ALCOHOL** to be able to drink alcohol without showing adverse effects (*informal*) **30.** *vt.* **PALM BALL IN BASKETBALL** to keep a hand in illegal contact with the ball in basketball ■ *n.* (*plural* **-ries**) **1. DISTANCE COVERED** the distance covered by sth struck, thrown, launched, or fired, or the reach of sth, e.g. a voice **2. ACT OF RUNNING WITH BALL** a sprint with the ball in American football ○ *a 50-yard carry that won the game* [14thC. Directly or via Anglo-Norman from Old North French *carier,* from *car* (see CAR).]

carry away *vt.* to make sb become less controlled, reasonable, or attentive by arousing his or her emotion or interest (*usually passive*) ○ *I was completely carried away by the beauty of it.*

carry back *vt.* to transfer sth such as a tax credit so that it is calculated against the previous year's income

carry forward *vt.* **1. TRANSFER ITEM IN ACCOUNT OR CALCULATION** to transfer an item to the next section or column in accounts or in a calculation **2. TRANSFER STH TO NEXT YEAR** to transfer sth, such as a tax credit or liability, so that it is calculated against the next year's income

carry off *vt.* **1. REMOVE SB OR STH** to take sth or sb away with determination or purpose, or by force ○ *carried him off, kicking and screaming, to his crib* **2. WIN** to win a prize (*informal*) ○ *She carried off the award for best newcomer.* **3. DO STH SUCCESSFULLY OR WELL** to succeed in doing sth well or producing a good effect ○ *He was nervous about chairing the meeting, but carried it off in style.* ○ *It's a very sophisticated outfit, but she can't quite carry it off.* **4. KILL SB** to kill sb (*usually passive*) ○ *Half the settlers were carried off by smallpox.*

carry on *v.* **1.** *vti.* **KEEP DOING STH** to continue to do sth ○ *Please just carry on with your work and pretend we're not here.* ○ *She carried on the business after her father retired.* **2.** *vt.* **BE INVOLVED IN STH** to engage in or be engaged in sth ○ *They were carrying on an intense conversation in a corner of the bar.* **3.** *vi.* **BEHAVE FOOLISHLY OR IMPROPERLY** to behave or talk in a way that is socially awkward or improper (*informal*) ○ *I'm ashamed of the way he's been carrying on in public.* **4.** *vi.* **HAVE AN AFFAIR** to have a casual affair with sb (*informal disapproving*)

carry out *vt.* **1. DO OR PERFORM** to perform or accomplish sth ○ *carry out research* **2. DO WHAT WAS ORDERED OR PLANNED** to do sth that has been ordered, planned, or stated as an aim ○ *We shall carry out your instructions to the letter.*

WORD KEY: SYNONYMS

See Synonyms at ***perform***.

carry over *v.* **1.** *vti.* **LEAVE STH TO BE FINISHED LATER** to leave the last part of sth to be done at a later date ○ *There were so many candidates that the ceremonies were carried over to the next morning.* **2.** *vt.* ACCT, ARITH **TRANSFER ITEM IN ACCOUNT OR CALCULATION** to transfer an item to the next group or column in accounts or in a calculation **3.** *vt.* **TRANSFER STH TO NEXT YEAR** to transfer an allowance or entitlement from one year or part of a year to the next **4.** *vi.* **CONTINUE TO EXIST** to continue to exist or produce an effect in changed circumstances ○ *The dislike he always felt for me has obviously carried over into our relationship at work.* **5.** *vt.* STOCK EXCH **POSTPONE DEAL ON STOCK EXCHANGE** to postpone a payment or settlement on the Stock Exchange until the next account day

carry through *v.* **1.** *vt.* **DO WHAT WAS PLANNED** to complete or accomplish sth planned ○ *We outlined our policy before the election, and we are determined to carry it through.* **2.** *vt.* **HELP SB SURVIVE** to give sb the support or strength needed to overcome a difficulty ○ *It was my family's support that carried me through.* ○ *Only his determination not to be humiliated carried him through the next five hours.* **3.** *vi.* **SURVIVE** to continue to exist ○ *It is an old tradition that has carried through into the information age.*

carryall /kárri awl/ *n.* **1.** *US* = **holdall 2. HORSE-DRAWN CARRIAGE** a covered horse-drawn carriage for four people [Early 18thC. Alteration of CARIOLE, by association with *carry all.*]

carryback /kárri bak/ *n.* an amount of money, e.g. a tax credit, that is transferred to the accounts for the previous year

carrycot /kárri kot/ *n.* a lightweight portable bed for a baby, often detachable from a wheeled base

carrying capacity (*plural* **carrying capacities**) *n.* **1. NUMBER OF ANIMALS LAND SUPPORTS** the number of animals a region can support **2. NUMBER OF PEOPLE AREA SUPPORTS** the number of individuals a region can support in terms of its resources

carrying charge *n.* **1. DELIVERY OR STORAGE CHARGE** a charge for storing or delivering a customer's goods **2. COST OF HOLDING ASSETS** the cost to a business of holding or storing assets from which it currently earns no income

carrying-on (*plural* **carryings-on**) *n.* behaviour regarded as immature or improper (*informal*) ○ *I won't have that kind of carrying-on in my house.*

carryon /kárri on/ *n.* **PASSENGER'S HAND LUGGAGE** a piece of luggage suitable for taking in the cabin of an aircraft ■ *adj.* **CARRIED ABOARD AN AIRCRAFT** used to describe or relating to luggage small enough to be carried and stowed aboard the cabin of an aircraft

carry-on *n.* an annoying incident involving unwise or over excited behaviour (*informal*) ○ *I've never heard such a carry-on.*

carryout /kárri owt/ *n.* **1.** *US, Scotland* **FOOD EATEN OFF THE PREMISES** an item of ready-to-eat food bought in a shop or restaurant and taken elsewhere to eat (*often used as a modifier*) ○ *a carryout pizza* **2.** *Scotland* **PLACE SELLING FOOD TO TAKE AWAY** a restaurant or shop that sells cooked food to be taken elsewhere to eat **3.** *Scotland* **ALCOHOL BOUGHT IN A SHOP** an amount of alcoholic drink bought from a shop and taken elsewhere, especially home, to drink

carryover /kárri ōvər/ *n.* **1.** ACCT, ARITH **ITEM TRANSFERRED IN ACCOUNT OR CALCULATION** an item transferred to the next group or column in accounts or in a calculation **2.** STOCK EXCH **POSTPONEMENT OF STOCK TRANSACTION** the postponement of a stock market transaction until the next day, in exchange for a fee

carse /kaarss/ *n.* *Scotland* a stretch of flat land beside a river [14thC. Origin uncertain: perhaps an alteration of the plural of CARR.]

car seat *n.* **1. CHILD'S SEAT IN CAR** a small seat for children, fitted or strapped inside a car **2. SEAT IN CAR** a driver's or passenger's seat in a car

carsick /kaar sik/ *adj.* feeling sick from the motion of a vehicle you are travelling in —**carsickness** *n.*

Carson /kaarss'n/, **Edward Henry, Baron Carson** (1854–1935) Irish-born British politician and lawyer. A UK cabinet minister (1915–18), he later led the Ulster Unionist resistance to Irish home rule.

Rachel Carson

Carson, Rachel (1907–64) US ecologist. In *Silent Spring* (1962) she argued that agricultural pesticides damage the food chain.

cart /kaart/ *n.* **1. HORSE-DRAWN VEHICLE CARRYING GOODS** an open horse-drawn vehicle, especially one with only two wheels, used for carrying goods or as a farm vehicle **2. HORSE-DRAWN CARRIAGE** a light horse-drawn carriage with two wheels **3. VEHICLE PUSHED BY HAND** a light vehicle or barrow pushed by hand **4.** *US* **WHEELED CARRIER FOR MERCHANDISE OR BAGGAGE** a container or platform on small wheels on which things are pushed along, e.g. supermarket items or airport baggage **5.** *US* **WHEELED TABLE** a small table on wheels, used for taking food and drinks to the table ■ *vt.* (**carts, carting, carted**) **1. CARRY STH ROUGHLY** to take or pull sb or sth roughly or with difficulty (*informal*) ○ *I had to cart the Christmas tree home myself.* ○ *Do you have to cart all those books around?* **2. CARRY OR TRANSPORT STH OR SB** to carry or transport sth or sb, especially in a cart ○ *carting the produce to market* [12thC. From Old Norse *kartr.*] —**cartable** *adj.* ◇ **put the cart before the horse** to do or say things in the wrong order

cartage /kaartij/ *n.* the cost of transporting or delivering goods by cart

Cartagena /kaartə jeenə/ **1.** capital of Bolívar Department in northwestern Colombia, a port on the Caribbean Sea's Bay of Cartagena. Population: 745,689 (1995). **2.** city, port, and naval base in the province and autonomous region of Murcia, southeastern Spain. Population: 180,553 (1995).

carte /kaart/ n. = **quarte**

carte blanche /kaart blaansh/ n. permission or authority given to sb to act with freedom or discretion ○ *She's been given carte blanche to make whatever changes she thinks necessary.* [From French, literally 'white card'. The underlying idea is of signing a blank sheet of paper on which anything might then be written.]

carte du jour /kaart də zhoor/ (*plural* **cartes du jour**) n. a restaurant menu showing what is available on a particular day [From French, literally 'card of the day']

cartel /kaar tél/ n. **1.** GROUP OF BUSINESSES CONTROLLING MARKET an alliance of business companies, formed to control production, competition, and prices **2.** ALLIANCE OF LIKE-MINDED POLITICAL GROUPS a political alliance among parties or groups having common aims [Mid-16thC. Via German *Kartell* and French *cartel* from Italian *cartello* 'placard', from, ultimately, Latin *c(h)arta* (see CARD¹). The underlying idea is of a written agreement.]

cartelise vt. = **cartelize**

cartelize /kaarti līz/ (**-izes, -izing, -ized**), **cartelise** (**-ises, -ising, -ised**) vti. to form a cartel of business companies or political groups ○ *The market leaders had every incentive to cartelize.*

carter /kaartər/ n. sb who uses a cart for transporting goods or for farm work

Carter /kaartər/, **Angela** (1940–92) English writer. Her novels include *The Magic Toyshop* (1967), *Nights at the Circus* (1984), and *Wise Children* (1991).

Carter, Howard (1873–1939) British archeologist and draughtsman. An Egyptologist, he was largely responsible for discovering the tomb of Tutankhamun in 1922.

The White House

Jimmy Carter

Carter, Jimmy (b. 1924) US statesman and 39th president of the United States. As president (1977–81) he negotiated the Panama Canal Treaty (1978) and the Camp David accords between Israel and Egypt (1978–79). Full name **James Earl Carter , Jr.**

Cartesian /kaar teezi ən/ adj. RELATING TO DESCARTES relating to the 17th-century French philosopher René Descartes, or his philosophical or mathematical writings or theories ■ n. BELIEVER IN DESCARTES'S WORK a supporter of Descartes's philosophical or mathematical theories and systems [Mid-17thC. From modern Latin *Cartesianus*, from *Cartesius*, the Latinized form of DESCARTES.]

Cartesian coordinate n. **1.** NUMBER SHOWING POSITION OF POINT ON PLANE one of a pair of coordinates giving the location of a point on a plane, relative to an origin and two perpendicular axes **2.** NUMBER SHOWING POSITION OF POINT IN SPACE one of three coordinates giving the location of a point in space, relative to an origin and three mutually perpendicular planes

Cartesianism /kaar teezi ənizzəm/ n. the philosophy of René Descartes, especially his belief in a distinction between the observing mind and the observed world

Cartesian plane n. a plane having all points defined by Cartesian coordinates

Cartesian product n. a set of all the pairs of elements from two sets that have their first element from the first set and the second from the second set

Carthage /kaarthij/ site of an ancient city, founded by the Phoenicians on the northern coast of Africa in 814 BC. The site is now in a suburb of Tunis, capital of Tunisia. —**Carthaginian** /kaarthə jínni ən/ n., adj.

carthorse /kaart hawrss/ n. a large strong horse bred to pull a cart or for other heavy work

Carthusian /kaar thyoozi ən/ n. MEMBER OF AUSTERE RELIGIOUS ORDER a member of a Catholic order of monks and nuns founded in Roman France early in the 11th century, who live by strict rules and in great austerity ■ adj. OF CARTHUSIANS relating to the order of Carthusians [Mid-16thC. From medieval Latin *Carthusianus*, from *Carthusia*, the Latin name of *Chartreuse* in southern France, where the order's first monastery was built.]

Cartier-Bresson /kaarti ay bréss oN/, **Henri** (b. 1908) French photographer. He was known for his black-and-white photographs of French life.

Cartier Island /kaarti ay-/ small uninhabited island off the northern coast of Western Australia

cartilage /kaartəlij, kaart'lij/ n. the tough elastic tissue that is found in the nose, throat, and ear and in other parts of the body and forms most of the skeleton in infancy, changing to bone during growth [15thC. Via French from Latin *cartilago*.]

cartilage of Santorini n. = **corniculate cartilage**

cartilaginous /kaartə lájjinəss/ adj. **1.** OF OR LIKE CARTILAGE resembling, made of, or relating to cartilage **2.** WITH MORE CARTILAGE THAN BONE having a skeleton composed mostly of cartilage

cartilaginous fish (*plural* **cartilaginous fish** *or* **cartilaginous fishes**) n. a fish with a skeleton made entirely of cartilage. Shark, rays, and ratfish are cartilaginous fish. Class: Chondrichthyes.

Cartland /kaartlənd/, **Dame Barbara** (b. 1901) English novelist. She has written more than 400 books, mostly popular romances. Born **Mary Barbara Hamilton**

cartload /kaart lōd/ n. the amount that a cart can carry

cartogram /kaartə gram/ n. a diagrammatic map showing the population and other statistics of a region [Late 19thC. From French *cartogramme*, from *carte* 'map'.]

cartographer /kaar tóggrəfər/ n. sb who makes maps

cartographic /kaartə gráffik/, **cartographical** /-k'l/ adj. **1.** OF MAPS relating to maps ○ *cartographic design* **2.** IN MAP FORM in the form of a map ○ *cartographic representation* —**cartographically** adv.

cartography /kaar tóggrəfi/ n. the science, skill, or work of making maps [Mid-19thC. From French *cartographie*, from *carte* 'map'.]

cartomancy /kaartō manssi/ n. fortune telling by using playing cards [Late 19thC. From French *cartomancie*, from *carte* 'card' (see CARD¹).]

carton /kaart'n/ n. **1.** CARDBOARD BOX a cardboard box in which sth, e.g. goods, movable property, or mail, is packaged **2.** PLASTIC OR CARD CONTAINER a container made of plastic or waxed card in which food or drink is sold **3.** CONTENTS OF CONTAINER the various contents, e.g. juice or milk, contained in a carton **4.** RIFLE SHOOTING TARGET CENTRE the white disc at the centre of a target in competitive shooting ■ vt. (**-tons, -toning, -toned**) PUT STH IN CARTON to put sth in a carton ○ *Most of our milk is sold cartoned.* [Early 19thC. Via French from Italian *cartone* (see CARTOON).]

Cartoon

cartoon /kaar toon/ n. **1.** ANIMATED FILM FROM DRAWINGS an animated film made up of drawings that are photographed and projected in sequence so that the figures in them appear to move, especially a humorous film intended primarily for children **2.** SEQUENCE OF DRAWINGS a sequence of drawings that tell a short story, published in a newspaper or magazine **3.** SATIRICAL DRAWING a humorous drawing published in a newspaper or magazine and commenting on a topical event or theme **4.** PREPARATORY DRAWING a drawing done, often in great detail, as a preliminary version of a painting or other art [Late 16thC. Via Italian *cartone*, literally 'pasteboard'(on which artists' preparatory drawings were made), from, ultimately, Latin *c(h)arta* (see CARD¹).]

cartoonish /kaar toonish/, **cartoony** /-tooni/ adj. resembling a humorous or animated cartoon —**cartoonishly** adv.

cartoonist /kaar toonist/ n. sb who draws cartoons for animated films or for newspapers or magazines

cartoony adj. = **cartoonish**

cartophily /kaar tóffəli/ n. collecting cigarette cards as a hobby [Mid-20thC. Coined from French *carte* 'card' or Italian *carta* + -PHILY.] —**cartophilist** n.

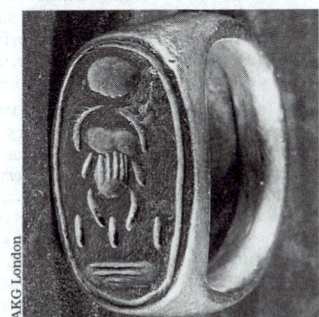
AKG London

Cartouche: Gold signet ring with cartouche of Tutankhamun (1346–37 BC)

cartouche /kaar toosh/ n. **1.** CASING FOR GUNPOWDER the paper casing of a firework or cartridge **2.** DECORATIVE PANEL a decorative panel in the form of a frame or unrolled scroll, sometimes containing writing forming an artistic or architectural feature **3.** FRAME FOR NAME an oval or oblong shape containing writing, especially one containing a king's name in Egyptian hieroglyphics [Early 17thC. Via French from Italian *cartoccio* 'paper cornet', from *carta* 'paper'.]

cartridge /kaartrij/ n. **1.** BULLET'S CASE a cylindrical case holding an explosive charge and a bullet or shot, which is put into a gun **2.** CONTAINER FOR LIQUID OR POWDER a container of liquid or powder that is loaded into a device, e.g. a removable ink container for a pen or printer ○ *toner cartridges* **3.** CASE FOR LOADING STH INTO MACHINE a plastic case containing sth that is loaded into a device, e.g. photographic film, a typewriter ribbon, a cassette, or a set of computer disks **4.** PART OF HI-FI PICKUP the part of the arm of a record-player that holds the needle [Late 16thC. Anglicization of French *cartouche* (see CARTOUCHE).]

cartridge belt n. a belt that holds gun cartridges or cartridge clips

cartridge case n. the casing of a gun cartridge

cartridge clip n. a container for bullets, loaded directly into an automatic weapon

cartridge paper n. thick drawing paper of a good quality with a grained or textured surface

cartridge pen n. a pen that holds a replaceable ink cartridge

cart track n. a rough track or narrow unsurfaced road used by farm vehicles

cartulary /kaartyoōləri/ (*plural* **-ies**) n. **1.** SET OF OFFICIAL RECORDS a collection of official records, especially those relating to a large estate or a religious community **2.** PLACE FOR RECORDS a room or building where official records are kept [Mid-16thC. From medieval Latin *c(h)artularium*, from Latin *c(h)artula* 'document', from *c(h)arta* (see CARD¹).]

cartwheel /kaart weel/ n. **1.** WOODEN WHEEL OF CART a large wooden spoked wheel for a cart **2.** ACROBATIC MOVEMENT an acrobatic movement in which the body is turned sideways onto the hands, then over onto the feet again ■ *vi.* **(cartwheels, cartwheeling, cartwheeled)** DO CARTWHEEL to perform a cartwheel

cartwright /kaárt rīt/ *n.* sb who makes carts

Cartwright /kaárt rīt/, **Edmund** (1743–1823) British inventor and clergyman. He is credited with the invention of the power loom for cotton-spinning (1785).

caruncle /kə rúngk'l/ *n.* **1.** ZOOL **FLESHY GROWTH** a fleshy growth on the head or body, e.g. a cock's comb **2.** BOT **GROWTH ON PLANT** a coloured outgrowth of tissue in some types of seed near the point of attachment to the plant [Late 16thC. Via obsolete French from Latin *caruncula* 'small piece of flesh', from *caro* (see CARRION).] —**caruncular** /kə rúngkyōōlər/ *adj.* —**carunculate** /-lət, -layt/ *adj.* —**carunculated** /-laytid/ *adj.* —**carunculous** /-ləsz/ *adj.*

Caruso /kə rōōssō/, **Enrico** (1873–1921) Italian operatic tenor. A powerful singer and actor, he appeared in the operas of Verdi and Puccini.

carvacrol /kaárvə krol/ *n.* an oily liquid with the smell of mint obtained from herbs such as savory, oregano, and thyme, used in flavourings, perfumes, and as a disinfectant [Mid-19thC. Coined from modern Latin *(Carum) carvi* 'caraway' + Latin *acer* 'sharp' + -OL.]

carve /kaarv/ **(carves, carving, carved)** *v.* **1.** *vti.* **MAKE STH BY CUTTING AND SHAPING** to make an object or design by cutting and shaping a hard material such as wood or stone ○ *statues carved from marble* ○ *I remembered carving her name on a tree, years ago.* **2.** *vt.* **CUT SUBSTANCE TO MAKE STH** to cut and shape a material such as wood or stone in order to make an object or design **3.** *vti.* **CUT MEAT** to cut cooked meat into slices **4.** *vti.* **MAKE SHAPE BY NATURAL FORCE** to make a shape by an eroding action ○ *dunes carved into strange shapes by the wind* [Old English *ceorfan*. Ultimately from a prehistoric Germanic word meaning 'to scratch'.]

carve out *vt.* to make or achieve sth through sustained hard work ○ *With unrelenting energy and ambition she had carved out a niche for herself in the world of investigative journalism.*

carve up *vt.* **1.** **DIVIDE STH UP** to divide sth, or ownership of sth, into rough or crude parts (*informal*) ○ *Their intention was to invade and carve up the kingdom among themselves.* **2.** **INJURE SB WITH KNIFE** to wound sb with a blade (*slang*)

carvel *n.* = **caravel**

carvel-built /kaáv'l-/ *adj.* used to describe a boat or ship made of planks of wood with their edges flush, not overlapping [Late 18thC. Via French *caravelle* and Portuguese *caravela* 'small ship' from, ultimately, Greek *karabos* 'light ship, crayfish'.]

carven /kaárv'n/ *adj.* carved (*archaic or literary*) ○ *thrones of carven onyx* ○ *Let the decree be carven in stone.* [14thC. Old past participle of CARVE, revived in the 19thC.]

carver /kaárvər/ *n.* **1.** **MEAT KNIFE** a knife for slicing cooked meat **2.** **SB OR STH THAT CARVES** a person or device that carves meat **3.** FURNITURE **DINING CHAIR WITH ARMS** a dining chair with arms designed to stand at the head of the table

carvery /kaárvəri/ (*plural* **-ies**) *n.* a restaurant or buffet where meat is freshly sliced to order for customers, sometimes offering unlimited servings for a fixed price

carving /kaárving/ *n.* **1.** **STH MADE BY CUTTING WOOD** an object or design formed by cutting and shaping a material, e.g. wood or stone ○ *The walls were covered with carvings depicting gods and heroes.* **2.** **ACT OF CARVING STH** the work or act of carving sth ○ *The carving of the panels was exquisite.*

carving knife *n.* a large knife for slicing meat

car wash *n.* **1.** **PLACE WHERE VEHICLES ARE WASHED** a site, often a tunnel-like building with drive-through conveyors, where motor vehicles are washed automatically by machine or can be washed manually **2.** **EQUIPMENT FOR WASHING VEHICLES** a shed or structure for washing motor vehicles automatically with revolving brushes and jets of water

Cary /káiri/, **Joyce** (1888–1957) Irish-born British novelist. His bittersweet humour characterizes such works as *The Horse's Mouth* (1944). Full name **Joyce Lunel Arthur Cary**

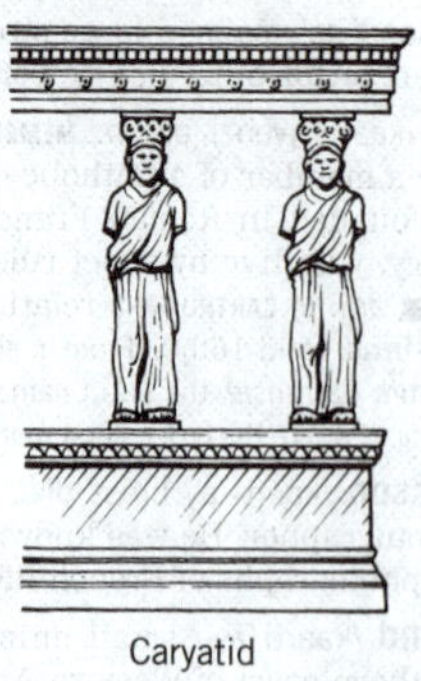

Caryatid

caryatid /kárri áttid/ (*plural* **-ids** *or* **-ides** /-áttideez/) *n.* a column in the shape of a draped female figure supporting a structure such as the frieze or porch of a classical Greek temple [Mid-16thC. Via French *caryatide* and Latin *caryatides* from Greek *karuatides*, literally 'maidens of Karuai'(now Caryae in southern Greece), the name given to the priestesses of Artemis there.] —**caryatidal** *adj.* —**caryatidean** /-átti dée ən/ *adj.* —**caryatidic** /-ə tíddik/ *adj.*

caryopsis /kárri ópsiss/ (*plural* **-ses** /-seez/ *or* **-sides** /-si deez/) *n.* a dry fruit that looks like a seed, borne by grasses and cereal crops such as wheat [Early 19thC. From modern Latin, formed from Greek *karuon* 'nut' + *opsis* 'appearance'.]

carzey *n.* = **karzy**

casaba /kə saábə/ *n.* a winter melon similar to the honeydew and cantaloupe, with whitish flesh. Latin name: *Cucumis melo* var. *inodorus.* [Late 19thC. Named for *Kasaba* (now Turgutlu), a city in western Turkey.]

Casablanca /kássə blángkə, kázzə-/ largest city and chief port in Morocco. It is situated on the Atlantic coast, about 80 km/50 mi. southwest of Rabat. Population: 2,943,000 (1993). Arabic **Dar el-Beida**

Casals /kə sáalz/, **Pablo** (1876–1973) Spanish cellist and composer. He was widely regarded as the greatest cellist of his generation.

Casanova /kássə nṓvə/ *n.* a charming seducer of women who moves quickly from one casual relationship to another, or who constantly pesters women in his pursuits [Early 20thC. Named for the Italian adventurer Giovanni Jacopo CASANOVA.]

Casanova /kássə nṓvə/, **Giovanni Jacopo, Chevalier de Seingalt** (1725–98) Italian adventurer and author. He was a soldier, diplomat, and spy whose amorous reputation rests on his 12-volume *History of My Life* (1826–38).

casbah *n.* = **kasbah**

cascade /ka skáyd/ *n.* **1.** **WATERFALL** a small waterfall or series of waterfalls **2.** **FLOWING LIQUID** a fast downward flow of liquid or small objects **3.** **HANGING MASS** a flowing mass of sth that hangs down or lies along a surface ○ *The bride carried a cascade of roses and baby's breath.* **4.** ELECTRON ENG, PHYS **SUCCESSION** a succession of things, e.g. chemical reactions or elements in an electrical circuit, each of which activates, affects, or determines the next ■ *v.* **(-cades, -cading, -caded)** **1.** *vti.* **FLOW** to flow fast and in large amounts, or to cause sth to flow this way **2.** *vi.* **HANG OR LIE** to hang or lie in a flowing mass (*literary*) ○ *Fine lace ruffles cascaded from his throat and sleeves.* **3.** *vt.* COMPUT **ARRANGE WINDOWS TO OVERLAP** to arrange the windows on a computer screen so that they overlap, with the title bar of each visible [Mid-17thC. Via French from Italian *cascata*, from, ultimately, Latin *cadere* (see CASE[1]).]

cascading menu *n.* COMPUT a menu in a computer program that opens when you select a choice from another menu

cascadura /káskə dōōrə/ (*plural* **-ras** *or* **-ra**), **cascadoo** /káskə dōō/ (*plural* **-doos** *or* **-doo**) *n. Carib* a small bony edible freshwater fish with thick scales that is considered a delicacy. According to a local legend, those who eat the cascadura will always return to Trinidad. [From Spanish *casca* 'shell' + Spanish *dura* 'hard']

cascara /ka skaárə/, **cascara buckthorn** *n.* **1.** **N AMERICAN SHRUB** a shrub or small tree of the northwestern United States. Latin name: *Rhamnus purshiana.* **2.** = **cascara sagrada** [Late 19thC. Shortening of CASCARA SAGRADA.]

cascara sagrada /-sə graádə/ *n.* the dried bark of the cascara shrub or tree, formerly used as a strong laxative but no longer prescribed medically [From Spanish, literally 'sacred bark']

cascarilla /káskə ríllə/ *n.* **1.** **AROMATIC BARK** an aromatic bark formerly used in medicine **2.** **W INDIAN SHRUB** a West Indian shrub from which cascarilla is obtained. Latin name: *Croton eluteria.* [Late 17thC. From Spanish, literally 'small cascara' (see CASCARA SAGRADA).]

case[1] /kayss/ *n.* **1.** **CIRCUMSTANCE** a situation or set of circumstances ○ *I don't think the usual rules apply in this case.* ○ *Sometimes anxiety causes weight loss, but that's not the case here.* **2.** **INSTANCE** an instance or example of sth ○ *This is nothing more than a case of mistaken identity.* **3.** **STH EXAMINED OR INVESTIGATED** a subject of investigation or scrutiny by a professional person, e.g. a doctor or police officer **4.** **ACTUAL FACT** what happens in reality or fact ○ *The case is that the witness has lied under oath.* **5.** LAW **STH EXAMINED IN LAW COURT** a matter examined or judged in a court of law ○ *It'll be some weeks before your case comes to trial.* **6.** LAW **ARGUMENTS** a set of arguments and evidence that supports a legal claim in court ○ *He presented his case calmly and with skill.* **7.** **ARGUMENT FOR OR AGAINST** an argument for or against sth ○ *You can make a good case for holding a referendum.* **8.** GRAM **GRAMMATICAL FORM OF WORD** a form of a noun, pronoun, or adjective that indicates its syntactical relation to surrounding words **9.** **KIND OF PERSON** sb of a particular kind or in a particular condition, especially an unfortunate one (*informal*) ○ *He's a hopeless case.* **10.** **ODD PERSON** an odd or eccentric person (*informal*) ■ *vt.* **(cases, casing, cased)** **INSPECT PLACE** to assess or survey a place with a view to robbing it (*slang*) [13thC. Via Old French *cas* 'event' from Latin *casus*, from *cadere* 'to fall' (source also of English *cadence* and *cascade*).] ◇ **a case in point** a relevant example ○ *A case in point for our discussion is the steady drop in unit sales.* ◇ **be on sb's case 1.** to use influence in order to help sb (*slang*) **2.** to persist in pestering sb to do sth (*slang*) ◇ **get off sb's case 1.** to stop using influence to help sb (*slang*) **2.** to stop pestering sb to do sth (*slang*) ○ *Please get off my case! I'll finish mowing the lawn later.* ◇ **in any case 1.** taking into account everything said or done before **2.** regardless of that ◇ **in case of sth** if sth happens ○ *In case of fire, leave by the nearest exit.* ◇ **(just) in case 1.** in preparation for an event that may possibly happen ○ *Take your umbrella, just in case.* **2.** used to introduce a piece of information and to explain your reason for giving it ○ *In case you're unaware of the fact, this is a nonsmoking area.*

case[2] /kayss/ *n.* **1.** **HOLDER OR OUTER COVERING** sth that serves as a container or covering **2.** **CONTAINER** a container with its contents ○ *bought a case of fizzy drinks* **3.** **PIECE OF LUGGAGE** an item of luggage, especially a suitcase **4.** PRINTING **KIND OF PRINTED CHARACTER** the function of a printed character as a capital or small letter **5.** PRINTING **TRAY HOLDING PRINTING TYPE** in hot-metal printing, a tray with compartments into which individual printing blocks are slotted **6.** **PAIR** a pair, especially of pistols **7.** = **casing** *n.* 3 ■ *vt.* **(cases, casing, cased)** **PUT COVERING ROUND STH** to enclose sth in a covering [13thC. Via Old French dialect *casse* from Latin *capsa* 'box', from *capere* 'to hold' (source of English *capacious, capable,* and *occupy*).]

CASE /kayss/ *abbr.* **1.** computer-aided software engineering **2.** computer-aided systems engineering

casease /káyssi ayss, -ayz/ *n.* an enzyme formed by certain bacteria that aids the breakdown of casein and is used in cheese ripening [20thC. From CASEIN + -ASE.]

caseate /káyssi ayt/ **(-ates, -ating, -ated)** *vi.* to undergo caseation [Late 19thC. Back-formation from CASEATION.]

caseation /káyssi áysh'n/ *n.* the process by which dead tissue decays into a firm and dry mass, characteristic of tuberculosis [Mid-19thC. From medieval Latin *caseatio*, from Latin *caseus* 'cheese'.]

casebearer /káyss bairər/ n. an insect whose larvae form a protective case around themselves

casebook /káyss book/ n. **1.** RECORD OF CASES DEALT WITH a record of legal or medical cases and their conduct **2.** SCHOLARLY COLLECTION a collection of academic writings on a subject

casebound /káyss bownd/ adj. = hardback. ◊ paperback, softback, clothbound

cased glass, **case glass** n. decorative glass consisting of several coloured layers with some areas cut away in different patterns

casefy /káyssi fī/ (-fies, -fying, -fied) vti. to develop, or cause sth to develop, a soft consistency like that of cheese [20thC. Formed from Latin caseus 'cheese'.]

case glass n. = cased glass

case grammar n. a system of grammar that analyses sentences in terms of the semantic relation of the noun or noun phrase and other elements to the main verb

case-harden (case-hardens, case-hardening, case-hardened) vt. **1.** HARDEN IRON to harden the surface of an iron alloy by heating and then cooling in water **2.** HARDEN SB'S ATTITUDE to make sb unsympathetic or unfeeling as a result of extended dealing with difficult and distressing problems

case history n. a record of sb's medical or social history kept by a doctor or social worker

casein /káyssi in, -een/ n. a protein formed in milk by the action of rennin or another agent, which is the main constituent of cheese. It is also used in plastics, adhesives, and paints. [Mid-19thC. Formed from Latin caseus 'cheese'.]

caseinate /káyssi i nayt, -ee nayt/ n. a casein salt formed by compounding casein with a metal such as calcium or sodium

caseinogen /kay seénəjin, káyssi ínn-/ n. the main protein in milk, from which casein is formed

case knife n. a sheath knife (archaic)

case law n. law established on the basis of previous verdicts according to the doctrine of binding precedent, rather than law established by legislation

caseload /káyss lōd/ n. the number of cases to be dealt with, e.g. by a doctor or a lawyer, at a particular time

casemate /káyss mayt/ n. a fortified compartment on an old sailing ship or a rampart, where a cannon was mounted [Mid-16thC. Directly or via French from Italian casamatta, of unknown origin.]

Casement

casement /káyssmənt/ n. a window that opens on hinges, as distinct from one that slides up and down [15thC. Via Anglo-Latin cassimentum, from, ultimately, Latin capsa (see CASE²). Originally in the meaning 'hollow moulding'.]

Casement /káyssmənt/, **Sir Roger** (1864–1916) Irish-born British consular official and rebel. Knighted for humanitarian work in Africa and South America, he became a militant Irish nationalist and was hanged for treason.

caseose /káyss ōss, -ōz/ n. a chemical produced in the digestion of cheese [20thC. Formed from Latin caseus 'cheese'.]

caseous /káyssi əss/ adj. used to describe firm, dry diseased tissue that has undergone caseation [Mid-17thC. Formed from Latin caseus 'cheese'.]

casern /kə zúrn/, **caserne** n. a barracks, especially a temporary one [Late 17thC. Via French caserne from, ultimately, Latin quarterna 'hut for four'.]

case shot n. an old kind of cannon shell containing shrapnel

case stated n. an outline of the circumstances of a legal case prepared by one court for another court to use in making its decision, e.g. in an appeal hearing or a retrial

case study n. an analysis of a particular case or situation used as a basis for drawing conclusions in similar situations

case system n. the teaching of law through the study of important and representative cases rather than by studying theory

casework /káyss wurk/ n. a system of making a social worker responsible for particular clients on a long-term basis

caseworker /káyss wurkər/ n. a professional social worker who is assigned a number of clients on a long-term basis

cash¹ /kash/ n. **1.** COINS AND BANKNOTES money in the form of coins and notes as distinct from money orders or credit **2.** CURRENCY OR CHEQUES money used as immediate payment in any form, e.g. currency or cheques (informal) ■ vt. (cashes, cashing, cashed) EXCHANGE STH FOR READY MONEY to exchange a cheque or money order for coins or banknotes ○ You can cash your pay cheque at the bank. [Late 16thC. Directly or via obsolete French casse from Italian cassa 'money-box, money', from Latin capsa (see CASE².)] —cashable adj.

cash in v. **1.** vt. TAKE WHAT IS OWED to withdraw from a business investment such as an insurance policy and take the money that is due **2.** vi. MAKE A LOT OF MONEY to make large amounts of money (slang) ○ When the stock was sold, she really cashed in.

cash in on vt. to exploit a situation in order to get personal benefit, especially money ○ It seemed that everyone who knew him wanted to cash in on his rise to fame.

cash out v. **1.** vti. SELL ASSET TO PROFIT to sell off an asset that has been held for a long time, e.g. land, in order to profit ○ He finally decided to cash out and sell the land that had been in his family for three generations. **2.** vi. US COMMIT SUICIDE to commit suicide (slang)

cash up vi. COMM to add up the day's takings of a shop or similar business ○ shopkeepers cashing up at the end of the day

cash² /kash/ (plural cash) n. any of several former small Asian coins of low value [Late 16thC. Via Portuguese caixa from Tamil kācu.]

Cash /kash/, **Martin** (1810–77) Irish-born Australian bushranger. The leader of a gang of outlaws based in Tasmania, he eventually reformed and was pardoned.

Cash, Pat (b. 1965) Australian tennis player. He won the Wimbledon men's singles championship in 1987. Full name **Patrick Hart Cash**

cash and carry n. (plural cash and carries) **1.** INEXPENSIVE WHOLESALE STORE a wholesale store selling inexpensive goods that are paid for in cash and taken away by the buyer **2.** POLICY OF SELLING WITHOUT DELIVERY SERVICE a policy of selling items for cash with no delivery service to customers ■ adj. CASH-ONLY AND WITHOUT DELIVERY sold, or operating, on a basis of cash-only payments by buyers who take their goods away at the time of purchase

cash bar n. a bar at a large party or reception at which drinks have to be paid for individually

cashbook /kásh book/ n. a book for keeping a record of cash spent and received

cash box n. a lockable box for cash, especially one holding the daily takings of a small business

cash card n. a coded plastic card that a bank customer uses to access an account by means of a cashpoint

cash cow n. a profitable business or product with low overheads often used to fund other businesses or investments (slang) ○ The grocery chain has been their cash cow for years.

cash crop n. a crop grown for direct sale rather than personal consumption

cash desk n. a counter for payment of goods in a shop

cash discount n. a reduction in price offered to a buyer who can pay in cash or pay immediately

cash dispenser n. = cashpoint

cashed up adj. Aus having plenty of money (informal) ○ I just got paid, so I'm cashed up for the weekend.

cashew /káshoo, ka shoo/ n. **1.** TREES TROPICAL TREE BEARING EDIBLE NUTS a tropical American evergreen tree grown for its edible nuts. Latin name: Anacardium occidentale. **2.** FOOD = cashew nut [Late 16thC. Via Portuguese from Tupi acajú.]

cashew apple n. the edible swollen stalk by which a cashew nut is attached to its stem, used to make preserves

cashew nut n. a kidney-shaped nut that grows on the tropical American cashew tree and is edible when roasted

cash flow n. **1.** MOVEMENT OF MONEY RECEIVED AND SPENT the pattern of income and expenses, and its consequences for how much money is available at a given time **2.** COMPANY'S MONEY RECEIVED AND SPENT the prediction or assessment of a company's income and expenditure over a period of time

cashier¹ /ka sheer/ n. **1.** BANK WORKER TAKING AND PAYING MONEY sb in a bank who deals directly with customers and handles routine account transactions **2.** SB RESPONSIBLE FOR FINANCIAL TRANSACTIONS an official in an organization who is responsible for receiving and paying out money and keeping financial records ■ vi. (cashiers, cashiering, cashiered) WORK AS CASHIER to work as a cashier, especially in a place of business such as a restaurant or bar ○ Who's cashiering tonight? US term checker [Late 16thC. Directly or via Dutch cassier from French caissier, from casse (see CASH¹).]

cashier² /ka sheer/ (-iers, -iering, -iered, cashiered) vt. to dismiss sb from the armed forces because of misconduct [Early 16thC. Via Middle Dutch kasseren 'to disband (soldiers)' and French casser 'to break, dismiss' from Latin quassare (see QUASH).]

cashier's cheque n. a guaranteed cheque issued by a bank against money taken from a customer's account or against cash provided for this purpose

cashless /káshləss/ adj. using an electronic means of exchanging money instead of dealing in cash

cash machine n. UK = cashpoint

cashmere /kásh meer/ n. **1.** GOAT'S SOFT WOOL the soft wool from a Himalayan goat **2.** FABRIC MADE FROM GOAT'S WOOL a woollen fabric made from cashmere **3.** IMITATION OF GOAT'S WOOL FABRIC a soft woollen fabric resembling the fabric made from cashmere [Late 17thC. An early spelling of KASHMIR.]

cashmere goat n. a Himalayan goat reared for the soft wool that grows under its coarse outer coat

cash on delivery adv. with full payment for ordered goods to be made by the buyer to the one delivering the goods ○ bought the coat cash on delivery

cashpoint /kásh poynt/ n. UK a machine that provides cash and account information on insertion of a machine-readable card

cash-poor adj. financially sound but having little readily available cash

cash ratio n. the ratio that a bank must maintain between available cash and total deposits

cash register n. a machine in a shop that records sales, calculates totals, and has a drawer for takings

cash-starved adj. having very little money or financial support

cash-strapped adj. having insufficient money (informal)

casimere n. = cassimere

Casimir III /kázzi meer/, **the Great, King of Poland** (1310–70). His reign (1333–70) as the 'Peasants' King' saw the introduction of fairer laws and peace through diplomacy. He founded Cracow University (1354).

casing /káyssing/ n. **1.** OUTER COVERING an outer covering, e.g. the sheath of an electrical cable or the skin of a sausage **2.** FRAME FOR DOOR OR WINDOW a frame containing a door, window, or stairway **3.** LINER PIPE IN WELL a liner pipe or tube in water, oil, or gas wells

casino /kə séenō/ (*plural* **-nos**) *n.* **1.** GAMBLING ESTABLISHMENT a private club, or a room in a club, hotel, or other establishment, where gambling takes place **2. casino, cassino** CARDS POINT-SCORING CARD GAME a point-scoring card game in which players combine cards exposed on the table with cards in their hands, with the 10 of diamonds being the highest-valued card [Mid-18thC. From Italian, literally 'small house', from, ultimately, Latin *casa* 'house'.]

Casino /kə séenō/ town in northern New South Wales, Australia, a centre of beef and dairy production. Population: 9,990 (1996).

cask /kaask/ *n.* **1.** BARREL CONTAINING ALCOHOL a wooden barrel containing alcoholic drink **2.** CONTAINER LIKE A BARREL any barrel-like container, whether or not of wood **3.** CONTENTS OF BARREL the contents of a barrel or similar container **4.** = **flask** *n.* 6 [Early 16thC. Via French *casque* or Spanish *casco* 'helmet, skull' from, ultimately, Latin *quassare* (see QUASH).]

casket /kaáskit/ *n.* **1.** FANCY BOX a decorative box for valuables **2.** *US* alternative for coffin [15thC. Origin uncertain: perhaps an alteration of French *cassette* (see CASSETTE).]

Caspian Sea /káspi ən-/ large landlocked salt lake lying between south-eastern Europe and Asia. It is the world's largest inland body of water. Area: 370,000 sq. km/143,000 sq. mi.

casque /kask/ *n.* **1.** KNIGHT'S HELMET a helmet from a suit of armour (*archaic*) **2.** ZOOL GROWTH ON ANIMAL'S HEAD a horny growth on the head of a bird, fish or reptile, resembling a helmet [Late 17thC. Via French from Spanish *casco* (see CASK).] —**casqued** *adj.*

Cassandra /kə sándrə/ *n.* sb whose warnings of impending disaster are ignored [Early 17thC. Named for *Cassandra*, the daughter of Priam, king of Troy, who was granted the gift of prophecy by Apollo but was condemned never to be believed.]

cassata /kə saátə/ *n.* **1.** ICE CREAM WITH CANDIED FRUIT brightly coloured Italian ice cream containing nuts and candied fruit and layers or streaks of different flavours **2.** SICILIAN CAKE WITH SOFT CHEESE a Sicilian sponge cake, layered and coated with sweet ricotta, flavoured with candied fruit and chopped chocolate, decorated with candied fruit, and eaten as a celebration cake or dessert [Early 20thC. From Italian.]

cassation /ka sáysh'n/ *n.* **1.** COURT OF APPEAL a court of appeal in countries that follow the Napoleonic code of civil law **2.** MUSIC SERENADE FOR INSTRUMENTS an 18th-century instrumental work similar in form to a divertimento [15thC. Formed from Latin *cassare* 'to annul'.]

cassava /kə saávə/ *n.* **1.** TROPICAL PLANT WITH EDIBLE ROOT a tropical plant with roots that are edible after processing. Latin name: *Manihot esculenta.* **2.** EDIBLE ROOT OF PLANT the root of the cassava plant, a large thick-skinned tuber like the potato when boiled, that is eaten in many tropical countries and is the source of tapioca. It is poisonous when raw and untreated. [Mid-16thC. From Taino *casávi*.]

Cassegrainian telescope /kássi gráyni ən-/ *n.* an astronomical telescope that uses a large concave mirror and a small convex mirror to form an image [Late 19thC. Named after its inventor, the French astronomer Giovanni *Cassegrain* (1625–1712).]

casserole /kássərōl/ *n.* **1.** COOKING POT a deep, heavy cooking pot suitable for use in an oven **2.** COOKED DISH a stew or other moist food dish, cooked slowly at a low heat in a covered pot or dish **3.** SCI LABORATORY CONTAINER a porcelain container used for heating substances in a laboratory ■ *vt.* (**-roles, -roling, -roled**) COOK FOOD IN LIQUID to cook food slowly at a low heat with liquid in a covered pot [Early 18thC. From French, literally 'small pan', from *casse* 'pan', from, ultimately, Greek *kuathos* 'cup'.]

cassette /kə sét/ *n.* **1.** CASE CONTAINING MAGNETIC TAPE a sealed plastic case containing a length of audio or video tape wound round spools ready for use **2.** SEALED PLASTIC CASE a sealed plastic case containing material for use in a machine, e.g. photographic film or ribbon for a printer [Late 18thC. From French, literally 'small box', from *casse* (see CASH[1]).]

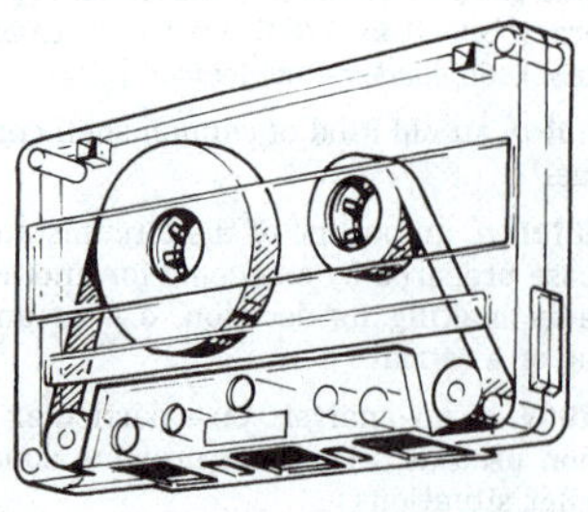

Cassette

cassette deck *n.* a tape deck that plays or records audio cassettes

cassette player *n.* a machine that plays cassettes, but does not record audio

cassette recorder *n.* a machine, especially a portable one, that plays and records audio cassettes

cassia /kássi ə/ *n.* an evergreen Asian tree with an aromatic bark. Latin name: *Cinnamomum aromaticum.* [Pre-12thC. Via Latin from, ultimately, Hebrew *qěṣī'āh*.]

cassimere /kássi meer/, **casimere** *n.* a plain or twill woollen fabric used for making suits [Mid-18thC. Alteration of CASHMERE.]

Cassini division /ka séeni-/, **Cassini's division** *n.* the dark area between the two brightest rings, the middle and outermost, of Saturn [Early 20thC. Named after its discoverer Giovanni Domenico *Cassini* (1625–1712), Italian-born French astronomer.]

cassino *n.* = **casino** *n.* 2

Cassiopeia /kássi ō pée ə/ *n.* a constellation shaped like the letter 'W' in the sky of the northern hemisphere near the Pole Star

cassis /ka séess/ *n.* a syrupy, usually alcoholic, cordial made in France from blackcurrants, often mixed with white wine to make kir [Late 19thC. Via French, 'blackcurrant', from, probably, Latin *cassia* CASSIA.]

cassiterite /kə síttə rīt/ *n.* a dark-coloured mineral found in igneous rocks that is an important ore of tin. Formula: SnO_2. [Mid-19thC. Coined from Greek *kassiteros* 'tin' + -ITE.]

Cassius /kássi əss/ (*fl.* 53–42 BC) Roman general and conspirator. A leader in the assassination of Julius Caesar (44 BC), he committed suicide when defeated by Mark Antony. Full name **Gaius Cassius Longinus**

cassock /kássək/ *n.* a full-length, usually black, robe worn by priests, their assistants, and singers in church choirs [Mid-16thC. Via French *casaque* 'long coat' from Italian *casacca* 'riding coat', perhaps from, ultimately, Turkic *kazak* 'vagabond, adventurer' (source of English *Cossack*).] —**cassocked** *adj.*

Casson /káss'n/, **Sir Hugh** (*b.* 1910) British architect. He was president of the Royal Academy of Arts (1976–84) and author of *Homes by the Million* (1947).

cassoulet /kássoo láy, kássoo lay/ *n.* a French stew consisting of haricot beans cooked in a casserole with pork, ham, sausage, or other meats and topped with a browned crust of breadcrumbs [Mid-20thC. From French, literally 'small stew-pan, tureen', from, ultimately, Greek *kuathos* 'cup, ladle' (source of English *casserole*).]

cassowary /kássə wairi/ (*plural* **-ies**) *n.* a large black flightless bird of northeastern Australia and New Guinea that resembles an ostrich or emu. It has colourful wattles and a large bony head shield. Genus: *Casuarius.* [Early 17thC. From Malay *kesuari*.]

cast /kaast/ *v.* (**casts, casting, cast**) **1.** *vt.* THROW STH OR SB to throw sth or sb, especially sth that or sb who is light in weight **2.** *vt.* THROW STH ASHORE to throw sth up on the seashore ○ *pieces of driftwood that had been cast up by the incoming tide* **3.** *vt.* FLING STH DOWN OR AWAY to throw sth away from yourself, usually with force **4.** *vt.* ANGLING THROW BAIT, HOOK, OR LINE to throw a line, baited hook, or fishing net into the water **5.** *vt.* CAUSE STH TO APPEAR SOMEWHERE to make sth, e.g. light or shadow, appear in a place ○ *The bulb cast an eerie green glow over everything.* **6.** *vt.* HAVE DISPIRITING EFFECT to introduce sth that reduces the enthusiasm, joy, or happiness of sb or sth ○ *Her mother's absence cast a shadow over the wedding plans.* **7.** *vt.* CREATE MISTRUST to generate a sense of uncertainty, distrust, or suspicion about sth ○ *an accident that has cast doubt over the whole future of the project* **8.** *vt.* DIRECT A LOOK to direct the eyes or a look towards sb or sth, often in a surreptitious, disapproving, or anxious manner ○ *casting a discreet glance at his watch* **9.** *vt.* DISMISS STH FROM THE MIND to remove or banish sth from your mind deliberately, decisively, and often with difficulty (*formal*) **10.** *vt.* PUT SB SOMEWHERE ROUGHLY to put or throw sb or sth somewhere, especially in a rough or brutal way (*formal*) ○ *cast into the dungeon* **11.** *vti.* ARTS SELECT PARTICIPANTS FOR PERFORMANCE to choose sb for a particular role in a drama, dance, or other performance, or choose people for all the roles in a production ○ *He was badly cast as Othello.* **12.** *vt.* DESCRIBE SB to classify or describe sb in a particular way ○ *I seem to have been cast as the villain in this affair.* **13.** *vt.* MANUF FORM STH USING MOULD to pour sth such as molten metal or plaster into a mould and allow it to solidify, or make an object in this way **14.** *vt.* SHED STH to shed sth, e.g. a skin ○ *a snake that had cast its skin* **15.** *vt.* DROP STH to drop or lose sth **16.** *vt.* ACCT CALCULATE STH to add sth up or calculate sth **17.** *vt. Scotland* REPROACH SB to reproach sb with sth (*informal*) ■ *n.* **1.** ACT OF THROWING the flinging, hurling, or throwing of sth, or an instance of that **2.** LENGTH OF THROW the distance that sth is thrown ○ *a 20-metre cast of a harpoon* **3.** ARTS PERFORMERS the actors or other performers who play the parts in a drama, dance, or other production (*takes a singular or plural verb*) **4.** MANUF MOULDED OBJECT an object that is made by pouring a molten substance, especially metal, into a mould and leaving it to solidify so that it takes on the shape of the mould **5.** MANUF MOULD a container of a particular shape into which a molten substance, especially metal, is poured and left to solidify **6.** MED SUPPORT FOR BROKEN BONE a stiff casing made from plaster of Paris or fibreglass that is used to hold a broken bone in place while it is mending ○ *He came back with his leg in a cast.* ◊ **plaster cast** **7.** MANUF, ARTS MOLTEN IMPRESSION an impression formed by pressing soft or molten material over or inside sth and letting it harden or dry ○ *a cast of the pianist's hands* **8.** GEOL, PALAEONT PRESERVED SEDIMENT preserved sediment made by the infilling of an impression such as a footprint **9.** EMOTIONAL OR PSYCHOLOGICAL TYPE the nature or quality of sb's character or mind **10.** PHYSICAL TYPE the nature or quality of sb's appearance ○ *I did not trust the sly cast of his face.* **11.** SQUINT a defect that causes one eye to look permanently sideways **12.** OVERSPREADING OF ONE THING ONTO ANOTHER the overspreading of sth, especially an added colour, that results in modification of the hue or general appearance of sth else **13.** TINGE a general suggestion of sth, e.g. a colour ○ *The mud gave a brown cast to the water.* **14.** ANGLING THROW OF LINE OR NET the throwing of a fishing line or net into the water **15.** ANGLING THROWN LINE OR NET a fishing line or net that is thrown into the water **16.** GAMBLING, GAME DICE THROW a throw of a dice, or the number that has been thrown **17.** BIOL STH SHED BY ORGANISM a part of an organism, e.g. an insect casing, a snake skin, or worm faeces, that has been shed in a natural recurring process [12thC. From Old Norse *kasta* 'to throw', of unknown origin. The theatrical senses are 17th-century developments, apparently based on the earlier meanings 'a plan, design' and 'to arrange, shape'.] —**castability** /kaàstə bíllәti/ *n.* —**castable** /kaástəb'l/ *adj.*

WORD KEY: SYNONYMS

See Synonyms at *throw.*

cast around, cast about *vi.* to search for sth or try to devise a solution to a problem

cast aside *vt.* **1.** ABANDON SB OR STH to reject and abandon sb or sth regarded as no longer interesting or useful ○ *You can't just cast him aside like that!* **2.** REJECT THOUGHT to abandon sth, e.g. a feeling or belief (*formal*) ○ *You must cast your doubts aside and trust in me.*

cast off *v.* **1.** *vt.* GET RID OF SB OR STH to reject or abandon sth or sb regarded as no longer useful or attractive ○ *cast off that old coat years ago.* **2.** *vti.* NAUT UNTIE MOORING LINES to untie the ropes securing a boat to its mooring so that it can move away **3.** *vti.* **FINISH KNITTING** to make the last row of stitches in a piece of knitting by looping each stitch over the next and removing it from the needle **4.** *vti.* PUBL **FIT TEXT** to calculate the amount of space a piece of text will take up when it has been typeset

cast on *vti.* to make the first row of stitches in a piece of knitting

cast out *v.* **1.** *vt.* **EJECT SB** to reject, abandon, or eject sb or sth (*formal*) **2.** *vi.* Scotland **HAVE DISAGREEMENT** to quarrel with sb (*informal*)

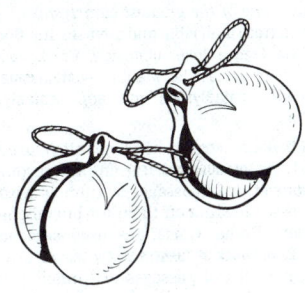

Castanets

castanet /kástə nét/ *n.* either of a pair of small curved pieces of hard wood or plastic that are joined at the top and used to make a rhythmic clicking sound. They are held in the palm of the hand and tapped together, traditionally by Spanish flamenco dancers and musicians. [Early 17thC. From Spanish *castañeta*, literally 'small chestnut', from *castaña* 'chestnut' from Latin *castanea* (source of English *chestnut*); from their likeness to chestnut shells.]

castaway /kástə way/ *n.* **SHIPWRECKED PERSON** sb who has been shipwrecked ■ *adj.* **SHIPWRECKED** shipwrecked or set adrift

caste /kaast/ *n.* **1.** SOC SCI **HINDU SOCIAL CLASS** any of the four main hereditary classes (**varnas**) into which Hindu society is divided and that dictate the social position and status of people according to their professions **2.** SOC SCI **HINDU CLASS SYSTEM** the Hindu system of organizing society into hereditary classes **3.** SOC SCI **CLASS SYSTEM** any system that divides people into classes according to their rank, wealth, or profession, or that of the family into which they were born **4.** **SOCIAL CLASS** the class and rank or position of sb in a society, based on birth, occupation, or some other criterion **5.** INSECTS **INSECT RANK** a rank within a colony or hive of social insects such as ants or bees. Members of a caste have a specialized role, e.g. as a soldier or worker. [Mid-16thC. Via Spanish and Portuguese *casta* 'unmixed, pure race' from Latin *castus* 'pure, chaste' (source of English *chaste* and *incest*), the underlying idea being 'racial purity'.] —**casteism** *n.*

Castel Gandolfo /káss tel gan dólfō/ village in Rome province, Lazio Region, just south of Rome, Italy. It contains a palace that is the summer residence of the pope. Population: 6,952 (1993).

Castella /ka stéllə/, **Robert de** (b. 1957) Australian marathon runner. He won gold medals at the Commonwealth Games in 1982 and 1986.

castellan /kástilən/ *n.* in former times, sb who governed or managed a castle [14thC. Via Old Northern French *castelain* from medieval Latin *castellanus*, from Latin *castellum* (see CASTLE).]

castellated /kástə laytid/ *adj.* **1.** ARCHIT **WITH BATTLEMENTS OR SERRATED TOP EDGE** with battlements or a serrated top edge like the walls of a castle **2.** **INDENTED OR SERRATED LIKE BATTLEMENTS** with indented or serrated edges resembling the top of a castle wall ○ *an ornate tablecloth with a castellated edge* **3.** **WITH CASTLE OR CASTLES** with a castle or castles as part of the surroundings or landscape (*literary*) ○ *the castellated French countryside* [Late 17thC. Formed from medieval Latin *castellatus* 'having a castle', from Latin *castellum* (see CASTLE).]

caste mark *n.* a mark, usually a painted dot on the forehead, that shows a Hindu person's caste

caster /kaástər/ *n.* **1.** **SB WHO CASTS** sb or sth that casts sth else **2.** = **castor**

caster sugar *n.* finely ground white sugar that is often used in baking. It is finer than granulated sugar but not as fine as icing sugar.

castigate /kásti gayt/ (**-gates, -gating, -gated**) *vt.* to criticize, rebuke, or punish sb severely (*formal; often passive*) ○ *They were strongly castigated for their refusal to act.* [Early 17thC. From Latin *castigat-*, the past participle stem of *castigare* 'to correct, chastise', from *castus* 'chaste, pure' (source of English *chaste* and *incest*).] —**castigation** /kásti gáysh'n/ *n.* —**castigator** /kásti gaytər/ *n.* —**castigatory** /kásti gáytəri/ *adj.*

WORD KEY: SYNONYMS
See Synonyms at *criticize.*

Castile /ka steél/ central region of Spain that formed the core of the Kingdom of Castile, under which Spain was united in the 15th and 16th centuries

Castile soap /ka steél-/ *n.* a type of hard white unperfumed soap made from olive oil and soda [Named after CASTILE, where it was first made]

Castilian /ka stílli ən/, **Castillian** *n.* **1.** LANG **SPANISH DIALECT** the dialect of the Spanish language that is spoken in the province of Castile **2.** LANG **SPANISH LANGUAGE** official, standard, and literary Spanish, based on the dialect spoken in the province of Castile **3.** PEOPLES **SB FROM CASTILE** sb who lives or was born or brought up in the province of Castile in Spain —**Castilian** *adj.*

casting /kaásting/ *n.* **1.** MANUF, ARTS **MAKING OF OBJECTS USING MOULDS** the making of a solid object by pouring molten metal, glass, or plastic into a mould and allowing it to cool **2.** MANUF, ARTS **OBJECT MADE WITH MOULD** an object made using a mould **3.** ANGLING **THROW OF FISHING LINE** the throwing out of a fishing line or net **4.** **STH THROWN** sth that is thrown out or thrown off **5.** ARTS **SELECTION PROCESS FOR PERFORMERS** the choosing of actors or other performers for a drama, dance, or other production, usually by audition, interview, or screen test **6.** ARTS **CHOICE OF PERFORMERS** the choice of actors or other performers for roles in a drama, dance, or other production ○ *The script was very sharp but the casting was terrible.*

casting couch *n.* the granting of usually sexual favours in return for work in a film, television, or other production (*informal humorous*) [From the idea of the sexual activity taking place on a couch in the office of sb with power over casting]

casting vote *n.* the deciding vote in a ballot or debate, cast by the chairperson or presiding officer when votes for and against sth are equally divided

cast iron *n.* iron with a high carbon content, making it hard but brittle, so that it must be shaped by casting rather than hammering or beating

cast-iron *adj.* **1.** METALL **OF CAST IRON** made from cast iron **2.** **VERY STRONG** extremely strong or resistant **3.** **ALLOWING NO CHANGE** not permitting any alteration of its terms ○ *a cast-iron agreement*

castle /kaás'l/ *n.* **1.** ARCHIT **FORTRESS** a large fortified building or complex of buildings, usually with tall solid walls, battlements, and a permanent garrison, built especially during the Middle Ages **2.** ARCHIT **MANOR HOUSE** a large magnificent house built, especially in the 18th and 19th centuries, to resemble the fortified castles of the past **3.** **PRIVATE REFUGE** the building, property, or place to which sb, especially the owner, turns for privacy or refuge **4.** CHESS = **rook** ■ *vti.* (**-tles, -tling, -tled**) CHESS **MOVE KING AND ROOK** in chess, to move the king two squares to the left or right and move the nearest rook over the king to the adjacent square on the opposite side [Pre-12thC. From Latin *castellum* 'fortified village' (source of English *castellated* and *chateau*), from *castrum* 'fortified place'. Later reborrowed from Anglo-Norman *castel* 'fortress' (also from Latin *castellum*).] ◇ **build castles in the air** or **in Spain** to have dreams or plans that are extremely unlikely to succeed or be realized

Castlebar /kaáss'l baar/ town in County Mayo, western Ireland. Population: 6,349 (1986). Irish **Caislen an Bharraigh**

castled /kaáss'ld/ *adj.* ARCHIT = **castellated** *adj.* 1

Castlereagh /kaáss'l ray/ **1.** river in northern New South Wales, Australia, that rises in the Warrumbungle Range and joins the Macquarie River

west of Walgett. Length: 550 km/342 mi. **2.** district in eastern Northern Ireland. Capital: Belfast. Population: 60,649 (1991). Area: 85 sq. km/33 sq. mi.

Castlereagh, Viscount, Robert Stewart, 2nd Marquis of Londonderry (1769–1822) Irish-born British statesman. As Foreign Secretary(1812–22), he secured long-lasting European peace at the Congress of Vienna (1814–15).

cast net *n.* a net used by anglers to catch fish for bait. In some cultures it is also used as a low energy way to catch fish for food.

castoff /kaást of/ *n.* **1.** **REJECTED THING OR PERSON** sth that or sb who has been rejected or abandoned because no longer considered useful or attractive (*often used in the plural*) ○ *I don't want your old cast-offs!* **2.** PUBL **CALCULATION OF TEXT LENGTH** a calculation of the length of a piece of text made before fitting copy into available space

castor[1] /kaástər/ *n.* **1.** **SMALL WHEEL UNDER FURNITURE** a small wheel on a mount that allows it to turn in all directions, attached under the corners of heavy furniture and other objects to make them easier to move **2.** **SMALL CONDIMENT CONTAINER** a small container with a perforated top or open mouth for sprinkling sugar, salt, or other condiments **3.** **CONDIMENT STAND** a small stand that holds condiment containers [Late 17thC. Alteration of CASTER, probably arising from confusion with CASTOR[2].]

castor[2] /kaástər/ *n.* **1.** INDUST **BEAVER OIL** a brown oily aromatic substance secreted from glands in a beaver's groin and used in medicine and perfumes **2.** INDUST **BEAVER FUR** the fur of a beaver **3.** CLOTHES **BEAVER HAT** a hat made of beaver fur or imitation beaver fur [14thC. Via French or Latin from Greek *kastōr* 'beaver'.]

Castor /kaástər/ *n.* **1.** ASTRON **BRIGHT STAR IN CONSTELLATION GEMINI** the second brightest star in the constellation Gemini **2.** MYTHOL ♦ **Castor and Pollux**

Castor and Pollux /-ənd pólləks/ *npl.* in classical mythology, the twin sons of Leda and the brothers of Helen of Troy and Clytemnestra

castor bean *n.* the poisonous seed of the castor-oil plant, from which castor oil is produced

castor oil *n.* a thin yellowish oil obtained from the seeds of the castor-oil plant, used medicinally as a laxative and industrially as a lubricant [*Castor* of uncertain origin: perhaps the same word as CASTOR[2], possibly because the oil has medical properties and a bitter taste similar to that of the beaver's secretion]

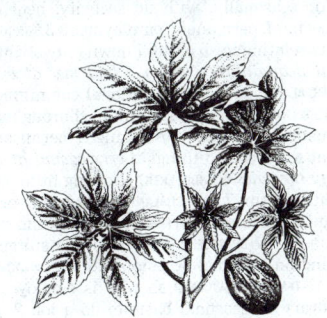

Castor-oil plant

castor-oil plant *n.* a tall tropical plant with large lobed leaves that is cultivated for ornament and for its seeds, from which castor oil is produced. Latin name: *Ricinus communis.*

castor steering *n.* a type of steering found in horse-drawn vehicles, steam wagons, traction engines, and trailers, in which the whole front axle swivels around a central point

castramentation /kástrə men táysh'n/ *n.* the creation and laying out of a military encampment [Late 17thC. From French *castramétation*, from Latin *castra metari* 'to measure or mark out a camp'.]

castrate /ka stráyt/ (**-trates, -trating, -trated**) *vt.* **1.** VET, MED **REMOVE TESTICLES FROM MALE** to remove the testicles of a man or male animal, making reproduction impossible. Animals are sometimes castrated to make them more docile and to prevent disease. **2.** **WEAKEN SB OR STH** to take away the strength, power, force, or vigour of sb or sth ○ *The department was castrated through heavy budget cuts.* **3.** VET, MED **REMOVE OVARIES FROM FEMALE** to remove the ovaries of a woman or female animal, making reproduction impossible [15thC. From Latin *castrat-*, the past participle stem of *castrare* 'to cut off, castrate', from, perhaps, assumed *castrum* 'knife'.] —**castrater** *n.* —**castration** /ka stráysh'n/ *n.*

castration complex *n.* according to Freudian psychology, a subconscious fear in men of having their genitals removed as a punishment for wanting to have sexual intercourse with their mother

castrato /ka straátō/ (*plural* **castrati** /-ti/ *or* **castratos**) *n.* a male singer who was castrated before puberty in order to retain a soprano or alto voice, a practice that ceased when it became illegal in the 19th century [Mid-18thC. From Italian, literally 'castrated one', from the past participle of Latin *castrare* (see CASTRATE).]

Castries /ka streéss/ capital city of St Lucia in the West Indies. Population: 11,147 (1991).

Fidel Castro

Castro /kástrō/, **Fidel** (*b.* 1926) Cuban statesman. He led the revolution that overthrew Fulgencio Batista and headed a Communist government as prime minister (1959–76) and president (from 1976).

Castroism /kástrō izzəm/ *n.* the communist political, social, and economic policies of Fidel Castro and his supporters [Mid-20thC. Named after Fidel CASTRO.] —**Castroist** *n., adj.* —**Castroite** *n., adj.*

casual /kázhyoo əl/ *adj.* **1. CHANCE OR UNPREMEDITATED** happening or done by chance or without prior thought or planning **2. OCCASIONAL OR TEMPORARY** relating to or taking on work that is available at irregular intervals or seasonally, with no security, benefits, or prospects of permanent employment **3. KNOWN ONLY SLIGHTLY** relating to sb or sth known only slightly ○ *a casual acquaintance whom I had met at work* **4. SUPERFICIAL** not involving emotional commitment or promises of loyalty, or lacking in thoroughness or seriousness **5. LENIENT** possessing a permissive or lenient approach to things ○ *very casual about enforcing the rules* **6. INDIFFERENT** showing little interest or enthusiasm **7. NONCHALANT** cool, calm, or nonchalant in manner **8. NOT FORMAL** informal and relaxed **9.** CLOTHES **COMFORTABLE** comfortable and suitable for wearing on informal occasions **10.** BIOL = **adventive** ■ *n.* **1. TEMPORARY WORKER** sb who is employed on a temporary or seasonal basis to do a job **2.** BIOL = **adventive** ■ **casuals** *npl.* **INFORMAL CLOTHES OR FOOTWEAR** informal comfortable clothes or shoes [14thC. Directly or via French *casuel* from Latin *casualis*, from *casus* 'chance, event, accident' (source of English *case* and *casuist*).] —**casually** *adv.* —**casualness** *n.*

casualization /kázhyoo ə lī záysh'n/, **casualisation** *n.* the changing of working practices so that workers are employed on a freelance and occasional basis rather than being offered full-time contracts ○ *the increasing casualization of labour*

casualty /kázhyoo əlti/ (*plural* **-ties**) *n.* **1. ACCIDENT VICTIM** sb who is seriously injured or killed in an accident **2.** MIL **INJURED OR DEAD SOLDIER** a member of the armed forces who is killed or injured during combat **3. VICTIM** sth or sb destroyed or suffering as an indirect result of a particular event or circumstances **4. HOSPITAL EMERGENCY DEPARTMENT** a hospital department that treats emergency patients who have had accidents or been injured (*informal*) (*often used before a noun*) ○ *rushed to casualty with multiple fractures.* US term **emergency room** [15thC. Alteration (on the model of words like PENALTY) of medieval Latin *casualitas* 'chance', from *casualis* (see CASUAL); the underlying idea is 'sb killed by accident'.]

casuarina /kázzyoo ə reénə, kázh-, -rínə/ (*plural* **-nas** *or* **-na**) *n.* a tree found mainly in Australia and some parts of Asia with needle-shaped leaves that form whorls at the end of short branches. Genus: *Casuarina.* [Late 18thC. From modern Latin, formed from *casuarius* 'cassowary' from the similarity of its branches to the bird's feathers.]

casuist /kázzyoo ist/ *n.* **1.** PHILOS, RELIG **SB CONSIDERING ETHICS AND MORALS** sb, especially a theologian, who tries to settle questions of ethics and morals by applying general rules and principles to them **2. SB USING MISLEADINGLY SUBTLE REASONING** sb who uses subtle and sophisticated reasoning, especially on moral issues, in order to justify sth or to mislead sb (*disapproving*) [Early 17thC. Via French from, ultimately, modern Latin, formed from Latin *casus* 'chance, event' (source of English *case* and *casual*).] —**casuistic** /kázzyoo ístik/ *adj.* —**casuistical** *adj.* —**casuistically** /-ikli/ *adv.*

casuistry /kázzyoo istri/ *n.* **1.** PHILOS, RELIG **APPLICATION OF PRINCIPLES TO MORAL QUESTIONS** the application of general rules and principles to questions of ethics and morals in order to resolve them **2. MISLEADINGLY SUBTLE REASONING** the use of sophisticated and subtle argument and reasoning, especially on moral issues, in order to justify sth or mislead sb (*disapproving*)

casus belli /kaássoòss béll ee/ (*plural* **casus belli**) *n.* a situation or event that causes, or is the pretext for starting, a war or other conflict (*formal*) [From modern Latin, literally 'occasion of war']

cat /kat/ *n.* **1.** ZOOL **FURRY ANIMAL THAT PURRS AND MEOWS** a small domesticated mammal that has soft fur, sharp claws, pointed ears, and, usually, a long furry tail. Cats are widely kept as pets or to catch mice. Latin name: *Felis catus.* **2.** ZOOL = **big cat 3. BAD-TEMPERED WOMAN** a spiteful or malicious woman (*informal insult*) **4.** *US* **MAN** a man (*dated slang*) ○ *He's a real cool cat.* **5.** *US* MUSIC **JAZZ PLAYER** a musician who plays jazz (*dated slang*) **6.** NAUT **ANCHOR TACKLE OR CATHEAD** a set of heavy tackle used for raising an anchor to the cathead, or the cathead itself **7.** = **cat-o'-nine-tails 8.** ZOOL = **catfish 9.** SAILING **CATAMARAN** a catamaran (*informal*) **10.** SAILING **CATBOAT** a catboat (*informal*) **11.** AUTOMOT **CATALYTIC CONVERTER** a catalytic converter (*informal*) ■ *v.* **(cats, catting, catted) 1.** *vt.* NAUT **RAISE ANCHOR** to raise the anchor to the cathead **2.** *vi.* **VOMIT** to vomit (*informal*) ■ *adj.* **BAD** devastatingly bad (*regional slang*) ○ *That game was cat! We lost 5 nil.* [Old English *catt, catte,* from prehistoric Germanic, perhaps ultimately from Egyptian; later reinforced by Anglo-Norman *cat* (probably ultimately from the same ancestor)] ◇ **bell the cat** to play the leading part in sth difficult or dangerous, usually when such action will be of help to a group ◇ **be raining cats and dogs** to be raining very heavily ◇ **has the cat got your tongue?** used, often to a child, to prompt sb to speak and to ask the reason for his or her silence ◇ **let the cat out of the bag** to disclose secret or confidential information ◇ **like a cat on hot bricks** extremely nervous or agitated ◇ **play cat and mouse with sb** to treat sb who is in your power in such a way that he or she does not know what you are going to do next ◇ **put** *or* **set the cat among the pigeons** to cause trouble ◇ **think that you are the cat's pyjamas** *or* **whiskers** to have an extremely high opinion of yourself ◇ **when the cat's away the mice will play** when sb in authority is absent, those he or she is in charge of will misbehave

CAT *abbr.* **1.** AIR clear-air turbulence **2.** MED computerized axial tomography **3.** EDUC College of Advanced Technology **4.** STOCK EXCH computer-aided trading

cat. *abbr.* catalogue

cata- *prefix.* down, apart ○ *catabolism* ○ *catalysis* [From Greek *kata* 'down, back, apart']

catabolise *v.* = **catabolize**

catabolism /kə tábbəlizəm/ *n.* a metabolic process in which energy is released through the conversion of complex molecules into simpler ones [Late 19thC. Formed (probably on the model of METABOLISM) from Greek *katabolē* 'throwing down', from *ballein* 'to throw'.] —**catabolic** /káttə bóllik/ *adj.* —**catabolically** /-bóllikli/ *adv.*

catabolite /kə tábbə līt/ *n.* a product of catabolism, especially a waste product

catachresis /káttə kreéssiss/ (*plural* **-ses** /-sseez/) *n.* the incorrect use of words, e.g. by mixing metaphors or applying terminology wrongly [Mid-16thC. Via Latin from Greek *katakhrēsis*, from *katakhrēsthai* 'to misuse'.] —**catachrestic** /-kréstik/ *adj.* —**catachrestical** *adj.* —**catachrestically** /-ikli/ *adv.*

cataclysm /káttəklizzəm/ *n.* **1. DISASTER** a sudden and violent upheaval or disaster that causes great changes in society, e.g. a war, earthquake, or drought ○ *one of the greatest cataclysms of the 20th century* **2. FLOOD** a terrible and devastating flood [Early 17thC. Via French from, ultimately, Greek *kataklusmos* 'deluge', from *kluzein* 'to wash'.] —**cataclysmal** /káttə klízm'l/ *adj.* —**cataclysmic** /-mik/ *adj.* —**cataclysmically** /-mikli/ *adv.*

catacomb /káttə koom, -kōm/ *n.* (*often used in the plural*) **1. UNDERGROUND CEMETERY** an underground cemetery consisting of passages or tunnels with rooms and recesses leading off them for burial chambers. In ancient Rome, Christians used catacombs for burial. **2. NETWORK OF TUNNELS BELOW GROUND** any underground network of passages or tunnels [Pre-12thC. Via Old French from late Latin *catacumbas*, the name of the subterranean cemetery of St Sebastian in Rome, which reputedly housed the bodies of St Peter and St Paul.]

catadromous /kə táddrəməss/ *adj.* used to describe fish that spend most of their lives in fresh water but migrate to salt water to breed, as eels do. ◊ **anadromous** [Late 19thC. Coined (on the model of ANADROMOUS) from CATA- 'down' + -DROMOUS 'running', in reference to migration from upper to lower water.]

catafalque /káttə falk/ *n.* a raised and decorated platform on which the coffin of a distinguished person lies in state before or during a funeral [Mid-17thC. Via French from Italian *catafalco*, probably from assumed Vulgar Latin *catafal(i)cum* (source of English *scaffold*), perhaps formed from *cata-* 'down' + *fala* 'scaffolding'.]

Catalan /káttə lan/ *n.* **1.** LANG **ROMANCE LANGUAGE** the regional language of Catalonia and the Balearic Islands, Spain, also spoken in Andorra and the French department of Roussillon. It belongs to the Romance group of Indo-European languages and is spoken by about seven million people. **2.** PEOPLES **SB FROM CATALONIA** sb who lives in or was born or brought up in the autonomous region of Catalonia, Spain —**Catalan** *adj.*

catalase /káttə layz, -layss/ *n.* an enzyme in living cells that aids the breakdown of hydrogen peroxide to oxygen and water [Early 20thC. Coined from CATALYSIS + -ASE.] —**catalatic** /káttə láttik/ *adj.*

catalepsy /káttə lepsi/ *n.* actual or apparent unconsciousness while muscles become rigid and remain in any position in which they are placed. The condition occurs naturally in diseases such as schizophrenia or epilepsy and can be induced by hypnosis or drugs. [14thC. Directly or via French from late Latin, from Greek *katalēpsis* 'seizure', from *katalambanein*, literally 'to seize upon', from *lambanein* 'to seize'.] —**cataleptic** /káttə léptik/ *adj.* —**cataleptically** /-léptikli/ *adv.*

catalexis /káttə léksiss/ *n.* the lack of one syllable in the final foot of a line of verse [Mid-19thC. From Greek *katalēxis* 'termination', from *katalēgein*, literally 'to leave off', from *legein* 'to cease'.] —**catalectic** /-léktik/ *adj.*

catalog *n., vt.* US = **catalogue**

catalogue *n.* (*plural* **-logues**) **1.** COMM **LIST OF GOODS FOR SALE** a list of goods for sale, with prices and illustrations, presented in book form or sometimes in other formats including CD-ROM or video, and often used for mail order **2.** ARTS **EXHIBITION GUIDE** a booklet that lists and often illustrates the objects on show at an exhibition **3.** LIBRARIES **LIST OF BOOKS** a list of the books and periodicals in a library, usually arranged according to subject, title, or author **4. SERIES OF THINGS** a long list of different things or events that all relate to a particular issue or person, especially things or events that are unpleasant or undesirable ○ *a catalogue of disorders* **5.** *US* UNIV = **prospectus** ■ *v.* **(-logues, -loguing, -logued) 1.** *vti.* **MAKE A CATALOGUE** to classify and list items to form a catalogue **2.** *vt.* **ENTER STH IN CATALOGUE** to enter sth in a catalogue ○ *I have catalogued all the new additions to the col-*

lection. **3.** *vt.* LIST SERIES OF THINGS OR EVENTS to list or describe a series of related events, items, or characteristics ○ *a history of the twentieth century that catalogues many examples of human ingenuity* [15thC. Via French from, ultimately, Greek *katalogos* 'list', from *katalegein*, literally 'to pick out', from *legein* 'to choose'.] —**cataloguer** *n.*

catalogue raisonné /kátta log ráyzə náy/ (*plural* **catalogues raisonnés** /kátta log ráyzə náy/) *n.* a detailed list of works by a particular artist, especially one produced to accompany an exhibition or collection [From French, literally 'reasoned catalogue']

Catalonia /kátta lóni ə/ autonomous region in northeastern Spain. It contains the provinces of Barcelona, Girona, Lléida, and Tarragona. Capital: Barcelona. Population: 6,226,869 (1995). Area: 31,930 sq. km/12,328 sq. mi. Catalan **Catalunya**. Spanish **Cataluña**. —**Catalonian** /kátta lóni ən/ *adj., n.*

catalyse /kátta líz/ (**-lyses, -lysing, -lysed**) *vt.* **1.** CHEM INCREASE CHEMICAL REACTION RATE to increase the rate of a chemical reaction by the action or use of a catalyst **2.** BRING STH ABOUT to cause a particular thing to happen or bring about a particular state of affairs ○ *The hearings have catalysed the passage of financial reforms.* [Late 19thC. Formed from CATALYSIS, on the model of ANALYSE.] —**catalyser** *n.*

catalysis /kə tálləssiss/ (*plural* **-ses** /-seez/) *n.* the increase in the rate of a chemical reaction by the introduction of a catalyst [Mid-17thC. Via modern Latin, 'dissolution' (the original sense in English), from Greek *katalusis*, from *kataluein* 'to dissolve', from *luein* 'to set free'.]

catalyst /káttəlist/ *n.* **1.** CHEM CHEMICAL THAT ACCELERATES CHEMICAL REACTION a substance that increases the rate of a chemical reaction without itself undergoing any change **2.** STIMULUS TO CHANGE sb or sth that makes a change happen or brings about an event ○ *The quarrel acted as a catalyst for the breakup of their partnership.* [Early 20thC. Formed from CATALYSIS, on the model of ANALYST.]

catalytic /kátta líttik/ *adj.* involving or causing an increase in the rate of a chemical reaction by the use of a catalyst [Mid-19thC. From Greek *katalutikos* 'able to dissolve', from *katalusis* (see CATALYSIS).] —**catalytically** *adv.*

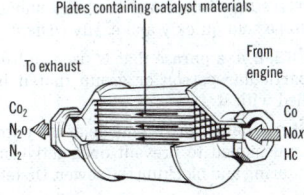

Catalytic converter

catalytic converter *n.* in the exhaust system of a motor vehicle, a chamber in which gases mix with air so that pollutants such as carbon monoxide can be oxidized. The chamber contains a platinum-iridium catalyst.

catalytic cracker *n.* an oil-refinery device that breaks down large molecules from crude oil into smaller ones that are useful as fuel, using heat and a catalyst to lower the required temperature

catalyze *vt.* US = catalyse

catamaran /káttəmə rán/ *n.* **1.** DOUBLE-HULLED CRAFT a sailing boat or engine-powered boat that has two identical hulls fixed together by a rigid framework **2.** LOG RAFT a simple raft made from logs or floats tied together [Early 17thC. From Tamil *kaṭṭumaram*, literally 'tied wood'.]

catamite /kátta mīt/ *n.* a boy or youth with whom a man has homosexual intercourse (*literary*) [Late 16thC. Via Latin *catamitus* from Greek *Ganumēdēs* GANYMEDE, a handsome youth in Greek mythology.]

catamount /kátta mownt/, **catamountain** /-mowntin/ *n.* = **puma** [Mid-17thC. From *cat of the mountain*.]

cat-and-mouse *adj.* cruel or sadistic, especially in exploiting, compounding, and enjoying sb else's suffering or fear

cataphora /kə táffərə/ *n.* the use of a word or phrase, usually a pronoun, that refers to sth mentioned later, as does 'it' in 'It's easy to make mistakes' [Late 20thC. Coined from CATA- + ANAPHORA.] —**cataphoric** /kátta fórrik/ *adj.*

cataphoresis /káttəfə reéssiss/ (*plural* **-ses** /-sseez/) *n.* = **electrophoresis** [Late 19thC. Coined from CATA- + Greek *phorēsis* 'being carried'.] —**cataphoretic** /káttəfə réttik/ *adj.* —**cataphoretically** /-réttikli/ *adv.*

cataplasia /kátta pláyzi ə/ *n.* the degeneration of cells or tissue to a more primitive or embryonic form —**cataplastic** /-plástik/ *adj.*

cataplasm /kátta plazzəm/ *n.* a poultice (*archaic*) [Mid-16thC. Via French *cataplasme* from, ultimately, Greek *kataplasma*, from *kataplassein*, literally 'to plaster over', from *plassein* 'to plaster, mould'.]

cataplexy /kátta pleksi/ *n.* sudden temporary paralysis caused by shock, fear, or ecstasy [Late 19thC. Formed from Greek *kataplēxis* 'stupefaction', from *kataplēssein*, literally 'to strike down', from *plēssein* 'to strike'.] —**cataplectic** /kátta pléktik/ *adj.*

catapult /kátta pult/ *n.* **1.** ARMS, HIST MEDIEVAL LAUNCHING WEAPON a large heavy war machine consisting of a wooden frame and a throwing device operated by levers, used in medieval times to hurl large stones at an enemy **2.** CHILDREN'S STONE-THROWER a Y-shaped device of wood, plastic, or metal with a piece of elastic stretched between the two top points of the Y, used for firing stones or pellets. US term **slingshot 3.** MIL PLANE OR MISSILE LAUNCHER a launching mechanism on an aircraft carrier or warship, used to propel planes or missiles at a speed sufficient for them to take off ■ *v.* (**-pults, -pulting, -pulted**) **1.** *vt.* HURL STH to throw sth with great force from a catapult (*often passive*) ○ *The fighters were catapulted from the carrier at 30-second intervals.* **2.** *vti.* FLING OR BE FLUNG to throw sb or sth violently into the air by collision, impact, or a force that has an effect like a catapult, or be thrown in this way ○ *They were catapulted out of their seats by the force of the impact.* **3.** *vt.* MAKE SB FAMOUS SUDDENLY to thrust sb unexpectedly and suddenly into a particular situation ○ *the hit that catapulted her to fame at the tender age of fifteen* [Late 16thC. Directly or via French from Latin *catapulta*, from Greek *katapeltēs*, from, ultimately, *pallein* 'to hurl'.]

cataract /kátta rakt/ *n.* **1.** OPHTHALMOL EYE DISEASE an eye disease in which the lens becomes covered in an opaque film that affects sight, eventually causing total blindness. The condition usually affects older people and is generally found in both eyes to varying degrees. It can be treated surgically by replacing the lens with an artificial implant. **2.** OPHTHALMOL FILM OVER EYE LENS the lens of the eye or the membrane surrounding it (**capsule**) that has become opaque as a result of disease **3.** GEOG WATERFALL a series of river rapids and small waterfalls with only moderate vertical drop (*literary*) **4.** FLOOD a heavy downpour of rain or a great flood (*literary*) ○ *Spring cataracts have flooded the low-lying farmlands.* [15thC. Via Latin *cataracta* 'waterfall, portcullis' (hence, 'sth that obstructs'), from Greek *kataraktēs* 'down-dashing', from *katarassein*, literally 'to dash down', from *arassein* 'to strike'.]

catarrh /kə taár/ *n.* inflammation of a mucous membrane, especially in the nose and throat, causing an increase in the production of mucus, as happens in the common cold [15thC. Via French *catarrhe* from, ultimately, Greek *katarrhous*, from *katarrhein*, literally 'to flow down', from *rhein* 'to flow' (see RHEUM).] —**catarrhal** *adj.* —**catarrhous** *adj.*

catarrhine /kátta rīn/ *adj.* WITH CLOSELY-SET NOSTRILS used to describe animals that have nostrils set close together and directed downwards. Humans, apes, and some monkeys are catarrhine. ■ *n.* PRIMATE WITH CLOSELY-SET NOSTRILS an animal with a catarrhine nose structure, e.g. a human or ape. Suborder: Catarrhini. [Mid-19thC. Coined from CATA- + Greek *rhinos* 'nose' (see RHINO-).]

catastasis /kə tástəssiss/ *n.* the intense part of the action in a classical tragedy, immediately preceding the tragic climax [Mid-16thC. From Greek *katastasis* 'settling, appointment', from *stasis* STASIS.]

catastrophe /kə tástrəfi/ *n.* **1.** DISASTER a terrible disaster or accident, especially one that leads to great loss of life **2.** HUMILIATING TOTAL FAILURE an absolute failure, often in humiliating or embarrassing circumstances **3.** THEATRE RESOLUTION OF PLOT the concluding part of the action in a drama, especially a classical tragedy, when the plot is resolved **4.** GEOL VIOLENT SEISMIC CHANGE a sudden and violent change in the earth's crust caused by an earthquake, flood, or any other natural process [Mid-16thC. Via Latin *catastropha* from Greek *katastrophē* 'overturning, sudden turn', from *katastrephein*, literally 'to overturn', from *strephein* 'to turn'.]

catastrophic /kátta stróffik/ *adj.* **1.** DISASTROUS causing or liable to cause widespread damage or death ○ *the uncontrolled spread of an infection that has had a catastrophic effect on livestock* **2.** AWFUL completely unsuccessful or very bad ○ *The party was a catastrophic affair, ending in a riot.* **3.** US MED LIFE-THREATENING AND REQUIRING EXPENSIVE TREATMENT so serious in nature as to require extensive, long-term, and expensive medical treatment ○ *cancer, Aids, and other catastrophic illnesses requiring excellent insurance coverage* —**catastrophically** *adv.*

catastrophism /kə tástrəfizzəm/ *n.* **1.** GEOL THEORY OF GEOLOGICAL VIOLENCE a theory, now discarded, that the geological features of the earth were formed by a series of sudden violent catastrophes rather than a gradual evolutionary process. A more recent version of this theory holds that the evolutionary process of geological development has on occasions been supplemented by such catastrophes. **2.** PESSIMISM an outlook or attitude that foresees disaster as the only possible outcome of any action or situation —**catastrophist** *n.*

catatonia /kátta tóni ə/ *n.* a condition, often associated with schizophrenia, characterized by periods of inertia or apparent stupor and rigidity of the muscles [Late 19thC. Coined from CATA- + Greek *tonos* 'tone, tension' (source of English *tone*) + -IA.]

catatonic /kátta tónnik/ *adj.* **1.** IN STATE RESEMBLING TRANCE in a state of inertia or apparent stupor often associated with schizophrenia and characterized by rigidity of the muscles **2.** IN DRUNKEN STUPOR in a stupefied or unconscious state, especially one caused by drunkenness (*informal*) —**catatonically** *adv.*

catboat /kát bōt/ *n.* a sailing boat that is broad across the beam and has a single sail on a forward-stepped mast [Late 19thC. *Cat* of uncertain origin: perhaps from obsolete *cat* 'merchant sailing vessel', from medieval Latin *catta* 'ship' or Old French *chat* 'merchant ship'.]

cat burglar *n.* a burglar who, using stealth and agility, breaks into properties, especially through high windows or small openings [From the burglar's catlike agility]

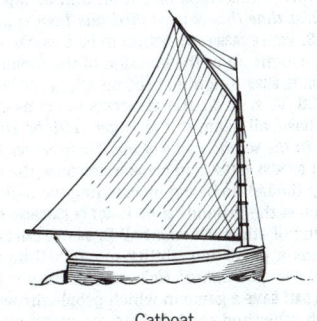

Catboat

catcall /kát kawl/ *n.* JEER a whistle or shout expressing disapproval or dislike, especially at a live performance ■ *vti.* (**-calls, -calling, -called**) UTTER JEERS to shout or whistle at sb as an expression of disapproval or dislike [Mid-17thC. From the resemblance to cats' nocturnal cries.]

catch /kach/ *v.* (**catches, catching, caught**) **1.** *vti.* STOP STH WITH THE HANDS to take hold of or stop sth that is travelling through the air **2.** *vt.* COLLECT FALLING OBJECTS FROM BELOW to collect sth falling, e.g. rain, from below **3.** *vt.* GRASP SB OR STH to take tight hold of sb or sth suddenly ○ *He caught me by the shoulder.* **4.** *vt.* HUNT CAPTURE ANIMAL to capture or trap an animal, bird, fish, or other living thing **5.** *vt.* CRIMINOL CAPTURE CRIMINAL to capture sb, especially a criminal or sb suspected of wrongdoing, after a search or chase ○ *Have they caught the culprit?* **6.** *vt.* REACH SB OR STH to reach or get alongside a person or vehicle moving ahead, usually at speed ○ *trying to catch the car in front* **7.** *vt.* TRANSP GET ON BOARD PUBLIC TRANSPORT to arrive in time to board a bus, train, or other form of public transport ○ *I have a plane to catch.* **8.** *vti.* MED GET DISEASE to become infected with a disease **9.** *vt.* SURPRISE SB DOING WRONG to surprise or stop sb who is in the act of doing sth illegal or forbidden ○ *He caught her taking money from the till.* **10.** *vt.* SURPRISE SB DOING STH EMBARRASSING to surprise or observe sb who is doing sth considered embarrassing, impolite, or private ○ *I caught him gazing at himself in the mirror.* **11.** *vt.* ATTRACT SB'S ATTENTION to attract the interest or attention of others ○ *a campaign that had caught the nation's imagination* **12.** *vti.* MANAGE TO HEAR STH to manage to hear what is being said ○ *I'm sorry, I didn't quite catch that.* **13.** *vt.* UNDERSTAND STH to understand the right meaning of sth **14.** *vt.* NOTICE STH SUBTLE OR FLEETING to notice sth subtle or fleeting, e.g. sth in the way sb is speaking that tells you how that person really feels ○ *I caught a note of sarcasm in his voice.* **15.** *vt.* ARTS SEE PERFORMER OR PRODUCTION to see a particular television programme, a film, or a play, or see a particular person performing in sth (*informal*) ○ *If you get the chance, try and catch the new production of 'Hamlet'.* **16.** *vt.* MANAGE TO MEET SB to manage to meet or talk to sb, especially sb who is very busy (*informal*) ○ *I was hoping to catch the doctor before she left.* **17.** *vt.* GET STH YOU NEED to get food, drink, or rest only hurriedly or in small amounts (*informal*) ○ *We can stop and catch a bite to eat.* **18.** *vt.* STRIKE SB to strike sb with a blow ○ *a blow that caught him on the side of the head* **19.** *vt.* TAKE IMPACT OF STH to receive the impact or force from sth such as a blow or the force of sb's anger or emotions ○ *He caught the full impact of the blast.* **20.** *vti.* ENTANGLE STH to entangle or hook sth such as clothing on sth sharp, or become entangled or hooked, sometimes resulting in damage ○ *She caught her blouse on a nail.* **21.** *vti.* TRAP STH to trap sth in an opening or door, or become trapped ○ *I caught my fingers in the letter box.* **22.** *vt.* DELAY SB to delay sb or hold sb up (*usually passive*) **23.** *vr.* STOP YOURSELF FROM DOING STH to stop yourself from saying or doing sth ○ *He was about to make a sarcastic remark but caught himself just in time.* **24.** *vt.* SURPRISE SB to take sb by surprise (*usually passive*) ○ *She got caught in the rain and was absolutely soaked.* **25.** *vt.* TRICK SB to trick or deceive sb **26.** *vt.* REPRODUCE ASPECTS OF STH OR SB to reproduce successfully the most typical aspects of sb or sth ○ *a novel that catches the mood of prewar Berlin* **27.** *vt.* CINEMA, TV, RECORDING RECORD STH ON FILM to record sb or sth on film or tape ○ *the very first time this elusive bird has been caught on film* **28.** *vti.* BE CARRIED BY EMOTION to be eager to do sth, or get caught up in the emotion of the moment **29.** *vi.* BEGIN TO BURN to ignite, become alight, or begin to burn **30.** *vi.* BASEBALL PLAY AS CATCHER to act as catcher on a baseball team ○ *Clevenger will be catching again in the second game of the World Series.* **31.** *vt.* CRICKET DISMISS BATSMAN in cricket, to cause the person hitting the ball to be out by catching the ball before it reaches the ground ■ *n.* **1.** ACT OF CATCHING STH the catching of sth, such as a ball **2.** SB WHO CAN CATCH sb who has a particular ability to catch things ○ *He missed the ball again! He's such a lousy catch!* **3.** SPORTS BALL GAME a game in which people throw a ball to each other and catch it **4.** SPORTS MOVE IN BALL GAMES a move in ball games such as cricket or rounders in which a player catches a ball hit by another before it touches the ground, forcing that person to retire **5.** NUMBER OF THINGS CAUGHT the amount or number of things caught, e.g. when fishing ○ *Not much of a catch today, I'm afraid.* **6.** IDEAL OR DESIRABLE PERSON sb or sth regarded as ideal or particularly desirable, especially as a marriage partner (*informal*) ○ *Her friends regarded Tom as quite a catch.* **7.** DEVICE THAT CLOSES OR FASTENS a device for fastening sth, e.g. a door, window, or piece of jewellery **8.** SNAG a hidden or unexpected problem, especially one suspected to exist because everything seems too good to be true (*informal*) ○ *Okay, it sounds great: where's the catch?* **9.** BREAK IN VOICE a brief moment when sb's voice becomes husky or unclear because of intense emotion ○ *There was a slight catch in his voice as he read out the letter.* **10.** MUSIC HUMOROUS SONG a type of round or canon with humorous, often risqué, words, popular in the 17th and 18th centuries [12thC. Via Anglo-Norman or Old French *cachier* 'to chase', variant of *chacier*, from, ultimately, Latin *captare* 'to try to catch', from *capere* 'to take'.] —**catchable** *adj.* ◇ **catch it** to get into trouble (*informal*) ◇ **catch sb with his** *or* **her pants** *or* **trousers down 1.** to expose sb in a very embarrassing situation, especially one that suggests hypocrisy or incompetence **2.** to surprise sb in a state of unpreparedness at a time when alertness is required

catch on *vi.* (*informal*) **1.** BECOME POPULAR OR WIDESPREAD to become popular or widely used **2.** GET THE IDEA to understand a new idea, task, or process ○ *pretty slow to catch on*

catch out *vt.* **1.** DEVISE WAY TO SHOW SB'S MISTAKES to find ways of exposing errors or ignorance in order to embarrass sb or show superiority (*informal*) ○ *He would try to catch me out by asking awkward questions during safety inspections.* **2.** EXPOSE WRONGDOER to catch sb doing sth wrong or illegal, especially when deliberately setting out to do so (*informal*) **3.** SPORTS CATCH BALL HIT BY SB to catch a ball hit by a player in baseball, rounders, or cricket while it is still in the air, forcing the player or the player's team to retire

catch up *v.* **1.** *vti.* REACH SB OR STH TRAVELLING AHEAD to reach or get alongside a person who or vehicle that was moving or had gone ahead **2.** *vt.* PICK STH UP to quickly pick sth or sb up in the hands or arms ○ *He caught up all the papers and strode off.* **3.** *vi.* GET UP TO DATE to make up for lost time by working harder in order to be up to date ○ *I really must make time to catch up on my reading.* **4.** *vt.* ENGROSS SB to absorb sb's attention completely (*usually passive*) ○ *I was so caught up in my work that I didn't have time for lunch.* **5.** *vt.* BECOME INVOLVED UNHAPPILY to become involved in sth undesirable (*usually passive*) ○ *They were caught up in the whole messy affair even though they tried to stay out of it.*

catch up on *vi.* to have a delayed effect on sb ○ *Three nights without sleep is beginning to catch up on me.*

catch up with *vt.* **1.** FIND WRONGDOER to find sb who has committed a crime or done sth wrong, especially after a search or chase ○ *By the time the police caught up with him, he had changed his name and moved to Brazil.* **2.** FINALLY AFFECT SB to finally have an effect after a period during which sb seemed free from the usual consequences of a particular way of behaving ○ *All those late nights will catch up with you eventually.*

catch-22 *n.* a situation in which whatever outcome sb desires is impossible to attain because the rules always work against it [Named after the 1955 novel *Catch-22* by Joseph Heller, in which the 'catch' was that an airman wishing to stop flying missions must be sane and therefore must continue]

WORD KEY: CULTURAL NOTE

Catch-22, a novel by US writer Joseph Heller (1961). The title of this dark satire relates to the skewed military logic that entraps the protagonist, Yossarian, a pilot serving in Italy during World War II. Although he has flown sufficient missions to be sent home, he is also obliged to obey orders, and his orders are to keep flying. The term ***Catch-22*** eventually took on the following meanings of its own: 'a situation or problem from which extrication is impossible because of built-in illogical rules and regulations', 'an absurd situation', 'a snag or catch', and 'a self-defeating course of action'.

catchall /kách awl/ *n.* sth that covers a wide range of possibilities, meanings, ideas, or situations (*often used before a noun*) ○ *one of those catchall phrases that doesn't really mean very much at all*

catch and release *n.* a conservation policy adopted by some anglers whereby they release some or all of the fish they catch in order to sustain fish populations

catch-as-catch-can *n.* NO-HOLDS-BARRED WRESTLING a style of wrestling in which most holds are permitted, including many that are not allowed in other wrestling styles ■ *adj. US* MAKING DO making do with whatever is available ○ *We took a catch-as-catch-can approach to our summer holiday.* ■ *adv. US* USING WHAT COMES TO HAND using whatever happens to be available ○ *The press conference was arranged catch-as-catch-can at very short notice.*

catch basin *n. US* **1.** = **catch pit 2.** DRAINAGE COLLECTION AREA OR RESERVOIR an area or reservoir for catching drainage water or runoff

catch crop *n.* a fast-growing crop grown between harvest and planting of two main crops, between the rows of a main crop, or as a substitute after a crop failure [From the idea of catching an opportunity to grow it]

catcher /káchər/ *n.* **1.** STH OR SB THAT CATCHES a person, animal, or device that catches things **2.** BASEBALL PLAYER POSITIONED BEHIND BATTER the baseball player who stands behind home plate, signals for pitches, and catches pitched balls that have not been hit by the batter

catchfly /kách flī/ (*plural* **-flies** *or* **-fly**) *n.* a plant related to the campion and ragged robin that exudes a sticky substance on the stem beneath each pair of leaves. Genus: *Silene* and *Lychnis.*

catching /káching/ *adj.* **1.** MED INFECTIOUS used to describe an illness that can be transmitted to other people because it is contagious or infectious ○ *Don't worry: it's not catching!* **2.** ATTRACTIVE so attractive as to be memorable **3.** AFFECTING ONE PERSON AFTER ANOTHER passed from one person to another like an infection ○ *a pessimism that seemed to be catching*

catchment /káchmənt/ *n.* **1.** RAINWATER RECEPTACLE a structure, reservoir, or container for collecting rainwater **2.** COLLECTED RAINWATER the rainwater that collects in a catchment **3.** COLLECTING OF RAINWATER the collecting or catching of rainwater

catchment area *n.* **1.** GEOG DRAINAGE AREA the area of land that drains rainfall into a river or lake **2.** EDUC, HEALTH AREA COVERED BY SERVICE the area from which a particular school, hospital, or doctor will accept pupils or patients

catchpenny /kách penni/ *adj.* FAST-SELLING AND SHODDY cheap and made to be sold quickly and easily without much regard for quality (*dated*) ■ *n.* (*plural* **-nies**) FAST-SELLING SHODDY ITEM a cheap shoddy item made to be sold quickly and easily (*dated*)

catch phrase *n.* a phrase that is used so frequently by a particular person or group that it becomes identified with it

catch pit *n.* a device or receptacle at the entrance of a sewer designed to prevent obstructive material from entering and blocking the sewer. US term **catch basin**

catch points *npl.* railway points designed to derail any train or part of a train that might cause a collision by running backwards, or forwards against a signal, to join another track

catchpole /kách pōl/ *n.* in England in former times, a sheriff's officer who collected money from debtors [Pre-12thC. From either assumed Anglo-Norman or Old French *cachepol* or Anglo-Latin *cacepollus*, both literally 'chicken-catcher'.]

catchup /kách up/ *n. US* = **ketchup**

catchwater drain /kách wawtər-/ *n.* a drain cut along the edge of high ground to catch water from it and divert it so that it does not fall onto low-lying ground

catchweight /kách wayt/ *adj.* used to describe a sporting contest, e.g. in wrestling or horse-racing, that has no weight restrictions [Early 19thC. Origin uncertain: perhaps from the idea of catching whichever weight you could.]

catchword /kách wurd/ *n.* **1.** POPULAR WORD a word or phrase that is so frequently used, often over a short period of time, that it comes to be identified with a particular feeling, quality, or idea ○ *catchwords of the 1980s such as 'upwardly mobile' and 'yuppie'* **2.** PUBL WORD MARKING RANGE OF MATERIAL COVERED a word printed at the top of a page in a dictionary or other reference book, usually the first or last entry for that page. US term **guideword 3.** PRINTING BINDER'S CUE the first word of a page of printed text repeated at the bottom right-hand corner of the previous page, originally placed there to draw the binder's attention to it **4.** THEATRE ACTOR'S CUE a cue for an actor to come on stage or to speak

catchy /káchi/ (**-ier, -iest**) adj. **1.** MEMORABLE easy to remember because of having a simple and effective melody or wording **2.** ATTRACTING ATTENTION tending to attract interest or attention because of a notable, unique, or pleasing character or quality ○ an attempt to come up with a catchy name for a new soft drink **3.** TRICKY designed to catch people out or trip them up ○ There were some catchy questions in the English paper. **4.** FITFUL coming in spasmodic or irregular bursts ○ light rain with catchy squalls of wind —**catchiness** n.

cat cracker n. = catalytic cracker

catechesis /kátti keéssiss/ (plural -**ses** /-seez/) n. oral religious instruction given in advance of baptism or confirmation [Early 17thC. Via ecclesiastical Latin from Greek katēkhēsis 'instruction by word of mouth', from katēkhein (see CATECHIZE).] —**catechetical** /kátti kéttik'l/ adj.

catechin /káttəkin/ n. a yellow crystalline substance used in tanning and dyeing [Mid-19thC. Coined from CATECHU + -IN.]

catechise vt. = catechize

catechism /káttəkizzəm/ n. **1.** CHR QUESTION-AND-ANSWER TEACHING instruction in the principles of Christianity using set questions and answers **2.** CHR RELIGIOUS QUESTIONS AND ANSWERS the series of questions and answers that are used to test people's religious knowledge in advance of Christian baptism or confirmation **3.** CHR QUESTION-AND-ANSWER BOOK a book containing questions and answers used to test the religious knowledge of people preparing for Christian baptism or confirmation **4.** BODY OF PRINCIPLES FOLLOWED UNTHINKINGLY a body of basic beliefs and principles followed slavishly or unthinkingly **5.** INTERROGATION a close and intense session of questioning on a particular subject, especially forming part of an examination or an interrogation [Early 16thC. Via ecclesiastical Latin catechismus from ecclesiastical Greek, from katēkhizein (see CATECHIZE).] —**catechismal** /kátti kízm'l/ adj.

catechist /káttəkist/ n. sb who instructs people in the basic principles of the Christian religion, especially people preparing for baptism or confirmation — **catechistic** /kátta kístik/ adj. —**catechistical** /-kístik'l/ adj.

catechize /káttə kīz/ (**-chizes, -chizing, -chized**), **catechise** (**-chises, -chising, -chised**) vt. **1.** CHR TEACH SB ABOUT CHRISTIANITY to instruct sb in the basic principles of the Christian religion using questions and answers **2.** INTERROGATE SB to question sb closely, e.g. in an examination or interrogation [15thC. Via ecclesiastical Latin catechizare from ecclesiastical Greek katēkhizein, from katēkhein 'to instruct orally' (literally 'to sound through'), from, ultimately, ēkhē 'sound'.] —**catechization** /káttə kī zaysh'n/ n. —**catechizer** /káttə kīzər/ n.

Catechol

catechol /kátti kol, -chol/ n. a colourless crystalline solid used as a photographic developer, as an antioxidant, and in the manufacture of dyes and pharmaceuticals. Formula: $C_6H_6O_2$. [Late 19thC. Coined from CATECHU + -OL.]

catecholamine /kátta kóllə meen/ n. an organic compound (**amine**) that affects the sympathetic nervous system. Dopamine and adrenaline are catecholamines.

catechu /kátta choo, -shoo/ n. an astringent water-soluble substance obtained especially from an Asian acacia tree and used in medicine and dyeing [Late 17thC. From modern Latin, formed from Malay kacu (source of English cachou).]

catechumen /kátta kyoó men, -mən/ n. sb who is receiving religious instruction in preparation for Christian baptism or confirmation [14thC. Directly or via French catéchumène from ecclesiastical Latin catechumenus, from Greek katēkhoumenos 'being instructed', the present participle passive of katēkhein (see CATECHIZE).] —**catechumenical** /kátta kyoo ménnik'l/ adj. —**catechumenism** /kátta kyoómənizzəm/ n.

categorical /kátta górrik'l/, **categoric** /-górrik/ adj. **1.** ABSOLUTE AND EXPLICIT absolute, certain, and unconditional, with no room for doubt, question, or contradiction ○ The press office has issued a categorical denial of these allegations. **2.** INVOLVING CATEGORIES involving or relating to the use of categories or categorization —**categorically** adv. —**categoricalness** n.

categorical imperative n. according to the moral philosophy of Immanuel Kant, an unconditional moral law applying to all rational beings. It is also independent of all personal desires and motives.

categorisation n. = categorization

categorise vt. = categorize

categorization /káttiga rī záysh'n/, **categorisation** n. **1.** SORTING INTO CATEGORIES the defining and grouping of people or things into categories **2.** CATEGORY a group of people or things regarded as being in or forming a particular category

categorize /káttiga rīz/ (**-rizes, -rizing, -rized**), **categorise** (**-rises, -rising, -rised**) vt. to place sb or sth in a particular category and define or judge the person or thing accordingly ○ It was originally categorized as a cactus, but it's actually a succulent. —**categorizable** adj.

category /káttəgəri/ (plural -**ries**) n. a group or set of things, people, or actions that are classified together because of common characteristics ○ There are choices available in the following categories: leisure, fitness, health. [15thC. Ultimately via late Latin from Greek katēgoria 'statement, accusation', from katēgorein 'to speak against'; the meaning developed from 'accusation' via 'assertion, naming' to 'list'.]

— **WORD KEY: SYNONYMS** —

See Synonyms at **type**.

catena /kə teénə/ (plural -**nae** /-nee/) n. a series of connected commentaries on or excerpts of writings, especially comments on the Bible written by early Christian theologians [Mid-17thC. From Latin, 'chain' (source also of English concatenation).]

catenaccio /kátta náchi ō/ n. a strongly defensive formation in football, involving one free defender positioned behind his or her teammates [Late 20thC. From Italian, 'door bolt' from, ultimately, Latin catena (see CATENA).]

catenary /kə teénəri/ (plural -**ies**) n. **1.** CURVE OF CABLE the curve adopted by a length of heavy cable, rope, or chain of uniform density, hanging between two points, or sth with this shape **2.** TROLLEY-WIRE SUPPORT CABLE a suspended overhead power cable that supplies current to trolleybuses, trams, and most electric trains [Mid-18thC. From modern Latin catenaria, from Latin catena (see CATENA).] —**catenary** adj.

catenate /kátti nayt/ (**-nates, -nating, -nated**) vt. **1.** MAKE STH INTO CHAIN to form sth into a chain or a series of chains **2.** CHEM FORM CHAIN OF ATOMS to form a chain of atoms of the same element held together by chemical bonds [Early 17thC. From Latin catenat-, the past participle stem of catenare 'to chain, bind together', from catena (see CATENA).]

cater /káytər/ (**-ters, -tering, -tered**) vti. **1.** PROVIDE WHAT IS WANTED to provide what is wanted or needed in a particular situation or by a particular group of people ○ We try to cater for all tastes in our bookshop. **2.** SUPPLY FOOD to provide food and drink for a number

of people, e.g. at a party or meeting ○ We can cater for up to a hundred people here. [Late 16thC. Shortening of obsolete acater 'caterer' (the original sense in English), from Anglo-Norman acateor, from ac(h)ater 'to buy' from, ultimately, Latin capere 'to take'.]

cater-cornered, **cater-corner**, **catty-cornered**, **catty-corner** adj. US DIAGONAL positioned or arranged diagonally ■ adv. **1.** US DIAGONALLY in a diagonal position or arrangement ○ He sits cater-cornered from me in history class. **2.** OPPOSITE diagonally opposite sth or sth else ○ Their office is cater-cornered from the bank. [Mid-19thC. Cater originally a dialect adverb meaning 'diagonally', from French quatre 'four'.]

caterer /káytərər/ n. a person who or company that provides and sometimes serves the food and drink for a social or business function, e.g. a wedding, party, or meeting

catering /káytəring/ n. the provision of food and drink for the people at a social or business function ○ a career in catering

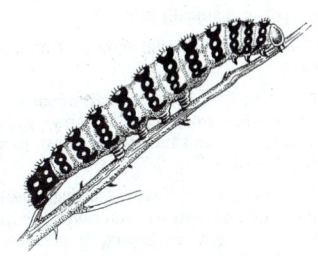

Caterpillar

caterpillar /káttər pillər/ n. the larva of a butterfly or moth. It has a long soft body, many short legs, and often brightly coloured or spiny skin. [15thC. Alteration (probably influenced by obsolete piller 'plunderer') of assumed Old Northern French catepelose, from assumed late Latin catta pilosa 'hairy cat'.]

Caterpillar /káttər pillər/ tdmk. **1.** a trademark for a continuous metal loop or belt made up of hinged links and fitted instead of wheels on tanks, bulldozers, and similar vehicles **2.** US a trademark for tractors that have continuous treads composed of chain

caterwaul /káttər wawl/ vi. (**-wauls, -wauling, -wauled**) YOWL OR ARGUE LOUDLY to make a loud howling noise like a cat on heat, or have a noisy argument ○ a street musician caterwauling in the background while we tried to talk ■ n. YOWL a loud howl or cry that sounds like a cat on heat [14thC. Origin uncertain: perhaps from Low German katerwaulen, or from an earlier form of CAT + a Middle English word meaning 'to yowl' of imitative origin.]

catfish /kát fish/ (plural -**fish** or -**fishes**) n. a scaleless, usually freshwater, fish with long whiskers (**barbels**) around its mouth that are sensitive to touch, taste, and smell. Order: Siluriformes. [From its barbels, likened to a cat's whiskers]

cat flap n. a piece of wood or plastic hinged at the top of an opening in an door to enable a pet cat to come and go as it pleases

catgut /kát gut/ n. a tough thin cord made from the dried intestines of sheep and other animals, used for stringing tennis rackets and musical instruments, and as surgical thread [Late 16thC. Origin uncertain: probably from CAT (for unknown reasons), or perhaps a contraction of 'cattle-gut'.]

cath. abbr. cathode

Cath. abbr. **1.** Cathedral **2.** Catholic

Cathar /káthər, -aar/ (plural -**ars** or -**ari** /káthərī, -aarī/) n. a member of a 12th- and 13th-century European heretical sect who believed the earth was ruled by Satan. They also believed that salvation lay in the renunciation of materialism and the adoption of a spiritual way of life. [Late 16thC. Via medieval Latin Cathari 'Cathars', from Greek katharoi 'the pure', from katharos 'pure' (see CATHARSIS).] —**Catharism** /káthərizzəm/ n. —**Catharist** /-rist/ n. —**Catharistic** /kátha rístik/ adj.

catharsis /kə tha'arssiss/ (plural **-ses** /-seez/) n. **1.** EMOTIONAL RELEASE an experience or feeling of spiritual release and purification brought about by an intense emotional experience **2.** THEATRE EMOTIONAL PURGING THROUGH GREEK TRAGEDY according to Aristotle, a purifying of the emotions that is brought about in the audience of a tragic drama through the evocation of intense fear and pity **3.** PSYCHIAT PURGING OF COMPLEXES the process of bringing to the surface repressed emotions, complexes, and feelings in an effort to identify and relieve them, or the result of this process **4.** MED PURGING OF BOWELS cleansing or purging of the bowels [Early 19thC. Via modern Latin from Greek *katharsis*, from *kathairein* 'to purge, cleanse', from *katharos* 'pure, clean'.]

cathartic /kə tha'artik/ adj. **1.** PURIFYING producing a feeling of being purified emotionally, spiritually, or psychologically as a result of an intense emotional experience or therapeutic technique ○ *a film that had a truly cathartic effect on me* **2.** MED HAVING PURGATIVE EFFECT ON BOWELS used to describe a medicine that causes emptying of the bowels ■ *n.* PHARM PURGATIVE MEDICINE a medicine that causes emptying of the bowels —**cathartically** adv.

Cathay /ka tháy/ n. a medieval name for China (archaic or literary)

cathead /kát hed/ n. a horizontal wooden or iron beam projecting from a ship's bow, where the anchor is carried and hoisted [From CAT 'to raise the anchor']

cathect /kə thékt, ka-/ (**-thects, -thecting, -thected**) vt. PSYCHOANAL to concentrate emotional or psychic energy on sth, e.g. an object, a person, or an idea [Mid-20thC. Back-formation from *cathectic*, formed from CATHEXIS.] —**cathectic** adj.

cathedra /kə theédrə/ (plural **-dras** or **-drae** /-dree/) n. **1.** BISHOP'S THRONE a bishop's official seat or throne. ◊ **ex cathedra 2.** BISHOP'S RANK OR OFFICE the official rank, office, or jurisdiction of a bishop [15thC. Via Latin from Greek *kathedra*, from *kata* 'down' + *hedra* 'seat'.]

cathedral /kə theédrəl/ n. BISHOP'S CHURCH a church that contains a bishop's throne and is the most important church in the bishop's diocese ■ *adj.* **1.** OF BISHOP OR CATHEDRAL relating to, belonging to, or having a bishop or cathedral **2.** LIKE A CATHEDRAL resembling or appropriate to a cathedral **3.** MADE BY BISHOP used to describe an official religious announcement made by a bishop or pope [13thC. Via Old French from late Latin *cathedralis*, from Latin *cathedra* 'bishop's throne' (source of English *chair*; see CATHEDRA).]

cathepsin /kə thépsin/ n. an enzyme that breaks down proteins after cell death or in some diseased conditions [Early 20thC. From German *Kathepsin*, from Greek *kathepsein* 'to digest', literally 'to boil down', from *hepsein* 'to boil'.]

Willa Cather

Cather /káthər/, **Willa** (1873–1947) US writer. Her novels include the Pulitzer Prize-winning *One of Ours* (1922). Full name **Willa Sibert Cather**

Catherine (of Aragon) /káth'rin/, **Catherine (of Aragón)** (1485–1536) Spanish-born English queen consort. The annulment of her marriage to King Henry VIII in 1533 precipitated the English Reformation.

Catherine (the Great) (1729–96) German-born Russian monarch. Empress from 1762 after deposing her husband, she extended and consolidated Russian power and culture.

Catherine the Great

Catherine de Médicis /káthrin də méddi chee, -me deéchi/, **Catherine de Medici, Queen of France** (1519–89) Italian-born widow of the French king Henry II. She was regent of France (1560–63) and may have instigated the St Bartholomew's Day Massacre (1572).

Catherine wheel n. **1.** SPINNING FIREWORK a flat spiral-shaped firework that is fastened to a vertical surface with a central pin, on which it spins, shooting out sparks or flame, after being lit. US term **pinwheel 2.** ARCHIT CIRCULAR WINDOW a circular window divided by ribs radiating from the centre [Late 16thC. Named after Saint *Catherine* of Alexandria, who was sentenced to be executed on a spiked wheel.]

catheter /káthitər/ n. a thin flexible tube that is inserted into a part of the body to inject or drain away fluid, or to keep a passage open. Catheters also have many diagnostic and surgical applications. [Early 17thC. Via late Latin from Greek *kathetēr*, from *kathienai* 'to send down', from *hienai* 'to send'.]

catheterize /káthitə rīz/ (**-izes, -izing, -ized**), **catheterise** (**-ises, -ising, -ised**) vt. to insert a catheter into a patient or a specific part of the body —**catheterization** n.

cathexis /ka théksis, kə-/ (plural **-es** /-seez/) n. PSYCHOANAL the concentration of a great deal of psychological and emotional energy on one particular person, thing, or idea [Early 20thC. From Greek *kathexis* 'holding' from *katekhein* 'to hold fast', from *ekhein* 'to hold'. Translation of German *Besetzung*.]

cathode /káthōd/ n. **1.** NEGATIVE ELECTRODE the negative electrode of an electrolytic cell **2.** ELECTRON SOURCE the negatively charged source of electrons in a valve **3.** POSITIVE TERMINAL the positive terminal of a cell that is producing electrical energy by a chemical process that cannot be reversed [Mid-19thC. From Greek *kathodos*, literally 'way down', from *kata* 'down' + *hodos* 'way'.] —**cathodal** /ka thŏd'l/ adj. —**cathodally** /-d'li/ adv.

cathode ray n. a stream of electrons that is emitted from a cathode in a vacuum tube

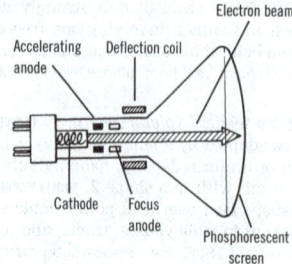

Cathode ray tube

cathode ray tube n. a vacuum tube in which a stream of electrons is produced and directed onto a fluorescent screen, e.g. in a television or visual display unit, creating images and text

cathodic /ka thóddik, ka thŏdik/ adj. relating to or involving a cathode —**cathodically** adv.

cathodic protection n. the prevention of electrolytic corrosion in sth metallic, e.g. an underground pipe or a ship, by making it the cathode in an electrolytic cell

cat hole n. either of two holes at the stern of a ship through which large ropes are passed

catholic /káthlik, káthəlik/ adj. **1.** ALL-INCLUSIVE including or concerned with all people **2.** USEFUL TO ALL useful or interesting to a wide range of people **3.** ALL-EMBRACING interested in or sympathetic to a wide range of things [14thC. Via Latin *catholicus* from, ultimately, Greek *katholikos* 'universal', from *katholou* 'in general', from *kata* 'in regard to' + *holos* 'whole'.] —**catholically** adv.

Catholic adj. **1.** ROMAN CATHOLIC belonging to or characteristic of the Roman Catholic Church **2.** CHRISTIAN belonging to the community of all Christian churches **3.** OF THE HISTORICAL UNITED CHURCH belonging to the united Christian church that existed before its separation into different churches, or to any church that regards itself as continuing the traditions of that united church ■ *n.* CHURCH MEMBER a member of the Roman Catholic Church [14thC. Via Christian Latin from Greek *katholikē (ekklēsia)* 'universal church', from *katholikos* (see CATHOLIC).]

Catholic Church n. **1.** = Roman Catholic Church **2.** CHURCH DESCENDED FROM ANCIENT CHRISTIAN CHURCH any church that regards itself as continuing the traditions of the Christian church before it was divided into separate churches

Catholic Epistles npl. the New Testament Epistles of James I and II, Peter, John, and Jude, addressed to the Christian churches as a whole rather than to a local church

catholicise, **Catholicise** vti. = catholicize, Catholicize

Catholicism /kə thóllisizzəm/ n. **1.** CATHOLIC BELIEFS the beliefs, doctrines, and rituals of a Catholic church, especially those of the Roman Catholic Church **2.** MEMBERSHIP OF CATHOLIC CHURCH membership of a Catholic church, especially that of the Roman Catholic Church

catholicity /káthə lissəti/ n. **1.** WIDENESS OF RANGE wideness of range of tastes or interests **2.** INCLUSIVENESS the quality of including or applying to everyone or everything

Catholicity /káthə lissəti/ n. = Catholicism

catholicize /kə thólli sīz/ (**-cizes, -cizing, -cized**), **catholicise** (**-cises, -cising, -cised**) vti. to broaden sth, e.g. an idea, classification, or range of things, to include or apply to many or all things or people, or become broader in this way

Catholicize (**-cizes, -cizing, -cized**), **Catholicise** (**-cises, -cising, -cised**) vti. to convert sb to Catholicism, or be converted to Catholicism

catholicon /kə thóllikən/ n. a remedy that is supposed to cure every ailment (archaic) [Early 17thC. Via French from modern Latin *catholicum* (remedium) 'universal (remedy)', from Greek *katholikos* (see CATHOLIC).]

Catiline /káttə līn/ (108?–62 BC) Roman conspirator. His plan to foment revolution by assassinating Marcus Cicero failed, and he was killed in battle with republican forces. Full name **Lucius Sergius Catilina**

cation /kátt ʃ ən/ n. an ion that has a positive electrical charge and is attracted towards the cathode in electrolysis [Mid-19thC. Coined from Greek *kata* 'down' + ION.] —**cationic** /kátt ʃ ónnik/ adj.

catkin /kátkin/ n. a long hanging furry cluster of tiny leaves and petal-less flowers, produced by trees such as willows, birches, alders, and poplars [Late 16thC. From obsolete Dutch *katteken* 'kitten'.]

Catlins /káttlinz/ scenic area of southeastern South Island, New Zealand, bounded by the Rata and Beresford ranges

cat litter n. absorbent material that is used to fill a box in which a cat can urinate and defecate indoors

catmint /kátmint/ n. a plant of the mint family that has greyish leaves, blue or white flowers, and a strong smell that attracts cats. Genus: *Nepeta*. US = catnip

catnap /kát nap/ n. SHORT SLEEP a short, light sleep ■ *vi.* (**-naps, -napping, -napped**) TAKE A SHORT SLEEP to take a short, light sleep, or several short light sleeps [From the cat's habit of sleeping lightly during the day] —**catnapper** n.

catnip /kátnip/ n. = **catmint** [Early 18thC. *Nip*, variant of obsolete *nep* 'catmint', via Old English *nepta* from Latin *nepeta*, of uncertain origin.]

cat-o'-nine-tails (*plural* **cat-o'-nine-tails**) n. a whip with several, usually nine, strands of knotted rope, used in the past for flogging prisoners and as a punishment in the armed forces

catoptric /kə tóptrik/, **catoptrical** /-trik'l/ adj. relating to or involving a mirror or reflection [Mid-16thC. From Greek *katoptrikos*, from *katoptron* 'mirror', literally 'sth that looks back'; related to *optos* 'seen' (see OPTIC).]

catoptrics /kə tóptriks/ n. the branch of optics that deals with mirrors and reflection (*takes a singular verb*)

Cato the Elder /káy tō-/, **Marcus Portius** (234–149 BC) Roman general and statesman. As censor he fought against Greek cultural influence and against the luxury and immorality of Rome. Known as **the Censor**

CAT scan n. = **CT scan**

CAT scanner n. = **CT scanner**

cat's cradle n. a children's game in which a loop of string is threaded between the fingers of both hands in variable complex patterns [Origin uncertain: perhaps an alteration of 'cratch cradle', the manger in which the infant Jesus was laid, from an alteration of French *crèche* 'CRECHE']

cat scratch disease, **cat scratch fever** n. an illness marked by fever and swollen lymph glands, thought to be caused by a bacterium transmitted to humans by the scratch of a cat

cat's eye /káts ī/ n. 1. SEMIPRECIOUS STONE any of various gemstones, especially chrysoberyl and chalcedony, that when cut in a rounded shape reflect a narrow silvery band of light that seems to come from within 2. GLASS MARBLE a clear glass marble with a core or swirl of colour at the centre

Catseye /káts ī/ tdmk. a trademark for a small reflecting device that is set into a road surface, kerb, or post to assist drivers at night in staying on the road or within lanes

cat's paw n. 1. SB USED AS A TOOL sb who is tricked or manipulated into doing sth for another person, without understanding what is happening, as in the fable of the fox and the cat 2. LOOPED KNOT a hitch with two loops, for attaching a rope to a hook

cat's pyjamas n. = **cat's whiskers** (*dated slang*)

catsuit /kát soot, -syoot/ n. a close-fitting one-piece garment that covers the whole body and has long sleeves and trouser legs [So called because it gives a sleek outline]

catsup /kátsəp/ n. = **ketchup**

cat's whiskers n. an excellent or special person or thing (*dated slang*)

cattalo /káttəlō/ n. (*plural* **-loes** *or* **-los**) n. = **beefalo** [Late 19thC. Blend of CATTLE and BUFFALO.]

cattery /káttəri/ n. (*plural* **-ies**) n. a place where cats are bred or boarded

cattish /káttish/ adj. = **catty** —**cattishly** adv. —**cattishness** n.

cattle /kátt'l/ npl. (*takes a plural verb*) 1. FARM ANIMALS OF THE OX FAMILY large domesticated mammals kept for the production of milk, meat, and hides, and also as draught animals. Cows and oxen are common types of cattle. Genus: *Bos*. 2. PEOPLE REGARDED AS ANIMALS people who are regarded as belonging to a low order, especially a crowd of people regarded as an unthinking mass (*disapproving*) [13thC. Via Anglo-Norman *catel* from, ultimately, Latin *capitale* 'funds'.]

cattle cake n. a manufactured food for cattle, concentrated and formed into blocks

cattle dog n. a breed of dog developed in Australia for herding and guarding cattle, with a blue-grey coat often speckled with black or brown, and black markings on the head

cattle egret n. a small, white, yellow-billed egret that often feeds on insects stirred up by cattle, native to Africa, southern Europe, and Asia and now widespread in the southeastern United States. Latin name: *Bubulus ibis*.

cattle grid n. a grid of metal bars over a shallow pit in a road, designed to stop animals, but not people or vehicles, leaving an enclosed area. US term **cattle guard**

cattle guard n. *US* = **cattle grid**

cattleman /kátt'lman, -mən/ (*plural* **-men** /-men/) n. sb who works with cattle, or who owns and raises cattle

cattle plague n. = **rinderpest**

cattle prod n. an electrified rod designed for driving and controlling cattle by giving them mild shocks

cattle stop n. *NZ* = **cattlegrid**

cattle truck n. a railway wagon for transporting livestock. US term **stock car**

cattleya /kátti ə/ n. (*plural* **-yas**) n. an orchid with decorative purple, pink, or white flowers that grows mainly as an epiphyte in tropical America and is also a popular greenhouse plant. Genus: *Cattleya*. [Early 19thC. From modern Latin, genus name, named after William *Cattley* (died 1832), English patron of botany.]

cat train n. *Canadian* in northern regions of Canada, a series of linked sled ges mounted on runners that is pulled over snow by a tractor with Caterpillar™ treads

catty /kátti/ (**-tier, -tiest**) adj. 1. SLYLY MEAN spiteful or malicious, especially in a subtle way 2. RESEMBLING CAT like a cat, especially in being cautious or secretive —**cattily** adv. —**cattiness** n.

catty-cornered, **catty-corner** adj. = **cater-cornered**

Catullus /kə túlləs/, **Gaius Valerius** (84?–54? BC) Roman poet. He wrote love poems addressed to 'Lesbia' and satirical attacks on Julius Caesar. —**Catullan** adj.

CATV abbr. community antenna television

catwalk /kát wawk/ n. 1. RAISED PLATFORM a long narrow raised platform along which the models walk in a fashion show 2. HIGH WALKWAY a narrow walkway high above the ground, e.g. along the side of a building or behind the stage in a theatre [So named because cats can walk safely along sth narrow]

Caucasia /kaw káyzi ə, -zhə/ region of southeastern Europe and southwestern Asia, divided by the Caucasian Mountains and containing Georgia, Armenia, Azerbaijan, and southern Russia. Area: 400,000 sq. km/150,000 sq. mi.

Caucasian /kaw káyzi ən, -zh'n/ adj. 1. ETHNOL OF FORMER ETHNIC GROUP belonging to or typical of the light-skinned peoples of Europe, North Africa, western Asia, and India, formerly considered as a distinct ethnic group (*no longer in technical use*) 2. WHITE-SKINNED relating to people who are white or of European origin 3. OF CAUCASIA belonging to or from Caucasia 4. LANG OF LANGUAGES OF CAUCASIA belonging or relating to either of two unrelated languages spoken in the area around the Caucasus Mountains ■ n. 1. ETHNOL MEMBER OF FORMER ETHNIC GROUP a member of the former Caucasian ethnic group (*no longer in technical use*) 2. WHITE PERSON sb white or of European origin 3. PEOPLES SB FROM CAUCASIA sb who lives in or comes from Caucasia 4. LANG LANGUAGES OF CAUCASIA either of two unrelated language families spoken in the area around the Caucasus Mountains, Kartvelian or South Caucasian, and North Caucasian [Early 17thC. Named after CAUCASIA, where the group of people was mistakenly thought to have originated.]

Caucasoid /káwkə soyd, -zoyd/ adj., n. = **Caucasian** adj. 1 ■ n. = **Caucasian** n. 1

Caucasus Mountains /káwkəssəss-/ mountain range that is considered a boundary between Europe and Asia, extending through Georgia, Armenia, Azerbaijan, and southwestern Russia. Its highest peak is El'brus 5,642 m/18,510 ft.

caucus /káwkəss/ n. 1. POLITICAL MEETING a closed meeting from one political party, especially a local meeting to select delegates or candidates, or a meeting of party representatives at national level to decide policy 2. SPECIAL-INTEREST GROUP a group of people, often within a larger group, e.g. a legislative assembly, who unite to promote a particular policy or particular interests ■ vi. (**-cuses, -cusing, -cused**) FORM A CAUCUS to hold or meet in a caucus [Mid-18thC.

Origin uncertain: perhaps from Algonquian *cau'-cau'-as'u* 'elder, adviser'.]

caudal /káwd'l/ adj. 1. OF A TAIL relating to, involving, typical of, or like a tail 2. IN HIND PART OF BODY situated in or extending towards the hind part of the body [Mid-17thC. From modern Latin *caudalis*, from Latin *cauda* 'tail'.] —**caudally** adv.

caudate /káw dayt/, **caudated** /-daytid/ adj. with a tail or an appendage like a tail [Early 17thC. From medieval Latin *caudatus*, from Latin *cauda* 'tail'.] —**caudation** /kaw dáysh'n/ n.

caudex /káw deks/ (*plural* **-dices** /-diseez/ *or* **-dexes**) n. 1. STEM a trunk of a tree that bears leaves only at its apex, as in a palm or tree fern 2. STEM BASE the swollen stem base of certain nonwoody perennial plants that survives over the winter and from which new growth is produced [Late 18thC. From Latin, 'tree trunk', a variant of *codex* (source of English *codex*), of unknown origin.]

caudillo /kow deé yō, -lyō/ (*plural* **-los**) n. a military or political leader, especially a dictator, in a Spanish-speaking country [Mid-19thC. Via Spanish, 'leader', from late Latin *capitellum* 'little head', from *caput* 'head'.]

caudle /káwd'l/ n. a drink made of hot ale or wine, with bread or oatmeal, sugar, and spices [13thC. Via Old Northern French from, ultimately, Latin *caldum* 'hot drink', from *calidus* 'hot'.]

caught past tense, past participle of **catch**

caul /kawl/ n. 1. MEMBRANE IN THE WOMB the membrane surrounding the amniotic fluid, a part of which sometimes covers a baby's head when it is born 2. = **omentum** [14thC. Origin uncertain.]

cauldron /káwldrən/, **caldron** n. a large metal pot in which liquids are boiled [13thC. Via Anglo-Norman and Old Norman French *caudron* from late Latin *calderia* 'cooking pot', from, ultimately, Latin *calidus* 'hot'.]

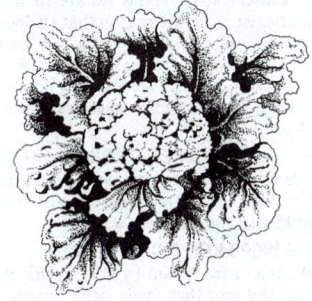

Cauliflower

cauliflower /kólli flowər/ n. 1. PLANTS VEGETABLE PLANT a plant that is related to the cabbage and has green leaves surrounding a large solid head of edible white or light-green flowers. Latin name: *Brassica oleracea* var. *botrytis*. 2. FOOD FLOWER HEAD EATEN AS VEGETABLE the flower head of the cauliflower plant, eaten as a vegetable [Late 16thC. Alteration of modern Latin *cauliflora*, from Latin *caulis* 'stem' + *flor-*, the stem of *flos* 'flower'.]

cauliflower cheese n. a hot dish of cauliflower with cheese sauce

cauliflower ear n. an ear that is permanently swollen and misshapen as a result of bleeding into the ear tissues after being repeatedly struck, usually in boxing

caulk /kawk/, **calk** vt. (**caulks, caulking, caulked; calks, calking, calked**) 1. MAKE BOAT WATERTIGHT to make a boat or the seams between its planks watertight by filling the seams with waterproof material, e.g. pitch 2. STOP STH UP to stop up the cracks or gaps in sth, e.g. a pipe or a window frame, with a waterproof material ■ n. STH USED TO FILL GAPS material used to make a boat watertight by filling in its seams, or to stop up the cracks or gaps in sth. US term **caulking** [15thC. Via Old Northern French *cauquer* 'to tread, stamp down' from Latin *calcare*, from *calc-*, the stem of *calx* 'heel' (source of English *inculcate*).] —**caulker** n.

caulking /káwking/ n. = **caulk**

caus. abbr. GRAM causative

causal /káwz'l/ *adj.* **1. BEING OR INVOLVING THE CAUSE** involving or being the cause of sth else or the relationship of cause and effect **2.** GRAM **EXPRESSING A CAUSE** expressing or indicating a cause or the relationship of cause and effect ■ *n.* GRAM **WORD EXPRESSING CAUSE** a word or other grammatical element that expresses the reason or cause of sth, or a relationship of cause and effect —**causally** *adv.*

causalgia /kaw záljə/ *n.* a persistent burning sensation of the skin, caused usually by injury to a peripheral nerve [Mid-19thC. Coined from Greek *kausos* 'burning' + -ALGIA.] —**causalgic** *adj.*

causality /kaw zálləti/ *n.* **1. PRINCIPLE OF CAUSE AND EFFECT** the principle that everything that happens must have a cause **2. QUALITY OF CAUSING EFFECT** the action that causes an effect, or the ability to cause an effect

causation /kaw záysh'n/ *n.* **1. CAUSE OR ACT OF CAUSING** the fact that sth causes an effect, or the action of causing an effect **2. CAUSE-AND-EFFECT RELATIONSHIP** the relationship between a cause and its effect

causative /káwzətiv/ *adj.* **1. INVOLVING CAUSE AND EFFECT** involving being the cause of sth or the relationship of the cause and effect **2.** GRAM **EXPRESSING CAUSE** used to describe verbs that express the action of sth causing sth else ■ *n.* GRAM **CAUSATIVE VERB** a causative verb, or a form or class of causative verbs —**causatively** *adv.* —**causativeness** *n.*

cause /kawz/ *n.* **1. WHAT MAKES STH HAPPEN** sth that or sb who makes sth happen or exist or is responsible for a certain result ○ *the cause of all the uproar* **2. REASON** a reason or grounds for doing or feeling sth ○ *no cause for complaint* **3. PRINCIPLE** a principle or idea that people believe in and work for **4. INTEREST** the interests and aims of a group of people **5.** LAW **LEGAL CASE** a lawsuit, or the reason that a suit is brought in a court of law **6. DISCUSSION SUBJECT** sth under discussion or to be decided (*old*) ■ *vt.* (**causes, causing, caused**) **BE THE REASON FOR STH** to make sth happen or exist or be the reason that sb does sth or sth happens [13thC. Via Old French from Latin *causa* 'reason, motive, lawsuit' (source of English *accuse* and *excuse*), of unknown origin.] —**causability** /káwzə bílləti/ *n.* —**causable** /káwzəb'l/ *adj.* —**causeless** /-ləss/ *adj.* —**causer** /-ər/ *n.*

WORD KEY: ORIGIN

Cause is derived from the Latin word *causa*, meaning 'reason', 'motive', or 'lawsuit', which is also the source of English *accuse* and *excuse*.

WORD KEY: CULTURAL NOTE

Rebel Without a Cause, a film by US director Nicholas Ray (1955). The film that made actor James Dean a symbol of an alienated generation, it is the story of Jim, a youth who seems unable to stay out of trouble. His attempts to win the affections of a local girl, Judy, lead to conflict with her boyfriend and, ultimately, tragedy.

'cause /kəz, koz/ *conj.* because (*informal*) [15thC. Shortening.]

cause célèbre /kőz sə lébbrə, káwz-/ (*plural* **causes célèbres** /kőz sə lébbrəz, káwz-/) *n.* a legal case or public controversy that arouses great interest and becomes famous, because of the issues or the people involved [From French, literally 'celebrated case']

causerie /kőzəri/ *n.* **1. CHAT** an informal conversation (*literary*) **2.** LITERAT **INFORMAL PIECE OF WRITING** a short piece of writing in a light informal style [Early 19thC. From French, via *causer* 'to chat' from Latin *causari* 'to discuss', from *causa* 'case, subject'.]

causeway /káwz way/ *n.* **1. RAISED PATH** a raised path or road through a marsh or water or across land that is sometimes covered by water **2. PAVED ROAD** a road or path with a paved or cobbled surface [15thC. Formed from CAUSEY + WAY.]

Causeway Coast /káwz way-/ area in northeastern Northern Ireland, that includes The Giant's Causeway, a World Heritage Site and one of Northern Ireland's top tourist sites

causey /káwzi/ (*plural* **-eys**) *n.* **1. CAUSEWAY** a causeway (*archaic*) **2.** *Scotland* **COBBLED STREET** a cobbled road or street [12thC. Via Anglo-Norman *caucie* from medieval Latin *calciata (via)* 'paved (road)', from Latin *calx* 'limestone'.]

caustic /káwstik/ *adj.* **1.** CHEM **CORRODING** corrosive or burning by chemical action **2. SARCASTIC** very sarcastic, in a way that is particularly bitter or cutting or causes intensely bad emotions ■ *n.* **1.** CHEM **SUBSTANCE THAT CORRODES** a substance that can corrode or burn away other substances by chemical action, especially a strong alkali **2.** OPTICS **CURVE FORMED BY REFLECTIONS** a peaked curve formed on a plane by parallel light rays reflected or refracted from a cylindrical or spherical surface. Caustics can sometimes be seen on the surface of drinks in glazed mugs or cups, or on the base of the mug or cup when empty. [14thC. Via Latin from Greek *kaustikos*, from *kaustos* 'combustible', from *kaiein* 'to burn' (see CAUTERY).] —**caustical** *adj.* —**caustically** *adv.* —**causticness** *n.*

WORD KEY: SYNONYMS

See Synonyms at ***sarcastic***.

caustic potash *n.* = **potassium hydroxide**

caustic soda *n.* = **sodium hydroxide**

cauterize /káwtə rīz/ (**-izes, -izing, -ized**), **cauterise** (**-ises, -ising, -ised**) *vt.* to seal a wound, or destroy abnormal or infected tissue, with a heated instrument, a laser, an electric current, or a caustic substance [14thC. Via French *cautériser* from, ultimately, late Latin *cauterium* (see CAUTERY).] —**cauterization** /káwtə rī záysh'n/ *n.*

cautery /káwtəri/ (*plural* **-ies**) *n.* **1. STH USED TO CAUTERIZE TISSUE** an instrument or substance used to seal a wound or to destroy abnormal or infected tissue by burning **2. CAUTERIZATION** the process or action of sealing a wound or destroying abnormal or infected tissue by burning [14thC. Via Latin from Greek *kautērion* 'branding iron', from *kaiein* 'to burn' (source of English *caustic, holocaust*, and *calm*).]

caution /káwsh'n/ *n.* **1. CAREFULNESS** care, thoughtfulness, lack of haste, and close attention that enable sb to avoid any risks involved in a task or procedure **2. WARNING** a warning to sb to be careful about sth or in doing sth **3.** LAW **LEGAL WARNING** a formal warning given instead of a penalty to sb who has done sth illegal, advising that punishment will follow if it is repeated **4.** LAW **POLICE WARNING ABOUT EVIDENCE** a formal warning given by a police officer to sb who has been arrested that anything he or she says may be used in evidence **5. UNUSUAL PERSON** a surprising or amusing person or thing (*dated*) ■ *vt.* (**-tions, -tioning, -tioned**) **1. WARN** to warn or advise sb that sth is risky or dangerous **2.** LAW **GIVE LEGAL WARNING** to give sb who has done sth illegal a formal warning, instead of a penalty, advising that punishment will follow if it is repeated **3.** LAW **GIVE WARNING ABOUT EVIDENCE** to give a formal warning to sb who has been arrested that anything he or she says may be used in evidence [Late 16thC. Via French from the Latin stem *caution-*, from *caut-*, the past participle stem of *cavere* 'to take heed' (source also of English *caveat*).] —**cautioner** *n.* ◇ **throw caution to the wind(s)** to be reckless

cautionary /káwsh'nəri/ *adj.* involving, giving, or being a warning

caution money *n.* money deposited as security for good behaviour, e.g. by a student to cover damage to accommodation, furniture, or equipment [From CAUTION in the early meaning 'security']

cautious /káwshəss/ *adj.* having or showing care, thoughtfulness, restraint, and lack of haste [Mid-17thC. From CAUTION, on the model of *ambitious*.] —**cautiously** *adv.* —**cautiousness** *n.*

WORD KEY: SYNONYMS

cautious, careful, chary, circumspect, prudent, vigilant, wary, guarded, cagey

CORE MEANING: attentive to risk or danger

cautious a general term for being aware of potential risk and modifying your behaviour accordingly; **careful** taking reasonable care to avoid risks; **chary** extremely cautious, often to the extent of being reluctant to act; **circumspect** taking into consideration all possible circumstances and consequences before acting; **prudent** a term suggesting cautiousness arising from good judgment or shrewdness; **vigilant** extremely alert and conscious of possible dangers; **wary** combining vigilance with feelings of suspicion; **guarded** cautious about sharing information with others; **cagey** an informal term for 'guarded', suggesting an element of craftiness.

Cauvery /káwvəri/, **Kāveri** river in southern India. It rises in the Western Ghats, Karnataka State, and flows to the Bay of Bengal. Length: 764 km/475 mi.

Cav., cav. *abbr.* cavalry

Cava /kaávə/ *n.* sparkling white wine produced in Spain

cavalcade /kávv'l káyd/ *n.* **1. PROCESSION** a procession, especially one of people on horses, in carriages, or in cars **2. SERIES** a series or procession of things or people, especially a spectacular or dramatic one [Late 16thC. Via French from Italian *cavalcata*, from *cavalcare* 'to ride on horseback', via medieval Latin *caballicare* from Latin *caballus* 'horse'.]

cavalier /kávvə léer/ *adj.* **CARELESS** showing an arrogant or jaunty disregard or lack of respect for sth or sb ■ *n.* **1. GENTLEMAN** a gallant or chivalrous gentleman, especially one escorting a lady (*formal*) **2. MOUNTED SOLDIER** a knight or soldier who fought on horseback (*archaic*) [Mid-16thC. Via French from Italian *cavaliere* 'knight' from medieval Latin *caballarius* 'horseman', from Latin *caballus* 'horse', of unknown origin.] —**cavalierly** *adv.*

Cavalier /kávvə léer/ *n.* a supporter of King Charles I in the English Civil War. ◊ **Roundhead**

cavalla /kə vállə/ (*plural* **-la** *or* **-las**) *n.* a tropical marine fish with a flattened body and forked tail. Family: Carangidae. [Early 17thC. From Spanish *caballa* 'horse mackerel', via late Latin from Latin *caballus* 'horse'.]

cavalry /kávəlri/ (*plural* **-ries**) *n.* **1. SOLDIERS ON HORSEBACK** the part of an army made up of soldiers trained to fight on horseback **2. MOBILE TROOPS** the more mobile part of a modern army, using armoured vehicles and helicopters [Mid-16thC. Via French from Italian *cavalleria* 'mounted militia', from *cavallo* 'horse', from Latin *caballus*, of unknown origin.]

cavalryman /kávvəlrimən/ (*plural* **-men** /-mən/) *n.* a soldier belonging to a regiment of cavalry

cavalry twill *n.* hard-wearing worsted fabric used for making tailored sporting jackets and trousers [From its use in making riding breeches for soldiers]

Cavan /kávv'n/ one of the three counties of the province of Ulster. Population: 52,903 (1996). Area: 1,891 sq. km/730 sq. mi.

cavatina /kávvə teénə/ (*plural* **-nas** *or* **-ne** /-teéni/) *n.* **1. SIMPLE SONG** a short and simple operatic song, especially a slow aria of 18th- and 19th-century Italian opera, usually followed by a livelier cabaletta **2. INSTRUMENTAL MUSIC** a melodious and expressive piece of instrumental music, based loosely on the operatic cavatina [Early 19thC. From Italian.]

cave /kayv/ (**caves, caving, caved**) *n.* a large, naturally hollowed-out place in the ground, or in rock above ground, that can be reached from the surface or from water [13thC. Via Old French from, ultimately, Latin *cavus* 'hollow' (source also of English *cavern, cavity, concave*, and *excavate*).]

cave in *v.* **1.** *vti.* **COLLAPSE** to collapse or cause sth to collapse because of pressure or because of being undermined **2.** *vi.* **YIELD** to yield to persuasion or threats, after trying to resist

caveat /kávvi at, káy-/ *n.* **1. WARNING OR PROVISO** sth said as a warning, caution, or qualification **2.** LAW **REQUEST TO A COURT** an official request to a court not to proceed with a case without notice to the person making the request [Mid-16thC. From Latin, literally 'let him or her beware', from *cavere* 'to heed' (source of English *caution*).]

caveat emptor /-émp tawr, káy-/ *n.* the commercial principle that the buyer is responsible for making sure that goods bought are of a reasonable quality, unless the seller is offering a guarantee of their quality [Early 16thC. From Latin, 'let the buyer beware'.]

cavefish /káyv fish/ (*plural* **-fish** *or* **-fishes**) *n.* a small North American freshwater fish that lives in subterranean waters and has underdeveloped eyes. Family: Amblyopsidae.

cave-in *n.* **1. COLLAPSE** a collapse of sth caused by pressure or undermining **2. ROOF FALL** a place where sth has collapsed because of pressure or being undermined **3. YIELDING** a yielding to persuasion or threats, after trying to resist

Cavell /kávv'l/, **Edith** (1865–1915) British nurse. She was executed by the Germans during World War I for helping Allied soldiers escape from occupied Belgium.

caveman /kávv man/ (plural **-men** /-men/) n. **1. STONE AGE MAN** sb living in a cave, especially a prehistoric human being of the Palaeolithic period **2. BRUTE** a man who behaves in a brutish or uncivilized way (informal)

Cavendish /kávvəndish/, **Henry** (1731–1810) British chemist and physicist. He identified hydrogen, discovered that water is a compound, and measured the earth's density.

cave painting n. any of the paintings made on the walls of caves by Palaeolithic peoples in different parts of the world

caver /káyvər/ n. sb who explores and climbs in underground caves and passages for sport

cavern /kávv'n/ n. **LARGE CAVE** a large underground cave, or a large chamber in an underground series of caves ■ vt. (**-erns, -erning, -erned**) **1. MAKE STH HOLLOW** to make a mountain, cliff, or area of ground hollow **2. ENCLOSE** to enclose sth in a cave or cavern (literary) [14thC. Directly or via French caverne from Latin caverna, from cavus 'hollow' (see CAVE).]

cavernous /kávvərnəss/ adj. **1. LIKE CAVERN** like or suggestive of a cavern, especially in being large, dark, deep, and hollow **2. HOLLOW-SOUNDING** with a hollow, resonating sound —**cavernously** adv.

cavesson /kávvissən/ n. a stiff noseband used in breaking horses [Late 16thC. Via French caveçon from, ultimately, medieval Latin capitium 'head covering', from Latin capit-, the stem of caput 'head'.]

cavetto /kə véttō/ (plural **-ti** /-tee/) n. a concave architectural moulding with a curve that is roughly a quarter circle [Mid-17thC. From Italian, a diminutive of cavo 'hollow', from Latin cavus (see CAVE).]

caviar /kávvi aar, kávvi aár/, **caviare** n. the salted roe of a large fish, particularly the sturgeon, eaten as a delicacy [Mid-16thC. Via French caviar from Italian caviaro from Turkish havyar, from Persian dialect khāvyār.]

cavil /kávv'l, kávvil/ vi. (**-ils, -illing, -illed**) **OBJECT FOR NO GOOD REASON** to make objections about sth on small and unimportant points ■ n. **CARPING CRITICISM** a trivial and unreasonable objection [Mid-16thC. Via French caviller from Latin cavillari, from cavilla 'scoffing, mockery'.] —**caviller** n.

caving /káyving/ n. the activity of exploring and climbing in underground caves and passages for sport

cavitand /kávvi tand/ n. **CHEM** a molecule, especially a synthetic receptor, that is hollow and has one open end [Late 20thC. Formed from CAVITY.]

cavitate /kávvi tayt/ (**-tates, -tating, -tated**) vt. to form bubbles or cavities in a substance [Early 20thC. Back-formation from CAVITATION.]

cavitation /kávvi táysh'n/ n. **1. PHYS DISTURBANCE OF LIQUID** the rapid formation and collapse of bubbles in a liquid, caused by the movement of sth in the liquid, e.g. a propeller, or by waves of high-frequency sound **2. PITTING OF SURFACE** the pitting of a solid surface as a result of the forces of repeated cavitation in a surrounding liquid **3. MED FORMATION OF CAVITIES IN TISSUE** the formation of cavities in body tissue caused by a disease, e.g. as an effect of tuberculosis on the lungs [Late 19thC. From CAVITY + -ATION.]

cavity /kávvəti/ (plural **-ties**) n. **1. HOLLOW PLACE** a hole or hollow space in sth **2. DENT HOLE IN TOOTH** a hole in a tooth, caused by decay **3. ANAT HOLLOW WITHIN THE BODY** a hollow area inside the body [Mid-16thC. Via French cavité from late Latin cavitas, from Latin cavus 'hollow' (see CAVE).]

cavity block n. a concrete construction block made with cavities inside it

cavity wall n. an external wall of a building that is made up of a two leaves of masonry, bricks, or blocks separated by a cavity. This prevents moisture penetration and improves thermal insulation.

cavo-relievo /kaávō ri leévō, káyvō-/ (plural **cavo-relievos** or **cavo-relievi** /-vi/), **cavo-rilievo** (plural **cavo-rilievos** or **cavo-rilievi**) n. a relief sculpture in which even the highest part lies below the level of the original surface, or this style of relief sculpture [Late 19thC. From Italian, 'hollow relief'.]

cavort /kə váwrt/ (**-vorts, -vorting, -vorted**) vi. to behave in a physically lively and uninhibited way [Late 18thC. Origin uncertain: perhaps an alteration of CURVET.]

Cavour /kə voór, -váwr/, **Camillo Benso, Conte di** (1810–61) Italian statesman. He was prime minister of Piedmont (1852–59, 1860–61) and chief architect of the unification of Italy (1861). Full name **Camilo Benso, Conte di Cavour**

cavy /káyvi/ (plural **-vies**) n. a short-tailed ground-living South American rodent of the family that includes the guinea pig. Family: Caviidae. [Late 18thC. Via modern Latin Cavia, genus name, from Galibi cabiai.]

caw /kaw/ vi. (**caws, cawing, cawed**) **MAKE BIRD CALL** to make the loud harsh cry of a crow or a related bird, or make a sound like this ■ n. **BIRD'S CRY** the loud harsh cry of a crow or a related bird, or a sound like this [Late 16thC. An imitation of the sound.]

Cawdor /káwdər/ parish in the Highland Region, northern Scotland, situated 8 km/5 mi. southwest of Nairn

Cawley /káwli/, **Evonne Fay** (b. 1951) Australian tennis player. She won the Wimbledon women's singles championship in 1971 and again in 1980. Born **Evonne Fay Goolagong**

Caxton /kákstən/, **William** (1422?–91) English printer. He established the first printing press in England (1477) and printed over 100 books, including The Canterbury Tales.

cay /kee, kay/ n. a small low island or reef in the sea, made of coral or sand, especially in the Caribbean [Late 17thC. Via Spanish cayo 'shoal', of uncertain origin: probably from Taino.]

Cayenne /kay én, kī én/ city and capital of French Guiana, situated in the northern coast of Cayenne Island. Population: 41,667 (1990).

cayenne pepper, **cayenne** n. a very hot-tasting red powder made of the dried and ground fruit and seeds of several kinds of chilli. It is used in cooking. [Early 18thC. Alteration of earlier kian (from Tupi kyynha), by association with CAYENNE.]

cayman /káymən/ (plural **caymans** or **cayman**), **caiman** (plural **caimans** or **caiman**) n. a Central and South American reptile of the alligator family that looks like a much smaller slimmer version of the alligator with a proportionally longer tail. Genus: Caiman.

Cayman Islands /káymən-/ group of three islands, situated in the northwestern Caribbean Sea, approximately 320 km/200 mi. northwest of Jamaica. Capital: George Town. Population: 25,355 (1990). Area: 306 sq. km/118 sq. mi.

Cayuga /kay oógə, kī yoógə/ (plural **-ga** or **-gas**) n. a member of a Native American people who originally occupied lands along Cayuga Lake, and whose members now live mainly in western New York State, Wisconsin, Ontario, and Oklahoma. The Cayuga were one of the five peoples who formed the Iroquois Confederacy, later known as the Six Nations. [Mid-18thC. From the Cayuga language, literally 'the place where locusts were taken out'.] —**Cayuga** adj.

Cayuga Lake one of the Finger Lakes, situated in Cayuga and Seneca counties, central New York State. Area: 171 sq. km/66 sq. mi.

cayuse /kī ooss/ n. Northwest US a small pony of a western North American breed [Mid-19thC. Shortening of Cayuse pony, named after the Cayuse, a Native American people of the Pacific Northwest.]

Cazaly /kázzəli/, **Roy** (1893–1963) Australian, Australian Rules footballer, noted for his ability to take high catches. He spent most of his career with St Kilda.

Cazneaux /káznō/, **Harold Pierce** (1878–1953) New Zealand-born Australian photographer. He was a leading figure in the Australian pictorialist school of photography.

CB abbr. **1. RADIO** Citizens' Band **2.** Companion of the (Order of the) Bath (used as a title)

CBA abbr. cost-benefit analysis

CBC abbr. Canadian Broadcasting Corporation

CBD abbr. **1. CBD, cbd** cash before delivery **2.** central business district

CBE abbr. Commander of the (Order of the) British Empire (used as a title)

CBI abbr. **1.** computer-based instruction **2.** Confederation of British Industry

CBR abbr. **ARMS, MIL** chemical, bacteriological, and radiation

CBS abbr. Columbia Broadcasting System

CBT abbr. computer-based training

CBW abbr. chemical and biological warfare

cc, c.c. abbr. **1. BUSINESS** (carbon) copy **2.** cubic centimetre **3. AUTOMOT, MEASURE** cubic capacity (used after a number to indicate the power of an internal-combustion engine)

CC abbr. **1.** City Council **2.** County Council **3.** Cricket Club

cc. abbr. chapters

CCA abbr. current-cost accounting

CCD abbr. **COMPUT** charge-coupled device

CCF abbr. Combined Cadet Force

CCK abbr. cholecystokinin

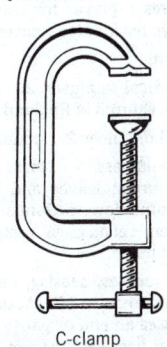

C-clamp

C-clamp n. a metal clamp shaped like a letter C, with horizontal flat pieces at the ends, that can be adjusted by a screw

C clef n. a symbol on a musical stave that shows the position of middle C. The alto and tenor clefs are the only commonly used C clefs today, and are used mostly in viola, cello, and bassoon music.

CCTV abbr. closed-circuit television

CCU abbr. coronary care unit

cd symbol. candela

Cd symbol. **1.** cadmium ■ abbr. **2. POL** command (paper) (used before a serial number)

CD abbr. **1.** compact disc **2.** Civil Defence **3.** Corps Diplomatique (often displayed on the backs of cars that belong to embassies)

c.d. abbr. cash discount

c/d abbr. **1. ACCT** carried down **2.** cum dividend

CDE n. a compact disk that can have its contents erased and sth else recorded onto it. Full form **compact disc erasable**. ◊ CDR

cdf abbr. **STATS** cumulative distribution function

CDI, CD-I n. an interactive compact disc containing text, video, and audio and accessed using a self-contained player plugged into a television set. Full form **compact disc interactive**

Cdn abbr. Canadian

CDN abbr. Canada (international vehicle registration)

cDNA abbr. complementary DNA

Cdr, CDR abbr. Commander

CDR n. a compact disc that can be used to record sth but cannot be erased. Full form **compact disc recordable**. ◊ CDE

Cdre abbr. Commodore

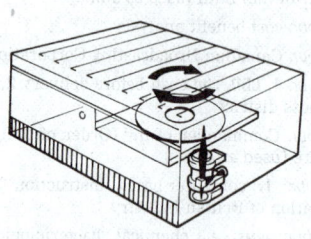

CD-ROM within a disk drive

CD-ROM /seé dee róm/ n. a compact disc containing a large amount of data, including text and images, that can be viewed using a computer but cannot be altered or erased. Full form **compact disc read-only memory**

CDT a school subject that can be studied to GCSE level. Full form **Craft, Design, and Technology**

CDU the Christian Democratic Union, a political party in Germany. Full form **Christlich-Demokratische Union**

CDV abbr. 1. CD-video 2. compact video disc

CD-video n. 1. COMPACT DISC WITH VIDEO IMAGES a compact disc used to store and play back video images 2. PLAYER FOR CD-VIDEOS a player for compact discs that stores and plays back video images

Ce symbol. cerium

CE abbr. 1. chemical engineer 2. chief engineer 3. Common Era 4. Church of England 5. civil engineer

C.E. abbr. 1. civil engineer 2. Common Era

ceanothus /seé ə nóthəss/ n. a North American shrub that has dark green leaves and tiny clusters of blue, white, or pink flowers. Genus: *Ceanothus*. [Late 18thC. Via modern Latin, genus name, from Greek *keanōthos*, a kind of thistle.]

cease /seess/ v. (ceases, ceasing, ceased) 1. vi. STOP HAPPENING to come to an end 2. vti. END to bring sth to an end ▪ n. ENDING an end or pause (archaic) [14thC. Via French *cesser* from Latin *cessare*, from *cedere* (see CEDE).] ◇ **without cease** without stopping, or without a break

ceasefire /seéss fīr/ n. 1. AGREEMENT TO STOP FIGHTING an agreement between opposing sides in a conflict that they will stop fighting, usually for a limited time during which they will try to reach a more permanent peace agreement 2. ORDER TO STOP FIRING a military order to stop firing

ceaseless /seéssləss/ adj. without pause or end — **ceaselessly** adv. —**ceaselessness** n.

Ceauşescu /chow shéskoo/, **Nicolae** (1918–89) Romanian former head of state. The Communist president of Romania (1967–89), he was overthrown and executed in a popular revolution.

Cebu /si boó/ island of the Philippines, in the Pacific Ocean, near the islands of Negros and Mindanao. Population: 2,646,000 (1990). Area: 4,422 sq. km/1,707 sq. mi.

Cecchetti /che kétti/, **Enrico** (1850–1928) Italian ballet dancer, choreographer, and teacher. Dancers trained by his technique included Anna Pavlova, Alicia Markova, and Leonide Massine.

Cecilia /sə seéli ə/, **St** (?–230?) Roman Christian martyr. She is regarded as the patron saint of music.

cecropia moth /si krópi ə-/ n. a large North American moth with red, white, and black wings that has a silkworm caterpillar. Latin name: *Hyalophora cecropia*. [Mid-19thC. Via modern Latin, species name, named after CECROPS.]

Cecrops /seé krops/ n. in Greek mythology, the first king of Attica and founder of Athens.

cecum n. US = caecum

CED abbr. Committee for Economic Development

cedar /seédər/ n. 1. TALL EVERGREEN TREE a tall evergreen tree of Europe, Asia, and Africa, with spreading branches, needles, and large rounded upright cones. Genus: *Cedrus*. 2. TREE LIKE TRUE CEDAR an evergreen tree that resembles a true cedar, e.g. a red cedar 3. WOOD FROM CEDAR the durable fragrant wood of a cedar tree [Pre-12thC. Via Old French *cedre* from, ultimately, Greek *kedros* 'cedar, juniper', of unknown origin.]

Cedar City city in southwestern Utah, north of Zion National Park and northeast of Saint George. Population: 17,811 (1996).

Cedar of Lebanon

cedar of Lebanon n. a tall long-lived cedar with horizontally spreading branches that grows in Lebanon and Turkey. Latin name: *Cedrus libari*.

cede /seed/ (cedes, ceding, ceded) vt. to surrender or give up sth, e.g. land, rights, or power, to another country, group, or person (formal) [Early 16thC. Via French *céder* from Latin *cedere* 'to give way' (source of English *concede, precede, excess,* and *ancestor*).]

─── WORD KEY: ORIGIN ───

Cede is derived from the Latin word *cedere*, meaning 'to give way', which is also the source of English *abscess, accede, ancestor, concede, decease, exceed, precede, predecessor, proceed, procession, recede,* and *succeed.*

cedi /seédi/ (plural **-di**) n. 1. UNIT OF GHANAIAN CURRENCY: the main unit of currency in Ghana, worth 100 pesewas see table at **currency** 2. COIN OR NOTE WORTH A CEDI a coin or note worth a cedi [Mid-20thC. Origin uncertain: possibly from Akan (Fanti) *sedī* 'small shell, cowrie'.]

cedilla /sə díllə/ (plural **-las**) n. a mark placed beneath the letters c (ç) and s (ş) in some languages. In French and Portuguese, it shows that c is pronounced like s, not k. In modern Turkish it shows whether c and s are voiced or voiceless. [Late 16thC. Via obsolete Spanish, literally 'little z', from Latin *zeta*.]

Ceefax /seé faks/ tdmk. a trademark for the teletext service of the BBC

CEGEP /sáy zhép/, **cegep** n. in Quebec, a post-secondary institution offering two-year programmes leading to university and three-year programmes qualifying students in a variety of professions and trades. Full form **Collège d'Enseignement Général et Professionel**

ceiba /sáybə/ (plural **-bas**) n. a large tropical tree that has seed pods containing a silky fibre from which kapok is obtained. Latin name: *Ceiba pentandra*. US term **silk-cotton tree** [Early 17thC. Via Spanish from Arawak, literally 'giant tree'.]

ceil /seel/ (ceils, ceiling, ceiled) vt. 1. PROVIDE WITH CEILING to construct a ceiling for a room 2. LINE A CEILING to line a ceiling with a material, e.g. plaster or wood [Early 16thC. Origin uncertain: perhaps via Old French, 'canopy', from Latin *caelum* 'heaven'; or via assumed Old French *celer* from Latin *caelare* 'to carve', from *caelum* 'chisel'.]

ceilidh n. 1. FOLK MUSIC AND STORYTELLING PARTY a social event with singing and dancing to Scottish or Irish traditional music and storytelling 2. Ireland EVENING VISIT an evening visit [Late 19thC. Via Irish *céilidhe* and Scots Gaelic *ceilidh* from Old Irish *célide* 'visit', from *céle* 'companion'.]

ceiling /seéling/ n. 1. BUILDING INSIDE TOP OF ROOM the overhead surface of a room, or the material used to line this surface 2. UPPER LIMIT a level above which sth is not allowed to rise, e.g. prices, rents, or wages 3. AIR FLYING HEIGHT the maximum height at which an aircraft can fly 4. METEOROL CLOUD LEVEL the highest point, usually the base of a layer of clouds, from which the surface of the Earth can be seen [Mid-16thC. Formed from CEIL.] —**ceilinged** adj. ◇ **go through the ceiling** to rise to a very high level ◇ **hit the ceiling** to become very angry

ceiling rose n. = **rose**[1] n. 8

ceilometer /see lómmitər/ n. an instrument for measuring the height of a cloud ceiling [Mid-20thC. Formed from CEILING.]

Cela /séllə, théllə/, **Camilo José** (b. 1916) Spanish novelist. A starkly realistic writer, he won the Nobel Prize for literature (1989) for such works as *The Family of Pascual Duarte* (1942) and *The Hive* (1951).

celadon /sél),ədən, -don/ n. 1. COLOURS PALE GREEN COLOUR a pale green colour tinged with grey 2. CERAMICS GREY-GREEN PORCELAIN a type of Chinese porcelain with a greyish-green glaze [Mid-18thC. From French *céladon*, from the name of a character in D'Urfé's romance *L'Astrée*.] —**celadon** adj.

Celaeno /se leénō/ n. in Greek mythology, one of the Pleiades

Celan /sél an/, **Paul** (1920–70) Romanian-born French poet. His best known poem, 'Death Fugue' (1948), takes as its subject the Nazi concentration camp at Auschwitz. Real name Paul Antschel

celandine /séllən dīn, -deen/ n. 1. SMALL YELLOW-FLOWERED PLANT a plant of the buttercup family found in woodland and damp locations in Europe and Asia. It has heart-shaped leaves and yellow flowers that grow on individual stems. Latin name: *Ranunculus ficaria*. US term **lesser celandine** 2. = **greater celandine** [Pre-12thC. Via Old French *celidoine* from, ultimately, Greek *khelidonion*, from *khelidōn* 'swallow'; so called because the plant flowered in spring, when swallows returned from migration.]

-cele suffix. tumour, swelling ○ *varicocele* [From Greek *kēlē*, of unknown origin]

celeb /si léb/ n. sb who is a celebrity (informal) [Early 20thC. Shortening.]

Celebes /séllə beez, se leé beez/ island in Indonesia, situated in the Malay Archipelago east of Borneo. Population: 13,732,500 (1995). Area: 189,040 sq. km/72,989 sq. mi.

Celebes Sea part of the Pacific Ocean, surrounded by the Philippines, Borneo, Celebes, the Sulu Archipelago, and the Sangihe Islands. Area: 427,000 km/165,000 sq. mi.

celebrant /sélləbrənt/ n. 1. OFFICIATING PRIEST a priest who is officiating at the Eucharist 2. WORSHIPPER sb who takes part in a religious ceremony 3. SB CELEBRATING sb who takes part in a celebration 4. ANZ SB WHO OFFICIATES a secular official who conducts civil ceremonies such as weddings and naming ceremonies [Mid-19thC. From Latin *celebrare* (see CELEBRATE).]

celebrate /séllə brayt/ (-brates, -brating, -brated) v. 1. vti. SHOW HAPPINESS to show happiness that sth good or special has happened, by doing such things as eating and drinking together or playing music ○ *I told them about my promotion, and we went out to celebrate.* ○ *a noisy crowd of fans celebrating the victory* 2. vt. MARK AN OCCASION to mark a special occasion or day by ceremonies or festivities 3. vti. PERFORM A RELIGIOUS CEREMONY to perform a religious ceremony according to the prescribed forms 4. vt. PRAISE STH to praise sth publicly or make it famous [Mid-16thC. From Latin *celebrare* 'to attend a festival', from *celeber* 'frequented, famous' (source of English *celebrity*).] —**celebrative** /sélləbrətiv/ adj. —**celebrator** /sélləb raytər/ n. —**celebratory** /sélləbrətəri, séllə bráytəri/ adj.

celebrated /séllə braytid/ adj. famous and admired

celebrity /sə lébbrəti/ (plural **-ties**) n. 1. FAMOUS PERSON sb who is famous during his or her own lifetime 2. FAME the state of being famous [14thC. Directly or via French *célébrité* from Latin *celebritas*, from *celeber* 'frequented, famous' (source of English *celebrate*).]

celeriac /sə lérri ak/ n. a vegetable that is a type of celery with an edible root that looks like an irregularly shaped turnip and is eaten cooked or raw. Latin name: *Apium graveolens* var. *rapaceum*. [Mid-18thC. Alteration of CELERY.]

celerity /sə lérrəti/ n. quickness in movement or in

doing sth (*formal*) [15thC. Via French *célérité* from Latin *celeritas*, from *celer* 'swift' (source of English *accelerate*).]

Celery

celery /sélləri/ *n.* **1.** LONG-STEMMED VEGETABLE a vegetable plant with long, crisp flattish stems that are eaten raw or cooked. Latin name: *Apium graveolens* var. *dulce.* **2.** CELERY STALKS celery stalks eaten as a vegetable **3.** SEASONING the seeds of the celery plant, which are used as a seasoning [Mid-17thC. Via French *céleri* from, ultimately, Greek *selinon* 'parsley'.]

celery pine *n.* a New Zealand tree that has shoots resembling celery and yields timber. Latin name: *Phyllocladus trichomanoides.*

celesta /sə léstə/ (*plural* **-tas**), **celeste** *n.* a musical instrument with keys that are played to make hammers strike metal plates, making a soft tinkling sound [Late 19thC. Alteration of French *céleste*, literally 'celestial', from Latin *caelestis* (see CELESTIAL).]

celestial /sə lésti əl/ *adj.* **1.** HEAVENLY belonging to, suitable for, in, or typical of heaven **2.** OF THE SKY relating to, involving, or observed in the sky or outer space [14thC. Via French from, ultimately, Latin *caelestis*, from *caelum* 'sky, heaven'.] —**celestially** *adv.*

celestial body *n.* any of the objects that are permanently present in the sky, e.g. a star or a planet

Celestial Empire *n.* a name for the former Chinese Empire (*archaic or literary*) [Translation of a Chinese term that stresses the divinity of the emperor and his importance in the universal scheme of things]

celestial equator *n.* the great circle in which the plane of the Earth's equator intersects the celestial sphere

celestial globe *n.* a globe showing the positions of the celestial bodies

celestial horizon *n.* = horizon *n.* 3

celestial mechanics *n.* the branch of astronomy concerned with the motions and positions of celestial bodies in gravitational fields (*takes a singular verb*)

celestial navigation *n.* the steering of a ship or aircraft by observing the positions of the stars by means of triangulation

celestial pole *n.* either of the two points where a line in continuation of the earth's axis intersects the celestial sphere

celestial sphere *n.* the imaginary sphere around the Earth on which the Sun, Moon, stars, and planets appear to be placed

celestite /séllə stīt/, **celestine** /sélləs teen, -stīn/ *n.* a mineral, consisting of strontium sulphate, that is the chief ore of strontium. It is usually white but occasionally brown, orange, red, or blue. Formula: $SrSO_4$. [Early 19thC. Formed from Latin *caelestis* 'of the sky' (see CELESTIAL).]

celiac *adj.* US = coeliac

celibacy /séllábəsi/ *n.* **1.** SEXUAL ABSTINENCE a state of sexual abstinence for religious reasons or as a personal choice **2.** LIFE WITHOUT MARRIAGE the condition of being unmarried [Mid-17thC. Formed from Latin *caelibatus* (see CELIBATE).]

celibate /séllábət/ *adj.* **1.** ABSTAINING abstaining from sex **2.** UNMARRIED unmarried, especially because of a religious vow ■ *n.* **1.** SB WHO ABSTAINS FROM SEX an adult who abstains from sex for religious reasons or as a personal choice **2.** SB UNMARRIED an unmarried person, especially one who has taken a vow of celibacy [Early

19thC. From Latin *caelibatus*, from *caelebs* 'unmarried', of unknown origin.] —**celibately** *adv.*

Céline /se léen, say-/, **Louis Ferdinand** (1894–1961) French novelist and doctor. Misogyny and anti-Semitism characterize such works as his *Journey to the End of the Night* (1932). Real name **Louis-Ferdinand Destouches**

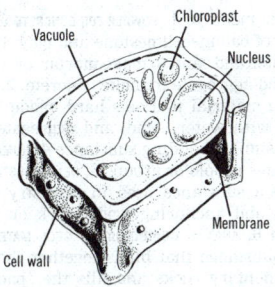
Cell: Structure of a plant cell

cell /sel/ *n.* **1.** ROOM FOR HOLDING PRISONER a room in a prison, in which one or more prisoners are confined, or a small room in a police station, used to confine sb who has been arrested **2.** SMALL ROOM a very small and simple room, especially in a monastery or convent **3.** BIOL BASIC UNIT OF LIVING THING the smallest independently functioning unit in the structure of an organism, usually consisting of one or more nuclei surrounded by cytoplasm and enclosed by a membrane. Cells also contain organelles, e.g. mitochondria, lysosomes, and ribosomes. **4.** SMALL ENCLOSED STRUCTURE a small contained or hollow unit in a structure, e.g. a compartment in a honeycomb or the reproductive organs of a plant, or an area on an insect's wing **5.** ELEC, ENG STH THAT PRODUCES ELECTRICITY a device that produces electrical energy by the chemical action of electrodes in an electrolyte **6.** = solar cell **7.** POL ACTIVIST GROUP a small group of people who work together and are part of a larger organization, especially members of a political organization who work in secret **8.** TELECOM RANGE OF MOBILE PHONE TRANSMITTER the area covered by one of the transmitters in a mobile telephone system that automatically switches a travelling user between short-range radio stations **9.** COMPUT SPACE IN TABLE a space for information in a table, e.g. in a computer spreadsheet, formed where a row and a column intersect **10.** CHR DEPENDENT RELIGIOUS HOUSE a small religious house that is dependent on a larger religious community [Pre-12thC. Via Old French *celle* from Latin *cella* 'small chamber' (see CELLA).]

cella /séllə/ (*plural* **-lae** /-lee/) *n.* the inner room of a classical Greek or Roman temple, which contained the shrine or statue of the god [Late 17thC. From Latin, 'small chamber'. Ultimately from an Indo-European base meaning 'to cover, conceal', which is also the ancestor of *hole, hell, helmet,* and *conceal*.]

cellar /séllər/ *n.* **1.** UNDERGROUND ROOM a room wholly or partly below ground level that is not suitable as living space and is usually used for storage **2.** PLACE FOR STORING WINE a room where wine is stored **3.** STOCK OF WINE a stock of wine ■ *vt.* (**-lars, -laring, -lared**) STORE WINE to store sth, especially wine, in a cellar [13thC. Via Anglo-Norman *celer* from late Latin *cellarium* 'group of storage chambers', from Latin *cella* (see CELLA).]

cellarage /séllərij/ *n.* **1.** STORAGE CHARGE a fee charged for storing sth in a cellar **2.** CELLAR SPACE a cellar or cellars, or the amount of space in a cellar

cellarer /séllərər/ *n.* sb who is in charge of stores of food and drink, especially in a monastery

cellaret /séllə rét/ *n.* a cabinet or sideboard for storing bottles of wine and glasses

cellarette *n.* US = cellaret

cellarman /séllərmən/ (*plural* **-men** /séllərmən/) *n.* a man who is in charge of the cellar in a pub or restaurant and is responsible for maintaining good storage conditions

cellblock /sél blok/ *n.* a group of cells forming a unit in a prison

cell division *n.* the process by which a cell divides to form two new cells, either to produce identical cells (**mitosis**) or to produce cells with half the number of chromosomes (**meiosis**)

Cellini /che léeni/, **Benvenuto** (1500–71) Italian sculptor and goldsmith. He wrote an autobiography considered a classic work of Renaissance literature.

cellist /chéllist/ *n.* a musician who plays the cello

cellmate /sél mayt/ *n.* a prisoner who shares a cell with another

cell membrane *n.* the membrane that surrounds the cytoplasm, through which substances pass in and out of the cell

cello /chéllō/ (*plural* **-los**) *n.* a large stringed instrument of the violin family that is held upright between a seated player's knees and played with a bow. The cello has a full deep sound. [Late 19thC. Shortening of VIOLONCELLO.]

cellobiose /séllō bí ōz/ *n.* a sugar obtained by the breakdown of cellulose. Formula: $C_{12}H_{22}O_{11}$. [Early 20thC. Coined from CELLULOSE + BI- + -OSE.]

Cellophane /séllə fayn/ *tdmk.* a trademark for a thin transparent waterproof material made from wood pulp, used for wrapping and covering things

Cellphone

cellphone /sélfōn/ *n.* a mobile telephone operated through a cellular radio network [Late 20thC. Contraction of *cellular telephone*.]

cellular /séllyōo lər/ *adj.* **1.** BIOL INVOLVING LIVING CELLS relating to or consisting of living cells **2.** CONTAINING SMALL PARTS OR GROUPS relating to small parts or groups making up a whole **3.** TELECOM ORGANIZED INTO CELLS organized as a system of cells, especially for radio communication **4.** INDUST, GEOL POROUS porous in texture and containing many small cavities **5.** TEXTILES OPEN-TEXTURED woven or knitted in a way that gives thickness of cloth and openness of texture [Mid-18thC. Via French *cellulaire* from modern Latin *cellularis*, from Latin *cellula* (see CELLULE).] —**cellularity** /séllyōo lárrəti/ *n.* —**cellularly** /séllyōo lərli/ *adv.*

cellular phone *n.* = cellphone

cellular radio *n.* the type of radio communication used for mobile phones that consists of a network of transmitters, each covering a small area. The travelling user is automatically switched between radio stations.

cellular telephone *n.* = cellphone

cellulase /séllyōo layz, -layss/ *n.* an enzyme found in certain microorganisms that converts cellulose to cellobiose [Early 20thC. Formed from CELLULOSE.]

cellule /séllyool/ *n.* a small cell in a living organism [Mid-19thC. Via French from Latin *cellula*, literally 'small cell', from *cella* (see CELLA).]

cellulite /séllyōol īt/ *n.* fatty deposits beneath the skin of the body that give a lumpy or grainy appearance to the skin surface, e.g. on the thighs and buttocks [Mid-20thC. From French, from *cellule* 'CELLULE'.]

cellulitis /séllyōo lítiss/ *n.* infection and inflammation of the tissues beneath the skin

celluloid /séllyōo loyd/ *n.* **1.** INDUST COLOURLESS PLASTIC a type of flammable transparent plastic, made from nitrocellulose and a plasticizer such as camphor **2.** CINEMA FILM the photographic film used for making films **3.** CINEMA CINEMA AS MEDIUM the cinema as a medium or art form ■ *adj.* INDUST OF OR WITH CELLULOID made of or treated with celluloid [Mid-19thC. Coined from CELLULOSE + -OID.]

cellulolytic /séllyŏlō líttik/ *adj.* used to describe a process or an organism that breaks down the plant material cellulose, e.g. in the stomachs of cows and other ruminants [Mid-20thC. Coined from CELLULOSE and -LYTIC.]

cellulose /séllyŏŏ lōss, -lōz/ *n.* the main constituent of the cell walls of plants and algae. Its derivatives are used for making plastics, lacquers, explosives, and synthetic fibres. [Mid-19thC. From French, from Latin *cellula*, literally 'small cell', from *cella* 'cell' (see CELL).] —**cellulosic** /séllyŏŏ lóssik, -lōzik/ *adj.*

cellulose acetate *n.* a chemical compound produced by the reaction of acetic or sulphuric acid on cellulose, used for making photographic film, plastics, textile fibres, and varnishes

cellulose nitrate *n.* nitrocellulose (*dated*)

cell wall *n.* the outermost layer of a cell in plants and certain fungi, algae, and bacteria, providing a supporting framework

celosia /sə lṓssi ə/ (*plural* -**sias** *or* -**sia**) *n.* a plant with feathery yellow to purplish-red flowers belonging to a genus that includes cockscomb. Genus: *Celosia.* [Early 19thC. From modern Latin, genus name, from Greek *kēlos* 'burnt, dry', from the appearance of the flowers of some species.]

Celsius /sélssi əss/ *adj.* using or measured on an international metric temperature scale on which water freezes at 0°C and boils at 100°C under normal atmospheric conditions. The term 'Celsius' is usually preferred to 'centigrade', especially in technical contexts. (*generally not used in scientific contexts apart from meteorology*) ◊ **Fahrenheit, kelvin**. Symbol **C** [Mid-19thC. Named after its inventor Anders Celsius (1701–44), a Swedish astronomer.]

—— **WORD KEY: USAGE** ——
See Usage note at *centigrade.*

celt /selt/ *n.* a prehistoric chisel or axe that has a metal or stone head with a bevelled edge [Early 18thC. From medieval Latin *celtis* 'chisel'.]

Celt /kelt, selt/, **Kelt** *n.* **1.** SB WHO SPEAKS CELTIC LANGUAGE sb who speaks or whose ancestors spoke a Celtic language **2.** MEMBER OF ANCIENT PEOPLE sb who belonged to an ancient Indo-European people who, in pre-Roman times, lived in central and western Europe. They were driven to the western fringes of the continent by the Romans and certain Germanic peoples, especially the Angles and Saxons. [Mid-16thC. Via Latin *Celtae* 'Celts' from Greek *Keltoi.* 'Descendant of ancient Celts, speaker of Celtic' came from French *Celte* 'Breton' (presumed representative of the ancient Gauls).]

Celt. *abbr.* Celtic

Celtiberian /kélti beéri ən, sélti-/ *n.* sb who belonged to a Celtic people who inhabited the Iberian peninsula during classical times [Early 17thC. Formed from Latin *Celtiberia* 'ancient province of Iberia', from *Celtae* 'Celts' (see CELT) + *Iberia* (see IBERIAN).] —**Celtiberian** *adj.*

Celtic *preferred form in England and Wales* /kéltik; *usual form in Scotland* /séltik/ *adj.* OF CELTS relating to or typical of the Celts or their cultures or languages ■ *n.* INDO-EUROPEAN LANGUAGE GROUP a group of languages that includes Irish, Scottish Gaelic, Welsh, and Breton. Part of the Indo-European family of languages, it has Brythonic and Goidelic subgroups. About one and a half million people speak a Celtic language.

Celtic cross *n.* a cross that has a broad ring around the intersection of the upright and crossbar

Celticism *preferred form in England and Wales* /kéltissizəm/; *usual form in Scotland* /séltissizəm/ *n.* **1.** LANGUAGE CELTIC WORD a word or idiom of Celtic origin that has become naturalized in another language. In English, examples include 'plaid' from Scottish Gaelic and 'leprechaun' from Irish Gaelic, and 'eisteddfod' from Welsh. **2.** CELTIC TRADITION a custom or belief of Celtic origin

Celticist *preferred form in England and Wales* /kéltissist/; *usual form in Scotland* /sélt-/, **Kelticist** /kéltissist/ *n.* sb who studies the Celts or their languages

Celtic Sea /kéltik-, sél-/ extension of the Atlantic Ocean between Ireland to the north and south-western England to the south

cembalo /chémbəlō/ (*plural* -**li** /-lee/ *or* -**los**) *n.* = **harpsichord** [Mid-19thC. From Italian, contraction of *clavicembalo*, from medieval Latin *clavicymbalum*, from Latin *clavis* 'key' (see CLAVICLE) + *cymbalum* 'cymbal' (see CYMBAL).] —**cembalist** *n.*

cement /si mént/ *n.* **1.** POWDER FOR CONCRETE a fine grey powder of calcined limestone and clay. It is mixed with water and sand to make mortar, or with water, sand, and aggregate to make concrete. **2.** CONCRETE a building material that sets hard, made by mixing cement with water, sand, and aggregate **3.** GLUE a glue or similar bonding substance **4.** HUMAN BOND sth that unites people or groups **5.** DENT SUBSTANCE USED IN DENTISTRY a substance used in dentistry for filling cavities and anchoring bridgework or crowns. ◊ amalgam **6.** ANAT = cementum **7.** GEOL MATERIAL BINDING ROCK a substance that binds together the particles in sedimentary rocks and fills the spaces ■ *vti.* (-**ments**, -**menting**, -**mented**) **1.** FIX OR BECOME FIXED WITH CEMENT to fix sth in place with cement or a similar substance, or become fixed in this way **2.** APPLY CEMENT TO STH to cover or fill sth with cement or a similar substance **3.** MAKE OR BECOME CLOSE FRIENDS to make a relationship between people very strong or permanent, or become very strong or permanent [14thC. Via French *ciment* from Latin *caementum* 'quarry stone', (in plural) 'stone chips (for making mortar)', from assumed *caedmentum*, from *caedere* 'to hew' (see CHISEL).] —**cementer** *n.*

cementation /seé men táysh'n/ *n.* **1.** CEMENTING the application of cement or a similar substance to sth **2.** CIV ENG CEMENTING OF ROCKS the injecting of cement into holes or fissures in rocks to make them watertight or strong **3.** METALL HEATING METAL WITH POWDER the modification of a solid, especially a metal, by heating it with one or more other substances that will diffuse into the surface, e.g. the production of steel by heating it with charcoal **4.** GEOL SEDIMENTARY ROCK FORMATION the process in which percolating groundwater deposits a cementing material to form a sedimentary rock

cementite /si mén tīt/ *n.* a hard brittle compound of iron and carbon that forms in some types of cast iron, in carbon steels, and in alloys of carbon and iron. Formula: Fe_3C.

cement mixer *n.* **1.** MACHINE FOR MAKING CONCRETE a transportable machine with a revolving drum in which cement powder, water, sand, and other materials can be mixed to make concrete, mortar, or stucco **2.** CONCRETE TRUCK a truck with a large revolving drum for mixing, transporting, and pouring concrete

cementum /si méntəm/ *n.* the thin layer of bony tissue that covers the dentine of the roots and neck of a tooth [Mid-19thC. From Latin *caementum* (see CEMENT).]

cemetery /sémmətri/ (*plural* -**ies**) *n.* an area of ground in which the dead are buried, especially one that is not in the grounds of a church [14thC. Via late Latin *coemeterium* from Greek *koimētērion* 'dormitory', from *koiman* 'to put to sleep'. Originally 'Roman catacombs'.]

CEMF *abbr.* counter-electromotive force

CEN *n.* = CENELEC

cen. *abbr.* **1.** central **2.** century

-cene *suffix.* HIST recent ◦ *Pliocene* [From Greek *kainos* 'new'. Ultimately related to Latin *recens*, the source of English *recent*.]

CENELEC /sénnə lek/, **CEN** *n.* an EU organization that controls the standard of electrical goods. Abbr of **Commission Européenne de Normalisation Electrique**

CEng *abbr.* chartered engineer

ceno- *prefix.* = **coeno-**

cenobite *n.* = **coenobite**

cenogenesis *n.* = **caenogenesis**

cenotaph /sénnə taaf, -taf/ *n.* a monument erected as a memorial to a dead person or dead people buried elsewhere, especially people killed fighting a war [Early 17thC. From, ultimately, Greek *kenotaphion*, literally 'empty tomb', from *kenos* 'empty' (see KENOSIS) +

taphos 'tomb' (see EPITAPH).] —**cenotaphic** /sénnə táffik/ *adj.*

Cenotaph *n.* a monument in London erected as a memorial to those killed in World War I. It also serves as a memorial to the dead of subsequent wars involving UK forces.

cenote /si nṓ tay/ *n.* a deep natural hole found in limestone, especially in Yucatán, Mexico. Cenotes were holy for the Mayans, who used them as places of sacrifice. [Mid-19thC. Via Yucatán Spanish from Maya *tzonot.*]

Cenozoic /seénō zṓ ik/, **Caenozoic, Cainozoic** /kī́nəzṓ ik, káynə-/ *adj.* OF MOST RECENT GEOLOGICAL ERA belonging or relating to the most recent era of geological time, covering the period from the present to about 65 million years ago, during which modern plants and animals evolved ■ *n.* MOST RECENT GEOLOGICAL ERA the era of geological time that covers the period from the present day to about 65 million years ago [Mid-19thC. Coined from Greek *kainos* (source of English *-cene*) + -ZOIC.]

cense /senss/ (**censes, censing, censed**) *vt.* **1.** BURN INCENSE TO DEITY to burn incense to a deity at an altar or shrine **2.** PERFUME STH WITH INCENSE to perfume a place or worshippers with incense [14thC. Shortening of French *encenser*, ultimately from Latin *incendere* 'to set fire to', from *candere* 'to glow' (source of English *candle*).]

Censer

censer /sénssər/ *n.* a container used for burning incense, especially one that is swung in a religious procession or ceremony [13thC. From, ultimately, Old French *censier*, shortening of *encensier*, from *encens* 'incense', from ecclesiastical Latin *incensum*, from the past participle of Latin *incendere* (see CENSE).]

censor /sénssər/ *n.* **1.** OFFICIAL REMOVING OBJECTIONABLE MATERIAL an official who examines plays, films, letters, and publications with a view to removing or banning content considered to be offensive or a threat to security **2.** SB THAT SUPPRESSES STH sb or sth that exercises suppressive control **3.** HISTORY ANCIENT ROMAN OFFICIAL either of two elected magistrates of ancient Rome who were responsible for holding the census, overseeing public morals, and controlling aspects of finance and taxation **4.** PSYCHIAT INHIBITING FORCE IN MIND a mechanism believed to be responsible for what can and cannot emerge from the subconscious to the conscious mind. It is thought to prevent harmful memories, ideas, and desires from reaching the conscious level. ■ *vt.* (-**sors**, -**soring**, -**sored**) **1.** REMOVE OFFENSIVE PARTS FROM STH to remove or change any part of a publication, play, or film considered offensive or a threat to security **2.** EXERCISE CONTROL OVER STH to suppress or control sth that may offend or harm others [Mid-16thC. From Latin *censere* (see CENSUS).] —**censorable** *adj.* —**censorial** /sens sáwri əl/ *adj.*

censorious /sen sáwri əss/ *adj.* **1.** HIGHLY CRITICAL inclined or eager to criticize people or things **2.** CONVEYING CRITICISM expressing strong disapproval or harsh criticism —**censoriously** *adv.* —**censoriousness** *n.*

censorship /sénssər ship/ *n.* **1.** SUPPRESSION OF PUBLISHED OR BROADCAST MATERIAL the suppression of all or part of a publication, play, or film considered offensive or a threat to security **2.** ANY SUPPRESSION the suppression or attempted suppression of sth regarded as objectionable **3.** HISTORY ANCIENT ROMAN OFFICE the office, authority, or term of an ancient Roman censor **4.** PSYCHIAT SUPPRESSION OF MEMORIES the suppression of potentially harmful memories, ideas, or desires from the conscious mind

censurable /sénshərəb'l/ *adj.* deserving severe criticism, or likely to be severely criticized —**censurability** /sénshərə bílləti/ *n.* —**censurableness** /sénshərəbəlnəss/ *n.* —**censurably** /sénshərəbli/ *adv.*

censure /sénshər/ *n.* **1. DISAPPROVAL** severe criticism **2. OFFICIAL CONDEMNATION** official expression of disapproval or condemnation ■ *vt.* (-**sures, -suring, -sured**) **1. CRITICIZE SB OR STH** to subject sb or sth to severe criticism **2. CONDEMN SB OR STH** to express official disapproval or condemnation of sb or sth [14thC. From, ultimately, Latin *censura* 'judgment', from *censere* (see CENSUS).] —**censurer** *n.*

— **WORD KEY: SYNONYMS** —
See Synonyms at **criticize**. See Synonyms at **disapprove**.

census /sénssəss/ (*plural* -**suses**) *n.* **1. COUNT OF POPULATION** an official count of a population carried out at set intervals **2. ANY COUNT** any systematic count or survey **3. HISTORY REGISTRATION OF ROMANS FOR TAXATION** in ancient Rome, a registration of the population and their property that was used for assessing taxes [Early 17thC. From Latin *censere* 'to appraise, assess' (source of English *censor* and *censure*). Originally 'tax'.]

cent /sent/ *n.* **1. UNIT OF CURRENCY IN THE US, ETC.** a subunit of currency in countries such as the United States, Canada, Australia, New Zealand or South Africa where the main currency is the dollar or, in the case of the Netherlands, the guilder. It is worth one hundredth of the main unit. See table at **currency 2. COIN WORTH ONE CENT** a coin worth one cent [14thC. Directly or via French, cent 'hundred', or Italian *cento*, 'hundred', from Latin *centum* 'hundred' (source of English *century*). Originally 'hundred' (still in PER CENT).]

cent. *abbr.* **1.** centigrade **2.** central **3.** century

cent- *prefix.* = **centi-**. symbol **c**

cental /sént'l/ *n.* a unit of mass equal to 100 lb (45.3 kg) [Late 19thC. Formed from Latin *centum* (see CENT; perhaps modelled on QUINTAL.]

centas /sén tass/ (*plural* -**tas**) *n.* **1.** see table at **currency 2. COIN WORTH ONE CENTAS** a coin worth one centas

Centaur

centaur /sén tawr/ *n.* in Greek mythology, a wild creature with the head, arms, and torso of a man joined to the body of a horse at its neck. [14thC. From, ultimately, Latin *centaurus* from Greek *kentauros*, of unknown origin. Originally, in Greek, 'a wild people of Thessaly', supposedly very fine horse riders.]

Centaurus /sen táwrəss/ *n.* a large conspicuous constellation in the southern hemisphere. It contains Alpha Centauri and Beta Centauri, two very bright stars.

centaury /sén tawri/ (*plural* -**ries**) *n.* a plant of the gentian family, with pink or purple flowers. It has been used in herbal medicine for centuries. Latin name: *Centaurium erythaea*. [14thC. From late Latin *centaurea*, from its having been, according to legend, discovered by the centaur Chiron.]

centavo /sen ta'avō/ (*plural* -**vos**) *n.* **1.** see table at **currency 2. COIN WORTH A CENTAVO** a coin worth one centavo [Late 19thC. From Spanish and Portuguese, literally 'hundredth', both formed from Latin *centum* (see CENT).]

centenarian /séntə náiri ən/ *n.* **100-YEAR-OLD PERSON** sb who has reached or passed the age of a hundred ■ *adj.* **1. 100 YEARS OLD** at least a hundred years of age

2. OF CENTENARIANS relating to or characteristic of a 100-year-old person

centenary /sen téenəri, -ténnə-/ *n.* (*plural* -**ries**) **1. 100-YEAR ANNIVERSARY** an anniversary of a hundred years, or its celebration. US term **centennial 2. CENTURY** a period of one hundred years ■ *adj.* **1. MARKING 100 YEARS** marking an anniversary of 100 years. US term **centennial 2. ONCE-A-CENTURY** occurring every 100 years **3. OF A CENTURY** relating to or involving a period of one hundred years [Early 17thC. From Latin *centenarius* 'containing a hundred', from *centeni* 'hundred each', from *centum* (see CENT).]

centennial /sen ténni əl/ *adj.* **1. OF CENTURY** relating to or involving a period of a hundred years **2. ONCE A CENTURY** occurring every hundred years **3.** *US* = **centenary** ■ *n.* *US* = **centenary** [Late 18thC. Formed from Latin *centum* (see CENT); modeled on BIENNIAL.] —**centennially** *adv.*

center *n., vti.* US = **centre**

centesimal /sen téssim'l/ *adj.* **1. IN 100THS** divided into hundredths **2. 100TH** constituting one-hundredth of sth **3. USING BASE OF 100** used to describe a number system that uses a base of 100 ■ *n.* **100TH PART** one hundredth of sth [Late 17thC. Formed from Latin *centesimus* 'hundredth', from *centum* 'hundred' (see CENT).] —**centesimally** *adv.*

centesimo /sen téssimō/ (*plural* -**mos** or -**mi** /-mi/ *n.* **1.** see table at **currency 2. COIN WORTH ONE CENTESIMO** a coin worth one centesimo [Mid-19thC. From Italian, from Latin *centesimus* (see CENTESIMAL).]

centi- *prefix.* **1.** hundredth ○ *centipoise* **2.** hundred ○ *centipede* [Via French from, ultimately, Latin *centum* 'one hundred' (see CENT)]

centigrade /sénti grayd/ *adj.* = **Celsius**. symbol **C** (*generally not used in scientific contexts apart from meteorology*) [Early 19thC. From French, from earlier forms of CENTI- + -GRADE.]

— **WORD KEY: USAGE** —
Celsius or **centigrade**? In denoting temperature, **Celsius** is now the more usual term in scientific and general contexts. **Centigrade** is a generic word applied to any scale based on a range of one hundred (and is not usually written with an initial capital letter), whereas **Celsius** applies specifically to the temperature scale with a freezing point of zero and a boiling point of one hundred degrees (and like *Fahrenheit* is written with an initial capital because it is derived from a personal name).

centigram /sénti gram/, **centigramme** *n.* a unit of mass equal to one hundredth of a gram. Symbol **cg**

centilitre /sénti leetər/ *n.* a unit of volume equal to one hundredth of a litre. Symbol **cl**

centillion /sen tílli ən/ (*plural* -**lions** or -**lion**) *n.* **1. ONE FOLLOWED BY 600 ZEROS** in the United Kingdom and Germany, the number represented by the figure 1 followed by 600 zeros **2.** *US* **ONE FOLLOWED BY 303 ZEROS** in the United States, Canada, and France, the number represented by the figure 1 followed by 303 zeros [Mid-19thC. Formed from CENTI-, the second element being modelled on words such as MILLION and BILLION.]

centime /són teem, sa'an-/ *n.* **1.** see table at **currency 2. COIN WORTH ONE CENTIME** a coin worth one centime [Early 19thC. Via French from, ultimately, Latin *centesimus* (see CENTESIMAL).]

centimetre /sénti meetər/ *n.* a unit of length equal to one hundredth of a metre. Symbol **cm**

centimetre-gram-second, **centimetre-gramme-second** *adj.* using or relating to an old metric measurement system that uses the centimetre as the basic unit for length, the gram for mass, and the second for time (*In scientific contexts the cgs system has been largely replaced by the SI system*) = **cgs**

centimo /séntimō/ (*plural* -**mos**) *n.* **1.** see table at **currency 2. COIN WORTH ONE CENTIMO** a coin worth one centimo [Late 19thC. Via Spanish from French *centime*, ultimately from Latin *centesimus* (see CENTESIMAL).]

centimorgan /sénti mawrgən/ *n.* a unit of measurement used to indicate how closely genes are linked together on the same chromosome [Mid-20thC. Coined from CENTI-+MORGAN, from the geneticist Thomas Hunt *Morgan*.]

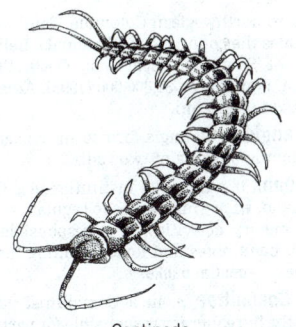

Centipede

centipede /sénti peed/ *n.* a small, fast-moving invertebrate animal with a long slender body divided into many segments, most of which bear one pair of legs. Centipedes eat other arthropods, e.g. small insects. Class: Chilopoda. [Mid-17thC. From, ultimately, Latin *centipeda*, literally 'with a hundred feet', from earlier forms of CENTI- + -PEDE, from its many legs.]

centipoise /sénti poyz/ *n.* a unit of measurement for viscosity in the cgs system that is equal to one hundredth of a poise [Early 20thC. From CENTI- and POISE.]

centr- *prefix.* = **centro-** (*used before a vowel*)

centra plural of **centrum**

central /séntrəl/ *adj.* **1. IN THE MIDDLE** in, near, or forming the middle of sth **2. EQUIDISTANT FROM OTHER POINTS** at approximately the same distance from a number of different points or places **3. IN MAIN PART OF TOWN** in the part of a town or city where the main shops, offices, and other facilities are situated **4. HAVING CONTROL OVER PARTS** controlling the activities of connected or subordinate parts ○ *a central authority* **5. HAVING LINKED COMPONENTS** used to describe a system of linked devices controlled by a single unit or at a single point **6. CRUCIAL** of critical importance or great influence ○ *the notion is central to their thinking on the subject* **7. DOMINANT** with a major or the principal role **8. ANAT RELATING TO CENTRUM** relating to the centrum of a vertebra **9. PHON SAID WITH TONGUE IN MIDDLE POSITION** used to describe a vowel articulated with the tongue at or near the middle of the hard palate, as is the final vowel in 'cola' [Mid-17thC. From, ultimately, Latin *centralis*, from *centrum* (see CENTRE).] —**centrally** *adv.*

Central /séntrəl/ former administrative region of Scotland from 1975 to 1996, bordered by Fife, Lothian, Tayside and Stathclyde. Population: 272,900 (1992). Area: 2,621/1,012 sq. mi.

Central African Federation federation from 1953 to 1963 of Nyasaland, Northern Rhodesia, and Southern Rhodesia, present-day Malawi, Zambia, and Zimbabwe

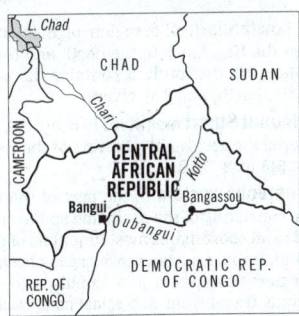

Central African Republic

Central African Republic landlocked country in central Africa. Formerly part of French Equatorial Africa, it became independent in 1960. It is bordered on the north by Chad, on the east by Sudan, on the south by the Democratic Republic of Congo, and on the west by Cameroon. Language: French. Currency: C.F.A. franc. Capital: Bangui. Population: 3,308,198 (1997). Area: 622,436 sq. km/240,324 sq. mi. Former name **Ubangi-Shari** (until 1958)

Central America the southern part of North America, extending from the southern border of

Mexico to northwestern Colombia, South America. It includes the countries of Guatemala, Belize, Honduras, El Salvador, Nicaragua, Costa Rica, and Panama. Population: 31,300,000 (1993). Area: 523,000 sq. km/201,930 sq. mi.

central angle *n.* an angle formed in the centre of a circle by the meeting of two radii

central bank *n.* a financial institution, e.g. the Bank of England, whose function is to regulate state fiscal and monetary activities. It is responsible for the issue of bank notes and for controlling the flow of currency. —**central banker** *n.*

Central Committee *n.* in a Communist party, the part of the bureaucracy responsible for party policy. ◊ Politburo, Agitprop

Central European Time *n.* the standard time adopted by most Western European countries, one hour ahead of Greenwich Mean Time

central government *n.* the area of government that is concerned with national issues such as taxation, defence, international relations, and trade

central heating *n.* a system designed to heat a whole building from a single source of heat by pumping hot water or air to room radiators or vents — **centrally heated** *adj.*

Central Intelligence Agency *n.* full form of **CIA**

centralisation *n.* = centralization

centralise *vti.* = centralize

centralism /séntrəlizzəm/ *n.* the concentration of control, especially political control, in a single authority —**centralist** *n., adj.* —**centralistic** /séntrə lístik/ *adj.*

centrality /sen trálləti/ *n.* **1.** CRITICAL ROLE the crucial importance of sb or sth **2.** POSITION IN MIDDLE the location of sb or sth in or near the middle of sth **3.** LOCATION IN MAIN PART OF TOWN the location of sth in the part of a town or city where the main shops, offices, and other facilities are situated

centralization /séntrə lī záysh'n/, **centralisation** *n.* **1.** CONCENTRATION OF POWER IN FEW HANDS the concentration of political or administrative power in a central authority with a resulting lack of power at local or subordinate levels **2.** APPROACHING MIDDLE OF STH the coming or bringing of sth to or towards the middle of sth

centralize /séntrə līz/ (-izes, -izing, -ized), **centralise** (-ises, -ising, -ised) *vti.* **1.** MOVE POWER TO A FEW HANDS to remove political or administrative power from local or subordinate levels and concentrate it in a central authority **2.** CONCENTRATE AT SINGLE PLACE to concentrate or collect sth at a single point —**centralizer** *n.*

central locking *n.* a system in which all the doors and the boot of a motor vehicle are automatically locked or unlocked when sb locks or unlocks one door

Central Lowlands fertile region of Scotland lying between the Highlands to the north and the Southern Uplands to the south. It contains the valleys of the Clyde, Forth, and Tay rivers.

Central Mount Stuart mountain in central Australia, considered the geographical centre of the continent. Height: 845 m/2,772 ft.

central nervous system *n.* the part of the nervous system, consisting of the brain and spinal cord, that controls and coordinates most functions of the body and mind. Impulses from sense organs travel to the central nervous system and impulses to muscles and glands travel from it. ◊ spinal cord, brain

central processing unit, **central processor** *n.* the part of a computer that performs operations and executes software commands

central reservation *n. UK* a narrow strip of land that separates lanes of traffic travelling in opposite directions on a dual carriageway or motorway. ◊ median strip

Central Standard Time, **Central Time** *n.* **1.** STANDARD TIME IN CENTRAL NORTH AMERICA the standard time in the zone that includes the central states of the United States and the central provinces of Canada. Central Standard Time is six hours behind Greenwich Mean Time. **2.** STANDARD TIME IN CENTRAL AUSTRALIA the standard time in the time zone centred on longitude 135° E, which includes the central part of Australia. It is nine-and-a-half hours behind Greenwich Mean Time.

central sulcus *n.* a deep groove in each of the hemispheres of the brain, separating the frontal and parietal lobes

Central Time *n.* = Central Standard Time

centre /séntər/ *n.* **1.** MIDDLE POINT OR AREA the middle point, area, or part of sth that is the same distance from all edges or opposite sides **2.** MATH MIDDLE OF CIRCLE OR SPHERE the interior point that is the same distance from all points on the circumference of a circle or the surface of a sphere or the vertices of a polygon **3.** MATH MIDDLE OF LINE the point on a line that is the same distance from both ends **4.** FOOD FOOD FILLING the filling of a chocolate, doughnut, or other food **5.** MAIN PART OF TOWN the part of a town or city where the main shops, offices, and other facilities are situated **6.** PLACE FOR PARTICULAR ACTIVITY a place where a particular activity is carried on ○ *a sports centre* **7.** FOCUS OF ATTENTION the point that is the focus of attention or interest ○ *the issue at the centre of the controversy* **8.** INFLUENTIAL PLACE OR ORGANIZATION a place, area, or group of people exerting control or influence over sth or sb else ○ *a centre of design innovation* **9.** CLUSTER OR CONCENTRATION a place or part where sth is concentrated or focused **10.** **centre, Centre** POL POLITICAL MODERATES those political parties or the section of a party holding views that are neither left-wing nor right-wing **11.** PIVOTAL POINT OR AXIS the point or line around which sth rotates **12.** PHYS POINT WHERE FORCE ACTS the point at or through which a force is considered to act **13.** ANAT GROUP OF NERVE CELLS REGULATING FUNCTION a group of nerve cells, especially within the central nervous system, that controls a particular function of the body **14.** MECH ENG CONICAL PART OF LATHE a part of a lathe that supports the work to be turned **15.** MECH ENG MARK TO GUIDE DRILL a dimple made in metal with a pointed tool (**centre punch**) to mark the centre of a larger hole to be drilled **16.** SPORTS ATTACKING PLAYER OR POSITION an attacking player or position in the middle of the field or court ■ *v.* (-tres, -tring, -tred) **1.** *vt.* PUT STH IN MIDDLE to position sth in the middle of sth **2.** *vti.* FOCUS ON THEME to have, or cause sth to have its focus on a theme or topic ○ *the debate centres on the possible health risks involved* **3.** *vti.* CONCENTRATE OR FOCUS to be concentrated, or cause sth to be concentrated, in a particular place or on a particular thing **4.** *vt.* SPORTS PASS BALL TOWARDS MIDDLE to pass, hit, or kick a ball or puck from the edge of the playing area towards the middle [14thC. From, ultimately, Greek *kentron* 'point', from *kentein* 'to prick' (source of English *eccentric*). 'Middle' came from 'stationary point of a pair of compasses'.]

centre back *n.* a player or position in the middle of the back line in various sports

centre bit *n.* a drill attachment or tool for boring or cutting with a pointed projection in the middle and cutters at the sides

centreboard /séntər bawrd/ *n.* a keel in a sailing boat that can be retracted upwards in shallow water

centred /séntərd/ *adj.* **1.** PLACED IN THE MIDDLE positioned at the same distance from all edges or opposite sides **2.** *US* WELL-BALANCED exhibiting confidence, self-awareness, and often a sense of determination — **centredness** *n.*

centrefold /séntər fōld/ *n.* **1.** PICTURE OR FEATURE ON CENTRE SPREAD a single illustration, advertisement, or feature that covers the two facing pages in the middle of a magazine or newspaper, especially a photograph of a nude model **2.** SB POSING IN CENTREFOLD sb who is photographed, especially naked or nearly naked, for a centrefold **3.** = centre spread

centre forward *n.* the player or position in the middle of the forward attacking line in games such as football and hockey

centre half (*plural* **centre halfs**) *n.* the player or position in the middle of the half-line in football and hockey

centreline /séntər līn/ *n.* **1.** LINE DOWN MIDDLE OF ROAD a solid or dashed line on a road that marks where traffic should flow, either separating lanes going in opposite directions or multiple lanes going the same way **2.** LINE DOWN MIDDLE a real or imaginary line through or along the middle of sth

centre of curvature *n.* the centre of a circle whose radius is perpendicular to a line tangent to any point on the concave side of a smooth curve. ◊ radius of curvature

centre of excellence *n.* a place where the highest standards of achievement are aimed for in a given sphere of activity

centre of gravity *n.* **1.** FOCUS OF GRAVITATIONAL FORCES the point through which the sum of gravitational forces on a body can be considered to act **2.** = centre of mass

centre of mass *n.* the point at which the total mass of a body or system is assumed to be centred and upon which the sum of external forces can be considered to act

centrepiece /séntər peess/ *n.* **1.** STH IN CENTRAL POSITION an object placed in the middle of sth as decoration or to attract attention **2.** MAIN FEATURE the most important part or feature

centre punch *n.* a pointed tool used in metalworking for making a dimple to guide a drill bit prior to drilling a hole

centre spread *n.* **1.** FACING MIDDLE PAGES the two pages that face each other in the middle of a magazine or newspaper **2.** ARTICLE ON MIDDLE PAGES a magazine or newspaper article featured in the middle to give it prominence

centre stage *n.* **1.** MIDDLE OF STAGE the middle area of a theatre stage **2.** FOCUS OF INTEREST the centre of people's attention or interest ■ *adv.* **1.** IN MIDDLE OF STAGE in or to the middle area of a theatre stage **2.** TO CENTRE OF ATTENTION at or to the centre of people's attention or interest

centre three-quarter *n.* **1.** MIDDLE OF THREE-QUARTER LINE in rugby, either of the two positions at the middle of the three-quarter line **2.** PLAYER AT CENTRE THREE-QUARTER in rugby, either of the two people who play in the middle of the three-quarter line

centri- *prefix.* = centro-

centric /séntrik/, **centrical** /-trik'l/ *adj.* **1.** AT OR AS THE MIDDLE at or constituting the middle of sth **2.** ANAT OF OR FROM NERVE CENTRE issuing from or relating to a nerve centre **3.** BOT WITH CONCENTRIC LAYERS OF TISSUE used to describe a plant's vascular bundles in which one type of sap-conducting tissue is surrounded by another **4.** BOT TAPERING AND CYLINDRICAL used to describe leaves that are tapering and cylindrical. ◊ terete **5.** BIOL OF A CLASS OF DIATOMS relating to a class of diatoms that have radial symmetry. Class: Centrales. — **centrically** *adv.* —**centricity** /sen tríssəti/ *n.*

-centric *suffix.* **1.** having a particular number or kind of centres ○ *hexcentric* ○ *acentric* **2.** having as its centre ○ *egocentric* [From medieval Latin *-centricus*, from Latin *centrum* (see CENTRE)]

centrifugal /séntri fyoóg'l, sen tríffyoōg'l/ *adj.* **1.** PHYS AWAY FROM CENTRE acting, moving, or pulling away from a centre or axis. ◊ centripetal **2.** TECH EMPLOYING CENTRIFUGAL FORCE using or operated by centrifugal force **3.** PHYSIOL = efferent **4.** BOT DEVELOPING OUTWARDS used to describe a plant part or tissue that develops from the centre outwards **5.** POL DECENTRALIZING POWER tending to disperse political or administrative power away from a central authority ■ *n.* TECH APPARATUS USING CENTRIFUGAL FORCE an apparatus that uses centrifugal force, or a rotating drum in such an apparatus —**centrifugalism** /séntri fyoógəlizzəm, sen tríffyoō-/ *n.* —**centrifugally** /séntri fyoógəli, sen tríffyoō-/ *adv.*

centrifugal force *n.* an apparent force that seems to pull a rotating or spinning object away from a centre

centrifuge /séntri fyooj, -fyoozh/ *n.* **1.** SEPARATION EQUIPMENT a device that rotates rapidly and uses centrifugal force to separate substances of different densities **2.** ROTATING DEVICE a rotating apparatus used to simulate the effects of gravity or acceleration on humans or animals ■ *vt.* (-fuges, -fuging, -fuged) SUBJECT STH TO CENTRIFUGAL ACTION to subject sth to the force of a centrifuge, especially in order to separate different substances [Early 18thC. From, ultimately, Latin *centrifugus* 'centrifugal', literally 'fleeing the centre',

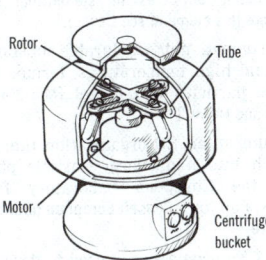

Rotor   Tube

Motor   Centrifuge bucket

Centrifuge

from *fugere* 'to flee' (see FUGITIVE).] —**centrifugation** /séntri fyoo gáysh'n/ *n.*

centriole /séntri ōl/ *n.* BIOL a two-part rod-shaped structure with the parts lying at right angles to each other, located in pairs near the nucleus of an animal cell. During cell division, centrioles move to opposite ends of the cell and form the poles of the spindle fibres that pull the chromosomes apart. [Late 19thC. From modern Latin *centriolum*, literally 'small centre', from *centrum* 'centre' (see CENTRE).]

centripetal /sen tríppit'l, séntri peét'l/ *adj.* **1.** PHYS TOWARDS CENTRE acting, moving, or pulling towards a centre or axis. ◊ **centrifugal 2.** TECH EMPLOYING CENTRIPETAL FORCE using or operated by centripetal force **3.** PHYSIOL = **afferent 4.** BOT DEVELOPING INWARDS used to describe a plant part or tissue that develops from the perimeter inwards **5.** CENTRALIZING POWER tending to concentrate political or administrative power in a central authority [Early 18thC. Formed from modern Latin *centripetus*, literally 'seeking the centre', from Latin *petere* 'to seek' (see PETITION).] —**centripetally** *adv.*

centripetal force *n.* a force that pulls a rotating or spinning object towards a centre or axis

centrism /séntrizzəm/ *n.* the holding or advocating of moderate political or other views —**centrist** *n.*, *adj.*

centro- *prefix.* centre ○ *centrosome* [From Latin *centrum* and Greek *kentron* (see CENTER)]

centrobaric /séntrō bárrik/ *adj.* relating to a centre of gravity [Early 18thC. From Greek *kentrobarikē*, literally 'centre-weight', from *baros* 'weight' (see BARO-).]

centroid /sén troyd/ *n.* PHYS = **centre of mass** [Late 19thC. Coined from CENTRO- + -OID.]

centrolecithal /séntrō léssithəl/ *adj.* used to describe an egg with the yolk in the middle. ◊ **isolecithal** [Late 19thC. Coined from CENTRO- + LECITHIN + -AL.]

centromere /séntrə meer/ *n.* BIOL the point at which two parts (**chromatids**) of a chromosome join and at which the spindle fibres are attached during cell division (**mitosis**) —**centromeric** /séntrə mérrik, -meérik/ *adj.*

centrosome /séntrə sōm/ *n.* BIOL a small region of cytoplasm near the nucleus of a cell, containing rod-shaped structures (**centrioles**) —**centrosomic** /séntrə sómmik/ *adj.*

centrum /séntrəm/ *n.* (*plural* **-trums** or **-tra** /-trə/) a thick mass of bone in a vertebra that is the point of attachment to the vertebrae above and below [Mid-19thC. From Latin (see CENTRE).]

centum /kéntəm/ *adj.* used to describe those ancient Indo-European language groups in which the /k/ sound, when preceding a front vowel, did not palatalize. ◊ **satem** [Early 20thC. From Latin 'hundred' (see CENT). The Latin and Sanskrit words for 'hundred', *centum* /k-/ and *satem* /s-/, exemplify the division and have given their names to the groupings.]

centurion /sen tyoóri ən, -choór-/ *n.* in ancient Rome, an officer in charge of a unit of foot soldiers (**century**) [14thC. From the Latin stem *centurion-*, from *centuria* 'century', from *centum* 'hundred' (see CENT).] —**centurial** *adj.*

century /sénchəri/ *n.* (*plural* **-ries**) *n.* **1.** 100 YEARS any period of a hundred years **2.** TIME 100-YEAR PERIOD IN DATING SYSTEM a period of a hundred years in a dating system, from a year numbered 1 or 00, e.g. 1901 or 2000, to one ending in 00 or 99, e.g. 2000 or 2099. Centuries are counted forwards or backwards from

a significant event, e.g. the birth of Jesus Christ. **3.** CRICKET 100 RUNS in cricket, 100 runs scored by one batsman **4.** HIST UNIT OF ROMAN SOLDIERS a group of foot soldiers in ancient Rome, originally comprising a hundred men but later between sixty and eighty. ◊ **maniple 5.** HIST GROUP OF ROMAN VOTERS a division of citizens in ancient Rome for voting purposes **6.** 100 THINGS any group of a hundred similar things **7.** LONG TIME a very long time (*informal*) (*usually used in the plural*) [14thC. From Latin *centuria*, literally 'group of a hundred', from *centum* (see CENT).]

—— **WORD KEY: USAGE** ——

When does a new century begin? Mathematicians will no doubt insist that a new *century* begins on 1 January of a year ending in 01, so that the 22nd century will begin on 1 January 2101. This is because the first *century* AD began with the year 1 (as did the first *century* BC – there was no year 0), and if that *century* is to have contained its requisite hundred years, the first year of any subsequent *century* must also end in 1. In most contexts, however, a new *century* is reckoned from the year ending in 00, since this is psychologically the more significant point. Similarly, a new millennium begins for practical purposes on 1 January of the year ending in 000, not 001.

century plant *n.* a plant found in Mexico and the southern United States, with greyish-green leaves and flowers on a tall stalk. It takes ten to thirty years to mature and flowers just once before dying. Latin name: *Agave americana*. [From the length of its maturation, likened to a hundred years]

CEO (*plural* **CEOs**) *abbr.* chief executive officer

ceorl /chairl/, churl /churl/ *n.* in Anglo-Saxon England, a freeman of the lowest class [Old English, from a prehistoric Germanic word that is also the ancestor of English *carl*]

cep /sep/, **cèpe** /sep, seep/ *n.* an edible woodland mushroom with a shiny brown cap and a creamy-coloured underside. It has a rich nutty flavour. Latin name: *Boletus edulis*. [Mid-19thC. Via French *cèpe* from Gascon *cep* 'tree trunk, mushroom', from Latin *cippus* 'stake'.]

cephal- *prefix.* = **cephalo-** (used before vowels)

cephalic /sə fállik/ *adj.* relating to the head, or in the region of the head [15thC. From, ultimately, Greek *kephalikos*, from *kephalē* (see CEPHALO-).] —**cephalically** *adv.*

-cephalic *suffix.* having a particular number or kind of heads ○ *monocephalic* ○ *brachycephalic* [Via Latin *cephalicus* from, ultimately, Greek *kephalē* 'head' (see CEPHALO-)]

cephalic index *n.* the ratio of the width to the length of a human skull, measured at the widest and longest points, and multiplied by 100

cephalin /séffəlin/, **kephalin** /kéff-/ *n.* a chemical found especially in the nervous tissue of the brain and spinal column and involved in controlling bleeding

cephalization /séffəlī záysh'n/, **cephalisation** *n.* the tendency for sensory, neural, and feeding organs to be concentrated at the front end of the body, leading to the development of a head in many organisms

cephalo- *prefix.* head, skull ○ *cephalometry* [Via modern Latin from, ultimately, Greek *kephalē*. Ultimately from an Indo-European word that is also the ancestor of English *gable*.]

cephalometer /séffə lómmitər/ *n.* an instrument used to measure the size of the human head

cephalometry /séffə lómmətri/ *n.* the measurement of human heads, especially using X-rays or ultrasound. It is practised in dentistry to determine if the mouth can accommodate new teeth and in obstetrics to gauge if a foetal head can pass through the birth canal. —**cephalometric** /séffə méttrik/ *adj.*

Cephalonia /séffə lōni ə/ largest of the Ionian islands in western Greece. Population: 32,474 (1991). Area: 750 sq. km/290 sq. mi. Greek **Kefallinía**

cephalopod /séffələ pod/ *n.* a marine animal with a large head and tentacles. Octopus, squid, and cuttlefish are cephalopods. Class: Cephalopoda. [Early 19thC. From modern Latin, class name, from, ultimately, earlier forms of CEPHALO- + -POD.] —**ceph-**

alopod *adj.* —**cephalopodan** /séffə lóppədən/ *adj.*, *n.* — **cephalopodic** /séffələ póddik/ *adj.* —**cephalopodous** /séffə lóppədəss/ *adj.*

cephalosporin /séffələ spáwrin/ *n.* an antibiotic derived from fungi, effective against a wide range of bacteria. ◊ **penicillin** [Mid-20thC. Formed from modern Latin *Cephalosporium*, from earlier forms of CEPHALO- + SPORE.]

cephalothorax /séffələ tháwraks/ (*plural* **-raxes** or **-races** /-rəsseez/) *n.* the fused head and thorax typical of spiders and other arachnids and many crustaceans

-cephalous *suffix.* having a particular number or kind of heads ○ *dicephalous* ○ *autocephalous* [Formed from Greek *-kephalos*, from *kephalē* 'head' (see CEPHALO-)]

-cephaly *suffix.* a particular condition of the head or skull ○ *microcephaly* [Formed from Greek *kephalē* 'head']

Cepheid /seéfi id/, **Cepheid variable** *n.* a star that has regular periods of varying brightness, usually lasting from one to fifty days [Early 20thC. Coined from CEPHEUS + -ID.]

Cepheus /seéf yooss, seéfi əss/ *n.* a constellation located in the northern hemisphere close to Draco and Cassiopeia

ceraceous /si ráyshəss/ *adj.* like wax in appearance or texture (*technical*) [Mid-18thC. Formed from Latin *cera* 'wax' (see CERE).]

ceramal /sə ráym'l/ *n.* = **cermet** [Mid-20thC. Blend of CERAMIC and ALLOY.]

ceramic /sə rámmik/ *n.* **1.** HARD FIRED CLAY a hard brittle heat-resistant material made by firing a mixture of clay and chemicals at high temperature **2.** FIRED CLAY OBJECT an object made from ceramic ■ *adj.* **1.** OF CERAMIC made of ceramic **2.** RELATING TO PRODUCTION OF CERAMICS relating to or involving the production of ceramic objects [Early 19thC. From Greek *keramikos* 'of pottery', from *keramos* 'potter's earth, pottery'.]

ceramic hob *n.* a flat cooking surface of ceramic with heating elements underneath

ceramicist *n.* = **ceramist**

ceramics /sə rámmiks/ *n.* the art, technology, or process of making ceramic objects (*takes a singular verb*)

ceramist /sérrəmist/, **ceramicist** /sə rámməsist/ *n.* sb who makes ceramic objects

Ceram Sea /sə rám-/ sea in the western Pacific Ocean, in central Moluccas, Indonesia, west of New Guinea. Area: 51,800 sq. km/20,000 sq. mi.

cerastes /sə ráss teez/ (*plural* **-tes**) *n.* a poisonous snake of northern Africa and southwestern Asia that has a projection like a horn above each eye. Genus: *Cerastes*. ◊ **horned viper** [14thC. From, ultimately, Greek *kerastēs*, literally 'horned', from *keras* 'horn' (source of English *keratin*).]

ceratoid /sérrə toyd/ *adj.* resembling the horn of an animal in appearance or substance [From Greek *keratoeidēs* 'hornlike', from earlier forms of CERAT- + -OID]

Cerberus /súrbərəss/ *n.* in Greek mythology, the fierce dog that guards the entrance to Hades, usually represented as having three heads —**Cerberean** /súrbə reé ən, sə beéri ən/ *adj.*

-cercal *suffix.* having a particular kind of tail ○ *diphycercal* [Formed from French *-cerque*, from Greek *kerkos* 'tail']

cercaria /sur káiri ə/ (*plural* **-ae** /-káiri ee/) *n.* the tadpole-shaped larva of various parasitic worms (**flukes**) [Mid-19thC. From modern Latin, from Greek *kerkos* 'tail' (see CERCUS).] —**cercarial** *adj.*

cercus /súrkəss/ (*plural* **-ci** /-see/) *n.* either of two sensory appendages at the end of the abdomen of the female mosquito and other insects [Early 19thC. Via modern Latin from Greek *kerkos* 'tail'.] —**cercal** *adj.*

cere /seer/ *n.* the thick skin at the base of the upper beak of some birds, e.g. parrots. The cere contains the bird's nostrils. [15thC. From Latin *cera* 'wax' (source of English *cerumen*), of uncertain origin: probably from Greek *kēros*.]

cereal /seéri əl/ *n.* **1.** CROP PLANT WITH EDIBLE GRAIN a plant belonging to the grass family that is cultivated for its nutritious grains. Cereals include oats, barley, rye, wheat, rice, and maize. **2.** GRAIN OF CEREAL PLANT the grain produced by a cereal plant **3.** BREAKFAST FOOD food made from cereal grain and eaten especially at breakfast, usually with milk [Early 19thC. Directly or via French *céréale* from Latin *cerealis* 'relating to the cultivation of grain', from CERES, the name of the Roman goddess of agriculture.]

cerebellum /sérrə béllәm/ (*plural* **-lums** *or* **-la** /-lə/) *n.* the part of the brain located directly behind the front part (**cerebrum**), typically consisting of two hemispheres connected by a thin central region. Its main function is to control and coordinate muscular activity and maintain balance. [Mid-16thC. From Latin, literally 'small brain', from *cerebrum* (see CEREBRUM).] —**cerebellar** *adj.*

cerebra *n.* plural of **cerebrum**

cerebral /sérrəbrəl, sə rée-/ *adj.* **1.** RELATING TO THE FRONT OF BRAIN relating to or located in the front part of the brain (**cerebrum**) **2.** RELATING TO WHOLE BRAIN relating to or involving the whole brain or any part of it **3.** INTELLECTUAL involving the psychological processes of thinking and reasoning rather than the emotions —**cerebrally** *adv.*

cerebral cortex *n.* the wrinkled outer layer of the front parts of the brain (**the cerebral hemispheres**). Its functions include the perception of sensations, learning, reasoning, and memory. Technical name **pallium**

cerebral dominance *n.* the normal tendency for one of the two sides of the brain (**cerebral hemispheres**) to have stronger control over some functions of the mind and body. When the left hemisphere is dominant sb is likely to be right-handed, and vice versa.

cerebral hemisphere *n.* either of the two symmetrical halves of the front part of the brain (**cerebrum**)

cerebral palsy *n.* a condition caused by brain damage around the time of birth and marked by lack of muscle control, especially in the limbs —**cerebral-palsied** *adj.*

cerebrate /sérrə brayt/ (**-brates, -brating, -brated**) *vi.* to use the mind to think or reason (*formal*) [Early 20thC. Origin uncertain: either formed directly from Latin *cerebrum* 'brain' (see CEREBRUM), or a back-formation from *cerebration*.] —**cerebration** /sérrə bráysh'n/ *n.*

cerebro- *prefix.* brain, cerebrum ○ *cerebrovascular* [From CEREBRUM]

cerebroside /sérrəbrō sīd, sə rée-/ *n.* a chemical substance (**lipid**) found in the brain and the covering (**myelin sheath**) of some nerves [Late 19thC. Coined from CEREBRO- + -OSE + -IDE.]

cerebrospinal /sérrəbrō spīn'l/ *adj.* relating to or involving the brain and spinal cord

cerebrospinal fluid *n.* the colourless fluid in and around the brain and spinal cord that absorbs shocks and maintains uniform pressure

cerebrospinal meningitis *n.* inflammation of the membranes (**meninges**) surrounding the brain and spinal cord, causing high fever and sometimes unconsciousness

cerebrovascular /sérrəbrō váskyoolər/ *adj.* relating to or involving the blood vessels that supply the brain

cerebrovascular accident *n.* any physical event, e.g. cerebral haemorrhage, that may lead to a stroke (*technical*)

cerebrum /sə réebrəm, sérrə-/ (*plural* **-brums** *or* **-bra** /-brə/) *n.* the front part of the brain, divided into two symmetrical halves (**cerebral hemispheres**). In humans, it is where activities including reasoning, learning, sensory perception, and emotional responses take place. [Early 17thC. From Latin, 'brain' (source of English *cerebellum, cerebral,* and *cerebrate*). Ultimately from an Indo-European base meaning 'head'.]

cerecloth /séer kloth/ *n.* fabric that has been coated with melted wax to make it waterproof [Mid-16thC. Alteration of *cered cloth*, literally 'waxed cloth', *cered* the past participle of *cere* 'to wax', from Latin *cerare*, from *cera* 'wax' (see CERE).]

Ceredigion /kérrə díggi on/ county and local council in Wales, occupying the area of the former county of Cardiganshire. Population: 70,200 (1995).

cerement /séermənt, sérrə-/ *n.* = **cerecloth** ■ **cerements** *npl.* BURIAL GARMENTS burial clothes [Early 17thC. Formed from *cere* 'to wax' (see CERECLOTH).]

ceremonial /sérrə mṓni əl/ *adj.* **1.** RELATING TO FORMAL OCCASIONS used on a formal occasion or at a ceremony **2.** INVOLVING CEREMONY involving or done as part of a ceremony ■ *n.* **1.** FORMAL ETIQUETTE the correct way to behave on formal occasions **2.** RITUAL a ceremony or set of ceremonies for an occasion **3.** CHR ORDER OF SERVICE the set order of rites or ceremonies in a Christian church, or a book containing this —**ceremonialism** *n.* —**ceremonialist** *n.* —**ceremonially** *adv.*

ceremonious /sérrə mṓni əss/ *adj.* **1.** VERY FORMAL excessively polite or formal **2.** ADHERING TO CONVENTION always careful to observe formalities and behave correctly **3.** INVOLVING CEREMONY involving ceremony or consisting of ceremony —**ceremoniously** *adv.* —**ceremoniousness** *n.*

WORD KEY: USAGE

ceremonial or **ceremonious**? ***Ceremonial*** is the more neutral word, describing things that have to do with ceremony or are a part of it, e.g. *ceremonial occasions.* It is not now used of people. ***Ceremonious*** is more judgmental, and is used of people: a *ceremonious person*, or sb with a *ceremonious manner*, is sb who likes and adheres to formalities, perhaps even overly so.

ceremony /sérrəməni/ (*plural* **-nies**) *n.* **1.** RITUAL FOR FORMAL OCCASION a formal event to celebrate or solemnize sth such as a wedding, an official opening, or an anniversary **2.** FORMAL ETIQUETTE the forms of behaviour that are expected or observed on a formal occasion **3.** SOCIAL GESTURE a polite social gesture or ritual performed for the sake of convention [14thC. From, ultimately, Latin *caerimonia* 'sacred rite, religious worship, ceremony', of unknown origin.] ◇ **stand on ceremony** to behave in a formal manner or insist on formality

Cerenkov effect /chə réngkof-/, **Cherenkov effect** *n.* the emission of light by a charged particle as it passes through a transparent medium at a speed greater than that of light in the same medium [Mid-20thC. Named after Pavel A. *Cherenkov* (1904–90), a Soviet physicist.]

Cerenkov radiation, **Cherenkov radiation** *n.* light emitted by a charged particle as it passes through a transparent medium at a speed greater than that of light in the same medium [Mid-20thC. See CERENKOV EFFECT.]

Ceres /séer eez/ *n.* **1.** MYTHOL GODDESS OF AGRICULTURE the Roman goddess of agriculture. Greek equivalent **Demeter 2.** ASTRON LARGEST ASTEROID the largest asteroid and the first to be discovered, in 1801, orbiting between Mars and Saturn [From Latin]

cereus /séeri əss/ *n.* **1.** SPINY RIBBED CACTUS any of several cacti with spiny ribbed stems, especially a Brazilian species that can reach a height of 13 m/40 ft. Genus: *Cereus.* **2.** CACTUS RELATED TO CEREUS any of several cacti related to the true cereus, e.g. the night-blooming cereus [Late 17thC. From modern Latin, genus name, from Latin, 'wax taper, candle', from *cera* 'wax' (see CERE); from its shape, likened to a candle.]

ceria /séeri ə/ *n.* = **ceric oxide** [From modern Latin, plural of *cerium* (see CERIUM)]

ceric /séerik/ *adj.* relating to or containing cerium with a valency of 4 [Mid-19thC. Coined from CERIUM + -IC.]

ceric oxide *n.* a white crystalline powder used in the manufacture of ceramics and to polish glass. Formula: CeO_2.

ceriph *n.* = **serif**

cerise /sə réez, -réess/ *n.* a deep, vivid red colour with a tinge of pink [Mid-19thC. Via French, 'cherry', from assumed Vulgar Latin *ceresia*, ultimately from Greek *kerasos* 'cherry tree' (source of English *cherry*).] —**cerise** *adj.*

cerium /séeri əm/ *n.* a grey malleable metallic chemical element that is the most abundant of the rare-earth group. Cerium is utilized in metallurgy, in the manufacture of glass and ceramics, and to make cigarette-lighter flints. Symbol **Ce** [Early 19thC. From modern Latin, from *Ceres* (the asteroid that was discovered just before this element; see CERES).]

cermet /súr met, -mit/ *n.* a durable substance that can withstand high temperatures, formed by bonding ceramic particles with metal [Mid-20thC. Blend of CERAMIC and METAL.]

CERN /surn/ *n.* an EU organization that carries out research into high-energy particle physics, now called the European Laboratory for Particle Physics. Full form **Conseil Européen pour la Recherche Nucléaire**

cernuous /súrnyoo əss/ *adj.* used to describe flowers and buds that droop naturally [Mid-17thC. Formed from Latin *cernuus* 'inclined forward'.]

cero /séerō, sírrō/ (*plural* **-ro** *or* **-ros**) *n.* a large edible marine fish found in warm western Atlantic waters that has silvery sides and large spiny fins. Latin name: *Scomberomorus regalis.* [Late 19thC. Alteration of Spanish *sierra* 'saw, sawfish', from Latin *serra* 'saw'.]

cerotic acid /si róttik-/ *n.* a white fatty acid found in natural waxes such as beeswax and carnauba wax. Formula: $CH_3(CH_2)_{24}COOH$. [Mid-19thC. *Cerotic* formed from Latin *cerotum* 'wax salve', from Greek *kērōton* 'waxed'.]

cerous /séerəss/ *adj.* relating to or containing cerium with a valency of 3 [Mid-19thC. Coined from CERIUM + -OUS.]

cert *n.* (*informal*) **1.** SB CERTAIN TO DO STH sb who is certain to do sth **2.** STH CERTAIN TO HAPPEN a foregone conclusion or certain outcome [Late 19thC. Shortening of CERTAIN or CERTAINTY.]

cert. /surt/ *abbr.* **1.** certificate **2.** certification **3.** certified

certain /súrt'n/ *adj.* **1.** WITHOUT DOUBT having no doubts about sth ○ *I'm certain he's the man I saw.* **2.** KNOWN OR SET definitely known, fixed, or settled **3.** INEVITABLE guaranteed to happen or to do sth ○ *they're certain to lose* **4.** RELIABLE able to be relied on **5.** NOT DEFINED undeniable but difficult to define, quantify, or express ○ *a certain hesitation in his manner* **6.** NOT NAMED able to be identified but not named ○ *A certain selfish person has used up all the milk.* **7.** UNKNOWN OR UNFAMILIAR used to indicate that only the name of the person, thing, or place mentioned is known ○ *A certain Mr Esposito was involved.* ■ *pron.* SOME of an imprecise but limited number (*formal*) [13thC. From, ultimately, assumed Vulgar Latin *certanus*, from Latin *certus* 'determined', originally a past participle of *cernere* 'to separate, decide'.] ◇ **certain of** some but not all of (*formal*) ◇ **for certain** without any doubt ◇ **make certain 1.** to check that sth has been done or is the case **2.** to take action to achieve sth

WORD KEY: ORIGIN

Certain is derived form the Latin word *cernere*, meaning 'to separate' or 'to decide', which is also the source of English *crime, decree, discern, discrete, discriminate, excrement, secret,* and *secretary.*

certainly /súrt'nli/ *adv.* **1.** DEFINITELY without any doubt or qualification on the part of the speaker ○ *It's certainly a big problem.* **2.** USED TO CONCEDE POINT used to concede a point that has been made ○ *That's certainly an area we could improve upon.* **3.** YES used to indicate unreserved assent ◇ **certainly not** used to indicate emphatic denial or refusal

certainty /súrt'nti/ (*plural* **-ties**) *n.* **1.** STH INEVITABLE a conclusion or outcome that is beyond doubt **2.** SB OR STH CERTAIN OF SUCCESS sb who or sth that is strongly expected to win or achieve sth **3.** CONFIDENCE a complete lack of doubt about sth ◇ **for a certainty** without any doubt

certifiable /súrti fī əb'l/ *adj.* **1.** DESERVING A CERTIFICATE authentic or good enough to be given a certificate **2.** THAT MUST BE CERTIFIED requiring to be reported to the appropriate authority (*informal*) ○ *a certifiable disease* **3.** REQUIRING PSYCHIATRIC TREATMENT legally or medically declared to be affected by a psychiatric disorder (*dated*) —**certifiably** *adv.*

certificate *n.* /sər tíffikət/ **1.** DOCUMENT PROVIDING OFFICIAL EVIDENCE an official document that gives proof and details of sth, e.g. personal status, educational achievements, ownership, or authenticity **2.** DOCUMENT SHOWING CONFORMITY TO STANDARD an official document awarded to sb who or sth that has passed a test or examination or conforms to a required standard **3.** DOCUMENT SHOWING QUALIFICATION an official document awarded to sb who has completed a course of study or training **4.** DOCUMENT GIVING STATE OF HEALTH an official document giving details of sb's state of health. It may be shown to an employer to confirm that the person is or is not fit for work. ■ *vt.* /sər tíffi kayt/ (**-cates, -cating, -cated**) **1.** GIVE CERTIFICATE TO SB OR STH to award a certificate to sb or sth **2.** AUTHORIZE OR PROVE STH WITH CERTIFICATE to authorize or provide evidence of sth with a certificate [15thC. From, ultimately, medieval Latin *certificatum*, from the past participle of late Latin *certificare* 'to certify' (see CERTIFY). The underlying idea is of a document that makes sth certain.] —**certification** *n.* —**certificatory** /sər tíffikətəri, súrtifi káytəri/ *adj.*

certificate of origin *n.* an official document stating what country a consignment of goods has come from

Certificate of Secondary Education *n.* full form of **CSE**

certified accountant *n.* an accountant who is a member of the Chartered Association of Certified Accountants and can therefore audit companies' accounts. ◊ **chartered accountant, certified public accountant**

certified mail *n.* *US* = **recorded delivery.** ◊ **registered mail**

certified public accountant *n.* a public accountant who has met the requirements of a particular US state and is therefore allowed to practise there

certify /súrti fī/ (**-fies, -fying, -fied**) *v.* **1.** *vti.* CONFIRM TRUTH OR ACCURACY OF STH to state or confirm that sth is true or correct **2.** *vt.* PROVE QUALITY OF SB OR STH to declare that sb or sth has passed a test or achieved a certain standard **3.** *vt.* ISSUE WITH A CERTIFICATE to award a certificate to sb or sth **4.** *vt.* DECLARE SB TO HAVE PSYCHIATRIC DISORDER to declare sb officially or legally to have a psychiatric disorder and require confinement in a mental health facility (*dated*) **5.** *vt.* *US* BANKING GUARANTEE PAYMENT OF CHEQUE to indicate on a cheque that there are sufficient funds to guarantee payment [14thC. Via French *certifier* from late Latin *certificare*, literally 'to make certain', from Latin *certus* (see CERTAIN).] —**certifier** *n.*

certiorari /súrti ə ráirī, súrti ə ráari/ *n.* LAW a writ issued by a higher court to obtain records on a case from a lower court so that the case can be reviewed. ◊ **mandamus, prohibition** [15thC. From late Latin, literally 'to be informed', the passive of Latin *certiorare* 'to inform', from, ultimately, *certus* 'sure'; the word occurs in the Latin version of the writ.]

certitude /súrti tyood/ *n.* **1.** FEELING OF CERTAINTY the feeling of conviction about sth, especially an opinion or religious faith **2.** DEFINITE TRUTH the definite truth of sth **3.** STH THAT IS CERTAIN sth that is certain to happen or about which sb can feel sure [15thC. From late Latin *certitudo*, from Latin *certus* (see CERTAIN).]

cerulean /sə róoli ən/ *adj.* of a deep blue colour, like the sky on a clear day (*literary*) [Mid-17thC. Formed from Latin *caeruleus* 'sky-blue, sea-blue', from *caelum* 'sky' (source of English *celestial*), of unknown origin.] —**cerulean** *n.*

ceruloplasmin /sə róolō plazmin/, **caeruloplasmin** *n.* a protein that helps the blood to store and transport copper [Mid-20thC. Coined from modern Latin *cerulo-* (from Latin *caeruleus*; see CERULEAN) + PLASMA + -IN. From its blue colour.]

cerumen /sə róomən/ *n.* the waxy secretion of glands lining the canal of the external ear (*technical*) [Late 17thC. From modern Latin, formed from Latin *cera* 'wax'.] —**ceruminous** /sə rOonənəss/ *adj.*

ceruse /sə róoss/ *n.* **1.** WHITE LEAD USED AS PIGMENT white lead used as a pigment and formerly in cosmetics **2.** COSMETIC CONTAINING WHITE LEAD a cosmetic containing white lead. Lead is now known to damage the skin and is no longer used in cosmetics. [14thC. Via French from Latin *cerussa*, of uncertain origin: perhaps ultimately from Greek *kēros* 'wax'.]

cerussite /séerə sīt/, **cerusite** *n.* a brittle colourless mineral, occurring mainly as crystals or granular aggregates in white to yellow and brown to black transparent or translucent forms. It is composed of lead carbonate and is used as a lead ore. [Mid-19thC. Coined from Latin *cerussa* (see CERUSE) + -ITE.]

Cervantes /sur vánt eez/, **Miguel de** (1547–1616) Spanish novelist and dramatist. His novel *Don Quixote* (1605–15) greatly influenced the development of the novel. Full name **Miguel de Cervantes Saavedra**

cervelat /súrvəlaa, -lat/ *n.* a German cured sausage made from pork and beef, usually smoked, with a mild flavour and a fine texture [Early 17thC. Via French from Italian *cervellata*, from *cervello* 'brain', from Latin *cerebellum* (see CEREBELLUM); from the fact that the sausage was originally made from brains.]

cervical /sər vík'l, súrvik'l/ *adj.* relating or belonging to the neck or any part of the body that resembles a neck, e.g. the cervix of the womb [Mid-19thC. Via French from Latin *cervic-*, the stem of *cervix* 'neck'.]

cervical cap *n.* = **diaphragm** *n.* 2

cervical smear *n.* a sample of tissue taken from the cervix of the womb for analysis, to enable early identification of cellular abnormalities that could lead to cervical cancer. US term **Pap smear**

cervices plural of **cervix**

cervicitis /súrvi sítiss/ *n.* inflammation of the cervix of the womb [Late 19thC. Coined from the Latin stem *cervic-* (see CERVIX) + -ITIS.]

cervid /súrvid/ *n.* any ruminant mammal, e.g. a deer, elk, or reindeer, characterized by the presence of antlers in the male or sometimes in both sexes. Family: Cervidae. [Late 19thC. From modern Latin *Cervidae* (plural), family name, from Latin *cervus* (see CERVINE).] —**cervid** *adj.*

cervine /súr vīn/ *adj.* relating to, resembling, or typical of a deer [Mid-19thC. From Latin *cervinus*, from *cervus* 'deer'. Ultimately from an Indo-European word meaning 'horn, head'.]

cervix /súrviks/ (*plural* **-vixes** *or* **-vices** /súrvi seez/) *n.* **1.** NECK OF WOMB the neck of the womb, consisting of a narrow passage leading to the vagina. The cervix widens greatly during childbirth to permit delivery of the baby. **2.** NECK the neck (*technical*) **3.** PART RESEMBLING NECK any part of the body that resembles a neck in shape or function [15thC. From Latin, 'neck'.]

cesarean *n.* US = **Caesarean**

České Budějovice /chéskay bóodə yawvit say/ city in southern Bohemia, Czech Republic. It is situated on the River Vltava, about 129 km/80 mi. south of Prague. Since the Middle Ages, it has produced Budvar beer. Population: 175,000 (1993).

cesium *n.* US = **caesium**

cespitose *adj.* = **caespitose**

cess[1] /sess/ *n.* **1.** LOCAL TAX a local tax or levy (*archaic*) **2.** OBLIGATION TO SUPPLY LORD DEPUTY'S SOLDIERS formerly in Ireland, a military assessment on a local population to provide food, lodgings, and supplies for the lord deputy's soldiers [Mid-16thC. Variant of earlier *sess*, from *assess* 'assessment', from the verb ASSESS.]

cess[2] /sess/ *n.* *Ireland* luck (*informal*) [Mid-19thC. Origin uncertain: either a shortening of SUCCESS, or from CESS[1].]

cessation /se sáysh'n/ *n.* a stop, pause, or interruption, especially a permanent discontinuation [15thC. From the Latin stem *cessation-*, from *cessat-*, the past participle stem of *cessare* 'to hold back, stop'.]

cession /sésh'n/ *n.* (*formal*) **1.** GIVING UP OR YIELDING the ceding or giving up of sth, especially land, property, or a right **2.** STH GIVEN UP sth ceded or given up, especially land, property, or a right [14thC. Directly or via French from the Latin stem *cession-*, from *cess-*, the past participle stem of *cedere* 'to yield' (see CEDE).]

Cessnock /séss nok/ town in New South Wales, southeastern Australia. Population: 43,849 (1991).

cesspit /sésspit/ *n.* **1.** PIT FOR WASTE MATTER a pit for the collection of waste matter and water, especially sewage **2.** FILTHY OR IMMORAL PLACE a foul and putrid place or situation, especially one linked with moral depravity [Mid-19thC. *Cess* from CESSPOOL.]

cesspool /séss pool/ *n.* **1.** UNDERGROUND CONTAINER FOR WASTE MATTER a covered underground tank or well for the collection of waste matter and water, especially sewage **2.** *US* = **cesspit** [Late 17thC. Origin uncertain: probably by folk etymology (from POOL) from earlier *cesperalle*, variant of *suspiral* 'cesspool', earlier 'drainpipe', from Old French *suspirail* 'breathing hole', from *souspirer* 'to breathe'.]

cesta /séstə/ *n.* a curved wicker basket for catching and throwing the ball in the Basque ball game jai alai [Early 20thC. Via Spanish, literally 'basket', from Latin *cista* 'chest' (see CHEST).]

c'est la vie /se laa vée/ *interj.* used to express philosophical acceptance of the way things are [Mid-20thC. From French, literally 'that's life'.]

cestode /séss tōd/ *n.* a tapeworm (*technical*) [Mid-19thC. From modern Latin *Cestoda* (plural), class name, from Latin *cestus* 'belt', from Greek *kestos*, originally 'stitched'.]

cestus[1] /séstəss/ (*plural* **-ti**), **cestos** (*plural* **-ti** /-tī/) *n.* a girdle or belt, especially one worn by women in ancient Greece [Mid-16thC. Via Latin from Greek *kestos* 'belt', originally 'stitched'.]

cestus[2] /séstəss/ (*plural* **-tuses** *or* **-tus**), **caestus** (*plural* **-tuses** *or* **-tus**) *n.* a studded gauntlet made of bull's hide worn by boxers in ancient Rome [Late 17thC. From Latin *caestus*, from *caedere* 'to hit'.]

cesura *n.* = **caesura**

CET *abbr.* **1.** Central European Time **2.** Common External Tariff

cetacean /si táysh'n/ *n.* a large aquatic mammal, e.g. a whale or a dolphin, that has a streamlined body with forelimbs modified as flippers, no hind limbs, and a blowhole on the back. Order: Cetacea. [Mid-19thC. Formed from modern Latin *Cetacea* (plural), order name, from Latin *cetus* 'whale', from Greek *kētos* 'sea-monster, huge fish, whale', of unknown origin.] —**cetaceous** *adj.*

cetane /sée tayn/ *n.* a colourless oily hydrocarbon found in petroleum. It is used in measuring the ignition quality of diesel fuels and as a solvent. Formula: $C_{16}H_{34}$. [Late 19thC. Coined from *cetyl* (see CETYL ALCOHOL) + -ANE.]

cetane number, **cetane rating** *n.* the performance rating of a diesel fuel expressed as the percentage of cetane in a mixture with 1-methylnaphthalene that shows the same ignition properties. The higher the cetane number, the better the performance.

cete /seet/ *n.* a group or company of badgers [15thC. Origin uncertain: perhaps from Latin *coetus* 'assembly, company', a variant of *coitus* 'combination'.]

ceteris paribus /káytəriss páaribəs, séttəriss párrəbəss/ *adv.* used to indicate that sth would be the case if everything else under consideration remains the same [Early 17thC. From modern Latin, literally 'other things being equal'.]

cetology /si tólləji/ *n.* the branch of zoology concerned with the study of whales, dolphins, and related mammals [Mid-19thC. Coined from Latin *cetus* 'whale' + -OLOGY.] —**cetological** /séetə lójjik'l/ *adj.* —**cetologist** /si tólləjist/ *n.*

Cetus /séetəss/ *n.* a constellation in the sky of the southern hemisphere near Aquarius and Eridanus that contains the bright star Mira

cetyl alcohol /séetīl-, sée't'l-/ *n.* a white waxy crystalline solid used in making cosmetics, pharmaceuticals, and detergents. Formula: $C_{16}H_{34}O$. [*Cetyl* coined from Latin *cetus* 'whale' + -YL. From the fact that the first compounds were isolated from spermaceti.]

Cévennes /say vén/ mountain range in France extending from the northern Ardèche Department to the southwestern Hérault Department. The highest peak is Mont Mézenc 1,754 m/5,755 ft.

ceviche /se véechay/, **seviche** *n.* a Latin American dish of raw fish marinated in lemon or lime juice and served as a type of salad with chopped onions and tomatoes [Mid-20thC. From American Spanish *seviche, ceviche*, from, apparently, Spanish *cebo* 'fodder, fish pieces used for bait', from Latin *cibus* 'food'.]

Ceylon /si lón/ former name for **Sri Lanka** (until 1972) —**Ceylonese** *adj., n.*

Ceylon moss *n.* a red seaweed of the East Indian Ocean that is a source of the gelatinous material agar. Latin name: *Gracilaria lichenoides.* [Because it grows in CEYLON]

Ceyx /see iks/ *n.* In Greek mythology, a king of Trachis in Thessaly who died in a shipwreck and whose wife, Alcyone, drowned herself in grief

Paul Cézanne: Self-portrait

Cézanne /si zán, say-/, **Paul** (1839–1906) French painter. His post-impressionist representation of nature in such paintings as *Rocky Landscape in Aix* (1887?) inspired cubism.

Cf *symbol.* californium

CF *abbr.* **1.** Chaplain to the Forces **2.** **CF, cf** cost and freight **3.** cystic fibrosis

cf. *abbr.* **1.** calfskin **2.** compare

c/f *abbr.* carried forward

CFA franc *n.* the unit of currency used in some African countries. See table at **currency** [*CFA* abbreviation of French *Communauté financière africaine* 'African financial community']

CFC *n.* a gas containing carbon, hydrogen, chlorine, and fluorine, used as a refrigerant and aerosol propellant. Some forms of CFC damage the ozone layer in the Earth's atmosphere. Full form **chlorofluorocarbon**

CFE *abbr.* **1.** College of Further Education **2.** Conventional Forces in Europe

CFI, cfi *abbr.* cost, freight, and insurance. ◊ **c.i.f.**

CFMEU *abbr.* Construction, Forestry, Mining and Energy Union

cg *abbr.* centre of gravity

CG *abbr.* **1.** captain general **2.** coastguard **3.** MIL Coldstream Guards **4.** Consul General

CGBR *abbr.* Central Government Borrowing Requirement

cge *abbr.* **1.** FREIGHT carriage **2.** BANKING charge

cgm *abbr.* centigram

CGM *abbr.* Conspicuous Gallantry Medal

cgs, CGS *abbr.* centimetre-gram-second

CGS *abbr.* **1.** centimetre-gram-second system **2.** Chief of General Staff

CGT *abbr.* capital gains tax

CH *abbr.* **1.** **CH, c.h.** clearing house **2.** Companion of Honour **3.** custom house

ch. *abbr.* **1.** MEASURE chain **2.** chapter **3.** CHESS check **4.** church **5.** BANKING charge

Ch. *abbr.* **1.** China **2.** BROADCAST channel

C/H *abbr.* central heating

chabazite /kábbə zīt/ *n.* a pink, yellow, white, or colourless mineral of the zeolite group, found in cavities in igneous rocks and as a deposit in hot springs. Chabazite is a hydrated silicate of calcium and aluminium. [Early 19thC. Formed from earlier *chabazie,* from Greek *khabazie,* a misspelling of *khalazie,* from, ultimately, *khalaza* 'hail' (see CHALAZA), from its form and colour.]

Chablis /shábli/, **chablis** *n.* a very dry white Burgundy wine made in the region around Chablis in central France

Chabrier /shábbri ay/, **Alexis Emmanuel** (1841–94) French composer. His light operas are rarely performed, but his orchestral rhapsody *España* (1883) remains popular.

Chabrol /sha bról/, **Claude** (*b.* 1930) French film director. He was a leader of the French New Wave in the 1950s. His films include *Story of Women* (1988).

cha-cha /chaá chaa/, **cha-cha-cha** /chaá chaa chaá/ *n.* **1.** RHYTHMIC LATIN AMERICAN DANCE a fast rhythmic ballroom dance of Latin American origin consisting of three steps and a hip-swaying shuffle **2.** DANCE MUSIC music written for the cha-cha ■ *vi.* (**cha-chas, cha-chaing, cha-chaed; cha-cha-chas, cha-cha-chaing, cha-cha-chaed**) DANCE to dance the cha-cha [From American Spanish (Cuban) *cha-cha-cha,* probably an imitation of the musical accompaniment]

chacma /chákmə/ (*plural* **-mas**) *n.* a ground-dwelling baboon of southern Africa that has a dark-grey coat and naked face with a long muzzle. Some authorities regard the chacma as a variety of savanna baboon rather than a distinct species. Latin name: *Papio ursinus.* [Mid-19thC. From Khoikhoi.]

chaconia /chə kóni ə/ (*plural* **-as** *or* **-a**) *n.* a red flower with large, conspicuous sepals that is the national flower of Trinidad and Tobago. Latin name: *Warszewiczia coccinea.*

chaconne /sha kón/ (*plural* **-connes**) *n.* **1.** DANCE ANCIENT DANCE an ancient, moderately slow dance that probably originated in Spain **2.** MUSIC MUSICAL FORM a musical composition consisting of variations on a fixed bass line continually repeated (**ground bass**) [Late 17thC. Via French from Spanish *chacona,* probably from Basque *chucun* 'pretty'.]

chacun à son gout /shákuN aa soN goó/ used to express the individuality or peculiarity of sb's taste or choice [From French, literally 'each to his or her own taste']

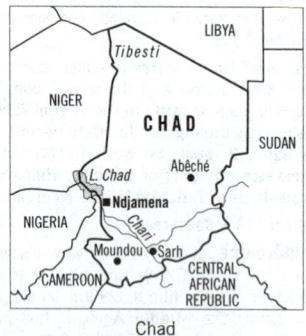

Chad

Chad /chad/ landlocked republic in north-central Africa, bordered on the north by Libya, on the east by Sudan, on the south by the Central African Republic, and on the west by Cameroon, Nigeria, and Niger. A former French territory, it became independent in 1960. Language: French. Currency: CFA franc. Capital: Ndjamena. Population: 7,166,023 (1997). Area: 1,284,000 sq. km/495,800 sq. mi. Official name **Republic of Chad** —**Chadian** *adj., n.*

Chad, Lake lake in central Africa, situated at the junction of Nigeria, Niger, and Chad. Area: approximately 10,360 to 25,900 sq. km/4,000 to 10,000 sq. mi.

chadar *n.* = chador

Chadic /cháddik/ *n.* a group of more than 100 languages spoken in west-central Africa. It is a branch of the Afro-Asiatic family of languages. There are about 25 million native speakers of Chadic languages, the most widespread being Hausa. —**Chadic** *adj.*

chador /chúddər/, **chadar, chuddar** *n.* **1.** DARK ROBE WORN BY MUSLIMS a dark traditional garment worn by Muslim and sometimes by Hindu women that covers almost all of the head and body **2.** CLOTH FOR MUSLIM TOMB a cloth that is used to cover a Muslim tomb [Early 17thC. Directly or via Urdu from Persian *čādar,* literally 'sheet, veil'.]

chaeta /keétə/ (*plural* **-tae** /-tee/) *n.* a bristle that occurs singly or in clusters in certain worms, e.g. earthworms and ragworms, and helps them to move [Mid-19thC. Via modern Latin from Greek *khaitē* 'long hair'.]

chaetognath /keétəg nath, keétə nath/ *n.* a torpedo-shaped invertebrate marine animal with an almost transparent body and fins running horizontally down both sides of the trunk and tail. Phylum: Chaetognatha. [Late 19thC. From modern Latin *Chaetognatha,* phylum name, from Greek *khaitē* (see CHAETA) + *gnathos* 'jaw'; from the spines on its head.] —**chaetognathous** /kee tógnəthəss/ *adj.*

chafe /chayf/ *v.* (**chafes, chafing, chafed**) **1.** *vti.* BECOME WORN OR MAKE STH WORN to become sore or worn by rubbing or make sth sore or worn in this way **2.** *vi.* CAUSE FRICTION to rub sth, causing friction **3.** *vt.* RUB STH TO WARM IT to warm sth, especially the hands or other parts of the body, by rubbing **4.** *vti.* BECOME ANNOYED OR ANNOY SB to be or make sb irritated, annoyed, or impatient ■ *n.* **1.** SORENESS OR WEAR soreness or wear caused by rubbing **2.** FEELING OF IRRITATION a feeling of irritation, annoyance, or impatience [13thC. Via Old French *chaufer* from Latin *calefacere* 'to make warm', from *calere* 'to be warm' (source of English *nonchalant*) + *facere* 'to make'.]

chafer[1] /cháyfər/ *n.* a large slow-moving scarab beetle, e.g. the cockchafer [Old English *ceafor.* Probably ultimately from an Indo-European word meaning 'jaw, mouth'. Related to German *Käfer* 'beetle'.]

chafer[2] /cháyfər/ *n.* = chafing dish [15thC. Via French *chauffoir* from Latin *calefactorium,* from *calefact-,* the past participle stem of *calefacere* (see CHAFE).]

chaff[1] /chaaf, chaf/ *n.* **1.** SEED COVERINGS REMOVED BY THRESHING the dry coverings (**bracts**) of grains and other grass seeds, which are separated by the process of threshing. When cereal crops are harvested mechanically, chaff is removed by the combine harvester and deposited with the straw in the field. **2.** WORTHLESS THING sth that is worthless or irrelevant **3.** MIL STRIPS OF METAL TO OBSTRUCT RADAR glass fibres or silvered nylon filaments dispersed into the air as an anti-radar measure [Old English *ceaf,* of uncertain origin: probably from a prehistoric Germanic base meaning 'chew'] —**chaffy** *adj.*

chaff[2] /chaaf, chaf/ *v.* (**chaffs, chaffing, chaffed**) **1.** *vt.* TEASE SB LIGHT-HEARTEDLY to tease sb in fun **2.** *vi.* BANTER to exchange light-hearted teasing or joking remarks ■ *n.* JOKING light-hearted joking or teasing [Early 19thC. Origin uncertain: perhaps an alteration of CHAFE.] —**chaffer** *n.*

chaffer /cháffər/ *vi.* (**-fers, -fering, -fered**) **1.** HAGGLE to haggle or bargain about sth **2.** BANDY WORDS to chatter idly ■ *n.* BARGAINING OR HAGGLING bargaining or haggling about sth [12thC. From Old English *ceap* 'bargain, sale' + *faru* 'faring, going', perhaps modelled on Old Norse *kaupför* 'trading-journey'.] —**chafferer** *n.*

chaffinch /cháffinch/ *n.* a finch, common in gardens and farmland of Europe and western Asia, that has white wing bars and a bluish hood, the males being more colourful. Latin name: *Fringilla coelebs.* [Old English *ceaffinc.* Because it pecks among farmyard chaff.]

chafing dish *n.* a shallow pan with a source of heat beneath it, used for cooking food or keeping food warm at the table

Chagall /sha gál/, **Marc** (1887–1985) Russian-born French painter and designer. His colourful fantasies, anticipating surrealism, stem largely from eastern European Jewish folklore.

Chagas' disease /shaágəss-/, **Chagas's disease** /-ssiz-/ *n.* an often fatal disease, occurring in South and Central America, that affects the heart and nervous system and is caused by a protozoan parasite transmitted by blood-sucking insects. ◊ **sleeping sickness** [Early 20thC. Named after Carlos *Chagas* (1879–1934), Brazilian physician, who first described it.]

chagrin /shággrin, shə grín/ *n.* ANGER AT BEING LET DOWN a feeling of vexation or humiliation due to disappointment about sth ■ *vt.* (**-grins, -grining, -grined**) VEX THROUGH FRUSTRATION to frustrate or annoy sb through disappointed hopes [Early 18thC. From French, 'sad, vexed', the original sense in English.]

chagrined /shággrind, shə grínd/ *adj.* frustrated, annoyed, or embarrassed through disappointed hopes

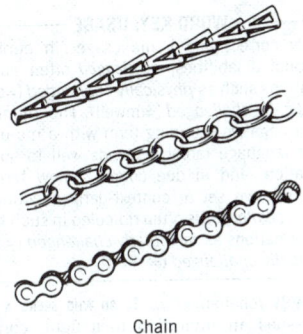

Chain

chain /chayn/ *n.* **1. SERIES OF JOINED METAL RINGS** a flexible interlinked series of usually metal links that may be used to support or restrain sth, as an ornament or decoration, or to drive or move sth **2. ACCESSORIES SERIES OF LINKS USED AS ACCESSORY** a series of rings, links, or discs used as a necklace, bracelet, or other piece of jewellery **3. BADGE OF OFFICE** a chain worn round the neck as a badge of office **4. STH RESEMBLING A CHAIN** a series of things or people linked or joined together for some purpose ○ *They stood hand in hand to form a human chain round the perimeter.* **5. COMM BUSINESSES UNDER ONE MANAGEMENT OR OWNERSHIP** a number of shops, hotels, restaurants, or other businesses that are owned by the same company and offer similar goods or services but are found in different locations **6. SEQUENCE OF RELATED EVENTS OR FACTS** a sequence of facts or events that happen one after the other and are connected in some way **7. UNIT OF LENGTH EQUAL TO 66 FT** a unit of length that is now rarely used, equal to 66 ft *(dated)* **8. CHEM SERIES OF ATOMS** a series of atoms, usually of a single element such as carbon, that are joined in a line or ring within a molecule **9. GEOG SERIES OF GEOGRAPHICAL FORMATIONS** a series of associated geographical features or formations, e.g. mountains, lakes, or islands ■ **chains** *npl.* **RESTRAINING CIRCUMSTANCES** feelings or circumstances that restrain or confine sb *(literary)* ■ *vt.* **(chains, chaining, chained)** **1. FASTEN STH WITH A CHAIN** to fasten, tie, or restrain sth or sb with a chain or chains **2. MEASURE WITH A CHAIN** to use a chain or tape to measure sth **3. RESTRICT SB'S MOBILITY** to restrict or confine sb's freedom of movement or action ○ *She was chained to the computer all day.* [13thC. Via Old French *chaeine* from Latin *catena* (source of English *concatenate*), of unknown origin.] —**chainless** *adj.*

Chain /chayn/, **Sir Ernst Boris** (1906–79) German-born British biochemist. With John Fleming and Howard Florey, his colleagues in the development of penicillin, he won the Nobel Prize in medicine in 1945.

chain drive *n.* an endless linked chain that meshes with the teeth of two sprocket wheels to transfer energy and motion from one to the other —**chain-driven** *adj.*

chaîné /sha náy/ *(plural* **-nés** */sha náy/) n.* a series of short, usually fast turns made by a ballet dancer moving in a straight line across a floor or stage [Mid-20thC. From French *chaîné*, literally 'chained, linked', the past participle of *chaîner* 'to chain', from, ultimately, Old French *chaeine* (see CHAIN).]

chained /chaynd/ *adj.* **1. FASTENED WITH CHAIN** tied up or fastened with a chain **2. LINKED** forming a chain

chain ferry *(plural* **chain ferries)** *n.* a river ferry that pulls itself along on one or more fixed chains, attached to each bank of the river. Chain ferries are used where there are strong currents and a shallow crossing.

chain gang *n.* a group of prisoners who work away from prison and are shackled together, usually with leg irons and a series of chains

chain grate, **chain grate stoker** *n.* a mechanism that stokes a large industrial furnace mechanically by supplying fuel on a conveyor that is driven by a chain

chain harrow *n.* a farm implement, consisting of a horizontal towing bar attached to heavy chains, that is trailed across soil or pasture to break up clods or disperse dung

chainlet /cháynlit/ *n.* a small chain

chain letter *n.* a letter sent to a number of people, each of whom is asked to send copies to the same number of new people, sometimes requesting and promising money to recipients

chainlink fence *n.* a fence formed from lengths of strong wire that are interwoven in a diamond pattern —**chainlink fencing** *n.*

chain mail *n.* interlinked rings of metal forming a flexible piece of armour, worn by knights in medieval times

chain of command *n.* a hierarchy of officials in the armed forces or in business, each reporting to and taking orders from the next most senior person

chainplate /cháyn playt/ *n.* a metal plate on the hull of a sailing vessel to which the ropes or cables supporting the mast are attached

chain reaction *n.* **1. CONNECTED SEQUENCE OF EVENTS** a series of events following quickly from each other, each of which causes the next one **2. NUCLEAR PHYS SELF-SUSTAINING NUCLEAR FISSION** a self-sustaining nuclear reaction in which each fission of an atomic nucleus causes neutrons and energy to be emitted, each collision of neutrons with other nuclei causing a further fission **3. CHEM SERIES OF CHEMICAL REACTIONS** a series of chemical reactions in which the product from one reaction helps to create the next one —**chain-react** *vi.*

chain saw *n.* a portable motor-driven saw with cutting teeth made of links that form a continuous chain, used for cutting wood

chain shot *n.* two cannonballs or half-balls connected by a chain, formerly used to destroy a ship's rigging

chain-smoke **(chain-smokes, chain-smoking, chain-smoked)** *vti.* to smoke cigarettes continuously, often lighting the next from the previous one as it is finished —**chain-smoker** *n.*

chain stitch *n.* a hand, machine, or crochet stitch in which each stitch forms a loop through the forward end of the previous one to resemble the links of a chain —**chain-stitch** *vti.*

chain store *n.* one of a series of retail shops, especially department stores or supermarkets, owned by the same company

chair /chair/ *n.* **1. SEAT WITH BACK AND SOMETIMES ARMRESTS** a seat with a back support, usually for one person. Most chairs have four legs or feet and some have rests for the arms. **2. CHAIRPERSON** sb presiding over sth such as a committee, board, or meeting, or the position of such a person **3. UNIV PROFESSORSHIP OR PROFESSOR** a university professorship, or the person holding such a position **4. MUSIC RANKED POSITION OF ORCHESTRAL MUSICIAN** the ranked position of a musician in an orchestra **5. ELECTRIC CHAIR** the electric chair *(informal)* **6. US BUILDING SUPPORTING DEVICE DURING POURING OF CONCRETE** a device to keep reinforcing rods in place during the pouring of concrete **7. RAIL METAL SOCKET ATTACHED TO SLEEPER CAR** a metal socket attached to a railway sleeper car in which a rail is locked into position **8. SEDAN CHAIR** a sedan chair *(archaic)* ■ *vt.* **(chairs, chairing, chaired)** **1. PRESIDE OVER STH** to preside over sth such as a committee, board, or meeting **2. CARRY WINNER ON SHOULDERS** to carry a victor or champion on the shoulders in triumph [13thC. Via Old French *chaiere* from Latin *cathedra* 'seat'.]

— **WORD KEY: USAGE** —
Chair has long been used to mean 'the authority or position of chairman', and has been extended to mean, more concretely, 'sb presiding over a meeting or committee',in order to avoid having to use the gender-specific terms *chairman* and *chairwoman*. An alternative is *chairperson*, though this is often thought to be a clumsy word.

chairborne /cháir bawrn/ *adj.* *(informal)* **1. HOLDING SEDENTARY OFFICE JOB** working at a desk in an office job rather than being more actively engaged **2. US HOLDING SEDENTARY MILITARY JOB** working at a desk in an office job in the armed forces, especially the air force, rather than having combat or field duties

Chair lift

chair lift *n.* a series of seats suspended from a moving cable, used to carry passengers up or down a mountain or other slope

chairman /cháirmən/ *(plural* **-men** */-mən) n.* **1. SB WHO PRESIDES OVER STH** the presiding officer of sth such as a committee or meeting **2. chairman, chairman of the board CHIEF PRESIDING OFFICER OF A COMPANY** the chief presiding officer of a business corporation, elected by its board of directors and responsible for corporate policy and supervision of upper management —**chairmanship** *n.*

— **WORD KEY: USAGE** —
See Usage note at **chair.**

chairperson /cháir purs'n/ *(plural* **-sons)** *n.* the presiding officer of sth such as a committee, board, or meeting

— **WORD KEY: USAGE** —
See Usage note at **chair.**

chairwoman /cháir woomən/ *(plural* **-en** */-wimmin/) n.* a woman who is the presiding officer of sth such as a committee, board, or meeting

— **WORD KEY: USAGE** —
See Usage note at **chair.**

chaise /shayz/ *(plural* **chaises** */shayz/) n.* **1. SMALL OPEN HORSE-DRAWN CARRIAGE** a light open two-wheeled carriage for one or more people, usually hooded and drawn by one horse **2.** = post chaise [Mid-17thC. From French, a variant of *chaire.*]

Chaise longue

chaise longue /shayz lóng/ *(plural* **chaise longues** */shayz lóng/ *or* **chaises longues** */shayz lóng/ *or* **chaises longues)** *n.* **1. CHAIR FOR LYING ON** a chair with an elongated seat, one armrest, and sometimes an adjustable back, designed for lying on **2. US FOLDABLE CHAIR WITH ADJUSTABLE BACK** a long low foldable chair with an adjustable back, used on a patio or beach [From French, literally 'long chair']

chakra /chúkrə, chaíakrə/ *(plural* **-ras)** *n.* in yoga, any one of the centres of spiritual power in the body. Each chakra is associated with a different god in Hinduism. [Late 18thC. From Sanskrit *cakra*, literally 'wheel'.]

chalaza /kə láyzə, kə lázzə/ *(plural* **-zas** *or* **-zae** */-zee/) n.* **1. ZOOL STRAND HOLDING EGG YOLK IN PLACE** a spiral chord of albumen that is attached at each end of the yolk to the lining membrane inside a bird's egg, holding it in position **2. BOT BASE OF IMMATURE SEED** the base of the immature seed of a plant [Early 18thC. Via modern Latin from Greek *khalaza* 'hail, small lump or knot like a hailstone' (source of English *chabazite*).] —**chalazal** *adj.*

chalazion /kə láyzi ən/ *n.* = **meibomian cyst** [Early 18thC. From Greek *khalazion*, literally 'small lump', formed from *khalaza* (see CHALAZA).]

Chalcedon /kálssidən/ *n.* an ancient Greek city on the Bosporus near modern-day Istanbul that was founded in 685 BC —**Chalcedonian** /kálssi dṓni ən/ *adj.*, *n.*

chalcedony /kal sédd'ni/ *n.* a translucent or greyish form of quartz in which the microscopic crystals are packed together in parallel bands, used as a gemstone and in ornaments. Formula: SiO_2. [13thC. Via Latin *c(h)alcedonius* from Greek *khalkēdōn*, a mystical stone, of uncertain origin: perhaps from *Khalkēdōn* (see CHALCEDON).] —**chalcedonic** /kálssi dónnik/ *adj.*

chalcid /kálssid/ *n.* a small wasp with bright metallic coloration whose larvae are often parasites of other insects in various stages of life. Superfamily: Chalcidoidea. [Late 19thC. Via modern Latin *Chalcid-*, the stem of *Chalcis*, genus name, from Greek *khalkos* 'copper', from its metallic colour and sheen.]

chalco- *prefix.* copper ○ *chalcopyrite* [From Greek *khalkos*]

chalcocite /kálkə sīt/ *n.* a grey to black brittle copper sulphide that is an important ore of copper. Formula: Cu_2S.

chalcography /kal kóggrəfi/ *n.* engraving on copper or brass —**chalcographer** *n.* —**chalcographist** *n.* —**chalcographic** /kálkə gráffik/ *adj.* —**chalcographical** /-gráffik'l/ *adj.*

chalcolithic /kálkə líthik/ *adj.* belonging or relating to the transitional period between the Neolithic and Bronze ages, beginning around 400 BC, when the use of copper became more prevalent

chalcopyrite /kálkə pī rīt/ *n.* a brassy yellow sulphide of copper and iron that is the commonest ore of copper. Formula: $CuFeS_2$.

Chaldea ancient region of Mesopotamia, between the Euphrates and the Persian Gulf, in modern-day southern Iraq

Chaldean /kal dée ən/, **Chaldaean** *n.* **1.** PEOPLES **MEMBER OF ANCIENT SEMITIC PEOPLE** a member of an ancient Semitic people who lived in Chaldea in southern Babylonia, where they were the dominant ethnic group during the 8th and 7th centuries BC **2.** LANG **ARAMAIC DIALECT** a dialect of the modern Aramaic language, spoken in Iraq and by communities now settled in the United States **3.** **SOOTHSAYER** an astrologer, fortune-teller, or enchanter (*archaic*) [Late 16thC. Formed from Latin *Chaldaeus*, from, ultimately, Assyrian *kaldū*.] —**Chaldaic** *n.*, *adj.* —**Chaldean** *adj.*

Chaldee /káldee, kal dée/ *n.* **1.** LANG **ARAMAIC** the Aramaic language (*dated*) **2.** PEOPLES = **Chaldean** *n.* 1 [14thC. Via Old French from Latin *Chaldaeus* (see CHALDEAN).]

chaldron /cháwldrən/ *n.* a former unit of capacity, especially a US unit equivalent to 1.268 m^3 used to measure solids or a British unit equivalent to 1.309 m^3 used to measure solids and liquids [Mid-16thC. Via Old French *chauderon* 'kettle', from, ultimately, Latin *caldarium* 'vessel containing warm water for bathing'.]

chalet /shállay/ *n.* **1.** **WOODEN HOUSE OF SWISS ORIGIN** a house or cottage traditionally made of wood with wide overhanging eaves, originally built in Switzerland **2.** **SMALL HUT IN HOLIDAY CAMP** a small hut, especially one used for living accommodation in a holiday camp [Late 18thC. From Swiss French, of uncertain origin: possibly formed from Old French *chasel* 'farmstead', from, ultimately, Latin *casa* 'hut, cottage'.]

chalice /chálliss/ *n.* **1.** **METAL CUP** a metal drinking cup or goblet (*literary*) **2.** CHR **CUP USED AT COMMUNION OR MASS** a gold or silver cup used in a church for serving the wine at Communion or Mass [14thC. Directly or via French from Latin *calic-*, the stem of *calix* 'cup' (source of English *calix*).]

chalicothere /kállikə theer/ *n.* an extinct mammal resembling a horse with clawed feet and forelimbs slightly longer than the hind limbs. It lived from about 55 million to about 10,000 years ago. Suborder: Chalicotheriidae. [Early 20thC. From modern Latin *Chalicotherium*, genus name, literally 'animal found in gravel', from the Greek stem *khalik-* 'pebble, gravel' + *thērion*, literally 'small animal', from *thēr* 'animal'.]

chalk /chawk/ *n.* **1.** GEOL **POWDERY WHITE ROCK** a soft white or grey fine-grained sedimentary rock consisting of nearly pure calcium carbonate that contains minute fossil fragments of marine organisms **2.** **SOFT MARKER MADE FROM CHALK** a piece of chalk or a similar substance, sometimes coloured, used for writing or drawing, e.g. on a blackboard **3.** CUE GAMES **CUBE OF CHALK FOR RUBBING CUE** a small cube of chalk or similar substance used for rubbing the tip of a billiard or snooker cue to increase friction between the cue and the ball ■ *v.* (**chalks, chalking, chalked**) **1.** *vti.* **DRAW OR MARK STH WITH CHALK** to draw, write, or mark sth with chalk **2.** *vi.* **BECOME POWDERY** to become powdery **3.** *vt.* CUE GAMES **RUB CHALK ON A CUE** to treat a billiard or snooker cue with chalk [Old English *cealc* 'lime(stone), chalk', via prehistoric Germanic from the Latin stem *calc-* 'lime(stone)', from Greek *khalix* 'small stone, pebble' (source of English *calcium* and *calculate*)] ◇ **as like** *or* **different as chalk and cheese** extremely different in important respects (*informal*) ◇ **by a long chalk** by a large margin ◇ **not by a long chalk** not by any means

chalk out *vt.* to sketch or outline a plan or proposal

chalk up *vt.* **1.** **SCORE OR KEEP SCORE OF STH** to score or achieve sth, or record a score or victory **2.** **CHARGE STH TO SB** to record the cost of sth and charge it to sb or sb's account **3.** **ATTRIBUTE TO STH** to credit or ascribe sth to sth or sb [From the custom at pubs or bars of writing up with chalk an account of credit given]

chalk and talk *n.* a traditional method of education in which the teacher addresses the students, using a blackboard to provide examples or illustrations

chalkboard /cháwk bawrd/ *n. US, Can* = **blackboard**

chalkface /cháwk fayss/ *n.* teaching in a classroom, as distinct from the other duties of a teacher (*informal*) [Modelled on COALFACE, from the idea of a blackboard at the front of a classroom]

chalkpit /cháwk pit/ *n.* a quarry where chalk is excavated

chalkstone /cháwk stōn/ *n.* a piece of chalk taken straight from the ground

chalky /cháwki/ (**-ier, -iest**) *adj.* containing chalk, or resembling chalk in colour or texture —**chalkiness** *n.*

challah /khaálə, haálə/ (*plural* **-lahs** *or* **-loth** /-lōt/), **hallah** (*plural* **-lahs** *or* **-loth**) *n.* white bread enriched with eggs, usually in a plaited loaf, traditionally eaten by Jews on Friday evening at the Sabbath meal [Early 20thC. From Hebrew *ḥallāh*, from, probably, *ḥll* 'to pierce', from its original shape.]

challenge /chállənj/ *vt.* (**-lenges, -lenging, -lenged**) **1.** **INVITE SB TO CONTEST STH** to invite sb to participate in a fight, contest, or competition **2.** **DARE** to dare sb to do sth **3.** **CALL STH INTO QUESTION** to call sth into question by demanding an explanation, justification, or proof **4.** **STIMULATE** to stimulate sb by making demands on the intellect **5.** **ORDER SB TO PRODUCE IDENTIFICATION** to order sb to stop and produce identification or a password **6.** LAW **OBJECT TO INCLUSION OF JUROR** to make a formal objection against the inclusion of a prospective juror on a jury **7.** IMMUNOL **TEST WHETHER STH PRODUCES ALLERGY** to expose a person or animal to a substance in order to determine whether an allergy or other adverse reaction will occur ■ *n.* **1.** **INVITATION TO TAKE PART IN CONTEST** an invitation to sb to compete in a fight, contest, or competition **2.** **STIMULATING TEST OF ABILITIES** a test of sb's abilities or a situation that tests sb's abilities in a stimulating way **3.** **QUESTIONING OF STH** a questioning of sth by demanding an explanation, justification, or proof **4.** **DEMAND FOR IDENTIFICATION** an order to sb to stop and produce identification or a password **5.** LAW **OBJECTION AGAINST JUROR** an objection against the inclusion of sb on a jury **6.** IMMUNOL **TESTING FOR ALLERGY** exposure of a person or animal to a substance in order to determine whether an allergy or other adverse reaction will occur [13thC. Via Old French *c(h)alengier* 'to accuse' from Latin *calumniare* 'to accuse falsely', from *calumnia* 'false accusation' (source of English *calumny*).] —**challengeable** *adj.*

challenged /chállənjd/ *adj.* **1.** **WITH SPECIFIED PROBLEM** having a specified handicap **2.** **LACKING IN STH** lacking in a specified quality or characteristic (*humorous*) ○ *vertically challenged*

WORD KEY: USAGE

Politically correct and ironic usage: In euphemisms for personal disabilities, ***challenged*** often appears in combinations such as *physically challenged* (=disabled) and *medically challenged* (=unwell). The intention is to replace a negative-sounding term with a more positive one. But language rarely responds well to such overt manipulation, and in due course a new terminology acquires its own set of context-derived connotations. The use of ***challenged*** is often ridiculed in such facetious ad hoc formations as *follicularly challenged* (= balding) and *vertically challenged* (= short).

challenger /chállənjər/ *n.* **1.** **SB WHO SEEKS A FIGHT** sb who issues an invitation to a fight, contest, or competition **2.** **SB WHO OPPOSES CHAMPION** sb who competes for a championship against the champion, especially in boxing

challenging /chállənjing/ *adj.* demanding physical or psychological effort of a stimulating kind —**challengingly** *adv.*

challis /shállis, -li/, **challie** /shálli/ *n.* a soft lightweight fabric for clothes, often patterned with a small print and made of wool, cotton, or synthetic fibres [Mid-19thC. Origin uncertain: perhaps from the surname *Challis*.]

chalone /káy lōn, kállōn/ *n.* a substance produced by cells that inhibits the division of cells of a similar type. Chalones are usually glycoproteins. [Early 20thC. Formed from Greek *khalōn*, the present participle of *khalan* 'to slacken', on the model of HORMONE.] —**chalonic** /ka lónik, kay-/ *adj.*

chalumeau /shállyōō mō/ (*plural* **-meaux** /shállyōō mō/) *n.* **1.** **EARLY MUSICAL INSTRUMENT** a woodwind instrument of the 17th and 18th centuries that developed into the clarinet **2.** **LOWEST REGISTER OF CLARINET** the lowest register of a clarinet, or its warm tone quality [Early 18thC. Via French from late Latin *calamellus*, literally 'small reed', from *calamus* 'reed', from Greek *kalamos* (source of English *calamus*, *caramel*, and *shawm*).]

chalutz /khaa lóots/ (*plural* **-lutzim** /kháa lóot séem/), **halutz** (*plural* **-lutzim**) *n.* a member of a group of Jewish immigrants to Palestine after 1917 who began or worked in agricultural or forestry projects [Early 20thC. From Hebrew *ḥaluṣ*, literally 'pioneer'.]

chalybeate /kə líbbi it/ *adj.* **1.** **CONTAINING IRON SALTS** containing iron salts **2.** **TASTING OF IRON** having a taste like iron [Mid-17thC. From modern Latin *chalybeatus*, from Latin *chalybs* 'steel', from Greek *khalups*.]

chalybite /kálli bīt/ *n.* = **siderite** [Mid-19thC. Coined from Greek *khalyb-*, the stem of *khalyps* 'steel' + -ITE.]

cham /kam/ *n.* a Tartar or Mogul khan (*archaic*) [15thC. Via French from Turkic *kān* 'lord, prince'.]

Cham /kam/ (*plural* **Chams** *or* **Cham**) *n.* **1.** **MEMBER OF VIETNAMESE PEOPLE** a member of a people who originally lived in Champa, a former kingdom in present-day Vietnam. After the Annamese invaded in the 17th century, many Chams fled to Cambodia. **2.** LANG **AUSTRONESIAN LANGUAGE** a language spoken in parts of Vietnam and Cambodia. It belongs to the Austronesian family of languages. Cham is spoken by about 230,000 people. —**Cham** *adj.*

Chamaeleon /kə méeli ən/, **Chameleon** *n.* a faint constellation lying near the south celestial pole

chamaephyte /kámmi fīt/ *n.* a perennial plant that produces buds on or close to the ground. The buds remain dormant during the winter. [Early 20thC. Coined from Greek *khamai* 'low, on the ground' (see CHAMELEON) + -PHYTE.]

chamber /cháymbər/ *n.* **1.** **BEDROOM** a bedroom or other room in sb's home (*archaic or literary*) **2.** **OFFICIAL RECEPTION ROOM** a reception room in an official residence or a palace **3.** **ROOM FOR SPECIFIC PURPOSE** a room used for a designated purpose **4.** **OFFICIAL ASSEMBLY OR MEETING PLACE** a legislative or judicial assembly, or the place where such a body meets **5.** **ORGANIZED BODY OF PEOPLE** a body of people organized into a group for a specific purpose **6.** **COMPARTMENT IN STH** an enclosed space, compartment, or cavity, e.g. one inside a machine, the body, or a plant **7.** ARMS **PLACE IN GUN FOR AMMUNITION** the compartment for a cartridge in a revolver or rifle, or for a shell in a cannon **8.** FIN **TREASURY** a treasury, especially for government funds (*archaic*) **9.** = chamber pot ■ **chambers** *npl.* **1.** LAWYERS' OFFICES a suite of rooms used by lawyers for consulting with clients **2.** JUDGE'S PRIVATE OFFICE a judge's private office for discussing cases or legal matters not taken up in open court **3.** FLAT OR SUITE OF ROOMS a flat or suite of private rooms ■ *adj.* OF CHAMBER MUSIC relating to, written as, or performing chamber music ■ *vt.* (**-bers, -bering, -bered**) **1.** ENCLOSE IN OR PROVIDE WITH CHAMBERS to put sth in or provide sth with a chamber or chambers **2.** ARMS PUT AMMUNITION IN WEAPON to insert a round of ammunition in the breech of a weapon [12thC. Via French *chambre* from Latin *camera* 'vault, arch, room' (source of English *camera*), from Greek *kamara* 'vault, sth with an arched cover'.]

chambered /cháymbərd/ *adj.* **1.** ENCLOSED enclosed or confined in a chamber or sth similar **2.** WITH CAVITIES containing a chamber or chambers

chambered nautilus *n.* = pearly nautilus

chamberlain /cháymbərlin/ *n.* **1.** MANAGER OF ROYAL OR NOBLE HOUSEHOLD an official who manages the household of a monarch or member of the nobility **2.** TREASURER OF MUNICIPALITY the treasurer of a municipality **3.** CHR PRIEST WHO IS PAPAL ATTENDANT a priest who is an attendant to the Pope, often an honorary position [12thC. Via Old French from assumed Frankish *kamarling*, literally 'little room', from, ultimately, Greek, 'vaulted room, vault'. The underlying meaning is 'bed-chamber attendant'.]

Chamberlain /cháymbərlin/, **Joseph** (1836–1914) British politician. An MP from 1876, he resigned from the Liberal Party in 1886 over Irish Home Rule and led the Liberal Unionists after 1891.

Chamberlain, Neville (1869–1940) British statesman. He resigned as prime minister (1937–40) after diplomatic and military failures, most notably his advocacy of appeasement towards Nazi Germany. Full name **Arthur Neville Chamberlain**

chambermaid /cháymbər mayd/ *n.* a woman employed to tidy and clean bedrooms in hotels or guest houses

chamber music *n.* classical instrumental music written for a small group e.g., a quartet or trio, and often originally intended for performance in a large room or a small concert hall

chamber of commerce *n.* an organization of local business people who work together to promote and protect common interests in trade

chamber of horrors *n.* an exhibition depicting macabre or gruesome objects and incidents [From the name given to a room in Madame Tussaud's waxwork exhibition in London, containing effigies of noted criminals]

chamber of trade *n.* a national organization representing local chambers of commerce

chamber orchestra *n.* a small orchestra, usually comprising fewer than 40 players, that performs classical music. A chamber orchestra can play at more modest-sized venues than a full symphony orchestra.

chamber pot *n.* a large bowl used in a bedroom for urination and defecation

Chambers Pillar /cháymbərz-/ sandstone monolith situated in Chambers Pillar Historical Reserve, approximately 162 km/100 mi. south of Alice Springs, central Australia. Height: 30 km/19 mi. Aboriginal **Itirkawara**

chambray /shám bray/ *n.* a fine lightweight cotton or linen fabric with coloured lengthwise fibres interlaced with white [Early 19thC. Alteration of the name of *Cambrai*, a city in northern France where the cloth was originally made.]

chameleon /kə meeli ən/ *n.* **1.** LIZARD THAT CHANGES COLOUR a tree-dwelling lizard found chiefly in Africa and Madagascar, with long thin legs, a strong curled tail, a long sticky tongue, and the ability to change colour. Family: Chamaeleonidae. **2.** SB WHO IS CHANGEABLE sb who easily and frequently changes personality or appearance [14thC. Via Latin from Greek *khamaileōn*, literally 'ground lion', from *khamai* 'low, on the ground' + *leōn* 'lion'.] —**chameleonic** /kə meeli ónnik/ *adj.*

Chameleon *n.* ASTRON = Chamaeleon

chametz /khaa méts, kháwmits/, **chometz, hametz, hometz** *n.* leavened bread or other food that may not

Chameleon

be eaten by Jews during Passover [Mid-19thC. From Hebrew *ḥāmēṣ*.]

chamfer /chámfər/ *n.* SHALLOW ANGLED CUT a shallow cut, edge, or groove made in wood, usually at an angle of 45 degrees to a corner ■ *vt.* (**-fers, -fering, -fered**) MAKE SHALLOW CUT IN WOOD to make a shallow cut, edge, or groove in wood, usually at an angle of 45 degrees to a corner [Mid-16thC. Back-formation from *chamfering* 'grooving', from French *chanfrein* 'bevelled edge', variant of *chanfreint*, past participle of *chanfraindre* 'to bevel', from *chant* 'edge' (from Latin *canthus* 'iron tyre') + *fraindre* 'to break'.] —**chamfered** *adj.*

chamfron /chámfrən/ *n.* a piece of armour used in medieval times to protect a horse's head in battle [15thC. From French *chanfrain*, of uncertain origin: perhaps from Old French *chafrener* 'to harness a horse', literally 'to put a bridle on', from *chief* 'head' + *frener* 'to bridle'.]

Chamois

chamois /shám waa/ *n.* (*plural* **-ois** /shám waa/ *or* **-oix**) **1.** EURASIAN GOAT ANTELOPE an agile goat antelope found in mountainous regions of Europe and southwestern Asia that has slender backward-curving horns and a tawny coat that darkens in winter. Latin name: *Rupicapra rupicapra.* **2.** chamois, chamois leather SOFT PLIABLE LEATHER soft pliable leather used for cleaning and polishing. Originally made from the hide of the chamois, it is now usually made from that of sheep or goats. **3.** CHAMOIS LEATHER CLOTH FOR POLISHING a piece of chamois leather, or a natural or synthetic substitute, used for cleaning and polishing **4.** COLOURS GREYISH-YELLOW a greyish-yellow colour, like that of chamois leather ■ *adj.* COLOURS GREYISH-YELLOW of a greyish-yellow colour ■ *vt.* (**-oises, -oising, -oised**) CLEAN OR POLISH STH WITH CHAMOIS to clean or polish sth with a chamois [Mid-16thC. Via French from late Latin *camox*, of uncertain origin: probably from a language spoken in the Alps before the Romans penetrated northwards.]

chamomile *n.* = camomile

champ[1] /champ/ *n.* **1.** MASHED POTATOES WITH SPRING ONIONS an Irish dish of mashed potatoes with milk and spring onions eaten with melted butter **2.** BITING, CHEWING, OR GRINDING STH the process of biting, chewing, or grinding sth vigorously, noisily, or impatiently, or the sound that this makes ■ *v.* (**champs, champing, champed**) **1.** *vti.* BITE STH VIGOROUSLY to bite, chew, or grind sth vigorously, noisily, or impatiently **2.** *vt.* Scotland MASH FOOD to mash sth, e.g. potatoes (*informal*) [Mid-16thC. Origin uncertain: probably an imitation of the sound.] —**champer** *n.*

Occasionally, the food of the poor becomes attractive to the more affluent and, in this way, a dialect word is often retained. In Ireland *champ* used to be boiled potatoes mashed with a little milk and butter and flavoured with nettles, leeks, or spring onions. It was the food of people who could rarely afford meat or fish. In later, more affluent, times it has featured as a delicacy in Irish restaurants and pubs, with the result that *champ* occurs more widely now than it did in the past.

champ[2] /champ/ *n.* a champion (*informal*) [Mid-19thC. Shortening.]

champac *n.* = champak

champagne /sham páyn/ *n.* **1.** WINE DRY WHITE SPARKLING WINE FROM CHAMPAGNE a dry white sparkling wine produced in the Champagne region of northeastern France, often drunk at special occasions **2.** WINE WHITE WINE RESEMBLING CHAMPAGNE any dry or semisweet white wine resembling champagne and made by a similar process **3.** COLOURS PALE BROWNISH GOLD a very pale brownish-gold colour ■ *adj.* **1.** EXTRAVAGANT involving luxury and indulgence ○ *a champagne lifestyle* **2.** PALE BROWNISH-GOLD of a very pale brownish-gold colour [Mid-17thC]

champagne socialist *n.* sb whose luxurious way of life appears to contradict that person's socialist principles (*informal*) —**champagne socialism** *n.*

champaign /chám payn/ *n.* a wide expanse of open countryside (*literary*) [14thC. Via French *champagne* from late Latin *campania* 'level country', from Latin, *Campania*, a province in Middle Italy (source of English *campaign*).]

Champaigne /sham páyn/, **Philippe de** (1602–74) Flemish-born French painter. Baroque portraiture, notably of his patron Cardinal Armand Richelieu, gives way to classicism in his later religious subjects.

champak /chúmpuk, chámpak/ (*plural* **-paks** *or* **-pak**), **champac** (*plural* **-pacs** *or* **-pac**) *n.* an Asian evergreen tree whose wood is used for furniture. It has fragrant orange-yellow flowers whose oil is used in perfumery and is sacred to Hindus and Buddhists. Latin name: *Michelia champaca.* [Late 18thC. Via Hindi from Sanskrit *chāmpākā*, from Dravidian (a non-Indo-European language family).]

champers /shámpərz/ *n.* champagne (*informal*)

champerty /chámpərti/ (*plural* **-ties**) *n.* LAW an agreement between a litigant and sb who aids or finances litigation in return for a share of the proceeds following a successful outcome [15thC. From Anglo-Norman *champartie*, from Old French *champart* 'field rent (a portion received by a feudal lord of the produce from land leased)', from *champ* 'field' + *part* 'portion'.] —**champertous** *adj.*

champignon /shámpin yoN, cham pínnyən/ *n.* a mushroom, especially one cultivated for eating [Late 16thC. From French, literally 'little country', formed from *champagne*, from late Latin *campania* 'level country'. The underlying idea is of sth that grows in the countryside.]

champion /chámpi ən/ *n.* **1.** SUPREME VICTOR IN CONTEST a person who or team that competes in and wins a contest, competition, or tournament **2.** SHOW WINNER sth, e.g. an animal or plant, that wins first place in a show **3.** DEFENDER sb who defends, supports, or promotes a person or cause **4.** REMARKABLE PERSON sb who exemplifies excellence or achievement **5.** HERO OR WARRIOR a hero or warrior, especially a knight who fights on behalf or or in defence of a monarch (*archaic or literary*) ■ *vt.* (**-ons, -oning, -oned**) DEFEND to defend, support, or promote a cause or person ■ *adj.* N England EXCELLENT very good or pleasing ■ *adv.* N England VERY WELL in a very good or pleasing way [12thC. Via Old French, 'combatant', from the late Latin stem *campion-* 'combatant in the arena or athletic field', from Latin *campus* 'field'.]

championship /chámpi ənship/ *n.* **1.** CONTEST TO DECIDE A CHAMPION a contest, competition, or tournament that is held to decide who will be the overall winner **2.** TITLE OR TIME OF BEING CHAMPION the designation or period of being a champion **3.** DEFENDING OR SUPPORTING SB OR STH the defence, support, or promotion of a person or cause

Champlain, Lake /sham pláyn/ lake situated between Vermont and New York, extending approximately 10 km/6 mi. into Canada. Area: 1,100 sq. km/430 s. mi. Depth: 122 m/399 ft.

champlevé /shámplə vay, sháaNlə váy/ *n.* enamel work in which coloured enamels are used to fill channels cut into a metal base [Mid-19thC. From French, literally 'raised field', from *champ* 'field' + *levé* 'raised'.] —**champlevé** *adj.*

Champollion /sham pố yoN/, **Jean François** (1790–1832) French Egyptologist. The founder of the study of ancient Egypt, he deciphered the Rosetta Stone to become the first person to decode Egyptian hieroglyphics (1822). Full name **Jean François Champollion Le Jeune**

Chanc. *abbr.* **1.** chancellor **2.** chancery

chance /chaanss/ *n.* **1. LIKELIHOOD THAT STH WILL HAPPEN** the degree of probability that sth will happen (*often used in the plural*) ○ *There's a strong chance we'll win.* **2. OPPORTUNITY OR OPPORTUNE TIME FOR STH** an opportunity or a set of circumstances that makes it possible for sth to happen ○ *I was given no chance to explain.* **3. SUPPOSED FORCE THAT MAKES THINGS HAPPEN** the supposed force that makes things happen in a particular way without any apparent cause **4. UNEXPECTED HAPPENING** an unexpected event **5. STH CAUSED BY LUCK** sth caused by luck or fortune ■ *v.* (**chances, chancing, chanced**) **1.** *vt.* **DO STH RISKY** to do sth knowing that it is risky **2.** *vi.* **DO STH UNPLANNED** to do sth or happen without a cause or plan [13thC. Via Anglo-Norman from, ultimately, late Latin *cadentia* 'falling', from the present participle of Latin *cadere* 'to fall'.] ◇ **by any chance** used to enquire if there is any possibility of sth ○ *Is there a copy you could lend me, by any chance?* ◇ **by chance** unexpectedly or without plan ◇ **chance your arm** to attempt sth despite unfavourable odds ◇ **fat chance** sth that is highly unlikely (*informal*)

chance on, **chance upon** *vt.* to find or encounter sb or sth unexpectedly

chancel /chaánssəl/ *n.* an area of a church near the altar for the use of clergy and choir, often separated from the nave by a screen or steps [14thC. Via Old French from Latin *cancelli*, literally 'little lattices' (source also of *chancellor*), from *cancer* 'lattice'. The underlying idea is of a place enclosed by a grating.]

chancellery /chaánssələri, chaánsslári/ (*plural* -**ies**), **chancellory** (*plural* -**ies**) *n.* **1. CHANCELLOR'S RESIDENCE** the official residence of a chancellor **2. CHANCELLOR'S RANK** the position or rank of a chancellor **3.** *US* = chancery

chancellor /chaánssələr, chaánsslər/, **Chancellor** *n.* **1. HEAD OF GOVERNMENT IN PARLIAMENTARY DEMOCRACY** the chief minister of government in some parliamentary democracies **2. Chancellor** = Chancellor of the Exchequer **3.** *UK, Can* **HONORARY HEAD OF UNIVERSITY** the honorary head of a university **4.** *US* **CHIEF ADMINISTRATIVE OFFICER OF UNIVERSITY** the chief administrative officer of some universities **5. EMBASSY SECRETARY** the main secretary of an embassy **6. HIGH-RANKING OFFICIAL** a high-ranking government or legal official **7. SECRETARY TO MONARCH OR NOBLE** a secretary to a monarch or noble (*archaic*) [Pre-12thC. Via Anglo-Norman *c(h)anceler* from Latin *cancellarius* 'court secretary' (originally the attendant at the grating that separated the public from the judges), from *cancelli* 'grating' (see CHANCEL).] —**chancellorship** *n.*

Chancellor of the Duchy of Lancaster (*plural* **Chancellors of the Duchy of Lancaster**) *n.* a member of the British government who legally represents a sovereign in matters concerning the Duchy of Lancaster. In practice, the title is honorary and held by a cabinet minister who does not have a department.

Chancellor of the Exchequer *n.* a member of the British government who is the chief minister of finance

chancellory *n.* = chancellery

chance-medley /chaanss/ *n.* **1. LAW KILLING IN SELF-DEFENCE** the killing of an assailant in self-defence during an unexpected brawl **2. STH HAPPENING BY CHANCE** a haphazard event or action, or the randomness of chance [15thC. From Anglo-Norman *chance medlee*, literally 'mixed chance'; from the idea of being only partly accidental.]

---

chancer /chaánssər/ *n.* sb who takes chances or risks in the interest of personal gain (*informal*)

chancery /chaánssəri/ (*plural* -**ies**), **Chancery** (*plural* -**ies**) *n.* **1. LAW LORD CHANCELLOR'S COURT** the Lord Chancellor's court, one of the five divisions of the High Court of Justice in England **2. LAW** = court of chancery **3. RELIG OFFICE ATTACHED TO EMBASSY** an office attached to an embassy or consulate, especially the political section. US term **chancellery 4. PUBLIC ARCHIVE** a public archive or record office **5.** = chancellery [14thC. Contraction of CHANCELLERY.]

Chancery Division *n.* = chancery

chancey *adj.* = chancy

chancre /shángkər/ *n.* **1. ULCER INDICATING SYPHILIS AND OTHER DISEASES** a small painless highly infectious ulcer or sore that is the first sign of syphilis and certain other infectious diseases **2. ULCER** a sore or ulcer at the point where a disease-causing organism (**pathogen**) enters the body [Late 16thC. Via French from Latin *cancer* 'ulcer'.] —**chancrous** *adj.*

chancroid /sháng kroyd/ *n.* **1. SEXUALLY TRANSMITTED DISEASE** a sexually transmitted disease that causes a painful ragged ulcer at the site of infection and is treated with antibiotics. It is caused by infection with a bacterium *Haemophilus ducreyi.* **2. ULCER** a painful ragged ulcer that is characteristic of the sexually transmitted disease chancroid —**chancroidal** /sháng króyd'l/ *adj.*

chancy /chaánssi/ (-**ier**, -**iest**), **chancey** (-**ier**, -**iest**) *adj.* **1. RISKY** involving risks or danger **2. RANDOM OR HAPHAZARD** occurring in a random or haphazard way — **chancily** *adv.* —**chanciness** *n.*

Chandelier

chandelier /shándə leér/ *n.* a decorative hanging light with several branches and holders for candles or light bulbs [Mid-18thC. From French, formed from *chandelle* 'candle' (originally the light in a chandelier), from Latin *candela* 'candle'.] —**chandeliered** *adj.*

chandelle /shan dél, shaaN-/ *n.* **STEEP CLIMBING TURN OF AIRCRAFT** a steep climbing turn in which an aircraft almost stalls as it uses momentum to increase the rate of climb ■ *vi.* (-**delles**, -**delling**, -**delled**) **EXECUTE CHANDELLE** to climb steeply in an aircraft, turning at the same time and almost stalling [Early 20thC. From French, literally 'candle'.]

Chandigarh /ch/, **Chandīgarh** /ndi gaár/ city situated in the northwestern part of India. It is the joint capital of Punjab and Haryana states. Population: 574,646 (1991).

chandler /chaándlər/ *n.* **1. SELLER OF SPECIFIED GOODS** a seller of specified supplies and goods ○ *a ship's chandler* **2. CANDLE MAKER AND SELLER** a seller or maker of candles **3. GROCER** sb who sells groceries and provisions (*archaic*) [14thC. From Anglo-Norman *chaundeler*, Old French *chandelier*, formed from Old French *c(h)andelle* 'candle', from Latin *candela*.]

Chandler /chaándlər, chánd-/, **Raymond** (1888–1959) US writer. He wrote gritty mystery and crime novels such as *The Big Sleep* (1939) and *Strangers on a Train* (1951). Full name **Raymond Thornton Chandler**

chandlery /chaándləri/ (*plural* -**ies**) *n.* the goods that a chandler deals in, or the place where they are stored or sold

Chandrasekhar limit /cháandrə séekə-/ *n.* the upper limit for the mass of a white dwarf star. A star above the limit, having exhausted its nuclear energy, would collapse to a neutron star or a black

---

Raymond Chandler

hole. [Named after Subrahmanyan *Chandrasekhar* (b. 1910), Pakistan astrophysicist, who formulated it]

Coco Chanel

Chanel /shə nél/, **Coco** (1883–1971) French couturier. Her name became synonymous with a distinctively elegant style of women's suit. Full name **Gabrielle Bonheur Chanel**

Chaney /cháyni/, **Lon** (1883–1930) US silent film actor. He specialized in horror roles, especially in *The Hunchback of Notre Dame* (1923) and *The Phantom of the Opera* (1925). Full name **Alonso Chaney**

Chang /chang/, **Victor Peter** (1937–91) Chinese-born Australian surgeon. He led the team that performed the first Australian heart-lung transplant (1986).

Changchun /cháng chóon/ transportation centre and capital city of Jilin province in northeastern China. Population: 2,110,000 (1991).

change /chaynj/ *v.* (**changes, changing, changed**) **1.** *vti.* **BECOME OR MAKE STH DIFFERENT** to become different, or make sth or sb different **2.** *vt.* **SUBSTITUTE OR REPLACE STH** to exchange, substitute, or replace sth ○ *If it doesn't fit, the shop will change it for another size.* **3.** **PASS FROM ONE STATE TO ANOTHER** to pass or make sth pass from one state or stage to another ○ *Water changes to ice when it freezes.* **4.** *vt.* **FIN CONVERT ONE CURRENCY INTO ANOTHER** to replace money of one currency with an equivalent amount in another currency, calculated according to an exchange rate **5.** *vt.* **FIN EXCHANGE MONEY FOR SMALLER UNITS** to exchange a unit of money for an equal amount of money in lower denominations ○ *Can you change me a £10 note for two fives?* **6.** *vti.* **MOVE FROM ONE VEHICLE TO ANOTHER** to get out of one vehicle or means of transportation and continue the journey in another **7.** *vti.* **REMOVE CLOTHES AND PUT ON OTHERS** to remove one or more articles of clothing and replace them with sth else ○ *Are you going to change for dinner?* **8.** *vt.* **REMOVE AND REPLACE STH** to remove sth dirty or used and replace it with another that is clean or unused **9.** *vti.* **OPERATE GEARS OF VEHICLE** to put a car or other vehicle into a different gear ■ *n.* **1. MAKING OR BECOMING DIFFERENT** alteration, variation, or modification, or the result of this ○ *There's been a change of plan.* **2. EXCHANGE OR REPLACEMENT** an exchange, substitution, or replacement of sth or sb **3. FIN MONEY GIVEN BACK** the balance of money given back to a customer who has handed over a larger sum than the cost of the goods or services purchased **4. COINS** coins collectively, especially coins of small denomination **5. FIN MONEY EXCHANGED FOR HIGHER DENOMINATION** a sum of money given or received as an equivalent of a higher denomination **6. TRANSITION FROM STH** a shift from one state, stage, or phase to another ○ *a change in* *attitude* **7.** VARIANCE FROM ROUTINE a variance from a routine or pattern, especially a welcome one ○ *She could do with a change.* **8.** FRESH SET OF STH a different, clean, or fresh set of sth, especially clothes **9.** MENOPAUSE the menopause (*dated informal*) **10.** MUSIC PROCEDURE FOR RINGING BELLS the order in which a set of tuned bells are rung. ◊ **change ringing** [12thC. Via Old French *changer* from late Latin *cambiare*, from Latin *cambire* 'to exchange, barter', of uncertain origin: probably from Celtic.] —**changer** *n.* ◇ **ring the changes** to repeat sth with variations

---

WORD KEY: SYNONYMS

change, alter, modify, convert, vary, shift, transform, transmute

CORE MEANING: to make or become different

change the most general term; **alter** a narrower term, often suggesting a change in an aspect of sth rather than in its entirety; **modify** to make minor changes or alterations, especially in order to improve sth; **convert** to change sth concrete such as a building from one form or function to another; **vary** to change within a range of possibilities, or in connection with sth else, with a suggestion of instability; **shift** to change from one position or direction to another; **transform** to make a radical and often very obvious change into a different form; **transmute** a more formal term for 'transform'.

---

change down *vi.* to change into a lower gear in a car or other vehicle. US term **downshift**

change off *vi. US* to alternate tasks, or tasks and work breaks, especially with sb else

change over *vi.* **1.** EXCHANGE OR REVERSE PLACES OR POSITIONS to exchange or reverse places, positions, or roles **2.** SUBSTITUTE STH FOR STH ELSE to replace one system, method, or product with another **3.** SPORTS EXCHANGE ENDS OF PLAYING FIELD in team sports, to switch to opposite ends of a playing field, usually halfway through a match **4.** SPORTS HAND OVER BATON IN RELAY RACE to pass on the responsibility for participation in a relay race to another team member by handing over a baton or touching

change round *vti.* to reverse or alter places, positions, or roles

change up *vi.* to change into a higher gear in a car or other vehicle

changeable /cháynjəb'l/ *adj.* **1.** LIABLE TO CHANGE capable of or liable to change ○ *his mood was changeable* **2.** VARIABLE IN COLOUR variable in colour according to viewpoint or lighting —**changeability** /cháynjə bílləti/ *n.* —**changeableness** /cháynjəb'lnəss/ *n.* —**changeably** /-əbli/ *adv.*

changeful /cháynjf'l/ *adj.* changing frequently —**changefully** *adv.* —**changefulness** *n.*

changeless /cháynjləss/ *adj.* not liable to change —**changelessly** *adv.* —**changelessness** *n.*

changeling /cháynjling/ *n.* in folklore, a child who is secretly substituted for another one by fairies

change of heart *n.* a profound change of attitude or opinion

change of life *n.* the menopause (*dated informal*)

change of venue *n.* **1.** LAW MOVE OF TRIAL TO ANOTHER LOCATION the removal of a trial to another jurisdiction **2.** MOVE OF EVENT TO ANOTHER PLACE a relocation of a public event, especially a play or concert

changeover /cháynj ōvər/ *n.* **1.** COMPLETE CHANGE FROM STH a conversion, reversal, or complete change from one position, situation, or system to another **2.** SPORTS EXCHANGE OF ENDS OF PLAYING FIELD in team sports, the switch of teams to opposite ends of a playing field **3.** SPORTS PASSING OF BATON IN RELAY RACE passing on responsibility for participation in a relay race from one team member to another by handing over the baton or touching, or the point at which this is done

change purse *n. US* = **purse**

change ringing *n.* the ordered ringing of a peal of bells in various combinations so that none of the combinations is repeated and all possible permutations are rung

changeround /cháynjə rownd/ *n.* a change to a different or opposite position

changing of the guard *n.* the action or ceremony in which one shift of guards takes up duty while

another leaves, especially outside Buckingham Palace

changing room *n.* an area in a sports or leisure centre where clothes can be changed and showers taken

Chang Jiang /cháng ji áng/ = **Yangtze**

Changsha /cháng sháa/ capital of the Hunan Province, situated north of Guangzhou, in southeastern China. Population: 1,330,000 (1991).

Changzhou /cháng jố/ city situated in the centre of the River Yangtze Delta, 162 km/100 mi. west of Shanghai. Population: 800,000 (1996).

channel[1] /chánn'l/ *n.* **1.** GEOG STRIP OF WATER SEPARATING LAND a wide passage of water between an island and a larger body of land **2.** NAUT NAVIGABLE PASSAGE a navigable route through a river or harbour, especially one that has been deepened by dredging **3.** GEOG ROUTE OF WATERWAY the course of a stream, river, canal, or other waterway **4.** TUBULAR PASSAGE FOR LIQUID a long narrow passage or tube along which a liquid can flow ○ *a drainage channel* **5.** MEANS OF COMMUNICATION a course or means of communication or expression (*often used in the plural*) ○ *the proper channels* **6.** BROADCAST FREQUENCY SPECTRUM USED IN TRANSMISSION the portion of a frequency spectrum that is set aside for a specific purpose, e.g. the broadcasting of a television or radio signal **7.** BROADCAST TV OR RADIO STATION a television or radio station broadcasting on a specified band of the frequency spectrum **8.** ELECTRON ENG PATH FOR ELECTRICAL CURRENT a path for an electrical current or signal **9.** GROOVE OR TRENCH a long narrow groove or furrow, e.g. in architecture or sculpture **10.** COMPUT PATH FOR COMPUTER ELECTRONIC SIGNALS a path for electronic signals within a computer or between a computer and a peripheral device **11.** PARANORMAL SPIRIT MEDIUM WHO ACTS AS GUIDE in spiritualism, sb who acts as a medium for receiving messages from the spirit world ■ *v.* (-nels, -nelling, -nelled) **1.** *vt.* DIRECT STH ALONG SPECIFIC ROUTE to direct, guide, or convey sth, e.g. money or information, through or along a specific route ○ *They channelled all their energies into the game.* **2.** *vti.* PARANORMAL SPEAK WITH A SPIRIT in spiritualism, to act as a medium for a spirit **3.** *vt.* MAKE CHANNEL IN LAND OR WATER to make a channel in land or water **4.** *vt.* MAKE GROOVE OR FURROW IN STH to cut a long narrow groove or furrow in a surface [14thC. Via Old French *chanel* from Latin *canalis* 'groove, waterpipe, canal', from *canna* 'pipe, reed', from Greek *kanna* 'reed' (source of English *cane, cannister,* and *canyon*).] —**channeller** *n.*

channel[2] /chánn'l/ *n.* a flat piece of wood or metal projecting horizontally from the side of a ship to increase the spread of the ropes or cables (**shrouds**) supporting the mast [Mid-18thC. Alteration of *chainwale*, from CHAIN + WALE.]

Channel /chánn'l/ = **English Channel**

Channel-hop *vi.* to cross the English Channel for a trip to mainland Europe, usually for shopping or sightseeing, and return on the same day —**Channel-hopper** *n.*

channel-hopping *n.* the use of a remote control device to move rapidly through many different television channels, either to see whether there is anything worth watching or without searching for anything in particular. US term **channel-surfing** —**channel-hop** *vi.* —**channel-hopper** *n.*

channeling *n. US* = **channelling**

channel iron *n.* an iron or steel bar with a U-shaped cross section

Channel Islands /chánn'l-/ group of islands in the English Channel, near the French coast. The islands Jersey, Guernsey, Alderney, and Sark are self-governing Crown dependencies. Language: English; Norman-French. Population: 143,534 (1991). Area: 195 sq. km/75 sq. mi.

channelize /chánn'l īz/ (-izes, -izing, -ized), **channelise** (-ises, -ising, -ised) *vt.* to make a channel for sth, or direct sth through a channel —**channelization** /chánnəl záysh'n/ *n.*

channelling /chánn'ling/ *n.* **1.** PARANORMAL SPIRITUAL COMMUNICATION THROUGH A MEDIUM in spiritualism, the practice of acting as a medium for receiving messages from the spirit world **2.** CREATION OF CHANNEL the making

of a channel in or on sth **3.** TUBING THAT PROTECTS WIRES a protective casing or container that carries one or more cables or wires inside or outside a building

channel-surf *vi. US* = **channel hopping** —**channel-surfer** *n.*

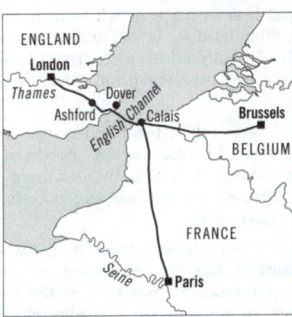

Channel Tunnel: Map showing railway routes using the Channel Tunnel

Channel Tunnel *n.* a railway tunnel, opened in 1994, that runs underneath the English Channel and links Folkestone in England with Coquelles near Calais in France. ◊ **Chunnel**

chanoyu /cháanaw yóo/ *n.* a Japanese ceremony in which tea is ritually prepared, served, and consumed [Late 20thC. From Japanese, literally 'hot water for tea'.]

chanson /shaaN són, shánssən/ *n.* a French song, e.g. a satirical cabaret song of the 20th century or a Renaissance song similar to the madrigal [15thC. Via French, 'song', from the Latin stem *cantion-*, from *cantare* 'to sing'.]

chanson de geste /shaaN sóN də zhést/ (*plural* **chansons de geste** /shaaN sóN də zhést/) *n.* a French epic poem written between the 11th and 14th centuries, usually celebrating the exploits of legendary events and figures [From French, literally 'song of heroic deeds']

chansonnier /shaaN soN nyáy, shánss'n yáy/ *n.* a cabaret performer or writer of chansons [Late 19thC. From French, from *chanson* (see CHANSON).]

chant /chaant/ *n.* **1.** PHRASE SPOKEN REPEATEDLY BY CROWD a phrase or slogan repeatedly and rhythmically spoken, often with a simple singsong intonation, especially in unison by a crowd or group **2.** MUSIC MUSIC FOR RELIGIOUS PASSAGE a musical passage in which words or syllables are sung on the same note, or a single word or syllable is sung on a series of notes. Chants are used in psalms, canticles, and other parts of a religious service. **3.** CHR HYMN OR PRAYER SUNG TO CHANT a psalm, hymn, or prayer sung to a chant **4.** STH SPOKEN MONOTONOUSLY OR REPETITIOUSLY a monotonous or repetitive song or intonation of the voice ■ *vti.* (chants, chanting, chanted) **1.** REPEAT SLOGAN CONTINUALLY to speak a slogan repeatedly and rhythmically with a simple singsong intonation **2.** CHR SING HYMN OR PRAYER AS CHANT to sing or intone part of a religious service as a chant **3.** UTTER MONOTONOUSLY to speak or sing sth monotonously [14thC. Via French, 'song', from Latin *cantus*, from the past participle of *canere* 'to sing' (source of English *accent* and *incentive*).] —**chantingly** *adv.*

chantecler *n.* = **chanticleer**

chanter /cháantər/ *n.* **1.** SB CHANTING SLOGAN sb who chants a slogan **2.** MUSIC, CHR SB WHO CHANTS PSALM OR HYMN sb who chants a musical passage, e.g. a priest or chorister **3.** MUSIC PIPE WITH FINGERHOLES ON BAGPIPE on a bagpipe, a pipe with fingerholes on which the melody is played **4.** MUSIC PIPE FOR PRACTISING BAGPIPE FINGERING a pipe used to learn or practise bagpipe fingering

chanterelle /sháantə rél, chaántə-/; /shántə-/ *n.* an edible mushroom found in temperate woodlands that has a yellow-to-orange trumpet-shaped cap. Latin name: *Cantharellus cibarius.* [Late 18thC. Via French from modern Latin *cantharellus*, literally 'little cup', from Latin *cantharus* 'drinking vessel', from Greek *kantharos*, of unknown origin.]

chanteuse /shaan túrz/ (*plural* **-teuses** /shaan túrz/) *n.* a woman singer, especially in a nightclub or cabaret [Mid-19thC. From French.]

---

chanticleer /chánti kleer, shánti-/, **chantecler** *n.* a cock, especially in fairy tales (*literary*) [13thC. From Old French *Chantecler*, from *chanter* 'to sing' + *cler* 'clear'.]

Chantilly[1] /shan tílli/ *n.* **1. Chantilly, Chantilly lace** TEXTILES **DELICATE LACE OFTEN USED FOR GOWNS** a delicate ornamental lace in black or white with an outlined design, often used for bridal and evening gowns **2. Chantilly, Chantilly cream** FOOD **TYPE OF WHIPPED CREAM** whipped cream, sweetened and often flavoured with vanilla

Chantilly[2] /shan tílli/ a town and resort in the Oise Department, Picardie region, northern France. Situated about 42 km/26 mi. north of Paris, it became famous for its lace and porcelain. Population: 11,341 (1990).

chantry /chaántri/ (*plural* **-tries**) *n.* **1. ENDOWMENT FOR PERFORMANCE OF MASS** an endowment to pay for the saying of masses for the soul of the founder or sb named by the founder **2. chantry, chantry chapel ENDOWED CHAPEL FOR CHANTRIES** a chapel or altar endowed for the performance of chantries [14thC. From Anglo-Norman *chaunterie*, Old French *chanterie*, formed from Old French *chanter* 'to sing'.]

Chanukah, **Chanukkah** *n.* = **Hanukkah**

chaology /kay óllәji/ *n.* the study of chaos theory and chaotic systems —**chaologist** *n.*

Chao Phraya /chów prә yaá/ river in Thailand. Length: 365 km/227 mi.

chaos /káy oss/ *n.* **1. DISORDER** a state of complete disorder and confusion **2. chaos, Chaos EARLIEST CONDITION OF UNIVERSE** the unbounded space and formless matter supposed to have existed before the creation of the universe **3.** PHYS **APPARENT DISORDER** the unpredictability inherent in a system such as the weather, in which apparently random changes occur as a result of the system's extreme sensitivity to small differences in initial conditions [15thC. Directly or via French from Latin, from Greek *khaos* 'void, abyss', the original sense in English (source of English *gas*).]

chaos theory *n.* a theory that complex natural systems obey certain rules but are so sensitive that small initial changes can cause unexpected final effects, thus giving an impression of randomness. ◊ **butterfly effect**

chaotic /kay óttik/ *adj.* **1. DISORDERED** completely disordered and out of control **2.** PHYS **INHERENTLY UNPREDICTABLE** used to describe the state of a system according to chaos theory [Early 18thC. Formed from CHAOS, modelled on words such as EROTIC and HYPNOTIC.] —**chaotically** *adv.*

chap[1] /chap/ *vti.* (**chaps, chapping, chapped**) **BECOME SORE AND ROUGHENED** to become or make skin sore and cracked by exposure to wind or cold ■ *n.* **1. AREA OF SORE SKIN** a sore cracked area of skin, caused by exposure to wind or cold **2.** GEOL **CRACK IN GROUND** a crack or fissure in dry ground [14thC. Origin unknown.] —**chapped** *adj.*

chap[2] /chap/ *n.* a man or youth, especially sb whose name is not known or not relevant (*informal*) [Late 16thC. Shortening of *chapman*. The word originally denoted a buyer or customer; the current meaning dates from the early 18thC.]

chap[3] /chap/ *n.* the lower exterior half of the jaw, especially the cheek [Mid-16thC. Origin unknown.]

chap. *abbr.* **1.** chapter **2.** chaplain

chaparral /sháppә rál/ *n.* a dense thicket of shrubs or small trees, especially of evergreen oaks in southern California [Mid-19thC. From Spanish, formed from *chaparra* 'dwarf evergreen oak' (source of English *chaps*).]

chapati /chә paáti, -pátti/ (*plural* **-tis** *or* **-ties**), **chapatti** (*plural* **-tis** *or* **-ties**) *n.* a thin round unleavened bread eaten with Indian dishes [Early 19thC. From Hindi *capātī*, from *capānā* 'to flatten, roll out'.]

chapbook /cháp bŏŏk/ *n.* a small booklet of poems, ballads, or stories, originally sold by travelling pedlars [Early 19thC. Blend of *chapman* and *book*.]

chape /chayp/ *n.* **1. TIP OF SCABBARD** the metal tip of a scabbard **2. TONGUE OF BUCKLE** the tongue of a buckle [14thC. Via French, 'cape, hood', from late Latin *cappa* (see CAP).]

chapeau /sha pṓ/ (*plural* **-peaux** /-pṓ, -pṓz/ *or* **-peaus** /-pṓ, -pṓz/) *n.* a hat as an item of high fashion or ceremonial dress (*formal*) [15thC. Via French from late Latin *cappellum*, literally 'small hooded cloak', from *cappa* (see CAP).]

chapel /chápp'l/ *n.* **1.** CHR **ROOM FOR WORSHIP** a place in a hospital, prison, or other institution, or in a large house, consecrated for Christian worship **2.** RELIG **SEPARATE AREA OF CHURCH** a separate area in a church, having its own altar and intended for private prayer **3.** CHR **PROTESTANT CHURCH** a place of worship used by a Nonconformist Protestant denomination such as the Methodists or Baptists **4.** CHR **SERVICE IN CHAPEL** a service held in a chapel, especially in a Nonconformist church **5.** CHR **SMALL ANGLICAN CHURCH** a small Anglican church that operates as a branch of a parish church **6.** PUBL **TRADE UNION BRANCH** a branch of a trade union in printing and journalism (*takes a singular or plural verb*) **7.** PUBL **MEETING OF PRINTERS' CHAPEL** a meeting of a printers' or journalists' chapel ■ *adj.* **BELONGING TO NONCONFORMIST CHURCH** belonging to a Nonconformist church [12thC. Via Old French *chapele* from medieval Latin *cappella*, literally 'small hooded cloak', from late Latin *cappa* (see CAP).]

chapel of ease *n.* a church built for people who live a long distance from a parish church

chapel of rest *n.* a place at an undertaker's where bodies are kept and may be visited by family and friends

chaperon /sháppәrōn/, **chaperone** *n.* **1. SUPERVISOR OF YOUNG WOMAN** sb, especially an older or married woman, who accompanies and supervises a young single woman at social events **2. GROUP SUPERVISOR** sb who accompanies and supervises a group of young people ■ *vti.* (**-ons, -oning, -oned; -ones, -oning, -oned**) **ACT AS A CHAPERON** to accompany a person or a group as a chaperon [12thC. Via French from late Latin *cappa* (see CAP). The word originally denoted a hood or cap.] —**chaperonage** /-rәnij/ *n.*

chapess /cha péss/ *n.* a woman (*dated or humorous*)

chapfallen /cháp fawlәn/ *adj.* unhappy and miserable (*archaic*) [Literally 'with a fallen chap' (lower jaw)]

chaplain /chápplin/ *n.* a member of the clergy employed to give religious guidance, e.g. to members of the armed services, schoolchildren, or prisoners [12thC. Via Anglo-Norman and Old French *chapelain*, from medieval Latin *cappellanus*, originally 'guardian of the cloak of St Martin of Tours', from *cappella* (see CHAPEL).] —**chaplainship** *n.*

chaplaincy /chápplinssi/ (*plural* **-cies**) *n.* **1. JOB AS CHAPLAIN** a post or position as chaplain **2. CHAPLAIN'S PLACE OF WORK** the place or building where a chaplain works

chaplet /chápplәt/ *n.* **1. HEAD DECORATION** a decorative circle of beads or flowers worn on the head **2.** CHR **PRAYER BEADS** a string of beads used by Roman Catholics for counting prayers. A chaplet has 55 beads, one third of the number on a rosary. **3.** ARCHIT **BEADED MOULDING** a small moulding resembling a string of beads [14thC. Via French *chapelet* from, ultimately, late Latin *cappa* (see CAP).] —**chapleted** *adj.*

Charlie Chaplin

Chaplin /chápplin/, **Charlie** (1889–1977) British-born US actor, director, and producer who is best known for the tramp character that he played in over seventy films. Full name **Sir Charles Spencer Chaplin**

chapman /chápmәn/ (*plural* **-men** /-mәn/) *n.* a wandering pedlar (*archaic*) [Old English *cēapman*, from *cēap* (see CHEAP)]

Chapman /chápmәn/, **George** (1559?–1634) English dramatist and translator who is known for his translations of Homer's *Iliad* and *Odyssey* (1616).

Chappell /chápp'l/, **Greg** (*b.* 1948) Australian cricketer. He was captain of the Australian Test team (1975–77 and 1979–83) and the country's second-highest scoring batsman, with 7,110 runs. Full name **Gregory Stephen Chappell**

Chappell, Ian Michael (*b.* 1943) Australian cricketer. He was captain of the Australian Test team (1971–75) and the Australian World Series Team (1977–78).

chappie /cháppi/ *n.* a chap (*informal*)

chaps /chaps/ *npl.* protective leather leggings, like a pair of trousers with no seat or crotch, worn on horseback over ordinary trousers by North American ranch workers, rodeo contestants, and cowboys [Late 19thC. Shortening of *chaparejos*, an alteration (probably influenced by Spanish *aparejo* 'equipment') of *chaparreras*, from *chaparra* (see CHAPARRAL); because chaps were worn when riding through chaparral.]

Chap Stick *tdmk.* a trademark for a lip balm in the form of a stick, applied to the lips to prevent or relieve chapping

chaptalize /cháptә līz/ (**-izes, -izing, -ized**), **chaptalise** (**-ises, -ising, -ised**) *vt.* to increase the alcohol content of wine by adding sugar before or during fermentation [Late 19thC. Named after the inventor of the process, the French chemist J. A. *Chaptal* (1756–1832).] —**chaptalization** /cháptә lī záysh'n/ *n.*

chapter /cháptәr/ *n.* **1. SECTION OF BOOK** one of the main sections of a text, usually having a title or number as a heading **2. PERIOD OF DEVELOPMENT** an identifiable period in the history or development of sth ○ *Their move to France began a new chapter in their lives.* **3. SERIES OF EVENTS** a series of events having a common characteristic ○ *a turbulent chapter in the movements of history* **4.** CHR **GROUP OF CANONS** the body of canons of a cathedral or collegiate church, or the body of members of an order of knighthood (*takes a singular or plural verb*) **5. BRANCH OF A GROUP** a branch of a society or organization (*takes a singular or plural verb*) **6.** RELIG **ASSEMBLY OF A CHAPTER** a meeting of a cathedral or church chapter [12thC. Via French *chapitre* from Latin *capitulum*, literally 'small head', from *caput* 'head' (source of English *capital*).] ◇ **give** *or* **quote chapter and verse** to give exact information and detailed references on a topic

chapter house *n.* **1.** CHR **BUILDING WHERE CHAPTER MEETS** a building used for meetings by a religious chapter **2.** *US* **COLLEGE MEETING PLACE** a building used by a fraternity or sorority at a North American college

char[1] /chaar/ (**chars, charring, charred**) *v.* **1.** *vti.* **BLACKEN BY BURNING** to blacken sth or become blackened by burning or scorching **2.** *vt.* **MAKE INTO CHARCOAL** to turn wood into charcoal by partial burning [Late 17thC. Back-formation from CHARCOAL.]

char[2] /chaar/ (*plural* **char** *or* **chars**), **charr** (*plural* **charr** *or* **charrs**) *n.* a trout that has light-coloured spots, found in northern waters [Mid-17thC. Origin uncertain: perhaps from Celtic.]

char[3] /chaar/ *n.* = **charwoman** ■ *vi.* (**chars, charring, charred**) **DO PAID HOUSEWORK** to do people's housework, especially cleaning, for pay (*dated informal*) [Old English *cierran* 'to turn', from a prehistoric Germanic word that also produced English *charwoman*. The current sense evolved via an earlier meaning 'to do a turn of work'.]

char[4] /chaar/ *n.* tea (*dated informal*) [Early 20thC. From Chinese (Mandarin) *chá*.]

charabanc /shárrә bang/ *n.* a bus or coach, often open-sided, used for pleasure trips or sightseeing (*dated*) [Early 19thC. From French *char-à-bancs*, literally 'carriage with benches'.]

characin /kárrәssin/ (*plural* **-cin** *or* **-cins**), **characid** /-sid/ (*plural* **-cid** *or* **-cids**) *n.* a small brightly coloured freshwater fish of Africa and South America, often kept in aquariums. Family: Characidae. [Late 19thC. Via modern Latin *Characinus*, genus name, from Greek *kharax* (see CHARACTER), used to denote a kind of fish.]

character /kárrәktәr/ *n.* **1. DISTINCTIVE QUALITIES** the set of qualities that make sb or sth distinctive, especially sb's qualities of mind and feeling ○ *It's just not in my character to behave like that.* **2. POSITIVE QUALITIES**

qualities that make sb or sth interesting or attractive ○ *an old house full of character* 3. **REPUTATION** sb's public reputation ○ *an attack on his good character that ended in court* 4. LITERAT, CINEMA **SB IN BOOK OR FILM** one of the people portrayed in a book, play, or film ○ *None of the central characters are particularly important.* 5. **UNUSUAL PERSON** sb who has an unusual or eccentric personality 6. **INDIVIDUAL** sb considered in terms of personality, behaviour, or appearance ○ *he was a flamboyant character* 7. **LETTER OR SYMBOL** any written or printed letter, number, or other symbol 8. COMPUT **COMPUTER UNIT OF DATA** a single letter, number, or symbol that can be displayed on a computer screen or printer and represents one byte of data 9. GENETICS **GENETICALLY CONTROLLED CHARACTERISTIC** a genetically controlled characteristic of an organism 10. **WRITTEN TESTIMONIAL** a written summary of sb's abilities and personality, written by an employer or other person who knows the person well 11. **CAPACITY OR POSITION** a particular role, position, or function that sb has in society or in an organization (*formal*) ○ *speaking in her character as chairperson* 12. **STYLE OF WRITING OR PRINTING** style of handwriting or printing ■ *vt.* (**-ters, -tering, -tered**) **WRITE** to write or carve words carefully and skilfully on paper, stone, or metal (*archaic*) [14thC. Via French *caractère* from, ultimately, Greek *kharaktēr* 'tool for marking', from *kharassein* 'to engrave', from *kharax* 'pointed stake'.] ◇ **in character** *or* **out of character** 1. typical (or untypical) of the behaviour of a particular person or thing 2. involved (or not involved) in the psychological preparations for acting out a particular role in a play, film, or other dramatic work

character actor *n.* an actor who specializes in playing the roles of unusual or distinctive characters

character assassination *n.* a deliberate and sustained attack on sb's reputation

characteristic /kárrəktə rístik/ *n.* 1. **DEFINING FEATURE** a feature or quality that makes sb or sth recognizable 2. MATH **WHOLE NUMBER IN LOGARITHM** the whole number (**integer**) found to the left of the decimal point in a common logarithm, e.g. the characteristic of 5.4321 is 5 ■ *adj.* **TYPICAL** distinguishing or typical of a particular person or thing —**characteristically** *adv.*

characterization /kárrəktər ī záysh'n/, **characterisation** *n.* 1. **PORTRAYAL OF FICTIONAL CHARACTER** the way in which the writer portrays the characters in a book, play, or film 2. **DESCRIPTION** a description of the character or nature or sb or sth

characterize /kárrəktə rīz/ (**-izes, -izing, -ized**), **characterise** (**-ises, -ising, -ised**) *vt.* 1. **DESCRIBE SB OR STH** to describe the character or characteristics of sb or sth 2. **BE TYPICAL OF SB OR STH** to be typical of the way a particular person or thing behaves or looks —**characterizable** /kárrəktə rīzəb'l/ *adj.* —**characterizer** /kárrəktə rīzə/ *n.*

characterless /kárrəktərləss/ *adj.* without any interesting or distinctive features ○ *a characterless view* —**characterlessly** *adv.* —**characterlessness** *n.*

character recognition *n.* a magnetic or optical process, by which written or printed letters, numbers, or symbols can be recognized and digitized for use in a computer

character set *n.* a set of letters, numbers, and symbols that can be coded for use by a computer or printer

character sketch *n.* a short description of sb's character and behaviour

character witness *n.* a witness who gives evidence of sb's good character in a court of law

charade /shə raád, -ráyd/ *n.* 1. **RIDICULOUS PRETENCE** an absurdly false or pointless act or situation 2. **CLUE IN CHARADES** a clue in the game of charades [Late 18thC. Via French from, ultimately, modern Provençal *charra* 'to chatter', perhaps an imitation of the sound.]

charades /shə raádz, -ráydz/ *n.* a game in which sb provides a visual or acted clue for a word or phrase, often the title of a book, play, or film, for others to guess (*takes a singular verb*)

charas /chaárəss/ *n.* = **hashish** [Mid-19thC. From Hindi *caras*.]

charbroil /chaár broyl/ (**-broils, -broiling, -broiled**) *vt.* *US* = **chargrill** [Mid-20thC. Blend of CHARCOAL and BROIL.] —**charbroiler** *n.*

charcoal /chaárkōl/ *n.* 1. CHEM **CARBON** a black or dark grey form of carbon, produced by heating wood or another organic substance in an enclosed space without air. Charcoal is used as a fuel, as an absorbent, in smelting, in explosives, and by artists for drawing. 2. DRAWING **DRAWING IMPLEMENT** sticks of charcoal used for drawing 3. DRAWING **DRAWING USING CHARCOAL** a drawing done with charcoal ■ *n., adj.* = **charcoal grey** [14thC. Origin of *char* uncertain: possibly from Old French *charbon* 'charcoal'; or literally 'turned (into charcoal)', from Old English *cierran* 'to turn'. *Coal* in the obsolete sense 'charcoal'.]

charcoal grey *adj.* of a dark grey colour —**charcoal grey** *n.*

charcuterie /shaar ko͝otəri/ *n.* 1. **COLD COOKED MEATS** cold cooked, cured, or processed meat and meat products 2. **SHOP SELLING CHARCUTERIE** a shop that specializes in charcuterie [Mid-19thC. From French, formed from obsolete *char cuite* 'cooked flesh'.]

chard /chaad/ *n.* PLANTS = **Swiss chard** [Mid-17thC. Via French *carde* (possibly by association with *chardon* 'thistle') from, ultimately, Latin *cardu(u)s* 'thistle, artichoke' (source of English *cardoon*).]

Chardin /shaar dáN/, **Jean Baptiste Siméon** (1699–1779) French painter. He was a master of lower-middle-class domestic and genre scenes, e.g. *The Benediction* (1740), now in the Louvre.

Chardonnay /shaárdə nay/, **chardonnay** *n.* 1. **WHITE GRAPE** a white grape used in making wine 2. **WHITE WINE** a dry white wine made from the Chardonnay grape [Early 20thC. From French.]

charge /chaarj/ *v.* (**charges, charging, charged**) 1. *vti.* COMM **ASK MONEY FOR STH** to ask sb for an amount as a price or fee 2. *vt.* **IMPOSE A FEE OR PENALTY** to hold a person or organization financially liable for sth 3. *vti.* FIN **DEBIT** to allow, and enter a record of, a deferred payment for sth 4. *vt.* LAW **ACCUSE SB OF CRIME** to accuse sb formally of having committed a crime 5. *vt.* **CRITICIZE** to criticize sb for doing sth wrong ○ *Her boss charged her with being lazy and incompetent.* 6. *vt.* **ORDER TO DO STH** to order or instruct sb formally to do sth ○ *The judge charged the jury to consider all the facts.* 7. *vti.* **ATTACK IN A RUSH** to attack sb or sth by rushing forwards, especially in a battle ○ *Police in riot gear charged the lines of demonstrators.* 8. *vi.* **RUSH** to run somewhere carelessly or clumsily ○ *He came charging in from the garden.* 9. *vti.* ELEC **RESTORE POWER IN BATTERY** to restore the power in a battery by connecting it to a supply of electricity 10. *vt.* **LOAD OR FILL STH** to load or fill sth, e.g. a gun with explosive, or a glass with drink (*formal*) 11. *vt.* **PERVADE A PLACE** to give an atmosphere of intense interest, excitement, or other strong emotion to a place (*usually passive*) ○ *The concert hall was charged with anticipation.* 12. *vt.* HERALDRY **PUT HERALDIC DEVICE ON STH** to put a heraldic device on sth such as a shield or banner ■ *n.* 1. COMM **AMOUNT OF MONEY ASKED** the price of sth that is for sale, or the fee asked for a service or in payment of a financial liability such as a tax ○ *We had to pay several extra charges before getting the vehicle back.* 2. **RESPONSIBILITY** the responsibility or duty of looking after sb or sth ○ *He took on the children's welfare as an extra charge.* 3. **SB BEING TAKEN CARE OF** sb, especially a child or a member of a minister's congregation, for whom sb else is responsible (*formal*) ○ *The nanny was keeping a close watch on her little charges.* 4. LAW **ACCUSATION** an accusation of wrongdoing, especially an official statement accusing sb of committing a crime 5. **RUSH TO ATTACK** a rush forward to attack, especially in a battle, or the signal for this 6. ELEC **POWER IN BATTERY** the power stored in a battery 7. PHYS **ELECTRIC PROPERTY OF MATTER** a fundamental characteristic of matter, responsible for all electric and electromotive forces, expressed in two forms known as positive and negative 8. PHYS **EXCESS OR LACK OF ELECTRONS** a quantity of electricity caused by an excess or lack of electrons 9. **ENOUGH EXPLOSIVE FOR DETONATION** the amount of explosive used to detonate a shell or cartridge 10. **ENOUGH TO FILL STH** the amount required to fill a container or to make a mechanism work 11. **AN ORDER TO DO STH** a formal order or instruction to do sth, e.g. a judge's instructions to a jury 12. **SUDDEN BURST OF EXCITEMENT** a sudden burst of excitement or interest 13. HERALDRY **HERALDIC DESIGN** a design or image used as part of a coat of arms [12thC. Via French *charger* 'to load, charge' from late Latin *car(ri)care*, from Latin *carrus* 'carriage'. The underlying idea is of 'loading, burdening'.]

chargeable /chaárjəb'l/ *adj.* 1. **ABLE TO BE CHARGED** liable or able to be charged 2. LAW **LIABLE TO RESULT IN CRIMINAL CHARGE** liable to result in or face a criminal charge 3. LAW **SUBJECT TO A CHARGE** used to describe property or land capable of being subject to a charge —**chargeability** /chaárjə bíllәti/ *n.*

charge account *n.* *US* COMM = **credit account**

charge-cap (**charge-caps, charge-capping, charge-capped**) *vt.* to put a limit on the amount of flat-rate tax that local authorities in the United Kingdom are allowed to charge people

charge card *n.* a card issued to customers by a shop, or other organization, used to charge purchases to an account for later payment

charge-coupled device *n.* a semiconductor device that converts light patterns into digital signals that can be read by a computer, used especially in digital cameras and optical scanners

chargé d'affaires /shaár zhay da fáir/ (*plural* **chargés d'affaires** /shaár zhay da fáir, shaár zhayz-/) *n.* a diplomat ranking immediately below an ambassador who deputizes in the ambassador's absence, or a diplomat who heads a minor diplomatic mission [Mid-18thC. From French, literally 'sb in charge of affairs'.]

charge density *n.* the amount of electric charge per unit of area or volume. Symbol ρ

charge hand *n.* a worker with supervisory responsibilities, ranking below a foreman

charge nurse *n.* a nurse in charge of a hospital ward, especially a male nurse having the same responsibilities as a ward sister

charger[1] /chaárjər/ *n.* 1. **LARGE HORSE** a large strong cavalry horse 2. ELEC = **battery charger** 3. **SB OR STH THAT CHARGES** sb or sth that charges

charger[2] /chaárjər/ *n.* a large flat serving dish of a kind now mainly collected for display [14thC. From Anglo-Norman *chargeour*, literally 'sth that loads', from Old French *charger* (see CHARGE).]

charge sheet *n.* a police document recording criminal charges and court appearances

chargrill /chaár gril/ (**-grills, -grilling, -grilled**) *vt.* to grill food over charcoal on a barbecue or on a ridged pan that produces a similar visual effect [From *char(coal)* + *grill*, modelled on CHARBROIL]

Chari /shaári/ the main tributary feeding Lake Chad in north-central Africa. It rises in the Central African Republic and flows about 1,400 km/870 mi.

chariot /chárri ət/ *n.* 1. **ANCIENT 2-WHEELED VEHICLE** a two-wheeled horse-drawn vehicle used in ancient times in races, warfare, or processions 2. **CEREMONIAL CARRIAGE** a four-wheeled horse-drawn carriage with rear seats only, used especially on ceremonial occasions [14thC. Via French from, ultimately, Latin *carrus* 'carriage'.]

charioteer /chárri ə teér/ *n.* a driver of a chariot

charisma /kə rízmə/ *n.* 1. **MAGNETIC PERSONALITY** the ability to inspire enthusiasm, interest, or affection in others by means of personal charm or influence 2. **charisma** (*plural* **-mata**) CHR **DIVINE GIFT** a gift or power thought to be divinely bestowed [Mid-17thC. Via ecclesiastical Latin from Greek *kharisma*, from *kharis* 'favour, grace'.]

WORD KEY: USAGE

Charisma meaning 'personal magnetism'. In their generalized meanings, ***charisma*** and ***charismatic*** have moved a long way from their original meanings in theology, where they referred to supernatural gifts of speaking, healing, and so on. The modern meanings have developed from a use in sociology, in which the sense is 'a power of leadership or authority', first used in translations of the German sociologist Max Weber (1864–1920).

charismatic /kárriz máttik/ *adj.* 1. **HAVING CHARISMA** possessing great powers of charm or influence 2. CHR **SEEKING DIRECT SPIRITUAL EXPERIENCE** used to describe

Christian groups or worship characterized by a quest for spontaneous and ecstatic experiences such as healing, prophecy, and speaking in tongues ■ *n.* CHR **MEMBER OF A CHARISMATIC GROUP** a member of a charismatic group

charitable /chárritəb'l/ *adj.* **1. GENEROUS** generous to people in need **2. SYMPATHETIC** sympathetic, favourable, or tolerant in judging **3. COLLECTIVELY DISPENSING HELP** dispensing assistance to needy people by means of a group or organization —**charitableness** *n.* —**charitably** *adv.*

charity /chárrəti/ (*plural* **-ties**) *n.* **1. PROVISION OF HELP** the voluntary provision of money, materials, or help to people in need **2. MATERIAL HELP** money, materials, or help voluntarily given to people in need **3. ORGANIZATION PROVIDING CHARITY** an organization that collects money and other voluntary contributions of help for people in need **4. TOLERANT ATTITUDE** the willingness to judge people in a tolerant or favourable way **5. IMPARTIAL LOVE** the impartial love of other people [12thC. Via French *charité* from Latin *caritas*, from *carus* 'dear' (source of English *cherish*).]

Charity Commission *n.* an organization that registers and regulates charities in the United Kingdom —**Charity Commissioner** *n.*

charity shop *n.* a shop that sells second-hand goods to raise money for a charity

charivari /shaàri vaàri/ *n.* **1. NOISY SERENADE FOR NEWLYWEDS** a noisy mock-serenade with the banging of saucepans, kettles, and similar objects, meant to wish newlyweds well. US term **shivaree 2. LOUD COMMOTION** a noise, commotion, or din (*formal*) [Mid-17thC. From French, of unknown origin.]

charkha /cháark ə/, **charka** *n.* a spinning wheel, especially for cotton, which is used in the Indian subcontinent [Late 19thC. Via Urdu *charka* from Persian *cark(a)*.]

charlady /chaàr laydi/ (*plural* **-dies**) *n.* = **charwoman** [Late 19thC. From the first element of CHARWOMAN + LADY.]

charlatan /shaàrlətən/ *n.* sb who falsely claims a special skill or expertise [Early 17thC. Via French from Italian *ciarlatano*, from *ciarlare* 'to babble, patter', an imitation of the sound of empty talk.] —**charlatanism** *n.* —**charlatanry** *n.*

Charlemagne /shaàrlə mayn/ (742–814) Frankish king and emperor. As emperor of the West (800–814), he inspired the 'Carolingian Renaissance' of European culture.

Charleroi /shaàrlə roy, -rwaa/ industrial city in Hainault Province, in south-central Belgium. It is situated about 48 km/30 mi. south of Brussels. Population: 205,591 (1996).

Charles /chaarlz/, **Prince of Wales** (*b.* 1948) British heir apparent and son of Elizabeth II. He was married to Diana, Princess of Wales, from 1981 to 1996.

Charles I, King of England, Scotland, and Ireland (1600–49). He succeeded James I in 1625. His determination to rule without Parliament's authority led to the Civil War (1642–48), which culminated in his execution.

Charles II, King of England, Scotland, and Ireland (1630–85). He was exiled during Oliver Cromwell's Protectorate (1653–59), but returned to England and formally ascended the throne after the restoration of the monarchy in 1660.

Charles V (1500–58) Belgian-born Spanish emperor. During his reign as Holy Roman Emperor (1519–58), he struggled to keep his Roman Catholic empire together and was finally forced to recognize Protestantism.

Charles, Bob (*b.* 1936) New Zealand golfer. He won the British Open in 1963 and the World Match Play Championship in 1969. Full name **Robert James Charles**

Charles, Ray (*b.* 1932) US singer and pianist whose rhythm-and-blues style took its roots from country and western and gospel music. Real name **Ray Charles Robinson**

Charles's law /chaàlziz-/ *n.* a law that holds that there is a direct relationship between the volume of a gas and its temperature, where its pressure is constant [Late 19thC. Named after the French physicist J. A. C. *Charles* (1746–1823), who discovered it.]

Charles's Wain /chaàlziz wayn/ *n.* ASTRON the Plough (*archaic*)

Charleston[1] /chaàlstən/ *n.* a lively North American dance, popular in the 1920s, characterized by kicking the feet out sideways while keeping the knees together [Early 20thC. Named after CHARLESTON in South Carolina.]

Charleston[2] /chaàrl stən/ city and port in south-eastern South Carolina where the Ashley, Cooper, and Wando rivers meet. Population: 71,052 (1996).

Charley *n.* = **charlie**[2]

charley horse /chaàrli-/ *n. US, Can* a severe muscular cramp, especially of the upper leg (*informal*) [Origin unknown]

charlie[1] /chaàrli/ *n.* cocaine used as an illicit drug (*slang*)

charlie[2] /chaàrli/ *n.* sb unintelligent or silly (*informal*) [Early 19thC. Pet form of the name *Charles*. Originally 'night-watchman' (for unknown reasons) and 'small triangular beard' (as worn by King Charles I).]

Charlie /chaàli/ *n.* **1. CODE WORD FOR LETTER 'C'** the NATO phonetic alphabet code word for the letter 'C', used in international radio communications **2. Charlie, Charley** *US, Aus* **VIET CONG** used to refer to a member of the Viet Cong during the Vietnam War, or the Viet Cong collectively (*slang dated*)

charlock /chaàr lok/ (*plural* **-lock** *or* **-locks**) *n.* a yellow-flowered Eurasian mustard plant that has hairy stems and leaves and is a common weed. Latin name: *Brassica kaber*. [Old English *cerlic*, of unknown origin]

charlotte /shaàrlət/ *n.* a sweet, cold or baked dish prepared in a deep straight-sided container and containing fruit surrounded by sponge cake, biscuits, or bread [Late 18thC. From French, probably from the name *Charlotte* (for unknown reasons).]

Charlotte Amalie /shaàrlət ə maàlyə/ seaport and capital of St Thomas Island and of the US Virgin Islands. Population: 12,331 (1990).

charlotte russe /-rooss/ (*plural* **charlottes russes** /-rooss/) *n.* a cold set dessert made with cream or custard surrounded by sponge fingers [From French, literally 'Russian charlotte']

Charlton /chaàrltən/, **Bobby** (*b.* 1937) British footballer. He scored 49 goals in 106 appearances for England from 1957 to 1973, and was on the World Cup-winning side in 1966. Real name **Sir Robert Charlton**

Charlton, 'Boy' (1907–75) Australian swimmer and winner of the gold medal in the 1,500 metres at the 1924 Olympic Games. Real name **Andrew Murray Charlton**

Charlton, Jack (*b.* 1935) British footballer and manager. He played for Leeds United (1965–75) and England (1965–70), and managed the Republic of Ireland national team from 1986 to 1996. Real name **John Charlton**

charm /chaarm/ *n.* **1. ATTRACTIVENESS** the power to delight or attract people **2. ATTRACTIVE FEATURE** a feature or quality that delights or attracts (*often used in the plural*) **3. STH SUPPOSED TO BRING LUCK** sth carried or worn because it is believed to bring good luck or ward off evil **4. TRINKET** a miniature metal animal, musical instrument, or similar trinket worn on a bracelet or around the neck **5. MAGIC SPELL** a special phrase or rhyme believed to have magical powers **6.** PHYS **CHARACTERISTIC OF ELEMENTARY PARTICLES** a quantum characteristic of elementary particles that accounts for the long lifetime of the J particle, lack of symmetry in hadron interactions, and failure of certain particles to react. Symbol **C** ■ *v.* (**charms, charming, charmed**) **1.** *vti.* **DELIGHT** to delight or attract people **2.** *vt.* **INFLUENCE PEOPLE** to influence sb or obtain sth from sb by using powers of persuasion and attraction **3.** *vti.* **CAST A SPELL** to affect sb or sth by, or as if by, the use of a supposed magic spell [13thC. Via French *charme* 'charm, song' from Latin *carmen* 'song, incantation', from *canere* 'to sing, chant' (source of English *chant* and *incantation*).] —**charmer** *n.*

charmed /chaarmd/ *adj.* **1. LUCKY** so pleasant or lucky as to suggest protection by a magic spell **2.** PHYS **HAVING CHARM** used to describe an elementary particle that has the property of charm

charmed circle *n.* a privileged group or elite

charming /chaàrming/ *adj.* **DELIGHTFUL OR FASCINATING** having the power to delight or attract people ○ *a charming village* ○ *a charming young man* ■ *interj.* **EXPRESSING DISPLEASURE** used ironically to express disapproval or distaste at sth just done or said (*informal*) —**charmingly** *adv.*

charm offensive *n.* a campaign, e.g. by a politician, to appear more pleasant, attractive, or reasonable, in order to gain popularity (*informal*)

charnel /chaàrn'l/ *n.* = **charnel house** ■ *adj.* **OF DEATH** suggestive of death or a tomb [14thC. Via Old French from medieval Latin *carnale*, from the Latin stem *carn-* 'flesh' (source of English *carnage*).]

charnel house *n.* a building or vault in which bones or dead bodies are placed

Charolais /shárrə lay/ (*plural* **-lais**), **Charollais** (*plural* **-lais**) *n.* a large white cow belonging to a breed originating in France and bred for beef [Late 19thC. Named after Monts du *Charollais* in eastern France.]

Charon /káirən/ *n.* **1.** MYTHOL **FERRYMAN IN GREEK UNDERWORLD** in Greek mythology, a ferryman who took the souls of the dead across the River Styx to Hades **2.** ASTRON **SATELLITE OF PLUTO** the only known satellite of Pluto, discovered in 1978

Charpentier /shaar páaNti ay/, **Gustave** (1860–1956) French composer. The opera *Louise* (1900) is the best-known work of this pupil of Jules Massenet.

Charpentier, Marc-Antoine (1645?–1704) French composer. He composed incidental music for his friend Molière's plays, as well as operas and oratorios. He is best known for his *Te Deum* (1692?).

charpoy /chaàr poy/ *n.* a light bedstead of webbing stretched across a frame, commonly used in the Indian subcontinent [Mid-17thC. Via Urdu *chārpāī* from Persian.]

charqui /chaàrki/ *n.* = **jerky** [Early 17thC. Via American Spanish (source of English *jerk*) from Quechua *cc'arki*.]

charr *n.* = **char**[2]

chart /chaart/ *n.* **1. DIAGRAM OR TABLE** a diagram or table displaying detailed information **2.** NAVIG **MAP TO NAVIGATE BY** a map for navigation by sea or air **3.** METEOROL **WEATHER MAP** an outline map that shows weather patterns **4.** ASTROL **BASIS FOR HOROSCOPE** a map that shows the relative positions of the planets at the time of sb's birth on which his or her horoscope is based **5.** MUSIC **MUSICAL SCORE** a musical score (*technical*) **6.** SEW **STITCHING PLAN** a squared grid marked with symbols indicating the placement of stitches in embroidery ■ **charts** *npl.* **LIST OF POPULAR RECORDS** a list of the musical recordings that have sold most copies during a specific period ■ *v.* (**charts, charting, charted**) **1.** *vt.* **MAKE A CHART OF STH** to make a map, graph, or diagram of sth **2.** *vt.* **MAKE A PLAN** to record or describe a plan **3.** *vi.* **BE IN THE CHARTS** to appear in the music charts [Late 16thC. Via French *charte* from Latin *charta* 'paper, papyrus-leaf, card, map' (source of English *card*). The verb dates from the 19thC.] —**chartable** *adj.*

charter /chaàrtər/ *n.* **1.** LAW **FORMAL DOCUMENT OF INCORPORATION** a formal document incorporating an organization, company, or educational institution **2.** LAW **CONSTITUTION** a formal written statement of the aims, principles, and procedures of an organization **3. STATEMENT OF RIGHTS AND RESPONSIBILITIES** a formal written statement describing the rights and responsibilities of a state and its citizens **4.** LAW **DOCUMENT OF AUTHORIZATION** a document from an organization or society that authorizes the setting up of a new branch **5.** LAW **SPECIAL PRIVILEGE** a special privilege, immunity, or exemption, granted to a particular person or group **6.** TRANSP **HIRE OR LEASE OF TRANSPORT** the hiring or leasing of transport vehicles for personal or special use, or a contract or agreement for this purpose **7.** TRANSP **HIRED OR LEASED TRANSPORT** a vehicle chartered for personal or special use **8.** LAW = **charter party** ■ *vt.* (**-ters, -tering, -tered**) **1.** TRANSP **HIRE OR LEASE TRANSPORT** to hire or lease a vehicle for a personal or special purpose **2.** LAW **GRANT A CHARTER** to grant a charter of incorporation to a group or organization [12thC. Via French *chartre* from, ultimately, Latin *charta* (see CHART).] —**charterer** *n.*

WORD KEY: SYNONYMS

See Synonyms at ***hire.***

chartered /chaártərd/ *adj.* **1. GRANTED A CHARTER** that has been granted a charter **2. FULLY QUALIFIED AS A PROFESSIONAL** having membership of a professional body that has been granted a royal charter

chartered accountant *n.* an accountant who has passed the examinations of one of the governing professional bodies and has been granted a royal charter

chartered engineer *n.* an engineer who is registered with the Engineering Council as having satisfied its professional and technical requirements

chartered surveyor *n.* a British surveyor who is a member of the Royal Institution of Chartered Surveyors

charter flight *n.* a flight that has been chartered for a specific journey, especially as part of a holiday package

Charterhouse /chaártər howss/ (*plural* **-houses**) *n.* a Carthusian monastery [14thC. Alteration (influenced by HOUSE) of Anglo-Norman *Chartrous* or French *Chartreuse* from, ultimately, medieval Latin *Cart(h)usia* 'La Grande Chartreuse', a monastery near Grenoble, France.]

Charteris /chaártəriss/, **Leslie** (1907–93) British-born US novelist who created the gentleman-crook, Simon Templar ('The Saint'). Real name **Leslie Charles Bowyer Yin**

charter member *n.* a founding or original member of a society or organization

Charter of Rights *n.* a section of the Canadian Constitution stating the rights conferred by Canadian citizenship

charter party *n.* a contractual arrangement by which the owner of a ship permits another person to use it to carry goods [Via French from medieval Latin *charta partita*, literally 'divided charter']

Charters Towers town in northern Queensland, Australia. Formerly a gold-mining town, it is now a centre of education and beef production. Population: 8,893 (1996).

Chartism /chaártizzəm/ *n.* the principles and practises of the movement advocating political and social reform in England between 1838 and 1848. Among its aims were improvement in the education and living conditions of the working classes, payment for Members of Parliament, adult male suffrage, equal electoral districts, and voting by ballot. [Mid-19thC. Named after the *People's Charter*.] —**Chartist** *n., adj.*

Chartres /shaártrə/ capital of the Eure-et-Loire Department in northwestern France. It is situated about 80 km/50 mi. southwest of Paris and is famous for its large Gothic cathedral. Population: 44,850 (1990).

chartreuse /shaar trúrz/ *n.* **1. YELLOW OR GREEN LIQUEUR** a yellow or green aromatic liqueur, flavoured with herbs and flowers **2. YELLOWISH-GREEN COLOUR** a bright yellowish-green colour ■ *adj.* **YELLOWISH-GREEN** having a bright yellowish-green colour [Early 19thC. From French (see CHARTERHOUSE).]

charwoman /chaár wŏŏmən/ (*plural* **-en** /-wimmin/) *n.* a woman employed to clean a house or office [Late 16thC. *Char* ultimately from Old English *c(i)err* 'turn', later 'turn of work, chore'.]

chary /cháiri/ (**-ier, -iest**) *adj.* **1. WARY** cautiously reluctant to do sth **2. SPARING** reluctant to share, give, or use sth **3. CONCERNED** fussily concerned **4. SHY** showing or characterized by shyness or modesty [Old English *cearig* 'sorrowful, anxious'. Ultimately from a prehistoric Germanic word that is also the ancestor of English *care*.] —**charily** *adv.* —**chariness** *n.*

WORD KEY: SYNONYMS

See Synonyms at ***cautious.***

Charybdis *n.* ➧ **Scylla and Charybdis**

chase[1] /chayss/ *v.* (**chases, chasing, chased**) **1.** *vti.* **PURSUE SB OR STH** to try to catch or overtake sb or sth **2.** *vt.* **MAKE SB RUN AWAY** to force a person or animal to run away ○ *The kids chased a black cat out of the garden.* **3.** *vi.* **RUSH ABOUT** to rush about ○ *They chased about all day.* **4.** *vt.* **INVESTIGATE STH** to follow up or investigate sth that has not been done or sb who has not done sth ○ *We need to chase up the plumber to find out when he's going to come.* **5.** *vti.* **TRY TO GET STH** to spend a lot of time and energy trying to acquire sth **6.** *vti.* **PAY PERSISTENT ATTENTION TO SB** to seek the company of sb for romantic or sexual purposes, especially in an obvious or unsubtle way ■ *n.* **1. PURSUIT** an act or situation in which sth or sb is being pursued **2.** HUNT **HUNTING FOR SPORT** the hunting of animals for sport **3. HUNTING LAND** a privately owned area of land where animals are confined or stocked for hunting purposes **4. RIGHT TO KEEP GAME OR HUNT** the right to keep game or to hunt on a particular area of land **5. STH PURSUED** sb who or sth, especially an animal, that is being pursued **6.** HORSERACING = **steeplechase 7.** MUSIC **JAZZ DUET** a jazz duet in which the players play alternate phrases and try to outdo each other in virtuosity and invention [13thC. Via Old French *chacier* 'to catch, seize' from, ultimately, Latin *captare* 'to try to seize, chase', from *capere* 'to seize, take'.] ◇ **cut to the chase** *US* to stop wasting time and get on with what needs to be dealt with (*informal*) ◇ **give chase** to pursue sth or sb forcefully (*formal*)

WORD KEY: SYNONYMS

See Synonyms at ***follow.***

chase[2] /chayss/ *n.* **1. PART OF GUN BARREL** the external part of a gun barrel just behind the muzzle **2. GROOVE** a channel, groove, or trench for sth such as a pipe to lie in or fit into ■ *vt.* (**chases, chasing, chased**) **1. CUT GROOVE IN STH** to cut or grind a channel, groove, or trench in sth **2. CUT THREAD IN SCREW** to cut a metal screw thread with a machine tool (**chaser**) [Late 16thC. Via French *châsse* from Latin *capsa* 'box, case' (source of English *capsule* and *case*). Early 17thC. Via French *chas* 'enclosed space' from, ultimately, Latin *capsum* 'thorax, church nave'.]

chase[3] /chayss/ (**chases, chasing, chased**) *vt.* to decorate metal or glass by engraving or embossing [15thC. Shortening of ENCHASE.]

chase[4] /chayss/ (*plural* **chases**) *n.* PRINTING a rectangular frame into which metal type or blocks are fitted so that a page or plate can be printed or made [Late 16thC. Via French *châsse* from Latin *capsa* 'box, case' (source of English *capsule* and *case*).]

chase plane *n.* an aeroplane that follows another aircraft carrying an important person such as a head of state

chaser[1] /cháyssər/ *n.* **1. SB OR STH THAT CHASES** sb or sth that forcefully pursues another person or thing **2.** BEVERAGES **DIFFERENT DRINK** a second drink, taken with or after one of a different kind, e.g. whisky taken after beer **3.** HORSERACING = **steeplechaser 4.** ARMS **NAVAL CANNON** a cannon located at the bow or stern of a vessel and used in pursuing an enemy

chaser[2] /cháyssər/ *n.* **1. ENGRAVER** sb who engraves metal or glass or who embosses metal **2. MACHINE TOOL** a machine tool for cutting screw threads

chasm /kázzəm/ *n.* **1. DEEP HOLE IN THE EARTH** a deep crack or hole in the ground **2. WIDE DIFFERENCE** a wide difference in feelings, ideas, or interests **3. GAP OR BREAK** a gap or break in the progress or continuity of sth [Late 16thC. Via Latin *chasma* from Greek *khasma* 'gaping hollow, gulf'.]

chasmogamous /kaz móggəməss/ *adj.* used to describe flowers that open to allow pollination

chasmogamy /kaz móggəmi/ *n.* the process by which a flower opens before it is pollinated [Early 20thC. Coined from CHASM and -GAMY.]

chassé /shá say/ *n.* **GLIDING STEP** a gliding step in dancing, especially in ballet or square dancing ■ *vi.* (**-sés, -séing, -séd**) **MAKE A CHASSÉ** to make a chassé [Early 19thC. From French, literally 'chasing, chase'.]

chasseur /sha súr/ *adj.* COOK **IN WINE AND MUSHROOM SAUCE** cooked in a rich white-wine and mushroom sauce ■ *n.* MIL **FRENCH SOLDIER** a soldier in a French special unit equipped and trained for rapid deployment [Mid-18thC. From French, literally 'hunter'.]

Chassid *n.* JUDAISM = **Hasid** —**Chassidism** *n.*

chassis /shássi/ (*plural* **-sis** /siz/) *n.* **1. MAIN FRAME OF VEHICLE** the frame and wheels that support the engine and body of a motor vehicle, or the frame and wheels of a carriage or wagon **2.** ELEC **MOUNTING FOR ELECTRONIC DEVICE** the mounting or supporting structure for the components of an electronic device, such as a television **3.** AIR **AIRCRAFT LANDING GEAR** the landing gear of an aircraft **4.** ARMS **MOUNTING FOR GUN CARRIAGE** a frame on which a gun carriage can move back and forth [Mid-17thC. Via French *châssis* from, ultimately, Latin *capsa* 'box, case' (source of English *capsule* and *case*).]

chaste /chayst/ *adj.* **1. ABSTAINING FROM SEX** abstaining from sex on moral grounds **2. SEXUALLY FAITHFUL** not having extramarital sexual relations **3. PURE IN THOUGHT AND DEED** behaving in a pure way, with no immoral thoughts **4. PLAIN** plain, simple, and unadorned in style [13thC. Via French from Latin *castus* 'pure' (source of English *caste, castigate*, and *incest*).] —**chastely** *adv.* —**chasteness** *n.*

chasten /cháyss'n/ (**-tens, -tening, -tened**) *vt.* **1. MAKE SB SUBDUED** to make sb less self-satisfied or self-assertive and more subdued **2. DISCIPLINE SB** to subject sb to discipline **3. MODERATE INTENSITY OF STH** to moderate the intensity of sth [Early 16thC. Formed from obsolete *chaste* (see CHASTISE).] —**chastened** *adj.* —**chastener** *n.* —**chastening** *adj.*

chaste tree *n.* a small ornamental Eurasian tree that has aromatic hairy leaves and fragrant clusters of light purplish flowers. Latin name: *Vitex agnus-castus.* [Translation of Latin *agnus castus* 'chaste agnus', reputedly because certain ancient Greek women maintaining their state of chastity spread its leaves on the ground at the feast of Ceres]

chastise /cha stíz/ (**-tises, -tising, -tised**) *vt.* to punish or scold sb (*formal*) [14thC. Formed from obsolete English *chaste* 'to chasten, reprove' (source of English *chasten*), via Old French *chastier* from Latin *castigare* (see CASTIGATE).] —**chastisable** *adj.* —**chastisement** *n.* —**chastiser** *n.*

chastity /chástəti/ *n.* **1. SEXUAL ABSTINENCE** the condition or practice of abstaining from sex on moral grounds **2. PLAINNESS** plainness or simplicity of style

chastity belt *n.* a locking device passing round the waist and between the legs, used in medieval times to prevent a woman from having sexual intercourse

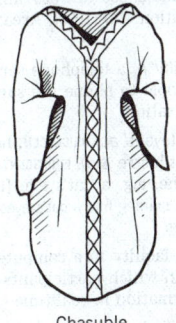

Chasuble

chasuble /cházyŏŏb'l/ *n.* a loose sleeveless outer garment worn by a priest when celebrating Mass or the Eucharist [13thC. Via French from, ultimately, Latin *casula* 'hooded cloak', literally 'little house', from *casa* 'house, hut'.]

chat /chat/ *vi.* (**chats, chatting, chatted**) **1. TALK INFORMALLY** to talk with sb in a relaxed informal way **2.** COMPUT **EXCHANGE MESSAGES BY COMPUTER** to exchange messages in real time with one or more other computer users ■ *n.* **1. INFORMAL TALK** a relaxed informal conversation with sb **2.** COMPUT **EXCHANGE OF MESSAGES BY COMPUTER** an informal exchange of messages in real time with one or more other computer users **3.** BIRDS **SONGBIRD** a small songbird related to the thrush with a harsh chattering cry. Subfamily: Turdinae. **4.** BIRDS = **yellow-breasted chat 5.** BIRDS **AUSTRALIAN WREN** any of several Australian wrens. Genus: *Ephthianura.* [15thC. Shortening of CHATTER.]

chat up *vt.* to talk to sb flirtatiously or flatteringly (*informal*)

zh vision In foreign words: kh German Bach; aN French vin; aaN French blanc; ö German schön, French feu; oN French bon; öN French un; ü French rue Stress marks: ´ as in secret \séek rət\; academic \ákə démmik\

Chateau: Chenonceaux, France

chateau /sháttō/ (*plural* **-teaux** /-tōz, -tō/ *or* **-teaus** /-tō, -tōz/), **château** (*plural* **-teaux** /-tō, -tōz/) *n.* a castle or large house in France, often one that has a vineyard attached and gives its name to wine produced there [Mid-18thC. Via French from Latin *castellum* (see CASTLE).]

Chateaubriand /sháttōbri óN/ *n.* a thick beefsteak cut from the widest middle part of the fillet [Late 19thC. Named after the French writer and statesman François René, Vicomte de *Chateaubriand* (1768–1848), whose chef is credited with creating a dish using the cut.]

chatelain /shátta layn/ *n.* in former times, a man who owned or controlled a castle or other large house [15thC. Via Old French *chastelain* (modern *châtelain*) from medieval Latin *castellanus* (see CASTELLAN).]

chatelaine /shátta layn/ *n.* **1.** MISTRESS OF LARGE HOUSE in former times, a woman who owned or controlled a castle or other large house **2.** WOMAN'S CHAIN KEY a chain and clasp formerly worn at the waist by a woman to hold keys and other small items [Mid-19thC. From French *châtelaine*, the feminine of *châtelain* (see CHATELAIN).]

chat group *n.* COMPUT a group of people who exchange messages online, especially people who share a common interest

Chatham /cháttam/ town and former naval dockyard on the estuary of the River Medway in northern Kent, England. Population: 71,691 (1991).

Chatham Islands group of islands in the southwestern Pacific Ocean forming part of New Zealand. They are situated 800 km/500 mi. east of South Island. Population: 739 (1996). Area: 963 sq. km/372 sq. mi.

chatline /chát līn/ *n.* a telephone service allowing a number of people to phone the same number and have a conversation

chatoyant /sha tóyent/ *adj.* IRIDESCENT having a changeable iridescent lustre ■ *n.* IRIDESCENT GEMSTONE a chatoyant gemstone, e.g. a cat's eye [Late 18thC. From French, literally 'shining like a cat's eyes'.] —**chatoyancy** /sha tóyanssi/ *n.*

chat room *n.* a facility in a computer network, e.g. the Internet, in which participants exchange comments or information in real time

chat show *n.* an informal TV or radio show in which the host interviews celebrities. US term **talk show**

Chattanooga /chátta nóoga, chátt'n óoga/ city and port in southeastern Tennessee, on the Tennessee River, near the Tennessee-Georgia border. Population: 150,425 (1996).

chattel /chátt'l/ *n.* MOVABLE PROPERTY an item of personal property that is not freehold land and that is not intangible. Chattels are typically movable property (**chattels personal**), such as furniture or cars, but may also be interests in property (**chattels real**), such as leases. ■ **chattels** *npl.* PERSONAL ITEMS personal possessions (*formal*) [13thC. Via Old French *chatel* 'property' (source of English *cattle*) from, ultimately, Latin *capitalis* (see CAPITAL).]

chatter /cháttar/ *vi.* (**-ters, -tering, -tered**) **1.** TALK RAPIDLY to talk or converse rapidly and informally about unimportant things **2.** MAKE HIGH-PITCHED SOUNDS to make a rapid series of short high-pitched sounds that seem to resemble speech (*refers to animals or machinery*) **3.** CLICK TOGETHER to click together rapidly because of movement of the jaw caused by fear or

cold (*refers to teeth*) **4.** VIBRATE DURING CUTTING to vibrate while cutting or being cut by a tool or machine, causing surface flaws (*refers to a sawblade or surface*) ■ *n.* **1.** TRIVIAL CONVERSATION rapid and informal talk or conversation, especially about unimportant things **2.** HIGH-PITCHED ANIMAL SOUNDS rapid short high-pitched sounds made by a bird, animal, or machine, that resemble human speech **3.** SURFACE FLAWS PRODUCED IN MACHINING imperfections in a surface, caused by vibration while being cut by a tool or machine [13thC. An imitation of the sound.]

chatterbox /cháttar boks/ *n.* sb who talks a lot, especially about unimportant things (*informal*)

chatterer /cháttarar/ *n.* **1.** VERY TALKATIVE PERSON sb who talks a lot, especially about unimportant matters **2.** BIRDS = cotinga

chattering classes *npl.* educated middle-class people with an interest in current affairs and culture, who like to make their views known to each other

chatter mark *n.* **1.** GEOL MARK ON ROCK a crack or groove on the surface of rock, caused by the abrasive action of a glacier on bedrock or by the collision of fragments in water **2.** ENG VIBRATION MARK a mark left on sth that has been machined, caused by vibration

Chatterton /cháttartan/, **Thomas** (1752–70) British poet and journalist. His pastiches of medieval literature were accepted as the work of a 15th-century monk. Poverty-stricken, he committed suicide. Pseudonym **Thomas Rowley**

chatty /chátti/ (**-tier, -tiest**) *adj.* **1.** FOND OF CHATTING fond of chatting about unimportant things **2.** FRIENDLY friendly and informal in tone —**chattily** *adv.* —**chattiness** *n.*

──── WORD KEY: SYNONYMS ────
See Synonyms at **talkative**.

chat-up line *n.* a prepared phrase or style of conversation that sb uses when trying to form a romantic or sexual relationship (*informal*)

Chatwin /cháttwin/, **Bruce** (1940–89) British writer. His novels, e.g. *On the Black Hill* (1983), and idiosyncratic travel writings show his distaste for the chaos of modern life.

Chaucer /cháwssar/, **Geoffrey** (1343?–1400) English poet and author of *The Canterbury Tales* (1387–1400), one of the finest early works in English. —**Chaucerian** *n., adj.*

chaudfroid /shō fwaa/ *n.* a hot béchamel sauce with aspic that sets when cold and is used to coat cold cooked savoury foods [Late 19thC. From French, literally 'hot-cold'.]

Chaudhuri /chówdari/, **Nirad Chandra** (b. 1897) Indian writer and critic of British cultural imperialism in India, notably in *Thy Hand Great Anarch* (1987).

chauffeur /shōfar/ *n.* HIRED DRIVER sb employed to drive a car ■ *vti.* (**-feurs, -feuring, -feured**) DRIVE SB to drive sb from place to place in a car, or be employed to drive a car for sb [Late 19thC. From French, literally 'stoker, fireman', (used to denote the stoker and sometimes the driver of an early steam car), from *chauffer* 'to heat'.]

chaulmoogra /chawl móogra/ *n.* a tropical tree of Southeast Asia with seeds that yield an oil once used to treat leprosy. Latin name: *Hydnocarpus kurzii*. [Early 19thC. From Bengali *cāul-mugrā*.]

Chauvel /shō vel/, **Charles Edward** (1897–1959) Australian film-maker. He was producer and director of films ranging from the silent *Moth of Moonbi* (1926) to *Jedda* (1955), one of the first colour films made in Australia.

chauvinism /shōvanizzam/ *n.* **1.** AGGRESSIVE PATRIOTISM unreasoning, overenthusiastic, and aggressive patriotism **2.** SENSE OF SUPERIORITY an excessive or prejudiced loyalty to a particular gender, group, or cause [Late 19thC. From French *chauvinisme*, which was coined from the name of Nicolas *Chauvin*, a French veteran of the Napoleonic wars.]

chauvinist /shōvanist/ *n.* **1.** SB WITH SENSE OF SUPERIORITY sb with an excessive or prejudiced loyalty to a particular gender, group, or cause **2.** UNREASONING PATRIOT an unreasoning, overenthusiastic, and aggressive patriot —**chauvinistic** /shōva nístik/ *adj.* —**chauvinistically** /-nístikli/ *adv.*

César Chávez

Chávez /cha véz/, **César** (1927–93) US trade unionist. He founded the National Farm Workers Association (1962) to help migrant farm workers.

chaw /chaw/ (**chaws, chawing, chawed**) *vti.* to chew (*regional*) [Early 16thC. Variant of CHEW.]

chayote /chī óti/ *n.* **1.** PLANTS TROPICAL CLIMBING PLANT a tropical American climbing plant of the gourd family. Latin name: *Sechium edule*. **2.** FOOD FRUIT OF CHAYOTE the pear-shaped, furrowed green or white fruit of the chayote that is cooked and eaten as a vegetable [Late 19thC. Via Spanish from Nahuatl *chayotli*.]

chazzen *n.* = chazan

ChB *abbr.* Bachelor of Surgery [Latin, *Chirurgiae Baccalaureus*]

cheap /cheep/ *adj.* **1.** COSTING LITTLE low in price or cost, or lower in price than might reasonably be expected **2.** CHARGING LITTLE charging low prices but offering good value **3.** POOR QUALITY inexpensive and of poor quality **4.** WORTH LITTLE worth little, or accorded little value ○ *In times of war, life is cheap.* **5.** UNDESERVING OF RESPECT not deserving of respect **6.** OFFENSIVE dishonourable, offensive, or unfair, especially in a way that seems obvious or calculated ○ *a cheap trick* **7.** US STINGY stingy or unwilling to give freely ■ *adv.* INEXPENSIVELY at low cost [Old English *cēap* 'trade, bargaining, a (good) bargain'. Ultimately via a prehistoric Germanic word from Latin *caupo* 'petty tradesman', 'innkeeper'.] —**cheapish** *adj.* —**cheaply** *adv.* —**cheapness** *n.* ◇ **on the cheap** at very low cost (*informal*)

cheapen /cheepan/ (**-ens, -ening, -ened**) *vti.* **1.** MAKE STH COST LESS to make sth less expensive, or become less expensive, especially in order to save money or increase profits, rather than to give better value **2.** DEGRADE SB OR STH to lower the quality or reputation of sb or sth, or become lower in quality or reputation

cheapie /cheepi/, **cheapy** (*plural* **-ies**) *n.* US (*informal*) **1.** STH CHEAP sth that is cheap **2.** STINGY PERSON sb who is mean or ungenerous

cheapjack /cheep jak/ *n.* SELLER OF INFERIOR GOODS sb who sells inferior goods ■ *adj.* INFERIOR inferior in value or quality [From the name *Jack*, used as a general term for a man]

cheapo /cheepō/ *adj.* cheap in price or cost (*informal*)

cheapskate /cheep skayt/ *n.* sb who is mean or ungenerous (*informal*)

cheapy *n.* = cheapie

cheat /cheet/ *v.* (**cheats, cheating, cheated**) **1.** *vt.* DECEIVE SB to deceive or mislead sb, especially for personal advantage **2.** *vi.* BREAK RULES TO GAIN ADVANTAGE to break the rules in a game, examination, or contest, in an attempt to gain an unfair advantage **3.** *vi.* BE UNFAITHFUL TO SB to have a sexual relationship with sb other than a spouse or regular sexual partner **4.** *vt.* ESCAPE HARM to avoid harm or injury by luck or cunning ■ *n.* **1.** DECEITFUL PERSON sb who uses deceit or trickery to gain an unfair advantage **2.** DISHONEST TRICK a dishonest or unfair trick **3.** LAW DISHONESTLY OBTAINING PROPERTY the obtaining of sb else's property by dishonest means **4.** US BOT = chess³ *n.* [14thC. Shortening of ESCHEAT. The sense development seems to have been from 'to confiscate (land and property) legally' via 'to deprive of sth dishonestly' to 'to deceive'.] —**cheater** *n.*

Chechen /ché chen/ *n.* **1.** PEOPLES SB FROM CHECHNYA sb who was born in or lives in Chechnya **2.** LANG MAJORITY LANGUAGE IN CHECHNYA the majority language in Chechnya, belonging to the Nakh group of North

Caucasian languages. Chechen is spoken by about one million people. —**Chechen** *adj.*

Chechnya /chéchni ə/ republic in southwestern Russia that formally separated from Ingushetia in 1992. In 1994, Russia refused to recognize Chechnya's independence, resulting in a conflict that ended formally in 1997. Capital: Grozny. Population: 1,500,000 (1994). Area: 15,000 sq. km/5,800 sq. mi.

check /chek/ *v.* (**checks, checking, checked**) **1.** *vti.* **EXAMINE STH** to examine sth in order to establish its state or condition ○ *Check the doors and windows to make sure they're locked.* **2.** *vti.* **CONFIRM TRUTH OR ACCURACY OF STH** to confirm or establish that sth is true or accurate ○ *We need to check with the insurance company to find out whether we're covered.* **3.** *vi.* **BE CONSISTENT WITH STH ELSE** to be the same as, or consistent with sth else ○ *What you're telling me now doesn't check with what you told me last week.* **4.** *vt.* **HALT OR SLOW STH** to stop or reduce the progress of some unwelcome process **5.** *vti.* **STOP SUDDENLY** to stop or pause suddenly, or make sb or sth stop suddenly ○ *In mid-sentence, he checked himself abruptly, looking terribly embarrassed.* **6.** *vt.* **PREVENT STH BEING EXPRESSED** to prevent sth from being expressed, or control the urge to express sth ○ *Checking the urge to laugh out loud, I buried my head in the newspaper.* **7.** *vt.* **REPRIMAND SB** to criticize sb for a fault or bad behaviour **8.** *vt.* SPORTS **BLOCK OPPONENT** in sports such as ice hockey, to move directly into the path of an opponent, usually making physical contact, in order to block his or her progress **9.** *vt.* = **tick 10.** *vt. US* **HAND OVER BAGGAGE** to hand over sth, especially baggage, so that it can be transported separately from passengers, usually in the same aircraft or vehicle ○ *You must check your luggage, sir.* **11.** *vt. US* **HAND STH OVER FOR TEMPORARY KEEPING** to hand over sth such as a coat in a restaurant or museum, so that it can be looked after ○ *Do you want to check your coat, ma'am?* **12.** *vt.* CHESS **PUT OPPONENT'S KING IN THREATENING SITUATION** to put an opponent's king in a situation in which one of your pieces directly threatens it ■ *n.* **1. EXAMINATION** an examination or investigation of sth, especially to verify its state or condition ○ *Routine checks should have revealed the cracks in the engine housing.* **2. STH THAT TESTS ACCURACY** sth that can be used or referred to in order to test the accuracy, truth, or safety of sth else **3. MEANS OF CONTROLLING OR RESTRAINING SB** a means of controlling or restraining sb or sth ○ *The United Nations was formed to act as a check on aggressive nations.* **4.** *US* = **cheque 5.** *US* = **bill**[1] *n.* 2 **6.** *US* **NUMBERED TICKET FOR DEPOSITED ITEM** a numbered ticket or token given out when an item is left at a cloakroom **7.** *US* = **tick**[1] *n.* 3 **8. PATTERN OF SQUARES** a pattern made up entirely of squares in at least two different colours that are arranged alternately **9. SQUARE IN CHECK PATTERN** a square in a pattern, in which at least two different colours are arranged alternately ○ *Every third check is red.* **10.** CHESS **MOVE ATTACKING KING** a move in chess by which a piece directly threatens the opposing king, or the position resulting from this move. The king must escape from this position to avoid checkmate. ○ *If you move your king there, you'll be in check.* **11.** SPORTS **BLOCKING MOVE** in sports, a move directly into the path of an attacking opponent ■ *adj.* = **chequered** ■ *interj.* CHESS **WARNING THAT KING IS IN CHECK** used to announce that an opponent's king is in check [14thC. Via Old French *eschec* 'check in chess', a warning that an opponent's king is under attack, from, ultimately, Persian *šāh* 'king' (see SHAH).] —**checkable** *adj.*
◇ **in check** restrained and under control ○ *managing to keep her anger in check*

check in *v.* **1.** *vti.* **REGISTER AT HOTEL** to register as a guest, or register a guest, on arrival at a hotel ○ *Has my colleague checked in yet?* **2.** *vti.* **ARRIVE FOR JOURNEY** to register and go through the necessary formalities before beginning a journey, especially by air ○ *All passengers should check in at least one hour before departure.* **3.** *vi.* **MAKE CONTACT** to make routine contact with a person or organization to exchange information ○ *The patrols are supposed to check in by radio at half-hourly intervals.*

check into *vt.* to investigate sth in order to get more information about it, or to establish its truth or accuracy ○ *When we checked into his background, we found that he had several convictions for fraud.*

check off *vt.* = **tick off**

check out *v.* **1.** *vi.* **LEAVE HOTEL** to pay the bill and leave a hotel or other place ○ *We'll be checking out later this morning.* **2.** *vi. US* **LEAVE** to leave a particular place or a person (*informal*) **3.** *vt.* **INVESTIGATE STH** to establish that sth is correct or valid ○ *The date is probably 1961. Check it out, will you?* **4.** *vt.* **TAKE A LOOK AT STH** to visit a place briefly to get information about it (*informal*) ○ *Let's check out the new pizza place down the High Street.* **5.** *vi.* **BE PROVED TRUE** to prove after investigation to be correct or valid ○ *If the DNA checks out, he's our man.* **6.** *vti. US* **PAY IN SUPERMARKET** to pay for sth in a supermarket ○ *When I went to check out, I realized I'd left my purse in the car.* **7.** *vt. US* **TAKE MONEY FOR GOODS AT SUPERMARKET** to calculate and take payment from a customer in a supermarket ○ *This person's in a hurry, so do you mind if I check her out first?*

check over *vt.* **1. EXAMINE STH** to examine sth to make sure that it is correct or satisfactory ○ *Could you check my essay over to make sure there are no errors, please?* **2. EXAMINE SB FOR HEALTH AND FITNESS** to examine sb carefully to establish his or her state of health ○ *I've checked her over, and there are no broken bones.*

check through *vt.* to examine or review systematically all the parts of sth to make sure that it is satisfactory

check up *vi.* to make enquiries to establish a point ○ *I checked up: no one of that name lives at that address.*

check up on *vt.* to make enquiries or obtain information about sb or sth, often secretly and usually because of suspicion or worry

checkbook *n.* US = **chequebook**

check box *n.* a small square on a computer screen that, when clicked on with a mouse, displays a small cross or check to show that an item has been selected

check digit *n.* in computing, a digit derived from and added to the other digits in a sequence, used to ensure that the sequence is correct

checked /chekt/ *adj.* having a pattern of small squares ○ *a red-and-white checked tablecloth*

checker /chékər/ *n.* **1. SB CHECKING STH** sb who carries out a check on sth **2.** *US* **CASHIER** a cashier in a supermarket or large store **3.** *US* BOARD GAMES = **draught**

checkerboard /chékərbawrd/ *n. US* = **chequerboard**

checkers /chékərz/ *n. US* BOARD GAMES = **draughts** (*takes a singular verb*)

check-in *n.* **1. CHECKING IN AT HOTEL OR AIRPORT** the process of registering on arrival at a hotel or airport **2. REGISTRATION DESK** a place where people check in at a hotel or airport **3.** *US* **SB CHECKING IN** sb who is checking in, e.g. a traveller at an airport, or a guest at a hotel ○ *Since the flight was overbooked, the five late check-ins had to wait.*

checking account *n. US* FIN = **current account**

checklist /chék list/ *n.* a list of names, items, or points for consideration or action

checkmate /chék mayt/ *n.* **1. WINNING POSITION IN CHESS** a move or position in chess, in which a player's king cannot escape check and the other player wins the game **2. MOVE THAT PRODUCES CHECKMATE** a move in chess that produces checkmate, or a game that ends in checkmate ○ *The series was declared a draw with three checkmates apiece.* **3. COMPLETE DEFEAT** a situation of defeat or deadlock ■ *vt.* (**-mates, -mating, -mated**) **1. PUT KING IN CHECKMATE** in chess, to put an opponent's king in checkmate **2. THWART SB** to make it impossible for sb to succeed or proceed further ■ *interj.* **ANNOUNCEMENT OF CHECKMATE** used in chess to announce that an opponent's king is in checkmate [15thC. Via Old French *eschec mat* from, ultimately, Persian *šāh māt* 'the king is dead'.]

checkout /chék owt/ *n.* **1. SUPERMARKET TILL** a point in a supermarket at which shoppers pay for their purchases ○ *Only three checkouts were open.* **2. DEPARTURE FROM A HOTEL** the procedure involved in paying a hotel bill and leaving ○ *We'd like to arrange for a later checkout.* **3.** *US* **SB CHECKING OUT** sb who is checking out, e.g. a traveller at an airport, or a guest at a hotel ○ *Apart from a couple of late checkouts, everyone seemed to be ready.*

checkpoint /chék poynt/ *n.* a place where police or other officials stop and check vehicles

Checkpoint Charlie *n.* a border crossing between East and West Berlin during the Cold War. Once situated on the Friedrichstrasse, it has now been demolished.

checkrail /chék rayl/ *n.* = **guardrail** *n.* 2

checkrein /chék rayn/ *n.* **1.** *US* RIDING = **bearing rein 2. REIN BETWEEN TWO HORSES** a rein used when driving a pair of horses, connecting the driving rein of one horse to the mouthpiece of the other

checksum /chék sum/ *n.* COMPUT a value transmitted with a data stream, derived from the other elements in the data stream and used to check for transmission errors in the data. If the transmitted checksum differs from the one derived by the receiving computer, a transmission error has probably occurred and the transmission is repeated.

checkup /chék up/, **check-up** *n.* a routine examination or inspection, especially one carried out by a doctor or dentist ○ *Regular checkups are required for all pilots.*

check valve *n.* a valve designed to allow liquids to flow in one direction only

chedarim plural of **cheder**

cheddar /chéddər/ *n.* a hard pale yellow or orange-red cheese with a flavour that ranges from mild to very strong, depending on its maturity [Mid-17thC. Named after the village of CHEDDAR, where it was originally made.]

Cheddar /chéddər/ village in Somerset, England, in the Mendip Hills. Population: 4,484 (1991).

Cheddar Gorge deep gorge in the Mendip Hills of Somerset, England. It has steep limestone cliffs, and caves with stalactites and stalagmites. Height: 137 m/450 ft (cliffs).

cheder /káydər/ (*plural* **-arim** /ke daárim/ *or* **-ers**) *n.* classes in Hebrew language and religious knowledge for younger Jewish children [Late 19thC. From Hebrew *ḥēder* 'room'.]

cheek /cheek/ *n.* **1. SOFT PART OF FACE** the soft side area of the face between the nose and ear **2. BUTTOCK** either side of the buttocks (*informal*) **3. BAD MANNERS** impertinent or precocious words or behaviour showing, or appearing to show, disregard for good manners or the feelings of others (*informal*) ○ *He had the cheek to ask me for a lift!* **4. DISRESPECT** deliberate disrespect or rudeness, especially by children towards adults (*informal*) ○ *I don't want to hear any more of your cheek, is that clear!* ■ *vt.* (**cheeks, cheeking, cheeked**) **SPEAK DISRESPECTFULLY TO SB** to speak disrespectfully or rudely (*informal*) [Old English *cēoce* related to English *choke* and *cackle*] ◇ **cheek by jowl** side by side or very close together ○ *living cheek by jowl in a tiny unheated flat* ◇ **turn the other cheek** to accept injury or insults without resisting or retaliating

cheekbone /cheék bōn/ *n.* an arch of bone in the face, below the eyes and above the cheeks

cheekpiece /cheék peess/ *n.* either of the two straps on a bridle that lie along the cheeks of a horse and join the bit to the crownpiece

cheek pouch *n.* a fold of skin in the mouth of some rodents and other mammals, e.g. squirrels and some monkeys, that acts as a pouch for storing food

cheek tooth *n.* a premolar or molar of a mammal, or any one of the teeth behind the canines

cheeky /cheéki/ (**-ier, -iest**) *adj.* **1. RUDE AND IMPERTINENT** insolently or playfully rude or disrespectful **2. AMUSING BUT MILDLY IMPROPER** amusing or endearing despite offending good manners, especially by being mildly sexually improper (*informal*) ○ *The stories are performed by a raconteur with warmth and a cheeky charm.* —**cheekily** *adv.* —**cheekiness** *n.*

cheep /cheep/ *n.* **SOUND MADE BY YOUNG BIRD** the high shrill sound made by a young bird ■ *vi.* (**cheeps, cheeping, cheeped**) **TO MAKE A HIGH SHRILL SOUND** to make a high shrill sound characteristic of young birds [Early 16thC. Originally from Scots dialect, as an imitation of the sound.]

cheer /cheer/ *n.* **1. SHOUT OF APPROVAL** a shout that expresses happiness, excitement, encouragement, or praise ○ *A huge cheer went up as the band walked onto the stage.* **2. WELL-BEING AND OPTIMISM** a sense of general well-being and optimism ○ *The latest sales figures will bring little cheer.* ■ *v.* (**cheers, cheering, cheered**) **1.** *vti.* **SHOUT ENCOURAGEMENT OR SUPPORT** to shout encouragement, support, or appreciation, especially to people who are performing or competing **2.** *vt.* **MAKE SB FEEL CHEERFUL** to make sb feel more cheerful, confident, or optimistic (*often passive*) ○ *very cheering news* [13thC. Via Anglo-Norman *chere* 'face, expression' from Latin *cara*, ultimately from Greek *kara* 'head'. The underlying meaning is 'mood, as shown in the face'.] —**cheerer** *n.* —**cheeringly** *adv.*

cheer on *vt.* to give active or vocal support, especially at a sports event ○ *We went to cheer our team on in the championships.*

cheer up *vti.* **1. MAKE SB FEEL LESS SAD** to become, or make sb feel, less sad ○ *She cheered up a little when I suggested lunch.* **2. MAKE PLACE BRIGHTER OR MORE ATTRACTIVE** to become, or make sth, brighter or more attractive and welcoming in appearance ○ *A coat of bright yellow paint will cheer up the dingiest of kitchens.*

cheerful /chéerf'l/ *adj.* **1. HAPPY AND OPTIMISTIC** in a happy and optimistic mood, or happy and optimistic by nature ○ *She remained her usual cheerful self despite recent setbacks.* **2. BRIGHT AND PLEASANT** causing people to feel cheerful ○ *a cheerful light blue* **3. WILLING AND UNRESENTFUL** showing willingness or good humour in complying ○ *They set to work cleaning up the mess with cheerful determination.* —**cheerfully** *adv.* —**cheerfulness** *n.*

cheerio /chéeri ó/ *interj.* **1. FAREWELL** used to say goodbye (*informal*) **2. TOAST** a word used to express good wishes when drinking (*dated informal*) [Early 20thC. Alteration of CHEER.]

cheerleader /chéer leedər/ *n.* **1. PERFORMER WHO MAKES CROWD CHEER** any of a group of uniformed performers who encourage the crowd to support a team at sports events in the United States and other places. Cheerleaders direct organized chants and songs, and often perform acrobatic routines. **2. UNCRITICAL ENTHUSIAST** an uncritically enthusiastic supporter (*disapproving*)

cheerless /chéerləss/ *adj.* lacking anything bright, pleasant, or encouraging ○ *a gloomy cheerless day* —**cheerlessly** *adv.* —**cheerlessness** *n.*

cheers /cheerz/ *interj.* **1. GOOD HEALTH** used to express good wishes just before drinking an alcoholic drink (*informal*) **2. GOOD BYE** good-bye or farewell **3. THANKS** thank you ○ *Cheers, you've been a big help!*

cheery /chéeri/ (**-ier, -iest**) *adj.* happy or in good spirits —**cheerily** *adv.* —**cheeriness** /chíərinəss/ *n.*

cheese /cheez/ *n.* **1. SOLID FOOD MADE FROM MILK** a food made from the milk of cows, sheep, goats, and some other animals. Cheese ranges in texture form hard to semisoft, and in flavour from mildly acidic to sharp. **2. BLOCK OF CHEESE** an individual block of cheese [Old English *cēse*. Ultimately from a prehistoric Germanic word that was borrowed from Latin *caseus*, of unknown origin.]

cheeseburger /chéez burgər/ *n.* a hamburger covered with melted cheese, served in a roll

cheesecake /chéez kayk/ *n.* **1. DESSERT MADE WITH SWEETENED SOFT CHEESE** a dessert consisting of a layer of sweetened soft cheese mixed with cream and eggs on a biscuit or pastry base **2. PHOTOGRAPHS OF ATTRACTIVE WOMEN** photographs of women that highlight their physical appearance, especially in a stereotypical way (*slang*) ◊ **beefcake**

cheesecloth /chéez kloth/ *n.* a light woven cotton material, originally used for wrapping or straining cheese and now used as a material for lightweight clothes

cheese cutter *n.* a board to which a piece of wire is attached for cutting cheese

cheesed off *adj.* annoyed, bored, or frustrated (*informal*)

cheesemonger /chéez mung gər/ *n.* a supplier of cheese and other dairy products (*dated*)

cheeseparing /chéez pairing/ *adj.* **STINGY** reluctant to spend money ■ *n.* **STINGINESS** reluctance to spend money [The word originally referred to 'a paring of cheese rind', sth only the most miserly would save]

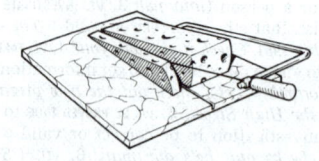

Cheese cutter

cheese straw *n.* a long thin biscuit of cheese-flavoured pastry, served as a snack

cheesy /chéezi/ (**-ier, -iest**) *adj.* **1. LIKE CHEESE** having the flavour or smell of cheese **2. TACKY** cheap and tawdry (*informal*)

Cheetah

cheetah /chéetə/ (*plural* **-tahs** *or* **-tah**) *n.* a large member of the cat family with a yellowish-brown, black-spotted coat, small head, slender body, and long legs, found mainly in Africa and southwestern Asia. It is the fastest land mammal, can reach speeds of up to 110km/h/68 mph while hunting, and is an endangered species. Latin name: *Acinonyx jubatus*. [Late 18thC. Via Hindi *cītā* from Sanskrit *citraka* 'leopard, tiger' (literally 'spotted, variegated'), from *citra-* 'spotted'.]

chef /shef/ *n.* a professional cook, especially the principal cook in a hotel or restaurant [Early 19thC. From French, shortening of *chef de cuisine* 'head of the kitchen'.]

chef-d'oeuvre /sháy dúrv/ (*plural* **chefs-d'oeuvre**) *n.* a masterpiece, especially one produced by a musician, writer, or artist (*formal*) ○ *He regarded that particular speech as his chef-d'oeuvre.* [From French, literally 'chief piece of work']

chef's salad *n.* US a tossed green salad with added tomatoes, sliced hard-boiled eggs, and thin strips of meat and cheese

Chekhov /chék of/, **Anton Pavlovich** (1860–1904) Russian writer. His plays and short stories reveal the emotional depth of ordinary lives and include *The Seagull* (1896) and *The Cherry Orchard* (1904). —**Chekhovian** /che kóvi ən/ *n., adj.*

Chekiang /chek ji áng/ coastal province in eastern China, and the smallest in China. Capital: Hangzhou. Population: 41,445,930 (1990). Area: 101,800 sq. km/39,305 sq. mi. Also known as **Zhejiang**

chela[1] /kéelə/ (*plural* **-lae** /-lee/) *n.* the opposable end joint that forms a claw on a limb of a lobster, crab, scorpion, or similar animal (**arthropod**) [Mid-17thC. Via modern Latin from Greek *khēlē* 'claw', of unknown origin.]

chela[2] /cháylə/ *n.* the pupil or disciple of a Hindu religious teacher [Mid-19thC. From Hindi *celā*.]

chelate[1] /kée layt/ *n.* **COMPOUND OF METAL AND NONMETAL** a chemical compound in which metallic and non metallic, usually organic, atoms are combined. These compounds are characterized by a ring structure in which a metal ion is attached to two non metal ions by covalent bonds. ■ *adj.* **RELATING TO CHELATES** in the form of or typical of a chelate ■ *v.* (**-lates, -lating, -lated**) **1.** *vti.* **CHEM COMBINE TO FORM CHELATE**

to combine, or combine sth, with a metal to form a chelate **2.** *vt.* **MED TREAT SB WITH CHELATING AGENT** to treat sb with a chelating agent in order to remove a heavy metal, such as lead, from the bloodstream —**chelatable** *adj.* —**chelation** *n.* —**chelator** /ki láytə/ *n.*

chelate[2] /kée layt/ *adj.* **ZOOL** having chelae, or shaped like chelae

chelating agent *n.* a chemical that combines with a metal to form a chelate. Chelating agents are often used to remove unwanted heavy metal ions from the body, e.g. in cases of metal poisoning.

chelicera /kə lissərə/ (*plural* **-ae** /-rī/) *n.* either of the first mouthparts of horseshoe crabs and spiders, resembling fangs or pincers and used to grab or poison prey [Mid-19thC. From modern Latin, coined from *chela* 'CHELA[1]' + Greek *keras* 'horn'.]

chelicerate /kə lissərət/ *n.* **INVERTEBRATE WITH PINCER-SHAPED MOUTHPARTS** an invertebrate with feeding appendages shaped like pincers. Spiders and crabs are chelicerates. Phylum: Chelicerata. ■ *adj.* **RELATING TO CHELICERATES** relating to or belonging to the chelicerates [Early 20thC. From modern Latin *chelicerata*, phylum name, formed from *chelicera* (see CHELICERA).]

cheliform /kéeli fawrm/ *adj.* used to describe an appendage shaped like a pincer or chela [Late 18thC. Coined from modern Latin *chela* 'CHELA[1]' + -FORM.]

Chelmsford /chélmzfərd/ cathedral town in Essex, England. Population: 152,418 (1991).

chelonian /ki lóni ən/ *n.* **REPTILE WITH SHELL** a reptile, such as a turtle or tortoise, that has most of its body enclosed in a hard bony shell. Order: Chelonia. ■ *adj.* **RELATING TO CHELONIANS** relating to or belonging to the chelonians [Early 19thC. Via modern Latin *Chelonia*, order name, from Greek *khelōnē* 'tortoise'.]

Chelsea bun /chélssi-/ *n.* a flat coil-shaped bun, made from yeasted dough, containing currants, and sometimes sprinkled with sugar [Early 18thC. Named after *Chelsea*, the district of London where it was first made.]

Chelsea pensioner *n.* a retired soldier who is an inmate of the Chelsea Royal Hospital in London. Chelsea pensioners wear a distinctive uniform with a red tunic.

Cheltenham /chélt'n əm/ spa and residential town in Gloucestershire, England, situated on the western edge of the Cotswold Hills. Population: 91,301 (1991).

Chelyabinsk /chel yaábinsk/ city and capital of Chelyabinsk Oblast, in western Russia, situated 201 km/125 mi. south of Yekaterinburg. Population: 1,143,000 (1992).

chem. *abbr.* **1.** chemical **2.** chemist **3.** chemistry

chem- *prefix.* = **chemo-**

chemi- *prefix.* = **chemo-**

chemical /kémmik'l/ *adj.* **1. RELATING TO CHEMISTRY** produced by or involved in the processes of chemistry **2. COMPOSED OF CHEMICALS** composed of or involving the use of chemicals ■ *n.* **SUBSTANCE USED OR MADE BY CHEMISTRY** a substance used in or produced by the processes of chemistry. A chemical has a defined atomic or molecular structure that results from, or takes part in, reactions involving changes in its structure, composition, and properties. [Late 16thC. Formed from modern Latin *chimicus* 'alchemist', a shortening of medieval Latin *alchimicus*, from *alchimia* (see ALCHEMY).] —**chemically** *adv.*

chemical bond *n.* a force resulting from the redistribution of energy contained by orbiting electrons, which tends to bind atoms together to form molecules

chemical dependency *n.* addiction to a chemical substance or drug

chemical engineering *n.* a branch of engineering that deals with the industrial applications of chemistry and chemical processes —**chemical engineer** *n.*

chemical equation *n.* a representation, using chemical symbols in a form resembling a mathematical equation, of the process involved in a chemical reaction

chemical free *adj.* US not addicted to drugs or refraining from the use of drugs (*informal*)

chemical reaction *n.* a process that changes the molecular composition of a substance by redistributing atoms or groups of atoms without altering the structure of the nuclei of the atoms

chemical toilet *n.* a portable toilet containing chemicals to neutralize human waste

chemical warfare *n.* military operations involving the use of weapons containing substances such as nerve gas or poison

chemical weapon *n.* a weapon containing a substance such as nerve gas or poison

chemiluminescence /kémmi loómi néss'nss/ *n.* emission of light as a result of a chemical reaction, without producing heat —**chemiluminescent** *adj.*

chemin de fer /shə máN də fáir/ *n.* a gambling card game, similar to and derived from baccarat [From French, 'railway', in reference to the speed at which the game is played]

chemise /shə meéz/ *n.* **1.** LONG LOOSE DRESS a type of long loose dress, sometimes loosely belted at the waist or hip **2.** LONG LOOSE UNDERGARMENT a long loose undergarment shaped like a dress [13thC. Via Old French from late Latin *camisia* 'shirt, nightgown' (source of English *camisado*).]

chemisette /shémmi zét/ *n.* a decorative undergarment made of lace or other fine material, worn to fill space left at the neckline of a low-cut dress [Early 19thC. From French, literally 'small chemise', from *chemise* (see CHEMISE).]

chemisorb /kémmi sawrb/ (**-sorbs, -sorbing, -sorbed**), **chemosorb** /keémō-/ (**-sorbs, -sorbing, -sorbed**) *vt.* to take up a substance by chemisorption [Mid-20thC. Back-formation from CHEMISORPTION.]

chemisorption /kémmi sáwrpsh'n/ *n.* the process of coating the surface of a substance rather than being absorbed by it, accompanied by chemical bonding between the surface of the material and the adsorbed substance [Mid-20thC. Blend of CHEMI- and ADSORPTION.] —**chemisorptive** *adj.*

chemist /kémmist/ *n.* **1.** SHOP SELLING MEDICINES AND TOILETRIES a shop where medicines, toiletries, and cosmetics are sold, and where prescriptions are dispensed. US term **drugstore 2.** = **pharmacist 3.** SCIENTIST SPECIALIZING IN CHEMISTRY a scientist who works in the field of chemistry [Mid-16thC. Via French *chimiste* from modern Latin *chimista*, a shortening of medieval Latin *alchimista* 'alchemist', from *alchimia* (see ALCHEMY).]

chemistry /kémmistri/ *n.* **1.** STUDY OF TRANSFORMATION OF MATTER a branch of science dealing with the structure, composition, properties, and reactive characteristics of substances, especially at the atomic and molecular levels. ◊ **inorganic chemistry, organic chemistry, physical chemistry 2.** CHEMICAL PROPERTIES OF STH the chemical composition, structure, and properties of a substance, or the chemical aspects of an activity ○ *the chemistry of wine-making* **3.** REACTION BETWEEN TWO PEOPLE the spontaneous reaction of individuals to each other, especially a mutual sense of attraction or understanding

Chemnitz /kémnits/ city in the state of Saxony, in east-central Germany. It is a major industrial city. Population: 278,700 (1994). Formerly **Karl Marx Stadt** (1953–90)

chemo /keémō/ *n.* chemotherapy (*informal*) [Mid-20thC. Shortening.]

chemo- *prefix.* chemical, chemistry ○ *chemoreceptor* [From CHEMICAL]

chemokinesis /keémō ki neéssiss, -kī-/ *n.* increased activity of cells or organisms caused by the presence of a chemical agent

chemolithotroph /keémō líthə trŏf, -trof/ *n.* a bacterium that obtains its energy from inorganic compounds containing iron, nitrogen, or sulphur, and not from living on decaying organisms [Late 20thC] —**chemolithotrophic** /keémō líthə trŏffik, -trŏffik/ *adj.*

chemoprophylaxis /keémō profə láksiss/ *n.* the use of chemical agents to prevent disease —**chemoprophylactic** *adj.*

chemoreception /keémō ri sépsh'n/ *n.* the physiological response of an organism or sense organ to a chemical stimulus —**chemoreceptive** *adj.* —**chemoreceptivity** /keémō ree sep tívvəti/ *n.*

chemoreceptor /keémō ri séptər/ *n.* a sense organ, e.g. a taste bud, that responds to a chemical stimulus

chemosorb *vt.* = **chemisorb**

chemosphere /kémmō sfiər, keémō-/ *n.* a variable region of the atmosphere, approximately 30 to 190 km/20 to 120 mi. above the Earth's surface, where photochemical reactions take place —**chemospheric** /kémmō sférrik, keémō-/ *adj.*

chemostat /keémō stat/ *n.* an apparatus designed to permit the growth of bacterial cultures at controlled rates [Mid-20thC. Coined from CHEMO-, on the model of *thermostat*.]

chemosurgery /keémō surjəri/ *n.* surgical removal of dead or diseased tissue by chemical means —**chemosurgical** /-srjik'l/ *adj.*

chemosynthesis /keémō sínthəssiss/ *n.* the synthesis of organic molecules by an organism using energy derived from chemical reactions, e.g. the synthesis of carbohydrates by bacteria —**chemosynthetic** /keémōsin théttik/ *adj.* —**chemosynthetically** /-théttikli/ *adv.*

chemotaxis /keémō táksiss/ *n.* movement or change in the position of a cell or organism in response to the presence of a chemical agent —**chemotactic** /-táktik/ *adj.* —**chemotactically** *adv.*

chemotaxonomy /keémō tak sónnəmi/ *n.* the identification and classification of plants and animals based on their biochemical composition —**chemotaxonomic** /keémō taksə nómmik/ *adj.* —**chemotaxonomically** /-nómmikli/ *adv.* —**chemotaxonomist** /keémō tak sónnəmist/ *n.*

chemotherapy /keémō thérrəpi/ (*plural* **-pies**) *n.* the use of chemical agents to treat diseases, infections, or other disorders, especially cancer —**chemotherapeutic** /keémō thérrə pyoótik/ *adj.* —**chemotherapeutically** /-pyoótikli/ *adv.* —**chemotherapist** /keémō thérrəpist/ *n.*

chemotropism /kémmō trŏpizzəm/ *n.* the movement or growth of an organism or part of an organism in response to a chemical stimulus —**chemotropic** /kémmō trŏppik/ *adj.* —**chemotropically** /-trŏppikli/ *adv.*

chemurgy /kémmurji/ *n.* US a branch of applied chemistry dealing with the industrial application of organic substances, especially of agricultural origin [Mid-20thC. Coined from CHEMICAL, on the model of 'metallurgy'.] —**chemurgic** /kem úrjik/ *adj.* —**chemurgical** /-úrjik'l/ *adj.*

chemzyme /kém zīm/ *n.* a substance that is a chemical but acts like an enzyme, often used to increase the effectiveness of a drug by accelerating its action [Late 20thC. Blend of CHEMO- and ENZYME.]

Chen /chen/ *n.* a Chinese dynasty that ruled from AD 557 to 589

Chenab /chi náb/, **Chenāb** river in northwestern India and eastern Pakistan. It flows about 960 km/600 mi. before discharging into the Sutlej, a tributary of the Indus.

Chengde /chúng dúr/, **Ch'eng-te** city and capital of the former Jehol Province, now Hebei Province, in northeastern China, situated on the River Luan, approximately 177 km/110 mi. northeast of Beijing. Population: 365,519 (1990).

Chengdu /chéng doó/ provincial capital, situated northwest of Chungking, in Szechwan, China. Population: 2,810,000 (1991).

chenille /shə neél/ *n.* **1.** SOFT THICK COTTON OR SILK FABRIC a soft thick fabric, usually made of cotton or silk with a raised pile, that is used to make furnishings and clothes **2.** THICK SILK, COTTON, OR WORSTED CORD a thick cord or yarn of silk, cotton, or worsted cord, used in embroidery and for fringes and trimmings [Mid-18thC. Via French, literally 'hairy caterpillar', from Latin *canicula*, literally 'little dog', from *canis* 'dog' (see CANINE).]

Chenin Blanc /shə naN blaáN/ *n.* a variety of white grape used for making light dry wine, especially in the Loire region of France and in South Africa [From French]

Chennai /chə ní/ capital of Tamil Nadu state, on the southeastern coast of India. It is also a major port and commercial city. Population: 5,421,985 (1991). Formerly called **Madras**

Cheongsam

cheongsam /chóng sám/ *n.* a straight dress with a small stand-up collar and a slit in the skirt, worn by Chinese women [Mid-20thC. From Chinese (Cantonese) (equivalent to Mandarin *chángshān*), literally 'long gown'.]

Chepstow /chépstō/ town on the River Wye in Monmouthshire, Wales. It has a racecourse. Population: 9,461 (1991).

cheque /chek/ *n.* a small printed form which, when filled in and signed, instructs a bank to pay a specified sum of money to the person named on it. US term **check** *n.* 4 [Early 18thC. Variant of CHECK, under the influence of *exchequer*.]

chequebook /chékboŏk/ *n.* a book of detachable cheques

chequebook journalism *n.* the payment of large sums of money to secure exclusive rights to a newspaper story (*disapproving*)

cheque card, **cheque guarantee card** *n.* UK a small plastic card issued by a bank to a customer that guarantees the customer's cheques up to a specified limit.

chequer /chékə/ *n.* **1.** = **check** *n.* 8, **check** *n.* 9 **2.** US = **draughtsman 3.** PIECE USED IN CHINESE CHEQUERS a peg, marble, or other piece used in the game of Chinese chequers ■ *vt.* (**chequers, chequering, chequered**) **1.** MARK STH WITH CHEQUER PATTERN to mark sth with a chequer pattern or with alternating areas of light and shade **2.** DISRUPT CONTINUOUS SUCCESS OF STH to affect sth adversely from time to time ○ *regrettable incidents that will chequer his career* [12thC. Shortening of EXCHEQUER, which originally denoted the checked chessboard in English.]

chequerboard /chékərbawrd/ *n.* a chessboard or game board with a pattern of alternate squares. US term **checkerboard**. = **draughtboard**

chequered /chékərd/ *adj.* **1.** = **checked 2.** UNEVEN OR INCONSISTENT uneven or inconsistent, and characterized by periods of trouble or controversy as well as periods of success

chequered flag *n.* a flag patterned with black and white squares that is waved as each participant in a motor race crosses the finishing line

Chequers /chékərz/ *n.* a country house in Buckinghamshire that is the official country residence of the Prime Minister

Cher /shair/ (*b.* 1946) US entertainer. She turned to acting after a successful singing career and won an Academy Award for *Moonstruck* (1987). Full name **Cherilyn LaPierre**

Cherbourg /sháir boorg/ city and port on the English Channel in the Manche Department of the Basse-Normandie Region, in northwestern France. Population: 28,773 (1990).

Cheremis /chérrəmiss/ *n., adj.* LANG = **Mari**

cherimoya /chérri móyə/ (*plural* **-as** *or* **-a**) *n.* **1.** TREES TROPICAL TREE WITH HEART-SHAPED FRUIT a tropical American tree of the custard apple family that has aromatic leaves, fragrant flowers, and edible fruit. Latin name: *Annona cherimola*. **2.** FOOD FRUIT OF CHERIMOYA TREE the heart-shaped fruit of the cherimoya tree, which has green skin turning purple-black when ripe and creamy-white scented flesh [Mid-18thC. Via

Spanish from Quechua *chirimuya*, from *chiri* 'cold, refreshing' + *muya* 'circle'.]

cherish /chérrish/ (**-ishes, -ishing, -ished**) *vt*. **1.** LOVE AND CARE FOR SB to feel or show great love or care for sb ○ *He cherishes that girl.* **2.** VALUE STH HIGHLY to value sth highly, e.g. as a right, freedom, or privilege ○ *I cherish my independence.* **3.** RETAIN IN THE MIND to retain a memory or wish in the mind as a source of pleasure or as an ambition [14thC. From French *chériss-*, the stem of *chérir* 'to hold dear', from *cher* 'dear', from Latin *carus* (see CHARITY).] —**cherishable** *adj*. —**cherisher** *n*. —**cherishingly** *adv*.

Chernenko /chur nyéngkõ/, **Konstantin** (1911–85) Soviet political leader. A long-time political ally of Leonid Brezhnev, he became general secretary of the Communist Party of the Soviet Union (1984–85).

Chernobyl /chər nõb'l, -nõbb'l/ *n*. the site of a nuclear power plant near Kiev, in Ukraine, where there was a catastrophic accident in 1986

chernozem /chúrnə zem/ *n*. fertile black or brown topsoil that is rich in humus and can support crops for long periods of time without the addition of fertilizers. It covers a large proportion of the Eurasian steppe, as well as a belt of land stretching from Saskatchewan in Canada through North Dakota into Texas in the United States. [Mid-19thC. From Russian, literally 'black earth'.] —**chernozemic** /chúrnə zémmik/ *adj*.

Cherokee /chérrə kee/ (*plural* **-kee** *or* **-kees**) *n*. **1.** MEMBER OF NATIVE AMERICAN PEOPLE OF SOUTH a member of a Native American people who originally occupied lands in southeastern parts of the United States and now live mainly in Oklahoma and North Carolina. The Cherokee were one of the Five Civilized Nations who, under the Removal Act of 1830, were sent to live on reservations in Oklahoma. **2.** CHEROKEE LANGUAGE the Iroquoian language of the Cherokee people. Cherokee is spoken by about 10,000 people. [Late 17thC. From Cherokee *tsalaki* (earlier *tsaraki*).] —**Cherokee** *adj*.

cheroot /shə rõot/ *n*. a cigar with two square-cut ends [Late 17thC. Via French *cheroute* from Tamil *curuttu* 'roll of tobacco'.]

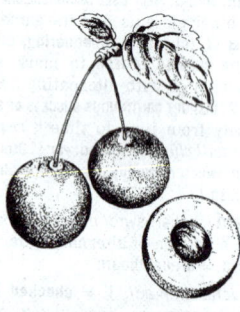

Cherry

cherry /chérri/ *n*. (*plural* **-ries**) **1.** TREES FRUIT TREE a common fruit tree or shrub that bears a small edible fruit in clusters with long thin stalks. Varieties include the sweet cherry, sour cherry, and morello cherry. Genus: *Prunus*. **2.** FOOD FRUIT OF CHERRY TREE the small round fruit of the cherry tree, which has a single hard stone and varies in colour from bright red or yellow to dark purplish-black **3.** INDUST WOOD OF CHERRY TREE the wood of the cherry tree, much valued as material for furniture and musical instruments **4.** VIRGINITY sb's virginity, or the hymen as a symbol of a woman's virginity (*slang taboo*) ■ *adj*. = **cherry red** [14thC. Via Old Northern French *cherise* (mistaken for a plural) from medieval Latin *ceresia*, ultimately from Greek *kerasos* 'cherry tree'.]

cherry bomb *n*. *US* a powerful round red firecracker that explodes with a loud bang

cherry laurel *n*. an evergreen Eurasian shrub cultivated for its white flowers and shiny leaves. Latin name: *Prunus laurocerasus*.

cherry-pick (**cherry-picks, cherry-picking, cherry-picked**) *vti*. to select only the most lucrative or profitable opportunities, especially in business (*disapproving*)

Cherry picker

cherry picker *n*. a mobile crane with an enclosed platform that can be raised to allow sb to work off the ground, e.g. on an overhead street light or cable

cherry plum *n*. a deciduous Eurasian plum tree that produces red or yellow fruit resembling cherries. Latin name: *Prunus cerasifera*.

cherry red *adj*. of a deep vivid red colour tinged with pink —**cherry red** *n*.

cherrystone /chérri stõn/ *n*. a half-grown quahog clam

cherry tomato *n*. a small tomato with a strong sweet flavour. Latin name: *Lycopersicon esculentum*. [So called because of its size and sweetness]

cherrywood /chérriwŏod/ *n*. = **cherry** *n*. 3

chersonese /kúrssə néess/ *n*. a peninsula (*literary*) [Early 17thC. Via Latin *chersonesus* from Greek *khersonēsos*, from *khersos* 'dry land' + *nēsos* 'island'.]

chert /churt/ *n*. a granular type of silica, usually found as bands of pebbles in sedimentary rock. It consists of microcrystalline quartz similar to flint, but more brittle. Formula: SiO_2. [Late 17thC. Origin unknown.] —**cherty** *adj*.

Cherub: Garden sculptures at Wendens Ambo, Essex, England

cherub /chérrəb/ *n*. **1.** (*plural* **-ubim** *or* **-ubs**) CHR ANGEL OF SECOND ORDER an angel, specifically one belonging to the second order in the celestial hierarchy whose distinctive attribute is knowledge **2.** ARTS DEPICTION OF ANGEL an angel depicted as a chubby-faced child with wings, sometimes simply as a child's head above a pair of wings **3.** WELL-BEHAVED CHILD a child whose behaviour, disposition, or appearance is attractively innocent and well-behaved [Pre-12thC. Via Latin *cherub* and Greek *kheroub* from Hebrew *kĕrūb* probably of Akkadian origin, but later mistakenly connected with Aramaic *kĕ-rabyā* 'like a child'.] —**cherubic** /chə rõobik/ *adj*. —**cherubically** /-bikli/ *adv*.

Cherubini /kérroo beeni/, **Luigi** (1760–1842) Italianborn French composer. A prolific composer of operas and sacred music, he was influential as director of the Paris Conservatoire (1821–41). Full name **Maria Luigi Carlo Zenobio Salvatore Cherubini**

chervil /chúrvil/ *n*. **1.** LEAFY HERB a herb cultivated for its leaves, which have a mild flavour of aniseed and resemble parsley. It is used to season and garnish food. Latin name: *Anthriscus cerefolium*. **2.** PLANT RELATED TO CHERVIL any plant related or similar to true chervil. Genera: *Anthriscus* and *Chaerophyllum*. [Pre-12thC. Via Latin *chaerephyllum* from Greek *khairephullon*, perhaps from *khairein* 'to delight in' + *phullon* 'leaf'.]

Chesapeake Bay /chéssə peek-/ largest inlet of the Atlantic Ocean on the East Coast of the United States, bounded by Virginia and Maryland. Area: 8,365 sq. km/3,320 sq. mi.

Cheshire[1] /chéshər/ *n*. a mild crumbly cheese that is usually white but sometimes red, originally made in Cheshire

Cheshire[2] /chéshər/ ancient county of northwestern England, between Manchester and the Welsh border. Population: 978,100 (1995). Area: 2,328 sq. km/900 sq. mi.

Cheshire cat *n*. the cat in Lewis Carroll's *Alice's Adventures in Wonderland*, whose broad grin remained suspended in the air after the cat itself had disappeared

Cheshvan /kesh vaan/ *n*. in the Jewish calendar, the eighth month of the year, consisting of 29 or 30 days and roughly corresponding to the Gregorian October to November

Chesil Beach /chézz'l-/, **Chesil Bank** narrow shingle ridge on the coast of Dorset, England. Length: 27 km/17 mi.

Chess

chess[1] /chess/ *n*. a game played on a chequered board by two players, each with 16 pieces representing a king and his attendants. The object is to capture (**checkmate**) the opponent's king. Each player begins with a king, a queen, two bishops, two knights, two rooks or castles, and eight pawns. [12thC. Shortening of Old French *esches*, plural of *eschec* 'check!' (see CHECK).]

chess[2] /chess/ *n*. a deck board or floorboard of a pontoon bridge [Early 19thC. Origin uncertain: perhaps via Old French *chasse* 'frame' from Latin *capsa* 'box' (see CAPSULE).]

chess[3] /chess/ *n*. *US* any one of several types of weedy bromegrass, especially an annual plant. Latin name: *Bromus secanilus*. [Mid-18thC. Origin unknown.]

chessboard /chéss bawrd/ *n*. a square board divided into 64 alternate light and dark squares, used for playing chess or draughts. The eight vertical rows of squares are called files, the eight horizontal rows are called ranks, and the squares that stretch diagonally across the board are called diagonals.

chessel /chéss'l/ *n*. a mould or vat used to make cheese [Late 17thC. Origin uncertain: possibly from CHEESE + WELL.]

chessman /chéss man/ (*plural* **-men** /-men/) *n*. any of the 32 pieces used in a game of chess

chesspiece /chéss peess/ *n*. = **chessman**

chessylite /chéssi līt/ *n*. *US* MINERALS = **azurite** [Mid-19thC. Named after the town of *Chessy*, near Lyons in France.]

chest /chest/ *n*. **1.** UPPER PART OF BODY the upper part of the body below the neck and above the stomach, covering the ribs and the organs that the ribs enclose **2.** FRONT PART OF BODY the front part of the body of a person or animal extending from the neck to the stomach ○ *the dog had a deep chest* **3.** STRONG RECTANGULAR BOX a strong rectangular box, usually with a lid and sometimes a lock, used for storage or transport **4.** CONTENTS OF CHEST the contents of a chest [Old English *cest* (related to Dutch *kist* 'coffin' and German *Kiste* 'box'). From a prehistoric West Germanic word borrowed from Latin *cista*, from Greek *kistē* 'basket'.] ◇ **get**

sth off your chest to talk openly about sth that has been making you feel guilty, embarrassed, worried, or angry, especially when talking about it helps to reduce or remove those feelings ◇ **keep** *or* **play sth** *or* **your cards close to your chest** to be discreet or secretive about current or future plans

Chester /chéstər/ ancient walled cathedral city that is the county town of Cheshire, England. Population: 115,000 (1991).

chesterfield /chéstərfeeld/ *n.* **1. SOFA** a large sofa with upright armrests at the same height as the back, usually upholstered in leather and with a rolled-over outward curve along the top **2.** *Can* **COUCH** any upholstered couch or sofa with back and arms **3. OVERCOAT** a style of overcoat, usually with concealed buttons and a velvet collar [Mid-19thC. Named after a 19thC earl of *Chesterfield*.]

Chesterfield /chéstər feeld/ town in Derbyshire, England, noted for the twisted spire of All Saints' Church. Population: 101,000 (1994).

Chesterfield, Philip Dormer Stanhope, 4th Earl of Chesterfield (1694–1773) British statesman and writer. Secretary of State to George III and a literary wit, he wrote *Letters to his Son* (1774).

Chester-le-Street /chéstər lə street/ mining town in County Durham, England. Population: 53,300 (1995).

Chesterton /chéstərtən/ **, G. K.** (1874–1936) British writer. His books include the Father Brown detective stories and volumes of literary criticism. Full name **Gilbert Keith Chesterton**

chestnut /chéss nut/ *n.* **1.** (*plural* **-nuts** *or* **-nut**) **TREES TREE WITH PRICKLY FRUIT** a tree or shrub with long toothed leaves, which bears edible nuts in a prickly case and is found in North America, Europe, Japan, and China. Genus: *Castanea*. ◊ **water chestnut, American chestnut 2. FOOD EDIBLE NUT** the edible nut of the chestnut tree, which grows inside a prickly case and has a glossy brown skin **3. INDUST WOOD** the coarse-grained durable wood of a chestnut tree **4. REDDISH-BROWN HORSE** a horse with a reddish-brown colour **5. ANAT CALLUS ON HORSE'S LEG** a small hard callus found in several places on the inner surface of a horse's leg. Chestnuts are thought to be vestigial toes. **6. STALE JOKE OR STORY** a joke or story that has lost its impact through overuse (*informal*) ■ *adj.* **COLOURS OF DEEP BROWN COLOUR** of a deep reddish-brown colour [Early 16thC. Formed from earlier *chesten*, via Old French *chastaine* from Latin *castanea* (see CASTANET).]

chestnut oak *n.* any North American deciduous oak tree whose leaves resemble those of the chestnut, especially one found in eastern North America that has shiny yellow leaves. Latin name: *Quercus prinus*.

chest of drawers *n.* a piece of furniture consisting of a set of drawers in a wooden frame with a flat top, used for storing clothes

chest voice *n.* the lowest register of sb's speaking or singing voice

chesty /chésti/ (**-ier, -iest**) *adj.* **1. HAVING PHLEGM IN THE LUNGS** showing the effects of a chest complaint, such as phlegm in the lungs **2. WITH LARGE CHEST** having a well-developed chest (*informal*) —**chestiness** *n.*

Chetnik /chétnik/ (*plural* **Chetniks** *or* **Cetniks**) *n.* a Serbian nationalist who was part of a group who fought the Turks before World War I, and was involved in guerrilla warfare in World War I and World War II [Early 20thC. From Serbo-Croat *četnik*, from *četa* 'band, troop'.]

chetrum /chétroōm/ (*plural* **-rum** *or* **-rums**) *n.* **1. UNIT OF CURRENCY IN BHUTAN** a subunit of currency in Bhutan. See table at **currency 2. COIN WORTH ONE CHETRUM** a coin worth one chetrum [Late 20thC. From Tibetan.]

cheval-de-frise /shə vál də freez/ (*plural* **chevaux-de-frise** /-vṓ-/) *n.* **1. OBSTACLE MADE OF BARBED WIRE** an obstacle consisting of barbed wire or spikes attached to a wooden frame, used to block an advancing enemy force **2. GLASS OR SPIKES TOPPING WALL** a line of jagged glass, nails, or spikes set into masonry on top of a wall to deter intruders [From French, literally 'horse of Friesland', in ironic reference to its use by the Friesians, who lacked cavalry, during the siege of Groningen in 1594]

chevalet /shə vállay, shévvə láy/ *n.* the bridge of a bowed musical instrument [Late 19thC. From French, literally 'small horse', from *cheval* 'horse', from Latin *caballus* (source of English *cavalier* and *chivalry*).]

cheval glass /shə vál-/ *n.* a long mirror that is mounted in a frame so that it can be tilted [From French *cheval* 'frame', literally 'horse']

chevalier /shə válli er/ *n.* **1. FRENCH TITLE OF HONOUR** used as the title of members of the French Legion of Honour and of other orders **2. FRENCH KNIGHT OR NOBLEMAN** a French knight or nobleman of the lowest rank [14thC. Via French from medieval Latin *caballarius*, from Latin *caballus* 'horse' (source of English *cavalcade*, *cavalier*, and *cavalry*).]

chevaux-de-frise plural of **cheval-de-frise**

chevet /shə váy/ *n.* a complex of elaborate architectural structures at the eastern end of a church, especially a French Gothic church, usually consisting of a semicircular or polygonal apse with radiating chapels and many buttresses [Early 19thC. From French, literally 'pillow'.]

Cheviot /chéevi ət, chévvi ət/ *n.* **1. ZOOL HORNLESS SHEEP** a hornless sheep with short thick wool, originally raised in the Cheviot Hills on the border between Scotland and England **2. Cheviot, cheviot TEXTILES COARSE WOOLLEN FABRIC** a woollen fabric with a coarse twill weave, used mainly for suits and overcoats, and originally made from the wool of Cheviot sheep

Cheviot Hills /chévvi ət, chéevi ət/ range of hills along the border of England and Scotland. The highest point is The Cheviot, 816 m/2,676 ft.

chèvre /shévrə/ *n.* any soft cheese made from goat's milk [Mid-20thC. Via French, 'goat' from, ultimately, Latin *capra*, feminine of *caper* 'goat' (source of English *caper²*, *cabriolet*, and *chevron*).]

chevrette /she vrét/ *n.* the skin of a young goat, or the leather made from this skin [Late 19thC. From French, literally 'small goat, kid', from *chèvre* (see CHÈVRE).]

Chevron

chevron /shévrən/ *n.* **1. V-SHAPED SYMBOL** a V-shaped symbol, especially one used as a sign of rank on military or police uniforms **2. HERALDRY HERALDIC ORNAMENT** a heraldic ornament in the form of a wide inverted V-shape ■ **chevrons** *npl.* **ROAD SIGN AT BEND** a large rectangular road sign with a pattern of horizontal black and white V-shapes, used to indicate a sharp bend [14thC. Via French, 'rafter', from, ultimately, Latin *caper* 'goat' (source of English *caper²* and *chèvre*).]

chevrotain /shévrə tayn, -tin/ (*plural* **-tains** *or* **-tain**) *n.* a small ruminant animal similar to a deer, native to the rain forests of west-central Africa and Southeast Asia. It is hornless and the male has projecting canine teeth. Family: Tragulidae. [Late 18thC. From French, literally 'small goat, kid', from *chèvre* (see CHÈVRE).]

chevy /chévvi/ *v.* = **chivvy**

chew /choo/ *v.* (**chews, chewing, chewed**) **1.** *vti.* **GRIND UP FOOD BEFORE SWALLOWING** to grind up food or other material with the action of the teeth and jaws **2.** *vti.* **DAMAGE STH BY BITING** to gnaw at sth repeatedly, usually causing damage ○ *chewing her nails* **3.** *vi.* **US CHEW TOBACCO** to bite into and chew tobacco ■ *n.* **1. ACT OF CHEWING STH** the act of chewing sth, or a period of chewing **2. SWEET** a sweet with a firm texture, which must be chewed before being swallowed ○ *fruit chews* **3.** **US PIECE OF CHEWING TOBACCO** a piece of dried tobacco for chewing [Old English *cēowan*, of prehistoric Germanic origin] —**chewable** *adj.* —**chewer** *n.*

chew out *vt.* *US* to tell sb off for doing sth wrong (*informal*) ○ *She really chewed me out for being late.*

chew over *vt.* to think about or discuss sth over a period of time ○ *We chewed the problem over for a couple of days before coming to a decision.*

chew up *vt.* **1. DAMAGE OR DESTROY STH** to damage or destroy sth, especially by passing it through machinery (*informal*) ○ *I'm afraid the machine chewed up your tape.* **2. DESTROY STH BY BITING** to destroy sth by biting or chewing it

Chewa /cháywə/ *n.* a language spoken in Malawi, Zambia, and Mozambique, and belonging to the Bantu group of Niger-Congo languages. There are over eight million Chewa speakers. —**Chewa** *adj.*

chewie /chóo i/ *n.* chewing gum (*informal*) [Early 20thC. Shortening.]

chewing gum *n.* a sweet flavoured substance that is chewed but not swallowed. The elastic ingredient in chewing gum used to be chicle from the sapodilla tree, but synthetic equivalents are now commonly used. ○ *a stick of chewing gum.* ◊ **bubble gum**

chewing louse *n.* = **biting louse**

chewy /chóo i/ (**-ier, -iest**) *adj.* having a consistency or texture that requires chewing —**chewiness** *n.*

Cheyenne /shT án/ (*plural* **-enne** *or* **-ennes**) *n.* **1. PEOPLES MEMBER OF NATIVE AMERICAN PEOPLE** a member of a Native American people who originally occupied lands in western parts of the Great Plains and now live mainly in Oklahoma and Montana. The Cheyenne, along with the Sioux, were instrumental in the defeat of Custer and his forces at the Battle of Little Bighorn. **2. LANG CHEYENNE LANGUAGE** the Algonquian language of the Cheyenne people. Cheyenne is spoken by about 2,000 people. [Late 18thC. Via Canadian French from Dakota *šahíyena*.] —**Cheyenne** *adj.*

Cheyne-Stokes respiration /cháyn stóks-/ *n.* an abnormal breathing pattern marked by shallow breathing alternating with periods of rapid heavy breathing, observed especially in comatose patients and often indicating impending death [Late 19thC. Named after the Scottish physician, John *Cheyne* (1777–1836) and the Irish physician, William *Stokes* (1804–78).]

chez /shay/ *prep.* at sb's home or business premises, especially a restaurant [Mid-18thC. Via French from, ultimately, Latin *casa* 'cottage' (source of *casino*, and *chasuble*).]

chg. *abbr.* **1.** change **2.** charge

chi[1] /kī/ (*plural* **chis**) *n.* the 22nd letter of the Greek alphabet, represented in English as 'ch' or 'kh' [15thC. From Greek *khi*.]

chi[2] /chee/ **, ch'i, Chi, Ch'i, qi, Qi** *n.* in Chinese medicine and philosophy, the energy or life force of the universe, believed to flow round the body and to be present in all living things. The manipulation of chi is the basis of acupuncture and Chinese martial arts. [From Chinese *qì*]

Chiang Kai-shek

Chiang Kai-shek /cháng kī shék/ (1887–1975) Chinese military leader and statesman. He helped to overthrow the imperial government (1912) and developed Taiwan's economy as its president (1949–75).

Chianti /ki ánti/ **, chianti** *n.* a light Italian red wine produced mainly from the Sangiovese grape in Tuscany in northwestern Italy [Mid-19thC. Named after the *Chianti* Mountains in Tuscany.]

Chiapas /chi áppəss/ state in southeastern Mexico. Capital: Tuxtla Gutiérrez. Population: 3,654,000 (1993). Area: 73,887 sq. km/28,528 sq. mi.

chiaroscuro /ki àarə skóorrō/ *n.* the use of light and shade in paintings and drawings, or the effect produced by this [Mid-17thC. From Italian, literally 'bright-dark', from *chiaro* 'bright, clear' + *oscuro* 'dark'.] —**chiaroscurism** *n.* —**chiaroscurist** *n.*

chiasma /kī ázmə/ (*plural* **-mas** *or* **-mata** /-zmətə/) *n.* **1.** ANAT **CROSSING OVER OF BODY PARTS** any crossing over of biological tissue, e.g. the intersection of the optic nerves **2.** GENETICS **CROSSING POINT OF CHROMOSOME PARTS** the point at which two chromatids join during the fusion and exchange of genetic material (**crossing-over**) in cell division [Mid-19thC. Via modern Latin from Greek *khiasma* 'crosspiece', from *khiazein* 'to mark with an X', from *khi* 'the letter chi'.] —**chiasmal** *adj.* —**chiasmic** *adj.*

chiasmus /kī ázməss/ (*plural* **-mi** /-mī/) *n.* a rhetorical construction in which the order of the words in the second of two paired phrases is the reverse of the order in the first. An example is 'grey was the morn, all things were grey'. [Mid-17thC. Via modern Latin from Greek *khiasmos*, from *khiazein* (see CHIASMA).]

chiastolite /kī ástə līt/ *n.* a variety of the mineral andalusite that contains carbon impurities arranged in an X-shape [Early 19thC. Coined from Greek *khiastos* 'marked with an X' (the past participle of *khiazein*; see CHIASMA) + -LITE.]

Chibcha /chíbchə/ (*plural* **-cha** *or* **-chas**) *n.* **1.** PEOPLES **MEMBER OF EXTINCT S AMERICAN PEOPLE** a member of an extinct Native South American people who lived in the Andes Mountains in the centre of Colombia. The Chibcha died out following their defeat by the Spanish conquistador, Gonzalo Jeménez de Quesada, in the 1530s. **2.** LANG **LANGUAGE OF CHIBCHA** the extinct Chibchan language of the Chibcha [Early 19thC. Via American Spanish from Chibcha *zipa* 'chief, hereditary leader'.]

Chibchan /chíbchən/ (*plural* **-chan** *or* **-chans**) *n.* **1.** **GROUP OF NATIVE CENTRAL AMERICAN LANGUAGES** a group of Native Central American languages spoken in Colombia and Panama. About 100,000 people speak a Chibchan language. **2.** **SB WHO SPEAKS CHIBCHAN LANGUAGE** a member of any of the peoples who speak a language belonging to the Chibchan group —**Chibchan** *adj.*

chic /sheek/ *adj.* **STYLISH** stylish and elegant ■ *n.* **STYLE** fashionable style or elegance [Mid-19thC. From French, of uncertain origin: probably from German *Schick* 'skill, elegance'.] —**chicness** *n.*

Chicago /shi kaágō/ city and port in northeastern Illinois, situated on Lake Michigan. It is the third largest city in the United States. Population: 2,731,743 (1994). —**Chicagoan** *n., adj.*

Chicago Board of Trade *n.* a major commodities exchange in Chicago, in the United States, that deals in grain and metal futures

Chicana /chi kaánə/ (*plural* **-nas**) *n.* a North American woman or girl of Mexican descent [Mid-20thC. From Spanish, feminine of *Chicano* (see CHICANO).]

chicane[1] /shi káyn/ *n.* **1.** MOTOR SPORTS **SHARP BEND ON MOTOR-RACING CIRCUIT** in motor-racing, a sharp double bend created by placing barriers on the circuit **2.** CARDS **HAND WITH NO TRUMPS** a bridge or whist hand without trumps or without cards of one suit [Late 19thC. From French, formed from *chicaner* see CHICANE[2].]

chicane[2] /shi káyn/ (**-canes, -caning, -caned**) *vi.* to practise chicanery [Late 17thC. From French *chicaner* 'to quibble, pursue at law', of unknown origin.] —**chicaner** *n.*

chicanery /shi káynəri/ (*plural* **-ies**) *n.* deception or trickery, especially by the clever manipulation of language

Chicano /chi kaánō/ (*plural* **-nos**) *n.* *US* a North American man or boy of Mexican descent [Mid-20thC. From American Spanish, a variant of Spanish *mexicano* 'Mexican', from *México* 'Mexico'.]

Chichester /chíchistər/ cathedral city in West Sussex, England, founded by the Romans. Population: 26,572 (1991).

Chichester, Sir Francis Charles (1901–72) British aviator and sailor. His feats included a solo Britain-Australia flight in 1929 and a solo round-the-world voyage in 1966–67, in *Gipsy Moth III*.

Chichewa /chi cháywə/ *n., adj.* = **Chewa**

chichi /shée shee/ *adj.* **SELF-CONSCIOUSLY STYLISH** trying too hard or too obviously to be chic or modish (*disapproving*) ○ *All this designer furniture – isn't it just a bit chichi?* ■ *n.* **SELF-CONSCIOUS STYLISHNESS** affected or self-conscious stylishness (*disapproving*) [Mid-20thC. From French.]

chick /chik/ *n.* **1.** **BABY BIRD** a young bird, especially a young chicken **2.** *US* **YOUNG WOMAN** an attractive girl or young woman (*slang*) (*considered offensive by some speakers*) **3.** **SMALL CHILD** a term of affection used to a baby or small child (*informal*) [14thC. Shortening of CHICKEN.]

chickabiddy /chíkə biddi/ (*plural* **-dies**) *n.* an affectionate term of address used by adults to children and babies (*archaic*) [Early 19thC. Formed from CHICK + BIDDY. Originally in the meaning 'chicken'.]

chickadee /chíkə dee/ (*plural* **-dees** *or* **-dee**) *n.* a small North American tit with a distinctive call. It has grey plumage and a darker-coloured crown on its head. Genus: *Parus*. [Mid-19thC. An imitation of the bird's call.]

chickaree /chíkə ree/ (*plural* **-rees** *or* **-ree**) *n.* a squirrel of western North America, related to the red squirrel. Latin name: *Tamiascurus douglasi*. [Early 19thC. An imitation of the animal's cry.]

Chickasaw /chíkə saw/ (*plural* **-saw** *or* **-saws**) *n.* **1.** PEOPLES **MEMBER OF NATIVE AMERICAN PEOPLE** a member of a Native American people who originally occupied lands in northeastern Mississippi and northwestern Alabama, and now live mainly in southern and central Oklahoma. The Chickasaw were one of the Five Civilized Nations who were sent to live on reservations in Oklahoma under the Removal Act of 1830. **2.** LANG **CHICKASAW LANGUAGE** the Muskogean language of the Chickasaw people. Chickasaw is spoken by approximately 10,000 people. [Late 17thC. From Chickasaw *čikaša*.] —**Chickasaw** *adj.*

chicken /chíkin/ *n.* **1.** **COMMON DOMESTIC FOWL** a domestic fowl, usually with brown or black feathers and a fleshy crest on its head, raised for its meat and eggs. Latin name: *Gallus domesticus*. ◊ **spring chicken** **2.** **MEAT FROM CHICKENS** meat obtained from chickens **3.** **COWARD** a cowardly or timid person (*informal*) ○ *You'll never do it – you're a chicken!* **4.** **DANGEROUS GAME** a game or challenge in which two or more people attempt a dangerous or daring feat (*informal*) ■ *adj.* **COWARDLY** showing a lack of courage (*informal*) ○ *Are you too chicken to do a high dive?* [Old English *cīcen* (related to Dutch *kuiken*). Ultimately from a prehistoric Germanic word related to the ancestor of English *cock*.] ◇ **a chicken-and-egg situation** a situation in which it is impossible to know which of two related circumstances occurred first and caused the other ○ *Stress causes mistakes, and mistakes cause stress: it's a chicken-and-egg situation.*

WORD KEY: SYNONYMS

See Synonyms at ***cowardly***.

chicken out (**chickens out, chickening out, chickened out**) *vi.* to fail in or withdraw from sth because of a lack of nerve (*slang*)

chicken breast *n.* = **pigeon breast** —**chicken-breasted** *adj.*

chicken feed *n.* an insignificant amount, especially an insignificant sum of money (*informal*)

chicken-fried steak *n.* *US* a cut of beef, usually round steak, that has been tenderized, dredged in flour, and then pan-fried

chicken-hearted, **chicken-livered** *adj.* easily frightened or lacking sufficient courage, boldness, or confidence (*insult*) —**chicken-heartedness** *n.*

chickenpox /chíkin poks/ *n.* a highly infectious viral disease, especially affecting children, characterized by a rash of small itching blisters on the skin and mild fever. Technical name **varicella** [Mid-18thC. Possibly so called because it is so much weaker than SMALLPOX.]

chickenshit /chíkin shit/ *n.* *US* **1.** **PETTY DETAILS OR TASKS** petty or tedious details or tasks (*slang offensive*) **2.** **COWARD** sb who is cowardly or timid (*slang or offensive*) ■ *adj.* *US* (*slang offensive*) **1.** **PETTY** petty or unimportant **2.** **COWARDLY** cowardly or frightened

chicken wire *n.* a lightweight flexible galvanized wire netting, usually made with a hexagonal mesh [From the use of the wire as a fence for enclosing chickens]

chickpea /chík pee/ *n.* **1.** **YELLOW EDIBLE SEED** an edible pale yellow seed about the size of a large pea. Chickpeas are the main ingredient of hummus. **2.** **CHICKPEA PLANT** an annual plant on which chickpeas grow, cultivated in Asia and Mediterranean regions. Latin name: *Cicer arietinum*. [Early 18thC. Alteration of earlier *chich pease*, via French *chiche* from Latin *cicer*, still the botanical Latin name for the plant.]

chickweed /chík weed/ *n.* a common European weed of cultivated land that produces small white flowers all year round. Latin name: *Stellaria media*. [Chick from the fact that chickens eat the plant]

Chiclayo /chi klī ō/ city in northwestern Peru, situated on the coast. Population: 410,486 (1993).

chicle /chík'l/ *n.* a gummy substance from the latex of the sapodilla tree, used as the main ingredient of chewing gum [Late 19thC. Via American Spanish from Nahuatl *tzictli*.] —**chicly** *adj.*

chicory /chíkəri/ (*plural* **-ries**) *n.* **1.** **PLANT CULTIVATED FOR LEAVES AND ROOTS** a perennial plant with blue flowers, native to Europe and northern Africa and naturalized in North America. It is cultivated for its leaves and roots. Latin name: *Cichorium intybus*. **2.** **CHICORY LEAVES USED IN SALAD** the leaves of the chicory plant, used in salads. US term **endive** **3.** **GROUND ROASTED ROOT OF CHICORY** the dried, roasted, and ground root of the chicory plant, used as a coffee additive or substitute [15thC. Via obsolete French *cicoré* 'endive'.]

chide /chīd/ (**chides, chiding, chided** *or* **chid, chided** *or* **chid** /chid/ *or* **chidden**) *vti.* to reproach or scold sb (*dated or literary*) [Old English *cīdan*, of unknown origin] —**chider** *n.* —**chidingly** *adv.*

chief /cheef/ *n.* **1.** **LEADER** the person with the most authority or highest rank in a group or an organization, who ultimately controls or commands all the others **2.** ANTHROP **CHIEFTAIN** the leader or titular head of a people or group **3.** NAUT **CHIEF PETTY OFFICER** a chief petty officer (*informal*) **4.** NAUT **SHIP'S PRINCIPAL ENGINEER** the principal engineer on a ship **5.** HERALDRY **TOP SECTION OF HERALDIC SHIELD** the upper third of the surface area of a heraldic shield ■ *adj.* **1.** **MOST IMPORTANT** most important, basic, or common **2.** **HIGHEST IN AUTHORITY** highest in authority, position, or rank [13thC. Via French *chef* from, ultimately, Latin *caput* 'head' (source of English *achieve*, *capital* and *captain*).] —**chiefdom** *n.* —**chiefship** *n.* ◇ **the big white chief** the most important person in an organization, often sb who makes his or her power and influence very obvious (*informal; used ironically*) ○ *The big white chief says that we all have to work overtime.*

chief constable *n.* in Britain, the police officer in overall command of a regional police force

chief education officer *n.* the chief administrative officer of a Local Education Authority

chief executive *n.* **1.** **HEAD OF EXECUTIVE BODY** the principal and highest-ranking member of an executive body, e.g. the head of a government or the governor of a US state **2.** **HIGHEST-RANKING EXECUTIVE** the executive director of a business or similar organization who holds the highest rank and has overall responsibility for its day-to-day management **3.** *US* **US PRESIDENT** the president of the United States

chief executive officer *n.* the highest-ranking executive officer within a company or corporation, who has responsibility for overall management of its day-to-day affairs under the supervision of the board of directors

chief justice *n.* **1.** **PRESIDING JUDGE** a judge who presides over a court that has several judges, especially the Supreme Court of the United States **2.** **SENIOR JUDGE** the senior judge in the High Courts of Australia and other Commonwealth countries

chiefly /chéefli/ *adv.* **1.** **ABOVE ALL** above all, especially, or most importantly ○ *We moved to this area of the city chiefly because it's convenient for getting to work.* **2.** **IN THE MAIN** for the most part ○ *The human body* *consists chiefly of water.* ■ *adj.* RELATING TO CHIEFS belonging or relating to chiefs, or befitting a chief

chief of staff *n.* **1.** US SENIOR RANKING OFFICER a high-ranking officer in the US Army or Air Force who is a member of the US Joint Chiefs of Staff **2.** SENIOR STAFF OFFICER the senior officer serving on a military staff, who has responsibility for managing it and for advising the commander

chief petty officer *n.* a noncommissioned officer ranking below fleet chief petty officer in the Royal Navy

Chief Rabbi *n.* the senior religious leader of the Jewish community in Great Britain and in some other countries

chieftain /chee´ftən/ *n.* the leader or titular head of a people or similar group [13thC. From Old French *chevetaine*, alteration (influenced by *chef* 'leader') of late Latin *capitaneus*, from Latin *capt-*, stem of *caput* 'head' (see CAPTAIN).] —**chieftaincy** *n.* —**chieftainship** *n.*

chief technician *n.* a noncommissioned officer ranking below a flight sergeant in the Royal Air Force

chief whip *n.* the most senior of a political party's whips, whose role is to maintain party discipline and ensure that party members attend and vote at debates in the Houses of Parliament

chiel /cheel/, **chield** /cheeld/ *n. Scotland* a boy or young man (*regional*) [Variant of CHILD]

chiffchaff /chíf chaf/ *n.* a small greyish-yellow Eurasian bird that has a characteristic repetitive song. Latin name: *Phylloscopus collybita.* [Late 18thC. An imitation of the bird's call.]

chiffon /shíffon/ *n.* **1.** TEXTILES FABRIC a very light thin sheer plain-woven fabric of nylon, rayon, or silk **2.** ACCESSORIES CLOTHING ACCESSORIES decorative accessories for women, e.g. laces or ribbons (*often used in the plural*) ■ *adj.* **1.** TEXTILES MADE OF CHIFFON made of chiffon, or resembling it in lightness and fineness **2.** COOK HAVING A FLUFFY TEXTURE having a light fluffy texture, usually created by adding whipped egg whites or gelatin [Mid-18thC. From French, from *chiffe* 'rag, flimsy stuff'.]

chiffonier /shíffə nee´r/ *n.* **1.** CABINET a low cabinet or cupboard with shelves above it **2.** CHEST OF DRAWERS a relatively tall narrow chest of drawers that often has a mirror attached to the back [Mid-18thC. From French. Originally 'rag-picker, collector of scraps', later 'piece of furniture for storing sewing and offcuts of fabric'.]

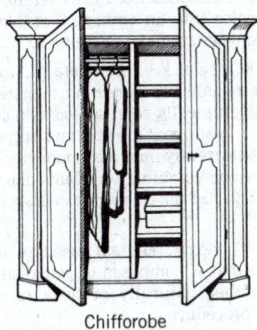

Chifforobe

chifforobe /shíffə rōb/, **chifferobe** /shíffrōb/, **chifrobe** *n. US* a tall piece of furniture with drawers and a hanging space for clothes (*dated*) [Early 20thC. Blend of CHIFFONIER and WARDROBE.]

Chifley /chíffli/, **Ben** (1885–1951) Australian statesman. He was Australian Labor Party politician and prime minister of Australia (1945–49). Full name **Joseph Benedict Chifley**

chigetai /chíggə tī/, **dziggetai** /jíg´ə tī/ *n.* a wild ass related to the onager and native to Mongolia. Latin name: *Equus hemionus.* [Late 18thC. From Mongolian *chikitei*, literally 'having ears', from *chiki* 'ear'.]

chigger /chíggər/ *n.* **1.** US, Can = **harvest mite 2.** = **chigoe** [Mid-18thC. From earlier CHIGOE.]

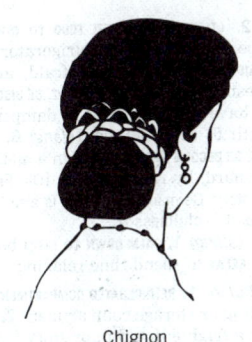

Chignon

chignon /shee´n yon, -yoN/ *n.* a knot or roll of hair, especially when worn at the nape of the neck [Late 18thC. From French, 'nape of the neck, chain', from, ultimately, Latin *catena* 'chain' (source of English *concatenation*).]

chigoe /chíggō/ *n.* a small tropical flea, the fertilized female of which burrows under the skin causing painful itching sores that easily become infected. Latin name: *Tunga penetrans.* [Mid-17thC. Via French *chique* from a West African language.]

Chihli, Gulf of /chee´ lee/ large inlet of the Yellow Sea, on the coast of northeastern China. Also known as **Bo Hai** or **Po Hai**

chihuahua /chi wa´awə/ *n.* a very small dog belonging to a breed originally from Mexico that has pointed ears, protruding eyes, and a tiny body with a disproportionally large head [Early 19thC. Named after CHIHUAHUA.]

Chihuahua /chi wa´a waa/ *n.* **1.** state in northern Mexico. Capital: Chihuahua. Population: 2,792,989 (1995). Area: 247,087 sq. km/95,401 sq. mi. **2.** city and capital of Chihuahua state in northern Mexico. Population: 530,487 (1990).

chilblain /chíl blayn/ *n.* a red itchy swelling on the ears, fingers, or toes, caused by exposure to damp and cold (*often used in the plural*) [Mid-16thC. From CHILL + BLAIN.] —**chilblained** *adj.*

child /chīld/ (*plural* **children** /chíldrən/) *n.* **1.** YOUNG HUMAN BEING a young human being between birth and puberty **2.** HUMAN OFFSPRING a son or daughter of human parents **3.** SB NOT YET OF AGE sb under a legally specified age who is considered not to be legally responsible for his or her actions **4.** BABY a baby or infant **5.** UNBORN BABY an unborn baby **6.** IMMATURE PERSON an adult who behaves in a childish or childlike way **7.** DESCENDANT OR MEMBER OF A PEOPLE a descendant of sb, or a member of a people founded by sb (*often used in the plural*) **8.** PRODUCT OR RESULT sb or sth considered to be either produced or strongly influenced by a particular environment, period, or historical figure ○ *a child of nature* ○ *a child of the 1960s* **9.** FEMALE CHILD a specifically female child or infant (*regional*) [Old English *cild*, of uncertain origin] ◇ **with child** pregnant (*archaic or literary*)

——— WORD KEY: SYNONYMS ———

See Synonyms at *youth.*

child abuse *n.* severe mistreatment of a child by a parent, guardian, or other adult responsible for his or her welfare, including physical violence, neglect, sexual assault, or emotional cruelty —**child abuser** *n.*

child-abuse register *n.* a register, maintained by a local authority, of people who have been found guilty of child abuse and who are considered likely to offend again

childbearing /chīld bairing/ *n.* the process of carrying a child in the womb and giving birth to it ○ *Her childbearing years are over.*

childbed /chīld bed/ *n.* the state of a woman in the process of giving birth to a child (*archaic*)

childbed fever *n.* MED puerperal sepsis (*archaic*)

child benefit *n.* in the UK and New Zealand, a regular payment made by the state to parents towards the maintenance of each child in a family below a certain age

---

childbirth /chīld burth/ *n.* the act or process of giving birth to a child ○ *natural childbirth methods*

childcare /chīld kair/ *n.* **1.** SUPERVISION OF CHILDREN the care and supervision of children by an adult, inside or outside the home and usually for pay, during times when the parents or guardians are at work **2.** CARE OF CHILDREN BY LOCAL AUTHORITY the care and supervision by a local authority of homeless children or children whose home life is severely disrupted

child-centred *adj.* adapted to the needs and concerns of children as opposed to adults

childe /chīld/ (*plural* **childes** /chīld/) *n.* a young person of noble birth (*archaic*) [Variant of CHILD]

Childe /chīld/, **V. Gordon** (1892–1957) Australian archaeologist. He was a pioneer of the study of prehistory and author of *The Dawn of European Civilisation* (1925). Full name **Vere Gordon Childe**

Childermas /chíldər mass/ *n.* the religious holiday of Holy Innocents' Day (*archaic*) [Old English *cildramæsse*, from *childra* 'of children' + *mæsse* 'mass']

Childers /chíldərz/, **Erskine** (1870–1922) British-born Irish nationalist and writer. Author of *The Riddle of the Sands* (1903), he joined the IRA and was executed.

child guidance *n.* the professional counselling of children who are emotionally disturbed, often also extended to their parents or guardians

childhood /chīld hood/ *n.* **1.** SB'S EARLIEST YEARS the state of being a child, or the period of sb's life when he or she is a child ○ *heard wonderful stories about her childhood.* **2.** EARLY STAGE an early period or stage in the development or existence of sth ○ *Interplanetary travel is still in its childhood.*

childish /chíldish/ *adj.* **1.** SOMEWHAT LIKE A CHILD like that of a child, or suitable for a child ○ *a childish voice* **2.** IMMATURE showing a lack of emotional restraint, seriousness, good sense, maturity, or similar adult qualities ○ *I don't have time for your childish tantrums.* —**childishly** *adv.* —**childishness** *n.*

child labour *n.* the full-time employment of children, especially of those who are legally too young to work

childless /chíldləss/ *adj.* not having had a child or children —**childlessness** *n.*

childlike /chīld līk/ *adj.* like a child, especially in having a sweet innocent unspoiled quality ○ *childlike innocence*

——— WORD KEY: USAGE ———

childish or **childlike**? Both words are used to describe people or behaviour that have qualities associated with children. The difference is that *childlike* is complimentary and even affectionate, whereas *childish* is a dismissive and disapproving term. *She spoke with a childlike directness about her holiday. His reaction to the criticism was childish and resentful.*

child minder *n.* sb who is employed to look after other people's children, especially when the parents or guardians are working —**child minding** *n.*

child prodigy *n.* a child who possesses extraordinary abilities or talents, often equal to those of adults

childproof /chīld proof/ *adj.* **1.** HARD FOR A CHILD TO OPEN designed to be difficult for children to open, tamper with, damage, or break **2.** MADE SAFE FOR CHILDREN made safe for young children to use or be in, e.g. through the removal of potential dangers and addition of extra safety devices ○ *Parents with toddlers should have at least one childproof room.* ■ *vt.* (**-proofs, -proofing, -proofed**) MAKE STH SAFE FOR CHILDREN to make sth safe for children to use, or safe against damage or tampering by children ○ *You'll need to childproof your house before the baby is born.*

children plural of **child**

——— WORD KEY: CULTURAL NOTE ———

The Man Who Loved Children, a novel by Australian writer, Christina Stead (1891). Through the story of the stormy domestic life of Sam and Henny Pollitt and their six children, Stead examines the ways in which human beings attempt, and often fail, to communicate with one other.

Children's Panel *n.* in Scotland, a hearing convened by representatives of the appropriate agencies to deal with a child who has committed a crime or is being mistreated by parents or guardians

child restraint *n.* a seat belt or detachable seat designed to protect a child travelling in a vehicle or a plane

child seat *n.* a detachable seat with a harness, attached to a car seat, used to protect a child too small to wear an adult seat belt

child's play *n.* sth that is very straightforward for sb to do ○ *Skiing these slopes will be child's play for her.*

Child Support Agency *n.* in the UK, a government-sponsored agency whose task is to ensure that absent parents, usually fathers, are making an adequate contribution to their children's maintenance

child tax benefit *n.* in Canada, an allowance or tax-free benefit given by the federal government or the province of Quebec to assist parents in the expense of rearing children below a specified age

Chile

Chile /chílli/ republic in southwestern South America bordered by Peru, Bolivia, Argentina, the Drake Passage, and the Pacific Ocean. Language: Spanish. Currency: peso. Capital: Santiago. Population: 14,508,131 (1997). Area: 756,626 sq. km/292,135 sq. mi. Official name **Republic of Chile** —**Chilean** /chílli ən/ *n., adj.*

Chile nitre *n.* CHEM = **Chile saltpetre**

Chile pine *n.* TREES = **monkey puzzle**

Chile saltpetre *n.* a form of sodium nitrate that occurs naturally in arid regions, especially in Chile and Peru. Formula: $NaNO_3$.

chili *n.* US = **chilli**

chiliasm /kílli azzəm/ *n.* = **millenarianism** [Early 17thC. From Greek *khiliasmos*, from *khilias* (stem *khiliad-*), from *khilioi* 'one thousand'.] —**chiliast** *n.* —**chiliastic** /kílli ástik/ *adj.*

chilidog /chílli dog/ *n. US* a hot dog topped with chilli

Chilkat blanket /chíl kat-/ *n. Northwest US, Can* among Native American peoples of the Pacific Northwest coast of North America, a blanket woven from mountain goat hair with a warp of shredded cedar bark, worn on ceremonial occasions [*Chilkat* from the name of an Aboriginal people of Canada]

chill /chil/ *n.* **1.** MODERATE COLDNESS a moderate but often unpleasant degree of coldness ○ *a chill in the air* **2.** MED SUDDEN SHORT FEVER a sudden short fever with shivering and a sensation of coldness **3.** COLDNESS CAUSED BY FEAR a sudden shuddering feeling of coldness caused by fear, anxiety, or excitement ○ *felt a chill run down my spine* **4.** DEPRESSING EFFECT a depressing or dampening effect on people or on an occasion ○ *The news cast a chill over the party.* **5.** LACK OF WARMTH an emotional coldness or unfriendliness in the atmosphere or in sb's manner **6.** METALL MOULD USED IN CASTING METAL a mould made of a highly conductive material such as iron, used to achieve a rapid even cooling of the material being cast. The chill may be watercooled to accelerate the cooling. ■ *adj.* **1.** MODERATELY COLD moderately cold, but usually cold enough to be unpleasant **2.** EMOTIONALLY COLD showing no friendliness or emotional warmth ■ *v.* (**chills, chilling, chilled**) **1.** *vt.* MAKE SB OR STH COLD to make sb or sth become cold, usually unpleasantly cold ○ *I was sitting in a freezing draught that chilled me to the bone.* **2.** *vti.* COOL OR FREEZE FOOD to cool food or drink, or be left to cool, in a refrigerator **3.** *vt.* MAKE SB FEEL AFRAID to make sb feel afraid, anxious, or horrified, especially suddenly **4.** *vt.* BE DISCOURAGING TO SB OR STH to have a discouraging or dampening effect on sb or sth **5.** *vi.* = **chill out** (*slang*) **6.** *vti.* METALL HARDEN METAL OR BECOME HARD to harden a metal surface, or become hard, by rapid cooling [Old English *ciele*, from a prehistoric Germanic word that is also the ancestor of English *cold*] —**chillness** *n.*

chill out *vi.* (*slang*) **1.** CALM DOWN to stop being angry or tense **2.** RELAX to spend time relaxing

chiller /chíllər/ *n.* **1.** REFRIGERATED COMPARTMENT a refrigerated cooling or storage compartment **2.** FRIGHTENING FILM OR STORY a frightening film or story (*slang*)

chill factor *n.* METEOROL = **wind-chill factor**

chilli /chílli/ (*plural* **-lies**) *n.* **1.** POD WITH STRONG FLAVOUR a narrow, tapering, usually red or green pod, produced by various types of capsicum pepper plant. Chillies have a very hot taste and are used for flavouring sauces and relishes. **2.** = **chilli powder 3.** = **chilli sauce 4.** = **chilli con carne** [Early 17thC. Via Spanish *chile* and *chili* from Nahuatl *chilli*.]

chilli con carne /chílli kon kaárni/ *n.* a highly spiced dish made of chopped or minced meat with beans and usually tomatoes, seasoned with chillies or chilli powder. Chilli con carne was originally a trail meal for Texas cowboys. [From American Spanish, literally 'chilli with meat']

chilling /chílling/ *adj.* causing a feeling of dread or horror ○ *a chilling account of his capture* —**chillingly** *adv.*

chilli pepper *n.* = **chilli** *n.* 1

chilli powder *n.* a seasoning consisting of ground chillies blended with several other seasonings, such as cumin, garlic, and oregano, often added to a dish to give it a hot taste

chilli sauce *n.* a highly spiced sauce made with tomatoes, ground dried chillies, and other seasonings

chillum /chílləm/ *n.* **1.** CANNABIS PIPE a short straight pipe, usually made of clay, for smoking cannabis or tobacco **2.** QUANTITY OF CANNABIS OR TOBACCO a quantity of cannabis or tobacco to be smoked [Late 18thC. From Hindi *chilam*.]

chilly /chílli/ (**-ier, -iest**) *adj.* **1.** MODERATELY COLD moderately or noticeably cold, usually enough to cause discomfort ○ *Bring a sweater to the park; it'll be chilly later.* **2.** FEELING RATHER COLD feeling cold enough to be uncomfortable **3.** UNFRIENDLY unfriendly or hostile ○ *a chilly reception* **4.** SENSITIVE TO COLD prone to feeling cold, or sensitive to the cold (*informal*) —**chillily** *adv.* —**chilliness** *n.*

chilly bin *n.* an insulated container for keeping food from spoiling and drinks cold, often small enough to be carried (*informal*)

chilopod /kílə pod/ *n.* any of a group of arthropods that includes the centipedes (*technical*) [Mid-19thC. From modern Latin *Chilopoda*, from Greek *kheilos* 'lip' + -POD.]

Chiltern Hills /chíltərn-/ range of chalk hills running north of London, England, from Oxfordshire to Bedfordshire for 72 km/45 mi., rising to 260 m/852 ft at Coombe Hill

Chiltern Hundreds *n.* a nominal office, in full, the Stewardship of the Chiltern Hundreds, that Members of Parliament apply for when they want to resign from the House of Commons (*takes a singular verb*) [13thC. Named after the CHILTERN HILLS.]

Chiluba /chi lóobə/, **Frederick, President of the Republic of Zambia** (*b.* 1943) Zambian head of state. In 1991, his Movement for Multiparty Democracy won a landslide victory over Kenneth Kaunda's UNIP in Zambia's first free elections since 1972.

Chi-lung /jee lóong/ seaport in northern Taiwan, one of the two ports of the capital, Taipei. Population: 356,501 (1992).

chimaera /kī meérə, ki-/ *n.* **1.** (*plural* **-ras** *or* **-ra**) DEEP-SEA FISH a deep-sea fish with a skeleton of cartilage, a smooth-skinned tapering body, and a tail that resembles a whip. Family: Chimaeridae. **2.** GENETICS = **chimera** [Early 19thC. From Latin (see CHIMERA).]

Chimaera *n.* = **Chimera**

chimb *n.* = **chime**[2]

Chimborazo /chímbə raázō/ mountain peak in central Ecuador, and the highest point in the Cordillera Real. Height: 6,310 m/20,702 ft.

Chimbote /chim bō tay/ seaport and town in western Peru, situated at the mouth of the River Santa and on the Pan-American Highway. Population: 296,600 (1990).

chime[1] /chīm/ *n.* **1.** SOUND OF BELL the musical ringing sound made by a bell or bells, or a similar sound made by some other object such as a doorbell **2.** DEVICE FOR STRIKING BELL a device for striking a bell or a set of bells in order to make a musical sound or play a tune (*often used in the plural*) **3.** NOTES SOUNDED BY A CLOCK a series of musical notes sounded by a clock before striking **4.** MUSIC PERCUSSION INSTRUMENT a set of hanging bells, metal bars, or tubes tuned to a scale, used to produce a musical sound when struck (*often used in the plural*) **5.** = **wind chime 6.** HARMONY an agreement or harmony among people or things (*literary*) ■ *v.* (**chimes, chiming, chimed**) **1.** *vi.* RING HARMONIOUSLY to make a harmonious ringing sound ○ *Did you hear the bells chiming?* **2.** *vt.* INDICATE STH BY CHIMING to indicate sth, especially the time, by chiming ○ *The clock chimed three o'clock.* **3.** *vt.* PRODUCE MUSICAL SOUND to strike a bell or bells so as to produce a musical sound **4.** *vi.* HARMONIZE to harmonize or be in agreement with sth else ○ *It was nice to find that her opinion chimed so perfectly with my own.* **5.** *vti.* SPEAK IN MUSICAL WAY to say or read sth aloud in a rhythmical or musical way [13thC. Of uncertain origin: perhaps from Old French *chimbe*, from, ultimately, Latin *cymbalum* (see CYMBAL).] —**chimer** *n.*

chime in *vi.* **1.** INTERRUPT OTHER PEOPLE'S CONVERSATION to interrupt or join in a conversation between other people, especially in order to voice an opinion **2.** COMBINE HARMONIOUSLY to agree or combine harmoniously with sth else

chime[2] /chīm/, **chimb, chine** /chīn/ *n.* an edge or lip around the rim of a barrel or cask [14thC. Origin uncertain: probably from assumed Old English *cim*.]

chimera /kī meérə, ki-/, **chimaera** *n.* **1.** STH TOTALLY UNREALISTIC OR IMPRACTICAL a figment of the imagination, e.g. a wildly unrealistic idea or hope or a completely impractical plan **2.** GENETICS ORGANISM WITH GENETICALLY DIFFERENT TISSUES an organism, or part of one, with at least two genetically different tissues resulting from mutation, the grafting of plants, or the insertion of foreign cells into an embryo **3.** EMBRYOL ORGANISM WITH DNA FROM DIFFERENT SOURCES an organism that has genetic material from a variety of sources as a result of the insertion of unspecialized cells (**stem cells**) from other species into an embryo [See CHIMERA] —**chimerism** /kī méerizzəm, kímərizzəm/ *n.*

Chimera /kī meérə, ki-/, **Chimaera** *n.* **1.** FIRE-BREATHING MONSTER a female fire-breathing monster in Greek mythology, typically represented as a combination of a lion's head, goat's body, and serpent's tail **2.** IMAGINARY MONSTER any imaginary monster whose body is a grotesque combination of mismatched animal parts [14thC. Via Latin *chimaera* from Greek *khimaira* 'she-goat'.]

chimeric /kī mérrik, ki-/ *adj.* used to describe an organism that is composed of genetically different tissues, either naturally or as a result of a laboratory procedure

chimerical /kī mérrik'l, ki-/ *adj.* **1.** IMAGINARY nonexistent, existing only in sb's imagination, or wildly improbable or unrealistic **2.** PRONE TO FANTASIZING having a tendency to indulge in unrealistic fantasies (*literary*) —**chimerically** *adv.* —**chimericalness** *n.*

chimney /chímni/ (*plural* **-neys**) *n.* **1.** STRUCTURE FOR VENTING GAS OR SMOKE a hollow vertical structure, usually made of brick or steel, that allows gas, smoke, or steam from a fire or furnace to escape into the atmosphere **2.** PART OF STRUCTURE RISING ABOVE ROOF the part of a chimney that rises above a roof **3.** SMOKE-VENTING PASSAGE INSIDE CHIMNEY a passage or pipe inside a chimney through which smoke or steam escapes **4.** ENG FUNNEL OF STEAM ENGINE a funnel on a railway engine or steamship. US term **smokestack 5.** GLASS TUBE PROTECTING LAMP FLAME a tube, usually made of glass, used to enclose the flame of a lamp in order to promote burning and exclude draughts **6.** MOUNTAINEERING **CLEFT IN ROCK FACE** a narrow vertical cleft in a rock face that is large enough for a climber to get inside and use as a means of ascending **7.** FIREPLACE a large fireplace or hearth, especially one that is very old (*regional*) [13thC. From Old French *cheminée*, from late Latin *caminata*, from Latin *camera caminata* 'room with a fireplace', from, ultimately, Greek *kaminos* 'oven, furnace'.]

chimney breast *n.* a projecting section of an interior wall surrounding a chimney or fireplace

chimney corner *n.* a recessed seat, beside or within a large old-fashioned open fireplace

chimneypiece /chímni peess/ *n.* = **mantelpiece**

chimney pot *n.* a short earthenware or metal pipe placed on the top of a chimney in order to increase the draught

chimney stack *n.* **1.** = **chimney** *n.* 2 **2.** TALL INDUSTRIAL CHIMNEY a tall, often cylindrical chimney attached to a factory or other large industrial building

chimney sweep *n.* sb whose job is removing soot from chimneys

chimney swift *n.* a small dark North American swift that nests in chimneys. Latin name: *Chaetura pelagica.*

chimp /chimp/ *n.* a chimpanzee (*informal*)

Chimpanzee

chimpanzee /chím pan zeé/ *n.* a medium-sized ape from the forests of equatorial Africa that has long dark-brown hair covering its body except for its naked face and ears. Chimpanzees are sociable and intelligent and are considered to be the closest living relatives of human beings. Latin name: *Pan troglodytes* and *Pan paniscus.* [Mid-18thC. Via French *chimpanzé* from Kikongo.]

chin /chin/ *n.* PART OF FACE the part of the face below the lips, including the usually protruding front portion of the lower jaw ■ *v.* (**chins, chinning, chinned**) **1.** *vti.* RAISE CHIN TO HIGH BAR to pull yourself up by the arms until your chin is level with the horizontal bar you are holding **2.** *vt.* HIT SB ON CHIN to hit sb on the chin or in the face (*slang*) [Old English *cin*, from prehistoric Germanic] ◇ **keep your chin up** to remain cheerful and hopeful in spite of difficulties or hardships ◇ **take it on the chin** to accept misfortune staunchly, without flinching

Chin /chin/ (*plural* **Chin** *or* **Chins**) *n.* **1.** PEOPLES **MEMBER OF PEOPLE OF SW MYANMAR** a member of a people living in southwestern Myanmar and neighbouring parts of India and Bangladesh **2.** LANG **GROUP OF SINO-TIBETAN LANGUAGES** a group of Sino-Tibetan languages spoken in southwestern Myanmar. About 800,000 people speak a Chin language. [Late 19thC. From Burmese, literally 'hill-man'.] —**Chin** *adj.*

Chin. *abbr.* Chinese

china[1] /chína/ *n.* **1.** PORCELAIN porcelain or a similar high-quality translucent or white ceramic material **2.** ARTICLES MADE OF CHINA articles made of china, especially dishes and decorative objects [Late 16thC. From Persian *čīnī* 'porcelain from China'.]

china[2] /chína/ *n.* Cockney a close and trusted friend (*slang*) [Late19thC. From *china plate*, rhyming slang for 'mate'.]

China

China /chína/ republic in eastern and central Asia. Language: Mandarin (official). Currency: renminbi (yuan). Capital: Beijing. Population: 1,226,274,731 (1997). Area: approximately 9,571,300 sq. km/ 3,695,500 sq. mi. Official name **People's Republic of China.** ◊ **Taiwan**

chinaberry /chínəbəri/ (*plural* **-ries**) *n.* **1.** TREE GROWN FOR SHADE a deciduous Asian tree of the mahogany family, widely grown in the United States for shade and its clusters of white or purple flowers. Latin name: *Melia azedarach.* **2.** = **soapberry** **3.** FRUIT FROM CHINABERRY OR SOAPBERRY TREE a fruit produced by either the chinaberry or soapberry tree

china clay *n.* = **kaolin**

Chinaman /chínəmən/ (*plural* **-men** /-mən/) *n.* **1.** OFFENSIVE TERM an offensive term for a man who was born in or who lives in China (*dated offensive*) **2.** CRICKET **METHOD OF BOWLING** in cricket, a slow off-break bowled by a left-handed bowler to a right-handed batsman

Chinan /chee nán/ industrial city and capital of Shandong province in northeastern China. Population: 1,430,000 (1986).

China rose *n.* **1.** CHINESE ROSE a rose that is native to China, has fragrant pink, red, or white flowers, and is the ancestor of many cultivated varieties. Latin name: *Rosa chinensis.* **2.** GARDEN ROSE a hybrid garden rose derived from the China rose, especially a dwarf rose with crimson flowers. Latin name: *Rosa semperflorens.* **3.** = **hibiscus**

China Sea part of the Pacific Ocean extending from Japan to the southern end of the Malay Peninsula. Area: East China Sea 752,000 sq. km/290,000 sq. mi. Depth: 2,717 m/8,913 ft.

china stone *n.* soft white clay formed from partially decomposed granite, used in ceramics and the paper and pharmaceutical industries

China syndrome *n.* a hypothetical accident in which the core of a nuclear reactor melts, allowing the radioactive fuel to burn through the floor of its container and straight down into the earth [From the idea of the molten core sinking through the earth and reaching China]

China tea *n.* tea produced in China that produces a light-coloured mild brew. China teas are sometimes smoke-cured and flavoured with flower petals.

Chinatown /chínə town/ *n.* an area of a city inhabited mainly by Chinese people, and containing businesses owned by them or selling Chinese products

China tree *n.* = **chinaberry** *n.* 1

chinaware /chínə wair/ *n.* plates, dishes, and other tableware made of china

chincherinchee /chínchə rínchi/ *n.* a South African plant of the lily family, with large fragrant flower heads that make it popular for use in flower arrangements. Latin name: *Ornithogalum thyrsoides.* [Early 20thC. An imitation of the sound created when stalks are rubbed together.]

chinchilla /chin chíllə/ *n.* **1.** (*plural* **-las** *or* **-la**) SMALL RODENT a South American rodent that is the size of a squirrel, with a bushy tail and large round ears. It is bred in captivity for its soft silvery-grey fur. Latin name: *Chinchilla laniger.* **2.** FUR OF CHINCHILLA the fur of the chinchilla **3.** WOOLLEN CLOTH a thick

Chinchilla

woollen fabric used to make overcoats [Early 17thC. Via Spanish from Aymara or Quechua.]

chin-chin /chín chín/ *interj.* used as a greeting, a way of saying goodbye, or as a toast when drinking (*dated informal*) [Late 18thC. From Chinese *qing qing.*]

Chindit /chíndit/ *n.* a soldier of the Allied forces in World War II, who fought behind the Japanese lines in Burma [Mid-20thC. From Burmese *cinthé*, a mythological lion-like creature used by the troops as their badge.]

Chindwin /chín dwín/ tributary of the River Irrawaddy, in Myanmar (Burma). It originates in a number of streams in the Indo-Myanmar region, before beginning its main course. Length: 837 km/520 mi.

chine[1] /chīn/ *n.* **1.** FOOD **JOINT OF MEAT** a cut of meat that includes part of the backbone **2.** NAUT **BOTTOM CORNER OF BOAT** the join between the bottom and sides of some boats, especially those with a flat or V-shaped bottom **3.** *S England* RAVINE a deep ravine in a cliff wall (*regional*) ■ *vt.* (**chines, chining, chined**) CUT MEAT FROM BACKBONE to cut meat along or across the backbone of the carcass [14thC. From Old French *eschine*, from a blend of the prehistoric Germanic ancestor of English *shin* and Latin *spina* 'spine'.]

chine[2] *n.* = **chime**[2]

Chinese /chī néez/ *npl.* PEOPLES **PEOPLE OF CHINA** people born or living in China, or whose family came from China ■ *n.* (*plural* **-nese**) **1.** GROUP OF LANGUAGES SPOKEN IN CHINA a group of related languages spoken across most of China and Taiwan, and by large communities in many other countries. They constitute a branch of the Sino-Tibetan language family. **2.** OFFICIAL LANGUAGE OF CHINA the standard language of China and Taiwan and an official language of Singapore. It belongs to the Chinese group of Sino-Tibetan languages. Chinese has about 800 million native speakers, which is more than any other language. **3.** FOOD, MEAL, OR RESTAURANT a restaurant or takeaway run by Chinese people and cooking food in styles from China, or food or a meal from one (*informal*) ■ *adj.* **1.** OF CHINA relating to or typical of China, its people, or culture **2.** OF THE CHINESE LANGUAGE relating to the language or language group Chinese

Chinese anise *n.* BOT = **star anise**

Chinese boxes *npl.* a set of matching boxes graduated in size so that each fits inside the next larger one, and as each opens it reveals another waiting to be opened

Chinese burn *n.* a way of inflicting pain, especially popular with children, that involves grasping sb's arm with both hands and twisting them in opposite directions

Chinese cabbage *n.* PLANTS **1.** VEGETABLE WITH WRINKLED LEAVES a plant with a long head of overlapping wrinkled leaves and broad stalks, popular as a salad vegetable. Latin name: *Brassica pekinensis.* **2.** = **pak-choi**

Chinese calendar *n.* the traditional calendar used in China that divides the year into 24 fifteen-day periods and is based on both the lunar and solar cycles. It has five months containing 29 days, six months of 30 days, and one month of 20 or 30 days.

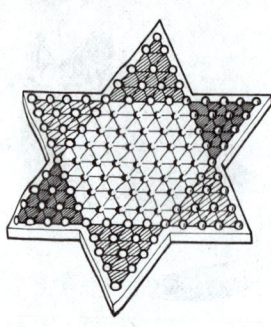

Chinese chequers

Chinese chequers *n.* a game played on a board marked with a six-pointed star studded with small holes. Players move or jump marbles hole by hole towards an opposite point of the star. (*takes a singular verb*)

Chinese chestnut *n.* a chestnut, originally native to China and Korea, that is resistant to a blight that affects other chestnuts. Latin name: *Castanea mollissima.*

Chinese copy *n.* an absolutely exact copy of an original, including any mistakes or defects it happens to contain

Chinese gooseberry *n.* = kiwi fruit

Chinese lantern

Chinese lantern *n.* **1.** PAPER LANTERN a lantern with a collapsible covering made of thin brightly coloured paper supported by thin wires **2.** PLANT WITH ORANGE SEED CASES a plant with papery orange-red seed cases. Latin name: *Physalis alkekengi.* US term **winter cherry**

Chinese leaves *npl.* = Chinese cabbage *n.* 1

Chinese New Year *n.* the first day of the Chinese month of Safar that falls between January 21 and February 19 and marks the start of two weeks of celebrations

Chinese puzzle *n.* a puzzle, either in the form of a game or a problem, that is extremely intricate, ingenious, and difficult to solve

Chinese red *n., adj.* = vermilion

Chinese restaurant syndrome *n.* a group of symptoms, including dizziness, headache, palpitations, and sweating, experienced by some people after eating food containing monosodium glutamate, an ingredient often used in preparing Chinese dishes

Chinese wall *n.* **1.** INSURMOUNTABLE BARRIER, ESPECIALLY TO COMMUNICATION a strong or insurmountable barrier, especially one that obstructs the exchange of information **2.** STOCK EXCH CONFIDENTIALITY BAR IN STOCK EXCHANGE BUSINESS a set of strict rules preventing the exchange of confidential information between different departments of a stock exchange business, which might lead to its illegal use for gain

Chinese water deer (*plural* **Chinese water deer**) *n.* a small Chinese or Korean deer without horns that has become naturalized in parts of Britain and France. The males have small tusks. Latin name: *Hydropotes inermis.*

Chinese water torture *n.* a method of psychological torture in which water is persistently dripped onto the victim's forehead

Chinese whispers *npl.* a game in which people in a circle pass a message by whispering it into the ear of the person next to them, the message becoming increasingly distorted on the way

Chinese windlass *n.* ENG = differential windlass

Chinese wood block *n.* a hollow slotted wooden block that, when struck, makes a sound similar to that of horses' hooves striking the ground

Chinese wood oil *n.* = tung oil

chink[1] /chingk/ *n.* NARROW OPENING a small narrow crack or slit ○ *Sunlight was coming through a chink in the curtains.* ■ *vt.* (**chinks, chinking, chinked**) *US* **1.** FILL CRACKS IN STH to fill up cracks or holes in sth **2.** MAKE CRACKS IN STH to make cracks in sth ○ *A flying pebble chinked my car's windshield.* [Early 16thC. Origin uncertain.] —**chinky** *adj.*

chink[2] /chingk/ *n.* SHARP RINGING SOUND a short sharp ringing sound such as that made when coins or glasses knock against each other ■ *vti.* (**chinks, chinking, chinked**) MAKE OR CAUSE METALLIC SOUND to make, or cause glass or metallic objects to make, a short sharp ringing sound ○ *We chinked glasses and said a toast.* [Late 16thC. An imitation of the sound.]

Chink /chingk/, **Chinky** /chíngki/ (*plural* **-ies**) *n.* an offensive term used to refer to a Chinese person (*slang offensive*) [Late 19thC. Formed from CHINA.]

chinless /chínləss/ *adj.* **1.** LACKING A PROJECTING CHIN having a lower jaw that recedes under the mouth instead of projecting in front of it **2.** WEAK lacking strength of character

chinless wonder *n.* sb, especially an upper-class man, who is considered weak or ineffectual (*informal insult*)

chino /cheenō/ *n.* COTTON TWILL FABRIC a durable coarse cotton twill fabric, often khaki-coloured, that is used to make military uniforms, but is also popular for making casual trousers ■ **chinos** *npl.* CHINO TROUSERS trousers made of chino [Mid-20thC. From American Spanish, literally 'toasted', from the original colour of the cloth.]

chinoiserie /shin waázəri/ *n.* **1.** ART STYLE WITH CHINESE INFLUENCE a style of art and interior design that reflects Chinese influence **2.** OBJECT IN CHINOISERIE STYLE an object or decoration in a style reflecting Chinese influence, or such objects and decorations collectively [Late 19thC. From French, from *chinois* 'Chinese'.]

chinook /chi nŏŏk/ *n.* **1.** WIND BLOWING ON NW US COAST a moist warm wind from the sea that affects weather along the northwestern coast of the United States **2.** WIND OFF ROCKY MOUNTAINS a dry warm wind that blows down the eastern slopes of the Rocky Mountains

Chinook /chi nŏŏk/ (*plural* **-nook** *or* **-nooks**) *n.* **1.** PEOPLES MEMBER OF NATIVE AMERICAN PEOPLE a member of a Native American people who originally occupied coastal lands around the estuary of the Columbia River in Oregon, but who now live in western Washington State **2.** LANG LANGUAGE OF CHINOOK PEOPLE the extinct language of the Chinook people that was possibly a separate branch of the Penutian group of languages [Early 19thC. From Salish *tsinúk.*] —**Chinook** *adj.*

Chinook Jargon *n.* a pidgin language, once used for trading along the western coast of North America, made up of words borrowed from Chinook, Nootka, various Salashian languages, French, and English

Chinook salmon *n.* a large salmon found in the northern Pacific Ocean that spawns in northern rivers of North America and North Asia. Its reddish flesh is highly prized. Latin name: *Oncorhyncus tshawytscha.*

chinquapin /chíngkəpin/, **chincapin, chinkapin** *n.* **1.** SMALL TREE OF EASTERN US a small deciduous tree found in the eastern United States. Latin name: *Castanea pumila.* **2.** LARGE EVERGREEN TREE a large evergreen tree found in western North America. Latin name: *Castanopsis chrysophylla.* **3.** EDIBLE NUT the edible nut of either of the chinquapin trees [Early 17thC. From Virginian Algonquian.]

chinstrap /chín strap/ *n.* a strap attached to a helmet or a hat that passes under the chin and is intended to keep the helmet or hat from falling off

chintz /chints/ *n.* a glazed fabric made of cotton and usually printed with a brightly coloured pattern [Early 17thC. Earlier *chints,* from *chint* 'calico cloth', from Hindi *chīṭ* 'stain', from Sanskrit *citra* 'variegated'.]

chintzy /chíntsi/ (**-ier, -iest**) *adj.* **1.** BRIGHTLY COLOURED AND PATTERNED brightly coloured and patterned, in a style associated with chintz fabric ○ *chintzy curtains* **2.** FUSSY OR QUAINT used to describe a fussy, quaint, or would-be genteel style of decor (*informal disapproving*) **3.** *US* PENNY-PINCHING mean and miserly ○ *He's so chintzy about money.* **4.** *US* TRASHY cheap and gaudy ○ *Don't buy that chintzy suit; it'll fall apart the first time you have it cleaned.*

chin-up *n.* an exercise performed by hanging from a horizontal bar and pulling the body up until the chin has been raised above the bar

chinwag /chín wag/ *n.* a chat or conversation, especially a long one (*informal*) —**chinwagger** *n.* —**chinwagging** *n.*

chionodoxa /kī ónnə dóksə/ *n.* (*plural* **chionodoxas** *or* **chionodoxa**) a hardy plant, native to Europe and Asia, that grows from a bulb and flowers in early spring. Genus: *Chionodoxa.* [Late 19thC. From modern Latin, from Greek *khiōn* 'snow' + *doxa* 'glory'.]

chip /chip/ *n.* **1.** SMALL PIECE BROKEN OR CUT OFF a small piece that has been broken, chopped, or cut off sth hard or brittle **2.** CRACK a space or crack left in sth hard or brittle after a small piece has been broken off or out of it ○ *This cup has a chip in it.* **3.** FOOD LONG PIECE OF FRIED POTATO a long finger-shaped wedge of potato traditionally fried in deep fat ○ *fish and chips* **4.** FOOD PIECE OF THIN CRISP SNACK FOOD a very thin crunchy slice made from a starchy food, usually potato or maize, that has been fried until it is crisp ○ *corn chips* **5.** GAMBLING COUNTER USED AS MONEY a token, often a small round plastic disc, used to represent money in poker and other gambling games **6.** ELECTRON ENG WAFER OF SEMICONDUCTOR MATERIAL a small wafer of semiconductor material, usually silicon, forming the base on which an integrated circuit is laid out, or such a wafer together with its integrated circuit **7.** SPORTS SHORT LOFTED SHOT in various sports, a short hit, kick, or shot that is lofted into the air over an obstacle or another player's head **8.** CRAFT WOOD CUT AS WEAVING MATERIAL wood, straw, or other material that has been dried and cut for use in weaving **9.** *US* DRIED DUNG a piece of dried animal dung, sometimes used for fuel ■ *v.* (**chips, chipping, chipped**) **1.** *vt.* BREAK OFF SMALL PIECE FROM STH to break one or more small pieces from sth hard or brittle **2.** *vi.* LOSE SMALL PIECES to become damaged by having a small piece or small pieces break off ○ *paint that will not chip easily* **3.** *vt.* SPORTS HIT STH IN HIGH ARC to hit or kick a ball or puck so that it travels a short distance in a high arc **4.** *vi.* GOLF PLAY A CHIP SHOT in golf, to play a chip shot **5.** *vt.* CARVE STH BY REMOVING SMALL PIECES to carve or shape sth by cutting small pieces off or out of it **6.** *vt.* CHOP STH INTO CHIPS to chop or cut up sth, e.g. a potato, to form chips ○ *Will you chip the ice for drinks?* [Pre-12thC. From Latin *cippus* 'stake'.] —**chipper** *n.* ◇ **cash in your chips** *US* to die (*informal*) ◇ **a chip off the old block** sb who looks and behaves very like one of his or her parents (*informal*) ◇ **have a chip on your shoulder** to feel inferior or badly treated and so act in an oversensitive and resentful manner (*informal*) ◇ **have had your chips** to fail, be defeated, or die (*informal*) ◇ **when the chips are down** at a time of crisis or when vital matters are at stake (*informal*)

chip in *v.* **1.** *vti.* CONTRIBUTE to contribute sth to a common fund or resource (*informal*) **2.** *vi.* INTERRUPT to interrupt a conversation in order to make a comment (*informal*) **3.** *vi.* PUT MONEY INTO POOL IN POKER in poker and other games, to put chips or money into the pool in order to play

chip basket *n.* a wire basket used to hold food such as chips when frying in deep fat

chipboard /chíp bawrd/ *n.* a construction material made from compressed wood chips held together by a synthetic resin and produced in the form of hard flat boards

Chipewyan /chíppə wī ən/ (*plural* **-an** *or* **-ans**) *n.* **1.** PEOPLES MEMBER OF NATIVE AMERICAN PEOPLE a member of a Native American people in Canada whose traditional territories are in northern Saskatchewan,

Manitoba, and the Northwest Territories. In the 18th century, they abandoned their nomadic life to settle and become fur traders. **2.** LANG **CHIPEWYAN LANGUAGE** the Athabaskan language of the Chipewyan people. Chipewyan is spoken by about 8,000 people. [Late 18thC. From Cree *cīpwayān*, literally '(wearing) pointed-skin (clothes)'.] —**Chipewyan** *adj.*

chiphead /chíp hed/ *n.* sb who is very interested in, and highly skilled at, computer use (*slang*)

chip log *n.* a wooden chip attached to a line marked off in measured sections that is thrown overboard in order to determine a ship's speed. The speed is calculated from the number of sections of line paid out in a period of twenty-eight seconds.

Chipmunk

chipmunk /chíp mungk/ (*plural* **-munks** *or* **-munk**) *n.* a striped rodent of the squirrel family, native to North America and Asia. It lives on the ground, collects nuts and fruit, and stores food in cheek pouches. Genera: *Tamias* and *Eutamias*. [Mid-19thC. From Ojibwa *ajidamoon*[?] 'squirrel', literally 'one that comes down trees headlong'.]

chipolata /chíppə láatə/ *n.* a small thin sausage, usually made of finely ground pork [Late 19thC. Via French from Italian *cipollata*, literally 'with onions', from *cipolla* 'onion', from Latin *cepa* (source of English *chive*).]

Chipp /chip/, **Don** (*b.* 1925) Australian politician. He was a Liberal government minister who resigned in order to found the centrist Australian Democrats party. Full name **Donald Leslie Chipp**

chip pan *n.* a deep pan, usually enclosing a wire basket, used for frying food, especially chips, in large quantities of oil or fat

Chippendale /chíppən dayl/ *adj.* **18THC ENGLISH FURNITURE STYLE** used to describe furniture made by, or in the style of, Thomas Chippendale, characterized by graceful flowing lines, cabriole legs, and elaborate ornamentation ■ *n.* **PIECE OF FURNITURE IN CHIPPENDALE STYLE** a piece of furniture in the Chippendale style [Named after Thomas CHIPPENDALE]

Chippendale /chíppən dayl/, **Thomas** (1718–79) British furniture designer. The influence of his neo-classical, increasingly eclectic style was spread through *The Gentleman and Cabinet Maker's Director* (1754).

chipper /chíppər/ *adj.* (*informal*) **1.** **CHEERFUL** cheerful and full of vitality **2.** **SMARTLY DRESSED** smartly dressed [Mid-19thC. Origin uncertain: perhaps a blend of dialect *kipper* and *chipper*, alteration of CHIRRUP.]

Chippewa /chíppə waa/ (*plural* **-was** *or* **-wa**) *adj.* = **Ojibwa** [Mid-18thC. Alteration of OJIBWA.]

chipping /chípping/ *n.* = **chip** *n.* 1 ■ **chippings** *npl.* **SMALL STONES FOR ROAD SURFACING** small stones used in surfacing roads

chipping sparrow *n.* a small North American sparrow with a grey breast, reddish-brown crown, and black-and-white stripes near its eyes. Latin name: *Spizella passerina*. [*Chipping* from *chipper*, alteration of CHIRRUP]

chippy[1] /chíppi/ (*plural* **-pies**), **chippie** *n.* (*informal*) **1.** **FISH AND CHIP SHOP** a fish and chip shop **2.** **CARPENTER** a carpenter

chippy[2] (**-pier**, **-piest**) *adj.* *Can* behaving in an aggressive or belligerent way [From *have a chip on your shoulder*]

chipset /chíp set/, **chip set** *n.* a group of microchips designed to perform one or more related functions as a unit, e.g. to update a computer screen display

chip shop *n.* a shop that sells fish and chips and various other fried foods

chip shot *n.* **1.** **SHORT HIGH HIT OR KICK** a short-range kick or shot in which the ball or puck rises sharply into the air **2.** **APPROACH SHOT** a short approach shot in golf, used to loft the ball onto the green

Chirac /sheer ak/, **Jacques** (*b.* 1932) French politician. He was prime minister (1974–76 and 1986–88) and, after two unsuccessful attempts, was elected president in 1995. Full name **Jacques René Chirac**

chiral /kírəl/ *adj.* used to describe a molecule whose arrangement of atoms is such that it cannot be superimposed on its mirror image [Late 19thC. Formed from Greek *kheir* 'hand'.] —**chirality** /kī rálləti/ *n.*

Chi-Rho

Chi-Rho /kí rố/ (*plural* **Chi-Rhos**) *n.* a monogram and symbol for Jesus Christ, formed by superimposing the Greek letters *chi* (X) and *rho* (P) [From the first two letters of Jesus Christ's name in Greek]

Chirico /kírrikō/, **Giorgio de** (1888–1978) Greek-born Italian painter. His metaphysical dreamscapes of 1910 onwards anticipated surrealism. From 1930, he disowned these works and denounced modernism.

chiro- *prefix.* hand ○ *chiromancy* [Via Latin from Greek *kheir* (source also of English *surgery*)]

chirography /kī róggrəfi/ *n.* = **calligraphy**

chiromancy /kírō manssi/ *n.* = **palmistry**

Chiron /kíron/ *n.* in Greek mythology, the centaur, known for his great wisdom, who was the tutor of Greek heroes such as Hercules, Achilles, and Jason

chironomid /kī rónnəmid/ *n.* a small nonbiting midge that gathers in large breeding swarms, especially near water. Family: Chironomidae. [Late 19thC. From modern Latin *Chironomidae*, from the genus name *Chironomus*, from Greek *kheironomos* 'pantomime dancer'.]

chiropody /ki róppədi, shi-/ *n.* the branch of medicine concerned with the care and treatment of the feet. US term **podiatry** —**chiropodist** *n.*

chiropractic /kírə práktik/ *n.* a medical system based on the theory that disease and disorders are caused by a misalignment of the bones, especially in the spine, that obstructs proper nerve functions [Late 19thC. Formed from CHIRO- and Greek *praktikos* 'effective'.] —**chiropractor** /kírō praktər/ *n.*

chiropteran /kī róptərən/, **chiropter** /kī róptər/ *n.* ZOOL a flying mammal, such as the bat, with forelimbs that have evolved as membranous wings (*technical*) [Mid-19thC. From modern Latin *Chiroptera*, from CHIRO- + Greek *pteron* 'wing'.]

chirp /churp/ *n.* **SHORT HIGH-PITCHED SOUND** a short high-pitched sound, especially as made by a bird ■ *v.* (**chirps, chirping, chirped**) **1.** *vi.* **MAKE A CHIRP** to make a short high-pitched sound **2.** *vti.* **SPEAK IN CHEERFUL MANNER** to speak, or say sth, in a cheerful, lively, or pert voice [15thC. An imitation of the sound.]

chirpy /chúrpi/ (**-ier, -iest**) *adj.* cheerful and lively (*informal*) —**chirpily** *adv.* —**chirpiness** *n.*

chirr /chur/ *n.* **SHRILL INSECT SOUND** a shrill harsh trilled sound made by some insects, e.g. grasshoppers ■ *vi.* (**chirrs, chirring, chirred**) **MAKE A CHIRR** to make a harsh trilled sound [Early 17thC. An imitation of the sound.]

chirrup /chírrəp/ *v.* (**-rups, -ruping, -ruped**) **1.** *vi.* **TWITTER** to utter a series of chirps **2.** *vti.* **SPEAK IN HIGH CHEERFUL VOICE** to speak or say sth in a high-pitched voice, and in a cheerful and lively fashion **3.** *vi.* **MAKE CLUCKING SOUND WITH LIPS** to make a clucking sound with the lips, e.g. when encouraging a horse to move faster ■ *n.* **CHIRP** a repeated series of chirping or clucking sounds [Late 16thC. Alteration of CHIRP.] —**chirrupy** *adj.*

Chisel

chisel /chízz'l/ *n.* **1.** **TOOL WITH FLAT BEVELLED BLADE** a tool for cutting and shaping wood or stone, consisting of a straight flat bevelled blade with a sharp square-cut bottom edge inserted in a handle. The chisel is often held in one hand and struck with a hammer or mallet, but is also used freehand. **2.** TECH, DIY = **cold chisel** ■ *v.* (**-els, -elling, -elled**) **1.** *vti.* **CARVE STH WITH CHISEL** to carve, cut, or work wood or stone using a chisel **2.** *vti.* **CHEAT SB** to cheat or swindle sb (*informal*) **3.** *vt.* **OBTAIN BY CHEATING** to obtain sth by cheating or deception (*informal*) [14thC. Via Old French from, ultimately, Latin *caes-*, stem of *caedere* 'to cut' (source of English *scissors*).]

chiselled /chízzəl'd/ *adj.* clear-cut or sharply defined in shape or profile ○ *a finely chiselled face*

chiseller /chízzələr/ *n.* **1.** **SWINDLER** a cheat or swindler (*informal*) **2.** *Ireland* **CHILD** a child (*regional slang*)

Chisholm /chízzəm/, **Caroline** (1808–77) British philanthropist. She was the creator of employment and welfare programmes for female immigrants to New South Wales.

Chişinău /kíshi nố/ *city* and capital of Moldova, situated on a tributary of the Dniester, 145 km/90 mi. northwest of Odessa, Ukraine. Population: 753,500 (1991). Former name **Kishinev** (1940–91)

chi-square *n.* a statistical calculation used to test how well the distribution of a set of observed data matches a theoretical probability distribution. The calculated value is equal to the sum of the squares of the differences divided by the expected values.

chi-square distribution *n.* a probability function widely used in testing a statistical hypothesis, e.g. the likelihood that a given statistical distribution of results might be reached in an experiment

chit[1] /chit/ *n.* **1.** **SLIP OF PAPER** a note, bill, or any small slip of paper with writing on it, especially a statement of money owed for food and drink (*dated*) **2.** **OFFICIAL NOTE OR DOCUMENT** an official note or document, usually signed by sb in authority, e.g. a receipt, order, or requisition form [Late 18thC. Shortening of *chitty*, via Hindi *ciṭṭhī*, from Sanskrit *citra* 'spot, mark', referring to the writing.]

chit[2] /chit/ *n.* a child, girl, or young woman, especially one whose physical slightness seems to be at odds with an impertinent, forceful, or self-confident manner

chit[3] /chit/ *vt.* to place a potato in a light place to cause it to produce shoots before planting in the ground

chital /cheet'l/ (*plural* **-tal** *or* **-tals**) *n.* = **axis deer** [Late 19thC. From Hindi *cittal*, from Sanskrit *citrala* 'spotted'.]

chitchat /chít chat/ *n.* **SMALL TALK** casual conversation or small talk, or a casual conversation with sb (*informal*) ■ *vi.* (**-chats, -chatting, -chatted**) **MAKE SMALL TALK** to engage in casual conversation or small talk (*informal*) ○ *What are you chitchatting about now?* [Late 17thC. A playful elaboration of CHAT.]

chitin /kítin/ n. a tough semitransparent substance that forms part of the protective outer casing (**cuticle**) of some insects and other arthropods, and the cell walls of some fungi [Mid-19thC. From French *chitine*, from Greek *khitōn* 'tunic, coat of mail'.] —**chitinoid** *adj.* —**chitinous** *adj.*

chitlins /chítlins/, **chitlings** /-lings/ npl. Southern US = **chitterlings** [Mid-19thC. Contraction of CHITTERLINGS.]

chiton /kít'n, -ton/ n. **1.** SMALL MARINE MOLLUSC a small primitive marine mollusc that lives on rocks and has an elongated body protected by a shell consisting of eight overlapping plates. Class: Polyplacophora. **2.** TUNIC OF ANCIENT GREECE AND ROME a loose knee-length woollen tunic worn by women and men in ancient Greece [Early 19thC. From Greek *khiton* 'tunic, coat of mail'.]

Chittagong /chítta gong/ chief port of Bangladesh and an important industrial city. It is situated on the southeastern coast of the country. Population: 1,364,000 (1991).

chitter /chítter/ (**-ters, -tering, -tered**) vi. Scotland to chatter or shiver with cold (*regional*) [12thC. An imitation of the sound.]

chitterlings /chítterlingz/ npl. the small intestines of pigs, especially when prepared as food [13thC. Origin unknown.]

chivalric /shívv'Irik/ adj. relating to knights, knighthood, and the knightly code of honour

chivalrous /shívv'lrəss/ adj. **1.** RELATING TO KNIGHTHOOD CODE relating to, or reflecting the values of, the medieval code of knighthood, especially courtesy, self-sacrifice, and a sense of fair play **2.** CONSIDERATE AND COURTEOUS considerate and courteous, especially towards women —**chivalrously** adv. —**chivalrousness** n.

chivalry /shívv'lri/ (plural **-ries**) n. **1.** QUALITIES OF IDEAL KNIGHT the combination of qualities expected of the ideal medieval knight, especially courage, honour, loyalty, and consideration for others, especially women **2.** CHIVALROUS BEHAVIOUR courteous and considerate behaviour, especially towards women **3.** MEDIEVAL KNIGHTHOOD the medieval concept of knighthood, and the customs, practices, social system, and religious and personal ideals associated with knights and their way of life **4.** GROUP OF KNIGHTS knights, noblemen, or armed mounted soldiers, collectively or in a group (*archaic*) [13thC. Via Old French *chevalerie* from medieval Latin *caballerius*, from Latin *caballus* 'horse' (source of English *cavalier*).]

chive /chīv/ n. a plant with long fine hollow leaves that has a strong onion flavour and purple ball-shaped flowers. Its leaves are used to season food. Latin name: *Allium schoenoprasum*. [14thC. From French dialect, variant of *cive*, from Latin *cepa* 'onion' (source of English *chipolata*).]

chivvy /chívvi/ (**-vies, -vying, -vied**), **chivy** (**-ies, -ying, -ied**), **chevy** /chévi/ (**-ies, -ying, -ied**) vt. to urge, pester, or harass sb, usually in order to make sb do sth or do it more quickly [Late 18thC. Origin uncertain: probably named after *Chevy Chase*, a place near the border between England and Scotland where a skirmish was fought in 1388.]

chlamydes plural of **chlamys**

chlamydia /klə míddi ə/ n. **1.** MICROBIOL PATHOGENIC BACTERIUM a spherical bacterium that causes several eye and urogenital diseases in humans and other animals, and psittacosis in pet birds. Genus: *Chlamydia*. **2.** MED SEXUALLY TRANSMITTED DISEASE a sexually transmitted disease, the most common in developed countries, caused by the bacterium *Chlamydia trachomatis*. Often producing no symptoms, it can cause infertility, chronic pain, or a tubal pregnancy if left untreated. [Mid-20thC. Via modern Latin from Greek *khlamyd-*, stem of *khlamus* 'mantle, chlamys'.]

chlamydial /kləmíddi əl/ adj. used to describe infections that are caused by a bacterium of the genus *Chlamydia*, e.g. trachoma and sexually transmitted infections such as urethritis

chlamydospore /klə mídda spawr/ n. an asexual thick-walled spore produced by some fungi. It is capable of remaining dormant for long periods and surviving adverse conditions. [Late 19thC. Coined from the Greek stem *khlamyd-* 'mantle' + SPORE.]

chlamys /klámmiss, kláy-/ (plural **-yses** or **-ydes** /klámmi deez/) n. a short cloak gathered and fastened at the shoulder, worn by men in ancient Greece [Late 17thC. From Greek *khlamus* 'mantle'.]

chloasma /klō ázmə/ (plural **-mata** /-mətə/) n. dark coloration on the skin of the face caused by hormonal changes related to pregnancy, liver disease, or the use of birth control pills. It is made worse by sunlight. [Mid-19thC. Formed from Greek *khloazein* 'to become green'.]

chlor- prefix. = **chloro-** (*used before vowels*)

chloral /kláwrəl/ n. a colourless oily toxic liquid with a strong odour, used in making chloral hydrate and DDT. Formula: CCl_3CHO. [Mid-19thC. Coined from CHLOR- + -AL.]

chloral hydrate n. a colourless crystalline solid that is soluble in water and is used as a sedative and hypnotic. Formula: $C_2H_3Cl_3O_2$.

chloramine /kláwrə meen/ n. an unstable colourless liquid with a pungent odour. It is used to make hydrazine. Formula: NH_2Cl.

chloramphenicol /kláwr am fénni kol/ n. a powerful antibiotic derived from a soil bacterium, the use of which is limited by its tendency to cause the failure of blood cell production (**aplastic anaemia**). Formula: $C_{11}H_{12}Cl_2N_2O_5$. [Mid-20thC. Coined from CHLOR- + AMIDE + PHEN- + NITRO- + GLYCOL.]

chlorate /kláwr ayt/ n. any salt of chloric acid [Early 19thC. Formed from CHLORIC.]

chlordiazepoxide /kláwr dī ázzə póksīd/ n. a yellow crystalline powder that is used as a tranquillizer and as a treatment for alcoholism. Formula: $C_{16}H_{14}ClN_3O$. [Mid-20thC. Coined from CHLOR- + DI- + AZO- + EPI- + OXIDE.]

chlorella /klə réllə/ n. a single-celled green alga that is often used in research. Genus: *Chlorella*. [Early 20thC. From modern Latin, literally 'little green (thing)', from Greek *khlōros* 'green'.]

chlorenchyma /klə réngkimə/ n. plant tissue that contains chloroplasts, found mainly in leaves [Late 19thC. Coined from CHLOROPHYLL + -ENCHYMA.]

chloric /kláwrik/ adj. containing chlorine, especially with a valency of 5 [Early 19thC. Formed from CHLORINE.]

chloric acid n. a toxic unstable acid, known only in solution and as chlorate salts. Formula: $HClO_3 \cdot 7H_2O$.

chloride /kláwr īd/ n. a compound containing chlorine and one other element [Early 19thC. Formed from CHLORINE.] —**chloridic** /klə ríddik/ adj.

chloride of lime n. a powder used as a bleach (*technical*)

chlorinate /kláwri nayt/ (**-nates, -nating, -nated**) vt. to combine or treat sth with chlorine, especially in order to kill harmful organisms —**chlorinated** adj. —**chlorination** /kláwri náysh'n/ n. —**chlorinator** /kláwri naytər/ n.

chlorine /kláwr een/ n. a gaseous, poisonous, corrosive, greenish-yellow chemical element of the halogen group that combines with nearly every other element. It is widely used to purify water and as a disinfectant. Symbol **Cl** [Early 19thC. Formed from Greek *khlōros* 'green', from the colour of the gas.]

chlorite[1] /kláwr īt/ n. a group of soft black or green aluminosilicate minerals found in metamorphic rocks. Formula: $(Mg,Fe,Al)_3(Si,Al)_4O_{10}(OH)_8$. [Late 18thC. Via Latin *chloritis* from Greek *khlōritis*, a green precious stone.]

chlorite[2] /kláwr īt/ n. any salt of chlorous acid [Mid-19thC. Formed from CHLORINE.]

chloro- prefix. **1.** green ○ *chlorophyll* **2.** chlorine ○ *chlorobenzene* [From Greek *khlōros* 'green']

chlorobenzene /kláwrō bén zeen/ n. a combination of chlorine and benzene that produces a colourless flammable liquid with an almond smell, used especially in the production of solvents and DDT. Formula: C_6H_5Cl.

chlorofluorocarbon /kláwrō flóorō ka'arbən, -fláwrō-/ n. full form of **CFC** [Mid-20thC. Coined from CHLORO- + FLUORO- + CARBON.]

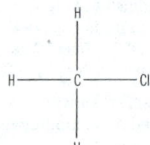

Chloroform

chloroform /kláwrə fawrm/ n. LIQUID CAUSING UNCONSCIOUSNESS a colourless sweet-smelling toxic liquid that rapidly changes to a vapour and causes unconsciousness if inhaled, used as a solvent and cleaning agent. It was formerly used as an anaesthetic for surgical operations and is still sometimes used as such in veterinary medicine. Formula: $CHCl_3$. ■ vt. RENDER UNCONSCIOUS WITH CHLOROFORM to make a person or animal breathe in chloroform in order to cause unconsciousness [Mid-19thC. Coined from CHLORO- + FORMIC.]

chloromethane /kláwrō mée thayn/ n. = **methyl chloride**

Chloromycetin /kláw rō mī séetin/ tdmk. a trademark for the antibiotic chloramphenicol

chlorophyll /klórrəfil/ n. the green or purple pigment found in plants, algae, and some bacteria that is responsible for capturing the light energy needed for photosynthesis. In plants and algae, chlorophyll is contained within numerous minute membranous sacs (**chloroplasts**) within cells of the stems and leaves. [Early 19thC. From French *chlorophylle*, from Greek *khlōros* (see CHLORO-) + *phullon* 'leaf'.] —**chlorophyllose** /klórrə fílləss/ adj.

chloropicrin /kláwrə píkrin/ n. a colourless toxic liquid that causes tears and vomiting and is used as a tear gas. It also has industrial uses as an insecticide, a disinfectant, and in dyes. Formula: CCl_3NO_2. [Mid-19thC. Coined from CHLORO- + PICRO- + -IN.]

chloroplast /kláwrə plast, -plaast/ n. a membranous sac (**plastid**) that contains chlorophyll and other pigments and is the place where photosynthesis occurs within the cells of plants and algae. Plant cells contain numerous chloroplasts, algal cells often have just one. Each consists of interconnected stacks of disc-shaped membranes in fluid, surrounded by a double membrane. [Late 19thC. Coined from CHLORO- + -PLAST.] —**chloroplastic** /kláw rə plástik/ adj.

chloroprene /kláwrə preen/ n. a colourless liquid used in the manufacture of the synthetic rubber, neoprene. Formula: C_4H_5Cl. [Mid-20thC. Coined from CHLORO- + ISOPRENE.]

chloroquine /kláwrə kwīn, -kween/ n. a synthetic drug that is taken orally and is used to treat malaria and amoebiasis. Formula: $C_{18}H_{26}ClN_3$. [Mid-20thC. Coined from CHLORO- + QUINOLINE, from which it is derived.]

chlorosis /klə róssiss/ n. **1.** LOSS OF GREENNESS THROUGH CHLOROPHYLL DEFICIENCY a yellowing or whitening of a plant's leaves and stems caused by a lack of the green pigment chlorophyll **2.** IRON-DEFICIENCY ANAEMIA severe iron-deficiency anaemia, formerly common in adolescent girls, that produces a greenish tint in the skin [Late 17thC. Coined from CHLORO- + -OSIS.] —**chlorotic** /klə róttik/ adj. —**chlorotically** /-róttikli/ adv.

chlorothiazide /kláwrō thī ə zīd/ n. a water-soluble powder used in the treatment of high blood pressure, swelling, and heart failure to relieve fluid retention in the body

chlorous /kláwrəss/ adj. relating to or containing chlorine with a valency of 3 [Mid-19thC. Coined from CHLORINE + -OUS.]

chlorpromazine /klawr prómə zeen/ n. a drug used as a sedative and tranquillizer in the treatment of psychiatric disorders such as schizophrenia [Mid-20thC. Coined from CHLOR- + PROMETHAZINE.]

chlorpropamide /klawr próppə mīd, -prṓpə-/ *n.* a drug that lowers blood sugar, used in the treatment of diabetes. Formula: $C_{10}H_{13}ClN_2O_3S$. [Mid-20thC. Coined from CHLOR- + PROPANE + AMIDE.]

chlortetracycline /klawr téttrə síklin, -kleen/ *n.* an antibiotic drug, derived from a soil bacterium, that is used to treat a wide range of infections in humans and to stimulate growth in livestock. Formula: $C_{22}H_{23}ClN_2O_8$.

ChM *abbr.* Master of Surgery [Latin *Chirurgiae Magister*]

chm., **Chm** *abbr.* chairman

Chmn, **chmn** *abbr.* chairman

choc /chok/ *n.* a chocolate-covered sweet, especially one from a box of chocolates (*informal*) [Shortening]

chocaholic *n.* = **chocoholic**

choccy /chóki/ (*plural* **-cies**) *n.* chocolate, or a chocolate-covered sweet (*informal*) ○ *a box of choccies* [Shortening]

choc ice *n.* a small block of ice cream coated in a thin layer of chocolate

chock /chok/ *n.* **1.** BLOCK TO STOP STH MOVING a block of wood or metal used to prevent a wheel from turning, an object from moving, or to support sth when it is raised off the ground **2.** SHIPPING SHIP'S HORN-SHAPED FITMENT FOR SECURING CABLES a heavy metal fitment attached to the deck of a ship that has two inward-curving horn-shaped projections around which a cable can be secured **3.** MOUNTAINEERING METAL ANCHOR FOR CLIMBING a metal device used to provide anchoring systems for climbing or caving ■ *vt.* USE CHOCK FOR BRACE to keep sth from turning, moving, or falling by using a chock to block or brace it ○ *chock the plane's wheels* [14thC. Probably from an assumed Old Norman French variant of Old French *ço(u)che* 'log', of unknown origin.]

chocka *adj.* = **chocker**

chock-a-block *adj.* **1.** PACKED FULL so crammed with things or crowded with people as to make it virtually impossible to get anything or anybody else in or to move about (*informal*) **2.** NAUT HAVING BLOCKS IN TIGHTEST POSITION having the two blocks in a block and tackle tight up against each other [Mid-19thC. Alteration of an earlier nautical term *block and block*, 'with pulleys drawn close together', influenced by CHOCK-FULL.]

chocker /chókər/, **chocka** /chókə/ *adj.* **1.** CHOCK-A-BLOCK chock-a-block (*slang*) **2.** COMPLETELY FULL completely full up after eating (*slang*) **3.** VERY FED UP OR IRRITATED very fed up or irritated (*dated slang*) ○ *I'm chocker with all this work.* [Mid-20thC. Shortening of CHOCK-A-BLOCK.]

chockers /chókərz/ *adj.* = **chocker** (*informal*)

chock-full *adj.* completely full, or containing an enormous number of things (*informal*) [14thC. *Chock* perhaps from CHOCK 'wooden block', hence, originally, 'stuffed with blocks of wood', or an alteration of CHEEK, hence, originally, 'full up to the cheeks'.]

chocoholic /chókə hóllik/, **chocaholic** *n.* sb who is extremely fond of or apparently addicted to chocolate, and who craves it or eats it in large quantities (*humorous*) [Late 20thC. Coined from CHOCOLATE + -AHOLIC.]

chocolate /chóklit/ *n.* **1.** FOOD SMOOTH SWEET BROWN FOOD a food or flavouring, typically a smooth sweet brown and rather brittle solid, made from roasted and ground cacao seeds usually sweetened and mixed with cocoa butter and dried milk. Chocolate is made into bars or sweets, or used to flavour other foods, especially cakes, desserts, sauces, and biscuits. (*often used before a noun*) ○ *a bar of chocolate* ○ *chocolate cake* **2.** FOOD SWEET COVERED IN CHOCOLATE a small chocolate-coated sweet with a hard or soft centre **3.** BEVERAGES CHOCOLATE DRINK a drink, usually served hot or warm, made from sweetened powdered chocolate mixed with water or milk **4.** COLOURS BROWN COLOUR a deep warm brown colour ■ *adj.* BROWN-COLOURED of a deep warm brown colour [Early 17thC. Directly or via French *chocolat* 'drinking chocolate', from Spanish *chocolate*, from Nahuatl *chocolatl*, literally 'bitter water'.] —**chocolatey** *adj.*

chocolate-box *adj.* depicting pretty scenes or pretty people in a stereotyped and usually sentimental or romanticized way ○ *chocolate-box portraits*

chocolate chip *n.* a small piece of chocolate, used especially in making biscuits and desserts ○ *chocolate chip cookies*

chocolate tree *n.* = **cacao** *n.* 1

chocolatier /chókə látti ər/ *n.* a maker or seller of chocolates

Choctaw /chók taw/ (*plural* **-taw** *or* **-taws**) *n.* **1.** PEOPLES MEMBER OF NATIVE AMERICAN PEOPLE a member of a Native American people who originally occupied lands in central and southern parts of Mississippi, and whose members now live mainly in Oklahoma and southern Mississippi. The Choctaw were one of the Five Civilized Nations who, under the Removal Act of 1830, were sent to live on reservations in Oklahoma. **2.** LANG CHOCTAW LANGUAGE the Muskogean language of the Choctaw people. Choctaw is spoken by about 10,000 people. [Early 18thC. From Choctaw *čahta*.] —**Choctaw** *adj.*

choice /choyss/ *n.* **1.** ACT OF CHOOSING STH OR SB a decision to choose one thing, person, or course of action in preference to others ○ *Think very carefully before you make a choice.* **2.** POWER TO CHOOSE the chance or ability to choose between different things ○ *They gave us no choice* **3.** SELECTION OF THINGS a variety of things, people, or possibilities from which to choose ○ *a wide choice of styles and colours* **4.** CHOSEN OBJECT a person, thing, or course of action chosen by sb from among a range of possibilities ○ *Red would not have been my choice.* **5.** BEST PART the best or most desirable part ■ *adj.* (**choicer, choicest**) **1.** HIGH-QUALITY being of particularly good quality **2.** RUDE OR EMPHATIC carefully chosen for effectiveness and usually expressing displeasure or dislike in a sufficiently emphatic way (*used euphemistically*) ○ *a few choice words* [13thC. From Old French *chois*, from *choisir* 'to choose', ultimately from a prehistoric Germanic word that is also the ancestor of English *choose*.] —**choiceness** *n.* ◇ **of choice** chosen from among several as being the best or most suitable ○ *the newspaper of choice*

choir /kwīr/ *n.* **1.** GROUP OF SINGERS an organized group of singers who perform together, typically combining smaller groups of singers who sing different parts at different pitches (*takes a singular or plural verb*) **2.** AREA WHERE CHOIR SINGS the part of a church where the choir performs **3.** INSTRUMENT GROUP a group of instruments of the same type **4.** = **choir organ** [13thC. Via Old French *quer*, from Latin *chorus* 'choral dance' (source of English *chorus*), on which the English spelling was modelled, from Greek *khoros* 'group of singers and dancers'.]

choirboy /kwīr boy/ *n.* a boy who sings in a church choir

choirgirl /kwīr gurl/ *n.* a girl who sings in a church choir

choir loft *n.* a raised gallery or part of the upper storey in a church, where the choir performs during services

choirmaster /kwīr maastər/ *n.* sb who instructs, trains, and conducts a choir

choir organ *n.* a manual or section of a large organ with sets of soft-toned pipes suitable for accompanying a choir. ◊ **great organ**

choir school *n.* a school where the members of a cathedral or church choir are educated and attend ordinary lessons as well as receiving special musical training

choke[1] /chōk/ *v.* (**chokes, choking, choked**) **1.** *vi.* STOP BREATHING THROUGH BLOCKAGE OF THROAT to stop breathing, or breathe with great difficulty, because of a blockage or restriction of the throat **2.** *vt.* PREVENT BREATHING BY CONSTRICTING THROAT to prevent sb from breathing by blocking or squeezing the throat **3.** *vt.* BLOCK PASSAGE OR CHANNEL to form an obstruction in a passage, channel, pipe, or roadway and prevent anything from passing along it **4.** *vt.* PREVENT PLANTS FROM GROWING to prevent plants from developing by growing over them and depriving them of light and air ○ *the bed was choked with weeds* **5.** *vti.* BE TOO MOVED TO SPEAK to be overcome with emotion and unable to speak, or make sb feel so much emotion that he or she cannot speak (*informal*) **6.** *vi.* US LOSE NERVE AND FALTER to lose nerve or confidence and falter in the middle of saying or doing sth (*informal*) ○ *He gets ahead, two sets to one, and then he chokes!* **7.** *vi.* US REFUSE TO COOPERATE to refuse to cooperate when presented with sth unacceptable (*informal*) ○ *We choked on their last demand.* ■ *n.* **1.** NOISE OF CHOKING a sound or movement made by sb choking, or indicative of sb choking **2.** FUEL MIXTURE REGULATOR FOR ENGINE a device that controls the ratio of air to fuel in the mixture supplied to an internal-combustion engine ○ *pull the choke out* [Old English *ācēocian* from, ultimately, *cēoce* 'cheek'. The underlying idea is of cutting off the air supply by constricting the cheeks.] —**choking** *adj.* —**chokingly** *adv.*

choke back *vt.* to stop the expression of an emotional response to sth by a deliberate effort of self-control ○ *I couldn't choke back my tears any longer.*

choke off *vt.* to stop the flow, supply, or development of sth, usually abruptly

choke[2] /chōk/ *n.* the bristly inner inedible part of an artichoke [Shortening]

chokebore /chṓk bawr/ *n.* **1.** TAPERING BORE a shotgun bore that tapers towards the muzzle to prevent wide scattering of the shot **2.** SHOTGUN WITH CHOKEBORE a shotgun with a bore that tapers towards the muzzle

choke chain *n.* a chain serving as a collar and short lead that fits in a sliding loop around an animal's neck, so that when the animal pulls away the chain gets tighter. Choke chains are used in obedience training for dogs and to restrain powerful animals.

chokecherry /chṓk cheri/ (*plural* **-ries**) *n.* **1.** (*plural* **-ries** *or* **-ry**) N AMERICAN WILD CHERRY a North American wild cherry that produces long clusters of small white flowers, followed by dark red or black bitter fruit. Latin name: *Prunus virginiana.* **2.** FRUIT OF CHOKECHERRY the fruit of the chokecherry

choke coil *n.* a type of induction coil used to limit or suppress the flow of alternating current without stopping the flow of direct current

choke collar *n.* = **choke chain**

choked /chōkt/ *adj.* overcome by emotion, usually unhappiness, disappointment, or resentment (*informal*) US term **choked up**

chokedamp /chṓk damp/ *n.* MINING = **blackdamp**

choked up *adj.* US = **choked** (*informal*)

chokehold /chṓk hōld/ *n.* = **stranglehold**

choke point *n.* **1.** AREA OF BLOCKAGE a congested or narrow part where a blockage can occur **2.** NAVY NARROW SHALLOW SEA CORRIDOR a place at sea where geography and water depth combine to create a narrow shallow corridor for submarines and surface ships **3.** *Can, US* STICKING POINT a point or situation that is an obstacle to an agreement or results in an impasse ○ *amnesty being the choke point in the political settlement*

choker /chṓkər/ *n.* **1.** NECK ORNAMENT a short length of cloth or ribbon, or a short necklace, that fastens closely around the neck and is worn as an ornament **2.** HIGH CLOSE-FITTING COLLAR a high close-fitting collar, e.g. a clerical collar

chokey *n.* = **choky**

choko /chṓkō/ (*plural* **-kos**) *n.* a light green, pear-shaped tropical fruit of a cayote plant, tasting like a cucumber, that is eaten as a vegetable in Australia, New Zealand, and the West Indies [Early 20thC. From Brazilian Indian *chuchu*.]

choky /chṓki/, **chokey** *n.* prison (*dated slang*) ○ *three months in choky* [Early 17thC. From Hindi *caukī* 'toll station, lock-up', influenced by CHOKE 'to restrict breathing'. Originally used by the British in India.]

cholangiography /kō lánji óggrəfi/ *n.* X-ray examination of the bile ducts to check for obstructions, carried out after the patient has swallowed a substance that shows up on an X-ray [Mid-20thC. Coined from CHOLE- + ANGIOGRAPHY.] —**cholangiogram** /kō lánji ə gram/ *n.* —**cholangiographic** /-ə gráffik/ *adj.*

chole- *prefix.* bile, bile ducts, gall bladder ○ *cholelithiasis* [From Greek *kholē*. Ultimately from an Indo-European base meaning 'yellow-coloured, bile', which is also the ancestor of English *bile*, *gall*, and *yellow*.]

cholecalciferol /kṓlə kal síffərol, kóllə-/ *n.* a type of vitamin D found naturally in fish-liver oils and egg yolks

cholecyst /kṓlə sist, kóllə-/ *n.* the gall bladder (*technical*)

cholecystectomy /kólə si stéktəmi, kóllə-/ (*plural* **-mies**) *n.* a surgical operation to remove the gall bladder

cholecystitis /kólə si stí tiss, kóllə-/ *n.* inflammation of the gall bladder, usually caused by a bacterial infection or gallstones

cholecystoduodenostomy /kólə sistō dyoŏ ŏdi nóstəmi, kóllə-/ (*plural* **-mies**) *n.* a surgical procedure in which the gall bladder is connected directly to the first part of the small intestine (**duodenum**)

cholecystography /kólə si stóggrəfi, kóllə-/ (*plural* **-phies**) *n.* X-ray examination of the gall bladder after the patient has swallowed a substance that shows up on an X-ray

cholecystokinin /kólə sistə kínin, kóllə-/ *n.* a hormone secreted by cells at the top of the small intestine that stimulates the gall bladder, making it contract and release bile [Early 20thC. Coined from CHOLECYST + KININ.]

cholelithiasis /kólə li thí əssiss, kóllə-/ *n.* the formation or presence of gallstones in the gall bladder or bile ducts

choler /kóllər/ *n.* **1.** BAD TEMPER anger or bad temper (*archaic or literary*) **2.** BODILY FLUID CAUSING BAD TEMPER one of the four basic fluids (**humours**) of the body according to medieval medicine, thought to make sb whose body contained too much of it prone to anger and irritability (*archaic*) [14thC. Via French *colère* from Latin *cholera* 'bile' (see CHOLERA), believed to cause bad temper.]

cholera /kóllərə/ *n.* an acute and often fatal intestinal disease that produces severe diarrhoea, vomiting, dehydration, and gastric pain, and is usually caused by swallowing food or water contaminated with a bacterium *Vibrio cholerae* [14thC. Via Latin, 'bile', originally 'illness caused by bile', from Greek *kholera*, from *kholē* 'bile'. Revived in its modern sense in the 17thC.] —**choleraic** /kóllə ráy ik/ *adj.* —**choleroid** /kóllə royd/ *adj.*

choleric /kóllərik/ *adj.* liable to become angry or irritated, or showing anger or irritation (*literary*) [14thC. Directly and via French *cholérique* from Latin *cholericus* 'bilious', from, ultimately, Greek *kholera* (see CHOLERA).] —**cholerically** *adv.*

cholestasis /kóli stáysiss, -stássiss, kólli-/ *n.* a stoppage or slowing of the flow of bile

cholesteatoma /kóli stee ə tṓmə, kólli-/ *n.* a potentially dangerous condition of the middle ear in which a mass of cholesterol and skin scales forms, grows, and invades the local structures, including bone

Cholesterol

cholesterol /kə léstə rol/ *n.* a steroid alcohol (**sterol**) found in animal tissue, bile, blood, eggs, and fats, high levels of which in the blood are linked to atherosclerosis, heart disease, and gallstones. Cholesterol is important to the body as a constituent of cell membranes, and is involved in the formation of bile acid and some hormones. Formula: $C_{27}H_{45}OH$. [Late 19thC. Coined from CHOLE- + Greek *stereos* 'stiff' + -OL.]

cholestyramine /kóli steərə meen, kō léstər ámmeen/ *n.* a synthetic resin used to lower cholesterol in the blood by binding it with bile acids [Mid-20thC. Coined from CHOLE- + STYRENE + -AMINE.]

choli /chóli/ (*plural* **-lis**) *n.* a short fitted top with short sleeves, worn underneath a sari [Early 20thC. From Hindi *colī*.]

choline /kṓ leen/ *n.* a soluble ammonia derivative (**amine**) that is found in animal and plant tissue and helps to prevent fat from being deposited in the liver. Choline is also involved in the formation of acetylcholine. Formula: $C_5H_{15}NO_2$. [Mid-19thC. Coined from CHOLE- + -INE.]

cholinergic /kóli núrjik/ *adj.* **1.** ACTIVATED BY OR RELEASING ACETYLCHOLINE used to describe nerve cells or fibres that are activated by acetylcholine or that release it **2.** RESEMBLING ACETYLCHOLINE used to describe drugs that resemble acetylcholine in the way they work or the effect they have [Mid-20thC. Coined from CHOLINE + Greek *ergon* 'work'.] —**cholinergically** *adv.*

cholinesterase /kólli néstə rayss, -rayz/ *n.* **1.** ENZYME an enzyme of the blood, brain, and heart that decomposes acetylcholine into acetic acid and choline, suppressing its stimulatory effect on nerves **2.** = acetylcholinesterase [Mid-20thC. Coined from CHOLINE + ESTERASE.]

cholla /chóy ə/ (*plural* **-las** *or* **-la**) *n.* a cactus of the southwestern United States and Mexico that has cylindrical stem segments and yellow spines. Some cultivated types have vividly coloured flowers. Genus: *Opuntia*. [Mid-19thC. From Mexican Spanish, from obsolete Spanish, 'top of the head', perhaps from Old French *cholle* 'round lump'.]

chomp /chomp/, **chump** *vti.* (**chomps, chomping, chomped; chumps, chumping, chumped**) CHEW NOISILY to take big bites of food and chew steadily, noisily, and with obvious satisfaction (*informal*) ■ *n.* (*informal*) **1.** NOISY BITE a big noisy bite into sth **2.** SOUND OF BITE the sound made by noisy energetic biting or chewing [Mid-17thC. Variant of CHAMP, and imitative of the sound.]

Chomsky /chómski/, **Noam** (*b.* 1928) US linguist. He is known for his transformational-generative grammar, which revolutionized linguistics, and for his political writings. Full name **Avram Noam Chomsky**

chon /chon/ (*plural* **chon**) *n.* **1.** KOREAN UNIT OF CURRENCY a subunit of currency in North and South Korea. See table at **currency 2.** COIN OR NOTE WORTH ONE CHON a coin note worth one chon [Mid-20thC. From Korean.]

chondr- *prefix.* = chondro-

chondral /kóndrəl/ *adj.* relating to or consisting of cartilage

chondri- *prefix.* = chondro-

chondrify /kóndri fī/ (**-fies, -fying, -fied**) *vti.* to change tissue into cartilage, or be changed into cartilage [Late 19thC. Formed from *khondros* 'cartilage'.] —**chondrification** /kóndri fi káysh'n/ *n.*

chondrite /kón drīt/ *n.* a stony meteorite that contains spherical masses (**chondrules**) of mainly silicate minerals [Mid-19thC. Coined from Greek *khondros* 'granule, cartilage' + -ITE.] —**chondritic** /kon dríttik/ *adj.*

chondro- *prefix.* **1.** cartilage ○ *chondrocranium* **2.** granule ○ *chondrule* [From Greek *khondros*]

chondrocranium /kón drō kráy ni əm/ (*plural* **-ums** *or* **-a** /-ni ə/) *n.* the part of an embryo's skull that consists of cartilage that later hardens into bone

chondroma /kon drṓmə/ (*plural* **-mas** *or* **-mata** /-mətə/) *n.* a benign abnormal growth of cartilage

chondrule /kón drool/ *n.* a small spherical mass of mineral matter from outer space, sometimes found in meteorites. Chondrules usually consist of olivine or pyroxene. [Late 19thC. Coined from CHONDRITE + -ULE.]

Chongqing /choŏng chíng/ city on the Yangtze River in southern Szechwan Province, south-central China. It was China's capital from 1937 to 1946. Population: 2,980,000 (1991).

Chonju /j/, **Chŏnju** /n joŏ/ town and capital of North Chŏlla Province, South Korea, situated 193 km/120 mi. south of Seoul. Population: 563,406 (1995).

choo-choo /choŏ choo/, **choo-choo train** *n.* a railway train or locomotive (*babytalk*) [Early 20thC. Imitation of the sound of a steam train.]

chook /choŏk, chook/ *n.* (*informal*) **1.** CHICKEN a hen or chicken **2.** ANZ WOMAN a woman, especially an older woman (*often used in a mildly contemptuous way*) [Mid-20thC. Alteration of earlier English dialect *chuck* 'chicken', an imitation of its clucking sound.]

choose /chooz/ (**chooses, choosing, chose** /chōz/, **chosen** /chōz'n/) *vti.* **1.** DECIDE FROM AMONG RANGE OF OPTIONS to decide which of a number of different things or people is best or most suitable **2.** MAKE A DELIBERATE DECISION to make a deliberate decision to do sth ○ *Jane has chosen to do the midwifery course.* [Old English *cēosan*. Ultimately from an Indo-European word that is also the ancestor of Latin *gustus* 'taste' (source of English *gusto*).] —**chooser** *n.*

choose up *vti.* US to pick the players wanted in a team for a game

choosy /choŏzi/ (**-ier, -iest**) *adj.* very precise or discriminating in preferences (*informal*) —**choosiness** *n.*

Cho Oyu /chṓ ố yoo/ mountain in the Himalaya range, one of the world's highest peaks. Height: 8,201 m/26,906 ft.

chop[1] /chop/ *v.* (**chops, chopping, chopped**) **1.** *vt.* CUT UP STH WITH SHARP TOOL to cut sth into pieces with downward strokes of an axe, knife, or other sharp-bladed tool ○ *a dish of chopped liver* **2.** *vt.* CUT OFF STH to use a quick sharp blow or blows to sever or fell sth ○ *chopped down the tree* **3.** *vi.* MAKE CHOPPING MOVEMENTS to make downward cutting movements with a tool or with the hand **4.** *vt.* FORM BY CHOPPING to make sth such as a hole or path by chopping with an axe or other tool ○ *He chopped his way through the undergrowth.* **5.** *vt.* GET RID OF STH OR SB to get rid of sth or sb, especially jobs or staff, put an end to sth, or curtail sth drastically (*informal*) ○ *Several junior members of staff have been chopped.* **6.** *vt.* SPORTS HIT BALL WITH SHARP DOWNWARD MOVEMENT to hit a ball with a quick sharp downward movement of the racket or bat, often in order to give the ball backspin **7.** *vt.* HIT SHARPLY DOWNWARDS to hit sb or sth with a sharp downward motion ■ *n.* **1.** FOOD SLICE OF MEAT WITH BONE a small piece of red meat cut from the ribs, loin, or shoulder, and usually with the bone still attached ○ *pork chops* **2.** SHARP STROKE DOWNWARDS a sudden strong downward blow with the hand or a cutting tool ○ *a karate chop* **3.** DISMISSAL dismissal from a job (*informal*) ○ *was given the chop* ○ *If the boss finds out, you'll be for the chop.* **4.** CLOSEDOWN the cancellation, closedown, or stoppage of sth (*informal*) ○ *Three of our rural offices are to get the chop.* **5.** IRREGULAR WAVE MOTION turbulent irregular motion in waves or water **6.** DISTURBED SEA a stretch of choppy water, especially on the sea [14thC. Variant of CHAP 'to crack open'.]

chop[2] /chop/ *v.* (**chops, chopping, chopped**) *vi.* to change direction or have a change of mind, especially suddenly or frequently [15thC. Variant of CHAP 'jaw'.] ◇ **chop and change** to have frequent changes mind, especially abruptly or in a way that disconcerts or irritates other people

chop[3] /chop/ *n.* a trademark, official stamp, or mark of quality, especially in the Far East ◇ **not much chop** not very good

chop-chop *interj.* used to indicate, often in a bossy or arrogant way, that sb should hurry or do sth quickly or right away (*informal*) [Mid-19thC. Repetition of Pidgin English *chop*, an alteration of Cantonese Chinese *gap* 'urgent'.] —**chop-chop** *adv.*

chophouse /chóp howss/ (*plural* **chophouses** /-howziz/) *n.* a restaurant serving grilled meat, e.g. chops and steaks, as its speciality, especially formerly

Frédéric François Chopin

Chopin /shóp aN, shŏp-/, **Frédéric François** (1810–49) Polish composer and pianist. His piano compositions include mazurkas, études, preludes, nocturnes, waltzes, polonaises, sonatas, and two concertos.

Chopin, Kate (1850–1904) US novelist, short-story writer, and poet. She wrote *The Awakening* (1899), a pioneering novel of female sexual discovery.

chopine /cho péen/, **chopin** /chóppin/ *n.* a type of high shoe with a very thick sole worn by European women in the 16th and 17th centuries [Late 16thC. Via Spanish *chapín* from Old French *chapin*.]

choplogic /chóp lojik/ *n.* the presentation of an argument in a way that is either illogical or pedantic and over-complicated [Early 16thC. *Chop* in the obsolete sense 'an exchange'.]

chopper /chóppər/ *n.* **1.** SMALL AXE a small axe **2.** CLEAVER a cutting tool with a handle and a sharp broad blade, used especially for chopping up meat **3.** HELICOPTER a helicopter (*informal*) **4.** BIKE WITH HIGH HANDLEBARS a motorcycle or bicycle with a lowered seat, raised handlebars, and lengthened forks holding the front wheel **5.** ELEC ENG INTERRUPTING DEVICE a device that regularly interrupts an electric current, a beam of light, or some other stream of radiation in order to produce a pulsing flow or beam **6.** PENIS the penis (*slang taboo*) ■ **choppers** *npl.* TEETH teeth, especially large or false ones (*slang*) ▪ *vti.* GO BY HELICOPTER to transport sth or sb by helicopter, or travel by helicopter (*informal*)

chopping board *n.* a piece of wood or plastic used for chopping food on. US term **cutting board**

choppy /chóppi/ (*-pier, -piest*) *adj.* rather rough, with the surface of the water broken up into many small waves made by strong winds —**choppily** *adv.* —**choppiness** *n.*

chops /chops/ *npl.* **1.** JAWS the jaws, or the skin covering the jaws (*informal*) **2.** MUSIC MUSICAL TALENT technique or virtuosity in playing an instrument, especially a wind instrument (*slang*)

chop shop *n.* US a workshop or garage where stolen vehicles are disguised or broken up for spare parts (*slang*)

chopsocky /chóp soki/ *n.* the genre of film in which martial arts, e.g. kung fu, feature prominently ○ *his latest chopsocky extravaganza* [Formed from CHOP + SOCK.]

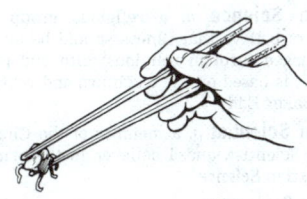

Chopsticks

chopstick /chóp stik/ *n.* either of a pair of narrow sticks that are held together in one hand and used when eating or preparing East Asian food [Late 17thC. *Chop* from Pidgin English, (see CHOP-CHOP). Translation of Chinese dialect *kuaizi*, literally 'nimble ones'.]

chop suey /chop soo i/ *n.* a Chinese-style dish made typically of shredded meat and mixed vegetables. It is Chinese-American rather than Chinese in origin. [Late 19thC. From Cantonese Chinese *tsaâp sui* literally, 'mixed bits'.]

choragus /kaw ráygəss/ (*plural* **-gi** /-jī, -gī/ *or* **-guses**) *n.* the leader of the chorus in ancient Greek drama [Early 17thC. Via Latin from Greek *khoragos*, literally 'to lead a chorus'.] —**choragic** /kaw rájjik, -ráyjik/ *adj.*

choral /káwrəl/ *adj.* **1.** PERFORMED BY CHOIR arranged for or performed by a chorus or choir ○ *choral singing* **2.** RELATING TO CHORUS OR CHOIR concerned with choral singing, choruses, or choirs ○ *a choral society* [Late 16thC. From medieval Latin *choralis*, from Latin *chorus* (see CHORUS).] —**chorally** *adv.*

chorale /ko ráal/ *n.* **1.** LUTHERAN HYMN TUNE a hymn tune, especially a slow and stately one, originally in-

tended for congregational singing in the Lutheran church **2.** PIECE OF MUSIC BASED ON CHORALE a piece of music, especially a choral work, based on a chorale tune or in a style reminiscent of traditional Lutheran church music **3.** US GROUP OF SINGERS a group of singers specializing in a particular style of music, especially church music [Mid-19thC. From German *Choral(gesang)*, a translation of Medieval Latin *(cantus) choralis* 'choral song'.]

chorale prelude *n.* an organ prelude based on a chorale tune, used to introduce congregational singing of the chorale on which it is based or performed as a separate piece

chord[1] /kawrd/ *n.* two or more musical notes played or sung simultaneously ○ *an F minor chord* [15thC. Shortening and alteration of ACCORD on the model of Latin *chorda*.]

WORD KEY: USAGE

chord or **cord**? In musical and mathematical contexts the spelling is *chord*, and this form is also used in figurative meanings that have to do with feelings: *They struck the right chord.* In anatomical contexts (*spinal cord, umbilical cord, vocal cords*), **cord** is more usual. **Cord** has to be used when referring to a kind of thick string.

chord[2] /kawrd/ *n.* **1.** GEOM LINE THROUGH ARC a straight line connecting two points on an arc or circle **2.** AIR AIRFOIL MEASURE the shortest distance between the leading and trailing edges of an airfoil **3.** ANAT = cord **4.** BUILDING HORIZONTAL CONNECTING PART the horizontal part of a truss designed to absorb tension, e.g. in a roof [Mid-16thC. Alteration of CORD, on the model of Latin *chorda*.] ◇ **strike** *or* **touch a chord** to produce an emotional, especially a sympathetic, response in sb, or jog sb's memory

chordal /káwrd'l/ *adj.* **1.** RELATING TO CHORDS consisting of chords, or played as a chord **2.** BASED ON CHORDS based principally on musical chords rather than linear melody

chordate /káwr dayt/ *n.* any animal that at some stage in its development has a main dorsal nerve cord, a skeletal rod (**notochord**), and gill slits. The chordates include all vertebrates and some primitive invertebrate marine animals. Phylum: Chordata. [Late 19thC. Formed from modern Latin *chordata*, from *chorda* 'cord'.] —**chordate** *adj.*

chordophone /káwrdə fōn/ *n.* a stringed instrument (*technical*) [Mid-20thC. Coined from CHORD + -PHONE.]

chord organ *n.* a small electronic organ with special keys to produce chords for accompanying a melody

chore /chawr/ *n.* **1.** ROUTINE TASK a task, especially an ordinary household task, that has to be done regularly (*often used in the plural*) **2.** UNENJOYABLE TASK sth that is unpleasant, difficult, awkward, or boring to do [Mid-18thC. Alteration of CHAR.]

-chore *suffix.* a plant distributed by a particular means ○ *anemochore* [From Greek *khōrein* 'to spread' (source also of English *anchorite*)]

chorea /ko ree ə/ *n.* jerky spasmodic movements of the limbs, trunk, and facial muscles, common to various diseases of the central nervous system [Late 17thC. Via Latin from Greek *khoreia* 'dance'. Probably a shortening of the Latin phrase *chorea sancti Viti* 'St Vitus's dance', a disease with this symptom.] —**choreal** *adj.* —**choreic** *adj.*

choreograph /kórri ə graaf/ *v.* **1.** *vti.* PLAN OUT DANCE ROUTINE to plan out the movements that dancers are to make to a piece of music **2.** *vt.* ORGANIZE to plan, coordinate, and supervise an event or activity ○ *His job is to choreograph royal weddings and other state occasions.* [Mid-20thC. Back-formation from CHOREOGRAPHY.] —**choreographer** /káw ri ógrəfər/ *n.*

choreography /kórri óggrəfi/ (*plural* **-phies**) *n.* **1.** COMPOSING DANCES the work or skill of planning dance movements to accompany music **2.** DANCE MOVEMENTS FOR PIECE the steps and movements planned for a ballet or dance routine, or a written record of them **3.** PLANNED MOVEMENT the carefully planned or executed organization of an event, or the manoeuvring of people or things [Late 18thC. From French *choreographie*, literally 'dance writing', from *choreo-* 'dance' (modelled on Greek *khoreia*) + *-graphie* 'writing'.] —**choreographic** /kórri ə gráffik/ *adj.* —**choreographically** /-gráffikli/ *adv.*

choriamb /kórri amb, -am/ *n.* a poetic foot consisting of two short syllables between two long ones, or two unstressed syllables between two stressed ones [Early 17thC. Via late Latin *choriambus* from Greek *khoriambos*, literally 'iamb of a chorus'.] —**choriambic** /kórri ámbik/ *adj.*

choric /kórrik/ *adj.* performed by or written for a chorus, especially a chorus in classical Greek theatre [Early 19thC. Via late Latin *choricus* from, ultimately, Greek *khoros*.]

chorioallantois /kórri ō ə lán tō iss, -állən tō iss/ *n.* a membrane surrounding the embryo and lying next to the shell in a bird's or reptile's egg. It is a fusion of the chorion and allantois membranes. In mammals, the chorioallantois of the egg forms a major part of the placenta. [Mid-20thC. Coined from CHORION + ALLANTOIS.] —**chorioallantoic** /kórri ō állən tố ik/ *adj.*

chorion /káw ri ən/ *n.* the outer membrane enclosing the embryo of mammals, reptiles, and birds. It has a dense concentration of blood vessels and aids in the formation of the placenta in mammals. ◊ **amnion** [Mid-16thC. From Greek *khorion*.] —**chorionic** /káwri ónnik/ *adj.*

chorionic gonadotrophin *n.* a hormone that stimulates the production of the oestrogen and progesterone needed for the maintenance of pregnancy

chorionic villus *n.* any of the tiny outgrowths from the outer membrane (**chorion**) surrounding an embryo that move into the womb wall to form the placenta (*often used in the plural*)

chorionic villus sampling *n.* a prenatal test for birth defects carried out by examining cells from the tiny hairy outgrowths (**villi**) of the outer membrane (**chorion**) surrounding an embryo, which have the same DNA as the foetus

chorister /kórristər/ *n.* a member of a chorus, choir, or other group of singers [14thC. Via an Anglo-Norman form of Old French *cuerist* from, ultimately, Latin *chorus* (see CHORUS). The spelling was changed in the 16thC on the model of CHOIR.]

chorizo /chə ree zō/ (*plural* **-zos**) *n.* a very spicy Mexican or Spanish pork sausage [Mid-19thC. From Spanish.]

C-horizon, C horizon *n.* the lowermost layer of soil immediately above bedrock

chorography /kə róggrəfi, kó-/ *n.* the preparation of maps in which specific areas or regions are delineated and often highlighted in some way, e.g. by colour-coding [Mid-16thC. Directly or via French from Latin *chorographia*, from Greek *khōrographia*, literally 'place writing'.] —**chorographer** *n.* —**chorographic** /kórrə gráffik/ *adj.* —**chorographically** /kórrə gráffikli/ *adv.*

choroid /káw royd/ *n.* choroid, choroid coat MEMBRANE OF THE EYE a brownish membrane between the retina and the white of the eye in vertebrates that contains blood vessels and large pigmented cells ■ *adj.* LIKE THE CHORION resembling the chorion in being vascular or membranous [Mid-17thC. From Greek *khoroeidēs*, from *khorion* 'chorion'.]

choroid plexus *n.* a membrane with many small blood vessels in the fluid spaces of the brain that secretes cerebrospinal fluid

chortle /cháwrt'l/ *n.* GLEEFUL LAUGH a noisy gleeful laugh ■ *vi.* (*-tles, -tling, -tled*) GIVE A CHORTLE to laugh in a noisy gleeful way [Late 19thC. Blend of CHUCKLE and SNORT, originated by Lewis Carroll in *Through the Looking-Glass* (1872).] —**chortler** *n.*

chorus /káwrəss/ *n.* **1.** MUSIC REPEATED PART OF A SONG a set of lines that are sung at least twice in the course of a song, usually being repeated after each verse **2.** THEATRE, ARTS GROUP OF PERFORMERS a group of people who appear, sing, and sometimes dance together as a unit in a performance, usually providing backing for the principal performers (*takes a singular or plural verb*) **3.** THEATRE GROUP OF ACTORS IN GREEK DRAMA a group of actors in ancient Greek drama who sing or speak in unison, generally commenting on the significance of the events that take place in the play **4.** THEATRE VERSE PASSAGE FOR GREEK DRAMA CHORUS any of the verse passages in an ancient Greek drama intended to be sung or spoken by the chorus **5.** THEATRE DRAMA ROLE a role in some Elizabethan and historical dramas for a solo actor, who speaks the introductory prologue, comments on the action, and delivers the epilogue **6.** MUSIC **MUSIC FOR GROUP** a musical composition written for a large group of singers, usually with different parts for the different voice types ○ *the Hallelujah Chorus* **7.** MANY VOICES TOGETHER the words spoken or feelings expressed by a group of people all giving voice at the same time ○ *a chorus of complaints* **8.** GROUP SPEAKING OR MAKING NOISE TOGETHER a group of people or animals all speaking or making a noise together ■ *vt.* (**-ruses, -rusing, -rused**) SAY TOGETHER to speak at the same time, saying the same thing or expressing the same feeling or opinion [Mid-16thC. Via Latin from Greek *khoros*.] ◇ **in chorus** all speaking or making a noise together

chorus boy *n.* a man or boy who sings and dances as one of the supporting group of performers in a stage or film production

chorus girl *n.* a woman or girl who sings and dances as one of the supporting group of performers in a stage or film production

chorus line *n.* the chorus of supporting singers and dancers in a musical or variety show

chorusmaster /káwrəss maastər/ *n.* sb who trains, rehearses, and directs a chorus

-chory *suffix.* = **-chore**

chose past tense of **choose**

chosen past participle of **choose** ■ *adj.* SELECTED picked out from or preferred to the rest ○ *one of the chosen few* ■ *npl.* RELIG = **elect**

chosen people *npl.* the Jews, who, according to the Bible and their own belief, were selected by God to play a unique role in world history

chou /shoo/ (*plural* **choux** /shoo/) *n.* **1.** FILLED SWEET PASTRY a small pastry with a fruit or cream filling **2.** = **choux pastry** [Early 18thC. From French, 'cabbage'.]

chouette /shoo ét/ *n.* a variation of backgammon in which one player plays against two or more opponents in one game [Late 19thC. From French, literally 'barn owl'.]

chough /chuf/ *n.* a Eurasian bird of the crow family, roughly the size of a pigeon, that has glossy black plumage, red legs and feet, and a red or yellow bill. Genus: *Pyrrhocorax*. [12thC. Probably an imitation of its call.]

Chouteau /shootó/, **René Auguste** (1749–1829) US pioneer. He founded St Louis, Missouri (1764), and was an important figure in the local fur trade.

choux pastry *n.* a soft glossy egg-rich pastry that puffs up into a hollow case when baked. It is used in making filled pastries such as cream puffs and éclairs.

chow[1] /chow/ *n.* food (*slang*) [Late 18thC. Shortening of Chinese Pidgin English *chow-chow* 'food, mixture', perhaps from Chinese *cha* 'mixed'.]

    chow down *vi.* US to eat food enthusiastically (*informal*)

chow[2] /chow/, **chow chow** *n.* a stocky thick-coated dog belonging to a breed originally from China, with a tail that curls over its back and a large dark purplish tongue [Late 19thC. From Pidgin English, possibly from Cantonese Chinese *gŏu* 'dog'.]

chow[3] /chow/ *n.* FOOD = **chow-chow**

chow chow *n.* ZOOL = **chow**[2]

chow-chow, **chow** *n.* **1.** TANGY SWEET MIXTURE IN SYRUP a Chinese mixture of fruit and candied peel in syrup, with stem ginger **2.** CHINESE MIXED VEGETABLE PICKLE a Chinese mixed vegetable pickle in a yellow sauce, similar to piccalilli

chowder /chówdər/ *n.* a thick soup, especially one made with seafood or fish [Mid-18thC. Probably via French *chaudière* 'stew pot', from, ultimately, Latin *calidarium* 'hot bath', source of English *cauldron*.]

chowderhead /chówdər hed/ *n.* US a fool or idiot (*informal*) [Mid-19thC. Alteration of English dialect *jolterhead*, by association with CHOWDER.] **—chowderheaded** *adj.*

chowhound /chów hownd/ *n.* US sb who especially enjoys eating (*informal*)

chow mein /chów máyn/ *n.* a Chinese-style dish of soft fried noodles, usually cooked with chopped meat and vegetables [From Mandarin Chinese *chăo miàn* 'fried noodles']

Chr. *abbr.* **1.** Christ **2.** Christian **3.** BIBLE Chronicles

chrestomathy /kre stómməthi/ (*plural* **-thies**) *n.* a collection of literary passages, especially one assembled for language study [Mid-19thC. Directly or via French *chrestomathie* from Greek *khrēstomatheia*, literally 'useful learning'.] **—chrestomathic** /krés tə máthik/ *adj.*

Chrétien /krétti aN/, **Jean** (*b.* 1934) Canadian politician. He became leader of the Liberal party and prime minister of Canada in 1990. Full name **Jean Joseph-Jacques Chrétien**

Chrétien de Troyes /krétti aN də tróyz/ (*fl.* 1170) French poet. His epics were the first to incorporate Arthurian legends and the quest for the Holy Grail.

chrism /krízzəm/ *n.* **1.** ANOINTING OIL consecrated oil, or a consecrated mixture of balsam and oil, used for anointing people at some ceremonies in the Roman Catholic, Anglican, and Orthodox churches **2.** ANOINTING WITH HOLY OIL a ceremonial anointing with holy oil, especially at confirmation in the Eastern Orthodox churches [Pre-12thC. Via medieval Latin *crisma* from Greek *khrisma* 'an anointing', from *khriein* 'to anoint' (source of English *Christ* and *cream*).] **—chrismal** /krízm'l/ *adj.*

chrismation /kriz máysh'n/ *n.* in the Eastern Orthodox tradition, the act of anointing sb, or being anointed, with holy oil in a religious ceremony such as confirmation [Mid-16thC. From the medieval Latin stem *chrismation-*, from *crisma* (see CHRISM).]

chrisom /krízzəm/ *n.* a white robe or shawl worn by an infant for his or her baptism (*formal*) [13thC. Alteration of CHRISM, which was popularly pronounced with two syllables.]

chrisom child *n.* a baby that dies within a month of its baptism (*archaic*)

Chrissie /kríssi/ *n.* Christmas (*informal*) [Late 20thC. From CHRISTMAS.]

Christ /krīst/ *n.* **1.** CHR = **Jesus Christ 2.** RELIG THE MESSIAH according to the Bible, a saviour who would come to deliver God's chosen people **3.** RELIG PAINTING OF JESUS CHRIST an artistic representation of Jesus Christ ■ *interj.* SWEARWORD used to express surprise, annoyance, exasperation, or alarm (*taboo*) [Pre-12thC. Via Latin *Christus* from Greek *Khristos*, literally 'anointed', from *khriein* 'to anoint' (source of English *chrism*), a translation of Hebrew *māšīāh* 'Messiah'.] **—Christhood** *n.* — **Christly** *adj.*

Christadelphian /krístə délfi ən/ *n.* a member of a religious group founded by John Thomas in the United States around 1848. Christadelphians reject the doctrine of the Trinity as not in the Bible and believe in the dead being resurrected with the Second Coming of Christ. [Mid-19thC. Formed from late Greek *Khristadelphos*, literally 'in brotherhood with Christ'.] **—Christadelphian** *adj.*

Christchurch /krīst church/ **1.** town and resort in Dorset, southern England, situated at the confluence of the Avon and Stour rivers, 37 km/23 mi. southwest of Southampton. Population: 40,500 (1991). **2.** city situated near the eastern coast of South Island, New Zealand, 13 km/8 mi. northwest of Lyttelton. Population: 331,443 (1996).

christen /kríss'n/ *vt.* **1.** BAPTIZE AND NAME to make sb, especially a baby, a member of the Christian church in a ceremony that includes a form of baptism and, usually, the giving of a Christian name or names **2.** GIVE NAME TO STH OR SB to give a name to sth or sb, with or without an accompanying ceremony ○ *christen a ship* **3.** USE FOR FIRST TIME to use or wear sth for the first time (*informal*) ○ *Shall we christen our new coffee pot?* [Pre-12thC. Formed from Old English *crīsten* 'Christian', from Latin *christianus*.] **—christener** *n.*

Christendom /kríss'ndəm/ *n.* **1.** CHRISTIAN COUNTRIES all the areas of the world where Christianity is accepted as the main religion **2.** CHRISTIANS AS A GROUP all Christian people considered as a group (*archaic* or *formal*) ◇ **Christianity** *n.* **3** [Old English *cristendom*, literally 'condition of being Christian', from *crīsten*]

christening /kríss'ning/ *n.* a ceremony in a Christian church in which sb, especially a baby, is baptized and usually given a Christian name or names

Christian /krísschən/ *n.* BELIEVER IN JESUS CHRIST AS SAVIOUR sb who believes that Jesus of Nazareth was sent to the world by God to save humanity, and who tries to follow his teachings and example ■ *adj.* **1.** CHR FROM THE TEACHINGS OF JESUS CHRIST based on or relating to a belief in Jesus of Nazareth as the son of God and Messiah, and acceptance of his teachings, contained in the Gospels **2.** RELATING TO CHRISTIANITY relating to Christianity, or belonging to or maintained by a Christian organization, especially a church ○ *Christian theology* ○ *a Christian school* **3.** KIND AND UNSELFISH showing qualities such as kindness, helpfulness, and concern for others (*dated*) [13thC. From Latin *Christianus*, from *Christus* (see CHRIST).] **— Christianly** *adv.*

Christian VIII /krísschən, krísti ən/ (1786–1848) Danish ruler who was elected to the Norwegian throne in 1814 but ousted the same year. During his Danish reign (1839–48), his Schleswig-Holstein policy precipitated war with Prussia (1848).

Christian Democrat *n.* a member or supporter of a political party of the moderate right, especially in continental Europe, known as the Christian Democratic Party

Christian Era *n.* the period of history dating from the year in which Jesus Christ is believed to have been born. Dates in the early Christian Era are often indicated by AD, and dates before the Christian Era by BC.

Christianise *vt.* = **Christianize**

Christianity /kríss ti ánnəti/ *n.* **1.** RELIGION THAT FOLLOWS JESUS CHRIST'S TEACHINGS the religion based on the life, teachings, and example of Jesus Christ **2.** HOLDING CHRISTIAN BELIEFS the fact of holding Christian beliefs or being a Christian **3.** CHRISTIANS AS A GROUP all Christian people considered as a group. ◇ **Christendom**

Christianize /krísschə nīz/ (**-izes, -izing, -ized**), **Christianise** (**-ises, -ising, -ised**) *vt.* **1.** CHANGE BELIEFS TO CHRISTIAN ONES to change the religious beliefs and practices of a person or group of people from another religion to Christianity **2.** MAKE CHRISTIAN to make sb or sth Christian by imbuing him, her, or it with Christian principles or a Christian spirit **—Christianization** /krísschə nī záysh'n/ *n.* **—Christianizer** /krísschə nīzər/ *n.*

Christian name *n.* a first name, especially one given at christening

Christian Science *n.* a religious group whose members believe that illness should be overcome or managed through religious faith and practice alone. It is based on the teachings and writings of Mary Baker Eddy.

Christian Scientist *n.* a member of the Church of Christ, Scientist, and a believer in the principles of Christian Science

Christian Scriptures *npl.* the New Testament of the Bible as opposed to the Old Testament (**Hebrew Scriptures**)

christie /krísti/, **christy** (*plural* **-ties**) *n.* in skiing, a type of turn used for stopping or rapidly changing direction, in which the skier twists sharply aside while keeping the skis parallel [Early 20thC. Shortening of *Christiania*, the former name of Norway's capital city, Oslo.]

AKG London

Dame Agatha Christie

Christie /krísti/, **Dame Agatha** (1891–1976) British novelist and playwright. She wrote over seventy detective novels featuring the sleuths Hercule Poirot and Miss Marple.

Christie, Linford (b. 1960) Jamaican-born British athlete. In 1993, he held the World, Olympic, Commonwealth, and European Cup titles for the 100 metres.

Christina /kri steenə/ (1626–89) Swedish monarch who, in 1644, negotiated the Peace of Westphalia, bringing to an end the Thirty Years' War.

christingle /krístng g'l/, **Christingle** n. a Christmas decoration made by children in some Christian churches, consisting of a candle in an orange symbolizing Jesus Christ as the light of the world [Mid-20thC. Probably an alteration of German *Christkindl* 'Christmas present, Christ-child', modelled on *Kriss Kringle*.]

Christmas /kríssməss/ n. **1. Christmas CHRISTIAN FESTIVAL CELEBRATING BIRTH OF JESUS CHRIST** an annual Christian festival on 25 December, celebrating the birth of Jesus Christ **2. SECULAR HOLIDAY ON 25 DECEMBER** a secular holiday on 25 December when people traditionally exchange presents and greetings. It is a public holiday in many countries. **3. CHRISTMAS PERIOD** the period around 25 December, or the church season extending from 24 December to 6 January **4. QUARTER DAY** in England, Wales, and Ireland, one of the four quarter days, falling on 25 December [Old English *Cristes mæsse*, literally 'mass of Christ']

Christmas beetle n. a greenish-gold scarab beetle common in Australia, particularly around Christmas time. Genus: *Anoplognathus*.

Christmas box n. a gift of money traditionally given by a householder or business, at Christmas, to workers who have provided a service throughout the year

Christmas bush n. an Australian tree belonging to any of the species whose colourful flowers are used as Christmas decorations

Christmas cactus n. a branching Brazilian cactus that is cultivated as an ornamental plant for its red, pink, white, or purplish-red flowers that appear in winter. Latin name: *Schlumbergera truncata*.

Christmas cake n. a rich dark fruitcake, usually with spice, nuts, and often brandy added, traditionally covered with marzipan and white icing. This cake is prepared in advance and then iced and decorated ready to be eaten at Christmastime.

Christmas card n. an illustrated greetings card sent at Christmas

Christmas carol n. a Christian song celebrating Christmas

Christmas club n. a savings account in which money is deposited regularly throughout the year in order to buy gifts and additional food and drink for Christmas

Christmas cracker n. = cracker

Christmas Day n. = Christmas n. 1, Christmas n. 2

Christmas disease n. a form of haemophilia caused by lack of a protein needed for blood clotting [Mid-20thC. Named after Stephen *Christmas*, a 20th-century Englishman who had the disease.]

Christmas Eve n. the day or evening of 24 December

Christmas Island /kríssməss-/ former name for **Kiritimati** (until 1981)

Christmas pudding n. a rich steamed pudding made with dried fruit, spices, and usually candied peel and brandy, prepared and cooked in advance, then reheated for serving at the main Christmas meal

Christmas rose n. an evergreen flowering plant, native to Europe and Asia, that has drooping white flowers during the winter. Latin name: *Helleborus niger*.

Christmas stocking n. a stocking or large sock hung up on Christmas Eve by children, in the belief that it will be filled with presents by Santa Claus during the night

Christmassy adj. suggesting the Christmas period or suitable for Christmas ○ *The decorations look really Christmassy.*

Christmastime /kríssməss tīm/ n. = **Christmas** n. 3

Christmas tree n. an evergreen tree, especially a conifer or an artificial version of one, that is decorated with lights and ornaments at Christmas

Christocentric /krístə séntrik, krístō–/ adj. **1. ASSUMING CHRISTIANITY** assuming, implying, or based on Christian values and beliefs, often where this is inappropriate **2. CENTRED ON JESUS CHRIST** concentrating or based strongly on Jesus Christ and his teachings

Christoff /kríst of/, **Boris** (1919–93) Bulgarian operatic singer. His repertoire spanned around 40 roles in six languages, including acclaimed performances in Modest Mussorgsky's *Boris Godunov*.

Christogram /krístə gram/ n. = **Chi-Rho**

Christology /kri stóllǝji/ n. the branch of theology concerned with the study of the nature, character, and actions of Jesus Christ —**Christological** /krístə lójjik'l/ adj. —**Christologist** /kri stóllǝjist/ n.

Christopher /krístəfər/, **St** (fl. 3rd century) According to legend, he carried Jesus Christ as a child across a river. He is the patron saint of travellers.

Christ's thorn, **Christ thorn** n. a thorny Asian shrub or tree, especially a jujube or a Jerusalem thorn, whose branches are popularly believed to have been used for Jesus Christ's crown of thorns

christy n. SKIING = **christie**

chrom- prefix. = **chromo-** (used before vowels)

chroma /krōmə/ n. = **saturation** [Late 19thC. From Greek *khrōma* 'colour'.]

chromaffin /krōməfin/ adj. used to describe cell components that can be easily and deeply stained with chromium salts, thereby indicating the presence of adrenaline or noradrenaline [Early 20thC. Coined from CHROMO- + Latin *affinis* 'related'.]

chromat- prefix. = **chromato-** (used before vowels)

chromate /krṓ mayt/ n. any salt or ester of chromic acid [Early 20thC. Formed from CHROMIC.]

chromatic /krō máttik/ adj. **1. MUSIC RELATING TO CHROMATIC SCALES** used to describe a musical scale that runs through all the semitones in an octave, e.g. using all the keys, black and white, on a keyboard **2. MUSIC HAVING FREQUENT ACCIDENTALS** used to describe music that is based on the chromatic scale or that makes frequent use of notes that are outside the key in which it is written **3. RELATING TO COLOUR** relating to colour and phenomena connected with it [15thC. Directly or via French *chromatique* from, ultimately, Greek *chrōmatikos*, from *khrōma* 'colour'.] —**chromatically** adv.

chromatic aberration n. an optical aberration in a lens, caused by a defect and leading to different coloured light being refracted differently

chromaticism /krō máttisizzəm/ n. the use in music of the chromatic scale, or of many notes and harmonies that are foreign to the basic key

chromaticity /krōmə tíssiti/ n. the colour quality of light precisely and uniquely defined in terms of three factors (**chromaticity coordinates**)

chromatics /krō máttiks/ n. the science or study of colour (*takes a singular verb*) —**chromatist** /krṓmətist/ n.

chromatid /krṓmətid/ n. either of the two strands into which a chromosome divides in the process of duplicating itself in cell division [Early 20thC. Formed from the Greek stem *khrōmat-*, from *khrōma* 'colour'.]

chromatin /krṓmətin/ n. the substance that forms chromosomes and contains DNA, RNA, and various proteins [Late 19thC. Formed from the Greek stem *khrōmat-*, from *khrōma* 'colour'.] —**chromatinic** /krṓmə tínnik/ adj.

chromato- prefix. **1.** colour ○ *chromatography* **2.** chromatin ○ *chromatolysis* [From Greek *khrōmat-*, the stem of *khrōma* 'colour']

chromatogram /krə máttə gram, krṓmətə gram/ n. a pattern formed by substances that have been separated by chromatography

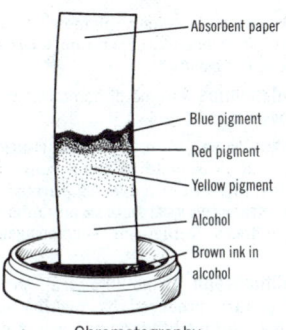

Chromatography

Labels: Absorbent paper; Blue pigment; Red pigment; Yellow pigment; Alcohol; Brown ink in alcohol

chromatography /krōmə tóggrəfi/ n. a method of finding out which components a gaseous or liquid mixture contains that involves passing it through or over sth that absorbs the different components at different rates —**chromatograph** /krə máttə graaf, –graf/ n. —**chromatographer** /krōmə tóggrəfər/ n. —**chromatographic** /krōmətə gráffik/ adj. —**chromatographically** /–gráffikli/ adv.

chromatolysis /krōmə tóllississ/ n. the breakdown of the substance that forms chromosomes (**chromatin**) within an injured cell nucleus [Late 19thC. Coined from CHROMATO- + -LYSIS.]

chromatophore /krə máttə fawr/ n. **1.** ZOOL **PIGMENT-CONTAINING CELL** a pigment-containing cell in many animals that, when it expands or contracts, causes a change in the animal's skin colouring. Octopus, squid, and some frogs and lizards contain these cells. **2.** BOT = **chromoplast** —**chromatophoric** /krə máttə fórrik/ adj.

chrome /krōm/ n. **1.** CHEM = **chromium 2. COMPOUND CONTAINING CHROMIUM** an alloy, dye, or pigment containing chromium **3. CHROMIUM-PLATED METAL** shiny chromium-plated metal, e.g. that used formerly to trim cars ■ vt. (**chromes, chroming, chromed**) **1. COAT WITH CHROMIUM** to electroplate a metal with chromium in order to make it shiny and protect it against corrosion **2. TREAT WITH CHROMIUM COMPOUND** to treat a substance with a chromium compound, usually when dyeing or tanning it [Early 19thC. Via French from Greek *khrōma* 'colour',; because compounds containing it are often brightly coloured.]

-chrome suffix. colour, pigment ○ *phytochrome* [From Greek *khrōma* 'colour']

chrome alum n. a red-violet crystalline solid used as a fixing agent in dyeing, tanning, and photography. Formula: $CrK(SO_4)_2.12H_2O$.

chrome green n. a brilliant green pigment containing chrome yellow and iron blue, used to dye fabrics

chrome red n. a bright red-orange pigment containing lead chromate and lead oxide, used in paints and dyes

chrome tape n. magnetic recording tape that is coated with chromium dioxide

chrome yellow n. a yellow pigment containing lead chromate and lead sulphate

chromic /krṓmik/ adj. relating to or containing chromium with a valency of 3

chromic acid n. an unstable oxidizing acid existing only in solution or in the form of a salt. Formula: H_2CrO_4.

chromite /krṓ mīt/ n. a brownish-black mineral ore consisting of an oxide of iron and chromium. It is the only commercial source of chromium. Formula: $FeCr_2O_4$.

chromium /krṓ mi əm/ n. a bluish-white metallic element used in alloys and electroplating to increase hardness and resistance to corrosion. Its compounds are used as pigments, as catalysts, and in tanning. Symbol **Cr**

chromium dioxide n. a black crystalline solid used to coat recording tape because of its magnetic properties. Formula: CrO_2.

chromo /krṓ mō/ (plural **-mos**) n. a chromolithograph [Mid-19thC. Shortening.]

chromo- *prefix.* **1.** colour, pigment ○ *chromolithograph* ○ *chromogen* **2.** chromium ○ *chromite* [From Greek *khrōma* 'colour']

chromodynamics /krṓ mō dī námmiks/ *n.* = **quantum chromodynamics**

chromogen /krṓmajən/ *n.* **1.** POTENTIAL PIGMENT any substance that is capable of being converted into a biological pigment or a dye, e.g. through oxidation **2.** PIGMENT-PRODUCING MICROORGANISM any microorganism that produces a pigment —**chromogenic** /krṓma jénnik/ *adj.*

chromolithograph /krṓmō líthə graaf, -graf/ *n.* a coloured picture produced by making and superimposing multiple lithographs, each of which adds a different colour —**chromolithographer** /krṓmali thóggrəfar/ *n.* —**chromolithographic** /krṓmō líthə gráffik/ *adj.* —**chromolithography** /krṓmōli thóggrəfi/ *n.*

chromomere /krṓma meer/ *n.* a small, dense, bead-shaped granule of chromatin, found at intervals along a chromosome during cell division —**chromomeric** /krṓma méerik, -mérrik/ *adj.*

chromonema /krṓma néemə/ (*plural* **-mata** /-mətə/) *n.* the coiled central filament that forms the core of a chromosome strand (**chromatid**) [Early 20thC. Coined from CHROMO- + Greek *nēma* 'thread'.] —**chromonemal** /krṓma néeməl/ *adj.*

chromophore /krṓma fawr/ *n.* a group of atoms in a molecule that produces colour in dyes and other compounds through selective absorption of light, e.g. the azo group —**chromophoric** /krṓma fórrik/ *adj.*

chromoplast /krṓma plast/ *n.* a membrane-surrounded structure (**plastid**) in a plant cell that contains pigment. Red, yellow, or orange chromoplasts contain carotenoid pigments, and green chromoplasts (**chloroplasts**) contain chlorophyll.

chromoprotein /krṓma prṓ teen/ *n.* any protein that contains a pigmented, nonprotein, metal-containing chemical group. Haemoglobins and carotenoids are chromoproteins.

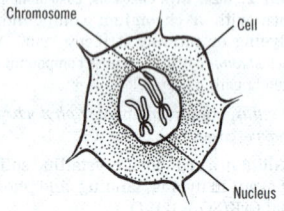

Chromosome

chromosome /krṓma sōm/ *n.* a rod-shaped structure in a cell nucleus carrying the genes that determine sex and the characteristics an organism inherits from its parents. A normal human body cell contains 46 chromosomes arranged in 23 pairs. [Late 19thC. From German *Chromosom*, formed from Greek *khrōma* 'colour' + *sōma* 'body',; because chromosomes readily take up dye.] —**chromosomal** /krṓma sṓm'l/ *adj.*

chromosome band *n.* a pattern produced in a chromosome by using a stain, making the chromosome identifiable from other chromosomes

chromosome map *n.* = **genetic map**

chromosome number *n.* the number of chromosomes present in the cell nucleus of a species of plant or animal. A normal human body has a chromosome number of 46.

chromosphere /krṓma sfeer/ *n.* **1.** LOWER REGION OF SUN'S ATMOSPHERE the lower region of the Sun's atmosphere, between the photosphere and the corona **2.** LOWER ATMOSPHERE OF STAR the lower region of the atmosphere of any star —**chromospheric** /krṓma sférrik/ *adj.*

chromous /krṓmass/ *adj.* relating to or containing chromium, especially chromium in its divalent state [Mid-19thC. Formed from CHROMIUM.]

chron. *abbr.* **1.** chronicle **2.** chronological **3.** chronology

Chron. *abbr.* BIBLE Chronicles

chron- *prefix.* = **chrono-** (*used before vowels*)

chronic /krónnik/ *adj.* **1.** MED LONG-LASTING used of an illness or medical condition that lasts over a long period and sometimes causes a long-term change in the body **2.** MED WITH LONG-TERM ILLNESS having a particular long-term illness or condition **3.** ALWAYS PRESENT always present or recurring **4.** HABITUAL repeatedly doing sth or behaving compulsively ○ *a chronic liar* **5.** DIRE terrible or appalling (*informal*) [15thC. Via French *chronique* from, ultimately, Greek *khronikos* 'to do with time', from *khronos* 'time'.] —**chronically** *adv.* —**chronicity** /krə níssəti/ *n.*

— **WORD KEY: USAGE** —
Meaning trap: *Chronic*, used both of illness and in general meanings (as in *a chronic problem*), essentially denotes continuation over a long period of time, as its origin in the Greek word for 'time' suggests, rather than severity, although this is often also the case. It should not be confused with *acute*, which denotes suddenness and intensity. So a *chronic* pain is one that lasts a long time whereas an *acute* pain is one that comes on suddenly and may last only a short time. In its informal meaning 'bad' or 'dreadful', *chronic* has lost all its sense of time, and for this reason and because of its apparent trivialization of a meaning used in serious contexts, many people dislike it: *Drink! my word! Something chronic* (G. B.Shaw, *Pygmalion*).

chronic fatigue syndrome *n.* = **ME**

chronicle /krónnik'l/ *n.* **1.** HISTORICAL ACCOUNT an account of events presented in chronological order **2.** NARRATIVE a narrative or fictional account ■ *vt.* (**-cles, -cling, -cled**) MAKE RECORD OF to record an event or series of events in chronological order [14thC. Via Anglo-Norman *cronicle* from, ultimately, Greek *khronika* (plural) 'annals', from *khronos* 'time'.] —**chronicler** *n.*

chronicle play *n.* a play based on historical events, especially one from the Elizabethan period

Chronicles /krónnik'lz/ *n.* either of two books of the Bible that tell the story of the Israelites from the creation of Adam to the middle of the 6th century BC (*takes a singular verb*)

chrono- *prefix.* TIME time ○ *chronograph* [From Greek *khronos* 'time']

chronobiology /krónnə bī ólləji, krṓnō-/ *n.* the study of recurring cycles of events in the natural world —**chronobiologic** /krónnə bī ə lójjik, krṓnō-/ *adj.* —**chronobiologist** /krónnə bī ólləjist, krṓnō-/ *n.*

chronogram /krónnə gram, krṓnə-/ *n.* a phrase or inscription containing letters indicating a date. Roman numerals are often used in this way. —**chronogrammatic** /krónnəgrə máttik, krṓnō-/ *adj.* —**chronogrammatically** /-máttikli/ *adv.*

chronograph /krónnə graf, -graaf, krṓnə-/ *n.* an instrument, e.g. a stopwatch, that records time with great accuracy —**chronographic** /krónnə gráffik, krṓnə-/ *adj.* —**chronographically** /-gráffikli/ *adv.*

chronol., chron. *abbr.* **1.** chronological **2.** chronology

chronological /krónnə lójjik'l, krṓnə-/ *adj.* **1.** IN ORDER OF TIME presented or arranged in the order in which events occur or occurred **2.** OF CHRONOLOGY relating to chronology —**chronologically** *adv.*

chronological age *n.* sb's real age, as opposed to the age suggested by mental or physical development

chronologist /krə nólləjist/ *n.* sb who studies, or is an expert in applying, the methods used for determining the correct sequence of events

chronology /krə nólləji/ (*plural* **-gies**) *n.* **1.** ORDER OF EVENTS the order in which events occur, or their arrangement according to this order **2.** LIST OF EVENTS a list or table of events arranged in order of occurrence **3.** STUDY OF ORDER IN TIME the study of, or the science of determining, the order in which things occur [Late 16thC. From modern Latin *chronologia*, formed from Greek *khronos* 'time'.]

chronometer /krə nómmitar/ *n.* any instrument designed to measure time accurately

chronometric /krónnə méttrik, krṓnə-/, **chronometrical** /-méttrik'l/ *adj.* relating to or designed for the accurate measurement of time —**chronometrically** *adv.*

chronometry /krə nómmətri/ *n.* the study or science of the accurate measurement of time

chronon /krṓ non/ *n.* a unit of time equal to the time that it would take for a photon to cross the diameter of an electron, taken as approximately 10^{-24} seconds [Coined from CHRONO- + -ON]

chronoscope /krónnə skōp, krṓnə-/ *n.* an electronic instrument that is designed to measure very small intervals of time with extreme precision —**chronoscopic** /krónnə skóppik, krṓnə-/ *adj.*

chrysalid /kríssəlid/ *adj.* AT THE CHRYSALIS STAGE used to describe the stage between larva and adult in an insect and the protective covering formed at this time ■ *n.* (*plural* **chrysalids** or **chrysalides**) = **chrysalis** [Late 18thC. From Latin *chrysa(l)lid-*, the stem of *chrysa(l)lis* (see CHRYSALIS).]

chrysalis /kríssəliss/ *n.* **1.** INSECT BETWEEN LARVA AND ADULT an insect at the stage of changing from larva to adult, during which it is inactive and encased in a hard cocoon **2.** INSECT COCOON the hard cocoon that protects a butterfly, moth, or other pupa during its change from larva to adult **3.** THING DEVELOPING anything in an early or intermediate stage of development (*literary*) [Early 17thC. Via Latin *chrysal(l)is* from Greek *khrūsalis*, from *khrūsos* 'gold', from the gold colour or metallic sheen of the pupae of some species.]

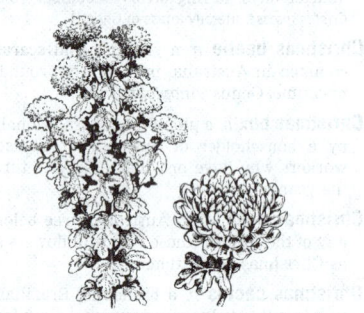

Chrysanthemum

chrysanthemum /krə sánthiməm, -zán-/ *n.* a plant with brightly coloured globe-shaped flowers and small densely clustered petals. Genus: *Chrysanthemum*. [Mid-16thC. From Greek *khrūsanthemon*, literally 'gold flower', from the colour of the corn marigold, a member of the species, to which the name was originally applied.]

Chryse /kríssi/ *n.* a lowland plain in the northern equatorial region of Mars where Viking 1 landed in 1976

chryselephantine /kríss eli fántīn/ *adj.* used to describe classical Greek sculptures that are made of or overlaid with gold and ivory [Early 19thC. From Greek *khrūselephantinos*, from *khrūsos* 'gold' + *elephas* 'elephant, ivory'.]

chryso- *prefix.* gold, golden ○ *chrysophyte* [From Greek *khrusos* 'gold', of Semitic origin]

chrysoberyl /kríssə berəl/ *n.* a green, yellow, or brown mineral used as a gemstone [Mid-17thC. From Latin *chrysoberyllus*, from Greek *khrūsos* 'gold' + *bērullos* 'beryl'.]

chrysolite /kríssə līt/ *n.* the mineral olivine (*no longer used technically*) [Middle English. Via Old French from, ultimately, Greek *khrūsolithos*, literally 'gold stone'.]

chrysoprase /kríssə prayz/ *n.* a bright green variety of chalcedony, used as a gemstone [13thC. Via Old French from, ultimately, Greek *khrūsoprasos*, literally 'golden leek'. The word originally denoted a golden-green variety of beryl.]

Chrysostom /kríssəstəm/, **John, St** (349?–407) Syrian theologian and orator. He was Bishop of Constantinople and a Church Father of both the Roman and the Orthodox Christian traditions.

chrysotile /kríssə tīl/ *n.* a green, grey, or white variety of the mineral serpentine. It is an important source of asbestos. [Mid-19thC. Coined from CHRYSO- + Greek *tilos* 'fibre', from *tillein* 'to pluck'.]

chthonic /thónnik, kthó-/, **chthonian** /thóni ən, kthó-/ *adj.* relating to the underworld as described in Greek mythology [Late 19thC. Formed from Greek *khthōn* 'earth'.]

chub /chub/ (*plural* **chubs** *or* **chub**) *n.* a minnow with a stout rounded body belonging to a family that includes some North American sea and river fishes and the European carp. Family: Cyprinidae. [15thC. Origin unknown.]

Chubb /chub/ *tdmk.* a trademark for a lock with a mechanism that makes the bolt immovable if an attempt is made to pick the lock

chubby /chúbbi/ (**-bier, -biest**) *adj.* pleasantly or charmingly plump, especially in the way that healthy babies and toddlers often are —**chubbily** *adv.* —**chubbiness** *n.*

chuck[1] /chuk/ *vt.* (**chucks, chucking, chucked**) **1. THROW CARELESSLY** to throw sth, especially in a careless or casual way (*informal*) **2. GET RID OF** to get rid of sth unwanted (*informal*) **3. FORCE TO LEAVE** to force sb to leave a place, or take away sb's membership of an organization (*informal*) **4. GIVE UP** to give sth up, especially a job (*informal*) **5. END RELATIONSHIP WITH** to end a relationship with a boyfriend or girlfriend (*informal*) **6. TICKLE AFFECTIONATELY UNDER CHIN** to give sb an affectionate pat or tickle under the chin ■ *n.* **1. CARELESS THROW** a throw, especially a careless or casual throw (*informal*) **2. AFFECTIONATE TICKLE UNDER THE CHIN** an affectionate pat or tickle under sb's chin [Early 16thC. Perhaps from Old French *chuquer* 'to knock, bump'. Originally in the sense 'to pat under the chin', hence 'to use a similar small movement to throw sth'.]

WORD KEY: SYNONYMS

See Synonyms at ***throw***.

chuck in *v.* (*informal*) **1.** *vt.* **GIVE UP** to give sth up, especially a job **2.** *vi.* **SHARE IN COST** to contribute to the cost of sth

chuck up *vti.* to vomit (*informal*). US term **upchuck**

chuck[2] /chuk/ *n.* **1.** TECH **CLAMP ON LATHE OR DRILL** a clamping device with three or four adjustable jaws, used to hold a piece of woodwork or metalwork in a lathe or a bit in a drill **2.** FOOD **CUT OF BEEF** a cut of beef that extends from the neck to the shoulder blade [Late 17thC. A variant of CHOCK.]

chuck[3] /chuk/ *vi.* (**chucks, chucking, chucked**) = **cluck** ■ *n.* = **cluck** (*archaic*) [14thC. An imitation of the sound.]

chuck[4] /chuk/ *n. N England* used as an affectionate way of addressing a man or a woman (*regional*) [Late 16thC. Alteration of CHICK.]

chuckie /chúki/ *n. Scotland* a small stone (*regional*) [Mid-18thC. Formed from CHUCK[1]; from the use of the stone for throwing in games.]

chuckle /chúk'l/ *vti.* (**-les, -ling, -led**) **LAUGH QUIETLY** to laugh quietly or to yourself ■ *n.* **QUIET LAUGH** a quiet or inward laugh [Late 16thC. Formed from CHUCK[3]. The word originally meant 'to laugh heartily'.] —**chuckler** *n.* —**chucklingly** /-lingli/ *adv.*

chufa /choófə/ *n.* an African plant of the sedge family with an edible tuber that looks like a nut. Latin name: *Cyperus esculentus*. [Mid-19thC. From Spanish, literally 'fluff, nonsense'.]

chuffed /chuft/ *adj.* very pleased or satisfied (*informal*) [Mid-20thC. Formed from northern English dialect *chuff* 'chubby, happy', of unknown origin.]

chug /chug/ *vi.* (**chugs, chugging, chugged**) **1. MAKE REPEATED THUDDING SOUND** to make a repetitive thudding sound like that of a small engine **2. MOVE WITH CHUGGING SOUND** to move along slowly with a chugging sound under the power of an engine **3. CONTINUE IN STEADY FASHION** to continue steadily doing the usual things (*informal*) ■ *n.* **CHUGGING NOISE** the chugging noise that an engine makes [Mid-19thC. An imitation of the sound.]

chukar /chu kaar, chŏŏ kaar/ *n.* a greyish-brown South Asian partridge with red legs and bill, introduced into the western United States as a game bird. Latin name: *Alectoris chukar*. [Early 19thC. From Hindi *cakor*; probably ultimately an imitation of the sound it makes.]

Chukchi /chŏŏk chee, chúk-/ (*plural* **-chi** *or* **-chis**), **Chukchee** (*plural* **-chee** *or* **-chees**) *n.* **1.** PEOPLES **MEMBER OF A SIBERIAN PEOPLE** a member of a people who live in the far northeastern corner of Siberia. The Chukchi were the first to breed huskies as working dogs. **2.** LANG **SIBERIAN LANGUAGE** a language spoken in the Chukchi Peninsula of northeastern Siberia. Chukchi is spoken by about 12,000 people. [Early 18thC. From Russian.] —**Chukchi** *adj.*

Chukchi Sea /chúkchi-, chŏŏk-/ part of the Arctic Ocean, situated north of the Bering Strait between Asia and North America

chukka /chúkə/ *n.* **1. chukka, chukka boot** CLOTHES **ANKLE-LENGTH BOOT** a casual ankle-high lace-up boot, typically made of suede **2.** SPORTS = **chukker**

chukker /chúkər/ (*plural* **-kers** *or* **-kas**) *n.* any of the six periods of continuous play in a polo match, each lasting for approximately 7.5 minutes [Late 19thC. From Hindi *cak(k)ar* 'circular course, turn', ultimately from an Indo-European word that is also the ancestor of English *cycle* and *wheel*.]

Chulalongkorn /chóolə lóng kawrn/, **Rama V** (1853–1910) Siamese monarch who ruled from 1868 until 1910, and was noted for his modernization programmes.

chum[1] /chum/ *n.* (*dated informal*) **1. FRIEND** a close friend **2. WAY OF ADDRESSING MAN** used as a term of address for a man ■ *v.* (**chums, chumming, chummed**) **1.** *vi.* **BE FRIENDS** to be friends with sb, or behave in a friendly way towards sb **2.** *vt. Scotland* **GO WITH** to accompany sb somewhere (*regional*) [Late 17thC. Origin uncertain: probably short for *chamber-fellow*. Originally the slang word for a roommate at Oxford University.]

chum[2] /chum/ *n.* **1. FISHBAIT** an angler's bait, especially chopped fish, scattered on the water **2. CHEAP TRINKETS** inexpensive trinkets such as cufflinks and pins bearing, e.g. the US Presidential seal (*slang*) ■ *vti.* (**chums, chumming, chummed**) **USE FISH CHUM** to fish using chum on the water [Mid-19thC. Origin unknown.]

chum[3] /chum/ (*plural* **chums** *or* **chum**) *n.* = **chum salmon** [Early 20thC. From Chinook Jargon *tzum (samun)*, literally 'spotted (salmon)'.]

chummy /chúmmi/ (**-mier, -miest**) *adj.* friendly or close (*informal*) —**chummily** *adv.* —**chumminess** *n.*

chump[1] /chump/ *n.* **1. UNWISE PERSON** an unwise person, especially sb whom the person using the term is rather fond of (*dated informal*) **2.** FOOD **THICK END OF MEAT** a thick end of a piece of meat, particularly of a leg of lamb or mutton (*often used before a noun*) ○ *a chump chop* **3.** INDUST **THICK PIECE OF WOOD** a short thick piece of wood **4. HEAD** sb's head or mind (*dated slang*) [Early 18thC. Origin uncertain: perhaps a blend of CHUNK and LUMP or STUMP. The word originally denoted a thick piece of wood; the sense 'fool' developed from this.]

chump[2] *vti., n.* = **chomp**

chum salmon *n.* a salmon with wavy vertical green streaks and blotches, found in northern Pacific waters. Latin name: *Oncorhynchus keta*.

chunder /chúndər/ *vti.* (**-ders, -dering, -dered**) **BE SICK** to vomit (*slang*) ■ *n.* **VOMIT** vomit, or the act of vomiting (*informal*) [Mid-20thC. Origin uncertain; probably shortening of *chunder loo*, British rhyming slang for *spew*, from *Chunder Loo of Akim Foo*, a cartoon character who appeared in boot-polish advertisements in Australia.]

chunk /chungk/ *n.* **1. PIECE** a thick squarish piece of sth, e.g. bread, wood, or meat **2. LARGE PORTION** a large amount or part of sth [Late 17thC. An alteration of CHUCK[2].]

chunky /chúngki/ (**-ier, -iest**) *adj.* **1. WITH LUMPS** containing lumps or bits **2. SQUARE AND SOLID** solid and squarish ○ *a chunky table* **3. SHORT AND BROAD** short, broad, and sometimes overweight (*informal*) **4. MADE OF THICK MATERIAL** made from thick material, especially wool —**chunkily** *adv.* —**chunkiness** *n.*

Chunnel /chúnn'l/ *n.* a nickname for the Channel Tunnel (*informal*) [Early 20thC. Blend of CHANNEL and TUNNEL.]

chunter /chúntər/ (**-ers, -ering, -ered**) *vi.* to say sth to yourself in a quiet grumbling voice (*informal*) [Late 17thC. Probably an imitation of the sound.]

chuppah /hŏŏppə/ (*plural* **chuppahs** *or* **chuppot** *or* **chupoth** /-poth/), **huppah** *n.* **1. JEWISH WEDDING CANOPY** the canopy under which a Jewish wedding ceremony is performed **2. JEWISH WEDDING** the Jewish wedding ceremony [Late 19thC. From Hebrew *ḥuppāh* 'cover, canopy'.]

church /church/ *n.* **1. RELIGIOUS BUILDING** a building for public worship, especially in the Christian religion **2. RELIGIOUS SERVICES** the religious services that take place in a church **3. CLERGY** the clergy as distinct from lay people **4. church, Church RELIGIOUS AUTHORITY** religious authority as opposed to the authority of the state **5. church, Church RELIGION'S FOLLOWERS AS GROUP** all the followers of a religion, especially the Christian religion, considered collectively **6. church, Church BRANCH OF CHRISTIAN RELIGION** any of several denominations of the Christian religion ■ *vt.* (**churches, churching, churched**) **GIVE CHURCH BLESSING TO** to give sb, especially a woman who has recently given birth, a blessing in church (*dated; often passive*) [Old English *cir(i)ce*, from a prehistoric Germanic word that is also the ancestor of German *Kirche*; ultimately from Greek *kuriakon doma* 'house of the lord', from *kurios* 'lord']

Church Army *n.* a voluntary organization founded by the Church of England in the 19th century to help parish priests evangelize

Church Commissioners *npl.* a group of representatives of church and state in England, who are responsible for the administration of the finances and property of the Church of England

church father *n.* any of the pre-8th century Christian scholars who set down the doctrines and practices of Christianity

churchgoer /chúrch gō ər/ *n.* sb who is attending a church service or who attends church services regularly —**churchgoing** *n., adj.*

Churchill /chúrchil/, **Charles** (1731–64) British poet. His satirical verse includes *The Rosciad* (1761).

Churchill /chúrchil/, **Randolph, Lord** (1849–95) British politician and father of Sir Winston Churchill, he was secretary for India (1885–86).

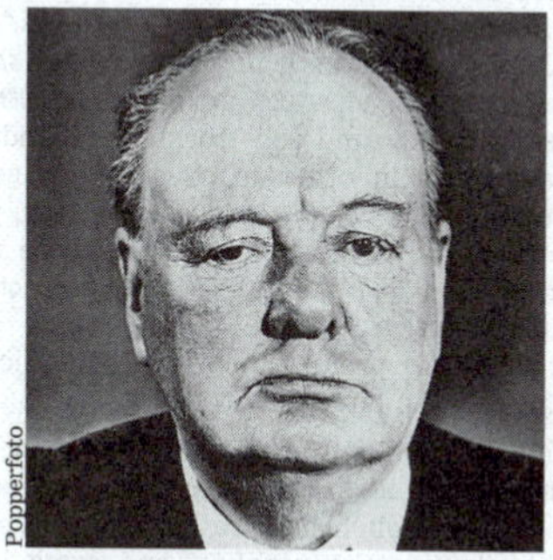

Sir Winston Churchill

Churchill, Sir Winston (1874–1965) British statesman and writer. As Prime Minister (1940–45, 1951–55) he led Britain through World War II. He wrote *The Second World War* (1948–54) and won the Nobel Prize in literature (1953). Full name **Sir Winston Leonard Spencer Churchill**

churchly /chúrchli/ *adj.* similar to, suitable for, or typical of a church —**churchliness** *n.*

churchman /chúrchmən/ (*plural* **-men** /-mən/) *n.* **1. CLERGYMAN** a male member of the clergy **2. CHURCH MEMBER** a man who is a practising member of a church —**churchmanship** *n.*

church mode *n.* any of the eight scales used for church music in the Middle Ages, e.g. the Dorian, Phrygian, or Lydian modes

Church of Christ, Scientist *n.* the official name of the Christian Science Church

Church of England *n.* the established church of England, ruled by a system of government by bishops and with the reigning monarch as its titular head

Church of Jesus Christ of Latter-Day Saints *n.* the official name of the Mormon Church

Church of Rome *n.* = **Roman Catholic Church**

Church of Scotland *n.* the official religion of Scotland, which is Presbyterian and is administered by selected members of the congregation (**elders**)

church parade *n.* a parade, in church, of members of the armed forces or other uniformed organizations as part of a special church service

church school *n.* a school that provides children with a general education, and was founded or is supported by the Church of England

Church Slavonic *n.* = **Old Church Slavonic**

church text *n.* a heavy ornamental Gothic typeface

churchwarden /chúrch wáwrd'n/ *n.* **1. LAYPERSON WITH CHURCH DUTIES** a layperson who manages secular matters in an Anglican church **2. PIPE WITH LONG STEM** a long-stemmed clay tobacco pipe

churchwoman /chúrch wòomən/ (*plural* **-en** /-wimin/) *n.* **1. CLERGYWOMAN** a woman member of the clergy **2. WOMAN MEMBER OF CHURCH** a woman who is a practising member of a church

churchy /chúrchi/ (**-ier, -iest**) *adj.* **1. OVERLY RELIGIOUS** overzealously or intolerantly religious **2. LIKE A CHURCH** resembling or suggesting a church

churchyard /chúrch yaard/ *n.* an area surrounding a church that is usually used as a graveyard

churl /churl/ *n.* **1. ILL-MANNERED PERSON** sb who has no manners **2.** HIST = **ceorl** [Old English *ceorl* 'man', specifically 'freeman of the lowest rank' (as opposed to a nobleman), from a prehistoric Germanic word that is also the ancestor of German *Kerl* 'fellow']

churlish /chúrlish/ *adj.* **1. CRASS** characteristic of sb who is ill-bred **2. UNKIND AND GRUMPY** surly, sullen, or miserly —**churlishly** *adv.* —**churlishness** *n.*

churn /churn/ *n.* **1. MILK CAN** a large metal container for transporting milk **2. BUTTER MAKER** a container or device in which milk or cream is stirred vigorously to produce butter ■ *v.* (**churns, churning, churned**) **1.** *vt.* **STIR TO MAKE BUTTER** to stir or beat milk or cream vigorously to make butter **2.** *vt.* **MAKE BUTTER** to make butter by beating milk or cream **3.** *vti.* **SPLASH VIOLENTLY** to move about violently, or cause a liquid or soft solid to move about violently **4.** *vi.* **FEEL UNSETTLED** to move unpleasantly, as if in a churn ○ *my stomach was churning* **5.** *vt.* STOCK EXCH **TRADE FREQUENTLY FOR COMMISSION** to buy and sell stocks and bonds on a frequent basis in order to earn brokerage commissions [Old English *cyrin*, of uncertain origin; perhaps from a prehistoric Germanic word that is also the ancestor of English *corn*, from the 'grainy' appearance of stirred cream] —**churner** *n.*

churn out *vt.* to produce or issue sth quickly or regularly and in large quantities

churr /chur/, **chirr** *vi.* (**churrs, churring, churred; chirrs, chirring, chirred**) **MAKE BIRDS' AND INSECTS' VIBRATING NOISE** to make the high-pitched vibrating sound typical of some birds, e.g. the nightjar, and some insects, e.g. the cicada ■ *n.* **CHURRING SOUND** a high-pitched vibrating sound [Mid-16thC. An imitation of the sound.]

chute[1] /shoot/ (**chutes, chuting, chuted**) *n.* **1. SLOPE TO DROP THINGS DOWN** an inclined channel or passage that sth can slide down **2.** LEISURE **CHILDREN'S SLIDE** a children's slide in a park or swimming pool **3.** SPORTS **SNOW-COVERED SLOPE** a snow- or ice-covered slope or channel for sports such as tobogganing or bobsleighing **4.** AGRIC **SLOPING PASSAGE FOR ANIMALS** a narrow passageway through which animals are driven to be branded, sheared, loaded, dipped, or sprayed **5.** SPORTS **SLOPE OR DROP ON WATERCOURSE** a waterfall, rapids, or steep descent in a river or stream [Early 19thC. From French, literally 'fall', ultimately from Latin *cadere* 'to fall'.]

chute[2] /shoot/ *n.* a parachute (*informal*) [Early 20thC. Shortening.] —**chutist** *n.*

chutney /chútni/ (*plural* **-neys**) *n.* FOOD a sweet and spicy relish made from fruit, spices, sugar, and vinegar [Early 19thC. From Hindi *caṭnī*.]

chutzpah /hòotspə, kh-/, **hutzpah, chutzpa** *n.* (*informal*) **1. SELF-CONFIDENCE** boldness coupled with supreme self-confidence **2. RUDENESS** impudent rudeness or lack of respect [Late 19thC. Via Yiddish from Aramaic *ḥuṣpā*.]

Chuvash /chòo vaásh/ *n.* a language spoken west of the Urals in central Russia, belonging to the Turkic family of Altaic languages. Chuvash is spoken by about two million people. [Via Russian from Chuvash *čăvaš*] —**Chuvash** *adj.*

chyle /kīl/ *n.* a milky fluid consisting of lymph and emulsified fat that forms in the small intestine during digestion [15thC. Via late Latin from Greek *khūlos* 'animal or plant juice'.] —**chylaceous** /kī láyshəss/ *adj.* —**chylous** /kīləss/ *adj.*

chylomicron /kīlō mīkron/ *n.* a microscopic particle, containing fats, cholesterol, phospholipids and protein, formed in the small intestine and absorbed into the blood during digestion

chyme /kīm/ *n.* a thick fluid mass of partially digested food and gastric secretions passed from the stomach to the small intestine [Early 17thC. Via late Latin from Greek *khūmos* 'animal or plant juice', ultimately 'tube through which sth flows', from an Indo-European word that is also the ancestor of English *funnel*.] —**chymous** *adj.*

chymopapain /kīmōpə páy in, -pī in/ *n.* an enzyme found in papaya juice that aids the breakdown of proteins and is used in medical procedures and as a meat tenderizer [Late 20thC. Formed from CHYME + PAPAIN.]

chymotrypsin /kīmō trípsin/ *n.* a digestive enzyme produced in the pancreas —**chymotryptic** *adj.*

chymotrypsinogen /kīmō trip sínnəjən/ *n.* the inactive form of chymotrypsin that is converted into chymotrypsin by the enzyme trypsin

chypre /sheéprə/ *n.* perfume made from sandalwood [Late 19thC. From French, literally 'Cyprus', perhaps where the perfume was originally made.]

Ci[1] *abbr.* METEOROL cirrus

Ci[2] *symbol.* MEASURE, PHYS curie

CI *abbr.* **1.** Channel Islands **2.** Cayman Islands

CIA *n.* a US federal bureau responsible for intelligence and counterintelligence activities outside the United States. In conjunction with the FBI, it is also involved in domestic counterintelligence. Full form **Central Intelligence Agency**

ciabatta /chə báttə/ (*plural* **-tas** *or* **-te** /-ttay/) *n.* a flat white Italian bread made with olive oil [Late 20thC. From Italian, literally 'slipper', from the shape of the loaf.]

ciao /chow/ *interj.* used to say hello or goodbye (*informal*) [Early 20thC. From Italian dialect, literally '(I am your) slave'.]

CIB *abbr.* **1.** Criminal Investigation Branch **2.** Chartered Institute of Bankers

ciborium /si báwri əm/ (*plural* **-a** /si báwri ə/) *n.* **1. ALTAR CANOPY** a canopy that stands on four pillars over the altar in some Christian churches **2. HOLY WAFER BOX** a small container with a lid, used to hold the consecrated wafers for Holy Communion [Mid-16thC. Via medieval Latin from Greek *kibōrion*, denoting the cup-shaped seed vessel of a species of water lily.]

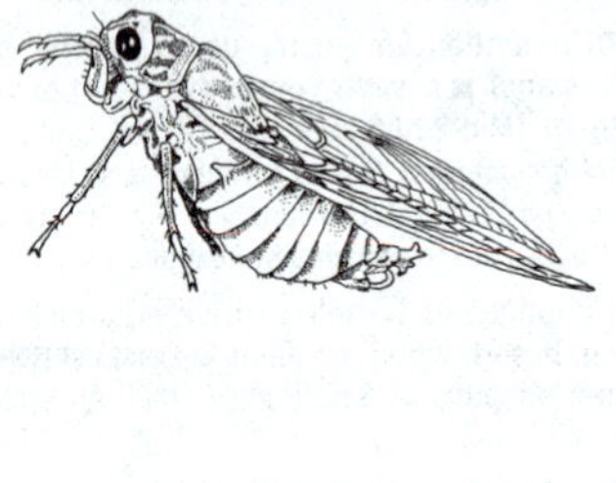

Cicada

cicada /si kaádə/ (*plural* **-das** *or* **-dae** /-dee/) *n.* a large winged insect that lives in trees and tall grass, the male of which makes a shrill sound. Family: Cicadidae. [15thC. From Latin, of uncertain ultimate origin.]

cicala /si kaálə/ (*plural* **-las** *or* **-le** /-lay/) *n.* = **cicada** [Late 18thC. Via Italian or directly from Latin, variant of *cicada*. The irregular plural comes from Italian.]

cicatrice *n.* = **cicatrix**

cicatrise *vti.* = **cicatrize**

cicatrix /síkətriks/ (*plural* **-trices** /síkə trī seez/), **cicatrice** *n.* **1.** MED **SCAR** a scar (*technical*) **2.** BOT **MARK OF LEAF ATTACHMENT** a scar left on a stem where a leaf used to be attached [Mid-17thC. From Latin, 'scar'.] —**cicatricial** /síkə trísh'l/ *adj.* —**cicatricose** /si kàttrikōss/ *adj.*

cicatrize /síkə trīz/ (**-trizes, -trizing, -trized**), **cicatrise** (**-trises, -trising, -trised**) *vti.* to heal, or cause a wound to heal, and form a scar (*technical*) [15thC. From French *cicatriser*, from *cicatrice* 'scar'.] —**cicatrization** /síkə trī záysh'n/ *n.*

cicely /síssəli/ *n.* = **sweet cicely**

cicero /síssərō/ *n.* a size of printed character slightly larger than the pica [From its first use (1458) for an edition of the works of CICERO]

Cicero /síssərō/, **Marcus Tullius** (106–43 BC) Roman philosopher, writer, and statesman. He was Rome's greatest orator during a long political career. His letters and essays are known for their rich prose style. —**Ciceronian** /síssə rṓni ən/ *adj.*

cicerone /chíchə rṓni, síssə-/ (*plural* **-nes** *or* **-ni** /-ni/) *n.* sb who guides and informs tourists [Early 18thC. From Italian, named after CICERO, because of the guide's knowledge and eloquence.]

cichlid /síklid/ *n.* a tropical freshwater fish with spiny fins, popular as an aquarium fish. Family: Cichlidae. [Late 19thC. From modern Latin *Cichlidae*, family name, from Greek *kikhlē*, denoting a kind of fish.]

cicisbeo /chíchiz báyō/ (*plural* **-bei** /-báyee/) *n.* a married woman's male escort or lover (*archaic or literary*) [Early 18thC. From Italian, of unknown origin.]

Cid /él sid/, **El** (1040?–99) Spanish military leader. Legend obscures the true nature of 'The Lord Champion' who fought both for and against Spain's Moorish rulers, and was virtual dictator of Valencia from 1094 to 1099. Born **Rodriguez Díaz de Vivar**

CID *n.* the detective branch of the UK police force. Full form **Criminal Investigation Department**

-cide *suffix.* **1.** killer ○ *fungicide* **2.** killing ○ *tyrannicide* [Via Old French from Latin *-cida* 'killer', and from Latin *-cidium* 'killing', both from Latin *caedere* 'to strike, kill' (source also of English *chisel, scissor, incise*, and *decide*)] —**-cidal** *suffix.*

cider /sídər/ *n.* **1. ALCOHOLIC DRINK MADE FROM APPLES** an alcoholic drink made by pressing and fermenting apples. ◊ **cyder 2.** *US* **NONALCOHOLIC FRESH APPLE DRINK** a nonalcoholic drink made from freshly-pressed apples **3.** *US, Can* **FERMENTED APPLE JUICE** an alcoholic drink made from fermented apple juice [13thC. Via Old French *sidre* from, ultimately, Hebrew *šēkār* 'alcoholic drink'.]

WORD KEY: CULTURAL NOTE

Cider With Rosie, a memoir by Laurie Lee (1959). An account of the author's childhood and youth in Gloucestershire, it is noted for its evocative descriptions of rural life and its affectionate portrayal of Lee's family and friends. Among his strongest memories is his first taste of cider, taken in a hay wagon with his friend, Rosie.

cider vinegar *n.* a light vinegar made from apple juice

ci-devant /see də vaáN/ *adj., adv.* used to indicate that what follows was sb's former name, office, or title (*formal*) [Early 18thC. From French, literally 'before this'.]

Cienfuegos /syen fwáy goss/ city and capital of Cienfuegos Province, central Cuba, situated on Cienfuegos Bay. Population: 132,038 (1993).

c.i.f., **CIF** *abbr.* cost, insurance, and freight. ◊ **CFI**

CIFE *abbr.* Colleges and Institutes for Further Education

cig /sig/ *n.* a cigarette (*informal*) [Late 19thC. Shortening.]

cigar /si gaár/ *n.* a cylindrical roll of tobacco leaves for smoking, with thin brown paper or a single tobacco leaf as an outer covering [Early 18thC. Directly or via French *cigare* from Spanish *cigarro*, probably from Mayan *sik'ar* 'smoking'.]

cigarette /síggə rét/ *n.* **1. ROLL OF SHREDDED TOBACCO** a cylindrical roll of shredded tobacco leaves for smoking, with an outer covering of thin, usually white, paper **2. ROLL OF ANY LEAVES FOR SMOKING** a roll of shredded leaves of any kind for smoking, e.g. marijuana leaves or leaves of herbs [Mid-19thC. From French, literally 'small cigar', from *cigare* (see CIGAR).]

cigarette card *n.* a small card with a picture and information on it, formerly given away free inside a cigarette packet, now considered a collector's item

cigarette holder *n.* a hollow cylindrical device for holding a smoking cigarette. Some cigarette holders include filters.

cigarette lighter *n.* = **lighter**

cigarette paper *n.* a sheet of thin paper with gum on one edge, used with loose tobacco to roll cigarettes

cigarillo /síggə rílló/ (*plural* **-los**) *n.* a slender cigar about the same size as a cigarette [Mid-19thC. From Spanish *cigarillo*, literally 'small cigar', from *cigarro* (see CIGAR).]

ciggy /síggi/ (*plural* **-gies**) *n.* a cigarette (*informal*)

CII *abbr.* Chartered Insurance Institute

cilantro /si lántrō/ *n. US* = **coriander** [Early 20thC. Via Spanish from, ultimately, Latin *coriandrum* 'coriander', source of English *coriander.*]

cilia plural of **cilium**

ciliary /sílli əri/ *adj.* **1.** BIOL used to describe the short threads (**cilia**) projecting from some cells and the beating movement they make **2.** ANAT used to describe the tissue and muscle that surrounds the lens of the eye [Late 17thC. Formed from CILIUM.]

ciliary body *n.* the ring-shaped part at the front of eye that connects the pigmented layer (**choroid**) of the eyeball with the iris diaphragm. It also contains the ciliary muscle, which alters the curvature of the lens.

ciliate /sílli ayt, -ət/ *n.* **ORGANISM PROPELLED BY THRASHING THREADS** a simple microscopic organism with projecting threads that thrash to help it to move along. Phylum: Ciliophora. ■ *adj.* = **ciliated** [Mid-18thC. Formed from CILIUM.]

ciliated /sílli aytid/, **ciliate** /sílli ayt, -ət/ *adj.* used to describe cells with projecting threads (**cilia**) or organisms with cells of this type —**ciliation** /sílli áysh'n/ *n.*

cilice /síliss/ *n.* **1.** TEXTILES = **haircloth 2.** CLOTHES **HAIRCLOTH GARMENT** a garment made of haircloth [Late 16thC. Via French from, ultimately, Greek *Kilikia*, Cilicia (an ancient district of Anatolia, now in southern Turkey), because the cloth was originally made of Cilician goats' hair.]

cilium /sílli əm/ (*plural* **-a** /-ə/) *n.* **1.** BIOL **MICROSCOPIC PROJECTION ON CELL** a tiny projecting thread, found with many others on a cell or microscopic organism, that beats rhythmically to aid the movement of a fluid past the cell or movement of the organism through liquid **2. EYELASH** an eyelash (*technical*) [Early 18thC. From Latin, literally 'eyelash'.]

Cimarosa /cheémə rózə/, **Domenico** (1749–1801) Italian composer. The most famous of his 60 operas is the light-hearted *The Secret Marriage* (1792).

cimbalom /símbələm, tsímb-/ *n.* a musical instrument similar to the hammered dulcimer. It is used especially in Hungarian folk and gypsy music. [Late 19thC. Via Hungarian from Italian *cimbalo* 'dulcimer'.]

Cimbri /símbri/ *npl.* a Germanic people who lived in parts of Jutland and the Rhine valley during the second century BC. They began to spread southwards, but were routed by the Romans in 101 BC. [From Latin]

cimetidine /sī métti deen/ *n.* a drug that limits the production of acid in the stomach and is used to treat peptic ulcers. Formula: $C_{10}H_{16}NS$. [Late 20thC. Coined from CYANO- + METHYL + -IDINE.]

cimex /símeks/ (*plural* **cimices** /sími seez/) *n.* a bedbug or related insect that feeds on birds, humans, and other mammals. Genus: *Cimex.* [Late 16thC. From Latin, 'bedbug'.]

Cimmerian /si meéri ən/ *adj.* **DARK** dark and gloomy (*literary*) ■ *n.* MYTHOL **INHABITANT OF DARK LAND** according to Greek mythology, a member of a people who lived in a land of perpetual darkness [Late 16thC. Formed from Latin *Cimmerius*, from Greek *Kimmerios.*]

C in C, C-in-C *abbr.* MIL Commander in Chief

cinch /sinch/ *n.* **1. STH EASILY DONE** sth that can be done or achieved with very little effort (*informal*) **2. STH CERTAIN** sth that is absolutely certain to happen (*informal*) **3.** *US* **FIRM GRIP** a firm grip (*archaic*) ■ *vt.* (**cinches, cinching, cinched**) **1.** *US* **GRASP STH ROUND MIDDLE** to grasp sth round the middle, as a belt does (*informal*) **2. MAKE CERTAIN OF** to make certain of sth (*dated informal*) [Mid-19thC. From Spanish *cincha* 'girth', ultimately from Latin *cingere* 'to gird' (see CINCTURE).]

cinchona /sing kṓnə/ *n.* **1. TREE WITH BARK PRODUCING QUININE** a South American evergreen tree or shrub whose bark is used to produce quinine and some other drugs. Genus: *Cinchona.* **2. cinchona, cinchona bark DRIED BARK OF THE CINCHONA** the dried bark of a cinchona tree, used to produce quinine and some other drugs [Mid-18thC. From modern Latin, named after the Countess of *Chinchón* (1576–1641), vicereine of Peru, who was cured of a fever by the drug and who introduced it into Spain.] —**cinchonic** /sing kónnik/ *adj.*

cinchonine /síng kə neen/ *n.* a colourless crystalline solid obtained from the dried bark of the cinchona tree, which has been used in treating malaria. Formula: $C_{19}H_{22}N_{20}$.

cinchonism /síngkənizzəm/ *n.* a condition resulting from the excessive use of quinine and other drugs derived from cinchona bark. The symptoms are headache, ringing in the ears, temporary deafness, and dizziness.

Cincinnati /sínssi nátti/ city in southwestern Ohio on the Ohio-Kentucky border, on the Ohio River, southwest of Dayton. Population: 345,818 (1996).

cincture /síngkchər/ *n.* **1. BELT** a girdle or belt, especially a cord or sash tied round a priest's, monk's, or nun's habit **2. ENCOMPASSING** the act of encircling sth, or sth that encircles (*archaic*) [Late 16thC. Via Latin *cinctura* 'girdle' from, ultimately, *cingere* 'to gird', source of English *cinch, precinct,* and *succinct.*]

cinder /síndər/ *n.* **BURNT WOOD OR FUEL** a small piece of charred wood or coal, especially one that continues to glow ■ **cinders** *npl.* **1. ASHES** the ashes that remain after a fire has burnt out **2.** INDUST **SLAG** waste material produced by smelting **3.** GEOL = **scoria** [Old English *sinder* 'slag', from prehistoric Germanic. The modern spelling arose by association with French *cendre* 'cinders, ash' (not related to the English word).] —**cindery** *adj.*

cinder block *n. US* = **breeze block**

Cinderella /síndə réllə/ *n.* **NEGLECTED PERSON OR THING** sb who or sth that suffers undeserved neglect ■ *adj.* **RAGS-TO-RICHES** achieving sudden recognition or success, or relating to sb who, or sth that, achieves this [Mid-19thC. Named after the fairy-tale character *Cinderella*, who is neglected by her sisters but enabled by her fairy godmother to attend a ball and meet a prince.]

cine- *prefix.* CINEMA film, motion picture ○ *cinephile* [From CINEMA]

cineaste /sínni ast/ *n.* **1. FILM BUFF** sb who is very interested in films and film-making **2. FILM-MAKER** sb who makes films [Early 20thC. From French, formed from *ciné* (shortening of *cinématographe*), modelled on *enthusiaste* 'enthusiast'.]

cine camera /sínni-/ *n.* a hand-held camera used for taking moving pictures rather than still photographs, before the introduction of video cameras. US term **movie camera** [*Cine* is a shortening of CINEMATOGRAPHIC]

cine film *n.* photographic film used for making moving films rather than still photographs. US term **movie film** [*Cine* is a shortening of CINEMATOGRAPHIC]

cinema /sínnəmə, sínni maa/ *n.* **1. PLACE TO WATCH FILMS** a building or room where films are shown **2. CINEMAS COLLECTIVELY** cinemas considered collectively **3. FILM INDUSTRY** the film industry or the business of making films **4. FILMS COLLECTIVELY** films considered collectively [Early 20thC. From French *cinéma*, shortening of *cinématographe*, from Greek *kinēma* 'movement'.]

cinemagoer /sínnəmə gō ər, sínni maa-/ *n.* sb who is watching a film at a cinema or who regularly goes to the cinema. US term **moviegoer**

Cinemascope /sínnəmə skōp/ *tdmk.* a trademark for a wide-screen film system that uses special lenses to squeeze the image onto a much narrower frame with partner lenses in the projector unsqueezing the image for projection

cinematheque /sínnəmə tek/ *n.* a small cinema, especially one showing artistic or classic films (*dated*) [Mid-20thC. From French, formed from *cinéma* (see CINEMA), modelled on *bibliothèque* 'library'.]

cinematic /sínnə máttik/ *adj.* **1. APPROPRIATE TO FILM** typical of the style in which films are made **2. OF FILMS** relating to films or film-making —**cinematically** *adv.*

cinematographer /sínnəmə tóggrəfər/ *n.* sb responsible for the lighting and camera work for a film and the general look of the film

cinematography /sínnəmə tóggrəfi/ *n.* the art or technique of photographing and lighting films —**cinematographic** /sínnə matə gráffik/ *adj.* —**cinematographically** /-gráffikli/ *adv.*

cinéma vérité /-vérri tay/ *n.* a style of film-making characterized by a search for an authentic documentary feel. The term was first applied to a series of French documentary films in the 1960s. [Mid-20thC. From French, literally 'cinema of truth'.]

cinephile /sínni fīl/ *n.* sb who is very interested in films and film-making

cineraria /sínə ráiri ə/ *n.* **1. PLANT WITH DAISY-LIKE FLOWERS** a plant native to the Canary Islands, cultivated as a houseplant for its mass of blue, purple, or red flowers resembling daisies. Latin name: *Senecio hybridus.* **2. GREY-LEAVED PLANT** a plant grown for its silver-grey, finely cut foliage. Latin name: *Cineraria maritima.* ■ plural of **cinerarium** [Late 16thC. From modern Latin, formed from the Latin stem *ciner-* 'ashes', from the fluffy grey leaves of the silver ragwort, the plant originally designated.]

cinerarium /sínnə ráiri əm/ (*plural* **-a** /-ráiri ə/) *n.* a place where the ashes of a corpse are stored [Mid-18thC. From late Latin, formed from the Latin stem *ciner-* 'ashes'.]

cinerary /sínnərəri/ *adj.* relating to ashes, especially human ashes [Mid-18thC. From Latin *cinerarius*, formed from the stem *ciner-* 'ashes'.]

cinereous /si neéri əss/ *adj.* (*literary*) **1. LIKE OR OF ASHES** resembling or consisting of ashes **2. ASH-GREY** of an ash-grey colour like ashes ■ *n.* **ASH-GREY** an ash-grey colour (*literary*) [15thC. Formed from Latin *cinereus*, from the stem *ciner-* 'ashes'.]

cinerin /sínnərin/ *n.* an oily liquid compound extracted from pyrethrum and used in insecticides [Mid-20thC. Formed from the Latin stem *ciner-* 'ashes'.]

cingulum /síng gyŏŏləm/ (*plural* **-la** /-lə/) *n.* **1.** ANAT **BODY PART ENCIRCLING ANOTHER** any part of the body that surrounds or encircles another part **2.** BIOL **STRIPE AROUND PLANT OR ANIMAL** a band or stripe that encircles a plant or animal [Early 19thC. From Latin, literally 'girdle', from *cingere* 'to gird' (see CINCTURE).] —**cingulate** /síng gyŏŏlət, -layt/ *adj.*

cinnabar /sínnə baar/ *n.* **1.** MINERALS **MINERAL SOURCE OF MERCURY** a reddish-brown mineral that is the principal source of mercury and is found near areas of volcanic activity **2.** CHEM **RED PIGMENT** red mercuric sulphide used as a pigment **3.** COLOURS **BRIGHT RED** a bright red colour tinged with orange ■ *adj.* **OF A BRIGHT RED COLOUR** of a bright red colour tinged with orange [Middle English. Via Latin from Greek *kinnabari*, ultimately from an oriental language.] —**cinnabarine** /sínnəbə rīn, -baarin/ *adj.*

cinnabar moth *n.* a large European moth that has orange-red wings. Latin name: *Hypocrita jacobaeae.*

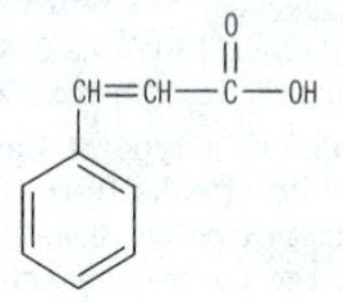

Cinnamic acid

cinnamic acid /si námmik-/ *n.* a white odourless acid that is insoluble in water, used in the perfume industry. Formula: $C_9H_8O_2$. [From its presence in cinnamon oil]

cinnamon /sínnəmən/ *n.* **1.** FOOD **SPICE OBTAINED FROM BARK** the dried bark of any of several Asian trees, used to spice foods and drinks **2.** TREES **ASIAN TREE WITH CINNAMON BARK** a small evergreen tree found in tropical regions of Asia whose dried bark is the source of cinnamon. Genus: *Cinnamomum.* **3.** COLOURS **REDDISH-BROWN COLOUR** a warm reddish-brown colour ■ *adj.* **OF A REDDISH BROWN COLOUR** of a warm reddish-brown colour [14thC. From French *cinnamome*, ultimately perhaps via Greek *kinnamon* from Malay.] —**cinnamic** /si námmik/ *adj.*

cinnamon bear *n.* a variety of the North American black bear that has reddish-brown fur

cinnamon fern *n.* a large fern common to wet sites that has narrow cinnamon-coloured inner pore-bearing fronds, surrounded by wider green sterile fronds. Latin name: *Osmunda cinnamomea.*

cinnamon stone *n.* = **essonite** [From its colour]

cinquain /sing káyn, síng kayn/ *n.* a stanza of poetry that consists of five lines [Late 19thC. From French, literally 'set of five', formed from *cinq* 'five'.]

cinque /singk/ *n.* the number five on cards or dice, or a throw of five in a dice game [14thC. From French, 'five'.]

cinquecento /chíngkwi chéntō/ *n.* the 16th century, especially with reference to Italian art and architecture [Mid-18thC. From Italian, literally '500', shortened from *milcinquecento* '1500', used to refer to the years 1500–99.]

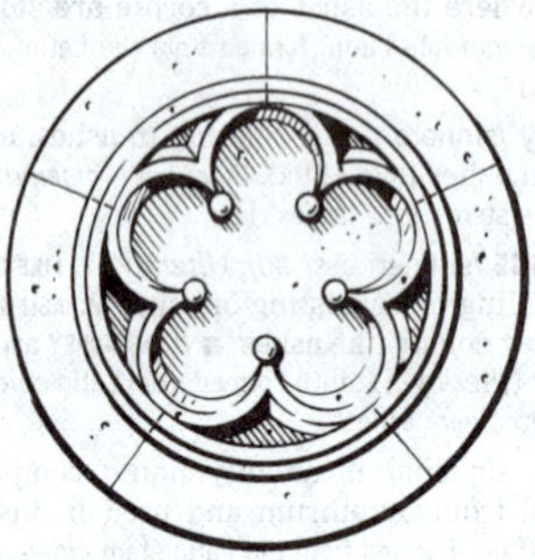

Cinquefoil

cinquefoil /síngk foyl, sángk-/ (*plural* **-foils** *or* **-foil**) *n.* **1.** PLANTS = **potentilla 2.** ARCHIT **FIVE-ARC DESIGN** an architectural design in the form of five arcs joined together [13thC. From Latin *quinquefolium*, literally 'five leaves'.]

Cinque Ports /síngk páwrts/ group of towns on the southeastern coast of England, which supplied the monarch with free ships for 15 days a year

Cipango /si páng gō/ *n.* in medieval mythology, an island off the eastern coast of Asia, perhaps modern-day Japan

cipher /sífər/, **cypher** *n.* **1.** **WRITTEN CODE** a written code in which the letters of a text are substituted according to a system **2.** **CIPHER KEY** the key to a cipher **3.** **TEXT IN CIPHER** a text written in cipher **4.** DESIGN **DESIGN OF INTERLACING INITIALS** a decorative design consisting of a set of interlaced initials **5.** MUSIC **FAULT IN ORGAN VALVE** a fault in an organ valve that causes a pipe to sound continuously without the key having been pressed ■ *v.* **1.** *vt.* **WRITE IN CODE** to write a text or message in cipher **2.** *vi.* MUSIC **SOUND OWING TO FAULT** to sound continuously because of a faulty valve (*refers to an organ or organ pipe*) [14thC. Via Old French *cif(f)re* from, ultimately, Arabic *ṣifr* 'zero', source of English *zero.*]

cipolin /síppəlin/ *n.* a type of Italian marble with green and white streaks [Late 18thC. Directly or via French from Italian *cipollino*, literally 'small onion', from *cipolla* 'onion', because the streaked structure resembles the layers of an onion.]

cir. *abbr.* **1.** circle **2.** circa **3.** circuit **4.** circulation **5.** circumference

circa /súrkə/ *prep.* used before a date to indicate that it is approximate or estimated [Mid-19thC. From Latin, ultimately from *circus* 'circle' (see CIRCUS).]

circadian /sur káydi ən/ *adj.* used to describe a pattern repeated approximately every 24 hours [Mid-20thC. Formed from Latin *circa* 'about, in' + *dies* 'day'.]

Circassian /sur kássi ən/ *n.* a group of languages spoken in southern Russia, northern Georgia, and by many émigré communities in Turkey. It belongs to the Abkhaz-Adyghean branch of North Caucasian languages. Circassian is spoken by about 1,500,000 people and its dialects include Adyghe and Kabardian. [Mid-16thC. Formed from *Circassia*, Latinized form of Russian *Cherkes.*] —**Circassian** *adj.*

Circe /súrssi/ *n.* in Greek mythology, the daughter of Hecate and the Sun, who lured sailors to her island where she made love with them and then turned them into pigs [12thC. Via Latin from Greek *Kirkē.*] —**Circean** *adj.*

circinate /súrssi nayt/ *adj.* used to describe leaves or fronds that are coiled with the tip in the centre, as in most ferns [Early 19thC. From Latin *circinatus*, past participle of *circinare* 'to make round', from *circinus* 'pair of compasses', from *circus* 'circle' (see CIRCUS).] —**circinately** *adv.*

Circinus /súrssinəss/ *n.* a small inconspicuous constellation in the southern hemisphere near Centaurus [Early 19thC. From Latin *circinus* 'pair of compasses'.]

circle /súrk'l/ *n.* **1.** GEOM **SHAPE OF PERFECT HOLLOW RING** a curved line surrounding a centre point, every point of the line being an equal distance from the centre point **2.** **AREA INSIDE CIRCLE** the area enclosed by a circle **3.** **CIRCLE-SHAPED THING** an area or object in the shape of a circle **4.** **CIRCLE-SHAPED PATTERN** an arrangement or pattern in the shape of a circle **5.** **GROUP OF PEOPLE** a group of people who share a common interest, profession, activity, or social background **6.** **CURVED ROUTE** a course or route that follows a curved path **7.** THEATRE **RAISED THEATRE SEATING** a section of tiered seating in a theatre that is above ground level **8.** **CYCLE** a process or series of events that ends at the point at which it began, or that repeats itself continuously **9.** ARCHAEOL **FORMATION OF ANCIENT STONES** any ring-shaped formation of large stones that dates from prehistoric times and is thought to have had a religious or astronomical use ■ *v.* (**-cles, -cling, -cled**) **1.** *vti.* **MOVE ALONG CURVING ROUTE** to move or move round sth, following a curving route or path that ends where it began and usually repeats its cycle **2.** *vt.* **MAKE MARK ROUND** to draw a ring round sth in order to mark it or draw attention to it **3.** *vt.* **SURROUND** to surround a place or an area with people [Pre-12thC. Via French from Latin *circulus*, literally 'small circle', from *circus* 'circle' (see CIRCUS).] —**circler** *n.* ◇ **come full circle** to return to an earlier or first position or situation after leaving it ◇ **go** *or* **run round in circles** to be very busy without actually achieving anything ◇ **square the circle** to try to do sth extremely difficult or impossible

WORD KEY: CULTURAL NOTE

The Caucasian Chalk Circle, a play by German dramatist Bertolt Brecht (1948). The central story of this play within a play, portrays a dispute for the custody of a young boy between his natural mother and the woman who has raised him at great personal cost. The work examines traditional values and the need to adapt them to changing historical circumstances.

circlet /súrklət/ *n.* **1.** **RING-LIKE DECORATION** a circular decoration, especially a decorative band worn on the head **2.** **SMALL CIRCLE** a small circle (*literary*)

circs /surks/ *npl.* circumstances (*informal*) [Mid-19thC. Contraction.]

circuit /súrkit/ *n.* **1.** **CIRCULAR PATH** a route or path that follows a curved course and finishes at the point at which it began **2.** **AREA BOUNDED BY CIRCULAR PATH** an area that lies inside a circular route or path **3.** **SINGLE JOURNEY ROUND CIRCULAR PATH** a single complete journey round a circular route or path **4.** **REGULAR JOURNEY** a journey that sb, e.g. a salesperson or circuit judge, regularly makes round an area **5.** **STOPS ON JOURNEY** the places visited by sb on a regular circuit **6.** **ROUND OF EVENTS** a series of events or places regularly attended or visited by the same group of people **7.** SPORTS **ONGOING SERIES OF COMPETITIONS** an ongoing series of competitions or tournaments regularly attended by the same group of people **8.** ELEC **ROUTE FOR ELECTRICITY** a route around which an electrical current can flow, beginning and ending at the same point **9.** MOTOR SPORTS **RACE TRACK FOR MOTORSPORTS** a race track for cars or motorcycles **10.** ARTS **CHAIN OF ARTS VENUES** a group of theatres, cinemas, or clubs, under the same management or showing the same performances or films in rotation **11.** SPORTS **SET OF EXERCISES** a complete round of exercises in circuit training **12.** CHR **LOCAL GROUP OF METHODIST CHURCHES** a group of Methodist churches that form a local division of the Church's national administration **13.** LAW **GEOGRAPHICAL DIVISION OF ENGLISH LEGAL SYSTEM** any of the six areas that England is divided into for the purposes of administering the law ■ *vti.* (**-cuits, -cuiting, -cuited**) **MOVE ROUND ALONG CIRCULAR PATH** to follow a circuit round sth (*formal*) [14thC. Via French from Latin *circuitus*, from *circuire* 'to go round', from *ire* 'to go'.]

circuit board *n.* COMPUT = **printed circuit board**

circuit breaker *n.* a device that can automatically stop the flow of electricity in a circuit if there is too much current to operate safely. Circuit breakers are easier to use than fuses because they just need to be reset instead of replaced.

circuit judge *n.* a judge who sits in different courts within a region

circuitous /sur kyoō itəss/ *adj.* lengthy because very indirect [Mid-17thC. From medieval Latin *circuitosus*, from Latin *circuire* (see CIRCUIT).] —**circuitously** *adv.* —**circuitousness** *n.*

circuitry /súrkitri/ *n.* **1.** **CIRCUIT COMPONENTS** the components of an electric circuit **2.** **ELECTRICAL SYSTEM** the system of circuits in an electrical or electronic device **3.** **ELECTRIC CIRCUIT'S LAYOUT** the design or layout of an electric circuit

circuit training *n.* a form of sports training that involves performing different exercises in rotation

circuity /sur kyoō əti/ (*plural* **-ties**) *n.* the indirect and lengthy nature of sth, especially the way sb speaks, argues, or reasons [Mid-16thC. From French *circuité*, ultimately from Latin *circuire* (see CIRCUIT).]

circular /súrkyoōlər/ *adj.* **1.** **LIKE A CIRCLE** shaped like, or resembling a circle **2.** **ENDING WHERE BEGINNING** following a curved route or path that ends at the point where it began **3.** LOGIC **NOT LOGICAL** used to describe an argument that does not move logically to a satisfactory conclusion because it assumes as true sth that needs to be proved or demonstrated **4.** **CIRCUITOUS** indirect and complicated **5.** **WIDELY DISTRIBUTED** intended for distribution to a large number of people ■ *n.* **WIDELY DISTRIBUTED NOTICE** a letter, advertisement, or other notice distributed to a large number of people [14thC. Via Anglo-Norman from, ultimately, late Latin *circularis*, from Latin *circulus* (see CIRCLE).] —**circularly** *adv.*

circular breathing *n.* the technique of using the cheeks to force air out of the mouth while breathing in through the nose, used by woodwind and brass players to hold long notes

circular function *n.* GEOM = **trigonometric function**

circularise *vt.* = **circularize**

circularity /súrkyoō lárrəti/ *n.* **1.** **CIRCULAR SHAPE** the quality or fact of being circular in shape **2.** LOGIC **ILLOGICAL NATURE** the illogical nature of sth such as an argument or piece of reasoning **3.** **COMPLEXITY AND INDIRECTNESS** the indirect and complicated nature of sth such as a method or route [Late 16thC. From medieval Latin *circularitas*, from *circularis* (see CIRCULAR).]

circularize /súrkyoōlə rīz/ (**-izes, -izing, -ized**), **circularise** (**-ises, -ising, -ised**) *vt.* **1.** **PUBLICIZE** to publicize sth by distributing leaflets or notices widely **2.** **CANVASS OR POLL** to ask people for support or to survey public opinion by sending out questionnaires, letters, or leaflets —**circularization** /súrkyoōlə rī záysh'n/ *n.*

circular measure *n.* the measurement of an angle by relating it to the angle formed in the centre of a circle by a sector, in units called radians

circular saw *n.* an electrically powered saw with a circular toothed blade that rotates at high speed

circulate /súrkyoō layt/ *v.* (**-lates, -lating, -lated**) **1.** *vi.* **MOVE ROUND CIRCULAR SYSTEM** to move freely through a circuit or to follow a circular route **2.** *vti.* **PASS ROUND** to distribute or pass sth from person to person or from place to place, or be passed in this way **3.** *vi.* **FLOW** to move or flow freely in an enclosed space or defined area **4.** *vi.* **MINGLE** to move from person to person or group to group at a social gathering in order to talk with different people (*informal*) [15thC. From Latin *circulat-*, past participle stem of *circulare*, from *circulus*, literally 'small circle'.] —**circulatable** *adj.* —**circulator** *n.*

circulating library *n.* = **mobile library**

circulating medium *n.* anything used as money, e.g. a valuable commodity, banknotes, or illegal drugs

circulation /súrkyoŏ láysh'n/ *n.* **1.** PHYSIOL **MOVEMENT OF BLOOD ROUND BODY** the movement of blood through the body **2. FLOW** the free movement of sth, e.g. air or water **3. DISTRIBUTION OR COMMUNICATION** the passing or communication of sth, e.g. news, information, or money, from place to place or from person to person **4.** PUBL **NUMBER DISTRIBUTED OF PUBLICATION** the number of copies of a publication that are sold or distributed to readers in a given period **5.** FIN **USE AS MONEY** valid use as currency **6.** LIBRARIES **LIBRARY DEPARTMENT** the department of a lending library that oversees the lending and retrieval of books and other items **7.** LIBRARIES **ITEM OR ITEMS BORROWED FROM LIBRARY** an item borrowed from a lending library, or the total number of items on loan at a given time

circulatory /súrkyoŏ láytəri, súrkyoŏlətəri/ *adj.* relating to the circulation of the blood

circulatory system *n.* the system consisting of the heart, blood vessels, and lymph vessels that pumps blood and lymph round the body

circum. *abbr.* circumference

circum- *prefix.* around ○ *circumlunar* [From Latin, formed from *circus* (see CIRCLE)]

circumambient /súrkəm ámbi ənt/ *adj.* surrounding (*literary*) —**circumambiently** *adv.*

circumambulate /súrkəm ámbyoŏ layt/ *v.* (**-lates, -lating, -lated**) **1.** *vti.* **WALK ROUND** to walk round sth, e.g. round the dead, a tomb, or a sacred site, as part of a ritual (*formal or humorous*) **2.** *vi.* **EVADE THE ISSUE** to avoid the point of a subject or discussion (*literary*) —**circumambulation** /súrkəm ambyoŏ láysh'n/ *n.*

circumcise /súrkəm sīz/ (**-cises, -cising, -cised**) *vt.* **1. REMOVE MALE'S FORESKIN** to remove all or part of the foreskin from the penis, either for hygiene reasons or as part of a religious ritual **2. REMOVE FEMALE'S CLITORIS OR PREPUCE** to cut away the skin (**prepuce**) covering the clitoris, or remove the clitoris, usually as part of a religious ritual [13thC. Via Old French from Latin *circumcidere* 'to cut round' (a literal translation of Greek *peritemnein*), from *caedere* 'to cut'.] —**circumciser** *n.*

circumcision /súrkəm sízh'n/ *n.* **1. REMOVAL OF MALE'S FORESKIN** the removal of all or part of the foreskin from the penis **2. REMOVAL OF CLITORIS OR ITS PREPUCE** the cutting away of the skin (**prepuce**) covering the clitoris, or the removal of the clitoris **3. RELIGIOUS CEREMONY WITH CIRCUMCISION** a religious ceremony during which a circumcision is performed, especially in Judaism or Islam

Circumcision *n.* a Roman Catholic festival held on 1 January to commemorate the circumcision of Jesus Christ

circumference /sər kúmfrənss/ *n.* **1.** GEOM **DISTANCE AROUND CIRCLE** the distance around the edge of a circle **2. DISTANCE AROUND STH** the distance around the edge of an object or a place that is roughly circular **3. EDGE** the edge of a round object or area [14thC. From, ultimately, Latin *circumferentia*, from *circumferens*, the present participle of *circumferre*, literally 'to carry round', from *ferre* 'to carry'.] —**circumferential** /sər kúmfə rénsh'l/ *adj.* —**circumferentially** /-rénsh'li/ *adv.*

circumflex /súrkəm fleks/, **circumflex accent** *n.* a mark ^ placed above a letter to indicate a specific pronunciation or a contraction, usually different from that of the unaccented letter. Circumflexes may be written over vowels as in French, or over consonants as in Esperanto. [Late 16thC. From Latin *circumflexus*, the past participle of *circumflectere*, literally 'to bend round', from *flectere* 'to bend'.]

circumfluent /sər kúmmfloŏ ənt/, **circumfluous** /-floŏ əss/ *adj.* flowing all around a thing or place (*literary*)

circumfuse /súrkəm fyoóz/ *vt.* (**-fuses, -fusing, -fused**) to surround or cover sth, especially with liquid (*formal or literary*) —**circumfusion** /-fyoózh'n/ *n.*

circumlocution /súrkəm lə kyoósh'n/ *n.* **1. INDIRECT WAY OF SAYING STH** the use of more words than necessary to express sth, especially to avoid saying it directly **2. INDIRECT EXPRESSION** sth said using more words than necessary, especially to avoid expressing it directly [15thC. Directly or via French from the Latin stem *circumlocution-*, literally 'speaking around', from the stem *locution-* 'speaking' (see LOCUTION).] —**circumlocutory** /súrkəm lókyoŏtəri/ *adj.*

circumlunar /súrkəm loónər/ *adj.* around or surrounding the moon

circumnavigate /súrkəm návvi gayt/ (**-gates, -gating, -gated**) *vt.* to sail or fly around sth, e.g. an island (*formal*) —**circumnavigable** /-návvigəb'l/ *adj.* —**circumnavigation** /súrkəm navi gáysh'n/ *n.* —**circumnavigator** /súrkəm návvi gaytər/ *n.*

circumpolar /súrkəm pólər/ *adj.* located or living near one or both poles of the Earth or some other planet (*technical*)

circumpolar star *n.* a star that is always visible above the horizon at a given latitude

circumscribe /súrkəm skrīb/ *v.* (**-scribes, -scribing, -scribed**) **1.** *vt.* **RESTRICT** to limit the power of sth or sb to act independently (*formal; often passive*) **2.** GEOM **ENCLOSE WITHIN GEOMETRICAL SHAPE** to draw one geometrical figure around another so that they touch at every corner (**vertex**) of the enclosed figure or at every side of the enclosing figure without cutting across each other [14thC. From Latin *circumscribere*, literally 'to write round', from *scribere* 'to write'.] —**circumscribable** /súrkəm skrībəb'l/ *adj.* —**circumscriber** /súrkəm skrībər/ *n.*

circumscription /súrkəm skrípsh'n/ *n.* **1. RESTRICTION OF POWER** the limiting of the power of sth or sb to act independently (*formal*) **2.** GEOM **ENCLOSING OF STH WITHIN GEOMETRICAL SHAPE** the act of drawing one geometrical figure around another so that they touch at every corner (**vertex**) of the enclosed figure or at every side of the enclosing figure without cutting across each other **3.** GEOM **DRAWN SHAPE** a shape drawn or enclosed by circumscription **4.** COINS **INSCRIPTION ROUND CIRCULAR EDGE** a circular inscription around the edge of a coin or medal —**circumscriptive** *adj.* —**circumscriptively** *adv.*

circumsolar /súrkəm sólər/ *adj.* around or surrounding the sun

circumspect /súrkəm spekt/ *adj.* showing unwillingness to act without first weighing up the risks or consequences [15thC. From, ultimately, the Latin stem *circumspect-*, the past participle of *circumspicere*, literally 'to look around', from *specere* 'to look'.] —**circumspective** /súrkəm spéktiv/ *adj.* —**circumspectly** /súrkəm spektli/ *adv.*

WORD KEY: SYNONYMS

See Synonyms at ***cautious***.

circumstance /súrkəmstəns, -staans/ *n.* **1. CONDITION AFFECTING SITUATION** a condition that affects what happens or how sb reacts in a particular situation (*usually used in the plural*) ○ *Under the circumstances, the team played well.* **2. UNCONTROLLABLE CONDITIONS** the conditions that affect sb's life and that are beyond his or her control **3. EVENT** an event or occurrence (*formal*) **4. WAY STH HAPPENS** the way an event happens or develops ■ **circumstances** *npl.* **CONDITIONS** the social, financial, material, or spiritual conditions that sb lives in [12thC. Via French or directly from Latin *circumstantia*, from *circumstant-*, the present participle stem of *circumstare*, literally 'to stand around', from *stare* 'to stand'.]

circumstanced /súrkəm staanst/ *adj.* living in a particular state or set of conditions (*formal*)

circumstantial /súrkəm stánsh'l/ *adj.* **1.** LAW **BASED ON INFERENCE** containing or based on facts that allow a court to deduce that sb is guilty without conclusive proof ○ *circumstantial evidence* **2. SPECIAL** related to particular circumstances **3. DETAILED** thorough and very detailed (*formal*) **4. FORMAL** with a great deal of formality and ceremony —**circumstantiality** /súrkəm stánshi álləti/ *n.* —**circumstantially** /-stánsh'li/ *adv.*

circumstantiate /súrkəm stánshi ayt/ (**-ates, -ating, -ated**) *vt.* to provide evidence to support an argument or allegation (*formal*) —**circumstantiation** /súrkəm stánshi áysh'n/ *n.*

circumstellar /súrkəm stéllər/ *adj.* around or surrounding a star

circumterrestrial /súrkəm tə réstri əl/ *adj.* around or surrounding the Earth

circumvallate /súrkəm vállayt/ (**-lates, -lating, -lated**) *vt.* to protect a town or camp by surrounding it with a rampart or a defensive wall (*archaic or formal*) [Mid-17thC. From Latin *circumvallare*, literally 'to fortify with a rampart round', from, ultimately, *vallum* 'rampart', from *vallus* 'stake'.] —**circumvallation** /súrkəm və láysh'n/ *n.*

circumvent /súrkəm vént/ (**-vents, -venting, -vented**) *vt.* **1. GET ROUND RESTRICTION** to find a way of avoiding restrictions imposed by a rule or law without actually breaking it ○ *an attempt to circumvent the ban* **2. OUTWIT SB** to anticipate and counter sb's plans [15thC. From Latin *circumvent-*, the present participle stem of *circumvenire*, literally 'to come round', from *venire* 'to come' (source of English *convene*).] —**circumventer** *n.* —**circumvention** /-vénsh'n/ *n.* —**circumventive** /-véntiv/ *adj.*

circumvolution /súrkəm və loósh'n/ *n.* a turning or winding movement around a central axis (*formal*) [15thC. From Latin *circumvolut-*, the past participle stem of *circumvolvere*, literally 'to turn around', from *volvere* 'to turn'.] —**circumvolutory** /súrkəm və loótəri/ *adj.*

circus /súrkəss/ *n.* **1. TRAVELLING SHOW** a group of travelling entertainers, including clowns, acrobats and sometimes animal trainers and their animals **2. SHOW** a performance given by circus entertainers, or the place where they perform **3. SELF-IMPORTANT EVENT** a confused, noisy, or overwhelming event or situation, especially one that seems full of self-importance (*informal*) ○ *a media circus* **4.** ARCHIT **ROMAN STADIUM** an open stadium built by the ancient Romans to stage chariot races or fights between gladiators **5. ROMAN SHOW** a performance staged in a Roman stadium **6. PLACE WHERE STREETS MEET** a round or roundish open space where several streets meet ○ *Piccadilly Circus* [14thC. From Latin, literally 'ring, circle' (source of English *circle* and *search*). Ultimately from an Indo-European word meaning 'to bend', which is also the ancestor of English *curve*.] —**circusy** *adj.*

WORD KEY: ORIGIN

Circus is derived from the Latin word *circus*, meaning 'ring' or 'circle', which is also the source of English *circle, circuit, circulate*, and *search*.

Circus Maximus /súrkəss máksiməss/ *n.* a stadium in Rome used to stage chariot races and fights between gladiators [From Latin, literally 'biggest racetrack']

ciré /séeray/ *adj.* **SHINY** used to describe fabric with a shiny highly glazed finish ■ *n.* **1. SHINY FINISH** a very shiny highly glazed finish achieved by treating a fabric with wax or with a heat process **2. SHINY FABRIC** a fabric with a shiny finish [Early 20thC. From French, from the past participle of *cirer* 'to wax', from *cire* 'wax', from Latin *cera*.]

Cirencester /sīrən sestər, síssitər/ ancient market town in Gloucestershire, England. Population: 15,221 (1991).

cire perdue /séer pair dyoó/ *n.* = **lost wax** (*technical*) [Late 19thC. From French, literally 'lost wax'.]

cirque /surk/ *n.* a semicircular hollow with steep walls formed by glacial erosion on mountains. It often forms the head of a valley. [Mid-19thC. From French, from Latin *circus* (see CIRCUS).]

cirrate /sírr ayt/ *adj.* **1.** BIOL **WITH TENTACLES** bearing structures resembling tentacles or tendrils (**cirri**) **2. SHAPED LIKE TENTACLE** like a tentacle or tendril in shape [Early 19thC. From the Latin stem *cirrat-* 'curled', from *cirrus* 'curl'.]

cirrhosis /sə róssiss/ *n.* a chronic progressive disease of the liver characterized by the replacement of healthy cells with scar tissue [Early 19thC. From modern Latin, formed from Greek *kirrhos* 'orange-coloured'. From the presence of yellowish granules.] —**cirrhotic** /sə róttik/ *adj.*

cirri plural of **cirrus**

cirriform /sírr i fawrm/ *adj.* shaped like a long slender tendril or tentacle [Early 19thC. Coined from Latin *cirrus* (see CIRRUS) + -FORM.]

cirriped /sírri ped/, **cirripede** /sírri peed/ *n.* a marine crustacean that lives fixed in one spot and draws food by means of slender hairs (**cirri**). Subclass: Cirripedia. [Mid-19thC. From modern Latin *Cirripedia*, literally 'with curly legs', subclass name, from Latin *cirrus* 'curl'.]

cirrocumulus /sírrō kyoŏmyoŏləss/ (*plural* **-li** /-lī/) *n.* a high-altitude cloud formed of icy particles that occurs in lines of small rounded clouds. Cirrocumulus clouds often make a pattern resembling fish scales, called a mackerel sky, indicating unsettled weather.

cirrose /sírr ōss/ *adj.* consisting of thin wisps, as formed by cirrus clouds

cirrostratus /sírrō stráatəss/ (*plural* **-ti** /-tī/) *n.* a cirrus cloud resembling a transparent white veil high in the sky. It indicates wet weather.

cirrus /sírrəss/ (*plural* **-ri** /-rī/) *n.* **1.** METEOROL **HIGH-ALTITUDE WISPY CLOUD** a thin wispy cloud, occurring as narrow bands of tiny ice particles, that forms at the highest and coldest point of the cloud region **2.** ZOOL **SLENDER TENTACLE** a slender tentacle with sensory or locomotive function, or a part resembling one [Early 18thC. From Latin, 'curl, fringe'.]

cis /siss/ *adj.* having two atoms or groups on the same side of a double bond between carbon atoms [Late 18thC. From Latin (see CIS-).]

CIS *abbr.* Commonwealth of Independent States

cis- *prefix.* GEOG on the near side of ○ *cisatlantic* [From Latin *cis*. Ultimately from an Indo-European base meaning 'this', which is also the ancestor of English *here*, *hither*, and *he*.]

cisalpine /siss álpīn/ *adj.* **1.** GEOG **SOUTH OF ALPS** situated south of the Alps **2.** CHR **LIMITING PAPAL POWER** relating to a movement in the Roman Catholic Church to limit papal power and encourage the independence of local churches [Mid-16thC. From Latin *cisalpinus* 'on this side of the Alps' (as viewed from Rome), from *alpinus* 'alpine'.]

cisatlantic /síss ət lántik/ *adj.* situated on the same side of the Atlantic Ocean as the writer or speaker

CISC *abbr.* complex instruction set computer

cisco /sískō/ (*plural* **-coes** or **-cos**) *n.* a silvery freshwater whitefish, found in deep lakes in North America. Genus: *Coregonus*. [Mid-19thC. Back-formation from Canadian French *ciscoette*, alteration (influenced by *-ette* 'small') of Ojibwa *bemidewiskawed*, literally 'that which has oily skin'.]

Ciskei /sís kī/ former homeland bordering the Indian Ocean in South Africa. South Africa declared Ciskei independent in 1981 and it was finally abolished in 1993, when the territory was reintegrated into South Africa.

cislunar /siss loŏnər/ *adj.* situated between the Earth and the Moon

cismontane /siss móntayn/ *adj.* on the same side of the mountains as the writer or speaker

cispadane /síss pə dayn/ *adj.* situated on the southern side of the River Po [Late 18thC. Formed from CIS- + Latin *Padus* 'the Po'.]

cissing /síssing/ *n.* the appearance of marks such as bubbles or pits in paintwork. This is a result of the paint not adhering properly to the surface. [Late 20thC. Origin unknown.]

cissus /síssəss/ *n.* an evergreen woody climbing plant, grown for its green foliage. Genus: *Cissus*. [Late 20thC. Via modern Latin from Greek *kissos* 'ivy', of uncertain origin; perhaps formed from *iskhein* 'to hold'.]

cist /sist/, **kist** /kist/ *n.* a wood or stone coffin, dating from the latter part of the Stone Age [Early 19thC. From Welsh, literally 'chest', from *cist faen* 'stone chest'.]

Cistercian /si stúrsh'n/ *adj.* **RELATING TO A RELIGIOUS GROUP** relating to an austere contemplative Christian order of monks and nuns founded by reformist Benedictines in 1098 ■ *n.* **MONK OR NUN** a member of the Cistercian order of monks and nuns [15thC. Via French from Latin *Cistercium* 'Cîteaux', near Dijon, France.]

cistern /sístərn/ *n.* **1.** CONSTR **WATER TANK** a tank for storing water, especially one in the roof of a house or connected to a toilet **2.** UNDERGROUND TANK an underground tank for storing rainwater **3.** ANAT = **cisterna** [13thC. Via French from Latin *cisterna*, from *cista* 'chest', from Greek *kistē* (source of English *chest*).]

cisterna /si stúrnə/ (*plural* **-nae** /-nee/) *n.* a pouch or cavity that contains a body fluid [Late 19thC. From, ultimately, Latin *cisterna* (see CISTERN).] —**cisternal** *adj.*

cistron /sísstrən, -tron/ *n.* a section of DNA containing the genetic code for a short chain of amino acids (**polypeptide**), the smallest functional unit carrying genetic information [Mid-20thC. Coined from CIS- + TRANS- + -ON.] —**cistronic** /siss trónnik/ *adj.*

cistus /sístəss/ *n.* an evergreen shrub grown for its white, red, or yellow flowers. Genus: *Cistus*. [Mid-16thC. From, ultimately, Greek *kistos* 'red-flowered shrub'.]

CIT *abbr.* Central Institute of Technology

cit. *abbr.* **1.** cited **2.** citizen

citadel /síttəd'l, -del/ *n.* **1.** FORTRESS a fortress or strongly fortified building in or near a city, used as a place of refuge **2.** DEFENDER a strong defender of a particular way of life or principle [Mid-16thC. Via French or directly from Italian *cittadella*, literally 'little city', from *cittade* 'city', variant of *città*, from Latin *civitas* (see CITY).]

citation /sī táysh'n/ *n.* **1.** OFFICIAL ACKNOWLEDGMENT OF MERIT an official document or speech that praises sb's actions, accomplishments, or character **2.** EXTRACT FROM WORK a quotation from an authoritative source, used, e.g., to support an idea or argument **3.** ACT OF CITING STH the act or process of citing sth **4.** US LAW ORDER TO APPEAR IN COURT a writ for sb to appear in a court of law **5.** LAW REFERENCE TO PREVIOUS DECISION a reference to a previous decision by a court or legal authority **6.** LAW USE OF PRECEDENT the legal practice or process of referring to precedent —**citational** *adj.* —**citatory** /sítətəri, sī táy-/ *adj.*

cite /sīt/ *vt.* (**cites**, **citing**, **cited**) **1.** QUOTE STH OR SB to mention sth or sb as an example to support an argument or help explain what is being said (*formal*) **2.** LAW NAME SB to name sb officially in a court case **3.** US LAW ORDER TO APPEAR IN COURT to order sb officially to appear in court **4.** MIL OFFICIALLY PRAISE SB to praise the actions of a member of the armed services in an official document (*often passive*) ■ *n.* US CITATION a citation (*informal*) [15thC. From, ultimately, Latin *citare*, literally 'to summon repeatedly', from *citus*, past participle of *ciere* 'to summon' (source of English *excite*).]

— **WORD KEY: ORIGIN** —

Cite is derived from the Latin word *ciere*, meaning 'to summon', which is also the source of English *excite*, *incite*, *recite*, and *solicit*.

cithara /síthərə/, **kithara** /kíthərə/ *n.* a stringed musical instrument similar to a lyre, played in ancient Greece [Late 18thC. Via Latin from Greek *kithara* (source of English *guitar* and *zither*).]

citified /sítti fīd/ *adj.* oversophisticated, in a way often associated with those who live in cities by those who do not (*disapproving*)

citify /sítti fī/ (**-fies**, **-fying**, **-fied**) *vt.* (*disapproving*) **1.** TURN PLACE INTO CITY to develop an area and make it more urban **2.** MAKE SB TOO SOPHISTICATED to make sb adopt the customs, behaviour, or dress of those who live in cities —**citification** /sítti fi káysh'n/ *n.*

citizen /síttiz'n/ *n.* **1.** LEGAL RESIDENT sb who has the right to live in a country because he or she was born there or because he or she has been legally accepted by that country **2.** SB WHO LIVES IN A CITY sb who lives in a city or town rather than in a rural area **3.** CIVILIAN a civilian, rather than a member of the armed forces, a police officer, or a public official [13thC. From Anglo-Norman *citezein*, from Old French *citeain*, from the Latin stem *civitat-* 'city'.] —**citizenly** *adj.*

— **WORD KEY: CULTURAL NOTE** —

Citizen Kane, a film by US director Orson Welles (1941). Repeatedly nominated as one of the greatest films of all time, it is the story of the rise and the tormented private life of a fictional media baron, Charles Foster Kane (supposedly based on the life of the billionaire publisher William Randolph Hearst). The film's many stylistic innovations include the use of mock-newsreel footage and striking deep-focus photography. The term *Citizen Kane* is often used as a description of real people and situations, for example in *a private life reminiscent of Citizen Kane*.

citizenry /síttiz'nri/ (*plural* **-ries**) *n.* the citizens of a place or area collectively (*formal*; *takes a singular or plural verb*)

citizen's arrest *n.* an arrest made by an ordinary citizen rather than by a police officer

citizens band *n.* radio frequencies used by the general public to talk to one another over short distances

citizenship /síttiz'nship/ *n.* **1.** LEGAL STATUS OF CITIZEN the legal status of being a citizen of a country **2.** SOCIAL CONDUCT the duties and responsibilities that come with being a member of a community

Citlaltépetl /seét lal táy pett'l/ volcanic peak in central Veracruz state, eastern Mexico, and the highest point in Mexico. Height: 5,700 m/18,700 ft.

citole /síttōl/ *n.* MUSIC = **cittern** [14thC. From French, of uncertain origin; probably literally 'little cithara', formed from Latin *cithara* 'cithara' (see CITHARA).]

citral /sítrəl/ *n.* a volatile pale yellow liquid with a pleasant odour found in lemon grass oil. Formula: $C_{10}H_{16}O$.

citrate /síttrayt/ *n.* a salt or ester of citric acid

citric /síttrik/ *adj.* relating to citrus fruit

Citric acid

citric acid *n.* a weak colourless acid present in citrus and other fruit. It is obtained commercially mainly from lemon, lime, or pineapple juice or from fermentation of sugars, and is used in flavourings.

citric acid cycle *n.* = Krebs cycle

citriculture /síttri kulchə/ *n.* the cultivation of citrus fruits [Early 20thC. From CITRUS + CULTURE.] —**citriculturist** /síttri kúlchərist/ *n.*

citrine /síttrin/ *n.* **1.** MINERALS YELLOW QUARTZ a brownish-yellow semiprecious variety of quartz **2.** COLOURS GREENISH-YELLOW COLOUR a greenish-yellow colour, like that of a lemon ■ *adj.* COLOURS GREENISH-YELLOW of a greenish-yellow colour, like that of a lemon [Late 16thC. From the colour of the citron or lemon.]

citron /síttrən/ *n.* **1.** TREES THORNY CITRUS TREE a small thorny evergreen citrus tree with edible fruit. Latin name: *Citrus medica*. **2.** FOOD CITRUS FRUIT LIKE LARGE LEMON the fruit of the citron tree, resembling a large lemon with a thick aromatic rind **3.** FOOD CANDIED RIND the candied rind of a fruit from a citron tree, used to decorate and flavour food **4.** PLANTS WATERMELON a small watermelon that has inedible white flesh and a hard rind. Latin name: *Citrullus lanatus* var. *citroides*. **5.** COLOURS = **citrine** *n.* 2 [Early 16thC. From French, alteration (influenced by *limon* 'lemon') of Latin *citrus* (see CITRUS).]

citronella /síttrə néllə/ *n.* **1.** citronella, citronella grass PLANTS LEMON-SCENTED GRASS a tropical Asian grass that has bluish-green lemon-scented leaves and contains an aromatic oil. Latin name: *Cymbopogon nardus*. **2.** citronella, citronella oil CHEM AROMATIC OIL a pale yellow aromatic oil obtained from citronella and used in perfumes and as an insect repellent [Mid-19thC. Via modern Latin from French *citronnelle* 'lemon oil', literally 'little citron', from *citron* 'citron', from Latin *citrus* (see CITRUS).]

citronellal /síttrə nélləl/ *n.* a colourless liquid, smelling like lemons, that is the main component of citronella oil. It is used in making perfumes and flavourings. Formula: $C_{10}H_{18}O$.

citronellol /síttrə néllol/ *n.* an alcohol derived from citronellal. Formula: $C_{10}H_{20}O$.

citron wood *n.* the wood of the citron tree or of the sandarac tree

citrulline /síttrəlin/ *n.* an amino acid found in watermelon and also formed in the liver as part of the process of urea production. Formula: $C_6H_{13}N_3O_3$. [Mid-20thC. From medieval Latin *citrullus* 'watermelon', literally 'little citron tree', from Latin *citrus* (see CITRUS).]

citrus /síttrəss/ *n.* **1.** FRUIT TREE WITH EDIBLE FRUIT a spiny evergreen tree with edible fruit of a genus that includes the orange, lemon, lime, grapefruit, and pomelo. Though native to southern and south-eastern Asia, citrus species are now grown throughout the world. Genus: *Citrus.* **2.** FOOD FRUIT the fruit of citrus trees collectively (*often used before a noun*) ○ *citrus flavour* [Early 19thC. From Latin, 'citron tree, citrus tree', of uncertain origin.]

cittern /síttərn/ *n.* a medieval stringed instrument similar to a lute but with wire strings and a flat back [Mid-16thC. Origin uncertain: probably a blend of Latin *cithara* and *gittern*, both ultimately from Greek *kithara* 'cithara'.]

city /sítti/ (*plural* **-ies**) *n.* **1.** VERY LARGE TOWN an extensive built-up area where large numbers of people live and work **2.** PEOPLE IN A CITY the inhabitants of a city collectively **3.** LARGE BRITISH TOWN a large town in Britain that has received the title of city from the Crown. It is usually the seat of a bishop, and so often has a cathedral. **4.** *US* US URBAN CENTRE OF GOVERNMENT an incorporated urban centre in the United States that has self-government, boundaries, and legal rights established by state charter **5.** *Can* CANADIAN URBAN AREA a Canadian town or urban area that has been incorporated and given the title of city by the provincial government **6.** *US* EXTREME THING a thing, place, or situation that is a good or extreme example of its type (*slang; used in combination*) ○ *It was panic city outside.* [12thC. Via Old French *cité* from Latin *civitas* 'citizenship, community', from *civis* 'citizen' (source of English *civil*).]

WORD KEY: SYNONYMS

city, conurbation, metropolis, town, municipality

CORE MEANING: an urban area where a large number of people live

city originally a town having a cathedral or having such a status conferred on it by the Crown; in the United States, a large municipal centre governed under a charter granted by the state; in Canada, a large municipal unit incorporated by the provincial government, but now used generally for any large urban area; **conurbation** an urban region formed or enlarged by the merging of adjacent cities and towns through expansion or development; **metropolis** a large or important city, sometimes the capital of a country, state, or region, often used ironically to indicate a fairly small town; **town** a populated area smaller than a city and larger than a village; **municipality** a city, town, or area with some degree of self-government.

City *n.* **1.** LONDON FINANCIAL CENTRE the important financial institutions of London. They include the Bank of England, the Stock Exchange, and the major international banks. **2.** = **City of London**

City and Guilds (*plural* **City and Guilds**) *n.* a technical or craft qualification awarded by the City and Guilds Institute (*informal*)

City and Guilds Institute *n.* a British examination body that awards qualifications for technical and craft skills

City Code *n.* a code established in the United Kingdom in 1968 to control takeover bids and mergers

city council *n.* a group of elected officials responsible for the government of a city or other municipality

city desk *n.* **1.** NEWSPAPER FINANCIAL NEWS DEPARTMENT the newspaper department that deals with financial news **2.** *US, Can* LOCAL NEWS DEPARTMENT a newspaper department that deals with local news

city editor *n.* **1.** FINANCIAL EDITOR the newspaper editor in charge of financial news **2.** *US, Can* LOCAL NEWS EDITOR the newspaper editor in charge of local news

city father *n.* a member of a city or town council or a local magistrate

city hall *n.* **1.** *US* CITY ADMINISTRATORS the administrators and elected officials who run a city **2.** *US* BUREAUCRACY the bureaucracy that runs a city, especially when regarded as insensitive or inflexible **3.** **city hall, City Hall** CITY COUNCIL BUILDING the building where a city council has its main administrative offices

city manager *n.* an administrator appointed by a municipal council to run its affairs

City of London the oldest part of London, and its business and financial heart. Its head of government is the Lord Mayor. Population: 4,142 (1991). Area: 2.6 sq. km/1 sq. mi.

cityscape /sítti skayp/ *n.* **1.** VIEW OF CITY a view of a city or town landscape **2.** PAINTING, PHOTOGRAPHY PHOTOGRAPH OR PAINTING OF CITY a photograph or painting of a view of part of a city or town

city slicker *n.* sb who lives in a city and is extremely or excessively sophisticated (*informal disapproving*)

city-state *n.* a independent state consisting of a sovereign city and its surrounding territory

city technology college *n.* in the United Kingdom, an inner-city secondary school specializing in technical subjects, with close links to and funding partly provided by private industry

citywide /sítti wīd/ *adj.* INVOLVING AN ENTIRE CITY involving the whole of a particular city ■ *adv.* ALL OVER A CITY so as to involve the whole of a particular city

Ciudad Real /syoo dád ray áal/ capital of Ciudad Real Province, in the Castile-La Mancha Region in south-central Spain. It is situated about 160 km/100 mi. south of Madrid. Population: 194,996 (1990).

civet /sívvit/ *n.* **1.** **civet, civet cat** ZOOL WILD ANIMAL LIKE CAT a small carnivorous African or Asian mammal that looks like a cat. It secretes from its anal glands a greasy substance that smells like musk. Family: Viverridae. **2.** COSMETICS SUBSTANCE USED IN PERFUME a yellow or brown substance of the consistency of butter and smelling strongly of musk, secreted by the civet. It is used in the manufacture of perfume. **3.** FUR the fur of a civet [Mid-16thC. Via French *civette* from Italian *zivetto*, from medieval Latin *zibethum*, from Arabic *zabād* 'civet perfume'.]

civic /sívvik/ *adj.* **1.** PUBLIC ADMIN CONNECTED WITH CITY ADMINISTRATION related to the government of a town or city ○ *civic reception* **2.** RELATING TO COMMUNITY connected with the duties and obligations of belonging to a community ○ *civic pride* [Mid-17thC. From, ultimately, Latin *civicus*, from *civis* 'citizen' (see CITY).] —**civically** *adv.*

civic centre *n.* **1.** PUBLIC ADMIN, LEISURE PUBLIC BUILDINGS a complex containing the public buildings of a particular town or city, e.g. the town hall, library, and recreational facilities **2.** *US* MUNICIPAL ENTERTAINMENT CENTRE a municipal entertainment complex containing an indoor arena that can be used for sports, concerts, and trade shows

civic-minded *adj.* taking an active interest in the community needs and affairs of a town or city —**civic-mindedness** *n.*

civics /sívviks/ *n.* the study of the rights and duties of citizens (*takes a singular verb*)

civic university (*plural* **civic universities**) *n.* a British university that was originally founded to provide higher education in a particular city

civil /sívv'l/ *adj.* **1.** RELATING TO CITIZENS relating to what happens within the state or between different citizens or groups of citizens ○ *civil war* **2.** NOT MILITARY connected with ordinary citizens and organizations as opposed to the armed forces ○ *the civil authorities* **3.** AS INDIVIDUAL CITIZEN relating to each citizen as an individual rather than as a member of a community or nation **4.** NOT RELIGIOUS performed by a state official such as a registrar rather than a member of the clergy ○ *civil marriage* **5.** LAW BETWEEN INDIVIDUALS involving individual people or groups in legal action other than criminal proceedings ○ *a civil action* **6.** = **civic** *adj.* 2 **7.** POLITE polite, but in a way that is cold and formal [14thC. From, ultimately, Latin *civilis*, from *civis* 'citizen' (see CITY).]

civil code *n.* the codified body of statutes in Quebec that derives from Roman and Napoleonic civil law

civil day *n.* = **calendar day** [*Civil* as in 'legally recognized' (as opposed to 'natural', 'astronomical', etc.)]

civil defence *n.* **1.** ORGANIZING OF CIVILIAN VOLUNTEERS the organization and training of civilian volunteers to help the armed forces, police, and emergency services in the event of a war, a national emergency, or a natural disaster **2.** VOLUNTEER GROUP civilian volunteers who take part in civil defence

civil disobedience *n.* the deliberate breaking of a law by ordinary citizens, carried out as nonviolent protest or passive resistance

civil engineering *n.* the branch of engineering concerned with the planning, design, and construction of such things as roads, bridges, and dams —**civil engineer** *n.*

civilian /sə vílli ən/ *n.* NONSOLDIER sb who is an ordinary citizen rather than a member of the armed forces ■ *adj.* RELATING TO CIVILIANS relating to ordinary citizens as opposed to members of the armed forces [Early 14thC. From Old French *civilien* 'of civil law', from *civil* 'civil', from Latin *civilis* (see CIVIL). Originally referring to 'civil law'; the modern sense dates from the early 19thC.]

civilianize /sə vílli ə nīz/ (**-izes, -izing, -ized**), **civilianise** (**-ises, -ising, -ised**) *vt.* to change sth from military to civilian use —**civilianization** /sə vílli ənī záysh'n/ *n.*

civilisation *n.* = **civilization**

civilise *vt.* = **civilize**

civility /sə víllәti/ (*plural* **-ties**) *n.* **1.** POLITENESS the rather formal politeness that results from observing social conventions **2.** POLITE ACT sth said or done in a formally polite way

civilization /sívvə lī záysh'n/, **civilisation** *n.* **1.** HIGHLY DEVELOPED SOCIETY a society that has a high level of culture and social organization **2.** ADVANCED DEVELOPMENT OF SOCIETY an advanced level of development in society that is marked by complex social and political organization, and material, scientific, and artistic progress **3.** ADVANCED SOCIETY IN GENERAL all the societies at an advanced level of development considered collectively **4.** POPULATED AREAS places where people live, rather than uninhabited areas **5.** COMFORT the level of material comfort that sb is used to **6.** CIVILIZING PROCESS the process of creating a high level of culture and ending barbaric or primitive practices in a particular society or region

civilize /sívvə līz/ (**-lizes, -lizing, -lized**), **civilise** (**-lises, -lising, -lised**) *vt.* **1.** TEACH ABOUT SOCIETY to create a high level of culture and end barbaric or primitive practices in a society or region **2.** MAKE MORE REFINED to teach sb to behave in a more socially and culturally acceptable way —**civilizable** *adj.* —**civilizer** *n.* —**civilizing** *adj.*

civilized /sívvə līzd/, **civilised** *adj.* **1.** CULTURALLY ADVANCED having advanced cultural and social development **2.** DECENT showing high moral development **3.** REFINED refined in tastes

civil law *n.* **1.** LAW OF CITIZENS' RIGHTS the law of a state dealing with the rights of private citizens **2.** ANCIENT ROMAN LAW the law of ancient Rome, especially the part concerned with private citizens **3.** LAW BASED ON ROMAN LAW a system of law based on Roman law rather than common law or canon law

civil liberties *npl.* the basic rights guaranteed to individual citizens by law, e.g. freedom of speech and action —**civil libertarian** *n.*

civil list *n.* in the United Kingdom, the money paid each year by the state to support the royal family [Originally 'list of the charges for the civil or administrative government of the state'. Most of the charges on that list have been moved to other accounts.]

civilly /sívvəli/ *adv.* showing politeness in a cold formal way

civil rights *npl.* rights that all citizens of a society are supposed to have, e.g. the right to vote or to receive fair treatment from the law

civil servant *n.* sb who works in a government department

civil service *n.* all the government departments of a state and the people who work in them

civil war *n.* a war between opposing groups within a country

Civil War *n.* **1.** 17C ENGLISH WAR the civil war fought between the Royalist supporters of Charles I and the Parliamentarians led by Oliver Cromwell, between 1642 and 1648 **2.** 19C US WAR the civil war fought in the United States from 1861 to 1865 between the North and the slave-owning states of the South

civil year *n.* = **calendar year** [See CIVIL DAY]

civvies /sívviz/ *npl.* ordinary clothes as opposed to a military uniform (*informal*) [Late 19thC. Shortening and alteration of CIVILIAN, in the plural probably because it is modelled on CLOTHES.]

civvy /sívvi/ (*plural* **-vies**) *n.* MIL a civilian (*informal*) [Early 20thC. Shortening and alteration.]

civvy street *n.* civilian life as referred to by military personnel (*informal*)

CJ *abbr.* **1.** Chief Justice **2.** *US* Chief Judge

CJD *abbr.* Creutzfeldt-Jakob disease

CKD *abbr. NZ* completely knocked down (*used of goods that are sold in parts to be assembled later*)

cl *abbr.* **1.** MEASURE centilitre **2.** class **3.** classification **4.** RELIG clergy **5.** FURNITURE closet **6.** CLOTHES cloth **7.** TRANSP carload

Cl *symbol.* chlorine

CL *abbr.* Sri Lanka (*international vehicle registration*)

clachan /klákhən, -kən/ *n. Scotland* a small village [15thC. From Gaelic *clachan* 'village, burying place', of uncertain origin: probably literally 'small stone', formed from *clach* 'stone'.]

clack /klak/ *v.* **1.** *vti.* MAKE NOISE to cause or make a short hard loud noise, or cause sth to make such a noise **2.** *vi.* CHATTER to chatter constantly or rapidly (*informal*) **3.** *vi.* = **cluck** ■ *n.* SHARP NOISE a short hard noise made by two things hitting each other [13thC. An imitation of the sound.]

clacker /klákər/ *n.* a rattle or toy that makes a clacking noise

Clackmannan /klak mánnən/ *parish and town in central Scotland, approximately 11 km/7 mi. east of Stirling. Population: 3,597 (1981).

Clackmannanshire /klak mánnən shər/ DISTRICT local government unitary council in Scotland, from 1996. It corresponds to the old county of this name, which was abolished in 1975. Population: 48,820 (1995).

clack valve *n.* a valve with a hinged flap that swings open

Clactonian /klak tóni ən/ *n.* a Lower Palaeolithic culture of northwestern Europe that made stone chopping tools [Named after CLACTON-ON-SEA] —**Clactonian** *adj.*

Clacton-on-Sea /kláktən-/ *popular seaside resort on the North Sea coast of Essex, England. Population: 45,065 (1991).

clad[1] /klad/ *adj.* **1.** DRESSED wearing particular clothes ○ *clad in blue* **2.** COVERED covered in a particular thing (*literary; often used in combination*) ○ *ironclad* [13thC. From Old English *clǣded*, the past participle of *clǣðian*, an earlier form of CLOTHE.]

clad[2] /klad/ (**clads, cladding, clad**) *vt.* **1.** BUILDING COVER WITH CLADDING to cover a wall or building with cladding **2.** TECH COVER METAL WITH METAL to cover or plate a metal with a layer of another metal, especially to make armour plating [Mid-16thC. Origin uncertain: probably from CLAD[1].]

clad- *prefix.* = **clado-**

Claddagh ring /kláddəkh-, kláddaak-/ *n.* an elaborate ring originally given in Ireland as a token of affection. The most common design is of two hands clasping a heart surmounted by a crown. [Late 20thC. From *Claddagh*, fishing village in Galway, Ireland, where the first Claddagh ring is said to have been made in the late 17thC.]

cladding /kládding/ *n.* **1.** BUILDING OUTER LAYER ON BUILDING a layer of stone, tiles, or wood added to the outside of a building to protect it or improve its insulation or appearance **2.** TECH METAL COATING a protective metal coating bonded onto another metal

clade /klayd/ *n.* a group of organisms, e.g. a species, that are considered to share a common ancestor [Mid-20thC. From Greek *klados* 'branch'.]

cladist /kláy dist/ *n.* a biologist who classifies organisms according to the principles of cladistics — **cladism** *n.*

cladistics /klə dístiks/ *n.* a system of biological classification that groups organisms on the basis of their observed shared characteristics in order to deduce the common ancestors (*takes a singular verb*) —**cladistic** *adj.* —**cladistically** *adv.*

clado- *prefix.* branch, shoot ○ *cladogram* [From Greek *klados*. Ultimately from an Indo-European base meaning 'to strike, cut', which is also the ancestor of English *holt*, *hilt*, and *gladiator*.]

cladoceran /klə dóssərən/ *n.* FRESHWATER CRUSTACEAN a tiny freshwater crustacean. Water fleas are cladocerans. Order: Cladocera. ■ *adj.* RELATING TO CLADOCERANS belonging to or relating to the cladocerans [Early 20thC. Formed from modern Latin *Cladocera*, order name, from Greek *klados* 'branch' + *keras* 'horn'.]

cladode /kláddōd/ *n.* BOT = **cladophyll** —**cladodial** /klə dódi əl/ *adj.*

cladogenesis /kláddō jénnəssiss, kláydó-/ *n.* evolutionary change regarded as taking place by the splitting of an ancestral species into two or more different descendant species —**cladogenetic** /kláddō jə néttik, kláy-/ *adj.* —**cladogenetically** /kláddō jə néttik'li, kláydó-/ *adv.*

cladogram /kláydə gram/ *n.* a tree-shaped evolutionary diagram in which the end of each branch represents one species. It shows evolutionary relationships and the points where species appear to have diverged from common ancestors.

cladophyll /kláydə fil/ *n.* a flattened stem similar to a leaf

clafoutis /kláffŏoti/ (*plural* **-tis**) *n.* a fruit and batter pastry, typically made with cherries [Late 20thC. From French *clafoutis*, from dialect *clafir* 'to stuff', originally 'to attach with nails' (from Latin *clavo figere*, from *clavus* 'nail' + *figere* 'to attach') + French *foutre* 'to stuff'.]

claim /klaym/ *v.* **1.** *vt.* MAINTAIN STH IS TRUE to say, without proof or evidence, that sth is true ○ *He claims we've already met.* **2.** *vt.* DEMAND STH AS ENTITLEMENT to demand sth that sb has a right to or owns **3.** *vti.* SOC WELFARE RECEIVE STATE MONEY to officially request and receive state money or other benefits **4.** *vt.* END SB'S LIFE to cause the loss of sb's life **5.** *vt.* WIN TITLE to take a title, prize, or record **6.** *vt.* DEMAND ATTENTION to force sb to give attention ■ *n.* **1.** STH THAT MAY BE TRUE an assertion that sth is true, unsupported by evidence or proof **2.** BASIS FOR GETTING STH the basis for demanding or getting sth **3.** DEMAND a demand for sth sb has a right to or owns **4.** INSUR, SOC WELFARE OFFICIAL REQUEST FOR MONEY an official request for money or other benefits from the state or an organization **5.** MONEY REQUESTED the amount of money requested in a claim **6.** LAW LEGAL RIGHT TO LAND the legal right to own a piece of land and to mine it for minerals **7.** LAW PIECE OF LAND the piece of land to which sb claims a legal right [14thC. From Old French *clamer* 'to call', from Latin *clamare* (source of English *clamour*). Ultimately from an Indo-European word that is also the source of English *éclair*.] —**claimable** *adj.* —**claimer** *n.* ◇ **lay claim to sth** to say that you have a right to sth, or take what you think you have a right to

─── **WORD KEY: ORIGIN** ───

Claim is derived from the Latin word *clamare*, meaning 'to call', which is also the source of English *acclaim*, *clamour*, *exclaim*, and *proclaim*.

claimant /kláymənt/ *n.* sb who is claiming or receiving sth, e.g. benefits or an inheritance

Clair /klair/, **René** (1898–1981) French film director and scriptwriter. *The Italian Straw Hat* (1927) established him as a master of light comedy. Real name **René-Lucien Chomette**

clair de lune /kláir də lŏon/ *n.* **1.** CERAMICS TYPE OF GLAZE a pale blue or greyish-blue glaze used on porcelain **2.** COLOURS PALE BLUISH-GREY a pale bluish-grey colour ■ *adj.* COLOURS OF A PALE BLUISH-GREY of a pale bluish-

grey colour [Late 19thC. From French, literally 'light of the moon'.]

claire-obscure /kláir əb skyŏor/ *n.* = **chiaroscuro** [Early 18thC. From French *clair-obscur*, literally 'light-dark', a translation of Italian *chiaroscuro*.]

clairvoyance /klair vóyəns/, **clairvoyancy** /-ənssi/ *n.* the supposed ability to see things beyond the range of normal human vision [Mid-19thC. From French, from *clairvoyant* 'clear-sighted', from *voyant*, the present participle of *voir* 'to see'.]

clairvoyant /klair vóyənt/ *n.* PSYCHIC PERSON sb supposedly able to see things beyond the range of normal human vision ■ *adj.* PSYCHIC supposedly able to see things beyond the range of normal human vision [Mid-19thC. See CLAIRVOYANCE.] —**clairvoyantly** *adv.*

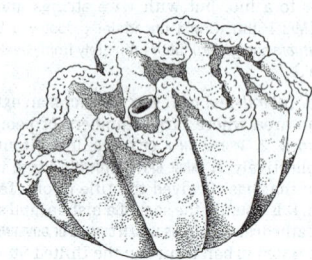

Clam

clam[1] /klam/ *n.* **1.** BURROWING SHELLFISH a freshwater or marine mollusc that has a muscular foot with which it can burrow into sand. Many are edible and the largest is nearly 1.5 m/5 ft long. Class: Pelecypoda. **2.** FOOD CLAM FLESH the soft edible flesh of the clam **3.** *US* SECRETIVE PERSON sb who is shy or secretive, especially sb who can keep a secret (*informal*) **4.** *US* DOLLAR a dollar (*slang*) ■ *vi.* (**clams, clamming, clammed**) *US* FOOD COLLECT CLAMS to gather clams [Early 16thC. From obsolete *clam-shell*, literally 'clamp-shell'; ultimately from an Indo-European word meaning 'to form into a ball'.]

clam up *vi.* to become suddenly secretive or unwilling to talk (*informal*)

clam[2] *vti.* = **clem** (*regional*)

clamant /kláymənt/ *adj.* **1.** LOUD loud or noisy (*archaic*) **2.** URGENT demanding attention (*literary*) [Mid-17thC. From Latin *clamant-*, the present participle stem of *clamare* (see CLAIM).] —**clamantly** *adv.*

clambake /klám bayk/ *n.* **1.** a picnic in which seafood such as clams and other foods are cooked and eaten **2.** *US* PARTY a relaxed party or other gathering (*informal*)

clamber /klámbər/ *vi.* CLIMB AWKWARDLY to climb quickly but awkwardly, using hands and feet ■ *n.* AWKWARD CLIMB a climb that involves clambering [14thC. Origin uncertain: probably literally 'to climb repeatedly', from *clamb*, former past tense of CLIMB.] —**clamberer** *n.*

clam chowder *n.* a thick soup made from clams and potatoes

clam-diggers *npl.* casual trousers reaching to the middle of the wearer's calf [From the fact that they were originally worn for digging clams]

clammy /klámmi/ (**-mier, -miest**) *adj.* **1.** COLD AND DAMP slightly damp and unpleasantly cold **2.** HUMID warm and damp [14thC. Origin uncertain: probably from *clam* 'to smear', a back-formation from *clamde*, past tense of Old English *clǣman*, from a prehistoric Germanic word meaning 'clay'.] —**clammily** *adv.* —**clamminess** *n.*

clamor *vi.*, *n. US* = **clamour**

clamorous /klámmərəss/ *adj.* **1.** DEMANDING ATTENTION demanding attention loudly and insistently **2.** LOUD loud and excited or angry **3.** NOISY making a loud noise —**clamorously** *adv.* —**clamorousness** *n.*

clamour /klámmər/ *vi.* **1.** DEMAND NOISILY to demand sth noisily or desperately **2.** SHOUT to shout at the same time as other people, and make a lot of noise ■ *n.* **1.** PERSISTENT DEMAND a persistent demand for sth, made in an excited or angry way **2.** LOUD NOISE a loud noise, especially one made by people shouting together [14thC. The verb came from the noun, from Old French *clamor*, from the Latin stem *clamor-*, from *clamare* (see CLAIM).] —**clamourer** *n.*

clamp /klamp/ *n.* **1. HOLDING DEVICE** a mechanical device with movable jaws used to hold two things firmly together or one object firmly in position **2.** CARS **WHEEL CLAMP** a wheel clamp ■ *vt.* **(clamps, clamping, clamped) 1. FASTEN THINGS TOGETHER** to fasten two or more things firmly together using a clamp **2. HOLD FIRMLY** to hold sth firmly and tightly in position **3.** CARS **PUT CLAMP ON CAR** to fix a clamp to the wheel of an illegally parked car. US term **boot** [15thC. Origin uncertain: probably from assumed Middle Dutch or Middle Low German *klampe*.]

clamp down *vi.* to take firm action to control or limit sth bad or sb doing sth bad ○ *police have clamped down on illegal parking in the area*

clampdown /klámpdown/ *n.* firm official action taken to control or limit sth bad or sb doing sth bad

clamper /klámpər/ *n.* a spiked metal frame fastened under a shoe to avoid slipping on ice or snow

clamshell /klám shel/ *n.* **1. SHELL** the shell of a clam **2.** *US* **DREDGING BUCKET** a dredging bucket that has two hinged jaws (*informal*) **3. HINGED DEVICE** any hinged device that opens like the shell of a clam (*informal*)

clamworm /klám wurm/ *n.* *US* = **ragworm** [*Clam* from the fact that clams live buried in sand or mud]

clan /klan/ *n.* (*takes a singular or plural verb*) **1.** ETHNOL **GROUP OF FAMILIES** a group of families related through a common ancestor or marriage **2.** SOC SCI **RELATED SCOTTISH FAMILIES** a group of Scottish families with common ancestors and surname and a single chief **3. LARGE FAMILY** a group of people who are all members of a particular family (*informal*) **4. GROUP WITH SHARED AIM** a group of people who act together because they have the same interests or aims (*informal*) [15thC. From Gaelic *clann* 'offspring', from Old Irish *cland*, from Latin *planta* 'sprout'.]

clandestine /klan déstin, klándestīn/ *adj.* secret or furtive, and usually illegal [Mid-16thC. From, ultimately, Latin *clandestinus*, from *clam* 'secretly'.] —**clandestinely** *adv.* —**clandestineness** *n.* —**clandestinity** /klánde stínnəti/ *n.*

WORD KEY: SYNONYMS

See Synonyms at ***secret***.

clang /klang/ *vti.* **1. MAKE LOUD RINGING NOISE** to make the ringing sound of two metal objects hitting each other **2. MOVE MAKING CLANGING SOUND** to move or operate with a clanging sound ■ *n.* **LOUD RINGING NOISE** a ringing sound made by two metal objects hitting each other [Late 16thC. From Latin *clangere* 'to emit a ringing sound'. Ultimately from an Indo-European word meaning 'to cry', an imitation of sounds made by people and animals.]

clanger /klángər/ *n.* an unwise or embarrassing mistake (*informal*) ○ *drop a clanger*

clangor *n.* *US* = **clangour**

clangour /kláng gər/ *n.* **1. CLANGING** a clang, or a repeated loud clanging **2. NOISE** a din or uproar —**clangorous** *adj.* —**clangorously** *adv.*

clanjamfry /klán jámfri/ *n.* *Scotland* a rabble or crowd of people (*informal or literary*)

clank /klangk/ *vti.* **1. MAKE METALLIC NOISE** to make the short loud sound of two heavy metal objects hitting each other **2. MOVE MAKING CLANKING SOUND** to move or operate with a clanking sound ■ *n.* **METALLIC NOISE** a short loud noise made by two heavy metal objects hitting each other [Mid-17thC. Origin uncertain: perhaps an imitation of the sound, with influence from CLANG and CLINK.] —**clankingly** *adv.* —**clanky** *adj.*

clannish /klánnish/ *adj.* inclined to stick together as a group and exclude outsiders —**clannishly** *adv.* —**clannishness** *n.*

clansman /klánzmən/ (*plural* **-men** /-mən/) *n.* a male member of a Scottish clan

clap[1] /klap/ *v.* **(claps, clapping, clapped) 1.** *vti.* **HIT HANDS TOGETHER** to hit the hands together quickly and loudly **2.** *vti.* **APPLAUD** to hit the hands together repeatedly to express approval **3.** *vti.* **HIT HANDS IN RHYTHM** to hit the hands together repeatedly in time with a beat **4.** *vt.* **PUT QUICKLY** to move sth to or against sth quickly **5.** *vt.* *Scotland* **PAT AN ANIMAL** to give a pat to an animal (*informal*) ■ *n.* **1. SUDDEN LOUD SOUND** the sound made by striking the palms together once, or any sudden loud sharp sound **2. EXPRESSION OF APPROVAL THROUGH APPLAUSE** an expression of approval by loud continuous clapping **3. CLAPPING RHYTHMICALLY** a session of rhythmic clapping **4.** *Scotland* **PAT** the act of patting an animal (*informal*) [Old English *clæppan*, from a prehistoric Germanic word that was an imitation of the sound]

clap on *vt.* to put clothing or equipment on hastily (*dated*)

clap[2] /klap/ *n.* gonorrhoea (*slang*) [Late 16thC. Origin uncertain: perhaps from French *clapoir* 'bubo', from Old French *clapiore* 'brothel'.]

clapboard /kláp bawrd/ *n.* a long narrow wooden board that has one edge thicker than the other, used to clad buildings. Boards are nailed to a wooden frame and overlap to form a wall or roof. [Mid-17thC. Partial translation of earlier *clapholt*, from Low German *klappholt*, from *klappen* 'to clap, split' + *holt* 'wood'.]

clapped-out *adj.* worn out and in very poor condition (*informal; not hyphenated after a verb*)

clapper /kláppər/ *n.* **1. PART MAKING BELL RING** a piece of metal inside a bell that strikes its side, making it ring **2. SB WHO CLAPS** sb who claps his or her hands ■ **clappers** *npl.* MUSIC **MUSICAL INSTRUMENT** a musical instrument consisting of two flat pieces of wood that are held between the thumb and forefinger and clapped together ◇ **like the clappers** extremely fast, or as fast as possible (*informal*)

Clapperboard

clapperboard /kláppər bawrd/ *n.* a pair of hinged boards filmed at the start of each take in a film and clapped together to help to synchronize the soundtrack with the film

Clapton /kláptən/, **Eric** (*b.* 1945) British guitarist, singer, and songwriter. The nickname indicating the rock-steady quality of this versatile bluesman graces his album *Slowhand* (1977).

claptrap /kláp trap/ *n.* pompous or important-sounding nonsense (*informal*) [Late 18thC. Originally, in the theatre, a device or line to elicit applause; that is, a trap to catch a clap.]

claque /klak/ *n.* (*takes a singular or plural verb*) **1. PAID AUDIENCE** a group of people hired to applaud a performance **2. ENTOURAGE** a group of people around a rich or famous person whom they praise and support uncritically [Mid-19thC. From French, from *claquer* 'to clap', an imitation of the sound.]

claqueur /klákər/ *n.* sb who goes around with a rich or famous person and gives him or her praise and uncritical support [Mid-19thC. From French, literally 'clapper', from *claquer* (see CLAQUE).]

clarabella /klárrə béllə/, **claribella** *n.* an eight-foot flute stop on an organ [Mid-19thC. From Latin *clara bella*, literally 'clear and beautiful'.]

Clare /kláir/ **1.** island off the western coast of Ireland, administratively part of County Mayo. Area: 16 sq. km/6.3 sq. mi. **2.** river in northeastern South Island, New Zealand. Length: 209 km/130 mi.

Clare /klair/, **John** (1793–1864) British poet and naturalist. He wrote *Poems Descriptive of Rural Life* (1820) and *The Shepherd's Calendar* (1827).

clarence /klárrənss/ *n.* an enclosed four-wheeled carriage that seats four and has a glass front [Mid-19thC. Named after the Duke of *Clarence*, later William IV.]

Clarence /klárrənss/ **1.** river in northeastern New South Wales, southeastern Australia. Length: 394 km/245 mi. **2.** river in northeastern South Island, New Zealand, which rises in the Spenser Mountains and flows into the Pacific Ocean 50 km/31 mi. north of Kaikoura. Length: 209 km/130 mi.

Clarenceux /klárrən sō/ *n.* the second King-of-Arms in England. The King-of-Arms is the highest rank of heraldic officer. [15thC. From Anglo-Norman, from English *Clarence*, an English dukedom, named after *Clare* in Suffolk.]

Clarendon /klárrəndən/ *n.* a style of boldface roman type [Mid-19thC. Origin uncertain; probably named after the *Clarendon* Press in Oxford.]

Clarendon /klárrəndən/, **Edward Hyde, 1st Earl of** (1609–74) English statesman and historian. Author of *History of the Rebellion in England* (1702–04), he was impeached for high treason.

Clarendon Code *n.* four acts passed by Parliament between 1661 and 1665 to deal with the religious problems caused by the Restoration of Charles II. Although the acts are named after the Earl of Clarendon, he did not support them.

Clare of Assisi /kláir əv ə séessi/, **Saint** (1194–1253) Italian nun. She was a follower of St Francis of Assisi, alongside her sister St Agnes. The three founded the order of the Poor Ladies of Damiano, or Poor Clares. Real name **Clara Offreducia**

claret /klárrət/ *n.* **1.** WINE **RED WINE** a red wine from the Bordeaux region of France **2.** COLOURS **DEEP RED** a deep purplish-red colour, like that of claret ■ *adj.* COLOURS **OF A DEEP RED COLOUR** of a deep purplish-red colour, like claret [Early 18thC. From Old French *(vin) claret* 'light-coloured (wine)', from Latin *vinum claratum* 'clarified wine', *claratum* a form of *clarare* 'to clarify', from *clarus* 'clear'.]

claret cup *n.* an iced summer drink made from claret, brandy, lemon, and sugar, sometimes with sherry or curaçao added

claribel flute *n.* = **clarabella**

claribella *n.* = **clarabella**

clarification /klárrifi káysh'n/ *n.* **1. EXPLANATION** a detailed explanation needed because sth is unclear **2.** COOK **PURIFYING OF FAT** the process of making butter or fat become clear by heating it gently and removing impurities **3. PURIFYING OF LIQUID** the process of making a liquid clear and pure

clarifier /klárri fī ər/ *n.* a device for removing impurities, e.g. from water

clarify /klárri fī/ *v.* **(-fies, -fying, -fied) 1.** *vt.* **MAKE STH CLEARER** to make sth clearer by explaining it in greater detail **2.** *vti.* COOK **MAKE BUTTER CLEAR** to make butter or fat clear, or become clear, by gently heating it to remove impurities **3.** *vti.* FOOD TECH **MAKE A LIQUID CLEAR** to make a liquid clear and pure, or become clear and pure, usually by filtering [14thC. Via Old French from late Latin *clarificare*, literally 'to make clear', from Latin *clarus* 'clear' (see CLARITY).]

clarinet /klárrə nét/ *n.* **1. WOODWIND INSTRUMENT** a musical instrument of the woodwind family, with a straight body and a single reed **2. CLARINET PLAYER** sb who plays the clarinet, especially in an orchestra or group [Mid-18thC. From French *clarinette*, literally 'little clarion', from *clarine* 'clarion', from, ultimately, Latin *clarus* 'clear' (see CLARITY).]

clarinettist /klárrə néttist/, **clarinetist** *n.* sb who plays the clarinet

clarion /klárri ən/ *n.* **1. ORGAN STOP** a four-foot organ stop that sounds like a trumpet **2. MEDIEVAL TRUMPET** a medieval trumpet with a clear high-pitched tone [14thC. From the medieval Latin stem *clarion-*, from Latin *clarus* 'clear' (see CLARITY).]

clarion call *n.* an urgent or inspiring appeal to people to do sth [From the use of the clarion as a signal in war]

clarity /klárrəti/ *n.* **1. CLEARNESS OF EXPRESSION** the quality of being clearly expressed **2. CLEARNESS OF THOUGHT** clearness in what sb is thinking **3. CLEARNESS OF REPRODUCTION** the quality of being clear in sound or image **4. TRANSPARENT QUALITY** the quality of being clear, pure, or transparent ○ *wine of great clarity* [Early 17thC. From the Latin stem *claritat-*, from *clarus* 'clear' (source of English *declare* and *chiaroscuro*).]

Clark /klaark/, **Helen Elizabeth** (*b.* 1950) New Zealand politician. She became leader of the New Zealand Labour Party in 1993.

Clark, Manning (1915–91) Australian historian. He wrote the six-volume *A History of Australia* (1962–87). Full name **Charles Manning Hope Clark**

Clark cell *n.* a standard battery cell with a mercury anode surrounded by a paste of mercury sulphate, and a zinc cathode immersed in saturated zinc sulphate solution [Late 19thC. Named after the English engineer Josiah Latimer *Clark* (1822–98), who invented it.]

Clarke /klaark/, **Sir Arthur C.** (*b.* 1917) British writer and scientist. His works of science fiction include the screenplay of *2001: A Space Odyssey* (1968), written with Stanley Kubrick. Full name **Arthur Charles Clarke**

Clarke, Austin (1896–1974) Irish poet and playwright. He followed William Butler Yeats in promoting verse drama and wrote the autobiographical *Twice Round the Black Church* (1962).

Clarke, Jeremiah (1669?–1707) English composer and organist. His best-known work, *The Prince of Denmark's March* or *Trumpet Voluntary*, was long attributed to Henry Purcell.

Clarke, John (*fl.* 1639) English scholar. He wrote *Paroemiologia Anglo-Latina* (1639), a collection of English and Latin proverbs.

Clarke, Marcus Andrew Hislop (1846–81) British-born Australian writer. He wrote *For the Term of His Natural Life* (1874).

claro /kláarō/ (*plural* **-ros** *or* **-roes**) *n.* a mild light-coloured cigar [Late 19thC. Via Spanish, literally 'clear, light', from Latin *clarus*.]

clarsach /kláar sakh, -sәkh/ *n.* a small harp of ancient Scotland and Ireland [15thC. From Irish *cláirseach* and Gaelic *clàrsach*.]

clarts /klaarts/ *npl. Scotland, N England* small lumps of mud, especially those stuck to shoes (*informal*) [Early 19thC. Origin unknown.]

clarty /kláarti/ (**-tier, -tiest**) *adj. Scotland, N England* muddy or dirty (*informal*)

clary /kláiri/ (*plural* **-ies**) *n.* a perennial plant of the mint family native to southern Europe. Some are cultivated for their violet, pink, or white flowers, or for an aromatic oil used in liquors and toiletries. Genus: *Salvia.* [14thC. Via obsolete French *clarie* from medieval Latin *sclarea*.]

clash /klash/ *v.* (**clashes, clashing, clashed**) **1.** *vi.* FIGHT OR ARGUE to come into verbal or physical conflict with sb ○ *Demonstrators clashed with police outside the headquarters this morning.* **2.** *vi.* BE AT ODDS WITH STH to be incompatible ○ *The conclusions clash with the evidence.* **3.** *vti.* MAKE LOUD NOISE to make a loud harsh metallic noise, or hit things together to make such a noise **4.** *vi.* NOT HARMONIZE to look unpleasant or inharmonious when together ○ *The orange of the upholstery clashes with the pink of the paintwork.* **5.** *vi.* CONFLICT WITH STH ELSE to conflict with sth else in terms of timing or appropriateness (*refers to events*) ○ *The final episode of the serial clashes with one of my husband's favourite programmes.* ■ *n.* **1.** FIGHT OR ARGUMENT verbal or physical conflict with another person or group ○ *There were several clashes between supporters outside the stadium.* **2.** LOUD METALLIC SOUND a loud harsh metallic noise **3.** LACK OF HARMONY a jarring or unpleasant juxtaposition of incompatible colours **4.** CONFLICT CAUSED BY DIFFERENCE a difference of opinions or qualities that causes conflict ○ *a clash of personalities* **5.** COINCIDENCE OF CONFLICTING EVENTS a conflict between two or more events due to occur at the same time [Early 16thC. An imitation of the sound.] —**clasher** *n.*

WORD KEY: SYNONYMS

See Synonyms at ***fight***.

clasp /klaasp/ *vt.* (**clasps, clasping, clasped**) **1.** HOLD WITH HANDS OR ARMS to hold sb or sth tightly with the hands or arms ○ *She clasped the baby tightly to herself in the surging crowd.* ○ *I clasped the handrail as the boat lurched.* **2.** FASTEN to fasten or hold two things together with a device designed for this purpose ■ *n.* **1.** SMALL BUCKLE OR FASTENING a small fastening for holding things, e.g. bags or jewellery, closed or together **2.** TIGHT ARM OR HAND HOLD a firm tight hold with the arms, a hand, or a device for fastening or holding things together **3.** MIL IDENTIFYING ATTACHMENT ON MILITARY MEDAL a small metal bar on the ribbon of a medal that identifies the military action or service for which the honour was awarded [14thC. Origin unknown.]

clasper /kláaspәr/ *n.* **1.** GRASPING ORGAN OF INSECTS either of a pair of structures located in the anal region of particular male insects and crustaceans and used to grasp a female during copulation **2.** REPRODUCTIVE ORGAN ON FIN either of a pair of elongated reproductive organs on the pelvic fins of male sharks and rays

clasp knife *n.* a pocket knife with one or more blades and sometimes other devices that can be folded back into the handle

class /klaass/ *n.* **1.** GROUP TAUGHT TOGETHER a group of students or pupils who are taught or study together **2.** PERIOD OF TEACHING a period when students meet to be taught a particular subject ○ *When's our next biology class?* **3.** SPECIFIC SUBJECT TAUGHT a specific course of instruction **4.** *US* STUDENTS WHO GRADUATE TOGETHER the group of students who leave or graduate from an institution in the same year **5.** GROUP WITHIN A SOCIETY a group of people within a society who share the same social and economic status **6.** STRUCTURE OF SOCIETY the structure of divisions in a society determined by the social or economic grouping of its members **7.** ELEGANCE IN STYLE elegance in appearance, behaviour, or lifestyle (*informal*) **8.** EXCELLENCE admirable skill or excellence in performance (*informal*) ○ *a player of real class* **9.** DIVISION ACCORDING TO QUALITY a categorization of services or goods according to quality ○ *This airline has several classes of seating.* **10.** UNIV UNIVERSITY HONOURS DEGREE GRADE a grade assigned to university honours degrees ○ *'What class is your degree?'—'First'.* **11.** GROUP OF SIMILAR ITEMS a group of things with at least one common characteristic **12.** BIOL SET OF RELATED ORGANISMS a major category in the taxonomic classification of related organisms, comprising a group of orders ○ *Elephants and dolphins both belong to the class Mammalia.* **13.** ETHNOL SOCIAL GROUP WITH SIMILAR OPPORTUNITIES a category of people who have a similar level of opportunity to obtain economic resources and prestige **14.** MATH, LOGIC = **set** ■ *vt.* (**classes, classing, classed**) ASSIGN TO A GROUP to assign sb or sth to a particular category or group ○ *It's not old enough to be classed as a vintage car.* [Mid-16thC. From Latin *classis* 'political class'.]

WORD KEY: SYNONYMS

See Synonyms at ***type***.

class. *abbr.* **1.** classic **2.** classical **3.** classification **4.** classified

class act *n.* a person or thing regarded as an example of excellence (*informal*)

class action *n.* a legal action brought by several litigants jointly, usually relying on one another to prove each individual's case

class-conscious *adj.* aware of your position in a social class system in relation to members of other classes —**class-consciousness** *n.*

classes /klássez/ plural of **classis**

classic /klássik/ *adj.* **1.** TOP QUALITY generally considered to be of the highest quality or lasting value, especially in the arts **2.** DEFINITIVE authoritative and perfect as a standard of its kind ○ *a classic example of mixed metaphor English* **3.** EXHIBITING STYLISTIC RESTRAINT AND REFINEMENT simple, restrained, and refined in style ○ *The new sports car, with its classic lines, was the hit of the motor show.* **4.** ALWAYS FASHIONABLE always fashionable and elegant, usually because of simplicity and restraint in style ○ *the classic 'little black dress'* **5.** GENERALLY ACCEPTED conforming to generally accepted principles or methods **6.** EXTREMELY AND USUALLY COMICALLY APROPOS apropos to an extreme degree, usually with a comical or ironic twist (*informal*) ■ *n.* **1.** WORK OF THE HIGHEST QUALITY sth created or made, especially a work of art, music, or literature, that is generally considered to be of the highest quality and of enduring value ○ *the novel has become a 20th-century classic* **2.** SIMPLE ELEGANT GARMENT a piece of clothing of a simple and enduring style **3.** TOP QUALITY ARTIST OR WRITER a creator of works of art or literature that have enduring excellence ○ *As a children's book illustrator she's a classic.* **4.** MAJOR SPORTING EVENT a major sporting event, e.g. a horse race or golf tournament **5.** STH COMICALLY APROPOS sth that is comically or ironically apropos (*informal*)

WORD KEY: USAGE

classic or **classical**? There is some overlap in the meanings of these words, but essentially ***classic*** is a judgmental or evaluative word that describes the value or status of sth (*a classic example of Art Deco*), whereas ***classical***, although often implying a judgment of value or worth, is a more factual reference to the literature, art, and culture of the ancient world or to the high period of an art form (*a classical education, classical music, classical ballet*). A ***classic*** is sth notable of its kind, and *classics* is the study of the language and culture of ancient Greece and Rome.

classical /klássik'l/ *adj.* **1.** RELATING TO ANCIENT GREECE OR ROME relating to or belonging to the ancient Greeks and Romans or their culture **2.** IN ANCIENT GREEK OR ROMAN STYLE in the style of ancient Greece or Rome, especially in architecture **3.** OF MUSIC CONSIDERED TO BE SERIOUS used to describe music that is considered serious or intellectual and is usually written in a traditional or formal style, as opposed to such genres as pop, rock, and folk music **4.** OF 18THC AND 19THC MUSIC used to describe the style of music composed in Europe in the 18th and 19th centuries **5.** STUDYING LATIN AND GREEK consisting of or involving the study of the ancient Greek and Latin languages and literature ○ *a classical education* **6.** KNOWLEDGEABLE ABOUT ANCIENT GREECE AND ROME highly knowledgeable about ancient Greek and Roman culture and art ○ *a classical scholar* **7.** ORTHODOX OR CONSERVATIVE considered as the traditional or authoritative form of sth ○ *a classical Freudianism* **8.** = **classic** *adj.* 2, **classic** *adj.* 3 **9.** PHYS EXCLUDING QUANTUM THEORY AND RELATIVITY not taking into account quantum theoretical or relativistic effects [Late 16thC. Formed from Latin *classicus* 'of the first class' (source of English *classic*).] —**classicality** /klássi kálləti/ *n.* —**classicalness** *n.*

WORD KEY: USAGE

See Usage note at ***classic***.

classical conditioning *n.* the teaching of a response to a new stimulus by pairing it repeatedly with a stimulus for which there is a biological reflex. The best-known example is Pavlov's experiment in which dogs heard a bell ring every time food appeared and eventually started salivating at the sound of the bell alone. ◊ **operant conditioning**

classicalism *n.* = **classicism**

classically /klássikli/ *adv.* **1.** SIMPLY STYLED in a simple and elegant style **2.** AS TRADITIONALLY ACCEPTED OR DONE in a manner that is traditionally accepted and belongs in the mainstream of the relevant art **3.** IN MANNER OF GRAECO-ROMAN CULTURE in the manner or style of ancient Greece or Rome **4.** AS USUALLY OCCURS used to indicate what usually or typically happens ○ *Classically, cases like this are solved through painstaking investigation.* **5.** AS TYPICAL EXAMPLE as a classic example of sth **6.** IN CLASSIC WAY in a classic or classical manner

classicise *vti.* = **classicize**

classicism /klássisizzәm/, **classicalism** /klássik'lizzәm/ *n.* **1.** RESTRAINED STYLE IN THE ARTS a style of art and architecture based on Greek and Roman models or principles, characterized by regularity of form and restraint of expression **2.** GREEK OR LATIN IDIOM a Greek or Latin phrase or expression **3.** STUDY OF GRAECO-ROMAN CULTURE the study or knowledge of ancient Greece and Rome

classicist /klássissist/ *n.* **1.** SCHOLAR OF ANCIENT GREEK AND LATIN sb who studies ancient Greek and Latin **2.** ADVOCATE OF ARTISTIC CLASSICISM a supporter of classicism in the arts

classicize /klássi sīz/ (**-cizes, -cizing, -cized**), **classicise** (**-cises, -cising, -cised**) *v.* **1.** *vt.* MAKE STH CLASSIC OR CLASSICAL to imbue sth with classical traits, qualities, or characteristics ○ *classicized the design of the windows* **2.** *vi.* BE STYLISTICALLY CLASSIC OR CLASSICAL to be in a classic or classical style

classics /klássiks/ *n.* **classics** STUDY OF ANCIENT GREECE AND ROME the academic study of the language, literature, and history of ancient Greece and Rome (*takes a singular verb*) ■ *npl.* COLLECTION OF ANCIENT GRAECO-ROMAN LITERATURE a body of ancient Greek and Roman literature (*takes a plural verb*) [So called because Greek and Roman culture was considered to be of the highest quality]

classification /klássifi káysh'n/ *n.* **1.** ORGANIZATION INTO GROUPS the allocation of items to groups according to type ○ *classification of members according to abilities and interests* **2.** CATEGORY a group or category within a system ○ *the classification 'history' can be further subdivided.* **3.** BIOL CATEGORIZATION OF LIVING THINGS the categorization of organisms into defined groups on the basis of identified characteristics. The Linnean classification groups organisms into species, genera, families, and higher taxonomic groups on the basis of visible resemblances, while other systems may determine, e.g. the molecular relationships among the groups. **4.** BIOL CATEGORY FOR LIVING THINGS each of several categories into which biologists organize living things based on structural resemblance or evolutionary relationships ○ *genus and species classifications* **5.** DESIGNATION AS SENSITIVE INFORMATION the restriction of sensitive government or military information to authorized individuals [Late 18thC. From French, formed from *classe* 'class', which came from Latin *classis* (see CLASS).] —**classificational** *adj.* —**classificatory** *adj.*

classification schedule *n.* the complete plan and content of a library's cataloguing system

classified /klássi fīd/ *adj.* **1.** SECRET OR SENSITIVE available only to authorized people for reasons of national security. The basic categories of classified information are confidential, secret, and top secret. **2.** GROUPED BY TYPE arranged in groups according to a classification system **3.** LISTED IN BRITISH ROAD SYSTEM classed as a motorway, an A-road, or a B-road in the British system of classifying roads ■ **classifieds** *npl.* GROUP OF ADVERTISEMENTS classified advertisements printed together in a newspaper or magazine (*informal*)

classified advertisement, **classified ad** *n.* a small advertisement positioned with others of similar content in a newspaper or magazine

classifier /klássi fī ər/ *n.* **1.** ASSIGNER TO CLASSIFICATIONS sb who assigns things to classes **2.** OFFICIAL WHO DETERMINES WHAT IS SECRET an official who decides if particular information is secret and thus available only to authorized people

classify /klássi fī/ (**-fies, -fying, -fied**) *vt.* **1.** CATEGORIZE THINGS OR PEOPLE to assign things or people to classes or groups **2.** DECLARE INFORMATION SENSITIVE AND THUS RESTRICTED to designate information as being available only to authorized people for reasons of security [Late 18thC. Back-formation from CLASSIFICATION.] —**classifiable** *adj.*

class interval *n.* any of the intervals into which adjacent discrete values of a variable are divided

classis /klássiss/ (*plural* **-ses** /-seez/) *n.* **1.** CHURCH GOVERNING BODY in some Reformed churches, a governing body composed of elders and pastors **2.** GROUP OF GOVERNED CHURCHES a district or group of churches governed by a classis [Late 16thC. From Latin *classis* 'political class'.]

classism /klaássizzəm/ *n.* discrimination or prejudice based on social or economic class —**classist** *adj., n.*

classless /klaássləss/ *adj.* **1.** LACKING SOCIAL CLASSES not having social or economic classes **2.** NOT HAVING A SOCIAL CLASS not belonging to or associated with a particular social or economic class —**classlessness** *n.*

class list *n.* a list of the classes of degree awarded in a British university

classmate /klaáss mayt/ *n.* sb who is or was in the same class as another at school

class number *n.* a series of letters and/or numbers on a book or other publication in a library identifying it, the category of its subject matter, and usually its shelf location

classroom /klaáss room, -rŏom/ *n.* a room, especially in a school or college, where classes are held

class struggle *n.* the Marxist principle of a continuous struggle for political and economic power between the ruling and working classes

classy /klaássi/ (**-ier, -iest**) *adj.* very stylish and elegant (*informal*) —**classily** *adv.* —**classiness** *n.*

clast /klast/ *n.* a fragment of rock produced by the breaking down of larger rocks [Mid-20thC. Back-formation from CLASTIC.]

clastic /klástik/ *adj.* **1.** ABLE TO BE TAKEN APART able to be separated into parts or have parts removed to enable better study ○ *Clastic models are often used to teach anatomy.* **2.** GEOL MADE FROM ROCK FRAGMENTS used to describe rock that is composed of fragments of other rocks [Late 19thC. Via French *clastique* from Greek *klastos* 'broken in pieces'.]

clathrate /kláth rayt/ *n.* CRYSTAL WITH EMBEDDED SUBSTANCE a solid compound with a physical structure in which molecules of one substance are fully enclosed within the crystal structure of another ■ *adj.* **1.** WITH CRYSTAL-EMBEDDED SUBSTANCE having molecules of one substance enclosed fully within the crystal structure of another substance **2.** LIKE A LATTICE resembling a lattice in structure or appearance [Mid-19thC. From Latin *clathrare* 'to fit with bars', from *clathri* 'lattice', from Greek *klēthra* 'bars'.]

clatter /kláttər/ *v.* (**-ters, -tering, -tered**) **1.** *vti.* MAKE RATTLING NOISE to make a loud rattling noise, or cause sth to make a rattling noise ○ *a clattering old lorry* **2.** *vi.* CHATTER NOISILY to chatter or prattle, especially noisily **3.** *vt.* N England, Scotland BOX SB'S EARS to hit sb on the ears, especially as a punishment ■ *n.* **1.** BANGING METALLIC SOUND a loud metallic banging or rattling noise ○ *the clatter of pots and pans in the kitchen* **2.** NOISY CHATTER noisy chatter and prattling talk **3.** LOUD COMMOTION a noisy disturbance [Assumed Old English *clatrian.* Ultimately from an ancient Germanic word thought to be an imitation of the sound.] —**clatterer** *n.* —**clatteringly** *adv.*

Claudel /klō dél/, **Paul Louis Marie** (1868–1955) French writer and diplomat. His symbolism and devout Catholicism inform such dramas as *The Satin Slipper* (1929).

claudication /kláwdi káysh'n/ *n.* **1.** LIMPING limping or lameness, especially as a result of reduced blood supply to the leg muscles **2.** = **intermittent claudication** [15thC. From the Latin stem *claudication-*, from *claudicare* 'to limp', from *claudus* 'lame'.]

Claudius I /kláwdi əss/ (10 BC–AD 54) Roman emperor. His reign (AD 41–54) was notable for the expansion of the Roman empire and the emperor's ambitious building programme. Full name **Tiberius Claudius Drusus Nero Germanicus**

clause /klawz/ *n.* **1.** GRAM GROUP OF WORDS a group of words consisting of a subject and its predicate. A clause usually contains a verb and may or may not be a sentence in its own right. The sentence 'she left before he arrived' contains two clauses, 'she left' and 'before he arrived'. **2.** LAW SECTION OF LEGAL DOCUMENT a distinct section of a document, especially a legal document, that is usually separately numbered [13thC. Via French and assumed Latin *clausa* 'close of a rhetorical period or legal argument' from, ultimately, *claudere* 'to close' (source of English *close* and *cloister*).] —**clausal** *adj.*

claustrophobe /kláwstrə fōb, klóstrə-/ *n.* = **claustrophobic** [Mid-20thC. Back-formation from CLAUSTROPHOBIA.]

claustrophobia /kláwstrə fóbi ə, klóstrə-/ *n.* an abnormal fear of being in a confined or enclosed space [Late 19thC. From modern Latin, coined from *claustrum* (see CLOISTER) + -PHOBIA.]

claustrophobic /kláwstrə fóbik, klóstrə-/ *adj.* **1.** CONFINED OR CRAMPED unpleasantly or uncomfortably confined ○ *The room is claustrophobic but painting the walls a light colour might help.* **2.** OF OR HAVING CLAUSTROPHOBIA affected by claustrophobia ■ *n.* SB WHO FEARS ENCLOSED SPACES sb who is affected by claustrophobia —**claustrophobically** *adv.*

clavate /kláy vayt/ *adj.* with one end thicker than the other ○ *Some protozoa have clavate cilia.* [Early 19thC. From modern Latin *clavatus*, from Latin *clava* 'club'.] —**clavately** *adv.*

clave /klaav, klayv/ *n.* either of a pair of hardwood sticks that are hit together to make a clicking sound [Early 20thC. Via American Spanish from Spanish, 'keystone', from Latin *clavis* 'key'.]

clavicembalo /klávvi chémbələ̄/ (*plural* **-los**) *n.* MUSIC = **harpsichord** [Mid-18thC. Via Italian from medieval Latin *clavicymbalum*, literally 'key cymbal'.]

Clavichord

clavichord /klávvi kawrd/ *n.* a keyboard instrument of the 15th to 19th centuries, a precursor of the modern piano, in which small wedges strike horizontal strings to produce a soft sound [15thC. From medieval Latin *clavichordium*, formed from Latin *clavis* 'key' + *chorda* 'string'.] —**clavichordist** *n.*

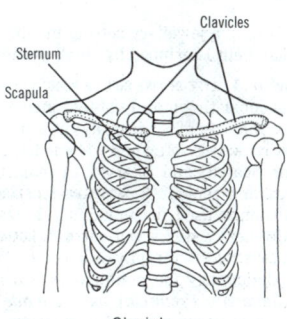

Clavicle

clavicle /klávvik'l/ *n.* **1.** ANAT BONE AT FRONT OF HUMAN SHOULDER the long curved bone that connects the upper part of the breastbone with the shoulder blade at the top of each shoulder in humans **2.** ZOOL BONE IN ANIMALS a bone or structure with a function similar to that of the human clavicle in some other animals. It is reduced or absent in many mammals. [Early 17thC. From Latin *clavicula*, literally 'small key', from *clavis* 'key'. From its shape.] —**clavicular** /klə víkyŏolər, kla-/ *adj.*

clavier /klə veér, klávvi ər/ *n.* **1.** STRINGED KEYBOARD INSTRUMENT any stringed keyboard musical instrument **2.** MUSICAL KEYBOARD the keyboard of a musical instrument [Early 18thC. Directly or via German *Klavier* from French, from medieval Latin *claviarius* 'key-bearer', from Latin *clavis* 'key'.]

clavius /klaávvi əss/ *n.* a large walled plain on the Moon near the south pole, approximately 225 km/140 mi. in diameter

claw /klaw/ *n.* **1.** ANIMAL'S SHARP NAIL a pointed curved nail on the end of each toe in birds, some reptiles, and some mammals **2.** PINCER an appendage used for grasping in crabs and other invertebrates **3.** APPENDAGE RESEMBLING CLAW sth resembling a claw in shape or function, e.g. a mechanical grabbing device ■ *v.* (**claws, clawing, clawed**) **1.** *vti.* ATTACK WITH CLAWS to scratch or dig at sth or sb with claws, fingernails, or sth similar ○ *The dogs had clawed at the door* **2.** *vt.* FORM STH BY SCRATCHING to form sth by digging or scratching with claws or sth similar ○ *Using our bare hands we clawed a hole in the sand* [Old English *clawu.* Ultimately from a prehistoric Germanic word that is also the ancestor of German *Klaue* 'claw'.] —**clawless** *adj.*

claw back *vt.* **1.** GET STH BACK WITH EFFORT to get sth back with difficulty ○ *She's slowly clawing back some of the respect she used to have.* **2.** RECOVER MONEY to recover money paid out in state benefits and in other ways

claw off *vi.* to avoid the dangers of a lee shore or other hazard by sailing as close to the wind as possible on alternate tacks

clawback /kláw bak/ *n.* **1.** RECOVERY OF MONEY the recovery of money, especially through taxation **2.** SUM RECOVERED a sum of money recovered, especially through taxation

clawed /klawd/ *adj.* having claws or similar projections for scratching or grasping

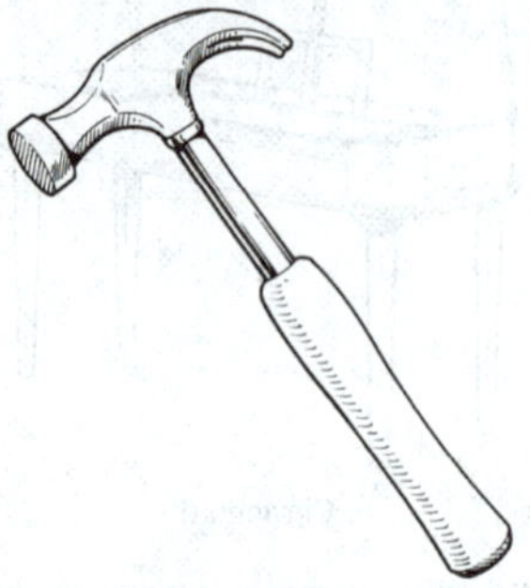

Claw hammer

claw hammer *n.* a hammer with a tapered fork at one end of its head for removing nails

claw hatchet *n.* a hatchet with a fork at one end of its head

claw setting *n.* a jewellery setting in which a stone or similar item is gripped by small prongs

clay /klay/ *n.* **1.** TYPE OF FINE SOIL OR ROCK a fine-grained material consisting mainly of hydrated aluminium silicates that occurs naturally in soil and sedimentary rock. It is soft when wet and hardens when dried or heated, and is used in making bricks, ceramics, and cement. **2.** MODELLING SUBSTANCE a clay-like substance used for modelling **3.** EARTH earth, especially heavy sticky wet earth **4.** HUMAN BODY AND ITS BASIC CONSTITUENTS the physical body of a human being, particularly the matter of which it is composed (*literary*) ○ *From clay we are made* **5.** = **clay court 6.** = **clay pigeon** *n.* 1 ■ *vt.* (**clays, claying, clayed**) COVER WITH CLAY to cover sth with clay [Old English *clǣg*. Ultimately from an Indo-European word that is also the ancestor of English *clammy, climb,* and *glue.*] —**clayey** *adj.*

Clay /klay/, **Cassius** ♦ **Muhammad Ali**

Clay, Henry (1777–1852) US statesman. He long served in the US Congress and was the architect of the Missouri Compromise (1820–21) and the Compromise of 1850 that temporarily averted civil war.

clay court *n.* a tennis court with a hard surface made of crushed clay or shale

Claymation /klay máysh'n/ *tdmk.* a trademark for an animated film process using clay figurines that are moved and filmed so as to create lifelike imagery and motion

clay mineral *n.* any of several hydrated aluminium silicates that constitute one of the main components of clay

claymore /kláy mawr/ *n.* **1.** LARGE SWORD a large double-edged broadsword formerly used by Scottish Highlanders **2.** = **claymore mine** [Early 18thC. From Gaelic *claidheamh mor*, literally 'great sword'.]

claymore mine *n.* a land mine in the shape of a convex disc that is placed above ground and detonates horizontally. It is designed to kill or maim approaching personnel.

claypan /kláy pan/ *n.* a layer of impervious clay close to the surface of the ground, which holds water after heavy rain

clay pigeon *n.* **1.** MOVING TARGET FOR SHOOTING a clay disc hurled into the air from a machine and used as a target for shooting **2.** *US* DEFENCELESS PERSON sb who is vulnerable to attack (*slang*)

claystone /kláy stōn/ *n.* a compact fine-grained rock containing primarily clay particles

cld *abbr.* STOCK EXCH called

clean /kleen/ *adj.* **1.** NOT DIRTY free from dirt or impurities ○ *clean hands* **2.** UNADULTERATED containing no foreign matter or pollutants ○ *a clean water supply* **3.** FREE OF DISEASE OR INFECTION not infected or diseased ○ *a clean wound* **4.** WASHED freshly laundered or washed after use ○ *fetch some clean shirts* **5.** taking pains over personal hygiene or grooming ○ *he is very clean in his habits* **6.** EMPTY containing nothing at all (*informal*) ○ *The flat was stripped clean by the previous tenants* **7.** MORALLY UPRIGHT morally pure and upright **8.** HONESTLY FAIR just and fair ○ *a clean verdict* **9.** NOT RUDE not rude or obscene **10.** BLANK without anything on it, especially anything written ○ *a clean sheet of paper* **11.** WITH NO POLICE RECORD having or showing no record of convictions or penalties, e.g. for driving offences ○ *Don's record is clean* **12.** FREE OF PROBLEMS without problems or difficulties ○ *The doctor gave me a clean bill of health.* **13.** SMOOTH-EDGED without rough or jagged edges ○ *a clean blow of the axe* **14.** STREAMLINED simple and flowing in design, without projections or additions ○ *the aircraft's clean silhouette* **15.** COMPLETE complete and unqualified ○ *made a clean break with the past* **16.** WITH NO FLAWS used to describe a gemstone that is free of flaws **17.** AGRIC FREE OF WEEDS cleared of weeds and unwanted undergrowth **18.** PRINTING NOT HEAVILY CORRECTED containing relatively few mistakes or corrections **19.** SPORTS PERFORMED PRECISELY precisely performed and in accordance with the best technique ○ *a clean jump* **20.** SPORTS WITH NO FOULS OR RULE-BREAKING played, fought, or won by strict compliance with the rules ○ *a clean victory for our team* **21.** NOT POLLUTING producing the least possible pollution ○ *a clean source of energy* **22.** MINIMALLY RADIOACTIVE producing the least possible radioactive fallout or contamination **23.** WITH NO CONCEALED ARMS not carrying concealed weapons (*slang*) ○ *A body search revealed that the suspect was clean.* **24.** WITH NO ILLEGAL DRUGS not containing or possessing illegal drugs (*slang*) **25.** UNADDICTED free from addiction to narcotic drugs or other substances (*slang*) **26.** INNOCENT not guilty of a particular crime (*slang*) **27.** JUDAISM RITUALLY UNDEFILED used to describe sb who is ritually undefiled according to Jewish law **28.** JUDAISM ABLE TO BE LAWFULLY EATEN used to describe food that may be eaten according to Jewish law **29.** CHR PURE IN SPIRIT spiritually pure or purified ■ *v.* (**cleans, cleaning, cleaned**) **1.** *vti.* RID STH OF DIRT to rid sth of dirt or impurities **2.** *vt.* ERADICATE UNWANTED DIRT to remove or eradicate unwanted dirt, stains, or marks ○ *we spent the day cleaning out the spare room* **3.** *vi.* GET FREE OF DIRT to become free of dirt, chiefly because of a content or structure that easily repels it ○ *This acrylic rug cleans easily.* **4.** *vt.* RID OF CORRUPTION to free sth of dishonest practices ○ *The commissioners were bent on cleaning the council of nepotism.* **5.** *vt.* PREPARE DEAD ANIMAL FOR COOKING to prepare a dead animal for cooking by removing its entrails **6.** *vt.* REMOVE CONTENTS to use up the contents of sth ○ *The children cleaned their plates and asked for more.* ■ *n.* SESSION OF CLEANING a spell of removing unwanted dirt or marks ■ *adv.* **1.** IN ORDER TO FREE OF DIRT so as to make sth free from dirt **2.** IN ORDER TO RID OF EVIDENCE so as to rid sth of incriminating evidence **3.** WITH NO OBSTRUCTION directly, especially without having any obstruction **4.** CLEANLY in a clean way ○ *Does this type of gas burn clean?* ○ *We wanted to play the game clean.* **5.** ENTIRELY completely or utterly (*informal*) ○ *I clean forgot to call.* [Old English *clǣne*. Ultimately from a prehistoric Germanic word meaning 'clear, pure'.] —**cleanability** /kleènə bíllәti/ *n.* —**cleanable** *adj.* —**cleanness** /kleén nəss/ *n.* ◇ **come clean** to confess or tell the truth about sth (*informal*)

clean out *vt.* to use up or steal all of sb's money or belongings (*informal*) ○ *Buying the new bike cleaned me out.*

clean up *v.* **1.** *vti.* MAKE CLEAN OR TIDY to make sb or sth clean or tidy ○ *Can you just give me a minute to clean up in here?* **2.** *vt.* ERADICATE STH UNPLEASANT to rid a place of sth unpleasant, e.g. pollution or crime **3.** *vi.* MAKE MONEY to acquire a large amount of money (*slang*) ○ *They really cleaned up on the stock market last year.* ◇ **clean up your act** to improve your behaviour or the way you conduct your life (*slang*)

clean and jerk *n.* a movement in weightlifting in which the weight is lifted to shoulder height, held there briefly, and then quickly pushed above the head

clean-cut *adj.* **1.** WITH SHARP OUTLINE distinctly outlined or designed **2.** NEAT-LOOKING neat in dress or appearance ○ *a clean-cut young officer in a spotless uniform* **3.** = **clear-cut** *adj.* 1

cleaner /kleénər/ *n.* **1.** SB EMPLOYED TO CLEAN INSIDE PLACES sb whose job is to clean the interior of a building **2.** STH USED IN CLEANING a chemical or machine used for cleaning ■ **cleaners** *npl.* SHOP PROVIDING DRY-CLEANING SERVICE a shop where clothes and other items are taken to be dry-cleaned ○ *My best suit is at the cleaners.* ◇ **take sb to the cleaners** to deprive sb of his or her money or possessions by dishonest means (*slang*)

clean-limbed *adj.* having a well-proportioned and youthful-looking body

cleanliness /klénnlinəss/ *n.* the degree to which sb keeps clean or a place is kept clean ○ *a small hotel noted for its cleanliness*

cleanly[1] /kleénli/ *adv.* **1.** EASILY OR EFFICIENTLY with ease or efficiency ○ *a cleanly executed triple jump on the ice* **2.** WITHOUT JAGGED EDGES in a manner that does not leave rough edges ○ *the saw cut cleanly* **3.** FAIRLY in a fair manner **4.** IN CLEAN WAY in a way that is clean ○ *work cleanly in the kitchen, avoiding spills*

cleanly[2] /klénli/ *adj.* habitually or fastidiously clean and neat (*archaic*)

clean room *n.* a room maintained with minimal contamination from dust or bacteria. Such rooms are used in the aerospace and electronics industries and in various kinds of scientific research.

cleanse /klenz/ (**cleanses, cleansing, cleansed**) *vt.* **1.** MAKE THOROUGHLY CLEAN to remove dirt from sb or sth, especially by washing thoroughly **2.** MAKE FREE FROM UNPLEASANTNESS to free a place, person, or society from sth wrong or unwelcome ○ *to cleanse the town council of corrupt influences* **3.** MAKE FREE FROM SIN to free sb or sth from sin or guilt [Old English *clǣnsian*, from *clǣne* (see CLEAN)] —**cleansing** *n.*

cleanser /klénzər/ *n.* **1.** CLEANING PRODUCT a substance for cleaning sth thoroughly, especially cream or another product for cleaning the skin **2.** a cosmetic product for cleaning the face

clean-shaven *adj.* with the facial hair shaved off

cleanskin /kleén skin/ *n. Aus* **1.** UNBRANDED ANIMAL an unbranded farm animal **2.** SB WITH NO CRIMINAL RECORD sb with no criminal record or untainted by corruption (*slang*) ○ *The latest developments threaten to damage his reputation as a cleanskin.*

cleanup /kleén up/ *n.* **1.** THOROUGH CLEANING a thorough cleaning ○ *This garage needs a good cleanup.* **2.** ELIMINATION OF STH BAD an elimination of sth unpleasant or unwanted **3.** *US* LARGE GAIN a large and often illicit acquisition of assets (*slang*)

clear /kleer/ *adj.* **1.** FREE FROM WHAT DIMS free from anything that darkens or obscures ○ *a clear stream* **2.** TRANSPARENT able to be seen through ○ *clear glass* **3.** FREE FROM CLOUDS free from clouds, mist, or airborne particles ○ *a clear blue sky* **4.** PURE IN HUE pure in colour or hue ○ *a clear red* **5.** PERFECT AND UNBLEMISHED free from any defect or impurity ○ *a clear complexion* **6.** EASILY HEARD OR SEEN easily heard or seen ○ *clear outlines* **7.** SOUNDING PLEASANT having a pleasant sound ○ *a clear singing voice* **8.** OUT-AND-OUT completely certain, allowing for no doubt ○ *clear evidence of collusion* **9.** UNAMBIGUOUS easy to understand and without ambiguity ○ *clear instructions* **10.** UNDERSTOOD PRECISELY understood without confusion or uncertainty ○ *Is it clear what you have to do when the bell rings?* **11.** EVIDENT so obvious as to need no further explanation or guidance ○ *After half an hour of trying it was clear that the engine would not work properly.* **12.** MENTALLY SHARP AND DISCERNING able to think without confusion ○ *You'll do better in the exam if you keep your mind clear.* **13.** WITHOUT GUILT free from feelings of guilt or blame ○ *a clear conscience* **14.** UNOBSTRUCTED free from obstructions or hindrances ○ *keep aisles clear* **15.** EMPTY empty, with all movable items removed **16.** NOT ATTACHED TO OR TOUCHING STH free of, or freed from, connection or contact ○ *they struggled to clear the wreckage* **17.** NET net of deductions or charges ○ *I earn a clear*

£500 a week. **18.** NOT FINANCIALLY OBLIGATED not having any debt or financial obligation **19.** SHOWJUMPING UNPENALIZED without any penalties being incurred ○ *jumped a clear round* ■ *adv.* **1.** OUT OF THE WAY completely away from sth ○ *Please stand clear of the doors until the vehicle has stopped.* **2.** ALL THE WAY totally or completely ○ *they moved clear across the country* ■ *v.* **(clears, clearing, cleared) 1.** *vi.* DISSIPATE AND DISPERSE to undergo the process of dissolving or dispersing, thereby disappearing ○ *By noon the fog had finally cleared.* **2.** *vi.* NO LONGER BE FOGGY OR DULL to brighten and become free of adverse conditions ○ *There will be rain in the morning but the skies will clear by the early afternoon.* **3.** *vti.* MAKE OR BECOME TRANSPARENT to become or make sth transparent or translucent ○ *The water cleared as the particles sank to the bottom.* **4.** *vt.* RID STH OF EXTRANEOUS MATTER to free sth of impurities or unwanted matter ○ *clear a drain of blockages* **5.** *vt.* RID THROAT OF OBSTRUCTIONS to rid the throat of phlegm or other obstructions by coughing **6.** *vt.* CLARIFY THOUGHTS to remove confusion or misunderstanding from the mind ○ *I'd like a few minutes to clear my head before going into the meeting.* **7.** *vi.* RETURN TO SENSES to become or make the mind free from the dulling effects of alcohol, drugs, illness, or a blow to the head ○ *After my head had cleared I was able to stand up again.* **8.** *vt.* PROVE SB INNOCENT to free sb from suspicion or blame ○ *anxious to clear her name* **9.** *vt.* REMOVE OBJECTS OR OBSTRUCTIONS FROM STH to empty a space of objects or obstructions ○ *the room had been cleared* **10.** *vt.* FORM SPACE FOR SB OR STH to form a route for sb or sth to pass by removing obstructions **11.** *vt.* REMOVE PEOPLE FROM A PLACE to empty a building or place of people, e.g. for security reasons ○ *police had to clear the area* **12.** *vt.* DISENTANGLE to straighten out sth that is snarled or otherwise in disarray or disorder ○ *Hurry up and clear that anchor line!* **13.** *vt.* MOVE PAST WITHOUT TOUCHING to move past or over sth and without touching it ○ *If we stay on this course we should clear the buoy.* **14.** *vti.* ALLOW TO UNLOAD OR DEPART to be allowed to unload or depart, or allow a vehicle or cargo to unload or passengers to depart, after customs and other formalities have been dealt with **15.** *vt.* AUTHORIZE SB TO DO OR GO to authorize sb to do sth or go somewhere ○ *You are now cleared to enter the restricted area.* **16.** *vt.* GIVE OR GET AUTHORIZATION to give or obtain authorization for an action **17.** *vt.* GAIN MONEY AS PROFIT to earn or acquire sth as profit (*informal*) ○ *We cleared £5000 on the deal.* **18.** *vt.* PAY OFF DEBT to settle a debt **19.** *vi.* BANKING MOVE BETWEEN ACCOUNTS to be authorized and credited to the account of the payee ○ *Cheques take three days to clear.* **20.** *vti.* BANKING SETTLE BANKING ACCOUNTS to settle the accounts of a banking transaction through a clearing house **21.** *vt.* SPORTS GET BALL OUT OF DEFENCE AREA to get the ball out of the defence area **22.** *vt.* COMPUT DELETE DATA to delete data from a computer display or storage device ■ *n.* OPEN SPACE an empty or open area or space ○ *The deer were standing in the clear.* [13thC. Via Old French *cler* from Latin *clarus* 'clear, bright'.] —**clearable** *adj.* —**clearer** *n.* —**clearness** *n.* ◇ **in the clear** free from suspicion or blame

WORD KEY: ORIGIN

Clear is derived from the Latin word *clarus*, meaning 'clear' or 'bright', which is also the source of English *claret, clarify, clarion, clerestory,* and *declare.*

clear away *vti.* to remove unwanted objects from a place and leave it tidy

clear off *vi.* to go away (*dated informal*) ○ *Clear off and don't come back!*

clear out *v.* **1.** *vi.* LEAVE FAST to leave a place quickly or urgently (*informal*) ○ *We cleared out as fast as we could.* **2.** *vt.* REMOVE STH to remove the contents of sth, e.g. a room or cupboard, or to tidy sth by removing some of its contents ○ *clearing out the attic* **3.** *vt.* USE ALL OF SB'S MONEY to leave sb without money or other resources (*slang*) ○ *It will clear us out if we have to pay all the legal expenses.*

clear up *v.* **1.** *vi.* BECOME BRIGHTER to become brighter, e.g. after rain **2.** *vti.* GET OR MAKE BETTER to alleviate or cure sth, or be alleviated or cured **3.** *vti.* PUT STH IN ORDER to tidy sth by removing or arranging disorganized contents ○ *Will you please clear up all this mess before you leave?* ■ SOLVE MYSTERY OR EXPLAIN MISUNDERSTANDING to solve a mystery or explain a misunderstanding ○ *Here is a big problem that has never been fully cleared up.*

clearance /kléerənss/ *n.* **1.** REMOVING UNWANTED OBJECTS the removal of obstructions or unwanted objects, e.g. dilapidated buildings or overgrown bushes, before building or cultivating **2.** PERMISSION FOR STH TO HAPPEN permission to do sth or for sth to take place ○ *several aircraft awaiting clearance to take off* **3.** WIDTH OR HEIGHT OF OPENING the width or height of an opening or passage **4.** CHEAP SALE OF GOODS a sale of goods at reduced prices in order to clear stock **5.** REMOVAL OF PEOPLE FROM LAND the forcible removal from an area of land of the people who have traditionally lived there **6.** BANKING PASSAGE OF COMMERCIAL DOCUMENTS the passage of commercial documents through a clearing house **7.** SPORTS GETTING BALL OUT OF DEFENCE AREA in games, the process of clearing the ball from the defence area **8.** FORESTRY = **clearing 9.** = **security clearance**

clear-cut *adj.* **1.** UNAMBIGUOUS so definite as to leave no possibility of ambiguity **2.** DISTINCTLY OUTLINED with a distinct outline or form ○ *a clear-cut silhouette of a naval frigate on the horizon* ■ *vt.* **(clear-cuts, clear-cutting, clear-cut)** = **clear-fell**

clear-eyed *adj.* **1.** DISCERNINGLY PERCEPTIVE able to discern things clearly **2.** SHARP-EYED having sharp sight **3.** BRIGHT-EYED having bright eyes

clear-fell **(clear-fells, clear-felling, clear-felled)** *vt.* to cut down and remove all of the trees from a wood or other land area

clear-headed *adj.* able to think clearly and decisively, especially in difficult circumstances —**clear-headedly** *adv.* —**clear-headedness** *n.*

clearing /kléering/ *n.* **1.** FORESTRY OPEN SPACE IN WOOD a space without trees in an area of land that is wooded or overgrown **2.** BANKING MOVEMENT OF CHEQUES BETWEEN ACCOUNTS exchange between banks of cheques, drafts, and notes, and the settlement of consequent differences

clearing bank *n.* any bank that uses a central clearing house for transferring credits and cheques between itself and other banks

clearing house *n.* **1.** BANKING INSTITUTION COORDINATING FINANCIAL DEALINGS BETWEEN BANKS an institution at which financial transactions between member banks are cancelled against each other, leaving only balances to be paid **2.** INSTITUTION COORDINATING INFORMATION INTERCHANGES an agency that collects and distributes information

clearly /kléerli/ *adv.* **1.** WITHOUT ANY PROBLEM IN HEARING in a way that is easy to hear **2.** WITHOUT ANY PROBLEM IN SEEING in a way that is easy to see **3.** WITHOUT ANY PROBLEM IN UNDERSTANDING in a way that is easy to understand ○ *a clearly phrased piece of legislation* **4.** LOGICALLY in a logical and unconfused manner ○ *a clearly written legal brief* **5.** OBVIOUSLY used to acknowledge that a statement is undeniably true ○ *Clearly, we must take immediate action.*

clear-out *n.* a session of removing the contents of sth, e.g. a room, or of tidying it by removing some of its contents ○ *We had a great clear-out at the weekend and now we've got room for the new table.*

clear-sighted *adj.* **1.** HAVING GOOD PERCEPTION OR JUDGMENT having or showing good perception or judgment **2.** WITH KEEN VISION having sharp vision —**clear-sightedly** *adv.* —**clear-sightedness** *n.*

clearstory *n.* ARCHIT = **clerestory**

clear-up *n.* a session of putting sth in order

clearway /kléer way/ *n.* a section of road where drivers may not normally stop

clearwing /kléer wing/ *n.* a moth with scaleless transparent wings that is active during the daytime. Family: Sesiidae.

cleat /kleet/ *n.* **1.** DEVICE FOR TYING BOAT TO a device with two projections pointing in opposite directions to which a rope can be tied to secure a boat **2.** HARD PIECE FIXED UNDER SHOE a small piece of metal or hard plastic fixed to the sole of a shoe to improve its grip or to reduce wear **3.** WEDGE-SHAPED SUPPORT wooden or other wedge attached to a structure in order to support it **4.** DEVICE ON BOOT FOR CLIMBING TREES a device with a blade or set of sharp projections that is attached to a boot to assist in climbing trees or poles ■ *vt.* **(cleats, cleating, cleated) 1.** PROVIDE WITH CLEATS to fix a cleat or cleats to sth **2.** SECURE ROPE TO CLEAT to tie a rope to a cleat **3.** SUPPORT WITH CLEAT to support sth using a cleat or cleats [14thC. Ultimately from a prehistoric Germanic word meaning 'firm lump', which is also the ancestor of English *clot.*]

cleavable /kléevəb'l/ *adj.* able to be split or divided

cleavage /kléevij/ *n.* **1.** ACT OF SPLITTING division or splitting **2.** SPLIT IN STH a split, division, or separation of sth **3.** CREASE VISIBLE BETWEEN BREASTS the hollow visible between a woman's breasts when a low-cut garment is worn **4.** GEOL, MINERALS ROCK OR MINERAL FRACTURE the splitting of minerals or rocks along natural planes of weakness. The angle of cleavage is one of the features used to identify minerals. **5.** EMBRYOL REPEATED DIVISION OF FERTILIZED EGG the repeated division of a fertilized ovum (**zygote**) before formation of the early embryo (**blastula**). The zygote does not increase in size during this process because the cells become progressively smaller after each division. **6.** CHEM SPLITTING OF A MOLECULE the splitting of a molecule into simpler molecules through the breaking of a chemical bond

cleave[1] /kleev/ **(cleaves, cleaving, cleaved** *or* **clove** *or* **cleft** /klōv/, **cleaved** *or* **cloven** *or* **cleft** /klṓv'n/) *vti.* **1.** SPLIT to split, or make sth split, especially along a plane of natural weakness **2.** CUT A PATH THROUGH to make a way through sth (*literary*) ○ *We watched the bows of the tall ships cleave through the waves* **3.** PENETRATE to penetrate or pierce sth deep or dense such as water or heavy undergrowth [Old English *clēofan*. Ultimately from an Indo-European word that is also the ancestor of Greek *gluphein* 'to carve' (source of English *hieroglyphics*).]

cleave[2] /kleev/ **(cleaves, cleaving, cleaved** *or* **clave** /klayv/, **cleaved)** *vi.* to cling closely, steadfastly, or faithfully to sth or sb (*literary*) ○ *Is it wrong to cleave to such fond memories?* [Old English *cleofian*. Ultimately from an Indo-European word that is also the ancestor of English *clay, climb,* and *glue.*]

cleaver /kléevər/ *n.* a heavy knife with a broad blade, used by butchers

cleavers /kléevərz/ *n.* = **goosegrass** (*takes a singular verb*) [Old English. From CLEAVE[2], because its bristles stick to whatever they come in contact with.]

cleck /klek/ *vi.* **(clecks, clecking, clecked)** *Wales* ENGAGE IN GOSSIP to gossip about or inform on sb ■ *n. Wales* PIECE OF GOSSIP a piece of gossip [From Welsh, from *clecan* 'to gossip' and *clec* 'gossip']

cleek /kleek/ *n.* a hickory-shafted iron golf club similar to the modern number 2 iron (*dated*) [15thC. Originally a northern English dialect verb meaning 'to clutch', of uncertain origin.]

Cleese /kleez/, **John** (*b.* 1939) British comic actor and writer, best known for the television series *Monty Python's Flying Circus* (1969–74) and *Fawlty Towers* (1975, 1979).

Cleethorpes /klée thawrps/ town in Humberside, eastern England, situated at the mouth of the Humber 29 km/18 mi. southeast of Hull. Population: 67,500 (1991).

clef /klef/ *n.* in written or printed music, a symbol placed at the beginning of each staff to indicate the pitch [Late 16thC. Via French from Latin *clavis* 'key'.]

cleft[1] /kleft/ *n.* **1.** SMALL INDENTATION a small indentation in a surface, e.g. skin or land **2.** GAP OR SPLIT a substantial gap or division separating two things (*formal*) ○ *the ever widening cleft between the parties in their approaches to state funding* [Old English *geclyft*. Ultimately from an ancient Germanic word that is also the ancestor of English *cleave.*]

cleft[2] /kleft/ *vti.* past tense, past participle of **cleave** ■ *adj.* SPLIT having been separated into two or more sections by division

cleft palate *n.* a congenital fissure along the midline of the roof of the mouth. It is caused by a failure of the two sides of the hard palate to meet and fuse during foetal development and is often associated with a cleft lip.

cleg /kleg/ *n. N England, Scotland* a horsefly of northern Europe and Asia. Genus: *Haematopota.* [15thC. From Old Norse *kleggi.*]

Cleisthenes /klísthə neez/ (570?–507 BC) Greek ruler. His constitutional reforms of 507 BC establishing a council of 500 citizens are seen as the foundation of Athenian democracy.

cleistogamous /klī stóggəməss/ *adj.* relating to or bearing small flowers that do not open, are self-pollinated in the bud, and appear in addition to brighter flowers on the same plant [Late 19thC. Coined from Greek *kleistos* 'closed' (from *kleiein* 'to close') + -GAMY.] —**cleistogamously** *adv.* —**cleistogamy** *n.*

Cleland /klélland/, **John** (1709–89) British government official and writer, author of the witty *Fanny Hill, the Memoirs of a Woman of Pleasure* (1750).

clem /klem/ (**clems, clemming, clemmed**), **clam** /klam/ (**clams, clamming, clammed**) *vti.* to be hungry or make a person or animal hungry (*regional*) [Mid-16thC. From Old English *beclemman* 'to confine'; ultimately from a prehistoric Germanic word that is also the ancestor of English *clamp*.]

---WORD KEY: CULTURAL NOTE---
The verb ***clem*** is still found in UK regional dialects, especially in the forms **clemmed** or **clammed**. Like many dialect words, this one is dying out because the hunger associated with it is no longer a regular occurrence for the poor. Rural dialects continue to preserve a number of words meaning 'extremely hungry', including *clemmed out, fammelled, starved,* and *thirly.*

clematis /klémmətiss, klə máytiss/ (*plural* **-tises** or **-tis**) *n.* a climbing plant, native chiefly to northern temperate regions, with fluffy seed heads. Some types have large flat colourful flowers, typically blue, purple, pink or white. Genus: *Clematis.* ◊ **old man's beard** [Mid-16thC. Via Latin, 'clematis, periwinkle', from Greek *klēmatis*, from *klēma* 'vine branch'.]

Clemenceau /klém aN sō/, **Georges** (1841–1929) French journalist and statesman. He was prime minister of France (1906–09, 1917–20) and helped to formulate the Treaty of Versailles, which ended World War I.

clemency /klémmənssi/ *n.* **1.** SHOWING MERCY an instance of showing mercy or leniency, or the tendency to do this **2.** MILDNESS IN WEATHER mildness or temperateness, especially in the weather ○ *the clemency of areas affected by the Gulf Stream*

Clemens /klémmənz/, **Samuel Langhorne** ♦ **Mark Twain**

clement /klémmənt/ *adj.* **1.** MILD AS REGARDS WEATHER showing or experiencing no extremes in weather conditions **2.** MERCIFUL showing mercy or leniency [15thC. From the stem of Latin *clemens* 'mild, gentle'.] —**clemently** *adv.*

Clement /klémmənt/ **Clement I, St** (?–101?) Roman pope. The third or fourth successor to St Peter, he probably wrote the *Epistle to the Corinthians* (95?), a vital document on papal authority. Known as **Clement of Rome**

Clement VII, Pope (1478–1534) During his papacy (1523–34) Rome was sacked (1527) by troops of the Holy Roman Emperor and the English church broke with Rome (1533). Real name **Giulio de' Medici**

clementine /klémmən tīn, -teen/ *n.* an orange-coloured citrus fruit, bred by crossing a tangerine with a Seville orange [Early 20thC. From French *clémentine*, of uncertain origin: perhaps named after Père *Clément*, a French missionary to Africa.]

clench /klench/ *v.* (**clenches, clenching, clenched**) **1.** *vt.* HOLD TEETH OR FIST TIGHTLY TOGETHER to close your teeth or fist tightly, e.g. when angry **2.** *vt.* CLUTCH STH to hold or grip sth tightly ○ *He clenched the rope in his teeth* **3.** *vti.* to contract suddenly, often as a result of sudden tension or emotion (*refers to muscles*) ○ *his jaw clenched as he waited* ■ *n.* **1.** TIGHT HOLD a tight grasp or hold ○ *She held the steering wheel in a tight clench.* **2.** DEVICE THAT GRIPS TIGHTLY a mechanical device that holds or grips sth firmly ■ *vt.* (**clenches, clenching, clenched**), *n.* NAUT = **clinch** *v.* 4 [Old English *beclencan.* Ultimately from a prehistoric Germanic word meaning 'to stick', which is also the ancestor of English *cling*.]

clenched /klencht/ *adj.* held tightly or firmly together ○ *clenched fists*

cleome /kli ómi/ *n.* an aromatic plant native to warm regions, often cultivated for its clusters of white or purplish flowers. Genus: *Cleome.* [Early 19thC. Via modern Latin from Greek, where it denoted a different plant.]

Cleon /klée on/ (?–422 BC) Greek politician and general. As leader of the Athenians, he spurned Spartan peace overtures during the Peloponnesian War (431–404 BC) and was killed in battle.

Cleopatra /klée ə páttrə/ (69–30 BC) Egyptian monarch. A queen (51–30 BC) of legendary beauty, she and her lover Mark Antony were defeated by Octavian's forces at Actium (31 BC).

Cleopatra's Needle *n.* either of two Egyptian obelisks originally erected at Heliopolis about 1500 BC. One was moved to the Thames Embankment, London (1878), the other to Central Park, New York (1880).

clepsydra /klépsidrə/ (*plural* **-dras** or **-drae** /-dree/) *n.* an ancient device used for measuring time by noting the amount of water or mercury that passes through a small aperture over a particular period [Mid-17thC. Via Latin from Greek *klepsudra*, from *kleptein* 'to steal' + *hudor* 'water'.]

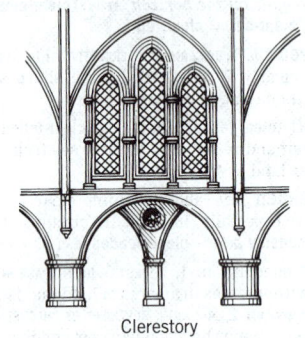

Clerestory

clerestory /kleér stawri, -stəri/ (*plural* **-ries**), **clearstory** (*plural* **-ries**) *n.* the upper part of the wall of a church nave that contains windows, or the upper part of a wall in other buildings that contains windows [*Clere* from an earlier spelling of CLEAR.]

clerestory coach *n.* a railway carriage or coach with a raised central section along its roof, containing small windows

clergy /klúrji/ (*plural* **-gies**) *n.* the body of people ordained for religious service, especially in the Christian Church (*takes a singular or plural verb*) [13thC. Partly from Old French *clergie* (from *clerc* 'cleric') and partly from *clergé* 'body of clerks', both from, ultimately, ecclesiastical Latin *clericus* (see CLERK).]

clergyman /klúrjimən/ (*plural* **-men** /-mən/) *n.* a man who is a member of the clergy

clergywoman /klúrji woomən/ (*plural* **-en** /-wimin/) *n.* a woman who is a member of the clergy

cleric /klérrik/ *n.* an ordained priest, minister, or rabbi [Early 17thC. From ecclesiastical Latin *clericus* (see CLERK).]

clerical /klérrik'l/ *adj.* **1.** OF OFFICE WORK relating or belonging to office work, especially of a routine administrative kind **2.** OF THE CLERGY relating or belonging to the clergy **3.** PROMOTING CLERICALISM advocating or supporting clericalism —**clerically** *adv.*

clerical collar *n.* a stiff white collar, continuous at the front, worn by some members of the clergy

clericalism /klérrik'lizzəm/ *n.* **1.** SUPPORT FOR CLERGY a policy of supporting the power or views of the clergy **2.** POWER OF CLERGY the power or influence of the clergy —**clericalist** *n.*

clericals /klérrik'lz/ *npl.* the characteristic clothing worn by some members of the clergy

clerihew /klérri hyoo/ *n.* a humorous or satirical verse consisting of two rhyming couplets in lines of irregular metre about sb who is named in the verse [Early 20thC. Named after the English writer Edmund *Clerihew* Bentley 1875–1956, who invented it.]

clerk /klaark/ *n.* **1.** GENERAL OFFICE WORKER a worker who performs general office duties, such as keeping records or sending out correspondence **2.** *US* = sales clerk **3.** *US* SERVICE DESK WORKER sb at a service desk who helps and advises other people **4.** GOVERNMENT WORKER WHO KEEPS RECORDS sb who keeps official transcripts and other records of a legislative or other official body **5.** LAW ADMINISTRATOR IN COURT OF LAW sb who administers the business of a court **6.** LAW COURT LEGAL ADVISER sb with legal qualifications who advises lay magistrates on points of law in court **7.** CHR CLERIC a member of the clergy (*formal*) **8.** SCHOLAR a scholar or learned person (*archaic*) ■ *vi.* (**clerks, clerking, clerked**) WORK AS CLERK to work as a clerk [Pre-12thC. Via ecclesiastical Latin *clericus* 'of the clergy' from Greek *klērikos*, from *klēros* 'heritage'. From the role of the clergy as scribes and record-keepers in the Middle Ages.] —**clerkdom** *n.* —**clerkish** *adj.* —**clerkship** *n.*

clerking /klaárking/ *n.* the taking and recording by a hospital of the medical history and other relevant details of a newly admitted patient

clerkly /klaárkli/ *adj.* behaving or looking like a clerk ○ *a clerkly attention to detail in the midst of a crisis* —**clerkliness** *n.*

clerk of the works (*plural* **clerks of the works**) *n.* an official who inspects the standard of construction of a new building

Clermont-Ferrand /kláir moN fe ráaN/ capital of Puy-de-Dôme Department, Auvergne Region, in south-central France. It is an industrial city, with a major rubber industry. Population: 140,167 (1990).

cleruch /kleéroŏk/ *n.* in ancient Athens, a citizen who received a land allotment in foreign territory and lived there without losing citizenship [Mid-19thC. From Greek *klēroūkhos*, literally 'lot-holder'.]

cleruchy /kleéroŏki/ (*plural* **-ies**) *n.* an ancient Athenian colony in foreign territory that remained dependent on Athens and whose settlers retained Athenian citizenship —**cleruchial** /kli roŏki əl/ *adj.*

cleveite /kleév īt/ *n.* a crystalline form of uraninite [Late 19thC. Named after the Swedish chemist Per T. *Cleve* (1840–1905).]

Cleveland /kleévlənd/ **1.** former county of north-eastern England, from 1974 until 1996. The name is retained in postal addresses. Area: 583 sq. km/225 sq. mi. **2.** city and port in northeastern Ohio on the southeastern shore of Lake Erie. Population: 498,246 (1996).

Cleveland, Grover (1837–1908) US statesman and 22nd and 24th president of the United States. As president (1885–89, 1893–97) he opposed special interests and the political spoils system. Full name **Stephen Grover Cleveland**

clever /klévvər/ *adj.* **1.** INTELLIGENT having sharp mental abilities **2.** SHOWING INTELLIGENCE demonstrating mental agility and creativity **3.** GLIBLY FACILE showing highly capable mental abilities in a showy or superficial way ○ *Don't give me one of your clever answers.* **4.** DEXTEROUS highly skilled in using the hands **5.** UNUSUAL AND EFFECTIVE produced by skill or ingenuity ○ *a clever idea* ○ *What a clever little gadget!* **6.** WELL in a state of good health (*regional*) [13thC. Origin uncertain. The present-day meaning evolved from 'deft' via 'sprightly' and 'agile'.] —**cleverly** *adv.* —**cleverness** *n.*

---WORD KEY: SYNONYMS---
See Synonyms at **intelligent**.

clever-clever *adj.* affectedly or ostentatiously clever (*informal*)

clever clogs (*plural* **clever clogs**) *n.* = clever Dick (*informal*)

clever Dick *n.* sb who is overconfidently or ostentatiously clever (*informal*)

clevis /klévviss/ *n.* a U-shaped device with a hole at the end of each prong through which a pin or bolt can be pushed to secure another part in place [Late 16thC. Origin uncertain.]

clew /kloo/ *n.* **1.** BALL OF THREAD OR YARN a wound ball of thread or yarn **2.** SAILING CORNER OF FORE-AND-AFT SAIL the rear lower corner of a triangular or four-sided sail set along the length of a boat **3.** SAILING CORNER OF SAIL SET ACROSS BOAT either of the two lower corners of a sail set parallel to the width of a boat, e.g. a square sail or a spinnaker ■ **clews** *npl.* NAUT HAMMOCK CORDS the cords by which a hammock is suspended ■ *vt.* (**clews, clewing, clewed**) ROLL YARN INTO BALL to roll thread or yarn into a ball [Old English *cliwen*, probably related to *claw*]

clew up *vt.* to furl a square sail by pulling on lines attached to its lower corners

clianthus /kli ánthəss, klī-/ (*plural* **-thuses** *or* **-thus**) *n.* a plant of Australia or New Zealand with drooping clusters of slender scarlet flowers. Genus: *Clianthus.* [Mid-19thC. From modern Latin, formed from Greek *kleos* 'glory' + *anthus* 'flower'.]

cliché /klée shay/ *n.* **1. OVERUSED EXPRESSION** a phrase or word that has lost its original effectiveness or power from overuse **2. OVERUSED IDEA** an overused activity or notion [Mid-19thC. From French, the past participle of *clicher* 'to stereotype', imitative of the sound made when a mould is dropped into molten metal to produce a stereotype plate.]

clichéd /klée shayd/ *adj.* full of clichés

Clichy /klée shee/ northern industrial suburb of Paris, France. Population: 48,204 (1990).

click[1] /klik/ *n.* **1. SHORT SHARP SOUND** a short sharp sound, often metallic but not resonant **2.** MECH ENG **MECHANICAL COMPONENT FOR LOCKING POSITION** a component of a mechanical device that holds a part in a locking position, or the movement of the part between adjacent positions **3.** PHON **SOUND PRODUCED BY SUCKING IN AIR** a consonant sound produced by sucking in air by movements of the tongue against the soft palate. It is part of the phonemic system of some African languages, e.g. Xhosa, but in English is used only for the sound represented by 'tut-tut' and the sound used for encouraging horses. Technical name **suction stop 4.** COMPUT **PRESS OF COMPUTER MOUSE BUTTON** a single action of pressing and releasing a button on a computer mouse ■ *v.* (**clicks, clicking, clicked**) **1.** *vti.* **MAKE OR CAUSE SHORT SHARP SOUND** to make a short sharp sound, or cause sth to make a short sharp sound **2.** *vti.* COMPUT **PRESS COMPUTER MOUSE BUTTON** to press and release a button of a computer mouse ○ *Click on 'yes'.* **3.** *vi.* **BECOME CLEAR FAST** to be understood suddenly (*informal*) ○ *The whole thing clicked: they had decided not to hire me.* **4.** *vi.* **EASILY COMMUNICATE OR WORK TOGETHER** to communicate or work together easily and readily (*informal*) ○ *It's too bad that the two venture partners in the deal just never clicked.* **5.** *vi.* **BE A SUCCESS** to be successful or popular (*informal*) ○ *The new show clicked from the very first performance.* [Late 16thC. An imitation of the sound.]

click[2] /klik/ *n.* a kilometre (*slang*) ○ *about twenty clicks from here* [Mid-20thC. Origin uncertain: possibly an alteration of KILOMETRE and TICK.]

click beetle *n.* a beetle that can right itself when inverted by springing into the air with a clicking sound. Family: Elateridae.

clicker /klíkər/ *n.* **1. SB OR STH THAT CLICKS** a person who or device that clicks **2. SUPERVISOR IN FACTORY** a foreman or forewoman at a printing press or shoe factory (*informal*)

clickstream /klík streem/ *n.* the path of mouse clicks that a computer user adopts to navigate the World Wide Web. Some Web sites trace and record their visitors' clickstreams as part of their marketing research.

client /klī ənt/ *n.* **1. SB USING PROFESSIONAL SERVICE** a person or organization taking advice from a lawyer, accountant, or other professional person **2. CUSTOMER** a person or organization to whom goods or services are provided and sold **3. USER OF SOCIAL SERVICE AGENCY** sb who uses the services of a social services agency **4. PERSON OR ENTITY HELPED BY ANOTHER** a person or entity dependent on the protection or patronage of another person or entity ○ *the former Soviet Union and its clients in the Middle East* **5.** COMPUT **COMPUTER PROGRAM THAT REQUESTS DATA** a computer program used to contact and obtain data from a program on another computer, often one linked on a network. A World Wide Web browser is a specific kind of client. [14thC. Via Latin *cliens* 'client, dependent' from, ultimately, *cluere* 'to listen, obey'.] —**cliental** *adj.* —**clientless** /klī əntləss/ *adj.*

clientage /klī əntij/ *n.* a social system in which free commoners receive the patronage of wealthy or influential aristocrats. It was common in ancient Rome and has become a feature of some modern societies.

client-centred therapy *n.* a form of psychotherapy in which the therapist seeks to elicit solutions to problems by gaining the trust of the patient through careful questioning. It was founded by Carl Rogers in the 1940s and is still used widely as a counselling method.

clientele /klée on tél, -ən-/ *n.* the clients or customers of a professional organization or business, considered as a group (*takes a singular verb*) ○ *The clientele of our family law firm consists mostly of big corporations.* [Mid-16thC. Directly, or later via French *clientèle*, from Latin *clientela*, from *cliens* (see CLIENT).]

client-server, client/server *adj.* designed for use on a computer network in which processing is divided between a client program running on a user's machine and a network server program. One server can provide data to, or perform storage-intensive processing tasks in conjunction with, one or more clients.

client state *n.* a country that depends on another for economic, political, or military support

cliff /klif/ *n.* a high steep rock or ice face, especially a rock face extending along a coastline [Old English *clif.* Ultimately from a prehistoric Germanic word that is also the ancestor of German *Klippe.*] —**cliffy** *adj.*

cliff dweller *n.* a member of any cliff-dwelling people, specifically of any of the Anasazi groups who constructed buildings on large ledges found in cliffs in the southwestern United States

Barnaby's

Cliff dwelling: Mesa Verde, Colorado, United States

cliff dwelling *n.* a building or group of buildings lived in by cliff dwellers

cliffhanger /klíf hangər/ *n.* **1.** ARTS, LITERAT **ENDING LEFT TEASINGLY UNRESOLVED** an unresolved ending in a serialized drama or book that leaves the audience or reader desperate to know what will happen in the next part **2.** ARTS **DRAMA SERIAL WITH SUSPENSEFUL ENDINGS** a drama serial that has episodes that often end in suspenseful unresolved endings **3. TENSE SITUATION** a situation full of tension or suspense because it is not clear what will happen next [From early serial films in which characters were left hanging off the edge of a cliff, their fate unresolved until the next episode] —**cliffhanging** *adj.*

cliff swallow *n.* a North American swallow with a dark throat patch. It builds its nest of mud on cliff faces or under eaves. Latin name: *Hyrundo pyrrhonota.*

Clift /klift/, **Charmian** (1923–69) Australian writer and author of *Peel Me a Lotus* (1958). She was married to George Johnston.

climacteric /klī máktərik, klī mak térrik/ *n.* **1. PERIOD OF IMPORTANT CHANGE** a period in which critically important changes take place **2.** PHYSIOL = **menopause 3.** PHYSIOL = **male menopause 4.** BOT **RIPENING STAGE IN FRUITS** a stage in the ripening of some fruits, e.g. apples, when the rate of respiration increases ■ *adj.* **1. IMPORTANT** crucially important **2.** PHYSIOL, BOT **RELATING TO CLIMACTERIC** relating to a physiological or botanical climacteric [Mid-16thC. Via French from, ultimately, Greek *klimaktēr* 'rung of a ladder', from *klimax* 'ladder' (see CLIMAX).] —**climacterically** /klī mak térrikli/ *adv.*

climactic /klī máktik/ *adj.* **1. EXCITING** extremely exciting or decisive **2. RELATING TO A CLIMAX** forming or relating to a climax [Late 19thC. Formed from CLIMAX, probably under the influence of CLIMACTERIC.] —**climactically** *adv.*

climate /klímət/ *n.* **1.** METEOROL **TYPICAL WEATHER IN REGION** the average weather or the regular variations in weather in a region over a period of years **2. PLACE WITH PARTICULAR WEATHER** a place with a particular kind of weather ○ *I prefer a warm climate* **3. SITUATION** the situation or atmosphere that prevails at a particular time or place **4. INDOOR ENVIRONMENT** the prevailing conditions or environment in an indoor setting such as an office [14thC. Via late Latin from Greek *klimat-*, the stem of *klima* 'slope, region of the earth'.] —**climatic** /klī máttik/ *adj.* —**climatically** /-máttikli/ *adv.*

climatic zone *n.* an area of the earth's surface that possesses a distinct type of climate. There are eight major climatic zones, roughly demarcated by lines of latitude.

climatology /klímə tólləji/ *n.* the scientific study of climates —**climatologic** /klímətə lójjik/ *adj.* —**climatological** /-lójjik'l/ *adj.* —**climatologically** /-lójjikli/ *adv.* —**climatologist** /klímə tólləjist/ *n.*

climax /klī maks/ *n.* **1. KEY MOMENT** the most exciting or important moment or point **2.** PHYSIOL **ORGASM** a sexual orgasm **3.** LING **EVER-INTENSIFYING SEQUENCE OF PHRASES** a sequence of phrases or sentences, each more forceful or intense than the last, or the conclusion of such a sequence **4.** ECOL **FINAL STAGE IN ECOLOGICAL COMMUNITY'S DEVELOPMENT** a late or final stage in the development of an ecological community in which the composition of plants and animals is relatively stable and well matched to environmental conditions ■ *v.* (**-maxes, -maxing, -maxed**) **1.** *vti.* **REACH THE KEY POINT** to reach the most important or exciting point in sth such as an event or a story, or bring sth to its most important or exciting point **2.** *vi.* PHYSIOL **HAVE AN ORGASM** to have a sexual orgasm [Mid-16thC. Via late Latin from Greek *klimax* 'ladder, progression'. Ultimately from an Indo-European base meaning 'to lean', which is also the ancestor of English *lean, incline,* and *ladder.*]

climb /klīm/ *v.* (**climbs, climbing, climbs, climbed**) **1.** *vti.* **GO UP USING HANDS AND FEET** to move towards the top of sth using the hands and feet ○ *climb a ladder* **2.** *vti.* **MOVE UPWARDS** to move upwards, or move towards the top of sth, by any means, and typically through continual or gradual effort ○ *climb the stairs* **3.** *vi.* **MOVE WITH EFFORT** to manoeuvre the body somewhere with effort or difficulty ○ *I managed to climb out of bed.* **4.** *vi.* **RISE STEEPLY IN AMOUNT** to rise sharply in value or amount **5.** *vi.* CLIMBING **BE A MOUNTAINEER** to go up mountains or rocks on foot or using hands and feet as a sport **6.** *vti.* **MOVE HIGHER SOCIALLY** to move to a higher social or professional position **7.** *vti.* BOT **GROW CLINGINGLY UPWARDS** to grow upwards by using plants or objects as a support, e.g. by producing shoots or tendrils that cling to them ■ *n.* **1. ACT OF CLIMBING** the process of moving to the top of sth ○ *It was a steep climb to the top.* **2.** CLIMBING **HILL OR MOUNTAIN** a route used to go up a hill, mountain, or rock, or the hill, mountain, or rock itself **3. RISE IN VALUE OR AMOUNT** a rise in the value or amount of sth [Old English *climban.* Ultimately from a prehistoric Germanic verb meaning 'to adhere', from assumed West Germanic *klimban*, a nasalized variant, that is, one introducing m or n, of an assumed word meaning 'to adhere' (source of English *cleave* 'to adhere' and *cleavers*).] —**climbable** *adj.*

climb down *vi.* to abandon forcefully or publicly expressed views or demands in the face of opposition from other people

climb into *vt.* to put on clothes, usually easy-to-wear ones (*informal*)

climb out of *vt.* to take off clothes, usually easy-to-wear ones (*informal*)

climb-down *n.* the act of abandoning forcefully or publicly expressed views or demands

climber /klímər/ *n.* **1.** CLIMBING **SB WHO CLIMBS MOUNTAINS** sb who climbs rocks or mountains as a sport **2.** BOT **PLANT THAT CLINGS** a plant that attaches itself to other plants or objects such as posts and walls as it grows **3. SB ADVANCING SOCIALLY** sb who rises to a higher social or professional position, especially an unscrupulous person obsessed with advancement (*usually used in combination*)

climbing /klíming/ *n.* the sport of climbing mountains or rocks

climbing fish *n.* a tropical freshwater fish found in Asia that can breathe out of water and that uses its gill plates and lower fins to pull itself along the ground. Latin name: *Anabas testudineus.*

climbing frame *n.* a framework of interlocking metal, wooden, or plastic bars designed for children to climb on. US term **jungle gym**

climbing iron *n.* a spike-covered metal frame that attaches to the sole of a boot to help sb climb up ice or trees

climbing perch *n.* = climbing fish

climbing rat *n.* = black rat

climbing wall *n.* a wall with handholds and footholds, often located indoors, that is designed to provide practice at rock-climbing

clime /klīm/ *n.* a place with a particular type of climate (*literary*) (*often plural*) ○ *off to sunnier climes* [Late 16thC. Via Latin from Greek *klima* (see CLIMATE).]

-clinal *suffix.* sloping, slanting ○ *isocline* [Formed from Greek *klinein* 'to lean' (see CLINE).]

clinandrium /kli nándri əm/ (*plural* **-a** /-dri ə/) *n.* a hollow in the upper column of the flower of an orchid, containing the anther [Mid-19thC. From modern Latin, literally 'stamen bed', coined from Greek *klinē* 'couch' + the modern Latin stem *-andrium* 'stamen'.]

clinch /klinch/ *v.* (**clinches, clinching, clinched**) **1.** *vt.* RESOLVE STH DECISIVELY to settle the outcome of sth that was uncertain, e.g. a business deal or an argument, in a positive way **2.** *vt.* DIY, CONSTR FLATTEN NAIL'S END to bend or flatten the protruding end of a nail or rivet, or fix sth together using nails or rivets in this way **3.** *vi.* SPORTS PUT ARMS AROUND OPPONENT in boxing or wrestling, to put your arms around an opponent's body so as to pin the arms and prevent an exchange of blows **4.** *vt.* NAUT FASTEN WITH A PARTICULAR KNOT to fasten or secure sth with a knot in a rope that is created by making a half hitch, the rope's end being fastened by seizing it ■ *n.* **1.** PASSIONATE EMBRACE a tight passionate embrace between lovers (*informal*) **2.** SPORTS TACTIC OF PINNING OPPONENT'S ARMS a tactic in boxing and wrestling designed to prevent an exchange of blows by putting your arms around an opponent's body, pinning the arms to the sides **3.** DIY, CONSTR BENT END OF NAIL a nail or rivet with its protruding end bent over, or a fastening made in this way **4.** NAUT KNOT IN ROPE a knot in a rope that is created by making a half hitch, the rope's end being fastened by seizing it [Mid-16thC. Origin uncertain: perhaps a blend of CLENCH and its dialectal (northern English and Scottish) variant *clink*.]

clincher /klínchər/ *n.* **1.** DECIDING FACTOR the factor that decides the outcome of sth, e.g. an argument or a contest (*informal*) **2.** DIY, CONSTR NAIL WITH END BENT a nail or rivet that has its protruding end bent over **3.** DIY, CONSTR TOOL FOR BENDING NAIL a tool for bending the ends of a nail or rivet

cline /klīn/ *n.* **1.** CONTINUUM a continuum between two extremes **2.** VARIATION IN CHARACTERISTICS OF A SPECIES a gradual variation in the characteristics of a plant or animal species that occurs when it is distributed over an area with differing environmental or geographic conditions [Mid-20thC. From Greek *klinein* 'to lean'.] —**clinal** *adj.* —**clinally** *adv.*

───── **WORD KEY: ORIGIN** ─────

The ultimate Indo-European source of *cline* is also the ancestor of English *client, clinic, decline, incline, ladder, lean,* and *recline.*

Cline /klīn/, **Patsy** (1932–63) US singer. Her slick, sentimental country songs such as 'Crazy' (1961) attracted huge popular audiences. She died in a plane crash at the peak of her career. Born **Virginia Patterson Hensley**

-cline *suffix.* slope ○ *syncline* [Back-formation from -CLINAL]

cling /kling/ *vi.* (**clings, clinging, clung** /klung/) **1.** HOLD TIGHTLY to hold onto sb or sth tightly with the hands or arms **2.** STICK TO STH to adhere to sth by sticking to it or staying very close to it **3.** RETAIN IDEAS OR CUSTOMS to refuse to give up sth, e.g. a belief or tradition, that you have grown fond of or used to **4.** NEED SB EMOTIONALLY to have a strong emotional

attachment to sb **5.** HOVER OVER AND SUFFUSE to linger, usually in the air, resisting dispersion or dissipation ■ *n.* **1.** STICKING QUALITY the tendency of sth to stick to surfaces **2.** BOT = clingstone [Old English *clingan* 'to adhere'. Ultimately from a prehistoric Germanic base that also produced English *clench*.] —**clingingly** *adv.*

clinger /klíngər/ *n.* sb who depends upon others for reassurance and a sense of security (*informal*)

cling film *n.* a clear plastic film that sticks to itself and to other surfaces, used to wrap food for storing

clingfish /klíng fish/ (*plural* **-fish** *or* **-fishes**) *n.* a small fish whose pelvic fins have been modified into a sucking disc that it uses to attach itself to rocks or other objects. Family: Gobiesocidae.

clingstone /klíng stōn/ *n.* a fruit with flesh that sticks to the stone. Some varieties of peach, nectarine, and plum have fruit of this type.

clingy /klíngi/ (**-ier, -iest**) *adj.* **1.** EMOTIONALLY DEPENDENT too dependent on the company or emotional support of other people **2.** STICKING TO THE BODY sticking closely to the body (*informal*) ○ *a clingy fabric* —**clinginess** *n.*

clinic /klínnik/ *n.* **1.** MED MEDICAL CENTRE a medical centre for outpatients, which may be attached to a hospital or form part of it **2.** MED SPECIALIZED MEDICAL CENTRE a medical centre that specializes in a particular condition or area of medicine **3.** MED GROUP MEDICAL PRACTICE a suite of offices or an office where a number of doctors practise general medicine as a partnership **4.** MED PRIVATE HOSPITAL a hospital that charges patients directly for their treatment, rather than one providing state-funded treatment **5.** MED MEDICINE TAUGHT AT THE BEDSIDE a teaching session during which student doctors are allowed to examine patients in hospital wards **6.** MED SESSION ATTENDED BY PATIENTS a session in a hospital that patients attend for specialized treatment or advice **7.** SPORTS SESSION OF PRACTICAL SPORTS INSTRUCTION a teaching session in which experts in specific sports give practical instruction and advice on improving technique and solving problems [Mid-19thC. Via French *clinique* from Greek *klinikē (tekhnē)* '(method of treating) the bedridden', from *klinikos* 'of a bed', from *klinē* 'bed', from *klinein* 'to lean, lie down' (see CLINE).]

-clinic *suffix.* having a particular number of obliquely intersecting axes ○ *triclinic* [From Greek *klinein* 'to lean' (see CLINE).]

clinical /klínnik'l/ *adj.* **1.** MED BASED ON MEDICAL TREATMENT OR OBSERVATION based on or involving medical treatment, practice, observation, or diagnosis **2.** UNEMOTIONAL practical and unemotional **3.** SEVERE IN DECOR OR DESIGN plain and severe in design, usually with the implication of lack of comfort —**clinically** *adv.*

clinical ecology *n.* MED the branch of medicine dealing with the supposed effects of the modern technological environment on human health, especially the relationship of allergies to the increase in chemicals in the environment

clinical nurse manager *n.* the administrative manager of the nursing staff in a hospital

clinical psychology *n.* a branch of psychology that deals with the diagnosis and treatment of psychological and behavioural problems —**clinical psychologist** *n.*

clinical thermometer *n.* a thermometer used for measuring the temperature of sb's body, which continues to register the observed temperature until reset

clinician /kli nísh'n/ *n.* **1.** MEDICAL PROFESSIONAL DOING PRACTICAL WORK a medical professional who works directly with patients, as distinct from one working in research **2.** DOCTOR WHO CONDUCTS CLINIC a medical professional who conducts or teaches in a clinic

clink[1] /klingk/ *vti.* (**clinks, clinking, clinked**) MAKE RINGING SOUND to make or cause sth to make the short high-pitched slightly ringing sound that metal or glass objects make when they knock against each other ■ *n.* RINGING SOUND the short high-pitched slightly ringing sound that metal or glass objects make when they knock against each other [14thC. Origin uncertain: possibly an imitation of the sound, or perhaps from Middle Dutch *klinken*.]

clink[2] /klingk/ *n.* a prison (*dated slang*) [Early 16thC. From the *Clink*, a noted former prison in Southwark, a borough of London.]

clinker /klíngkər/ *n.* **1.** BALL OF COAL RESIDUE a hard mass of ash and partially fused coal that remains after coal is burnt in a fire or furnace **2.** HARD BRICK a very hard brick, or an overhard brick that has been fired in a kiln for too long ■ *vi.* (**-ers, -ering, -ered**) FORM LUMPY BURNT RESIDUE to form hard lumps of partially fused coal and ash after burning [Mid-17thC. Alteration of obsolete *clincard*, from obsolete Dutch *klinckaerd* 'brick', from *klinken* 'to sound, ring'; from the sound made by a brick when struck.]

clinker-built /klíngkər/ *adj.* used to describe a boat that has a hull made of overlapping planks [From *clinker* 'clinched nail', from *clink* 'to secure a nail', a variant of CLENCH]

clinkety-clank *n.* the dull short ringing sounds produced when sth metallic hits a surface repeatedly [Early 20thC. From CLINK and CLANK, an imitation of the sound.]

clinkstone /klíngk stōn/ *n.* = phonolite [Translation of German *Klingstein*, literally 'ringing stone'; from its metallic resonance when struck]

clino- *prefix.* slope, slant ○ *clinometer* [Formed from Greek *klinein* 'to lean, slope' (see CLINE)]

clinometer /klī nómmitər/ *n.* any instrument used in surveying or geology to measure the angle of a slope or incline —**clinometric** /klīnə méttrik/ *adj.* —**clinometrical** /-méttrik'l/ *adj.* —**clinometry** /klī nómmətri/ *n.*

clinopyroxene /klīnō pī rók seen/ *n.* a silicate mineral of the pyroxene group, containing calcium, iron, and magnesium and forming monoclinic crystals, e.g. augite

clinostat /klínō stat/ *n.* a piece of laboratory equipment with a turntable that allows a plant placed on it to be exposed to a stimulus, e.g. light, equally on all sides

-clinous *suffix.* **1.** having stamens and pistils in a particular number of flowers ○ *diclinous* **2.** descending from a particular line ○ *matriclinous* [Origin uncertain: ultimately from Greek *klinein* 'to lean, decline' (see CLINE)]

clint /klint/ *n.* a limestone block separated from others by cracks, forming a limestone pavement. ◊ **grike** [14thC. Via Danish and Swedish *klint* from Old Swedish *klinter* 'rock'.]

Bill Clinton and Hillary Rodham Clinton

Clinton /klíntən/, **Bill** (b. 1946) US statesman and 42nd president of the United States (1993-). Before his election to the White House he was Democratic Governor of Arkansas (1979–81, 1983–92). In 1999 he was impeached and acquitted by the US senate for perjury and obstruction of justice. Full name **William Jefferson Clinton**

Clinton, Hillary Rodham (b. 1947) US lawyer and first lady. In 1994, her proposals for the first national health care program were blocked by Congress.

clintonia /klin tóni ə/ *n.* a broad-leafed perennial plant of the lily family with white, yellow, or purplish flowers and blue or purple berries. Genus: *Clintonia.* [Mid-19thC. From modern Latin, genus name, named after de Witt *Clinton* (1769–1828), US politician.]

Clio /klī ō/ *n.* in Greek mythology, the muse of history

cliometrics /klī ō méttriks/ *n.* the study of economic history using statistics, advanced methods of data processing, analysis of mathematical data, and economic modelling (*takes a singular verb*) [Mid-20thC. Coined from CLIO + -METRICS, modelled on such words as *econometrics*.] —**cliometric** *adj.* —**cliometrician** /klī ō mə trísh'n/ *n.*

clip[1] /klip/ *v.* (**clips, clipping, clipped**) **1.** *vt.* **CUT OR TRIM STH** to cut or trim sth, or cut it off, e.g. with scissors or shears **2.** *vt.* **CUT STH OUT** to remove sth from sth else by cutting **3.** *vt.* **SHORTEN TIME TAKEN FOR STH** to reduce the time taken to complete sth, especially travelling time **4.** *vt.* PHON **TRUNCATE SPEECH SOUND** to shorten a speech sound **5.** *vt.* LING **ABBREVIATE WORD** to shorten a word or other expression by abbreviating it or dropping a syllable **6.** *vt.* **CURTAIL** to reduce or diminish power or influence **7.** *vi.* **GO FAST** to move at a brisk pace (*informal*) **8.** *vt.* **SIDESWIPE** to make physical contact with sb or sth else with a light glancing slapping blow (*informal*) **9.** *vt.* **SWINDLE SB** to cheat or swindle sb, especially by overcharging (*slang*) ■ *n.* **1.** CINEMA, TV **FILM OR TV EXTRACT** an extract, especially a short piece from film or television footage **2.** PRESS **EXTRACT FROM PRINT MEDIA** a news story or other article cut out of a print publication and used, e.g., as a sample of work **3.** **THING OR AMOUNT CUT** sth cut or removed, especially the amount of wool cut from a flock of sheep at one shearing **4.** **GLANCING BLOW** a sideswiping blow **5.** **RATE OF MOTION** the speed at which sb or sth moves (*informal*) [13thC. Origin uncertain: probably from Old Norse *klippa* 'to cut short', which may be an imitation of the sound.]

clip[2] /klip/ *n.* **1.** **GRIPPING DEVICE** any of numerous devices that grip or clasp loose things together or that hold things firmly (*often used in combination*) **2.** ACCESSORIES **PIECE OF JEWELLERY** a piece of jewellery with a gripping device fitted that attaches to clothing **3.** ARMS **BULLET-HOLDER** a container for bullets, slotted directly into an automatic firearm ■ *vti.* (**clips, clipping, clipped**) **HOLD STH WITH GRIPPING DEVICE** to hold loose things together, or attach one thing to another, using a clip, or be attached in this way [Old English *clyppan* 'to embrace, fasten', of prehistoric West Germanic origin. The noun evolved from the verb in the 15thC. Ultimately from an Indo-European word meaning 'to form into a ball'. See CLING.]

clip art *n.* prepackaged artwork, available on graphics or desktop publishing software, for use in documents produced on computer [So called because it originally came in the form of *clip sheets*, pages of drawings that graphic designers could cut out and paste into layouts]

clipboard /klíp bawrd/ *n.* a small portable board with a clip fitted to the top, used for securing papers and providing a hard writing surface for sb on the move

clip-clop *n.*, *interj.* **SOUND OF HOOVES** used to represent or imitate the rhythmic sound made by a walking horse's hooves as they strike hard ground ■ *vi.* (**clip-clops, clip-clopping, clip-clopped**) **GO CLIP-CLOP** to make the sound of hooves striking hard ground [Early 20thC. An imitation of the sound.]

clip joint *n.* a shop or club that habitually overcharges its customers (*slang*) [From CLIP[1] 'to swindle']

clip-on *adj.* **ATTACHING BY GRIPPING** used to describe sth, especially an item of clothing, that is attached by means of a clip ■ *n.* **ACCESSORY THAT ATTACHES WITH CLIP** an accessory, e.g. an earring or a tie, that is attached with a clip

clipped /klipt/ *adj.* **1.** **NEATLY TRIMMED** trimmed or cut back neatly **2.** **WITH EACH WORD SPOKEN CLEARLY** spoken with each word pronounced separately and distinctly in a way that sounds terse or upper-class

clipper /klíppər/ *n.* **1.** NAUT **FAST SAILING SHIP** a mid-19th-century tall ship with a sharp bow, designed for fast speeds **2.** **SB WHO USES CUTTING TOOL** sb who uses a cutting or shearing tool **3.** ELECTRON ENG = **limiter** ■ **clippers** *npl.* **TOOL FOR CLIPPING STH** a hand tool for cutting or clipping sth. Clippers include the tool for trimming very short hair, that for trimming fingernails, and that for shearing sheep.

clippie /klíppi/ *n.* a woman bus or tram conductor (*dated informal*)

clipping /klípping/ *n.* = **cutting** *n.* 2 ■ **clippings** *npl.* **TRIMMED-OFF HAIR OR GRASS** pieces of grass or hair that have been cut or clipped off

Clipper

clique /kleek/ *n.* a close group of friends or colleagues having similar interests and goals, and whom outsiders regard as excluding them [Early 18thC. From French, formed from *cliquer* 'to click, clap', an imitation of the sound. The underlying meaning is apparently 'a group of people who applaud one another'.] —**cliquey** *adj.* —**cliquish** *adj.* —**cliquishly** *adv.* —**cliquishness** *n.*

clishmaclaver /klíshmə kláyvər/ *n. Scotland* casual chat or gossip (*informal*) [Early 18thC. From *clish* (apparently from Scottish *clish-clash* 'idle gossip') + CLAVER.]

clitellum /klī téllәm/ (*plural* **-la** /-téllə/) *n.* a glandular section, similar in shape to a saddle, in the body wall of some worms, e.g. earthworms and leeches, that secretes a sticky substance during copulation. The substance is later used to form a sac in which the eggs are deposited. [Mid-19thC. Via modern Latin from Latin *clitellae* 'packsaddle' (from its shape), literally 'little litters'.]

clitic /klíttik/ *adj.* used to describe a word that cannot be stressed and is pronounced as part of the word that follows or precedes it, e.g. in 've' in 'I've' [Mid-20thC. Back-formation from ENCLITIC and PROCLITIC.] —**clitic** *n.*

clitoridectomy /klíttəri déktəmi/ (*plural* **-mies**) *n.* the cutting off of all or part of a woman's or girl's clitoris, practised in some societies as a social or cultural rite of passage

clitoris /klíttəriss/ (*plural* **clitorises** *or* **clitorides** /klíttə rī deez/) *n.* a small highly sensitive erectile organ at the front junction of the labia minora in the vulva [Early 17thC. Via modern Latin from Greek *kleitoris*, literally 'little hill'.] —**clitoral** *adj.*

Clive /klīv əv plássi/, **Robert, Baron Clive of Plassey** (1725–74) British soldier and colonial administrator who was instrumental in establishing British rule in India. He served as governor of Bengal from 1765 to 1767 but became embroiled in scandal and committed suicide. Known as **Clive of India**

clk *abbr.* clerk

Cllr *abbr.* Councillor

clm *abbr.* column

cloaca /klō áykə/ (*plural* **-cae** /-kee/) *n.* the terminal region of the gut in reptiles, amphibians, birds, and many fishes as well as in some invertebrates. The intestinal, urinary, and genital canals open into it. [Late 16thC. From Latin, 'sewer, canal'. Ultimately from an Indo-European word meaning 'to flush out', which is also the ancestor of English *cataclysm* and *clyster*).] —**cloacal** *adj.*

cloak /klōk/ *n.* **1.** CLOTHES **OUTER GARMENT** a loose sleeveless outer garment that fastens at the neck **2.** **ENSHROUDING OBJECT OR FORCE** sth that covers or conceals things (*literary*) ■ *vt.* (**cloaks, cloaking, cloaked**) **ENSHROUD STH** to cover or conceal sth (*often passive*) [13thC. Via Old Northern French *cloke, cloque*, variants of Old French *cloche*, from medieval Latin *clocca* 'bell, cape worn by travellers' (see CLOCK); from its bell-like shape.]

cloak-and-dagger *adj.* involving secrecy or intrigue, often as part of an espionage operation [Translation of French *de cape et d'épée* and Spanish *de capa y espada*, literally 'of cape and sword', symbols of the rank of the chief characters in dramas of domestic intrigue]

cloakroom /klōk room, -rōom/ *n.* **1.** **PLACE FOR DEPOSITING BELONGINGS** a room in a public building, e.g. a theatre, club, or restaurant, where customers can leave coats, umbrellas, and other belongings during their stay. US term **coat check** **2.** **CUPBOARD FOR COATS** a walk-in cupboard in a house, where coats and other outdoor items are stored **3.** **LAVATORY** a lavatory, especially one in a public building, or downstairs in a house with an upstairs bathroom (*informal*) US term **restroom**

clobber /klóbbər/ *vt.* (**-bers, -bering, -bered**) (*informal*) **1.** **HIT SB OR STH** to hit sb or sth with great force **2.** **UTTERLY DEFEAT SB** to defeat sb heavily **3.** **CRITICIZE SEVERELY** to criticize sth or sb severely ○ *The scheme has been clobbered in the national press.* ■ *n.* **SB'S BELONGINGS OR CLOTHES** sb's belongings or clothes, usually those intended for a particular activity (*informal*) [Mid-20thC. Origin unknown.]

cloche /klosh/ *n.* **1.** CLOTHES **WOMAN'S HAT** a woman's or girl's close-fitting hat with a very narrow brim, or no brim at all, especially popular in the 1920s and 1930s **2.** GARDENING **PROTECTIVE COVER FOR PLANTS** a small structure made of glass or clear plastic, placed over cold-sensitive garden plants in cold weather [Late 19thC. Via French, literally 'bell', from medieval Latin *clocca* (see CLOCK); from the shape.]

clock[1] /klok/ *n.* **1.** TIME **DEVICE DISPLAYING THE TIME** a free-standing device that measures and records time, which it displays by a pointer on a dial or by a digital readout **2.** TECH **MEASURING INSTRUMENT WITH DISPLAY** a measuring instrument with a dial or a digital display, e.g. any of a vehicle's control gauges, especially the mileometer **3.** BUSINESS = **time clock** **4.** BOT **SEED HEAD OF DANDELION** the fluffy white seed head of a dandelion **5.** COMPUT **ELECTRONIC CIRCUIT THAT SYNCHRONIZES COMPUTER PROCESSES** an electronic circuit that generates pulses at a constant rate in order to synchronize the internal operations in a computer ■ *vt.* (**clocks, clocking, clocked**) **1.** **RECORD SB'S OR STH'S TIME** to measure or record the time sb or sth takes, using a stopwatch or an electronic timing device **2.** **PUNCH SB** to punch sb (*slang*) ○ *He clocked him one.* **3.** **NOTICE STH** to notice sth (*slang*) ○ *We clocked him going into the betting shop.* **4.** CARS **TAMPER WITH VEHICLE'S MILEOMETER** to turn back the mileometer on a used car so that the mileage appears much lower than it is (*slang*) [14thC. Via Middle Dutch and Middle Low German *klocke* from, ultimately, medieval Latin *clocca* 'bell' (source of English *cloak*).] ◇ **against the clock** with limited time to finish sth ◇ **around the clock, round the clock** day and night, without stopping ◇ **turn the clock(s) back, put the clock(s) back** to return to the conditions of an earlier time

clock in, clock on *vi.* to arrive for work, or record arrival for work by inserting a personalized card into a time clock

clock out, clock off *vi.* to leave work, or record departure from work by inserting a personalized card into a time clock

clock up *vt.* to reach a particular total

clock[2] /klok/ *n.* a design on the ankle or side of a stocking or sock [Mid-16thC. Origin uncertain: perhaps the pattern originally consisted of bell-shaped ornaments (see CLOCK[1]).]

clock golf *n.* a putting game in which the ball is played from each of several points on the edge of a circular lawn towards a single hole in the centre

clockmaker /klók maykər/ *n.* sb who makes and repairs clocks and watches for a living

clock radio *n.* an electronic device that incorporates a digital clock, an alarm clock, and a radio

clock speed *n.* the speed of a microprocessor's internal clock that controls how fast a computer can make calculations, usually measured in megahertz (MHz)

clock-watcher *n.* sb who is more interested in going home or to lunch on time than getting a job done —**clock-watching** *n.*

clockwise /klók wīz/ *adv.*, *adj.* in the same direction that the hands of a clock move around a clockface

clockwork /klók wurk/ *n.* **1.** **MECHANICAL POWERING SYSTEM** a mechanism consisting of cogs and a wound spring, used to drive a traditional clock or a moving toy **2.** **UNVARYING REGULARITY** precise unvarying regularity

clod /klod/ *n.* **1.** LUMP OF EARTH a large lump of earth or clay **2.** UNINTELLIGENT PERSON sb who is unintelligent and stupid (*insult*) [14thC. Variant form of CLOT.] — **cloddish** *adj.* — **cloddishly** *adv.* — **cloddishness** *n.* — **cloddy** *adj.*

clodhopper /klód hopər/ *n.* AWKWARD UNSOPHISTICATED PERSON sb who is awkward and unsophisticated and behaves insensitively or clumsily (*insult*) ■ **clod-hoppers** *npl.* CLOTHES BIG HEAVY SHOES OR BOOTS a pair of large heavy shoes or boots (*informal*) [Early 18thC. Originally 'a ploughman or other agricultural worker', from the idea of sb who 'hops' or walks over ploughed land with clods of earth.]

clog /klog/ *v.* (**clogs, clogging, clogged**) **1.** *vti.* BLOCK GRADUALLY to block a tube or opening gradually with dirt or dust, or become gradually blocked with dirt or dust **2.** *vt.* TRANSP HINDER MOVEMENT IN STH to block sth such as a road or tunnel, making movement difficult ■ *n.* **1.** CLOTHES HEAVY SHOE a heavy shoe traditionally made of wood, or a shoe with a heavy, traditionally wooden, sole **2.** OBSTRUCTION sth that works against sb as an obstacle or hindrance **3.** WEIGHT RESTRICTING ANIMAL'S MOVEMENT a wooden block fastened to an animal's leg to restrict its movement [14thC. Origin unknown. The original meaning of the word was 'block, lump'. The verb developed from the idea of impeding an animal with a wooden block.] ◇ **pop your clogs** to die (*slang*)

clog up *vti.* = **clog**

clog dance *n.* a dance performed by dancers wearing clogs, who tap or stamp in time to the music

cloggy /klóggi/ *adj.* sticky, or lumpy in texture — **clogginess** *n.*

cloisonné /klwaa zónn ay/ *adj.* DECORATED WITH PATTERN OF ENAMEL decorated with a pattern formed by pieces of enamel in various colours separated by strips of flattened wire ■ *n.* CLOISONNÉ WORK decorative work with a cloisonné pattern [Mid-19thC. From French, literally 'partitioned', the past participle of *cloisonner*, from Old French *cloison* 'partition', from, ultimately, Latin *claudere* (see CLOSE).]

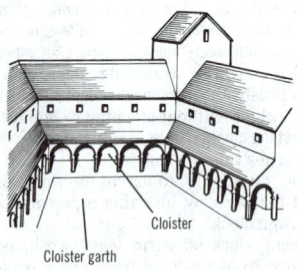

Cloister garth

Cloister

cloister /klóystər/ *n.* **1.** ARCHIT COVERED WALKWAY ROUND COURTYARD a continuous covered outdoor walkway built against buildings surrounding a central courtyard or quadrangle, especially in a monastery or college. The inner side of the walkway may be open or colonnaded. **2.** RELIG MONASTERY OR CONVENT a place where people live a life of religious seclusion and contemplation, e.g. a monastery or convent **3.** RELIG LIFE OF RELIGIOUS SECLUSION the life of religious seclusion lived by a monk or nun ○ *He chose the cloister rather than the secular world.* **4.** PLACE OF SECLUSION a place where people can be private or secluded ■ *vr.* (**-ters, -tering, -tered**) FIND PRIVATE PLACE to find a quiet private place where you can remain undisturbed [13thC. Via Old French *cloistre* from medieval Latin *claustrum*, from Latin, 'bar, bolt', formed from *claudere* (see CLOSE). The underlying idea is of an enclosed place.]

cloistered /klóystərd/ *adj.* **1.** SECLUDED secluded, or sheltered from the harsh realities of life ○ *had led a cloistered life* **2.** RELIG IN A MONASTERY living or occurring in a monastery or convent **3.** ARCHIT WITH A CLOISTER having a cloister for walking in

cloistral /klóystrəl/ *adj.* **1.** RELIG OF RELIGIOUS SECLUSION relating to a life of religious seclusion **2.** LEADING A SHELTERED LIFE sheltered from the harsh realities of life

clomiphene /klómi feen/ *n.* a synthetic drug used to induce ovulation and treat infertility. Formula: $C_{26}H_{28}ClNO$. [Mid-20thC. Coined from CHLORO- + AMINE + PHENYL.]

clomp *n.*, *vti.* = **clump**[2]

Cloncurry /klon k/ town in northwestern Queensland, Australia, a centre of mining and cattle grazing. Population: 2,459 (1996).

Clone: First clone of an adult animal ('Dolly'), Roslin Institute, Edinburgh (1997)

clone /klōn/ *n.* **1.** GENETICS GENETICALLY IDENTICAL ORGANISM a plant, animal, or other organism that is genetically identical to its parent, having developed by vegetative reproduction, e.g. from a bulb or a cutting, or experimentally from a single cell **2.** GENETICS GROUP OF GENETICALLY IDENTICAL PROGENY a collection of organisms, cells, or molecular segments that are genetically identical direct descendants of a single parent by asexual reproduction, e.g. plant cuttings or grafts. Some plant varieties are clones. **3.** COMPUT NEAR COPY OF HARDWARE OR SOFTWARE a hardware device, e.g. a PC, or a piece of software that is a functional copy of another, popular, more expensive product developed by another manufacturer ■ *v.* (**clones, cloning, cloned**) **1.** *vti.* GENETICS PRODUCE GENETICALLY IDENTICAL ORGANISMS to produce an organism that is genetically identical to its parent, by vegetative reproduction or a laboratory technique, or be produced in this way **2.** *vt.* MAKE COPY OF STH to produce an exact or near copy of an object or product [Early 20thC. From Greek *klōn* 'twig'.] — **clonal** *adj.* — **clonally** *adv.* — **cloner** *n.*

— **WORD KEY: SYNONYMS** —
See Synonyms at *copy*.

clonk /klongk/ *n.*, *interj.* DULL HOLLOW SOUND used to represent or imitate the dull hollow sound of sth heavy, usually metal, ceramic, or glass, hitting a surface hard ■ *v.* (**clonks, clonking, clonked**) **1.** *vti.* MAKE THUDDING NOISE to make a heavy hollow thud, or make sth produce such a noise **2.** *vt.* HIT SB HEAVILY to hit sb with a heavy blow, usually on a particular part of the body (*informal*) [Mid-19thC. An imitation of the sound.]

Clonmel /klon mél/ town and sporting centre in County Tipperary, Ireland. Population: 11,737 (1986). Irish **Cluain Meala**

clonus /klónəss/ *n.* a series of rapid repetitive contractions and relaxations in a muscle during movement, which is characteristic of certain nervous disorders. Spontaneous clonus is a principal feature of grand-mal epilepsy seizures but is otherwise uncommon. [Early 19thC. Via Latin from Greek *klonos* 'turmoil, agitation'.] — **clonic** /klónnik/ *adj.* — **clonicity** /klō níssəti/ *n.*

Clooney /klóoni/, **George** (b. 1961) US film and television actor. He played Dr Douglas Ross in the 1990s' US television series *ER*.

cloot /kloot/ *n.* Scotland **1.** HOOF a hoof, or either half of a cloven hoof **2.** CLOTH a cloth (*nonstandard*) [Late 18thC. Variant of CLOUT.]

clootie dumpling /klóoti-/ *n.* Scotland a sweet pudding, full of currants or raisins, that is boiled in a cloth. It is rather like Christmas pudding. [From CLOOT]

clop /klop/ *n.*, *interj.* SOUND OF HOOVES used to represent or imitate the sound that a walking horse's hooves

make when they strike hard ground ■ *vi.* (**clops, clopping, clopped**) MAKE SOUND OF HOOVES to make the sound of a walking horse's hooves striking hard ground [Mid-19thC. An imitation of the sound.]

cloque /klo káy, klókay/, **cloqué** *n.* fabric with a raised woven or embossed pattern that gives it a quilted look [Early 20thC. Via French *cloqué*, literally 'blistered', from dialectal *cloque* 'blister', from medieval Latin *clocca* 'bell'.]

close[1] /klōss/ *adj.* (**closer, closest**) **1.** NEAR near in space or time ○ *The deadline was getting closer all the time.* **2.** ABOUT TO HAPPEN about to happen, or about to do sth ○ *close to collapse* **3.** KNOWING AND LIKING SB knowing sb very well and liking him or her very much ○ *close friends* **4.** CLOSELY RELATED being a member of sb's immediate family **5.** INVOLVING REGULAR CONTACT involving or having regular contact because of a shared interest in sth **6.** THOROUGH involving great care and thoroughness ○ *give it close inspection.* **7.** DECIDED BY A SMALL MARGIN decided by, or likely to be decided by, a small margin ○ *a close contest* **8.** TEXTILES ALLOWING LITTLE SPACE BETWEEN so densely packed or woven as to allow only little spaces between **9.** VERY SIMILAR very similar to an original ○ *a close copy* **10.** NEARLY CORRECT nearly correct or exact ○ *You're not quite right, but you're pretty close.* **11.** NEARLY A NUMBER OR QUANTITY approximately the same as a particular number or quantity **12.** SECRETIVELY SILENT unwilling to talk about sth or to reveal feelings **13.** CUT VERY SHORT cut so as to be very short **14.** STINGY unwilling to spend or give money **15.** HARD TO GET difficult to obtain **16.** CLOSELY GUARDED kept closely guarded **17.** STUFFY oppressively hot and airless **18.** US SPORTS DEFENSIVE, WITH SHORT PASSES involving short passes only, so as to retain possession **19.** AIRLESS warm and uncomfortable because there seems to be no fresh air **20.** PHON PRODUCED WITH TONGUE NEAR PALATE used to describe a vowel sound that is produced with the tongue near the palate, e.g. the 'ee' in 'tee' ■ *adv.* (**closer, closest**) **1.** NEAR TO STH near in space or time **2.** TIGHTLY in a snug tight way [13thC. Via French *clos* from Latin *clausus*, the past participle of *claudere* 'to close'. The sense 'near' developed from the idea of the closing off of the gap between two things if they are brought together.]

close[2] /klōz/ *v.* (**closes, closing, closed**) **1.** *vti.* COVER AN OPENING to move or move sth so that an opening or hole is covered or blocked **2.** *vti.* COME OR BRING TOGETHER to come together, or bring the edges or ends of sth together, e.g. the eyelids **3.** *vti.* SHUT DOWN BUSINESS FOR SHORT TIME to stop working or operating, or shut a shop or business, for a short period of time or overnight **4.** *vti.* = **close down 5.** *vt.* = **close off 6.** *vti.* TERMINATE to come to an end, or bring sth to an end, e.g. an activity, period of time, or spoken or written text **7.** *vti.* REDUCE THE DISTANCE to reduce the distance between two people or things, especially in a race or chase **8.** *vt.* COMM BRING DEAL TO CLOSURE to complete a transaction successfully, e.g. a business deal or a house purchase **9.** *vi.* STOCK EXCH HAVE AN END-OF-DAY VALUE to have a particular value at the end of a day's trading on a stock exchange **10.** *vt.* COMPUT DEACTIVATE AND STORE FILE OR PROGRAM to perform the series of operations necessary to deactivate a file or program and store it for later use **11.** *vt.* ELEC ENG COMPLETE AN ELECTRICAL CIRCUIT to complete an electrical circuit ■ *n.* **1.** END OF AN ACTIVITY the end of an activity, period of time, or spoken or written text ○ *The meeting drew to a close.* **2.** MUSIC = **cadence** [13thC. From French *clos-*, the stem of *clore* 'to close', from Latin *claudere* (see CLOSE[1]).] — **closable** *adj.* — **closer** *n.*

— **WORD KEY: ORIGIN** —

Close is derived from the Latin word *claudere*, meaning 'to close', which is also the source of English *clause, cloister, closet, conclude, include, preclude, recluse,* and *seclude.*

close down *v.* **1.** *vti.* STOP OPERATING PERMANENTLY to stop operating or trading permanently, or shut a factory, business, or school so that it stops operating permanently **2.** *vi.* BROADCAST STOP BROADCASTING to stop broadcasting at the end of the day

close in *vi.* **1.** APPROACH AND SURROUND STH to move closer and eventually surround sb or sth **2.** HAVE SHORTER DAYLIGHT PERIOD to become progressively shorter, with fewer hours of daylight

close off *vt.* to prevent people from reaching a place

or using a route by blocking access to it (*often passive*)
close up *v.* **1.** *vti.* LOCK BUILDING to lock the doors of a building at the end of a working or trading session **2.** *vti.* MOVE CLOSER TOGETHER to move closer together, or make people or things move closer together **3.** *vti.* BRING TOGETHER to come together, or bring the ends or edges of sth together **4.** *vi.* HIDE EMOTIONS to hide your true emotions deliberately because you do not want sb to know or understand you
close with *vt.* to enter into physical conflict or a fight with sb ○ *The two boxers closed with one another.*

close[3] /klōss/ *n.* **1.** CUL-DE-SAC a residential road, often a cul-de-sac in a modern housing estate (*often used in street names*) ○ *Brookside Close* **2.** AREA ROUND CATHEDRAL the area immediately surrounding a cathedral, including the buildings, many of which are often cathedral property **3.** *Scotland* COURTYARD an outdoor area enclosed by buildings, e.g. a courtyard, or a passageway leading to one (*often used in street names*) ○ *Lady Stair's Close* **4.** *Scotland* PASSAGEWAY INSIDE TENEMENT BUILDING in the West of Scotland, especially Glasgow, a passage inside a tenement building that leads from the street to the common stairway **5.** LAW PARCEL OF LAND an individual parcel of land, whether marked off by fencing or only having invisible boundaries [13thC. Via French *clos* from Latin *clausum* 'closed place, enclosure', from the neuter form of *clausus* (see CLOSE[1]).]

Close /klōss/, **Glenn** (*b.* 1947) US stage and film actor. She won an Academy Award for her role in *The World According to Garp* (1982).

close call *n.* a dangerous situation that could have resulted in death or injury, but from which sb just manages to escape

close company (*plural* **close companies**), **closed company** (*plural* **closed companies**) *n.* a company that is controlled by its directors

close-cropped *adj.* cut very short

closed /klōzd/ *adj.* **1.** WHERE WORK HAS STOPPED where work, operation, or trading has temporarily or permanently stopped **2.** DENYING ACCESS where access or passage is denied **3.** NO LONGER TO BE DISCUSSED about which there is to be no further discussion or investigation ○ *The subject is closed.* **4.** RIGIDLY EXCLUDING OTHERS' IDEAS rigidly rejecting ideas, beliefs, opinions, and influence from or by others ○ *He has a closed mind to all arguments.* **5.** NOT ADMITTING OUTSIDERS allowing no outsiders in, or tending not to meet with outsiders **6.** CONFIDENTIAL AND PRIVATE carried on or conducted in the strictest confidentiality or secrecy **7.** MATH FULLY ENCLOSING AN AREA OR VOLUME used to describe a curve, especially a circle, that fully encloses an area, or to describe a solid every surface of which is such a curve **8.** LING HAVING LIMITED NUMBER OF MEMBERS used to describe a word class that has a limited number of members, e.g. pronouns or conjunctions **9.** PHON ENDING IN CONSONANT used to describe a syllable that ends in a consonant

closed circuit *n.* an electrical circuit in which there is an uninterrupted endless path for current to flow when voltage is applied

closed-circuit television, closed-circuit TV *n.* a television transmission system in which cameras transmit pictures by cable to connected monitors. Surveillance systems are based on this type of transmission.

closed company *n.* = **close company**

closed couplet *n.* a pair of rhymed lines that form a complete sentence or unit of meaning

closed-door *adj.* restricted to members or those directly involved, and not open to the general public or the news media

closed-end fund *n.* an investment company with a fixed number of shares trading on the stock exchange

closed-end investment company *n. US* a corporation whose capitalization is fixed, whose capital is invested in other companies, and whose own shares are traded by outside investors

closed interval *n.* a set consisting of all the numbers between two given numbers (**end points**), including the given numbers. All the whole numbers greater than or equal to 5 and less than or equal to 10 constitute a closed interval.

closed loop *n.* a system, usually computer-controlled, that adjusts itself to varying conditions by feeding output information back as input

closedown /klōz down/ *n.* **1.** STOPPAGE OF WORK a temporary or permanent stopping of work or operations **2.** END OF BROADCASTING the end of a broadcasting day or period

closed scholarship *n.* a scholarship for which only certain people may apply, e.g. students from a particular school or college

closed season *n.* US = **close season**

closed set *n.* a set that includes the limits by which the set is defined, e.g. all the points within and on a circle

closed shop *n.* a place of work in which the employer has agreed to employ only members of a particular trade union. ◊ **open shop, union shop**

closed stance *n.* a stance, e.g. in baseball or golf, in which the front foot is closer to the line of play than the rear foot

close-fisted *adj.* reluctant to spend money (*informal*) —**close-fistedness** *n.*

close-fitting *adj.* fitting tightly on the body

close-grained *adj.* used to describe wood that has dense fibres and as a result a smooth texture

close harmony *n.* the arrangement of chord tones so that they are as close together as possible, used especially in music for vocal ensembles

close-hauled *adj., adv.* with the sails set for sailing towards the direction from which the wind is blowing

close-knit *adj.* supportive and loyal to the other members of a community or group

close-lipped *adj.* unwilling to talk or to reveal anything

closely /klōssli/ *adv.* **1.** CAREFULLY AND THOROUGHLY in a careful and thorough way ○ *listening closely* **2.** IN A VERY SIMILAR WAY in a way that is very similar or strongly linked to sth ○ *She closely resembles you.* **3.** SO AS TO BE NEAR in a way that is near sth in space or time ○ *We heard a bang, closely followed by another.* **4.** INTIMATELY in an intimate manner ○ *worked closely with her*

closemouthed /klōss mówthd, -mówtht/ *adj.* unwilling to talk or to reveal anything

closeness /klōssnəss/ *n.* **1.** NEARNESS the quality or state of being close to sb or sth in space, time, relationship, or intimacy **2.** STUFFY AIRLESSNESS stuffy airlessness

close-order drill *n.* a formation or movement that is conducted with soldiers at close intervals

close punctuation *n.* punctuation in which a large number of commas, semicolons, and colons are used

close-run *adj.* having a very close result

close season *n.* **1.** PERIOD OF NO HUNTING the time of the year when it is illegal to hunt and kill certain animals, birds, or fish **2.** PERIOD BETWEEN SEASONAL SPORTS COMPETITIONS the period between the end of one annual seasonal sports competition, e.g. a football season, and the start of the next one

close shave *n.* = **close call**

closestool /klōss stool/ *n.* a stool or chair containing a chamber pot, used in former times [15thC. Literally 'enclosed stool'.]

closet /klózzit/ *n.* **1.** *US* LARGE CUPBOARD a walk-in wardrobe or walk-in cupboard in which clothes and linen are stored **2.** SMALL PRIVATE ROOM a small private room (*archaic*) **3.** TOILET a water closet (*archaic*) ■ *adj.* SECRET having beliefs or behaviour that is not openly acknowledged but kept secret ■ *vt.* (**-ets, -eting, -eted**) PUT SB IN PRIVATE PLACE to put people in a small room where they can have privacy (*often passive*) [14thC. From Old French, literally 'small enclosure', formed from *clos* 'enclosure' (see CLOSE[3]).] —**closetful** *n.* ◇ **come out of the closet** to acknowledge openly sth previously kept secret, especially the fact of being homosexual

closet queen *n.* an offensive term for a homosexual man who does not reveal his homosexuality openly, or who actively conceals or denies it (*slang offensive*)

close-up *n.* **1.** PHOTOGRAPHY, CINEMA, TV CLOSE-RANGE PHOTO OR SHOT a photograph, film, or television shot taken from a position very close to the subject **2.** DETAILED LOOK AT STH a detailed view or examination of sth ■ *adj.* AT CLOSE RANGE seen from a position very near sb or sth else

closing /klōzing/ *adj.* FINAL forming or connected with the final part of an activity or period of time ■ *n.* **1.** STH THAT CLOSES sth that closes, e.g. a fastening on clothes **2.** *US* COMM, LAW TRANSFER OF PROPERTY OWNERSHIP a meeting among principals in a real estate transaction, during which legal papers related to the sale and purchase are signed and financial arrangements are made final and binding

closing price *n.* the price of a share or bond on a stock exchange recorded at the official close of trading

closing time *n.* the time that an establishment such as a shop, library, or bar closes and people have to leave

clostridium /klo stríddi əm/ (*plural* **-ums** *or* **-a** /-di ə/) *n.* a rod-shaped, usually motile, Gram-positive bacterium that can cause serious illnesses including botulism, tetanus, and gas gangrene. Genus: *Clostridium.* [Late 19thC. From modern Latin, genus name, literally 'little spindle', coined from Greek *klōstēr* 'spindle'.] —**clostridial** *adj.*

closure /klōzhər/ *n.* **1.** PERMANENT END OF BUSINESS the permanent ending of a business or activity **2.** BARRING OF ACCESS blocking the access to a place or blocking a route **3.** STH THAT CLOSES AN OPENING a device for closing an opening, e.g. a zip or a cap on a bottle, or the place where the opening closes **4.** CLOSING STH an act or process of closing sth, e.g. closing an opening or terminating an activity **5.** POL PROCEDURE FOR CUTTING DEBATE SHORT a parliamentary procedure that allows a debate to be cut short and a vote to be taken immediately **6.** GEOL VERTICAL DISTANCE OF ROCK FORMATION the distance measured vertically between the top of a rock formation (**anticline**) and the lowest contour **7.** *US* POL = **cloture 8.** PHON CONTACT BETWEEN VOCAL ORGANS PRODUCING SOUND a contact made between vocal organs, e.g. the tongue and the soft palate, that produces a speech sound **9.** MATH BEING A CLOSED SET IN MATHEMATICS the characteristic of a set in which the application of a given mathematical operation to any member of the set always results in another member of that set ■ *vt.* (**-sures, -suring, -sured**) *US* POL = **cloture**

clot /klot/ *n.* **1.** STICKY LUMP a mass of thickened liquid, especially blood **2.** IDIOT a stupid person (*informal*) ■ *vti.* (**clots, clotting, clotted**) THICKEN AND FORM LUMPS to thicken, or make a liquid thicken, and form lumps [Old English *clott.* Ultimately from an Indo-European word meaning 'to form into a ball'.] —**clottish** *adj.*

cloth /kloth/ *n.* **1.** FABRIC fabric made by weaving, knitting, or felting thread or fibres **2.** PIECE OF FABRIC a piece of fabric used for a particular purpose, e.g. a dishcloth (*often used in combination*) **3.** CHR CLERGY the clergy, or the clothes worn by its members **4.** SAILING SAIL a sail of a boat **5.** THEATRE PIECE OF FABRIC SCENERY a painted piece of fabric used as scenery [Old English *clāþ.* Ultimately from a prehistoric Germanic word (related to Danish *klæde* 'cloth' and German *Kleid* 'garment').]

clothbound /klóth bownd/ *adj.* used to describe a book that has a cloth-lined hardback cover

cloth cap *n.* a flat cap, usually made of tweed, with a stiffened peak. It is regarded as a symbol of the working class.

clothe /klōth/ (**clothes, clothing, clothed** *or* **clad** *literary or archaic* /klad/, **clothed** *or* **clad** *literary or archaic*) *vt.* **1.** DRESS SB to put clothes on sb (*often passive*) **2.** PROVIDE CLOTHING FOR SB to provide sb with clothes **3.** COVER STH to completely cover an area ○ *The hills were clothed in mist.* **4.** COVER STH UP to obscure or conceal sth as if wrapping sth round it **5.** ENDOW SB OR STH to endow or invest sb or sth with some quality (*usually passive*) [Old English *clāþian,* from *clāþ* 'cloth' (see CLOTH)]

cloth-eared *adj.* unable or unwilling to hear (*informal*)

clothes /klōthz/ *npl.* **1.** **THINGS WORN ON THE BODY** garments that cover the body **2.** **BEDCLOTHES** sheets and blankets used to cover a bed (*dated*) [Old English *clāpas*, the plural of *clāp* 'cloth' (see CLOTH)]

clotheshorse /klōthz hawrss/ *n.* **1.** **FRAME FOR CLOTHES** a frame on which clothes are hung to dry indoors **2.** **SB WHO DRESSES FASHIONABLY** sb who insists on wearing the latest fashions or who wears conspicuously fashionable clothing (*informal*)

clothesline /klōthz līn/ *n.* a cord or wire on which clean laundry is hung to dry

clothes moth *n.* any of the small moths whose larvae feed on wool and fur. Family: Tineidae.

clothes peg *n.* a small clip of plastic or wood used to secure laundry to a clothesline. US term **clothespin**

clothespin /klōthz pin/ *n. US* = **clothes peg**

clothes press *n.* a piece of furniture for storing clothes, with hanging space and sometimes drawers or shelves

clothes prop *n.* a long pole for raising a clothesline

clothier /klōthi ər/ *n.* sb who sells clothes or cloth retail [14thC. Alteration of obsolete *clother*, from CLOTH.]

clothing /klōthing/ *n.* **1.** **CLOTHES** clothes collectively **2.** **COVERING** a covering for sth

Clotho /klō thō/ *n.* one of the three Fates of classical mythology. She holds the distaff and spins the thread of life. ◊ **Lachesis, Atropos** [From Greek *Klōthō*, literally 'I spin']

cloth of gold *n.* a luxury fabric of the Middle Ages woven from silk, or sometimes wool, intermixed with gold thread

clotrimazole *n.* an antifungal drug, used to treat yeast and fungal infections [Late 20thC]

clotted cream *n.* a thick cream made by removing the cream from the top of heated milk

clotting factor *n.* any substance in the blood that is essential for blood to coagulate

cloture /klōchər/ *n. US* **CLOSING OF DEBATE IN US SENATE** the process of closing a debate in the US Senate by calling for a vote ■ *vt.* (**-tures, -turing, -tured**) *US* **CLOSE DEBATE IN US SENATE** to close a debate in the US Senate by calling for a vote [Late 19thC. From French *clôture*, literally 'closing'.]

cloud /klowd/ *n.* **1.** **MASS OF WATER IN SKY** a visible mass of water or ice particles in the atmosphere from which rain and other forms of precipitation fall **2.** **MASS OF PARTICLES IN AIR** a mass of particles in the air, e.g. dust or smoke ○ *a cloud of smoke* **3.** **FLYING MASS** an airborne mass of insects or birds **4.** **DARKER PART** a dark or dim area on sth such as jewellery **5.** **STH WORRYING** sth that causes anxiety or fear ○ *Lack of financial independence was a cloud hanging over our future.* **6.** **GLOOMY CONDITION** a condition of gloom or despondency ○ *a cloud of despair* ■ *v.* (**clouds, clouding, clouded**) **1.** *vti.* **BECOME CLOUDY** to become covered with cloud or mist, or make sth cloudy **2.** *vt.* **CONFUSE STH** to make sth more confusing ○ *cloud the issue* **3.** *vt.* **DETRACT FROM STH** to make sth appear less good ○ *It clouded their reputation.* **4.** *vt.* **IMPAIR STH** to diminish a mental faculty **5.** *vti.* **LOOK TROUBLED** to become or cause sth to become troubled or gloomy ○ *His face clouded with disappointment.* **6.** *vti.* **BECOME OR MAKE STH OPAQUE** to become or cause sth to become opaque or murky ○ *The water was clouded with particles.* [Old English *clūd* 'mass of rock, hill'. The modern meaning (13thC) probably came from the supposed resemblance between cumulus clouds and lumps of rock.] ◊ **on cloud nine** extremely happy (*informal*) ◊ **under a cloud** in disgrace

cloud over, cloud up *vi.* **1.** **BECOME CLOUDY** to become covered with cloud or mist **2.** **GROW TROUBLED** to become troubled

cloudberry /klowdbəri/ *n.* (*plural* **-ries**) a creeping perennial plant of the rose family found in Europe, North America, and Asia. It has white flowers and yellowish edible berries. Latin name: *Rubus chamaemorus*. [From CLOUD + BERRY, but the reason for the name is unknown]

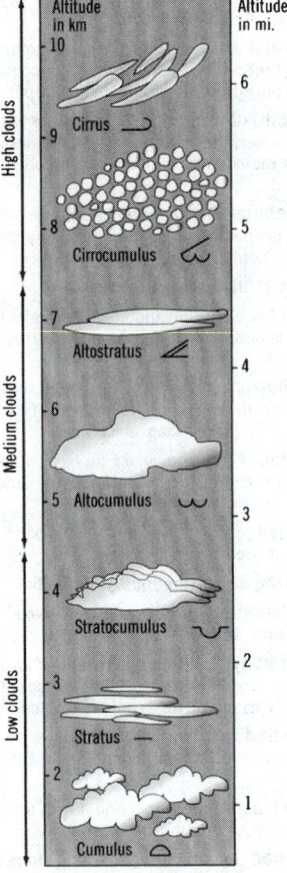

Cloud

cloudburst /klowd burst/ *n.* a sudden heavy rain shower

cloud chamber *n.* a device in which the movement of high-energy particles is detected as they pass through a chamber of supersaturated vapour. Observable tracks are formed when droplets condense on the ionized molecules left by the high-energy particle.

cloud-cuckoo-land *n.* an imaginary place in which problems do not exist [Translation of Greek *Nephelokokkygia*, an imaginary city in the air built by the birds in the comedy *Birds* by Aristophanes]

clouded /klowdid/ *adj.* **1.** **TROUBLED** appearing troubled **2.** **OPAQUE** opaque or murky

clouded leopard *n.* a rare medium-sized cat that lives in forests from Nepal to Borneo and has short legs and a greyish to yellowish coat with darker irregular markings. It hunts by jumping from trees as well as by stalking. Latin name: *Neofelis nebulosa*.

clouded yellow *n.* a butterfly that has yellowish wings with brownish or blackish margins and migrates between continental Europe and Great Britain. Latin name: *Colias croceus*.

cloud forest *n.* a high-altitude tropical forest that is usually covered by cloud. Clinging plants (**epiphytes**), especially mosses and ferns, grow on the trees in profusion, encouraged by the moisture.

cloudless /klowdləss/ *adj.* **1.** **BRIGHT AND CLEAR** bright and sunny without clouds ○ *a cloudless sky* **2.** **WITHOUT PROBLEMS** free of trouble —**cloudlessly** *adv.* —**cloudlessness** *n.*

cloud rack *n.* a group of clouds moving across the sky

cloudscape /klowd skayp/ *n.* a view or depiction of clouds

cloud seeding *n.* the technique or process of scattering substances such as silver iodide into clouds from an aircraft in order to precipitate rain

cloudy /klowdi/ (**-ier, -iest**) *adj.* **1.** **WITH CLOUDS** covered with some clouds, usually a great deal **2.** **OPAQUE** opaque or murky ○ *a cloudy liquid* **3.** **RESEMBLING CLOUDS** having the appearance of clouds **4.** **TROUBLED** seeming troubled or gloomy **5.** **NOT CLEAR** obscure or difficult to understand —**cloudily** *adv.* —**cloudiness** *n.*

clough /kluf/ *n.* a ravine, or the sloping side of a ravine (*regional*)

clout /klowt/ *n.* **1.** **POWER AND INFLUENCE** the power to direct, shape, or otherwise influence things (*informal*) **2.** **PUNCH** a blow with the hand or fist **3.** **ARCHERY TARGET** in archery, a mark or target, especially at a long distance **4.** **PIECE OF CLOTH** a rag or piece of cloth (*regional*) ○ *a dish clout* ■ *vt.* (**clouts, clouting, clouted**) **HIT SB WITH HAND** to hit sb or sth hard with the hand [Old English *clūt* 'patch made of cloth, plate of metal'. The reason behind the meaning 'to hit', which dates from the 14thC, is unknown, and this group of senses may represent a different word.]

clove[1] /klōv/ *n.* **1.** **AROMATIC SPICE** a strongly aromatic spice that is the dried flower bud of a tropical tree, used in both savoury and sweet dishes **2.** **SPICE-YIELDING TROPICAL TREE** an evergreen tree of the myrtle family, native to the Moluccas but grown in other tropical regions, with flower buds that are used dried as a spice. The buds, stalks, and leaves also yield aromatic oil of cloves. Latin name: *Syzygium aromaticum*. [12thC. From Old French *clou (de girofle)*, literally 'nail (of the clove-tree)', from Latin *clavus* 'nail' from the resemblance of a single clove-tree bud, with its stalk, to a nail.]

clove[2] /klōv/ *n.* one of the segments of a compound bulb ○ *a clove of garlic* [Old English *clufu*, from a prehistoric Germanic word that is also the ancestor of English *cleave* 'to cut']

clove[3] past tense of **cleave**

clove hitch *n.* a knot made of two half-hitches, used to attach a rope to a post or to another, thicker, rope [*Clove* is an old past participle of CLEAVE[1]]

Clovelly /klō vélli/ village in Devon, southwestern England, situated approximately 18 km/11 mi. southwest of Bideford. Population: 500 (1989).

cloven /klōv'n/ *v.* past participle of **cleave** ■ *adj.* **SPLIT IN TWO** split or divided into two parts (*archaic or literary*)

cloven hoof, **cloven foot** *n.* **1.** **SPLIT HOOF OF ANIMAL** the divided hoof of such animals as cattle, sheep, and pigs. Order: Artiodactyla. **2.** **MARK OF DEVIL** an indication of the presence of the Devil, traditionally represented in Christianity with a cloven hoof —**cloven-hoofed** *adj.*

clove oil *n.* = oil of cloves

clove pink *n.* = carnation [From CLOVE[1]; from the fact that the flower smells like the spice]

clover /klōvər/ (*plural* **-ver** or **-vers**) *n.* **1.** **PLANT WITH THREE-LOBED LEAVES** a plant with three-lobed leaves and small rounded flower heads. Clover is often cultivated as a forage plant, for erosion control, and to provide nectar for bees. Genus: *Trifolium*. **2.** **FORAGE PLANT** any forage plant similar to clover. Genera: *Meliotus* and *Lespedeza* and *Medicago*. [Old English *clāfre*, ultimately from a prehistoric Germanic compound whose first part is also the ancestor of German *Klee* 'clover'] ◊ **in clover** financially well off

cloverleaf /klōvər leef/ (*plural* **cloverleaves** /-leevz/) *n.* **1.** **THREE-LOBED LEAF** the three-lobed leaf of a clover plant (*often used before a noun*) ○ *a cloverleaf motif* **2.** **ROAD INTERCHANGE** an arrangement of major roads resembling a four-leaf clover, with entrance and exit roads enabling traffic to change direction at speed without intersections

Clovis /klōviss/ *adj.* used to describe a prehistoric North American culture characterized by leaf-shaped flint points that were used as parts of weapons to hunt game [Mid-20thC. Named after the city of Clovis in eastern New Mexico in the US, where remains were first found.]

clown /klown/ *n.* **1.** **ARTS COMIC CIRCUS PERFORMER** a comic performer, usually in a circus, who does not speak and wears an outlandish costume and heavy makeup **2.** **SB FUNNY** sb who behaves comically **3.** **PRANKSTER** sb who plays practical jokes **4.** **ILL-MANNERED**

PERSON an ill-mannered or ineffectual person (*informal*) ■ *vi.* (**clowns, clowning, clowned**) **1.** BEHAVE COMICALLY to behave in a silly or funny way **2.** PLAY PRANKS to play practical jokes **3.** ARTS PERFORM AS CLOWN to perform as a circus clown [Mid-16thC. Origin uncertain. Originally 'peasant'.] —**clownery** /klównəri/ *n.*

clown anemone *n.* = **anemone fish**

clown fish *n.* = **anemone fish**

clownish /klównish/ *adj.* resembling or characteristic of a clown —**clownishly** *adv.* —**clownishness** *n.*

cloy /kloy/ (**cloys, cloying, cloyed**) *vti.* to sicken sb or become sickened with too much sweetness or sensation from sth initially pleasing [Mid-16thC. Shortening of obsolete *accloy*, via French *encloer* 'to drive in a nail' from medieval Latin *inclavare*, from, ultimately, Latin *clavus* 'nail'.] —**cloyingly** *adv.* —**cloyingness** *n.*

clozapine /klṓzə peen/ *n.* PHARM an antipsychotic drug used especially to alleviate symptoms of schizophrenia [Mid-20thC. Contraction of CHLORO- + BENZODIAZEPINE.]

cloze test /klṓz-/ *n.* a test of comprehension and grammar in which a language student supplies appropriate missing words omitted from a text [*Cloze* shortening and alteration of CLOSURE]

CLU *abbr.* Chartered Life Underwriter

club /klub/ *n.* **1.** THICK STICK USED AS WEAPON a stout stick used as a weapon **2.** SPORTS STICK FOR HITTING BALL a stick or bat used in certain sports, especially golf, to hit a ball ○ *a golf club* **3.** SPORTS = **Indian club 4.** ASSOCIATION FOR PARTICIPATING IN INTEREST an association of people with a common interest ○ *a gardening club* **5.** SPORTS ORGANIZATION FOR SPORT an organization formed for the pursuit of a sport on an amateur or a professional basis ○ *a football club* **6.** PREMISES OF CLUB the premises where the activities of a club are pursued ○ *See you at the club tonight!* **7.** BUILDING PROVIDING FACILITIES TO MEMBERS a building that offers facilities and refreshment to members of the organization that owns or occupies it ○ *a gentlemen's club* **8.** COMM ORGANIZATION GIVING DISCOUNTS a scheme or organization in which members receive price reductions in return for regular purchases ○ *a book club* **9.** FIN SAVINGS SCHEME a savings scheme organized as a means of saving for sth ○ *a Christmas club* **10.** NATIONS SHARING STH a group of nations or people who have a particular thing in common ○ *the nuclear club* **11.** = **nightclub 12.** CARDS BLACK SYMBOL ON PLAYING CARD a black symbol shaped like a three-leaved clover on a playing card ■ *v.* (**clubs, clubbing, clubbed**) **1.** *vt.* HIT SB WITH CLUB to hit a person or animal with a club ○ *The animal had been clubbed to death.* **2.** *vi.* FORM CLUB to join or form a club for social purposes or to pursue a common interest **3.** *vi.* NAUT DRIFT WITH ANCHOR LOWERED to drift with an anchor that drags to reduce the speed of the vessel [12thC. From Old Norse *klubba* 'heavy stick', alteration of *klumpa*. With reference to cards, a translation of Spanish *basto* or Italian *baston*, from the stick on Spanish cards.] ◇ **in the club, in the pudding club** pregnant (*slang*) ◇ **join the club!** used to tell sb that you are in the same position as he or she is

club together *vi.* **1.** CONTRIBUTE TO GROUP FUND to contribute money collectively for some purpose **2.** JOIN IN A GROUP to collaborate as a group

clubbable /klúbbəb'l/, **clubable** *adj.* sociable, and enjoying belonging to clubs —**clubbability** /klúbbə bíllәti/ *n.*

clubbed /klubd/ *adj.* used to describe an appendage with a swelling at one end, like a club ○ *clubbed antennae*

clubber /klúbbər/ *n.* **1.** NIGHTCLUB GOER sb who frequently goes to nightclubs (*informal*) **2.** MEMBER OF CLUB sb who belongs to a club **3.** CLUB WIELDER sb who uses a club

clubbing /klúbbing/ *n.* **1.** GOING TO NIGHTCLUBS the activity of going to nightclubs **2.** MED THICKENING OF FINGERS AND TOES a medical condition in which the tips of the fingers and toes become thickened, especially at the base of the nail. It may be associated with certain lung or heart diseases.

clubby /klúbi/ (**-bier, -biest**) *adj.* **1.** SOCIABLE enjoying the friendliness associated with clubs **2.** TYPICAL OF CLUB typical of a social club **3.** SNOBBISH socially exclusive and snobbish —**clubbily** *adv.* —**clubbiness** *n.*

club chair *n.* a heavily upholstered chair with a low back and thick arms [From its use in gentlemen's clubs]

club class *n.* a class of travel on an aircraft between first class and economy class

clubface /klúbb fayss/ *n.* the surface of the head of a golf club with which the player strikes the ball

club foot (*plural* **club feet**) *n.* **1.** DEFORMITY OF FOOT a congenital deformity of the foot, especially one in which the foot is twisted and turned inwards **2.** DEFORMED FOOT a foot that is deformed by club foot —**club footed** *adj.*

club hand *n.* **1.** DEFORMITY OF HAND a congenital deformity in which the hand is twisted and turned inwards or outwards **2.** DEFORMED HAND a hand deformed by club hand —**club handed** *adj.*

clubhaul /klúb hawl/ (**-hauls, -hauling, -hauled**) *vti.* to force a sailing vessel to change tack by dropping the lee-anchor and hauling in the anchor cable to swing the stern to windward

clubhouse /klúb howss/ *n.* the premises of a club, especially a sports club

clubland /klúb land/ *n.* an area in central London in which many exclusive social clubs and nightclubs are located

clubman /klúb mən/ (*plural* **-men** /-mən/) *n.* a man who belongs to one or more exclusive social clubs

club moss *n.* a nonflowering plant that typically has creeping stems with small overlapping leaves and reproduces by spores, often borne in club-shaped organs (**strobili**). Order: Lycopodiales.

clubroom /klúb room, -rŏŏm/ *n.* a room in which members of a club meet

clubroot /klúb root/ *n.* a disease affecting plants of the cabbage family, in which the roots become swollen and distorted. Latin name: *Plasmodiophora brassicae.*

clubs /klubz/ *n.* one of the four suits used in cards, with a black shape similar to a three-leaved clover as its symbol (*takes a singular or plural verb*)

club sandwich *n.* a sandwich consisting of two layers of fillings between three slices of bread [Origin uncertain: perhaps from the variety of ingredients combined into one mass]

club soda *n. US, Can* = **soda water** *n.* 1 [Originally a proprietary name]

cluck /kluk/ *interj.* USED TO REPRESENT HEN'S CALL used to imitate the short low clicking sound made by a hen ■ *v.* (**clucks, clucking, clucked**) **1.** *vi.* MAKE HEN'S SOUND to make natural short low clicking sounds (*refers to hens*) **2.** *vti.* EXPRESS STH WITH CLICKING SOUND to show disapproval or concern by making short clicking sounds ■ *n.* **1.** HEN'S CALL a hen's short low clicking call **2.** *US* UNINTELLIGENT PERSON a person who is considered mildly unintelligent (*informal*) [15thC. An imitation of the sound.]

clucked /klukt/ *adj.* AGRIC used to describe a hen that is broody (*regional*)

clucky /klúki/ *adj. Aus* keen to have children (*slang*) [From the idea of a broody hen]

clue /kloo/ *n.* **1.** AID IN SOLVING MYSTERY sth that helps to solve a mystery or crime **2.** AID IN SOLVING CROSSWORD one of the numbered items of information used to solve a crossword puzzle **3.** EXPLANATION FOR BEHAVIOUR an explanation or reason for sth that is difficult to understand ■ *vt.* (**clues, cluing, clued**) GIVE SB INFORMATION to supply sb with useful information [Late 16thC. Alteration of CLEW. From the Greek myth of Theseus, who used a *clew* ('ball') of thread to escape from the Minotaur's labyrinth.] ◇ **not have a clue about sth 1.** to know nothing about sth (*informal*) **2.** to be very bad at sth (*informal*)

clue in *vt. US* to provide sb with useful information ○ *She clued me in about office politics.*

clued-up *adj.* well-informed about sb or sth (*informal*) (*not hyphenated when used after a verb*) ○ *She's quite clued up about food additives.* [Alteration (modelled on CLUE) of *clewed up*, literally 'furled up', from CLEW 'lower corner of a sail']

clueless /kloōləss/ *adj.* incompetent or ignorant (*informal*)

Cluj-Napoca /kloōzh nə pṓkə/ industrial city and capital of Cluj County in Transylvania, northwestern Romania. Population: 326,017 (1994).

clumber spaniel /klúmbər-/, **clumber** *n.* a thickset short-legged spaniel with a dense silky coat belonging to an English breed [Named after *Clumber* Park in Nottinghamshire]

clumble-fisted /klúmb'l fistid/ *adj. SW England* heavy-handed

clump[1] /klump/ *n.* **1.** CLUSTER OF THINGS a compact cluster or group of growing things ○ *a clump of moss* **2.** MASS OF SIMILAR THINGS an undifferentiated mass of sth **3.** IMMUNOL CLUSTER OF CELLS a cluster of cells, e.g. bacteria or red blood cells, especially one formed during an immune response or when blood of incompatible blood groups is mixed ■ *v.* (**clumps, clumping, clumped**) **1.** *vti.* COMBINE THINGS INTO MASS to be gathered or gather things into a mass **2.** IMMUNOL CAUSE MASSING OF CELLS to cause cells, e.g. bacteria or red blood cells, to combine into a mass, especially as part of an immune response [13thC. Origin uncertain: probably from Low German *klump.*]

clump[2] /klump/, **clomp** /klomp/ *n.* **1.** THUMPING SOUND a heavy thumping sound **2.** HEAVY BLOW a heavy blow or punch (*informal*) ■ *v.* (**clumps, clumping, clumped; clomps, clomping, clomped**) **1.** *vi.* MOVE WITH CLUMP to walk or move with a heavy thumping sound **2.** *vt.* THUMP SB to give sb a heavy thump or punch (*informal*) [Mid-17thC. An imitation of the sound.]

clumpy /klúmpi/ (**-ier, -iest**) *adj.* **1.** LARGE AND UNGAINLY large, heavy, and ungainly **2.** CHARACTERIZED BY CLUMPS composed of or growing in clumps —**clumpily** *adv.* —**clumpiness** *n.*

clumsy /klúmzi/ (**-sier, -siest**) *adj.* **1.** MOVING AWKWARDLY poorly coordinated physically **2.** SAID OR DONE AWKWARDLY said or done in an awkward or insensitive way ○ *a clumsy remark* [Late 16thC. Origin uncertain: perhaps formed from obsolete *clumse* 'to be numb with cold', perhaps from Scandinavian.] —**clumsily** *adv.* —**clumsiness** *n.*

Clunies-Ross /kloōniz róss/, **Sir Ian** (1899–1959) Australian veterinary scientist. He was prominent in the development of the Australian sheep.

clunk /klungk/ *n.* **1.** DULL SOUND a dull sound like that of a heavy piece of metal hitting sth **2.** BLOW OR SOUND IT MAKES a blow, or the sound made by a blow (*informal*) **3.** UNINTELLIGENT PERSON sb who is considered unintelligent or dull-witted (*informal*) ■ *vti.* (**clunks, clunking, clunked**) MAKE DULL SOUND to make a dull heavy sound [Late 18thC. An imitation of the sound.]

clunker /klúngkər/ *n. US* a dilapidated old motor vehicle or piece of machinery (*informal*)

clunky /klúngki/ (**-ier, -iest**) *adj.* solid, or bulky and heavy

Cluny lace /kloōni-/ *n.* a strong white lace made of silk, linen, or cotton [Late 19thC. Named after *Cluny*, a town in the Saône-et-Loire Department of France.]

clupeid /kloōpi id/ *n.* a soft-finned bony fish that has oily flesh, a narrow body, and a forked tail. Herrings, sardines, and shad are clupeids. Family: Clupeidae. [Late 19thC. From modern Latin *Clupeidae*, family name, from, ultimately, Latin *clupea*, a small river fish.]

cluster /klústər/ *n.* **1.** DENSE BUNCH a small group of people or things that are closely packed together ○ *a cluster of diamonds* ○ *a little cluster of onlookers* **2.** ASTRON STARS THAT APPEAR NEAR EACH OTHER a group of galaxies or stars that are gravitationally interacting in space and appear to an observer on earth to be close together **3.** PHON GROUP OF CONSONANTS a group of consecutive consonants in the same syllable **4.** STATS SUBSET IN STATISTICAL SAMPLE a statistically significant subset within a population, used in sampling **5.** MUSIC CHORD OF THREE OR MORE NOTES a chord consisting of three or more notes spaced a semitone apart **6.** *US* ARMY DESIGN INDICATING MILITARY AWARDS in the US Army, a small metal design indicating that a medal has been awarded before to the same individual **7.** MIL GROUP OF BOMBS a group of bombs dropped together **8.** MIL SET OF MINES a basic unit of mines used in laying a minefield **9.** COMPUT NETWORK OF SMALL COMPUTERS a network of computers under the control of a larger, more powerful computer ■ *vti.* (**-ters, -tering, -tered**)

FORM INTO CLUSTER to gather sth into or form a small group [Old English *clyster*, of uncertain origin: probably from the same prehistoric Germanic source as English *clot*] —**clustered** *adj.* —**clustery** *adj.*

cluster analysis *n.* a statistical technique that compares multiple characteristics of a population to determine whether individuals fall into different groups

cluster bomb *n.* a canister dropped from an aircraft to release a number of small bombs over a wide area

cluster controller *n.* COMPUT a computer that sorts and files data transmitted by other smaller computers in a network

cluster headache *n.* a severe recurring headache associated with the release of histamine in the bloodstream, and marked by sudden sharp pain behind one eye or nostril

clutch[1] /kluch/ *v.* (**clutches, clutching, clutched**) 1. *vt.* **HOLD STH TIGHTLY** to grip sth tightly 2. *vi.* **MAKE GRABBING MOVEMENT** to try to grab hold of sth ∎ *n.* 1. ENG **MECHANISM THAT CONNECTS SHAFTS** a device that enables two rotating shafts to be connected and disconnected smoothly, especially one in a motor vehicle that transmits power from the engine to the gearbox 2. AUTOMOT **PEDAL ACTIVATING CLUTCH** the pedal that activates the clutch in a motor vehicle 3. **GRIP ON STH** a tight grip on sth 4. **CONTROLLING POWER** control and influence (*often used in the plural*) ○ *We were plainly in his clutches.* [14thC. Variant of obsolete *clitch* 'to bend, grasp', from Old English *clyccan* 'to grasp', of uncertain origin.]

——— **WORD KEY: SYNONYMS** ———
See Synonyms at *catch*.

clutch[2] /kluch/ *n.* 1. BIRDS **GROUP OF EGGS HATCHED TOGETHER** the number of eggs hatched by a bird or a pair of birds at one time 2. BIRDS **GROUP OF CHICKENS HATCHED TOGETHER** all the chickens hatched together from one clutch of eggs 3. **GROUP OF SIMILAR THINGS** a number of similar people or things (*informal*) [Early 18thC. Origin uncertain: probably a variant of dialectal *cletch*, from *cleck* 'to hatch', from Old Norse *klekja*.]

clutch purse *n.* US = **clutch bag**

Clutha /kloŏtha/ the longest river in South Island, New Zealand. It issues from Lake Wanaka and flows southeastwards, reaching the coast southeast of Balclutha. Length: 322 km/200 mi.

clutter /klúttar/ *n.* 1. **UNTIDY STUFF** an untidy collection of objects 2. **DISORGANIZED MESS** a condition of disorderliness or overcrowding 3. MIL **CONFUSING RADAR IMAGES** images on a radar screen that hinder observation ∎ *vt.* (**-ters, -tering, -tered**) **FILL STH WITH CLUTTER** to make a place untidy or overfilled with objects [Mid-16thC. Origin uncertain: probably a variant of obsolete *clotter*, literally 'to clot repeatedly', from CLOT.]

Clwyd /kloŏ id/ former county of Wales from 1974 to 1996. The name is retained for postal addresses. Area: 2,427 sq. km/937 sq. mi.

Clyde /klīd/ the most important river of Scotland. It flows westwards through Glasgow to the Firth of Clyde, where it joins the Atlantic Ocean. Length: 171 km/106 mi.

Clydebank /klíd bangk/ town in western Scotland on the north bank of the River Clyde. Population: 44,658 (1991).

Clydesdale /klídz dayl/ *n.* a strong heavy horse belonging to a breed originally developed in Scotland as draught animals [Late 18thC. Named after *Clydesdale*, the area of the river Clyde in Scotland where the horses originally were bred.]

clype /klīp/ *vi.* (**clypes, clyping, clyped**) *Scotland* **INFORM ABOUT SB'S MISDEEDS** to inform sb in authority of a person's wrongdoings as a way of getting that person into trouble (*informal*) ∎ *n. Scotland* **INFORMER** a telltale or informer (*informal*) [Early 18thC. Origin uncertain: probably a variant of obsolete *clepe* 'to call', from Old English *clipian*.]

clyster /klístar/ *n.* an enema (*archaic or literary*) [14thC. Directly or via French from Latin *clyster*, from Greek *klustēr* 'syringe', from *kluzein* 'to wash out' (source of English *cataclysm*).]

cm *symbol.* centimetre

Cm *symbol.* curium

c.m. *abbr.* 1. PHYS centre of mass 2. court martial

CMA *abbr.* 1. Canadian Medical Association 2. certified medical assistant

cmdg *abbr.* MIL commanding

Cmdr *abbr.* MIL Commander

CMEA *abbr.* Council for Mutual Economic Assistance

CMG *abbr.* Companion of the Order of St Michael and St George

cml *abbr.* commercial

c'mon /kəm ón/ *contr.* come on (*nonstandard*)

CMOS /seé moss/ *abbr.* COMPUT complementary metal oxide semi-conductor

CMV *abbr.* cytomegalovirus

C/N *abbr.* 1. credit note 2. INSUR cover note

CNAA *abbr.* Council for National Academic Awards

CNAR *abbr.* FIN compound net annual rate

CND *abbr.* Campaign for Nuclear Disarmament

cnidarian /nī daíri ən/ *n.* 1. MARINE BIOL **MARINE ANIMAL WITH TENTACLES** any marine invertebrate animal that has tentacles surrounding the mouth. Sea anemones, corals, and jellyfishes are cnidarians. Phylum: Cnidaria. 2. ZOOL = **coelenterate** [Early 20thC. From modern Latin *Cnidaria*, phylum name, from Greek *knidē* 'nettle', from *knizein* 'to cause to itch'.] —**cnidarian** *adj.*

CNN *abbr.* Cable News Network

CNS *abbr.* central nervous system

CORBIS/Michael S. Yamashita
CN Tower, Toronto, Canada

CN Tower *n.* a tall tower in central Toronto, Canada. It is more than 553 m/1800 ft high and was the world's tallest free-standing structure when it was built in 1976.

Co *symbol.* cobalt

CO *abbr.* 1. Commanding Officer 2. Commonwealth Office 3. conscientious objector 4. Colorado 5. Colombia (*international vehicle registration*)

Co. /kō/ *abbr.* 1. Company (*used in names of businesses*) 2. County (*used in place names*) 3. Colorado

c.o. *prefix.* 1. together, jointly ○ *coauthor* 2. associate, alternate ○ *copilot* 3. to the same degree ○ *coeternal* 4. complement of an angle ○ *cotangent*

c/o[1] *abbr.* care of (*used in addresses*)

c/o[2] *abbr.* 1. care of 2. ACCT carried over

CoA *abbr.* coenzyme A

coach /kōch/ *n.* 1. TRANSP **LONG-DISTANCE BUS** a bus designed for long-distance travel or sightseeing 2. TRANSP **HORSE-DRAWN CARRIAGE** a large enclosed horse-drawn carriage 3. RAIL **RAILWAY CARRIAGE** a railway carriage 4. SPORTS **SB WHO TRAINS SPORTS PLAYERS** sb who trains sports players and athletes 5. ARTS **SB WHO TRAINS PERFORMER** sb who trains people in acting or singing 6. EDUC **TUTOR** sb who instructs an individual in a specified subject 7. EDUC **TUTOR FOR EXAMINATIONS** a private tutor who prepares students for examinations 8. US, Can TRANSP **INEXPENSIVE TRAVEL CATEGORY** an inexpensive class of passenger accommodation on a bus, train, or aircraft ∎ *v.* (**coaches, coaching, coached**) 1. *vt.* SPORTS **TRAIN ATHLETE** to train sb in a sport 2. *vt.* ARTS **TRAIN PERFORMER** to train sb in acting or singing 3. *vt.* EDUC **TRAIN STUDENT** to give sb private tuition in a particular subject or towards examinations 4. *vti.* **TRANSPORT PEOPLE IN COACH** to carry passengers in a horse-drawn coach, or travel by coach [Mid-16thC. Via French *coche* from German *Kutsche*, *Kotsche*, from Hungarian *kocsi (szekér)*, literally '(wagon) of Kocs', named after *Kocs*, a village in Hungary where carriages, carts, and suchlike were made.] —**coachable** *adj.*

——— **WORD KEY: SYNONYMS** ———
See Synonyms at *teach*.

coach bolt *n.* a bolt for timber with a shank that at one end is square in section with a rounded head. This end grips the timber while the nut is turned by a spanner. US term **carriage bolt**

coach box *n.* the driver's seat on a horse-drawn carriage

coach dog *n.* a Dalmatian dog (*archaic*) [From the former practice of the dogs being kept to run in attendance on a carriage]

coaching /kóching/ *n.* training in how to deal with emotional problems and interpersonal relationships

coaching inn *n.* a roadside inn formerly used by horsedrawn coach services to provide refreshments and accommodation for passengers, to pick up and set down passengers, and to change horses, often with stabling facilities

coachload /kóch lōd/ *n.* the total number of people who are travelling in or who fill a coach ○ *coachloads of tourists*

coachman /kóchmən/ (*plural* **-men** /-mən/) *n.* the driver of a horse-drawn coach or carriage

coachwood /kóch woŏd/ (*plural* **-woods** *or* **-wood**) *n.* a medium-sized Australian tree with a straight trunk, small crown, and white flowers that provides a light versatile wood used in cabinetmaking. Latin name: *Ceratopetalum apetalum*.

coachwork /kóch wurk/ *n.* the painted bodywork of a road vehicle or railway carriage

coaction /kō áksh'n/ *n.* joint or reciprocal action [Early 17thC. Via French from the Latin stem *coaction-*, from *coact-*, the past participle stem of *coagere*, literally 'to drive together', from *agere* 'to drive'.] —**coactive** *adj.* —**coactively** *adv.* —**coactivity** /kó ak tívvəti/ *n.*

coadaptation /kó ə dap táysh'n/ *n.* the mutually advantageous development of characteristics in two or more species of organisms —**coadapted** *adj.*

coadjutant /kō ájjətənt/ *n.* sb who helps another

coadjutor /kō ájjoŏtər/ *n.* 1. **ASSISTANT** a helper for sb (*formal*) 2. CHR **BISHOP WHO HELPS ANOTHER** a bishop who assists a diocesan bishop [15thC. Via French from late Latin, literally 'helper with', formed from Latin *adjutor* 'helper', from *adjuvare* 'to help'.]

coagula plural of **coagulum**

coagulant /kō ággyoŏlənt/ *n.* a substance that causes or assists coagulation of the blood, e.g. a natural clotting factor or a drug —**coagulant** *adj.*

coagulase /kō ággyoŏ layz, -layss/ *n.* an enzyme, especially one produced by some bacteria, that causes coagulation of the blood [Early 20thC. Coined from COAGULATE + -ASE.]

coagulate /kō ággyoŏlayt/ *vti.* (**-lates, -lating, -lated**) 1. **MAKE OR BECOME SEMISOLID** to thicken, or cause liquid to thicken, into a soft semisolid mass 2. CHEM **GROUP TOGETHER IN LARGER MASS** to group together as a mass, or cause the particles in a colloid to group together, as, e.g., egg white does when heated ∎ *n.* CHEM **COAGULATED MASS** a soft semisolid mass produced by coagulation of a colloid [15thC. From Latin *coagulat-*, the past participle stem of *coagulare* 'to coagulate', from, ultimately, *coagere* 'to drive together'.] —**coagulability** /kō ággyoŏlə bílləti/ *n.* —**coagulable** /kō ággyoŏləb'l/ *adj.* —**coagulator** /-laytər/ *n.*

coagulation /kō ággyoŏ láysh'n/ *n.* 1. **BECOMING SEMISOLID** the thickening of a fluid into a soft semisolid mass 2. **CLOT** a clot or coagulum 3. CHEM **CHEMICAL FORMATION OF MASS** grouping together of the particles of a colloid to form a larger mass

coagulation factor *n.* = **clotting factor**

coagulum /kō ággyoŏləm/ (*plural* **-la** /-lə/) *n.* a clot or coagulated mass of sth, especially blood [Mid-16thC. From Latin, formed from *coagere* (see COAGULATE).]

coal /kōl/ *n.* **1.** BLACK ROCK USED AS FUEL a hard black or dark brown sedimentary rock formed by the decomposition of plant material, widely used as a fuel **2.** PIECE OF COAL a piece of coal **3.** SMALL PIECE OF BURNABLE MATERIAL any small piece of combustible material **4.** = **charcoal** ■ *v.* **(coals, coaling, coaled) 1.** *vt.* CONVERT STH INTO CHARCOAL to burn sth combustible and convert it into charcoal **2.** *vti.* PROVIDE OR TAKE ON COAL to supply sth with coal or take on coal [Old English *col.* Ultimately from an Indo-European word meaning 'glowing ember'. The modern meaning 'black fossil fuel' dates from the 13thC.] —**coaly** *adj.* ◇ **carry coals to Newcastle** to do sth superfluous or supply sth already plentiful

coal black *adj.* **1.** VERY BLACK completely black **2.** VERY DARK very dark black in colour

coaler /kṓlər/ *n.* a ship or train that transports coal

coalesce /kṓ ə léss/ **(-lesces, -lescing, -lesced)** *vti.* to merge or cause things to merge into a single body or group [Mid-16thC. From Latin *coalescere*, literally 'to grow up together', from *alescere* 'to grow up', from *alere* 'to nourish' (source of English *adolescent* and *alumnus*).] —**coalescence** *n.* —**coalescent** *adj.*

coalface /kṓl fayss/ *n.* **1.** SEAM OF COAL BEING WORKED the newly exposed rock surface in a mine, from which coal is being cut **2.** WHERE WORK GETS DONE the site of physical or practical work, as opposed to management or administration

coalfield /kṓl feeld/ *n.* an area with coal deposits

coalfish /kṓl fish/ (*plural* **coalfish** *or* **coalfishes**) *n.* a black-backed or dark-coloured edible fish, e.g. sablefish or pollack

coal gas *n.* **1.** METHANE AND HYDROGEN MIXTURE a flammable mixture of gases obtained by distilling coal, consisting mainly of methane and hydrogen. It is sometimes used as a fuel. **2.** GAS BURNED OFF COAL the gas produced when coal is burned

coalhole /kṓl hōl/ *n.* a small cellar or a similar place for storing coal, especially for a domestic fire

coalification /kṓlifi káysh'n/ *n.* the process in which coal is formed by the action of pressure and heat on buried plant material. The moisture content of the plants is progressively removed and the material remaining is solidified.

coalition /kṓ ə lísh'n/ *n.* **1.** POLITICAL ALLIANCE a temporary union between two or more groups, especially political parties **2.** MERGING INTO SINGLE ENTITY the merging of things into one body or mass [Early 17thC. From the medieval Latin stem *coalition-*, from Latin *coalit-*, the past participle stem of *coalescere* 'to grow together' (see COALESCE).] —**coalitionist** *n.*

Coalition *n.* in Australia, a long-standing political coalition between the Liberal Party and the National Party

coal measures *npl.* a series of strata containing economically workable coal deposits, e.g. the upper Carboniferous rocks of northwestern Europe

coalmine /kṓl mīn/ *n.* a mine where coal is dug from the ground —**coalminer** *n.*

coalminer's lung *n.* = **anthracosis** [From the fact that the disease frequently affects coalminers]

Coalport /kṓl pawrt/ *n.* a variety of white, strongly patterned bone china made in Coalport, near Shrewsbury, England, in the 19th century

Coalsack /kṓl sak/ *n.* **1.** INTERSTELLAR CLOUD SEEN IN SOUTHERN HEMISPHERE a dark cloud of interstellar dust (**nebula**) that is part of the Crux constellation and is visible in the southern hemisphere in front of the Milky Way **2.** INTERSTELLAR CLOUD SEEN IN NORTHERN HEMISPHERE a dark interstellar cloud (**nebula**) visible in the northern hemisphere near the constellation Cygnus

coal scuttle *n.* a metal container for holding and pouring coal for a domestic fire

coal tar *n.* a thick black liquid obtained as a by-product in the production of coke. It yields chemicals that are used in making dyes, drugs, and soap.

coal-tar pitch *n.* a by-product of the distillation of coal tar, used especially in making road surfaces, in carbon electrodes, and in binding fuel briquettes

coal tit, **coletit** *n.* a small songbird of Europe and Asia belonging to the tit family, with a black-crowned head, white cheeks, and a white patch on the nape of the neck. Latin name: *Parus ater*.

coaming /kṓming/ *n.* a raised edging round the cockpit or hatchway of a boat for keeping out water [Early 17thC. Origin unknown.]

co-anchor /kō ángkər/ *n.* *US* JOINT BROADCASTER OF NEWS either of two broadcasters who jointly present a television programme ■ *vti.* **(co-anchors, co-anchoring, co-anchored)** *US* BE CO-ANCHOR to be co-anchor of a television programme, especially a news programme

coapt /kō ápt/ **(-apts, -apting, -apted)** *v.* to join or bring displaced parts close together in their correct alignment, e.g. the edges of a wound or broken bone [Late 16thC. From late Latin *coaptare*, literally 'to fit together', from, ultimately, Latin *aptus* 'fastened, suitable'.] —**coaptation** /kṓ ap táysh'n/ *n.*

coarctate /kō áark tayt/ *adj.* **1.** MED CONSTRICTED used to describe any vessel or canal in the body that has become constricted, narrowed, or pressed together **2.** ZOOL IN HARD SHELL used to describe a pupa that is enclosed in a horny oval case ■ *vi.* **(-tates, -tating, -tated)** CONSTRICT to become narrow, constricted, or pressed together (*refers to blood vessels or other body passages*) [15thC. From Latin *coar(c)tatus*, the past participle of *coar(c)tare*, literally 'to press close together', from *artare* 'to press close', from *artus* 'confined, narrow'.] —**coarctation** /kṓ aark táysh'n/ *n.*

coarse /kawrss/ **(coarser, coarsest)** *adj.* **1.** ROUGH harsh or rough to the touch **2.** WITH THICK GRAINS OR STRANDS consisting of large grains or thick strands **3.** INDELICATE OR TASTELESS lacking taste or refinement **4.** VULGAR vulgar or obscene **5.** UNREFINED not refined ○ *coarse metal* **6.** INFERIOR of inferior quality [14thC. Originally *corse*, *course*, meaning 'ordinary' (used of cloth); of uncertain origin: perhaps from COURSE (as in 'of course' or 'matter of course').] —**coarsely** *adv.* —**coarseness** *n.*

coarse fish (*plural* **coarse fish** *or* **coarse fishes**) *n.* any freshwater fish that does not belong to the salmon family —**coarse fishing** *n.*

coarse-grained *adj.* **1.** WITH ROUGH GRAIN having a large or rough grain **2.** VULGAR coarse or vulgar in speech or manner

coarsen /káwrss'n/ **(-ens, -ening, -ened)** *vti.* to become or make sth coarse or coarser

coast /kōst/ *n.* **1.** LAND NEXT TO SEA land beside the sea ○ *sailed along the coast* **2.** = **seaside 3.** *US, Can* SLOPE FOR SLEDGING a slope suitable for sledging **4.** FRONTIER a frontier (*archaic*) ■ *v.* **(coasts, coasting, coasted) 1.** *vti.* MOVE BY MOMENTUM to move forwards by momentum, without applying power or cause sth to move in this way **2.** *vi.* SUCCEED EFFORTLESSLY to progress with very little effort **3.** *vti.* NAUT TRAVEL ALONG SHORE to sail along a shore [14thC. Via Old French *coste* from Latin *costa* 'rib, side' (source of English *accost* and *cutlet*).]

coastal /kṓst'l/ *adj.* along, near, or relating to a coast —**coastally** *adv.*

coaster /kṓstər/ *n.* **1.** SHIPPING SHIP TRADING ALONG COAST a ship that sails along a coast to trade **2.** MAT FOR GLASS a mat placed under a glass in order to protect a surface **3.** TRAY FOR PASSING BOTTLE a small tray, sometimes on wheels, for passing a bottle or decanter round a table **4.** STH THAT COASTS sth that coasts of its own momentum

coastguard /kṓst gaard/ *n.* **1.** SERVICE DEALING WITH COASTAL MATTERS an emergency service that rescues people in difficulties at sea and acts against smuggling **2.** MEMBER OF COASTGUARD a member of the coastguard

Coast Guard *n.* a US military service that enforces maritime laws, acts in marine emergencies, and maintains navigational aids, in wartime supplementing the navy

coastline /kṓst līn/ *n.* the outline of a coast as viewed from the sea or on a map

coast-to-coast *adj.* from one coast to another of a continent, or a nation that is an island ○ *The debate had coast-to-coast coverage on the news media.*

coat /kōt/ *n.* **1.** WARM OUTER GARMENT an item of clothing with long sleeves that is usually at least knee-length and is worn outdoors over other clothes **2.** *US, NZ* SUIT JACKET a jacket worn as part of a suit, with a skirt or trousers (*dated*) **3.** COVERING ON ANIMAL the fur, wool, or hair that covers an animal **4.** THIN COVERING any thin layer that covers sth ■ *vt.* **(coats, coating, coated) 1.** INDUST COVER SURFACE to cover a surface with a thin layer of sth (*often passive*) **2.** PROVIDE SB WITH COAT to provide sb with a coat (*usually used in the passive*) [14thC. From Old French *cote*, from prehistoric Germanic.] —**coater** *n.*

Coatbridge /kṓt brij/ industrial town in Strathclyde Region, Scotland. Population: 43,617 (1991).

coat check *n.* *US* = **cloakroom**

coat dress *n.* a tailored dress that is shaped like a coat and fastened in front from the neck to the hem, usually with buttons

coated /kṓtid/ *adj.* **1.** WITH OUTER LAYER covered with a layer of sth **2.** PAPER PREPARED FOR WRITING OR PRINTING ON treated with a fine layer of a mineral to make paper suitable for writing or printing on **3.** TEXTILES TREATED AGAINST MOISTURE with a treated surface or plastic coating that resists moisture ○ *coated fabric*

coatee /kṓtee, kō tée/ *n.* **1.** BABY'S COAT a baby's knitted coat **2.** COAT WITH SHORT COAT-TAILS a military cutaway coat with shortened coat-tails

Coates /kōts/, **Joseph Gordon** (1878–1943) New Zealand statesman. He was a Reform Party politician and prime minister of New Zealand (1925–28).

coat hanger *n.* a curved frame with a hook, used to hang clothes

coati /kō áati/ (*plural* **-tis** *or* **-ti**), **coatimundi** /kō áati mṓondi/ (*plural* **-dis** *or* **-di**) *n.* a South or Central American omnivorous mammal related to the raccoon, that has a narrow flexible snout and a striped tail. Genus: *Nasua*. [Early 17thC. Via Portuguese from Tupi *kua'ti*.]

coating /kṓting/ *n.* **1.** THIN LAYER a thin layer that covers sth ○ *a coating of dust* **2.** CLOTH FOR COATS cloth used in making coats

Coat of arms

coat of arms *n.* **1.** DESIGN ON SHIELD a design on a shield that signifies a particular family, university, or city **2.** GARMENT WITH COAT OF ARMS a garment that is decorated with a coat of arms [Translation of French *cote d'armes*]

coat of mail *n.* a protective garment of armour worn in medieval times, consisting of linked metal rings

coatrack /kṓt rak/ *n.* a stand or rack fitted with hooks, used for hanging clothes on

coat stand *n.* a stand with hooks for hanging, used for hanging coats on. US term **coat tree**

coat-tail *n.* the part below the waist at the back of a coat, especially one of the parts when it is divided into two (*usually used in the plural*) ◇ **on sb's coat-tails** helped by sb else rather than succeeding alone

coat tree *n.* *US* = **coat stand**

coauthor /kṓ áwthər/ *n.* JOINT AUTHOR sb who writes sth jointly with one or more other authors ■ *vt.* **(-thors, -thoring, -thored)** WRITE STH JOINTLY to write sth jointly with one or more other authors

coax /kōks/ **(coaxes, coaxing, coaxed)** *v.* **1.** *vti.* PERSUADE GENTLY to persuade sb gently to do sth **2.** *vt.* OBTAIN STH BY GENTLE PERSUASION to get sth from sb by gentle persuasion **3.** *vt.* GENTLY MAKE STH WORK to manipulate sth patiently until it moves or works ○ *I finally coaxed the sticky drawers open.* [Late 16thC. Alteration of *cokes*, from obsolete *cokes* 'simpleton', of uncertain origin. 'To persuade gently' developed via 'to treat as a simpleton or pet' and 'to fondle'.] —**coaxingly** *adv.*

coax cable /kó aks-/ *n.* = **coaxial cable** [*Coax* shortening of COAXIAL.]

coaxial /kō áksi əl/ *adj.* **1.** SHARING AXIS having a common axis **2.** ELEC OF COAXIAL CABLE belonging or relating to a coaxial cable —**coaxially** *adv.*

coaxial cable *n.* a cable consisting of an inner core and outer flexible braided tube, both of conductive material separated by an insulator, used to transmit high-frequency signals at high speeds

cob[1] /kob/ *n.* **1.** CORE OF MAIZE EAR the hard core to which individual kernels of maize are attached **2.** ROUND BREAD a rounded loaf of bread **3.** = **cobnut 4.** ZOOL MALE SWAN a male swan **5.** RIDING SHORT-LEGGED RIDING HORSE a sturdy short-legged riding horse **6.** SMALL PIECE a small lump or mass of sth hard, especially coal [15thC. Partly ultimately from a prehistoric Germanic word meaning 'round, lumpy object', and partly a variant of dialect *cop* 'head, top'.]

cob[2] /kob/ *n.* a building material consisting of clay, gravel, and straw [Early 17thC. Origin uncertain: perhaps from COB[1] in the sense 'lump'.]

cob[3] /kob/ *n.* a crude often irregularly shaped gold or silver coin that circulated in Spanish colonies in the Americas between the 16th and 18th centuries [From Spanish *cabo de barra*, literally 'end of bar' from the crudely cut silver or gold coin-sized planchets that were sliced from the cast bar]

cobalamin /kə bólləmin/ *n.* = **vitamin B**$_{12}$ [Mid-20thC. Blend of COBALT and VITAMIN.]

cobalt /kó bawlt, -bolt/ *n.* a tough brittle silvery-white metallic chemical element found in iron, nickel, and copper ores. It is used to colour ceramics and in alloys. Symbol **Co** [Late 17thC. From German *Kobalt*, variant of *Kobold* 'harmful goblin', from the belief of miners that the cobalt ore was harmful to neighbouring silver ores.]

cobalt 60 *n.* a naturally radioactive isotope of cobalt that has a mass number of 60, spontaneously emits strong gamma radiation, and is used in radiotherapy and in industry

cobalt bloom *n.* = **erythrite** [Translation of German *Kobaltblüte*]

cobalt blue *adj.* of a deep blue colour with a tinge of green —**cobalt blue** *n.*

cobalt bomb *n.* a device containing cobalt 60, used in radiotherapy

cobaltic /kō báwltik, -ból/ *adj.* relating to or containing cobalt, especially with a valency of 3

cobaltite /kō báwl tīt, -ból/ *n.* a rare silvery-white or greyish mineral consisting of cobalt sulphide and arsenide. It is used in ceramics.

cobaltous /kō báwltəs, -ból/ *adj.* relating to or containing cobalt, especially with a valency of 2

cobber /kóbbər/ *n.* ANZ a friend or companion (*dated informal*) [Late 19thC. Origin uncertain: perhaps formed from dialectal *cob* 'to take a liking to'.]

Cobbett /kóbbit/, **William** (1763–1835) British writer, journalist, and reformer. He wrote *History of the Protestant Reformation* (1824–27) and *Rural Rides* (1830).

cobble[1] /kóbb'l/ *n.* **1.** TRANSP = **cobblestone 2.** GEOL ROCK FRAGMENT a naturally rounded rock fragment between 64 and 256 mm in diameter ■ *vt.* (**cobbles, cobbling, cobbled**) TRANSP PAVE ROAD WITH COBBLESTONES to pave a road with cobblestones [Early 17thC. Shortening of earlier *cobelstone*, from assumed *cobel* (perhaps literally 'little lump', formed from COB[1] (+ STONE).]

cobble together *vt.* to assemble or make sth roughly and quickly

cobble[2] /kóbb'l/ (**cobbles, cobbling, cobbled, cobbling**) *vt.* to make, mend, or patch footwear [15thC. Back-formation from COBBLER.]

cobbled /kóbb'ld/ *adj.* paved with cobblestones

cobbler[1] /kóbblər/ *n.* sb who makes, mends, or patches footwear [13thC. Origin unknown.]

cobbler[2] /kóbblər/ *n.* **1.** DESSERT WITH CRUST a baked fruit dessert with a soft thick crust **2.** ICED ALCOHOLIC DRINK an iced drink made of wine, rum or whisky, and sugar, often garnished with fruit and mint [Early 19thC. Origin uncertain: probably representing uses of COBBLER.]

cobblers /kóbblərz/ *npl.* **1.** NONSENSE nonsense (*slang*) **2.** TESTICLES testicles (*slang offensive*) [Mid-20thC. Shortening of *cobbler's awls*, rhyming slang for BALLS 'testicles'.]

cobbler's wax *n.* a resin used to wax thread

cobblestone /kóbb'l stōn/ *n.* a small rounded stone used for paving streets [15thC. See COBBLE[1].] —**cobblestoned** *adj.*

Cobden /kóbdən/, **Richard** (1804–65) British economist and politician. An outstanding orator and advocate of free trade, he formed, with John Bright, the Anti-Corn Law League (1838).

cobelligerent /kó bə líjjərənt/ *n.* a country that or individual who is an ally in a fight or war

cobia /kóbi ə/ (*plural* **cobia** or **cobias**) *n.* a large bony dark-striped fish found in tropical and subtropical seas that is related to the perch and sea bass. Latin name: *Rachycentron canadum*. [Mid-19thC. Origin unknown.]

coble /kób'l/ *n.* Scotland, N England a small flat-bottomed boat for fishing, usually used near a coast or in an estuary [Pre-12thC. Probably of Celtic origin.]

cobnut /kób nut/ (*plural* **cobnuts** or **cobs**) *n.* a variety of hazelnut [Late 16thC. From earlier *cobill nut*, *cobill*, of uncertain origin: perhaps from COBBLE[1], or from COB[1].]

COBOL /kó bol/, **Cobol** *n.* a high-level computer programming language, widely adopted for corporate business applications [Mid-20thC. Acronym formed from *common business-oriented language*.]

Cobra

cobra /kóbrə/ *n.* a venomous snake found in tropical Asia and Africa that, when excited, rears up and spreads the skin behind its head to form a hood. Genus: *Naja* and *Ophiophagus*. [Early 19thC. Shortening of *cobra de capello*, literally 'snake with a hood'; *cobra* ultimately from Latin *cubra* 'snake'.]

coburg /kóburg/ *n.* **1.** TEXTILES THIN TWILLED FABRIC a thin fabric made of wool and cotton or silk, twilled on one surface and used as a dress fabric or lining cloth **2.** FOOD TYPE OF ROUND LOAF a round loaf with a cross cut on the top of the dough before baking [Early 19thC. Named after Prince Albert of Saxe-Coburg (1819–61), consort of Queen Victoria.]

Coburg /kó burg/ city in the state of Bavaria, southeastern Germany, near the Czech border. It was the seat of the Dukes of Saxe-Coburg-Gotha, whose line supplied many of Europe's monarchs. Population: 44,246 (1991).

cobweb /kób web/ *n.* **1.** DUSTY SPIDER'S WEB a fine thread or web of fine threads spun by spiders, especially when covered with dust **2.** STH RESEMBLING COBWEB sth that resembles a cobweb in being flimsy and insubstantial or in acting as a trap or snare ■ **cobwebs** *npl.* SLUGGISH MENTAL STATE mental sluggishness and tiredness ○ *I need to blow the cobwebs away.* [14thC. Cob from obsolete *coppe* 'spider', ultimately from Old English *ātorcoppe*, probably literally 'poison-head', from the idea that spiders are venomous.] —**cobwebbed** *adj.* —**cobwebby** *adj.*

coca /kókə/ (*plural* **-ca**) *n.* **1.** PLANTS SHRUB YIELDING COCAINE a shrub, native to the Andes, that has yellow flowers and whose leaves yield cocaine and other alkaloids. Latin name: *Erythroxylum coca*. **2.** DRIED LEAVES OF COCA the dried leaves of coca, chewed as a stimulant or processed for cocaine and other alkaloids [Late 16thC. Via Spanish from Aymara *kuka* or Quechua *koka*.]

Coca-Cola /kókə kólə/ *tdmk.* a trademark for a cola-flavoured soft drink

cocaine /kō káyn/ *n.* an addictive narcotic drug obtained from the leaves of the coca plant, taken illegally as a stimulant. It is now only used medicinally as a surface anaesthetic. Formula: $C_{17}H_{21}NO_4$. [Mid-19thC. Coined from COCA + -INE.]

cocainise *vt.* = **cocainize**

cocainism /kō káy nizzəm/ *n.* an addiction to or overuse of cocaine, resulting in physical or mental impairment (*dated*)

cocainize /kō káy nīz/ (**-izes, -izing, -ized**), **cocainise** (**-ises, -ising, -ised**) *vt.* to anaesthetize sb using cocaine as a surface (**topical**) application in paste form in the nose. Cocaine is no longer used in this way, having been succeeded by synthetic analogues. —**cocainization** /kókay nī záysh'n/ *n.*

cocarcinogen /kó kaar sínnəjən, kō ka'arsin-/ *n.* a substance that does not cause cancer on its own but can increase the effect of carcinogenic factors or substances when acting together with them —**cocarcinogenic** /kō ka'arssinə jénnik/ *adj.*

cocci plural of **coccus**

coccid /kóksid/ *n.* any insect that folds its wings over its back when not flying. Scale insects and mealybugs are coccids. Family: Coccidae. [Late 19thC. Formed from modern Latin *Coccus*, genus name (see COCCUS).] —**coccid** *adj.*

coccidia plural of **coccidium**

coccidioidomycosis /kok síddi óydōmī kóssiss/ *n.* a respiratory disease of humans and domestic animals in North America, marked by flu-like symptoms, that is caused by inhalation of spores from a fungus. Latin name: *Coccidioides immitis*.

coccidiosis /kok síddi óssiss/ *n.* a disease of domestic animals and birds, and occasionally humans, caused by coccidia in the intestines, and causing diarrhoea

coccidium /kok síddi əm/ (*plural* **-a** /-ə/) *n.* a parasitic sporozoan that can cause disease in the gut of humans and animals. Order: Coccidia. [Mid-19thC. From modern Latin, from the Greek stem *kokkid-*, literally 'little berry', from *kokkos* 'berry'.] —**coccidial** *adj.*

coccolith /kókə lith/ *n.* a microscopic calcareous platelet that forms the covering for some marine plankton, one form of which makes up chalk deposits [Mid-19thC. From modern Latin *Coccolithus*, genus name, coined from Greek *kokkos* 'grain' + *lithos* 'stone'.]

coccus /kókəss/ (*plural* **-ci** /kóksī/) *n.* **1.** MICROBIOL TYPE OF BACTERIUM a spherical or nearly spherical microorganism, especially a bacterium **2.** BOT PART OF FRUIT CONTAINING SEED a subdivision of a fruit that contains a single seed and resembles a berry [Early 19thC. Via modern Latin from Greek *kokkos* 'grain, berry'.] —**coccal** *adj.* —**coccoid** /kókoyd/ *adj.* —**coccous** *adj.*

-coccus *suffix.* a spherical microorganism ○ *pneumococcus* [From COCCUS]

coccyx /kók siks/ (*plural* **-cyges** /kok sí jeez/ *or* **-cyxes**) *n.* a small triangular bone at the base of the spinal column [Late 16thC. Via Latin from Greek *kokkux*, originally 'cuckoo'; from its resemblance to a cuckoo's beak.] —**coccygeal** /kok síjji əl/ *adj.*

Cochabamba /kóchə bámbə/ city and capital of Cochabamba Department, central Bolivia, situated approximately 129 km/80 mi. northeast of Oruro. Population: 404,102 (1992).

co-channel /kō chán'l/ *adj.* relating to a transmission occupying the same frequency band as another

Cochin /kó chin/ major port and town in Kerala State, southwestern India. Population: 564,000 (1991).

cochineal /kóchi nee'l/ *n.* a red dye obtained from the crushed dried bodies of female cochineal insects, used to colour food and drinks and to dye fabrics [Late 16thC. Via French *cochenille* or Spanish *cochinilla* from Latin *coccinus* 'scarlet', from, ultimately, Greek *kokkos* 'berry', because the dried body of the insect was believed to be a berry.]

cochineal insect *n.* a small red scale insect found in Mexico and the West Indies that feeds on cacti. The dye cochineal is derived from the crushed bodies of cochineal insects. Latin name: *Coccus cacti*.

cochlea /kókli ə/ (*plural* **-ae** /-ī, -ee/ *or* **-as**) *n.* a spiral structure in the inner ear that looks like a snail shell and contains over 10,000 tiny hair cells that move in response to sound waves. These movements stimulate nerve cells to send messages to the brain, which the brain interprets as sound. [Mid-16thC. Via Latin *coc(h)lea* 'snail shell, screw' from Greek *kokhlias* 'snail'.] —**cochlear** /kókliər/ *adj.*

cochlear implant *n.* a device implanted under the skin that picks up sounds and converts them to impulses transmitted to electrodes placed in the cochlea, restoring some hearing to people with a hearing impairment

cochleate /kókli ət/ *adj.* shaped in a spiral like the shell of a snail

cock[1] /kok/ *n.* **1.** ADULT MALE CHICKEN an adult male of a domestic fowl, normally only kept for breeding **2.** MALE BIRD the adult male of a bird **3.** MALE ANIMAL an adult male salmon, crab, or lobster **4.** ARMS PART OF GUN the hammer of a gun that, when released by the action of the trigger, makes the gun fire **5.** ARMS RAISED POSITION OF HAMMER OF GUN the raised position of the hammer of a gun when it is ready to fire **6.** OFFENSIVE TERM an offensive term for a man's penis (*slang taboo*) **7.** STOPCOCK a stopcock **8.** WEATHERCOCK a weathercock **9.** TILTED POSITION the tilt or angle in the position of sb's head or hat, often suggesting that he or she is in a good mood **10.** CHUM OR MATE used as a friendly or familiar way of addressing a man, especially among Cockneys (*regional dated informal*) **11.** NONSENSE sth sb has said or written that you consider to be nonsense (*dated informal*) ■ *vt.* (**cocks, cocking, cocked**) **1.** ARMS PREPARE GUN FOR FIRING to pull back the hammer of a gun so that it is ready to be fired when the trigger is pulled **2.** TURN EARS OR EYES to turn one or both ears or eyes in a particular direction to listen for or look out for sb or sth **3.** TILT BACK OR ANGLE STH to tilt or raise sth, often as a way of expressing that you are full of confidence or in good humour **4.** RAISE LIMB IN AIR to lift or raise a part of the body **5.** SET STH TO OPERATE to set a device or mechanism so that it will release sth, e.g. a camera shutter [Pre-12thC. Origin uncertain, probably from medieval Latin *coccus*, ultimately an imitation of a cock's crow.]

cock[2] /kok/ *n.* CONE-SHAPED PILE OF GRAIN straw, hay, or grain piled in the shape of a cone (*dated*) ■ *vt.* (**cocks, cocking, cocked**) AGRIC PILE GRAIN INTO CONE-SHAPED STACK to pile grain, straw, or hay into a cone-shaped stack (*dated*) [14thC. From Scandinavian.]

cockade /ko káyd/ *n.* a rosette, ribbon, or other ornament worn, usually on a hat, as an identifying badge or as part of a livery [Mid-17thC. From French *bonnet à la coquarde*, literally 'bonnet worn proudly', from obsolete *coquard* 'proud, saucy', from *coq* 'cock'.] —**cockaded** *adj.*

cock-a-doodle-doo /kók ə dood'l doŏ/ *n., interj.* used as a description or imitation of the sound a cock makes when it crows —**cock-a-doodle-doo** *vi.*

cock-a-hoop *adj.* **1.** ELATED extremely happy or excited about sth **2.** VERY PROUD OF STH boastful about sth that has been achieved [From *set the cock on the hoop* 'to celebrate', of uncertain origin: perhaps referring to a wine-barrel tap, or a cock eating *hoop* 'grain']

cock-a-leekie /kók ə leèki/, **cockieleekie** *n.* a Scottish soup made from a whole chicken and leeks and sometimes containing prunes

cock-and-bull story (*plural* **cock-and-bull stories**), **cock-and-bull** *n.* a ridiculous and scarcely credible story that sb tries to convince people is true, usually either to impress them or as an excuse for sth [Origin uncertain: perhaps from the popularity of fables with animal characters. The theory involving stories exchanged by travellers near the Bull Inn and Cock Inn is folk etymology.]

cockatiel /kóka teél/, **cockateel** *n.* a small grey Australian parrot with a white patch on its wing and a prominent crest that is yellow in males. Latin name: *Nymphicus hollandicus*. [Late 19thC. From Dutch *kaktielje*, of uncertain origin: probably a diminutive of *kaketoe* (see COCKATOO).]

cockatoo /kóka toó/ (*plural* **-toos**) *n.* **1.** AUSTRALASIAN PARROT a parrot with a prominent crest, found in Australia, New Guinea, the East Indies, and the Philippines. Many have white or light-coloured plumage. Genera: *Cacatua* and *Callocephalon* and

Cockatoo

Calyptorhynchus. **2.** *Aus* SMALL-SCALE FARMER a farmer who owns a small piece of land [Mid-17thC. Via Dutch *kaketoe* from Malay *kakatua*; influenced by COCK.]

cockatrice /kóka trīss/ *n.* a mythological serpent that was supposed to have hatched from a cock's egg, and to be able to kill with its stare [14thC. Via Old French *cocatris* from medieval Latin *calcatrix* 'tracker', from Latin *calcare* 'to track', from *calx* 'heel' (see CAULK).]

Cockayne /ko káyn/, **Leonard** (1855–1934) British-born New Zealand botanist. He was a pioneer of field botany and ecology.

cockboat /kók bōt/ *n.* a small rowing boat, especially one that belongs to a larger ship. Cockboats are often used to ferry stores and provisions between ship and shore. [15thC. *Cock* via Old French *coque* from, ultimately, Latin *codex* 'block of wood' (source of English *code*).]

cockchafer /kók chayfər/ *n.* INSECTS a large European beetle with larvae that destroy trees and other plants. Family: Scarabaeidae.

cockcrow /kók krō/ *n.* the time of day when the sun begins to show above the horizon (*archaic or literary*)

cocked hat *n.* a two- or three-cornered hat with a wide turned up brim, popular in the 18th century. A cocked hat was especially worn as part of a uniform or livery. ◇ **knock sb** *or* **sth into a cocked hat** **1.** to be much better than sb or sth else (*informal*) **2.** to ruin or damage sth utterly

cocker[1] /kókər/ *n.* **1.** = **cocker spaniel** **2.** TRAINER OF GAMECOCKS sb who raises and trains cocks for fighting **3.** SB INVOLVED IN COCKFIGHTING sb who is involved in cockfighting either as a breeder or as a trainer of cocks, or as a regular spectator

cocker[2] /kókər/ *vt.* (**-ers, -ering, -ered**) PAMPER OR CODDLE SB to treat sb in an over-protective or indulgent way ■ *n.* CHUM used to refer to a close friend (*informal*) [15thC. Origin unknown.]

cockerel /kókərəl/ *n.* a young male chicken, usually one that is less than a year old [15thC. Literally 'small cock', formed from COCK.]

Cockerell /kókərəl/, **Sir Christopher** (b. 1910) British radio and marine engineer. His experiments in 1953–59 led to the invention of the Hovercraft.

cocker spaniel *n.* ZOOL a small dog with long floppy ears and a soft wavy coat, belonging to a breed of spaniel originally bred for flushing out game [So called because the breed was developed for rousing woodcock for shooting]

cockeye /kók ī/ *n.* an eye that is turned inwards or outwards from the nose, making parallel vision impossible (*informal offensive*)

cockeyed /kók īd/ *adj.* **1.** FOOLISH not sensible or properly thought out (*informal*) **2.** NOT ALIGNED positioned at an awkward or crooked angle **3.** AFFECTED BY A SQUINT having one eye that turns inwards or outwards from the nose (*informal offensive*) **4.** VERY DRUNK so drunk that it is impossible to see straight (*informal*) ○ *Boy, did I get cockeyed last night!*

cock feather *n.* the feather on an arrow positioned at right-angles to the notch into which the bow string fits [*Cock* from COCK in the sense 'to stick up']

cockfight /kók fīt/ *n.* an organized fight between two cocks, each of which is fitted with sharp metal spurs

cockfighting /kók fīting/ *n.* the practice of setting two cocks to fight each other in front of spectators who often make bets on the outcome. The cocks are equipped with metal spurs designed to inflict the maximum harm on the opposing bird, and the sport is illegal in many countries.

cockhorse /kók hawrss/ *n.* a rocking horse or a stick with an imitation horse's head on one end

cockieleekie *n.* = **cock-a-leekie**

cockle[1] /kók'l/ *n.* **1.** MOLLUSC WITH HEART-SHAPED SHELL a small mollusc that has a rounded or heart-shaped ridged shell in two parts. Family: Cardiidae. **2.** = **cockleshell** *n.* 1 **3.** = **cockleshell** *n.* 2 **4.** WRINKLE a crease or pucker in a piece of material such as paper or cloth ■ *vti.* (**-les, -ling, -led**) BECOME OR MAKE WRINKLED to become wrinkled or puckered or make sth such as a piece of material wrinkled or puckered [14thC. Via French *coquille* 'shell' from, ultimately, Greek *kogkhē* 'conch' (source of English *conch*).] ◇ **warm the cockles of sb's heart** to give sb a feeling of well-being or sentimental contentment

cockle[2] /kók'l/ *n.* a weedy plant that belongs to the pink family, especially the corn cockle, which grows in cornfields [Pre-12thC. Origin uncertain: perhaps from assumed medieval Latin *cocculus*, literally 'small berry', from Latin *coccus* (see COCOON).]

cockleboat /kók'l bōt/ *n.* NAUT = **cockboat** [Early 17thC. *Cockle* from COCKLE[1].]

cocklebur /kók'l bur/ *n.* a coarse annual plant with prickly seed husks that attach easily to people's clothes or animals' fur. Genus: *Xanthium*. [Mid-19thC. *Cockle* from COCKLE[2].]

cockleshell /kók'l shel/ *n.* **1.** SHELL OF COCKLE a shell of a marine cockle, or any similar mollusc **2.** NAUT SMALL BOAT a small, light shallow boat

cockloft /kók loft/ *n.* a small room beneath the roof of a building

cockney /kókni/ (*plural* **-neys**) *n.* **1.** cockney, Cockney SB FROM LONDON'S EAST END sb born in London, traditionally within a two-mile radius of the bells of St Mary-le-Bow church in London's East End. Cockneys are considered to be the 'true' Londoners. **2.** cockney, Cockney LONDON DIALECT the accent or dialect of native Londoners from the East End **3.** *Aus* YOUNG AUSTRALIAN SNAPPER a young Australian snapper. Latin name: *Chrysophrys guttulatus*. [14thC. Middle English *coken* generative plural of *cok* (see COCK[1]) + obsolete *ey* 'egg', from Old English *æg*. Originally 'small or misshapen egg' (supposedly laid by a cock), 'pampered child'; hence 'town-dweller' (originally pejorative).] —**cockneyism** *n.*

cock-of-the-rock (*plural* **cocks-of-the-rock**) *n.* a tropical South American bird, the males of which have bright orange or red plumage and crests that extend over the bill. Genus: *Rupicola*. [From the bird's practice of nesting on rocks]

cockpit /kók pit/ *n.* **1.** AEROSP PILOT'S PART OF AIRCRAFT the compartment in an aircraft or spacecraft where the pilot and other crew members sit **2.** MOTOR SPORTS AREA FOR DRIVER IN RACING CAR a space for the driver in a racing car **3.** SPORTS PLACE FOR COCKFIGHTING an enclosed place where cockfights are held **4.** NAUT ENCLOSURE FOR WHEEL OR TILLER an enclosure at the stern of a ship for the wheel or tiller **5.** MIL FREQUENT BATTLEGROUND a place where many battles have been fought [Late 16thC. Originally 'pit for cockfighting', later 'place for treating wounded below decks in warship' (from the association of blood and noise), later 'well at yacht stern where helm is'.]

cockroach /kók rōch/ *n.* a nocturnal insect with a flat

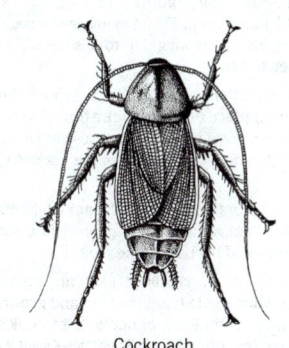
Cockroach

oval body, long antennae, and chewing mouthparts, some species of which are household pests. Order: Blattodea. [Early 17thC. From Spanish *cucaracha*, changed by assimilation with COCK and ROACH.]

cockscomb /kóks kōm/ *n.* **1.** CREST OF DOMESTIC COCK the red fleshy crest that grows on the top of a domestic cock's head **2.** PLANT WITH CREST OF RED FLOWERS a tropical plant with a broad crest or plume of orange or red flowers resembling a cockscomb, often grown as a houseplant. Latin name: *Celosia cristata*. **3.** = coxcomb n. 1

cockshot /kók shot/ *n.* = cockshy n. 2

cockshy /kók shī/ (*plural* **-shies**) *n.* (*dated*) **1.** TARGET a target or mark for throwing things in a contest **2.** THROW AT TARGET a throw at a cockshy [Early 19thC. So called because originally a cock was the target and prize; contestants had to catch the cock or break a pot containing the bird.]

cockspur /kók spur/ *n.* a spur on the foot of some male birds

cocksucker /kóksukə/ *n. US* (*taboo offensive*) **1.** OFFENSIVE TERM a highly offensive term of abuse for a man **2.** OFFENSIVE TERM sb who performs fellatio

cocksure /kok sháw/ *adj.* arrogantly confident and self-assured [Early 16thC. From *cock* as a euphemism for 'God'. Originally 'absolutely sure, safe'; later associated with the bird, regarded as swaggering in front of the hens.] —**cocksurely** *adv.* —**cocksureness** *n.*

cockswain *n.* = coxswain

cocktail /kók tayl/ *n.* **1.** MIXED BEVERAGE a drink that is made up of a mixture of different beverages, e.g. fruit juice or soda and usually alcohol, and served iced or chilled **2.** LIGHT SNACK a light appetizer before a main meal, consisting usually of seafood or fruit served with a sauce (*usually used in combination*) ○ *a prawn cocktail* **3.** MIXTURE OF THINGS a mixture of different things or elements combined together ○ *a malicious cocktail of lies and gossip* **4.** MED COMBINATION TREATMENT a combination of two or more drugs or therapeutic agents given as a single treatment ■ **cocktails** *npl.* GATHERING TO CONSUME ALCOHOLIC BEVERAGES a gathering where alcoholic beverages are consumed, sometimes with light snacks, often taking place early in the evening before another planned event ■ *adj.* SMALL extra small, designed to be eaten as a snack with the fingers or on a cocktail stick ○ *cocktail sausage* [Early 17thC. Originally 'having a tail like a cock', later 'horse with docked tail (that sticks up)' (used for carthorses), hence 'non-thoroughbred racehorse', hence 'mixture'.]

cocktail lounge *n.* a bar, sometimes a room in a large hotel, where cocktails and other drinks are served

cocktail party *n.* a party where cocktails and light snacks are served, often taking place early in the evening before another social event

cocktail stick *n.* a small pointed wooden or plastic stick on which olives or cherries are placed in cocktails, or small items of food, e.g. sausages or cubes of cheese, are served

cock-teaser, **cock-tease** *n.* an offensive term used to describe sb who makes sexual advances towards a man (*slang offensive*)

cockup /kók up/ *n.* a blunder, or piece of mismanagement (*informal*) [Mid-20thC. Formed from COCK.]

cocky[1] /kóki/ (**-ier**, **-iest**) *adj.* confident and sure of yourself to the point of being arrogant (*informal*) [Mid-16thC. From the image of a cock strutting about, apparently showing off to his hens.] —**cockily** *adv.* —**cockiness** *n.*

cocky[2] /kóki/ (*plural* **-ies**) *n. Aus* a farmer who owns a very small piece of land (**cockatoo**) (*informal*) [Late 19thC. Shortening of COCKATOO, perhaps because the farmer is thought to encroach on land as the cockatoo plunders corn.]

coco /kŏkō/ (*plural* **-cos**) *n.* = coconut [Mid-16thC. From Spanish and Portuguese, literally 'grinning face' (because of the appearance of the base of the shell).]

cocoa /kŏkō/ *n.* **1.** CHOCOLATE BASE an unsweetened brown powder made from roasted and ground cacao beans, used in making chocolate, in cooking, and as the base for a hot drink **2.** HOT DRINK MADE WITH COCOA

POWDER a hot drink made with milk or water, cocoa powder, and sugar **3.** LIGHT TO MEDIUM BROWN COLOUR a light to medium brown colour [Early 18thC. Alteration of CACAO.]

cocoa bean *n.* the bean-shaped seed of the cacao tree, used to make cocoa powder and chocolate

cocoa butter *n.* a thick oily solid obtained from cocoa beans and used in making chocolate, cosmetics, and suntan oils

coco-de-mer /kŏkō də máir/ (*plural* **cocos-de-mer** /kŏkō də máir/) *n.* **1.** LARGE FAN PALM a fan palm, now found only in nature reserves in the Seychelles, that produces the largest seed in the world. Latin name: *Lodoicea maldivica*. **2.** COCO-DE-MER NUT the edible two-lobed fruit of the coco-de-mer palm [Early 19thC. From French, literally 'coco from the sea' (because it was first known from nuts found floating in the sea).]

Coconut

coconut /kŏkə nut/ (*plural* **-nut** *or* **-nuts**), **coco** (*plural* **-cos**) *n.* **1.** HARD-SHELLED FRUIT CONTAINING SWEET JUICE the fruit of the coconut palm, consisting of a hard fibrous husk surrounding a single-seeded nut with firm white flesh and a hollow core containing sweet-tasting liquid (**coconut milk**). The flesh is eaten raw or is dried to make copra, and the husk fibres are used for matting and compost. **2.** WHITE FLESH OF COCONUT FRUIT the sweet white flesh of the coconut fruit, used widely in cooking and confectionery in the form of small dried flakes **3.** TREES = coconut palm

coconut butter *n.* solidified coconut oil used in the manufacture of soap and candles

coconut crab *n.* a large hermit crab that lives on islands in the Pacific and Indian oceans. It burrows in the ground, can climb trees, and feeds on coconuts and other vegetation as well as carrion. Latin name: *Birgus latro*.

coconut matting *n.* coarse floor matting made from the fibres that grow on coconut shells

coconut milk *n.* the sweet watery juice that is contained within a coconut and is used in drinks and cookery

coconut oil *n.* a thick sweet-smelling oil extracted from the flesh of the coconut and used widely in food and cosmetics

coconut palm *n.* a tall palm tree widely cultivated in tropical countries for its large fruit and from which beverages, oil, fibre, utensils, and thatch are produced. Latin name: *Cocos nucifera*.

cocoon /kə kóon/ *n.* **1.** ZOOL SHEATH FOR CATERPILLAR the silky covering with which a caterpillar or other insect larva encloses itself during its transition to an adult state **2.** ZOOL EGG COVERING a protective covering on the eggs of spiders, leeches, and other invertebrates **3.** ZOOL SHEATH FOR SPIDER'S PREY a sheath in which spiders wrap their prey **4.** TECH COVERING THAT PROTECTS STH FROM WATER a cover or protective spray used to seal machinery and make it waterproof, especially military equipment for storage or transport **5.** STH SIMILAR TO COCOON sth that resembles a cocoon in the way that it provides protection or a sense of safety ■ *v.* (**-coons**, **-cooning**, **-cooned**) **1.** *vt.* WRAP STH OR SB SAFELY to cover or envelop sth or sb for warmth or protection ○ *cocooned in a pile of bedclothes* **2.** *vt.* KEEP SAFE FROM STH to protect sb from unpleasantness or danger **3.** *vi. US* WITHDRAW INTO PRIVACY to withdraw into a state of personal privacy in order to escape stressful everyday life (*informal*) [Late 17thC. Via French *cocon* from, ultimately,

Latin *coccus* 'berry', from Greek *kokkos* (source of English *cochineal*).] —**cocooned** *adj.*

coco plum *n.* a tropical American and African tree, cultivated for its edible fruit that is usually eaten preserved and, in West Africa, for an oil obtained from its seeds. Latin name: *Chrysobalanus icaco*.

Cocos Islands /kŏkəss-/ group of 27 small islands in the Indian Ocean that belong to Australia, situated approximately 930 km/580 mi. southwest of Java. Population: 655 (1996). Area: 14.2 sq. km/5.5 sq. mi.

cocos wood *n.* = cocuswood n. 2

cocotte /kə kót/ *n.* **1.** PROSTITUTE a promiscuous woman or prostitute (*literary*) **2.** SMALL HEATPROOF DISH FOR COOKING FOOD a heatproof dish in which food can be cooked and served in small portions [Early 20thC. Via French *cocasse* from Latin *cucuma* 'cooking-pot'.]

co-counselling *n.* a form of counselling in which participants receive training as counsellors and work alternately as counsellor and client

cocoyam /kŏkō yam/ *n.* in West Africa, a plant with edible tubers. Genus: *Colocasia*. [Early 20thC. Origin uncertain: probably from a Caribbean English sense of COCO 'tarot root' + YAM.]

Jean Cocteau

Cocteau /kóktō/, **Jean** (1889–1963) French writer and film director. His works include the novel *Les enfants terribles* (1929) and the film *La belle et la bête* (1945).

cocuswood /kŏkəss wŏod/ (*plural* **-wood**) *n.* **1.** WEST INDIAN HARDWOOD TREE a West Indian tree that yields a hard wood. Latin name: *Brya ebenus*. **2.** WOOD OF COCUSWOOD TREE the hard wood of the cocuswood tree, which turns black with age and is used to make musical instruments, backs of brushes, and inlays [Mid-17thC. *Cocus* of unknown origin.]

Cocytus /kō kítəss, -sítəss/ *n.* one of the tributaries of the river Styx that, in Greek mythology, flowed through the underworld [From Greek *Kōkutos*, literally 'wailing']

cod[1] /kod/ (*plural* **cod** *or* **cods**) *n.* **1.** MARINE FOOD FISH a saltwater food fish that has three dorsal fins and slender feelers like whiskers (**barbels**) on its jaw and lives close to the seabed. Family: Gadidae. **2.** *ANZ* AUSTRALIAN FISH any of various fish found in fresh and salt water throughout Australia, including Murray cod (*Maccullochella peeli*) and estuary rock cod (*Epinephelus tauvina*) [14thC. Origin unknown.]

cod[2] /kod/ *n.* (*archaic*) **1.** BAG a bag **2.** SAC CONTAINING TESTES a sac of skin that contains the testes of male mammals [Old English *cod(d)*, from a prehistoric Germanic word that is also the ancestor of English *cuttlefish*.]

cod[3] *n. Ireland* MILDLY UNINTELLIGENT PERSON sb who behaves in an unintelligent or silly way ■ *vti.* (**cods**, **codding**, **codded**) *Ireland* FOOL AROUND to fool around or play a trick on sb [Late 17thC. Origin unknown.]

COD *abbr.* cash on delivery

cod., **Cod.** *abbr.* codex

coda /kŏdə/ *n.* **1.** FINAL SECTION OF MUSICAL PIECE in some pieces of music, a final section that adds dramatic energy to the work as a whole, usually through intensified rhythmic activity **2.** EXTRA TEXT an additional section at the end of a text, e.g. a literary work or speech, that is not necessary to its structure but gives additional information [Mid-18thC. Via Italian from Latin *cauda* 'tail' (source of English *cue* and *queue*).]

coddle / kódd'l/ (**-dles, -dling, -dled**) *vt.* **1. BE OVER-PROTECTIVE OF SB** to treat sb in an overprotective and indulgent way **2. COOK EGG GENTLY** to cook an egg in water just below the boiling point [Late 16thC. Origin uncertain: perhaps a variant of CAUDLE.] —**coddler** /1kód'lə/ *n.*

code /kōd/ *n.* **1. SYSTEM OF LETTERS, NUMBERS, OR SYMBOLS** a system of letters, numbers, or symbols into which normal language is converted to allow information to be communicated secretly, briefly, or electronically **2. INFORMATION SYSTEM OF LETTERS OR NUMBERS** a system of letters or numbers that gives information about sth, e.g. postal or telephone areas **3. COMPUT COMPUTER INFORMATION** a system of symbols, numbers, or signals that conveys information to a computer **4. LAW, PUBLIC ADMIN RULES AND REGULATIONS** a system of accepted laws and regulations that govern procedure or behaviour in particular circumstances or within a particular profession **5. WAY OF BEHAVING** a set of unwritten rules concerning acceptable standards of behaviour ■ *v.* (**codes, coding, coded**) **1.** *vt.* **PUT STH IN CODE** to put a message or text into code **2.** *vi.* **GENETICS PROVIDE GENETIC INFORMATION** to act as or provide the genetic information that enables a polypeptide, RNA molecule, or one of their constituent groups to be produced (*refers to codons or genes*) **3.** *vt.* **COMPUT WRITE COMPUTER PROGRAM** to write a computer program that provides instructions to a computer [Late 16thC. From, ultimately, Latin *codex* 'block of wood, block split into waxed tablets for writing on, book', hence 'set of statutes'.]

codebook /kódbŏok/ *n.* a book containing a key to a code or codes

Codeine

codeine /kṓ deen/ *n.* a white crystalline drug derived from opium, but milder in action, used as a painkiller and to relieve coughing [Mid-19thC. Coined from Greek *kōdeia* 'poppy head' + -INE.]

code name *n.* a name used to disguise the identity or nature of sb or sth, e.g. a military operation —**code-name** *vt.*

Code Napoléon /kōd na pṓlay óN/ *n.* the codification of French laws drawn up under Napoleon between 1804 and 1810 and forming the basis of modern French civil law

code of conduct *n.* a set of unwritten rules according to which people in a particular group, class, or situation are supposed to behave

code of practice *n.* a set of rules according to which people of a particular profession are expected to behave

codependency /-dənsi/, **codependence** /kṓdi péndənss/ *n.* **1. MUTUAL NEED** the dependence of two people, groups, or organisms on each other, especially when this reinforces mutually harmful behaviour patterns **2. COUNSELLING RELATIONSHIP OF MUTUAL NEED** a situation in which one person feels a need to be needed by another person, e.g. the partner of an alcoholic or a parent of a drug-addicted child —**codependent** *n., adj.*

coder /kṓdər/ *n.* **1. CONVERTER OF STH INTO CODE** sb or sth that converts texts, messages, or symbols into code **2. DEVICE TRANSFORMING SIGNALS INTO CODE** an electronic device that transforms signals into coded form

codetermination /kódi túrmi náysh'n/ *n.* cooperation between management and employees in making decisions

code word *n.* **1. SECRET WORD IDENTIFYING SB OR STH** a secret word or phrase that is used to identify a person, operation, or organization whose true identity is to be kept hidden, or is used as a password in a secret operation **2. EUPHEMISM** a word or phrase used to describe sth in a euphemistic way ○ *corporate re-engineering is often just a code word for layoffs*

codex /kṓ deks/ (*plural* **-dices** /-di seez/) *n.* a collection of ancient manuscript texts, especially of the Scriptures, in book form [Late 16thC. From Latin (see CODE).]

Codex Juris Canonici /kṓ deks jóoriss sə nónni sī/ *n.* the official code of canon law of the Roman Catholic Church since 1918, when it replaced the Corpus Juris Canonici. It was revised in 1983. [From ecclesiastical Latin, 'Code of Canon Law']

codfish /kódfish/ (*plural* **-fish** *or* **-fishes**) *n.* = **cod**[1] *n.* 1

codger /kójjər/ *n.* a man, especially a man of advanced years who is seen as slightly eccentric or amusing (*informal*) [Mid-18thC. Origin uncertain: perhaps a variant of CADGER.]

codices plural of **codex**

codicil /kṓdissil/ *n.* **1. EXTRA PART OF WILL** an additional part of a will that either modifies it or revokes part of it **2. APPENDIX TO TEXT** an appendix or supplement to a text (*formal*) [15thC. From Latin *codicillus*, diminutive of *codex* (see CODE).] —**codicillary** /kṓdi sílləri/ *adj.*

codicology /kṓdi kólləji/ *n.* the study of manuscripts [Mid-20thC. From French *codicologie*, literally 'science of books', from Latin *codic-*, stem of *codex* (see CODE).] —**codicological** /kṓdikə lójjik'l/ *adj.*

codification /kṓdifi káysh'n/ *n.* the act of arranging laws, rules, or codes of behaviour into organized systems, or any arrangement of these

codify /kṓdi fī/ (**-fies, -fying, -fied**) *vt.* to arrange things, especially laws, rules, or principles, into an organized system or code —**codifier** *n.*

codling /kódling/ (*plural* **-lings** *or* **-ling**) *n.* a small or young codfish

codling moth, **codlin moth** *n.* a small stout-bodied moth whose larvae feed on apples, pears, and other fruit. Latin name: *Laspeyresia pomonella.*

cod-liver oil *n.* an oil rich in vitamins A and D that is extracted from the liver of the codfish and is often used as a food supplement

codominant /kō dómminənt/ *adj.* **1. GENETICS WITH EQUAL GENETIC EFFECT** used to describe genes that each have equal effect in making the character they control appear in offspring. The genes for A and B blood groups are codominant and give rise to the AB blood group if they are both inherited. **2. ECOL INFLUENCING WHICH SPECIES ARE PRESENT** determining the kinds of species that exist in an ecological community —**codominance** *n.*

codon /kṓ don/ *n.* a unit in messenger RNA consisting of a set of three consecutive nucleotides, which specifies a particular amino acid in protein synthesis [Mid-20thC. Coined from CODE + -ON.]

codpiece /kód peess/ *n.* a decorative pouch attached to the crotch of breeches or hose worn by men in the 15th and 16th centuries [15thC. *Cod* from COD[2].]

co-driver *n.* sb who does a share of the driving on a car journey or in a rally

codswallop /kódz woləp/ *n., interj.* nonsense (*informal*) [Mid-20thC. Origin uncertain: perhaps literally '(small, contemptible) testicles of the codfish'; or named after Hiram Codd, inventor of bottle for carbonated drinks (*wallop* 'beer').]

Coe /kō/, **Sebastian** (*b.* 1956) British athlete and politician. He broke eight world middle-distance track records and was a Conservative MP (1992–97).

co-ed *n.* **1. SCHOOL FOR BOTH SEXES** a school where boys and girls are educated together (*informal*) **2. US WOMAN AT MIXED COLLEGE** a woman student who attends a college or university where men and women are educated together (*dated*) ■ *adj.* **EDUCATING MEN AND WOMEN TOGETHER** with both male and female students (*informal*) [Late 19thC. Shortening of COEDUCATIONAL.]

co-edition *n.* a book published by two or more publishers jointly

coeducation /kṓ eddyŏo káysh'n/ *n.* the education of both sexes together —**coeducational** *adj.* —**coeducationally** *adv.*

coef. /kṓ if/ *abbr.* coefficient

coefficient /kṓ i físh'nt/ *n.* **1. MATH NUMERICAL PART OF ALGEBRAIC TERM** the number placed before a letter that represents a variable in algebra, e.g. the '3' of '3x' in the equation '3x = 6' **2. PHYS FIGURE MEASURING PROPERTY OF SUBSTANCE** a constant that is a measure of a property of a substance [Mid-17thC. From modern Latin *coefficient-*, stem of *coefficiens* 'combining to produce a result', from Latin *efficiens*.]

coefficient of correlation *n.* = correlation coefficient

coefficient of expansion *n.* PHYS the change in length or area of a material per unit length or unit area that accompanies a change in temperature of one degree

coefficient of friction *n.* PHYS the ratio of the force needed to make two surfaces slide over each other to the force that holds them together. Symbol μ

-coel *suffix.* cavity, chamber ○ *pseudocoel* [Via modern Latin *-coela* from Greek *koilos* 'hollow'. Ultimately from an Indo-European base that is also the ancestor of English *cave* and *concave*.]

Coelacanth

coelacanth /sée'lə kanth/ *n.* a fish found off the east coast of Africa that crawls on the sea bottom using its fins to move. Coelacanths, ancient forms of which are believed to be ancestors of the vertebrates, were considered to have been extinct for 70 million years until a living species was discovered in 1938. Latin name: *Latimeria chalumnae.* [Mid-19thC. From modern Latin *Coelacanthus*, genus name, from Greek *koilos* 'hollow' + *akantha* 'spine' (because the fins of the fish have hollow spines).] —**coelacanthine** /sée'lə kán thin/ *adj.* —**coelacanthous** /-kánthəss/ *adj.*

-coele *suffix.* = **-coel**

coelentera plural of **coelenteron**

coelenterate /si léntə rayt/ *n.* a marine invertebrate animal that has an internal body cavity (**coelenteron**), e.g. sea anemones, corals, jellyfish, or comb jellies. Phyla: *Cnidaria* and *Ctenophora.* Now called **cnidarian** [Late 19thC. From modern Latin *Coelenterata*, from Greek *koilos* 'hollow' + *enteron* 'intestine'.] —**coelenteric** /sée len térrik/ *adj.*

coelenteron /si léntə ron/ (*plural* **-tera** /-tərə/) *n.* the internal body cavity of a marine invertebrate animal (**coelenterate**)

coeliac /sée'li ak/ *adj.* relating to, involving, or contained in the abdomen [Mid-17thC. Via Latin from Greek *koiliakos*, from *koilia* 'abdomen', from *koilos* 'hollow'.]

coeliac disease *n.* a disorder caused by a sensitivity to gluten that makes the digestive system unable to deal with fat. Symptoms include diarrhoea and anaemia.

coelom /sée'ləm, -lōm/ (*plural* **-loms** *or* **-lomata** /si lṓmətə/) *n.* the cavity between the body wall and the gut of many animals, formed when the embryonic mesoderm is divided into two layers [Late 19thC. Via German *Koelom* from Greek *koilōma* 'a hollow'.] —**coelomic** /si lómmik/ *adj.*

coelomate /sée'lə mayt, si lṓmit/ *adj.* having a cavity between the body wall and the digestive tract —**coelomate** *n.*

coelostat /sée'lə stat/ *n.* an instrument with a mirror that rotates parallel to the Earth's axis in order to reflect light from a celestial body onto a second mirror aimed at a fixed telescope [Late 19thC. Coined from Latin *caelum* 'sky' + -STAT.]

coemption /kō émpsh'n/ *n.* the purchase of all available supplies of a particular commodity [14thC. From the Latin stem *coemption-*, literally 'buying up' from, ultimately, *emere* 'to take or buy' (source of English *exempt*).]

Coen /koon/, **Jan Pieterszoon** (1587–1629) Dutch colonial administrator. He secured the East Indies for Holland and founded its capital in Batavia, present-day Jakarta (1618).

coen- *prefix.* = **coeno-** (*used before vowels*)

coeno- *prefix.* general, common ○ *coenocyte* [From Greek *koinos*. Ultimately from an Indo-European base meaning 'together', which is also the ancestor of English *com-* and *contra-*.]

coenobite /séénō bīt/, **cenobite** *n.* sb who belongs to a convent, monastery, or other religious community [15thC. Via French *cénobite* or ecclesiastical Latin *coenobita*, from, ultimately, Greek *koinobion*, literally 'common life'.]

coenocyte /séénō sīt/ *n.* a cell, part, or organism that contains many nuclei not separated by cell walls, e.g. the threads (**hyphae**) of many fungi or the bodies of some algae —**coenocytic** /séénō síttik/ *adj.*

coenzyme /kō én zīm/ *n.* a non-protein compound or molecule that combines with a protein (**apoenzyme**) to form an active enzyme

coenzyme A *n.* a complex compound derived from vitamin B₅ that acts together with specific enzymes in the metabolism of carbohydrates and fats

coenzyme Q *n.* = ubiquinone

coequal /kō éékwəl/ *adj.* EQUAL TO SB OR STH of the same size or belonging to the same rank or status ■ *n.* SB OF SAME STATUS sb who belongs to the same rank or status as another [14thC. From Latin *coaequalis* 'of the same age', from *aequalis* (see EQUAL).] —**coequality** /kō i kwólləti/ *n.* —**coequally** /kō éékwəli/ *adv.* —**coequalness** /-éékwəlnəss/ *n.*

coerce /kō úrss/ (**-erces, -ercing, -erced**) *vt.* to force sb to do sth that he or she does not want to do [15thC. From Latin *coercere*, literally 'to shut in together', from *arcere* 'to shut in' (source of English *arcane* and *exercise*).] —**coercer** *n.* —**coercible** *adj.*

coercion /kō úrsh'n/ *n.* **1.** FORCING SB TO DO STH the use of force or threats to make people do things against their will **2.** FORCE USED TO COMPEL SB force used to make sb do sth against his or her will —**coercionary** *adj.* —**coercionist** *n., adj.*

coercive /kō úrssiv/ *adj.* using force, or having the power to use force, to make people do things against their will —**coercively** *adv.* —**coerciveness** *n.*

coercive force *n.* the magnetic force necessary to demagnetize a substance

coercivity /kō ur sívvəti/ *n.* = coercive force

coessential /kō i sénsh'l/ *adj.* with the same essence or nature [Late 15thC. From ecclesiastical Latin *co-essentialis* 'of the same substance' (used as an attribute of the persons of the Trinity), from late Latin *essentialis* (see ESSENTIAL).] —**coessentiality** /kō i senshi álləti/ *n.* —**coessentially** /kō i sénshəli/ *adv.* —**coessentialness** /-sh'lnəss/ *n.*

coetaneous /kō i táyni əss/ *adj.* having the same age, duration, or period (*formal*) [Early 17thC. From Latin *coaetaneus*, literally 'of the same age', from *aetas* 'age'.] —**coetaneously** *adv.* —**coetaneousness** *n.*

coeternal /kō i túrn'l/ *adj.* existing together throughout eternity (*formal*) [14thC. From ecclesiastical Latin *coaeternus*, from Latin *aeternus* (see ETERNAL).] —**coeternally** *adv.*

coeternity /kō i túrnəti/ *n.* eternal existence with sb or sth else [Late 16thC. From late Latin *coaeternitas*, from Latin *aeternitas* (see ETERNITY).]

Coetzee /kúrt zee/, **J. M.** (*b.* 1940) South African novelist. His works, reflecting turmoil in his homeland, include *The Life and Times of Michael K* (1983), which won Britain's Booker Prize. Full name **John Michael Coetzee**

coeval /kō éev'l/ *adj.* having the same age, duration, or date of origin (*formal*) [Early 17thC. From late Latin *coaevus*, from Latin *aevum* 'age', from Greek *aion* (source of English *aeon* and *age*).] —**coevality** /kō i válləti/ *n.* —**coevally** /kō éevəli/ *adv.*

coevolution /kō éevə loósh'n/ *n.* the joint development of two or more interdependent species, e.g. parasites and the animals they live on, such that they adapt to external changes together —**coevolutionary** *adj.*

coevolve /kō i vólv/ (**-volves, -volving, -volved**) *vi.* to evolve and adapt together, e.g. in the way that parasites and host organisms do (*refers to two different species*)

coexist /kō ig zíst/ (**-ists, -isting, -isted**) *vi.* **1.** BE IN EXISTENCE TOGETHER to exist together at the same time and in the same place **2.** LIVE TOGETHER PEACEFULLY to occupy the same place in a peaceful way —**coexistence** *n.* —**coexistent** *adj.*

coextend /kō ik sténd/ (**-tends, -tending, -tended**) *vti.* to extend or make things extend in or through the same space or length of time —**coextension** /kō ik sténsh'n/ *n.*

coextensive /kō ik sténssiv/ *adj.* sharing the same limits, boundaries, or scope —**coextensively** *adv.*

cofactor /kō faktər/ *n.* a substance, e.g. a coenzyme or metal ion, that acts with and is essential to the activity of an enzyme

C of C *abbr.* chamber of commerce

C of E *abbr.* Church of England

Coffee

coffee /kóffi/ *n.* **1.** STRONG CAFFEINE-RICH DRINK a drink made from ground or processed coffee beans that contains caffeine and has a mildly stimulating effect. Coffee may be drunk hot, often with cream or milk and sweetened with sugar, or iced. **2.** BEANS FOR MAKING COFFEE the beans used to make coffee. They are either roasted and ground, or made into powder or granules that dissolve in hot water. **3.** BUSH YIELDING COFFEE BEANS a bush cultivated as a source of the beans used in making coffee. Genus: *Coffea*. **4.** PALE BROWN COLOUR a pale brown colour, like that of milky coffee [Late 16thC. Via Turkish *kahve* from, ultimately, Arabic *kahwa*.]

coffee bag *n.* a small porous bag containing ground coffee powder that is steeped in boiling water to make coffee

coffee bar *n.* a small café where coffee, other drinks, and snacks are served

coffee bean *n.* a seed of the coffee tree that is roasted and ground, or processed in other ways, to make coffee

coffee break *n.* a short break for coffee or other refreshment

coffee cup *n.* a cup intended for drinking coffee, usually smaller than a teacup but sometimes much larger and generally with a saucer underneath

coffee grinder *n.* an electrical or hand-operated device for grinding roasted coffee beans

coffee mill *n.* a device for grinding roasted coffee beans to make coffee

coffee morning *n.* an informal social gathering where coffee and snacks are served, often to raise money for charity or a cause

coffeepot /kóffi pot/ *n.* a tall narrow pot with a curved spout and lid designed for serving or brewing coffee

coffee shop *n.* a place where coffee and snacks are served and coffee beans are sold

coffee table *n.* a low table, for use in a living room

coffee-table book *n.* a large, typically expensive book with lavish illustrations, usually used for display or casual perusal rather than reading

coffer /kóffər/ *n.* **1.** STRONGBOX a strong chest or box used for keeping valuables or money safe **2.** ARCHIT CEILING PANEL an ornamental sunken panel in a ceiling or dome **3.** CONSTR = cofferdam *n.* 1 ■ **coffers** *npl.* FUNDS a supply or store of money, often belonging to an organization ■ *vt.* (**-fers, -fering, -fered**) **1.** STORE STH VALUABLE IN STRONGBOX to put money or valuables in a coffer **2.** DECORATE CEILING WITH COFFERS to decorate sth, especially a ceiling, with coffers [13thC. Via French *coffre* from Latin *cophinus* (see COFFIN).]

cofferdam /kóffər dam/ *n.* **1.** CONSTR UNDERWATER CONSTRUCTION AREA a temporary watertight structure that is pumped dry to enclose an area underwater and allow construction work on a ship, bridge, or rig to be carried out **2.** BUFFER ON SHIP an empty space that acts as a protective barrier between two floors or bulkheads on a ship

coffin /kóffin/ *n.* **1.** BOX FOR CORPSE a long oblong container, usually made of wood, in which a dead body is placed for burial or cremation **2.** PART OF HOOF the horny part of a horse's hoof that contains the coffin bone **3.** PRINTING TYPE OF PRINTING FRAME a frame that holds electrotype or stereotype printing plates ■ *vt.* (**-fins, -fining, -fined**) PUT STH IN A COFFIN to place sb or sth in a coffin or in sth resembling a coffin [14thC. From Old French *cof(f)in* 'little basket or case', from Latin *cophinus* 'basket', from Greek *kophinos*.]

coffin block *n.* = coffin *n.* 3

coffin bone *n.* the main bone in a horse's hoof

coffin nail *n.* a cigarette (*dated slang*)

Coffs Harbour /kófs-/ coastal town in eastern New South Wales, Australia, which is a tourist resort and fruit-growing centre. Population: 22,177 (1996).

C of S *abbr.* chief of staff

Cog

cog[1] /kog/ *n.* **1.** TOOTH ENGAGING WITH WHEEL FOR MOTION a projection on the edge of a gearwheel that engages with corresponding parts on another wheel to transfer motion from one wheel to the other **2.** = cogwheel [13thC. Origin uncertain: probably of Scandinavian origin.] —**cogged** *adj.*

cog[2] /kog/ (**cogs, cogging, cogged**) *vti.* to cheat in a gambling game by loading the dice (*slang*) [Mid-16thC. Origin unknown.]

cog[3] /kog/ *n.* TIMBER BEAM JOINT a piece that projects from the end of a timber beam and is designed to fit into an opening in another beam to form a joint ■ *vt.* (**cogs, cogging, cogged**) JOIN TIMBER BEAMS to join two timber beams with a cog [Early 19thC. Origin uncertain: probably a variant of *cock* 'to pamper', shortening of COCKER[2].]

cog. *abbr.* GRAM cognate

cogency /kójənssi/ *n.* the power of an argument or piece of reasoning to convince sb on an intellectual and rational level (*formal*)

cogeneration /kō jenə ráysh'n/ *n.* the production of two types of energy, such as heat or electricity, from one source in such a way that both are usable rather than one being treated as waste energy —**cogenerator** /kō jénnə raytə/ *n.*

cogent /kṓjənt/ *adj.* forceful and convincing to the intellect and reason ○ *a cogent argument* [Mid-17thC. From Latin *cogent-*, present participle stem of *cogere* 'to drive together', from *agere* 'to drive' (source of English *agent*).] —**cogently** *adv.*

WORD KEY: SYNONYMS

See Synonyms at ***valid***.

cogitate /kójji tayt/ (**-tates, -tating, -tated**) *vti.* to think deeply and carefully about sth (*formal*) [Late 16thC. From, ultimately, Latin *cogitare*, literally 'to disturb together', from *agitare* 'to disturb' (see AGITATE).]

cogitation /kójji táysh'n/ *n.* (*formal*) **1.** DEEP THOUGHT deep thought or consideration that sb gives to a particular problem or subject **2.** ACT OF DEEP THOUGHT an act of thinking deeply about sth

cogitative /kójjitətiv/ *adj.* thinking deeply about or seriously considering sth (*formal*) —**cogitatively** *adv.* —**cogitativeness** *n.*

cognac /kón yak/ *n.* a high-quality brandy distilled from white grapes in Cognac, western France

Cognac /kón yak/ town in Charente Department, in the Poitou-Charentes administrative region of western France, about 97 km/60 mi. north of Bordeaux. It is known for the brandy distilled there. Population: 19,932 (1990).

cognate /kóg nayt/ *adj.* **1.** LING DERIVED FROM SAME ROOT OR ORIGIN having the same linguistic root or origin **2.** WITH SAME ANCESTOR related by blood or having an ancestor in common (*formal*) ■ *n.* **1.** LING WORD WITH SAME ORIGIN AS ANOTHER one of two or more words that have the same root or origin **2.** SB IN SAME FAMILY sb who is related by blood to sb else or shares a common ancestor with sb else [14thC. From Latin *cognatus*, literally 'born together', from *gnatus*, past participle of *(g)nasci* 'to be born' (source of English *native*).] —**cognation** /kog náysh'n/ *n.*

cognate object *n.* a noun that functions as the object of a verb that is from the same etymological root, as in 'to dream a dream' or 'to think a thought'

cognisable *adj.* = **cognizable**

cognisance *n.* = **cognizance**

cognisant *adj.* = **cognizant**

cognition /kog nísh'n/ *n.* **1.** ABILITY TO ACQUIRE KNOWLEDGE the mental faculty or process of acquiring knowledge by the use of reasoning, intuition or perception **2.** KNOWLEDGE ACQUIRED knowledge that is acquired through processes such as reasoning, intuition or perception [15thC. From the Latin stem *cognition-*, from *cognoscere* 'to get to know', from *(g)noscere* 'to know' (see NOTION).] —**cognitional** *adj.*

cognitive /kógnitiv/ *adj.* **1.** CONCERNED WITH ACQUISITION OF KNOWLEDGE relating to the process of acquiring knowledge by the use of reasoning, intuition, or perception **2.** RELATING TO THOUGHT relating to thought processes [Late 16thC. From medieval Latin *cognitivus*, from Latin *cognoscere* (see COGNITION).] —**cognitively** *adv.*

cognitive dissonance *n.* a state of psychological conflict or anxiety resulting from a contradiction between a person's simultaneously held beliefs or attitudes

cognitive map *n.* a map of three-dimensional space maintained in the brain

cognitive psychology *n.* the branch of psychology concerned with the study of mental states

cognitive science *n.* the scientific study of knowledge and how it is acquired, combining elements of philosophy, psychology, linguistics, anthropology, and artificial intelligence

cognitive therapy *n.* a treatment of psychiatric disorders such as anxiety or depression that encourages patients to confront and challenge the distorted way of thinking that characterizes their disorder

cognitivism /kógnitivizzəm/ *n.* the theory that moral judgments are statements of fact and can therefore be classed as true or false

cognizable /kógnizəb'l/, **cognisable** *adj.* **1.** ABLE TO BE KNOWN able to be known or perceived by the human mind (*formal*) **2.** LAW WITHIN LAW COURT'S JURISDICTION falling within the jurisdiction of a particular court of law and therefore able to be tried by that court —**cognizably** *adv.*

cognizance /kógnizənss/, **cognisance** *n.* **1.** KNOWLEDGE knowledge or awareness of sth (*formal*) **2.** SB'S SCOPE OF KNOWLEDGE the extent or range of what sb can know and understand (*formal*) **3.** COURT'S RIGHT TO DEAL WITH STH the right of a court of law to deal with a particular matter **4.** TAKING NOTICE OF A FACT notice of a fact or facts taken by a court of law **5.** HERALDRY DISTINGUISHING SIGN a badge or other sign that is worn to distinguish the wearer [14thC. Via Old French *conis(s)aunce* from, ultimately, Latin *cognoscere* (see COGNITION).]

cognizant /kógnizənt/, **cognisant** *adj.* being fully aware or having knowledge of sth (*formal*)

WORD KEY: SYNONYMS

See Synonyms at ***aware***.

cognize /kóg nīz/ (**-nizes, -nizing, -nized**), **cognise** (**-nises, -nising, -nised**) *vt.* to become aware of or know sth (*formal*) [Mid-17thC. Back-formation from COGNIZANCE, modelled on *recognizance, recognize*.] —**cognizer** *n.*

cognomen /kog nṓ men/ (*plural* **-nomens** *or* **-nomina** /kog nómminə/) *n.* **1.** NICKNAME a nickname or name that describes sb, e.g. 'Ethelred the Unready' (*formal*) **2.** HIST ROMAN SURNAME a surname or family name, especially the third name given to a citizen of ancient Rome, e.g., 'Cicero' in 'Marcus Tullius Cicero' [Early 17thC. From Latin, literally 'added name', from *(g)nomen* 'name' (source of English *noun*).] —**cognominal** /kog nómminəl/ *adj.*

cognoscenti /kónnyōshénti, kógnə-/ (*singular* **-te** /-shéntay/) *npl.* people who have a refined and superior knowledge of a subject, especially the arts [Mid-18thC. From Italian, literally 'person who knows', a Latinized form of *conoscente*, from Latin *cognoscent-*, present participle stem of *cognoscere* (see COGNITION).]

cogon /kṓ gōn/ *n.* a coarse tall grass used, especially in the Philippines, as thatching. Genus: *Imperata*. [Late 19thC. Via Spanish from Tagalog *kúgon*.]

cog railway *n.* = **rack railway**

cogwheel /kóg weel/ *n.* a wheel with a series of projections around the rim that enable it to engage with projections on another wheel or rack to create traction and so produce motion

cohabit /kō hábbit/ (**-its, -iting, -ited**) *vi.* to live together, especially without being formally married (*formal*) [Mid-16thC. From Late Latin *cohabitare*, from *habitare* 'to dwell', literally 'to have usually' (see INHABIT).] —**cohabitant** *n.* —**cohabitee** /kṓ habi tée/ *n.* —**cohabiter** /kō hábbitər/ *n.*

cohabitation /kṓ habi táysh'n/ *n.* the state or practice of living with another person, especially without being formally married (*formal*) —**cohabitational** *adj.*

cohen /kṓ in/ (*plural* **-hens** *or* **-hanim** /kṓ ə neem/), **kohen** *n.* in Judaism, a person recognized as a descendant of Aaron. The cohens were priests in the Temple in ancient Jerusalem, and a male identified as a cohen still retains certain obligations in Orthodox Judaism today.

Cohen /kṓ in/, **Leonard** (*b.* 1934) Canadian poet, novelist, singer, and songwriter. His albums include *The Songs of Leonard Cohen* (1967) and *I'm Your Man* (1988).

cohere /kō héer/ (**-heres, -hering, -hered**) *vi.* **1.** STICK TOGETHER to stick or hold together in a mass that is not easily separated (*formal*) **2.** BE LOGICALLY CONSISTENT to be logically consistent so that all the separate parts fit together and add up to a harmonious or believable whole (*formal*) **3.** PHYS BE HELD TOGETHER BY MOLECULAR FORCES to be held together by the molecular forces of cohesion [Mid-16thC. From Latin *cohaerere*, from *haerere* 'to stick' (source of English *adhere*).]

coherence /kō héeranss/, **coherency** *n.* **1.** LOGICAL OR AESTHETIC CONSISTENCY the quality of being logically or aesthetically consistent, with all separate parts fitting together to form a harmonious or credible whole **2.** PHYS = **cohesion** *n.* 2

coherent /kō héerənt/ *adj.* **1.** LOGICALLY OR AESTHETICALLY CONSISTENT logically or aesthetically consistent and holding together as a harmonious or credible whole **2.** SPEAKING LOGICALLY able to speak clearly and logically ○ *He was so confused and dazed he was barely coherent.* **3.** STICKING TOGETHER being able to hold together to form an inseparable mass (*formal*) **4.** PHYS DESCRIBING ELECTROMAGNETIC WAVES used to describe electromagnetic waves that have the same wavelength and a fixed phase relationship. Coherent light is produced by lasers. **5.** FORMING UNITS WITHOUT INTRODUCING CONSTANTS forming a system of units, such as SI units, in which the product or quotient of two units gives the unit of the derived quantity —**coherently** *adv.*

cohesion /kō héezh'n/ *n.* **1.** STICKING OR WORKING TOGETHER the state or condition of joining or working together to form a united whole, or the tendency to do this **2.** PHYS MOLECULAR ATTRACTION the force of attraction by which the molecules of a solid or liquid tend to remain together [Mid-17thC. From Latin *cohaes-*, past participle stem of *cohaerere* (see COHERE).]

cohesive /kō héessiv/ *adj.* sticking, holding, or working together to form a united whole ○ *She had welded the team into a cohesive unit.* [Early 18thC. From Latin *cohaes-*, present participle stem of *cohaerere* (see COHERE).] —**cohesively** *adv.* —**cohesiveness** *n.*

coho /kṓhō/ (*plural* **-hos** *or* **-ho**) *n.* = **coho salmon** [Mid-19thC. Origin unknown.]

cohort /kṓ hawrt/ *n.* **1.** HIST UNIT OF ROMAN ARMY an ancient Roman military unit that formed one tenth of a legion and that consisted of 300 to 600 men **2.** GROUP OF PEOPLE a united group of people **3.** *US* SUPPORTER a supporter, accomplice, or associate of a leader, especially one to whom special treatment and preference is given (*disapproving*) **4.** SOLDIERS a group of soldiers or warriors **5.** STATS GROUP WITH STATISTICAL SIMILARITIES a group of people sharing a common factor, e.g. the same age or the same income bracket, especially in a statistical survey [15thC. From, ultimately, the Latin stem *cohort-*, literally 'enclosure', thus 'people within an enclosure', hence 'company of infantry', variant of *cort-*.]

WORD KEY: USAGE

What is a **cohort**? The common plural use of ***cohorts*** to mean 'people banded together in a cause' has given rise to an erroneous singular use in which a ***cohort*** is a single assistant or supporter: *His most trusted cohort was an Englishman, David Hall (The Independent).* This use, which is more common in American English, is probably influenced by the coincidence of the first syllable with the prefix *co-*.

coho salmon /kṓ hō/ *n.* a small Pacific salmon with light-coloured flesh. The coho salmon has been successfully introduced in the Great Lakes of North America and other inland waters. Latin name: *Oncorhynchus kisutch.*

cohune /kō hóon/ *n.* a Central American palm with feathery leaves that produces a nut yielding an oil similar to coconut oil, often used in soaps and cosmetics. Latin name: *Orbignya cohune.* [Mid-18thC. From Miskito.]

coif *n.* /koyf/ **1.** TYPE OF SKULLCAP FOR WOMEN a close-fitting linen cap worn by women in the Middle Ages, and now worn by some nuns under their veils **2.** LAWYER'S SKULLCAP a close-fitting white cap worn in the past by English serjeants-at-law (*archaic*) **3.** LEATHER SKULLCAP a thick, close-fitting leather cap formerly worn under a hood of chain mail ■ *vt.* /kwaaf/ (**coifs, coifing, coifed**) **1.** COVER HEAD WITH COIF to cover sb's head with a coif or with sth like a coif **2.** ARRANGE HAIR to arrange or style sb's hair (*formal*) [14thC. Via Old French *coife* 'headdress' from late Latin *cofia* 'helmet', ultimately from prehistoric Germanic.]

coiffeur /kwaa fúr/ (*plural* **-feurs**) *n.* a male hairdresser (*formal or humorous*) [Mid-19thC. From French, ultimately from Old French *coife* (see COIF).]

coiffeuse /kwaa fúrz/ (*plural* **-feuses** /kwaa fúrz/) *n.* a female hairdresser (*formal or humorous*) [Late 18thC. From French, feminine of COIFFEUR.]

coiffure /kwaa fyóor/ *n.* SB'S HAIRSTYLE the way sb wears his or her hair (*formal or humorous*) ■ *vt.* (**-fures, -furing, -fured**) STYLE SB'S HAIR to style or arrange sb's hair (*formal or humorous*) [Mid-17thC. From French, where it was formed from *coiffer* 'to arrange the hair', ultimately from Old French *coife* (see COIF).] —**coiffured** *adj.*

coign of vantage /kóyn-/ *n.* a good position from which to be able to observe sb or sth or to take action (*literary*) [*Coign* is a variant of COIN or QUOIN]

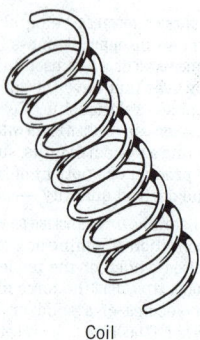

Coil

coil /koyl/ *n.* **1.** SERIES OF LOOPS a series of connected loops into which sth has been wound or gathered **2.** LOOP one of a series of loops into which sth has been wound or gathered **3.** SPIRAL sth that curls or is curled into a spiral shape **4.** PIPES ARRANGED IN ROWS OR SPIRAL a series of pipes arranged in rows or in a spiral, e.g. in a radiator or condenser **5.** ELEC ENG WIRE SPIRAL FOR ELECTRIC CURRENT a spiral of wire through which an electric current is passed to create a magnetic field or to function as an inductor **6.** ELEC ENG DEVICE SUPPLYING ELECTRICITY TO SPARKING PLUGS a device that supplies a high voltage to the sparking plugs in an internal-combustion engine **7.** MED CONTRACEPTIVE DEVICE a coil-shaped device made of plastic or metal that is placed inside the womb to prevent a woman from becoming pregnant **8.** ROLL OF STAMPS a roll of postage stamps dispensed by a vending machine ■ *v.* (**coils, coiling, coiled**) **1.** *vti.* WIND STH INTO LOOPS to wind sth into a series of connected loops or form a series of connected loops ○ *The rope had coiled itself around the propeller.* **2.** *vi.* CURVE OR BEND to move in a curving, sinuous way [Early 16thC. Via Old French *coillir* 'to gather' from Latin *colligere* (see COLLECT).] — **coiler** *n.*

coil pot *n.* a pot formed from a structure of coils or ropes of clay laid one on top of the other in a spiral

Coimbatore /kóymbə táwr/ industrial town and administrative headquarters of Coimbatore district, Tamil Nadu state, southeastern India. Population: 816,000 (1991).

Coimbra /kwímbrə, kweéNbrə/ historic city and capital of Coimbra District in west-central Portugal. Population: 96,140 (1991).

coin /koyn/ *n.* **1.** PIECE OF METAL MONEY a usually circular flat piece of metal stamped with its value as money **2.** METAL MONEY money in the form of coins rather than banknotes or cheques **3.** PAPER OR METAL MONEY money in whatever form, as opposed to such things as cheques ■ *vt.* (**coins, coining, coined**) **1.** MINT COINS to make a coin or coins **2.** MAKE METAL INTO COINS to make a metal, e.g. gold or silver, into coins **3.** CREATE EXPRESSION to invent or devise a word or phrase ■ *adj.* COIN-OPERATED requiring a coin or coins to be inserted to make it operate (*usually used in combination*) [14thC. From Old French *coin(g)*, literally 'wedge, cornerstone', later 'die (usually wedge-shaped) for stamping coins', from Latin *cuneus* 'wedge'.] — **coiner** *n.* ◇ **coin it (in)** to earn a great deal of money (*informal*) ◇ **the other side of the coin** the contrasting or contrary aspect of sth

coinage /kóynij/ *n.* **1.** COINS currency in the form of coins **2.** CURRENCY a system or type of coins in use as currency ○ *decimal coinage* **3.** MAKING OF METAL MONEY the act or process of minting coins **4.** INVENTION OF NEW WORD OR PHRASE the invention of a new word or phrase **5.** NEW WORD OR PHRASE a newly used word or phrase ○ *'Cyberspace' was a popular coinage of the 1980s.*

coin box *n.* a box into which coins are inserted to get sth from a coin-operated machine

coincide /kó in síd/ (**-cides, -ciding, -cided**) *vi.* **1.** HAPPEN AT SAME TIME to happen at or around the same time **2.** BE SAME IN POSITION OR FORM to occupy the same place or be exactly alike in position or form **3.** AGREE to agree exactly [Early 18thC. From medieval Latin *coincidere*, literally 'to fall upon together', from Latin *incidere* 'fall upon', from *cadere* 'to fall' (see CADENCE).]

coincidence /kō ínssidənss/ *n.* **1.** CHANCE HAPPENING sth that happens by chance in a surprising or re-

markable way **2.** HAPPENING WITHOUT PLANNING the fact of happening by chance ○ *It was pure coincidence that we met.* **3.** HAVING IDENTICAL FEATURES the fact or condition of happening at the same time or place or being identical (*formal*)

coincident /kō ínssidənt/ *adj.* (*formal*) **1.** SHARING SAME PLACE OR TIME happening at the same time or occupying the same position in space **2.** AGREEING EXACTLY being in exact agreement or matching —**coincidently** *adv.*

coincidental /kō ínssi dént'l/ *adj.* **1.** HAPPENING BY CHANCE happening by chance rather than intentionally **2.** OCCURRING AT SAME TIME happening or existing at the same time —**coincidentally** *adv.*

Cointreau /kwóntrō/ *tdmk.* a trademark for a colourless orange-flavoured liqueur

coir /kóyə/ *n.* a kind of coarse fibre that comes from the husk of the coconut and is used to make matting and rope [Late 16thC. From Malayalam *kayaru* 'cord, coir'.]

coition /kō ísh'n/ *n.* = **coitus** [Mid-16thC. From the Latin stem *coition-*, from *coire* (see COITUS).]

coitus /kṓ itəss/ *n.* sexual intercourse (*formal or technical*) [Mid-19thC. From Latin, past participle of *coire*, literally 'to go together', from *ire* 'to go'.] —**coital** *adj.* —**coitally** *adv.*

coitus interruptus /-íntə rúptəss/ *n.* during sexual intercourse, the deliberate withdrawal of the penis from the vagina before semen is ejaculated, used as a method of contraception [From modern Latin, 'interrupted coitus']

coke[1] /kōk/ *n.* CARBON FUEL a solid residue consisting mainly of carbon, left after the volatile elements have been driven from bituminous coal or other petroleum material. Coke is used as a fuel and in steel-making. ■ *vti.* (**cokes, coking, coked**) CHANGE INTO COKE to change sth, e.g. bituminous coal, into coke, or to become coke or like coke [Mid-17thC. Origin unknown.]

coke[2] /kōk/ *n.* cocaine used as an illicit drug (*slang*) [Early 20thC. Contraction.]

Coke /kōk/ *tdmk.* a trademark for a cola-flavoured soft drink

cokehead /kṓk hed/ *n.* sb who takes cocaine frequently or is addicted to it (*slang*)

col /kol/ *n.* **1.** LOW POINT OF MOUNTAIN RIDGE a low point in a ridge of mountains, often forming a pass between two peaks **2.** REGION OF LOW ATMOSPHERIC PRESSURE a pattern of atmospheric pressure distribution that develops between two anticyclones and two depressions arranged alternately, characterized by light variable winds and often thundery weather in summer and foggy conditions in winter [Mid-19thC. Via French from Latin *collum* 'neck'.]

COL *abbr.* **1.** cost of living **2.** computer-oriented language

col. *abbr.* **1.** college **2.** colony **3.** colour **4.** column

Col. *abbr.* **1.** BIBLE Colossians **2.** Columbia **3.** Columbian **4.** Colonel **5.** **Col., Colo.** Colorado

col-[1] *prefix* = **colo-** (*used before vowels*)

col-[2] *prefix* = **com-** (*used before l*)

cola[1] /kṓlə/, **kola** *n.* **1.** TYPE OF FIZZY DRINK a sweet carbonated drink that is flavoured with cola nuts **2.** cola, kola TROPICAL TREE BEARING COLA NUTS a tropical evergreen tree cultivated for its reddish seeds (**cola nuts**). Genus: *Cola*. [Early 17thC. From Temni *k'ola* 'cola nut'.]

cola[2] plural of **colon**

Colac /kṓ lak/ town in central Victoria, Australia, that is an agricultural and pastoral centre. Population: 9,793 (1996).

colander /kúlləndər/ *n.* a bowl-shaped dish with holes in it, used for draining food that has been cooked in water or for washing vegetables or fruit [14thC. Origin uncertain: perhaps via Old Provençal *colador* from, ultimately, Latin *colare* 'to strain', from *colum* 'sieve' (source of English *percolate*).]

cola nut, **kola nut** *n.* the small hard seed of the cola tree, which contains caffeine and theobromine and is used in carbonated drinks and medicines

Colander

colatitude /kō látti tyood/ *n.* the difference between a latitude and 90°

Colbert /kól bair/, **Jean-Baptiste** (1619–83) French statesman. He reformed the French economy as Louis XIV's comptroller general of finance from 1665.

colcannon /kəl kánnən/ *n.* an Irish dish made of cabbage and potatoes boiled and mashed together and served with butter or cream [Late 18thC. Origin uncertain: perhaps from COLE, or Irish *cál ceannan*, literally 'white-headed cabbage'.]

Colchester /kólchistər/ historic town in Essex, England. Population: 141,100 (1991).

colchicine /kólchi seen, kólk-/ *n.* a poisonous pale yellow extract obtained from autumn crocus plants, used in plant breeding to inhibit cell division and cause chromosome doubling, and in medicine to treat gout. Formula: $C_{22}H_{25}NO_6$.

colchicum /kólchikəm, kólk-/ *n.* a European flowering bulb with pink or white flowers that appear separately from the leaves, especially in the autumn. Genus: *Colchicum*. [Late 16thC. Via Latin, from Greek *kolkhikon* 'product of Colchis', ultimately from *Kolkhis* 'Colchis' (east of the Black Sea), legendary home of the sorceress Medea; the plant was considered poisonous.]

cold /kōld/ *adj.* **1.** AT LOW TEMPERATURE at or with a low, relatively low, uncomfortably low, or unusually low temperature ○ *The weather turned colder.* ○ *a cold drink* **2.** MAKING PLACE SEEM COOLER giving a place a feeling of coolness rather than warmth ○ *blue is a cold colour* **3.** COOK COOKED HOT THEN COOLED cooked or prepared as a hot food and then cooled ○ *Serve the pie cold, with ice cream.* **4.** TACITURN AND EMOTIONLESS showing no emotion, sympathy, or kindness **5.** UNFRIENDLY AND UNCARING feeling or exhibiting no friendship or sense of caring **6.** STRONG BUT CONTROLLED intense but expressed or shown in a controlled way ○ *cold fury* **7.** SEXUALLY FRIGID giving or feeling no sexual response **8.** HARD TO FOLLOW no longer recent or fresh and so difficult to track or follow ○ *The trail had gone cold.* **9.** NOT NEAR OBJECT OF SEARCH not close to the correct answer or to sth being searched for (*informal*) **10.** DEAD dead, especially from a long time before **11.** METALL PROCESSED AT LOW TEMPERATURE processed at a temperature below that at which recrystallization takes place ■ *n.* **1.** MED VIRAL INFECTION OF NOSE AND THROAT a viral infection of the nose, throat, and bronchial tubes, characterized by coughing, sneezing, headaches, and nasal congestion **2.** COLD WEATHER low-temperature weather or conditions ○ *The cold made me shiver.* **3.** CONDITION CAUSED BY LOW TEMPERATURE the state of being subjected to low temperatures, or the condition caused by being subjected to low temperatures ■ *adv.* **1.** EXTEMPORANEOUSLY without any preparation ○ *sang the part cold* **2.** US, Can COMPLETELY completely and without any possibility of a change of mind ○ *turned the proposal down cold* [Old English *cald, ceald*. Ultimately from an Indo-European word that is also the ancestor of English *chill* and *cool*. Perhaps originally a past participle meaning 'cooled'.] —**coldness** *n.* ◇ **left out in the cold** ignored or denied benefits that other people are getting ◇ **out cold** unconscious or in a deep sleep ◇ **blow hot and cold** to have wide extremes of attitude or mood ◇ **catch a cold** to experience financial loss (*informal*) ◇ **the cold light of day** conditions when things are seen for what they really are rather than being seen in an unrealistically favourable light ◇ **come** *or* **be brought in from the cold** to be allowed to take part in sth after being previously excluded ◇ **leave sb cold** to fail to impress or excite sb

cold-blooded /-blúddid/ *adj.* **1.** ZOOL WITH VARYING BODY TEMPERATURE used to describe an animal with an internal body temperature that varies according to the temperature of the surroundings **2.** LACKING IN PITY OR WARMTH showing a total lack of kindness, pity, or care for sb's suffering —**cold-bloodedly** *adv.* —**cold-bloodedness** *n.*

coldboot (**-boots, -booting, -booted**) *vt.* to restart a computer by switching it off and on. ◊ **warmboot**

cold call *n.* a telephone call or personal visit made to sb not known to the caller or visitor, in order to try to sell that person goods or services [From the fact that the call is unsolicited and comes *cold*] —**cold-call** *vt.*

cold chisel *n.* a tool consisting of a solid metal shaft with a sharply bevelled point or edge that is struck with a hammer or mallet to break up or shape hard materials such as metal or stone [From the chisel's being so tempered as to be able to cut cold metal when struck with a hammer]

cold comfort *n.* sth intended as encouraging or reassuring that does not help in practice

cold cream *n.* a thick cream used for cleaning and softening the skin, especially on the face

cold cuts *npl.* slices of cooked meat that are served cold

cold drink *n.* a chilled drink of water, juice, or sth similar

cold duck *n.* a cocktail made with sparkling burgundy and champagne [Translation of German *kalte Ente*, by folk etymology from *kaltes Ende* 'cold end', supposedly because leftover champagne and burgundy were poured by waiters into a single bottle]

cold feet *npl.* a loss of nerve about sth planned, causing a person not to go ahead as originally intended [From the fact that a soldier with cold or frozen feet is prevented from fighting]

cold fish *n.* sb who shows no warmth or friendship

cold frame *n.* a box with glass or clear plastic sides and an opening roof, used in gardens for protecting seedlings and other plants from cold weather

cold front *n.* the boundary zone of an advancing cold-air mass as it replaces warmer air

cold fusion *n.* a hypothetical form of nuclear fusion held to take place at room temperature

cold-hearted /-haártid/ *adj.* showing no sympathy or warmth to other people —**cold-heartedly** *adv.* —**cold-heartedness** *n.*

Colditz /kóldits/ site of Colditz Castle, a German prisoner-of-war camp during World War II, from which many prisoners made daring escapes. It is situated about 48 km/30 mi. southwest of Leipzig.

cold light *n.* light produced from a low-temperature source, e.g. phosphorescence, containing no infrared wavelengths and therefore having no heating effects

coldly /kóldli/ *adv.* without emotion, affection, friendliness, or sympathy

cold pack *n.* **1.** MED STH COLD PRESSED ON BODY a bag, cloth, or sheet that is soaked with water or filled with sth cold and applied to the body to relieve pain or inflammation **2.** FOOD TECH CANNING PROCESS the packing and sterilization of uncooked food in jars or tins

cold-pressed *adj.* used to describe high-grade olive oil produced from the first pressing of the raw olives. The pressed olives are subsequently heated to extract further amounts of oil.

cold-rolled *adj.* used to describe metal that is rolled into sheets under pressure at room temperature in order to retain the crystalline structure of the metal and produce a smooth surface —**cold-rolling** *n.*

cold rubber *n.* a durable synthetic rubber made through polymerization at low temperature and used for retreading tyres

cold shoulder *n.* a refusal to behave in a friendly or pleasant way towards sb ○ *He gave me the cold*

shoulder. [From the former practice of giving only a cold shoulder of mutton to an unwelcome guest]

coldshoulder /kóld shóldər/ (**-ders, -dering, -dered**) *vt.* to ignore sb or behave in an unfriendly way towards sb

cold snap *n.* a sudden short period of very cold weather

cold sore *n.* a small painful blister on or near the lips, or sometimes the nose, caused by a virus *Herpes simplex* [From the fact that the sores often accompany colds]

cold storage *n.* chilled or refrigerated conditions in which perishable objects, especially food or furs, are kept to preserve them ◇ **in cold storage** ready to be put into action at some later date, but not being currently being acted on

cold store *n.* a refrigerated building or area for keeping goods, especially food or furs, in cold conditions to preserve them

Coldstream /kóld streem/ small town on the River Tweed in Scottish Borders, Scotland. Population: 1,746 (1995).

cold sweat *n.* a very nervous, anxious, or frightened state, often with sweating and cold clammy skin

cold turkey *n.* **1.** ABRUPT WITHDRAWAL OF ADDICTIVE DRUGS a method of stopping drug addiction by not taking any further drugs and not having any other treatment to protect the addict from the withdrawal symptoms **2.** WITHDRAWAL SYMPTOMS the unpleasant symptoms, usually including nausea and shivering, that accompany a sudden withdrawal from an addictive drug [Origin uncertain; perhaps from the goose pimples, suggesting turkey flesh, experienced by addicts withdrawing from drugs]

cold type *n.* typesetting that is done without casting metal

cold war *n.* a relationship between two people or groups that is unfriendly or hostile but does not involve actual fighting or military combat. ◊ **hot war** [From the fact that the antagonism stops short of military conflict and so never heats up into an actual war]

Cold War *n.* the hostile yet nonviolent relations between the former Soviet Union and the United States, and their respective allies, from around 1946 to 1989

cold wave *n.* **1.** METEOROL COLD PERIOD a sudden fall in temperature associated with the passage of air of continental polar origin **2.** HAIR PERMANENT WAVE IN HAIR a permanent wave in hair that is produced using chemicals, rather than heat (*dated*)

cold-weld (**cold-welds, cold-welding, cold-welded**) *vt.* to join two metal surfaces using pressure rather than heat —**cold-welding** *n.*

cole /kōl/ *n.* a member of the cabbage family. Genus: *Brassica*. (*archaic*) [Pre-12thC. From Latin *caulis* 'stem, stalk, cabbage' (source of English *cauliflower* and *kohlrabi*).]

colectomy /kō léktəmi/ (*plural* **-mies**) *n.* an operation in which part or all of the colon is removed [Late 19thC. Coined from COLON + -ECTOMY.]

colemanite /kólmən ìt/ *n.* a milky white or colourless crystalline mineral consisting of hydrous calcium borate. It is a source of borax. [Late 19thC. Named after William T. *Coleman* (1824–93), US mine owner.]

coleopteran /kólli óptərən/ *n.* an insect with modified forewings that function as tough covers for the membranous hind wings. Beetles, fireflies, and weevils are coleopterans. Order: Coleoptera. —**coleopterous** *adj.*

coleoptile /kólli óp tìl/ *n.* BOT the first leaf in some grasses that forms a protective sheath around the stem tip (**plumule**) [Mid-19thC. Coined from Greek *koleos* 'sheath' (see COLEUS) + *ptilon* 'feather, down'.]

coleorhiza /kólli ə rízə/ (*plural* **-zae** /-zee/) *n.* BOT a protective sheath surrounding the young root of a germinating grass seed [Mid-19thC. Coined from Greek *koleos* 'sheath' (see COLEUS) + *rhiza* 'root'.]

Coleraine /kōl ráyn/ city and county seat of Coleraine district, northern Northern Ireland, situated on the River Bann. Population: 48,600 (1990).

Coleridge /kólərij/, **Samuel Taylor** (1772–1834) British poet. His collection *Lyrical Ballads* (1798), published with William Wordsworth, launched romanticism in English poetry.

coleslaw /kól slaw/ *n.* a salad made with shredded raw cabbage and carrot in a mayonnaise dressing [Late 18thC. From Dutch *koolsla*, literally 'cabbage salad', from *kool* 'cabbage' + *sla* 'salad'.]

coletit /kól tit/ *n.* = **coal tit**

Colette

Colette /ko lét/ (1873–1954) French novelist. Among the best known of her many novels are *Chéri* (1926) and *Gigi* (1945). Full name **Sidonie Gabrielle Claudine Colette**

coleus /kó li əss/ *n.* a plant grown for its brightly coloured variegated leaves. Genus: *Coleus*. [Mid-19thC. Via modern Latin from Greek *koleos* 'sheath', from the way the plant's filaments are joined.]

coley /kóli/ (*plural* **-ley** *or* **-leys**) *n.* an edible white-fleshed fish, especially a coalfish [Mid-20thC. Probably from COALFISH.]

coli- *prefix.* = **colo-** (*used before vowels*)

colic /kóllik/ *n.* **1.** MED PAIN IN ABDOMEN a sudden attack of abdominal pain, often caused by spasm, inflammation, or obstruction **2.** MED CRYING IN BABIES excessive crying and irritability in infants from a variety of causes, especially stomach or intestinal discomfort **3.** VET SERIOUS DIGESTIVE DISEASE IN HORSES a serious disease of the digestive system in horses, sometimes leading to fatal intestinal blockage [15thC. Via French from Latin *colicus*, from Greek *kolikos* 'suffering in the large intestine', from *kolon* 'large intestine' (source of English *colon*^{2}), of unknown origin.]

colicky /kólliki/ *adj.* experiencing bouts of abdominal pain (**colic**)

coliform /kóli fawrm, kólli-/ *adj.* used to describe rod-shaped bacteria that are normally found in the colons of humans and animals and become a serious contaminant when found in the food or water supply. ◊ **E coli** [Early 20thC. Coined from modern Latin *coli*, species name, literally 'of the large intestine' (a form of Latin *colon, colum* 'large intestine') + -FORM.]

colinear /kó línni ər/ *adj.* **1.** ARRANGED IN LINEAR ORDER with corresponding parts arranged in a regular linear order **2.** MATH = **collinear** [Early 20thC. Coined from CO- + LINEAR.] —**colinearity** /kólinni árrəti/ *n.*

coliseum /kólli seé əm/ *n.* a large building used as a theatre or for sports events [Early 16thC. Via medieval Latin *coliseum*, literally 'sth colossal', from Latin *colosseus* 'colossal', from *colossus* 'colossus' (source of English *colossal*).]

colistin /kə lístin, kō lístin/ *n.* an antibiotic effective against a wide range of organisms and used to treat gastrointestinal infections. It is obtained from a soil bacterium. [Mid-20thC. From modern Latin (*Bacillus*) *colistinus*, scientific name for the bacterium that produces it, from *coli* (see COLIFORM).]

colitis /kō lítis, ko-/ *n.* inflammation of the colon, characterized by lower-bowel spasms and upper abdominal cramps [Mid-19thC. Coined from COLON^2 + -ITIS.] —**colitic** /kō líttik, ko-/ *adj.*

coll. *abbr.* **1.** COMM collateral **2.** colleague **3.** MAIL collect **4.** MAIL collection **5.** MAIL collector **6.** EDUC college **7.** EDUC collegiate **8.** LANG colloquial

coll- *prefix.* = **collo-** (*used before vowels*)

collaborate /kə lábbə rayt/ (**-rates, -rating, -rated**) *vi.* **1.** WORK WITH OTHERS to work with another person or group in order to achieve sth **2.** MIL WORK WITH ENEMY to betray others by working with an enemy, especially an occupying force [Late 19thC. From late Latin *collaborat-*, the past participle stem of *collaborare*, literally 'to work together', ultimately from Latin *labor* 'toil' (see LABOUR).]

collaboration /kə lábbə ráysh'n/ *n.* **1.** A WORKING TOGETHER the act of working together with one or more people in order to achieve sth **2.** MIL A WORKING WITH ENEMY the betrayal of others by working with an enemy, especially an occupying force —**collaborationist** *n., adj.* —**collaborationism** *n.*

collaborative /kə lábbərətiv/ *adj.* achieved by working together or with others —**collaboratively** *adv.*

collaborator /kə lábbə raytər/ *n.* **1.** SB WORKING WITH OTHERS sb working with one or more other people to achieve sth **2.** MIL SB WORKING WITH ENEMY sb who betrays others by working with an enemy, especially an occupying force

collage /ko laázh, kóllaazh/ *n.* **1.** CRAFT PICTURE WITH PIECES STUCK ON SURFACE a picture made by sticking cloth, pieces of paper, photographs, and other objects onto a surface **2.** CRAFT ART OF MAKING COLLAGES the art of making pictures by sticking cloth, pieces of paper, photographs, and other objects onto a surface **3.** COMBINATION OF DIFFERENT THINGS a combination of different things [Early 20thC. From French, from *coller* 'to glue', from *colle* 'glue', from, ultimately, Greek *kolla* (see COLLO-).] —**collagist** *n.*

collagen /kólləjən/ *n.* a fibrous protein found in skin, bone, cartilage, tendon, and other connective tissue that yields gelatin when boiled in water [Mid-19thC. From French *collagène*, from Greek *kolla* 'glue' (see COLLO-).] —**collagenic** /kóllə jénnik/ *adj.* —**collagenous** /kə lájjənəss/ *adj.*

collagenase /kə lájjə nayz, -nayss/ *n.* any enzyme that assists in the breakdown of collagen and gelatin

collapsar /kə láp saar/ *n.* ASTRON = **black hole** [Late 20thC. Coined from COLLAPSE (verb), on the model of PULSAR and QUASAR.]

collapse /kə láps/ *v.* (**-lapses, -lapsing, -lapsed**) **1.** *vi.* FALL DOWN to fall down suddenly, generally as a result of damage, structural weakness, or lack of support ○ *A section of cliff had collapsed into the sea.* **2.** *vi.* FAIL ABRUPTLY to fail or come to an end suddenly ○ *Their partnership nearly collapsed under the strain.* **3.** *vi.* MED FALL SUDDENLY to fall or faint because of illness, exhaustion, or weakness ○ *He collapsed from overwork.* **4.** *vi.* SUDDENLY SIT OR LIE DOWN to sit or lie down suddenly and relax completely or give way to emotion ○ *I collapsed into an armchair.* **5.** *vi.* BEND DOUBLE WITH EMOTION to bend over double or otherwise contort the body, typically in the throes of emotion such as laughter or crying **6.** *vti.* DEFLATE to fold up or become flat from lack of pressure or loss of air, or to cause sth such as a parachute to do this ○ *The left lung had collapsed.* **7.** *vti.* FOLD STH TO MAKE SMALLER to fold sth up so that it is smaller or takes up less space, or to fold up in this way ■ *n.* **1.** FAILURE OR END a failure or sudden end to sth ○ *The abrupt collapse of the campaign.* **2.** A FALLING DOWN the act of falling down suddenly, generally as a result of damage, structural weakness, or lack of support ○ *The roof was in danger of collapse.* **3.** DECREASE IN VALUE a sudden reduction or decrease in value ○ *the threatened collapse of the yen* **4.** MED SUDDEN ILLNESS a sudden onset of severe illness, resulting in hospitalization or bed rest ○ *in a state of nervous collapse* [Mid-18thC. Back-formation from *collapsed*, from Latin *collapsus*, the past participle of *collabi*, literally 'to fall together', from *labi* 'to fall'.]

collapsible /kə lápsəb'l/ *adj.* designed to fold up so as to be smaller or take up less space —**collapsibility** /kə lápsə bíllǝti/ *n.*

collar /kóllər/ *n.* **1.** CLOTHES GARMENT'S NECKBAND the upright or turned-over neckband of a coat, jacket, dress, shirt, or blouse **2.** BAND ROUND NECK OF AN ANIMAL a stiff band of leather, plastic, strong fabric, or metal placed round the neck of an animal to identify it or attach it to a lead **3.** AREA RESEMBLING A COLLAR an area around the neck of a bird or animal that has a colour or marking different from the rest **4.** AGRIC PART OF A HARNESS the cushioned ring or other part of a harness that presses against a draught animal's shoulders **5.** MECH ENG RING-SHAPED DEVICE OR PART a ring-shaped device or part on a shaft that guides, seats, or restricts another mechanical part **6.** ACCESSORIES NECKLACE a close-fitting necklace or one that lies flat over the shoulders **7.** ORNAMENTAL INSIGNIA OF OFFICE an ornamental chain or band worn round the neck as a badge of office or insignia of knighthood **8.** FOOD MEAT FROM NECK a cut of meat, especially bacon, taken from an animal's neck **9.** POLICE ARREST an arrest made by a police officer (*slang*) ■ *vt.* (**-lars, -laring, -lared**) **1.** FIND OR STOP SB to find or stop sb you want to talk to (*informal*) **2.** CATCH SB to catch sb and hold him or her to prevent escape (*slang*) **3.** MAKE A POLICE ARREST to arrest a criminal suspect in your capacity as a police officer (*slang*) **4.** PUT A COLLAR ON STH to put a collar on sth, e.g. an animal, a garment, or a machine part **5.** COOK PICKLE AND ROLL MEAT to pickle meat by soaking it in salt or brine with seasonings and flavouring ingredients, then rolling, boiling, and pressing it [14thC. Via Old French *colier* from Latin *collare*, from *collum* 'neck'. Ultimately from an Indo-European word meaning 'to turn around', which is also the ancestor of English *cycle*, *wheel*, and *palindrome*.] —**collared** *adj.* —**collarless** *adj.* ◇ **hot under the collar** angry, irritated, or generally agitated (*informal*)

collarbone /kóllər bōn/ *n.* = **clavicle** *n.* 1

collard /kóllərd/ *n.* *US* a variety of kale with a crown of smooth edible leaves [Mid-18thC. An alteration of *colewort*.]

collat. *abbr.* collateral

collate /kə láyt, ko láyt/ (**-lates, -lating, -lated**) *vt.* **1.** COMM PUT PAGES IN ORDER to assemble pages in the correct order **2.** COMPARE INFORMATION to bring together pieces of information and compare them in detail **3.** PRINTING EXAMINE SHEETS OR PAGES to examine sheets or pages so as to put them into the proper sequence prior to binding **4.** PRINTING VERIFY PAGE SEQUENCING to verify the correct sequencing and completeness of the pages in a book **5.** CHR ADMIT CLERIC TO BENEFICE to admit a member of the clergy to a benefice [Mid-16thC. From Latin *collat-*, used as the past participle stem of *conferre*, literally 'to bring together', from *ferre* 'to bring' (source of English *confer*).]

collateral /kə láttərəl/ *n.* **1.** FIN PROPERTY AS SECURITY AGAINST LOAN property or goods used as security against a loan and forfeited if the loan is not repaid **2.** SOC SCI DESCENDANT FROM DIFFERENT LINE a relative descended from the same ancestor as another person but through a different set of parents, grandparents, and other forebears ■ *adj.* **1.** PARALLEL running side by side in parallel or corresponding in some way, e.g. in size **2.** SOC SCI DESCENDED FROM SAME ANCESTOR having the same ancestor but descended through a different set of parents, grandparents, and other forebears **3.** ADDITIONAL additional to and in support of sth **4.** ACCOMPANYING accompanying or additional but secondary **5.** FIN WITH PROPERTY AS SECURITY obtained by putting up property or goods as security, to be forfeited if the loan cannot be paid [14thC. From medieval Latin *collateralis*, literally 'side by side with', from Latin *lateralis* 'on the side' (see LATERAL).] —**collaterality** /kə lattə rálləti/ *n.* —**collaterally** /kə láttərəli/ *adv.*

collateral damage *n.* unintended damage to civilian life or property during a military operation

collation /kə láysh'n/ *n.* **1.** COMPARISON OF INFORMATION a detailed comparison between different items or forms of information **2.** PRINTING ASSEMBLY OF PAGES IN ORDER the assembling of pieces of paper in the right order, particularly the sections of a book prior to binding **3.** PRINTING TECHNICAL DESCRIPTION OF BOOK the technical description of a book, including its bibliographical details and information about its physical construction, or the act of compiling a description **4.** COOK LIGHT MEAL a light meal or refreshment ○ *a cold collation* **5.** CHR APPOINTMENT OF CLERGY the appointment of clergy to a benefice **6.** CHR READING OF RELIGIOUS TEXT the reading of a religious text to a gathering of monks [14thC. From medieval Latin and Latin *collation-* 'a bringing together' from *collat-* (see COLLATE).]

collative /kə láytiv/ *adj.* CHR used to describe an ecclesiastical benefice to which a member of the clergy is appointed [Early 17thC]

collator /kə láytər/ *n.* a person or machine that reads, compares, and sorts pages, e.g. of a book [Early 17thC. Directly or via French from medieval Latin *collator*, from Latin, 'contributor', literally 'one who brings together', from the stem *collat-* 'brought together' (see COLLATE).]

colleague /kólleeg/ *n.* a person sb works with, especially in a professional or skilled job [Early 16thC. Via French from Latin *collega*, literally 'someone one commissions with', from *legare* 'to commission, entrust', from *lex* 'law' (source of English *privilege*).] —**colleagueship** *n.*

collect[1] /kə lékt/ *v.* (**-lects, -lecting, -lected**) **1.** *vt.* BRING THINGS TOGETHER to gather things and bring them together ○ *I collected up my belongings and left.* **2.** *vt.* KEEP THINGS OF SAME TYPE to obtain and keep objects of a similar type because of their interest, value, or beauty **3.** *vt.* FETCH AND BRING SB OR STH to fetch people or objects and bring them somewhere ○ *They collected me from the airport.* **4.** *vt.* TAKE MONEY OR PRIZE to take the money or prize to which a person is entitled **5.** *vti.* ASK FOR DONATIONS to ask for money from people for a particular purpose **6.** *vti.* ACCUMULATE SOMEWHERE to gather and gradually accumulate in a place **7.** *vi.* GRADUALLY ASSEMBLE to come together gradually in a place and form a group or crowd of people ○ *By now an angry crowd had collected.* **8.** *vr.* GET CONTROL OF YOURSELF to gain or regain control of yourself and deliberately calm yourself or prepare yourself psychologically **9.** *vi.* GET MONEY FROM STH to obtain money that is due, e.g. from an insurance policy **10.** *vt.* *ANZ* TRANSP COLLIDE to be in collision with another vehicle (*informal*) ■ *adv.* *US* TELECOM = **reverse charges** ■ *adj.* *US* TELECOM = **reverse-charge** [Mid-16thC. Directly or via French from medieval Latin *collectare*, from Latin *collect-*, past participle stem of *colligere*, literally 'to gather together', from *legere* 'to gather, read' (source of English *lecture*).]

WORD KEY: SYNONYMS

collect, accumulate, gather, amass, assemble, stockpile, hoard

CORE MEANING: to bring dispersed things together in a group or mass

collect a general term, with the additional sense that the things brought together have been selected or arranged in an orderly way, especially as a hobby; **accumulate** to collect over a period of time; **gather** to collect or accumulate, with the suggestion of bringing together things from various locations; **amass** to accumulate, with the suggestion of a large amount; **assemble** to bring things together in an orderly way for a specific purpose; **stockpile** to collect and keep for future use, or permanently; **hoard** a term similar to 'stockpile', often suggesting greed or secrecy.

collect[2] /kóllekt/ *n.* a short formal prayer that can vary according to the day, said before the reading of the epistle in certain Christian church services [13thC. Via Old French from late Latin *collecta* 'assembly', from Latin, a form of *collectus* 'gathered together' (see COLLECT[1]).]

collectable /kə léktəb'l/, **collectible** *n.* COLLECTING OBJECT VALUED BY COLLECTORS an object of a type that is valued or sought after by collectors ■ *adj.* POPULAR WITH COLLECTORS good for collecting or popular with collectors and much sought after

collectanea /kóllek táyni ə/ *npl.* a selection of pieces of writing by an author or by several authors [Mid-17thC. From Latin, literally 'things collected', a form of *collectaneus* 'collected', from *collectus* 'gathered together' (see COLLECT[1]).]

collected /kə léktid/ *adj.* **1.** CALM AND COMPOSED calm and in control of yourself **2.** LITERAT BROUGHT TOGETHER AS WHOLE gathered together in one book or set of volumes as the whole of an author's work or work of a particular type **3.** EQU CONTROLLED IN GAIT moving with a controlled gait [Early 17thC. The underlying idea is of having pulled yourself together.] —**collectedly** *adv.* —**collectedness** *n.*

collectible *n., adj.* = **collectable**

collection /kə léksh'n/ *n.* **1.** GROUP OF THINGS OR PEOPLE a group of things or people together in one place **2.** SEVERAL DIFFERENT WORKS TOGETHER a number of different pieces of writing or music together in one book, CD, or record **3.** OBJECTS HELD BY COLLECTOR a set of objects collected for their interest, value, or beauty **4.** PAINTINGS OR OBJECTS IN MUSEUM all the paintings or objects of one kind held by an art gallery or museum **5.** TAKING OF DONATIONS the act of taking money due or given ○ *They took up a collection for him when he was in hospital.* **6.** CHR TAKING OF MONEY IN CHRISTIAN CHURCH the act of accepting money from worshippers in a Christian church service, or the money collected **7.** FASHION RANGE OF NEW CLOTHES a range of newly designed clothes for a particular season ○ *the spring collection* **8.** MAIL TAKING OF STH the taking of sth on a regular basis, e.g. letters from postboxes by the Post Office, or refuse from buildings **9.** GATHERING TOGETHER the act of gathering things together (*formal*) [14thC. Via Old French from the Latin stem *collection-*, from the stem *col-lect-* 'gathered together' (see COLLECT[1]).]

collective /kə léktiv/ *adj.* **1.** SHARED BY ALL made or shared by everyone in a group **2.** COLLECTED TO FORM WHOLE collected together to form a whole or added up to form a total from different sources or groups **3.** APPLYING TO MANY applying to a number of individuals taken together ○ *staff training was the collective responsibility of the three personnel officers* **4.** BUSINESS, POL WORKER-RUN UNDER STATE SUPERVISION used to describe a business or other enterprise run by the people who work in it but under the jurisdiction of the state ■ *n.* **1.** BUSINESS, POL WORKER-RUN ENTERPRISE an enterprise, such as a farm or factory, that is run by its workers under state control **2.** BUSINESS, POL MEMBERS OF COLLECTIVE the members of a collective who work in and run the business **3.** GRAM = **collective noun** —**collectively** *adv.* —**collectiveness** *n.*

collective agreement *n.* a contract of employment negotiated between a management and union

collective bargaining *n.* negotiations between a management and union about pay and conditions of employment on behalf of all the workers in the union [Coined by Beatrice Webb of the Fabians]

collective farm *n.* a farm that is state-supervised but operated by its workers

collective noun *n.* a noun that refers to a group of people or things considered as a single unit. 'Committee' and 'government' are collective nouns.

WORD KEY: USAGE

Collective nouns: Examples of collective nouns are *audience, clergy, committee, crowd, flock, government, jury,* and *orchestra*, all of which are singular in form but plural in the sense of being made up of a number of individuals or individual things. Nouns that denote a class of objects, for example *furniture* and *luggage*, are always singular: *My luggage is missing.* Other collective nouns are generally treated as singular unless there is an evident reason to treat them otherwise. Thus *The audience was absolutely silent* but *It was so warm the audience were stripping off their jackets.* It is important to avoid inconsistency in your choice of verb and pronoun number when using collective nouns. For instance, this example contains inconsistencies: *The committee has [singular] decided to reject the proposal and will give their [plural] reasons in writing tomorrow.*

collective security *n.* the maintenance of peace and security through the united action of nations

collective unconscious *n.* the inherited part of unconscious thought, memories, and instinct, which, according to Jungian principles, is common to members of a people and is observable through dreams and behaviour

collectivise *vt.* = **collectivize**

collectivism /kə léktivizzəm/ *n.* the system of control and ownership of factories and farms and of the means of production and distribution of products by a nation's people [Mid-19thC. From COLLECTIVE, on the model of French *collectivisme.*] —**collectivist** *n.* —**collectivistic** /kə lékti vístik/ *adj.* —**collectivistically** /-vístikli/ *adv.*

collectivity /kóllek tívvəti/ (*plural* **-ties**) *n.* **1.** STATE OF BEING TOGETHER a state or situation in which people or things are together or work together to form a whole **2.** POL AGGREGATE a group regarded as an aggregate, especially a people [Mid-19thC]

collectivize /kə lékti vīz/ (**-izes, -izing, -ized**), **collectivise** (**-ises, -ising, -ised**) *vt.* to run or organize sth such as a farm according to principles of collective control —**collectivization** /kə lékti vī záysh'n/ *n.*

collector /kə léktər/ *n.* **1.** SB WHO COLLECTS OBJECTS sb who collects objects of a particular type for their interest, value, or beauty ○ *a stamp collector* **2.** SB WHO COLLECTS STH sb whose job is to collect sth, e.g. money owed, tickets, or refuse **3.** CONTAINER WHERE THINGS COLLECT sth in which things are collected intentionally or where unwanted things collect **4.** ELECTRON ENG TRANSISTOR REGION the region of a transistor towards or through which charge carriers flow **5.** *S Asia* PUBLIC ADMIN INDIAN ADMINISTRATOR in India, the chief administrator of a district [14thC] —**collectorship** *n.*

collectorate /kə léktərət/ *n.* *S Asia* in India, the district over which a collector presides

collector's item *n.* an object that is sought after or valued highly by collectors

colleen /kə léen, kólleen/ *n.* **1.** *Ireland* GIRL a girl, especially a young girl **2.** IRISH GIRL a girl living or born in Ireland or a girl of Irish descent [Early 19thC. From Irish *cailín*, literally 'little girl', from *caile* 'girl'.]

college /kóllij/ *n.* **1.** INSTITUTION OF HIGHER LEARNING an institution of higher or further education, especially one offering courses in specialized or practical subjects **2.** PART OF BRITISH UNIVERSITY a division of some British universities, e.g. Oxford or Cambridge **3.** SCHOOL a school for senior students **4.** BRITISH SCHOOL used as part of the name of some British private schools **5.** COLLEGE BUILDING OR BUILDINGS the building or buildings of a college **6.** COLLEGE STAFF AND STUDENTS the staff and students of a college **7.** PROFESSIONAL BODY a group of people, usually of the same profession, who have agreed duties and rights **8.** *US* UNIVERSITY SCHOOL OR DIVISION a school or a division of a university that usually has its own dean and other administrators and whose faculty teaches and confers degrees in specific academic fields **9.** CHR BODY OF CLERGY a group or body of clergy who live together [14thC. Directly or via Old French from Latin *collegium* 'association, corporation', from *collega* 'colleague' (see COLLEAGUE).]

College of Arms *n.* a British institution that specializes in matters relating to heraldry, the granting of arms, and tracing genealogies

College of Cardinals *n.* the body of cardinals who elect popes, assist the pope in church governance, and manage the Holy See in the absence of a living or elected pope [Shortening of *Sacred College of Cardinals*, its official name]

College of Justice *n.* the Scottish Court of Session, Scotland's highest civil court

college pudding *n.* a steamed or baked suet pudding containing spices and dried fruit

collegia plural of **collegium**

collegial /kə léeji əl/ *adj.* **1.** OF COLLEGE OR UNIVERSITY involving, typical of, or belonging to a college or university **2.** POWER-SHARING with power shared equally between colleagues **3.** CHR OF POWER-SHARING BY BISHOPS relating to a situation or system in the Roman Catholic Church in which the bishops share equal power [14thC. Directly or via Old French from late Latin *collegialis*, from Latin *collegium* (see COLLEGE).] —**collegiality** /kə léeji állәti/ *n.* —**collegially** /kə lée ji əli/ *adv.*

collegian /kə léeji ən/ *n.* a college undergraduate, graduate student, or recent graduate [15thC. From medieval Latin *collegianus*, from Latin *collegium* 'association, corporation' (see COLLEGE).]

collegiate /kə léeji ət/ *adj.* **1.** OF COLLEGE involving, belonging to, appropriate to, or being a college, including its students and their pursuits **2.** WITH SEPARATE COLLEGES consisting of separate university colleges [15thC. From medieval Latin *collegiatus* '(member) of a college', from Latin *collegium* (see COLLEGE).] —**collegiately** *adv.*

collegiate church *n.* **1.** CHURCH WITH CANONS a Roman Catholic or Anglican church that has a chapter of canons but is not a cathedral **2.** CHURCH WITH TWO MINISTERS in Scotland, a church with two or more ministers of equal seniority **3.** *US* GROUP OF CHURCHES a group or association of churches that have pastors in common

collegiate institute *n.* in some Canadian provinces, a secondary school that offers a high level of courses and facilities

collegium /kə léeji əm/ (*plural* **-ums** *or* **-a** /-ə/) *n.* **1.** SOVIET COMMITTEE in the former Soviet Union, a committee of equally empowered members in charge of a department or industry **2.** = **College of Cardinals** [From Latin (see COLLEGE)]

col legno /kol lég nō, -láy nyō/ *adv.* to be played by tapping the strings of a stringed instrument with the back of the bow (*used as a musical direction*) [20thC. From Italian, literally 'with the wood'.]

collembolan /kə lémbələn/ *n.* INSECTS = **springtail** [Late 19thC. From modern Latin *Collembola*, order name, from Greek *kolla* 'glue' + *embolon* 'peg, stopper'. From its ventral tube, which can secrete an adhesive substance.] —**collembolous** *adj.*

collenchyma /kə léngkimə/ *n.* a layer of supportive plant tissue that consists of elongated living cells that have walls unevenly thickened with cellulose and pectin [Mid-19thC. Coined from COLLO- + -ENCHYMA.] —**collenchymatous** /kóllən kímmətəss/ *adj.*

Colles' fracture /kólliz-/ *n.* a fracture of the radius bone in which a piece broken off at the end is displaced towards the back of the wrist. The fracture is commonly caused by falling on the palm of the hand. [Late 19thC. Named after Abraham *Colles* (1773–1843), Irish surgeon.]

collet /kóllit/ *n.* **1.** CONE-SHAPED MECHANICAL PIECE a slotted cone-shaped piece that encloses and grips a rod or shaft when inserted into the sleeve of a lathe or other machine **2.** SETTING FOR GEMSTONE a band or claw that holds a gemstone **3.** BAND ATTACHED TO SPRING IN WATCH a ring that holds the hairspring in a watch [16thC. From French *collet*, literally 'little collar', from *col* 'collar', from Latin *collum* 'neck' (see COLLAR).]

colleterial gland /kóllə téeri əl-/ *n.* a reproductive gland in female insects that secretes a sticky material that binds eggs together or to a surface [Late 19thC. *Colleterial* from modern Latin *colleterium*, from Greek *kollan* 'to glue' (see COLLO-).]

collide /kə líd/ (**-lides, -liding, -lided**) *vi.* **1.** CRASH INTO STH to hit a person or object moving towards you or a person or object you are moving towards ○ *I collided with her in the corridor.* **2.** COME INTO CONFLICT WITH SB to come into conflict with sb else or another group [Early 17thC. From Latin *collidere* 'to shatter', literally 'to strike together', from *laedere* 'to strike, injure' (source of English *elide* and *lesion*).]

collider /kə lídər/ *n.* a particle accelerator in which two oppositely moving particle beams are made to collide. This allows the particles to use more of their energy to create new particles than when they collide with a fixed target.

Collie

collie /kólli/ *n.* ZOOL a dog with a long narrow muzzle, originally bred to herd sheep. There are short-haired (smooth) and long-haired (rough) collies. ◊ **Border collie** [Mid-17thC. Origin uncertain; perhaps formed from COAL, from its colour.]

collier /kólli ər/ *n.* **1.** MINING COAL MINER a coal miner (*dated*) **2.** SHIPPING COAL-TRANSPORT VESSEL a ship designed to transport coal [13thC. Formed from COAL. Originally in the meaning of 'charcoal burner'.]

colliery /kóllyəri/ (*plural* **-ies**) *n.* a coal mine and the buildings associated with it

collinear /ko línni ər/, **colinear** /kō-/ *adj.* MATH lying on or passing through a single straight line [Mid-19thC.

Coined from COL- + LINEAR.] —**collinearity** /ko línni árrəti/ *n.*

collins /kóllinz/ (*plural* **-linses**) *n.* an iced drink made with spirits such as gin or vodka and fruit juice such as lemon or lime [Mid-19thC. Origin uncertain; possibly from the name of the bartender who originally dispensed it.]

Collins /kóllinz/, **Jackie** (*b.* 1939) British novelist. Her popular novels include *The Bitch* (1978).

Michael Collins

Collins, Michael (1890–1922) Irish politician. A creator of the Irish Free State (1922), he was shot by Republicans who opposed the Anglo-Irish Treaty.

Collins, Wilkie (1824–89) British novelist. His *The Woman in White* (1860) and *Moonstone* (1868) were pioneering mystery novels. Full name **William Wilkie Collins**

Collins Street Farmer *n. Aus* a city person who has money invested in rural properties, often for tax reasons (*regional*) [Named after *Collins Street*, an important business street in Melbourne, Australia]

collision /kə lízh'n/ *n.* **1.** CRASH the action of two moving vehicles, ships, aircraft, or other objects hitting each other **2.** CONFLICT BETWEEN IDEAS a conflict between people or their ideas or beliefs **3.** PHYS EXCHANGE OF ENERGY BETWEEN PARTICLES an encounter between two or more particles that come together or close to each other, and exchange or transfer energy [15thC. From the late Latin stem *collision-*, from Latin *collis-*, the past participle stem of *collidere* ‘to smash together’ (see COLLIDE).] —**collisional** *adj.* —**collisionally** *adv.*

collision course *n.* a path or course of action that inevitably leads to conflict ○ *The two of them were clearly headed on a collision course.*

collision zone *n.* an extensive linear feature marking the collision of two continental plates, characterized by young fold mountains and earthquakes

collo- *prefix.* glutinous, gelatinous ○ *collotype* [Via modern Latin from Greek *kolla* ‘glue’ (source of English *collage* and *protocol*)]

collocate *v.* /kólla kayt/ (**-cates, -cating, -cated**) **1.** *vi.* LING OCCUR FREQUENTLY WITH ANOTHER WORD to occur frequently in conjunction with another word. For example, ‘vast’ collocates with ‘majority’ in the phrase ‘vast majority’. **2.** *vt.* PUT STH NEXT TO STH to arrange sth so that it is next to or close to sth else (*formal*) ■ *n.* /kólləkət/ LING WORD THAT OCCURS WITH ANOTHER a word that is frequently or typically used with another word [Early 16thC. From Latin *collocat-*, the past participle stem of *collocare*, literally ‘to place together’, from *locare* ‘to place’.]

collocation /kóllə káysh'n/ *n.* **1.** LING CO-OCCURRENCE OF WORDS the association between two words that are typically or frequently used together **2.** CLOSENESS OF THINGS an arrangement in which things are placed next to each other or close together [Early 17thC] —**collocational** *adj.*

collodion /kə lódi ən/ *n.* a thick colourless solution of pyroxylin, ether, and alcohol. It is used in medicine to treat wounds and hold surgical dressings, and formerly in photography to make plates. [Mid-19thC. From Greek *kollōdēs* ‘gluelike’, from *kolla* ‘glue’ (see COLLO-).]

colloid /kólloyd/ *n.* **1.** CHEM SUSPENSION OF SMALL PARTICLES a suspension of small particles dispersed in another

substance **2.** CHEM PARTICLES IN COLLOID the particles that are suspended in a colloid solution **3.** PHYSIOL SUBSTANCE IN THYROID GLAND a thick gelatinous substance that is produced in the thyroid gland and stores hormones ■ *adj.* CHEM OF COLLOID relating to or resembling a colloid [Mid-19thC. Coined from Greek *kolla* ‘glue’ (see COLLO-) + -OID).] —**colloidal** /ko lóyd'l/ *adj.*

collop /kólləp/ *n.* **1.** FOOD SLICE OF MEAT a slice of meat, especially fried bacon **2.** PIECE a small piece of sth [14thC. From Scandinavian.]

colloq. *abbr.* colloquial

colloquia plural of **colloquium**

colloquial /kə lókwi əl/ *adj.* **1.** INFORMAL said more usually in informal conversation than in formal speech or writing **2.** BY WAY OF CONVERSATION expressed by way of conversation (*archaic*) [Mid-18thC. Formed from Latin *colloquium* (see COLLOQUIUM).] —**colloquiality** /kə lókwi álləti/ *n.* —**colloquially** /kə lókwi əli/ *adv.* —**colloquialness** /-əlnəss/ *n.*

colloquialism /kə lókwi əlizzəm/ *n.* an informal word or phrase that is more usual in conversation than in formal speech or writing

colloquium /kə lókwi əm/ (*plural* **-ums** *or* **-a** /-ə/) *n.* **1.** UNIV ACADEMIC SEMINAR an academic conference or seminar in which a particular topic is discussed, often with guest speakers **2.** DISCUSSION MEETING an informal meeting to discuss sth [Late 16thC. From Latin, ‘conversation’, formed from *colloqui*, literally ‘to speak with’, from *loqui* ‘to speak’ (source of English *eloquent*).]

colloquy /kólləkwi/ (*plural* **-quies**) *n.* **1.** DISCUSSION a formal conversation or discussion (*formal*) **2.** LITERAT WRITTEN DIALOGUE a literary or other written work in the form of a dialogue [15thC. Formed from Latin *colloquium* (see COLLOQUIUM).]

collotype /kóllə tīp/ *n.* **1.** PRINTING PROCESS a process for making lithographic prints **2.** PRINT MADE BY COLLOTYPE a print that is made by use of the collotype process [Late 19thC. Coined from Greek *kolla* ‘glue’ (see COLLO-) + -TYPE.]

collude /kə lood/ (**-ludes, -luding, -luded**) *vi.* to co-operate with sb secretly in order to do sth illegal or undesirable [Early 16thC. From Latin *colludere*, literally ‘to play with’, from *ludere* ‘to play’, from *ludus* ‘game, play’ (source of English *ludicrous*).] —**colluder** *n.*

collusion /kə loozh'n/ *n.* secret cooperation between people in order to do sth illegal or underhand [14thC. Directly or via Old French from the Latin stem *collusion-*, from *collus-*, past participle stem of *colludere* (see COLLUDE).]

collusive /kə loossiv/ *adj.* secretly cooperating or involving secret cooperation in order to do sth illegal or underhanded [Late 17thC. From Latin *collus-*, past participle stem of *colludere* (see COLLUDE).] —**collusively** *adv.* —**collusiveness** *n.*

colluvium /kə loovi əm/ (*plural* **-a** /-ə/ *or* **-ums**) *n.* loose rock and soil at the base of a cliff or steep slope [Mid-20thC. From Latin, formed from *colluvies*, from *colluere*, literally ‘to wash thoroughly’, from *lavere* ‘to wash’ (source of English *lotion*).] —**colluvial** *adj.*

collywobbles /kólli wobb'lz/ *npl.* a feeling of nervousness about sth (*informal*) [Early 19thC. Origin uncertain: probably formed from COLIC and WOBBLE, the underlying idea being of intestines wobbling.]

Colo. *abbr.* Colorado

colo- *prefix.* intestine ○ *colorectal* [From COLON]

coloboma /kóllə bṓmə/ *n.* a structural defect in the retina, iris, or other tissue of the eye, usually present at birth [Mid-19thC. Via modern Latin from Greek *koloboma* ‘part removed in mutilation’, from *kolobos* (see COLOBUS).] —**colobomatous** *adj.*

colobus /kólləbəss/ (*plural* **-buses** *or* **-bi** /-bī/), **colobus monkey** *n.* a large slender monkey native to Africa that has a long tail and long silky fur but lacks developed thumbs. Genus: *Colobus*. [Late 19thC. Via modern Latin from Greek *kolobos* ‘docked, maimed’. Ultimately from an Indo-European word meaning ‘to cut’, which is also the ancestor of English *calamity*.]

colocynth /kóllə sinth/ *n.* **1.** PLANTS VINE WITH BITTER FRUIT a European vine related to the pumpkin and squash that bears bitter yellow fruit about the size of a lemon but speckled with green. Latin name: *Citrulus colocynthis*. **2.** PLANTS, PHARM FRUIT OF COLOCYNTH

the spongy bitter fruit of the colocynth that yields a powerful laxative or purgative [Mid-16thC. Via Latin from Greek *kolokunthis*, from *kolokunthē* ‘pumpkin, round gourd’.]

cologne /kə lṓn/ *n.* a scented liquid that is lighter than perfume [Early 19thC. Named after the city of *Cologne*, Germany, where it was first made.]

Cologne /kə lṓn/ river port and largest city in the North Rhine-Westphalia state of Germany. Population: 958,600 (1992).

Colombia

Colombia /kə lúmbi ə/ republic in northwestern South America surrounded by the Caribbean Sea, Venezuela, Brazil, Peru, Ecuador, Panama, and the Pacific Ocean. Language: Spanish. Currency: peso. Capital: Bogotá. Population: 37,852,050 (1997). Area: 1,141,748 sq. km/440,831 sq. mi. Official name **Republic of Colombia** —**Colombian** *n., adj.*

Colombo /kə lúm bō/ commercial capital of Sri Lanka, situated on the west coast. It is also a port with a large artificially created harbour. Population: 615,000 (1990).

colon[1] /kṓlən, -lon/ *n.* **1.** LANG PUNCTUATION MARK the punctuation mark (:) used to divide distinct but related elements, e.g. clauses in which the second elaborates on the first, or to introduce a list, quotation, or speech **2.** MARK (:) USED IN PHONETICS a mark (:) after a vowel in a system of phonetic writing that shows that the vowel is lengthened **3.** (*plural* **cola**) LITERAT UNIT OF CLASSICAL POETRY in Greek or Roman verse, a rhythmic unit consisting of two to six metrical feet with one main accent [Mid-16thC. Via Latin from Greek *kōlon*, originally ‘limb’, hence ‘unit of verse’, hence ‘clause’.]

colon[2] /kṓlən, -lon/ (*plural* **-lons** *or* **-la** /-lə/) *n.* the section of the large intestine that runs from the caecum to the rectum [14thC. Via Latin from Greek *kolon* ‘large intestine, food, meat’, of unknown origin.]

colon[3] /ko lṓn/ (*plural* **-lons** *or* **-lones** /ko lṓness/) *n.* **1.** see table at **currency 2.** COIN OR NOTE WORTH ONE COLON a coin or note worth one colon [Late 19thC. Named after Cristóbal *Colón*, Spanish name of Christopher Columbus.]

colonel /kúrn'l/ *n.* **1.** MILITARY RANK IN UK an officer whose rank in the British Army or Royal Marines is between a brigadier and a lieutenant colonel **2.** *US* MILITARY RANK IN UNITED STATES an officer whose rank in the US Army, Marine Corps, or Air Force is between a brigadier general and a lieutenant colonel **3.** MILITARY RANK IN CANADA a high-ranking commissioned officer in the army or air force of Canada, ranking above lieutenant colonel and below brigadier general, equivalent in rank to a commander in the navy **4.** *US* HONORARY US TITLE an honorary title in an official state militia, given to respected citizens by the governor in some southern and central US states. This practice is most closely associated with the state of Kentucky, but also occurs in the states of Louisiana and Tennessee. [Mid-16thC. Via obsolete French *coronel* from Italian *colonnella*, literally ‘little column’, from *colonna* ‘column’, from Latin *columna* (see COLUMN).] —**colonelship** *n.*

Colonel Blimp /-blímp/ *n.* = **Blimp** [A cartoon character created by British cartoonist David Low after World War I. His name came from the nickname for observation balloons used during the war.]

colonelcy /kúrn'lssi/ (*plural* **-cies**) *n.* the rank or commission of a colonel in the armed forces

colones plural of **colon**[3]

colonia /kə lóni ə/ n. US a poor Hispanic-American community, especially along the border between the United States and Mexico [Late 20thC. From Spanish, literally 'colony'.]

colonial /kə lóni əl/ adj. **1.** RELATING TO COLONY possessing, ruling over, living in, or relating to a colony **2.** **colonial, Colonial** HIST RELATING TO BRITISH COLONIES IN AMERICA relating to the 13 original British colonies in North America before their independence in 1776 **3. colonial, Colonial** HIST OF THE BRITISH EMPIRE relating to the colonies of the former British Empire, or to the Empire as a whole **4.** ARCHIT, FURNITURE IN STYLE OF NORTH AMERICAN COLONIES dating from or in a style typical of British North America from the late 17th to the early 19th centuries **5.** ANZ HIST FROM AUSTRALIAN TIME AS COLONY dating from or related to the period before the Federation of Australia in 1901 **6.** ZOOL LIVING IN COLONIES used to describe animals that live in groups or colonies and are dependent on each other. Some, e.g. corals, are physically joined, while others, e.g. insects, show social organization and specialized functions. ■ n. **1.** SB WHO LIVES IN COLONY sb who lives in a colony but who is a national of the colonizing country **2.** SB FROM A COLONY sb whose native country is a colony [Late 18thC. From COLONY, perhaps on the model of French colonial.] —**colonially** adv. —**colonialness** n.

—————— **WORD KEY: CULTURAL NOTE** ——————
The Wild Colonial Boy, an anonymous song from the 1860s. It tells the story of Jack Doolan, an Irish boy transported to Australia for theft, who becomes an outlaw before being hunted down and killed by police. In Australia, the phrase came to mean 'bushranger'.

colonialism /kə lóni əlizzəm/ n. a policy in which a country rules other nations and develops trade for its own benefit —**colonialist** n. —**colonialistic** /kə lóni ə lístik/ adj.

colonic /kō lónnik/ adj. MED, ANAT OF COLON relating to or situated in the colon ■ n. MED, ALTERN MED CLEANSING OF COLON a medical treatment in which fluids are injected through the anus into the colon to clean it out

colonise vt. = colonize

colonist /kóllənist/ n. **1.** SB LIVING IN NEW COLONY sb who goes to live in a new colony or is among the founders of a colony **2.** **colonist, Colonist** HIST EUROPEAN SETTLER OF NORTH AMERICA one of the early European settlers of North America before it became the United States **3.** BIOL ORGANISM MOVING INTO NEW ECOSYSTEM an organism, including a plant such as a weed, that moves into and establishes itself in a new ecosystem

colonitis /kóllə nítiss/ n. = colitis

colonize /kóllə nīz/ (-nizes, -nizing, -nized), **colonise** (colonises, colonising, colonised) v. **1.** vti. ESTABLISH COLONY to establish a colony in another country or place **2.** vt. GO TO NEW LAND to go to and live in a colony or other civilized setting established in a foreign, hitherto sparsely inhabited or virtually unsettled land **3.** vti. BIOL BECOME ESTABLISHED IN NEW ECOSYSTEM to establish plants or animals, or become established, in a biological colony in a new ecosystem —**colonizable** adj. —**colonization** /kóllə nī záysh'n/ n. —**colonizationist** /-sh'nist/ n. —**colonizer** /kóllə nīzər/ n.

Colonnade

colonnade /kóllə náyd/ n. a row of columns, usually supporting a roof or arches [Early 18thC. From French, formed on the model of Italian colonnato from French

colonne 'column', from Latin columna (see COLUMN).] —**colonnaded** adj.

colonoscope /kə lónnə skōp/ n. a long flexible instrument (**endoscope**) for viewing the interior of the colon, and often equipped with a device that can remove tissue for biopsy

colonoscopy /kóllə nóskəpi/ (plural -pies) n. a medical examination of the colon using a colonoscope [Coined from COLON[2] + -SCOPY] —**colonoscopic** /kə lónnə skóppik/ adj.

colony /kólləni/ (plural -nies) n. **1.** COUNTRY RULED BY ANOTHER a country or area that is ruled by another country **2.** HIST SETTLEMENT IN NORTH AMERICA one of the early settled areas in North America that formed the 13 founding states of the United States after independence (often used in the plural) **3.** GROUP OF COLONISTS the group of people who have gone to live in a colony **4.** GROUP OF SIMILAR PEOPLE a group of people of the same nationality or ethnic group, doing the same work, or living in the same circumstances, who reside together or near one another ○ a colony of artists **5.** AREA WHERE GROUP LIVES the area, e.g. in a city, where a group of people of the same or similar ethnicity or interests or jobs lives **6.** BIOL GROUP OF ANIMALS OR PLANTS a group of animals, insects, or organisms of the same kind that are living together and dependent on each other, or a group of plants growing in the same place **7.** MICROBIOL MASS OF ORGANISMS a localized mass or growth of organisms, e.g. bacteria, in or on a nutrient medium [14thC. From Latin colonia 'farm, settlement', from colonus 'tiller, settler', from colere 'to cultivate, dwell'.]

colophon /kóllə fon/ n. **1.** PUBLISHER'S EMBLEM ON BOOK the symbol or emblem that is printed on a book and represents a publisher or publisher's imprint **2.** PUBLICATION DETAILS IN BOOKS the details of the title, printer, publisher, and publication date given at the end of a book. Colophons are commonly found in early printed books and in modern private press editions. [Early 17thC. Via late Latin from Greek kolophōn 'summit, finishing touch'.]

colophony /ko lóffəni/ (plural -ies) n. = rosin [14thC. From Latin colophonia, from Colophonia resina 'resin of Colophon', named after a city in the ancient kingdom of Lydia, in what is now Turkey.]

color n., vti. US = colour

Colorado

Colorado /kóllə ráadō/ **1.** state in the western United States bordering on seven other states, including Utah to the west. Capital: Denver. Population: 3,892,644 (1997). Area: 269,618 sq. km/104,100 sq. mi. **2.** major North American river, rising in northern Colorado and flowing southwest through the Grand Canyon. Length: 2,330 km/1,450 mi.

Colorado beetle n. a small black-and-yellow striped beetle that is a serious agricultural pest and feeds on the leaves of potato plants. Latin name: Leptinotarsa decemlineata. US term **Colorado potato beetle** [From the fact that the beetle is native to the state of COLORADO]

Colorado potato beetle n. = Colorado beetle

Colorado Springs city in central Colorado, south of Denver and east of Pikes Peak. Population: 345,127 (1996).

Colorado topaz n. **1.** TOPAZ FOUND IN COLORADO a brownish-yellow topaz found in the state of Colorado **2.** BROWNISH-YELLOW QUARTZ a type of brownish-yellow quartz that resembles true Colorado topaz

coloration /kúllə ráysh'n/, **colouration** n. **1.** COLOUR APPEARANCE the appearance or pattern of colour on an object **2.** COLOURING OF AN ORGANISM the pattern of colours naturally occurring on an insect, bird, animal, or plant [Early 17thC]

coloratura /kóllərə tóorə/ n. a passage or piece of vocal music characterized by florid and demanding ornamentation, usually consisting of a rapid succession of notes. Coloratura passages are frequent in 18th- and 19th-century arias. [Mid-18thC. From obsolete Italian, literally 'colouring'.]

coloratura soprano n. a soprano with a light versatile voice capable of performing coloratura roles

colorectal /kōlō rékt'l/ adj. relating to both the colon and rectum [Mid-20thC. Coined from COLO- + RECTAL.]

colorific /kúllə ríffik/ adj. producing or giving colour to sth

colorimeter /kúllə rímmitər/ n. **1.** INSTRUMENT THAT MEASURES COLOUR an instrument for measuring and specifying colours by comparison with an established set of standard colours **2.** INSTRUMENT FOR MEASURING COLOURED SOLUTION CONCENTRATION an instrument that determines the concentration of a solution of a coloured substance by reference to standard solutions or standard colour slides [Mid-19thC. Coined from Latin color (see COLOUR) + -METER.] —**colorimetric** /kúlləri méttrik/ adj. —**colorimetrically** /-métrikli/ adv. —**colorimetry** /k/ n.

colossal /kə lóss'l/ adj. **1.** VERY LARGE unusually or impressively large **2.** VERY GREAT very great or impressive ○ a colossal increase in consumer spending **3.** SCULPTURE TWICE LIFE SIZE used to describe sculptures that are twice life size —**colossally** adv.

colosseum n. = coliseum

Colosseum, Rome

Colosseum /kóllə seé əm/ n. a large amphitheatre in Rome, built in the 1st century AD for sport and entertainment

Colossians /kə lósh'nz/ n. the twelfth book of the New Testament, a letter from St Paul to the church in the Phrygian city of Colossae written between 55 and 63 AD. See table at **Bible** [Early 16thC]

colossus /kə lóssəss/ (plural -si /-sī/ or -suses) n. **1.** SCULPTURE HUGE STATUE a statue that is several times larger than life size **2.** STH ENORMOUSLY LARGE OR POWERFUL an enormously large or powerful person or thing ○ a colossus among contemporary fashion designers [14thC. Via Latin from Greek kolossos, of uncertain origin: possibly from a non-Indo-European Mediterranean language.]

colostomy /kə lóstəmi/ (plural -mies) n. **1.** OPERATION CREATING AN ARTIFICIAL ANUS a surgical operation that creates an artificial anus through an opening made in the abdomen from the colon **2.** ARTIFICIAL ANUS an opening surgically created in the abdomen that functions as an anus [Late 19thC. Coined from COLO- + -STOMY.]

colostrum /kə lóstrəm/ n. a yellowish fluid rich in antibodies and minerals that a mother's breasts produce after giving birth and before the production of true milk. It provides newborns with immunity to infections. [Late 16thC. From Latin, of unknown origin.]

colour /kúllər/ n. **1.** PROPERTY CAUSING VISUAL SENSATION the property of objects that depends on the light that they reflect and that is perceived as red, blue, green, or other shades **2.** PAINTING PIGMENT a pigment used in painting **3. NOT BLACK OR WHITE** a colour such as red or green, as opposed to black, white, or grey **4. STH THAT ADDS COLOUR** sth such as paint, cosmetics, or dye that is used to add colour to sth **5. NATURAL SHADE OF COMPLEXION** the natural shade or colour of sb's skin as characteristic of race, especially of sb who is not white ○ *a person of colour* **6. NON-CAUCASIAN** a skin colour other than that normally described as white **7. HEALTHY LOOK TO SKIN** the normal look of a person's skin, especially in the face, when healthy **8. EXTRA FACIAL REDNESS** an extra redness in sb's face, e.g. caused by embarrassment or exposure to cold wind **9. VARIETY OF COLOURS** brightness and variety in the colours sth such as a room or picture has **10. INTEREST OR VIVIDNESS** a quality in sth that gives it interest or immediacy **11.** PAINTING **USE OF COLOUR IN PAINTING** the use of colour in painting, as distinct from line, form, or composition ○ *liked her handling of colour* **12.** MUSIC **SOUND QUALITY** the quality of a particular sound **13.** LAW **CLAIM OF LEGALITY** a claim or appearance of legal right ○ *by colour of law* **14.** PHYS **HYPOTHETICAL QUANTUM CHARACTERISTIC** a hypothetical property of quarks that takes three forms designated red, blue, and green **15.** OPTICS **ABILITY TO SEE COLOURS** the aspect of visual perception by which an observer recognizes colours **16.** *US* MINING **GOLD FOUND IN GRAVEL** a particle of gold found in gravel or sand ■ **colours** *npl.* **1. NATIONAL OR MILITARY FLAG** the flag of a nation or military unit **2. COLOURS REPRESENTING TEAM OR GROUP** the colours that are used to represent a team, school, or other group **3. CLOTHING WORN IN SPORT** the clothing worn by a jockey or an athlete that indicates the horse's owner or the team to which the athlete belongs **4.** HERALDRY **HERALDIC COLOUR** the main heraldic colours (**tinctures**) of azure, vert, sable, gules, and purpure **5.** SPORTS **TEAM MEMBERS' BADGE** a badge or other symbol given to members of a sports team ○ *In her second year she got her rowing colours.* **6. SB'S REAL SELF** sb's real beliefs, opinions, ethics, and principles ○ *It showed her up in her true colours.* ■ *v.* (**colours, colouring, coloured**) **1.** *vt.* **CHANGE OR ADD TO STH'S COLOUR** to change or add to the colour of sth using paint, dye, cosmetics, or a similar agent **2.** *vi.* **TAKE ON COLOUR** to take on a particular colour or change colour **3.** *vi.* **BLUSH** to have more red in the cheeks or face than normal, generally because of embarrassment **4.** *vt.* **SKEW OPINION OR JUDGMENT** to skew the way sb thinks about sth, making an opinion or judgment less objective [13thC. Via Old French from Latin *color.* Ultimately from an Indo-European word meaning 'to cover', which is also the ancestor of English *holster* and *calypso.*] ◇ **with flying colours** with the greatest of ease and to an excellent standard ◇ **nail your colours to the mast** to make it obvious what your opinions or intentions are ○ *They've nailed their colours to the mast and announced that they will not sell their property for redevelopment.*

colour in *vti.* to colour shapes or areas that have been left white or blank, especially in a special book of outline drawings for children ○ *I gave him a box of crayons so he could do some colouring in.* US term **color**

colour up *vi.* to become red in the face because of embarrassment or annoyance ○ *If you so much as look at him he colours up.* US term **color**

colourable /kúllərəb'l/ *adj.* (*formal*) **1. LOOKING REASONABLE BUT NOT SO** appearing to be reasonable or true, but in fact being neither ○ *a colourable explanation* **2. FEIGNING VALIDITY** pretending to be true or valid [14thC. From Old French *colorable* 'brightly coloured', from *color* (see COLOUR).] —**colourability** /kùllərə bílləti/ *n.* —**colourableness** /kúllərəb'lnəss/ *n.* —**colourably** /-bli/ *adv.*

colourant /kúllərənt/ *n.* a dye, pigment, ink, or similar agent that is used to add or change colour

colouration /kùllə ráysh'n/ *n.* = **coloration**

colour bar *n.* the legal, social, and traditional barriers that separate people of different ethnic groups. US term **colour line**

colour-blind *adj.* **1. UNABLE TO DISTINGUISH BETWEEN CERTAIN COLOURS** partially or completely unable to see or to distinguish between certain colours because of a defect in vision **2. NOT DISCRIMINATING** not discriminating between people on the grounds of their ethnic group or the colour of their skin [Mid-19thC. Coined by Sir David Brewster (1781–1868), the inventor of the kaleidoscope.] —**colour blindness** *n.*

colour-code (**colour-codes, colour-coding, colour-coded**) *vt.* to classify different types of things by different colours

colour contrast *n.* the perceived difference in a colour that occurs when it is surrounded by another colour

coloured /kúllərd/ *adj.* **1. HAVING COLOUR** having a particular colour or colours (*often used in combination*) ○ *dark coloured* ○ *honey coloured* **2. OFFENSIVE TERM** an offensive term meaning belonging to an ethnic group whose members have dark-coloured skin (*dated offensive*) **3. Coloured, coloured** *S Africa* **OF MIXED ETHNIC ORIGIN** belonging to a group of mixed ethnic origin (*dated*) ◊ **Cape Coloured 4. DISTORTED OR BIASED** biased or sensationalized ○ *a highly coloured account* ■ *n.* (*dated offensive*) **1. OFFENSIVE TERM** an offensive term for sb who belongs to an ethnic group that is predominantly dark-skinned **2. coloured, Coloured** *S Africa* **SB OF MIXED ETHNIC ORIGIN** sb whose ancestors were of both African and non-African descent

colourfast /kúllər faast/ *adj.* containing a dye that will not fade or wash out [Early 20thC. From FAST 'firm'.] —**colourfastness** *n.*

colour filter *n.* a filter made of coloured glass or gelatin that absorbs light of a given colour before it reaches the camera lens. It is used to achieve artistic effects or to compensate for weather conditions.

colourful /kúllərf'l/ *adj.* **1. WITH BRIGHT COLOURS** having bright or varied colours ○ *colourful costumes* **2. INTERESTING** interesting and exciting ○ *one of the most colourful periods in our history* ○ *She has a colourful past.* **3. NOT ORDINARY OR PREDICTABLE** likely to behave in unusual and unexpected ways ○ *The grandfather was certainly a colourful character.* **4. FULL OF SWEARWORDS** characterized by coarse words or obscenities (*informal*) (*used euphemistically*) ○ *colourful language* —**colourfully** *adv.* —**colourfulness** *n.*

colouring /kúlləring/ *n.* **1. ACT OF GIVING COLOUR** the act of giving colour to sth ○ *Children often enjoy colouring.* **2. COLOURING SUBSTANCE** a substance that gives colour to sth, e.g. a food dye **3. TYPE OF COMPLEXION** the shade of sb's skin or hair colour **4. CHARACTERISTIC COLOURS** the characteristic colours of a bird's plumage or an animal's coat

colouring book *n.* a book with drawings for a child to colour

colourist /kúllərist/ *n.* **1. ARTIST KNOWN FOR USE OF COLOURS** a painter whose technique involves special use of colour **2. COLOURER** sb whose work involves colouring things [Late 17thC. Formed from COLOUR, on the model of Italian *colorista.*] —**colouristic** /kùllə rístik/ *adj.* —**colouristically** /-rístikli/ *adv.*

colourize /kúllər īz/ (**-izes, -izing, -ized**), **colourise** (**-ises, -ising, -ised**) *vt.* to add colour to a black and white film, e.g. by using computer techniques

colourless /kúllərləss/ *adj.* **1. WITHOUT COLOUR** lacking colour **2. CHARACTERLESS** not interesting or exciting ○ *a colourless personality* **3. PALE** pale or lacking distinct colour ○ *It looks rather colourless; how about adding some parsley?* —**colourlessly** *adv.* —**colourlessness** *n.*

colour line *n.* = **colour bar**

colour phase *n.* **1. SEASONAL VARIATION IN COLOUR** a seasonal variation in the colour of a bird's plumage or an animal's coat **2. PERMANENT VARIATION IN COLOUR** a distinct and permanent colour variation shown by a group of animals within a species

colourpoint cat *n.* a long-haired cat with the markings of a Siamese cat, bred by crossing a Persian cat with a Siamese cat. US term **Himalayan cat**

colourpoint shorthair /k/ *n.* a domestic cat belonging to a breed with a light-coloured coat and darker markings on the face, ears, feet, and tail

colour scheme *n.* a combination of colours used in interior decoration

colour subcarrier *n.* the component of a television signal that transmits colour information to the receiver

colour supplement *n.* a magazine printed in colour and forming a section of a newspaper

colourwash *n.* coloured distemper —**colourwash** (**colourwashes, colourwashing, colourwashed**) *vt.*

colourway *n.* one of range of possible colours available ○ *The shirt comes in three exciting colourways, taupe, red, and navy.*

colourway *n.* one of various colours or combinations of colours on, or in which a pattern is printed when making fabric or wallpaper

colour wheel *n.* the spectrum represented as a circular diagram that shows how colours are related to one another

colpitis /kol pítiss/ *n.* MED = **vaginitis** (*technical*)

colpo- *prefix.* vagina ○ *colposcope* [From Greek *kolpos* (source also of English *gulf*)]

colposcope /kólpəskōp/ *n.* a magnifying and photographic instrument used to examine the vagina [Mid-20thC. From Greek *kolpos* 'womb'.] —**colposcopic** /kòlpə skóppik/ *adj.* —**colposcopy** /kol póskəpi/ *n.*

colt /kōlt/ *n.* **YOUNG MALE HORSE** a young uncastrated male horse, usually under four years of age ■ **colts** *npl.* **JUNIOR TEAM** a team made up of young or inexperienced players, often the junior team representing a club or school [Old English. Origin unknown.]

Colt /kōlt/ *tdmk.* a trademark for a brand of firearm

coltish /kóltish/ *adj.* energetic and playful in nature [14thC. From the wild behaviour of a colt.] —**coltishly** *adv.* —**coltishness** *n.*

Coltrane /kol tráyn/, **John** (1926–67) US saxophonist and composer. He was a leading proponent of free-form jazz in the 1960s. His compositions include *'Giant Steps'.*

coltsfoot /kóltsfòot/ (*plural* **-foots** *or* **-foot**) *n.* a plant of the daisy family found in Europe, Asia, and North America, with yellow flowerheads and large hoof-shaped leaves. The dried leaves and flowers are used in herbal medicine to treat coughs. Latin name: *Tussilago farfara.* [Mid-16thC. From the shape of the leaves.]

colubrid /kóllyòobrid/ (*plural* **-brid** *or* **-brids**) *n.* a snake belonging to a family of mostly nonvenomous snakes. Grass snakes and whip snakes are colubrids. Family: Colubridae. [Late 19thC. From modern Latin *Colubridae,* family name, which was coined from Latin *colubrid-,* the stem of *coluber* 'snake' (see COBRA).]

colubrine /kóllyòo brīn/ *adj.* **1. LOOKING LIKE A SNAKE** resembling a snake **2. RELATING TO COLUBRIDS** belonging or relating to the colubrid snakes [Early 16thC. From Latin *colubrinus,* from *coluber* 'snake' (see COLUBRID).]

colugo /kə lóogō/ (*plural* **-gos** *or* **-go**) *n.* = **flying lemur** [Early 18thC. From Malay.]

Colum /kóllәm/, **Padraic** (1881–1972) Irish poet and dramatist. He was an early supporter of Dublin's Abbey Theatre, where his plays, including *The Land* (1905), were presented.

Columba /kə lúmbə/ *n.* a small faint constellation of the southern hemisphere between Canis Major and Pictor

Columba /kə lúmbə/, **St** (521–597) Irish missionary. He travelled from the monastery he founded on the Hebridean island of Iona to spread Christianity through Scotland. Alternative names **Colmcille, Columcille, Columbanus**

columbarium /kòlləm báiri əm/ (*plural* **-a** /-báiri ə/) *n.* **1. PLACE FOR STORING FUNERAL URNS** a chamber or wall in which urns containing the ashes of the dead are stored **2. NICHE FOR FUNERAL URN** one of the niches in a building used to store funeral ashes [Mid-18thC. From Latin, formed from *columba* 'dove' (see COLUMBINE[1]).]

Columbian /kəlúmbi ən/ *adj.* relating to or typical of the United States, or its people or culture. ◊ **pre-Columbian**

columbine[1] /kólləm bīn/ (*plural* **-bines** *or* **-bine**) *n.* = **aquilegia** [14thC. Via Old French from medieval Latin *columbina (herba),* literally 'dovelike (plant)', from Latin *columbinus* (see COLUMBINE[2]); from the resemblance of the flower to a cluster of pigeons.]

columbine[2] /kólləm bīn/ *adj.* resembling or relating to doves [14thC. Via Old French from Latin *columbinus* 'dovelike', which was formed from *columba* 'dove, pigeon'.]

columbite /kə lúmm bīt/ n. a black, reddish-brown, or transparent mineral that is an ore of niobium and is made up of iron and manganese. Formula: $(Fe,Mn)(Nb,Ta)_2O_6$. [Early 19thC. Coined from COLUMBIUM + -ITE.]

columbium /kə lúmbi əm/ n. the element niobium (no longer in technical use) Symbol **Cb** [Early 19thC. Formed from modern Latin Columbia 'America', named after Christopher Columbus (from the fact that the element was discovered in ore from Massachusetts).] —**columbic** adj. —**columbous** adj.

Columbus /kə lúmbəss/, **Christopher** (1451–1506) Italian explorer. He reached the West Indies in 1492, thereby opening the Americas to European trade and colonization.

Columbus Day n. a US holiday, falling on October 12, that celebrates Christopher Columbus's first voyage to the Americas in 1492

columella /kólyŏŏ méllə/ (plural -lae) n. a tiny bone in the middle ear of all land vertebrates that transmits sound waves from the eardrum to the inner ear and corresponds to the stapes in mammals [Late 16thC. From Latin, literally 'little column', formed from columna 'column' (see COLUMN).] —**columellar** /kólyŏŏ méllə/ adj. —**columellate** /-méllət/ adj.

column /kólləm/ n. **1. ROUND PILLAR** an upright support shaped like a long cylinder ○ a Corinthian column **2. STH SHAPED LIKE A COLUMN** sth compared to a column in form ○ a column of smoke **3. LINE OF PEOPLE OR THINGS** a long line of people or vehicles **4. SECTION OF PAGE** one of two or more vertical sections of printed material on a page **5. REGULAR ARTICLE** an item in a newspaper or magazine that is always written by the same person, or is always about the same subject **6. VERTICAL ARRANGEMENT OF NUMBERS** a vertical arrangement of figures or mathematical terms **7.** ANAT, BOT **PART SHAPED LIKE COLUMN** any long part of a plant or animal ○ spinal column [15thC. Directly or via Old French from Latin columna (source of English colonel), of uncertain origin; probably formed from columen, culmen 'top, summit' (source of English culminate).] —**columned** adj.

column inch n. an area on a page one column wide and one inch deep, used to measure the amount of type that would fill that space

columnist /kólləmnist/ n. sb who writes a regular column for a newspaper or magazine ○ a gossip columnist

colure /kə loŏr/ n. either of two great circles on the celestial sphere that intersect at the celestial poles, one of which connects the equinoctial points on the ecliptic while the other connects the solstitial points [14thC. Via late Latin coluri from Greek kolourai (grammai) 'truncated (lines)', from kolouros, from kolos 'docked' + oura 'tail'.]

Colwyn Bay /kólwin-/ coastal resort in Conwy, North Wales. Population: 29,883 (1991).

coly /kó li/ (plural -ies or -y) n. a gregarious African bird that has soft hairy plumage, a crest on its head, and a very long tail. Family: Coliidae. [Mid-19thC. Via modern Latin Colius, genus name, from Greek kolios 'green woodpecker', of uncertain origin; from the bird's pecking.]

com /kom/ abbr. company (used in e-mail addresses)

COM /kom/ n. a process of converting computer output directly to microfilm. Full form **computer output on microfilm**

com. abbr. **1.** comedy **2.** comic **3.** commerce **4.** commercial **5.** committee **6.** commune

Com. abbr. **1.** Commander **2.** Commodore **3.** Communist

com- prefix. together, with, jointly (used before b, n, or p) ○ commix [From Latin com. Ultimately from an Indo-European base meaning 'together', which is also the ancestor of English contra- and coeno-.]

coma[1] /kómə/ n. a prolonged state of deep unconsciousness [Mid-17thC. Via modern Latin from Greek kōma 'deep sleep', of uncertain origin: perhaps related to Greek koiman 'to put to sleep' (source of English cemetery).]

coma[2] /kómə/ (plural -mae /-mee/) n. **1.** ASTRON **CLOUD AROUND HEAD OF COMET** a luminous cloud of gas and dust surrounding the head of a comet **2.** OPTICS **DISTORTION OF IMAGE** a lens defect that produces a blurred, comet-shaped image of a point, or the image produced [Early 17thC. Via Latin from Greek komē 'hair of the head', of unknown origin.] —**comal** adj.

Coma Berenices /kómə bérri nī seez/ n. a faint constellation in the sky of the northern hemisphere between Virgo and the Plough

Comanche /kə mán chi/ (plural -che or -ches) n. **1.** MEMBER OF NATIVE AMERICAN PEOPLE a member of a Native American people who formerly led a nomadic life in areas of Kansas, Oklahoma, and Texas and who now live mainly in Oklahoma **2.** COMANCHE LANGUAGE the Shoshonean language of the Comanche people. Comanche is spoken by about 500 people. [Early 19thC. Via Spanish from Southern Paiute or another Numic language.] —**Comanche** adj.

Comanchean /kə mán chi ən/ n. US a part of the early Cretaceous period in North America, which lasted from 140 to 100 million years ago [Named after Comanche, a county in Texas where limestone rocks of this period were first found] —**Comanchean** adj.

Comaneci /kómmə néchi/, **Nadia** (b. 1961) Romanian-born US gymnast. At the age of 14 she was the youngest person to win an Olympic gold medal in gymnastics and the first to attain a perfect 10 mark (1976).

comatose /kómətōss/ adj. **1.** IN A COMA in a coma **2.** UNABLE TO FUNCTION in a very tired or drunken state (informal) [Late 17thC. Formed from Greek kōmat-, the stem of kōma 'deep sleep' (see COMA[1]).] —**comatosely** adv.

comatulid /kə máttyŏŏlid/ (plural -lids or -lid), **comatula** /kə máttyŏŏlə/ (plural -lae /-lee/ or -la) n. a marine invertebrate animal that is free-swimming when it reaches maturity. Feather stars are comatulids. Order: Comatulida. [Late 19thC. From modern Latin Comatulidae, family name, from late Latin comatulus 'with neatly curled hair', from Latin comatus 'having hair'.]

comb /kōm/ n. **1.** INSTRUMENT FOR NEATENING HAIR an instrument with a row of long thin teeth, used to make hair tidy **2.** FASTENING FOR HAIR a piece of plastic or wood with long thin teeth, used to fasten back the hair **3.** TEXTILES TOOL FOR CLEANING WOOL a tool or part of a machine with long slender teeth, used for cleaning wool or other materials **4.** EQU = currycomb **5.** NEATENING OF HAIR an act of neatening the hair with a comb (informal) **6.** ZOOL CREST OF COCK the fleshy red growth on the head of a cock or other bird **7.** ZOOL HONEYCOMB a honeycomb ■ vt. (combs, combing, combed) **1.** NEATEN HAIR WITH COMB to tidy hair or fur with a comb **2.** TEXTILES CLEAN OR ARRANGE FIBRES to clean or arrange the fibres of wool or other materials using a comb **3.** SEARCH PLACE THOROUGHLY to search an area thoroughly ○ We combed the house for his keys. [Old English camb, comb. Ultimately from an Indo-European word meaning 'tooth, nail', which is also the ancestor of English gem.] ◇ **go over sth with a fine-tooth(ed) comb, go through sth with a fine-tooth(ed) comb** to study or search sth extremely carefully

comb. abbr. **1.** combination **2.** combining **3.** combustion

combat /kóm bat/ n. **1.** FIGHTING fighting between groups or individuals, especially between soldiers (often used before a noun) ○ He had never seen combat. ○ combat troops **2.** FIGHT OR STRUGGLE a struggle between opposing individuals or forces ○ a combat between good and evil ■ vt. (-bats, -bating or -batting, -bated or -batted) **1.** TRY TO DESTROY STH DANGEROUS to attempt to destroy or control sth harmful ○ measures to combat pollution **2.** RESIST STH to resist sb or sth actively [Mid-16thC. Via French combattre 'to fight' from assumed late Latin combattere, literally 'to fight with', from, ultimately, Latin battuere 'to beat' (see BATTER).] —**combatable** /kom báttəb'l/ adj. —**combater** /-báttər/ n.

combatant /kómmbətənt/ n. **1.** SB TAKING PART IN WAR a person or group taking part in a war **2.** SB INVOLVED IN ARGUMENT sb who is involved in a struggle or argument

combat fatigue n. a psychological disorder resulting from the stress of being involved in a battle and characterized by acute anxiety, depression, and loss of motivation. = **battle fatigue**

combative /kómmbətiv/ adj. eager to fight or argue —**combatively** adv. —**combativeness** n.

combe /koom/ n. primarily in southern England, a small valley with steep sides that seldom has running water in it [Pre-12thC. Of Celtic origin.]

comber /kómər/ n. **1.** TEXTILES SB OR STH THAT COMBS YARN a person or machine that combs wool or other materials **2.** US = beachcomber

combination /kómbi náysh'n/ n. **1.** MIXTURE a mixture of different things or factors, or the act of mixing them ○ We were saved by a combination of skill and good luck. **2.** COMBINED SET two or more things or people that are combined to form a set ○ The red shirt and navy waistcoat make a striking colour combination. **3.** ALLIANCE an association between groups or individuals established in order to accomplish sth **4.** NUMBERS THAT OPEN A LOCK a series of numbers or letters needed to open a combination lock **5.** MATH ARRANGEMENT OF NUMBERS IN SUBSETS an arrangement of the numbers or symbols in a mathematical set into smaller subsets without regard to the order in which those numbers or symbols appear **6.** MATH SUBSET a subset containing a specified number of the elements of a given set, selected without regard to the order in which they were chosen **7.** CHEM FORMATION OF A COMPOUND the union of substances in the formation of a chemical compound **8.** CHESS SEQUENCE OF MOVES INVOLVING SEVERAL PIECES a series of tactical moves involving two or more chess pieces **9.** BOXING SERIES OF PUNCHES in boxing, two or more punches quickly delivered one after the other ■ **combinations** npl. UNDERWEAR a piece of underwear with long sleeves and legs (dated) —**combinational** adj.

——— **WORD KEY: SYNONYMS** ———
See Synonyms at **mixture**.

combination lock n. a lock that operates by means of a set of wheels, each having a sequence of numbers from 0 to 9. It opens only when the wheels are aligned to give a specific sequence of numbers.

combination tone n. MUSIC = resultant tone

combinatorial analysis /kómbinə táwr iəl-/ n. a branch of mathematics dealing with combinations and permutations, especially those relating to probability and statistics

combine v. /kəm bīn/ (-bines, -bining, -bined) **1.** vti. JOIN OR MIX TOGETHER to join or mix together, or join or mix people or things together ○ Combine the ingredients in a large mixing bowl. ○ All these factors combine to make for a truly successful product. **2.** vt. DO THINGS SIMULTANEOUSLY to undertake two or more activities at the same time ○ It can be difficult to combine having a career with being a mother. **3.** vti. CHEM UNITE CHEMICALLY to join together or to make substances join together to form a chemical compound **4.** vti. AGRIC HARVEST CROPS WITH MACHINE to harvest crops using a combine harvester ■ n. /kóm bīn/ **1.** ASSOCIATION an association of business organizations **2.** AGRIC = combine harvester [15thC. From late Latin combinare, literally 'to put two things together', from Latin bini 'two at a time', from bi- 'twice' (see BI-).] —**combinable** adj. —**combinative** /kómbinaytiv, -nətiv/ adj. —**combiner** /kəm bīnər/ n.

combined /kəm bīnd/ n. SKIING a skiing event involving competition in downhill and slalom runs that are slightly less arduous than either run as a single event

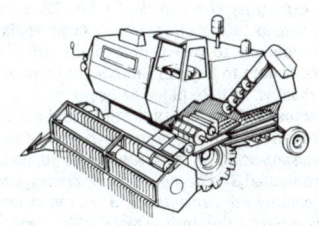

Combine harvester

combine harvester /kóm bīn-/ n. a large farm machine that is used to harvest crops

combings /kṓmingz/ *npl.* small loose pieces of hair, wool, or other fibre that are collected during combing

combo /kómbō/ (*plural* **-bos**) *n.* **1.** JAZZ GROUP a small jazz or dance band **2.** *US* SB OR STH JOINED a combination of several people or elements (*informal*) ○ *a burger, fries, and shake combo* [Early 20thC. Formed from COMBINATION.]

comb-over *n.* a man's hairstyle designed to conceal baldness by allowing the hair to grow long on one side of the head and combing it over the top (*informal*)

combust /kəm búst/ (**-busts, -busting, -busted**) *vti.* to react vigorously with oxygen to produce heat and light, seen as a flame [15thC. Partly from obsolete *combust* 'burnt', from Latin *combustus* (see COMBUSTION); partly a back-formation from COMBUSTION.]

combustible /kəm bústəb'l/ *adj.* **1.** LIKELY TO CATCH FIRE able or likely to catch fire and burn **2.** CHEM REACTING WITH OXYGEN TO PRODUCE FLAME able to react vigorously with oxygen to produce heat and light, seen as a flame —**combustibility** /kəm bústə bíllәti/ *n.* —**combustibly** /-bústəb li/ *adv.* —**combustible** /-b/ *n.*

combustion /kəm búschən/ *n.* **1.** IGNITION the burning of fuel in an engine to provide power **2.** CHEMICAL REACTION a chemical process in which a substance reacts vigorously with oxygen to produce heat and light, seen as a flame [15thC. From Latin *combustos*, the past participle of *comburere* 'burn up', from, ultimately, *urere* 'burn'.] —**combustive** *adj.*

combustion chamber *n.* an enclosed space in which combustion takes place, e.g. in a jet engine or internal-combustion engine

combustor /kəm bústər/ *n.* a combustion system in a jet engine or gas turbine, consisting of the fuel injection system, the igniter, and the combustion chamber

comd *abbr.* MIL command

comdg *abbr.* MIL commanding

Comdr *abbr.* Commander

Comdt *abbr.* Commandant

come (**comes, coming, came**) CORE MEANING: a basic intransitive verb expressing movement towards a specified place or person. This verb often expresses the concept of movement coupled with the arrival at a place where an activity will take place. ○ *Come and sit by me.* ○ *Come to my house tomorrow.*

1. *vi.* REACH to reach or extend to a particular point or place ○ *Her hair came down to her waist.* **2.** *vi.* REACH A STATE to reach or be brought into a particular state or situation ○ *It just came apart in my hands.* **3.** *vi.* ARRIVE OR HAPPEN to happen or exist at a particular point or time ○ *I never thought this day would come.* **4.** *v. vti.* OCCUR IN THE MIND to occur in the mind ○ *An afterthought came to me while I was shaving.* **5.** *vi.* ORIGINATE FROM to originate from a place or thing ○ *The meat came from Canadian herds.* **6.** *vi.* RESULT FROM to result from sth ○ *We hoped some good would come of it.* **7.** *vi.* BE PRODUCED to be produced in a particular size, colour, or style ○ *This model also comes in red.* **8.** *vi.* AMOUNT TO to add up to a particular total ○ *That comes to £14.50.* **9.** *vi.* HAVE AN ORGASM to reach sexual climax (*slang*) (*considered offensive by some speakers*) **10.** *vt.* ADOPT BEHAVIOUR to adopt a certain kind of attitude or behaviour (*informal*) ○ *Don't come the smart aleck with me, son.* **11.** *prep.* by a particular time in the future ○ *Come July there will be an extra fifty cases to deal with.* **12.** *n.* SEMEN a man's semen (*slang offensive*) ◇ **come again?** used to ask someone to repeat or explain sth (*informal*) ◇ **come to pass** to happen (*archaic or literary*)

come about *vi.* to take place or occur

come across *v.* **1.** *vt.* FIND SB OR STH to find sth or meet sb by chance ○ *I came across a reference to her in the newspaper.* **2.** *vi.* BE COMMUNICATED to be clearly communicated ○ *The point came across loud and clear: cutbacks are inevitable.* **3.** *vi.* GIVE AN IMPRESSION to give a particular impression ○ *She comes across as honest and sincere.*

come along *vi.* **1.** APPEAR to appear or arrive ○ *We'll deal with whatever comes along.* **2.** PROGRESS to progress or develop (*only used in continuous tenses, usually in questions or with an adverb*) ○ *How's the new recruit coming along?* **3.** ACCOMPANY SB ELSE to go somewhere with sb **4.** HURRY UP to move or act more quickly ○ *Come along or we'll be late for dinner.* **5.** USED TO ENCOURAGE OR REPRIMAND SB used to encourage or reprimand sb who is tired, unhappy, unwilling, or uncooperative (*usually used in the imperative*) ○ *Come along, dry your eyes.*

come apart *vi.* to tear or disintegrate ○ *The dress just came apart when I washed it.*

come around *vi.* US = **come round**

come at *vt.* **1.** ARRIVE AT STH to reach or discover sth with difficulty ○ *The only way to come at the facts is to ask pertinent questions.* **2.** ATTACK SB to set upon and attack sb ○ *He came at his opponent on a dark side street.* **3.** *Aus* AGREE TO DO STH to agree to do sth (*slang*) **4.** *Aus* BE UNABLE TO TOLERATE STH to be unable or unwilling to tolerate sth, e.g. obnoxious behaviour (*slang*) **5.** *Aus* ASSUME STH to assume or suppose sth (*slang*)

come away *vi.* to become detached from sth ○ *The handle came away in my hand.*

come back *vi.* **1.** BE POPULAR AGAIN to become popular again ○ *Seventies fashions came back briefly during the mid-nineties.* **2.** COME INTO SB'S MIND to appear or become clear again from sb's memory ○ *I can't remember the address, but give me a moment and it'll come back to me.* **3.** *US* RETORT to reply energetically or aggressively to sb ○ *She came back at him immediately with a counterblast.*

come back to *vt.* **1.** CONSIDER STH AGAIN to reconsider or refer to sth again (*informal*) ○ *I'll come back to that question in a moment.* **2.** REPLY AFTER INTERVAL to speak to sb again about sth at a later time ○ *Do you mind if I come back to you on that one?*

come before *vt.* be submitted for consideration or judgment before a group of people with authority ○ *The proposal comes before the committee next week.*

come between *vt.* **1.** INTERFERE IN SB'S RELATIONSHIP to disrupt a relationship ○ *I won't let anything come between us.* **2.** STOP SB GETTING OR DOING STH to prevent sb from having or doing sth ○ *He won't let anything come between him and his Saturday football.*

come by *vt.* to manage to acquire sth ○ *Jobs are not so easy to come by nowadays.*

come down *vi.* **1.** DECREASE to decrease in value or amount ○ *Prices are coming down.* **2.** REACH A DECISION to make a decision or judgment ○ *The judge came down in favour of the plaintiff's motion.* **3.** BE HANDED DOWN to be passed down from one generation to another ○ *written records that have come down to us from that period* **4.** LEAVE UNIVERSITY to leave a university, especially Oxford or Cambridge **5.** RETURN TO NORMAL CONSCIOUSNESS to return to a normal state of consciousness after being affected by drugs (*informal*) ◇ **come down in the world** to have less money or power than previously ◇ **come down to earth** to come back to reality after a period of happiness or unrealistic hopes

come down on *vt.* to punish or criticize sb severely

come down to *vt.* to mean or represent sth fundamentally, when all nonessential detail has been disregarded

come down with *vt.* to catch a cold, flu, or another minor illness

come for *vt.* **1.** PICK SB UP to arrive at a place to pick sb or sth up **2.** MOVE TOWARDS SB THREATENINGLY to move towards sb in a threatening way ○ *The dog came for me.*

come forward *vi.* to present yourself and show that you are willing to undertake sth ○ *She came forward with a rather good suggestion.*

come from *v.* **1.** *vi.* BE DESCENDED FROM be descended from a particular line, family, or stock **2.** *vti.* ORIGINATE OR ARISE to have a particular place as your original home or a particular source of sth ○ *She came from Manchester.*

come in *vi.* **1.** FINISH IN A PARTICULAR POSITION to finish a race in a particular position ○ *The British yacht came in fifth.* **2.** ARRIVE to arrive or be received and become available for use, sale, or communication ○ *The spring fashions will be coming in next month.* **3.** BECOME FASHIONABLE to become fashionable ○ *Long hair for men came in during the 1960s.* **4.** PARTICIPATE to become involved in sth ○ *There are three other companies interested in coming in on the deal.* **5.** RADIO BEGIN SPEAKING to begin speaking during a discussion or in reply to a radio signal ○ *Perhaps I could ask you to come in on that point, Professor Witz.* **6.** PROVE to turn out to have a particular level of usefulness ○ *That little knife came in very handy when we went camping.* **7.** TRANSP APPROACH DESTINATION to approach or arrive at a destination **8.** BECOME HIGHER to become higher, driving water up over the shore (*refers to the tide*)

come in for *vt.* to be the object of criticism or scrutiny ○ *The policy has come in for scathing attacks by the media.*

come into *vt.* to inherit money or property

come of *vt.* to be the result of sth

come off *v.* **1.** *vt.* FALL OFF to fall from sth ○ *She came off at the water jump.* **2.** *vt.* COME LOOSE to become detached or to be detachable from sth ○ *The top comes off easily.* **3.** *vi.* HAPPEN to take place as planned or predicted (*informal*) ○ *Let's hope the trip comes off.* **4.** *vi.* SUCCEED to be successful (*informal*) ○ *It was a risky thing to try, but it came off.* **5.** *vt.* BE DEDUCTED FROM STH to be deducted from sth **6.** *vt.* STOP TAKING MEDICINE to stop taking a drug or a medicine ○ *When I came off the painkillers, the doctor put me on aspirin.*

come on *v.* **1.** *vi.* START TO OPERATE to become available for use or to begin to function (*refers to a power source or machine*) ○ *The street lights come on at dusk.* **2.** *vi.* HURRY to hurry up (*usually used in the imperative*) ○ *Come on, I haven't got all day!* **3.** *vi.* USED TO ENCOURAGE SB used to encourage sb who is tired or unwilling (*usually used in the imperative*) ○ *Come on, you can do it if you try.* **4.** *vi.* USED TO SHOW DISBELIEF used to tell sb to stop exaggerating or lying ○ *Come on! You don't expect me to believe that, do you?* **5.** *vi.* TO TELL SB TO STOP PRETENDING used to tell sb to drop a pretence or stop behaving in a superior way (*usually used in the imperative*) ○ *Come on! You know you can't afford that car.* **6.** *vi.* PROGRESS to develop well or in the stated way ○ *How's the book coming on?* **7.** *vi.* ADVANCE to move forward, especially in battle ○ *Our cannon fire tore huge holes in their ranks, but still they came on.* **8.** *vi.* DEVELOP GRADUALLY to develop gradually ○ *It grew chilly as night came on.* **9.** *vi.* THEATRE ENTER DURING PLAY to go onto the stage as part of the action ○ *The villain doesn't come on until Act 2.* **10.** *vt.* APPEAR OR SPEAK ON BROADCAST MEDIUM to appear or speak on television, radio, or the telephone ○ *I noticed her voice when she came on the phone.* **11.** *vi.* BEGIN AT SCHEDULED TIME to begin at a particular time (*refers to radio or television programmes or a stage performer*) ○ *Her favourite show is coming on in an hour, and she never misses it.*

come on to *vt.* **1.** MOVE ON TO STH to begin to deal with sth ○ *We now come on to the most controversial item on our agenda.* **2.** MAKE SEXUAL ADVANCES to make sexual advances to sb (*slang*)

come out *vi.* **1.** REVEAL OR BE REVEALED to reveal sth or be revealed ○ *The true facts only came out when journalists began to dig a little deeper.* **2.** PUBL BE PUBLISHED to be published ○ *Her new novel is coming out next month.* **3.** DECLARE STH to state sth openly ○ *The majority came out in favour of raising the age limit.* **4.** REVEAL STH SECRET ABOUT YOURSELF to reveal to other people sth about yourself that you have kept secret **5.** ACKNOWLEDGE SEXUALITY to declare openly that one is gay or lesbian **6.** BECOME ACTIVE IN SAME-SEX RELATIONSHIPS to become active in sexual relationships with others of the same sex for the first time ○ *I think she came out when she was 17, with her best friend.* **7.** MAKE DEBUT IN SOCIETY to make a first appearance in society **8.** BE UTTERED to be uttered involuntarily or with an unintended effect ○ *We had no intention of revealing the story; it came out by accident.* **9.** BECOME VISIBLE IN SKY to become visible in the sky ○ *The sun came out from behind a cloud.* **10.** BE REMOVABLE to disappear after cleaning ○ *Even the toughest stains come out with this new detergent.* **11.** STRIKE to begin a strike ○ *The train drivers came out in sympathy.*

come out in *vt.* to have sth such as spots or a rash appear on the skin

come out of *vt.* **1.** SURVIVE HAZARD OR ILLNESS to survive a hazard or illness ○ *I'd say she came out of the ordeal in pretty good shape.* **2.** BE DEDUCTED to be deducted from an amount of money ○ *The new window will have to come out of your allowance.*

come out with *vt.* to say sth surprising ○ *never know what children will come out with*

come over *v.* **1.** *vi.* CHANGE SIDES to change an opinion or allegiance ○ *She says she'll come over if we guarantee her a seat on the board.* **2.** *vi.* BE COMMUNICATED to be clearly communicated ○ *The message came over loud and clear: he isn't going to change his mind.* **3.** *vi.* GIVE IMPRESSION to give a particular impression ○ *She comes over as much less forceful and ambitious than her sister.* **4.** *vt.* AFFECT SB to affect or overcome sb ○ *A feeling of giddiness came over her, and she nearly fell over.* **5.** *vi.* BEGIN TO FEEL STH to begin to feel a strange sensation (*informal*) ○ *I came over all peculiar and had to sit down.*

come round *vi.* **1.** VISIT to visit sb ○ *Why don't you come round this evening?* **2.** REGAIN CONSCIOUSNESS to regain consciousness after being knocked out, e.g. ○ *When I came round, I was in hospital.* **3.** CHANGE YOUR OPINION to change your opinion to that of sb else ○ *They soon came round to our way of thinking.* **4.** RECUR to happen again at the expected time ○ *The same questions come round year after year at these meetings .*

come through *v.* **1.** *vi.* SURVIVE to survive a dangerous or unpleasant experience **2.** *vi.* BE RECEIVED to be received or heard, usually through a telecommunications medium ○ *A fax has come through from head office.* **3.** *vti.* MOVE THROUGH A PLACE to move between one place and another ○ *The porch was so crowded, we had to come through the kitchen.* ○ *Coming through! Coming through! These plates are hot!*

come to *v.* **1.** *vi.* REGAIN CONSCIOUSNESS to regain consciousness or wake up ○ *The patient came to in the recovery room.* **2.** *vi.* NAUT SLOW DOWN OR STOP to slow down or stop (*refers to a ship*) **3.** *vt.* TOTAL to amount to a particular total ◇ **come to that** used when adding sth to what has just been said

come under *vt.* **1.** BE CLASSIFIED to be classified under a particular heading ○ *Hawthorne comes under American authors.* **2.** BE UNDER SB'S AUTHORITY to be subject to the authority of sb or sth ○ *Which department do we come under?* **3.** UNDERGO STH to be subjected to sth ○ *She came under attack from members of her own party.*

come up *vi.* **1.** EMERGE FROM WATER to rise to the surface of water ○ *She'll have to come up for air in a minute.* **2.** APPEAR ABOVE HORIZON to appear above the horizon ○ *I enjoy watching the sun come up.* **3.** BE MENTIONED to be mentioned or discussed ○ *a topic that came up in conversation* **4.** OCCUR UNEXPECTEDLY to happen unexpectedly ○ *I won't be able to make lunch; something's come up at work.* **5.** BE HAPPENING SOON to be going to happen in the near future ○ *Coming up next, the news.* **6.** APPEAR IN COURT to be tried by a judge or a court of law ○ *Her case comes up next week.* **7.** BE SELECTED AS WINNER to win a prize in a game involving luck ○ *if my numbers come up*

come up against *vt.* to meet with sth that has to be faced or dealt with ○ *He has come up against fierce criticism.*

come up for *vt.* to become due for sth ○ *The case is coming up for review.*

come upon *vt.* to find sth or meet sb by chance

come up to *vt.* to be as good as sb's expectations

come up with *vt.* to produce or discover sth, in response to a need or challenge ○ *She's come up with a brilliant solution.*

comeback /kúm bak/ *n.* **1.** RETURN TO SUCCESS a return to a successful position or activity ○ *Rumour has it that she's planning a comeback.* **2.** SHARP REPLY a sharp or witty reply ○ *He's always been one for the quick comeback.* **3.** COMPLAINT OR CLAIM FOR COMPENSATION a complaint about sth, or a claim for compensation ○ *I don't want any comebacks from dissatisfied customers.*

Comecon /kómi kon/, **COMECON** *n.* an organization of the former USSR and satellite Communist countries aimed at encouraging economic development. It existed between 1949 and 1991. Full form **Council for Mutual Economic Assistance** [Mid-20thC]

comedian /kə méedi ən/ *n.* **1.** COMIC ENTERTAINER a humorous entertainer **2.** COMIC ACTOR an actor who plays comic roles **3.** AMUSING PERSON sb who is or tries to be amusing (*often used ironically*) ○ *Some comedian put salt in the sugar bowl.*

comedienne /kə méedi én/ *n.* **1.** FEMALE COMIC ENTERTAINER a female entertainer who tells jokes **2.** COMIC ACTRESS a female actor who takes comic roles **3.** AMUSING WOMAN a woman who is, or tries to be amusing (*often used ironically*)

comedo /kómmidō/ (*plural* **-dones** /-dō neez/ *or* **-dos**) *n.* MED a blackhead [Mid-19thC. From Latin, 'glutton, worm that devours the body', formed from *comedere* 'to devour' (see COMESTIBLE). From the shape of the contents when squeezed out.]

comedown /kúm down/ *n.* a decline in status or position (*informal*)

comedy /kómmədi/ (*plural* **-dies**) *n.* **1.** FUNNY PLAY, FILM, OR BOOK a play, film, or book depicting amusing events **2.** COMIC GENRE comic works, especially plays, considered as a literary genre **3.** COMIC ENTERTAINMENT entertainment that is amusing **4.** COMIC ELEMENT the humorous elements of a situation or work of art [14thC. Via French *comédie* from, ultimately, Greek *kōmōidia*, from *kōmōidos* 'comic actor, comic poet', from *kōmos* 'revel' (see COMIC) + *aoidos* 'singer', from *aeidein* 'to sing'.] —**comedic** /kə méedik/ *adj.* —**comedically** /-méedikli/ *adv.*

come from away *n. Can* sb who is a newcomer to the Atlantic region of Canada (*informal*)

comely /kúm li/ (**-lier, -liest**) *adj.* physically attractive (*archaic or literary*) (*refers to women*) [13thC. Origin uncertain: probably shortening of obsolete *becomely* 'becoming, fitting', from BECOME 'to be suitable to'.] —**comeliness** *n.*

come-on *n.* **1.** ENTICEMENT sth that arouses interest or desire, e.g. a free gift intended to encourage purchasers (*informal*) **2.** COMMENT OR ACTION a comment or action intended to indicate sb's sexual interest in another person

comer /kúmmər/ *n.* sb or sth that is likely to succeed (*informal*)

comestible /kə méstəb'l/ *n.* FOOD sth edible, usually a cooked food (*formal*) ■ *adj.* EDIBLE edible (*formal*) [15thC. Via French from medieval Latin *comestibilis*, from Latin *comestus*, past participle of *comedere*, literally 'to eat completely', from *edere* 'to eat' (see EDIBLE).]

Comet: Hale-Bopp comet, photographed over Bulgaria (1997)

comet /kómmit/ *n.* a celestial body that is composed of a mass of ice and dust and has a long luminous tail produced by vaporization when its orbit passes close to the Sun [12thC. Directly or via Old French from Latin *(stella) cometa* 'long-haired (star)', from Greek *(astēr) komētēs*, from, ultimately, *komē* 'hair of the head'.] —**cometary** *adj.* —**cometic** /kə méttik/ *adj.*

comeuppance /kúm úppənss/ *n.* sth unpleasant, regarded as a just punishment for sb (*informal*) ○ *He got his comeuppance in the end.* [Mid-19thC. Formed from COME UP, probably in the sense 'to be tried before a court'.]

comfit /kúmfit/ *n.* a sweet consisting of a piece of fruit, a seed, or a nut in a sugar coating [14thC. Via Old French from Latin *confectum, confecta*, from *confectus* 'prepared, made ready' (see CONFECT).]

comfort /kúmfərt/ *n.* **1.** STATE OF BEING COMFORTABLE conditions in which sb feels physically relaxed ○ *Enjoy the comfort of your own home.* **2.** COMFORTABLE THING sth that makes you feel physically relaxed (*often used in the plural*) ○ *the comforts of home* **3.** RELIEF FROM PAIN relief from pain or anxiety ○ *They brought comfort to the wounded.* **4.** STH PROVIDING RELIEF sb or sth that provides relief from pain or anxiety ○ *The family has been such a comfort to me since my wife died.* ■ *vt.* (**-forts, -forting, -forted**) **1.** CHEER SB to bring sb relief from distress or anxiety ○ *The victim's parents were being comforted at home by relatives.* **2.** MAKE SB COMFORTABLE to make sb feel pleasantly relaxed ○ *She was comforted by the warmth.* [12thC. Via Old French *confort* from, ultimately, late Latin *confortare*, literally 'to strengthen completely', from Latin *fortis* 'strong' (see FORCE). Originally 'to encourage, support'.]

comfortable /kúmftəb'l, -fərtəb'l/ *adj.* **1.** RELAXED feeling comfort or ease ○ *Sit down and make yourselves comfortable.* **2.** MAKING SB RELAXED making sb feel physically relaxed ○ *I changed into something more comfortable.* **3.** NOT ANXIOUS free from stress or anxiety ○ *I don't feel comfortable with that idea.* **4.** MED STABLE PHYSICALLY in a stable physical condition ○ *The patient is comfortable.* **5.** ADEQUATE OR LARGE large enough to prevent anxiety or risk ○ *The government won by a comfortable majority.* **6.** WITH ADEQUATE INCOME having enough income ○ *They're not what you'd call well-off, but they're certainly comfortable.* —**comfortableness** *n.*

comfortably /kúmftəbli, -fərtəbli/ *adv.* **1.** AT EASE with a feeling of comfort or ease ○ *Are you sitting comfortably?* **2.** HAVING NO PROBLEMS having enough of sth to stave off worry, especially enough money to live on without worrying about providing essentials ○ *We can manage comfortably on what we earn together.*

comforter /kúmfərtər/ *n.* **1.** SB WHO COMFORTS sb who relieves other people's grief or anxieties **2.** *US, Can* = **duvet 3.** BABY'S DUMMY a baby's dummy (*dated*)

Comforter *n.* the Holy Spirit [14thC. From Old French *confortere*, translation of Latin *consolator*, translation in turn of Greek *paraklētos* 'advocate, intercessor' (see PARACLETE). The proper Latin translation would have been *advocatus*.]

comfort food *n.* FOOD easily prepared unsophisticated food that is psychologically comforting, especially food that is high in carbohydrates (*informal*)

comforting /kúmfərting/ *adj.* relieving anxiety or pain —**comfortingly** *adv.*

comfortless /kúmfərtləss/ *adj.* affording no comfort ○ *a sterile, comfortless room* —**comfortlessly** *adv.* —**comfortlessness** *n.*

comfort level, **comfort zone** *n.* the set of physical or psychological circumstances in which sb feels most at ease and free from physical discomfort or stress (*informal*) ○ *He said that the task was outside his workplace comfort zone.*

comfort station *n. US* a public toilet (*used euphemistically*)

comfrey /kúmfri/ (*plural* **-frey** *or* **-freys**) *n.* a plant native to Europe and Asia, with hairy leaves and stems and clusters of pink, white, or blue flowers. Herbalists used its grated roots in poultices to heal broken bones, or in linctuses for back pain and coughs. Genus: *Symphytum*. [13thC. Via Anglo-Norman and Old French from, ultimately, Latin *conferva*, from *confervere* 'to heal', literally 'to boil together', from *fervere* 'to boil' (see FERVENT).]

comfy /kúmfi/ (**-fier, -fiest**) *adj.* comfortable (*informal*) [Early 19thC. Formed from a shortening of COMFORTABLE.]

comic /kómmik/ *adj.* **1.** FUNNY so amusing that it induces smiles or laughter **2.** THEATRE RELATING TO COMEDY appearing in or characteristic of comedy ○ *a great comic routine* ■ *n.* **1.** THEATRE COMEDIAN a comedian or comedienne **2.** PUBL MAGAZINE a magazine that consists of stories told in a series of coloured panels. US term **comic book** [Late 16thC. Via Latin from Greek *kōmikos*, from *kōmos* 'revel' (source of English *comedy*), of unknown origin.]

WORD KEY: USAGE

comic or **comical**? The two words are close in meaning, but ***comic*** generally denotes intention (*a comic act, a comic poet*) whereas ***comical*** denotes effect or result, whether intentional or not (*a comical performance; his attempts at skiing were comical*).

WORD KEY: SYNONYMS

See Synonyms at ***funny***.

comical /kómmik'l/ *adj.* so amusing that it elicits smiles or laughter ○ *comical facial expressions* —**comicality** /kómmi kálləti/ *n.* —**comicalness** /kómmik'lnəss/ *n.* —**comically** /kómmikli/ *adv.*

WORD KEY: USAGE
See Usage note at *comic.*

WORD KEY: SYNONYMS
See Synonyms at *funny.*

comic book *n. US* = comic

comic opera *n.* 1. OPERA WITH COMIC LIBRETTO an opera with a humorous plot and a happy ending 2. MUSICAL GENRE comic operas considered as a musical genre

comic strip *n.* a series of cartoons that tell a story or a joke

coming /kúmming/ *adj.* 1. HAPPENING SOON about to happen or start ○ *She was dreading the coming winter.* 2. PROBABLY SUCCESSFUL likely to be successful in the near future ○ *She's the coming power in this company.* ■ *n.* ARRIVAL the arrival of a person or an event

coming of age *n.* 1. REACHING ADULTHOOD the reaching of the official age of adulthood and legal responsibility 2. ADVANCED DEVELOPMENT the reaching of an advanced stage of development ○ *the coming of age of the computer*

comings and goings *npl.* busy activity in which people arrive and depart frequently

Comintern /kómmin turn/ *n.* an international organization of Communist parties set up by Lenin in 1919 and abolished in 1943 [Early 20thC. From Russian *Komintern*, which was coined from *kommunisticheskii internatsional'nyi* 'communist international'.]

comitia /kə míshi ə/ (*plural* **-a**) *n.* a legislative assembly of citizens in ancient Rome [Early 17thC. From Latin, the plural of *comitium* 'assembly', literally 'going together', from *itus*, the past participle of *ire* 'to go' (see ITINERARY).]

comity of nations /kómmiti-/ *n.* the mutual recognition among nations of one another's laws, customs, and institutions

comm. *abbr.* 1. commerce 2. commercial 3. committee 4. commonwealth

comma /kómmə/ *n.* 1. GRAM PUNCTUATION MARK a punctuation mark (,) that represents a slight pause in a sentence or is used to separate words and figures in a list 2. MUSIC BRIEF PAUSE OR INTERVAL a short pause or interval in a piece of music 3. ZOOL = **comma butterfly** [Late 16thC. Via Latin from Greek *komma* 'piece cut off, short clause', from *koptein* 'to cut'. The original English meaning was 'short clause'.]

comma butterfly *n.* an orange and brown butterfly that has a comma-shaped white mark on the underside of each hind wing. Latin name: *Polygonia c-album.*

command /kə maánd/ *n.* 1. ORDER an order or instruction given by sb in authority ○ *On the command to mount up, the crews scrambled into their tanks.* 2. CONTROL control over sb or sth that is gained by personal power or authority ○ *She sized up the situation and took command.* 3. THOROUGH KNOWLEDGE thorough knowledge of sth, especially a language ○ *a fluent command of French* 4. COMPUT OPERATING INSTRUCTION TO COMPUTER an instruction to a computer to carry out an operation 5. MIL AUTHORITY the authority to control and direct the actions of a group of people, especially a military unit ○ *A new officer arrived to take command of the regiment.* 6. MIL MILITARY CONTROL the ability to control an area militarily ○ *Our primary objective is to gain command of the high ground.* 7. MIL STH UNDER OFFICER'S JURISDICTION troops or a particular area that are controlled by an officer ○ *My new command consists of a mechanized unit.* 8. MIL GROUP OF OFFICERS IN CONTROL a group of officers who control part of an army ○ *the enemy command* 9. MIL MILITARY GROUP WITH SPECIFIC FUNCTION a section of an army or air force that has a particular function ■ *v.* (**-mands, -manding, -manded**) 1. *vti.* ORDER SB to give sb an order or instruction ○ *I command you to let these men go.* 2. *vti.* MIL HAVE AUTHORITY OVER STH to control a military unit or a specific area ○ *an officer who commands a special operations battalion* 3. *vt.* MIL CONTROL OR DOMINATE AREA to control an area using military force ○ *a fort that commanded the single pass through steep mountains* 4. *vt.* BE ABLE TO OBTAIN STH to deserve or be entitled to sth ○ *With your qualifications you can command a high salary.* 5. *vt.* LOOK OVER STH to be in a position that has a wide view over sth ○ *The observation deck commands a breathtaking view of San Francisco Bay.* [13thC. Via Anglo-Norman and Old French from assumed late Latin *commandare*, literally 'to enjoin strongly', from Latin *mandare* 'to entrust, order' (see MANDATE).] —**commandable** *adj.*

command and control *n.* 1. SYSTEM DIRECTING A MISSILE a system that directs the course of a missile 2. COMMANDER'S EXERCISE OF AUTHORITY AND DIRECTION a military commander's exercise of authority and direction of operations

commandant /kómmən dant/ *n.* an officer in command of a military establishment

command car *n.* an armoured vehicle that can travel over rough terrain

command economy *n.* an economy in which resources and business activity are controlled by the government

commandeer /kómən deér/ (**-deers, -deering, -deered**) *vt.* 1. FORCE SB INTO MILITARY SERVICE to force sb to serve in the armed forces 2. SEIZE STH FOR MILITARY PURPOSES to take sth from its owner for official or military purposes 3. TAKE STH OVER to take or use sth, sometimes using force (*disapproving*) [Early 19thC. Via Afrikaans *kommandeer* from Dutch *kommanderen* 'to command', from French *commander* (see COMMAND).]

commander /kə maándər/ *n.* 1. MILITARY OFFICER an officer in command of a military unit 2. NAVAL RANK a naval rank below captain and above lieutenant commander, or an officer holding this rank 3. SENIOR POLICE OFFICER an officer in charge of a police district in London 4. MEMBER WITH HIGH RANK a high-ranking member of some knightly and fraternal orders —**commandership** *n.*

commander in chief (*plural* **commanders in chief**) *n.* an officer who has supreme command of military forces

Commander in Chief *n.* used as an honorific title to denote the President of the United States, as commander of the nation's armed forces

Command Group *n.* a group of officers and security personnel who accompany a commander

commanding /kə maánding/ *adj.* 1. IMPRESSIVE able to control or dominate ○ *a commanding presence* 2. BEING HIGHER IN POSITION dominating a landscape or view 3. DOMINATING demonstrating clear superiority ○ *a commanding lead* —**commandingly** *adv.*

commanding officer *n.* an officer in command of a military unit or establishment

command-line *adj.* COMPUT using letters or words instead of codes to instruct a computer to perform a task [From the fact that such instructions are entered all on a single line after a prompt character called the 'command prompt']

commandment /kə maándmənt/ *n.* a command from God, especially one of the Ten Commandments

command module *n.* the part of a spacecraft that houses the controls and the crew's living quarters

commando /kə maándō/ (*plural* **-dos** *or* **-does**) *n.* 1. SPECIALLY TRAINED SOLDIER a member of a military force specially trained to make dangerous raids 2. UNIT a military unit made up of commandos 3. BOER FIGHTING UNIT a force of Boer troops during the Boer War [Late 18thC. From Portuguese, 'raiding party', literally 'commanded (squad)', from *commandar* 'to command'.]

command paper *n.* a government document presented to Parliament, historically by royal command

command performance *n.* a performance of a play or film given by command of a ruler or state

command post *n.* 1. FIELD HEADQUARTERS a military headquarters for a command group and its officers during an operation 2. TEMPORARY COMMUNICATIONS CENTRE a temporary headquarters for a team of people involved in an operation

commedia dell'arte /ko máydi ə del aár tay/ *n.* an Italian form of popular comedy developed during the 16th and 17th centuries, characterized by the use of stock characters and familiar plots [Late 19thC. From Italian, literally 'comedy of art'.]

commemorate /kə mémmə rayt/ (**-rates, -rating, -rated**) *vt.* 1. REMEMBER STH CEREMONIALLY to honour the memory of sb or sth in a ceremony ○ *a service held to commemorate the dead* 2. BE MEMORIAL TO STH to serve as a memorial to sth [Mid-17thC. From Latin *commemoratus*, the past participle of *commemorare* 'to call to mind clearly', from *memorare* 'to remind, speak of', from *memor* 'mindful' (see MEMORY).] —**commemorator** *n.* —**commemoratory** /-mémmərətəri/ *adj.*

commemoration /kə mémmə ráysh'n/ *n.* 1. CEREMONY HONOURING SB OR STH a ceremony or religious service to commemorate a person or an event 2. ACT OF HONOURING the act of honouring the memory of a person or an event —**commemorational** *adj.*

commemorative /kə mémmərətiv/ *adj.* honouring the memory of a person or an event —**commemoratively** *adv.*

commence /kə ménss/ (**-mences, -mencing, -menced**) *vti.* to begin happening or to begin sth (*formal*) [14thC. Via Old French *com(m)encier* from assumed Vulgar Latin *cominitiare*, from Latin *initiare* 'to begin' (see INITIATE).] —**commencer** *n.*

commencement /kə ménssmənt/ *n.* 1. THE BEGINNING OF STH the beginning of sth (*formal*) ○ *the commencement of open hostilities* 2. *US* GRADUATION CEREMONY a ceremony during which degrees and diplomas are conferred at US high schools, colleges, and universities, or the day on which this ceremony takes place

commend /kə ménd/ (**-mends, -mending, -mended**) *vt.* 1. PRAISE SB OR STH to praise sb or sth in a formal way ○ *She was commended for her bravery.* 2. PROVE STH WORTHWHILE to prove sth to possess worthwhile qualities ○ *The plan has much to commend it.* 3. SURRENDER SOUL FOR SAFEKEEPING to entrust sb, yourself, or your soul to sb's safekeeping [14thC. From Latin *commendare*, literally 'to entrust completely', from *mandare* 'to entrust, commit' (see MANDATE).] —**commender** *n.*

commendable /kə méndəb'l/ *adj.* worthy of praise —**commendableness** *n.* —**commendably** *adv.*

commendation /kómmen dáysh'n/ *n.* 1. ACT OF COMMENDING praise of sb's abilities 2. RECOGNITION OF ACCOMPLISHMENT an award or citation given to sb in recognition of an outstanding achievement

commendatory /kə méndətəri/ *adj.* expressing praise

commensal /kə ménss'l/ *adj.* used to describe a relationship between organisms of two different species in which one derives food or other benefits from the association while the other remains unharmed and unaffected [Late 19thC. Directly or via French from medieval Latin *commensalis*, literally 'at table together', from Latin *mensa* 'table'.] —**commensal** *n.* —**commensality** /kómmen sálləti/ *n.* —**commensally** /kə ménss'li/ *adv.*

commensurable /kə ménshərəb'l/ *adj.* 1. RELATED BY MEASUREMENT related by virtue of sharing the same system of measurement or by being measurable using the same units 2. COMMENSURATE equal in terms of sth else (*formal*) ○ *His salary is commensurable to his ability.* 3. MATH DESCRIBING TWO QUANTITIES divisible by the same unit an even number of times [Mid-16thC. From late Latin *commensurabilis*, literally 'completely measurable', from *mensurabilis* 'measurable' (see MENSURABLE).] —**commensurability** /kə ménshərə bílləti/ *n.* —**commensurably** /kə ménshərəbli/ *adv.*

commensurate /kə ménshərət/ *adj.* 1. EQUAL IN SIZE of the same size or extent 2. IN PROPORTION properly or appropriately proportionate ○ *The rewards will be commensurate with the efforts made.* 3. MEASURED USING COMPATIBLE UNITS measured in or related by units that are compatible [Mid-17thC. From late Latin *commensuratus*, literally 'measured with', from, ultimately, Latin *mensura* 'measure' (source of English *measure*).] —**commensurately** *adv.* —**commensurateness** *n.* —**commensuration** /kə ménshə ráysh'n/ *n.*

comment /kómment/ *n.* 1. REMARK a remark that states a fact or expresses an opinion ○ *Comments are invited from all participants.* 2. OBSERVATION an implied or indirect judgment ○ *The incident attracted a great deal of press comment.* 3. EXPLANATORY NOTE a note that explains a passage in a text 4. COMPUT NOTE EXPLAINING PROGRAM CODE a note embedded in a computer program that describes how the programming code that follows works ■ *vti.* (**-ments, -menting, -mented**) MAKE A COMMENT to state a fact or give an opinion [14thC. From, ultimately, Latin *commentum* 'invention, fiction', from the past participle stem *comment-* of *comminisci* 'to invent', literally 'to think together'.]

commentary /kómmantəri/ *n.* (*plural* **-ies**) **1.** SPORTS **SPOKEN DESCRIPTION OF EVENT** a spoken description of an event as it happens, especially of a sporting event being broadcast on radio or television. US term **play-by-play 2. CLARIFICATION OF A SITUATION** an example illustrating a situation **3. SERIES OF EXPLANATORY NOTES** a series of notes explaining or interpreting a written text **4. EXPLANATORY ESSAY** an essay or book that explains a text ■ **commentaries** *npl.* **RECORD OF EVENTS** a record of events, usually written by sb who participated in them —**commentarial** /kómmən táiri əl/ *adj.*

commentary box *n.* a booth at a sports stadium where a television or radio commentator broadcasts from

commentate /kómmən tayt/ (**commentates, commentating, commentated**) *vi.* to act as a commentator, either in radio or television broadcasting or on texts [Mid-19thC. Back-formation from COMMENTATOR.]

commentator /kómmən taytər/ *n.* **1. PERSON PROVIDING BROADCAST COMMENTARY** a broadcaster for radio or television who describes events, especially sporting events, as they happen **2. REPORTER ANALYSING EVENTS** sb who reports on and analyses events in the news for radio, television, or a newspaper [14thC. From Latin, formed from *commentari* 'to comment', from *comminisci* (see COMMENT).]

commerce /kómm urss/ *n.* **1. TRADE IN GOODS AND SERVICES** the large-scale buying and selling of goods and services **2. STUDY OF COMMERCE** the study of the principles and practices of commerce [Mid-16thC. From, ultimately, Latin *commercium*, literally 'mutual trade'.]

commercial /kə múrsh'l/ *adj.* **1. RELATING TO COMMERCE** relating to the buying and selling of goods or services **2. SUITABLE FOR TRADING** appropriate or sufficient for the purposes of trade **3. FOR INDUSTRIAL USE** produced in bulk for industrial use and often unrefined **4. DONE FOR PROFIT** done with the primary aim of making money **5. PAID FOR WITH ADVERTISING** supported by revenue from advertising ■ *n.* **ADVERTISEMENT ON RADIO OR TELEVISION** an advertisement broadcast on radio or television [Late 16thC. The noun first meant 'commercial traveller', the current sense being a mid-20th-century development.] —**commerciality** /kə múrshi álləti/ *n.*

commercial art *n.* graphic art produced for purposes such as advertising and packaging —**commercial artist** *n.*

commercial bank *n.* a bank whose primary business is providing financial services to companies

commercial break *n.* an interval during a radio or television programme for the purpose of broadcasting advertisements

commercial college *n.* a college that teaches primarily business-related subjects

commercialese /kə múrsh'l éez/ *n.* the kind of language or jargon used by people who work in business

commercialism /kə múrsh'lizzəm/ *n.* **1. COMMERCIAL PRINCIPLES** the principles and methods of commerce **2. ACTING FOR PROFIT** excessive emphasis on profit-making —**commercialist** /kə múrsh'list/ *n.* —**commercialistic** /-ístik/ *adj.*

commercialize /kə múrsh'l īz/ (**-izes, -izing, -ized**), **commercialise** (**-ises, -ising, -ised**) *vt.* **1. APPLY COMMERCIAL PRINCIPLES TO STH** to apply business principles to sth or run it as a business **2. USE FOR PROFIT ONLY** to exploit sth for financial gain —**commercialization** /kə múrsh'l ī záysh'n/ *n.*

commercially /kə múrshəli/ *adv.* in commercial terms or from a profit-making point of view

commercial traveller *n.* a travelling company sales representative (*dated*)

commercial vehicle *n.* a road vehicle designed to transport goods or passengers

commère /kómmair/ *n.* a woman who introduces acts on a television, radio, or stage show [Early 20thC. From French, 'godmother', literally 'mother with', from, ultimately, Latin *mater* 'mother' (see MATERNAL).]

commesse /kómmess/ *n.* *Carib* in Trinidad, any kind of scandal, conflict, or illegal behaviour (*informal*)

commie /kómmi/, **commy** *n.* (*plural* **-mies**) **COMMUNIST** sb who is a Communist (*informal disapproving*) ■ *adj.* **SUPPORTING COMMUNISM** holding or advocating Communist or left-wing views (*informal disapproving*) [Mid-20thC. Coined from COMMUNIST + -IE.]

commination /kómmi náysh'n/ *n.* **1. ACT OF DENOUNCING** a formal denunciation of sb or sth (*formal*) **2. THREAT OF PUNISHMENT** a warning of punishment or vengeance, especially punishment by God (*formal*) **3. LIST OF GOD'S WARNINGS** a recital of God's warnings to sinners, read out in the Ash Wednesday service in Anglican churches [15thC. From, ultimately, Latin *comminat-*, past participle stem of *comminari*, literally 'to threaten with', from *minari* 'to threaten' (see MENACE).] —**comminatory** /kómminətəri/ *adj.*

commingle /ko míng g'l/ (**-gles, -gling, -gled**) *v.* **1.** *vti.* **MIX STH OR BECOME MIXED** to blend or mix two or more things, or become mixed or blended (*literary*) **2.** *vt.* FIN **COMBINE FUNDS OR PROPERTIES** to put a number of funds or properties into a single fund or stock

comminute /kómmi nyoot/ (**-nutes, -nuting, -nuted**) *v.* **1.** *vti.* MED **BREAK BONE INTO FRAGMENTS** to break, or cause a bone to break, into small parts **2.** *vt.* **PULVERIZE STH** to crush or grind sth into a powder **3.** *vt.* **DIVIDE STH INTO SMALL PARTS** to divide sth, especially property, into small parts (*formal*) [Late 16thC. From, ultimately, Latin *comminuere*, literally 'to lessen greatly', from *minuere* 'to lessen'.] —**comminuted** *adj.* —**comminution** /kómmi nyóosh'n/ *n.*

comminuted fracture *n.* a fracture in which the bone is broken into fragments

commis /kómmi/ (*plural* **-mis**) *n.* an agent or deputy [Late 16thC. From French, from the past participle of *commettre* 'to entrust', from Latin *committere* (see COMMIT).]

commis chef *n.* a trainee chef who has the most junior position in the kitchen

commiserate /kə mízzə rayt/ (**-ates, -ating, -ated**) *vi.* to express sympathy or sorrow [Late 16thC. From, ultimately, Latin *commiserari*, literally 'to lament with, be miserable with', from, ultimately, *miser* 'miserable'.] —**commiserative** /-rətiv/ *adj.* —**commiseratively** /-rətivli/ *adv.*

commiseration /kə mízzə ráysh'n/ *n.* **SYMPATHY** feelings of sympathy or compassion ■ **commiserations** *npl.* **SYMPATHETIC WORDS** expressions of sympathy or sorrow

commissar /kómmi saar/ *n.* **1. FORMER SOVIET DEPARTMENT HEAD** in the former Soviet Union, the chief minister in a government department **2. COMMUNIST PARTY OFFICIAL** in the former Soviet Union, a Communist Party official, often attached to a military unit, responsible for providing political education [Early 20thC. From Russian *komissar*, from, ultimately, medieval Latin *commissarius* 'officer in charge', from Latin *commiss-*, past participle stem of *committere* 'to entrust' (see COMMIT).] —**commissarial** /kómmi sáiri əl/ *adj.*

commissariat /kómmi sáiri ət/ *n.* **1.** ARMY **ARMY SUPPLY DEPARTMENT** an army department responsible for organizing food and supplies **2.** ARMY **ARMY SUPPLIES** food and other supplies given to soldiers **3. FORMER SOVIET GOVERNMENT DEPARTMENT** a government department in the former Soviet Union. The term was used until 1946, after which it was called a ministry. [Late 16thC. From, ultimately, assumed medieval Latin *commissariatus*, from *commissarius* (see COMMISSAR).]

commissary /kómmissəri/ (*plural* **-ies**) *n.* a deputy or representative, especially of a bishop [14thC. From medieval Latin *commissarius* (see COMMISSAR).] —**commissaryship** *n.*

commission /kə mísh'n/ *n.* **1.** COMM **FEE PAID TO AGENT** a fee paid to an agent for providing a service, especially a percentage of the total amount earned by the agent **2. TASK** a job or task given to an individual or group, especially an order to produce a particular product or piece of work **3.** POL **GOVERNMENT GROUP** a government agency that has judicial or legislative powers **4. GROUP WITH TASK** a group of people authorized or directed to carry out a duty or task **5.** MIL **APPOINTMENT AS MILITARY OFFICER** an appointment to the rank of officer in the armed forces, or a document conferring such a rank **6. AUTHORITY TO ACT AS AGENT** the authority granted to an individual or organization to act as an agent for another **7. AUTHORITY OR INSTRUCTION** the authority to do sth, or an instruction to do it (*formal*) **8. ACT OF COMMITTING STH** the committing of a crime or other offence ■ *vt.* (**-sions, -sioning, -sioned**) **1. ASSIGN** to assign a duty or task to sb **2. ORDER STH SPECIAL** place an order for sth that must be specially made or created ○ *have commissioned a new architectural firm to design the building* **3.** MIL **MAKE SB OFFICER** to confer the rank of officer on sb in the armed forces **4. BRING OR COME INTO OPERATION** to become operative or bring equipment or machinery into operation **5.** SHIPPING **EQUIP SHIP** to bring a ship into active service **6. START OPERATING** to bring a new project or facility such as a nuclear facility into operation [14thC. From, ultimately, Latin *commiss-* (see COMMISSAR).] —**commissional** *adj.* —**commissionary** *adj.* ◇ **on commission** with a percentage of the value of sales being full or partial payment for the work of selling ◇ **in commission** in operational use or in working order ◇ **out of commission** not in operational use or not in working order

commissionaire /kə míshə náir/ *n.* **1. UNIFORMED WORKER** a uniformed attendant or usher at a cinema, hotel, or theatre **2. MEMBER OF CANADIAN VETERANS' ORGANIZATION** in Canada, a veteran of the armed forces who belongs to the Corps of Commissionaires, an organization whose uniformed members can be hired to watch or protect buildings and property [Mid-17thC. From, ultimately, medieval Latin *commissionarius*, from the Latin stem *commission-* 'commission', from *commiss-* (see COMMISSAR).]

commissioned officer *n.* a military officer who holds rank by appointment above subordinate ranks such as, in the army, sergeant or corporal

commissioner /kə mísh'nər/ *n.* **1. COMMISSION MEMBER** a member of a commission **2. SB WORKING FOR COMMISSION** sb authorized by a commission to carry out prescribed duties or tasks **3. GOVERNMENT OFFICIAL** a government representative in an administrative area —**commissionership** *n.*

commissioner for oaths (*plural* **commissioners for oaths**) *n.* a solicitor authorized to authenticate oaths for people making affidavits

Commission for Racial Equality *n.* in the United Kingdom, the official body appointed by the Home Secretary to enforce the Race Relations Act of 1976

commissure /kómmi syoor/ *n.* **1.** ANAT **PLACE WHERE CELLS OR ORGANS MEET** a line or point where two cells, organs, or body parts meet or connect **2.** ANAT **LINKING BAND OF NERVE TISSUE** a band of nerve tissue that connects opposite sides of the central nervous system, e.g. the tissue connecting the left and right sides of the brain **3.** BOT **PLACE WHERE PLANT PARTS JOIN** a junction or seam between two organs or parts, such as that between the carpels of a flower [15thC. From Latin *commissura* 'juncture', from *commiss-* (see COMMISSAR).] —**commissural** /kə míssyoorəl, kómmi syóorəl/ *adj.*

commit /kə mít/ (**commits, committing, committed**) *v.* **1.** *vi.* **PROMISE DEVOTION** to pledge devotion or dedication to sb or sth ○ *he wasn't yet ready to commit to the relationship* **2.** *vt.* **PROMISE RESOURCES** to devote or pledge sth, e.g. time or money, to an undertaking **3.** *vt.* **DO WRONG** to do sth wrong or illegal ○ *commit a felony* **4.** *vt.* **ENTRUST TO** to entrust sth or sb to sb else for protection **5.** *vt.* **RECORD FOR THE FUTURE** to consign or record sth in order to preserve it **6.** *vt.* **ASSIGN FOR DESTRUCTION** to give sth over for destruction or disposal **7.** *vt.* **INSTITUTIONALIZE** to legally confine sb to an institution, e.g. to prison or a mental health facility. ◊ **section 8.** *vt.* LAW **SEND FOR TRIAL** to send sb for trial in a higher court **9.** *vt.* POL **REFER PROPOSED LAW FOR REVIEW** to refer a bill to a parliamentary committee for review [14thC. From Latin *committere*, literally 'to put together', from *mittere* 'to put, send' (source of English *missile*).] —**committable** *adj.* —**committer** *n.*

commitment /kə mítmənt/ *n.* **1. RESPONSIBILITY** sth that takes up time or energy, especially an obligation **2. LOYALTY** devotion or dedication, e.g. to a cause, person or relationship **3. PREVIOUSLY PLANNED ENGAGEMENT** a planned arrangement or activity that cannot be avoided

committal proceedings *npl.* legal proceedings in a

magistrates' court to decide whether a case should be tried in a crown court

committed /kə míttid/ *adj.* devoted to sb or sth such as a cause or relationship —**committedly** *adv.*

committee /kə mítti/ *n.* a group of people appointed or chosen to perform a function on behalf of a larger group [15thC. Originally 'person to whom sth is committed'.]

committee stage *n.* the stage in British parliamentary proceedings in which a bill is closely examined by members of parliament sitting in relevant committees, between the second and third readings of the bill

commode /kə mṓd/ *n.* **1. CHAIR WITH CHAMBER POT** a chair or box-shaped piece of furniture holding a chamber pot covered by a lid **2. PORTABLE WASHSTAND** a movable washstand with a cupboard underneath containing a chamber pot or washbasin **3. DECORATED CABINET** a low cabinet or chest of drawers, usually elaborately decorated [Late 17thC. From French, originally 'suitable', from Latin *commodus*, literally 'conforming with due measure, quite fit', from *modus* 'measure' (see MODE).]

commodious /kə mṓdi əss/ *adj.* pleasantly spacious —**commodiously** *adv.* —**commodiousness** *n.*

commodity /kə móddəti/ (*plural* **-ties**) *n.* **1.** FIN **TRADED ITEM** an item that is bought and sold, especially a raw material or manufactured item **2. USEFUL THING** sth that people value or find useful [15thC. From, ultimately, Latin *commodus* 'useful' (see COMMODE).]

commodore /kómmə dawr/ *n.* **1.** NAVY **NAVAL OFFICER** an officer in the navy ranked above a captain and below a rear admiral **2.** SHIPPING **MERCHANT NAVY CAPTAIN** a senior captain in charge of a fleet of merchant ships **3.** SAILING **PRESIDENT OF YACHT CLUB** the head of a yacht or boat club [Late 17thC. Origin uncertain: probably an alteration of Dutch *komandeur* 'commander', from French *commandeur*, ultimately from Old French *comander* 'to command' (see COMMAND).]

common /kómmən/ *adj.* **1. SHARED** belonging to or shared by two or more people or groups ○ *they shared a common goal* **2. OF OR FOR ALL** relating or belonging to the community as a whole ○ *the common good* **3. EVERYDAY** often occurring or frequently seen ○ *a common sight in cities* **4. WIDELY FOUND** used to describe a widely found species of plant or animal **5. NONSPECIALIST** used by ordinary people who have no specialist knowledge ○ *The common name for 'Viscum album' is 'mistletoe'.* **6. GENERAL** done, used, or held by most people ○ *common practice* **7. ORDINARY** without special privilege, rank, or status ○ *the common man* **8. OF AN EXPECTED STANDARD** of the standard that most people expect ○ *common courtesy* **9. VULGAR** considered to be lower-class, illbred or vulgar ○ *a common accent* **10.** MATH **WITH EQUAL MATHEMATICAL RELATIONSHIP** having an equal relationship to two or more mathematical entities **11.** POETRY **OF VARYING STRESS OR LENGTH** used to describe a syllable that, in a line of poetry, can be either long or short, or stressed or unstressed **12.** CHR **USEFUL FOR SEVERAL RELIGIOUS FESTIVALS** capable of being used as a service for any of a number of similar religious festivals ■ *n.* **1. PIECE OF PUBLIC LAND** an area of land available for anybody to use, e.g. as a public recreation area or as pasture for cattle **2.** LAW **RIGHT TO USE SB'S LAND** the legal right to use sb else's land or waters in a particular way, usually for grazing or fishing **3.** CHR **SERVICE FOR SEVERAL RELIGIOUS FESTIVALS** a religious service that can be used for any of a number of similar festivals **4. COMMON SENSE** common sense (*slang*) ■ *npl.* COMPUT **SHARED DATA STORE** data stored in the memory of one computer that is available to all computers linked to it by a network [13thC. From, ultimately, Latin *communis*, literally 'duties together', from *munia* (plural) 'duties'. Ultimately from an Indo-European word meaning 'exchange', which is also the ancestor of English *immune*.] —**commonness** *n.*

WORD KEY: USAGE

See Usage note at ***mutual***.

commonage /kómmənij/ *n.* **1. RIGHT TO USE JOINTLY** the legal right to use sth, especially a pasture, in common with other people, or the use that is made of it **2. PUBLIC OWNERSHIP OF LAND** the status of sth, usually land, that is publicly owned and available **3. LAND FOR ALL TO USE** land that is publicly owned and available **4.** = **commonalty**

commonality /kómmə nálləti/ (*plural* **-ties**) *n.* **1. POSSESSION OF COMMON ATTRIBUTES** the sharing of characteristics or qualities with other individuals **2. COMMON ATTRIBUTE** a shared characteristic or quality **3.** = **commonalty** [Late 16thC. Alteration of COMMONALTY.]

commonalty /kómmənəlti/ *n.* (*takes a singular or plural verb*) **1. COMMON PEOPLE** the ordinary people as distinct from the upper classes, especially when considered as a political class **2. GROUP** a group or society or its membership [13thC. Via Old French from medieval Latin *communalitas*, from Latin *communis* (see COMMON).]

common bile duct *n.* the duct formed by the joining of the duct from the liver and and that from the gall bladder

common blue *n.* a common European butterfly, the male of which is blue and the female usually brown with orange markings. Latin name: *Polyommatus icarus.*

common carrier *n.* an individual or company in the business of transporting goods or passengers

common chord *n.* a major or minor musical chord of three notes (**triad**) that contains a perfect fifth

common cold *n.* = **cold** *n.* **1**

common denominator *n.* **1. NUMBER DIVISIBLE BY BOTTOM FRACTION PART** a whole number that can be divided exactly by the lower numbers (**denominators**) of two or more fractions. For example, 8 is a common denominator of $\frac{1}{4}$ and $\frac{1}{2}$. **2. STH IN COMMON** a shared belief or characteristic

common difference *n.* the difference between successive terms in an arithmetic series. For example, 3 is the common difference in the series 2, 5, 8, 11.

common divisor *n.* = **common factor**

commoner /kómmənər/ *n.* **1. ORDINARY PERSON** an ordinary member of society who does not belong to the nobility **2.** EDUC **STUDENT WITHOUT SCHOLARSHIP** in some British universities and colleges, a student who does not receive a college scholarship **3.** POL **MEMBER OF HOUSE OF COMMONS** a member of the House of Commons, the lower house in the United Kingdom and Canadian parliaments

Common Era *n.* the Christian Era, especially as used in reckoning dates. ◊ **Christian Era**

common factor *n.* a number that two or more other numbers can be divided by exactly. For example, 4 is a common factor of 8, 12, and 20. US term **common divisor**

common fraction *n.* = **simple fraction**

common gender *n.* **1. GENDER OF NOUN FOR BOTH SEXES** in English, the gender of a noun that can refer to a person or animal of either sex, e.g. 'leader' and 'fox' **2. GENDER THAT EXCLUDES NEUTER** in some languages, the gender of those nouns that can be either masculine or feminine but not neuter

common good *n.* the advantage or benefit of everyone

common ground *n.* sth mutually agreed upon especially as a basis for negotiation

common knowledge *n.* sth that is generally known

common law *n.* **1. EVOLVED LAW** the body of law developed as a result of custom and judicial decisions, as distinct from the law laid down by legislative assemblies. Common law forms the basis of all law that is applied in England and most of the United States. **2. NATIONAL LAW** law that is applied consistently throughout a place and is not subject to regional variations [A translation of Latin *jus commune*]

common-law *adj.* **1.** LAW **WITHOUT OFFICIAL CEREMONY** used to describe a partner in a marriage that is recognized in some jurisdictions when both parties declare themselves married without an official ceremony. Common-law marriages are recognized, e.g., in some states in the United States. **2. OF UNMARRIED COUPLE LIVING TOGETHER** used to describe a partner in a marriage so called because of the length of time the two unmarried people have lived together as husband and wife **3. OF COMMON LAW** based on or relating to common law

common logarithm *n.* a logarithm with ten as its base number

common loon *n.* *US* = **great northern diver**

commonly /kómmənli/ *adv.* by most people or in most circumstances ○ *The measure was commonly held to be a success.*

common market *n.* any economic association established, typically between nations, with the aim of removing or reducing trade barriers

Common Market *n.* a term used in the 1960s and 1970s to refer both to the European Community and the European Economic Community

common measure *n.* **1.** MUSIC = **common time 2.** POETRY **4-LINE STANZA FORM FOR BALLADS** the stanza form used for ballads, with four iambic lines rhymed 'abab' or 'abac' **3.** MATH = **common factor**

common metre *n.* **1.** POETRY = **common measure 2.** MUSIC **4-LINE VERSE FORM FOR HYMNS** the verse form used in many hymns, consisting of four-line verses that alternate lines of eight and six syllables

common multiple *n.* a number that can be divided exactly by two or more other numbers. For example 12 is a common multiple of 2, 3, and 4.

common noun *n.* a noun that refers to any of a class of people or things, e.g. 'singer' and 'place', as distinct from a proper noun, e.g. 'Lennon' or 'Washington'. Common nouns can be preceded by words that modify their meaning, such as 'some' and 'any'.

common or garden *adj.* of the ordinary, everyday kind [From an original application to the common horticultural variety of a plant]

commonplace /kómmən playss/ *adj.* **1. EVERYDAY** encountered or happening often **2. DULL** uninteresting as a result of being unoriginal ■ *n.* **1. DULL REMARK** an unoriginal remark **2. STH ORDINARY** sth that is encountered or seen often, or that happens often [Mid-16thC. Originally two words; a translation of Latin *locus communis*, a translation of Greek *koinos topos* 'general theme'.] —**commonplaceness** *n.*

commonplace book *n.* a personal notebook used for copying down quotations and memorable passages from other books

Common Pleas *n.* LAW = **Court of Common Pleas** (*takes a singular verb*)

common prayer, **Common Prayer** *n.* standard prayers for public worship in the Church of England, as recorded in the Book of Common Prayer

Common Riding *n.* *Scotland* a traditional ceremony carried out annually in certain towns in Scotland, especially in the Borders when mounted men inspect the boundaries of the common land

common room *n.* **1. ROOM FOR THE RELAXATION OF RESIDENTS** a lounge available to everyone living in a residential community or institution **2.** EDUC **LOUNGE IN COLLEGE** a sitting room in a college or university where staff or students can relax

commons /kómmənz/ *npl.* **1. COLLEGE DINING HALL** a dining hall in a college or university (*takes a singular verb*) **2. commons, Commons MASSES** the common people as distinct from the ruling classes (*takes a singular or plural verb*)

Commons *npl.* (*takes a singular or plural verb*) **1. PARLIAMENTARY REPRESENTATIVES** the politicians who are elected to the lower house of the UK and Canadian parliament and represent all the people **2. LOWER PARLIAMENTARY HOUSE** the House of Commons in the parliaments of the United Kingdom and Canada

common salt *n.* = **salt** *n.* **1**

common seal *n.* a grey seal with dark blotches on its skin that lives in northern Atlantic and Pacific waters. Latin name: *Phoca vitulina.*

common sense *n.* sound practical judgment derived from experience rather than study

commonsense /kómmən senss/ *adj.* based on common sense —**commonsensical** /-sénssik'l/ *adj.* —**commonsensically** /-sénssikli/ *adv.*

common stock *n.* *US* a stock that pays the holder a fluctuating dividend after the holders of preferred stock have been paid

common time *n.* a musical metre with four crotchet beats to the bar, commonly referred to as four-four time

common touch *n.* the ability of a celebrity or sb in public life to behave towards members of the general public in a naturally friendly, informal, and uncondescending way

commonwealth /kómmən welth/ *n.* **1. NATION OR ITS PEOPLE** a nation or its people considered as a political entity **2. REPUBLIC** a nation or state in which the people govern **3. ASSOCIATION OF STATES** a group of states that have formed an association for the political and economic benefit of all members **4. PEOPLE WITH COMMON INTEREST** a group of people linked by sth that they all have in common

Commonwealth /kómmən welth/ *n.* **1.** RELIG = **Commonwealth of Nations 2.** HIST **REPUBLIC IN 17C ENGLAND** the state and republican government in England from the death of Charles I in 1649 until the restoration of the monarchy in 1660 **3.** POL **FEDERATED STATES OF AUSTRALIA** the official designation of the federated states of Australia, often used to refer to the federal government as opposed to the state governments **4. TERRITORY ASSOCIATED WITH UNITED STATES** a self-governing territory voluntarily associated with the United States. Puerto Rico and the Northern Mariana Islands are Commonwealths. **5. TITLE FOR SOME US STATES** an official title used by the US states of Kentucky, Massachusetts, Pennsylvania, and Virginia

Commonwealth Day *n.* a holiday observed in some countries of the Commonwealth of Nations, formerly on the anniversary of Queen Victoria's birth on May 24 but now on the second Monday in March. It was formerly known as Empire Day.

Commonwealth Games *n.* a sports contest held every four years involving participants from British Commonwealth countries

Commonwealth of Independent States *n.* an association formed in 1991 by most of the republics of the former Soviet Union, with ceremonial headquarters in Minsk, Belarus

Commonwealth of Nations *n.* an association consisting of Britain and sovereign states that were formerly British colonies or are ruled by Britain. The British monarch is acknowledged by member states as its head.

common year *n.* an ordinary year of 365 days, as distinct from a leap year

commotion /kə mṓsh'n/ *n.* a scene of noisy confusion or activity [14thC. From the Latin stem *commotion-*, literally 'intensive motion', from the stem *motion-* 'motion' (see MOTION).] —**commotional** *adj.*

comms /komz/ *npl.* communications, especially in the military sense (*informal*) [Shortening]

communal /kómmyŏŏn'l, kə myŏŏn'l/ *adj.* **1. SHARED** used or owned by all members of a group or community **2. OF COMMUNITIES** relating to communities or to living in communities **3. OF A COMMUNE** belonging or relating to a commune **4. RELATING TO DIFFERENT SOCIAL GROUPS** relating to or involving different groups within a society [Early 19thC. From, ultimately, late Latin *communalis*, from Latin *communis* (see COMMON).] —**communally** /kómmyŏŏn'li, kə myŏŏn'li/ *adv.*

communalism /kómmyŏŏn'lizzəm/ *n.* **1. COMMUNAL LIVING** the principles and practices of communal living or ownership or support for a communal society **2. ALLEGIANCE TO AN ETHNIC GROUP** a greater loyalty to an ethnic or religious group than to society in general —**communalist** /kómmyŏŏn'list/ *n.* —**communalistic** /kómmyŏŏn'l ístik/ *adj.*

communality /kómmyŏŏ nálləti/ *n.* **1. SHARING** shared use or ownership **2. SPIRIT OF TOGETHERNESS** the spirit of cooperation and solidarity that exists among members of a community or commune

communalize /kómmyŏŏn'l īz/ (**-izes, -izing, -ized**), **communalise** (**-ises, -ising, -ised**) *vt.* to put sth into joint ownership among the members of a community

communard /kómmyŏŏ naard/ *n.* sb living in a commune

Communard /kómmyŏŏ naard/ *n.* a member or supporter of the Paris Commune of 1871 [Late 19thC. From French, from *commune* 'group of citizens, Commune', from medieval Latin *communia*, the neuter plural of Latin *communis* 'common' (see COMMON).]

commune[1] /kóm yoon/ *n.* **1. COMMUNAL GROUP** a mutually supportive community in which possessions and responsibilities are shared **2. PEOPLE LIVING IN COMMUNE** a group of families or individuals living in a commune **3. SMALLEST ADMINISTRATIVE DISTRICT OF VARIOUS COUNTRIES** the smallest administrative district of some countries, e.g. France, Italy, and Switzerland, governed by a mayor and a council [Late 17thC. Via French from medieval Latin *communia*, from Latin *communis* (see COMMON).]

commune[2] /kə myŏŏn, kóm yoon/ (**-munes, -muning, -muned**) *vi.* to experience a deep emotional or spiritual relationship with sth [14thC. From Old French *comuner* 'to share', from *comun* 'common', from Latin *communis* (see COMMON).]

Commune /kóm yoon/ *n.* **1.** = **Paris Commune 2. COMMUNE OF FRENCH-REVOLUTION PARIS** the insurrectionary committee that governed Paris at the height of the French Revolution in 1792, originally the driving force behind the executions of members of the previous ruling classes. More moderate forces gradually gained control and by 1795 it had been suppressed.

communicable /kə myŏŏnikəb'l/ *adj.* **1. READILY TRANSMITTABLE** able to be passed from one person, animal, or organism to another ○ *a communicable disease* **2. EASILY EXPLAINED** easily communicated or capable of being communicated [14thC. From, ultimately, late Latin *communicabilis*, from Latin *communicare* (see COMMUNICATE).] —**communicability** /kə myŏŏnikə bílləti/ *n.* —**communicably** /-myŏŏnikəbli/ *adv.*

communicant /kə myŏŏnikənt/ *n.* **1.** CHR **SB WHO RECEIVES COMMUNION** sb who receives the Christian sacrament of Communion **2. SB OR STH THAT INFORMS** sb or sth such as a service that provides information [15thC. From the Latin present participle stem *communicant-* of *communicare* (see COMMUNICATE).]

communicate /kə myŏŏni kayt/ (**-cates, -cating, -cated**) *v.* **1.** *vti.* **EXCHANGE INFORMATION** to give or exchange information, e.g. by speech or writing ○ *We communicate by e-mail.* **2.** *vt.* **CONVEY** to transmit or reveal a feeling or thought by speech, writing, or gesture so that it is clearly understood **3.** *vi.* **UNDERSTAND ONE ANOTHER** to share a good personal understanding **4.** *vi.* **HAVE COMMON ACCESS** to be connected or provide access to each other **5.** *vt.* MED **TRANSMIT DISEASE** to pass a disease or infection on to sb **6.** *vi.* CHR **GIVE OR RECEIVE COMMUNION** to give or receive the Christian sacrament of Communion [Early 16thC. From, ultimately, Latin *communicare* 'to share', from *communis* (see COMMON).] —**communicatory** /-kətəri/ *adj.*

communication /kə myŏŏni káysh'n/ *n.* **1. EXCHANGE OF INFORMATION** the exchange of information between individuals, e.g. by means of speaking, writing, or using a common system of signs or behaviour **2. MESSAGE** a spoken or written message **3. ACT OF COMMUNICATING** the communicating of information **4. RAPPORT** a sense of mutual understanding and sympathy **5. ACCESS** a means of access or communication, e.g. a connecting door —**communicational** *adj.*

communication cord *n.* a cord, or handle in a railway carriage that a passenger can pull to stop a train in an emergency. US term **emergency cord**

communications /kəmyooni káysh'nz/ *n.* **1. SYSTEMS FOR COMMUNICATING** the technology and systems used for sending and receiving messages, e.g. postal and telephone networks **2. EFFECTIVE VERBAL EXPRESSION** the effective use of words to convey ideas or information (*takes a singular or plural verb*) **3. TRANSPORTATION OF TROOPS** a system of routes and transportation for moving troops and supplies **4. STUDY OF HUMAN COMMUNICATION** the study of the different means people use to communicate with each other, e.g. by gesture, speech, telecommunications, and writing (*takes a singular or plural verb*)

communications satellite *n.* an artificial satellite used to relay data such as radio, telephone, and television signals around the world. Signals may be reflected, but more often they are strengthened using a solar-powered transponder. Satellites often follow a geostationary orbit, remaining in the same position relative to Earth.

communication theory, **communications theory** *n.* the study of all forms of human communication, including branches of linguistics such as semantics, as well as telecommunications and other non-linguistic forms

communicative /kə myŏŏnikətiv/ *adj.* **1. TALKATIVE** inclined or ready to talk **2. OF COMMUNICATION** relating to communication or to systems for communication **3. STRESSING PRACTICAL COMMUNICATION** in foreign language teaching, stressing the importance of language as a tool for communicating information and ideas —**communicatively** *adv.* —**communicativeness** *n.*

communicator /kə myŏŏni kaytər/ *n.* **1. SB COMMUNICATING** sb or sth that communicates **2. SB WHO CAN MAKE STH CLEAR** sb who has a particular ability to express things effectively ○ *She's a highly effective communicator.*

communion /kə myŏŏni ən/ *n.* **1. INTIMACY** a feeling of emotional or spiritual closeness **2. CONNECTION** an association or relationship **3.** CHR **RELIGIOUS GROUP WITH COMMON FAITH** a religious group with its own set of beliefs and practices, especially a Christian denomination **4.** CHR **FELLOWSHIP BETWEEN RELIGIOUS GROUPS** a sense of shared religious identity and fellowship, especially between members of different Christian denominations [14thC. From the Latin stem *communion-*, from *communis* (see COMMON).] —**communional** *adj.* —**communionally** *adv.*

Communion /kə myŏŏni ən/ *n.* **1. CHRISTIAN SACRAMENT** a Christian sacrament that commemorates Jesus Christ's Last Supper, with the priest or minister consecrating bread and wine that is consumed by the congregation **2. PART OF THE COMMUNION SERVICE** the celebration of the sacrament of Communion **3. CONSECRATED BREAD AND WINE** the consecrated bread and wine received by worshippers at a Communion service

communiqué /kə myŏŏni kay/ *n.* an official announcement, especially to the press or public [Mid-19thC. From French, from the past participle of *communiquer* 'to communicate', from Latin *communicare* (see COMMUNICATE).]

communism /kómmyŏŏnizzəm/ *n.* the political theory or system in which all property and wealth is owned in a classless society by all the members of a community. ◊ **Communism** [Mid-19thC. From French *communisme*, from *commun* 'common', from Latin *communis* (see COMMON).]

Communism /kómmyŏŏnizəm/ *n.* **1. Communism, communism MARXIST-LENINIST SYSTEM** the Marxist-Leninist version of a classless society in which capitalism is overthrown by a working-class revolution that gives ownership and control of wealth and property to the state **2. ONE-PARTY STATE** any system of government in which a single, usually totalitarian, party holds power, and the state controls the economy

Communism Peak /kómmyŏŏ nizzəm-/ mountain situated in central Tajikistan, and the highest peak in the country. Height: 7,495 m/24,590 ft. Also known as **Mount Communism**

communist /kómmyŏŏnist/ *n.* **1. SUPPORTER OF COMMUNISM** an advocate or supporter of any type of communism **2. SB LEFT-WING** sb with left-wing views, especially sb denounced as revolutionary or subversive **3. PRACTISER OF COMMUNAL LIVING** sb who practises communal living ■ *adj.* **OF COMMUNISM** relating to communism or its supporters [Mid-19thC. From French *communiste*, from *commun* 'common', from Latin *communis* (see COMMON).] —**communistic** /kómmyŏŏ nístik/ *adj.*

Communist /kómmyŏŏnist/, **communist** *n.* a supporter of Communism or a member of an organization that supports or practises Communism —**Communist** *adj.*

communitarian /kə myŏŏni táiri ən/ *n.* **ADVOCATE OF COLLECTIVE WAY OF LIVING** a member or supporter of a collectivist or cooperative community or system ■ *adj.* **OF COMMUNITARIANS** relating to communitarians or a collectivist or cooperative way of life [Mid-19thC. Coined from COMMUNITY + -ARIAN, modelled on words such as UNITARIAN.] —**communitarianism** *n.*

community /kə myoˊonəti/ (*plural* **-ties**) *n.* **1.** PEOPLE IN AREA a group of people who live in the same area, or the area in which they live ○ *a close-knit fishing community* **2.** PEOPLE WITH COMMON BACKGROUND a group of people with a common background or with shared interests within society ○ *the financial community* **3.** NATIONS WITH COMMON HISTORY a group of nations with a common history or common economic or political interests ○ *the international community* **4.** SOCIETY the public or society in general ○ *a useful member of the community* **5.** INTERACTING PLANTS AND ANIMALS all the plants and animals that live in the same area and interact with one another [14thC. Via Old French *communeté* from the Latin stem *communitat-*, from *communis* (see COMMON).]

community centre *n.* a building used for a range of community activities

community charge *n.* a flat-rate tax formerly levied in Britain on all adults to part-finance local government. It was introduced in the late 1980s as a replacement for domestic rates, but was replaced in 1993 by a charge known as the Council Tax, based on property value.

community college *n.* **1.** = village college **2.** *NZ* ADULT TECHNICAL COLLEGE an adult education college that offers courses in practical or technical subjects

community education *n.* educational and recreational programmes provided by local governments for people in their communities

community home *n.* a home provided by a local authority or voluntary organization for children who cannot live with relatives or foster parents

community medicine *n.* the branch of medicine devoted to the care of public health provision

community policing *n.* policing that seeks to integrate officers into the local community in order to reduce crime and foster good community relations

community relations *npl.* **1.** RELATIONSHIPS BETWEEN GROUPS IN AREA the relationships between different cultural, ethnic, political, or religious groups who live in an area and may come into conflict **2.** MEDIATION BETWEEN GROUPS mediation between different cultural, ethnic, political, or religious groups living in an area

community school *n.* a state primary or secondary school for which a Local Education Authority has staffing, premises, and admissions responsibilities. ◊ **foundation school**

community service *n.* a penalty requiring that an offender convicted of a relatively minor crime do unpaid work that is beneficial to the community as an alternative to imprisonment

community-service order *n.* a court order requiring a convicted offender to do community service for a specified number of hours

communize /kómmyoŏ nīz/ (**-nizes, -nizing, -nized**), **communise** (**-nises, -nising, -nised**) *vt.* **1.** MAKE PUBLICLY OWNED to transfer sth, e.g. land or property, from private to public ownership **2.** RUN ON COMMUNIST PRINCIPLES to apply communist principles of organization to a government or people [Late 19thC. From Latin *communis* 'common' (see COMMON) + -IZE.] —**communization** /kómmyoŏ nī záysh'n/ *n.*

commutable /kə myoˊotəb'l/ *adj.* **1.** LAW CAPABLE OF BEING REDUCED capable of being shortened or made less severe ○ *a commutable sentence* **2.** EXCHANGEABLE FOR MONEY able to be converted or exchanged, especially into or for money **3.** TRANSP WITHIN COMMUTING DISTANCE close enough to make a daily journey to and from work practical —**commutability** /kə myoˊotə bílləti/ *n.*

commutate /kómmyoŏ tayt/ (**-tates, -tating, -tated**) *vt.* to convert alternating electric current to direct current or vice versa

commutation /kómmyoŏ táysh'n/ *n.* **1.** LAW REDUCTION IN SEVERITY OF LEGAL PENALTY the reduction of a prison sentence or other legal penalty to a less severe one **2.** ELEC CONVERSION OF ELECTRIC CURRENT the converting of an electric current from alternating to direct current or vice versa **3.** CONVERSION any exchange or substitution, e.g. the substituting of one kind of payment for another (*formal*) **4.** *US* TRANSP COMMUTER'S TRAVEL the travelling undertaken by a commuter

commutation ticket *n.* *US* = season ticket

commutative /kə myoˊotətiv/ *adj.* **1.** OF SUBSTITUTION involving or relating to exchanges or substitutions **2.** MATH NOT DEPENDENT ON ORDER giving the same result in mathematics or logic irrespective of the order in which two or more terms or quantities are placed. For example, addition and multiplication are commutative processes, while subtraction and division are not. —**commutatively** *adv.* —**commutativity** /kə myoŏtə tívvəti/ *n.*

commutator /kómmyoŏ taytər/ *n.* a device that maintains the direction of flow of electric current in a generator or reverses it in an electric motor

commute /kə myoˊot/ (**commutes, commuting, commuted**) *v.* **1.** *vi.* TRANSP TRAVEL REGULARLY BETWEEN PLACES to travel regularly from one place to another, especially between home and work **2.** LAW REDUCE SEVERITY OF PENALTY to reduce a legal sentence to a less severe one **3.** *vti.* REPLACE WITH STH ELSE to be changed or substituted or to change or substitute one thing for another, e.g. one form of payment for another **4.** *vi.* BE REPLACEMENT to compensate or act as a substitute **5.** *vt.* ELEC = commutate **6.** *vi.* MATH GIVE SAME RESULT WITH DIFFERENT ORDER to give the same mathematical result irrespective of the order in which two or more quantities are placed, e.g. as in addition but not subtraction [15thC. From Latin *commutare*, literally 'to change altogether', from *mutare* 'to change' (source of English *mutant*). First used of travelling in the 19thC.]

commuter /kə myoˊotər/ *n.* **1.** REGULAR TRAVELLER FROM HOME TO WORK sb who travels regularly from one place to another, especially between home and work and usually between a suburb and a city **2.** *US* INTERCITY AIRLINE an airline that provides short flights between major cities

commuter belt *n.* a residential area from where many people commute

commy /kómmi/ *n.* = commie

Como /kóˊmō/ resort town and capital of Como Province, in Lombardy Region, northern Italy, on the southwestern extremity of Lake Como. Population: 89,600 (1990).

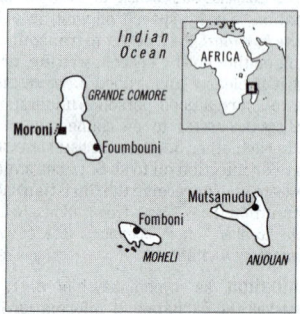

Comoros

Comoros /kómmə rōz, kə máwrōz/ an independent state consisting of a group of islands in the Indian Ocean, 290 km/180 mi. from Mozambique and 320 km/200 mi. from Madagascar. Language: French, Arabic. Currency: Comorian Franc. Capital: Moroni. Population: 528,893 (1997). Area: 1,862 sq. km/719 sq. mi. Official name **Federal Islamic Republic of the Comoros**

comp[1] /komp/ *n.* (*informal*) **1.** JAZZ ACCOMPANIMENT an accompaniment, especially a jazz accompaniment played on piano or guitar **2.** ACCOMPANIST an accompanist ■ *vti.* (**comps, comping, comped**) PLAY JAZZ ACCOMPANIMENT to play a musical accompaniment, often improvised, especially in jazz (*informal*) [Mid-20thC. Shortening.]

comp[2] /komp/ *n.* COMPETITION a competition (*informal*) ■ *vi.* (**comped**) ENTER COMPETITION to enter a competition (*informal*)

comp. *abbr.* **1.** companion **2.** comparative **3.** compare **4.** compensation **5.** compilation **6.** compiled **7.** complete **8.** composer **9.** composite **10.** composition **11.** compound **12.** comprehensive **13.** comprising

compact[1] *adj.* /kəm pákt/ **1.** PACKED TIGHTLY closely clustered or packed together ○ *a compact bundle of papers* **2.** SMALL AND EFFICIENTLY ARRANGED small, with

efficient use of available space **3.** SHORT AND STURDY short and stocky **4.** CONCISE brief and concise ■ *v.* /kəm pákt/ (**-pacts, -pacting, -pacted, -pacted** *or* **-pact**) **1.** *vti.* PACK STH TIGHTLY to become, or make sth, more dense or firmly packed **2.** *vt.* METALL COMPRESS METAL POWDER to compress metal powder in a die so that it bonds into a single component ready for heat-treatment (**sintering**) ■ *n.* /kóm pakt/ **1.** COSMETICS CASE FOR MAKE-UP a small flat case containing make-up, usually face powder, with a mirror inside the lid **2.** PHOTOGRAPHY COMPACT CAMERA a compact camera **3.** *US, Can* SMALLISH CAR a medium-sized car that is economical to run **4.** METALL METAL POWDER READY FOR PRESSING a mass of metal powders in a die, ready for the compression and heat-treatment (**sintering**) that will consolidate it into a useable article [14thC. From Latin *compactus*, the past participle of *compingere*, literally 'to fasten together', from *pangere* 'to fasten'.] —**compactible** *adj.* —**compactly** *adv.* —**compactness** *n.*

compact[2] /kóm pakt/ *n.* an agreement , especially an informal or private agreement [Late 16thC. From Latin *compactum*, from the past participle of *compacisci*, literally 'to make an agreement together', from *pacisci* 'to make an agreement' (see PACT).]

compact camera *n.* a small camera with an integral lens

compact disc *n.* a hard plastic disc approximately 12 cm/4¾ in in diameter on which information, e.g. music or computer data, is digitally encoded in a format readable by laser beam

Compact Disc-Interactive *n.* full form of **CDI**

compact disc player *n.* a machine for playing compact discs

compacter /kəm páktər/ *n.* *US* = compactor

compaction /kəm páksh'n/ *n.* **1.** COMPRESSING the pressing together of particles to make a denser mass, or the compressed state of the resulting mass **2.** GEOL PROCESS OF ROCK FORMATION a process in the formation of sedimentary rock in which pressure from overlying sediment forces water from unconsolidated sediment, reducing its volume and yielding solid rock

compactor /kəm páktər/, **compacter** *n.* *US* a machine used in the home to compress rubbish into small bundles for easy disposal

compact video disc *n.* a compact disc that plays both sound and pictures

companion[1] /kəm pánnyən/ *n.* **1.** SB TO BE WITH sb who accompanies you, spends time with you, or is a friend **2.** SB WHOSE JOB IS ACCOMPANYING ANOTHER sb, usually a woman, employed to live with another, especially in former times **3.** MATCH FOR STH an article that goes with another to make a pair **4.** PUBL HANDBOOK a guide or handbook on a particular subject **5.** ASTRON FAINTER OF TWO STARS the fainter of the stars that make up a double-star or multiple-star system ■ *vt.* (**-ions, -ioning, -ioned**) ACCOMPANY SB to be a companion to sb [13thC. From, ultimately, the late Latin stem *companion-*, literally 'one who shares bread', from Latin *panis* 'bread' (source of English *pantry*).]

companion[2] /kəm pánnyən/ *n.* a companionway, or a covering above a companionway [Mid-18thC. Alteration of obsolete Dutch *kompanje* 'quarterdeck', from, ultimately, Italian *compagna* 'storeroom (for) provisions', literally '(eaten) with bread', from, ultimately, Latin *panis* 'bread' (see PANTRY).]

Companion /kəm pánnyən/, **companion** *n.* a member of the lowest rank in a British order of knighthood

companionable /kəm pánnyənəb'l/ *adj.* friendly, sociable, and good company ○ *They sat in a companionable silence.* —**companionability** /kəm pánnyənə bílləti/ *n.* —**companionableness** /kəm pánnyənəb'lnəss/ *n.* —**companionably** /-əbli/ *adv.*

companionate /kəm pánnyənət/ *adj.* **1.** FITTING FOR A COMPANION appropriate for a companion **2.** WELL SUITED right for each other

companionate marriage *n.* SOCIOL marriage based on mutual affection and shared interests as opposed to purely economic or dynastic considerations

companion cell *n.* a type of cell found in flowering plants that lies alongside a sap-conducting sieve-tube element, whose function is thought to influence. Companion cells have a prominent nucleus and dense cytoplasm, and form fine cytoplasmic connections (**plasmodesmata**) with the adjacent sieve-tube element.

companion piece *n.* a work, especially of music or literature, that is closely related to another, often by the same composer or author

companion set *n.* a set of implements for tending a fire

companionship /kəm pánnyən ship/ *n.* **1.** RELATIONSHIP OF FRIENDS the company of friends and the relationship that exists between them **2.** GROUP an organized group of people

companionway /kəm pánnyən way/ *n.* a stairway or ladder between decks on a boat or ship

company /kúmpəni/ *n.* (*plural* **-nies**) **1.** BUSINESS BUSINESS a business enterprise **2.** BEING WITH SB being together with others ○ *He didn't feel at ease in company.* **3.** GROUP a gathering of people **4.** COMPANIONS the people that sb associates with **5.** PARTICULAR TYPE OF COMPANION sb seen as providing a particular type of companionship ○ *he can be very good company* **6.** GUEST a guest or visitor, especially for a meal or overnight stay ○ *We're having company this weekend.* **7.** BUSINESS BUSINESS PARTNERS the partners of a business enterprise whose names are not included in the firm's title **8.** THEATRE TROUPE a group of performing artists, e.g. actors **9.** MIL GROUP OF TROOPS a unit of soldiers, usually consisting of two or more platoons **10.** NAVY SHIP'S CREW the crew and officers of a ship **11.** SCOUTING GROUP OF GUIDES a unit of Girl Guides **12.** BUSINESS, HIST TRADE GUILD a medieval trade guild ■ *vi.* (**-nies, -nying, -nied**) JOIN to associate with sb (*archaic*) [13thC. From Anglo-Norman *compainie*, ultimately from the late Latin *companion-* (see COMPANION).]

company car *n.* a car owned or leased by a business for use by an employee, often as a fringe benefit of a job or position

company doctor *n.* **1.** DOCTOR EMPLOYED BY COMPANY a doctor employed by a company to look after the health of its employees **2.** PERSON WHO HELPS AILING COMPANIES a person who specializes in making unprofitable businesses efficient and profitable

company-grade officer *n.* = company officer

company man *n.* an employee who puts loyalty to an employer before friendship or personal beliefs (*disapproving*)

company officer *n.* a commissioned officer who holds the rank of captain or below

compar. *abbr.* comparative

comparable /kómpərəb'l/ *adj.* **1.** CAPABLE OF BEING COMPARED similar enough for a fair comparison to be made ○ *We ate a meal comparable to that of the finest restaurant.* **2.** SIMILAR as good as another or each other ○ *They both have comparable skills.* —**comparability** /kómpərə bílləti/ *n.* —**comparableness** /kómpərəb'lnəss/ *n.* —**comparably** /kómpərəbli/ *adv.*

━━━━ **WORD KEY: USAGE** ━━━━

comparable to or **comparable with**? *Comparable* mimics the verb *compare* in being followed either by *to* or *with*, depending on whether a likening to or a contrasting with is intended: *The agency provides a service comparable to that of a good library. The air raid was comparable with the ones on Dresden or Hiroshima.* See Usage note at **compare**.

━━━━ **WORD KEY: USAGE** ━━━━

Pronunciation trap. The most acceptable pronunciation in British English is with the stress on the first syllable, although stress on the second syllable is also heard and is more usual in American usage.

comparable worth *n.* the belief that men and women should receive equal pay for jobs requiring comparable responsibility and skills

comparatist /kəm párrətist/ *n.* sb who uses a comparative method, e.g. in the study of linguistics [Mid-20thC. From French, formed from *comparatif* 'comparative'.]

comparative /kəm párrətiv/ *adj.* **1.** INVOLVING COMPARISONS based on or using comparisons of different elements or types in the investigation of sth ○ *comparative linguistics* **2.** COMPARED TO OTHERS considered relative to sth known, mentioned, or expected ○ *He passed*

the test with comparative ease. **3.** GRAM IN A FORM EXPRESSING INCREASE used to describe the form of an adjective or adverb that expresses an increase in quality, quantity, or degree e.g. 'quicker' and 'more importantly' ■ *n.* GRAM COMPARATIVE FORM OF WORD a comparative form of an adjective or adverb [15thC. Formed from Latin *comparat-*, the past participle stem of *comparare* (see COMPARE).] —**comparatively** *adv.* —**comparativeness** *n.*

comparatively /kəm párrətivli/ *adv.* in comparison to sth else ○ *the costs were comparatively high*

compare /kəm páir/ *v.* (**-pares, -paring, -pared**) **1.** *vt.* EXAMINE FOR SIMILARITIES to examine two or more people or things in order to discover similarities and differences between them **2.** *vt.* LIKEN to consider or represent sb or sth as similar to another ○ *'Shall I compare thee to a summer's day?'* (William Shakespeare, *Sonnet*; 1564–1616) **3.** *vi.* BE AS GOOD AS to be equal or similar in quality or standing, especially to be as good as another ○ *As an athlete she can compare with the best in the sport.* **4.** *vi.* CONTRAST to have a particular relationship with sth or sb else ○ *Its performance compares badly with that of rival engines.* **5.** *vi.* MAKE COMPARISON to make a comparison **6.** *vt.* GRAM GIVE ALL ADJECTIVE'S OR ADVERB'S FORMS to give the positive, comparative, and superlative forms of an adjective or adverb ■ *n.* COMPARISON comparison (*literary*) ○ *a painting beautiful beyond compare* [15thC. From, ultimately, Latin *comparare*, from *compar*, literally 'equal with', from *par* 'equal'.] —**comparer** *n.* —**comparison** *n.*

━━━━ **WORD KEY: USAGE** ━━━━

Compare to or **compare with**? *Compare to* is used when things are being likened in general ways: *He compared her skin to ivory. Compare with* is used when the comparison is more specific and implies differences as well as similarities: *Tourists find its hotels poor value compared with those of other European capitals.* When *compare* is used intransitively (i.e. without an object), *with* should always be used: *The new model compares well with others in the same price range.*

compartment /kəm páartmənt/ *n.* **1.** PARTITIONED SPACE one of the areas into which an enclosed space is divided **2.** TRAIN CARRIAGE SECTION a subdivision of a passenger train carriage, with a door and features such as two facing rows of seats or sleeping accommodation **3.** SMALLER PART a separate part of sth larger ○ *He liked to divide his life into different compartments.* [Mid-16thC. Via French *compartiment* from, ultimately, late Latin *compartiri*, literally 'to divide up', from Latin *partiri* 'to divide', from *pars*.] —**compartmental** /kóm paart mént'l/ *adj.* —**compartmentally** /-mént'li/ *adv.*

compartmentalize /kóm paart mént'l īz/ (**-izes, -izing, -ized**), **compartmentalise** (**-ises, -ising, -ised**) *vt.* to divide sth into separate areas, categories, or compartments, often in a way that makes the separate parts too isolated ○ *She had to compartmentalize her home life and work.* —**compartmentalization** /kóm paart mént'l ī záysh'n/ *n.*

compass /kúmpəss/ *n.* **1.** DIRECTION FINDER a device for finding directions, usually with a magnetized pointer that automatically swings to magnetic north **2.** PERSONAL DIRECTION a sense of personal direction ○ *a leader who was devoid of moral compass* **3.** SCOPE the scope of sth such as a subject or area ○ *beyond the compass of the enquiry* ■ *vt.* (**-passes, -passing, -passed**) **1.** UNDERSTAND STH to understand sth fully and completely (*formal*) ○ *far more than the average mind can compass* **2.** = encompass **3.** ACHIEVE STH to achieve or attain sth (*literary*) [14thC. Via French *compas* 'scope, circle' and *compasser* 'to measure' from assumed Vulgar Latin *compassare*, literally 'to step off', from Latin *passus* 'step' (see PACE).] —**compassable** *adj.*

compass card *n.* the circular diagram in a direction-finding compass over which the needle rotates

compasses /kúmpəssiz/ *npl.* a device for drawing circles or measuring distances, e.g. on a map that consists of two rods, one pointed, the other often holding a pencil, joined by an adjustable hinge [Mid-16thC]

compassion /kəm pásh'n/ *n.* sympathy for the suffering of others, often including a desire to help [14thC. Via French from, ultimately, Latin *compass-*,

the past participle stem of *compati* (see COMPATIBLE).] —**compassionless** *adj.*

compassionate /kəm pásh'nət/ *adj.* showing feelings of sympathy for the suffering of others, often with a desire to help —**compassionately** *adv.* —**compassionateness** *n.*

compassionate leave *n.* exceptional leave granted to sb, especially in the armed forces, for personal reasons, e.g. the death of a close relative

compassion fatigue *n.* a loss or lessening of sympathy for the misfortune of others because too many demands have been made on your feelings

compass plant *n.* a plant found in prairie regions of the central United States, with yellow flowers similar to daisies and leaves that tend to point north and south. Latin name: *Silphium laciniatum.*

compass rose *n.* a circular diagram printed on a chart or map to show the direction of north and other main points of the compass [So called because its many-pointed design was thought to resemble a rose]

compass saw *n.* a handsaw with a tapering blade, used for cutting curved shapes

compass window *n.* a semicircular bay window

compatible /kəm páttəb'l/ *adj.* **1.** HARMONIOUS able to exist, live, or work together without conflict ○ *a highly compatible couple* **2.** CONSISTENT consistent or in keeping with sth else ○ *an observation not compatible with the facts* **3.** COMPUT ABLE TO BE USED WITH STH able to be used together with or substituted for another piece of hardware or software ○ *The software isn't PC-compatible* **4.** BOT ABLE TO CROSS-POLLINATE used to describe plant varieties that are able to cross-pollinate successfully **5.** BOT ABLE TO BE GRAFTED used to describe plants that are able to be grafted onto each other successfully **6.** FUNGI ABLE TO MATE used to describe fungal strains that are able to mate successfully **7.** MED ACCEPTABLE TO THE BODY used to describe blood, organs, or tissue that can be transplanted or transfused into a person's body without being rejected [Mid-16thC. Via French from, ultimately, Latin *compati*, literally 'to suffer together', from *pati* (see PATIENT).] —**compatibility** /kəm páttə bílləti/ *n.* —**compatibleness** /kəm páttəb'lnəss/ *n.* —**compatibly** /-páttəbli/ *adv.*

compatriot /kəm páttri ət/ *n.* sb from the same country as another [Late 16thC. Via French from late Latin *compatriota*, literally 'fellow countryman', from *patriota* (see PATRIOT).]

compd *abbr.* compound

compeer /kóm peer/ *n.* (*formal*) **1.** EQUAL sb who is the equal or peer of sb else **2.** COMPANION a person who is a close companion or associate of sb else [Via Old French *comper* from Latin *compar* 'equal with' (see COMPARE).]

compel /kəm pél/ (**-pels, -pelling, -pelled**) *vt.* **1.** FORCE SB to force sb to do sth ○ *I felt compelled to listen.* **2.** FORCE STH TO HAPPEN to make sth happen by force [14thC. From Latin *compellere*, literally 'to drive together', from *pellere* (see PULSE).] —**compellable** *adj.* —**compellably** *adv.* —**compeller** *n.*

compelling /kəm pélling/ *adj.* **1.** HOLDING THE ATTENTION attracting strong interest and attention ○ *a compelling account of a major scientific discovery* **2.** MAKING SB DO STH tending to make sb do sth, make sth happen, or be necessary ○ *I felt a compelling need to explain my actions.* —**compellingly** *adv.*

compendious /kəm péndi əss/ *adj.* containing a wide range of information in a concise form —**compendiously** *adv.* —**compendiousness** *n.*

compendium /kəm péndi əm/ (*plural* **-ums** or **-a** /-di ə/) *n.* **1.** SHORT ACCOUNT a comprehensive but brief account of a subject, especially in book form **2.** TWO BOOKS IN ONE a book in which two or more previously published books are brought together **3.** COLLECTION a collection of things, especially several different board games in one box [Late 16thC. From Latin, formed from *compendere*, literally 'to weigh together', from *pendere* (see PENSIVE).]

compensable /kəm pénssəb'l/ *adj.* qualifying for compensation —**compensability** /kəm pénssə bílləti/ *n.*

compensate /kómpən sayt/ (**-sates, -sating, -sated**) *v.* **1.** *vt.* PAY SB FOR LOSS to pay sb for work done or for sth lost ○ *adequately compensated for their efforts* **2.** *vti.* COUNTERBALANCE to counterbalance a force or quality **3.** *vi.* MAKE AMENDS to make amends or make up for sth ○ *Nothing can compensate for the loss of a child.* **4.** *vi.* PSYCHOL STRESS STH TO MAKE UP DEFICIENCY to stress the development of one aspect of your personality to make up for deficiency in another. ◊ **overcompensate** [Mid-17thC. From Latin *compensat-*, the past participle stem of *compensare*, literally 'to weigh together', from *pensare* (see PENSIVE).] —**compensative** /kómpən saytiv, kəm pénssətiv/ *adj.* —**compensator** /kómpən saytər/ *n.*

compensation /kómpən sáysh'n/ *n.* **1.** MONEY PAID TO REPAIR A LOSS an amount of money or sth else given to pay for loss, damage, or work done ○ *claimed compensation for loss of earnings* **2.** PAYMENT OF MONEY TO COVER LOSS the giving of sth to sb to pay for work done, loss, or damage **3.** AMENDS sth that makes amends or makes up for sth else ○ *one of the compensations of living abroad* **4.** PSYCHOL STRESSING A QUALITY the stressing of one aspect of the personality to make up for deficiency in another —**compensational** *adj.*

compensation order *n.* LAW an order from a court instructing sb convicted of an offence to pay compensation to the victim for

compensatory /kómpən sáytəri/ *adj.* serving to offset the negative effects or results of sth else

compensatory growth *n.* the growth in size of one part or organ of the body to make up for the failure or loss of another

compere /kóm pair/ *n.* HOST a host of an entertainment show, especially on television ■ *vti.* (**-peres, -pering, -pered**) ACT AS COMPERE to act as a compere [Mid-18thC. Via French *compère*, literally 'godfather', from medieval Latin *compater*, from Latin *pater* 'father'.]

compete /kəm peét/ (**-petes, -peting, -peted**) *vi.* **1.** TRY TO WIN to do sth with the goal of outperforming others or of winning sth **2.** PUT UP REASONABLE CONTEST to be able to put up a contest against sb or sth else and have a chance of winning ○ *This product just can't compete.* [Early 17thC. From late Latin *competere*, literally 'to strive together', from Latin *petere* (see PETITION).]

competence /kómpitənss/, **competency** /-tənssi/ *n.* **1.** ABILITY the ability to do sth well or to a required standard ○ *I don't doubt his competence for a moment.* **2.** SUFFICIENT INCOME an income that is enough to live on (*formal*) **3.** LAW BEING LEGALLY QUALIFIED the condition of being accepted by a court as legally qualified to be a party or witness **4.** LING LANGUAGE KNOWLEDGE a person's internalized knowledge of the rules of a language that enables them to speak and understand it. ◊ **performance, parole 5.** EMBRYOL ABILITY OF CELL TO SPECIALIZE the ability of embryonic cells to respond to an outside stimulus in a way that affects their development into specialized tissue

WORD KEY: SYNONYMS

See Synonyms at ***ability***.

competent /kómpitənt/ *adj.* **1.** ABLE having enough skill or ability to do sth **2.** ADEQUATE good enough or suitable for sth **3.** LAW LEGALLY CAPABLE accepted by a court as credible, legally qualified, or within sb's capacity **4.** MED, BIOL FUNCTIONING NORMALLY able to carry out its normal functions effectively ○ *a competent cervix* [14thC. Via French from Latin *competent-*, the present participle stem of *competere* (see COMPETE). The underlying sense is 'adequate for the purpose'.] —**competently** *adv.*

competition /kómpə tísh'n/ *n.* **1.** TRYING TO BEAT OTHERS the activity of doing sth with the goal of outperforming others or winning sth ○ *several firms are in competition for the contract* **2.** CONTEST an activity in which people try to do sth better than others or win sth **3.** OPPOSITION those against whom one is competing, or the level of opposition they give ○ *keep one step ahead of the competition* **4.** ECOL STRUGGLE FOR RESOURCES the struggle between organisms of the same or different species for limited resources such as food or light [Early 17thC. From the late Latin stem *competition-*, from Latin *competit-*, the past participle stem of *competere* (see COMPETE).]

competitive /kəm péttitiv/ *adj.* **1.** INVOLVING BEATING OTHERS involving or decided by trying to do sth better than others or win sth ○ *a highly competitive sport* **2.** WANTING TO BEAT OTHERS inclined towards wanting to do sth better than others **3.** ATTRACTIVE more attractive than others because of being good value or worth more ○ *competitive prices* —**competitiveness** *n.*

competitive exclusion *n.* ECOL the concept that two or more species with identical requirements cannot coexist on the same limited resources because one will compete more successfully than the other

competitively /kəm péttitivli/ *adv.* **1.** SO AS TO BEAT OTHERS in a way that involves trying to do sth better than others or win sth ○ *You will have to play competitively to win.* **2.** ATTRACTIVELY in an attractive way because of being good value or worth more than sth else ○ *competitively priced*

competitor /kəm péttitər/ *n.* **1.** PARTICIPANT IN COMPETITION a person or animal taking part in a competition **2.** MARKETPLACE OPPONENT an opponent that sb is competing against in a commercial market [Early 16thC. From Latin, formed from *competere* (see COMPETE).]

compilation /kómpi láysh'n/ *n.* **1.** GATHERING the activity of gathering things together from various places **2.** STH CREATED BY GATHERING sth created by gathering things together from various places ○ *a compilation of new poems*

compile /kəm píl/ (**-piles, -piling, -piled**) *vt.* **1.** PUT THINGS TOGETHER to gather things together from various places to form a whole **2.** CREATE STH BY GATHERING THINGS to create sth by gathering things together **3.** COMPUT TRANSLATE COMPUTER LANGUAGE to convert a computer program written in a high-level language into an intermediate language (**machine language**) using a special program (**compiler**) [14thC. From French *compiler*, of uncertain origin: probably from Latin *compilare* 'to plunder, plagiarize', literally 'to heap together', from *pila* (see PILE[1]).]

compiler /kəm pílər/ *n.* **1.** GATHERER sb who gathers things together, especially to create a whole **2.** COMPUT PROGRAM a computer program that converts another program from a high-level language into an intermediate language (**machine language**)

complacent /kəm pláyss'nt/ *adj.* **1.** SATISFIED self-satisfied, usually in an unreflective way and without being aware of possible dangers **2.** EAGER TO PLEASE eager to please (*old*) [Mid-17thC. From Latin *complacent-*, the present participle stem of *complacere*, literally 'to please very much', from *placere* (see PLACID). The word's original sense was 'pleasing'.] —**complacency** *n.* —**complacently** *adv.*

WORD KEY: USAGE

complacent or **complaisant**? Both words are used of people and their actions. The difference is that ***complacent*** refers to sb's feeling about himself or herself, whereas ***complaisant*** refers to feelings or attitudes about sb else. A ***complacent*** smile is a smile of self-satisfaction, whereas a ***complaisant*** smile is one that is intended to please. It is possible for a smile, or for sb showing the smile, to be both ***complacent*** and ***complaisant***.

complain /kəm pláyn/ (**-plains, -plaining, -plained**) *vi.* **1.** EXPRESS UNHAPPINESS ABOUT STH to express unhappiness about sth **2.** DESCRIBE SYMPTOMS OF STH to say that you are experiencing sth, especially pain or an illness ○ *complaining of chest pains* **3.** ACCUSE to accuse sb of doing sth illegal or undesirable, or make a protest about sth ○ *The neighbours complained to the police about the noise.* [14thC. Via French *complaign-*, the stem of *complaindre*, from assumed Vulgar Latin *complangere*, from Latin *plangere* (see PLAINT).]

WORD KEY: SYNONYMS

complain, object, protest, grumble, grouse, carp, gripe, whine, nag

CORE MEANING: to indicate dissatisfaction with sth

complain a general and neutral term; **object** to indicate dissatisfaction with and opposition to sth; **protest** a more forceful term for *object*; **grumble** a term suggesting a moderate degree of dissatisfaction, and suggesting that the complaint is repeated or continual; **grouse** to complain regularly and continually, often in a way that is not constructive; **carp** to complain continually, especially about unimportant things; **gripe** an informal term for *complain*; **whine** to complain in an unreasonable, repeated, or irritating way; **nag** to find fault with sb regularly and repeatedly.

complainant /kəm pláynənt/ *n.* a person or organization that takes legal action against another

complainer /kəm pláynər/ *n.* sb who is unhappy about sth and expresses this, especially habitually

complaint /kəm pláynt/ *n.* **1.** STATEMENT OF UNHAPPINESS a statement expressing dissatisfaction with sth ○ *If you've any complaints, talk to the manager.* **2.** STH MAKING SB UNHAPPY sth that makes sb unhappy or dissatisfied **3.** EXPRESSING OF DISSATISFACTION the act of expressing dissatisfaction with sth ○ *has cause for complaint* **4.** AILMENT a physical disorder, usually sth minor **5.** LAW STATEMENT a statement setting out the reasons for a legal action [14thC. From French *complainte*, the feminine past participle of *complaindre* (see COMPLAIN).]

complaisant /kəm pláyz'nt/ *adj.* showing a willingness to please others by carrying out, or allowing them to carry out, their wishes [Mid-17thC. Via French, the present participle of *complaire* 'to agree in order to please', from Latin *complacere* (see COMPLACENT).] —**complaisance** *n.* —**complaisantly** *adv.*

WORD KEY: USAGE

See usage note at ***complacent***.

compleat /kəm pleét/ *adj.* having or exhibiting full knowledge of a particular field or skill (*literary*) [14thC. Variant of COMPLETE.]

complement *n.* /kómplimənt/ **1.** COMPLETING PART sth that completes or perfects sth else **2.** ONE OF TWO either of two things that form a unit **3.** FULL QUANTITY a quantity of things or people that is considered complete ○ *the full complement of warships and replenishing vessels* **4.** LING SENTENCE PART the predicate part of a sentence that refers to the subject, not counting the verb **5.** MATH, LOGIC ITEMS EXCLUDED FROM A SUBSET the elements of a set that are not included in a particular subset of that set **6.** GEOM = **complementary angle 7.** IMMUNOL GROUP OF BLOOD PROTEINS a set of proteins in the bloodstream that, together with antibodies, recognize and attack foreign cells such as bacteria **8.** MUSIC NOTE INTERVAL an interval that, when added to a given interval, equals an octave ■ *vt.* /kómpli ment/ (**-ments, -menting, -mented**) COMPLETE STH to complete, perfect, or accompany sth else pleasingly ○ *a light dessert that complements a rich meal* [14thC. From Latin *complementum*, literally 'sth that fills up' from *complere* (see COMPLETE).] —**complemental** /kómpli mént'l/ *adj.* —**complementally** /-mént'li/ *adv.*

WORD KEY: USAGE

complement or **compliment**? The two words are close in spelling but their meanings are quite different. A ***complement*** is sth added to enhance a thing and make it complete, whereas a ***compliment*** is an expression of praise. *A fine wine is the perfect complement to good cooking. The cook received many compliments from the guests that evening.* Both words are also used as verbs, and both have adjectival forms: ***complementary*** and ***complimentary***. ***Complimentary*** has the special meaning 'given free of charge'; and so a ***complimentary*** copy of a book is one given without charge, whereas a ***complementary*** copy is one that completes a set of books.

complementarity /kómpli men tárrəti/ (*plural* **-ties**) *n.* **1.** RELATION OF PARTS the condition of things that complement one another **2.** PHYS PRINCIPLE GOVERNING EXPLANATION OF ATOMIC SYSTEMS the concept that two different models may be necessary to describe an atomic or subatomic system, e.g. electrons may be regarded as particles or waves in different circumstances

complementary /kómpli méntəri/ *adj.* **1.** COMPLETING completing sth else **2.** GENETICS INTERDEPENDENT used to describe genes that are interdependent and produce their effect only when present together **3.** MATH NOT IN SUBSET used to describe the elements of a mathematical set that are not included in a particular subset of that set **4.** GEOM = **complementary angle 5.** MED RELATING TO COMPLEMENTARY MEDICINE used in or using complementary medicine —**complementarily** *adv.* —**complementariness** *n.*

WORD KEY: USAGE

See Usage note at ***complement***.

complementary angle *n.* GEOM either of two angles that together make up a right angle

a at; aa father; aw all; ay day; air hair; ə about, edible, item, common, circus; e egg; ee eel; hw when; i it, happy; ī ice; 'l apple; 'm rhythm; 'n fashion; o odd; ō open; ŏŏ good; oo pool; ow owl; oy oil; th thin; th this; u up; ur urge;

complementary colour *n.* PHYS a colour or coloured light that, when combined with another, produces white or grey

complementary DNA *n.* single-stranded DNA made in a laboratory so that its base sequence is complementary to a messenger RNA template. It is assembled by the enzyme reverse transcriptase, and may be used in gene cloning or as a gene probe.

complementary gene *n.* a gene that produces an observable effect in an organism only in conjunction with another gene

complementary medicine *n.* a range of therapies based on the holistic treatment of physical disorders, generally addressing the causes of diseases rather than their symptoms and also taking steps in the prevention of disease. The term embraces therapies such as acupuncture, herbalism, and homeopathy. ◊ **alternative medicine**

complement fixation *n.* the process in which a group of blood proteins (**complement**) is bound to a specific combined antibody-antigen pair as part of the immune reaction to foreign cells

complementizer /kómplimən tīzər/ *n.* a word introducing a clause that acts as a complement ○ *'For' in 'for Sam to be late is unusual' is a complementizer.*

complete /kəm pléet/ *adj.* **1.** WHOLE having every necessary part or everything that is wanted ○ *a complete set of Dickens* **2.** FINISHED having reached the normal or expected end ○ *The washing machine stops when the last spin cycle is complete.* **3.** ABSOLUTE being the greatest degree of sth ○ *a complete waste of time* **4.** ACCOMPLISHED having all the necessary qualities or abilities for a particular role ○ *She is the complete diplomat.* **5.** BOT HAVING ALL PRINCIPAL FLOWER PARTS used to describe flowers that have all the principal flower parts, that is carpels, petals, sepals, and stamens. ◊ **incomplete** ■ *vt.* (**-pletes, -pleting, -pleted**) **1.** MAKE STH WHOLE to make sth whole by including every necessary part or everything that is wanted ○ *one more goblet to complete the set* **2.** FINISH STH to finish sth or bring sth to an end ○ *You have 20 minutes to complete the quiz.* **3.** ACCOMPLISH STH to carry out or accomplish sth ○ *The terms of the sale have been completed.* [14thC. Directly or via French from Latin *completus*, the past participle of *complere*, literally 'to fill up', from *plere* 'to fill' (source also of English *supply*).] —**completely** *adv.* ◇ **complete with** including a particular thing as a feature

WORD KEY: ORIGIN

Complete comes from the Latin word *plere*, meaning 'to fill', which is also the source of English *accomplish, complement, compliment, comply, deplete, expletive, implement, replete, supplement,* and *supply.*

complete blood count *n.* a diagnostic test used to identify the levels of all blood-cell types in a quantity of blood

completely /kəm pléetli/ *adv.* used to emphasize the extent of sth ○ *completely wrong* ○ *I completely forgot about it*

complete metamorphosis *n.* metamorphosis that involves the four stages of egg, larva, pupa, and adult in insects such as butterflies, beetles, flies, and bees

completeness /kəm pléetnəss/ *n.* the condition of being full, entire, or finished

completion /kəm pléesh'n/ *n.* **1.** FINISHING the finishing of sth or making sth whole **2.** STATE OF BEING FINISHED the state of being finished or brought to an end ○ *the building is nearing completion* **3.** LAW FINAL STAGE OF SALE the final stage of the sale of land or real property, when ownership changes hands **4.** AMERICAN FOOTBALL CAUGHT PASS a forward pass that has been successfully caught

completist /kəm pléetist/ *n.* sb who collects a particular kind of thing and wants to obtain an example of everything available, even of inferior items (*informal*) [Late 20thC]

complex *adj.* /kóm pleks, kəm pléks/ **1.** COMPLICATED difficult to analyse, understand, or solve **2.** HAVING MANY PARTS made up of many interrelated parts ■ *n.* /kóm pleks/ **1.** INTERCONNECTED BUILDINGS a group of interconnected buildings functioning as a whole ○ *a sports complex* **2.** INFLUENCE ON BEHAVIOUR a set of related feelings, ideas, or impulses that may be repressed but that continues to influence thoughts and behaviour ○ *a guilt complex* **3.** EXAGGERATED FEELINGS an exaggerated or obsessive set of feelings about sth (*informal*) ○ *He has a complex about eating in restaurants.* **4.** CHEM COMPOUND OF NONMETAL AND METAL ATOMS a compound in which nonmetal molecules or ions form weak bonds (**coordinate bonds**) with a central metal atom [Mid-17thC. Directly and via French from Latin *complexus*, the past participle of *complecti*, literally 'to weave together', from *plectere* 'to plait'(see PLEXUS).] —**complexly** *adv.* —**complexness** *n.*

complex conjugate *n.* MATH a complex number in a pair that have the same real components but opposite imaginary components. The complex conjugate of a + ib is a – ib.

complex fraction *n.* MATH a fraction with a mixed number or fraction in its numerator or denominator, or in both

complexion /kəm pléksh'n/ *n.* **1.** SKIN TYPE the quality and colour of the skin, especially of the face **2.** CHARACTER the character of sth or the way it appears ○ *This development puts an entirely new complexion on the matter.* [14thC. Via French, 'bodily constitution', from, ultimately, Latin *complecti* 'to entwine' (see COMPLEX). The original underlying sense was the 'combination' of a person's bodily humours.] —**complexional** *adj.*

complexioned /kəm pléksh'nd/ *adj.* having a particular type of skin, especially on the face (*usually used in combination*) ○ *fair-complexioned*

complexity /kəm pléksəti/ (*plural* **-ties**) *n.* **1.** COMPLICATED NATURE the condition of being difficult to understand, or being made up of many interrelated things ○ *the increasing complexity of computing systems* **2.** COMPLICATED THING any one of the interrelated problems or difficulties involved in a complicated matter (*often used in the plural*)

complex number *n.* a number in the form $a + ib$, where $i = \sqrt{-1}$, that may be either real or imaginary

complex plane *n.* MATH a plane whose coordinates are expressed as single complex numbers

complex sentence *n.* a sentence containing one or more subordinate clauses

compliance /kəm plī ənss/, **compliancy** /-ənssi/ *n.* **1.** CONFORMITY the state or act of conforming with or agreeing to do sth ○ *in compliance with the court order* **2.** READINESS TO COMPLY readiness to conform or agree to do sth

compliance documentation *n.* the documents that a company issuing shares must publish to comply with regulatory requirements governing new share issues and related matters

compliance legislation *n.* legislation enacted to ensure compliance with a legal agreement or requirement, e.g. a treaty or mandate

compliance officer *n.* a person employed by a financial organization to ensure that conflicts of interest do not arise in companies with wide-ranging, complex financial dealings and that regulations are not broken

compliancy *n.* = **compliance**

compliant /kəm plī ənt/ *adj.* **1.** READY TO CONFORM ready to conform or agree to do sth **2.** CONFORMING TO REQUIREMENTS made or done according to requirements or instructions (*often used in combination*) ○ *compliant with the general statutes* ○ *Y2K-compliant* —**compliantly** *adv.*

complicacy /kómplikəssi/ (*plural* **-cies**) *n.* (*formal*) **1.** COMPLICATEDNESS the condition of being complex or complicated **2.** STH COMPLICATED a complicated matter or situation

complicate /kómpli kayt/ *vt.* (**-cates, -cating, -cated**) MAKE STH MORE COMPLEX to make sth complex or difficult ○ *Further delay will only complicate matters.* ○ *a complicating factor* ■ **adj. 1.** FOLDED used to describe things that are folded lengthwise, e.g. leaves or insect wings **2.** = **complicated** [Early 17thC. From Latin *complicat-*, the past participle stem of *complicare*, literally 'to fold together', from *plicare* (see PLY[2]).]

complicated /kómpli kaytid/, **complicate** *adj.* **1.** HAVING MANY INTERRELATED PARTS composed of many interrelated parts and so difficult to understand or deal with ○ *a complicated diagram* **2.** DIFFICULT difficult to deal with because of the need to take different relationships or points of view into consideration ○ *Life is complicated enough as it is.* —**complicatedly** *adv.* —**complicatedness** *n.*

complication /kómpli káysh'n/ *n.* **1.** DIFFICULT STATE a difficult or confused state caused by many interrelated factors **2.** DIFFICULTY sth that makes sth else more difficult or complex ○ *Far from being helpful, this is just a further complication.* **3.** PLOT DEVICE an event or character whose introduction into a story causes difficulty **4.** MEDICAL PROBLEM a disease or problem that arises in addition to the initial condition or during a surgical operation **5.** INTRODUCTION OF DIFFICULTY the act of making sth complex or difficult

complice /kómpliss/ *n.* sb who helps another, especially in doing sth illegal (*archaic*) [15thC. Via French from late Latin *complic-*, the stem of *complex* 'close associate', from *plicare* (see PLY[2]). The underlying meaning is 'sb who is bound together with you'.]

complicity /kəm plíssəti/ *n.* involvement with another in doing sth illegal or wrong [Mid-17thC. Formed from COMPLICE.]

compliment *n.* /kómplimənt/ **1.** STATEMENT OF PRAISE sth said to express praise and approval **2.** ACT OR GESTURE sth done to show respect and honour ■ *vt.* /kómpli ment/ (**-ments, -menting, -mented**) **1.** SAY STH NICE TO SB to say sth that expresses praise and approval to sb **2.** GIVE STH TO SB to give sb a gift as a sign of respect or affection **3.** CONGRATULATE SB to congratulate sb [Mid-17thC. Via French from, ultimately, Latin *complere* (see COMPLETE). The underlying sense is 'to fulfil the demands of courtesy'.] ◇ **return the compliment** to respond to a gesture sb has made towards you with a similar gesture

WORD KEY: USAGE

See Usage note at ***complement.***

complimentary /kómpli méntəri/ *adj.* **1.** ADMIRING expressing praise or approval ○ *a complimentary glance* **2.** FREE given free as a courtesy or favour ○ *complimentary seats* —**complimentarily** *adv.*

WORD KEY: USAGE

See Usage note at ***complement.***

compline /kómplin, -līn/, **complin** /-lin/ *n.* the last of the seven separate hours (**canonical hours**) that are set aside for prayer each day in the Roman Catholic Church [12thC. An alteration (probably influenced by 'matins') of Old French *complie*, from medieval Latin *(hora) completa* 'final (hour)', from Latin *completus* (see COMPLETE).]

comply /kəm plī/ (**-plies, -plying, -plied**) *vi.* to obey or conform to sth, e.g. a rule, law, wish, or regulation [Late 16thC. Via obsolete French *complire* from Latin *complere* (see COMPLETE). The underlying sense is 'to carry out completely, fulfil'.] —**complier** *n.*

compo[1] /kóm pō/ *n.* a material mixed from various ingredients, especially a mix of cement mortar (*slang*) [Early 19thC. Shortening of COMPOSITION.]

compo[2] /kómpō/ *n.* *ANZ* compensation, usually that paid to workers for injury or during ill health (*informal*) [Mid-20thC. Shortening and alteration of COMPENSATION.]

component /kəm pōnənt/ *n.* **1.** PART a part of sth, usually of sth bigger ○ *a manufacturer of vehicle components* ○ *one of several major components of our research* **2.** ELEC ELECTRIC PART a device, e.g. a resistor or transistor, that is part of an electronic circuit **3.** MATH VECTOR any one of a set of vectors whose combination (**resultant**) is another vector **4.** CHEM CONSTITUENT SUBSTANCE any one of the substances necessary to describe each phase of a chemical system ■ *adj.* FORMING PART forming part of a whole [Mid-16thC. From Latin *component-*, the present participle stem of *componere*, literally 'to put together', from *ponere* (see POST).] —**componential** /kómpə nénsh'l/ *adj.*

compo rations *npl.* food in a dried and compressed form, meant for use by soldiers when no fresh food is available

comport /kəm páwrt/ (**-ports, -porting, -ported**) *v.* (*formal*) **1.** *vr.* BEHAVE to behave in a particular way **2.** *vi.* BE CONSISTENT to agree or be consistent with sth ○ *This does not comport with the established facts.* [14thC. From Latin *comportare*, literally 'to bring together', from *portare* (see PORT⁵). The underlying meaning is 'to collect yourself'.]

comportment /kəm páwrtmənt/ *n.* the way in which sb behaves (*formal*)

compose /kəm pṓz/ (**-poses, -posing, -posed**) *v.* **1.** *vt.* BE THE PARTS OF STH to make sth by combining together ○ *fertilizer composed of organic compounds* **2.** *vt.* PUT ELEMENTS TOGETHER to put things together to form a whole ○ *compose a light lunch, using cold meats and salads* **3.** *vt.* ARRANGE ITEMS to arrange things in order to achieve an effect ○ *compose objects for a still life in oils* **4.** *vti.* CREATE to create sth, especially a piece of music or writing ○ *She is trying to compose a rather difficult letter to her client.* **5.** *vt.* CALM to make sb become calm ○ *please compose yourself* **6.** *vt.* RECONCILE ARGUMENT to settle a quarrel or dispute (*archaic*) **7.** *vti.* SET TYPE to set type in preparation for printing [14thC. From French *composer*, an alteration (influenced by *poser* 'to place') of Latin *componere* (see COMPONENT).]

WORD KEY: USAGE

See Usage note at ***comprise***.

composed /kəm pṓzd/ *adj.* not agitated or distracted —**composedly** /kəm pṓzidli/ *adv.* —**composedness** /kəm pṓzidnəss/ *n.*

WORD KEY: SYNONYMS

See Synonyms at ***calm***.

composer /kəm pṓzər/ *n.* sb who composes, especially a writer of music

composite /kómpəzit/ *adj.* **1.** COMPOUND made up of different parts **2.** BOT BELONGING TO DAISY FAMILY used to describe any plant belonging to a large family that has flower heads resembling a single flower but composed of many smaller flowers. Dandelions and daisies are composite plants. Family: Compositae. ■ *n.* **1.** STH MADE OF PARTS sth made from different parts ○ *The new law is a composite of previous suggested legislation.* **2.** *US* CRIMINOL IMAGE OF SUSPECT an image of a suspect's face that is created by a police artist or photographer, based on input from witnesses (*informal*) **3.** BOT PLANT OF DAISY FAMILY a composite plant **4.** BUILDING BUILDING MATERIAL any building material made up of different ingredients ■ *vt.* (**-posites, -positing, -posited**) COMBINE PROPOSALS to combine motions from various local branches of an organization, e.g. a political party or a trade union, for discussion at a higher level [14thC. Directly or via French from Latin *compositus*, the past participle of *componere* (see COMPONENT).] —**compositely** /kómpəzitli/ *adv.* —**compositeness** *n.*

Composite *adj.* belonging to a Classical order of architecture that combines elements of the Ionic and Corinthian orders [Mid-16thC]

composite construction *n.* a building technique that combines the use of steel and concrete to make supporting columns, resulting in stronger, lighter, and less costly supports

composite photograph *n.* an image or scene made up of two or more original images placed side by side, overlapped, or superimposed

composite school *n.* in some Canadian provinces, a secondary school in which academic, business, and vocational programmes are offered

composition /kómpə zísh'n/ *n.* **1.** CONSTITUENTS the way in which sth is made, especially in terms of its different parts **2.** ARRANGEMENT the way in which the parts of sth are arranged, especially the elements in a visual image ○ *the artist's masterly composition of a group portrait* **3.** PUTTING TOGETHER the act or process of combining things to form a whole, or of creating sth such as a piece of music or writing **4.** ARTS ARTISTIC CREATION sth created as a work of art, especially a piece of music **5.** PIECE OF WRITING a short piece of writing, especially a school exercise **6.** PRODUCT a thing created by combining separate parts **7.** LAW SETTLEMENT a settlement whereby creditors agree to accept partial payment of debts by a bankrupt party, typically in return for a consideration such as immediate payment of a lesser amount **8.** LING WORD FORMATION the formation of compound words from separate words **9.** PRINTING TYPESETTING the setting of type in preparation for printing **10.** LOGIC FALLACY the fallacy of arguing that what is true of parts of a whole is true of the whole [14thC. Via French from, ultimately, Latin *composit-*, the past participle stem of *componere* (see COMPONENT).] —**compositional** *adj.* —**compositionally** *adv.*

compositor /kəm pózzitər/ *n.* sb who sets text in type [Mid-16thC. From Latin, 'compiler', formed from *composit-*, the past participle stem of *componere* (see COMPONENT).]

compos mentis /kómpəss méntiss/ *adj.* sane or of sound mind [From Latin, literally 'in control of one's mind']

compost /kóm post/ *n.* **1.** DECAYED PLANT MATTER a mixture of decayed plants and other organic matter used by gardeners for enriching soil **2.** SOIL MIXTURE FOR POT PLANTS any mixture, e.g. based on peat or soil, used in pots for growing plants ○ *a rich potting compost* ■ *v.* (**-posts, -posting, -posted**) **1.** *vti.* DECAY to convert organic matter to compost, or to be converted to compost **2.** *vt.* TREAT SOIL to treat soil or an area of ground by adding compost [14thC. Via Old French *composte* 'mixture' (source of English *compote*) from Latin *composita*, from *composit-*, the past participle stem of *componere* (see COMPONENT).] —**compostable** *adj.*

composter /kóm postər/ *n.* a device, often shaped like a box or barrel, used to collect organic materials to be used later in composting

compost heap *n.* a pile of organic matter left to rot for use as fertilizer, especially by a gardener or farmer

composure /kəm pṓzhər/ *n.* calm and steady control over the emotions

compote /kóm pōt/ *n.* fruit cooked in sugar or syrup, served as a hot or cold dessert [Late 17thC. Via French, literally 'mixture', from Old French *composte* (see COMPOST).]

compound[1] *n.* /kóm pownd/ **1.** MIXTURE sth made by the combination of two or more different things **2.** GRAM WORD MADE UP OF OTHER WORDS a word that is formed from two or more identifiable words, e.g. 'blackbird', 'cookbook', or 'bullheaded', or, in some analyses, 'mother-in-law' or 'fire drill' ■ *adj.* /kóm pownd/ **1.** HAVING PARTS made by the combination of two or more different things **2.** GRAM MADE FROM TWO OR MORE WORDS used to describe a word that is made up of two or more words or word parts **3.** BOT DIVIDED INTO PARTS used to describe a leaf that is divided into two or more parts (**leaflets**) attached to a single stalk. ◊ **simple** ■ *v.* /kəm pównd, kom-/ (**-pounds, -pounding, -pounded**) **1.** *vti.* ADD TOGETHER to add together, or add one thing to another or others, to form a whole ○ *hatred that was compounded with fear and revulsion* **2.** *vt.* MAKE STH BY COMBINING PARTS to make sth by the adding together of different parts ○ *a medication compounded from several constituent elements* **3.** *vt.* INTENSIFY STH to make sth more extreme or intense by adding sth to it ○ *Further financial reverses compounded his despair.* **4.** *vt.* LAW TAKE BRIBE TO IGNORE CRIME to accept a bribe in return for not prosecuting or informing about a crime **5.** *vti.* SETTLE DEBT to settle a debt by paying a lesser amount owed, typically right away in a lump sum [14thC. Originally the past participle of earlier *compoune* 'to put together', via Old French *compoun-*, the stem of *compondre*, from Latin *componere* (see COMPOSE).] —**compoundable** /kəm pówndəb'l/ *adj.* —**compounder** /kəm pówndər/ *n.*

WORD KEY: SYNONYMS

See Synonyms at ***mixture***.

compound[2] /kóm pownd/ *n.* an enclosed group of buildings for the segregation or restraint of a particular group of people [Late 17thC. Alteration of Malay *kampong* 'enclosure, village'.]

compound eye *n.* the eye that most insects and some crustaceans have, made up of several separate light-sensitive parts

compound fault *n.* GEOL a series of faults that lie closely together, following the same general direction

compound fraction *n.* MATH = **complex fraction**

compound fracture *n.* a bone fracture in which a broken bone pierces the skin or comes into contact with an open wound

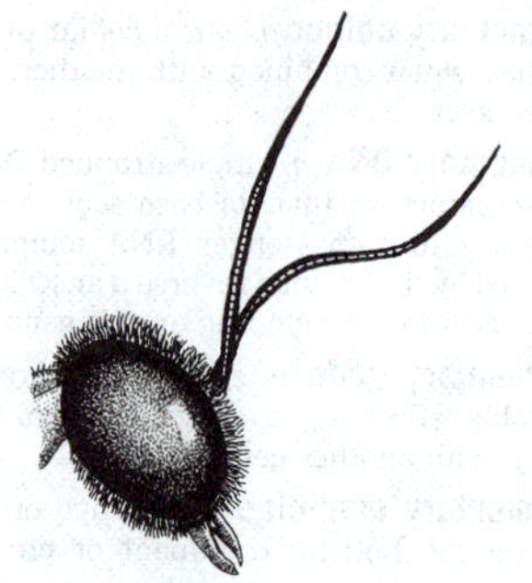

Compound eye

compound interest *n.* interest that is calculated on the combined total of the original sum borrowed (**principal**) and the interest it has already accrued

compound meter *n. US* MUSIC = **compound time**

compound microscope *n.* a microscope consisting of two lenses or lens systems and an eyepiece, mounted in a tube

compound sentence *n.* a sentence containing two or more clauses that can stand independently. The clauses are often linked by a conjunction that is sometimes preceded by a comma, as in 'We waited for over an hour, but she didn't show up'.

compound time *n.* MUSIC musical time in which the number of beats to the bar is a multiple of three. US term **compound meter**

comprehend /kómpri hénd/ (**-hends, -hending, -hended**) *v.* **1.** *vti.* UNDERSTAND to grasp the meaning or nature of sth ○ *It was hard to comprehend the sheer scale of the problem.* **2.** *vt.* INCLUDE STH to include sth as a part of sth else (*formal*) [14thC. From Latin *comprehendere*, literally 'to grasp fully', from *prehendere* 'to seize'.]

comprehensible /kómpri hénssəb'l/ *adj.* capable of being understood [15thC. Directly or via French from Latin *comprehensibilis*, from *comprehens-*, the past participle stem of *comprehendere* (see COMPREHEND).] —**comprehensibility** /kómpri hénssə bílləti/ *n.* —**comprehensibleness** /kómpri hénssəb'lnəss/ *n.* —**comprehensibly** /-hénssəbli/ *adv.*

comprehension /kómpri hénsh'n/ *n.* **1.** UNDERSTANDING the grasping of the meaning of sth **2.** INTELLECTUAL ABILITY the ability to grasp the meaning of sth ○ *It's beyond my comprehension.* **3.** EDUC SET OF QUESTIONS ON TEXT an exercise consisting of a set of questions on a short text, designed to test students' understanding of it [15thC. Directly or via French from the Latin stem *comprehension-*, from *comprehens-*, the past participle stem of *comprehendere* (see COMPREHEND).]

comprehensive /kómpri hénssiv/ *adj.* **1.** INCLUSIVE covering many things or a wide area ○ *a comprehensive survey of public opinion* **2.** INCLUDING ALL including everything, so as to be complete ○ *comprehensive knowledge of the subject* **3.** COVERING MANY EVENTUALITIES used to describe insurance policies that provide coverage or benefit in most areas **4.** EDUC FOR ALL CHILDREN for all children of a local area, no matter what their level of ability **5.** ABLE TO UNDERSTAND able to understand, or using the power of understanding (*archaic*) ○ *an unusually comprehensive mind* ■ *n.* EDUC = **comprehensive school** [17thC. Directly or via French from Latin *comprehensivus*, from *comprehens-*, the past participle stem of *comprehendere* (see COMPREHEND).] —**comprehensively** *adv.*

comprehensiveness /kómpri hénssivnəss/ *n.* the state of including a great deal or everything

comprehensive school *n.* a local secondary school for children of all ability levels

compress *v.* /kəm préss/ (**-presses, -pressing, -pressed**) **1.** *vti.* SHRINK to make sth smaller by applying pressure or by some analogous process **2.** *vt.* PRESS THINGS TOGETHER to press things, e.g. the lips, together **3.** *vt.* COMPUT MAKE FILES SHORTER to reduce the size of computer files or transmissions by means of algorithms ■ *n.* /kóm pres/ **1.** MED TREATMENT PAD a cloth pad, often moistened or medicated, pressed firmly against a part of the body as a treatment, e.g. to stop bleeding **2.** MACHINE a machine for compressing material, especially cotton that is being packed [14thC. Via Old

French from late Latin *compressare*, literally 'to keep pressing together', from Latin *comprimere*, from *premere* (see PRESS).] —**compressible** *adj.* —**compressibility** /kəm préssə bílləti/ *n.* —**compressibleness** *n.*

compressed /kəm prést/ *adj.* squeezed or condensed and made smaller or shorter

compressed air *n.* air that is kept in a container under pressure, often used to power machines

compression /kəm présh'n/ *n.* **1.** REDUCTION IN SIZE the reduction of the volume or mass of sth by applying pressure, or the state of having been treated in this way **2.** PHASE IN ENGINE a phase in the working of an internal-combustion engine in which a combination of fuel and air is compressed in a cylinder before being ignited [14thC. Via French from, ultimately, Latin *compress-*, the past participle stem of *comprimere* (see COMPRESS).] —**compressional** *adj.*

compression ratio *n.* the ratio between the largest and smallest possible volumes in the cylinder of an internal-combustion engine that contains a combination of fuel and air being compressed

compression wave *n.* a longitudinal wave created in a fluid by a compressing force, e.g. a sound wave in air

compressive /kəm préssiv/ *adj.* having the power or tendency to compress [14thC. Via French from, ultimately, Latin *compress-*, the past participle stem of *comprimere* (see COMPRESS).] —**compressively** *adv.*

compressor /kəm préssər/ *n.* **1.** MACHINE THAT COMPRESSES GAS a machine that compresses gas so that the power produced when the gas is released can be used to power another machine, e.g. a pneumatic drill **2.** ANAT MUSCLE a muscle that compresses or flattens a part of the body

comprimario /kómpri máiri ō/ *n.* a secondary role in an opera or ballet, or sb who performs such a role [From Italian, literally 'co-primary']

comprise /kəm príz/ (-prises, -prising, -prised) *vt.* **1.** INCLUDE STH to incorporate or contain sth **2.** CONSIST OF STH to be made up of sth **3.** CONSTITUTE STH to make up the whole of sth [15thC. Formed from French *compris*, the past participle of *comprendre* 'to include', from Latin *comprehendere* (see COMPREHEND).] —**comprisable** *adj.*

————————— WORD KEY: USAGE —————————

comprise, consist of, include, compose, or **constitute**? *Comprise* and *consist of* are concerned with a whole having a number of parts. They are used in the active voice, with the whole as their subject and the parts as their object: *the house comprises three bedrooms, a bathroom, a kitchen, and a living room. The meal consisted of several small dishes that everybody dipped into and shared.* If some rather than all the parts are mentioned, *include* may be used instead: *the house includes a kitchen and a living room on the first floor. Consist of* is more usual than *comprise* when the parts, or some of them, are mass nouns, as opposed to count nouns: *Breakfast consists of bread, jam, cereal, and coffee. Compose* and *constitute* are concerned with parts making up a whole. *Compose* is normally used in the passive and *constitute* in the active: *The team is composed of several experts in the field. The following commodities constitute the average household diet.*

————————————————————————————————

compromise /kómprə mīz/ *n.* **1.** AGREEMENT a settlement of a dispute in which two or more sides agree to accept less than they originally wanted ○ *After hours of negotiations a compromise was reached.* **2.** STH ACCEPTED RATHER THAN WANTED sth that sb accepts because what was wanted is unattainable **3.** POTENTIAL DANGER OR DISGRACE exposure to danger or disgrace ■ *v.* (-mises, -mising, -mised) **1.** *vi.* AGREE BY CONCEDING to settle a dispute by agreeing to accept less than what was originally wanted **2.** *vt.* LESSEN VALUE OF STH to undermine or devalue sth or sb by making concessions ○ *Don't compromise your integrity by telling half-truths.* **3.** *vt.* EXPOSE TO DANGER to expose sb or sth to danger or risk ○ *This scandal could compromise his chances of re-election.* ○ *drugs that can compromise the immune system* [15thC. Via French *compromis* from Latin *compromissum* 'mutual agreement', from the past participle of *compromittere*, literally 'to make mutual promises', from *promittere* (see PROMISE).] —**compromiser** *n.*

compromising /kómprə mīzing/ *adj.* liable to expose sb to disgrace or humiliation —**compromisingly** *adv.*

compt. *abbr.* compartment

Compton /kómptən, kúmp-/, **Sir Denis** (1918–98) British cricketer and footballer. An international player in both his sports, he set an all-time batting record in the 1947 season with 3,816 runs, including 18 centuries.

Compton-Burnett /kómptən bər nét/, **Ivy, Dame** (1884–1969) British novelist. She wrote *Pastors and Masters* (1925) and *Brothers and Sisters* (1929).

Compton effect *n.* the decrease in energy and increase in wavelength experienced by a photon after colliding or interacting with an electron [Early 20thC. Named after the US physicist A. H. Compton 1892–1962.]

comptroller /kən trólər/ *n.* FIN = **controller** *n.* 2 [15thC. Variant of CONTROLLER, by association with *compt*, an older spelling of *count*.] —**comptrollership** *n.*

compulsion /kəm púlsh'n/ *n.* **1.** FORCE a force that makes sb do sth **2.** COMPELLING an act of compelling or the state of being compelled ○ *You are under no compulsion to leave.* **3.** PSYCHOL PSYCHOLOGICAL FORCE a psychological and usually irrational force that makes sb do sth, often unwillingly ○ *felt an irresistible compulsion* [14thC. Via French from, ultimately, Latin *compuls-*, the past participle stem of *compellere* (see COMPEL).]

compulsive /kəm púlsiv/ *adj.* **1.** DRIVEN driven by an irresistible inner force to do sth ○ *a compulsive liar* **2.** POWERFULLY INTERESTING exerting a powerful attraction or interest ■ *n.* SB UNDER PSYCHOLOGICAL COMPULSION sb whose actions are driven by a usually irrational psychological force —**compulsively** *adv.* —**compulsiveness** *n.*

compulsory /kəm púlssəri/ *adj.* **1.** NECESSARY required by law or an authority ○ *attendance at the lecture is compulsory* **2.** FORCED caused by force, or using force to make sb do sth ■ *n.* (*plural* -ries) REQUIRED ROUTINE an exercise or routine that participants in a sport such as gymnastics or figure skating must perform as part of a competition (*often used in the plural*) [Early 16thC. From medieval Latin *compulsorius*, from Latin *compuls-*, the past participle stem of *compellere* (see COMPEL).] —**compulsorily** *adv.* —**compulsoriness** *n.*

compulsory purchase *n.* a situation in which sb is obliged by law to sell property to the government or a local authority because it is wanted for public use

compunction /kəm púngksh'n/ *n.* feelings of shame and regret about doing sth wrong [14thC. Via French *componction* from, ultimately, Latin *compunct-*, the past participle stem of *compungere*, literally 'to sting strongly', from *pungere* (see PUNGENT).] —**compunctious** *adj.* —**compunctiously** *adv.*

compurgation /kóm pur gáysh'n/ *n.* formerly, a way of proving that sb is innocent by collecting a number of oaths from his or her friends and colleagues [Mid-17thC. Via the medieval Latin stem *compurgation-*, from, ultimately, Latin *compurgare*, literally 'to cleanse completely', from *purgare* (see PURGE). The underlying meaning is 'to clear of suspicion.'] —**compurgator** /kóm pur gaytər/ *n.*

computable /kəm pyóotəb'l/ *adj.* capable of being worked out by calculation, especially using a computer —**computability** /kəm pyóotə bílləti/ *n.*

computation /kómpyŏŏ táysh'n/ *n.* **1.** USE OF COMPUTER the use of a computer, especially for calculation, or sth calculated using a computer **2.** CALCULATION the calculating of sth, or the result of a calculation —**computational** *adj.*

computational /kómpyŏŏ táysh'nəl/ *adj.* relating to or involving the use of computers ○ *computational linguistics* —**computationally** *adv.*

compute /kəm pyóot/ (-putes, -puting, -puted) *v.* **1.** *vt.* CALCULATE STH to calculate an answer or result, especially using a computer **2.** *vi.* USE COMPUTER OR CALCULATOR to use a computer or calculator **3.** *vi.* YIELD RESULT to yield a result, especially a correct result, from calculation ○ *These numbers just don't compute.* [Early 17thC. From Latin *computare*, literally 'to reckon together' source of COUNT[1].]

computed tomography *n.* MED a technique for producing images of cross-sections of the body. A computer processes data from X-rays penetrating the body from many directions and projects the results on a screen. This is the technology used when conducting a CT scan.

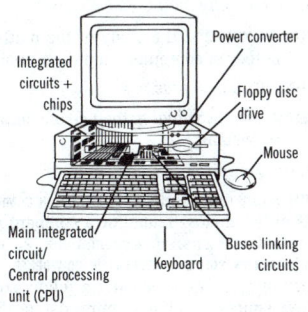

Integrated circuits + chips — **Power converter** — **Floppy disc drive** — **Mouse** — **Main integrated circuit/ Central processing unit (CPU)** — **Keyboard** — **Buses linking circuits**

Computer

computer /kəm pyóotər/ *n.* **1.** ELECTRONIC DATA PROCESSOR AND STORER an electronic device that accepts, processes, stores, and outputs data at high speeds according to programmed instructions **2.** SB WHO COMPUTES a person who calculates figures or amounts using a machine

computer conferencing *n.* the use of computers to allow people at distant sites to exchange text and graphic messages as they would at a meeting

computer crime *n.* illegal activities carried out on or by means of a computer. Computer crime includes criminal trespass into another's computer system, theft of computerized data, and the use of an on-line system to commit or aid in the commission of fraud.

computer dating *n.* the business or practice of putting people's personal details and preferences into a computer that then matches apparently compatible couples

computerese /kəm pyóotə réez/ *n.* the technical language used by people involved with computers (*humorous*)

computer game *n.* a game in the form of computer software, run on a personal computer or games machine and played by one or more people using a keyboard, mouse, control pad, or joystick. Computer games usually combine sound and graphics and range from traditional games such as chess to fast-moving action games or complex puzzles.

computer graphics *n.* GENERATION OF PICTURES ON COMPUTER the use of a computer and specialized software to produce and manipulate pictorial images for purposes of animation, business presentations, and scientific research. The graphic images may be stored as mathematical representations called 'vector graphics', which may be sized and scaled as desired, or as 'bit-mapped graphics', which are patterns on the screen (**pixels**). (*takes a singular verb*) ■ *npl.* COMPUTER-GENERATED IMAGES the images produced by computer graphics

computerize /kəm pyóotə rīz/ (-izes, -izing, -ized), **computerise** (-ises, -ising, -ised) *vt.* **1.** CONVERT TO COMPUTER-BASED SYSTEM to install or start using a computer system to organize, control, or automate sth, such as a mechanical process or calculations **2.** PUT DETAILS OF STH ON COMPUTER to store information in a computer system or process it by computer —**computerizable** *adj.* —**computerization** /kəm pyóotə rī záysh'n/ *n.*

computerized /kəm pyóotə rīzd/, **computerised** *adj.* **1.** RUN BY COMPUTER operated, organized, controlled, or performed by computer **2.** KEPT ON COMPUTER processed by or stored in a computer or computer system

computerized axial tomography, computerised axial tomography *n.* = computed tomography

computerized tomography, computerised tomography *n.* = computed tomography

computer language *n.* = programming language

computer literacy *n.* the ability to use computers competently and to understand computer terminology

computer literate *adj.* having a good understanding and experience of working with a computer or computer system

computerphobe /kəm pyóotərfōb/ *n.* sb who dislikes, avoids, or worries about using computers (*informal*) —**computerphobia** /kəm pyóotər fóbi ə/ *n.* —**computerphobic** /-fóbik/ *adj.*

computer science *n.* the study of the mathematics and technology of computers and their applications

computer virus *n.* = **virus** *n.* 3

computing /kəm pyóoting/ *n.* the use of computers or computing systems

Comr *abbr.* Commissioner

comrade /kóm rayd, -rid/ *n.* **1.** FRIEND OR COMPANION sb who is either a close friend or a companion, often resulting from shared experiences **2. comrade, Comrade** FELLOW SOLDIER, MEMBER, OR CO-WORKER a fellow member of a group, especially a fellow soldier or a fellow supporter of a Communist or Socialist party [Mid-16thC. Via French *camerade* from Spanish *camarada* 'barracks mate', from *camara* 'room', from Latin *camera* (see CAMERA).] —**comradely** *adj.* —**comradeship** *n.*

comrade-in-arms (*plural* **comrades-in-arms**) *n.* sb who is fighting on the same side in a war, battle, or other armed struggle (*formal*)

Comrades Marathon *n. S Africa* a long distance race held annually between Pietermaritzburg and Durban in South Africa

Comsat[1] /kóm sat/ *tdmk.* a trademark for a communications satellite

Comsat[2] /kóm sat/ *n.* a communications satellite that channels digital and analog signals within a carrier frequency for earth-based stations

Comstockery /kóm stokəri, kúm stokəri/ *n. US* the removal of, or strong opposition to, anything that could be seen as immoral or obscene in literary, artistic, or broadcast material [Early 20thC. Named after the US moral crusader Anthony *Comstock* 1844–1915, who founded the New York Society for the Suppression of Vice.]

Comte /komt, koNt/, **Auguste** (1798–1857) French philosopher. He was a pioneer of 'positivism' who, through his theories of social evolution, both named and established the science of sociology. Full name **Isidore Auguste Marie François Xavier Comte** —**Comtian** /kómti ən, kóNti ən/ *n., adj.* —**Comtism** /kómtizəm, kóNtizəm/ *n.*

Comus /kṓməss/ *n.* the Roman god of revelry

con[1] /kon/ *vt.* (**cons, conning, conned**) **1.** TRICK SB to cheat sb, usually out of money or property, by first convincing the victim of sth that is untrue **2.** LIE to tell sb sth untrue or misleading **3.** PERSUADE SB to get sb to agree to sth (*informal*) ○ *See if you can con him into babysitting tonight.* ■ *n.* DISHONEST TRICK a trick or dishonest business ploy that takes advantage of sb's trust, such as telling lies in order to get money or property unfairly [Late 19thC. Shortening of CONFIDENCE TRICK.]

con[2] /kon/ *n.* **1.** REASON NOT TO DO STH an argument against doing sth, or evidence or an opinion stating that sth should not be done ○ *the pros and cons* **2.** PERSON NOT IN FAVOUR sb who opposes or votes against sth [Late 16thC. Shortening of Latin *contra* 'against'.]

con[3] /kon/ *n.* a convict (*slang*) [Late 19thC. Shortening.]

con[4] /kon/ (**cons, conning, conned**) *vt.* (*archaic*) **1.** EXAMINE STH to study sth with great care and attention **2.** LEARN OR MEMORIZE to learn or memorize sth [Partly from Old English *cunnan* 'to know how' (source of English *can*); partly from Old English *cunnian* 'to explore'. Both ultimately from an Indo-European word that also produced English *know*.]

con[5] /kon/, **conn** *vt.* (**cons, conning, conned; conns, conning, conned**) DIRECT STEERING OF SHIP to control or direct the steering of a ship ■ *n.* DIRECTING OF SHIP'S STEERING control of the steering of a ship, or the controls so used [Early 17thC. Shortened from French *conduire*, from Latin *conducere* 'conduct'.]

con[6] /kon/ *prep.* used to mean 'with' in a musical direction [From Italian, 'with']

con. *abbr.* **1.** MUSIC concerto **2.** LAW conclusion **3.** connection **4.** consolidated **5.** continued **6.** contra

Con. *abbr.* **1.** Consul **2.** Conformist **3.** Conservative

con- *prefix.* = **com-** (*used before sounds other than b, l, m, or p.*)

Conakry /kónnə kri, kónnə kree/ capital, largest city, and chief Atlantic port of Guinea, in western Africa. Population: 705,280 (1983).

con amore /kón a máwray, -máwri/ *adv.* with tender feeling (*used as a musical direction*) [From Italian, literally 'with love']

conation /kō náysh'n/ *n.* in psychology, a mental process involving the will, such as impulse, desire, or resolve [Mid-19thC. From the Latin stem *conation-*, from *conat-*, the past participle stem of *conari* 'to endeavour'.] —**conational** *adj.* —**conative** /kṓnətiv, kónn-/ *adj.*

con brio /kon brée ō/ *adv.* with spirit or vigour (*used as a musical direction*) [From Italian, literally 'with vigour']

conc. *abbr.* **1.** concentrated **2.** concentration **3.** concerning **4.** concerto **5.** concession

concatenate /kon káttə nayt, kən-/ *vt.* (**-nates, -nating, -nated**) **1.** BRING TOGETHER to connect separate units or items into a linked system **2.** COMPUT LINK UNITS TOGETHER to link two or more information units, such as character strings or files, so that they form a single unit ■ *adj.* COMPUT LINKED TOGETHER linked together in a sequence or chain [15thC. From late Latin *concatenat-*, the past participle stem of *concatenare*, literally 'to chain together', from *catena* 'chain' (source of English *chain* and *catenary*).]

concatenation /kon káttə náysh'n, kən-/ *n.* **1.** PROCESS OR STATE OF BEING LINKED the linking of things together or the state of being interconnected **2.** COMPUT LINKING OF UNITS the linking of characters, strings, or files in a specified order to form a single entity equal to the sum of the lengths of the original entities

concave /kón kayv, kon káyv/ (**-caves, -caving, -caved**) *adj.* **1.** CURVED INWARD curved inward like the inner surface of a bowl or sphere **2.** MATH CONTAINING AN ANGLE GREATER THAN 180° used to describe a polygon with an interior angle greater than 180° [From Latin *concavus*, literally 'hollowed out', from *cavus* (see CAVE)] —**concavely** *adv.* —**concaveness** *n.*

concavity /kon kávvəti/ (*plural* **concavities**) *n.* **1.** STATE OF BEING CONCAVE the state of being concave **2.** CONCAVE PART OR SURFACE a concave part or surface

concavo-concave /kon káyvō kon káyv/ *adj.* OPTICS used to describe a lens that is concave on both surfaces

concavo-convex /kon káyvō-/ *adj.* OPTICS used to describe a lens that is concave on one surface and convex on the other

conceal /kən séel/ (**-ceals, -cealing, -cealed**) *vt.* **1.** HIDE PERSON OR THING to put or keep sth or sb out of sight or prevent the person or thing from being found ○ *he was found carrying a concealed weapon on him* **2.** HIDE FACT OR FEELING to keep sth secret or prevent it from being known [13thC. Via Old French *conceler* from Latin *concelare* 'to hide well', from *celare* 'to hide'.] —**concealable** *adj.*

concealer /kən séelər/ *n.* **1.** MAKEUP FOR HIDING BLEMISHES flesh-coloured makeup that can be applied to the skin to hide blemishes **2.** SB OR STH THAT CONCEALS sb or sth that conceals

concealment /kən séelmənt/ *n.* **1.** HIDING STH OR SECRECY secrecy, or the act of hiding sb or sth **2.** MIL MILITARY COVER the protection of troops from observation in combat, or sth that provides such protection

concede /kən séed/ (**-cedes, -ceding, -ceded**) *v.* **1.** *vt.* RELUCTANTLY ACCEPT STH TO BE TRUE to admit or acknowledge sth, often grudgingly or with reluctance **2.** *vti.* POL ADMIT FAILURE BEFORE END to accept and acknowledge defeat in a contest, debate, election, or fight, often without waiting for the final result **3.** *vt.* SPORTS GIVE STH AWAY to allow your opponent or opposing team to gain sth valuable, usually a goal or points **4.** *vt.* RELIG GRANT RIGHTS TO to allow or yield sth such as a right or privilege to another person or country [15thC. Via French from Latin *concedere*, literally 'to yield completely', from *cedere* (see CEDE).] —**conceder** *n.*

conceit /kən séet/ *n.* **1.** TOO MUCH PRIDE IN YOURSELF a high opinion of your own qualities or abilities, especially one that is not justified **2.** LITERAT EXAGGERATED COMPARISON IN LITERATURE an imaginative poetic image, or writing that contains such an image, especially a comparison that is extreme or far-fetched **3.** WHIMSICAL OBJECT an object created from the imagination **4.** IMAGINATIVE IDEA an idea, opinion, or theme, especially one that is fanciful or unusual in some way **5.** WITTY EXPRESSION a witty, inventive, or amusing expression (*archaic*) ■ *vt.* (**-ceited**) **1.** *N England* LIKE STH to like or tolerate sth **2.** APPREHEND MENTALLY to think of, to consider, to imagine, or to understand sth (*archaic*) [14thC. Formed from CONCEIVE, on the model of 'deceit'. The underlying sense is 'sth conceived in the mind'.]

conceited /kən séetid/ *adj.* **1.** TOO PROUD having or showing an excessively high opinion of your own qualities or abilities **2.** CREATIVELY WITTY imaginative, fanciful, witty, or ingenious (*archaic*) —**conceitedly** *adv.*

WORD KEY: SYNONYMS

See Synonyms at *proud*.

conceitedness /kən séetidnəss/ *n.* = **conceit** *n.* 1

conceivable /kən séevəb'l/ *adj.* possible to imagine, understand, or believe ○ *we tried every means conceivable to contact her* —**conceivability** /kən séevə bílləti/ *n.* —**conceivableness** /kən séevəb'lnəss/ *n.*

conceivably /kən séevəbli/ *adv.* possibly, even if only a remote possibility ○ *you could just conceivably be wrong*

conceive /kən séev/ (**-ceives, -ceiving, -ceived**) *v.* **1.** *vti.* THINK OF OR IMAGINE STH to form an idea or concept of sth in your mind **2.** *vt.* INVENT, DEVISE, OR ORIGINATE STH to think up sth that could be put into action such as a plan or an invention ○ *Conceived and written by John Sander* **3.** START TO EXPERIENCE to produce sth from the mind such as an emotion **4.** *vti.* BECOME PREGNANT to become pregnant with a child or with young **5.** *vt.* UNDERSTAND to understand sth [13thC. Via Old French *conceiv-*, the stem of *concevoir*, from Latin *concipere*, literally 'to take in', from *capere* (see CAPTURE).] —**conceiver** *n.*

concelebrant /kən séllibrənt/ *n.* a priest who celebrates the Christian Mass or Holy Communion together with one or more other priests

concelebrate /kən sélli brayt/ (**-brates, -brating, -brated**) *vti.* to celebrate the Christian Mass or Holy Communion jointly with one or more other priests [Late 16thC. From Latin *concelebrat-*, the past participle stem of *concelebrare*, literally 'to celebrate together', from *celebrare* (see CELEBRATE).] —**concelebration** /kən sélli bráysh'n/ *n.*

concentrate /kónss'n trayt/ *v.* (**-trates, -trating, -trated**) **1.** *vti.* SILENTLY AND INTENSELY THINK ABOUT STH to focus all of your thoughts or mental activity on one subject or activity, usually in silence ○ *I found myself unable to concentrate on my work* **2.** *vti.* DEVOTE EFFORTS TO ONE THING to direct attention, time, and resources to one particular area or activity, usually over a period of time **3.** *vti.* CLUSTER TOGETHER to bring things to a common centre or close together in the same area, or to come together in the same place **4.** *vt.* MAKE PURER to make a substance purer by the removal of another substance, especially by removing a liquid **5.** *vti.* COOK MAKE THICKER OR STRONGER to remove water from a substance, usually a liquid, leaving a smaller quantity that is thicker in consistency and stronger in flavour **6.** *vti.* BIOL ACCUMULATE IN TISSUE to accumulate or be stored, or to cause to accumulate or be stored, in biological tissue over a period of time **7.** *vt.* MINERALS PURIFY ORE to remove rock and other material from ore to purify it ■ *n.* **1.** PURE SUBSTANCE a substance made purer by the removal of another, especially a liquid **2.** FOOD THICK FOOD SUBSTANCE a food substance, especially a liquid, made thicker or stronger in flavour by the removal of liquid [Mid-17thC. Formed from CONCENTRE.] —**concentrative** *adj.* —**concentratively** *adv.*

concentrated /kónss'n traytid/ *adj.* **1.** CHEM, FOOD STRONG used to describe a substance, especially a liquid, made thicker or stronger by the removal of water **2.** FOCUSED involving or characterized by the focusing or intensifying of an activity or process —**concentratedly** *adv.*

concentration /kónss'n tráysh'n/ *n.* 1. FOCUS OF MIND OR RESOURCES the direction of all thought or effort towards one particular task, idea, or subject 2. CLUSTER OR NUMBER a large number of things or amount of sth collected together in one area ○ *the concentration of computing talent in one part of the country* 3. CHEM STRENGTH OF SOLUTION the amount of a substance dissolved in another. Symbol *c* 4. CHEM, COOK MAKING A LIQUID THICKER OR STRONGER the removal of water from sth, usually a liquid, to make it thicker or stronger

concentration camp *n.* 1. HIST NAZI CAMP FOR EXTERMINATING PRISONERS one of the prison camps used under the rule of Hitler in Nazi Germany 2. PRISON CAMP FOR CIVILIANS IN WAR a prison camp used for the incarceration of political prisoners or civilians. An example is the type of camp used by Great Britain during the Boer War to move civilians out of the war zone. [Originally used in the Boer War to denote camps into which civilians were 'concentrated' so that they did not hinder military operations]

concentrator /kónss'n traytər/ *n.* 1. COMPUT TELECOMMUNICATIONS DEVICE a telecommunications device that combines outgoing messages into one message, or extracts individual messages from one transmission into which they have been combined 2. MINERALS FACTORY THAT PROCESSES MINERAL ORE an industrial plant that produces purified or concentrated mineral ore 3. ENERGY MIRROR SYSTEM FOR PRODUCING SOLAR ENERGY a set of mirrors used to concentrate sunlight in the collection of energy from the sun

concentre /kon séntər/ (**-tres, -tring, -tred**) *vti.* MATH to direct things to a common centre or to converge at a common centre [Late 16thC. From French *concentrer*, from *con-* 'together' and *centre* 'centre'.]

concentric /kən séntrik, kon-/ *adj.* 1. WITH COMMON MIDDLE POINT used to describe circles and spheres of different sizes with the same middle point 2. WITH COMMON AXIS with a common axis, as when rotating elements are mounted on shafts that have a common centre line [14thC. From Medieval Latin *concentricus*, literally 'having the same centre', formed from Latin *centrum* (see CENTRE).] —**concentrically** *adv.* —**concentricity** /kónss'n tríssəti/ *n.*

Concepción /kən sépsi ón/ city and capital of Bío-Bío Region, central Chile, situated on the River Bío-Bío, 418 km/260 mi. southwest of Santiago. Population: 326,784 (1992).

concept /kón sept/ *n.* 1. STH THOUGHT OR IMAGINED sth that sb has thought up, or that sb might be able to imagine 2. BROAD PRINCIPLE AFFECTING PERCEPTION AND BEHAVIOUR a broad abstract idea or a guiding general principle, such as one that determines how a person or culture behaves, or how nature, reality, or events are perceived ○ *the concept of time* 3. UNDERSTANDING OR GRASP the most basic understanding of sth 4. WAY OF DOING OR PERCEIVING STH a method, scheme, or type of product or design [Mid-16thC. From late Latin *conceptus*, from the past participle of Latin *concipere* (see CONCEIVE).]

concept art *n.* = **conceptual art**

conception /kən sépsh'n/ *n.* 1. BROAD UNDERSTANDING a general understanding of sth 2. STH CONCEIVED IN THE MIND a result of thought, such as an idea, invention, or plan 3. BIOL CONCEIVING OF YOUNG the fertilization of an egg by a sperm at the beginning of pregnancy 4. BIOL EMBRYO OR FOETUS an embryo or foetus (*technical*) 5. ORIGIN OR BEGINNINGS the beginnings or origin of sth 6. FORMULATION OF IDEA the process of arriving at an abstract idea or belief or the moment at which such an idea starts to take shape or emerge 7. = **concept** *n.* 1 [14thC. Via French from, ultimately, Latin *concipere* (see CONCEIVE).] —**conceptional** *adj.* —**conceptive** *adj.* —**conceptively** *adv.*

conceptual /kən séptyoo əl/ *adj.* coming from or belonging to the concepts, ideas, or principles sth is based on —**conceptually** *adv.*

conceptual art, concept art *n.* art designed to present an idea rather than to be appreciated for its creative skill or beauty, and that often makes use of unconventional media instead of painting or sculpture

conceptual artist *n.* an artist specializing in conceptual art

conceptualise *vti.* = **conceptualize**

conceptualism /kən séptyoo əlizzəm/ *n.* 1. THEORY THAT MENTAL CONCEPTS DETERMINE REALITY the philosophical theory that the existence of sth is dependent on our having a mental concept of it 2. ARTS THEORY OF ART FOCUSING ON IDEAS a school of art concerned primarily with the ideas behind a work of art rather than the artwork itself —**conceptualistic** /-lístik/ *adj.* —**conceptualistically** /-lístikli/ *adv.*

conceptualist /kən séptyoo əlist/ *n.* 1. PHILOS BELIEVER IN CONCEPTUALISM a person who believes in conceptualism 2. ARTS = **conceptual artist**

conceptualize /kən séptyoo ə līz/ (**-izes, -izing, -ized**), **conceptualise** (**-ises, -ising, -ised**) *vti.* to arrive at a concept or generalization as a result of things seen, experienced, or believed —**conceptualization** /kən séptyoo ə lī záysh'n/ *n.* —**conceptualizer** /kən séptyoo ə līzər/ *n.*

conceptus /kən séptəss/ (*plural* **-tuses**) *n.* an embryo or foetus along with all the tissues that surround it throughout pregnancy, including the placenta, amniotic sac and fluid, and the umbilical cord [Mid-18thC. From Latin, literally 'sth conceived', from the past participle of *concipere* (see CONCEIVE).]

concern /kən súrn/ *vt.* (**-cerns, -cerning, -cerned**) 1. MAKE SB WORRIED to give sb an uneasy or anxious feeling 2. INVOLVE SB OR GET INVOLVED to require sb to be involved with sth, or to get involved with or interested in sth 3. BE INTERESTING OR IMPORTANT TO SB to have a direct effect on, or be a matter of significance to, sb or sth 4. BE ON THE SUBJECT OF to be about a particular topic ■ *n.* 1. WORRY OR STH CAUSING IT a reason to worry, or sth that causes worry ○ *His condition is giving rise to concern* 2. AFFAIR THAT SHOULD INVOLVE SB a matter that affects sb, or that sb has the right to be involved with ○ *it's no concern of yours* 3. CARING FEELINGS emotions such as worry, compassion, sympathy, or regard for sb or sth 4. BUSINESS a commercial enterprise 5. OBJECT a gadget or trivial object (*dated*) [Late 14thC. Via French from late Latin *concernere*, literally 'to sift together', from Latin *cernere* (see CERTAIN). The meaning evolved from 'to sort out' through 'decide' to 'relate to'.]

concerned /kən súrnd/ *adj.* 1. ANXIOUS OR WORRIED worried or apprehensive, particularly about sth such as a situation that is developing or that has newly arisen 2. INTERESTED caring and interested in general, or giving care and attention to a particular thing or area 3. INVOLVED having an active role in sth, or anything to do with sth ○ *a message was conveyed to the families concerned*

concerning /kən súrning/ *prep.* to do with or involving sth or sb

concernment /kən súrnmənt/ *n.* (*archaic*) 1. CONCERN a concern or matter of interest 2. IMPORTANCE importance, relevance, or weight

concert /kónsərt/ *n.* 1. MUSIC PUBLIC MUSICAL PERFORMANCE an event where an individual musician or a group of musicians, such as a choir or an orchestra, performs in front of an audience 2. AGREEMENT harmony or accord, e.g. in purpose or action 3. UNIFIED PAIR OR GROUP a combination of people or things in agreement or harmony, especially one resulting from a consensus of opinions and ideas ■ *vti.* (**-certs, -certing, -certed**) ACT IN AGREEMENT OR UNITY to do or plan sth in cooperation or in harmony with another person or group [Late 16thC. Via French from Italian *concerto* 'harmony, agreement' (see CONCERTO).] ◇ **in concert** 1. MUSIC playing music or singing at a live concert 2. working or acting together, especially in a united or harmonious way ◇ **in concert with** working or conspiring together

concertante /kónchər tántay, -ti/ *adj.* 1. RELATING TO BAROQUE CONCERTO relating to or resembling a concerto, especially one in the Baroque style 2. WITH SOLO PASSAGES relating to a symphonic work that highlights individual instruments within the orchestra [Early 18thC. From Italian, the present participle of *concertare* 'to be in harmony', from *concerto* (see CONCERTO).]

concerted /kən súrtid/ *adj.* 1. ACHIEVED OR PERFORMED TOGETHER planned or carried out by two or more people working together or with the same aim 2. MUSIC ARRANGED FOR ORCHESTRA OR CHAMBER ENSEMBLE written for several soloists to perform together in an ensemble, or within the context of a larger-scale work —**concertedly** *adv.* —**concertedness** *n.*

concertgoer /kónssərt gō ər/ *n.* sb who is or will be attending a concert, or who often goes to concerts —**concertgoing** *adj.*

concert grand *n.* the largest size of grand piano, between 2.74 m/9 ft and 3.66 m/12 ft long, designed for use in a concert hall

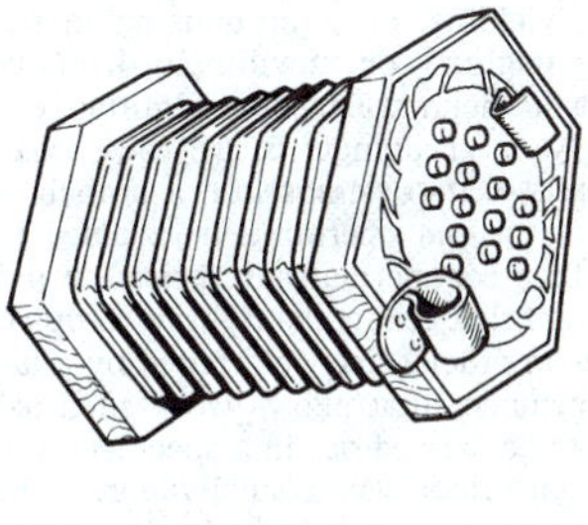

Concertina

concertina /kónssər téénə/ *n.* MUSICAL INSTRUMENT RESEMBLING ACCORDION a small octagonal accordion with button keys ■ *vi.* (**-nas, -naing, -naed**) COLLAPSE IN FOLDS to collapse in a series of folds like an accordion [Mid-19thC. Formed from CONCERT + the Italian suffix *-ina*.] —**concertinist** *n.*

concertino /kón chər téénō/ (*plural* **-nos** *or* **-ni** /-nee/) *n.* 1. SOLOIST GROUP the solo instrumental group in a piece of music played by a small group of soloists and a larger ensemble (**concerto grosso**) 2. SMALL-SCALE CONCERTO a small-scale concerto for a single solo instrument [Late 18thC. From Italian, literally 'little concerto', from *concerto* 'CONCERTO'.]

concertize /kónssər tīz/ (**-tizes, -tizing, -tized**), **concertise** (**-tises, -tising, -tised**) *vi.* MUSIC to perform in concerts (*refers to a soloist or conductor*)

concertmaster /kónssərt maastər/ *n.* US MUSIC the leader of the first violin section of an orchestra, usually next in rank below the conductor [Late 19thC. Translation of German *Konzertmeister*.]

concertmistress /kónssərt mistrəss/ *n.* US a woman who is the leader of the first violin section of an orchestra, usually next in rank below the conductor

concerto /kən cháirtō, kən chúrtō/ (*plural* **-tos** *or* **-ti** /kən cháirti, kən chúrti/) *n.* 1. MUSICAL COMPOSITION FOR SOLOIST AND ORCHESTRA an instrumental work for orchestra that highlights a soloist or group of soloists 2. ORGAN-ACCOMPANIED VOICES in music before 1650, a work for voices with organ or continuo [Early 18thC. From Italian, of uncertain immediate origin: possibly from Latin *concertus*, the past participle of *concernere* (see CONCERN).]

concerto grosso /kən cháirtō grṓssō/ (*plural* **concerti grossi** /-tee grósseе/ *or* **concerto grossos**) *n.* a genre of orchestral composition, popular in the 17th century, that contrasts a small group of soloists (**concertino**) with a larger ensemble (**ripieno**) [From Italian, literally 'big concerto']

concert overture *n.* a short orchestral composition similar to an opera overture but intended for concert performance on its own

concert party (*plural* **concert parties**) *n.* 1. SMALL GROUP OF MUSICIANS a small number of performers working together to entertain the public, e.g. in a seaside town. Concert parties were especially popular in the early 20th century. (*dated*) 2. FIN GROUP OF SHAREBUYERS a group of people buying shares (*slang*)

concert pitch *n.* 1. MUSIC STANDARD PITCH TO WHICH INSTRUMENTS TUNED the internationally agreed standard pitch to which orchestral instruments are tuned, typically using the A above middle C as a reference. In an instrument tuned to concert pitch, the A above middle C is at a pitch of 440 hertz per second. 2. MUSIC PITCH OF NOTE IN TRANSPOSED MUSIC the sounding pitch of a note played by an instrument when transposing a piece of written music to a different key, as opposed to the written pitch **3.** READINESS a state of readiness for action

concertstück /kən súrt shtŏŏk/ *n.* a short character piece, usually for piano [From German *Konzertstück*, literally 'concert piece']

concession /kən sésh'n/ *n.* **1.** SPECIAL PRIVILEGE sth such as a particular privilege, right, or kindness, that is allowed or granted to a individual or group, usually in view of special circumstances **2.** CHEAP TICKET a special reduced price at which tickets for travel or entertainment are sold to some groups of people, such as senior citizens, students, or the unemployed **3.** RELUCTANT YIELDING an act or an example of conceding, yielding, or compromising in some way, often grudgingly or unwillingly **4.** STH UNWILLINGLY ADMITTED sth acknowledged or admitted, even if unwillingly or grudgingly **5.** *US* COMM SMALL BUSINESS OUTLET INSIDE ANOTHER ESTABLISHMENT a branch of a business set up and operating in a place belonging to another commercial enterprise, or a business agreement that grants the right to do this **6.** RIGHT TO USE LAND an official licence granted by a landowner or government that allows work such as drilling for oil to be carried out in a specified area of land **7.** *Can* LAND SUBDIVISION a subdivision of land in a township survey, mainly in Ontario and Quebec, that was formerly one of the rows of 32 200-acre lots into which each new township was divided [Early 17thC. Directly or via French from, ultimately, Latin *concess-*, the past participle stem of *concedere* (see CONCEDE).] —**concessible** /kən séssəb'l/ *adj.* —**concessional** /-sésh'nəl/ *adj.*

concessionaire /kən sésh'n áir/, **concessionnaire, concessioner** /kən sésh'nər/ *n.* sb who has been given land by a government concession or who has a concession to operate a business or sell a product in a specific place [Mid-19thC. From French, formed from *concession* (see CONCESSION).]

concessionary /kən sésh'nəri/ *adj.* **1.** CUT-PRICE describes special advantages, particularly price reductions, that exist only for certain groups of people **2.** CREATED AS COMPROMISE created or executed as a compromise or goodwill gesture, especially within a negotiating process

concessioner *n.* = **concessionaire**

concessive /kən séssiv/ *adj.* **1.** GRAM SHOWING WILLINGNESS TO CONCEDE STH relating to a word or part of a sentence that expresses concession, e.g. the word 'although' **2.** WITH CONCESSION relating to or containing a concession [Early 18thC. From late Latin *concessivus*, from Latin *concess-*, the past participle stem of *concedere* (see CONCEDE).] —**concessively** *adv.*

conch /kongk, konch/ (*plural* **conches** *or* **conchs**) *n.* **1.** TROPICAL SEA ANIMAL WITH SHELL a tropical marine mollusc with a large, often brightly coloured, spiral shell **2.** LARGE SPIRAL SHELL the large spiral shell of a conch, often used as a horn or trumpet, as an ornament, or to make jewellery **3.** ANAT = **concha** *n.* [14thC. Via Latin *concha* from Greek *kogkhē* 'shell, shellfish' (source of English *cockle*).]

conch- *prefix.* = **concho-** (*used before vowels*)

concha /kóngkə/ (*plural* **-chae** /-ki/) *n.* ANAT a part of the body shaped like a conch shell, such as the external ear or the central cavity of the ear [Late 16thC. From Latin, 'shell' (see CONCH).] —**conchal** /kóngk'l/ *adj.*

conchi- *prefix.* = **concho-**

conchie /kónchi/, **conchy** (*plural* **-chies**) *n.* a conscientious objector (*dated informal*) [Early 20thC. Shortening.]

conchiglie /kon kéeli/ *n.* FOOD pasta formed into small shell shapes [Via Italian, literally 'little shells', from, ultimately, Latin *concha* 'shell' (see CONCH)]

conchiolin /kong kī əlin/ *n.* BIOCHEM a fibrous protein that makes up the inner part of the shell of a mollusc [Late 19thC. Formed from modern Latin *conchiola*, literally 'little shell', from Latin *concha* (see CONCH).]

concho- *prefix.* shell ○ *conchology* [From Latin *concha* 'shell' (see CONCH)]

conchology /kong kólləji/ *n.* a branch of zoology dealing with the study of sea shells and the animals that inhabit them —**conchological** /kóng kə lójjik'l/ *adj.* —**conchologist** /kong kólləjist/ *n.*

concierge /kónssi airzh, kóN-/ (*plural* **-cierges**) *n.* **1.** CARETAKER OF BLOCK OF FLATS especially in France, sb whose job is to staff or watch the entrance to a large residential building, and who usually also lives on the premises (*dated*) **2.** *US* CHIEF HOTEL PORTER a person employed at a hotel or apartment building to help the guests or residents, e.g. by dealing with luggage, making travel arrangements, or delivering messages [Mid-16thC. Via French from, ultimately, Latin *conservus* 'fellow slave', from *servus* 'slave' (source also of English *serve*, *serf*, and *sergeant*).]

conciliar /kən sílli ər/ *adj.* belonging to, issued by, or relating to a council, especially a church council [Late 17thC. Formed from Latin *concilium* (see COUNCIL).] —**conciliarly** *adv.*

conciliate /kən sílli ayt/ (**-ates, -ating, -ated**) *vti.* **1.** BRING DISPUTING SIDES TOGETHER to work with opposing parties with the aim of bringing them to an agreement or reconciliation, especially in an industrial dispute **2.** GET SB'S SUPPORT OR FRIENDSHIP BACK to bring a disagreement with sb to an end, or to overcome sb's anger, suspicion, or hostility **3.** BE CHARMING TO GAIN STH to gain sth, especially sb's friendship, goodwill, or respect, by behaving pleasantly [Mid-16thC. From Latin *conciliat-*, the past participle stem of *conciliare*, from *concilium* (see COUNCIL).] —**conciliable** *adj.* —**conciliative** *adj.*

conciliation /kən sílli áysh'n/ *n.* action taken to reach agreement or restore trust, friendship, or goodwill that has been lost, especially as a deliberate process involving an independent negotiator in an industrial dispute

conciliator /kən sílli aytər/ *n.* sb who works to overcome disagreement between other parties, or who tries to overcome sb's anger or distrust with friendly actions and discussion

conciliatory /kən sílli ətəri/ *adj.* done or said to appease sb, to bring about agreement, or to restore trust or goodwill —**conciliatorily** *adv.* —**conciliatoriness** *n.*

concinnity /kən sínnəti/ (*plural* **-ties**) *n.* **1.** LITERAT PLEASING STYLISTIC ARTISTIC HARMONY a balanced, graceful, polished quality, particularly in a literary work **2.** GENERALLY HARMONIOUS STRUCTURE a harmonious structuring of all parts of sth in terms of the whole [Mid-16thC. Formed from Latin *concinnitas*, from *concinnus* 'skilfully put together'.] —**concinnous** *adj.*

concise /kən sīss/ *adj.* using as few words as possible to give the necessary information, or compressed in order to be brief [Late 16thC. Directly or via French from Latin *concisus*, the past participle of *concidere*, literally 'to cut down', from *caedere* (see CAESURA).] —**concisely** *adv.* —**conciseness** *n.* —**concision** *n.*

conclave /kóng klayv/ *n.* **1.** SECRET MEETING a private gathering of a select group of people, where discussions are kept secret **2.** CHR MEETING TO SELECT ROMAN CATHOLIC POPE the secret meeting at which Roman Catholic cardinals elect a new pope **3.** CHR ROOMS WHERE POPE IS ELECTED the private rooms in which the college of Roman Catholic cardinals assembles to elect a new pope [14thC. Via French from Latin 'locked room', formed from *clavis* 'key' (see CLEF).] —**conclavist** *n.*

conclude /kən klóod/ (**-cludes, -cluding, -cluded**) *v.* **1.** *vt.* COME TO A CONCLUSION to form an opinion or make a logical judgment about sth after considering everything known about it **2.** *vti.* FINISH to come to an end or bring sth to an end **3.** *vt.* SETTLE STH to make a formal agreement complete and fixed, especially after detailed or prolonged discussions or arrangements **4.** *vti. US* DIVIDE to reach a decision about sth (*dated*) [13thC. From Latin *concludere*, literally 'to close completely', from *claudere* (see CLOSE).] —**concluder** *n.*

WORD KEY: SYNONYMS

See Synonyms at ***deduce***.

conclusion /kən klóozh'n/ *n.* **1.** DECISION BASED ON FACTS a decision made or an opinion formed after considering the relevant facts or evidence **2.** FINAL PART OF STH an ending or the part that brings sth to a close (*formal*) **3.** FINAL SETTLEMENT OF STH the completion of a formal agreement or deal, especially after long or detailed discussions and arrangements **4.** LOGIC PART OF ARGUMENT DEDUCED FROM EVIDENCE the portion of an argument for which evidence is presented [14thC. Via French from, ultimately, Latin *conclus-*, the past participle stem of *concludere* (see CONCLUDE).]

conclusive /kən klóossiv/ *adj.* being such that what is specified proves a matter beyond all doubt [Late 16thC. From late Latin *conclusivus*, from Latin *conclus-*, the past participle stem of *concludere* (see CONCLUDE).] —**conclusively** *adv.* —**conclusiveness** *n.*

concoct /kən kókt/ (**-cocts, -cocting, -cocted**) *vt.* **1.** MIX INGREDIENTS TO MAKE STH NEW to create sth by mixing or combining various ingredients in a new way, especially in cooking **2.** MAKE STH UP to think up a story or plan, especially sth ingenious or imaginative [Mid-16thC. From Latin *concoct-*, the past participle stem of *concoquere*, literally 'to cook together', from *coquere* (see COOK).] —**concocter** *n.* —**concoctive** *adj.*

concoction /kən kóksh'n/ *n.* **1.** NEW AND UNUSUAL MIXTURE sth that has been concocted, especially a drink or dish created by mixing together ingredients **2.** CONCOCTING A MIXTURE the act or process of mixing or combining ingredients to create sth new and unusual **3.** LIE OR TRICK sth such as a story or plan devised to be deceitful

concomitance /kən kómmitənss/ *n.* **1.** EXISTENCE OR OCCURRENCE TOGETHER the existence or occurrence of sth at the same time as, or in connection with, sth else **2.** STH CONNECTED WITH STH ELSE sth that exists at the same time, or in connection with, sth else **3.** CHR CHRISTIAN BELIEF REGARDING EUCHARIST the Christian doctrine that the body and blood of Jesus Christ are embodied in the elements of the Eucharist

concomitant /kən kómmitənt/ *adj.* HAPPENING AT THE SAME TIME happening or existing along with or at the same time as sth else ○ *parenthood and all its concomitant responsibilities* ■ *n.* STH THAT ACCOMPANIES STH ELSE sth that happens or exists along with or at the same time as sth else [Early 17thC. From late Latin *concomitant-*, the present participle stem of *concomitari* 'to accompany', from *comit-*, the stem of *comes* 'companion', source of English *count*[2].] —**concomitantly** *adv.*

concord /kóng kawrd/ *n.* **1.** PEACEFUL COEXISTENCE agreement, friendly relations, or peace **2.** PEACE TREATY a peace treaty **3.** MUSIC PLEASING COMBINATION OF SOUNDS a pleasing sound made when two or more notes are played together **4.** GRAM = **agreement** [13thC. Via Old French from, ultimately, Latin *concord-*, the stem of *concors*, literally 'of one heart', from *cor* 'heart' (see CORDIAL).]

concordance /kən káwrd'nss/ *n.* **1.** SIMILARITY OR AGREEMENT similarity or agreement between two or more things **2.** LITERAT INDEX OF WORDS USED BY AUTHOR an index of words, e.g. of all the words contained in a single work, or in the combined works of an author, or in any body or bank of text, arranged in alphabetical order. A concordance often gives information about the meaning and context of a listed word. [14thC. Via French from medieval Latin *concordantia*, from Latin *concordant-*, the stem of *concordare* (see CONCORDANT).]

concordant /kən káwrd'nt/ *adj.* showing harmony, unity, or agreement [15thC. Via French from Latin *concordant-*, the present participle stem of *concordare*, literally 'to bring into harmony', from *concord-*, the stem of *concors* (see CONCORD).] —**concordantly** *adv.*

concordat /kon káwr dat, kən-/ *n.* an official agreement, especially a formal contract between the Pope and a national government concerning the religious affairs of a country [Early 17thC. Via French from Latin *concordatum*, the past participle of *concordare* (see CONCORDANT).]

Concorde /kóng kawrd/ *tdmk.* a trademark for a supersonic commercial passenger aircraft developed jointly by the British and French governments

concourse /kóng kawrss/ *n.* **1.** LARGE OPEN SPACE a large space where people can gather in a public place or building, e.g. at an airport or train station **2.** CROWD a large number of people who have gathered for a special event **3.** GATHERING TOGETHER coming or moving together, or an example of this [14thC. Via French from Latin *concursus* 'assembly', from *concurs-*, the past participle stem of *concurrere* (see CONCUR).]

a at; aa father; aw all; ay day; air hair; ə about, edible, item, common, circus; e egg; ee eel; hw when; i it, happy; ī ice; 'l apple; 'm rhythm; 'n fashion; o odd; ō open; ŏŏ good; oo pool; ow owl; oy oil; th thin; th this; u up; ur urge;

concrescence /kən kréss'nss/ *n.* **1.** BIOL **GROWING TOGETHER OF PARTS** the growing or coming together of body parts or organs, especially in the normal early formation of an embryo **2.** MED = **concretion** [Early 17thC. Formed from Latin *concrescent-*, the present participle stem of *concrescere* (see CONCRETE).] —**concrescent** *adj.*

concrete /kóng kreet/ *n.* **1.** CONSTR **HARD CONSTRUCTION MATERIAL** a mixture of cement, sand, aggregate, and water in specific proportions that hardens to a strong stony consistency over varying lengths of time **2.** PHYS **MASS FORMED WHEN PARTICLES COALESCE** a mass formed when particles coalesce ■ *adj.* **1. SOLID AND REAL, NOT IMAGINARY** able to be seen or touched because it exists in reality, not just as an idea **2. DEFINITE** certain and specific rather than vague or general ○ *concrete proposals for reform* **3.** PHYS **SOLIDIFIED** made solid by coalescence ■ *vt.* (**-cretes, -creting, -creted**) **COVER WITH CONCRETE** to cover an area with concrete [14thC. Via French from Latin *concretus*, the past participle of *concrescere*, literally 'to grow together', from *crescere* (see CRESCENT).] —**concretely** *adv.* —**concreteness** *n.*

concrete jungle *n.* an urban area completely covered with walkways, roads, and buildings, and perceived as a hostile environment

concrete music *n.* electronic music assembled from recordings of live sounds, usually including natural and mechanical sources, manipulated for effect [Translation of French *musique concrète*, literally 'real music', so called because it is created from real-life sounds]

concrete noun *n.* a noun that refers to a physical, and usually visible or touchable, object or substance, e.g. 'clock' or 'elephant'

concrete poetry *n.* verse that uses physical arrangement of the words on the page to add to its meaning and effect

concretion /kən kréesh'n/ *n.* **1. FORMATION OF WHOLE FROM PARTS** the act or process of separate parts or particles coming together into a solid mass **2. SOLID FORMED BY UNIFICATION OF PARTS** a hard solid mass formed by parts uniting into a whole **3.** GEOL **ROUNDED MASS** a rounded mass of compact concentric layers within a sediment, built up round a nucleus such as a fossil **4.** MED **INORGANIC MASS IN BODY** a mass of inorganic material in a body organ or tissue, usually caused by disease [Mid-16thC. Via French from, ultimately, Latin *concret-*, the past participle stem of *concrescere* (see CONCRETE).] —**concretionary** *adj.*

concretise *vt.* = **concretize**

concretism /kóng kreet izzəm/ *n.* the creation of physical things to represent abstract ideas, especially by the use of concrete poetry —**concretist** *n.*

concretize /kóng kreet īz/ (**-tizes, -tizing, -tized**), **concretise** (**-tises, -tising, -tised**) *vt.* to make sth solid, real, or specific —**concretization** /kóng kree tī záysh'n/ *n.*

concubinage /kon kyóobinij, kən-/ *n.* the state of being or keeping a concubine

concubine /kóng kyoo bīn/ *n.* **1.** HIST **OFFICIAL MISTRESS IN SOME CULTURES** a woman who is the lover of a wealthy married man but with the social status of a subordinate form of wife, often kept in a separate home. The term usually refers to such a woman in imperial China. **2. MAN'S FEMALE LIVE-IN LOVER** a woman who lives with a man and has a sexual relationship with him but is not married to him [13thC. Via Old French from Latin *concubina*, literally 'bed-mate', from *cubare* 'to lie down' (see CUBICLE).] —**concubinary** /kóng kyoo bīnəri, kon kyóobinəri/ *adj.*

concupiscence /kən kyóopiss'nss, kon-/ *n.* powerful feelings of physical desire (*literary*) [14thC. Via French from, ultimately, late Latin *concupiscere*, literally 'to start longing for', from *cupere* (see COVET).] —**concupiscent** *adj.*

concur /kən kúr/ (**concurs, concurring, concurred**) *v.* **1.** *vti.* **AGREE** to have the same opinion or reach agreement on a specified point **2.** *vi.* **COINCIDE** to happen at the same time **3.** *vi.* **COOPERATE OR COMBINE** to work or act together, especially cooperatively [14thC. From Latin *concurrere*, literally 'to run together', from *currere* (see CURRENT).] —**concurringly** *adv.*

WORD KEY: SYNONYMS

See Synonyms at ***agree***.

concurrent /kən kúrrənt/ *adj.* **1. HAPPENING TOGETHER** taking place or existing at the same time, or running in parallel **2.** GEOM = **convergent** [14thC. From Latin *concurrent-*, the present participle stem of *concurrere* (see CONCUR).] —**concurrently** *adv.* —**concurrence** *n.*

concuss /kən kúss/ (**-cusses, -cussing, -cussed**) *vt.* to cause concussion, usually by a blow to the head or a jarring fall or jolt [Late 16thC. From Latin *concuss-*, the past participle stem of *concutere*, literally 'to strike together', from *quatere* 'to strike' (source of English *discuss*, *percussion*, and *rescue*).]

concussion /kən kúsh'n/ *n.* **1.** MED **MILD TO MODERATE BRAIN INJURY** an injury to the brain, often resulting from a blow to the head, that can cause temporary disorientation, memory loss, or unconsciousness **2.** MED **INJURY TO A BODILY ORGAN** an injury to an organ of the body, usually caused by a violent blow or shaking **3. SUDDEN JOLT OR SHOCK** any sudden violent jolting or shaking —**concussive** /-kússiv/ *adj.*

condemn /kən dém/ (**-demns, -demning, -demned**) *vt.* **1. PRONOUNCE STH OR SB AS BAD** to state that sth or sb is in some way wrong or unacceptable **2. GIVE SB A LEGAL SENTENCE** to make a judicial pronouncement stating what punishment has been imposed on a person found guilty of a crime, especially in the case of a heavy penalty or a death sentence **3. CONSIDER SB GUILTY** to judge that a person or thing is to blame for sth **4. MAKE SB EXPERIENCE STH** to force or oblige sb to experience sth very unpleasant, especially sth permanent or long-lasting **5. BAN USE OR CONSUMPTION OF STH** to issue an official order saying that sth such as a building is unfit to be used **6. PROVE GUILTY** to serve as proof of guilt [14thC. Via French *condemner* from Latin *condemnare*, literally 'to pass final sentence', from *damnare* 'to sentence' (see DAMN).] —**condemnable** *adj.* —**condemnation** /kón dem náysh'n, kóndəm-/ *n.* —**condemnatory** /kən démnətəri, kón dem náytəri/ *adj.*

WORD KEY: SYNONYMS

See Synonyms at ***criticize*** and ***disapprove***.

condemned cell *n.* a prison cell where a person who has been sentenced to death is kept before the execution is carried out. US term **death row cell**

condensate /kón den sayt, kóndən sayt, kən dén sayt/ *n.* a substance resulting from condensation, especially a liquid from a vapour

condensation /kón den sáysh'n, kóndən sáysh'n/ *n.* **1.** PHYS **CONVERSION OF GAS TO LIQUID** the process by which a vapour loses heat and changes into a liquid **2. FILM OF WATER DROPLETS** tiny drops of water that form on a cold surface such as a window when warmer air comes into contact with it **3. MAKING STH SHORTER** the state of being compressed or made briefer, or the act or result of summarizing or compressing sth **4.** CHEM **FORMATION OF DENSER MOLECULES** the bonding of molecules of a substance to form a larger denser molecule, usually with the release of simpler substances, such as water —**condensational** *adj.*

condensation trail *n.* AIR = **vapour trail**

condense /kən dénss/ (**-denses, -densing, -densed**) *v.* **1.** *vti.* PHYS **CHANGE FROM GAS TO LIQUID** to lose heat and change from a vapour into a liquid, or to make a vapour change to a liquid **2.** *vt.* **MAKE STH SHORTER** to reduce the length of a text by removing unnecessary words or passages or by expressing the content more concisely **3.** *vti.* CHEM **FORM DENSER MOLECULES** to bond together to form a larger denser molecule, or to make molecules undergo this process **4.** *vti.* COOK **THICKEN BY REMOVING WATER** to make sth, especially a food, denser by removing water, or to become denser in this way [15thC. Via French from Latin *condensare* 'to thicken', from *condensus* 'very dense', from Latin *densus* (see DENSE).] —**condensability** /kən dénssə bílləti/ *n.* —**condensable** /kən dénssəb'l/ *adj.*

condensed milk *n.* milk thickened by evaporating most of the water content and then sweetened. ◊ **evaporated milk**

condenser /kən dénssər/ *n.* **1.** PHYS **CONVERTER OF GAS TO LIQUID** a device that converts a gas to a liquid to obtain either the substance or the released heat **2.** OPTICS **LENS OR MIRROR FOR CONCENTRATING LIGHT** a lens or mirror used to concentrate light onto, e.g., a transparency or specimen **3.** ELEC = **capacitor**

Conder /kóndər/, **Charles Edward** (1868–1909) British painter. He was trained in Australia, where he was part of the impressionist Heidelberg School. Among his best-known works is *'A Holiday at Mentone'* (1888).

condescend /kón di sénd/ (**-scends, -scending, -scended**) *vi.* **1. ACT IN A SUPERIOR WAY** to behave towards other people as though they are less important or less intelligent than you are **2. MAKE CONCESSIONS FOR OTHERS** to do sth that you would normally consider yourself too important or dignified to do [14thC. Via French *condescendre* from ecclesiastical Latin *condescendere* 'to lower oneself', from Latin *descendere* (see DESCEND).] —**condescender** *n.*

condescending /kón di sénding/ *adj.* behaving towards other people in a way that shows you consider yourself socially or intellectually superior to them, especially when explaining or giving sth —**condescendingly** *adv.*

condescension /kón di sénsh'n/ *n.* behaviour or an example of behaviour that implies that sb is graciously lowering himself or herself to the level of people less important or intelligent

condign /kən dīn/ *adj.* well deserved and completely appropriate (*formal*) [14thC. Via French from Latin *condignus*, literally 'wholly worthy', from *dignus* (see DIGNITY).] —**condignly** *adv.*

condiment /kóndimənt/ *n.* salt, pepper, mustard, relish, or a similar substance added to food to improve or adjust its flavour. Condiments are usually served at table and added in modest amounts according to individual taste. [15thC. Via French from Latin *condimentum*, from *condire* 'to preserve, pickle'.]

condition /kən dísh'n/ *n.* **1. STATE OF REPAIR** the particular state of repair or ability to function of an object or piece of equipment ○ *The meter is still in good condition.* **2. STH STATED AS NECESSARY FOR AGREEMENT** sth that is necessary for sth else to happen, e.g. to bring a situation about or make a contract valid **3. WAY OF BEING** a general state or mode of existence, especially one characterized by hardship or suffering **4. STATUS** position, rank, or social status (*formal*) **5. STATE OF HEALTH** a state of physical fitness or general health ○ *out of condition* **6. DISORDER** a physical disorder **7. STATE OF PREGNANCY** the state of being pregnant (*informal*) ○ *A woman in her condition shouldn't be dancing!* ■ *npl.* **1. conditions FACTORS AFFECTING PEOPLE** the factors or circumstances that affect the situation sb is living or working in ○ *poor working conditions* **2. STATE OF WEATHER** the state of the weather ■ *vt.* (**-tions, -tioning, -tioned**) **1.** PSYCHOL **TRAIN SB** to make people or animals act or react in a certain way by gradually getting them used to a certain pattern of events **2. MAKE STRONG, HEALTHY, OR READY** to give sb or sth a treatment to improve general health, soundness, readiness for use, appearance, or performance **3.** HAIR **IMPROVE HAIR'S CONDITION** to put conditioner or a similar substance on the hair in order to improve its appearance and texture **4. SPECIFY A REQUIREMENT OR PREREQUISITE** to state a requirement that must be fulfilled, or to make sth dependent on a requirement, especially in a legal contract (*formal*) **5. ADAPT TO STH** to become accustomed to specific conditions or activities, or to make yourself adapt to these **6. COOL** to make air cooler ○ *Heat pumps condition the air on the first floor.* [13thC. Via Old French from the Latin stem *condition-* 'agreement, stipulation', from *condicere*, literally 'to talk together', from *dicere* (see DICTATE).] —**conditionable** *adj.*

conditional /kən dísh'nəl/ *adj.* **1. DEPENDENT ON STH ELSE BEING DONE** used to describe sth that will be done or will happen only if and when another thing is done or happens **2.** GRAM **STATING A CONDITION OR LIMITATION** used to describe a clause, conjunction, verb form, or sentence that expresses a condition or limitation **3.** MATH **TRUE ONLY FOR CERTAIN MATHEMATICAL VALUES** true only for certain values of one or more variables in a mathematical equation **4.** MATH **DESCRIBING SERIES OF NUMBERS** used to describe a convergent series of numbers that becomes a divergent series when its terms are converted to their absolute values ■ *n.* GRAM **CONDITIONAL CLAUSE, CONJUNCTION, OR VERB FORM** a conditional clause, conjunction, verb form, or sentence —**conditionable** *adj.* —**conditionality** /kən dísh'n álləti/ *n.*

conditional access *n.* the coding of television transmissions in order to limit reception to subscribers who have decoding devices

conditional discharge *n.* a judgment of a criminal court that finds sb guilty but lets the person go unpunished subject to certain conditions, e.g. to keep the peace for a year

conditionalization /kən dísh'n'l ī záysh'n/, **conditionalisation** *n.* the process of turning a statement into a conditional statement, e.g. changing 'It will rain' into 'If it is cloudy, then it will rain'

conditionally /kən dísh'nəli/ *adv.* with the proviso that all valid conditions be met

conditional probability *n.* the probability that one event will occur, given that another event has occurred or is certain to occur

condition codes *npl.* a signal, usually in the form of a number, that indicates the status of a previous arithmetic, logic, or input/output operation

conditioned /kən dísh'nd/ *adj.* **1. AT SPECIFIED PERFORMANCE OR QUALITY LEVEL** having reached or been brought to a specified or high level of fitness, quality, or performance **2.** PSYCHOL **INVOLUNTARILY PRODUCED AS LEARNED RESPONSE** brought on unconsciously by a stimulus that triggers a reaction because of a learned association with sth else

conditioned response, conditioned reflex *n.* PSYCHOL a response to a new second stimulus as a result of association with a prior stimulus. The classic example is Pavlov's experiment in which dogs began to salivate at the sound of a bell, having previously been fed when the bell was rung.

conditioned stimulus *n.* in classical psychological conditioning, an otherwise ineffective stimulus that, when paired with an unconditioned stimulus, is able to evoke a conditioned response

conditioner /kən dísh'nər/ *n.* **1.** HAIR **PRODUCT FOR IMPROVING HAIR TEXTURE** a liquid or cream applied to hair, either after or with shampoo and usually while the hair is still wet, to make it more manageable or healthier **2. STH THAT CONDITIONS** a substance that makes sth, e.g. bread dough or soil, easier to manage

conditioning /kən dísh'ning/ *n.* **1.** PSYCHOL **GRADUAL TRAINING PROCESS** a method of controlling or influencing the way people or animals behave or think by using a gradual training process **2. GETTING SB OR STH FIT** the work or programme used to bring a person or thing to a good physical state

condo /kóndō/ (*plural* **-dos**) *n.* *US* ARCHIT a condominium (*informal*) [Mid-20thC. Shortening.]

condole /kən dṓl/ (**-doles, -doling, -doled**) *vi.* to express sympathy to sb who is experiencing grief, loss, or pain, especially over a death (*formal*) [Late 16thC. From Christian Latin *condolere*, literally 'to grieve together', from *dolere* 'to suffer' (source of English *doleful* and *indolent*).] —**condolatory** *adj.* —**condoler** *n.* —**condolingly** *adv.*

WORD KEY: USAGE

condole or **console**? These words are easy to confuse because they are both connected with reassuring people in distress. The more common word is ***console***, which takes an object and means 'to comfort'. *He tried to console his father when his mother died.* ***Condole*** means 'to express sympathy', and does not take an object but uses *with* instead. *He condoled with his father over the death of his mother.*

condolence /kən dṓlənss/ *n.* an expression of sorrow and sympathy, usually to sb who is grieving over a death (*often used in the plural*) —**condolent** *adj.* —**condolently** *adv.*

con dolore /kón do láwray, -ri/ *adv.* in a sad or sorrowful way (*used as a musical direction*) [From Italian, literally 'with sorrow'] —**con dolore** *adj.*

condom /kóndəm, -dom/ *n.* a close-fitting rubber covering worn by a man over the penis during sexual intercourse to prevent pregnancy or the spread of sexually transmitted disease. ◊ **female condom** [Early 18thC. Origin unknown.]

condominium /kóndə mínni əm/ *n.* **1.** *US* ARCHIT **INDIVIDUALLY OWNED FLAT** an individually owned unit of real estate, especially a flat or townhouse, in a building or on land that is owned in common by the owners of the units **2.** *US* ARCHIT **BUILDING CONTAINING CONDOMINIUMS** a building or complex containing condominium flats or townhouses **3.** POL **STATE RULED BY FOREIGN COUNTRIES** a country governed by two or more different countries with joint responsibility **4.** POL **JOINT GOVERNMENT OF TERRITORY** the system under which a country or state is ruled by two or more other nations [Early 18thC. From modern Latin, literally 'joint right of ownership', from Latin *dominium* 'property' (see DOMINION).] —**condominial** *adj.*

condone /kən dṓn/ (**-dones, -doning, -doned**) *vt.* to regard sth that is considered immoral or wrong in a tolerant way, without criticizing it or feeling strongly about it [Mid-19thC. From Latin *condonare*, literally 'to give up', from *donare* (see DONATE). The underlying meaning is 'to give up your objections'.] —**condonable** *adj.* —**condonation** /kóndə náysh'n, kón dō-/ *n.* —**condoner** *n.*

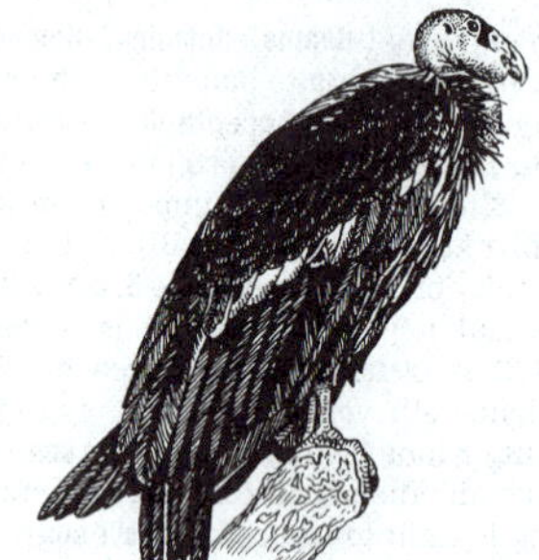

Condor

condor /kón dawr, kóndər/ *n.* a large vulture of the Andes that has dull black plumage with white around the neck. Latin name: *Vultur gryphus.* [Early 17thC. Via Spanish *cóndor* from Quechua *kuntur.*]

condottiere /kón doti áiray, -ri/ (*plural* **-ri** /-ri/) *n.* **1. CAPTAIN OF MERCENARY SOLDIERS DURING RENAISSANCE** a man who led a group of hired soldiers, or one of the hired soldiers in such a group, especially during the period of the Italian Renaissance, between the 13th and 16th centuries **2. MERCENARY** a hired soldier [Late 18thC. From Italian, literally 'contractor'.]

conduce /kən dyóoss/ (**-duces, -ducing, -duced**) *vi.* to help, contribute, or lead to bringing about an action or event (*formal*) [14thC. From Latin *conducere*, literally 'to bring together', from *ducere* (see DUCT).] —**conducer** *n.* —**conducible** *adj.* —**conducingly** *adv.*

conducive /kən dyóossiv/ *adj.* tending to encourage or bring about a good or intended result

conduct *v.* /kən dúkt/ (**conducts, conducting, conducted**) **1.** *vti.* **LEAD INSTRUMENTAL OR VOCAL GROUP** to lead a group of musicians or a musical performance by signalling the beat with a baton or hand gestures, giving cues, and offering suggestions for interpretation or expression **2.** *vt.* **DO OR RUN STH** to carry out, manage, or control sth **3.** *vr.* **BEHAVE** to behave in a specified way ○ *He conducted himself with great dignity.* **4.** PHYS, ELEC **TRANSMIT ENERGY** to transmit energy, e.g. heat, light, sound, or electricity **5.** *vt.* **GUIDE SB ALONG** to lead a person or group of people by going along with them ■ *n.* /kón dukt/ **1. BEHAVIOUR** the way a person behaves, especially in public **2. HOW SB DOES OR HANDLES STH** the management or execution of matters such as work or official affairs **3. LEADER OR GUIDE** sb who leads, guides, or escorts another or others (*archaic*) [15thC. Directly and via *conduit* from Latin *conduct-*, the past participle stem of *conducere* (see CONDUCE).] —**conductibility** /kən dúktə bílləti/ *n.* —**conductible** /kən dúktəb'l/ *adj.*

WORD KEY: SYNONYMS

See Synonyms at ***guide***.

conductance /kən dúktənss/ *n.* a measure of the ability of an object to transmit electricity. ◊ **conductivity** *n.* 1. Symbol *G*

conduction /kən dúksh'n/ *n.* **1.** PHYS **TRANSMISSION OF ENERGY** the passage of energy through sth, particularly heat or electricity **2. TRANSMISSION THROUGH A NERVE FIBRE** the transmission of biochemical or electrical energy through a nerve fibre **3. CONVEYANCE THROUGH PASSAGE** the passage of sth through or along sth, e.g. water through a pipe

conductive /kən dúktiv/ *adj.* **1.** PHYS **CONDUCTING ENERGY** transmitting or able to transmit energy, particularly heat or electricity **2.** BIOL **TRANSMITTING NERVE IMPULSE** used to describe a cell that allows a physiological disturbance, e.g. a nerve impulse, to pass through it

conductive education *n.* a system of education that teaches children and adults with motor disorders to function independently

conductivity /kón duk tívvəti/ *n.* **1.** ELEC **ABILITY TO TRANSMIT ELECTRICITY** a mathematical relationship between the dimensions of an object and its ability to transmit electricity. ◊ **conductance**. Symbol ' **2.** BIOL **TRANSMISSION OF NERVE IMPULSES** the ability of tissue to transmit nerve impulses

conductor /kən dúktər/ *n.* **1.** TRANSP **SB WHO COLLECTS FARES ON BUS** sb who takes money for tickets on a bus or tram **2.** *US, Can* TRANSP = **guard 3.** MUSIC **DIRECTOR OF ORCHESTRA OR CHOIR** sb in charge of an orchestra or choir who marks time and signals to musicians or singers when and how to play or sing **4.** PHYS **STH THAT CONVEYS HEAT OR ELECTRICITY** a substance, body, or medium that allows heat, electricity, light, or sound to pass along it or through it. Metals are good conductors of heat because of the high concentration of free electrons they contain. **5.** ENG = **lightning conductor** —**conductorial** /kón duk táwri əl/ *adj.* —**conductorship** /kən d/ *n.*

conductress /kən dúktrəss/ *n.* a woman who collects fares on a bus or tram

conduit /kóndyoo it, kóndit/ *n.* **1.** UTIL **CHANNEL FOR LIQUID** a pipe or channel that carries liquid to or from a place **2.** CONSTR **PROTECTIVE COVER FOR CABLE** a pipe or tube that covers and protects electrical cables **3. CONVEYER OF INFORMATION** sb or sth that conveys information, especially if in secret [14thC. Via French *conduit* from, ultimately, Latin *conduct-*, stem of *conducere*, literally 'to lead with' (source of English *conduct*).]

condyle /kóndil, -dīl/ *n.* a rounded part at the end of a bone that forms a moving joint with a cup-shaped cavity in another bone. The ball part of a ball-and-socket joint, such as the hip or shoulder joint, is a condyle. [Mid-17thC. Via French from, ultimately, Greek *kondulos* 'knuckle'.] —**condylar** *adj.*

condyloid /kóndi loyd/ *adj.* rounded like the protruding surface at the end of a bone

condyloma /kóndi lṓmə/ (*plural* **-mas** *or* **-mata** /-mətə/) *n.* a growth resembling a wart on the skin or a mucous membrane, usually of the genitals or anus [14thC. Via Latin from Greek *kondulōma* 'callous knob or lump', from *kondulos* 'knuckle'.]

cone /kōn/ *n.* **1. POINTED OBJECT WITH ROUND BASE** any object or shape that has a circular base and tapers to a point at the top, or has a circular top and tapers to a point at the bottom **2.** GEOM **POINTED FIGURE WITH CURVED FLAT BASE** a three-dimensional geometric figure formed by straight lines through a fixed point (**vertex**) to the points of a fixed curve (**directrix**). A circular cone has a directrix that is a circle. **3.** FOOD = **cornet 4.** TRANSP **PLASTIC CONE-SHAPED ROAD MARKER** a plastic cone-shaped object used as a temporary road marker or barrier, e.g. to close off part or all of a road during repairs or after an accident **5.** BOT **SEED-BEARING STRUCTURE OF PINES AND FIRS** a tightly packed cluster of scales that bears the reproductive organs of coniferous plants such as pines and firs. Male cones produce pollen, and female cones bear seeds. Technical name **strobilus 6.** BOT **REPRODUCTIVE PART OF NONFLOWERING PLANTS** a club-shaped, umbrella-shaped, or poker-shaped cluster of fertile leaves that bears the spore-producing organs of a clubmoss or horsetail **7.** ANAT **LIGHT RECEPTOR CELL IN EYE** a cone-shaped cell sensitive to light and colour in the retina of the eye of a human being or any other vertebrate animal. There are three different types of cone cells, responding to blue, green, or red light. **8.** MARINE BIOL **SEA SNAIL WITH CONE-SHAPED SHELL** a sea snail found in the South Pacific and Indian oceans that has a cone-shaped, vividly marked shell and a poisonous, sometimes fatal, sting. Family: Conidae. **9.** GEOG **VOLCANO** a cone-shaped mountain, especially a volcano ■ *vt.* **(cones, coning, coned) MAKE STH INTO CONE SHAPE** to shape sth into the form of a cone [15thC. Via French from, ultimately, Greek *kōnos* 'pine cone, cone'.]

cone off *vt.* to close off a part or all of a road with traffic cones because of road repairs or an accident

coneflower /kṓn flowər/ *n.* a plant, originally from North America, with variously coloured flowers that have a brown or black cone-shaped centre. Genera: *Echinacea* and *Rudbeckia*.

cone shell *n.* = **cone** *n.* **8**

con espressione /kón ess pressi ṓni/ *adv.* **EXPRESSIVELY** with feeling and expression (*used as a musical direction*) ■ *adj.* **PLAYED WITH GREAT FEELING** to be played with great feeling and expression [From Italian, literally 'with expression']

coney /kṓni/ *n.* = **cony**

Coney Island /kṓni-/ formerly a resort, now an amusement area in southern Brooklyn, New York City, New York. It was an island, but has become part of Long Island since the silting up of Coney Island Creek.

conf *abbr.* **1.** confer **2.** conference **3.** LAW confessor **4.** confidential

confab /kón fab/ *n.* **TALK** a chat or casual discussion (*informal*) ■ *vi.* **(-fabs, -fabbing, -fabbed) TALK ABOUT STH** to have a chat or discussion about sth (*informal*) [Early 18thC. Shortening of CONFABULATION.]

confabulate /kən fábbyōō layt/ **(-lates, -lating, -lated)** *vi.* **1. CONFER ABOUT STH** to discuss or have a chat about sth (*formal*) **2.** PSYCHOL **CREATE MEMORY OF SUPPOSED PAST EVENTS** to give fictitious accounts of past events, believing they are true, in order to cover a gap in the memory caused by a medical condition such as dementia or Korsakoff's syndrome [Early 17thC. From Latin *confabulat-*, stem of *confabulari*, literally 'to talk together', from, ultimately, *fabula* 'story' (see FABLE).] —**confabulation** /kən fábbyōō láysh'n/ *n.* —**confabulator** /kən fábbyōō laytər/ *n.* —**confabulatory** /kən fábbyōōlətəri, kən fábbyōō láytəri/ *adj.*

confect /kən fékt/ **(-fects, -fecting, -fected)** *vt.* **1.** COOK **MAKE SWEETS OR PRESERVES** to make sweets by combining ingredients such as sugar, fruit, and nuts, or make preserves (*formal*) **2. MAKE** to create sth by combining different materials or items ○ *Using scrap lumber, they succeeded in confecting a house of sorts.* [14thC. From Latin *confect-*, stem of *conficere*, literally 'to put or make together', from *facere* 'to make'.]

confection /kən féksh'n/ *n.* **1.** FOOD **STH SWEET** a sweet food made by combining ingredients such as fruit, nuts, and sugar **2. COMBINATION** a combining of elements or materials or its result ○ *a confection of lies and half-truths* **3. ELABORATE CREATION** an often elaborate piece of craftsmanship and skill, e.g. an ornate piece of women's clothing ○ *Her gown was a marvellous confection of lace and tulle.* **4.** PHARM **SWEET MEDICINE** a medicine that has been sweetened with honey or sugar (*archaic*)

confectionary /kən féksh'nəri/ *n.* (*plural* **-ies**) FOOD = **confectionery** *n.* **1**, **confectionery** *n.* **3** ■ *adj.* **RELATING TO CONFECTIONERY** relating to confectionery and confectioners (*formal*)

confectioner /kən féksh'nər/ *n.* sb who makes or sells sweets

confectioners' sugar *n.* *US* = **icing sugar**

confectionery /kən féksh'nəri/ (*plural* **-ies**) *n.* **1.** FOOD **CONFECTIONS** sweets, considered collectively **2.** COOK **SWEET-MAKING** the skill, technique, or practice of making sweets **3.** COMM **CONFECTIONER'S SHOP** a shop where sweets are sold

confed *abbr.* POL **1.** confederation **2.** confederate *or* Confederate

confederacy /kən féddərəssi/ *n.* **1. POLITICAL UNION** an alliance of people, states, or parties for some common purpose, or the people, states, or parties in an alliance **2. GROUP DOING STH UNLAWFUL TOGETHER** a group of people who have joined together to do sth unlawful

Confederacy /kən féddərəssi/ *n.* = **Confederate States of America**

confederal /kən féddərəl/ *adj.* **1. OF A CONFEDERATION** relating to a confederation **2. CONCERNING TWO OR MORE NATIONS** relating to the activities of two or more nations —**confederalist** *n.*

confederate *n.* /kən féddərət/ **1. ALLY** one of two or more people, groups, or nations that have formed an alliance for some common purpose **2. ACCOMPLICE** sb who is part of a plot or conspiracy ■ *adj.* /kən féddərət/ **ASSOCIATED** joined in common purpose ■ *vti.* /kən féddə rayt/ **(-ates, -ating, -ated) UNITE PEOPLE OR THINGS** to form people, groups, or nations into a confederacy, or become part of a confederacy [14thC. From late Latin *confoederat-*, the past participle stem of *confoederare*, literally 'to league together', from, ultimately, the stem *foeder-* 'league' (see FEDERAL).] —**confederative** /kən féddərətiv/ *adj.*

Confederate /kən féddərət/ *n.* **SUPPORTER OF CONFEDERATE STATES OF AMERICA** a supporter or soldier of the Confederate States of America during the American Civil War ■ *adj.* **RELATING TO CONFEDERATE STATES OF AMERICA** relating to the Confederate States of America during the American Civil War

confederation /kən féddə ráysh'n/ *n.* **1. GROUP OF LOOSELY ALLIED STATES** a group of states that are allied together to form a political unit in which they keep most of their independence but act together for certain purposes such as defence **2. BODY REPRESENTING INDEPENDENT ORGANIZATIONS** a body comprising representatives of independent organizations that wish to cooperate for some common beneficial purpose **3.** *Can* **FEDERATION** a federation **4. CONFEDERATING** the formation of or state of being a confederation —**confederationism** *n.* —**confederationist** *n.*

Confederation /kən féddə ráysh'n/ *n.* **1. ORIGINAL UNITED STATES** the union of the original 13 states of the United States under the Articles of Confederation from 1781 to 1789 **2. CANADA IN 1867** the original union of Ontario, Quebec, New Brunswick, and Nova Scotia in 1867 into the federation of Canada, afterwards joined by the six other provinces

confer /kən fúr/ **(-fers, -ferring, -ferred)** *v.* **1.** *vi.* **DISCUSS STH WITH SB** to talk to sb in order to compare opinions or make a decision **2.** *vt.* **GIVE HONOUR OR TITLE TO SB** to give sth such as a title, honour, or favour to sb (*formal*) ○ *The university conferred an honorary degree on the president.* **3.** *vt.* **GIVE SB OR STH SOME CHARACTERISTIC** to give sb or sth a certain status or characteristic ○ *His demeanor conferred a sense of dignity on the whole affair.* [15thC. From Latin *conferre*, literally 'to bring together', from *ferre* 'to bring'.] —**conferment** *n.* —**conferrable** *adj.* —**conferral** *n.* —**conferrer** *n.*

WORD KEY: SYNONYMS

See Synonyms at ***give***.

conferee /kónfə reé/, **conferree** *n.* **1. PARTICIPANT AT CONFERENCE** sb who takes part in a conference **2. SB HONOURED** sb who is given a title, honour, or favour

conference /kónfərənss/ *n.* **1. MEETING FOR LECTURES AND DISCUSSION** a meeting, sometimes lasting for several days, in which people with a common interest participate in discussions or listen to lectures to obtain information **2. MEETING FOR SERIOUS DISCUSSION** a meeting to discuss serious matters, e.g. policy or business **3. MEETING OF REPRESENTATIVES OF ORGANIZATION** a usually annual gathering of local representatives of an organization, such as a political party, trade union, or church, where policy matters and other issues are discussed or decided ○ *I would ask conference to throw out this motion.* ○ *the Conservative Party Conference* **4.** POL **MEETING OF TWO LEGISLATIVE COMMITTEES** a meeting of select members or committees from two legislative bodies, for the purpose of settling differences in bills they have passed **5.** CHR **AREA ORGANIZATION OF CHURCHES** in some Protestant churches, a regional or national body to which a number of local churches belong ○ *the Friends General Conference* **6.** SPORTS **SPORTS LEAGUE** an association or league of athletic teams that compete with each other ○ *the Vauxhall Conference* **7. CONFERRING OF STH** the conferring of sth such as a degree or honour on sb (*archaic*)

conference call *n.* a conversation involving three or more people linked together by telephone

Conference pear *n.* a longish sweet and juicy variety of pear with a dark green skin [Named after the late 19th-Century horticultural conference]

conferencing /kónfərənssing/ *n.* the holding of a conference, meeting, or discussion in which the participants are linked by telephone (**audioconferencing**), by telephone and by video equipment (**videoconferencing**), or by computer (**computer conferencing**)

conferree *n.* = **conferee**

confess /kən féss/ **(-fesses, -fessing, -fessed)** *v.* **1.** *vti.* **ADMIT HAVING DONE STH WRONG** to admit openly a wrongdoing, crime, or error ○ *She confessed to having taken the watch.* ○ *I eventually confessed that I had made the call that night.* **2.** *vt.* **ACKNOWLEDGE TO BE TRUE** to admit the truth of sth, e.g. sth that might reflect badly or be embarrassing ○ *I confess I didn't really want to come here tonight.* ○ *I confess myself unworthy of the honor you are bestowing on me.* **3.** *vt.* **STATE BELIEF ABOUT YOURSELF** to say that you believe sth to be the case, especially sth about yourself and especially sth bad ○ *I confess myself quite unworthy of the honour you are bestowing on me.* **4.** *vti.* CHR **ADMIT SINS** to reveal sins to a priest or to God and ask for forgiveness ○ *It had been some months since I had confessed.* **5.** *vt.* CHR **HEAR SB'S CONFESSION** to listen to sb's confession of sins ○ *A priest visited her to confess her every day.* **6.** *vt.* **ACKNOWLEDGE FAITH IN** to declare faith or belief in sth or sb (*archaic*) ○ *On that day everyone will confess him Lord and God.* [14thC. Via French *confesser* from Latin *confess-*, past participle stem of *confiteri* 'to acknowledge', literally 'to declare utterly', from *fateri* 'to declare'.] —**confessable** *adj.*

confessant /kən féss'nt/ *n.* sb who makes a confession to a priest

confessed /kən fést/ *adj.* openly admitted ○ *a confessed admirer of your films*

confessedly /kən féssidli/ *adv.* used to indicate that sth is admitted to be the case

confession /kən fésh'n/ *n.* **1. ADMISSION OF WRONGDOING** an admission of having done sth wrong or embarrassing **2.** LAW **ADMISSION OF GUILT** a voluntary written or verbal statement admitting the commission of a crime **3. OPEN ACKNOWLEDGMENT OF FEELINGS** a profession of emotions or beliefs such as love, loyalty, or faith **4.** CHR **DECLARATION OF SINS** a formal declaration of sins confidentially to a priest or to God **5.** RELIG **DECLARATION OF BELIEFS OR DOCTRINES** a declaration of the beliefs or doctrines of a religious body **6.** CHR **RELIGIOUS GROUP SHARING BELIEFS** a religious group that has a specific set of beliefs and practices

confessional /kən fésh'nəl/ *adj.* **RESEMBLING CONFESSION** suited to, typical of, or resembling an act of confession ■ *n.* CHR **PLACE FOR CONFESSION IN CHURCH** a small wooden stall in a Roman Catholic church with a partition behind which a priest sits to hear confession —**confessionally** *adv.*

confessionalism /kən fésh'nəl izzəm/ *n.* **1. DEVOTION TO CONFESSION OF FAITH** strong devotion to a church's confession of faith **2. BELIEF IN CONFESSION OF FAITH** support for the view that a church should have a confession of faith

confessor /kən féssər/ *n.* **1.** CHR **PRIEST** a priest who hears confessions and sometimes acts as a spiritual adviser **2.** CHR **SPIRITUAL ADVISOR** a priest who acts as sb's spiritual advisor as well as hearing his or her confessions **3.** CHR **CHRISTIAN NOT DETERRED BY PERSECUTION** sb who demonstrates Christian faith by living a holy life, especially in the face of persecution but without being a martyr (*archaic*) **4. SB WHO CONFESSES** sb who makes a confession

confetti /kən fétti/ *n.* **COLOURED PAPER PIECES FOR THROWING** small pieces of coloured paper or dried flowers thrown over the bride and groom at a wedding ■ *adj.* **RESEMBLING CONFETTI** similar to confetti in shape or colour [Early 19thC. From Italian, plural of *confetto* 'small sweet thrown at carnivals', from, ultimately, Latin *conficere* (see CONFECT).]

confidant /kónfi dánt, kónfi dant/ *n.* a trusted person with whom personal matters and problems are discussed [Mid-17thC. Alteration of CONFIDENT.]

confidante /kónfi dánt, kónfi dant/ *n.* a trusted woman with whom personal matters and problems are discussed [Mid-17thC. Alteration of CONFIDENT.]

confide /kən fíd/ (**-fides, -fiding, -fided**) *v.* **1.** *vti.* **TELL STH SECRET TO SB** to tell sb sth that is to remain secret or private ○ *He later confided to me that he had not wanted the position at all.* **2.** *vt.* **GIVE STH OVER TO SB'S CARE** to entrust sb with sth such as a valuable object or an important task (*archaic*) ○ *He had been confided with the task of taking the message to the king.* **3.** *vi.* **TRUST IN SB** to have trust or confidence in sb (*archaic*) [15thC. From Latin *confidere* 'to put your trust in', from *fidere* 'to trust', from *fides* 'trust' (source of English *faith*).] —**confider** *n.*

confidence /kónfid'nss/ *n.* **1. BELIEF IN OWN ABILITIES** a belief or self-assurance in your ability to succeed **2. FAITH IN SB TO DO RIGHT** belief or assurance in sb or sth or the ability of sb or sth to act in a proper, trustworthy, or reliable manner **3. SECRET** sth told to sb that is to be kept private **4. TRUSTING RELATIONSHIP** a relationship based on trust and intimacy ○ *He took me into his confidence.*

confidence game *n.* US = **confidence game**

confidence interval *n.* a range of statistical values within which a result is expected to fall with a specific probability

confidence level *n.* a measure of how reliable a statistical result is, expressed as a percentage that indicates the probability of the result being correct

confidence limit *n.* the highest and lowest values of a confidence interval

confidence trick *n. US* = **confidence trick**

confident /kónfidənt/ *adj.* **1. SELF-ASSURED** certain of having the ability, judgment, and resources needed to succeed **2. CONVINCED** sure about the nature or facts of sth ○ *We are confident that the market for our products is expanding.* **3. EXCESSIVELY FORWARD** bold and presumptuous in manner [Late 16thC. Via French from *confidere* (see CONFIDE).] —**confidently** *adv.*

confidential /kónfi dénsh'l/ *adj.* **1. PRIVATE AND SECRET** carried out or revealed in the expectation that anything done or revealed will be kept private **2. FOR A SELECT GROUP** not available to the public, e.g. because it is commercially or industrially sensitive or concerns matters of national security **3. DEALING WITH PRIVATE AFFAIRS** entrusted with sb's personal or private matters **4. SUGGESTING A CLOSE RELATIONSHIP** suggesting familiarity or intimacy that may not exist ○ *a confidential whisper* —**confidentiality** /kónfi denshi álləti/ *n.* —**confidentially** /kónfi dénsh'li/ *adv.*

confiding /kən fíding/ *adj.* **1. TRUSTING** willing to trust others with the knowledge of private or personal matters **2. AS IF TELLING SB STH SECRET** in a manner or tone appropriate for telling sb sth secret or that suggests that a secret is being told —**confidingly** *adv.*

configuration /kən fíggə ráysh'n, -fígyŏŏ-/ *n.* **1. ARRANGEMENT OF PARTS** the way the parts or elements of sth are arranged and fit together ○ *I don't quite grasp the configuration of this engine.* **2. SHAPE OR OUTLINE** the shape or outline of sth, determined by the way its parts or elements are arranged ○ *Geese fly in a V-shaped configuration.* **3.** COMPUT **COMPUTER SYSTEM'S SETUP** the manner in which the software and internal and external hardware components of a computer system are arranged and interconnected, so that the system functions correctly **4.** CHEM, PHYS **ARRANGEMENT OF ATOMS IN MOLECULE** the fixed stable spatial arrangement of atoms within a molecule **5.** PSYCHOL = **gestalt** —**configurative** /kən fíggərətiv, -fíggyŏŏ-/ *adj.* —**configurational** /kən fíggə ráysh'nəl, -fíggyŏŏ-/ *adj.* —**configurationally** /kən fíggə ráysh'nəli, -fíggyŏŏ-/ *adv.*

configure /kən fíggər/ (**-ures, -uring, -ured**) *vt.* to set up, design, or arrange the parts of sth for a specific purpose [14thC. From Latin *configurare* 'to fashion after a pattern', literally 'to form together', from *figura* 'shape' (source of English *figure*).]

confine /kən fín/ *vt.* (**-fines, -fining, -fined**) **1. KEEP SB OR STH WITHIN LIMITS** to keep within certain limits or boundaries ○ *Please confine your comments to the matter in hand.* **2. KEEP IN SOME PLACE** to keep sb or sth from leaving an enclosed or limited space such as a prison, room, or bed ■ *n.* **1. LIMITATION** restriction within limits (*archaic literary*) **2. PRISON** a place of confinement (*archaic*) ■ **confines** *npl.* **BOUNDARIES OR SCOPE** the boundaries, limits, or scope that restricts sb or sth ○ *Their goals were defined by the confines of the project requirements.* [15thC. From French *confiner*, from *confins* (plural) 'boundaries', from, ultimately, Latin *confinis* 'ending with', from *finis* 'end' (see FINAL).] —**confinable** *adj.* —**confiner** *n.*

confined /kən fínd/ *adj.* **1. LIMITED** restricted in scope or application ○ *a problem that is not confined to the inner cities* **2. CONSTRICTED** small, cramped, and completely enclosed **3.** MED **IN PROCESS OF GIVING BIRTH** giving birth, or about to give birth, to a child (*dated*) —**confinedness** /kən fínidnəss/ *n.*

confinement /kən fínmənt/ *n.* **1.** MED **PROCESS OR TIME OF GIVING BIRTH** the period of time or the process of giving birth, beginning when a woman goes into labour and ending when a child is born (*dated*) **2. RESTRAINT** restriction or limitation within the boundaries or scope of sth

confirm /kən fúrm/ (**-firms, -firming, -firmed**) *v.* **1.** *vt.* **PROVE TO BE TRUE** to verify the truth or validity of sth thought to be true or valid **2.** *vti.* **MAKE STH DEFINITE** to make certain that a tentative arrangement or one made earlier is firm ○ *call to confirm the booking* **3.** *vt.* **LEGALLY APPROVE** to ratify or make sth valid with a formal or legal act ○ *confirmed his appointment to the post with a unanimous vote* **4.** *vt.* JUD-CHR **ADMIT INTO RELIGIOUS BODY** in Judaism and Christianity, to admit sb into full membership of a religious body or community **5.** *vt.* **STRENGTHEN** to make sth stronger (*formal*) [13thC. Via Old French *confermer* from Latin *confirmare*, literally 'to strengthen together', from *firmare* 'to strengthen'.] —**confirmability** /kən fúrmə bílləti/ *n.* —**confirmable** /kən f/ *adj.* —**confirmatory** /kən fúrmətəri, kónfər máytəri/ *adj.* —**confirmer** /kən f/ *n.*

confirmand /kónfər mand/ *n.* sb who is being confirmed in a religious ceremony (*formal*) [Mid-18thC. From Latin *confirmandus* 'fit to be confirmed', from *confirmare* (see CONFIRM).]

confirmation /kónfər máysh'n/ *n.* **1. CONFIRMING STH** verification that sth has been or will be done **2. STH THAT CONFIRMS STH ELSE** sth that supports, validates, or verifies sth ○ *a confirmation of my worst fears* **3.** CHR **ACCEPTANCE INTO CHURCH** a religious ceremony that marks sb's formal acceptance into a Christian church **4.** JUDAISM **CEREMONY MARKING BEGINNING OF RESPONSIBLE ADULTHOOD** in Reform Judaism, a ceremony that marks the completion of sb's religious training and entry into full adult membership of the community —**confirmational** *adj.*

confirmed /kən fúrmd/ *adj.* **1. SETTLED AND UNLIKELY TO CHANGE** firmly settled in a particular habit and unlikely to change **2. ESTABLISHED AS TRUE** having been found or shown to be true or definite ○ *confirmed cases of infection* **3.** CHR **MADE MEMBER OF CHURCH** received into a Christian church as a full member

confirmedly /kən fúrmidli/ *adv.* to an extent or in a way that is unlikely to change

confiscable /kən fískəb'l/ *adj.* at risk of being confiscated (*formal*) ○ *confiscable goods*

confiscate /kónfi skayt/ *vt.* (**-cates, -cating, -cated**) **1. TAKE AWAY FROM SB** to take sb's property with authority, or appropriate it for personal use as if with authority ○ *I'll confiscate that ruler if you don't stop playing with it.* **2. TAKE PROPERTY AS LEGAL PENALTY** to seize property legally forfeited to the public treasury as a penalty ○ *The goods were confiscated by customs.* ■ *adj.* (*formal*) **1. TAKEN BY AUTHORITY** taken legally or forfeited **2. HAVING FORFEITED PROPERTY** having had property taken away legally or by forfeiture [Mid-16thC. From Latin *confiscare* 'to appropriate for the public treasury', from *fiscus* (see FISCAL).] —**confiscatable** *adj.* —**confiscator** *n.* —**confiscatory** /kən fískətəri/ *adj.*

confiscation /kónfi skáysh'n/ *n.* the seizing of property either legally for the public treasury or by appropriation for personal use

confit /kónfee/ *n.* meat cooked and preserved in its own fat, e.g. goose, duck, or pork [Mid-20thC. From French, originally the past participle of Old French *confire* 'to prepare', from Latin *conficere* 'to put together' (see CONFECT).]

Confiteor /kən fítti awr/ *n.* a Roman Catholic prayer of confession and plea for forgiveness [13thC. From Latin, 'I confess', from the opening words *Confiteor Deo Omnipotenti...* 'I confess to Almighty God...'.]

confiture /kónfi tyoor/ *n.* fruit jam or preserve [Mid-16thC. From French, where it was formed from *confit* (see CONFIT).]

conflagrant /kən fláygrənt/ *adj.* burning intensely (*literary*) [Mid-17thC. From Latin *conflagrant-*, present participle stem of *conflagrare* (see CONFLAGRATION).]

conflagration /kónflə gráysh'n/ *n.* a large fire that causes a great deal of damage [15thC. From the Latin stem *conflagration-*, ultimately from *conflagrare* 'to burn up', from *flagrare* 'to blaze' (source of English *flagrant*).]

WORD KEY: SYNONYMS

See Synonyms at ***fire***.

conflate /kən fláyt/ (**-flates, -flating, -flated**) *vti.* to join or merge two or more things into a unified whole (*formal*) [15thC. From Latin *conflat-*, past participle stem of *conflare* 'to melt together', from *flare* 'to blow' (source of English *flavour* and *soufflé*).] —**conflation** /kən fláysh'n/ *n.*

conflict *n.* /kón flikt/ **1.** MIL **WAR** a continued struggle or battle, especially open warfare between opposing forces ○ *news that the conflict had reached the outskirts of the capital* **2. DIFFERENCE** a disagreement or clash between ideas, principles, or people ○ *The two sides came into conflict over the proposed contract.* **3.** PSYCHOL **MENTAL STRUGGLE** a psychological state resulting from the often unconscious opposition between simultaneous but incompatible desires, needs, drives, or impulses **4.** LITERAT **PLOT TENSION** opposition between or among characters or forces in a literary work that shapes or motivates the action of a plot ■ *vi.* /kən flíkt/ (**-flicts, -flicting, -flicted**) **DIFFER** to be incompatible, in opposition, or in disagreement ○ *The latest findings conflict with those of the original report.* [15thC. From Latin *conflictus*, past participle of *confligere* 'to strike together, fight', from *fligere*, to strike (source of English *profligate* and *inflict*).] —**confliction** /kən flíksh'n/ *n.* —**conflictive** /kən flíktiv/ *adj.* —**conflictory** /kən flíktəri/ *adj.* —**conflictual** /kən flíkchoo əl/ *adj.*

WORD KEY: SYNONYMS

See Synonyms at ***fight***.

conflicting /kən flíkting/ *adj.* **1. DIFFERENT AND INCOMPATIBLE** inconsistent or contradictory and unable to be reconciled ○ *We've been receiving conflicting reports about the whereabouts of the kidnappers.* **2. REQUIRING DIFFERENT AND INCOMPATIBLE ACTIONS** not able to be followed or acted on, because each requires different and incompatible actions ○ *In the confusion, the men were ordered to do conflicting and impossible things.* —**conflictingly** *adv.*

conflict of interest *n.* a conflict between the public and private interests of sb in an official position or conflicts between a number of public positions

confluence /kón floo ənss/ *n.* **1.** GEOG **MEETING OF STREAMS** a flowing together of two or more streams, a point at which streams combine, or a stream formed by their combining **2. MEETING OF TWO OR MORE THINGS** a meeting or gathering together of two or more things, or the place where two or more things meet or join

confluent /kón floo ənt/ *adj.* **1.** GEOG **MERGING INTO ONE** used to describe streams that blend or flow into one **2.** MED **MERGING TOGETHER** used to describe skin eruptions that merge or spread into one another ■ *n.* GEOG **STREAM** one of two or more streams that flow together [15thC. From Latin *confluent-*, present participle stem of *confluere* 'to flow together', from *fluere* 'to flow' (see FLUID).]

confocal /kon fók'l/ *adj.* having the same focus or foci [Mid-19thC. Coined from Latin *con-* 'with' + FOCAL.] —**confocally** *adv.*

conform /kən fáwrm/ (**-forms, -forming, -formed**) *v.* **1.** *vi.* **BEHAVE ACCEPTABLY** to behave or think in a socially acceptable or expected way ○ *the constant pressure to conform* **2.** *vi.* **FOLLOW A STANDARD** to comply with a fixed standard, regulation, or requirement ○ *a transformer that doesn't conform to UK standards* **3.** *vi.* **FIT IN WITH IDEA OR IDEAL** to be or fit in with a person's idea of what sb or sth should be like ○ *He certainly doesn't conform with my expectations of a diplomat.* **4.** *vti.* **MATCH PATTERN OR SAMPLE** to match, or make sb or sth match, a pattern or sample **5.** *vti.* AGREE to be in accord or to bring sth into accord with sth else ○ *As soon as possible, the revolutionary government conformed the country's laws with those of the Soviet Union.* **6.** *vti.* BE OR MAKE SIMILAR to be the same as or very similar to sth or sb, or make sth similar ○ *The Assyrian account of the great flood conforms closely with the biblical account.* **7.** *vi.* CHR FOLLOW PRACTICES OF ESTABLISHED NATIONAL CHURCH to follow the practices of the established church of a country, especially, in the past, to belong to the Anglican Church in England and Wales (*archaic*) [14thC. Via French *conformer* from Latin *conformare* 'to shape after', from *forma* 'shape' (source of English *form*).] —**conformer** *n.*

conformable /kən fáwrməb'l/ *adj.* **1.** IN AGREEMENT consistent with sth ○ *This gradual increase in the number of species in a group is conformable with the theory.* **2.** SIMILAR similar in form or shape ○ *I think this software is conformable with what you already have on your system.* **3.** COMPLIANT eager to obey or comply with the wishes of others ○ *I've always found him a conformable sort of person.* **4.** GEOL LYING ABOVE LAYER DEPOSITED IMMEDIATELY BEFORE used to describe a layer of rock that lies on the stratum that was deposited immediately before it, so there is no break in stratigraphic sequence or intervening erosion —**conformability** /kən fáwrmə bílləti/ *n.* —**conformableness** *n.* —**conformably** /-əbli/ *adv.*

conformal /kən fáwrm'l/ *adj.* **1.** MATH MAINTAINING THE SAME ANGLES used to describe a mathematical transformation that leaves the angles between intersecting curves unchanged **2.** MAPS WITH ACCURATE SHAPE AND SCALE used to describe a map that shows the correct shape and scale of a small area [Late 19thC. Formed from German *conform*, literally 'of the same shape', ultimately from Latin *forma* 'shape' (see FORM).]

conformance /kən fáwrmənss/ *n.* the act of conforming or bringing about accord or compliance

conformation /kón fawr máysh'n/ *n.* **1.** STH'S STRUCTURE the shape, outline, or form of sth, determined by the way in which its parts are arranged ○ *He attempted to discover whether different conformations of bodily organs caused alterations to the state of the mind.* **2.** SYMMETRY the symmetrical arrangement of parts or elements of sth ○ *That sculpture shows excellent conformation.* **3.** CHEM MOLECULAR ARRANGEMENT any of the arrangements of a molecule that result from atoms being rotated about a single bond **4.** CREATION OF CONFORMITY a bringing of one thing into accord with another —**conformational** *adj.* —**conformationally** *adv.*

conformist /kən fáwrmist/ *n.* **1.** SB WHO FOLLOWS CUSTOMS AND RULES sb who behaves or thinks in a socially acceptable or expected way **2.** CHR SB BELONGING TO ESTABLISHED NATIONAL CHURCH sb who adheres to the doctrines and practices of an established national church, especially the Church of England ■ *adj.* SOCIALLY ACCEPTABLE characterized by adherence to accepted norms of behaviour or thought —**conformism** *n.*

conformity /kən fáwrməti/ *n.* **1.** DOING AND THINKING AS OTHERS behaving or thinking in a socially acceptable or expected way ○ *a certain lack of conformity in his attitudes* **2.** FOLLOWING A STANDARD compliance with a fixed standard, regulation, or requirement **3.** AGREEMENT IN FORM agreement, correspondence, or similarity in structure, manner, or character **4.** CHR COMPLIANCE acceptance and adherence to the doctrines of an established national church, especially the Church of England

confound /kən fównd/ (**-founds, -founding, -founded**) *vt.* **1.** GET THINGS MIXED UP to fail to distinguish between two or more things ○ *He often confounds fact and opinion.* **2.** BEWILDER to puzzle or confuse sb **3.** REFUTE to prove sb or sth to be wrong **4.** MAKE SITUATION WORSE to cause a confused situation to become even more confused ○ *Shouting at her like that only confounded the problem.* **5.** EXPRESSING ANGER a word used to express anger at sth or sb ○ *Confound his insolence!* **6.** PUT TO SHAME to cause sb to feel ashamed or embarrassed ○ *Her presentation confounded everyone who had criticized her.* **7.** BRING TO RUIN to ruin or destroy sb or sth (*archaic*) [13thC. Via Anglo-Norman *conf(o)undre* from, ultimately, Latin *confundere*, literally 'to pour together', hence 'to mix up', from *fundere*, 'to melt, pour' (see FOUND).] —**confounder** *n.* —**confoundingly** *adv.*

confounded /kən fówndid/ *adj.* **1.** EXPRESSING ANNOYANCE used to express annoyance or irritation (*dated informal*) **2.** BEWILDERED puzzled or confused by sth ○ *'I don't know what's happened', he spluttered, completely confounded.* **3.** SHOWN TO BE WRONG not sure what to say or do because of having been shown to be wrong (*archaic*) ○ *His invention actually worked, which left his critics quite confounded.* **4.** humiliated by sth such as being beaten (*archaic*) —**confoundedly** *adv.* —**confoundedness** *n.*

confraternity /kónfrə t/ (*plural* **-ties** /rnəti/) *n.* a group of people united in a common profession or for some purpose, often a group of Christians who have joined together to perform charitable acts [15thC. Via French *confraternité* from, ultimately, Latin *confrater*, literally 'brother with', hence 'colleague'.]

confrère /kón frair/ *n.* a fellow member of a professional, charitable, or other group (*formal*) [15thC. Via French from, ultimately, Latin *confrater* (see CONFRATERNITY).]

confront /kən frúnt/ (**-fronts, -fronting, -fronted**) *vt.* **1.** CHALLENGE FACE TO FACE to come face to face with sb, especially in a challenge, and usually with hostility, criticism, or defiance **2.** MAKE AWARE OF STH to bring sb face to face with sth such as contradictory facts or evidence **3.** ENCOUNTER DIFFICULTY to meet sth face to face, especially an obstacle that must be overcome ○ *This is just one of the difficulties students confront these days.* **4.** BE MET BY DIFFICULTY to be met face to face by sth that must be overcome ○ *The hardships that would confront the settlers were blissfully unknown when they started out.* [Mid-16thC. Via French *confronter* from medieval Latin *confrontare*, from Latin *front-*, stem of *frons* 'forehead, face, front'.] —**confronter** *n.*

confrontation /kón frun táysh'n/ *n.* **1.** ENCOUNTER a face-to-face meeting or encounter with sb or sth **2.** fighting or a fight or battle **3.** RELIG HOSTILITY WITHOUT WARFARE hostility between nations often involving armed forces, yet stopping short of actual warfare **4.** CONFLICT BETWEEN IDEAS OR PEOPLE conflict between ideas, beliefs, or opinions, or between the people who hold them ○ *This country is headed for a confrontation over natural resources and whether exploiting them is a right or a privilege.* **5.** FACING UP TO OR ENCOUNTERING STH the act or state of facing up to sth or encountering sth face to face —**confrontational** *adj.* —**confrontationist** *n., adj.*

Confucian /kən fyóosh'n/ *adj.* RELATING TO CONFUCIUS'S TEACHINGS relating to the teachings of Confucius or his followers, emphasizing personal control, adherence to a social hierarchy, and social and political order ■ *n.* FOLLOWER OF CONFUCIUS'S TEACHINGS sb who follows the teachings of Confucius —**Confucianism** *n.* —**Confucianist** *n.*

Confucius /kən fyóoshəss/ (551?–479? BC) Chinese philosopher, administrator, and moralist. His social and moral teachings, collected in the *Analects*, tried to replace former religious observances.

con fuoco /kon foo ōkō/ *adv.* to be played with energy, passion, and fire (*used as a musical direction*) [From Italian, literally 'with fire'] —**con fuoco** *adj.*

confuse /kən fyóoz/ (**-fuses, -fusing, -fused**) *vt.* **1.** MAKE UNABLE TO THINK INTELLIGENTLY to make sb unable to think or reason clearly or act sensibly **2.** MAKE HARD TO UNDERSTAND to make sth hard or harder to understand **3.** GET THINGS MIXED UP to mistake one person or thing for another **4.** EMBARRASS to make sb feel embarrassed or ill at ease **5.** UPSET THE ORDER OF to cause disorder in sth or sb ○ *The dense fog utterly confused traffic on the motorway.* [14thC. Via French *confus* 'perplexed' from Latin *confusus* 'mixed up', from *confundere* 'to mix together' (see CONFOUND).] —**confusability** /kən fyóozə bílləti/ *n.* —**confusable** *adj.*

confused /kən fyóozd/ *adj.* **1.** UNABLE TO THINK INTELLIGENTLY unable to think or reason clearly or act sensibly **2.** DISORDERED in no logical or sensible order **3.** EMBARRASSED embarrassed and not knowing what to say or how to act **4.** NOT DIFFERENTIATED mistaken for each other **5.** DISORIENTATED having impaired psychological capacity to the extent of being forgetful and no longer able to carry out simple everyday tasks —**confusedly** /kən fyóozidli, kən fyóozdli/ *adv.* —**confusedness** /-fyóozidnəss/ *n.*

confusing /kən fyóozing/ *adj.* unclear and difficult to understand —**confusingly** *adv.*

confusion /kən fyóozh'n/ *n.* **1.** BEWILDERMENT the act of confusing sb or sth, or the state of being confused or perplexed **2.** LACK OF CLARITY misunderstanding of a situation or the facts **3.** MISTAKING ONE FOR ANOTHER a failure to distinguish between people or things **4.** DISORDER a chaotic or disordered state **5.** EMBARRASSMENT self-consciousness or embarrassment **6.** DISORIENTED STATE OF MIND a psychological state in which sb is disoriented and unable to think clearly —**confusional** *adj.*

confutation /kónfyoo táysh'n/ *n.* (*formal*) **1.** PROVING STH WRONG proving that sb is wrong or that sth is false, invalid, or faulty ○ *The lawyer's confutation of the witness's testimony was decisive.* **2.** STH THAT REFUTES STH ELSE a fact, observation, or piece of evidence proving that sb is wrong or that sth is false, invalid, or faulty (*often used in the plural*) —**confutative** /kən fyóotətiv/ *adj.*

confute /kən fyóot/ (**-futes, -futing, -futed**) *vt.* to prove conclusively that sb is wrong or that sth is false, invalid, or faulty (*formal*) [Early 16thC. From Latin *confutare* 'to restrain, answer conclusively'.] —**confutable** *adj.* —**confuter** *n.*

cong. *abbr.* **1.** POL congress **2.** POL congressional **3.** RELIG congregational

Cong. *abbr.* **1.** POL Congress **2.** POL Congressional **3.** RELIG Congregational

conga /kóng gə/ *n.* **1.** DANCE DONE IN A LINE a Latin American dance in which people form a line and, holding the waist of the person ahead, move three steps forward rhythmically, then kick out a leg **2.** MUSIC FOR CONGA a piece of music to which people dance the conga **3.** = **conga drum** ■ *vi.* (**-gas, -gaing, -gaed**) DANCE to dance the conga [Mid-20thC. Via American Spanish (*danza*) *Conga* 'dance from the Congo' from Spanish *Congo*.]

conga drum *n.* a tall tapering drum, played with both hands and used in Latin American and African music

congé /kón zhay, kón zhay/ (*plural* **-gés**) *n.* **1.** PERMISSION formal permission for sb to leave (*formal*) **2.** LEAVE-TAKING a departure (*formal*) **3.** BOW a formal bow (*formal*) **4.** ARCHIT CONCAVE MOULDING an architectural moulding that is concave in shape [14thC. Via French *congié* from, ultimately, Latin *commeare* 'to come and go'.]

congeal /kən jéel/ (**-geals, -gealing, -gealed**) *vti.* **1.** BECOME OR MAKE LIQUID THICK to become thick and solid or cause a liquid to thicken and solidify **2.** BECOME OR MAKE FIRM to become, or cause to become, firm and strong ○ *Let's act before opposition to our plan congeals.* [14thC. Via French *congeler* from Latin *congelare*, literally 'to freeze together', from *gelu* 'frost' (see GEL).] —**congealer** *n.* —**congealment** *n.*

congelation /kónji láysh'n/ *n.* **1.** SOLIDIFYING OR SOLIDIFIED STATE the process of turning from a liquid into a solid, or the state of being solid as a result of congealing (*formal*) **2.** CONGEALED LIQUID a liquid that has solidified [15thC. Directly or via French from the Latin stem *congelation-*, from *congelare* (see CONGEAL).]

congener /kən jéenər, kónjinər/ *n.* sb or sth that belongs to the same class, group, or type, e.g. an animal or plant of the same genus as another animal or plant, or two elements belonging to the same group [Mid-18thC. Formed from Latin *congenus* 'of the same race', from *genus* 'race' (see GENUS).]

congeneric /kónji nérrik/ *adj.* used to describe organisms belonging to the same class, group, or type —**congenerous** /kon jénnərəss, kən jénnərəss/ *adj.*

congenial /kən jéeni əl/ *adj.* **1.** AGREEABLE pleasant and suitable to sb's character or taste or to a situation ○ *a very congenial atmosphere* **2.** KINDRED OR SIMILAR compatible in tastes, interests, attitudes, or backgrounds **3.** FRIENDLY having an outgoing pleasant character ○ *Her congenial nature makes her well-loved in the town.* [Early 17thC. Formed from Latin *con-* + GENIAL.] —**congeniality** /kən jéeni álləti/ *n.* —**congenially** /kən jéeni əli/ *adv.* —**congenialness** /-ələnəss/ *n.*

congenic /kən jénnik/ *adj.* used to describe animal cells that are genetically identical except for the arrangement of genes in a single restricted chromosome region (**locus**)

congenital /kən jénnit'l/ adj. **1.** MED EXISTING AT BIRTH used to describe an abnormal condition present at birth **2.** INGRAINED IN SB'S CHARACTER firmly established as part of sb's character or beliefs [Late 18thC. Formed from Latin *congenitus*, literally 'born with', from *genitus* 'born' (see GENITAL).] —**congenitally** adv. —**congenitalness** n.

congenital anomaly n. a birth defect (*technical*)

conger eel /kóng gər-/, **conger** n. a large scaleless eel found in temperate and tropical coastal waters of the Atlantic Ocean. Latin name: *Conger oceanicus*.

congeries /kən jéereez, kónjə reez/ (*plural* -ries) n. a collection or assortment of things (*takes a singular verb*) [Mid-16thC. From Latin, 'heap, pile', from *congerere* (see CONGEST).]

congest /kən jést/ (-gests, -gesting, -gested) vti. **1.** BLOCK OR BECOME BLOCKED to overcrowd a street or area, or become overcrowded so that movement is slow or difficult **2.** MED HAVE TOO MUCH FLUID to accumulate an abnormal amount of blood or fluid in an organ or body part, as a result of disease or infection [15thC. From Latin *congest-*, past participle stem of *congerere* 'to collect, heap up', literally 'to carry together', from *gerere* 'to carry' (see GESTURE).] —**congestible** adj. —**congestive** adj.

congested /kən jéstid/ adj. **1.** PACKED WITH TRAFFIC OR PEOPLE overcrowded with traffic or people, making movement slow and difficult **2.** MED CONTAINING TOO MUCH FLUID having an abnormal amount of blood or other fluid in a vessel or organ, as a result of disease or infection

congestion /kən jéschən/ n. **1.** EXCESSIVE TRAFFIC OR PEOPLE a state of overcrowding in a street or other area, making movement slow or difficult **2.** MED ABNORMAL ACCUMULATION OF FLUID the condition of having an abnormal amount of blood or fluid accumulate in an organ or body part, as a result of disease or infection **3.** COMPUT HAVING TOO MUCH INFORMATION TO TRANSFER in computing, a situation that arises when the amount of information to be transferred is greater than the data communication path can carry

congestive heart failure n. a form of heart failure in which the heart is unable to pump away the blood returning to it fast enough, causing congestion in the veins

conglobate /kóng glō bayt/ vti. (-bates, -bating, -bated) MAKE OR BECOME BALL-SHAPED to form or be formed into a globe or ball (*formal*) ■ adj. BALL-SHAPED shaped like a ball (*archaic*) [Mid-17thC. From Latin *conglobat-*, past participle stem of *conglobare* 'to make into a ball', from *globus* 'ball' (source of English *globe*).] —**conglobation** /kóng glō báysh'n/ n.

conglobe /kon glób/ (-globes, -globing, -globed) vti. = **conglobate** v. (*formal*)

conglomerate n. /kən glómmərət/ **1.** BUSINESS BUSINESS ORGANIZATION INVOLVED IN MANY AREAS a large business organization that consists of a number of companies that deal with a variety of different business, manufacturing, or commercial activities **2.** STH MADE BY COMBINING THINGS sth formed from gathering together a number of dissimilar materials or elements **3.** GEOL ROCK COMPRISING PIECES OF OTHER ROCKS coarse-grained sedimentary rock containing fragments of other rock larger than 2 mm/0.08 in diameter, held together with another material such as clay ■ adj. /kən glómmərət/ FORMED BY COMBINING DIFFERENT THINGS consisting of a mass or accumulation of dissimilar materials or elements ■ vti. /kən glómmə rayt/ (-ates, -ating, -ated) BRING THINGS TOGETHER TO FORM MASS to gather together materials or elements, or to be gathered together into a mass [Late 16thC. From Latin *conglomeratus* 'wound into a ball', from *glomer-*, stem of *glomus* 'ball'.] —**conglomeratic** /kən glómmə ráttik/ adj. —**conglomeritic** /-ríttik/ adj. —**conglomerator** /kən glómmə raytər/ n.

conglomerated /kən glómmə raytid/ adj. made up of and controlling many parts of an industry ○ *a conglomerated corporation*

conglomeration /kən glómmə ráysh'n/ n. **1.** MASS OF DIFFERENT THINGS an accumulation or mass of dissimilar materials or elements **2.** FORMATION OF A MASS

the gathering together of different materials or elements, or the state of being gathered together into a mass —**conglomerative** /kən glómmərətiv/ adj.

conglutinate /kən glooti nayt/ (-nates, -nating, -nated) vti. to become stuck together, or cause two or more things to become stuck together (*formal*) [15thC. From Latin *conglutinat-*, past participle stem of *conglutinare* 'to glue together', from *gluten* 'glue' (source of English *glue*).] —**conglutinative** /-nətiv/ adj.

Congo /kóng gō/ Africa's second longest river, which provides a major transportation network. It rises in the north of the Democratic Republic of Congo and empties into the Atlantic Ocean. Length: 4,374 km/2,710 mi. Former name **Zaire River**

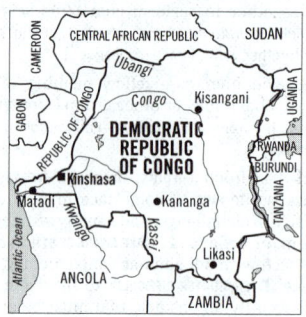

Democratic Republic of Congo

Congo, Democratic Republic of large equatorial country of Central Africa with a coastline on the Atlantic Ocean. Language: French. Currency: new zaire. Capital: Kinshasa. Population: 447,589,551 (1997). Area: 2,344,885 sq. km/905,365 sq. mi. Official name **Democratic Republic of the Congo**. Former name **Congo Free State** (1880s-1908), **Belgian Congo** (1908-60), **Zaire** (1971–97) —**Congolese** /kóng gə léez/ adj., n.

Republic of Congo

Congo, Republic of republic in West Africa, on the coast of the Atlantic Ocean. Language: French. Currency: CFA franc. Capital: Brazzaville. Population: 2,599,713 (1997). Area: 342,000 sq. km/132,000 sq. mi. Former name **People's Republic of the Congo** —**Congolese** /kóng gə léez/ adj., n.

congo dye n. any of a number of dyes containing nitrogen, usually derived from benzidine [*Congo* from the perception that it is associated either with the region of the Congo, or with African Americans from this region]

Congo eel n. an amphibian of the southeastern United States that has a long body with gill slits and two pairs of rudimentary limbs that enable it to travel on land. Latin name: *Amphiuma means*. [As CONGO DYE]

Congo Free State former name for **Congo** [Democratic Republic of]

Congo red n. a dye that is red in alkaline solutions and blue in acid solutions. It is used as a chemical indicator, a biological stain, and a dye for cotton and wool. [As CONGO DYE]

Congo snake n. = **Congo eel**

congou /kóng goo, kóng gō/ n. a fine grade of Chinese black tea, made from the largest leaf gathered from the tip of a shoot on a tea plant [Early 18thC. Shortening of Cantonese Chinese *kungfúch'a* and Mandarin *gōngfu chá* 'tea made for refined tastes', literally 'effort tea'.]

congrats /kən gráts/ npl., interj. an expression of congratulations (*informal*) [Early 20thC. Shortening.]

congratulate /kən gráttyōō layt, -gráchoo-/ (-lates, -lating, -lated) v. **1.** vt. EXPRESS PLEASURE AT SB'S GOOD FORTUNE to express pleasure or approval to sb for an achievement or good fortune or on a special occasion **2.** vr. FEEL PLEASED WITH STH to feel self-satisfied in having success or good fortune ○ *I was congratulating myself on my driving skills, when I skidded into a snow bank.* [Mid-16thC. From Latin *congratulat-*, past participle stem of *congratulari* 'to rejoice with', from *gratus* 'pleasing, thankful' (source of English *grateful*).] —**congratulative** /kən gráttyōōlətiv, -gráchoo-/ adj. —**congratulator** /kən gráttyōō laytər, -gráchoo-/ n. —**congratulatory** /kən gráttyōōlətəri, -gráchoo-/ adj.

congratulation /kən gráttyōō láysh'n, -gráchoo-/ n. ACT OF CONGRATULATING SB the expressing of pleasure to sb for an achievement or good fortune or on a special occasion ○ *The bride's father made a short speech of congratulation to the newly married couple.* ■ npl., interj. **congratulations** EXPRESSION OF JOY FOR SB'S ACHIEVEMENT an expression of pleasure or acknowledgment of sb's success or good fortune or on a special occasion

congregant /kóng grigənt/ n. a member of a religious congregation, especially in a Jewish synagogue [Late 19thC. From Latin *congregant-*, present participle stem of *congregare* (see CONGREGATE).]

congregate vti. /kóng gri gayt/ (-gates, -gating, -gated) ASSEMBLE PEOPLE OR ANIMALS to come together in a group, or gather people or animals together in a group ■ adj. /kóng gri gət, kóng gri gayt/ (*formal*) **1.** HAVING COME TOGETHER gathered or assembled in a group **2.** RELATING TO A GATHERING relating to an assembled group [15thC. From Latin *congregat-*, past participle stem of *congregare* 'to collect together', from *greg-*, stem of *grex* 'flock' (source of English *egregious*).] —**congregative** adj. —**congregator** n.

congregation /kóng gri gáysh'n/ n. **1.** RELIG GROUP OF WORSHIPPERS a group of people who have gathered together for a religious service **2.** RELIG MEMBERS OF SAME CHURCH the members of a particular church **3.** CHR ROMAN CATHOLIC RELIGIOUS BODY a Roman Catholic religious body whose members follow a common rule of life and are bound by simple vows (*formal*) **4.** CHR DIVISION OF ROMAN CATHOLIC CENTRAL ADMINISTRATION a section of the central administrative organization (**Curia**) of the Roman Catholic Church **5.** CHR COMMITTEE OF ROMAN CATHOLIC BISHOPS a committee of Roman Catholic bishops responsible for handling the business of a general council (*formal*) **6.** GATHERING a group of people or things gathered together ○ *A congregation of reporters waited outside the courthouse.* **7.** EDUC SENIOR MEMBERS OF UNIVERSITY STAFF an assembly of the senior members of the academic staff of a university **8.** COMING TOGETHER the act of gathering together or assembling (*formal*) ○ *Congregation in the halls is not allowed.*

congregational /kóng gri gáysh'nəl/ adj. relating to a congregation

Congregational /kóng gri gáysh'nəl/ adj. relating to Congregationalism or its followers

Congregational Church n. a Protestant denomination in which each church is self-governing

congregationalism /kóng gri gáysh'nəlizzəm/ n. a system of church organization in which each church is self-governing —**congregationalist** n., adj.

Congregationalism /kóng gri gáysh'nəlizzəm/ n. a Protestant denomination with a system of government in which each local church governs itself —**Congregationalist** n., adj.

congress /kóng gress/ n. **1.** CONFERENCE OR MEETING OF REPRESENTATIVES a conference or formal meeting of delegates or representatives, such as the representatives of a group of nations, to discuss matters of interest or concern **2.** ORGANIZED GROUP a society or organization of people with common interests and concerns **3.** GATHERING FOR A MEETING the act of meeting, especially a single occurrence for a special purpose (*dated formal*) **4.** SEXUAL INTERCOURSE sexual intercourse (*dated formal*) [15thC. From Latin *congressus*, past participle of *congredi* 'to go together', from *gradi* 'to proceed, step' (source of English *aggressive*).]

Congress *n.* **1.** US PARLIAMENT the national legislative body of the United States, consisting of the House of Representatives and the Senate **2.** SESSION OF CONGRESS OR ITS MEMBERS a two-year term of the US Congress, or the members of Congress during such a term ○ *the 22nd Congress* **3.** GOVERNING AND LAW-MAKING BODY the governing and law-making body in some countries ○ *the National People's Congress* **4.** NAME OF CERTAIN POLITICAL PARTIES shortened name of a number of political parties whose name includes the word 'Congress', e.g. the African National Congress or the Indian Congress Party

congressional /kən grésh'nəl/ *adj.* relating to a congress —**congressionalist** *n.* —**congressionally** *adv.*

Congressional /kən grésh'nəl/ *adj.* relating to the US Congress or its members

congressional district *n.* a district within a US state that is entitled to elect one representative to the House of Representatives

Congressional Medal of Honor *n.* the highest military decoration in the United States, awarded by Congress for outstanding bravery in action

Congressional Record *n.* a government journal in the United States that records and publishes the proceedings of Congress

congressman /kóng gressmən/ (*plural* **-men** /-mən/) *n.* a man who is a member of the US Congress, especially of the House of Representatives

Congress of Industrial Organizations *n.* a federation of industrial trades unions formed in the United States in 1935 and merged with the American Federation of Labor in 1955 to form the AFL-CIO

Congress of Vienna *n.* a congress held in Vienna between 1814 and 1815 to deal with the territorial and jurisdictional problems remaining after the defeat of Napoleon in the Napoleonic Wars

congressperson /kóng gress purs'n/ (*plural* **-people** /-peep'l/) *n.* a member of the US Congress, especially of the House of Representatives

congresswoman /kóng gress wo͝omən/ (*plural* **-en** /-wimin/) *n.* a woman who is a member of the US Congress, especially of the House of Representatives

Congreve /kóng greev/, **William** (1670–1729) English playwright and poet. He wrote*The Double Dealer* (1693), *Love for Love* (1695) and *The Way of the World* (1700).

congruence /kóng groo ənss/ *n.* **1.** AGREEMENT a coinciding, agreeing, or being in harmony **2.** MATH STATEMENT ABOUT NUMBERS OR GEOMETRICAL SHAPES a statement that two quantities or geometrical structures are congruent

congruent /kóng groo ənt/ *adj.* **1.** IN AGREEMENT corresponding to or consistent with each other or sth else (*formal*) ○ *We receive congruent sensations from the world around us.* **2.** GEOM WITH THE SAME SHAPE with identical geometric shapes **3.** MATH DIFFERING BY EXACTLY DIVISIBLE AMOUNT used to describe two numbers whose difference is exactly divisible by a third number (**modulus**) [15thC. From Latin *congruent-*, present participle stem of *congruere* 'to meet together, agree', from *ruere* 'to fall'.] —**congruently** *adv.*

congruity /kən gro͞o əti/ *n.* (*formal*) **1.** AGREEMENT OR CONSISTENCY the state or fact of agreeing or being consistent with each other or with sth else **2.** APPROPRIATENESS the quality or fact of being suitable or appropriate for sth

congruous /kóng groo əss/ *adj.* **1.** APPROPRIATE appropriate to or suitable for a particular thing or situation (*formal*) **2.** CORRESPONDING OR CONSISTENT corresponding to or consistent with each other or sth else [Late 16thC. Formed from Latin *congruus* 'agreeing, suitable', from *congruere* (see CONGRUENT).] —**congruously** *adv.* —**congruousness** *n.*

conic /kónnik/ *adj.* = **conical** ■ *n.* = **conic section** [Late 16thC. Via modern Latin *conicus* from Greek *kōniko*, from *kōnos* (see CONE).]

conical /kónnik'l/ *adj.* **1.** CONE-SHAPED shaped like a cone **2.** GEOM OF A CONE relating to or having the form of a geometrical cone

conic projection *n.* a method of making a map by projecting the globe onto a surrounding cone whose point is above one of the poles and then flattening the cone, or a map so made. On a conic projection, the parallels of latitude appear as concentric circles, and the lines of longitude radiate from the centre as equal radii.

conics /kónniks/ *n.* the branch of geometry involving the study of conic sections

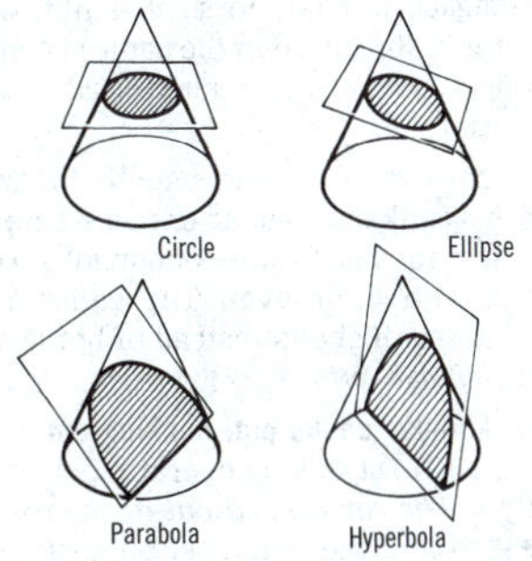

Conic section

conic section *n.* a curve produced by the intersection of a plane with a circular cone, e.g. a circle, ellipse, hyperbola, or parabola

conidia plural of **conidium**

conidiophore /kō níddi ə fawr/ *n.* a simple or branched part (**hypha**) of a fungus that produces spores asexually [Late 19thC. Coined from CONIDIUM + -PHORE.] —**conidiophorous** /kō níddi óffərəss/ *adj.*

conidium /kō níddi əm/ (*plural* **-a** /-ə/) *n.* an asexually produced spore of certain types of fungi [Late 19thC. From modern Latin, from Greek *konis* 'dust'.] —**conidial** *adj.*

conifer /kónnifər, kṓnifər/ *n.* any tree that has thin leaves (**needles**) and produces cones. Many types are evergreen. Pines, firs, junipers, larches, spruces, and yews are conifers. Order: Coniferales. [Mid-19thC. From Latin, literally 'cone-bearing', from Greek *kōnos* 'cone'.] —**coniferous** /kə nífərəs/ *adv.*

coniine /kṓni een, kō neen/ *n.* a colourless substance with poisonous properties found in hemlock. Formula: $C_8H_{17}N$. [Mid-19thC. Coined from *conium* 'hemlock' from Latin+ -ine.]

Coniston Water /kónnistən-/ lake in southern Cumbria, England, where several water speed records have been set. Area: 7 sq. km/2.75 sq. mi. Depth: 56 m/184 ft.

conj. *abbr.* **1.** GRAM conjugation **2.** ASTRON, GRAM conjunction **3.** GRAM conjunctive

conjectural /kən jékchərəl/ *adj.* **1.** BASED ON GUESSWORK based on or involving conjecture **2.** INCLINED TO SPECULATE inclined to make guesses or speculations —**conjecturally** *adv.*

conjecture /kən jékchər/ *n.* **1.** GUESSWORK the formation of judgments or opinions on the basis of incomplete or inconclusive information **2.** STH BASED ON GUESSWORK a conclusion, judgment, or statement based on incomplete or inconclusive information ■ *vti.* (**-tures, -turing, -tured**) GUESS to form an opinion or judgment based on incomplete or inconclusive information [14thC. Directly or via French from Latin *conjectura*, from, ultimately, *conjicere*, literally 'to throw together', from *jacere* 'to throw'.] —**conjecturable** *adj.* —**conjecturably** *adv.* —**conjecturer** *n.*

conjoin /kən jóyn/ (**-joins, -joining, -joined**) *vti.* to join two or more things together, or become joined together (*formal*) [14thC. Via French *conjoindre* from Latin *conjungere*, literally 'to join together', from *jungere* 'to join' (see JOIN).] —**conjoiner** *n.*

conjoint /kən jóynt/ *adj.* **1.** BY TWO COMBINED THINGS done by, involving, or relating to two or more combined entities ○ *a conjoint project* **2.** LINKED joined together or combined —**conjointly** *adv.*

conjugal /kónjo͝og'l/ *adj.* relating to marriage or to husbands and wives [Early 16thC. From Latin *conjugalis*, from *conjugare* (see CONJUGATE).] —**conjugality** /kónjo͝o gálləti/ *n.* —**conjugally** /kónjo͝ogəli/ *adv.*

conjugal rights *npl.* the rights that husbands or wives are entitled to in a marriage, especially the right to have sexual relations with their spouse

conjugal visit *n.* a visit to a jail by the husband or wife of a prisoner, during which the couple is allowed some privacy, e.g. to allow them to have sexual relations

conjugant /kónjo͝ogənt/ *n.* either of a pair of organisms, cells, or gametes in the process of reproducing [Early 20thC. From Latin *conjugant-*, present participle stem of *conjugare* (see CONJUGATE).]

conjugate *v.* /kónjo͝o gayt/ (**-gates, -gating, -gated**) **1.** *vti.* GRAM STATE DIFFERENT GRAMMATICAL FORMS OF VERB to state systematically the different forms a verb has according to tense, mood, person, and number **2.** *vi.* GRAM HAVE DIFFERENT GRAMMATICAL FORMS to have different grammatical forms according to tense, mood, number, and person (*refers to verbs*) **3.** *vt.* CHEM JOIN SUBSTANCES to join two substances together in such a way that they can easily be separated again, especially in chemical reactions **4.** *vi.* BIOL REPRODUCE to reproduce by physically joining in order to transfer genetic information (*refers to organisms that normally reproduce by division*) ■ *adj.* /kónjo͝ogət, kónjo͝o gayt/ **1.** CHEM EXISTING TOGETHER IN STATE OF EQUILIBRIUM used to describe a state of chemical equilibrium in which two liquids coexist in separate forms, one being the solute and the other the solvent **2.** CHEM DIFFERING BY ONE PROTON used to describe substances that have such similar molecular structures that one becomes the other through the gain or loss of a proton **3.** MATH ADDING UP TO 360 DEGREES used to describe a pair of angles that together add up to 360 degrees **4.** PAIRED joined together in pairs (*formal*) ■ *n.* /kónjo͝o gət/ **1.** GRAM VERB FORM one of the different forms of a verb according to tense, mood, person, or number **2.** RESULT OF JOINING TWO THINGS a product of joining or union **3.** MATH = **conjugate complex number** [15thC. From Latin *conjugatus*, past participle of *conjugare*, literally 'to yoke together', hence 'to marry'. The grammatical sense comes from the idea of a set of verbs belonging together.] —**conjugable** /kónjo͝ogəb'l/ *adj.* —**conjugately** /kónjo͝ogitli, -gaytli/ *adv.* —**conjugateness** /-gətnəss, -gaytnəss/ *n.* —**conjugative** /-gətiv, -gaytiv/ *adj.* —**conjugator** /-gaytər/ *n.*

conjugate complex number *n.* either of a pair of complex numbers that are symmetrically located on either side of an x-axis, differing only in the sign of the imaginary component

conjugated /kónjo͝o gaytid/ *adj.* **1.** CONTAINING ALTERNATING CHEMICAL BONDS containing two or more double or triple bonds in alternation with single bonds **2.** SEPARATED BY SINGLE CHEMICAL BOND used to describe a double chemical bond separated by a single bond

conjugated protein *n.* a compound containing a series of amino acids that form a simple protein attached to a nonprotein, e.g. a carbohydrate or lipid group

conjugation /kónjo͝o gáysh'n/ *n.* **1.** GRAM INFLECTION OF VERB the different patterns of inflection of a given verb **2.** GRAM GROUP OF VERBS WITH SAME INFLECTIONS a group of verbs that use the same patterns of inflection **3.** GRAM SET OF VERB INFLECTIONS the complete set of inflections for a given verb **4.** ACT OF JOINING TOGETHER the act of joining together or uniting, or the state of being joined together **5.** BIOL REPRODUCTION IN SIMPLE ORGANISMS the simplest form of reproduction, in which two single-celled organisms, e.g. bacteria or protozoans, link together, exchange genetic information, and then separate **6.** BIOL FUSION OF NUCLEI the fusion of the nuclei of a male and a female gamete in algae and fungi **7.** GENETICS PAIRING OF CHROMOSOMES the distribution of pairs of chromosomes into the four nuclei produced by the division of a parent nucleus **8.** CHEM ALTERNATION OF NUMBER OF BONDS the occurrence of two or more double or triple bonds in alternation with single bonds in a molecule —**conjugational** *adj.* —**conjugationally** *adv.*

conjunct /kón jungkt/ *adj.* **1.** ATTACHED OR JOINED attached or joined very close to sth **2.** LING ADJACENT TO CONSONANT used to describe consonants that are next to each other within a word without a vowel or vowels between **3.** MUSIC CONSISTING OF SINGLE STEPS IN SCALE relating to or consisting of adjacent notes in a musical scale ■ *n.* LOGIC EITHER PROPOSITION IN CONJUNCTION either of the two propositions or formulas in a conjunction in logic [15thC. From Latin *conjunctus*, the past participle of *conjungere* (see CONJOIN).] —**conjunctly** *adv.*

conjunction /kən júngksh'n/ *n.* **1.** COMBINING OF SEVERAL THINGS the joining together or combining of two or more things **2.** SIMULTANEOUS OCCURRENCE a simultaneous occurrence of events or circumstances **3.** GRAM CONNECTING WORD a word that is used to link sentences, clauses, phrases, or words, e.g. 'and', 'but', or 'if' **4.** ASTRON ALIGNMENT WITH SUN the position of a planet or the Moon when aligned with the Sun, as seen from Earth **5.** ASTRON CLOSE PROXIMITY OF PLANETS the appearance of two planets very close to each other or in the same place on the celestial sphere **6.** ASTROL ASPECT OF 0° BETWEEN PLANETS in astrology, an aspect of 0° between two planets **7.** LOGIC TYPE OF COMPOUND STATEMENT a proposition in logic of the form 'A and B' that is true only if both A and B are true [14thC. From the Latin stem *conjunction-*, from *conjunct-*, the past participle stem of *conjungere* (see CONJOIN).] —**conjunctional** *adj.* —**conjunctionally** *adv.* ◇ **in conjunction with** together with or combined with sth

conjunctiva /kón jungk tívə/ (*plural* **-vas** *or* **-vae** /-vee/) *n.* a delicate mucous membrane that covers the internal part of the eyelid and is attached to the cornea [14thC. From medieval Latin *(tunica) conjunctiva* 'connective (membrane)', from Latin *conjunct-*, the past participle stem of *conjungere* (see CONJOIN).] —**conjunctival** *adj.*

conjunctive /kən júngktiv/ *adj.* **1.** CONNECTIVE serving to join things together **2.** COMBINED joined together or combined with sth else **3.** GRAM OF GRAMMATICAL CONJUNCTIONS relating to conjunctions or their grammatical function, or consisting of conjunctions ■ *n.* GRAM CONJUNCTION a conjunction (*archaic*) [15thC. From late Latin *conjunctivus*, from Latin *conjunct-*, the past participle stem of *conjungere* (see CONJOIN).] —**conjunctively** *adv.*

conjunctive eye movement *n.* a simultaneous movement of both eyes in the same direction

conjunctivitis /kən júngkti vítiss/ *n.* inflammation of the conjunctiva caused by infection, injury, or allergy

conjuration /kónjoo ráysh'n/ *n.* **1.** MAGIC SPELL a word or phrase that a magician says when casting a spell (*literary*) **2.** INVOCATION OF SUPERNATURAL FORCE a summoning or invoking, usually of a supernatural force, by pronouncing a sacred name (*literary*) **3.** MAGIC TRICK a magic or supernatural occurrence achieved by pronouncing a spell or chanting **4.** PERFORMANCE OF TRICKS the performance of illusions or tricks (*archaic*) **5.** BEGGING pleading or begging (*archaic*)

conjure /kúnjər/ (**-jures, -juring, -jured**) *v.* **1.** *vi.* PERFORM MAGIC TRICKS to perform illusions and magic tricks that require agile hand movements, usually for entertainment **2.** *vti.* INVOKE SUPERNATURAL FORCES to call upon or order a supernatural force or being by reciting a spell ○ *He was struck dumb by the very demons he was conjuring.* **3.** *vt.* INFLUENCE WITH SPELL to change or influence sth by reciting a spell or invocation **4.** *vt.* IMPLORE to implore sb to do sth (*archaic*) ○ *I conjure you to show me mercy.* **5.** *vt.* COMMAND SOLEMNLY to command sb solemnly to do sth (*archaic*) [13thC. Via Old French from, ultimately, Latin *conjurare* 'to bind with an oath', literally 'to swear together', from *jurare* (see JURY).] ◇ **a name to conjure with** a person or organization considered to be influential, powerful, or extremely famous

conjure up *vt.* **1.** EVOKE to create sth in the mind ○ *This music conjures up images of rural scenes.* **2.** PRODUCE AS IF BY MAGIC to produce or create sth difficult or unexpected as if by magic ○ *She conjured up a delicious meal from the most basic ingredients.* **3.** SUMMON SUPERNATURAL BEING to call upon a supernatural force or being by reciting a spell or chanting magic words

conjurer /kúnjərər/, **conjuror** *n.* **1.** ENTERTAINER WHO PERFORMS TRICKS sb who performs tricks involving manual agility and the illusion of magic, as an entertainment **2.** SORCERER sb who is believed to practise magic or conjure supernatural forces or beings

conjuring /kúnjəring/ *n.* the performance of tricks that involve manual agility or the illusion of magic, as an entertainment

conjuror *n.* = **conjurer**

conk /kongk/ *n.* (*slang*) **1.** HEAD OR NOSE the head or the nose **2.** BLOW TO THE HEAD a blow, especially on the head or, less commonly, the nose ■ *vt.* (**conks, conking, conked**) HIT ON HEAD OR NOSE to hit sb, especially on the head or nose (*slang*) [Early 19thC. Origin uncertain: possibly an alteration of CONCH.]

conker /kóngkər/ *n.* *UK* a horse chestnut, without its spiny outer casing, used in the game of conkers [Mid-19thC. Origin uncertain: apparently a blend of CONCH, CONK, and CONQUER.]

conkers /kóngkərz/ *n.* a game, usually for two people, each with a conker threaded onto a string, in which players try to smash the opponent's conker by hitting it with their own. The game used to be played with snail shells instead of horse chestnuts. (*takes a singular verb*)

conk out /kongk/ (**conks out, conking out, conked out**) *vi.* (*informal*) **1.** FAIL to stop operating or break down suddenly ○ *The car conked out at the traffic lights.* **2.** COLLAPSE to collapse or fall asleep, usually through exhaustion ○ *I conked out the minute I got home.* [Early 20thC. Origin unknown.]

con man (*plural* **con men**) *n.* sb who uses deception and persuasive speech to get people to part with their money (*informal*) [*Con* shortening of CONFIDENCE, shortening of CONFIDENCE MAN]

con moto /kon mṓt ō/ *adv.* to be performed in a lively or brisk way (*used as a musical direction*) [Early 19thC. From Italian, literally 'with movement'.]

Connacht /kónnət, -nəkht/ area comprising the counties of Galway, Leitrim, Mayo, Roscommon and Sligo on the western coast of the Republic of Ireland. Population: 423,031 (1991). Area: 17,122 sq. km/6,611 sq. mi. Also spelled **Connaught**

connate /kónn ayt/ *adj.* **1.** BOT UNITED BY GROWTH used to describe parts that have grown closely joined to a single structure in a plant or animal **2.** GEOL FORMED SIMULTANEOUSLY WITH SURROUNDING ROCK used to describe water, usually very saline, that has been trapped in sedimentary rock since the original deposits were laid down [Mid-17thC. From late Latin *connatus*, the past participle of *connasci*, literally 'to be born with', from Latin *nasci* (see NATIVE).] —**connately** *adv.* —**connateness** *n.*

connect /kə nékt/ (**-nects, -necting, -nected**) *v.* **1.** *vti.* LINK TWO THINGS to link or join two or more parts, things, or people together ○ *All you have to do is connect these two wires, and it should work.* ○ *A flagstone walk connected the main house with the toolshed.* **2.** *vt.* ASSOCIATE WITH STH ELSE to make a psychological or emotional association between people, things, or events ○ *She always connected that house with family celebrations.* ○ *There was no evidence to connect them to the robbery.* **3.** *vt.* TELECOM ESTABLISH TELECOMMUNICATION to set up a communication link between people, organizations, or places ○ *All my friends are connected to the Internet.* **4.** *vt.* PUBL LINK UP TO UTILITY to link people or equipment to a source of electricity, water, or gas ○ *Have the gas board connected you yet?* ○ *The appliance should not be connected to the mains.* **5.** *vi.* TRANSP ALLOW TIME FOR PASSENGERS TO TRANSFER to arrive shortly before another vehicle or vessel departs, or shortly after another arrives, so as to allow passengers to change from one to the other ○ *This train connects with another one going to the city centre.* **6.** *vi.* TRANSP MAKE TRANSPORT CONNECTION to change from one vehicle or vessel to another ○ *those wishing to connect to a long-haul flight* **7.** *vi.* HIT STH FIRMLY to strike, punch, or kick firmly, with good contact between the striking surface and the object struck (*informal*) ○ *The punch connected, and he sank to the ground.* **8.** *vi.* GET ON WELL WITH SB to have a good rapport with sb ○ *The interview was a disaster – we never really connected.* [15thC. From Latin *connectere*, literally 'to tie together', from *nectere* (see NEXUS).] —**connectible** *adj.*

connect up *vti.* = **connect**

connected /kə néktid/ *adj.* **1.** JOINED TOGETHER joined or linked firmly together **2.** WITH WEALTHY RELATIVES with upper-class or wealthy relatives (*often used in combination*) ○ *Her husband is well connected.* **3.** WITH BENEFICIAL SOCIAL CONNECTIONS with useful business or social connections (*often used in combination*) **4.** LOGICAL AND INTELLIGIBLE ordered in a logical and intelligible way **5.** MATH DESCRIBING MATHEMATICAL RELATION used to describe a mathematical relation for which either the relation or its converse is true for any two members in a set —**connectedly** *adv.* —**connectedness** *n.*

connecter *n.* = **connector**

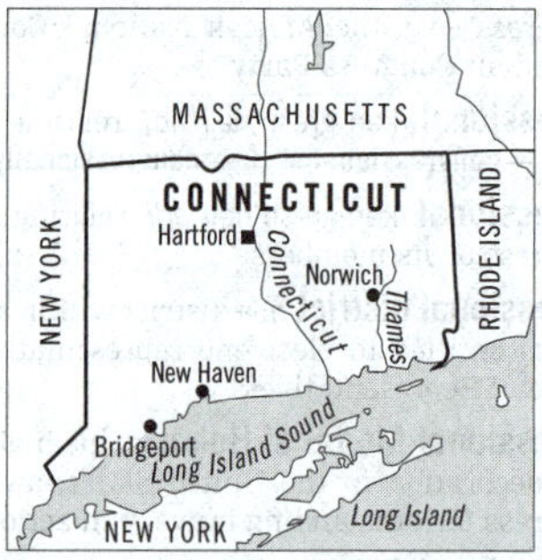

Connecticut

Connecticut /kə néttikət/ **1.** southernmost state in New England, US. It is bordered on the north by Massachusetts, on the east by Rhode Island, on the south by the Long Island Sound, and on the west by New York State. Population: 3,287,116 (1990). Area: 14,359 sq. km/5,544 sq. mi. **2.** longest river of New England, flowing southwards from Massachusetts to enter Long Island Sound. Length: 655 km/407 mi.

connecting rod *n.* a rod that transmits motion, especially the rod that connects the crankshaft to the piston in an internal combustion engine

connection /kə néksh'n/, **connexion** *n.* **1.** LINKING THINGS TOGETHER the linking or joining of two or more parts, things, or people **2.** PHYSICAL LINK sth that links two or more things ○ *check for a loose connection* **3.** LOGICAL LINK a linking association between people, things, or events **4.** CONTEXT the relationship of sth with its context ○ *In this connection, we need to tighten up safety procedures in general.* **5.** INFLUENTIAL CONTACT a friend, relative, or associate who either has or has access to influence or power (*often used in the plural*) ○ *She used her connections to wangle an interview with the lead singer.* **6.** RELATION sb who is related to another person, usually distantly or by marriage (*often used in the plural*) ○ *The family's English but they have Spanish connections.* **7.** TRANSPORT LINK an opportunity for passengers to use any of a variety of transport options, or to change from one form of transport to another ○ *If we don't hurry, we'll miss our connection in Paris.* **8.** VEHICLE SCHEDULED TO PERMIT TRANSFER a particular bus, train, ferry, or plane that is scheduled to arrive at such a time as to allow passengers to transfer onto it from another scheduled form of transport ○ *Your connection will arrive on platform ten at 9.15.* **9.** COMMUNICATION LINK a communication link, especially between telephones **10.** SUPPLIER OF ILLEGAL SUBSTANCES a supplier of illegal substances, usually drugs (*slang*) ■ **connections** *npl.* CONTROLLERS OF A RACEHORSE the owners or controllers of a racehorse [14thC. From the Latin stem *connexion-*, from *connex-*, the past participle stem of *connectere* (see CONNECT). The spelling was influenced by CONNECT.] —**connectional** *adj.*

connective /kə néktiv/ *adj.* LINKING linking or joining two or more parts, things, or people ■ *n.* **1.** LINK sth that links or joins two or more parts, things, or people **2.** LING LINKING WORD a word that links sentences, phrases, clauses, or words **3.** BOT STAMEN TISSUE the tissue that joins the two lobes of an anther in the stamen of a plant —**connectively** *adv.*

connective tissue *n.* animal tissue that supports, connects, and surrounds organs and other body parts. It may consist mainly of collagen, elastic and reticular fibres, fatty tissue, cartilage, or bone.

connectivity /kónn ek tívvəti/ *n.* the ability to connect with sth, especially to communicate with another machine, e.g. a computer or computer system

connector /kə néktər/, **connecter** n. sth that connects things, especially two pieces of equipment, or components of a single device or structure

connect-the-dots adj. US (slang) **1.** BUSINESS SKILFULLY ASSEMBLED gathering information or facts from different sources to make a coherent whole ○ *The article was a model of connect-the-dots journalism.* **2.** EASY TO DO straightforward or obvious ○ *It's a connect-the-dots problem, easily solvable.* [From the method of producing a picture by connecting printed dots in order to form its outline]

connect time n. the period of time a user is logged on to a remote computer, e.g. when browsing the Internet

Connemara /kónnə maàrə/ mountainous coastal area of Galway in the west of the Republic of Ireland

Connery /kónnəri/, **Sean** (b. 1930) Scottish film actor. He played the starring role in several James Bond films and won an Academy Award for best supporting actor for *The Untouchables* (1987). Full name **Thomas Sean Connery**

connexion n. = connection

conning tower n. **1.** SUBMARINE CONTROL DECK a structure on the top of a submarine that is used as the navigation bridge and main point of entrance **2.** ARMOURED PILOT HOUSE the armoured pilot house in the shape of a low dome found on the deck of a warship [Formed from CONN]

conniption /kə nípsh'n/ n. US a hysterical fit caused by extreme excitement or anger (*informal*) (*often used in the plural*) [Mid-19thC. Origin unknown.]

connivance /kə nívənss/ n. **1.** SECRET PLOTTING secret joint conspiracy or plotting **2.** TACIT ENCOURAGEMENT OF WRONGDOING unspoken encouragement of, or consent to, sb else's wrongdoing

connive /kə nív/ (-nives, -niving, -nived) vi. **1.** PLOT to plan secretly to do sth, usually sth wrong or illegal **2.** GIVE TACIT CONSENT TO STH WRONG to pretend not to know about or do nothing to stop a wrongful or illegal act, thus showing encouragement of or consent to the act ○ *suspected of conniving in the leaking of a sensitive document* [Early 17thC. Via French from Latin *connivere* 'to close your eyes', (related to *nictare* 'to wink', the source of English *nictitate*).] —**conniver** n. —**connivery** n.

connivent /kə nív'nt/ adj. used to describe insect wings and flower petals or stamens that converge and touch but remain separate and not fused

conniving /kə nívíng/ adj. devious and scheming —**connivingly** adv.

connoisseur /kónnə súr/ n. sb who has specialist knowledge of or training in a particular field of the fine or domestic arts, or whose taste in such a field is considered to be discriminating [Early 18thC. From French, formed from *connoistre* 'to know', from Latin *cognoscere* (see COGNITION).]

Connolly /kónnəli/, **Maureen** (1934–69) US tennis player. She was the first woman to win all four grand slam tournaments in one year (1953). Full name **Maureen Catherine Connolly.** Known as **Little Mo**

Connors /kónnərs/, **Jimmy** (b. 1952) US tennis player. He won 109 professional singles titles, including eight grand slam tournaments, during the 1970s and 1980s. Full name **James Scott Connors.** Known as **Jimbo**

connotation /kónnə táysh'n/ n. **1.** IMPLIED ADDITIONAL MEANING an additional sense or senses associated with or suggested by a word or phrase. Connotations are sometimes, but not always, fixed, and are often subjective. ○ *Patriotism has different connotations for different people.* **2.** SUGGESTING MEANING FOR WORD the implying or suggesting of an additional meaning for a word or phrase apart from the explicit meaning **3.** DEFINING CHARACTERISTIC in logic, the characteristic or set of characteristics that makes up the meaning of a term and thus defines the objects to which a term can be applied —**connotative** /kónnə taytiv, kə nótətiv/ adj. —**connotatively** /kónnə taytivli/ adv.

connote /kə nót/ (-notes, -noting, -noted) vt. **1.** HAVE AS ADDITIONAL IMPLIED MEANING to imply or suggest sth in addition to the main or literal meaning ○ *The word 'hearth' often connotes cosiness and warmth.* **2.** IMPLY STH ELSE to mean that sth else is necessarily either a condition or a consequence ○ *His reluctance to act connotes cowardice.* [Mid-17thC. From medieval Latin *connotare*, literally 'to mark along with', from Latin *notare* 'to mark', from *nota* 'sign' (source of English *note* and *annotate*).]

connubial /kə nyoóbi əl/ adj. dealing with or relating to marriage (*formal*) [Mid-17thC. From Latin *connubialis* 'concerning marriage', from *connubium* 'marriage', from *nubere* 'to marry' (source of English *nubile* and *nuptial*).] —**connubially** adv.

conodont /kónə dont, kónnə-/ n. a very small tooth-shaped fossil thought to be the remains of a marine organism. Conodonts are commonly found in marine limestone beds from the Palaeozoic era and are used by geologists to date rock layers. [Mid-19thC. Coined from Greek *kōnos* 'cone' + -DONT.]

conquer /kóngkər/ (-quers, -quering, -quered) v. **1.** vt. SEIZE AREA BY MILITARY FORCE to take control of a place by force of arms ○ *The Normans conquered England in 1066.* **2.** vt. DEFEAT PEOPLE IN WAR to win a victory over a people in war **3.** vt. MASTER STH DIFFICULT to overcome or gain control of sth that is difficult to overcome ○ *the first woman to conquer Everest* ○ *conquered inflation by controlling public expenditure* **4.** vt. WIN SB'S ADMIRATION to win sb's love, affection, or admiration, often through strength of character or seduction, and sometimes somewhat against the person's will ○ *By the end of the last song, she had conquered their hearts.* **5.** vi. WIN to be victorious [13thC. Via Old French *conquerre* from assumed Vulgar Latin *conquaerere*, literally 'to seek diligently', from *quaerere* (see QUERY).] —**conquerable** adj.

— **WORD KEY: SYNONYMS** —
See Synonyms at **defeat**.

— **WORD KEY: CULTURAL NOTE** —
She Stoops to Conquer, a play by Oliver Goldsmith (1773). An enduringly popular comedy of manners, it is the story of a shy young gent, Marlow, who reluctantly travels to the country to woo a young woman. Mistaking her home for an inn, he assumes she is the maid, treats her accordingly, and wins her heart with his frankness.

conqueror /kóngkərər/ n. **1.** VICTOR OVER ENEMY sb who has enjoyed great success at war and has defeated an enemy or enemies **2.** VICTOR IN CONTEST sb who has beaten an opponent in a contest

conquest /kóng kwest/ n. **1.** SUBJUGATION OF ENEMY AFTER FIGHTING taking control of a place or people by force of arms **2.** STH ACQUIRED BY CONQUERING sth that has been acquired through force of arms, e.g. land, people, or goods **3.** ADMIRER GAINED BY PERSISTENT ATTENTION sb whose love, affection, or admiration has been won, often through strength of character or seduction, and sometimes somewhat against the person's will ○ *boasting about his conquests* [13thC. Via Old French from assumed Vulgar Latin *conquaesita*, the feminine past participle of *conquaerere* (see CONQUER).]

conquistador /kon kwístə dawr/ (*plural* **-dors** *or* **-dores** /-dáwr ayz/) n. a Spanish conqueror or adventurer, especially one of those who conquered Mexico, Peru, and Central America in the 16th century [Mid-19thC. Via Spanish from, ultimately, Latin *conquirere* 'to conquer'.]

AKG London
Joseph Conrad

Conrad /kónn rad/, **Joseph** (1857–1924) Polish-born British writer. His novels and stories include *Nos-*
tromo (1904), *Lord Jim* (1900), and *Heart of Darkness* (1902).

Conran /kónnrən/, **Sir Terence** (b. 1931) British designer and retailer. The opening of his first Habitat shop in 1964 marked a significant change in British attitudes to design and the marketing of household wares. Full name **Terence Orby Conran**

cons. abbr. **1.** consigned **2.** consignment **3.** consecrated **4.** consonant **5.** cons., cons constitution **6.** constitutional

Cons. abbr. **1.** Conservative **2.** Constable **3.** Cons Constitution **4.** Consul

consanguineous /kón sang gwínni əss/, **consanguine** /kon sáng gwin/ adj. descended from the same family or ancestors [Early 17thC. Formed from Latin *consanguineus*, literally 'of the same blood', from *sanguineus* (see SANGUINE).] —**consanguineously** adv.

consanguinity /kón sang gwínnəti/ n. **1.** RELATIONSHIP BY BLOOD relationship by descent from the same ancestor, rather than by marriage or affinity **2.** CLOSE CONNECTION a close relationship or connection

conscience /kónsh'nss/ n. **1.** SENSE OF RIGHT AND WRONG the internal sense of what is right and wrong that governs sb's thoughts and actions, urging him or her to do right rather than wrong ○ *Let your conscience be your guide.* **2.** OBEDIENCE TO CONSCIENCE behaviour in compliance with what your internal sense of right and wrong tells you is right ○ *a person of strict conscience* **3.** SHARED MORAL VIEWPOINT a shared concern for moral issues ○ *a social conscience* **4.** PSYCHOANAL PART OF SUPEREGO the part of the superego that passes judgments on thought and behaviour to the ego for further consideration [13thC. Via Old French from Latin *conscientia* 'consciousness', from *conscire* 'to be conscious', literally 'to know thoroughly', from *scire* (see SCIENCE).] ◇ **in (all) (good) conscience 1.** while being fair and reasonable **2.** used to emphasize that what you are saying is truly the case ◇ **on sb's conscience** causing sb to feel guilty or anxious about sth

conscience clause n. a clause in an act, law, or contract that exempts those who have moral or religious objections from complying

conscience money n. money paid voluntarily in compensation for a previous act of wrongdoing by which sb has been harmed

conscience-stricken, **conscience-smitten**, **conscience stricken**, **conscience smitten** adj. feeling guilty or anxious about having done sth wrong

conscientious /kónshi énshəss/ adj. **1.** PAINSTAKING thorough and diligent in performing a task **2.** IN ACCORDANCE WITH SB'S CONSCIENCE governed by or done according to sb's sense of right and wrong ○ *a conscientious decision to dedicate an hour a week to charity* [Early 17thC. Via French *consciencieux* from, ultimately, Latin *conscientia* (see CONSCIENCE).] —**conscientiously** adv. —**conscientiousness** n.

— **WORD KEY: SYNONYMS** —
See Synonyms at **careful**.

conscientious objector n. sb who, for moral or religious reasons, believes it is wrong to wage war and therefore refuses to join any branch of the armed services

conscionable /kónsh'nəb'l/ adj. acceptable according to sb's conscience (*archaic*) [Mid-16thC. Formed from *conscions*, a variant of CONSCIENCE.] —**conscionableness** n. —**conscionably** adv.

conscious /kónshəss/ adj. **1.** AWAKE awake and responsive to stimuli ○ *He's been seriously injured but he's still conscious.* **2.** KEENLY AWARE OF STH aware of sth, and attaching importance to it ○ *I'm conscious of all that you've done for us.* **3.** CONSIDERED AND DELIBERATE considered and deliberate, or done with critical awareness ○ *a conscious effort not to lose her temper* **4.** AWARE AND WELL-INFORMED aware of issues relating to a particular topic of serious significance (*often used in combination with adverbs*) ○ *environmentally conscious* **5.** CONCERNED WITH STH aware of and interested in a specified topic (*used hyphenated in combination with nouns*) ○ *fashion-conscious* **6.** PSYCHOL FUNCTIONING WITH INDIVIDUAL'S KNOWLEDGE concerned with or relating to a part of the mind that is capable of thinking, choosing, or perceiving ■ *n.* PSYCHOL **AREA OF MIND AWARE OF SURROUNDINGS** the part of the human mind that is aware of the feelings, thoughts, and surroundings [Late 16thC. From Latin *conscius* 'knowing', from *scire* (see SCIENCE).] —**consciously** *adv.*

WORD KEY: SYNONYMS

See Synonyms at ***aware***.

consciousness /kónshəssnəss/ *n.* **1. BEING AWAKE AND AWARE OF SURROUNDINGS** the state of being awake and aware of what is going on around you **2. SB'S MIND** sb's mind and thoughts ○ *In time, this experience will fade from your consciousness.* **3. SHARED FEELINGS AND BELIEFS** the set of opinions, feelings, and beliefs of a group **4. BEING AWARE OF SPECIFIC ISSUES** awareness of or sensitivity to issues in a particular field

consciousness-raising *n.* **1. IMPROVING GROUP UNDERSTANDING OF ISSUE** the aim of increasing people's awareness of a moral or social issue with a view to encouraging them to take action **2. INCREASING SELF-AWARENESS** increasing self-awareness, usually through group therapy —**consciousness-raiser** *n.*

conscript *vt.* /kən skrípt/ (**-scripts, -scripting, -scripted**) **COMPEL TO DO MILITARY SERVICE** to enrol sb compulsorily in the armed forces or for military service ■ *n.* /kón skript/ **MILITARY RECRUIT** sb who has been enrolled compulsorily for service, usually in the armed forces [15thC. From Latin *conscript-*, the past participle stem of *conscribere* 'to enrol', literally 'to write down', from *scribere* (see SCRIBE).]

conscription /kən skrípsh'n/ *n.* obligatory enrolment of citizens for a period of national service, usually in the armed forces

consecrate /kónssi krayt/ (**-crates, -crating, -crated**) *vt.* **1. DECLARE PLACE HOLY** to declare or set apart a building, area of ground, or specific spot as holy or sacred ○ *The cathedral was consecrated in the 12th century.* **2. BLESS COMMUNION BREAD AND WINE** to sanctify the bread and wine for use in the Eucharist or Communion service, as symbols of the body and blood of Jesus Christ **3. ORDAIN AS BISHOP** to ordain a priest as a bishop **4. DEDICATE TO SPECIFIC PURPOSE** to dedicate sth or sb to a specific purpose **5. MAKE CUSTOM REVERED** to cause a custom to be revered [14thC. From Latin *consecrat-*, the past participle stem of *consecrare*, literally 'to make sacred', from *sacer* (see SACRED).] —**consecrative** *adj.* —**consecrator** *n.* —**consecratory** /kónssi kráytəri/ *adj.*

consecration /kónssi kráysh'n/ *n.* **1. CONSECRATING CEREMONY** the ceremony in which sb or sth is consecrated **2. Consecration SANCTIFICATION OF COMMUNION BREAD AND WINE** the process or ceremony of sanctifying the bread and wine during Communion, as symbols of the body and blood of Jesus Christ

consecutive /kən sékyōōtiv/ *adj.* **1. SUCCESSIVE** following one after another without interruption or break ○ *He's been off work now for three consecutive days.* **2. FOLLOWING LOGICAL SEQUENCE** following a logical or chronological sequence [Early 17thC. Via French from, ultimately, Latin *consecut-*, the past participle stem of *consequi* (see CONSEQUENT).] —**consecutively** *adv.* —**consecutiveness** *n.*

consensual /kən sénsyōō əl/ *adj.* **1. BY MUTUAL CONSENT** involving the agreement of all involved **2.** LAW **REQUIRING CONSENT ONLY** requiring only the consent of the parties involved to make it binding **3.** PHYSIOL **RESPONDING INVOLUNTARILY TO INDIRECT STIMULUS** used to describe an involuntary response to a voluntary movement from another body part, e.g. the pupil of one eye constricting when the other eye is exposed to light [Mid-18thC. Formed from Latin *consens-*, the past participle stem of *consentire* (see CONSENT).] —**consensually** *adv.*

consensus /kən sénssəs/ *n.* **1. BROAD UNANIMITY** general or widespread agreement among all the members of a group ○ *The consensus of opinion amongst journalists was that the vote could make or break this government.* **2. VIEW OF SOCIETY IN EQUILIBRIUM** a concept of society in which the absence of conflict is seen as the equilibrium state of society [Mid-17thC. From Latin, from the past participle of *consentire* (see CONSENT).]

WORD KEY: USAGE

Tautology trap: Since ***consensus*** already means 'a view or opinion that is generally shared', expressions such as *general consensus* and *consensus of opinion* are, strictly speaking, tautologies (i.e. they say the same thing twice), in which 'general' and 'of opinion' are redundant. However, occasionally a modifier such as 'of opinion' can be justified, as in *There was a consensus of feeling, but no consensus of opinion.* It is always best to begin by considering whether or not the word without modifiers expresses what you mean.

WORD KEY: USAGE

The word ***consensus*** is often misspelt *concensus*, probably from the erroneous influence of the word *census*.

consent /kən sént/ *vi.* (**-sents, -senting, -sented**) **1. GIVE PERMISSION FOR STH** to give permission or approval for sth to happen ○ *As soon as they met Robert, her parents consented to the marriage.* ○ *I will never consent to do that.* **2. AGREE ABOUT STH** to be of the same opinion (*archaic*) ■ *n.* **1. PERMISSION FOR STH** acceptance of or agreement to sth proposed or desired by another **2. CONSENSUS** agreement on an opinion or course of action ○ *It was by common consent the best.* [13thC. Via Old French from Latin *consentire*, literally 'to feel with', from *sentire* (see SENTIENT). The underlying meaning is 'to feel the same'.] —**consenter** *n.*

WORD KEY: SYNONYMS

See Synonyms at ***agree***.

consenting adult *n.* sb who is no longer a minor, or is above the legal permitted age for any specific activity, who is willing to participate in that activity, especially sexual activities

consequence /kónssikwənss/ *n.* **1. RESULT** sth that follows as a result ○ *This is a direct consequence of your negligence.* **2. RELATION BETWEEN RESULT AND CAUSE** the relation between a result and its cause **3. IMPORTANCE** importance or significance (*formal*) (*often used in negative statements*) ○ *Your opinion is of no consequence whatsoever to me.* **4. LOGICAL CONCLUSION** a conclusion reached through valid deductive reasoning ■ **consequences** *npl.* **NEGATIVE RESULTS** the unpleasant or difficult results of a previous action [14thC. Via French from Latin *consequentia*, from *consequi* (see CONSEQUENT).] ◇ **in consequence** as a result of sth (*formal*)

consequences /kónssikwənssiz/ *n.* a game in which each player in turn writes down a line of a story about two people, their meeting, and its consequences, without knowing what the previous lines are. The intention is to produce incongruous and therefore humorous juxtapositions, which are discovered when the completed stories are read out loud. (*takes a singular verb*)

consequent /kónssikwənt/ *adj.* **1. FOLLOWING AS RESULT** following as a result or effect ○ *weeks of rain and the consequent flooding* **2.** LOGIC **AS LOGICAL CONCLUSION** following as a logical conclusion ■ *n.* **1.** LOGIC **RESULT OF STH** sth that follows as a result **2.** LOGIC **SECOND HALF OF CONDITIONAL SENTENCE** the part of a conditional sentence that expresses the result and is the q clause in a proposition of the form 'if p then q' **3.** MATH **SECOND TERM OF RATIO** the second term in a mathematical ratio [15thC. Via Old French from Latin *consequent-*, the present participle stem of *consequi*, literally 'to follow along with', from *sequi* (see SEQUENCE.]

consequential /kónssi kwénsh'l/ *adj.* **1.** INSUR **ARISING AS INDIRECT COST** used to describe costs, loss, or damage beyond the market value of the object lost or damaged, including other indirect costs arising **2. IMPORTANT** of considerable importance, significance, or value ○ *a consequential figure on the classical music circuit* **3. TOO SELF-IMPORTANT** having an exaggerated opinion of your own importance —**consequentiality** /kónssi kwénshi álləti/ *n.* —**consequentially** /kónssi kwénsh'li/ *adv.* —**consequentialness** /-sh'lnəss/ *n.*

consequentialism /kónsi kwénsh'lizzəm/ *n.* the tenet by which an action is considered right or wrong depending on whether its outcome is good or bad

consequently /kónssikwəntli/ *adv.* as a result or in view of this (*formal*) ○ *The joke backfired and the relationship consequently deteriorated.*

conservancy /kən súrv'nssi/ (*plural* **-cies**) *n.* a commission, court, or board with authority to regulate and protect a waterway, port, or area of countryside, and often also its wildlife. In England the former 'Nature Conservancy Council' is now renamed 'English Nature'. ○ *the Thames Conservancy*

conservation /kónssər váysh'n/ *n.* **1. PROTECTION FROM CHANGE** the keeping or protecting of sth from change, loss, or damage **2. PROTECTION OF VALUED RESOURCES** the preservation, management, and care of natural and cultural resources —**conservational** *adj.*

conservationist /kónssər váysh'nist/ *n.* sb who campaigns for, supports, or works towards the preservation, management, and care of the environment, especially of natural resources in the countryside

conservation of charge *n.* the principle that the total electric charge of an isolated system remains constant no matter what internal changes take place

conservation of energy *n.* the principle that the amount of energy in an isolated system remains the same, even though the form of energy may change

conservation of mass, conservation of matter *n.* the principle that the total mass of an isolated system remains constant, no matter what physical or chemical changes take place

conservation of momentum *n.* the principle that the total linear or angular momentum of an isolated system remains the same

conservatism /kən súrvətizzəm/ *n.* **1. RELUCTANCE TO ACCEPT CHANGE** unwillingness or slowness to accept change or new ideas **2. RIGHT-WING POLITICAL VIEWPOINT** a right-of-centre political philosophy based on a tendency to support gradual rather than abrupt change and to preserve the status quo **3. DESIRE TO PRESERVE CURRENT SOCIETAL STRUCTURE** an ideology that views the existing form of society as worthy of preservation

Conservatism *n.* the principles and practice of Conservative politicians or supporters, e.g. in the United Kingdom or Canada

conservative /kən súrvətiv/ *adj.* **1. RELUCTANT TO ACCEPT CHANGE** in favour of preserving the status quo and traditional values and customs, and against abrupt change **2. OF CONSERVATISM** associated with, characteristic of, or displaying conservatism **3. CAUTIOUS AND ON THE LOW SIDE** cautiously moderate and therefore often less than the final outcome ○ *Several hundred pounds is probably a very conservative estimate.* **4. CONVENTIONAL IN APPEARANCE** conventional or restrained in style and avoiding showiness ○ *a conservative business suit* **5. USING MINIMUM MEDICAL INTERVENTION** designed to help relieve symptoms or preserve health with a minimum of medical intervention ■ *n.* **1. TRADITIONALIST PERSON** sb who is reluctant to consider new ideas or accept change **2. SUPPORTER OF CONSERVATISM** sb who supports the doctrine or beliefs of conservatism —**conservatively** *adv.* —**conservativeness** *n.*

Conservative *adj.* **1. OF CONSERVATIVE PARTY** supporting, belonging to, or associated with a Conservative Party, e.g. in the United Kingdom or Canada **2. OF CONSERVATIVE JUDAISM** relating to, associated with, or characteristic of Conservative Judaism ■ *n.* **SUPPORTER OF CONSERVATIVE PARTY** sb who is a member of or supports a Conservative Party, e.g. in the United Kingdom or Canada

Conservative Judaism *n.* a form of Judaism that accepts most of the principles and practices of traditional Judaism but supports the modification and relaxing of certain laws. The movement arose around the turn of the 20th century as a reaction against the more liberal Reform Judaism.

Conservative Party *n.* (*takes a singular or plural verb*) **1. MAIN UK RIGHT-WING POLITICAL PARTY** in the United Kingdom, the principal right-of-centre political party. It supports low personal taxation, home ownership, and the maintenance of the present form of government. It was founded in the early 1830s as a successor to the Tory Party. **2. CANADIAN RIGHT-WING POLITICAL PARTY** in Canada, the Progressive Conservative Party, which originally derived its political principles from British Toryism. It added Progressive to its name in 1942. **3. POLITICAL PARTY OPPOSED TO CHANGE** in countries other than the United

Kingdom and Canada, a political party that is opposed to change

conservatoire /kən súrvə twaar/ *n.* = **conservatory** *n.* 2 [Late 18thC. Via French from Italian *conservatorio*, originally a home for orphans that provided an education in music, from late Latin *conservatorium* (see CONSERVATORY).]

conservator /kən súrvətər/ *n.* **1.** RESTORER OF WORKS OF ART sb who is responsible for looking after or restoring exhibits in a museum or collection, or other works of art **2.** PROTECTOR OF INTERESTS OF INCOMPETENT PERSON a person or institution responsible for protecting the interests of an incompetent, e.g. under a protective trust —**conservatorial** /kən súrvə táwri əl/ *adj.*

conservatorium /kən súrvə táwri əm/ *n.* *Australian* = **conservatory** *n.* 2 [Mid-19thC. Via German from late Latin *conservatorium* (see CONSERVATORY).]

conservatory /kən súrvətəri/ (*plural* **-ries**) *n.* **1.** GREENHOUSE a room with glass walls and roof where plants are grown or displayed, often built onto the side of a house **2.** ADVANCED MUSIC OR DRAMA SCHOOL an institution or school where students are taught one of the arts, most commonly music or drama, to a professional standard [Mid-16thC. From late Latin *conservatorium*, from Latin *conservare* (see CONSERVE).]

conserve *vt.* /kən súrv/ (**-serves, -serving, -served**) **1.** PROTECT FROM HARM OR DECAY to keep sth, especially an important environmental or cultural resource, from harm, loss, change, or decay ○ *the importance of conserving our national heritage* **2.** USE SPARINGLY to use sth sparingly so as not to exhaust supplies ○ *some drastic measures to conserve water* **3.** PRESERVE FOOD IN SUGAR to preserve food, especially fruit, in sugar **4.** KEEP MATTER OR ENERGY CONSTANT to keep sth constant through physical changes or chemical reactions ■ *n.* /kón surv, kən súrv/ FRUIT IN SYRUP a food consisting of fruit in a thick sugar syrup, like jam but less firmly set and usually containing larger pieces of fruit [14thC. Via French from Latin *conservare*, literally 'to preserve well', from *servare* (see SERVE).] —**conservable** *adj.* —**conserver** *n.*

Consett /kónssit/ former mining and steel town in County Durham, England. Population: 20,148 (1991).

consider /kən síddər/ (**-ers, -ering, -ered**) *v.* **1.** *vti.* THINK CAREFULLY to think carefully about sth ○ *You should consider your next move carefully.* ○ *time to consider whether this is what you really want* **2.** *vt.* JUDGE to have sth as an opinion or point of view ○ *He considers himself lucky to be alive.* ○ *I consider it unlikely that they'll accept your proposal.* **3.** *vt.* RESPECT to show respect for or be thoughtful of sb's feelings or position ○ *They never seem to consider the feelings of others.* **4.** *vt.* WEIGH UP POSSIBILITIES BEFORE DECIDING to weigh up the pros and cons of the situation before making a decision on a course of action ○ *I'm considering my options.* ○ *They're considering buying a new house.* **5.** *vt.* EXAMINE to examine a problem and discuss it in detail ○ *On this week's show, we're going to consider the following question.* **6.** *vt.* TAKE INTO ACCOUNT to take sth into account, often in a sympathetic way ○ *We've done rather well, all things considered.* **7.** *vt.* LOOK CAREFULLY AT to look at sth carefully and with concentration (*formal*) [14thC. Via French *considérer* from Latin *considerare*, of uncertain origin: probably formed from *sidus* 'star', the underlying idea being one of examining the stars carefully to divine the future.] —**considerer** *n.*

considerable /kən síddərəb'l/ *adj.* **1.** LARGE large enough to be important ○ *needs a considerable income to afford this flat* **2.** MUCH with a far from negligible amount of sth ○ *a woman of considerable influence* **3.** SIGNIFICANT worthy of consideration or respect ○ *a considerable figure in the art world*

considerably /kən síddərəbli/ *adv.* to a significant degree ○ *He's considerably older than I am.*

considerate /kən síddərət/ *adj.* mindful of the needs, wishes, and feelings of others —**considerately** *adv.* —**considerateness** *n.*

consideration /kən síddə ráysh'n/ *n.* **1.** CAREFUL THOUGHT careful thought or deliberation (*formal*) ○ *Your application will be given the fullest consideration.* **2.** OPINION a carefully thought-out opinion ○ *It is my consideration that you are not suitable for this post.* **3.** RESPECT thoughtful concern for or sensitivity towards the feelings of others **4.** RELEVANT FACTOR IN ASSESSING STH sth to be taken into account when weighing up the pros and cons before making a decision ○ *Value for money is one of the most important considerations for our customers.* **5.** DETAILED EXAMINATION detailed discussion or scrutiny ○ *The issue for consideration on today's show is cosmetic surgery.* **6.** PAYMENT a payment or fee in return for a service (*formal*) **7.** HIGH REGARD high regard or esteem (*formal*) ○ *She has always been held in great consideration by this congregation.* **8.** STH MAKING CONTRACT BINDING sth done by one of the parties as part of a contractual arrangement that makes it binding, e.g. the payment of the price in a contract of sale ◇ **take sth into consideration** to take account of special circumstances, often in a sympathetic way ◇ **of little consideration, of no consideration** not important or significant (*formal*) ◇ **in consideration of 1.** because of (*formal*) **2.** as payment for (*formal*)

considered /kən síddərd/ *adj.* **1.** THOUGHT OUT carefully thought out ○ *my considered opinion* **2.** REGARDED regarded in a particular way (*formal*) (*usually used in combination*) ○ *highly considered*

considering /kən síddəring/ *prep., conj.* TAKING INTO ACCOUNT taking sth into account ○ *It's a tremendous bargain, considering the price and how much we need one.* ■ *adv.* ALL IN ALL taking everything into account, often in a sympathetic way (*usually used at the end of a phrase or sentence*) ○ *We've done a really good job, considering.*

consign /kən sín/ (**-signs, -signing, -signed**) *vt.* **1.** ENTRUST to hand sb or sth over to the care of another ○ *The children were consigned to the care of the nanny.* **2.** GET RID OF to dispose of sth or sb, usually for a very long time if not permanently, and often to somewhere unpleasant or difficult ○ *Before fleeing, they consigned the documents to the flames.* **3.** DELIVER to address, deliver, or hand over for later delivery sth for sale, safekeeping, or disposal [15thC. Via French from Latin *consignare* 'to certify with a seal', from *signum* (see SIGN).] —**consignable** *adj.*

consignee /kón sī neé/ *n.* the person, people, or organization to whom sth is delivered or addressed (*formal*)

consigner *n.* = **consignor**

consignment /kən sínmənt/ *n.* **1.** DELIVERY a quantity or package of goods delivered or to be delivered **2.** DISPOSAL TO SOMEWHERE DISAGREEABLE the disposing of sb or sth, or being disposed, to an unpleasant or difficult place or task, usually for a very long time if not forever **3.** ENTRUSTING OF SB TO ANOTHER'S CARE the handing over of sb or sth to the care of another ◇ **on consignment** on the understanding that payment will be made only when the goods have been sold and that any remaining unsold articles can be returned

consignor /kən sínər/, **consigner** *n.* a person who or organization that delivers goods

consist /kən síst/ (**-sists, -sisting, -sisted**) *vi.* **1.** BE MADE UP OF STH to be made up of diverse elements ○ *This dressing consists of oil, lemon juice, and mustard.* **2.** BE BASED ON STH to be based on or defined by sth ○ *Her talent consists in her superb musicianship.* [Early 16thC. From Latin *consistere* 'to be made of', literally 'to stand together', from *sistere* 'to make stand', from *stare* 'to stand' (see STATION).]

WORD KEY: USAGE

See Usage note at ***comprise***.

consistency /kən sístənssi/ (*plural* **-cies**), **consistence** /kən sístənss/ *n.* **1.** CONSTANCY the ability to maintain a particular standard or repeat a particular task with minimal variation ○ *Consistency is important in performing this job.* ○ *'A foolish consistency is the hobgoblin of small minds'.* (Ralph Waldo Emerson *Self-Reliance*; 1841) **2.** COHERENCE reasonable or logical harmony between parts ○ *The plot lacked consistency.* **3.** LEVEL OF THICKNESS OR SMOOTHNESS level of thickness or smoothness of a mixture ○ *Blend the mixture until it reaches the consistency of thick cream.*

consistent /kən sístənt/ *adj.* **1.** COHERENT reasonably or logically harmonious ○ *The evidence is consistent with the defendant's statement.* ○ *Their accounts of the incident just aren't consistent.* **2.** RELIABLE able to maintain a particular standard or repeat a particular task with minimal variation ○ *He's one of the most consistent strikers in the league.* **3.** WITH COMMON SOLUTIONS with a set of solutions in common, especially for two or more equations or inequalities **4.** FREE OF CONTRADICTION containing no provable contradiction [Late 16thC. From Latin *consistent-*, the present participle stem of *consistere* (see CONSIST).] —**consistently** *adv.*

consistory /kən sístəri/ (*plural* **-ries**) *n.* **1.** RELIG ASSEMBLY OF CARDINALS AND POPE in the Roman Catholic Church, an assembly of cardinals convoked and led by the Pope **2.** RELIG ANGLICAN DIOCESAN COURT in the Anglican Church, the court of any diocese except Canterbury **3.** RELIG CONGREGATIONAL GOVERNING BODY in certain Reformed churches, the governing body of a congregation **4.** RELIG REGULATORY COURT IN LUTHERAN CHURCHES in Lutheran state churches, a court appointed to regulate ecclesiastical affairs **5.** HIST HISTORICAL COUNCIL OR ASSEMBLY a council or assembly, e.g. in the Roman Empire [13thC. Via Anglo-Norman from late Latin *consistorium* 'place of assembly', from Latin *consistere* 'to stand together' (see CONSIST).] —**consistorial** /kónssi stáwri əl/ *adj.*

consociate *vti.* /kən sṓshi ayt, -sṓssi-/ (**-ates, -ating, -ated**) JOIN OR WELCOME ASSOCIATION to enter or welcome sb into a friendly association (*formal*) ■ *adj.* /kən sṓshi ət, -sṓssi-/ ASSOCIATED associated or united (*formal*) ■ *n.* /kən sṓshi ət, -sṓssi-/ PARTNER an associate or partner (*formal*) [15thC. From Latin *consociat-*, the past participle stem of *consociare* 'to associate', from *socius* 'companion' (see SOCIAL).]

consociation /kən sṓshi áysh'n, -sṓssi-/ *n.* **1.** FRIENDLY ASSOCIATION a friendly association or alliance (*formal*) **2.** ECOL ECOLOGICAL COMMUNITY WITH ONE MAIN SPECIES an ecological community that has one dominant species, e.g. a wood consisting predominantly of beech trees **3.** POL POLITICAL COALITION a grouping of political parties or pressure groups within a region or country that work together to share power —**consociational** *adj.*

consocies /kən sṓsh eez/ (*plural* **-cies**) *n.* an ecological community that has one dominant species. = **consociation** *n.* 2 [Early 20thC. Formed from CONSOCIATION, on the model of SPECIES.]

consolation /kónssə láysh'n/ *n.* **1.** SOURCE OF COMFORT a source of comfort to sb who is upset or disappointed ○ *The fortune she left was little consolation for him.* **2.** COMFORT TO SB IN DISTRESS comfort to sb who is distressed or disappointed ○ *Most of those at the funeral murmured some words of consolation as they left.* **3.** GAME FOR EARLIER LOSERS a game or contest held for people or teams who have lost earlier in a tournament

consolation prize *n.* a prize given to comfort the loser or losers in a game or competition

console[1] /kən sṓl/ (**-soles, -soling, -soled**) *vt.* to be or provide a source of comfort to sb who is distressed or disappointed [Mid-17thC. Via French from Latin *consolare*, from *solari* 'to soothe' (see SOLACE).] —**consolable** *adj.* —**consolatory** *adj.* —**consoler** *n.* —**consolingly** *adv.*

WORD KEY: USAGE

See Usage note at ***condole***.

console[2] /kón sōl/ *n.* **1.** CABINET FOR TELEVISION OR HI-FI a free-standing cabinet, especially one used to house a television or hi-fi system **2.** ORGAN CONTROLS the part of an organ that houses the keyboards or manuals, pedals, and stops **3.** ORNAMENTAL BRACKET an ornamental bracket, often in the shape of a scroll, used for decoration and for supporting wall fixtures **4.** CONTROL PANEL a desk, table, display, or keyboard onto which the controls of an electronic system or some other machine are fixed **5.** = **console table** [Mid-17thC. From French, of uncertain origin: perhaps a shortening of *consolider* 'to consolidate'.]

console table /kón sōl t-b'l/ *n.* a small table with curved legs designed to stand against a wall

consolidate /kən sólli dayt/ (**-dates, -dating, -dated**) *vti.* **1.** UNITE BUSINESS ACTIVITIES to bring businesses or business activities together, or come together, into a single unit **2.** STRENGTHEN YOUR POSITION to increase the strength, stability, or depth of your success or position ○ *This excellent performance has enabled* *her to consolidate her lead.* **3.** **COMBINE INTO SINGLE MASS** to combine separate items or scattered material into a single mass [Early 16thC. From Latin *consolidat-*, the past participle stem of *consolidare*, literally 'to make solid', from *solidus* (see SOLID).] —**consolidator** *n.*

consolidated fund *n.* in the United Kingdom, a government fund made up of revenue from taxes, used to cover regular costs, especially interest payments on the national debt

consolidation /kən sólli dáysh'n/ *n.* **1.** **COMBINING OF BUSINESS ACTIVITIES** the bringing together of two or more businesses or business activities into a single unit **2.** **STRENGTHENING** increasing of the strength, stability, or depth of a person's or group's success ○ *The final six weeks saw a consolidation of their position at the top of the league.* **3.** **COMBINATION INTO SINGLE MASS** the combination of separate items or scattered material into a single mass **4.** POL **COMBINING SEVERAL ACTS INTO SINGLE STATUTE** combination of two or more Acts of Parliament into a single statute **5.** GEOL **COMPACTION INTO ROCK** any process by which a loose deposit is compacted into hard rock **6.** PSYCHOL **PSYCHOLOGICAL PROCESS THAT RETAINS MEMORY** the process in the brain that enables sb to have a lasting memory of a particular event

consols /kən sólz, kón səlz/ *npl.* in the United Kingdom, government bonds with a fixed interest rate and no date of maturity [Late 18thC. Contraction of *consolidated annuities*.]

consommé /kon sómm ay/ *n.* a thin clear soup made from meat or chicken stock. It can be eaten hot, or cold in the form of a jelly. [Early 19thC. From French, from the past participle of *consommer* 'to use up', from Latin *consummare* (see CONSUMMATE).]

consonance /kónss'nənss/, **consonancy** /kónss'nənsi/ (*plural* **-cies**) *n.* **1.** **AGREEMENT** agreement or harmony (*formal*) **2.** **SIMILARITY BETWEEN CONSONANTS** a close similarity between consonants or groups of consonants, especially at the ends of words, e.g. between 'strong' and 'ring' **3.** **PLEASANT COMBINATION OF MUSICAL NOTES** a combination of notes that sounds pleasing when played simultaneously

consonant /kónss'nənt/ *n.* **SPEECH SOUND OTHER THAN VOWEL** a speech sound produced by partly or totally blocking the path of air through the mouth, or the corresponding letter of the alphabet ■ *adj.* **1.** **IN AGREEMENT WITH STH** in agreement or harmony with sth (*formal*) ○ *I was delighted to learn that their views were consonant with my own.* **2.** **PLEASING IN HARMONY** containing chords or harmonies that are pleasing to hear **3.** **HAVING SIMILAR SOUNDS** having similar sounds or showing consonance [14thC. Via French from Latin *consonant-*, the stem of *consonans*, literally 'sounding together', from *sonare* (see SONANT).] —**consonantly** *adv.*

consonantal /kónssə nánt'l/ *adj.* **1.** **OF CONSONANT** consisting of, relating to, or functioning like a consonant **2.** **CONTAINING CONSONANTS** containing consonants or nothing but consonants —**consonantally** *adv.*

con sordino /kon sawr deén ō/ *adv.* to be played with a mute or the mute pedal (*used as a musical direction*) [Early 19thC. From Italian, literally 'with a mute'.]

consort *vi.* /kən sáwrt/ (**-sorts, -sorting, -sorted**) **ASSOCIATE WITH UNDESIRABLES** to associate with or spend time in the company of undesirable people (*formal*) ○ *consorting with known criminals* ■ *n.* /kón sawrt/ **1.** **consort, Consort** **SPOUSE OF REIGNING MONARCH** the husband or wife of a reigning monarch **2.** **PARTNER** a partner or companion (*formal*) **3.** **SHIP THAT ESCORTS ANOTHER** a ship that accompanies or escorts another on a journey **4.** **CHAMBER GROUP SPECIALIZING IN EARLY MUSIC** a small group of musical instruments, often of the baroque or other early period, or a group of players of such instruments [15thC. Via French from Latin *consort-*, the stem of *consors*, literally 'having the same fate', from *sors* 'fortune' (see SORT).] ◇ **in consort with** in association or together with others (*archaic or formal*)

consortium /kən sáwrti əm/ (*plural* **-a** /-ti ə/) *n.* **1.** **COMBINATION OF ORGANIZATIONS FOR COMMON PURPOSE** an association or grouping of institutions, businesses, or financial organizations, usually set up for a common purpose that would be beyond the capabilities of a single member of the group **2.** **RIGHT TO MARITAL COMPANY AND AFFECTION** the right of husbands or wives to the company, affection, and help of their spouses (*archaic*) [Early 19thC. From Latin, 'fellowship', from *consors* 'fellow' (see CONSORT).] —**consortial** *adj.*

conspecific /kónspə siffik/ *adj.* **OF SAME SPECIES** of the same species as another organism ■ *n.* **ORGANISM OF SAME SPECIES** an organism of the same species as another

conspectus /kən spéktəss/ *n.* **1.** **MENTAL OVERVIEW OF STH** a general mental survey or overview of sth **2.** **SYNOPSIS OF STH** an overview of sth in outline or synopsis (*technical*) [Mid-19thC. From Latin, formed from *conspect-*, the past participle stem of *conspicere* (see CONSPICUOUS).]

conspicuous /kən spíkyoo əss/ *adj.* **1.** **EASILY VISIBLE** easily or clearly visible ○ *The building's most conspicuous feature is its dome-shaped roof.* **2.** **ATTRACTING ATTENTION** attracting attention through being unusual or remarkable ○ *He felt uncomfortably conspicuous, since he was the only man in evening dress.* [Mid-16thC. Formed from Latin *conspicuus*, from *conspicere*, literally 'to observe carefully', from *specere* (see SPECTACLE).] —**conspicuously** *adv.* —**conspicuousness** *n.*

conspicuous consumption *n.* spending large quantities of money, often extravagantly, to impress others [The term was introduced by Thorstein Veblen in his *Theory of the Leisure Class*, 1899]

conspiracist /kən spírrəssist/ *n.* sb who believes in a conspiracy theory about some event

conspiracy /kən spírrəssi/ (*plural* **-cies**) *n.* **1.** **PLAN TO COMMIT ILLEGAL ACT TOGETHER** a plan or agreement between two or more people to commit an illegal or subversive action **2.** **AGREEMENT AMONG CONSPIRATORS** the making of an agreement or plot to commit an illegal or subversive action **3.** **GROUP OF CONSPIRATORS** a group of conspirators [14thC. Via Anglo-Norman *conspiracie* from, ultimately, Latin *conspirat-*, the past participle stem of *conspirare* (see CONSPIRE).]

conspiracy of silence *n.* an agreement among a group of people to say nothing in public about sth of public interest or importance, in order to protect or promote selfish interests

conspiracy theory *n.* a belief that a particular event is the result of a secret plot rather than the actions of an individual or chance —**conspiracy theorist** *n.*

conspirator /kən spírrətər/ *n.* a member of a group of people planning or agreeing to commit an illegal or subversive act

conspiratorial /kən spírrə táwri əl/ *adj.* indicating or betraying knowledge of or involvement in a secret plot —**conspiratorially** *adv.*

conspire /kən spír/ (**-spires, -spiring, -spired**) *vi.* **1.** **PLAN SECRETLY TO ACT ILLEGALLY** to plan or agree in secret with others to commit an illegal or subversive act ○ *In court, the three defendants admitted to conspiring against the government.* **2.** **JOINTLY CAUSE TROUBLE** to combine so as to cause harm, inconvenience, or difficulty ○ *Rain and tears conspired to smudge her carefully applied mascara.* [14thC. Via French from Latin *conspirare* 'to agree', literally 'to breathe or whisper together', from *spirare* (see SPIRIT).] —**conspiringly** *adv.*

conspiriologist /kən spírri óllәjist/ *n.* *US* POL sb who engages in conspiracy theories

con spirito /kon spírritō/ *adv.* to be performed in a lively or spirited way (*used as a musical direction*) [Late 19thC. From Italian, literally 'with spirit'.]

const. *abbr.* **1.** constant **2.** constitution

constable /kúnstəb'l, kón-/ *n.* **1.** LAW **POLICE OFFICER** a police officer of the lowest rank **2.** LAW **OFFICER BELOW SHERIFF** a low-ranking law officer in some towns or townships in the United States and, historically, in British towns and boroughs **3.** **CASTLE WARDEN** the warden of a royal castle or fortress **4.** **ROYAL HOUSEHOLD OFFICIAL IN MIDDLE AGES** the chief administrative and military officer in a royal household, especially in medieval France and England [12thC. From Old French *conestable*, from late Latin *comes stabilis*, literally 'count of the stable', later 'chief household officer of the Frankish kings'.] —**constableship** *n.*

Constable /kúnstəb'l/, **John** (1776–1837) British landscape painter. His paintings such as *The Haywain* (1821) came to symbolize rural England.

constabulary /kən stább yoolәri/ *n.* (*plural* **-ies**) **1.** LAW **POLICE FORCE** a police force for a city or a district **2.** **FORCE OF CONSTABLES** an organized force of constables operating in a city or district ■ *adj.* **OF POLICE FORCE OR OFFICERS** relating to a police force or involved in being a police officer

Constance, Lake /kónstənss/ lake in central Europe on the borders of Austria, Germany, and Switzerland, in the Alps. Area: 540 sq. km/210 sq. mi. Depth: 827 ft/252 m. Length: 74 km/46 mi. Also known as **Bodensee**

constancy /kónstənssi/ *n.* **1.** **LOYALTY** the quality of remaining faithful to a person, belief, or decision, especially in the face of difficulties ○ *The church would never have been finished if not for the constancy of a few citizens over the past six years.* **2.** **UNCHANGING QUALITY** the quality or fact of remaining the same despite change or variation in other things

constant /kónstənt/ *adj.* **1.** **EVER PRESENT** always present or available ○ *constant whining* **2.** **HAPPENING OR DONE REPEATEDLY** occurring or made again and again ○ *constant visits to the doctor* **3.** **NOT CHANGING OR VARYING** remaining the same and not varying with change in other things ○ *kept at a constant pressure* **4.** **FAITHFUL** faithful and loyal, especially to a husband, wife, or loved one ■ *n.* **1.** **STH UNCHANGING** an object, quality, or fact that is invariable ○ *This preoccupation has become a constant in our daily lives.* **2.** MATH **QUANTITY WITH FIXED VALUE** a quantity that retains a fixed value in any circumstances or throughout a particular set of calculations. Pi, the ratio of the circumference to the radius of any circle, is a constant. **3.** PHYS **UNVARYING PROPERTY** a property, condition, or quantity that is assumed not to vary for the purposes of a theory or experiment, e.g. the speed of light [14thC. Via French from Latin *constant-*, present participle stem of *constare* 'to stand together', from *stare* 'to stand' (see STAGE).]

constantan /kónstən tan/ *n.* an alloy of copper and nickel whose electrical resistance is unaffected by changes in temperature. It is used mainly in resistors and thermocouples. [Early 20thC. Formed from CONSTANT.]

Constantine II /kónstən tīn, -teen/, **King of the Hellenes** (*b.* 1940). Succeeding in 1964, he was exiled in 1967 by a military junta and deposed in 1973. A referendum abolished the Greek monarchy in 1974.

Constantine (the Great), Emperor of Rome (274–337). He converted to Christianity in 312 and made it a state religion in 324. He moved his capital to Byzantium, renamed Constantinople in 330. Real name **Flavius Valerius Aurelius Constantinus**

Constantinople /kón stanti nóp'l/ former name for **Istanbul**

constantly /kónstənstli/ *adv.* always and without interruption, or again and again without end ○ *She's been on my mind constantly since I heard the news.*

constellate /kónstə layt/ (**-lates, -lating, -lated**) *vti.* to form clusters, in or as if in constellations (*formal*) [Late 16thC. From late Latin *constellatus*, literally 'stars together', from, ultimately, Latin *stella* 'star'.]

constellation /kónstə láysh'n/ *n.* **1.** ASTRON **GROUP OF STARS FORMING SHAPE** a group of stars visible from Earth that forms a distinctive pattern and has a name linked to its shape, often derived from Greek mythology. There are 88 constellations and the groupings are historical rather than scientific. **2.** ASTRON **AREA OF SKY CONTAINING CONSTELLATION** the area of the sky within and around a constellation **3.** **GATHERING OF CELEBRITIES** a gathering of famous or important people ○ *a glittering constellation of Hollywood stars* **4.** **GROUP OF RELATED THINGS** a group of things or circumstances felt to be related to each other in some way ○ *Problems tend to occur not singly, but in constellations.* **5.** ZODIAC **ASTROLOGICAL ARRANGEMENT OF PLANETS** the arrangement of the planets in the zodiac at a particular time, believed by astrologers to influence human character or events on earth —**constellational** *adj.* —**constellatory** /kən stéllətəri/ *adj.*

consternate /kónstər nayt/ (**-nates, -nating, -nated**) *vt.* to fill sb with alarm, confusion, or dismay (*formal*) [Mid-17thC. From Latin *consternat-*, past participle stem of *consternare*, literally 'to make prostrate with fear', from *sternare* 'to lay low'.]

consternation /kónstər náysh'n/ *n.* a feeling of bewilderment and dismay, often caused by sth unexpected ○ *The news caused worldwide consternation and a panic on the stock exchange.*

constipate /kónsti payt/ (**-pates, -pating, -pated**) *vt.* to cause sb or sth to become constipated [Mid-16thC. From Latin *constipat-*, past participle stem of *constipare* 'to cram together', from *stipare* 'to press'.]

constipated /kónsti paytid/ *adj.* **1.** HAVING DIFFICULTY WITH DEFECATION having difficulty in eliminating solid waste from the body with faeces being hard and dry **2.** BLOCKED OR OBSTRUCTED unable to flow or produce at the normal rate because of blockage or obstruction

constipation /kónsti páysh'n/ *n.* **1.** DIFFICULTY IN DEFECATION a condition in which a person or animal has difficulty in eliminating solid waste from the body and the faeces are hard and dry **2.** BLOCKAGE OR OBSTRUCTION a state in which the normal flow of sth is blocked or obstructed

constituency /kən stíttyoo ənssi, -stíchyoo-/ (*plural* **-cies**) *n.* **1.** POL ELECTORAL DISTRICT one of the areas into which a country is divided for election purposes, from which a representative is elected to serve in a legislative body **2.** POL VOTERS IN A CONSTITUENCY the voters or residents in a particular electoral district **3.** GROUP WITH COMMON OUTLOOK a group of people thought to have common aims or views, and therefore sometimes appealed to for support ○ *people outside his usual constituency of young married couples* **4.** CUSTOMERS CONSIDERED AS A GROUP a group of people served by an organization, especially a business ○ *enlarging its constituency via a website*

constituent /kən stíttyoo ənt, -stíchyoo-/ *n.* **1.** POL RESIDENT OF CONSTITUENCY a person living in an electoral district, especially one having the right to vote **2.** INGREDIENT one of the materials or elements that make up sth ○ *one of the constituents of cement* **3.** GRAM WORD, PHRASE, OR CLAUSE a word, phrase, or clause in a larger construction such as a sentence. ◊ **immediate constituent, ultimate constituent 4.** LAW CLIENT sb who appoints another person to act on his or her behalf (*formal*) ■ *adj.* **1.** FORMING A PART forming a part of sth (*formal*) ○ *a constituent part of sth* **2.** POL WITH POWER TO DRAW UP CONSTITUTION having the power to draw up or alter a constitution [15thC. Directly or via French *constituant*, from Latin *constituent-*, present participle stem of *constituere* (see CONSTITUTE).] —**constituently** *adv.*

constitute /kónsti tyoot/ (**-tutes, -tuting, -tuted**) *vt.* **1.** BE to be, amount to, or have the status of a particular thing ○ *This letter does not constitute an offer of employment.* **2.** BE INGREDIENT OF to make up the whole or a stated part of sth ○ *a panel constituted of four individuals* **3.** FORMALLY ESTABLISH to create and establish sth formally, especially an official body (*formal*) ○ *constitute an assembly* **4.** FORMALLY APPOINT to appoint sb formally to a position (*formal*) [15thC. From Latin *constitut-*, past participle stem of *constituere* 'to establish, appoint', from *statuere* 'to set up'.] —**constituter** *n.*

WORD KEY: USAGE

See Usage note at ***comprise***.

constitution /kónsti tyóosh'n/ *n.* **1.** POL STATEMENT OF FUNDAMENTAL LAWS a written statement outlining the basic laws or principles by which a country or organization is governed **2.** POL DOCUMENT CONTAINING FUNDAMENTAL LAWS the document or statute setting out the fundamental laws or bylaws of a country or organization **3.** SB'S HEALTH sb's general condition of health, especially the body's ability to remain healthy and withstand disease or hardship **4.** COMPOSITION OF STH the parts or members of sth, or the way in which they combine to form it **5.** ACT OR PROCESS OF ESTABLISHING STH the formal creation or establishment of sth

Constitution *n.* POL the Constitution of the United States, containing seven articles and 26 amendments, that has been in effect since its adoption in 1789

constitutional /kónsti tyóosh'nəl/ *adj.* **1.** POL INVOLVING CONSTITUTION involving the constitution of a country or an organization **2.** POL GOVERNED BY CONSTITUTION governed or regulated by a constitution **3.** POL IN ACCORDANCE WITH A CONSTITUTION authorized by a constitution ○ *The US Supreme Court has to decide whether such punishments are constitutional.* **4.** RELATING TO BODY AND HEALTH being part of, or a consequence of, a person's physical and sometimes psychological make-up **5.** HEALTH-GIVING beneficial to a person's health (*dated*) ■ *n.* WALK a short walk, taken regularly for health reasons

constitutionalism /kónsti tyóosh'nəlizzəm/ *n.* **1.** GOVERNMENT BY CONSTITUTION the principles or practice of government regulated by a constitution, especially a written one **2.** BELIEF IN IDEA OF CONSTITUTION belief in constitutional government —**constitutionalist** *n., adj.*

constitutionality /kónsti tyóosh'n álləti/ *n.* validity or permissibility in terms of the provisions or principles of a constitution

constitutionalize /kónsti tyóosh'nə līz/ (**-izes, -izing, -ized**), **constitutionalise** (**-ises, -ising, -ised**) *vt.* **1.** INCORPORATE INTO CONSTITUTION to incorporate a piece of legislation into a constitution, or to authorize a practice through a constitution **2.** SUBJECT TO CONSTITUTION to make a form of government, a country, or an organization subject to a constitution —**constitutionalization** /kónsti tyóosh'nə lī záysh'n/ *n.*

constitutionally /kónsti tyóosh'nəli/ *adv.* POL in accordance with a political constitution

constitutional monarchy (*plural* **constitutional monarchies**) *n.* **1.** POLITICAL SYSTEM a political system in which the head of state is a king or queen ruling to the extent allowed by a constitution **2.** ROYAL-RULED COUNTRY a country with a constitutional monarchy —**constitutional monarch** *n.*

constitutive /kən stíttyootiv/ *adj.* **1.** POL HAVING POWER TO ESTABLISH INSTITUTION having the power to create or establish a system of government, legislative body, or other institution, or to appoint members of official bodies **2.** FORMING A PART forming a part of sth **3.** ESSENTIAL essential to the particular nature or character of sth **4.** BIOCHEM FORMED CONTINUOUSLY used to describe enzymes that are formed continuously and at a constant rate within the body regardless of the physiological demands of the cell —**constitutively** *adv.*

constr. *abbr.* construction

constrain /kən stráyn/ (**-strains, -straining, -strained**) *vt.* **1.** FORCE TO ACT to force sb to do sth, especially through pressure of circumstances or a sense of obligation ○ *Many companies have been constrained to lay off workers.* **2.** LIMIT to limit or restrict sb or sth, especially to prevent the free expression of sth ○ *We felt constrained by the presence of the others.* **3.** RESTRAIN to hold sb or sth back from an action [14thC. Via Old French *constraindre* from Latin *constringere* 'to bind tightly together', from *stringere* 'draw tight'.] —**constrainable** *adj.* —**constrainer** *n.*

constrained /kən stráynd/ *adj.* lacking naturalness or spontaneity because of self-consciousness, reserve, or inhibiting circumstances —**constrainedly** /kən stráynidli/ *adv.*

constraint /kən stráynt/ *n.* **1.** LIMITING FACTOR sth that limits the freedom to act spontaneously ○ *Even in a free society individual liberty must be subject to certain constraints.* **2.** LACK OF SPONTANEITY a lack of warmth and spontaneity in sb's manner, or in the atmosphere on a particular occasion **3.** STATE OF RESTRICTION a state in which freedom of action is severely restricted **4.** FORCE OR COMPULSION physical, moral, or other force that compels sb to do sth or that limits sb's freedom of action ○ *Constraint was needed to get the parties to agree to negotiate.* [14thC. From French *costreinte*, feminine past participle of *constraindre* (see CONSTRAIN).]

constrict /kən stríkt/ (**-stricts, -stricting, -stricted**) *v.* **1.** *vti.* NARROW to make sth, especially a blood vessel, narrower, or to become narrower **2.** *vt.* LIMIT OR RESTRICT to limit the movement of a person or part of the body in an uncomfortable way **3.** *vt.* RESTRICT FLOW to stop or slow down the flow of sth, e.g. air, liquid, or blood **4.** *vt.* SUFFOCATE PREY BY SQUEEZING to squeeze prey animals until they suffocate, as many snakes do [Mid-18thC. From Latin *constrict-*, past participle stem of *constringere* (see CONSTRAIN).] —**constrictive** *adj.* —**constrictively** *adv.* —**constrictiveness** *n.*

constriction /kən stríksh'n/ *n.* **1.** BECOMING CONSTRICTED the process of becoming narrower, or of making sth narrower, e.g. blood vessels **2.** COMPRESSION BY SQUEEZING the process of squeezing or compressing sth, e.g. the prey of a snake **3.** NARROW PLACE a narrow place or part ○ *A constriction in the tube prevents the mercury from returning to the bulb.* **4.** FEELING OF TIGHTNESS a feeling of tightness or pressure, especially in the chest or throat **5.** RESTRICTION sth that severely restricts a person's freedom of movement, action, or expression **6.** CONSTRICTING THING sth that constricts sb or sth

constrictor /kən stríktər/ *n.* **1.** ZOOL SNAKE THAT SQUEEZES PREY TO DEATH a large non-venomous snake, such as an anaconda, boa, or python, that coils itself around its prey and crushes it to death **2.** ANAT MUSCLE a muscle that tightens to make a part of the body narrower **3.** STH THAT CONSTRICTS sth that constricts

constringe /kən strínj/ (**-stringes, -stringing, -stringed**) *vt.* to cause sth to contract or grow narrower (*archaic*) [Late 16thC. From Latin *constringere* (see CONSTRAIN).] —**constringency** *n.* —**constringent** *adj.*

construct *vt.* /kən strúkt/ (**-structs, -structing, -structed**) **1.** BUILD to build or assemble sth by putting together separate parts in an ordered way **2.** CREATE IN THE MIND to create sth, such as a theory, as a result of systematic thought **3.** GEOM DRAW ACCURATELY to draw sth accurately using given measurements ■ *n.* /kónstrukt/ CONSTRUCTED THING OR CONCEPT sth that has been systematically put together, usually in the mind, especially a complex theory or concept [15thC. From Latin *construct-*, past participle stem of *construere*, literally 'to pile together', from *struere* 'to pile, build'.] —**constructible** *adj.* —**constructor** *n.*

WORD KEY: SYNONYMS

See Synonyms at ***build***.

construction /kən strúksh'n/ *n.* **1.** BUILDING ACT OR PROCESS OF CONSTRUCTING the building of sth, especially a large structure such as a house, road, or bridge **2.** BUILDING BUILT STRUCTURE a structure or thing that has been built **3.** WORKMANSHIP AND MATERIALS the way in which sth has been built, especially with regard to the type and quality of the structure, materials, and workmanship **4.** BUILDING BUILDING INDUSTRY the building industry regarded as a whole **5.** CREATION OF STH the creation of sth such as a system or concept from a number of different elements **6.** GRAM COMBINATION OF WORDS a group of words governed by particular grammatical rules **7.** GEOM GEOMETRIC SHAPE a geometric figure drawn accurately in accordance with given measurements **8.** ARTS WORK OF ART a visual work of art that is put together from a variety of different materials, abstract in design, and usually three-dimensional —**constructional** *adj.* —**constructionally** *adv.*

constructive /kən strúktiv/ *adj.* **1.** USEFUL carefully considered and meant to be helpful ○ *constructive criticism* **2.** LAW BASED ON INFERENCE based on what sb infers from other statements or circumstances **3.** BUILDING STRUCTURAL involved in construction, especially forming part of the basic structure of a building —**constructively** *adv.* —**constructiveness** *n.*

constructive dismissal *n.* action by an employer intended to make continuing in a job intolerable for an unwanted employee, thus forcing the employee to resign

constructive margin *n.* a boundary between two tectonic plates at which new crust is formed, e.g. the mid-ocean ridges

constructivism /kən strúktivizzəm/ *n.* ARTS a modern art movement originating in Moscow in the 1920s that produced large non-representational structures made of industrial materials such as plastic, glass, and sheet metal. Its leading figures were Naum Gabo and Antoine Pevsner. [Early 20thC. Formed from CONSTRUCTIVE, modelled on Russian *konstruktivism*.] —**constructivist** *n.*

construe /kən stróo, kón stroo/ *v.* (**-strues, -struing, -strued**) **1.** *vt.* INTERPRET to interpret or understand the meaning of a word, gesture, or action in a particular way ○ *His silence could be construed as an admission of guilt.* **2.** *vti.* GRAM ANALYZE SYNTAX to analyze the grammar of a piece of text, such as text that is to be translated **3.** *vt.* GRAM **USE WORD IN PARTICULAR WAY** to use a word in a grammatical structure, e.g. by making it singular or plural ○ *'Folk' is construed as plural, except when it means 'folk music'.* **4.** *vti.* EDUC **TRANSLATE ALOUD** to translate sth aloud, often word for word and especially from Latin or Greek (*dated*) ■ *n.* **LITERAL TRANSLATION** a word for word translation, especially from Latin or Greek, or the act of making such a translation (*archaic*) [14thC. From Latin *construere* (see CONSTRUCT), used in late Latin to mean 'to parse'.] —**construable** *adj.* —**construability** /kən stro͞o ə bíllәti/ *n.* —**construer** /kən stro͞o ər/ *n.*

consubstantial /kónsəb stánsh'l/ *adj.* CHR having the same substance as sth else, e.g. another member of the Holy Trinity [14thC. From ecclesiastical Latin *consubstantialis*, literally 'substance together', from Latin *substantia* 'substance'.] —**consubstantiality** /kónsəb stánshi állәti/ *n.*

consubstantiate /kónsəb stánshi ayt/ (**-ates, -ating, -ated**) *vti.* CHR to become united, or to unite two things, in one single substance, as the body and blood of Jesus Christ are believed to become one with bread and wine in the Christian doctrine of transubstantiation [Late 16thC. From late Latin *consubstantiatus* 'united in one substance', from *substantiat-*, past participle stem of *substantiare* (see SUBSTANTIATE).]

consubstantiation /kónsəb stánshi áysh'n/ *n.* **1.** **CHRISTIAN EUCHARISTIC DOCTRINE** the Christian belief that the body and blood of Jesus Christ coexist in the bread and wine consecrated at Holy Communion with the natural elements of which bread and wine are made. This belief is held mainly by High-Church Anglican Christians. ◊ **transubstantiation** **2.** **PROCESS IN CHRISTIAN COMMUNION SERVICE** the process by which the body and blood of Jesus Christ are believed by some Christians to become present in the bread and wine consecrated at Holy Communion

consuetude /kónswi tyood/ *n.* a long-standing custom or right, particularly one that has acquired legal force (*formal*) [14thC. Directly or via French from Latin *consuetudo*, literally 'complete accustomedness', from, ultimately, *suescere* 'to become accustomed'.] —**consuetudinary** /kónswi tyo͞odinəri/ *adj.*

consul /kónss'l/ *n.* **1.** POL **GOVERNMENT OFFICIAL WORKING ABROAD** a government official living in a foreign city to promote the commerce of the official's own state and protect its citizens **2.** HIST **ANCIENT ROMAN MAGISTRATE** one of the two chief magistrates who were elected annually to govern ancient Rome **3.** HIST **FORMER FRENCH OFFICIAL** one of the three chief magistrates of the first French Republic between 1799 and 1804 [14thC. From Latin, from or related to consultive 'to seek advice'.] —**consulship** /kónss'lship/ *n.* —**consular** /kón syo͞olar/ *adj.*

consulate /kónssyo͞olət/ *n.* **1.** RELIG **CONSUL'S OFFICE** a consul's office or official residence **2.** **SCOPE OF CONSUL'S RESPONSIBILITIES** the political office or period of office of a consul, or the jurisdiction of a consul **3.** HIST **ANCIENT ROMAN GOVERNMENT** the ancient Roman government administered by consuls

Consulate /kónssyo͞olət/ *n.* HIST **1.** **FORMER FRENCH GOVERNMENT** the government, consisting of three consuls, that ruled France from 1799 to 1804 **2.** **PERIOD IN FRENCH HISTORY** the period from 1799 to 1804 during which France was ruled by three consuls

consulate general (*plural* **consulate generals** *or* **consulates general**) *n.* the building where a consul general lives or works

consul general (*plural* **consul generals** *or* **consuls general**) *n.* a consul of the highest rank, usually based in a major foreign city that is important for trade

consult /kən súlt/ *v.* (**-sults, -sulting, -sulted**) **1.** *vti.* **ASK FOR SPECIALIST ADVICE** to ask for specialist advice or information, especially from a professional ○ *If symptoms persist, consult a doctor.* **2.** *vti.* **DISCUSS** to ask for sb's opinion or permission before taking action ○ *You'd be wise to consult the boss before you make any major changes.* **3.** *vt.* **REFER TO FOR INFORMATION** to look at sth, such as a reference book, in order to get information **4.** *vi.* **GIVE PROFESSIONAL ADVICE** to provide specialist advice for a fee ○ *After 15 years in computer programming, I now consult from home.* ■ *n.* **CONSULTATION** a consultation or discussion about sth (*informal*) [Early 16thC. Via French *consulter*, from Latin *consultare* 'to confer', from *consulere* 'to seek advice'.] —**consultable** *adj.* —**consulter** *n.*

consultancy /kən súltənssi/ (*plural* **-cies**) *n.* **1.** **WORK OF BEING A CONSULTANT** the work or business of offering expert advice or services in a particular field ○ *We charge £75 per hour for consultancy.* **2.** **COMPANY PROVIDING SPECIALIST ADVICE** a business or professional practice that provides expert advice in a particular field **3.** **CONSULTANT'S POSITION** a position as a consultant

consultant /kən súltənt/ *n.* **1.** **PROFESSIONAL ADVISER** an expert who charges a fee for providing advice or services in a particular field **2.** MED **SENIOR DOCTOR** a senior doctor who is fully qualified in a particular branch of medicine —**consultantship** *n.*

consultation /kónss'l táysh'n, kónsul-/ *n.* **1.** **EXCHANGE OF OPINIONS** a discussion, especially in order to ascertain opinions or reach an agreement ○ *After a quick consultation with his wife, he signed the paper.* **2.** **MEETING** a meeting with an expert in a particular field to obtain advice ○ *an appointment for a consultation with the heart surgeon* **3.** **DISCUSSION FOR ADVICE** the process of discussing sth either with experts or with other participants and asking for their opinions or advice ○ *Insufficient time was allowed for consultation before the project began.* **4.** **REFERENCE TO STH** the act of referring to a book or person for information or advice ○ *Consultation of the manual confirmed the problem was the gearbox.*

consultative /kən súltətiv/ *adj.* available for consultation or involved in consultation —**consultatively** *adv.*

consulting /kən súlting/ *adj.* **1.** **PROVIDING SPECIALIST ADVICE** providing specialist advice to other people who work in the same field **2.** **OF CONSULTANTS OR CONSULTATION** relating to a consultant or consultation ○ *a consulting fee* ■ *n.* **BUSINESS OF CONSULTATION** the business of being a consultant

consulting room *n.* the room in which a doctor sees patients, mainly in a hospital

consultor /kən súltər/ *n.* sb, usually a priest, who advises a Roman Catholic bishop or the Curia

consumable /kən syo͞oməb'l/ *adj.* **ABLE TO BE CONSUMED** able or intended to be used up or discarded after use rather than saved ■ **consumables** *npl.* **CONSUMABLE GOODS** goods that have to be bought regularly because they wear out or are used up, such as food and clothing

consume /kən syo͞om/ (**-sumes, -suming, -sumed**) *v.* **1.** *vt.* **EAT OR DRINK** to eat or drink sth, especially in large amounts **2.** *vt.* **USE UP** to use sth in such a way that it cannot be reused or recovered afterwards ○ *The newer models consume less petrol.* **3.** *vt.* **ENGROSS OR OVERCOME** to fill sb's mind or attention fully (*usually passive*) ○ *consumed by a desire for new experiences* **4.** *vt.* **DESTROY COMPLETELY** to destroy sth or sb completely, especially by fire or disease **5.** *vti.* **BUY FROM OTHERS** to buy goods or services produced by other people [14thC. Directly or via French *consumer* from Latin *consumere* 'to take up completely, devour', from *sumere* 'to take'.]

consumedly /kən syo͞omidli/ *adv.* extremely or excessively, usually to an annoying or distressing degree (*archaic*) ○ *I'd have been fine if it weren't so consumedly hot!*

consumer /kən syo͞omər/ *n.* **1.** **BUYER** sb who buys goods or services **2.** **SB OR STH THAT CONSUMES STH** sb or sth that consumes sth, by eating it, drinking it, or using it up ○ *The country is one of the largest consumers of paper products.* **3.** ECOL **ORGANISM THAT FEEDS ON OTHERS** in an ecological community or food chain, an organism that feeds on other organisms, or on material derived from them. Consumers include herbivorous and carnivorous animals, which feed on plants and other animals respectively, and also organisms such as worms, fungi, and bacteria, which feed on nonliving organic material. —**consumership** *n.*

consumer credit *n.* money lent by financial institutions to enable members of the public to buy consumer goods or services. Hire-purchase agreements, credit cards, and charge accounts are all forms of consumer credit.

consumer durables *npl.* items such as computers or washing machines, that last a relatively long time and are purchased infrequently

consumer goods *npl.* goods that are bought by consumers and are not used to produce other goods

consumerism /kən syo͞omərizzəm/ *n.* **1.** ECON **BELIEF IN BENEFITS OF CONSUMPTION** the belief that the buying and selling of large quantities of consumer goods is beneficial to an economy or a sign of economic strength **2.** **PROTECTION OF CONSUMERS' RIGHTS** the protection of the rights and interests of consumers, especially with regard to price, quality, and safety **3.** **MATERIALISTIC ATTITUDE** an attitude that values the acquisition of material goods (*disapproving*) —**consumerist** /kən syo͞omərist/ *n.*, *adj.*

consumer price index *n.* **1.** **LIST OF CURRENT RETAIL PRICES** a government-issued list of the retail prices of basic household goods and services **2.** *ANZ* **COST OF GOODS** the average cost of a basket of goods during a specific period, used as an indicator of economic inflation

consuming /kən syo͞oming/ *adj.* so intense as to take up all of sb's attention, time, and energy ○ *a consuming interest in horses* —**consumingly** *adv.*

consummate /kónssə mayt, kónssyo͞o-/ *v.* (**-mates, -mating, -mated**) **1.** *vt.* **COMPLETE MARRIAGE** to make a marriage legally complete and fully valid by having sexual intercourse **2.** *vt.* **FULFILL RELATIONSHIP THROUGH SEX** to bring a relationship to completion or to gratify desire, especially by having sexual intercourse (*often passive*) **3.** *vti.* **CONCLUDE** to bring sth such as a business deal to a conclusion, or to be brought to a conclusion (*formal*) ○ *Leaving her business partner to consummate the deal, she boarded a flight for New York.* **4.** *vt.* **ACHIEVE** to achieve or fulfil sth, especially sth long sought (*formal; often passive*) ○ *Twelve years of effort and struggle were consummated when the foundation stone for the new theatre was laid.* **5.** *vti.* **BRING TO PERFECTION** to develop a skill to the point of perfection, or to be brought to the point of perfection (*literary*) ■ *adj.* **1.** **SUPREME OR PERFECT** excellent, skilful, or accomplished ○ *with consummate ease* **2.** **UTTER OR TOTAL** possessing or showing a bad quality to an extreme degree ○ *consummate arrogance* [15thC. From Latin *consummat-*, past participle stem of *consummare* 'to accomplish, to finish', from *summa* 'the highest thing'.] —**consummately** /kən súmmətli/ *adv.* —**consummative** /kən súmmətiv/ *adj.* —**consummator** /kónssə maytər, kónssyo͞o-/ *n.* —**consummatory** /kən súmmətəri/ *adj.*

consummation /kónsə máysh'n, kónsyo͞o máysh'n/ *n.* **1.** **PERFECT ENDING** the bringing of sth to a satisfying conclusion, or the final satisfying completion or achievement of sth ○ *The publication of her book was a consummation of her whole life's work.* **2.** **LEGAL COMPLETION OF MARRIAGE BY SEX** the legal completion of a marriage by an act of sexual intercourse between the spouses **3.** **COMPLETION OF DEAL** the completion of sth, such as a business deal

consumption /kən súmpsh'n/ *n.* **1.** **ACT OF EATING OR DRINKING** the eating or drinking of sth, or the amount that a person eats or drinks ○ *unfit for human consumption* **2.** **ACT OF USING STH UP** the use of natural resources or fuels or the amount of resources or fuels used ○ *consumption of fossil fuels* **3.** **CONSUMER EXPENDITURE** the purchase and use of goods and services by consumers, or the quantity of goods and services purchased **4.** **WASTING DISEASE** any condition that causes progressive wasting of the tissues, especially tuberculosis of the lungs (*dated*) [14thC. Via French *consomption* from the Latin stem *consumption-*, from *consumere* (see CONSUME).]

consumptive /kən súmptiv/ *adj.* **1.** **AFFECTED BY TUBERCULOSIS** affected by a wasting disease, especially tuberculosis of the lungs, or connected with such a disease (*dated*) **2.** **ENGAGED IN OR CAUSING CONSUMPTION** engaged in, causing, or encouraging the consumption of food, materials, or goods, especially in a wasteful or destructive way ■ *n.* **SB WITH TUBERCULOSIS** sb affected by a wasting disease, particularly tuberculosis of the lungs (*dated*) ○ *a chronic consumptive* [Mid-17thC. From medieval Latin *consumptivus*, from Latin *consumere* (see CONSUME).] —**consumptively** *adv.* —**consumptiveness** *n.*

cont. *abbr.* **1.** containing **2.** PUBL contents **3.** GEOG continent **4.** GEOG continental **5.** continued **6.** MED, GRAM contraction **7.** GRAM continuous **8.** control

contact /kón takt/ *n.* **1.** STATE OF COMMUNICATION a state or relationship in which communication happens or is possible ○ *Our only means of contact with the base was a small radio receiver.* **2.** ACT OF COMMUNICATING an act of communicating with sb ○ *All my contacts with him to date have been about business.* **3.** PHYSICAL CONNECTION a situation or state in which two or more things or people actually touch or strike against one another ○ *White phosphorus ignites on contact with the air.* **4.** INTERACTION a state in which sb has access to, and can be affected or influenced by, people, situations, ideas, or information ○ *You'll come into contact with a number of people.* **5.** SB WHO CAN HELP sb who may be useful either professionally or socially by providing a connection to a professional field or social circle **6.** MED INFECTIOUS PERSON sb associated with and seen as a possible carrier of an infectious disease **7.** ELEC DEVICE MAKING ELECTRICAL CONNECTION a movable part, such as a component of a switch, that can be made to touch another conductive part in order to enable an electrical current to pass **8.** ELEC ELECTRICAL CONNECTION a connection between, or the connection of, two or more electrical conductors so that current flows between them ■ **contacts** *npl.* CONTACT LENSES a set of contact lenses (*informal*) ■ *v.* (**-tacts, -tacting, -tacted**) **1.** *vt.* REACH IN ORDER TO COMMUNICATE to send a message to sb, or reach sb, e.g. by telephone or letter, in order to communicate ○ *You can contact me at this number.* **2.** *vti.* TOUCH to touch or strike against sth ■ *adj.* **1.** USED FOR COMMUNICATING WITH SB used as a means to contact sb ○ *a contact address* **2.** WORKING BY TOUCHING working or happening by touching or being touched by sth or sb **3.** CAUSED BY TOUCH caused by touching sth that irritates ○ *contact dermatitis* [Early 17thC. From Latin *contactus*, past participle of *contingere*, literally 'to touch with', from *tangere* 'to touch'.] —**contactual** /kon táktyoo əl/ *adj.* —**contactually** /-táktyoo əli/ *adv.*

contactable /kon táktəb'l/ *adj.* able to be contacted by sb wishing to send a message or communicate

contact flight, **contact flying** *n.* navigation of an aircraft by observing landmarks and other visible guides without the use of navigational aids

contact group *n.* a group of people who are neutral in a dispute and meet both sides to try to resolve disagreements through discussion

contact inhibition *n.* the normal cessation of cell division and growth caused by physical contact with other cells. This normal end to cell division does not function when cancer is present, resulting in uncontrolled reproduction of cells.

contact language *n.* a simplified language variety retaining features of other languages contributing to it, used as a means of communication in regions where the majority of speakers share no common language

contact lens *n.* a small plastic or glass lens placed directly onto the front of the eye to correct defective vision or make the iris appear a different colour

contactor /kón taktər/ *n.* a switch that controls the flow of electric current by repeatedly opening and closing a circuit

contact print *n.* a photographic print made by placing a negative directly on top of photosensitive paper and exposing it to light. This is usually done to check the images on a roll of film before making enlargements from individual negatives.

contact sport *n.* a sport such as boxing, rugby, or hockey in which physical contact between players is an integral part of the game

contagion /kən táyjən/ *n.* **1.** SPREAD OF DISEASE BY PHYSICAL CONTACT the transmission of disease, especially by physical contact between persons or contact with infected objects such as bedding or clothing **2.** DISEASE SPREAD BY PHYSICAL CONTACT an illness that spreads from one person to another, especially by physical contact between persons or contact with infected objects **3.** HARMFUL INFLUENCE a harmful or corrupting influence with a tendency to spread **4.** SPREAD OF FEELING the spreading of an attitude or emotion from person to person among a number of people (*literary*) ○ *the contagion of happiness* [14thC. From the Latin stem *contagion-*, from *contingere* (see CONTACT).]

contagious /kən táyjəss/ *adj.* **1.** ABLE TO BE PASSED BY CONTACT transmitted from one person to another either by direct contact, such as touching an infected person, or indirect contact **2.** CAPABLE OF TRANSMITTING DISEASE affected by or carrying a disease that can be transmitted by direct or indirect contact **3.** LIKELY TO AFFECT OTHERS quickly spread from one person to another ○ *Laughter is contagious.* [14thC. From late Latin *contagiosus*, from Latin *contingere* (see CONTACT).] —**contagiously** *adv.* —**contagiousness** *n.*

contagious abortion *n.* VET a contagious or infectious disease of farm animals, e.g. brucellosis, that is characterized by abortion

contain /kən táyn/ (**-tains, -taining, -tained**) *vt.* **1.** HAVE WITHIN to have sth inside, or to hold sth **2.** BE CAPABLE OF HOLDING PARTICULAR AMOUNT to be capable of holding sth within, especially a particular amount **3.** INCLUDE OR CONSIST OF to include sth as part of its contents or makeup **4.** CONTROL EMOTION to keep an emotion under control ○ *I couldn't contain myself any longer.* **5.** HOLD BACK OR RESTRICT to restrict the movement, spread, or influence of a strong enemy, force, disease, or idea **6.** MATH BE DIVISIBLE BY to be divisible by a number, leaving no remainder **7.** GEOM FORM SIDES OF ANGLE to form the boundaries that define an angle [13thC. Via French *contenir* from Latin *continere* 'to hold together', from *tenere* 'to hold'.] —**containable** *adj.*

container /kən táynər/ *n.* **1.** OBJECT USED TO HOLD STH an object such as a box, jar, or bottle that is used to hold sth, especially when it is being stored or transported **2.** FREIGHT BOX FOR CARGO a large box of a standard size into which goods are packed so that they can be transported securely and efficiently from departure point to destination by road, ship, or rail, without having to be repacked in any way

containerize /kən táynə rīz/ (**-izes, -izing, -ized**), **containerise** (**-ises, -ising, -ised**) *vt.* **1.** MOVE CARGO IN LARGE CONTAINERS to pack sth in freight containers for transportation by sea, road, or rail, especially commercially **2.** MODERNIZE TO ACCEPT CONTAINERS to convert a port, transport system, or industry so that it can use or handle standard-sized cargo containers —**containerization** /kən táynə rī záysh'n/ *n.*

container ship *n.* a ship specially designed to carry cargo that is packed in freight containers

containment /kən táynmənt/ *n.* **1.** ATTEMPT TO STOP SPREAD OF STH action taken to restrict the spread of sth hostile such as an enemy, or sth undesirable such as a disease **2.** NUCLEAR PHYS CONTROL MEASURE IN NUCLEAR REACTIONS the use of magnetic fields to prevent the reacting particles from touching the containing vessel's walls in a reactor **3.** ACT OR PROCESS OF CONTAINING STH the act or process of being contained or of containing sth

contaminant /kən támminənt/ *n.* a substance, such as a toxin in food, that contaminates sth else

contaminate /kən támmi nayt/ (**-nates, -nating, -nated**) *vt.* **1.** MAKE DIRTY OR IMPURE to make sth impure, unclean, or polluted, especially by mixing harmful impurities into it or by putting it in contact with sth harmful **2.** NUCLEAR PHYS MAKE RADIOACTIVE to make sth radioactive by mixing it or putting it in contact with a radioactive substance [15thC. From, ultimately, Latin *contaminare*, from *contamen* 'contact, pollution', literally 'touching with', from *tangere* 'to touch'.] —**contaminable** *adj.* —**contaminative** /-nətiv/ *adj.* —**contaminator** /-naytər/ *n.*

contamination /kən támmi náysh'n/ *n.* **1.** ACT OF CONTAMINATING STH the act or process of contaminating sth or becoming contaminated, or the unclean or impure state that results from this **2.** STH THAT CONTAMINATES sth that physically contaminates a substance or that corrupts a person morally ○ *The investigators found considerable contamination in the rivers.* **3.** LING ALTERATION OF WORD OR PHRASE the process by which a word or phrase changes as a result of mistaken association with another word or phrase

contango /kən táng gō, kon-/ *n.* (*plural* **-gos**) **1.** POSTPONEMENT OF STOCK DELIVERY formerly the postponement of the delivery of stock to a broker and payment for it, from one account day to the next **2.** INTEREST PAYABLE ON CONTANGO interest payable by a broker when the delivery of and payment for stock is postponed ■ *vt.* (**-gos, -going, -goed**) ARRANGE A CONTANGO to arrange for delivery and payment to be postponed when transferring stock in a stock exchange [Mid-19thC. Origin uncertain: perhaps an alteration of CONTINUE, or of Latin *contingo*, first person singular present tense of *contingere* (see CONTACT).]

contd *abbr.* continued

conte /koNt/ *n.* **1.** SHORT STORY a short story (*literary*) **2.** LITERAT MEDIEVAL NARRATIVE a narrative tale from the Middle Ages [Late 19thC. From French, where it was formed from Old French *counter* (see COUNT[1]).]

conté /kón tay/ *n.* a hard drawing crayon made of clay and graphite [Mid-19thC. Named after the French inventor Nicolas Jacques *Conté* (1755–1805), who developed a method of making pencils.]

contemn /kən tém/ (**-temns, -temning, -temned**) *vt.* to view or treat sb with contempt (*literary*) [15thC. Directly or via Old French *contemner* from Latin *contemnere* (see CONTEMPT).] —**contemner** *n.* —**contemnible** *adj.* —**contemnibly** *adv.*

contemp. *abbr.* contemporary

contemplate /kóntəm playt, -tem-/ (**-plates, -plating, -plated**) *v.* **1.** *vt.* LOOK AT THOUGHTFULLY to look at sth thoughtfully and steadily **2.** *vt.* CONSIDER to think about sth seriously and at length, especially in order to understand it more fully ○ *I sat there, contemplating what she'd said.* **3.** *vt.* HAVE AS POSSIBLE INTENTION to think about sth as a possible course of action ○ *contemplating moving house* **4.** *vi.* THINK ABOUT SPIRITUAL MATTERS to think calmly and at length, especially as a religious or spiritual exercise [Late 16thC. From Latin *contemplat-*, past participle stem of *contemplari* 'to observe carefully', from *templum* 'space for observing omens'.] —**contemplator** *n.*

contemplation /kóntəm pláysh'n, -tem-/ *n.* **1.** THOUGHT ABOUT STH long and attentive consideration or observation of sth **2.** DEEP SPIRITUAL THOUGHT OR MEDITATION concentration of the mind on spiritual matters such as achieving closer unity with God

contemplative /kən témplətiv/ *adj.* MEDITATIVE calm and thoughtful, or inclined to be this way ■ *n.* SB WHO PRACTISES CONTEMPLATION sb who practises contemplation as a spiritual exercise, especially a member of a Christian monastic order —**contemplatively** *adv.* —**contemplativeness** *n.*

contemporaneous /kən témpə ráyni əss, kon-/ *adj.* existing, occurring, or beginning at the same time or during the same period of time as sth else [Mid-17thC. Formed from Latin *contemporaneus*, literally 'time together', from *tempor-* (see CONTEMPORARY).] —**contemporaneity** /kən témpərə née əti, kon-/ *n.* —**contemporaneously** /kən témpə ráyni əssli, kon-/ *adv.* —**contemporaneousness** /-əssnəss/ *n.*

contemporary /kən témprəri/ *adj.* **1.** OF THE SAME TIME existing or occurring at, or dating from, the same period of time as sth or sb else **2.** EXISTING in existence now **3.** MODERN IN STYLE distinctively modern in style ○ *a variety of favourite contemporary styles* **4.** OF THE SAME AGE of the same, or approximately the same, age as sb else ○ *She and I are more or less contemporary.* ■ *n.* (*plural* **-ies**) **1.** SB OR STH OF SAME TIME sb who lived or sth that existed during the same general span of time as sb or sth else ○ *This 18th-century table is a contemporary of the Shaker furniture in the other room.* **2.** SB OF SAME AGE sb who is approximately the same age as sb else ○ *It was nice to spend time with my Dad's contemporaries.* **3.** MODERN PERSON OR THING sb or sth in existence at the present time **4.** PRESS, PUBL RIVAL NEWSPAPER OR MAGAZINE a newspaper or magazine that is regarded as a rival or competition by another paper or periodical [Mid-17thC. From medieval Latin *contemporarius*, from Latin *tempor-*, stem of *tempus* 'time' (source of English *tempo*, *temporary*, and *tense*).] —**contemporarily** *adv.* —**contemporariness** *n.*

contemporize /kən témpə rīz/ (**-rizes, -rizing, -rized**), **contemporise** (**-rises, -rising, -rised**) *vt.* **1.** MAKE MODERN to make sth modern or fashionable **2.** DATE THINGS FROM SAME PERIOD to place sb or sth in the same period as sb or sth else [Mid-17thC. Formed from late Latin *contemporare* 'to make contemporary', from Latin *tempor-*

(see CONTEMPORARY).] —**contemporization** /kən témpə rī záysh'n/ *n.*

contempt /kən témpt/ *n.* **1.** ATTITUDE OF UTTER DISGUST OR HATRED a powerful feeling of dislike towards sb or sth considered to be worthless, inferior, or undeserving of respect **2.** LAW = **contempt of court** [14thC. From Latin *contemptus* 'scorn', from *contemnere* 'to despise utterly', from *temnere* 'to scorn'.]

contemptible *adj.* deserving to be treated with contempt —**contemptibility** /kən témptə bílləti/ *n.* —**contemptibleness** /kən témptəb'lnəss/ *n.* —**contemptibly** /-témptəbli/ *adv.*

contempt of court *n.* the crime of deliberately failing to obey or respect the authority of a court of law or legislative body

contemptuous /kən témptyoo əss/ *adj.* feeling, expressing, or demonstrating a strong dislike or utter lack of respect for sb or sth [Early 16thC. From medieval Latin *contemptuosus*, from Latin *contemnere* (see CONTEMPT).] —**contemptuously** *adv.* —**contemptuousness** *n.*

contend /kən ténd/ (**-tends, -tending, -tended**) *v.* **1.** *vi.* STATE STH to argue or claim that sth is true **2.** *vti.* COMPETE to compete for sth, especially a prize or trophy ○ *the teams contending for the cup* **3.** *vi.* STRUGGLE OR DEAL WITH STH to fight with, struggle against, or deal with sb or sth ○ *Their lawyers have a number of awkward issues to contend with.* **4.** *vi.* DEBATE WITH SB to debate or dispute with sb (*literary*) [15thC. Directly or via French *contendre* from Latin *contendere* 'to strive together', from *tendere* 'to strive, stretch'.]

contender /kən téndər/ *n.* a competitor, especially sb who has a good chance of winning

WORD KEY: SYNONYMS

See Synonyms at ***candidate***.

content[1] /kón tent/ *n.* **1.** AMOUNT OF STH IN STH ELSE the amount of sth contained in sth else **2.** SUBJECT MATTER the various issues, topics, or questions dealt with in speech, discussion, or a piece of writing **3.** LITERAT MEANING OR MESSAGE the meaning or message contained in a creative work as distinct from its appearance, form, or style **4.** COMPUT INFORMATION AVAILABLE ELECTRONICALLY information made available by an electronic medium or product **5.** CAPACITY the capacity of a container ■ **contents** *npl.* **1.** STH CONTAINED everything that is inside a particular container ○ *picked up the file and emptied its contents onto the desk* **2.** SUBJECT OF TEXT the subject matter of a publication **3.** LIST OF SUBJECT OR CHAPTER HEADINGS a list at the front of a publication that gives the title and number of the first page of each new chapter, article, or part [15thC. From medieval Latin *contentum* 'sth contained', a form of Latin *contentus*, past participle of *continere* (see CONTAIN).]

content[2] /kən tént/ *adj.* **1.** QUIETLY SATISFIED AND HAPPY reasonably happy and satisfied with the way things are **2.** READY TO ACCEPT STH willing to accept or comply with a situation or course of action ■ *v.* (**-tents, -tenting, -tented**) **1.** *vt.* CAUSE TO FEEL CONTENT to make sb feel happy or satisfied with sth **2.** *vr.* ACCEPT OR MAKE DO WITH STH to accept or make do with sth, rather than taking further action or making more demands ○ *He contented himself with a few cutting remarks about lack of discipline and did not take the matter further.* ■ *n.* = **contentment** *n.* 1 ■ *interj.* HOUSE OF LORDS EXPRESSION OF AGREEMENT used by a member of the House of Lords to express formal agreement to a bill. Disagreement is expressed by the phrase 'not content'. (*formal*) [15thC. Via French from Latin *contentus*, past participle of *continere* (see CONTAIN). The underlying sense is of having your desires limited to what you have.] —**contently** *adv.*

contented /kən téntid/ *adj.* peacefully happy and satisfied with the way things are, or with what you have done or achieved —**contentedly** *adv.* —**contentedness** *n.*

contention /kən ténsh'n/ *n.* **1.** ASSERTION IN AN ARGUMENT an opinion or claim stated in the course of an argument ○ *It is my contention that the scheme was bound to fail.* **2.** DISAGREEMENT angry disagreement between people ○ *a lot of contention over the quality of the goods* **3.** RIVALRY competition between rivals or opponents ○ *fierce contention for the title* [14thC. Directly or via French from the Latin stem *contention-*, from *contendere* (see CONTEND).]

contentious /kən ténshəss/ *adj.* **1.** CREATING DISAGREEMENT causing or likely to cause disagreement and disputes between people with differing views ○ *It should have been possible to word the statement in a less contentious way.* **2.** ARGUMENTATIVE frequently engaging in and seeming to enjoy arguments and disputes **3.** LAW SUBJECT TO LITIGATION contested by another interested party ○ *a contentious will* [15thC. Via French *contentieux* from Latin *contentiosus*, from *contendere* (see CONTEND).] —**contentiously** *adv.* —**contentiousness** *n.*

contentment /kən téntmənt/ *n.* **1.** SATISFACTION a feeling of calm satisfaction **2.** STH THAT MAKES SB CONTENTED a circumstance, or a feature or characteristic of sth, that gives rise to satisfaction (*formal or literary*)

content word *n.* LING a word that refers to a real world object and primarily conveys meaning. ◊ **function word**

conterminous /kon túrminəss, kən-/, **coterminous** /kō-/ *adj.* **1.** INSIDE SAME BOUNDARY enclosed inside a common boundary **2.** ADJACENT next to and sharing a common boundary with sth **3.** MEETING IN TIME OR PLACE meeting end to end, so that where or when one finishes the next begins [Mid-17thC. From Latin *conterminus*, literally 'boundary with', from *terminus* 'boundary'.] —**conterminously** *adv.* —**conterminousness** *n.*

contessa /kon téssə/ *n.* an Italian countess [Early 19thC. Via Italian from medieval Latin *comitissa*, feminine of *comes* (see COUNT[2]).]

contest *n.* /kóntest/ **1.** COMPETITION TO FIND THE BEST an organized competition for a prize or title, especially one in which the entrants appear or demonstrate their skills individually and the winner is chosen by a group of judges **2.** STRUGGLE FOR CONTROL a struggle between rival or opposing individuals, organizations, or forces for victory or control ■ *vt.* /kən tést/ (**-tests, -testing, -tested**) **1.** CHALLENGE to challenge or question sth **2.** TAKE PART IN CONTEST to take part in a contest or competition, especially an election [Late 16thC. Directly or via French from Latin *contestari* 'to begin a lawsuit by calling witnesses together', from *testari* 'to be a witness'.] —**contestable** /kən téstəb'l/ *adj.* —**contestably** /-téstəbli/ *adv.* —**contester** /-téstər/ *n.*

contestant /kən téstənt/ *n.* **1.** SB COMPETING IN CONTEST sb who takes part in a competition **2.** LAW FORMAL CHALLENGER sb who enters a formal challenge to sth such as a will, verdict, or decision

WORD KEY: SYNONYMS

See Synonyms at ***candidate***.

context /kón tekst/ *n.* **1.** TEXT SURROUNDING A WORD OR PASSAGE the words, phrases, or passages that come before and after a particular word or passage in a speech or piece of writing and help to explain its full meaning **2.** SURROUNDING CONDITIONS the circumstances or events that form the environment within which sth exists or takes place [15thC. From Latin *contextus* 'cohering, connected', from *contexere* 'to weave together', from *texere* 'to weave'.] —**contextless** *adj.*

contextual /kən tékstyoo əl/ *adj.* forming, relating to, or contained in the context of a word or event —**contextually** *adv.*

contextualize /kən tékstyoo ə līz/ (**-izes, -izing, -ized**) *vt.* to place a word, phrase, or idea within a suitable context —**contextualization** /kən tékstyoo ə lī záysh'n/ *n.*

contexture /kən tékschər/ *n.* **1.** WEAVING TOGETHER the process of weaving together separate strands, e.g. of an argument, to form a complex but coherent whole **2.** INTERWOVEN STRUCTURE a structure resulting from the complex interweaving of separate strands or parts [Early 17thC. From French, literally 'weaving together', from, ultimately, Latin *textura* 'weaving'.] —**contextural** *adj.*

Conti /kónti/, **Tom** (*b.* 1942) Scottish-born British stage and film actor. He is a versatile character actor whose success dates from his Tony award for the Broadway production of *Whose Life Is It Anyway?* (1974).

contiguity /kónti gyoō əti/ (*plural* **-ties**) *n.* (*formal*) **1.** CLOSENESS OR CONTACT closeness in space or time to sth, or actual contact with it along one side **2.** STH CONTINUOUS a continuous line, mass, or series ○ *a contiguity of roofs*

contiguous /kən tíggyoo əss/ *adj.* (*formal*) **1.** ADJOINING sharing a boundary or touching each other physically **2.** NEIGHBOURING situated next to sth else or to each other **3.** CONTINUOUS connected together so as to form an unbroken sequence in time or an uninterrupted expanse in space [Early 16thC. Formed from Latin *contiguus* 'touching together', from *contingere* (see CONTACT).] —**contiguously** *adv.* —**contiguousness** *n.*

continence /kóntinənss/ *n.* **1.** CONTROL OVER URINATION AND DEFECATION the ability to prevent involuntary urination and defecation **2.** SELF-RESTRAINT control over physical, especially sexual, impulses leading to self-restraint, moderation, or abstinence [14thC. Directly or via French from Latin *continentia*, from *continere* (see CONTAIN).]

continent[1] /kóntinənt/ *n.* **1.** LAND MASS any one of the seven large continuous land masses that constitute most of the dry land on the surface of the earth. They are Africa, Antarctica, Asia, Australia, Europe, North America, and South America. **2.** GEOG LAND ABOVE SEA LEVEL the part of the earth's crust that rises above the oceans [Mid-16thC. From Latin *terra continens* 'continuous land', from the present participle of *continere* (see CONTAIN).]

continent[2] /kóntinənt/ *adj.* **1.** ABLE TO CONTROL URINATION AND DEFECATION able to exercise control over urination and bowel movements **2.** MODERATE OR CELIBATE restrained, especially abstaining from sexual activity [14thC. From Latin *continent-*, present participle stem of *continere* (see CONTAIN).]

Continent *n.* the mainland of Europe, not including the British Isles

continental /kónti nént'l/ *adj.* RELATING TO EARTH'S CONTINENTS relating to, typical of, or belonging to the continents of the earth ■ *n.* HIST BANKNOTE a banknote issued by the Continental Congress during the American War of Independence —**continentalism** *n.* —**continentalist** *n.* —**continentally** *adv.*

Continental *adj.* **1. Continental, continental** OF MAINLAND EUROPE from or relating to mainland Europe **2.** HIST OF THE ORIGINAL 13 AMERICAN COLONIES from or relating to the 13 colonies that later became the United States. ◊ **Continental Congress** ■ *n.* **1. Continental, continental** MAINLAND EUROPEAN sb from mainland Europe (*informal*) **2.** HIST AMERICAN SOLDIER DURING REVOLUTION a soldier in the American army during the American War of Independence

continental breakfast *n.* a light breakfast usually consisting of fruit juice, a roll, croissant, or pastry with jam and butter, or sometimes with slices of cold meat or cheese, and coffee or tea [Continental from the fact that this kind of breakfast is common on the Continent]

continental climate *n.* the climate characteristic of the interior of a continent, with hot summers, cold winters, and little rainfall

Continental Congress *n.* HIST the congress of delegates from the American colonies held before, during, and after the American War of Independence. It issued the Declaration of Independence (1776) and drafted the Articles of Confederation (1777).

continental crust *n.* GEOG the part of the outer shell of the solid earth that constitutes the continents and the rocks beneath them as deep as the mantle. It is approximately 35 km/22 mi. thick in most areas and is composed of sedimentary rocks near the surface and metamorphic rocks at a lower depth.

continental divide *n.* GEOG a massive area of high ground in the interior of a continent, from either side of which a continent's river systems flow in different directions

Continental Divide *n.* the series of mountain ridges running from Alaska to Mexico and including the Rocky Mountains that forms the main watershed of North America

continental drift *n.* a theory that explains the formation, alteration, and extremely slow movement of the continents across the earth's crust. The continents are thought to have been formed from one large land mass that split, drifted apart, and in places collided again. ◊ **plate tectonics**

continental quilt *n.* = **duvet**

continental shelf *n.* the gently sloping undersea area surrounding a continent at depths of up to 200 m/656 ft, at the edge of which the continental slope drops steeply to the ocean floor

continental slope *n.* the steep slope from the continental shelf down to the ocean floor

contingence /kən tínjənss/ *n.* **1.** CONTACT physical contact between objects **2.** = **contingency** *n.* 1

contingency /kən tínjənssi/ (*plural* **-cies**) *n.* **1.** STH THAT MAY HAPPEN an event that may occur in the future, especially a problem, emergency, or expense that might arise unexpectedly, needs to be dealt with, and therefore must be prepared for **2.** STH INCIDENTAL OR DEPENDENT sth that occurs or exists only as a result of sth else or that depends on sth else **3.** DEPENDENCE UPON CHANCE dependence upon chance or factors and circumstances that are presently unknown **4.** GRAM CHANGE IN MEANING PRODUCED BY CLAUSE in systemic grammar, a change in the meaning of the main clause brought about by the addition of a bound clause introduced by 'if', 'when', 'though', or 'since'

contingency fee *n.* a payment for professional services, such as those of a lawyer, that is made only if the client receives a satisfactory result

contingency force *n.* MIL = **rapid-deployment force**

contingent /kən tínjənt/ *adj.* **1.** DEPENDENT ON WHAT MAY HAPPEN dependent on or resulting from a future and as yet unknown event or circumstance ○ *Payment is contingent upon winning the case.* **2.** POSSIBLE BUT NOT CERTAIN possible, but not certain to happen ○ *'...all the advantages of a long slow ramble with Elfride, without the contingent possibility of the enjoyment being spoilt by her becoming weary'.* (Thomas Hardy, *A Pair of Blue Eyes*; 1889) **3.** CHANCE happening by chance **4.** LOGIC TRUE ONLY UNDER CERTAIN CONDITIONS true only under certain conditions or under existing conditions, and therefore not universally true or valid ■ *n.* **1.** GROUP OF PEOPLE a group of people representing a particular organization or belief, or from a particular region or country, and forming part of a larger group **2.** MIL GROUP OF MILITARY PERSONNEL a group, particularly of soldiers, forming part of a larger force **3.** = **contingency** *n.* 1 [14thC. From Latin *contingent-*, present participle stem of *contingere* 'to happen, have contact with'. The underlying idea is of being affected by things happening.] —**contingently** *adv.*

contingent fee *n.* = **contingency fee**

contingent worker *n.* US a temporary employee, often employed for a specific task

continual /kən tínnyoo əl/ *adj.* **1.** RECURRING VERY FREQUENTLY happening again and again, especially regularly **2.** UNINTERRUPTED continuing without interruption or ending [14thC. From French *continuel*, from *continuer* (see CONTINUE).] —**continually** *adv.* —**continualness** *n.*

WORD KEY: USAGE

continual or **continuous**? Something ***continual*** stops from time to time but continues intermittently over a long period, whereas sth ***continuous*** goes on without a break. So a ***continual*** noise is one that is constantly repeated, like a dog's barking, and a ***continuous*** noise is one that continues unbroken, like the roar of a waterfall. The same distinction applies to the adverbs *continually* and *continuously*: *The speaker was continually interrupted by hecklers. She drove continuously for ten hours.*

continuance /kən tínnyoo ənss/ *n.* **1.** CONTINUATION OF STH the fact or quality of continuing to be in a particular situation, to exist, or to occur beyond the present time into the future **2.** LENGTH OF TIME STH LASTS the period of time that sth lasts or continues **3.** US LAW ADJOURNMENT a postponement of legal proceedings until a later date

continuant /kən tínnyoo ənt/ *n.* a speech sound, such as 'l', 'f', or 's', made with the vocal passage partly open for breath to pass through, thus enabling the sound to be prolonged at will. ◊ **stop**

continuation /kən tínnyoo áysh'n/ *n.* **1.** PROCESS OF CONTINUING the process of continuing sth without interruption **2.** ADDITION OR EXTENSION an additional part that extends sth that already exists or has already begun **3.** STARTING AGAIN AFTER INTERRUPTION the renewal of an action, event, or process after it has been interrupted

continuative /kən tínnyoo ətiv/ *adj.* **1.** AIDING CONTINUITY causing or helping sth to continue (*formal*) **2.** GRAM EXPRESSING CONTINUATION expressing the continuation of an action ■ *n.* GRAM WORD EXPRESSING CONTINUATION a continuative clause, phrase, or word —**continuatively** *adv.*

continuator /kən tínnyoo aytər/ *n.* sb who continues sth, especially work started by another person

continue /kən tínnyoo/ (**-ues, -uing, -ued**) *v.* **1.** *vti.* KEEP GOING to last, or to make sth last, beyond the present **2.** *vti.* LAST to last or to make sth last throughout a particular period of time **3.** *vti.* NOT STOP to keep up an activity or state already begun **4.** *vti.* START STH AGAIN to start, or to start doing sth again after an interruption or pause **5.** *vti.* UTTER OR BEGIN SPEAKING AGAIN to begin speaking again, or to say sth, after an interruption or pause **6.** *vti.* MAKE STH LONGER to extend, or to extend sth, beyond a particular point or beyond its original length **7.** *vi.* MOVE FURTHER to move or travel further in a particular direction **8.** *vt. US, Scotland* LAW POSTPONE CASE to postpone legal proceedings [14thC. Via French *continuer* from Latin *continuare* 'to make or be continuous', from, ultimately, *continere* (see CONTAIN).] —**continuable** *adj.* —**continuer** *n.*

continued /kən tínnyood/ *adj.* uninterrupted or unchanged from its beginning up to the present time

continued fraction *n.* a fraction with a whole number as numerator, a number plus a fraction as denominator, which in turn has a number plus a fraction as its denominator. If there is a finite number of terms, it is said to be terminating, otherwise it is non-terminating.

continuing /kən tínnyoo ing/ *adj.* having existed for some time, currently in existence, and likely to remain so in the future —**continuingly** *adv.*

continuing education *n.* **1.** LIFELONG ADULT EDUCATION adult education, usually in the form of short or part-time courses, continuing throughout an individual's life **2.** US SPECIALIST COURSES TO UPDATE PROFESSIONALS regular courses or training designed to bring professionals up to date with the latest developments in their particular field

continuity /kónti nyóō əti/ (*plural* **-ties**) *n.* **1.** UNCHANGING QUALITY the fact of staying the same, of being consistent throughout, or of not stopping or being interrupted ○ *measures to ensure continuity of care* **2.** CONSISTENT WHOLE sth that remains consistent or uninterrupted throughout **3.** CINEMA, BROADCAST CONSISTENCY BETWEEN FILM OR BROADCAST PARTS consistency in the details from one part of a film or broadcast to another ○ *discrepancies in continuity* **4.** CINEMA, BROADCAST SEAMLESSNESS OF NARRATIVE smoothness in the narrative flow in a film or broadcast **5.** CINEMA DETAILED SCRIPT a comprehensive script that includes full details of the contents of each shot or scene, including such items as camera positions and settings and costume features **6.** BROADCAST SPOKEN LINK IN BROADCASTING things said by a television or radio announcer to fill the time between the end of one programme and the beginning of the next, or between parts of programmes

continuo /kən tínnyoo ō/ (*plural* **-os**) *n.* an instrumental bass accompaniment, usually played on a keyboard, with numbers written beneath the notes so that musicians can improvise and provide harmony [Early 18thC. From Italian, literally 'continuous', from Latin *continuus* (see CONTINUOUS).]

continuous /kən tínnyoo əss/ *adj.* **1.** UNCHANGED OR UNINTERRUPTED continuing without changing, stopping, or being interrupted ○ *three days of continuous rain* **2.** UNBROKEN having no gaps, holes, or breaks ○ *a continuous line* **3.** GRAM = **progressive 4.** MATH RELATING TO DIFFERENCE OF FUNCTION VALUES relating to a line or curve along which the difference between function values at any two points within a given interval will approach zero if the interval is decreased sufficiently **5.** RELATING TO UNINTERRUPTED CHEMICAL MANUFACTURING relating to chemical manufacturing in which material is processed in an uninterrupted stream. Continuous processes are usually advantageous for large-scale chemical production. [Mid-17thC. Formed from Latin *continuus* 'uninterrupted', from *continere* (see CONTAIN).] —**continuousness** *n.*

WORD KEY: USAGE

See Usage note at ***continual***.

continuous creation theory *n.* ASTRON = **steady-state theory**

continuously /kən tínnyooəssli/ *adv.* **1.** WITHOUT INTERRUPTION without any break or interruption ○ *It had rained continuously for three days.* See Usage note at **continual 2.** RECURRENTLY frequently or regularly

continuous spectrum *n.* a sequence of frequencies that is without breaks over a relatively wide range of wavelengths

continuous wave *n.* an electromagnetic wave generated as an unbroken train of constant frequency and amplitude, rather than in pulses

continuum /kən tínnyoo əm/ (*plural* **-a** /-nyoo ə/ *or* **-ums**) *n.* **1.** CONTINUOUS SEAMLESS SERIES a link between two things, or a continuous series of things, that blend into each other so gradually and seamlessly that it is impossible to say where one becomes the next ○ *A rainbow forms a continuum of colour.* **2.** MATH SET OF NUMBERS a set of real numbers between any two of which a third can always be found, and in which there are no gaps [Mid-17thC. From Latin, a form of *continuus* (see CONTINUOUS).]

contort /kən táwrt/ (**-torts, -torting, -torted**) *v.* **1.** *vti.* TWIST OUT OF NATURAL SHAPE to become so twisted as to take on an unnatural or grotesque shape or to twist sth, especially a part of the body, in this way ○ *Fear had contorted their faces.* **2.** *vt.* MAKE UNRECOGNIZABLE to change sth so greatly that it becomes unrecognizable [15thC. From Latin *contort-*, past participle stem of *contorquere* 'to twist violently', from *torquere* 'to twist'.] —**contortive** *adj.*

contorted /kən táwrtid/ *adj.* **1.** VERY TWISTED greatly or violently twisted out of shape **2.** OVERLAPPING used to describe plant parts such as sepals or leaves whose margins overlap in the bud like playing cards in a hand, so that they appear to be twisted —**contortedly** *adv.* —**contortedness** *n.*

contortion /kən táwrsh'n/ *n.* **1.** TWISTED SHAPE OR POSITION a twisting of sth, especially a part of the body, out of its natural shape **2.** COMPLEX MANOEUVRE a bewilderingly complex manoeuvring or manipulation of sth ○ *verbal contortions that tie his opponents in knots*

contortionist /kən táwrsh'nist/ *n.* **1.** SB WHO PERFORMS BENDING FEATS sb who bends his or her body into unnatural shapes as an entertainment ○ *You'd have to be a contortionist to get into those jeans.* **2.** SKILFUL MANIPULATOR OR MANOEUVRER sb who twists or distorts things, e.g. things people say, or who wriggles out of things, e.g. difficult situations ○ *a debater skilled as a logical contortionist* —**contortionistic** /kən ta-wrsh'n ístik/ *adj.*

contour /kón toor/ *n.* **1.** SHAPE'S OUTLINE an outline, especially of sth curved or irregular (*often used in the plural*) ○ *The contours of the hills were characteristically rounded.* **2.** GENERAL NATURE the general character or nature of sth ○ *scenes that establish the contour of the play* **3.** = **contour line** ■ *adj.* **1.** SHAPED OR FITTED shaped to fit sth, especially the shape of sb's body ○ *contour furniture* **2.** FOLLOWING LAND'S SHAPE following the lie of the land, rather than cutting through or across it ○ *contour farming* ■ *vt.* (**-tours, -touring, -toured**) **1.** SHAPE TO FIT to shape one thing so that it fits the outlines of another ○ *furniture that is contoured to the human body* **2.** PUT CONTOUR LINES ON to mark contour lines on sth such as a map **3.** CAUSE TO FIT LAND'S SHAPE to build or operate sth so that it follows the natural shape of the land ○ *roads that are sensitively contoured* [Mid-17thC. Via French from, ultimately, Italian *contornare* 'to draw in outline', literally 'to turn with', from Latin *tornare* 'to turn (in a lathe)' (see TURN).]

contour feather *n.* a medium-sized feather of a bird, excluding those on the wings and tail, that makes up its external covering and determines its shape

contour interval *n.* the interval between contour lines on a map, or the altitude the interval represents ○ *at contour intervals of 10 metres*

contour line *n.* a line on a map connecting points on a land surface that are the same elevation above sea level

contour map *n.* a map that uses contour lines to show the shapes and elevations of land surfaces

contr. *abbr.* **1.** GRAM contraction **2.** MUSIC contralto **3.** control

contra /kóntrə/ *n.* a member of the United States-backed counter-revolutionary force whose aim was to bring down the Nicaraguan government in the 1980s [From Spanish *contrarevolucionario* 'counter-revolutionary']

contra- *prefix.* **1.** against, opposite, contrasting ○ *contraindicate* **2.** lower in pitch ○ *contrabass* [From Latin *contra* 'against'. Ultimately from an Indo-European base meaning 'together', which is also the ancestor of English *com-*.]

contraband /kóntrə band/ *n.* **1.** ILLEGAL IMPORTS AND EXPORTS goods that are illegally imported or exported, e.g. goods that evade duty or are prohibited by law from being taken into or out of a country ○ *dealers in contraband* **2.** ILLEGAL TRADE illegal trade, especially the illegal importing or exporting of goods **3.** SUPPLIES FORBIDDEN TO WARRING SIDES goods that a neutral country must not supply to either side in a war ■ *adj.* **1.** ILLEGALLY TRADED bought or sold, especially imported or exported, illegally ○ *truckloads of contraband cigarettes* **2.** FORBIDDEN FROM BEING IMPORTED OR EXPORTED forbidden by law from being traded, especially as an import or export [Late 16thC. Via Spanish *contrabanda* from Italian *contrabbando*, literally 'against proclamation', from *bando* 'proclamation', ultimately from prehistoric Germanic.] —**contrabandage** *n.* —**contrabandist** *n.*

contrabass /kóntrə bayss/ *n.* **1.** DOUBLE BASS a double bass **2.** INSTRUMENT PITCHED LOWEST OF ITS FAMILY an instrument pitched an octave below the usual range for that family of instruments **3.** CONTRABASSIST an instrumentalist in an orchestra or band who plays the contrabass ■ *adj.* PITCHED AN OCTAVE BELOW pitched an octave below the usual range of that instrument ○ *contrabass clarinet* [Early 19thC. From Italian *contrabbasso*, from *basso* 'bass'.] —**contrabassist** /kóntrə báyssist/ *n.*

contrabassoon /kóntrə bə sóon/ *n.* **1.** LARGEST INSTRUMENT OF OBOE FAMILY a U-shaped woodwind instrument that is the largest in the oboe family and has a pitch an octave below the bassoon **2.** CONTRABASSOONIST an instrumentalist in an orchestra or chamber group who plays the contrabassoon —**contrabassoonist** *n.*

contraception /kóntrə sépsh'n/ *n.* a way of avoiding pregnancy, using either artificial methods such as condoms and contraceptive pills or natural methods such as avoiding sex during the woman's known fertile periods [Late 19thC. Coined from CONTRA- + CONCEPTION.]

contraceptive /kóntrə séptiv/ *n.* DEVICE PREVENTING FERTILIZATION a device used to prevent fertilization of an egg, e.g. a condom worn by a man during intercourse or a pill taken regularly by a woman ■ *adj.* PREVENTING INSEMINATION designed to prevent sperm from fertilizing an egg ○ *various contraceptive methods and devices*

contract *n.* /kón trakt/ **1.** FORMAL AGREEMENT a formal or legally binding agreement, such as one for the sale of sth, or one setting out terms of employment ○ *Such actions would be in breach of contract.* **2.** DOCUMENT RECORDING AGREEMENT a document that records a formal or legally binding agreement ○ *sign a contract* **3.** AGREEMENT TO MARRY a formal agreement to marry (*dated*) **4.** PAID ASSASSIN'S ASSIGNMENT a hiring of an assassin to kill sb (*informal*) **5.** BRIDGE HIGHEST BRIDGE BID IN ONE HAND a winning bid in a single hand of bridge, in which partners agree regarding the number of tricks they can take **6.** BRIDGE NUMBER AND SUIT OF CONTRACT the number and suit of the tricks agreed on by the highest bidders **7.** BRIDGE = **contract bridge 8. contracts** LAW BRANCH OF LAW the branch or category of law and legal education that deals with contracts ○ *She made a career in contracts.* ■ *v.* /kən trákt/ (**-tracts, -tracting, -tracted**) **1.** *vti.* SHRINK OR LESSEN to shrink or become smaller, or make sth shrink or become smaller ○ *metals expanding and contracting as temperatures change* **2.** *vti.* TIGHTEN OR DRAW TOGETHER to become tighter or draw together, or make sth tighter or draw sth together ○ *see the muscles contracting under the skin* **3.** *vi.* FORMALLY OR LEGALLY AGREE to make a formal or legally binding agreement to do sth, especially work (*often passive*) ○ *I'm not contracted to work on Sundays.* **4.** *vt.* GET ILLNESS to become affected by an illness or disease **5.** *vt.* SHORTEN WORD OR PHRASE to shorten a word by leaving out letters or syllables, or a phrase by leaving out words **6.** *vt.* ARRANGE MARRIAGE to arrange a marriage formally (*dated*) [14thC. Directly or via French from Latin *contractus*, past participle of *contrahere* 'to draw together', from *trahere* 'to draw' (see TRACTOR).] —**contractibility** /kən tráktə bílləti/ *n.* —**contractible** /kən tráktəb'l/ *adj.* —**contractibleness** /-əb'lnəss/ *n.* —**contractibly** /-əbli/ *adv.*

contract out /kón trakt ówt/ *v.* **1.** *vt.* GIVE WORK TO OUTSIDERS to offer work to outside companies or individuals **2.** *vi.* WITHDRAW FORMALLY to withdraw from sth by making a formal or legally binding declaration ○ *employees contracting out of the state pension scheme*

contract bridge *n.* the most common variety of bridge, in which points are awarded only for tricks bid as well as won

contractile /kən trákt īl/ *adj.* able or tending to shrink, tighten, or become narrower —**contractility** /kón trak tílləti/ *n.*

contractile vacuole *n.* BIOL a membrane-surrounded cavity within a cell that regulates the water content of the cell by absorbing water and then contracting to expel it

contraction /kən tráksh'n/ *n.* **1.** REDUCTION IN SIZE a shrinking or reducing ○ *alternate expansion and contraction* **2.** CONTRACTING OF BODY PART a tightening or narrowing of a muscle, organ, or other body part **3.** TIGHTENING OF WOMB MUSCLES EFFECTING CHILDBIRTH a tightening of the muscles of the womb that occurs at increasingly frequent intervals immediately before childbirth and eventually pushes the baby out of the womb **4.** SHORTENED WORD a shortened form or shortening of a word or phrase, e.g. 'he'll' for 'he will', or 'Dr' for 'Doctor'. In English the omitted letter or letters may be marked with an apostrophe, depending on the type of contraction. —**contractional** *adj.* —**contractionary** *adj.* —**contractive** /-tráktiv/ *adj.*

contractor /kən tráktər/ *n.* **1.** COMPANY OR PERSON UNDER CONTRACT a company or individual with a formal contract to do a specific job, supplying labour and materials and providing and overseeing staff if needed **2.** THING THAT CONTRACTS sth that contracts, e.g. a muscle **3.** SB WHO MAKES A CONTRACT one of the parties to a contract

contractual /kən trákchoo əl/ *adj.* contained in, arising from, or in the form of a formal or legally binding agreement ○ *fulfilling your contractual obligations* —**contractually** *adv.*

contracture /kən trákchər/ *n.* a permanent abnormal tightening or shortening of a body part, such as a muscle, a tendon, or the skin, often resulting in deformity

contradance *n.* = **contredanse**

contradict /kóntrə díkt/ (**-dicts, -dicting, -dicted**) *vt.* **1.** DISAGREE WITH to argue against the truth or correctness of sb's statement or claim **2.** SHOW TO BE WRONG to show that sth is not true, or show that the opposite is true ○ *The results contradicted all previously held theories.* [Late 16thC. From Latin *contradict-*, past participle stem of *contradicere* 'to speak against', from *dicere* 'to speak' (source of English *dictate* and *diction*).] —**contradictable** *adj.* —**contradicter** *n.* —**contradictive** *adj.* —**contradictively** *adv.* —**contradictiveness** *n.*

WORD KEY: SYNONYMS

See Synonyms at ***disagree***.

contradiction /kóntrə díksh'n/ *n.* **1.** STH ILLOGICAL sth that contains parts or elements that are illogical or inconsistent with each other ○ *a contradiction in terms* **2.** OPPOSING STATEMENT a statement or the making of a statement that opposes or disagrees with sb or sth ○ *I can say without fear of contradiction that she is our best worker.*

contradictory /kóntrə díktəri/ *adj.* **1.** INCONSISTENT inconsistent either within itself or in relation to one or more others **2.** OPPOSING holding or consisting of an opposite view in relation to sth **3.** ARGUMENTATIVE fond of or given to taking opposite views —**contradictorily** *adv.* —**contradictoriness** *n.*

contradistinction /kóntrədi stíngksh'n/ *n.* differentiation between two things by identifying their contrasting qualities —**contradistinctive** *adj.* —**contradistinctively** *adv.*

contraflow /kóntrəflō/ *n.* a temporary two-way traffic system on one carriageway of a motorway

contrail /kón trayl/ *n.* = **vapour trail** [Mid-20thC. Contraction of condensation trail.]

contraindicate /kóntrə índi kayt/ (**-cates, -cating, -cated**) *vt.* to state sth to be inadvisable while taking certain medication because of a likely adverse reaction ○ *Taking aspirin with this drug is contraindicated.* —**contraindicant** *n.* —**contraindication** /kóntrə índi káysh'n/ *n.* —**contraindicative** /kóntrə in díkətiv/ *adj.*

contralateral /kóntrə láttərəl/ *adj.* used to describe a body part on the opposite side of the body or that acts in conjunction with such a part

contralto /kən traáltō/ (*plural* **-tos**) *n.* **1.** LOWEST FEMALE VOCAL RANGE the lowest vocal range for women's voices, below soprano and mezzo-soprano **2.** SB WITH CONTRALTO SINGING VOICE a singer, usually a woman, with a contralto voice **3.** PART FOR CONTRALTO a singing part for a contralto [Mid-18thC. From Italian, literally 'below alto'.]

contraposition /kóntrəpə zísh'n/ *n.* **1.** POSITION OPPOSITE a position opposite to or against sth ○ *took up a stand in contraposition to government policy* **2.** LOGIC ANTITHESIS the relation of a proposition to its contrapositive [Mid-16thC. From the late Latin stem *contraposition-*, from Latin *contraponere* 'to place opposite', from *ponere* 'to place' (see POSE).]

contrapositive /kóntrə pózzətiv/ *n.* LOGIC a conditional proposition that negates another conditional proposition and also reverses its clauses. The proposition 'if not q then not p' is the contrapositive of the proposition 'if p then q'.

contrapposto /kóntrə póstō/ (*plural* **-tos**) *n.* a relaxed asymmetrical pose of the human body in art, especially sculpture, in which the shoulders and hips are turned in different planes [Early 20thC. From Italian, past participle of *contrapporre*, from Latin *contraponere* (see CONTRAPOSITION).]

contraption /kən trápsh'n/ *n.* a device or machine, especially one that appears strange or improvised ○ *They'd rigged up a contraption for opening the door.* [Early 19thC. Origin uncertain: perhaps a blend of CONTRIVE and TRAP.]

contrapuntal /kóntrə púnt'l/ *adj.* used to describe polyphonic music with very active and strongly differentiated parts [Mid-19thC. From Italian *contrapunto* 'counterpoint', from *punto* 'point, note', from Latin *punctum* (see POINT).] —**contrapuntally** *adv.*

contrapuntist /kóntrə púntist/ *n.* MUSIC sb who writes counterpoint or who composes in a contrapuntal style [Late 18thC. From Italian *contrapuntista*, from *contrapunto* 'counterpoint'.]

contrariety /kóntrə rī əti/ (*plural* **-ties**) *n.* **1.** OPPOSITENESS the state or quality of opposing or being contrary **2.** POINT OF DIFFERENCE a point of difference or inconsistency **3.** OBSTACLE TO PROGRESS sth that obstructs or hinders progress ○ *battling against the contrarieties of the weather*

contrarious /kən tráiri əss/ *adj.* **1.** UNCOOPERATIVE wilfully disobedient or uncooperative **2.** OBSTRUCTIVE obstructing or hindering progress ○ *beset by contrarious circumstances* —**contrariously** *adv.* —**contrariousness** *n.*

contrariwise /kən tráiri wīz/ *adv.* **1.** IN THE OPPOSITE WAY in the opposite way or direction or on the opposite side **2.** ON THE OTHER HAND used to introduce a statement in direct opposition to what has already been said **3.** UNHELPFULLY in a way that obstructs or hinders progress ○ *Unfortunately, things turned out contrariwise, and we had to give up the idea.*

a at; aa father; aw all; ay day; air hair; ə about, edible, item, common, circus; e egg; ee eel; hw when; i it, happy; ī ice; 'l apple; 'm rhythm; 'n fashion; o odd; ō open; ŏŏ good; oo pool; ow owl; oy oil; th thin; th this; u up; ur urge;

contrary /kóntrəri/ *adj.* **1. CONFLICTING** not at all in agreement with sth ○ *Such arrangements were contrary to his moral code.* **2. OPPOSITE** opposite in direction **3. OBSTRUCTING OR HINDERING PROGRESS** making forward motion extremely hard ○ *slowed by contrary winds* **4. DELIBERATELY DISOBEDIENT** wilfully disobedient or uncooperative ○ *a contrary child* **5.** LOGIC **UNABLE TO BE TRUE AT ONCE** used to describe a pair of propositions that cannot both be true, though they may both be false ■ *n.* **THE OPPOSITE** the opposite of sth ○ *Actually, the contrary is true.* [13thC. Via Anglo-Norman *contrarie* from Latin *contrarius*, from *contra* 'against'.] —**contrarily** /kən tráirəli/ *adv.* —**contrariness** /kən tráirinəss/ *n.* ◇ **contrary to** differently from ◇ **on** *or* **to the contrary** quite the reverse is true

contrast *n.* /kón traast/ **1. MARKED DIFFERENCE** a difference, or sth that is different, compared with sth else ○ *in stark contrast to the luxury they formerly enjoyed* **2. JUXTAPOSITION OF DIFFERENT THINGS** an effect created by placing or arranging very different things, e.g. colours, shades, or textures, next to each other **3. DEGREE OF LIGHTNESS AND DARKNESS** the difference or the use of differences between the lightest and the darkest parts of sth, e.g. to create a special effect in a painting, photograph, or television image ■ *vti.* /kən tráast/ (**-trasts, -trasting, -trasted**) **BE OR SHOW TO BE DIFFERENT** to compare different things or arrange them in a way that highlights their differences, or to be markedly different when compared with sth ○ *These poems have a mature voice when contrasted with her earlier work.* [15thC. Via French from Italian *contrastare* 'to stand against', from Latin *stare* 'to stand' (source of English *statue*).] —**contrastable** /kən tráastəb'l/ *adj.* —**contrastably** /-əb'li/ *adv.* —**contrasting** /-ing/ *adj.* —**contrastingly** /-ingli/ *adv.*

contrastive /kən tráastiv/ *adj.* forming a contrast, or using contrasting colours, tones, or textures —**contrastively** *adv.* —**contrastiveness** *n.*

contrast medium *n.* a substance opaque to X-rays that is used to fill a body cavity, making the outline of the body part easier to see on an X-ray photograph. Barium is frequently used as a contrast medium.

contrasty /kón traasti/ *adj.* showing sharp contrast between the lightest and darkest areas in a photograph or television or movie image

contravene /kóntrə véen/ (**-venes, -vening, -vened**) *vt.* **1. VIOLATE RULE OR LAW** to break a rule or law ○ *outdated equipment that contravenes the safety regulations* **2. CONTRADICT STH** to disagree with or oppose a statement or decision ○ *There was no question of contravening the committee's findings.* [Mid-16thC. From late Latin *contravenire*, literally 'to come against', from Latin *venire* 'to come'.] —**contravener** *n.* —**contravention** /-vénsh'n/ *n.*

contrecoup /kóntrə koo/ *n.* an injury to one side of an organ, especially the brain, as a result of a blow that causes it to swing inside the retaining cavity [Mid-18thC. From French, literally 'a blow opposite', from *coup* (see COUP).]

contredanse /kóntrə daanss/, **contradance** *n.* **1. KIND OF FOLK DANCE** a folk dance for pairs of dancers who face each other in groups of two pairs **2. MUSIC FOR CONTREDANSE** music that is written for or in the rhythm of contredanse [Early 19thC. From French, by folk etymology (by association with *contre* 'against') from English *country dance*.]

contretemps /kóntrə ton/ *n.* **1. A QUARREL** a dispute or minor disagreement (*formal*) **2. MISHAP** a mishap, especially an awkward or embarrassing one [Late 17thC. From French, literally 'against the time'.]

contrib. *abbr.* **1.** contribution **2.** contributor

contribute /kən tríbbyoot/ (**-utes, -uting, -uted**) *v.* **1.** *vti.* **GIVE MONEY FOR SPECIFIC PURPOSE** to give money to sth, such as a fund or charity, for a specific purpose, along with others ○ *Some organizations contribute thousands to political parties.* **2.** *vti.* **DO OR GIVE STH WITH OTHERS** to do or give sth, along with others, that helps to achieve a specific purpose or goal ○ *I felt I had nothing to contribute to the discussion.* **3.** *vi.* **BE PARTIAL CAUSE OF STH** to be one of the factors that causes sth ○ *a heart condition that contributed to his early death* **4.** *vti.* **PROVIDE WORKS FOR PUBLICATION** to supply material for a publication or broadcast [Mid-16thC. From Latin *contribut-*, past participle stem of *contribuere* 'to bring in together', from *tribuere* 'to grant' (source of English *tribute*).] —**contributive** /kən tríbbyŏŏtiv/ *adj.* —**contributively** /-li/ *adv.* —**contributiveness** /-nəss/ *n.*

WORD KEY: USAGE

Pronunciation trap The traditional pronunciation is with the stress on the second syllable; stress on the first syllable is increasingly heard but is widely disliked.

contribution /kóntri byóosh'n/ *n.* **1. STH GIVEN** sth given, such as money or time, especially to a common fund or for a specific purpose **2. MATERIAL SUPPLIED FOR PUBLICATION OR BROADCAST** a piece of material that forms part of a publication or broadcast **3. REGULAR PAYMENT** a regular fixed amount paid, e.g., to a pension fund, often deducted from sb's wage ○ *national insurance contributions*

contributor /kən tríbbyŏŏtər/ *n.* **1. ONE OF THE PEOPLE GIVING STH** sb who gives money to a common fund, or who, with others, gives their time and effort to a project **2. SB SUPPLYING MATERIAL PUBLISHED OR BROADCAST** one of the people supplying material for a publication or broadcast **3.** one of the causes of sth ○ *Smoking is also a major contributor to heart disease.*

contributory /kən tríbbyŏŏtəri/ *adj.* **1. HELPING STH HAPPEN** partly responsible for sth ○ *Poor diet is often a contributory factor.* **2. GIVEN ALONG WITH OTHERS** given with others to a common fund or project **3. REQUIRING EMPLOYEE TO PAY IN PART** used to describe a pension or insurance scheme that requires premiums to be paid by the employee as well as by the employer ■ *n.* (*plural* **-ries**) **GIVER OF MONEY OR TIME** sb who donates money or effort

contributory negligence *n.* a victim's share in the responsibility for an accident, when care to prevent it could have been taken by the victim as well as the other party

con trick *n.* a confidence trick (*informal*)

contrite /kón trīt, kən trít/ *adj.* **1. VERY SORRY** genuinely and deeply sorry about sth ○ *She was suitably contrite.* **2. ARISING FROM SENSE OF GUILT** done or said out of a sense of guilt or remorse ○ *full of contrite promises* **3. ASHAMED OF OWN SIN** deeply ashamed of past sins and determined not to sin in future [13thC. Via French *contrit* from Latin *contritus*, past participle of *conterere* 'to rub together', from *terere* 'to rub or grind' (source of English *trite*).] —**contritely** *adv.* —**contriteness** *n.*

contrition /kən trísh'n/ *n.* **1. REPENTANCE** deep and genuine feelings of guilt and remorse **2. SHAME OVER PAST SINS** a deep sense of shame over past sins and a firm resolve not to sin in future ○ *acts of contrition*

contrivance /kən trív'nss/ *n.* **1. GADGET** a cleverly made device or machine, especially one that is unusual ○ *a clumsy-looking contrivance for keeping your back straight* **2. DEVIOUS PLOT** a plan intended to deceive **3. SCHEMING** the making of clever or deceitful schemes

contrive /kən trív/ (**-trives, -triving, -trived**) *v.* **1.** *vti.* **DO STH CREATIVELY** to accomplish sth by being clever and creative ○ *She contrived a meeting between the warring factions.* **2.** *vt.* **MAKE STH INGENIOUS** to make or invent sth clever, especially from whatever materials are available ○ *A tree house had been contrived from bits of scrap.* **3.** *vt.* **DO CLEVERLY** to accomplish sth with cleverness and skill ○ *She somehow contrived to be both an effective and a well-liked teacher.* **4.** *vti.* **PLOT** to formulate clever or deceitful schemes ○ *The gang contrived a way to hack into the main computer system.* [13thC. Via Old French *contro(u)ver* 'to invent' from medieval Latin *contropare* 'to compare', from Latin *tropus* 'turn, manner', from Greek *tropos* (source of English *trope*).] —**contrivable** *adj.* —**contriver** *n.*

contrived /kən trívd/ *adj.* **1. NOT SPONTANEOUS** intended to appear spontaneous or genuine but really planned or affected ○ *Her apology was very contrived.* **2. UNLIKE REALITY** unrealistic and unconvincing ○ *a film with a contrived ending* —**contrivedly** /kən trívidli/ *adv.*

control /kən tról/ *vt.* (**-trols, -trolling, -trolled**) **1. OPERATE MACHINE** to work or operate sth such as a vehicle or machine ○ *Computers control many of the safety features on board.* **2. RESTRAIN OR LIMIT** to limit or restrict the occurrence or expression of sb or sth, especially to keep it from appearing, increasing, or spreading ○ *The last administration set out to control inflation.* **3. MANAGE** to exercise power or authority over sth such as a business or nation ○ *The company is controlled largely by foreign interests.* **4. OVERSEE FINANCIAL AFFAIRS** to regulate the financial affairs of a business or other large organization **5. VERIFY ACCOUNTS** to examine financial accounts and verify them as correct ■ *n.* **1. ABILITY TO RUN STH** ability or authority to manage or direct sth ○ *circumstances beyond our control* **2. OPERATING SWITCH** a mechanical or electronic device used to operate a vehicle or machine ○ *a pilot at the controls of a plane* **3. SKILL** skill in using sth or in performing (*often used in combination*) ○ *players with excellent ball control* **4. LIMITS AND RESTRICTIONS** the limiting or restricting of sth, or the methods used in restricting sth ○ *an era of price and wage controls* **5. PLACE OF INSPECTION OR DIRECTION** a place where sth is checked or inspected, or from which sth is directed (*usually used in combination*) ○ *passengers filing through passport control* **6. COMPARATIVE STANDARD IN EXPERIMENT** a subject taking part in an experiment or survey who is not involved in the procedures affecting the rest of the experiment, thus acting as the standard against which the results are compared **7. SUPERVISING PERSON OR GROUP** sb or a group that supervises or monitors operations or operatives ○ *Their intelligence agents report to control twice a week* **8.** COMPUT **SPECIAL COMPUTER KEY** a computer key pressed in conjunction with others to perform any of a set of functions **9. SPIRIT THAT GUIDES SÉANCE** a spirit that is believed to help a medium gain access to other spirits being called up in a séance [15thC. Via Anglo-Norman *contreroller* from medieval Latin *contrarotulare* 'to check against a duplicate register' (the original sense in English), from *rotulus* 'roll' (see ROLL).] —**controllability** /kən trōlə bílləti/ *n.* —**controllable** /kən trṓləb'l/ *adj.* —**controllably** /-əbli/ *adv.*

control freak *n.* sb who feels an excessive need to exert control over people and over his or her own life (*slang*)

control gene *n.* one of the group of genes that regulates the development and specialization of cells

control grid *n.* = **grid** *n.* **6**

control group *n.* in an experiment, the group of test subjects left untreated or unexposed to some procedure and then compared with treated subjects in order to validate the results of the test

controlled /kən tróld/ *adj.* **1. DONE WITH SKILL AND DISCIPLINE** showing the skill, judgment, and discipline needed in order to achieve a desired result, without doing too little or too much ○ *His controlled performance as Lear was masterful.* **2. CAREFULLY REGULATED** carefully measured and regulated, especially in relation to medical treatments or scientific experiments ○ *They tested the effectiveness of controlled doses of the drug.* **3. KEPT UNDER CONTROL** kept in check and not expressed fully or at all ○ *She spoke with scarcely controlled fury.*

controlled substance *n.* a substance subject to statutory control, especially a drug that can be obtained legally only with a doctor's prescription

controlled user *n.* sb who maintains a normal lifestyle while being addicted to drugs

controller /kən trólər/ *n.* **1. SB WHO CONTROLS OR ORGANIZES STH** sb in a managing, supervising, or monitoring position **2. controller, comptroller** FIN **FINANCIAL SUPERVISOR** sb whose job is to oversee financial matters in a business or government department **3. CONTROLLING DEVICE** a device or mechanism that controls sth, such as part of an operation —**controllership** *n.*

controlling interest *n.* ownership of enough of a company's shares to allow the holder to control the business

control rod *n.* a rod or cylinder made of or containing neutron-absorbing material such as graphite, used to control the rate of fission in a nuclear reactor

control surface *n.* a movable surface, such as a rudder or elevator, that controls the direction of an aircraft, rocket, or missile

control tower *n.* a high building at an airport, from which air-traffic controllers organize the movements of incoming and outgoing aircraft by radioing to their pilots

controversial /kóntrə v/ *adj.* **1.** CAUSING DISAGREEMENT provoking strong disagreement or disapproval, e.g. in public debate ○ *The CEO heading up the company is a controversial figure.* **2.** ARGUMENTATIVE enjoying or habitually engaging in controversy ○ *a controversial writer* —**controversialism** *n.* —**controversialist** *n.* —**controversiality** /kóntrə v/ *n.* —**controversially** /kóntrə v/ *adv.*

controversy /kóntrə vurssi, kən tróvvərsi/ (*plural* **-sies**) *n.* disagreement on a contentious topic, strongly felt or expressed by all those concerned [14thC. From Latin *controversia*, from *controversus* 'disputed', literally 'turned against', from *vertere* 'to turn' (source of English *versus*).]

WORD KEY: USAGE

Pronunciation trap: The traditional pronunciation is with the stress on the first syllable (on the analogy of words such as *acrimony* and *matrimony*); stress on the second syllable is increasingly heard, and although it follows a better established pattern in English pronunciation it is widely disliked.

controvert /kóntrə vúrt/ (**-verts, -verting, -verted**) *vt.* to argue strongly against sth (*formal*) [Mid-16thC. From Latin *contro-* 'against' + *vertere* 'to turn' (see CONTROVERSY).] —**controverter** /kóntrə vúrtər/ *n.* —**controvertible** /kóntrə vúrtəb'l/ *adj.* —**controvertibly** /-vl/ *adv.*

contumacious /kóntyoo máyshəss/ *adj.* **1.** VERY RESISTANT TO AUTHORITY flagrantly insubordinate or rebellious **2.** LAW DISOBEYING COURT OF LAW persistently refusing to appear in court or to obey a court order without good reason —**contumaciously** *adv.* —**contumaciousness** *n.*

contumacy /kóntyoŏməssi/ *n.* **1.** DEFIANCE OF AUTHORITY flagrant disobedience or rebelliousness **2.** LAW REFUSAL TO SUBMIT TO COURT'S AUTHORITY persistent refusal to appear in court or to obey a court order without good reason [13thC. From Latin *contumacia*, from *contumac-*, stem of *contumax* 'insolent'.]

contumelious /kóntyoŏ méeli əss/ *adj.* having or showing an insulting, scornful, or contemptuous attitude (*archaic or literary*) —**contumeliously** *adv.* —**contumeliousness** *n.*

contumely /kón tyoomli/ (*plural* **-lies**) *n.* (*archaic or literary*) **1.** CONTEMPT insulting, scornful, or contemptuous language or treatment **2.** DERISIVE REMARK an openly insulting, scornful, or contemptuous remark [14thC. Via Old French *contumelie* from Latin *contumelia*.]

contuse /kən tyoóz/ (**-tuses, -tusing, -tused**) *vt.* to bruise a body part (*technical*) [14thC. From Latin *contus-*, past participle stem of *contundere* 'to beat small, bruise', from *tundere* 'to beat'.]

contusion /kən tyoózh'n/ *n.* an injury to the body in which skin and bone are not broken, but damage is done to tissues under the skin, causing a bruise or bruises (*technical*)

conundrum /kə núndrəm/ *n.* **1.** WORD PUZZLE a riddle, especially one with an answer in the form of a play on words **2.** STH CONFUSING sth puzzling, confusing, or mysterious [Early 17thC. Origin unknown.]

WORD KEY: SYNONYMS

See Synonyms at ***problem***.

conurbation /kón ur báysh'n/ *n.* a large urban area created when neighbouring towns spread into and merge with each other [Early 20thC. Coined from CON- + the Latin stem *urb-* 'city' (see URBAN) + -ATION.]

WORD KEY: SYNONYMS

See Synonyms at ***city***.

Conv. *abbr.* Conventual

convalesce /kónvə léss/ (**-lesces, -lescing, -lesced**) *vi.* to spend time recovering from an illness or medical treatment, especially by resting [15thC. From Latin *convalescere*, from *valescere* 'to grow strong', from *valere* 'to be strong' (source of English *valid*).]

convalescence /kónvə léss'nss/ *n.* gradual return to good health after an illness or medical treatment, or the period spent recovering

convalescent /kónvə léss'nt/ *n.* sb who is recovering after a period of illness or medical treatment such as surgery —**convalescent** *adj.*

convection /kən véksh'n/ *n.* **1.** CIRCULATORY MOTION IN LIQUID OR GAS circulatory movement in a liquid or gas, resulting from regions of different temperatures and different densities rising and falling in response to gravity **2.** METEOROL HEAT TRANSFER LEADING TO CLOUD FORMATION heat transfer within the atmosphere involving the upward movement of huge volumes of warm air, leading to subsequent condensation and cloud formation [Mid-19thC. From the late Latin stem *convection-*, from Latin *convehere* 'to bring together', from *vehere* 'to carry' (source of English *vehicle*).] —**convectional** *adj.* —**convective** *adj.* —**convectively** /-tivli/ *adv.*

convection heater *n.* = **convector**

convection oven *n.* an oven with a fan that circulates heat throughout the oven, so that food on all levels cooks uniformly

convector /kən véktər/ *n.* a heater that depends on convection of air to transfer heat from the heating element [Early 20thC. Formed from CONVECTION.]

convenance /kóNvə naaNss/ *n.* suitable or acceptable behaviour (*literary*) [15thC. From French, where it was formed from *convenir* 'to be suitable, to agree', from Latin *convenire* (see CONVENE).]

convene /kən véen/ (**-venes, -vening, -vened**) *v.* **1.** *vti.* GATHER FOR A MEETING to come together for or arrange a formal meeting ○ *A meeting of the working group has been convened for tomorrow* **2.** *vt.* LAW CALL BEFORE COURT to order sb to appear before a court, tribunal, or other decision-making body [15thC. From Latin *convenire* 'to come together, to agree or suit', from *venire* 'to come'.] —**convenable** *adj.* —**convener** *n.*

convenience /kən véeni ənss/ *n.* **1.** QUALITY OF BEING CONVENIENT the quality of being easy, useful, or suitable ○ *have the convenience of working at home* **2.** SB'S PERSONAL COMFORT personal comfort, or circumstances that promote sb's personal comfort ○ *All rooms have cooking facilities, for our guests' convenience.* **3.** STH PROVIDING EASE OR COMFORT sth that makes life easier or more comfortable, especially a labour-saving device ○ *apartments supplied with every modern convenience* **4.** LAVATORY a lavatory, especially in a public place

convenience food *n.* packaged food that can be prepared quickly and easily, e.g. tinned foods and cook-chill meals

convenient /kən véeni ənt/ *adj.* useful or suitable, because it makes things easier, is close by, or does not involve much effort or trouble ○ *Choose a time convenient for you.* [14thC. From Latin *convenient-*, present participle stem of *convenire* (see CONVENE).] —**conveniently** *adv.*

convent /kónvənt/ *n.* **1.** RELIGIOUS COMMUNITY a community of women who live a life devoted largely to religious worship **2.** RELIGIOUS COMMUNITY'S BUILDING the building occupied by a community of religious women [13thC. Via Anglo-Norman *covent* from Latin *conventus* 'assembly, company', from *convenire* (see CONVENE). Originally covent, now only in place names such as Covent Garden, London.]

conventicle /kən véntik'l/ *n.* an unlawful or secret religious gathering or the building where it is held (*formal*) [14thC. From Latin *conventiculum*, literally 'small assembly', ultimately from *convenire* (see CONVENE).] —**conventicler** *n.*

convention /kən vénsh'n/ *n.* **1.** GATHERING a gathering of people who have a common interest or profession ○ *He's attending a sales convention in Manchester.* **2.** PEOPLE ATTENDING FORMAL MEETING the people present at a convention **3.** FORMAL AGREEMENT an agreement between groups, especially an international agreement slightly less formal than a treaty ○ *under the terms of the Geneva Convention* **4.** USUAL WAY OF DOING THINGS the customary way in which things are done within a group ○ *designs that flout convention* **5.** FAMILIAR DEVICE a standard technique or well-used device, especially in the arts ○ *Her style does not follow the usual literary conventions.* **6.** BRIDGE CODED BID a bid in bridge intended for a partner to understand differently from its face value, because of a pre-arranged bidding system [15thC. Via French from the Latin stem *convention-*, from, ultimately, *convenire* (see CONVENE).]

conventional /kən vénsh'nəl/ *adj.* **1.** SOCIALLY ACCEPTED conforming to socially accepted customs of behaviour or style, especially in a way that lacks imagination ○ *the conventional white wedding dress* **2.** USUAL OR ESTABLISHED using well-established methods or styles ○ *conventional cooking in a stove rather than a microwave* **3.** RELATING TO A GATHERING relating to a large gathering of people with a common interest or purpose **4.** ARMS ENGAGED IN WITHOUT NUCLEAR ENERGY not involving the use of nuclear weapons or energy **5.** LAW BASED ON CONSENT based or dependent on the consent of the various parties —**conventionalism** *n.* —**conventionalist** *n.* —**conventionally** *adv.*

conventionalise *vt.* = **conventionalize**

conventionality /kən vénshənállәti/ (*plural* **-ties**) *n.* **1.** ADHERENCE TO SOCIAL CONVENTIONS adherence to social conventions in behaviour, tastes, or methods **2.** STH CONVENTIONAL a socially accepted way of behaving or of doing sth ○ *the conventionalities of a formal occasion*

conventionalize /kən vénsh'nə līz/ (**-izes, -izing, -ized**), **conventionalise** (**-ises, -ising, -ised**) *vt.* to make conventional, especially in style or taste ○ *His flights of fancy had become conventionalized as the Gothic style.* —**conventionalization** /kən vénsh'nə lī záysh'n/ *n.*

conventional wisdom *n.* a generally held view, notion, or opinion ○ *Conventional wisdom dictates that such skills merit high rewards.*

conventioneer /kən vénshənéer/ *n.* sb who attends and participates in a convention

conventual /kən vénchoo əl/ *adj.* RELATING TO A CONVENT relating to or resembling a convent in quietness, simplicity, or discipline ○ *living a quiet conventual life* ■ *n.* SB LIVING IN CONVENT a woman who lives in a convent —**conventually** *adv.*

Conventual *n.* a member of a branch of a Franciscan order of friars who live a less austere life than in other branches

converge /kən vúrj/ (**-verges, -verging, -verged**) *vi.* **1.** MEET to reach the same point coming from different directions ○ *the place where the roads converge* **2.** BECOME THE SAME to become gradually less different and eventually the same ○ *rapidly converging political parties* **3.** ARRIVE AT SAME DESTINATION to gather or meet at the same destination ○ *Delegates from all over the world are converging on the city of New York.* **4.** MATH APPROACH FINITE LIMIT to approach a finite limit as the number of terms in an infinite series increases **5.** BIOL DEVELOP SIMILAR CHARACTERISTICS to independently develop superficially similar characteristics in response to a set of environmental conditions, e.g. the development of wings in birds and insects [Late 17thC. From late Latin *convergere* 'to lean together', from Latin *vergere* 'to bend or turn' (source of English *verge*).]

convergence /kən vúrjənss/ *n.* **1.** **convergence, convergency** COMING TOGETHER a coming together from different directions, especially a uniting or merging of groups or tendencies that were originally opposed or very different **2.** **convergence, convergency** MATH SERIES WITH CONSTANT OR INCREASING DIFFERENCES the characteristic of a series or sequence of numbers in which the difference between each term and the following term remains constant or increases. ◊ **divergence** **3.** BIOL SIMILAR EVOLUTIONARY DEVELOPMENT the tendency of different species to develop similar characteristics in response to a set of environmental conditions. ◊ **divergence** **4.** METEOROL MEETING OF AIR MASSES the meeting of different air masses, often resulting in vertical air currents **5.** OPHTHALMOL TURNING THE EYES INWARDS the turning inwards of both eyes in order to look at sth nearer than the previous object viewed —**convergent** *adj.*

convergent evolution *n.* BIOL = **convergence** *n.* 3

convergent margin *n.* a boundary between two tectonic plates that are moving together, one dipping under the other

conversance /kən vúrs'nss/, **conversancy** /-s'nssi/ *n.* knowledge of or familiarity with sth

conversant /kən vúrs'nt/ *adj.* knowing about sth, or familiar with it, from experience or study ○ *not* *conversant with local customs* [14thC. From French, present participle of *converser*, from Latin *conversare* 'to live or associate with' (see CONVERSE).] —**conversantly** *adv.*

conversation /kónvər sáysh'n/ *n.* **1.** CASUAL TALK an informal talk with sb, especially about opinions, ideas, feelings, or everyday matters ○ *a telephone conversation* **2.** TALKING the activity of talking to sb informally ○ *in conversation with one of the cleaners* **3.** COMPUT REAL-TIME INTERACTION WITH COMPUTER an interaction with a computer carried on in real time **4.** NON-VERBAL EXCHANGE a non-verbal exchange that is perceived to have the qualities of conversation ○ *Critics spoke of the conversation between the new building and its neighbours.* [14thC. Via French from the Latin stem *conversation-*, from *conversari* (see CONVERSE[1]).]

conversational /kónvər sáysh'nəl/ *adj.* **1.** CONNECTED WITH CONVERSATION relating to informal talking, especially to the ability to say interesting things **2.** INFORMAL IN LANGUAGE informal in language and style, and usually dealing with simple subjects ○ *She writes in an easy conversational style.* **3.** APPROPRIATE FOR INFORMAL TALK suitable in style and vocabulary for informal talk on simple subjects, usually applied to skill in a foreign language ○ *conversational German* —**conversationally** *adv.*

conversationalist /kónvər sáysh'nəlist/, **conversationist** /-sáysh'nist/ *n.* sb who enjoys talking to people or has the ability to converse in an interesting engaging manner ○ *Her husband's not much of a conversationalist.*

conversation piece *n.* **1.** OBJECT USED AS CONVERSATION TOPIC sth that attracts people's interest and leads to conversation ○ *I don't think much of the sculpture in their front garden, but it makes a good conversation piece.* **2.** GROUP PORTRAIT a portrait painting of a group of stylish people in a domestic or landscape setting

conversazione /kónvə satsi óni/ (*plural* **-ni** /-óni/ *or* **-nes**) *n.* a social gathering to hear a talk on or discuss a topic related to the arts (*formal*) [Mid-18thC. From Italian, literally 'conversation', ultimately from Latin *conversare* (see CONVERSE[1]).]

converse[1] *vi.* /kən vúrss/ (**-verses, -versing, -versed**) **1.** TALK to have a conversation ○ *a place where they can converse uninterrupted* **2.** COMPUT INTERACT WITH COMPUTER to interact with a computer as if engaged in a dialogue **3.** INTERACT SOCIALLY WITH SB to be in sb's company or associate with him or her socially (*archaic*) **4.** ENGAGE IN SEXUAL INTERCOURSE to have sexual intercourse with sb (*archaic*) ■ *n.* /kón vurss/ **1.** CONVERSATION conversation with sb ○ *They were deep in converse with one another.* **2.** SOCIAL ASSOCIATION being with sb socially (*archaic*) ○ *Their converse was always cordial.* **3.** SEXUAL RELATIONS sexual relations (*archaic*) [14thC. Via French *converser* from Latin *conversare* 'to live or associate with', from *versari* 'to occupy yourself', ultimately from *vertere* 'to turn'.] —**converser** /kən vúrsər/ *n.*

converse[2] /kón vurss/ *n.* **1.** POLAR OPPOSITE the opposite of sth ○ *Actually, the converse is true.* **2.** LOGIC REVERSED CATEGORICAL SENTENCE a categorical sentence in which the subject and predicate have been reversed, e.g., 'all dogs are collies' from 'all collies are dogs' ■ *adj.* OPPOSITE opposite or reverse [14thC. From Latin *conversus*, past participle of *convertere* (see CONVERT).] —**conversely** *adv.*

conversion /kən vúrsh'n/ *n.* **1.** ALTERATION a change in the nature, form, or function of sth ○ *a conversion of waste land into a sports field* **2.** STH ALTERED sth that has been changed in nature, form, or function, especially a building or room ○ *a loft conversion* **3.** CHANGE OF MEASURING SYSTEM a change from one measuring or calculating system to another, or a calculation done to bring about the change ○ *the conversion from miles to kilometres* **4.** CHANGING OF SB'S BELIEFS an adoption of new opinions or beliefs, especially in religion ○ *his conversion to Islam* **5.** FOOTBALL an act of converting following a touchdown or a down. A conversion by kick earns one point, but a conversion by run or pass into the end zone earns two. **6.** RUGBY, AMERICAN FOOTBALL KICK FOLLOWING TRY OR TOUCHDOWN a kicking of the ball over the crossbar following a try or touchdown, and the score made with a successful kick **7.** LOGIC REVERSING TERMS IN CATEGORICAL SENTENCE the reversing of the subject and predicate in a categorical sentence, forming a new sentence, e.g. 'all dogs are collies' from 'all collies are dogs' **8.** LAW UNLAWFUL HOLDING OF ANOTHER'S PROPERTY unlawful treating of sb else's property as your own **9.** LAW CHANGING OF PROPERTY CLASSIFICATION the changing of one type of property to another, e.g. from real to personal property [14thC. Via French from the Latin stem *conversion-*, from *convers-*, past participle stem of *convertere* (see CONVERT).] —**conversional** *adj.* —**conversionary** *adj.*

conversion disorder *n.* a neurosis marked by the appearance of physical symptoms, such as partial paralysis, without physical cause but in the presence of psychological conflict

convert *v.* /kən vúrt/ (**-verts, -verting, -verted**) **1.** *vti.* CHANGE STH'S CHARACTER to change the nature or form of sth, or to be changed in nature or form ○ *a process for converting waste into usable fuel* **2.** *vti.* CHANGE THING'S FUNCTION to change the function or use of sth or be able to change in function or use ○ *sofas that convert into beds* **3.** *vt.* CHANGE MEASURING OR CALCULATING UNITS to change units of one measuring or calculating system into units of another ○ *the formula for converting litres into gallons* **4.** *vti.* CHANGE SB'S BELIEFS to adopt new opinions or beliefs or to change the opinions or beliefs of another, especially religious beliefs ○ *His wife converted to Judaism.* **5.** *vti.* RUGBY KICK TO ADD ON POINTS to add to the points awarded for a try by following it with a successful kick of the ball over the crossbar **6.** *vt.* LOGIC REVERSE TERMS IN CATEGORICAL SENTENCE reverse the subject and predicate in a categorical sentence, forming a new sentence, e.g. 'all dogs are collies' from 'all collies are dogs' **7.** *vt.* LAW UNLAWFULLY HOLD ANOTHER'S PROPERTY to unlawfully treat sb else's property as your own **8.** *vt.* LAW CHANGE CLASSIFICATION OF PROPERTY to change the classification of property, e.g. from real to personal property, in the course of certain transactions ■ *n.* /kón vurt/ SB WITH CHANGED BELIEFS sb who has changed from one way of perceiving or understanding sth, such as a belief system, to another ○ *ex-conservative converts to liberalism* [13thC. Via Old French *convertir* from, ultimately, Latin *convertere* 'to turn around or transform', from *vertere* 'to turn' (source of English *verse*).] ◇ **preach to the converted** to advocate a viewpoint to people who already have it

WORD KEY: SYNONYMS

See Synonyms at ***change***.

convertaplane *n.* = **convertiplane**

converter /kən vúrtər/, **convertor** *n.* **1.** TECH DEVICE THAT CONVERTS a device that converts sth, e.g. an electrical device that converts alternating current into direct current **2.** PHYS FREQUENCY CHANGER an electronic component for changing one frequency to another **3.** METALL FURNACE a furnace for refining molten metal **4.** COMPUT DATA CODE CHANGER a device for changing data from one form to another, e.g. from analogue to digital **5.** PHYS = **converter reactor**

converter reactor *n.* a type of nuclear reactor that converts one nuclear fuel into another, especially fertile into fissile material

convertible /kən vúrtəb'l/ *adj.* **1.** CAPABLE OF BEING CONVERTED capable of being changed from one form, function, or use to another **2.** FIN EXCHANGEABLE FOR GOLD OR ANOTHER CURRENCY able to be legally exchanged for gold or for another currency **3.** FIN EXCHANGEABLE FOR STOCK exchangeable for other assets, especially a fixed number of shares in ordinary stock ■ *n.* CAR WITH REMOVABLE ROOF a car with a roof that can be folded back or taken off ○ *a flashy red convertible* —**convertibility** /kən vúrtə bíllәti/ *n.* —**convertibly** /kən vúrtəbli/ *adv.*

convertiplane /kən vúrtə playn/, **convertaplane, convertoplane** *n.* an aeroplane that takes off and lands vertically by altering the direction of its engines' thrust, reconverting to normal horizontal thrust for forward flight [Mid-20thC. Blend of CONVERTIBLE and AEROPLANE.]

convertor *n.* = **converter**

convex /kón veks, kon véks/ *adj.* **1.** OUTWARDLY CURVING with a surface that curves outwards rather than inwards **2.** OPTICS SHAPED LIKE A SPHERE'S EXTERIOR shaped like the exterior of a sphere, paraboloid, ellipsoid,

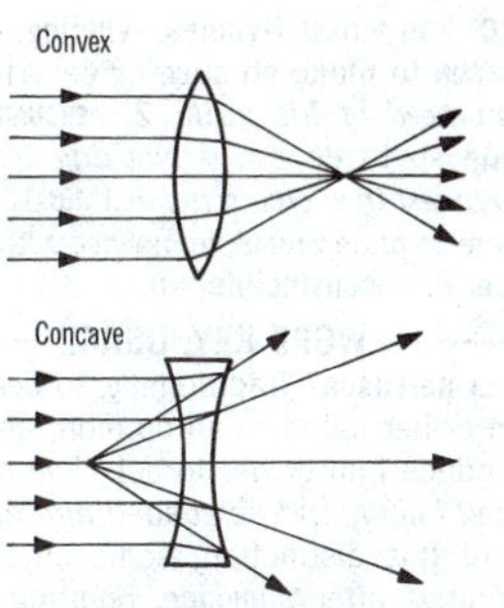

Convex: convex and concave lenses

or any other outwardly curved surface ○ *a convex lens* **3.** MATH CONTAINING NO ANGLE ABOVE 180° used to describe a polygon with no interior angle greater than 180° ■ *vti.* (**-vexes, -vexing, -vexed**) CURVE OUTWARDS to curve outwards, or make sth curve outwards [Late 16thC. From Latin *convexus* 'vaulted, arched'.] —**convexly** /kón veksli/ *adv.*

convexity /kon véksəti/ (*plural* **-ties**) *n.* **1.** CURVING OUTWARDS outwardly curving quality **2.** STH THAT CURVES OUTWARDS an outwardly curving surface or part

convexo-concave /kon véksō konkáyv/ *adj.* used to describe a lens that is convex on one side and concave on the other

convexo-convex *adj.* used to describe a lens that is convex on both sides

convey /kən váy/ (**-veys, -veying, -veyed**) *vt.* **1.** TAKE SOMEWHERE to take sb or sth somewhere (*formal*) **2.** COMMUNICATE to communicate sth and make it known ○ *a look that conveyed all the tenderness he felt for her* **3.** MEAN have sth as a meaning or connotation ○ *'Majesty' conveys grandeur.* **4.** TRANSFER THROUGH CARRIER to transfer or transmit sth along a wire, pipe, tube, or other carrier **5.** LAW TRANSFER OWNERSHIP to transfer ownership of sth ○ *The title to the property was conveyed last June.* [14thC. Via Old French *conveier* (source of English *convoy*) from medieval Latin *conviare*, literally 'to go together on the road', from Latin *via* 'road'.] —**conveyable** *adj.*

conveyance /kən váyənss/ *n.* **1.** MOVING STH the conveying of sth, especially the transportation or transmission of sth from one place to another ○ *the conveyance of information from the mainland to the islands* **2.** VEHICLE a vehicle or other means of transportation (*formal*) ○ *public conveyances* **3.** LAW TRANSFER OF OWNERSHIP a document that legally transfers ownership or the transfer itself —**conveyancer** *n.* —**conveyancing** *n.*

conveyor /kən váyər/ *n.* **1.** CONVEYING DEVICE a device that transports or transmits sth, especially a conveyor belt **2.** MEANS OF TRANSMITTING sb or sth that transmits sth, especially news ○ *conveyor of good tidings*

conveyor belt *n.* a device that consists typically of a continuous wide flat rubber loop moved by electrically operated rollers, used to move objects from one place to another nearby

convict *v.* /kən víkt/ (**-victs, -victing, -victed**) **1.** *vt.* STATE THAT SB IS GUILTY to declare sb guilty of a crime in a court of law (*often passive*) ○ *had been previously convicted of fraud* **2.** *vi.* ARRIVE AT GUILTY VERDICT to reach a verdict of guilty ○ *juries who will convict on the slimmest evidence* **3.** *vt.* SHOW TO BE AT FAULT to show that sb is in the wrong in some respect ○ *actions that convicted her of selfishness* ■ *n.* /kón vikt/ SB IN PRISON sb serving a prison sentence ○ *an escaped convict* [14thC. From Latin *convict-*, past participle stem of *convincere* (see CONVINCE).] —**convictable** /kən víktəb'l/ *adj.*

conviction /kən víksh'n/ *n.* **1.** FIRMLY HELD BELIEF a belief or opinion that is held firmly ○ *my conviction that they are lying* **2.** FIRMNESS OF BELIEF firmness of belief or opinion ○ *said with complete conviction* **3.** GUILTY VERDICT the finding or an instance of finding sb guilty or of being found guilty of a crime ○ *The accused has no previous convictions.* —**convictional** *adj.*

convictive /kən víktiv/ *adj.* powerful enough to convince or persuade (*formal*) —**convictively** *adv.*

convince /kən vínss/ (**-vinces, -vincing, -vinced**) *vt.* **1.** MAKE CERTAIN to make sb sure or certain of sth ○ *We are convinced of his guilt.* **2.** PERSUADE TO DO STH to persuade sb to do sth ○ *Nothing would convince them to invest in such a scheme.* [Mid-16thC. From Latin *convincere* 'to prove wrong', from *vincere* 'to overcome'.] —**convincer** *n.* —**convincible** *adj.*

WORD KEY: USAGE

convince or **persuade**? Traditionally, to ***convince*** sb is to bring him or her round to an opinion, and to ***persuade*** sb is to induce him or her to act: *She convinced him that he had talent, and persuaded him to study music.* Because of this distinction, some object to the use of an infinitive after ***convince,*** pointing out that *She convinced him to . . . .* will tend to involve action. All the same, sb who is ***persuaded*** to act has probably also been ***convinced*** of the merit of doing so. In many contexts the two words are completely interchangeable, and in others are nearly so.

convincing /kən vínssing/ *adj.* **1.** PERSUASIVE persuading sb to believe sth is true or real ○ *The special effects were very convincing.* **2.** ABLE TO PERSUADE PEOPLE skilled at making people believe sth ○ *a convincing impostor* **3.** BEYOND DOUBT impressively clear or definite ○ *a convincing victory* —**convincingly** *adv.*

WORD KEY: SYNONYMS

See Synonyms at ***valid.***

convivial /kən vívvi əl/ *adj.* **1.** PLEASANT enjoyable because of its friendliness ○ *spent many a convivial evening at the pub* **2.** SOCIABLE enjoying the company of others ○ *He was famously convivial.* [Mid-17thC. From Latin *convivialis*, from *convivium* 'feast', from *vivere* 'to live' (source of English *vivid*).] —**convivialist** *n.* —**conviviality** /kən vívvi álləti/ *n.* —**convivially** /kən vívvi əli/ *adv.*

convocation /kónvə káysh'n/ *n.* **1.** FORMAL ASSEMBLY a large formal assembly, e.g., the senior members of a church or the members of a university council **2.** CALLING A MEETING the arranging or calling of a formal meeting [14thC. From the Latin stem *convocation-*, from *convocare* (see CONVOKE).] —**convocator** /kónvə kaytər/ *n.*

convoke /kən vṓk/ (**-vokes, -voking, -voked**) *vt.* to call a formal meeting or call people together for such a meeting [Late 16thC. From Latin *convocare* 'to call together', from *vocare* 'to call' (source of English *vocation*).] —**convocative** /-vókətiv/ *adj.* —**convoker** /kən vṓkər/ *n.*

convolute /kónvə loot/ *vti.* (**-lutes, -luting, -luted**) TWIST to twist or coil sth in folds ○ *The snake's coils were tightly convoluted.* ■ *adj.* BOT TIGHTLY TWISTED used to describe petals or leaves that are rolled from the sides so that one side is wrapped around the other [Late 17thC. From Latin *convolut-*, past participle stem of *convolvere* 'to twist or coil round', from *volvere* 'to roll'.] —**convolutely** *adv.*

convoluted /kónvə lootid/ *adj.* **1.** EXTREMELY INTRICATE too complex or intricate to understand easily ○ *convoluted sentences* **2.** VERY TWISTED having many twists, coils, or whorls ○ *the brain's convoluted surface* —**convolutedly** *adv.* —**convolutedness** *n.*

convolution /kónvə lo͞osh'n/ *n.* **1.** TWISTED SHAPE a curve, coil, or twist **2.** TWISTED RIDGE ON BRAIN SURFACE any of the ridges on the brain's surface **3.** INTRICACY a complexity or intricacy, especially one of many ○ *The plot had so many convolutions it was difficult to follow.* —**convolutional** *adj.* —**convolutionary** *adj.*

convolvulus /kən vólvyo͝oləss/ (*plural* **-luses** *or* **-li** /-lī/) *n.* a plant of the morning-glory family with trumpet-shaped flowers. Most types are twining plants and some are cultivated. Genus: *Convolvulus.* [Mid-16thC. From Latin, where it was formed from *convolvere* (see CONVOLUTE).]

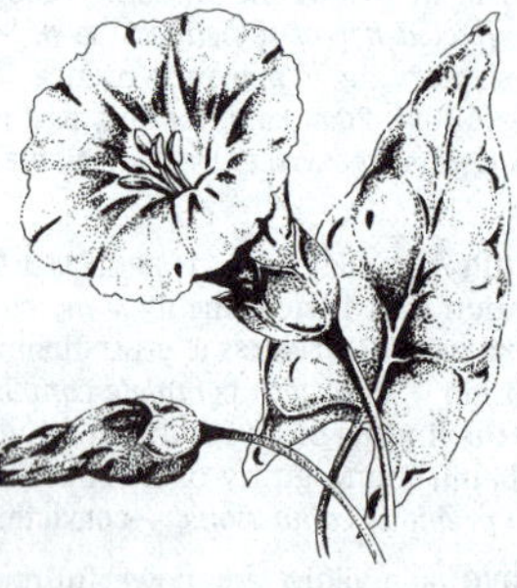

Convolvulus

convoy /kón voy/ *n.* **1.** VEHICLES OR SHIPS TRAVELLING TOGETHER a group of vehicles or ships travelling together, often with an escort for protection ○ *travelling in convoy* **2.** VEHICLES' OR SHIPS' ESCORT a protective escort for a group of vehicles or ships ■ *vt.* (**-voys, -voying, -voyed**) ESCORT VEHICLES OR SHIPS to travel as an escort to protect a group of vehicles or ships [14thC. Via French *convoi* from Old French *conveier* (see CONVEY).]

convulsant /kən vúlss'nt/ *adj.* CAUSING CONVULSIONS causing convulsions ■ *n.* DRUG CAUSING CONVULSIONS a drug that causes convulsions

convulse /kən vúlss/ (**-vulses, -vulsing, -vulsed**) *v.* **1.** *vti.* SHAKE UNCONTROLLABLY to jerk or shake violently and uncontrollably, or to make a muscle or body part go into repetitive spasm **2.** *vt.* CAUSE TO SHAKE to make sb shake with laughter or a strong emotion (*often passive*) ○ *convulsed with panic* **3.** *vt.* DISRUPT to cause extreme disruption or disturbance in sth ○ *Problems in the Far Eastern economies convulsed the London markets.* [Mid-17thC. From Latin *convuls-*, past participle stem of *convellere* 'to wrench or pull violently', from *vellere* 'to pluck or pull' (source of English *svelte*).]

convulsion /kən vúlsh'n/ *n.* (*often used in the plural*) **1.** UNCONTROLLABLE SHAKING a violent shaking of the body or limbs caused by uncontrollable muscle contractions, which can be a symptom of brain disorders and other conditions **2.** DISTURBANCE an extreme disruption or disturbance (*literary*) ■ **convulsions** *npl.* LAUGHTER fits of laughter —**convulsionary** *adj.*

convulsive /kən vúlssiv/ *adj.* **1.** JERKY sudden, jerky, or uncontrollable **2.** HAVING OR PRODUCING CONVULSIONS undergoing or producing uncontrollable jerking of the body or limbs —**convulsively** *adv.* —**convulsiveness** *n.*

Conwy /kónwi/ town and local government district in North Wales. Population: town 3,627 (1991); district 111,200 (1995).

cony (*plural* **-nies**), **coney** (*plural* **-neys**) *n.* **1.** *US* ZOOL EUROPEAN RABBIT a rabbit, especially the common domesticated European rabbit **2.** INDUST RABBIT FUR rabbit fur used for coats and other articles of clothing **3.** ZOOL = **hyrax 4.** ZOOL = **pika** [14thC. Via Anglo-Norman from, ultimately, Latin *cuniculus* 'rabbit, burrow', of uncertain origin: perhaps from *cunus* 'female pudenda'.]

coo /koo/ *v.* (**coos, cooing, cooed**) **1.** *vi.* MAKE SOUND OF PIGEON to make the soft warbling sound that is characteristic of pigeons **2.** *vti.* SPEAK VERY TENDERLY to speak or say sth with affected or exaggerated admiration ■ *n.* (*plural* **coos**) BIRD'S SOUND the soft warbling sound that pigeons make ■ *interj.* EXPRESSING SURPRISE used to express surprise or wonder (*informal*) ○ *Coo! Look at all that money!* [Mid-17thC. An imitation of the sound.]

Coober Pedy /ko͝obər pēēdi/ town in central-southern South Australia, a centre of opal mining. It is noted for its underground dwellings, built by miners seeking to escape the heat. Population: 1,762 (1996).

co-occur (**co-occurs, co-occurring, co-occurred**) *vi.* **1.** HAPPEN TOGETHER to happen at the same time and place **2.** LING SHARE SAME LINGUISTIC CONTEXT to appear together in the same contexts (*refers to linguistic elements, for example sound*) —**co-occurrence** *n.*

cooee /ko͞o ee/ *interj.* used to attract sb's attention. Originally a high-pitched cry used by Australian aboriginals, it was later adopted by settlers in Australia and subsequently spread throughout most of the English-speaking world. (*informal*) [Late 18thC. An imitation of the cry.]

cook /ko͝ok/ *v.* (**cooks, cooking, cooked**) **1.** *vti.* PREPARE FOOD to prepare food for a meal **2.** *vti.* MAKE OR BECOME HOT to make food safe and appetizing by heating it, or to become ready to eat by heating ○ *The onions have been cooking for a while.* ○ *Cook the beef until it is tender.* **3.** *vi.* BE UNCOMFORTABLE IN HEAT to feel extreme discomfort in hot conditions (*informal*) ○ *cooking in an overcrowded bus* **4.** *vt.* CHANGE IN ORDER TO DECEIVE to alter or tamper with information or evidence fraudulently (*informal*) **5.** *vi.* HAPPEN to be happening or developing (*informal*) ○ *I had the feeling that something was cooking.* **6.** *vt.* HEAT ILLEGAL DRUG to heat an illegal drug, e.g. heroin (*slang*) ■ *n.* SB WHO PREPARES FOOD sb who prepares food, or whose job is preparing food [Pre-12thC. Via assumed Vulgar Latin *cocus* 'a cook' from Latin *coquus*, from *coquere* 'to cook' (source of English *kitchen, concoct,* and *biscuit*).] —**cookable** *adj.*

cook up *vt.* **1.** PREPARE MEAL QUICKLY to prepare or improvise a meal quickly **2.** INVENT to invent sth untrue or dishonest such as an excuse (*informal*) **3.** = **cook** *v.* 6 (*slang*)

Cook, Mount /ko͝ok/ the highest mountain in New Zealand, situated in the Southern Alps on the South Island. Height: 3,754 m/12,316 ft.

Cook, James, Captain (1728–79) British explorer and cartographer. During three great voyages (1768–71, 1772–75, 1776–79) he charted New Zealand and Australia and explored the Antarctic and the northwestern coast of North America.

Cook, Sir Joseph (1860–1947) British-born Australian statesman. He was a Liberal Party politician and prime minister of Australia (1913–14).

Cook, Peter (1937–95) British actor and comedian. He appeared in *Beyond the Fringe* (1959–64) and wrote for the satirical magazine *Private Eye.* Full name **Peter Edward Cook**

Cook, Thomas (1808–92) British travel agent. In 1841 he organized a railway excursion for a temperance group and so began his creation of tourism in its modern form.

cookbook /ko͝ok bo͝ok/ *n.* = **cookery book**

cook-chill *adj.* PRECOOKED AND REFRIGERATED used to describe food that is cooked, packaged, and refrigerated, and then reheated before serving ■ *n.* PRECOOKING AND PACKAGING OF FOOD the preparation of cook-chill food

cooker /ko͝okər/ *n.* **1.** *UK* APPLIANCE FOR COOKING a box-shaped kitchen appliance for cooking food, powered by electricity, gas, or solid fuel, and including an oven, grill, and hob **2.** APPLE FOR COOKING a type of apple, usually large and sour, that is more suitable for cooking than for eating raw (*informal*)

cookery /ko͝okəri/ *n.* **1.** PREPARATION OF FOOD the skill or activity of preparing food **2.** STYLE OF PREPARING FOOD a type or style of cooking, such as a national variety or one that meets specific dietary requirements

cookery book *n.* a book containing recipes for preparing food

cookie /ko͝oki/, **cooky** (*plural* **-ies**) *n.* **1.** *US* = **biscuit 2.** TYPE OF PERSON sb who has a particular characteristic (*informal*) ○ *She's a tough cookie.* **3.** COMPUT COMPUTER FILE CONTAINING USER INFORMATION on the Internet or in a computer network, a file containing information about a user that is sent to the central computer each time a request is made. The server uses this information to customize data sent back to the user and to log the user's requests. [Early 18thC. From Dutch *koekje*, literally 'little cake', from *koek* 'cake'.]

cookie cutter *n. US, Can* a shaped template with a sharp edge, used for pressing into a sheet of dough to make biscuit shapes

cookie-cutter *adj. US* seemingly mass-produced without distinctive features

cookie sheet *n. US* = **baking tray**

cooking /ko͝oking/ *n.* **1.** PREPARATION OF FOOD the skill or practice of preparing food **2.** PREPARED FOOD food that has been prepared for eating ○ *She doesn't like my cooking.* ■ *adj.* USED IN COOKING intended for use in cooking rather than for consumption on its own

Cook Islands /ko͝ok ~/ group of islands in the South Pacific that are in free association with New Zealand. They are self-governing and predominantly volcanic. Population: 18,617 (1991). Area: 240 sq. km/90 sq. mi.

Cookson /ko͝oks'n/, **Dame Catherine Ann** (1906–98) British novelist. Her novels of working-class life in northeastern England have sold 90 million copies worldwide. Pseudonym **Catherine Merchant, Catherine Fawcett**

Cook's tour /ko͝oks ~/ *n.* a quick tour or survey, with attention only to the main features (*informal*) ○ *The*

book doesn't aim to give anything more than a Cook's tour of European history. [Named after Thomas COOK]

Cookstown /ko͝oks town/ local government district in County Tyrone, Northern Ireland. Population: 31,300 (1995). Area: 622 sq. km/240 sq. mi.

Cook Strait /ko͝ok ~/ area of ocean separating the North Island and the South Island of New Zealand, noted for its treacherous currents. At its narrowest, it is 22 km/14 mi. wide.

cooktop /ko͝ok top/ *n. US* a flat cooking area on a stove that includes heating units and a surface that can be used for food preparation

Cooktown /ko͝ok town/ coastal town in northern Queensland, Australia. Formerly a mining town, it is now a tourist centre. Population: 1,411 (1996).

cook-up *n.* a Caribbean dish of mixed meats, seafood, and rice

cookware /ko͝ok wair/ *n.* utensils, e.g. pots, pans, and dishes, used in cooking

cooky *n.* = **cookie**

cool /kool/ *adj.* **1.** COLDISH somewhat cold, usually pleasantly so **2.** KEEPING TEMPERATURE LOW made of fabric that keeps the body at a pleasant temperature in hot conditions **3.** SEEMING COLD giving an impression of coldness ○ *a cool mint green* **4.** STAYING CALM staying calm or not showing emotions, especially nervousness or fear **5.** UNFRIENDLY unfriendly or unenthusiastic ○ *They gave us a rather cool reception.* **6.** FASHIONABLE fashionable and sophisticated ○ *looking cool* **7.** EXCELLENT very good (*slang*) ○ *a cool idea* **8.** EMPHASIZING SUM OF MONEY used to emphasize how large a sum of money is (*informal*) ○ *a cool £3.2 million* **9.** MUSIC HAVING RELAXED RHYTHM used to describe a style of jazz, popular in the mid-20th century, characterized by a relaxed rhythm ■ *vti.* (**cools, cooling, cooled**) **1.** MAKE OR BECOME LESS WARM to become or cause sb or sth to become less warm ○ *Wait until the mixture cools* **2.** MAKE OR BECOME LESS INTENSE to make sb or sth less intense, or to become less intense ○ *anything that might cool his anger* ■ *n.* **1.** SLIGHT CHILL moderate coldness, especially in relation to greater heat or coldness ○ *the cool of our hotel room* **2.** CALMNESS the ability to remain calm in difficult circumstances (*informal*) **3.** STYLISHNESS stylishness that is attractive without being ostentatious (*informal*) ■ *adv.* CALMLY in a calm self-controlled way (*informal*) ○ *Just act cool.* ■ *interj.* EXPRESSING PLEASURE used to express delight or excitement at a prospect or event (*informal*) ○ *You're coming too? Cool!* [Old English *cōl*. Ultimately from an Indo-European word denoting 'cold' that is also the ancestor of English *chill*, *congeal*, and *glacier*.] —**coolingly** *adv.* —**coolness** *n.* ◇ **keep your cool** to remain calm ◇ **lose your cool** to become angry and excitable

cool down *vti.* **1.** MAKE OR BECOME LESS WARM to make sb or sth less warm, or to become less warm ○ *Wait till the engine cools down before you lift the bonnet.* **2.** MAKE OR BECOME CALM to make sb or sth calm or calmer after strong feeling or excitement, or become calm or calmer ○ *The political situation has cooled down a lot.*

cool off *v.* **1.** *vi.* BECOME COOL AGAIN to become comfortably cool again ○ *I went for a swim to cool off.* **2.** *vti.* REGAIN CALMNESS to become calm again after being angry (*informal*)

cool out *vi. Carib* to relax (*informal*)

coolabah *n.* = **coolibah**

coolamon /ko͝olə mon/ *n. ANZ* an oblong wooden container used by Australian aboriginals for holding food or water [Mid-19thC. From Kamilaroi *gulaman*.]

Coolangatta /ko͝olən gáttə/ coastal town in southeastern Queensland, Australia, a commercial centre and tourist resort. Population: 3,778 (1996).

coolant /ko͝olənt/ *n.* a substance, usually a liquid, used to prevent overheating in an engine or other mechanism

cool bag, cool box *n.* a portable insulated container used to keep food cool outdoors. US term **cooler**

cooler /ko͝olər/ *n.* **1.** COOL PLACE OR CONTAINER a compartment or container in which sth is cooled or kept cool **2.** *US* = **cool bag 3.** LONG DRINK a long refreshing drink, especially an iced mixture of wine, fruit juice, and soda water **4.** PRISON a prison or prison cell (*dated slang*)

Coolgardie /kool gaárdi/ gold-mining town in southern Western Australia. It was once the third largest town in the state. Population: 1,258 (1996).

cool-headed *adj.* staying calm in tense situations

coolibah /ko͝olə baa/ (*plural* **-bahs** *or* **-bah**), **coolabah** (*plural* **-bahs** *or* **-bah**) *n.* a smooth-barked eucalyptus tree with long leaves containing oil glands. It grows near rivers and water holes in the interior of Australia. Latin name: *Eucalyptus microtheca.* [Late 19thC. From Kamilaroi *gulubaa*.]

Coolidge /ko͝olij/, **Calvin** (1872–1933) US statesman and 30th President of the United States. A pro-business Republican, he presided over a period of prosperity, but his presidency (1923–29) ended with the Wall Street Crash. Full name **John Calvin Coolidge**

coolie /ko͝oli/ *n.* an offensive term in India, China, and other parts of Asia for a local man hired cheaply to do labouring or portering work (*offensive*) [Mid-17thC. From Hindi *kulī*, of uncertain origin: possibly a blend of Telugu *kūli* 'hire' and Urdu *kulī* 'slave', or from *Kulī*, a Gujarati people.]

cooling-off period /ko͝oling-/ *n.* **1.** BREAK IN DISPUTE an agreed pause in a dispute to allow tempers to cool and peaceful solutions to be examined **2.** TIME TO RECONSIDER a period of reflection allowed before making a legally binding commitment

cooling tower *n.* a tall chimney in which the steam produced by an industrial process is condensed

cool jazz *n.* a kind of jazz with a lighter tone and more relaxed character, popular in the 1940s and 1950s, especially on the West Coast of the United States

coolly /ko͝ol li/ *adv.* **1.** CALMLY in a calm or relaxed way ○ *She coolly marched up to the desk and demanded to see the manager.* **2.** IN COLD MANNER without friendliness or enthusiasm ○ *He greeted her coolly.*

coolth /koolth/ *n.* pleasant coolness or coldness relative to greater heat or cold (*informal or humorous*) [Mid-16thC. Formed from COOL, on the model of WARMTH.]

coom /koom/ *n.* dusty or greasy dirt, e.g. coal dust (*regional*) [Late 16thC. Origin uncertain: possibly a variant of CULM[1].]

Cooma /ko͝omə/ town in southeastern New South Wales, Australia. Formerly the administrative centre of the Snowy Mountains Hydroelectric Scheme, it is the gateway to the New South Wales ski fields. Population: 7,150 (1996).

Coomaraswamy /koo maárə swaámi/, **Ananda Kentish** (1877–1947) Sri Lankan-born Indian Orientalist. His many works on Asian culture, including *The Transformation of Nature in Art* (1934), stimulated scholarship in Asian studies.

coomb /koom/, **coombe** *n.* GEOL = **combe** (*regional*)

Coombs /koomz/, **Nuggett** (1906–97) Australian economist. The head of Australia's Reserve Bank (1959–68), he was an active supporter of environmental causes and Aboriginal land rights. Real name **Herbert Cole Coombs**

coon[1] /koon/ *n. US* a raccoon (*informal*) [Mid-18thC. Shortening of RACCOON.]

coon[2] /koon/ *n.* **1.** OFFENSIVE TERM a highly offensive term for a Black person (*offensive taboo*) **2.** *ANZ* OFFENSIVE TERM a highly offensive term for an Australian aboriginal (*offensive slang*) [Mid-19thC. Shortening of Portuguese *barracoos* 'buildings specially constructed to hold slaves for sale'.]

Coonabarabran /ko͝onə bárrə bran/ town in northern New South Wales, Australia, near the Siding Spring Anglo-Australian Observatory. Population: 3,012 (1996).

cooncan /ko͝on kan/ *n.* a card game from Mexico that is similar to rummy and played with one or two packs [Late 19thC. By folk etymology from American Spanish *conquián*, from Spanish *con quién?* 'with whom?'.]

coonskin /ko͝on skin/ *n. US* the skin of a raccoon, or clothing made from it

coop /koop/ *n.* **1.** ENCLOSURE FOR POULTRY an enclosure or hut in which poultry is kept **2.** FISHING BASKET a wicker basket used for catching fish **3.** PRISON a prison or prison cell [13thC. Origin uncertain: possibly via Middle Dutch *kūpe* 'basket, tub' from, ultimately, Latin *cupa* 'cask'. The earliest meaning in English was 'basket'.]

coop up *vt.* to keep sb in a confined space

co-op /kó op/, **coop** *n.* a cooperative organization or venture, especially a marketing enterprise (*informal*) [Mid-19thC. Shortening.]

cooper /ko͝opər/ *n.* BARREL-MAKER sb skilled in making and repairing wooden barrels ■ *vti.* (**-ers, -ering, -ered**) MAKE BARRELS to make or repair wooden barrels [15thC. From Middle Dutch *kūper*, from *kūpe* 'cask' (see COOP).]

Cooper /ko͝opər/, **Gary** (1901–61) US film actor. He starred in Westerns, winning Academy Awards for *Sergeant York* (1941) and *High Noon* (1952).

Cooper, Henry (*b.* 1934) British boxer. British and sometime European heavyweight champion (1959–69, 1970–71), he was noted for his powerful left hook, 'Enry's 'ammer.

Cooper, James Fenimore (1789–1851) US writer. Among his Leather-Stocking Tales about frontier life is the novel *The Last of the Mohicans* (1826).

Cooper, Samuel (1609–72) English miniaturist. His portraits in oils, including those of Oliver Cromwell and John Milton, brought new vivacity and realism to the miniature style.

cooperage /ko͝opərij/ *n.* **1.** COOPER'S CRAFT the craft of making and repairing wooden barrels **2.** COOPER'S WORKPLACE a place where wooden barrels are made and repaired **3.** COOPER'S FEE the fee charged by a cooper for making or repairing barrels

cooperate /kō óppə rayt/ (**-ates, -ating, -ated**) *v.* **1.** *vi.* WORK TOGETHER to work or act together to achieve a common aim **2.** COMPLY to do what is asked or required [Late 16thC. From ecclesiastical Latin *cooperat-*, past participle stem of *cooperari*, literally 'to work together', from Latin *operari* 'to work'.] —**cooperator** *n.*

cooperation /kō óppə ráysh'n/ *n.* **1.** WORKING TOGETHER the act of working together to achieve a common aim **2.** COMPLIANCE doing what is asked or required —**cooperationist** *n.*

cooperative /kō óppərətiv/ *adj.* **1.** WILLING TO HELP doing, or willing to do, what is asked or required ○ *She's a good worker and very cooperative.* **2.** WORKING TOGETHER working or acting together with others, or done by people working or acting together ○ *a cooperative effort* **3.** OPERATED COLLECTIVELY owned jointly by all its members or workers, who share all profits equally ○ *a cooperative farm* ■ *n.* BUSINESS OWNED BY WORKERS a business that is jointly owned by the people who run it, with all profits shared equally ○ *a workers' cooperative* —**cooperatively** *adv.* —**cooperativeness** *n.*

cooperative society (*plural* **cooperative societies**) *n.* a commercial organization distributing goods to its members who participate in profit-sharing schemes

Cooper Creek /ko͝opər ~/ river in central Australia that runs from the junction of the Barcoo and Thomson rivers in Queensland to Lake Eyre in South Australia. Length: 800 km/500 mi.

co-opt /kō ópt/ (**co-opts, co-opting, co-opted**) *vt.* **1.** APPOINT BY AGREEMENT to appoint sb to a body by agreement with the other members **2.** TAKE INTO LARGER GROUP to absorb an opponent or opposing group into a larger group or society by making promises and concessions **3.** ADOPT OR APPROPRIATE to adopt or appropriate sth, e.g. a political issue or idea, as your own [Mid-17thC. From Latin *cooptare*, literally 'to choose mutually', from *optare* 'to choose' (source of English *opt* and *adopt*).] —**co-optation** /kō op táysh'n/ *n.* —**co-option** *n.* —**co-optative** *adj.* —**co-optive** *adj.*

Coopworth /ko͝op wərth/ *n. ANZ* a sheep belonging to a breed developed in New Zealand by crossing the Border Leicester with the Romney

coordinate *v.* /kō áwrdi nayt/ (**-nates, -nating, -nated**) **1.** *vt.* ORGANIZE STH COMPLEX to organize a complex enterprise in which numerous people are involved and bring their contributions together to form a unified whole ○ *responsible for coordinating the campaign* **2.** *vti.* MAKE PARTS MOVE TOGETHER to make moving parts, e.g. parts of the body, work together in sequence or in time with one another, or to work together in this way ○ *hand and eye coordinating perfectly for the overhead shot* **3.** *vt.* **PUT TOGETHER** to place or class things together ○ *Before we can proceed, all of our files have to be coordinated.* **4.** *vi.* **WORK TOGETHER** to work together as a unit ○ *members of the team coordinating brilliantly* **5.** *vti.* **GO WELL TOGETHER** to make a pleasing combination or match ○ *outfit and accessories that coordinate stylishly* ■ *n.* /kō áwrdinət/ **1.** **GEOM** **NUMBER SPECIFYING POSITION** each of a set of numbers that together describe the exact position of sth such as a place on a map with reference to a set of axes ○ *Did you receive the coordinates for your target?* **2.** **SB OR STH EQUAL** sb or sth that is equal in rank or importance ○ *We need the faculties of the college as coordinates in this endeavour.* **3.** **CHEM, PHYS** **VARIABLE** a variable used with others to describe the state of a physical or chemical system ■ **coordinates** *npl.* **MATCHING CLOTHES** clothes that are designed to be worn together ■ *adj.* /kō áwrdinət/ **1.** **EQUAL** equal in rank or importance ○ *The district offices should work as coordinate elements of the company.* **2.** **CHEM, PHYS** **INVOLVING SET OF VARIABLES** involving the use of coordinates [Mid-17thC. Coined from CO- + Latin *ordinare* 'to set in order', on the model of SUBORDINATE.] —**coordinated** /kō áwrdi naytid/ *adj.* —**coordinately** /-nətli/ *adv.* —**coordinateness** /-nətnəss/ *n.* —**coordinative** /kō áwrdinətiv/ *adj.*

coordinate bond *n.* a chemical bond between two atoms created by the sharing of a pair of electrons, both supplied by one atom. A coordinate bond is a type of covalent bond.

coordinate clause *n.* any of two or more clauses in a sentence that have the same grammatical function or status, usually joined by a coordinating conjunction such as 'and' or 'but'. ◊ **subordinate clause, main clause**

coordinate geometry *n.* = **analytic geometry**

coordinating conjunction *n.* a word such as 'and' or 'but' that joins two words or clauses with the same grammatical function or status

coordination /kō áwrdi náysh'n/ *n.* **1.** **COMING OR WORKING TOGETHER** the combining of diverse parts or groups to make a unit, or the way these parts work together **2.** **MOVEMENT OF PARTS TOGETHER** the skilful and balanced movement of different parts, especially parts of the body, at the same time

coordination complex, **coordination compound** *n.* a chemical compound containing one or more ions, atoms, or molecules bound by coordinate bonds to a central metallic atom

coordination number *n.* the number of ions, atoms, or molecules attached by coordinate bonds to the metallic atom in a complex

coordinator /kō áwrdi naytər/ *n.* **1.** **SB BRINGING TOGETHER DIFFERENT ELEMENTS** sb responsible for organizing diverse parts of an enterprise or groups into a coherent or efficient whole **2.** = **coordinating conjunction**

Coorong /koo róng/ long narrow salt lagoon on the southeastern coast of South Australia. It was declared a national park in 1966. Area: 4,000 sq. km/1,500 sq. mi.

Coot

coot /koot/ (*plural* **coots** *or* **coot**) *n.* **1.** **WATER BIRD** an aquatic bird of Europe, Asia, and North America that has long toes, darkish plumage, and a white bill and forehead. Genus: *Fulica*. **2.** **UNCONVENTIONAL**

PERSON an odd, eccentric, or unreasonably stubborn person [13thC. Origin uncertain: possibly from Middle Dutch *coet*.]

Cootamundra /koōtə múndrə/ city in New South Wales, Australia, northwest of Canberra. Population: 6,314 (1986).

cootie /koōti/ *n. US, NZ* a louse of the kind that infests people (*informal*) [Early 20thC. Origin uncertain: probably from Malay *kutu*.]

cop¹ /kop/ *n.* **POLICE OFFICER** a police officer (*slang*) ■ *vt.* (**cops, copping, copped**) **1.** **GRAB** to seize or grab sth (*informal*) **2.** **RECEIVE PUNISHMENT** to receive or undergo sth unpleasant, especially punishment (*informal*) **3.** **DRUGS OBTAIN DRUGS** to obtain illegal drugs (*slang*) [Early 18thC. 'Police officer': related to COPPER², literally 'grabber'. Verb senses from a variant of *cap* 'to catch', which came via French *caper* from Latin *capere* 'to seize, take'.] ◊ **a fair cop** a fair or just arrest ◊ **cop a plea** *US* to negotiate with a prosecutor in order to avoid prosecution for a serious crime by agreeing to plead guilty to a lesser crime (*slang*) ◊ **cop it sweet** *ANZ* to accept a penalty or punishment without resisting or complaining ◊ **not much cop** not very good or useful (*informal*)

cop out *vi.* to withdraw from an activity because of lack of nerve or inclination (*slang*)

cop² /kop/ *n.* a cone-shaped roll of thread on a spindle [Old English *coppe* 'summit', of unknown origin]

COP a pass in a university subject. Abbr of **Certificate of Proficiency**

cop. *abbr.* copyright

Copacabana /kópə kə bánnə/ beach resort and residential area in southern Rio de Janeiro, Brazil

copacetic /kópə seétik/, **copasetic** *adj. US, Can* excellent or very good (*slang*) [Early 20thC. Origin unknown.]

copal /kóp'l/ *n.* a hard resin from various tropical trees, used to make varnish [Late 16thC. Via Spanish from Nahuatl *copalli*.]

Copán /kō pán/ ancient city of the Mayan people, in northwestern Honduras. It is an important archaeological site.

co-parenting *n.* **1.** **SHARED RESPONSIBILITY FOR CHILDREN** the care and bringing up of children by two people who have divorced or separated **2.** **BRINGING UP CHILDREN TOGETHER** shared responsibility for bringing up children between two people who are not legally married, especially a same-sex couple —**co-parent** *n.*

copartner /kō paátnər/ *n.* a close partner or associate, especially one who has an equal stake in a company —**copartnership** *n.*

copasetic *adj.* = **copacetic**

co-payment *n.* an arrangement by which two or more parties make matching payments on a loan or other financial obligation, or a payment made in this way

cope¹ /kōp/ (**copes, coping, coped**) *vi.* to deal successfully with a difficult problem or situation [14thC. Via French *couper* 'to strike, cut' from, ultimately, Greek *kolaphos* 'a blow'. The underlying meaning is 'to come to blows or contend with'.] —**coper** *n.*

cope² /kōp/ *n.* a long sleeveless ceremonial cape worn by priests in some Christian Churches [13thC. Via medieval Latin *capa* 'cloak, hood' from late Latin *cappa* (source of English *cape* and *chaperone*).] —**coped** *adj.*

cope³ /kōp/ *n.* = **coping** ■ *vt.* (**copes, coping, coped**) **1.** **PROVIDE WALL WITH COPING** to lay a protective top course of brick or stone (**coping**) on a wall **2.** **JOIN TIMBER** to join two pieces of moulded timber [16thC. From COPE².]

copeck *n.* = **kopeck**

Copenhagen /kópən háygən, -haágən/ capital and largest city of Denmark, situated on the eastern coast of Sjælland Island and the northern coast of Amager Island. Population: 1,339,395 (1994). Danish **København**

Copenhagen blue *adj.* of a greyish-blue colour — **Copenhagen blue** *n.*

copepod /kópə pod/ (*plural* **-pods** *or* **-pod**) *n.* a tiny marine or freshwater crustacean that lives among plankton and is an important food source for many

fish. Subclass: Copepoda. [Late 19thC. From modern Latin *Copepoda*, subclass name, from Greek *kōpē* 'oar' + -POD, because of its paddle-shaped feet.]

coper /kópər/ *n.* a trader or merchant, especially one who deals in horses [Mid-16thC. Formed from *cope* 'to buy', from Middle Dutch or Low German *kōpen*.]

Copernican /kə púrnikən/ *adj.* **1.** **OF COPERNICUS** relating to Copernicus, especially to his theory that the Earth and other planets revolve around the sun **2.** **FAR-REACHING** profoundly important or far-reaching (*literary*) ○ *a Copernican change in attitudes*

Copernican system *n.* the theory of Copernicus regarding the mechanics of the solar system, published in 1543, in which he argued that the Earth and other planets revolve around the Sun. This theory challenged the Ptolemaic system of astronomy that had prevailed since the second century.

Copernicus /kə púrnikəss/ *n.* a large crater on the Moon in the northwest quadrant, 93 km/58 mi. in diameter. It is the centre of a major system of rays on the lunar surface.

AKG London

Nicolaus Copernicus

Copernicus, Nicolaus (1473–1543) Polish astronomer. His major work, *De Revolutionibus Orbium Coelestium* (1543), postulated that the Earth orbited the Sun and laid the foundations of modern astronomy. Born **Mikołaj Kopernik**

copestone /kóp stōn/ *n.* one of the stones that form the top edge of a wall [Mid-16thC. Formed from COPE³.]

copier /kóppi ər/ *n.* **1.** **DEVICE FOR MAKING COPIES** a device, especially a photocopier, that makes copies of documents **2.** **SB WHO MAKES COPIES** sb who makes copies of things, especially handwritten copies of manuscripts in former times

copilot /kó pīlət/ *n.* a second pilot in an aircraft, who shares the flying but is not in command

coping /kóping/ *n.* the top, often sloping, course of brick or stone on top of a wall that forms a protective cap against the weather [Mid-16thC. Formed from COPE³.]

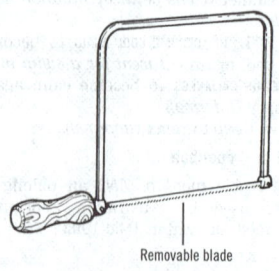

Removable blade

Coping saw

coping saw *n.* a saw with a thin flexible blade held tight in a U-shaped frame that is used for cutting curves in wood

copious /kópi əss/ *adj.* **1.** **ABUNDANT** produced or existing in large quantities **2.** **USING WORDY STYLE** using many words in writing or speech (*archaic*) [14thC. Directly or via French from Latin *copiosus*, from *copia* 'abundance' (source of English *cornucopia* and *copy*).] —**copiously** *adv.* —**copiousness** *n.*

copita /kō peétə/ n. a traditional Spanish tulip-shaped sherry glass, or a drink of sherry served in one [Mid-19thC. From Spanish, literally 'little cup'.]

coplanar /kō pláynər/ adj. lying in the same plane — **coplanarity** /kṓ play nárrəti/ n.

Aaron Copland

Copland /kṓplənd/, **Aaron** (1900–90) US composer whose music was often based on folk themes. He won the Pulitzer Prize in music for *Appalachian Spring* (1944).

copolymer /kō póllimər/ n. a substance with a high molecular weight that results from chemically combining two or more monomers —**copolymeric** /kṓ poli mérrik/ adj.

copolymerize /kō póllimə rīz/ (-**izes**, -**izing**, -**ized**), **copolymerise** (-**ises**, -**ising**, -**ised**) vt. to unite two or more monomers chemically to form a copolymer — **copolymerization** /kō pólimə rī záysh'n/ n.

cop-out n. (slang) **1. EVASION OF RESPONSIBILITY** a feeble avoidance of a responsibility or commitment **2. EXCUSE FOR NOT TAKING ACTION** a feebly transparent excuse or explanation for refusing to face up to sth **3. SB WHO BACKS OUT OF STH** sb who refuses to follow through on or fulfil a commitment ○ *What a bunch of cop-outs!*

copper[1] /kóppər/ n. **1. REDDISH-BROWN METAL** a reddish-brown metallic chemical element that bends easily and is a good conductor of electricity and heat. Symbol **Cu 2. REDDISH-BROWN COLOUR** a reddish-brown colour, like that of polished copper **3. SMALL COIN** a low-value coin made of copper or brass (informal) ○ *a pocketful of coppers* **4. POT FOR BOILING WATER** a large pot, formerly made of copper, used to boil water **5.** ZOOL **REDDISH-BROWN BUTTERFLY** a small reddish-brown butterfly. Genera: *Lycaena* and *Heodes.* ■ vt. (-**pers**, -**pering**, -**pered**) **COVER WITH COPPER** to cover or coat sth with copper (often passive) ■ adj. **OF REDDISH-BROWN COLOUR** of a reddish-brown colour, like that of polished copper [Pre-12thC. Via late Latin *cuprum* from, ultimately, Greek *Kupros* 'Cyprus', an important ancient source of copper.] —**coppery** adj.

copper[2] /kóppər/ n. a police officer [Mid-19thC. Formed from COP[1].]

copperas /kóppərəss/ n. = **ferrous sulphate** [15thC. Via French from medieval Latin *cuperosa*, of uncertain origin: probably an alteration of assumed *aqua cuprosa* 'copper water', from late Latin *cuprum* (see COPPER).]

Copper Belt n. an area in Central Africa that has rich deposits of copper ore

copper-bottomed adj. **1. HAVING COPPER BOTTOM** having a copper coating on the base **2. SOUND** certain or reliable, especially financially

copper-fasten (**copper-fastens**, **copper-fastening**, **copper-fastened**) vt. to make an agreement binding [From the use of copper fastenings on ships to prevent corrosion]

copperhead /kóppər hed/ (plural -**heads** or -**head**) n. **1. REDDISH-BROWN SNAKE** a reddish-brown poisonous snake of the viper family found in the eastern and central United States. Latin name: *Agkistrodon contortrix.* **2.** ANZ **AUSTRALIAN SNAKE** a large poisonous Australian snake of the cobra family with pale brown to black skin and a copper-coloured band round the back of its head. Latin name: *Denisonia superba.* [Late 18thC]

copperplate /kóppər playt/ n. **1. PRINTING PLATE** a polished copper printing plate with a design etched or engraved on it **2. PRINT** a print made from a cop-

perplate **3. NEAT HANDWRITING** neat handwriting, especially in the style of copybooks produced from copper plates

copper pyrites n. = **chalcopyrite**

coppersmith /kóppər smith/ n. **1. SB WHO MAKES COPPER ARTICLES** sb who makes or repairs articles of copper **2. ASIAN BIRD WITH METALLIC CALL** a small greenish bird of Southeast Asia belonging to the barbet family that has a distinctive metallic call. Latin name: *Megalaima haemacephala.*

copper sulphate n. a poisonous blue compound containing copper and sulphur that is used in dyeing and as a fungicide. Formula: $CuSO_4$.

copperware /kóppər wair/ n. objects made of copper, especially cooking pots and pans

coppice /kóppiss/ n. **GROVE OF SMALL TREES** an area of densely growing small trees, especially one in which the trees are regularly cut back to encourage more growth ■ vt. (-**pices**, -**picing**, -**piced**) **PRUNE TREES** to cut back trees periodically to encourage young growth [Mid-14thC. From Old French *copeīz*, from *coper* 'to cut' (see COPE[1]).]

Francis Ford Coppola

Coppola /kóppələ/, **Francis Ford** (b. 1939) US film director. He directed the *Godfather* trilogy (1972, 1974, 1990).

copra /kóprə/ n. the dried flesh of the coconut from which coconut oil is obtained [Late 16thC. Via Portuguese from Malayalam *koppara*.]

Coprates /kóprə teez/ n. a giant canyon on Mars running east–west to the equatorial region. It is over 800 km/500 mi. long and 95 km/60 mi. wide in places.

copro- prefix. dung, excrement ○ *coprophilous* [From Greek *kopros* 'dung']

coprocessor /kṓ prṓ sessər/ n. a second processor in a computer, designed to improve performance time by handling specialized tasks

coprolalia /kóprə láyli ə/ n. the uncontrolled use of violent and obscene language, especially as a result of an illness such as Tourette's syndrome

coprolite /kóprə līt/ n. fossilized dung from which information about eating patterns in prehistoric times can be discovered —**coprolitic** /kóprə líttik/ adj.

coprology /ko prólləji/ n. an obsession with defecation especially as expressed in art and literature

coprophagy /ko próffəji/ n. the eating of dung by certain species of insects or animals —**coprophagous** /-gəss/ adj.

coprophilia /kóprə fílli ə/ n. an obsessive and often sexual interest in faeces and defecation —**coprophiliac** n. —**coprophilic** adj.

coprophilous /kə próffiləss/ adj. used to describe organisms such as some insects or fungi that live on or in dung

copse /kops/ n. = **coppice** [Late 16thC. Alteration of COPPICE.]

Copt /kopt/ n. **1. MEMBER OF COPTIC CHURCH** a member of the Coptic Church **2. NON-ARAB EGYPTIAN** an Egyptian of non-Arab descent [Early 17thC. Via French or modern Latin from Arabic *al-kibt* 'the Copts', from Coptic *Gyptios* 'Egyptian', from Greek *Aiguptios*.]

Copt. abbr. Coptic

copter /kóptər/ n. a helicopter (informal) [Mid-20thC. Shortening.]

Coptic /kóptik/ n. **FORMER EGYPTIAN LANGUAGE** a language formerly spoken in Egypt, a later form of ancient Egyptian and one of the Afro-Asiatic languages. Coptic survives as the liturgical language of Egyptian Monophysite Christians. ■ adj. **OF THE COPTS** relating or belonging to the Copts, Coptic, or Egyptian Monophysite Christian Church

Coptic Church n. the Egyptian Christian Church, established in the 6th century and adhering to the doctrine of the Monophysites

copula /kópp yōōlə/ (plural -**las** or -**lae** /-lee/) n. **1.** GRAM **LINKING VERB** a verb such as 'be' or 'seem' that links the subject of a sentence with an adjective or noun phrase (**complement**) relating to it (technical) **2.** LOGIC **LINK BETWEEN SUBJECT AND PREDICATE** a form of the verb 'to be' linking the subject and the predicate in certain propositions, such as 'are' in 'Some dogs are poodles' (technical) **3. LINK BETWEEN TWO THINGS** anything that provides a link between two things (formal) [Early 17thC. From Latin, 'link' (source of English *couple*). Ultimately from an Indo-European word meaning 'to reach' that is also the ancestor of English *apt*, *apex*, and *attitude*.] —**copular** adj.

copulate /kópp yōō layt/ (-**lates**, -**lating**, -**lated**) vi. to have sexual intercourse (formal) [Early 17thC. From Latin *copulat-*, past participle stem of *copulare* 'to join together', from *copula* (see COPULA).] —**copulation** /kópyōō láysh'n/ n. —**copulatory** /-láytəri/ adj.

copulative /kóppyōōlətiv/ adj. **1. LINKING** linking or joining (formal) **2.** GRAM **RELATING TO LINKING VERB** relating to a verb that links the subject with its complement, or to the function of such a verb —**copulatively** adv.

copy /kóppi/ n. (plural -**ies**) **1. REPRODUCTION** sth that is made exactly like sth else in appearance or function **2. ONE OF MANY** any of many identical specimens of sth that is produced in large numbers, especially sth printed or published **3. WRITTEN TEXT** the written text to be published in a book, newspaper, or magazine, as distinct from visual material or graphics ■ v. (-**ies**, -**ying**, -**ied**) **1.** vt. **MAKE IDENTICAL VERSION** to make another example or specimen that is exactly the same as sth **2.** vt. **DO SAME AS** to do exactly what sb else does **3.** vti. **CHEAT BY DOING SAME** to reproduce the work of another fraudulently [14thC. Via French from, ultimately, Latin *copia* 'abundance, power, right' (see COPIOUS), in phrases meaning 'the right to transcribe'.] —**copyable** adj.

── **WORD KEY: SYNONYMS** ──

copy, reproduce, duplicate, clone, replicate, recreate
CORE MEANING: to make sth that resembles sth else to a greater or lesser degree

copy the most general term; **reproduce** to make a copy that is careful and exact; **duplicate** to copy sth two or more times; **clone** to produce a copy that is very nearly identical to the original, particularly a piece of equipment or an organism; **replicate** to copy sth repeatedly and exactly; **recreate** to make sth that appears to be the same as sth that no longer exists, or that exists in a different place.

───────────────

copy down vt. to make a written copy of sth ○ *Journalists copied down his every word.*

copybook /kóppi book/ n. **BOOK OF HANDWRITING SPECIMENS** a book containing models of handwriting for young students to copy ■ adj. **1. EXCELLENT** so good that it could be used as a model for others to copy **2. UNORIGINAL** following guidelines slavishly and showing no originality ◊ **blot your copybook** to do sth that spoils your previously good record or reputation

copycat /kóppi kat/ n. **SB WHO IMITATES OTHERS** sb, especially a child, who slavishly imitates another (informal) ■ adj. **DONE IN IMITATION** done in close imitation of sb or sth else (informal)

copy desk n. a desk at which written material is edited for publication

copy-edit (**copy-edits**, **copy-editing**, **copy-edited**) vti. to read written material and correct it for publication

copy editor n. sb who reads written material and corrects it for publication

copygraph /kóppi graaf, -graf/ n. = **hectograph**

copyhold /kóppi hōld/ n. a tenure of land held at the will of a landowner, originally a lord (dated) [15thC.

From the fact that it was recorded in a transcript of the manorial court rolls.]

copyholder /kóppi hōldər/ *n.* **1.** DOCUMENT STAND a stand that holds documents upright while they are being read or keyed **2.** ASSISTANT TO PROOFREADER sb who reads written material aloud to a proofreader **3.** HOLDER OF ESTATE a holder of a tenement (**copyhold**) that consisted of an estate held at the will of a land-owner, originally a lord (*dated*)

copyist /kóppi ist/ *n.* **1.** SB WHO MAKES WRITTEN COPIES sb whose job is making copies of handwritten documents or music **2.** UNIMAGINATIVE IMITATOR sb who merely imitates others

copy protection *n.* a means of preventing un-authorized duplication of computer software — **copy-protected** *adj.*

copyreader /kóppi reedər/ *n. US* = **subeditor**

copyright /kóppi rīt/ *n.* CREATIVE ARTIST'S CONTROL OF ORIGINAL WORK the legal right of creative artists or publishers to control the use and reproduction of their original works ■ *adj.* PROTECTED BY COPYRIGHT controlled or restricted by a copyright ■ *vt.* (**-rights, -righting, -righted**) GET COPYRIGHT OF to secure the copyright on a creative work —**copyrightable** *adj.* —**copyrighter** *n.*

copyright deposit library *n.* any of a small number of libraries that receives a free copy of every book published in the UK

copy typist *n.* a typist who works from written or typed drafts, rather than from dictation

copywriter /kóppi rītər/ *n.* sb who writes the texts for advertisements and other publicity material — **copywriting** *n.*

coq au vin /kók ō ván, -ván/ (*plural* **coqs au vin** /kók ō ván, -ván/ *or* **coq au vins**) *n.* a French dish of chicken cooked in red wine with other ingredients [From French, literally 'cock in wine']

coquet /ko két/ *vi.* (**-quets, -quetting, -quetted**) (*literary*) **1.** FLIRT to act coyly and flirtatiously **2.** ACT FRIVOLOUSLY to act casually or frivolously ■ *n.* MAN WHO FLIRTS a flirtatious man (*literary*) [Late 17thC. From French, literally 'little cock', from *coq* 'cock' (see COCKADE).]

coquetry /kókitri/ (*plural* **-ries**) *n.* flirtatious behaviour (*literary*)

coquette /ko két/ *n.* a flirtatious woman (*literary*) [Mid-17thC. From French, the feminine form of *coquet* 'COQUET'.] —**coquettish** *adj.* —**coquettishly** *adv.* —**coquettishness** *n.*

coquilla nut /ko kéelyə-/ *n.* the nut of a Brazilian palm tree, with a thick hard shell used for carving [Coquilla of uncertain origin: possibly an alteration of Portuguese *coquilho*, literally 'little coconut', from *cóco* 'coconut' (see COCO)]

coquille /ko kée/ *n.* **1.** SEAFOOD DISH a dish of seafood baked and served in a scallop shell or a scallop-shaped dish **2.** SHELL OR SHELL-SHAPED DISH a scallop shell or a scallop-shaped dish **3.** FENCING GUARD ON FOIL a bell-shaped guard on a fencing foil [From French, 'cockle shell' (see COCKLE)]

coquina /kō kéenə/ *n.* **1.** SOFT LIMESTONE a soft limestone formed largely from crushed shells and coral, used as a building material in the West Indies and the southeastern United States **2.** SEA CLAM a small clam common in the seas around the eastern and southern United States. Genus: *Donax*. [Mid-19thC. From Spanish, 'cockle shell', of uncertain origin: probably via *concha* 'mollusc shell' from Latin, 'mussel'.]

coquito /ko kéetō/ (*plural* **-tos** *or* **-to**) *n.* a Chilean palm tree with edible nuts and a sweet sap that is used to make wine. Latin name: *Jubaea chilensis*. [Mid-19thC. Via Spanish, literally 'little coco shell', from, ultimately, Portuguese *cóco* 'coconut' (see COCO).]

cor /kawr/ *interj.* used to express amazement or admiration (*informal*) [Mid-20thC. Shortening of COR BLIMEY.]

cor. *abbr.* **1.** corner **2.** cornet **3.** correction **4.** correspondence **5.** PRESS correspondent

Cor. *abbr.* BIBLE Corinthians

coracle /kórrək'l/ *n.* a small round boat made from animal skins stretched over a wicker frame [Mid-16thC. Via Welsh *corwgl* from Middle Irish *curach* 'currach' (see CURRACH).]

coracoid /kórrə koyd/ *n.* a bony projection on the shoulder blade in most mammals [Mid-18thC. Via modern Latin from Greek *korakoeidēs* 'crow-like' (from its resemblance to a crow's beak), from *korax* 'raven, crow'.]

Coral

coral /kórrəl/ *n.* **1.** MARINE ORGANISM a marine organism that lives in colonies and has an external skeleton. Class: Anthozoa. **2.** HARD MARINE DEPOSIT a hard deposit consisting of coral skeletons, often forming marine reefs **3.** STH MADE OF CORAL a piece of coral or an article made from it **4.** DEEP REDDISH-ORANGE COLOUR a deep reddish-orange colour **5.** LOBSTER'S OR CRAB'S EGGS the unfertilized eggs of a crab or lobster that turn pinkish-orange when cooked ■ *adj.* DEEP REDDISH-ORANGE of a deep reddish-orange colour [14thC. Via Old French from, ultimately, Greek *korallion*.]

coralberry /kórrəl berri/ (*plural* **-ries** *or* **-ry**) *n.* **1.** PLANT WITH RED BERRIES a North American shrub of the honeysuckle family that produces dark red berries. Latin name: *Symphoricarpos orbiculatus*. **2.** EASTERN ASIAN SHRUB an evergreen shrub of eastern Asia. Genus: *Ardisia*.

coralline /kórrə līn/ *adj.* **1.** OF OR LIKE CORAL relating to or resembling coral **2.** PINKISH-RED OR PINKISH-ORANGE of the pinkish-red or pinkish-orange colour of coral ■ *n.* **1.** CALCIUM-COVERED RED ALGA a red alga whose fronds are covered or impregnated with calcium deposits. Genus: *Corallina*. **2.** ORGANISM THAT RESEMBLES CORAL a sponge or other organism that resembles coral

coralloid /kórrə loyd/ *adj.* relating to or resembling coral

coral reef *n.* a marine reef composed of the skeletons of living coral, together with minerals and organic matter

coralroot /kórrəl root/ (*plural* **-roots** *or* **-root**) *n.* a leafless orchid with small insignificant flowers that feeds through roots that resemble coral. Genus: *Corallorhiza*.

Coral Sea sea in the southwestern Pacific Ocean bounded by Australia, New Guinea, the Solomon Islands, and Vanuatu

Coral Sea Islands Territory island group and external dependency of Australia, east of Queensland state, in the South Pacific

coral snake *n.* **1.** POISONOUS SNAKE OF N AND S AMERICA a poisonous snake of North and South America that is strikingly marked with red, black, and yellow or white bands. Coral snakes are mostly nocturnal and feed on other snakes and lizards. Genera: *Micrurus* and *Micruroides*. **2.** AUSTRALIAN POISONOUS SNAKE a poisonous snake of eastern Australia that is red with yellow and black bands. Latin name: *Brachyurophis australis*.

coral tree *n.* a thorny shrub or small tree of tropical and subtropical regions with large red or orange flowers that are pollinated by birds and brightly coloured seeds that grow in long pods. Genus: *Erythrina*.

coral trout (*plural* **coral trout** *or* **coral trouts**) *n. ANZ* a fish of northern Australia that has a scarlet body covered with blue spots. Latin name: *Plectropoma maculatum*.

coram populo /káw ram póppyoŏlō/ *adv.* where other people can see what is being done (*literary*) [From Latin, literally 'before the people']

cor anglais /káwr óng glay/ (*plural* **cor anglais** *or* **cors anglais** /káwrz-/) *n.* a woodwind instrument like an oboe but larger and lower-pitched. US term **English horn** [From French, literally 'English horn']

coranto /ko rántō/ (*plural* **-tos**) *n.* = **courante** [Mid-16thC. Alteration of French *courante* (see COURANTE), influenced by Italian *corranta* (also from French).]

corban /káwr ban/ *n.* **1.** HEBREW OFFERING TO GOD an offering to God made by the ancient Hebrew people **2.** TEMPLE TREASURY the treasury of the Temple of Jerusalem, or an offering made to it [14thC. Via Greek from Hebrew *qorbān* 'offering', from *qārab* 'to approach'.]

corbeil /káwrb'l/, **corbeille** *n.* a stone carving of a basket of fruit or flowers as a feature on a building [Mid-18thC. Via French from late Latin *corbicula*, literally 'small basket', from Latin *corbis* 'basket'.]

Corbel

corbel /káwrb'l/ *n.* SUPPORTING STONE BRACKET a bracket of brick or stone that juts out of a wall to support a structure above it ■ *vt.* (**-bels, -belling, -belled**) **1.** LAY MASONRY UNITS TO FORM PROJECTION to lay stones or bricks in layers so that each juts out above the one below to form a supporting bracket **2.** SUPPORT WITH CORBELS to support a cornice or other structure on corbels [14thC. From Old French, literally 'little raven', from *corp* 'raven', from Latin *corvus* (see CORVINE); from its original beak-like profile from being cut slantwise.]

corbelling /káwrbəling/ *n.* a structural system using corbels as supports

corbel step *n.* = **corbie-step**

Corbett /káwrbit/ *n. Scotland* a Scottish mountain between 762 m/2500 ft and 914.4 m/3000 ft [Named after J. R. *Corbett*, who listed such mountains.]

corbie /káwrbi/ (*plural* **-bies** *or* **-bie**) *n. Scotland* a crow, especially a raven [15thC. Via Old French *corbin* from late Latin *corvinus* 'raven-like' (see CORVINE).]

corbie gable *n.* a gable with top edges shaped like a series of steps [Corbie from CORBIE-STEP]

corbie step, **corbel step** *n.* each of a series of decorative steps going up the side of a gable [Corbie from the idea that only crows can reach them]

cor blimey, **gorblimey** *interj.* used to express amazement or admiration (*informal*) [Alteration of *God blind me!*]

Corby /káwrbi/ former steel town in Northamptonshire, England. It was designated a new town in 1950. Population: 52,300 (1995).

cord /kawrd/ *n.* **1.** STRING OR ROPE thick strong string or thin rope ○ *hands and feet tied with cords* **2.** FASTENING OR BELT a length of cord used as a fastening or belt **3.** ELECTRICAL CABLE flexible insulated electric cable **4.** BODY PART RESEMBLING ROPE a part of the body resembling cord, e.g. the spinal cord or the umbilical cord **5.** RIBBED FABRIC any fabric that has a ribbed surface, especially corduroy **6.** UNIT OF VOLUME FOR CUT TIMBER a unit of volume for cut timber, equal to 128 ft³ (approximately 3.6 m³) ■ **cords** *npl.* TROUSERS corduroy trousers (*informal*) ○ *a pair of cords* ■ *vt.* (**cords, cording, corded**) **1.** TIE WITH CORD to fasten or tie sth with cord or rope ○ *Are the packages corded and ready to ship?* **2.** STACK WOOD IN CORDS to stack wood in units with a volume of one cord [13thC. Via Old French and Latin from Greek *khordē* 'string'. Ultimately from an Indo-European word meaning 'gut, entrail' that is also the ancestor of English *yarn*, *chord*, and *hernia*.] —**corder** *n.*

— **WORD KEY: USAGE** —

See Usage note at *chord*.

cordage /káwrdij/ *n.* **1. CORDS AS GROUP** ropes or cords collectively, especially the lines and rigging of a ship **2. AMOUNT OF WOOD** the amount of wood in a stack, measured in cords

cordate /káwrd ayt/ *adj.* BOT used to describe a leaf that is heart-shaped [Mid-18thC. Via modern Latin *cordatus* from the Latin stem *cord-* (see CORDIAL).] —**cordately** *adv.*

Corday /káwrd ay/, **Charlotte** (1768–93) French assassin. She supported the moderate Girondins during the Revolution, and was guillotined after murdering the Jacobin extremist Jean Paul Marat. Full name **Marie Anne Charlotte Corday d'Armont**

corded /káwrdid/ *adj.* **1. TIED UP** securely tied up with string or rope **2. RIBBED** used to describe a fabric with a ribbed surface **3. WITH TIGHT MUSCLES** having tensed or well-developed muscles visible as ridges or ripples

Cordelia /kawr deéli ə/ *n.* a small natural satellite of Uranus, discovered in 1986 by the Voyager 2 planetary probe. Its gravitational influence appears to help stabilize the outer ring of Uranus.

cord grass *n.* a coarse grass found on coastal salt marshes or mudflats. Genus: *Spartina.*

cordial /káwrdi əl/ *adj.* **1. WARM** friendly and affectionate **2. DEEPLY FELT** sincere or profound (*literary*) **3. REFRESHING** stimulating or invigorating (*literary*) ■ *n.* **1. FRUIT DRINK** a fruit drink, especially one sold in concentrated form and diluted with water **2. TONIC** a stimulating or medicinal drink **3.** *US* = **liqueur** [14thC. Via medieval Latin *cordialis* 'of the heart' from the Latin stem *cord-* from *cor* 'heart' (source of English *courage* and *accord*).] —**cordially** *adv.* —**cordialness** *n.*

cordiality /káwrdi állati/ *n.* friendliness and affection ○ *We were surprised by the cordiality of their response.*

cordierite /káwrdi ə rīt/ *n.* a purplish-blue or grey mineral that is a silicate of magnesium, aluminium, and iron and is found in metamorphic rock [Early 19thC. Named after the French geologist, Pierre L. *Cordier* (1777–1861) who discovered it.]

cordillera /káwdil yáirə/ (*plural* **-ras**) *n.* a system of mountain ranges consisting of approximately parallel ridges [Early 18thC. From Spanish, from *cordilla*, literally 'small cord', from *cuerda* 'cord', from Latin *chorda* (see CORD).]

cordite /káwrd īt/ *n.* a smokeless explosive, usually made of gunpowder and nitroglycerin [Late 19thC. Formed from CORD, because of its stringy appearance.]

cordless /káwrdləss/ *adj.* powered by an internal battery and not needing to be continuously attached by a cable to an external electricity supply

cordless telephone *n.* a telephone, powered by a recharging battery, with a portable handset that can be removed from its base unit and has a short-range radio link to it

córdoba /káwrdəbə/ *n.* **1.** see table at **currency 2. COIN WORTH ONE CÓRDOBA** a coin worth one córdoba [Early 20thC. Named after the Spanish explorer, Francisco Fernández de *Córdoba* (1475–1526).]

Córdoba /káwrdəbə/ city in Andalusía, southern Spain. It is the capital of Córdoba Province. Population: 300,229 (1991). English **Cordova**

cordon /káwrd'n/ *n.* **1. PEOPLE OR VEHICLES ENCIRCLING AREA** a chain of police officers or soldiers, or their vehicles, surrounding an area to control access to it **2. RIBBON** a piece of ribbon worn for decoration or as a sign of rank or a mark of honour **3.** GARDENING **FRUIT TREE WITH NO SIDE BRANCHES** a fruit tree grown as a main stem with spurs, but with its side branches removed **4.** ARCHIT = **string course** [Late 16thC. From Old French, literally 'small cord', from *corde* (see CORD).]
cordon off (**cordons off, cordoning off, cordoned off**) *vt.* to surround an area with a line of police officers, soldiers, or their vehicles, to control access to it

cordon bleu /káwr dón blúr/ *adj.* **1. OF HIGHEST CLASS** used to describe a cook or cooking of the highest class **2. WITH CHEESE AND HAM** used to describe a way of preparing meat, especially veal, by rolling a thin slice around cheese and ham and then coating in breadcrumbs ■ *n.* (*plural* **cordon bleus**) **1. MASTER CHEF** a cook of the very highest class, especially a master chef **2.** HIST **KNIGHT'S RIBBON** a blue ribbon worn by knights of the highest order in Bourbon France [Early 18thC. From French, literally 'blue ribbon'.]

cordon sanitaire /káwr don sani táir/ *n.* **1. DISEASE-CONTROLLING BARRIER** a barrier erected to control the spread of a disease by restricting movement to and from the infected area **2. AREA SEPARATING WARRING NATIONS** a neutral state, or a string of neutral states, lying between two states that are hostile to each other [Mid-19thC. From French, literally 'sanitary line'.]

cordovan /káwrdəvən/ *n.* a fine soft leather originally made from goatskin and now usually made from horsehide [Late 16thC. From Spanish *cordován*, named after the Spanish city of CÓRDOBA where it was made.]

corduroy /káwdə roy, -dyōō-/ *n.* **RIBBED COTTON FABRIC** a heavy cotton fabric with a ribbed nap running lengthways ■ **corduroys** *npl.* **TROUSERS** trousers made of corduroy [Late 18thC. Origin uncertain: probably coined from CORD + *duroy*, a kind of coarse woollen fabric.]

corduroy road *n.* a road made of logs across muddy or swampy ground [*Corduroy* from the resemblance of its surface to corduroy fabric]

cordwain /káwrd wayn/ *n.* = **cordovan** (*archaic*) [14thC. Via Old French *cordewan* from Spanish *cordován* (see CORDOVAN).]

cordwainer /káwrd waynər/ *n.* sb who makes shoes and other articles from fine soft leather (**cordovan**) (*archaic*) —**cordwainery** *n.*

cordwood /káwrd wŏŏd/ *n.* wood in stacks with a volume of one cord, or cut into lengths of 1.2 m/ 4 ft for stacking in cords

core /kawr/ *n.* **1. CENTRAL PART OF FRUIT** the fibrous central part of some kinds of fruit, containing the seeds **2. ESSENTIAL PART** the central or most important part of sth **3.** GEOL **CENTRE OF EARTH** the central part of the Earth, or the corresponding part of another celestial body. The Earth's core is molten in parts and is composed of an alloy of iron and nickel. **4.** PHYS **CENTRAL PART OF NUCLEAR REACTOR** the central part of a nuclear reactor in which fission takes place **5.** ELEC **IRON IN TRANSFORMER** a block of iron in a coil or transformer, used to intensify and direct the magnetic field produced by a current in surrounding coils **6.** GEOL **SAMPLE OBTAINED BY DRILLING** a tubular segment of rock, ice, or other material obtained as a study sample by drilling **7. STONE USED TO MAKE TOOLS** a block of stone from which tools or flakes are chipped **8.** COMPUT **PIECE OF COMPUTER MEMORY** a ring-shaped piece of magnetic material formerly used to store digital data in a computer, each core representing one binary digit (**bit**) **9.** COMPUT **COMPUTER MEMORY** the main memory of a computer, which was composed of arrays of ring-shaped magnets, before the introduction of semiconductor memories ■ *adj.* **ESSENTIAL** of central or fundamental importance ■ *vt.* (**cores, coring, cored**) **TAKE CORE OUT OF** to remove the core from a piece of fruit [13thC. Origin unknown.]

CORE /kawr/ *abbr.* Congress of Racial Equality

core competency *n.* an area of expertise that is fundamental to a particular job or function

core curriculum *n.* the subjects that all students are required to study at school

core dump *n.* **1. TRANSFER OF DATA** a transfer of data stored in the core memory of a computer, usually to external storage **2. LONG-WINDED ANSWER** a long-winded response to a simple question (*informal humorous*)

coreferential /kō refə rénsh'l/ *adj.* referring to the same person or thing ○ *In the sentence 'Mary lost her purse', 'Mary' and 'her' are coreferential.*

coreligionist /kō ri líjjənist/ *n.* sb who practises the same religion as another person

Corelli /kə rélli, ko-/, **Arcangelo** (1653–1713) Italian composer and violinist. He was a virtuoso violinist. His chamber music set a baroque style that influenced Johann Sebastian Bach.

core memory *n.* = **core** *n.* **9** (*technical*)

coreq *n.* a corequisite (*informal*)

corer /káwrər/ *n.* a utensil with a near-cylindrical blade used for removing the cores of apples and other fruit

co-respondent, **corespondent** *n.* **ALLEGED SEXUAL PARTNER** sb named in a divorce suit as the alleged adulterous sexual partner of the respondent ■ **co-respondents** *npl.* = **co-respondent shoes** —**co-respondency** *n.*

co-respondent shoes *npl.* men's shoes having a striking black- or brown-and-white pattern (*humorous*)

core subject *n.* any of a number of subjects that all students are required to study at school

core time *n.* the part of the working day during which workers on flexitime must be present at work

corf /kawrf/ (*plural* **corves** /kawrvz/) *n.* MINING a wagon used inside a mine for transporting mined coal or ore [15thC. Via Middle Dutch or Middle Low German *korf* 'basket' from Latin *corbis.* Its earliest meaning in English was 'basket'.]

Corfam /káwr fam/ *tdmk.* a trademark for a synthetic water-resistant substitute for leather, used in the making of shoes

Corfu /kawr fóo, -fyóo/ most northerly island in the Ionian Islands, west of Greece. It is a major tourist centre. Population: 107,592 (1991). Area: 641 sq. km/247 sq. mi.

corgi /káwrgi/ (*plural* **-gis**) *n.* a small dog with short legs and smooth hair. There are two breeds of corgi, the Cardigan Welsh corgi and the Pembroke Welsh corgi. [Early 20thC. From Welsh, formed from *cor* 'dwarf' + *ci* 'dog'.]

CORGI /káwrgi/ *abbr.* Council for Registered Gas Installers

coriaceous /kórri áyshəss/ *adj.* like leather in texture or appearance [Late 17thC. From late Latin *coriaceus*, from Latin *corium* 'leather'.]

coriander /kórri ándər/ *n.* **1. AROMATIC PLANT** an annual plant native to Asia and the Mediterranean, grown for its aromatic leaves and seeds that are used as a flavouring in cooking. Latin name: *Coriandrum sativum.* **2. FOOD FLAVOURING** the leaves or seeds of the coriander plant, or a powder made from the crushed seeds, used to season food [13thC. Via Old French from, ultimately, Greek *koriandron.*]

Corinth /kórrinth/ ancient Greek city and modern town 5 km/3 mi. to the northeast. The ruins of the ancient city are about 80 km/50 mi. west of Athens. Population: 29,600 (1995).

Corinthian /kə rínthi ən/ *adj.* **1. OF CORINTH** relating to or typical of the ancient or modern Greek city of Corinth **2.** ARCHIT **SLENDER AND ORNATE AT TOP** used to describe a slender column with an ornate capital **3. DEBAUCHED** debauched or ostentatiously luxurious (*literary*) ■ *n.* **1. SB FROM CORINTH** sb from the city of Corinth **2. WEALTHY SPORTSPERSON** a wealthy amateur sportsperson, especially sb fond of yachting (*humorous*) **3. MAN ABOUT TOWN** a man who enjoys good living

Corinthian order *n.* an ancient Greek order of architecture characterized by a slender column with an ornate capital [Corinthian from the origin of the order in CORINTH, Greece]

Corinthians /kə rínthi ənz/ *n.* either of two books in the New Testament, originally written as letters by St Paul to the church at Corinth. See table at **Bible**

Coriolanus /kórri ō láynəss/ *n.* in Roman legend the defeater of the Volsci in the 5th century BC. He later joined his former enemies, and was dissuaded from leading a Volscian attack on Rome by the pleas of his wife and mother.

Coriolis effect /kórri ṓliss-/ *n.* the observed deflection of sth such as a missile in flight relative to the Earth's surface, caused by the Earth's rotation beneath the object. The deflection is to the right in the northern hemisphere and to the left in the southern hemisphere. [Named after the French mathematician Gaspard de *Coriolis* 1792–1843]

Coriolis force *n.* an apparent but nonexistent force used to describe the effect of the Earth's rotation on the motion of moving objects

corium /káwri əm/ (*plural* **-a** /-ri ə/) *n.* **1.** MED = **dermis 2.** INSECTS **PART OF INSECT'S WING** the leathery middle part of the forewing of some insects [Early 19thC. From Latin, 'hide, leather' (source of English *excoriate*).]

corival n. = corrival

corixid /kə ríksid/ n. = **water boatman** n. 1

cork /kawrk/ n. **1.** INDUST OUTER BARK OF CORK OAK the light, flexible, outer bark of the cork oak tree commonly used to make bottle stoppers and as an insulator **2.** BOTTLE STOPPER a usually cylindrical piece of cork or other material used as a bottle stopper **3.** ANGLING FLOAT USED IN ANGLING a small float used in angling to maintain a hook or net suspended in the water **4.** BOT LAYER OF PLANT TISSUE dead tissue that forms a protective outer layer on plants and is part of the bark in woody plants ■ vt. (corks, corking, corked) **1.** SEAL CONTAINER WITH CORK to stop or seal sth, especially a bottle, with a cork **2.** RESTRAIN FEELINGS to restrain feelings, especially strong negative ones such as anger or grief [13thC. Origin uncertain: probably via Middle Dutch from, ultimately, Arabic dialect *kurk* 'cork-soled sandal', which may have been borrowed from Latin *quercus* 'oak tree'.]

Cork /kawrk/ county town of County Cork, southern Ireland. It is a port on the River Lee and the second largest city in the Republic of Ireland. Population: 127,024 (1991).

corkage /káwrkij/ n. a fee charged at some restaurants for serving wine and other alcoholic drinks that guests bring in from elsewhere

corkboard /káwrk bawrd/ n. **1.** THIN SHEET OF COMPRESSED CORK GRANULES a thin sheet made from compressed cork granules, typically used as a floor covering and as wall insulation before plastic was available **2.** US = notice board

cork cambium n. a zone of actively dividing tissue near the outer surface of a woody plant that produces cork

corked /kawrkt/ adj. **1.** SEALED sealed or stopped with a cork or other object **2.** WINE TAINTED BY CORK given an unpleasant flavour by substances from a tainted cork ○ *Waiter, this wine's corked!*

corker /káwrkər/ n. **1.** PARTICULARLY STRIKING PERSON OR THING sb or sth particularly striking or special (*dated slang*) ○ *It was a corker of a day.* **2.** PERSON OR MACHINE THAT FITS CORKS a person or machine that fits corks, especially into bottles

corking /káwrking/ adj. excellent or splendid (*dated slang*)

cork oak (*plural* **cork oaks** or **cork oak**) n. a Mediterranean evergreen oak tree whose thick bark is a source of cork. Latin name: *Quercus suber*.

corkscrew /káwrk skroo/ n. DEVICE FOR REMOVING CORKS FROM BOTTLES a device for taking corks out of bottles, usually a pointed spiral of metal attached to a handle or simple lever ■ v. (-screws, -screwing, -screwed) **1.** vi. MOVE IN SPIRAL PATH to move in a spiral path ○ *watched anxiously as the plane corkscrewed towards the ground* **2.** vt. WIND IN SPIRAL to wind or twist sth in a spiral ■ adj. SPIRAL-SHAPED shaped like a spiral ○ *corkscrew curls*

cork tree n. = cork oak

corkwing /káwrk wing/ n. a European fish of the wrasse family. Latin name: *Ctenolabrus melops*.

corkwood /káwrk wŏod/ (*plural* **-woods** or **-wood**) n. TREES a deciduous shrub or small tree that grows in wetlands of the southeastern United States and has light porous wood. Latin name: *Leitneria floridana*.

corky /káwrki/ (-ier, -iest) adj. **1.** OF OR LIKE CORK made from or resembling cork **2.** TASTING OR SMELLING OF CORK having the taste or smell of cork —**corkiness** n.

corm /kawrm/ n. a short swollen underground stem base in some plants, e.g. crocus and gladiolus, that stores food over the winter and produces new foliage in the spring. New corms often form on top of old ones and are used as a means of propagating new plants. [Mid-19thC. Via modern Latin *cormus* from Greek *kormos* 'lopped-off tree trunk'.] —**cormous** adj.

cormorant /káwrmərənt/ n. a large marine diving bird with webbed feet, a hooked bill, and a long neck that can expand to swallow fish. Family: Phalacrocoracidae. [13thC. Alteration of Old French *cormaran*, literally 'sea raven', from *corp* 'raven' (source of English *corbel*) + *marenc* 'of the sea' (from Latin *marinus*, source of English *marine*).]

Cormorant

corn[1] /kawrn/ n. **1.** US = maize **2.** UK, Ireland CEREAL CROP any cereal crop, especially wheat, barley, or oats **3.** US = maize **4.** UK, Ireland GRAIN OF CORN the grains produced by corn plants, especially when collected together by harvesting **5.** BEVERAGES = corn whisky **6.** CORNY ITEM OR MATERIAL sth trite or overly sentimental (*informal*) [Old English. Ultimately from an Indo-European word meaning 'grain' that is also the ancestor of English *grain, kernel, granite*, and *grenade*.]

corn[2] /kawrn/ n. MED a hardened or thickened, often painful, area of skin, usually on a toe, caused by friction or pressure [Late 14thC. Via French, from Latin *cornu* 'horn'. Ultimately from an Indo-European base that is also the ancestor of English *horn, cranium, reindeer*, and *carrot*.]

Corn. abbr. Cornwall

cornball /káwrn bawl/ n. US SB VERY SENTIMENTAL sb who is very sentimental or unsophisticated ■ adj. US VERY SENTIMENTAL trite or overly sentimental ○ *a cornball movie* [Mid-20thC. Originally used for a ball of popcorn and molasses or syrup, often sold at carnivals and circuses. The underlying meaning is 'sth popular with unsophisticated rural audiences'.]

corn borer n. ZOOL a moth whose larvae bore into maize. Family: Pyralidae.

corn bunting n. a stout-billed songbird with brown plumage and a speckled breast, found in Europe and Asia. Latin name: *Emberiza calandra*.

corn chip n. a crisp thin piece of fried maize meal batter, eaten as a savoury snack food

corn circle n. = crop circle

corncob /káwrn kob/ n. **1.** EAR OF SWEETCORN OR MAIZE an ear of sweetcorn or maize **2.** CORE OF MAIZE EAR the hard core of an ear of maize, on which the kernels grow

corncockle /káwrn kok'l/ (*plural* **-les** or **-le**) n. an annual Mediterranean plant of the pink family with reddish-purple flowers and poisonous seeds, once common as a weed in cornfields. Latin name: *Agrostemma githago*. [Early 18thC. From *corn*[1] + *cockle* 'corncockle', from Old English *coccul*.]

corncrake /káwrn krayk/ n. a speckled bird with a harsh call, a short bill, and reddish wings that lives in fields and meadows in Europe and Asia. It has become rare in the British Isles. Latin name: *Crex crex*.

corncrib /káwrn krib/ n. Can, US a ventilated building used for the storage and drying of maize ears

corn dolly (*plural* **corn dollies**) n. a small ornamental object made from plaited straw

cornea /káwrni ə, kawr née ə/ (*plural* **-as** or **-ae** /-ee/) n. the transparent convex membrane that covers the pupil and iris of the eye [14thC. From medieval Latin *cornea tela* 'horny tissue', because of its fibrous consistency, from, ultimately, Latin *cornu* 'horn' (source of English *corn*[2]).] —**corneal** adj.

corn earworm n. a large striped American moth larva that feeds destructively on maize, tomatoes, cotton bolls, and many other plants. Latin name: *Helicoverpa zea*.

corned /kawrnd/ adj. cooked and then preserved in salt or brine ○ *corned mutton* [Early 17thC. From corn 'to preserve with grains of salt', from CORN[1].]

corned beef n. beef that has been cooked, preserved in salt or brine, and often canned

Corneille /kawr náy/, Pierre (1606–84) French playwright. His plays include the tragedies *Le Cid* (1637), *Horace* (1640), and *Polyeucte* (1643).

cornel /káwrn'l/ (*plural* **-nels** or **-nel**) n. **1.** any plant related to dogwood. Genus: *Cornus*. **2.** = cornelian cherry [Mid-16thC. Via French *corneille* or German *Kornelbaum* from, ultimately, Latin *cornus*.]

cornelian n. = carnelian

cornelian cherry /kawrneélian-/ n. a small deciduous tree that is native to southern Europe but is widely cultivated for its clusters of bright yellow flowers, which it bears in early spring, and its small red fruits. The fruits are edible but sour, and were formerly used in jellies and preserves. Latin name: *Cornus mas*.

corner /káwrnər/ n. **1.** MEETING OF LINES OR SURFACES the angle formed where two or more lines or surfaces meet ○ *a corner of the room* **2.** AREA ENCLOSED BY CONVERGING LINES the area enclosed where two lines or surfaces meet **3.** PROJECTING PART OF STH a projecting angular part of sth **4.** PLACE WHERE TWO ROADS MEET the place where two roads or streets meet **5.** DIFFICULT SITUATION a difficult or embarrassing position, especially one from which there is no easy way of escape ○ *got himself into a corner about his previous statements* **6.** QUIET PLACE a secluded, peaceful, or secret place **7.** REMOTE PLACE any area or place, especially one that is remote **8.** OBJECT FITTED OVER CORNER an object made to fit over a corner of sth, especially to protect it ○ *a diary with metal corners* **9.** COMM CONTROL OF A MARKET a monopoly of a particular commodity acquired in order to control its market price **10.** SPORTS PART OF PLAYING FIELD OR SURFACE in various sports, part of the playing field or surface where two boundaries meet **11.** SOCCER, HOCKEY KICK OR SHOT FROM CORNER in some games, a free kick or shot from a corner of the field given to the attacking team when a defending player plays the ball over the goal line **12.** BOXING, WRESTLING PART OF RING in boxing and wrestling, any of the four parts of a ring where the ropes are attached to the posts, especially the two where the competitors rest between rounds ■ adj. **1.** LOCATED ON CORNER situated on a street corner ○ *a corner shop* **2.** INTENDED FOR CORNER intended to be put in a corner ○ *a corner cabinet* **3.** IN CORNER OF STH at or in a corner of sth ○ *sat at a corner table* ■ v. (-ners, -nering, -nered) **1.** vt. FORCE INTO DIFFICULT POSITION to force a person or an animal into a position from which escape is difficult **2.** vt. PUT IN CORNER to place sb or sth in a corner **3.** vt. PROVIDE WITH CORNERS to give corners to sth **4.** vt. COMM ACQUIRE MONOPOLY OF to acquire a monopoly of a particular commodity and so be able to control its market price **5.** vi. TURN CORNER to turn a corner (*refers to vehicles or their drivers*) **6.** vti. SOCCER, HOCKEY TAKE CORNER KICK in some games, to take a free kick or hit from a corner of the field on an opponents' goal line [13thC. Via Anglo-Norman from, ultimately, Latin *cornua* 'horns, points', the plural of *cornu* 'horn, point' (source of English *corn*[2]).] ◇ **cut corners** to do sth in a quicker, cheaper, or less careful way than is desirable or wise ◇ **turn the corner** to get past the worst part of a difficult or dangerous situation

Corner /káwrnər/ n. Aus the part of Australia where the borders of Queensland, New South Wales, and South Australia meet

cornerback /káwrnər bak/ n. in American football, either of two defensive halfbacks placed behind the linebackers and near the sidelines

cornered /káwrnərd/ adj. **1.** IN DIFFICULT POSITION in a difficult or embarrassing position, especially when there is no easy way of escape **2.** WITH PARTICULAR CORNERS with a particular number or type of corners (*usually used in combination*) **3.** WITH NUMBER OF CONTENDERS with a specified number of contenders ○ *a three-cornered struggle for the championship*

corner kick n. SOCCER in football, a free kick from a corner of the field given to the attacking team when a defending player plays the ball over the goal line

cornerman /-man/ (*plural* **-men** /-men/) n. US sb who provides support and advice, especially to a political candidate (*slang*)

corner shop n. a small shop, especially one at the corner of two streets, where a limited range of groceries and general goods is sold

cornerstone /káwrnər stōn/ n. **1. FUNDAMENTALLY IMPORTANT PERSON OR THING** sb or sth that is fundamentally important to sth **2. BUILDING STONE AT CORNER OF TWO WALLS** a stone joining two walls where they meet at a corner **3. BUILDING FIRST STONE OF NEW BUILDING** the first stone laid at a corner where two walls begin and form the first part of a new building [13thC. Modelled on Latin *lapis angularis*.]

cornerwise /káwrnər wīz/, **cornerways** /-wayz/ adv., adj. diagonal or diagonally, or with a corner at the front

cornet /káwrnit/ n. **1. MUSIC BRASS INSTRUMENT LIKE TRUMPET** a three-valved brass instrument shaped like a compressed trumpet. Its tubing is more conical than a trumpet and it has a softer warmer sound. **2. MUSIC = cornetist 3. FOOD CONICAL WAFER FOR ICE CREAM** a wafer shaped into a cone for holding ice cream, or one of these filled with ice cream **4. FOOD PAPER CONE FOR HOLDING SWEETS** a piece of paper folded into a cone shape and used to hold small edible things, especially sweets **5. ARMY OBSOLETE CAVALRY RANK** an obsolete military rank, in the past the lowest commissioned rank in a cavalry regiment **6. CLOTHES WOMAN'S HEADDRESS** a headdress of starched cloth worn by women from the 12th to the 15th centuries **7. CLOTHES, CHR NUN'S HEADDRESS** a large white headdress worn by some Christian nuns **8. S Africa ARMY = field cornet** [14thC. From French, literally 'small horn', from *corne* 'horn', from, ultimately, Latin *cornu* 'horn' (source of English corn[2]).]

cornetfish /káwrnit fish/ (plural -fish or -fishes) n. a tropical or subtropical sea fish that has a long tubular snout ending in a small mouth and a forked tail with a long trailing extension from its centre. Family: Fistulariidae.

cornetist /kawr néttist/, **cornettist** n. sb who plays a cornet

cornett /kawr nétt/ n. Renaissance and Baroque wooden horn with six keys and a cup mouthpiece [Late 19thC. Variant of CORNET, modelled on Italian *cornetto*, literally 'small horn'.]

corn exchange n. a market where corn was bought or sold, or the building where such transactions took place

corn factor n. sb who trades in corn

corn-fed adj. fed or fattened on maize

cornfield /káwrn feeld/ n. a field in which cereal crops such as wheat, barley, or oats are growing

cornflakes /káwrn flayks/ npl. a breakfast cereal consisting of small pieces of toasted maize, usually eaten with cold milk

cornflour /káwrn flowər/ n. fine-grained starchy flour made from maize, used especially as a thickener in sauces and soups. US term **cornstarch**

cornflower /káwrn flowər/ n. an annual plant found in Europe and Asia and naturalized in North America, with blue, pink, white, or purple flowers when cultivated. It was formerly common as a blue-flowered weed in cultivated fields. Latin name: *Centaurea cyanus*.

cornflower blue n. a deep brilliant blue colour with a tinge of purple

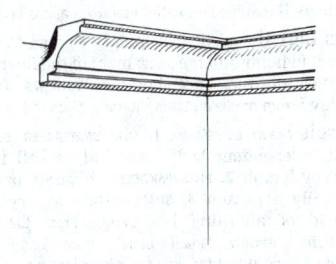

Cornice

cornice /káwrniss/ n. **1. ARCHIT PROJECTING MOULDING ALONG WALL** a projecting horizontal moulding along the top of a wall or building **2. ARCHIT DECORATIVE PLASTER MOULDING** a decorative plaster moulding around a room where the walls and ceiling meet **3. ARCHIT PART OF CLASSICAL BUILDING** the top projecting section of the part of a classical building that is supported by the columns (**entablature**) **4. MOUNTAINEERING OVERHANG OF SNOW** an overhanging mass of snow or ice formed by wind action ■ vt. (-nices, -nicing, -niced) ARCHIT **DECORATE WALL WITH CORNICE** to decorate or finish a wall or building with a cornice [Mid-16thC. From French and Italian, of uncertain origin: perhaps from the Latin stem *cornic-* 'crow' (because it resembles a crow's beak), influenced by Greek *korōnis* 'copestone'.]

corniche /kawr nèesh/ n. a coast road, especially one cut into a cliff [Mid-19thC. From French, a variant of *cornice* 'CORNICE'.]

corniculate /kawr níkyoŏlət/ adj. **1. HAVING HORNS** having horns or projections like horns **2. OF HORNS** relating to or resembling a horn [Mid-17thC. Formed from Latin *cornicula*, literally 'little horn', from *cornu* 'horn' (see CORN[2]).]

cornification /káwrnifi káysh'n/ n. the conversion of skin cells into keratin or other horny material, such as nails or scales [Mid-19thC. Coined from Latin *cornu* 'horn' (see CORN[2] + -FICATION).]

Corning /káwrning/ city in southern New York State, northwest of Elmira, on the Cohocton River. Population: 11,356 (1996).

Cornish /káwrnish/ adj. **OF CORNWALL** relating to or typical of Cornwall or its people, language, or culture ■ npl. **PEOPLES PEOPLE OF CORNWALL** the people of Cornwall ■ n. (plural -nish) LANG, HIST **EXTINCT CELTIC LANGUAGE** a Celtic language spoken in Cornwall until the late 18th century. Breton is the living language most closely related to Cornish.

Cornishman /káwrnishmən/ (plural -men /-mən/) n. a man who was born in or lives in Cornwall

Cornish pasty (plural **Cornish pasties**) n. a baked food made of a circle of pastry filled with beef and vegetables, with the pastry edges pinched together over the filling, eaten as a savoury snack or light meal

Cornishwoman /káwrnish woŏmən/ (plural -women /-wimin/) n. a woman who was born in or lives in Cornwall

Corn Laws npl. HIST a group of laws introduced in Great Britain in 1804 and repealed in 1846 that were designed to restrict the importation of foreign corn by imposing duty on it. This caused bread prices to rise and led to riots.

corn lily n. a southern African plant of the iris family, widely grown for its ornamental flowers of various colours that resemble lilies. Genus: *Ixia*.

corn marigold n. an annual plant with flowers like yellow daisies that was formerly a common weed in cultivated fields. Latin name: *Chrysanthemum segetum*. [Because it grows in cornfields]

cornmeal /káwrn meel/, **corn meal** n. flour made from maize

corn oil n. oil extracted from maize, used in cooking, in margarine, as salad oil, and in some soaps

corn on the cob n. an ear of maize that is cooked and served whole

corn pone /-pōn/ n. Southern US **MAIZE MEAL BREAD** bread made with maize meal but often without eggs or milk, shaped into ovals, then fried or baked ■ adj. **cornpone** US **TYPICAL OF COUNTRY LIFE** typical of country life and people in being simple, unpretentious, and homely (informal)

corn poppy n. a common wild plant of Europe and Asia that has large scarlet flowers and often grows in cultivated fields. Latin name: *Papaver rhoeas*.

cornrow /káwrn rō/ n. **BRAIDED ROW OF HAIR** any of a group of narrow parallel braids of hair lying flat against the scalp ■ vt. (-rows, -rowing, -rowed) **FIX HAIR INTO CORNROWS** to style hair in cornrows [Late 20thC. Because the braids resemble rows of maize.]

corn salad n. = lamb's lettuce

corn snow n. US, Can fallen snow that has a grainy surface because it has thawed and refrozen

cornstarch /káwrn staarch/ n. US = cornflour

cornu /káwrnyoo/ (plural -nua /-nyoŏ əl/) n. a part that resembles a horn or has a horn-shaped pattern [Late 17thC. From Latin, 'horn' (see English CORN[2]).] —**cornual** adj.

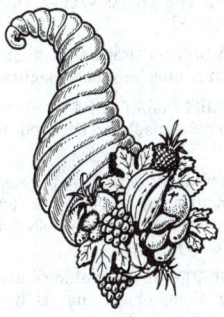

Cornucopia

cornucopia /káwrnyoŏ kōpi ə/ n. **1. ABUNDANCE** a great abundance of sth **2. ARTS GOAT'S HORN OVERFLOWING WITH PRODUCE** a painting or other representation of a goat's horn overflowing with fruits, flowers, and vegetables, used to symbolize plenty or prosperity **3. HORN-SHAPED CONTAINER** an ornament or container shaped like a goat's horn **4. MYTHOL HORN OF GOAT THAT SUCKLED ZEUS** in Greek mythology, the horn of the goat that suckled Zeus [Early 16thC. Via late Latin from Latin *cornu copiæ*, literally 'horn of plenty'.] —**cornucopian** adj.

cornute /kawr nyoōt/, **cornuted** /-nyoōtid/ adj. resembling a horn, or having horns or horny parts [Early 17thC. From Latin *cornutus* 'horned', from *cornu* 'horn' (see English CORN[2]).]

Cornwall /káwrn wəl, -wawl/ southwesternmost county of England, bordered on three sides by the sea. It used to be a major tin-mining area. Population: 482,700 (1995).

corn whisky (plural **corn whiskies**) n. whisky distilled from mash made mostly of maize

corny /káwrni/ (-ier, -iest) adj. unsophisticated and trite ○ a corny love scene [Late 16thC. Formed from CORN[1].] —**cornily** adv. —**corniness** n.

corol., **coroll.** abbr. corollary

corolla /kə róllə/ n. the petals of a flower collectively, forming a ring around the reproductive organs and surrounded by an outer ring of sepals [Mid-18thC. From Latin, 'garland', literally 'little crown', from *corona* 'crown, wreath' (source of *crown*).]

corollary /kə rólləri/ n. (plural -ies) **1. NATURAL CONSEQUENCE** sth that is a natural consequence of or accompaniment to sth else **2. LOGIC STATEMENT EASILY PROVED FROM ANOTHER** a proposition that follows, with little or no further reasoning, from the proof of another **3. LOGIC OBVIOUS DEDUCTION** sth that is very obviously or easily deduced from sth already proven **4. STH ADDED** sth added to sth else, e.g. sth appended to a document ■ adj. **FOLLOWING** following as a consequence or result [14thC. From Latin *corollarium* 'money paid for a garland, gratuity, deduction', from *corolla* (see COROLLA).]

coromandel /kórrə mánd'l/ n. = calamander [Mid-19thC. Named after the *Coromandel* Coast, where it is found.]

Coromandel Coast southern part of the eastern Indian coastline in the states of Tamil Nadu and Andhra Pradesh, on the Bay of Bengal

Coromandel Peninsula peninsula on the northeastern coast of North Island, New Zealand. Rugged and heavily forested, it is 112 km/70 mi. long and, on average, 32 km/20 mi. wide.

corona /kə rónə/ (plural -nas or -nae /-nee/) n. **1. ASTRON RING OF LIGHT AROUND MOON** a ring of light visible around a luminous body, especially the Moon, typically as a result of optical effects caused by thin cloud, water droplets or ice in the Earth's atmosphere **2. ASTRON OUTERMOST PART OF SUN'S ATMOSPHERE** the outermost part of the Sun's atmosphere **3. BOT LIP OF FLOWER TRUMPET** the prominent, sometimes frilly lip of the petal tube or trumpet corolla of some flowers such as daffodils and narcissi **4. ANAT TOP OF BODY PART** the top of a part of the body such as the crown of the head or a tooth **5. PHYS = corona discharge 6. ARCHIT PART OF CORNICE** the flat vertical surface of a cornice just above the bottom surface (**soffit**) **7. LONG CIGAR** a long cigar with a blunt rounded mouth end **8.** CIRCULAR CHANDELIER a circular hanging chandelier, especially in a church [Mid-16thC. From Latin *wreath crown* (see CROWN).]

Corona Australis /-o stráyliss/ *n.* a constellation in the southern hemisphere near Sagittarius

Corona Borealis /-báwri áyliss/ *n.* a constellation in the northern hemisphere between Hercules and Boötes

coronach /kórrənəkh/ *n. Scotland, Ireland* a dirge or funeral lament sung or played on bagpipes [Early 16thC. From Gaelic *corranach*, literally 'outcry together', from *rànach* 'outcry'.]

corona discharge *n.* a luminous discharge from the surface of an object that is highly charged electrically, caused by ionization of the surrounding gas

Coronado /kórrō naádō/, **Francisco Vásquez de** (1510–54) Spanish explorer. He led the first European expeditions to what is now the southwestern United States.

coronagraph /kə rṓnnə graaf, -graf/, **coronograph** *n.* a telescope that masks the bright disc of the Sun so that the Sun's corona can be studied

coronal /kórrən'l/ *adj.* **1.** OF TOP OF BODY PART relating to the top of a body part (**corona**) **2.** RELATING TO JOINT OF SKULL BONES relating to the top of the skull where the bony plates join **3.** OF IMAGINARY PLANE DIVIDING BODY relating to, involving, or in the direction of an imaginary plane dividing the body into front and back parts [Mid-16thC. Via French from, ultimately, Latin *corona* 'crown' (source also of English *crown*).]

coronal suture *n.* a junction extending side-to-side across the crown of the skull between the two parietal bones and the frontal bone

coronary /kórrənəri/ *n.* (*plural* **-ies**) **1.** = **coronary thrombosis 2.** HEART ATTACK a heart attack (*informal*) ■ *adj.* **1.** SUPPLYING OR DRAINING BLOOD FROM HEART used to describe the arteries that supply blood to the muscle tissue of the heart, or the veins that take blood away from it **2.** INVOLVING THE CORONARY ARTERIES AND VEINS relating to disease of the coronary arteries and veins, and conditions associated with it ○ *coronary care* [Early 17thC. From Latin *coronarius* 'crownlike', from *corona* 'crown' (source of English *crown*). The underlying idea is sth that encircles, like the arteries of the heart.]

coronary artery *n.* an artery supplying blood to the muscles of the heart, one of a pair arising from the aorta. The left artery divides into two almost immediately, giving rise to the common assumption that there are three coronary arteries.

coronary bypass *n.* an operation in which a new blood vessel is grafted onto the heart to replace a blocked coronary artery

coronary thrombosis *n.* the blocking of a coronary artery by a blood clot, which obstructs the blood supply to the heart muscle, resulting in death of the muscle and, often, a heart attack

coronary vein *n.* any of the veins that drain blood from the muscles and other tissues of the heart

coronation /kórrə náysh'n/ *n.* the ceremony or act of crowning a monarch [14thC. Via Old French from the medieval Latin stem *coronation-*, from, ultimately, Latin *corona* 'crown' (source also of English *crown*).]

coroner /kórrənər/ *n.* a public official responsible for investigating deaths that appear not to have natural causes [13thC. From Anglo-Norman *coruner* 'officer of the crown', from *coroune* 'crown' (source also of English *crown*).] —**coronership** *n.*

coronet /kórrənit/ *n.* **1.** SMALL CROWN a small crown, especially one worn by a prince or a peer rather than a reigning monarch **2.** WOMAN'S HEAD DECORATION a circular ornamental band worn by women on the head **3.** VET TOP OF HORSE'S HOOF the upper part of a horse's hoof, where the horn of the hoof meets the skin of the pastern **4.** ZOOL BASE OF DEER'S ANTLER the rosette of bone at the base of a deer's antler [14thC. From French, literally 'little crown', from *corone* (see CROWN).]

coronograph *n.* = **coronagraph**

Corot /kórrō/, **Jean Baptiste Camille** (1796–1875) French landscape and portrait painter. His freely handled landscapes influenced the Barbizon School and impressionism. Postimpressionists admired the tonal contrasts of his earlier, classical work.

corp. *abbr.* corporation

Corp. *abbr.* MIL Corporal

corpora plural of **corpus**

corporal[1] /káwrpərəl/ *adj.* relating or belonging to the body ○ *corporal punishment* [14thC. Via French from Latin *corporalis*, 'bodily', from *corpus* (see CORPUS).] —**corporally** *adv.*

WORD KEY: USAGE

corporal or **corporeal**? ***Corporal*** means 'relating to the human body' and is mainly used in the expression *corporal punishment*, in reference to physical abuse. ***Corporeal*** means 'bodily or physical as distinct from spiritual': *The gods of antiquity were not just spirits but enjoyed a corporeal existence.*

corporal[2] /káwrpərəl/ *n.* **1.** NONCOMMISSIONED OFFICER ABOVE PRIVATE a noncommissioned officer in various armed forces, ranking immediately below sergeant, or, in Canada, a master corporal **2.** PETTY OFFICER a petty officer in the Royal Navy, immediately junior to the master-at-arms [Mid-16thC. Via French from, ultimately, Italian *caporale*, literally 'of the head', from *capo* (see CAPO). The underlying meaning is 'head of a company of troops'.] —**corporalcy** *n.* —**corporalship** *n.*

corporal[3] /káwrpərəl/, **corporale** /káwrpə ráyli/ *n.* a white, usually linen, cloth on which the consecrated bread and wine are placed in the Christian sacrament of Communion [14thC. Directly or via French from medieval Latin *(pallium) corporale*, literally '(cloth) for the body'.]

corporality /káwrpə rálləti/ *n.* the state of being in physical or bodily form rather than spiritual form

Corporal of Horse *n.* a noncommissioned officer in the (**Household Cavalry**) ranking above sergeant and below staff sergeant

corporal punishment *n.* the striking of a person's body as punishment

corporate /káwrpərət/ *adj.* **1.** INVOLVING A CORPORATION relating or belonging to a corporation **2.** OF CORPORATE EMPLOYEES designed for, suitable for, or typical of people who work for large corporations ○ *corporate fashions* **3.** INCORPORATED legally united to form a body that can act as a unit **4.** OF GROUP AS A WHOLE relating to or involving a group as a whole (*formal*) [16thC. From Latin *corporatus*, the past participle of *corporare* 'to form a body', from *corpus* 'body' (see CORPUS).] —**corporately** *adv.*

corporation /káwrpə ráysh'n/ *n.* **1.** GROUP REGARDED AS INDIVIDUAL BY LAW a company recognized by law as a single body with its own powers and liabilities, separate from those of the individual members. Corporations perform many of the functions of private business, governments, educational bodies, and the professions. **2.** LOCAL GOVERNING AUTHORITY the governing authority of an incorporated municipality, e.g. a city or town ○ *working for the corporation* ○ *corporation transport* **3.** GROUP ACTING AS SINGLE ENTITY a group of people acting as a single entity **4.** a paunch, especially a large one (*dated informal humorous*) [15thC. From late Latin *corporation-*, from *corporatus* (see CORPORATE).]

corporation tax *n.* a tax on the profits of a company

corporatism /káwrpərətizzəm/ *n.* a system of running a state using the power of organizations like businesses and trade unions that act, or purport to act, for large numbers of individuals —**corporatist** *adj., n.*

corporator /káwrpə raytər/ *n.* a member of a corporation, especially a founding member (*archaic*) [Late 18thC. Back-formation from CORPORATION.]

corporeal /kawr páwri əl/ *adj.* **1.** CONCERNING THE PHYSICAL BODY relating to or involving the physical body rather than the mind or spirit **2.** MATERIAL material or physical rather than spiritual [Early 17thC. From late Latin *corporealis*, from, ultimately, Latin *corpus* (see CORPUS).] —**corporeality** /kawr páwri álləti/ *n.* —**corporeally** /kawr páwri əli/ *adv.*

WORD KEY: USAGE

See Usage note at ***corporal***.

corporeity /káwrpə reé əti/ *n.* the state of existing as sth material or physical [Early 17thC. From French *corporéite*, from, ultimately, Latin *corpus* (see CORPUS).]

corposant /káwrpə zant/ *n.* St. Elmo's fire. (*archaic*) [Mid-16thC. From Old Spanish or Italian *corpo santo*, literally 'holy body'.]

corps /kawr/ (*plural* **corps**) *n.* **1.** MIL SPECIALIZED MILITARY FORCE a military force that carries out specialized duties **2.** MIL TACTICAL UNIT a tactical military unit that is made up of two or more divisions with additional supporting services **3.** GROUP OF ASSOCIATED PEOPLE a group of people who work together or are associated [Late 16thC. Via French from Latin *corpus* (see CORPUS).]

corps de ballet /káwr də bállay/ (*plural* **corps de ballet**) *n.* the dancers of a ballet company who perform as a group rather than individually [From French, literally 'dance company']

corps diplomatique /káwr díplō ma teék/ (*plural* **corps diplomatiques**) *n.* = **diplomatic corps** [From French]

corpse /kawrps/ *n.* DEAD BODY a dead body, especially of a human being ■ *vti.* (**corpses, corpsing, corpsed**) THEATRE TO LAUGH OR MAKE LAUGH INVOLUNTARILY to become unable to speak lines because of involuntary laughing, or make an actor on stage unable to speak his or her lines because of involuntary laughing (*slang*) [14thC. Directly and via French *cors* from Latin *corpus* (see CORPUS).]

corpsman /káwrmən/ (*plural* **-men** /-mən/) *n. US* in the US armed forces, an enlisted person with training in giving first aid and basic medical treatment

corpulence /káwrpyŏŏlənss/, **corpulency** /-lənssi/ *n.* obesity (*formal or literary*)

corpulent /káwrpyŏŏlənt/ *adj.* obese (*formal or literary*) [15thC. From Latin *corpulentus*, literally 'abundant in body', from *corpus* (see CORPUS).] —**corpulently** *adv.*

cor pulmonale /káwr púlmə naáli/ *n.* a disease in which the right ventricle of the heart becomes enlarged and fails, caused by disease of the lungs or pulmonary blood vessels [From modern Latin, literally 'pulmonary heart']

corpus /káwrpəss/ (*plural* **-pora** /-pərə/) *n.* **1.** BODY OF WRITINGS a body of writings by a particular person, on a particular subject, or of a particular type ○ *one of the most popular works in the Shakespearean corpus* **2.** MAIN PART the main part of sth **3.** ANAT PART OF ORGAN the main portion of sth, such as an organ or other body part, or a mass of tissue with a distinct function ○ *the corpus of the uterus* **4.** FIN CAPITAL the capital or principal of a sum of money **5.** LING COLLECTION OF LANGUAGE USE a large collection of written, and sometimes spoken, examples of the usage of a language, used for linguistic analysis [Early 18thC. From Latin, 'body'. Ultimately from an Indo-European word that is also the ancestor of English *corpse, corset, corsage*, and possibly *midriff*.]

corpus callosum /-kə lṓssəm/ (*plural* **corpora callosa** /-kə lṓsə/) *n.* the thick band of nerve fibres that connects the two hemispheres of the brain in higher mammals and allows the hemispheres to communicate [From modern Latin, literally 'callous body']

Corpus Christi /-krísti/ *n.* a mainly Roman Catholic festival in honour of the sacrament of the Eucharist, observed on the Thursday that follows Trinity Sunday [From medieval Latin, literally 'body of Christ']

corpuscle /káwr puss'l/ *n.* **1.** ANAT UNATTACHED CELL any small independent body, especially a cell in the blood or lymph **2.** PHYS PARTICLE a discrete particle, especially a photon **3.** SMALL PARTICLE a very small particle of anything [Mid-17thC. From Latin *corpusculum*, literally 'small body', from *corpus* (see CORPUS).] —**corpuscular** /kawr púskyŏŏlər/ *adj.*

corpuscular theory *n.* the theory that light consists of a stream of particles. The theory was originally introduced by Newton and although it cannot be used to explain all the properties of light it has applications in quantum physics.

corpus delicti /-di lík tī/ *n.* the body of facts that show that a crime has been committed, including physical evidence such as a corpse [From modern Latin, literally 'body of the crime']

corpus luteum /-lóoti əm/ (*plural* **corpora lutea** /-lóoti ə/) *n.* a yellow mass of tissue that forms in part of the ovary (**Graafian follicle**) after ovulation in mammals and secretes the hormone progesterone. If no pregnancy is established, the corpus luteum degenerates, whereas it continues to secrete the hormone if pregnancy occurs. [From modern Latin, literally 'yellow body']

corpus striatum /-strī áytəm/ (*plural* **corpora striata** /-strī áytə/) *n.* a mass of striped grey and white nervous tissue, one of which occurs in each hemisphere of the brain [From modern Latin, literally 'striated body']

corral /kə ráal/ *n.* *US* **1.** AGRIC **PLACE FOR KEEPING LIVESTOCK** a fenced area in which livestock or horses are kept **2.** HIST **CIRCLE OF WAGONS** a temporary defensive enclosure formed by wagons arranged in a circle, used in the past by people travelling through regions of North America where they might be attacked ■ *vt.* (**-rals, -ralling, -ralled**) *US* **1.** AGRIC **DRIVE ANIMALS INTO CORRAL** to gather animals together and drive them into a corral **2.** HIST **PUT WAGONS IN CIRCLE** to form wagons into a corral **3. GATHER AND CONTROL** to gather together and take control of people or things ○ *hopes to corral sufficient funding for the project* [Late 16thC. From Spanish, of uncertain origin: perhaps from Khoisan, or perhaps from, ultimately, Latin *currus* 'vehicle' (source of English *car*).]

corrasion /kə ráyzh'n/ *n.* the mechanical erosion of a surface by fragments of rock carried by water, wind, or ice [Late 19thC. From Latin *corras-*, the past participle stem of *corradere* 'to scrape together', from *radere* 'to scrape' (source of English *raze*).] —**corrasive** /kə ráyssiv/ *adj.*

correct /kə rékt/ *vt.* (**-rects, -recting, -rected**) **1. REMOVE ERRORS FROM** to take the errors out of sth **2. POINT OUT ERRORS IN** to point out or mark the errors in sth **3. RECTIFY DEFECT** to rectify a defect in sth or counteract sth wrong or undesirable ○ *wears glasses to correct his astigmatism* **4. MODIFY** to modify sth, e.g. behaviour, to make it acceptable or bring it up to a particular standard **5. PUNISH TO GAIN IMPROVEMENT** to punish or scold sb, especially a child, to bring about improvement or reform (*dated*) ■ *adj.* **1. ACCURATE** accurate or without errors ○ *the correct time* **2. ACCEPTABLE** acceptable or meeting a particular standard ○ *correct dress* [14thC. From Latin *correct-*, the past participle stem of Latin *corrigere*, literally 'to rule completely', from *regere* 'to rule' (source of English *regent*).] —**correctable** *adj.* —**correctly** *adv.* —**correctness** *n.* —**corrector** *n.*

correction /kə réksh'n/ *n.* **1. ALTERATION THAT IMPROVES** an alteration that removes an error **2. WRITTEN COMMENT ON ERROR** sth written beside an error in a text to point out what should be there instead **3. REMOVING OF ERRORS** the removing of errors from sth or the indicating of errors in sth **4. MODIFICATION TO CALCULATION** an adjustment made to a calculation or measurement to compensate for an observed deviation from ideal conditions **5. PUNISHMENT MEANT TO IMPROVE** punishment, especially when meant to improve or reform the person punished (*dated*) —**correctional** *adj.*

correctional facility *n.* *US* a prison or other institution where criminals are held and treated

correctitude /kə rékti tyood/ *n.* the fact of being correct, especially in behaviour and manners (*formal*) [Late 19thC. Blend of CORRECT and RECTITUDE.]

corrective /kə réktiv/ *adj.* **CORRECTING** acting to correct or intended to correct sth ○ *corrective action* ■ *n.* **STH INTENDED TO CORRECT** sth that corrects or is meant to correct sth —**correctively** *adv.*

corrective shoe *n.* *US* = **surgical boot**

Corregidor /kə réggi dawr/ island at the entrance to Manila Bay in the Philippines. Area: 5 sq. km/2 sq. mi.

correl. *abbr.* correlative

correlate /kórrə layt/ *v.* (**-lates, -lating, -lated**) **1.** *vti.* **HAVE OR SHOW MUTUAL RELATIONSHIP** to have a mutual or complementary relationship, or show two or more things, e.g. a cause and an effect, to have a mutual or complementary relationship ○ *How do these results correlate with your findings?* **2.** *vt.* **GATHER AND COMPARE THINGS** to gather together and compare related things, e.g. results or reports ○ *Her job is to correlate the statistics from a range of sources and prepare a report.* ■ *adj.* **HAVING SHARED PROPERTIES** having mutual or complementary properties ■ *n.* **1. COMPLEMENTARY THING** sth that shares mutual or complementary properties with sth else **2.** STATS **VARIABLE RELATED TO ANOTHER VARIABLE** either of two variables that are related with the result that a variation in one is accompanied by a linear variation of the other [Mid-18thC. Back-formation from CORRELATION.] —**correlatable** *adj.* —**correlator** *n.*

correlation /kórrə láysh'n/ *n.* **1. MUTUAL OR COMPLEMENTARY RELATIONSHIP** a relationship in which two or more things are mutual or complementary, or one is caused by another ○ *the close correlation between the two factors* **2. ACT OF CORRELATING** the act of correlating, or the state of being correlated **3.** STATS **RELATEDNESS OF VARIABLES** the degree to which two or more variables are related and change together [Mid-16thC. From the medieval Latin stem *correlation-*, literally 'mutual relationship', from Latin *relation-*, (see RELATION).] —**correlational** *adj.*

correlation coefficient *n.* a number or function indicating the degree of correlation between two variables. It ranges between 1 for high positive correlation to –1 for high negative correlation, with 0 indicating a purely random relationship.

correlative /kə rélləti v/ *adj.* **1. BEING CORRELATES** in a mutual or complementary relationship **2.** GRAM **TOGETHER BUT NOT ADJACENT** often used together but not usually adjacent, as are the conjunctions 'either' and 'or' ■ *n.* **1.** = **correlate** *n.* 1 **2.** GRAM **CORRELATIVE WORD** a word, especially a conjunction, that is often used together with but not usually adjacent to another —**correlatively** *adv.* —**correlativeness** *n.* —**correlativity** /kə rélla tívvəti/ *n.*

correspond /kórri spónd/ (**-sponds, -sponding, -sponded**) *vi.* **1. CONFORM OR BE CONSISTENT** to conform, be consistent, or be in agreement with sth else **2. BE SIMILAR** to be similar or equivalent **3. WRITE TO ONE ANOTHER** to communicate with sb by exchanging written messages [Early 16thC. Via French from medieval Latin *correspondere*, literally 'to respond to each other', from Latin *respondere* (see RESPOND).]

correspondence /kórri spóndənss/ *n.* **1. WRITTEN COMMUNICATION** communication by means of exchanged written messages, e.g. letters or e-mail **2. WRITTEN MESSAGES** written messages, especially letters **3. CONFORMITY** conformity, consistency, or agreement between two or more things **4. SIMILARITY** similarity or equivalence between two or more things

correspondence column *n.* a part of a newspaper or magazine where letters from readers are printed

correspondence course *n.* an educational course in which the teaching organization sends lessons and tests to students by post and students return completed work in the same way

correspondence school *n.* an educational organization that carries out teaching by post

correspondent /kórri spóndənt/ *n.* **1. SB COMMUNICATING BY WRITING** sb who communicates in writing or electronically ○ *Most of my correspondents have e-mail now.* **2.** PRESS **SB PROVIDING SPECIAL REPORTS** sb employed by a news organization, especially a newspaper or broadcasting company, to provide reports from a particular place or on a particular subject ○ *our Paris correspondent* **3.** BUSINESS **BUSINESS DEALING WITH A DISTANT BUSINESS** a person or company that regularly does business with another, especially one that is distant **4. STH THAT CORRESPONDS** sth that conforms or agrees with, or is similar to, sth else (*formal*) ■ *adj.* = **corresponding**

corresponding /kórri spónding/ *adj.* **1. CONSISTENT** consistent, conforming, or in agreement with sth else ○ *Line up the prongs on one half with the corresponding sockets on the other.* **2. ANALOGOUS** similar or equivalent to sth else in one or more important respects ○ *the corresponding word in her own language* **3. WORKING FROM A DISTANCE** interacting or contributing from a distance, e.g. by post ○ *a corresponding member based in China* **4. DEALING WITH CORRESPONDENCE** handling correspondence, or assigned to handle correspondence

corresponding angles *npl.* the angles formed on the same side of two lines and a third line (**transversal**) that intersects them, each of the four angles at each intersection corresponding to the four angles at the other

correspondingly /kórri spóndingli/ *adv.* in a way that is consistent, equivalent, or similar ○ *A large company has correspondingly large problems.*

corrida /ko reédə/ *n.* a programme of bullfights [Late 19thC. From Spanish, literally 'running' (of bulls), from, ultimately, Latin *currere* 'to run' (source also of English *current*).]

corridor /kórri dawr/ *n.* **1.** ARCHIT **PASSAGE INSIDE BUILDING** a passage between parts of a building, often with a series of rooms opening onto it **2.** RAIL **PASSAGEWAY IN RAILWAY CARRIAGE** a passageway in a railway carriage giving access to cabins or compartments **3.** GEOG **STRIP OF LAND** a narrow strip of land belonging to one country and projecting through another, e.g. to give a landlocked country access to a port **4.** AIR **REGION OF AIRSPACE FOR AIR TRAFFIC** a particular region of airspace designated for use by air traffic **5.** AEROSP **SPACECRAFT FLIGHT PATH** a predetermined flight path that a spacecraft follows upon re-entry into the earth's atmosphere [Late 16thC. Via French and Italian from, ultimately, Latin *currere* 'to run' (source also of English *current*). The underlying meaning is 'a place to run'.]

corrie /kórri/ *n.* = **cirque** [Mid-16thC. Via Scots Gaelic *coire* 'hollow' from Old Irish, 'cauldron'.]

Corriedale /kórri dayl/ (*plural* **-dales** *or* **-dale**) *n.* a sheep belonging to a breed without horns developed in New Zealand and kept for both wool and meat [Early 20thC. Named after *Corriedale*, an estate in northern Otago, New Zealand.]

corrigenda /kórri jén də/ *n.* = **errata** (*takes a singular or plural verb*)

corrigendum /kórri jéndəm/ (*plural* **-da**) *n.* an error to be corrected [Early 19thC. From Latin, literally 'thing to be corrected'.]

corrival /kō rív'l/, **corival** *n.* a rival (*archaic*) [Late 16thC. Directly and via French from Latin *corrivalis*, literally 'completely rivalling', from *rivalis* 'rivalling' (see RIVAL).] —**corrivalry** *n.*

corroborate /kə róbbə rayt/ (**-rates, -rating, -rated**) *vt.* to give or represent evidence of the truth of sth ○ *The photographs corroborate the verbal account.* [Mid-16thC. From Latin *corroborat-*, the past participle stem of *corroborare*, literally 'to strengthen together', from *roborare* 'to strengthen'.] —**corroborative** /kə róbbərətiv/ *adj.* —**corroboratively** /-tivli/ *adv.* —**corroboratory** /kə róbbə ráytəri/ *adj.* —**corroborator** /kə róbbə raytər/ *n.*

corroboration /kə róbbə ráysh'n/ *n.* **1. CONFIRMATION** sth that supports or confirms sth else **2. ACT OF CONFIRMING** the supporting or confirming of sth else

corroboree /kə róbbəri/ *n.* *Aus* **1. ABORIGINAL GATHERING** a gathering of an Aboriginal people **2. NOISY GATHERING** any noisy gathering of people, especially a party (*informal*) [Late 18thC. From Dharuk (an Australian Aboriginal language) *garaabara*.]

corrode /kə ród/ (**-rodes, -roding, -roded**) *v.* **1.** *vti.* CHEM **DESTROY PROGRESSIVELY BY CHEMICAL ACTION** to destroy sth progressively, or be destroyed progressively, by chemical action **2.** *vt.* **UNDERMINE** to undermine or destroy sth gradually ○ *His continual scorn had corroded her pride.* [14thC. From Latin *corrodere*, literally 'to gnaw away', from *rodere* 'to gnaw' (source of English *rodent*).] —**corrodant** *n.* —**corroder** *n.* —**corrodibility** /kə ródə bílləti/ *n.* —**corrodible** /kə ródəb'l/ *adj.* —**corrosible** /kə róssəb'l/ *adj.*

corrosion /kə rózh'n/ *n.* **1.** CHEM **DESTRUCTION BY CHEMICAL ACTION** a process in which sth, especially a metal, is destroyed progressively by chemical action, as iron is when it rusts **2. MATERIAL PRODUCED BY CORROSION** material produced by corrosion, e.g. rust **3. GRADUAL DESTRUCTION** the gradual destruction or undermining of sth ○ *the steady corrosion of civil rights* **4. RESULT OF CORROSION** the condition produced by corrosion [14thC. Via French and late Latin from, ultimately, Latin *corros-*, the past participle stem of *corrodere* (see CORRODE).]

corrosive /kə rṓssiv/ *adj.* **1.** CHEM **PROGRESSIVELY DESTRUCTIVE** able to destroy sth progressively by chemical action **2. DESTROYING GRADUALLY** destroying sth gradually **3. VERY SARCASTIC** very strongly sarcastic or bitter ○ *a corrosive review* ■ *n.* CHEM **DESTRUCTIVE SUBSTANCE** a substance that is able to destroy sth progressively by chemical action, e.g. an acid [14thC. Via French, ultimately from Latin *corros-*, the past participle stem of *corrodere* (see CORRODE).] —**corrosively** *adv.* —**corrosiveness** *n.*

corrosive sublimate *n.* = **mercuric chloride**

corrugate /kórrə gayt/ *vti.* (**-gates, -gating, -gated**) **FOLD INTO RIDGES AND TROUGHS** to become folded into parallel ridges and troughs, or fold sth, e.g. a sheet of cardboard, into parallel ridges and troughs ■ *adj.* = **corrugated** [Early 17thC. From Latin *corrugat-*, the past participle stem of *corrugare*, literally 'to wrinkle completely', from *rugare* 'to wrinkle'.]

corrugated /kórrə gaytid/ *adj.* **1. WITH RIDGES AND TROUGHS** folded into parallel ridges and troughs **2. MADE FROM STH CORRUGATED** made from a corrugated material ○ *a shed with a corrugated roof*

corrugation /kórrə gáysh'n/ *n.* **1. FOLD IN CORRUGATED SURFACE** any of the folds in a corrugated surface **2. PARALLEL RIDGES AND TROUGHS** parallel ridges and troughs formed by folding

corrugator /kórrə gaytər/ *n.* a muscle that wrinkles the skin when it contracts

corrupt /kə rúpt/ *adj.* **1. IMMORAL OR DISHONEST** immoral or dishonest, especially as shown by the exploitation of a position of power or trust for personal gain **2. DEPRAVED** extremely immoral or depraved **3.** COMPUT **CONTAINING ERRORS** unusable because of the presence of errors that have been introduced unintentionally ○ *a corrupt file* **4. CONTAINING COPYING ERRORS** containing undesirable changes in meaning or errors made in copying ○ *a corrupt transcription of the manuscript* **5. CONTAMINATED** contaminated or tainted by sth else (*archaic*) ○ *a corrupt fountain* **6. ROTTEN** putrid or decomposing (*archaic*) ○ *corrupt flesh* ■ *v.* (**-rupts, -rupting, -rupted**) **1.** *vti.* **MAKE OR BECOME DISHONEST** to become dishonest, or destroy or compromise sb's morality or honesty **2.** *vti.* **MAKE OR BECOME DEPRAVED** to become or cause sb to become immoral or depraved **3.** *vt.* COMPUT **INTRODUCE ERRORS INTO DATA** to introduce unintentional errors into data or a program, making it unusable or unreliable **4.** *vt.* **SPOIL TEXT WITH COPYING ERRORS** to make undesirable changes in meaning or errors in a text during copying **5.** *vt.* **CONTAMINATE** to contaminate or taint sth or sb (*archaic*) **6.** *vt.* **CAUSE TO ROT** to make sth rot or become putrid (*archaic*) [14thC. From Latin *corruptus*, the past participle of *corrumpere*, literally 'to break completely', from *rumpere* 'to break' (source of English *rupture*).] —**corrupter** *n.* —**corruptly** *adv.* —**corruptness** *n.*

corruptible /kə rúptəb'l/ *adj.* capable of or susceptible to being corrupted —**corruptibility** /kə rúptə bíllәti/ *n.* —**corruptibleness** /kə rúptəb'lnas/ *n.* —**corruptibly** /-bli/ *adv.*

corruption /kə rúpsh'n/ *n.* **1. DISHONESTY FOR PERSONAL GAIN** dishonest exploitation of power for personal gain **2. DEPRAVITY** extreme immorality or depravity **3.** LING **WORD OR PHRASE ALTERED FROM ORIGINAL** a word or phrase that has been altered from its original form **4. UNDESIRABLE CHANGE** an undesirable change in meaning or error introduced into a text during copying **5. CORRUPTING OF STH** the corrupting of sth or sb, or the state of being corrupt **6. ROTTING** rotting or putrefaction, or the state of being rotten or putrid (*archaic*)

corruptionist /kə rúpsh'nist/ *n.* sb who takes part in corruption or defends it, especially in politics

corruptive /kə rúptiv/ *adj.* having a bad effect on sb's character or behaviour —**corruptively** *adv.*

corsac /káwr sak/ *n.* a small yellowish or reddish brown fox from Central Asia. Latin name: *Vulpes corsac.* [Mid-19thC. Via Russian *korsak* from Turkic *karsak*.]

corsage /kawr saázh, káwrss aazh/ *n.* **1. FLOWERS ON DRESS** a small bouquet worn on the bodice of a dress or the lapel of a jacket **2. BODICE** the bodice of a dress (*archaic*) [Early 19thC. From French, formed from Old French *cors* 'body'.]

corsair /káwrss air, kawr sáir/ *n.* **1. PIRATE** a pirate, especially one based on the northern African coast between the 16th and 19th centuries **2. OFFICIAL PIRATE SHIP** a privately owned ship commissioned by a government to attack foreign ships, especially one based on the coast of northern Africa **3. OWNER OF PIRATE SHIP** the owner of a ship commissioned by a government to attack ships of other countries [Mid-16thC. Via French from medieval Latin *cursarius*, from Latin *cursus*,'hostile incursion, plunder' from the past participle of *currere* 'to run' (see COURSE).]

corselet /káwrsslət, -it/ *n.* **1. corselet, corselette FOUNDATION GARMENT** a garment combining a corset and a bra **2. corselet, corslet** ARMS **BREASTPLATE** armour covering the upper body [15thC. From French, formed from Old French *cors* 'body'.]

corset /káwrssit/ *n.* **1. STIFF GARMENT** a stiffened garment worn by women to shape the waist and breasts **2. STIFF UNDERGARMENT** a stiff undergarment with laces to fasten it tightly, worn in former times to shape and support the body **3.** MED **INJURY SUPPORT** a garment like a corset worn by men or women for support when injured [13thC. From French, formed from Old French *cors* 'body'.] —**corseted** *adj.*

corsetière /káwrss eti áir/ *n.* sb who makes or fits corsets [Mid-19thC. From French, formed from *corset* 'CORSET'.]

corsetry /káwrssitri/ *n.* **1. CORSETS** corsets in general **2. MAKING OF CORSETS** the process or business of making corsets

Corsica /káwrssikə/ mountainous island in the Mediterranean Sea, an administrative region of France. Population: 249,237 (1990). Area: 8,680 sq. km/3,351 sq. mi. —**Corsican** *adj., n.*

cortege /kawr táyzh, -tézh/, **cortège** *n.* **1. PROCESSION** a procession, especially a funeral procession **2. ATTENDANTS** a retinue of servants or attendants [Mid-17thC. Via French from Italian *corteggio*, from *corteggiare* 'to attend court', from *corte* 'court', from Latin *cohors* (see COHORT).]

Cortés /káwr tez/, **Hernán** (1485–1547) Spanish explorer. He conquered Mexico in 1521 for Spain, and served as its governor (1523–28).

cortex /káwr teks/ (*plural* **-tices** /-ti seez/ *or* **-texes**) *n.* **1.** ANAT **OUTER LAYER OF BODY PART** the outer layer of a solid organ or part of the body, e.g. the outer covering of the kidney or brain (**cerebral cortex**) **2.** BOT **TISSUE LAYER** the tissue in plant stems and roots between the outer layer (**epidermis**) and the central core (**stele**) [Mid-17thC. From Latin, literally 'bark'. Ultimately from an Indo-European base meaning 'to cut', which is also the ancestor of English *shear, shirt, carnage*, and *corm*.] —**cortical** /káwrtik'l/ *adj.*

cortic- *prefix.* = **cortico-** (*used before vowels*)

cortico- *prefix.* cortex, cortical ○ *corticospinal* [From Latin *cortic-*, the stem of *cortex* (see CORTEX)]

corticoid /káwrti koyd/ *n.* a drug that acts in a similar way to the hormone produced by the outer layer of the adrenal gland

corticospinal /káwrtikō spīn'l/ *adj.* relating to or connecting the outer covering of the brain (**cerebral cortex**) and the spinal cord

corticosteroid /káwrtikō stérroyd, -stéer-/ *n.* **1.** MED **NATURAL STEROID** a steroid hormone produced by the adrenal gland and involved in metabolism and immune response **2.** PHARM **SYNTHETIC STEROID** a synthetic drug similar or identical to a natural corticosteroid, used to reduce inflammation, control allergic disorders, and prevent graft rejection

corticotrophin /káwrtikō trṓfin/, **corticotropin** /-pin/ *n.* = **ACTH** [Mid-20thC. Contraction of *adrenocorticotrophic hormone*.]

cortisol /káwrti sol, -zol/ *n.* = **hydrocortisone** [Mid-20thC. Coined from CORTISONE + -OL.]

cortisone /káwrti zōn/ *n.* a hormone secreted by the adrenal gland and used to treat rheumatoid arthritis and allergies [Mid-20thC. Contraction of *corticosterone*, a type of CORTICOSTEROID.]

corundum /kə rúndəm/ *n.* a hard mineral of aluminium oxide, with crystals in a range of colours and used as an abrasive or a gemstone. The best-known varieties are ruby and sapphire. [Early 18thC. From Tamil *kuruntam*.]

coruscant /kə rúskənt/ *adj.* sparkling or glittering (*literary*)

coruscate /kórrə skayt/ (**-cates, -cating, -cated**) *vi.* (*literary*) **1. GLITTER** to give off flashes of bright light **2. BE BRILLIANT** to show brilliance or virtuosity ○ *a journalist renowned for her coruscating wit* [Early 18thC. From Latin *coruscat-*, the past participle stem of *coruscare* 'to glitter'.] —**coruscating** *adj.* —**coruscation** /kórrə skáysh'n/ *n.*

corvée /káwr vay/ *n.* **1. FEUDAL SERVICE** a day of unpaid labour required of a serf for a manorial lord **2. SERVICE FOR GOVERNMENT** a period of labour sometimes required by the state in lieu of taxes [14thC. Via French from, ultimately, Latin *corrogata*, the past participle of *corrogare*, literally 'to summon together', from *rogare* 'to ask, beg'.]

corves plural of **corf**

corvette /kawr vét/ *n.* **1. NAVAL ESCORT SHIP** an armed naval escort vessel, smaller than a destroyer **2. SMALL WARSHIP** in former times, a small wooden warship with one tier of guns [Mid-17thC. Via French from, ultimately, Dutch *korf* 'small ship', literally 'basket', from Latin *corbis* (source also of English *corf*).]

corvid /káwrvid/ *n.* a bird of the family that includes crows, jays, and magpies. Family: Corvidae. [Mid-20thC. From modern Latin *Corvidae*, family name, from Latin *corvus* (see CORVINE).]

corvine /káwr vīn/ *adj.* belonging to the crow family, or characteristic of birds of the crow family such as crows and ravens (*formal or literary*) [Mid-17thC. From Latin *corvinus*, from *corvus* 'raven'. Ultimately from an Indo-European word that is also the ancestor of English *screech, shrike, raven*, and *rook*.]

Corvus /káwrvəss/ *n.* a small constellation situated in southern skies between Virgo and Hydra

Corybant /kórri bant/ (*plural* **-bants** *or* **-bantes** /-bán teez/) *n.* **1.** RELIG **PRIEST OF CYBELE** in ancient Phrygia, a priest of the goddess Cybele who performed wild ecstatic dances **2.** MYTHOL **ATTENDANT OF GODDESS CYBELE** in ancient mythology, any of the goddess Cybele's attendants [15thC. From Latin *Corybant-*, the stem of *Corybas*, from Greek *Korubas*.] —**Corybantic** /kórri bántik/ *adj.*

corymb /kórrimb, -im/ *n.* a flat flower head (**inflorescence**) consisting of flowers whose stalks grow from different points on the flower stem but reach approximately the same height [Early 18thC. Via French from, ultimately, Greek *korumbos* 'summit'. Ultimately from an Indo-European base meaning 'head, horn'.] —**corymbed** *adj.* —**corymbose** /kórrimbōss/ *adj.* —**corymbous** /kórrim bəss/ *adj.*

coryphée /kórri fáy/ *n.* a leading dancer in a ballet company who usually performs with a small group of other dancers [Early 19thC. Via French from, ultimately, Greek *koruphaios* 'chorus leader', from *koruphe* 'head top'.]

coryza /kə rīzə/ *n.* **1.** MED **NASAL CONGESTION** severe nasal congestion **2.** MED **COLD** a common cold (*technical*) **3.** VET **BIRD DISEASE** a respiratory disease of chickens and turkeys, caused by bacteria [Early 16thC. Via Latin from Greek *koruza* 'nasal mucus, catarrh', of unknown origin.] —**coryzal** *adj.*

cos[1] /koss/ (*plural* **coses** *or* **cos**) *n.* a lettuce with long crisp leaves. US term **romaine** [Late 17thC. Named after the island of *Cos* in Greece, from which it was introduced.]

cos[2] /koz/ *abbr.* cosine. ◊ **sin, tan**

'cos /koz/ *conj.* because (*informal*) [Early 19thC. Shortening and alteration of BECAUSE.]

Cos /koss/ second largest of the Greek Dodecanese Islands, off the coast of Turkey in the Aegean Sea. Population: 20,350 (1981). Area: 287 sq. km/111 sq. mi. Greek **Kos**

COS /koss/ *abbr.* **1.** cash on shipment **2.** chief of staff

c.o.s. /koss/ *abbr.* cash on shipment

Cosa Nostra /kṓssə nóstrə, kṓzə-/ *n.* a criminal organization in the United States, linked with the Mafia of Sicily [Mid-20thC. From Italian, literally 'our concern'.]

cosec /kṓ sek/ *abbr.* cosecant

cosecant /kō séekənt/ *n.* for a given angle in a right-angled triangle, a trigonometric function equal to the length of the hypotenuse divided by that of the side opposite the angle

coseismal /kō sízm'l/ *n.* a line on a map that connects places where the effects of an earthquake were felt at the same time

Cosenza /kō zénzə, -zéntsə/ capital of Cosenza Province in Calabria Region, in southern Italy. Population: 104,483 (1990).

Cosgrave /kóz grayv/, **Liam** (*b.* 1920) Irish politician and lawyer. The son of William Thomas Cosgrave, he led the Fine Gael party from 1965 to 1977 and was prime minister of the Republic of Ireland from 1973 to 1977.

Cosgrave, William Thomas (1880–1965) Irish politician. A republican, he co-founded Sinn Fein (1905), fought in the Easter Rising (1916), and became president of the Irish Free State (1922–32).

cosh /kosh/ *n.* BLUNT WEAPON a blunt weapon usually made of rubber or metal ■ *vt.* **(coshes, coshing, coshed)** HIT WITH A COSH to attack sb using a cosh [Mid-19thC. Origin uncertain: possibly from Romany *kosh* 'stick'.]

COSHH regulations /kosh-/ *npl.* in the UK, legal requirements concerning the storage and use of hazardous chemicals in the workplace [*COSHH* an acronym formed from *Control of Substances Hazardous to Health*]

cosignatory /kō sígnətəri/ (*plural* **-ries**) *n.* a person, government, or organization that signs a document or treaty jointly with others

cosine /kṓ sīn/ *n.* for a given angle in a right-angled triangle, a trigonometric function equal to the length of the side adjacent to the angle divided by the hypotenuse

cosmetic /koz méttik/ *n.* (*often used in the plural*) **1.** BEAUTIFYING SUBSTANCE a preparation, e.g. lipstick, that is applied to the face or the body to make it more attractive **2.** *US* SUPERFICIALLY ATTRACTIVE ASPECT sth added or done to sth else to cover up defects ■ *adj.* **1.** BEAUTIFYING intended to improve sb's physical appearance ○ *cosmetic surgery* **2.** ONLY FOR APPEARANCES done to make sth seem better but having no real value ○ *The changes to the code of conduct were purely cosmetic, since attitudes remained fundamentally the same.* **3.** DECORATIVE designed or added for decorative purposes rather than for any real function [Early 17thC. Via French *cosmétique* from Greek *kosmētikos* 'skilled in ornamenting', from *kosmein* 'to arrange', from *kosmos* (see COSMOS[1]).] —**cosmetically** *adv.*

cosmetician /kózmə tísh'n/ *n.* sb who makes or sells cosmetics, or who applies them professionally

cosmetologist /kózmə tólləjist/ *n.* an expert in cosmetics and their use

cosmetology /kózmə tólləji/ *n.* the study of cosmetics or the art or profession of using them [Mid-19thC. From French *cosmétologie*, from *cosmétique*.]

cosmic /kózmik/ *adj.* **1.** OF WHOLE UNIVERSE relating to the whole universe **2.** ASTRON OF UNIVERSE APART FROM EARTH used to describe outer space or a part of the universe other than the Earth **3.** GREAT very great in size or significance ■ *interj.* EXPRESSING AMAZEMENT used to express amazement or wonder [Mid-17thC. From Greek *kosmikos*, from *kosmos* (see COSMOS[1]).] —**cosmically** *adv.*

cosmic dust *n.* small particles of solid matter found in outer space, often collected in clouds

cosmic ray *n.* a stream of high-energy radiation that reaches the earth from outer space

cosmic string *n.* an extremely long and thin astronomical object theorized to be a space-time defect formed when the universe began

cosmo- *prefix.* the universe, space ○ *cosmochemistry* [From Greek *kosmos* 'order, the world' (source of English *microcosm*)]

cosmogony /koz móggəni/ (*plural* **-nies**) *n.* **1.** STUDY OF UNIVERSE'S ORIGIN the study of the origin of the universe or a part of it **2.** THEORY OF UNIVERSE'S ORIGIN a theory that explains the origin of the universe [Late 17thC. From Greek *kosmogonia* 'creation of the world', from *kosmos* 'COSMOS[1]'.] —**cosmogonic** /kózmə gónnik/ *adj.* —**cosmogonical** /-gónnik'l/ *adj.* —**cosmogonically** /-gónnikli/ *adv.* —**cosmogonist** /koz móggənist/ *n.*

cosmography /koz móggrəfi/ (*plural* **-phies**) *n.* the study and description or mapping of the entire world or the universe [14thC. Via late Latin from Greek *kosmographia*, from *kosmos* 'COSMOS[1]'.] —**cosmographer** *n.* —**cosmographic** /kózmə gráffik/ *adj.* —**cosmographical** /-gráffik'l/ *adj.* —**cosmographically** /-gráffikli/ *adv.*

cosmological argument *n.* a logical argument that tries to prove the existence of God from empirical information about the universe

cosmological principle *n.* the principle that the universe would look the same to observers at any point in it as it does to us

cosmology /koz mólləji/ (*plural* **-gies**) *n.* **1.** PHILOS STUDY OF UNIVERSE the philosophical study and explanation of the nature of the universe **2.** COSMOL SCIENTIFIC STUDY OF UNIVERSE the scientific study of the origin and structure of the universe [Mid-17thC. From modern Latin *cosmologia*, from, ultimately, Greek *kosmos* 'COSMOS[1]'.] —**cosmologic** /kózmə lójjik/ *adj.* —**cosmological** /-lójjik'l/ *adj.* —**cosmologically** /-lójjikli/ *adv.* —**cosmologist** /koz mólləjist/ *n.*

cosmonaut /kózmə nawt/ *n.* an astronaut in the space programmes of Russia and the former Soviet Union [Mid-20thC. From Russian *kosmonavt*, coined from Greek *kosmos* 'COSMOS' + *nautēs* 'sailor', on the model of *aeronavt* 'aeronaut'.]

cosmopolis /koz móppəliss/ *n.* a large city where people from many different countries and cultures live [Mid-19thC. Coined from COSMOS-, on the model of METROPOLIS.]

cosmopolitan /kózmə póllitən/ *adj.* **1.** WITH FEATURES OF DIFFERENT COUNTRIES composed of or containing people from different countries **2.** WELL-TRAVELLED familiar with many different countries and cultures **3.** UNPREJUDICED free from national prejudices **4.** KNOWLEDGEABLE AND REFINED showing a breadth of knowledge and refinement from having travelled widely **5.** ECOL OCCURRING WORLDWIDE growing or occurring in many different parts of the world ■ *n.* WELL-TRAVELLED PERSON sb who has travelled to many different countries around the world [Mid-17thC. Formed from COSMOPOLITE.] —**cosmopolitanism** *n.*

cosmopolite /koz móppə līt/ *n.* = **cosmopolitan** [Early 17thC. Via French from Greek *kosmopolitēs*, literally 'citizen of the world'.] —**cosmopolitism** *n.*

cosmos[1] /kóz moss/ *n.* **1.** PHILOS, COSMOL WHOLE UNIVERSE the universe thought of as an ordered and integrated whole **2.** ORDERED SYSTEM an ordered system or harmonious whole [13thC. From Greek *kosmos* 'order, universe, ornament' (source also of English *microcosm*).]

cosmos[2] /kóz moss/ (*plural* **-moses** *or* **-mos**) *n.* a tropical American plant with flowers of various colours that resemble large daisies. Genus: *Cosmos.* [Early 19thC. Via modern Latin from Greek *kosmos* 'ornament' (source of English COSMOS[1]). So called because of its elegant foliage.]

Cossack /kóss ak/ *n.* **1.** HIST RUSSIAN PEASANT a peasant of Polish or Russian descent living in southeastern Russia, Ukraine, or Siberia. Cossacks were noted for their skill in horsemanship. **2.** MIL COSSACK SOLDIER a member of a Russian army unit whose soldiers are Cossacks [Late 16thC. Via Russian *kazak* (source of English *Kazakh*) from Turkic, literally 'nomad, adventurer'. The spelling was influenced by French *Cosaque*.]

cosset /kóssit/ **(-sets, -seting, -seted)** *vt.* to give sb or sth excessive care and protection [Mid-16thC. Origin uncertain: perhaps via Anglo-Norman *coscet* 'lamb reared by hand' from Old English *cotsǣta*, literally 'cottage-dweller'.]

cossie /kózzi/, **cozzie** *n.* a swimming costume (*informal*) [Early 20thC. Shortening.]

cost /kost/ *v.* **(costs, costing, cost) 1.** *vt.* BE PRICED AT to require the payment of a particular sum **2.** *vti.* BE EXPENSIVE to require payment of a large sum of money (*informal*) **3.** *vt.* CAUSE LOSS OF to cause sb or sth to lose, sacrifice, or suffer sth **4.** (*past and past participle* **costed**) *vt.* CALCULATE MONEY REQUIRED to calculate the price or expense of sth ■ *n.* **1.** AMOUNT PAID FOR STH the amount of money required to be paid for sth **2.** MONEY SPENT DOING STH the amount of money spent in producing or doing sth **3.** LOSS OR EFFORT the loss, sacrifice, suffering, or effort involved in doing sth **4.** = **cost price** ■ **costs** *npl.* LAW LEGAL EXPENSES the amount of money that is spent pursuing a legal action, especially those expenses that the losing party is required to pay [14thC. Via Old French from, ultimately, Latin *constare* 'to be fixed'.] —**costless** *adj.* —**costlessly** *adv.* —**costlessness** *n.*

costa /kóstə/ (*plural* **-tae** /-tee/) *n.* **1.** ANAT RIB a rib (*technical*) **2.** BIOL PART LIKE RIB a part of sth, e.g. a leaf or a wing, that resembles a rib [Mid-19thC. From Latin, 'rib' (source also of English *accost*, *coast* and *cutlet*).] —**costal** *adj.*

Costa Brava /kóstə braávə/ resort region on the Mediterranean coast of northeastern Spain, north of Barcelona

cost accountant *n.* an accountant who calculates and provides detailed information on the cost of producing sth or carrying out some operation in a business, and compares actual costs with expected costs

cost accounting *n.* accounting that is concerned with providing detailed information on the cost of producing sth or carrying out an operation in a business

Costa del Sol /kóstə del sól/ tourist coastal region on the Mediterranean coast of southern Spain

costae plural of **costa**

co-star /kṓ staar/, **costar** *n.* JOINT STAR sb who stars jointly with another person or other people in a production ■ *v.* **(co-stars, co-starring, co-starred) 1.** *vi.* STAR JOINTLY WITH OTHERS to star jointly with another actor or actors in a production **2.** *vt.* FEATURE AS JOINT STAR to include or feature sb as a co-star

costard /kústərd, kós-/ *n.* a large English cooking apple [13thC. From Anglo-Norman, formed from *coste* 'rib', from Latin *costa* (see COSTA). So called because of its prominent ridges.]

Costa Rica

Costa Rica /kóstə reékə/ republic in southern Central America between the Caribbean Sea and the Pacific Ocean. Language: Spanish. Currency: colón. Capital: San José. Population: 3,534,174 (1997). Area: 51,060 sq. km/19,714 sq. mi. Official name **Republic of Costa Rica** —**Costa Rican** *n., adj.*

costate /kóst ayt/ *adj.* BOT used to describe a leaf that has ridges or is ribbed [Early 19thC. From Latin *costatus*, formed from *costa* (see COSTA).]

cost-effective *adj.* economically worthwhile in terms of what is achieved for the amount of money spent —**cost-effectively** *adv.* —**cost-effectiveness** *n.*

costermonger /kóstər mung gər/, **coster** *n.* sb who sells fruit and vegetables or other things from a barrow or stall in the street (*archaic*) [Early 16thC. From COSTARD + *monger* 'seller'.]

costing /kósting/ *n.* **1.** CALCULATION OF COSTS the process of calculating the cost involved in undertaking a project **2.** CALCULATED COST OF STH the cost that has been calculated for undertaking a project (*often used in the plural*)

costive /kóstiv/ *adj.* **1.** MED CONSTIPATED constipated, or causing constipation (*technical*) **2.** HESITANT slow to act or speak [14thC. Via Old French from Latin *constipatus*, the past participle of *constipare* (see CONSTIPATE).] —**costively** *adv.* —**costiveness** *n.*

costly /kóstli/ **(-lier, -liest)** *adj.* **1.** EXPENSIVE costing a lot of money to buy **2.** LUXURIOUS using expensive and luxurious materials **3.** INVOLVING TIME OR EFFORT involving a great deal of effort, time, or sacrifice **4.** **DAMAGING** causing great loss, damage, or suffering — **costliness** *n.*

Costner /kóstnər/, **Kevin** (*b.* 1955) US film actor and director. He won seven Academy Awards for *Dances With Wolves* (1990), a film about the Sioux.

cost of living *n.* the amount of money spent on food, clothing, accommodation, and other basic necessities (*hyphenated when used before a noun*)

cost-of-living index *n.* = consumer price index

cost-plus *n.* a pricing system that calculates the price of a product by adding a specified percentage as profit to the production cost

cost price *n.* the price that sb selling sth paid for it

costume /kós tyoom/ *n.* **1.** **SPECIAL CLOTHES** clothes worn to make sb look like sb or sth else, e.g. when performing in a play **2.** **CLOTHES OF PERIOD OR GROUP** the clothes worn during a specific period of time or in a specific location **3.** **CLOTHES FOR CERTAIN ACTIVITY** the clothing appropriate for a particular activity, e.g. swimming **4.** **WOMEN'S SKIRT SUIT** women's clothes comprising a matching jacket and skirt (*dated*) ■ *vt.* (**-tumes, -tuming, -tumed**) **1.** **DRESS IN A COSTUME** to provide sb with a costume **2.** **PROVIDE COSTUMES** to provide costumes for a production [Early 18thC. Via French from Italian *costume*, literally 'custom, fashion', from Latin *consuetudo* (see CUSTOM).]

costume drama, **costume piece** *n.* a dramatic production in which the actors wear clothes appropriate for the period during which the drama takes place

costume jewellery *n.* jewellery that is decorative but cheap

costumier /ko styoomi ər, -i ay/, **costumer** /-mər/ *n.* sb who makes or supplies costumes for a play, show, or festivity [Mid-19thC. From French, from *costumer* 'to provide with a costume'.]

co-survivor *n.* PSYCHOL a close relative or friend of sb who has experienced a traumatizing event, e.g. a rape victim, AIDS patient, or victim of a disaster

cosy /kós zee/ *adj.* **1.** **SNUG** warm, comfortable, and snug **3.** **FRIENDLY** friendly and intimate **3.** **UNETHICALLY CLOSE** close and friendly, but for mutually beneficial or underhanded purposes ■ *n.* **COVERING TO KEEP STH WARM** a covering, often knitted or padded, put over sth, especially a teapot, to keep it or its contents warm —**cosily** *adv.* —**cosiness** *n.*

cosy up *v.* **1.** *vi.* **CUDDLE UP** to sit or lie as close as possible to sb for warmth or affection **2.** **INGRATIATE YOURSELF** to try to ingratiate yourself, or become friendly or intimate, with sb

cot[1] /kot/ *n.* **1.** **BABY'S BED** a small bed designed for a baby or young child, often with high sides. US term **crib 2.** *US* **= camp bed 3.** **SAILING HAMMOCK-LIKE BED** a kind of hammock with a stiff frame, used on board ship [Mid-17thC. From Hindi *khāṭ*, a framework strung with rope and used as a bed or seat, via Sanskrit *khaṭvā* from Tamil *kaṭṭu* 'to tie'.]

cot[2] /kot/ *n.* **1.** **COTTAGE** a small cottage (*archaic or literary*) **2.** **MED COVER FOR SORE FINGER** a cover for an injured finger, shaped like the finger of a glove [Old English, from prehistoric Germanic (see COTE)]

cot[3] /kot/ *abbr.* cotangent

cot[4] *n.* = cote

CoT *abbr.* college of technology

cotan /kó tan/ *abbr.* cotangent

cotangent /kō tánjənt/ *n.* for a given angle in a right-angled triangle, a trigonometric function equal to the length of the side adjacent to the angle divided by that of the side opposite —**cotangential** /kó tan jénsh'l/ *adj.*

cot case *n.* **1.** *ANZ* **VERY DRUNK PERSON** sb who has drunk so much that he or she is fit only for bed (*informal*) **2.** *NZ* **SICK PERSON** sb who has to stay in bed as a result of illness

cot death *n.* the sudden and unexplained death of a baby while sleeping. US term **crib death**

cote /kōt/, **cot** /kot/ *n.* a small shelter, especially one for birds or animals (*usually used in combination*) [Old English. Ultimately from a prehistoric Germanic word that is also the ancestor of English *cot*[2].]

Côte d'Azur /kót da zyoor/ part of the French Riviera near the Italian border, including the communities of Cannes, Nice, and Monaco

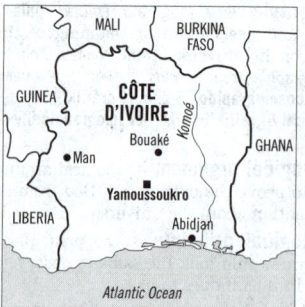

Côte d'Ivoire

Côte d'Ivoire /kót dee vwaár/ republic in western Africa, situated north of the Gulf of Guinea and east of Liberia. Language: French. Currency: CFA franc. Capital: official, Yamoussoukro; seat of government, Abidjan. Population: 15,074,684 (1997). Area: 322,462 sq. km/124,503 sq. mi. Official name **Republic of Côte d'Ivoire**

Côte d'Or /-dáwr/ administrative region and major wine-producing area in Bourgogne, eastern France. The main city in the region is Dijon. Population: 497,917 (1991). Area: 8,765 sq. km/3,384 sq. mi.

coterie /kótəri/ *n.* a small exclusive group of people who share the same interests [Early 18thC. Via French from, ultimately, Middle Low German *kote* 'cottage'. In Old French, the word meant 'tenants'.]

coterminous *adj.* = conterminous

Côte-Rôtie BEVERAGES a full-bodied red wine produced in the northern Rhône valley, France

Côtes-du-Nord /kót dyoo náwr/ area of northwestern France in Bretagne region. Population: 538,594 (1991). Area: 6,876 km/2,655 mi.

Côtes du Rhône /kót dyoo rṍn/ *n.* a red or white wine produced in the Rhône valley, France

coth /koth/ *abbr.* hyperbolic cotangent [Late 19thC. From COT[3] + *h* for HYPERBOLIC.]

cotidal /kō tíd'l/ *adj.* used to describe a line that joins together locations on a coastal map where tides occur simultaneously

cotillion /kə tíllyən, kō-/, **cotillon** *n.* **1.** **FRENCH DANCE** a complicated French dance popular in the 18th century **2.** *US* **BALL** a formal ball **3.** *US* **DANCE LIKE QUADRILLE** a dance similar to a quadrille **4.** **MUSIC MUSIC** the music for a cotillion [Early 18thC. From French *cotillon*, literally 'petticoat', from *cotte* (see COAT).]

cotinga /kō tíng gə, kə-/ *n.* a brightly coloured bird of Central and South America. Family: Cotingidae. [Late 18thC. Via French from Tupi *cutinga*.]

Cotman /kótmən/, **John Sell** (1782–1842) British painter, etcher, and founder, with John Crome, of the Norwich School. Most of his watercolours show Norfolk landscapes.

coton à broder /kótton aa bródday/ *n.* fine flat cotton thread with a slight sheen, used for embroidery [From French, literally 'cotton for embroidery']

cotoneaster /kə tóni ástər/ *n.* a shrub of European or Asian origin with small white or pink flowers and black or red berries. Genus: *Cotoneaster*. [Mid-18thC. From modern Latin, genus name, from Latin *cotoneum* (see QUINCE).]

Cotonou /kótə noo/ city, port, and capital of Atlantique Province, southern Benin, on the coast of West Africa. Population: 350,000 (1989).

coton perlé /kótton púr lay/ *n.* shiny twisted two-ply thread available in various thicknesses, used for embroidery [From French, literally 'pearly cotton']

Cotopaxi /kótə páksi/ volcano in central Ecuador, in the Andes Mountains. It is the highest active volcano in the world. Height: 5,897 m/19,347 ft.

co-trimoxazole /kótri móksə zōl/ *n.* an antibiotic used mainly to treat urinary tract infections, that consists of a mixture of trimethoprim and sulpha-

---

methoxazole [Late 20thC. Coined from CO- + a blend of *trimethoprim* and *sulphamethoxazole*.]

Cotswold /kóts wold/ *n.* a sheep with fine long wool of a breed originating in the Cotswolds ■ *adj.* relating to the Cotswolds

Cotswolds /kóts wōldz/ range of limestone hills in southwestern England, extending 80 km/50 mi. from near Bath to northern Oxfordshire

cotta /kóttə/ *n.* a short surplice reaching to just above the waist, worn by clergy, acolytes and choristers, in the Roman Catholic Church and in some Anglican and Lutheran churches [Mid-19thC. From Italian, ultimately from an ancient Germanic word that is also the ancestor of English *coat*.]

cottage /kóttij/ *n.* **1.** **SMALL RURAL HOUSE** a small house, usually situated in the countryside **2.** *US, Can* **HOLIDAY HOME** in North America, a small holiday home in the country or beside the sea **3.** *US* **SMALL RESIDENTIAL UNIT** in the United States, a small residential unit, e.g. at a camp, in which residents can be housed in groups **4.** **PUBLIC TOILET** a public toilet, especially one used by homosexuals for sexual encounters (*dated informal*) [14thC. From either Anglo-Norman *cotage* or Anglo-Latin *cotagium*, both of prehistoric Germanic origin.] —**cottagey** *adj.*

cottage cheese *n.* a soft white low-fat cheese with a distinctive lumpy texture and mild flavour

cottage hospital *n.* a small rural hospital that does not have any resident medical staff

cottage industry *n.* a small-scale business where people mostly work at home

cottage loaf *n.* a loaf of bread consisting of a large round piece with a smaller one on top

cottage pie *n.* = shepherd's pie

cottager /kóttijər/ *n.* **1.** **OCCUPANT OF COTTAGE** a person who lives in a cottage **2.** *US* **SB WHO HOLIDAYS IN A COTTAGE** sb who takes his or her holidays in a holiday cottage **3.** **SB WHO ENGAGES IN COTTAGING** sb who has homosexual sex or looks for homosexual partners in public toilets (*slang*)

cottaging /kóttijing/ *n.* homosexual sex or looking for homosexual partners in public toilets, a practice that was especially prevalent in the years when homosexual sex was a criminal offence (*slang*)

cottar /kóttər/, **cotter** *n.* **1.** **FARM WORKER OCCUPYING COTTAGE** formerly in Scotland, a farm worker who was allowed to occupy a cottage in return for labour **2.** **=** cottier [Mid-16thC. Origin uncertain: perhaps from medieval Latin *cotarius* (from Old English *cotsæta*, literally 'cottage-dweller'), or formed from COT[2] + a Scots variant of -ER.]

Cottbus /kót booss/ city in Cottbus District, in the state of Brandenburg in eastern central Germany, near the Polish border. Population: 126,400 (1990).

cotter[1] /kóttər/ *n.* **1.** **WEDGE OR BOLT KEEPING THINGS TOGETHER** a wedge, key, or bolt used to keep two parts of sth, e.g. machinery, together **2.** **=** cotter pin [14thC. Origin unknown.] —**cottered** *adj.* —**cotterless** *adj.*

cotter[2] *n.* = cottar

cotter pin *n.* a split pin inserted through a hole in a machine part and then bent so it holds the part in place

cottier /kótti ər/ *n.* formerly in Ireland, a tenant who farmed land he had acquired as the highest bidder [14thC. From Old French *cotier*. Ultimately of prehistoric Germanic origin.]

cotton /kótt'n/ *n.* **1.** **PLANTS BUSH PRODUCING DOWNY FIBRE** a tropical or subtropical bush producing soft white downy fibres and oil-rich seeds. Genus: *Gossypium*. **2.** **INDUST SOFT FIBRE** the soft white downy fibre that grows on the seed pods of the cotton plant, used for making textiles **3.** **TEXTILES FABRIC MADE FROM COTTON** fabric woven or knitted from spun cotton fibre **4.** **SEW YARN OR THREAD** yarn or thread made from cotton fibre, or a synthetic substitute **5.** **STH MADE OF COTTON** sth made of cotton (*often used in the plural*) **6.** **INDUST SUBSTANCE RESEMBLING COTTON** a substance that resembles cotton fibre but is produced by another plant, e.g. kapok [14thC. Via French *coton* from, ultimately, Arabic *kuṭun*.]

cotton on (**cottons on, cottoning on, cottoned on**) *vi.* to grasp the meaning of what is being said or done

---

(informal) [From the obsolete verb cotton 'to prosper', which is said to have come from success in raising the nap of cotton and so increasing its value]

Cotton Belt n. an extensive agricultural area in the southeast United States where cotton is the main crop

cotton bud n. a short stick with a small amount of absorbent cotton wound tightly onto one or both ends, used, e.g., to clean ears or apply makeup

cotton bush n. Aus a downy shrub used to feed livestock in Australia. Latin name: Kochia aphylla.

cotton cake n. a hard cake produced as a residue after the extraction of oil from cottonseeds and used as a feed for livestock. It is usually ground for feeding.

cotton candy n. US, Can = candy floss

cotton grass n. a reed-like bog plant of northern temperate areas that has white tufted cottony flower heads. Genus: Eriophorum.

cottonmouth /kótt'n mowth/ (plural -mouths /-thz, -ths/) n. = water moccasin [Mid-19thC. From the whitish colour inside its mouth.]

cotton-picking adj. US used to indicate disapproval or annoyance, or simply for emphasis (informal) [From the fact that cotton-picking was done by only the poorest labourers]

cottonseed /kótt'n seed/ n. the seed of the cotton plant, used to give oil and make meal

cotton stainer n. an insect that pierces cotton seed pods (bolls) and stains the fibres. Genus: Dysdercus.

cotton swab n. US = cotton bud

cottontail /kótt'n tayl/ n. a small North American rabbit with brown or grey fur and a tail with a white cottony underside. Genus: Sylvilagus.

cotton waste n. waste cotton yarn used as a cleaning material

cottonwood /kótt'n wood/ (plural -woods or -wood) n. a North American poplar tree that has seeds with cottony tufts. Latin name: Populus deltoides.

cotton wool n. 1. COTTON FIBRE soft fluffy cotton fibre that has been purified and bleached, used for tasks such as cleaning wounds or removing makeup (hyphenated when used before a noun) US term absorbent cotton 2. UNPROCESSED COTTON raw unprocessed cotton

cottony /kótt'ni/ adj. looking or feeling like cotton

cottony-cushion scale n. a small sap-sucking insect, native to Australia, that damages citrus crops in California and elsewhere. Latin name: Icerya purchasi.

-cotyl suffix. cotyledon ○ hypocotyl [From COTYLEDON]

cotyledon /kótti leed'n/ n. 1. FIRST LEAF the first leaf, or one of the first pair of leaves, produced by the seed of a flowering plant. They may serve as food stores, remaining in the seed at germination, or produce food by photosynthesis. 2. TUFT ON MAMMALIAN PLACENTA a tuft of projections (villi) on the placenta of a mammal [Mid-16thC. Via Latin, literally 'navelwort', from Greek kotulēdōn 'cup-shaped cavity', from kotulē 'cup, socket'.] —**cotyledonal** adj. —**cotyledonary** adj. —**cotyledonous** adj.

cotylosaur /kóttilə sawr, kə tíllə-/ n. an extinct reptile with a heavy body and short legs. The cotylosaurs were probably the first land vertebrates. Order: Cotylosauria. [Early 20thC. Coined from Greek kotulē 'cup, socket' + sauros 'lizard'. So called from its vertebrae, which are concave at both ends.]

coucal /koo kal, -k'l/ n. a tropical bird of the cuckoo family with a large hooked beak and long broad tail, found in Africa, southern Asia, and Australasia. Genus: Centropus. [Early 19thC. From French, said to be a blend of coucou 'cuckoo' and alouette 'lark'.]

couch[1] /kowch/ n. 1. LONG SEAT a piece of upholstered furniture on which two or more people can sit side by side. It usually has a back and arms. 2. DOCTOR'S LONG SEAT a long seat with a headrest that a patient lies on, e.g. during a medical examination 3. MALTING FRAME a frame on which barley grain is spread during malting 4. PAINTING FIRST COAT OF PAINT a layer of paint or varnish applied to a canvas as a first coat

■ v. (couches, couching, couched) 1. vt. PHRASE IN CERTAIN WAY to express sth using a particular style or choice of words 2. vt. SPREAD FOR MALTING to spread barley on a frame for malting 3. vti. LIE OR LAY DOWN to lie down, or lay sb or sth down (archaic or literary) (often passive) 4. vi. LIE IN AMBUSH to lie in ambush (archaic or literary) 5. vt. ARMS LOWER LANCE to lower a lance into position for an attack 6. vt. SURG REMOVE CATARACT to remove a cataract by pushing down the lens of the eye 7. vt. SEW EMBROIDER BY HOLDING DOWN THREADS to embroider a pattern by holding down threads by means of other threads passed through the material [14thC. The noun is via French couche, the verb directly from coucher 'to lie or set down', from Latin collocare, literally 'to place together'.] —**coucher** n.

couch[2] n. = couch grass [Late 16thC. Variant of QUITCH.]

couchant /kówchənt/ adj. used in heraldry to describe an animal lying down with its head raised [15thC. From French, the present participle of coucher (see COUCH[1]).]

couchette /koo shét/ n. 1. SEAT CONVERTIBLE TO BED a seat in a compartment on a continental European train that can be converted into a sleeping berth 2. COMPARTMENT WITH COUCHETTES a compartment of a train containing couchettes [Early 20thC. From French, literally 'small bed', from couche (see COUCH[1]).]

couch grass /kówch-, kooch-/ n. a type of grass with rapidly spreading underground roots, that is a troublesome weed in gardens. Latin name: Agropyron repens.

couch potato n. an inactive person who spends too much time sitting watching television (disapproving informal) [A pun on the idea that sb who watches the 'boob tube' (television) is a 'tuber'; also with reference to snacking on potato crisps]

coudé /koo dáy/, **coudé telescope** n. an astronomical telescope that reflects light from a main mirror onto a detector to one side [Late 19thC. From French, the past participle of couder 'to bend at right angles', from coude 'elbow', from Latin cubitum 'elbow, forearm, cubit'.]

Cougar

cougar /koogər, -aar/ (plural -gars or -gar) n. = puma [Late 18thC. Via French couguar from, ultimately, Guarani cuguaçuarana.]

cough /kof/ v. (coughs, coughing, coughed) 1. vi. EXPEL AIR FROM LUNGS NOISILY to release air through the windpipe and mouth sharply and noisily 2. vt. EXPEL BY COUGHING to expel sth from the lungs or windpipe by coughing 3. vi. MAKE COUGHING NOISE to make a noise that is similar to the sound of sb coughing ■ n. 1. ACT OR SOUND OF COUGHING a sudden noisy release of air through the windpipe and mouth, often expelling an obstruction 2. MED ILLNESS CAUSING COUGHING an illness causing coughing because of an infection in the lungs [14thC. Ultimately from a prehistoric Germanic word that imitated the sound.] —**cougher** n.

cough up vti. to give sth such as money or information reluctantly (informal)

cough drop n. a medicated sweet for soothing a cough or sore throat

cough mixture n. a medicated, often sweet-tasting, syrup that is taken to soothe or suppress a cough

could /kood/ CORE MEANING: a modal verb used to form the past tense of 'can' ○ My mother did the best she could for my brother and me, often against very stiff odds. ○ She could perform illusions and she was a trapeze artist. ○ His feet had swollen so he could

hardly walk. ○ We were so tired we couldn't stay awake.

vi. 1. EXPRESSING POSSIBILITY used to express that sth is possibly true or happening in the future ○ She thinks that medical technology could be the field for her. 2. EXPRESSING REQUEST used when making polite requests ○ Could you close the window please? 3. INDICATING A POSSIBLE PAST SITUATION used to indicate a possible situation in the past that did not happen ○ We could have gone. 4. EXPRESSING POLITE OFFER used to make polite offers and suggestions 5. FOR EMPHASIS used in questions to emphasize strong feelings about sth ○ How could you do that? [Old English cūpe, past tense of cunnan 'to know' (see CAN[2]; altered on the model of SHOULD and WOULD]

couldn't /koodd'nt/ contr. could not

could've /kooddəv/ contr. could have

coulee /kooli, -lay/ n. 1. GEOL LAVA FLOW a thick short flow of viscous molten lava 2. Northwest US, Can GEOG DEEP GULLY DRY IN SUMMER a deep gully formed by rain or melting snow and usually dry in the summer [Early 19thC. From French, literally 'flow', from the feminine past participle of couler 'to flow', from Latin colare 'to strain' (see COLANDER).]

coulis /kooli/ (plural -lis /-li/) n. a thin puree of fruit or vegetables used as a garnish [Late 20thC. Via French from Old French coleïs, literally 'flowing'.]

coulisse /koo leess/ n. in the theatre, a piece of side scenery on a stage or the space between two of these pieces (often used in the plural) [Early 19thC. From French, from (porte) coulisse 'sliding (door)', from Old French (see PORTCULLIS).]

couloir /kool waar/ n. a broad mountain gully, especially one prone to avalanches [Early 19thC. From French, literally 'channel', from couler 'to flow' (see COULEE).]

coulomb /koo lom/ n. the SI unit of electric charge equal to the amount of charge transported by a current of one ampere in one second. Symbol **C** [Late 19thC. Named after the French physicist Charles Augustin de Coulomb (1736–1806), because of his work in electrostatics.]

Coulomb's law n. a law of electricity stating that the force of attraction or repulsion between two electric charges is proportional to their product and inversely proportional to the square of the distance between them [Mid-19thC. Named after the physicist who formulated it (see COULOMB).]

coulometry /koo lómmitri/ n. a means of analysing the results of a process of electrolysis by measuring the amount of electricity used in the process to determine the amount of the substance produced [Mid-20thC. Coined from COULOMB + -METRY.] —**coulometric** /koolə méttrik/ adj. —**coulometrically** /-méttrikli/ adv.

coulter /kóltər/ n. a vertical blade attached to a plough that cuts into the soil in front of a ploughshare [Pre-12thC. From Latin culter 'knife, ploughshare' (source of English cutlass and cutlery). Ultimately from an Indo-European word meaning 'to cut', which also produced English shell, scale, and skill.]

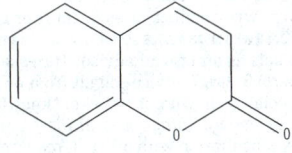

Coumarin

coumarin /koomərin/ n. a fragrant compound found naturally in plants or made synthetically, used in perfumes and in medicine. Formula: $C_9H_6O_2$. [Mid-19thC. Via French from, ultimately, Tupi cumarú 'tonka bean tree', one of the plants from which coumarin is obtained.] —**coumaric** adj.

council /kównss'l/ *n.* **1.** PUBLIC ADMIN **PEOPLE RUNNING LOCAL AFFAIRS** a group of people elected to run the administrative affairs of a local district **2. COMMITTEE** an appointed or elected body of people with an administrative, advisory, or representative function **3.** CHR **CHURCH ASSEMBLY** an assembly of church representatives who meet to decide matters of discipline and doctrine **4.** *Aus* PUBLIC ADMIN **AUSTRALIAN PARLIAMENT'S UPPER HOUSE** the upper house of a state parliament in Australia **5. COUNCIL MEETING** a meeting of a council **6. MEETING FOR DISCUSSION** a meeting to discuss or decide sth [Pre-12thC. Via Anglo-Norman *cuncile* from Latin *concilium*, literally 'calling together'. Ultimately from an Indo-European word meaning 'to call', which also produced English *low, claim,* and *calendar.*]

WORD KEY: USAGE

council or **counsel**? ***Council*** is a noun only, meaning an assembly or a body of persons or their deliberations. ***Counsel*** is both a noun and a verb, and has to do with advice, particularly of a professional nature, and the giving of it. The noun ***counsel*** most often means a lawyer or lawyers dealing with a legal case, whereas a ***counsellor*** gives some other kind of professional advice. The verb describes the activity of such advisers: *The company psychologist counsels employees having stress problems. International financial analysts counselled caution.*

council estate *n. UK* an estate of houses and flats built by the local council and available at a subsidized rent

council house (*plural* **council houses**) *n. UK* a house owned by a local council and let at a relatively low rent —**council housing** *n.*

councillor /kównsələr/ *n.* **1. MEMBER OF LOCAL GOVERNMENT COUNCIL** a member of a council elected to run the administrative affairs of a local district **2. MEMBER OF ADVISORY COUNCIL** an elected or appointed member of an advisory council [14thC. Alteration of COUNSELLOR by association with COUNCIL.] —**councillorship** *n.*

councilman /kównss'lmən/ (*plural* **-men** /-mən/) *n. US* a man who is a member of a council, especially of a local authority

Council of Europe *n.* an organization of European states founded in 1949 to further political unity

Council of Trent *n.* a Roman Catholic Church council held in Trento, Italy, from 1545 to 1563 to respond to the threat from Protestantism. The council reaffirmed and defined Roman Catholic beliefs and laid the foundation for the Counter-Reformation.

council of war *n.* **1. STRATEGIC WARTIME MEETING** a wartime meeting of military officers to discuss a plan of action **2. EMERGENCY MEETING** a meeting called to formulate a plan of action in an emergency

councilor *n.* US = **councillor**

council tax *n.* in the UK, a local tax that is levied on the basis of the estimated value of a property. The tax was introduced in 1993 to replace the short-lived community charge and the earlier rates system.

councilwoman /kównss'l wŏŏmən/ (*plural* **-en** /-wimmin/) *n. US* a woman member of a council, especially of a local authority

counsel /kównss'l/ *n.* **1. COURT LAWYER** a lawyer or group of lawyers who conduct cases in court or give legal advice **2. SB WHO GIVES ADVICE** sb whose advice is sought, or who acts as an official advisor (*takes singular or plural verb*) **3. ADVICE** advice sought from or given by sb, especially sb who is wise or knowledgeable (*formal or literary*) (*often used in the plural*) **4. CONSULTATION** consultation with others (*archaic or literary*) ■ *vt.* (**-sels, -selling, -selled**) **1. ADVISE TO DO STH** to advise sb on a particular course of action (*formal or literary*) **2. ADVISE ON PERSONAL PROBLEMS** to give sb advice and support on personal or psychological matters, usually in a professional context [12thC. Via Old French *conseil* from, ultimately, Latin *consilium* 'consultation, deliberating body', from *consulere* 'to seek advice'.] ◇ **keep your own counsel** to keep your thoughts and intentions secret

WORD KEY: USAGE

Counsel, meaning a lawyer, is often mispronounced 'consul', the latter word meaning a foreign service officer attached to and running a consulate. See also Usage note at ***council.***

WORD KEY: SYNONYMS

See Synonyms at ***recommend.***

counseling /kównss'ling/ *n.* US = **counselling**

counsellee /kównss' lée/ *n.* sb who is receiving counselling

counselling /kównss'ling/ *n.* **1. HELP WITH PERSONAL PROBLEMS** help with personal or psychological matters usually given by a professional **2. MEETINGS WITH COUNSELLOR** meetings with a counsellor to receive help with personal or psychological problems

counsellor /kównss'lər/ *n.* **1. SB WHO GIVES ADVICE** sb, e.g. a friend, who gives advice **2.** SOC WELFARE **ADVISER ON PERSONAL PROBLEMS** sb, usually a professional, who helps others with personal, social, or psychological problems **3.** EDUC, MED **ADVISER ON SPECIAL SUBJECT** a professional who gives advice on such matters as careers, education, or health **4. counsellor, counsellor-at-law** (*plural* **counsellors-at-law**) *US* LAW **LAWYER** a lawyer, especially one who acts for a client in a trial **5. counsellor, counsellor-at-law** (*plural* **counsellors-at-law**) LAW **ADVISORY BARRISTER** in Ireland, a barrister who acts in an advisory capacity **6.** PUBLIC ADMIN **SENIOR DIPLOMAT** an officer of senior grade in the diplomatic service **7.** *US* PUBLIC ADMIN **HIGH-RANKING DIPLOMAT** a diplomat ranking below an ambassador or minister **8.** *US* LEISURE **CHILDREN'S SUPERVISOR** sb who supervises young people at a summer camp [12thC. Partly from French *conseiller* (from Latin *consiliarius*), and partly from French *conseilleur* (from Latin *consiliator*), both ultimately from Latin *consilium* (see COUNSEL).] —**counsellorship** *n.*

counselor *n.* US = **counsellor**

count[1] /kownt/ *v.* (**counts, counting, counted**) **1.** *vti.* **SAY NUMBERS** to say numbers in order, usually starting at one **2.** *vti.* **ADD UP** to add things up to see how many there are or to find the value of an amount of money **3.** *vt.* **INCLUDE** to include sb or sth in a calculation **4.** *vti.* **CONSIDER OR BE CONSIDERED** to consider sb or sth, or be considered, in a particular way or as a particular thing **5.** *vi.* **BE OF IMPORTANCE** to be of importance or value **6.** *vi.* **HAVE A VALUE** to have a specific value **7.** *vti.* MUSIC, DANCE **KEEP TIME** to keep time by counting beats ■ *n.* **1. SAYING OF NUMBERS** an act of saying numbers in order **2. FINDING OF TOTAL** an addition of people or things to find a total **3. TOTAL** a total that is reached by adding up **4. ONE OF MANY POINTS** any one of a number of points, e.g. in a discussion **5.** LAW **CHARGE AGAINST SB** a charge against sb who is on trial **6.** BOXING **BOXING REFEREE'S COUNT** a count to ten by the referee in a boxing match during which a boxer who has been knocked down must stand up or lose the match **7.** WRESTLING **WRESTLING REFEREE'S COUNT** a count to three by the referee at a wrestling match during which a wrestler being held on the floor must break the hold or lose the point [14thC. The noun is via old French *conte*; the verb directly from Old French *conter* 'to reckon', from Latin *computare*, literally 'to reckon together'.] ◇ **keep count** to count and remember the number of people or things counted ◇ **lose count** to fail to count accurately or remember the number of people or things counted ◇ **out for the count 1.** unconscious or deeply asleep and unlikely to wake again for some time (*informal*) **2.** BOXING unable to stand up, after being knocked down, within the ten-second count given by the referee, and therefore losing the match

count against *vt.* to be detrimental to sb's interests or prospects

count down *vi.* to count backwards from a number to zero, or from a given time to sth such as the launch of a rocket

count in *vt.* to include sb in a plan

count on *vt.* **1. RELY ON** to rely on sb to do sth **2. BE SURE OF** to be sure that sth will happen

count out *vt.* **1. COUNT ONE BY ONE** to count sth, e.g. money, one item at a time **2. NOT INCLUDE** to exclude sb from a plan **3.** BOXING **DECLARE BOXER DEFEATED BY COUNTING TEN** to disqualify a boxer who has been knocked down and fails to get up within ten seconds

count towards, count toward *vt.* to be included as part of sth

count upon *vt.* = **count on**

count[2] /kownt/ *n.* a nobleman in certain European countries, with a rank equal to that of a British earl [14thC. Via old French *conte* from Latin *comit-*, the stem of *comes* 'companion', later 'member of the imperial court', literally 'sb who goes with'.]

countable /kówntəb'l/ *adj.* **1. THAT CAN BE COUNTED** able to be counted **2.** GRAM **ABLE TO FORM A PLURAL** used to describe a noun that can be used with 'a' or 'an' and with a plural verb, usually in a distinct plural form —**countability** /kówntə bílləti/ *n.* —**countably** /-bli/ *adv.*

countdown /kównt down/ *n.* **1. BACKWARDS COUNT** a count in descending order before an event such as a rocket launch **2. ACTIVITIES BEFORE AN EVENT** the activities carried on during the period of time before sth such as a rocket launch **3. PREPARATORY PERIOD** the period immediately preceding an important event

countenance /kówntənənss/ *n.* **1. FACE OR EXPRESSION** sb's face, or the expression on it **2. COMPOSURE** composure or self-control ■ *vt.* (**-nances, -nancing, -nanced**) **TOLERATE OR APPROVE** to tolerate, accept, or give approval to sth (*formal*) [13thC. From old French *contenance* 'demeanour', literally 'contents', from *contenir* (see CONTAIN).] —**countenancer** *n.*

counter[1] /kówntər/ *n.* **1. FLAT SURFACE** a flat surface on which food or drink is served, goods are displayed, or business is transacted **2. FLAT SURFACE IN KITCHEN** a kitchen worktop **3.** LEISURE **SMALL MARKER** a small object, often a flat disc, used in games to mark a player's position or to keep score **4. IMITATION COIN** an object, usually a flat disc, used as a substitute for a coin [14thC. Via Anglo-Norman *counteor* from medieval Latin *computatorium*, literally 'place for counting', from Latin *computare* (see COUNT[1]).] ◇ **under the counter** secretly and unofficially, usually because there is sth illegal about what is being done

counter[2] /kówntər/ *vti.* (**counters, countering, countered**) **1. CONTRADICT OR OPPOSE** to say sth that contradicts or opposes what sb has said **2. DO STH IN OPPOSITION** to do sth in opposition to what sb is doing, to make it less effective **3.** BOXING **PUNCH OPPONENT IN RETURN** to defend yourself against a punch from an opponent and deliver a punch in return ■ *adv.* **1. OPPOSITE** in the opposite direction **2. CONTRARILY** in a contrary manner ■ *adj.* **CONTRADICTING** contradicting or opposing sth ○ *a counter blow* ■ *n.* **1. RESPONSE** a response made in retaliation to sth that has been said **2. OPPOSITE** sth that is the opposite of sth else or that is done in opposition to sth else **3.** BOXING **RETURN PUNCH** a punch that counters a punch aimed by an opponent **4.** FENCING **PARRY** in fencing, a parry in which the foils make a circular movement **5.** NAUT **END OF SHIP'S STERN** the part of the stern of a ship or boat that juts out above the waterline **6.** PRINTING **HOLLOW PART OF TYPEFACE** a hollow part of a piece of type, such as the inner parts of the letters 'p' and 'd' **7.** CLOTHES **LEATHER AROUND HEEL OF SHOE** a piece of leather around the heel of a shoe or boot [14thC. From COUNTER-. The underlying meaning is 'to go against'.]

counter[3] /kówntər/ *n.* **1. DEVICE THAT COUNTS** a device that counts automatically **2. SB WHO COUNTS** sb whose job is to count sth, e.g. votes

counter- *prefix.* **1.** contrary, opposing ○ *counterattack* **2.** complementary, corresponding ○ *counterpart* [Via Anglo-Norman *countre-* from, ultimately, Latin *contra* (see CONTRA-)]

counteract /kówntər ákt/ (**-acts, -acting, -acted**) *vt.* to prevent sth having an effect, or lessen its effect —**counteraction** *n.* —**counteractive** *adj.* —**counteractively** *adv.*

counterargument /kówntər aargyŏŏmənt/ *n.* a fact or opinion that challenges the reasoning behind sb's proposal and shows that there are grounds for taking an opposite view

counterattack /kówntər ə tak/ *n.* **RESPONSE TO ATTACK** an attack made in response to an attack by an enemy or opponent ■ *vti.* (**-tacks, -tacking, -tacked**) **LAUNCH COUNTERATTACK** to launch a counterattack against an enemy or opponent

counterattraction /kówntər ə tráksh'n/ *n.* sth set up to draw people away from another attraction

counterbalance /kówntər ballənss/ *vt.* (**-ances, -ancing, -anced**) **1. HAVE EQUAL AND OPPOSING EFFECT ON** to be or have an equal and opposing force or effect on

a at; aa father; aw all; ay day; air hair; ə about, edible, item, common, circus; e egg; ee eel; hw when; i it, happy; ī ice; 'l apple; 'm rhythm; 'n fashion; o odd; ō open; ŏŏ good; oo pool; ow owl; oy oil; th thin; th this; u up; ur urge;

sth **2.** BALANCE WITH EQUAL WEIGHT to make sth balance by putting equal weight on the opposite side ■ *n.* **1.** COUNTERBALANCING PERSON OR THING sb who or sth that is or has an equal and opposing force or effect **2.** WEIGHT THAT BALANCES ANOTHER a weight that exactly balances another weight

counterbattery fire /kówntər battəri-/ *n.* firing weapons with the aim of destroying enemy artillery

counterblast /kówntər blaast/ *n.* **1.** ANGRY REPLY an attack on sb in speech or writing, made in response to an attack by that person **2.** COUNTERACTING BLAST a blast that counters the effect of a preceding blast

counterchange /kówntər chaynj/ **(-changes, -changing, -changed)** *v.* **1.** *vti.* INTERCHANGE to interchange the parts or positions of two things **2.** *vt.* CHEQUER to chequer or dapple sth with colours (*literary*)

countercharge /kówntər chaarj/ *n.* **1.** ACCUSATION AGAINST ACCUSER a charge or accusation made against the person or group who has accused another of sth **2.** MIL CHARGE COUNTERING ENEMY'S CHARGE a military charge made to counter an enemy's charge ■ *vt.* **(-charges, -charging, -charged)** CHARGE ACCUSER WITH STH to bring a charge against an accuser

countercheck /kówntər chek/ *n.* **1.** SECOND CHECK a check made to ensure that a previous check was correct **2.** RESTRAINT ON STH sth that acts to block or restrain sth else ■ *v.* **(-checks, -checking, -checked) 1.** *vti.* CHECK AGAIN to carry out a second check on sth, in order to ensure that the first was accurate **2.** *vt.* RESTRAIN to act in order to block the force or action of sth

counterclaim /kówntər klaym/ *n.* CLAIM ENTERED BY DEFENDANT a claim entered by the defendant in a court of civil law, as a response to the original claim that was entered against the defendant by the plaintiff ■ *vti.* **(-claims, -claiming, -claimed)** RESPOND TO ONE CLAIM WITH ANOTHER to make a claim in response to, or as a defence against, an earlier claim —**counterclaimant** /kówntər kláymənt/ *n.*

counterclockwise /kówntər klók wīz/ *adv. US, Can* = **anticlockwise** ■ *adj. US, Can* = **anticlockwise**

counterconditioning /kówntər kən dísh'ning/ *n.* a process of psychological conditioning that attempts to replace sb's undesired habitual response to a particular situation with a desired learned response

countercoup /kówntər koo/ *n.* a coup made against a group that has seized political power in an earlier coup

counterculture /kówntər kulchər/ *n.* a culture that has ideas and ways of behaving that are consciously and deliberately very different from the cultural values of the larger society that it is part of —**countercultural** *adj.* —**counterculturist** *n.*

countercurrent /kówntər kurrənt/ *n.* CURRENT FLOWING OPPOSITE WAY a current that flows in the opposite direction to another current ■ *adj.* **1.** FLOWING IN OPPOSITE DIRECTION flowing in the opposite direction to another current **2.** USING OPPOSING CURRENTS involving the flow of two currents in opposite directions —**countercurrently** *adv.*

counterdemonstration /kówntər deman stráysh'n/ *n.* a public demonstration that is held to oppose the purpose of another demonstration that was recently held or is currently being held —**counterdemonstrator** /-démən straytər/ *n.*

counterespionage /kówntər éspi ə naazh/ *n.* government activity designed to detect and prevent spying by agents of other countries who are operating against that government's country

counterexample /kówntər ig zaamp'l/ *n.* a fact or argument that indicates that a theory, scientific hypothesis, or mathematical theorem is not true

counterfactual /kówntər fákchoo əl/ *adj.* **1.** CONTRARY TO THE FACTS not reflecting or taking into account the facts **2.** LOGIC EXPRESSING WHAT MIGHT HAVE HAPPENED expressing what has not actually happened but might have happened in other circumstances ■ *n.* LOGIC STATEMENT OF WHAT MIGHT HAVE HAPPENED a statement expressing sth that did not happen but might have

counterfeit /kówntərfit/ *adj.* **1.** FORGED made as a copy of sth, especially money, in order to defraud or deceive people **2.** FALSE pretended in order to deceive sb ○ *counterfeit geniality* ■ *vti.* **(-feits, -feiting, -feited) 1.** FORGE to make realistic copies of sth, especially money, in order to defraud or deceive people **2.** PRETEND to pretend to have an emotion in order to deceive sb ■ *n.* FORGERY a copy of sth, especially money, made in order to defraud or deceive people [14thC. From Anglo-Norman *countrefet*, the past participle of *countrefaire* 'to counterfeit', from medieval Latin *contrafacere*, from Latin *contra-* 'against'+ *facere* 'to make' (see FACT).] —**counterfeiter** *n.*

counterfoil /kówntər foyl/ *n.* the part of a cheque, ticket, or other paper used in a financial transaction that is detached and kept by the issuer as a record

counterfort /kówntər fawrt/ *n.* a type of buttress that sticks out at right angles from a wall [Late 16thC. From French *contrefort*, from Old French *contreforcier* 'buttress'.]

counterglow /kówntər glō/ *n.* = **gegenschein** [Mid-19thC. Translation of German *Gegenschein*.]

counterhegemonic *adj. US* contrary to the prevailing fashion, especially in intellectual matters [Late 20thC. Formed from COUNTER- + HEGEMONY.]

counterinsurgency /kówntər in súrjənssi/ *n.* military and political activities undertaken by a government to defeat a rebellion or guerrilla movement —**counterinsurgent** *n.*

counterintelligence /kówntər in téllijənss/ *n.* government and military activities designed to gather information about enemy spies, thwart their activities, and supply them with false information

counterintuitive /kówntər in tyoó itiv/ *adj.* not in accordance with what would naturally be assumed or expected ○ *I know it's counterintuitive, but the highest grade in this system is D and the lowest is A.* —**counterintuitively** *adv.*

counterirritant /kówntər írritənt/ *n.* a substance applied to the skin in the belief that the irritation produced will reduce the inflammation of underlying tissue —**counterirritation** /kówntər írri táysh'n/ *n.*

countermand /kówntər maánd, kówntər maand/ *vt.* **(-mands, -manding, -manded) 1.** CANCEL A COMMAND to give an order or instruction that a previous order or instruction should not be followed **2.** RECALL to recall sb or sth sent somewhere by a previous order ■ *n.* ORDER CANCELLING ANOTHER an order cancelling a previous order [15thC. From old French *contremander*, from, ultimately, Latin *mandare* 'to command' (see MANDATE).]

countermarch /kówntər maarch/ *n.* **1.** RETURN MARCH a march, especially one undertaken by soldiers, back from a position following the same route as that taken on the outward march **2.** CHANGE IN MARCHING DIRECTION a marching manoeuvre in which soldiers change the direction they are marching in while retaining their positions within a formation **3.** COMPLETE CHANGE OF APPROACH a complete change in sb's behaviour or way of doing things ■ *v.* **(-marches, -marching, -marched) 1.** *vti.* MARCH BACK to return from a position by marching back along the same route, or to make soldiers do this **2.** *vi.* CHANGE DIRECTION OF MARCHING to change the direction of a formation of marching soldiers without altering the positions of the individual soldiers

countermeasure /kówntər mezhər/ *n.* sth that is done in reaction to and as defence against a hostile action by sb else, or is done in order to deal with a threatening situation

countermine /kówntər mīn/ *v.* **(-mines, -mining, -mined) 1.** *vti.* EXPLODE ENEMY'S MINES IN AN AREA to place explosive mines in an area in order to explode mines placed there by an enemy **2.** *vti.* DIG TUNNELS AGAINST ENEMY'S TUNNELS to dig underground tunnels in order to intercept or destroy tunnels dug by an enemy **3.** *vt.* SECRETLY FOIL PLOT to take secret action against sb's plans ■ *n.* **1.** TUNNEL DUG AGAINST ENEMY'S TUNNELS a tunnel dug to intercept or destroy tunnels dug by an enemy **2.** SECRET ACTION TO FOIL PLOT a secret action designed to undermine or destroy a plot or scheme

countermove /kówntər moov/ *n.* RESPONSE a move made in response to an opponent's move, e.g. in a game ■ *vi.* **(-moves, -moving, -moved)** RESPOND to act in response to an opponent's action, e.g. in a game —**countermovement** *n.*

counteroffensive /kówntər ə fenssiv/ *n.* a major attack or series of attacks made by a military force in response to the attacks made by an enemy

counteroffer /kówntər ofər/ *n.* an offer made by sb selling sth, usually a reduction in what was first asked, made to persuade the buyer to improve a previous unsatisfactory offer

counterpane /kówntər payn/ *n.* a cover for a bed and its bedding (*dated*) [15thC. Alteration, under the influence of pane 'panel', of earlier *counterpoint*, via Old French from, ultimately, medieval Latin *culcita puncta*, literally 'stitched quilt'.]

counterpart /kówntər paart/ *n.* **1.** SB OR STH CORRESPONDING TO ANOTHER sb who or sth that has very similar characteristics to another person or thing, or plays a very similar part in a different system or organization **2.** MATCHING PART OR THING either of two parts that fit together, or either of two things that complement each other ○ *I identified bolt A but could not find its counterpart, socket B.* **3.** ARTS ACTOR PLAYING OPPOSITE ANOTHER sb who plays opposite another person in a play or film **4.** LAW COPY OF LEGAL DOCUMENT a copy of a lease, contract, or other legal document that is held by one party to a transaction and that duplicates the copy held by the other party

counterplan /kówntər plan/ *n.* **1.** OPPOSING PLAN a plan made to defeat or respond to another plan **2.** ALTERNATIVE PLAN a plan prepared as an alternative or substitute for the primary plan

counterplea /kówntər plee/ *n.* a plea made by the plaintiff in a court of law in response to the plea made by the defendant

counterplot /kówntər plot/ *n.* PLOT MADE AGAINST PLOT a plot made in order to defeat an enemy's or opponent's plot ■ *vi.* **(-plots, -plotting, -plotted)** MAKE COUNTERPLOT to make a plot designed to defeat an enemy's or opponent's plot

counterpoint /kówntər poynt/ *n.* **1.** SOUNDING TOGETHER OF MELODIES the sounding together of two or more melodic lines in a piece of music, each of which displays an individual and differentiated melodic contour and rhythmic profile **2.** MELODY COMBINED WITH ANOTHER in a piece of music, a melodic line or part that is sung or played at the same time as another **3.** CONTRASTING ELEMENT a theme or element in a work of art that forms a contrast with another ■ *vt.* **(-points, -pointing, -pointed) 1.** CONTRAST WITH to make an effective contrast with sth, especially in a work of art ○ *Richard's social ease counterpoints his sister's awkwardness.* **2.** ARRANGE MUSIC IN COUNTERPOINT to add one or more melodic lines in counterpoint in a piece of music [15thC. Via French from, ultimately, medieval Latin *(cantus) contrapunctus*, literally '(song) with notes marked opposite (the melody)'.]

counterpoise /kówntər poyz/ *n.* **1.** COUNTERACTING WEIGHT a weight that balances another weight **2.** COMPENSATING FACTOR sth that has the effect of diminishing or compensating for the effect of sth else ○ *The government had covertly encouraged the fascists as a counterpoise to the reformers.* **3.** BALANCED STATE a state of balance ■ *vt.* **(-poises, -poising, -poised) 1.** OPPOSE AND BALANCE STH to counteract or compensate for sth by providing an equal force, influence, or weight **2.** MAKE BALANCED to bring sth into a state of balance [15thC. Alteration, under the influence of *poise* 'balance', of French *contrepeis*, literally 'counterweight'.]

counterproductive /kówntər prə dúktiv/ *adj.* producing problems or difficulties instead of helping to achieve a goal ○ *A direct challenge to her authority is likely to be counterproductive.* —**counterproductively** *adv.*

counterproof /kówntər proof/ *n.* an impression taken from a new print of an engraving while it is still wet, producing a reversed image of the print

counterproposal /kówntər prə pōz'l/ *n.* a suggestion made in response to, and with the hope of modifying or replacing, another suggestion in a negotiation

counterpunch /kówntər punch/ *n.* COUNTERATTACKING PUNCH a punch made by a boxer in response to an opponent's punch ■ *vi.* **(-punches, -punching, -punched)** BOX BACK to punch in response to an opposing boxer's punches —**counterpuncher** *n.*

counter-reformation *n.* a reform or reform movement that seeks to reverse the effects of earlier reforms

Counter-Reformation *n.* the movement of reform and regeneration instituted by the Roman Catholic Church in 1545 to counter the increasing strength of Protestantism in Europe as a result of the Reformation

counter-revolution *n.* **1.** REVOLUTION OPPOSING PREVIOUS REVOLUTION a revolution with the aim of undoing the effects of a previous revolution and overthrowing the government or social system that it produced **2.** ACTIVITY AGAINST RESULTS OF REVOLUTION subversive activity aimed at undoing the results of a revolution and overthrowing the government or social system that it produced —**counter-revolutionist** *n.*

counter-revolutionary *n.* (*plural* **counter-revolutionaries**) **1.** SB FIGHTING REVOLUTIONARY GOVERNMENT sb, especially a member of a military force, who seeks to overthrow a national government or social system established by a revolution **2.** SB OPPOSED TO REVOLUTION sb who is opposed to revolution as a means of political and social change ■ *adj.* OPPOSED TO REVOLUTION opposed to a specific revolution or to revolution as a means of political and social change

countersank past tense of **countersink**

counterscarp /kówntər skaarp/ *n.* the slope or bank on the outer side of the ditch outside a fort [Late 16thC. Via French *contrescarpe* from Italian *controscarpa*, from *scarpa* (see SCARP).]

countershading /kówntər shayding/ *n.* a pattern of colouring on an animal's skin or coat where the upper parts are darker than the lower, counteracting the effects of sun and shade and camouflaging the animal

countershaft /kówntər shaaft/ *n.* an intermediate shaft that transmits power from the main shaft to a working part but rotates in the opposite direction, especially in a belt drive or gear drive

countersign /kówntər sīn/ *vt.* (**-signs, -signing, -signed**) SIGN DOCUMENT ALREADY SIGNED to sign a document that sb else has signed, e.g. as a witness to the signature or to confirm an authorization ■ *n.* **1.** MIL SECRET PASSWORD an agreed and secret sign, word, or signal given as a password to a military sentry in order to pass **2.** = **countersignature**

countersignature /kówntər signəchər/ *n.* a signature added to a document that has already been signed, e.g. to witness the first signature or to confirm an authorization

countersink /kówntər singk/ *vt.* (**-sinks, -sinking, -sank** /-sangk/, **-sunk** /-sungk/) **1.** MAKE SCREW HEADS LEVEL WITH SURFACE to place screws, bolts, or nails in wood or another material so that their heads are level with or below the surface of the material **2.** MAKE HOLE TO INCLUDE SCREW HEAD to widen the top of the hole for a screw or bolt so that the head will fit into the hole and be flush with or below the surface ■ *n.* **1.** HOLE THAT ACCEPTS SCREW HEAD a hole for a screw or bolt that is wider at the top so that the head will fit into the hole and be flush with or below the surface **2.** COUNTERSINKING TOOL a special drill bit or other tool for countersinking holes for screws or bolts

counterspy /kówntər spī/ (*plural* **-spies**) *n.* a spy who spies on and seeks to thwart enemy spies

counterstain /kówntər stayn/ *n.* ADDITIONAL STAIN FOR MICROSCOPE SPECIMEN an additional stain applied to a specimen to be examined under a microscope, in order to bring out features not revealed by the primary stain ■ *vt.* (**-stains, -staining, -stained**) ADD COUNTERSTAIN to use a counterstain on a microscope specimen

countersubject /kówntər sub jekt/ *n.* a second theme or melodic line that contrasts with the main one in a fugue or other piece of music employing counterpoint

countersue /kówntər syoo/ (**-sues, -suing, -sued**) *vti.* to bring a lawsuit against sb who is suing you

countersunk past participle of **countersink**

countertenor /kówntər tenər/ *n.* **1.** HIGH MALE SINGING VOICE an adult male singing voice that is higher than tenor and covers the alto range, produced by singing in falsetto **2.** MAN WITH HIGH SINGING VOICE a man whose singing voice is a countertenor [14thC. Via French *contrateneur* from obsolete Italian *contratenore*, literally 'against the tenor'.]

counterterrorism /kówntər térrərizzəm/ *n.* **1.** ACTIVITIES TO COMBAT TERRORISM military or political activities intended to combat or prevent terrorism **2.** TERRORIST ACTIVITIES AGAINST TERRORISM terrorist activities undertaken in revenge for or in retaliation against terrorism —**counterterrorist** *adj., n.*

countertop /kówntər top/ *n.* *US, Can* the surface of a worktop, especially in a kitchen, or of the top of a counter in a shop

countertrade /kówntər trayd/ *n.* a system of international trade in which countries exchange goods or services, rather than paying for imports with currency —**countertrader** *n.*

countertransference /kówntər transfərənss/ *n.* a process that sometimes occurs in psychoanalytic therapy where repressed emotions in the therapist are awakened by identification with the experiences and feelings of the patient

countertype /kówntər tīp/ *n.* **1.** OPPOSITE TYPE a type that is the complete opposite of another type **2.** CORRESPONDING TYPE a type that corresponds with or is equivalent to another type

countervail /kówntər váyl/ (**-vails, -vailing, -vailed**) *v.* **1.** *vti.* EXERT COUNTERACTING EFFECT to exert a counteracting power or influence against sth, especially against a harmful force, idea, or influence **2.** *vt.* OFFSET to offset or compensate for sth [14thC. From Anglo-Norman *contrevaloir*, literally 'to be worth against'.]

countervailing duty (*plural* **countervailing duties**) *n.* an import duty on commodities that can be produced very cheaply in their country of origin, e.g. because of a subsidy, imposed in order to protect domestic producers

counterweigh /kówntər wáy/ (**-weighs, -weighing, -weighed**) *vt.* to counterbalance sth, or use sth to counterbalance sth

counterweight /kówntər wayt/ *n.* **1.** COUNTERBALANCING WEIGHT a weight that balances another weight **2.** STH WITH COMPENSATORY EFFECT sth that counteracts or compensates for sth else, e.g. a force, idea, or influence —**counterweighted** *adj.*

counterwork /kówntər wurk/ *n.* **1.** WORK COUNTERACTING OTHER WORK work or action undertaken to counteract other work or another action **2.** MIL FORTIFICATIONS fortifications against an attack

countess /kówntiss, -ess, kown téss/ *n.* **1.** WIFE OF COUNT OR EARL a woman who is married to a count or an earl, or who is the widow of a count or an earl **2.** FEMALE EQUIVALENT OF COUNT OR EARL a woman who holds the rank of count or earl in her own right [12thC. Via Old French *contesse* from medieval Latin *comitissa*, the feminine form of *comes* (see COUNT²).]

counting house (*plural* **counting houses**) *n.* the place where the financial work of a business is done or where its accounts are kept (*archaic*)

countless /kówntləss/ *adj.* many more than it is possible or convenient to count ○ *I've told him countless times to be more careful.* —**countlessly** *adv.*

count noun *n.* a noun that refers to one thing rather than a mass of sth and that can be used with 'a' or 'an', with a number, and in the plural. Examples of English count nouns are 'cat', 'sheep', and 'child'.

count palatine /-pállə teen/ (*plural* **counts palatine**) *n.* **1.** LOCAL RULER IN HOLY ROMAN EMPIRE a count who ruled over his own domain (**county palatine**) in the Holy Roman Empire, or an official who ruled an area of the empire as the emperor's representative **2.** SB WITH JUDICIAL POWER OVER COUNTY in former times, an earl or other nobleman in England or Ireland who held the highest judicial authority and other supreme powers within his own domain (**county palatine**) **3.** ROMAN PALACE OFFICIAL a palace official with judicial authority in the late Roman Empire

countrified /kúntri fīd/, **countryfied** *adj.* **1.** WITH A COUNTRY AIR having a style or quality appropriate to the country ○ *a pretty, countrified row of houses* **2.** UNSOPHISTICATED not fashionable or sophisticated and of a style or quality that is typical of rural areas

country /kúntri/ *n.* (*plural* **-tries**) **1.** SEPARATE NATION a nation or state that is politically independent, or a land that was formerly independent and remains separate in some respects **2.** HOMELAND the nation or state where sb was born or is a citizen **3.** GEOGRAPHICALLY DISTINCT AREA a large area of land regarded as distinct from other areas, e.g. because of its natural boundaries or because it is inhabited by a particular people ○ *The country was settled by Europeans in the 16th century.* **4.** FARMED AND UNDEVELOPED AREA an area that is farmed or remains in a relatively undeveloped state, as distinct from cities, towns, and other built-up areas ○ *a house in the country* **5.** REGION WITH SPECIAL CHARACTER a region that is distinguished by particular characteristics or is associated with a particular activity, person, or group of people ○ *This was chapel country, and all the pubs were closed.* **6.** NATION'S PEOPLE the people of a nation or state, especially when affected as a group by political or other events ○ *a scandal that rocked the country* **7.** = **country music** ■ *adj.* **1.** TYPICAL OF RURAL AREAS typical of rural areas or the people living there **2.** OF COUNTRY MUSIC typical of, similar to, or performing country music [13thC. Via Old French *cuntrée* from assumed Vulgar Latin *(terra) contrata*, literally '(land) lying opposite', from Latin *contra* 'against'.] —**countryish** *adj.* ◇ **go to the country** to hold a general election

country and western *n.* = **country music** (*hyphenated when used before a noun*)

country bumpkin *n.* = **bumpkin**

country club *n.* a club for social and leisure activities that has facilities for golf, tennis, or other outdoor sports, usually located in the suburbs or the country

country code *n.* a code of conduct for people spending leisure time in the country, suggesting how to respect the natural environment and avoid causing damage and harm

country cousin *n.* sb from the country whose unsophisticated reactions to town life are amusing (*dated*)

country dance *n.* a folk dance in which several couples form a square, a circle, or two lines, and perform a set of movements —**country dancing** *n.*

countryfied *adj.* = **countrified**

country gentleman *n.* a man who owns an estate in the country

country house *n.* a large house in the country, often with a large area of land attached

countryman /kúntrimən/ (*plural* **-men** /-mən/) *n.* **1.** SB FROM THE COUNTRY sb who lives in the country, especially sb brought up there and familiar with rural life and pursuits **2.** SB FROM SAME NATION sb who was born in or has become a citizen of the same nation as sb else **3.** SB FROM PARTICULAR NATION sb who is from or is a citizen of a particular nation

country music *n.* a type of American popular music, based on the traditional music of the rural South and the cowboy music of the West, whose songs express strong personal emotions. Country musicians typically play such instruments as the guitar and fiddle. —**country musician** *n.*

country park *n.* an area of countryside in Britain that has been set aside for public recreational use through the agency of the Countryside Commission

country rock *n.* **1.** MUSIC COUNTRY-INFLUENCED ROCK MUSIC a type of rock music that is strongly influenced by American country music **2.** GEOL ROCK SURROUNDING OTHER ROCK rock that has been intruded by magma or that surrounds veins of mineral ore

country seat *n.* an estate or a large house in the country that is the hereditary property of a particular family

countryside /kúntri sīd/ *n.* **1.** RURAL LAND an area of land that is farmed or in a relatively undeveloped state ○ *a village set in wooded countryside* **2.** COUNTRY PEOPLE the people who live in a country area ○ *The entire countryside was up in arms against the proposed development.*

Countryside Commission *n.* a British organization concerned with the preservation of the countryside in England and Wales and with setting up country parks for public recreation

Countryside Commission for Scotland *n.* a British organization concerned with the preservation of the countryside in Scotland and with setting up country parks for public recreation

countrywide /kúntri wīd/ *adj., adv.* throughout an entire nation ○ *a countrywide organization for professional women* ○ *rates that were increased countrywide*

countrywoman /kúntri wŏŏmən/ (*plural* **-en** /-wimin/) *n.* **1.** WOMAN FROM THE COUNTRY a woman who lives in the country, especially one brought up there and familiar with rural life and pursuits **2.** WOMAN FROM SAME NATION a woman who was born in or is a citizen of the same nation as sb else **3.** WOMAN FROM PARTICULAR NATION a woman who was born in or is a citizen of a particular nation

county /kównti/ *n.* (*plural* **-ties**) **1.** LOCAL GOVERNMENT AREA a unit of local government and one of the administrative subdivisions that the states of the United States and, excepting major cities, all of England and Wales are divided into **2.** PEOPLE OF A COUNTY the people who live in a county **3.** COUNT'S OR EARL'S DOMAIN the lands controlled by a count or an earl (*archaic*) ■ *adj.* SUGGESTIVE OF RICH COUNTRY FAMILIES belonging to or typical of long-established British upper-class or wealthy families who live in the country (*informal*) ○ *girls from county families* [13thC. Via Anglo-Norman *counté* from, ultimately, Latin *comitatus*, literally 'group of companions', from *comes* (see COUNT[2]).]

county borough *n.* any town with a local government that is independent of the surrounding county, including many towns in England and Wales before 1974 and the four largest boroughs in the Republic of Ireland

county council *n.* a local government body administering a county in the United Kingdom and some parts of the United States

county court *n.* a local court in England with limited powers to decide civil cases, usually those concerning less than a given amount of money

county palatine (*plural* **counties palatine**) *n.* **1.** COUNT PALATINE'S DOMAIN the lands governed by a nobleman or imperial official with the rank of count palatine in the Holy Roman Empire **2.** EARL'S OR COUNT'S DOMAIN in England and Ireland in former times, the lands administered by an earl or other nobleman who exercised judicial authority [See COUNT PALATINE]

county seat *n. US* = **county town**

county town *n.* a town that is the seat of local government in a county. US term **county seat**

countywide /kównti wīd/ *adj., adv.* throughout an entire county

coup /koo/ *n.* **1.** SUCCESSFUL ACTION a success that is unexpected and achieved with exceptional skill ○ *Getting the author to come and speak was quite a coup.* **2.** SEIZURE OF POLITICAL POWER the sudden overthrow of a government and seizure of political power, especially in a violent way and by the military [Late 18thC. Via French, 'blow', from, ultimately, Greek *kolophos* 'blow with the fist'.]

coup de foudre /kŏŏ də fŏŏdrə/ (*plural* **coups de foudre** /kŏŏ də fŏŏdrə/) *n.* sth that happens suddenly and is amazing and overwhelming, especially a sudden feeling of admiration or love [From French, literally 'stroke of lightning']

coup de grâce /kŏŏ də graáss/ (*plural* **coups de grâce** /kŏŏ də graáss/) *n.* **1.** DEATH BLOW a final stroke or shot that kills a person or animal, especially one intended to end suffering **2.** ACT THAT ASSURES VICTORY the final action that assures victory or success, especially in a sporting event [From French, literally 'stroke of mercy']

coup de main /kŏŏ də máyn/ (*plural* **coups de main** /kŏŏ də máyn/) *n.* a sudden, fierce, and successful surprise attack against an enemy [From French, literally 'blow of the hand']

coup d'état /kŏŏ day taá/ (*plural* **coups d'état** /kŏŏz day taá/) *n.* = **coup** *n.* 2 [From French, literally 'stroke of state']

coup de théâtre /kŏŏ də tay aátrə/ (*plural* **coups de théâtre** /kŏŏ də tay aátrə/) *n.* **1.** SURPRISING TURN OF EVENTS sth that occurs in a very dramatic way, especially a sensational and unexpected turn of events **2.** THEATRE EFFECTIVE PIECE OF THEATRE a strongly dramatic moment in a play or other theatrical production, produced by an exceptional piece of writing, performance, or staging **3.** THEATRE SUCCESSFUL PLAY a play or other theatrical performance that is very successful [From French, literally 'stroke of theatre']

coup d'oeil /koo dőy/ (*plural* **coups d'oeil** /koo dőy/) *n.* a quick look at sth, especially one that provides an overall general impression (*literary*) [From French, literally 'stroke of the eye']

coupe[1] /koop/ *n.* **1.** ICE CREAM WITH FRUIT a dessert of ice cream and fruit **2.** GLASS DISH a small shallow glass bowl, often with a stem, for fruit and ice cream [Late 19thC. Via French, literally 'goblet', from medieval Latin *cuppa* (see CUP).]

coupe[2] /koop, kŏŏ pay/ *n. US* = **coupé** [Early 20thC. Variant of COUPÉ.]

coupé /kŏŏ pay/ *n.* **1.** CARS CAR WITH TWO DOORS a car with two doors, a sloping back, and a hard fixed roof **2.** TRANSP TWO-SEATER CARRIAGE a closed four-wheeled carriage that has two inside seats for passengers and a driver's seat outside in the front **3.** RAIL END COMPARTMENT IN RAILCAR an end compartment in an old type of European railway carriage, with seats on one side only [Mid-19thC. From French *(carrosse) coupé*, literally 'cut-down (carriage)' (because it was smaller than earlier models), the past participle of *couper* 'to cut' (see COPE).]

Couperin /kŏŏpə ran/, **François** (1668–1733) French composer and organist. The best-known member of a musical family, his baroque keyboard compositions greatly influenced Johann Sebastian Bach. Known as **Le Grand**

couple /kúpp'l/ *n.* **1.** TWO SIMILAR THINGS two things of the same kind that are together or are considered as a pair ○ *found a couple of mugs in the cupboard* **2.** SEVERAL a few things of the same kind ○ *There are a couple of things I'm not sure about.* **3.** TWO PEOPLE SHARING LIVES two people who are married, are living together, or have an intimate relationship **4.** TWO PEOPLE DOING STH TOGETHER two people, especially a man and a woman, who are sitting, walking, dancing, or working together ○ *There were only a few couples on the dance floor.* **5.** STH THAT JOINS sth that links or joins two similar things **6.** ENG SYSTEM OF OPPOSING FORCES a system of two equal forces that are parallel and in opposite directions **7.** HUNT PAIR OF DOGS a pair of hunting dogs attached to each other by a leash, or the double collar and leash on which they are held **8.** PHYS ELECTRICAL CONTACT a connection of two dissimilar metals that develops an electric current in the presence of an electrical conductor (**electrolyte**) ■ *v.* (**-ples, -pling, -pled**) **1.** *vt.* ASSOCIATE TWO THINGS to associate or combine sth or sb with another ○ *High prices coupled with poor living conditions made their lives difficult.* **2.** *vt.* JOIN TWO THINGS to join or link two things or people ○ *to couple freight cars* **3.** *vi.* HAVE SEXUAL INTERCOURSE to have sexual intercourse (*formal*) [13thC. Via Old French from Latin *copula* (see COPULA).]

WORD KEY: USAGE

Singular or plural? When ***couple*** refers to two married people or partners, it may be treated as either singular or plural: *The couple wants to be married before the end of the year* but *The couple have not reconciled, and continue to live apart.* If there is a pronoun referring to the word, it is almost always plural (*their*), and then any verb should be plural as well: *The couple have repeatedly asked that their privacy be respected.* In other uses, the word is often followed by *of* and a plural noun, in which case it is treated as plural: *A couple of books were on the table.* In informal uses the idea of 'two' may be very approximate. If sb says, e.g. *A couple of us are going out for coffee*, no one should be surprised if three people go.

coupledom /kúpp'ldəm/ *n.* the state of living together as a couple, or the condition of a society in which most adult people are assumed to live together as couples

coupler /kúpplər/ *n.* **1.** *US, Can* RAIL = **coupling** *n.* 5 **2.** ENG = **coupling** *n.* 4 **3.** MEANS OF COUPLING THINGS sth or sb that joins or combines two things together **4.** MUSIC DEVICE CONNECTING KEYBOARDS a mechanical or electronic device that connects two keyboards on an organ or harpsichord so that all the keys can be played from one keyboard

couplet /kúpplət/ *n.* two lines of verse that form a unit alone or as part of a poem, especially two that rhyme and have the same metre [Late 16thC. From French, literally 'little couple', from *couple* 'COUPLE'.]

coupling /kúppling/ *n.* **1.** STH THAT JOINS TWO THINGS sth that joins two things, especially a device for connecting two pieces of pipe, hose, or tube **2.** JOINING TWO THINGS TOGETHER a joining together or linking of two persons or things ○ *a disastrous coupling of two very unlike singers* **3.** ACT OF SEXUAL INTERCOURSE an act of sexual intercourse **4.** MECH ENG LINK THAT TRANSFERS POWER a part of a mechanical system by which power is transmitted from one rotating part to another part **5.** RAIL CONNECTOR FOR RAILWAY CARRIAGES a device on railway carriages that is used to link them in a train. US term **coupler** **6.** ZOOL TRUNK OF ANIMAL'S BODY the part of the body of a four-legged animal between the forequarters and hindquarters **7.** ELECTRON ENG CONNECTION OF ELECTRICAL CIRCUITS a means of connecting two electrical circuits so that power can be passed between them, or the process of connecting electrical circuits in this way

coupon /kŏŏ pon/ *n.* **1.** VOUCHER REDEEMED BY STORE OR COMPANY a voucher that entitles sb to a discount, refund, gift, or place in a draw, typically issued as a sales promotion **2.** ORDER FORM a printed form, e.g. in an advertisement, that may be filled in and returned to order a product or request information **3.** FORM FOR PAYMENT BY INSTALMENTS a form or card showing the payment due on a certain date for sth that was bought by hire purchase. The card is returned with the payment. **4.** FIN CERTIFICATE OF INTEREST ON BOND a detachable part of a bond that indicates a date and the amount of interest paid on that date. It must be presented to receive payment of the interest. **5.** TICKET IN RATIONING SYSTEM a ticket issued in a rationing system that entitles sb to a certain amount of a rationed item and that must be handed over to buy or receive that item **6.** ENTRY FORM FOR FOOTBALL POOLS an entry form for the football pools, with lists of fixtures against which entrants can mark their bets of a draw or a home or away win [Early 19thC. From French, literally 'piece cut off', from *couper* (see COPE).]

couponing /kŏŏpəning/ *n.* the use of coupons as a means of promoting a product's sales or of saving money on purchases

courage /kúrrij/ *n.* the ability to face danger, difficulty, uncertainty, or pain without being overcome by fear or being deflected from a chosen course of action ○ *He showed great courage throughout this difficult time.* [13thC. From Old French *corage*, from, ultimately, Latin *cor* 'heart' (the source also of English *cordial* and *discord*).]

WORD KEY: SYNONYMS

courage, bravery, fearlessness, nerve, guts, pluck, mettle

CORE MEANING: personal resoluteness in the face of danger or difficulties

courage the most general term, indicating fearlessness and determination, whether physical, mental, or moral, against a wide range of difficulties or dangers; **bravery** a slightly narrower term, emphasizing a lack of physical fear; **fearlessness** a term similar to *bravery*, but less commonly used; **nerve** coolness and steadiness, sometimes with the suggestion of calculated risk-taking; **guts** a widely used slang term suggesting boldness or fortitude when faced with a difficult or potentially dangerous situation; **pluck** a dated rather formal term similar to *guts*, suggesting resolution and a willingness to continue struggling against the odds; **mettle** a rather literary term similar to *pluck*, suggesting a spirited determination.

WORD KEY: CULTURAL NOTE

The Red Badge of Courage, a novel by US writer Stephen Crane (1895). Set during the American Civil War, it tells the story of an idealistic soldier, Henry Fleming, who panics in battle and temporarily deserts. During a scuffle with another deserter, he receives a minor wound. Returning to battle bearing this 'badge of courage', he performs with heroism but is wracked by guilt.

courageous /kə ráyjəss/ *adj.* acting with or showing courage —**courageously** *adv.* —**courageousness** *n.*

courante /koŏ raánt/ *n.* **1.** MUSIC **PIECE OF FAST MUSIC** a musical composition in quick time with three beats to the bar, frequently a part of a baroque suite **2.** DANCE **QUICK DANCE** a dance of French and Italian origin with short quick steps, performed to music in quick time with three beats to the bar [Late 16thC. From French, literally 'running'.]

Courbet /koŏr bay/, **Gustave** (1819–77) French painter. He was a leading French realist with such controversial works as *Burial at Ornans* (1850). A supporter of the Paris Commune (1871), he died in exile.

coureur de bois /koo rúr də bwaá/ (*plural* **coureurs de bois** /koo rúr də bwaá/) *n.* sb of French or French and Native American descent who trapped and traded furs in the 18th and 19th centuries in the north and northwest of what is now Canada [Early 18thC. From French, literally 'woods runner'.]

courgette /kawr zhét/ *n. UK* a kind of small vegetable marrow that is eaten cooked or sometimes raw in salads. ◊ **zucchini** [Mid-20thC. From French, literally 'small gourd', via Old French *cohourde* from Latin *cucurbita* (source of English *gourd* and *zucchini*).]

courier /koŏri ər/ *n.* **1.** **SB PROVIDING DELIVERY SERVICE** a person or company that delivers documents or small and valuable packages by hand **2.** **OFFICIAL MESSENGER** a diplomat, soldier, or other person with the responsibility of carrying and delivering official documents **3.** **SECRET MESSENGER** sb who carries and delivers sth secretly, e.g. illegal drugs, smuggled goods, or information gained by espionage **4.** **TRAVELLERS' GUIDE** a paid guide and helper who accompanies a group of travellers and makes arrangements for them, especially sb employed by a travel agency to do this ■ *vt.* (**-ers, -ering, -ered**) **SEND BY COURIER** to send a document or package by a commercial courier service [14thC. From French, literally 'runner', from, ultimately, Latin *currere* 'to run' (see CURRENT).]

courlan /koŏrlən/ *n.* BIRDS = **limpkin** [Late 19thC. From French, of uncertain origin: probably ultimately from Galibi *kurliri*.]

Courrèges /koŏ rézh, -ráyzh/, **André** (*b.* 1923) French fashion designer. Alongside Pierre Cardin and Mary Quant, he was a creator of the space age look of the 1960s, characterized by miniskirts (1964), white boots, and trouser suits.

course /kawrss/ *n.* **1.** **SEQUENCE OF EVENTS** the progression or development of a sequence of events, especially a development that is normal or expected ○ *events that changed the course of history* **2.** **PERIOD OF TIME** the progression or development of a period of time ○ *in the course of the afternoon* **3.** **DIRECTION TRAVELLED** the direction or route along which sth travels **4.** **ACTION CHOSEN** an action or series of actions that sb decides to take ○ *The simplest course would be to say nothing.* **5.** EDUC **PROGRAMME OF STUDY** a programme of study or training, especially one that leads to a qualification from an educational institution **6.** EDUC **UNIT IN EDUCATIONAL PROGRAMME** one of several distinct units that together form the programme of study leading to a qualification such as a degree **7.** **PART OF MEAL** one of two or more different dishes or types of food that are served in sequence during a meal **8.** **PATH OF RIVER** the route followed by a river or stream or by sth very long such as a road or boundary **9.** **ONWARD MOVEMENT** swift onward movement ○ *Nothing could interrupt his headlong course.* **10.** MED **ESTABLISHED SEQUENCE OF TREATMENT** a sequence of treatment, exercise, or medication that is followed over a period of time **11.** SPORTS **PLACE FOR RACE OR SPORT** an area where a race is run or where a sport in which players progress over the area is played **12.** BUILDING **LAYER OF BRICKS** one of the layers of bricks that make up a wall **13.** SAILING **LOWEST SAIL ON SHIP** the lowest sail or row of sails on a square-rigged ship **14.** SPORTS **GREYHOUND CHASE** a chase or race by dogs such as greyhounds ■ **courses** *npl.* **MENSTRUAL PERIOD** a woman's menstrual period (*archaic*) ■ *v.* (**courses, coursing, coursed**) **1.** *vi.* **RUN FAST** to flow or run swiftly **2.** *vi.* **TRAVEL** to travel or range over an area (*archaic*) **3.** *vti.* HUNT **HUNT ANIMALS WITH GREYHOUNDS** to hunt animals, especially hares, with greyhounds or other dogs that hunt by sight **4.** *vt.* HUNT **USE GREYHOUNDS FOR HUNTING** to use greyhounds or other dogs that hunt by sight [13thC. Via French *cours* from Latin *cursus*, the past participle of *currere* (see CURRENT).] ◇ **be par for the course** to be what would be expected ◇ **in due course** after the lapse of an appropriate period of time ◇ **of course 1.** without any question or doubt **2.** used to show that the speaker has just understood sth **3.** used to point out a possibility that sb may not have considered

course book *n.* a book that is used by students and teachers as the basis of a course of study

courser[1] /káwrssər/ *n.* **1.** **DOG THAT HUNTS BY SIGHT** a dog that is trained to hunt its quarry by sight instead of by scent **2.** **HUNTER WITH COURSERS** sb who hunts with coursers [Early 17thC. Formed from COURSE.]

courser[2] /káwrssər/ *n.* a strong swift horse (*literary*) [13thC. From Old French *corsier*, from, ultimately, Latin *cursus* 'course' (see COURSE).]

courser[3] /káwrssər/ *n.* a bird related to the plovers that lives in arid regions of Africa and Asia and is a swift runner. Subfamily: Cursoriinae. [Mid-18thC. Anglicization of modern Latin *Cursorius*, genus name, from Latin *cursor* 'runner' (see CURSOR).]

coursework /káwrss wurk/ *n.* work that is assigned to students as part of an educational course and counts towards the assessment given for the course

coursing /káwrssing/ *n.* the sport of hunting with dogs such as greyhounds that follow their quarry using sight instead of scent

court[1] /kawrt/ *n.* **1.** **MEETING WHERE LEGAL JUDGMENTS ARE MADE** a session of an official body that has authority to try criminals, resolve disputes, or make other legal decisions **2.** **JUDGE** the constituted authority presiding over a court of law **3.** **COURTROOM OR COURTHOUSE** a place where a court of law is held **4.** **PEOPLE IN COURTROOM** all those present in a courtroom ○ *The court shall rise.* **5.** **OPEN SPACE WITHIN WALLS** an open space surrounded by buildings and walls, or a roofless area within a building **6.** **AREA FOR BALL GAME** an area marked out for playing a sport such as tennis or basketball, or a walled area where squash or a similar sport is played **7.** **MONARCH'S ATTENDANTS** the ministers, courtiers, and officials of the royal household who attend a king or queen **8.** **MEETING OF MONARCH AND ATTENDANTS** an occasion when a king or queen and the ministers, courtiers, and officials of the royal household are assembled **9.** **PLACE WHERE MONARCH LIVES** the place where a king or queen and the court are usually in residence **10.** **IMPORTANT PERSON'S FOLLOWERS** a group of people who devote their time to the service and flattery of a noble, rich, or important person **11.** **SHORT STREET** a short street of houses that is closed at one end **12.** **GROUP OF HOUSES** a group of houses built around an open space **13.** **BLOCK OF FLATS** a large building containing many flats or offices **14.** **LARGE HOUSE** a large and imposing house and the land surrounding it (*often used in placenames*) **15.** **GOVERNING BODY** the governing body or council of an organization such as a corporation or academic institution [13thC. From Anglo-Norman *curt*, ultimately from Latin *cohort-*, the stem of *cohors* 'enclosed space, retinue'.] ◇ **be laughed out of court** to be ridiculed so severely that what you have to say is not considered seriously ◇ **pay court to sb 1.** to try to win influence with sb or to win sb's approval or favour through flattery or attentiveness **2.** to try to gain sb's love (*dated*) ◇ **rule sth out of court** to refuse absolutely to allow sth to take place

court[2] /kawrt/ (**courts, courting, courted**) *v.* **1.** *vt.* **BE ATTENTIVE TO** to try to win influence with sb or to win sb's approval or favour through flattery or attentiveness **2.** *vt.* **TRY TO GAIN** to try to gain sth, e.g. sb's attention or admiration, by behaving in ways that are intended to attract or encourage it **3.** *vt.* **RISK EXPERIENCING STH BAD** to behave in a way that increases the likelihood of failure, injury, or other trouble **4.** *vti.* **TRY TO GAIN SB'S LOVE** to try to gain sb's love (*dated*) **5.** *vti.* ZOOL **TRY TO ATTRACT MATE** to engage in behaviour that is designed to attract another animal or bird as a mate **6.** *vi.* **BE SWEETHEARTS** to spend time together in a romantic relationship as a prelude to getting married (*dated*) ○ *We used to come here when we were courting.* [Early 16thC. From Old Italian *corteare*, which came from Latin *cohors* (see COURT[1]).]

Court /kawrt/, **Margaret Jean** (*b.* 1942) Australian tennis player. She was the winner of the Wimbledon women's singles championship in 1963, 1965, and 1970. In 1970 she also completed the grand slam. Born **Margaret Jean Smith**

court bouillon /káwrt boŏ yon/ *n.* a liquid used for poaching fish, made with water flavoured with vegetables, herbs, and wine or vinegar. The liquid is discarded after the fish is poached. [From French, literally 'short broth']

court card *n.* any of the kings, queens, and jacks in a pack of playing cards. US term **face card**

court circular *n.* an account of what a country's monarch will be doing that day, along with other news of the royal family, published in a leading national newspaper

court cupboard *n.* a sideboard or cabinet with some open shelves for display, used especially in the 16th and 17th centuries

court dress *n.* the type and style of clothing that is officially approved for wear at a royal court

Courtenay /káwrtni/, **Bryce** (*b.* 1931) Australian writer. He wrote the best-selling novel *The Power of One* (1989). Full name **Arthur Bryce Courtenay**

courteous /kúrti əss/ *adj.* polite in a way that shows consideration of others or good manners [13thC. From Old French *corteis* 'courtly', from *cort* 'court' (see COURT[1]).] —**courteously** *adv.* —**courteousness** *n.*

courtesan /káwrti zán, káwrti zan/ *n.* a prostitute or mistress, especially one associated with a rich, powerful, or upper-class man who provides her with luxuries and status [Mid-16thC. Via French *courtisane* from a dialect form of Italian *cortigiana* 'female courtier', from *corte* 'court', from the Latin stem *cohort-* (see COHORT).]

courtesy /kúrtəssi/ *n.* (*plural* **-sies**) **1.** **POLITE OR CONSIDERATE BEHAVIOUR** politeness that shows consideration for other people or good manners ○ *He didn't even have the courtesy to offer me a seat.* **2.** **POLITE OR CONSIDERATE ACTION** sth done out of politeness or consideration for another person ○ *We should certainly go, if only as a courtesy to Helen.* ■ *adj.* **1.** **FOR SAKE OF POLITENESS** given or done as a courtesy ○ *a courtesy call* **2.** **PROVIDED FREE** provided free of charge ○ *Your courtesy limousine will take you to the airport.* [13thC. From Old French *curtesie* (source also of English *curtsey*), from *corteis* 'courtly' (see COURTEOUS).]

courtesy card *n.* a card given to customers of a supermarket or other business that entitles them to special benefits or privileges

courtesy light *n.* a light inside the passenger compartment of a vehicle that turns on automatically when the door is opened

courtesy title *n.* a personal title that is used to address sb out of politeness or as a social convention even though the person is not professionally or socially entitled to it

court hand *n.* a style of handwriting formerly used by legal clerks

courthouse /káwrt howss/ *n.* a building where a court of law is held

courtier /káwrti ər/ *n.* **1.** **SB AT ROYAL COURT** sb who spends time at a royal court or attends a king or queen **2.** **FLATTERER OF IMPORTANT PERSON** sb who is insincerely polite or flattering to a more important person [13thC. Alteration of Anglo-Norman *courteour*, from Old French *courtoyer* 'to be at court', from *cort* 'court' (see COURT).]

court-leet *n.* = **leet**

courtly /káwrtli/ (**-lier, -liest**) *adj.* **1.** **WITH REFINED MANNERS** showing great delicacy and refinement in behaviour **2.** **OF THE HIGHEST QUALITY** rich or fine and suitable for a royal court **3.** **INSINCERELY POLITE** insincerely polite or deferential in order to win sb's favour —**courtliness** *n.*

courtly love *n.* a medieval code of behaviour that idealized the love of a knight for a usually married noblewoman and prescribed how they should act towards each other

court martial (*plural* **courts martial** *or* **court martials**) *n.* **1.** MILITARY COURT a military court that tries members of the military and others for offences under military law **2.** MILITARY TRIAL a trial by court martial

court-martial (**court-martials, court-martialling, court-martialled**) *vt.* to try sb by a military court for an offence under military law

Court of Appeal *n.* the branch of the Supreme Court in England and Wales that hears civil and criminal appeals from other courts

court of chancery *n.* in the United States, a court of equity, ruling on matters not covered by common law

Court of Chancery *n.* a division of the High Court in England and Wales, presided over by the Lord Chancellor

Court of Common Pleas *n.* a former higher court with jurisdiction over civil cases in England and Wales

court of equity *n.* a court belonging to a separate system of courts organized under the Lord Chancellor that dispenses judgments on the basis of principles of equity, e.g., in cases of wills and trusts

Court of Exchequer *n.* a former civil court in the United Kingdom with jurisdiction over revenue cases

court of first instance (*plural* **courts of first instance**) *n.* a court in which legal proceedings are started, in particular one attached to the European Court of Justice

court of honour *n.* a military court that investigates questions involving personal honour

court of inquiry *n.* **1.** INVESTIGATING BODY a group specially set up to inquire into a matter of public concern such as the cause of a disaster **2.** MILITARY INVESTIGATING BODY a military tribunal that investigates a matter of concern, especially in order to determine whether official charges should be brought

Court of Justiciary *n.* = High Court of Justiciary

court of law *n.* a court that hears legal cases and issues rulings based on legal statutes or common law

court of record *n.* a court that has its proceedings placed on an official permanent record and has the power to give penalties for contempt of court

Court of Saint James's *n.* the court of the monarch of the United Kingdom, to which ambassadors are accredited (*technical*)

Court of Session *n.* the highest civil court in Scotland

court order *n.* an official order issued by the judge of a court, requiring or forbidding sb to do sth

court plaster *n.* cloth treated on one side with isinglass or another adhesive substance, formerly used to bandage small cuts, hide skin blemishes, and simulate beauty spots [So called because of its use by ladies at court]

Courtrai /koor tráy/ city in West Flanders, western Belgium. It is known for its textile industries. Population: 75,951 (1996). Flemish **Kortrijk**

court recorder *n.* sb who records the proceedings of a law court and prepares a verbatim report of them. US term **court reporter**

court reporter *n.* US = court recorder

court roll *n.* the register of the lands held by a medieval manor

courtroom /káwrt room, -rŏŏm/ *n.* a room used for holding a session of a court of law

courtship /káwrt ship/ *n.* **1.** TRYING TO GAIN SB'S LOVE the act of paying attention to sb with a view to developing a more intimate relationship **2.** PRELUDE TO MARRIAGE the period of a romantic relationship before marriage **3.** INGRATIATING BEHAVIOUR friendly and often ingratiating attention for the purpose of winning a favour or establishing an alliance or other relationship **4.** ZOOL MATING BEHAVIOUR behaviour designed to attract another animal or bird as a mate, or the time during which an animal or bird engages in this

court shoe *n.* a woman's shoe that is plain and cut low in front and has a moderately high heel. US term **pump**[2] *n.* 1

courtside /káwrt sīd/ *adj., adv.* at the side of an athletic court where a match or game such as tennis or basketball is being played

court tennis *n.* US = real tennis

courtyard /káwrt yaard/ *n.* an area of ground that is surrounded by buildings, lies inside a large building, or is adjacent to a building and enclosed by walls

couscous /kŏŏss kooss/ *n.* **1.** SAVOURY FOOD MADE OF SEMOLINA a food made from semolina and resembling tiny grains. It is cooked by steaming or briefly soaking in boiling water, and is served in the same way as rice. **2.** DISH OF STEW AND COUSCOUS a North African dish consisting of a spicy stew of meat and vegetables served with couscous [Late 16thC. Via French from Arabic *kuskus*, from *kaskasa* 'to pulverize'.]

cousin /kúzz'n/ *n.* **1.** UNCLE'S OR AUNT'S CHILD a child of sb's uncle or aunt **2.** DISTANT RELATIVE sb to whom sb is related through the brother or sister of a grandparent, great-grandparent, or even older ancestor **3.** SB WITH MUCH IN COMMON sb with whom sb feels connected because of similar ancestry or ethnic background, or interests ○ *our Canadian cousins* **4.** TERM OF ADDRESS BETWEEN SOVEREIGNS used by European sovereigns as a term of address for another sovereign or a member of a royal family [13thC. Via Old French from Latin *consobrinus* 'mother's sister's child', from *sobrinus* 'maternal cousin'.] —**cousinhood** *n.* —**cousinly** *adj.*

Cousin /koo záN/, **Victor** (1792–1867) French philosopher. He wrote studies of Pascal and Kant. His original works include *Philosophical Fragments* (1826).

cousin german (*plural* **cousins german**) *n.* = cousin *n.* 1 [14thC. from French *cousin germain*; *germain* from Latin *germanus* 'having the same parents' (see GERMANE).]

Cousteau /kŏŏstố/, **Jacques** (1910–97) French film director and underwater explorer. He invented the aqualung (1943). His films include the Oscar-winning *The Golden Fish* (1960).

couth /kooth/ *adj.* showing very good manners or great social sophistication (*humorous*) [Late 19thC. Back-formation from UNCOUTH. In Scots it survives from Old English *cúp* (see UNCOUTH).]

couthie /kŏŏthi/, **couthy** (**couthier, couthiest**) *adj.* Scotland **1.** FRIENDLY friendly or sociable **2.** COMFORTABLE comfortable and homely **3.** HOMESPUN plain or homespun [Early 18thC. Formed from COUTH.]

couture /koo tyŏŏr/ *n.* **1.** FASHION DESIGN the design and production of fashionable high-quality custom-made clothes **2.** HIGH-FASHION CLOTHING high-quality clothing made to order by a fashion designer [Early 20thC. Via French from late Latin *consutura*, literally 'sewing together', from Latin *suere* 'to sew' (see SUTURE).]

couturier /koo tyŏŏri ay/ *n.* a designer of fashionable high-quality custom-made clothes [Late 19thC. From French, 'dressmaker', formed from *couture* 'COUTURE'.]

couturière /koo tyŏŏri áir/ *n.* a woman who is a designer of fashionable high-quality custom-made clothes [Early 19thC. From French, the feminine form of *couturier* 'COUTURIER'.]

couturify /koo tyŏŏri fī/ (**-fies, -fying, -fied**) *vt.* to make a garment more stylish or fancier by using fine fabrics, unusual colours, handwork, and other elements of designer clothing (*informal*) [Late 20thC. Formed from COUTURE.]

couvade /koo vaad/ *n.* the mimicking of childbirth by the father while it is taking place, a custom in some Native South American societies [Mid-19thC. From French, literally 'hatching', from *couver* 'to hatch', from Latin *cubare* 'to lie down' (see CUBICLE).]

Cov., COV. *abbr.* STATS covariance

covalence /kō váylənss/ *n.* US = covalency

covalency /kố váylənssi/ *n.* chemical valency involving the sharing of electrons. US term **covalence**

covalent /kō váylənt/ *adj.* used to describe a chemical bond in which the attractive force between atoms

is created by the sharing of electrons —**covalently** *adv.*

covalent bond *n.* a chemical bond between two atoms created by the sharing of a pair of electrons

covariance /kō váiri ənss/ *n.* a statistical measure of the tendency of two variables to change in conjunction with each other. It is equal to the product of their standard deviations and correlation coefficients.

covariant /kō váiri ənt/ *adj.* exhibiting a tendency to change in conjunction with another statistical variable

cove[1] /kōv/ *n.* **1.** BAY IN SHORELINE a small bay on the shore of the sea or a lake, especially one that is enclosed by high cliffs **2.** NOOK IN CLIFF a small semicircular recessed valley in the side of a hill or cliff **3.** CURVE AT TOP OF WALL an inwardly curved surface at the point where a wall meets a ceiling **4.** CURVED MOULDING a moulding that curves inwards ■ *vti.* (**coves, coving, coved**) MAKE WITH OR HAVE INWARD CURVE to have a cove, or design or build a wall with a cove [Old English *cofa* 'bedchamber, alcove'. Ultimately from a prehistoric Germanic word meaning 'hollow place providing shelter', which is also the ancestor of English *cubby*.]

cove[2] /kōv/ *n.* a man (*dated slang*) [Mid-16thC. Probably from Romany *kova* 'person, thing'.]

covellite /kō vél īt/ *n.* a purple mineral consisting of thin sheets of copper sulphide [Mid-19thC. Named after the Italian mineralogist Nicolò *Covelli* (1790–1829).]

coven /kúvv'n/ *n.* a meeting or group of witches, usually 13 in number [Mid-17thC. From Anglo-Norman 'assembly' (see CONVENT) from, ultimately, Latin *convenire* (see CONVENE).]

covenant /kúvvənənt/ *n.* **1.** SOLEMN AGREEMENT a solemn agreement that is binding on all parties **2.** LAW LEGALLY BINDING AGREEMENT a formal and legally binding agreement or contract such as a lease, or one of the clauses in an agreement of this kind. A covenant is often used to require an owner or user of a piece of land to do or refrain from doing sth. **3.** LAW LAWSUIT FOR BREACH OF AGREEMENT a lawsuit for damages that is brought because of the breaking of a legal covenant **4.** BIBLE MUTUAL PROMISES OF GOD AND ISRAELITES the promises that were made in the Bible between God and the Israelites, who agreed to worship no other gods ■ *vti.* (**-nants, -nanting, -nanted**) AGREE IN COVENANT to promise sth in a covenant, especially a legal one promising regular payments of a stated amount to a charity [13thC. From Old French, the present participle of *convenir* 'to agree' (see CONVENE).] —**covenantal** /kúvvə nánt'l/ *adj.* —**covenantally** /-nánt'li/ *adv.*

Covenant *n.* any of several agreements in the 17th century by which Scottish Presbyterians united to defend their church

covenantee /kúvvənən teé/ *n.* sb to whom sth is promised in a covenant

covenanter /kúvvənəntər/, **covenantor** *n.* sb who joins in a covenant or undertakes an obligation in a covenant

Covenanter *n.* sb who joined in a Covenant during the 17th century to defend the Scottish Presbyterian church

Coventry /kóvvəntri/ historic cathedral city in Warwickshire, England, and the home of Warwick University. It has also been a car manufacturing centre. Population: 303,600 (1995).

co-venture, coventure *vti.* UNDERTAKE AS JOINT VENTURE to undertake a business venture in partnership with another individual or company ■ *n.* BUSINESS PARTNERSHIP a business agreement, deal, partnership involving two or more companies

cover /kúvvər/ *v.* (**covers, covering, covered**) **1.** *vt.* PUT STH OVER to put sth over the whole of or the upper surface of sth, e.g. in order to hide, protect, or decorate it **2.** *vt.* BE ALL OVER to lie across or in a layer over the whole or the upper surface of sth ○ *rocks covered with seaweed* **3.** *vt.* KEEP WARM to put sth such as a blanket over or around sb for warmth ○ *She covered him with the quilt.* **4.** *vt.* BE WRAPPED AROUND to be lying over or wrapped around sb to provide warmth ○ *He was covered only by a thin blanket.* **5.** *vt.* PUT CLOTHING ON to put a piece of clothing on part of your own or sb else's body ○ *Keep your head covered if you are going out.* **6.** *vt.* **BE WORN ON** to be worn on part of the body **7.** *vt.* **PUT LID ON** to put a lid or protective covering over sth **8.** *vt.* **TALK OR WRITE ABOUT** to deal with a subject in a discussion, speech, book, or article ○ *His talk covered several aspects of company law.* **9.** *vt.* **PROVIDE NEWS OF** to be responsible for reporting, videotaping, or photographing an event or a particular class of events for a newspaper or a broadcasting company ○ *We cover everything that has a financial angle.* **10.** *vt.* **INCLUDE PARTICULAR INSTANCE** to take sth into account and provide an adequate treatment of it ○ *Unfortunately, the law does not cover cases of this sort.* **11.** *vt.* **EXTEND OVER** to include the whole of a particular area, either physically or as a field of operations or responsibility ○ *an office complex covering three blocks* ○ *a police operation that covered the whole of the city* **12.** *vt.* **TRAVEL CERTAIN DISTANCE** to travel a particular distance **13.** *vt.* **HIDE STATE OF** to conceal a feeling, action, or situation by presenting a different appearance or directing attention elsewhere ○ *I managed to cover my mistake by changing the subject.* **14.** *vt.* INSUR **INSURE** to provide insurance protection to sb **15.** *vt.* INSUR **INSURE AGAINST** to provide insurance protection against a type of hazard or risk **16.** *vt.* **PAY FOR** to be sufficient to pay for sth **17.** *vt.* **PROTECT FROM ATTACK** to protect sb, a part of an army, or a piece in chess or another game from attack by occupying a position nearby from which a counterattack can be made **18.** *vt.* **AIM GUN AT** to have a person or place in the aim or range of a gun, especially in order to provide protection against a possible attack **19.** *vt.* **PATROL** to maintain a watch on or a patrol of sth, e.g. to track sb's movements ○ *One police officer covered the rear exit while the others knocked at the front door.* **20.** *vt.* **INFUSE WITH A QUALITY** to bring an overwhelming amount of some quality upon yourself or sb else (*often passive*) **21.** *vi.* **DO SB'S JOB** to do the work of sb who is absent for a time **22.** *vi.* **TELL LIES FOR SB** to keep people from learning sth about sb that is not as it should be ○ *to cover for him by lying* **23.** *vt.* ZOOL **COPULATE WIH FEMALE** to copulate with a female animal, especially a mare **24.** *vt.* CARDS **PLAY HIGHER CARD** to play a card that has a higher value than one already played by another person **25.** *vti.* FIN **BUY REPLACEMENT STOCK** to buy shares of stock or commodities to replace others that were borrowed from a broker and sold with the expectation that the price would fall **26.** *vt.* GAMBLING **MATCH ANOTHER'S BET** to match the amount of money bet by another gambler **27.** *vt.* MUSIC **RECORD NEW VERSION OF SONG** to record a new version of a song that was first sung or made popular by another performer **28.** *vt.* SPORTS **DEFEND AREA AGAINST OPPONENT** to play in defence against an opponent or in a particular position or area on a sports field **29.** *vt.* BIRDS **SIT ON EGGS** to sit on eggs in a nest to hatch them ■ *n.* **1. STH THAT COVERS STH** sth that hides, protects, or covers sth, or is used to cover sth **2. LID** sth that covers the top of a container, e.g. a lid **3. BINDING OF BOOK OR MAGAZINE** the protective binding, thick paper, or boards at the front and back of a book or magazine **4. CLOTH THAT COVERS FURNITURE** a cloth or plastic covering for a piece of furniture or bedding **5. SHELTER FROM WEATHER** sth that provides shelter from the weather **6. HIDING PLACE** sth that provides concealment or protection, especially undergrowth where animals can hide or a shelter from attack **7. VEGETATION** the plants that cover an area of land **8. DEFENCE AGAINST ATTACK** protection provided, especially to an attacking force, by other forces located nearby or in the air ○ *air cover* **9. PROTECTIVE PRETENCE** a false identity or a pretext that provides protection for sb such as a spy or a detective **10. SUBSTITUTES FOR WORKERS** people who are available to do other people's jobs when they are absent ○ *We no longer have enough staff to provide cover in emergencies.* **11. PLACE LAID AT TABLE** a place laid at table, especially in a restaurant **12.** = **cover charge 13.** CRICKET = **cover point 14. INSURANCE PROTECTION** the amount or type of protection provided by an insurance policy. US term **coverage 15.** FIN **ENOUGH MONEY** sufficient funds or guaranteed income to meet a liability or cover a planned expenditure **16.** MUSIC **NEW RECORDING OF WELL-KNOWN SONG** a recording by a performer of a song that was first sung or popularized by another performer **17.** MUSIC **UNDERSTUDY** an understudy for a musical role **18.** STAMPS **ENVELOPE** a postmarked envelope ■ **covers** *npl.* **1. COVERINGS ON BED** the sheets, blankets, and other coverings on a bed **2.** SPORTS **WATERPROOF COVERS PROTECTING SPORTS FIELD** sheets of waterproof material spread over a playing surface to protect it against rain (*usually plural*) US term **groundcloth 3.** CRICKET **OFF-SIDE FIELD** the area of a cricket field in front of the batsman on the off side that is between cover point and extra cover [13thC. Via Old French *covrir* from Latin *cooperire*, literally 'to cover completely', from *operire* 'to cover'.] —**coverable** *adj.* —**coverer** *n.* —**coverless** *adj.* ◇ **blow sb's cover** to expose a disguise, lie, or pretence that sb was using to conceal sth ◇ **under cover of sth** hidden or protected by sth ◇ **under separate cover** in another envelope or package

cover up *v.* **1.** *vti.* **COVER STH COMPLETELY** to cover sb or sth completely **2.** *vti.* **CONCEAL STH BAD** to try to conceal that sth illegal, immoral, or undesirable has happened or how or why it happened **3.** *vi.* BOXING **PROTECT HEAD AND UPPER BODY** to hide the head and upper body behind the arms as protection against another boxer's blows

coverage /kúvvərij/ *n.* **1. MEDIA ATTENTION** the attention given to an event or topic by newspapers, radio, and television in their reporting **2.** *US* INSUR = **cover** *n.* **15 3. MEDIA AUDIENCE** the percentage of all the people in a given area who are reached by a newspaper or radio or television station **4. DEGREE OF COVERING** the degree to which sth is covered by sth else ○ *the coverage of the ground by the snow* **5.** FIN **AVAILABLE FUNDS** the amount of funds available to cover financial liabilities or commitments

coveralls /kúvvər awlz/ *npl.* a one-piece outer garment that covers and protects the clothes

cover charge *n.* a fixed charge that is added per head to the cost of drinks and food in a nightclub or restaurant, e.g. for bread or entertainment

cover crop *n.* a crop planted between main crops to prevent erosion or to plough in to enrich the soil

cover girl *n.* a young woman, usually a glamorous model, whose picture is on the cover of a magazine

cover glass *n.* = **cover slip**

covering /kúvvəring/ *n.* sth that protects, hides, or covers sth

covering fire *n.* weapon fire used to protect friendly troops from direct fire from the enemy's weapons

covering letter *n.* a letter sent with another document or a package, providing necessary or additional information. US term **cover letter.** = **covering letter**

coverlet /kúvvərlət/ *n.* a usually decorative cover for a bed, placed over the other bedclothes when the bed is not being used [13thC. From Old French *couvre lit* 'bed cover'.]

cover letter *n.* = **covering letter**

covermount /k/ *n.* PRESS a gift fixed to the cover of a magazine, such as a diary or recipe book [Late 20thC]

cover note *n.* a document given by an insurance company to a person who has taken out a policy, acting as a temporary certificate of insurance until the full policy is issued

cover page, **cover sheet** *n.* a form sent along with a fax that gives information about the sender, e.g. the name, address, telephone number, and fax number

cover point *n.* in cricket, a position in the covers to the right of the fielder at point, or a fielder who takes up this position

cover slip *n.* a piece of thin glass used to cover a specimen on a microscope slide

cover story *n.* **1. MAIN FEATURE IN MAGAZINE** a magazine feature that is illustrated on the front cover and is the most important article in the issue **2. FALSE STORY** a story made up to deceive sb, e.g. to provide a false identity for an undercover investigator

covert /kúvvərt/ *adj.* **SECRET** not intended to be known, seen, or found out ■ *n.* **1. UNDERGROWTH PROVIDING COVER** a thicket or undergrowth in which game can shelter or hide **2. SHELTER** a shelter or hiding place **3. SMALL FEATHER** a small feather around the base of a quill on the wing or tail of a bird **4. TWILLED CLOTH** a hard-wearing twilled cloth often used for making suits **5.** TECH **FLOCK OF COOTS** a flock of coots [13thC. From Old French, 'covered', from the past participle of *covrir* 'to cover' (see COVER).] —**covertly** *adv.* —**covertness** *n.*

WORD KEY: SYNONYMS

See Synonyms at ***secret***.

coverture /kúvvərchər/ *n.* **1. SHELTER** a shelter or covering **2.** LAW **CONDITION OF BEING MARRIED WOMAN** the condition of being a married woman considered to be under the protection and guidance of a husband [13thC. From Old French, formed from *covrir* (see COVER).]

cover-up *n.* **1. CONCEALMENT OF STH UNFAVOURABLE** a concealment of sth illegal, immoral, or undesirable **2. OUTER GARMENT** a loose item of clothing worn over another garment, e.g. a wrap over an evening dress or a T-shirt over a swimsuit

cover version *n.* = **cover** *n.* **16**

covet /kúvvət/ (**-ets, -eting, -eted**) *v.* **1.** *vti.* **WANT SB ELSE'S PROPERTY** to have a strong desire to possess sth that belongs to sb else **2.** *vt.* **YEARN TO HAVE** to want to have sth very much (*formal*) [13thC. From Old French *coveitier*, from, ultimately, Latin *cupiditas* 'cupidity'.] —**covetable** *adj.* —**coveter** *n.* —**covetingly** *adv.*

WORD KEY: SYNONYMS

See Synonyms at ***want***.

covetous /kúvvətəss/ *adj.* **1. WANTING SB ELSE'S PROPERTY** having a strong desire to possess sth that belongs to sb else **2. YEARNING FOR STH** wanting to have sth very much —**covetously** *adv.* —**covetousness** *n.*

covey /kúvvi/ (*plural* **-eys**) *n.* **1. GROUP OF GAME BIRDS** a small group of game birds such as partridge, grouse, or quail **2. GROUP OF PEOPLE OR THINGS** a small group of people or things [14thC. From French *covée* 'brood', from, ultimately, Latin *cubare* 'to lie down' (source of English *cubicle*).]

coving /kṓving/ *n.* a pre-fabricated curved moulding used as a decorative cover for the join between a wall and a ceiling [Early 18thC]

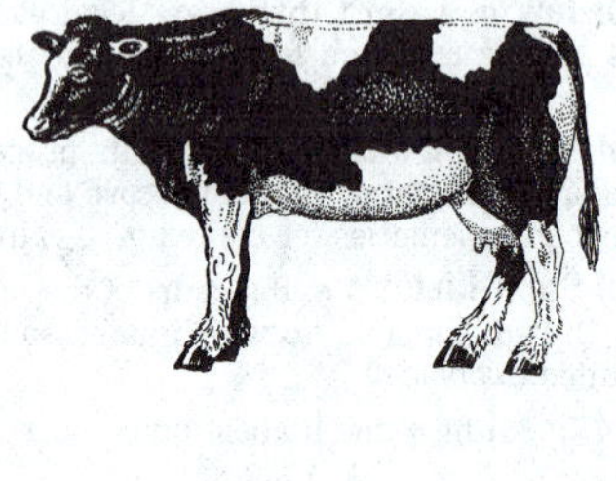

Cow

cow[1] /kow/ *n.* **1. LARGE FEMALE MAMMAL KEPT FOR MILK** an adult female grass-eating quadruped, kept as a farm animal for the milk it produces or for breeding. Genus: *Bos.* **2. MALE OR FEMALE OF DOMESTIC CATTLE** a male or female, whether adult or not, belonging to any breed of domestic cattle **3. LARGE FEMALE MAMMAL** an adult female of a large mammal species other than cattle, e.g. the whale, elephant, seal, or moose **4. OFFENSIVE TERM** an offensive term that deliberately insults a woman (*slang offensive*) [Old English *cū*. Ultimately from an Indo-European word that is also the ancestor of English *beef*, *bovine* and *bulge*.] ◇ **have a cow** *US* to become suddenly and greatly excited or angry (*slang*) ◇ **till the cows come home** until an extremely long time has elapsed

cow[2] /kow/ (**cows, cowing, cowed**) *vt.* to frighten sb into submission or obedience [Late 16thC. Probably from Old Norse *kúga* 'to tyrannize over, oppress'.]

cowal /kówəl/ *n. Aus* a small swampy hollow in the Australian interior [Late 19thC. From Kamilaroi.]

Cowan /kówən/ salt lake in southern Western Australia. Area: 940 sq. km/359 sq. mi.

coward /kówərd/ *n.* sb who is too easily or too greatly frightened [13thC. From Old French *cuard*, from Latin *cauda* 'tail', the underlying idea probably being the same as in 'to turn tail' or 'run away with your tail between your legs'.]

Coward /kówərd/, **Sir Noel** (1899–1973) British drama-tist, actor, and songwriter. He was the author of *The Vortex* (1924), *Private Lives* (1930), *Blithe Spirit* (1941), and *Brief Encounter* (1946).

cowardice /kówərdiss/ *n.* a lack of courage, or be-haviour that shows such a lack

cowardly /kówərdli/ *adj.* **1.** NOT BRAVE caused by a lack of courage, or lacking courage **2.** CRUEL AND SPINELESS showing meanness or cruelty to those who are weaker and fear of those who are equal or stron-ger —**cowardliness** *n.* —**cowardly** *adv.*

WORD KEY: SYNONYMS
---
cowardly, faint-hearted, spineless, gutless, pusillanimous, craven, yellow, chicken
CORE MEANING: lacking in courage
cowardly the most general and widely used term, applied to people and their actions; **faint-hearted** a less strong term than *cowardly*, suggesting timidity and lack of resolve; **spineless** a disapproving term suggesting con-temptible weakness of character; **gutless** a slang term for *spineless*; **pusillanimous** a formal term suggesting an extreme and contemptible degree of cowardice; **craven** a formal or literary term suggesting an extreme and contemptible degree of cowardice and weakness of will; **yellow** an insulting slang term suggesting extreme cow-ardice and implying utter contempt; **chicken** an informal term, often used by children and young people of peers who refuse to take part in sth daring.

cow bail *n.* ANZ a frame placed around a cow's head to keep it still during milking

cowbane /ków bayn/ (*plural* **-bane**) *n.* **1.** POISONOUS EUR-ASIAN PLANT a poisonous Eurasian marsh plant of the carrot family, e.g. the water hemlock. Genus: *Cicuta*. **2.** POISONOUS N AMERICAN PLANT a poisonous North American marsh plant of the carrot family. Latin name: *Oxypalis rigidior*.

cowbell /ków bel/ *n.* **1.** BELL ON COW'S NECK a bell that is fastened to a collar round a cow's neck and clangs as the cow moves, making the animal easier to find **2.** PERCUSSION INSTRUMENT a bell without a clapper, played as a percussion instrument by being struck with a drumstick

cowberry /kówbəri/ *n.* **1.** (*plural* **-ries** or **-ry**) CREEPING SHRUB a creeping flowering shrub that grows in northern temperate areas and produces edible berries. Latin name: *Vaccinium vitis-idaea*. **2.** (*plural* **-ries**) EDIBLE BERRY the edible berry of the cowberry plant

cowbird /ków burd/ *n.* a North American blackbird belonging to either of two species that lay their eggs in the nests of other birds and often feed alongside grazing cattle. Genus: *Molothrus*.

cowboy /ków boy/ *n.* **1.** MAN WHO LOOKS AFTER CATTLE a man employed to look after cattle, especially in the western United States. Cowboys traditionally work on horseback, but now also use motor vehicles. **2.** MALE CHARACTER IN WESTERNS a male character in stories and films about the West of the United States in the late 1800s, often shown fighting Native Americans or outlaws **3.** UNRELIABLE WORKER an unskilled or un-scrupulous person working in a trade or business who carries out cheap but inferior work (*informal*)

cowboy boot *n.* a high-heeled boot, like those ori-ginally worn by cowboys, usually with pointed toes and ornamental stitching

cowboy hat *n.* a hat, usually felt, with a high crown and a wide brim, originally worn by cowboys, now widely worn in the southwestern and midwestern United States

cowboys and Indians *n.* a children's game involving two sides, pretending to be cowboys and Native Americans fighting against each other (*takes a sin-gular verb*)

cowcatcher /ków kachər/ *n.* an angled metal frame formerly fixed to the front of a steam railway engine to clear animals and other obstructions from the track

Cowdrey /kówdri/, **Colin, Baron Cowdrey of Tonbridge** (*b.* 1932) Indian-born British cricketer. As a batsman, he scored 107 centuries in a playing career spanning almost 25 years. He played for England

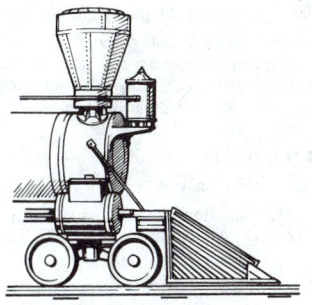
Cowcatcher

114 times, 27 times as captain. Full name **Michael Colin Cowdrey**

Cowen /ków ən/, **Sir Zelman** (*b.* 1919) Australian lawyer and statesman. He was a professor of law and governor-general of Australia (1977–82).

cower /kówər/ (**-ers, -ering, -ered**) *vi.* to cringe or move backwards defensively in fear [13thC. From Middle Low German *kūren* 'to lie in wait', of unknown origin.]

Cowes /kowz/ resort and yachting centre on the Isle of Wight. A regatta is held there every August. Population: 16,335 (1991).

cowfish /ków fish/ (*plural* **-fish** or **-fishes**) *n.* **1.** FISH WITH SPINES ABOVE EYES a small brightly coloured warm-water marine fish with spines that resemble horns above the eyes. Family: Ostraciidae. **2.** DOLPHIN, POR-POISE, OR MANATEE an aquatic mammal, e.g. certain species of dolphin or porpoise, or a manatee

cowgirl /ków gurl/ *n.* **1.** US WOMAN WHO LOOKS AFTER CATTLE a woman employed to look after cattle, especially in the western United States **2.** WOMAN CHARACTER IN WESTERNS a woman character in stories and films about the West of the United States in the late 1800s, usually accompanying or assisting a cowboy in his exploits **3.** US FEMALE RODEO PERFORMER a woman who performs or competes in shows such as rodeos

Cow Gum *tdmk.* a trademark for a colourless liquid adhesive made from rubber

cowhand /ków hand/ *n.* US sb employed to look after cattle

cowherd /ków hurd/ *n.* sb who tends cattle, usually on foot (*archaic or literary*)

cowhide /ków hīd/ *n.* **1.** SKIN OF COW the skin of a cow or bull, especially removed and processed **2.** LEATHER leather made from a cowhide **3.** LEATHER WHIP a whip made of braided leather or rawhide ■ *vt.* (**-hides, -hiding, -hided**) WHIP SB to beat sb with a whip made of braided leather or rawhide

Cowl

cowl /kowl/ *n.* **1.** MONK'S HOOD the hood on a monk's cloak or a monk's hooded cloak **2.** = cowl neck **3.** HOOD FOR CHIMNEY a hood-shaped, sometimes revolving, cover fitted to a chimney or vent to improve ven-tilation and prevent downward draughts **4.** PART OF VEHICLE BODY the part of the body of a motor vehicle to which the windscreen, bonnet, and dashboard are attached **5.** ENG = cowling [Pre-12thC. Via prehistoric Germanic from, ultimately, Latin *cucullus* 'hood'.]

cowled /kowld/ *adj.* fitted with or wearing a hood or hooded cloak

Cowley /kówli/, **Abraham** (1618–67) English poet. A royalist secret agent and author of *The Mistress* (1647) and *Pindarique Odes* (1656).

cowlick /ków lik/ *n.* a tuft of hair growing in a different direction from the rest of the hair on sb's head and usually sticking up [From its resemblance to a ridge of hair on a cow's hide where hair growing in different directions meets, thought to be caused by the animal licking itself]

cowling /kówling/ *n.* a streamlined removable metal covering for an aircraft engine, fuselage, or nacelle

cowl neck *n.* a collar on a woman's garment, e.g. a jersey, that drapes in large folds around the neck (*hyphenated when used before a noun*)

cowman /kówmən/ (*plural* **-men** /-mən/) *n.* **1.** MAN WHO TENDS DAIRY HERD a man who tends cattle, especially sb responsible for the milking and other aspects of managing a dairy herd **2.** US, Can CATTLE OWNER a man who owns cattle or a cattle ranch **3.** US = cowherd

coworker /kố wurkər/ *n.* sb who works along with one or more other people

cow parsley *n.* a tall European herbaceous plant with umbrella-shaped clusters of white flowers, that grows on roadsides and in hedgerows. Latin name: *Anthriscus sylvestris*.

cow parsnip *n.* a tall perennial plant that grows in northern temperate regions and has a thick stem and flattened clusters of tiny white and purple flowers. Genus: *Heracleum*.

cowpat /ków pat/ *n.* a circular flat mass of dung excreted by a cow

cowpea /ków pee/ *n.* = black-eyed bean

Cowper /koopər, ków-/, **William** (1731–1800) British poet. His works include the ballad *John Gilpin* (1783) and the rural idyll *The Task* (1785).

Cowper's gland /kooʻpərz-, ków-/ *n.* either of two small glands, just below the prostate, that secrete into the urethra a lubricant fluid that is released just prior to ejaculation of semen. ◊ **Bartholin's gland** [Mid-18thC. Named after the English anatomist William *Cowper* (1666–1709), who first described it.]

cowpox /ków poks/ *n.* a mild viral skin disease in cattle, usually affecting the udder with a pustular rash. Cowpox virus was once used to inoculate humans against smallpox. Technical name **vaccinia**

Cowra /kówrə/ town and agricultural centre on the Lachlan River in central New South Wales, Aus-tralia. Population: 8,416 (1991).

cowrie /kówri/, **cowry** (*plural* **-ries**) *n.* **1.** BRIGHTLY COLOURED MOLLUSC a tropical marine mollusc that has a glossy brightly coloured shell with a long central toothed opening. Family: Cypraeidae. **2.** SHELL USED AS MONEY the shell of the cowrie, formerly used as money in parts of Africa and Asia [Mid-17thC. From Hindi *kaurī*.]

cowrite /kố rīt/ (**-writes, -writing, -written, -wrote**) *vt.* to write sth, e.g. a screenplay or report, jointly with sb —**cowriter** *n.*

cowry /kówri/ *n.* = cowrie

cow shark *n.* a large flabby bottom-dwelling shark that has a weak jaw and small teeth and lives in warm and temperate seas. Family: Hexanchidae.

cowshed /ków shed/ *n.* a building in which cattle are housed

cowslip /kówslip/ *n.* a common primrose with long-stemmed fragrant yellow flowers that grows in grassy areas in temperate regions of Europe, Africa, and Asia. Latin name: *Primula veris*. [Old English *cūslyppe* 'cow dung', probably from a belief that it grew where a cowpat had fallen]

cox /koks/ *n.* SB IN CHARGE OF ROWING BOAT the member of a rowing crew who faces forward, steers the boat, and directs the speed and rhythm of the rowers. US term **coxswain** *n.* **1** ■ *vti.* (**coxes, coxing, coxed**) STEER ROWING BOAT to act as the cox of a rowing boat, es-pecially in a race. US term **coxswain** *v.* [Late 19thC. Shortening of COXSWAIN.] —**coxless** *adj.*

Cox /koks/ *n.* = Cox's Orange Pippin (*informal*)

Cox /koks/, **David** (1783–1859) British artist. He is known for his watercolours of landscapes in northern Wales, characterized by broad washes and atmospheric effects.

Cox, Paul (b. 1940) Dutch-born Australian film director. He wrote and directed *Man of Flowers* (1983) and *Cactus* (1986).

Cox, Philip (b. 1939) Australian architect. He is noted for his use of awnings and curved steel frames in buildings such as the Yulara Resort at Uluru and the Sydney Exhibition Centre.

coxa /kóksə/ (plural **-ae** /-seeǐ/) n. **1.** ANAT HIP the hipbone or hip joint (technical) **2.** ZOOL PART OF INSECT LEG the base segment of the leg of most insects and other arthropods [Early 19thC. From Latin, 'hip'.] —**coxal** adj.

coxalgia /kok sálji ə, -jə/ n. pain in the hip, or a disease of the hip —**coxalgic** adj.

coxcomb /kóks kōm/ n. (archaic) **1.** DANDY a conceited man with an excessive interest in clothes and fashion **2.** JESTER'S CAP the cap worn by a medieval jester, shaped like a cockscomb [Mid-16thC. Alteration of COCKSCOMB.]

coxcombry /kóks kōmri/ (plural **-ries**) n. foolishly excessive conceit or concern about clothes and fashion, or an instance of this (archaic)

Coxsackie virus /kok sáki-, kŏŏk saáki-/, **coxsackie virus** n. an enterovirus belonging to a group that occurs in the human intestinal tract and causes diseases such as viral meningitis and a condition similar to poliomyelitis [Mid-20thC. Named after *Coxsackie* in New York State, USA, where the first cases were identified.]

Cox's Orange Pippin n. a small variety of eating apple with a yellowish-green skin flecked or patched with red [Mid-19thC. Named after Richard *Cox* (c.1776–1845), an English amateur fruit-grower who first grew it.]

coxswain /kóks'n, -swayn/, **cockswain** n. **1.** ROWING = COX **2.** SB IN CHARGE OF LIFEBOAT sb who is in charge of a lifeboat and its crew, and who usually steers it **3.** SENIOR PETTY OFFICER the senior petty officer of a small ship ■ vti. (**-swains, -swaining, -swained**) = cox [14thC. From COCK 'ship's boat' + SWAIN.]

coy /koy/ adj. **1.** PRETENDING TO BE SHY pretending, in a teasing or provocative way, to be reserved or modest **2.** SHY shy or reserved in social situations **3.** UNCOMMUNICATIVE unwilling to reveal information about sb or sth, especially in a way that teases or annoys sb who wants the information [14thC. Via French *coi* 'quiet' from, ultimately, Latin *quietus* (source of English *quiet*).] —**coyish** adj. —**coyly** adv. —**coyness** n.

Coy. abbr. MIL company

coyote /koy óti, kī-, kóyōt, kī'-/ (plural **-tes** or **-te**) n. a carnivorous North American canine mammal, similar to but smaller than the wolf. Coyotes are known for their howling and yapping at night and are considered pests in crowded residential and farming areas. Latin name: *Canis latrans*. [Mid-18thC. Via Mexican Spanish from Nahuatl *coyotl*.]

coyotillo /kóyō teé lyō/ (plural **-los**) n. a thorny shrub that grows in Mexico and the southwestern United States, with small green flowers and poisonous black berries. Latin name: *Karwinskia humboldtiana*. [Late 19thC. From Mexican Spanish, literally 'little coyote'.]

Coypu

coypu /kóy poo/ (plural **-pus** or **-pu**) n. a large semi-aquatic rodent with webbed feet and a long tail, native to South America. It is reared in captivity for its fur. [Late 18thC. From Araucanian.]

coz /kuz/ n. a cousin (old) [Mid-16thC. Shortening.]

cozen /kúzz'n/ (**-ens, -ening, -ened**) vti. to deceive, cheat, or defraud sb (archaic) [Late 16thC. Perhaps from obsolete Italian *cozzonare* 'to cheat' or Old French *coçoner* 'to act as a middle man', both from, ultimately, Latin *coctio* 'dealer'.] —**cozener** n.

cozenage /kúzz'n ij/ n. trickery or deception (archaic)

cozy adj., n. US = **cosy**

CP abbr. **1.** Canadian Press **2.** chemically pure **3.** command post **4.** Communist Party **5.** Aus Country Party

cp. abbr. compare

CPA abbr. COMPUT critical path analysis

cpd abbr. compound

cpi abbr. characters per inch

Cpl abbr. Corporal

CPO abbr. Chief Petty Officer

CPR abbr. **1.** cardiopulmonary resuscitation **2.** Canadian Pacific Railway

cps abbr. **1.** COMPUT characters per second **2.** PHYS cycles per second

CPS abbr. Crown Prosecution Service

CPSA abbr. Civil and Public Services Association

CPSU abbr. **1.** Communist Party of the Soviet Union **2.** Aus Community and Public Service Union

Cpt. abbr. Captain

CPU abbr. central processing unit

CQ[1] n. the code letters transmitted at the start of a radio message indicating that the message is meant for all receivers and requesting a response

CQ[2] abbr. charge of quarters

Cr symbol. **1.** chromium ■ abbr. **2.** Councillor

CR abbr. **1.** Community of the Resurrection **2.** PSYCHOL conditioned reflex **3.** PSYCHOL conditioned response

cr. abbr. **1.** credit **2.** creditor **3.** creek

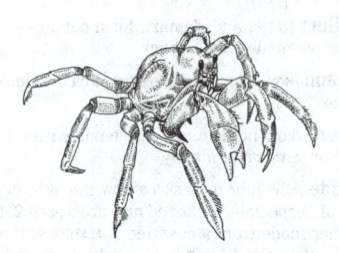

Crab

crab[1] /krab/ n. **1.** FLAT CRUSTACEAN a crustacean with a broad flat shell, antennae, a small abdomen, and five pairs of legs, the front pair of which are in the form of grasping pincers. Suborder: Brachyura. **2.** CRUSTACEAN RESEMBLING CRAB an animal similar or related to the true crab, e.g. the hermit crab, horseshoe crab, and king crab **3.** FLESH OF CRAB the flesh of a crab when used as food **4.** PARASITIC LOUSE IN PUBIC HAIR a parasitic louse resembling a tiny crab that infests the pubic hair of humans, causing inflammation and itching of the skin. Latin name: *Phthirius pubis*. **5.** MECH ENG CRANE a machine similar to a crane designed to lift and move heavy weights **6.** AIR FLYING MANOEUVRE a flying manoeuvre in which an aircraft is steered into a crosswind slightly to compensate for drifting off course ■ **crabs** npl. LICE INFESTATION an infestation of crab lice (informal) ■ v. (**crabs, crabbing, crabbed**) **1.** vti. SCURRY SIDEWAYS to move sideways as a crab does, or to cause sth to move in this way **2.** vi. CATCH CRABS to go fishing or hunting for crabs **3.** vti. AIR FLY INTO CROSSWIND to fly an aircraft slightly into a crosswind to compensate for drifting off course **4.** vi. NAUT SAIL WITH SIDEWAYS DRIFT to sail forwards with a slight sideways drift caused by a current [Old English *crabba*. Ultimately from an Indo-European word meaning 'scratch', which also produced English *carve* and *graffito*.] ◇ **catch a crab** in rowing, to make a faulty stroke by failing to make contact

with the water or plunging the oar blade in too deeply

crab[2] /krab/ n. = **crab apple** [15thC. Origin uncertain: possibly an alteration by folk etymology (because a bad-tempered crab was likened to a sour apple) of dialect *scrab*, from a Scandinavian language.]

crab[3] /krab/ n. SB BAD-TEMPERED sb who is bad-tempered or disagreeable by nature (informal insult) ■ v. (**crabs, crabbing, crabbed**) (informal) **1.** vi. CRITICIZE to criticize or grumble about sb or sth **2.** vt. SPOIL to ruin or spoil sth through interference [Late 16thC. Probably a back-formation from CRABBED.]

Crab n. ZODIAC = **Cancer**

crab apple n. **1.** SMALL SOUR APPLE the small sour fruit of a type of apple tree. Crab apples are too sour to eat but are used in preserves. **2.** APPLE TREE an apple tree with white, pink, or red flowers that produces small sour fruit. Genus: *Malus*.

Crabbe /krab/, **George** (1754–1832) British poet and clergyman. He was the author of *The Village* (1783), *The Parish Register* (1807), and *The Borough* (1810).

crabbed /krábbid/ adj. **1.** GROUCHY bad-tempered, irritable, or disagreeable by nature **2.** HARD TO READ hard to read, because the words and letters are compressed **3.** COMPLICATED complicated and hard to follow (dated) ○ *crabbed logic* [13thC. Formed from CRAB[1] because the way crabs threaten with their claws and their sideways walk suggest bad temper; reinforced by the idea of 'sourness' found in CRAB[2].] —**crabbedly** adv. —**crabbedness** n.

crabber /krábbər/ n. **1.** CATCHER OF CRABS sb who fishes for crabs **2.** CRAB BOAT a boat used in fishing for crabs

crabbing /krábbing/ n. fishing or hunting for crabs

crabby /krábbi/ (**-bier, -biest**) adj. bad-tempered or irritable in character [Mid-16thC. Formed from both CRAB[1] and CRAB[2].] —**crabbily** adv. —**crabbiness** n.

crab grass (plural **crab grasses** or **crab grass**) n. a coarse grass that grows in warm regions, has creeping stems that root freely, and is considered a weed in lawns and gardens. Genus: *Digitaria*.

crab louse n. = **crab**[1] n. 4

crabmeat /kráb meet/ n. the flesh of a crab when used as food

Crab Nebula n. the gaseous remains of an exploded star in the constellation Taurus, about 5000 light-years from the Earth

crab stick n. a stick-shaped piece of processed fish that has been flavoured and coloured to resemble crabmeat

crabstick /kráb stik/ n. **1.** SB BAD-TEMPERED sb bad-tempered or irritable (informal) **2.** STICK OF CRAB APPLE WOOD a stick or club made from the wood of a crab apple

crabwise /kráb wīz/ adv., adj. **1.** SIDEWAYS sideways, as crabs usually move **2.** BY INDIRECT MEANS in roundabout and cautious way

CRAC /krak/ abbr. Careers Research and Advisory Centre

crachach /krákh akh/ npl. Wales upper class people (informal) [Late 20thC. From Welsh.]

crack /krak/ v. (**cracks, cracking, cracked**) **1.** vti. BREAK WITHOUT COMING FULLY APART to break, or make sth break, in such a way that a fine split or splits appear but the split sections do not come apart **2.** vti. BREAK INTO PIECES to break into pieces, or to break sth into pieces **3.** vti. BREAK WITH SHARP NOISE to break, or make sth break, with a sudden sharp noise **4.** vti. MAKE SHARP NOISE to make a loud sharp sound, or to cause sth, e.g. a whip or a rifle, to make such a sound **5.** vt. HIT HARD to hit sth with a powerful impact **6.** vti. BREAK OPEN UNDER PRESSURE to break open because of pressure, or to make sth, e.g. a nut, break or open by pressure **7.** vti. FAIL OR MAKE STH FAIL to fail, give way, or break down, or to make sb or sth do so **8.** vti. BREAK DOWN PSYCHOLOGICALLY to break down psychologically, or to cause sb to break down psychologically, e.g. under stress or torture **9.** vi. BECOME HOARSE OR CHANGE IN PITCH to become slightly hoarse or suffer from uncontrollable changes in pitch, especially because of emotion or stress (refers to the voice) **10.** vt. TELL JOKE to tell sth, especially a joke (informal) **11.** vt. DECODE OR SOLVE to decipher or solve sth, e.g. a code, puzzle, or problem (*informal*) **12.** *vt.* **BREAK INTO** to force a way into sth, especially a safe (*informal*) **13.** *vt.* **OPEN STH TO DRINK** to open sth such as a bottle in order to drink its contents (*informal*) **14.** *vi. Scotland* **TO CHAT** to chat or gossip ○ *We haven't got time to crack with you just now.* **15.** *vt.* INDUST **BREAK DOWN INTO SMALLER MOLECULES** to break down sth, especially the heavier hydrocarbons in petroleum, into smaller molecules by using heat or catalysis ■ *n.* **1. THIN BREAK** a break or flaw in sth, e.g. a mirror, that is visible as a fine line **2. LONG NARROW OPENING** a relatively long and narrow break, hole, or opening in sth **3. SHARP NOISE** a sudden loud sharp noise **4. WEAKNESS** a flaw, defect, or weak spot **5. BLOW** a hard blow from sb or sth (*informal*) **6. SARCASTIC COMMENT** a sarcastic, funny, or rude remark, especially at sb's expense (*informal*) **7. ATTEMPT** an attempt at sth (*informal*) **8. UNEVEN VOICE TONE** a hoarseness or uncontrollable change in pitch in sb's voice **9. EXACT MOMENT** the exact moment when sth happens or begins ○ *at the crack of dawn* **10.** *Scotland* **CONVERSATION** chat, conversation, gossip, or news **11.** *Ireland, Scotland* **ENJOYMENT** entertainment, fun, or enjoyment, especially when experienced in a group or in a particular place ○ *The crack was fierce in Heraghty's last night!* ○ *We took turns at driving, and the crack was great all the way down.* **12. SB OR STH THAT EXCELS** sb or sth that is outstandingly good, talented, or skilled (*informal*) **13. crack PURIFIED FORM OF COCAINE** a purified and extremely addictive form of cocaine (*slang*) ■ *adj.* **EXCELLENT** excellent, expert, or trained to a high degree of efficiency (*informal*) [Old English *cracian*, from the same prehistoric Germanic ancestor as Dutch *kraken* and German *krachen*. The original idea was of making a loud noise, the idea of breaking coming from this.] ◇ **a fair crack of the whip** an equal chance, or fair treatment ◇ **be not all he's** *or* **she's** *or* **it's cracked up to be** to be not as good as promised or reputed ◇ **crack it** to achieve sth or be successful (*informal*) ◇ **paper over the cracks** to try to hide the fact that sth is wrong and pretend that everything is all right ◇ **the crack of doom** the moment when the world ends and God's final judgment of humankind **(the Last Judgment)** begins (*literary*)

crack down *vi.* to take strong and decisive action against sth undesirable or illegal or against sb involved in such activity (*informal*)

crack on *vi.* to work hard or harder at sth (*informal*)

crack onto *vt. Aus* to start a sexual relationship with sb (*informal*)

crack up *v.* **1.** *vi.* **HAVE BREAKDOWN** to experience a psychological or, sometimes, physical breakdown, usually because of stress (*informal*) **2.** *vi.* **BREAK INTO PIECES** to crack and break into pieces **3.** *vti.* **LAUGH UNCONTROLLABLY** to laugh, or cause sb to laugh, uncontrollably (*informal*)

crackbrained /krák braynd/ *adj.* extremely irrational or eccentric

crack cocaine *n.* = **crack** *n.* 13

crackdown /krák down/ *n.* a strong and decisive measure taken against sth undesirable or illegal, or against sb involved in such activity

cracked /krakt/ *adj.* **1. HAVING CRACKS** marked with a crack or cracks **2. IRRATIONAL** extremely irrational (*informal*) **3. COARSELY CRUSHED** broken or crushed into coarse pieces ○ *cracked wheat* **4. HOARSE** sounding rough or hoarse vocally, often because of emotion or stress

cracked wheat *n.* whole grains of wheat that have been chopped into little pieces

cracker /krákər/ *n.* **1. DECORATED TUBE WITH TRINKET** a cardboard tube, containing a small toy, trinket, joke, or paper hat, that is wrapped in coloured paper and opens with an explosive noise when both its ends are pulled **2.** = **firecracker 3. FLAT CRISP BISCUIT** a thin crisp, usually unsweetened, and sometimes salted biscuit, often eaten with cheese **4. SB OR STH THAT CRACKS** sb who or sth that cracks sth (*often used in the plural*) **5. SB OR STH EXCELLENT** sb or sth that is excellent or a fine example of its kind (*informal*) **6.** INDUST **DEVICE FOR CRACKING PETROLEUM COMPOUNDS** a device in which petroleum oils and tars are broken down to yield more valuable light fuels

crackerjack /krákər jak/ *adj.* outstanding in quality or ability (*dated informal*) [Late 19thC. From CRACKER 'excellent' + JACK 'man'.] —**crackerjack** *n.*

crackers /krákərz/ *adj.* mildly irrational or eccentric (*informal*)

crackhead /krák hed/ *n.* sb who is addicted to crack cocaine (*slang*)

crack house *n.* a house or flat where crack cocaine is sold to addicts and where, sometimes, it is also made (*slang*)

cracking /kráking/ *adj.* (*informal*) **1. QUICK** very fast ○ *at a cracking pace* **2. EXCELLENT** excellent or impressive ■ *adv.* **VERY** extremely (*informal*) ■ *n.* **BREAKING DOWN INTO SMALLER MOLECULES** the breaking down of sth, especially the heavier hydrocarbons in petroleum, into smaller molecules using heat or catalysis ◇ **get cracking** to start moving or doing sth quickly or more quickly (informal)

crackle /krák'l/ *v.* (**-les, -ling, -led**) **1.** *vti.* **MAKE RAPID SNAPPING NOISE** to make, or cause sth to make, repeated short sharp snapping or popping noises, such as dry wood makes when burning **2.** *vi.* **SCINTILLATE** to be lively, energetic, or scintillating ○ *The play crackles with wit.* **3.** *vt.* **DECORATE WITH CRACKS** to decorate a piece of pottery or porcelain with a network of fine cracks in the surface of its glaze ■ *n.* **1. REPEATED SNAPPING NOISES** a series of repeated short sharp snapping or popping noises **2. FINE DECORATIVE CRACKS** a network of fine cracks created as decoration in the surface of the glaze of pottery or porcelain **3. crackle, crackleware PORCELAIN DECORATED WITH FINE CRACKS** pottery or porcelain decorated with a network of fine cracks in the surface of its glaze

crackling /krákling/ *n.* **1. SNAPPING OR POPPING NOISES** a series of repeated short sharp snapping or popping noises **2. CRISPLY COOKED PORK SKIN** the crisp skin of roast pork **3. OFFENSIVE TERM** an offensive term for women (*offensive slang*)

crackly /krákli/ (**-lier, -liest**) *adj.* **1. BRITTLE** brittle or crisp **2. MAKING SNAPPING NOISES** making or consisting of a series of repeated short sharp snapping or popping noises

cracknel /krákn'l/ *n.* a hard light brittle biscuit [14thC. Via Old French *craquelin* from Middle Dutch *krākeline*, a type of small cake, from *kraken* 'to crack'.]

Cracknell /krákn'l/, **Ruth Winifred** (*b.* 1925) Australian actor. She is noted for her performances in classic theatrical works as well as television dramas and situation comedies.

crackpot /krák pot/ *n.* **SB UNCONVENTIONAL** sb who has unconventional or wild ideas (*informal insult*) ■ *adj.* **UNREALISTIC** extremely eccentric or unrealistic (*informal*) ○ *another of his crackpot money-making schemes*

cracksman /kráksmən/ (*plural* **-men** /-mən/) *n.* a burglar, especially one who breaks into safes (*slang*)

crack-up *n.* (*informal*) **1. BREAKDOWN** a psychological or sometimes a physical breakdown **2. CRASH** a motor vehicle or aircraft crash

Cracow /krákow, -ō, -of/ university city on the River Vistula in southern Poland. Its medieval architecture attracts many tourists, but it is also an important industrial centre. Population: 745,400 (1995).

-cracy *suffix.* rule, government, power ○ *technocracy* [Via French *-cratie* from, ultimately, Greek *kratos* 'power, strength'. Ultimately from an Indo-European word meaning 'hard', which is also the ancestor of English *hard* and *hardy*.]

cradle /kráyd'l/ *n.* **1. BABY'S BED** a small bed, usually on rockers, with enclosing sides, used for a baby **2. STARTING PLACE** the place where sth begins or develops in its early stages ○ *the cradle of civilization* **3. MECHANIC'S BOARD ON WHEELS** a flat board on wheels or casters on which a mechanic can slide under a vehicle **4. SUPPORTING FRAMEWORK** a framework for supporting sth, e.g. a ship that is being built or repaired **5. HANGING PLATFORM** a movable platform or cage hung on the side of sth, e.g. a building or ship, to hold sb who is working there **6. SUPPORT FOR TELEPHONE HANDSET** the part of a telephone on which the handset rests or hangs **7. PROTECTIVE FRAME SUPPORTING BEDCLOTHES** a frame placed beneath bedclothes covering a patient to keep them from touching a sensitive part of the body, e.g. after injury or an operation **8. PANNING DEVICE** a rocking device like a box used in panning for gold ■ *vt.* (**-dles, -dling, -dled**) **1. HOLD CAREFULLY** to hold or support sb or sth tenderly, carefully, or protectively, especially in a hollow formed with the arms or hands **2. PUT INTO CRADLE** to put sb or sth into a cradle or sth like a cradle **3. SUPPORT IN FRAMEWORK** to support sth in a framework, e.g. a ship that is being built or repaired **4. NURTURE** to look after a young child, or support sth in the early stages of its development **5. HANG UP PHONE** to put the handset of a telephone on its cradle **6. WASH SOIL** to wash gold-bearing soil in a cradle [Old English *cradol*, of uncertain origin: possibly from a prehistoric Germanic word that is also the ancestor of German *Kratte* 'basket'] —**cradler** *n.* ◇ **rob the cradle** *US* to be romantically or sexually involved with sb who is much younger (*informal*)

cradle cap *n.* a skin condition that commonly affects the scalp of young babies, causing thick scaling and flaking

Cradle Mountain /kráyd'l-/ mountain in central Tasmania, Australia, now part of Cradle Mountain-Lake St Clair National Park. Height: 1,545 m/5,069 ft.

cradle snatcher *n.* sb who has a romantic or sexual relationship with a much younger person (*informal*)

cradlesong /kráyd'l song/ *n.* = **lullaby**

cradling /kráydling/ *n.* a wooden or iron framework, especially one used to support a ceiling while it is being installed

Crafers-Bridgewater /kráyfərz bríj wawtər/ town in South Australia, in Oceania, near Adelaide in the Mount Lofty Ranges. Population: 11,879 (1991).

craft /kraaft/ *n.* **1. SKILFUL CREATIVE ACTIVITY** a profession or activity such as weaving, pottery, or wood carving, involving the skilful making of decorative or practical objects by hand (*often used in combination*) **2. OBJECT PRODUCED BY SKILFUL HANDWORK** sth such as a piece of pottery or carving produced skilfully by hand, especially in a traditional manner **3. SKILL** skill in making or doing things, especially by hand **4. SKILLED PROFESSION OR ACTIVITY** a profession or activity that requires skill and training, or experience, or specialized knowledge (*often used in combination*) **5. TRADE ASSOCIATION** the people engaged in a skilled trade or profession, considered as a group (*dated*) **6. DEVIOUSNESS** skill in trickery or deceiving others **7.** (*plural* **craft**) **VESSEL** a vessel used for travelling, e.g. a boat, ship, aeroplane, or space vehicle (*often used in combination*) ■ *vt.* (**crafts, crafting, crafted**) **MAKE WITH SKILL** to produce or create sth with skill and care [Old English *cræft* of prehistoric Germanic origin. Originally 'strength, power'; this sense died out in the 16thC.] —**crafter** *n.*

WORD KEY: SYNONYMS

See Synonyms at ***boat***.

craft apprenticeship *n.* a period of practical training undertaken by sb who is learning a skilled trade such as plumbing or carpentry

craft-brewed *adj. US* made by a small-scale brewery in small quantities

craftsman /kraáftsmən/ (*plural* **-men** /-mən/) *n.* **1. SKILLED WORKER** a man who works at a skilled trade or profession **2. SKILFUL MAN** a man who does sth with great skill and expertise —**craftsmanlike** *adj.* —**craftsmanly** *adj.* —**craftsmanship** *n.*

craftswoman /kraáfts wòomən/ (*plural* **-en** /-wimmin/) *n.* **1. SKILLED FEMALE WORKER** a woman who works at a skilled trade or profession **2. SKILFUL WOMAN** a woman who does sth with great skill and expertise

craft union *n.* a labour union for people who work at a particular skilled trade, as distinct from an organization for everyone employed in a particular industry

crafty /kraáfti/ (**-ier, -iest**) *adj.* using cunning or trickery to deceive other people —**craftily** *adv.* —**craftiness** *n.*

crag /krag/ *n.* a steep rough mass of rock forming part of a cliff or mountain peak [14thC. From a Celtic word, probably either Welsh *craig* or Gaelic *creagh*.] —**cragged** *adj.*

craggy /krággi/ (**-gier, -giest**) *adj.* **1.** ROCKY AND STEEP steep and rocky, and forming part of a cliff or mountain peak **2.** RUGGED rugged-looking with strong prominent masculine features —**craggily** *adv.* —**cragginess** *n.*

cragsman /krágzmən/ (*plural* **-men** /-mən/) *n.* a skilled and experienced rock climber

Craig /krayg/, **Sir Edward Gordon** (1872–1966) British actor, director, and stage designer. He was the author of *On the Art of the Theatre* (1911) and published the theatrical journal *The Mask* (1908–29).

Craigavon /krayg ávv'n/ administrative district in County Armagh, Northern Ireland. Population: 77,900 (1995).

Craigieburn /kráygi burn/ town in central Victoria, Australia. It is an industrial and residential centre. Population: 12,919 (1996).

Craiova /krī óvə/ city and capital of Dolj County, southwestern Romania. It is an important industrial centre. Population: 306,825 (1994).

crake /krayk/ *n.* a short-billed long-legged Eurasian marsh bird of the rail family, e.g. the corncrake or spotted crake [14thC. From Old Norse *kráka, krákr* used of several birds, including the raven; probably an imitation of their sound.]

cram /kram/ *v.* (**crams, cramming, crammed**) **1.** *vt.* FORCE INTO STH to force people or objects into a space or container that is too small to hold them comfortably **2.** *vti.* EAT GREEDILY to eat hastily and greedily **3.** *vt.* FORCE TO EAT to encourage or force a person or animal to eat more than is necessary **4.** *vti.* STUDY INTENSIVELY to study a subject intensively for an imminent examination (*informal*) **5.** *vt.* TUTOR INTENSIVELY to tutor sb intensively for an examination (*informal*) ■ *n.* **1.** TIGHTLY PACKED STATE a situation in which a group of people or things is crushed, crowded, or tightly packed together **2.** PERIOD OF INTENSIVE STUDY a period of intensive study, especially for an imminent examination (*informal*) [Old English *(ge)crammian*, from a prehistoric Germanic base that also produced English *grapnel* and *crampon*]

Cram /kram/, **Steve** (*b.* 1960) British middle-distance runner and 1984 Olympic silver medallist in the 1,500 metres. Over 19 days in 1985, he set new world records for the mile, the 1,500 metres, and the 2,000 metres. Full name **Steven Cram**

crambo /krámbō/ (*plural* **-boes**) *n.* a game in which one player gives a word or a line of verse for which the other players must find a rhyming word or line (*dated*) [Mid-17thC. Alteration of obsolete *crambe* 'cabbage, distasteful repetition', via Latin from Greek *krambē* 'cabbage' (usually referring to Latin *crambe repetita* 'sth unpleasant to have repeated', literally 'warmed-up cabbage').]

cram-full *adj.* absolutely full

crammer /krámmər/ *n.* a school or tutor that prepares students intensively for an examination, especially one that they have failed before

cramp[1] /kramp/ *n.* **1.** PAINFUL MUSCLE CONTRACTION a sudden painful involuntary contraction of a muscle **2.** MUSCLE PARALYSIS the temporary paralysis of a muscle or muscle group caused by repetitive use or overexertion ○ *writer's cramp* ■ **cramps** *npl.* ABDOMINAL PAIN severe pain in the abdomen or adjoining areas, usually of gastrointestinal or uterine origin ■ *vi.* (**cramps, cramping, cramped**) BE AFFECTED WITH CRAMP to experience cramp [14thC. Via Old French *crampe* from Middle Dutch *krampe*.]

cramp[2] /kramp/ *n.* **1.** DEVICE FOR HOLDING THINGS TOGETHER an adjustable clamp for temporarily holding or pressing objects together **2.** RESTRICTION sth that confines, restricts, or restrains, e.g. a set of shackles **3.** CONFINED PLACE a confined or restricted position or place **4.** BAR WITH BENT ENDS a metal bar with ends bent at right angles, used in building to hold objects together, e.g. bricks or timbers ■ *vt.* (**cramps, cramping, cramped**) **1.** HOLD TOGETHER to fasten, hold, or press sth together with a cramp **2.** CONFINE to confine or enclose sb or sth in a small space (*usually passive*) **3.** HAMPER to hamper or obstruct sb or sth [14thC. From Middle Dutch *krampe*. Ultimately from a prehistoric Germanic word meaning 'bending, compression', which also

produced English *cramp*[1], *crimp*, and *cripple*.] ◇ **cramp sb's style** to restrict or hinder sb from doing sth freely (*informal*)

cramped /krampt/ *adj.* **1.** LACKING SPACE inconveniently or uncomfortably small and confining **2.** PACKED IN packed into too small a space for comfort **3.** HARD TO READ written or printed in small characters that are close together and hard to read

cramp iron *n.* = cramp[2] *n.* 4

Crampon

crampon /krám pon, krámpən/ *n.* **1.** SPIKES ON CLIMBING BOOT a set of metal spikes fastened to the sole of a boot or shoe to provide better traction on ice or snow (*usually used in the plural*) **2.** GRAPPLING IRON a grappling iron (*archaic*) (*often used in the plural*) [13thC. Via Old French from Frankish.]

Cranach /kráa nakh/, **Lucas, the Elder** (1472–1553) German painter and engraver. Despite his stylized sensuous nudes, he was a friend of Martin Luther, whose portrait he painted. He was also a propagandist for the Reformation. Real name **Lucas Müller**

cranage /kráynij/ *n.* the use of a crane, or the fee paid for such use

cranberry /kránbəri/ (*plural* **-ries**) *n.* **1.** RED BERRY a sour red or reddish berry, used especially to make a sauce to accompany roast turkey **2.** PLANT PRODUCING RED BERRIES a low-growing evergreen plant of the heath family that yields cranberries. Genus: *Vaccinium*. [Mid-17thC. From German *Kranbeere*, literally 'crane berry', because the stamens are said to look like a crane's beak.]

cranberry bush, cranberry tree *n.* a North American shrub that produces acid red fruit. Latin name: *Viburnum trilobum.*

Cranborne Chase /kránbawrn-/ ancient royal forest in Wiltshire and Dorset, England, that is still partly wooded. It forms part of an Area of Outstanding Natural Beauty along with West Wiltshire Downs. Area: 983 sq. km/379 sq. mi.

Cranbourne /krán bawrn/ town in southeastern Australia. It is a suburb of Melbourne, in the state of Victoria. Population: 18,890 (1991).

Crane

crane /krayn/ *n.* **1.** LIFTING MACHINE a large machine used to lift and move heavy objects by means of a hook attached to cables suspended from a supporting, usually movable, beam **2.** MOVING SUPPORT FOR CAMERA a moving platform with a long support for a film or television camera **3.** MOVABLE SUPPORT WITH LONG ARM a device with a long arm for supporting sth, e.g. one for swinging and holding a pot or kettle over a fire **4.** BIRDS LONG-LEGGED BIRD a large long-necked long-

legged short-tailed bird that lives on plains and in marshes. Family: Gruidae. ■ *v.* (**cranes, craning, craned**) **1.** *vti.* STRETCH NECK TO SEE to stretch the neck in order to get a better view of sth **2.** *vt.* MOVE BY CRANE to lift or move sth using a crane [Old English *cran*. Ultimately from an Indo-European word that was probably an imitation of the sound of the bird, and which also produced English *geranium*.]

Crane /krayn/, **Hart** (1899–1932) US poet. His work celebrated modern civilization in poems such as *The Bridge* (1930). Full name **Harold Hart Crane**

Crane, Stephen (1871–1900) US writer. He is known for his novel *The Red Badge of Courage* (1895) and other fiction and poetry.

crane fly *n.* a large two-winged fly with a long thin body and long legs. Family: Tipulidae.

cranesbill /kráynz bil/ *n.* = geranium *n.* 2

crani- *prefix.* = cranio-

crania plural of cranium

cranial /kráyni əl/ *adj.* relating to, involving, or in the skull, especially the part covering the brain

cranial index *n.* = cephalic index

cranial nerve *n.* one of a pair of nerves that originate in the brainstem and pass out of the skull to the surface of the body. There are 12 pairs of cranial nerves in mammals, birds, and reptiles, and usually 10 in fish and amphibians.

craniate /kráyni it, -ayt/ *adj.* having a skull or cranium

cranio- *prefix.* cranium, skull ○ *craniofacial* [From CRANIUM]

craniofacial /kráyni ō fáysh'l/ *adj.* relating to or involving both the cranium and the face

craniology /kráyni ólləji/ *n.* the scientific study of the shapes, sizes, and other characteristics of human skulls —**craniological** /kráyni ə lójjik'l/ *adj.* —**craniologically** /-ə lójjikli/ *adv.* —**craniologist** /-óllǝjist/ *n.*

craniometer /kráyni ómmitər/ *n.* an instrument used to take measurements of the skull

craniometry /kráyni ómmətri/ *n.* the scientific measurement of skulls —**craniometric** /kráyni ə méttrik/ *adj.* —**craniometrical** /-ə méttrik'l/ *adj.* —**craniometrically** /-ə méttrikli/ *adv.* —**craniometrist** /-óm mətrist/ *n.*

craniosacral /kráyni ō sáykrəl, -sák-/ *adj.* = parasympathetic

craniosacral therapy *n.* gentle manipulation of the bones of the face, skull, and spine, intended to relieve conditions including migraine, sinusitis, and musculoskeletal problems

craniotomy /kráyni óttəmi/ (*plural* **-mies**) *n.* cutting open the skull to expose the brain, especially for brain surgery

cranium /kráyni əm/ (*plural* **-ums** or **-a** /-ni ə/) *n.* the skull of a vertebrate, especially the part that covers the brain [15thC. Via medieval Latin from Greek *kranion*.]

crank[1] /krangk/ *n.* **1.** MECHANICAL DEVICE FOR TRANSMITTING MOTION a device consisting of an arm or handle that is connected to a shaft at right angles, enabling the transmission of motion to or from the shaft. A crank may be used for changing rotary motion to reciprocating motion or vice versa. **2.** crank, crank handle HANDLE FOR STARTING MOTOR a handle with two or four right-angled bends, used to start an engine **3.** SB ECCENTRIC sb who has unusual or eccentric ideas and opinions, especially ones that are strongly held (*informal*) ■ *v.* (**cranks, cranking, cranked**) **1.** *vti.* USE CRANK TO DO STH to start, move, or operate sth by turning a crank **2.** *vt.* FORM INTO CRANK SHAPE to form sth into the shape of a crank ■ *adj.* ECCENTRIC typical of or done by sb who has unusual or eccentric, often strongly held, ideas and opinions (*disapproving*) [Old English *cranc*, from a prehistoric Germanic word meaning 'bent, crooked']

crank out *vt.* to produce sth, especially quickly, mechanically, regularly, and in large quantities (*informal*)

crank up *v.* **1.** *vti.* START WITH CRANK to start sth, especially an engine, with a crank **2.** *vt.* INCREASE to increase the force, volume, or intensity of sth (*informal*) **3.** *vt.* START to get sth started (*informal*) **4.** *vi.* INJECT DRUG to take or inject an illegal drug (*slang*)

crank[2] /krangk/ *adj.* unsteady on the water and likely to capsize [Early 17thC. Origin uncertain: possibly from CRANK[1].]

crankcase /krángk kayss/ *n.* the metal casing that encloses the crankshaft in some engines, especially internal-combustion engines

crank handle *n.* = **crank**[1] *n.* 2

crankpin /krángk pin/ *n.* a short cylindrical bearing piece in the arm of a crank, attached to a connecting rod

crankshaft /krángk shaaft/ *n.* a shaft driving or driven by a crank, e.g. one attached to a connecting rod in an internal-combustion engine

cranky[1] /krángki/ (**-ier, -iest**) *adj.* **1.** ECCENTRIC eccentric or obsessive (*informal*) **2.** GROUCHY disagreeable and easily irritated (*informal*) **3.** NOT IN WORKING ORDER not in good working order and likely to break down or operate unreliably **4.** CROOKED characterized by turns and twists **5.** UNWELL unwell or infirm (*regional*) —**crankily** *adv.* —**crankiness** *n.*

cranky[2] /krángki/ (**crankier, crankiest**) *adj.* SAILING = **crank**[2] *adj.*

Cranmer /kránmər/, **Thomas** (1489–1556) English archbishop. He was Archbishop of Canterbury (1533) and largely responsible for *The Book of Common Prayer* (1549, 1552). He annulled Henry VIII's marriages to Catherine of Aragon and Anne Boleyn, and divorced him from Anne of Cleves. Under Queen Mary he was burnt at the stake.

crannog /krànnəg/ *n.* an ancient Celtic settlement in Scotland or Ireland, usually fortified, built on a natural or constructed island in a lake or bog [Early 17thC. From Irish *crannóg* or Gaelic *crannag* 'timber structure', formed from *crann* 'tree, beam'.]

cranny /kránni/ (*plural* **-nies**) *n.* a small narrow crack, hole, or opening in a wall or rock [15thC. From French *crané* 'notched', from, ultimately, popular Latin *crena* 'small notch' (source of English *crenate*).] —**crannied** *adj.*

crap[1] /krap/ *n.* (*slang offensive*) **1.** EXCREMENT solid waste matter passed out of the body through the anus **2.** NONSENSE rubbish, nonsense, or sth worthless or annoying **3.** DEFECATION an act of passing solid waste matter out of the body through the anus ■ *adj.* WORTHLESS OR USELESS worthless, useless, or lacking in ability (*slang offensive*) ■ *vti.* (**craps, crapping, crapped**) DEFECATE to pass solid waste matter out of the body through the anus (*slang offensive*) [Late 19thC. From Middle English *crap* 'chaff', of uncertain origin: perhaps from Dutch *krappe* 'sth separated'; or via French *crape* 'siftings' from medieval Latin *crappa* 'chaff'.]

crap[2] *n.* **1.** DICE GAME a US gambling game played with two dice (*takes a singular verb*) **2.** *US* LOSING THROW a losing throw of the dice in the game of craps (*takes a singular or plural verb*) [Early 18thC. Origin uncertain: probably from French, variant of *crabs* 'score of two ones at dice', from English, plural of CRAB[1], the black dots perhaps being likened to a crab's eyes.]

crap out *vi.* (*slang*) **1.** AVOID DOING STH to avoid or discontinue an activity, especially out of fear **2.** *US* MAKE LOSING THROW to make a losing throw in the game of craps

crap[3] (**crap, crapping, crapped**) *vt.* to be afraid of doing sth (*slang*) [Late 19thC. See CRAPS.]

crape /krayp/ *n.* **1.** = **crêpe 2.** BLACK SILK FOR CLOTHES black silk used in the past to make mourning clothes **3.** BLACK BAND INDICATING MOURNING a band of crape worn as a sign of mourning round the arm or, in the past, round a hat [Early 16thC. From French *crêpe* (see CRÊPE).]

crape myrtle *n.* a deciduous Asian shrub or tree, cultivated for its white, pink, or red flowers. Latin name: *Lagerstroemia indica.*

crapper /kráppər/ *n.* a toilet (*slang offensive*)

crappie /kráppi/ (*plural* **-pies** *or* **-pie**) *n.* a freshwater sunfish, with equal-sized anal and dorsal fins, found in lakes and ponds in North America. Genus: *Pomoxis.* [Mid-19thC. Origin unknown.]

crappy /kráppi/ (**-pier, -piest**) *adj.* worthless, useless, of poor quality, or badly made or done (*slang*)

crapulent /krápyŏŏlənt/, **crapulous** /-ləss/ *adj.* (*dated*) **1.** REGULARLY OVERINDULGING regularly overindulging in both alcoholic drink and food **2.** SICK FROM OVERINDULGENCE suffering from the effects of overindulgence in both alcoholic drink and food [Mid-17thC. From late Latin *crapulentus* 'very drunk', from, ultimately, Greek *kraipalē* 'drunken headache, hangover'.] —**crapulence** *n.* —**crapulently** *adv.* —**crapulousness** *n.*

craquelure /krákə loor/ *n.* a network of small cracks that sometimes appear on the surface of an oil painting as it ages [Early 20thC. From French.]

crash[1] /krash/ *n.* **1.** VEHICLE COLLISION a collision involving a moving vehicle or aircraft **2.** LOUD NOISE a loud noise such as that made by thunder or by sth breaking violently into pieces **3.** COMPUTER BREAKDOWN a sudden complete failure of a computer system, device, or program, usually with an accompanying loss of data ○ *a system crash* **4.** FINANCIAL COLLAPSE the financial collapse or failure of sth such as a stock market, involving a massive drop in share prices, or the collapse of a commercial business ■ *v.* (**crashes, crashing, crashed**) **1.** *vti.* COLLIDE VIOLENTLY to strike against sth with great force, causing damage or destruction, or to cause sth, e.g. a car, to strike against sth in this way **2.** *vti.* MAKE LOUD NOISE to make a loud noise, or to cause sth to make such a noise **3.** *vti.* BREAK IN PIECES NOISILY to break into pieces violently and noisily, or break an object in this way **4.** *vti.* MOVE NOISILY to move, or cause sth to move, noisily, destructively, or violently **5.** *vti.* HAVE OR CAUSE COMPLETE COMPUTER FAILURE to experience a sudden complete failure, or cause a computer system to have a sudden complete failure **6.** *vi.* COLLAPSE FINANCIALLY to suffer financial collapse or failure **7.** *vi.* DROP SHARPLY to decrease in value rapidly and steeply **8.** *vi.* BE HEAVILY DEFEATED to be heavily defeated, e.g. in a sports match (*informal*) **9.** *vti.* ATTEND UNINVITED to attend an event, such as a party, without an invitation (*informal*) **10.** *vi.* SLEEP to sleep, especially somewhere other than usual when exhausted, or stay temporarily somewhere other than home (*informal*) ■ *adj.* **1.** RAPID AND INTENSIVE done intensively over a short period of time in order to achieve the desired results quickly **2.** SUDDEN AND STRONG abrupt and forceful ○ *a perfectly timed crash tackle* [14thC. Origin uncertain: possibly an imitation of the sound of a crash, perhaps influenced by DASH and CRAZE.] —**crasher** *n.*

crash out *vi.* (*informal*) **1.** = **crash**[1] **2.** BECOME UNCONSCIOUS to lose consciousness suddenly

crash[2] /krash/ *n.* a coarse linen or cotton cloth used for towels and curtains and in the bindings of books [Early 19thC. From Russian *krashenina* 'dyed coarse linen'.]

crash barrier *n.* a safety barrier, usually metal, at the edge of a road or racetrack or between the carriageways of a motorway

crash box *n.* a theatrical sound-effects device consisting of a box filled with various objects that, when shaken or dropped, will simulate the sound of a crash

crash dive *n.* a steep rapid dive from the surface of a body of water by a submarine

crash-dive (**crash-dives, crash-diving, crash-dived**) *vti.* **1.** DESCEND AND CRASH to dive steeply through the air and crash, or cause an aircraft to do this **2.** MAKE RAPID DIVE IN WATER to make a steep rapid descent from the surface of a body of water, or cause a submarine to do this

crash gearbox *n.* a gearbox without synchromesh, so that changing gears demands considerable skill and care by the driver, to ensure that engine and wheel speed are aligned

crash helmet *n.* a hard padded helmet worn by motorcyclists, racing drivers, and others to protect the head in case of an accident

crashing /kráshing/ *adj.* complete and utter (*informal*) ○ *a crashing bore*

crash-land (**crash-lands, crash-landing, crash-landed**) *vti.* to make an emergency landing in an aircraft, usually causing damage to the aircraft, or to cause an aircraft to make such a landing

crash landing *n.* an emergency landing by an aircraft, usually causing damage to the aircraft

crash pad *n.* **1.** PROTECTIVE PADDING IN VEHICLE padding inside a vehicle to protect the occupants in a crash **2.** PLACE TO SLEEP a place, other than home, where sb sleeps or stays temporarily (*dated informal*)

crash-test (**crash-tests, crash-testing, crash-tested**) *vt.* **1.** TEST TO BREAKING POINT to establish the safety and reliability of sth by subjecting it to tests, e.g. using heat, pressure, or strain, until it reaches its breaking point **2.** TEST VEHICLE IN CRASH to test a vehicle by deliberately crashing it into a wall to learn how it and its occupants will be affected in an accident

crashworthy /krásh wurthi/ *adj.* able to withstand a crash —**crashworthiness** *n.*

crass /krass/ *adj.* **1.** THOUGHTLESS AND VULGAR so thoughtless, vulgar, and insensitive as to lack all refinement or delicacy **2.** UTTER extreme or flagrant ○ *crass stupidity* [15thC. From Latin *crassus* 'thick, solid, fat' (source of English *grease* and *cresset*).] —**crassitude** *n.* —**crassly** *adv.* —**crassness** *n.*

-crat *suffix.* sb who supports or is a member of a particular kind of government ○ *technocrat* [Via French *-crate* from, ultimately, Greek *kratos* (see -CRACY)]

cratch /krach/ *n.* a rack for hay or other livestock fodder [13thC. Via Old French *creche* 'manger, crib' from a prehistoric Germanic word that is also the ancestor of English *crib.*]

crate /krayt/ *n.* **1.** BOX OR BASKET a large basket or a large open sturdy box used to carry or store objects **2.** OLD VEHICLE an old rickety aeroplane, car, or lorry (*dated informal*) ■ *vti.* (**crates, crating, crated**) PUT IN CRATE to put or pack sth in a crate [14thC. Origin uncertain: perhaps from Latin *cratis* 'wickerwork' or Dutch *krat* 'tailboard of a wagon'. Originally 'hurdle, grillwork'.]

crater /kráytər/ *n.* **1.** VOLCANO SUMMIT a circular funnel-shaped depression produced by volcanic eruption **2.** METEORITE IMPACT AREA a bowl-shaped hole on the surface of the Moon or a planet caused by the impact of a meteorite **3.** EXPLOSION HOLE a large hole in the ground or a surface caused by an explosion **4.** ANCIENT GREEK WINE BOWL in ancient Greece, a large shallow bowl with two handles, used to mix wine and water. US term **krater** ■ *vti.* (**-ters, -tering, -tered**) FORM CRATERS to form craters or make craters form in sth [Early 17thC. Via Latin from Greek *kratēr* '(mixing) bowl'.]

Crater *n.* a small constellation in the southern hemisphere near Hydra and Virgo

crathur *n. Ireland* = **cratur**

craton /kráy ton/ *n.* the extensive interior of a large block of the earth's crust that has been relatively stable for many millions of years [Mid-20thC. Origin uncertain: either an alteration of *kratogen*, from Greek *kratos* 'strength' + -GEN ; or from German *Kraton*, alteration of Greek *kratos.*] —**cratonic** /krə tónnik/ *adj.*

cratur /kréttər/, **crathur, craythur** *n. Ireland, Scotland* **1.** WHISKY whisky, often distilled illegally (*informal*) ○ *a drop of the cratur* **2.** PERSON a person [Variant of CREATURE, used humorously]

cravat /krə vát/ *n.* a scarf or band of fabric worn around a man's neck and tied in front [Mid-17thC. From French *cravate*, from *Cravate* 'Croatian', from German *Krabat(e)*, from Serbo-Croat *Hrvāt* 'a Croat'. From the linen scarfs worn by Croatian mercenaries in French service.]

crave /krayv/ (**craves, craving, craved**) *v.* **1.** *vti.* DESIRE to have a strong desire for sth **2.** *vt.* BEG FOR to beg or implore sth from sb (*archaic*) [Old English *crafian* 'to demand', from a prehistoric Germanic word perhaps meaning 'to force', which may also be the ancestor of English *craft*] —**craver** *n.* —**cravingly** *adv.*

WORD KEY: SYNONYMS

See Synonyms at ***want***.

craven /kráyv'n/ *adj.* COWARDLY so lacking in courage as to be worthy of contempt ■ *n.* UTTER COWARD a despicable coward (*archaic*) [12thC. Origin uncertain: perhaps via Anglo-Norman from Old French *cravanté* 'defeated', past participle of *cravanter* 'to crush', from Latin *crepant-*, the present participle stem of *crepare* 'to break'.] —**cravenly** *adv.* —**cravenness** *n.*

WORD KEY: SYNONYMS

See Synonyms at ***cowardly***.

craving /kráyving/ *n.* a strong desire for sth

craw /kraw/ *n.* **1.** = **crop** *n.* 7, **crop** *n.* 8 **2.** STOMACH the stomach of an animal (*informal*) **3.** *Ireland* THROAT the throat or gullet [14thC. From or related to Middle Low German *krage* or Middle Dutch *crāghe* 'neck, throat'.] ◇

stick in your craw to go against your sense of what is right, making you feel anger or resentment (*informal*)

crawfish /kráw fish/ (*plural* **-fish** *or* **-fishes**) *n. US* = **crayfish** [Early 17thC. Variant of CRAYFISH.]

Joan Crawford

Crawford /kráwfərd/, **Joan** (1908–77) US actor. She starred in over 70 films, including the Academy Award-winning *Mildred Pierce* (1945). Real name **Lucille Le Sueur**

crawl /krawl/ *vi.* (**crawls, crawling, crawled**) **1.** MOVE CLOSE TO GROUND to move slowly along on hands and knees or with the body close to the ground or a surface **2.** MOVE VERY SLOWLY to move forward at a slow pace **3.** BE SERVILE to try to please sb by behaving in a servile way (*informal*) **4.** BE OVERRUN to be filled with large numbers of moving people or things **5.** FEEL CREEPY to feel a sensation of being covered with moving insects, usually in reaction to sth frightening or disgusting ■ *n.* **1.** SLOW SPEED a very slow pace **2.** SWIMMING OVERARM SWIMMING STROKE a fast swimming stroke in which the swimmer lies face down and uses a flutter kick and an overarm stroke **3.** PROGRESS ON HANDS AND KNEES slow movement on hands and knees or with the body close to the ground [14thC. Origin uncertain: probably from Old Norse *krafla* 'to paw with the hands'.] —**crawlingly** *adv.*

crawler /kráwlər/ *n.* **1.** STH THAT CRAWLS an insect or other animal that crawls **2.** SB ACTING INGRATIATINGLY sb who behaves in a servile way in order to gain favour (*informal*) **3.** VEHICLE WITH TRACKS a vehicle that has continuous tracks of linked plates instead of wheels

crawler lane *n.* an extra lane on an uphill section of a main road for slow-moving vehicles

Crawley town in West Sussex, southeastern England. It was designated a new town in 1947. Population: 88,500 (1992).

crawling peg *n.* a method of controlling exchange rates or prices by limiting their fluctuation for a time and later allowing them to change in small increments

crawl space *n. US* a low unfinished space under a floor or above a ceiling in a building that gives access to plumbing, wiring, and ductwork [From having to crawl through it because of its restricted height]

crawly /kráwli/ (**-ier, -iest**) *adj.* causing a shuddery disgust or unease

craw-thumper *n. Ireland* sb who makes a great show of being very pious (*informal*) [*Craw* from such a person being typified as a 'breast-beater']

Craxi /kráksi/, **Bettino** (b. 1934) Italian politician. He was Italy's first socialist prime minister (1983–87). Indicted for corruption in 1993, he was convicted and sentenced to 14 years' imprisonment.

crayfish /kráyfish/ (*plural* **-fish** *or* **-fishes**) *n.* **1.** ANIMAL RESEMBLING LOBSTER a freshwater crustacean with large claws like those of a lobster. It is prized for its tail meat. Superfamily: Astacoidea. **2.** = **spiny lobster** [14thC. By folk etymology (influenced by FISH) from French *crevice* 'crayfish', from, ultimately, an Indo-European word meaning 'to scratch', which is also the ancestor of English *crawl*.]

crayon /kráy on/ *n.* **1.** COLOURED DRAWING STICK a stick of coloured wax, chalk, or charcoal, sometimes enclosed in wood like a pencil, used for drawing and colouring **2.** DRAWING a drawing made using crayons

Crayfish

■ *vti.* (**-ons, -oning, -oned**) USE CRAYONS to draw or colour sth with crayons [Mid-17thC. From French, 'pencil', from *craie* 'chalk', from Latin *creta* 'chalk, clay' (source of English *cretaceous*).] —**crayonist** /kráyənist/ *n.*

craythur *n. Ireland* = **cratur**

craze /krayz/ *n.* **1.** FAD a fashion that is extremely popular for a short time **2.** PERSONAL OBSESSION a short-lived obsession or enthusiasm that sb has for sth **3.** CERAMICS FINE CRACK a fine crack in the glaze of pottery. It happens when the glaze cools and contracts at a different temperature from the clay. ■ *vti.* (**crazes, crazing, crazed**) **1.** MAKE OR BECOME UNBALANCED to become or make sb become psychologically unbalanced or unstable **2.** PRODUCE CRACKS IN to produce fine cracks in the glaze of pottery, or to become covered with such cracks [14thC. Origin uncertain: probably from assumed Old Norse *krasa* 'to shatter', perhaps an imitation of the sound.]

crazed /krayzd/ *adj.* **1.** PSYCHOLOGICALLY UNBALANCED driven wild or uncontrollable, or showing signs of psychological disturbance **2.** CERAMICS WITH SURFACE CRACKS with fine cracks on the surface

crazing /kráyzing/ *n.* fine cracks in the glaze of a piece of pottery, produced when the glaze cools and contracts at a different temperature from the clay. When the effect is deliberate, it is often called crackle.

crazy /kráyzi/ *adj.* (**-zier, -ziest**) (*informal*) **1.** UNBALANCED affected by psychological disturbance or instability, or produced by an unbalanced mind **2.** RIDICULOUS not showing good sense or practicality **3.** EXCESSIVELY FOND excessively fond of sb or sth ■ *n.* (*plural* **-zies**) *US* UNBALANCED PERSON sb whose behaviour shows signs of psychological disturbance or instability (*informal*) —**crazily** *adv.* —**craziness** *n.*

Crazy Horse (1849?–77) Native American leader. As leader of the Oglala Sioux, he opposed and fought against European settlement. Original name **Ta-shunca Witco**

crazy paving *n.* a pavement of irregularly shaped pieces of paving stone fitted together, often used for garden paths

crazy quilt *n.* a quilt made of irregularly shaped and patterned pieces of cloth sewn together

CRE *abbr.* Commission for Racial Equality

creak /kreek/ *vi.* (**creaks, creaking, creaked**) **1.** SQUEAK to make a prolonged squeaking noise **2.** MOVE WITH SQUEAKING to move along while making prolonged squeaking noises ■ *n.* PROLONGED SQUEAK a prolonged squeaking noise [14thC. An imitation of the sound.] —**creakingly** *adv.*

creaky /kreéki/ (**-ier, -iest**) *adj.* **1.** CREAKING making a prolonged squeaking noise **2.** STIFF not able to move easily, especially as a result of ageing (*informal*) **3.** OLD OR OLD-FASHIONED showing signs of having deteriorated over time or of being old-fashioned (*informal*) —**creakily** *adv.* —**creakiness** *n.*

cream /kreem/ *n.* **1.** FATTY PART OF MILK a high-fat liquid product separated from milk and used in cooking and as an accompaniment to desserts **2.** CREAMY LOTION a cosmetic or medicinal preparation that has a thick smooth consistency like cream **3.** FOOD CREAMY FOOD a food that contains cream or has a consistency like cream **4.** FOOD SOFT-CENTRED CHOCOLATE a chocolate with a soft smooth filling **5.** BEST PART the best part of sth **6.** COLOURS WHITE TINGED WITH YELLOW a white colour with a faint yellowish tinge ■ *adj.* WHITE WITH SOME

YELLOW white with a tinge of yellow ■ *v.* (**creams, creaming, creamed**) **1.** *vt.* MAKE CREAMY to mix ingredients together to soften and combine them **2.** *vt.* PREPARE WITH CREAM to add cream to sth while cooking it or on serving it **3.** *vti.* FORM FOAM ON TOP to form, or cause sth to form a frothy layer resembling cream on the surface **4.** *vt.* to remove the cream from milk **5.** *vti.* FORM CREAM to form cream, or leave milk to form cream **6.** *vti.* EJACULATE ON STH to have an orgasm and ejaculate on sth (*slang taboo*) [14thC. From French *creme*, blend of late Latin *cramum* (of uncertain origin: perhaps from Gaulish) and ecclesiastical Latin *chrisma* 'ointment' (from Greek *khrisma*).]

cream off *vt.* **1.** REMOVE AS BEING THE BEST to take away the best part of sth **2.** *US* TAKE ILLICITLY to take and use sth for an illicit or unintended purpose (*informal*)

cream cheese *n.* a soft white unmatured cheese with a high fat content

cream cracker *n.* a crisp savoury biscuit usually eaten with cheese

creamer /kreémər/ *n.* **1.** CREAM SUBSTITUTE a cream substitute, used especially in coffee or tea **2.** SMALL JUG a small jug for serving cream

creamery /kreéməri/ (*plural* **-ies**) *n.* **1.** PLACE PRODUCING DAIRY PRODUCTS a place where milk is processed and dairy products are produced **2.** BUSINESS SELLING DAIRY PRODUCTS a business that sells dairy products [Mid-19thC. Formed from CREAM on the model of French *créme-rie*.]

cream of tartar *n.* potassium bitartrate, used as a raising agent in cooking, usually in baking powder

cream puff *n.* **1.** CREAM-FILLED PASTRY a sweet pastry made of a flaky shell filled with whipped cream and dusted with icing sugar **2.** EFFEMINATE MAN a weak effeminate man (*slang offensive*)

cream sherry *n.* a type of smooth sweet sherry

cream soda *n.* a carbonated soft drink flavoured with vanilla

cream tea *n.* a British afternoon meal of tea served with scones, jam, and thick, traditionally clotted, cream

creamware /kreém wair/ *n.* glazed earthenware of a deep creamy colour, first produced in Britain about 1720

creamy /kreémi/ (**-ier, -iest**) *adj.* **1.** LIKE CREAM with a texture, colour, taste, or consistency like cream **2.** CONTAINING CREAM containing a large amount of cream —**creamily** *adv.* —**creaminess** *n.*

crease /kreess/ *n.* **1.** FOLD PUT IN FABRIC a straight line formed in clothing or fabric by pressing **2.** UNWANTED FABRIC FOLD an unwanted line in clothing or fabric that has been crushed or folded **3.** SKIN WRINKLE a line or wrinkle on the skin **4.** CRICKET LINE NEAR WICKET a line that marks the position of the bowler or batsman in cricket **5.** ICE HOCKEY GOAL AREA the rectangular area in front of an ice hockey goal **6.** LACROSSE GOAL AREA the semicircular area surrounding a lacrosse goal ■ *v.* (**creases, creasing, creased**) **1.** *vti.* MAKE OR ACQUIRE CREASES to form lines, folds, or wrinkles in sth, or to become lined, folded, or wrinkled **2.** *vt.* GRAZE to graze the skin and inflict a superficial wound [Late 16thC. Origin uncertain: probably an alteration of *creaste* 'furrow, ridge', perhaps a variant of CREST, the ridges in creased cloth being likened to crests.] —**creaser** *n.* —**creasy** *adj.*

crease up *vti.* to laugh or make sb laugh uncontrollably (*informal*) [From the appearance of the face when laughing]

create /kri áyt/ (**-ates, -ating, -ated**) *v.* **1.** *vt.* MAKE to bring sb or sth into existence **2.** *vt.* GIVE RISE TO to produce sth as a result, or make sth happen **3.** *vti.* PRODUCE ART OR INVENT to use imagination to invent things or produce works of art **4.** *vt.* APPOINT to give sb a new title, role, or office **5.** *vt.* ARTS PERFORM FOR FIRST TIME to be the first person to perform a particular role in a production **6.** *vi.* CAUSE TROUBLE to become upset and make a fuss (*informal*) [14thC. From Latin *creat-*, the past participle stem of *creare* 'to bring forth, produce' (source of English *creature*), of uncertain origin: perhaps formed from *crescere* 'to grow'.]

— **WORD KEY: SYNONYMS** —
See Synonyms at *make*.

Creatine

$H_2N-C-N-CH_2-C-OH$ with CH_3, O groups and NH

Creatine

creatine /kreé ə teen/, **creatin** /-tin/ n. an amino acid formed during metabolism and used as an energy-storage molecule in vertebrate muscle tissue, usually as phosphocreatine. Formula: $C_4H_9O_2N_3$. [Mid-19thC. Coined from assumed Greek *kreat-* the stem of assumed *kreas* 'flesh' (source of English *pancreas*) + -INE.]

creatine kinase n. an enzyme that aids the breakdown of phosphocreatine into creatine and phosphoric acid, with a release of energy

creatine phosphate n. = phosphocreatine

creatinine /kri áttə neen/ n. a derivative of creatine found in muscle, blood, and urine. Formula: $C_4H_7ON_3$. [Mid-19thC. Coined from CREATINE + -INE.]

creation /kri áysh'n/ n. 1. MAKING STH the bringing of sth into existence 2. EARTH AND ITS INHABITANTS the world and everything on it 3. STH CREATED BY SB a product of human imagination or invention 4. ELABORATE GARMENT an elaborate or striking article of clothing —**creational** adj.

Creation n. 1. GOD'S MAKING OF UNIVERSE the act of God that, according to the Bible, brought the universe and all living beings into existence 2. UNIVERSE the universe as created by God, according to the Bible

creationism /kri áysh'nizzəm/ n. the belief that the Bible's account of the Creation is literally true —**creationist** adj., n.

creation science n. the attempt to provide scientific proof for the account of God's creation of the world that is described in the Bible

creative /kri áytiv/ adj. 1. NEW AND ORIGINAL using or showing use of the imagination to create new ideas or things ○ *a creative approach to the problem of space* 2. ABLE TO CREATE able to create things 3. RESOURCEFUL making imaginative use of the limited resources available 4. FIN INTENTIONALLY DECEPTIVE ABOUT FINANCIAL INFORMATION employing deceptive methods to distort financial records (*ironic*) ○ *creative accounting* ○ *creative bookkeeping* ■ n. IDEAS PERSON sb who is responsible for coming up with new ideas and concepts for sales campaigns (*informal*) ○ *ad agency creatives hard at work on a TV infomercial series* —**creatively** adv. —**creativeness** n.

creative writing n. the writing of fiction, poetry, or drama, often as an exercise, or the work written

creativity /kreé ay tívvəti/ n. 1. IMAGINATIVE ABILITY the ability to use the imagination to develop new and original ideas or things, especially in an artistic context 2. BEING CREATIVE the quality of being creative

creator /kri áytər/ n. sb who brings sth into existence —**creatorship** n.

Creator n. God regarded as creator of the universe

creature /kreéchər/ n. 1. LIVING BEING any living person or animal 2. UNPLEASANT LIVING BEING an unpleasant or frightening living thing 3. CREATED THING sth or sth that has been created ○ *a creature of your imagination* 4. TYPE OF PERSON sb of a particular type ○ *He's a harmless creature.* 5. SUBSERVIENT PERSON sb who is under the influence of sb or sth else [13thC. Directly or via French from late Latin *creatura*, from Latin *creat-* (see CREATE).] —**creatural** adj.

creature comforts npl. things considered necessary to a comfortable life

crèche /kresh, kraysh/ n. 1. CHILDCARE FACILITY a place where small children are looked after while their parents or guardians are working or doing sth else 2. NATIVITY SCENE a three-dimensional representation of the scene at the birth of Jesus Christ [Late 18thC. Via French, 'crib', from assumed Vulgar Latin *creppia*, from a prehistoric Germanic word that is also the ancestor of English *crib*.]

cred /kred/ n. credibility (*informal*) [Late 20thC. Shortening.]

credence /kreéd'nss/ n. 1. ACCEPTANCE acceptance based on the degree to which sth is believable 2. TRUSTWORTHINESS the power to inspire belief or trust 3. **credence, credence table** CHR CHURCH TABLE FOR BREAD AND WINE a small shelf or table in a church where the bread, wine, and vessels used for the Eucharist are kept [14thC. Directly or via French from medieval Latin *credentia* 'belief', from Latin *credent-*, the present participle stem of *credere* 'to believe'.]

credential /krə dénsh'l/ n. 1. PROOF OF ABILITY OR TRUSTWORTHINESS a certificate, letter, or experience that qualifies sb to do sth 2. AUTHENTICATION anything that provides authentication for a claim ■ **credentials** npl. OFFICIAL IDENTIFICATION a letter, badge, or other official identification that confirms sb's position or status [15thC. From medieval Latin *credentialis* 'entitling confidence', from *credentia* belief (see CREDENCE).] —**credentialed** adj.

credenza /krə dénzə/ n. a low sideboard, usually without legs [Late 19thC. Via Italian from medieval Latin *credentia* 'side table' (see CREDENCE).]

credibility /kréddə bílləti/ n. 1. BELIEVABILITY the ability to inspire belief or trust 2. WILLINGNESS TO BELIEVE a willingness to accept sth as true 3. STATUS sb's status as an acceptable person among a group of people

credibility gap n. 1. DISTRUST OF OFFICIAL STATEMENTS a situation in which the public distrusts the accuracy of official statements 2. LACK OF TRUST any situation in which a lack of trust exists between two groups 3. DISCREPANCY BETWEEN CLAIM AND TRUTH an apparent difference between what is claimed to be true and what is in fact true

credible /kréddəb'l/ adj. 1. BELIEVABLE easy to believe 2. TRUSTWORTHY inspiring trust and confidence [14thC. From Latin *credibilis*, from *credere* 'to believe' (source of English *creed*, and *miscreant*).] —**credibly** adv. —**credibleness** n.

— **WORD KEY: USAGE** —
credible, **creditable**, or **credulous**? These three adjectives, and the corresponding nouns *credibility*, *credit*, and *credulity*, are sometimes confused. Something or sb is **credible** when it (or he or she) can be easily or readily believed. Somebody is **credulous** when he or she is all too ready to believe. *My story may sound barely credible but I assure you it's true. Only the most credulous person would believe such a story.* **Credible** has the special newer meaning 'inspiring confidence': *The government needs to develop a credible monetary policy.* **Creditable** is connected with the word *credit* and means 'bringing credit': *An excellent squash player, she plays a creditable game of tennis as well.*

credit /kréddit/ n. 1. COMM DELAYED PAYMENT an arrangement by which a buyer can take possession of sth now and pay for it later or over time ○ *offer credit* ○ *buy on credit* 2. COMM TIME TO PAY the time allowed for payment of sth by credit 3. COMM SPENDING ENTITLEMENT AT SHOP money that a customer is owed by a shop and is entitled to spend there 4. COMM BALANCE IN ACCOUNT the amount of money in an account after debts have been charged against it 5. FIN MONEY PAID INTO ACCOUNT an amount of money paid into an account 6. FIN AMOUNT BANK WILL LEND the amount of money that a financial institution is prepared to lend sb 7. FIN FINANCIAL STATUS sb's financial status or reputation 8. RECOGNITION praise or recognition for sth done or achieved 9. SOURCE OF PRIDE sb or sth that is a source of pride or honour 10. ACKNOWLEDGMENT OF SB'S ROLE a mention of the role that sb played in an endeavour, especially an artistic one 11. ACCT DEDUCTION OF PAYMENT FROM OWED AMOUNT the deduction from a business account of an amount owed paid from the amount 12. ACCT ACCOUNT PAYMENTS COLUMN the right-hand side of an account record, where payments to the account are recorded 13. ACCT PAYMENT RECORDED a payment recorded against an amount owed 14. EDUC COURSE UNIT a completed unit of study in a course of higher education 15. US EDUC RECOGNITION OF COURSE COMPLETION official recognition that a student has satisfactorily completed a course of study ○ *get credit for a course* 16. EDUC EXAMINATION GRADE a mark above a basic pass in an exam 17. EDUC EXAM MARK a mark awarded in one examination that usually counts towards an overall grade ■ **credits** npl. CINEMA, TV LIST OF ACKNOWLEDGMENTS a listing of the people involved in a film or television production, together with their roles or jobs ■ vt. (-its, -iting, -ited) 1. BELIEVE to accept that sth is true 2. RECOGNIZE to recognize sb as the person responsible for an achievement 3. ATTRIBUTE to ascribe sth such as a personal quality to sb 4. FIN ADD TO BANK ACCOUNT to add an amount of money to sb's account 5. ACCT RECORD PAYMENT OF to record an amount of money as a payment in an accounting record 6. ACCT RECORD PAYMENT TO to enter a credit in the record of sb's account 7. EDUC MAKE EDUCATIONAL AWARD TO to award a credit to a student for successful completion of a course of study [Mid-16thC. From French, ultimately from Latin *creditum* 'loan', from the past participle of *credere* 'to entrust, believe'. The underlying idea is of sth entrusted.] —**creedal** adj. ◇ **to sb's credit** commendable of sb

— **WORD KEY: ORIGIN** —
Credit is derived from Latin *credere*, meaning 'to believe', which is also the source of English *credible*, *creed*, *grant*, and *miscreant*.

creditable /kréddităb'l/ adj. bringing credit or worthy of praise —**creditability** /kréddită bílləti/ n. —**creditableness** /kréddităb'l'nəss/ n. —**creditably** /-əbli/ adv.

— **WORD KEY: USAGE** —
See Usage note at **credible**.

credit account n. an account that allows you to buy goods and services and pay for them later. US term **charge account**

credit bureau n. US = credit-reference agency

credit card n. a card issued by a bank or business that allows sb to purchase goods and services and pay for them later, often with interest

credit line n. 1. FIN = line of credit 2. WRITTEN RECOGNITION a printed acknowledgment of the author or source of sth that was included in a publication

credit note n. a slip of paper stating that sb is owed an amount of money by a shop and is entitled to goods to that value

creditor /kréddităr/ n. a person or organization owed money by another

credit rating n. an estimate of sb's ability to repay money given on credit

credit-reference agency n. a business that provides information concerning sb's creditworthiness to companies or banks. = credit-reference agency

credit squeeze n. a reduction in the availability of credit or an increase in the interest charged for credit

credit standing n. the reputation that sb has for paying off financial obligations

credit transfer n. a transfer of money between bank accounts

credit union n. a cooperative savings association that makes loans to its members at reduced interest rates

creditworthy /kréddit wurthi/ adj. considered to be financially reliable enough to be given credit or lent money —**creditworthiness** n.

credo /kráydō/ (*plural* -dos) n. a statement of principles or beliefs, especially one that is professed formally [12thC. From Latin, literally 'I believe' (first words of the Apostles' and Nicene creeds), a form of *credere* (see CREDIBLE).]

Credo (*plural* -dos) n. 1. STATEMENT OF CHRISTIAN BELIEFS the Apostles' Creed or Nicene Creed, both of which are ancient statements of the basic doctrines of Christianity 2. MUSICAL SETTING OF THE CREDO a musical setting, especially in a Mass, of the Credo

credulity /krə dyóoləti/ n. the tendency to believe sth too readily

credulous /kréddyŏoləss/ adj. 1. GULLIBLE too easily convinced that sth is true 2. DUE TO READINESS TO BELIEVE resulting from a tendency to believe things too readily [Late 16thC. Formed from Latin *credulus*, from *credere* (see CREDIBLE).] —**credulously** *adv.* —**credulousness** *n.*

WORD KEY: USAGE

See Usage note at ***credible***.

WORD KEY: SYNONYMS

See Synonyms at ***naive***.

Cree /kree/ (*plural* **Cree** *or* **Crees**) *n.* **1.** PEOPLES **MEMBER OF NATIVE N AMERICAN PEOPLE** a member of a Native North American people who originally occupied lands in central Canada, and whose members continue to live there, with another substantial community in Montana. The Cree are the largest group of the Native Americans in Canada. **2.** LANG **CREE LANGUAGE** the Algonquian language of the Cree people. Cree is spoken by about 62,000 people. [Mid-18thC. From Canadian French *Cris*, shortening of earlier *C(h)ristinaux*, alteration of an Algonquian word (modern *kinistiono*).] —**Cree** *adj.*

creed /kreed/ *n.* **1.** **STATEMENT OF BELIEFS** a formal summary of the principles of the Christian faith **2.** **RELIGION** a set of religious beliefs **3.** **SET OF PRINCIPLES** any set of beliefs or principles [Pre-12thC. From Latin *credo* (see CREDO).]

creek /kreek/ *n.* **1.** *US Canada ANZ* **STREAM** a stream, especially one that flows into a river **2.** **NARROW TIDAL INLET** a narrow tidal inlet or bay on a sea coast, especially in a saltmarsh [15thC. Directly or via French *crique* from Old Norse *kriki* 'nook, corner'. Perhaps also partly from Middle Dutch *krēke*.] ◇ **up the creek (without a paddle)** in a difficult situation, or in trouble (*informal*)

Creek (*plural* **Creek** *or* **Creeks**) *n.* **1.** PEOPLES **MEMBER OF NATIVE N AMERICAN PEOPLE** a member of a Native North American people who originally occupied lands in Alabama, Georgia, and Florida, and whose members now live mainly in central Oklahoma and southern Alabama. The Creek were one of the Five Civilized Nations who, under the Removal Act of 1830, were sent to live on reservations in Oklahoma. **2.** LANG **CREEK LANGUAGE** the Muskogean language of the Creek people. Creek is spoken by about 50,000 people. [Early 18thC. From CREEK; from the large number of creeks in their country.] —**Creek** *adj.*

creel /kreel/ *n.* **1.** **WICKER BASKET FOR FISH** a wicker basket used by anglers for holding fish **2.** **WICKER FISH TRAP** a wicker trap for catching fish or lobsters **3.** **BOBBIN HOLDER** a framework in a spinning machine that holds the bobbins [14thC. Origin uncertain: perhaps via assumed Old French *creille* 'grill' from Latin *craticula* 'fine wickerwork', from *cratis* 'wickerwork' (source of English *griddle*).]

creep /kreep/ *vi.* (**creeps, creeping, crept** /krept/ *or* **creeped**) **1.** **MOVE QUIETLY** to move along silently and stealthily **2.** **MOVE NEAR THE GROUND** to move along with the body close to the ground **3.** **PROCEED SLOWLY** to move along very slowly **4.** **GRADUALLY DEVELOP** to appear, approach, or develop gradually **5.** **SHIVER WITH DISGUST** to tingle uncomfortably as if covered with crawling insects, especially from fear or disgust **6.** BOT **SPREAD OVER A SURFACE** to grow along a surface by sending out tendrils, suckers, or roots **7.** **BE DISPLACED SLIGHTLY** to move slightly from the original or proper position **8.** **BE OBSEQUIOUS** to behave in a servile manner to sb in authority (*informal*) **9.** INDUST **DEFORM FROM HEAT OR STRESS** to become deformed over a period of time due to stress or heat ■ *n.* **1.** **CREEPING MOVEMENT** a slow or stealthy pace or movement **2.** **SB REPELLENT** sb obnoxious or disliked (*informal*) **3.** **OBSEQUIOUS PERSON** sb who behaves in a servile manner to sb in authority (*informal*) **4.** **SLIGHT DISPLACEMENT** the slight movement of sth **5.** GEOL **MOVEMENT OF ROCK** a gradual movement of rock and debris down a slope **6.** GEOL **DEFORMATION OF ROCKS UNDER STRESS** a slow deformation of rocks and minerals in response to prolonged stress **7.** METALL **DEFORMATION OF METAL UNDER STRESS** a gradual deformation of a hard material, especially metal, as a result of heat or stress ■ **creeps** *npl.* **UNEASY FEELING** an uneasy or unnerving feeling usually caused by fear or disgust (*informal*) [Old English *crēopan*, from a prehistoric Germanic word that may also be the ancestor of English *cripple*. The underlying idea would be of moving with back bent.]

creep up on *vt.* **1.** **MAKE QUIET APPROACH TO** to approach sb or sth stealthily **2.** **GRADUALLY DAWN ON** to enter sb's consciousness or feelings gradually

creepback /kreep bak/ *n.* the tendency for employers to recruit new staff surreptitiously after making over-enthusiastic redundancies

creeper /kreepər/ *n.* **1.** BOT **CLINGING PLANT** any plant that grows by means of tendrils, suckers, or roots that anchor it to a surface **2.** **SB OR STH THAT CREEPS** a person or animal that moves by creeping **3.** *US, Can* BIRDS = **tree creeper** **4.** CARS = **cradle** *n.* 3 **5.** INSUR **UNDERWATER GRAPPLING DEVICE** a device with hooks that is used to drag for submerged objects in deep water

creeping /kreeping/ *adj.* **1.** **SLOWLY DEVELOPING** developing or advancing gradually over a period of time **2.** BOT **GROWING BY CLINGING** growing and spreading by sending out tendrils, suckers, or roots

creeping eruption *n.* a skin disease caused by hookworm or roundworm larvae, producing itching and eruptions in the form of spreading red lines on the skin

creeping Jennie /-jénni/, **creeping Jenny** *n.* an evergreen creeping plant of Europe and eastern North America that has coin-shaped leaves and yellow flowers. Latin name: *Lysimachia nummularia*. US term **moneywort**

creeping thistle *n.* a thistle that has pinkish-purple to white flowers and grows 90 cm/3 ft tall. It is a troublesome weed. Latin name: *Cirsium arvense*. US term **Canada thistle**

creepy /kreepi/ (**-ier, -iest**) *adj.* (*informal*) **1.** **UNNERVING THROUGH FEAR** unsettling because it causes fear, disgust, or uneasiness **2.** **REPELLENT** repellent because of annoying, unpleasant, or disturbing qualities — **creepily** *adv.* —**creepiness** *n.*

creepy-crawly (*plural* **creepy-crawlies**) *n.* a crawling insect or small animal (*informal*)

cremate /krə máyt/ (**-mates, -mating, -mated**) *vt.* to burn a dead body until nothing remains but ashes [Late 19thC. Either formed from Latin past participle stem *cremat-* (see CREMATION), or a back-formation from CREMATION.] — **cremator** *n.*

cremation /krə máysh'n/ *n.* **1.** **INCINERATION OF DEAD BODY** the burning of a dead body until only ashes are left **2.** **FUNERAL** a funeral ceremony during which the body is cremated [Early 17thC. From the Latin stem *cremation-*, from *cremat-*, the past participle stem of *cremare* 'to burn'.]

crematorium /krémmə táwri əm/ (*plural* **-ums** *or* **-a** /-ri ə/) *n.* a building or furnace where bodies are incinerated [Late 19thC. From modern Latin, where it was formed from Latin *cremat-* (see CREMATION).]

crematory /krémmətəri/ *n.* (*plural* **-ries**) *US* = **crematorium** ■ *adj.* **RELATING TO CREMATION** relating to or used for cremation

crème brûlée /krém broo láy/ (*plural* **crème brûlées** /-broo láyz/ *or* **crèmes brûlées** /krém broo láy/) *n.* a rich baked custard with caramelized sugar on top. It is served chilled. [From French, literally 'burnt cream']

crème caramel /krém kárrə mél/ (*plural* **crème caramels** *or* **crèmes caramel** /krémz kárrə mél/) *n.* a custard cooked in a mould coated with caramelized sugar, which forms a sauce. It is chilled and removed from the mould before serving. [From French, literally 'caramel cream']

crème de cacao /-də kə káā ō/ (*plural* **crème de cacaos** *or* **crèmes de cacao** /krém də kə káā ō/) *n.* a sweet chocolate-flavoured liqueur [From French, literally 'cream of cacao']

crème de la crème /-də la krém/ *n.* the very best of a group of people or things [From French, literally 'cream of the cream']

crème de menthe /-də mónth/ (*plural* **crème de menthes** *or* **crèmes de menthe** /krém də mónth/) *n.* a sweet mint-flavoured liqueur [From French, literally 'cream of mint']

crème fraîche /-frésh/ *n.* thickened French soured cream, used in cooking or served with other foods [From French, literally 'fresh cream']

Cremona /kri mṓnə/ capital of Cremona Province, Lombardy Region, in northern Italy. It is situated on the River Po, about 72 km/45 mi. southeast of Milan. Population: 75,500 (1990).

crenate /kree nayt/, **crenated** /kree naytid/ *adj.* with a scalloped edge or a surface with rounded projections [Late 18thC. From modern Latin *crenatus*, from Latin *crena* 'small notch' (source of English *cranny*), of unknown origin.] —**crenately** *adv.*

crenation /kri náysh'n/ *n.* **1.** **ROUNDED PROTRUSION** a rounded protrusion from the edge or surface of sth **2.** **SCALLOPED EDGE OR SURFACE** a scalloped edge or a surface with rounded projections **3.** MED **SHRINKAGE OF RED BLOOD CELLS** a medical condition in which the red blood cells shrink and develop multiple indentations and protrusions

crenature /krénnəchər/ *n.* = **crenation** *n.* 1, **crenation** *n.* 2 (*technical*)

crenel /krénn'l/, **crenelle** /krə nél/ *n.* **1.** **OPENING IN BATTLEMENTS** any of the rectangular openings in the top of a castle wall or parapet **2.** **ROUNDED PROTRUSION** a rounded protrusion from the edge or surface of sth [15thC. From Old French, literally 'small notch', from Latin *crena* (see CRENATE).]

crenelate *adj.* US = **crenellate**

crenellate (**-lates, -lating, -lated**) *vt.* **1.** **BUILD WITH BATTLEMENTS** to provide a structure with battlements or decorative features resembling battlements **2.** **MAKE WITH SQUARE INDENTATIONS** to make sth with square indentations like the openings (**crenels**) of a battlement [Early 19thC. Formed from French *créneler*, from Old French *crenel* (see CRENEL).] —**crenellated** *adj.* — **crenellation** *n.*

crenelle *n.* = **crenel**

crenulate /krénnyoo layt/, **crenulated** /-laytid/ *adj.* with a finely scalloped or notched wavy edge [Late 18thC. From modern Latin *crenulatus*, from *crenula*, literally 'small notch', from Latin *crena* (see CRENATE).]

crenulation /krénnyoo láysh'n/ *n.* **1.** **TINY NOTCH** a very small notch or indentation **2.** **FINELY NOTCHED EDGING** very fine notching or indentation along an edge

creodont /kree ə dont/ (*plural* **-donts** *or* **-donta** /kree ə dóntə/) *n.* an extinct carnivorous mammal that lived during the Tertiary period. Suborder: Creodonta. [Late 19thC. From modern Latin *Creodonta*, literally 'flesh-toothed ones', from Greek *kreas* 'flesh' (source of English *pancreas*)+ *rodont-*, from *odous* 'tooth'.]

creole /kree ōl/ *n.* LING **LANGUAGE OF MIXED ORIGIN** a language that has evolved from the mixture of two or more languages and has become the first language of a group ■ *adj.* COOK **COOKED AS IN NEW ORLEANS** cooked in a spicy highly-flavoured way typical of the French Creoles of New Orleans. Tomatoes, hot peppers, onions, and rice are characteristic ingredients. [Late 19thC. From CREOLE.]

Creole *n.* **1.** **SB OF FRENCH ANCESTRY** an inhabitant of the southern United States, especially southern Louisiana, who is descended from the early French settlers **2.** **LANGUAGE OF LOUISIANA** the creolized French language spoken by the Creoles of New Orleans and southern Louisiana **3.** **LANGUAGE OF CARIBBEAN ISLANDS** a group of creolized languages, based on English and French, spoken on many of the islands of the Caribbean **4.** **HAITIAN LANGUAGE** the creolized language spoken in Haiti **5.** **WEST INDIAN OF EUROPEAN ANCESTRY** sb who was born in or is a citizen of a West Indian or Latin American country, and who is of European, especially Spanish, descent **6.** **CREOLE SPEAKER** sb of both European and African ancestry who speaks a form of Creole [Mid-18thC. From French, from Spanish *criollo* 'native', from Portuguese *crioulo*, from *criar* 'to bring up', from Latin *creare* (see CREATE).] —**Creole** *adj.*

creolize /kree ə līz/ (**-olizes, -olizing, -olized**), **creolise** (**-olises, -olising, -olised**) *vt.* to form a new mixed language from two or more other languages — **creolization** /kreeō lī záyshən/ *n.*

creolized /kree ə līzd/, **creolised** *adj.* combining elements of two or more separate languages to form the new mixed language of a group of people

Creon /kree ən/ *n.* in Greek mythology, the brother of Jocasta and the successor of Oedipus as king of Thebes. He was also the uncle of Antigone and issued an edict forbidding the burial of the body of her brother Polynices, which she defied.

creosol /kree ə sol/ *n.* a pale yellow or colourless oily liquid that is a component of creosote. Formula: $C_8H_{10}O_2$. [Mid-19thC. Coined from CREOSOTE + -OL.]

a at; aa father; aw all; ay day; air hair; ə about, edible, item, common, circus; e egg; ee eel; hw when; i it, happy; ī ice; 'l apple; 'm rhythm; 'n fashion; o odd; ō open; oo good; oo pool; ow owl; oy oil; th thin; th this; u up; ur urge;

creosote /kreé ə sōt/ *n.* **1.** WOOD PRESERVATIVE a thick yellowish to brown oily substance derived from coal tar, used as a wood preservative **2.** ANTISEPTIC a yellow to colourless oily substance derived from wood tar, used as an antiseptic ■ *vt.* **(-sotes, -soting, -soted)** APPLY CREOSOTE TO to apply creosote to wood as a preservative [Mid-19thC. From German *Kreosote*, literally 'flesh-saving', from Greek *kreas* 'flesh' (source of English *pancreas*) + *sōtēr* 'preserver'; from its antiseptic properties.]

creosote bush *n.* a resinous evergreen shrub that is native to the deserts of the southwestern United States and Mexico and has leaves that smell like creosote. Latin name: *Larrea tridentata.*

crêpe /krayp/, **crepe** *n.* **1. crêpe** TEXTILES LIGHT CRINKLED FABRIC a light fine fabric with a crinkled surface **2.** COOK THIN PANCAKE a thin pancake usually served rolled up or folded with a filling **3.** = **crepe paper 4.** = **crepe rubber** [Late 18thC. From French, from Old French *crespe* 'curled', from Latin *crispus* (the source also of English *crisp*).] —**crepy** /kráypi/ *adj.*

crepe de Chine /kráyp də sheén/ (*plural* **crepes de Chine** /kráyp də sheén/ *or* **crepe de Chines** /kráyp də sheénz/), **crêpe de Chine** (*plural* **crêpes de Chine** *or* **crêpe de Chines**) *n.* a light smooth silk fabric, used to make delicate articles of clothing [From French, literally 'crepe of China']

crepe paper, **crêpe paper** *n.* a thin, slightly stretchy, crinkled coloured paper, used for wrapping presents or making decorations (*hyphenated when used before a noun*)

creperie /kráypəri, krép-/, **crêperie** *n.* a restaurant that specializes in thin pancakes (**crepes**) with fillings [From French *crêperie* from *crêpe* (see CREPE)]

crepe rubber, **crêpe rubber** *n.* rubber in the form of thin crinkled sheets, used especially for the soles of shoes

crêpe suzette /-soo zét/ (*plural* **crêpes suzettes** /kráyp soo zéts/) *n.* a pancake prepared with orange sauce and flambéed with an orange-flavoured liqueur or brandy [From French, said to be named after the French actress *Suzanne* Reichenberg (1853–1924)]

crepitate /kréppi tayt/ **(-tates, -tating, -tated)** *v.* **1.** *vi.* CRACKLE to make a crackling or grating sound (*formal or literary*) **2.** MED CRACKLE OR GRATE to make the crackling or grating sound of crepitus [Early 17thC. From Latin *crepitat-*, the past participle stem of *crepitare* 'to crackle', from *crepare* 'to rattle' (source of English *crevice*) an imitation of the sound.] —**crepitant** *adj.* —**crepitation** /kréppi táysh'n/ *n.*

crepitus /kréppitəss/ *n.* MED **1.** GRATING SOUND OF BROKEN BONE the grating sound heard when the broken ends of a bone rub together **2.** CRACKLING CHEST NOISE a crackling sound heard in the chest of sb who has a lung disease, e.g. pneumonia [Early 19thC. From Latin, 'rattling', from *crepare* (see CREPITATE).]

crept past tense, past participle of **creep**

crepuscular /kri púskyŏolər/ *adj.* **1.** LIKE TWILIGHT relating to or resembling the fading light of dusk (*literary*) **2.** ZOOL ACTIVE IN LOW LIGHT used to describe fish and land mammals that are active at dusk and dawn, when the light level is low [Mid-17thC. Formed from Latin *crepusculum* 'twilight'.]

Cres. *abbr.* Crescent (*used in addresses*)

cresc. *abbr.* crescendo

crescendo /krə shéndō/ *n.* (*plural* **-dos** *or* **-does** *or* **-di** /-dee/) **1.** MUSIC INCREASING LOUDNESS a gradual increase in the volume of a passage of music **2.** MUSIC MUSIC PLAYED INCREASINGLY LOUD a passage of music in which there is a gradual increase in volume **3.** INTENSIFICATION an increase in volume or intensity similar to a crescendo in music **4.** CLIMAX the climax of an increase in volume or intensity ■ *adj.* INTENSIFYING gradually increasing in volume or intensity ■ *adv.* MUSIC WITH GREATER VOLUME with increasing loudness ■ *vi.* **(-does, -doing, -doed)** BECOME LOUDER OR STRONGER to increase in volume or intensity [Late 18thC. From Italian, the present participle of *crescere* 'to increase', from Latin *crescere* (see CRESCENT).]

WORD KEY: USAGE

A ***crescendo*** is properly a process and not the end of a process. This is usually well understood in musical contexts, because the word is a technical term. In figurative uses, though, it tends to be used as an alternative for *climax*, which is indeed the end point or culmination of a process. A noise or feeling can increase *to* a climax but it does so *in* a ***crescendo***. Correct: *The bird's calls rose in a crescendo and then subsided again.* Avoid: *The abusive calls reached a crescendo the following week.*

crescent /kréss'nt, krézz'nt/ *n.* **1.** ARC SHAPE a curved shape like that of the moon when it is less than half illuminated **2.** ARC-SHAPED THING sth shaped like a crescent **3. crescent, Crescent** ISLAM ISLAMIC SYMBOL the emblem of Islam or Turkey, shaped like a crescent moon **4. crescent, Crescent** ISLAM ISLAMIC OR TURKISH POWER Islamic or Turkish power **5. crescent, Crescent** TRANSP ARC-SHAPED STREET a curved street, especially one that opens onto the same street at each end **6.** HERALDRY SYMBOL FOR SECOND SON a crescent moon, used in heraldry to signify a second son ■ *adj.* **1.** ARC-SHAPED shaped like a crescent **2.** GROWING gradually increasing in size (*literary*) [14thC. Via Anglo-Norman *cressaunt* from, ultimately, Latin *crescent-*, the present participle stem of *crescere* 'to grow'.] —**crescentic** /krə séntik, krə zéntik/ *adj.*

WORD KEY: ORIGIN

As well as being the source of ***crescent***, the Latin word *crescere*, meaning 'to grow', is also the source of English *accretion, concrete, create, crescendo, crew, croissant, increase,* and *recruit.*

cresol /kreé sol/ *n.* a colourless compound derived from wood or coal tar, used as an antiseptic and disinfectant. Formula: C_7H_8O. [Mid-19thC. Alteration of CREOSOL.]

cress /kress/ (*plural* **cress** *or* **cresses**) *n.* a plant of the mustard family with small pungently flavoured leaves that are used in salads or as a garnish [Old English *cressa*, from prehistoric Germanic]

cresset /kréssit/ *n.* a metal cup or basket mounted on a pole and filled with oil or pitch that was burned to give light [14thC. From Old French *cresset*, from *craisse*, variant of *graisse* 'oil, grease', from, ultimately, Latin *crassus* 'solid, fat' (source of English *crass*).]

Cressida[1] /kréssidə/ *n.* in medieval retellings of the Trojan War, a Trojan woman captured by the Greeks who is unfaithful to her Trojan lover, Troilus, by giving herself to the Greek Diomedes

Cressida[2] *n.* a small natural satellite of Uranus, discovered by the Voyager 2 planetary probe in 1986

crest /krest/ *n.* **1.** TOP OF CURVE OR SLOPE the top part of sth that slopes or rises upwards, e.g. a wave or a hill **2.** CULMINATION the highest stage or culminating point in an activity or achievement **3.** ZOOL TUFT ON ANIMAL'S HEAD a tuft or other growth on the top of the head of a bird or other animal **4.** STH RESEMBLING CREST sth resembling the crest of a bird or other animal **5.** ARMS HELMET ORNAMENT a plume or other decoration on top of a helmet **6.** ZOOL NECK RIDGE a ridge along the neck of a horse, lion, or other animal, from which hair grows **7.** HERALDRY SYMBOL OF FAMILY OR OFFICE a small animal, bird, or other heraldic symbol of a family or office, placed above the shield in a coat of arms or used alone on a helmet **8.** HERALDRY = **coat of arms** ■ *v.* **(crests, cresting, crested) 1.** *vi.* RISE to reach or rise to a crest **2.** *vt.* REACH TOP OF to reach the top of sth **3.** *vt.* TOP STH to be at the top of sth [14thC. Via French *creste* from Latin *crista* 'tuft, plume'.]

crested /kréstid/ *adj.* **1.** CLOTHES WITH FUR OR FEATHER CREST used to describe an item of headgear that has a knot or row of hairs or feathers on its top **2.** ZOOL TUFTED used to describe a bird or other animal with a tuft or other growth on its head

crested dog's-tail (*plural* **crested dog's-tail** *or* **crested dog's-tails**) *n.* a European grass with flower spikes that resemble a long-haired dog's tail. Latin name: *Cynosurus cristatus.*

crestfallen /krést fawlən/ *adj.* disappointed or humiliated, especially after being enthusiastic or confident [From the drooping of a sb's head when disappointed] —**crestfallenly** *adv.*

cresting /krésting/ *n.* **1.** ARCHIT DECORATIVE ROOF RIDGE an ornamental ridge on a roof **2.** FURNITURE FURNITURE ORNAMENT an ornamental carving or rail on the top of a piece of furniture

cresylic /kri síllik/ *adj.* relating to or containing creosol or creosote

cresylic acid *n.* = **cresol**

cretaceous /kri táyshəss/ *adj.* resembling or consisting of chalk (*technical*) [Late-17thC. Formed from Latin *cretaceus* 'chalklike, chalky', from *creta* 'chalk' (source of English *crayon*).] —**cretaceously** *adv.*

Cretaceous *adj.* belonging to or dating from the end of the Mesozoic era, 144 to 65 million years ago

Cretan /kreét'n/ *n.* SB FROM CRETE sb who was born or brought up in Crete ■ *adj.* RELATING TO CRETE relating to or typical of Crete, or its people or culture

Crete /kreet/ the largest Greek island in the southern Aegean Sea. The chief town is Iráklion. Population: 540,054 (1991). Area: 8,335 sq. km/3,218 sq. mi.

cretic /kreétik/ *n.* POETRY = **amphimacer** [Late 16thC. Via Latin *creticus*, literally 'Cretan', from Greek *krētikos*, from *Krētē* 'Crete'.]

cretin /kréttin/ *n.* **1.** OFFENSIVE TERM an offensive term that deliberately insults sb's supposed intellectual capacity (*offensive*) **2.** MED SB WITH THYROID HORMONE DEFICIENCY sb affected by congenital myxoedema (*dated*) [Late 18thC. Via French from Swiss French *creitin* 'Christian mentally challenged', from Latin *Christianus* 'Christian', from *Christus* 'Christ'.] —**cretinism** *n.* —**cretinoid** *adj.* —**cretinous** *adj.*

cretonne /kre tón/ *n.* a heavy fabric made from cotton, linen, or rayon and usually printed with a colourful design, used for upholstery [Late 19thC. From French, from *Creton*, name of a village in Normandy, France, where it was first made.]

Creutzfeldt-Jakob disease /króytsfelt yák ob-/ *n.* a rare fatal brain disease, a form of spongiform encephalopathy, that develops slowly, causing dementia and loss of muscle control. An abnormal protein (**prion**) is the suspected cause. A new variant of the disease, that develops rapidly and affects younger people, appeared in the late 1980s. [Late 20thC. Named after the German neurologists H. G. *Creutzfeldt* (1885–1964) and A. M. *Jakob* (1884–1931).]

crevasse /krə váss/ *n.* **1.** DEEP CRACK a deep crack, e.g. in the ice of a glacier **2.** *US* CRACK IN EMBANKMENT a crack in a river embankment or dyke ■ *vti.* **(-vasses, -vassing, -vassed)** FORM CREVASSES to develop or make sth develop crevasses [Early 19thC. From French, from Old French *crevace* (see CREVICE).]

crevice /krévviss/ *n.* a narrow crack or opening, especially in rock [14thC. From Old French *crevace* 'a burst, split', from *crever* 'to burst', from Latin *crepare* 'to rattle' (source of English *decrepit*), an imitation of the sound.] —**creviced** *adj.*

crew[1] /kroo/ *n.* **1.** ONBOARD STAFF the people who work on a boat, ship, aircraft, or spacecraft **2.** SHIP'S STAFF EXCLUDING OFFICERS the members of a ship's crew who are not officers **3.** SPECIALIZED STAFF ON CRAFT a smaller group within the crew of a ship, aircraft, or spacecraft who are assigned a specific task **4.** PEOPLE WORKING TOGETHER a group of people who work together on a project or task **5.** GROUP OF FRIENDS a group of people who spend a lot of time together or are somehow associated with each other (*informal*) **6.** ROWERS the coxswain and oarsmen or oarswomen of a racing boat ■ *v.* **(crews, crewing, crewed) 1.** *vi.* BE ON CREW to be a member of a crew **2.** *vt.* BE ON CREW OF to serve as a member of the crew of a boat, ship, aircraft, or spacecraft (*often passive*) [15thC. From French *creüe* 'increase, recruit', from the past participle of *croistre* 'to grow', from Latin *crescere* (see CRESCENT). Originally 'company of soldiers'.]

crew[2] past tense of **Crow**

crew chief *n. US* AIR FORCE a noncommissioned officer in the air force who is in charge of the maintenance and ground handling of an aircraft

crew cut *n.* a haircut, usually worn by men and boys, with the hair cut close to the head [Thought to be from its original adoption by boat crews at the US universities of Harvard and Yale in the mid-20thC]

Crewe /kroo/ town and major rail junction in Cheshire, England. Population: 63,351 (1991).

crewel /kroó əl/ *n.* **1.** WOOL EMBROIDERY YARN a loosely twisted woollen yarn used in embroidery **2.** = **crewelwork** [15thC. Origin unknown.]

crewelwork /kroo̅ əl wurk/ *n.* embroidery work done with crewel yarn

crewmate /kroo̅ mayt/ *n.* a fellow member of a crew, especially on board a boat or spacecraft

crew neck *n.* **1.** ROUND NECKLINE a close-fitting round neckline on a sweater, sweatshirt, or other garment **2.** CREW-NECK SWEATER a sweater with a close-fitting round neck [From the sweaters with such a neckline worn by boat crews] —**crew-neck** *adj.*

crib /krib/ *n.* **1.** *US* = **cot** (*dated*) **2.** EDUC CRIB SHEET a crib sheet (*informal*) **3.** PLAGIARISM a theft of sth from an intellectual or artistic work **4.** AGRIC ANIMAL'S STALL a stall for cattle or horses **5.** AGRIC HAY RACK a trough or box for hay or other fodder from which livestock can feed **6.** CHR MODEL OF MANGER a model of the manger in which Jesus lay after his birth, **7.** PROSTITUTE'S ROOM a run-down house or room used by a prostitute **8.** BASKET a wicker basket **9.** CARDS DEALER'S CARDS the cards used by the dealer in cribbage, consisting of cards discarded by the other players **10.** CARDS CRIBBAGE cribbage (*informal*) **11.** *ANZ* SNACK a light snack (*informal*) ■ *v.* (**cribs, cribbing, cribbed**) **1.** *vti.* PLAGIARIZE to steal sb's ideas or work (*informal*) **2.** *vi.* EDUC USE CRIB SHEET to use a crib sheet in an examination (*informal*) **3.** *vt.* PUT IN CRIB to put sb or sth in a crib **4.** *vt.* PROVIDE CRIB FOR to construct or provide a crib for sth [Old English *crib(b)* 'manger, trough for fodder', from a prehistoric Germanic word that is also the ancestor of English *crèche*. Plagiarize came via thieves' slang 'pilfer from basket'.] —**cribber** *n.*

cribbage /kríbbij/ *n.* a card game for two to four players in which the score is kept by moving pegs along rows of holes in a small board [Mid-17thC. Origin uncertain: probably from CRIB + -AGE.]

cribbage board *n.* a board with holes in which pegs are placed for scoring in cribbage

cribbing /kríbbing/ *n.* **1.** EDUC CHEATING IN EXAMINATION using a crib sheet to cheat in an examination (*informal*) **2.** CONSTR BEAMS FOR MINESHAFT the timbers used for a framework, e.g. of a mineshaft or foundation **3.** VET = **crib-biting**

crib-biting *n.* a behavioural abnormality in horses in which animals kept in stables chew their stalls and salivate excessively. The disorder is partly an inherited condition and partly an expression of boredom. —**crib-biter** *n.*

crib death *n. US, Can* = **cot death**

cribellum /kri bélləm/ (*plural* -**bella** /-béllə/) *n.* an oval perforated plate just in front of the silk-secreting organs (**spinnerets**) in some spiders, through which the emerging silk is combed [Late 19thC. From late Latin, literally 'small sieve', from *cribrum* 'sieve'.]

cribriform /kríbbri fawrm/ *adj.* with small holes like a sieve (*technical*) [Mid-18thC. Coined from Latin *cribrum* 'sieve' + -FORM.]

crib sheet *n.* a list of answers or translation of a foreign text used for cheating in examinations or lessons

cricetid /krī seetid/ (*plural* -**tids** *or* -**tid**) *n.* a small rodent of the family that includes the hamster, gerbil, muskrat, and vole. Family: Cricetidae. [Mid-20thC. From modern Latin *Cricetidae*, from *Cricetus* (genus name of hamsters), from medieval Latin *cricetus* 'hamster', from or related to Old Czech *křeček*.] —**cricetid** *adj.*

crick /krik/ *n.* PAINFUL STIFFNESS a painful stiffness or muscle spasm in the neck or back ■ *vt.* (**cricks, cricking, cricked**) CAUSE CRICK IN to cause a painful stiffness or muscle spasm in the neck or back [15thC. Origin unknown.]

cricket[1] /kríkit/ *n.* a leaping insect that has biting mouthparts, long legs, and antennae. The male produces a chirping sound by rubbing its forewings together. Family: Gryllidae. [14thC. From French *criquet* 'grasshopper, locust', from Old French *criquer* 'to click', an imitation of the sound.]

Cricket: A batsman is bowled

cricket[2] /kríkit/ *n.* BAT-AND-BALL GAME an outdoor sport played by two teams of 11 players using a flat bat, a small hard ball, and wickets. A player scores by batting the ball and running, while the defenders can get a player out by bowling and hitting the wicket, catching a hit ball, or running the player out. ■ *vi.* to play cricket [Late 16thC. Origin uncertain: perhaps from Old French *criquet* 'stick (used in a bowling game)', or Flemish *krick* 'stick' or *krickstoel* 'low stool' (resembling early wickets).] ◇ **not cricket** unfair and not honourable (*dated informal*)

cricket[3] /kríkit/ *n.* a wooden footstool [Mid-17thC. Origin unknown.]

cricketer /kríkitər/ *n.* sb who plays cricket

cricoid /krík oyd/ *adj.* relating to or in the region of the lowermost cartilage of the larynx [Mid-18thC. Via modern Latin *cricoides* 'ring-shaped' from Greek *krikoeidēs*, from *krikos* 'ring'.]

cricoid cartilage *n.* the lowermost cartilage of the voice box (**larynx**), which has a shape like a signet ring

cri de coeur /kree də kúr/ (*plural* **cris de coeur** /kree də-/) *n.* a heartfelt, usually anguished appeal [From French, literally 'cry from the heart']

crier /krī ər/ *n.* **1.** SB OR STH THAT CRIES a person or animal that cries **2.** = **town crier**. **3.** LAW COURT ANNOUNCER an official who makes public announcements of the orders of a court of law **4.** VENDOR SHOUTING WARES a pedlar who makes public announcements about the goods he or she has for sale (*old*)

crim /krim/ *n. ANZ* a criminal (*informal*) [Early 20thC. Shortening.]

crim. *abbr.* criminal

crim. con. *abbr.* LAW criminal conversation

crime /krīm/ *n.* **1.** ILLEGAL ACT an action prohibited by law, or a failure to act as required by law **2.** ILLEGAL ACTIVITY activity that involves breaking the law **3.** IMMORAL ACT any act considered morally wrong **4.** UNDESIRABLE ACT a shameful, unwise, or regrettable act (*informal*) ○ *It's a crime the way some people mistreat their pets.* [13thC. Via French from Latin *crimen* (stem *crimin-*) 'judgment', from *cernere* 'to decide' (source of English *certain* and *decree*).] —**crimeless** *adj.*

— WORD KEY: CULTURAL NOTE —

Crime and Punishment, a novel by Russian writer Fyodor Dostoevsky (1866). Set in St Petersburg, it describes how a young student, Raskolnikov, plans and carries out the murder of a woman pawnbroker, ostensibly for money but in reality to prove that certain individuals are above the law. Ultimately, however, his conscience forces him to confess his crime.

Crimea /krī mee ə/ peninsula in southeastern Ukraine between the Black Sea and the Sea of Azov. Area: 25,993 sq. km/10,036 sq. mi. —**Crimean** *n., adj.*

crime against humanity *n.* a cruel and immoral act, e.g. torture, murder, or expulsion, committed against a large number of people

crime of passion *n.* a crime that is motivated by an extreme emotion, especially sexual jealousy

crime passionnel /kreem passi ə nél/ (*plural* **crimes passionnels** /kreem passi ə nél/) *n.* = **crime of passion** [From French, literally 'crime of passion']

crime sheet *n.* a record that lists a person's breaches of military regulations

crime wave *n.* a period during which more crimes than usual are committed

criminal /krímminəl/ *n.* SB ACTING ILLEGALLY sb who has committed a crime ■ *adj.* **1.** PUNISHABLE AS CRIME punishable as a crime under the law **2.** PROSECUTING CRIMINALS involved in or relating to the prosecution and punishment of people accused of committing crimes **3.** RELATING TO CRIMINALS relating to or typical of criminals **4.** MORALLY WRONG morally wrong whether illegal or not **5.** UNWISE OR REGRETTABLE not showing good sense or fairness (*informal*) [15thC. Directly or via French *criminel* from late Latin *criminalis* 'of crime', from the Latin stem *crimin-* (see CRIME).] —**criminally** *adv.*

— WORD KEY: SYNONYMS —
See Synonyms at ***bad***.

criminal conversation *n.* adultery considered as a legal breach of the marriage contract (*technical*)

criminalise *vt.* = **criminalize**

criminality /krímmi nálləti/ *n.* **1.** CRIMINAL QUALITY a criminal character or quality **2.** TENDENCY TO LAWBREAKING a tendency to commit crimes **3.** CRIME a criminal act or practice (*often used in the plural*)

criminalize /krímminə līz/ (-**izes**, -**izing**, -**ized**), **criminalise** (-**ises**, -**ising**, -**ised**) *vt.* **1.** MAKE ILLEGAL to make an action punishable as a crime under the law **2.** MAKE INTO CRIMINAL to make sb become or treat sb as a criminal —**criminalization** /krímminə lī záysh'n/ *n.*

criminol. *abbr.* criminology

criminology /krímmi nólləji/ *n.* the sociological study of crime, criminals, and the punishment of criminals —**criminological** /krímminən lójjik'l/ *adj.* —**criminologically** /-lójjikli/ *adv.* —**criminologist** /krímmi nólləjist/ *n.*

crimp /krimp/ *vt.* (**crimps, crimping, crimped**) **1.** FOLD OR PRESS TOGETHER to fold or press the ends or edges of sth together **2.** PLEAT to press or gather sth into small folds, e.g. a piece of fabric **3.** HAIR CURL to make sb's hair wavy with curling tongs **4.** COOK PINCH DECORATIVELY to pinch or press together the edges of pastry to form a seal or for decoration **5.** MANUF MOULD to mould or form leather into a shape **6.** METALL JOIN INTO SEAM to bend or fold the edges of sheet metal to form a seam for a tube or between two pieces ■ *n.* **1.** CRIMPING ACTION a pinching, folding, or other action that crimps sth **2.** HAIR TIGHT HAIR WAVE a tight artificial wave in sb's hair, usually made with curling tongs **3.** PINCHED EDGE a fold or crease made by pinching together two edges, e.g. of fabric or pastry **4.** CREASE FORMED BY BENDING a fold or crease formed by bending sth, e.g. sheet metal **5.** CURL OF WOOL FIBRES the curl or wave of wool fibres [Late 17thC. Origin uncertain: probably via Dutch or Low German *krimpen* 'to shrink, crimp' from a prehistoric Germanic word that is also the ancestor of English *cram*.] —**crimper** *n.*

Crimplene /krím pleen/ *tdmk.* a trademark for a crease-resistant synthetic clothing fabric

crimpy /krímpi/ (-**ier**, -**iest**) *adj.* with many small waves, folds, or wrinkles

crimson /krímz'n/ *adj.* OF DEEP RICH RED COLOUR of a deep rich red colour with a tinge of purple ○ *crimson lips* ■ *n.* a deep rich red colour tinged with purple ■ *v.* (-**sons**, -**soning**, -**soned**) **1.** *vti.* MAKE OR BECOME CRIMSON to become a vivid or deep red colour, or make sth become this colour **2.** *vi.* BLUSH to blush, with embarrassment, shyness, or shame [15thC. Via Old Spanish *cremesín* from Arabic *kirmizī* 'red colour', from *kirmiz* 'kermes insect'.]

cringe /krinj/ *vi.* (**cringes, cringing, cringed**) **1.** CROUCH OR MOVE BACK SUDDENLY to pull the head and body quickly away from sth or sb in a frightened or servile way **2.** BE EMBARRASSED OR UNCOMFORTABLE to react to sth with embarrassment or discomfort, often showing this by physically flinching (*informal*) ○ *We always cringe at his jokes.* **3.** ACT HUMBLY to behave in a very humble or servile way (*disapproving*) ■ *n.* **1.** COWERING MOVEMENT a quick pulling away of the head and body from sth or sb in a frightened or servile way **2.** EMBARRASSED REACTION an embarrassed or uncomfortable reaction, often shown by physically flinching (*informal*) [13thC. Origin uncertain: probably from Old English *crincan* 'to yield'. Ultimately from a prehistoric Germanic word meaning 'to bend, curl', which is also the ancestor of English *crank*.] —**cringer** *n.*

cringe-making *adj.* so embarrassing or painful that people wince at it (*informal*) —**cringe-makingly** *adv.*

cringle /kríng g'l/ *n.* a piece of rope with a metal ring (**thimble**) in it, fitted into the main rope (**boltrope**) around the edge of a sail [Early 17thC. From Low German *kringel*, literally 'small ring'. Ultimately from a prehistoric Germanic base meaning 'to bend', which is also the ancestor of English *crinkle* and *cringe*.]

crinkle /kríngk'l/ *vti.* **1. CREASE UP** to become, or make sth become, finely folded, wrinkled, or wavy, e.g. by crushing or pressing it **2. MAKE SOFT CRACKLING SOUND** to make little crunching or rustling noises, like the sound of paper being crushed, or cause sth to make these noises ■ *n.* **TINY FOLD OR WAVE** a little fold or wave, especially in paper or cloth [14thC. Origin uncertain: perhaps formed from Old English *crincan* (see CRINGE).]

crinklecut /kríngk'l kut/ *adj.* cut in wavy shapes or with wavy edges

crinkly /kríngkli/ *adj.* (**-klier, -kliest**) **1. WAVY OR CREASED UP TIGHTLY** covered in or full of fine creases or folds ○ *made of some kind of crinkly material.* **2. MAKING RUSTLING NOISES** making little crunching or rustling noises ■ *n.* (*plural* **-klies**) **OLDER PERSON** a person of advanced years (*slang*)

crinoid /krī noyd, krínnoyd/ *n.* a type of primitive marine invertebrate animal (**echinoderm**) with a cup-shaped body and five feathery radiating arms. These animals are related to the starfish and the sea urchin. Class: Crinoidea. [Mid-19thC. From Greek *krinoeidēs* 'lily-like', from *krinon* 'lily'.] —**crinoid** *adj.*

crinoline /krínnəlin/ *n.* **1. FABRIC FOR STIFFENING THINGS** a stiff fabric made of horsehair and cotton or linen, used in the past for linings and petticoats **2. STIFF PETTICOAT** a petticoat of crinoline fabric or net, worn to expand a skirt **3. HOOPED SKIRT** a skirt or petticoat containing wire hoops, worn to expand the skirt [Mid-19thC. Via French from Italian *crinolino*, from *crino* 'horsehair' + *lino* 'flax'.] —**crinolined** *adj.*

crinum /krīnəm/ (*plural* **-num** *or* **-nums**) *n.* a tropical plant that grows from a bulb and has long thin leaves and clusters of flowers in various colours. Genus: *Crinum.* [Via modern Latin, genus name, from Greek *krinon* 'lily', of unknown origin]

criollo /kri ólō/ *n.* (*plural* **-los**) **1. LATIN AMERICAN OF EUROPEAN DESCENT** sb who was born in or is a citizen of a Latin American country, and who is of European, especially Spanish, descent **2. ANIMAL OF LATIN AMERICAN BREED** any Latin American breed of domestic animal ■ *adj.* **1. OF LATIN AMERICANS OF EUROPEAN DESCENT** relating to or typical of Latin American people of European, especially Spanish, descent, or their language, or their culture **2. BEING LATIN AMERICAN ANIMAL** belonging to a Latin American breed of domestic animal ○ *a criollo pony* [Late 19thC. From Spanish (see CREOLE).] —**criollo** *adj.*

criosphinx /krée ō sfingks/ (*plural* **-sphinxes** *or* **-sphinges** /-sfin jeez/) *n.* in ancient Egyptian mythology and art, a figure that is like a sphinx in having a lion's body but has the head of a ram rather than a human head [Mid-19thC. Coined from Greek *krios* 'ram' + SPHINX.]

cripes /krīps/ *interj.* used to express surprise or concern (*slang*) ○ *Cripes! That's torn it!* [Early 20thC. Alteration of CHRIST.]

Crippen /kríppin/, **Hawley Harvey** (1861–1910) US-born British dentist and murderer who poisoned his wife and fled to Canada with his lover. The first British police use of an early form of radio communication resulted in his arrest and execution. Pseudonym **Mr Robinson**

cripple /kripp'l/ *n.* **1. DISABLED PERSON** sb whose use of a limb or limbs is impaired (*offensive*) **2. INCAPABLE PERSON** sb who is deficient in a particular area (*informal*) ○ *an emotional cripple* **3. STH DAMAGED** sth that does not work properly (*informal*) ■ *vt.* (**-ples, -pling, -pled**) **1. MAKE SB PHYSICALLY CHALLENGED** to hurt or damage sb seriously and often permanently, especially impairing the ability to move ○ *crippled by arthritis* **2. DAMAGE SERIOUSLY** to cause major problems to sth, e.g. a machine or a business, so that it cannot operate properly ○ *a business crippled by debts and bad publicity* [Old English *crypel*. Ultimately from a prehistoric Germanic word denoting 'bent', which was also the ancestor of English *creep*.] —**crippled** *adj.* —**crippling** *adj.* —**cripplingly** *adv.*

crisis /krī siss/ (*plural* **-ses** /-seez/) *n.* **1. DANGEROUS OR WORRYING TIME** a situation or period in which things are very uncertain, difficult, or painful, especially a time when action must be taken to avoid complete disaster or breakdown **2. CRITICAL MOMENT** a time when sth very important for the future happens or is decided **3.** MED **TURNING POINT IN DISEASE** a point in the course of a disease when the patient suddenly begins to get worse or better [15thC. Via Latin from Greek *krisis* 'decisive moment', from *krinein* 'to decide' (source of English *critic* and *criterion*).]

crisis centre *n.* an office or meeting-place where people can go in a time of great personal difficulty or distress for advice and support, often from voluntary staff

crisis management *n.* the business or process of working through a crisis to solve or cope with problems as they arise

crisp /krisp/ *adj.* **1. HARD BUT EASILY BROKEN** dry and firm, and of a texture that breaks easily **2. FRESH AND CRUNCHY** fresh and firm enough to snap when bitten into ○ *nice crisp lettuce* **3. SMOOTH, FIRM, AND CLEAN** with a stiff, uncreased, or unspoilt surface ○ *a crisp white tablecloth* **4. DISTINCT** distinct and clear, without ambiguity or distortion ○ *She was pleased with the crisp image of the print.* **5. SHARP AND CONCISE** sharp and concise, often to the point of brusqueness ○ *crisp responses* **6. INVIGORATING** invigorating and fresh ○ *It was a beautiful crisp December morning.* ■ *n.* **1. FRIED POTATO SLICE** a very thin slice of fried potato, eaten as a snack, usually salted and often flavoured ○ *cheese and onion crisps.* ◊ **potato chip 2.** *US* = **crumble** ■ *vti.* (**crisps, crisping, crisped**) **MAKE OR BECOME CRISP** to become or make sth crisp or crisper, usually in the oven [Mid-16thC. Originally in the sense 'curly', from Latin *crispus* (the source also of English *crêpe*).] —**crisply** *adv.* —**crispness** *n.* ◇ **to a crisp** until it has become hard and crunchy, usually when it should not be (*informal*) ○ *toast burned to a crisp*

crispate /kríss payt/ *adj.* used to describe leaves that have curled or wavy edges [Mid-19thC. From Latin *crispatus*, the past participle of *crispare* 'to curl', from *crispus* 'curled'.]

crispation /kriss páysh'n/ *n.* **1. ACT OF CURLING** the act of curling or the condition of being curled (*formal*) **2. MUSCLE CONTRACTION** a minor convulsive muscle contraction that produces a creeping feeling in the skin [Early 17thC. Formed from Latin *crispat-*, the past participle stem of *crispare* (see CRISPATE).]

crispbread /krísp bred/ *n.* a flat, crisp, usually rectangular cracker or biscuit made from rye, wheat, corn, or other grain

crispen /kríspən/ (**-ens, -ening, -ened**) *vti.* to become or make sth crisp or crisper

crisper /kríspər/ *n.* a covered compartment in a refrigerator, where fruits and vegetables are placed to keep them fresh and crisp

crispy /kríspi/ (**-ier, -iest**) *adj.* with a pleasantly light, crunchy texture ○ *Do you like your bacon crispy?* —**crispily** *adv.* —**crispiness** *n.*

crissa plural of **crissum**

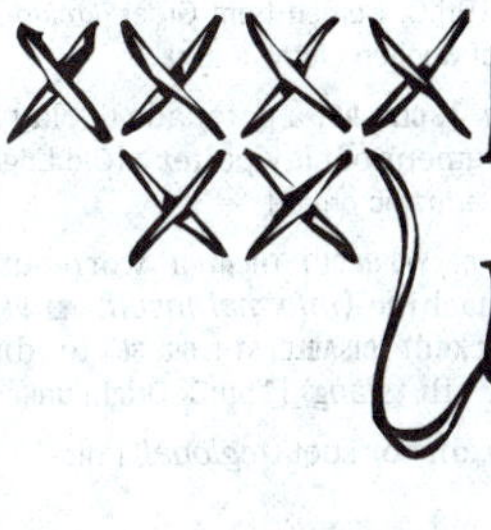

Crisscross

crisscross /kríss kross/ *n.* **CROSS OR LATTICE ARRANGEMENT** a pattern of lines that cross each other ■ *adj.* **WITH CROSSED VERTICAL AND HORIZONTAL LINES** running in different directions across each other, or made up of lines like this ■ *adv.* **BACK AND FORTH** in a way that makes a crisscross pattern of crossing lines ■ *v.* (**-crosses, -crossing, -crossed**) **1.** *vti.* **MAKE PATTERN OF CROSSED LINES** to create a crisscross pattern on sth **2.** *vt.* **GO TO AND FRO ACROSS STH** to travel or move backwards and forwards or in all different directions over sth [Early 17thC. Alteration of *cristcross* 'sign of cross'.]

crissum /kríssəm/ (*plural* **-sa** /-sə/) *n.* the feathers beneath the tail of a bird [Late 19thC. From modern Latin, formed from Latin *crissare* 'to wiggle the hips'.] —**crissal** *adj.*

crista /krístə/ (*plural* **-tae** /-tī/) *n.* **1.** ANAT **CREST** a crest or ridge, e.g. the border of a bone **2.** CELL BIOL **FOLD** a fold in the inner membrane of a mitochondrion, providing a large surface area over which the enzymes responsible for energy metabolism are located [Mid-19thC. From Latin, 'tuft of hair, ridge' (source of English *crest*).] —**cristate** *adj.*

cristobalite /kris tṓbəlīt/ *n.* a white mineral form of silica that occurs in volcanic rocks. Formula: SiO_2. [Late 19thC. Named after the hill of San *Cristóbal*, near the town of Pachuca de Soto in Mexico.]

crit /krit/ *n.* a critique (*informal*) ○ *I haven't seen the film but I've read a couple of crits.* [Early 20thC. Shortening.]

crit. *abbr.* 1. critic 2. critical 3. criticism

criterion /krī téeri ən/ (*plural* **-a** /-téeri ə/) *n.* an accepted standard used in making decisions or judgments about sth (*often used in the plural*) [Early 17thC. From Greek *kritērion*, from *kritēs* 'judge' (see CRITIC).] —**criterial** /krī téeri əl/ *adj.*

WORD KEY: USAGE

criterion or **criteria**? ***Criterion*** is singular, and ***criteria*** is plural; it is incorrect to use ***criteria*** as a singular noun (with *criterias* as a bogus plural), although this is commonly seen and heard in the print and electronic media, and in some law contexts as well: *In two cases … the courts expressly adopted that criteria* (P. P. Craig, *Administrative Law*). To form a correct singular noun, the phrase *set of criteria* is often used.

critic /kríttik/ *n.* **1. SB JUDGING STH** sb who makes a judgment about or an appraisal of sth or sb and gives comments ○ *an eminent critic of postwar government* **2. WRITER OF REVIEWS** sb, especially a journalist, who writes or broadcasts opinions on the quality of things such as drama productions, art exhibitions, and literary works ○ *the newspaper's TV critic* **3. SB WHO FINDS FAULT** sb who does not like sth or sb, or who finds fault with sth or sb [Mid-16thC. Via Latin from Greek *kritikos* 'discerning', from *kritēs* 'judge', from *krinein* (see CRISIS).]

critical /kríttik'l/ *adj.* **1. NOT APPROVING** tending to find fault with a particular person or thing, or with people and things in general **2. GIVING COMMENTS OR JUDGMENTS** containing or involving comments and opinions that analyse or judge sth, especially in a detailed way ○ *a critical analysis of modern economic theory* **3. CRUCIAL** extremely important because of being a time or happening at a time of special difficulty, trouble, or danger, when matters could quickly get either worse or better ○ *The decision was a critical one for the country.* **4. ESSENTIAL** absolutely necessary for the success of sth ○ *The army's immediate response is critical to our campaign.* **5. LIFE-THREATENING** life-threatening as a medical condition, or in danger from such a condition ○ *a patient in critical condition* **6. UNDERGOING CHANGE** relating to a property of a system that is undergoing a sudden change ○ *critical temperature* **7. SUSTAINING NUCLEAR CHAIN REACTION** designed to or having the mass to sustain a nuclear chain reaction —**critically** *adv.* —**criticalness** *n.*

critical angle *n.* **1. ANGLE PRODUCING COMPLETE REFLECTION** the angle between a ray of light and a surface at which the ray will be completely reflected by the surface **2.** = **stalling angle**

criticality /krítti kálləti/ *n.* **1. CRUCIALNESS** the condition of being crucial, decisive, or extremely serious **2. STAGE OF NUCLEAR REACTION** the point in an intensifying nuclear reaction at which it becomes self-sustaining

critical mass *n.* **1. AMOUNT OF FISSIONABLE MATERIAL** the smallest amount of fissionable material needed to maintain a nuclear chain reaction **2. NECESSARY SIZE**

zh vision In foreign words: kh German Bach; aN French vin; aaN French blanc; ö German schön, French feu; oN French bon; öN French un; ü French rue Stress marks: ´ as in secret \séek rət\; academic \àkə démmik\

OR AMOUNT the size or amount of sth that is required before sth can take place ○ *The service fell below the critical mass of subscribers and was suspended.*

critical point *n.* **1. POINT OF EQUILIBRIUM BETWEEN TWO STATES** a point at which two or more phases of a substance, e.g. liquid and gas, are identical or in equilibrium **2.** *US* = **stationary point**

critical region *n.* the possible results of a statistical test that are outside the range of acceptable probabilities and, if observed, would lead to their rejection

critical state *n.* = **critical point** *n.* 1

critical thinking *n.* disciplined intellectual criticism that combines research, knowledge of historical context, and balanced judgment

criticise *vti.* = **criticize**

criticism /kríttissizzəm/ *n.* **1. ACT OF CRITICIZING** a spoken or written opinion or judgment of what is wrong or bad about sb or sth **2. DISAPPROVAL** spoken or written opinions that point out one or more faults of sb or sth **3. ASSESSMENT OF CREATIVE WORK** considered judgment of or discussion about the qualities of sth, especially a creative work **4.** = **critique** *n.* 1

criticize /krítti sīz/ (**-cizes, -cizing, -cized**), **criticise** (**-cises, -cising, -cised**) *vti.* **1. COMPLAIN ABOUT STH WRONG** to comment on or point out the faults of people or things, or find sth wrong or bad about them **2. GIVE CONSIDERED OPINION ON STH** to make a considered assessment of the qualities of sth, especially a creative work —**criticizable** *adj.* —**criticizer** *n.* —**criticizingly** *adv.*

WORD KEY: SYNONYMS

criticize, censure, castigate, blast, condemn, find fault with, pick holes in, nitpick

CORE MEANING: to express disapproval or dissatisfaction with sb or sth

criticize the most wide-ranging term; **censure** to make a formal, often public or official statement of disapproval; **castigate** to criticize severely, often with a suggestion of reprimanding; **blast** an informal term for 'castigate'; **condemn** to give an unfavourable, absolute, and final judgment; **find fault with** to enumerate specific grounds for dissatisfaction; **pick holes in** to point out flaws in sth, particularly an argument; **nitpick** to engage in petty fault-finding.

---

critique /kri teˈek/ *n.* **1. REVIEW OF SB'S WORK** a written or broadcast assessment of sth, usually a creative work, with comments on its good and bad qualities **2.** = **criticism** *n.* 3 ■ *vt.* (**-tiques, -tiquing, -tiqued**) **GIVE REVIEW OF** to discuss or comment on sth, e.g. an artist's work or a political policy, giving an assessment of its good and bad features [Mid-17thC. Via French from Greek *kritikē (tekhnē)*, literally 'art of criticism', from *kritikos* (see CRITIC).]

CRO *abbr.* **1.** cathode-ray oscilloscope **2.** Community Relations Officer **3.** Criminal Records Office

Croagh Patrick /krō páttrik/ a holy mountain said to have been visited by St Patrick. It is situated west of Westport and south of Clew Bay, in County Mayo, Ireland. Height: 765 m/2,510 ft.

croak /krōk/ *n.* **CRY OF ANIMAL OR BIRD** a rough, usually low-pitched, vibrating sound, especially made by a frog or a crow, or the rough-sounding voice of sb with a dry or sore throat ■ *v.* (**croaks, croaking, croaked**) **1.** *vi.* **GIVE HARSH GRATING CALL** to make a rough, usually low-pitched, vibrating call **2.** *vti.* **SPEAK HOARSELY** to speak or say sth in a rough low unnatural voice **3.** *vti.* **DIE OR KILL** to die, or to kill sb (*slang*) **4.** *vi.* **GRUMBLE** to grumble or mutter gloomily (*informal*) [Mid-16thC. Origin uncertain: probably an imitation of the sound.] —**croakily** *adv.* —**croaky** *adj.*

croaker /krōˈkər/ *n.* **1. FISH THAT MAKES CROAKING SOUND** a fish that makes croaking or grunting noises. Family: Sciaenidae. **2. CROAKING ANIMAL** a bird or other animal that croaks when it calls

Croat /krōˈat/ *n.* **1. PEOPLES SB FROM CROATIA** sb who was born or brought up in Croatia, or who has Croatian citizenship **2. LANG** = **Croatian** *n.* 1 [Mid-17thC. Via modern Latin *Croata* from Serbo-Croatian *Hrvāt* (source of English *cravat*).] —**Croat** *adj.*

Croatia

Croatia /krō áyshə/ formerly one of the six republics that made up the former Federal People's Republic of Yugoslavia, Croatia declared itself an independent republic in 1991. Language: Croatian. Currency: kuna. Capital: Zagreb. Population: 4,664,710 (1997). Area: 56,510 sq. km/21,819 sq. mi. Official name **Republic of Croatia**

Croatian /krō áysh'n/ *adj.* **OF CROATIA** relating to or typical of Croatia, its people, culture, or language ■ *n.* **1. LANG OFFICIAL LANGUAGE OF CROATIA** the official language of Croatia, a variety of Serbo-Croat written in the Latin alphabet. Croatian is spoken by about five million people. **2. PEOPLES** = **Croat** *n.* 1

croc /krok/ *n.* a crocodile (*informal*) ○ *Any crocs in this river?* [Late 19thC. Shortening.]

crocein /krṓssi in/ *n.* a red or orange acid azo dye [20thC. Formed from Latin *croceus* 'saffron-coloured', from *crocus* (see CROCUS).]

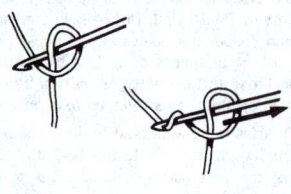

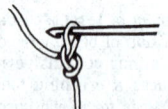

Crochet: Hooked needle is used to catch thread (top), which is twisted and pulled to create loop (centre and bottom)

crochet /krṓ shay/ *n.* **TYPE OF KNITTING USING HOOK** a form of needlework used to make clothes or decorative items from wool or thread, by looping it through itself with a special hooked needle (**crochet hook**) ■ *vti.* (**-chets** /-shayz/, **-cheting** /-shaying/, **-cheted, -cheted** /-shayd/) **USE CROCHET TO MAKE STH** to make things, or a particular item, in crochet work [Mid-19thC. From French *crochet*, literally 'little hook', from *croche* 'hook', of Germanic origin.] —**crocheter** /krṓ shayər/ *n.*

crocidolite /krō síddə līt/ *n.* a fibrous purplish blue form of the mineral riebeckite. It is a type of asbestos. [Mid-19thC. Coined from Greek *krokid-*, the stem of *krokis* 'nap of woollen cloth' + -LITE.]

crock¹ /krok/ *n.* **1. CLAY POT** a pot made of clay **2. POTTERY FRAGMENT** a fragment of clay pottery [Old English *crocc*, of prehistoric Germanic origin]

crock² /krok/ *n.* **WORN-OUT THING** a worn-out person, vehicle, or machine (*informal insult*) ■ *vt.* (**crocks, crocking, crocked**) **DISABLE STH OR SB** to disable or weaken sb or sth (*slang*) [15thC. Origin unknown.]

crock³ /krok/ *n.* dirt or soot (*regional*) [Mid-17thC. Origin unknown.]

crocked /krokt/ *adj.* (*slang*) **1. INJURED** physically incapacitated by an injury ○ *I'm too crocked to play this week.* **2.** *US* **DRUNK** drunk [Early 20thC. Origin uncertain: possibly from CROCK².]

crockery /krṓkəri/ *n.* plates, cups, saucers, and other household items made of china or earth-

---

enware [Early 18thC. Formed from earlier *crocker* 'potter', from CROCK¹.]

crocket /krókit/ *n.* any of various leaf shapes carved as decorations in Gothic architecture, often projecting along the angles on a spire or gable [Late 17thC. From Old French dialect *croquet* 'shepherd's crook', a variant of Old French *crochet* (see CROCHET).]

Crockett, Davy (1786–1836) US frontiersman. He fought against the Creek Native Americans, and joined Congress in 1827. Full name **David Crockett**

Crocodile

crocodile /krókə dīl/ (*plural* **-diles** *or* **-dile**) *n.* **1. LARGE REPTILE WITH STRONG JAWS** a large tropical or subtropical carnivorous reptile that lives near water. It has a long, thick-skinned, body and a broad head with strong jaws. Crocodiles have longer and more tapering snouts than alligators. Family: Crocodylidae. **2.** = **crocodilian 3. LEATHER FROM CROCODILE SKIN** leather made from the skin of a crocodile ○ *crocodile shoes* **4. LINE OF CHILDREN** a procession of schoolchildren walking in pairs (*informal*) ○ *A neat crocodile of schoolgirls filed into the museum.* [13thC. Via Old French *cocodril* from, ultimately, Greek *krokodilos*, a kind of small lizard.]

crocodile bird *n.* a long-legged black-and-white African bird that lives near the sandy banks of rivers and lakes and feeds on insects parasitic to the crocodile. Latin name: *Pluvianus aegyptius.*

crocodile clip *n.* a metal clip with serrated jaws held closed by a spring, used for making temporary electrical connections. US term **alligator clip**

crocodile tears *npl.* false tears or an insincere show of grief [Because crocodiles were once believed to have made sounds like weeping to attract prey, and to shed hypocritical tears over their victims]

crocodilian /krókə dílli ən/ *n.* any large predatory reptile belonging to a group that includes the alligator, cayman, crocodile, gavial, and related extinct animals. Order: Crocodylia. —**crocodilian** *adj.*

crocoite /krṓkō īt, krṓ kō-/, **crocoisite** /krṓ kō i sīt/ *n.* a rare orange or red mineral consisting of lead chromate. Formula: PbCrO₄. [Mid-19thC. Alteration of French *crocoise*, from Greek *krokoeis* 'saffron-coloured', from *krokos* 'saffron'.]

crocosmia /krə kózmi ə/ (*plural* **-mias** *or* **-mia**) *n.* a South African plant cultivated for its orange to red ornamental flower sprays. Montbretia is a hybrid of two species of crocosmia. Genus: *Crocosmia.*

crocus /krṓkəss/ *n.* **1. SPRING FLOWER** a small perennial that grows from a corm and has white, purple, or yellow flowers in early spring. Genus: *Crocus.* **2. FLOWER SIMILAR TO CROCUS** any plant that has a flower like a true crocus, e.g. the autumn crocus **3.** *US* = **jeweller's rouge** [14thC. Via French and Latin from Greek *krokos* 'saffron, crocus'.]

Croesus /kréessəss/ *n.* a name used for a very wealthy man [From CROESUS]

Croesus, King of Lydia (*fl.* 6th century BC) Lydian monarch who was a proverbially wealthy ruler whose reign from about 560 to 546 BC ended in defeat and probable capture by Cyrus the Great

croft /kroft/ *n.* a small plot of land, often with a house on it, that the owner or occupier works, especially in Scotland [Old English. Of unknown origin.]

crofter /króftər/ *n.* sb who owns or rents and works a

small plot of land, often living in a house on it, especially in Scotland

crofting /króftin̲g/ *n.* the occupation of working a small plot of land, especially in Scotland, or the system of using land in this way

Crohn's disease /krōnz-/ *n.* a chronic inflammatory disease, usually of the lower intestinal tract, marked by scarring and thickening of the intestinal wall and obstruction [Mid-20thC. Named after the US pathologist B. B. *Crohn* (1884–1983), who identified it.]

croissant /krwáss oN/ *n.* a piece of baked dough or pastry shaped into a crescent, usually moist, flaky, and very rich in fat, originally made in France [Late 19thC. From French, literally 'crescent'.]

Croix de Guerre /krwaa də gáir/ (*plural* **Croix de Guerre**) *n.* a French military medal awarded for bravery in war [Early 20thC. From French, literally 'war cross'.]

Cro-Magnon /krō mánn yon/ *n.* the earliest known type of modern human being found in Europe and dating from between about 50,000 and 30,000 years ago [Mid-19thC. From the name of the *Cro-Magnon* hill in the Dordogne, France, where Cro-Magnon skeletons were first discovered.]

crombie /krómbi/ *n.* a type of overcoat made of woollen material (*informal*) [Mid-20thC. Named after J & J *Crombie* Ltd, Scottish clothmakers.]

Crome /krōm/, **John** (1768–1821) British landscape painter who was instrumental in forming the Norwich School (1803?-33). Most of his works depict the Norfolk countryside.

cromlech /króm lek/ *n.* **1.** STONE CIRCLE a group of prehistoric standing stones arranged in a circle **2.** BURIAL CHAMBER an ancient stone burial chamber [Late 17thC. From Welsh, formed from *crwm* 'arched' and *llech* 'flat stone'.]

Crompton /krómptən/, **Samuel** (1753–1827) British inventor. His 'spinning mule' (1779?) greatly improved muslin manufacture, but he was too poor to patent it and profited little.

Cromwell /króm wel/, **Oliver** (1599–1658) English soldier and statesman. He led the Parliamentarians to victory in the Civil War (1642–48) and, after the execution of Charles I, ruled as Lord Protector of England (1653–58).

Cromwell, Thomas, Earl of Essex (1485?–1540) English statesman. He carried out the dissolution of the monasteries for Henry VIII, but was later beheaded.

crone /krōn/ *n.* an offensive term that deliberately insults a woman's age, appearance, and temperament (*offensive*) [14thC. Via Old Northern French *carogne* 'withered old woman', literally 'carrion', from assumed Vulgar Latin *caronia*, from Latin *caro* 'flesh'.]

Cronin /krṓnin/, **A. J.** (1896–1981) Scottish novelist and physician. His bestsellers, including *The Stars Look Down* (1935), drew on his medical background, as did the television series *Dr Finlay's Casebook* (1960s). Full name **Archibald Joseph Cronin**

Cronus /krṓnəss/, **Cronos, Kronos** *n.* in Greek mythology, one of the Titans who ruled the world until his son Zeus dethroned him. Roman equivalent **Saturn**

crony /krṓni/ (*plural* **-nies**) *n.* a close friend, sometimes one to whom special treatment and preference is given (*disapproving*) [Mid-17thC. From Greek *khronios* 'long-lasting', from *khronos* 'time' (source of English *chronic*). The word was originally Cambridge University slang.]

cronyism /krṓni izzəm/ *n.* special treatment and preference given to friends or colleagues, especially the giving of political posts to people because of friendship rather than their ability (*informal disapproving*)

crook /kröök/ *n.* **1.** HOOK-SHAPED DEVICE a curved or hooked tool, instrument, or part in a mechanism **2.** AGRIC SHEPHERD'S HOOKED STICK a long stick with a curved end used by a shepherd to catch or guide a sheep **3.** CHR = **crosier** *n.* 1 **4.** DISHONEST PERSON sb who steals, cheats, or is involved in criminal activities (*informal*) **5.** BEND IN STH a bent or curved part of sth, e.g. the curve made by sb's arm when the elbow is bent **6.** TUBE INSERTED IN INSTRUMENT a tube inserted into a brass instrument to increase its length and lower its fundamental pitch ■ *vti.* (**crooks, crooking, crooked**) BEND STH to curve, or make sth, e.g. a finger, take on a hooked or curved shape ■ *adj.* *ANZ* (*informal*) **1.** ill or unwell ○ *I'm feeling a bit crook today.* **2.** NOT WORKING PROPERLY not working properly, or in a poor state of repair ○ *It's a bit crook this door; doesn't shut properly.* **3.** UNPLEASANT nasty or unpleasant ○ *It was real crook that time we had our money stolen.* [12thC. From Old Norse *krókr* 'hook'.]

crooked /kröökid/ *adj.* **1.** WITH BENT SHAPE sharply curved, bent, or twisted, often in more than one place **2.** AT ANGLE not aligned properly, or at an angle ○ *That picture is crooked.* **3.** NOT LEGAL illegal or dishonest (*informal*) —**crookedly** *adv.* —**crookedness** *n.*

crookery /kröökəri/ *n.* illegal or dishonest activities

Crookes /krööks/, **William, Sir** (1832–1919) British chemist and physicist. His work on the vacuum electron tube furthered the development of X-rays, television, and radar. He discovered the metal thallium.

croon /kroon/ *vti.* (**croons, crooning, crooned**) **1.** SING OR MURMUR GENTLY to sing or murmur sth in a soft, low voice, especially to yourself or to a sleepy child **2.** SING SENTIMENTALLY to perform a song or songs in a smooth sentimental style ■ *n.* GENTLE SINGING a singing in a soft low way, or sth sung in this way [15thC. From Middle Dutch *krōnen* 'to lament' (perhaps ultimately an imitation of the sound).]

crooner /kroonər/ *n.* a singer who favours slow songs, especially ballads, and whose style is generally sentimental

crop /krop/ *n.* **1.** AGRIC, BOT PLANT GROWN FOR USE any group of plants grown by people for food or other use, especially on a large scale in farming or horticulture **2.** AGRIC AMOUNT PRODUCED the amount harvested from a plant or area of land, during one particular period of time ○ *a good crop of tomatoes* **3.** AGRIC ANIMALS REARED FOR PRODUCE a group of animals reared in farming, or sth produced from them ○ *a poor crop of lambs* **4.** GROUP OF PEOPLE OR THINGS a number of things occurring, or people doing or being sth, at the same time ○ *last year's crop of students* **5.** EQU WHIP HANDLE the handle of a whip **6.** HAIR SHORT HAIRSTYLE a short hairstyle, usually for a woman **7.** BIRDS POUCH IN GULLET OF BIRDS a pouch in the gullet of many birds in which they store or partially digest food before regurgitating it to feed their young **8.** ZOOL POUCH IN DIGESTIVE SYSTEM a pouch in the digestive tract of an insect or earthworm ■ *v.* (**crops, cropping, cropped**) **1.** *vti.* AGRIC GRAZE to eat the top parts of growing plants, especially grass **2.** *vt.* CUT STH SHORT to cut sth short, e.g. hair or a lawn **3.** *vti.* AGRIC GATHER PRODUCE to cut or gather the produce of plants or of a cultivated area ○ *crop a field* **4.** *vti.* AGRIC PRODUCE CROP to produce a crop, or make an area of land produce a crop ○ *The tomatoes cropped well this summer.* **5.** *vt.* PHOTOGRAPHY CUT PART OF PHOTO to cut off or conceal unwanted parts of an image, especially a photograph [Old English *cropp* 'ear of grain'. Ultimately from a prehistoric Germanic word meaning 'round mass', which is also the ancestor of English *croup* and *group*.]

crop out *vi.* = **outcrop**

crop up *vi.* to appear or arrive, especially unexpectedly or from time to time (*informal*) ○ *Her name keeps cropping up in conversation.*

crop circle *n.* an area in a field of crops where the plants have been mysteriously flattened, usually overnight, into the shape of a circle or a more complex pattern

crop-dusting *n.* the spraying of powdered fungicide or insecticide onto crops from the air

cropper /kroppər/ *n.* **1.** *US* = **sharecropper 2.** PLANT GIVING YIELD a plant described in terms of its ability to yield produce ◇ **come a cropper 1.** to experience a hurtful or embarrassing fall (*informal*) **2.** to fail completely (*informal*)

crop rotation *n.* a system of farming in which a piece of land is planted with different crops in succession, in order to improve soil fertility and control crop pests and diseases

crop top *n.* a piece of clothing for women or girls, covering the upper body but cut short to end above the navel

croquet /krṓ kay, -ki/ *n.* **1.** LAWN GAME WITH BALLS AND MALLETS an outdoor game, usually played on a lawn, in which the players use long-handled wooden mallets to hit large wooden balls through a series of hoops (**wickets**) **2.** STROKE IN CROQUET a stroke played in the game of croquet whereby a player knocks away an opponent's ball by hitting his or her own ball when the two are touching ■ *vti.* (**-quets** /-kayz, -kiz/, **-queting** /-kaying, -ki ing/, **-queted, -queted** /-kayed, -kid/) KNOCK SB'S CROQUET BALL AWAY to knock away an opponent's ball in the game of croquet by hitting your own ball when the two are touching [Mid-19thC. Origin uncertain: possibly from French dialect *croquet* 'shepherd's crook', a variant of French *crochet* (see CROCHET).]

croquette /kro két/ *n.* a little flat cake, cylinder, or ball of a savoury mixture, e.g. containing potato, meat, or fish, coated in egg and breadcrumbs, and fried [Early 18thC. From French, formed from *croquer* 'to crunch', ultimately an imitation of the sound.]

crore /krawr/ (*plural* **crores** *or* **crore**) *n.* *S Asia* ten million, especially ten million rupees or the equivalent, one million pounds, in sterling [Early 17thC. Via Hindi *kroṛ* from Sanskrit *koṭiḥ*.]

Crosby /krózbi/, **Bing** (1904?–77) US singer and actor. Famous for songs such as 'White Christmas' (1942), he also starred in many films, including *High Society* (1956). Real name **Harry Lillis Crosby**

crosier /krṓzi ər, -zhər/, **crozier** *n.* **1.** CHR ROD CARRIED BY BISHOP a staff with a hooked end like a shepherd's crook, carried by Christian bishops, archbishops, or abbots, symbolizing their roles of caring for their congregations as shepherds tend flocks **2.** BOT CURLED PLANT PART a part of a plant that has a curled end, e.g. the frond of a fern [13thC. Via Old French *crosier* 'crook bearer' from *croce* 'crook' (also influenced by *crois* 'cross'). Ultimately of Germanic origin.]

cross /kross/ *n.* **1.** TWO INTERSECTING LINES a sign or mark (X) made of two straight lines that bisect each other, used to mark or cancel sth, or, in the past, as a signature by people who could not write **2.** CHRISTIAN SYMBOL a long vertical bar intersected at right angles, usually about two-thirds up, by a shorter horizontal bar, used as a symbol of Christianity, or of the crucifixion. The shape refers to the cross on which Jesus Christ was crucified. **3. Cross, cross** WOODEN STRUCTURE JESUS CHRIST DIED ON the specific wooden cross on which Jesus Christ was crucified **4.** CROSS-SHAPED DECORATION a medal or emblem shaped like a cross **5.** WOODEN EXECUTION POST WITH CROSSBAR an upright wooden post with a shorter post fixed across it at right angles towards the top, on which, in the past, people were nailed or hanged in public executions **6.** STONE MONUMENT an upright stone or structure in the shape of a cross or holding a cross, erected to commemorate sb or sth (*often used in placenames*) **7.** STH TO BE BORNE a difficulty in sb's personal life that is particularly testing, troubling, or painful ○ *What's happened to him is a shame, but we all have a cross to bear.* **8.** MIXTURE a thing or person that results from blending two different kinds together and is neither one of them nor the other but sth in between ○ *a cross between a mystery and a historical novel* **9.** GENETICS PRODUCTION OF HYBRID the process of producing a crossbreed or hybrid from genetically different individuals **10.** GENETICS HYBRID INDIVIDUAL an animal or plant produced by interbreeding two genetically different individuals **11.** SOCCER PASSING OF BALL ACROSS PITCH in soccer, a kicked pass that sends the ball across the field, usually in the air **12.** BOXING SIDEWAYS BLOW IN BOXING a punch thrown at an opponent from the side, in response to and evading the opponent's jab or lead **13.** SPORTS PASS ACROSS GOAL a pass that sends the ball across the field, e.g., in hockey **14.** CONSTR PIPE CONNECTION a cross-shaped joint used to connect four pipes ■ *vti.* (**crosses, crossing, crossed**) MEET AT ONE POINT to meet at a particular place or time and then continue separately again ○ *A settlement grew up where two trade routes crossed.* ■ *n.* STH DISHONEST sth dishonest or fraudulent, especially a sports contest in which the outcome has been dishonestly decided before it begins (*slang*) ■ *v.* (**crosses, crossing, crossed**) **1.** *vt.* BANKING MAKE CHEQUE PAYABLE ONLY THROUGH BANK to draw two parallel lines across the front of a cheque, diagonally or vertically, meaning that it has to be paid into a bank

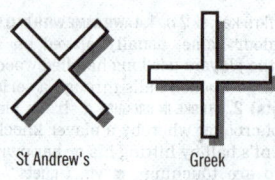

St Andrew's   Greek

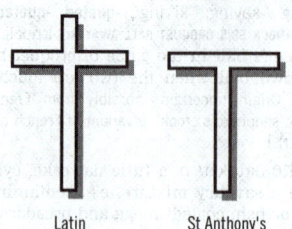

Latin   St Anthony's

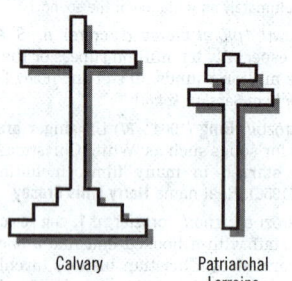

Calvary   Patriarchal Lorraine

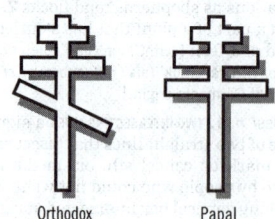

Orthodox   Papal

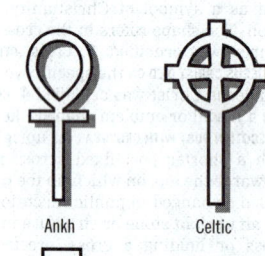

Ankh   Celtic

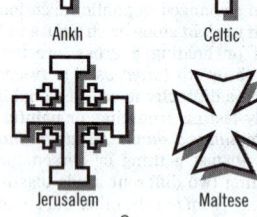

Jerusalem   Maltese

Cross

account **2.** *vti.* **GO ACROSS** to move or move sb or sth from one side of sth to the other ○ *We've already crossed the border.* ○ *The river's too swift to cross the horses here.* **3.** *vt.* **PLACE THINGS ONE ACROSS THE OTHER** to put two things so that one lies across the other ○ *crossed her legs* **4.** *vi.* **COMMUNICATION BE EN ROUTE AT ONE TIME** to be travelling in opposite directions between the same two correspondents at the same time (*refers to letters and other forms of communication*) **5.** *vti.* **TELECOM CONNECT TELEPHONE LINES WRONGLY AND CONFUSINGLY** to make an incorrect connection between telephone numbers or lines, so that two or more conversations intermingle with each other, or to be connected in this way (*often passive*) **6.** *vt.* **GENETICS INTERBREED PLANTS OR ANIMALS** to interbreed or hybridize plants or animalsthat are genetically different **7.** *vt.* **CHR MAKE CHRISTIAN BLESSING GESTURE WITH HAND** to draw the shape of a Christian cross in the air over sb or sth as a symbol of God's blessing **8.** *vti.* **SPORTS PASS BALL ACROSS PITCH** in soccer and some other games, to make a pass that sends

the ball across, rather than up or down, the field **9.** *vt.* **THWART SB** to do sth that goes against sb's wishes, or that annoys or frustrates sb (*formal*) ○ *I wouldn't cross her; she gets nasty when she's angry.* **10.** *vt.* **WRITE LINE ACROSS LETTER T** to draw a horizontal line across the vertical line of a letter t, to complete the letter ■ *adj.* **ANGRY** angry and upset ○ *exchanged a few cross words* [Pre-12thC. Via Old Norse *kross* and Old Irish *cros* from Latin *crux* (source of English *crucify*, *crucible*, *cruise*, and *crusade*). Perhaps ultimately of Phoenician origin.] —**crosser** *n.* —**crossly** *adv.* —**crossness** *n.*

cross off *vt.* to remove sth, especially a name or item written on a list, by drawing a line through it

cross out *vt.* to cancel sth, especially a word or item that is wrong or not wanted, by drawing a line through it

cross- *prefix.* **1.** crossing ○ *crossover* **2.** opposing, opposite ○ *crosscurrent* **3.** reciprocal, mutual ○ *crosslink* [From CROSS]

crossable /króssəb'l/ *adj.* possible, easy, or safe to pass across from one side to the other —**crossability** /króssə bílləti/ *n.*

cross action *n.* **LAW** a legal proceeding brought by a person who has been sued against the person who brought the original action, or against a fellow defendant

crossbar /króss baar/ *n.* **1.** **LEVEL POLE** a bar that runs horizontally between two vertical posts, e.g. between goalposts or the uprights of a jump **2.** **LEVEL BAR IN BICYCLE FRAME** a horizontal metal bar that runs from below the handlebars to below the saddle in a man's or boy's bicycle

crossbeam /króss beem/ *n.* a beam that passes between two supports in the structure of a building

crossbearer /króss bairər/ *n.* sb who carries a cross in front of a bishop or archbishop in a ceremonial procession

cross bedding *n.* layering of geological strata in which deposits were laid down at an angle with respect to those above and below, commonly seen in sandstone deposited as dunes —**cross-bedded** *adj.*

cross bench *n.* one of the benches in the House of Commons and House of Lords where members sit if they belong to neither the governing party nor one of the main opposition parties. The cross benches are set at right angles to the government and opposition benches. (*hyphenated when used before a noun*) ○ *a cross-bench MP*

crossbencher /króss benchər/ *n.* a member of the House of Commons or House of Lords who belongs to neither the governing party nor any of the main opposition parties

crossbill /króss bil/ *n.* (*plural* **-bills** *or* **-bill**) *n.* a large finch that lives in coniferous forests and has a beak with crossed tips that it uses to extract seeds from conifer cones. Genus: *Loxia.*

crossbones /króss bōnz/ *npl.* a representation of two human thighbones crossing each other in the middle, traditionally placed beneath a skull as a symbol of death. The image of crossbones lying below a skull was traditionally used by pirates on their flag (**Jolly Roger**) and in modern times to show that sth is poisonous. ♦ **skull and crossbones**

crossbow /króss bō/ *n.* a medieval weapon, or its modern sports successor, consisting of a bow attached crosswise to a stock with a cranking mechanism and a trigger. A crossbow fires short, heavy arrows called bolts or quarrels. —**crossbowman** *n.*

crossbred /króss bred/ *adj.* **HYBRID** produced by hybridization of genetically different individuals ■ *n.* = **crossbreed**

crossbreed /króss breed/ *vti.* (**-breeds, -breeding, -bred** /-bred/, **-bred**) **BREED FROM GENETICALLY DIFFERENT INDIVIDUALS** to breed new strains of plants or animals from genetically different individuals ■ *n.* **PRODUCT OF CROSSBREEDING** an animal or plant produced by crossbreeding

cross-buttock *n.* a wrestling throw in which the hip is used to pivot the opponent

cross-Channel *adj.* going across the English Channel ○ *cross-Channel ferries*

crosscheck /króss chék/ (**-checks, -checking, -checked**) *vt.* **1.** **VERIFY STH IN ANOTHER WAY** to make sure that sth such as a fact or figure is correct by looking it up in other sources or asking another person **2.** **OBSTRUCT OPPONENT USING STICK** in hockey, ice hockey, and lacrosse, to obstruct an opposing player by using both hands to thrust a playing stick across his or her body —**crosscheck** *n.*

cross-claim *n.* a claim made against another party on the same side of a lawsuit, e.g. a fellow defendant

cross-country *adj.* **NOT ON ROAD OR TRACK** done over fields or hills, or through woods, not on roads or a specially prepared area ○ *a cross-country run* ■ *n.* **RACING OVER FIELDS** running, sporting activity, or a race or event, done cross-country ■ *adj.* **1.** **ACROSS A COUNTRY** from one side of a country to another, or throughout a country ○ *The band embarked on a cross-country tour.* **2.** **OPERATING OFF ROADS** designed or able to operate without roads ○ *a cross-country vehicle*

cross-country skiing *n.* skiing on long narrow skis across open countryside on fairly level ground

crosscourt /króss kawrt/ *adj.* hit or thrown from one side of a playing court towards the other, especially in tennis or basketball

cross cousin *n.* a cousin who is related to sb through a brother and sister, being either a father's sister's child or a mother's brother's child. ♦ **parallel cousin**

cross-cultural *adj.* relating to or comparing two or more different cultures —**cross-culturally** *adv.*

crosscurrent /króss kurrənt/ *n.* **1.** **CONTRARY FLOW** a current that flows across another current, mainly in water but also in air **2.** **OPPOSITE TENDENCY** a movement or trend that conflicts with the general one, especially a trend in people's ideas or opinions

crosscut /króss kut/ *adj.* **1.** **CUT AT ANGLE** used to describe sth such as wood, meat, or fabric that is cut across its main grain **2.** **FOR CUTTING ACROSS** made or used for cutting across the grain of wood ■ *vti.* (**-cuts, -cutting, -cut**) **CINEMA MOVE FROM ONE SHOT TO ANOTHER** to alternate repeatedly brief scenes from one filmed sequence with scenes from another to give the impression that the events they show are happening at the same time ■ *n.* **1.** **CUT ACROSS** a cut made across sth, e.g. a long piece of timber **2.** **TUNNEL ACROSS VEIN OF ORE** a tunnel in a mine that cuts across a vein of ore **3.** **CINEMA EXAMPLE OF FILM TECHNIQUE** an example of the film technique in which short segments of two or more scenes are alternated **4.** **SHORTCUT** a shorter and more direct route to place

crosscut saw *n.* a saw used for cutting wood across the grain

cross-dress (**cross-dresses, cross-dressing, cross-dressed**) *vi.* to wear clothes usually worn by sb of the opposite sex —**cross-dresser** *n.* —**cross-dressing** *n.*

crosse /kross/ *n.* a wooden stick used in the game of lacrosse, curved at the top into a triangular frame that supports a tough leatherwork net [Mid-19thC. From French, 'bishop's crook'. See CROSIER.]

cross-examine (**cross-examines, cross-examining, cross-examined**) *vt.* **1.** **QUESTION OPPOSING WITNESS** to question a witness for the opposing side in a hearing or trial **2.** **QUESTION SB RELENTLESSLY** to ask sb a lot of detailed questions in a persistent or aggressive way (*informal*) —**cross-examiner** *n.* —**cross-examination** *n.*

cross-eyed *adj.* having an eye alignment that makes one or both eyes turn in towards the nose

cross-fade (**cross-fades, cross-fading, cross-faded**) *vti.* to gradually introduce a new sound or picture while causing another one to disappear

cross-fertilization, cross-fertilisation *n.* **1.** **FERTILIZATION BY FUSION** the fertilization of a female sex cell (**gamete**) of one individual by a male sex cell from a different individual, usually of the same species. ♦ **self-fertilization 2.** = **cross-pollination 3.** **EXCHANGE OF IDEAS** the exchange of ideas between two groups, especially cultures, that produces benefits for both —**cross-fertile** *adj.* —**cross-fertilize** *vti.*

crossfield /króss feeld/ *adj.* kicked or thrown from one side of a playing field towards the other, especially in soccer or rugby ○ *a crossfield pass*

crossfire /króss fīr/ *n.* **1. GUNFIRE FROM DIFFERENT DIRECTIONS** shots that come from more than one place, in such a way that the lines of fire converge **2. FIERCE CLASH OF OPINIONS** heated or lively conversation, with different and opposing views and ideas being put forward, or an example of this

cross-grained *adj.* **1. WITH GRAIN RUNNING CROSSWISE** with an irregular grain or a grain that runs across the length **2. BAD-TEMPERED AND DIFFICULT** difficult to deal with because of stubbornness, contrariness, or bad temper (*informal*)

cross hairs /króss hairz/, **crosshairs** *npl.* a pair of fine lines or wires that cross at right angles inside a lens or sight, used, e.g. in focusing an optical instrument or in aiming a rifle

crosshatch /króss hátch/ **(-hatches, -hatching, -hatched)** *vti.* to draw parallel or intersecting lines across part of a drawing or diagram, usually diagonally, especially to give the effect of shadow or different texture —**crosshatching** *n.*

crosshead /króss hed/ *n.* a sliding metal block securing one end of a piston rod to a connecting rod

cross-index **(cross-indexes, cross-indexing, cross-indexed)** *v.* **1.** *vt.* **CROSS-REFER ITEM IN INDEX** to give a particular item one or more additional entries in an index, under different headings, as cross-references to it **2.** *vti.* **GIVE CROSS-REFERENCES** to supply cross-references in sth

crossing /krόssing/ *n.* **1. SOMEWHERE WHERE SB CAN CROSS** a place that has been specially constructed, chosen, or marked out as somewhere where sth, e.g. a road or a border, may be crossed **2. POINT WHERE ROUTES CROSS** a place where a railway line and a road, two railway lines, roads, paths, or similar lines go across each other **3. JOURNEY ACROSS WATER** a journey across a body of water **4. CENTRAL AREA OF CROSS-SHAPED CHURCH** the place in a cross-shaped church where the nave and the transept meet

crossing-over *n.* GENETICS the interchange of segments between homologous chromosomes during cell division **(meiosis)**, resulting in new combinations of gene types **(alleles)** and therefore variability in inherited characteristics. ◊ **recombination**

crossjack /króss jak/ *n.* a sail on the mizzenmast of a ship

cross-legged /-légd, -léggid/ *adj.* **WITH KNEES APART AND ANKLES CROSSED** in a sitting position with the legs bent so that the knees are apart and the ankles are crossed in front ■ *adv.* **WITH ONE LEG OVER OTHER** with one leg lying over the other ○ *sitting cross-legged*

crosslet /krósslit/ *n.* on coats of arms, a cross that has a smaller cross at the end of each of its arms [15thC. Modelled on Anglo-Norman *croiselet*, literally 'small cross'.]

cross-link *n.* **cross-link, cross-linkage CONNECTING LINK IN MOLECULE** a transverse connecting element, such as an atom, chemical group, or covalent bond, between parallel chains of a complex organic molecule, especially a polymer or protein ■ *vt.* **(cross-links, cross-linking, cross-linked) JOIN STH BY CROSS-LINK** to join polymer chains by a cross-link

cross matching *n.* the process of testing for the compatibility of a donor's and recipient's tissues before blood transfusion or tissue transplantation —**cross-match** *vt.*

cross-multiply **(cross-multiplies, cross-multiplying, cross-multiplied)** *vi.* to multiply each numerator of two fractions by the denominator of the other —**cross-multiplication** *n.*

cross of Lorraine *n.* a cross with two horizontal bars, a short bar near the top and a longer one near the bottom [Mid-19thC. Named after the former French province of *Lorraine*.]

Cross of Valour *n.* the highest Canadian decoration for courage

crossopterygian /kro sóptə ríjji ən/ (*plural* **-ans** *or* **-an**) *n.* a bony fish with paired fleshy pectoral fins like limbs that is thought to be ancestral to amphibians and other land vertebrates. All except the coelacanth are extinct. Subclass: Crossopterygii. [Mid-19thC. From modern Latin *Crossopterygii*, subclass name, from Greek *krossoi* 'fringe' and *pterux* 'wing, fin'.] —**crossopterygian** *adj.*

crossover /króss ōvər/ *n.* **1. CROSSING OR TRANSFER POINT** a place for crossing from one side of sth to the other, or from one line, system, or vehicle to another **2.** GENETICS = **crossing-over 3. WIDENING OF POPULARITY** the process by which an artistic work becomes popular outside the category in which it originated **4. STH NOW POPULAR WITH DIFFERENT AUDIENCE** an artist, musician, artistic creation, or piece of music that has become popular outside one original category ■ *adj.* **MIXING TWO DIFFERENT STYLES** resulting from a mixture of two different artistic categories or styles, or from elements of one category becoming popular in another

cross-party *adj.* involving two or more political parties ○ *Members of both government and opposition are arriving for cross-party talks.*

crosspatch /króss pach/ *n.* a bad-tempered, touchy person [Late 17thC. Formed from CROSS in the sense 'annoyed' + PATCH, with the early meaning 'fool'.]

crosspiece /króss peess/ *n.* a piece that crosses a structure or implement from one side to the other, e.g. a beam in a building or part of the handle of a tool

cross-ply *adj.* used to describe tyres made with the strands of the fabric crossing each other diagonally

cross-pollination *n.* the transfer of pollen from an anther of one flower to the stigma of another —**cross-pollinate** *vti.*

cross product *n.* = **vector product**

cross-purpose *n.* a conflicting or contrary purpose ◇ **at cross-purposes** not understanding each other, usually through not realizing that the other person means or intends sth different

cross-question *vt.* = **cross-examine** ■ *n.* **QUESTION TO WITNESS IN COURT** a lawyer's question to a witness being cross-examined in a court case —**cross-questioning** *n.* —**cross-question** *vt.*

cross-reaction *n.* the immunological reaction of one antigen with the antibodies developed against another similar antigen —**cross-react** *vi.* —**cross-reactive** *adj.* —**cross-reactivity** *n.*

cross-refer **(cross-refers, cross-referring, cross-referred)** *vti.* to give a note that tells a reader of a book, index, or card catalogue to look in another specified part of the same work

cross-reference *n.* **DIRECTION TO READER TO LOOK ELSEWHERE** a note, especially one printed in a book, index, or card catalogue, that tells a reader to look in another specified place for information ■ *v.* **(cross-references, cross-referencing, cross-referenced) 1.** *vt.* **PUT NOTES INTO TEXT** to provide a text, index, or card catalogue with cross-references **2.** *vti.* = **cross-refer**

cross-resistance *n.* resistance developed by an organism to the effects of a toxin as a result of being exposed to a similar toxin

crossroads /króssrōdz/ *npl.* (*takes a singular verb*) **1. ROAD JUNCTION** a place where two or more roads meet or cross each other **2. DECISIVE MOMENT** a time when an important decision must be made

crossruff /króss ruf/ *n.* **PLAN BETWEEN PARTNERS AT CARDS** a tactic used in the games of whist and bridge, in which two partners alternately trump each other's first card **(lead)** in each round ■ *vti.* **(-ruffs, -ruffing, -ruffed) TAKE TURNS TO TRUMP PARTNER** to play a crossruff, or to trump the card led by your partner or from the dummy in a crossruff [Late 16thC. Formed from CROSS + RUFF² 'to trump'.]

cross section *n.* **1. PLANE CUTTING THROUGH AN OBJECT** a plane surface formed by cutting through an object at right angles to an axis, especially the longest axis **2. STH CUT IN CROSS SECTION** a piece cut as part of a cross section, or an image of such a piece ○ *draw a cross-section of a cone* **3. REPRESENTATIVE SAMPLE** a sample of sth that represents all or most of the different elements that the whole contains **4. PROBABILITY OF PARTICLE INTERACTION** a measure of the probability of any specific interaction such as fission or ionization occurring between two elementary particles —**cross-sectional** *adj.*

cross-stitch *n.* **1. EMBROIDERY STITCH** a stitch made up of two diagonal stitches crossing each other **2. EMBROIDERY IN CROSS-SHAPED STITCHES** pictures, designs, or items of needlework sewn using cross-stitches ■ *vti.* **(cross-stitches, cross-stitching, cross-stitched) SEW USING CROSS-STITCH** to do embroidery using cross-stitches, or to make sth in cross-stitch

crosstalk /króss tawk/ *n.* **1. UNWANTED SIGNALS** unwanted sounds or other signals picked up by one channel of an electronic communications system from another channel, e.g. between telephones or loudspeakers **2. CLEVER FAST-MOVING TALK** conversation full of quick and witty lines and replies (*informal*) ○ *He sat quietly at the dinner table, too shy to take part in the scintillating crosstalk that flowed to and fro.*

cross-tolerance *n.* = **cross-resistance**

cross-town, **crosstown** *adj.* travelling or extending across a city or town —**crosstown** *adv.*

cross-train **(cross-trains, cross-training, cross-trained)** *vi.* SPORTS to train for more than one competitive sport at a time

crosstrainer /króss traynər/ *n.* SPORTS **1. SB TRAINING FOR DIFFERENT SPORTS** an athlete who trains for more than one competitive sport simultaneously **2. SPORTS SHOE** a sports shoe designed for more than one sporting activity

cross training *n.* SPORTS fitness training in different sports, e.g. running and weightlifting, usually undertaken to enhance performance in one of the sports

cross-training *adj.* SPORTS designed to be used for more than one kinds of sporting activity ○ *a cross-training bike*

crosstree /króss tree/ *n.* either of a pair of horizontal pieces of wood or metal at the top of a ship's mast to which ropes are fixed to support the mast

cross vault, **cross vaulting** *n.* a ceiling created by the crossing of two or more simple arched vaults **(barrel vaults)**

crosswalk /króss wawk/ *n. US* = **pedestrian crossing**

crossways /króss wayz/ *adv.* **1.** = **crosswise 2. DIAGONALLY** from one side or corner to another, in a slanting line

crosswind /króss wind/ *n.* a wind that blows across a particular route, flight path, or direction of travel

crosswise /krósswīz/ *adv.* **1. SIDEWAYS ACROSS STH** in such a way as to cross sth or be positioned across it **2. IN A CROSS SHAPE** in the shape of a cross ■ *adj.* **TRANSVERSE** crossing or lying across sth else

crossword /króss wurd/, **crossword puzzle** *n.* a puzzle in which numbered clues are solved and words that form the answers entered horizontally or vertically into a correspondingly numbered grid of squares. Crossword puzzles are often printed in newspapers and magazines, usually with black squares in the grid amongst the blank squares.

crotch /kroch/ *n.* **1. PLACE WHERE LEGS JOIN BODY** the part of the human body where the legs join the trunk **2. PART OF GARMENT COVERING GENITALS** the area of a pair of trousers or underpants that covers sb's genitals **3. PLACE WHERE TREE DIVIDES** a part of a tree where it forks into two branches **4. FORKED STICK** a pole or stick with a forked end, or the fork itself. ◊ **crutch** [Mid-16thC. Probably a variant of CRUTCH, but influenced by Old North French *croche* 'crook', ultimately of Germanic origin. (See CROZIER).] —**crotched** *adj.*

crotchet /króchit/ *n.* **1. SHORT MUSICAL NOTE WITH STEM** a musical note lasting a quarter of the time-length of a semibreve, shown as a black note-head with a stem. A crotchet lasts half as long as a minim and twice as long as a quaver. US term **quarter note 2. WHIM** a whim, or a perverse idea or opinion (*dated*) [14thC. From Old French *crochet*, literally 'small hook' (see CROCHET).]

crotchety /króchəti/ *adj.* irritable and difficult to please (*informal*) —**crotchetiness** *n.*

croton /krṓt'n/ (*plural* **-ton** *or* **-tons**) *n.* **1. TROPICAL PLANT** a tropical plant belonging to the spurge family. Most are shrubs or trees, and some are noted for their medicinal properties . Genus: *Croton.* **2. TROPICAL EVERGREEN PLANT** a tropical evergreen plant, grown for its leathery, variegated foliage. Latin name: *Codiaeum variegatum.* [Mid-18thC. Via modern Latin, genus name, from Greek *krotōn* 'sheep-tick', because of the shape of the plant's seeds.]

crotonic acid /krō tónnik-/ *n.* a colourless, crystalline, organic acid used in organic synthesis and the manufacture of drugs and resins. Formula: $C_4H_6O_2$. [Formed from CROTON]

croton oil *n.* a yellowish brown oil used in the past as a purgative and counterirritant, extracted from the seeds of a croton plant

crouch /krowch/ *v.* (**crouches, crouching, crouched**) **1.** *vi.* **BEND DOWN LOW** to squat down on the balls of the feet with knees bent and body hunched over ○ *I had to crouch to get under the table.* **2.** *vi.* **BEND IN PREPARATION TO POUNCE** to stay down close to the ground with legs bent, waiting to spring or run forwards (*refers to animals*) ○ *The mountain lion crouched in readiness to pounce.* **3.** *vti.* **CRINGE** to bow the head or bend the body down in a humble or frightened way (*dated*) ■ *n.* **SQUATTING POSITION** the position of a human squatting with back and knees bent, or the position of an animal with the body pressed low to the ground in readiness to spring [14thC. Origin uncertain: probably from a variant of Old French *crochir* 'to be crooked', from *croche* 'hook' (see CROCHET).]

croup[1] /kroop/ *n.* an inflammatory condition of the larynx and trachea, especially in young children, marked by a cough, hoarseness, and difficult breathing [Mid-18thC. From *croup* 'to croak', probably an imitation of the sound.] —**croupous** *adj.* —**croupy** *adj.*

croup[2] /kroop/, **croupe** *n.* the hindquarters of a four-legged animal, especially a horse. ◊ **crupper** [13thC. From Old French *croupe* (source also of English *crupper*).]

croupier /kroōpi ər/ *n.* sb in charge of a gaming table who collects and pays out the players' money and chips, and deals the cards or spins the roulette wheel [Mid-18thC. From French, literally 'person who rides behind'. The modern English meaning developed from 'adviser standing behind a gambler'.]

croustade /kroo stáad/ *n.* an edible casing, usually of fried bread or pastry, for holding a savoury filling e.g. fish, poultry, meat, or vegetables [Mid-19thC. Via French from, ultimately, Latin *crusta* (see CRUST).]

crouton /kroō ton/ *n.* a small piece, usually a cube, of fried bread used as a garnish for soups, salads, and other dishes (*usually used in the plural*) [Early 19thC. From French, literally 'little crust', from *croûte* (see CRUST).]

crow /krō/ *n.* **1.** **LARGE BLACK BIRD** a large bird with shiny black feathers and a raucous cry, belonging to a family whose members are found in most parts of the world. Rooks and ravens are crows. Genus: *Corvus.* **2.** = **crowbar** *n.* **3.** **OFFENSIVE TERM** an offensive term for a woman that deliberately insults the pitch of her voice (*slang offensive*) **4.** **COCK'S LOUD CRY** a long shrill call made by a bird, especially a cock ■ *vi.* (**crows, crowing, crowed** *or* **crew** /kroo/, **crowed**) **1.** **CRY LIKE COCK** to give the loud shrill cry of a cock **2.** **CRY OUT HAPPILY** to cry out with pleasure in the way that babies do **3.** **BRAG ABOUT STH** to boast about personal success or celebrate about sth another person has failed to do in a noisy and exuberant way [The noun is from Old English *crāwe*; the verb from Old English *crāwan*. Ultimately from a prehistoric Germanic word that was also the ancestor of English *crack* and *croon*.] ◇ **eat crow** *US* to be forced to admit that you have been wrong or have been humiliatingly defeated (*informal*) ◇ **as the crow flies** in a straight line

Crow /krō/ (*plural* **Crow** *or* **Crows**) *n.* **1.** **MEMBER OF NATIVE AMERICAN PEOPLE** a member of a Native North American people who used to live on the plains of North Dakota but who now inhabit areas of southern Montana and Wyoming **2.** **CROW LANGUAGE** the Siouan language of the Crow people. Crow is spoken by about five thousand people. [Early 19thC. Translation of French *(gens de) corbeaux*, literally 'raven people', which in turn was a translation of the Native American name.] —**Crow** *adj.*

crowbar /krō baar/ *n.* **STRONG METAL LEVER** an iron or steel bar with one flattened, often bent or forked end that is used to lever things up or off ■ *vt.* (**-bars, -barring, -barred**) **USE CROWBAR ON STH** to prise or force sth using a crowbar (*informal*) [Mid-18thC. So called because the flattened end resembles a crow's foot.]

crowberry /krōbəri/ (*plural* **-ries**) *n.* **1.** **EVERGREEN SHRUB** a low-growing evergreen shrub found in colder regions that has tiny pink or purple flowers and small black berries. Latin name: *Empetrum nigrum.* **2.** **BERRY OF CROWBERRY SHRUB** the flavourless edible berry of the crowberry shrub [Late 16thC. Probably a translation of German *Krähenbeere*.]

crowd[1] /krowd/ *n.* **1.** **PEOPLE GATHERED TOGETHER** a large group of people gathered in one place **2.** **SET OF PEOPLE** a group of people with sth in common **3.** **AUDIENCE OR SPECTATORS** a group of people attending the same public event or entertainment **4.** **THE MASSES** the mass or majority of people **5.** **LARGE GROUP OF THINGS** a large number of things put or found together ■ *v.* (**crowds, crowding, crowded**) **1.** *vi.* **THRONG TOGETHER** to assemble or move in large numbers **2.** *vt.* **FILL OR PACK STH** to fill or cover sth or a place in large numbers or to capacity **3.** *vti.* **PRESS NEAR SB** to stand or move uncomfortably close to sb **4.** *vti.* **HERD OR CRAM** to urge, herd, or force a closely packed group of people, animals, or things into a place **5.** *vti.* **ADVANCE BY SHOVING** to move forward by pushing and shoving, or shove past sb **6.** *vt.* **PRESSURIZE SB** to put pressure on sb to do sth, or make sb feel forced into sth [Old English *crūdan* 'to press'. The underlying sense is 'pressing against sth or into a space'.] —**crowded** *adj.* —**crowdedness** *n.* —**crowder** *n.*

crowd out *vt.* to exclude or push out sb or sth by force of numbers

crowd[2] /krowd/ *n.* MUSIC an ancient Celtic stringed instrument that was bowed or plucked [14thC. From Welsh *crwth*.]

crowd pleaser *n.* a person, object, event, or occasion that has great popular appeal —**crowd-pleasing** *adj.*

crowd puller *n.* a person, object or event that is popular enough to draw a large audience or body of spectators

Crowe /krō/, **Russell** (*b.* 1964) Australian actor. He came to prominence in *Romper Stomper* (1992) and subsequently appeared in US films such as *L.A. Confidential* (1997).

crowfoot /krō fŏŏt/ *n.* **1.** PLANTS **PLANT WITH LEAVES LIKE CROW'S FOOT** a plant related to the buttercup that has small yellow or white flowers and divided leaves resembling the feet of a crow. Some species grow in water. Genus: *Ranunculus.* **2.** PLANTS **PLANT RESEMBLING CROWFOOT** any of various plants that have leaves resembling a bird's foot **3.** (*plural* **-feet**) NAUT **ROPES SUPPORTING AWNING** a set of ropes to support an awning

crown /krown/ *n.* **1.** ACCESSORIES **HEADDRESS SYMBOLIZING ROYALTY** an ornate headdress worn as a symbol of sovereignty, often made of gold and set with gems **2.** **SYMBOL OF ACHIEVEMENT** a wreath or circlet worn on the head as a symbol of victory, success, or high achievement **3.** POL **MONARCH** the reigning monarch of a country **4.** **Crown, crown** POL **MONARCH'S POWER** the power or authority vested in a monarch **5.** **EMBLEM RESEMBLING CROWN** an emblem or ornament resembling or representing a crown **6.** **TOP-RANKING TITLE** a title or distinction that signifies victory or supreme achievement **7.** **PINNACLE** the highest point of quality, achievement, or fame **8.** **UPPERMOST PART** the top part of sth, especially a hill **9.** ANAT **TOP OF HEAD** the top part of the head **10.** ACCESSORIES **TOP OF HAT** the top part of a hat **11.** DENT **VISIBLE PART OF TOOTH** the visible part of a tooth, covered by enamel **12.** DENT **ARTIFICIAL TOOTH** an artificial replacement for the visible part of a tooth that has decayed or been damaged **13.** TRANSP **CENTRE OF ROAD** the middle of a road, especially a cambered one **14.** HIST, MONEY **BRITISH COIN** a former British coin worth five shillings, equivalent to 25 pence, now issued only to commemorate special events **15.** MONEY **EUROPEAN COIN** any of several European coins, such as the Norwegian and Danish krone or the Swedish krona, whose name is translated as 'crown' **16.** BOT **UPPER PART OF PLANT** the upper part of a tree or shrub, consisting of the foliage and branches **17.** BOT **ROOTS AND LOWER STEM OF PLANT** the roots and lower stem of a plant, or a plant consisting only of these parts, used especially for propagation **18.** BOT = **corona 19.** BIRDS **BIRD'S CREST** the crest of a bird **20.** **TOP OF GEMSTONE** the upper part of a cut gemstone **21.** NAUT **JUNCTION OF ANCHOR ARMS AND SHANK** the junction where the arms of an anchor join the shank **22.** ACCESSORIES **WINDING KNOB ON WATCH** a ridged winding knob on a watch **23.** PAPER **SIZE OF PAPER** a size of paper equal to 38 by 51 cm/15 by 20 in ■ *vt.* (**crowns, crowning, crowned**) **1.** POL **CONFER ROYAL STATUS** to make sb royal or place a crown on sb's head to symbolize this **2.** **REWARD SB WITH CROWN** to place a crown on sb's head, especially in recognition of a victory, success, or achievement **3.** **RANK HIGHEST** to confer the top rank on sb **4.** **BE SUMMIT OF STH** to be or form the top of sth **5.** **PUT FINISHING TOUCH TO STH** to complete or be the consummation or confirmation of sth **6.** DENT **FIT CROWN TO TOOTH** to fit an artificial crown to a damaged or decayed tooth **7.** **TOP STH WITH STH ELSE** to put sth on or at the top of sth else **8.** **HIT SB ON HEAD** to hit sb over the head (*informal*) **9.** BOARD GAMES **MAKE INTO KING IN DRAUGHTS** to promote an ordinary draughts piece to the status of king [12thC. Via Anglo-Norman *corune* or Old French *corone* from Latin *corona* 'wreath, garland' (source of English *corona*), from Greek *korōnē* 'sth curved' from *koronis* 'curved'.]

crown agent *n.* a solicitor in Scotland engaged to prepare prosecution cases

Crown Agent *n.* sb appointed by the Minister for Overseas Development to sit on a board that provides financial, commercial, and other services to some foreign governments and international organizations

Crown attorney *n.* a lawyer who undertakes criminal prosecutions in Canada on behalf of a federal, provincial, or territorial government

crown cap *n.* a metal cap with a corrugated edge, used to seal bottles of beer and other drinks

crown colony *n.* a British colony in which the Crown has a whole or partial governing power

crown court *n.* a court presided over by circuit judges that hears criminal cases in England and Wales

Crown Derby *n.* a soft-paste porcelain manufactured in the city of Derby from 1784–1848 and usually marked with the letter 'D' surmounted by a crown

crowned head *n.* a reigning monarch

crown gall *n.* a disease of fruit and roses that results in swellings on the roots or stems and is caused by a bacterium *Agrobacterium tumefaciens*

crown glass *n.* **1.** **OLD WINDOW GLASS** a traditional window glass made by spinning a bubble of molten glass on the end of a rod until it forms a flat disc **2.** **GLASS FOR LENSES** high-quality glass with a low refractive index used for making lenses

crown green *n.* a bowling green that is higher in the middle than it is at the edges

crown imperial (*plural* **crown imperials** *or* **crown imperial**) *n.* a garden plant that has a cluster of bell-shaped orange or yellow flowers at the top of a single tall stem. The bulbs have a strong musky smell. Latin name: *Fritillaria imperialis.*

crowning /krówning/ *n.* **1.** POL **INVESTITURE OF MONARCH** the process or ceremony of making sb a monarch **2.** MED **STAGE IN LABOUR** the stage in giving birth at which an infant's head passes through the vaginal opening ■ *adj.* **1.** **ULTIMATE IN ACHIEVEMENT** representing supreme achievement or the ultimate moment in sth **2.** **FORMING SUMMIT** forming a crown or summit

crown jewels *npl.* **1.** **ROYAL JEWELLERY AND REGALIA** the jewellery and regalia that a monarch wears on state occasions **2.** the male genitalia, especially the testicles (*humorous slang*)

crown lens *n.* a lens made of crown glass, especially the converging component of an achromatic lens

Crown Office *n.* an office of the Queen's Bench Division of the High Court in England, responsible for administration

crown of thorns *n.* **1.** ZOOL **SPINY STARFISH** a spiny Pacific starfish that feeds on live coral. Latin name: *Acanthaster planci.* **2.** PLANTS **SHRUB WITH SCARLET BRACTS** a Madagascan shrub, grown as a house plant or as a hedge in tropical areas, whose flowers have scarlet bracts. Latin name: *Euphorbia milii.* **3.** **HEAVY BURDEN** a painful or onerous burden [From the biblical accounts of the wreath of thorns placed on the head of Jesus Christ]

crownpiece /krówn peess/ *n.* **1.** **TOP-FITTING PART OF STH** the part that fits over or forms the top of sth **2.** RIDING **BRIDLE STRAP** a bridle strap that fits over a horse's head behind the ears

crown prince *n.* the principal male heir in a monarchy

crown princess *n.* the principal female heir in a monarchy, or the wife of the male heir

Crown Prosecution Service *n.* an independent body set up in 1986 to determine whether cases prepared by the police in England and Wales should be brought to trial

Crown prosecutor *n.* = **Crown attorney**

crown roast *n.* a meat joint consisting of two rib sections sewn together to form a circle

crown saw *n.* a cylindrical saw with a row of teeth along one edge, designed for cutting round holes

crown vetch *n.* a European leguminous plant with small pink or white flowers. Latin name: *Coronilla varia.*

crown wheel *n.* a wheel in a clock or watch next to the winding knob, formed from two sets of teeth at right angles to each other

crow's feet *npl.* a network of wrinkles radiating from the outer corner of the human eye [Because they resemble the footprints of crows]

crow's foot (*plural* **crow's feet**) *n.* **1.** SEW **THREE-POINT STITCH** a sewing stitch with three points, used especially for finishing off a seam **2.** AIR **SET OF ROPES** a set of short ropes, used in airships and ballooning, that redistributes the pull of a single rope **3.** MIL = **caltrop** [From the shape]

crow's-nest *n.* **1.** NAUT **SHIP'S LOOKOUT POINT** a lookout point consisting of a railed platform at the top of a ship's mast or superstructure **2.** ARCHIT **LOOKOUT POINT ON LAND** a high enclosed lookout point on land

crow step *n.* = **corbie-step** [Because only a small or perching animal could use it]

Croydon /króyd'n/ a borough in South London, England. At one time it had London's main airport. Population: 330,900 (1995).

croze /krōz/ *n.* **1. GROOVE ON BARREL** a groove at the top of a barrel or cask into which the head is fitted **2. TOOL TO CUT CROZE** a cooper's tool used to cut grooves at the top of barrels and casks [Early 17thC. From French *creux* 'hollow, groove', probably ultimately of Celtic origin.]

crozier *n.* = **crosier**

CRP *abbr.* Central Reserve Police (in India)

CRT[1] *abbr.* cathode-ray tube

CRT[2] (*plural* **CRTs**) *n.* a computer monitor containing a cathode-ray tube

cru /kroo/ *n.* **1. FRENCH VINEYARD** a vineyard or wine-growing area in France that meets specified standards of quality. The French government sometimes classifies a cru either as a 'grand cru' or a 'premier cru'. **2. OFFICIAL CLASS OF FRENCH WINE** an official grade of French wine such as grand or premier cru [Early 19thC. Formed from French *crû*, past participle of *croître* 'to grow', from, ultimately, Latin *crescere* (source of English *accretion* and *crescent*).]

crucial /kroósh'l/ *adj.* **1. VITAL TO SOLUTION** vital to the outcome of sth **2. IMPORTANT** very important or significant (*informal*) **3.** great or excellent (*slang*) **4.** shaped like a cross (*archaic*) [Early 18thC. Via French, from Latin *cruc-*, the stem of *crux* 'cross' (source of English *crux*).]

WORD KEY: USAGE

Meaning trap: ***Crucial*** has been trivialized to the point that it often means nothing more than 'important'. This is especially true in media reports in which a hard-hitting word is often more attractive to the reporter: *If proportional representation is adopted, it is crucial to choose the best method.* ***Crucial*** would better be reserved for sth decisive: *Her tie-breaking vote was crucial* and *Her vote was nearly crucial* are correct; *Her tie-breaking vote was very crucial* and *Her vote was somewhat crucial* are not, because the meanings of ***crucial*** are 'of the greatest significance' and 'most vital', thus admitting no comparatives or superlatives.

crucially /kroósh'li/ *adv.* in a way that determines the outcome of sth or has great impact and importance

crucian /kroósh'n/ (*plural* **-cians** *or* **-cian**), **crucian carp** *n.* a carp that lives in Europe and Asia and has a dark-green back, golden-yellow sides, and reddish fins. Latin name: *Carassius carassius.* [Mid-18thC. Via an alteration of Low German *karu(s)se*, *karutze* from, ultimately, Latin *coracinus*, denoting a black fish of the River Nile, from Greek *korax* 'raven'.]

cruciate /kroóshi ət, kroóshi ayt/ *adj.* **1.** = **cruciform 2.** INSECTS **FORMING CROSS SHAPE** used to describe insect wings that form a cross shape when at rest [Late 17thC. From medieval Latin *cruciata*, from Latin *crux* 'cross'.]

crucible /kroóssib'l/ *n.* **1.** METALL **CONTAINER FOR MELTING STH** a heat-resistant container in which ores or metals are melted **2.** METALL **BOTTOM OF FURNACE** the hollow part at the bottom of a furnace where molten metal collects **3. ORDEAL** a severe trial or ordeal **4. TESTING CIRCUMSTANCES** a place or set of circumstances where people or things are subjected to forces that test them and often make them change [15thC. From medieval Latin *crucibulum* 'nightlight, crucible' of uncertain origin: perhaps from Latin *crux* 'cross' or from Old French *croisel* 'cresset'.]

WORD KEY: CULTURAL NOTE

The Crucible, a play by US dramatist Arthur Miller (1953). Intended as a metaphor for the 'un-American' McCarthy hearings of the 1950s, is set in Salem, Massachusetts, in 1692 and describes how the social fabric of a small town is ripped apart when a group of young girls starts to denounce townsfolk to witch-hunters. It was made into a film by Nicholas Hytner in 1996.

crucible steel *n.* a high-grade steel made by mixing steel and additives in a furnace

crucifer /kroóssifər/ *n.* **1.** PLANTS **PLANT WITH FOUR-PETALLED FLOWERS** a plant that has flowers with four petals in the shape of a cross and long narrow seed pods. Crucifers include cabbages, turnips, broccoli, and wallflowers. Family: Cruciferae. **2.** CHR **SB CARRYING CROSS** sb who carries a cross, especially in a religious ceremony [Mid-16thC. From ecclesiastical Latin, from Latin *cruc-* (the stem of *crux* 'cross') + *-fer* 'bearer'.]

cruciferous /kroo síffərəss/ *adj.* used to describe a plant that is a crucifer [Mid-17thC. Formed from Christian Latin *crucifer.*]

crucifix /-ifiks/ *n.* a model or image of Jesus Christ on the Cross [12thC. Via French from Ecclesiastical Latin *crucifixus*, from Latin *cruci fixus* 'fixed to a cross'.]

crucifixion /kroóssi fíksh'n/ *n.* **1. EXECUTION BY HANGING ON CROSS** a form of execution used in ancient times that involved binding or nailing sb to an upright cross until death **2. EXECUTION** an execution involving crucifixion **3. ORDEAL** a painful ordeal or victimization [15thC. From the ecclesiastical Latin stem *crucifixion-*, which was formed from *crucifigere* (see CRUCIFY).]

Crucifixion *n.* **1. AGONY AND DEATH OF JESUS CHRIST** the agony and death of Jesus Christ on the Cross at Calvary **2. DEPICTION OF THE CRUCIFIXION** a depiction of Jesus Christ on the Cross

cruciform /kroóssi fawrm/ *adj.* shaped like a cross [Mid-17thC. Coined from Latin *cruc-*, the stem of *crux* 'cross' + -FORM.] —**cruciformly** *adv.*

crucify /kroóssi fī/ (**-fies, -fying, -fied**) *v.* **1.** *vt.* **EXECUTE BY CRUCIFIXION** to execute sb by crucifixion **2.** *vt.* **TREAT SB CRUELLY** to defeat, torment, or victimize sb in a thorough or cruel way **3.** *vr.* **SEVERELY DISCIPLINE YOUR BODY** to severely punish your body as a form of self-discipline [14thC. Via French *crucifier* from, ultimately, Ecclesiastical Latin *crucifigere*, from Latin *cruci figere* 'to fix to a cross'.] —**crucifier** *n.*

cruck /kruk/ *n.* one of a pair of curved wooden timbers that supported the roof of some medieval English buildings [Late 16thC. Probably a variant of CROOK.]

crud /krud/ *n.* **1. FILTH** a messy, dirty, or sticky substance (*slang*) **2.** MANUF **WASTE PRODUCT** an unwanted by-product, especially in the nuclear industry **3. SB OR STH CONTEMPTIBLE** sb or sth that is disgusting or worthless (*informal*) **4.** SKIING **SLUSHY SNOW** slushy snow that is unfit for good skiing (*informal*) **5. NONSENSE** absolute nonsense (*informal*) [14thC. An earlier form of CURD, surviving in this sense in dialect; current senses date from the 20thC.] —**cruddy** *adj.*

crude /krood/ *adj.* (**cruder, crudest**) **1. IN RAW STATE** in an unprocessed state or condition ○ *crude ore* **2. APPROXIMATE** not precisely accurate ○ *a crude estimate* **3. UNSKILFUL** roughly or unskilfully made or conceived ○ *a crude model of a ship* **4. UNCORRECTED OR UNEMBELLISHED** used to describe numerical results or collected data that have not been organized, analysed, adjusted, or altered in any way ○ *crude data* ○ *crude facts* **5. VULGAR** vulgar or obscene ○ *a crude gesture* ■ *n.* = **crude oil** [14thC. From Latin *crudus* 'raw, rough, cruel'.] —**crudely** *adv.* —**crudeness** *n.* —**crudity** *n.*

crude oil *n.* petroleum that has not yet been refined

crudités /kroódi tay/ *npl.* small pieces of raw vegetables such as carrots and cucumber eaten as an appetizer or snack, often served with a dip [Mid-20thC. From French, plural of *crudité* from Latin *cruditas*, from *crudus* 'raw, rough, cruel'.]

cruel /kroó əl/ (**-eller, -ellest**) *adj.* **1. MERCILESS** deliberately and remorselessly causing pain or anguish, or insensitive to the pain and anguish of others **2. BRINGING ABOUT PAIN** bringing about pain and distress, or painful to bear [12thC. Via French from Latin *crudelis*. Ultimately, from an Indo-European word that also produced English *raw* and Latin *crudus* (source of English *crude*).] —**cruelly** *adv.* —**cruelness** *n.*

cruelty /kroó əlti/ (*plural* **-ties**) *n.* **1. DELIBERATELY CRUEL ACT** an act that deliberately causes pain and distress **2. STATE OF BEING CRUEL** the quality or condition of being cruel **3.** LAW **PSYCHOLOGICAL OR PHYSICAL PAIN** the infliction of pain, distress, or anguish, especially when it is long-term and considered extreme enough to be grounds for divorce [13thC. Via Old French *crualté* from, ultimately, Latin *crudelitas*, from *crudelis* (see CRUEL).]

cruelty-free *adj.* used to describe manufactured goods, especially cosmetics, that have been developed without being tested on animals

cruet /kroó it/ *n.* **1.** HOUSEHOLD **CONDIMENT CONTAINER** a small container for holding salt, pepper, oil, or vinegar **2.** HOUSEHOLD **CONDIMENT SET** a set of matching cruets on a stand **3.** CHR **SMALL BOTTLE USED IN EUCHARIST** either of two containers that hold the water and wine used in the Eucharist [13thC. From Anglo-Norman, literally 'little flask', formed from Old French *crue* 'flask'. Ultimately from a prehistoric Germanic word that is also the ancestor of English *crock* 'earthenware pot'.]

Cruikshank /kroŏk shangk/, **George** (1792–1878) British caricaturist and illustrator. He was famous for his satirical etchings and wood engravings. He also illustrated works by Charles Dickens and William Thackeray, among others.

cruise /krooz/ *v.* (**cruises, cruising, cruised**) **1.** *vti.* LEISURE, NAUT **TRAVEL BY SEA** to travel by ship over a sea or other large body of water on a pleasure trip, usually calling at several places **2.** *vi.* **TRAVEL AT EASY RATE** to travel at a steady efficient rate, below top speed **3.** *vti.* **SEEK SEXUAL PARTNER** to go out looking for a sexual partner, or frequent a public place in search of a sexual partner (*slang*) **4.** *vi.* **PROCEED CASUALLY** to proceed in a leisurely casual way or with no particular destination **5.** *vi.* NAVY **PATROL SEA** to patrol an area of sea on the lookout for enemy vessels ■ *n.* LEISURE, NAUT **PLEASURE TRIP BY SEA** a journey by ship for pleasure [Mid-17thC. From Dutch *kruisen* 'to cross', from *kruis* 'cross' from, ultimately, Latin *crux* (source of English 'cross').]

Cruise /krooz/, **Tom** (*b.* 1962) US actor and star of many Hollywood films, including *Jerry Maguire* (1996). Real name **Thomas Cruise Mapother IV**

cruise control *n.* an electronic device in a motor vehicle that allows a selected speed to be maintained consistently

cruise missile *n.* a long-range jet-propelled guided missile that flies low

cruiser /kroózər/ *n.* **1.** NAVY **SMALL WARSHIP** a fast and easily manoeuvrable warship that is smaller and less heavily armoured than a battleship **2.** NAUT = **cabin cruiser 3. STH OR SB THAT CRUISES** a vehicle that cruises, e.g. a ship, aircraft, or motor vehicle, or a person that cruises (*slang*) **4. SB SEEKING SEXUAL PARTNER** sb who goes out looking for a sexual partner in a public place (*slang*) **5.** BOXING = **cruiserweight** ■ BOXING = **cruiserweight** [Late 17thC. From Dutch *kruiser*, from *kruisen* (see CRUISE).]

cruiserweight /kroózər wayt/ *n.* a light heavyweight boxer with a maximum weight of 86 kg/190 lb

cruising radius *n.* the maximum distance that a vessel or aircraft can travel without needing to refuel

cruller /krúllər/, **kruller** *n.* *US* a small ring-shaped deep-fried cake [Early 19thC. From Dutch *kruller*, from *krullen* 'to curl'.]

crumb /krum/ *n.* **1.** SMALL FRAGMENT OF BAKED FOOD a very small fragment of bread, cake, biscuit, or similar food **2.** SMALL AMOUNT any tiny amount of sth **3.** COOK INNER PART OF LOAF the soft middle part of a loaf of bread **4.** CONTEMPTIBLE PERSON sb who is unworthy of respect (*dated slang*) ■ *v.* **(crumbs, crumbing, crumbed) 1.** *vt.* COOK PUT CRUMBS ON OR IN FOOD to coat or thicken food with crumbs, especially breadcrumbs **2.** *vti.* COOK CRUMBLE to break bread, cake, or biscuits into small bits **3.** *vt.* CLEAN CRUMBS FROM STH to clear away crumbs from sth [Old English *cruma*, of prehistoric Germanic origin. The final 'b' was added in the 16thC.]

crumble /krúmb'l/ *v.* **(-bles, -bling, -bled) 1.** *vti.* REDUCE TO TINY BITS to break or make sth break into tiny bits **2.** *vi.* DISINTEGRATE to disintegrate or fall apart ■ *n.* PUDDING WITH CRUMB TOPPING a baked pudding made from fruit topped with a mixture of flour, fat, and sugar baked until the top is crunchy. US term **crisp** [15thC. Probably ultimately from Old English *gecrymmian* 'to break into crumbs', which was formed from *cruma* (see CRUMB).]

crumbly /krúmbli/ *adj.* **(crumblier, crumbliest) 1.** EASILY CRUMBLED tending to crumble readily **2.** WITH MANY CRUMBS containing or covered with many crumbs ■ *n.* (*plural* **crumblies**) OLDER PERSON a mildly insulting term for an older person (*informal*) —**crumbliness** *n.*

crumbs /krumz/ *interj.* used to express dismay or shock (*dated informal*) [Late 19thC. Alteration, to avoid giving offence, of CHRIST.]

crumby /krúmmi/ **(-ier, -iest)** *adj.* **1.** FULL OF CRUMBS full of or covered with crumbs **2.** SOFT-TEXTURED soft and spongy in texture, like the inside of a loaf of bread **3.** = **crummy**

crumhorn /krúm hawrn/, **krummhorn** *n.* a double-reed medieval woodwind instrument with an upward curving tube [Late 17thC. From German, literally 'crooked horn'.]

crummy /krúmmi/ **(-mier, -miest)**, **crumby (-ier, -iest)** *adj.* (*informal*) **1.** OF LITTLE VALUE inferior and of little worth **2.** MISERABLE miserable or unwell [Mid-19thC. Variant of CRUMBY.]

crump /krump/ *n.* SOUND OF BURSTING BOMB the thudding sound of an exploding shell or bomb ■ *vi.* **(crumps, crumping, crumped) 1.** MAKE THUDDING NOISE to make a thudding noise like the sound of an exploding shell or bomb **2.** MAKE CRUNCHING NOISE to make a crunching noise like the sound of footsteps in crisp snow [Mid-17thC. An imitation of the sound.]

Crump /krump/, **Barry John** (*b.* 1935) New Zealand writer and author of the comic novel *A Good Keen Man* (1960).

crumpet /krúmpit/ *n.* **1.** CAKE COOKED ON GRIDDLE a griddle cake with a slightly elastic texture and small holes that is made from a batter risen with yeast. Crumpets are usually eaten toasted with butter. **2.** *Scotland* THIN PANCAKE a large thin pancake **3.** OFFENSIVE TERM an offensive term for a woman, or women collectively, regarded as sexually desirable or available (*informal offensive*) [Late 17thC. Origin uncertain: perhaps from the earlier phrase *crompid cake*, literally 'curled-up cake'; *crompid* 'crooked'.]

crumple /krúmp'l/ *v.* **(-ples, -pling, -pled) 1.** *vti.* CREASE AND WRINKLE to become or make sth become full of irregular creases and wrinkles **2.** *vti.* COLLAPSE to collapse, or make sth collapse **3.** *vi.* LOOK UPSET OR DISAPPOINTED to lose the appearance of equanimity and control, especially when upset or disappointed and close to tears ■ *n.* WRINKLE a crease or wrinkle in sth [14thC. Formed from Old English *crump* 'to curl up'.] —**crumply** *adj.*

crumple zone *n.* a part of a motor vehicle designed to absorb the impact of a collision by crumpling easily

crunch /krunch/ *v.* **(crunches, crunching, crunched) 1.** *vt.* MUNCH NOISILY to crush crisp foods audibly with the teeth **2.** *vti.* MAKE CRUSHING SOUND to make or cause sth to make a noisy crushing sound ○ *the crunch of footsteps on gravel* **3.** *vt.* COMPUT RAPIDLY PROCESS DATA to process data or numbers at high speed (*informal*) ■ *n.* **1.** CRUSHING NOISE a loud short sound made when sth is crushed **2.** DECISIVE MOMENT a critical time or situation, especially one when a decision or action must be taken ○ *when it comes to the crunch* ■ *adj.* NEEDING DECISIVE ACTION requiring a decision or action [Early 19thC. A variant of earlier *cranch* (an imitation of the sound), by association with MUNCH and CRUSH.] —**crunchable** *adj.* —**cruncher** *n.*

crunchy /krúnchi/ **(-ier, -iest)** *adj.* crisp and making a crunching sound when eaten or walked upon — **crunchily** *adv.* —**crunchiness** *n.*

crunode /kroōnōd/ *n.* = **node** [Late 19thC. Coined from Latin *crux* 'cross' + NODE.]

crupper /krúppər/ *n.* **1.** RIDING STRAP HOLDING ON SADDLE a strap that passes under the tail of a horse and is attached to a saddle or harness to prevent it from sliding forwards **2.** ZOOL HORSE'S HINDQUARTERS the hindquarters of a horse. ◊ **croup** [14thC. From Anglo-Norman *cropere* or Old French *cropiere*. Ultimately, from a prehistoric Germanic word that is also the ancestor of English *crop* and *croup* 'rump'.]

crura plural of **crus**

crural /kroōrəl/ *adj.* belonging or relating to the leg, or an elongated part resembling a leg [Late 16thC. Directly or via French from Latin *cruralis*, from *crus* 'leg'.]

crus /kruss, krooss/ (*plural* **crura** /kroōrə/) *n.* **1.** SECTION OF LEG the leg between the knee and ankle **2.** ELONGATED BODY PART a body part shaped like a leg or pair of legs [Late 16thC. From Latin, literally 'leg'.]

crusade /kroo sáyd/ *n.* **1.** **crusade, Crusade** HIST, CHR RELIGIOUS WAR any of several military expeditions made by European Christians in the 11th to 13th centuries to retake areas captured by Muslim forces **2.** RELIG RELIGIOUSLY MOTIVATED EFFORT a war or campaign that is religiously motivated, e.g. one with papal sanction **3.** CONCERTED EFFORT a vigorous concerted action to promote or eliminate sth ■ *vi.* **(-sades, -sading, -saded) 1.** CAMPAIGN to make a vigorous or concerted effort to promote or eliminate sth **2.** HIST, RELIG FIGHT TO RETAKE HOLY LAND to go on a religious crusade, especially one to retake the Holy Land in the 11th to 13th centuries [15thC. Ultimately, from Latin *crux* 'cross'. Originally via Medieval Latin *cruciata*, later via French *croisade* or Spanish *cruzada*.]

crusader /kroo sáydər/ *n.* **1.** **crusader, Crusader** SOLDIER IN CRUSADES a soldier who took part in any of the crusades **2.** CAMPAIGNER sb who campaigns vigorously for or against sth

crusado /kroo sáydō, kroo zaádō/ (*plural* **-does** *or* **-dos**) *n.* a gold or silver coin with a cross imprinted on it that was a unit of currency in Portugal between the 15th and 20th centuries [Mid-16thC. From Portuguese *cruzado* (see CRUZADO).]

cruse /krooz/ *n.* a small earthenware container used to hold liquids (*archaic*) [Old English *crūse*, of prehistoric Germanic origin]

crush /krush/ *v.* **(crushes, crushing, crushed) 1.** *vti.* COMPRESS STH to compress sb or sth, or become compressed, causing injury, damage, or distortion **2.** *vti.* CREASE STH to compress a fabric or item of clothing, or become compressed, causing creasing or crumpling **3.** *vti.* GRIND STH to grind sth, or become ground, into bits **4.** *vt.* QUELL PROTEST to put down a protest or movement using force **5.** *vt.* OVERWHELM SB OR STH to defeat, subdue, or suppress sb or sth overwhelmingly **6.** *vt.* MASH FRUIT to reduce fruit or vegetables to juice and pulp by pressing **7.** *vt.* SQUASH SB to exert physical pressure on sb by hugging, pressing, or pushing **8.** *vt.* OPPRESS SB to oppress or burden sb severely **9.** *vt.* HUMILIATE SB to humiliate sb by the force of a remark, criticism, or argument **10.** *vi.* CROWD TOGETHER to move in a mass or crowd ■ *n.* **1.** CROWD a crowd or mass, especially of people **2.** CROWDING a crowded situation or mass especially of people, or an action that results in this **3.** FOOD FRUIT DRINK a drink containing the juice from crushed fruit **4.** TEMPORARY ROMANTIC ATTRACTION a temporary romantic infatuation (*informal*) ○ *a teenage crush* **5.** OBJECT OF SB'S CRUSH the person who is the object of sb's romantic infatuation (*informal*) [14thC. From Anglo-Norman *crussier* or Old French *croissir*, of uncertain origin: perhaps from the prehistoric Germanic language.] —**crushable** *adj.* —**crusher** *n.* —**crushing** *adj.* —**crushingly** *adv.*

WORD KEY: SYNONYMS

See Synonyms at ***love***.

crush bar *n.* a bar in a theatre where drinks are served before performances and during intervals

crush barrier *n.* a barrier, especially a temporary one, put up to restrain crowds and prevent people from being crushed

crushed /krusht/ *adj.* used to describe a fabric or material that has been manufactured or treated to create permanent creases in it ○ *crushed velvet*

crushproof /krúsh proof/ *adj.* made to resist being crushed, creased, or wrinkled

crust /krust/ *n.* **1.** FOOD OUTER PART OF BREAD the thin, usually hard or crisp, outer part of a loaf or slice of bread **2.** FOOD PIECE OF BREAD a piece of bread that is mostly crust or is stale and dry **3.** FOOD PASTRY FOR PIE the pastry that wholly or partly encases a pie or tart **4.** HARD UPPER LAYER a crisp, hard, or thick outer layer or coating that develops on sth **5.** MED SCAB a dry hardened outer layer of blood, pus, or other bodily secretion that forms over a cut or sore **6.** GEOL SOLID OUTER LAYER OF EARTH the thin outermost layer of the Earth, approximately one per cent of the Earth's volume, that varies in thickness and has a different composition from the interior. Other terrestrial planets are believed to have crusts. **7.** WINE LAYER OF POTASSIUM TARTRATE a thin layer of potassium tartrate that forms on the inside of some wine and port bottles as the contents mature **8.** BIOL BODY COVERING the hard outermost body covering in some living organisms such as lichens and crustaceans **9.** INCOME a living (*informal*) ○ *just trying to earn a crust* **10.** IMPUDENCE impudent or impertinent attitude or behaviour (*dated informal*) ■ *vti.* **(crusts, crusting, crusted) 1.** FORM CRUST to form into or develop a crust **2.** MAKE OR BECOME ENCRUSTED to cover sth or become covered with a crust [14thC. Via Old French *crouste* (source of English *crouton* and *custard*) from Latin *crusta* 'rind, shell, incrustation' (source of English *crustacean* and *encrust*).]

crustacean /kru stáysh'n/ *n.* an arthropod with several pairs of jointed legs, a hard protective outer shell, two pairs of antennae, and eyes at the ends of stalks. Lobsters, crabs, shrimps, crayfish, waterfleas, barnacles, and woodlice are crustaceans. Subphylum: Crustacea. [Mid-19thC. Formed from Modern Latin *Crustacea*, neuter plural of *crustaceus* 'having a shell', from Latin *crusta* (see CRUST).] —**crustacean** *adj.* —**crustaceous** *adj.*

crustal /krúst'l/ *adj.* used to describe the crust of the Earth or another celestial body [Mid-19thC. From Latin *crusta* (see CRUST).]

crustie *n.* = **crusty**

crustose /krústōss/ *adj.* used to describe lichens or algae that resemble a crust on the surface they adhere to [Late 19thC. From Latin *crustosus*, from *crusta* (see CRUST).]

crusty /krústi/ *adj.* **(-ier, -iest) 1.** WITH CRUST with a crisp crust ○ *crusty bread* **2.** CURT gruff, curt, and candid in speech ■ *n.* **crusty, crustie** (*plural* **crusties**) UNKEMPT PERSON a dirty, unkempt person who leads an unconventional, unmaterialistic life, often in borrowed or temporary accommodation (*slang informal*) —**crustily** *adv.* —**crustiness** *n.*

crutch /kruch/ *n.* **1.** MED WALKING AID a staff with a handgrip and a rest for the forearm or armpit, used to help sb who is lame or injured to walk **2.** STH PROVIDING HELP OR SUPPORT sth that sustains or supports sb or sth liable to collapse, fail, or falter **3.** ANAT = **crotch 4.** NAUT FORKED SUPPORT a forked supporting piece for a boom, oar, or spar ■ *vt.* **(crutches, crutching, crutched)** SUPPORT WITH CRUTCH to support sth with a crutch or similar object [Old English *cryc(c)*. Ultimately, from a prehistoric Germanic word that is also the ancestor of English *crook, crochet, crotch,* and *encroach*).]

crux /kruks/ (*plural* **cruxes** *or* **cruces** /kroō seez/) *n.* **1.** CRUCIAL POINT an essential or deciding point or element in sth, e.g. in an argument **2.** PUZZLING PROBLEM an extremely difficult or puzzling problem **3.** MOUNTAINEERING ARDUOUS PART OF CLIMB the most demanding part of a climb [Mid-17thC. From Latin, literally 'cross' (source of English *cross*).]

Crux *n.* the Southern Cross (*formal*)

crux ansata /krúks an sáatə/ (*plural* **cruces ansatae** /króo seez an sáatee/) *n.* = **ankh** [From Latin, literally 'cross with a handle']

Cruyff /kroyf/, **Johan** (*b.* 1947) Dutch footballer. As captain of Holland and the Dutch team Ajax, he led them respectively to the World Cup final in 1974 and three European Cups (1971–73).

Celia Cruz

Cruz /krooz/, **Celia** (*b.* 1924) Cuban-born US vocalist. She is one of the leading singers of the popular Latin dance music called salsa.

cruzado /kroo záadō/ (*plural* **-does** *or* **-dos**) *n.* **1.** FORMER BRAZILIAN UNIT OF CURRENCY a unit of currency used in Brazil between 1986 and 1990, equivalent to 100 centavos **2.** COIN OR NOTE WORTH ONE CRUZADO a coin or note worth one cruzado **3.** = **crusado** [Mid-16thC. From Portuguese, literally 'marked with a cross', from the past participle of *cruzar* 'to mark with a cross', from, ultimately, Latin *crux* 'cross'.]

cruzeiro /kroo záirō/ (*plural* **-ros**) *n.* **1.** FORMER BRAZILIAN UNIT OF CURRENCY a unit of currency formerly used in Brazil **2.** COIN WORTH ONE CRUZEIRO a coin worth one cruzeiro [Early 20thC. From Portuguese, literally 'large cross', (from the figure on the coin), from, ultimately, Latin *crux* 'cross'.]

crwth /krooth/ *n.* MUSIC = **crowd**[2] [Mid-19thC. From Welsh, source also of *crowd* 'stringed instrument'.]

cry /krī/ *v.* (**cries**, **crying**, **cried**) **1.** *vti.* SHED TEARS to shed tears as the result of a strongly felt emotion **2.** *vti.* SHOUT to call or shout out loudly **3.** *vi.* ZOOL MAKE DISTINCTIVE SOUND to make a natural high-pitched call (*refers to a bird or animal*) **4.** *vt.* ANNOUNCE FOR SALE to proclaim sth publicly as being for sale (*archaic*) **5.** *vt.* GIVE STH AS REASON to plead or profess sth as a reason or explanation ■ *n.* (*plural* **cries**) **1.** INARTICULATE SOUND a loud inarticulate expression of rage, pain, or surprise **2.** SHOUT a loud shout or call **3.** ZOOL CALL OF BIRD OR ANIMAL the natural high-pitched call of a bird or animal **4.** PERIOD OF WEEPING an act or period of shedding tears **5.** PUBLIC DEMAND a public demand, especially an urgent one **6.** HUNT BAYING OF HOUNDS the sound of hounds baying as they chase their quarry **7.** HUNT HOUNDS a pack of hounds **8.** PROCLAMATION an announcement or advertisement called out in public (*archaic*) [13thC. Via French *crier* from Latin *quiritare* 'to raise a public outcry', literally 'to call for the help of the Roman citizens', which was formed from *Quirites* 'Roman citizens'.] ◇ **in full cry** in enthusiastic pursuit of sth

cry down *vt.* to say disparaging or belittling things about sb or sth

cry off *vi.* to withdraw from sth you had previously agreed to do (*informal*)

cry out *v.* **1.** *vti.* SHOUT LOUDLY to exclaim loudly because of pain, shock, or fear **2.** *vi.* BE IN NEED to be in obvious and urgent need ◇ **for crying out loud!** used to express annoyance, impatience, frustration, or surprise (*informal*)

cry up *vt.* to praise sb or sth highly

crybaby /krī báybi/ (*plural* **-bies**) *n.* sb, especially a child, who cries or complains a lot

crying /krī ing/ *adj.* desperate or deplorable and demanding a remedy ◇ *a crying shame*

cryo- *prefix.* freezing, cold ◇ *cryosurgery* [From Greek *kruos* 'icy cold'. Ultimately from an Indo-European base

meaning 'to freeze over', which is also the ancestor of English *crust* and *crystal*.]

cryobank /krī ō bangk/ *n.* a place where biological material such as semen and body tissues can be stored at extremely low temperatures

cryobiology /krī ō bī óllaji/ *n.* the branch of biology that studies how extremely low temperatures affect organisms —**cryobiological** /krī ō bī ə lójjik'l/ *adj.* —**cryobiologically** /-lójjikəli/ *adv.* —**cryobiologist** /-bī óllajist/ *n.*

cryogen /krī ō jen/ *n.* a substance, e.g. liquid nitrogen, used in producing extremely low temperatures

cryogenic /krī ō jénnik/ *adj.* having or relating to extremely low temperatures —**cryogenically** *adv.*

cryogenics /krī ō jénniks/ *n.* a branch of physics that studies the causes and effects of extremely low temperatures (*takes a singular verb*)

cryolite /krī ə līt/ *n.* an uncommon white mineral that consists of a fluoride of sodium and aluminium. It is used in the production of aluminium. Formula: Na_3AlF_6. [Early 19thC. Coined from CRYO- 'cold' (because it was first found in Greenland) + -LITE.]

cryometer /krī ómmitər/ *n.* a thermometer that measures very low temperatures —**cryometry** *n.*

cryonics /krī ónniks/ *n.* FREEZING OF CORPSE the study or practice of keeping a newly dead body at an extremely low temperature in the hope of restoring it to life later with the help of future medical advances (*takes a singular verb*) ■ *npl.* CRYOGENIC TECHNIQUES the collective techniques involved in cryogenics (*takes a plural verb*) [Mid-20thC. Contraction of CRYOGENICS.] —**cryonic** *adj.*

cryophilic /krī ō fíllik/ *adj.* capable of living at low temperatures

cryophyte /krī ə fīt/ *n.* an organism that can live or grow on snow or ice. Most cryophytes are algae.

cryoprecipitate /krī ō pri síppitət/ *n.* a substance that is precipitated at low temperatures, especially a precipitate of blood containing a blood-clotting factor

cryopreservation /krī ō prézzər váysh'n/ *n.* the process of storing semen, ova, corneas, embryos, or body tissue at extremely low temperatures for future use —**cryopreserve** /krī ō pri zúrv/ *vt.*

cryoprobe /krī ō prōb/ *n.* an instrument used in cryosurgery for cooling body tissue to low temperatures

cryoprotectant /krī ō prə téktənt/ *n.* a substance, e.g. glycerol, used to protect stored living tissue from the effects of freezing

cryoscope /krī ə skōp/ *n.* an instrument used for determining the temperature at which a liquid freezes

cryoscopy /krī óskəpi/ *n.* the study or practice of determining the freezing point of liquids —**cryoscopic** /krī ə skóppik/ *adj.*

cryostat /krī ə stat/ *n.* a regulating device for maintaining a constant low temperature

cryosurgery /krī ō súrjəri/ *n.* surgery in which low temperatures are applied, e.g. to destroy diseased tissue, or to seal down detached retinas —**cryosurgeon** /krī ō súrjən/ *n.* —**cryosurgical** /-súrjik'l/ *adj.*

cryotherapy /krī ō thérrəpi/ (*plural* **-pies**) *n.* medical treatment that involves cooling the body, especially by applying ice packs

crypt /kript/ *n.* **1.** ARCHIT UNDERGROUND CHAMBER an underground room or vault, often below a church, used as a burial chamber or chapel, or for storing religious artefacts **2.** ANAT SMALL BODY CAVITY a small recess, tubular gland, or follicle in the body [Late 18thC. Via Latin *crypta* from Greek *kruptē* 'vault', feminine of *kruptos* 'hidden'.]

crypt- *prefix.* = **crypto-**

cryptanalyse /krip tánnə līz/ (**-analyses**, **-analysing**, **-analysed**) *vt.* to decipher coded texts or messages

cryptanalysis /krīptə nálləssiss/ *n.* the process or science of deciphering coded texts or messages —**cryptanalyst** /kriptánnə list/ *n.* —**cryptanalytic** /krīpt anə líttik/ *adj.* —**cryptanalytical** /-líttik'l/ *adj.*

cryptanalyze *vt.* US = **cryptanalyse**

cryptic /kríptik/ *adj.* **1.** AMBIGUOUS OR OBSCURE deliberately mysterious and seeming to have a hidden meaning **2.** SECRET secret or hidden in some way **3.** LEISURE INDICATING SOLUTION INDIRECTLY with an indirect solution or clue, e.g. crosswords, puzzles, or anagrams **4.** USING CODES using or relating to codes and similar techniques **5.** ZOOL PROTECTIVE used to describe body markings and colour that camouflage an animal [Early 17thC. Via late Latin *crypticus* from Greek *kruptikos*, from *kruptē* (see CRYPT).] —**cryptically** *adv.* —**crypticness** *n.*

——————— **WORD KEY: SYNONYMS** ———————
See Synonyms at *obscure*.

crypto- *prefix.* secret, hidden ◇ *cryptogram* [From Greek *kruptos*, from *kruptein* 'to hide']

cryptoclastic /kríptə klástik/ *adj.* used to describe rock composed of microscopic mineral fragments

cryptococcosis /kríptōkə kóssiss/ *n.* an infectious disease that affects parts of the body, especially the brain and central nervous system, with lesions or abscesses caused by the fungus *Cryptococcus neoformans* [Mid-20thC. Coined from modern Latin *Cryptococcus* + -OSIS.]

cryptococcus /kríptō kókəss/ (*plural* **-cocci** /-kókī/) *n.* a budding fungus that resembles a yeast, some types of which cause illnesses, e.g. cryptococcosis. Genus: *Cryptococcus*. [Early 20thC. From modern Latin, literally 'hidden coccus'.]

cryptocrystalline /kríptō krístəlīn/ *adj.* used to describe rocks that are composed of crystals too small to be seen with a petrological microscope

cryptogam /kríptə gam/ *n.* a plant that reproduces by means of spores instead of seeds. Ferns, moss, algae, and fungi are cryptogams. (*dated*) [Late 18thC. Via French *cryptogame* from, ultimately, modern Latin *cryptogamus*, literally 'hidden marriage' (because the means of reproduction is not apparent).] —**cryptogamic** /kríptə gámmik/ *adj.* —**cryptogamous** /krip tóggəməss/ *adj.*

cryptogenic /kríptō jénnik/ *adj.* = **idiopathic**

cryptogram /kríptə gram/ *n.* **1.** CODED MESSAGE a text or message that is in code or cipher **2.** SECRET SYMBOL a symbol with a secret meaning or significance

cryptograph /kríptə graaf, -graf/ *n.* **1.** = **cryptogram 2.** ENCODING OR DECODING MACHINE a machine for writing or deciphering encoded messages

cryptographer /krip tóggrəfər/, **cryptographist** /-fist/ *n.* sb who writes, transcribes, or decodes cryptograms, or studies such methods

cryptography /krip tóggrəfi/ *n.* **1.** STUDY OF ENCODING the study or analysis of codes and coding methods **2.** SECRET WRITING coded or secret writing —**cryptographic** /kríptə gráffik/ *adj.* —**cryptographical** /-gráffik'l/ *adj.* —**cryptographically** /-gráffikli/ *adv.*

cryptology /krip tólləji/ *n.* **1.** = **cryptography** *n.* **2.** = **cryptanalysis** —**cryptologic** /kríptə lójjik/ *adj.* —**cryptological** /-lójjik'l/ *adj.* —**cryptologist** /krip tólləjist/ *n.*

cryptomeria /kríptō meéri ə/ *n.* a tall coniferous tree native to China and Japan that has curved needle-shaped leaves arranged in spirals. Latin name: *Cryptomeria japonica*. [Mid-19thC. From modern Latin, literally 'hidden part', because its seeds are hidden by scales.]

cryptorchid /krip táwrkid/ *n.* a male human or animal with one or both testicles that have failed to descend into the scrotum [Late 19thC. From CRYPTORCHISM.]

cryptorchism /krip táwrkizzəm/, **cryptorchidism** /krip táwrkidizzəm/ *n.* a developmental condition affecting humans or animals in which one or both testicles fail to descend into the scrotum [Late 19thC. Coined from CRYPTO- + Latin *orchis* 'testicle' (from Greek *orkhis*) + -ISM.]

cryptosporidiosis /kríptōspə riddi óssiss/ *n.* an infectious condition of humans and domestic animals, characterized by fever, diarrhoea, and stomach cramps. It is spread by a protozoan of the genus *Cryptosporidium*. [Formed from CRYPTOSPORIDIUM]

cryptosporidium /kríptōspə riddi əm/ (*plural* **-a** /-riddi ə/) *n.* MICROBIOL a water-borne protozoan parasite that contaminates drinking water supplies, causing intestinal infections in human beings and domestic animals [Late 20thC. From Modern Latin, genus name, from Greek *kruptos* (see CRYPTO-) + *sporidium*, literally 'little spore', from *spora* (see SPORE).]

cryptozoic /kríptō zṓ ik/ *adj.* used to describe invertebrates that live in dark or concealed places, such as under stones or in caves or holes

Cryptozoic *adj.* OCCURRING BEFORE COMPLEX ORGANISMS belonging to a geological time in which only a few very primitive organisms existed ■ *n.* GEOLOGICAL ERA the Cryptozoic era of geological time

cryptozoite /kríptō zṓ īt/ *n.* a malarial parasite at the stage in its life cycle when it is present in the host's body tissue but before it invades the red blood cells [Coined from CRYPTO-+ Greek *zōion* 'animal' + -ITE]

cryptozoology /kríptō zoo ólləji/ *n.* the study of legendary creatures like the Loch Ness monster or the Yeti —**cryptozoological** /kríptō zóo ə lójjik'l/ *adj.* —**cryptozoologist** /kríptō zoo óllǝjist/ *n.*

cryst. *abbr.* 1. crystalline 2. crystallography

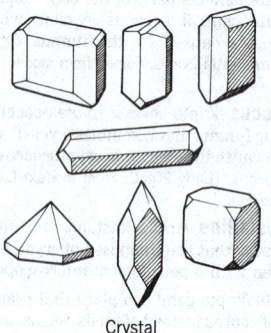

Crystal

crystal /kríst'l/ *n.* 1. MINERALS QUARTZ a clear colourless mineral, especially quartz 2. MINERALS PIECE OF CRYSTAL a piece of a mineral in crystal form 3. CHEM SOLID WITH REPETITIVE INTERNAL STRUCTURE a solid containing an internal pattern of atoms, molecules, or ions that is regular, repeated, and geometrically arranged 4. STH LIKE CRYSTAL sth that has the form of a crystal, e.g. a frozen snowflake or a grain of salt 5. CRAFT HEAVY GLASS a heavy transparent sparkling glass 6. HOUSEHOLD CRYSTAL GLASS OBJECTS things made from crystal 7. ELECTRON ENG ELECTRONIC COMPONENT a crystalline substance that has semiconducting or piezoelectric properties and is used as an electronic component, or the electrical device using it 8. = watch-glass ■ *adj.* VERY CLEAR clear and sparkling [Pre-12thC. Via French *cristal* and Latin *crystallum* from Greek *krustallos* 'ice' (the original sense in English). Ultimately, from an Indo-European word meaning 'to freeze over' which is also the ancestor of English *crust* and cryo-.]

crystal ball *n.* 1. FORTUNE TELLER'S GLOBE a clear solid sphere of glass or rock crystal that is used by a fortune teller to predict the future 2. MEANS TO PREDICT FUTURE any means used to predict future events

crystal clear *adj.* 1. VERY CLEAN clean and sparkling 2. OBVIOUS OR UNDERSTOOD clear or obvious to the understanding

crystal gazing *n.* predicting the future by any questionable means, most commonly by staring into a crystal ball in the belief that images of future events will appear —**crystal gazer** *n.*

crystal healing *n.* use of pieces of crystal that are supposed to promote health and increase well-being

crystall. *abbr.* crystallography

crystall- *prefix.* = crystallo- (used before vowels)

crystal lattice *n.* the regular array of points in space that are occupied by the atoms, ions, or molecules that make up a crystal

crystalline /krístə līn/ *adj.* 1. LIKE OR BEING CRYSTALS relating to, made of, containing, or resembling crystals 2. VERY CLEAR clear and sparkling —**crystallinity** /krístə línnəti/ *n.*

crystalline lens *n.* the transparent lens behind the iris in the eyes of vertebrates

crystallite /krístə līt/ *n.* a tiny rudimentary crystal, e.g. those found in some igneous rocks —**crystallitic** /krístə líttik/ *adj.*

crystallize /krístə līz/ (-lizes, -lizing, -lized), **crystallise** (-lises, -lising, -lised) *vti.* 1. MAKE OR BECOME WELL DEFINED to become or make an idea or feeling become fixed or definite 2. FORM CRYSTALS to form or make sth form crystals 3. COOK COAT WITH SUGAR CRYSTALS to coat or impregnate sth, or become coated or impregnated, with crystals, especially sugar crystals —**crystallizability** /krístə līzə bílləti/ *n.* —**crystallizable** /krístə līzəb'l/ *adj.* —**crystallization** /krístə līf záysh'n/ *n.* —**crystallizer** /krístə līzər/ *n.*

crystallo- *prefix.* crystal, crystalline ○ *crystallography* [From Greek *krustallos* (see CRYSTAL)]

crystallography /krístə lóggrəfi/ *n.* a branch of science dealing with the formation and properties of crystals —**crystallographer** *n.* —**crystallographic** /krístələ gráffik/ *adj.* —**crystallographically** /-gráffikli/ *adv.*

crystalloid /krístə loyd/ *adj.* LIKE CRYSTAL with the structure, properties, or appearance of a crystal ■ *n.* 1. SUBSTANCE FORMING CRYSTALS a substance that can form crystals and in solution can pass through a semipermeable membrane 2. BOT PROTEIN IN PLANT CELL a mass of protein resembling a crystal that commonly occurs in seeds and other storage organs —**crystalloidal** /krístə lóyd'l/ *adj.*

Crystal Palace *n.* a large glass building designed by Joseph Paxton for the Great Exhibition in Hyde Park, London, in 1851. It was later moved to the area of South London now called Crystal Palace, and was destroyed by fire in 1936.

crystal pleat *n.* one of a series of permanently pressed pleats of varying widths, often in a sheer fabric

crystal set *n.* an early form of radio receiver that used a quartz crystal as a detector

Cs *symbol.* caesium

CS *abbr.* 1. POL civil service 2. CIV ENG chartered surveyor 3. LAW Court of Session 4. FIN capital stock 5. CHR Christian Science 6. CHR Christian Scientist 7. chief of staff

cs. *abbr.* case

CSA *n.*, *abbr.* Child Support Agency

CSB *abbr.* chemical stimulation of the brain

csc *abbr.* cosecant

CSC *abbr.* Civil Service Commission

CSE *n.* a school-leaving certificate in England and Wales that was replaced in 1988 by the GCSE. Abbr of **Certificate of Secondary Education**

CSEU *abbr.* Confederation of Shipbuilding and Engineering Unions

CSF *abbr.* cerebrospinal fluid

CS gas *n.* a gas, used to control crowds, that causes tears, salivation, and painful breathing. Formula: $C_6H_5ClN_2$. [Abbreviation of *Corson-Stoughton*, named after the US chemists B. B. Corson (1896–) and R. W. Stoughton (1906–57), who developed it.]

CSIRO *abbr.* Commonwealth Scientific and Industrial Research Organization

CSM *abbr.* Company Sergeant-Major

CSO *abbr.* Central Statistical Office

CSS *abbr.* Certificate in Social Service

CST *abbr.* 1. Central Standard Time 2. convulsive shock treatment

CSU *abbr.* Civil Service Union

CSYS *abbr.* Scotland Certificate of Sixth Year Studies

ct *abbr.* 1. cent 2. certificate

CT *abbr.* 1. TIME Central Time 2. MED computerized tomography. ♦ CT scan 3. *US* Connecticut

Ct. *abbr.* 1. *US* Connecticut 2. Count (used in titles)

CTC *n.*, *abbr.* 1. City Technology College 2. Cyclists' Touring Club

CTD *abbr.* MED cumulative trauma disorder

ctenidium /ti níddi əm/ (*plural* -a /-di ə/) *n.* a gill found in molluscs that has a central axis with a fringe of filaments on either side. It is used in gas exchange and filter feeding. [Late 19thC. Via modern Latin from Greek *ktenidion*, literally 'little comb', from *kteis* 'comb'.]

ctenoid /teén oyd, ténnoyd/ *adj.* used to describe fish scales that have tiny projections like the teeth of combs, or fish that have such scales [Mid-19thC. Coined from Greek *kten-*, the stem of *kteis* 'comb' +-OID.]

ctenophore /ténnə fawr, teénə fawr/ *n.* a marine invertebrate resembling a jellyfish but with eight rows of undulating filaments used for swimming. Sea gooseberries and sea walnuts are ctenophores. Phylum: Ctenophora. [Late 19thC. Formed from modern Latin *ctenophorus*, from the Greek stem *kten-* (see CTENOID).] —**ctenophoran** /ti nóffərən/ *adj.*, *n.*

ctn *abbr.* 1. cotangent 2. carton

ctr. *abbr.* centre

Ctrl *abbr.* COMPUT control

CT scan *n.* a diagnostic medical scan in which cross-sectional images of the body part are formed through computerized axial tomography and shown on a computer screen. US term **CAT scan**

CT scanner *n.* the radiological diagnostic scanning equipment used to make a CT scan. US term **CAT scanner**

CTV *abbr.* Canadian Television Network Limited

Cu *symbol.* copper

cu. *abbr.* cubic

cuadrilla /kwaa dreéyə/ *n.* a group of three banderilleros and two picadors who assist a matador in the bullring [Mid-19thC. From Spanish, literally 'little square' (from a formation used), from *cuadra* 'square', from, ultimately, the Latin stem *quadr-* (source of English *quadrille*).]

cub /kub/ *n.* 1. ZOOL YOUNG OF CARNIVOROUS MAMMAL an offspring of some carnivorous mammals, e.g. a bear, lion, or tiger 2. NOVICE an inexperienced person or apprentice (*dated*) 3. YOUNG PERSON a cheeky young person (*dated*) 4. *Ireland* a boy (*regional informal*) ■ *vi.* (**cubs, cubbing, cubbed**) 1. PRODUCE YOUNG to give birth to an animal cub 2. HUNT FOX CUBS to hunt fox cubs [Mid-16thC. Origin unknown.] —**cubbish** *adj.* —**cubbishly** *adv.*

Cub /kub/ *n.* = Cub Scout ■ **Cubs** *npl.* CUB SCOUT MEETING a Cub Scout meeting

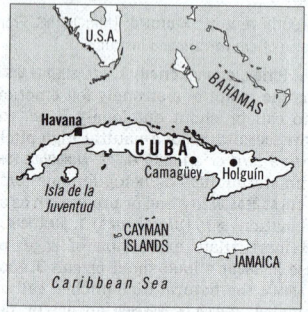

Cuba

Cuba /kyooba/ independent republic in the Caribbean Sea comprising two main islands and over 1,000 islets. Language: Spanish. Currency: peso. Capital: Havana. Population: 10,999,139 (1997). Area: 114,525 sq. km/44,218 sq. mi. Full name **Republic of Cuba**

cubage /kyoóbij/ *n.* the cubic content or volume of a solid. US = **cubature**

Cuba libre /kyooba leébrə/ *n.* a drink made by mixing rum, cola, ice, and lime juice [From American Spanish, literally 'free Cuba', used as a toast during the Cuban War of Independence, 1895–98]

Cuban /kyoóbən/ *n.* 1. SB FROM CUBA sb who was born or brought up in Cuba, or who is a citizen of Cuba 2. CIGAR a Cuban cigar ■ *adj.* RELATING TO CUBA relating to or typical of the Republic of Cuba, or its people or culture

Cuban heel *n.* a straight broad heel of medium height for a shoe

Cuban sandwich *n.* *Southern US* a long narrow sandwich of Cuban origin, filled with ham, pork, cheese, and pickles, and often grilled

cubature /kyoóbəchər/ *n.* 1. DETERMINATION OF VOLUME OF SOLID the process of working out the cubic content or volume of a solid **2.** = **cubage** [Late 17thC. Formed from CUBE, modelled on *quadrature*.]

cubbyhole /kúbbi hōl/, **cubby** (*plural* **-bies**) *n.* **1.** SMALL AREA a small space or room **2.** STORAGE COMPARTMENT a small storage compartment

cubbyhouse /kúbbi howss/ (*plural* **cubbyhouses** /-howziz/) *n. Aus* a playhouse for a child

cube[1] /kyoob/ *n.* **1.** GEOM SOLID FIGURE OF SIX EQUAL SIDES a solid figure of six equal square plane faces, each set at right angles to the four sides adjacent to it **2.** CUBE-SHAPED OBJECT any solid shaped like a cube **3.** MATH PRODUCT OF THREE EQUAL NUMBERS the product of three equal numbers or quantities multiplied together, usually written in mathematical notation as a raised 3, e.g. 4^3 means $4 \times 4 \times 4$ ■ *vt.* (**cubes, cubing, cubed**) **1.** COOK DICE to cut or shape food into cubes **2.** MATH MULTIPLY ITEM BY ITSELF TWICE to multiply a number or quantity by itself twice, e.g. 6 cubed is 6 multiplied by 6 and then multiplied by 6 again **3.** MATH WORK OUT CUBIC CONTENT to calculate the cubic content of sth [Mid-16thC. Directly or via French from Latin *cubus*, from Greek *kubos* 'cube' (and also 'pelvis' because of its shape).] —**cuber** *n.*

cube[2] /kyoō bay, koō-/, **cubé** *n.* **1.** PLANTS TROPICAL AMERICAN PLANT a tropical American leguminous woody plant that is cultivated as a source of rotenone. Genus: *Lonchocarpus*. **2.** BIOCHEM POISONOUS EXTRACT FROM CUBE ROOTS an extract containing roteneone from the roots of the cube plant, used in insecticides and as fish poison [Early 20thC. From American Spanish.]

cubeb /kyoō beb/ *n.* **1.** ASIAN CLIMBING PLANT a climbing plant of Southeast Asia that has heart-shaped leaves, spikes of small flowers, and brownish berries. Latin name: *Piper cubeba*. **2.** BERRY OF CUBEB PLANT a small unripe spicy berry of the cubeb plant, used in the past to treat respiratory and urinary disorders [13thC. Via French *cubèbe* from, ultimately, Arabic *kubāba*.]

cube root *n.* a number or quantity that, when multiplied by itself twice, equals a given number or quantity

cube van *n. Can* a small lorry with a cube-shaped storage compartment at the rear

cubic /kyoōbik/ *adj.* **cubic, cubical 1.** CUBE-SHAPED shaped like a cube **2.** WITH THREE DIMENSIONS with three measurable dimensions **3.** DESCRIBING VOLUME BY COMPARING WITH CUBE used to describe a volume or capacity that is equal to that of a specified cube **4.** MATH RELATING TO OR CONTAINING CUBED VARIABLE used to describe a mathematical expression or equation in which at least one variable is cubed but no variable is to be multiplied by itself more than two times ○ *a cubic equation* **5.** CRYSTALS WITH THREE EQUAL AXES used to describe a crystal that has three equal perpendicular axes. Symbol **c** ■ *n.* MATH MATHEMATICAL EQUATION a cubic expression, equation, or curve —**cubically** *adv.*

cubicle /kyoōbik'l/ *n.* a small partitioned area for private use in a larger, more public room, e.g. a changing room or dormitory [15thC. From Latin *cubiculum* 'bedroom' (the original sense in English), from *cubare* 'to lie down'.]

cubic measure *n.* a unit or system for measuring volume or capacity

cubic zirconia *n.* a synthetic gemstone used as a substitute for diamonds in costume jewellery. It is formed by heating zirconia together with a stabilizing metallic oxide. Formula: ZrO_2.

cubiform /kyoōbi fawrm/ *adj.* shaped like a cube

cubism /kyoōbizzəm/, **Cubism** *n.* an artistic style, chiefly in painting and sculpture, that developed in the early 20th century and emphasized the representation of natural forms as geometric shapes seen from several angles [Early 20thC. From French *cubisme*, from *cube* (see CUBE).] —**cubist** *n.* —**cubistic** /kyoo bístik/ *adj.* —**cubistically** *adv.*

cubit /kyoōbit/ *n.* an ancient unit of length, equal to the distance from the elbow to the tip of the middle finger, approximately 17–22 in or 43–56 cm [14thC. From Latin *cubitum* 'elbow, forearm, cubit'.]

cubital /kyoōbit'l/ *adj.* relating to the elbow, ulnar bone, or forearm [15thC. From Latin *cubitalis*, from *cubitum* 'elbow, forearm, cubit'.]

cuboid /kyoō boyd/ *n.* **1.** GEOM SOLID FIGURE OF SIX RECTANGULAR PLANES a solid figure of six rectangular plane faces, each set at right angles to the four sides adjacent to it **2.** ANAT BONE IN FOOT the outermost tarsal bone of the foot in vertebrates ■ *adj.* GEOM CUBE-SHAPED shaped like a cube —**cuboidal** /kyoo bóyd'l/ *adj.*

cub reporter *n.* a young inexperienced newspaper reporter

Cub Scout *n.* a member of the branch of the Scout Association for younger children, generally 8 to 11 years of age

cucking stool /kúking-/ *n.* a punishment used in medieval times in which sb was tied to a stool and pelted with rotting food [14thC. *Cucking* 'defecating' (from obsolete *cuck* 'to defecate', of Scandinavian origin), because a commode was sometimes used for this purpose.]

cuckold /kúkōld/ *n.* MAN WHOSE WIFE IS UNFAITHFUL a husband whose wife has been unfaithful to him (*archaic*) ■ *vt.* (**-olds, -olding, -olded**) MAKE CUCKOLD OF SB to make a cuckold of a husband (*archaic*) [Pre-12thC. From Old Northern French, a variant of Old French *cucuault*, from *cucu* 'cuckoo', perhaps from the analogy that other birds' nests are invaded by cuckoos.] —**cuckoldry** *n.*

Cuckoo

cuckoo /kóokoo/ *n.* (*plural* **-oos**) **1.** BIRDS BIRD LAYING IN OTHERS' NESTS a European songbird that lays its eggs in the nests of other birds who bring the nestlings up as their own. Latin name: *Cuculus canorus*. **2.** BIRDS RELATED BIRD a bird related to the European cuckoo **3.** BIRDS CUCKOO'S CALL the characteristic two-note call of the European cuckoo **4.** ECCENTRIC PERSON sb who is very eccentric, strange, or extremely unconventional (*informal*) ■ *adj.* STRANGE very eccentric, strange, or extremely unconventional (*informal*) ■ *vi.* (**-oos, -ooing, -ooed**) GIVE THE CALL OF THE CUCKOO to make the characteristic two-note call of the cuckoo [13thC. From Old French *cucu*, an imitation of its call.]

WORD KEY: CULTURAL NOTE

One Flew Over the Cuckoo's Nest, a film by US director Milos Forman (1975). Based on Ken Kesey's 1962 novel, it describes how mischievous convict Randle McMurphy inspires his fellow inmates at a psychiatric hospital to rebel against their disciplinarian nurse, Ratched. The film can be seen as a metaphor for the conflict between individuality and creativity and society's pressure to conform.

cuckoo clock *n.* a clock that indicates the hour with sounds like a cuckoo's call, usually accompanied by the appearance of a mechanical bird from behind a door

cuckooflower /kóo koo flowər/ *n.* a plant often found in moist meadows, with light purple or occasionally white flowers and yellow anthers in April to June. Latin name: *Cardamine pratensis*. [Late 16thC. Because the plant is in flower at about the time of year when the bird is first heard.]

cuckoopint /kóo koo pīnt/ *n.* a perennial European plant, with leaves shaped like arrowheads and flowering stems consisting of a yellowish-green cone around a reddish-purple spike that later carries poisonous scarlet berries. Latin name: *Arum maculatum*. [15thC. Shortening of earlier *cuckoo pintle*, literally 'cuckoo penis', from the shape of the spadix.]

cuckoo shrike (*plural* **cuckoo shrikes** *or* **cuckoo shrike**) *n.* a smallish bird of Africa, Asia, and Australasia with a long rounded tail. Cuckoo shrikes feed on insects and are often noisy. Family: Campephagidae.

cuckoo spit *n.* a white frothy secretion found on the stems and leaves of plants, produced by the larva of insects like the frog-hopper [Because it was believed to have been spat out by cuckoos]

cuckoo wasp *n.* a solitary wasp known for laying its eggs in the nests of other wasps and bees. Family: Chrysididae.

cucumber /kyoō kumbər/ *n.* **1.** PLANTS PLANT WITH LONG GREEN FRUIT a climbing or trailing annual plant of the gourd family that is grown for its edible long green fruit. Latin name: *Cucumis sativus*. ◊ **squirting cucumber 2.** FOOD FRUIT OF CUCUMBER PLANT the long fruit of the cucumber plant that has dark green peel and crisp white watery flesh and is usually eaten raw in salads and sandwiches or pickled [14thC. From Latin *cucumer-*, the stem of *cucumis*, by association with Old French *cocombre*.] ◇ **cool as a cucumber** calm and composed, especially under pressure

cucumber fish (*plural* **cucumber fish** *or* **cucumber fishes**) *n.* a small slender tropical fish that drills its tail into sea cucumbers and other marine invertebrates to make a home for itself. Family: Carapidae.

cucurbit /kyoo kúrbit/ *n.* a tropical or subtropical climbing or trailing plant of the gourd family with large, fleshy, tough- or hard-skinned fruits, many of which are edible, e.g. cucumber, watermelon, or pumpkin. Family: Cucurbitaceae. [14thC. Via French *curcurbite* from Latin *cucurbita* 'gourd'.]

cud /kud/ *n.* ZOOL partly digested food that cows and other ruminants return to the mouth, after it has passed into the first stomach, to chew again as an aid to digestion [Old English *cudu*. Ultimately from an Indo-European word that probably also produced the first syllable of English *bitumen* (the underlying idea being 'sticky substance').]

cudbear /kúd bair/ *n.* a violet dye extracted from some lichens [Mid-18thC. Alteration of *Cuthbert*, named after an 18th-century Scottish chemist *Cuthbert* Gordon, who patented it.]

cuddle /kúdd'l/ *v.* (**-dles, -dling, -dled**) **1.** *vti.* TENDERLY HUG OR NESTLE to nestle together or hold sb or sth close for affection, warmth, or comfort **2.** *vi.* ASSUME COMFORTABLE POSITION to get into a warm comfortable position ■ *n.* TENDER HUG a prolonged hug or embrace given to comfort or show affection [Early 16thC. Origin uncertain: perhaps formed from earlier *couth* (see UNCOUTH), in the sense 'familiar, comfortable, cosy'.] —**cuddler** *n.* **cuddle up** *vi.* to assume a relaxed comfortable position

cuddlesome /kúdd'lsəm/ *adj.* = **cuddly**

cuddly /kúdd'li/ (**-dlier, -dliest**) *adj.* **1.** pleasant to hold because of being soft, warm, or endearingly attractive **2.** given to or fond of cuddling

cuddy[1] /kúddi/ (*plural* **-dies**) *n.* **1.** NAUT SMALL CABIN ON BOAT a small cabin or galley on a boat **2.** NAUT OFFICERS' MESS the officers' mess on a ship **3.** SMALL ROOM a small room or closet [Mid-17thC. Origin uncertain: probably via early modern Dutch *kajute* from French *cahute* 'shanty', of unknown origin.]

cuddy[2] (*plural* **-dies**) *n. Scotland* a donkey or horse (*informal*) [Early 18thC. Origin uncertain: perhaps a pet form of the name *Cuthbert*.]

cudgel /kújjəl/ *n.* SHORT HEAVY CLUB a heavy stick used as a weapon ■ *vt.* (**-els, -elling, -elled**) BEAT WITH CUDGEL to beat sb with a cudgel [Old English *cycgel*, of unknown origin] ◇ **take up the cudgels** to defend or support sb or sth actively and energetically

cudweed /kúd weed/ (*plural* **-weeds** *or* **-weed**) *n.* a plant of the daisy family that has woolly leaves and clusters of white or yellow flowers and is found in temperate regions worldwide. Genera: *Gnaphalium* and *Filago*.

cue[1] /kyoo/ *n.* **1.** SIGNAL TO SPEAK OR ACT sth said or done that provides the signal for sb, especially an actor or performer, to say or do sth **2.** PROMPT OR REMINDER sth that prompts or reminds sb to do sth ○ *I took my cue from my brother and said nothing.* **3.** PSYCHOL RESPONSE-PRODUCING STIMULUS a stimulus or pattern of stimuli, often not consciously perceived, that results in a specific learned behavioural response

4. **SB'S ROLE** a part or function assigned to or expected of a person (*archaic*) ■ *vt.* **(cues, cueing, cued) GIVE SIGNAL OR PROMPT TO** to give sb, especially an actor or performer, a signal to say or do sth [Mid-16thC. Origin uncertain: perhaps standing for *qu*, an abbreviation of Latin *quando* 'when', written on actors' scripts to remind them to come in.]

cue in *vt.* **1. GIVE SIGNAL TO** to signal that it is now time for sb, especially a performer, to say or do sth ○ *The conductor will cue you in.* **2. INSTRUCT OR REMIND** to give sb information, instructions, or a reminder **3. INSERT INTO PERFORMANCE** to insert sth, such as a speech or song, into a performance

cue[2] /kyoo/ *n.* **1.** CUE GAMES **STICK USED TO KNOCK BALL** a long tapering stick used to strike the cue ball in games such as billiards or pool (*often used before a noun*) **2.** = **queue** *n.* 4 ■ *vt.* **(cues, cueing, cued) 1.** CUE GAMES **STRIKE WITH CUE** to strike a cue ball with a cue in such games as pool and billiards **2. TIE IN PLAIT** to tie the hair at the back of the head in a plait [Mid-18thC. Variant of QUEUE.]

cue ball *n.* the white ball struck with the cue in games such as billiards or pool, which strikes the object ball in turn

cue bid *n.* BRIDGE in bridge, a bid made to show a partner that the bidder has either an ace or no cards in a particular suit

cue card *n.* in broadcasting, a large card containing the words that sb is to say, held up out of sight of the viewing audience

cued speech *n.* a series of hand movements used to differentiate ambiguous mouth positions as an aid in lip reading

cuesta /kwéstə/ *n.* a ridge with a steep face on one side and a gentle slope on the other, especially in the southwestern United States [Early 19thC. Via Spanish, literally 'slope', from Latin *costa* 'rib, side' (source of English *coast* and *accost*).]

cuff[1] /kuf/ *n.* **1. END OF SLEEVE NEAREST WRIST** the part of a sleeve that covers the wrist, either turned back or with a band of fabric attached **2.** *US, Can, ANZ* **FOLD AT BOTTOM OF TROUSER** a turned-up fold at the bottom of a trouser leg **3. PART OF GLOVE COVERING LOWER ARM** the part of a glove or gauntlet that extends up the arm beyond the wrist **4.** MED **BAND USED IN MEASURING BLOOD PRESSURE** an inflatable band fastened around a patient's arm when measuring blood pressure ■ *npl.* **HANDCUFFS** a pair of handcuffs (*slang*) ■ *vt.* **(cuffs, cuffing, cuffed) 1.** *US, Can, Aus* **PUT TURN-UPS ON TOUSERS** to put turn-ups on a pair of trousers **2. PUT HANDCUFFS ON** to put handcuffs on sb (*slang*) [14thC. Origin unknown.]

cuff[2] *vt.* **(cuffs, cuffing, cuffed) HIT WITH OPEN HAND** to hit sb lightly with an open hand ■ *n.* **OPEN-HANDED BLOW** a blow with an open hand [Mid-16thC. Probably an imitation of the sound of hitting.]

cuff link *n.* each one of a pair of ornamental fasteners for shirt cuffs used as an alternative to buttons (*often used in the plural*)

Cuiaba /kòoyə baá/ city in southwestern Brazil on the River Cuiaba, capital of the state of Mato Grosso. Population: 389,070 (1990).

cui bono /kwee bốnō/ *n.* **1. LEGAL PRINCIPLE** the legal principle that sb who would gain sth from a particular action or event is probably responsible for it **2. USEFULNESS AS MEASURE OF VALUE** the usefulness of sth used to measure its value [Early 17thC. From Latin, literally 'to whom is the benefit'.]

Cuillin Hills /kòolin-/ range of hills on the Isle of Skye, northwestern Scotland. The highest peak is Sgurr Alasdair, 1,009 m./3,309 ft. Length: 24 km/15 mi. Also spelt **Coolin Hills**

cuirass /kwi ráss/ *n.* **1. ARMOUR FOR UPPER BODY** a piece of body armour made of metal or leather, covering the chest and sometimes the back **2. PROTECTION** a protective covering, or any means of protection **3.** ZOOL **ANIMAL'S HARD PROTECTIVE COVERING** a protective outer covering on some animals, e.g. scales or a shell [15thC. Via Old French *cuirace* from, ultimately, Latin *coriaceus* 'made of leather', from *corium* 'leather'.]

cuirassier /kwírrə seér/ *n.* a mounted soldier wearing a cuirass, especially in 16th-century Europe [Mid-16thC. From French, from *cuirasse*, from Old French *cuirace* (see CUIRASS).]

Cuisenaire /kwízzi náir-/ *tdmk.* a trademark for a set of rods of different colours and lengths used by teachers to illustrate concepts of basic arithmetic

cuish *n.* = **cuisse**

cuisine /kwi zeén/ *n.* **1. COOKING STYLE** a specified style of cooking, especially one that is notable for high quality. ◊ **haute cuisine 2. RANGE OF FOOD** the range of food prepared by a particular restaurant, country, or individual [Late 18thC. Via French, literally 'kitchen', from Latin *coquina*, from *coquere* 'to cook' (source of English *concoct*, *decoct*, and *precocious*).]

cuisine minceur /-maN súr/ *n.* a low-calorie form of cooking originating in France [From French, literally 'slimness cooking']

cuisse /kwiss/, **cuish** /kwish/ *n.* a piece of armour formerly worn in battle to protect the thigh [13thC. Via Old French *cuiss(i)eus*, plural of *cuissel*, from late Latin *coxale*, from Latin *coxa* 'hip' (source of English *cushion*).]

cuke /kyook/ *n.* a cucumber (*informal*) [Early 20thC. Shortening.]

culchie /kúlchi/ *n. Ireland* a farm labourer (*informal insult*) [Mid-20thC. Origin uncertain: perhaps an alteration of the first syllable of *Kiltimagh*, name of a town in County Mayo, Ireland.]

cul-de-sac /kúl də sak, kòol-/ (*plural* **culs-de-sac** *or* **cul-de-sacs**) *n.* **1. STREET CLOSED AT ONE END** a road with no exit at one end, often in a residential area **2. IMPASSE** a situation in which further progress is impossible **3.** ANAT **BODY CAVITY RESEMBLING POUCH** a body cavity or tubular structure open at one end only [From French, literally 'bottom of a sack']

culet /kyòolət/ *n.* the flat face at the back or base of a faceted gemstone [Late 17thC. From French, literally 'little base', from *cul* (see CULOTTES).]

culinary /kúlli nəri/ *adj.* relating to food or cooking [Mid-17thC. From Latin *culinarius*, from *culina* 'kitchen' (source of English *kiln*).] —**culinarily** *adv.*

cull /kul/ *vt.* **(culls, culling, culled) 1.** VET **REDUCE BY KILLING MEMBERS** to reduce the size of a herd, flock, or population by killing some of the animals in it **2.** VET **REMOVE FROM HERD** to remove an animal, especially a sick or weak one, from a herd or flock **3. REMOVE AS WORTHLESS** to remove an inferior thing or person from a larger group **4. SELECT** to select or gather things or people, especially those that are good examples of their kind ○ *The following cases are culled from the police reports.* ■ *n.* **1.** VET **REDUCTION OF ANIMAL NUMBERS** a reduction of the numbers of an animal population achieved by killing some of its members **2. STH WITHOUT VALUE** sth regarded as worthless, especially an unwanted or inferior animal removed from a herd [12thC. Via Old French *coillier* from Latin *colligere* 'to gather together', from *legere* 'to gather' (source of English *select*).]

cullet /kúlit/ *n.* broken or waste glass returned for recycling [Early 19thC. Variant of COLLET in the obsolete sense 'glass left on the end of a blowing iron when the finished article has been removed'.]

cullion /kúlli ən/ *n.* a contemptible or despicable person (*archaic*) ○ *'For such a one as leaves a gentleman, And makes a god of such a cullion'* (William Shakespeare, *The Taming of the Shrew*; 1593) [14thC. From Old French *coillon*, from, ultimately, Latin *coleus* 'bag, testicle' (the original sense in English), from Greek *koleos* 'sheath'.]

Culloden Moor /kə lódd'n-/ stretch of moorland near Inverness, in northeastern Scotland. Charles Edward Stuart was defeated there in 1746, ending the second Jacobite Rebellion.

cully /kúlli/ *n.* (*plural* **-lies**) **1. FRIEND** a friend (*slang*) **2. GULLIBLE PERSON** sb who is easily tricked (*archaic*) ■ *vt.* **(-lies, -lying, -lied) DECEIVE** to cheat or deceive sb (*archaic*) [Mid-17thC. Origin uncertain: perhaps a contraction of CULLION.]

culm[1] /kulm/ *n.* **1. COAL MINE WASTE** waste from a coal mine **2. INFERIOR ANTHRACITE** anthracite coal of poor quality [14thC. Origin uncertain: probably ultimately from Old English *col* (see COAL).]

culm[2] /kulm/ *n.* the jointed hollow stem of a grass or similar plant [Mid-17thC. From Latin *culmus*.]

culminant /kúlminənt/ *adj.* **1.** ASTRON **AT HIGHEST POINT** used to describe a planet or other celestial body that is at its highest altitude **2. CULMINATING** reaching its climax or point of highest development [Early 17thC. From late Latin *culminant-*, the present participle stem of *culminare* (see CULMINATE).]

culminate /kúlmi nayt/ **(-nates, -nating, -nated)** *v.* **1.** *vti.* **COME OR BRING TO HIGHEST POINT** to reach a climax or point of highest development, or to bring sth to this point ○ *a general feeling of dissatisfaction that culminated in his resignation* **2.** *vti.* **FINISH SPECTACULARLY** to come or bring sth to a climax ○ *The festivities culminated in a procession through the town.* **3.** *vi.* **HAVE STH AT HIGHEST END** to have sth at its apex ○ *The tower culminates in a point.* **4.** *vi.* ASTRON **REACH HIGHEST OR LOWEST POINT** to reach the highest or, less commonly, the lowest point in the sky relative to an observer's horizon (*refers to celestial bodies*) [Mid-17thC. From late Latin *culminat-*, the past participle stem of *culminare* 'to exalt or extol', from *culmen* 'summit'.]

culmination /kúlmi náysh'n/ *n.* **1. HIGHEST POINT** the highest, most important, or final point of an activity **2. ACT OF CULMINATING** the arrival at, or the bringing of sth to, a climax **3.** ASTRON **HIGHEST OR LOWEST ALTITUDE** the highest or, less commonly, the lowest point that a celestial body reaches relative to an observer's horizon

culottes /kyoo lóts/ *npl.* a pair of women's knee-length shorts, cut to resemble a skirt [Mid-19thC. From French, literally 'small bottom', later 'knee breeches' (the original sense in English), from *cul* 'bottom, rump' (source of English *tutu*), from Latin *culus*.]

culpable /kúlpəb'l/ *adj.* deserving blame or punishment for a wrong [13thC. Via French *coupable* from Latin *culpabilis*, from *culpare* 'to blame', from *culpa* 'fault, blame'.] —**culpability** /kúlpə bílləti/ *n.* —**culpably** /-bli/ *adv.*

culpable homicide *n. Scotland* CRIMINAL LAW the crime of manslaughter

Culpeper /kúl pepər/, **Nicholas** (1616–54) English physician and astrologer. He was a Puritan and compiled an influential manual on herbal medicine, *The English Physician Enlarged* (1653).

culprit /kúl prit/ *n.* **1. WRONGDOER** sb who is responsible for or guilty of an offence or misdeed **2.** CRIMINAL LAW **ACCUSED PERSON** sb charged with a crime and awaiting trial, especially sb who has pleaded not guilty **3. ORIGIN OF PROBLEM** a cause of a problem (*informal*) ○ *A faulty connection proved to be the culprit.* [Late 17thC. Origin uncertain: perhaps from an earlier abbreviation *cul. prist* (mistakenly taken as a form of address), from Anglo-Norman *Culpable; prest d'averer*, literally 'You are guilty; we are ready to prove it'.]

cult /kult/ *n.* **1. RELIGION** a system of religious or spiritual beliefs, especially an informal and transient belief system regarded by others as misguided or unorthodox **2. RELIGIOUS GROUP** a group of people who share religious or spiritual beliefs **3. IDOLIZATION OF SB OR STH** extreme or excessive admiration for a person, philosophy of life, or activity (*often used before a noun*) ○ *a cult following* **4. OBJECT OF IDOLIZATION** a person, philosophy, or activity regarded with extreme or excessive admiration **5. FAD** sth popular or fashionable among a devoted group of enthusiasts (*often used before a noun*) ○ *cult status* **6.** ETHNOL **SYSTEM OF SUPERNATURAL BELIEFS** a body of organized practices and beliefs supposed to involve interaction with and control over supernatural powers **7. ELITE GROUP** a self-identified group of people who share a narrowly defined interest or perspective [Early 17thC. Directly or via French from Latin *cultus* 'worship' (the original sense in English), from *colere* (see CULTURE).] —**cultic** *adj.* —**cultish** *adj.* —**cultism** *n.* —**cultist** *n.*

culti plural of **cultus**

cultivable /kúltivəb'l/, **cultivatable** /-vaytə-/ *adj.* used to describe land that is capable of being cultivated —**cultivability** /kúltivə bílləti/ *n.*

cultivar /kúlti vaar/ *n.* a variety of a cultivated plant that is developed by breeding and has a designated name [Early 20thC. Blend of CULTIVATE and VARIETY.]

cultivatable *adj.* = **cultivable**

cultivate /kúlti vayt/ **(-vates, -vating, -vated)** *vt.* **1. PREPARE LAND FOR CROPS** to work land or prepare soil for growing crops **2. GROW PLANTS** to grow a plant or crop **3. LOOSEN SOIL** to break up soil with a tool or machine, especially before sowing or planting **4. NURTURE** to improve or develop sth, usually by study or education ○ *cultivating her interest in science* **5. DEVELOP, OFTEN SELFISHLY** to develop an acquaintance or intimacy with sb, often for personal advantage **6. MAKE CULTURED** to civilize or educate a person or group [Mid-17thC. From medieval Latin *cultivat-*, the past participle stem of *cultivare*, from *cultivus* 'cultured', from Latin *cult-* (see CULTURE).]

cultivated /kúlti vaytid/ *adj.* **1. KNOWLEDGEABLE** well-educated, knowledgeable, and well-mannered **2. FOR CROPS** prepared or used for growing crops **3. PRODUCED BY HORTICULTURAL OR AGRICULTURAL METHODS** developed or improved by horticultural or agricultural techniques

cultivation /kúlti váysh'n/ *n.* **1. PREPARATION OF LAND OR GROWING CROPS** planting, growing, and harvesting crops or plants, or preparing land for this purpose **2. IMPROVEMENT** improvement or development, especially through study or education **3. SOPHISTICATION** educated taste or sophistication [Via French, from *cultiver* 'to cultivate', from, ultimately, Latin *cult-* (see CULTURE)]

cultivator /kúlti vaytər/ *n.* any gardening or farm tool or machine for breaking up soil [Mid-19thC. From CULTIVATE, modelled on French *cultivateur.*]

cultural /kúlchərəl/ *adj.* **1. OF SPECIFIC CULTURE** relating to a particular culture or civilization **2. OF THE ARTS** relating to the arts and intellectual activity —**culturally** *adv.*

cultural anthropology *n.* the scientific study of human culture or the culture of specific societies, including social structure, language, religion, art, and technology. ◊ **social anthropology** —**cultural anthropologist** *n.*

cultural cringe *n. Aus* a sense of embarrassment caused by a feeling that your national culture is inferior to others

cultural lag, **culture lag** *n.* SOCIOL a slower rate of change in one part of a culture or one society compared with another

cultural materialism *n.* the anthropological theory that environment, resources, technology, and other material things are the major influences on cultural change

cultural relativism *n.* the principle that we should not judge the behaviour of others using the standards of our own culture, and that each culture must be analysed on its own terms

Cultural Revolution *n.* a political and cultural reform movement in China from 1965 to 1968 that was intended to revolutionize political opinion and behaviour and was characterized by social upheaval. The Red Guard played a prominent role in the movement, which was aimed at restoring principles associated with Mao Zedong.

cultural weapon *n. S Africa* a traditional African weapon sometimes carried by participants at political rallies

culturati /kúlchə raáti/ *npl.* people who have a passion for the arts (*informal*) [Mid-20thC. From CULTURE, modelled on *literati.*]

culture /kúlchər/ *n.* **1. THE ARTS COLLECTIVELY** art, music, literature, and related intellectual activities ○ *Culture is necessary for a healthy society.* **2. KNOWLEDGE AND SOPHISTICATION** enlightenment and sophistication acquired through education and exposure to the arts ○ *They are people of culture.* **3. SHARED BELIEFS AND VALUES OF A GROUP** the beliefs, customs, practices, and social behaviour of a particular nation or people ○ *Southeast Asian culture* **4. PEOPLE WITH SHARED BELIEFS AND PRACTICES** a group of people whose shared beliefs and practices identify the particular place, class, or time to which they belong **5. SHARED ATTITUDES** a particular set of attitudes that characterizes a group of people ○ *The company tries hard to avoid a blame culture.* **6. DEVELOPMENT OF TOOLS AND LANGUAGE** the development and use of artefacts and symbols in the advancement of a society **7. GROWING BIOLOGICAL MATERIAL IN SPECIAL CONDITIONS** the growing of biological material, especially plants, microorganisms, or animal tissue, in a nutrient substance in specially controlled conditions for scientific, medical, or commercial purposes **8.** BIOL **BIOLOGICAL MATERIAL GROWN IN SPECIAL CONDITIONS** biological material, especially plants, microorganisms, or animal tissue, grown in a nutrient substance (**culture medium**) in specially controlled conditions for scientific, medical, or commercial purposes **9. TILLAGE** the cultivation of the land or soil in preparation for growing crops or plants **10. IMPROVEMENT** the development of a skill or expertise through training or education ○ *physical culture* ■ *vt.* (**-tures, -turing, -tured**) **1. GROW IN SPECIAL CONDITIONS** to grow biological material, especially plants, microorganisms, or animal tissue, in a nutrient substance in specially controlled conditions, for scientific, medical, or commercial purposes **2.** AGRIC **CULTIVATE** to cultivate plants or crops [13thC. Via French from Latin *cultura* 'tillage', from *cult*, the past participle stem of *colere* 'to inhabit, cultivate, worship'. Originally in English 'piece of tilled land'.]

cultured /kúlchərd/ *adj.* **1. EDUCATED AND SOPHISTICATED** generally educated and informed about the arts and related intellectual activity **2.** BIOL **GROWN IN NUTRIENT SUBSTANCE** grown in a nutrient substance in a laboratory **3. ARTIFICIALLY PRODUCED** created artificially rather than by natural or organic processes

cultured pearl *n.* a pearl created artificially by introducing a foreign body into an oyster or clam shell to attract layers of mother-of-pearl around it

culture lag *n.* SOCIOL = **cultural lag**

culture shock *n.* the feelings of confusion and anxiety experienced when an individual or a group suddenly finds itself in an unfamiliar cultural environment

culture vulture *n.* sb who has a strong or obsessive interest in the arts (*informal*)

cultus /kúltəss/ (*plural* **-tuses** *or* **-ti** /-tī/) *n.* a religious group (*formal*) [Early 17thC. From Latin *cultus*, 'worship' (source of English *cult*), from *cult-* (see CULTURE).]

culverin /kúlvərin/ *n.* **1. HEAVY CANNON** a type of long-range cannon used in the 15th to 17th centuries **2. MEDIEVAL MUSKET** a type of musket used in the 15th and 16th centuries [15thC. From French *coulevrine*, from *couleuvre* 'snake', from, ultimately, Latin *colubra.*]

culvert /kúlvərt/ *n.* **1. UNDERGROUND DUCT** a covered channel that carries water or cabling underground **2. STRUCTURE COVERING DRAINAGE CHANNEL** an arch, bridge, or part of a road that covers a culvert [Late 18thC. Origin unknown.]

cum /kum/ *prep.* together with, along with, in combination with, or functioning as (*informal*) ○ *He lives and works in an apartment cum office.* [Late 19thC. From Latin, 'with'.]

cum. *abbr.* cumulative

Cumb. *abbr.* Cumbria

cumber /kúmbər/ *vt.* (*archaic or literary*) **1. HAMPER** to hamper or hinder **2. BURDEN** to burden or encumber ■ *n.* **ENCUMBRANCE** an obstruction or hindrance (*archaic or literary*) [14thC. Origin uncertain: probably a shortening of ENCUMBER.]

Cumberland /k/ former county in northwestern England on the Scottish border, now part of Cumbria. Carlisle was its county town.

Cumberland sausage *n.* a large sausage containing coarse-cut pork, originally made in Cumberland

Cumbernauld /k/ town and former local government region in Scotland (1973–96), now in North Lanarkshire. It was built as a new town in 1955. Population: 48,760 (1991).

cumbersome /kúmbərsəm/ *adj.* **1. HEAVY OR BULKY** awkward to carry or handle because of weight, size, or shape **2. COMPLICATED OR PROBLEMATIC** difficult to use or deal with because of length or complexity —**cumbersomely** *adv.* —**cumbersomeness** *n.*

Cumbria /kúmbri ə/ county in northwestern England, formed in 1974, incorporating mainly the former counties of Cumberland and Westmorland. Carlisle is the county town. Population: 490,300 (1995). Area: 6,810 sq. km/2,629 sq. mi. —**Cumbrian** *n., adj.*

cumbrous /kúmbrəss/ *adj.* large and unwieldy (*archaic or literary*) ○ *'this cumbrous and creaking structure'* (Thomas Hardy, *Tess of the d'Urbervilles*; 1891) —**cumbrously** *adv.* —**cumbrousness** *n.*

cum div. *abbr.* cum dividend

cum dividend /kúm dívvidənd/ *adv.* with a right to the current dividend when buying a security

cumin /kúmmin/, **cummin** *n.* **1. PLANT WITH AROMATIC SEEDS** a Mediterranean plant of the carrot family with small white or pink flowers, often grown for its aromatic seeds. Latin name: *Cuminum cyminum.* **2. SEEDS USED COOKING** the aromatic seeds of the cumin plant, used whole or ground as a spice [Pre-12thC. Via Latin *cuminum* from Greek *kuminon*, of Semitic origin.]

cum laude /kúm lów day/ *adv., adj. US, Can* with the lowest of the three grades of academic distinction awarded above the general pass [From Latin, literally 'with praise']

cummerbund /kúmmər bund/ *n.* a brightly coloured pleated sash worn around the waist by men as part of formal dress [Early 17thC. From Urdu *kamar-band*, literally 'loin-band, waistband'.]

cummin *n.* = **cumin**

cummings /kúmmingz/, **e. e.** (1894–1962) US poet. He is known for his experimental poetry, which was written only in lower case. Full name **Edward Estlin Cummings**

Cummings /kúmmingz/, **Bart** (*b.* 1927) Australian racehorse trainer. He has won ten Melbourne Cups and numerous classic races including the Caulfield Cup and the Golden Slipper Stakes. Real name **James Bartholomew Cummings**

cum new *adv.* with a right to any shares that may be issued free or on favourable terms to existing shareholders when buying a security. ◊ **cum dividend**

cumquat *n.* = **kumquat**

cumshaw /kúm shaw/ *n.* a tip or gift, originally one given to Chinese beggars (*dated*) [Early 19thC. From Chinese dialect *gǎmsiâ*, an expression of thanks used by beggars.]

cumulate /kyoōmyoō layt/ *v.* (**-lates, -lating, -lated**) **1.** *vti.* = **accumulate** *v.* **2.** *vt.* **MERGE** to combine two or more items into one ■ *adj.* **HEAPED OR AMASSED** heaped up in a pile or mass [Mid-16thC. From Latin *cumulat-*, the past participle stem of *cumulare* 'to gather in a heap' (the original sense in English), from *cumulus* 'a heap'.] —**cumulation** /kyoō myoō láysh'n/ *n.*

cumulative /kyoōmyoōlətiv/ *adj.* **1. GRADUALLY BUILDING UP** becoming successively larger, stronger, or more effective ○ *Many drugs have a cumulative effect on the body.* **2. CREATED BY GRADUAL ADDITIONS** resulting from successive additions **3.** FIN **ADDED TO NEXT PAYMENT** used to describe an interest or dividend payment that is added to the next payment rather than being paid out when it falls due **4.** STOCK EXCH **ENTITLING SHAREHOLDER TO CLAIM DIVIDEND ARREARS** used to describe preferred shares whose holder has the right to claim dividend arrears before dividends are distributed to holders of common shares **5.** LAW **MORE SEVERE FOR REPEAT OFFENDER** used to describe a more severe punishment imposed on sb who has previously committed the same crime **6.** LAW **CONSECUTIVE** following consecutively on from another sentence or term of imprisonment **7.** STATS **INCLUDING ALL GIVEN VALUES OF VARIABLE** relating to the sum of the number of times a variable has a particular value totalled over all the values of the variable that are less than a given value **8.** STATS **INCREASING WITH SUCCESSIVE MEASUREMENTS** used to describe an error that increases as more measurements are taken —**cumulatively** *adv.* —**cumulativeness** *n.*

cumulative distribution function *n.* a procedure that assigns to each possible value of a random variable the probability that this value will be found. If each value is equally likely to be found, the distribution is said to be uniform.

cumulative trauma disorder *n.* MED = **repetitive strain injury**

cumuli plural of **cumulus**

cumulonimbus /kyoōmyoō lō nímbəss/ (*plural* **-bi** /-bī/ *or* **-buses**) *n.* a tall dark cumulus cloud in the shape of an anvil, often bringing thunderstorms

cumulous /kyo͞omyo͞oləss/ *adj.* having a piled up shape similar to a cumulus cloud

cumulus /kyo͞omyo͞oləss/ (*plural* **-li** -lī/) *n.* **1. LARGE FLUFFY CLOUD** a large white or grey cloud with a flat base and a rounded fluffy top, or a mass of such clouds, developing as a result of rising hot air currents **2. HEAP** a mass or heap [Mid-17thC. From Latin, literally 'heap, pile' (the original sense in English).]

cunctation /kúngk táysh'n/ *n.* hesitation or procrastination in the performance of sth (*formal*) [Late 16thC. From the Latin stem *cunctation-*, from *cunctare* 'to delay'.] —**cunctative** /kúngktətiv/ *adj.* —**cunctator** /-táytər/ *n.*

cuneal /kyo͞oni əl/ *adj.* having the shape of a wedge [Late 16thC. Directly or via modern Latin, from medieval Latin *cunealis*, from Latin *cuneus* 'wedge'. Probably obsolete by the 18thC and revived in the 19th.]

cuneate /kyo͞oni it, -ayt/ *adj.* BOT used to describe a leaf that is more or less triangular with the narrowest point of the triangle forming the tip [Early 19thC. Formed from Latin *cuneus* 'wedge'.] —**cuneately** *adv.*

Cuneiform: Sumerian clay tablet (18th century BC)

cuneiform /kyo͞oni fawrm/ *adj.* **1. USED IN ANCIENT WRITING SYSTEM** relating or belonging to any of several writing systems of the ancient Near East, e.g. Sumerian or Linear B, in which wedge-shaped impressions were made in soft clay **2. USED FOR CUNEIFORM WRITING** used to describe the clay tablets on which cuneiform script was written **3. WEDGE-SHAPED** with the narrowly triangular shape of a wedge **4. ANAT OF ANKLE** used to describe any of three wedge-shaped bones of the ankle ■ *n.* **1. CUNEIFORM SCRIPT** writing that uses small wedge-shaped characters **2. ANAT WEDGE-SHAPED ANKLE BONE** any of the three cuneiform bones of the ankle (*informal*) [Late 17thC. From French *cunéiforme* or modern Latin *cuneiformis*, from Latin *cuneus* 'wedge'.]

cunjevoi /kúnjə voy/ *n. Aus* MARINE BIOL = **sea squirt** [Early 19thC. From an Australian Aboriginal language, probably of New South Wales.]

cunnilingus /kúnni líng gəss/ *n.* sexual stimulation of a woman's genitals using the tongue and lips [Late 19thC. From Latin, literally 'vulva-licker'.]

cunning /kúnning/ *adj.* **1. CRAFTY AND DECEITFUL** clever or artful in a way that is intended to deceive **2. CLEVERLY THOUGHT OUT** showing skill, shrewdness, and ingenuity in planning or doing sth **3.** *US* **CUTE** attractive in a pleasant delicate way (*informal*) ■ *n.* **1. CRAFTINESS AND DECEITFULNESS** the ability to deceive in a clever subtle way **2. SKILFUL PERFORMANCE** skilful ingenuity or grace in doing sth [13thC. Probably ultimately from Old Norse *kunna* 'to know'. Originally in the sense 'learned, knowledgeable'.] —**cunningly** *adv.* —**cunningness** *n.*

Cunningham /kúnningəm/, **Allan** (1791–1839) English-born Australian botanist and explorer. An early collector of Australian plants, he was the first European to explore the Darling Downs region of Eastern Australia.

Cunningham, Merce (b. 1919) US dancer and choreographer. He invented the 'choreography by chance' technique and has played an important role in the development of avant-garde dance.

cunt /kunt/ *n.* (*taboo offensive*) **1. OFFENSIVE TERM** a highly offensive term for a woman's genitals **2. OFFENSIVE TERM** a highly offensive term for a woman **3. OFFENSIVE TERM** a highly offensive term for sb who is viewed

Merce Cunningham

with great dislike or contempt, especially a man **4. OFFENSIVE TERM** a highly offensive term for sexual intercourse with a woman [13thC. Ultimately of prehistoric Germanic origin. First recorded in *Gropecuntlane*, a street in Oxford where prostitutes worked; there were similar names in London, Norwich, and York.]

cup /kup/ *n.* **1. DRINKING CONTAINER** a small container, usually with a handle, used to hold liquids for drinking **2. CONTENTS OF CUP** the contents of a cup ○ *Will you have another cup?* **3. COOK VOLUME MEASURE USED IN COOKING** a unit of volume used esp. in cooking, equal to 8 fluid ounces (approximately 237 millilitres in the US and approximately 227 millilitres in the UK). **4. WINNER'S PRIZE IN SPORTS** an ornamental trophy, typically a large two-handled silver goblet, awarded as a prize in a competition **5. SPORTS COMPETITION** a sporting competition in which the winner's prize is a large ornamental goblet **6. BOWL-SHAPED OBJECT** sth that has an open hollow rounded shape **7. PART OF BRA** either of the shaped sections of a bra that support and cover the breasts **8. BOWL-SHAPED PLANT OR BODY PART** an open hollow rounded part or structure in a plant or in the body **9. PARTY PUNCH** a mixed drink with a particular ingredient as its base, usually served from a large bowl at parties ○ *a champagne cup* **10. DISH SERVED IN CUP-SHAPED CONTAINER** a dessert or appetizer served in a small bowl or glass dish **11. COMMUNION CHALICE OR WINE** in Christian services, the vessel from which the consecrated wine is drunk during Holy Communion, or the wine itself **12. GOLF GOLF HOLE** the hole on a green that is the target in golf, or the metal lining of such a hole **13. SB'S LOT IN LIFE** what a person is destined to receive, suffer, or enjoy in life (*literary*) ■ *vt.* (**cups, cupping, cupped**) **1. FORM INTO CUP SHAPE** to form one or both of the hands into an open hollow rounded shape, usually to hold or receive sth, e.g. water **2. HOLD IN HANDS** to hold sth in cupped hands **3. DRAW TO SURFACE OF SKIN** formerly, to use a cupping glass to increase the blood supply to an area of the skin [Pre-12thC. From Latin *cuppa*, probably from Latin *cupa* 'tub' (source of English *coop* and *cupola*).] ◇ **in your cups** drunk (*archaic*)

cup-and-saucer plant *n.* a Mexican climbing plant with large brightly coloured flowers. Latin name: *Cobaea scandens.*

cupbearer /kúp bairər/ *n.* a servant who pours wine, especially one employed in a royal household (*formal*)

cupboard /kúbbərd/ *n.* a piece of furniture, either built-in or freestanding, or a small room used for storing food and other kitchen necessities [14thC. Originally used for a table or sideboard on which cups and other crockery were displayed.]

cupboard love *n.* affection that is motivated by self-interest [From CUPBOARD in the obsolete sense 'food, provisions']

cupcake /kúp kayk/ *n.* a small individual iced cake, baked in a paper or foil case or in a cup-shaped mould

cupel /kyo͞op'l/ *n.* **CONTAINER FOR SEPARATING PRECIOUS METALS** a small container in which precious metals are refined, especially in which gold and silver are separated from base metals during assaying ■ *vt.* (**-pels, -pelling, -pelled**) **REFINE IN A CUPEL** to separate gold or silver from a base metal using a cupel [Early 17thC. From French *coupelle*, literally 'little cup', from *coupe* 'cup', from late Latin *cuppa* (see CUP).] —**cupeller** *n.*

cupellation /kyo͞oə láysh'n/ *n.* the recovery of precious metals in a cupel by exposure to a blast of hot air that oxidizes the unwanted base metals, such as lead, which are partly absorbed

Cup Final, **cup final** *n.* the final match in a knockout sports competition, especially the FA Cup or the Scottish Cup

cupful /kúp fo͝ol/ *n.* the amount held by a cup ○ *There's only about a cupful of water left.*

cup fungus *n.* a cup-shaped and often bright red, orange, or yellow fungus with a spore-bearing often stalkless structure. Subdivision: *Ascomycotina.*

cupid /kyo͞opid/ *n.* a representation of the god Cupid as a symbol of love in painting or sculpture

Cupid *n.* the Roman god of love, the son of Venus, usually represented as a young boy with wings and a bow and arrow. Greek equivalent **Eros** [14thC. From Latin *Cupido*, literally 'desire', from *cupere* 'to desire'.]

cupidity /kyoo píddəti/ *n.* greed, especially for money or possessions (*formal*) [15thC. Directly or via French from Latin *cupiditas* (source also of English *covet*), from *cupere* 'to desire'.]

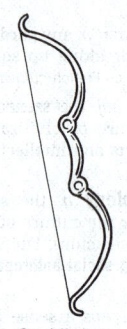

Cupid's bow

Cupid's bow *n.* **1. DOUBLE CURVE** a double curve, especially the curves of the upper lip **2. ARCHERY DOUBLE-CURVED BOW** a bow with two curves used in archery [From the shape of the bow used by Cupid]

cup of tea *n.* **1. PREFERRED THING** what sb likes or prefers ○ *This is more my cup of tea.* **2.** *US* **STH TO DEAL WITH** sth to be dealt with

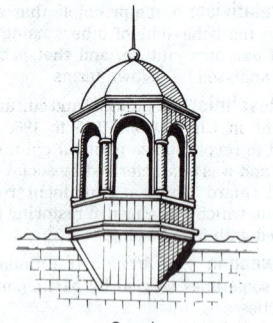

Cupola

cupola /kyo͞opələ/ *n.* **1. ARCHIT DOME-SHAPED ROOF** a roof or ceiling in the form of a dome **2. ARCHIT DOME ON ROOF** a small dome on a roof, sometimes made of glass and providing natural light inside **3.** MIL **GUN TURRET** a domed structure protecting a gun, e.g. on a warship **4. SMALL OBSERVATION DOME** a glass observation dome on the roof of an armoured vehicle or railway van **5. BLAST FURNACE** a cylindrical blast furnace used in foundries for remelting iron or other metals [Mid-16thC. Via Italian from late Latin *cupula* 'little cask, vault', from *cupa* 'cask'.]

cuppa /kúppə/ *n.* a cup of tea (*informal*) ○ *Let's have a cuppa.* [Mid-20thC. Representing an informal pronunciation of *cup of*.]

cupped /kupt/ *adj.* formed into the open hollow shape of a cup

cupping /kúpping/ *n.* MED a historical medical practice in which a cupping glass was used to increase the blood supply to an area of the skin

cupping glass *n.* MED a glass container in which a partial vacuum is created by heat or suction that is applied to the skin to increase the blood supply in the tissues below

cuppy /kúppi/ (**-pier, -piest**) *adj.* **1.** CUP-SHAPED with the shape of a cup **2.** FULL OF SHALLOW DEPRESSIONS with many small shallow hollows in the surface

cupr- *prefix.* = **cupro-** (*used before vowels*)

cupreous /kyóopri əss/ *adj.* **1.** COPPERY consisting of or containing copper **2.** OF REDDISH-BROWN COLOUR having a reddish-brown colour, like that of polished copper [Mid-17thC. Formed from late Latin *cupreus*, from *cuprum* 'copper'.]

cupri- *prefix.* = **cupro-**

cupric /kyóoprik/ *adj.* containing copper with a valency of two. ◊ **cuprous** [Late 18thC. Formed from Late Latin *cuprum* 'copper'.]

cupriferous /kyoo prífferəss/ *adj.* having copper as a constituent [Late 18thC. Coined from late Latin *cuprum* 'copper' + -IFEROUS.]

cuprite /kyóo prīt/ *n.* a reddish-brown or black mineral consisting of copper oxide. It is an ore of copper. [Mid-19thC. Formed from Late Latin *cuprum* 'copper'.]

cupro- *prefix.* copper ○ *cupronickel* [From late Latin *cuprum* (see COPPER)]

cupronickel /kyóo prō ník'l/ *n.* a corrosion-resistant alloy of copper containing up to 40 per cent nickel

cuprous /kyóoprəss/ *adj.* containing copper with a valency of 1. ◊ **cupric** [Mid-17thC. Formed from late Latin *cuprum* 'copper'.]

cup tie *n.* a match in a knockout competition for which the prize is a cup

cup-tied *adj.* **1.** UNABLE TO PLAY IN CUP TIE unable to play in a cup tie for some reason, e.g. disqualification or injury **2.** NOT FREE BECAUSE OF CUP TIE not free to play another fixture because of participation in a cup tie

cupulate /kyóopyoo layt/, **cupular** /-lər/ *adj.* **1.** SMALL AND CUP-SHAPED shaped like a small cup or dome **2.** HAVING CUPULES having a cupule or cupules

cupule /kyóo pyool/ *n.* a cup-shaped body part or plant part, such as that enclosing the base of an acorn [15thC. From late Latin *cupula* 'little cask, vault', from *cupa* 'cask'.]

Cuquenan Waterfall /kóo kay nán-/ waterfall in Venezuela, one of the highest in the world. Height: 610 m/2,000 ft.

cur /kur/ *n.* **1.** MONGREL DOG a mixed-breed dog, especially an ill-natured or worthless one **2.** CONTEMPTIBLE PERSON a mean, cowardly, or otherwise unpleasant person (*dated insult*) [12thC. Originally in *cur-dog*; perhaps ultimately from Old Norse *kurr* 'grumbling'.]

cur. *abbr.* current

curable /kyóorəb'l/ *adj.* **1.** ABLE TO BE TREATED MEDICALLY capable of being treated by medical procedures **2.** ABLE TO BE HEALED capable of being healed by medical procedures —**curability** /kyóorə bílləti/ *n.* —**curably** /-bli/ *adv.*

curaçao /kyóorə sō/ *n.* an orange-flavoured liqueur that originated on the Caribbean island of Curaçao

Curaçao /kóorə sow, -sō, kyóorə-/ island in the Netherlands Antilles, in the Caribbean Sea, and the largest of the island group. Area: 444 sq. km/171 sq. mi.

curacy /kyóorəssi/ (*plural* **-cies**) *n.* the position or term of office of a curate

curare /kyoo ráari/, **curari** *n.* **1.** PLANT RESIN CAUSING PARALYSIS a dark resin obtained from certain South American plants, used by indigenous hunters to poison their arrows and in medicine as a muscle relaxant **2.** SOURCE OF CURARE a tropical South American vine from which curare is obtained. Genera: *Strychnos* and *Chondodendron.* [Late 18thC. Via Spanish and Portuguese from Carib *kurari.*]

curarize /kyóorə rīz/ (**-rizes, -rizing, -rized**), **curarise** (**-rises, -rising, -rised**) *vt.* to treat sb with curare —**curarization** /kyóorə rī záysh'n/ *n.*

curassow /kyóorə sow/ *n.* a large crested game bird of South and Central America with a long tail and a brightly coloured bill. Genus: *Crax.* [Late 17thC. Alteration of CURAÇAO.]

curate[1] /kyóorət/ *n.* **1.** PRIEST'S ASSISTANT a member of the clergy who assists a vicar, rector, or priest **2.** SB RESPONSIBLE FOR PARISH a member of the clergy in charge of a parish [14thC. From medieval Latin *curatus* 'sb who cares for a parish', from Latin *cura* 'care' (source of English *cure*).]

curate[2] /kyoo ráyt/ (**-rates, -rating, -rated**) *vti.* to be the curator of a museum, gallery, or other collection [Early 18thC. Back-formation from CURATOR.]

curate's egg *n.* sth that may be described as only partly bad, especially when this makes the whole thing unacceptable [From a cartoon in *Punch* magazine, 1895, in which a curate when served a bad egg at the bishop's table assured his host that 'parts of it are excellent']

curative /kyóorətiv/ *adj.* CAPABLE OF CURING able to restore health ■ *n.* MEDICINE OR MEDICAL TREATMENT a substance or treatment that can restore health —**curatively** *adv.* —**curativeness** *n.*

curator /kyoo ráytər/ *n.* **1.** HEAD OF MUSEUM OR OTHER COLLECTION the administrative head of a museum, gallery, or other collection **2.** *Scotland* LAW MINOR'S GUARDIAN the legal guardian of a minor [14thC. From Latin, from *curare* 'to care for' (see CURE).] —**curatorial** /kyóorə táwri əl/ *adj.* —**curatorship** /kyoo ráytərship/ *n.*

curb /kurb/ *n.* **1.** IMPOSED LIMITATION sth that controls or limits sth else **2.** HORSE'S BIT AND ATTACHED CHAIN a horse's bit with a chain or strap attached, passed under the horse's jaw (*often used before a noun*) ○ *a curb chain* **3.** EDGING FOR LAWN a line of stones that forms the edge of an area of lawn **4.** RAISED PART THAT SURROUNDS STH an enclosing frame or raised margin, e.g. around a skylight or a well **5.** *US, Can* = **kerb** ■ *vt.* (**curbs, curbing, curbed**) **1.** RESTRAIN to restrain, control, or limit sth **2.** *US* = **kerb** [15thC. Probably a variant of earlier *courb* 'to curve' (the underlying sense in English), which came via French *courber*, from Latin *curvare*. Originally, 'horse's bit' (that bends the horse's neck).]

curb bit *n.* a horse's bit attached to a chain or strap

curbing /kúrbing/ *n. US* = **kerbing**

curb roof *n.* a roof that has two or more different angles of slope on each side, e.g. a mansard or gambrel roof

curbside /kúrb sīd/ *n. US* = **kerbside**

curbside service *n.* = **curb service**

curbstone /kúrb stōn/ *n. US* = **kerbstone**

curcuma /kúrkyoomə/ *n.* a tropical plant from which turmeric and zedoary are obtained. Genus: *Curcuma.* [15thC. Via medieval Latin from Arabic *kurkum* 'turmeric', from Sanskrit *kuṇkuma* 'saffron'. The change of meaning from 'saffron' to 'turmeric' presumably occurred because of the yellow colouring of both.]

curd /kurd/ *n.* **1.** SOLID PART OF SOUR MILK the solid substance formed when milk coagulates, used to make cheese **2.** SUBSTANCE RESEMBLING MILK CURD a food substance with a consistency similar to milk curd ■ *vti.* (**curds, curding, curded**) CURDLE to turn sth into curd, or to become curd [14thC. Origin uncertain: perhaps from Celtic.] —**curdy** *adj.*

curd cheese *n.* a mild soft cheese made from skimmed milk curds

curdle /kúrd'l/ (**-dles, -dling, -dled**) *vti.* **1.** COAGULATE OR MAKE STH COAGULATE to separate, or cause a liquid such as milk, to separate into curds and whey, e.g. by permitting or encouraging bacterial action **2.** GO BAD OR SPOIL STH to go bad or wrong, or to spoil sth (*informal*) [Late 16thC. Formed from CURD. Literally 'to keep on making into curd'.]

cure /kyoor/ *v.* (**cures, curing, cured**) **1.** *vti.* HEAL to restore a sick person or animal to health ○ *Six months later she was completely cured.* **2.** *vt.* TREAT SUCCESSFULLY to bring about recovery from an illness, disorder, or injury ○ *Diseases like this are not easily cured.* **3.** *vt.* SOLVE PROBLEM to solve a problem ○ *curing unemployment* **4.** *vti.* PRESERVE FOOD to preserve food, especially meat or fish, usually by smoking, drying, or salting it, or to be preserved by one of these methods **5.** *vt.* PRESERVE BY DRYING to preserve a substance, especially leather or tobacco, by drying it **6.** *vt.* FINISH WITH CHEMICAL PROCESS to finish a material by applying chemicals **7.** *vt.* MAKE RUBBER STRONGER to strengthen rubber with additives in the presence of heat and pressure **8.** *vti.* HARDEN to make a material, especially concrete or cement, harden ■ *n.* **1.** STH THAT RESTORES HEALTH a medication or treatment that brings about a full recovery from an illness or injury ○ *working to find a cure for the disease* **2.** RECOVERY restoration or return to health ○ *I managed to achieve a complete cure.* **3.** PROBLEM'S SOLUTION sth that resolves a problem **4.** FOOD PRESERVATION PROCESS the preservation of meat or fish, especially by smoking, drying, or salting **5.** SPIRITUAL CARE the spiritual and pastoral responsibility of the clergy for laypeople **6.** *N Ireland* FOLK REMEDY a folk practice supposed to cure an illness, and handed down as a secret in a family because of some peculiarity such as having married sb of the same name [13thC. Via Old French from Latin *curare* 'to care for', or its source *cura* 'care, concern' (the original sense in English). Current senses evolved via the obsolete sense 'medical care'.] —**curer** *n.*

WORD KEY: ORIGIN

Cure is derived from the Latin word *cura*, meaning 'care' or 'concern', which is also the source of English *curate*, *curious*, *scour*, *secure*, and *sinecure*.

curé /kyóoray/ *n.* a parish priest in a French-speaking country [Mid-17thC. Via French from medieval Latin *curatus* (see CURATE[1]).]

cure-all *n.* a treatment or remedy that is believed to be able to cure every ailment or problem

curet *n., vt.* = **curette**

curettage /kyóorə táazh, kyoo réttij/, **curettement** /kyoo rétmənt/ *n.* a surgical procedure that involves scraping the inside surface of a body cavity with an instrument shaped like a spoon (**curette**) to remove abnormal growths or other tissue [Late 19thC. From French, from *curette* (see CURETTE).]

curette /kyoo rét/, **curet** *n.* SURGICAL INSTRUMENT FOR SCRAPING a spoon-shaped surgical instrument used to remove tissue from the inner surface of a body cavity ■ *vt.* (**-rettes,** *or* **-rets, -retting, -retted**) REMOVE TISSUE BY SCRAPING to scrape tissue from the inner surface of a body cavity using a curette [Mid-18thC. From French, from *curer* 'to clean out', from Latin *curare* 'to care for'.]

curettement *n.* = **curettage**

curfew /kúr fyoo/ *n.* **1.** RESTRICTION ON PEOPLE'S MOVEMENTS an official restriction on people's movements, requiring them to remain indoors after a specified time at night **2.** TIME OR SIGNAL FOR CURFEW the time at which a curfew takes effect, or the signal given at this time **3.** LENGTH OF CURFEW the duration of a curfew **4.** MEDIEVAL REMINDER TO EXTINGUISH LIGHTS in the Middle Ages, the ringing of a bell in the evening as a reminder to put out fires and lights ○ *'The curfew tolls the knell of parting day'* (Thomas Gray, *Elegy written in a Country Churchyard*; 1751) [13thC. From Anglo-Norman *coeverfu* or Old French *cuevrefeu*, literally 'cover fire'.]

curia /kyóori ə/ (*plural* **-ae** /-ri ee/) *n.* **1.** PAPAL COURT the administrative body at the Vatican, by which the Pope governs the Roman Catholic Church **2.** SUBDIVISION OF ANCIENT ROMAN TRIBE in ancient Rome, a subdivision of each tribe, or the place where it met **3.** ANCIENT ROMAN SENATE the senate or senate house in an ancient Roman city **4.** MEDIEVAL COURT a medieval monarch's court of justice [Early 17thC. From Latin, literally 'council', perhaps formed from *co-* 'together' + *vir* 'man' (source of English *virile*).] —**curial** *adj.*

curie /kyóori/ *n.* a unit of radioactivity equal to 3.7 times 10^{10} disintegrations per second [Early 20thC. Named after the French physicists Pierre *Curie* (1859–1906) and Marie CURIE, who studied radioactivity.]

Curie /kyóori/, **Marie** (1867–1934) Polish-born French chemist and physicist. She pioneered research into radioactivity and was awarded the Nobel Prize in 1903 and 1911. She died of leukaemia. Her husband Pierre Curie collaborated with her and was jointly awarded the 1903 Nobel Prize. Born **Marja Sklodowska**

Curie point, **Curie temperature** *n.* the temperature at which in some substances, such as iron, there is a change in the magnetic characteristics, from ferromagnetic to paramagnetic behaviour [Named after Pierre *Curie* (see CURIE), who discovered the laws that relate some magnetic properties to changes in temperature]

Marie Curie

Curie's law *n.* the law of physics stating that there is an inverse proportionality between the effect of a magnetic field on a paramagnetic material and its absolute temperature [Named after Pierre *Curie* (see CURIE), who formulated it]

Curie-Weiss law /-víss-/ *n.* a variation of Curie's law in which the temperature term is reduced by an amount equal to the Curie point [Named after Pierre *Curie* (see CURIE) and the French physicist Pierre Ernest *Weiss* (1865–1940), who constructed a mathematical description of phenomena such as the Curie point]

curio /kyoóri ō/ (*plural* **-os**) *n.* an object that is valued and often collected for its interest or rarity [Mid-19thC. Shortening of CURIOSITY.]

curiosa /kyoóri óssə, -ózə/ *npl.* **1. WRITINGS ON UNUSUAL SUBJECTS** books or other texts dealing with unusual topics, especially erotica **2. UNUSUAL OBJECTS** interesting and unusual objects [Late 19thC. From Latin, neuter plural of *curiosus* (see CURIOUS).]

curiosity /kyoóri óssəti/ (*plural* **-ties**) *n.* **1. DESIRE TO KNOW STH** eagerness to know about sth or to get information **2. TENDENCY TO PRY** an excessive interest in other people's affairs **3. SB OR STH THOUGHT STRANGE** an interesting and unusual object, person, or phenomenon [14thC. Via French *curiosité* from Latin *curiositas*, from *curiosus* (see CURIOUS).]

curious /kyoóri əss/ *adj.* **1. EAGER TO KNOW STH** eager to know about sth or to get information ○ *I'm curious to know how they found out about the party.* **2. TOO INQUISITIVE** excessively eager to find out about other people's affairs **3. ODD** strange, unexpected, or hard to explain ○ *several curious events* **4. VERY INTRICATE** intricate or detailed (*archaic or literary*) [14thC. Via Old French *curios* from Latin *curiosus* 'careful, assiduous, inquisitive', from *cura* 'care, concern, solicitude' (source of English *cure*).] —**curiously** *adv.* —**curiousness** *n.*

curium /kyoóri əm/ *n.* a silvery-white metallic radioactive chemical element produced artificially from plutonium. Symbol **Cm** [Mid-20thC. Named after Pierre and Marie *Curie* (see CURIE), because of their research into radioactivity.]

curl /kurl/ *v.* (**curls, curling, curled**) **1.** *vti.* **MAKE HAIR CURLY** to make naturally straight hair curly, usually by twisting it around sth while it is damp, or to grow in ringlets naturally **2.** *vti.* **MAKE OR BECOME CURVED OR COILED** to bend, twist, or wind sth into a curved or spiral shape, or to become curved or coiled ○ *He curled the silver ribbon into spirals.* ○ *The paper had begun to curl at the edges.* **3.** *vi.* **MOVE IN A SPIRAL MOTION** to move in a curve or spiral ○ *Smoke curled into the sky.* **4.** *vi.* **PARTICIPATE IN CURLING** to play the game of curling ■ *n.* **1. CURVED OR COILED HAIRS** a lock of hair curved into a round or spiral shape (*often used in the plural*) **2. TENDENCY TO CURL** the tendency of hair to grow or stay in ringlets ○ *My hair doesn't have much curl.* **3. CURVED OR COILED THING** sth with a curved or coiled shape, e.g. a wood shaving or the crest of a breaking wave **4. CURLING OF STH** the forming of sth into a curved or round shape **5. GYM WEIGHTLIFTING MANOEUVRE** a weightlifting move in which a barbell is held at thigh height with the underarms facing outwards, then raised to the chest, and lowered without moving the shoulders, upper arms, or legs **6. MARKING ON WOOD** a curved or spiral marking in wood grain [14thC. From Middle Dutch *krul* 'curly', of prehistoric Germanic origin.]

curl up *v.* **1.** *vi.* **CURVE BODY AND DRAW UP LEGS** to sit or lie with the body curved and the legs tucked up, usually in order to relax ○ *curl up into bed with a good novel* **2.** *vti.* **MAKE OR BECOME CURVED OR COILED** to become curved or coiled, or to bend, twist, or wind sth into a curved or spiral shape ○ *The paper curled up in the fire before it burst into flames.* **3.** *vi.* **FEEL EXTREMELY EMBARRASSED** to be overcome with embarrassment, revulsion, or some other strong feeling (*informal*) ○ *When I realized my mistake I just wanted to curl up and disappear.*

curled paperwork *n.* = rolled paperwork

curler /kúrlər/ *n.* **1. DEVICE FOR CURLING HAIR** a roller or other device used to curl hair **2. SB PLAYING CURLING** sb who takes part in the game of curling

Curlew

curlew /kúr lyoo/ *n.* a large shore bird with brownish plumage, long legs, and a long slender bill that curves downwards. Genus: *Numenius*. [14thC. From Old French *courlieu*, a variant, probably influenced by *courliu* 'courier, messenger', of *courlis*, an imitation of the bird's cry.]

Curlewis /kúrlyooz/, **Sir Adrian Herbert** (1901–85) Australian judge. He was a prominent figure in the development of lifesaving services for swimmers.

curlicue /kúrli kyoo/ *n.* a curly ornamental twist, especially in calligraphy or design [Mid-19thC. From CURLY + CUE² (in the obsolete sense 'pigtail').] —**curlicued** *adj.*

curling /kúrling/ *n.* a team game played on an ice rink, in which a heavy polished stone with a handle is slid towards a circular target (**tee**) [Early 17thC. From the curving path of the stone as it reaches the target.]

curling iron *n.* = curling tongs

curling stone *n.* a heavy polished stone with a handle used in the game of curling

curling tongs *npl.* a device consisting of a heated rod round which the hair is twisted to form a curl

curlpaper /kúrl paypər/ *n.* a small piece of paper rolled round a lock of hair, which is then twisted and left to set into a curl

curly /kúrli/ (**-ier, -iest**) *adj.* **1. WITH CURLS** arranged in curls, or curling naturally **2. CURVED OR COILED** bent or twisted into a wavy, curved, or spiral shape ○ *The paper has gone all curly.* **3. WITH CURVES IN GRAIN** used to describe wood that has irregular curved or wavy markings in the grain **4. TRICKY** difficult to answer or deal with (*informal*) ○ *had to fend off a few curly questions* —**curliness** *n.*

curly-coated retriever *n.* a dog with a short curly black or brown coat, belonging to a breed used for hunting

curly endive *n.* = endive 1

curly top *n.* a viral disease of beets, tomatoes, beans, and other plants that makes the leaves curl

curmudgeon /kur mújjən/ *n.* a bad-tempered, disagreeable, or stubborn person (*disapproving*) [Late 16thC. Origin uncertain: perhaps thought to suggest the sound of grumbling.] —**curmudgeonly** *adj.* —**curmudgeonry** *n.*

Curnow /k/, **Allen** (*b.* 1911) New Zealand poet and author of *Valley of Decision* (1933). Full name **Thomas Allen Curnow**

currach /kúrrəkh, -rə/, **curragh** *n.* *Ireland, Scotland* a boat like a coracle, formerly used on Scottish and Irish lakes and rivers [15thC. From Irish and Gaelic *curach* 'small boat'. Ultimately from a Celtic word which is also the ancestor of English *coracle*.]

currant /kúrrənt/ *n.* **1. SMALL DRIED GRAPE** a small dark dried seedless grape originally from the Mediterranean, used in cookery **2. SMALL FRUIT-BEARING SHRUB** a small deciduous shrub cultivated in temperate regions that bears a small round edible fruit, especially the redcurrant or blackcurrant. Genus: *Ribes*. **3. FRUIT OF CURRANT BUSH** the small round juicy fruit of a currant bush, especially a redcurrant or blackcurrant [Early 16thC. Shortening of Anglo-Norman *raisins de Corauntz*, a variant of Old French *raisins de Corinthe*, literally 'grapes from Corinth', where they originated.]

currawong /kúrrə wong/ *n.* a large Australian bird resembling a crow, with black and white plumage and a strong pointed bill. Currawongs feed on carrion and live in noisy flocks. Genus: *Strepera*. [Early 20thC. From Yagara *garraway* (also found in neighbouring languages).]

currency /kúrrənssi/ (*plural* **-cies**) *n.* **1. MONEY** a system of money, or the notes and coins themselves, used in a particular country **2. ACCEPTANCE OF IDEA OR TERM** widespread acceptance or use of an idea, theory, word, or phrase **3. CIRCULATION** the transmitting of sth, especially money, from person to person **4. TIME WHEN STH IS CURRENT** the period of time during which sth is current **5.** *Aus* **INDIGENOUS AUSTRALIAN** an Australian-born resident of Australia, as opposed to a British-born immigrant (*dated slang*) [Mid-17thC. Formed from CURRENT. In the financial sense, from the idea of being currently in circulation.]

current /kúrrənt/ *adj.* **1. EXISTING NOW** happening, existing, or in force at the present ○ *In my current job, I am in charge of 25 people.* **2. VALID** accepted as legally valid **3. PRESENTLY ACCEPTED** widely known, accepted, or believed ○ *The theory is no longer current.* ■ *n.* **1. FLOW OF WATER OR AIR** the steady flow of water or air in a particular direction **2. STREAM** a mass of water or air flowing steadily in a particular direction **3. FLOW OF ELECTRIC CHARGE** the flow of electricity through a cable, wire, or other conductor **4. RATE OF FLOW OF ELECTRICITY** the rate of flow of an electric charge through a conductor **5. TENDENCY** a trend or tendency ○ *going against the current and moving to a farm* [13thC. From Old French *corant*, the present participle of *courre* 'to run', from Latin *currere*. The original and underlying sense is 'running, flowing'.] —**currentness** *n.*

—— WORD KEY: ORIGIN ——

Current is derived from the Latin word *currere*, meaning 'to run', which is also the source of English *corridor*, *courier*, *course*, *occur*, and *succour*.

current account *n.* BANKING an account at a bank or building society from which money may be drawn on demand. US term **checking account**

current affairs *npl.* important political and social events or issues of the present time (*often used before a noun*)

current assets *npl.* available cash and other assets that could be converted to cash within a year

current-cost accounting *n.* a method of accounting that assesses the value of assets as the cost of replacing them rather than as their original cost

current density *n.* the ratio of the amount of current flowing through a conductor to the cross-sectional area of the conductor. Symbol j, J

current efficiency *n.* in an electrolytic process, the mass of the substance liberated by a given current divided by the theoretical mass, as predicted by Faraday's law

current events *npl.* = current affairs (*often used before a noun*)

current liabilities *npl.* business liabilities that are due to be cleared before the end of the financial year

currently /kúrrəntli/ *adv.* at the present time ○ *They are currently living abroad.*

current ratio *n.* the ratio of current assets to current liabilities

curricle /kúrrik'l/ *n.* a light two-wheeled open carriage drawn by a pair of horses side by side [Mid-18thC. From Latin *curriculum*, in the sense 'racing chariot'.]

CURRENCY: UNITS AND SUBUNITS

Country	Unit	Subunit
Afghanistan	afghani	100 puls
Albania	lek	100 qindars
Algeria	dinar	100 centimes
Andorra	peseta	100 centimos
	franc	100 centimes
Angola	readjusted kwanza	100 lwei
Antigua and Barbuda	dollar	
Argentina	peso argentino	
Armenia	dram	100 humma
Australia	dollar	100 cents
Austria*	schilling	100 groschen
Azerbaijan	manat	100 gyapiks
The Bahamas	dollar	100 cents
Bahrain	dinar	1000 fils
Bangladesh	taka	100 paisas
Barbados	dollar	100 cents
Belarus	ruble	
Belgium*	franc	100 centimes
Belize	dollar	100 cents
Benin	franc	
Bhutan	ngultrum	100 chetrums
Bolivia	boliviano	100 centavos
Bosnia-Herzegovina	dinar	
Botswana	pula	100 thebe
Brazil	real	100 centavos
Brunei	dollar/ringgit	100 cents
Bulgaria	lev	100 stotinki
Burkina Faso	franc	
Burundi	franc	100 centimes
Cambodia	riel	100 sen
Cameroon	franc	
Canada	dollar	100 cents
Cape Verde	escudo	100 centavos
Central African Republic	franc	
Chad	franc	
Chile	peso	100 centavos
China	yuan	10 jiao
Hong Kong	dollar	100 cents
Macao	pataca	100 avos
Colombia	peso	100 centavos
Comoros	franc	100 centimes
Democratic Republic of Congo	new zaire	100 makuta
Republic of Congo	franc	
Costa Rica	colón	100 centimos
Côte d'Ivoire	franc	
Croatia	kuna	100 lipa
Cuba	peso	100 centavos
Cyprus	pound/lira	
Czech Republic	koruna	100 haler
Denmark	krone	100 øre
Djibouti	franc	100 centimes

Country	Unit	Subunit
Dominica	dollar	
Dominican Republic	peso	100 centavos
Ecuador	sucre	100 centavos
Egypt	pound	100 piastres
El Salvador	colon	100 centavos
Equatorial Guinea	franc	
Eritrea	nakfa	100 cents
Estonia	kroon	100 sents
Ethiopia	birr	100 cents
Fiji	dollar	100 cents
Finland*	markka	100 pennis
France*	franc	100 centimes
Gabon	franc	
The Gambia	dalasi	100 bututs
Georgia	lari	
Germany*	mark	100 pfennig
Ghana	new cedi	100 pesewas
Greece	drachma	100 lepta
Grenada	dollar	
Guatemala	quetzal	100 centavos
Guinea	franc	100 centimes
Guinea-Bissau	franc	
Guyana	dollar	100 cents
Haiti	gourde	100 centimes
Honduras	lempira	100 centavos
Hungary	forint	100 fillér
Iceland	króna	100 aurar
India	rupee	100 paisa
Indonesia	rupiah	100 sen
Iran	rial	
Iraq	dinar	1000 fils
Ireland*	punt	100 pence
Israel	shekel	100 agorot
Italy*	lira	100 centesimi
Jamaica	dollar	100 cents
Japan	yen	100 sen
Jordan	dinar	1000 fils
Kazakhstan	tenge	
Kenya	shilling	100 cents
Kiribati	dollar	100 cents
Kuwait	dinar	1000 fils
Kyrgyzstan	som	100 tyiyn
Laos	new kip	
Latvia	lat	100 santims
Lebanon	pound	100 piastres
Lesotho	loti	100 lisente
Liberia	dollar	100 cents
Libya	dinar	1000 dirhams
Liechtenstein	franc	100 centimes

Country	Unit	Subunit
Lithuania	litas	100 centas
Luxembourg*	franc	100 centimes
Macedonia	denar	100 deni
Madagascar	franc	
Malawi	kwacha	100 tambala
Malaysia	ringgit	100 sen
Maldives	rufiyaa	100 laari
Mali	franc	
Malta	lira	100 cents
Marshall Islands	dollar	100 cents
Mauritania	ouguiya	5 khoums
Mauritius	rupee	100 cents
Mexico	peso	100 centavos
Micronesia	dollar	100 cents
Moldova	leu	
Monaco	franc	100 centimes
Mongolia	tugrik	100 mongo
Morocco	dirham	100 centimes
Mozambique	metical	100 centavos
Myanmar	kyat	100 pyas
Namibia	dollar	100 cents
Nauru	dollar	100 cents
Nepal	rupee	100 paisas
Netherlands*	guilder	100 cents
New Zealand	dollar	100 cents
Nicaragua	córdoba	100 centavos
Niger	franc	
Nigeria	naira	100 kobo
North Korea	won	100 chon
Norway	krone	100 øre
Oman	riyal	1000 baiza
Pakistan	rupee	100 paisas
Palau	dollar	100 cents
Panama	balboa	100 centesimos
Papua New Guinea	kina	100 toea
Paraguay	guarani	100 centimos
Peru	nuevo sol	100 centimos
Philippines	peso	100 centavos
Poland	zloty	100 groszy
Portugal*	escudo	100 centavos
Qatar	riyal	100 dirhams
Romania	leu	100 bani
Russia	ruble	100 kopeks
Rwanda	franc	100 centimes
St Kitts and Nevis	dollar	
St Lucia	dollar	
San Marino	lira	
St Vincent and the Grenadines	dollar	
Samoa	tala	100 sene

Country	Unit	Subunit
Sao Tome and Principe	dobra	100 centimos
Saudi Arabia	riyal	100 halalah
Senegal	franc	
Seychelles	rupee	100 cents
Sierra Leone	leone	100 cents
Singapore	dollar	100 cents
Slovakia	koruna	100 haliers
Slovenia	tolar	100 stotinas
Solomon Islands	dollar	100 cents
Somalia	shilling	100 cents
South Africa	rand	100 cents
South Korea	won	100 chon
Spain*	peseta	100 centimos
Sri Lanka	rupee	100 cents
Sudan	pound	100 piastres
Suriname	guilder	100 cents
Swaziland	lilangeni	100 cents
Sweden	krona	100 öre
Switzerland	franc	100 centimes
Syria	pound	100 piastres
Taiwan	dollar	100 cents
Tajikistan	ruble	100 tanga
Tanzania	shilling	100 cents
Thailand	baht	100 satang
Togo	franc	
Tonga	pa'anga	100 seniti
Trinidad and Tobago	dollar	100 cents
Tunisia	dinar	1000 millimes
Turkey	lira	100 kurus
Turkmenistan	manat	100 tenesi
Tuvalu	dollar	100 cents
Uganda	shilling	100 cents
Ukraine	hryvnia	
United Arab Emirates	dirham	100 fils
United Kingdom	pound	100 pence
United States	dollar	100 cents
Uruguay	peso	100 centesimos
Uzbekistan	soum	
Vanuatu	vatu	
Vatican City	lira	
Venezuela	bolivar	100 centimos
Vietnam	new dong	100 xu
Yemen	riyal	100 fils
Yugoslavia	new dinar	100 para
Zambia	kwacha	100 ngwee
Zimbabwe	dollar	100 cents

* Indicates member states of the European Union in which the Euro was introduced in 1999

curriculum /kə ríkyŏŏləm/ (*plural* **-la** /-lə/ *or* **-lums**) *n.* the subjects taught at an educational institution, or the elements taught in a particular subject [Early 19thC. From Latin, literally 'running, course', from *currere* 'to run' (source of English *current*).] —**curricular** *adj.*

curriculum vitae /-veé tī, -vī́ tee/ (*plural* **curricula vitae**) *n.* a summary of a person's educational qualifications, skills, and professional history [Early 20thC. From Latin, literally 'course of life'.]

currier /kúrri ər/ *n.* sb who dresses and finishes leather after it has been tanned [14thC. Via Old French *corier* from Latin *coriarius*, from *corium* 'leather'.]

currish /kúrish/ *adj.* having a very hostile or disagreeable disposition [15thC. Formed from CUR.] —**currishly** *adv.* —**currishness** *n.*

curry[1] /kúrri/ *n.* (*plural* **-ries**) (*often used before a noun*) **1. HIGHLY SPICED SAVOURY DISH** a dish containing meat, fish, or vegetables in a highly spiced sauce ○ *chicken curry* **2. SEASONING FOR CURRY** a mixture of spices in any of various forms, such as sauce, paste, or powder, used to prepare curry ○ *curry paste* ■ *vt.* (**-ries, -rying, -ried**) **COOK IN HIGHLY SPICED SAUCE** to cook meat, fish, or vegetables in a highly spiced sauce [Late 16thC. From Tamil *kari* 'sauce'.]

curry[2] /kúrri/ (**-ries, -rying, -ried**) *vt.* **1. GROOM** to groom a horse **2. PUT THROUGH FINISHING PROCESS** to make leather flexible and waterproof as the final stage in its processing [13thC. Via Old French *correier*, 'to arrange, prepare' from an assumed Vulgar Latin verb formed from Latin *con* 'with' and a prehistoric Germanic base that is also the ancestor of English *ready*.]

currycomb /kúrri kōm/ *n.* **COMB USED TO GROOM HORSES** a comb with metal or rubber teeth, used to groom horses ■ *vt.* (**-combs, -combing, -combed**) **GROOM WITH CURRYCOMB** to groom a horse with a currycomb [Late 16thC. From CURRY[2] + COMB.]

curry powder *n.* a mixture of finely ground spices, usually turmeric, cumin, coriander, chilli, and ginger, used to make curry

curse /kurss/ *n.* **1. SWEARWORD** a swearword, obscenity, or blasphemous oath **2. EVIL PRAYER** a malevolent appeal to a supernatural being for harm to come to sb or sth, or the harm that is thought to result from this **3. SOURCE OF HARM** a cause of unhappiness or harm ○ *the curse of poverty* **4. MENSTRUATION** menstruation or a menstrual period (*dated slang*) **5. RELIGIOUS BAN** an ecclesiastical pronouncement of censure or excommunication ■ *interj.* **CURSES USED AS OATH** used to express irritation or annoyance ■ *v.* (**curses, cursing, cursed** *or* **curst** /kurst/) **1.** *vi.* **SWEAR** to utter swearwords or obscenities **2.** *vt.* **SWEAR AT** to swear at sb **3.** *vt.* **WISH EVIL ON** to appeal malevolently to a supernatural being for harm to come to sb or sth **4.** *vt.* **CAUSE SUFFERING TO** to inflict sth unpleasant on sb ○ *cursed with a succession of mediocre assistants* [Old English *curs*, of unknown origin] —**curser** *n.*

cursed /kúrssid, kurst/ *adj.* **1. HAVING BEEN WISHED EVIL** afflicted with harm thought to result from a curse **2. WICKED OR HATEFUL** evil to the point of being despicable **3. ANNOYING OR FRUSTRATING** stubborn to the point of causing irritation or annoyance (*informal*) —**cursedly** /kúrssidli/ *adv.* —**cursedness** /kúrssidnəss/ *n.*

cursive /kúrssiv/ *adj.* **WRITTEN IN FLOWING STYLE** written in a flowing style with the letters joined together ■ *n.* **1. FLOWING SCRIPT** cursive writing **2. MANUSCRIPT WRITTEN IN FLOWING STYLE** a piece of cursive handwriting, especially an ancient manuscript **3.** PRINTING **TYPEFACE** a cursive typeface [Late 18thC. From medieval Latin *cursivus*, from Latin *currere* 'to run'.] —**cursively** *adv.* —**cursiveness** *n.*

cursor /kúrssər/ *n.* COMPUT **MARKER ON COMPUTER SCREEN** a moving marker on a computer screen, e.g. a flashing horizontal or vertical bar, that marks the point at which keyed characters will appear, be deleted, or be corrected ■ *vi.* COMPUT **MOVE CURSOR** to move the cursor in a particular direction on the screen of a computer or VDU ○ *As we cursor down, the hierarchy changes.* [14thC. From Latin (see CURSORY). Originally, 'runner, messenger'; later used to denote part of a scientific instrument which slides backwards and forwards, specifically the slide of a sliderule.]

cursorial /kur sáwri əl/ *adj.* ZOOL having a body or body parts that are particularly well-adapted for running [Mid-19thC. Formed from Latin *cursor* (see CURSORY).]

cursory /kúrssəri/ *adj.* done in a quick or superficial way [Early 17thC. From Latin *cursorius*, from *cursor* 'runner', from *currere* 'to run'. The underlying sense is 'running rapidly over sth'.] —**cursorily** *adv.* —**cursoriness** *n.*

curt /kurt/ *adj.* **1. RUDELY BRIEF** rude or abrupt **2. TERSE** using few words [14thC. From Latin *curtus* 'cut short'.] —**curtly** *adv.* —**curtness** *n.*

curtail /kur táyl/ (**-tails, -tailing, -tailed**) *vt.* to reduce the length or duration of sth [15thC. By folk etymology from CURTAL, by association with TAIL and probably also with French *tailler* 'to cut'.] —**curtailment** *n.*

curtail step *n.* a wider lowest step on some flights of stairs, often rounded at one or both ends

curtain /kúrt'n/ *n.* **1. CLOTH HUNG TO COVER STH** a piece of cloth hung at a window, in a doorway, or round a bed, usually for privacy or to exclude light or draughts **2. CLOTH AT FRONT OF STAGE** in a theatre, a hanging cloth that is raised and lowered at the front of the stage **3. BEGINNING OR END OF SHOW** the beginning or end of a performance, act, or scene, as marked by the raising or lowering of the curtain **4. BARRIER OR SCREEN** sth that acts as a barrier or screen to divide, protect, or conceal sth **5. STH RESEMBLING CURTAIN** sth that resembles a curtain in appearance ○ *a curtain of water* **6.** ARCHIT **WALL CONNECTING OTHER STRUCTURES** a length of wall, especially one that connects two towers or gates ■ *vt.* (**-tains, -taining, -tained**) **1. COVER OR DIVIDE WITH CURTAIN** to surround, separate, or conceal sth with a curtain **2. FIT WITH CURTAINS** to provide sth, especially a window, with curtains [13thC. Via Old French from Latin *cortina* 'cauldron', mistakenly rendering Greek *aulaia* 'curtain', perhaps from association of *aulaia* (formed from *aulē* 'court') with Latin *cohort-* 'court'.] ◇ **curtain raiser** any preliminary event

curtain call *n.* an appearance by actors, dancers, or singers at the front of the stage to receive the audience's applause at the end of a performance

curtain lecture *n.* a private reprimand given to a man by his wife (*archaic*) [From its originally being delivered within the privacy of drawn bed curtains]

curtain raiser *n.* **1. PRELIMINARY PERFORMANCE** a short performance put on immediately before the main performance **2. PRELIMINARY EVENT** a smaller or less important event that takes place before a bigger or more important one

curtain speech *n.* **1. TALK AFTER PLAY** a speech addressed to the audience by sb in front of the curtain after a play has ended **2. LAST SPEECH** the speech before the final curtain of an act or play

curtain wall *n.* **1. NON-BEARING WALL** an external wall that does not bear any of the load of the building it is attached to **2. LOW CASTLE WALL** a low wall outside a castle built for defence

curtal /kúrt'l/ *n.* an animal whose tail has been docked (*archaic*) [Early 16thC. From obsolete French *courtault*, from *court* 'short' + the pejorative suffix *-ault*.]

curtilage /kúrtəlij/ *n.* an enclosed area occupied by a dwelling, grounds, and outbuildings [14thC. From Old French *co(u)rtillage*, from *co(u)rtil* 'kitchen garden', literally 'small court', from *cort*.]

Curtin /kúrtin/, **John Joseph** (1885–1945) Australian statesman. He was an Australian Labor Party politician and prime minister of Australia (1941–45).

Curtiz /kúrtiz/, **Michael** (1888–1962) Hungarian-born US film director. He won an Oscar for *Casablanca* (1943) and directed over 125 Hollywood films.

curtsy /kúrtsi/, **curtsey** *vi.* (**-sies, -sying, -sied; -seys, -seying, -seyed**) **BEND KNEES IN RESPECT** to bend the knees, with one foot behind the other, as a gesture of respect. Women curtsy in formal situations where men bow, e.g. when acknowledging the applause of an audience after performing on stage, or when meeting royalty. ■ *n.* (*plural* **-sies;** *or* **-seys**) **WOMAN'S RESPECTFUL MOVEMENT** a movement made by a woman as a sign of respect for sb in which she bends her knees with one foot behind the other [Early 16thC. A variant of COURTESY.]

curule /kyŏŏr ool/ *adj.* in ancient Rome, having the status to sit on an official chair (**curule chair**) and the privileges associated with this status [Mid-16thC. From Latin *curulis*, from *currus* 'chariot', from *currere* 'to run' (see CURRENT); from the conveying of the chief Roman magistrate in a chariot.]

curule chair *n.* a folding chair with heavy legs and no back, used by high officials of ancient Rome

curvaceous /kur váyshəss/ *adj.* having an attractive body with rounded hips and breasts [Mid-20thC. The suffix -ACEOUS is mainly botanical, here used humorously.] —**curvaceously** *adv.* —**curvaceousness** *n.*

curvature /kúrvəchər/ *n.* **1. BEING CURVED** the quality of being curved **2. DEGREE OF CURVE** the degree of curving in a line or surface ○ *the slight curvature of the land* **3.** GEOM **RECIPROCAL OF RADIUS** the reciprocal of the radius of the circle that best matches a curve at a given point [15thC. From Latin *curvatura* 'bending', from *curvus* (see CURVE).]

curve /kurv/ *n.* **1. ROUNDED LINE** a line that bends smoothly and regularly from being straight or flat, like part of a circle or sphere **2. STH SHAPED IN A CURVE** sth with a smooth round shape, such as a rounded part of a woman's body or a bend in a road **3.** STATS **PLOTTED LINE** a line plotted on a graph from statistical data **4.** MATH **LINE REPRESENTING EQUATION** a line whose points are defined by an equation and whose coordinates are functions of an independent variable **5.** BASEBALL = **curve ball** ■ *v.* (**curves, curving, curved**) **1.** *vi.* **MOVE IN CURVE** to move or bend in a curve **2.** *vt.* **CAUSE TO CURVE** to make sth move or bend in a curve [15thC. From Latin *curvus* 'curved, crooked'. English adopted the word as an adjective, and it was not used as a noun until the late 17thC.] ◇ **ahead of the curve** forward-thinking and ahead of a trend or trends ◇ **behind the curve** reacting, or slow to react, to a trend or trends

curve ball *n.* in baseball, a ball that when pitched drifts to the left if thrown by a right-handed pitcher and to the right if thrown by a left-handed pitcher

curved /kurvd/ *adj.* with a rounded or bending shape

curvet /kur vét/ *n.* **HORSE'S LEAP** a leap by a horse in dressage in which its hind legs are raised just before the forelegs touch the ground ■ *vi.* (**-vets, -veting** *or* **-vetting, -veted** *or* **-vetted**) **PERFORM CURVET** to execute a curvet in dressage [Late 16thC. From Italian *corvetta*, literally 'small curve', from *corve*, from, ultimately, Latin *curvus* 'curved'.]

curvilinear /kúrvi línni ər/, **curvilineal** /kúrvi línni əl/ *adj.* **1. CURVED** being a curve or having a curved part or parts ○ *a curvilinear polygon* **2. MOVING IN CURVE** moving along a curved path or line ○ *The ball followed a curvilinear trajectory.* [Early 18thC. Modelled on RECTILINEAR.] —**curvilinearity** /kúrvilinni árrəti/ *n.* —**curvilinearly** /kúrvi línni ərli/ *adv.*

curvy /kúrvi/ (**-ier, -iest**) *adj.* **1. ROUNDED** with a rounded shape **2. WINDING** having many curves or bends

Curzon /kúrz'n/, **Clifford Michael, Sir** (1907–82) British concert pianist. His repertoire ranged from W. A. Mozart to Alan Rawsthorne. He also gave recitals with Benjamin Britten.

Curzon, George Nathaniel, Lord (1859–1925) British statesman. As Viceroy of India (1898–1905), he partitioned Bengal. He was Lord Privy Seal during World War I.

Cusack /kyŏŏss ak, kyŏŏz-/, **Cyril** (1910–93) South African-born Irish actor and stage director. He made his name at Dublin's Abbey Theatre (1932–45), toured with his own company (1946–61), acted with major British companies, and appeared in many films.

cuscus /kúss kuss/ *n.* a tree-dwelling nocturnal mammal inhabiting rainforests in northeastern Australia and New Guinea. Cuscuses have round heads, large eyes, large curved claws, and thick fur, and can grip with their tails. Genus: *Phalanger*. [Mid-17thC. Via French *couscous* or modern Latin *cuscus* from Dutch *koeskoes*, ultimately from a native word in New Guinea.]

cusec /kyŏŏ sek/ *n.* a dated unit of flow equal to one cubic foot per second [Early 20thC. Shortening of *cubic foot per second*.]

a at; aa father; aw all; ay day; air hair; ə about, edible, item, common, circus; e egg; ee eel; hw when; i it, happy; ī ice; 'l apple; 'm rhythm; 'n fashion; o odd; ō open; ŏŏ good; oo pool; ow owl; oy oil; th thin; th this; u up; ur urge;

CUSeeMe *n.* a computer program, developed at Cornell University, in Ithaca, New York, that enables users to engage in real-time video conferencing over the Internet

Cush /kŏosh/, **Kush** *n.* **1.** BIBLE **CANAAN'S BROTHER** in the Bible, the oldest son of Ham and brother of Canaan (Genesis 10:6) **2. ANCIENT AFRICAN REGION** a region of northeastern Africa thought to be where the descendants of Cush settled. It is roughly equivalent to modern Ethiopia, part of northern Sudan, and southern Egypt.

cushat /kúshət/ *n. Scotland* a wood pigeon [Old English *cuscute*, of unknown origin]

Cushing /kúshing/, **Peter** (1913–94) British actor. He was noted for his Baron Frankenstein and other roles in Hammer Studio's gothic horror films (1957–73).

Cushing's disease *n.* a form of Cushing's syndrome caused by excessive production of the hormone ACTH by the pituitary gland [Mid-20thC. Named after the US surgeon Harvey *Cushing* (1869–1939), who described the condition.]

Cushing's syndrome *n.* a condition caused by excessive production of corticosteroids by the adrenal cortex or pituitary gland and marked by obesity, muscular weakness, hypertension, striated skin, and fatigue [Mid-20thC. Named after Harvey Williams Cushing, who described the syndrome.]

cushion /kŏosh'n/ *n.* **1. SOFT FILLED BAG FOR SITTING ON** a fabric case filled with soft material, used to sit or lean on **2. SOFT PROTECTIVE PAD** a pad that is used for support, to rest against, to protect against damage, or as a shock absorber **3. STH SOFT AND YIELDING** sth that gives slightly when pressed ○ *a cushion of moss at the foot of the tree* **4. STH HELPFUL** sth that limits the effect of an unpleasant situation ○ *An unexpected legacy provided a cushion when her savings ran out.* **5.** CUE GAMES **BILLIARD TABLE RIM** the raised rim around the top of a billiard table that borders its playing surface **6.** = **air cushion 7.** SEW **LACEMAKING ACCESSORY** a pillow used to support the tools used in lacemaking **8.** ARCHIT **BOWL-SHAPED CAPITAL** a type of bowl-shaped capital with a square top ■ *vt.* **(-ions, -ioning, -ioned) 1. PROTECT AGAINST IMPACT** to protect sb or sth against the effects of physical impact ○ *A pile of sand cushioned his fall.* **2. REDUCE UNPLEASANT EFFECT OF** to lessen the effect of an unpleasant situation, especially one involving money ○ *a generous pension to cushion the blow of early retirement* **3. SUPPORT OR PLACE ON CUSHION** to support or rest sth on a cushion or other soft object **4. PAD** to pad sth with cushions or some other soft spongy material [14thC. Via French *coussin* from, ultimately, assumed Vulgar Latin *coxinum*, literally '(support for the) hip', from Latin *coxa* 'hip'.] —**cushiony** *adj.*

Cushitic /kŏo shíttik/ *n.* a branch of the Afro-Asiatic family of languages including about 30 languages spoken in areas of Ethiopia, Somalia, and Kenya [Early 20thC. Formed from CUSH.] —**Cushitic** *adj.*

cushy /kŏoshi/ **(-ier, -iest)** *adj.* providing a good salary, many perks, and little or no hard work (*informal*) ○ *a cushy job* [Early 20thC. Formed from Hindi *khūsh* 'pleasant'.] —**cushily** *adv.* —**cushiness** *n.*

cusk /kusk/ (*plural* **cusk** *or* **cusks**) *n. US* **1.** = **torsk 2.** = **burbot** [Early 17thC. Origin unknown.]

cusp /kusp/ *n.* **1.** ZODIAC **BORDER BETWEEN ZODIAC SIGNS** the border between two astrological star signs **2.** ASTRON **POINTED END OF CRESCENT MOON** either of the pointed ends of a crescent moon, or of any celestial body appearing with the same curved shape **3.** DENT **RIDGE ON MOLAR TOOTH** a ridge on the grinding surface of a molar tooth that helps in grinding and chewing food **4.** ANAT **FLAP OF VALVE** a triangular fold or flap of a valve in the heart or in lymph vessels that allows the flow of blood or lymph in one direction only **5.** BOT **POINTED END** a pointed end of a leaf or other plant part **6.** GEOM **POINT OF INTERSECTION** a point where two arcs or branches of a curve intersect and the two tangents to the curve coincide **7.** ARCHIT **POINTED PROJECTION IN GOTHIC ARCHITECTURE** a pointed projection formed by the intersection of two arcs, used especially in Gothic architecture [Late 16thC. From Latin *cuspis* 'point, spear, pointed end of anything', of unknown origin.] —**cusped** *adj.*

cuspid /kúspid/ *n.* DENT = **canine** [Mid-18thC. From Latin *cuspid-*, the stem of *cuspis* (see CUSP).]

cuspidate /kúspi dayt/ *adj.* **1.** ANAT **WITH CUSP** ending in or having a cusp or cusps **2.** BOT **POINTED** used to describe a leaf that ends in a sharp point [Late 17thC. From Latin *cuspidatus*, the past participle of *cuspidare* 'to make pointed', from *cuspid*, the stem of *cuspis* 'point' (source of English *cusp* and *bicuspid*).]

cuspidor /kúspi dawr/ *n. US* = **spittoon** [Mid-18thC. From Portuguese, formed from *cuspir* 'to spit', from Latin *conspuere*, from *spuere* 'to spit'.]

cuss /kuss/ *vti.* **(cusses, cussing, cussed) USE BAD LANGUAGE** to use vulgar and offensive language (*informal*) ■ *n.* (*informal*) **1. SB ANNOYING** sb with a particular, usually irritating trait ○ *an awkward cuss* **2. VULGAR OATH** an instance of vulgar or offensive language [Late 18thC. Colloquial variant of CURSE.]

cussed /kússid/ *adj.* (*informal*) **1. ANNOYING** causing annoyance and anger, especially by being uncooperative **2. CURSED** cursed [Mid-19thC. Variant of CURSED.] —**cussedly** *adv.* —**cussedness** *n.*

cussword /kúss wurd/ *n. US* a swearword (*informal*)

custard /kΙ *n.* **1. SWEET SAUCE** a sweet sauce made with eggs, milk, sugar, and a thickening agent, or with milk and custard powder **2. SWEET DISH** a cooked mixture of sugar, eggs, and milk [15thC. Originally 'open pie of meat or fruit', from Anglo-Norman *crustade*, from Old French *crouste* 'crust' (source of English *crust*).] —**custardy** *adj.*

WORD KEY: ORIGIN

A ***custard*** was originally an open pie of meat or fruit, and the reference in the name is to the pie's pastry shell. The filling included stock or milk, often thickened with eggs. By around 1600 the term indicated a dish in its own right made of eggs beaten into milk and cooked.

custard apple *n.* **1.** FOOD **HEART-SHAPED GREEN FRUIT** a large heart-shaped fruit with large black seeds and soft whitish flesh inside a green skin **2.** TREES **WEST INDIAN TREE** a small West Indian tree that bears custard apples. Latin name: *Annona reticulata.* **3.** TREES **FRUIT TREE RELATED TO CUSTARD APPLE** a fruit-bearing tree related to the custard apple tree, such as the papaw and sweetsop

custard pie *n.* a pie filled with custard, whipped cream, or a substance resembling either of these, that is traditionally thrown at people in slapstick comedy routines

custard powder *n.* a powder containing cornflour, colouring, and sugar, used as a basis for making custard

Custer /kústər/, **George Armstrong** (1839–76) US military leader. He was killed fighting against Native North Americans at the Battle of Little Bighorn (1876).

custodial /ku stṓdi əl/ *adj.* **1. INVOLVING DETENTION** involving or consisting of detention in a prison ○ *a custodial sentence* **2. RELATING TO LEGAL CUSTODY** relating to the legal custody of, and responsibility for, a child ○ *a custodial parent* **3. RELATING TO A CUSTODIAN** connected with the work of a custodian ■ *n.* FIN **SB THAT SAFEGUARDS INVESTORS' FUNDS** an organization such as a bank that holds in safekeeping the securities and other assets of an investment company or individual investor

custodian /ku stṓdi ən/ *n.* **1.** LAW **SB RESPONSIBLE FOR STH VALUABLE** sb responsible for holding or looking after valuable property on behalf of a company or another person **2.** FIN **SB THAT SAFEGUARDS INVESTORS' FUNDS** an organization such as a bank that holds in safekeeping the securities and other assets of an investment company or individual investor **3. UPHOLDER OF STH VALUABLE** sb who wants to protect and uphold sth seen as valuable and endangered, e.g. traditions or moral values **4. CARETAKER** sb who looks after a building **5. SB LOOKING AFTER VALUABLE COLLECTION** sb who looks after the contents of a museum, library, or other public institution [Late 18thC. Formed from *custody*, on the model of GUARDIAN.] —**custodianship** *n.*

custody /kústədi/ *n.* **1.** CRIMINOL **DETENTION** the state of being detained by the police or other authorities ○ *arrested and in custody* **2.** LAW **RIGHTS OVER CHILD** the legal right to look after a child **3. PROTECTION** the state of being held under the protection of sb or sth or being in sb's care [15thC. From Latin *custodia* 'guarding, keeping', from *custos* 'guardian', of unknown origin.]

custom /kústəm/ *n.* **1. TRADITION** sth that people always do or always do in a particular way by tradition **2. HABIT** the way sb normally or routinely behaves in a situation **3. REGULAR BUYING FROM A SHOP** the regular buying of goods from a particular shop or business ○ *The manager and staff would like to thank you for your custom.* US term **patronage 4. SHOP'S CUSTOMERS** all the customers of a particular shop or business **5. TRADITION LIKE LAW** a traditional practice that is so long-established and universal that it has acquired the force of law ○ *custom and practice* **6.** HIST **FEUDAL RENT** a tribute, rent, or other obligation paid by a feudal vassal to a lord ■ *adj.* **1. MADE TO ORDER** made or built to order **2. MAKING GOODS TO ORDER** making or selling custom-made goods ○ *a custom tailor* **3. CHANGED TO SUIT BETTER** altered in order to fit sb's requirements better [12thC. Via Old French *costume* 'habitual practice' (source of English *costume*) from the Latin stem *consuetudin-*, from *consuescere*, literally 'to accustom completely', from *suescere* 'to become accustomed'.]

WORD KEY: SYNONYMS

See Synonyms at ***habit***.

customable /kústəməb'l/ *adj.* liable to import or export duties

customary /kústəməri/ *adj.* **1. USUAL** conforming to what is usual or normal **2. TYPICAL** usual for sb or typical of sb's normal behaviour ○ *his customary good humour* **3.** LAW **BY CUSTOM** based on tradition and custom rather than written law ■ *n.* LAW **BODY OF CUSTOMARY PRACTICES** a listing of customary practices that have the force of law —**customarily** *adv.* —**customariness** *n.*

WORD KEY: SYNONYMS

See Synonyms at ***usual***.

custom-built *adj.* designed and built to meet the requirements of one individual customer —**custom-build** *vt.*

customer /kústəmər/ *n.* **1. BUYER OR BROWSER** a person or company who buys goods or services **2. TYPE OF PERSON** a person who interacts with others in a characteristic way (*informal*) ○ *a tough customer* [15thC. From the idea of 'customary business practice'.]

customer service *n.* a department of a business that deals with complaints from or disputes with customers, or that handles routine inquiries from callers ○ *a free customer-service line*

custom house /kústəm howss/, **customhouse, customs house** (*plural* **customs houses**) *n.* an office at a port where customs are collected and where ships are given permission to enter or leave

customize /kústə mīz/ **(-izes, -izing, -ized), customise (-ises, -ising, -ised)** *vt.* to alter sth in order to make it fit sb's requirements better ○ *She has customized the software to suit our needs.* —**customization** /kústə mī záysh'n/ *n.* —**customizer** /kústə mīzər/ *n.*

custom-made *adj.* designed and made to meet the requirements of one individual customer ○ *custom-made shoes*

customs /kústəmz/ *n.* (*takes a singular or plural verb*) **1. customs, Customs PLACE WHERE DUTIABLE GOODS ARE EXAMINED** the place where goods and baggage are examined on entering a country to see what duty is payable on them and to check for smuggled goods ○ *pass through customs* **2. customs, Customs GOVERNMENT AGENCY** the government department responsible for collecting taxes on imports and for prevention of illegal imports **3. DUTIES ON GOODS** taxes payable on imports and exports [14thC. From the term used for the 'customary tax' levied by a lord or local authority on goods bound for market.]

Customs and Excise *n.* the department of the United Kingdom government responsible for collecting customs and VAT and for preventing the import of illegal goods

customs house (*plural* **customs houses**) *n.* = **custom house**

customs union *n.* an association of countries that enjoy free trade among themselves and agree on tariffs for nonmembers

cut /kut/ *v.* (**cuts, cutting, cut**) **1.** *vti.* **DIVIDE STH WITH SHARP TOOL** to divide sth into pieces using a knife, scissors, or a similar sharp-edged tool **2.** *vt.* **SEVER USING SHARP TOOL** to sever sth or separate a part of sth using a sharp-edged tool such as a knife, scissors, or a saw ○ *cut a slice of bread* **3.** *vti.* **MAKE HOLE IN STH** to pierce sth or make a hole in sth using a sharp instrument **4.** *vi.* **BE SHARP** to be sharp enough to slice or pierce things easily ○ *These scissors won't cut.* **5.** *vt.* MED **INJURE WITH SHARP EDGE** to injure yourself or sb with sth sharp, usually enough to draw blood **6.** *vt.* **SHORTEN WITH SHARP TOOL** to make sth shorter by removing some of it with a sharp tool such as scissors ○ *I'm having my hair cut this afternoon.* **7.** *vt.* FASHION **FASHION A GARMENT** to shape fabric in a particular way in order to fashion a garment ○ *You can tell a jacket that has been nicely cut.* **8.** *vi.* **TAKE OR BE A SHORTCUT** to cross, travel, or make a line through or across an area, especially in order to save time ○ *This path cuts through the woods.* **9.** *vt.* **REDUCE A QUANTITY** to reduce an amount, e.g. of money or time, or remove an amount from sth ○ *The budget cannot be cut any further without reducing services.* **10.** *vt.* **SHORTEN BY EDITING** to make a film, text, play, broadcast, or speech shorter by removing parts of it, or remove a part to make it shorter **11.** *vti.* COMPUT **DELETE DATA** to delete data from one place, usually with the intention of inserting it in another **12.** *vti.* CINEMA, BROADCAST **EDIT FILM OR VIDEO** to edit a film or other work intended for performance or broadcast **13.** *vi.* CINEMA **STOP FILMING** to stop filming a particular scene (*usually used as a command*) **14.** *vi.* CINEMA **CHANGE SCENE** to switch suddenly from one scene to another when filming or showing a film **15.** *vt.* **STOP PROVIDING** to stop providing a service or supply of sth ○ *cut the food supply to the refugee camps* **16.** *vt.* **SWITCH OFF** to stop sth operating ○ *cut the engine* **17.** *vt.* **CASTRATE** to castrate or geld a male animal **18.** *vti.* CARDS **DIVIDE PACK OF CARDS** to divide a pack of cards in two, usually after shuffling them **19.** *vt.* RECORDING **MAKE A RECORDING** to make a recording of a song or group of songs ○ *The band cut 12 new tracks for the album.* **20.** *vti.* **REMOVE GRIME** to dissolve or clean sth such as dirt or grease from sth else **21.** *vti.* **INTERSECT** to cross sth or cross each other at a particular point ○ *The road cuts the river in three places.* **22.** *vi.* **CHANGE DIRECTION SHARPLY** to make a sharp change in direction ○ *You need to cut to the right here.* **23.** *vt.* **NOT ATTEND** to not go to a place you are supposed to be, such as school (*informal*) ○ *expelled for cutting classes* **24.** *vt.* DENT **GROW TEETH THROUGH GUMS** to produce a tooth through the surface of the gums ○ *The baby's cutting a tooth.* **25.** *vt.* **SNUB** to pay no attention to sb publicly or obviously, or stop a social relationship with sb **26.** *vti.* **UPSET SB** to hurt sb's feelings ○ *a cruel remark that cut me to the quick* **27.** *vt.* **DILUTE** to add a substance to another, especially to a drug or an alcoholic drink, usually in order to make it weaker or cheaper **28.** *vt.* **STOP DOING** to stop doing sth that is annoying sb ○ *Cut that racket!* **29.** *vt.* RACKET GAMES **HIT A BALL SO IT SPINS** to hit a ball in such a way that it spins as it flies through the air **30.** *vt.* CRICKET **HIT WITH BAT HORIZONTAL** to strike a cricket ball square on the offside with the bat more or less parallel to the ground ■ *n.* **1.** MED **WOUND IN SKIN** an injury made when sth sharp pierces the skin **2.** **INCISION** an incision made in sth with a knife or other sharp-edged tool **3.** **REDUCTION** a reduction in the amount of sth ○ *cuts in taxes and interest rates* **4.** HAIR **HAIRCUT** a haircut or hairstyle **5.** FASHION **GARMENT STYLE** the way of cutting a garment from fabric that determines its shape and fit **6.** **PRUNING OF TEXT** a removal of a section of a film, text, play, broadcast, or speech in order to make it shorter or improve it, or a section removed ○ *The editor advised me to make some cuts in the final chapter.* **7.** CINEMA **VERSION** a particular edited version of a film ○ *the director's cut of 'Blade Runner'* **8.** **SHARE** sb's share from an amount of money or sth else to be divided (*informal*) **9.** **STOPPING OF SUPPLY** a stopping of the supply of sth such as electricity or water ○ *power cuts* **10.** FOOD **PIECE OF MEAT FOR COOKING** a piece of meat cut in a standard way, ready to be cooked ○ *The chef only buys the more expensive cuts.* **11.** CRICKET **CRICKET STROKE** a cricket stroke square on the offside where the bat is swung more or less parallel to the gound **12.** RECORDING **SINGLE RECORDING** a track on a musical recording **13.** BASEBALL **SWING OF BASEBALL BAT** a swing of a baseball bat **14.** RACKET GAMES **SPIN ON A BALL** the spin given to a struck ball **15.** CARDS **DIVIDING OF PACK OF CARDS** the action of dividing a pack of cards in two **16.** **ITEMS FOR DRAWING LOTS** one of several pieces of paper or straws used to draw lots **17.** PRINTING **PRINTING DEVICE** a block for printing that has a design engraved, incised, or cut in relief on it (*often used in combination*) **18.** **HURTFUL WORDS** words or action intended to insult or hurt **19.** **SNUB** a snub (*archaic*) **20.** CIV ENG = **cutting 21.** **ALLEY** a narrow alley or passageway (*archaic*) **22.** CIV ENG **CANAL** a stretch of canal or a channel made for a river **23.** *Ireland* **LOOKS** sb's personal appearance (*informal*) **24.** *Ireland* **MESS** a messy condition ■ *adj.* **1.** MED **INJURED WITH STH SHARP** injured or damaged by sth sharp, usually enough to draw blood ○ *nursing a cut finger* **2.** **SEPARATED WITH KNIFE** separated or severed using a knife, scissors, or similar sharp tool **3.** **DRUNK** totally drunk (*informal*) **4.** BOT **DIVIDED** used to describe a leaf that is divided into segments [13thC. From assumed Old English *cytan*.] ◇ **a cut above** sb or sth superior to sb or sth ◇ **cut a deal** to negotiate an agreement ◇ **cut a fine** *or* **sorry figure** to look impressive *or* unimpressive ◇ **cut and run** to leave a place quickly to avoid being caught or detained ◇ **cut both ways** to have both advantages and disadvantages ◇ **cut it fine** to allow barely enough of sth, often time, for what has to be done ◇ **cut loose** *US, ANZ* to behave in an unrestrained and relatively uncontrolled way (*informal*) ◇ **cut sb dead** to ignore sb deliberately and completely ◇ **not cut it, not be able to cut it** to fall short of requirements or be unable to cope with a situation (*informal*) ○ *His usual excuses just don't cut it with me.*

cut across *vt.* to affect a widely differing group of people or things equally

cut along *vi.* go somewhere promptly (*informal dated; usually used as a command*)

cut back *v.* **1.** *vti.* **REDUCE STH** to reduce the amount of sth ○ *cut back on spending* **2.** *vt.* GARDENING **REMOVE TOP OF PLANT** to cut the tops or all of the stems or branches off a plant in order to remove dead growth or produce bushier growth ○ *cut back the roses*

cut down *v.* **1.** *vti.* **REDUCE STH** to consume, use, or do less of sth, especially because it is considered harmful ○ *The doctor says I have to cut down on fried foods.* **2.** *vt.* **FELL OR CLEAR AWAY PLANTS** to cut through the trunk or stem of a plant so that it can be harvested or removed **3.** *vt.* **KILL** to kill sb, especially suddenly or unexpectedly (*informal; usually passive*) **4.** *vt.* CLOTHES **MAKE CLOTHING SMALLER** to alter a piece of clothing so that it will fit sb smaller **5.** *vt.* CARS **REMODEL BY REMOVING EXTRAS** to remodel a car by removing unnecessary extras, especially to make it more suitable for racing

cut in *v.* **1.** *vti.* **INTERRUPT** to interrupt when sb is speaking **2.** *vi.* TRANSP **JOIN TRAFFIC DANGEROUSLY** to join a lane of traffic too close in front of another car so that it has to brake sharply **3.** *vti.* **JOIN MIDDLE OF QUEUE** to enter a queue of people by pushing in front of others who have been waiting **4.** *vi.* TECH **START TO OPERATE** to start working as part of a machine or electrical device **5.** *vt.* **ALLOW TO SHARE** to allow sb to have a share in sth, especially money ○ *cut us in on the profits* **6.** *vi.* DANCE **PARTNER SB ALREADY DANCING** to interrupt a couple who are dancing and take one of them as your own partner **7.** *vi.* CARDS **REPLACE A CARD PLAYER** to take the place of a person who has abandoned a card game **8.** *vt.* COOK **MIX FAT WITH FLOUR** to mix fat into flour using a metal blade in order to ensure that it is evenly distributed

cut off *v.* **1.** *vt.* **REMOVE PART OF STH** to remove sth that is part of sth else by cutting it **2.** *vt.* **STOP SUPPLY** to stop supplying sth ○ *cut off the electricity* **3.** *vt.* **ISOLATE** to separate a person, place, or group from normal communication or contact ○ *a town cut off by the blizzard* **4.** *vt.* **STOP SB TALKING** to interrupt what sb is saying and stop him or her talking ○ *cut him off in mid-sentence* **5.** *vt.* UTIL **DISCONNECT TELEPHONE CONNECTION** to disconnect people who are talking on the telephone **6.** *vt.* **DISINHERIT** to exclude sb from an inheritance ○ *They cut their son off without a penny.* **7.** *vt.* **BRING TO ABRUPT END** to bring sth to an abrupt end or sb to an early death (*often passive*) ○ *She was cut off in her prime.* **8.** *vi.* **CEASE ABRUPTLY** to come to an abrupt end ○ *The noise cut off suddenly.*

cut out *v.* **1.** *vt.* **REMOVE BY CUTTING** to remove part of sth using a cutting tool **2.** *vt.* **CUT SHAPE** to cut a shaped piece from a larger part or whole **3.** *vt.* **STOP DOING** to stop consuming, using, or doing sth, especially because it is considered harmful ○ *I've cut out all dairy products.* **4.** *vt.* **REMOVE PART FROM TEXT** to remove part of a text or broadcast **5.** *vt.* **OMIT** to exclude, eliminate, or omit sth ○ *I followed the recipe but cut out the walnuts.* **6.** *vt.* **EXCLUDE** to exclude or eliminate sb from a group or activity ○ *cut them out of future negotiations* **7.** *vt.* **DISINHERIT** to change a will so that sb will no longer inherit **8.** *vi.* **STOP WORKING** to stop functioning suddenly, especially to stop providing power ○ *The engine cut out.* **9.** *vt.* **STOP STH ANNOYING** to stop doing sth that is annoying sb (*informal; often used as a command*) ○ *Cut out the wisecracks.* **10.** *vt.* AGRIC **SEPARATE ANIMAL FROM HERD** to separate an animal or animals, particularly cows, from a herd **11.** *vi.* **END** to finish or come to an end (*informal*) ○ *The road cuts out at the creek.* ■ *adj.* **NATURALLY SUITED** naturally suited for a particular activity or profession ○ *I wasn't cut out to be a driving instructor.*

cut over *vt.* COMPUT to transfer existing data, functions, or users of a system to new facilities or equipment in a synchronized manner, to ensure continuity and minimize disruption

cut through *vt.* to deal with an obstacle in a way that reduces or eliminates it ○ *Can't we cut through the formalities?*

cut up *v.* **1.** *vt.* **CUT IN PIECES** to cut sth into pieces **2.** *vt.* MED **INJURE** to injure sb, especially enough to draw blood ○ *He was badly cut up after the fight and had to be taken to hospital.* **3.** *vt.* **UPSET** to upset and distress sb greatly (*informal; usually passive*) ○ *all cut up over his mother's death* **4.** *vt.* **ENDANGER TRAFFIC** to endanger fellow road users by driving suddenly in front of them or across their path **5.** *vi. US* **MISBEHAVE** to behave in a humorous and disruptive way (*slang*) ○ *cutting up in class* **6.** *vt.* **CRITICIZE** to criticize sb severely (*dated informal*) ◇ **cut up rough** to become very angry or unpleasant

cut-and-cover *adj.* used to describe a method of constructing a tunnel by digging a trench down from ground level and then roofing it

cut-and-dried *adj.* **1.** **DECIDED AND FIXED** clear, settled, and not needing changes or causing further problems **2.** **PREDICTABLE** obvious or conforming to what is expected ○ *a cut-and-dried press conference* [From the earlier sense 'prepared in advance, not spontaneous', from the idea of dried rather than fresh herbs offered for sale]

cut-and-paste *n.* COMPUT a facility of computers allowing data to be deleted in one place and inserted in another ○ *Use cut-and-paste to move that paragraph into the new document.*

cut-and-shut *n.* a car created by welding together the bodies of two cars that have been damaged in an accident [Late 20thC] —**cut-and-shut** *vt.*

cut and thrust *n.* **DRAMATIC EXCHANGES** fast, aggressive, or dramatic exchanges between people ○ *the cut and thrust of parliamentary debate* ■ *adj.* **FOR CUTTING AND POKING** used to describe swords designed for using both the blade and the tip

cutaneous /kyoō táyni əss/ *adj.* relating to the skin [Late 16thC. Formed from modern Latin *cutaneus*, from Latin *cutis* 'skin'.] —**cutaneously** *adv.*

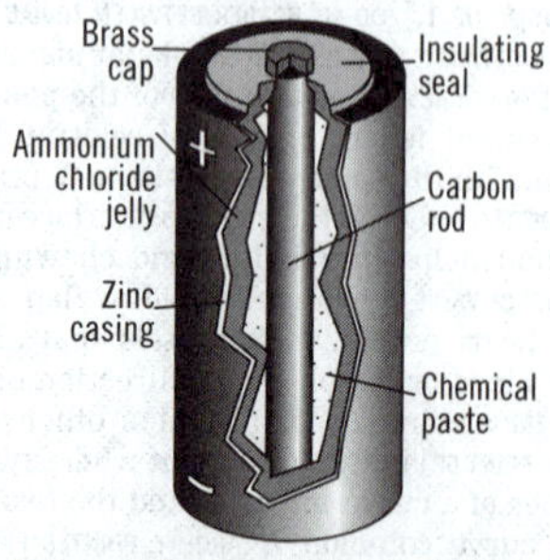

Cutaway: Cutaway view of a battery

cutaway /kúttə way/ *n.* **1.** **MODEL WITH INSIDE VIEW** a drawing or model of sth with part of its outside removed to give a view of the inside **2.** CINEMA, VIDEO

SECONDARY SHOT WITH CAMERA a cut to a camera shot of an action separate from the main action ■ adj. 1. GIVING INSIDE VIEW constructed or represented so as to give a view of the inside 2. CLOTHES CUT DIAGONALLY with the front cut diagonally away from the centre, e.g. in the part of a tailcoat below the waist

cutback /kút bak/ n. a reduction in the amount of sth ○ *cutbacks in public spending*

cutch /kuch/ n. = **catechu** [Mid-18thC. From Malay *kachu* 'astringent vegetable extract' (source of English *catechu*), ultimately of Dravidian origin.]

cute /kyoot/ (cuter, cutest) adj. 1. ATTRACTIVE IN CHILDLIKE WAY endearingly attractive in the way that some children and young animals are 2. US PHYSICALLY ATTRACTIVE young and physically attractive 3. PLEASING smaller than the usual size but nicely arranged or appointed ○ *an apartment with a cute little kitchen* 4. SHREWD sharply clever, shrewd, or wily (dated) [Early 18thC. Colloquial shortening of ACUTE.] —**cutely** adv. — **cuteness** n. ◇ **get cute (with sb)** to show insolence to sb

cutes plural of **cutis**

cutesy /kyóotsi/ (-sier, -siest) adj. too obviously attempting to be charming —**cutesiness** n.

cutey n. = **cutie**

cut glass n. glass with a decorative pattern cut into its surface

cut-glass adj. 1. MADE OF CUT GLASS made of glass with a decorative pattern cut into its surface 2. UPPER CLASS sounding extremely upper class ○ *a cut-glass accent*

Cuthbert /kúthbərt, St (630?–687) English missionary. He preached throughout Northumbria and lived as a hermit on Farne Island for over a decade. Many miracles are attributed to him.

Cuthbert, Betty (b. 1938) Australian sprinter. Her three gold medals at the 1956 Olympics and another at the 1964 Olympics gained her the nickname of 'the Golden Girl'.

cuticle /kyóotik'l/ n. 1. ANAT SKIN AT BASE OF NAILS an edge of hard skin at the base of a fingernail or toenail 2. ANAT = **epidermis** ANAT DEAD EPIDERMIS dead or hardened epidermis 4. BOT PROTECTIVE PLANT LAYER the thin outermost noncellular layer covering the aboveground parts of plants and helping to prevent water loss 5. ZOOL HARD COVERING OF INVERTEBRATES a hardened noncellular layer secreted by and covering the epidermis in many invertebrates [15thC. From Latin *cuticula*, literally 'little skin', from *cutis* 'skin'.] —**cuticular** /kyoo tíkyŏolər/ adj.

cutie /kyóoti/, **cutey** (plural -eys) n. an endearingly attractive person (informal)

cutin /kyóotin/ n. a waterproof mixture of waxy material containing derivatives of fatty acids, soaps, and other resinous substances that forms the protective layer (**cuticle**) of the aboveground parts of a plant [Mid-19thC. Coined from CUTIS + -IN.]

cut-in n. a camera shot that focuses in on a smaller portion of a scene already established

cutinize /kyóoti nīz/ (-izes, -izing, -ized), **cutinise** (-ises, -ising, -ised) vti. to deposit cutin in the cell walls of aboveground plant parts —**cutinization** /kyóoti nī záysh'n/ n.

cutis /kyóotiss/ (plural -tes /kyóo teez/) n. = **dermis** [Early 17thC. From Latin, 'skin'.]

cutlass /kútləss/ n. a short thrusting sword with a

Cutlass

flat and slightly curved blade used in the past, especially by sailors [Late 16thC. Via French *cutelas* 'large knife', from, ultimately, Latin *cultellus*, literally 'small knife', from *culter* 'knife, ploughshare' (see COULTER).]

cutlass fish n. US = **hairtail**

cutler /kútlər/ n. 1. MAKER OF CUTLERY sb who makes cutlery for a living 2. MAKER OF KNIVES sb whose job is to make, repair, or sell knives and other bladed tools (archaic) [14thC. From French *coutelier*, from *coutel* (see CUTLASS).]

cutlery /kútləri/ n. 1. EATING UTENSILS knives, forks, and spoons used for eating. US term **flatware** 2. TOOLS WITH BLADES knives and other instruments with a blade 3. JOB OF CUTLER the job of making knives and other bladed instruments (dated) [14thC. From French *coutellerie*, from *coutel* (see CUTLASS).]

cutlet /kútlət/ n. 1. CUT OF MEAT a piece of lamb or veal taken from the neck of the animal 2. CHOPPED FRIED FOOD a mixture of chopped meat, fish, nuts, vegetables, or other foods, made into a flat round shape, covered with breadcrumbs, and fried [Early 18thC. From French *côtelette*, literally 'little rib', from, ultimately, Latin *costa* 'rib' (source of English *coast*). The modern spelling reflects the idea of a 'small cut' (of meat).]

cut lunch n. ANZ a packed lunch (informal)

cutoff /kút of/ n. 1. LIMIT a limit or date, beyond which sth is stopped 2. END OF SUPPLY an end to the supply of sth ○ *a cutoff in oil imports* 3. ENG VALVE a valve that controls the flow of fluid or gas through a pipe 4. MUSIC BREAK IN MUSIC the end of a note, passage, or piece of music, especially when indicated by a sign from the conductor 5. MUSIC SIGNAL FROM MUSIC CONDUCTOR a sign given by a conductor to indicate a cutoff in the music 6. ELECTRON ENG ELECTRICAL THRESHOLD the value of voltage, frequency, or other variable that represents a minimum or maximum for effective operation 7. GEOG NEW RIVER CHANNEL a short channel cut by a river across a bend in the river, forming an oxbow lake ■ **cutoffs** npl. CLOTHES SHORTS MADE FROM TROUSERS shorts made by cutting off the legs of a pair of trousers, especially jeans

cutout /kút owt/ n. 1. SHAPE OF SB OR STH a two-dimensional shape of sb or sth usually made from stiff cardboard 2. STH CUT OUT sth that has been cut out from sth else 3. ELEC SAFETY DEVICE FOR ELECTRIC CIRCUIT a device that switches off an electric circuit or supply, e.g. to a machine, as a safety measure 4. UNORIGINAL PERSON an unoriginal or characterless person, or an unimaginative imitation of another person (disapproving) ○ *a cardboard cutout* 5. RECORDING OUTDATED AUDIO RECORDING a recording sold at a discount because it is out-of-date and supply exceeds demand

cutover /kút ōvər/ n. COMPUT the synchronized transfer of data, functions, or users to new facilities or equipment in order to ensure continuity and minimize disruption

cut-price adj. 1. CHEAPER THAN USUAL on sale for less than the standard price 2. SELLING CHEAP GOODS selling goods or services at a cheaper price than is standard ○ *a cut-price chemist*

cutpurse /kút purss/ n. a pickpocket (archaic)

CUTS /kuts/ abbr. Computer Users' Tape System

cut string n. = **bridgeboard**

cuttable /kúttəb'l/ adj. capable of being shortened or divided by cutting

Cuttack /k/ city in eastern Orissa State, in eastern India. It is situated at the head of a delta formed by the River Mahanadi on the Bay of Bengal. Population: 439,273 (1991).

cutter /kúttər/ n. 1. SHARP TOOL a tool used to cut through sth (often used in the plural) ○ *wire cutters* 2. SB WHO CUTS STH sb whose work involves cutting things, e.g. fabrics to be made into clothing 3. SB WHO REDUCES STH sb who makes sth shorter or reduces sth in amount 4. SAILING SINGLE-MASTED SAILING BOAT a single-masted sailing vessel on which the mast is positioned further aft than on a sloop 5. NAUT BOAT FOR TRANSPORTING PASSENGERS a ship's boat, powered by a motor or by oars that is used for transporting passengers and light cargo

cutthroat /kút thrōt/ adj. 1. WITH NO HOLDS BARRED aggressive and merciless in striving for supremacy 2. FOR 3 PLAYERS used to describe games for three players that are adapted from games for four partnered players ○ *cutthroat bridge* 3. MURDEROUS capable of murder or characteristic of a murderer (archaic) ■ n. 1. DANGEROUS PERSON a murderer or a very aggressive dangerous person 2. = **cutthroat razor** 3. (plural -throat or -throats) ZOOL = **cutthroat trout**

cutthroat razor n. a razor with a long blade and a handle that the blade can be folded into. US term **straight razor**

cutthroat trout n. a trout of western North America that resembles the rainbow trout but has reddish-orange markings on either side of the throat. Latin name: *Salmo clarkii*.

cutting /kútting/ n. 1. PART OF PLANT FOR PROPAGATION a piece taken from a stem, leaf, or root that will grow into a new whole plant 2. ARTICLE CUT FROM NEWSPAPER an article or photograph that has been cut out of a newspaper or magazine. US term **clipping** n. 3. CIV ENG OPEN TRENCH THROUGH HIGH GROUND an open trench cut through a hill or high ground to avoid a steep incline for a railway, road, or canal 4. EDITING PROCESS the process of editing a text, film, or recording 5. CINEMA CHANGING OF SHOTS IN FILM the technique of changing from one shot to another in the editing of a film ■ **cuttings** npl. PILE OF SMALL FRAGMENTS small fragments that are brought up during rock drilling or that accumulate during coal cutting ■ adj. 1. ABRASIVE AND HURTFUL sharply expressed and likely to upset sb's feelings ○ *a cutting remark* 2. VERY COLD piercingly cold ○ *a cutting wind* —**cuttingly** adv.

cutting board n. US = **chopping board**

cutting edge n. the most advanced and modern stage of sth (hyphenated when used before a noun)

cutting room n. a room where cinema film is edited, normally by hand and by being physically cut

cuttlebone /kútt'l bōn/ n. the white internal shell of a cuttlefish, used whole as a mineral supplement for caged birds and in powdered form for polishing [Late 16thC. *Cuttle* from Old English *cudele* 'cuttlefish' (see CUTTLEFISH).]

Cuttlefish

cuttlefish /kútt'l fish/ (plural -fish or -fishes) n. a marine mollusc that lives on the seabed and has ten arms, a flattened body, and an internal shell. Cuttlefish eject a dark inky fluid as a defensive mechanism. Genus: *Sepia*. [Late 16thC. *Cuttle* from Old English *cudele*; related to *cod(d)* 'bag' (see CODPIECE); so called because of the animal's shape.]

cutty /kútti/ (plural -ties) n. Northern Ireland a girl (informal) [Early 19thC. Formed from CUT. The original meaning was 'short woman'.]

cutty grass n. a New Zealand grass with sharp-edged leaves. Latin name: *Cyperus ustulatus*. [Formed from CUT]

cutty sark n. Scotland a woman's short shirt or undergarment, or a woman wearing one (archaic) [From obsolete *cutty* 'short' (formed from *cut*, the past participle of CUT) + SARK]

cutup /kút up/ n. US sb known for telling jokes, showing off, and doing pranks (informal)

cutwater /kút wawtər/ n. 1. NAUT FRONT OF SHIP'S PROW the foremost part of a ship's prow 2. CIV ENG BUFFER PART OF BRIDGE SUPPORT a pointed or wedge-shaped upstream face of a bridge pier at water level, designed to minimize the effects of moving water, ice floes, and debris

cutwork /kút wurk/ n. a form of openwork embroidery in which each part of the design is outlined in buttonhole stitch, then some parts of the fabric within the outlines are cut away

cutworm /kút wurm/ n. a nocturnal moth caterpillar that feeds on and eats through the base of young plant stems. Family: Noctuidae.

cuvée /koo váy/ n. a single batch of wine [Mid-19thC. From French, 'vatful', from *cuve* 'cask, vat', from Latin *cupa* (source of English *coop*).]

cuvette /kyoo vét/ n. a transparent tubular laboratory vessel or dish for holding a liquid [Late 17thC. From French, literally 'small cask', from *cuve* (see CUVÉE).]

Cuvier /kyoʻovi ay/, **Georges, Baron** (1769–1832) French zoologist and anatomist. He devised animal classification systems and established the fields of comparative anatomy and palaeontology. Full name **Georges Léopold Chrétien Frédéric Dagobert, Baron Cuvier**

Cuzco /kóoss kō, kóoss-/ city in southern Peru, and capital of Cuzco Department. It was the capital of the Inca empire until 1533. Population: 255,568 (1993).

CV abbr. **1. CV, cv** curriculum vitae **2.** MIL Cross of Valour

cv. abbr. BOT cultivar

CVA abbr. cerebrovascular accident

CVO abbr. Commander of the Royal Victorian Order

CVS abbr. **1.** Council of Voluntary Service **2.** chorionic villus sampling

CW abbr. continuous wave

CW abbr. **1.** continuous wave **2.** chemical warfare **3.** chemical weapons **4.** Morse code (*informal*)

cw. abbr. clockwise

CWA abbr. Aus Country Women's Association

Cwlth abbr. Commonwealth

cwm /koŏm, koom/ n. **1.** Wales VALLEY a valley (*often used in placenames*) **2.** = **cirque** [Mid-19thC. From Welsh, 'valley'.]

Cwmbran /koŏm braán/ town in Monmouthshire, Wales. It was designated as a new town in 1949. Population: 46,021 (1991).

CWO abbr. MIL Chief Warrant Officer

c.w.o., **CWO** abbr. cash with order

CWS abbr. Cooperative Wholesale Society

cwt abbr. hundredweight [Early 16thC. *C* is the roman numeral that denotes one hundred.]

CY abbr. calendar year

-cy suffix. **1.** condition, quality ○ *buoyancy* **2.** action ○ *advocacy* **3.** rank, office ○ *baronetcy* [Via Old French *-cie, -tie* from Latin *-cia, -tia* and Greek *-k(e)ia, -t(e)ia*]

cyan /sí ən, sí an/ n. a deep greenish-blue colour that, together with yellow and magenta, is one of the three primary colours used in printing and photographic processing [Late 19thC. From Greek *kuan(e)os* 'dark blue', of unknown origin.] —**cyan** adj.

cyan- prefix. = **cyano-** (used before vowels)

cyanamide /sí ánnə mīd/, **cyanamid** /-mid/ n. **1.** CAUSTIC COMPOUND a white crystalline caustic compound. Formula: CH_2N_2. **2.** = **calcium cyanamide**

cyanate /sí ə nayt/ n. a salt or ester of cyanic acid

cyanic /sī ánnik/ adj. COLOURS of a greenish-blue colour

cyanic acid n. a weak colourless unstable acid. Formula: HOCN.

cyanide /sí ə nīd/ n. **1.** POISONOUS SALT a poisonous salt of hydrocyanic acid that contains the radical CN **2.** = **potassium cyanide 3.** = **sodium cyanide** ■ vt. (**-nides, -niding, -nided**) **1.** METALL HARDEN METAL WITH CYANIDE to treat sth, e.g. a metal surface, with cyanide to increase its hardness **2.** MINING TREAT ORE WITH SODIUM CYANIDE to treat ore with a weak solution of sodium cyanide to remove gold or silver [Early 19thC. Coined from CYANOGEN + -IDE.] —**cyanidation** /sí ə nī dáysh'n/ n.

cyanide process n. MINING a process for extracting gold or silver from ore by treating the ore with a weak solution of sodium cyanide and recovering the metal particles from the resulting solution

cyanine /sí ə neen/ n. a chemical belonging to a group of blue dyes used to improve the sensitivity of photographic film to green, yellow, red, and infra-red light

cyanite /sí ə nīt/ n. = **kyanite**

cyano- prefix. **1.** blue ○ *cyanosis* **2.** cyanogen ○ *cyanic* **3.** cyanide ○ *cyanogen* [From Greek *kuanos* 'dark blue']

cyanoacrylate /sí ə nō ákri layt/ n. a liquid acrylate monomer belonging to a group with adhesive properties, used in industry and medicine

cyanobacteria /sí ənō bak teéri ə/ npl. bacteria belonging to a large group that have a photosynthetic pigment, carry out photosynthesis, and were classified in the past as blue-green algae. Family: Cyanophyta.

cyanocobalamin /sí ə nō kō bálləmin/ n. = **vitamin B₁₂**

cyanogen /sī ánnəjən/ n. **1.** POISONOUS GAS a flammable colourless poisonous gas used in organic synthesis. Formula: C_2N_2. **2.** CHEMICAL RADICAL a univalent radical found in cyanide compounds. Formula: CN. [Early 19thC. From French *cyanogène*, from, ultimately, Greek *kuan(e)os* 'dark blue'; from its being a constituent of Prussian blue.]

cyanogenesis /sí ə nō jénnississ/ n. the natural generation and release of hydrogen cyanide that occurs in some plants —**cyanogenic** adj. —**cyanogenetic** /sí ə nō ji néttik/ adj.

cyanohydrin /sí ə nō hídrin/ n. an organic compound containing both cyano and hydroxyl groups, usually linked to the same carbon atom

cyanosis /sí ə nóssiss/ n. a condition in which the skin and mucous membranes take on a bluish colour because there is not enough oxygen in the blood [Mid-19thC. Via modern Latin from Greek *kuanōsis* 'blueness', from *kuan(e)os* 'dark blue'.] —**cyanotic** /sí ə nóttik/ adj.

cyanotype /sī ánnə tīp/ n. = **blueprint**

Cybele /síbbəli/ n. the Phrygian goddess of nature. She was worshipped by the Romans as the Great Mother of the Gods.

cyber- prefix. computers and information systems ○ *cyberphobia* [From CYBERNETICS and CYBERSPACE]

cybercafé /síbər kaffay/ n. **1.** COFFEE HOUSE OFFERING INTERNET ACCESS a coffee house that provides patrons with computer terminals for browsing the Internet for a fee **2.** VIRTUAL MEETING PLACE a virtual gathering place on the Internet where people communicate using a chat program or by posting messages on a BBS

cybernate /síbər nayt/ (**-nates, -nating, -nated**) vt. to control a manufacturing process with a servomechanism or computer [Mid-20thC. Coined from CYBERNETICS.] —**cybernated** adj. —**cybernation** /síbər náysh'n/ n.

cybernetician /síbərni tísh'n/, **cyberneticist** /síbər néttissist/ n. a specialist in cybernetics

cybernetics /síbər néttiks/ n. (*takes a singular verb*) **1.** STUDY OF AUTOMATIC CONTROL SYSTEMS the science or study of communication in organisms, organic processes, and mechanical or electronic systems **2.** REPLICATION OF NATURAL SYSTEMS the replication or imitation of biological control systems with the use of technology [Mid-20thC. Formed from Greek *kubernētēs* 'steersman, governor', from *kubernan* 'to steer' (source of English *govern*). Coined by the US mathematician Norbert Wiener (1894–1964).] —**cybernetic** adj. —**cybernetical** adj. —**cybernetically** adv.

cyberphobia /síbər fóbi ə/ n. a pathological fear of computers and information technology

cyberpunk /síbər pungk/ n. a type of science fiction featuring characters living in a darkly frightening, futuristic world dominated by computer technology

cyberspace /síbər spayss/ n. **1.** IMAGINED PLACE WHERE ELECTRONIC DATA GOES the notional realm in which electronic information exists or is exchanged ○ *an e-mail message lost in cyberspace* **2.** VIRTUAL REALITY the imagined world of virtual reality

cybersurfer /síbər surfər/, **cybertraveller** /-travvələr/ n. COMPUT sb who spends a lot of time surfing the Internet (*slang*)

cyborg /sí bawrg/ n. a fictional being that is part human, part robot [Mid-20thC. Coined from CYBERNETICS + ORGANISM.]

cycad /sí kad/ n. a tropical tree that has a thick trunk, sharp pointed leaves like palm leaves, and cones. Order: Cycadales. [Mid-19thC. Via modern Latin *Cycad-*, the stem of *Cycas*, genus name, from Greek *kukas*, a miswriting of *koikas*, a plural form of *koix*, a type of palm tree.]

cycl- prefix. = **cyclo-**

Cyclades /síklə deez/ large group of Greek islands in the southern Aegean Sea. The largest island is Naxos and the chief town is Hermoupolis on the island of Syros. Population: 257,481 (1991). Area: 2,572 sq. km/993 sq. mi.

cyclamate /síklə mayt/ n. a salt or ester of cyclamic acid, especially sodium cyclamate, a compound approved for use in some countries as an artificial sweetener [Mid-20thC. Contraction of *cyclohexylsulphamate*, its chemical name.]

cyclamen /síkləmən/ n. **1.** FLOWERING PLANT a small plant with heart-shaped leaves that grows wild under trees in parts of Europe, and is also cultivated in gardens for its white or pink flowers. Bigger, large-flowered types are cultivated as houseplants. Genus: *Cyclamen*. **2.** COLOURS DEEP PINK a bright deep pink colour [Mid-16thC. Via Latin *cyclaminos* from Greek *kuklaminos*, which was probably formed from *kuklos* 'circle', with reference to the flower's bulbous root.]

cyclamic acid /síkləmik-/ n. a synthetic crystalline acid used to produce cyclamates and as a food additive. Formula: $C_6H_{13}NO_3S$. [Contraction of *cyclohexylsulfamic acid*]

cyclase /-klayz, -klayss/ n. an enzyme that aids the formation of hydrocarbon rings (**cyclization**) in a compound

cycle /sík'l/ n. **1.** REPEATED SEQUENCE OF EVENTS a sequence of events that is repeated again and again, especially a causal sequence **2.** TIME BETWEEN REPEATED EVENTS a period of time between repetitions of an event or phenomenon that occurs regularly ○ *a seven-year economic cycle* **3.** TECH COMPLETE PROCESS a complete process or sequence of processes in a machine or electronic device, or the time that this takes **4.** CYCLING BICYCLE a bicycle or tricycle **5.** BICYCLE RIDE a ride on a bicycle or tricycle ○ *go for a cycle* **6.** US MOTORCYCLES = **motorcycle 7.** PHYS ONE COMPLETE OSCILLATION one complete continuous change in the magnitude of an oscillating quantity or system that brings the system back to its original energy state ○ *running at 100 cycles per second* **8.** ARTS LINKED ARTWORKS a series of linked songs, poems, stories, plays, or operas that deal with the same story, events, or characters ○ *Wagner's Ring cycle* **9.** TIME LONG TIME a very long period of time **10.** ASTRON ORBIT one complete orbit of a celestial body **11.** COMPUT SET OF OPERATIONS a set of instructions completed as a unit by a computer, or the time that completion takes ■ v. (**-cles, -cling, -cled**) **1.** vi. RIDE BICYCLE to ride a bicycle or tricycle **2.** vti. GO THROUGH CYCLE to put sth through or go through a sequence of events ○ *programmed to cycle every hour* [14thC. Directly or via French from Latin *cyclus*, from Greek *kuklos* 'circle' (source also of English *cyclone* and *encyclopedia*).]

cycle lane n. a lane of a road for the use of cyclists

cycle of erosion n. the development of landforms from mountains to plains

cycle path n. a route or path for the use of cyclists. US term **bikeway**

cyclic /síklik/, **cyclical** /síklik'l/ adj. **1.** IN CYCLES occurring or repeated in cycles **2.** CHEM ARRANGED IN RING used to describe organic compounds that are composed of a closed ring of atoms **3.** MUSIC WITH RECURRENT THEME containing a recurrent theme or motif —**cyclicality** /síkli kálləti/ n. —**cyclically** /síklikli/ adv. —**cyclicity** /sik líssəti/ n.

cyclic AMP n. a cyclic form of adenosine monophosphate that is a constituent of plant and animal cells and is responsible for activating enzymes and enhancing hormonal processes within the cell

cyclisation n. = **cyclization**

cyclist /síklist/ n. sb who rides a bicycle or tricycle

cyclization /sī klīt záysh'n, síklīt-/, **cyclisation** n. the formation of one or more hydrocarbon rings in an organic compound

cyclo- prefix. 1. circle, cycle ○ cyclometer 2. cyclic compound ○ cyclopropane [From Greek kuklos (see CYCLE)]

cyclo-cross /síklō-/ n. the sport of racing bicycles across rough country, or a race of this kind [Coined from CYCLE + MOTOCROSS]

cyclogenesis /sī klō jénnəssiss, sí klō-/ n. the formation and development of a cyclone [Mid-20thC. Coined from CYCLONE + -GENESIS.]

Cyclohexane

cyclohexane /sī klō hék sayn, sí klō-/ n. a pungent flammable colourless liquid hydrocarbon derived from benzene and used as a paint thinner and solvent, and in organic synthesis. Formula: C_6H_{12}.

cycloheximide /sī klō héksə mīd/ n. a colourless crystalline compound derived from a bacterium and used as a fungicide in agriculture. Formula: $C_{15}H_{23}NO_4$.

cycloid /sī kloyd/ adj. 1. LIKE CIRCLE resembling a circle 2. ZOOL CIRCULAR used to describe fish scales that are circular and thin with smooth edges 3. PSYCHOL MOODY changing between states of depression and elation (technical) ■ n. 1. GEOM GEOMETRIC CURVE a geometric curve formed by a point on the circumference of a circle that rolls along a straight line 2. ZOOL FISH WITH CYCLOID SCALES a fish with scales that are circular and thin with smooth edges —**cycloidal** adj. —**cycloidally** adv.

cyclometer /sī klómmitər/ n. an instrument that counts the number of a times a wheel rotates and can, therefore, show the distance a vehicle has travelled —**cyclometric** /síklō méttrik/ adj. —**cyclometry** /sī klómmətri/ n.

cyclone /sī klōn/ n. 1. METEOROL LARGE-SCALE STORM SYSTEM a large-scale storm system with winds that rotate anticlockwise in the Northern Hemisphere and clockwise in the Southern Hemisphere about and towards a low pressure centre. ◊ anticyclone 2. METEOROL VIOLENT STORM a violent rotating windstorm or tornado 3. TECH ROTATING DEVICE a device that rotates rapidly, using centrifugal force to separate materials, e.g. particles from a gas [Mid-19thC. From Greek kuklōma 'wheel, serpentine coil', from kuklos 'circle' (see CYCLE).] —**cyclonic** /sī klónnik/ adj. —**cyclonical** adj. —**cyclonically** /-ikli/ adv.

Cyclone /síklōn/ tdmk. ANZ a trademark for a type of fence made from panels of wire grid

cyclopaedia n. = cyclopedia

cyclopean /sī klō peé ən, sī klópi ən/ adj. 1. MYTHOL LIKE THE CYCLOPS relating to or resembling the Cyclops 2. ARCHIT MADE OF BIG STONES constructed of massive irregular stone blocks 3. OPTICS DESCRIBING VISION used to describe the phenomenon of apparent unity in binocular vision

cyclopedia /sī klō peédi ə/, **cyclopaedia** n. = encyclopedia [Early 18thC. Shortening.] —**cyclopedic** adj. —**cyclopedist** n.

cyclopentane /sī klō pén tayn, sí klō pén tayn/ n. a colourless, flammable, pungent, liquid cycloalkane used as a paint remover, fuel, and solvent. Formula: C_5H_{10}.

cyclopes plural of **cyclops**

Cyclopes plural of **Cyclops**

cyclophosphamide /síklō fósfə mīd/ n. a toxic drug used to suppress the body's immune system in the treatment of leukaemia, lymphoma, Hodgkin's disease, and tumours

cycloplegia /sī klō pleéjə, sí klō-/ n. paralysis of the eye muscles that adjust the size of the lens and are used for focusing —**cycloplegic** adj.

Cyclopropane

cyclopropane /sī klō prṓ payn, sí klō-/ n. a flammable hydrocarbon gas used in medicine as a general anaesthetic and in organic synthesis. Formula: C_3H_6.

cyclops /sī klops/ (plural -clopes /sī klṓ peez/ or -clops) n. ZOOL an aquatic crustacean (copepod) with a single eye. Genus: Cyclops. [Mid-19thC. From modern Latin, genus name, from Latin (see CYCLOPS); from its characteristically centrally placed eye.]

Cyclops (plural -clopes or -clops or -clopses) n. MYTHOL one of a race of giants in Greek mythology who had only one eye in the middle of the forehead [Early 16thC. Via Latin from Greek Kuklōps, literally 'round-eyed', from kuklos 'circle' + ōps 'eye'.]

cyclorama /sī klō raámə/ n. 1. PAINTING CIRCULAR MURAL a picture painted all the way round the wall of a circular room 2. THEATRE STAGE BACKDROP a large concave curtain or wall behind a stage [Mid-19thC. Coined from CYCLO- on the model of PANORAMA.] —**cycloramic** /-rámmik/ adj.

cyclosis /sī klṓssiss/ n. the rotary flow of protoplasm within some cells and protozoans [Mid-19thC. From Greek kuklōsis 'encirclement'.]

cyclosporine /sī klō spáw reen, -spáwrin/, **cyclosporin** /-rin/ n. a drug obtained from a soil fungus and used to suppress the body's immune system in order to prevent tissue rejection in transplant surgery [Late 20thC. Coined from CYCLO- + polysporum, name of the fungus that produces the drug + -INE.]

cyclostome /síklə stōm, síklə-/ n. ZOOL a jawless fish with a circular sucking mouth and without true teeth. Lampreys and hagfish are cyclostomes. Class: Cyclostomata. [Mid-19thC. Coined from CYCLO- + Greek stoma 'mouth'.] —**cyclostomate** /sī klóstəmət/ adj. —**cyclostomatous** /síklō stómmətəss, -stṓmətəss, síklō-/ adj.

cyclostyle /sī klō stīl/ n. a now obsolete duplication method using perforated stencils, or the special pen used in this process. The pen had a tiny toothed perforating wheel and was used to create stencils on sheets of waxed paper. ◊ mimeograph [Late 19thC. Coined from CYCLO- + STYLE 'stylus'.] —**cyclostyled** adj.

cyclothymia /sī klō thími ə, síklō thími ə/ n. a psychiatric disorder in which the patient has frequent, relatively mild mood swings between elation and depression [Early 20thC. Coined from CYCLO- + Greek thumos 'mind, temper'.] —**cyclothymic** adj.

cyclotron /sī klō tron/ n. a circular particle accelerator in which charged particles are confined by a vertical magnetic field and accelerated by an alternating high-frequency applied voltage, in order to study the way they interact [Mid-20thC. Coined from CYCLO- + -TRON.]

cyder /sídər/ n. cider, especially of a brand made to a traditional recipe or by a traditional manufacturing process [16thC. Variant of CIDER.]

cygnet /sígnət/ n. a young or baby swan [15thC. Literally 'little swan', formed from Old French cigne 'swan' from, ultimately, Greek kuknos.]

Cygnus /sígnəss/ n. a constellation in the northern hemisphere between Lyra and Pegasus and containing the star Deneb

cyl. abbr. 1. cylinder 2. cylindrical

cylinder /síllindər/ n. 1. TUBE SHAPE a shape with straight sides and circular ends of equal size 2. GEOM GEOMETRICAL SOLID a solid bounded by two equal parallel circles and a curved surface formed by moving a straight line so that its ends lie on the circles 3. GEOM GEOMETRICAL SURFACE a surface formed by a straight line moving in a circle round and parallel to a fixed straight line, forming a hollow tube shape 4. TUBE-SHAPED OBJECT any object with straight sides and circular ends of equal size 5. LONG THIN CONTAINER a long thin sealed container, such as one in which gas is kept under pressure 6. HOUSEHOLD = hot-water tank 7. ENG CHAMBER FOR PISTON a chamber in an internal combustion engine or a pump within which a piston moves back and forth 8. PRINTING ROTATING PART OF PRINTING PRESS any one of the revolving drums of a printing press that produce or receive the impression 9. ARMS ROTATING PART OF REVOLVER the rotating part of a revolver, containing chambers into which cartridges are loaded 10. ARCHAEOL ANCIENT CYLINDRICAL CLAY OBJECT a hollow barrel-shaped object of baked clay covered in cuneiform script 11. HIST = cylinder seal [Late 16thC. Via Latin cylindrus from Greek kulindros 'roller', from kulindein 'to roll'.] —**cylindered** adj.

cylinder barrel n. a metal casting enclosing a cylinder of an internal combustion engine

cylinder block n. a metal casting enclosing the cylinders of an internal combustion engine. US term engine block

cylinder head n. the closed detachable end of a cylinder in an internal-combustion engine

cylinder press n. a printing press in which a flat bed holding the type matter moves under a revolving cylinder carrying the paper. = flat-bed press

cylinder seal n. an engraved cylindrical clay or stone object used in ancient times, especially in Mesopotamia, as a seal that was rolled in wet clay to leave an impression

cylindrical /si líndrik'l/, **cylindric** /-drik/ adj. with straight sides, circular ends of equal size, and constant circular cross section —**cylindricality** /si líndri kálləti/ n. —**cylindrically** /-kli/ adv.

cylindroid /si lín droyd/ n. GEOM a solid with straight sides and an elliptical cross section [Mid-17thC. Coined from CYLINDER + -OID.] —**cylindroid** adj.

cyma /símə/ (plural -mae /-mee/ or -mas) n. ARCHIT a projecting moulding with an S-shaped profile [Mid-16thC. Via modern Latin from Greek kuma 'billow, wave, wavy moulding' from kuein 'to become pregnant'.]

cymar /si maár/, **cimar, simar** n. a loose jacket or robe for women that originated in the Renaissance and was popular in the 17th and 18th centuries [Mid-17thC. Via French from Italian cimarra 'long robe'.]

cymatium /sī máyti əm/ (plural -a /-ti ə/) n. ARCHIT 1. = cyma n. 2. TOP CORNICE MOULDING the top moulding of a classical cornice [Mid-16thC. Via Latin, 'ogee', from Greek kumation, literally 'little cyma', from kuma (see CYMA).]

cymbal /símb'l/ n. a circular brass percussion instrument played with a stick or by striking two of them together [Pre-12thC. Directly or via Old French cymbale from Latin cymbalum, from Greek kumbalon, from kumbē 'bowl, drinking cup'.] —**cymbaleer** /símbə leér/ n. —**cymbaler** /símb'lər/ n. —**cymbalist** /símbəlist/ n.

cymbidium /sim bíddi əm/ (plural -a /-di ə/ or -ums) n. an orchid native to tropical Asia and Australia whose brightly coloured flowers have a boat-shaped lower petal. Genus: Cymbidium. [Early 19thC. From modern Latin, genus name, formed from Greek kumbē 'cup'; because of a depression resembling a cup in the flower lip.]

cyme /sīm/ n. a flower cluster in which each flower stem ends in a single flower and other flower stems form below and to the side [Early 18thC. Via French, 'summit, top', from Latin cyma (see CYMA).] —**cymiferous** /sī mífferəss/ adj.

cymene /símeen/ *n.* a colourless liquid benzene derivative, existing in three isomers, used as a solvent and in making resins. Formula: $(CH_3)_2CHC_6H_4CH_3$. [Mid-19thC. Coined from Greek *kummon* 'cumin' + -ENE.]

cymogene /síma jeen/ *n.* US a flammable gaseous mix of petroleum derivatives consisting mainly of butane and used to produce low temperatures [Mid-19thC. Coined from CYMENE + GENE.]

cymograph /síma graaf, -graf/ *n.* ARCHIT an instrument used to trace the outline of an architectural moulding [Mid-19thC. Coined from CYMA + -GRAPH.] —**cymographic** /síma gráffik/ *adj.*

cymoid /sí moyd/ *adj.* **1.** BOT LIKE CYME resembling a cyme **2.** ARCHIT LIKE CYMA resembling a cyma

cymophane /síma fayn/ *n.* chrysoberyl, especially an opalescent variety used as a gemstone [Early 19thC. From Greek *kuma* (see CYMA) + -*phanēs*, 'showing, shining'.]

cymose /sí môss, -môz, sī môss/, **cymous** /símass/ *adj.* relating to, like, or being a cyme —**cymosely** *adv.*

Cymric /kímmrik/ *n.* **1.** WELSH LANGUAGE the Welsh language (*dated*) ■ *adj.* OF WALES relating to or typical of Wales, or its people or culture [Mid-19thC. Formed from Welsh *Cymry* 'the Welsh', from *Cymru* 'Wales'.]

Cymru /kúmri, kóŏmri/ ♦ **Wales**

Cymry /kúmri, kóŏmri/ *npl.* **1.** BRYTHONIC CELTS members of the Brythonic branch of the Celtic peoples, which now comprises the Welsh, Cornish, and Breton peoples **2.** WELSH PEOPLE people who are born in or are citizens of Wales [Mid-19thC. See CYMRIC.]

Cynewulf /kínniwoŏlf/, **Cynwulf** /kín-/ (*fl.* 750?) English poet and probable author of four important Old English poems in the *Exeter Codex* and *Vercelli Codex*. He may have been a Northumbrian monk.

cynic /sínnik/ *n.* **1.** BELIEVER THAT PEOPLE ARE INSINCERE sb who believes that human actions are insincere and motivated by self-interest **2.** SB SARCASTIC sb sneering and sarcastic ■ *adj.* = **cynical** [Late 16thC. From CYNIC.]

Cynic /sínnik/ *n.* ANCIENT GREEK PHILOSOPHER a member of a group of ancient Greek philosophers who believed that virtue is the only good and that the only means of achieving it is self-control. The sect was founded by Antisthenes in the 4th century BC. ■ *adj.* RELATING TO CYNICS belonging to, characteristic of, or relating to the Cynics [Mid-16thC. Via Latin from Greek *Kunikos*.]

cynical /sínnik'l/, **cynic** /sínnik/ *adj.* **1.** DISTRUSTFUL OF HUMAN NATURE doubting or contemptuous of human nature or of the motives, goodness, or sincerity of others ○ *Many people have developed a cynical distrust of politicians.* **2.** SARCASTIC mocking, scornful, or sneering ○ *cynical remarks to cover up disappointment* **3.** IGNORING ACCEPTED STANDARDS OF BEHAVIOUR acting with disregard or contempt for accepted standards of behaviour ○ *a cynical disregard for the welfare of employees* —**cynically** *adv.* —**cynicalness** *n.*

cynicism /sínnisizzam/ *n.* **1.** CYNICAL QUALITY OR DISPOSITION cynical attitude, beliefs, character, or quality **2.** CYNICAL REMARK a cynical action, comment, or idea

Cynicism /sínnisizzam/ *n.* the beliefs or philosophy of the ancient Greek Cynics

cynipid /sínnipid/ *n.* a gall wasp (*technical*)

cynosure /sína syoor, sínna-, -zyoor/ *n.* **1.** CENTRE OF ATTENTION sb or sth that is the centre of admiration, attention, or attraction ○ *Guidebooks are the cynosure of the inexperienced traveller.* [Late 16thC. Via Latin *Cynosura* 'the constellation Ursa Minor, containing the Pole Star' (hence 'guiding star', hence 'centre of attention') from Greek *kunosoura*, literally 'dog's tail'.] —**cynosural** /sína syoorəl, sínna-, -zyoŏrəl/ *adj.*

Cynthia /sínthi ə/ *n.* **1.** MOON the Moon personified as a goddess (*literary*) **2.** = **Diana** [Late 16thC. Because the goddess Diana was said to have been born on Mount *Cynthus* in Delos.]

cypher *n.* = **cipher**

cypherpunk /sífər pungk/ *n.* an experienced computer user who is adept at breaking codes and entering secure computer systems [Late 20thC. Coined from CYPHER + PUNK on the model of CYBERPUNK.]

cy pres /sée práy/ *adv.* LAW as nearly as possible to the will or intention of a person whose wishes

cannot be executed literally [Via Anglo-Norman from French *si près* 'as near as']

Cypress

cypress[1] /síprəss/ *n.* **1.** CONIFER a coniferous evergreen tree, native to Eurasia and North America, that has hard wood and dark green leaves resembling scales. Genus: *Cupressus.* **2.** TREE OR SHRUB RESEMBLING CYPRESS a coniferous tree or shrub that is similar or related to the cypress, e.g. the bald or swamp cypress **3.** WOOD the hard wood of a cypress tree **4.** CYPRESS BRANCHES AS SYMBOL OF MOURNING the branches of a cypress tree used as a symbol of mourning [12thC. Via Old French *cipres* and late Latin *cypressus* from Greek *kuparissos.*]

cypress[2] /síprəss/, **cyprus** *n.* a fine silk or cotton fabric, usually black, used for mourning clothes [15thC. Via Anglo-Norman *cipres* from Old French *Cipre* 'Cyprus', because the fabric was originally brought from Cyprus.]

cypress pine *n.* a conifer native to Australia that is grown for timber. Genus: *Callitris.*

cypress vine *n.* a tropical American climbing plant related to morning glory that has leaves divided into many thin segments and scarlet, orange, or white tubular flowers. Latin name: *Ipomoea quamoclit.*

Cyprian /síppri ən/, St (200?–258) African-born Roman lawyer, bishop, and martyr. He was a Carthaginian bishop whose works, including *De Unitate Catholicae Ecclesiae* (251), influenced St Augustine. Full name **Thascius Caecilius Cyprianus**

cyprinid /si prínid, sípprinid/ (*plural* -**nid** *or* -**nids**) *n.* a freshwater fish of the family that includes the carps and minnows, typically with rounded scales, soft fins, and toothless jaws. Family: Cyprinidae. [Late 19thC. Formed from Latin *cyprinus* 'carp', from ultimately, Greek *kuprinos*.] —**cyprinid** *adj.*

cyprinodont /si prínnə dont, -prínə-/ *n.* a small freshwater fish of North America, Eurasia, and Africa with soft fins and a toothed jaw. Killifishes and guppies are cyprinodonts. Family: Cyprinodontidae. [Mid-19thC. Coined from CYPRINOID + -ODONT.] —**cyprinodont** *adj.*

cyprinoid /síppri noyd/ *n.* any fish belonging to a large group that includes the carp [Mid-19thC. Formed from Latin *cyprinus* 'carp', from ultimately, Greek *kuprinos.*] —**cyprinoid** *adj.*

Cypriot /síppri ət/, **Cypriote** *n.* SB FROM CYPRUS sb who was born or brought up in Cyprus or who has Cypriot citizenship ■ *adj.* **1.** OF CYPRUS relating to or typical of Cyprus, or its peoples or cultures **2.** OF THE LANGUAGES OF CYPRUS belonging or relating to the dialects of Greek and Turkish that are spoken on Cyprus [Late 16thC. From Greek *Kupriōtēs*, from *Kupros* 'Cyprus'.]

cyproheptadine /síprō héptə deen/ *n.* an antihistamine drug used especially to treat asthma, allergies, and skin disorders [Late 20thC. Coined from CYCLIC + PROPYL + HEPTA + PIPERIDINE.]

cyprus *n.* = **cypress**[2]

Cyprus /síprəss/ island republic in the eastern Mediterranean Sea. Since 1974, it has been partitioned between the Greek Cypriot south and the officially unrecognized Turkish Republic of Northern Cyprus. Language: Greek, Turkish. Currency: Cyprus pound. Capital: Nicosia. Population: 752,808 (1997). Area: 9,251 sq. km/3,572 sq. mi. Official name **Republic of Cyprus**

Cyprus

cypsela /sípsilə/ (*plural* -**lae** /-lee/) *n.* a small hard one-seeded fruit with an attached calyx that does not split during seed dispersal. Plants with cypselae include daisies and dandelions. Family: Compositae. [Late 19thC. Via modern Latin from Greek *kupselē* 'hollow vessel, chest'.]

Cyrano de Bergerac /sírrənō də búrzhə rak/, **Savinien** (1619–55) French poet and dramatist who fought in over 1,000 duels, often on account of insults relating to his extraordinarily long nose. His satirical accounts of journeys to the sun and the moon suggested the character of Gulliver to Swift.

Cyrenaic /sírə náy ik/ *adj.* **1.** PEOPLES OF CYRENE relating to or typical of the ancient Greek city of Cyrene in North Africa, or its people or culture **2.** PEOPLES OF CYRENAICA relating to or typical of the ancient Cyrenaica, or its people or culture **3.** PHILOS OF THE PHILOSOPHY OF PLEASURE relating to or advocating the doctrines of the school of philosophy founded in the 4th century BC by Aristippus of Cyrene, who believed pleasure is the sole or supreme good ■ *n.* **1.** PEOPLES SB FROM CYRENE sb who was born in or was a citizen of ancient Cyrene **2.** PHILOS BELIEVER IN CYRENAIC PHILOSOPHY an adherent of the Cyrenaic school of philosophy **3.** PHILOS HEDONIST sb who believes that pleasure is the sole good in life [Late 16thC. Via Latin *Cyrenaicus* from Greek *Kurēnaikos*, from *Kurēnē*, 'Cyrene'.] —**Cyrenaicism** /sírə náy issizzəm/ *n.*

Cyrenaica /sírə náy ikə, sírrə-/ historic region settled by the ancient Greeks that occupied the eastern half of Libya

Cyrene /sī réeni/ ancient Greek town in Libya and the original capital of Cyrenaica, founded in about 630 BC. The ruins are situated about 225 km/140 mi. from Benghazi in northeastern Libya.

Cyril /sírrəl/, St (827–869) Greek missionary. With his brother Methodius he brought Christianity to the Slavs of southeastern Europe, and is said to have devised the Cyrillic alphabet. Born **Constantine**

Cyrillic /si ríllik/ *adj.* OF ALPHABET USED IN SLAVONIC LANGUAGES relating or belonging to the old alphabet derived from Greek script and attributed to St Cyril, or a modified form used in modern Slavonic languages such as Bulgarian and Russian. The Cyrillic alphabet is also used in the non-Slavonic languages of some republics of the former Soviet Union. ■ *n.* SLAVONIC ALPHABET the Cyrillic alphabet [Early 19thC. Named after ST CYRIL.]

cyst /sist/ *n.* **1.** ANAT ABNORMAL SPHERICAL SWELLING a closed, usually spherical, membranous sac that develops abnormally in human or other animal tissue and contains fluid or semisolid material. Some types of cyst form when glands are blocked, and most cysts are benign. **2.** ANAT HOLLOW ORGAN OR CAVITY a thin-walled bladder, sac, or vesicle in an animal **3.** BOT, FUNGI RESTING SPORE a spore that is not undergoing cell division, in some algae and fungi **4.** ZOOL PROTECTIVE SAC ENCLOSING ORGANISM a sac or capsule that encloses and protects some organisms in a dormant or larval stage **5.** ZOOL PROTECTIVE COVERING AROUND PARASITE a protective covering around a parasite, produced by a host or by the parasite itself **6.** BOT AIR-FILLED CAVITY IN SEAWEEDS a small air-filled cavity resembling a bladder that occurs in some seaweeds, e.g. the bladderwrack [Early 18thC. Via late Latin *cystis* from Greek *kustis* 'bladder, cyst'.]

cyst- *prefix.* = **cysto-** (*used before vowels*)

cystectomy /si stéktəmi/ (*plural* **-mies**) *n.* **1.** OPERATION TO REMOVE CYST surgical removal of a cyst **2.** OPERATION TO REMOVE BLADDER surgical removal of the urinary bladder

Cysteine

cysteine /sísti een, sístayn/ *n.* a crystalline sulphur-containing amino acid that is converted to cystine during metabolism. Formula: $C_2H_7NO_2S$. [Late 19thC. Coined from CYSTINE + -*eine*, a variant of - EIN.]

cystic /sístik/ *adj.* **1.** RELATING TO CYST used to describe a cyst or material that forms, contains, or is enclosed in a cyst **2.** CONTAINING CYST consisting of or containing a cyst or cysts **3.** WITHIN CYST enclosed within a cyst **4.** RELATING TO BLADDER relating to a bladder, especially the urinary bladder

cystic duct *n.* the duct of the gall bladder that joins the bile duct from the liver to form the common bile duct

cysticercus /sísti súrkəss/ (*plural* **-ci** /-sī/) *n.* the larva of some tapeworms that consists of a folded inverted head encapsulated in a fluid-filled sac. It is found in the body tissues of infested people and animals. [Mid-19thC. From modern Latin *cysticercus*, from Greek *kustis* 'bladder' (see CYST) + *kerkos* 'tail'.]

cystic fibrosis /-fī bróssiss/ *n.* a hereditary disease starting in infancy that affects various glands and results in secretion of thick mucus that blocks internal passages, including those of the lungs, causing respiratory infections. The pancreas is also affected, resulting in a deficiency of digestive enzymes and impaired nutrition.

cystine /sís teen/ *n.* a crystalline amino acid found in many proteins, especially keratin. Formula: $C_6H_{12}N_2O_4S_2$. [Mid-19thC. Coined from Greek *kustis* 'bladder'+-IN.]

cystinuria /sísti nyoóri ə/ *n.* the excessive excretion of cystine in the urine and the formation of cystine stones in the kidney, characteristic of an inherited disorder of the metabolism

cystitis /si stítiss/ *n.* inflammation of the urinary bladder, often caused by infection

cysto- *prefix.* hollow structure, sac, cyst ○ *cystocarp* [Via modern Latin *cystis* 'bladder' from Greek *kustis* (see CYST)]

cystocarp /sístə kaarp/ *n.* the reproductive body of red algae produced after fertilization and consisting of a mass of asexual spores borne on filaments

cystocoele /sístə seel/ *n.* a hernia of the urinary bladder that protrudes through the vaginal wall

cystography /si stóggrəfi/ *n.* X-ray examination of the urinary bladder after the introduction of a liquid that is partially opaque to X-rays

cystoid /sís toyd/ *adj.* LIKE A CYST resembling a cyst ■ *n.* STRUCTURE RESEMBLING CYST a structure or mass of tissue that resembles a cyst but lacks an enclosing capsule

cystolith /sístə lith/ *n.* **1.** BOT MINERAL DEPOSIT IN PLANT CELLS a hard mineral deposit, usually of calcium carbonate, that occurs in the epidermal cells of some plants, e.g. figs or stinging nettles **2.** MED BLADDER STONE a stone that occurs in the bladder

cystoscope /sístə skōp/ *n.* a narrow tubular instrument that is passed through the urethra to examine the interior of the urethra and the urinary bladder —**cystoscopic** /sístə skóppik/ *adj.* —**cystoscopy** /si stóskəpi/ *n.*

cystostomy /si stóttəmi/ (*plural* **-mies**) *n.* the surgical construction of an opening into the urinary bladder to permit the removal of stones

cyt- *prefix.* = cyto- (*used before vowels*)

cytaster /sī tástər, sī tastər/ *n.* = aster *n.* 2 [Late 19thC. Coined from CYTO- + ASTER.]

-cyte *suffix.* cell ○ *phagocyte* [Via modern Latin -*cyta* from Greek *kutos* 'hollow vessel']

Cytherea /síthə reé ə/ *n.* = Aphrodite

Cytherean /síthə reé ən/ *adj.* **1.** OF CYTHEREA relating to Cytherea **2.** OF VENUS relating to the planet Venus

cytidine /sítti deen/ *n.* a compound (**nucleoside**) formed from cytosine and ribose. Formula: $C_9H_{13}N_3O_5$. [Early 20thC. Coined from CYTO- + -IDINE.]

cytidylic acid /sítti díllik-/ *n.* a nucleotide derived from cytosine and found in DNA and RNA. Formula: $C_9H_{14}N_3O_8P$. [Mid-20thC. Coined from CYTIDINE + -YL + -IC.]

cyto- *prefix.* cell ○ *cytotoxin* [From Greek *kutos* 'hollow vessel'. Ultimately from an Indo-European word meaning 'thing that hides', which is also the ancestor of English *hide* and *cuticle*.]

cytochalasin /sítō kə láyzin/ *n.* a substance derived from fungi that inhibits the formation of microscopic filaments within living cells, thereby interfering with various cell activities such as the cleavage of cytoplasm following nuclear division. Cytochalasins are used in cell biology to investigate various phenomena, such as cytoplasmic movement and cell motility. [Mid-20thC. Coined from CYTO- + Greek *khalasis* 'dislocation'.]

cytochemistry /sítō kémmistri/ *n.* a branch of biochemistry dealing with the chemistry of the cells of organisms —**cytochemical** *adj.* —**cytochemically** *adv.*

cytochrome /sítō krōm/ *n.* a compound containing protein and iron that plays a role in cell respiration

cytochrome oxidase *n.* an enzyme containing iron and porphyrin that is important in cell respiration

cytogenesis /sítō jénnəssiss/ *n.* the origin, development, and variation of cells

cytogenetics /sítō jə néttiks/ *n.* the study of the relationship between inheritance and the structure and function of cell components (*takes a singular verb*) —**cytogenetic** *adj.* —**cytogenetically** *adv.* —**cytogeneticist** *n.*

cytogeny /sī tójjəni/ *n.* = cytogenesis

cytokine /sítō kīn/ *n.* a protein secreted by cells of the lymph system that affects the activity of other cells and is important in controlling inflammatory responses. Interleukins and interferons are cytokines. [Mid-20thC. Coined from CYTO- + kinein 'to move'.]

cytokinesis /sítō kī néessiss, -ki-/ *n.* division of the cytoplasm of a cell during mitosis or meiosis —**cytokinetic** /sítō kī néttik, -ki-/ *adj.*

cytokinin /sítō kínin/ *n.* a plant hormone that regulates cell division and growth. Kinetin and zeatin are cytokinins.

cytology /sī tólləji/ *n.* **1.** STUDY OF CELLS a branch of biology dealing with the study of cells, especially their structures and functions **2.** MED EXAMINATION OF CELLS the examination of cells obtained from body tissue or fluids, especially to establish if they are cancerous —**cytologic** /sítə lójjik/ *adj.* —**cytological** /-lójjik'l/ *adj.* —**cytologically** /-lójjikli/ *adv.* —**cytologist** /sī tólləjist/ *n.*

cytolysin /sī tólləssin/ *n.* a substance that can destroy or dissolve cells [Early 20thC. Coined from CYTOLYSIS + -IN.]

cytolysis /sī tólləssiss/ *n.* the destruction or dissolution of cells, e.g. by the immune system —**cytolytic** /sítō líttik/ *adj.*

cytomegalic /sítō mə gállik/ *adj.* characterized by, producing, or relating to enlarged cells [Mid-20thC. Coined from CYTO- + MEGALO- + -IC.]

cytomegalic inclusion disease *n.* a serious disease of newborn babies affecting the brain, liver, kidneys, and lungs. It is caused by cytomegalovirus infection of pregnant mothers and leads to enlargement of the affected cells.

cytomegalovirus /sítō méggəlō vīrəss/ *n.* a virus that causes enlargement of epithelial cells, usually resulting in mild infections. It causes more serious disorders in AIDS patients and in newborn babies. [Mid-20thC. Coined from CYTO- + MEGALO- + VIRUS.]

cytopathogenic /sítō pathə jénnik/, **cytopathic** /-páthik/ *adj.* relating to or causing damage or disease to cells [Mid-20thC. Coined from CYTO- + PATHOGENIC.] —**cytopathogenicity** /sítō pathəjə níssəti/ *n.*

cytopathology /sítō pə thólləji/ (*plural* **-gies**) *n.* **1.** PATHOLOGY OF CELL DISEASE a branch of pathology dealing with cell disease and damage **2.** FEATURES OF DISEASED CELL the set of features or conditions associated with a diseased cell or cells

cytopathy /sī tóppəthi/ *n.* deterioration or disease in a living cell

cytopharynx /sítō fárringks/ (*plural* **-pharynges** /-fə rín jeez/ or **-pharynxes**) *n.* a tube in some protozoans, extending from the cytoplasm into the endoplasm

cytophotometer /sítō fə tómmitər/ *n.* an instrument that utilizes the variations in light intensity produced by stained cell cytoplasm to identify and locate chemical compounds within cells —**cytophotometric** /sítō fōtō méttrik/ *adj.* —**cytophotometrically** /-méttrikli/ *adv.* —**cytophotometry** /sítō fə tómmitri/ *n.*

cytoplasm /sítō plazəm/ *n.* the complex of chemical compounds and structures within a plant or animal cell excluding the nucleus. Cytoplasm contains the cytosol, organelles, vesicles, and cytoskeleton. —**cytoplasmic** /sítō plázmik/ *adj.* —**cytoplasmically** /-plázmikli/ *adv.*

cytoplasmic inheritance *n.* the inheritance of genes from the female parent that are not in the nucleus but in organelles such as mitochondria that are found in the cytoplasm. This type of inheritance is not controlled by Mendel's laws.

cytoplast /sítō plaast, -plast/ *n.* a plant or animal cell that has had the nucleus removed —**cytoplastic** /sítō plástik/ *adj.*

cytosine /sítə seen/ *n.* a component of nucleic acids that pairs with guanine to carry hereditary information in DNA and RNA in cells. Chemically, it is a pyrimidine base. Formula: $C_4H_5N_3O$. Symbol **C** [Late 19thC. Coined from CYTO- + -OSE^1 + -INE.]

cytoskeleton /sítō skéllitən/ *n.* the internal network of protein filaments and microtubules in an animal or plant cell that controls the cell's shape and movement —**cytoskeletal** *adj.*

cytosol /sítə sol/ *n.* the fluid component of a cell's cytoplasm excluding organelles and other structures —**cytosolic** /sítə sóllik/ *adj.*

cytosome /sítəsōm/ *n.* the cytoplasm in a cell, excluding the nucleus

cytostatic /sítə státtik/ *adj.* STOPPING CELL GROWTH suppressing cell growth and multiplication ■ *n.* CYTOSTATIC AGENT a cytostatic agent —**cytostatically** *adv.*

cytotaxis /sítō táksiss/ *n.* the movement of cells or cell masses in relation to one another

cytotaxonomy /sítō tak sónnəmi/ *n.* the classification of organisms according to cell structure, especially the number, structure, and shape of chromosomes —**cytotaxonomic** /sítō taksə nómmik/ *adj.* —**cytotaxonomically** /-nómmikli/ *adv.* —**cytotaxonomist** /-tak sónnəmist/ *n.*

cytotechnologist /sítō tek nólləjist/ *n.* sb trained to prepare cell samples and identify abnormalities —**cytotechnology** *n.*

cytotoxic /sítō tóksik/ *adj.* **1.** PREVENTING CELL DIVISION used to describe a drug that prevents cell division, often used in cancer treatment **2.** BIOL KILLING CELLS used to describe a type of cell in the immune system that destroys other cells —**cytotoxicity** /sítō tok síssəti/ *n.*

cytotoxic T cell *n.* a killer cell (*technical*)

cytotoxin /sítō tóksin/ *n.* a substance, e.g. an antibody, that has a toxic effect on living cells

cytotropic /sítō tróppik/ *adj.* used to describe motile cells that are mutually attracted to each other

cytotropism /sítō trópizzəm/ *n.* the movement or turning of cells or cell masses towards or away from one another

czar /zaar, tsaar/ *n.* HIST = **tsar** [Mid-16thC. Via Russian *tsar'* from Old Slavic *cēsarĭ*, ultimately (perhaps via Germanic) from Latin *Caesar* (source of English *Kaiser* and *caesarean*).] —**czardom** *n.* —**czarism** *n.* —**czarist** *adj., n.*

czardas /chaárdash/, **csardas** *n.* **1.** HUNGARIAN DANCE a Hungarian dance composed of a slow section followed by a faster one **2.** HUNGARIAN DANCE MUSIC a piece of music composed for a czardas [Mid-19thC. From Hungarian *csárdás*, from *csárda* 'inn'.]

czarevitch *n.* = **tsarevitch**

czarevna *n.* = **tsarevna**

czarina *n.* = **tsarina**

czaritza *n.* = **tsarina**

Czech /chek/ *n.* **1.** SB FROM CZECH REPUBLIC sb who was born or brought up in, or is a citizen of the Czech Republic **2.** SB FROM CZECHOSLOVAKIA sb who was born or brought up in, or who was a citizen of the former Czechoslovakia **3.** OFFICIAL LANGUAGE OF CZECH REPUBLIC the official language of the Czech Republic, belonging to the West Slavonic group of Indo-European languages. About 10 million people speak Czech. [Early 19thC. Via Polish from Czech *Čech*.] —**Czech** *adj.*

Czechoslovak /chékō slóvak/ *n.* sb who was born or brought up in, or who was a citizen of the former Czechoslovakia [Early 20thC. Back-formation from CZECHOSLOVAKIA.] —**Czechoslovak** *adj.* —**Czechoslovakian** /chékə slə váki ən/ *n., adj.*

Czechoslovakia /chékəslə vaáki ə, -vák-, chékō slō váki ə/ former country in eastern Europe that was divided into the Czech Republic and the Slovak Republic, or Slovakia, on January 1, 1993

Czech Republic /chék-/ republic created in 1993 when the former Czechoslovakia was divided into the Czech Republic and the Slovak Republic, or Slovakia. Language: Czech. Currency: Czech koruna. Capital: Prague. Population: 10,298,324 (1997). Area: 78,864 sq. km/30,450 sq. mi.

Czerny /chúrni/, **Karl** (1791–1857) Austrian pianist and composer. He was a pupil of Ludwig van Beethoven

Czech Republic

and the teacher of Franz Liszt. Of his many compositions, his teaching studies for the piano are best known.

Częstochowa /chéNstə khốvə, chénstə kốvə/ city in south-central Poland that contains the Jasna Góra monastery. It is situated about 64 km/40 mi. north of Katowice. Population: 259,500 (1995).

Dd

d[1] /dee/ (*plural* **d's**), **D** (*plural* **D's** *or* **Ds**) *n*. **1.** LING **4TH LETTER OF ENGLISH ALPHABET** the fourth letter of the English alphabet **2.** MUSIC **2ND NOTE OF SCALE IN C** the second note of a scale in C major **3.** MUSIC **STH THAT PRODUCES A D** a string, key, or pipe tuned to produce the note D **4.** MUSIC **SCALE BEGINNING ON D** a scale or key that starts on the note D **5.** MUSIC **WRITTEN SYMBOL OF D** a graphic representation of the tone of D **6.** LING **PRINTED OR WRITTEN D OR d** a representation of the letter D or d in written or printed form **7.** PHON **SOUND REPRESENTED BY D OR d** a speech sound represented by the letter D or d **8.** **4TH ITEM** the fourth item in a series **9.** **STH D-SHAPED** sth shaped like a letter D **10.** EDUC **GRADE INDICATING POOR QUALITY** a grade or mark indicating that a student's work is of poor quality **11.** SPORTS **SEMICIRCLE ROUND HOCKEY GOAL** in hockey, the semicircle surrounding the goal from which an attacker may try to score

d[2] *symbol*. **1.** deci- **2.** PHYS relative density **3.** PHYS deuteron **4.** PHYS down (*used of quark flavours*) **5.** the fourth vertical row of squares from the left on a chessboard

'd /d/ *contr*. **1.** DID did ○ *Where'd she get that hat?* **2.** HAD had ○ *We'd already finished supper.* **3.** SHOULD OR WOULD should or would ○ *I'd like to stop at the shop.*

D[1], **d** *n*. the Roman numeral for 500

D[2] *symbol*. **1.** PHYS dispersion *or* drag **2.** MATH the first derivative of a function **4.** deuterium

D[3] *abbr*. **1.** diameter **2.** drive (*used on gear levers of automatic transmissions*)

d. *abbr*. **1.** ZOOL dam **2.** date **3.** daughter **4.** day **5.** degree **6.** departs **7.** depth **8.** diameter **9.** died **10.** dollar **11.** drachma **12.** denarius (*used of old-style currency in Great Britain before 1971*) **13.** denarii (*used of old-style currency in Great Britain before 1971*)

D. *abbr*. **1.** December **2.** Department **3.** Deus **4.** D., d. dinar **5.** OPTICS dioptre **6.** Director **7.** JUD-CHR Dominus **8.** Don **9.** Duchess **10.** Duke

da *symbol*. deca-

DA[1] *abbr*. **1.** COMM deed of arrangement **2.** ARMS delayed action **3.** district attorney

DA *n*. a man's hairstyle popular in the 1950s in which the hair is slicked back and drawn into a point at the back of the neck to look like a duck's tail (*informal*) Full form **duck's arse**

Da. *abbr*. Danish

d.a. *abbr*. **1.** deposit account **2.** documents against acceptance

D/A *abbr*. **1.** COMM days after acceptance **2.** COMM delivery on acceptance **3.** FIN deposit account **4.** COMPUT digital-to-analogue **5.** COMM documents against acceptance

daal *n*. FOOD = **dahl**

dab[1] /dab/ *vti*. (**dabs**, **dabbing**, **dabbed**) **1.** TAP GENTLY to pat or touch sth lightly or gently ○ *She dabbed the tears from her eyes.* **2.** APPLY GENTLY to apply a substance using a quick light tapping action ○ *The nurse dabbed some ointment on the cut.* ■ *n*. **1.** SMALL QUANTITY a small quantity, especially of a moist or soft substance ○ *a dab of butter* **2.** GENTLE TAP a light or gentle tap, e.g. with the hand or a soft material **3.** CRIMINOL FINGERPRINT a fingerprint, especially of a suspected criminal (*slang; often used in the plural*) [13thC. Thought to suggest the action. The modern

meaning, 'to pat gently', evolved from 'to strike a blow with a weapon' through 'to strike lightly'.]

dab[2] /dab/ (*plural* **dabs** *or* **dab**) *n*. a small brown European flatfish eaten as food. Latin name: *Limanda limanda*. [15thC. Origin unknown.]

dab[3] /dab/ *n*. = **dab hand** (*informal*) [Late 17thC. Origin uncertain: perhaps from DAB[1] with the meaning, 'person who has a deft touch'.]

dabber /dábbər/ *n*. a pad used by engravers and printers to apply ink or colour

dabble /dább'l/ (**-bles**, **-bling**, **-bled**) *v*. **1.** *vi*. SPLASH to paddle, play, or splash in water **2.** *vt*. DIP to wet sth by dipping it in a liquid ○ *We sat by the pool, dabbling our feet in the water.* **3.** *vt*. SPLASH WITH LIQUID to daub, splash, or spatter sb or sth with a liquid **4.** *vi*. BECOME INVOLVED SUPERFICIALLY to have a casual or superficial interest in sth ○ *He dabbled in local politics for a few years.* **5.** *vi*. ZOOL MOVE UNDER WATER FOR FOOD to move the bill to the bottom of shallow water in order to reach food (*refers to ducks*) [Mid-16thC. Origin uncertain: probably from Dutch *dabbelen*, literally 'to keep tapping', from *dabben* 'to tap'.]

dabbler /dább'lər/ *n*. sb whose involvement with sth is superficial rather than serious

dabchick /dáb chik/ *n*. a small bird of the grebe family. Family: Podicipedidae.

dab hand *n*. a person with a special talent in some activity (*informal*) [See DAB[3]]

daboia /də bóyə/ *n*. a colourful adder of Southeast Asia. Latin name: *Vipera russelii*. [Late 19thC. From Hindi *daboyā*, literally 'lurker', from *dabnā* 'to lurk'.]

dabster /dábstər/ *n*. sb with a special talent in some activity (*regional informal*)

da capo /daa ka'apō/ *adv*. MUSIC to be played or sung again from the beginning of the passage or piece (*used as a musical direction*) ◊ **dal segno** [Early 18thC. From Italian, literally 'from the head'.] —**da capo** *adj*.

Dacca = **Dhaka**

dace /dayss/ (*plural* **dace** *or* **daces**) *n*. **1.** SMALL EUROPEAN FISH a small European freshwater fish with a slim olive-green body. Latin name: *Leuciscus leuciscus*. **2.** N AMERICAN FRESHWATER FISH a small freshwater fish of North America. Family: Cyprinidae. [15thC. From Old French *dars*, 'dace, dart'. Because of its darting motion in the water.]

dacha /dáchə/, **datcha** *n*. a cottage or house in the suburbs or countryside in Russia [Mid-19thC. From Russian, literally 'grant of land'.]

Dachau /dákow, dákh-/ site of a World War II Nazi concentration camp (1939–45) in Bavaria, about 16 km/10 mi. northwest of Munich, southwestern Germany. It is now a memorial to those who died there.

dachshund /dáksənd, dásh-, -hŏond/ *n*. a small dog of a breed that has a long body, short legs, and drooping ears [Late 19thC. From German, literally 'badger dog'. Because the breed was originally developed to hunt badgers.]

dacoit /də kóyt/, **dakoit** *n*. a member of a gang of armed robbers in India and Myanmar (Burma), especially in the past [Late 18thC. From Hindi *dakait*, from *dākā*, 'gang robbery'.]

dacoity /də kóyti/ (*plural* **-ies**), **dakoity** (*plural* **-ies**) *n*. robbery by a gang of armed robbers in India or

Dachshund

Myanmar (Burma), especially in the past [Early 19thC. From Hindi *dakaitī*.]

dactyl /dáktil/ *n*. **1.** dactyl, dactylic POETRY METRICAL FOOT OF THREE SYLLABLES a metrical foot consisting of one long syllable followed by two short syllables in classical verse, or one stressed syllable followed by two unstressed syllables in modern verse **2.** ZOOL FINGER OR TOE a finger, toe, or related body part [14thC. Via Latin *dactylus* from Greek *daktulos*, 'finger'. *Metrical foot* from the length of the three joints in a finger.]

dactyl- *prefix*. = **dactylo-** (*used before vowels*)

-dactyl *suffix*. having fingers or toes of a particular kind or number ○ *polydactyl* [From Greek *daktulos* 'finger'] —**dactylous** *suffix*.

dactylic /dak tíllik/ *adj*. OF OR CONTAINING DACTYLS relating to a dactyl or containing dactyls ■ *n*. = **dactyl** *n*. 1 —**dactylically** *adv*.

dactylic hexameter *n*. a line of verse consisting of six feet, the fifth of which is a dactyl, the first four dactyls or spondees, and the sixth a spondee or trochee. It is the metre of Greek and Roman epic and some other poetry.

dactylo- *prefix*. finger, toe ○ *dactylology* [From Greek *daktulos* 'finger' (see -DACTYL)]

dactylography /dákti lóggrəfi/ *n*. the scientific examination of fingerprints for identification purposes [Coined from Greek *daktulos* 'finger' + -OGRAPHY] —**dactylographic** /dak tíllə gráffik/ *adj*.

dactylology /dákti lólləji/ *n*. communication using signs made with the hands, often used by the deaf [Coined from Greek *daktulos* 'finger' + -O- + -LOGY]

dad /dad/ *n*. used especially by a child or as a term of address, to refer to a father (*informal*) [Mid-16thC. Origin uncertain: perhaps an imitation of young children's speech.]

Dada /da'a daa/, **dada, Dadaism** /-izəm/, **dadaism** *n*. a European artistic and literary movement of the early 20th century founded on a rejection of traditional artistic and cultural values. Its work was characterized by anarchy, irrationality, and irreverence. [Early 20thC. From French, literally 'hobbyhorse'. Said to have been chosen because of its meaningless sound and childish connotations.] —**Dadaist** *n*., *adj*.

daddy /dáddi/ (*plural* **-dies**) *n*. (*informal*) **1.** FATHER used especially by a young child or as a term of address, to refer to a father **2.** US, Can, Aus SUPREME EXAMPLE the earliest or finest example of sth ○ *He was a fine trumpet player, the daddy of them all.* [Early 16thC. Formed from DAD.]

daddy longlegs /-lóng legz/ (plural **daddy longlegs**) n. **1.** LONG-LEGGED FLY a long-legged, slender-winged fly. Family: Tipulidae. US term **crane fly 2.** US LONG-LEGGED ARACHNID a long-legged arachnid with an oval body. Order: Opiliones.

daddy track n. US a career route taken by a man whereby he reduces his chances of career advancement by working flexitime or fewer hours in order to look after a child or children (informal) ◊ **mommy track**

dado /dáydō/ n. (plural **-does** or **-dos**) **1.** = **die**² n. 5 **2.** LOWER PART OF INTERIOR WALL the lower part of an interior wall, decorated or faced in a different manner from the upper part, usually with panels, paint, or wallpaper **3.** RECTANGULAR GROOVE IN BOARD a rectangular groove cut into a board so that a matching piece can be fitted into it to form a joint ▪ vt. (**-does, -doing, -doed**) **1.** PROVIDE WITH DADO to fit a wall with a dado **2.** CUT DADO IN STH to cut a rectangular groove in sth so that a matching piece can be fitted into it to form a joint **3.** INSERT INTO DADO to insert sth into a rectangular groove to form a joint [Mid-17thC. From Italian, literally 'die, cube'.]

daedal /deéd'l/, **dedal** adj. (literary) **1.** INTRICATE complex or intricate **2.** INGENIOUS skilful or ingenious [Late 16thC. Via Latin dædalus from Greek daidalos, 'skilful'; as noun, Daidalos 'Daedalus', literally 'skilful worker'.]

Daedalus /deéd ələs/ n. in Greek mythology, a craftsman and inventor who built a labyrinth on the island of Crete to house a half-bull, half-man monster (**Minotaur**). He made wings so that he could escape from Crete with his son (**Icarus**), but his son perished during the flight. —**Daedalian** /di dáyli ən/ adj.

daemon /deémən, dī́-, dáy-/, **daimon** /dī́mōn/ n. **1.** MYTHOL DEMIGOD mythological being that is part-god and part-human **2.** MYTHOL GUARDIAN SPIRIT a guardian spirit **3.** DEMON a demon (archaic) [Variant of DEMON] —**daemonic** /di mónnik/ adj.

daff¹ /daf/ n. a daffodil (informal) [Early 20thC. Shortening.]

daff² /daf/ (**daffs, daffing, daffed**) vt. (archaic) **1.** THRUST ASIDE to thrust sb or sth aside **2.** PUT SB OR STH OFF to put sb or sth off, e.g. with an excuse [Late 16thC. Variant of DOFF.]

Daffodil

daffodil /dáffədil/ n. **1.** SPRINGTIME PLANT WITH TRUMPET-SHAPED FLOWERS a European plant that has yellow trumpet-shaped flowers and long slender leaves growing from a bulb. Latin name: Narcissus pseudonarcissus. **2.** BRIGHT YELLOW COLOUR a brilliant yellow colour, like that of a daffodil ▪ adj. BRIGHT YELLOW of a brilliant yellow colour, like a daffodil [Mid-16thC. From medieval Latin affodilus, 'asphodel'. The modern spelling may have been influenced by Dutch de affodil, 'the daffodil'.]

daffy /dáffi/ (**-fier, -fiest**) adj. silly in an amusing or harmless way (informal) [Late 19thC. Blend of DAFT and -Y.] —**daffily** adv. —**daffiness** n.

daft /daaft/ adj. (informal) **1.** NOT SENSIBLE obviously silly or unreasonable ◊ a daft idea . **2.** NOT HEALTHY IN MIND psychiatrically disordered **3.** VERY ENTHUSIASTIC extremely enthusiastic about sth **4.** Scotland THOUGHTLESS OR FRIVOLOUS thoughtless or frivolous [Old English gedæfte, 'fitting', from a prehistoric Germanic word meaning 'fit, suitable'. The modern meaning, 'silly', evolved from 'suitable' via 'compliant, gentle'.] —**daftly** adv. —**daftness** n.

Dafydd ap Gwilym /dávvith ap gwíllim/ (1320?–80?) Welsh poet. Considered one of the greatest medieval poets, he wrote poems about love and the beauty of nature.

dag¹ /dag/ n. **1.** = **daglock** n. **2.** DECORATIVE EDGING a decorative edging on garments, used especially in medieval times ▪ vti. (**dags, dagging, dagged**) REMOVE SOILED WOOL FROM SHEEP to cut off dung-coated wool from a sheep's coat [Early 17thC. Shortening of DAGLOCK.]

dag² /dag/ n. ANZ (informal) **1.** SLOVENLY PERSON a dirty or untidy person **2.** SURPRISING TURN OF EVENTS a surprising thing or interesting turn of events ◊ I got a real job. What a dag! **3.** UNFASHIONABLE PERSON an unfashionable person **4.** UNUSUAL CHARACTER an odd person, often with amusing characteristics or unconventional habits [Early 20thC. From DAG¹.]

Dagan /dáagən/ n. the god of the Earth in Babylonian mythology

Dagestanian /daágə stáyni ən/ n. **1.** LANG CAUCASIAN LANGUAGE GROUP a group of North Caucasian languages spoken in Dagestan, an autonomous republic in southwestern Russia. The main member of the group is Avar. No more than a few thousand people speak a Dagestanian language. **2.** PEOPLES SB FROM DAGESTAN sb who was born or brought up in Dagestan, or who is a citizen of Dagestan [Formed from Dagestan in southwestern Russia] —**Dagestanian** adj.

dagga /dúkhə, daágə/ n. S Africa Indian hemp smoked as a narcotic [Late 17thC. Via Afrikaans from Nama daxa.]

dagger /dággər/ n. **1.** SHORT POINTED KNIFE a short pointed knife used as a weapon **2.** IRRITATION sth that torments or wounds sb ◊ Such cutting words were a dagger to my heart. **3.** PRINTING SIGN USED AS REFERENCE MARK a sign (†) that is used as a reference mark, especially to a footnote ▪ vt. (**-gers, -gering, -gered**) **1.** MARK STH WITH REFERENCE SIGN to mark sth with a dagger sign **2.** STAB to stab sb or sth with a dagger (archaic) [14thC. Origin uncertain: perhaps formed from obsolete dag 'to stab'; or ultimately from Old Provençal or Old Italian daga, literally 'Dacian knife', ultimately from Latin Dacia (see DACIA).] ◊ **be at daggers drawn** to be hostile and ready to fight with sb ◊ **look daggers at sb** to look at sb in an angry or hostile way

daggy /dággi/ (**-gier, -giest**) adj. ANZ (informal) **1.** UN-FASHIONABLE used to describe clothing or behaviour that is considered unfashionable, especially by young people **2.** MESSY untidy, dirty, and unpleasant ◊ Her bedsit was so daggy. **3.** unusual or unconventional [Early 20thC. Formed from DAG².]

daglock /dág lok/ n. a lock of dung-coated wool on a sheep's hindquarters [Early 17thC. From earlier dag, 'hanging part of sth' + LOCK, 'piece of hair'.]

dago /dáygō/ (plural **-gos** or **-goes**), **Dago** (plural **-gos** or **-goes**) n. a highly offensive term that refers to sb of Italian, Spanish, or Portuguese birth or descent (taboo insult) [Mid-19thC. Variant of the name Diego.]

dagoba /daágəbə/ n. a dome-shaped shrine that contains Buddhist relics [Early 19thC. Via Sinhalese dāgaba from Pali dhātu-gabbha, 'receptacle for relics'.]

Dagon /dáygən/ n. the chief god in Philistine mythology, often depicted as half man and half fish

Daguerre /da gáir/, **Louis Jacques** (1789–1851) French painter and inventor. Originally a scene painter, he became a pioneer photographer who, working initially with French physicist Joseph Niepce (1829), perfected the daguerreotype process (1837). Full name **Louis Jacques Mandé Daguerre**

daguerreotype /də gérrō tīp/ n. **1.** EARLY PHOTOGRAPHIC PROCESS an early photographic process in which an image was produced on a light-sensitive silver or silver-coated plate and developed in mercury vapour **2.** EARLY PHOTOGRAPH a photograph produced by the daguerreotype process ▪ vt. (**-types, -typing, -typed**) TAKE PHOTOGRAPH OF make a daguerreotype of sth or sb [Mid-19thC. From French, named after Louis-Jacques Mandé Daguerre.] —**daguerreotyper** n. —**daguerreotypist** n. —**daguerreotypy** /də gérrō tīpi/ n.

dah /daa/ n. COMMUNICATION the spoken representation of a dash in Morse code and other telegraphic codes [Mid-20thC. An imitation of the sound made by a Morse code transmitter.]

dahabeah /daáhə beé ə/, **dahabeeyah, dahabiah** n. a passenger boat or houseboat with sails and sometimes an engine, used on the Nile. It has a very shallow draught. [Mid-19thC. From Arabic dahabīya 'golden (boat)'.]

dahl n. = **dhal**

Dahl /daal/, **Roald** (1916–90) British writer. He is best known for his many children's books, including James and the Giant Peach (1961) and Charlie and the Chocolate Factory (1964). His books for adults include Kiss, Kiss (1960).

Dahlia

dahlia /dáyli ə/ n. a tall perennial plant native to Central America and Mexico that has large brightly coloured flowers and tuberous roots. Many different varieties of dahlia are cultivated as garden plants. Genus: Dahlia. [Early 19thC. Named after Andreas Dahl (1751–89), a Swedish botanist who discovered this genus of plants in Mexico in 1788.]

Dahomey /də hómi/ former name for **Benin**

daikon /dī́kən/ n. = **mooli** [Late 19thC. From Japanese, literally 'big root'.]

Dáil Eireann /dóyl áirən, daál-/, **Dáil** n. the lower house of the parliament of the Republic of Ireland [Early 20thC. From Irish, literally 'Irish Assembly'.]

daily /dáyli/ adj. **1.** DONE EVERY DAY done or occurring every day **2.** FOR EACH DAY for each day or for a period of a day **3.** LASTING A DAY for the duration of or during a day ▪ adv. EVERY DAY on each day ▪ n. (plural **-lies**) PRESS NEWSPAPER PUBLISHED EVERY DAY a newspaper published every day, or every day except Sunday (often used in the plural) ▪ **dailies** npl. CINEMA DAY'S SHOOTING OF FILM SCENES unedited prints of a day's shooting of scenes from a film prepared each day for the director to view the following day [15thC. Formed from DAY.]

daily double n. **1.** BET ON TWO RACES a bet, e.g. in horse-racing, won by correctly choosing the winners of two specified races taking place on the same day **2.** TWO RACES the two races specified for a daily double bet

daily dozen n. a set of physical exercises done each day (informal)

daimio n. = **daimyo**

Daimler /dáymlər/, **Gottlieb** (1834–1900) German engineer and inventor. His high-speed petrol-burning internal-combustion engine powered the first motorcycle and one of the earliest successful cars (1887).

daimon n. = **daemon**

daimyo /dī́myō/ (plural **-o** or **-os**), **daimio** (plural **-o** or **-os**) n. a great Japanese feudal lord who was a vassal of the emperor [Early 18thC. From Japanese, literally 'great name'.]

Daintree /dáyn tree/ river in northern Queensland, Australia, that rises near the town of Mossman and flows into the Pacific Ocean near Cape Tribulation. Length: 108 km/67 mi.

Daintree River National Park /dáyn tree-/ national park in north-eastern Queensland, Australia, that forms part of the Wet Tropics of Queensland World Heritage Area. Area: 7,000 sq. km/2,734 sq. mi.

dainty /dáynti/ adj. (**-tier, -tiest**) **1.** PRETTY delicate and pretty ◊ dainty slippers **2.** TASTY choice, delicious, or tasty ◊ a dainty morsel **3.** REFINED IN TASTE having refined taste or manners **4.** OVERLY NICE excessively fastidious or particular ■ *n.* (*plural* **-ties**) DELICACY sth delicious, especially a small piece of food [13thC. Via Anglo-Norman *dainte* and Old French *daintie* from Latin *dignitas* (see DIGNITY). 'Delicate' evolved from 'esteem' through 'pleasure' and 'luxury' to 'delightful'.] —**daintily** *adv.* —**daintiness** *n.*

daiquiri /dîkəri, dák-/ (*plural* **-ris**) *n.* an iced cocktail made from rum, lemon or lime juice, and sugar or syrup [Early 20thC. Named after *Daiquiri*, a Cuban rum-producing district.]

dairy /daíri/ *n.* (*plural* **-ies**) **1.** PLACE TO STORE MILK AND CREAM a room or building where milk and cream are stored **2.** PLACE TO MAKE BUTTER AND CHEESE a room or building where butter and cheese are made **3.** ESTABLISHMENT THAT SELLS OR PROCESSES MILK a commercial establishment that processes, sells, or distributes milk and milk products **4.** FARM FOR MILK PRODUCTION a farm that produces milk and milk products **5.** *NZ* GROCERY STORE a small local grocery store that sells milk, newspapers, and other provisions **6.** DAIRY PRODUCTS dairy products collectively ■ *adj.* **1.** RELATING TO MILK PRODUCTS relating to, producing, or containing milk or milk products **2.** CONCERNING FOODS IN JEWISH DIETARY LAW relating to those foods, including milk products, eggs, fish, and vegetables, that Jewish dietary law allows on occasions when milk is consumed [13thC. Via *deie* 'woman servant' (hence 'place where she works') from Old English *dæge*, 'kneader (of bread)' (source of English *lady*).]

dairy cattle *npl.* cattle bred and raised for milk production

dairy farm *n.* a farm that produces milk and milk products

dairying /daíri ing/ *n.* the business of operating a dairy or dairy farm

dairyman /daírimən, -man/ (*plural* **-men**) *n.* sb who owns or works in a dairy (*dated*)

dais /dáy iss, dayss/ *n.* a raised platform at the end of a hall or large room [13thC. Via Old French *deis* from Latin.]

daishiki *n.* CLOTHES = **dashiki**

Daisy

daisy /dáyzi/ (*plural* **-sies**) *n.* **1.** LOW-GROWING FLOWERING PLANT a plant of European origin that has short stems and flowers with white or pinkish-white petals radiating from a round yellow centre. Latin name: *Bellis perennis*. **2.** TALL PLANT a tall plant of Europe, Asia, and North America that has flowers with white petals radiating from a round yellow centre. Latin name: *Chrysanthemum leucanthemum*. [Old English *dæges eage*, literally 'day's eye'. Because the flower opens in daylight and closes at night.]

daisy bush *n.* a shrub or tree found in Australia, New Zealand, and New Guinea that has clusters of white flowers resembling those of the daisy. Genus: *Olearia*.

daisy chain *n.* **1.** GARLAND OF DAISIES a garland made by threading the stems of daisies together **2.** SERIES a series of connected things, events, or people (*slang*)

daisycutter /dáyzi kuttər/ *n.* **1.** CRICKET BALL THAT SKIMS GROUND a ball bowled or struck so that it skims the ground **2.** MIL FRAGMENTATION BOMB a bomb that detonates just above ground level, used against personnel and to destroy vegetation in order to create a landing zone for helicopters

daisy ham *n.* *US* a small cut of pork shoulder that has been boned, salted, and smoked

daisy wheel *n.* a wheel with type elements at the ends of spokes radiating from a central hub, used in some electronic typewriters and printers

dak /daak, dak/, **dawk** /dawk/ *n.* **1.** TRANSPORT SYSTEM IN INDIA a system of mail delivery or passenger transportation using relays of horses or bearers, used in the past in India **2.** MAIL IN INDIA letters, parcels, and other mail in India [Early 18thC. Via Hindi *dāk* from Sanskrit *drāk*, 'quickly'.]

Dak. *abbr.* Dakota

Dakar /dák aar, -ər/ capital and largest city of Senegal. It is situated on Cape Verde Peninsula, close to the westernmost tip of mainland Africa, and is one of western Africa's leading ports. Population: 1,729,823 (1992).

dak bungalow *n.* a house for travellers, originally on the route of a dak

dakoit *n.* = **dacoit**

dakoity *n.* = **dacoity**

Dakota /də kṓtə/ (*plural* **-tas** or **-ta**) *n.* **1.** MEMBER OF NATIVE AMERICAN PEOPLE a member of a Native North American people who originally lived in the upper Mississippi River valley **2.** DAKOTA LANGUAGE a Siouan language spoken in the United States and the Canadian province of Manitoba. Dakota is spoken by between 10,000 and 20,000 people. [Early 19thC. From Dakota *Dakhóta*, literally 'allies'.] —**Dakota** *adj.*

daks /daks/ *npl.* ANZ trousers (*informal*)

dal[1] /daal/ *n.* = **dhal**

dal[2] *symbol.* decalitre

Dalai Lama /dálī laamə/ *n.* the highest priest of Tibetan Buddhism and, until the Chinese occupation of Tibet in 1959, the traditional spiritual and secular ruler of Tibet [Late 17thC. From Mongolian, literally 'ocean lama'. See LAMA.]

dalasi /də laássi/ (*plural* **-sis**) *n.* the basic monetary unit of Gambia, divided into 100 bututs. See table at **currency** [Late 20thC. From the name of an earlier Gambian coin.]

dale /dayl/ *n.* **1.** LOWLAND VALLEY a broad lowland valley, especially in northern England ○ *walked over hill and dale* **2. dales, Dales** = **Yorkshire Dales** [Old English *dæl*. Ultimately from an Indo-European word meaning 'bend, curve', which is also the ancestor of English *dell* and *dollar*.]

Dale /dayl/, **Sir Henry Hallett** (1875–1968) British physiologist and pharmacist. With Otto Loewi, he established the role of the chemical acetylcholine in the transmission of nerve impulses. He and Loewi were joint Nobel laureates in 1936.

Dalek /daálek/, **dalek** *n.* an alien creature in a metal casing, like a robot, with a harsh monotonous voice, from the British science fiction television series *Dr Who* [Mid-20thC]

Dales, Yorkshire national park and series of deep river valleys in the Pennine uplands in Yorkshire, England

dalesman /dáylzmən/ (*plural* **-men** /-mən/) *n.* sb who lives in or was born in a dales region, especially the Yorkshire Dales in England

daleth /daálit/, **daled** /-lid/, **dalet** /-lit/ *n.* the fourth letter of the Hebrew alphabet, transliterated into English as 'd'. See table at **alphabet**

Dalgarno /dal gaárnō/, **George** (1626?–87) Scottish educationalist. His *Didascalocophus* (1680) was perhaps the first attempt at codifying a sign language for the deaf.

Dali /daáli/, **Dalí, Salvador** (1904–89) Spanish surrealist painter. He is known for the dreamlike imagery and almost photographic realism of his work. After settling in New York (1940), he adopted other styles and wrote *The Secret Life of Salvador Dalí* (1942). —**Daliesque** *adj.*

Dalian /daályən/ industrial seaport on the southern peninsula in Liaoning Province, northeastern China. Population: 2,416,000 (1991).

Dalit *n.* a member of the lowest caste within the traditional caste system in India

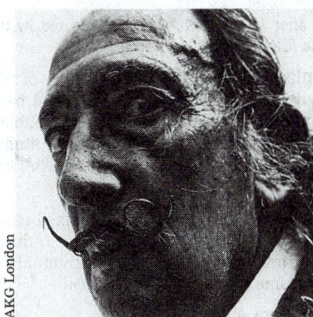

AKG London

Salvador Dali

Dallapiccola /dállə píkələ/, **Luigi** (1904–75) Italian composer and teacher. His works, including the opera *The Prisoner* (1948), blend traditional Italian lyricism with modern serial techniques.

Dallas /dálləss/ city in northeastern Texas, on the Trinity River, east of Fort Worth. It is an important commercial, financial, and distribution centre. Population: 1,053,292 (1996).

dalliance /dálli ənss/ *n.* **1.** TRIFLING frivolous or idle wasting of time (*literary*) **2.** FLIRTATION a flirtation or flirtatious episode (*old*) [14thC. Coined from DALLY + -ANCE.]

dally /dálli/ (**-lies, -lying, -lied**) *v.* **1.** *vi.* FLIRT to act in an amorous, flirtatious, or playful manner **2.** *vi.* TOY WITH STH OR SB to trifle or deal lightly with sth or sb **3.** *vti.* WASTE TIME to dawdle, loiter, or waste time [14thC. From Anglo-Norman *dalier*, 'to amuse yourself', of ultimately unknown origin. The modern meaning, 'to flirt', evolved from 'to talk, converse' through 'to chat idly'.] —**dallier** *n.*

Dalmatia /dal máyshə/ region of Croatia, consisting of a coastal area and offshore islands. It is bordered inland by the Dinaric Alps and includes the major cities of Dubrovnik and Split. Area: 12,950 sq. km/5,000 sq. mi.

Dalmatian /dal máysh'n/ *n.* **1. Dalmatian, dalmatian** ZOOL SPOTTED DOG a dog belonging to a breed that has a white coat with black or brown spots **2.** PEOPLES SB FROM DALMATIA sb who was born in or who lives in the Adriatic coastal region of Dalmatia **3.** LANG EXTINCT ROMANCE LANGUAGE an extinct language once spoken along the Adriatic coast in the region of Dubrovnik. It belongs to the Romance group of Indo-European languages and became extinct at the end of the 19th century. [Late 16thC. In the meaning of 'dog', named after *Dalmatia*, because the breed supposedly originated there.] —**Dalmatian** *adj.*

Dalmatian coast *n.* GEOG a coastline characterized by chains of islands close to the mainland, formed when rising sea-levels flood a series of valleys and ridges parallel to the coast

dalmatic /dal máttik/ *n.* **1.** CHR VESTMENT WORN BY PRIEST a vestment with slit sides and wide sleeves, worn by a priest or deacon of the Roman Catholic Church **2.** HIST CORONATION ROBE a robe with slit sides and wide sleeves, worn by British sovereigns at their coronation [15thC. From Old French *dalmatique* or Latin *dalmatica*, '(robe) made of Dalmatian wool', formed from *Dalmaticus* 'of Dalmatia', from *Dalmatia*.]

d'Alpuget, Blanche (b. 1944) Australian writer. She wrote the novel *Turtle Beach* (1981), and *Robert J. Hawke: A biography* (1982). Full name **Josephine Blanche d'Alpuget**

dal segno /dal sényō/ *adv.* to be played or sung again from the point marked with the sign ※ to the point marked 'fine' (*used as a musical direction*) ◊ **da capo** [Late 19thC. From Italian, literally 'from the sign'.]

dalton /dáwltən/ *n.* = **atomic mass unit** [Mid-20thC. Named after John *Dalton*.]

Dalton /dáwltən/, **John** (1766–1844) British physicist and meteorologist. His experiments with gases (1803) laid the foundations of modern atomic theory. He also first described colour blindness (1794).

daltonism /dáwltənizəm/, **Daltonism** *n.* colour blindness, especially an inability to distinguish between red and green [Mid-19thC. From French *daltonisme*, named after John *Dalton*, who was affected by this.] — **daltonic** /dawl tónnik/ *adj.*

Dalton plan, **Dalton scheme** *n.* a system of teaching and learning whereby the student must be free to continue without interruption on any subject that may arise in the course of his or her study [Early 20thC. Named after *Dalton, Massachusetts, USA*, where this was first implemented.]

Dalton's law *n.* the principle that mixed gases in a given volume exert a pressure equal to the sum of the pressures they would exert individually in the same volume [Named after John *Dalton*]

Dalton system *n.* = **Dalton plan**

Dam: Hoover Dam (completed 1936), Arizona

dam[1] /dam/ *n.* **1.** BARRIER CONTROLLING FLOW OF WATER a barrier of concrete or earth that is built across a river or stream to obstruct or control the flow of water, especially in order to create a reservoir **2.** RESERVOIR CONFINED BY DAM a reservoir of water created, confined, or controlled by a dam **3.** STH RESEMBLING DAM a barrier that resembles or acts as a dam ■ *vt.* (**dams, damming, dammed**) **1.** CONFINE WITH DAM to confine, provide, or restrain sth with a dam **2.** OBSTRUCT to block, obstruct, or restrict sth [14thC. From Middle Dutch, ultimately of unknown origin.]

dam[2] /dam/ *n.* the female parent of an animal, especially of four-legged domestic livestock [14thC. Variant of DAME.]

dam[3] *symbol.* decametre

Dam /dam/, **Henrik** (1895–1976) Danish biochemist. Working with Edward A. Doisy, he isolated vitamin K, a fat-soluble substance necessary for blood coagulation. The pair shared a Nobel Prize in 1943. Full name **Carl Peter Henrik Dam**

damage /dámmij/ *n.* **1.** HARM OR INJURY physical harm or injury that makes sth less useful, valuable, or able to function ○ *Damage to the vehicle was slight* ○ *The scandal did considerable damage to his reputation.* **2.** ADVERSE EFFECT a harmful effect on sb or sth **3.** COST the cost or price of sth (*informal*) ○ *What's the damage?* ■ **damages** *npl.* LAW MONEY PAID AS COMPENSATION money paid or claimed as compensation for harm, loss, or injury ■ *v.* (**-ages, -aging, -aged**) **1.** *vt.* CAUSE HARM to cause damage to sth or sb **2.** *vi.* BE HARMED to suffer damage ○ *Soft fruit damages easily.* [13thC. Via Old French, 'loss through injury', from *dam*, 'loss, damage', from Latin *damnum* (source of English *damn* and *indemnity*).] — **damageability** /dámmijə bílləti/ *n.* — **damageable** /dámmijəb'l/ *adj.* — **damager** *n.*

—— **WORD KEY: SYNONYMS** ——
See Synonyms at *harm.*

damage control *n.* **1.** NAVY QUICK CONTAINMENT OF PHYSICAL DAMAGE shipboard measures to control, contain, and offset damages to a vessel by, e.g. collision, attack, fire, or an explosion **2.** CONTAINMENT OF NONPHYSICAL DAMAGE containment and neutralization of, e.g. public relations problems caused by a scandal, legal case, or other controversial matter (*informal*) ○ *As soon as the scandal broke, the Party's damage control kicked in.*

damaging /dámmijing/ *adj.* causing or capable of causing harm, injury, or loss ○ *a damaging report —* **damagingly** *adv.*

damar *n.* = **dammar**

Damara /də maárə/ (*plural* **-as** *or* **-a**) *n.* **1.** PEOPLES MEMBER OF AFRICAN PEOPLE a member of a people living in southwestern Africa, mainly in the Republic of Namibia **2.** LANG = **Nama** [Early 19thC. From Nama.] — **Damara** *adj.*

Damaraland /də maárə land/ historical region in north-central Namibia, named after the Damara people

damascene /dámmə seen, -seén/ *vt.* (**-cenes, -cening, -cened**) DECORATE METAL WITH WAVY PATTERNS to decorate metal such as iron or steel with wavy patterns of etching or inlay of precious metals, especially gold or silver ■ *n.* DESIGN OR OBJECT CREATED BY DAMASCENING a design or object created by the process of damascening ■ *adj.* **1.** RELATING TO DAMASCENING relating to the art or process of damascening metal **2.** OF OR LIKE DAMASK made of or resembling damask [From Latin *Damascenus* 'of Damascus', a city of Syria famous for its steel and silk fabrics, from Greek *damaskēnos*] — **damascener** *n.*

Damascus /də máskəs, -maáskəs/ capital city of Syria on the River Baradá in the southwestern part of the country. Thought to have been inhabited since 2000 BC, it is one of the oldest cities in the world. Population: 1,451,000 (1992). — **Damascene** /dámmə seen, -seén/ *n., adj.*

damask /dámməsk/ *n.* **1.** PATTERNED FABRIC a reversible fabric, usually of cotton, linen, or silk, with a pattern woven into it. It is used especially for table linen. **2.** TABLE LINEN table linen made from damask **3.** COLOURS GREYISH-PINK COLOUR a greyish-pink colour, like that of the damask rose ■ *adj.* PINK pink or greyish-pink ■ *vt.* (**-asks, -asking, -asked**) DECORATE WITH PATTERN to decorate or weave a fabric with an elaborate pattern [14thC. From Latin *Damascus*, named after that city because the fabric was originally produced there.]

damask rose *n.* a large hardy rose native to Asia and cultivated for its fragrant pink or red flowers that are used to make a fragrant essential oil (**attar**). Latin name: *Rosa damascena.* [*Damask* from earlier English *Damask* 'Damascus', from Latin *Damascus*]

Damavand /dámmə vand/ mountain in Iran, northeast of Teheran, that is the highest point in the Elburz Mountains and in the country. Height: 5,771 m/18,934 ft.

Dama wallaby *n.* = **tammar**

Dam Busters *npl.* a squadron of the Royal Air Force that destroyed dams in Germany during World War II using bouncing bombs [Mid-20thC. From the title of a film based on a history of the squadron by Paul Brickhill.]

dame /daym/ *n.* **1.** US, Can a term, often considered offensive, that refers to a woman or girl (*informal*) **2.** the woman in charge of a household (*archaic*) **3.** WOMAN a married or matronly woman who is no longer young (*archaic*) **4.** SENIOR NUN used as the formal title of the superior of a nunnery **5.** THEATRE PANTOMIME ROLE the pantomime role of an ill-tempered comic woman of advanced years, traditionally played by a man [13thC. Via Old French and late Latin *domna* from Latin *domina*, 'woman in charge of the house'.]

Dame *n.* **1.** WOMAN AWARDED ORDER OF CHIVALRY the title of a woman awarded any of various orders of chivalry or merit, e.g. the Order of the British Empire, by a sovereign or government **2.** WIFE OF BARONET OR KNIGHT the official title of the wife of a baronet or knight

dame school *n.* a small school, often in a rural area, where in the past children were taught the basics of reading, writing, and arithmetic, usually by a woman of advanced years in her home (*archaic*)

dame's rocket *n.* = **dame's violet** [*Dame's* a translation of Latin (*Hesperis*) *matronalis*]

dame's violet /dáymz-/ (*plural* **dame's violets** *or* **dame's violet**) *n.* a perennial Eurasian plant of the mustard family, cultivated for its fragrant purple or white flowers. Latin name: *Hesperis matronalis.* [Translation of the Latin name in the old herbals, *Viola matronalis*]

damiana /dáymi aánə/ *n.* a drug used as a stimulant and diuretic that is extracted from the leaves of a tropical American plant. Latin name: *Turnera diffusa.* [Late 20thC. From American Spanish.]

Damietta /dámmi éttə/ city in the northeastern corner of the Nile delta, Egypt. It is situated on the Damietta, a tributary of the Nile, about 13 km/8 mi. from the Mediterranean coast. Population: 113,000 (1991).

dammar /dámmər/, **damar, dammer** *n.* a hard resin obtained from various trees of Southeast Asia, used in inks, lacquers, oil paints, and varnishes [Late 17thC. From Malay *damar*, 'resin'.]

dammit /dámmit/ *interj.* used as a swearword to show annoyance [Mid-19thC. Variant of *damn it*.]

damn /dam/ *interj.* EXCLAMATION OF ANNOYANCE used as a mild swearword to emphasize irritation, displeasure, disappointment, or frustration ■ *adj.* USED TO EXPRESS ANNOYANCE used emphatically or as a swearword to express annoyance, disappointment, or frustration with sb or sth ■ *v.* (**damns, damning, damned**) **1.** *vt.* DECLARE TO BE BAD to express disapproval of sth or sb, especially in public **2.** *vt.* DOOM TO FAILURE to cause sb or sth to fail **3.** *vt.* RELIG CONDEMN TO HELL to condemn sb to hell or to eternal punishment **4.** *vti.* CURSE OR SWEAR AT to curse or swear at sb or sth, using the word 'damn' [13thC. Via Old French *damner*, 'to condemn', from Latin *damnare*, from *damnum* 'damage' (see DAMAGE).] — **damner** *n.* ◇ **damn all** nothing at all (*slang*) ◇ **not give** *or* **care a damn** to be not at all concerned or worried about sth

damnable /dámnəb'l/ *adj.* (*dated*) **1.** HEINOUS deserving divine condemnation or damnation **2.** DETESTABLE detestable, hateful, or extremely bad — **damnably** *adv.* — **damnability** /dámnə bílləti/ *n.* — **damnableness** *n.*

damnation /dam náysh'n/ *n.* **1.** CONDEMNATION condemnation to hell or eternal punishment **2.** SIN sth that causes condemnation to hell or eternal punishment **3.** PUNISHMENT eternal punishment in hell ■ *interj.* ANGRY EXCLAMATION used as a swearword to express anger or disappointment

damnatory /dámnətəri/ *adj.* causing, expressing, or threatening condemnation

damned /damd/ *adj.* **1.** RELIG CONDEMNED condemned to hell or to eternal punishment **2.** EXPRESSION OF ANNOYANCE used emphatically or as a swearword to express annoyance ■ *adv.* VERY extremely (*informal*) ○ *a damned good saxophone player* ■ *npl.* RELIG THE CONDEMNED those condemned to hell or doomed to suffer eternal punishment

damnedest /dámdist/ *adj.* US MOST AMAZING most amazing or extraordinary ○ *It was the damnedest thing I'd ever seen.* ■ *n.* UTMOST everything possible ○ *She did her damnedest to persuade them to stay.*

damnify /dámnifí/ (**-fies, -fying, -fied**) *vt.* in law, to cause damage or loss to sb or sth [Early 16thC. Via Old French *damnifier* from Latin *damnificare*, 'injure, condemn', from *damnare*. See DAMN.] — **damnification** /dámnifi káysh'n/ *n.*

damning /dámming/ *adj.* **1.** HIGHLY CRITICAL very critical or unfavourable **2.** PROVING GUILTY, WRONG, OR BAD proving or showing that sb or sth is guilty, wrong, or very bad — **damningly** *adv.* — **damningness** *n.*

Damoclean /dámmə klée ən/ *adj.* under the threat of imminent disaster [Late 19thC. Named after *Damocles*.]

Damocles /dámmə kleez/ (fl. 4th century BC) Syracusan Greek courtier. Dionysius of Syracuse, tired of his envious flattery, had him seated beneath a sword hanging from a hair, thus symbolizing the perils of the powerful.

Damodar /dámmə daar/ river that rises in the Chota Nagpur plateau in the Indian state of Bihar, flows through West Bengal, then joins the River Hoogly southwest of Calcutta. Length: 592 km/368 mi.

damp /damp/ *adj.* **1.** MOIST slightly wet ○ *damp laundry* **2.** HALF-HEARTED unenthusiastic or indifferent **3.** MELANCHOLY dejected or melancholy (*archaic*) ■ *n.* **1.** SLIGHT WETNESS humidity, moisture, or slight wetness ○ *patches of damp* **2.** MINING HARMFUL GAS poisonous gas or rank air, especially in a mine **3.** STH THAT DEPRESSES a feeling of gloom or melancholy ○ *The host's low spirits cast a damp over the party.* **4.** MELANCHOLY dejection, melancholy, or lowness of spirits (*archaic*) ■ *vt.* (**damps, damping, damped**) **1.** DAMPEN to make sb or sth slightly wet **2.** EXTINGUISH to extinguish a fire or make it burn more slowly by reducing its supply of air **3.** MUSIC **STOP** to stop the vibration of a string on a musical instrument **4.** STIFLE to discourage or stifle sb or sth ○ *Rain damped the picnickers' enthusiasm.* **5.** PHYS **REDUCE OSCILLATION** to decrease the amplitude of an oscillation or wave **6.** MUSIC **MUFFLE** to deaden or muffle the sound of a musical instrument [14thC. Via Middle Low German *damp* from prehistoric Germanic. 'Moist' evolved from 'vapour', through 'noxious gas', 'mist', and 'moisture'.] — **damply** *adv.* —**dampness** *n.*

——— **WORD KEY: SYNONYMS** ———
See Synonyms at **wet**.

damp down, dampen down *vt.* **1.** CAUSE TO BURN MORE SLOWLY to cause a fire to burn more slowly by adding ash or by reducing the flow of air **2.** REDUCE to control, restrain, or reduce the intensity of sth **3.** COVER WITH WATER to cover a surface with a small quantity of water ○ *Bill damped down his hair.*

damp off, dampen off *vi.* to decline in power, wealth, or strength

dampcourse /dámp kawrss/ *n.* a layer of waterproof material near the ground in a brick wall that prevents damp from rising

dampen /dámpən/ (**-ens, -ening, -ened**) *vti.* **1.** MOISTEN to make sth slightly wet, or to become slightly wet **2.** DEADEN to deaden or stifle sth, or to become deadened or stifled [14thC. Formed from DAMP.] —**dampener** *n.*

damper /dámpər/ *n.* **1.** SB OR STH DISCOURAGING sb or sth that causes discouragement or inhibition **2.** PLATE TO CONTROL FIRE a metal plate that controls the draught in a furnace or stove **3.** MUSIC PIANO MUTE a felt-covered block in a piano that stops the vibration of strings **4.** MUSIC HORN OR WOODWIND MUTE a mute to muffle the sound of a brass or woodwind instrument **5.** *Aus* FOOD UNLEAVENED BREAD bread made from a simple flour and water dough and often cooked over an open fire. It is a traditional bush food in Australia. **6.** ELEC ENG DEVICE TO CONTROL VIBRATION a device for controlling the excessive vibration of a suspended magnetic needle **7.** ELEC ENG DEVICE TO REDUCE HUNTING a piece of copper embedded in or near the poles of an electric motor to reduce any tendency it might have to pulsate to speeds above or below its intended speed ◇ **put a damper on sth** to make sth less fun and more inhibited ○ *The sudden arrival of the adults put a damper on the kids' party.*

Dampier /dámpi ər/ coastal town in northwestern Western Australia that serves as a port for nearby mining and industrial centres. Population: 1,424 (1996).

Dampier /dámpi ə/, **William** (1652–1715) English explorer. He was one of the first Europeans to visit Australia and published numerous surveys, logs, and charts of his voyages around the world.

damping off *n.* a fatal disease of seedlings grown under very damp conditions that is caused by various fungi

damp-proof *adj.* RESISTANT TO MOISTURE impervious or resistant to damp or moisture ■ *vt.* (**damp-proofs, damp-proofing, damp-proofed**) MAKE RESISTANT TO MOISTURE to make sth such as a building damp-proof

damp-proof course *n.* = damp course

damp squib *n.* sth that is intended or expected to be effective or impressive, but fails or disappoints (*informal*)

damsel /dámz'l/ *n.* a girl or young unmarried woman, originally one of noble birth (*archaic or literary*) [13thC. From Old French *dameisele*, by folk etymology (from *dame*) from *donsele*, from Vulgar Latin *dominicella*, 'little lady', ultimately from Latin *domina*, 'woman in charge of the house' (see DAME).]

damselfish /dámz'l fish/ *n.* (*plural* **-fish** *or* **-fishes**) *n.* a small brightly-coloured marine fish that lives along coral reefs. Family: Pomacentridae.

damselfly /dámz'l flī/ (*plural* **-flies**) *n.* a slender insect related to the dragonfly but smaller in size that folds its wings together above its body when resting. Damselflies are often brightly coloured and have eyes that face sideways. Suborder: Zygoptera.

damson /dámz'n/ *n.* **1.** PLUM TREE a fruit tree related to the plum, cultivated for its edible dark purple fruit. Latin name: *Prunus insititia.* **2.** SMALL PURPLE PLUM the

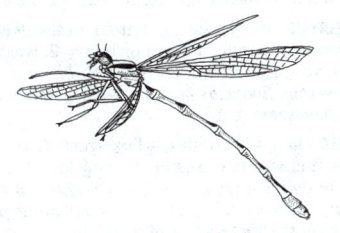
Damselfly

small sour dark purple fruit of the damson tree, usually eaten cooked or made into jam [15thC. Alteration of DAMASCENE, translating Latin (*prunum*) *damascenus*, '(plum) from Damascus'.]

dan[1] /dan/, **Dan** *n.* **1.** PROFICIENCY LEVEL IN MARTIAL ARTS any one of the numbered black-belt levels of proficiency in martial arts such as judo and karate **2.** SB PROFICIENT IN A MARTIAL ART a person who has achieved a dan [Mid-20thC. From Japanese.]

dan[2] /dan/, **dan buoy** *n.* a small buoy, often with a flag attached, used as a marker [Late 17thC. Origin unknown.]

Dan *n.* a title of honour, equivalent to 'Master' or 'Sir', used in the past before the personal names of respected men such as clerics or poets (*archaic*) [13thC. Via Old French from Latin *dominus*, 'master'.]

Dan. *abbr.* **1.** BIBLE Daniel **2.** Danish

Dana /dáynə/, **Richard Henry** (1815–82) US writer and lawyer. He is known for his maritime narrative *Two Years Before the Mast* (1840).

Danaides /də náy i deez/, **Danaïdes** *npl.* in Greek mythology, the fifty daughters of Danaüs, who killed their bridegrooms

Danby /dánbi/, **Francis** (1793–1861) Irish-born British painter. He is known for his dramatic biblical and historical subjects as well as his romantic landscapes.

dance /daanss/ *v.* (**dances, dancing, danced**) **1.** *vi.* MOVE RHYTHMICALLY TO MUSIC to move the feet and body rhythmically, usually in time to music **2.** *vt.* DO A DANCE to perform or participate in a specified dance ○ *to dance a lively polka* **3.** *vt.* CAUSE TO DANCE to make sb dance or lead sb in a dance ○ *He danced her across the floor.* **4.** *vt.* REACH BY DANCING to get to a particular state by dancing ○ *She danced her way to fame and adulation.* **5.** *vi.* JUMP UP AND DOWN to leap or skip, especially in an emotional manner ○ *The children danced with glee.* **6.** *vi.* MOVE ABOUT QUICKLY to bob up and down or move quickly about ○ *The leaves danced across the lawn.* **7.** *vi.* BACKGAMMON FAIL TO ROLL RE-ENTRY NUMBER to fail to roll a number that re-enters a backgammon piece from the bar ○ *He rolled a 6–6 and danced.* ■ *n.* **1.** RHYTHMICAL BODY MOVEMENTS TO MUSIC a series of rhythmical steps and body movements, usually performed in time to music **2.** ACTION OF DANCING a session of dancing **3.** OCCASION FOR DANCING a party or social gathering for dancing **4.** ART OF DANCING dancing as a performance art **5.** MUSIC FOR DANCING a piece of music in the rhythm of a particular type of dance **6.** ZOOL PATTERN OF ANIMAL MOVEMENTS a pattern of animal movements used, e.g. in courtship by birds or by bees to give information about food ■ *adj.* OF OR FOR DANCING relating to, involving, or created for dancing [13thC. From Old French, of uncertain origin: perhaps via Vulgar Latin from Frankish.]

danceable /daánssəb'l/ *adj.* suitable for or conducive to dancing

dance band *n.* a band that plays music for dancing

dance card *n.* a card on which people wrote the names of their dancing partners at a formal dance or ball in the past

dance floor *n.* an area of uncarpeted floor for dancing

dance hall *n.* **1.** PLACE WHERE DANCES ARE HELD a building or large room where public dances are held **2.** *US* MUSIC DANCE MUSIC ACCOMPANIED BY DISC JOCKEY elec-

tronically produced dance music that combines different kinds of popular music styles with continuous accompaniment by a disc jockey talking or rapping to the rhythm

dance music *n.* **1.** MUSIC FOR DANCING any music suitable for dancing **2.** ELECTRONIC POP MUSIC pop music that is typically characterized by repeated electronic rhythms

dance of death, Dance of Death *n.* an allegorical representation in medieval art, literature, and music of a dance in which Death, personified as a skeleton, leads people to the grave

dancer /daánssər/ *n.* **1.** PERSON DANCING a person who dances, usually in a specified way, or who is dancing **2.** PERSON PAID TO DANCE a person who dances as a professional artist

dancercise /daánssər sīz/ *n. US* aerobic exercise in the form of dance [Mid-20thC. Blend of DANCE and EXERCISE.]

dancewear /daánss wair/ *n.* clothing, such as leotards and leg-warmers, worn for dance practice

dancing /daánssing/ *n.* the activity of performing or taking part in a dance

dancy /daánssi/ (**-cier, -ciest**) *adj.* conducive to dancing, especially in a lively manner

D and C *n.* a gynaecological surgical procedure in which the cervix is widened and some of the womb lining is scraped out, for diagnostic or treatment purposes or in an abortion. Full form **dilatation and curettage**

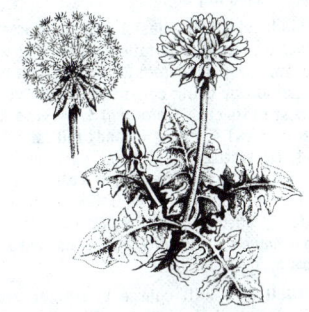
Dandelion

dandelion /dándi lī ən/ *n.* a common plant that has bright yellow flowers on a hollow stalk. Its seed head is white and fluffy and its leaves are used in salads, medicine, and winemaking. Latin name: *Taraxacum officinale.* [15thC. From French *dent de lion*, 'lion's tooth', translating Latin *dens leonis*. Because of the plant's toothed leaves.]

Dandenong Ranges[1] /dándə nong ráynjiz/ densely forested range of hills near Melbourne in Victoria, Australia. The highest peak is Mount Dandenong, 634 m./2080 ft.

Dandenong Ranges[2] /dándə nong ráynjiz/ densely forested range of hills near Melbourne in Victoria, Australia. The highest peak is Mount Dandenong, 634 m/2,080 ft.

dander[1] /dándər/ *n.* **1.** SCALES OF HAIR OR FEATHERS minute particles or scales that are shed from the feathers, hair, or skin of various animals. They may be the cause of some allergies, especially asthma. **2.** *Ireland* = dandruff [Late 18thC. Origin uncertain.] ◇ **get sb's dander up** to make sb angry

dander[2] /dándər/, **daunder** /dáwndər/ *n. N England, Scotland* CASUAL WALK a saunter or stroll ■ *vi.* (**-ders, -dering, -dered**) *N England, Scotland* SAUNTER to dawdle, saunter, or stroll [Late 16thC. Origin unknown.]

Dandie Dinmont /dándi dínmont/, **Dandie Dinmont terrier** *n.* a small terrier of a breed from the Scottish borders with a long body, short legs, drooping ears, and a long wiry greyish or brownish coat [Early 19thC. Named after a character who owned six such dogs in *Guy Mannering*, a novel by Sir Walter Scott.]

dandified /dándi fīd/ *adj.* dressed as or made to resemble a dandy or fop

dandify /dándifī/ (**-fies, -fying, -fied**) *vt.* to dress sb as or

Dandie Dinmont

cause sb to resemble a dandy or fop —**dandification** /dándifi káysh'n/ n.

dandiprat /dándi prat/ n. **1.** 16C ENGLISH COIN a small English coin of the 16th century **2.** BOY a small boy (archaic) **3.** INSIGNIFICANT PERSON a small or insignificant person (archaic) [Early 16thC. Origin unknown.]

dandle /dánd'l/ (-dles, -dling, -dled) vt. **1.** MOVE GENTLY UP AND DOWN to move a baby or small child gently up and down in your arms or on your knees **2.** FONDLE OR PET to fondle or pet sb or sth [Mid-16thC. Origin uncertain: perhaps a variant of DANGLE.] —**dandler** n.

dandruff /dándrəf, -druf/ n. loose dry scales of dead skin that are shed from the scalp [Mid-16thC. From dand-, of unknown origin, and -ruff, of uncertain origin: probably from English dialect huff 'scab', from Scandinavian.] —**dandruffy** adj.

dandy /dándi/ n. (plural -dies) **1.** MAN TOO CONCERNED WITH APPEARANCE a man who is much concerned with his elegant appearance (dated) **2.** US EXCELLENT PERSON OR THING a person or thing considered to be very good or the best in its class (informal) **3.** SAILING SAILING BOAT a ketch or yawl **4.** PAPER = dandy roll ■ adj. (-dier, -diest) **1.** US EXCELLENT very good, excellent, or first-rate (informal) **2.** CHARACTERISTIC OF A DANDY dressed or acting like a dandy [Late 18thC. Shortening of Scottish Jack-a-dandy, 'affected man', from Dandy, a Scots form of the name Andrew.] —**dandily** adv. —**dandyish** adj. —**dandyism** n.

dandy-brush n. a stiff coarse brush for grooming animals, especially horses

dandy roll, **dandy** (plural -dies), **dandy roller** n. a wire cylinder used in papermaking to produce a watermark

Dane /dayn/ n. **1.** SB FROM DENMARK sb who was born or brought up in or is a citizen of Denmark **2.** SB OF DANISH DESCENT a person of Danish descent [14thC. From Old Norse Danir (plural) 'Danes'.]

Danegeld /dáyn geld/, **Danegelt** /-gelt/ n. **1.** HISTORY HISTORICAL TAX an annual tax first levied in the 10th century in England to buy off Danish invaders. It continued until the 12th century as a land tax. **2.** PROTECTION MONEY a payment made in order to avoid trouble or to prevent attack from a stronger enemy [Pre-12thC. From assumed Old Norse Danagiald, literally 'payment of the Danes', from Danir (plural) 'Danes' + giald 'payment'.]

Danelaw /dáyn law/ n. **1.** LAWS ENFORCED BY DANES IN ENGLAND the body of laws established in the parts of England settled in the 9th century by Danish invaders **2.** ANGLO-SAXON ENGLAND UNDER DANISH LAW the parts of Anglo-Saxon England that came under Danish law and where Danish customs were observed [Old English Dena lagu 'Danes' law'.]

dang /dang/ interj., adj., adv., vti. (**dangs, danging, danged**) US = damn [Late 18thC. Euphemistic alteration.]

danged /dangd/ adj., adv. US = damned [Late 19thC. Euphemistic alteration.]

danger /dáynjər/ n. **1.** EXPOSURE TO HARM exposure or vulnerability to harm, injury, or loss ○ Their lives were in danger. **2.** SB OR STH THAT CAUSES HARM sb or sth that may cause harm, injury, or loss (often used in the plural) **3.** POWER power or domain (archaic) [13thC. Via Anglo-Norman daunger from, ultimately, assumed Vulgar Latin domniarium 'power to do harm', from Latin dominium 'sovereignty', which was in turn derived from dominus, 'lord'.]

danger money n. additional payment made for doing a job that involves danger. US term **hazard pay**

dangerous /dáynjərəss/ adj. **1.** LIKELY TO CAUSE HARM likely to cause or result in harm or injury **2.** INVOLVING RISK involving risk or difficulty ○ The business is in a dangerous financial position. —**dangerously** adv. —**dangerousness** n.

dangle /dáng g'l/ v. (-gles, -gling, -gled) **1.** vti. HANG OR CAUSE TO HANG LOOSELY to hang or hang loosely or cause sth to swing or hang loosely ○ The children dangled their legs over the side of the swimming pool. **2.** vt. OFFER AS INDUCEMENT to offer or display sth as an enticement or inducement ○ The possibility of promotion was dangled before her. ■ n. DANGLING THING sth that dangles [Late 16thC. Thought to suggest the action.] —**dangler** n. —**dangly** adj.

dangling participle n. a participle that is not grammatically linked to the word it is intended to modify. In 'Driving down the street, the house came into view', 'driving' is a dangling participle.

— **WORD KEY: USAGE** —
Dangling participles: Also called 'misplaced' or 'un-attached participles', these typically occur at the beginning of sentences and modify either the wrong thing or nothing in particular: Startled by the noise, her book fell to the floor (it was she, not her book, who was startled). Lying in the sun, it was hard to imagine the winter back home (who was lying in the sun?). Such mismatches should be corrected by rephrasing: Startled by the noise, she dropped her book and lying in the sun, he found it hard to imagine the winter back home. A number of dangling participles, however, are well established and idiomatic, for example given, granting, and speaking: Given that dividends depend on earnings, what determines earnings? Other similar words, including considering and regarding, are so well established in such contexts that they are generally thought of as independent of the verbs from which they sprang and are now said to be prepositions.

dan grade n. = dan[1] n. 1

Daniel /dánnyəl/ n. **1.** BIBLICAL PROPHET a biblical prophet whose faith in God protected him in the lion's den **2.** BOOK OF BIBLE the book of the Bible that tells the story of Daniel **3.** WISE PERSON sb who is wise and honourable [Late 16thC. 'Wise person' from the presentation of Daniel as a wise judge in the apocryphal Book of Susanna.]

Daniel /dányəl/, **Samuel** (1562–1619) English poet. His works include the sonnet collection Delia (1592) and his famous masque Hymen's Triumph (1615).

danio /dáyni ō/ (plural -os) n. a brightly-coloured freshwater fish native to India and Sri Lanka that is kept as an aquarium fish. Genera: Danio and Brachydanio. [Late 19thC. From modern Latin, the genus name.]

Danish /dáynish/ adj. OF DENMARK relating to or typical of Denmark or its people, culture, or language ■ n. LANG LANGUAGE OF DANES the language of Denmark, also an official language of the Faroe Islands and Greenland. It belongs to the North Germanic group of Indo-European languages. Danish is spoken by over five million people. ■ npl. PEOPLES PEOPLE FROM DENMARK people who were born or brought up in or are citizens of Denmark ■ n. Danish, danish FOOD = Danish pastry [14thC. Formed from Danes (plural) 'Danes', from Old Icelandic Danir.]

Danish blue n. a blue-veined cheese with a strong taste, originally produced in Denmark

Danish pastry n. a rich puff pastry made from a yeast dough with a sweet filling containing fruit or nuts

dank /dangk/ adj. unpleasantly damp and cold [14thC. Origin uncertain: probably from Scandinavian.] —**dankly** adv. —**dankness** n.

— **WORD KEY: SYNONYMS** —
See Synonyms at **wet**.

Dankworth /dángk wurth/, **Johnny** (b. 1927) British jazz musician, bandleader, and composer. From 'trad' in the 1950s, he moved through bebop to chamber jazz. With his wife, the singer Cleo Laine, he established the Wavendon All Music Plan (1969). Full name **John Philip William Dankworth**

D'Annunzio /da noʻonssi ō/, **Gabriele** (1863–1938) Italian novelist, poet, and playwright. A supporter of Italian fascism, he headed an unofficial Italian occupation of Fiume, now called Rijeka, in Croatia (1919–20).

danse macabre /daʻanss mə kaʻabrə/ (plural danses macabres) n. = dance of death [Late 19thC. From French, literally 'macabre dance'.]

danseur /doN súr, daan súr, daaN sőr/ n. a male ballet dancer [Early 19thC. From French, 'male dancer'.]

danseuse /doN súrz, daan súrz, daaN sőrz/ n. a woman ballet dancer [Early 19thC. From French, 'woman dancer'.]

Dante Alighieri /dánti alli gyáiri/ (1265–1321) Italian poet. One of the greatest poets in world literature, he is best known for his epic masterpiece The Divine Comedy, which he began writing in 1307 and completed shortly before his death. He was involved in the political struggles of his time, which forced him to leave his native Florence. He finally settled in Ravenna.

Dantean /dánti ən, dan teé ən/ adj. **1.** OF OR BY DANTE relating to Dante Alighieri or his works **2.** DANTESQUE in the style of the works of Dante Alighieri ■ n. ADMIRER OR STUDENT OF DANTE ALIGHIERI a person who admires, studies, or is an expert on Dante Alighieri

Dantesque /dan tésk/ adj. in the style of the works of Dante Alighieri

danthonia /dan thóni ə/ n. a perennial tufted grass native to Australia and New Zealand, which has narrow leaves and small flowers growing closely together along the stem. Genus: Danthonia. [Early 20thC. From modern Latin, named after Étienne Danthoine, 19th-century French botanist.]

Danton /dántən, daaN toN/, **Georges Jacques** (1759–94) French lawyer. Minister of Justice in Revolutionary France, he was overthrown in the Reign of Terror (1793) and guillotined the following year.

Danube /dán yoob/ the longest river in western Europe. It rises in the Black Forest in southwestern Germany and flows through Austria, the Czech Republic, Slovakia, Hungary, Croatia, Yugoslavia, Bulgaria, Romania, and Ukraine. It empties into the Black Sea. Length: 2,850 km/1,770 mi. —**Danubian** /də nyoóbi ən/ adj.

Danzig /dánsig/ former name for **Gdansk**

dap /dap/ (daps, dapping, dapped) v. **1.** vi. ANGLING FISH WITH BOBBING BAIT to fish by bobbing the bait lightly on the surface of the water **2.** vi. DIP QUICKLY to dip gently or quickly into water **3.** vti. BOUNCE OR SKIP to bounce or skip, or cause sth to bounce or skip, especially across the surface of water **4.** vt. WOODWORK JOIN WITH A NOTCH to cut a notch in timber in order to join it to another piece [Mid-17thC. Thought to suggest the action.]

daphne /dáfni/ (plural -nes or -ne) n. a European and Asian shrub that is often cultivated as an ornamental garden plant for its glossy evergreen leaves and fragrant bell-shaped pink or purplish flowers. Genus: Daphne. [15thC. From Greek daphnē, 'laurel, bay tree'. Named after Daphne, a nymph in Greek mythology who was changed into such a tree to escape Apollo's attentions.]

daphnia /dáfni ə/ (plural -as or -a) n. a tiny freshwater flea with a transparent shell and branched antennae for swimming. Some types are used as food for aquarium fish. Genus: Daphnia. [Mid-19thC. From modern Latin, where it was formed from daphne, genus name, named after Daphne (see DAPHNE).]

Da Ponte /da pónti/, **Lorenzo** (1749–1838) Italian librettist and poet. He wrote the libretto for Wolfgang Amadeus Mozart's Don Giovanni (1787) and other operas. He moved to New York in 1805. Real name **Emanuele Conegliano**

dapper /dáppər/ adj. **1.** TRIM neat and elegant (refers to men) **2.** LIVELY alert and lively or brisk **3.** NIMBLE small and active or nimble [15thC. From Middle Dutch or Middle Low German dapper, 'bold, heavy'. The modern meanings, 'elegant, nimble', evolved from 'stolid, sturdy', perhaps ironically.] —**dapperly** adv. —**dapperness** n.

dapple /dápp'l/ vti. (-ples, -pling, -pled) MARK WITH PATCHES OF COLOUR to mark sth with patches or spots of a different colour or with light and shade, or to be marked in this way ○ *Sunlight dappled the path through the trees.* ■ *adj.* = **dappled** ■ *n.* **1.** COLOURED MARKINGS spots or patches of a different colour, especially on a horse, or of light and shade **2.** SPOT OF COLOUR an individual spot or patch of colour, light, or shade **3.** ZOOL DAPPLED ANIMAL an animal, especially a horse, with a dappled coat [Late 16thC. Back-formation from DAPPLED.]

dappled /dápp'ld/, **dapple** *adj.* marked with spots or patches of a different colour or with light and shade ○ *in the dappled shade of the chestnut tree* [15thC. Origin uncertain: perhaps formed from DAPPLE 'blotch', or perhaps ultimately from APPLE (compare French *gris-pommelé* and German *apfelgrau* 'dapple-grey', literally 'apple-grey'), perhaps from the shape of the fruit.]

dapple-grey *adj.* OF A LIGHT-GREY COLOUR used to describe a horse or pony of a light-grey colour with darker grey spots or patches ■ *n.* (*plural* **dapple-greys**) HORSE a dapple-grey horse or pony [14thC. Origin uncertain: perhaps from DAPPLED (of later date, but the dates are close enough to be ignored) + GREY; or from assumed *apple-grey* (see DAPPLED).]

daps /daps/ *npl. W Country, Wales* light shoes for gymnastics or sport with canvas uppers and rubber soles [Early 20thC. Origin uncertain: perhaps from *dap* 'bounce of a ball', or *dap* 'to bounce, hop, skip', with the underlying idea of 'shoes for bouncing or skipping'.]

Dapsang /dáp sang/ = **K2**

dapsone /dáp sōn/ *n.* an antibacterial drug containing sulphur, used in the treatment of leprosy and some forms of dermatitis [Mid-20thC. Contraction of *di(para-amino-phenyl)sulphone*, its technical name.]

DAR *abbr.* Daughters of the American Revolution

darbies /daárbiz/ *npl.* a pair of handcuffs (*archaic slang*) [Late 16thC. Shortening of *Father Darby's bands*, a kind of restraint for those arrested for debt, perhaps named after a legendary moneylender, John *Derby*.]

Darby and Joan *n.* a contented and devoted couple who have long lived together in domestic harmony [Late 18thC. From the names of a contented long-married couple in a poem published in the *Gentleman's Magazine* in 1735.]

Darby and Joan club *n.* a social club for people of advanced years

Darcy /daárssi/, **Les** (1895–1917) Australian boxer. He was a winner of the Australian lightweight, middleweight, and heavyweight championships. Full name **James Leslie Darcy**

Dard /daard/ *n.* a member of any of the peoples who speak a Dardic language [Mid-19thC. From Dardic.]

Dardan /daárd'n/, **Dardanian** *adj.* TROJAN a word meaning 'Trojan', used mainly in poetry (*archaic literary*) ■ *n.* A TROJAN a word meaning 'Trojan person', used mainly in poetry (*archaic literary*) [Early 17thC. From Latin *Dardanus*, an adjective used in poetry for 'Trojan'.]

Dardanelles /daárdə nélz/ strait that separates Asian Turkey from the Gallipoli peninsula of European Turkey, and links the Aegean Sea with the Sea of Marmara. Its ancient name is Hellespont. Length: 60 km/38 mi.

Dardic /daárdik/ *n.* a subgroup of Indic languages spoken in the mountainous northern regions of India and Pakistan. Kashmiri is the best known of the Dardic languages, of which there are about seven million speakers. —**Dardic** *adj.*

dare /dair/ *vt.* (**dares** *or* **dare, daring, dared**) **1.** HAVE ENOUGH COURAGE FOR STH to have the courage needed to do sth (*sometimes used as an auxiliary*) ○ *wanted to ask but then didn't dare* ○ *'We must dare to think about "unthinkable things" because when things have become unthinkable, thinking stops and action becomes mindless'.* (William Fulbright *US Senate Speech*; 27 March, 1965) **2.** HAVE AUDACITY TO DO STH to do sth that angers or outrages sb (*sometimes used as an auxiliary*) ○ *Don't you dare do that!* ○ *How dare you?* **3.** CHALLENGE SB to challenge sb to do sth, usually sth dangerous or frightening ○ *daring each other to jump first* ■ *n.* A CHALLENGE a challenge to sb to do sth dangerous or frightening, or a response to such a challenge ○ *did it for a dare* [Old English *darr, dearr*, first and third person present singular forms of *durran* 'to dare', from prehistoric Germanic] —**darer** *n.*

daredevil /dáir devv'l/ *n.* SB WHO DOES RISKY THINGS sb who is daring and takes risks, especially sb who performs dangerous stunts ■ *adj.* **1.** UNMINDFUL OF DANGER showing a carefree disregard for risk or danger, especially by performing dangerous stunts **2.** DANGEROUS with a high degree of risk or danger ○ *a daredevil stunt*

daredevilry /dáir devv'lri/, **daredeviltry** /dáir devv'ltri/ *n.* **1.** FEARLESS ATTITUDE a carefree disregard for danger **2.** RISK-TAKING dangerous acts or stunts performed by a daring person

daresay /dáir sáy/ ◇ **I daresay, I dare say 1.** used, often in an irritable tone, to express the fact that the speaker considers sth to be likely or possible **2.** used crossly or impatiently to dismiss sth that is true but irrelevant

Dar es Salaam /daár ess sə laám/ largest city, leading port, and former capital of Tanzania. The name means 'haven of peace'. Population: 1,360,850 (1988).

darg /daarg/ *n.* **1.** *Scotland* DAY'S WORK a day's work **2.** *Aus* SPECIFIC AMOUNT OF WORK a specific amount of work [Mid-16thC. Shortening and alteration of *daywork*, from Old English *dæg-weorc*, literally 'a day's work'.]

dargah /daárgə/ *n.* **1.** TOMB OF MUSLIM SAINT a site where a Muslim holy man was buried or cremated **2.** SHRINE TO SAINT a shrine built at a dargah [From Persian]

daric /dárrik/ *n.* a gold or silver coin used in ancient Persia [Mid-16thC. From Greek *Dareikos* 'of Darius (I)', King of Persia, denoting that the coin was of the realm of Darius and his successors.]

daring /dáiring/ *adj.* **1.** BRAVE AND ADVENTUROUS showing a courageous or reckless disregard for danger ○ *The officer led a daring assault on the enemy machine-gun post.* **2.** RISKY involving an element of risk or danger ○ *a daring move* **3.** SHOCKING unconventional or ahead of its time and therefore likely to shock, upset, or offend ■ *n.* BOLDNESS courage combined with a willingness to take risks or attempt difficult or unconventional things —**daringness** *n.*

WORD KEY: SYNONYMS

See Synonyms at ***bold***.

daringly /dáiringli/ *adv.* in a way that involves taking a risk and is likely to be exciting or shocking ○ *She daringly decided to break with tradition.*

dariole /dárri ōl/ *n.* **1. dariole, dariole mould** COOKING MOULD a small cup-shaped mould in which individual portions of savoury or sweet dishes can be cooked and then served **2.** DISH COOKED IN SMALL MOULD a dish cooked and served in a dariole [14thC. From French, 'custard tart'.]

Darius I /də rī́ əss/, **King of Persia** (558–486 BC). He reorganized the administration of the Persian Empire during his reign (521–486 BC). His army invaded Greece in 490 but was defeated at the battle of Marathon.

Darius III /dərīəs/, **King of Persia** (380?–330 BC). He was defeated by Alexander the Great at the battles of Issus (333 BC) and Guagamela (331 BC) and was assassinated by one of his own satraps.

Darjeeling[1] /daar jeéling/ *n.* a high-quality black tea grown around Darjeeling in India, or the hot drink made from its leaves

Darjeeling[2] /daar jeéling/ town in northern West Bengal, India, close to the border with Nepal. Under British rule it was the summer capital of the government of Bengal. It is famous for its tea estates. Population: 73,078 (1991).

dark /daark/ *adj.* **1.** NOT LIGHT OR LIT with little or no light ○ *It's getting dark; do you mind if I put the light on?* ○ *It was a dark and stormy night.* **2.** NOT LIGHT IN COLOUR reflecting less light than other colours or shades and therefore appearing deeper, richer, or more sombre ○ *The curtains are dark green.* **3.** BROWNISH OR BLACKISH not pale or fair, but brown to black in hair or eye colour ○ *She has darker eyes than her brother.* **4.** MISERABLE characterized by unhappiness, misfortune, or pessimism ○ *in the dark days of the Depression* **5.** ANGRY suggesting hostility or anger ○ *dark looks* **6.** NASTY evil or wicked ○ *the dark side of his character* **7.** MYSTERIOUS little known or kept hidden from others ○ *dark secrets* **8.** UNENLIGHTENED lacking enlightenment, learning, and artistic or scientific achievement (*formal*) **9.** THEATRE CLOSED not presenting theatrical performances **10.** MELLOW deep and rich in sound ■ *n.* **1.** LACK OF LIGHT a place, time, or situation in which there is too little light to see properly ○ *I don't like driving in the dark.* **2.** NIGHTFALL the beginning of night ○ *We left early to be home before dark.* **3.** SHADED AREA a darker colour or a darker-coloured or shaded part ○ *the contrast between the darks and the lights in the picture* [Old English *deorc*. Ultimately from an Indo-European word that also produced German *tarnen* 'to mask, screen', which is related via Old French to English *tarnish*.]

Dark /daark/, **Eleanor** (1901–85) Australian writer. She wrote a trilogy of historical novels about the early years of European settlement in Australia, the first of which was *The Timeless Land* (1941). Born **Eleanor O'Reilly**

dark adaptation /-ə dápsh'n/, **dark adaption** *n.* the reflex changes, such as dilation of the pupil and increased sensitivity of the retina, that enable the eye to continue to see in dim light

dark-adapted /daárk ə dáptid/ *adj.* ANAT having made the physical and chemical changes involved in dark adaptation and adjusted for seeing in relative darkness

Dark-Age *adj.* dating from, belonging to, or typical of the Dark Ages

Dark Ages *npl.* **1.** HIST PERIOD BEFORE MIDDLE AGES the period of European history between the fall of the Roman Empire in AD 476 and about AD 1000, for which there are few historical records and during which life was comparatively uncivilized **2.** UNDEVELOPED STATE an undeveloped state, way of life, or way of doing things (*informal*) ○ *Computers were in their Dark Ages a few decades ago.*

dark chocolate *n.* chocolate that has no added milk and is darker and less sweet than milk chocolate

Dark Continent *n.* a term formerly used to refer to Africa before large areas of the continent had been explored (*archaic*) [Probably taken from the title of Henry Stanley's *Through the Dark Continent* (1878), most of central Africa being unknown and mysterious to Europeans of the time]

darken /daárkən/ (**-ens, -ening, -ened**) *vti.* **1.** GET DARKER OR COLOUR STH DARKER to become darker, or to make sth darker ○ *I mixed a little blue and brown with the red to darken it.* **2.** BECOME UNHAPPY OR MAKE SB UNHAPPY to become unhappy, less hopeful, or angry, or to cause such a change in sb or sth ○ *The outlook has darkened considerably since the last update.* —**darkener** *n.*

darkey *n.* = **darky**

dark-field illumination *n.* the lighting of a specimen in a microscope from the side so that it can be seen against a dark background

dark-field microscope *n.* = **ultramicroscope**

dark glasses *npl.* spectacles with dark-tinted lenses, especially sunglasses

dark horse *n.* **1.** UNKNOWN QUANTITY sb about whom very little is known or who tends to be reticent, especially sb who subsequently reveals unexpected talents **2.** POL UNEXPECTEDLY SUCCESSFUL CANDIDATE a candidate who gains an unexpected amount of support in an electoral campaign **3.** SPORTS UNEXPECTEDLY SUCCESSFUL CONTESTANT a little-known competitor who achieves unexpected success in a race or other sporting contest [From the image of a little-known racehorse who makes a surprisingly good showing in a race]

darkish /daárkish/ *adj.* fairly dark in colour or shading ○ *a woman with darkish hair*

dark lantern *n.* a lantern with a sliding panel that is used to dim or hide its light

darkle /daárk'l/ (**-kles, -kling, -kled**) *vi.* (*archaic or literary*) **1.** BECOME DARK to grow dark **2.** BE FAINT to appear indistinctly [Early 19thC. Back-formation from DARKLING, adverb, mistaken for a present participle and adjective.]

darkling /daárkling/ *adv.* IN DARKNESS in the dark (*archaic literary*) ○ *'Darkling I listen, and full many a time...'* (John Keats, *Ode to a Nightingale*; 1820)

■ *adj.* (*archaic or literary*) **1.** WITHOUT CLARITY dark, dim, or obscure **2.** OCCURRING IN DARKNESS done or happening in the night [15thC. Formed from DARK + the obsolete adverbial suffix *-ling*, denoting position or condition.]

darkling beetle *n.* a beetle with a hard black or brown body whose larvae feed on decaying vegetable matter, living plants, and grain. Family: Tenebrionidae. [Probably from the beetle's habit of living in dark or hidden places]

darkly /daʹarkli/ *adv.* **1.** THREATENINGLY in a way that conveys a threat or a sense of foreboding **2.** IN BLACK OR A DARK COLOUR in or with black, or as a dark-coloured shape ○ *trees darkly outlined against the horizon*

dark matter *n.* matter postulated to exist in the universe because of observed gravitational effects. It is thought to comprise a substantial part of the mass of the universe but remains as yet undetected by direct observation. [From the nonluminous and mysterious nature of the matter]

dark meat *n.* meat from the legs and thighs of poultry, which is a darker colour than the meat of the breast

darkness /daʹarknəs/ *n.* **1.** DARK the absence or lack of light ○ *He flicked a switch and the room was plunged into darkness.* **2.** NIGHT night time **3.** DEPTH OF COLOUR the comparative depth of a colour or its closeness to black [Old English *deorcnes*]

dark reaction *n.* the second phase of photosynthesis, during which light is not required and carbon dioxide is reduced

darkroom /daʹark room, -room/ *n.* a room from which natural light is excluded so that light-sensitive photographic materials can be safely handled and photographs can be developed

dark rum *n.* rum that is brown in colour

darksome /daʹarksəm/ *adj.* without light and gloomy or unpleasant (*archaic or literary*) ○ *doomed to die in a darksome dungeon*

dark star *n.* a star that is not visible and is usually detectable only by its radio or infrared emissions or by its gravitational effect on other bodies. It is often a component of a binary star and can cause the brightness of its visible partner to vary periodically.

darky /daʹarki/ (*plural* **-ies**), **darkey** (*plural* **-eys**), **darkie** *n.* a highly offensive term formerly used to refer to a Black person (*dated taboo insult*)

darling /daʹarling/ *n.* **1.** LOVING TERM OF ADDRESS used as an affectionate form of address to a loved one, or as a general, informal, and sometimes slightly affected form of address to social acquaintances **2.** SB CONSIDERATE a kind, helpful, or likable person **3.** INFORMAL TERM OF ADDRESS an extremely informal and typically suggestive term of address, often to a stranger (*informal*) **4.** FAVOURITE sb who is very popular with another person or with a particular group of people ○ *She's the darling of the literary reviews.* **5.** BELOVED PERSON a much-loved person or sweetheart (*dated*) ○ *She is my darling.* ■ *adj.* **1.** DEARLY LOVED loved very much **2.** NICE pretty and charming (*informal*) **3.** darling, darlin' *Ireland* SWEET-NATURED lovable, kind, pleasant, or sweet-natured (*informal*) [Old English *deorling*, literally 'dear person, dear one', formed from an earlier form of DEAR]

Darling /daʹarling/ river in southeastern Australia that rises near Toowoomba in southern Queensland and joins the River Murray in New South Wales, forming the country's longest river system. Length: 2,736 km/1,700 mi.

Darling, Grace (1815–42) British heroine. The daughter of a lighthouse keeper on the Farne Islands, she rowed with her father in a storm to rescue shipwrecked mariners (1838). Full name **Grace Horsley Darling**

Darling Downs /daʹarling-/ fertile tableland 160 km/100 mi. east of Brisbane in southeastern Queensland, Australia. Area: 70,000 sq. km/27,000 sq. mi.

Darling Range range of hills near Perth in Western Australia. The range is 320 km/200 mi. long, and the highest peak is Mount Cooke, 582 m/1,910 ft.

Darlington town and borough in County Durham, England. The Stockton and Darlington Railway, the

world's first public steam railway line, opened in 1825. Population: 100,600 (1995).

darn[1] /daarn/ *vti.* (**darns, darning, darned**) REPAIR STH WITH THREAD to mend a hole in a piece of clothing or fabric using long interwoven stitches to fill the gap ○ *sat there darning socks.* ■ *n.* REPAIR OF HOLE a repair to a piece of clothing or fabric using long interwoven stitches [Early 17thC. Origin uncertain: probably from French dialect *darner* 'to mend', from *darne* 'piece', ultimately of Celtic origin.] —**darner** *n.*

darn[2] /daarn/ *interj.* EXCLAMATION used instead of a swearword to express irritation, displeasure, or surprise (*informal*) ■ *adj., adv.* **darn, darned** EMPHATIC TERM used instead of a swearword to give emphasis or to indicate irritation or displeasure with sb or sth (*informal*) ○ *a darn good movie* ■ *vt.* (**darns, darning, darned**) CONDEMN STH used to express annoyance or frustration with sth or sb (*informal*) ○ *Darn it, I told you not to go in there.* [Late 18thC. From US English, alteration of DAMN, perhaps influenced by regional US English 'tarnal', alteration of ETERNAL.]

darned /daarnd/ *adj.* TERM OF DENIAL used instead of a swearword to express surprise, bafflement, disavowal, or refusal (*informal*) ○ *I'll be darned if I know.* ■ *adj., adv.* = **darn**[2] (*informal*)

darnedest /daʹarndist/ *adj.* used to emphasize or draw to sb's attention sth that is unusual or out of the ordinary (*informal*)

darnel /daʹarn'l/ *n.* a type of grass commonly found growing as a weed in grain fields in Europe and Asia. Genus: *Lolium*. [Early 14thC. Origin uncertain: perhaps from Walloon *darnelle*, a form found in a regional dialect.]

darning /daʹarning/ *n.* **1.** MENDING HOLES IN CLOTHES the work of repairing holes in clothes with long interwoven stitches **2.** CLOTHING IN NEED OF MENDING clothes that need to be darned

darning egg *n.* an egg-shaped piece of wood or plastic, used to support the fabric around a hole that is being darned

darning mushroom *n.* a mushroom-shaped support made of wood or plastic, placed under a hole that is being darned

darning needle *n.* a long needle with a large eye, used in darning

Darnley /daʹarnli/, **Henry Stewart, Lord** (1545–67) Scottish nobleman. He was the second husband of Mary, Queen of Scots, and father of James VI of Scotland, who later became James I of England.

darogha /dárrōgə/ *n. S Asia* a person in charge of a group of police officers [Mid-17thC. From Persian and Urdu *daroga*, literally, 'governor'.]

dart /daart/ *n.* **1.** DARTS MISSILE USED IN DARTS a short weighted arrow with a long slender point, a tapered tubular body, and plastic or metal fins that is thrown at a dartboard in the game of darts **2.** ARMS MISSILE USED AS WEAPON a small arrow with a point at one end and feathers or fins at the other that can be thrown, shot from a blowgun, or scattered by an exploding bomb **3.** ZOOL POINTED, PROJECTING PART OR ORGAN a pointed, projecting part used, e.g. to penetrate tissue, or, in some species of snail, in mating **4.** FAST MOVE a sudden quick movement ○ *He made a dart for the door.* **5.** SEW STITCHED TAPERING FOLD a tapering fold sewn into a garment to make it fit, e.g. at the waist or bust ■ *v.* (**darts, darting, darted**) **1.** MOVE SWIFTLY to move suddenly and quickly ○ *The little fish darted under a stone.* **2.** *vt.* MAKE STH MOVE QUICKLY to move, extend, or direct sth quickly and suddenly ○ *She darted a meaningful glance at her husband across the table.* [14thC. Via Old French from a prehistoric Germanic word, from, ultimately, an Indo-European word meaning 'sharp'.]

dartboard /daʹart bawrd/ *n.* a round piece of wood or similar material marked with twenty radiating numbered segments and a bull's eye in the centre, used as a target in the game of darts

darter /daʹartər/ *n.* **1.** N AMERICAN FISH a small brightly-coloured fast-moving freshwater fish of the perch family, found in eastern North America. Family: Percidae. **2.** TROPICAL FISH-EATING BIRD a fish-eating diving bird with a long neck and sharp bill that inhabits the warmer freshwater regions of North and South

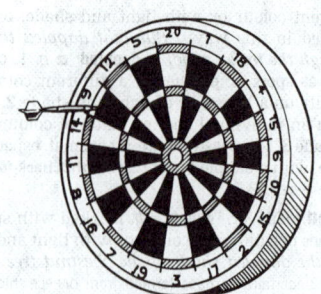

Dartboard

America, Africa, Asia, and Australia. Family: Anhingidae. US term **anhinga 3.** SB or STH THAT DARTS sb or sth that moves quickly and suddenly

Dartford /daʹartfərd/ town and local government district in northern Kent, England. Population: 83,600 (1995).

darting /daʹarting/ *adj.* swift and sudden, or making swift and sudden movements ○ *His darting runs down the left flank frequently opened up the Scottish defence.* —**dartingly** *adv.*

Dartmoor /daʹart moor/ *n.* **1.** HARDY SHEEP a sheep belonging to a hardy coarse-woolled breed originating in Dartmoor in Devon **2.** = **Dartmoor pony** [Mid-19thC. Named after *Dartmoor*, now called DARTMOOR NATIONAL PARK.]

Dartmoor National Park national park in Devon, southwestern England, established in 1951. The highest point of this moorland region is High Wilhays, 621 m/2,038 ft. Area: 954 sq. km/368 sq. mi.

Dartmoor pony (*plural* **Dartmoor ponies**) *n.* a pony belonging to a hardy long-haired breed originating in Dartmoor and still found living wild there [Mid-19thC. Named after *Dartmoor*, now called DARTMOOR NATIONAL PARK.]

Dartmouth /daʹartməth/ town and seaport in Devon, England. The Royal Naval College is located there. Population: 5,750 (1994).

darts /daarts/ *n.* an indoor game in which players take turns throwing arrow-shaped missiles (**darts**) from a set distance at a circular board (**dartboard**) placed at about eye level on a wall (*takes a singular verb*)

Darvon *tdmk.* a trademark for propoxyphene hydrochloride

Darwin /daʹarwin/ coastal city in northern Australia, capital of the Northern Territory. It was devastated by Cyclone Tracy in 1974. Population: 70,251 (1996).

Darwin, Charles (1809–82) British scientist. He laid the foundation of modern evolutionary theory and wrote the highly controversial *On the Origin of Species by Means of Natural Selection* (1859). He wrote many other books on the natural sciences, including *The Volcanic Islands* (1844) and *The Descent of Man* (1871). Full name **Charles Robert Darwin**

Darwinian /daar winni ən/ *adj.* relating to the 19th-century British naturalist Charles Darwin or his theory of evolution —**Darwinian** *n.*

Darwinian theory *n.* the theory, first developed by the 19th-century British naturalist Charles Darwin, that species of living things originate, evolve, and survive through natural selection in response to environmental changes

Darwinism /daʹarwinizəm/ *n.* **1.** = **Darwinian theory 2.** SUPPORT FOR DARWIN'S THEORY belief in or advocacy of Charles Darwin's theory of evolution —**Darwinist** *n.*, *adj.*

Darwin's finches *npl.* the birds of the Galapagos Islands on which Charles Darwin based his theory of evolution through observation of their feeding habits and corresponding differences in bill structure. Subfamily: Geospizinae.

dash /dash/ *n.* **1.** GRAM PUNCTUATION MARK a short horizontal line used as a punctuation mark, often in place of a comma or colon, or as a sign that certain letters or words have been omitted **2.** COMMUNICATION MORSE SYMBOL a short horizontal line representing a long sound or flash of light in written transcriptions of Morse code **3. RUSH** a quick purposeful movement by a person or a group of people in any direction ○ *There was a dash for the exit as soon as the alarm was raised.* **4.** ATHLETICS **RACE** a short-distance running race **5. SMALL QUANTITY ADDED** a small quantity of sth added to sth else, e.g. to improve the flavour of food or drink or to enliven speech or writing ○ *A dash of common sense would make his arguments a lot more convincing.* **6. VIGOUR AND VERVE** a combination of vigour, daring, and style in the way a person acts ○ *She carried it off with a certain amount of dash.* **7.** CARS **DASHBOARD** the instrument panel of a car (*informal*) **8. QUICK STROKE** a quick and often violent movement, blow, or stroke ○ *with a dash of her arm* ■ *v.* **(dashes, dashing, dashed) 1.** *vi.* **HURRY** to run, move, or travel fast or hastily ○ *He dashed off to catch his plane.* **2.** *vt.* **KNOCK OR THROW STH VIOLENTLY** to knock or throw sth with a sudden violent sweep or blow (*formal*) ○ *She dashed the papers down on the desk in anger.* **3.** *vti.* **SMASH** to break or throw sth or to be broken or thrown, usually against a hard surface (*formal*) ○ *The waves were dashing against the sea wall.* **4.** *vt.* **RUIN STH** to frustrate or destroy sth (*often passive*) ○ *The new crisis has dashed all hopes of a speedy return to democratic government.* **5.** *vt.* **DISCOURAGE SB** to make sb feel discouraged or intimidated (*usually passive*) ○ *I felt more than a little dashed by the ease with which she had refuted my arguments.* **6.** *vt.* **ADD SMALL AMOUNT TO STH** to alter, improve, or flavour with a small amount of another substance (*often passive*) ○ *tonic water dashed with bitters* **7.** *vt.* **EXCLAIM AGAINST STH OR SB** used to express annoyance or dissatisfaction with sth or sb (*dated informal*) ○ *Dash it, I've already paid the man!* [13thC. Origin uncertain: perhaps from Old Norse (compare Swedish *daska* 'to slap, beat'). Originally a verb meaning 'to smash to pieces'; the meaning evolved via the idea of quick movement.] ◇ **cut a dash** to be dressed smartly and stylishly so as to attract attention (*dated*)

dash off *vt.* to write, draw, or compose sth in a great hurry (*informal*) ○ *She dashed off a note to her secretary before leaving the office.*

dashboard /dásh bawrd/ *n.* **1. PANEL IN FRONT OF DRIVER** a panel in front of the driver of a vehicle or the pilot of a small aircraft or boat that contains various indicator dials, switches, and controls **2. MUDGUARD ON CARRIAGE** a board, panel, or screen to protect the driver of a horse-drawn carriage from being splashed with mud [Mid-19thC. From DASH in the obsolete sense 'to splash, spatter'.]

dashed /dasht/ past participle of **dash** ■ *adv.* **VERY** used, usually with affectation, to add emphasis to an adjective or adverb (*dated informal*) ○ *You see it's dashed awkward, because I've already promised to take Emmy.* ■ *adj.* **VERY BOTHERSOME** used to express annoyance or dissatisfaction with sth or sb (*dated informal*) ○ *Dashed cartridges got wet, dashed gun wouldn't fire!*

dasheen /da sheen/ *n. Carib* **1.** = **taro 2. BOILED TUBERS** tubers of the dasheen plant, usually boiled for eating [Late 19thC. Origin uncertain: perhaps an alteration of French *(chou) de Chine* 'Chinese (cabbage)'.]

dasher /dáshər/ *n.* a device that agitates or stirs the contents of a churn or ice-cream maker

dashi /dáshi/ *n.* a clear broth or stock, usually made from fish [Mid-20thC. From Japanese.]

dashiki /də sheeki/, **daishiki, dasheki** *n.* a man's brightly coloured loose-fitting buttonless garment resembling a long shirt, worn mainly in Africa, the Caribbean, and the United States [Mid-20thC. Origin uncertain: probably from Yoruba *danshiki*.]

dashing /dáshing/ *adj.* **1. SPIRITED** confident and full of bravado and spirit (*dated*) ○ *a dashing young officer* **2. SMART** smart and stylish ○ *That's a rather dashing outfit, if I may say so.* —**dashingly** *adv.* —**dashingness** *n.*

dashpot /dásh pot/ *n.* a device consisting of a piston inside a fluid-filled cylinder that absorbs or dampens vibrations in a mechanism

dassie /dássi/ *n.* ZOOL = **hyrax** [Late 18thC. Via Afrikaans from Dutch *dasje*, literally 'small badger', from *das* 'badger'.]

dastard /dástərd/ *n.* sb who is cowardly, mean, and treacherous (*archaic*) [15thC. Origin uncertain: probably formed from Middle English *dast*, a form of the past participle of DAZE + -ARD. The original meaning was 'unintelligent person'.]

dastardly /dástərdli/ *adj.* used to refer humorously or melodramatically to sb or sth mean, treacherous, and cowardly ○ *a dastardly deed* —**dastardliness** *n.*

dasyure /dássi yoor/ *n.* a small usually carnivorous marsupial found in Australia, Tasmania, and neighbouring islands. Subfamily: Dasyurinae. [Mid-19thC. Via French from modern Latin *dasyurus*, from Greek *dasus* 'rough, hairy' + *oura* 'tail'.]

DAT /dee ay tee, dat/ *abbr.* digital audio tape

dat. *abbr.* dative

data[1] /dáytə, daatə/ *n.* (*takes a singular or plural verb*) **1. FACTUAL INFORMATION** information, often in the form of facts or figures obtained from experiments or surveys, used as a basis for making calculations or drawing conclusions **2.** COMPUT **INFORMATION FOR COMPUTER PROCESSING** information, e.g. numbers, text, images, and sounds, in a form that is suitable for storage in or processing by a computer [Mid-17thC. From the plural of Latin *datum*, neuter past participle of *dare* 'to give, grant' (source of English *condone* and *vendor*). The original English meaning was 'accepted assumptions, premises'.]

WORD KEY: USAGE

Singular or plural? Use of the term ***data*** has grown apace with the use of computer technology and of statistical methods. Because the word's meaning is much like that of the singular noun *information*, and because its Latin *-a* plural announces the word's plural status to us less plainly than a final *s* would, it is often treated as if it were singular. This use is extremely common, and few perceive it as wrong these days, especially given the word's connotation of a collection or single unit made up of many informational subunits. All the same, in highly formal English, use of ***data*** as a singular is best avoided. According to the traditional view, *Our data have been assembled over a number of years* would be correct, and constructions such as *very little data, The data shows...,* and *a great deal of data* would be regarded as incorrect.

data[2] plural of **datum**

data bank *n.* **1. STORE OF INFORMATION** a large store of information, especially one that is kept in or available to a computer, sometimes consisting of a number of databases **2.** = **database**

database /dáytə bayss/ *n.* a systematically arranged collection of computer data, structured so that it can be automatically retrieved or manipulated

database management system *n.* a computer program devised to design, create, manipulate, update, control, and interrogate one or more databases, often containing a proprietary query language for extracting data

data capture *n.* the collecting of data and entering of it in a computer, or the conversion of data into a form that can be input into a computer

data compression *n.* the encoding of data so that it requires less disk space for storage and transmission

dataglove /dáytə gluv/ *n.* a glove equipped with sensors that feed spatial and tactile data to a computer, allowing the wearer to manipulate and explore environments in virtual reality

data mining *n.* the locating of previously unknown patterns and relationships within data using a database application, e.g. the locating of customers with common interests in a retail establishment's database

data processing *n.* the entering, storing, updating, and retrieving of information, using a computer

data protection *n.* **1. PREVENTION OF MISUSE OF COMPUTER DATA** legal safeguards to prevent the misuse of information stored on a computer, particularly information relating to individuals **2. INSTALLATION OF SAFEGUARDS FOR COMPUTER DATA** the adoption of administrative, technical, or physical deterrents to safeguard the privacy, integrity, and security of computer data

data warehouse *n.* a database or collection of databases from different areas of a commercial organization used as a tool for analysing overall business strategy as opposed to routine operations

datcha /dáchə/ *n.* ARCHIT = **dacha**

date[1] /dayt/ *n.* **1.** TIME **DAY, MONTH, AND YEAR** a phrase or string of numbers that denotes a particular day of the month or year. It usually consists of the number of the day, the name or number of the month, and the number of the year. **2.** TIME **TIME OF AN EVENT** a date used to locate a past or future event in time ○ *The concert has been postponed to a later date.* **3. VISUAL REPRESENTATION OF DATE** the words or numbers of a date in the form of a written statement or inscription, e.g. on a document or coin ○ *There's no date on this letter.* **4. PERIOD** the period during which sth such as a work of art was created ○ *This has much in common with other artefacts of that date.* **5. APPOINTMENT** an appointment to meet sb for a social or business activity ○ *I've got a dinner date with a client.* **6. ROMANTIC APPOINTMENT** a social or romantic engagement with a person ○ *I thought we had a date tonight.* **7. PARTNER ON DATE** sb with whom a date has been arranged ○ *My date stood me up.* **8.** ARTS **COMMITMENT TO PERFORM** an engagement to give a performance ○ *Our band has a date to play at the Coliseum.* ■ **dates** *npl.* **DATES OF BIRTH AND DEATH** the years of sb's birth and death ○ *Do you happen to know Van Gogh's dates?* ■ *v.* **(dates, dating, dated) 1.** *vt.* **PUT DATE ON STH** to mark sth with a date, usually the current date ○ *Please sign and date the contract.* **2.** *vt.* **ASSIGN DATE TO STH** to find out or state the time or period when sth was made ○ *The early works of Shakespeare are rather difficult to date precisely.* **3.** *vi.* **ORIGINATE** to have an origin in a particular time in the past ○ *We have records dating back to the 16th century.* **4.** *vi.* **GO OUT OF STYLE** to become old-fashioned ○ *This is a classic style and won't date.* **5.** *vt.* **MAKE SB OR STH SEEM OLD** to reveal the age of sb or sth, or to make sb or sth seem old-fashioned ○ *The shape of the headlights dates the car.* **6.** *vti.* **GO ON DATES WITH SB** to go out regularly with sb as a social or romantic partner ○ *We dated for a few months.* [14thC. Ultimately from medieval Latin *data*, literally 'given', past participle of Latin *dare* (see DATA[1]); from '(epistola) data Romae', literally '(letter) given at Rome', with the day and month appended.] —**dateable** *adj.* ◇ **to date** up to the present time

date[2] /dayt/ *n.* **1.** FOOD **SMALL OVAL FRUIT** the dark-coloured oval edible fruit of the date palm tree. It has sweet flesh and a single hard narrow seed. **2.** TREES = **date palm 3.** *Aus* **ANUS** the anus (*taboo offensive*) [13thC. Via Old French from, ultimately, Greek *daktulos* 'finger or toe, date'; from the resemblance of dates to fingers or toes or of the date palm's leaves to a hand.]

dated /dáytid/ *adj.* **1. OLD-FASHIONED** no longer used or in vogue, often having been current or fashionable in the recent past **2. SHOWING A DATE** with a date marked or written on it

Datel /dáy tel/ *tdmk.* a trademark for a British Telecom service providing data connections between computers

dateless /dáytləss/ *adj.* **1. TIMELESS** unlikely to become old-fashioned or obsolete **2. LIMITLESS** with no limit in time (*archaic or literary*) ○ *'For precious friends hid in death's dateless night'* (William Shakespeare, *Sonnets*; 1609)

dateline /dáyt līn/ *n.* a line at the head of a newspaper article or similar item giving the date and place of writing

Date Line *n.* = **International Date Line**

date palm *n.* a tall palm tree with feathery fronds, originally from North Africa and West Asia, cultivated for its edible fruit. Latin name: *Phoenix dactylifera.*

date rape *n.* an act of rape committed on a person after a date

date-rape **(date-rapes, date-raping, date-raped)** *vt.* to rape a person after a date

date stamp *n.* a rubber stamp used to mark the date on sth, or the date marked by such a stamp —**date-stamp** *vt.*

Datin *n.* the title of a woman member of a senior order of chivalry in Malaysia

dating agency (*plural* **dating agencies**) *n.* an agency whose business is to establish personal contacts between similar or compatible people

dative /dáytiv/ *n.* **1.** GRAMMATICAL FORM a grammatical form (**case**) of nouns, pronouns, and other parts of speech in some languages that indicates the indirect object of a verb or is used after certain prepositions **2.** WORD a word in the dative ■ *adj.* IN THE DATIVE in or relating to the dative [15thC. From Latin *dativus* 'of giving' (formed from *dat-*, past participle stem of *dare* 'to give'; see DATA[1]), used in the phrase *dativus casus* 'dative case'.]

dative bond *n.* CHEM = **coordinate bond** [From the fact that one of the atoms gives up or yields electrons to another atom to form the bond]

datolite /dáttə līt/ *n.* a hydrated silicate of calcium and boron found in cavities in basalt and other igneous rocks. Formula: $CaBSiO_4(OH)$. [Early 19thC. Coined from Greek *dateisthai* 'to divide' + -O- + -LITE; from the divisions between its crystals.]

Datuk *n.* the title of a man member of a senior order of chivalry in Malaysia [Mid-19thC. From Malay *dato'*, *datok*, variants of the same word.]

datum /dáytəm, daá-/ (*plural* **-ta** /-tə/) *n.* **1.** ITEM OF INFORMATION a single piece of information **2.** LOGIC GIVEN FACT a known or assumed fact that is used as the basis for a theory, conclusion, or inference **3.** MAPS POINT OF REFERENCE a point, line, or surface used as a basis for measurement or calculation in mapping or surveying [Mid-18thC. From Latin (see DATA[1]).]

datum line, **datum level**, **datum plane** *n.* the horizontal plane or line from which all other heights and depths are measured or calculated on a map or chart

DATV *abbr.* digitally assisted television

daub /dawb/ *v.* (**daubs, daubing, daubed**) **1.** *vt.* PUT STH ON BLOTCHILY to put or spread a semiliquid substance, e.g. mud, paint, or cream, on a surface in a crude, hurried, or irregular way ○ *They had daubed slogans all over the walls.* **2.** *vti.* PAINTING PAINT CRUDELY to paint or apply paint crudely and inexpertly ■ *n.* **1.** BLOTCH a crude patch, splash, or smear of a semiliquid substance on sth **2.** BAD PAINTING a painting that is considered to be badly or inexpertly done ○ *'When he first came to Rome he painted worthless daubs and gave no promise of talent'.* (Henry James, *Roderick Hudson*; 1876) **3.** CONSTR SUBSTANCE FOR DAUBING a mixture of clay, lime, and chopped straw plastered onto interwoven rods or twigs to make a wall. ◊ **wattle and daub** [14thC. Via Old French *dauber* from Latin *dealbare* 'to whiten over, plaster', from *albare* 'to whiten', from *albus* 'white' (source of English *album*).] —**dauby** *adj.*

daube /dōb/ *n.* a dish of braised meat or vegetables, especially a traditional French dish of beef braised in wine [Early 18thC. By folk etymology (from DAUB) from French *daube*, via Italian *dobba* from Catalan *a la adoba* 'stewed', ultimately from a prehistoric Germanic word meaning 'to strike'.]

dauber /dáwbər/ *n.* a very bad or inexpert painter

Daubigny /dóō bee nyee/, **Charles-François** (1817–78) French painter and etcher. He was a landscape painter associated with the Barbizon school whose work influenced the impressionists.

daud /dawd/ *n.* Scotland LUMP OF STH a lump, chunk, or stiff dollop of sth ■ *vt.* (**dauds, dauding, dauded**) Scotland KNOCK OR THUMP STH to knock or thump sth [Late 16thC. Probably an imitation of the sound.]

Daudet /dō day/, **Alphonse** (1840–97) French writer. His works include *Letters from My Mill* (1869). Full name **Louis Marie Alphonse Daudet**

daughter /dáwtər/ *n.* **1.** FEMALE CHILD sb's female child **2.** WOMAN OR GIRL CONNECTED WITH PLACE a woman or girl considered as a product of a place or institution (*formal*) ○ *Daughters of the American Revolution* **3.** PRODUCT OF STH sth produced by or issuing from sth else (*literary*) ○ *Truth is the daughter of time.* **4.** DESCENDANT a woman or girl descendant (*literary*) ○ *a daughter of Eve* **5.** PHYS NUCLIDE FORMED BY RADIOACTIVE DECAY a nuclide formed from an element by radioactive decay ■ *adj.* **1.** FORMED FROM STH ELSE formed by or from a similar thing, usually retaining close links with it and sometimes remaining subordinate to it **2.** SCI BEING AN OFFSPRING produced by a process of

reproduction, replication, or division [Old English *dohtor*. Via a prehistoric Germanic word, which also produced Dutch *dochter*, German *Tochter*, and Swedish *dotter*, from an Indo-European word with descendants in Sanskrit *duhitir* and Greek *thugatēr*.] —**daughterless** *adj.*

daughterboard /dáwtər bawrd/ *n.* a printed circuit board that plugs into the motherboard of a computer, usually to improve the performance of a system

daughter cell *n.* either of the identical cells produced when a living cell divides

daughter-in-law (*plural* **daughters-in-law**) *n.* the wife of your son

daughterly /dáwtərli/ *adj.* typical or expected of a daughter ○ *She came to regard the distinguished professor with an almost daughterly affection.* —**daughterliness** *n.*

Daughters of the American Revolution *npl.* in the United States, a women's patriotic society founded in 1890 by descendants of those who fought in the War of American Independence. It has about 200,000 members and is based in Washington.

Daumier /dō mi ay/, **Honoré** (1808–79) French painter and caricaturist. He is known for his satirical caricatures of contemporary society and politics.

daunt /dawnt/ (**daunts, daunting, daunted**) *vt.* to make sb feel anxious, intimidated, or discouraged (*usually passive*) ○ *The scale of the task would have daunted even the most experienced organizer.* [13thC. Via Anglo-Norman *daunter* from Latin *domitare* 'to tame'.] —**daunter** *n.*

daunting /dáwnting/ *adj.* likely to discourage, intimidate, or frighten sb ○ *You'll find the task less daunting if you divide it up into manageable sections.* —**dauntingly** *adv.*

dauntless /dáwntləss/ *adj.* unlikely or unable to be frightened or discouraged (*literary*) ○ *We remember with admiration their dauntless courage and optimism.* —**dauntlessly** *adv.* —**dauntlessness** *n.*

dauphin /dáwfin, dō-/ *n.* in former times, the eldest son of the king of France and the direct heir to the throne [15thC. Via French, literally 'dolphin', from Old French *daulphin* (see DOLPHIN).]

━━ WORD KEY: ORIGIN ━━
The title *dauphin* originally belonged to the lords of the Viennois, an area in the southeast of France, whose coat of arms incorporated three dolphins. After the Viennois province of Dauphiné was sold by Charles of Valois to the French crown in 1343, the king gave it to his eldest son, and from then on all eldest sons of the French monarch inherited it, along with the title *dauphin.*

dauphine /dáw feen, dō-/, **dauphiness** /dáwfinəss/ *n.* the wife of the dauphin [Mid-19thC. From French, the feminine form of *dauphin* (see DAUPHIN).]

daven /daá ven/ (**-ens, -ening, -ened**) *vi.* JUDAISM **1.** RECITE JEWISH PRAYERS to recite prayers from the Jewish liturgies **2.** LEAD PRAYERS to lead Jewish prayers [Mid-20thC. From Yiddish *davnen* 'to pray'.]

Davenant /dávvənənt/, **Sir William** (1606–68) English poet and dramatist. His works include the comic play *The Wits* (1633), and the epic poem *Gondibert* (1651). His notable theatrical innovations include an early English opera, movable scenery, and the introduction of women actors. He was appointed poet laureate in 1638.

davenport /dávv'n pawrt/ *n.* **1.** WRITING DESK an ornamental writing desk with a sloping top and drawers in its sides **2.** *US* LARGE SOFA a large well-upholstered sofa, especially one that can be converted into a bed [Mid-19thC. Origin uncertain: perhaps named after the craftsman who produced it, or one Captain *Davenport*, said by some to have ordered a writing desk with these features.]

David /dáy vid/, **King of Judah** (d. 961 BC). During his reign (1000 BC-962 BC), he defeated the Philistines, conquered Jerusalem, and became the ruler of Israel.

David, St (520?–589?) patron saint of Wales. A missionary in Wales and southwestern England, he is thought to have founded 12 monasteries, including Glastonbury in Somerset.

David /dáyvid/, **Sir Edgeworth** (1858–1934) Welsh-born Australian geologist and explorer. He was a member of Shackleton's 1907 Antarctic expedition and leader of the first party to reach the South Magnetic Pole (1908). Full name **Sir Tannatt William Edgeworth David**

David /dáy vid/, **Elizabeth** (1913–92) British food researcher and writer. Her many books include *Mediterranean Food* (1950) and *English Bread and Yeast Cookery* (1977).

David /da veéd/, **Jacques-Louis** (1748–1825) French painter. His neoclassical romantic style, e.g. in his *Death of Marat* (1793), made him the favoured painter of French Revolutionary leaders and of Napoleon I.

Davies /dáy viss/, **Paul Charles William** (b. 1946) British-born Australian physicist. He was Professor of Natural Philosophy at the University of Adelaide, and author of *The Mind of God* (1992).

Davies, Sir Peter Maxwell (b. 1934) British composer and conductor. His works, such as the operas *The Lighthouse* (1980) and *Resurrection* (1987), often deal with black, apocalyptic themes.

Davies, Robertson (1913–95) Canadian novelist, essayist, and playwright. His books include *The Salterton Trilogy* (1951–58), *The Deptford Trilogy* (1970–75), and *The Cornish Trilogy* (1981–88). *What's Bred in the Bone* (1985) was shortlisted for the Booker Prize.

Davies, W. H. (1871–1940) British poet. His works include *The Soul's Destroyer* (1905) and *The Autobiography of a Super Tramp* (1907). As a young man he spent some years living as a tramp in Britain and the United States before settling down to writing. Full name **William Henry Davies**

Bette Davis

Davis /dáyviss/, **Bette** (1908–89) US film actor. She won the Academy Award for best actress for *Dangerous* (1935) and *Jezebel* (1938). Full name **Ruth Elizabeth Davis**

Davis, Judy (b. 1955) Australian actor. She is noted for her performances on stage and in films, including *My Brilliant Career* (1979) and *Husbands and Wives* (1992).

Popperfoto
Miles Davis

Davis, Miles (1926–91) US trumpet player and band leader. A consummate improviser, he pioneered a more understated form of bebop know as 'cool jazz'. He was also noted for incorporating electronic instruments into jazz and combining jazz and rock. Full name **Miles Dewey Davis III**

Davis Cup *n.* **1.** INTERNATIONAL MEN'S TENNIS COMPETITION an annual international men's tennis competition for which a trophy is awarded to the winning nation **2.** TROPHY GIVEN AS PRIZE the trophy awarded to the winning nation in the Davis Cup competition [Early 20thC. Named after Dwight Filley *Davis*, US tennis player and government official, who donated the trophy.]

Davison /dáyviss'n/, **Emily** (1872–1913) British suffragette. Protesting against women's exclusion from the franchise, she died after throwing herself in front of a racehorse owned by King George V during the Epsom Derby.

davit /dávvit/ *n.* a small crane at the side of a ship's deck, especially one of a pair of curved metal posts with tackle attached for suspending and lowering a lifeboat [15thC. From Anglo-Norman *daviot, daviet*, literally 'little David', from the male name *Davi* 'David'.]

Davitt /dávvit/, **Michael** (1846–1906) Irish nationalist leader. He was imprisoned (1870–77) for nationalist activities, and founded the anti-absentee landlord Land League (1879).

Davos /dávvoss/ mountain resort in Graubünden Canton, eastern Switzerland. Population: 10,500 (1992).

Davy /dáyvi/, **Sir Humphry** (1778–1829) British chemist. He is best known as the inventor of the miner's safety lamp (1815). He also discovered the use of nitrous oxide as an anaesthetic and identified several metallic elements.

Davy Jones *n.* the personification of the sea [Origin unknown]

Davy Jones's locker *n.* the bottom of the sea, especially considered as the final resting place of drowned sailors or sunken ships (*informal*) [Early 18thC. *Davy Jones* 'Evil Spirit of the Sea' (in sailors' parlance); *locker* is a sea-chest; the phrase 'laid in the lockers' was a nautical metaphor for 'dead'.]

Davy lamp

Davy lamp /dáyvi-/ *n.* MINING a portable oil-burning lamp, formerly used by miners, in which the flame is protected by metal gauze to prevent it from igniting explosive gases underground [Early 19thC. Named after Sir Humphry DAVY, who invented it.]

daw /daw/ *n.* a jackdaw (*archaic or regional*) [15thC. Origin uncertain: probably from assumed Old English *dawe*, which came from a prehistoric Germanic word that also produced German *Dohle* 'jackdaw'.]

dawdle /dáwd'l/ (-**dles**, -**dling**, -**dled**) *vi.* **1.** MOVE SLOWLY to walk or move slowly and reluctantly or idly ○ *We'll get there in time if you don't dawdle.* **2.** WASTE TIME to spend far more time than is necessary in doing sth ○ *We dawdled over lunch and it was three o'clock before we left the restaurant.* [Mid-17thC. Origin uncertain: perhaps from a dialectal form of *daddle*, from *dadder* 'to walk unsteadily, walk like a child, dawdle'.] —**dawdler** *n.* —**dawdling** *n., adj.* —**dawdlingly** *adv.*

dawk /dawk/ *n.* = **dak**

Dawkins /dáwkinz/, **Richard** (*b.* 1941) British evolutionary biologist. He is best known for his book *The Selfish Gene* (1976), which describes the gene's strategy for survival. He developed his arguments in *The Blind Watchmaker* (1988).

dawn /dawn/ *n.* **1.** DAYBREAK the first appearance of light in the sky as the sun rises at the beginning of a new day **2.** BEGINNING the beginning of sth, especially a period of time or history ○ *the dawn of the industrial era* ■ *vi.* (**dawns, dawning, dawned**) **1.** BEGIN to begin, as the sun rises and light appears in the sky ○ *The day dawned cloudy and wet.* **2.** BECOME APPARENT to begin to be perceived ○ *The realization dawned that few of them would survive.* **3.** COMMENCE to begin to develop (*literary*) [15thC. The verb is a back-formation from DAWNING; the noun arose from the verb in the late 16thC.]

dawn on *vt.* to come into sb's mind or consciousness ○ *It was some time before the seriousness of the situation dawned on them.*

dawn alert *n.* taking defensive precautions on a ship just before first light if an enemy attack seems likely ○ *All hands went to their battle stations for dawn alert.*

dawn chorus *n.* **1.** BIRDSONG AT DAYBREAK the loud singing of many birds as the first light of day appears in the sky **2.** NOISE IN EARLY MORNING any loud sound, especially from a number of different sources, occurring very early in the morning (*humorous*) ○ *a dawn chorus of power drills and hammering*

dawning /dáwning/ *n.* BEGINNING OF DAY OR AGE the beginning of a new day or of a new period of time or history ○ *with the dawning of the computer age* ■ *adj.* DEVELOPING beginning to appear, develop, or be perceived [13thC. Alteration of obsolete *dawing*, from obsolete *daw* 'to dawn', literally 'to become day' (related to English *day*).]

dawn raid *n.* **1.** MIL SURPRISE ATTACK a surprise attack on enemy troops at dawn **2.** STOCK EXCH TAKEOVER STRATEGY a surprise attempt to buy a large number of a company's shares at the start of a day's trading, especially as a first stage in a takeover bid

dawn redwood *n.* a deciduous tree with flat leaves and small round cones that is native to China and widely grown elsewhere as an ornamental. Latin name: *Metasequoia glyptostroboides*.

Dawson river in eastern Queensland, Australia, that rises in the Carnarvon Range and flows into the Mackenzie and Fitzroy rivers near the town of Duaringa. Length: 640 km/398 mi.

DAX *n.* a share index on the Frankfurt Stock Exchange. Full form **Deutsche Aktienindex**

day /day/ *n.* **1.** TIME 24 HOURS a period of 24 hours, usually beginning and ending at midnight **2.** SUNRISE TO SUNSET the part of a 24-hour period when it is light, between sunrise and sunset **3.** TIME NOT ASLEEP the part of a 24-hour period when sb is working or active ○ *I work an 8-hour day.* **4.** INDEFINITE PERIOD OR POINT IN TIME a time or period of time in the past, present, or future ○ *One of these days we'll get round to painting the house.* **5.** TIME OF FAME the time when a particular person or thing is well-known, popular, successful, or effective ○ *In her day she was one of our best-known Shakespearean actresses.* **6.** LIFE OR EXISTENCE the time when a particular person or thing is active or in existence ○ *In my day we had to work on Saturday mornings.* **7.** ASTRON, TIME PERIOD OF EARTH'S ROTATION ABOUT AXIS a unit of time equal to the Earth's period of rotation about its axis, measured either relative to the Sun (**solar day**) or the stars (**sidereal day**) **8.** ASTRON PERIOD OF PLANET'S ROTATION ABOUT AXIS the period of time in which a planet revolves once on its axis [Old English *dæg*. Ultimately from an Indo-European root that is also the ancestor of Latin *fovere* 'to warm'. The underlying sense is 'time when the sun is hot'.] ◇ **call it a day** to finish work or stop doing sth ◇ **carry** or **win the day** to gain a victory ◇ **day after day** for several or many days in a row ◇ **day by day 1.** each consecutive day **2.** progressively ◇ **day in, day out** every day without exception and all day long ◇ **in this day and age** nowadays, as opposed to past times and customs ◇ **it's early days** it is too soon to know how things will turn out ◇ **make sb's day** to make sb very happy ◇ **name the day** to set a date for sth, typically a wedding ◇ **save the day** to prevent defeat or disaster ◇ **sb's** or **sth's days are numbered** sb or sth will not survive much longer ◇ **that'll be the day!** an exclamation used to express the opinion that sth is most unlikely to happen (*informal*) ○ *You think they'll offer me Mike's job? That'll be the day!* ◇ **the other day** not long ago ◇ **those were the days!** used with affection and nostalgia about past times

Day /day/, **Doris** (*b.* 1924) US film actor and singer. She came to fame in the late 1950s with roles in light musicals and romantic comedies such as *Calamity Jane* (1953) and *Pillow Talk* (1959), for which she received an Academy Award nomination. Born **Doris von Kappelhoff**

Dayak /dī ak/ (*plural* -**aks** /dī ak/ *or* -**ak**) *n.* = **Dyak**

Dayan /dī án/ *n.* the title of the judge of the Beth Din, a Jewish religious court [Late 19thC. From Hebrew, formed from *dān* 'to judge'.]

day bed *n.* a couch or bed for reclining on during the day

day blindness *n.* the inability to see clearly in bright light with comparatively good vision in dim light. Technical name **hemeralopia**

daybook /dáy book/ *n.* a book in which financial transactions are recorded day by day

dayboy /dáy boy/ *n.* a boy who is a pupil at a residential school but does not board there

daybreak /dáy brayk/ *n.* the time when light first appears in the sky at the beginning of a day

daycare /dáy kair/ *n.* daytime supervision and recreational, training, or medical facilities for preschool children, physically challenged people, or seniors wishing special assistance

day centre *n.* a place providing nonresidential care or recreation for senior citizens, physically challenged people, or people with psychiatric disorders

daydream /dáy dreem/ *n.* **1.** DREAM EXPERIENCED WHILE AWAKE a series of often distracting and usually pleasant thoughts and images that pass through the mind while awake **2.** UNREALIZABLE HOPE OR FANTASY a pleasant wish or hope that is unlikely to be fulfilled ■ *vi.* (-**dreams**, -**dreaming**, -**dreamt** *or* -**dreamed** /-dremt/, -**dreamt** *or* -**dreamed**) THINK DISTRACTING THOUGHTS to have or indulge in daydreams —**daydreaming** *n.* —**daydreamy** *adj.*

daydreamer /dáy dreemər/ *n.* sb who is often inattentive or has unrealistic ideas

dayflower /dáy flowər/ *n.* a tropical plant with narrow pointed leaves and blue or purplish flowers that soon wilt. Genus: *Commelina*. [Late 17thC. From the fact that the flowers last for only one day.]

dayfly /dáy flī/ (*plural* -**flies**) *n.* = **mayfly** [Early 17thC. From the fact that the fly lives for only one day.]

daygirl /dáy gurl/ *n.* a girl who is a pupil at a residential school but does not board there

Day-Glo /dáy glō/ *tdmk.* a trademark for fluorescent dyes and colouring agents

day hospital *n.* a non-residential hospital or part of a hospital where patients go for treatment or therapy during the daytime

day job *n.* US a job that sb does merely to earn an income while trying to achieve success in another field, especially the arts (*informal*)

day labourer *n.* a manual worker who is hired and paid on a day-to-day basis

Day-Lewis /day loóis/, **C.** (1904–72) Irish-born British poet and novelist. His poetry includes *A Time to Dance* (1935) and *Poems in Wartime* (1940). He was poet laureate (1968–72), wrote works of literary criticism, and published detective stories under the name Nicholas Blake. Full name **Cecil Day-Lewis**

Day-Lewis, Daniel (*b.* 1957) British-born Irish stage and film actor. He won an Academy Award for best actor in *My Left Foot* (1989).

daylight /dáy līt/ *n.* **1.** SUNLIGHT natural light from the sun ○ *Open the curtains and let in a bit of daylight.* **2.** DAYTIME the part of the day when it is light **3.** DAYBREAK the time when light first appears in the sky at the beginning of a day **4.** PUBLIC AWARENESS public knowledge, notice, or scrutiny ○ *There are some secrets that they would prefer not to have exposed to daylight.* **5.** VISIBLE GAP a visible gap between competitors in a race, showing the lead that one has over the other ○ *There's definitely daylight now between the two boats as they approach the halfway mark.*

daylight lamp *n.* a lamp that gives light with a range of wavelengths similar to natural light

daylight robbery *n.* charging prices that seem far too high (*informal*) US term **highway robbery** [From the idea that the price charged is outrageous enough to be considered a crime committed in full public view]

daylight-saving time n. an adjustment of clock time to allow more hours of normal daylight. Clocks are usually set one hour ahead of standard time to achieve this.

day lily n. a perennial plant with large yellow, red, or orange flowers resembling those of the lily. The individual flowers usually die after one day but are produced over a period of time. Genus: *Hemerocallis*.

daylong /dáy long/ adj., adv. throughout the entire day

day-neutral adj. used to describe plants that mature and flower unaffected by the length of the daylight period they grow in

day-night match n. a one-day cricket match that begins in the early afternoon in natural light and continues into the evening under artificial light

day nursery n. a place where preschool children are looked after during the daytime, usually while their parents are at work

Day of Atonement n. = Yom Kippur

day off (plural **days off**) n. a day on which sb does not have to work

Day of Judgment n. = Judgment Day

day of reckoning n. a time when sb is made to answer for crimes or mistakes

day one n. the first day or the very beginning of sth ○ *It's day one of the electoral campaign.*

day out (plural **days out**) n. a day of leisure spent away from home

daypack /dáy pak/ n. a small rucksack or bag for carrying things needed during the day

day release n. a system that allows employees to take days off work without loss of pay to continue their education or training (hyphenated when used before a noun)

day return n. a ticket, or the fare charged, to travel to a place and back again on the same day, usually at a reduced price ○ *Two day returns to Glasgow, please.*

day room n. a communal recreation room in an institution such as a hospital or barracks

days /dayz/ adv. during the day or every day ○ *I work days one week and nights the next.* [Old English *dæges*, the genitive singular of *dæg* 'day', later re-interpreted as the plural of DAY]

day sailer n. a small sailing boat without sleeping accommodation

day school n. **1.** PRIVATE SCHOOL a private school that does not take boarders **2.** SCHOOL WITH DAYTIME CLASSES ONLY a school that holds classes during the daytime but not during the evening

day shift n. **1.** DAYTIME WORK PERIOD a shift that is worked during the day or part of the day **2.** WORKERS a group of employees who work during the day at a place where others work during the night

Days of Awe npl. JUDAISM = High Holidays

days of grace npl. the extra days, customarily three, allowed for the settlement of a note or bill after it falls due [From GRACE 'favour shown by granting immunity from a penalty']

dayspring /dáy spring/ n. the first light of day (archaic or literary)

daystar /dáy staar/ n. **1.** = morning star (literary) **2.** SUN the sun (archaic or literary) [Old English *dægsteorra*]

day student n. sb who studies at a school, college, or university but who does not board there

daytime /dáy tīm/ n. SUNLIT PART OF DAY the part of the day when there is natural light ■ adj. OF OR FOR DAYTIME occurring, done, or used during the daytime

day-to-day adj. **1.** EVERYDAY occurring or tending to be the same every day ○ *the day-to-day business of earning a living* **2.** ONE DAY AT A TIME planning or providing for one day at a time ○ *We do everything on a day-to-day basis – we can never plan ahead.*

Dayton /dáyt'n/ city in Ohio on the Great Miami River, southwest of Columbus and northeast of Cincinnati. Population: 172,947 (1996).

Dayton Accords npl. an agreement reached in November 1995 at Wright-Patterson Air Force Base among representatives for Bosnia, Croatia, and Serbia, containing measures to end hostilities in the former Yugoslavia. It was signed in Paris, France, on December 14, 1995, by the presidents of the three warring nations. [Mid-20thC. From *Dayton*, Ohio, where the agreement was reached.]

day trip n. a journey or outing to and from a place within a day

day tripper n. sb who goes on a day trip

daywear /dáy wair/ n. clothes for wearing during the day

daze /dayz/ n. CONFUSED STATE a state of confusion and unclear thinking, often the result of a blow or shock ○ *Things happened so quickly I was left in a daze.* ■ vt. (**dazes, dazing, dazed**) **1.** STUN SB to leave sb wholly or partly unconscious or unable to think clearly, especially as a result of a blow or shock ○ *The blow seemed to have dazed her.* **2.** BEWILDER SB to leave sb feeling confused or amazed [14thC. Back-formation from DAZED.]

dazed /dayzd/ adj. **1.** PUZZLED bewildered, confused, or amazed **2.** STUNNED not fully conscious or able to think clearly, often as a result of a blow or shock [14thC. From Old Norse *dasaðr* 'weary from cold or exertion'.] —**dazedly** /dáyzidli/ adv.

dazzle /dázz'l/ vti. (**-zles, -zling, -zled**) **1.** DEPRIVE OF SIGHT TEMPORARILY to make sb temporarily unable to see ○ *The glare of the oncoming headlights dazzled me.* **2.** AMAZE SB to amaze sb with brilliance or skill or with a wonderful spectacle or display (often passive) ○ *She dazzled the spectators with a triple somersault.* ■ n. LIGHT THAT DAZZLES very bright light that deprives sb of sight temporarily ○ *a lot of dazzle from the white-painted walls of the house* [15thC. Formed from DAZE, probably in the now obsolete sense 'to become confused or stupefied'.]

dazzling /dázzling/ adj. **1.** VERY BRIGHT bright enough to deprive sb of sight temporarily **2.** STRIKING spectacularly skilful or impressive ○ *a dazzling line-up of stars* —**dazzlingly** adv.

Db symbol. dubnium

DB, **D/B** abbr. ACCT daybook

DBA abbr. Doctor of Business Administration

d.b.a. abbr. doing business as

DBE abbr. Dame Commander of the Order of the British Empire

dbh, **DBH** abbr. FORESTRY diameter at breast height

DBib abbr. Douay Bible

dbl., **dble** abbr. double

DBMS abbr. COMPUT database management system

DBS abbr. **1.** direct broadcasting by satellite **2.** direct broadcasting satellite

DC, **D.C.** abbr. **1.** MUSIC da capo **2.** ELEC ENG direct current. ◊ AC **3.** District Commissioner **4.** Detective Constable

D.C. abbr. District of Columbia

DCB abbr. Dame Commander of the Order of the Bath

DCC abbr. digital compact cassette

DCD abbr. digital compact disc

DCF abbr. ACCT discounted cash flow

DCL abbr. Doctor of Civil Law

DCM abbr. Distinguished Conduct Medal

DCMG abbr. Dame Commander of the Order of St Michael and St George

DCMS abbr. Department of Culture, the Media, and Sport

DCVO abbr. Dame Commander of the Royal Victorian Order

dd abbr. **1.** delivered **2.** dated

DD abbr. **1.** BANKING demand draft **2.** direct debit **3.** dishonourable discharge **4.** Doctor of Divinity

D/D abbr. direct debit

D-day n. **1.** HIST BEGINNING OF LIBERATION OF EUROPE June 6, 1944, the day on which Allied forces landed in northern France to begin the liberation of occupied Europe in World War II **2.** DAY WHEN OPERATION IS TO BEGIN a day chosen for the beginning of a military operation or other major venture [Origin uncertain; the initial 'D' is perhaps from DAY, the phrase thus being modelled on H-HOUR; another possibility is that the 'D' is from 'designated']

DDR abbr. HIST Deutsche Demokratische Republik

DDS abbr. **1.** LIBRARIES Dewey Decimal System **2.** DENT Doctor of Dental Science **3.** DENT Doctor of Dental Surgery

DDSc abbr. Doctor of Dental Science

DDT n. an insecticide effective especially against malaria-carrying mosquitoes that has been banned in many countries since 1974 because of its toxicity, its persistence in the environment, and its ability to accumulate in living tissue. Formula: $C_{14}H_9Cl_5$. Full form **dichlorodiphenyltrichloroethane**

DE abbr. Delaware

de- prefix. **1.** opposite, reverse ○ *decertify* **2.** remove ○ *decaffeinate* ○ *delist* **3.** derived from ○ *denominative* **4.** reduce ○ *declass* **5.** to get off ○ *deplane* **6.** formed by removing one or more atoms from a particular element ○ *deoxy-* [Via Old French *de-* and *des-* from, ultimately, Latin *de-* 'apart, away' and *dis-* (see DIS-)]

deaccession /deé ək sésh'n/ (**-sions, -sioning, -sioned**) vti. to remove a book or work of art from the collection of a library or museum and sell it

deacidify /deé ə síddi fī/ (**-fies, -fying, -fied**) vt. to remove the acid from sth or reduce the acid content of sth —**deacidification** /deé əsíddifi káysh'n/ n.

deacon /deékən/ n. **1.** ORDAINED PERSON RANKING BELOW A PRIEST in the Roman Catholic, Orthodox, and Anglican Churches, an ordained member of the clergy with a rank immediately below that of a priest **2.** LAY PERSON ASSISTING MINISTER in many Protestant churches, a lay person who is appointed or elected to assist the minister [Pre-12thC. Via Latin *diaconus* from Greek *diakonos*, literally 'servant, messenger'.]

deaconess /deékənəss/ n. a woman who ranks below a priest or who is appointed to assist a minister [Mid-16thC. Formed from DEACON on the model of medieval Latin *diaconissa* 'deaconess'.]

deaconry /deékənri/ (plural **-ries**) n. **1.** POST OF DEACON the position or rank of a deacon **2.** DEACONS COLLECTIVELY deacons considered as a group

deactivate /di ákti vayt/ (**-vates, -vating, -vated**) vt. **1.** MAKE STH INACTIVE OR HARMLESS to prevent sth that is active or live, especially an explosive device, from operating **2.** BIOCHEM STOP ACTIVE COMPOUND FROM WORKING to render a biologically active compound, e.g. an enzyme, inactive or ineffective **3.** US MIL END ACTIVE MILITARY STATUS to make a military unit no longer active —**deactivation** /dá akti váysh'n/ n. —**deactivator** /di ákti vaytər/ n.

dead /ded/ adj. **1.** NO LONGER ALIVE having passed from the living state to being no longer alive ○ *a dead bird* **2.** INANIMATE never having been alive and having none of the characteristics of a living thing **3.** WITHOUT LIVING THINGS IN IT having no living things, or unable to support life **4.** WITHOUT PHYSICAL SENSATION having lost normal sensitivity to touch or pain, e.g. from the effects of cold, disease, or anaesthesia ○ *My fingers have gone completely dead.* **5.** INSENSITIVE unable or unwilling to respond to, understand, or appreciate sth **6.** LACKING ANY SPARK OF LIFE showing little indication of feeling or vitality ○ *His eyes were dead.* **7.** LIKE A CORPSE having the appearance of a dead person **8.** LACKING ACTIVITY OR INTEREST without human activity or anything interesting or entertaining ○ *This town is dead after seven o'clock at night.* **9.** NO LONGER CURRENT no longer in use, or no longer relevant, appropriate, or important ○ *That issue is now well and truly dead, despite attempts to revive it.* **10.** TECH BROKEN DOWN no longer able to operate because of a fault, breakdown, or loss of power ○ *The phone went dead.* **11.** NOT BURNING no longer burning or able to burn **12.** ACOUSTICS NONRESONANT not resonant, or producing sounds that are not resonant ○ *'... To where Saint Mary Woolnoth kept the hours*

With a dead sound on the final stroke of nine ...' (T. S. Eliot, *The Waste Land*; 1922) **13.** TOTALLY QUIET unbroken by any sound or movement ○ *There was dead silence for a few seconds; then everyone started cheering.* **14.** TOTAL sudden, abrupt, and complete ○ *came to a dead stop in the middle of the road* **15.** EXACT precise or exact in position or character **16.** EXHAUSTED very tired or completely without energy (*informal*) **17.** DOOMED certain to face a very unpleasant fate (*informal*) ○ *If I don't get this report in by tomorrow, I'm dead.* **18.** EMPTY empty and ready to be cleared away (*informal*) **19.** COMM WITH NO RETURN producing or yielding no return **20.** SPORTS OUT OF PLAY used to describe a ball that has crossed the boundary of the playing area in some games **21.** GOLF LANDING CLOSE TO HOLE used to describe a golf shot in which the ball comes to rest so close to the hole that the next shot cannot miss ■ *npl.* DEAD PEOPLE people who have died or been killed (*takes a plural verb*) ○ *respect for the dead* ■ *adv.* **1.** PRECISELY used to emphasize that an approximate-sounding description or instruction, e.g. concerning a time, a position, or a straight line, is in fact precise or to be followed precisely ○ *Keep going dead ahead for another 300 yards.* **2.** ENTIRELY completely or absolutely ○ *You can be dead sure that he won't make the same mistake again.* **3.** WITH SUDDENNESS abruptly or immediately ○ *stopped dead in her tracks* **4.** VERY used in informal contexts to add emphasis to an adjective or adverb (*informal*) ○ *I was dead scared.* [Old English *dēad*. Ultimately from the past participle of the prehistoric Germanic verb that is also the ancestor of English *die*, so the underlying meaning is 'died'.] ◇ **the dead of night** *or* **winter** the most extreme point of night or winter

WORD KEY: SYNONYMS

dead, deceased, departed, late, lifeless, defunct, extinct

CORE MEANING: no longer living, functioning, or in existence

dead the most general term, used of organisms that are no longer alive, physical objects that no longer function or exist, and abstract entities that are no longer valid or relevant; **deceased** a formal term restricted to people, most commonly used in legal or other technical contexts, or as a euphemism; **departed** a euphemistic term restricted to people, used to suggest that the dead person has gone away rather than died; **late** a term restricted to people, usually applied to sb who has died fairly recently or whose death is within living memory. It is always followed by a proper name or a noun indicating a particular relationship or status; **lifeless** a literary term used to describe the body of a dead person or animal; **defunct** a neutral term used of sth such as a machine or a system that has ceased to exist or function. In current usage, it is used to describe people only for comic effect; **extinct** a technical term used of animal and plant species that no longer exist, or of sth such as a volcano that is no longer active. It is sometimes used to describe institutions, customs, or ways of life that no longer exist.

dead air *n.* an unintentional period of silence during a broadcast

dead-air space *n.* a space that is sealed or has no ventilation

dead-and-alive *adj.* lacking any interest or vitality (*informal*) ○ *something more than this dead-and-alive existence* [From the association of boredom with a 'living death']

dead beat *adj.* completely exhausted (*informal*)

deadbeat /déd beet/ *n.* (*slang*) **1.** LOAFER sb who is lazy and disreputable **2.** *US* SB WHO DOES NOT PAY DEBTS sb who does not pay money that is owed ■ *adj.* PHYS DAMPED AND NOT OSCILLATING used to describe an instrument that gives a true reading without oscillation

dead bolt /déd bōlt/, **deadbolt** *n.* a bolt that is operated directly by the turning of a key or knob and not by a spring mechanism

dead cat bounce *n.* FIN an apparent recovery from a major decline in share prices resulting from speculators rebuying stock that they previously sold rather than from a genuine upturn in the market (*slang*)

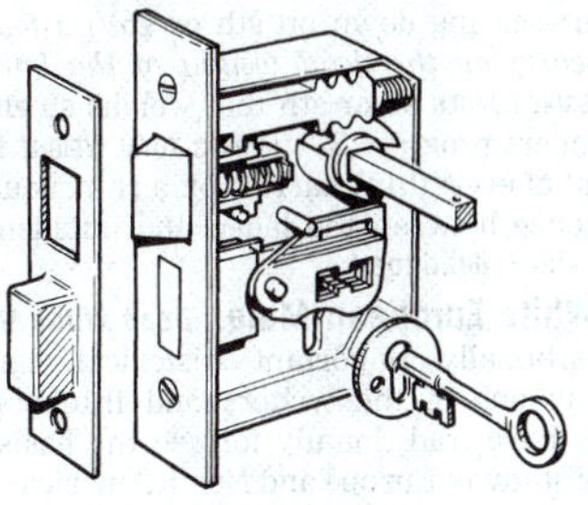

Dead bolt

dead centre *n.* **1.** MIDDLE the exact centre of sth **2.** MECH ENG TOP OR BOTTOM OF A PISTON STROKE the position at the top or bottom of a piston stroke in a reciprocating engine or pump, at which point the piston and the connecting rod are in a straight line **3.** TECH POINTED ROD IN A LATHE a nonrotating pointed shaft mounted at both ends or one end of a lathe to support the workpiece and hold it in place

dead duck *n.* sth or sb with no chance of success or survival (*slang*) [Origin uncertain: perhaps based on an early 19th-century US proverb about the futility of shooting a duck that is already dead]

deaden /dédd'n/ (**-ens, -ening, -ened**) *vt.* **1.** MAKE STH LESS INTENSE to lessen the intensity of sth, such as pain or sound ○ *The snow deadened the sound of their footsteps.* **2.** DESENSITIZE SB OR STH to make sth or sb less sensitive to pain or other stimuli ○ *A local anaesthetic will deaden the nerves.* **3.** ACOUSTICS MAKE STH LESS RESONANT to make an area soundproof or less resonant —**deadener** *n.*

dead end *n.* **1.** POINT AT WHICH STH ENDS ABRUPTLY an end of a street, path, road, or passage beyond which it is impossible to proceed **2.** PASSAGE THAT ENDS ABRUPTLY a street, path, or passage beyond which sb or sth cannot proceed ○ *Our road is a dead end, so we don't get much traffic.* **3.** SITUATION THAT LEADS NOWHERE a situation or course of action in which further progress or development is impossible ○ *a line of research that proved to be a dead end*

dead-end (**dead-ends, dead-ending, dead-ended**) *adj.* **1.** WITH CLOSED END with no exit at one end **2.** WITHOUT PROSPECTS offering no prospects of progress, development, or improvement ○ *stuck in a dead-end job* **3.** *US* ROWDY AND TOUGH used to describe young people, usually from underprivileged backgrounds, whose behaviour makes them unlikely to succeed in life (*informal*)

deadening /dédd'ning/ *n.* material used to make a room or building soundproof or less resonant

deadeye /déd ī/ *n.* **1.** NAUT WOODEN BLOCK WITH THREE HOLES a rounded block of wood pierced by three holes that has a groove around its edge. Deadeyes are usually used in pairs to tighten stays or shrouds on sailing vessels. **2.** *US* EXPERT SHOT sb who always aims accurately and hits the target (*informal*)

deadfall /déd fawl/ *n.* a simple trap consisting of a heavy weight that falls on and crushes its victim when a support is removed

dead fingers *n.* a condition that can affect people who work with pneumatic drills, causing loss of sensation and reduced blood circulation in the fingers (*takes a singular verb*)

dead hand *n.* **1.** OPPRESSIVE INFLUENCE a negative or oppressive influence or control exerted over an activity or a group of people ○ *remove the dead hand of bureaucracy* **2.** = **mortmain**

deadhead /déd hed/ *n.* **1.** SB INCOMPETENT an unintelligent, useless, or ineffectual person (*informal insult*) **2.** TRANSP SB WITH A FREE TICKET sb who uses a free ticket for travel, accommodation, or some form of entertainment (*informal*) **3.** *US* VEHICLE WITH NO PASSENGERS a vehicle or aircraft that is carrying no passengers or freight (*informal*) ■ *v.* (**-heads, -heading, -headed**) **1.** *vt.* REMOVE DEAD FLOWERS FROM PLANT to remove dead flower heads from a plant to improve its appearance or stimulate further flowering **2.** *vti.* *US* DRIVE EMPTY VEHICLE to drive or pilot a vehicle or aircraft that is carrying no passengers or freight ○ *Williams deadheaded it from New Jersey to California last weekend.*

dead heat *n.* a race or other competition in which two or more contestants finish together or with the same score

dead-heat (**dead-heats, dead-heating, dead-heated**) *vi.* to finish a race or other competition together or with the same score

dead letter *n.* **1.** MAIL LETTER THAT CANNOT BE DELIVERED a letter that the postal service cannot deliver, usually because the address is inadequate or the addressee does not claim it **2.** UNENFORCED OR INEFFECTIVE RULE a law or regulation that still applies but is not enforced or uniformly obeyed **3.** STH NOW IRRELEVANT OR UNIMPORTANT sth that is no longer considered relevant or important

dead letter box, **dead letter drop** *n.* a place where a message or other item can be left in secret by one person and collected later by another, so that the two people do not meet

dead lift *n.* a weightlifting event in which a weight is raised from the floor to the level of the hips and lowered again in a controlled manner [From the idea of lifting a dead weight]

deadlight /déd līt/ *n.* **1.** PROTECTIVE SHUTTER OVER PORTHOLE a protective shutter or plate fastened over a porthole or cabin window in bad weather **2.** THICK WINDOW IN DECK OR HULL a thick glass window set in the deck or side of a ship to let light into a cabin

deadline /déd līn/ *n.* **1.** TIME LIMIT the time by which sth must be done or completed **2.** LINE MARKED IN PRISON in former times, a line in a prison or prison camp marking a boundary beyond which prisoners were forbidden to go on pain of death

dead load *n.* the permanent weight of a structure, e.g. a bridge, exclusive of its load

deadlock /déd lok/ *n.* **1.** BLOCK TO PROGRESS a situation in which no further progress is possible in a dispute, usually because the people involved are unwilling to change their positions or to compromise ○ *try to break the deadlock in negotiations* **2.** BUILDING TYPE OF LOCK a type of lock that can only be opened or closed with a key ■ *vti.* (**-locks, -locking, -locked**) CAUSE DEADLOCK to reach a situation in which no further progress is possible, or to bring sth into such a situation ○ *The talks are deadlocked.*

dead loss *n.* **1.** COMPLETELY USELESS PERSON OR THING sth or sb that is completely useless and not worth spending any further time, effort, or money on (*informal*) **2.** COMM COMPLETE LOSS a complete loss for which no form of compensation is available

deadly /déddli/ *adj.* (**-lier, -liest**) **1.** CAUSING DEATH able or likely to cause death **2.** PRECISE very accurate, or able to aim or shoot very accurately **3.** EXTREMELY HOSTILE involving or having an intense desire for the defeat, downfall, or death of sb ○ *deadly enemies* **4.** CAUSING OFFENCE causing or intended to cause great offence to another person **5.** COMPLETE used to emphasize the intensity of sth ○ *in deadly earnest* **6.** DULL extremely boring (*informal*) ○ *back to the deadly routine of daily life* ■ *adv.* **1.** = **deathly 2.** COMPLETELY to the greatest extent possible ○ *I was being deadly serious when I made that suggestion.* [Old English *dēadlic*] —**deadliness** *n.*

WORD KEY: SYNONYMS

deadly, fatal, mortal, lethal, terminal

CORE MEANING: causing death

deadly likely or designed to cause death, or having caused death; **fatal** a more commonly used term than *deadly*, used especially to describe accidents or illnesses that have resulted in death; **mortal** a more literary or formal term used to describe sth that seems likely to cause death or that has already caused death; **lethal** a term used to describe sth that is certain to cause death, especially sth that is expressly intended to cause death; **terminal** used to describe illnesses that cause death.

deadly nightshade *n.* a poisonous Eurasian plant with drooping purplish flowers and small black berries, commonly found in hedgerows. Latin name: *Atropa belladonna.* US term **belladonna**

deadly sins *npl.* the sins that lead to damnation according to some Christian beliefs. The seven deadly sins are anger, avarice, envy, gluttony, lechery, pride, and sloth. [Translation of Latin *peccata mortalia*]

deadman /déd man/ (*plural* **-men** /-men/) *n.* **1.** CIV ENG **ANCHORING BLOCK** a heavy block or plate buried in the ground and connected to another structure, e.g. a retaining wall, by means of a tie, thereby anchoring the structure firmly **2.** MOUNTAINEERING **TYPE OF BELAY** a belaying point for use in firm snow, consisting of a metal plate with a wire loop attached to it

dead man's float *n.* a floating position in which a swimmer is face down with arms extended forward and legs kept together

dead man's handle, dead man's pedal *n.* a safety device on a train that automatically cuts off the power and applies the brakes when the driver releases pressure on it

dead march *n.* a piece of solemn music played to accompany a procession at a funeral, especially a military funeral

dead men's shoes *npl.* a situation in which the only prospect of promotion is the death or retirement of more senior employees

deadness /dédnəss/ *n.* **1. DULLNESS** lack of activity, liveliness, or interest ○ *Young people complain about the deadness of the town.* **2. NUMBNESS** lack or loss of sensation in a part of the body **3. INABILITY TO OPERATE** lack of power or ability to operate

dead nettle *n.* a flowering plant that resembles a nettle but does not have stinging hairs on its leaves. Genus: *Lamium.*

dead-on *adj.* very accurate or correct (*informal; not hyphenated after verb*) ○ *a dead-on prediction*

deadpan /déd pan/ *adj.* **1. PURPOSELY INEXPRESSIVE** deliberately showing no expression or emotion **2. SAID EXPRESSIONLESSLY** spoken or delivered with no expression or emotion ■ *adv.* **EXPRESSIONLESS** without showing any expression or emotion ○ *delivered the line absolutely deadpan* ■ *n.* **EXPRESSIONLESS FACE OR PERFORMER** an expressionless face or sb with an expressionless face ■ *vti.* **(-pans, -panning, -panned) SPEAK OR ACT IN DEADPAN MANNER** to say sth or do sth in a deliberately expressionless way [Early 20thC. From US slang PAN 'face'.]

dead reckoning *n.* a simple method of determining the position of a ship or aircraft by charting its course and speed from a previously known position [Origin uncertain; probably from DEAD 'absolute' or 'exact', although 'dead' may be by folk etymology from *ded.*, a shortening of DEDUCE or DEDUCTION.]

dead ringer *n.* sb who looks exactly like sb else (*informal*)

Dead Sea /déd-/ salt lake on the border between Israel and Jordan, in southwestern Asia. Its surface, at 400 m/1,312 ft below sea level, marks the lowest point on earth. Area: 1,049 sq. km/405 sq. mi.

Dead Sea Scrolls *npl.* a collection of ancient manuscripts discovered in caves near the Dead Sea that provide important evidence for biblical scholars and historians. They were discovered between 1947 and 1956, and are generally held to have been written between 100 BC and AD 68.

dead set *n.* **DOG'S POINTING POSE** the rigid motionless position of a hunting dog pointing with its muzzle at game ■ *interj. Aus* **HONESTLY** used to emphasize the truth of sth said (*informal*)

dead shot *n.* sb who always aims accurately and hits the target

dead soldier *n.* a bottle whose alcoholic contents have been drunk (*dated slang*) [Origin uncertain: perhaps from the former associations of alcohol with liveliness and life itself (compare WHISKY)]

dead spot *n.* an area within the range of a radio transmitter where reception of the signal is weak or dead

dead time *n.* an interval during which an electrical device or component, having just responded to one stimulus, is unable to respond to another

dead weight *n.* **1. A HEAVY WEIGHT** a heavy motionless weight bearing down on sth or sb ○ *a foundation slab carrying the dead weight of the building* **2. OPPRESSIVE BURDEN** sb or sth that weighs sb else down or hinders progress **3.** SHIPPING **TOTAL WEIGHT** the total weight of everything carried on a ship, equal to the difference between the laden and unladen weight **4.** CIV ENG = **dead load**

Dead White European Male, Dead White Male *n.* a conventionally important historical figure, especially one of the writers and thinkers whose works have traditionally formed the basis of academic study in Europe and North America (*informal disapproving*)

deadwood /déd wŏŏd/ *n.* **1. DEAD TREE PARTS** dead trees and branches **2. SB OR STH UNNECESSARY** useless or superfluous people or things **3.** NAUT **PLANKS BETWEEN KEEL AND STERN** vertical planks filling the gap between the keel and the stern of a sailing vessel

deaf /def/ *adj.* **1. HEARING-IMPAIRED** completely or partially unable to hear in one or both ears **2. UNRESPONSIVE OR INDIFFERENT** unwilling to respond to sth as if unable to hear it ○ *They remained deaf to all our entreaties.* ■ *npl.* **HEARING-IMPAIRED PEOPLE** people who cannot hear (*takes a plural verb*) [Old English *dēaf*. Ultimately from an Indo-European word that also produced English *dumb* and Greek *taphlos* 'sightless'.]

deaf aid *n.* a hearing aid. See usage note at **deaf**

deafen /déff'n/ (**-ens, -ening, -ened**) *vt.* **1. MAKE SB UNABLE TO HEAR** to make sb temporarily or permanently unable to hear ○ *I was momentarily deafened by the noise of the explosion.* **2.** ACOUSTICS **SOUNDPROOF STH** to soundproof a room, wall, or building [Late 16thC]

deafening /déff'ning/ *adj.* extremely or unbearably loud ○ *She turned up the volume until the noise was absolutely deafening.* —**deafeningly** *adv.*

deaf-mute *adj.* **OFFENSIVE TERM FOR IMPAIRED CONDITION** an obsolete and nowadays offensive term meaning unable to hear or speak ■ *n.* **OFFENSIVE TERM FOR PERSON WITH IMPAIRMENT** an obsolete and nowadays offensive term meaning sb who is unable to hear or speak

deafness /défnəss/ *n.* a partial or total hearing impairment in one or both ears [Old English *dēafnis*]

deaf without speech *adj.* hearing-impaired and able to utter sounds but not words, usually because of being born hearing-impaired or having become so before learning how to talk

Deák /dáy aak/, **Ferenc** (1803–76) Hungarian statesman. He oversaw the restoration of Hungary's constitution and the establishment of the Dual Monarchy of Austria-Hungary (1867).

Deakin /deékin/, **Alfred** (1856–1919) Australian statesman. A Liberal Party politician, he was prime minister of Australia (1903–04, 1905–08, and 1909–10).

deal[1] /deel/ *n.* **1.** BUSINESS **BUSINESS TRANSACTION** an agreement, arrangement, or transaction, usually one that has benefits for all the parties involved **2.** COMM **BARGAIN** sth offered for sale on favourable terms (*informal; often used in the plural*) **3. TREATMENT** the treatment given to sb or received from sb (*informal*) ○ *They got a pretty raw deal from their employer.* **4.** CARDS **DISTRIBUTION OF CARDS** the distribution of the cards needed to play a game **5.** CARDS **PLAYER'S TURN TO DISTRIBUTE CARDS** a particular player's right or turn to distribute the cards ○ *Whose deal is it?* **6.** CARDS **ROUND OF GAME** a round of a game following a particular distribution of the cards **7.** CARDS **CARDS DISTRIBUTED OR RECEIVED** the cards distributed or received for a particular round of a game ■ *v.* **(deals, dealing, dealt) 1.** *vti.* CARDS **DISTRIBUTE CARDS** to distribute the cards for a round of a game ○ *You deal seven cards to each player.* **2.** *vti.* CARDS **GIVE OUT A PARTICULAR CARD** to give a particular card or cards to a player when distributing them ○ *I was dealt five clubs and no hearts.* **3.** *vti.* DRUGS **SELL ILLEGAL DRUGS** to sell sth, especially illegal drugs **4.** *vt.* **MAKE SB EXPERIENCE STH** to cause sb to experience or suffer sth, often as a reward or punishment ○ *The latest opinion poll has dealt a severe blow to her hopes of re-election.* [Old English *dǣl* 'part, share, amount', and *dǣlan* 'to divide', from a prehistoric Germanic word that also produced English *dole* and *ordeal*] ◇ **a done deal** sth that has already been settled or finalized ◇ **make a big deal out of sth** to make a fuss about sth unimportant (*informal*)

deal in *vt.* **1. TRADE IN STH** to buy and sell sth as a business ○ *We deal mainly in second-hand goods.* **2. INCLUDE SB** to let sb join in a card game or some other form of joint activity (*informal*) ○ *Deal me in.*

deal out *vt.* to give sth, or a share of sth, to each of a number of people ○ *She dealt out compliments to all the actors.*

deal with *vt.* **1. HANDLE STH** to take action with regard to sth or sb, e.g. to solve a problem or to help sb **2. BE ABOUT STH** to write or speak about sth or to have sth as the subject of written or spoken material ○ *I was intending to deal with the Metaphysical poets in my next lecture.* **3. TREAT SB IN PARTICULAR WAY** to treat or behave towards sb in a specified way, especially in a business context ○ *People who break the regulations will be dealt with severely.* **4. HAVE BUSINESS DEALINGS WITH SB** to do business with sb or an organization

deal[2] *n.* **1. SOFTWOOD TIMBER** fir or pine wood, especially when cut to a standard size **2. BOARD OF SOFTWOOD** a plank or board of deal [15thC. From Middle Low German or Middle Dutch *dele* 'plank'. Ultimately from a prehistoric Germanic word that also produced English *thill* 'shaft'.]

Deal harbour and fishing port in Kent, England, on the English Channel. Population: 28,504 (1991).

dealate /deé ay layt, -lit/, **dealated** /-laytid/ *adj.* used to describe an insect such as an ant or termite that has lost or shed its wings, usually after mating [Early 20thC. Formed from ALATE.] —**dealation** /deé ay láy sh'n/ *n.*

dealcoholize /di álkə hol īz/ (**-izes, -izing, -ized**), **dealcoholise** (**-ises, -ising, -ised**) *vt.* to remove some or all of the alcohol from a drink —**dealcoholization** /di álkə hol ī záysh'n/ *n.*

dealer /deélər/ *n.* **1.** COMM **SELLER OR TRADER** an individual or company whose business is buying and selling, especially in a particular commodity **2.** DRUGS **SELLER OF DRUGS** sb who sells illegal drugs **3.** CARDS **SB WHO DEALS CARDS** sb who distributes the cards for a game or whose turn it is to distribute the cards [Old English *dǣlere* 'distributor']

dealership /deélərship/ *n.* **1. FRANCHISE TO SELL STH** a franchise to sell a particular brand of product or service **2. DEALER'S PREMISES** the premises from which a dealer, especially a car dealer, operates

dealfish /deel fish/ (*plural* **-fish** *or* **-fishes**) *n.* a deep-sea Atlantic fish with a long flat silvery body. Genus: *Trachipterus.* [Mid-19thC. *Deal* from the resemblance of the fish to a thin plank (see DEAL[2]).]

dealing /deéling/ *n.* **CONDUCT OR TREATMENT** conduct towards or treatment of other people, especially in business matters ○ *The firm's reputation for fair dealing is at stake.* ■ **dealings** *npl.* **TRANSACTIONS AND RELATIONS** contact and interaction with other people or organizations for business purposes

dealmaker /deél maykər/ *n.* sb who makes deals, especially in business or politics —**dealmaking** *n.*

dealt past tense, past participle of **deal**[1]

deaminase /di ámmə nayss, -nayz/ *n.* an enzyme that breaks down amino compounds such as amino acids [Early 20thC. Coined from DE- + AMINE + -ASE.]

deaminate /di ámmə nayt/ (**-nates, -nating, -nated**), **deaminize** (**-nizes, -nizing, -nized**), **deaminise** (**-nises, -nising, -nised**) *v.* to remove an amino group from an organic compound in a chemical reaction [Early 20thC. Coined from DE- + AMINE + -ATE.] —**deamination** /di ámmə náysh'n/ *n.* —**deaminization** /di ámmə nī záysh'n/ *n.*

dean /deen/ *n.* **1.** EDUC **ACADEMIC ADMINISTRATOR** a senior member of the academic staff of a university or college who manages the whole institution or a department, faculty, or group of students **2.** EDUC **COLLEGE ADVISER OR RULE-ENFORCER** a member of the academic staff of a university or college responsible for the counselling and welfare of students, and sometimes, as at Oxford and Cambridge universities, for discipline **3.** CHR **SENIOR CLERIC** a senior member of the clergy who holds an administrative position in a cathedral or collegiate church, or in a division in a diocese [14thC. Via Old French *deien* from late Latin *decanus* 'person in charge of ten others', from Latin *decem* 'ten' (source of English *doyen*).] —**deanship** *n.*

Dean, Forest of /deen/ wooded area and National Park in western Gloucestershire, England. Population: 75,400 (1995).

Dean, Christopher (*b.* 1958) British ice dancer, partnered with Jane Torvill. Together they won four world championships (1981–84) and were Olympic gold medallists in 1984. Full name **Christopher Colin Dean**

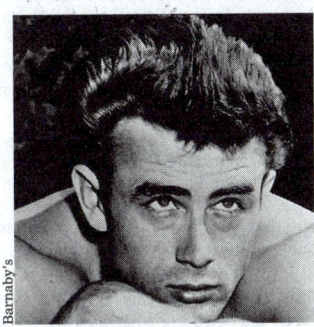

James Dean

Dean, James (1931–55) US film actor. He became a symbol of misunderstood youth through his roles in *East of Eden* (1955) and *Rebel Without a Cause* (1955).

Deane /deen/, **Sir William Patrick** (*b.* 1931) Australian judge and statesman. He became Governor-General of Australia in 1996.

deanery /déenəri/ (*plural* **-ies**) *n.* **1.** OFFICE OF DEAN a dean's jurisdiction, office, or residence **2.** RURAL DEAN'S PARISHES a group of parishes administered by a rural dean

Dean of Faculty *n.* **1.** HEAD OF FACULTY OF ADVOCATES the president of the Faculty of Advocates in Scotland **2.** HEAD OF UNIVERSITY FACULTY sb who is in charge of a university or college faculty

dean of guild *n.* formerly, a public official in Scotland who had jurisdiction over buildings and building work in a royal burgh

dear /deer/ *adj.* **1.** BELOVED loved or especially valued ○ *a dear friend* **2.** COSTLY high in price ○ *Prices are dear at that shop.* **3.** CHARGING A LOT charging high prices ○ *That's a dear place for food.* ■ *n.* **1.** SB WHO IS LOVED sb who is loved and valued, especially for being a kind or thoughtful person **2.** TERM OF ENDEARMENT used as an affectionate term of address ■ *interj.* USED TO EXPRESS SHOCK used to express shock or consternation ■ *adv.* DEARLY at a high cost ○ *This will cost you dear.* [Old English *deore*, from prehistoric Germanic. The two senses 'loved' and 'expensive' developed from an underlying idea of 'highly valued'.] —**dearness** *n.* ◇ **dear knows!** used to express ignorance about sth

Dear *adj.* used before a name or title to begin a letter

dearie /déeri/, **deary** (*plural* **-ies**) *n.* used to address sb in an affectionate way (*informal*)

Dear John letter, **Dear John** *n.* a letter from a woman ending a romantic or sexual relationship [From the salutation opening such a letter, 'John' being a common male forename]

dearly /déerli/ *adv.* **1.** WITH STRONG FEELINGS with great affection or intensity **2.** AT GREAT COST at a high cost ○ *He paid dearly for his mistake.*

dearth /durth/ *n.* a scarcity or lack of sth ○ *a dearth of new ideas* [13thC. Formed from DEAR, probably originally with the idea of sth being 'expensive', which developed via 'expensive because scarce' to 'scarce'.]

—— **WORD KEY: SYNONYMS** ——
See Synonyms at *lack*.

deary *n.* = **dearie**

deasil /déss'l, dyésh'l/ *adv. Scotland* in a clockwise direction [Late 18thC. From Gaelic *deiseil*.]

death /deth/ *n.* **1.** END OF BEING ALIVE the ending of all vital functions or processes in an organism or cell **2.** WAY OF DYING a way of dying ○ *an easy death* **3.** SB'S DYING an instance of sb's dying **4.** END OF STH the destruction or extinction of sth ○ *Losing the job marked the death of his ambitions.* **5.** CONDITION OF BEING DEAD the condition or quality of being dead ○ *In death she looked peaceful and composed.* [Old English *dēað*, from a prehistoric Germanic base that also produced English *die*] ◇ **be in at the death** to be present at the end or culmination of sth ◇ **be the death of sb** to cause sb's death ◇ **bored to death with sth** so bored as to be unable to stand it ◇ **catch your death (of cold)** to get a very bad cold ◇ **flog sth to death** to continue talking or arguing about sth needlessly ◇ **like death warmed up** looking very ill ◇ **sick to death of sth** tired of hearing about sth or having to deal with it ◇ **to the death** until sb or sth dies, or until sth ends ◇ **hold on for grim death, hang on like grim death** to keep hold of sb or sth very tightly and determinedly (*informal*)

Death *n.* a personification of death, usually represented as a ghostly form or skeleton holding a scythe

death adder *n.* a poisonous Australian snake with a body like an adder. Latin name: *Acanthopis antarcticus.*

death angel *n.* FUNGI = **death cap**

deathbed /déth bed/ *n.* BED WHERE SB DIES the bed on which sb dies ■ *adj.* WHILE DYING said, done, or made by sb while near death ○ *deathbed confessions*

death benefit *n.* a sum of money that is paid to the beneficiary of sb's life insurance policy after the death of the insured

deathblow /déth blō/ *n.* **1.** FATAL ACTION OR EVENT an action or event that destroys or ends sth **2.** KILLING BLOW a blow that kills sb

death camas /-kámməss/ *n.* a plant of the lily family found in western North America. It has clusters of greenish-white flowers and roots that are poisonous to livestock. Genus: *Zigadenus.*

death camp *n.* a place where prisoners are systematically killed, or where harsh conditions make survival unlikely

death cap *n.* a poisonous fungus of European and North American woodlands that has a pale cap and a structure resembling a cup at its base. Latin name: *Amanita phalloides.*

death cell *n.* a prison cell in which sb who has been sentenced to death is kept before execution

death certificate *n.* an official document completed and signed by a doctor, stating that sb is dead and giving the cause of death if known

death chamber *n.* a room where prisoners condemned to death are executed

death cup *n.* FUNGI = **death cap**

death-dealing *adj.* causing or liable to cause death (*literary*)

death-defying *adj.* taking the risk of being killed

death duty (*plural* **death duties**) *n.* the former name for a tax paid in the United Kingdom on inherited property, now called inheritance tax

death futures *npl.* a financial investment in the form of the purchase at a reduced rate of the life insurance of sb who has a terminal illness, which provides necessary income for the dying person to meet medical costs and guarantees a good return for the purchaser (*hyphenated before a noun*) ○ *the growth in death-futures companies*

death grant *n.* a sum of money paid under the British National Insurance scheme when sb has died, in order to cover funeral expenses

death house *n.* a building where prisoners condemned to death are housed prior to execution

death instinct *n.* an inherent and unconscious tendency, proposed in some theories of the mind, towards self-destruction

death knell *n.* **1.** SIGNAL THAT STH IS DEAD a sign that sth is dead, destroyed, or coming to an end ○ *The bankruptcy notice was the company's death knell.* **2.** BELL ANNOUNCING A DEATH the ringing of a bell to announce that sb has died

deathless /déthləss/ *adj.* immortal, usually because of being excellent —**deathlessly** *adv.* —**deathlessness** *n.*

deathly /déthli/ *adj.* LIKE DEATH resembling death or sb who is dead ○ *deathly pale* ■ *adv.* EXTREMELY extremely or intensely —**deathliness** *n.*

Death mask: 'Mask of Agamemnon', discovered in a grave at Mycenae, Greece, in 1876

death mask *n.* a cast made of sb's face soon after death

death metal *n.* a type of heavy metal music characterized by satanic and horror film iconography

death notice *n.* an official notification from the British War Office of the death of a member of the armed forces, sent to the next of kin during World Wars I and II

death penalty *n.* = **capital punishment**

death rate *n.* the proportion of deaths to the population of a particular area or group

death rattle *n.* a rough gurgling noise that sometimes comes from sb's throat at the moment of death, caused by breath passing through mucus

death ray *n.* an imaginary power beam that can kill

death row *n.* a row of prison cells, or an area in a prison, housing prisoners that have been sentenced to death

death seat *n. Aus, US* the seat next to the driver in a motor vehicle, considered to be especially dangerous (*informal*)

death sentence *n.* **1.** PUNISHMENT OF DEATH the punishment of death, received in a court of law **2.** STH WITH FATAL RESULT an event or decision that has a fatal effect

death's head *n.* a human skull or its representation in art, often a symbol of mortality

death's head moth, **death's head hawkmoth** *n.* a large European hawkmoth with pale markings on the back of its thorax that look like a human skull. Latin name: *Acherontia atropos.*

death squad *n.* an unofficial but organized group of people who seek out and murder political opponents or other people they consider as enemies (*takes a singular or plural verb*)

death stroke *n.* = **deathblow**

deathtrap /déth trap/ *n.* a building, structure, or vehicle that is extremely unsafe (*informal*)

Death Valley National Park national park in southeastern California and southwestern Nevada. It contains the lowest point in the United States, 86 m/282 ft below sea level. Area: 13,765 sq. km/8,554 sq. mi.

death warrant *n.* **1.** LEGAL ORDER TO EXECUTE SB an official document that authorizes sb's execution **2.** STH THAT IS FATAL sth that ends hope or expectation

deathwatch /déth woch/ *n.* **1.** TIME SPENT WATCHING AT DEATHBED a vigil near a dead or dying person, sometimes a traditional or religious custom **2.** ZOOL = **deathwatch beetle**

deathwatch beetle *n.* a small beetle whose larva bores into wood and makes a ticking sound. Latin name: *Xestobium rufovillosum.*

death wish *n.* a desire to die or, less commonly, a desire for the death of sb else

deattribution /di áttri byóosh'n/ *n.* a change in an official or agreed opinion about the attribution of a work of art (*formal*)

deave /deev/ (**deaves**, **deaving**, **deaved**) *vt.* (*informal*) **1.** *Scotland, N England, Ireland* WORRY OR BOTHER SB to weary or confuse sb, especially by making a lot of noise or fuss **2.** CAUSE INABILITY TO HEAR to cause sb to be unable to hear, especially temporarily [Old English *dēafian* 'to deafen', from DEAF]

WORD KEY: REGIONAL NOTE

Deave meaning 'to deafen' was once widespread, but is now confined to the north of England, Scotland, and Ireland. The *v* is a vestige of a feature of English pronunciation from earliest times. When *f* occurred before a vowel, it was pronounced /v/. We have relics of this in *hoof* and *hooves*, *wife* (once *wif*) and *wives*, and *wolf* and *wolves*.

deb /deb/ *n.* a debutante (*informal*) [Early 20thC. Shortening.]

deb. *abbr.* **1.** FIN debenture **2.** BANKING debit

debacle /day ba̋ak'l, di-/ *n.* **1.** CHAOTIC FAILURE sth that becomes a disaster, defeat, or humiliating failure **2.** BREAKUP OF RIVER ICE a sudden breakup of river ice in the spring thaw, causing a violent rush of flow water and ice [Early 19thC. From French, formed from *débâcler*, literally 'to unbar' (used of ice breaking on a river), from, ultimately, Latin *bacculus* 'stick' (source of English *bacillus* and *bacterium*).]

debag /dee bág/ (**-bags, -bagging, -bagged**) *vt.* to take off sb's trousers by force as a joke or humiliation (*slang*) [Early 20thC. Formed from BAGS 'trousers'.]

debar /di ba̋ar/ (**-bars, -barring, -barred**) *vti.* to exclude sb from entering or taking part in sth [15thC. From Old French *desbarrer, barrer* 'to bar'.] —**debarment** *n.*

debark[1] /di ba̋ark/ (**-barks, -barking, -barked**) *v.* **1.** *vi.* = **disembark 2.** *vt. US* UNLOAD STH to take sth off a vehicle after transporting it (*formal*) [Mid-17thC. From French *débarquer* 'to get out of a boat'.] —**debarkation** /dee baar káysh'n/ *n.*

debark[2] /dee ba̋ark/ (**-barks, -barking, -barked**) *vt.* to remove the bark from wood

debase /di báyss/ (**-bases, -basing, -based**) *vt.* **1.** MAKE STH INFERIOR to reduce sth in value or quality **2.** REDUCE IN RANK to reduce sb in status, significance, or moral worth —**debasedness** /di báyssidnəss/ *n.* —**debaser** *n.*

debasement /di báyssmənt/ *n.* a reduction in value, quality, or significance

debatable /di báytəb'l/ *adj.* **1.** SUBJECT TO ARGUMENT liable to be questioned or disputed ○ *Whether it's actually an improvement is debatable.* **2.** CLAIMED BY TWO SIDES claimed by more than one country or party (*formal*)

debate /di báyt/ *vti.* (**-bates, -bating, -bated**) **1.** TALK OR ARGUE ABOUT STH to talk about sth at length and in detail, especially as part of a formal exchange of opinion **2.** THINK ABOUT STH to ponder sth carefully ■ *n.* **1.** PUBLIC MEETING FOR DISCUSSION an organized or public discussion of sth **2.** CONSIDERATION a prolonged consideration of sth **3.** ARGUMENT argument or prolonged discussion ○ *The matter is not open to debate.* [13thC. Via Old French *debat* from, ultimately, Latin *battere* 'to fight'.] —**debater** *n.*

debating society *n.* an organization whose main purpose is to hold regular formal debates on various topics

debauch /di báwch/ *vt.* (**-bauches, -bauching, -bauched**) (*formal*) **1.** LEAD SB INTO IMMORAL BEHAVIOUR to persuade sb to behave in an immoral way **2.** SEDUCE SB to seduce sb ■ *n.* EPISODE OF DISSIPATION a period of indulgence in drunkenness or immoral behaviour (*formal*) [Late 16thC. From French *débaucher*, of unknown origin.]

debauched /di báwcht/ *adj.* unrestrainedly and immorally self-indulgent —**debauchedly** /di báwchtli, -chidli/ *adv.* —**debauchedness** /di báwchtnəss, -chidnəss/ *n.*

debauchee /débbaw chee/ *n.* sb who leads an immoral, unrestrained, and self-indulgent life (*formal*)

debaucher /di báwchər/ *n.* sb who corrupts people by encouraging them to behave immorally, especially in an unrestrained and self-indulgent way (*formal*)

debauchery /di báwchəri/ (*plural* **-ies**) *n.* unrestrained self-indulgent behaviour, or an instance of this

de Beauvoir, Simone ➧ **Beauvoir**

debenture /di bénchər/ *n.* **1. debenture, debenture bond** BOND BACKED ONLY BY CREDIT RATING a bond backed only by the credit standing of the issuer, sometimes convertible into stock **2.** CERTIFICATE OF DEBT a certificate that acknowledges the existence of a debt of a specified amount owed to sb **3.** CUSTOMS REFUND CERTIFICATE a certificate issued by customs officials to sb providing for a refund of a duty previously paid [15thC. From Latin *debentur*, literally 'they are owed', a form of the verb *debere* 'to owe' (source of English *debt*). Probably originally used on certificates of indebtedness.] —**debentured** *adj.*

debilitate /di bílli tayt/ (**-tates, -tating, -tated**) *vt.* to sap strength of sb or sth [Mid-16thC. From Latin *debilitat-*, the past participle stem of *debilitare* 'to weaken', from *debilitas* 'weakness' (see DEBILITY).] —**debilitation** /di bílli táysh'n/ *n.* —**debilitative** /di bíllitətiv/ *adj.*

debilitated /di bílli taytid/ *adj.* with diminished strength and energy

WORD KEY: SYNONYMS

See Synonyms at ***weak***.

debilitating /di bílli tayting/ *adj.* reducing sb's strength or energy

debility /di bílləti/ (*plural* **-ties**) *n.* a general lack of energy and strength [15thC. Via French *débilité* from Latin *debilitas*, from *debilis* 'weak'.]

debit /débbit/ *n.* **1.** RECORDED DEBT OR EXPENSE an entry showing a debt or expense in a record of accounts **2.** SUM OF MONEY DEDUCTED an amount of money taken out of an account **3.** TOTAL OF DEBTS OR EXPENSES the total of individual debit entries in an account **4.** COLUMN FOR RECORDING DEBTS OR EXPENSES a column on the left of an accounting statement where debts and expenses are recorded **5.** DRAWBACK sth that is disadvantageous or unfavourable ○ *The pay's better, but on the debit side there's a lot more work to do.* ■ *vt.* (**-its, -iting, -ited**) **1.** RECORD DEBIT to make, enter, or record a debit in an account **2.** CHARGE SB MONEY to remove a sum of money from sb's account in payment for sth [15thC. From Latin *debitum* 'debt' (see DEBT).]

WORD KEY: ORIGIN

As well as giving rise to ***debit***, Latin *debere* is also the source of English *debenture, debt, due, duty*, and *endeavour*.

debit card *n.* a plastic card that the holder can use to pay for purchases, the money being transferred directly from the holder's account to the seller

debonair /débbə náir/ *adj.* **1.** ELEGANT looking well-dressed, sophisticated, and at ease **2.** SHOWING ELEGANCE showing ease of manner, elegance, or sophistication [13thC. From Old French, from *de bon aire* 'of good disposition'.] —**debonairly** *adv.* —**debonairness** *n.*

debone /dee bṓn/ (**-bones, -boning, -boned**) *vt.* to remove the bones from meat or fish

de Bono /də bṓ nō/, **Edward** (*b.* 1933) Maltese-born British psychologist. Director of the Cognitive Research Trust since 1971, he has published widely on thought processes and lateral thinking.

debouch /di bówch, di bo͞osh, dee-/ (**-bouches, -bouching, -bouched**) *vi.* **1.** MOVE INTO LESS CONFINED AREA to move from an enclosed or confined area into more open terrain **2.** EMERGE INTO A WIDER PLACE to widen out, or flow out, from a valley or ravine into a wider area (*refers to a geographical feature such as a valley or a flow of water*) [Mid-18thC. From French *déboucher*, literally 'to come out of the mouth', modelled on Italian *sboccare*, both ultimately from Latin *bucca* 'cheek, mouth'.]

débouché /débboo sháy/ *n.* an exit or outlet for troops in fortifications [Mid-18thC. From French, from the past participle of *déboucher* (see DEBOUCH).]

debouchment /di bówchmənt, di bo͞osh-/ *n.* an act of debouching, or a place where this happens

Debrecen /débbre tsen/ capital of Hajdú-Bihar County, eastern Hungary. It is situated about 32 km/20 mi. from the border with Romania. Population: 211,000 (1995).

Debrett /də brét/, **Debrett's Peerage** *n.* a publication that lists members of the British aristocracy [Mid-19thC. Named after John *Debrett* (1705–1822), a London publisher who wrote and published the first edition in 1803.]

débridement /di breedmənt, day breed moN/ *n.* the removal of dead, damaged, or infected tissue from a wound in order to expose healthy tissue and allow the wound to heal [Mid-19thC. From French, literally 'unbridling'.]

debrief /dee breef/ (**-briefs, -briefing, -briefed**) *v.* **1.** *vt.* INTERROGATE SB AFTER STH HAS ENDED to question sb closely after a task, mission, or event has ended **2.** *vi.* MAKE REPORT to supply information about a task, mission, or event after it has ended

debriefing /dee breefing/ *n.* an interview in which sb is asked about or reports on an event or mission after it has ended

debris /déb ree, dáy bree/ (*plural* **-bris**), **débris** (*plural* **-bris**) *n.* **1.** FRAGMENTS fragments of sth that has been destroyed or broken down **2.** BROKEN FRAGMENTS OF ROCK fragments of rock broken by a powerful or destructive natural force such as the action of a glacier [Early 18thC. Via French *débris*, literally 'broken up', from, ultimately, Old French *brisier* 'to break'.]

debris flow *n.* a slow-moving body of sediment in which rock particles are suspended in a slurry of mud

de Broglie wavelength /də brṓgli-, də brṓli-/ *n.* the wavelength of the wave associated with the motion of an atomic or subatomic particle (**de Broglie wave**) that produces diffraction. The de Broglie wavelength is given by Planck's constant divided by the mass and velocity of the particle. [Early 20thC. Named after the French physicist Louis Victor *de Broglie* (1892–1987).]

debt /det/ *n.* **1.** STH THAT IS OWED an amount of money, a service, or an item of property that is owed to sb **2.** OBLIGATION an obligation or borrowing ○ *the criminal must repay his debt to society* **3.** STATE OF OWING STH the condition of owing sth to sb **4.** SIN a sin or trespass (*archaic*) [13thC. Via French *dette* from Latin *debitum* (which probably influenced the modern spelling of DEBT), from the past participle of *debere* 'to owe' (source of English *due* and *duty*).] —**debtless** *adj.*

debt of honour *n.* a debt that sb is morally, but not legally, obliged to pay

debtor /déttər/ *n.* sb who or sth that owes a debt

debt swap *n.* an exchange of financial obligations with sb or sth in order to gain profit or a more convenient repayment schedule

debud /dee búd/ (**-buds, -budding, -budded**) *vt.* = **disbud**

debug /dee búg/ (**-bugs, -bugging, -bugged**) *vt.* **1.** COMPUT FIND AND REMOVE ERRORS to find and remove errors in sth, especially in a computer program or system **2.** REMOVE SECRET LISTENING DEVICES to find and take away any electronic listening devices that are concealed in a place **3.** CLEAR PLACE OF INSECTS to remove or destroy insects that are in a place (*informal*)

debugger /dee búggər/ *n.* **1.** COMPUT COMPUTER PROGRAM THAT FINDS SOFTWARE ERRORS a computer utility program that helps to find software errors by allowing the user to access the source code as the program runs **2.** BUG REMOVER sb who or sth that removes bugs

debunk /dee búngk/ (**-bunks, -bunking, -bunked**) *vt.* to show that sth is wrong or false [Early 20thC. Formed from BUNK[2].] —**debunker** *n.*

deburr /dee búr/ (**-burrs, -burring, -burred**) *vt.* to remove rough edges (**burrs**) from a piece of machined metal

debus /dee búss/ (**-busses** *or* **-buses, -bussing** *or* **-busing, -bussed** *or* **-bused**) *vti.* to leave a bus or unload people or supplies from it

Debussy /də byo͞ozsi/, **Claude** (1862–1918) French composer. His works include the opera *Pelléas et Mélisande* (1902) and the orchestral poem *La Mer* (1905). He developed a style known as musical impressionism.

debut /dáybyoo, débb-/ *n.* **1.** FIRST PUBLIC APPEARANCE the first public appearance or presentation of a performer, programme, or performance **2.** YOUNG WOMAN'S FIRST OFFICIAL SOCIAL ENGAGEMENT a young woman's first appearance in public at a formal social event ■ *vti.* (**-buts, -buting, -buted**) MAKE FIRST FORMAL PUBLIC APPEARANCE to show or perform sth formally and publicly for the first time [Mid-18thC. From French, from *débuter* 'to lead off', from *de-* 'from' + *but* 'goal, target'.]

debutante /débbyoo taant/ *n.* a young woman who is being introduced formally into society by appearing at a public event such as a dance or party [Early 19thC. From French, literally 'leading off', from the present participle of *débuter* (see DEBUT).]

dec. *abbr.* **1.** deceased **2.** declaration **3.** GRAMMAR declension **4.** declination **5.** decrease

Dec. *abbr.* December

dec- *prefix.* = **deca-**. symbol **da** (*used before vowels*)

deca- *prefix.* ten ○ *decagram.* Symbol **da** [From Greek *deka.* Ultimately from the Indo-European word for 'ten', which is also the ancestor of English *ten* and *-teen,* and *decimal.*]

decade /dék ayd/ *n.* **1.** TEN YEARS a period of ten years **2.** GROUP OF TEN a group, set, or series of ten [15thC. Via French from the late Latin stem *decad-*, from, ultimately, Greek *deka* 'ten'.] —**decadal** /dékəd'l/ *adj.*

WORD KEY: USAGE

Pronunciation. The pronunciation with a stress on the second syllable is increasingly heard, but the traditional pronunciation with stress on the first syllable is preferable.

decadence /dékədənss/, **decadency** /-dənssi/ *n.* **1.** PROCESS OF CIVILIZATION'S DECLINE a process of decline or decay in a society, especially in its morals **2.** STATE OF DECLINE the condition of a civilization in decline **3.** IMMORALITY a state of uninhibited self-indulgence [Mid-16thC. Via French *décadence* from, ultimately, Latin *decadere* 'to fall down or away', from *cadere* 'to fall' (see DECAY).]

decadent /dékədənt/ *adj.* **1.** IN DECLINE in a process of decline or decay, especially in morals **2.** IMMORAL showing uninhibitedly self-indulgent behaviour ■ *n.* DEGENERATE PERSON sb who behaves in an immoral or uninhibitedly self-indulgent way [Mid-19thC. From French *décadent,* a back-formation from *décadence* (see DECADENCE).] —**decadently** *adv.*

decaf /dée kaf/ *n.* DECAFFEINATED DRINK a decaffeinated drink, especially coffee, tea, or a soft drink (*informal*) ■ *adj.* DECAFFEINATED decaffeinated (*informal*) [Late 20thC. Shortening.]

decaffeinate /dee káffi nayt, di-/ (**-ates, -ating, -ated**) *vt.* to remove all or most of the caffeine from a substance —**decaffeination** /dee káffi náysh'n, di-/ *n.*

decaffeinated /dee káffi naytid, di-/ *adj.* WITHOUT CAFFEINE with all or most of the caffeine taken out ■ *n.* DRINK WITHOUT CAFFEINE a drink from which all or most of the caffeine has been removed

decagon /dékəgən, -gon/ *n.* a polygon with ten straight sides and ten angles [Mid-17thC. Via medieval Latin from Greek *dekagōnos,* literally 'ten-angled'.] —**decagonal** /də kággən'l/ *adj.* —**decagonally** /-n'li/ *adv.*

decahedron /dékə heédrən/ *n.* a solid geometrical figure with ten flat outer surfaces [Early 19thC. Coined from DECA- + -HEDRON.] —**decahedral** /dékə heédrəl/ *adj.*

decal /di kál, dée kal/ *n.* **1.** *US* DECORATIVE STICKER a decorative paper or plastic sticker **2.** PICTURE FOR TRANSFER a picture or design on specially treated paper that allows it to be transferred to a surface such as glass, wood, or metal [Mid-20thC. Shortening of DECALCOMANIA.]

decalcification /dee kálssifi káysh'n/ *n.* the loss of calcium or calcium compounds from bone or teeth

decalcify /dee kálssi fī/ (**-fies, -fying, -fied**) *vti.* to lose calcium or a calcium compound from the bones or teeth —**decalcifier** *n.*

decalcomania /di kálkə máyni ə/ *n.* **1.** PROCESS OF TRANSFERRING PICTURE FROM PAPER the process of fixing a picture or design to the surface of sth, e.g. glass, pottery, or textiles, by transferring it from a prepared type of paper **2.** = **decal** [Mid-19thC. From French *décalcomanie,* from *décalquer* 'to transfer a tracing' + *-manie* 'mania, craze', from its popularity in the 19thC.]

decalescence /deekə léssənss/ *n.* the absorption of heat without temperature increase at specific conditions during the heating of a metal, caused by changes in the crystalline composition [Late 19thC. Formed from *calescence* 'increasing warmth or heat'.] —**decalescent** *adj.*

decalitre /dékə leetər/ *n.* **1.** 10 LITRES a unit of volume equal to ten litres. Symbol **dal 2. decaliter** US = **decalitre** [Early 19thC. From French *décalitre.*]

Decalogue /dékə log/ *n.* = **Ten Commandments** [14thC. Either directly or via French from ecclesiastical Latin *decalogus,* from Greek *dekalogos (biblos)* '(book of) ten pronouncements', from *deka* 'ten' + *logos* 'word, pronouncement'.]

decametre /dékə meetər/ *n.* **1.** 10 METRES a unit of length equal to ten metres. Symbol **dam 2. decameter** US = **decametre** [Early 19thC. From French *décamètre.*]

decametric /dékə méttrik/ *adj.* having radio waves of high frequency, between 10 and 100 metres

decamp /di kámp/ (**-camps, -camping, -camped**) *vi.* **1.** SUDDENLY OR SECRETLY LEAVE to leave a place abruptly or secretly **2.** LEAVE A CAMP to pack up and leave a camp or camping site [Late 17thC. From French *décamper,* from *camp* 'camp'.] —**decampment** *n.*

decanal /di káyn'l, dékənəl/ *adj.* relating to a dean or deanery (*formal*) [Early 18thC. From medieval Latin *decanalis,* from late Latin *decanus* (see DEAN).]

decani /di káyn ī/ *adj.* connected with or sung by the half of a choir that sits on the south side of the chancel. ◊ **cantoris** [Mid-18thC. From Latin, literally 'of the dean' (see DEAN), referring to the side of the church the dean usually sits on.]

decanoic acid /dékə nō ik-/ *n.* = **capric acid**

decant /di kánt/ (**-cants, -canting, -canted**) *vt.* **1.** POUR STH GENTLY INTO ANOTHER CONTAINER to pour a liquid gently and carefully from one container to another so as not to disturb sediment **2.** MOVE PEOPLE TEMPORARILY to move people temporarily from their houses or areas to another to allow work to be done on their own houses [Mid-17thC. From medieval Latin *decanthare,* from Latin *canthus* 'lip of a jug', from Greek *kanthos* 'corner of the eye' (from the supposed similarity in shape).]

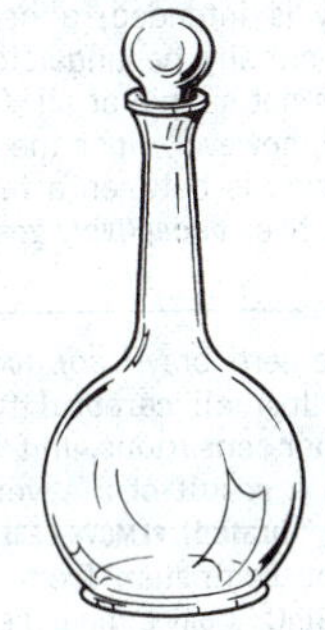

Decanter

decanter /di kántər/ *n.* a decorative bottle with a stopper, used for holding and serving drinks, especially wine

decapitate /di káppi tayt/ (**-tates, -tating, -tated**) *vt.* to cut off the head of sb or sth [Early 17thC. From late Latin *decapitat-*, the past participle stem of *decapitare,* from Latin *caput* 'head' (source of English *capital, chieftain, mischief,* and *biceps*).] —**decapitator** *n.*

decapitation /di káppi táysh'n/ *n.* the act, practice, or process of cutting the head off sb or sth

decapod /dékə pod/ *n.* **1.** INVERTEBRATE ANIMAL WITH 10 LEGS an invertebrate animal with stalked eyes and five pairs of legs, one or more with pincers, attached to the thorax. Many decapods are marine crustaceans and they include shrimps, lobsters, and crabs. Order: Decapoda. **2.** MARINE INVERTEBRATE ANIMAL WITH 10 TENTACLES a marine mollusc with ten tentacles, e.g. the cuttlefish or squid. Class: Cephalopoda. [Early 19thC. Via French *décapode* from modern Latin, literally 'ten legs'.] —**decapodal** /də káppəd'l/ *adj.* —**decapodan** /-dən/ *adj.* —**decapodous** /-dəss/ *adj.*

decapsulate /dee kápsyoo layt/ (**-lates, -lating, -lated**) *vt.* to remove a capsule from a body part or organ such as the kidney —**decapsulation** /dee kápsyoo láysh'n/ *n.*

decarbonate /dee kaárbə nayt/ (**-ates, -ating, -ated**) *vt.* to remove carbon dioxide or carbonic acid from sth —**decarbonation** /dee kaárbə náysh'n/ *n.* —**decarbonator** /-kaárbə naytər/ *n.*

decarbonize /dee kaárbə nīz/ (**-izes, -izing, -ized**), **decarbonise** (**-ises, -ising, -ised**) *vt.* to remove the carbon from sth, e.g. the carbon deposits from an internal-combustion engine —**decarbonization** /dee kaárbə nī záysh'n/ *n.* —**decarbonizer** /-kaárbə nīzər/ *n.*

decarboxylase /dee kaar bóksi layz, -layss/ *n.* an enzyme that helps to remove a carboxyl group from an organic compound, e.g. an amino acid [Mid-20thC. Coined from DE- + CARBOXYL + -ASE.]

decarboxylation /dee kaar bóksi láysh'n/ *n.* the removal or loss of a carboxyl group from an organic compound

decarburize /dee kaárbyoo rīz, -kaárbə-/ (**-rizes, -rizing, -rized**), **decarburise** (**-rises, -rising, -rised**) *vt.* = **decarbonize**

decastyle /dékə stīl/ *n.* PORTICO WITH 10 COLUMNS a portico that has ten columns ■ *adj.* WITH 10 COLUMNS consisting of or having ten columns [Early 18thC. From Greek *dekastulos* 'having ten columns'.]

decasyllable /dékə silab'l/ *n.* a line of verse, or sometimes a word, made up of ten syllables —**decasyllabic** /dékə si lábbik/ *adj.*

decathlete /di káth leet/ *n.* an athlete who competes in the decathlon

decathlon /di káth lon, -lən/ *n.* a contest for men in which the athletes compete in ten different events and are awarded points for each to find the best all-round athlete. The events are long jump, high jump, pole vault, shot put, discus, javelin, 110 metre hurdles, and running over 100 metres, 400 metres, and 1500 metres. ◊ **heptathlon, pentathlon, triathlon** [Early 20thC. Coined from DECA- + Greek *athlon* 'contest'.]

decay /di káy/ *v.* (**-cays, -caying, -cayed**) **1.** *vti.* BIOL GO ROTTEN OR DETERIORATE to decompose, or make sth decompose, and become soft, crumbly, or liquefied **2.** *vti.* DECLINE OR CAUSE STH TO DECLINE to decline in quality gradually and steadily, or cause sth to undergo such a decline **3.** *vi.* NUCLEAR PHYS DISINTEGRATE to undergo spontaneous disintegration (*refers to radioactive material*) **4.** *vi.* PHYS DECREASE to decrease gradually in magnitude (*refers to a physical quantity or effect*) **5.** *vi.* ASTRON DESCEND to decrease gradually in altitude (*refers to an artificial satellite in orbit*) ■ *n.* **1.** DECLINE a decline in quality ○ *'A state too extensive in itself, or by virtue of its dependencies, ultimately falls into decay'.* (Simón Bolívar, *Letter from Jamaica*; 1815) **2.** BIOL PROCESS OF BIOLOGICAL DETERIORATION the process of rotting and decomposition that affects plant material and the bodies of animals after they die and are invaded by bacteria or fungi **3.** BIOL ROTTEN OR SPOILED PART the areas of sth that are decomposed or rotted ○ *cut out the decay* **4.** NUCLEAR PHYS DISINTEGRATION OF RADIOACTIVE MATERIAL the spontaneous disintegration of a radioactive material along with the emission of one or more elementary particles or radiation **5.** PHYS GRADUAL DECREASE a gradual decrease in the magnitude of a physical quantity or effect, such as current, stored charge, or phosphorescence **6.** ASTRON DESCENT OF ARTIFICIAL SATELLITE the gradual decrease in altitude of an orbiting artificial satellite **7.** MUSIC DECLINE IN SOUND OF NOTE the fading away of a musical note [15thC. Via French *decair* from, ultimately, Latin *decidere,* literally 'to fall off or away' (source of English *deciduous*), from *cadere* 'to fall' (source of English *case, accident,* and *chance*).] —**decayable** *adj.*

Deccan /dékən/ triangular plateau that makes up much of southern India, south of the Sātpura Range. It is bordered by the mountainous Eastern and Western Ghats ranges.

decd *abbr.* deceased

decease /di seéss/ *n.* DEATH death, especially the death of sb (*formal*) ■ *vi.* (**-ceases, -ceasing, -ceased**) DIE to die (*formal*) [14thC. Via French *décès* from Latin *decessus* 'death, departure', from the past participle of *decedere* 'to go away' (source of English *predecessor*), from *cedere* 'to go' (see CEDE).]

deceased /di seést/ *n.* DEAD PERSON sb who has died recently (*formal*) ■ *adj.* DEAD no longer living (*formal*)

WORD KEY: SYNONYMS

See Synonyms at ***dead.***

deceit /di seét/ *n.* **1.** DISHONEST PRACTICE the act or practice of deceiving or misleading sb **2.** STH DONE TO MISLEAD sth that is done to trick or mislead sb [13thC. From Old French, formed from *deceveir* (see DECEIVE).]

deceitful /di sḗetf'l/ *adj.* intentionally misleading or fraudulent in lying to people or not telling them the whole truth —**deceitfully** *adv.*

deceitfulness /di sḗetf'lnəss/ *n.* = **deceit** *n.* 1

deceive /di sḗev/ (**-ceives, -ceiving, -ceived**) *v.* **1.** *vt.* **INTENTIONALLY TRICK OR MISLEAD SB** to mislead sb or hide the truth deliberately **2.** *vr.* **FOOL YOURSELF** to convince yourself of sth that is not true **3.** *vt.* **BE SEXUALLY UNFAITHFUL TO SB** to be sexually unfaithful to a spouse or sexual partner [13thC. Via Old French *deceveir* from, ultimately, Latin *decipere* 'to ensnare, take in', from *capere* 'to take, seize' (source of English *capture* and *receive*).] —**deceivability** /di sḗevə bíllәti/ *n.* —**deceivable** /di sḗevәb'l/ *adj.* —**deceiver** *n.*

deceiving /di sḗeving/ *adj.* liable or meant to mislead —**deceivingly** *adv.*

decelerate /dḗe séllə rayt/ (**-ates, -ating, -ated**) *vti.* to reduce speed, or make sth go more slowly [Late 19thC. Coined from DE- + ACCELERATE.] —**decelerator** *n.*

deceleration /dḗe séllə ráysh'n/ *n.* the act or process of reducing speed or making sth go more slowly

December /di sémbər/ *n.* the 12th month of the year in the Gregorian calendar. It is 31 days long. [13thC. Via French *décembre* from Latin *december*, from *decem* 'ten', because it was the tenth month of the Roman year.]

Decembrist /di sémbrist/ *n.* a member of a group of Russian officers who tried unsuccessfully to overthrow Tsar Nicholas I of Russia in December 1825

decemvir /di sémvər/ (*plural* **-virs** *or* **-viri** /-və ree, -və rī/) *n.* **1. ONE OF 10 OFFICIALS** a member of an official body that consists of ten people (*archaic*) **2. ROMAN LAW-MAKER** any one of a group of ten ancient Roman magistrates, especially those who drew up the laws of the Twelve Tables in 451–450 BC [15thC. From Latin *decem viri* (plural) 'ten men'.] —**decemviral** *adj.*

decemvirate /di sémvərət/ *n.* a group of ten people who hold power or office together (*formal*)

decency /dḗess'nssi/ *n.* (*plural* **-cies**) **1. CONFORMITY WITH MORAL STANDARDS** behaviour or an attitude that conforms to the commonly accepted standards of what is right and respectable **2. MODESTY** modesty or propriety ■ **decencies** *npl.* **MORAL BEHAVIOUR** the commonly accepted standards of good behaviour (*formal*)

decennary /di sénnəri/ *n.* (*plural* **-ries**) **DECADE** a ten-year period (*formal*) ■ *adj.* = **decennial** [Early 19thC. Formed from DECENNIUM.]

decennial /di sénni əl/ *adj.* **IN OR EVERY 10 YEARS** lasting for, consisting of, or happening every ten years ■ *n.* **10TH ANNIVERSARY** an anniversary celebrated ten years after sth or every ten years —**decennially** *adv.*

decennium /di sénni əm/ (*plural* **-ums** *or* **-a** /-ni ə/) *n.* a ten-year period (*formal*) [Late 17thC. From Latin, formed from *decennis*, from *decem* 'ten' + *annus* 'year'.]

decent /dḗess'nt/ *adj.* **1. MORAL** conforming to accepted standards of moral behaviour **2. GOOD** above average in quality or quantity ○ *one of the few decent restaurants around here* **3. QUITE GOOD** adequate or sufficient in quality ○ *did a decent job* **4. SUFFICIENTLY DRESSED** fully dressed, as opposed to being naked or in underwear only (*informal*) ○ *Don't come in; I'm not decent!* **5. KIND** kind, considerate, or generous [Mid-16thC. Either via French *décent* or directly from Latin *decent-*, the present participle stem of *decere* 'to be fitting'.] —**decentness** *n.*

decently /dḗess'ntli/ *adv.* in a way that conforms to accepted standards of conduct or appearance

decentralize /dee séntrə līz/ (**-izes, -izing, -ized**), **decentralise** (**-ises, -ising, -ised**) *vti.* to reorganize sth such as a political unit so that power is shifted from a central or upper location to another, less central place —**decentralization** /dḗe sentrə lī záysh'n/ *n.*

deception /di sépsh'n/ *n.* **1. PRACTICE OF MISLEADING SB** the practice of deliberately making sb believe things that are not true **2. STH INTENDED TO MISLEAD SB** an act, trick, or device intended to deceive sb [15thC. Either directly or via French from the Latin stem *deception-*, from *decept-*, the past participle stem of *decipere* (see DECEIVE).]

Deception Bay /di sépsh'n-/ coastal town near the city of Brisbane in southeastern Queensland, Australia. It is located on the bay of the same name. Population: 13,163 (1996).

deceptive /di séptiv/ *adj.* **1. MISLEADING** liable or meant to mislead sb **2. ABLE TO BE MISTAKEN** capable of being mistaken for sth else ○ *a deceptive barking noise* [Early 17thC. Either directly or via French from late Latin *deceptivus*, from Latin *decept-* (see DECEPTION).] —**deceptiveness** *n.*

deceptively /di séptivli/ *adv.* in a way that misleads people or is contrary to appearances ○ *a deceptively easy task*

WORD KEY: USAGE

Although *deceptively simple* almost invariably means 'complex despite apparent simplicity', that is not a model from which to generalize about the meaning of ***deceptively***. When people are asked whether, for example, *a deceptively dangerous place to stand* is a place that is more or less dangerous than it appears, they respond variously, with a substantial minority admitting they have no idea what ***deceptively*** is intended to convey. Sometimes context clarifies the meaning: *It was a small house, but it had deceptively large rooms.* Where this is not the case, ***deceptively*** is best avoided.

WORD KEY: USAGE

A house with deceptively spacious rooms. There is a logical flaw in coupling ***deceptively*** with the adjective it is meant to imply rather than the one it is meant to contradict, but it would be pedantic to insist on the alternative *A house with deceptively small rooms* (let alone the true opposite *A house with deceptively cramped rooms!*). In general use, if you refer to *a deceptively tall man*, no one will understand that to mean a short man. Usage therefore follows the analogy of *surprisingly* or *unexpectedly* (which denote the reality) rather than of *apparently* or *seemingly* (which denote appearances). A possible exception is the phrase *deceptively simple*, in which the context normally makes it clear that irony is intended; a *deceptively simple explanation* will normally be understood to mean an explanation that is not simple at all. (This may not be an exception at all, however, since the rule seems to be that when the choice is between a favourable and an unfavourable adjective, ***deceptively*** goes with the more favourable one.).

decerebrate /dee sérri brayt/ *adj.* **HAVING LOST CEREBRAL FUNCTION** having lost all cerebral function, vision, hearing, and other sensations, and voluntary motor activity, e.g. as a result of a severe stroke ■ *vt.* (**-brates, -brating, -brated**) **REMOVE CEREBRUM** to remove the cerebrum or brainstem from an animal surgically [Late 19thC. Coined from DE- + CEREBRUM + -ATE.] —**decerebration** /dee sérri bráysh'n/ *n.*

decern /di súrn/ (**-cerns, -cerning, -cerned**) *vti. Scotland* to give a judgment or make an official decision about sth or sb in a court of law. In order to make a binding decree in Scots law, this technical term must be used. (*technical*) ○ *They decern and decree the said John Smith to be returned to prison.* [15thC. Via French *décerner* from Latin *decernere* 'to decide, pronounce a decision', from *cernere* 'to separate, sift' (source of English *crime* and *secret*).]

decertify /dee súrti fī/ (**-fies, -fying, -fied**) *vt.* to withdraw certification from sb or sth —**decertification** /dee súrtifi káysh'n/ *n.*

dechannelise /dee chánn'l īz/ (**-ises, -ising, -ised**) *vt.* to reroute a river to its original location and configuration of flow [Late 20thC]

deci- *prefix.* a tenth ○ *decigram.* Symbol **d** [Via French from Latin *decimus* (see DECIMAL)]

decibel /déssi bel, déssib'l/ *n.* a unit of relative sound loudness, electric voltage, or current equal to ten times the common logarithm of the ratio of two readings. For sound, the decibel scale runs from zero for the least perceptible sound to 130 for sound that causes pain. Symbol **dB**

decide /di sīd/ (**-cides, -ciding, -cided**) *v.* **1.** *vti.* **CHOOSE WHAT TO DO** to make a choice or come to a conclusion about sth ○ *We decided not to go in the end.* **2.** *vt.* **LEAD SB TO CHOOSE** to make sb choose what to do or come to a conclusion about sth (*informal*) ○ *His encouraging letter decided me against giving up the course.* **3.** *vt.* **END STH CLEARLY** to bring sth to an end in a definite or obvious way **4.** *vi.* **ARRIVE AT A VERDICT** to come to a verdict or judgment [14thC. Directly or via French *décider* from Latin *decidere*, literally 'to cut off', from *caedere* 'to cut' (source of English *chisel*); the underlying idea being to cut through a problem.] —**decidable** *adj.*

decided /di sīdid/ *adj.* **1. OBVIOUS** clearly seen, felt, or noticed **2. FIRM OR CERTAIN** free of uncertainty or doubt —**decidedness** *n.*

decidedly /di sīdidli/ *adv.* without any doubt or question

decider /di sīdər/ *n.* sth that settles the outcome of a contest or argument, especially, in sport, a game played to determine the ultimate winner

deciding /di sīding/ *adj.* acting to settle the result of a contest or debate, or to make clear what must be done next

decidua /di síddyoo ə/ (*plural* **-as** *or* **-ae** /-ee/) *n.* a specialized part of the mucous membrane (**endometrium**) that lines the womb during pregnancy and is shed with the placenta at birth [Late 18thC. From modern Latin *decidua (membrana)* 'deciduous (membrane)', so called because it is shed (see DECIDUOUS).] —**decidual** *adj.* —**deciduate** /-ət/ *adj.*

deciduous /di síddyoo əss/ *adj.* **1. SHEDDING LEAVES IN AUTUMN** used to describe trees and shrubs that shed their leaves in the autumn **2. WITH DECIDUOUS TREES** used to describe a forest or wood that is composed mostly of deciduous trees **3. SHED AFTER DEVELOPMENTAL STAGE** shed after a stage of development, as are the teeth, antlers, or wings of animals and birds, or shed easily or at intervals, as are the scales of fish [Mid-17thC. From Latin *deciduus*, from *decidere* 'to fall down', from *cadere* 'to fall, die' (see DECAY).] —**deciduously** *adv.* —**deciduousness** *n.*

deciduous tooth *n.* = **milk tooth**

decile /déss īl, -il/ *n.* **1. ANY OF 10 GROUPS** any one of ten groups containing an equal number of the items that make up a frequency distribution **2. VALUE DIVIDING UP A FREQUENCY DISTRIBUTION** any of the nine values that divide the total number of items in a frequency distribution into ten groups, each containing an equal number of items [Late 19thC. Coined from DECI- + -ILE.]

decilitre /déssi leetər/ *n.* **1. TENTH OF A LITRE** a unit of volume equal to 0.1 litre. Symbol **dl 2. deciliter** US = **decilitre** [Early 19thC. From French *décilitre*.]

decimal /déssim'l/ *adj.* **COUNTED IN GROUPS OF 10** using the number ten as a base and counted or ordered in units of ten, or belonging to a system organized in this way ■ *n.* **NUMBER IN DECIMAL SYSTEM** a number expressed in a counting system that uses units of ten, especially a decimal fraction [Early 17thC. From modern Latin *decimalis*, from Latin *decimus* 'tenth', from *decem* 'ten'.] —**decimally** *adv.*

decimal classification *n.* = **Dewey Decimal System**

decimal currency *n.* a type of currency based on units of ten or multiples of ten, now used in most countries

decimal fraction *n.* a numerical fraction with ten as its denominator, written showing the fractional elements after a decimal point

decimalize /déssimə līz/ (**-izes, -izing, -ized**), **decimalise** (**-ises, -ising, -ised**) *vti.* to convert sth, e.g. a country's currency or measurement system, into a decimal or metric system or convert to this — **decimalization** *n.*

decimal place *n.* the place or a specific number of digits to the right of the decimal point in a line of numbers

decimal point *n.* a printed or written dot in a decimal number that divides the whole numbers from the tenths, hundredths, and smaller divisions of ten

decimal system *n.* a numerical system that has the number ten as the basic unit from which the other counting units are formed as multiples. The metric system of measurement and most currency systems are based on a decimal system, using a basic unit of ten with larger units as multiples of it.

decimate /déssi mayt/ (**-mates, -mating, -mated**) *vt.* **1. DESTROY LARGE PROPORTION OF STH** to kill off or remove a large proportion of a group of people, animals, or things, or of the population of a place **2. VIRTUALLY DESTROY STH** to inflict so much damage on sth that it is very nearly destroyed or rendered beyond repair

3. KILL ONE PERSON IN 10 to kill one out of every ten people, especially in a body of mutinous soldiers (*archaic*) [Late 16thC. From Latin *decimat-*, the past participle stem of *decimare*, literally 'to take a tenth', from *decimus* 'tenth' (see DECIMAL).] —**decimator** *n.*

WORD KEY: USAGE

Extension of meaning: No doubt *his cat decimated the neighbourhood's mouse population* does not mean that the creature limited its destruction to one mouse in ten. The popular meaning of ***decimate*** is effectively the reverse of its historical meaning, and now predominates because the need for a word meaning 'to kill one person in ten' has greatly diminished. Even so, the popular meaning is not accepted by everyone, and it is often better to use an alternative such as *annihilate*, *exterminate*, *destroy*, or *devastate*.

decimation /déssə máysh'n/ *n.* **1. WIDESPREAD DESTRUCTION** the act, process, or result of destroying, removing, or damaging a large proportion of sth **2. KILLING ONE IN 10** the execution of one person out of every ten, especially as a punishment on a body of mutinous soldiers (*archaic*)

decimetre /déssi meetər/ *n.* **1. TENTH OF A METRE** a unit of length equal to 0.1 metre. Symbol **dm 2. decimeter** US = **decimetre**

decipher /di sífər/ (**-phers, -phering, -phered**) *vt.* **1. MAKE OUT WHAT STH SAYS** to establish what a word or piece of writing says when it is difficult or almost impossible to read **2. WORK OUT MEANING OF STH** to study sth that is written in code or in an unknown form of writing until it can be understood and read normally —**decipherer** *n.* —**decipherment** *n.*

decipherable /di sífərəb'l/ *adj.* capable of being read and understood —**decipherability** /di sífərə bílləti/ *n.*

decision /di sízh'n/ *n.* **1. STH SB HAS SETTLED ON** sth that sb chooses or makes up his or her mind about, after considering it and other possible choices ○ *It was a tough decision to make.* **2. FIRMNESS IN CHOOSING STH** the ability to choose or decide about things in a clear and definite way without too much hesitation or delay ○ *a man of decision* **3. PROCESS OF CHOOSING** the process of coming to a conclusion or determination about sth **4.** BOXING **BOXING VICTORY DECIDED ON POINTS** a win in a boxing match that is awarded to the fighter with the higher total of points given by a majority of one or more judges ○ *He won a 10-round decision.* [15thC. Either directly or via French from the Latin stem *decision-*, from the past participle stem of *decidere* 'to decide' (see DECIDE).] —**decisional** *adj.*

decision-making *n.* the process of making choices or reaching conclusions, especially on important political or business matters —**decision-maker** *n.*

decision theory *n.* the study of the best possible outcomes for decisions made under varying conditions

decision tree *n.* a diagram set out like the branches of a tree that shows the consequences of a decision, each decision entailing a course of action that requires various other decisions

decisive /di sīssiv/ *adj.* **1. SETTLING STH** settling or ending sth, e.g. a debate, controversy, or contest ○ *a decisive victory* **2. ABLE TO MAKE DEFINITE DECISIONS** showing an ability to make decisions quickly, firmly, and clearly [Early 17thC. Via French from, ultimately, Latin *decidere* 'to decide' (see DECIDE).] —**decisiveness** *n.*

decisively /di sīssivli/ *adv.* in a way that brings a clear and definite decision or a recognizable end

deck /dek/ *n.* **1.** NAUT **FLOOR SURFACE ACROSS A SHIP** a level surface that runs from one side of a ship to the other and along all or part of its length, forming a floor **2.** TRANSP **VEHICLE SECTION ON ONE LEVEL** a floored, self-contained area of a ship or of a passenger vehicle, e.g. a bus or tram **3.** ELEC **AUDIO UNIT** a wide, flat piece of audio equipment that contains a player for tapes, records, cassettes, or compact discs **4.** CIV ENG **FLOOR OF ROADWAY OR BRIDGE** the floor or platform of a roadway or bridge **5.** *US, Can* CARDS **PLAYING CARDS** a pack of playing cards **6.** *US, Can* ARCHIT **TERRACE OF HOUSE** an open unroofed area of floor extending from the back of a house ○ *They had a barbecue on the deck.* **7. GROUND** the ground or floor (*informal*) ■ *vt.* (**decks, decking, decked**) **1. DECORATE STH OR SB** to decorate or ornament sth or sb (*literary*) ○ *deck the hall with boughs of holly* **2. KNOCK SB DOWN** to strike and knock sb down deliberately (*informal*) **3. BUILD DECK FOR STH** to make a deck for a ship or other structure [15thC. From Middle Dutch *dec* 'roof, covering, cloak', ultimately from a prehistoric Germanic word that is the ancestor of English *thatch*.] —**decker** *n.* ◇ **clear the deck** *or* **decks** to get rid of all obstacles, especially pending work, prior to beginning a new task ◇ **hit the deck** to fall on the floor or ground, often as self-protection (*informal*) ◇ **on deck** NAUT on the top, external surface of a ship or boat

deck out *vt.* to decorate sth, or dress sb up in fancy clothes

deck over *vt.* to complete the construction of an upper deck on a ship or boat

deck bridge *n.* a bridge designed so that the roadway or track is supported by the upper horizontal part of the structural framework

deck chair *n.* a collapsible adjustable outdoor chair with a wooden framework and a seat made from a piece of strong fabric suspended between the top and bottom of the central frame. Deck chairs are usually made with striped or plain canvas in bright colours and used on the beach, around a pool, or on the deck of a ship.

decked /dekt/ *adj.* **1. DONE UP DECORATIVELY** colourfully or attractively set out, draped, or decorated (*literary*) **2. WITH A DECK** having or fitted with a deck (*usually used in combination*)

deck hand *n.* sb who does general manual work on a ship, yacht, or other vessel

deckhouse /dék howss/ (*plural* **-houses** /-howziz/) *n.* a structure built on the main deck of a ship or other vessel, used as a room or several rooms

deckle /dék'l/ *n.* **1. PAPER-MAKING FRAME** a metal frame used to contain pulp in a mould during the making of handmade paper **2.** = **deckle edge** [Mid-18thC. From German *Deckel*, literally 'little covering', from *Decke* 'covering'.]

deckle edge *n.* a rough, irregular, or feathery edge on handmade paper —**deckle-edged** *adj.*

deck officer *n.* an officer responsible for tasks such as navigation that take place on a ship's main deck

deck tennis *n.* a game based on lawn tennis, using a small court with a net and a ring made of rubber or rope that the players throw back and forth

decl. *abbr.* GRAM declension

declaim /di kláym/ (**-claims, -claiming, -claimed**) *v.* **1.** *vti.* **SPEAK FORMALLY AND DRAMATICALLY** to make a formal forceful speech about sth, or say sth in a formal and dramatic way **2.** *vi.* **RECITE** to deliver a recitation [14thC. Directly or via French *déclamer* from Latin *declamare* 'to cry out', from *clamare* 'to cry, call' (source of English *claim* and *clamour*).] —**declaimer** *n.*

declamation /déklə máysh'n/ *n.* **1. FORMAL DRAMATIC SPEECH** a speech or presentation spoken in a formal and theatrical style **2. PROCESS OF DECLAIMING** the art or process of declaiming ○ *'The air of the New World seems favourable to the art of declamation'.* (Joseph Conrad, *Nostromo*; 1904)

declamatory /di klámmətəri/ *adj.* **1. DRAMATIC** formal and dramatic in public speech **2. RHETORICAL** loud and rhetorical but without very meaningful content —**declamatorily** *adv.*

declarant /di kláirənt/ *n.* sb who makes a formal, often legal, statement [Late 17thC. From French *déclarant*, the present participle of *déclarer* 'to declare'.]

declaration /déklə ráysh'n/ *n.* **1. FORMAL STATEMENT** a formal document giving explicit details, e.g. the terms of a business agreement or plan, or information on goods or assets for tax purposes **2. OFFICIAL PROCLAMATION** an emphatic formal public statement, especially by a government or public body **3. PROCESS OF MAKING A DECLARATION** the process or act of declaring sth in an official or public way **4.** LAW **UNSWORN BUT SOLEMN EVIDENCE** a formal statement of facts that is allowed in a legal case in place of a statement made under oath **5.** LAW **PLAINTIFF'S OFFICIAL WRITTEN CLAIM** a formal document in which a plaintiff lays out precise details of the circumstances leading to the legal action being taken **6. RULING ON QUESTIONS OF LAW** a ruling by a judge or court on the legal position of contesting parties **7.** CARDS **ANNOUNCEMENT OF BID** the act of naming a particular suit as trumps, or of declaring no-trumps, by the player who makes the final bid of a hand of bridge

Declaration of Human Rights *n.* a United Nations document approved on 10 December, 1948 by the General Assembly, affirming the dignity of all human beings. It proclaimed their right to free movement in search of truth and justice and their right to live their lives in dignity.

declaration of independence *n.* a proclamation by which a country, group, or people asserts firmly and publicly that it has become independent of a governing power

Declaration of Independence *n.* a written statement issued and adopted by the Continental Congress in 1776 proclaiming that the 13 North American colonies henceforward would govern themselves rather than be ruled by Great Britain. The Declaration of Independence was adopted by the Congress on 2 July, 1776 and formally endorsed on 4 July. ○ *'If the American Revolution had produced nothing but the Declaration of Independence, it would have been worthwhile.'* (Samuel Eliot Morison, *The Oxford History of the American People*; 1965)

declarative /di klárrətiv/ *adj.* containing a statement, or in the form of a statement —**declaratively** *adv.*

declarator /di klárrətər/ *n.* a legal action brought in Scotland by sb who wants a particular right or status to be clarified and stated judicially

declaratory /di klárrətəri/ *adj.* **1. STATING A PRECISE LEGAL POSITION** stating and clarifying sth, especially a legal right, status, decree, or judgment **2.** = **declarative** —**declaratorily** *adv.*

declare /di kláir/ (**-clares, -claring, -clared**) *v.* **1.** *vti.* **ANNOUNCE CLEARLY OR LOUDLY** to state sth in a plain, open, or emphatic way **2.** *vt.* **STATE STH FORMALLY OR OFFICIALLY** to make an official or public announcement about sb or sth, especially on a legal or medical matter ○ *The doctors declared her fit to work.* ○ *The chairperson declared the meeting open.* **3.** *vti.* **REVEAL STH AS DUTIABLE OR TAXABLE** to inform customs or tax authorities about goods on which duty is owed, or about income that is taxable **4.** *vt.* **STATE AN INTENT OFFICIALLY** to state an official intention to undertake a particular course of action or adopt a particular status ○ *to declare independence* **5.** *vi.* **MAKE A DECISION KNOWN** to announce a choice or decision formally and publicly (*formal*) **6.** *vti.* CARDS **SAY WHICH SUIT IS TRUMPS** to announce to the other players in bridge the suit that has been chosen as trumps or no-trumps for the next hand **7.** *vi.* CRICKET **CHOOSE TO END INNINGS** to end an innings in cricket before all the batsmen have been dismissed, having decided, as the batting side or the captain of it, that the team has probably made enough runs **8.** *vti.* CARDS **LAY CARDS ON THE TABLE** to show that you have a particular score in bezique and other card games by displaying the cards face up on the table and claiming your score **9.** *vr.* **PROPOSE MARRIAGE** to make a formal or open statement of love for and a wish to marry sb (*dated*) [14thC. From Latin *declarare* 'to make clear', from *clarus* 'clear' (source of English *clear* and *claret*).] —**declarable** *adj.* —**declarer** *n.* ◇ **declare war 1.** to make a formal public announcement that the country represented is now at war with another country and will begin military action against it ○ *'Older men declare war, but it is the youth that must fight and die'.* (Herbert Hoover, *Speech, Republican National Convention*; 27 June, 1944) **2.** to begin a fierce campaign to get rid of or defeat sth, or start fighting it in earnest

declarer /di kláirər/ *n.* CARDS sb who announces either no-trumps or which suit is to be trumps in the next hand, and, in bridge, plays his or her own cards and those of the dummy for that hand

declass /deé klaáss/ (**-classes, -classing, -classed**) *vt.* to give sb a lower status or class in society

déclassé /day kláss ay, -klaáss-, dáy kla sáy/ *adj.* reduced to a lower class or status in society [Late 19thC. From French, the past participle of *déclasser* 'to declass'.]

declassify /dee klássi fī/ (**-fies, -fying, -fied**) *vt.* to remove sth from an official list of confidential or top-secret material so that anyone may see it — **declassifiable** *adj.* —**declassification** /dee klássifi káysh'n/ *n.*

declaw /deé kláw/ (**-claws, -clawing, -clawed**) *vt.* to remove the claws from an animal's paws, often to prevent it from injuring or catching other animals, or from scratching or climbing

declension /di klénsh'n/ *n.* **1.** GRAM SET OF WORDS THAT BEHAVE SIMILARLY a group of nouns, adjectives, or pronouns that all change their form or word-endings in the same way according to gender, number, or grammatical case **2.** GRAM PROCESS OF ENDING WORDS the process by which some sets of nouns, adjectives, and pronouns vary in form to show gender, number, or grammatical case **3.** WORSENING OR FALLING AWAY the process of gradually declining or deteriorating (*formal*) **4.** GEOL DOWNWARD SLOPE a downward slope, especially of terrain [15thC. Via French *déclinaison* from the Latin stem *declination-*, from *declinare* 'to fall away' (see DECLINE), from the idea that grammatical endings were a falling away from the pure form.] —**declensional** *adj.* —**declensionally** *adv.*

declination /dékli náysh'n/ *n.* **1.** ASTRON ANGULAR DISTANCE FROM CELESTIAL EQUATOR the angular distance of an astronomical body measured in degrees from the celestial equator along the great circle passing through it and the celestial poles **2.** PHYS, GEOG = magnetic declination —**declinational** *adj.*

decline /di klín/ *v.* (**-clines, -clining, -clined**) **1.** *vti.* REFUSE INVITATION to give a polite refusal to an invitation **2.** *vt.* REFUSE PARTICIPATION to refuse to respond or take part in sth **3.** *vi.* DIMINISH to become fewer or less ◦ *shares declining in value* **4.** *vi.* GET WEAKER to become physically or mentally less vigorous, especially because of illness or mature years ◦ *his health had declined* **5.** *vti.* GRAM SHOW VARIOUS FORMS to state the grammatical forms of a noun, adjective, or pronoun, or have various grammatical forms. ◊ **declension 6.** *vti.* SLOPE DOWN to bend sth downwards, or slope downwards ■ *n.* **1.** DETERIORATION a deterioration in quality, strength, or degree, or a reduction in amount **2.** PERIOD NEAR END the terminal period of sb or sth, ending in death or disappearance ◦ *at the decline of the empire* **3.** DOWNWARD SLOPE a downward slope or movement [14thC. Directly and via French *decliner* from Latin *declinare* 'to turn aside', literally 'to bend away', from *clinare* 'to bend'.] —**decliner** *n.* ◇ **be on the decline 1.** show a gradual lessening of quality, amount, or degree **2.** show a gradual worsening of health

declinometer /dékli nómmitər/ *n.* an instrument that measures the difference between magnetic north or south and true north or south at a particular point on the Earth's surface [Mid-19thC. Coined from DECLINATION + METER.]

declivitous /di klívvətəs/ *adj.* sloping downwards

declivity /di klívvəti/ (*plural* **-ties**) *n.* **1.** STH SLOPING sth, especially a piece of land, that slopes downwards **2.** INCLINATION DOWNWARDS a downward inclination, especially of a piece of land [Early 17thC. Via Latin *declivitas* from, ultimately, *clivus* 'slope'. Ultimately from an Indo-European word meaning 'to lean, bend over', which is also the ancestor of English *client* and *ladder*.]

declutch /deé klúch/ (**-clutches, -clutching, -clutched**) *vi.* to disengage the clutch of a motor vehicle (*technical*)

Deco /dékō/, **deco** *adj.* = Art Deco

decoct /di kókt/ (**-cocts, -cocting, -cocted**) *vt.* to extract the essence or active ingredient from a substance by boiling it [15thC. From Latin *decoct-*, the past participle stem of *decoquere*, literally 'to boil down', from *coquere* 'to cook'.]

decoction /di kóksh'n/ *n.* **1.** EXTRACTING PROCESS the extraction of an essence or active ingredient from a substance by boiling **2.** CONCENTRATED SUBSTANCE a concentrated substance that results from decoction

decode /deé kōd/ (**-codes, -coding, -coded**) *v.* **1.** *vt.* DECIPHER MESSAGE to transform an encoded message or signal into a usable form **2.** *vt.* INTERPRET MESSAGE to find the direct meaning of cryptic or indirect language **3.** *vti.* LING TRANSLATE STH to understand the meaning of a word or phrase in a foreign language —**decodable** *adj.*

decoder /deé kōdər/ *n.* a person, device, or computer program that decodes sth

decoke /deé kōk/ (**-cokes, -coking, -coked**) *vt.* to remove the carbon deposits from an internal combustion engine

decollate /deé kə láyt, dékə layt/ (**-lates, -lating, -lated**) *vt.* **1.** SEPARATE PAPER to separate continuous paper into single sheets **2.** DECAPITATE to decapitate (*archaic*) — **decollation** /deékə láysh'n, dékə-/ *n.* —**decollator** /deé kə láytər, dékə laytər/ *n.*

decollectivize /deé kə lékti vīz/ (**-izes, -izing, -ized**), **decollectivise** (**-ises, -ising, -ised**) *vti.* to modify a socialist production system or economy to work on free market principles —**decollectivization** /deé kə lekti vī záysh'n/ *n.*

décolletage /dáy kol taázh, day kóllə taazh/ *n.* **1.** LOW NECKLINE the top front part of a woman's low-cut garment **2.** LOW-CUT GARMENT a piece of women's clothing with a décolletage [Late 19thC. From French, formed from *décolleté* (see DÉCOLLETÉ).]

décolleté /day kól tay, -kóllə tay/ *n.* CHEST AREA the upper part of a woman's chest, below the neck ◦ *a décolleté moisturizing treatment* ■ *adj.* **1.** CLOTHES WITH LOW NECKLINE having a low-cut front neckline ◦ *a décolleté dress* **2.** WEARING LOW-CUT GARMENT wearing a décolleté garment [Mid-19thC. From French, the past participle of *décolleter* 'to lower the neckline', from *collet* 'collar', from, ultimately, Latin *collum* 'neck'.]

decolonize /deé kóllə nīz/ (**-nizes, -nizing, -nized**), **decolonise** (**-nises, -nising, -nised**) *vt.* to grant a colony its independence —**decolonization** /dee kóllə nī záysh'n/ *n.*

decolorant /deé kúllərənt/ *n.* a chemical that removes the colour from a fabric or other substance — **decolorant** *adj.*

decolorize /deé kúllə rīz/ (**-izes, -izing, -ized**), **decolorise** (**-ises, -ising, -ised**) *vt.* to remove the colour from a fabric or other substance, e.g. by chemical means —**decolorization** /dee kúllə rī záysh'n/ *n.*

decolour /deé kúllər/ (**-ours, -ouring, -oured**) *vt.* = decolorize —**decoloration** /dee kúllə ráysh'n/ *n.*

decommission /deé kə mísh'n/ (**-sions, -sioning, -sioned**) *vt.* to remove sth, e.g. a ship, nuclear power station, machinery, or weapons, from service

decompensation /deé kom pen sáysh'n/ *n.* **1.** MED HEART CONDITION the failure of the heart to maintain adequate circulation because of various stresses upon it **2.** PSYCHIAT WORSENING PSYCHIATRIC CONDITION the deterioration of existing psychological defences in a patient already exhibiting pathological behaviour

decompose /deékəm pōz/ (**-poses, -posing, -posed**) *vti.* **1.** BIOL ROT to break down organic matter from a complex to a simpler form, mainly through the action of fungi and bacteria, or undergo this process **2.** BREAK DOWN INTO PIECES to break sth down, or be broken down, into smaller or simpler parts **3.** CHEM BREAK DOWN INTO CONSTITUENT PARTS to separate or cause sth to separate into constituent parts —**decomposability** /deékəm pōzə bílləti/ *n.* —**decomposable** /-pōzəb'l/ *adj.* —**decomposition** /deé kompə zísh'n/ *n.*

decomposer /deékəm pōzər/ *n.* an organism, especially a bacterium or fungus, that causes organic matter to rot or decay

decompress /deékəm préss/ (**-presses, -pressing, -pressed**) *vti.* **1.** REDUCE PRESSURE to cause or experience a reduction in the atmospheric pressure of an enclosed space **2.** ALLOW EXPANSION to allow a substance to expand to normal dimensions or volume by the removal of pressure, or to undergo this process **3.** COMPUT EXPAND DATA to expand compressed data to its normal extent, or to undergo this process — **decompressive** *adj.*

decompression /deékəm présh'n/ *n.* **1.** PRESSURE DECREASE a decrease in surrounding or inherent pressure, especially the controlled decrease in pressure that divers undergo to prevent decompression sickness **2.** COMPUT DATA EXPANSION the expansion to full size of compressed computer data ◦ *decompression must precede installation* ◦ *decompression software* **3.** SURG SURGERY TO REDUCE PRESSURE IN ORGAN a surgical procedure to reduce pressure in an organ or part of the body caused, e.g. by fluid on the brain, or to reduce the pressure of tissues on a nerve

decompression chamber *n.* a sealed room where decompression is carried out

decompression sickness, decompression illness *n.* a condition marked by joint pain, nausea, loss of motion, and breathing difficulties experienced by divers and workers in caissons who emerge too quickly from a pressurized environment. It is caused by the formation of nitrogen bubbles in the blood and tissues.

decon /deé kon/ (**-cons, -conning, -conned**) *vt.* ◆ decontaminate (*informal*)

decondition /deékən dísh'n/ (**-tions, -tioning, -tioned**) *vt.* to cause or teach a person or animal to stop exhibiting a conditioned response

decongest /deé kənjést/ (**-gests, -gesting, -gested**) *vt.* **1.** UNBLOCK NOSE to loosen mucus in the nasal passages, sinuses, or bronchi **2.** LOOSEN to increase the flow in sth that is compacted or congested

decongestant /deé kənjéstənt/ *n.* an agent that reduces or relieves nasal congestion, e.g. during a cold or chest infection —**decongestant** *adj.*

deconsecrate /dee kónssi krayt/ (**-crates, -crating, -crated**) *vt.* to convert a sacred place, building, or object to secular use —**deconsecration** /deé konsi kráysh'n/ *n.*

deconstruct /deékən strúkt/ (**-structs, -structing, -structed**) *vt.* to subject a text to critical analysis using the theories of deconstruction

deconstruction /deékən strúksh'n/ *n.* a method of analysing texts based on the ideas that language is inherently unstable and shifting and that the reader rather than the author is central in determining meaning. It was introduced by the French philosopher Jacques Derrida in the late 1960s. — **deconstructionism** *n.* —**deconstructionist** *n.*

decontaminate /deékən támmi nayt/ (**-nates, -nating, -nated**) *vt.* to remove unwanted chemical, radioactive, or biological impurities or toxins from land or a person or object —**decontamination** /deé kən támmi náysh'n/ *n.*

decontrol /deékən trōl/ (**-trols, -trolling, -trolled**) *vt.* to remove official restraints or regulations on sth, especially rents

decor /dáy kawr, dék-/, **décor** *n.* **1.** FURNISHING STYLE the style of furniture and furnishings chosen for a room or house **2.** STAGE SCENERY the scenery of a stage [Late 19thC. From French, formed from *décorer* 'to decorate', from Latin *decorare* (see DECORATE).]

decorate /dékə rayt/ (**-rates, -rating, -rated**) *v.* **1.** *vt.* MAKE STH ATTRACTIVE to make sth more attractive by adding ornate or stylish elements to it **2.** *vti.* CHANGE APPEARANCE OF ROOM to paint or wallpaper a building or a room **3.** *vt.* AWARD SB A MEDAL to give a medal or other honour or award to sb to acknowledge bravery, dedication, or achievement [Mid-16thC. From Latin *decoratus*, the past participle of *decorare* 'to beautify', from *decus* 'ornament'.]

Decorated architecture, Decorated style *n.* the second, more ornate stage of English Gothic architecture that is characterized by an increased use of geometric tracery and floral motifs

decoration /déka ráysh'n/ *n.* **1.** ATTRACTIVE ITEM an item, usually one of a group, attached to sth to make it look more attractive or to mark a special occasion **2.** ORNAMENTATION the addition of ornaments to make sth more attractive **3.** PAINTING AND PAPERING the painting and wallpapering in a room or building **4.** AWARD a medal or other honour or award given to sb to acknowledge bravery, dedication, or achievement

decorative /dékərətiv/ *adj.* **1.** ATTRACTIVE serving merely to look attractive rather than having a functional purpose **2.** OF DECORATION relating to the decoration of a room or home ◦ *added some nice decorative touches* **3.** ORNAMENTAL serving to make sth look more attractive, especially by the addition of nonfunctional embellishments —**decoratively** *adv.* —**decorativeness** *n.*

decorative art *n.* any art concerned with the design and production of functional but decorative items for home use, e.g. ceramics, furniture, and fabrics (*often used in the plural*)

decorator /dékə raytər/ *n.* **1.** PAINTER OR WALLPAPERER sb whose job is painting and wallpapering houses and other buildings **2.** SB WHO DECORATES sb whose job is to decorate sth (*often used in combination*)

decorous /dékərəss/ *adj.* **1.** SEEMLY conforming to what is acceptable or expected in formal or solemn settings, especially in dress or behaviour ○ *'They began to talk politely, in decorous half-completed sentences, with little gasps of agreement'.* (William Faulkner, *Sanctuary*; 1931) **2.** DIGNIFIED understated and dignified [Mid-17thC. Formed from Latin *decorus*, 'seemly', from *decor* 'attractiveness'. Ultimately from an Indo-European word meaning 'to accept', which is also the ancestor of English *decent, docile, dogma,* and *disciple.*] —**decorously** *adv.* —**decorousness** *n.*

decorticate /dee káwrti kayt/ *vt.* (**-cates, -cating, -cated**) **1.** BOT REMOVE OUTER LAYER FROM A PLANT to remove an outer layer such as bark, rind, or a husk from a plant or part of a plant **2.** SURG REMOVE STH FROM AN ORGAN to remove surgically the outer layer of an organ or structure such as the brain or kidney ■ *adj.* MED WITHOUT CORTEX FUNCTION used to describe a brain that has lost the function of its cerebral cortex as a result of disease or surgery [Early 17thC. From Latin *decorticare*, from *cortex* (see CORTEX).] —**decortication** /dee káwrti káysh'n/ *n.* —**decorticator** /dee káwrti kaytər/ *n.*

decorum /di káwrəm/ *n.* **1.** DIGNITY dignity or correctness that is socially expected **2.** APPROPRIATENESS OF ARTISTIC ELEMENT the compatibility of an element in a literary or artistic work, e.g. character, form, style, or plot, with the work as a whole **3.** CONVENTION a socially accepted or expected convention or requirement (*archaic*) [Mid-16thC. From Latin, formed from *decorus* (see DECOROUS).]

decoupage /dáy koo paázh/, **découpage** *n.* **1.** PAPER DECORATION METHOD a technique for decorating sth in which a design is made of pieces of printed paper cut out and stuck on a flat base, then coated with varnish **2.** DECOUPAGE PICTURE a picture or other form of decoration that is made using decoupage [Mid-20thC. From French, formed from *découper* 'to cut up, cut out', from *couper* 'to cut'.]

decouple /dee kúpp'l/ (**-ples, -pling, -pled**) *vt.* **1.** SEPARATE OBJECTS to separate or disengage one thing from another **2.** ELEC REDUCE INTERDEPENDENCE to remove or weaken the interaction between two electronic circuits, subsystems, or systems so that there is little or no transfer or feedback of energy between them —**decoupler** *n.*

decoy /dee koy, di kóy/ *n.* **1.** HUNT HUNTING LURE a bird or animal, or a realistic replica, used by hunters to attract an animal or bird to a place for trapping or shooting **2.** DISTRACTER sth or sb used to deceive or divert attention, especially in order to lure sb into a trap **3.** ENTRAPMENT AREA an enclosed area or stretch of water that game or fowl are driven or lured into so that they can be easily shot or captured **4.** MIL FAKE EQUIPMENT a fake tank, ship, aircraft, or other military apparatus meant to deceive the enemy ■ *vt.* (**-coys, -coying, -coyed**) DECEIVE to deceive or entrap a person or animal by using a decoy [Mid-16thC. From Dutch *de kooi*, literally 'the cage', ultimately from Latin *cavea* 'cage' (source of English cage).] —**decoyer** *n.*

decoy duck /dee koy-/ *n.* **1.** TAMED DUCK a wild duck that has been tamed so it can be used for attracting other ducks **2.** MODEL DUCK a model duck, typically carved from wood, for use as a decoy or decoration

decrease /di kreess/ *vti.* (**-creases, -creasing, -creased**) DIMINISH to lessen or cause sth to lessen in size, strength, or amount ■ *n.* **1.** PROCESS OF DECREASING the process of becoming less, fewer, or smaller ○ *street crime is on the decrease* **2.** REDUCTION a reduction in the amount or rate of sth ○ *a 2% decrease in customers* [14thC. Via the Old French stem *decreiss-*, from, ultimately, Latin *decrescere*, from *crescere* 'to grow'.] —**decreasing** *adj.* —**decreasingly** *adv.*

decree /di kree/ *n.* **1.** OFFICIAL ORDER an order with the power of legislation issued by a ruler or other person or group with authority **2.** LAW COURT RULING a ruling given by a court, especially a divorce court **3.** RELIG DIVINE WILL the will or purpose of God, interpreted through events considered to be God's doing ■ *vt.* (**-crees, -creeing, -creed**) MAKE ORDER to make an official order, pronouncement, or legal ruling to effect sth [14thC. Via Old French *decré* from Latin *decretum*, the neuter past participle of *decernere* 'to decide, pronounce a decision'.] —**decreeable** *adj.* —**decreer** *n.*

decree absolute (*plural* **decrees absolute**) *n.* the final divorce court ruling that officially ends a marriage, leaving both parties free to marry again

decree nisi /-ní sī/ (*plural* **decrees nisi**) *n.* an interim ruling of a divorce court that will become absolute in the absence of objections arising

decreet /di kreet/ *n. Scotland* the final judgment in a court case

decrement /dékrimənt/ *n.* **1.** AMOUNT OF DECREASE the amount by which a quantity or quality gradually decreases **2.** DECREASING the process of becoming less or fewer (*formal*) [Late 16thC. From Latin *decrementum*, from *decrescere* from *crescere* 'to grow'.] —**decremental** /dékri mént'l/ *adj.* —**decrementally** /-mént'li/ *adv.*

decreolization /dee kree əlī záysh'n/, **decreolisation** *n.* the gradual adoption by speakers of a creole of a form of speech that is closer to the standard language from which the creole had originated

decrepit /di kréppit/ *adj.* **1.** OLD AND IN POOR CONDITION in poor condition, especially old, overused, or not working efficiently **2.** NOT YOUNG OR STRONG with strength lessened by the effects of age (*archaic or humorous*) [15thC. From Latin *decrepitus*, from *crepitus*, the past participle of *crepare* 'to crack, creak'. Ultimately from an imitative Indo-European base that is also the ancestor of English *raven* and *retch.*] —**decrepitly** *adv.* —**decrepitude** *n.*

WORD KEY: SYNONYMS

See Synonyms at ***weak***.

decrepitate /di kréppi tayt/ (**-tates, -tating, -tated**) *vti.* to heat a substance, especially a salt, until it crackles or stops crackling, or to be heated in this way [Mid-17thC. Coined from DE- + Latin *crepitare* 'to crackle', from *crepitus* 'cracked' (see DECREPIT).] —**decrepitation** /di kréppi táysh'n/ *n.*

decresc. *abbr.* decrescendo

decrescendo /deekrə shéndō/ *adv.* = **diminuendo** (*used as a musical direction*) ■ *n.* (*plural* **-dos**) = **diminuendo** *n.* [Early 19thC. From Italian, 'decreasing'.] —**decrescendo** *adj.*

decrescent /di kréss'nt/ *adj.* used to describe the moon when it is waning (*technical*) [Early 17thC. Formed from Latin *decrescere*, from *crescere* 'to grow'.] —**decrescence** *n.*

decretal /di kreet'l/ *n.* a papal decree or edict that relates to an aspect of church law or doctrine [14thC. Via late Latin *decretale*, from, ultimately, Latin *decret-*, the past participle stem of *decernere*, from *cernere* 'to separate, sift'.] —**decretal** *adj.*

decretory /di kreetəri/ *adj.* relating to or having the force of a decree [Late 16thC. From Latin *decretorius*, from *decret-*, the past participle stem of *decernere* (see DECERN).]

decriminalize /dee krímminə līz/ (**-izes, -izing, -ized**), **decriminalise** (**-ises, -ising, -ised**) *vt.* to make legal an action or substance that was formerly illegal —**decriminalization** /dee krimminə lī záysh'n/ *n.*

WORD KEY: SYNONYMS

See Synonyms at ***legal***.

decry /di krī/ (**-cries, -crying, -cried**) *vt.* to express strong disapproval of or openly criticize sb or sth (*formal*) ○ *critics decrying lowered standards in education* [Early 17thC. Modelled on French *décrier* 'to cry down'.] —**decrial** *n.* —**decrier** *n.*

decrypt /dee kript/ (**-crypts, -crypting, -crypted**) *vt.* render an encoded text or message into plain language. = **decode** *v.* 1, **decode** *v.* 2 [Mid-20thC. Coined from DE- + CRYPT(OGRAM).] —**decryption** /dee krípsh'n/ *n.*

decubitus /di kyóobitəss/ *n.* the particular position of sb's body when lying down, usually on the front, back, or side (*technical*) [Late 19thC. From modern Latin, formed from Latin *decumbere* 'to lie down', on the model of *accubitus* 'reclining at table'.] —**decubital** *adj.*

decubitus ulcer *n.* a bedsore (*technical*)

decumbent /di kúmbənt/ *adj.* **1.** BOT GROWING ALONG THE GROUND used to describe plants that lie along the ground but have a tip growing upwards **2.** ZOOL GROWING FLAT used to describe hair or bristles that lie or grow flat along a surface [Early 17thC. From Latin *decumbere* 'to lie down', from *cubare* 'to lie down'.] —**decumbence** *n.* —**decumbently** *adv.*

decuple /dékyoop'l/ *adj.* increasing by ten times (*formal*) [15thC. From late Latin *decuplus* 'tenfold', from Latin *decem* 'ten' + *-plus* '-fold'.]

decurion /de kyóori ən/ *n.* **1.** ROMAN OFFICER in ancient Rome, an officer in command of ten soldiers **2.** ROMAN COUNCILLOR a councillor in the Roman Empire [14thC. From the Latin stem *decurion-*, from *decuria* (see DECURY) on the model of *centurion.*]

decurrent /di kúrrənt/ *adj.* used to describe plant leaves that curve down at the edges, or trees with a rounded shape [15thC. From Latin *decurrere*, literally 'to run down', from *currere* 'to run'.] —**decurrently** *adv.*

decury /dékyoori/ (*plural* **-ies**) *n.* in ancient Rome, a company of ten soldiers [Mid-16thC. From Latin *decuria*, from *decem* 'ten', on the model of *centuria* 'century'.]

decussate /di kússayt/ *adj.* **1.** SHAPED LIKE A CROSS having the shape of a cross **2.** BOT FORMING OPPOSITE PAIRS used to describe leaves that form pairs opposite each other and at right angles to the pair above and the pair below, as in the horse chestnut [Early 19thC. From Latin *decussatus*, the past participle of *decussare* 'to divide crosswise', from *decussis*, the numeral ten (written X), from *decem* 'ten' + *assis*, a type of coin.] —**decussately** *adv.* —**decussation** /dee kuss áysh'n/ *n.*

dedans /də daaN/ *n.* (*plural* **-dans**) SPECTATING AREA in real tennis, the open end of the court just behind the serving area where spectators can watch the match ■ *npl.* SPECTATORS the spectators who watch from the dedans [Early 18thC. From French, 'inside, interior'.]

Dedham Vale /déddəm-/ Area of Outstanding Natural Beauty on the border of Essex and Suffolk, England. Area: 90 sq. km/35 sq. mi.

dedicate /déddi kayt/ (**-cates, -cating, -cated**) *vt.* **1.** DEVOTE ATTENTION TO STH to spend time or energy doing sth **2.** COMMIT YOURSELF TO STH to commit yourself or your life to sth **3.** SET STH ASIDE AS SPECIAL to set sth aside for a particular purpose ○ *an entire TV series dedicated to birds* **4.** ADDRESS WORK OF ART TO SB to associate a book, piece of music, or other art form with sb as a token of friendship or esteem or as an acknowledgment of help received **5.** RELIG SET STH APART AS HOLY to set sth apart for a sacred purpose or to the memory of a holy person, saint, or god, especially in a ceremony for this purpose ○ *'We cannot dedicate – we cannot consecrate – we cannot hallow – this ground. The brave men...who struggled here have consecrated it.'* (Abraham Lincoln, *Gettysburg Address*; 19 November, 1863) **6.** BROADCAST PLAY MUSIC ADDRESSED TO SB to play a piece of music, or request the playing of a piece of music, as a tribute, especially on the radio [15thC. From Latin *dedicare* 'to consecrate', from *dicare* 'to proclaim'.] —**dedicatee** /déddikə tee/ *n.* —**dedicative** /déddikətiv, -kaytiv/ *adj.* —**dedicator** /déddi kaytər/ *n.* —**dedicatory** /déddikətəri, -kaytəri/ *adj.*

dedicated /déddi kaytid/ *adj.* **1.** DEVOTED wholeheartedly devoted or committed to an aim, cause, or job **2.** INTENDED ONLY FOR ONE PURPOSE designed to carry out only one task, or set aside for a purpose ○ *relayed via a dedicated satellite link*

dedication /déddi káysh'n/ *n.* **1.** DEVOTION the quality of being devoted or committed to sth ○ *her dedication to duty* **2.** INSCRIPTION a short printed text at the beginning of a written or musical work associating it with sb esteemed by the author **3.** MUSIC PIECE OF MUSIC a piece of music played or requested as a tribute, especially on the radio **4.** SETTING ASIDE an act or process of setting sth aside for a particular purpose, especially in a ceremony that achieves this —**dedicational** *adj.*

dedifferentiation /dee difə renshi áysh'n/ *n.* CELL BIOL = **anaplasia**

deduce /di dyóoss/ (**-duces, -ducing, -duced**) *vt.* **1.** REACH A CONCLUSION to come to a conclusion, often without all the necessary or relevant information, but using what is known in a logical way **2.** LOGIC INFER STH

FROM A GENERAL PRINCIPLE to come to a conclusion by inference from a general principle [15thC. From Latin *deducere*, literally 'to lead out', from *ducere* 'to lead'.] —**deducibility** /di dyóossə bíllәti/ *n.* —**deducible** /di dyóosəb'l/ *adj.* —**deducibleness** /-nəss/ *n.*

WORD KEY: SYNONYMS

deduce, infer, assume, reason, conclude, work out, figure out

CORE MEANING: to reach a logical conclusion on the basis of information

deduce a general term for reaching a conclusion based on evidence; **infer** to draw a conclusion from specific circumstances or evidence; **assume** to take a premise or information as true without checking or confirming; **reason** to consider information and use it to reach a conclusion in a logical way; **conclude** a term used to suggest that a conclusion has been reached in a logical way after much consideration; **work out** an informal term suggesting some careful thought or reasoning, possibly working with limited information; **figure out** the most informal term, emphasizing the application of sb's own intelligence to the solving of a problem.

deduct /di dúkt/ (**-ducts, -ducting, -ducted**) *vt.* to subtract an amount for some purpose [15thC. From Latin *deduct-*, the past participle stem of *deducere*, literally 'to lead out', from *ducere* 'to lead'.]

deductible /di dúktəb'l/ *adj.* **1.** LIABLE TO DEDUCTION capable of being, or liable to be, subtracted from sth for some purpose **2.** *US, Can* ALLOWABLE AGAINST TAX allowed by tax authorities as a legitimate expense not liable to tax ■ *n. US* = **excess** —**deductibility** /di dúktə bíllәti/ *n.*

deduction /di dúksh'n/ *n.* **1.** CONCLUSION DRAWN a conclusion drawn from available information **2.** DRAWING A CONCLUSION the process of drawing a conclusion from available information **3.** LOGIC LOGICAL CONCLUSION a conclusion reached by applying the rules of logic to a premise **4.** AMOUNT DEDUCTED an amount that is subtracted from sth, especially as an allowance against tax **5.** SUBTRACTION OF AN AMOUNT the subtracting of an amount for some particular purpose **6.** LOGIC REASONING the forming of conclusions by applying the rules of logic to a premise

deductive /di dúktiv/ *adj.* based on logical or reasonable deduction —**deductively** *adv.*

deed /deed/ *n.* **1.** STH DONE an intentional act ○ *'The last temptation is the greatest treason / To do the right deed for the wrong reason'.* (T.S. Eliot, *Murder in the Cathedral*; 1935) **2.** NOTEWORTHY ACTION an action that is outstanding in a particular way **3.** LAW DOCUMENT a signed document that outlines the terms of an agreement, especially one that details a change in ownership of property **4.** LAW = **title deed** ■ **deeds** *npl.* ACTIONS action in general, especially as contrasted with speech ■ *vt.* (**deeds, deeding, deeded**) *US* LAW TRANSFER PROPERTY TO SB to sign over or transfer sth, especially property, to another person [Old English *dēd*. From a prehistoric Germanic word meaning 'a doing', ultimately from the same Indo-European ancestor as English *do*.]

deed box *n.* a lockable strongbox where deeds and other important documents can be safely kept

deeded /déedid/ *adj. US, Can* associated with a deed that shows clear ownership ○ *a ranch consisting of 640 deeded acres*

deed of covenant *n.* a signed document by which sb formally agrees to make payments for a period of several years to a charity or other organization

deed poll *n.* an official document, especially one that makes a change in a sb's name, that is signed and executed by one person only [From POLL 'cut off cleanly', as opposed to notched at the edge as with a contract drawn up in multiple copies]

deejay /dée jay/ *n.* a disc jockey (*informal*) [Mid-20thC. Respelling.] —**deejay** *vi.*

deem /deem/ (**deems, deeming, deemed**) *vt.* to judge or consider sth in a particular light (*formal; often used in the passive*) ○ *a plan that was deemed impractical from the very start* [Old English *dēman*. Ultimately from a prehistoric Germanic word meaning 'to judge', the ancestor of English *doom*.]

de-emphasize /dee émfə sīz/ (**de-emphasizes, de-emphasizing, de-emphasized**), **de-emphasise** (**de-emphasises, de-emphasising, de-emphasised**) *vt.* to make sth seem or be less important or central — **de-emphasis** /dee émfəssiss/ *n.*

deemster /déemstər/, **dempster** /démpstər/ *n.* the title given to either of the two justices serving on the Isle of Man [13thC. Formed from DEEM.] —**deemstership** *n.*

de-energize /dee énnər jīz/ (**de-energizes, de-energizing, de-energized**), **de-energise** (**de-energises, de-energising, de-energised**) *v.* **1.** *vt.* CUT OFF POWER to cut off an electrical circuit from its source of power **2.** *vti.* LOSE ENERGY to have or cause sb to have less energy or vitality —**de-energization** /dee énnər jī záysh'n/ *n.*

deep /deep/ *adj.* **1.** DOWN FROM A SURFACE extending from a surface downwards or inwards ○ *a deep wound* **2.** FAR FROM TOP TO BOTTOM extending a long way from top to bottom ○ *a deep well* ○ *'The deep dark-shining / Pacific leans on the land'.* (Robinson Jeffers, *Night*; 1925) **3.** FAR FROM FRONT TO BACK extending a long way from front to back ○ *a cupboard with deep shelves* **4.** FAR FROM AN EDGE extending a long way from a surface or boundary inwards ○ *deep wood* **5.** MADE UP OF UNITS standing or lining up in rows of a particular number ○ *people six deep on the pavement* **6.** FAR DOWN OR IN relatively far down, in, or inside sth ○ *a nagging pain deep in his chest* **7.** COMING FROM OR REACHING FAR INSIDE coming from or reaching far down inside the body ○ *take a deep breath* **8.** LOW IN PITCH low in pitch and rounded in tone ○ *a deep booming voice* **9.** DARK IN COLOUR relatively dark, rich, or intense in colour ○ *deep purple* **10.** INTENSE intensely held, kept, or experienced ○ *deep suspicion* **11.** PROFOUND intellectually profound ○ *no evidence of deep thinking* ■ *adj., adv.* **1.** SPORTS NEAR OWN GOAL nearer to the goal a team is defending than the goal it is attacking ○ *Aberdeen played with two deep defenders.* ○ *deep in their own territory* **2.** CRICKET NEAR BOUNDARY in cricket, playing or played near the boundary of the playing area, relatively far from the batsman ○ *deep mid-on* ■ *adv.* FAR far, especially from a surface or point of entry ○ *The expedition went deep into the jungle.* ■ *n.* **1.** SEA the ocean depths **2.** CRICKET POSITION FAR FROM BATSMAN the fielding position relatively far from the batsman **3.** INTENSE PART the middle or most intense part of sth (*literary*) ○ *the deep of night* [Old English *dēop*. Ultimately from an Indo-European word meaning 'deep, hollow', which is also the ancestor of English *dip* and *dive*.] —**deepness** *n.* ◇ **deep down (inside)** in your innermost being ◇ **deep in** completely overwhelmed by or absorbed in sth ○ *deep in a new novel* ◇ **in deep** very involved ◇ **in deep water, in deep shit** *taboo*, **in deep doodoo** *humorous* in a lot of trouble

deep-discount bond *n.* FIN a bond sold at a large discount because it bears little or no interest. It will, however, provide a capital gain on redemption.

deep-dish *adj.* baked in a deep dish and so thicker than normal ○ *deep-dish pizza*

deep-dyed *adj.* **1.** TEXTILES NONFADING used to describe fabric that has been dyed with a concentrated fade-resistant dye **2.** = **dyed-in-the-wool**

deepen /déepən/ (**-ens, -ening, -ened**) *vti.* **1.** GET DEEPER to become or make sth deep or deeper **2.** MAKE OR BECOME INTENSE to become or make sth more intense ○ *the recession was deepening* —**deepener** *n.*

deep end *n.* the part of a swimming pool, lake, or other body of water where the water is deepest ◇ **be thrown in at the deep end** to have to learn sth new or difficult with very little experience or warning ◇ **go off (at) the deep end** to fly into a rage or lose your emotional equilibrium

deep-fat fryer *n.* = **deep fryer**

deepfreeze /déep freez/ *n.* **1.** = **freezer 2.** STORAGE OF STH IN EXTREME CONDITIONS the storage of sth in very cold or hostile conditions **3.** SUSPENSION OF ACTIVITY the suspension or delay of further activity (*informal*)

deep-freeze (**deep-freezes, deep-freezing, deep-froze, deep-frozen**) *vt.* **1.** FREEZE STH QUICKLY to freeze sth such as food quickly in order to prolong its freshness or nutritional value **2.** KEEP STH VERY COLD to store sth at very low temperatures **3.** SUSPEND ACTIVITY to put off or suspend activity (*informal*) —**deep-frozen** *adj.*

deep-fry (**deep-fries, deep-frying, deep-fried**) *vt.* to cook food in fat or oil that is deep enough to cover the food completely —**deep-fried** *adj.*

deep kiss *n.* a French kiss (*dated*) —**deep-kiss** *vti.*

deep-laid *adj.* carefully worked out and highly confidential ○ *a deep-laid plan*

deep-litter *adj.* **1.** USING STRAW LAYER using a thick layer of straw or other natural material for farm animals, especially poultry, to move about in **2.** FROM DEEP-LITTER FARM from or produced by animals raised in deep-litter conditions

deeply /déepli/ *adv.* **1.** INTENSELY profoundly or intensely ○ *deeply offended* **2.** DEEP INSIDE far down inside ○ *breathe deeply* ○ *deeply felt pain*

deep-pan *adj.* used to describe a pizza with a deep filling baked in a dish with raised sides

deep pocket *n.* a seemingly unlimited supply of money (*informal*)

deep-rooted *adj.* **1.** FIRMLY HELD firmly held or established, usually over a long period of time, and so unlikely to change **2.** BOT WITH DEEP ROOTS having roots that grow deep in the soil

deep-sea *adj.* relating to the deep waters of the ocean far away from land

deep-seated *adj.* firmly established and difficult to change or eradicate ○ *deep-seated fear*

deep-set *adj.* used to describe eyes with deep sockets

deep soul *n.* soul music of the 1960s and 1970s that took the form of slow and emotionally sung ballads

deep space *n.* space beyond the Earth's gravitational influence or beyond the orbit of the Moon

deep structure *n.* LING the underlying form of a language, conceived as containing all the information needed to make any sentence in that language. ◊ **surface structure**

deep-water *adj.* **1.** ACCOMMODATING LARGE SHIPS used to describe a harbour or anchorage that is deep enough to accommodate large ocean-going vessels **2.** *US* SEAGOING designed or trained to travel on the oceans (*regional*)

deer /deer/ (*plural* **deer**) *n.* a mammal distinguished by the branched antlers on males. More than forty species of deer exist, of different sizes and with different markings, and they are found wild on all continents except Australia and Antarctica. Family: Cervidae. [Old English *dēor* 'animal'. From a prehistoric Germanic word meaning literally 'breathing creature', ultimately from an Indo-European base denoting 'breath, vapour', which is also the ancestor of English *fume, dust*, and *thyme*.]

deer-culler *n. NZ* a professional hunter of wild deer

deer fly *n.* a biting fly that infests deer and other animals, sucking blood and spreading the infectious disease tularemia. It also delivers a stinging bite to humans. Genus: *Chrysops.*

deergrass /déer graass/ (*plural* **-grass**) *n.* a perennial flowering grassy plant that grows in thick tufts in temperate peat bogs. Latin name: *Trichophorum caespitosum.*

deerhound /déer hownd/ *n.* a large long-legged greyhound with a very shaggy coat, originally bred in Scotland as a hunting dog from a Mediterranean strain of greyhound

deer lick *n.* a naturally occurring or artificial salty patch of ground where deer come to lick

deer mouse *n.* an agile mouse native to North and Central America. Genus: *Peromyscus.* ◊ **white-footed mouse**

deerskin /déer skin/ *n.* the treated hide of a deer used as a fabric

deerstalker /déer stawkər/ *n.* **1.** **deerstalker, deerstalker hat** FLAPPED HAT a type of tweed hat with peaks at the front and back and earflaps that can either be tied together on its crown or fastened under the chin **2.** HUNT HUNTER OF DEER sb who hunts deer on foot

deerstalking /déer stawking/ *n.* the activity of hunting wild deer by stealthily following them on foot

deer tick *n.* a tick that is a parasite of humans and other mammals. It carries and transmits the bacterium causing Lyme disease. Latin name: *Ioxides dammini.*

de-escalate /dee éskə layt/ (**de-escalates, de-escalating, de-escalated**) *vt.* to reduce the level or intensity of a difficult or dangerous situation —**de-escalation** /deè eskə láysh'n/ *n.*

Deeside and Lochnagar /deè sīd ənd lókhnə gaar/ designated Natural Scenic Area in Scotland, on the banks of the River Dee in Aberdeenshire. Area: 400 sq. km/250 sq. mi.

deet /deet/ *n.* an oily colourless insect repellent. Formula: $C_{12}H_{17}NO$. Full form **diethyl toluamide** [Mid-20thC. Probably from the initial letters of its chemical name.]

def /def/ *adj.* excellent (*slang*) [Late 20thC. Shortening of DEFINITIVE.]

def. *abbr.* **1.** defence **2.** defendant **3.** deferred **4.** GRAM definite **5.** definition

deface /di fáyss/ (**-faces, -facing, -faced**) *vt.* to spoil the appearance of sth, especially intentionally [14thC. From French *défacer*, from *face* (see FACE).] —**defaceable** *adj.* —**defacer** *n.*

defacement /di fáyssmənt/ *n.* the deliberate spoiling of the appearance of sth

de facto /day fáktō/ *adv.* IN FACT in fact, whether with a legal right or not ■ *adj.* AS THOUGH RIGHTFUL acting or existing in fact but without legal sanction ○ *the de facto rules of the country* ■ *n.* (*plural* **de factos**) *ANZ* PARTNER sb not married to sb else but living with the person as if they are married (*informal*) [Early 17thC. From Latin, 'in fact', literally 'from what is done'.]

defaecate *vi.* = **defecate**

defalcate /deè fal kayt, -fawl-/ (**-cates, -cating, -cated**) *vt.* to misuse sth, especially money or property, that belongs to sb else and is held in trust [Mid-16thC. From medieval Latin *defalcare* 'to deduct', literally 'to mow off', from Latin *falx* 'scythe', of unknown origin.] —**defalcator** *n.*

defalcation /deè fal káysh'n, -fawl-/ *n.* **1.** EMBEZZLEMENT the misuse of sb else's money, property, or funds **2.** SUM EMBEZZLED an amount of money obtained by defalcation

defamation /déffə máysh'n/ *n.* an attack on sb's good name, character, or reputation

defamatory /di fámmətəri/ *adj.* harmful to sb's good name, character, or reputation —**defamatorily** *adv.*

defame /di fáym/ (**-fames, -faming, -famed**) *vt.* to attack sb or sb's reputation, character, or good name by making slanderous or libellous statements [14thC. Via Old French *deffamer* from Latin *diffamare* 'to spread about as an insulting report', from *fama* (see FAME).] —**defamer** *n.*

WORD KEY: SYNONYMS

See Synonyms at *malign.*

defang /deè fáng/ (**-fangs, -fanging, -fanged**) *vt.* to remove the fangs from a snake or other animal

defat /deè fát/ (**-fats, -fatting, -fatted**) *vt.* to remove the fat or fats from sth

default /di fáwlt/ *n.* **1.** COMPUT PRESET OPTION an option that will automatically be selected by a computer if the user does not choose one **2.** FAILURE TO DO STH a failure to meet an obligation, especially a financial one **3.** LAW NONAPPEARANCE IN COURT a failure to make a summoned court appearance **4.** SPORTS NON-PARTICIPATION IN COMPETITION a failure to appear for or complete a competition ■ *vi.* (**-faults, -faulting, -faulted**) **1.** FAIL TO PAY to fail to pay a debt or other financial obligation **2.** LAW FAIL TO APPEAR IN COURT to fail to make an appearance in court although summoned to do so **3.** SPORTS FAIL TO COMPETE to fail to appear for a match or contest **4.** COMPUT USE PRESET OPTION to use a device, command, or file when no other is specified [13thC. From Old French *defaute*, the past participle of *defaillir* 'to fail', from *faillir* (see FAIL).] ◇ **by default 1.** having come about because some other thing, often sth expected, did not happen **2.** having come about because sb failed to appear as expected **3.** according to a computer's preset configuration ◇ **in default of sth** *or* **sb** because of a lack of or the absence of sth or sb (*formal*)

defaulter /di fáwltər/ *n.* **1.** NONPAYER sb who fails to comply with a financial obligation **2.** LAW ABSENTEE FROM COURT sb who fails to appear when summoned to court **3.** SPORTS ABSENTEE FROM COMPETITION a person or team failing to appear for a match or contest **4.** ARMY MILITARY OFFENDER a soldier who commits a military offence

defeasance /di feèz'nss/ *n.* **1.** MAKING VOID the declaration of sth as null and void **2.** LEGAL CLAUSE a clause in a legal document that states that, in the event of a condition or conditions being fulfilled, the document will become null and void **3.** LEGAL DOCUMENT a document containing a defeasance [15thC. From Old French *defesance*, from *defaire*, from medieval Latin *disfacere* , literally 'to unmake'.]

defeasible /di feèzəb'l/ *adj.* LAW **1.** VOIDABLE capable of being made or declared null and void **2.** SUBJECT TO FORFEIT liable to be forfeited —**defeasibility** /di feèzə bíllәti/ *n.* —**defeasibleness** /di feèzəb'l nəss/ *n.*

defeat /di feèt/ *vt.* (**-feats, -feating, -feated**) **1.** MIL BEAT AN ENEMY to win a victory over enemy forces in a battle or war **2.** BEAT A COMPETITOR to win a victory over a competitor, e.g. in sport or business **3.** WIN A VOTE to win a victory over another in a debate or vote **4.** CAUSE FAILURE to cause sth to fail or to fall short of realization ○ *The truck defeated all my attempts to get it to start.* **5.** BAFFLE SB to leave sb in a baffled or uncomprehending state ○ *His logic defeats me.* **6.** LAW MAKE STH VOID to make or declare sth null and void ■ *n.* **1.** LOSING TO AN OPPONENT the fact or an instance of losing to an enemy in battle or an opponent in a competition **2.** FAILURE failure to win or to realize a goal ○ *She refused to admit defeat and appealed.* [14thC. Via Anglo-Norman *defeter* 'to disfigure, destroy' from, ultimately, medieval Latin *disfacere*, literally 'to unmake', from Latin *facere* 'to do, make' (see FACT).] —**defeater** *n.* ◇ **defeat the object, defeat the purpose** make the desired or expected outcome ridiculous or possible

WORD KEY: SYNONYMS

defeat, beat, conquer, vanquish, overcome, triumph over, thrash, trounce

CORE MEANING: to win a victory

defeat the most general and wide-ranging term, used to talk about both real events and situations and abstract concepts; **beat** a slightly less formal term for *defeat*, commonly used to talk about real events or situations as well as successfully dealing with serious problems or surviving serious illnesses; **conquer** a term suggesting a convincing victory, often used in a military context, but also used with reference to abstract concepts; **vanquish** a formal or literary term for *conquer*; **overcome** a term suggesting that victory was gained after a struggle, often used with reference to abstract concepts; **triumph over** a fairly formal term suggesting decisive victory with cause for celebration; **thrash** an informal term used of an easy victory in a contest or athletic match, particularly one with a large margin of victory; **trounce** a more formal word for *thrash*.

defeatist /di feètist/ *adj.* EXPECTING FAILURE showing a tendency to expect failure or accept it too readily ■ *n.* SB WHO EXPECTS FAILURE sb who expects or accepts failure as a matter of course —**defeatism** *n.*

defecate /déffə kayt/ (**-cates, -cating, -cated**), **defaecate** (**-cates, -cating, -cated**) *v.* **1.** *vi.* EXPEL FAECES to expel faeces from the bowel through the rectum (*formal or technical*) **2.** *vt.* CHEM REMOVE IMPURITIES to remove impurities from a solution, especially a solution that contains sugar [15thC. From Latin *defaecare* 'to remove waste', from *faex* 'dregs, waste' (source of English *faeces*).] —**defecation** /déffə káysh'n/ *n.* —**defecator** /déffə kaytər/ *n.*

defect *n.* /deè fekt/ **1.** FLAW a failing, blemish, or flaw, especially one that still allows the affected thing to function, however imperfectly **2.** PERSONAL FLAW a personal failing, weakness, or shortcoming, especially in character **3.** CRYSTALS IMPERFECTION IN CRYSTAL an imperfection in the internal structure of a crystal, e.g. an atom of a different substance ■ *vi.* /di fékt/ (**-fects, -fecting, -fected**) **1.** REJECT YOUR HOMELAND to leave your native country or the country you are living in and refuse to return there, usually for political or moral reasons **2.** ABANDON AN ALLEGIANCE to abandon allegiance to a cause or party, especially when this also involves supporting sth previously opposed [15thC. From Latin *defect-*, the past participle stem of *deficere* 'to be wanting, desert', from *facere* 'to do, make' (see FACT).] —**defection** /di féksh'n/ *n.*

WORD KEY: SYNONYMS

See Synonyms at *flaw.*

defective /di féktiv/ *adj.* **1.** FAULTY faulty, especially in having sth missing or broken and so not functioning properly or at all **2.** OFFENSIVE TERM FOR LEARNING DIFFICULTIES highly objectionable term that means with learning difficulties or problems in coping with emotions (*offensive insult*) **3.** GRAM INCOMPLETE lacking the usual or expected range of grammatical inflections ■ *n.* OFFENSIVE TERM REFERRING TO LEARNING DIFFICULTIES highly objectionable term that means sb who has learning difficulties or problems in coping with emotions (*offensive insult*) —**defectively** *adv.* —**defectiveness** *n.*

WORD KEY: USAGE

defective or **deficient**? ***Defective*** is normally used in reference to machines or to other functional things such as the human senses: *If the workmanship is defective, they'll replace the shoes with a new pair. As he grew very old his hearing became defective.* ***Deficient*** is used to describe things that lack a quality or an attribute, without this amounting to actual failure to work or function: *Her voice is beautiful but a little deficient in power. Their diet is deficient in vitamin D.*

defector /di féktər/ *n.* **1.** POLITICAL EMIGRANT sb who rejects his or her native country in favour of another, usually for political or moral reasons **2.** CONVERTED PERSON sb who, because of a clash in ideology, rejects one cause or political group in favour of another

defeminize /dee fémmi nīz/ (**-nizes, -nizing, -nized**), **defeminise** (**-nises, -nising, -nised**) *vt.* to remove or diminish characteristics of sb or sth that are traditionally regarded as associated with women or girls

defence /di fénss/ *n.* **1.** PROTECTION the protection of sth, especially from attack by an enemy **2.** STH THAT PROTECTS a method or object for protecting sth ○ *a castle with strong defences* **3.** MIL ARMED FORCES a country's armed forces **4.** JUSTIFICATION an excuse or justification for sth ○ *spoke in defence of the motion* **5.** LAW REASONS OFFERED the set of reasons that a defendant offers in court in denial of a charge **6.** LAW DEFENDANT'S CASE the facts and their presentation as they relate to the defendant in a court case **7.** LAW LAWYER AND DEFENDANT the lawyer or lawyers and the defendant in a court case **8.** SPORTS DEFENSIVE PLAY in sports, the method or manoeuvres that prevent the other team from scoring **9.** SPORTS DEFENSIVE PLAYERS the sports team members who have responsibility for defence ■ **defences** *npl.* **1.** PROTECTIVE QUALITIES the qualities of the body or mind that protect sb from attack, injury, or illness **2.** FORTIFICATIONS the fortifications that protect a place from enemies or the forces of nature ○ *Roman defences that are now a tourist attraction* ○ *sea defences* [14thC. Via Old French from, ultimately, Latin *defens-*, the past participle stem of *defendere* (see DEFEND).]

defenceless /di fénsslәss/ *adj.* UNPROTECTED lacking any form of protection and therefore vulnerable ■ *npl.* UNPROTECTED PEOPLE people who are unable to defend themselves and their interests ○ *working as a shield for the defenceless* —**defencelessly** *adv.* —**defencelessness** *n.*

defence mechanism *n.* **1.** PROTECTIVE MENTAL ACTIVITY any means of avoiding emotional distress, destructive impulses, or a threat to self-esteem, especially by the suppression of unwanted thoughts or memories **2.** PROTECTIVE PHYSICAL ACTIVITY any of the natural protective responses to danger or attack used by an organism, e.g. when faced with a predator or invaded by a disease agent

defence-minded *adj.* giving emphasis to building a team with strong defensive skills

defend /di fénd/ (**-fends, -fending, -fended**) *v.* **1.** *vt.* PROTECT SB OR STH to protect sb or sth from attack, harm, or danger **2.** *vti.* LAW REPRESENT IN COURT to represent and speak on behalf of an accused person in court **3.** *vt.* **SUPPORT A POSITION** to offer support for sth or sb, especially by arguing against the objections or criticism of others **4.** *vi.* SPORTS **RESIST AN OPPONENT** to resist the attacks of an opposing side and try to prevent from scoring **5.** *vt.* SPORTS **TRY TO KEEP A TITLE** to try to retain a title, especially a sporting one, by competing in the relevant competitions **6.** *vt.* SPORTS **PROTECT GOAL** to protect the goal and goal area from the attacks of the opposition [13thC. Via French *défendre* from Latin *defendere* 'to ward off'. Ultimately from an Indo-European word meaning 'to strike, kill', which is also the ancestor of English *bane* and *gun*.] —**defendable** *adj.*

WORD KEY: SYNONYMS

See Synonyms at ***safeguard***.

defendant /di féndənt/ *n.* a person, party, or company required to answer criminal or civil charges in a court

defender /di féndər/ *n.* **1. PROTECTOR** sb who protects a person or place against attack **2. SUPPORTER** sb who offers support, justification, or an explanation for sth or sb **3.** SPORTS **DEFENSIVE PLAYER** sb whose role is to try to prevent the opposition from scoring or getting into a scoring position **4.** SPORTS **HOLDER OF TITLE** sb who holds a title that is subject to recurring competition

Defender of the Faith *n.* a title given by Pope Leo X in 1521 to King Henry VIII and held by English and British monarchs ever since. It was bestowed in recognition of the stance Henry took against Martin Luther after the king wrote a pamphlet denouncing Luther's doctrines and supporting the sacraments of the Roman Catholic Church.

defending /di fénding/ *adj.* SPORTS holding a title that is subject to recurring competition ○ *the defending champions*

defenestrate /dee fénni strayt/ (**-trates, -trating, -trated**) *vt.* to throw sth or sb out of a window (*formal or humorous*) [Early 17thC. Coined from DE- + Latin *fenestra* 'window' (source of English *fenestrated*), of unknown origin.] —**defenestration** /dee fénni stráysh'n/ *n.*

defense *n.* US = **defence**

defensible /di fénssəb'l/ *adj.* **1. ABLE TO BE PROTECTED** capable of being protected from attack **2. JUSTIFIABLE** able to be explained, justified, or excused —**defensibility** /di fénssə bílləti/ *n.* —**defensibleness** /di fénssəb'l nəss/ *n.* —**defensibly** /-bli/ *adv.*

defensin /di fénssin/ *n.* any of three peptides present in human white blood cells that appear to play a role in the prevention or elimination of infection

defensive /di fénssiv/ *adj.* **1. QUICK TO JUSTIFY** aiming to deflect or avoid perceived criticism **2. SERVING TO PROTECT** designed or intended for protection or defence **3.** SPORTS **FAVOURING DEFENCE AS PLAYING STRATEGY** concentrating more on preventing an opponent from gaining an advantage than on scoring **4.** *US* SPORTS **OF A DEFENCE PLAYER** relating to those players who have responsibility for defence —**defensiveness** *n.* ◇ **on the defensive 1.** expecting criticism or aggression and prepared to respond **2.** SPORTS having assumed a position that indicates readiness to play defensively

defensively /di fénssivli/ *adv.* **1. IN DEFENSIVE WAY** in a defensive way **2. AS REGARDS DEFENCE** as regards defence, especially defensive play ○ *Defensively they played well, but they couldn't manage to score.*

defensive medicine *n.* *US* medical treatment that involves carrying out extensive diagnostic testing in order to minimize the chances of a patient's suing the doctor or hospital for negligence

defer[1] /di fúr/ (**-fers, -ferring, -ferred**) *vti.* to put sth off until a later time [14thC. From French *différer* 'to put aside, differ'.] —**deferment** *n.* —**deferrable** *adj.* —**deferrer** *n.*

defer[2] /di fúr/ (**-fers, -ferring, -ferred**) *vi.* to give way to, and usually acknowledge the merit of, sb else's judgment, opinion, wishes, or action ○ *I defer to your superior knowledge.* [15thC. Via French *déférer* from Latin *deferre*, literally 'to carry away', from *ferre* 'to carry' (see FERTILE).] —**deferrer** *n.*

deference /déffərənss/ *n.* **1. RESPECT** polite respect, especially putting another person's interests first **2. SUBMISSION** submission to the judgment, opinion, or wishes of another person [Mid-17thC. Formed from DEFER[2].] ◇ **in deference to** out of respect or courtesy to sb or sth

deferent[1] /déffərənt/ *adj.* = **deferential**

deferent[2] /déffərənt/ *adj.* PHYSIOL used to describe a duct, nerve, or vessel in the body that is capable of carrying impulses or fluid away, down, or outwards

deferential /déffə rénsh'l/ *adj.* showing or expressing polite respect or courtesy —**deferentially** *adv.*

deferral /di fúrəl/ *n.* an instance or the process of putting sth off until a later date

deferred annuity *n.* a type of investment that does not pay out until at least one year after the final premium has been paid. ◊ **immediate annuity**

deferred sentence *n.* a sentence that is not passed until a specified period has elapsed in order to allow the court time to assess the behaviour of the convicted person

defervescence /deéfər véss'nss/ *n.* **1. DECREASE IN FEVER** a decrease in a fever **2. STAGE OF ILLNESS WHEN FEVER DECREASES** the stage of an illness during which fever subsides [Early 18thC. Via Latin *defervescere* 'to stop boiling' from, ultimately, *fervere* 'to be hot, boil'.] —**defervesce** *vti.* —**defervescent** *adj.*

defiance /di fí ənss/ *n.* open, bold, or hostile refusal to obey or conform ◇ **in defiance of** with complete disregard for a rule, law, or person in authority

defiant /di fí ənt/ *adj.* **1. CHALLENGING AGGRESSIVELY** tending to confront and challenge **2. DISOBEDIENT** deliberately and openly disobedient [Late 16thC. From French *défiant*, the present participle of *défier*, from assumed Vulgar Latin *disfidare* 'to renounce your faith'.] —**defiantly** *adv.*

defibrillate /dee fíbbri layt/ (**-lates, -lating, -lated**) *vt.* to apply an electric shock to the chest, or sometimes directly to the heart itself, in order to restore a regular heartbeat after a critically irregular beat has developed —**defibrillation** /dee fíbbri láysh'n/ *n.*

defibrillator /dee fíbbri laytər/ *n.* a machine that administers a controlled electric shock to the chest or heart to correct a fluttering heartbeat that cannot drive the circulation

deficiency /di físh'nssi/ (*plural* **-cies**) *n.* **1. SHORTAGE** a lack or shortage of sth **2. AMOUNT LACKING** the amount by which sth falls short of being complete

WORD KEY: SYNONYMS

See Synonyms at ***lack***.

deficiency disease *n.* a disease resulting from lack of a nutrient or other substance required by a human or other animal or plant for growth, development, or general health. The deficiency may be caused either by an inadequate supply of the required substance or an inability to process it.

deficient /di físh'nt/ *adj.* **1. LACKING** lacking a particular quality, element, or ingredient, especially one that is expected or necessary **2. INADEQUATE** inadequate or not good enough [Late 16thC. From Latin *deficient-*, the present participle stem of *deficere* 'to leave undone, fail', from *facere* 'to do, make' (see FACT).] —**deficiently** *adv.*

WORD KEY: USAGE

See Usage note at ***defective***.

deficit /déffəssit/ *n.* **1. EXCESSIVE AMOUNT SPENT** the amount by which expenditure exceeds income or budget **2. SHORTFALL** the amount by which a total is less than it should be [Late 18thC. Via French *déficit* from Latin *deficit* 'it is lacking', from *deficere* 'to leave undone, fail'.]

WORD KEY: SYNONYMS

See Synonyms at ***lack***.

deficit financing *n.* the practice of deliberately allowing government spending to exceed its revenues in order to try to boost economic activity and lower unemployment

deficit spending *n.* government spending that is financed by borrowing money rather than through money raised by taxation

defier /di fí ər/ *n.* sb who openly refuses to obey or conform to a rule, regulation, or authority

defilade /déffi láyd/ *n.* **DEFENCE CONFIGURATION** fortifications or protection designed to guard against enemy gunfire that might be aimed at a line of troops. ◊ **enfilade** ■ *vt.* (**-lades, -lading, -laded**) **PROTECT TROOPS** to set up protective fortifications to protect troops or a position [Early 19thC. Formed from French *défiler* (see DEFILE[2]), on the model of 'enfilade'.]

defile[1] /di fíl/ (**-files, -filing, -filed**) *vt.* **1. CORRUPT STH** to corrupt or ruin sth (*formal*) ○ *'The dust is his original sin and inward corruptions, that have defiled the whole man'.* (John Bunyan, *Pilgrims Progress*; 1678) **2. DAMAGE REPUTATION** to damage sb's reputation or good name **3.** RELIG **DESTROY SANCTITY OF STH** to make a holy or sacred thing or place no longer fit for ceremonial use **4. POLLUTE STH** to make sth dirty or polluted (*formal*) **5. DEPRIVE WOMAN OF VIRGINITY** to be the first man to have sexual intercourse with a woman, usually outside marriage (*archaic*) [14thC. An alteration (influenced by an obsolete word meaning 'to befoul') of French *defouler* 'to trample', from *fouler* 'to trample under foot'.] —**defilement** *n.* —**defiler** *n.*

defile[2] /di fíl/ *n.* **1. NARROW MOUNTAIN PASS** a narrow pass between mountains **2. NARROW PASSAGE** a passage only wide enough for people to pass single-file ■ *vi.* (**-files, -filing, -filed**) **MARCH SINGLE-FILE** to march or go in single file, especially when the way is too narrow to march in any other formation [Late 17thC. From French *défiler* 'to march in a line', from *file* 'FILE[1]'.]

define /di fín/ (**-fines, -fining, -fined**) *v.* **1.** *vti.* **GIVE MEANING OF WORD** to give the precise meaning of a word or expression **2.** *vt.* **STATE** to state or describe sth clearly **3.** *vt.* **CHARACTERIZE SB OR STH** to identify sb or sth by a distinctive characteristic quality or feature ○ *The age we live in is defined by a deep sense of uncertainty.* **4.** *vt.* **SHOW STH CLEARLY** to show sth clearly, especially in shape or outline (*usually passive*) ○ *The tyre marks were clearly defined in the snow.* **5.** *vt.* **MARK** to mark a boundary, edge, or limit ○ *That row of trees defines the eastern boundary of the estate.* [14thC. Via Old French *definer* from Latin *definire* 'to limit, determine', from *finis* (see FINAL).] —**definability** /di fínə bílləti/ *n.* —**definable** /di fínəb'l/ *adj.* —**definably** *adv.* —**definer** *n.*

definiendum /di fínni éndəm/ (*plural* **-da** /-də/) *n.* the word or expression defined by a definition, e.g. in a dictionary or glossary (*technical*) [Late 19thC. From Latin, literally 'thing to be defined', formed from *definire* (see DEFINE).]

definiens /di fínni enz/ (*plural* **-entia** /-énshə/) *n.* the words used to define a particular word or expression, e.g. in a dictionary or glossary (*technical*) [Late 19thC. From medieval Latin, literally 'sth that defines', from the present participle of *definire* (see DEFINE).]

defining /di fíning/ *adj.* giving a distinctive character to sth, or encapsulating its character ○ *That was the defining moment of the election campaign.*

definite /déffənət/ *adj.* **1. WITH CLEAR LIMITS** precise and distinct in describing the limits of sth ○ *with a definite age range for the junior chess club* **2. WITH CLEAR OUTLINE** with a clearly distinct shape or outline ○ *the definite outline of a building amongst the trees* **3. OBVIOUS** unquestionable and unmistakable ○ *a definite turn for the better* **4. FIXED** fixed, certain, and not to be altered ○ *Have we got a definite date for the meeting?* **5. ABSOLUTELY SET ON STH** certain about sth and unlikely to have a change of plan ○ *I'm definite about this.* **6.** BOT **WITH TERMINAL FLOWER** used to describe a flower head in which the first-formed flower is at the stalk's end with subsequent flowers developing lower down on one or both sides of the stalk [Mid-16thC. From Latin *definitus*, the past participle of definire (see DEFINE).] —**definiteness** *n.*

WORD KEY: USAGE

definite or definitive? ***Definite*** describes sth as being clear or exact without making any strong judgment about it: *He has definite ideas on the subject.* ***Definitive*** denotes sth that is authoritative, conclusive, or decisive, and is therefore a more judgmental word: *She wrote the definitive book on the subject.*

definite article *n.* a word, e.g. 'the' in English, that designates a noun as being specific and identifiable

definite integral *n.* a determination of the difference in values of an integral between two specified limits, expressed using symbols

definitely /déffənətli/ *adv.* **1. CERTAINLY** without a doubt ○ *He definitely had a Swedish accent.* **2. FINALLY AND**

UNCHANGEABLY as a conclusion after some thought or hesitation ○ *Once she had definitely decided to go, she started packing.* **3.** EXACTLY in a precise way ○ *Without knowing definitely what it was, he just felt that something was wrong.* **4.** CLEARLY in a distinct and unmistakable way ○ *Her attitude suddenly became more definitely critical.* **5.** ABSOLUTELY with no exceptions ○ *The notice said 'Definitely no bikers'.* ■ *interj.* YES used to say 'yes' in an emphatic and enthusiastic way ○ *'Are you going to come to the party?' 'Definitely!'*

definition /déffə nísh'n/ *n.* **1.** MEANING OF WORD a brief precise statement of what a word or expression means, e.g. in a dictionary **2.** ACT OF DEFINING A WORD the act or process of defining what a word or expression means, e.g. in writing a dictionary **3.** MAKING STH CLEAR the act of describing or stating sth clearly and unambiguously **4.** TV, PHOTOGRAPHY DEGREE OF CLARITY the clarity of a photograph, television picture, or other reproduced image. It is related to the sharpness and degree of contrast in the image. **5.** RECORDING CLARITY OF RECORDED SOUND the degree of sharpness or clarity in recorded sound **6.** EMBODIMENT OF STH sb or sth believed to represent or embody a particular idea or quality (*formal*) ○ *His behaviour has always seemed to me the very definition of courtesy.* [14thC. Via French from, ultimately, Latin *definire* (see DEFINE).] —**definitional** *adj.* ◇ **by definition** used to emphasize that sb or sth is considered to have a particular quality as part of his, her, or its nature

definitive /di fínnətiv/ *adj.* **1.** CONCLUSIVE AND FINAL providing a final decision that will not be questioned or changed ○ *We need a definitive answer.* **2.** MOST AUTHORITATIVE recognized as being the most authoritative and of the highest standard ○ *the definitive study of the subject* **3.** STAMPS SOLD FOR LONG TIME used to describe stamps sold for an extended or indefinite period and often part of a set sharing common design elements **4.** BIOL FULLY GROWN fully formed or completely developed ■ *n.* STAMPS DEFINITIVE STAMP a postage stamp sold for an extended or indefinite period [14thC. Via French *définitif* from, ultimately, Latin *definire* (see DEFINE).] —**definitively** *adv.* —**definitiveness** *n.*

WORD KEY: USAGE

See Usage note at ***definite***.

definitive host *n.* the plant or animal in or on which a parasitic organism reaches sexual maturity. ◊ **intermediate host**

definitude /di fínni tyood/ *n.* the quality of being exact and precise (*formal*) [Mid-19thC. Formed from DEFINITE, on the model of infinitude.]

deflagrate /défflə grayt/ (**-grates, -grating, -grated**) *vti.* to burn or make sth burn violently (*literary or technical*) [Early 17thC. From Latin *deflagrare*, literally 'to burn up', from *flagrare* (see FLAGRANT).] —**deflagration** /défflə gráysh'n/ *n.*

deflate /di fláyt/ (**-flates, -flating, -flated**) *v.* **1.** *vti.* LET AIR OUT to let out or lose air or gas from an inflatable object with the result that it shrinks or collapses **2.** *vt.* MAKE SB LESS CONFIDENT to destroy sb's confidence, or make sb less self-assured or conceited **3.** *vt.* DESTROY THEORY to show that a theory or argument is wrong **4.** *vt.* ECON CAUSE DEFLATION to bring about deflation in the economy or the money supply [Late 19thC. Coined from DE- + INFLATE.] —**deflator** *n.*

deflated /di fláytid/ *adj.* **1.** LESS SELF-ASSURED with less confidence, self-assurance, or conceit than before because of sth sb has said or done **2.** WITH NO AIR IN IT without enough air or gas to keep fully expanded **3.** ECON AFTER DEFLATION having undergone economic deflation

deflation /di fláysh'n/ *n.* **1.** COLLAPSE BECAUSE OF AIR LOSS the releasing or escaping of air or gas from sth, resulting in its shrinking or collapsing **2.** LOSS OF SELF-ESTEEM a sudden loss of confidence, self-assurance, or conceit **3.** ECON REDUCED ECONOMIC ACTIVITY the reduction of general economic activity, including lower prices and a reduced supply of money and credit **4.** GEOL EROSION the erosion of land by wind

deflationary /di fláysh'nəri/ *adj.* undergoing or creating a lower level of general economic activity

deflationist /di fláysh'nist/ *adj.* ADVOCATING DEFLATION in favour of economic deflation ■ *n.* SUPPORTER OF DEFLATION sb who advocates deflation of an economy

deflect /di flékt/ (**-flects, -flecting, -flected**) *v.* **1.** *vti.* CHANGE COURSE to change course because of hitting sth, or change sth's course by coming into contact with it **2.** *vt.* DIRECT ATTENTION AWAY to direct people's attention or criticism away from a particular subject or issue to sth else **3.** *vt.* FORCE ALTERATION OF PLANS to force sb to change from what he or she usually does or planned to do [Mid-16thC. From Latin *deflectere*, literally 'to bend away', from *flectere* (see FLEXIBLE).] —**deflectable** *adj.* —**deflective** *adj.* —**deflector** *n.*

deflection /di fléksh'n/, **deflexion** *n.* **1.** CHANGING OF COURSE a change of course after hitting sb or sth, or a changing of sth's course by being hit by it **2.** AMOUNT STH DEFLECTS the amount or distance by which sth is deflected **3.** DIVERTING OF ATTENTION the act of directing people's attention or criticism away from sth **4.** MEASURE MOVEMENT OF NEEDLE AWAY FROM ZERO a definite movement of the indicator on a measuring instrument **5.** ENG MOVEMENT OF STRUCTURE UNDER LOAD the movement of a structure or a part of a structure when it is bearing a load

deflexed /di flékst, dée-/ *adj.* BOT used to describe petals or leaves that bend sharply downwards [Late 18thC. Formed from Latin *deflexus*, the past participle of *deflectere* (see DEFLECT).]

deflexion = **deflection**

defloration /dée flaw ráysh'n, défflə-/ *n.* ending of a woman's or girl's virginity (*literary*) [14thC. Via French from, ultimately, late Latin *deflorare* (see DEFLOWER).]

deflower /dee flówər/ (**-ers, -ering, -ered**) *vt.* **1.** HAVE SEX WITH VIRGIN to end the virginity of a girl or woman (*formal*) **2.** GARDENING STRIP PLANT OF FLOWERS to remove some or all of the flowers from a plant [14thC. Via Old French *defflourer* from late Latin *deflorare*, from Latin *flos* (see FLOWER).] —**deflowerer** *n.*

deflowering /dee flówəring/ *n.* **1.** ENDING OF VIRGINITY the ending of a woman's or girl's virginity (*formal*) **2.** GARDENING REMOVAL OF FLOWERS the removal of some or all of the flowers from a plant

defocus /dee fókəss/ *v.* (**-cuses, -cusing** *or* **-cussing, -cused** *or* **-cussed**) **1.** *vt.* PHOTOGRAPHY SOFTEN PICTURE BY SHIFTING FOCUS to soften or blur an image by focusing away from the exact plane of focus of the object in the image **2.** *vti.* STOP FOCUSING to stop focusing on sth, or cause the eyes to stop focusing on sth ■ *n.* CONDITION OF DEFOCUSING the condition or state caused by defocusing, e.g. the blurring of a photographic image

Defoe /di fó/, **Daniel** (1660?–1731) English novelist and journalist. His first and most famous novel is *The Life and Adventures of Robinson Crusoe* (1719), and he wrote *Moll Flanders* (1722) late in life.

defog /dée fóg/ (**defogs, defogging, defogged**) *vti.* **1.** *US* CARS = **demist 2.** PHOTOGRAPHY GET RID OF CONDENSATION FROM LENS to remove condensation from the lens of a camera or other optical equipment, especially by allowing it to warm up, or lose condensation in this way —**defogger** *n.*

defoliant /dee fóli ənt/ *n.* a chemical that strips trees and plants of their leaves and is sometimes used in warfare to deny cover to enemy forces

defoliate /dee fóli ayt/ (**-ates, -ating, -ated**) *vti.* to strip trees and plants of their leaves, e.g. by using chemicals or through pollution or attack by pests, or to lose leaves in any of these ways [Late 18thC. From late Latin *defoliare*, from *folium* (see FOLIO).] —**defoliation** /dee fóli áysh'n/ *n.* —**defoliator** /dee fóli aytər/ *n.*

deforce /dee fáwrss/ (**-forces, -forcing, -forced**) *vt.* to keep the rightful owner of property away from it, or keep the property away from its owner, by force or violence (*formal*) [14thC. From Anglo-Norman *deforcer*, literally 'to force away from', from *forcier* (see FORCE).] —**deforcement** *n.*

deforest /dee fórrist/ (**-ests, -esting, -ested**) *vt.* to remove the trees from an area of land —**deforestation** /dee fórri stáysh'n/ *n.* —**deforester** /dee fórristər/ *n.*

deform /di fáwrm/ (**-forms, -forming, -formed**) *vti.* **1.** MAKE OR BECOME DISTORTED to become, or make sth become, distorted, damaged, or disfigured **2.** SPOIL STH OR BECOME SPOILED to spoil the appearance of sth and make it ugly, or become spoiled and ugly ○ *The new office buildings have deformed the whole area.* **3.** PHYS CHANGE SHAPE BY STRESS to change the shape of sth through stress, or become changed in this way [15thC. Via Old French *deformer* from Latin *deformare*, literally 'to un-form', from *forma* (see FORM).] —**deformability** /di fáwrmə bílləti/ *n.* —**deformable** *adj.* —**deformer** *n.*

deformalize /dee fáwrmə līz/ (**-izes, -izing, -ized**), **deformalise** (**-ises, -ising, -ised**) *vt.* to make sth such as a meeting or report less formal —**deformalization** /dee fáwrmə lī záysh'n/ *n.*

deformation /dée fawr máysh'n/ *n.* **1.** ACT OF DEFORMING OR BEING DEFORMED the act or process of damaging, disfiguring, or spoiling the look of sth, or the condition of being damaged, disfigured, or spoiled **2.** CHANGE IN SHAPE a change in the shape of sth, especially one that suggests damage or disfigurement **3.** UNPLEASANT RESULT OF CHANGE the harmful or disfiguring result of a change in form **4.** PHYS CHANGE IN SHAPE BECAUSE OF STRESS a change in shape resulting from the application of stress

deformed /di fáwrmd/ *adj.* **1.** BADLY FORMED abnormal or unnatural in shape, and often unattractive to look at **2.** NOT NORMAL not normal in outlook or temperament, especially in a way that is considered dangerous or depraved **3.** PHYS DISTORTED changed in shape as a result of stress —**deformedly** /di fáwrmidli, di fáwrmdli/ *adv.* —**deformedness** *n.*

deformity /di fáwrməti/ (*plural* **-ties**) *n.* **1.** DISFIGUREMENT the condition of being disfigured or badly formed ○ *the deformity of the pine trees at such a high altitude in the mountains* **2.** ANAT STRUCTURAL CHANGE FROM NORMAL a permanent change from normal body structure **3.** STH WITH SHAPE FAR FROM NORMAL sth that has a shape not normal for its kind or nature

defrag /dée frag/ (**-frags, -fragging, -fragged**) *vt.* ➧ **defragment** (*informal*)

defragment /dée frag mént/ (**-ments, -menting, -mented**) *vt.* to reorganize the storage space on a hard disk by consolidating similar files thereby optimizing the performance of the hard disk

defraud /de fráwd/ (**-frauds, -frauding, -frauded**) *vt.* to deprive sb of money or property by dishonest means [14thC. Directly or via Old French from Latin *defraudare*, from *fraudare* 'to cheat'.] —**defraudation** /dée fraw dáysh'n/ *n.* —**defrauder** *n.* —**defraudment** *n.*

defray /di fráy/ (**-frays, -fraying, -frayed**) *vt.* to provide money to pay for part or all of the cost of sth (*formal*) ○ *The company will defray the cost of your training course.* [Mid-16thC. From French *défrayer*, from *frais* 'expenses'.] —**defrayable** *adj.* —**defrayal** *n.* —**defrayer** *n.* —**defrayment** *n.*

defrock /dée frók/ (**-frocks, -frocking, -frocked**) *vt.* to take away the status, job, and authority of a priest or other member of the clergy, especially as a punishment for wrongdoing [Early 17thC. From French *défroquer*, from *froc* (see FROCK).]

defrost /di fróst, dee-/ (**-frosts, -frosting, -frosted**) *vti.* **1.** REMOVE ICE FROM to remove frost or ice from sth, or become free of frost or ice **2.** THAW to thaw frozen food, or become thawed

deft /deft/ *adj.* **1.** QUICK AND SKILFUL moving or acting in a quick, smooth, and skilful way **2.** CLEVER showing good sense and skill in achieving or acquiring things [13thC. An early variant of DAFT.] —**deftly** *adv.* —**deftness** *n.*

defunct /di fúngkt/ *adj.* **1.** NOT OPERATING NOW no longer operative, valid, or functional **2.** DEAD no longer alive or in existence [Mid-16thC. From Latin *defunctus*, the past participle of *defungi* 'to finish', literally 'to perform completely', from *fungi* 'to perform' (source of English *function* and *perfunctory*).] —**defunctness** *n.*

WORD KEY: SYNONYMS

See Synonyms at ***dead***.

defuse /dee-/ (**-fuses, -fusing, -fused**) *vt.* **1.** ARMS MAKE BOMB HARMLESS to make a bomb or mine harmless by removing its detonating device **2.** EASE DIFFICULT SITUATION to make a situation less tense, dangerous, or uncomfortable ○ *The diplomats tried to defuse the escalating crisis.*

defy /di fī/ (**-fies, -fying, -fied**) *vt.* **1. CHALLENGE AUTHORITY OR POWER** to challenge openly sb's or sth's authority or power by refusing to obey a command or regulation ○ *He defied all orders from head office.* **2. CHALLENGE SB TO DO STH** to challenge or dare sb to do sth ○ *I defy you to find a better deal than this.* **3. NOT BE EXPLAINED BY STH** to fail to be explained or clarified by sth such as logic or analysis ○ *a decision that defies all logic* [14thC. Via French *défier* from assumed Vulgar Latin *disfidare* 'to renounce your faith', from Latin *fides* (see FAITH).]

dégagé /dáy gaa zháy/ *adj.* (*formal*) **1. RELAXED** casual and relaxed **2. NOT INVOLVED** detached and without emotional involvement [Late 17thC. From French, literally 'disengaged'.]

degas /dee gáss/ (**degases** *or* **degasses, degassing, degassed**) *vt.* to remove gas from a liquid or solid or from a vacuum system

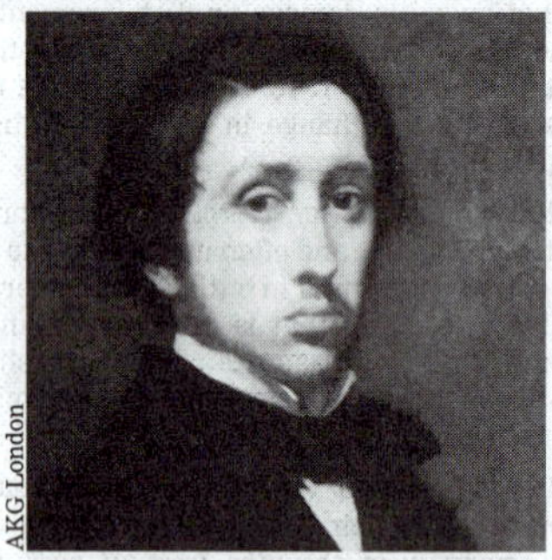

Edgar Degas: Self-portrait (1854–5)

Degas /dáy gaa/, **Edgar** (1834–1917) French painter and sculptor. A genius of modern art in the late 19th century, he often depicted the human figure in movement, particularly ballet dancers. Full name **Hilaire Germain Edgar Degas**

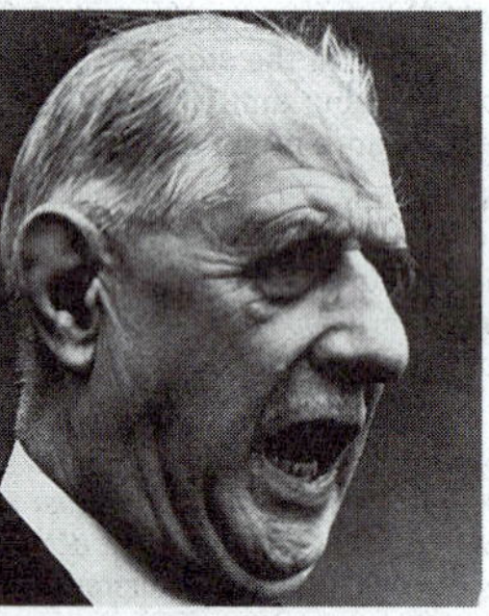

Charles De Gaulle

De Gaulle /də gṓl/, **Charles, General** (1890–1970) French general and statesman. He became leader of the Free French in London after the fall of France in World War II, taking over as head of the provisional government in 1945. He served as French President from 1959 to 1969. Full name **Charles André Joseph Marie de Gaulle**

degauss /dee gówss/ (**degausses, degaussing, degaussed**) *vt.* to remove or counteract a magnetic field in sth, e.g. electrical equipment or a ship's hull. The hull of a ship can be degaussed as a protection against magnetic mines. —**degausser** *n.*

degenderize /dee jéndə rīz/ (**-izes, -izing, -ized**), **degenderise** (**-ises, -ising, -ised**), **degender** /dee jéndə/ (**-ders, -dering, -dered**) *vt.* to remove references to people's gender from language or a text in order to make it more neutral or less biased —**degenderization** /dee jéndə rī záysh'n/ *n.*

degeneracy /di jénnərəssi/ *n.* **1. WORSENING OF CONDITION** the process of becoming physically, morally, or mentally worse **2. WORSENED CONDITION** a condition that is worse than normal or worse than before **3.** (*plural* **-cies**) **BAD BEHAVIOUR** immoral, depraved, or corrupt behaviour **4.** QUANTUM PHYS **STATE OF EQUAL ENERGY** the condition of two or more quantum states that have the same energy

degenerate /di jénnə rayt/ *vi.* (**-ates, -ating, -ated**) **1. BECOME WORSE** to develop into a condition that is worse than before, worse than normal, or not as good as it should be **2.** BIOL **BECOME USELESS** to become less specialized or lose the ability to function (*refers to organisms or body parts*) ■ *adj.* **1. IN A WORSENED CONDITION** in a condition that is worse than normal or worse than before **2. INFERIOR** in a condition that is worse than an original or previous state **3.** PHYS **EQUAL IN ENERGY** used to describe a system in which different quantum states have equal energy **4.** BIOL **WITH REDUCED OR ABSENT PART** used to describe a part, or an organism with a part, that has become reduced in size or function, or lost completely, during the history of its species or compared to related species ■ *n.* **SB IMMORAL OR CORRUPT** sb who is in a bad condition, especially as a result of immoral behaviour [15thC. From Latin *degenerare*, literally 'to depart from your own kind', from *genus* 'kind'.] —**degenerately** /-rətli/ *adv.* —**degenerateness** /-rətnəss/ *n.*

degenerate matter *n.* PHYS highly compressed matter consisting of elementary particles that are not combined to form atoms, occurring in the final stage of a star's development into a white dwarf

degeneration /di jénnə ráysh'n/ *n.* **1.** = **degeneracy** *n.* 1 **2.** MED **DETERIORATION** a disease process that causes a gradual deterioration in the structure of a body part with a consequent loss of the ability to function **3.** BIOL **BIOLOGICAL LOSS OVER GENERATIONS** the gradual loss of the biological function, specialization, or adaptation of a part of the body over many generations

degenerative /di jénnərətiv/ *adj.* causing or showing a gradual deterioration in the structure of a body part with a consequent loss of the part's ability to function

degenerative joint disease *n.* = **osteoarthritis**

deglamorize /dee glámmə rīz/ (**-izes, -izing, -ized**), **deglamorise** (**-ises, -ising, -ised**) *vt.* to make sth less attractive or exciting than it sometimes appears —**deglamorization** /dee glámmə rī záysh'n/ *n.*

deglutinate /dee glóoti nayt/ (**-nates, -nating, -nated**) *vt.* to remove the gluten from cereal or flour [Late 19thC. Coined from DE- + Latin *glutin-*, the stem of *gluten* 'GLUTEN'.] —**deglutination** /dee glóoti náysh'n/ *n.*

deglutition /dée gloo tísh'n/ *n.* the act or process of swallowing (*technical*) [Mid-17thC. Via French from, ultimately, Latin *deglutire*, literally 'to swallow down', from *glutire* (see GLUTTON).]

degradable /di gráydəb'l/ *adj.* **1. ABLE TO ROT AWAY** able to undergo chemical or biological decomposition **2. ABLE TO BE DEGRADED** able to be degraded in any way —**degradability** /di gráydə bílləti/ *n.*

degradation /déggrə dáysh'n/ *n.* **1. GREAT HUMILIATION** great humiliation brought about by loss of status, reputation, or self-esteem ○ *suffered the degradation of overwhelming defeat at the polls* **2. HUMILIATING SB** the humiliating of sb, causing him or her a loss of status, reputation, or self-esteem ○ *the constant degradation and undermining of other members of staff* **3. BAD LIVING CONDITIONS** way of life without dignity, health, or social comforts **4. LOSS OF QUALITY** a decline in sth's quality or performance ○ *a rapid degradation in the engine's horsepower* **5. PROCESS OF DECLINE** the process by which a decline in quality or performance is brought about **6.** GEOL, GEOG **EROSION** erosion of the Earth's land surface by water, wind, or ice **7.** CHEM **BREAKDOWN OF COMPOUND** the breakdown of a chemical compound into atoms or simpler compounds **8.** PHYS **DECREASE OF ENERGY** the process by which the energy available for doing work is irreversibly decreased

degrade /di gráyd/ (**-grades, -grading, -graded**) *v.* **1.** *vt.* **TREAT HUMILIATINGLY** to cause sb or sth a humiliating loss of status or reputation, or cause sb a humiliating loss of self-esteem **2.** *vt.* **LOWER IN GRADE** to lower sb or sth in rank, grade, or level **3.** *vti.* **BECOME OR MAKE WORSE** to become worse, or make sth become worse, especially in quality or performance ○ *Using the wrong fuel had significantly degraded the engine's power.* **4.** *vti.* GEOL, GEOG **ERODE LAND** to erode the land surface or a river bed, or be eroded by the action of wind, ice, or water. ◊ **aggrade 5.** *vt.* ENVIRON **DESTROY ENVIRONMENT** to cause damage or destruction to part of the environment as a result of human activity **6.** *vti.* PHYS **REDUCE AVAILABLE ENERGY IN** to reduce irreversibly the energy available in matter, or be reduced irreversibly [14thC. Via French *dégrader* from ecclesiastical Latin *degradare* 'to reduce in rank', from Latin *gradus* (see GRADE).] —**degrader** *n.*

degraded /di gráydid/ *adj.* **1. HUMILIATED** humiliated and suffering a loss of status, reputation, or self-esteem **2. SQUALID** existing in poverty and squalor **3. WITH POORER PERFORMANCE** showing a decline in quality, standard, or performance **4. OF LOWER RANK** made lower in rank, grade, or level —**degradedly** *adv.* —**degradedness** *n.*

degrading /di gráyding/ *adj.* causing sb to feel shame and humiliation —**degradingly** *adv.*

degrease /dee grées/ (**-greases, -greasing, -greased**) *vt.* to remove grease from sth such as an engine, especially using chemicals —**degreaser** *n.*

degree /di grée/ *n.* **1. EXTENT OR AMOUNT** the relative extent, amount, intensity, or level of sth, especially when compared with other things **2.** EDUC **EDUCATIONAL QUALIFICATION** a qualification awarded by a university or college following successful completion of a course of study or period of research, or a similar qualification granted as an honour **3.** PHYS, MEASURE **UNIT OF TEMPERATURE MEASUREMENT** a unit of measurement for temperature on a scale such as Celsius or Fahrenheit. Symbol ° **4.** GEOM, MEASURE **UNIT FOR MEASURING ANGLES** a unit of measurement for planar angles, equal to $\frac{1}{360}$ of a full revolution. Symbol ° **5.** GEOG, MEASURE **UNIT OF LATITUDE OR LONGITUDE** a unit of latitude or longitude, equal to $\frac{1}{360}$ of a circle, used to locate and designate places on the earth ○ *27 degrees north.* Symbol ° **6.** *US* LAW **CLASSIFICATION OF MURDER** a level of classification of murder according to its seriousness. First-degree murder is the most serious. **7.** MED **SEVERITY OF BURNS ON BODY** a level of classification of the seriousness of the damage to tissue caused by a burn. Third-degree burns are the most serious. **8.** MEASURE **UNIT OF MEASUREMENT ON SCALE** one of various units used on different measurement scales, such as that used to measure specific gravity or that used to specify the alcohol content of drinks. Symbol ° **9.** GRAM **STATE OF ADJECTIVE OR ADVERB** any one of the three states that an adjective or adverb can exist in when used to describe sth. 'Red' and 'quickly' are in the positive degree, 'redder' and 'more quickly' in the comparative degree, and 'reddest' and 'most quickly' in the superlative degree. **10.** SOC SCI **CLOSENESS OF RELATIONSHIP** an indication of the closeness of a relationship within a family **11.** SOC SCI **STATUS** rank, position, or status in society (*formal or literary*) ○ *of high degree* **12.** MUSIC **POSITION OF NOTE ON MUSICAL SCALE** the relative position of a note on a musical scale **13.** MATH **HIGHEST EXPONENT OF DERIVATIVE** in a differential equation, the exponent of the derivative of highest order, e.g. $4x^2y^2$ is of degree four **14.** MATH **SUM OF POLYNOMIAL VARIABLE EXPONENTS** in a polynomial equation, the sum of the exponents of the variables in the term with the highest power, e.g. $4x^3y^2 + 3y^2 + 2$ is of degree five [13thC. Via French *degré* from assumed Vulgar Latin *degradus*, literally 'step down', from Latin *gradus* (see GRADE).]

degree day *n.* the day on which students receive their degrees at a university award ceremony

degree-day *n.* a unit of measurement for heating systems, used to estimate fuel requirements and representing one degree of variation from the mean daily temperature out of doors

degree of freedom *n.* **1.** STATS **INDEPENDENT VARIABLE** an independent variable in a statistical measure or frequency distribution **2.** PHYS, CHEM **VARIABLE SPECIFYING ENERGY** an independent variable needed to specify the energy state of an atom, molecule, or system **3.** CHEM **VARIABLE SPECIFYING STATE** any of the independent variables such as pressure that are needed to specify the state of a system according to the phase rule

degression /di grésh'n/ *n.* **1. DECREASE** a gradual decrease or downward movement (*formal*) **2.** FIN **GRADUAL DECREASE IN TAXATION** a gradual lowering of the tax rate on sums below a specified amount [15thC. Via medieval Latin from Latin *degress-*, the past participle stem of *degredi*, literally 'to step down', from *gradus* (see GRADE).] —**degressive** *adj.*

degust /di gúst/ (**-gusts, -gusting, -gusted**), **degustate** /di gú stayt/ (**-tates, -tating, -tated**) *vt.* to taste food with great enjoyment and appreciation (*formal*) [Early 17thC. Directly and via French *déguster* from Latin *degustare*, literally 'to taste thoroughly', from *gustare* 'to taste'.] —**degustation** /dée gústáysh'n/ *n*.

De Havilland /də hávviländ/, **Sir Geoffrey** (1882–1965) British aviation pioneer and aircraft designer. Aircraft designed by him include the Tiger Moth (1930), Mosquito (1941), and Comet airliner (1952).

De Havilland /di hávviländ/, **Olivia** (*b*. 1916) British-born US film actor. She won Academy Awards for *To Each His Own* (1946) and *The Heiress* (1949). Full name **Olivia Mary De Havilland**

dehisce /di híss/ (**-hisces, -hiscing, -hisced**) *vi*. **1.** BOT BURST OPEN to burst open, releasing seeds, pollen, or spores (*refers to dry fruits, seed pods, anthers, or spore-bearing structures*) **2.** MED BREAK OPEN to open along the joined edges (*technical*) (*refers to a wound that has been stitched*) [Mid-17thC. From Latin *dehiscere*, literally 'to open up', from *hiscere*, literally 'to begin opening', from *hiare* (see HIATUS).] —**dehiscence** *n*. —**dehiscent** *adj*.

dehorn /dee háwrn/ (**-horns, -horning, -horned**) *vt*. VET to remove or prevent the growth of an animal's horns by surgery or cauterization —**dehorner** *n*.

Dehra Dūn /dáirə doón/ city in northern India, in Uttar Pradesh State, and the capital of Dehra Dūn District. Population: 367,411 (1991).

dehumanize /dee hyoómə nīz/ (**-izes, -izing, -ized**), **dehumanise** (**-ises, -ising, -ised**) *vt*. **1.** MAKE LESS HUMAN to take away sb's individuality, the creative and interesting aspects of his or her personality, or his or her compassion and sensitivity towards others **2.** TAKE AWAY PEOPLE-FRIENDLY FEATURES OF to take away the qualities or features of sth that make it able to meet human needs and desires or enhance people's lives ○ *The very design of these tower blocks dehumanizes them.* **3.** MAKE ROUTINE to take away all creativity and interest from some process and make it dull, routine, and mechanical —**dehumanization** /dee hyoómə nī záysh'n/ *n*. —**dehumanized** *adj*. —**dehumanizing** *adj*.

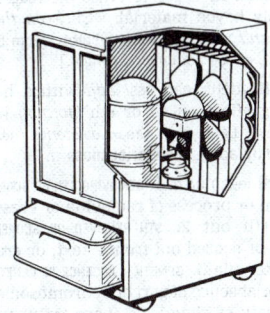

Dehumidifier: Cutaway view showing filters for removal of moisture from the air

dehumidifier /dee hyoo míddi fīr/ *n*. an electrical appliance for removing excess humidity from the air in a room or building

dehumidify /dee hyoo míddi fī/ (**-fies, -fying, -fied**) *vt*. to remove moisture from the air in a room or building

dehydrate /dee hī drayt, dée hī dráyt, dée hī drayt/ *v*. **1.** *vt*. FOOD TECH PRESERVE FOOD BY DRYING to remove moisture from food as a way of preserving it **2.** *vti*. MED LOSE BODY FLUIDS to remove or lose water or fluids from the body or its tissues **3.** *vti*. CHEM TAKE AWAY WATER FROM to deprive a chemical compound of water or of the proportion of hydrogen and oxygen atoms that are present in water

dehydrated /dee hī draytid, dée hī dráytid, dée hī draytid/ *adj*. **1.** FOOD TECH DRIED preserved by the removal of all moisture **2.** MED EXPERIENCING FLUID LOSS lacking water in the body, as the result of loss of bodily fluids, or from being deprived of liquid **3.** CHEM WITH WATER MOLECULES REMOVED used to describe a chemical compound that has had water molecules removed or the proportion of hydrogen and oxygen atoms that would be present in a water molecule removed

— WORD KEY: SYNONYMS —
See Synonyms at *dry*.

dehydration /dee hī dráysh'n/ *n*. **1.** FOOD TECH REMOVAL OF MOISTURE FROM FOOD the removal of moisture from food as a way of preserving it **2.** MED LOSS OF BODY FLUID a dangerous lack of water in the body resulting from inadequate intake of fluids or excessive loss through sweating, vomiting, or diarrhoea **3.** CHEM LOSS OF WATER BY CHEMICAL COMPOUND the process by which a chemical compound loses water molecules or the proportion of hydrogen and oxygen atoms that would be present in water

dehydrator /dee hī draytər, dée hī dráytər, dée hī draytər/ *n*. HOUSEHOLD, FOOD TECH an electrical appliance for drying food, consisting of a stack of interlocking trays through which heated air is circulated

dehydrochlorinase /dee hī drō kláwri nayz, -nayss/ *n*. an enzyme that removes hydrogen and chlorine from chlorinated hydrocarbons. Its presence accounts for the resistance shown by some insects to DDT.

dehydrochlorinate /dee hī drō kláwri nayt/ (**-ates, -ating, -ated**) *vt*. to chemically remove hydrogen and chlorine or hydrogen chloride from a substance —**dehydrochlorination** /dee hī drō kláwri náysh'n/ *n*.

dehydrogenase /dee hī drójjə nayz, -nayss, dee hī́drəjə-/ *n*. an enzyme that speeds up the removal and transfer of hydrogen atoms between organic compounds

dehydrogenate /dee hī drójjə nayt, dee hī́drəjə nayt/ (**-ates, -ating, -ated**) *vt*. to remove hydrogen from a compound, e.g. by means of a catalyst or in an enzyme-controlled process in cells —**dehydrogenation** /dee hī drójjə náysh'n, dee hī́drəjə-/ *n*.

dehydrogenize /dee hī drójjə nīz, dee hī́drəjə nīz/ (**-izes, -izing, -ized**), **dehydrogenise** (**-ises, -ising, -ised**) *vt*. = dehydrogenate —**dehydrogenization** /dee hī drójjə nī záysh'n, dee hī́drəjə nī-/ *n*.

dehypnotize /dee hípnə tīz/ (**dehypnotizes, dehypnotizing, dehypnotized**), **dehypnotise** (**-tises, -tising, -tised**) *vt*. to bring sb out of a hypnotic state —**dehypnosis** /dee híp nóssiss/ *n*. —**dehypnotization** *n*.

de-ice /dee íss/ (**de-ices, de-icing, de-iced**) *vt*. to remove ice from sth such as a windscreen, or prevent ice from forming on it

de-icer *n*. a device or chemical substance that removes ice or prevents it forming, e.g. on the windscreen of a motor vehicle or the wings of an aircraft. One of the commonest de-icers is ethylene glycol, which is used in antifreeze.

deicide /dée i sīd, dáy-/ *n*. LITERAT **1.** KILLING A GOD OR GODDESS the act of killing a god or goddess **2.** SB WHO KILLS A GOD OR GODDESS sb who kills a god or goddess [Early 17thC. Partly from ecclesiastical Latin *deicida* 'god-killer', and partly coined from Latin *deus* 'god' + -CIDE.] —**deicidal** /dáy i sī́d'l, dée i-/ *adj*.

deictic /díktik/ *adj*. depending for its full meaning on the context in which it is used. Words such as 'you', 'this', 'now', and 'there' are deictic. [Early 19thC. From Greek *deiktikos*, from *deiknunai* 'to show'. Ultimately from an Indo-European word meaning 'to point out' that is also the ancestor of English *dictate, index, digit*, and *token*.] —**deictically** *adv*.

deid /deed/ *adj. Scotland* dead [15thC. Variant of DEAD.]

deific /dee íffik, day-/ *adj*. (*formal*) **1.** MAKING SB A GOD OR GODDESS making sb divine or giving him or her the status of a god or goddess **2.** LIKE A GOD OR GODDESS with a divine nature or the status of a god or goddess [15thC. From ecclesiastical Latin *deificus*, from Latin *deus* (see DEITY).]

deification /dee ifi káysh'n, dáy ifi káysh'n/ *n*. (*formal*) **1.** MAKING SB A GOD OR GODDESS the action or process of making a god or goddess **2.** STATE OF HAVING BEEN MADE A GOD OR GODDESS the condition of having been made a god or goddess

deiform /dée i fawrm, dáy-/ *adj*. like a god or goddess in appearance [Mid-17thC. From medieval Latin *deiformis*, from *deus* (see DEITY).]

deify /dée i fī, dáy-/ (**-fies, -fying, -fied**) *vt*. **1.** MAKE DIVINE to make sb into a god **2.** ADORE to honour or adore

sb or sth as if he, she, or it were divine [14thC. Via French *déifier* from, ultimately, Latin *deus* (see DEITY).] —**deifier** *n*.

Deighton /dáyt'n/, **Len** (*b*. 1929) British writer. He is best known for spy thrillers, including *The Ipcress File* (1962). He has also written on cookery and military history. Full name **Leonard Cyril Deighton**

deign /dayn/ (**deigns, deigning, deigned**) *vti*. to do sth in a way that shows that you consider it a great favour and almost beneath your dignity to do it ○ *I don't suppose he'll deign to accept our invitation.* [13thC. Via Old French *deignier* from Latin *dignare* 'to deem worthy', from *dignus* 'worthy'.]

Dei gratia /dáy i gráati ə, dée T gráyshə/ *adv*. by the grace of God (*formal*) [From Latin, 'by the grace of God']

deil /deel/ *n. Scotland* a devil [15thC. Variant of DEVIL.]

Deimos /dáy moss/ *n*. the outermost of the two natural satellites of Mars, both of which are small. It was discovered in 1877 and there is evidence suggesting that it is a captured asteroid. ◊ **Phobos**

deindustrialization /dee in dústri ə lī záysh'n/, **deindustrialisation** *n*. the removal or reduction of industrial activity in a country or region, especially heavy industry or manufacturing industry

deindustrialize /dee in dústri ə līz/ (**deindustrializes, deindustrializing, deindustrialized**), **deindustrialise** (**deindustrialises, deindustrialising, deindustrialised**) *vti*. to take away or lose industries, especially the heavy industries and manufacturing industries, that a particular country or region has

deinstitutionalize /dée insti tyóosh'nə līz/ (**-izes, -izing, -ized**), **deinstitutionalise** (**-ises, -ising, -ised**) *vt*. to discharge sb from institutional care, often in order to treat him or her in the community where he or she lives —**deinstitutionalization** /dée insti tyóosh'nə lī záysh'n/ *n*.

deionize /dee í ə nīz/ (**deionizes, deionizing, deionized**), **deionise** (**-ises, -ising, -ised**) *v*. to remove ions from a solution —**deionization** /dee í ə nī záysh'n/ *n*. —**deionizer** /dee í ə nīzər/ *n*.

deism /dée izzəm, dáy-/ *n*. a belief in God based on reason rather than revelation, and involving the view that God has set the universe in motion but does not interfere with how it runs. Deism was especially influential in the 17th and 18th centuries. [Late 17thC. Formed from Latin *deus* 'god' (see DEITY).] —**deist** *n*. —**deistic** /dee ístik, day-/ *adj*. —**deistically** /-ístikli/ *adv*.

deity /dée i ti, dáy-/ (*plural* **-ties**) *n*. **1.** GOD OR GODDESS a god, goddess, or other divine being **2.** SB OR STH LIKE GOD sb or sth that is treated like a god **3.** DIVINE STATE the condition or status of a god or goddess [14thC. Via French *déité* from ecclesiastical Latin *deitas* 'divine nature', from *deus* 'god'.]

Deity /dée i ti, dáy-/ *n*. God in monotheistic belief [14thC]

deixis /díksiss/ *n*. the use of a word such as 'he', 'that', 'now', or 'here', whose full meaning depends on the context in which it is used [Mid-20thC. From Greek, 'reference', formed from *deiknunai* 'to show' (see DEICTIC).]

déjà vu /dáy zhaa voó/ *n*. **1.** PSYCHOL FEELING OF RELIVING STH a feeling of having experienced sth before although in fact it is the first time that it has been experienced **2.** BOREDOM boredom resulting from sth that has happened many times before [Early 20thC. From French, literally 'already seen'.]

— WORD KEY: USAGE —
Extension of meaning: *déjà vu* once referred exclusively to the illusion of having been somewhere before or done sth before: *As she entered the house, so far from any place she had ever been, she had an eerie sense of déjà vu.* Recently, however, it has come to encompass as well the reality of repetitiveness in events or actions: *The opening of yet another Italian restaurant in that spot gave her a distinct sense of déjà vu.*

deject /di jékt/ (**-jects, -jecting, -jected**) *vt*. to make sb or sth miserable or disheartened (*archaic*) ○ *'Nor once deject the courage of our minds'* (William Shakespeare, *Troilus and Cressida*; 1601) [15thC. From Latin *deject-*, the past participle stem of *dejicere*, literally 'to throw down', from *jacere* 'to throw'.]

dejected /di jéktid/ *adj.* feeling or showing sadness and lack of hope, especially because of disappointment —**dejectedly** *adv.* —**dejectedness** *n.*

dejection /di jéksh'n/ *n.* **1.** GREAT UNHAPPINESS unhappiness and lack of hope, especially caused by disappointment **2.** MED DEFECATION the act of passing solid waste matter out of the anus (*technical*) **3.** MED EXCREMENT solid waste matter that is passed out through the anus (*technical*)

de jure /dee joóri, day yoó ray/ *adv., adj.* by right according to the law [Mid-16thC. From Latin, literally 'from the law'.]

deka- *prefix.* = **deca-**

Dekker /dékər/, **Thomas** (1572?–1632) English dramatist and pamphleteer. He wrote over 40 plays, including *The Honest Whore, or a Converted Courtesan* (1604, 1630). He also wrote in collaboration with other Elizabethan dramatists including Philip Massinger, Thomas Middleton, and William Rowley.

dekko /déko/ (*plural* **-kos**) *n.* a quick look or glance (*informal*) ○ *Come and have a dekko at this!* [Late 19thC. From Hindi *dekho* 'look!'.]

de Klerk /də klúrk/, **F. W.** (*b.* 1936) South African politician. He introduced reforms during his presidency (1989–94) that led to the end of apartheid. He shared the Nobel Peace Prize with Nelson Mandela in 1993. Full name **Frederik Willem de Klerk**

del *abbr.* delete

del. *abbr.* **1.** delegate **2.** delegation **3.** delete

Del. *abbr.* Delaware

Delacroix /déllə krwaa/, **Eugène** (1798–1863) French painter and lithographer. His romantic works, such as *Liberty Guiding the People* (1830), are characterized by Byronic melodrama and vivid colour. Full name **Ferdinand Victor Eugène Delacroix**

Delagoa Bay /délla gố ə-/ bay on the southern Mozambique coast. Mozambique's capital, Maputo, is situated near the head of the bay.

delaine /di láyn/ *n.* a fine fabric resembling muslin but made of wool or wool and cotton [Mid-19thC. Shortening of MOUSSELINE DE LAINE.]

de la Mare /də lə máir/, **Walter** (1873–1956) British poet, anthologist, and novelist. A prolific writer, his work includes verse, *The Listeners and Other Poems* (1912), and prose, *Memoirs of a Midget* (1921).

delaminate /dee lámmi nayt/ (**delaminates**, **delaminating**, **delaminated**) *vti.* to separate or peel off in thin layers, or cause sth to do this

delamination /dee lámmi náysh'n/ *n.* the process of separating sth into, or peeling off in, thin layers, or the state of being separated into thin layers

Delaroche, **Paul** (1797–1856) French painter. His historical subjects, such as his huge mural (1834–41) in the École des Beaux-Arts, Paris, are painstaking classical-romantic works. Full name **Hippolyte-Paul Delaroche**

Delaunay /də láw nay/, **Robert** (1885–1941) French painter. A cubist-influenced painter, he developed a new style called orphism. He was later a pioneer of pure abstract art, as shown in his *Windows* series (1912).

Delaunay, **Sonia** (1885–1980) Russian-born French painter and designer. Her paintings and designs for textiles, bookbindings, and theatrical costumes in the 1920s were characterized by bright colours and geometric forms. Born **Sonia Terk**

Delaware[1] /déllə wair/ (*plural* **-ware** *or* **-wares**) *n.* PEOPLES a member of a group of Native North American peoples who used to live between the Delaware and Hudson rivers, and who now live mostly in Oklahoma, Ontario, Wisconsin, and Kansas [Early 18thC. Named after the *Delaware* River in the eastern United States.]

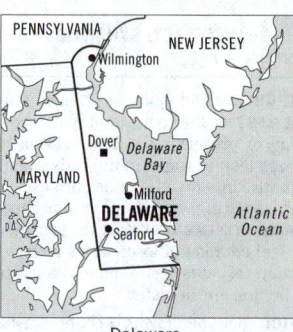
Delaware

Delaware[2] /déllə wair/ the first US state, bordered by the Atlantic Ocean, Maryland, Pennsylvania, and New Jersey. Capital: Dover. Population: 731,581 (1997). Area: 6,206 sq. km/2,396 sq. mi. —**Delawarean** /déllə wáiri ən/ *n., adj.*

De La Warr, **Thomas West**, **3rd Baron** (1577–1618) English-born governor of the colony of Virginia. In 1610 he arrived at Jamestown in time to save the settlement from being disbanded. The state of Delaware is named for him. Known as **Lord Delaware**

delay /di láy/ *v.* (**-lays**, **-laying**, **-layed**) **1.** *vti.* PUT STH OFF TILL LATER to postpone sth or wait until later before doing sth **2.** *vt.* MAKE LATE to make sb or sth late by slowing or stopping him, her, or it ○ *I was delayed at the office.* **3.** *vi.* PROCRASTINATE to hesitate, or fail to do sth quickly enough ○ *Don't delay, book today.* ■ *n.* **1.** LATENESS a situation in which sth does not happen or start at the time it was meant to ○ *All services are subject to delay or cancellation.* **2.** EXTENT OF LATENESS the extent of the period of time by which sb or sth is made late or slowed down ○ *long delays on the M1* **3.** PROCRASTINATION procrastination, or failure to do sth quickly enough ○ *This must be done without delay.* [13thC. From Anglo-Norman *delaier* 'to leave off', from *laier* 'to leave', of uncertain origin: probably from prehistoric Germanic.] —**delayer** *n.*

delay action *n.* = delayed action *n.* 1

delayed /di láyd/ *adj.* **1.** MADE LATE made to happen, start, arrive, or leave later than intended or later than usual **2.** LATER THAN USUAL happening at some time after the usual or expected time ○ *delayed language development* **3.** HAPPENING LATER happening after a period of time ○ *causing delayed damage to the kidneys*

delayed action *n.* **1.** EFFECT DEFERRED FOR A PERIOD the activation of a mechanism a short time after it has been set (*hyphenated when used before a noun*) **2.** DELAY MECHANISM a mechanism used to produce delayed action

delayed neutron *n.* a neutron emitted after a measurable time delay in the process of nuclear fission

delayering /dee láy ə ring/ *n.* the process of simplifying the structure of an organization to make it more efficient —**delayer** *vti.*

delaying action, **delaying operation** *n.* a manoeuvre used to gain time or allow a retreat when there are not enough resources to confront an opponent directly

delaying tactic *n.* a deliberate attempt to delay sth in order to gain time or some other advantage

delay line *n.* a device designed to cause a delay in transmitting an electronic signal

Delbrück, **Max** (1906–81) German-born US biologist. In 1969 he shared the Nobel Prize in physiology or medicine for his work on the replication of viruses and their genetic structure.

dele /deéli/ *n.* MARK TO SHOW DELETION a mark used in the margin of printed material to show that sth is to be deleted (*informal*) ■ *vt.* (**-les**, **-leing**, **-led**) MARK MATERIAL FOR DELETION to mark a passage of printed material for deletion (*informal*) [Early 18thC. From Latin, 'delete!', from *delere* (see DELETE).]

delectable /di léktəb'l/ *adj.* **1.** DELICIOUS with a delicious taste **2.** DELIGHTFUL absolutely delightful, very pleasing, or very attractive ■ *n.* STH VERY TASTY an appetizing food or dish [14thC. Via French *délectable* from, ultimately, Latin *delectare* 'to please' (see DELIGHT).] —

delectability /di léktə bí lləti/ *n.* —**delectableness** *n.* —**delectably** /-əbli/ *adv.*

delectation /deé lek táysh'n/ *n.* pleasure or enjoyment (*formal*) [14thC. Via Old French from, ultimately, Latin *delectare* (see DELIGHT).]

delegate *n.* /délligət, délli gayt/ **1.** REPRESENTATIVE OR DEPUTY sb chosen to represent or given the authority to act on behalf of another person, group, or organization, e.g. at a meeting or conference **2.** POL MEMBER OF HOUSE OF DELEGATES a member of a US House of Delegates, the lower house of the legislature in Maryland, Virginia, or West Virginia **3.** POL REPRESENTATIVE OF US TERRITORY a representative of a territory in the US House of Representatives, who may speak on issues but not vote ■ *v.* /délli gayt/ (**-gates**, **-gating**, **-gated**) **1.** *vti.* GIVE TASK TO to give a task to sb else with responsibility to act on your behalf **2.** *vti.* GIVE POWER OR AUTHORITY TO to give sb the power to act, make decisions, or allocate resources on your behalf ○ *an executive who was unafraid to delegate* **3.** *vt.* US LAW, FIN SEND DEBTOR TO CREDITOR to appoint one of your debtors to represent you to your creditor [15thC. From Latin *delegare*, literally 'to send away', from *legare* 'to send'.] —**delegable** /délligəb'l/ *adj.* —**delegator** *n.*

delegation /délla gáysh'n/ *n.* **1.** GROUP REPRESENTING OTHERS a group of people chosen to represent or act on behalf of others **2.** GIVING OF RESPONSIBILITY TO SB ELSE the giving of some power, responsibility, or work to sb else **3.** BEING GIVEN TO SB ELSE the condition of being given to sb else as a duty or responsibility **4.** POL STATE REPRESENTATIVES all the members of the US Congress who represent one state

delegitimize /deéla jítta mīz/ (**-mizes**, **-mizing**, **-mized**), **delegitimise** (**-mises**, **-mising**, **-mised**) *vt.* to take away the legitimacy or legal status of sb or sth —**delegitimization** /deéla jítta mī záysh'n/ *n.*

delete /di leét/ *vt.* (**-letes**, **-leting**, **-leted**) REMOVE OR ERASE to remove or score out sth that is printed or written, or erase sth from a computer file or disk ■ *n.* KEY FOR REMOVAL OF DATA a key on a computer keyboard that is depressed in order to erase or destroy files of previously keyed material ○ *Click on the icon for that file and then hit delete.* [15thC. From Latin *delere* 'to blot out, efface', of unknown origin.]

deleterious /délli teéri əss/ *adj.* with a harmful or damaging effect on sb or sth (*formal*) [Mid-17thC. Via medieval Latin from Greek *dēlētērios* 'noxious'.] —**deleteriously** *adv.* —**deleteriousness** *n.*

deletion /di leésh'n/ *n.* **1.** REMOVING STH OR SCORING STH OUT the action or process of removing or erasing sth or scoring sth out **2.** STH REMOVED OR SCORED OUT sth removed or scored out from a text, or erased from a computer file **3.** GENETICS ABSENCE OF GENETIC MATERIAL the loss or absence of part of a chromosome, ranging from a pair of chemicals (**base pair**) to a whole arm. Some medical conditions are the result of deletion.

deleverage /dee leévərij/ (**-ages**, **-aging**, **-aged**) *vti.* to reduce the amount of debt that a company owes, usually by laying off workers, selling off unprofitable divisions, and other cost-cutting measures

delft /delft/, **Delft**, **delftware** /délft wair/, **Delftware** *n.* earthenware with an opaque white glaze, usually with blue decoration [Late 17thC. Named after the town of DELFT where such pottery was originally made.]

Delft city in the province of Zuid-Holland, in the western Netherlands, known as a centre of production of glazed earthenware. Population: 92,241 (1994).

delftware, **Delftware** *n.* = delft

Delgado, Cape /del gaádo/ cape in northeastern Mozambique, just south of the border with Tanzania

Delhi /délli/ city in northern India and capital of the Union Territory of Delhi. It is a major transportation, commercial, and industrial centre. Population: 8,375,188 (1991). ◊ **New Delhi**

deli /délli/ (*plural* **-is**) *n.* a delicatessen (*informal*) [Mid-20thC. Shortening.]

Delian /deéli ən/ *n.* SB FROM DELOS sb who lives on or was born or brought up on the Greek island of

Delos ■ *adj.* **OF DELOS** relating to the Greek island of Delos, its people, or its culture

Delian League /deéli ən leég/, **Delian Confederacy** *n.* an alliance of Greek states set up in 478 BC to oppose Persia

deliberate *adj.* /di líbbərət/ **1. INTENTIONAL** carefully thought out and done intentionally **2. CAREFUL** slow, careful, and methodical ■ *vti.* /di líbbə rayt/ **(-ates, -ating, -ated) THINK** to consider sth carefully and in detail [15thC. From Latin *deliberare*, literally 'to weigh carefully', from *librare* 'to weigh', from *libra* 'balance' (source of English *level* and *equilibrium*).] —**deliberateness** /di líbbərətnəss/ *n.* —**deliberator** /di líbbə raytər/ *n.*

deliberately /di líbbərətli/ *adv.* **1. INTENTIONALLY** in a way that is intentional and thought out in advance ○ *The police believe that the fire was started deliberately.* **2. CAREFULLY** with care and thought ○ *He spoke slowly and deliberately.*

deliberation /di líbbə ráysh'n/ *n.* (*formal*) **1. CAREFUL THOUGHT** long careful consideration of sth **2. DISCUSSION** formal or official discussion or debate ○ *The planning committee's deliberations seemed to last all night.* **3. CARE** slowness and methodical carefulness

deliberative /di líbbərətiv/ *adj.* (*formal*) **1.** POL **INVOLVED IN DISCUSSION** involved in or organized for careful discussion and debate **2. RESULTING FROM DISCUSSION** relating to or resulting from discussion and debate —**deliberatively** *adv.* —**deliberativeness** *n.*

Delibes /də leéb/, **Léo** (1836–91) French composer. His grand operas include *Lakmé* (1883), and his masterpiece ballet is *Coppélia* (1870). Full name **Clément Philibert Léo Delibes**

delicacy /déllikəssi/ (*plural* **-cies**) *n.* **1.** FOOD **STH NICE TO EAT** a delicious, rare, or highly prized item of food **2. SENSITIVITY** sensitivity to the feelings of others **3. NEED FOR TACT** the quality of requiring great tact or sensitivity ○ *a matter of extreme delicacy* **4. GREAT SENSITIVITY IN FEELINGS** extreme and perhaps unnecessary fussiness or squeamishness in the way sb responds to sth offensive or embarrassing ○ *his delicacy on matters of a medical nature* **5. SUBTLETY AND REFINEMENT** pleasing subtlety in sth, e.g. taste, smell, or colour ○ *the delicacy of her perfume* **6. FINENESS** fineness and subtlety of feeling, observation, or execution ○ *the delicacy of the brushwork in his later paintings* **7. FRAGILITY** the quality of being easily damaged or broken **8. LACK OF PHYSICAL STRENGTH** lack physical strength or health **9. SENSITIVITY OF RESPONSE IN EQUIPMENT** sensitivity in the way sth e.g. scientific equipment or a musical instrument, responds to use

delicate /déllikət/ *adj.* **1. FRAGILE** easily damaged or broken **2. FRAIL** without much resistance to illness or injury ○ *in delicate health* **3. SUBTLE** mild, gentle, pale, or soft, and pleasant to the senses ○ *a delicate shade of blue.* **4. FINE** finely made and with small parts or detail in its design **5. SKILFUL** showing sb's skill or craft, especially in producing finely detailed intricate work or gentle or adroit movements ○ *a filigree of delicate, shimmering brushstrokes* **6. NEEDING TACT** needing to be dealt with using tact and sensitivity ○ *The negotiations were at a delicate stage.* **7. REFINED** having or showing a refined and sensitive taste **8. EASILY OFFENDED** easily shocked or upset by offensive or embarrassing things **9.** TECH **ACCURATE** used to describe instrumentation that is very precise and able to give exact readings **10. NOT WELL** uncomfortable as the result of over-indulgence (*humorous*) ○ *I'm feeling a bit delicate this morning.* ■ **delicates** *npl.* CLOTHES **CLOTHES NEEDING SPECIAL WASHING AND DRYING** clothes that need careful washing and drying, e.g. using a special washing machine programme [14thC. Directly or via French *délicat* from Latin *delicatus*, related to *delicere* (see DELIGHT).] —**delicateness** *n.*

WORD KEY: SYNONYMS

See Synonyms at ***fragile***.

delicately /déllikətli/ *adv.* **1. FINELY** in a way that shows skill in producing fine detail **2. SUBTLY** in a pleasingly mild and subtle way ○ *delicately flavoured* **3. GENTLY AND CAREFULLY** gently and carefully, with no rough or sudden movements **4. WITH TACT** tactfully and sensitively ○ *a matter that must be handled very delicately* **5. UNSTABLY** in a way that seems precarious or sensitive to even a slight change or disturbance ○ *delicately balanced on its edge*

delicatessen /déllikə téss'n/ *n.* **1.** FOOD, COMM **SPECIALIZED FOOD SHOP** a shop specializing in imported or unusual foods and ingredients, e.g. cooked meats, cheeses, and pickles **2. PREPARED FOOD SOLD IN DELICATESSEN** prepared food sold in a delicatessen, e.g. cooked meats, cheeses, pickles, and salads [Late 19thC. Via German and French from Italian *delicatezza* 'delicacy', from Latin *delicatus* 'pleasing, choice'.]

delicious /di líshəss/ *adj.* **1. GOOD TO EAT** with an appealing or enjoyable taste or smell **2. DELIGHTFUL** highly amusing, pleasing, or enjoyable [13thC. Via Old French from, ultimately, Latin *delicia* 'pleasure', from *delicere* 'to allure' (see DELIGHT).] —**deliciousness** *n.*

deliciously /di líshəssli/ *adv.* **1. TASTILY** in a way that appeals to the sense of taste or smell ○ *a deliciously sweet and crunchy apple* **2. APPETIZINGLY** in an appetizing way ○ *king prawns sizzling away deliciously on the barbecue* **3. VERY SATISFYINGLY** to a great and very satisfying degree ○ *a deliciously ironic twist of fate* **4. ENJOYABLY** in an enjoyable and pleasant way

delict /di líkt/ *n.* LAW in Scottish civil law, a wrong or injury done to sb [Early 16thC. From Latin *delictum*, the neuter past participle of *delinquere* 'to offend' (see DELINQUENT).]

delight /di lít/ *n.* **1. JOY** great joy and pleasure ○ *To my delight, he accepted.* **2. SB OR STH GIVING JOY** sb or sth that brings sb great joy and pleasure ○ *That's one of the delights of having children.* ■ *v.* **(-lights, -lighting, -lighted) 1.** *vti.* **GIVE SB JOY** to give sb great joy and pleasure **2.** *vi.* **GAIN ENJOYMENT FROM STH** to gain great enjoyment or pleasure from sth ○ *She delighted in outwitting her competitors.* [13thC. Via Old French *delit* from, ultimately, Latin *delectare*, literally 'to keep enticing' (source of English *delectable*), from *delicere* 'to allure', from *lacere* 'to entice'.] —**delighter** *n.*

delighted /di lítid/ *adj.* extremely pleased or filled with delight ○ *I was delighted to hear about your good news!* —**delightedly** *adv.* —**delightedness** *n.*

delightful /di lítf'l/ *adj.* giving great pleasure and joy, especially by being pleasant, good to look at, or amusing —**delightfulness** *n.*

delightfully /di lítfəli/ *adv.* in a way or to an extent that gives a lot of pleasure

delimit /di límmit/ **(-its, -iting, -ited)**, **delimitate** /di límmi tayt/ **(-tates, -tating, -tated)** *vt.* to set out or establish the limits or boundaries of sth (*formal*) [Mid-19thC. Via French *délimiter* from Latin *delimitare*, from *limit-*, the stem of *limes* (see LIMIT).] —**delimitation** /di límmi táysh'n/ *n.* —**delimitative** /di límmitətiv/ *adj.*

delimiter /di límmitər/ *n.* COMPUT a character or blank space that marks the beginning or end of a data element

delineate /di línni ayt/ **(-ates, -ating, -ated)** *vt.* **1. DESCRIBE** to describe or explain sth in detail (*formal*) **2.** DRAWING **DRAW** to sketch or draw sth in outline **3. PORTRAY VISUALLY** to represent sth visually using sth such as a chart or graph [Mid-16thC. From Latin *delineare*, literally 'to sketch out', from *linea* (see LINE).] —**delineable** *adj.* —**delineation** /di línni áysh'n/ *n.* —**delineative** /di línni ətiv/ *adj.*

delineator /di línni aytər/ *n.* **1.** TEXTILES **TAILOR'S ADJUSTABLE PATTERN** an adjustable pattern that a tailor uses to cut garments of different sizes **2. SB OR STH THAT DELINEATES** sb or sth that outlines or describes sth

delinquency /di língkwənssi/ *n.* **1.** LAW, CRIMINOL **UNLAWFUL BEHAVIOUR** antisocial or illegal behaviour or acts, especially by young people **2. NEGLECT OF OBLIGATION** failure to fulfil an obligation, commitment, or pledge (*formal*) **3.** *US* FIN **STH OVERDUE** sth that is overdue, e.g. a debt or tax (*formal*)

delinquent /di língkwənt/ *n.* LAW, CRIMINOL **LAWBREAKER, ESPECIALLY YOUNG OFFENDER** sb, especially a young person, who has acted antisocially or broken the law ■ *adj.* **1.** LAW, CRIMINOL **ANTISOCIAL OR UNLAWFUL** relating to antisocial behaviour or lawbreaking **2. IGNORING DUTY** neglecting a duty, commitment, or responsibility (*formal*) **3.** FIN **UNPAID** with unpaid sums of money due [15thC. From Latin *delinquere* 'to offend', from *linquere* 'to leave'. Ultimately from an Indo-European base that is also the ancestor of English *lend* and *eclipse*.] —**delinquently** *adv.*

WORD KEY: SYNONYMS

See Synonyms at ***bad***.

deliquesce /délli kwéss/ **(-quesces, -quescing, -quesced)** *vi.* **1.** CHEM **ABSORB MOISTURE** to dissolve gradually by absorbing moisture from the air **2.** BOT **FORM BRANCHES** to form many branches without a main stem **3.** FUNGI **BECOME LIQUID** to become soft or liquid after the release of spores [Mid-18thC. From Latin *deliquescere*, literally 'to start melting away', from *liquere* 'to be liquid'.] —**deliquescence** *n.* —**deliquescent** *adj.*

delirious /di lírri əss/ *adj.* **1.** MED **IRRATIONAL THROUGH ILLNESS** irrational as a temporary result of a physical condition, e.g. fever, poisoning, or brain injury. ◊ **delirium 2. EXCITED** extremely excited or emotional ○ *delirious with joy* [Late 16thC. Formed from DELIRIUM.] —**deliriousness** *n.*

deliriously /di lírri əssli/ *adv.* **1.** MED **BECAUSE OF BEING DELIRIOUS** as a result of being delirious, e.g. due to poisoning, fever, or brain injury ○ *muttering and shouting out deliriously* **2. EXCITEDLY** in an almost uncontrollably excited or emotional way ○ *deliriously happy at passing her driving test*

delirium /di lírri əm/ (*plural* **-ums** *or* **-a** /-ri ə/) *n.* **1.** MED **TEMPORARY MENTAL DISTURBANCE** a state marked by extreme restlessness, confusion, and sometimes hallucinations, caused by fever, poisoning, or brain injury **2. GREAT EXCITEMENT** a condition of extreme excitement or emotion [Mid-16thC. From Latin, formed from *delirare* 'to be deranged', literally 'to be out of your track', from *lira* 'ridge between furrows'.]

delirium tremens /di lírri əm trémmenz, -treé menz/ *n.* agitation, tremors, and hallucinations caused by alcohol dependence and withdrawal [From Latin, literally 'trembling delirium']

delish /di lísh/ *adj.* very delicious (*slang*) [Early 20thC. Shortening.]

delist /dee líst/ **(-lists, -listing, -listed)** *vt.* **1. TAKE OFF LIST** to remove sb or sth from a list **2.** *US* STOCK EXCH **REMOVE SECURITY FROM LISTING** to remove a security from a listing on a stock exchange

Delius /deéli əss/, **Frederick** (1862–1934) English composer. His music is characterized by rich orchestration and the subtle evocation of moods, e.g. in *On Hearing the First Cuckoo in Spring* (1912).

deliver /di lívvər/ **(-ers, -ering, -ered)** *v.* **1.** *vti.* COMM, MAIL **CARRY STH TO SB** to take sth, e.g. mail, goods that have been bought, or a message, to a particular person or address **2.** *vt.* OBSTET, VET **ASSIST DURING BIRTH** to give medical help when a baby or other offspring is being born **3.** *vt.* GYN **PRODUCE BABY** to give birth to a baby (*often passive*) **4.** *vt.* **MAKE SPEECH** to make a speech or give a talk to an audience **5.** *vt.* **ANNOUNCE** to announce sth formally, e.g. an opinion, decision, or judgment ○ *The jury delivered its verdict.* **6.** *vt.* SPORTS **THROW BALL OR PUNCH** to toss or throw a ball or aim a punch at sb or sth **7.** *vti.* **DO AS PROMISED** to do what has been promised ○ *He has yet to deliver anything that was promised in his speeches.* **8.** *vt.* *US* POL **ACHIEVE SUPPORT FOR SB** to organize and produce the support of a place or people for sb (*informal*) **9.** *vt.* **PRODUCE** to provide or produce sth ○ *Note the total dosage of antibiotics delivered.* **10.** *vt.* **RELEASE** to free or save sb from captivity or hardship (*literary*) **11.** *vt.* **GIVE SB STH** to hand sb or sth over to sb else ○ *You have 48 hours to deliver the payment.* [13thC. Via French *délivrer* from Latin *deliberare*, literally 'to free completely', from *liberare* (see LIBERATE).] —**deliverability** /di lívvərə bílləti/ *n.* —**deliverable** /di lívvərəb'l/ *adj.*

deliverance /di lívvərənss/ *n.* **1. RESCUE FROM STH** rescue from captivity, hardship, or domination by evil (*formal*) ○ *He sought deliverance from his imprisonment.* **2. ANNOUNCEMENT** a formal announcement of a decision, judgment, or opinion

WORD KEY: CULTURAL NOTE

Deliverance, a film by British director John Boorman (1972) Based on the novel by James Dickey (1972), it is the story of a canoe trip through the Appalachian Mountains undertaken by four city businessmen. The journey turns into a struggle for survival when the men are exposed to unexpected dangers and harried by sinister mountain people. In the famous 'Dueling Banjos' sequence, one of the men and a boy attempt to outplay each other on their banjos.

deliverer /di lívvərər/ n. **1.** SB WHO DELIVERS STH sb who delivers sth, such as a message or goods that have been bought **2.** RESCUER sb who rescues sb or sth from captivity or evil (archaic or literary)

delivery /di lívvəri/ (plural **-ies**) n. **1.** COMM, MAIL TAKING STH TO SB the carrying of sth to a particular person or a particular address ○ We can arrange delivery of any items purchased. **2.** COMM, MAIL VISIT BY SB BRINGING STH one of the regular visits made to a person, address, or area by a postal worker or a vendor's vehicle ○ We only get one delivery a day. **3.** COMM, MAIL ITEM BROUGHT TO SB sth brought by a postal worker or a vendor, e.g. the post or goods that have been bought **4.** GYN GIVING BIRTH the process of giving birth to a baby **5.** MANNER OF SPEAKING the action or manner in which sb speaks to an audience ○ She needs to work on her vocal delivery. **6.** RESCUE the rescue or saving of sb from captivity, hardship, or evil ○ He prayed for delivery from his oppressors. **7.** SPORTS WAY OF PUTTING BALL IN MOTION the action or manner of throwing, tossing, or rolling a ball or aiming a punch **8.** LAW ACTION NEEDED TO EFFECT PROPERTY TRANSFER a formal action needed to accomplish a transfer of property

delivery room n. a specially equipped room in a hospital where women give birth

dell /del/ n. a small usually wooded valley or hollow (literary) [Old English. Ultimately from the same prehistoric Germanic word that was the ancestor of DALE.]

Della Robbia /déllə róbbi ə/, **Luca** (1400?–82) Italian sculptor and ceramicist. He is best known for his early Renaissance panels in Florence Cathedral. He invented a technique for making glazed terracotta figures.

Delmarva Peninsula /del maárvə-/ peninsula in the US states of Delaware, Maryland, and Virginia. Length: 290 km/180 mi.

delocalize /dee lōkə līz/ (**-izes, -izing, -ized**), **delocalise** (**-ises, -ising, -ised**) vt. to remove sth from its locality —**delocalization** /dee lōkə līzáysh'n/ n.

Delon /də lóN/, **Alain** (b. 1935) French actor, producer, director, and screenwriter. His notable films include the film noir classic The Godson (1967).

Delors /də láwr/, **Jacques** (b. 1925) French politician, economist, and statesman. As president of the European Commission (1985–94), he oversaw moves towards a free European Community market in 1992. Full name **Jacques Lucien Jean Delors**

Delors Plan n. a plan for closer European union, originated by Jacques Delors and presented in 1989

Delos /dée loss/ island of Greece, the smallest island of the Cyclades group in the southern Aegean Sea, now almost uninhabited. In classical times it was considered sacred to Apollo, and was the birthplace of Apollo and Artemis. Area: approximately 3 sq. km/1 sq. mi.

delouse /dee lówss/ (**-louses, -lousing, -loused**) vt. to give a person or animal treatment to remove lice

Delphi /délfi/ ancient Greek town on the southern slopes of Mount Parnassus, about 9.5 km/6 mi. north of the Gulf of Corinth. It is the site of the Temple of Apollo and the Delphic oracle.

Delphic /délfik/, **Delphian** /délfi ən/ adj. **1.** RELATING TO DELPHI relating to Delphi, or its temple or oracle **2.** Delphic, delphic AMBIGUOUS obscure and open to more than one interpretation

Delphic oracle n. the oracle of great authority and notorious ambiguity at Delphi, where it was believed the god Apollo spoke through a priestess

delphinium /del fínni əm/ (plural **-ums** or **-a** /-ni ə/) n. a plant cultivated for its variously coloured flower spikes, especially those species with tall blue or white flower spikes. Genus: Delphinium. [Early 17thC. Via modern Latin from Greek delphinion 'larkspur', literally 'little dolphin', from delphis 'dolphin' (because of the shape of the flower).]

Delphinus /del fínəss/ n. a small faint constellation of the northern hemisphere lying on the Milky Way, situated between Pegasus and Aquila

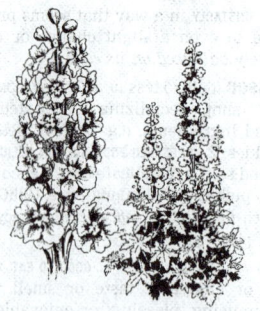
Delphinium

delt /delt/ n. US a deltoid (informal) [Shortening of DELTOID]

delta /déltə/ n. **1.** GEOG TRIANGULAR LAND AREA AT RIVER MOUTH a triangular deposit of sand and soil at the mouth of a river or inlet **2.** delta, Delta GEOG AREA IN RIVER DELTA an area in or around the delta of a river **3.** 4TH LETTER OF GREEK ALPHABET the fourth letter of the Greek alphabet, represented in the English alphabet as 'd'. See table at **alphabet 4.** STH LIKE DELTA sth shaped like a triangle or delta **5.** MATH CHANGE IN VARIABLE an increase or decrease in the value of a variable. Symbol Δ [Pre-12thC. Via Latin from Greek; ultimately of Phoenician origin.]

Delta /déltə/ n. **1.** ASTRON FOURTH BRIGHTEST STAR the fourth brightest star in a constellation **2.** SPACE TECH US ROCKET a rocket used by the United States to launch satellites into orbit above the Earth **3.** COMMUNICATION CODE WORD FOR LETTER 'D' the NATO phonetic alphabet code word for the letter 'D', used in international radio communications

Delta Force n. the US Army 1st Special Forces Operational Detachment, a military and counter-terrorist force similar to the SAS

delta ray n. a low-energy particle such as an electron, emitted by matter when subjected to ionizing radiation

delta wave, **delta rhythm** n. a brain wave that is produced by adults in deep sleep. Delta waves are produced in the front of the brain and are slow waves with a frequency of 3.5 cycles per second.

delta wing n. an aeroplane wing that has a triangular, swept-back shape

deltiology /délti óllǝji/ n. the collection and study of postcards [Mid-20thC. Formed from Greek deltion, literally 'little writing tablet', from deltos 'writing tablet'.] —**deltiologist** n.

deltoid /dél toyd/ n. SHOULDER MUSCLE a thick triangular muscle that covers the shoulder joint ■ adj. TRIANGULAR triangular in shape (technical) [Mid-18thC. Directly or via French deltoïde from modern Latin deltoides, literally 'delta-shaped', from Greek delta (see DELTA).]

delude /di lood/ (**-ludes, -luding, -luded**) vt. **1.** LEAD INTO FALSE BELIEF to persuade sb to believe in sth that is untrue or unreal **2.** FRUSTRATE HOPES to frustrate sb's hopes or expectations (archaic) [15thC. From Latin deludere, literally 'to play to your detriment', from ludere 'to play' (see LUDICROUS).] —**deludable** adj. —**deluder** n. —**deludingly** adv.

deluded /di lóodid/ adj. firmly believing in sth that is untrue or unreal

deluge /déllyooj/ n. **1.** SUDDEN HEAVY DOWNPOUR a sudden heavy downpour of rain or torrent of water **2.** VAST QUANTITY an overwhelming amount of sth ■ vt. (**-uges, -uging, -uged**) **1.** OVERWHELM WITH STH to inundate sb suddenly with a large amount of sth **2.** OVERWHELM WITH WATER to flood or soak sb or sth with heavy rain or a sudden torrent of water [15thC. From Old French, from, ultimately, Latin diluere 'to wash away' (source of English dilute), from lavare 'to wash' (see LAVATORY).]

Deluge n. BIBLE = Flood

delusion /di loozh'n/ n. **1.** PSYCHOL FALSE BELIEF a persistent false belief held in the face of strong contradictory evidence, especially as a symptom of psychiatric disorder **2.** MISTAKEN NOTION a false or mistaken belief or idea about sth [15thC. From the Latin

stem delusion-, from the past participle stem of deludere (see DELUDE).] —**delusional** adj.

— WORD KEY: USAGE —
See Usage note at **allusion**.

delusions of grandeur npl. gross and false overestimation of personal worth, importance, powerfulness, or attractiveness

delusive /di loóssiv/ adj. leading to a belief in sth untrue or unreal [Early 17thC. Formed from Latin delus-, past participle stem of deludere (see DELUDE).] —**delusively** adv. —**delusiveness** n.

delusory /di loóssəri/ adj. so deceptive in nature or character as to be likely to mislead or delude sb [15thC. From late Latin delusorius, from the past participle stem of Latin deludere (see DELUDE).]

deluxe /də lúks/, **de luxe** adj. of a luxurious standard and surpassing all others in its class [Early 19thC. From French de luxe, literally 'of luxury'.]

delve /delv/ (**delves, delving, delved**) v. **1.** vi. DIG INTO STH AND SEARCH AROUND to thrust your hand deeply into sth to find a hidden or hard-to-reach item or items **2.** vi. DIG FOR INFORMATION to investigate or research sth thoroughly to obtain information **3.** vt. EXCAVATE to dig sth such as a ditch, hole, or burrow (archaic) [Old English delfan 'to dig', from prehistoric Germanic] —**delver** n.

dely abbr. delivery

Dem /dem/ n. a member of the Democratic Party in the United States (informal) [Late 19thC. Shortening.]

dem. abbr. GRAM demonstrative

Dem. abbr. **1.** Democrat **2.** Democratic

demagnetize /dee mágnə tīz/ (**-izes, -izing, -ized**), de-**magnetise** (**-netises, -netising, -netised**) vt. to remove the magnetic properties from sth —**demagnetization** /dee mágnə tī záysh'n/ n. —**demagnetizer** n.

demagogic /démmə góggik'l/, **demagogical** /démmə góggik'l/ adj. making an appeal to people's emotions, instincts, and prejudices in a way that is considered to be politically manipulative and dangerous [Mid-19thC. From Greek dēmagōgikos, from dēmagōgos (see DEMAGOGUE).] —**demagogically** adv.

demagogue /démmə gog/ n. **1.** EMOTIVE DICTATOR a political leader who gains power by appealing to people's emotions and prejudices rather than their rationality **2.** POPULAR LEADER IN ANCIENT TIMES in ancient times, a popular leader who represented the ordinary people [Mid-17thC. From Greek dēmagōgos, literally 'leader of the people', from agōgos 'leader', from agein 'to lead' (source of English stratagem).]

demagoguery /démmə goggəri/, **demagogy** /démmə goggi/, **demagoguism** /-gogizəm/ n. the character, behaviour, tactics, or rhetoric of a demagogue

demand /di maánd/ n. **1.** FORCEFUL REQUEST a clear and firm request that is difficult to ignore or deny **2.** ECON CUSTOMER INTEREST IN ACQUIRING STH the level of desire or need that exists for particular goods or services ○ Demand for that particular model is outstripping supply. **3.** NEED FOR RESOURCES OR ACTION an urgent requirement for time, facilities, resources, or action **4.** LAW LEGALLY ENFORCEABLE REQUEST a formal request that must be complied with by law ■ v. (**-mands, -manding, -manded**) **1.** vt. ASK FORCEFULLY to request sth firmly in a way that is difficult to ignore or deny **2.** vt. ASK TO KNOW AT ONCE to ask a question in an extremely forceful way **3.** vti. CALL FOR RESOURCES to require sth such as time, resources, facilities, or action in order to function or succeed [14thC. Via Old French demander from Latin demandare, literally 'to entrust completely', from mandare 'to entrust, order' (see MANDATE).] —**demandable** adj. —**demander** n. ◇ **in demand** wanted or sought by many people ◇ **on demand** promptly, whenever a request is received

demand deposit n. a bank deposit that can be withdrawn at any time without notice

demand feeding n. the practice of feeding a baby when it cries to be fed, rather than at set times

demanding /di maánding/ adj. requiring a lot of time, attention, energy, or resources

demandingly /di maándingli/ adv. in a highly insistent manner

demand loan *n.* FIN = **call loan**

demand note *n.* a bill or draft stating that a particular amount of money will be paid when it is asked for

demand-pull, **demand-pull inflation** *n.* inflation caused by demand for goods and services outstripping supply. ◊ **cost-push**

demand-side *adj.* relating to an economic policy that emphasizes the importance of demand and consumption

demantoid /di mán toyd/ *n.* a transparent green variety of garnet used as a gemstone [Late 19thC. From German, literally 'diamond-shaped', from *Demant* 'diamond'.]

demarcate /deé maar kayt/ (**-cates, -cating, -cated**) *vt.* **1.** DETERMINE AND SET OFFICIAL BORDERS to decide on and fix land boundaries **2.** SET DOWN NONPHYSICAL BOUNDS to state in a clear way where sth begins and ends [Early 19thC. Back-formation from DEMARCATION.] —**demarcator** *n.*

demarcation /deé maar káysh'n/ *n.* **1.** SETTING OF BORDERS the process of deciding on and fixing land boundaries **2.** IDENTIFIABLE SEPARATION OF THINGS the division of sth so that its divided parts are separate and identifiable **3.** CLEAR DIVISION OF WORK DUTIES the division of work duties into clearly identifiable parts to be carried out by different workers [Early 18thC. From Spanish *demarcación*, literally 'marking off', from *marcar* 'to mark', from, ultimately, a prehistoric Germanic word that is also the ancestor of English *margin*.]

demarcation dispute *n.* **1.** LAND-BOUNDARY DISPUTE a disagreement over where a land boundary lies **2.** INDUSTRIAL DISAGREEMENT ABOUT WORK ROLES in industrial relations law, a dispute as to which workers are to perform which tasks, especially when different trade unions are involved

démarche /dáy maarsh/ (*plural* **-marches** /dáy maarsh/) *n.* **1.** DIPLOMATIC REPRESENTATION a diplomatic representation, especially a move, manoeuvre, or protest made orally **2.** CITIZENS' PROTEST STATEMENT a statement of protest made by or on behalf of the citizens of a nation to their government or to a controlling authority **3.** MOVE OR COUNTERMOVE a move, step, or countermove [Mid-17thC. From French *démarcher* 'to take steps', from *marcher* 'to march'.]

dematerialize /deémə teéri ə līz/ (**-izes, -izing, -ized**), **dematerialise** (**-ises, -ising, -ised**) *vti.* to disappear or cause sth to disappear physically or apparently —**dematerialization** /deémə teéri ə lī záysh'n/ *n.*

deme /deem/ *n.* **1.** HIST TOWNSHIP IN ATTICA a township in Attica in ancient Greece **2.** ECOL POPULATION OF RELATED SPECIES a local population of closely related interbreeding species [Mid-19thC. From Greek *dēmos* 'district', hence, 'people living in a district' (see DEMOS).]

demean[1] /di meén/ (**-means, -meaning, -meaned**) *vt.* to reduce sb to a much lower status in a humiliating way [Early 17thC. Coined from DE- 'down' + MEAN 'inferior in rank'.] —**demeaning** *adj.*

demean[2] /di meén/ (**-means, -meaning, -meaned**) *vr.* to behave in a particular way (*dated*) [14thC. From Old French *demener*, literally 'to lead away', from, ultimately, Latin *minare* 'to drive a herd of animals'.]

demeanor *n.* US = **demeanour**

demeanour /di meénər/ *n.* sb's behaviour, manner, or appearance, especially as it reflects on character

demented /di méntid/ *adj.* **1.** ENTIRELY IRRATIONAL completely unreasonable or without any sense of consequences (*informal*) **2.** PSYCHIAT AFFECTED WITH DEMENTIA affected by the loss of intellectual functions that is associated with dementia [Mid-17thC. Originally the past participle of obsolete *dement* 'to deprive of reason', from Latin *dementare*, literally 'to take the mind away', from, ultimately, the stem *ment-* 'mind' (see MENTAL).] —**dementedly** *adv.* —**dementedness** *n.*

dementia /di ménshə/ *n.* PSYCHIAT the usually progressive deterioration of intellectual functions such as memory that can occur while other brain functions such as those controlling movement and the senses are retained. ◊ **senile dementia** [Late 18thC. From Latin, from the stem *dement-*, literally 'mind away', from *ment-* 'mind' (see MENTAL).]

dementia praecox /-preé koks/ *n.* schizophrenia (*archaic*) [From Latin, literally 'premature loss of mind']

demerara /démmə ráirə/, **demerara sugar** *n.* a type of sugar with yellowish-brown crystals that feel slightly moist [Mid-19thC. From *Demerara*, a region of Guyana where it originally came from.]

demerge /deé múrj/ (**-merges, -merging, -merged**) *vti.* to separate a company from a larger company so that it becomes an individual concern, or divide a large company into a number of smaller companies

demerger /deé múrjər/ *n.* a merger between two or more companies that is dissolved, or the separation of one company from a larger company or group

demerit /dee mérrit/ *n.* **1.** NEGATIVE FEATURE a negative feature or disadvantage of sth, especially when contrasted with its positive features or advantages (*often used in the plural*) **2.** US MIL, EDUC MARK FOR DEFICIENCY OR MISCONDUCT a mark against sb such as a student or cadet for a deficiency or misconduct [14thC. Directly or via Old French *desmerite* from Latin *demeritum*, from, ultimately, *demereri*, literally 'to deserve thoroughly', from *mereri* 'to deserve'. The original English meaning was 'merit, worth'. The modern meanings are derived from the negative connotations of DE-.] —**demeritorious** /dee mérri táwri əss/ *adj.* —**demeritoriously** /-əssli/ *adv.*

Demerol /démmə rol/ *tdmk.* a trademark for a medicinal preparation of the painkiller meperidine

demersal /di múrss'l/ *adj.* living or found in the deepest part of a body of water [Late 19thC. Formed from Latin *demersus*, the past participle of *demergere* 'to submerge', from *mergere* 'to plunge' (see MERGE).]

demesne /di máyn/ *n.* **1.** POSSESSION OF OWN LAND possession and use of your own land, as opposed to ownership of land that is occupied by tenants (*formal*) **2.** PRIVATE GROUNDS WITH MANSION the estate attached to a mansion for the private use of the owner (*archaic*) **3.** HIST FEUDAL MANORIAL LAND manorial land that a feudal lord kept for his own private use (*formal*) **4.** ESTATE an extensive landed property (*formal*) **5.** REALM OF MONARCH the realm under the rule of a monarch (*formal*) [14thC. Via Old French *demeine* 'belonging to a lord' from Latin *dominicus* 'of a lord' (source of English *domain*).]

Demeter /di meétər/ *n.* in Greek mythology, the goddess of corn and the harvest, daughter of Cronus and Rhea and mother of Persephone. Roman equivalent **Ceres**

demi- *prefix.* **1.** half ○ *demirep* **2.** partly ○ *demigod* [Via Old French from, ultimately, Latin *dimidius* 'split in two', from *dis-* 'apart' and *medius* 'half']

demibastion /démmi básti ən/ *n.* a two-sided fortification that consists of a wall facing forward and a wall facing a flank

demigod /démmi god/ *n.* **1.** SB TREATED LIKE GOD sb who is very important or highly revered and is treated like a god **2.** HUMAN WITH POWERS OF A GOD a mythological being who is half human and half god **3.** MINOR GOD a god regarded as minor in a hierarchy of other gods [Mid-16thC. Translation of Latin *semideus*.]

demigoddess /démmi goddess/ *n.* **1.** SB TREATED LIKE A GOD sb who is very important or highly revered and is treated like a god **2.** WOMAN WITH POWERS OF A GODDESS a mythological being who is half woman and half goddess **3.** SB TREATED LIKE A GOD sb who is very important or highly revered and is treated like a god

demijohn /démmi jon/ *n.* a large bottle that has a short narrow neck and is often used for making wine [Mid-18thC. By folk etymology from French *dame-jeanne*, literally 'Lady Jane', its popular name in France.]

demilitarize /dee míllitə rīz/ (**-rizes, -rizing, -rized**), **demilitarise** (**-rises, -rising, -rised**) *vt.* to remove or prohibit the presence of soldiers, weapons, and military installations in an area after an agreement has been made to stop fighting —**demilitarization** /deé millitə rī záysh'n/ *n.*

demilitarized zone, **demilitarised zone** *n.* an officially recognized area from which all soldiers, weapons, and military installations have been removed after an agreement to stop fighting

demimondaine /démmi mon dáyn/ *n.* a woman who is financially supported by a wealthy lover (*literary*) [Late 19thC. From French, from *demi-monde* (see DEMIMONDE).]

demimonde /démmi mónd/ *n.* (*literary*) **1.** PEOPLE OF QUESTIONABLE RESPECTABILITY people who are not considered to be completely respectable **2.** WOMEN SUPPORTED BY LOVERS a class of women who were financially supported by wealthy lovers, especially in the 19th and early 20th centuries [Mid-19thC. From French *demi-monde*, literally 'half world'.]

demineralise *vt.* = **demineralize**

demineralization /dee mínnərə lī záysh'n/, **demineralisation** *n.* the loss of mineral salts from the body, especially in the teeth and bones

demineralize /dee mínnərə līz/ (**-izes, -izing, -ized**), **demineralise** (**-ises, -ising, -ised**) *vt.* to remove minerals or mineral salts from sth such as bone or a liquid —**demineralizer** *n.*

demi-pension /démmi pa͞aN syoN/ *n.* = **half board**

Demirel /démmi rél/, **Süleyman** (*b.* 1924) Turkish statesman. He served four terms as prime minister (1965–93) and became the ninth president of Turkey in 1993.

demirelief /démmiri leef/ *n.* sculptural relief made of modelled forms that are half-raised from the background

demirep /démmi rep/ *n.* sb who is disreputable, especially a woman who acts in a way considered sexually improper (*archaic*) [Mid-18thC. Coined from DEMI- + *rep*, shortening of REPUTABLE.]

demise /di mīz/ *n.* (*formal*) **1.** SB'S DEATH the death of a person, especially when it happens slowly and predictably **2.** END OF STH the end of sth that used to exist, especially when it happens slowly and predictably ■ *vti.* (**-mises, -mising, -mised**) BE LEGALLY TRANSFERRED to transfer sth or undergo transfer through a line of descent or according to a will (*formal*) [15thC. Via Anglo-Norman from Old French *demis* 'sent away', from, ultimately, Latin *dimittere* (see DEMIT).] —**demisable** *adj.*

demi-sec /démmi sék/ *adj.* used to describe champagne or sparkling wine that is more sweet than dry [From French, literally 'half-dry'] —**demi-sec** *n.*

demisemiquaver /démmi semi kwayvər/ *n.* a note with the time value of one thirty-second of a semibreve. It is represented by a solid note-head with a stem and three 'tails'. US term **thirty-second note**

demission /di mísh'n/ *n.* resignation from an important official post [Mid-16thC. Via French *démission* from, ultimately, the Latin stem *dimission-* 'dismissal', from the past participle of *dimittere* (see DEMIT).]

demist /dee míst/ *vti.* to remove mist or condensation from sth, especially a car windscreen. US term **defog**

demister /dee místər/ *n.* a piece of equipment that clears away mist or condensation, especially a device that channels warm air over the inside of a car windscreen. US term **defogger**

demit /di mít/ (**-mits, -mitting, -mitted**) *vti.* to resign from or give up an important official post [15thC. Via Old French *desmettre*, from, ultimately, Latin *dimittere* 'to send away', from *mittere* 'to send'.]

demitasse /démmi tass/ *n.* a small cup of strong black coffee, or the cup in which such coffee is served [Mid-19thC. From French, literally 'half-cup', from *tasse* 'cup', from, ultimately, Persian *tāsht*.]

demiurge /démmi urj/ *n.* **1.** POWERFUL FORCE OR PERSONALITY a very strong, driving, and influential force or personality (*formal*) **2.** HIST ANCIENT GREEK MAGISTRATE a public magistrate in some ancient Greek states [Early 17thC. Via ecclesiastical Latin *demiurgus* from Greek *dēmiourgos* 'skilled person', from *dēmios* 'of the people' + *-ergos* 'working'.] —**demiurgeous** *adj.* —**demiurgic** *adj.* —**demiurgical** *adj.* —**demiurgically** *adv.*

Demiurge /démmi urj/ *n.* PHILOS in Gnostic and Platonic philosophies, the creator and controller of the material world

demivierge /démmi vi áirzh/ *n.* a young woman who takes part in sexual activity without ending her virginity (*literary*) [Early 20thC. From French, literally 'half virgin'.]

demivolte /démmi volt/, **demivolt** *n.* in dressage, a half turn made by a horse with its forelegs raised [Mid-17thC. From French, literally 'half turn', from *volte* 'turn'.]

demiworld /démmi wurld/ *n.* = demimonde *n.* 1

demo /démmō/ *n.* (*plural* demos) (*informal*) **1. PUBLIC PROTEST** a public event in which people protest against sth, often by marching through the streets **2. COMPUT TRIAL SOFTWARE** a trial version of software that demonstrates its principle features **3. MUSIC MUSIC SAMPLE** a recorded sample of music produced for promotional purposes **4. DEMONSTRATION OF PRODUCT** a demonstration, especially of a new product ■ *vt.* (demos, demoing, demoed) **SHOW HOW STH WORKS** to explain, describe, or give a demonstration of how sth works or how to do sth (*informal*) [Mid-20thC. Shortening of DEMONSTRATION.]

demob /dee mób/ (-mobs, -mobbing, -mobbed) *vti.* to demobilize armed forces (*informal*) [Early 20thC. Shortening of DEMOBILIZE.]

demobilize /di mṓbə līz/ (-izes, -izing, -ized), de-mobilise (-ises, -ising, -ised) *vti.* to discharge personnel from the armed forces and send them home, usually after a war —**demobilization** /di mṓbə līzáysh'n/ *n.*

demob suit *n.* a new suit given to servicemen when their employment in the armed forces is ended, especially at the end of World War I and World War II

democracy /di mókrəssi/ (*plural* -cies) *n.* **1. REPRESENTATION OF PEOPLE** the right to a form of government in which power is invested in the people as a whole, usually exercised on their behalf by elected representatives ○ *'Democracy is like the experience of life itself – always changing, infinite in its variety, sometimes turbulent and all the more valuable for having been tested for adversity'.* (Jimmy Carter, *Speech to Parliament of India; 2 June, 1978*) **2. DEMOCRATIC NATION** a country with a democratically elected government **3. DEMOCRATIC GOVERNMENTAL SYSTEM** a system of government based on the principle of majority decision-making **4. ORGANIZATIONAL CONTROL BY MEMBERS** the control of an organization by its members, who have a right to participate in decision-making processes [Late 16thC. Directly and via Old French *democratie* from medieval Latin *democratia*, from, ultimately, Greek *dēmokratia*, literally 'rule of the people', from *dēmos* 'people' (see DEMOS) + *kratos* 'rule'.]

democrat /démmə krat/ *n.* sb who believes in democracy and the democratic system of government and argues in favour of them

Democrat /démmə krat/ *n.* **1. MEMBER OF US DEMOCRATIC PARTY** a member of the Democratic Party, one of the two major political parties in the United States **2. MEMBER OF AUSTRALIAN DEMOCRATIC PARTY** a member of the Australian Democrats, a centre-left minority political party

democratic /démmə kráttik/ *adj.* characterized by democracy in government or in the decision-making processes of an organization or group —**democratically** *adv.*

Democratic /démmə kráttik/ *adj.* belonging or relating to or associated with the Democratic Party of the United States

democratic deficit *n.* a situation in which political structures, organizations, or decision-making processes lack democratic legitimacy, especially as discussed in the European Union

Democratic Party *n.* one of the two major political parties in the United States. It was formed after a split in the former Democratic-Republican Party under Andrew Jackson in 1828.

democratize /di mókrə tīz/ (-tizes, -tizing, -tized), de-mocratise (-tises, -tising, -tised) *vt.* **1. GIVE GOVERNMENT CONTROL TO THE PEOPLE** to make a country into a democracy **2. INTRODUCE DEMOCRACY TO STATE** to take steps towards establishing the features of liberal democracy in a state **3. GIVE ORGANIZATIONAL CONTROL TO MEMBERS** to put an organization under the control of its members by giving them free and equal decision-making powers **4. GIVE STH POPULAR APPEAL** to make sth accessible to everybody —**democratization** /di mókrə tī záysh'n/ *n.*

Democritus /di mókritəss/ (460?–370? BC) Greek philosopher. A prolific writer, he first propounded the

atomic theory of the universe. Only a few fragments of his work remain.

démodé /day mṓd ay/ *adj.* no longer fashionable [Late 19thC. From French, the past participle of *démoder* 'to go out of fashion', from *mode* 'fashion' (see MODE).]

demodulate /deé móddyoō layt/ (-lates, -lating, -lated) *vt.* to extract a signal carrying information from a radio wave (**carrier**) —**demodulator** *n.*

demographer /di móggrəfər/ *n.* sb who studies human populations, including their size, growth, density, and distribution, and statistics regarding birth, marriage, disease, and death

demographic /démmə gráffik/ *adj.* relating to demography or demographics —**demographical** *adj.* —**demographically** *adv.*

demographics /démmə gráffiks/ *npl.* the characteristics of a human population or part of it, especially its size, growth, density, distribution, and statistics regarding birth, marriage, disease, and death (*takes a plural verb*)

demography /di móggrəfi/ *n.* the study of human populations, including their size, growth, density, and distribution, as well as statistics regarding birth, marriage, disease, and death [Late 19thC. Coined from Greek *dēmos* 'people' + -GRAPHY.] —**demographist** *n.*

demoiselle /dém waa zél/ *n.* **1. YOUNG WOMAN** a young woman or girl, especially one who is French (*formal*) **2.** = damselfish (*formal*) **3.** = damselfly [Early 16thC. From French, 'damsel', from Old French *dameisele* (see DAMSEL).]

Demoiselle crane

demoiselle crane *n.* a small crane of North Africa and Asia that has a slender grey body, black plumes, and white ear tufts. Latin name: *Anthropoides virgo*. ['Demoiselle' from its ladylike form]

demolish /di móllish/ (-ishes, -ishing, -ished) *vt.* **1. WRECK A BUILDING** to destroy a building or other structure completely **2. DAMAGE IRREPARABLY** to damage sth so severely that it cannot be repaired or restored **3. BEAT OPPONENT SOUNDLY** to beat an opponent very convincingly, especially in sport or debate (*informal*) **4. EAT FAST AND GREEDILY** to eat a lot of food very quickly (*informal*) [Mid-16thC. From Old French *démoliss-*, a stem of *démolir*, from Latin *demolire*, literally 'to undo construction of a mass', from, ultimately, *moles* 'mass' (see MOLECULE).] —**demolisher** *n.*

demolition /démmə lísh'n/ *n.* **1. WRECKING OF BUILDING** the total destruction of a building or other structure ○ *The old hospital is scheduled for demolition.* **2. DESTRUCTION OR ANNIHILATION** the destruction or annihilation of sth or sb ■ **demolitions** *npl.* **EXPLOSIVES** explosives, especially those used by the military [Mid-16thC. Via French *démolition* from the Latin stem *demolition-*, from *demolire* (see DEMOLISH).]

demolition derby (*plural* demolition derbies) *n.* US an entertainment and sporting event held at a fair or on a speedway, during which drivers crash old cars, the winner being the driver of the last car running

demolitionist /démmə lísh'nist/ *n.* a person or company whose job it is to demolish buildings

demon /deémən/ *n.* **1. EVIL SPIRIT** an evil supernatural being such as a ghost or spirit **2. PERSONAL FEAR OR ANXIETY** a fear or anxiety that torments sb **3. EXPERT** sb who is extremely good at sth (*informal*) [13thC. Via Latin *daemon* and medieval Latin *demon* 'evil spirit' from Greek *daimōn* 'divine power, guiding spirit' (see DAEMON).]

demonetize /dee múnni tīz/ (-tizes, -tizing, -tized), de-monetise (-tises, -tising, -tised) *vt.* **1. CEASE MINTING COINS IN SPECIFIC METAL** to stop using a particular metal to make coins **2. WITHDRAW MONEY FROM CIRCULATION** to withdraw units of money from circulation [Mid-19thC. From French *démonétiser*, literally 'to refrain from using money', from Latin *moneta* 'money' (see MONEY).] —**demonetization** /dee múnni tī záysh'n/ *n.*

demoniac /di móni ak/ *adj.* **1. DEMONIACAL RESEMBLING A DEMON** resembling or characteristic of an evil spirit **2. demoniac, demoniacal EVIL OR WICKED** evil or wicked in character or nature **3. demoniac, demoniacal INTENSE OR FRANTIC** intense, frantic, or wild, as if driven or possessed by a demon ■ *n.* **SB INFLUENCED BY DEMON** sb believed to be possessed by an evil supernatural being (*archaic*) [14thC. From late Latin *daemoniacus*, from, ultimately, Greek *daimōn* (see DEMON).]

demonic /di mónnik/ *adj.* **1. OF OR RESEMBLING DEMON** relating to or resembling a demon, especially in wickedness **2. INTENSE OR FRANTIC** intense, frantic, or wild, as if driven or possessed by a demon —**demonically** /di mónnikli/ *adv.*

demonise *vt.* = demonize

demonism /deémənizəm/ *n.* **1. WORSHIP OF OR BELIEF IN DEMONS** the worship of or belief in demons **2.** = demonology —**demonist** *n.*

demonize /deémə nīz/ (-izes, -izing, -ized), demonise (-ises, -ising, -ised) *vt.* to cause sb or sth to appear evil or wicked in the eyes of others —**demonization** /deémə nī záysh'n/ *n.*

demonolatry /deémə nóllətri/ *n.* worship of demons or of the devil —**demonolater** *n.*

demonology /deémə nólləji/ *n.* the study of demons, especially those that are frequent in folklore of certain societies —**demonological** /deémənə lójjik'l/ *adj.* —**demonologist** /deémə nólləjist/ *n.*

demonstrable /di mónstrəb'l/ *adj.* **1. EASILY SHOWN TO BE SO** so obvious as to be readily provable **2. PROVABLE** capable of being shown to exist or be true [14thC. Directly or via Old French from Latin *demonstrabilis*, from *demonstrare* (see DEMONSTRATE).] —**demonstrability** /di mónstrə bílləti/ *n.* —**demonstrableness** /di món strəb'lnəss/ *n.* —**demonstrably** /-bli/ *adv.*

demonstrate /démmən strayt/ (-strates, -strating, -strated) *v.* **1. *vt.* EXPLAIN WORKINGS** to explain or describe how sth works or how to do sth **2. *vt.* SHOW CONVINCINGLY** to show or prove sth clearly and convincingly **3. *vi.* PROTEST OR SUPPORT SB OR STH** to make a public show as a group for or against an issue, cause, or person, often by marching through the streets [Mid-16thC. From Latin *demonstrat-*, the past participle stem of *demonstrare*, from *monstrare* 'to show', from *monstrum* 'omen' (source of English *monster*).]

demonstration /démmən stráysh'n/ *n.* **1. DISPLAY SHOWING HOW TO DO STH** a display given to others of how sth is done or how sth works **2. CONCLUSIVE PROOF** evidence or proof that allows no doubt as to its validity or soundness **3. GROUP DISPLAY OF OPINION** a public show as a group for or against an issue, cause, or person **4. MIL ATTACK OR SHOW OF FORCE** a show of military force or a movement towards an enemy —**demonstrational** *adj.* —**demonstrationist** *n.*

demonstration sport *n.* a sport that is contested in the Olympics on a trial basis even though it is not a permanent medal sport

demonstrative /di mónstrətiv/ *adj.* **1. OBVIOUSLY AFFECTIONATE** unrestrained in showing love and affection towards sb **2. PROVING** serving to show proof of truth **3. GRAM SPECIFYING WHICH PERSON OR THING** referring to a particular person or thing, e.g. 'this', 'that', 'these', and 'those' ■ *n.* **GRAM WORD SPECIFYING WHICH PERSON OR THING** a demonstrative word or phrase, e.g. 'this', 'that', 'these', or 'those' —**demonstratively** *adv.* —**demonstrativeness** *n.*

demonstrator /démmən straytər/ *n.* **1. SUPPORTER OR PROTESTER** sb who protests or supports sth publicly, usually as a member of a group **2. EXPLAINER OF DEVICES** sb who shows people how do sth or explains how sth works **3. STH DEMONSTRATING FEATURES** sth, e.g. a motor vehicle or an electrical appliance, made available for testing by potential buyers. US term **demo** *n.* 1

demoralize /di mórrə līz/ (**-izes, -izing, -ized**), **demoralise** (**-ises, -ising, -ised**) *vt.* **1. ERODE ANOTHER'S MORALE** to erode or destroy the courage, confidence, or hope of a person or group **2. MAKE DISORDERED** to throw sth into disorder or chaos **3. CORRUPT SB'S MORALS** to corrupt sb's morals —**demoralization** /di mórrə lī záysh'n/ *n.* —**demoralizer** /di mórrə līzər/ *n.*

demos /démmoss/ *n.* **1. POPULACE** the ordinary people of a community or nation (*formal*) **2. HIST GREEK CITY-STATE POPULACE** the common people in an ancient Greek city-state [Late 18thC. From Greek *dēmos* 'district', hence 'people living in a district'.]

demote /dee mṓt/ (**-motes, -moting, -moted**) *vt.* to reduce sb or sth to a lower rank, status, or position [Late 19thC. Blend of DE- and PROMOTE.]

demotic /di móttik/ *adj.* **1. OF THE POPULACE** relating to or involving ordinary people (*formal*) **2. USING SIMPLIFIED HIEROGLYPHICS** relating to a simplified form of hieroglyphics, the writing system used in ancient Egypt [Early 19thC. From Greek *dēmotikos* 'popular, common', literally 'of the people', from *dēmos* (see DEMOS).]

Demotic *n.* **1. MODERN SPOKEN GREEK** the colloquial form of modern Greek, used in conversation and in literature and now adopted as the official variety of the language. ◊ **Katharevusa 2. LATE EGYPTIAN LANGUAGE** the later form of the ancient Egyptian language, written in demotic script, which was current in the first millennium BC —**Demotic** *adj.*

demotion /dee mṓsh'n/ *n.* a reduction in the rank, status, or position of sb or sth

demount /dee mównt/ (**-mounts, -mounting, -mounted**) *vt.* **1. REMOVE DEVICE FROM SUPPORTS** to take a piece of equipment away from its supports **2. DISMANTLE STH** to take sth apart, usually with the intention of reassembling it later

demountable /dee mówntəb'l/ *adj.* **1. REMOVABLE FROM SUPPORTS** used to describe a piece of equipment that can be removed from its supports **2. REMOVABLE FROM CAB OF LORRY** relating to the storage part of a lorry that can be removed from the cab without the use of a crane

demulcent /di múls'nt/ *n.* a substance that is used to soothe irritated or inflamed skin or internal parts of the nose, mouth, or throat. Lanoline and glycerine are demulcents. [Mid-18thC. From Latin *demulcent-*, present participle stem of *demulcere*, literally 'to soothe down', from *mulcere* 'to soothe'.] —**demulcent** *adj.*

demulsify /di múlssi fī/ (**-fies, -fying, -fied**) *vti.* to break an emulsion down permanently into its components, or be broken down permanently —**demulsification** /di múlssifi káysh'n/ *n.* —**demulsifier** /di múlssi fī ər/ *n.*

demur /di múr/ (**-murs, -murring, -murred**) *v.* **1.** *vi.* **SHOW RELUCTANCE TO DO STH** to delay or try to avoid doing sth because of personal reservations or objections ○ *'While I acknowledged it might come to that (the use of force in the Persian Gulf), I demurred, saying it was too early to contemplate such action'.* (George Bush, *A World Transformed*; 1998) **2.** *vi.* **OBJECT MILDLY** to object mildly to sth that you do not want to do but have been asked to do **3.** *vti.* LAW **MAKE LEGAL OBJECTION** to admit the facts of an opposing argument, but object that those facts alone are not by themselves adequate to make the case [13thC. From Old French *demorer* 'to delay, stay', from Latin *demorare*.] —**demurrable** *adj.*

WORD KEY: SYNONYMS

See Synonyms at ***object***.

demure /di myŏŏr/ (**-murer, -murest**) *adj.* **1. LOOKING SHYLY MODEST** looking or behaving in a modest manner with reserve or seriousness **2. AFFECTEDLY SHY OR MODEST** acting in an affectedly shy or modest way [14thC. From the past participle of Old French *demorer* (see DEMUR). The modern meaning evolved via the sense of 'calmness'.] —**demurely** *adv.* —**demureness** *n.*

demurrage /di múrrij/ *n.* **1. DETENTION OF CARGO CARRIER** detention or delay of a cargo carrier during its loading or unloading process, beyond its scheduled time of departure **2. COMPENSATION FOR LOADING OR UNLOADING DELAY** compensation paid when there is a delay in loading or unloading a carrier causing a delay in the carrier's departure [Mid-17thC. From Old French *demo(u)rage*, from *demorer* (see DEMUR).]

demurral /di múrrəl/ *n.* a mild indication of hesitation, refusal, or objection

demurrer /di múrrər/ *n.* LAW a legal objection that admits the facts of an opposing argument but asserts that those facts alone are not adequate to make the case [Early 16thC. From French *demorer* (see DEMUR).]

demy /di mī/ *adj.* used to describe printing paper that is 444.5 mm/17.5 in by 571.5 mm/22.5 in or writing paper that is 393.7 mm/15.5 in by 508 mm/20 in [15thC. Alteration of DEMI-.]

demyelination /dee mī əli náysh'n/ *n.* loss of the fatty covering (**myelin**) of nerve fibres, which is characteristic of multiple sclerosis and other neurological disorders —**demyelinate** /dee mīəli nayt/ *vt.*

demystify /dee místi fī/ (**-fies, -fying, -fied**) *vt.* to remove the mystery surrounding sth, e.g. by explaining it in simple language —**demystification** /daa místifi káysh'n/ *n.* —**demystifier** /dee místi fī ər/ *n.*

demythologize /deemi thóllə jīz/ (**-gizes, -gizing, -gized**), **demythologise** (**-gises, -gising, -gised**) *vt.* to reveal and understand the true character, nature, or meaning of sth by ridding it of all mythical or mysterious aspects —**demythologization** /deemi thóllə jī záysh'n/ *n.* —**demythologizer** /deemi thóllə jīzər/ *n.*

den /den/ *n.* **1. WILD ANIMAL'S LAIR** the hidden home of a wild animal **2. PLACE OF CRIME** a place where illegal or secret activities take place **3. CHILDREN'S HIDEOUT** a secret place where children play **4. QUIET ROOM** a small quiet retreat in a house, especially a study (*dated*) **5.** *US* **ROOM FOR RELAXING** a room in a house where family members and guests relax **6. SQUALID ROOM** a squalid small room or place to live **7.** *US* **CUB SCOUT GROUP** a group of Cub Scouts that is typically made up of eight to ten youths [Old English *denn* 'wild animal's lair', from, ultimately, an Indo-European word meaning 'flat surface']

DEN *abbr.* District Enrolled Nurse

Den. *abbr.* Denmark

denarius /di náiri əss/ (*plural* **-i** /-ri ī/) *n.* **1. OLD ROMAN SILVER COIN** an ancient Roman silver coin originally worth ten asses **2. OLD ROMAN GOLD COIN** an ancient Roman gold coin that was worth 25 silver denarii [14thC. From Latin, literally 'containing ten', from *deni* 'ten at a time'.]

denary /deenəri/ *adj.* relating to a number system, or a number belonging to it, that has ten as its base, as in the decimal system [Mid-19thC. From Latin *denarius* (see DENARIUS).]

denationalize /dee násh'nə līz/ (**-izes, -izing, -ized**), **denationalise** (**-ises, -ising, -ised**) *vt.* **1. SELL STATE-OWNED ASSETS** to sell industries or other major assets owned by the state to private buyers **2. DEPRIVE OF NATIONAL RIGHTS** to deprive a people or nation of national rights and characteristics —**denationalization** /dee nash'nə lī záysh'n/ *n.*

denaturalize /dee náchərə līz/ (**-izes, -izing, -ized**), **denaturalise** (**-ises, -ising, -ised**) *vt.* **1. REVOKE CITIZENSHIP OF** to take away a naturalized citizen's citizenship, e.g. for illegal entry into the country **2. MAKE UNNATURAL** to take away the original nature of sth ○ *once verdant jungles that were denaturalized by defoliants* —**denaturalization** /dee náchərə lī záysh'n/ *n.*

denature /dee náychər/ (**-tures, -turing, -tured**) *vt.* **1. MAKE UNPALATABLE** to make food or drink, especially alcohol, unsuitable for human consumption, by adding poison, dye, or unpleasant flavours **2.** BIOCHEM **MODIFY MOLECULAR STRUCTURE** to change the molecular structure of a protein or nucleic acid by chemical or physical means, so that some of its original biological properties are reduced or lost **3.** PHYS **REMOVE WEAPON POTENTIAL OF NUCLEAR MATERIAL** to make nuclear material unsuitable for use in a weapon by adding an isotope that cannot be split —**denaturant** *n.* —**denaturation** /dee náychə ráysh'n/ *n.*

denazify /dee naatsi fī/ (**-fies, -fying, -fied**) *vt.* to remove connection with or hint of Nazism from sth, or to remove Nazis from official positions [Mid-20thC. Coined from DE- + NAZI + -FY.] —**denazification** /dee naatsifi káysh'n/ *n.*

Denbighshire /dénbishər/ county in northeastern Wales. It was divided between the counties of Clywd and Gwynedd between 1974 and 1994. Population: 91,600 (1995).

Dench /dench/, **Dame Judi** (*b.* 1934) British actor. She has played leading roles with Britain's major stage companies and in award-winning films such as *Mrs Brown* (1997). She won an Academy Award for her performance in *Shakepeare in Love* (1999). Full name **Dame Judith Olivia Dench**

dendr- *prefix.* = **dendro-**

dendri- *prefix.* = **dendro-**

dendriform /déndri fawrm/ *adj.* shaped like a tree

dendrite /dén drīt/ *n.* **1.** MINERALS **TREE-SHAPED MINERAL** a mineral that crystallizes in the shape of a tree or branch **2.** ANAT **BRANCHED EXTENSION OF NERVE CELL** a branched extension of a nerve cell (**neuron**) that receives electrical signals from other neurons and conducts those signals to the cell body [Early 18thC. Directly or via French from Greek *dendritēs* 'of a tree', from *dendron* 'tree'.] —**dendritic** /den dríttik/ *adj.* —**dendritical** /-tik'l/ *adj.* —**dendritically** /-tikli/ *adv.*

dendro- *prefix.* tree, treelike ○ *dendrology* ○ *dendrite* [From Greek *dendron*. Ultimately from an Indo-European base meaning 'to be solid', which is also the ancestor of English *tree*, *deodar*, and *druid*.]

dendrochronology /dén drōkrə nólləji/ *n.* the study of the annual growth rings in trees or wooden objects, especially as a way of dating wooden remains or determining past climatic conditions —**dendrochronological** /dén drō krónnə lójjik'l/ *adj.* —**dendrochronologist** /dén drōkrə nólləjist/ *n.*

dendrogram /déndrə gram/ *n.* a diagram showing the relationships of items arranged like the branches of a tree

dendroid /dén droyd/, **dendroidal** /den dróyd'l/ *adj.* **1. WITH STEM RESEMBLING TREE TRUNK** used to describe plants with an erect main stem like a tree trunk **2. MULTIBRANCHED** used to describe plants with many branches, like a tree **3. RESEMBLING A TREE** generally resembling a tree in shape or form

dendrology /den drólləji/ *n.* the study of trees and other woody plants —**dendrologic** /déndrə lójjik/ *adj.* —**dendrological** /-lójjik'l/ *adj.* —**dendrologist** /den drólla jist/ *n.* —**dendrologous** *adj.*

dendron /dén dron/ *n.* = **dendrite** *n.* 2 (*dated*) [Late 19thC. Coined from DENDRITE + -ON.]

dene /deen/ *n.* a narrow wooded valley (*often used in placenames*) [Old English *denu* 'valley', from prehistoric Germanic (ancestor of English *den*)]

Dene /dénni, dénnay/ *npl.* the First Nations people of the Northwest Territories in Canada [Late 19thC. Via Canadian French from Athabaskan.]

denegation /dénni gáysh'n/ *n.* a refusal to accede to or grant sth that is asked for (*archaic*) [15thC. Via French *dénégation* from the late Latin stem *denegation-*, from *negare* (see NEGATE).]

dene hole *n.* in chalky areas of southern England and northern France, an ancient excavation consisting of a deep shaft leading to one or more cavities resembling rooms [*Dene* of uncertain origin: perhaps from DANE, influenced by *dene* 'beach, sand-hill' and *den*]

denervate /dee núr vayt, dénnər vayt/ (**-vates, -vating, -vated**) *vt.* to deprive an organ or body part of nerves, either by cutting them or by blocking them with drugs, e.g. to control pain

denervation /dee nur váysh'n/ *n.* interruption in nerve supply to muscles or skin, with loss of motion and sensation, caused by surgical or drug treatment, e.g. to control pain

Deneuve /də nṓv/, **Catherine** (*b.* 1943) French film actor. Her films include *Repulsion* (1965) and *Belle de Jour* (1967). Born **Catherine Dorléac**

DEng. *abbr.* Doctor of Engineering

dengue /déng gi, -gay/, **dengue fever** *n.* a tropical disease caused by a virus that is transmitted by mosquitoes and marked by high fever, rash, headache, and severe muscle and joint pains [Early 19thC. From West Indian Spanish, of uncertain origin: perhaps from, ultimately, Kiswahili.]

Deng Xiaoping

Popperfoto

Deng Xiaoping /dúng shów píng/ (1904–97) Chinese Communist leader. Despite a turbulent relationship with the Communist Party, he became its leader in 1978. He introduced reforms that led to greater economic freedom in China.

deniable /di nî əb'l/ adj. referring to sth that can be disclaimed or declared untrue —**deniably** adv.

denial /di nî əl/ n. **1.** DISAVOWAL a statement saying that sth is not true or not correct **2.** REFUSAL TO GRANT STH a refusal to allow people to have sth that they want or that they believe they have a right to **3.** REFUSAL TO ACKNOWLEDGE EXISTENCE OF STH an inability or a refusal to admit that sth exists **4.** PSYCHOL REFUSAL TO FACE UNPLEASANT FACTS a state of mind marked by a refusal or an inability to recognize and deal with a serious personal problem ○ *She's in denial.* **5.** LAW OPPOSITION TO AN ALLEGATION in a court of law, saying that you did not do sth that you are accused of

denier /dénni ər/ n. **1.** TEXTILES MEASURE OF FIBRE FINENESS a unit of fineness of silk and some artificial fibres, such as nylon, equal to one gram per 9,000 metres of yarn. Now largely superseded by other units. **2.** OLD SILVER COIN a small silver coin used in several European countries between the 8th and 18th centuries [15thC. Via Old French from Latin *denarius* (see DENARIUS).]

denigrate /dénni grayt/ (**-grates, -grating, -grated**) vt. **1.** DEFAME to defame sb's character or reputation **2.** DISPARAGE AND BELITTLE to disparage or criticize sb or sth, to lower sb's self-esteem or to make sth seem unimportant **3.** CRITICIZE HARSHLY to criticize sth harshly, while attempting to make others think it has no importance [15thC. From Latin *denigrat-*, the past participle of stem *denigrare*, literally 'to blacken completely', from *niger* 'black'.] —**denigration** /dénni gráysh'n/ n. —**denigrator** /dénni graytər/ n.

— **WORD KEY: USAGE** —

Denigrate In its best-established sense **denigrate** means 'ruin a reputation' or 'defame'. However, it is now often found in sentences like *I don't mean to denigrate the problem*, where its meaning is more like "belittle". In this, it is following in the footsteps of *deprecate*, whose traditional meaning is "express disapproval of", but which, particularly in *self-deprecating*, has taken on the additional sense of "belittle".

denim /dénnim/ n. JEANS FABRIC a hard-wearing woven cotton cloth that is typically used to make jeans ■ **denims** npl. DENIM GARMENTS clothes made of denim, especially jeans, jackets, shirts, or skirts [Late 17thC. From French (*serge*) *de Nîmes*, literally '(serge) of Nîmes', the town in France where it was primarily manufactured.]

De Niro /də neêrō/, **Robert** (b. 1943) US actor. He has won Academy Awards for *The Godfather II* (1974) and *Raging Bull* (1980).

denitrate /dee nî trayt/ (**-trates, -trating, -trated**) vti. to remove a nitro or nitrate group, nitrogen compound, or nitrous acid from a chemical compound, or lose such components —**denitration** /dée nî tráysh'n/ n.

denitrify /dee nîtri fî/ (**-fies, -fying, -fied**) vt. **1.** REMOVE NITROGEN FROM SUBSTANCE to remove nitrogen or a nitrogen compound from a substance **2.** CONVERT NITRATES to convert nitrates to nitrites, ammonia, and nitrogen —**denitrification** /dee nîtrifi káysh'n/ n.

denizen /dénniz'n/ n. **1.** RESIDENT OF PLACE sb who lives in a particular place or area **2.** HABITUAL VISITOR TO PLACE a habitual visitor to a place ○ *denizens of*

cyberspace chat rooms **3.** FOREIGNER WITH RIGHTS OF RESIDENCE sb who has taken up permanent residence in a foreign country and is given some rights there **4.** ECOL NONNATIVE PLANT OR ANIMAL a nonnative plant or animal that grows or lives in an area [15thC. From Anglo-Norman *deinzein*, from Old French *deinz* 'inside', from Latin *de intus*, literally 'from inside'.]

Denmark

Denmark /dén maark/ smallest country in Scandinavia, comprising the Jutland peninsula and about 480 islands. Language: Danish. Currency: krone. Capital: Copenhagen. Population: 5,305,048 (1997). Area: 43,094 sq. km/16,639 sq. mi. Official name **Kingdom of Denmark**

Denning /dénning/, **Alfred, Baron Denning of White-church** (1899–1999) British judge. In 1963 he led the inquiry into John Profumo's resignation as secretary of state for war.

Dennis /dénniss/, **C. J.** (1876–1938) Australian writer. He is the author of humorous verse written in colloquial language. His best-known work is *The Songs of a Sentimental Bloke* (1915). Full name **Clarence Michael James Dennis**

denom. abbr. RELIG denomination

denominal /di nómminəl/ adj. used to describe parts of speech that are formed from or have the same form as a noun, e.g. the verb 'to butter'

denominate /di nómmi nayt/ (**-nates, -nating, -nated**) vt. **1.** EXPRESS IN MONETARY UNITS to define sth in terms of a specific unit of currency **2.** GIVE NAME TO to give sth a particular name or description (*formal*) [Mid-16thC. From Latin *denominat-*, the past participle stem of *denominare*, literally 'to name completely', from *nominare* 'to name'.] —**denominable** /di nómminəb'l/ adj.

denomination /di nómmi náysh'n/ n. **1.** RELIG RELIGIOUS GROUPING a religious grouping within a faith, e.g. a section of the Christian church that has specific beliefs and practices that differ from those of other groupings and its own system of organization **2.** UNIT OF MONETARY VALUE a unit in the scale of value (especially monetary value), weight, measure, or size **3.** NAME OR DESIGNATION a name or designation given to a class, group, or type

denominational /di nómmi náysh'nəl/ adj. relating to a religious grouping within a faith —**denominationally** adv.

denominative /di nómminətiv/ adj. denominal (*dated*) —**denominative** n. —**denominatively** adv.

denominator /di nómmi naytər/ n. **1.** MATH NUMBER BELOW LINE IN FRACTION the number below the line in a fraction, which indicates the number of parts making up the whole **2.** COMMON CHARACTERISTIC sth held in common **3.** AVERAGE LEVEL an average standard, degree, or level of quality or taste

denotation /deenō táysh'n/ n. **1.** LING BASIC MEANING the most specific or literal meaning of a word, as opposed to its figurative senses or connotations **2.** LOGIC REFERENCE OF TERM the reference of a term in logic

denotative /di nôtətiv/ adj. designating or showing sth —**denotatively** adv.

denote /di nôt/ (**-notes, -noting, -noted**) vt. **1.** MEAN to have sth as a specified meaning ○ *The name actually denotes 'lightning bolt' in Italian.* **2.** REFER TO to designate or refer to sb or sth specified ○ *The term 'caregiver' will be used to denote those providing unpaid family care.* **3.** SIGNIFY to be a sign or representation of sth ○ *The specks of light denote*

planets. [Late 16thC. Via French *dénoter* from Latin *denotare* 'to mark completely', from *notare* 'to mark' (see NOTATION).] —**denotive** adj.

denouement /day noō moN/ (*plural* **-ments**) n. a final part in which everything is made clear and no questions or surprises remain (*formal*) [Mid-18thC. From French, from *dénouer* 'to untie', from *nouer* 'to tie', from, ultimately, Latin *nodus* 'knot' (see NODE).]

denounce /di nównss/ (**-nounces, -nouncing, -nounced**) vt. **1.** CRITICIZE PUBLICLY AND HARSHLY to express harsh criticism or condemnation of sth or sb, usually in public **2.** ACCUSE PUBLICLY to accuse sb publicly of sth such as disloyalty, or inform against sb **3.** ANNOUNCE TERMINATION OF to make a formal announcement of the end of a treaty or other agreement (*formal*) [14thC. Via Old French *denoncier* from Latin *denuntiare*, from *nuntiare* 'to proclaim, announce', from *nuntius* 'messenger', of uncertain origin.] —**denouncement** n. —**denouncer** n.

— **WORD KEY: SYNONYMS** —
See Synonyms at *disapprove*.

de novo /di nôvō/ adv. LAW anew, afresh, or over again from the beginning [Mid-16thC. From Latin, literally 'from new'.]

Denpasar /den paâ saar/ city in Indonesia and capital of the island province of Bali, located near Bali's southernmost point. Population: 367,000 (1993).

dense /denss/ (**denser, densest**) adj. **1.** TIGHTLY PACKED so close together that there is not much sense of room or open space **2.** VERY THICK so thick that it is difficult or impossible to see through **3.** PHYS WITH HIGH MASS with a relatively high mass per unit volume **4.** HARD TO PENETRATE INTELLECTUALLY so complex and intricate that it is difficult to assimilate and understand **5.** SLOW TO LEARN OR UNDERSTAND lacking the ability to learn and understand quickly (*disapproving*) [15thC. Directly or via French from Latin *densus* 'thick'.] —**densely** adv. —**denseness** n.

densimeter /den símmitər/ n. an instrument that measures density or specific gravity [Mid-19thC. Coined from Latin *densus* 'dense' + -METER.] —**densimetric** /dénssi méttrik/ adj. —**densimetry** /den símmətri/ n.

densitometer /dénssi tómmitər/ n. **1.** DEVICE MEASURING OPTICAL DENSITY an instrument for measuring optical density, e.g. that of a photographic negative **2.** = densimeter [Early 20thC. Coined from DENSITY + -METER.] —**densitometric** /dénssitə méttrik/ adj. —**densitometry** /dénssi tómmətri/ n.

density /dénssəti/ (*plural* **-ties**) n. **1.** HOW FULL AN AREA IS concentration of people or things within an area in relation to its size **2.** PHYS RELATIVE MASS a measure of a quantity such as mass or electric charge per unit volume. Symbol ρ **3.** ELEC = charge density **4.** ELEC = current density

density function n. STATS = probability density function n. 2

dent /dent/ v. (**dents, denting, dented**) **1.** vti. MAKE DEPRESSION BY HITTING to make a shallow depression in the surface of sth by hitting it or putting pressure on it **2.** vt. HARM STH ABSTRACT to do nonphysical, usually minor, damage to sth ○ *His reputation was somewhat dented.* ■ n. **1.** BENT AREA IN STH a shallow depression in the surface of sth that is made by hitting it or putting pressure on it **2.** NONPHYSICAL DAMAGE nonphysical, usually minor, damage, e.g. to sb's reputation **3.** ADVANCE progress in reaching a goal (*informal*) ○ *a dent in the team's lead* **4.** REDUCTION a reduction in an amount of sth such as resources (*informal*) ○ *a dent in the budget* [13thC. Variant of DINT 'stroke, blow'; hence, 'indentation made by blow'.]

dent. abbr. **1.** dental **2.** dentistry

dent- prefix. = denti- (used before vowels)

dental /dént'l/ adj. **1.** OF DENTISTRY relating to or used in dentistry **2.** OF TEETH relating or belonging to the teeth **3.** DENT NEAR TOOTH affecting or located in or near a tooth ○ *dental abscess* **4.** PHON MADE BY TONGUE AND TEETH used to describe a consonant that is formed by placing the tongue against the back of the top front teeth [Late 16thC. From late Latin *dentalis*, from the Latin stem *dent-* 'tooth' (see DENTIST).]

dental caries n. decay of teeth that is caused by the action of acid-forming bacteria and improper dental care

dental floss *n.* thread that is used to remove food and plaque from between the teeth

dental hygiene *n.* the care people take of their teeth and gums to prevent tooth and gum disease

dental hygienist *n.* sb who provides certain kinds of dental care under the supervision of a dentist, especially cleaning and scaling teeth

dental nurse *n.* a dentist's assistant, who prepares materials and equipment and helps the dentist during the treatment of a patient

dental surgeon *n.* = dentist (*formal*)

dental technician *n.* sb trained to make dental appliances such as caps, dentures, and bridges

dentate /dén tayt/ *adj.* edged with pointed or tooth-shaped projections [15thC. From Latin *dentatus*, from the stem *dent-* 'tooth' (see DENTIST).] —**dentately** *adv.*

dentation /den táysh'n/ *n.* a pointed or tooth-shaped projection on sth such as a leaf

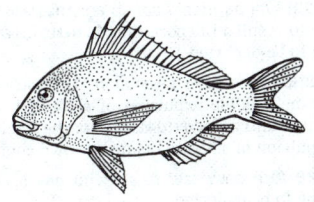

Dentex

dentex /dén teks/ (*plural* -**texes** *or* -**tex**) *n.* a red game fish, about 1.2 m/4 ft long, that is found in seas off the Cape of Good Hope, South Africa. Latin name: *Dentex rupestris*. [Mid-19thC. Via modern Latin from Latin, name of a type of fish.]

denti- *prefix.* tooth, dental ○ *dentiform* [From Latin *dent-*, the stem of *dens*. Ultimately from an Indo-European word that is also the ancestor of English *tooth*, *tusk*, *indent*, and *dandelion*.]

denticle /déntik'l/ *n.* **1.** BIOL SMALL TOOTH-SHAPED PART a small tooth or tooth-shaped projection **2.** ZOOL SMALL FISH SCALE a small tooth-shaped scale with a projecting spine, typical of cartilaginous fish [15thC. From Latin *denticulus*, literally 'small tooth', from the stem *dent-* 'tooth' (see DENTIST).] —**denticular** /den tíkyoōlər/ *adj.*

denticulate /den tíkyoōlət, -layt/ *adj.* **1.** WITH FINE TOOTH-SHAPED PROJECTIONS with fine teeth or pointed projections **2.** ARCHIT DECORATED WITH TOOTH-SHAPED BLOCKS decorated with small rectangular blocks (**dentils**) that look like a row of teeth [Mid-17thC. From Latin *denticulatus*, from *denticulus* (see DENTICLE).] —**denticulately** *adv.*

dentiform /dénti fawrm/ *adj.* shaped like a tooth

dentifrice /déntifriss/ *n.* a paste or similar compound for cleaning teeth [15thC. Via French from Latin *dentifricium*, from the stem *dent-* 'tooth' (see DENTIST) + *fricare* 'to rub'.]

dentil /déntil/ *n.* ARCHIT a rectangular block that is arranged with others to look like a row of teeth, used as a form of architectural decoration [Late 16thC. Via either Italian *dentello* or obsolete French *dentille*, literally 'small tooth', from, ultimately, the Latin stem *dent-* 'tooth' (see DENTIST).]

dentilingual /dénti líng gwəl/ *adj.* pronounced or articulated with the tongue touching the teeth on the top jaw

dentine /dén teen/, **dentin** /-tin/ *n.* the part of a tooth that is hard, contains calcium, lies underneath the enamel, and surrounds the pulp and root canals [Mid-19thC. Coined from the Latin stem *dent-* 'tooth' (see DENTIST) + -INE.] —**dentinal** /-tinəl/ *adj.*

dentist /déntist/ *n.* sb trained and licensed to practise general dentistry or a branch of dentistry such as orthodontics or dental surgery [Mid-18thC. From French *dentiste*, from *dent* 'tooth', from the Latin stem

dent-. Ultimately from an Indo-European word that is also the ancestor of English *tooth*.]

dentistry /déntistri/ *n.* the medical science concerned with the prevention and treatment of tooth and gum disorders and diseases

dentition /den tísh'n/ *n.* **1.** ARRAY OF TEETH the type, number, and arrangement of a set of teeth **2.** DEVELOPING OF TEETH the process of developing and cutting new teeth [Late 16thC. From the Latin stem *dent-* 'tooth' (see DENTIST).]

Denton /déntən/ city in northern Texas, north of Fort Worth and northwest of Dallas. Population: 73,483 (1996).

denture /dénchər/ *n.* a partial or complete set of artificial teeth for the upper or lower jaw, usually attached to a plate [Late 19thC. From French, from *dent* 'tooth' (see DENTIST).]

denuclearize /dee nyoōkli ə rīz/ (-**izes**, -**izing**, -**ized**), **denuclearise** (-**ises**, -**ising**, -**ised**) *vt.* to remove, ban, or eliminate nuclear weapons or nuclear power sources from a place, industry, or organization —**denuclearization** /dee nyoōkli ə rī záysh'n/ *n.*

denude /di nyoōd/ (-**nudes**, -**nuding**, -**nuded**) *vt.* **1.** STRIP BARE to strip sb or sth bare **2.** ECOL STRIP AWAY GROUND COVER to strip away the vegetation that covers an area **3.** GEOL STRIP BY EROSION to remove soil from an area or expose underlying layers of rock by weathering and erosion [15thC. From Latin *denudare*, literally 'to strip away', from *nudare* 'to strip', from *nudus* 'nude' (see NUDE).] —**denudation** /deé nyoo dáysh'n/ *n.* —**denuder** /di nyoōdər/ *n.*

denumerable /di nyoómərəb'l/ *adj.* able to form a one-to-one correspondence with the positive integers [Early 20thC. Formed from late Latin *denumerare* 'to count out', from Latin *numerare* 'to number' (see NUMERATION).] —**denumerability** /di nyoōmərə bílləti/ *n.* —**denumerably** /di nyoómərəbli/ *adv.*

denunciate /di núnssi ayt/ (-**ates**, -**ating**, -**ated**) *vt.* to accuse or condemn sb or sth publicly (*formal*) [Late 16thC. From the medieval Latin stem *denunciat-*, from, ultimately, Latin *denuntiare* 'to denounce' (see DENOUNCE).]

denunciation /di núnssi áysh'n/ *n.* a public accusation or condemnation of sth or sb

Denver /dénvər/ capital city and commercial centre of the US state of Colorado, in the Rocky Mountains. Population: 467,610 (1990).

Denver boot *n.* *US* = wheel clamp [Named after DENVER, one of the first cities to adopt the clamp]

deny /di ní/ (-**nies**, -**nying**, -**nied**) *v.* **1.** *vt.* SAY STH IS NOT TRUE to declare that sth is not true or not the case **2.** *vt.* REFUSE to refuse sth to sb **3.** *vt.* REFUSE TO ACKNOWLEDGE to refuse to acknowledge sth **4.** *vr.* NOT ALLOW YOURSELF to refuse to gratify your needs or desires [13thC. Via Old French *deneier* from Latin *denegare*, literally 'to negate completely', from *negare* 'to deny'.]

deoch an doris /dókh ən dórriss, dyókh-/ *n.* Scotland a parting drink [From Scots Gaelic *deoch an doruis* 'a drink at the door']

deodar /deé ō daar/ (*plural* -**dars** *or* -**dar**) *n.* **1.** HIMALAYAN CEDAR TREE a Himalayan cedar with dark blue-green leaves and drooping branches, that is highly valued as a timber tree in India. Latin name: *Cedrus deodara*. **2.** DEODAR WOOD the hard sweet-smelling wood of the deodar [Early 19thC. Via Hindi *deodār* from Sanskrit *devadāru*, literally 'divine wood' (perhaps because of its durability).]

deodorant /di ōdərənt/ *n.* **1.** BODY ODOUR MASK a spray, cream, or liquid that people apply under their arms to mask body odour **2.** SUBSTANCE TO DISGUISE SMELLS a substance that is used to disguise unpleasant smells

deodorize /di ōdə rīz/ (-**izes**, -**izing**, -**ized**), **deodorise** (-**ises**, -**ising**, -**ised**) *vt.* to disguise or eliminate unpleasant smells —**deodorization** /di ōdə rī záysh'n/ *n.* —**deodorizer** *n.*

Deo gratias /dáy ō gráati əss/ *interj.* thanks be to God, used in various Christian choral and liturgical contexts [From Latin, literally 'thanks to God']

deontic /di óntik/ *adj.* relating to the concept of moral obligation [Mid-19thC. Formed from Greek *deont-*, present participle stem of *dein* 'to be wanting, be needful'.]

deontological /di óntə lójjik'l/ *adj.* relating to philosophical theories that state that the moral content of an action is not wholly dependent on its consequences —**deontologically** *adv.*

deontology /deé on tólləji/ *n.* the study of what is obligatory, permissible, right, or wrong, in moral terms [Early 19thC. Coined from Greek *deont-*, the present participle stem of *dein* 'to be wanting, be needful' + -LOGY.] —**deontologist** *n.*

deorbit /dee áwrbit/ (-**bits**, -**biting**, -**bited**) *vti.* to put sth out of orbit or go out of orbit

Deo volente /dáy ō və lénti/ *interj.* God willing [From Latin, 'God willing']

deoxidize /dee óksi dīz/ (-**dizes**, -**dizing**, -**dized**), **deoxidise** (-**dises**, -**dising**, -**dised**) *vt.* **1.** REMOVE OXYGEN FROM MOLECULE to remove the oxygen from a compound or molecule **2.** = reduce —**deoxidization** /dee óksi dī záysh'n/ *n.* —**deoxidizer** /dee óksi dīzər/ *n.*

deoxy- *prefix.* containing less oxygen than a related compound ○ *deoxyribose* [From DE- + OXY-]

deoxygenate /dee óksijə nayt/ (-**ates**, -**ating**, -**ated**) *vt.* to remove dissolved oxygen from a substance —**deoxygenation** /dee óksijə náysh'n/ *n.*

deoxygenize /dee óksijə nīz/ (-**izes**, -**izing**, -**ized**), **deoxygenise** (-**ises**, -**ising**, -**ised**) *vt.* = deoxygenate

deoxyribonuclease /deé oksi ríbō nyoōkli ayz/ *n.* full form of **DNAase** [Mid-20thC. Formed from DE-OXYRIBONUCLEIC ACID.]

deoxyribonucleic acid /deé oksi ríbō nyoo kláyik-, -kláy-/ *n.* full form of **DNA** [Mid-20thC. Coined from DEOXYRIBOSE + NUCLEIC.]

deoxyribonucleotide /deé oksi ríbō nyoōkli ə tīd/ *n.* a nucleotide composed of deoxyribose, a phosphate group and a base, that is a component of DNA [Mid-20thC. Coined from DEOXYRIBOSE + NUCLEOTIDE.]

deoxyribose /deé oksi ríbōss/ *n.* a five-carbon simple sugar that is a structural component of DNA [Mid-20thC. Coined from deoxy- 'having fewer oxygen atoms' (from DE- + OXY-) + RIBOSE.]

dep. *abbr.* **1.** department **2.** departs **3.** departure **4.** GRAM deponent **5.** deposed **6.** deposit **7.** depot **8.** dep., Dep. deputy

Depardieu /dé paar djő/, **Gérard** (b. 1948) French actor. His films include *The Last Metro* (1980), *Cyrano de Bergerac* (1990), and *Green Card* (1990).

depart /di paárt/ (-**parts**, -**parting**, -**parted**) *v.* **1.** *vi.* SET OFF to leave, especially at the beginning of a journey **2.** *vi.* CHANGE to change or vary from a pattern **3.** *vt.* DIE to end your life (*formal*) ○ *depart this life* [13thC. From French *départir* 'to end your life', from, ultimately, Latin *partire* 'to divide into parts' (the original sense of English *depart*), from *pars* 'part'.]

departed /di paártid/ *adj.* DEAD having died (*formal or literary*) ■ *n.* (*plural* -**ed**) DEAD PERSON sb who has died especially recently (*formal or literary*)

— WORD KEY: SYNONYMS —

See Synonyms at **dead**.

department /di paártmənt/ *n.* **1.** SECTION OF ORGANIZATION a specialized section of a large organization such as a university or store **2.** POL PART OF GOVERNMENT a major division of government that is responsible for dealing with a particular area of policy or administration **3.** SPECIALITY sb's speciality or particular area of responsibility (*informal*) **4.** CATEGORY a specified quantifiable or qualifiable category (*informal*) **5.** POL FRENCH DISTRICT an administrative district in France

departmental /deé paart mént'l/ *adj.* relating to or for a department in a government or an organization —**departmentally** *adv.*

departmentalism /deé paart mént'lizəm/ *n.* **1.** POLICY OF MAKING DEPARTMENTS the division of organizations into departments, particularly as a deliberate policy that is taken to excess **2.** TENDENCY TO CONSIDER ONLY OWN DEPARTMENT the tendency of government departments to follow their own interests

departmentalize /deé paart mént'l īz/ (-**izes**, -**izing**, -**ized**), **departmentalise** (-**ises**, -**ising**, -**ised**) *vt.* to divide an organization into departments, especially as a

department store

policy or to an excessive extent —**departmentalization** /dèe paart mént'l ɪ záysh'n/ n.

department store n. a large store that sells a wide range of goods in separate departments

departure /di páarchər/ n. **1.** SETTING OFF the action of setting off on a journey **2.** CHANGE FROM USUAL a change from the usual or expected way **3.** COURSE a course of action or the beginning of one **4.** SAILING EAST OR WEST TRAVEL the distance travelled due east or west by a ship

departure lounge n. an area where departing passengers can wait until their aircraft or other transport is ready

depasture /dèe páaschər/ (-tures, -turing, -tured) vt. **1.** = overgraze **2.** PUT ANIMALS TO PASTURE to allow animals to graze on a particular area

depauperate /di páwpərət/ adj. **1.** NOT FULLY GROWN less than fully grown or developed **2.** LACKING SPECIES VARIETY lacking or depleted in the variety of plant or animal species [Mid-19thC. From medieval Latin depauperatus, the past participle of depauperare 'to impoverish', from Latin pauper (see PAUPER).]

depend /di pénd/ (-pends, -pending, -pended) vi. **1.** BE CONTINGENT to be affected or decided by other factors **2.** VARY to vary according to the circumstances **3.** HANG DOWN to hang down or be suspended from sth (archaic) [15thC. Via French dépendre from Latin dependere, literally 'to hang down', from pendere 'to hang'.] **depend on, depend upon** vt. **1.** REQUIRE to need sth in order to exist or survive **2.** RELY ON to have complete confidence in sb or sth

dependable /di péndəb'l/ adj. able to be trusted to act in the way required or expected —**dependability** /di péndə bílləti/ n. —**dependably** /di péndəbli/ adv.

dependant /di péndənt/ n. a family member or other person who is supported financially by another, especially one living in the same house. US term **dependent**

dependence /di péndənss/ n. **1.** NEED FOR STH a need for sth or sb to be available in order to exist or survive ○ financial dependence ○ dependence on public transport **2.** PHYSICAL OR PSYCHOLOGICAL NEED a physical or psychological need to use a drug or other substance regularly, despite the fact that it is likely to have a damaging effect

dependency /di péndənssi/ (plural -cies) n. **1.** POL TERRITORY a country or state that belongs to another non-adjacent country **2.** ARCHIT LESSER BUILDING a building near to and associated with a larger main building **3.** = dependence

dependency theory n. POL a theory of international relations that major states influence other states though their economic power

dependent /di péndənt/ adj. **1.** NOT SELF-RELIANT not able to live without support from other people, especially financial support from a parent or child **2.** PSYCHOL NEEDING STH needing to use sth, especially a drug (usually used in combination) **3.** CONTINGENT affected or decided by stated factors or circumstances (often used in combination) ○ age-dependent **4.** SUSPENDED hanging down (archaic or literary) ■ n. US = dependant —**dependently** adv.

dependent clause n. = subordinate clause

dependent variable n. an element in a mathematical expression that changes its value according to the value of other elements present

depersonalization /dèe púrss'nəl ɪ záysh'n/, **depersonalisation** n. **1.** MAKING IMPERSONAL a process or act of depersonalizing sb or sth **2.** PSYCHOL ALIENATED STATE a psychological state in which sb loses a sense of personal identity and of the reality of the world

depersonalize /dèe púrss'nəl ɪz/ (-izes, -izing, -ized), **depersonalise** (-ises, -ising, -ised) vt. **1.** MAKE IMPERSONAL to take away or omit personal qualities from sb or sth **2.** PSYCHOL ALIENATE SB to make sb lose a sense of personal identity and of the reality of the world

depict /di píkt/ (-picts, -picting, -picted) vt. **1.** PORTRAY to describe or portray sth in words **2.** ARTS SHOW IN A PICTURE to show sth in a picture, painting, or sculpture [15thC. From Latin depict-, the past participle stem of depingere 'to portray', from pingere 'to paint'.] —**depicter** n. —**depictive** adj.

depiction /di píksh'n/ n. a picture, description, or other representation of sth

depicture /di píkchər/ (-tures, -turing, -tured) vt. to depict (archaic) [Late 16thC. Formed from DE- + PICTURE.]

depigmentation /dèe pígmən táysh'n/ n. partial or total absence of the body colouring pigment melanin, especially in the skin, hair, and eyes

depilate /déppi layt/ (-lates, -lating, -lated) vti. to remove hair from the body, usually from the legs or underarms [Mid-16thC. From Latin depilare, from pilus 'hair'.] —**depilator** n.

depilation /déppi láysh'n/ n. the removal of hair, including its roots, from the body or from hides or leather

depilatory /di píllətəri/ adj. HAIR-REMOVING used for removing hair from the body ■ n. (plural -ries) HAIR REMOVER an agent or substance that can be used to remove hair from the body

deplane /dèe pláyn/ (-planes, -planing, -planed) vi. US, Can to disembark from an aeroplane

deplete /di pléet/ (-pletes, -pleting, -pleted) vt. **1.** REDUCE to use up or reduce sth, e.g. supplies, resources, or energy **2.** EMPTY to empty sth [Early 19thC. From Latin deplet-, the past participle stem of deplere 'to empty out', literally 'to un-fill', from plere 'to fill'.] —**depletable** adj. —**depletion** /di pléesh'n/ n. —**depletive** adj.

depleted uranium n. uranium containing an abnormally low amount of the U-235 isotope, usually as a result of having been used as fuel in a nuclear reactor

depletion layer n. a layer in a semiconductor that has few charge carriers transporting electric charge between zones of different conductivity

deplorable /di pláwrəb'l/ adj. **1.** EXTREMELY UNACCEPTABLE worthy of severe condemnation **2.** WRETCHED wretched because of neglect, poverty, or other misfortune —**deplorableness** /di pláwrə bíllati/ n. —**deplorableness** /di pláwrəb'lnəss/ n. —**deplorably** /-əbli/ adv.

deplore /di pláwr/ (-plores, -ploring, -plored) vt. **1.** FIND EXTREMELY UNACCEPTABLE to condemn sth or disapprove of it strongly **2.** REGRET to regret or feel grief about sth [Mid-16thC. Via French déplorer or Italian deplorare from Latin deplorare 'to lament, regret', from plorare 'to wail' (source also of English implore).] —**deplorer** n. —**deploringly** adv.

—————— WORD KEY: SYNONYMS ——————
See Synonyms at **disapprove**.

deploy /di plóy/ (-ploys, -ploying, -ployed) v. **1.** vti. MIL READY MILITARY FORCE to position troops, weapons, or resources in a specific area in readiness for action, or take up position in this way **2.** vt. USE to put sth to use [15thC. Via French déployer from Latin displicare, literally 'to unfold', from plicare (see PLY².)] —**deployable** adj. —**deployer** n.

deployment /di plóymənt/ n. the act of deploying troops, resources, or equipment

deplume /dèe plóom/ (-plumes, -pluming, -plumed) vt. to remove the feathers from a bird [15thC. Via French déplumer from medieval Latin deplumare, from Latin pluma (see PLUME).] —**deplumation** /dèe ploo máysh'n/ n.

depolarize /dèe pôlə rīz/ (-izes, -izing, -ized), **depolarise** (-ises, -ising, -ised) vti. to remove or lose polarization or polarity —**depolarization** /dèe pôlə rɪ záysh'n/ n. —**depolarizer** /dèe pôlə rīzər/ n.

depoliticize /dèepə lítti sīz/ (-cizes, -cizing, -cized), **depoliticise** (-cises, -cising, -cised) vt. to remove the political aspect of sth —**depoliticization** /dèepə lítti sɪ záysh'n/ n.

depollution /dèepə lóosh'n/ n. the removal of pollution from sth —**depollute** /-lóot/ vt.

depolymerize /dèe póllimə rīz/ (-izes, -izing, -ized), **depolymerise** (-ises, -ising, -ised) vti. to break down a polymer into simpler monomers or to undergo this process —**depolymerization** /dèe póllimə rɪ záysh'n/ n.

depone /di pôn/ (-pones, -poning, -poned) vti. LAW to testify or declare sth under oath [15thC. From medieval Latin deponere 'to testify' from Latin, 'to put down' from ponere (see DEPOSE).]

deponent /di pônənt/ n. **1.** LAW TESTIFYING WITNESS sb who makes an affidavit or who testifies under oath **2.** GRAM DEPONENT VERB a deponent verb ■ adj. GRAM PASSIVE AND ACTIVE inflecting like a passive verb but active in meaning

depopulate /dèe póppyoö layt/ (-lates, -lating, -lated) vt. to cause a reduction in the number of residents in an area through, e.g. disease, war, famine, or enforced relocation [Mid-16thC. From Latin depopulare, 'to ravage completely', later 'to reduce in population', from populari 'to lay waste', from populus (see PEOPLE).] —**depopulation** /dèe póppyoö láysh'n/ n. —**depopulator** /de póppyoö laytər/ n.

deport¹ /di páwrt/ (-ports, -porting, -ported) vt. **1.** FORCIBLY REPATRIATE to force a foreign national to leave a country **2.** BANISH to expel or banish sb from their own country [Mid-17thC. Via French déporter from Latin deportare, literally 'to carry off', from portare 'to carry'.]

deport² /di páwrt/ (-ports, -porting, -ported) vr. to conduct yourself in a particular way [15thC. From Old French deporter 'to behave, conduct oneself', from porter, from Latin portare 'to carry'.]

deportable /di páwrtəb'l/ adj. **1.** RESULTING IN DEPORTATION liable to result in deportation **2.** LIABLE TO DEPORTATION liable to be deported

deportation /dèe pawr táysh'n/ n. **1.** EXPULSION OF FOREIGNER the forcible expulsion of a foreign national from a country **2.** EXPELLING NATIONAL the banishment or expulsion of sb from his or her own country

deportee /dèe pawr tée/ n. sb who has been or is waiting to be deported

deportment /di páwrtmənt/ n. the way that you stand, sit, or move, especially whether you have a straight back, move smoothly, and carry yourself well (formal) [Early 17thC. From French déportement, from Old French deporter (see DEPORT²).]

depose /di pôz/ (-poses, -posing, -posed) v. **1.** vt. REMOVE FROM OFFICE to remove sb from office or from a position of power **2.** vti. LAW GIVE EVIDENCE to give evidence or testify on oath, either in a written or verbal form [13thC. From French déposer, an alteration (influenced by poser 'to put') of Latin deponere 'to put down', later 'to testify', from ponere (see POSITION).] —**deposable** adj. —**deposer** n.

deposit /di pózzit/ v. (-its, -iting, -ited) **1.** vt. PUT STH SOMEWHERE to put or drop sth somewhere ○ She deposited her coat on the couch. **2.** vti. GEOG FORM LAYER to form a layer of sand, sediment, or other substance, as a gradual process in one place ○ layers of silt deposited by the river **3.** vt. BANKING PUT MONEY IN BANK to pay money into a bank or other financial institution **4.** vt. LEAVE SAFELY to leave sth somewhere for safekeeping ○ deposit valuables in the hotel safe **5.** vt. COMM GIVE AS SECURITY to give a sum of money as part-payment or security ○ deposited £500 as a down payment ■ n. **1.** BANKING PUTTING MONEY IN BANK an act of placing money or a valuable item in a bank or other institution ○ make a monthly deposit **2.** BANKING MONEY IN BANK an amount of money or a valuable item that is paid into or left in a bank or other institution ○ Deposits made after 2 pm are credited the following day. **3.** COMM SECURITY MONEY a partial payment or security on sth you wish to buy ○ You need to pay a deposit. **4.** SURETY MONEY money that is given as security against possible damage or loss, e.g. on sth rented **5.** GEOG ACCUMULATION OF NATURAL MATERIALS an accumulation of sand, sediment, minerals, or other substances that has built up over a period of time through a natural process ○ a land rich in mineral deposits **6.** POL ELECTION CANDIDATE'S MONEY money that candidates in a parliamentary election must deposit to show that their standing is serious and which they forfeit if they fail to win a given percentage of votes **7.** COATING a coating or crust that is left on a surface by a process such as evaporation or electrolysis **8.** DEPOSITED THING sth put or left in a place [Late 16thC. From Latin depositum, from deposit-, the past participle stem of deponere (see DEPOSE).]

deposit account n. a bank account that earns interest

depositary /di pózzitəri/ (plural -ies) n. **1.** SAFEKEEPER a person or institution that is entrusted with sth for safekeeping **2.** = depository n. ɪ

deposition /déppə zísh'n, de̅epə-/ *n.* **1.** WITNESS'S TESTIMONY testimony that is given under oath, especially a statement given by a witness that is read out in court in the witness's absence **2.** OUSTING FROM OFFICE the act of removing sb from high office or power **3.** STH DEPOSITED sth that has been deposited somewhere **4.** BUILD-UP OF DEPOSITS the accumulation of natural materials by a gradual process [14thC. Via French *déposition* from the Latin stem *deposition-*, from, ultimately, *deponere* (see DEPOSE).] —**depositional** *adj.*

depositor /di pózzitər/ *n.* sb who deposits or has money in a bank or similar institution

depository /di pózzitəri/ (*plural* **-ries**) *n.* **1.** STOREHOUSE a place where sth is kept for safekeeping or storage, such as a warehouse or store for furniture or valuables **2.** = **depositary** *n.* 1

depot /déppō/ *n.* **1.** WAREHOUSE a warehouse or other place used for storing things **2.** TRANSP VEHICLE BASE a building where buses, trains, or lorries are based and serviced **3.** *US, Can* TRANSP STATION a railway or bus station **4.** MIL MILITARY STORE a place where military supplies are stored **5.** MIL MILITARY TRAINING BASE a place where military recruits are gathered together and trained [Late 18thC. Via French *dépôt* from, ultimately, Latin *depositum* (see DEPOSIT). The underlying sense is 'a place where things are deposited'.]

deprave /di práyv/ (**-praves, -praving, -praved**) *vt.* to have a morally bad influence on sb (*often passive*) [14thC. Directly or via French from Latin *depravare* 'to corrupt', literally 'to distort completely', from *pravus* 'crooked', of unknown origin.] —**depraver** *n.*

depraved /di práyvd/ *adj.* showing great moral corruption or wickedness —**depravedly** /di práyvidli, -práyvd-/ *adv.* —**depravedness** /di práyvidnəss, -práyvd-/ *n.*

depravity /di právvəti/ (*plural* **-ties**) *n.* **1.** CORRUPTION a state of moral corruption **2.** CORRUPT ACT a morally corrupt or wicked act [Mid-17thC. Alteration (by association with DEPRAVE), of earlier *pravity*, from Latin *pravitas*, from *pravus* 'crooked'.]

deprecate /déppri kayt/ (**-cates, -cating, -cated**) *vt.* to express condemnation of sth or sb [Early 17thC. From Latin *deprecari*, literally 'to pray against', from *precari* (see PRAY).] —**deprecation** /déppra káysh'n/ *n.* —**deprecator** *n.*

WORD KEY: USAGE

deprecate or **depreciate**? These two words are easily confused, but those who use English carefully try to maintain the distinction between them. To ***deprecate*** sth is to deplore or condemn it as wrong in itself: *We deprecate the use of public money for nonessential purposes.* To ***depreciate*** sth is to belittle or disparage it, although it may not be wrong or bad in itself: *They were constantly depreciating our attempts to speak Italian.* Admittedly, *self-deprecate* goes a long way towards blurring the distinction, for it means 'belittle yourself', not 'condemn yourself'; in this sense it is well established, but it may be best regarded as an exception rather than a precursor. Both words have more common synonyms: *condemn, deplore,* and *disapprove of* for ***deprecate***, and *belittle, disparage,* and *decry* for ***depreciate***. ***Depreciate*** is also used intransitively, in financial contexts: *The value of the yen depreciated 20 per cent in real terms.*

deprecating /déppra kayting/ *adj.* showing or expressing disapproval —**deprecatingly** *adv.*

deprecatory /déppri kaytəri, -kətəri/, **deprecative** /-kətiv/ *adj.* **1.** CRITICAL disapproving and critical **2.** APOLOGETIC showing or expressing apology —**deprecatorily** *adv.*

depreciable /di pre̅eshi əb'l/ *adj.* capable of being or becoming depreciated

depreciate /di pre̅eshi ayt/ (**-ates, -ating, -ated**) *v.* **1.** *vti.* LOSE VALUE to lessen in value or to become less valuable **2.** *vt.* ACCT DECREASE FOR TAX PURPOSES to consider sth as having less value each year over a fixed period, for the calculation of income tax **3.** *vt.* BELITTLE to speak critically or disparagingly about sth or sb [15thC. From late Latin *depreciare*, an alteration of Latin *depretiare* 'to lower the price of', from *pretium* (see PRICE).] —**depreciatingly** *adv.* —**depreciator** *n.*

WORD KEY: USAGE

See Usage note at ***deprecate***.

depreciation /di pre̅eshi áysh'n/ *n.* **1.** DROP IN VALUE the decrease in value of an item over time **2.** AMOUNT OF DECREASE the amount or percentage by which sth decreases in value over time, usually one year **3.** BELITTLEMENT critical commentary or strong disparagement of sb or sth

depreciative /di pre̅eshi ətiv/ *adj.* **1.** REDUCING IN VALUE reducing or tending to reduce sth in value **2.** LOSING VALUE losing or tending to lose value

depreciatory /di pre̅eshi ətəri/ *adj.* **1.** = **depreciative 2.** CRITICAL belittling or critical

depredate /déppra dayt/ (**-dates, -dating, -dated**) *vti.* to ransack or plunder a place after attacking and overrunning it (*formal*) [Early 17thC. From Latin *depraedari*, literally 'to plunder thoroughly', from *praedari* (see PREDATORY).] —**depredator** *n.* —**depredatory** /déppra daytəri, di préddətəri/ *adj.*

depredation /déppra dáysh'n/ *n.* an attack involving plunder and pillage

depress /di préss/ (**-presses, -pressing, -pressed**) *vt.* **1.** MAKE SAD to make sb feel very sad or hopeless ○ *'There's nothing that depresses me more than seeing a planet being destroyed'.* (Douglas Adams, *Life, The Universe, and Everything*; 1982) **2.** WEAKEN to weaken sth or make sth less active **3.** REDUCE to decrease the value of sth **4.** PRESS to press sth, e.g. a button or lever [14thC. Via Old French from, ultimately, Latin *depress-*, the past participle stem of *deprimere* 'to press down', from *premere* 'to press'.] —**depressible** *adj.*

depressant /di préss'nt/ *n.* SEDATIVE a drug or agent that has the effect of slowing the rate of the body's vital functions ■ *adj.* WITH SLOWING EFFECT able to sedate or lower the rate of the body's vital functions

depressed /di prést/ *adj.* **1.** UNHAPPY unhappy or hopeless **2.** PSYCHIAT HAVING DEPRESSION having the psychiatric disorder depression **3.** ECON ECONOMICALLY LACKING lacking economic resources or activities **4.** WEAK less active or strong than usual **5.** LOWER lower than the surrounding area **6.** BIOL FLATTENED flattened, as if from downward pressure

depressing /di préssing/ *adj.* making sb feel sad or disheartened —**depressingly** *adv.* —**depressingness** *n.*

depression /di présh'n/ *n.* **1.** UNHAPPINESS a state of unhappiness and hopelessness **2.** PSYCHIAT PSYCHIATRIC DISORDER a psychiatric disorder showing symptoms such as persistent feelings of hopelessness, dejection, poor concentration, lack of energy, inability to sleep, and, sometimes, suicidal tendencies **3.** ECON ECONOMIC SLUMP a period in which an economy is greatly affected by unemployment, low output, and poverty **4.** REDUCED ACTIVITY a lowering of activity, quality, vitality, or force **5.** HOLLOW an area on the surface of sth that is lower than the surface surrounding it **6.** METEOROL LOW PRESSURE AREA an area of low barometric pressure that often brings rain

depressive /di préssiv/ *adj.* **1.** CAUSING DEPRESSION relating to or causing depression ○ *the depressive atmosphere of a grey, cold marshland* **2.** PSYCHIAT HAVING DEPRESSION experiencing or with a history of depression ■ *n.* PSYCHIAT DEPRESSED PERSON sb who regularly experiences periods of depression —**depressively** *adv.* —**depressiveness** *n.*

depressor /di préssər/ *n.* **1.** MED MEDICAL INSTRUMENT a medical or surgical instrument that is used to move aside or press down an organ or part of the body **2.** ANAT PULLING MUSCLE a muscle that acts to pull down a part of the body **3.** SB OR STH THAT PRESSES DOWN sb or sth that presses down

depressor nerve *n.* a nerve that, when stimulated, decreases activity in an organ, lowers blood pressure, or slows the heart

depressurize /dee préshə rīz/ (**-izes, -izing, -ized**), **depressurise** (**-ises, -ising, -ised**) *vt.* to reduce the pressure of air or gas within a container, cabin, or other enclosed space —**depressurization** /dee préshə rī záysh'n/ *n.*

deprivation /déppri váysh'n/ *n.* **1.** STATE OF POVERTY the state of being without or denied sth, especially of lacking adequate food or shelter **2.** TAKING AWAY the act of taking sth away from sb or preventing sb from having sth

WORD KEY: SYNONYMS

See Synonyms at ***poverty***.

deprive /di prīv/ (**-prives, -priving, -prived**) *vt.* **1.** NOT ALLOW TO HAVE to prevent sb from having sth **2.** TAKE AWAY to take sth away from sb ○ *They have no right to deprive you of your own property.* **3.** DEPOSE to depose sb from high rank or office (*archaic*) [14thC. Via Old French from medieval Latin *deprivare*, literally 'to deprive completely', from Latin *privare* (see PRIVATION).] —**deprivable** *adj.* —**depriver** *n.*

deprived /di prīvd/ *adj.* lacking adequate food and shelter

de profundis /dáy prə fo̅o̅ndiss/ *adv.* out of the depths of misery or despair (*literary*) [13thC. From Latin, literally 'out of the depths', the first words of Psalm 130 in the Bible.]

deprogramme /dee prō gram/ (**-grammes, -gramming, -grammed**) *vt.* to undo the effects of indoctrination on an individual, especially sb under the influence of a religious group —**deprogrammer** *n.*

dept *abbr.* department

depth /depth/ *n.* **1.** HOW DEEP STH IS the distance or measurement from the top of sth to its bottom, from front to back, or from the outside in **2.** BEING DEEP the quality of being deep **3.** INTENSITY the intensity or strength of a feeling or emotion **4.** COMPLEXITY complexity or profundity of character ○ *a woman of great depth* ○ *hidden depths of knowledge* **5.** BREADTH wideness in scope **6.** COLOUR QUALITY the intensity or richness of a colour **7.** LOWNESS the low tone or pitch of a sound ■ *npl.* **1. depths** LOWEST POINT the lowest or worst point or moment ○ *the depths of despair* **2. depths** DEEP PART a deep or remote part of sth ○ *the ocean depths* **3. depths** MIDDLE PART the middle part of sth long, monotonous, and possibly unpleasant ○ *in the depths of tedious research* **4.** DEBASEMENT a state of great moral debasement ○ *having fallen to such depths* [14thC. Formed from DEEP.] ◇ **out of your depth 1.** unable to stand because the water is too deep **2.** unable to understand or do sth because it is outside the range of your knowledge or skills

depth charge, depth bomb *n.* a bomb that is designed to explode at a particular depth under water, often used against submarines

depth gauge, depth finder *n.* an instrument that measures the depth of water or other liquid

depth of field *n.* the total focused area in front of and behind an object held in the focus of a camera or lens

depth of focus *n.* the distance that a camera lens can be moved closer to or further from the film, without the resulting image being blurred

depth perception *n.* the ability to perceive objects and their spatial relationship in three dimensions

depth psychology *n.* the study and psychology of the unconscious mind

depth sounder *n.* an ultrasonic instrument that measures the depth of water under a ship

depurate /déppyo̅o̅ rayt/ (**-rates, -rating, -rated**) *vt.* to cleanse or purify sth, especially by removing toxins [Early 17thC. From medieval Latin *depurare*, from Latin *purus* 'pure'.] —**depuration** /déppyo̅o̅ ráysh'n/ *n.* —**depurator** /déppyo̅o̅ raytər/ *n.*

depurative /déppyo̅o̅rətiv/ *adj.* purifying sth by the removal of toxins (*technical*)

deputation /déppyo̅o̅ táysh'n/ *n.* **1.** REPRESENTATIVES a group of people who have been chosen to represent a larger group of people and act on their behalf **2.** APPOINTMENT OF DEPUTY the act of appointing a deputy or deputation

depute /di pyo̅o̅t/ *vt.* (**-putes, -puting, -puted**) (*formal*) **1.** CHOOSE REPRESENTATIVE to choose sb to be your agent, substitute, or representative **2.** DELEGATE to delegate one's work, authority, or duties to sb else ■ *adj. Scotland* DEPUTY acting as deputy (*formal*) ○ *headmaster depute* [14thC. Via French *députer* from, ultimately, Latin *deputare* 'to assign', from *putare* 'to consider'.]

deputize /déppyŏŏ tīz/ (-tizes, -tizing, -tized), **deputise** (-tises, -tising, -tised) v. 1. vi. BE DEPUTY to act as sb's deputy 2. vt. SELECT DEPUTY to choose sb to act as a deputy to sb —**deputization** /déppyŏŏ tī záysh'n/ n.

deputy /déppyŏŏti/ (plural **-ties**) n. 1. SB'S REPRESENTATIVE sb who has been authorized or appointed to act on behalf of sb else with full authority 2. SECOND-IN-COMMAND an assistant who is authorized to act in a superior's place 3. MEMBER OF PARLIAMENT a parliamentary representative in some countries, e.g. France, Germany, or Italy 4. US LAW = **deputy sheriff** [15thC. From French député, the past participle of députer (see DEPUTE).]

── **WORD KEY: SYNONYMS** ──
See Synonyms at **assistant**.

deputy head n. EDUC a senior member of a school staff, second in status to the head

deputy minister n. Can the most senior civil servant in a Canadian government department

deputy sheriff n. a sheriff's assistant in the United States, authorized to take charge when the sheriff is absent

De Quincey /də kwínssi/, **Thomas** (1785–1859) British essayist and critic. He was a friend of Wordsworth and Coleridge, and author of Confessions of an English Opium Eater (1821).

deracinate /dee rássi nayt/ (-nates, -nating, -nated) vt. to remove sb or sth from a natural environment, especially people from their native culture (formal) [Late 16thC. Formed from French déraciner, from racine 'root', which came via late Latin radicina from Latin radix 'root' (see RADIX).] —**deracination** /dee rássi náysh'n/ n.

deraign /diráyn/ (-raigns, -raigning, -raigned) vt. (archaic) 1. LAW CONTEST CASE to dispute a claim or suit 2. MIL ARRANGE SOLDIERS to line soldiers up ready for battle [14thC. Via Anglo-Norman derainer from assumed Vulgar Latin disrationare 'to settle an account', from Latin ratio 'reckoning' (see RATIO).] —**deraignment** n.

derail /dee ráyl/ (-rails, -railing, -railed) vti. 1. COME OFF RAILS to make a train or tram come off the rails, or to come off the rails 2. SEND OR GO OFF COURSE to send sth off course, or to go off course [Mid-19thC. From French dérailler, from rail 'rail' (see RAIL¹).] —**derailment** n.

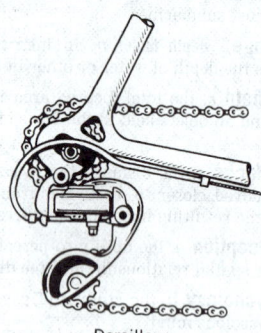

Derailleur

derailleur /di ráylyər/ n. a device for changing gears on a bicycle that lifts the chain from one sprocket wheel to another [Mid-20thC. From French dérailleur, literally 'derailer', from dérailler (see DERAIL).]

Derain /də ráN/, **André** (1880–1954) French painter, illustrator, and stage designer. A leader in several art movements of the early 20th century, he is particularly noted for the paintings of his 'fauve' period (1905–08).

derange /di ráynj/ (-ranges, -ranging, -ranged) vt. 1. MAKE IRRATIONAL to make sb irrational or extraordinarily angry 2. DISTURB to disturb the normal way in which sth works 3. THROW INTO DISORDER to throw sth into disorder and confusion [Late 18thC. From French déranger, literally 'to put out of line', from rang 'line'.]

deranged /di ráynjd/ adj. completely unreasonable, especially as a result of great emotional excitement

derangement /di ráynjmənt/ n. 1. COMPLETE IRRATIONALITY a complete lack of rationality, especially with great emotional excitement 2. DISORDER disorder and con-

fusion 3. ACT OF DERANGING the act of disturbing or confusing sth

derate /dee ráyt/ (-rates, -rating, -rated) vt. 1. ELEC ENG LOWER RATED CAPABILITY OF APPARATUS to lower the rated capability of an electrical apparatus 2. LOWER RATES to lower or abolish the rates on a property

deration /dee rásh'n/ (-tions, -tioning, -tioned) vt. to stop rationing a commodity, usually because the supply has become adequate

derby /daarbi/ (plural **-bies**) n. 1. HORSERACING HORSERACE any of a number of horseraces run annually, usually for three year olds 2. RACE a race or contest, open to qualified competitors 3. US, Can CLOTHES = **bowler hat** [Late 19thC. Named after DERBY. In sense 3, supposedly from the wearing of such hats at the Derby horserace.]

Derby¹ /daarbi/ n. a flat horserace for three year olds, run annually at Epsom Downs, Surrey, England or one held each spring at Churchill Downs in Louisville, Kentucky, in the United States [Early 19thC. Named after Edward Stanley 1752–1834, 12th Earl of Derby, who founded the English race in 1780.]

Derby² /daarbi/ (plural **-by** or **-bies**) n. a close-textured pale-coloured cheese, sometimes flavoured with sage [Named after DERBYSHIRE, where most of it is made]

Derby³ /daarbi/ 1. cathedral city in Derbyshire, England. Population: 225,400 (1997). 2. port in northwestern Western Australia, situated on King Sound near the mouth of the River Fitzroy. Population: 3,236 (1996).

Derby, 14th Earl of (1799–1869) British statesman. Three times prime minister (1852, 1858–59, and 1866–68), he carried the second Reform Act for the emancipation of West Indian slaves (1867) through Parliament. Full name **Edward George Geoffrey Smith Stanley**

Derbyshire /daarbishər/ county in central England, including most of the Peak District. Matlock is the administrative centre. Population: 726,000 (1995). Area: 2,631 sq. km/1,016 sq. mi.

derecognize /dee rékəg nīz/ (-nizes, -nizing, -nized), **derecognise** (-nises, -nising, -nised) vt. to stop accepting the legitimacy of sth, especially a trade union or diplomatic mission —**derecognition** /dee rekəg nísh'n/ n.

deregister /dee réjjistər/ (-ters, -tering, -tered) vti. to remove sth or sb from a register or official list —**deregistration** /dee rejji stráysh'n/ n.

deregulate /dee réggyŏŏ layt/ (-lates, -lating, -lated) vt. to free sth such as an organization or industry from regulation —**deregulation** /dee réggyŏŏ láysh'n/ n. —**deregulator** /dee réggyŏŏ laytər/ n. —**deregulatory** /-lətəri/ adj.

derelict /dérrəlikt/ adj. 1. DESERTED no longer lived in 2. NEGLECTED in poor condition because of neglect 3. LAW ABANDONING NEGLECTFUL of your duty or obligations ■ n. 1. HOMELESS PERSON sb who has no home, employment, or family care 2. ABANDONED BUILDING a building, ship, or other property that has been abandoned or deserted 3. LAW NEGLECTFUL PERSON a person who is neglectful of duty or obligations [Mid-17thC. From Latin derelictus, the past participle of derelinquere, literally 'to abandon utterly', from relinquere (see RELINQUISH).]

dereliction /dérrə líksh'n/ n. 1. LAW NEGLECT OF DUTY deliberate neglect of duty or obligations 2. ABANDONMENT the act of abandoning or deserting a building 3. STATE OF NEGLECT a state of abandonment or neglect 4. LAW LAND GAINED FROM THE SEA land gained when water has receded from it

derepress /dee ri préss/ (-presses, -pressing, -pressed) vt. to activate a gene by deactivating the repressor —**derepression** /-présh'n/ n.

derequisition /dee rékwi zísh'n/ (-tions, -tioning, -tioned) vt. to return sth to civilian use that was earlier requisitioned by the military or a government

derestrict /dee ri stríkt/ (-stricts, -stricting, -stricted) vt. to remove the restrictions from sth —**derestriction** /-stríksh'n/ n.

Derg, Lough /durg/ LAKES stretch of water in western Ireland, in counties Tipperary, Galway, and Clare.

Area: 96 sq. km/37 sq. mi. Depth: 36 m/118 ft. Length: 32 km/20 mi.

deride /di rīd/ (-rides, -riding, -rided) vt. to ridicule or show contempt for sb or sth [Mid-16thC. From Latin deridere, literally 'to laugh down', from ridere 'to laugh'.] —**derider** n. —**deridingly** adv.

── **WORD KEY: SYNONYMS** ──
See Synonyms at **ridicule**.

de rigueur /də ri gúr/ adj. strictly required by the current fashion or by etiquette (formal) [Mid-19thC. From French, literally 'of strictness'.]

derisible /di rízzəb'l/ adj. deserving contempt or ridicule (formal) [Mid-17thC. From late Latin derisibilis, from, ultimately, Latin deridere (see DERIDE).]

derision /di rízh'n/ n. contempt and mockery [14thC. Via French dérision from, ultimately, Latin deridere (see DERIDE).]

derisive /di ríssiv, -ziv/ adj. showing contempt or ridicule [Mid-17thC. Formed from DERISION.] —**derisively** adv. —**derisiveness** n.

── **WORD KEY: USAGE** ──
derisive or **derisory**? Derisive means 'showing derision' (that is, scornful, contemptuous): He gave a derisive laugh. Derisory means 'deserving derision' (that is, ridiculous, contemptible): a derisory offer.

derisory /di ríssəri, -ríz-/ adj. 1. RIDICULOUSLY SMALL so small or inadequate for the purpose intended that it is ridiculous 2. = **derisive** [Early 17thC. From late Latin derisorius from, ultimately, Latin deridere (see DERIDE).]

── **WORD KEY: USAGE** ──
See Usage note at **derisive**.

deriv. abbr. 1. derivation 2. derivative

derivate n., adj. = **derivative** [15thC. From Latin derivatus, the past participle of derivare (see DERIVE).]

derivation /dérri váysh'n/ n. 1. SOURCE the origin or source of sth, e.g. a word or someone's name 2. LING WORD FORMATION the formation of a word or term from another, or from a base form 3. MATH, LOGIC PROOF a mathematical or logical argument whose steps show that a conclusion follows necessarily from initial assumptions 4. ACT OF DERIVING STH the act of obtaining sth from a source or issuing from a source —**derivational** adj.

── **WORD KEY: SYNONYMS** ──
See Synonyms at **origin**.

derivative /di rívvətiv/, **derivate** /dérrivət/ adj. UNORIGINAL copied from somewhere and not original ■ n. 1. DERIVED THING an idea, language, term, or other thing that has developed from sth else that is similar to it 2. LING DERIVED WORD a word that is formed from another word, e.g. 'quickly' from 'quick' 3. CHEM RELATED CHEMICAL PRODUCT a chemical substance that is formed from a related substance 4. MATH CHANGE OF FUNCTION the limit approached in the ratio of a function and its variable, as the variable is changed ever more infinitesimally 5. FIN FINANCIAL PRODUCT a tradable financial product whose value depends on the value of some other asset or combination of assets —**derivatively** adv. —**derivativeness** n.

derive /di rív/ (-rives, -riving, -rived) v. 1. vti. GET OR COME FROM STH to obtain sth or come from a source 2. vt. LOGIC DEDUCE to reach a conclusion about sth by reasoning 3. vt. CHEM MAKE COMPOUND to create a chemical substance from another 4. vti. LING COME FROM SOURCE to develop from another word or a source word or term 5. vt. MATH OBTAIN FUNCTION to obtain a function by differentiation [14thC. Directly or via French dériver from Latin derivare 'to draw off water through a channel', from rivus 'stream' (see RIVAL).] —**derivable** adj. —**deriver** n.

derm- prefix. = **derma-** (used before vowels)

-derm suffix. skin ○ ectoderm [From Greek derma (see DERMA-)]

derma n. COOK = **kishke** [Origin uncertain: probably via Yiddish gederem 'intestines' from, ultimately, Old High German darm 'gut'.]

derma- prefix. skin ○ dermatome [Early 18thC. Via modern Latin from Greek, 'skin'. Ultimately from an Indo-

European word meaning 'to peel', which is also the ancestor of English tear¹.]

dermabrasion /dúrmə bráyzh'n/ n. a surgical process that removes scars or other imperfections of the skin by scraping the skin's surface with wire brushes or very fine sandpaper [Mid-20thC. Coined from Greek *derma* 'skin' + ABRASION.]

dermal /dúrm'l/, **dermic** /-mik/ adj. involving, located in, or made up of skin or its main layer (**dermis**) [Early 19thC. Formed from Greek *derma* 'skin'.]

dermapteran /dur máptərən/ n. an insect, e.g. an earwig, that has strong sharp sensory appendages coming from the end of its abdomen [Late 19thC. Formed from modern Latin *Dermaptera*, order name, from Greek *derma* 'skin' + *pteron* 'wing'. So called because of their membranous wings.] —**dermapteran** adj.

dermat- prefix. = **dermato-** (used before vowels)

dermatitis /dúrmə títiss/ n. inflammation of the skin from any cause, resulting in a range of symptoms such as redness, swelling, itching, or blistering

dermato- prefix. skin ○ *dermatoplasty* [From Greek *dermat-*, the stem of *derma* (see DERMA-)]

dermatoglyphics /dúrmətō glíffiks/ npl. **SKIN PATTERNS** the lines that form a pattern on the skin, e.g. on the fingers and palms of the hands ■ n. **STUDY OF SKIN PATTERNS** the study of dermatoglyphics (takes a singular verb) [Early 20thC. Coined from DERMATO- + Greek *gluphē* 'carving, inscription' (see GLYPH).] —**dermatoglyphic** adj.

dermatoid /dúrmə toyd/ adj. resembling skin

dermatology /dúrmə tólləji/ n. the branch of medicine that deals with the skin and diseases affecting the skin —**dermatological** /dúrmətə lójjik'l/ adj. —**dermatologist** /dúrmə tólləjist/ n.

dermatome /dúrmətōm/ n. 1. ANAT **SKIN SERVED BY ONE SPINAL NERVE** an area of skin that has nerve fibres coming from a single spinal nerve 2. MED **SURGICAL INSTRUMENT** an instrument used to slice thin layers of skin for skin grafting [Late 19thC. Coined from DERMATO- + -TOME.] —**dermatomic** /dúrmə tómmik/ adj.

dermatophyte /dur máttə fīt/ n. a parasitic fungus that affects the skin, hair, or nails —**dermatophytic** /dur máttō fíttik/ adj.

dermatophytosis /dúrmətō fī tóssiss/ n. a fungal infection of the skin, hair, or nails

dermatoplasty /dúrmətō plasti/ n. any operation on the skin, especially skin grafting (technical) —**dermatoplastic** /dúrmətō plástik/ adj.

dermatosis /dúrmə tóssiss/ (plural **-ses** /-seez/) n. any disease affecting the skin

-dermatous suffix. having a particular kind of skin ○ *sclerodermatous* [Formed from Greek *dermat-*, the stem of *derma* (see DERMA-)]

dermestid /dur méstid/ n. a beetle that has clubbed antennae and eats and destroys organic materials such as meat, fur, wool, fabric, or museum specimens. Cabinet and carpet beetles are dermestids. Family: Dermestidae. [Late 19thC. From modern Latin *Dermestidae*, family name, from Greek *derma* 'skin' + *esthien* 'to eat'.]

dermic /dúrmik/ adj. = **dermal** [Mid-19thC. Formed from Greek *derma* 'skin'.]

dermis /dúrmiss/ n. the thick sensitive layer of skin or connective tissue beneath the epidermis that contains blood, lymph vessels, sweat glands, and nerve endings [Mid-19thC. From modern Latin, back-formation from EPIDERMIS.]

-dermis suffix. skin ○ *endodermis* [Back-formation from EPIDERMIS]

dermoid /dúr moyd/, **dermoid cyst** n. a benign tumour that contains skin or skin derivatives, found in the ovaries or on the face, especially round the eyes [Early 19thC. Formed from Greek *derma* 'skin'.]

dernier cri /dúrni ay krée/ n. the latest thing in fashion [Late 19thC. From French, literally 'latest cry'.]

derogate /dérrə gayt/ (**-gates, -gating, -gated**) v. 1. vi. **DEVIATE FROM CONDITIONS** to deviate from a norm, rule, law, or set of conditions, e.g. by refusing to be bound by part of a treaty 2. vi. **MAKE SEEM INFERIOR** to make sth seem inferior or less significant (formal)

○ *conduct that will derogate from your good name* 3. vt. **CRITICIZE** to criticize sb or sth negatively 4. vt. LAW **REPEAL PARTIALLY** to repeal or abolish part of a law or decree [15thC. From Latin *derogare* 'to repeal a law', later 'to detract from, impair', from *rogare* 'to ask, propose a law' (see ROGATION).]

derogation /dérrə gáysh'n/ n. 1. LAW **DEVIATION** a deviation from a rule or law, especially one specifically provided for 2. INTERNAT REL **EXEMPTION FROM RULE** an exemption from a law or ruling given to a state 3. **DISPARAGEMENT** the act of belittling or negatively criticizing sb or sth

derogative /di róggətiv/ adj. 1. = **derogatory** 2. **RELATING TO DEROGATION** relating to a derogation —**derogatively** adv.

derogatory /di róggətəri/ adj. expressing a low opinion or negative criticism —**derogatorily** adv. —**derogatoriness** n.

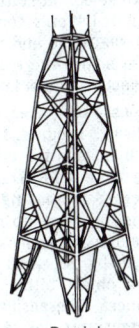

Derrick

derrick /dérrik/ n. 1. **LOADING CRANE** a simple crane that is often used for moving cargo onto or from a ship 2. INDUST **OIL STRUCTURE** a structure placed over an oil well that is used to raise and lower piping, drills, and other boring equipment [Early 17thC. From an earlier sense 'hangman, gallows', after a London hangman called *Derrick* who was working at Tyburn at about this time.]

Derrida /de réedə/, **Jacques** (b. 1930) Algerian-born French philosopher. He introduced deconstruction, a controversial technique for textual analysis.

derrière /dérri air, dérri áir/ n. sb's bottom (humorous) [Late 18thC. Via French, literally 'behind', from, ultimately, Latin *de retro*.]

derring-do /dérring dóo/ n. boldness, or acts of great daring (literary) [Late 16thC. Alteration of earlier *dorring don* 'daring to do', which was erroneously printed in 16th-century editions of medieval works as *derrynge do* and interpreted as a noun.]

derringer /dérrinjər/ n. a pocket-sized short-barrelled large-calibre pistol [Mid-19thC. Named after the US gunsmith Henry *Deringer*, 1786–1868, who designed it.]

derris /dérriss/ n. 1. PLANTS **E INDIAN CLIMBING PLANT** a woody climbing plant that grows in East India. Genus: *Derris*. 2. GARDENING **INSECTICIDE** an insecticide made from the powdered roots of the derris plant, that contain the natural insecticide rotenone [Mid-19thC. Via modern Latin, genus name, from Greek, literally 'leather covering'. So called because of its leathery pod.]

derry /dérri/ (plural **-ries**) n. a derelict house (dated slang) [Mid-20thC. Shortening.]

Derry /dérri/ district council in County Londonderry, Northern Ireland. Population: 101,700 (1995).

derv /durv/ n. diesel oil used as a fuel for road vehicles [Mid-20thC. An acronym formed from *diesel-engined road vehicle*.]

dervish /dúrvish/ n. 1. **MEMBER OF MUSLIM RELIGIOUS GROUP** a member of any of several ascetic Muslim religious groups, some of which are known for their practices of very energetic dancing, whirling, chanting, or singing 2. **FRENZIED PERSON** sb who behaves very energetically [Late 16thC. Via Turkish *derviş* from Persian *darvīš* 'poor, mendicant'.]

Derwent /dúrwənt/ river in southern Tasmania, Australia, that rises in Lake St Clair and flows southwest to the Tasman Sea at Storm Bay near Hobart. Length: 190 km/118 mi.

Derwentwater /dúrwənt wawtər/ lake in Cumbria, northeastern England. It contains several wooded islands. Length: 4.8 km/3 mi.

DES abbr. 1. diethylstilboestrol 2. data encryption standard

desacralize /deé sákrə līz/ (**-izes, -izing, -ized**), **desacralise** (**-ises, -ising, -ised**) vt. to remove the sacred, religious, or supernatural qualities or status from sth

Desai /de sī/, **Morarji Ranchhodji** (1896–1995) Indian statesman. Five times imprisoned under British rule, and in 1975–77 by Indira Gandhi, he was prime minister (1977–79), heading the Janata party.

desalinate /dee sálli nayt/ (**-nates, -nating, -nated**) vt. to remove the salt from sth —**desalinator** n.

desalination /deé sálli náysh'n/ n. the process of removing salt from sth, especially from seawater to produce drinking water. The main methods used are distillation and reverse osmosis.

desalinize /dee sálli nīz/ (**-nizes, -nizing, -nized**), **desalinise** (**-nises, -nising, -nised**) vt. = **desalinate** —**desalinization** /dee sálli nī záysh'n/ n.

desalt /dee sáwlt, -sólt/ (**-salts, -salting, -salted**) vt. = **desalinate** —**desalter** n.

desaturation /dee sácha ráysh'n/ n. the addition of white to a saturated colour in order to achieve a paler shade

desc. abbr. descendant

descale /deé skáyl/ (**-scales, -scaling, -scaled**) vt. to remove the limescale that has accumulated in a household appliance, e.g. a kettle

descant /déss kant, díss-/, **discant** /díss-/ n. 1. MUSIC **HIGH MELODY** a melody that is sung or played above the basic melody of a piece of music 2. **COMMENT** a comment, remark, or criticism on a particular subject (archaic) ■ adj. MUSIC **HIGH-TONED** highest in range of a family of musical instruments ○ *descant recorder* ■ vi. (**-cants, -canting, -canted**) 1. MUSIC **MAKE MUSIC** to sing, play, or compose a descant part for a piece of music 2. **DISCOURSE ON STH** to comment at length on a particular subject (literary) [14thC. Via Anglo-Norman *descaunt* from medieval Latin *discantus* 'part-song, refrain', from Latin *cantus* 'song' (see CANTO).] —**descanter** /des kántər, dis-/ n.

Descartes /dáy kaart/, **René** (1596–1650) French philosopher and mathematician. He is often called the father of modern philosophy, and his *Discourse on Method* (1637) introduced his technique of philosophical enquiry. His work on analytical geometry resulted in the Cartesian system of coordinates.

descend /di sénd/ (**-scends, -scending, -scended**) v. 1. vti. **GO DOWN** to go down a staircase, hill, valley, or other downward incline 2. vi. **COME NEARER GROUND** to come nearer the ground, especially in an aircraft in preparation for landing 3. vi. **SLOPE** to slope downwards 4. vti. **BE RELATED** to be connected by blood to an ancestor ○ *Our family descends from French royalty.* ○ *be descended from* 5. vi. **BE INHERITED** to be inherited from or passed down by parents or ancestors 6. vi. **LOWER ONESELF** to behave in a way that is disappointing and below sb's normal standards 7. vi. **ARRIVE SUDDENLY** to arrive at a place suddenly, especially in large numbers ○ *tourists descending on unspoilt areas* 8. vi. **BECOME ESTABLISHED** to become more evident or established, suddenly or by degrees ○ *An atmosphere of gloom descended on the assembled crowd.* [14thC. Via French *descendre* from Latin *descendere*, literally 'to climb down', from *scandere* 'to climb'.] —**descendable** adj.

descendant /di séndənt/ n. 1. **SB OR STH RELATED TO ANCESTOR** a person, animal, or plant related to one that lived in the past 2. **RELATED MODEL** sth that is based in design, form, or concept on an earlier thing ■ adj. = **descendent**

descendent /di séndənt/, **descendant** adj. 1. **MOVING DOWN** moving downwards 2. **DESCENDING FROM ANCESTOR** descending from an ancestor

descender /di séndər/ n. 1. PRINTING **BOTTOM PART OF LETTER** the tail part of a letter, e.g. on a 'y' or 'g', that extends below the baseline of other letters 2. **STH DESCENDING** sb or sth that descends

descendeur /déssaaN dúr/ *n.* a mechanical device that can be tightened or loosened on a rope, enabling a climber to control the speed of his or her descent [Late 20thC. From French, literally 'descender', from *descendre* (see DESCEND).]

descendible /di séndəb'l/ *adj.* **1.** LAW HERITABLE able to be inherited **2.** ALLOWING DESCENT allowing descent or downward movement

descending /di sénding/ *adj.* going or arranged from highest to lowest, greatest to smallest, or latest to earliest ○ *in descending order*

descent /di sént/ *n.* **1.** GOING DOWN an act of going from the top to the bottom, or from a higher position to a lower position **2.** WAY DOWN a path or other way down sth, e.g. a mountain **3.** DECLINE a decline or change from sth better to sth worse **4.** ANCESTRAL BACKGROUND the connection sb has to an ancestor or group of ancestors **5.** SUDDEN ARRIVAL the sudden arrival of a person or group of people **6.** INHERITED DEVELOPMENT characteristics or developments that can be traced to an earlier source **7.** ONE GENERATION a step of one generation in a lineage **8.** LAW INHERITANCE the transmission of property by inheritance [13thC. From French *descente*, from *descendre* (see DESCEND).]

Deschamps /day shaaN/, **Eustache** (1340?–1407?) French poet. He wrote many ballads and poems, and the first treatise on French versification.

deschool /dée skóol/ (-schools, -schooling, -schooled) *v.* **1.** *vt.* TAKE OUT OF SCHOOL to remove children from school to educate them at home **2.** *vti.* DEEMPHASIZE SCHOOL to reduce sb's involvement with education within the school system, or to undergo this process —**deschooling** *n.*

descramble /dée skrámb'l/ (-bles, -bling, -bled) *vt.* to make intelligible a message transmitted in code form

descrambler /dée skrámblər/ *n.* a device that decodes scrambled messages or signals

describe /di skríb/ (-scribes, -scribing, -scribed) *vt.* **1.** EXPLAIN to give an account of sth by giving details of its characteristics **2.** LABEL to label or typify sb or sth **3.** DRAW SHAPE to make a shape or outline in the air (*formal*) ○ *The plane described a perfect figure of eight.* **4.** REPRESENT to represent sth pictorially or with a model [15thC. From Latin *describere*, literally 'to write down', from *scribere* 'to write'.] —**describable** *adj.* —**describer** *n.*

description /di skrípsh'n/ *n.* **1.** EXPLANATION a written or verbal account, representation, or explanation of sth **2.** PROCESS OF DESCRIBING the process of giving an account or explanation of sth **3.** SORT a kind or variety of sth ○ *cars of every description* [14thC. Via French from the Latin stem *description-* from *descript-*, the past participle stem of *describere* (see DESCRIBE).]

descriptive /di skríptiv/ *adj.* **1.** BEING DESCRIPTION containing or consisting of description **2.** CLASSIFYING serving mainly to label, describe, or classify **3.** GRAM ATTRIBUTIVE expressing an attribute or quality of a noun [Mid-18thC. From late Latin *descriptivus*, from, ultimately, Latin *describere* (see DESCRIBE).] —**descriptively** *adv.* —**descriptiveness** *n.*

descriptive clause *n.* = nonrestrictive clause

descriptive linguistics *n.* the study of a language limited to a comprehensive account of its grammar at a given time, omitting historical or comparative features and not attempting to formulate prescriptive rules

descriptivism /di skríptivizəm/ *n.* **1.** LING SUPPORT FOR DESCRIPTIVE LINGUISTICS adherence to the practices and tenets of descriptive linguistics **2.** PHILOS BELIEF IN DESCRIPTION the notion or thesis that descriptive statements can be true and accurate reflections of phenomena —**descriptivist** *n.*, *adj.*

descriptor /di skríptər/ *n.* COMPUT sth, e.g. a word or phrase, used as a key to categorize records in a database so that all records containing the key can be retrieved together [Mid-20thC. From Latin, literally 'describer', formed from *describere* (see DESCRIBE).]

descry /di skrí/ (-scries, -scrying, -scried) *vt.* **1.** SEE to catch sight of sth (*archaic or formal*) **2.** DISCOVER to detect or discover sth (*archaic or humorous*) [14thC. From Old French *descrier* 'to cry out, proclaim' (source also of English *decry*), from *crier* (see CRY). Its modern meaning

developed by association with obsolete *descry* 'to describe, perceive' which came via Old French *descrire* from Latin *describere* (see DESCRIBE).] —**descrier** *n.*

Desdemona /dézdi mốnə/ *n.* a small satellite of Uranus, discovered in 1986 by Voyager 2

desecrate /déssi krayt/ (-crates, -crating, -crated) *vt.* to damage sth sacred, or do sth that is offensive to the religious nature of sth [Late 17thC. Coined from DE- + CONSECRATE.] —**desecrater** /déssi kráytər/ *n.* —**desecration** /déssi kráysh'n/ *n.* —**desecrator** /déssi kráytər/ *n.*

desegregate /dée séggri gayt/ (-gates, -gating, -gated) *vti.* to put an end to a customary or enforced separation of ethnic or racial groups, e.g. in a workplace or school —**desegregation** /dée seggri gáysh'n/ *n.* —**desegregationist** /-gáysh'nist/ *n.*

deselect /dée si lékt/ (-lects, -lecting, -lected) *vt.* **1.** POL REJECT MP to refuse to select a serving MP, councillor, or party member for reelection **2.** COMPUT REMOVE SELECTION to remove selection status from an option or data on a menu or list on a computer monitor **3.** *US* MANAGEMT LET TRAINEE GO to end the training of an unsuitable trainee before the training program is completed —**deselection** /dée si léksh'n/ *n.*

desensitize /dée sénssə tīz/ (-tizes, -tizing, -tized), **desensitise** (-tises, -tising, -tised) *vt.* **1.** MAKE LESS SENSITIVE to make sb or sth insensitive or less sensitive **2.** MAKE LESS ALLERGIC to make sb less sensitive to a known allergen by injecting increasing amounts of the allergen over time, building up resistance **3.** MAKE LESS SENSITIVE TO FEAR to make sb less responsive to an overwhelming fear by repeated exposure to the feared situation or object, either in natural or artificial circumstances —**desensitization** /dee sénssə tī záysh'n/ *n.* —**desensitizer** /dee sénssə tīzər/ *n.*

WORLD'S LARGEST DESERTS

#	Desert	Area	Location
1	Sahara Desert	[3.5 million sq. mi. / 9.1 million sq. km]	North Africa
2	Rub' al-Khali Desert	[0.9 million sq. mi. / 2.3 million sq. km]	Southwestern Asia /Arabia
3	Gobi Desert	[0.5 million sq. mi. / 1.3 million sq. km]	Central Asia / Mongolia
4	Patagonian Desert	[0.3 million sq. mi. / 0.8 million sq. km]	South America / Argentina
5	Kalahari Desert	[0.27 million sq. mi. / 0.71 million sq. km]	Southwestern Africa
6	Great Victoria Desert	[0.25 million sq. mi. / 0.65 million sq. km]	Australia
7	Great Basin Desert	[0.2 million sq. mi. / 0.5 million sq. km]	North America
8	Great Sandy Desert	[0.15 million sq. mi. / 0.4 million sq. km]	Australia
9	Sonoran Desert	[0.12 million sq. mi. / 0.31 million sq. km]	North America
10	Garagum Desert	[0.11 million sq. mi. / 0.28 million sq. km]	Central Asia / Turkmenistan

desert[1] /dézzərt/ *n.* **1.** ARID AREA an area of land, usually in very hot climates, that consists only of sand, gravel, or rock with little or no vegetation, no permanent bodies of water, and erratic rainfall **2.** DEPRIVED PLACE a place or situation that is devoid of some desirable thing, or overwhelmed by an undesirable thing ○ *a cultural desert* **3.** LIFELESS PLACE a place devoid of life **4.** BARREN LAND a wild, bleak, and uncultivated place (*archaic*) [12thC. Via French *désert* from late Latin *desertum* 'abandoned place', from the past participle of Latin *deserere* (see DESERT[2]).]

desert[2] /di zúrt/ (-serts, -serting, -serted) *v.* **1.** *vt.* ABANDON PLACE to leave a place with no one staying behind **2.** *vt.* ABANDON PERSON to leave or abandon sb, especially when you have some kind of duty or obligation towards him or her **3.** *vti.* MIL LEAVE ARMY WITHOUT PERMISSION to run away from an armed force or military post without permission and intending never to go back **4.** *vt.* LEAVE to be absent when needed ○ *Her sense of humour appeared to have deserted her.* [14thC. Via French *déserter* from, ultimately, Latin *desert-*, the past participle stem of *deserere* 'to abandon', from *serere* 'to join'.]

desert[3] /di zúrt/ *n.* sth deserved, either punishment or reward (*usually used in the plural*) ○ *He'll get his just deserts.* [13thC. From Old French, literally 'what is deserved', from the past participle of *deservir* (see DESERVE).]

WORD KEY: USAGE

desert or **dessert?** *Dessert* is a noun, is pronounced with the stress on the second syllable, and has only one meaning: 'a sweet course of a meal'. *Desert* is pronounced with the stress on the first syllable when it is a noun meaning 'a dry barren area of land', and with the stress on the second syllable when it is a noun meaning 'what sb deserves', in *just deserts* and similar expressions. The stress is also on the second syllable when *desert* is used as a verb, meaning 'abandon' or 'abscond'.

deserted /di zúrtid/ *adj.* empty after being abandoned by people

deserter /di zúrtər/ *n.* a member of the armed forces who leaves his or her post without permission and does not intend to go back

desertification /di zúrtifi káysh'n/ *n.* a process by which land becomes increasingly dry until almost no vegetation grows on it, making it a desert

desertion /di zúrsh'n/ *n.* the act or an instance of deserting from the armed forces

desert island *n.* a small isolated unpopulated tropical island

desert lynx *n.* = caracal

desert pavement *n.* GEOG a layer of gravel that remains when the finer-grained particles of a desert soil have been blown away

desert pea *n.* an Australian trailing plant with bright red flowers. It is the floral emblem of South Australia. Latin name: *Clianthus formosus*.

desert rat *n.* **1.** ZOOL DESERT RODENT any rodent that lives in a desert **2.** ARMY UK SOLDIER IN N AFRICA a soldier who served in the British 7th Armoured Division in North Africa during World War II (*informal*)

desert varnish *n.* GEOG a very thin dark surface coating of iron and manganese oxides that forms on exposed rock surfaces in deserts

deserve /di zúrv/ (-serves, -serving, -served) *vt.* to have earned or be worthy of sth [13thC. Via Old French *deservir* from Latin *deservire* 'to serve well', from *servire* (see SERVE).] —**deserver** *n.*

deserved /di zúrvd/ *adj.* justly earned or merited —**deservedness** /di zúrvidnəss/ *n.*

deservedly /di zúrvidli/ *adv.* in a way that is justly and fully earned or merited ○ *She was deservedly popular as a teacher.*

deserving /di zúrving/ *adj.* worthy to receive sth because of need, merit, or justice ○ *The charity was thought to be a deserving cause.* —**deservingly** *adv.* —**deservingness** *n.*

desex /dee séks/ (-sexes, -sexing, -sexed) *vt.* **1.** VET, MED REMOVE SEX ORGANS to remove the sex organs from an animal or person **2.** = desexualize

desexualize /dee sékshoo əlīz/ (-izes, -izing, -ized), **desexualise** (-ises, -ising, -ised) *vt.* to suppress or diminish the sexual characteristics of an animal or person —**desexualization** /dee sékshoo əlī záysh'n/ *n.*

deshabille /dáysə beél/, **dishabille** /díssə-/ *n.* **1.** STATE OF CASUAL DRESS a state in which sb is partially undressed or dressed very casually or incompletely (*formal*) **2.** CASUAL CLOTHING very casual clothes or clothes worn very casually (*archaic*) [Late 17thC. From French *déshabillé*, past participle of *déshabiller* 'to undress', from *habiller* 'to dress'.]

De Sica /də séekə/, **Vittorio** (1901–74) Italian film director and actor. He made Italian neorealism internationally known through his *Bicycle Thieves* (1948).

desiccant /déssikənt/ *n.* a substance that absorbs water and can be used to remove moisture [Late 17thC. From Latin *desiccant-*, the present participle stem of *desiccare* (see DESICCATE).]

desiccate /déssi kayt/ (**-cates, -cating, -cated**) *v.* **1.** REMOVE OR LOSE MOISTURE to remove the moisture from sth or become free of moisture **2.** *vt.* PRESERVE FOOD BY DRYING to preserve food by removing its moisture [Late 16thC. From Latin *desiccat-*, the past participle stem of *desiccare* 'to dry out', from *siccus* 'dry'.] —**desiccation** /déssi káysh'n/ *n.* —**desiccative** /déssikətiv, -kaytiv/ *adj.*

desiccated /déssi kaytid/ *adj.* **1.** DRIED dried and often pulverized **2.** WITHOUT VITALITY lacking in energy or vitality

WORD KEY: SYNONYMS

See Synonyms at ***dry***.

desiccator /déssi kaytər/ *n.* an airtight apparatus that removes water from a substance either by heat or vacuum, or by using a chemical agent

desiderata plural of **desideratum**

desiderate /di zíddə rayt, -sídd-/ (**-ates, -ating, -ated**) *vt.* to wish or long for sth (*archaic*) [Mid-17thC. From Latin *desiderat-*, the past participle stem of *desiderare* (see DESIRE).] —**desideration** /di zíddə ráysh'n, -sídd-/ *n.*

desiderative /di zíddərətiv, -sídd-/ *adj.* **1.** DESIRING having a desire for sth (*formal*) **2.** GRAM EXPRESSING DESIRE TO DO STH used to describe a verb that, in some languages, expresses a desire to perform the action indicated by a related verb

desideratum /di zíddə ráatəm, -síddə-/ (*plural* **-ta** /-ráatə/) *n.* sth that is desired or felt to be essential (*formal*) [Mid-17thC. From Latin, a form of the past participle of *desiderare* (see DESIRE).]

design /di zín/ *v.* (**-signs, -signing, -signed**) **1.** *vti.* CREATE DETAILED PLAN OF STH to work out or create the form or structure of sth **2.** *vti.* PLAN AND MAKE STH to plan and make sth in a skilful or artistic way **3.** *vt.* INTEND FOR A USE to intend sth for a particular purpose ○ *The scholarship was designed to aid foreign students.* **4.** *vt.* INVENT to contrive, devise, or plan sth ○ *They designed a scheme to get rich quick.* ■ *n.* **1.** WAY STH IS MADE the way in which sth is planned and made ○ *The basic design of the ship was sensible.* **2.** PICTURE OF STH'S FORM AND STRUCTURE a drawing or other graphical representation of sth that shows how it is to be made **3.** DECORATIVE PATTERN a pattern or shape, sometimes repeated, used for decoration **4.** PROCESS OF DESIGNING the process and techniques of designing things **5.** SCHEME a plan or scheme for sth **6.** STH PLANNED sth that is planned or intended ■ **designs** *npl.* SELFISH OR DISHONEST PLAN a secretive plan undertaken for selfish or dishonest motives [14thC. From, ultimately, Latin *designare* (see DESIGNATE).] —**designable** *adj.* ◇ **by design** intentionally or on purpose

designate /dézzig nayt/ *vt.* (**-nates, -nating, -nated**) **1.** DESCRIBE FORMALLY to give sb or sth a formal description or name (*often passive*) **2.** CHOOSE FOR A USE to choose sth for a particular purpose (*usually passive*) **3.** NAME TO A POSITION to formally choose sb for a job, position, or duty **4.** MARK to mark or indicate sth ○ *Coloured pins on the map designated the new buildings.* ■ *adj.* CHOSEN FOR FUTURE POST chosen for a particular position, while not yet actually in office [Late 18thC. From Latin *designat-*, the past participle stem of *designare* 'to mark out', from, ultimately, *signum* 'mark'.] —**designative** /dézzig naytiv/ *adj.* —**designatory** /dézzig náytəri, -nətəri/ *adj.* —**designator** /dézzig naytər/ *n.*

designated driver *n.* sb who goes to a social occasion and decides in advance not have any alcoholic drinks so as to be able to drive other people safely

designation /dézzig náysh'n/ *n.* **1.** NAME a name, label, or description given to sth or sb **2.** FACT OF BEING SPECIFIED the act or process of being named or specified

designedly /di zínidli/ *adv.* intentionally or on purpose

designer /di zínər/ *n.* SB WHO DESIGNS sb who makes and executes designs ■ *adj.* **1.** TRENDY used to describe sth to suggest that it is trendy and popular ○ *designer foods* **2.** DESIGNED BY SB FAMOUS created or produced by a famous designer

designer drug *n.* a drug that has been chemically altered to enhance its properties or to evade a legal prohibition

designer gene *n.* a gene that is introduced into an organism to control the presence or absence of a specific characteristic

designer label *n.* a label attached to clothing to display the name of the designer

designer stubble *n.* beard growth that is kept deliberately short to look as if the person has not shaved recently rather than as if trying to grow a beard (*informal*)

designing /di zíning/ *adj.* tending to scheme and make secret plans for personal benefit —**designingly** *adv.*

desinence /déssinənss/ *n.* an ending or suffix of a word (*technical*) [Late 16thC. Via French *désinence* from medieval Latin *desinentia*, from Latin *desinere* 'to leave off, end', from *sinere* 'to leave'.] —**desinential** /déssi nénsh'l/ *adj.*

desirable /di zírəb'l/ *adj.* **1.** WORTHY OF DESIRE worth having or doing **2.** ATTRACTIVE sexually attractive or pleasing ■ *n.* SB OR STH DESIRED sb who or sth that is desired —**desirability** /di zírə bíllәti/ *n.* —**desirably** /di zírəbli/ *adv.*

desire /di zír/ *vt.* (**-sires, -siring, -sired**) **1.** WISH FOR to want sth very strongly **2.** FIND SEXUALLY ATTRACTIVE to want to have sexual relations with sb **3.** REQUEST to wish for and request sth (*formal*) ■ *n.* **1.** CRAVING a wish, craving, or longing for sth **2.** STH WISHED FOR sth that or sb who is wished for (*formal*) **3.** SEXUAL CRAVING a strong wish for sexual relations with sb (*formal*) ○ *'Is it not strange that desire should so many years outlive performance?'* (William Shakespeare, *Henry IV, Part 2*) [13thC. Via Old French from Latin *desiderare*, perhaps originally 'to wish upon a star', from the stem *sider-* 'star' (source of English *consider* and *sidereal*).] —**desirer** *n.*

WORD KEY: SYNONYMS

See Synonyms at ***want***.

desirous /di zírəss/ *adj.* seeking or wishing for sth very much (*formal*) —**desirously** *adv.* —**desirousness** *n.*

desist /di síst, -zíst/ (**-sists, -sisting, -sisted**) *vi.* to cease or stop doing sth [15thC. Via Old French from Latin *desistere*, from *sistere* 'to bring to a standstill', from *stare* 'to stand' (source of English *stance*).] —**desistance** *n.*

desk /desk/ *n.* **1.** FURNITURE TABLE USED FOR WORK a table with a broad flat or sloping top, often with drawers and compartments, used for writing, reading, drawing, or computing **2.** COUNTER OFFERING SERVICE TO CUSTOMERS a counter where a service is provided, e.g. in a hotel or an airport **3.** DEPARTMENT OF ORGANIZATION a division of a communications company or other organization that specializes in a particular area of interest **4.** MUSIC STAND FOR SUPPORTING MUSIC a stand for supporting a musical score that is shared by two players in an orchestra, or the two players who share it **5.** CHR BOOK STAND IN CHURCH a stand for the book from which a service is read in church ■ *adj.* OF A DESK at, for, done on, or taking place at a desk [14thC. Via medieval Latin *desca* from, ultimately, Latin *discus* 'disc, dish, tray' (see DISH). The underlying idea is of a tray set on legs.]

deskbound /désk bownd/ *adj.* working at a desk rather than at a physically active or practical task

desk clerk *n. US, Can* a hotel receptionist

desk editor *n.* sb who prepares text for typesetting or publishing, corrects proofs, and passes corrected proofs for printing

deskill /dee skíl/ (**-skills, -skilling, -skilled**) *vt.* to remove the need for skill or judgment in the performance of a task, often because of increasingly sophisticated production methods

desktop /désk top/ *n.* **1.** SURFACE OF DESK the working surface of a desk **2.** GRAPHICAL COMPUTER REPRESENTATION OF OFFICE DESK a visible portion of a software program that forms a background on which icons representing equipment, programs, and files are displayed ■ *adj.* USABLE ON TOP OF DESK small and compact enough to be used on the top of a desk, especially as a piece of computer equipment

desktop publishing *n.* the use of a personal computer and specialist software to design, lay out, and produce typeset-quality documents for output on a computer printer or for commercial printing

desm- *prefix.* = **desmo-** (*used before vowels*)

desman /déssmən/ *n.* **1.** PYRENEAN AMPHIBIOUS MAMMAL an amphibious mammal resembling a mole that has dense fur, webbed feet, and a flat scaly tail and lives in the Pyrenees. Latin name: *Galemys pyrenaicus.* **2.** RUSSIAN AMPHIBIOUS MAMMAL an amphibious mammal related to the Pyrenean desman that is found in Russia. Latin name: *Desmana moschata.* [Late 18thC. Shortening of Swedish *desmanråtta* 'muskrat', from *desman* 'musk' (from, ultimately, medieval Latin *bisamum*) + *råtta* 'rat'.]

desmid /déssmid, déz-/ *n.* a green, usually one-celled, freshwater alga composed of two symmetrical half-cells. It forms branching matlike colonies and is found in unpolluted water. Family: Desmidiaceae. [Mid-19thC. From modern Latin *Desmidium*, genus name, which was coined from Greek *desmos* 'bond, chain'.] —**desmidian** /dess míddi ən, dez-/ *adj.*

desmo- *prefix.* ligament, bond ○ *desmosome* [From Greek *desmos*, from *dein* 'to bind' (source of English *diadem*)]

Des Moines /di móyn/ capital, largest city, and commercial centre of the US state of Iowa, situated where the Raccoon River meets the Des Moines River in the south-central part of the state. Population: 193,422 (1996).

Desmoulins /dáy moo láN/, **Camille** (1760–94) French revolutionary and journalist. An effective pamphleteer and orator, he incurred the wrath of Robespierre and was guillotined. Full name **Lucie-Simplice-Camille-Benoist Desmoulins**

desolate *adj.* /déssələt/ **1.** EMPTY bare, uninhabited, and deserted **2.** ALONE solitary, joyless, and without hope ○ *'And I was desolate and sick of an old passion'* (Ernest Dowson, *Non Sum Qualis Eram Bonae Sub Regno Cynarae*; 1896) **3.** GRIM dismal and gloomy ■ *vt.* /déssə layt/ (**-lates, -lating, -lated**) **1.** DEVASTATE PLACE to make a place barren or deserted **2.** MAKE WRETCHED to make sb feel sad and lonely [14thC. From Latin *desolatus*, the past participle of *desolare*, literally 'to leave alone', from *solus* 'alone' (source of English *solitary*).] —**desolater** /déssə laytər/ *n.* —**desolately** /déssələtli/ *adv.* —**desolateness** /-lətnəss/ *n.*

desolation /déssə láysh'n/ *n.* **1.** WRETCHED FEELING a feeling of loneliness and despair **2.** DESOLATE CONDITION a condition of devastation or ruin in a place **3.** ACT OF DEVASTATING PLACE the act or process of devastating or laying waste to a place

desorption /dee sáwrpsh'n, -záwrp-/ *n.* the action or process of releasing an absorbed substance from sth, e.g. gas from rocks [Early 20thC. Coined from DE- + ABSORPTION.]

despair /di spáir/ *n.* **1.** FEELING OF HOPELESSNESS a profound feeling that there is no hope **2.** CAUSE OF HOPELESSNESS sb or sth that makes sb feel hopeless or exasperated ■ *vi.* (**-spairs, -spairing, -spaired**) LOSE HOPE to feel that there is no hope [13thC. Via Old French from Latin *desperare*, literally 'to stop hoping', from *sperare* 'to hope', from *spes* 'hope'.]

despairing /di spáiring/ *adj.* feeling or showing loss of hope ○ *a despairing look* —**despairingly** *adv.*

despatch *vti., n.* = **dispatch**

desperado /déspə ráadō/ (*plural* **-does** *or* **-dos**) *n.* a reckless and violent criminal [Early 17thC. Alteration of obsolete *desperate* 'desperate person', modelled on Spanish *desesperado*.]

desperate /désspərət/ *adj.* **1.** DESPAIRING overwhelmed with urgency and anxiety, to the point of losing hope ○ *Desperate because of his financial situation, he took his own life.* **2.** AS LAST RESORT so drastic or reckless as to be suitable only for a last resort ○ *The firefighters made a last desperate attempt to rescue the children.* **3.** EXTREME extremely difficult, serious, or dangerous ○ *a desperate shortage of food and water* **4.** IN GREAT NEED wanting or needing sth very much ○ *Desperate for an answer, she phoned again.*

5. BEYOND HOPE so wicked as to allow no hope of redemption **6.** AWFUL extremely bad or deplorable [14thC. From Latin *desperatus*, past participle of *desperare* (see DESPAIR).] —**desperately** *adv.* —**desperateness** *n.*

desperation /déspə ráysh'n/ *n.* **1.** RECKLESSNESS recklessness brought on by great urgency and anxiety ○ *In desperation people were jumping from the windows of the blazing building.* **2.** HOPELESSNESS a condition of being without hope

despicable /di spíkəb'l/ *adj.* fully deserving of contempt [Mid-16thC. From late Latin *despicabilis*, from Latin *despicari* 'to look down on'.] —**despicability** /di spíkə bílləti/ *n.* —**despicableness** /di spíkəb'lnəss/ *n.* —**despicably** /-əbli/ *adv.*

Despina /de spéenə/ *n.* a small natural satellite of Neptune, discovered in 1989 by the Voyager 2 planetary probe

despise /di spíz/ (**-spises, -spising, -spised**) *vt.* to look down on and feel contempt for sb or sth [13thC. From Old French *despis-*, the stem of *despire*, from Latin *despicere*, literally 'to look down on', from *specere* 'to look' (source of English *spectacle*).] —**despiser** *n.*

despite /di spít/ *prep.* **1.** REGARDLESS OF notwithstanding or regardless of sth ○ *A mission to investigate the rings of Saturn blasted off today despite bad weather.* **2.** CONTRARY TO indicates that sth is done unexpectedly or unintentionally ○ *She blushed deeply despite herself.* [13thC. Via Old French *despit* 'spite' from Latin *despect-*, the past participle stem of *despicere* (see DESPISE).] ◇ **in despite of** in spite of or notwithstanding (*archaic*)

despiteful /di spítf'l/ *adj.* spiteful (*archaic*)

despoil /di spóyl/ (**-spoils, -spoiling, -spoiled**) *vt.* to rob a place, often using force, of everything of value ○ *Thieves had despoiled the palace.* [13thC. Via Old French *despoillier* from Latin *despoliare* 'to strip entirely of booty', from *spolium* 'booty'.] —**despoiler** *n.* —**despoilment** *n.*

despoliation /di spōli áysh'n/ *n.* the plundering of everything of value in a place

despond /di spónd/ *vi.* (**-sponds, -sponding, -sponded**) GIVE UP HOPE to become discouraged or lose hope (*archaic or literary*) ○ *began to despond in their minds* ■ *n.* HOPELESSNESS a feeling of extreme unhappiness and hopelessness (*archaic or literary*) [Mid-17thC. From Latin *despondere* 'to give up (one's vitality)', literally 'to promise away', from *spondere* 'to promise' (source of English *sponsor*).] —**despondingly** *adv.*

despondent /di spóndənt/ *adj.* extremely unhappy and discouraged —**despondence** *n.* —**despondency** *n.* —**despondently** *adv.*

despot /déss pot, -pət/ *n.* **1.** POL ABSOLUTE RULER a tyrant or ruler with absolute powers **2.** TYRANNICAL PERSON sb who acts in a tyrannical way towards people **3.** HIST ROMAN, BYZANTINE, OR OTTOMAN RULER a minor emperor or prince of the later Roman, Byzantine, or Ottoman empires [Mid-16thC. Via French *despote* from, ultimately, Greek *despotēs* 'absolute ruler'.]

despotic /di spóttik/, **despotical** /-k'l/ *adj.* relating to, typical of, or behaving like a despot —**despotically** *adv.*

despotism /déspətizəm/ *n.* **1.** RULE BY DESPOT rule by a despot or tyrant **2.** ABUSE OF POWER cruel and arbitrary use of power

despumate /di spyoō mayt, désspyoō-/ (**-mates, -mating, -mated**) *v.* **1.** *vi.* CHEM FORM FROTH to form froth or scum on the surface of a liquid **2.** *vt.* INDUST REMOVE FROTH OR SCUM to remove the scum or froth on the surface of a liquid [Mid-17thC. From Latin *despumat-* the past participle stem of *despumare* 'to skim off (scum)', from *spuma* 'foam, scum' (source of English *spume*).] —**despumation** /désspyoō máysh'n/ *n.*

desquamate /déskwə mayt/ (**-mates, -mating, -mated**) *v.* **1.** *vi.* PHYSIOL SCALE OR PEEL OFF to flake or peel off naturally in small pieces (*refers especially to skin*) **2.** *vt.* DERMAT REMOVE LAYER OF SKIN to remove a thin layer of skin, especially as a treatment for acne [Early 18thC. From *desquamat-*, the past participle stem of Latin *desquamare* 'to scale off', from *squama* 'scale'.] —**desquamation** /déskwə máysh'n/ *n.*

des res /déz réz/ *n.* a house or flat that is considered, especially by an estate agent, as highly desirable (*informal*) [Late 20thC. Shortening of *desirable residence*.]

Dessau /déssow/ industrial city in Halle District, Saxony-Anhalt State, east-central Germany. It is situated about 64 km/40 mi. north of Leipzig. Population: 97,800 (1990).

dessert /di zúrt/ *n.* **1.** SWEET DISH CONCLUDING MEAL a sweet course eaten at the end or towards the end of a meal **2.** FRUIT AND NUTS fresh or dried fruit and nuts served at the end of a meal (*dated*) [Mid-16thC. From French, literally '(course following) clearing the table', from the past participle of *desservir*, literally 'to remove what has been served', from *servir* (see SERVE).]

WORD KEY: USAGE

See Usage note at ***desert***.

dessertspoon /dizúrt spoon/ *n.* **1.** MEDIUM-SIZED SPOON FOR EATING DESSERT a medium-sized spoon, larger than a teaspoon but smaller than a tablespoon and used for eating dessert **2.** **dessertspoon, dessertspoonful** AMOUNT HELD BY DESSERTSPOON the amount a dessertspoon contains

dessert wine *n.* a sweet wine served with dessert or after a meal

destabilize /dee stáybə līz/ (**-lizes, -lizing, -lized**), **destabilise** (**-lises, -lising, -lised**) *vt.* to make sth, particularly a government or economy, unstable in order to impair its functioning or bring about its collapse —**destabilization** /dee stáybə lī záysh'n/ *n.*

destination /désti náysh'n/ *n.* **1.** PREDETERMINED END OF TRIP the place to which sb or sth is going or must go **2.** INTENDED OR DESTINED END a purpose for which sb or sth is intended [14thC. From the Latin stem *destination-* 'appointment', literally 'sth determined', from *destinare* (see DESTINE).]

destine /déstin/ (**-tines, -tining, -tined**) *vt.* to preordain or intend sb or sth for a particular fate or use (*formal*) [14thC. Via French from Latin *destinare* 'to set up, decree, determine', from the base *-stinare* 'to cause to stand'.]

destined /déstind/ *adj.* **1.** SURE sure, preordained, or intended ○ *From an early age he was destined to follow his father in the family business.* **2.** HEADING TOWARDS bound or travelling towards a particular destination

destiny /déstini/ (*plural* **-nies**) *n.* **1.** SB'S PREORDAINED FUTURE the apparently predetermined and inevitable series of events that happen to sb or sth ○ *No one could have foreseen that the child's destiny was to rule an empire.* **2.** INNER REALIZABLE PURPOSE OF A LIFE the inner purpose of a life that can be discovered and realized ○ *He decided that his destiny was to go into show business.* **3.** **destiny, Destiny** STH THAT PREDETERMINES EVENTS a force or agency that predetermines what will happen ○ *Destiny had decided her future.* [14thC. From Old French *destinee*, from, ultimately, Latin *destinare* (see DESTINE).]

destitute /désti tyoot/ *adj.* **1.** LACKING THE NECESSITIES OF LIFE lacking all money, resources, and possessions necessary for subsistence **2.** LACKING STH lacking or without sth [14thC. From Latin *destitutus*, the past participle of *destituere* 'to set down, abandon', from *statuere* 'to set', from *status* 'position'.] —**destituteness** *n.*

destitution /désti tyoōsh'n/ *n.* lack of the necessary means of subsistence

WORD KEY: SYNONYMS

See Synonyms at ***poverty***.

destrier /déstri ər/ *n.* a warhorse or charger, especially of a medieval knight (*archaic*) [14thC. Via Anglo-Norman *destrer* and Old French *destrier* from, ultimately, Latin *dexter* 'right' (because the horse was led by the squire's right hand).]

destroy /di stróy/ (**-stroys, -stroying, -stroyed**) *v.* **1.** *vti.* DEMOLISH to demolish or reduce sth to fragments **2.** *vti.* RUIN to ruin or make sth useless **3.** *vti.* ABOLISH to abolish, rescind, or end sth **4.** *vt.* DEFEAT to defeat sb in a crushing way **5.** *vt.* KILL ANIMAL to kill sth or sb, especially an animal (*usually passive*) ○ *Afterwards, the dog could not be cured and so had to be destroyed.* [12thC. Via Old French *destruire* from, ultimately, Latin *destruere*, literally 'to undo results of building' from *struere* 'to build' (source of English *structure*).] —**destroyable** *adj.*

destroyer /di stróyər/ *n.* **1.** NAVY SMALL FAST WARSHIP a fast highly manoeuvrable warship, smaller than a cruiser and bigger than a frigate, that is used to escort convoys and attack submarines **2.** SB OR STH THAT DESTROYS sb or sth that causes destruction

destroyer escort *n.* a smaller, slower form of destroyer that is mainly used to escort convoys of merchant ships

destroying angel *n.* a highly poisonous large white mushroom with a frill near the top of its stalk. It grows in moist woodlands in temperate regions. Latin name: *Amanita virosa.*

destruct /di strúkt/ *n.* INTENTIONAL DESTRUCTION OF ROCKET OR MISSILE the intentional destruction of a malfunctioning missile or rocket after its launch ■ *vti.* (**-structs, -structing, -structed**) DESTROY MALFUNCTIONING MISSILE OR ROCKET to intentionally destroy a malfunctioning missile or rocket after its launch, or be destroyed in this way [Mid-20thC. Back-formation from DESTRUCTION.]

destructible /di strúktəb'l/ *adj.* capable of being destroyed or liable to be destroyed [Mid-18thC. Via French from late Latin *destructibilis*, from Latin *destruct-* (see DESTRUCTION).] —**destructibility** /di strúktə bílləti/ *n.*

destruction /di strúksh'n/ *n.* **1.** PROCESS OF DESTROYING the act or process of destroying sth **2.** DESTROYED STATE the condition of having been destroyed **3.** MEANS OF DESTROYING a cause or means of destroying sth [13thC. From the Latin stem *destruction-*, from *destruct-*, the past participle stem of *destruere* (see DESTROY).]

destructive /di strúktiv/ *adj.* **1.** DESTROYING causing or capable of causing destruction **2.** MEANT TO DAMAGE intended to damage or hurt rather than be helpful or instructive [15thC. Via French from late Latin *destructivus*, from Latin *destruct-* (see DESTRUCTION).] —**destructively** *adv.* —**destructivity** /di strúk tívvəti, dée-/ *n.* —**destructiveness** /di strúktivnəss/ *n.*

destructive distillation *n.* the process of heating solid substances in the absence of air to decompose them in order to obtain useful products from the vapour and residues

destructor /di strúktər/ *n.* **1.** INDUST INCINERATOR an incinerator used to burn rubbish **2.** AEROSP EXPLOSIVE DEVICE FOR MISSILE OR ROCKET an onboard explosive device used to destroy a missile or rocket if it malfunctions dangerously after its launch

desuetude /désswi tyood/ *n.* the condition of not being in use (*formal*) [Early 17thC. Via French *désuétude* from, ultimately, Latin *desuescere* 'to become unaccustomed', from *suescere* 'to be accustomed' (source of English *custom*).]

desulfurize *vti.* US = **desulphurize**

desulphurize /dee súlfə rīz/ (**-izes, -izing, -ized**), **desulphurise** (**-phurises, -phurising, -phurised, -phurised**) *vti.* to remove sulphur and its compounds from sth, typically from petroleum products or from flue gases when coal or another fuel is burned, or to lose sulphur in this way —**desulphurization** /dee súlfə rī záysh'n/ *n.* —**desulphurizer** /dee súlfə rīzər/ *n.*

desultory /déss'ltəri/ *adj.* **1.** PASSING FROM ONE THING TO ANOTHER aimlessly passing from one thing to another **2.** RANDOM happening in a random, disorganized, or unmethodical way ○ *The soldiers were subject to desultory fire from the enemy position.* [Late 16thC. From Latin *desultorius* 'leaping', from *desilire* 'to leap down', from *salire* 'to leap' (source of English *salient*).] —**desultorily** *adv.* —**desultoriness** *n.*

det., **det** *abbr.* GRAM determiner

detach /di tách/ (**-taches, -taching, -tached**) *v.* **1.** *vti.* SEPARATE to separate, disconnect, or unfasten sth, or become separated, disconnected, or unfastened **2.** *vt.* MIL SEND ON SPECIAL ASSIGNMENT to separate a military unit or an individual from the normal, larger unit for special duties [Late 17thC. Via French *détacher* from Old French *destachier*, from *attachier* 'to attach' (see ATTACH).] —**detacher** *n.*

detachable /di táchəb'l/ *adj.* capable of being taken off, disconnected, or removed —**detachability** /di táchə bílləti/ *n.*

detached /di tácht/ *adj.* **1.** NOT ATTACHED not attached to sth **2.** BUILDING SEPARATE standing on its own and not joined to another building **3.** FREE FROM EMOTIONAL INVOLVEMENT unaffected by emotional involvement or any form of bias —**detachedly** /di táchidli, di táchtli/ *adv.* —**detachedness** /di táchtnəss/ *n.*

detached retina *n.* an eye condition in which the retina becomes separated from the eyeball, causing loss of vision

detachment /di táchmənt/ *n.* **1.** ALOOFNESS AND INDIFFERENCE lack of interest in or involvement with other people, or indifference to worldly concerns **2.** DISINTERESTEDNESS a lack of bias, prejudice, or emotional involvement **3.** CONDITION OR PROCESS OF SEPARATION the condition of being separated from sth, or the process of separating one thing from another **4.** MIL MILITARY UNIT SENT ON SPECIAL ASSIGNMENT a military unit separated from its normal, larger unit for special duties **5.** SPECIALIZED GROUP any specialized and separately employed unit of a group or organization **6.** *Can* CANADIAN POLICE UNIT an organizational unit of the Royal Canadian Mounted Police

detail /dee tayl/ *n.* **1.** INDIVIDUAL PART an individual separable part of sth, especially one of several items of information ○ *No details of the proposed legislation are available yet.* **2.** EACH AND EVERY ELEMENT all of the individual elements that together make up a whole **3.** INCLUSION OF ALL ELEMENTS treatment of and inclusion of all of the individual elements that make up sth ○ *Your description of the item needs more detail.* **4.** INSIGNIFICANT PART sth that is insignificant or a minor part of sth else ○ *Safety in the sport is not a mere detail.* **5.** ARTS, ARCHIT SMALL ELEMENT OF ART OR BUILDING STRUCTURE a small element of a work of art or building structure, considered separately **6.** GROUP WITH SPECIAL TASK a group of people, especially in the armed services, given a specific task ■ **details** *npl.* PERSONAL FACTS facts about sb, e.g. his or her name and address ■ *vt.* (**-tails, -tailing, -tailed**) **1.** LIST THINGS to list or enumerate a series of items or events ○ *Please detail all the things that were stolen.* **2.** DECORATE to add refinements or decorations to sth **3.** AUTOMOT CLEAN CAR COMPLETELY to clean and polish a motor vehicle so thoroughly inside and out that it is spotless **4.** MIL GIVE MILITARY UNIT SPECIALIZED ASSIGNMENT to assign a military unit to a specialized task (*often passive*) [Early 17thC. From French *détail*, literally 'piece cut off', from *détaillir* 'to cut up', from *taillier* 'to cut'.] ◇ **go into detail** to be very specific and include all of the particulars ◇ **in detail** covering every item or particular

detail drawing *n.* a large-scale drawing that shows part of a machine, device, or building

detailed /dee tayld/ *adj.* including all or many of the particular elements of sth

detain /di táyn/ (**-tains, -taining, -tained**) *vt.* **1.** DELAY PROGRESS to hold back or delay sb or sth **2.** LAW HOLD IN CUSTODY to restrain or keep sb or sth in custody [15thC. Via Old French *detenir* from, ultimately, Latin *detinere*, literally 'to hold back', from *tenere* 'to hold' (see TENANT).] —**detainable** *adj.* —**detainment** *n.*

detainee /dee tay née, di-/ *n.* sb who is held in custody

detainer /di táynər/ *n.* **1.** WRIT AUTHORIZING EXTENDED DETENTION a writ authorizing that sb in custody may be confined for a further period **2.** WRONGFUL DETENTION the wrongful withholding of sb's property or freedom

detect /di tékt/ (**-tects, -tecting, -tected**) *vt.* **1.** PERCEIVE THE EXISTENCE OF to notice or discover the existence of sth **2.** ELECTRON ENG = **demodulate** [15thC. From Latin *detect-*, the past participle stem of *detegere* 'to uncover', from *tegere* 'to cover'.] —**detectable** *adj.*

detection /di téksh'n/ *n.* **1.** PERCEPTION OF STH'S EXISTENCE the act of noticing or discovering the existence of sth, or the state of having been detected **2.** CRIMINOL DETECTIVE WORK the work of a detective in investigating crime or wrongdoing **3.** ELECTRON ENG = **demodulation**

detective /di téktiv/ *n.* SB WHO INVESTIGATES WRONGDOING sb who investigates and gathers evidence about crimes or possible wrongdoing, either for a police force or privately for a client ○ *I became a detective last year.* ■ *adj.* DETECTING STH acting to detect sth ○ *detective devices*

detector /di téktər/ *n.* **1.** TECH SENSING DEVICE a device for sensing the presence of or changes in sth, e.g. radiation or pressure **2.** SB OR STH THAT DETECTS sb who or sth that detects

detent /di tént/ *n.* a locking device, e.g. a lever or spring-loaded catch, that permits movement of a machine part in one direction only [Late 17thC. From French *détente* 'release', literally 'opposite of stretching', from, ultimately, Latin *tendere* 'to stretch' (source of English *tension*).]

détente /day tónt, -taánt/ *n.* a relaxation of tension or hostility between nations [Early 20thC. From French, 'relaxation' (see DETENT).]

detention /di ténsh'n/ *n.* **1.** CRIMINOL PROCESS OF BEING DETAINED the act keeping sb in custody, or the state of being kept in custody **2.** EDUC PUNISHMENT BY BEING DETAINED AFTER SCHOOL a form of punishment for school students in which they are made to stay in class at a break or at school after normal hours [15thC. From the late Latin stem *detention-*, from, ultimately, Latin *detinere* (see DETAIN).]

detention centre *n.* a place where young people can be confined for a brief period by order of a court

detention home *n. US* = **remand home**

deter /di túr/ (**-ters, -terring, -terred**) *vti.* to discourage sb from taking action or prevent sth happening, especially by making people feel afraid or anxious ○ *New laws to deter speeding will be enforced at the end of the month.* [Mid-16thC. From Latin *deterrere*, literally 'to scare off', from *terrere* 'to scare' (source of English *terror*).] —**determent** *n.*

deterge /di túrj/ (**-terges, -terging, -terged**) *vt.* to cleanse sth, especially a wound (*technical*) [Early 17thC. Directly or via French *déterger* from Latin *detergere*, literally 'to wipe off', from *tergere* 'to wipe'.]

detergency /di túrjənssi/, **detergence** /di túrjənss/ *n.* the ability of a substance to cleanse (*technical*)

detergent /di túrjənt/ *n.* CLEANSING SUBSTANCE a cleansing substance, especially a synthetic liquid that dissolves dirt and oil ■ *adj.* CLEANSING with the properties of a detergent

deteriorate /di teéri ə rayt/ (**-rates, -rating, -rated**) *vti.* to become or make sth worse in quality, value, or strength [Late 16thC. From *deteriorat-*, the past participle stem of late Latin *deteriorare*, from Latin *deterior* 'worse', from, ultimately, *de* 'down'.] —**deteriorative** /di teéri ə raytiv/ *adj.*

deterioration /di teéri ə ráysh'n/ *n.* **1.** DECLINE a decline in quality, value, or strength **2.** PROCESS OF DETERIORATING the act or process of deteriorating **3.** DETERIORATED CONDITION the condition of having deteriorated

determinable /di túrminəb'l/ *adj.* **1.** CAPABLE OF BEING DETERMINED able to be worked out, decided, or found **2.** ABLE TO BE ENDED subject to being terminated —**determinability** /di túrminə bílləti/ *n.* —**determinably** /di túrminəbli/ *adv.*

determinant /di túrminənt/ *n.* **1.** CAUSE a factor that causes or influences sth **2.** MATH SQUARE ARRAY OF MATHEMATICAL ELEMENTS a square array of elements that is used in various mathematical processes, e.g. solving simultaneous equations and studying linear transformations, and which itself has a numerical value ■ *adj.* CAUSAL influencing or causing sth

determinate /di túrminət/ *adj.* **1.** LIMITED with exact and definite limits **2.** DETERMINED determined (*formal*) **3.** BOT WITH STEMS ENDING IN A BUD used to describe a pattern of flowering in which primary and secondary stems end in a flower bud and stop growing. ◊ **indeterminate** —**determinately** *adv.* —**determinateness** *n.*

determination /di túrmi náysh'n/ *n.* **1.** FIRMNESS OF PURPOSE firmness of purpose, will, or intention ○ *full of ambition and determination* **2.** FIXED PURPOSE a fixed purpose or resolution ○ *her determination to succeed* **3.** ACT OF DISCOVERING STH an act of finding out or ascertaining sth, especially as a result of investigation or research (*formal*) ○ *determination of the cause of death* **4.** DECISION ON COURSE OF ACTION decision-making on, or the establishment of, a course of action (*formal*) ○ *They were entrusted with the determination of future policy.* **5.** SETTLEMENT OF DISPUTE OR CONTEST the authoritative settlement of a dispute, especially by a judicial body **6.** END OF ESTATE, INTEREST, OR RIGHT the conclusion or termination of an estate, interest, or right **7.** LOGIC QUALIFYING OF CONCEPT the qualifying of a concept or proposition by defining its attributes **8.** EMBRYOL STAGE IN DEVELOPMENT OF EMBRYONIC TISSUE the stage in the development of embryonic tissue after which it can only develop as one specific type of tissue and no longer has the potential to develop into different types

determinative /di túrminətiv/ *adj.* ACTING TO DETERMINE able to determine sth ■ *n.* **1.** DETERMINING FACTOR a factor that determines sth **2.** GRAM = **determiner** —**determinatively** *adv.* —**determinativeness** *n.*

determine /di túrmin/ (**-mines, -mining, -mined**) *v.* **1.** *vt.* DECIDE to decide or settle sth conclusively **2.** *vt.* FIND OUT to find out or ascertain sth, usually after investigation **3.** *vt.* INFLUENCE to influence or give form to sth **4.** *vt.* FIX LIMITS to fix the limits or form of sth **5.** *vti.* ADOPT OR CAUSE TO ADOPT PURPOSE to adopt a set purpose, or make sb do this ○ *determined to leave as soon as possible* **6.** *vti.* END to end sth, or come to an end [14thC. Via Old French from Latin *determinare*, literally 'to set the limits of', from *terminus* 'limit, boundary'. Originally in the sense 'to bring to an end'.]

determined /di túrmind/ *adj.* feeling or showing firmness or a fixed purpose —**determinedly** *adv.* —**determinedness** *n.*

determiner /di túrminər/ *n.* **1.** GRAM WORD THAT DETERMINES NOUN USE a word such as 'a', 'the', 'this', 'each', 'some', 'either', 'my', and 'your' that appears before any descriptive adjective and decides the kind of reference that a noun has **2.** STH OR SB THAT DETERMINES sth that or sb who determines

determining /di túrmining/ *adj.* causing or deciding sth

determinism /di túrminizəm/ *n.* the doctrine or belief that everything, including every human act, is caused by sth and that there is no real free will —**determinist** *n.* —**deterministic** /di túrmi nístik/ *adj.*

deterrence /di térrənss/ *n.* **1.** ACT OF DETERRING the act of deterring sb or sth **2.** STH THAT DETERS a means of deterring sb or sth **3.** DEFENSIVE POLICY the policy of discouraging enemy attack by maintaining sufficient military force to retaliate

deterrent /di térrənt/ *adj.* ACTING TO DETER capable of deterring sb or sth ■ *n.* **1.** STH THAT DETERS sth that deters sb or sth **2.** WEAPONS THAT DETER AN ATTACK weapons, particularly nuclear weapons, held as a retaliatory threat

detersive /di túrssiv/ *adj.* with the properties of a detergent (*technical*) [Late 16thC. From French *détersif*, from Latin *deters-*, the past participle stem of *detergere* (see DETERGE).]

detest /di tést/ (**-tests, -testing, -tested**) *vt.* to dislike sb or sth very much [15thC. Via French *détester* from Latin *detestari* 'to bear witness against, denounce', from *testis* 'witness' (source of English *testify*).] —**detester** *n.*

detestable /di téstəb'l/ *adj.* causing or deserving intense dislike —**detestability** /di téstə bílləti/ *n.* —**detestably** /-əbli/ *adv.*

detestation /dee te stáysh'n/ *n.* **1.** GREAT DISLIKE an intense loathing or hatred **2.** DETESTED PERSON OR THING sth that or sb who is detested ○ *Apples are a real detestation for him.*

dethrone /dee thrṓn/ (**-thrones, -throning, -throned**) *vt.* **1.** POL REMOVE RULER FROM POWER to remove a ruler, especially a monarch, from power **2.** REMOVE FROM POSITION to remove sb from a high or powerful position —**dethronement** *n.* —**dethroner** *n.*

detonate /déttə nayt/ (**-nates, -nating, -nated**) *vti.* to explode, or make sth explode [Early 18thC. From *detonat-*, the past participle stem of Latin *detonare* 'to thunder down', from *tonare* 'to thunder' (source of English *stun*).] —**detonative** /déttə naytiv/ *adj.*

detonation /déttə náysh'n/ *n.* **1.** EXPLOSION an explosion, or an act of making sth explode **2.** AUTOMOT PREMATURE COMBUSTION INSIDE ENGINE a premature spontaneous burning of a fuel-air mixture inside an internal-combustion engine

detonator /déttə naytər/ *n.* a device or small quantity of explosive used to make a bomb or larger quantity of explosive explode

detour /dee t-r, day t-r/ *n.* **1.** DEVIATION FROM MORE DIRECT ROUTE a deviation from a shorter, more direct route **2.** *US* TRANSP = **diversion** ■ *vti.* (**-tours, -touring, -toured**) DEVIATE OR MAKE DEVIATE to deviate or make sb or sth deviate from a shorter route [Mid-18thC. From French *détour*, from, ultimately, Old French *destorner* 'to turn away', from *torner* 'to turn' (see TURN).]

detox /dée toks/ *n.* = **detoxification** ▪ *vti.* (**-toxes, -toxing, -toxed**) = **detoxify** [Late 20thC. Shortening of DE-TOXIFICATION and DETOXIFY.]

detoxicate /dee tóksi kayt/ (**-cates, -cating, -cated**) *vt.* = **detoxify** —**detoxicant** /dee tóksikənt/ *n., adj.*

detoxification /dee tóksifi káysh'n/, **detoxication** /dee tóksi káysh'n/ *n.* **1.** BIOCHEM PROCESS OF REMOVING OR TRANS-FORMING POISON the process of removing toxic substances or transforming them into sth harmless **2.** MED TREATMENT FOR ADDICT the treatment of an alcoholic or drug addict by controlled withdrawal of the toxic addictive substance

detoxify /dee tóksifī/ (**-fies, -fying, -fied**) *v.* **1.** *vt.* BIOCHEM REMOVE OR TRANSFORM TOXIC SUBSTANCE to remove a poison from sth or counteract its toxic effects **2.** *vti.* MED RID SB OF TOXIC SUBSTANCES to subject sb to or undergo the withdrawal of a toxic or addictive substance such as alcohol or a drug [Early 20thC. Coined from DE- + TOXIC + -FY.]

detract /di trákt/ (**-tracts, -tracting, -tracted**) *v.* **1.** *vti.* TAKE STH AWAY to reduce the quality, value, or importance of sth by taking sth away **2.** *vt.* DISPARAGE to disparage sb or sth (*archaic*) [15thC. From Latin *detract-*, the past participle stem of *detrahere* 'to take or pull away', from *trahere* 'to pull' (see TRACTOR).] —**detractingly** *adv.* —**detractive** *adj.* —**detractively** *adv.* —**detractory** *adj.*

DETR *abbr.* Department of the Environment, Transport, and the Regions

detraction /di tráksh'n/ *n.* **1.** SLANDERING the act of damaging sb's reputation, especially by making discrediting comments (*formal*) **2.** DETRACTING PERSON OR THING sb or sth that detracts from the quality, value, or importance of sth

detractor /di tráktər/ *n.* sb who disparages or devalues sth or sb

detrain /dee tráyn/ (**-trains, -training, -trained**) *vti.* to get out of or remove people from a railway train —**detrainment** *n.*

detribalize /dee tríbə līz/ (**-izes, -izing, -ized**), **de-tribalise** (**-ises, -ising, -ised**) *vti.* to abandon or make people abandon tribal practices, usually by exposure to another culture —**detribalization** /dee tríbə lī záysh'n/ *n.*

detriment /déttrimənt/ *n.* **1.** DISADVANTAGE damage, harm, or disadvantage **2.** HARMFUL THING sth that causes harm or injury (*formal*) [15thC. Via French from Latin *detrimentum*, from *deterere* 'to wear away', from *terere* 'to rub, wear' (source of English *attrition*).]

detrimental /déttri mént'l/ *adj.* causing harm or damage —**detrimentally** *adv.*

detrition /di trísh'n/ *n.* the process of wearing sth away by friction [Late 17thC. From the medieval Latin stem *detrition-*, from Latin *deterere* (see DETRIMENT).]

detritivore /di trītə vawr/, **detritovore** /n.* an organism that feeds on decaying animal or plant material. Detritivores such as bacteria, earthworms, and many insects aid in breaking down soil. [Mid-20thC. coined from DETRITUS + -VORE.]

detritus /di trítəss/ *n.* **1.** DEBRIS debris or discarded material **2.** GEOL ROCK FRAGMENTS fragments of rock that have been worn away **3.** ECOL ORGANIC MATTER organic debris formed by the decomposition of plants and animals [Late 18thC. From Latin, from the past participle of *deterere* (see DETRIMENT).] —**detrital** *adj.*

Detroit /di tróyt/ largest city in southeastern Michigan, US, on the Detroit River and Lake St Clair. Population: 1,000,272 (1996).

Detroit techno *n.* a type of techno music with a warm emotional feel, often using strings, that originated in Detroit in the late 1980s

de trop /də tró/ *adj.* superfluous or excessive [Mid-18thC. From French, literally 'excessive'.]

detrude /di trood/ (**-trudes, -truding, -truded**) *vt.* to force sth down, out, or away (*formal*) [Mid-16thC. From Latin *detrudere* 'to thrust down', from *trudere* 'to thrust'.] —**detrusion** /di troózh'n/ *n.*

detumescence /dee tyoo méss'nss/ *n.* a gradual reduction in a swelling, especially of a penis [Late

17thC. Formed from Latin *detumescere* 'to stop swelling', from *tumere* 'to swell' (source of English *tumour*).] —**detumesce** *vi.*

detumescent /dee tyoo méss'nt/ *adj.* flaccid and no longer erect

deuce[1] /dyooss/ *n.* **1.** RACKET GAMES TIE-BREAKING SITUATION in tennis, badminton, and other racket games, a situation in which a player must score two successive points to win after the score is tied **2.** CARDS DICE OR CARD WITH TWO SPOTS a playing card or the face of a dice that has two spots [15thC. Via Old French *deus* 'two' from Latin *duos*. Ultimately from an Indo-European word that is also the ancestor of English *two*.]

deuce[2] /dyooss/ *interj.* USED TO SHOW DISPLEASURE used instead of a swearword to show displeasure, irritation, or surprise (*dated slang*) ▪ *n.* BAD THING sth that is bad or unpleasant (*dated slang*) [Mid-17thC. Via Dutch or Low German *duus* 'throw of two on two dice' (the lowest score) from, ultimately, Latin *duus* 'two' (see DEUCE[1]).]

deuced /dyóossid, dyoóst/ *adj.* USED FOR EMPHASIS used instead of a swearword to give emphasis or to show irritation or displeasure (*dated slang*) ▪ *adv.* VERY decidedly or extremely (*dated slang*) —**deucedly** /dyóossidli, dyoóstli/ *adv.*

Deus /dáyōoss/ *n.* God [13thC. From Latin. From an Indo-European word that is also the ancestor of *deity, divine,* and *July.*]

deus ex machina /dáyōoss eks mákinə/ *n.* **1.** GOD WHO RESOLVES PLOT in ancient Greek and Roman theatre, a god introduced to resolve a complicated plot **2.** UNCONVINCING CHARACTER WHO RESOLVES PLOT an improbable character or unconvincing event used to resolve a plot [From modern Latin, literally 'god from the machinery'; the *machina* was a device used in Greek theatre to lower actors onto the stage]

Deut. *abbr.* Deuteronomy

deuter- *prefix.* = **deutero-** (*used before vowels*)

deuteragonist /dyoótə rággənist/ *n.* a character second in importance to the leading character (**protagonist**) in ancient Greek drama [Mid-19thC. From Greek *deuteragōnistēs*, from *deuteros* 'second' + *agōn-istēs* 'actor' (see PROTAGONIST).]

deuteranopia /dyoótərə nốpi ə/ *n.* colour blindness in which red and green are confused [Early 20thC. Coined from DEUTERO- + AN- + -OPIA. From the fact that green is regarded as the second component of colour vision.] —**deuteranopic** /-nóppik/ *adj.*

deuterate /dyoótə rayt/ (**-ates, -ating, -ated**) *vt.* to add deuterium, an isotope of hydrogen with double the normal mass, to a chemical compound [Mid-20thC. Coined from DEUTERIUM + -ATE.] —**deuteration** /dyoótə ráysh'n/ *n.*

deuteride /dyoótə rīd/ *n.* a compound of hydrogen (**hydride**) in which hydrogen has been replaced by its heavier isotope deuterium [Mid-20thC. Coined from DEUTERIUM + -IDE.]

deuterium /dyoo teéri əm/ *n.* an isotope of hydrogen that has double the mass of ordinary hydrogen because it contains a neutron in its nucleus. It is often used as a tracer in experiments. Symbol **D** [Mid-20thC. Coined from Greek *deuteros* 'second' (see DEUTERO-) + -IUM. From the fact that it is second in the series of possible hydrogen isotopes.]

deuterium oxide *n.* = **heavy water**

deutero- *prefix.* second, secondary ○ *deutero-plasm* [From Greek *deuteros*]

deuterocanonical /dyoótərōkə nónnik'l/ *adj.* part of a secondary, less well regarded, or disputed collection of religious scripture, especially the Apocrypha and the Antilegomena, or constituting or relating to one of these secondary canons

deuteron /dyoótə ron/ *n.* the nucleus of a deuterium atom, consisting of one proton and one neutron. It is mainly used as a bombarding particle in particle accelerators such as cyclotrons. Symbol **D**[+] [Mid-20thC. Formed from DEUTERO-, on the model of PROTON.]

Deuteronomist /dyoótə rónnəmist/ *n.* one of the authors of Deuteronomy, the fifth book of the Bible

Deuteronomy /dyoótə rónnəmi/ *n.* the fifth book of the Bible [14thC. Via late Latin from Greek *Deuteronomion,*

literally 'second law' (because the book contains a repetition of the Decalogue and of parts of *Exodus*).] —**Deuteronomic** /dyoótə rə nómmik/ *adj.*

deutoplasm /dyoótə plazzəm/ *n.* nutrient matter contained in certain reproductive cells, e.g. the yolk in a bird's egg [Late 19thC] —**deutoplasmic** /dyoótə plázmik/ *adj.*

Deutschmark /dóychə maárk/, **Deutsche Mark** *n.* the standard currency unit of Germany. Symbol **DM**. See table at **currency** [Mid-20thC. From German, 'German mark', from *deutsch* 'German' (see DUTCH) + *Mark* MARK.]

deutzia /dyoótsi ə/ (*plural* **-as** *or* **-a**) *n.* a shrub in the saxifrage family, native to Asia and Central America, that has clusters of white to pink or lavender flowers. Genus: *Deutzia.* [Mid-19thC. From modern Latin, genus name; named after Johann van der *Deutz,* 18th-century Dutch patron of botany.]

dev *abbr.* deviation

Dev /dev/, **Kapil** (b. 1959) Indian cricketer. He played in 131 test matches, scoring 5,248 runs and taking a world record 434 wickets.

deva /dáyvə/ *n.* a Hindu or Buddhist god [Early 19thC. From Sanskrit, 'god', originally 'bright or shining one'. Ultimately from an Indo-European word meaning 'to shine', which is also the ancestor of English *divine*.]

Popperfoto

Eamon De Valera

De Valera /dévvə láirə/, **Eamon** (1882–1975) US-born Irish statesman. He was a key figure in establishing the Irish Republic. He formed a dissident faction of Sinn Fein, the Fianna Fáil party (1926), was prime minister (1937–48, 1951–54, and 1957–59), and served as president (1959–73).

De Valois /də vál waa/, **Dame Ninette** (1898–1998) Irish-born British ballet dancer and choreographer. A soloist (1923–26) with Diaghilev, she founded the Vic-Wells Ballet in 1931, chartered in 1956 as the Royal Ballet. Real name **Edris Stannus**

devaluate /deé vályoo ayt/ (**-ates, -ating, -ated**) *vti.* = **devalue** *v.* 1

devaluation /deé valyoo áysh'n/ *n.* **1.** LOWERING OF CURRENCY'S VALUE a lowering by the government of the value of a nation's currency relative to that of foreign currencies **2.** REDUCTION IN IMPORTANCE a reduction in the importance or value of sth

devalue /dee vályoo/ (**-ues, -uing, -ued**) *v.* **1.** *vti.* LOWER CURRENCY'S VALUE to lower the value of a nation's currency by a governmental action, or to become lowered in value **2.** *vt.* MAKE OR BECOME LESS VALUABLE to cause the value or importance of sb or sth to be reduced, or to become reduced in value or importance

Devanagari /dáyvə naágəri/ *n.* the alphabet that is used to write many of the modern languages of India as well as ancient Sanskrit [Late 18thC. From Sanskrit, from *deva* DEVA + *Nāgarī,* an earlier name for the script, apparently literally 'of the city, urbane'.]

devastate /dévvə stayt/ (**-tates, -tating, -tated**) *vt.* **1.** DAMAGE SEVERELY to cause severe or widespread damage to sth ○ *an area devastated by floods* **2.** UPSET ENORMOUSLY to shock or upset sb enormously, producing a feeling of being overwhelmed or helpless (*often passive*) ○ *We were devastated by the news of his death.* [Mid-17thC. From Latin *devastat-,* the past participle stem of *devastare,* literally 'to lay waste completely', from *vastare* 'to lay waste', from *vastus* 'waste' (source of English *waste* and *vast*).] —**devastation** /dévvə stáysh'n/ *n.* —**devastative** /dévvə staytiv/ *adj.* —**devastator** /-staytər/ *n.*

devastating /dévvə stayting/ *adj.* **1. DAMAGING** causing severe or widespread damage ○ *policies that have a devastating effect on economic growth* **2. VERY UPSETTING** causing enormous shock or upset ○ *The news was devastating.* **3. SHARPLY CRITICAL** containing criticism that is very sharp and very effective or damaging, often as a result of its precise detail or caustic wit **4. REMARKABLE** startlingly impressive or attractive (*informal*) ○ *the devastating speed of her forehand return* —**devastatingly** *adv.*

devein /dée váyn/ (**-veins, -veining, -veined**) *vt.* to remove the dark threadlike gut (**vein**) from the back of the tail meat of a prawn

develop /di vélləp/ (**-ops, -oping, -oped**) *v.* **1.** *vti.* **CHANGE AND GROW** to change, or cause to change, and become larger, stronger, or more impressive, successful, or advanced ○ *The business has developed from humble beginnings into a multinational concern.* **2.** *vi.* **ARISE AND INCREASE** to arise and then increase or progress to a more complex state ○ *Tension was developing between the two nations.* **3.** *vt.* **ACQUIRE FEATURE, HABIT, OR ILLNESS** to acquire a particular feature, habit, or illness that then becomes more marked or extreme ○ *The baby is developing a cold.* **4.** *vt.* **ENLARGE ON** to add details to a basic plan or idea **5.** *vti.* **PRESENT OR BE REVEALED IN STAGES** to present the sequential events or successive stages of a story or argument, or to have such events or stages revealed ○ *The theory is developed at length in her new book.* **6.** *vt.* **USE RESOURCES FOR HUMAN PURPOSES** to use or make available land, minerals, or other natural resources for human purposes such as housing **7.** *vt.* **BUILD STRUCTURES** to plan and construct buildings, roads, or other technological structures ○ *develop a global communications system* **8.** *vt.* **TURN FILM INTO NEGATIVES OR PRINTS** to treat photographic film with chemicals in order to produce a negative or print (*often passive*) ○ *Send the films off to be developed.* **9.** *vi.* **ACHIEVE SEXUAL MATURITY** to become sexually mature **10.** *vt.* CHESS **BRING PIECE INTO PLAY** to bring a chess piece into play **11.** *vt.* MUSIC **VARY MUSICAL THEME** to add to a musical theme by using variation or ornamentation, especially by breaking it down into motifs and using other musical techniques [Mid-17thC. From French *développer*, literally 'to unwrap' (the original sense in English), from, ultimately, Old French *voloper* 'to wrap' (source of English *envelope*).] —**developable** *adj.*

developed /di véllәpt/ *adj.* ECON wealthy and technologically advanced, with sophisticated manufacturing and service industries

developer /di vélləpər/ *n.* **1. SB WHO DEVELOPS** sb who or sth that develops sth ○ *the developer of a new manufacturing process* **2. BUYER OF LAND FOR BUILDING** a person or company that buys land in order to build on it or sell it to others who want to build on it **3.** PHOTOGRAPHY **CHEMICAL FOR MAKING NEGATIVES OR PRINTS** a chemical used to turn exposed film into negatives or prints

developing /di vélləping/ *adj.* ECON using or involving small-scale agriculture and industry of the kind that characterized the earlier economic stages of technologically advanced nations

developing agent *n.* PHOTOGRAPHY = **developer**

development /di vélləpmənt/ *n.* **1. EVENT CAUSING CHANGE** an incident that causes a situation to change or progress (*often used in the plural*) ○ *Have there been any political developments since last week?* **2. DEVELOPING OF STH** the process of developing, developing sth, or of being developed, e.g. by growth, change, or elaboration ○ *sustained economic development* **3. BEING DEVELOPED** a state in which the developing of sth is not yet completed ○ *The prototype is in development.* **4. GROUP OF BUILDINGS** a group of buildings of the same kind that are built as a single construction project **5.** MUSIC **ELABORATION OF MUSICAL THEME** the process of varying and elaborating the rhythm and melody of a musical theme **6.** MUSIC **MUSICAL SECTION WHERE THEME IS DEVELOPED** one of the three main sections of the sonata form, in which the musical themes presented in the exposition are rhythmically and melodically elaborated

developmental /di vélləp mént'l/ *adj.* **1. INVOLVING DEVELOPMENT** representing or involving a development of some kind **2. TYPICAL OF DEVELOPMENT** characteristic of or resulting from the way sth develops **3. CONCERNED WITH DEVELOPMENT** concerned with development or a development **4.** EDUC, PSYCHOL **DEVELOPING AS CHILD GROWS** changing or growing as a child grows ○ *an educational programme that takes into account a student's developmental capacity* **5.** EDUC **REFLECTING AGE-RELATED ABILITIES** taking into account the age-related capacities of children ○ *a developmental approach to the education of children* —**developmentally** *adv.*

developmental psychology *n.* the branch of psychology that deals with the ways that personality, cognitive ability, and behaviour change during a person's lifespan, concentrating particularly on childhood development

development area *n.* an area of high unemployment that receives government money to help develop new industry there

development education *n.* a subject of study intended to give school pupils a basic knowledge of world politics

développé /dáyvəllə pay, di véll/ *n.* a ballet movement in which the foot of one leg is drawn up to the knee of the other and then extended slowly out into the air [Early 20thC. From French, the past participle of *développer* (see DEVELOP).]

deverbative /dee vúrbətiv/, **deverbal** /dee vúrb'l/ *adj.* GRAM derived from a verb, such as the noun 'driver', which is derived from the verb 'drive', and the adjective 'clingy', from the verb 'cling' [Early 20thC. Coined from DE- + VERB + -ATIVE.]

Devi /dáyvi/ *n.* the supreme Hindu goddess, wife of the god Shiva, manifested in the different forms and characters of Durga, Kali, Parvati, and Sati [Late 20thC. From Sanskrit, the feminine of *deva* (see DEVA).]

deviance /déevi ənss/, **deviancy** /-ənssi/ *n.* behaviour that is sharply different from the norm or the accepted standard

deviant /déevi ənt/ *adj.* **DIFFERENT FROM TRADITIONAL NORM** diverging sharply from a customary or traditional norm or accepted standard, or displaying sharply divergent behaviour ○ *abstract paintings, once thought deviant, now worth millions* ■ *n.* **SB BEHAVING DIFFERENTLY OR UNACCEPTABLY** sb whose behaviour is different from the norm or from accepted standards [14thC. From late Latin *deviant-*, the present participle stem of *deviare* (see DEVIATE).]

deviate *vi.* /déevi ayt/ (**-ates, -ating, -ated**) **1. BE DIFFERENT** to be different or behave differently **2. TURN FROM** to turn off from a course or path ■ *adj.* /déevi ət/ **BEHAVING DIFFERENTLY OR UNACCEPTABLY** exhibiting behaviour that diverges sharply from a norm or accepted standards ■ *n.* /déevi ət/ **SB BEHAVING DIFFERENTLY FROM TRADITIONAL NORM** sb whose behaviour differs sharply from the customary or traditional norm or accepted standards [Mid-17thC. From late Latin *deviat-*, the past participle stem of *deviare* 'to depart from the way', from Latin *via* 'way, road'.] —**deviator** /déevi aytər/ *n.* —**deviatory** /déevi ətəri, -aytəri/ *adj.*

deviation /déevi áysh'n/ *n.* **1. CHANGE OR DIFFERENCE** a change or difference from what is normal, accepted, expected, or planned ○ *These rituals represented a deviation from established practices.* **2. UNACCEPTABLE BEHAVIOUR OR ATTITUDE** behaviour or an attitude that is sharply different from what is normal or acceptable **3.** STATS **DIFFERENCE FROM STATISTICAL AVERAGE** the difference between any particular value and a fixed value, such as the average of all the other values in its series **4.** NAVIG **COMPASS ERROR** an error in a compass reading caused by local magnetic fields, especially on a ship at sea

deviationism /déevi áysh'nizəm/ *n.* departure from accepted or established political views, especially from orthodox communism —**deviationist** *n., adj.*

device /di vís/ *n.* **1. TOOL OR MACHINE** a tool or machine designed to perform a particular task or function **2. PLOY** a way of achieving sth, especially a clever or dishonest way **3. BOMB** a bomb or sth that causes an explosion or fire **4. LITERARY OR DRAMATIC TOOL** sth designed to create a particular effect in a story or drama or to evoke a particular response from a reader, listener, or viewer ○ *a familiar cinematic device* **5. EMBLEM OR MOTTO** an emblem, motto, or combination of the two, especially when used in heraldry ○ *a heraldic device* **6. ORNAMENTAL DESIGN** an ornamental pattern or design, e.g. in embroidery [13thC. From Old French *devis* 'division, contrivance' and *devise* 'plan', both from, ultimately, Latin *dividere* (see DIVIDE). The sense 'simple machine' evolved in the 16thC.] ◇ **leave sb to his** *or* **her own devices** to let sb do as he or she wishes, instead of giving the person direction or assistance

devil /dévv'l/ *n.* **1. devil, Devil GOD'S ENEMY** in Christianity and some other religions, the enemy of God, who rules Hell, tempts people to sin, and as Satan personifies the spirit of evil **2. EVIL SPIRIT** an evil spirit, particularly a subordinate of Satan **3. EVIL PERSON OR ANIMAL** an unpleasant, violent, or evil person or animal **4. MISCHIEVOUS PERSON OR ANIMAL** a mischievous, troublesome, or high-spirited person or animal **5. PERSON OR ANIMAL** a person or animal of the sort described ○ *You lucky devil!* **6. NAME FOR TOOL** a name given to various tools or machines, especially ones that cut or tear **7.** = **dust devil 8. DIFFICULT OR UNPLEASANT CASE** an extremely difficult or unpleasant instance of sth (*informal*) **9. INTENSIFIER** used as an intensifier in questions and exclamations (*slang*) ○ *Who the devil does he think he is, talking to his boss like that?* **10.** PRINTING = **printer's devil** (*archaic*) **11. JUNIOR BARRISTER** a person who works as an assistant for a barrister in order to gain experience (*archaic informal*) ■ *vt.* (**-ils, -illing, -illed**) **1. MAKE FOOD SPICY** to cook or prepare a food with spicy seasonings **2.** *US* **PESTER** to annoy, worry, or pester sb, especially by making repeated requests for sth (*informal*) ○ *He's been devilling me with requests for an interview.* [Old English *dēofol*, from, ultimately, Greek *diabolus* 'the Devil, Satan' (see DIABOLIC)] ◇ **between the devil and the deep blue sea** faced with two equally undesirable choices

devilfish /dévv'l fish/ (*plural* **-fish** *or* **-fishes**) *n.* a fish that is thought to have an evil or frightening appearance, such as a manta ray or octopus

devilish /dévv'lish/ *adj.* **1. SINISTER OR CRUEL** so sinister, cruel, or evil as to be considered like or worthy of the devil ○ *some devilish scheme to get what they want* **2. MISCHIEVOUS** full of or indicating mischievousness ○ *a devilish grin* **3. GREAT** extremely great or intense (*informal*) ○ *the devilish midday heat* ■ *adv.* **VERY** extremely (*informal*) —**devilishly** *adv.* —**devilishness** *n.*

devil-may-care *adj.* **1. RECKLESS** foolishly lighthearted about risk or danger **2. CHEERFULLY UNCONCERNED** tending to enjoy the present and not think or worry about the future

devilment /dévv'lmənt/ *n.* troublesome, mischievous, or devilish behaviour ○ *always getting up to some devilment or other*

devilry /dévv'ltri/ (*plural* **-ries**) *n.* **1. EVIL BEHAVIOUR** cruel or evil behaviour or actions **2. BLACK MAGIC** evil act or acts supposedly performed by calling on the powers of the devil or evil spirits **3. MISCHIEF** mischief or a mischievous act (*archaic*) ○ *the endearing devilry of young puppies*

devil's advocate *n.* **1. OPPONENT FOR THE SAKE OF IT** sb who criticizes or opposes sth purely in order to provoke a discussion or argument **2. CATHOLIC OFFICIAL OPPOSING CANONIZATION** a Roman Catholic official appointed to argue against the canonization or beatification of a candidate [Translation of Latin *advocatus diaboli*]

devil's coach-horse (*plural* **devil's coach-horses**) *n.* a large fierce black beetle with long jaws. Family: Staphylinidae. ◊ **rove beetle** [From the rearing and defiant attitude that it assumes when disturbed]

devil's darning needle *n.* = **damselfly** (*informal*) [From its long, needlelike body]

devil's food cake *n.* a rich dark chocolate cake [From the contrast with the paleness of ANGEL FOOD CAKE]

Devil's Island /dévv'lz-/ rocky islet off the coast of French Guiana in the Atlantic Ocean. It was used as a penal colony from 1852 to 1946.

Devil's Marbles /dévvəlz-/ mound of granite boulders and sacred Aboriginal site in central Australia, near Tennant Creek in the Northern Territory. The boulders are about 1,500 million years old.

deviltry /dévv'ltri/ *n.* = **devilry** (*archaic*)

devious /deévi əss/ *adj.* **1.** SECRETIVE AND CALCULATING not straightforward, sincere, and honest in or about your intentions or motives **2.** UNFAIR OR UNDERHAND not adhering to the right or usual course, procedures, or standards **3.** RAMBLING circuitous and roundabout, usually changing direction many times ○ *got here by a devious route* [Late 16thC. From Latin *devius* 'out of the way', from *via* 'way, road' (see DEVIATE).] —**deviously** *adv.* —**deviousness** *n.*

devisal /di vīz'l/ *n.* **1.** CONTRIVING the inventing or contriving of sth **2.** LAW PROPERTY TRANSFER BY WILL the handing down of property through a will

devise /di vīz/ *vt.* (**-vises, -vising, -vised**) **1.** THINK UP to conceive of the idea for sth and work out how to make it or put it into practice **2.** LAW PASS ON PROPERTY to pass on property through a will ■ *n.* LAW **1.** WILL CLAUSE BEQUEATHING PROPERTY a clause in a will stating that an item of property is to be given to sb or sth **2.** BEQUEATHING PROPERTY the bequeathing of an item of property **3.** PROPERTY BEQUEATHED an item of property bequeathed through a will [13thC. From French *deviser* 'to divide, order' (the first senses in English), hence 'to form a plan', from, ultimately, Latin *dividere* (see DIVIDE).] —**devisable** *adj.*

devisee /di vī zeé/ *n.* LAW sb to whom property has been bequeathed in a will

deviser /di vīzər/ *n.* sb who conceives of sth and works out how to make it or put it into practice

devisor /di vīzər/ *n.* LAW sb who leaves property to another in a will [15thC. From Anglo-Norman *devisour* and Old French *deviseor*, both from Old French *deviser* (see DEVISE).]

devitalize /dee vītə līz/ (**-izes, -izing, -ized**), **devitalise** (**-ises, -ising, -ised**) *vt.* to deprive sth of its strength or vigour (*formal*) —**devitalization** /dee vītə lī záysh'n/ *n.*

DeVito /də veétō/, **Danny** (*b.* 1944) US film actor and director. He starred as Louie De Palma in the US television series *Taxi* (1978–83). Full name **Daniel Michael DeVito**

devitrify /dee vítri fī/ (**-fies, -fying, -fied**) *vti.* to change, or cause a material to change, from a glassy to a crystalline state and become brittle and opaque —**devitrification** /deé vitrifi káysh'n/ *n.*

Devizes /di vīziz/ market town in Wiltshire, southern England. Population: 13,205 (1991).

devocalize /dee vōkə līz/ (**-izes, -izing, -ized**), **devocalise** (**-ises, -ising, -ised**) *vt.* = **devoice** —**devocalization** /deévōkə lī záysh'n/ *n.*

devoice /dee vóyss/ (**-voices, -voicing, -voiced**) *vt.* to make a usually voiced speech sound without vibration of the vocal cords

devoid /di vóyd/ *adj.* completely lacking in or without sth ○ *a house devoid of charm* [14thC. From the past participle of obsolete *devoid* 'to remove, vacate', from Old French *devoidier*, literally 'to empty out', from *vuidier* 'to empty', from, ultimately, Latin *vacare* (see VACATION).]

devoirs /də vwaá/ *npl.* expressions or acts of courtesy and respect (*archaic or literary*) [15thC. From Old French *deveir*, literally 'to owe', from Latin *debere* 'to owe' (source of English *debt* and *duty*).]

devolatilize /dee vóllətə līz/ (**-izes, -izing, -ized**), **devolatilise** (**-ises, -ising, -ised**) *vt.* to remove volatile material from a substance, usually by means of heat or a vacuum and sometimes by both —**devolatilization** /dee vóllətə lī záysh'n/ *n.*

devolution /deévə lóosh'n/ *n.* **1.** DELEGATING OF RESPONSIBILITIES the delegation of responsibilities from a superior to a subordinate, deputy, or substitute **2.** DELEGATING POWER the transfer of power from a central to a subordinate level or organization, particularly from a central government to regional or local governments **3.** INHERITANCE OF PRIVILEGES the transfer or inheritance of authority, rights, or property, e.g. from a monarch to his or her successors **4.** = **degeneration** *n.* 3 [15thC. From the late Latin stem *devolution-* from, ultimately, Latin *devolvere* (see DEVOLVE).] —**devolutionary** *adj.*

devolutionist /deévə lóosh'nist/ *n.* sb who favours transferring power from a central government to regional or local governments —**devolutionist** *adj.*

devolve /di vólv/ (**-volves, -volving, -volved**) *v.* **1.** *vti.* TRANSFER OR BE TRANSFERRED TO ANOTHER to transfer power, responsibility, or rights to sb or sth, e.g. from a central government to a regional government, or to be transferred in this manner ○ *the government's pledge to devolve powers to local communities* **2.** *vi.* BECOME ANOTHER PERSON'S OBLIGATION to become the duty or responsibility of another person ○ *Many childcare responsibilities have devolved on husbands.* **3.** *vi.* RELY OR DEPEND to be decided by sth or depend on sth for its validity (*formal*) ○ *Their case devolved on witnesses' willingness to testify.* **4.** *vi.* LAW BE GIVEN OR BEQUEATHED to be given to sb under the terms of a will or other legal instruction [15thC. From Latin *devolvere*; literally 'to roll down' (the original sense in English), from *volvere* 'to roll' (source of English *involve* and *volume*.] —**devolvement** *n.*

WORD KEY: USAGE

devolve on or **to**? The traditional distinction is that powers, authority, etc., devolve or are devolved *on* (or *upon*) sb, whereas a right or benefit devolves *to* sb. However, this is not widely observed in current usage. The two constructions are used more or less interchangeably, though the use of *to* is somewhat more common: *The point of devolving power to provincial assemblies . . . was to give these provinces some control over their own affairs* (*Economist*). *On* or *upon* is used when the right or authority is regarded as a kind of inheritance (actually or figuratively): *In 1912 the leadership of the expedition's remnant at Cape Evans devolved upon Atkinson, the sole remaining officer* (*Dictionary of National Biography*).

devon /dévvən/ *n. Aus* a bland processed meat in the form of a large sausage, usually sold in slices [Mid-19thC. Probably from *Devon*, a breed of cattle named after DEVON, where it was first bred.]

Devon /dévv'n/ county in southwestern England, bordered on the north by the Bristol Channel and on the south by the English Channel. It is a popular holiday area. Population: 378,900 (1995). Area: 6,711 sq. km/2,591 sq. mi.

Devonian /de vṓni ən/ *n.* **1.** **Devonian, Devonian period** GEOLOGICAL PERIOD the geological period that extended from 410 to 360 million years ago, when forests and amphibians first appeared and fish became abundant **2.** SB FROM DEVON sb who was born in or resides in the county of Devon ■ *adj.* **1.** BELONGING TO GEOLOGICAL PERIOD belonging or relating to the geological period that extended from 410 to 360 million years ago **2.** CHARACTERISTIC OF DEVON typical of or relating to the English county of Devon, its people, or its culture [Early 17thC. Formed from medieval Latin *Devonia*, from Old English *Defenascīr* 'Devonshire', the former name of the county of Devon. Originally, the name given to a geological formation of rocks particularly prevalent there.]

Devonport /dévv'n pawrt/ city on the northern coast of Tasmania, Australia. It is a busy cargo and ferry port. Population: 22,299 (1996).

Devonshire cream /dévv'nshər-/ *n.* = **clotted cream** [From the fact that the cream was a speciality of the county of DEVON, formerly known as *Devonshire*]

dévoré /də váw ray/ *n.* the use of a chemical paste to create patterns in specially structured fabrics such as velvet by dissolving the natural fibres and revealing the synthetic warp and weft threads [From French *dévorer* (see DEVOUR)]

devote /di vṓt/ (**-votes, -voting, -voted**) *vt.* to commit yourself to, or allot or use sth for, a particular activity, aim, or purpose ○ *She devoted her whole life to the cause.* [Late 16thC. From Latin *devot-*, the past participle stem of *devovere* 'to dedicate by a vow', from *vovere* 'to vow' (source of English *vow* and *vote*).]

devoted /di vṓtid/ *adj.* **1.** LOVING AND COMMITTED feeling or showing great love, commitment, or loyalty to sb or sth, especially over a long period of time **2.** DEDICATED feeling or showing great dedication to sth —**devotedly** *adv.* —**devotedness** *n.*

devotee /dévvō teé/ *n.* **1.** KEEN ENTHUSIAST a very keen enthusiast or follower of sth **2.** RELIGIOUS PERSON a dedicated member of a religious or spiritual group

devotion /di vṓsh'n/ *n.* **1.** COMMITTED LOVE deep love and commitment **2.** DEDICATION great dedication and loyalty **3.** ENTHUSIASM strong enthusiasm and admiration for sb or sth **4.** RELIGIOUS FERVOUR fervent religious or spiritual feeling **5.** ACT OF DEVOTING the act of devoting sth or being devoted to a particular purpose ■ **devotions** *npl.* PRAYERS prayers or other religious observances, especially sb's private prayers or observances

devotional /di vṓsh'nəl/ *adj.* EXPRESSING RELIGIOUS DEVOTION expressing or relating to religious feeling, prayer, or worship ○ *devotional literature* ■ *n.* SHORT RELIGIOUS SERVICE a short religious service usually consisting of special prayers (*often used in the plural*) —**devotionality** /di vṓshə nálləti/ *n.* —**devotionally** /di vṓsh'nəli/ *adv.*

devour /di vówər/ (**-vours, -vouring, -voured**) *vt.* **1.** EAT QUICKLY to eat sth quickly and hungrily ○ *They devour in minutes what it's taken you all afternoon to prepare.* **2.** TAKE IN EAGERLY to read, look at, watch, or listen to sth eagerly ○ *Young children seem to devour her stories.* **3.** DESTROY to destroy sth rapidly and completely (*literary*) (*often passive*) ○ *a house devoured by the flames* **4.** WASTE to use up sth unwisely or wastefully (*literary*) **5.** OVERWHELM to become an overwhelming and destructive passion or obsession for sb (*literary*) (*usually passive*) [14thC. Via Old French *devour-*, the stressed stem of *devorer*, from Latin *devorare*, literally 'to swallow down', from *vorare* 'to swallow' (source of English *voracious*).] —**devourer** *n.* —**devouring** *adj.* —**devouringly** *adv.*

devout /di vówt/ *adj.* **1.** VERY RELIGIOUS deeply and faithfully religious **2.** VERY SINCERE deeply and sincerely felt or meant (*formal*) **3.** DEVOTED TO STH devoted to a particular personal interest or cause ○ *a devout sports fan* [12thC. Via French *dévot* from Latin *devotus*, the past participle of *devovere* (see DEVOTE).] —**devoutly** *adv.* —**devoutness** *n.*

De Vries /də vreéss/, **Hugo** (1848–1935) Dutch botanist and geneticist. He independently rediscovered the laws of heredity and introduced the theory of mutation in plant evolution. Full name **Hugo Marie De Vries**

dew /dyoo/ *n.* **1.** WATER DROPLETS ON COOL OUTDOOR SURFACES moisture from the air that has condensed as tiny drops on outdoor objects and surfaces that have cooled, especially during the night **2.** SMALL DROPS drops of moisture of any kind, e.g. tears or sweat (*literary*) **3.** FRESHNESS AND PURITY a fresh and pure or refreshing quality in sth (*literary*) ■ **dews** *npl.* DEWDROPS drops of dew (*literary*) ■ *vt.* (**dews, dewing, dewed**) COAT WITH DEW to coat or moisten sth with drops of dew (*literary*) [Old English *dēaw*]

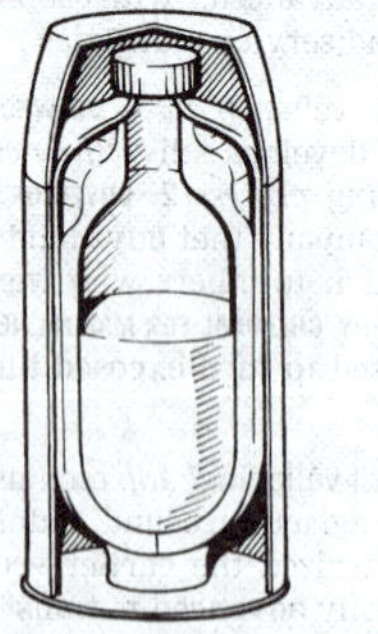

Dewar flask

Dewar flask /dyoó ər-/, **Dewar vacuum flask** *n.* a double-walled silvered glass or metal flask with a vacuum between the walls, providing thermal insulation. It is frequently used to store liquefied gases. [Mid-20thC. Named after Sir James *Dewar* (1824–1923), British physicist and chemist, who invented it.]

dewater /dee wáwtər/ (**-ers, -ering, -ered**) *vt.* to remove water from a substance, especially sewage or crude oil, or from a place

dewberry /dyoóbəri/ (*plural* **-ries**) *n.* **1.** TRAILING BLACKBERRY PLANT a variety of the blackberry bramble with trailing stems and bluish-black fruit. Genus: *Rubus*. **2.** BLUE-BLACK BERRY the edible blue-black fruit of a dewberry plant

dewclaw /dyoó klaw/ *n.* a functionless shorter digit or claw on the foot of a dog or other mammal [Late 16thC. Origin uncertain: perhaps from the fact that while the other claws touch the soil, or press the grass to the ground, this only brushes the dewy surface.] —**dewclawed** *adj.*

dewdrop /dyoó drop/ *n.* **1.** DROP OF WATER a drop of water that has condensed on a cool outdoor surface **2.** DROP OF NOSE MUCUS a drop of mucus hanging from a person's nostril (*informal*) (*used euphemistically*)

De Wet /də vét/, **Christiaan** (1854–1922) South African general and politician. He was a guerrilla leader in both Anglo-Boer Wars (1880–81, 1899–1902) and helped form the Afrikaner Nationalist Party (1912–13). Full name **Christiaan Rudolph De Wet**

Dewey /dyoó i/, **Melvil** (1851–1931) US librarian and educator. He formulated the Dewey Decimal System (1876), which revolutionized the way books were catalogued.

Dewey Decimal System, **Dewey decimal classification** *n.* a system of classifying library books that divides them into ten main classes, divided in turn into categories with three-digit numbers and sub-categories with numbers after a decimal point [Late 19thC. Named after Melvil DEWEY.]

dewfall /dyoó fawl/ *n.* **1.** TIME DEW FORMS the formation of dew, or the time when dew begins to form **2.** AMOUNT OF DEW the amount of dew that has condensed on objects and surfaces

de Wint /də wínt/, **Peter** (1784–1849) English painter. His watercolour landscapes and architectural and genre studies recorded contemporary life in eastern England.

dewlap /dyoó lap/ *n.* **1.** HANGING FLAP OF SKIN ON ANIMAL'S NECK a loose fold of skin hanging from the neck of certain animals such as cows **2.** LOOSE SKIN ON PERSON'S THROAT a loose fold of skin on the throat of a person, often forming later in life [14thC. From obsolete English *dewe*, of uncertain meaning and origin + LAP 'loose piece'. The first element was associated by folk etymology with DEW, from the idea that the 'lap' touches the dewy ground.] —**dewlapped** *adj.*

DEW line /dyoó-/ *n.* a line of radar stations across the Arctic regions of North America, designed to give an early warning of approaching enemy aircraft and missiles [*DEW* is an acronym formed from *Distant Early Warning*]

deworm /dee wúrm/ (**-worms**, **-worming**, **-wormed**) *vt.* to cure an animal of an infestation of worms —**dewormer** *n.*

dew point *n.* the temperature at which the air cannot hold all the moisture in it and dew begins to form. If objects and surfaces have cooled to below freezing point when the moisture in the air begins to condense, frost is formed instead.

dew pond *n.* a small shallow pond on high ground that is regularly refreshed by heavy rainfall and condensing fog

dew worm *n. US, Can* a common earthworm used as fishing bait [Origin uncertain: perhaps from the fact that the worm comes out when the earth is moist]

dewy /dyoó i/ (**-ier**, **-iest**) *adj.* **1.** COVERED WITH DEW covered with dew or characterized by the presence of dew **2.** MOIST moist or moist-looking **3.** LIKE DEW like dew, especially in having a fresh, pure, or refreshing quality (*literary*) —**dewily** *adv.* —**dewiness** *n.*

dewy-eyed *adj.* childishly innocent, inexperienced, or trusting ○ *full of dewy-eyed optimism*

dex /deks/ *n.* dextroamphetamine or a tablet containing it (*slang*) [Mid-20thC. Shortening.]

dexamethasone /déksə méthəson/ *n.* a synthetic steroid used to treat inflammatory conditions and hormonal imbalances [Mid-20thC. Coined from dexa- (a blend of HEXA- and DECA-) + METHYL + CORTISONE.]

Dexedrine /déksi dreen/ *tdmk.* a trademark for a sulphate of dextroamphetamine used as a pharmaceutical drug

dexie /déksi/ *n.* a tablet containing dextroamphetamine (*slang*) [Mid-20thC. Shortening.]

dexter /dékstər/ *adj.* placed on the right-hand side of a coat of arms, that is, on the left from the point of view sb looking at it (*technical*) (*usually used after the noun*) [Mid-16thC. From Latin, 'on the right side' (see DEXTEROUS).]

dexterity /dek stérrəti/ *n.* **1.** PHYSICAL SKILL ease and skill in physical movement, especially in using the hands and manipulating objects ○ *manual dexterity* **2.** QUICK WITS sharpness or quickness of mind

dexterous /dékstərəss/, **dextrous** /dékstrəss/ *adj.* **1.** PHYSICALLY SKILFUL characterized by ease and skill in movement, especially in the use of the hands to carry out tasks **2.** QUICK-WITTED mentally sharp or quick [Early 17thC. From Latin *dexter* 'skilful', literally 'on the right side' (source of English *ambidextrous* and *destrier*). The right hand was viewed as the stronger, hence the meaning 'skilful'.] —**dexterously** *adv.* —**dexterousness** *n.*

dextr- *prefix.* = dextro- (*used before vowels*)

dextral /dékstrəl/ *adj.* (*technical*) **1.** ON THE RIGHT on or relating to the right-hand side, especially of the body **2.** RIGHT-HANDED right-handed **3.** SPIRALLING TO THE RIGHT used to describe the clockwise spiralling of the shell of a marine invertebrate animal [Mid-17thC. Via medieval Latin *dextralis* from Latin *dextra* 'right hand', from *dexter* (see DEXTEROUS).] —**dextrality** /dek strálləti/ *n.* —**dextrally** /dékstrəli/ *adv.*

dextran /dékstrən/ *n.* a glucose polymer (**polysaccharide**) produced by the action of bacteria on sucrose and used as a blood plasma substitute, food additive, and in confections and lacquers [Late 19thC. Coined from DEXTRO- + -AN.]

dextrin /dékstrin/, **dextrine** /-streen, -strin/ *n.* a product formed from the heating of starch that is an intermediate in the formation of maltose, and is used as an adhesive and a size, and in syrups and beers. Formula: $(C_6H_{10}O_5)_n$. [Mid-19thC. Coined from DEXTRO- + -IN.]

dextro /dékstrō/ *adj.* = dextrorotatory [Early 20thC. Shortening.]

dextro- *prefix.* **1.** right, on the right ○ *dextrocardia* **2.** dextrorotatory ○ *dextroglucose* [From Latin *dexter* 'on the right' (source of English *dexterity* and *ambidextrous*)]

dextroamphetamine /dékstrō am féttə meen/ *n.* a form of amphetamine sulphate, used as a stimulant and antidepressant

dextrocardia /dékstrō kaárdi ə/ *n.* a medical condition in which the heart inclines to the right side of the centre of the chest instead of the left, often with a similar reversal of all abdominal organs

dextroglucose /dékstrō glóokōz/ *n.* = dextrose

dextrorotary *adj.* = dextrorotatory

dextrorotation /dékstrō rō táysh'n/ *n.* a rotation to the right, particularly of the plane of polarization of light passing through a crystal or solution. Substances that cause dextrorotation are said to be optically active.

dextrorotatory /dékstrō rō táytəri/, **dextrorotary** /-rótəri/ *adj.* rotating the plane of polarization of light passing through it to the right or clockwise

dextrose /dékstrōz/ *n.* a sugar produced during cellular metabolism in plant and animal tissue. It is found in many fruits, especially grapes, and is a major component of honey.

dextrous *adj.* = dexterous

dey /day/ (*plural* **deys**) *n.* **1.** GOVERNOR OF ALGIERS the governor of Algiers under the Ottoman Empire **2.** RULER OF TUNIS OR TRIPOLI a title sometimes used for ruling officials in Tunis and Tripoli in North Africa under the Ottoman Empire [Mid-17thC. Via French from Turkish *dayi* 'maternal uncle', also a courtesy title.]

DF *abbr.* **1.** Defender of the Faith **2.** TELECOM direction finder

D/F *abbr.* TELECOM direction finder

DFC *abbr.* Distinguished Flying Cross

DfEE *abbr.* Department for Education and Employment

DFID *abbr.* Department for International Development

DFM (*plural* **DFMs**) *n.* a medal awarded to members of the RAF below officer rank for acts of bravery carried out when flying but not in action. Full form **Distinguished Flying Medal**

dg *abbr.* decigram

DG *abbr.* **1.** Deo gratias **2.** director-general

DH *abbr.* **1.** Department of Health **2.** DH, dh *US* designated hitter

DHA (*plural* **DHAs**) *abbr.* District Health Authority

Dhaka /dáka/, **Dacca** capital and largest city of Bangladesh. It is situated in the centre of the country, on the Buriganga, one of the tributary rivers of the Ganges delta. Population: 3,397,190 (1991).

dhal /daal/, **dahl**, **daal**, **dal** *n.* a thick Indian stew made from pulses, onions, and spices

dhansak *n.* an Indian curry that is made from meat or vegetables mixed with lentils [Late 20thC. From Gujarati.]

dharma /daárma/ *n.* **1.** PERFORMING OF DUTIES OF HINDUISM in Hinduism, a person's duty to behave according to strict religious and social codes, or the righteousness earned by performing religious and social duties **2.** ETERNAL TRUTH IN BUDDHISM in Buddhism, the truth about the way things are, and will always be, in the universe or in nature, especially when contained in scripture [Late 18thC. From Sanskrit, 'sth established, decree, custom'.] —**dharmic** *adj.*

dharna /daárna/, **dhurna** /dúrnə/ *n.* in India, the practice of protesting against an injustice by sitting and fasting outside the door of the offender [Late 18thC. From Hindi, 'placing, act of sitting in restraint'.]

Dhaulagiri /dówlə geéri/ one of the world's highest mountains. It is situated in the Himalayas in northern Nepal. Height: 8,163 m/26,811 ft.

dhobi /dóbi/ *n.* a washerman in India, some other parts of Asia, and East Africa [Mid-19thC. From Hindi, from *dhob* 'washing'.]

dhobi itch /dóbbee-/ *n.* a fungal infection of the skin in the groin area, especially in men in the tropics (*informal*) US term **jock itch** [Because the British servicemen who first used the term blamed the disease on the carelessness of their *dhobi* or washerman, although inadequate personal hygiene was often the real reason]

dhole /dōl/ *n.* a wild dog found in South Asia that has a reddish coat and bushy tail, and hunts large animals in packs. Latin name: *Cuon alpinus*. [Early 19thC. Origin uncertain: perhaps from Canarese *tōla* 'wolf'.]

dhoti /dóti/, **dhootie** /dóoti/, **dhotie** /dóti/, **dhuti** /dóoti/ *n.* **1.** INDIAN MAN'S LOINCLOTH a loincloth worn by some men in India **2.** COTTON CLOTH the cotton cloth used in India to make the loincloths called dhotis [Early 17thC. From Hindi.]

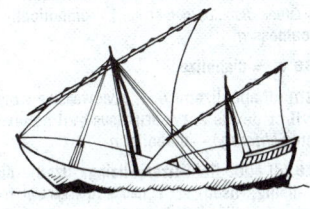

Dhow

dhow /dow/ *n.* a low-sided, one- or two-masted ship with triangular curving sails, used by Arab sailors in the Indian Ocean [Late 18thC. Origin uncertain: probably from Persian.]

Dhu al-Hijjah /dóo əl híjjaa/, **Dhu'l-Hijjah** *n.* in the Islamic calendar, the 12th lunar month of the year during which the holiday of Yom Arafat is celebrated [Late 18thC. From Arabic, literally 'the one of the pilgrimage'.]

Dhu al-Qadah /dóo əl ka´a daa/, **Dhu'l-Qadah** *n.* in the Islamic calendar, the 11th lunar month of the year [Late 18thC. From Arabic, literally 'the one of the sitting'.]

dhurna *n.* = dharna

dhuti *n.* = dhoti

di. *abbr.* diameter [Shortening]

di-[1] *prefix.* **1.** two, twice, double ○ *dicephalous* **2.** containing two atoms, radicals, or groups ○ *dimethyl* [From Greek. Ultimately from a form of the Indo-

European word for 'two' that is also the ancestor of English *twin, twilight,* and *bi-*.]

di-² *prefix.* = dia- (used before vowels)

dia. *abbr.* diameter

dia- *prefix.* through, across ○ *diachronic* ○ *diadromous* [From Greek *dia*]

diabase /díˈə bayss/ *n. US* = dolerite [Mid-19thC. From French, of uncertain origin: probably from Greek *diabasis* 'act of crossing over', from, ultimately, *bainein* 'to go'.] —**diabasic** /dī ə báyssik/ *adj.*

diabetes /dí ə bee´ teez/ *n.* a medical disorder that causes the body to produce an excessive amount of urine, especially diabetes mellitus [Mid-16thC. Via Latin from Greek, literally 'passer through, siphon', from *diabainein,* literally 'to go through'. The underlying idea, from the symptomatic excessive urination, is 'passing through'.]

diabetes insipidus /-in síppidəss/ *n.* a disorder of the pituitary gland that causes the body to produce large amounts of urine [From modern Latin, literally 'bland diabetes']

diabetes mellitus /-mə lítəss/ *n.* a disorder in which there is no control of blood sugar, through inadequate insulin production (Type 1) or decreased cellular sensitivity to insulin (Type 2), causing kidney, eye, and nerve damage. Type 1 develops in childhood and requires lifelong injection of insulin, while Type 2 develops in middle age and can usually be controlled by diet and drugs. [From modern Latin, literally 'honey-sweet diabetes']

diabetic /dí ə béttik/ *adj.* **1.** HAVING DIABETES having diabetes, especially diabetes mellitus **2.** RELATING TO DIABETES relating to or caused by diabetes, especially diabetes mellitus ○ *diabetic symptoms* **3.** INTENDED FOR DIABETICS made without sugar and therefore suitable for people who have diabetes mellitus ■ *n.* SB WITH DIABETES sb who has diabetes, especially diabetes mellitus

diablerie /di aáblə ri/ *n.* **1.** MAGIC witchcraft or magic **2.** THINGS CONNECTED WITH WITCHCRAFT OR EVIL stories, traditions, and practices associated with magic or devil worship **3.** MISCHIEF mischief (*literary*) [Mid-18thC. From French, from *diable* 'devil', from Latin *diabolic* (see DEVIL).]

diabolical /dí ə bóllik´l/ *adj.* **1.** VERY BAD extremely bad or unpleasant (*informal*) **2.** USED FOR EMPHATIC DISAPPROVAL a word used for emphasis when disapproving of sth, especially sb's behaviour (*slang*) [14th c. Via French *diabolique* from late Latin *diabolicus,* from, ultimately, Greek *diabolos* (see DEVIL).] —**diabolically** *adv.* —**diabolicalness** *n.*

diabolise *vt.* = diabolize

diabolism /dī ábbəlizəm/ *n.* **1.** DEVIL WORSHIP worship of the devil or devils **2.** EVIL BEHAVIOUR evil behaviour or character (*literary*) —**diabolist** *n.*

diabolize /dī ábbə līz/ (-**lizes, -lizing, -lized**), **diabolise** (-**lises, -lising, -lised**) *vt.* **1.** CAUSE TO SEEM EVIL to cause sb or sth to appear evil **2.** MAKE EVIL to make sb or sth evil

diabolo /dī ábbəlō/ (*plural* **-los**) *n.* **1.** GAME WITH SPINNING TOP the game of spinning a top with a narrow waist and two heads on a string tied to two sticks held in the hands **2.** KIND OF TOP a top designed to be used in the game of diabolo [Early 20thC. Via Italian *diabolo,* literally 'devil', from late Latin *diabolus* (see DIABOLIC). Originally called *devil on two sticks* (the top being the devil).]

diacetylmorphine /dī ássətil máwr feen/ *n.* heroin (*technical*) [Late 19thC. Coined from DI- + ACETYL + MORPHINE.]

diachronic /dí ə krónnik/ *adj.* involving, or relating to the study of, the development of sth, especially a language, through time ○ *diachronic linguistics* [Mid-19thC. Coined from DIA- + Greek *khronos* 'time' (source of English *chronic, chronicle,* and *chronological*).] —**diachronically** *adv.*

diachronism /dī ákrənizəm/ *n.* the existence within a single geological formation of regions of rock that were laid down at different times, e.g. by a sea that gradually covered a landmass —**diachronous** *adj.*

diachrony /dī ákrəni/ *n.* change or development over time (*formal*)

---

diacid /dī ássid/ *adj.* HAVING TWO ACIDIC HYDROGEN ATOMS having two acidic hydrogen atoms that may be replaced by metal or acid ions to form a salt or an ester ■ *n.* ACID WITH TWO ACIDIC HYDROGEN ATOMS an acid that has two acidic hydrogen atoms [Mid-19thC. Coined from DI- + ACID, on the model of DIBASIC.]

diaconal /dī ákənəl/ *adj.* relating to a deacon or deaconess or to the position of deacon or deaconess [Early 17thC. From late Latin *diaconalis,* from *diaconus* (see DEACON).]

diaconate /dī ákə nayt/ *n.* the position of deacon or deaconess, or the period of time during which it is held by a particular person [Early 18thC. From late Latin *diaconatus,* from *diaconus* (see DEACON).]

COMMON DIACRITICAL MARKS

Name	Mark		Word/Phrase
grave	À	à	à la mode
acute	Á	á	Cádiz
circumflex	Â	â	château
tilde	Ã	ã	São Paulo
umlaut	Ä	ä	fräulein
angstrom	Å	å	smörgåsbord
cedilla	Ç	ç	façade
grave	È	è	crèche
acute	É	é	purée
circumflex	Ê	ê	fête
umlaut	Ë	ë	noël
grave	Ì	ì	Forlì
acute	Í	í	Valparaíso
circumflex	Î	î	maître d'hôtel
umlaut	Ï	ï	faïence
eth	Ð	ð	Hamðir
tilde	Ñ	ñ	mañana
acute	Ó	ó	Kraków
circumflex	Ô	ô	maître d'hôtel
umlaut	Ö	ö	danke schön
Danish/Norwegian 0	Ø	ø	øre
acute	Ú	ú	Setúbal
circumflex	Û	û	croûtons
umlaut	Ü	ü	führer
thorn	Þ	þ	þ ingeyrar

diacritic /dí ə kríttik/ *adj.* = diacritical ■ *n.* PHONETIC MARK ADDED TO LETTER a mark above or below a printed letter that indicates a change in the way it is to be pronounced or stressed. Acute and grave accents, tildes, and cedillas are examples of diacritics. [Late 17thC. From Greek *diakritikos* 'that distinguishes or separates', from, ultimately, *krinein* 'to separate, decide' (source of English *crisis, critic,* and *hypocrisy*).] —**diacritically** *adv.*

diacritical /dí ə kríttik´l/, **diacritic** /dīə kríttik/ *adj.* indicating a change or modification in sth, especially in the way a printed letter is to be pronounced or stressed

diacritical mark *n.* = diacritic

diadelphous /dí ə délfəss/ *adj.* used to describe stamens or flowers that have the stamen filaments grouped into two bundles [Early 19thC. Coined from DI- + Greek *adelphos* 'brother'.]

diadem /dí ə dem/ *n.* **1.** CROWN a jewelled headband used as a royal crown **2.** JEWELLED HEADBAND any jewelled headband **3.** REGAL POWER royal power or dignity (*literary*) [14thC. Via Old French from, ultimately, Greek *diadēma* 'headband', especially the regal headband of Persian kings, adopted by Alexander the Great, from *diadein* 'to bind around', from *dein* 'to bind'.]

diadem spider *n.* a harmless spider common in Europe and Asia. Latin name *Araneus diadematus.* [Diadem from the orb webs that it spins]

Diadochi /dī áddəkī/ *npl.* the six Macedonian generals who divided up and then fought over the empire of Alexander the Great after his death

diadochy /dī áddəki/ *n.* the replacement of one element by another within the structure of a crystal [Early 18thC. From Greek *diadokhē* 'succession', from *diadekhesthai* 'to succeed', from *dekhesthai* 'to take, accept'.]

diadromous /dī áddrəməss/ *adj.* ZOOL used to describe fish that migrate between fresh and salt water [Mid-20thC. Coined from DIA- + 'running', from, ultimately, Greek -*dromous dromos*.]

diaeresis /dī eˈərəssiss/ (*plural* -**ses** /-seez/), **dieresis** (*plural* -**ses**) *n.* **1.** LING MARK MAKING ADJACENT VOWEL SEPARATE SYLLABLE a mark consisting of two dots, printed above the second of two adjacent vowels to show that it should be pronounced as a separate syllable, as in the word 'naïve' **2.** LANG MARK CHANGING PRONUNCIATION OF VOWEL a mark consisting of two dots, placed above certain vowels in some languages to show that they are to be pronounced in a particular way **3.** POETRY PAUSE IN POETRY a pause in a line of poetry that occurs when the end of a metrical foot coincides with the end of a word [Late 16thC. Via Latin from, ultimately, Greek *diairein* 'to separate, divide', literally 'to take apart', from *hairein* 'to take' (source of English *heresy*).] —**diaeretic** /dí ə réttik/ *adj.*

diag. *abbr.* **1.** diagonal **2.** diagram

diagenesis /dí ə jénnəssiss/ *n.* the changes that take place in a sediment as a result of increased temperatures and pressures, causing solid rock to form, e.g. as sand becomes sandstone —**diagenetic** /dīə je néttik/ *adj.*

diageotropism /dí əji óttrəpizəm/ *n.* a response of a plant to gravity in which a part of the plant adopts a horizontal position —**diageotropic** /dí ə jee ə tróppik/ *adj.*

Diaghilev /di ággə lef/, **Sergei** (1872–1929) Russian ballet impresario. His Ballets Russes company, founded in 1909, revolutionized ballet as an art; unifying dance, music, drama, and painting. Full name **Sergei Pavlovich Diaghilev**

diagnose /dí əgnōz/ (-**noses, -nosing, -nosed**) *vt.* **1.** IDENTIFY ILLNESS IN PATIENT to identify an illness or disorder in a patient through an interview, physical examination, and medical tests and other procedures ○ *The doctor diagnosed rheumatism.* **2.** IDENTIFY CAUSE OF STH to identify the nature or cause of sth, especially a problem or fault [Mid-19thC. Back-formation from DIAGNOSIS.] —**diagnosable** /dí əg nōzəb´l/ *adj.*

WORD KEY: USAGE

Diagnose means 'discover' or 'identify'. Thus *flu was diagnosed* is correct, and *she was diagnosed with flu* is not correct.

diagnosis /dí əg nōssiss/ (*plural* -**ses** /-seez/) *n.* **1.** IDENTIFICATION OF ILLNESS the identifying of an illness or disorder in a patient through an interview, physical examination, and medical tests and other procedures ○ *a doctor with vast experience of diagnosis* **2.** IDENTIFICATION OF PROBLEM the identifying of the nature or cause of sth, especially a problem or fault ○ *mechanics specializing in fault diagnosis* **3.** DECISION REACHED BY DIAGNOSIS a decision or conclusion reached by medical or other diagnosis ○ *The diagnosis is flu.* [Late 17thC. Via modern Latin from Greek *diagnōsis,* from *diagignōskein* 'to distinguish', literally 'to know apart', from *gignōskein* 'to know, perceive' (source of English *physiognomy* and *gnostic*).]

diagnostic /dí əg nóstik/ *adj.* FOR IDENTIFYING ILLNESSES OR PROBLEMS identifying, or used in identifying, the nature or cause of an illness, disorder, or problem ■ *n.* TEST TO IDENTIFY STH a test, procedure, or instrument used to identify the nature or cause of an illness, disorder, or problem —**diagnostically** *adv.*

diagnostician /dí əg no stísh´n/ *n.* **1.** DOCTOR SKILLED AT DIAGNOSIS a doctor with special skills in identifying illnesses or disorders **2.** PROBLEM IDENTIFIER sb with special skills in identifying the cause or nature of a problem ○ *an excellent diagnostician of engine problems*

diagnostics /dī əg nóstiks/ *n.* the art of, or procedures for, identifying illnesses or disorders in patients through diagnosis (*takes a singular verb*)

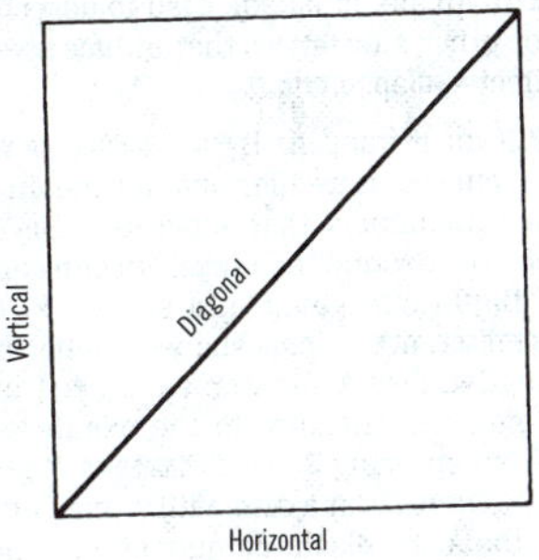

Diagonal

diagonal /dī ággənəl/ *adj.* **1.** SLANTING OR OBLIQUE running from one side to another in a slanting or oblique way **2.** WITH SLANTING LINES having slanting lines or markings **3.** GEOM JOINING ANGLES OR CORNERS used to describe a line that joins two opposite or nonadjacent angles or corners of a straight-sided geometric figure ■ *n.* **1.** SLANTING LINE a slanting line or direction **2.** GEOM LINE JOINING ANGLES a line that joins two opposite or nonadjacent angles or corners of a straight-sided geometric figure **3.** PRINTING = **slash** [Mid-16thC. From Latin *diagonalis*, from Greek *diagōnios* 'from angle to angle', from *gōnia* 'angle' (source of English *polygon* and *amblygonite*).] —**diagonally** *adv.*

diagram /dī ə gram/ *n.* **1.** SIMPLE EXPLANATORY DRAWING a simple drawing showing the basic shape, layout, or workings of sth **2.** CHART a chart or graph that illustrates sth such as a statistical trend **3.** MATHEMATICAL DRAWING a line drawing that presents mathematical information ■ *vt.* (**-grams, -gramming, -grammed**) ILLUSTRATE STH to make a diagram that represents or illustrates sth [Early 17thC. Via Latin from Greek *diagramma* 'geometrical figure, written list, scale in music', from *diagraphein* 'to mark out by lines, draw', from *graphein* 'to write' (see GRAPH).] —**diagrammable** *adj.*

diagrammatic /dī əgrə máttik/ *adj.* in the form of an explanatory drawing or chart —**diagrammatically** *adv.*

diagraph /dī ə graf, -graaf/ *n.* a mechanical instrument used for producing scale copies of diagrams and maps [Late 19thC. Via French from Greek *diagraphein* (see DIAGRAM).]

diakinesis /dī əki neéssiss, -kī-/ *n.* the final stage in cell reduction division (**meiosis**) during which the paired chromosomes begin to shorten, thicken, and separate [Early 20thC. Via modern Latin from German *Diakinese*, from Greek *kinēsis* 'motion' (see KINESIOLOGY).] —**diakinetic** /-néttik/ *adj.*

dial /dī əl/ *n.* **1.** INDICATOR WITH MOVEABLE POINTER an instrument with a movable pointer that displays a measurement, e.g. the current speed of a vehicle or the level of steam pressure inside a boiler **2.** CONTROL KNOB a round control knob or disc turned with the fingers to adjust a piece of electrical or mechanical equipment, e.g. a radio **3.** STATION INDICATOR ON RADIO a numbered panel with a movable pointer on a radio that is used for tuning in to different stations **4.** CLOCK FACE the round face of a traditional clock **5.** DISC WITH HOLES ON TELEPHONE a disc with numbered finger holes on the front of an old telephone, turned with a finger to select the required telephone number **6.** SUNDIAL a sundial or its face (*dated or literary*) ■ *vti.* (**-als, -alling, -alled**) CONTACT ON TELEPHONE to contact a number or a person by telephone ○ *She must have dialled the wrong number.* [14thC. Via Old French, 'wheel in clockwork that makes a revolution once a day', from, ultimately, Latin *dies* 'day'. The underlying idea is 'recording a day's passage'.] —**dialler** *n.*

dial. *abbr.* **1.** dialect **2.** dialectal

dial-a-ride *n.* a bus service that can be called to the door by telephone, generally intended for people in need of assistance in moving about

dialect /dī ə lekt/ *n.* **1.** REGIONAL VARIETY OF LANGUAGE a regional variety of a language, with differences in vocabulary, grammar, and pronunciation **2.** LANGUAGE SPOKEN BY CLASS OR PROFESSION a form of a language spoken by members of a particular social class or profession **3.** NONSTANDARD SPEECH nonstandard spoken language **4.** MEMBER OF LANGUAGE FAMILY one of a family of related languages ○ *Romance dialects such as French and Italian* [Mid-16thC. Directly or via French from Latin *dialogus*, 'way of speaking, dialect', from Greek *dialektos* 'conversation, language, local speech', from *dialegesthai* (see DIALOGUE).] —**dialectal** /dī ə lékt'l/ *adj.* —**dialectally** /-lékt'li/ *adv.*

WORD KEY: REGIONAL NOTE

The word ***dialect*** has been used in so many different ways that linguists often prefer to avoid it and use a term such as *lect*, which has no class, social, regional, or ethnic overtones. Many speakers use ***dialect*** when they mean 'accent', forgetting that a dialect comprehends pronunciation, vocabulary, and grammar. Somebody who says 'boot' for 'but' is speaking with a local accent. Somebody who says 'I were reet chuffed tha come, lass' is speaking dialect.

dialect atlas *n.* = **linguistic atlas**

dialect geography *n.* = **linguistic geography** —**dialect geographer** *n.*

dialectic /dī ə léktik/ *n.* **1.** TENSION BETWEEN CONFLICTING IDEAS the tension that exists between two conflicting or interacting forces, elements, or ideas **2.** INVESTIGATION OF TRUTH THROUGH DISCUSSION the investigation of the truth through discussion, or the art of investigating truths through discussion **3.** **dialectic, dialectics** DEBATE RESOLVING CONFLICT debate intended to resolve a conflict between two contradictory or apparently contradictory ideas or elements logically, establishing truths on both sides rather than disproving one argument (*takes a singular verb*) **4.** HEGELIAN PROCESS the process, in Hegelian and Marxist thought, in which two apparently opposed ideas, the thesis and antithesis, become combined in a unified whole, the synthesis **5.** SOCRATIC METHOD FOR REVEALING TRUTH the methods used in Socratic philosophy to reveal truth through disputation [Late 16thC. Via Latin *dialectica* from Greek *dialektikē* (*tekhnē*) '(art) of discussion or debate', from *dialektikos* 'of conversation', from *dialektos* (see DIALECT).]

dialectical /dī ə léktik'l/ *adj.* **1.** ACHIEVED BY DIALECTIC achieved or attempted by dialectic **2.** INVOLVING DIALECTIC involving or depending upon dialectic **3.** RELATING TO DIALECT relating to or belonging to a dialect —**dialectically** *adv.*

dialectical materialism *n.* the Marxian concept of reality in which material things are in the constant process of change brought about by the tension between conflicting or interacting forces, elements, or ideas —**dialectical materialist** *n.*

dialectician /dī ə lek tísh'n/ *n.* **1.** STUDENT OF DIALECTS sb who studies or is a specialist in language dialects **2.** PHILOSOPHER SKILLED AT DIALECTIC a person who practises dialectic or has special skills in dialectic

dialectics *n.* = **dialectic** *n.* 3

dialectology /dī ə lek tólləji/ *n.* the study of language dialects —**dialectological** /dī ə lektə lójjik'l/ *adj.* —**dialectologically** /-lójjikli/ *adv.* —**dialectologist** /dī ə lek tólləjist/ *n.*

dial gauge *n.* a sensitive measuring device that indicates small displacements of a plunger by means of a pointer moving over a circular scale. It is usually used for measuring pressure or a vacuum.

dialling code *n.* digits indicating a particular area or country that are dialled before the local number in calls made from outside that area or country

dialling tone *n.* a continuous sound that is heard when a telephone receiver is lifted, signalling that a number can be dialled. US term **dial tone**

dialogic /dī ə lójjik/ *adj.* **1.** WRITTEN AS CONVERSATION written in the form of a conversation **2.** ABOUT DIALOGUES relating to dialogues

dialogise *vi.* = **dialogize**

dialogist /dī álləjist/ *n.* **1.** WRITER OF DIALOGUE sb who writes dialogue for films, television, or radio **2.** SB WHO TAKES PART IN DIALOGUE sb who engages in a dialogue —**dialogistic** /dī allə jístik/ *adj.*

dialogize /dī állə jīz/ (**-gizes, -gizing, -gized**), **dialogise** (**-gises, -gising, -gised**) *vi.* to take part in a dialogue (*archaic or formal*)

dialogue /dī ə log/ *n.* **1.** CHARACTERS' WORDS the words spoken by characters in a book, a film, or a play, or a section of a work that contains spoken words ○ *pages of dialogue* **2.** FORMAL DISCUSSION a formal discussion or negotiation, especially between opposing sides in a political or international context **3.** CONVERSATION talk of any kind between two or more people (*formal*) **4.** LITERARY WORK IN CONVERSATION FORM a work of literature in the form of a conversation ■ *vi.* (**-logues, -loguing, -logued**) TAKE PART IN TALK to take part in a conversation, discussion, or negotiation [12thC. Via Old French from, ultimately, Greek *dialogos*, from *dialegesthai*, literally 'to speak with each other', from *legein* 'to speak' (source of English *dialect* and *eclectic*).] —**dialoguer** *n.*

dialogue box *n.* a small rectangular window displayed on a computer screen that conveys information to, or requires a response from, the user

dial tone *n. US, Can* = **dialling tone**

dial-up *adj.* COMPUT requiring the use of a computer modem and telephone line to establish communication with another computer or a network

dialyse /dī ə līz/ (**-lyses, -lysing, -lysed**) *vti.* **1.** MED REMOVE WASTE PRODUCTS to remove the accumulated waste products of metabolism from the blood of a patient whose kidneys are not functioning, or to undergo such a procedure **2.** CHEM SEPARATE SUBSTANCES FROM SOLUTION to separate dissolved substances from a solution by diffusing it through a semi-permeable membrane, or to be subjected to this process [Mid-19thC. Formed from DIALYSIS, on the model of ANALYSE.] —**dialysability** /dī ə līzə bílləti/ *n.* —**dialysable** /dī ə līzəb'l/ *adj.* —**dialysation** /dī ə lī záysh'n/ *n.*

dialyser *n.* **1.** MED KIDNEY MACHINE a machine used to carry out dialysis of the blood of a patient whose kidneys are not functioning **2.** CHEM MEMBRANE SEPARATING SUBSTANCES FROM SOLUTION an apparatus used in chemical dialysis, especially a semi-permeable membrane used to separate dissolved substances from a solution

dialysis /dī álləssiss/ *n.* **1.** MED MEDICAL FILTERING PROCESS the process of filtering the accumulated waste products of metabolism from the blood of a patient whose kidneys are not functioning properly, using a kidney machine **2.** CHEM SEPARATION OF SUBSTANCES FROM SOLUTION the separation of dissolved substances from a solution by allowing the solution to diffuse through a semi-permeable membrane [Mid-19thC. Via Latin, 'set of propositions without a connecting conjunction' (the original sense in English), from Greek *dialusis* 'separation, loosening' from, ultimately, *luein* 'to loosen'.] —**dialytic** /dī ə líttik/ *adj.* —**dialytically** /-líttikli/ *adv.*

dialyze *v.* MED, CHEM US = **dialyse**

diam. *abbr.* diameter

diamagnet /dī ə magnət/ *n.* a substance that is repelled by magnetic fields, such as noble gases, halogens, and alkali and alkaline earth metals —**diamagnetic** /dī ə mag néttik/ *adj.* —**diamagnetically** /-néttikli/ *adv.*

diamagnetism /dī ə mágnətizəm/ *n.* a tendency in materials with a relative permeability of less than one to be repelled by a magnetic field and align themselves at right angles to it

diamanté /deé ə mónt ay, dī ə-/ *adj.* RHINESTONE-COVERED decorated with colourless imitation gems (**rhinestones**) that look like diamonds ■ *n.* RHINESTONES colourless imitation gems that look like diamonds, used for costume jewellery and decorating clothing [Early 20thC. From French, originally the past participle of *diamanter* 'to set with diamonds', from *diamant* (see DIAMOND).]

Diamantina /dī əmən teénə-/ river in eastern Australia that rises near the town of Cloncurry in Queensland and flows south into Lake Eyre in South Australia. Length: 800 km/500 mi.

diamantine /dī ə mán tīn/ *adj.* **1.** LOOKING LIKE DIAMONDS resembling diamonds **2.** MADE OF DIAMONDS made of diamond or consisting of diamonds [Early 17thC. From French *diamantin*, from *diamant* (see DIAMOND).]

diameter /dī ámmitər/ *n.* **1. LINE THROUGH CENTRE OF CIRCLE** a straight line running from one side of a circle or other rounded geometric figure through the centre to the other side, or the length of this line **2. WIDTH** the width or thickness of sth, especially sth circular or cylindrical ○ *in diameter* [14thC. Via Old French *diametre* from Latin, from Greek *diametros (grammē)*, literally '(line) which measures through' from *metron* 'measure' (source of English *meter* and *geometry*).]

diametral /dī ámmitrəl/ *adj.* GEOM relating to or forming a diameter —**diametrally** *adv.*

diametric /dī ə méttrik/, **diametrical** /dī ə méttrik'l/ *adj.* complete (refers to opposites, differences, etc.)

diametrically /dī ə méttrikli/ *adv.* used to emphasize that a difference or contrast is as great as it can be ○ *diametrically opposite concepts*

diamine /dī ə meen/ *n.* an organic chemical compound that contains two amino **(nitrogen-containing)** groups [Mid-19thC. Coined from DI- + AMINE.]

diamond /dī əmənd/ *n.* **1.** MINERALS **HARD COLOURLESS MINERAL** a transparent form of carbon that is the hardest known mineral, with many applications in cutting tools and abrasives. It is also the most highly prized gemstone. **2. SHAPE LIKE SQUARE RESTING ON CORNER** a four-sided shape like a square standing on one of its corners **3.** CARDS **CARD WITH DIAMOND-SHAPED SYMBOL** a playing card with a diamond-shaped symbol on it. ◊ **diamonds 4.** BASEBALL **PART OF PLAYING AREA IN BASEBALL** the area of a baseball field bounded by the home plate and the three bases **5.** BASEBALL **BASEBALL PLAYING AREA** an area for playing baseball including the infield and the outfield **6.** *N Ireland* **IRISH MARKET SQUARE** the market square of a town in Northern Ireland (*regional*) ■ *vt.* **(-monds, -monding, -monded) DECORATE WITH DIAMONDS** to decorate sth with diamonds or similar gemstones [13thC. Via Old French *diamant* 'hardest metal' from the medieval Latin stem *diamant-*, an alteration of the Latin stem *adamant-* (see ADAMANT).]

diamond anniversary *n.* an anniversary celebrating 60, or sometimes 75, years of sth, e.g. marriage [From the custom of marking the occasion with gifts containing diamonds]

diamondback /dī əmənd bak/ *n.* **1. RATTLESNAKE WITH DIAMOND-SHAPED MARKINGS** a large poisonous rattlesnake found in the southwestern United States and Mexico that has diamond-shaped markings on its back. Latin name: *Crotalus adamantus* and *Crotalus atrox.* **2. TERRAPIN WITH DIAMOND-SHAPED MARKINGS** a terrapin with diamond-shaped markings on its shell that lives in the salt marshes of the Atlantic and the Gulf coasts of North America. Genus: *Malaclemys.*

diamondback moth *n.* a brightly coloured moth with diamond-shaped markings on the underside of the front wings, visible when the wings are folded. Family: Plutellidae.

diamondiferous /dī əmən dífferəss/ *adj.* containing diamond or diamonds

diamond in the rough *n. US* = **rough diamond**

diamond jubilee *n.* = **diamond anniversary**

diamond point *n.* a cutting tool in which two cutting edges meet at an acute angle, forming a diamond shape

diamond python *n.* a greenish-yellow python with yellow diamond-shaped markings along its side, found in Australia, New Zealand, and New Guinea. Latin name: *Morelia argus.*

diamonds /dī əməndz/ *n.* one of the four suits used in cards, with a red diamond shape as its symbol (*takes a singular or plural verb*)

diamond wedding *n.* the celebration of 60 years of marriage [From the custom of marking the occasion with gifts containing diamonds]

diamorphine /dī ə máwr feen/ *n.* heroin (*technical*) [Early 20thC. Contraction of *diacetylmorphine*, its chemical name.]

Diana /dī ánnə/ *n.* in Roman mythology, the goddess of hunting, virginity and the moon. Greek equivalent **Artemis**

Diana, Princess of Wales (1961–97) British princess. She married Prince Charles in 1981, had two sons,

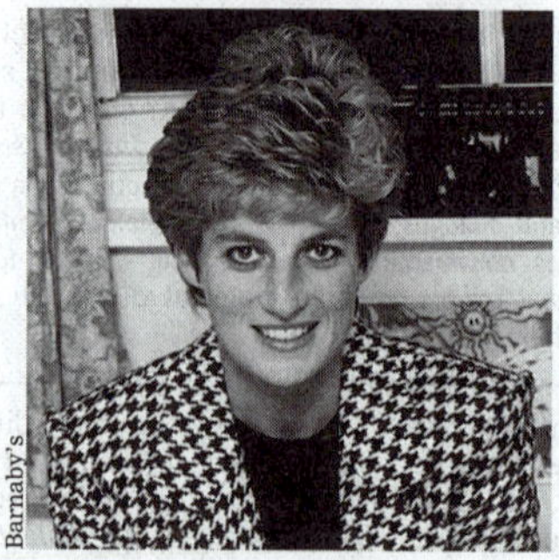

Barnaby's

Diana, Princess of Wales

and was divorced in 1996. She was killed in a car crash in Paris. Born **Diana Frances Spencer**

diandrous /dī ándrəss/ *adj.* used to describe flowers that have two stamens, or fungi and non-seeding plants that have two antheridia [Late 18thC. Coined from DI- + the Greek stem *andr-* 'man' + -OUS.]

dianthus /dī ánthəss/ *n.* a flowering plant belonging to the group that includes carnations, pinks, and sweet william. Genus: *Dianthus.* [Late 18thC. From modern Latin, genus name, from Greek *Dios* 'of Zeus' + *anthos* 'flower'.]

diapason /dī ə páyz'n, -páyss'n/ *n.* **1. PIPE ORGAN'S MAIN STOP** either of the two main stops on a pipe organ that control the organ's tone and give the instrument its characteristic sound **2. RANGE OF SINGER OR MUSICAL INSTRUMENT** the complete range of a musical instrument or a person's singing voice (*technical*) **3. TUNING DEVICE** a tuning fork or pitch pipe (*technical*) [14thC. Via Latin from, ultimately, Greek *dia pasōn khordōn*, literally 'across all the notes of the scale'.] —**diapasonal** *adj.* —**diapasonic** /dī ə pay zónnik, -sónnik/ *adj.*

diapause /dī ə pawz/ *n.* a period during which the metabolism of certain animals or insects slows down, temporarily suspending their bodily development and growth. Such periods are linked to seasonal or environmental changes.

diapedesis /dī əpə deessiss/ *n.* a condition in which blood leaks through the apparently unruptured walls of blood vessels into surrounding tissue, as a reaction to severe inflammation or injury [Early 17thC. From modern Latin, formed from Greek *dia-* 'through' + *pēdan* 'to leap'.] —**diapedetic** /dī əpə déttik/ *adj.*

diapente /dī ə pénti/ *n.* in ancient Greek music, the interval of a perfect fifth [14thC. Via Old French from, ultimately, Greek *dia pente*, literally 'through five'.]

diaper /dī əpər/ *n.* **1.** *US, Can* = **nappy 2.** CRAFT **PATTERN OF SMALL MOTIFS** a pattern, especially woven into or printed on fabric, consisting of a small motif, often a diamond, repeated over and over to cover an entire surface **3.** TEXTILES **FABRIC WITH DIAPER PATTERN** cotton or linen fabric with a diaper pattern woven into or printed on it ■ *vt.* **(-pers, -pering, -pered) 1.** TEXTILES **DECORATE WITH DIAPER PATTERN** to decorate sth, especially fabric, with a diaper pattern **2.** *US, Can* **PUT NAPPY ON BABY** to put a nappy on a baby [14thC. Via Old French *diapre* 'ornamental cloth', from, ultimately, medieval Greek *diaspros* 'thoroughly white', originally applied to silver coins, from, ultimately, Latin *asper* 'rough', used for the surface of coins.]

diaper rash *n. US, Can* = **nappy rash**

diaphanous /dī áffənəss/ *adj.* **1. TRANSPARENT** delicate or gauzy, so as to be transparent ○ *the insect's diaphanous wings* **2. INSUBSTANTIAL** fragile or insubstantial because extremely faint or slight (*literary*) ○ *diaphanous imaginings* [Early 17thC. Via Latin *diaphanus* from Greek *diaphanēs*, literally 'shown through', from *phainein* 'to show' (source of English *fantasy*).] —**diaphaneity** /dī əfə neé əti/ *n.* —**diaphanously** /-nəsli/ *n.* —**diaphanousness** *adv.*

diaphone /dī ə fōn/ *n.* **1.** PHON **SET OF PRONUNCIATION VARIANTS** a set of all the different ways that a particular speech sound is pronounced in all the dialects of a language, or a member of this set **2. FOGHORN SOUNDING TWO NOTES** a foghorn with a two-note sound

diaphoresis /dī əfə reéssiss/ *n.* sweating, especially sweating induced for medical reasons (*technical*) [Late 17thC. Via late Latin from, ultimately, Greek *diaphorein* 'to dissipate by sweating', literally 'to carry away', from *phorein* 'to carry'.]

diaphoretic /dī əfə réttik/ *adj.* used to describe drugs, herbs, or other substances that induce sweating, or their effect —**diaphoretic** *n.*

diaphragm /dī ə fram/ *n.* **1.** ANAT **MUSCULAR WALL BELOW RIBCAGE** a curved muscular membrane in humans and other mammals that separates the abdomen from the area around the lungs. Hiccups are caused by the diaphragm going into spasm. **2.** GYN **DOME-SHAPED CONTRACEPTIVE** a dome-shaped rubber or plastic contraceptive device for women, placed inside the vagina over the entrance to the womb to prevent sperm from entering **3.** OPTICS **CAMERA'S MECHANISM CONTROLLING OPENING FOR LIGHT** a disc with a fixed or variable opening that controls the amount of light that enters a camera or other optical instrument **4.** COMMUNICATION **VIBRATING DISC IN SOUND EQUIPMENT** a thin disc in a microphone, telephone receiver, or other sound device that vibrates in response to sound waves or electrical signals, converting one into the other **5. ANY THIN MEMBRANE** any thin separating membrane, e.g. the porous plate dividing the sections of an electrolytic cell or the plate of cells across the stems of some water plants [14thC. From late Latin *diaphragma*, from, ultimately, Greek *diaphrassein* 'to barricade', literally 'to fence across', from *phrassein* 'to fence in'.] —**diaphragmatic** /dī ə frag máttik/ *adj.* —**diaphragmatically** /-máttikli/ *adv.*

diaphysis /dī áffəssiss/ (*plural* **-ses** /-seez/) *n.* the central section of a long bone, between the growth areas at each end. ◊ **epiphysis** [Mid-19thC. From Greek *diaphusis*, literally 'growing through', from *phusis* 'growth'.] —**diaphysial** /dī ə fízzi əl/ *adj.*

diapir /dī ə peer/ *n.* a dome-shaped body of rock that migrates upwards through denser overlying rock, e.g. a salt deposit [Early 20thC. From Greek *diapeirainein* 'to pierce through', from *peirainein* 'to pierce'.] —**diapiric** /dī ə pírrik/ *adj.*

diapositive /dī ə pózzitiv/ *n.* a photographic slide [Late 19thC. Coined from DIA- 'through' (from its transparency) + POSITIVE.]

diarchy /dī aarki/ (*plural* **-chies**), **dyarchy** (*plural* **-chies**) *n.* **1. GOVERNMENT BY TWO RULERS OR BODIES** a form of government in which power is held by two supreme rulers or two governing bodies **2. COUNTRY RULED BY TWO RULERS** a country ruled or run by two supreme rulers or two governing bodies [Mid-19thC. Formed from DI- on the model of MONARCHY.] —**diarchal** /dī áark'l/ *adj.* —**diarchic** *adj.* —**diarchical** *adj.*

diarist /dī ərist/ *n.* sb who writes a diary, especially one that is published

diarrhoea /dī ə reé ə/, **diarrhea** *n.* **1. FREQUENT AND EXCESSIVE BOWEL MOVEMENTS** frequent and excessive discharging of the bowels producing abnormally thin watery stools, usually as a symptom of gastro-intestinal upset or infection **2. WATERY STOOLS** abnormally thin watery faeces [Early 16thC. Via Latin *diarrhoea*, from Greek *diarrhoia*, from *diarrhein* 'to flow through', from *rhein* 'to flow'.] —**diarrhoeal** *adj.* —**diarrhoeic** *adj.*

diarthrosis /dī aar thróssiss/ (*plural* **-ses** /-seez/) *n.* **1. JOINT THAT MOVES IN MULTIPLE DIRECTIONS** a joint of the body that is able to move freely in various directions, e.g. the shoulder, hip, knee, or elbow **2. JOINT'S MOVEMENT IN MULTIPLE DIRECTIONS** the ability of some joints of the body to move in several directions [Late 16thC. From Greek, formed from *diarthroun* 'to fasten by a joint', which in turn was formed from *arthroun* 'to fasten'.] —**diarthrodial** /-thrṓdi əl/ *adj.*

diary /dī əri/ (*plural* **-ries**) *n.* **1. PERSONAL RECORD OF LIFE'S EVENTS** a personal record of events in sb's life, often including personal thoughts and observations **2. BLANK BOOK** a book with blank or lined paper for keeping a diary in **3. BOOK FOR APPOINTMENTS** a book, usually with pages labelled according to the days of a given year, in which people keep notes of appointments ○ *a desk diary* ○ *I'll check my diary to see if I'm free.* US term **appointment book 4. LIST OF EVENTS** a list of events taking place in a particular place during a particular period of time ○ *a diary of October's events* [Late 16thC. From Latin *diarium*, from *dies* 'day'. The Latin word originally meant 'daily allowance of food or pay'.]

diaspora /dī áspərə/ *n.* a dispersion of a people, language, or culture that was formerly concentrated in one place ○ *the African diaspora* [Late 19thC. From Greek, formed from *diaspeirein* 'to disperse', from *speirein* 'to sow, scatter' (source of English *sperm*).]

Diaspora /dī áspərə/ *n.* JUDAISM **1.** EXILE OF THE JEWS FROM ISRAEL the dispersion of the Jews from Palestine following the Babylonians' conquest of the Judean Kingdom in the 6th century BC and again following the Romans' destruction of the Second Temple in AD 70 **2.** JEWS LIVING OUTSIDE ISRAEL the Jewish communities living outside either the present-day state of Israel or the ancient biblical kingdom of Israel

diaspore /dī́ ə spawr/ *n.* **1.** MINERALS WHITE OXIDE OF ALUMINIUM a white, grey, or pink form of aluminium oxide that is found in bauxite and corundum. It is useful for its abrasive and heat-resistant properties. **2.** BOT REPRODUCTIVE STRUCTURE a seed or spore that is dispersed from a plant [Early 19thC. From Greek *diaspora* (see DIASPORA); from its dispersion when heated.]

diastase /dī́ ə stayz, -stayss/ *n.* BIOCHEM now called **amylase** [Mid-19thC. Coined from modern Latin *diastasis* (see DIASTASIS) + -ASE.] —**diastasic** /dī́ ə stáyzik, -stáysik/ *adj.*

diastasis /dī ástəssiss/ (*plural* **-ses** /-seez/) *n.* MED the dislodging of the end (**epiphysis**) of a long bone from its shaft without a fracturing of the bone itself (*technical*) [Early 18thC. Via modern Latin from Greek, 'separation', from *stasis* 'placing'.] —**diastatic** /dī́ ə státtik/ *adj.*

diastema /dī́ ə steémə/ (*plural* **-mata** /-mətə/) *n.* DENT a larger than usual gap between two adjacent teeth (*technical*) [Mid-19thC. Via late Latin from Greek, 'gap', from *diistanai* 'to place apart', from *histanai* 'to place'.] —**diastematic** /dī́ əstə máttik/ *adj.*

diastereoisomer /dī́ ə stérri ō íssəmər/, **diastereomer** /dī́ ə stérri əmər/ *n.* CHEM a molecule that has the same formula and structure as another (**stereoisomer**), but is arranged differently in space and is therefore not a mirror image of the other (**enantiomer**)

diastole /dī ásstəli/ *n.* the rhythmic expansion of the chambers of the heart at each heartbeat, during which they fill with blood [Late 16thC. Via late Latin from Greek, 'separation, expansion', from *diastellein*, literally 'to place apart', from *stellein* 'to place'.] —**diastolic** /dī́ ə stóllik/ *adj.*

diastyle /dī́ ə stīl/ *adj.* HAVING WIDELY SPACED COLUMNS used to describe classical buildings with columns set at intervals equal to three or sometimes four times the diameter of a column, slightly farther apart than in the Doric order ■ *n.* DIASTYLE STRUCTURE a diastyle building or colonnade [Mid-16thC. Directly or via Latin from Greek *diastulos*, literally 'between columns', from *stulos* 'column'.]

diatessaron /dī́ ə téssə ron/ *n.* **1.** BIBLE GOSPELS AS ONE STORY the combination of all four Gospels of the Bible to make a single narrative **2.** MUSIC ANCIENT GREEK INTERVAL OF A FOURTH in ancient Greek music, the interval of a perfect fourth [Late 16thC. Via late Latin from Greek *dia tessarōn*, literally 'composed of four'.]

diathermia *n.* MED = **diathermy** [Early 20thC. From modern Latin, literally 'heat across', formed from Greek *thermē* 'heat'.]

diathermic /dī́ ə thúrmik/ *adj.* **1.** MED RELATING TO DIATHERMY relating to diathermy **2.** PHYS CONDUCTING HEAT able to conduct or transmit heat or infrared radiation [Early 20thC. From French *diathermique*, from Greek *thermē* 'heat'.]

diathermy /dī́ ə thurmi/, **diathermia** /dī́ ə th/ *n.* MED the treatment of organs or tissues by passing high-frequency electric currents through them in order to generate heat, thus increasing circulation [Early 20thC. From modern Latin *diathermia* (see DIATHERMIA).]

diathesis /dī áthississ/ (*plural* **-ses** /dī áthisseez/) *n.* a susceptibility to a particular disease or set of diseases, e.g. allergies or gout [Mid-17thC. Via modern Latin from, ultimately, Greek *diatithenai* 'to arrange, dispose', literally 'to put in different directions', from *tithenai* 'to put'.] —**diathetic** /-ə théttik/ *adj.*

diatom /dī́ ə tom/ *n.* a microscopic one-celled alga that has silica-filled cell walls or shells divided into two halves. Diatoms are responsible for the formation of diatomite in water. Class: Bacillariophyceae. [Mid-19thC. From modern Latin *Diatoma*, genus name, from Greek *diatomos* 'cut in two', from *diatemnein* 'to cut through', from *temnein* 'to cut'.]

diatomaceous /dī́ ətə máyshəss/ *adj.* containing diatoms or their skeletal remains

diatomaceous earth *n.* **1.** = **diatomite 2.** POWDERED ROCK USED AS NONTOXIC INSECTICIDE a form of unrefined diatomite that is used as an insecticide. It is used indoors as an alternative to chemical insecticides because it is virtually nontoxic to humans, although it can be a lung irritant if inhaled.

diatomic /dī́ ə tómmik/ *adj.* having two atoms per molecule [Mid-19thC. Coined from DI- 'two' + ATOMIC.] —**diatomicity** /dī́ ətə míssəti/ *n.*

diatomite /dī áttə mīt/ *n.* a soft powdery porous rock made from the accumulated shells of diatoms. It is resistant to heat and chemical action and has many industrial uses, e.g. as an ingredient in fireproof cements and insulating materials, as well as in dynamite. [Late 19thC. Coined from DIATOM + -ITE.]

diatonic /dī́ ə tónnik/ *adj.* RELATING TO SIMPLE MUSICAL SCALES relating to or based on musical scales consisting of five tones and two semitones, e.g. the major or minor scale, with no sharps or flats added ■ *n.* INTERVAL IN A DIATONIC SCALE the interval between any two notes of a diatonic scale [Early 17thC. Via French *diatonique* or late Latin *diatonicus*, from Greek *diatonikos* 'at intervals of a tone', from *tonos* 'tone'.] —**diatonically** *adv.* —**diatonicism** /-tónnissizəm/ *n.*

diatribe /dī́ ə trīb/ *n.* a bitter verbal or written attack on sb or sth ○ *a diatribe against falling standards* [Late 16thC. Via French from, ultimately, Greek *diatribē* 'act of spending time (in discourse)'. Originally, in English, 'learned discourse'; its connotations of 'bitter resentment' date from the 19thC.]

diatropism /dī áttrəpizəm/ *n.* the tendency of a plant or plant part to grow at right angles in response to an external stimulus, e.g. light —**diatropic** /dī́ ə tróppik/ *adj.*

diaz- *prefix.* = **diazo-** (*used before vowels*)

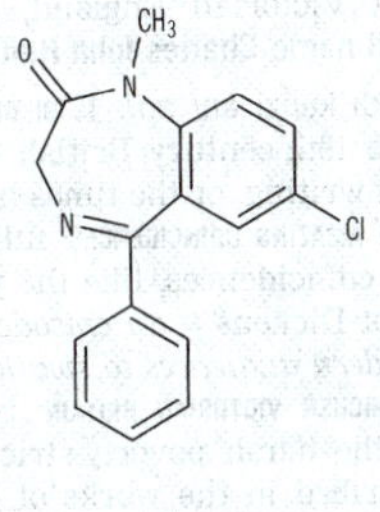

Diazepam

diazepam /dī áyzə pam, -ázzə-/ *n.* a tranquillizing drug used to reduce anxiety and tension, and as a muscle relaxant and sedative. Formula: $C_{16}H_{13}ClN_2O$. [Mid-20thC. Coined from a shortening of BENZODIAZEPINE + a shortening of AMIDE.]

diazine /dī́ ə zeen/, **diazin** /-zin, dī ázzin/ *n.* CHEM a chemical compound in which the molecules contain a hexagonal ring of four carbon atoms and two nitrogen atoms. It has three different molecular structures (**isomers**). Formula: $C_4N_2H_4$. [Early 20thC. Coined from DI- 'two' + AZINE.]

diazo /dī áy zō/ *adj.* CHEM CONTAINING TWO ADJACENT NITROGEN ATOMS used to describe any organic compound containing two adjacent nitrogen atoms, e.g. an azo compound or a diazonium salt. ◊ **azo** ■ *n.* (*plural* **-azos** *or* **-azoes**) PRINTING, PHOTOGRAPHY DOCUMENT COPY MADE WITH DIAZO COMPOUND a photograph or photocopy made using the diazotype process [Late 19thC. Coined from DI- + AZO-. The noun is a shortening of DIAZOTYPE.]

diazo- *prefix.* containing a pair of carbon atoms bonded to an aromatic hydrocarbon ○ *diazonium* [Coined from DI-[1] + AZO-]

diazole /dī áy zōl/ *n.* CHEM an organic chemical compound with a five-sided ring structure containing three carbon atoms and two nitrogen atoms

diazotize /dī áyzə tīz/ (**-tizes, -tizing, -tized**), **diazotise** (**-tises, -tising, -tised**) *v.* CHEM to use nitrous acid to transform an amine into a diazo compound —**diazotization** /dī áyzə tī záysh'n/ *n.*

diazotype /dī áyzə tīp/ *n.* a printing or photographic process that exploits the light-sensitive properties of diazo compounds

dib /dib/ (**dibs, dibbing, dibbed**) *vi.* to fish by causing the bait to bob on the surface of the water [Early 17thC. Alteration of DAB.]

dibasic /dī báyssik/ *adj.* CHEM **1.** WITH TWO REPLACEABLE HYDROGEN ATOMS used to describe an acid that has two replaceable hydrogen atoms **2.** FORMED WITH TWO ATOMS OF METAL used to describe a salt or an acid that is formed with two atoms of a univalent metallic element —**dibasicity** /dī bay síssəti/ *n.*

dibber /díbbər/ *n.* a small pointed gardening tool used to make holes in the soil for planting seeds, bulbs, or seedlings [Mid-18thC. Formed from DIB, in the dialect sense 'to dibble'.]

dibble /díbb'l/ *n.* = **dibber** ■ *vt.* (**-bles, -bling, -bled**) MAKE HOLES IN SOIL to make planting holes in soil with a pointed tool, or put plants or seeds in such holes [14thC. Origin uncertain: possibly formed from Old English *dyppan* 'to dip'.] —**dibbler** *n.*

dibbuk *n.* = **dybbuk**

dibranchiate /dī brángki ət/ *n.* a mollusc with two gills. Octopus, squid, and cuttlefish are dibranchiates. Order: Dibranchiata. [Mid-19thC. Coined from DI- 'two' + Greek *bragkhia* 'gills' + -ATE.]

dibromide /dī brṓ mīd/ *n.* a chemical compound whose molecules contain two bromine atoms

dibs /dibz/ *npl.* **1.** MONEY money, especially in small amounts (*dated informal*) **2.** = **jacks 3.** CLAIM OF RIGHTS a claim of exclusive rights to take or use sth (*informal*) ○ *called dibs on the front seat* [Early 19thC. From *dibs* 'game played with pebbles', hence 'counters used in a game', shortening of *dibstones*, probably from DIB in the obsolete sense 'to tap'.]

dicarboxylic acid /dī kaar bok síllik-/ *n.* any acid that contains two carboxyl groups

dicast /dík ast/ *n.* in ancient Athens, a citizen who was among the six thousand chosen by lot each year to act as jurors and judges in the popular law courts [Early 19thC. From Greek *dikastes* 'judge, juryman', from *dikazein* 'to judge'.] —**dicastic** /di kástik/ *adj.*

dice /dīss/ *npl.* **1.** GAME GAMBLING GAME PLAYED WITH DICE a gambling game played with dice, e.g. craps (*often takes a singular verb*) **2.** CHUNKS cube-shaped pieces, especially of meat ■ *v.* (**dices, dicing, diced**) **1.** *vt.* CUT INTO CUBES to cut food into cubes ○ *diced carrots* **2.** *vti.* GAME GAMBLE WITH DICE to gamble using dice, or win or lose sth playing dice **3.** *vi.* TAKE RISKS to challenge or take risks with sb or sth dangerous ○ *dicing with death* **4.** *vt.* DECORATE WITH SQUARE PATTERN to decorate sth with a pattern of squares or cubes **5.** *vt. Aus* ABANDON to abandon or discard sth (*informal*) [14thC. Plural of DIE[2], from French *dé* (plural *dés*), from Latin *datum*, past participle of *dare* 'to give', also 'to play'.] —**dicer** *n.* ◇ **no dice** used to indicate that there is no chance of sth happening

WORD KEY: USAGE

Dice – singular or plural? The singular form ***die***, of which ***dice*** was originally the plural, is now seldom used other than in the idiom *The die is cast.* ***Dice***, used with a singular verb, means a small cube marked with one to six dots, used in gambling games (its plural in this use is ***dice***), or a gambling game in which these cubes are used. ***Dice*** (plural) can also refer to any small cubes, especially cube-shaped pieces of food (*Cut the cheese into dice*).

dicentra /dī séntrə/ *n.* a perennial plant with arching sprays of small drooping flowers that grows best in shade. Genus: *Dicentra.* [Mid-19thC. Via modern Latin, genus name, from Greek *dikentros*, literally 'two-pointed', from *kentron* 'centre, point'; from the shape of its leaves.]

dicey /dī́ssi/ (**-ier, -iest**), **dicy** (**-ier, -iest**) *adj.* uncertain and involving danger or risk (*informal*) [Mid-20thC. From the riskiness of gambling with dice.]

dich- *prefix.* = **dicho-** (*used before vowels*)

dichasium /dī káyzi əm/ (*plural* **-a** /-zi ə/) *n.* a flowering stem that has a single flower growing on the end (**cyme**) and later sprouts two single-flower branches, one on each side of and below the first flower [Late 19thC. Coined from Greek *dikhasis* 'division' formed from *dikha* 'apart' + -IUM.] —**dichasial** *adj.* —**dichasially** *adv.*

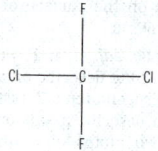

Dichlorofidfuoromethane

dichlorodifluoromethane /dī kláwr ō dī floŏr ō meéth ayn/ *n.* a colourless, nonflammable, gaseous CFC. It is easily liquified under pressure and is therefore used as a propellant in aerosols, as a refrigerant, and in fire extinguishers. Formula: CCl_2F_2.

dichlorodiphenyltrichloroethane /dī kláwr ō dī feén īl trī kláwr ō eé thayn/ *n.* full form of **DDT**

dichloromethane /dī kláwr ō meéth ayn/ *n.* a colourless, nonflammable, toxic gas used in paint strippers, degreasing, and in plastics processing. Formula: CH_2Cl_2. [Mid-20thC]

dichlorophenoxyacetic acid /dī kláwr ō fə nóksi ə seétik ássid/ *n.* CHEM = **2,4-D**

dicho- *prefix.* having two parts ○ *dichogamy* [From Greek *dikha* 'in two'; related to *di-* 'two']

dichogamy /dī kóggəmi/ *n.* a plant's production of male and female parts at different times, in order to prevent self-pollination and ensure cross-fertilization [Mid-19thC. Coined from Greek *dikho-* 'apart' + *gamos* 'marriage'.] —**dichogamic** *adj.* —**dichogamous** /dī kō gámmik/ *adj.*

dichondra /dī kóndrə/ *n.* a low-growing plant of the morning glory family that is often planted in place of lawn grass in warm parts of the United States. Genus: *Dichondra*. [Mid-20thC. From modern Latin, genus name, literally 'two grains', formed from Greek *dikho-* 'apart' + *khondros* 'grain'.]

dichoptic /dī kóptik/ *adj.* with eyes clearly separated from each other [Late 19thC. Coined from Greek *dikho-* 'apart' + OPTIC.]

dichotic /dī kóttik/ *adj.* involving or relating to the simultaneous stimulation of each ear with different sounds [Mid-20thC. Coined from Greek *dikho-* 'apart' + the Greek stem *ōt-* 'ear' + -IC.]

dichotomize /dī kóttə mīz/ (**-mizes, -mizing, -mized**), **dichotomise** (**-mises, -mising, -mised**) *vti.* to divide sth, or become divided, into two classes or groups (*formal*) —**dichotomization** /dī kóttə mī záysh'n/ *n.*

dichotomy /dī kóttəmi/ (*plural* **-mies**) *n.* **1.** SEPARATION OF DIFFERENT OR CONTRADICTORY THINGS a separation into two divisions that differ widely from, or contradict each other **2.** BOT BRANCHING OF PLANTS the division of each of a plant's branches into two more branches **3.** ASTRON MOON PHASE WHEN HALF VISIBLE the phase of the moon or a planet when half of its surface appears illuminated by the sun [Late 16thC. Via modern Latin from Greek *dikhotomia*, literally 'cutting in two', from *dikho-* 'apart, in two' + *temnein* 'to cut'.] —**dichotomic** /dī kō tómmik/ *adj.* —**dichotomous** /dī kóttəməss/ *adj.* —**dichotomously** /-məssli/ *adv.*

dichroic /dī krō ik/, **dichroitic** /dī krō íttik/ *adj.* used to describe a crystal that appears to be a different colour when viewed along a different axis [Mid-19thC. Formed from Greek *dikhroos* 'two-coloured', from *khrōs* 'colour'.] —**dichroism** *n.*

dichroite /dī krō īt/ *n.* = **cordierite**

dichromate /dī krō mayt/ *n.* a salt of dichromic acid. Dichromates are a characteristic orange-red colour.

dichromatic /dī krō máttik/ *adj.* **1.** WITH TWO COLOURS having two colours **2. dichromatic, dichromic** OPHTHALMOL PARTIALLY COLOUR-BLIND able to distinguish only two of the three primary colours and their combinations **3.** ZOOL WITH DIFFERENT COLOUR PHASES used to describe animals, especially birds, that have two different colours in phases that are not associated with the normal variations in colour that occur with sex and age

dichromatism /dī krōmətizzəm/ *n.* **1.** COLOURING WITH TWO COLOURS ONLY the presence of only two colours in sth **2.** OPHTHALMOL PARTIAL COLOUR-BLINDNESS a type of colour-blindness in which only two of the three primary colours and their combinations can be distinguished

dichromic *adj.* = **dichromatic** *adj.* 2 [Mid-19thC. Formed from Greek *dikhrōmos* 'two-coloured' (from *khrōma* 'colour'.]

dichromic acid *n.* an unstable acid found only in solution and in the form of dichromate salts. Formula: $H_2Cr_2O_7$.

dichromism /dī krōm izzəm/ *n.* = **dichromatism** *n.* 2

dicht /dikht/ *vti. Scotland* CLEAN to wipe or rub dirt or dust from sth (*nonstandard*) ■ *n. Scotland* ACT OF CLEANING a wipe or rub to clean dirt or dust away (*nonstandard*) [Late 17thC. Variant of DIGHT.]

dick[1] /dik/ *n.* (*slang offensive*) **1.** OFFENSIVE TERM offensive term for the penis **2.** OFFENSIVE TERM a highly offensive term for a very thoughtless boy or man [Mid-16thC. From the male first name *Dick*.]

dick[2] /dik/ *n. US* a detective (*dated slang*) [Early 20thC. Origin uncertain: perhaps a shortening of DETECTIVE, or from slang *dick* 'look'.]

dickens /díkinz/ *n.* exclamation used for emphasis in a variety of expressions, especially expressions of surprise or annoyance (*informal*) ○ *What the dickens is going on here?* ○ *scared the dickens out of me* [Late 16thC. Origin uncertain: probably from the surname *Dickens*.]

Dickens /díkinz/, **Charles** (1812–70) British novelist. His career began with magazine sketches, written under the pseudonym 'Boz', before *Pickwick Papers* (1837) brought him greater popularity. His many subsequent novels, appearing in monthly instalments and often depicting poverty and social injustice in Victorian England, have remained popular. Full name **Charles John Huffam Dickens**

Dickensian /di kénzi ən/ *adj.* **1.** OF CHARLES DICKENS relating to the 19th-century British author, Charles Dickens, his writing, or the times he lived in **2.** FULL OF TWISTS AND AMAZING COINCIDENCES full of twists and remarkable coincidences, like the plots of some of the novels of Dickens ○ *an episode too Dickensian for most modern audiences to swallow* **3.** REMINISCENT OF POVERTY-STRICKEN VICTORIAN BRITAIN typical or reminiscent of the harsh poverty-stricken living conditions described in the works of Dickens **4.** JOLLY AND GENIAL jolly and cordial, like some of the scenes and characters featured in the novels of Dickens

dicker /díkər/ *vi.* (**-ers, -ering, -ered**) HAGGLE to bargain for goods or services ○ *collectors dickering at antique sales* ■ *n.* BARGAINING bargaining in general, or sth settled, achieved, or obtained through bargaining [Early 19thC. Origin uncertain: probably from, ultimately, Latin *decuria* 'group of ten, ten hides for sale', from *decem* 'ten' + *vir* 'man'. Originally in English 'a quantity of ten'.]

dickhead /dík hed/ *n.* an offensive term for an unintelligent or inattentive man (*slang insult*)

Dickinson /díkins'n/, **Emily** (1830–86) US poet. She is considered one of America's greatest writers. Most of her poems were published posthumously. Full name **Emily Elizabeth Dickinson**

Dick test *n.* a skin test used to determine whether sb is immune or susceptible to scarlet fever [Early 20thC. Named after George Frederick Dick (1881–1967), the US biologist who invented the test.]

dicky[1] /díki/ (*plural* **-ies**), **dickey** (*plural* **-eys**) *n.* **1.** CLOTHES FALSE SHIRT FRONT OR NECK a garment that is only the front or neck of a shirt, worn under a shirt, jacket, or jumper **2.** ACCESSORIES = **dicky bow** (*informal*)

Emily Dickinson

3. DONKEY a donkey, especially a male **4.** AUTOMOT OUTSIDE CAR SEAT a folding outside seat on the back of some early cars. US term **rumble seat** [Mid-18thC. Of uncertain origin; probably representing different words, some of which may have been inspired by the male name *Dicky*, a pet form of *Richard*.]

dicky[2] /díki/ (**-ier, -iest**) *adj.* (*informal*) **1.** UNWELL not well in health **2.** NOT RELIABLE faulty or unreliable ○ *The doctor says I have a dicky heart.* [Late 18thC. Origin unknown.]

dicky bird /díki burd/, **dickeybird** *n.* **1.** SMALL BIRD a small bird (*babytalk*) **2.** WORD a single word (*slang*) ○ *did not say a dicky bird* [In sense 2, rhyming slang]

dicky bow *n.* a bow tie (*informal*) [*Dicky* probably from the male name, a pet form of *Richard*, or perhaps from DICKY, 'false shirt front']

diclinous /díklinəss, dī klínəss/ *adj.* used to describe plants that have stamens and pistils in separate flowers, rather than in the same flower [Early 19thC. Formed from modern Latin *diclines*, literally 'two beds', from Greek *klinē* 'bed'.] —**diclinism** /dī klinnizəm/ *n.* —**dicliny** /díklini, dī klíni/ *n.*

dicotyledon /dī kotti leéd'n/ *n.* a flowering plant with two seed leaves (**cotyledons**) that appear from the seed at germination and subsequent leaves with a network of veins. Most herbaceous plants, trees, and shrubs are dicotyledons. Subclass: Dicotyledonae. [Early 18thC. From modern Latin *Dicotyledonae*, subclass name, literally 'two cotyledons'.] —**dicotyledonous** *adj.*

dicrotism /díkrətizzəm/ *n.* a physiological condition in which each heartbeat produces a double pulse, as occurs, e.g., in typhoid fever [Mid-19thC. Formed from Greek *dikrotos* 'double-beating'.] —**dicrotal** /díkrətəl/ *adj.* —**dicrotic** /dī króttik/ *adj.*

dict. *abbr.* **1.** dictation **2.** dictator **3.** dictionary

dicta plural of **dictum**

Dictaphone /díktəfōn/ *tdmk.* a trademark for a small hand-held tape recorder used for dictation

dictate *v.* /dik táyt/ (**-tates, -tating, -tated**) **1.** *vti.* SPEAK ALOUD WORDS TO BE WRITTEN to speak the words of a text or letter to be written, either to sb writing it down as it is spoken, or into a tape recorder for later transcription **2.** *vti.* RULE OR CONTROL OTHER PEOPLE to rule over or make decisions for others with absolute authority, or attempt to do so ○ *dictates their every move* **3.** *vt.* CONTROL to have control over sth (*usually passive*) ○ *The possibility of play today will be dictated largely by the weather.* ■ *n.* /dík tayt/ **1.** COMMAND GIVEN an order telling people what they must do ○ *dictates received from their superiors* **2.** GOVERNING PRINCIPLE a rule or principle that governs how people behave ○ *the dictates of fashion* [Late 16thC. From Latin *dictat-*, the past participle stem of *dictare* 'to say often', from *dicere* 'to say' (see DICTION).]

dictation /dik táysh'n/ *n.* **1.** ACT OF DICTATING the act of dictating a text or letter, or of writing down what is being dictated **2.** EDUC STUDENTS' WRITING OF WORDS SPOKEN a test or exercise of language comprehension in which pupils write down words spoken aloud by a teacher ○ *a French dictation* —**dictational** *adj.*

dictator /dik táytər/ *n.* **1.** POL TYRANT a leader who rules a country with absolute power, usually by force **2.** BOSSY PERSON sb who behaves in a tyrannical way **3.** AUTHORITY ON A SUBJECT sb whose opinions on a subject are listened to and followed by society at large ○ *one of the great dictators of modern music* **4.** HIST

TEMPORARY ROMAN RULER in ancient Rome, a temporary appointed leader with absolute power to deal with a crisis or an emergency

dictatorial /dìktə táwri əl/ *adj.* **1.** IMPOSING WILL ON OTHERS fond of telling others what to do, or of using power or authority to make them do it **2.** POL OF DICTATORS relating to or ruled by dictators —**dictatorially** *adv.*

dictatorship /dik táytər ship/ *n.* **1.** DICTATOR'S POWER OR RULE a dictator's power or authority, or the period of time during which a dictator rules **2.** GOVERNMENT BY DICTATOR government by a dictator **3.** COUNTRY RULED BY DICTATOR a state ruled by a dictator **4.** ABSOLUTE AUTHORITY absolute power or authority

diction /díksh'n/ *n.* **1.** SPOKEN CLARITY the clarity with which sb pronounces words when speaking or singing **2.** CHOICE OF WORDS choice of words to fit their context ○ *'a tendency to identify the poetic impulse with melancholy moods and sonorous diction'* (Northrop Frye, *The Bush Garden*; 1972) [Mid-16thC. From the Latin stem *diction-*, from *dicere* 'to say'.] —**dictional** *adj.* —**dictionally** *adv.*

WORD KEY: ORIGIN

As well as giving rise to ***diction***, Latin *dicere* is also the source of English *addict, condition, dictate, ditto, ditty, edict, index, indicate, judge, predict,* and *verdict.*

dictionary /díksh'nəri/ (*plural* **-ies**) *n.* **1.** BOOK OF WORD MEANINGS a reference book that contains words listed in alphabetical order and gives explanations of their meanings, often with additional information about grammar, pronunciation, and etymology **2.** FOREIGN-LANGUAGE REFERENCE BOOK OF WORDS a reference book that gives equivalents of words and phrases in two or more languages, often with translations from each language to the other in separate sections ○ *a Spanish-English dictionary* **3.** SPECIALIZED REFERENCE BOOK a reference book that gives the meanings of, and often other information about, terms relating to a particular subject or field, arranged alphabetically ○ *a dictionary of music* **4.** LIST OF INFORMATION a book that contains a list of examples or information arranged either alphabetically or in some other way, e.g. by author ○ *a dictionary of quotations* **5.** COMPUT ALPHABETICAL LIST OF COMPUTER CODES an alphabetized list of keys or code names used in a program, together with a brief description of the meaning of each **6.** COMPUT WORD-PROCESSING REFERENCE a file used as a reference by a word-processing program for correct spelling and hyphenation [Early 16thC. From medieval Latin *dictionarius* 'of words', from the Latin stem *diction-* (see DICTION).]

dictum /díktəm/ (*plural* **-tums** *or* **-ta** /-tə/) *n.* **1.** PRONOUNCEMENT an authoritative saying, statement, or pronouncement (*formal*) **2.** SAYING a popular saying **3.** LAW = **obiter dictum** [Late 16thC. From Latin, from the past participle of *dicere* (see DICTION).]

dictyopteran /dìkti óptərən/ *n.* an insect with, typically, a flattened body, long legs, and leathery front wings held flat over the membranous hind wings. Dictyopterans include cockroaches and mantises. Order: Dictyoptera.

dicynodont /dī sínnə dont/ *n.* an extinct plant-eating reptile with teeth like tusks. Suborder: Dicynodontia. [Mid-19thC. From modern Latin *Dicynodontia*, suborder name, literally 'two canine teeth', from the Greek stems *kun-* 'dog' and *odont-* 'tooth'.]

did past tense of **do**

didact /dī dakt/ *n.* sb who speaks or writes in a didactic way (*formal*) [Mid-20thC. Back-formation from DIDACTIC.]

didactic /dī dáktik, di dáktik/ *adj.* **1.** WITH MESSAGE containing a political or moral message ○ *didactic theatre* **2.** FOND OF INSTRUCTING OR ADVISING OTHERS tending to give instruction or advice, even when it is not welcome or not needed [Mid-17thC. From Greek *didaktikos*, from *didaskein* 'to teach'.] —**didactically** *adv.*

didacticism /dī dáktisizəm, di-/ *n.* the instructional quality of sth, e.g. a piece of writing, or the attitude of sb who likes to instruct others or give them advice ○ *the welcome absence of didacticism in modern poetry*

didactics /dī dáktiks, di dáktiks/ *n.* the science or profession of teaching (*formal*) (*takes a singular verb*)

diddle[1] /dídd'l/ (**-dles, -dling, -dled**) *vt.* (*informal*) **1.** CHEAT to cheat or swindle sb (*often passive*) **2.** COMPUT MANIPULATE DATA ILLEGALLY to manipulate computer data illegally **3.** COMPUT MANIPULATE PROGRAM to manipulate a computer program in an informal or a not particularly serious manner [Early 19thC. Origin uncertain: perhaps a back-formation from *Diddler*, the surname of a swindler in *Raising the Wind*, a play by James Kenney (1803).] —**diddler** *n.*

diddle[2] /dídd'l/ (**-dles, -dling, -dled**) *v.* **1.** *vi.* SPEND TIME IDLY to spend time doing nothing in particular (*informal*) ○ *spent the morning diddling about* **2.** *vt.* *US* OFFENSIVE TERM to have sexual intercourse with a woman (*slang offensive*) **3.** *vt.* JERK REPEATEDLY to jerk sth up and down or back and forth (*informal*) [Mid-17thC. Origin uncertain: perhaps formed from dialect *didder* 'to quiver'.] —**diddler** *n.*

diddlysquat /dídli skwot/, **diddly** *n.* *US* nothing at all (*informal*) ○ *And what did I get? Diddlysquat!* [Mid-20thC. Origin uncertain: probably alteration of *doodlysquat*.]

diddy /díddi/ (**-dier, -diest**) *adj.* tiny (*informal*) ○ *a diddy little travelling manicure set* [Mid-20thC. Origin uncertain: probably alteration of *tiddy* 'small'.]

Diderot /deédə rō/, **Denis** (1713–84) French encyclopedist and philosopher. He was chief editor of the 35-volume *Encyclopédie* (1751–80), one of the major works of the Enlightenment.

didgeridoo /díjjəri dóo/ (*plural* **-doos**), **didjeridoo** (*plural* **-doos**) *n.* an Australian Aboriginal musical instrument consisting of a long thick wooden pipe that the player blows into, creating a deep reverberating humming sound [Early 20thC. An Aboriginal word imitating the sound of the instrument.]

didn't /díd'nt/ *contr.* did not ○ *I didn't want to go.*

Dido /dīdō/ in Roman mythology, the queen and founder of Carthage who killed herself when abandoned by her lover, Aeneas

didst /didst/ *contr.* second person present singular of 'did', used with 'thou' (*archaic*)

didymium /dī dímmi əm/ *n.* a mixture of metallic elements from the rare-earth, or lanthanide, series of elements, consisting chiefly of neodymium and praseodymium, used in the production of coloured glass and optical filters [Mid-19thC. Coined from Greek *didumos* 'twin' + -IUM.]

die[1] /dī/ (**dies, dying, died**) *v.* **1.** *vi.* STOP LIVING to cease to be alive (*refers to a person, plant, or animal*) **2.** *vi.* STOP EXISTING to cease to exist, especially gradually ○ *feelings I thought had died long ago* **3.** *vi.* STOP WORKING to stop functioning ○ *The engine suddenly died.* **4.** *vti.* DIE AS STATED to cease to live in a particular way ○ *The villain, of course, dies a gruesome death.* [12thC. Origin uncertain: probably from Old Norse *deyja* 'to die', from, ultimately, an Indo-European base that also produced English *death* and *dead*.] ◇ **to die for** highly desirable and hence worth sacrificing sth to obtain ◇ **die hard** give up or come to an end only after long, difficult, and sustained resistance. ◊ **diehard**
die away *vi.* to fade or grow faint
die back *vi.* to wither or die from the tips of new shoots back to the established stem or old wood of the plant, as a result of disease, seasonal change, or poor conditions
die down *vi.* to become quieter, weaker, or less intense
die off *vi.* to die gradually one by one, till none are left (*refers to plants or animals*)
die out *vi.* **1.** CEASE GRADUALLY TO EXIST to become extinct or cease to exist gradually ○ *entire species that have died out in our century* **2.** DISAPPEAR GRADUALLY to fade and finally disappear gradually ○ *Over the years, opposition to the plan had died out.*

die[2] /dī/ *n.* **1.** GAME DICE a dice for use in games of chance (*formal*) **2.** ENG STAMPING OR PRESSING TOOL the metal tool on a stamping or pressing machine that gives the finished article its shape and design **3.** ENG MOULD tool for moulding substances such as metal or plastic **4.** ENG TOOL FOR CUTTING a tool that cuts screw threads on metal rods, consisting of a metal block with an internally threaded hole into which blank rods are screwed to cut external threads **5.** ARCHIT PART OF PEDESTAL the part of a pedestal that lies between the base and the cornice, especially when it is cubic in shape [12thC. From French *dé* (see DICE).] ◇ **as straight as a die** completely honest and trustworthy (*informal*)

dieback /dī bak/ *n.* gradual decay that sets in at a plant's young shoots then works back to established stems or old wood, as a result of disease, seasonal change, or poor conditions

die-cast (**die-casts, die-casting, die-cast**) *vt.* to make a metal or plastic object by pouring or forcing molten metal or plastic into a mould —**die-cast** *adj.*

die casting *n.* a manufacturing process in which objects are formed by pouring or forcing molten metal or plastic into a die

diecious *adj.* = **dioecious**

dieffenbachia /deéf'n báki ə/ *n.* an evergreen plant with poisonous sap, native to tropical America but widely cultivated as a house plant for its large many-coloured leaves. Dumb cane is a type of dieffenbachia. Genus: *Dieffenbachia.* [Late 19thC. From modern Latin, genus name, named after Ernst *Dieffenbach* (1794–1855), a German botanist.]

diehard /dī haard/ *adj.* STUBBORNLY RESISTANT TO CHANGE resistant to any kind of change, and reluctant to give up beliefs, positions, or attitudes ○ *diehard fans* ■ *n.* STUBBORNLY RESISTANT PERSON sb who resists change or who clings to a belief, attitude, or position in the face of all opposition ○ *with the old diehards holding out to the bitter end* —**diehardism** *n.*

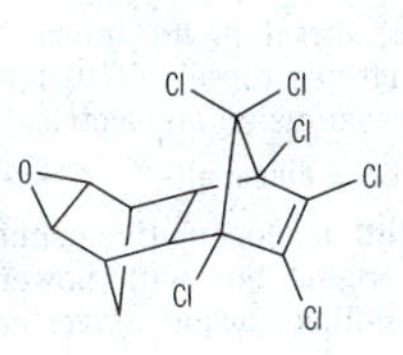

Dieldrin

dieldrin /deéldrin/ *n.* a contact insecticide based on a chlorinated naphthalene derivative. Its effects are cumulative and long lasting in humans and animals, therefore it is now widely banned. Formula: $C_{12}H_{10}OCl_6$. [Mid-20thC. Named after Otto *Diels* (1876–1954), German chemist + ALDRIN.]

dielectric /dī iléktrik/ *adj.* NOT CONDUCTING DIRECT ELECTRIC CURRENT not able to conduct direct electric current and therefore useful as an insulator ■ *n.* DIELECTRIC SUBSTANCE a dielectric substance [Mid-19thC. Coined from DIA- 'through' + ELECTRIC.] —**dielectrically** *adv.*

dielectric constant *n.* PHYS = **relative permittivity**

dielectric heating *n.* ELEC ENG the heating of an insulating material by placing it in a rapidly changing electric field. The technique is used in the manufacture of foam rubber, plastics, and other materials.

dielectric lens *n.* a lens made of insulating material that deflects radio waves passing through it in the way that a glass lens deflects light. It is used to shape the beams emitted from radar and microwave antennas.

Diels-Alder reaction /deélz áwldər-/ *n.* a chemical reaction in which an organic compound with two double bonds between carbon atoms (**diene**) and a compound containing a double or triple bond, combine to form a ring compound [Mid-20thC. Named after the German chemists Otto *Diels* (see DIELDRIN) and Kurt *Alder* (see ALDRIN).]

diencephalon /dī en séffə lon/ *n.* the area in the centre of the brain just above the brain stem that includes the thalamus and hypothalamus [Late 19thC. Coined from DIA- 'across' + Greek *enkephalos* 'brain'.] —**diencephalic** /dī ensso fállik/ *adj.*

diene /dī een/ *n.* an unsaturated hydrocarbon (**alkene**) containing two carbon-to-carbon double bonds [Early 20thC. Coined from DI- + -ENE.]

Dieppe /di ép/ seaport and resort on the English Channel in the Seine-Maritime Department, Haute-Normandie Region, in northwestern France. It is situated about 97 km/60 mi. west of Amiens. Population: 36,600 (1990).

dieresis n. = diaeresis

diesel /déez'l/ n. 1. = diesel engine 2. **VEHICLE WITH DIESEL ENGINE** a vehicle such as a car or train that is powered by a diesel engine 3. = diesel oil [Late 19thC. Named after Rudolf Diesel (1858–1913), the German engineer who designed the engine.]

diesel-electric n. a locomotive in which a diesel engine drives an electric generator that provides current to the traction motors driving the wheels

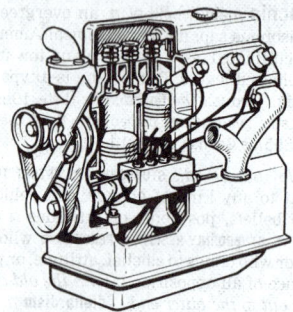

Diesel engine: Cutaway view showing compression chambers

diesel engine, **diesel** n. an internal combustion engine that ignites diesel oil using compression alone, rather than using an electrical spark

diesel fuel n. US = diesel oil

diesel-hydraulic n. a locomotive primarily powered by a diesel engine but with power transmitted through an oil-filled torque converter or infinitely variable gear

diesel oil n. a thick oily fuel that is obtained from the distillation of petroleum. It has an ignition temperature of 540°C and is ignited by the heat of compression. US term **diesel fuel**

Dies Irae /dée ayz eér ī/ n. 1. **CHR CHRISTIAN HYMN FOR DEAD IN LATIN** a thirteenth-century Latin hymn that describes the Last Judgment, used in a Christian Mass for the dead 2. **MUSIC PART OF REQUIEM MASS** a musical setting of the Dies Irae, used as part of a Requiem Mass [From Latin, literally 'day of wrath']

diesis /dí əsiss/ (plural **-ses** /-seez/) n. **PRINTING** = **double dagger**

dies non /dí eez nón/ n. a day on which no legal business is transacted [Early 19thC. Shortening of Latin dies non juridicus, literally 'day not judicial'.]

diestock /dí stok/ n. a device for holding the dies that are used for cutting threads on screws

diestrus n. US = dioestrus

diet[1] /dí ət/ n. 1. **WHAT A PERSON OR ANIMAL EATS** the food that a person or animal usually consumes 2. **CONTROLLED INTAKE OF FOOD** a controlled intake of food and drink designed for weight loss, for health or religious reasons, or to control or improve a medical condition ○ a wheat-free diet 3. **REGULAR INTAKE OF STH** a continuous or daily experience of, or indulgence in, sth other than food ○ living on a diet of soap operas and game shows ■ adj. **DESIGNED OR PROMOTED FOR WEIGHT LOSS** used to describe a food or drink that is intended for people trying to lose weight, usually because it is low in calories or fat, or contains a sugar substitute ○ a diet soda ■ vi. (**-ets, -eting, -eted**) **EAT LESS** to follow a restricted pattern of eating or drinking in order to lose weight [Pre-12thC. Via Old French diete from, ultimately, Greek diaita 'course of life'.]

diet[2] /dí ət/ n. 1. **POL PARLIAMENT** a legislative assembly in certain countries, e.g. Japan 2. **LAW COURT SESSION IN SCOTLAND** a session of a court, or the date fixed for a court hearing 3. **HIST ASSEMBLY IN HOLY ROMAN EMPIRE** a general assembly of the estates of the Holy Roman Empire [15thC. From medieval Latin dieta 'day's journey, work', associated with Latin dies 'day', hence 'day for a meeting (of legislators)', probably from, ultimately, Greek diaita (see DIET[1].)]

dietary /dí ətəri/ adj. **OF EATING HABITS** relating to what people or animals eat ■ n. (plural **-ies**) **DIET** a diet or system of dieting (archaic)

dietary fibre n. = fibre

dieter /dí ətər/ n. sb who is on a diet, particularly sb who is trying to lose weight

dietetic /dí ə téttik/ adj. 1. **RELATING TO DIETS** relating to what people eat and drink 2. **PREPARED WITH SPECIAL DIETS IN MIND** specially prepared to suit the requirements of a particular diet —**dietetically** adv.

dietetics /dí ə téttiks/ n. the study of food and nutrition and its relation to people's health (takes a singular verb.)

diethylcarbamazine citrate /dī éthil kaar bámmə zeen-, dī ée thīl-/ n. a drug used to treat intestinal worms in humans, and roundworm in dogs and cats [Diethylcarbamazine coined from DI- + ETHYL + CARBO- + AMIDE + AZINE]

diethyl ether /dī éthil-/ n. **CHEM** = **ether**

diethylstilbestrol n. US = diethylstilboestrol

diethylstilboestrol /dī éthil stil béstrol, dī ée thīl-/ n. **PHARM** a form of synthetic oestrogen once widely used as a hormone replacement [Mid-20thC. Coined from DI- + ETHYL + STILBENE + OESTRUS + -OL.]

diethyl toluamide /dī éthil tóllyoŏ ámmīd, dī ée thīl-/ n. full form of **DEET**

dietitian /dí ə tísh'n/, **dietician** n. sb who specializes in the study of food and nutrition in relation to health

Marlene Dietrich

Dietrich /dée trik/, **Marlene** (1901–92) German-born US singer and film actor. She starred in films from the 1930s to the 1970s, including *The Devil Is a Woman* (1935) and *Witness for the Prosecution* (1957). Full name **Maria Magdalene Dietrich von Losch**

Dieu et mon droit /dyŏ ay mon drwaá/ n. 'God and my right', the motto written under the coat of arms of the British Royal Family [From French]

diff. abbr. 1. difference 2. different

differ /díffər/ (**-fers, -fering, -fered**) vi. 1. **BE UNLIKE** to be dissimilar or unlike ○ new models that differ greatly from the early prototypes 2. **DISAGREE** to have different opinions about sth ○ We agreed to differ. [14thC. Via French différer 'to differ, defer' from Latin differre 'to differ', literally 'to carry apart', from ferre 'to carry' (see -FER).]

— **WORD KEY: SYNONYMS** —

See Synonyms at *disagree*.

difference /díffrənss/ n. 1. **STATE OF BEING UNLIKE OTHERS** the quality of being different from or unlike sth or sb else ○ There's no real difference between going by train and going by car. 2. **DISTINGUISHING FEATURE** a feature that distinguishes one person or thing from another ○ Can you spot the differences between the two? 3. **SIGNIFICANT CHANGE** a change that has an effect ○ a noticeable difference in her moods 4. **DISAGREEMENT** a disagreement, argument, or divergence of opinions ○ settle our differences 5. **MATH ANSWER TO SUBTRACTION EQUATION** the amount by which one quantity is greater or smaller than another ○ What's the difference between 16 and 6? 6. **LOGIC DEFINING FEATURE** a distinguishing feature that marks out a thing that is being defined or discussed, from others that are more general ○ being divisible by two is the difference between even numbers and other whole numbers 7. **HERALDRY ADDITION TO COAT OF ARMS** an addition to a family's coat of arms that represents a younger branch

of the family ◇ **make all the difference** have an enormous, usually positive, effect or influence ◇ **make no difference** be of no importance or not matter ◇ **split the difference** take the average of two amounts, or agree on sth that is halfway between two extremes ◇ **tell the difference** distinguish or figure out the particular features that make things unlike each other

different /díffrənt/ adj. 1. **UNLIKE STH OR SB ELSE** not the same as sth or sb else ○ The two places are very different to each other. 2. **DISTINCT** separate or distinct from another or others ○ She wears a different pair of shoes every day. 3. **UNUSUAL** contrary to norms or expectations ○ What do you think of my hat? – Well, it's certainly different. [14thC. Via French from the Latin stem different-, present participle stem of differre (see DIFFER).] —**differently** adv.

— **WORD KEY: USAGE** —

Different from or different than? No one objects to *different from* (on the analogy of *differ from*: *His attitude towards women was quite different from that of his contemporaries*. *Different to* is not so generally accepted, although it is commonly used in British English. *Different than* is also seen and heard, especially in US English. Although some object to it as a matter of principle (the analogous *This differs than that* is obviously unacceptable), it can at times serve as a useful shortcut. Compare *The book has a title different from the one I thought it had* with *The book has a different title than I thought*.

differentia /díffə rénshi ə/ (plural **-ae** /-shi ee/) n. an element that separates one thing from another, especially a trait that distinguishes one subclass from another, e.g. one species from another in the same genus

differentiable /-əb'l/ adj. recognizable as different or distinct from sth else —**differentiability** /díffə rénshi ə bílləti/ n.

differential /díffə rénsh'l/ n. 1. **DIFFERENCE BETWEEN POINTS ON A SCALE** a difference between two values on a scale, e.g. a difference in the rates of pay for different jobs in the same line of work 2. **AUTOMOT** = **differential gear** 3. **MATH INFINITESIMAL CHANGE IN VARIABLE** an infinitesimal change in a variable ■ adj. 1. **OF DIFFERENCES** relating to or based on differences 2. **MATH RELATING TO INFINITESIMAL CHANGES** relating to a function of one or more variables that exhibits an infinitesimal change as a consequence of a small change in the variables

differential calculus n. the branch of mathematics dealing with continuously varying quantities, with applications in the determination of maximum and minimum points, and with rates of change through the use of derivatives and differentials

differential coefficient n. **MATH** = **derivative**

differential equation n. a mathematical equation that relates functions and their derivatives

differential gear n. an arrangement of gears that allows two shafts driven by a third to turn at different speeds, e.g. in a motor vehicle

differentiate /díffə rénshi ayt/ (**-ates, -ating, -ated**) v. 1. vti. **SEE DIFFERENCES BETWEEN THINGS** to see or show the differences between two or more things 2. vt. **BE A DIFFERENCE** to establish a difference between two things or among several things 3. vti. **MAKE OR BECOME DIFFERENT** to make sth different or specialized by modifying it, or to become different or specialized by being modified 4. vti. **EDUC PROVIDE ACTIVITIES MATCHED TO ABILITY** to provide school work and activities that are suited to the individual abilities of each student 5. vi. **EMBRYOL BECOME SPECIALIZED** to change from a generalized form into a form specialized for a certain tissue, organ, or other body part (refers to embryo cells) 6. vt. **MATH CALCULATE DERIVATIVE** to calculate the mathematical derivative of a function [Early 19thC. From medieval Latin differentiat-, the past participle stem of differentiare, from, ultimately, Latin differre (see DIFFER).] —**differentiability** /-əb'l/ adj. —**differentiation** /-áysh'n/ n. —**differentiator** /-aytər/ n.

difficult /díffik'lt/ adj. 1. **HARD TO DO** requiring a lot of planning or effort to accomplish ○ a difficult job 2. **FULL OF PROBLEMS** full of problems, trouble, or aspects that are hard to endure ○ a difficult birth 3. **HARD TO**

UNDERSTAND hard to understand, learn, or solve ○ *a difficult subject* **4.** HARD TO ANSWER hard to answer, deal with, or fulfil ○ *a difficult question* **5.** HARD TO MANAGE hard to cope with or control ○ *a difficult plant to grow indoors* **6.** HARD TO PLEASE hard to please or satisfy ○ *a difficult audience* **7.** HARD TO CONVINCE hard to convince or persuade ○ *If they're difficult, offer them more.* **8.** FULL OF HARDSHIP containing great hardship, especially of a financial kind [14thC. Back-formation from DIFFICULTY.] —**difficultness** *n.*

WORD KEY: SYNONYMS

See Synonyms at ***hard***.

difficulty /díffik'lti/ *n.* (*plural* **-ties**) **1.** QUALITY OF BEING DIFFICULT the quality of being hard to do, understand, or deal with **2.** STH NOT EASILY DONE sth that is hard to do, understand, or deal with **3.** EFFORT a great effort or struggle to do sth **4.** A DISPUTE a dispute or controversy ■ **difficulties** *npl.* **1.** TROUBLE a situation full of trouble, danger, or embarrassment ○ *Even a strong swimmer can get into difficulties in this river.* **2.** OBJECTIONS objections, or attempts to prevent the progress of sth ○ *You're supposed to be here to help, not make difficulties.* [14thC. From Latin *difficultas*, from *difficilis*, literally 'not easy', from *facilis* 'easy' (see FACILE).]

diffidence /díffidənss/ *n.* **1.** LACK OF SELF-CONFIDENCE a lack of self-confidence or hesitation caused by lack of confidence **2.** RESERVED MANNER a reserved or restrained manner

diffident /díffidənt/ *adj.* **1.** LACKING SELF-CONFIDENCE lacking self-confidence and rather shy **2.** RESERVED OR RESTRAINED reserved or restrained in the way you behave [15thC. From Latin *diffident-*, the present participle stem of *diffidere* 'to distrust', from *fidere* 'to trust'. The original English meaning was 'distrustful'.] —**diffidently** *adv.*

diffract /di frákt/ (**-fracts, -fracting, -fracted**) *vti.* to produce or undergo diffraction [Early 19thC. From Latin *diffract-*, the past participle stem of *diffringere*, literally 'to break apart', from *frangere* 'to break'.] —**diffractive** *adj.* —**diffractively** *adv.* —**diffractiveness** *n.*

diffraction /di fráksh'n/ *n.* the bending or spreading out of waves, e.g. of sound or light, as they pass round the edge of an obstacle or through a narrow aperture

diffraction grating *n.* a glass plate or metal mirror engraved with a large number of parallel lines or grooves, used to produce a spectrum by diffraction or interference

diffractometer /díffrak tómmitər/ *n.* an instrument that uses diffraction, typically of X-rays or electrons by crystals, to investigate the atomic structure of a material

diffuse[1] /di fyóoz/ (**-fuses, -fusing, -fused**) *v.* **1.** *vti.* SPREAD THROUGH to spread sth throughout sth else, or to become spread throughout sth else **2.** *vti.* SCATTER OR BECOME SCATTERED to scatter sth over an area, or become scattered over an area **3.** *vt.* MAKE LESS INTENSE to make sth, especially light, less bright or intense **4.** *vti.* PHYS UNDERGO OR SUBJECT TO DIFFUSION to undergo or subject sth to diffusion [14thC. From Latin *diffus-*, the past participle stem of *diffundere*, literally 'to pour in every direction', from *fundere* 'to pour' (see FOUND).]

WORD KEY: SYNONYMS

See Synonyms at ***wordy***.

diffuse[2] /di fyóoss/ *adj.* **1.** SPREAD THROUGHOUT AREA spread throughout a wide area **2.** LACKING CONCISENESS lacking organization and conciseness, especially in writing or speech [15thC. Directly or via French *diffus* from Latin *diffusus* 'spread out', from the past participle of *diffundere* (see DIFFUSE[1]).] —**diffusely** *adv.* —**diffuseness** *n.*

diffuser /di fyóozər/, **diffusor** *n.* **1.** HOUSEHOLD DEVICE THAT DIFFUSES LAMP LIGHT a piece of translucent or reflective material fixed to a light source, such as a lamp, in order to soften or spread the light over a wide area **2.** PHOTOGRAPHY, CINEMA DEVICE THAT SOFTENS LIGHT a cloth screen, piece of frosted glass, or other material that is used to soften the brightness of the lighting in photography or cinematography **3.** HAIR HAIRDRYER ATTACHMENT an attachment for a hairdryer that slows down and spreads the air flow, making the drying action gentler **4.** ACOUSTICS CONE TO DISPERSE SOUND WAVES a device, such as a cone or wedge, fixed inside a loudspeaker to diffuse sound waves

diffusible /di fyóozəb'l/ *adj.* capable of being diffused —**diffusibility** /di fyóozə bílləti/ *n.*

diffusion /di fyóozh'n/ *n.* **1.** PROCESS OF DIFFUSING a process during which sth diffuses or is diffused **2.** RESULT OF DIFFUSING the result of sth diffusing or being diffused, or a situation where sth is diffused **3.** ANTHROP SPREAD OF CULTURAL FEATURES the spread of tools, practices, or other features from one culture to another **4.** PHYS SCATTERING OF LIGHT the scattering of light in many directions as the result of reflection from an uneven surface or passage though a translucent material **5.** PHYS INTERMINGLING OF SUBSTANCES the random movement of atoms, molecules, or ions from one site in a medium to another, resulting in complete mixing —**diffusional** *adj.*

diffusionism /di fyóozh'nizəm/ *n.* the theory that similarities in tools, practices, or other features between cultures, result from their being spread from one culture to another rather than being arrived at independently —**diffusionist** *adj., n.*

diffusive /di fyóossiv/ *adj.* **1.** INVOLVED IN DIFFUSION involved in diffusion **2.** SPREADING in which diffusion is important or characteristic **3.** = **diffuse**[2] *adj.* 2 —**diffusively** *adv.* —**diffusiveness** *n.*

diffusor *n.* = **diffuser**

dig /dig/ *v.* (**digs, digging, dug** /dug/) **1.** *vti.* BREAK UP OR REMOVE EARTH to break up, turn, or remove sth, especially earth, with the hands, paws, a tool, or a machine ○ *The excavator dug the rock out of the hole.* **2.** *vt.* CREATE BY DIGGING to make sth by removing material, especially earth, with the hands, paws, a tool, or a machine ○ *digging a hole* **3.** *vti.* OBTAIN OR FREE BY DIGGING to obtain, uncover, or free sth by removing the material covering it using a shovel, the hands, paws, a tool, or a machine **4.** *vi.* SEARCH BY DIGGING to try to find sth by digging ○ *dig for buried treasure* **5.** *vi.* MOVE THROUGH STH BY DIGGING to move through sth by digging a way through it **6.** *vt.* DISCOVER BY RESEARCH to find out sth by research or questioning ○ *See what you can dig up about her past.* **7.** *vi.* SEARCH CAREFULLY to search sth carefully or persistently ○ *digging through the papers in a file* **8.** *vti.* PUSH INTO STH FORCEFULLY to push sth into sth else with force, or be pushed forcefully into sth ○ *He dug his teeth into the steak.* **9.** *vti.* POKE to push sb with sth fairly sharp ○ *She dug her elbow into my side.* **10.** *vti.* UNDERSTAND to understand sth fully or with sympathy (*dated slang*) ○ *I dig what you're saying.* **11.** *vt.* LIKE to like or appreciate sth (*dated slang*) ○ *They don't dig jazz.* **12.** *vt.* LOOK AT to look at, notice, or pay attention to sth (*dated slang*) ○ *Now dig this, honey.* ■ *n.* **1.** PROD a push with sth fairly sharp ○ *a dig in the ribs* **2.** CUTTING REMARK a remark that is meant to hurt or make fun of sb ○ *a dig about her new hairstyle* **3.** ARCHAEOL ARCHAEOLOGICAL EXCAVATION an archaeological or palaeontological excavation ○ *a dig in Egypt* **4.** SOCCER POWERFUL BLOW a powerful blow, especially a kick at a football (*slang*) ○ *It was a well-placed free kick and he really gave it quite a dig.* **5.** ACT OF DIGGING the act of digging or excavating sth ■ **digs** *npl.* LODGINGS a room or rooms that sb rents in another person's house (*dated informal*) [12thC. Origin uncertain: perhaps literally 'to make a ditch', formed from Old English *dīc*, an earlier form of DITCH.]

dig in *v.* **1.** *vti.* MIL TAKE UP POSITIONS to prepare trenches or other defensive structures, or to establish a force or equipment in a defensive position **2.** *vi.* MIL RESIST ATTACK to put up a stubborn resistence to an attack **3.** *vi.* FIGHT STUBBORNLY to stick to an established position, e.g. in an argument, and fight stubbornly to maintain it **4.** *vi.* START EATING to start eating, especially in an enthusiastic way (*informal*) **5.** *vt.* AGRIC, GARDENING BURY PLANTS to cover plants or the remains of a crop by turning over the soil in which they are growing and burying them

dig out *vt.* **1.** UNCOVER to obtain, uncover, or free sth by removing the material covering it using a shovel, the hands, paws, a tool, or a machine **2.** RETRIEVE to retrieve sth from where it is kept, or find out sth by research or questioning (*informal*)

dig up *vt.* **1.** TAKE OUT OF GROUND to dig for sth that is buried in the ground and remove it **2.** TURN OVER EARTH to dig into and turn over the earth in an area **3.** INVESTIGATE to find out sth by research or investigation (*informal*)

dig. *abbr.* PUBL digest

digamma /dī gamə/ *n.* a letter of the ancient Greek alphabet, Ϝ, that was already obsolete in the classical period [Late 17thC. Via Latin from Greek, literally 'double gamma', from *gamma* 'gamma'; from its resemblance to two capital gammas, set one above the other.]

digamy /díggəmi/ (*plural* **-mies**) *n.* a second marriage that, unlike bigamy, is legal because the first husband or wife is dead or has been divorced (*formal*) [Early 17thC. Via late Latin *digamia* from Greek, from *digamos* 'married to two people', from *gamos* 'marriage'.] —**digamous** *adj.*

digastric /dī gástrik/ *adj.* used to describe a muscle, especially the muscle on either side of the lower jaw, in which two fleshy parts are connected by a tendon [Early 18thC. From modern Latin *digastricus*, from *gastricus* 'gastric' (see GASTRIC); from an analogy between 'fleshy parts' and 'bellies'.]

digerati /díjjə raati/ *npl.* people who have or claim to have a sophisticated expertise in the area of computers, the Internet, and the World Wide Web [Late 20thC. Formed from DIGITAL on the model of LITERATI.]

digest *v.* /dī jést, di jést/ (**-gests, -gesting, -gested**) **1.** *vti.* PROCESS FOOD to process food in the body into a form that can be absorbed and used or excreted **2.** *vt.* ABSORB MENTALLY to think about sth and come to understand or appreciate what it means **3.** *vt.* ORGANIZE SYSTEMATICALLY to organize sth into a system, often through selective condensing of the various items, so that essential information is readily available **4.** *vt.* ABRIDGE to make a summary of sth, often a written work **5.** *vti.* CHEM BREAK DOWN to soften or break down a substance through exposure to heat, water, or chemicals, or to be broken down in this way **6.** *vt.* BEAR PATIENTLY to put up with sth without reacting (*archaic*) ■ *n.* /dījest/ **1.** SUMMARY a shortened version of a work that contains the most important or interesting information from the original version **2.** COLLECTION OF ABRIDGED PIECES a magazine, book, or broadcast that contains shortened versions of articles or stories originally from different sources **3.** LAW COLLECTION OF LEGAL OPINIONS a systematic compilation of laws or legal opinions [14thC. From Latin *digest-*, the past participle stem of *digerere*, literally 'to carry apart', from *gerere* 'to carry'.]

Digest /dī jest/ *n.* a 50-volume compilation of Roman civil law, created by the order of Emperor Justinian in the 6th century

digester /dī jéstər, di-/ *n.* **1.** SB OR STH THAT DIGESTS sb or sth that digests sth **2.** CHEM VESSEL FOR CHEMICAL DIGESTION a vessel or device in which chemical digestion takes place

digestible /dī jéstəb'l, di-/ *adj.* easily digested —**digestibility** /dī jéstə bílləti, di-/ *n.* —**digestibly** /-əbli/ *adv.*

digestif /di zhe steéf/ *n.* an alcoholic drink, e.g. a brandy or liqueur, drunk after a meal supposedly to help the digestion of food [Early 20thC. From French, literally 'digestive', from Latin *digestivus*, from, ultimately, *digerere* (see DIGEST).]

digestion /dī jéschən, di-/ *n.* **1.** PHYSIOL PROCESSING OF FOOD IN BODY the breaking down of foodstuffs in the body into a form that can be absorbed and used or excreted **2.** PHYSIOL ABILITY TO DIGEST FOOD the ability to process food in the body into a form that can be absorbed and used or excreted **3.** ABILITY TO ABSORB IDEAS the ability to think about sth and come to understand or appreciate its content, or the process of doing so **4.** CHEM BREAKING DOWN the softening or breaking down of a substance through exposure to heat, water, chemicals, enzymes, or bacteria —**digestional** *adj.*

digestive /dī jéstiv, di-/ *adj.* RELATING TO DIGESTION associated with or aiding in the digestion of food ■ *n.* **1.** STH THAT AIDS DIGESTION sth that aids or promotes the digesting of food **2.** = **digestive biscuit** —**digestively** *adv.*

digestive biscuit *n.* a semi-sweet round biscuit that is made from wholemeal flour

digestive gland *n.* any gland that secretes digestive enzymes, e.g. the pancreas in vertebrates

digestive tract *n.* ANAT = alimentary canal

digger /dígger/ *n.* **1.** SB OR STH THAT DIGS sb or sth that digs **2.** TOOL FOR DIGGING a tool, machine, or part of a machine that is used for digging or excavation

Digger[1] /dígger/ *n.* member of the English Puritan religious group, the Diggers, active in 1649 and 1650, that believed in communal land ownership [Mid-17thC. From the group's cultivation of land.]

Digger[2] /dígger/, **digger** *n.* **1.** MIL SB FROM AUSTRALIA OR NEW ZEALAND sb from Australia or New Zealand, especially a soldier who served in World War I (*informal*) **2.** *Aus* MAN IN LATER LIFE a man who has lived for a long time (*informal*) **3.** PEOPLES NATIVE AMERICAN PERSON a member of any of various Native American peoples who gathered food mainly by digging for roots (*sometimes used disparagingly*) **4.** FORM OF ADDRESS used as a friendly form of address between men (*informal*) [Mid-19thC. In sense 1, from DIGGER 'miner', reinforced by the idea of trench-digging in World War I.]

diggings /díggingz/ *n.* MINING LOCATION a place where sth is mined, especially precious metals or gems ■ *npl.* **1.** MATERIAL EXCAVATED material that has been dug out of a hole or mine **2.** LODGINGS a room or rooms that sb rents in another person's house (*dated informal*)

dight /dīt/ (**dights, dighting, dight** *or* **dighted**) *vt.* to equip, dress, or adorn sb (*archaic*) [Old English *dihtan*. From a prehistoric Germanic word borrowed from Latin *dictare* 'to say often', (see DICTATE).]

digit /díjit/ *n.* **1.** MATH NUMERAL USED IN DECIMAL SYSTEM any of the ten Arabic numerals, 0 to 9, that are used to represent numbers in the decimal system **2.** MATH NUMERAL IN ANY NUMBER SYSTEM a symbol that represents a number in any number system, such as the hexadecimal system **3.** ANAT HUMAN FINGER OR TOE a finger or toe of a human **4.** ZOOL ANIMAL TOE OR FINGER a finger, toe, or similar part on a terrestrial vertebrate [14thC. From Latin *digitus* 'finger, toe', from assumed *dicitus* 'pointer'. The numerical senses come from the counting of numbers on the fingers.]

Digital: Clock displaying the time in numerical form

digital /díjit'l/ *adj.* **1.** REPRESENTING DATA AS NUMBERS processing, operating on, storing, transmitting, representing, or displaying data in the form of numerical digits, as in a digital computer. ◊ **analogue** *adj.* **2.** REPRESENTING SOUND/LIGHT WAVES AS NUMBERS representing a varying physical quantity, such as sound or light waves, by means of discrete signals interpreted as numbers, usually in the binary system, as in a digital recording or digital television **3.** LIKE A FINGER like a finger or toe **4.** DONE WITH THE FINGERS using the fingers, or operated by a finger or fingers [15thC. From Latin *digitalis*, from *digitus* (see DIGIT).] —**digitally** *adv.*

digital audio tape *n.* a magnetic tape used in the digital recording of music

digital computer *n.* a computer that stores and performs a series of mathematical and logical operations on data expressed as discrete signals interpreted as numbers, usually in the form of binary notation

digital imagery, **digital imaging** *n.* the process of transforming or altering a digital image by manipulating it on a computer

digitalize /díjitə līz/ (**-izes, -izing, -ized**), **digitalise** (**-ises, -ising, -ised**) *vt.* **1.** = digitize 2. MED TREAT WITH DIGITALIS to treat sb with digitalis —**digitalization** /díjitə līt záysh'n/ *n.*

digital recording *n.* **1.** SOUND STORED AS DIGITS a form of audio recording in which sounds are stored as numbers, producing a purer sound **2.** RECORDING MADE DIGITALLY a recording made using the digital method

digital signature *n.* a digital signal or pattern that serves to identify the user or the habits of the user

Digital Subscriber Line *n.* a high-speed telephone line that can supply television, video, Internet access, and video telephoning, often over standard copper wire

digital tablet *n.* COMPUT = graphics tablet

digital television *n.* **1.** TELEVISION USING DIGITAL TRANSMISSION television broadcasting in which the picture is transmitted as a digital signal that is decoded by a device in or attached to the viewer's television set **2.** BROADCASTING SIGNALS INTERPRETED AS NUMBERS a system of broadcasting pictures and sounds as discrete signals represented as numbers, or a television set specially constructed or adapted for receiving such signals

digital video disc, **digital versatile disc** *n.* full form of **DVD**

digital video disc-ROM *n.* full form of **DVD-ROM**

digital watch *n.* a watch that shows the time in numerical form, rather than by hands on a dial

digitate /díjji tayt/, **digitated** /-tàytid/ *adj.* **1.** HAVING FINGERS OR TOES having fingers or toes, or having parts that are like fingers or toes **2.** BOT SPREADING FROM CENTRE having divisions or parts arrayed from a central point like the spread fingers of a hand, e.g. in the leaves of certain trees —**digitately** *adv.* —**digitation** /díjji táysh'n/ *n.*

digiti- *prefix.* finger or toe ◦ *digitigrade* [From Latin *digitus* (see DIGIT)]

digitiform /díjjiti fawrm/ *adj.* shaped or looking like a finger

digitigrade /díjjiti grayd/ *adj.* WALKING ON THE TOES used to describe the gait of those animals that walk with only the tips of the digits touching the ground, the rest of the foot being raised, e.g. cats and deer ■ *n.* ANIMAL THAT WALKS ON ITS TOES an animal, such as a deer or cat, that walks with its weight on its digits and the back of its foot raised [Mid-19thC. From French, literally 'toe-stepping', from Latin *digitus* (see DIGIT) + *gradus* 'step' (see GRADE).]

digitize /díjji tīz/ (**-tizes, -tizing, -tized**), **digitise** (**-tises, -tising, -tised**) *vt.* to convert an image, graph, or other data into digital form for processing on a computer —**digitization** /díjjitī záysh'n/ *n.* —**digitizer** /díjji tīzər/ *n.*

digizine /díjji zeen/ *n.* a magazine that is delivered in digital form either on the Internet or on a CD-ROM (*informal*) ◊ **e-zine** [Combination of DIGITAL + MAGAZINE]

diglossia /dī glóssi ə/ *n.* the existence of a formal literary form of a language, considered higher and more prestigious, along with a colloquial form used by most speakers and considered of lower status [Mid-20thC. Formed from Greek *diglōssos* 'bilingual', from *glōssa* 'language']

dignified /dígni fīd/ *adj.* showing self-respect or behaving in a proper and respectable way —**dignifiedly** *adv.*

dignify /dígni fī/ (**-fies, -fying, -fied**) *vt.* **1.** GIVE DISTINCTION TO to give honour or a sense of importance to sth **2.** GIVE UNDESERVED ATTENTION TO to treat sb or sth as honourable or worthy of attention when this treatment is undeserved **3.** MAKE NOBLE to award an honour to sb, or raise a person to noble rank [15thC. Via obsolete French *dignifier* from late Latin *dignificare*, literally 'to make worthy', from *dignus* (see DIGNITY).]

dignitary /dígnitəri/ (*plural* **-ies**) *n.* a person who holds a high rank or position

dignity /dígnəti/ (*plural* **-ties**) *n.* **1.** PRIDE AND SELF-RESPECT a proper sense of pride and self-respect **2.** SERIOUSNESS IN BEHAVIOUR seriousness, respectfulness, or formality in a person's behaviour and bearing **3.** WORTHINESS the condition of being worthy of respect, esteem, or honour **4.** DUE RESPECT the respect or honour that a high rank or position should be shown **5.** HIGH OFFICE a high rank, position, or honour **6.** DIGNITARY a dignitary (*archaic*) [12thC. Via Old French *digneté* from Latin *dignitas*, from *dignus* 'worthy'].

— WORD KEY: ORIGIN —
As well as giving rise to **dignity**, Latin *dignus* is also the source of English *condign*, *dainty*, *deign*, *disdain*, and *indignant*.

digoxin /dī jóksin/ *n.* a glycoside extracted from foxglove leaves and used as a heart stimulant. Formula: $C_{41}H_{64}O_{14}$. [Mid-20thC. Contraction of *digitoxin*, name of a glycoside similar to digoxin, coined from DIGITALIS + TOXIN.]

digraph /dī graaf, -graf/ *n.* **1.** TWO LETTERS REPRESENTING ONE SOUND a pair of letters that represents a single speech sound, such as 'ng' in 'ring' or 'ch' in 'child' **2.** = ligature —**digraphic** /dī gráffik/ *adj.* —**digraphically** /-gráffikli/ *adv.*

digress /dī gréss/ (**-gresses, -gressing, -gressed**) *vi.* to move away from the central topic or line of argument in speaking or writing, usually temporarily [Early 16thC. From Latin *digress-*, past participle stem of *digredi*, literally 'to step aside', from, ultimately, *gradus* 'step' (see GRADE).]

digression /dī grésh'n/ *n.* **1.** DEPARTURE FROM CENTRAL TOPIC an act or instance of departing from the central topic or line of argument while speaking or writing **2.** TEXT OR SPEECH OFF THE SUBJECT a part of sth spoken or written that departs from the central topic or line of argument —**digressional** *adj.* —**digressionary** *adj.*

digressive /dī gréssiv/ *adj.* tending to depart from the main subject or line of argument —**digressively** *adv.* —**digressiveness** *n.*

dihedral /dī heédrəl/ *n.* **1.** dihedral, dihedral angle MATH ANGLE MADE BETWEEN SURFACES the angle contained between two planes that intersect, measured by the angle made by any two lines at right angles to the two planes **2.** AEROSP ANGLE OF AN AIRCRAFT WING the angle between an upwardly inclined aircraft wing and a horizontal line ■ *adj.* MATH TWO-SIDED made by intersecting planes and having two sides or two faces [Late 18thC. Coined from DI- + Greek *hedra* 'seat' (see -HEDRON).]

dihybrid /dī híbrid/ *n.* an organism that is heterozygous for two genes, so that each gene is represented by two variant forms (**alleles**) —**dihybridism** *n.*

dihydric /dī hídrik/ *adj.* containing two hydroxyl groups

Dijon /deé zhoN/ capital of the Côte d'Or Department on the Bourgogne Canal in east-central France. It is situated at the foot of the Côte d'Or hills, about 249 km/155 mi. southeast of Paris. Population: 151,636 (1990).

Dik-dik

dik-dik /dík dik/ (*plural* **dik-diks** *or* **dik-dik**) *n.* a small long-muzzled antelope that lives in arid regions of eastern Africa. Genus: *Madoqua*. [Late 19thC. From an East African language; an imitation of the animal's cry.]

dike *n.*, *v.* = dyke

diktat /dík taat/ *n.* **1.** DICTATORIAL STATEMENT a statement or order that cannot be opposed **2.** HARSH IMPOSED SETTLEMENT a harsh settlement imposed on a defeated opponent or enemy [Mid-20thC. From German, from Latin *dictatum*, from the past participle of *dictare* (see DICTATE).]

dilapidate /di láppi dayt/ (**-dates, -dating, -dated**) *vti.* to become or make sth become partially ruined or decayed, especially through neglect [Early 16thC. From Latin *dilapidat-*, past participle stem of *dilapidare* 'to squander', literally 'to scatter like stones', from, ultimately, *lapis* 'stone'.] —**dilapidation** /di láppi dáysh'n/ *n.*

dilapidated /di láppi daytid/ *adj.* in a condition of disrepair or partial decay

dilatancy /dī láyt'nssi, di-/ *n.* CHEM the tendency of a substance to become more viscous or solid when affected by an outside force or agitation

dilatant /dī láyt'nt, di-/ *adj.* **1.** ABLE TO EXPAND able or likely to expand **2.** CHEM BECOMING MORE VISCOUS tending to become more viscous or solid when affected by an outside force or agitation ■ *n.* SUBSTANCE CAUSING EXPANSION a substance that causes another to expand

dilatation /dīlə táysh'n, dìllə-/ *n.* **1.** PROCESS OF EXPANDING the act or process of widening or being widened, stretching or being stretched, or enlarging or being enlarged **2.** EXPANDED CONDITION a condition in which sth is enlarged, expanded, or stretched **3.** DILATED THING sth, especially a part of sth else, that has become enlarged, expanded, or stretched **4.** LENGTHY EXPLANATION a lengthy detailed explanation or discussion of a subject by a speaker or writer **5.** MED = **dilation** *n.* 3 —**dilatational** *adj.*

dilatator /dīlə taytər, dìllə-/ *n.* = **dilator** *n.* 1

dilate /dī láyt, di-/ (**-lates, -lating, -lated**) *v.* **1.** *vti.* EXPAND OR MAKE EXPAND to become or cause sth to become wider or larger **2.** *vi.* TALK OR WRITE AT LENGTH to talk or write about sth at great length [14thC. Via French *dilater* from Latin *dilatare*, literally 'to spread widely apart', from *latus* 'wide'.] —**dilatability** /dī láytə bílləti, di-/ *n.* —**dilatable** /dī láytəb'l, di-/ *adj.* —**dilatableness** /-b'lnəss/ *n.* —**dilative** *adj.*

dilation /dī láysh'n, di-/ *n.* **1.** EXPANDING OF STH the act or process of widening or being widened, stretching or being stretched, or enlarging or being enlarged **2.** DILATED CONDITION a condition in which sth is enlarged, expanded, or stretched **3.** MED ENLARGEMENT OF BODY PART the stretching or enlargement of a hollow organ or body cavity

dilation and curettage *n.* full form of **D and C**

dilatometer /dìllə tómmitər/ *n.* an instrument used to measure expansion, e.g. in the volume of a liquid —**dilatometric** /dìllətə méttrik/ *adj.* —**dilatometry** /dìllə tómmətri/ *n.*

dilator /dī láytər, di-/ *n.* **1.** MED THING THAT DILATES sth that makes sth else wider or larger, especially a medical instrument used to widen a body passage **2.** ANAT MUSCLE THAT DILATES STH a muscle or muscle group that expands a part of the body

dilatory /dìllətəri/ *adj.* **1.** SLOW tending to waste time or move slowly **2.** INTENDED TO DELAY intended to cause a delay or waste time [15thC. From late Latin *dilatorius*, from, ultimately, Latin *dilat-*, the past participle stem of *differre* 'to delay' (see DEFER).] —**dilatorily** *adv.* —**dilatoriness** *n.*

dildo /díl dō/ (*plural* **-dos**), **dildoe** (*plural* **-does**) *n.* an object shaped like a penis, used in sexual activity [Late 16thC. Origin uncertain: perhaps an alteration of Italian *diletto* 'delight', from, ultimately, Latin *delectare* 'to allure, delight' (see DELIGHT).]

dilemma /di lémmə, dī-/ *n.* **1.** SITUATION WITH UNSATISFACTORY CHOICES a situation in which sb must choose one of two or more unsatisfactory alternatives **2.** LOGIC ARGUMENT LEADING TO UNDESIRABLE CHOICE in logic, a form of reasoning that, though valid, leads to two undesirable alternatives [Early 16thC. From, ultimately, Greek *dilēmma*, literally 'double proposition', from *lēmma* 'proposition' (see LEMMA).]

dilettante /dìlli tánti, -taánti/ *n.* (*plural* **-tantes** *or* **-tanti** /-ti/) **1.** DABBLER IN ART OR KNOWLEDGE sb who is interested in an art or a specialized field of knowledge but who has only a superficial understanding of it **2.** ART LOVER sb who has a passionate interest in the fine arts (*dated*) ■ *adj.* SUPERFICIAL typical of sb who has only a superficial understanding of sth [Mid-18thC. From Italian, from *dilettare* 'to delight', from Latin *delectare* (see DELIGHT).] —**dilettantish** *adj.* —**dilettantism** *n.*

diligence[1] /dìllijənss/ *n.* **1.** PERSISTENT EFFORT persistent and hard-working effort in doing sth **2.** LEGAL CAREFULNESS the care or attention expected by the law in doing sth, such as fulfilling the terms of a contract [14thC. Via French from Latin *diligentia*, from *diligent-* (see DILIGENT).]

diligence[2] /dìllijənss/ *n.* a stagecoach, especially in France (*literary*) [Late 17thC. From French, a shortening of *carrosse de diligence*, literally 'coach of speed' (see DILIGENCE[1]).]

diligent /dìllijənt/ *adj.* showing persistent and hard-working effort in doing sth [14thC. Via French from Latin *diligent-*, the present participle stem of *diligere* 'to value highly, love' (literally 'to single out'), from *legere* 'to choose'.] —**diligently** *adv.*

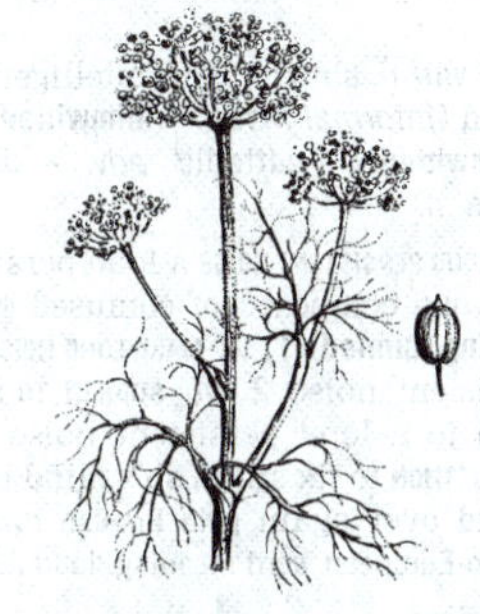

Dill

dill[1] /dil/ *n.* **1.** AROMATIC PLANT an aromatic plant with fine feathery leaves and flat flowerheads, grown as a herb. Latin name: *Anethum graveolens.* **2.** DILL LEAVES OR SEEDS the feathery leaves or seeds of the dill plant, used as a flavouring in foods [Old English *dile*] —**dilly** *adj.*

dill[2] /dil/ *n.* ANZ a fool or idiot (*informal*) [Mid-20thC. Back-formation from *dilly* 'fool', of uncertain origin: perhaps a blend of DAFT and SILLY.]

dill pickle *n.* a cucumber that has been pickled in dill-flavoured vinegar or brine, or a portion of such a pickled cucumber. ◊ **gherkin**

dilly bag /dìlli-/ *n.* Aus a bag traditionally made of plaited grass or reeds, used by Aborigines for carrying food and other belongings [From Aboriginal *dili* 'coarse grass']

dilly-dally /dìlli-/ (**dilly-dallies, dilly-dallying, dilly-dallied**) *vi.* to waste time by being too slow, doing nothing, or being unable to decide what to do [Doubled form (with alteration) of DALLY]

diluent /dìllyoo ənt/ *n.* DILUTING SUBSTANCE a substance that dilutes another substance ■ *adj.* USED TO DILUTE used for diluting sth [Early 18thC. From Latin *diluent-*, the present participle stem of *diluere* (see DILUTE).]

dilute /dī lo͞ot, -lyo͞ot/ *vti.* (**-lutes, -luting, -luted**) **1.** MAKE THINNER to make sth thinner or weaker by adding water or another liquid, or to become thinner or weaker by the addition of water or another liquid **2.** LESSEN STRENGTH to lessen the strength or effect of sth, or to become weaker in strength or effect ■ *adj.* THINNED thinner or weaker than at full concentration because of the addition of water or another liquid [Mid-16thC. From Latin *dilut-*, the past participle stem of *diluere* 'to wash away', from *lavare* 'to wash'.] —**diluteness** *n.* —**diluter** *n.*

dilution /dī lo͞osh'n, -lyo͞osh'n/ *n.* **1.** A THINNING OR WEAKENING a thinning or weakening of a substance, usually a liquid, by the addition of another substance, such as water **2.** LESSENING OF STRENGTH a lessening of the strength or effect of sth **3.** THINNED OR WEAKENED STATE a thinned or weakened condition **4.** LESS CONCENTRATED LIQUID a substance, especially a liquid, that has been made thinner or weaker by the addition of water or another liquid

diluvial /dī lo͞ovi əl, di-/, **diluvian** /-vi ən/ *adj.* about, involving, typical of, deposited by, or caused by the great Flood described in the Bible [Mid-17thC. *Diluvial* from late Latin *diluvialis*, from Latin *diluvium* 'flood' (source of English *deluge*, from *diluere* (see DILUTE).]

dim /dim/ *adj.* (**dimmer, dimmest**) **1.** NOT WELL LIT not easy to see in or into because of inadequate light **2.** PRODUCING LITTLE LIGHT not producing very much light, or less bright than is usual **3.** DULL IN COLOUR dull or subdued in colour or brightness **4.** NOT CLEARLY VISIBLE not clearly visible or distinct **5.** NOT EASY TO PERCEIVE difficult to understand or perceive with the senses **6.** NOT CLEAR TO THE MIND not clearly recalled or perceived **7.** NOT SEEING CLEARLY not able to see clearly **8.** IMPROBABLE unlikely to be successful or fulfilled **9.** UNINTELLIGENT lacking in intelligence or mental sharpness (*informal*) ■ *v.* (**dims, dimming, dimmed**) **1.** *vti.* MAKE OR BECOME DIM to make or become less bright, clear, or keen **2.** *vt.* US = **dip** *v.* 4 [Old English, from a prehistoric Germanic word that is also the ancestor of English *damp*] —**dimly** *adv.* —**dimmable** *adj.* —**dimness** *n.*

dim. *abbr.* **1.** dimension **2.** MUSIC diminuendo **3.** diminutive

Dimbleby /dímb'lbi/, **Richard** (1913–65) British broadcaster and journalist. He was a war correspondent on British radio during World War II, and later became a television commentator specializing in state occasions. Full name **Richard Frederick Dimbleby**

dime /dīm/ *n.* US a US or Canadian coin worth ten cents [14thC. Via French, 'tithe, tenth part', from Latin *decima*, a form of *decimus* 'tenth', from *decem* 'ten' (source of English *decimal*).] ◇ **a dime a dozen** US = **two a penny**

dime bag *n.* US a quantity of an illegal drug sold for a set price, originally ten dollars (*slang*)

dimenhydrinate /dī men hīdri nayt/ *n.* a white bitter antihistamine drug used to treat travel sickness. Formula: $C_{24}H_{28}ClN_5O_3$. [Mid-20thC. Coined from DIMETHYL + AMINE + HYDR- + AMINE + -ATE.]

dimension /di ménsh'n, dī-/ *n.* **1.** MEASUREMENT OF THE SIZE OF STH a measurement of sth in one or more directions, e.g. its length, width, or height **2.** SIZE the size or extent of sth (*usually used in plural*) **3.** ASPECT a feature or distinctive part of sth **4.** LIFE-LIKE QUALITY a roundedness that gives a convincingly life-like quality **5.** LEVEL OF REALITY a level of consciousness, existence, or reality **6.** MATH COORDINATE FOR SPACE AND TIME a coordinate used with others to locate a point in space and time **7.** PHYS PROPERTY DEFINING PHYSICAL QUANTITY any of a group of properties or magnitudes, such as mass or time, that collectively define a physical quantity ■ *vt.* US **1.** MAKE TO REQUIRED DIMENSIONS to cut or make sth to a specified size **2.** INDICATE THE DIMENSIONS OF to specify the size of sth [14thC. Via Old French from the Latin stem *dimension-*, from, ultimately, *dimetiri* 'to measure out', from *metiri* 'to measure'.] —**dimensional** *adj.* —**dimensionality** /di ménshə nálləti, dī-/ *n.* —**dimensionally** /di ménsh'nəli, dī-/ *adv.* —**dimensionless** /-sh'nləss/ *adj.*

dimer /dīmər/ *n.* a molecule made up of two simpler identical molecules [Early 20thC. Coined from DI- + -MER.] —**dimeric** /dī mérrik/ *adj.*

dimercaprol /dīmər ká prol/ *n.* a clear thick compound used as an antidote to poisoning by heavy metals such as arsenic and mercury, or by substances containing such toxic metals. Formula: $C_3H_8OS_2$. [Mid-20thC. Coined from DI- + MERCAPTAN + PROPANE + -OL.]

dime store *n.* US a shop that sells a range of inexpensive goods [From the maximum price of goods sold there being, originally, one dime]

dime-store *adj.* US **1.** INEXPENSIVE not costing very much money **2.** SECOND-RATE of low or second-rate quality

dimeter /dímmitər/ *n.* **1.** LINE OF POETRY a line of poetry consisting of two metrical feet **2.** TYPE OF VERSE verse made up of lines consisting of two metrical feet [Late 16thC. Via late Latin from Greek *dimetros* 'having two measures', from *metron* 'measure, poetic metre' (see METRE).]

dimethoate /dī méthō ayt/ *n.* a crystalline compound used as an insecticide. Formula: $C_5H_{12}NO_3PS_2$. [Mid-20thC. Coined from DIMETHYL + THIO- + -ATE.]

dimethyl /dī mēe thīl, -méth'l/ *adj.* with two methyl groups in a molecule

dimethylsulphoxide /dī mēe thīl sul fók sīd, -méth'l-/ *n.* full form of **DMSO**

dimidiate /di míddi it/ *adj.* **1.** DIVIDED IN TWO divided into halves **2.** BIOL ASYMMETRICAL having one part or side developed more than, or differently from, the other ■ *vt.* (**-ates** /di míddi ayt/, **-ating, -ated**) HERALDIC EMBLEM to halve each of two heraldic emblems so that both can appear on one shield (*technical*) [Late 16thC. From Latin *dimidiat-*, the past participle stem of *dimidiare* 'to halve', from *dimidium* 'half', literally 'middle apart', from *medium* 'middle' (see MEDIUM).] —**dimidiation** /di míddi áysh'n/ *n.*

dimin. *abbr.* **1.** MUSIC diminuendo **2.** diminutive

diminish /di mínnish/ (**-ishes, -ishing, -ished**) *v.* **1.** *vti.* **MAKE OR BECOME SMALLER** to make sth smaller or less important, or to become smaller or less important **2.** *vti.* **APPEAR SMALLER** to appear smaller or to make sth appear smaller **3.** *vti.* ARCHIT **TAPER FROM BOTTOM TO TOP** to taper or make sth taper from the lower part to the upper part **4.** *vt.* MUSIC **CONTRACT AN INTERVAL** to contract a perfect or minor interval by one semitone [15thC. Blend of obsolete *diminue* (literally 'to lessen completely', from, ultimately, Latin *minuere* 'to lessen') and *minish* 'to diminish' (from, ultimately, Latin *minutia* 'smallness').] —**diminishable** *adj.* —**diminishment** *n.* —**diminishingly** *adv.*

diminished /di mínnisht/ *adj.* **1. REDUCED** reduced in quantity, size, or importance **2.** MUSIC **REDUCED BY A SEMITONE** used to describe a musical interval or chord reduced by one semitone

diminished responsibility *n.* a partial defence in criminal law where the defendant seeks to argue reduced culpability on the grounds that a psychiatric disorder reduced responsibility for his or her actions

diminishing returns *npl.* additional increases in sth produced, e.g. profits or benefits, that do not rise in proportion to the additional effort or investment necessary to produce them

diminuendo /di mínnyoo éndō/ *adv.* **GRADUALLY DECREASING IN VOLUME** having a gradual decrease in volume (*used as a musical direction*) US term **decrescendo** ■ *n.* (*plural* **-dos**) **DIMINUENDO PIECE OF MUSIC** a piece of music, or a section of a piece, played diminuendo. US term **decrescendo** [Late 18thC. From Italian, present participle of *diminuire* 'to diminish', from Latin *deminuere*, literally 'to lessen completely', from *minuere* 'to lessen'.] —**diminuendo** *adj.*

diminution /dímmi nyóosh'n/ *n.* **1. REDUCTION** a lessening, decreasing, or reduction of sth, or the result of such a reduction **2.** MUSIC **REPETITION OF MUSICAL PHRASE** the repetition of a musical phrase, using notes that are of a shorter duration than in the original phrase [14thC. From, ultimately, Latin *diminut-*, the past participle stem of *diminuere* 'to break into small pieces', from *minuere* 'to lessen'.] —**diminutional** *adj.*

diminutive /di mínnyōotiv/ *adj.* **1. VERY SMALL** very small or much smaller than is usual **2.** GRAM **INDICATING SMALLNESS** used to describe a suffix that indicates small size, youth, familiarity, or fondness, e.g. '-ette' or 'let' ■ *n.* **1. WORD INDICATING SMALLNESS OR FONDNESS** a word or name that indicates small size, youth, familiarity, or fondness, e.g. 'kitchenette' or 'booklet' **2.** GRAM **SUFFIX INDICATING SMALLNESS OR FONDNESS** a suffix, e.g. '-ette', or 'let' that indicates small size, youth, familiarity, or fondness **3. VERY SMALL PERSON OR THING** a person or thing that is very small or much smaller than is usual [14thC. From French *diminutif*, from, ultimately, Latin *diminut-* (see DIMINUTION).] —**diminutively** *adv.* —**diminutiveness** *n.*

dimity /dímmiti/ (*plural* **-ties**) *n.* a thin cotton fabric with a striped or checked texture produced by weaving together yarn of different thicknesses [15thC. Alteration of *demyt*, which came via medieval Latin *dimitum* from Greek *dimitos*, literally 'of double thread', from *mitos* 'warp thread'.]

dimmer /dímmər/ *n.* **1. dimmer, dimmer switch DEVICE FOR VARYING LIGHT'S BRIGHTNESS** a device, such as a variable resistor, that can be used to vary the brightness of a light by regulating the amount of current supplied to it **2.** *US* = **dip switch**

dimorphism /dī máwrfizəm/ *n.* **1.** BIOL **DIFFERENT FORMS WITHIN SINGLE BIOLOGICAL SPECIES** the existence of two or more different forms within a biological species. In sexual dimorphism, male and female may vary in colour, size, or some other trait. **2.** BOT **DIFFERENT FORMS OF THE SAME ORGAN** the existence of two different forms of the same organ or part in a plant, such as leaves or flower forms **3.** CHEM **DIFFERENT CRYSTALLINE FORMS** the existence of a substance in two different crystalline forms —**dimorphic** *adj.* —**dimorphous** *adj.*

dimple /dímp'l/ *n.* **1. INDENTED AREA IN SKIN** a naturally occurring slightly indented area in the skin and flesh of the cheek, chin, or other part of the body **2. INDENTED SURFACE AREA** an indented, hollowed, or depressed area in the surface of sth ■ *v.* (**-ples, -pling, -pled**) **1.** *vti.* **FORM DIMPLE** to form or have a dimple ○ *This mould dimples the surface of the golf ball.* **2.** *vt.* **PRODUCE DIMPLES IN** to smile, causing dimples to appear in the cheeks [14thC. From assumed Old English *dympel*, from a prehistoric Germanic base that may also be the ancestor of English *deep* and *dip*.] —**dimply** *adj.*

dim sum /dím súm/ *n.* dumplings, spring rolls, and various other traditional Chinese dishes served in small portions as a meal (*takes a singular or plural verb*) [From Chinese (Cantonese) *tím sam*, literally 'small centre']

dimwit /dím wit/ *n.* sb who is unintelligent or slow to understand (*informal insult*) —**dimwitted** /dím wíttid/ *adj.* —**dimwittedly** /-wíttedli/ *adv.* —**dimwittedness** /-wíttedniss/ *n.*

din /din/ *n.* **LOUD PERSISTENT NOISE** a loud persistent noise, especially one composed of confused sounds ■ *v.* (**dins, dinning, dinned**) **1.** *vi.* **MAKE LOUD NOISE** to make a loud persistent noise **2.** *vt.* **SUBJECT TO LOUD NOISE** to subject sb to a loud persistent noise **3.** *vt.* **INSTIL THROUGH REPETITION** to fix sth in sb's mind by repeating it over and over again [Old English *dyne*. Ultimately from an Indo-European word meaning 'loud noise'.]

Din *symbol.* dinar

DIN /din/ *n.* **1.** PHOTOGRAPHY a system of numbers used to express the speed of a photographic film **2.** ELEC **STANDARD ELECTRICAL CONNECTION SYSTEM** a system of standard electrical connections, especially used with television and audio equipment [Acronym formed from German *Deutsche Industrie-Norm* 'German Industry Standard']

Dinant /dée naaN/ town in Namur Province in southern Belgium, situated on the River Meuse, about 24 km/15 mi. south of Namur. Population: 12,461 (1995).

dinar /dée naar/ *n.* **1. IRANIAN CURRENCY UNIT** a subunit of currency in Iran, 100 of which are worth one rial. See table at **currency 2. NOTE OR COIN WORTH DINAR** a note or coin worth a dinar **3. OLD MIDDLE EASTERN COIN** a coin, especially gold, used in the past in the Middle East [Mid-17thC. From, ultimately, late Greek *dēnarion*, from Latin *denarius* 'DENARIUS'.]

Dinaric Alps /di nárrik-, dī-/ southeastern extension of the Eastern Alps that runs parallel to the Adriatic Sea coast through Slovenia, Croatia, Bosnia-Herzegovina, and Yugoslavia, as far south as Albania, rising to a height of 2,522 m/8,274 ft

din-din, din-dins *n.* a meal, especially dinner (*babytalk*) [Late 19thC. Childish or humorous shortening and doubling of DINNER.]

d'Indy /dáN dee/, **Vincent** (1851–1931) French composer, teacher, and writer. He was a disciple of César Franck, whose ideals guided his influential direction of the Schola Cantorum, the Paris conservatory that d'Indy co-founded in 1894. Full name **Paul Marie Théodore Vincent d'Indy**

dine /dīn/ (**dines, dining, dined**) *v.* **1.** *vi.* **EAT DINNER** to eat dinner ○ *We dine early.* **2.** *vi.* **EAT** to eat or have a particular food or type of food in a meal ○ *We dined on vegetables and rice.* **3.** *vt.* **PROVIDE DINNER FOR** to provide dinner for sb or take sb out to dinner (*informal*) ○ *wined and dined their guests* [13thC. From Old French *di(s)ner*, of uncertain origin: probably ultimately from assumed Vulgar Latin *disjejunare* 'to break a fast', from, ultimately, Latin *jejunus* 'fasting' (source of English *jejune*).]

dine out *vi.* to eat dinner somewhere other than at home, especially in a restaurant

diner /dīnər/ *n.* **1. PERSON WHO EATS** a person eating a meal, especially dinner **2.** *US* **INEXPENSIVE RESTAURANT** a small inexpensive restaurant where customers eat at the counter or in booths

Dinesen /dínniss'n/, **Isak** (1885–1962) Danish writer. A much-travelled author, she is best known for her short stories, such as *Seven Gothic Tales* (1934), and her semi-autobiographical work, *Out of Africa* (1938). Real name **Karen Blixen-Finecke, Baroness Karen Christence.** Born **Karen Christence Dinesen**

dinette /dī nét/ *n.* an alcove or part of a room where meals are eaten, especially in or near a kitchen

ding[1] /ding/ *v.* (**dings, dinging, dinged**) **1.** *vti.* **RING OR MAKE RING** to ring or make sth ring with a high-pitched sound **2.** *vi.* **TALK REPEATEDLY** to talk repeatedly or wearyingly about sth ■ *n.* **RINGING** a ringing sound, especially made by a bell [Mid-16thC. Partly an imitation of the sound of metal ringing, and partly an alteration of DIN; influenced by DING[2].]

ding[2] /ding/ *v.* (**dings, dinging, dinged**) (*informal*) **1.** *vti. regional* **STRIKE** to strike sth or strike against sth **2.** *vt. US, Aus* **MAKE A DENT IN** to make a dent or other surface damage in sth ■ *n. US, Aus* **DENT** a dent or other surface damage in sth (*informal*) [14thC. Origin uncertain: probably from an Old Norse source.]

ding[3] /ding/ *n. Aus* an offensive term for an Italian or Greek person (*slang offensive*) [Mid-20thC. Shortening of DINGBAT.]

ding-a-ling *n.* **1. TINKLE OF BELL** the sound of a bell, especially a small hand-held bell, being rung **2. SILLY PERSON** a person with very odd, irrational ideas or behaviour (*insult*) [Late 19thC. An imitation of the sound of a bell.]

dingbat /díng bat/ *n.* **1. SILLY PERSON** a person with very odd, irrational ideas or behaviour (*informal*) **2.** *US* **THING WHOSE NAME IS NOT KNOWN** an object whose name has been forgotten or is not known (*slang*) **3. PRINTER'S SYMBOL** a symbol or ornamental character, such as a star or pointing hand, used in a printed work [Mid-19thC. Origin uncertain: perhaps from DING[2] + BAT.]

dingbats /díng bats/ *n. Aus* **THE DT'S** delirium tremens (*slang*) ■ *adj.* **SILLY** odd or irrational (*slang*) [Mid-20thC. Plural of DINGBAT.] ◇ **give sb the dingbats** *Aus* to make sb nervous or annoyed (*slang*)

ding-dong *n.* **1. SOUND OF BELL** a sound of a bell being struck two or more times **2. SOUND IMITATIVE OF BELL SOUND** any ringing or repeated sound that is similar to that made by a bell **3. ARGUMENT** a fierce argument (*informal*) ■ *adj.* **FIERCELY CONTESTED** fiercely contested, with advantage shifting continually from one side to another (*informal*) ○ *a ding-dong battle of wills* ■ *vi.* (**ding-dongs, ding-donging, ding-donged**) **MAKE RINGING SOUND** to make a ringing sound like a bell [Mid-16thC. An imitation of the sound.]

dinge /dinj/ *n.* a condition of dirtiness, shabbiness, or dullness [Early 19thC. Origin uncertain: probably a back-formation from DINGY.]

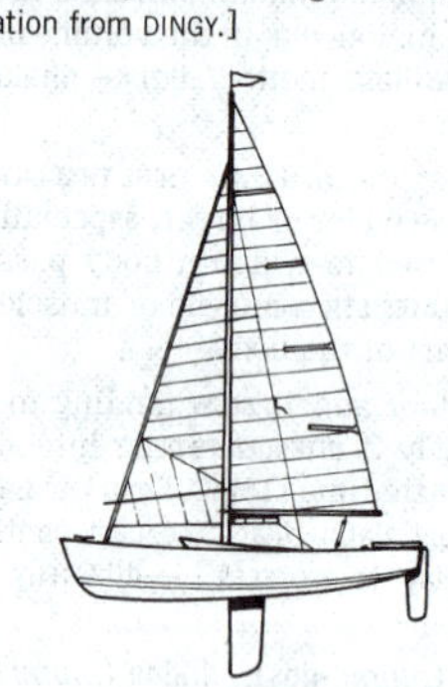

Dinghy

dinghy /díngi, díng gi/ (*plural* **-ghies**) *n.* **1. SMALL BOAT** any small boat, especially one that is towed behind or carried on a larger boat **2. INFLATABLE LIFE RAFT** an inflatable life raft [Early 19thC. From Hindi *dīgī*, literally 'small boat', from *dēgā* 'boat'.]

dingle /díng g'l/ *n.* a wooded valley (*literary*) [13thC. Origin uncertain. The original sense was 'abyss'.]

dingleberry /díng g'l berri/ (*plural* **-ries**) *n.* a small piece of dried faeces that clings to the hair or fur near the anus (*slang*) [Mid-20thC. *Dingle* of unknown origin.]

dingo /díng gō/ (*plural* **-goes**) *n.* an Australian wild dog with a reddish brown coat. Latin name: *Canis dingo.* [Late 18thC. From Aboriginal *dingu*.]

Dingo /díng gō/, **Ernie** (*b.* 1956) Australian actor and television presenter. His films include *The Fringe Dwellers* (1986).

dingy /dínji/ (**-gier, -giest**) *adj.* **1. DIRTY OR FADED** dirty-looking, discoloured, or faded **2. SHABBY** shabby, dirty, and uninviting [Mid-18thC. Origin uncertain: perhaps an alteration of DUNGY; or perhaps ultimately from

Old English *dynge* 'dung, manured land', from *dung* 'DUNG'.] —**dingily** *adv.* —**dinginess** *n.*

dining car *n.* = **restaurant car**

dining room *n.* a room where meals are eaten, especially in a home or hotel

dinitrobenzene /dī nī trō bén zeen/ *n.* a yellow crystalline compound that occurs in three isomeric forms and is used in making dyes and plastics. Formula: $C_6H_4(NO_2)_2$. [Late 19thC. Coined from DI- + NITROBENZENE.]

dink /dingk/ *n.* SPORT = **drop shot** [Mid-20thC. An imitation of the sound of the ball being hit.]

DINK /dingk/, **dink** *n.* US = **dinky**[2] *n.* [Late 20thC. Acronym formed from *dual* (or *double*) *income, no kids.*]

Dinka /díngkə/ (*plural* **-kas** *or* **-ka**) *n.* **1.** PEOPLES **MEMBER OF AFRICAN PEOPLE** a member of a tall people who live as herders in the Nile Valley in southern Sudan **2.** LANG **NILO-SAHARAN LANGUAGE** a language of the Nilo-Saharan family, spoken in southern Sudan. About 1,350,000 people speak Dinka. [Mid-19thC. From Dinka *Jieng* 'people'.] —**Dinka** *adj.*

dinkie *n.* = **dinky**[1] *adj.*

dinkum /díngkəm/ *adj.* genuine, real, or honest (*informal*) ◊ **fair dinkum** [Late 19thC. From earlier dialect *dinkum* '(hard) work, share of work', of unknown origin.]

dinky[1] /díngki/ *adj.* (**-kier, -kiest**) **SMALL AND COMPACT** small and compact or neat (*informal*) ■ *n.* (*plural* **-kies**) *S African* BEVERAGES **SMALL BOTTLE OF WINE** a small bottle of wine, usually containing 250 ml (*informal*) [Late 18thC. Formed from Scots dialect *dink* 'finely dressed, trim', of unknown origin. The original sense was 'neat, dainty'.]

dinky[2] (*plural* **-kies**), **dinkie** *n.* a member of a couple who both have careers, usually in well-paid fields, and who have no children. US term **DINK** [Late 20thC. Formed from DINK.]

dinky-di *adj. Aus* genuine, real, or typical (*informal*) [Early 20thC. Doubling and alteration of DINKUM.]

dinna /dínnə/, **dinnae** /dínni/ *vi. regional* do not [Early 18thC. Contraction.]

dinner /dínnər/ *n.* **1. MAIN MEAL** the main meal or one of the main meals of the day. Depending on geographical and social factors, *dinner* may either refer to a midday meal or an evening meal. **2. BANQUET** a formal evening meal given in honour of sb or sth **3. FULL-COURSE RESTAURANT MEAL** a meal that is eaten in a restaurant and consists of all the usual courses often offered together for a set price **4. FOOD SERVED FOR DINNER** the food served during or for a dinner [13thC. From Old French *di(s)ner* 'to dine' (see DINE), used as a noun.]

dinner-dance *n.* a formal social occasion at which dancing follows a dinner

dinner jacket *n.* a man's jacket without tails that is worn on formal occasions, especially in the evening. US term **tuxedo**

dinner lady *n.* a woman who supervises children during the midday meal break in a primary school (*dated informal*)

dinner party *n.* a social gathering where dinner is served at sb's home

dinner service, **dinner set** *n.* a matching set of all the plates, dishes, cups, and saucers needed to serve a meal to a number of people

DIN number *n.* a number that indicates the speed of a photographic film, as expressed in the DIN system

dinoflagellate /dī nō flájjələt/ *n.* a tiny single-celled marine organism with two long slender appendages (**flagella**) that lie in surface grooves at right-angles to each other. Most are constitutents of plankton. Some types are luminescent and some are toxic, especially when multiplying prolifically to cause colourful blooms (**red tide**). Latin name: *Dinoflagellata.* [Late 19thC. From modern Latin *Dinoflagellata*, order name, from Greek *dinos* 'a whirling' + Latin *flagellum* 'whip' (see FLAGELLUM).]

dinosaur /dínə sawr/ *n.* **1. EXTINCT REPTILE** an extinct, chiefly terrestrial reptile that lived in the Mesozoic Era. Some dinosaurs were the largest known land animals. Order: Ornithischia and Saurischia. **2. OUTMODED PERSON OR THING** a person or thing that is hopelessly out of date or incapable of adapting to change [Mid-19thC. From modern Latin *dinosaurus*, from Greek *deinos* 'terrible' (ultimately from an Indo-European word that is also the ancestor of English *dire*) + *sauros* 'lizard' (source of English *saurian*).] —**dinosaurian** /dīnə sáwri ən/ *adj.*

dint /dint/ *n.* **DENT** a dent ■ *vt.* (**dints, dinting, dinted**) **MAKE A DENT IN** to make a dent in sth [Old English *dynt* 'blow, stroke (especially of a weapon)'; influenced by related Old Norse *dyntr*] ◇ **by dint of** using sth, or by the force of sth

dioc. *abbr.* diocese

diocesan /dī óssiss'n/ *adj.* **RELATING TO DIOCESE** relating to, belonging to, or established by a diocese, its bishop, or its churches ■ *n.* **BISHOP OF DIOCESE** the bishop in charge of a diocese

diocese /dí əssiss/ *n.* the churches that are under the authority of one bishop, or the district containing those churches [14thC. From, ultimately, Greek *dioikēsis* 'administration', from *dioikein* 'to manage', literally 'to inhabit a house thoroughly', from *oikos* 'house'.]

Diocletian /dí ə kleesh'n/, **Emperor of Rome** (245–313). Proclaimed emperor in 284, his administrative reforms succeeded, but his attempt to restore traditional religion by persecuting Christians failed. He abdicated in 305. Full name **Gaius Aurelius Valerius Diocletianus**

diode /dí ōd/ *n.* an electronic device that has two electrodes and is used to convert alternating current to direct current. The older valve diodes have been replaced by more reliable semiconductor devices. [Early 20thC. Coined from DI- + -ODE, the underlying sense being 'double way'.]

dioecious /dī éeshəss/, **diecious, dioicous** /dī óykəss/ *adj.* having male and female flowers on different plants of the same species [Mid-18thC. Formed from modern Latin *Dioecia*, class name, literally 'two houses', from Greek *oikos* 'house'.] —**dioeciously** *adv.* —**dioeciousness** *n.* —**dioecism** /dī ée sizəm/ *n.*

dioestrus /dī éestrəss/ *n.* a stage of the oestrous cycle, following oestrus, in which the ovary is functional and the predominant ovarian hormone produced is progesterone [Early 20thC. Coined from DI- 'twice, doubly' + OESTRUS.] —**dioestrous** *adj.*

Diogenes /dī ójjə neez/ (412?–323 BC) Greek philosopher. He was a founder of Cynicism, an ancient school of philosophy. He is said to have lived in a tub in Athens and to have wandered the streets with a lamp, seeking an honest man.

diol /dí ol/ *n.* an alcohol with two hydroxyl groups in each molecule [Early 20thC. Coined from DI- + -OL.]

Dione /dī óni/ *n.* a natural satellite of Saturn discovered in 1684. It has a radius of 560 km/348 mi. and the surface exhibits several distinct terrain types.

Dionysia /dí ə nízzi ə, -níssi-/ *npl.* the celebrations held in ancient Greece in honour of the god Dionysus, which included the performance of plays [Early 19thC. From Greek *Dionusia*, from *Dionusos* 'Dionysus'.]

Dionysiac *adj.* = **Dionysian** [Early 19thC. From Latin *Dionysiacus*, from, ultimately, Greek *Dionusos* 'Dionysus'.]

dionysian /dí ə nízzi ən, -níssi-/ *adj.* **1. ORGIASTIC** involving drunkenness and sexual activity **2.** PHILOS **NOT RATIONAL** in the philosophical writings of Nietzsche, spontaneous and intuitive rather than rational

Dionysian /dí ə nízzi ən, -níssi-/, **Dionysiac** /dí ə nízzi ak, -níssi-/ *adj.* **1. RELATING TO DIONYSUS** relating to the Greek god Dionysus **2. RELATING TO DIONYSIA** connected with the worship of the Greek god Dionysus [Early 17thC. Formed from Greek *Dionusos* 'Dionysus'.]

Dionysius Exiguus /dí ə níssi əss eg zíggyoo͝ əss/ (500?–556) Scythian Roman scholar. He introduced the Christian era of dating in his *Cyclus Paschalis* (525). He adopted the name *Exiguus* 'little' as a token of humility.

Dionysius the Areopagite /-árri óppə gīt/ (*fl.* 1st century AD) Greek religious leader. He converted to Christianity through the preaching of St Paul, recorded in Acts 17:34, and is thought to have been the first bishop of Athens. He was formerly thought to be the author of influential theological texts that were actually written in about AD 500.

Dionysus /dí ə níssəss/ *n.* MYTHOL ➧ **Bacchus**

Diophantine equation /dí ō fán tīn-/ *n.* an algebraic equation that contains two or more variables, has only whole number (**integral**) coefficients and has integral solutions for the variables [Named after DIOPHANTUS the 3rd-century Greek mathematician, who invented these equations]

Diophantus /dí ə fántəss/ (*fl.* 3rd century AD) Greek mathematician. His *Arithmetica* was the first work to apply algebraic rather than geometrical methods to solving mathematical problems.

diopside /dī óp sīd/ *n.* a pale green mineral calcium magnesium silicate that is a common component of some types of igneous rock. Formula: $CaMgSi_2O_6$. [Early 19thC. Coined from DI- + Greek *opsis* , literally 'two aspects', later interpreted as a derivative of Greek *diopsis* 'a view through'.]

dioptre /dī óptər/ *n.* a unit of measurement for the power of a lens, especially a spectacle lens, equal to the reciprocal of the focal length of the lens in metres. Symbol **D** [Late 19thC. Via French from Latin *dioptra* 'instrument for measuring angles', from Greek, from *dia-* 'through' + *optos* 'visible' (see OPTIC).] —**dioptral** /dī óptrəl, dí optrəl/ *adj.*

dioptric /dī óptrik/, **dioptrical** /-óptrik'l/ *adj.* **1. RELATING TO BRANCH OF OPTICS** relating to the study of how images are formed by lenses **2. RELATING TO LIGHT'S REFRACTIVE POWERS** relating to the refractive powers of light or the measurement of the refractive power of a lens [Mid-17thC. From Greek *dioptrikos* 'of the dioptre', from *dioptra* (see DIOPTRE).] —**dioptrically** *adv.*

dioptrics /dī óptriks/ *n.* the branch of optics that studies the refraction of light by lenses or within the eye

Dior /dée awr/, **Christian** (1905–57) French couturier. In 1946 he founded the fashion house bearing his name. He achieved worldwide fame by introducing the 'New Look' in 1947, featuring narrow shoulders and calf-length skirts.

diorama /dí ə raámə/ *n.* **1. DISPLAY CASE** a three-dimensional representation of a scene, e.g. in a museum, in which objects or models are arranged in a natural setting against a realistic background **2. MINIATURE REPLICA OF SCENE** a representation of a scene that is made to appear three-dimensional, e.g. one in which the viewer looks through a hole at objects painted on layers of translucent material [Early 19thC. From French, literally 'sight through'; formed from Greek *dia-* 'through' on the model of *panorama*.] —**dioramic** /-rámmik/ *adj.*

diorite /dí ə rīt/ *n.* a dark granular igneous rock that consists of plagioclase and a ferromagnesian mineral such as hornblende. Diorite is used in materials for surfacing roads. [Early 19thC. Formed from Greek *diorizein* 'to distinguish', literally 'to limit through', from *orizein* 'to limit'.] —**dioritic** /dí ə ríttik/ *adj.*

Dioscuri /dī óskyoo͝ri, -óskyoo͝ rī, dí o skyoo͝ri, -skyoo͝r ī/ *npl.* the twin gods Castor and Polydeuces, or Pollux, who in Greek mythology were the sons of Zeus and Leda [Early 20thC. From Greek *Dioskouroi*, from *Dios* 'of Zeus' + *kouros* 'boy, son'.]

dioxane /dī ók sayn/, **dioxan** /dī óks'n/ *n.* a toxic flammable colourless liquid used as a solvent for waxes and resins, paints, lacquers, cosmetics, and deodorants, and in textile manufacture. Formula: $C_4H_8O_2$. [Early 20thC. Coined from DI- + OX- + -ANE.]

dioxide /dī ók sīd/ *n.* an oxide that has two oxygen atoms in each molecule

dioxin /dī óksin/ *n.* any derivative of dibenzo-*p*-dioxin, produced as a toxic byproduct of combustion processes, the manufacture of some herbicides and bactericides, and in chlorine bleaching of paper. The best-known dioxin is the extremely carcinogenic and mutagenic 2,3,7,8-tetrachlorodibenzo-*p*-dioxin (TCDD). [Early 20thC. Coined from DI- + OX- + -IN.]

dip /dip/ *v.* (**dips, dipping, dipped**) **1.** *vt.* **PUT BRIEFLY IN LIQUID** to put sth briefly into a liquid and take it out again ○ *She dipped her fingers in the water.* **2.** *vi.* **MOVE DOWNWARDS** to sink to a lower level ○ *The plane dipped and then flew on.* **3.** *vt.* **LOWER** to lower sth and raise it again ○ *The horse dipped its head.* **4.** *vi.* **BECOME LESS** to fall to a lower amount, especially for a short time ○ *Prices dipped at the beginning of October.* **5.** *vti.* **PUT YOUR HAND IN** to put your hand into sth in order to take sth out ○ *He dipped his hand into his pocket.* **6.** *vt.* **SCOOP** to take up liquid or small pieces of a substance with sth such as a spoon or cup ○ *She was dipping soup from the pot.* **7.** *vt.* **LOWER HEADLIGHTS** to alter a car's headlights so that they shine downwards and slightly towards the kerb in order to avoid dazzling oncoming vehicle drivers ○ *driving with dipped headlights.* US term **dim 8.** *vt.* **DISINFECT ANIMAL** to put an animal, such as a sheep or dog, into a bath of disinfectant in order to clear or prevent infection by insects, parasites, or fungi **9.** *vi.* **SLOPE DOWNWARDS** to slope downwards from the horizontal **10.** *vt.* **MAKE FROM WAX** to make a candle by repeatedly putting a wick into melted wax ○ *dip a candle* ■ *n.* **1.** **LOWERING** an act of sinking lower, of lowering sth, or of putting sth in liquid ○ *She acknowledged him with a dip of her head.* **2.** **PUTTING HAND IN** the action of putting the hand into sth to take sth out, or of scooping up liquid or small pieces of a substance **3.** **SWIM** a quick swim ○ *There's time for a dip before lunch.* **4.** **SLIGHT DECREASE** a temporary decrease in the amount or level of sth ○ *a dip in sales* **5.** **LOWER PLACE** a place where the ground slopes, especially to form a hollow ○ *We came to a dip in the road.* **6.** **FOOD MIXTURE FOR DIPPING FOOD INTO** a creamy mixture into which pieces of food can be dipped, often served with crisps ○ *an avocado dip* **7.** **AGRIC DISINFECTANT FOR ANIMALS** a mixture of chemicals used to disinfect animals ○ *sheep dip* **8.** **INDUST LIQUID CHEMICAL PREPARATION** a chemical mixture in which sth can be immersed, such as a dye or preservative **9.** *US* **UNINTELLIGENT PERSON** an unintelligent or unsophisticated person (*slang insult*) **10.** **GEOG ANGLE OF MAGNETIC NEEDLE** the angle that a magnetic needle makes with the horizontal plane **11.** **GEOL ANGLE OF ROCK LAYER** the angle a sloping rock layer makes to the horizontal ○ *The rock bed has a dip of ten degrees.* **12.** **CANDLE** a candle made by dipping a wick repeatedly in wax **13.** **GYMNASTICS PARALLEL BARS EXERCISE** an exercise on parallel bars in which the elbows are bent until the gymnast's chin is level with the bars, and the body is raised by straightening the arms **14.** **PICKPOCKET** a pickpocket (*slang*) [Old English *dyppan*, from a prehistoric Germanic word that is also the ancestor of English *deep*]

dip into *vt.* **1.** **READ PARTS OF BOOK** to read parts of a text, such as a book or magazine, rather than the whole of it **2.** **USE SAVED MONEY** to use some of the money that has been saved

Dip., dip. *abbr.* diploma

DipEd /dip éd/ *abbr.* Diploma in Education

dipeptidase /dī pépti dayz, -dayss/ *n.* an enzyme that aids the breakdown of proteins as part of the process of protein digestion

dipeptide /dī pép tīd/ *n.* a chemical compound consisting of two linked amino acids

diphasic /dī fáyzik/, **diphase** /dī fayz/ *adj.* relating to parasites that have an independent stage in their life cycle

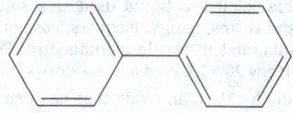

Diphenyl

diphenyl /dī feén'l, -fénn'l/ *n.* a white crystalline substance used as a fungicide, in organic synthesis, and as a heat transfer agent. Formula: $C_{12}H_{10}$.

diphenylamine /dī feén'l ə meen, -fénn'l-/ *n.* a colourless toxic crystalline substance used in solid rocket propellants, dyes, and the manufacture of plastics. Formula: $(C_6H_5)_2NH$.

---

diphenylketone /dī feén'l keétōn, -fénn'l-/ *n.* CHEM = benzophenone

diphosgene /dī fóz jeen/ *n.* a colourless oily liquid with an extremely poisonous vapour, used in gas warfare during World War I. Formula: $ClCOOCCl_3$.

diphosphate /dī fóss fayt/ *n.* a chemical compound that contains two phosphate groups per molecule

diphosphoglyceric acid /dī fósfō gli sérrik-/ *n.* an abundant compound found in the red blood cells of most mammals that decreases the affinity of haemoglobin for oxygen

diphtheria /dif théeri ə, dip-/ *n.* a serious infectious disease, caused by a bacterium *Corynebacterium diphtheriae*, that attacks the membranes of the throat and releases a toxin that damages the heart and the nervous system. The main symptoms are fever, weakness, and severe inflammation of the affected membranes. [Mid-19thC. From modern Latin, ultimately from Greek *diphthera* or *diphtheris* 'hide, skin', indicating the tough membrane developed in the throat.] — **diphtherial** *adj.* —**diphtheric** *adj.* —**diphtheritic** /díftho ríttik, díp-/ *adj.* —**diphtheroid** /díftho royd, díp-/ *adj.*

diphthong /díf thong, díp-/ *n.* **1.** **TWO VOWELS AS ONE SYLLABLE** a complex vowel sound in which the first vowel is gradually raised by a second vowel so that both vowels form one syllable, such as 'a' and 'i' in 'rail' **2.** **JOINED LETTERS** a character formed by joining the two letters 'a' and 'e' as 'æ' or the two letters 'o' and 'e' as 'œ' [15thC. Via French from Latin *diphthongus*, literally 'two sounds', from, ultimately, Greek *phthoggos* 'sound'.] —**diphthongal** /dif thóng g'l, dip-/ *adj.*

diphthongize /díf thong īz, díp-/ (**-izes, -izing, -ized**), **diphthongise** (**-ises, -ising, -ised**) *vti.* to become a diphthong or make a vowel into a diphthong —**diphthongization** /díf thong ī záysh'n, díp-/ *n.*

Diphycercal

diphycercal /díffi súrk'l/ *adj.* used to describe a fish's tail fin that is divided into two equal parts [Mid-19thC. From the Greek stem *diphu-* 'of double form' + *kerkos* 'tail'.]

diphyodont /dī fī ə dont/ *adj.* used to describe a mammal that grows two sets of teeth in a lifetime [Mid-19thC. Coined from the Greek stem *diphu-* 'double form' + the Greek stem *odont-* 'tooth'.]

dipl. *abbr.* **1.** diplomat **2.** diplomatic

dipl- *prefix.* = diplo- (*used before vowels*)

diplegia /dī pleéjə/ *n.* inability to move corresponding parts on both the right and left sides of the body [Late 19thC. Coined from DI- on the model of PARAPLEGIA.] —**diplegic** *adj.*

diplex /dī pleks/ *adj.* capable of simultaneously transmitting or receiving two signals in the same direction along a telecommunications channel [Late 19thC. Alteration of DUPLEX.] —**diplexer** *n.*

diplo- *prefix.* **1.** double, twin ○ *diplopod* **2.** having twice the basic number of chromosomes ○ *diplont* [From Greek *diploos* 'double' (see DIPLOMA)]

diploblastic /dípplō blástik/ *adj.* used to describe an invertebrate animal in which the adult tissues are derived from just two layers of embryonic germ tissue, endoderm and ectoderm. Cnidarians are diploblastic.

diplodocus /di plóddəkəss, dípplō dōkəss/ *n.* a large herbivorous dinosaur of the late Jurassic Period that had four legs and a very long neck and tail. It had nostrils near the top of the head, indicating that it spent time in deep water. Genus: *Diplodocus.* [Late

---

19thC. From modern Latin, genus name, from Greek *diploos* 'double' + *dokos* 'beam'. The underlying sense is of a creature twice as large as the widest part of anything.]

diploë /dípplō ee/ *n.* a layer of spongy bone tissue found between the harder inside and outside bone layers of the cranium [Late 16thC. From Greek *diploë* 'doubling', from *diploos* 'double'.]

diploid /díp loyd/ *adj.* possessing two matched sets of chromosomes in the cell nucleus, one set from each parent. There is a characteristic diploid number of chromosomes for each species. —**diploidic** /di plóydik/ *adj.* —**diploidy** /díp loydi/ *n.*

diploma /di plṓmə/ *n.* **1.** **COURSE CERTIFICATE** a certificate given by a college, university, or professional organization, indicating that sb has completed a course of education or training and reached the required level of competence **2.** **OFFICIAL PAPER DESCRIBING RIGHTS AND PRIVILEGES** a written document or charter, especially one that confers specific rights or privileges [Mid-17thC. Via Latin from Greek, 'folded paper', from *diploun* 'to fold, make double', from *diploos* 'double'.]

diplomacy /di plṓməssi/ *n.* **1.** **INTERNATIONAL RELATIONS** the management of communication and relationships between nations by members and employees of each nation's government **2.** **SKILL IN INTERNATIONAL DEALINGS** skill in managing communication and relationships between nations **3.** **TACT** skill and tact in dealing with other people

diplomat /dípplə mat/ *n.* **1.** **GOVERNMENT REPRESENTATIVE ABROAD** a member or employee of a government who represents his or her country in dealings with other nations, especially by working in an embassy or consulate abroad **2.** **TACTFUL PERSON** sb who is tactful and good at dealing with people [Early 19thC. From French *diplomate*, back-formation from *diplomatique* 'diplomatic'.]

diplomate /dípplə mayt/ *n.* sb who holds a diploma granted by a professional organization

diplomatic /dípplə máttik/ *adj.* **1.** **INVOLVING DIPLOMACY** concerned with or involving international diplomacy or the work of diplomats **2.** **TACTFUL** showing tact and skill in dealing with people **3.** **RELATING TO DIPLOMATICS** relating to the study of old documents **4.** **BEING EXACT COPY** having been copied from an original document [Early 18thC. Partly from French *diplomatique*, and partly from modern Latin *diplomaticus*, from *diploma* (see DIPLOMA). Originally 'relating to official documents'.]

diplomatic bag *n.* a bag in which official correspondence travels between a government office and an embassy of that government in another country. The case is carried by a special messenger and is not subject to the regulations governing ordinary mail.

diplomatic corps *n.* all the diplomats from other countries who reside in another nation

diplomatic immunity *n.* the legal status of diplomats, who are not subject to the legal and taxation systems of a country in which they are resident as accredited representatives

diplomatics /dípplə máttiks/ *n.* the study and verification of very old documents (*takes a singular verb*)

diplomatist /di plṓmətist/ *n.* a professional diplomat

diplont /dī plont/ *n.* an organism whose cells, other than reproductive cells, have a diploid number of chromosomes in their nuclei [Early 20thC. Coined from DIPLO- + -ONT.] —**diplontic** /di plóntik/ *adj.*

diplopia /di plṓpi ə/ *n.* double vision (*technical*) [Early 19thC. Coined from DIPLO- + -OPIA.] —**diplopic** /di plóppik/ *adj.*

diplopod /dípplə pod/ *n.* a millipede that has two pairs of legs on each body segment. Class: Diplopoda. [Mid-19thC. From modern Latin Diplopoda, class name, from Greek *diploos* 'double' + the stem *pod-* 'foot'.] —**diplopodous** /di plóppədəss/ *adj.*

diplotene /dípplō teen/ *n.* a stage in the first part of reproductive cell division (**meiosis**) in which paired chromosomes start to move apart from one another but remain connected at points. At these connecting points, genetic information is exchanged. [Early 20thC. Coined from DIPLO- + *-tene*, from Greek *tainia* 'band, ribbon']

---

a at; aa father; aw all; ay day; air hair; ə about, edible, item, common, circus; e egg; ee eel; hw when; i it, happy; ī ice; 'l apple; 'm rhythm; 'n fashion; o odd; ō open; oo good; oo pool; ow owl; oy oil; th thin; <u>th</u> this; u up; ur urge;

dipody /díppədi/ (*plural* **-dies**) *n.* a unit of poetry that consists of two stressed units or feet [Late 19thC. Formed from the Greek stem *dipod-* 'two-footed'.]

dipole /dí pōl/ *n.* two equal and opposite magnetized or electrically charged poles that are separated by a short distance —**dipolar** /dī pṓlər/ *adj.*

dipole moment *n.* **1.** PRODUCT OF EQUAL BUT OPPOSITE CHARGES the product of one of the equal but opposite charges on two atoms in a molecule, and the distance separating them **2.** RESULT OF MAGNETIC DIPOLE the product of two equal and opposite magnetic poles or electric charges that are separated by a short distance

dipper /díppər/ *n.* **1.** SCOOP a cup or ladle for dipping into liquid **2.** BIRDS SMALL WATER BIRD a small plain-coloured bird that lives beside rivers and can swim and dive. Family: Cinclidae. **3.** STH THAT DIPS sb or sth, such as a machine, that dips objects in a liquid, e.g. in an industrial process

dipropellant /dīprə péllənt/ *n.* SPACE TECH = **bipropellant**

diprotic /dī próttik/ *adj.* with two transferable hydrogen protons [Coined from DI- + PROTON + -IC]

diprotodont /dī prṓtə dont/ *adj.* WITH ENLARGED INCISORS used to describe a mammal that has the first pair of incisor teeth in each jaw enlarged ■ *n.* MARSUPIAL WITH ENLARGED INCISORS a marsupial that has enlarged incisors. Kangaroos and wallabies are diprotodonts. Order: Diprotodontia. [Late 19thC. Coined from DI- + PROTO- + -ODONT.]

dipso /díp sō/ (*plural* **-sos**) *n.* a dipsomaniac (*slang insult*) [Late 19thC. Shortening.]

dipsomania /dípsō máyni ə/ *n.* a habitual and uncontrollable craving for alcohol (*dated*) [Mid-19thC. From Greek *dipsa* 'thirst' + MANIA.]

dipsomaniac /dípsō máyni ak/ *n.* sb with a habitual and uncontrollable craving for alcohol (*dated*) —**dipsomaniacal** /dípsō mə nī́ ək'l/ *adj.*

dipstick /díp stik/ *n.* **1.** MEASURING ROD a measuring rod that is dipped into a container to indicate the depth of liquid in it, especially one used to measure the amount of oil in a car's engine **2.** INCOMPETENT PERSON an unintelligent and incompetent person (*informal*) [20thC. The sense meaning 'fool' is said to be a euphemism for *dipshit*.]

dip switch /díp-/ *n.* **1.** SWITCH FOR DIMMING HEADLIGHTS a control used to dip a car's headlights or raise them to full beam. US term **dimmer 2.** = **DIP switch**

DIP switch, **dip switch** *n.* one or more tiny switches used to turn optional settings on or off on a computer component [Late 20thC. *DIP* an acronym formed from *dual in-line package*.]

dipteran /díptərən/, **dipteron** /-ron/ *n.* a two-winged fly. Order: Diptera. [Mid-19thC. Formed from modern Latin *Diptera*, order name, from Greek *dipteros* 'two winged'.] —**dipteral** *adj.*

dipterous /díptərəss/ *adj.* characteristic of or relating to the order Diptera of two-winged insects that includes flies, gnats, mosquitoes, and midges

diptych /díptik/ *n.* **1.** PAIRED PAINTINGS a pair of paintings, especially religious paintings on two hinged panels **2.** WRITING TABLETS a pair of writing tablets joined by a hinge and having wooden backs and waxed writing surfaces, used especially in ancient Greece and Rome [Early 17thC. Via late Latin *diptycha* from late Greek *diptukha* 'pair of writing tablets', plural of *diptukhos* 'folded in two', from *ptukhē* 'fold'.]

dipyridamole /dí pī ríddə mōl/ *n.* a vasodilator drug used to treat angina pectoris and to prevent clots in blood vessels. Formula: $C_{24}H_{40}N_8O_4$. [Mid-20thC. Coined from DI- + PYRIMIDINE + PIPERIDINE + AMINO- + -OL.]

diquat /dí kwot/ *n.* a biodegradable herbicide used to control weeds in water [Mid-20thC. Coined from DI- + QUATERNARY; from its being based on a quaternary amine.]

dir. *abbr.* director

Dirac /di rák/, **Paul** (1902–84) British theoretical physicist. He worked on quantum theory and predicted the existence of the positron. He shared the Nobel Prize in physics (1933). Full name **Paul Adrien Maurice Dirac**

Dirac constant *n.* a constant used in quantum mechanics that is Planck's constant divided by 2π [Named after Paul DIRAC]

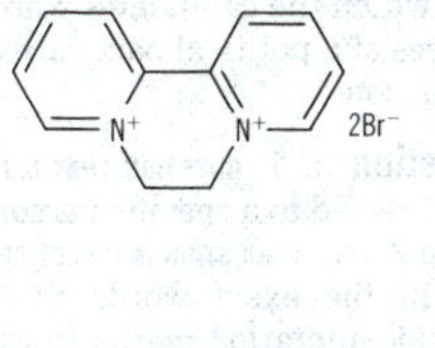

Diquat

Dirac equation *n.* an equation in quantum mechanics that describes the wave behaviour of an electron in an electromagnetic field, in a manner consistent with special relativity [Named after Paul DIRAC]

dire /dīr/ (**direr, direst**) *adj.* **1.** VERY BAD characterized by severe, serious, or desperate circumstances **2.** THREATENING DISASTER warning of a future disaster or serious consequences [Mid-16thC. From Latin *dirus* 'fearful, awful, boding ill'. Ultimately from an Indo-European word that is also the ancestor of English *dinosaur*.] —**direly** *adv.* —**direness** *n.*

direct /di rékt, dī-/ *v.* (**-rects, -recting, -rected**) **1.** *vt.* SUPERVISE to organize and control the work of an organization or a group of people ○ *I found her directing the efforts of a team of rescue workers.* **2.** *vt.* INSTRUCT to tell sb to do sth (*formal*) ○ *The medicine should be taken only as directed.* **3.** *vt.* FOCUS ATTENTION ON STH to focus attention or concentrate activities on sth ○ *Please direct your attention towards the figures at the right of the screen.* **4.** *vt.* AIM to aim, point, or send sth in a particular direction ○ *Direct the extinguisher at the base of the flames.* **5.** *vt.* ADDRESS LETTER to write an address on sth to be delivered ○ *The envelope was directed to our offices.* **6.** *vt.* GIVE DIRECTIONS to tell sb how to get to a place ○ *Can you direct me to the station?* **7.** *vt.* ADDRESS to say sth to sb specifically ○ *The remarks were directed to his sister.* **8.** *vti.* ARTS SUPERVISE FILMS OR PLAYS to be responsible for supervising the creative aspects of a film, play, or television programme, giving instructions and guidance to the actors and other people involved ○ *He has directed several films.* **9.** *vt.* US MUSIC = **conduct** *v.* 1 ■ *adj.* **1.** NOT STOPPING OR DEVIATING going straight from one place or point to another ○ *a direct flight from Paris to Miami* **2.** IMMEDIATE lacking the influence of any other factors ○ *No direct link between the two events has been established.* **3.** PERSONAL not having a person, action, or process intervene ○ *We are in direct contact with them.* **4.** STRAIGHTFORWARD easy to understand or respond to ○ *The author makes a direct appeal to our emotions.* **5.** PRECISE having the characteristics of accuracy and precision ○ *a direct quotation* **6.** IMMEDIATELY RELATED connected by a straight and unbroken line of descent from parent to child ○ *a direct descendant of George Washington* **7.** COMPLETE OR EXACT showing complete contradiction or opposition ○ *Their conclusions were in direct contradiction to ours.* **8.** POL DIRECTLY INVOLVING THE ELECTORATE involving participation in government from the electorate rather than through electoral representatives ○ *direct democracy* **9.** MATH, LOGIC WORKING FROM PREMISE TO CONCLUSION working immediately from the premise to the conclusion in proving sth **10.** ASTRON MOVING WEST TO EAST moving from west to east as observed from celestial north ■ *adv.* **1.** STRAIGHT WITHOUT DIVERSION straight from one place or person to another, without a stop or diversion ○ *You can fly direct from Amsterdam to Chicago.* **2.** DIRECTLY by an immediate connection, without sb or sth intervening ○ *You can dial Calcutta direct.* [14thC. From Latin *directus*, past participle of *dirigere* 'to set straight, guide'.] —**directness** *n.*

WORD KEY: SYNONYMS

See Synonyms at ***guide***.

WORD KEY: ORIGIN

As well as giving rise to ***direct***, Latin *dirigere* is also the source of English *address*, *dirigible*, and *dress*.

direct access *n.* the ability to retrieve information directly from any part of a storage device without referring to the preceding data

direct action *n.* a political or industrial action, such as a strike, a boycott, or civil disobedience, intended to have an immediate and noticeable effect that will influence a government or employer

direct coupling *n.* direct connection of one part of a circuit to another without the use of transformers or capacitors, allowing both direct current and alternating current to flow along the connection —**direct-coupled** *adj.*

direct current *n.* electrical current that flows in only one direction and has a fairly constant average value. ◊ **alternating current**

direct debit *n.* an arrangement by which sums of varying amounts that are owed at regular intervals, such as bills, are paid to the creditor directly from the payer's bank account

direct discourse *n.* US GRAM = **direct speech**

direct dye *n.* a dye that can be used directly on a fabric without needing an extra chemical (**mordant**) to fix the colour

direct evidence *n.* evidence, such as a photograph, a document, or a witness's account, that provides direct factual information in a trial

direct free kick *n.* a free kick in football that is awarded as compensation for a foul and can be taken as a direct shot at the opponent's goal

direct injection *n.* the injection of fuel in liquid form into the cylinders of an internal-combustion engine, without previously passing it through a carburettor

direction /di réksh'n, dī-/ *n.* **1.** MANAGEMENT the management or control of sb or sth by providing instructions **2.** WAY the way in which sb or sth goes, points, or faces ○ *They shook hands and walked off in opposite directions.* **3.** SUPERVISION OF STH the control and supervision of a group, person, or organization **4.** DEVELOPMENT the way in which sth develops ○ *The organization has begun to take a new direction.* **5.** ARTS ART OF DIRECTING the art or practice of directing a film or play **6.** SENSE OF PURPOSE a feeling of having a definite goal or purpose ○ *He's a nice boy, but seems to lack a sense of direction.* **7.** MUSIC INSTRUCTION IN MUSIC an instruction in a piece of music that shows how it should be played **8.** MUSIC CONDUCTING PERFORMERS the process of conducting an orchestra or choir ■ **directions** *npl.* INSTRUCTIONS instructions on how to get to a place or how to do sth ○ *I need to stop the car and ask for directions.*

directional /di réksh'nəl, dī-/ *adj.* **1.** RELATING TO DIRECTION showing, concerned with, or dependent on direction ○ *Use your directional lights to indicate the way you plan to turn.* **2.** ELECTRON ENG MORE EFFICIENT IN ONE DIRECTION more efficient in a specific direction for transmitting and receiving sound waves, nuclear particles, light, or radio waves **3.** RELATING TO CONTROL OF STH showing or relating to the management or control of sb's work, behaviour, or way of thinking **4.** INDICATING TREND showing the future direction in which sth might go —**directionality** /di rékshə nálləti, dī-/ *n.*

directional antenna *n.* an antenna in which the transmitting and receiving characteristics are concentrated in certain directions, used when transmitting or receiving over very long distances, e.g. when receiving signals from space

directional drilling *n.* a method of drilling for oil or gas in which special assemblies are used to turn a drill hole in the required direction

direction finder *n.* a device used especially in navigation to determine the direction of a transmitted radio signal —**direction finding** *n.*

directive /di réktiv, dī-/ *n.* **1.** ORDER an order or official instruction **2.** EU LAW PASSED IN MEMBER COUNTRIES a law passed by the European Union that is then applied through the domestic law of its member states ■ *adj.* **1.** PROVIDING GUIDANCE giving explicit guidance or instructions ○ *directive utterances* **2.** SHOWING DIRECTION indicating a direction ○ *directive signals*

direct labour *n.* labour that is directly involved in

the production of goods or the provision of services rather than, e.g. in administration or sales

direct lighting *n.* a method of lighting in which a large percentage, usually not less than 90 per cent, of the emitted light is directed downwards

directly /di réktli, dī-/ *adv.* **1.** STRAIGHT straight to a place or a person, or straight in a direction ○ *She went directly to the filing cabinet.* ○ *Your letter was sent directly to me.* **2.** WITH NOTHING IN BETWEEN without any person, thing, or event intervening ○ *I prefer to deal directly with senior management.* ○ *I hold you directly responsible for what has happened.* **3.** COMPLETELY in every respect ○ *I am directly opposed to everything that they stand for.* **4.** CLEARLY in a clear and unambiguous manner ○ *She refuses to say directly what the trouble is.* **5.** IMMEDIATELY at once ○ *I'll deal with it directly.* **6.** *US* SOON in a short while (*regional*) ○ *Please take a seat, and I'll be with you directly.* ■ *conj.* IMMEDIATELY AFTER as soon as sth happens ○ *I left directly I heard the news.*

direct mail, **direct mail shot** *n.* the use of mail addressed to potential customers as a way of advertising, or the promotional material that is mailed —**direct mailer** *n.*

direct marketing, **direct selling** *n.* methods of marketing by which a company deals directly with its end customers, including mail order by catalogue, direct mail, telephone sales, or the advertising of goods

direct object *n.* the word or phrase in a sentence that indicates sb or sth directly affected by the action of the verb, such as 'cat' in 'she fed the cat'

director /di réktər, dī-/ *n.* **1.** BUSINESS HEAD OF MANAGEMENT sb who is at the head of an organized group, such as a government department, or in charge of a programme of activity, e.g. in social services **2.** BUSINESS SB WHO RUNS A COMPANY a member of the board that controls the affairs of a company. A board may be made up of executive directors, who manage the company, and nonexecutive directors, who contribute advice. **3.** CINEMA, TV FILMMAKER sb who has control over, and responsibility for, the actual making of a film or television programme, and its artistic and technical content **4.** MUSIC MUSICAL CONDUCTOR sb who is responsible for the work of a group of musicians, especially the conductor of an orchestra [15thC. From Anglo-Norman *directour*, from, ultimately, Latin *direct-*, past participle stem of *dirigere* (see DIRECT).] —**directorial** /dī rek táwri əl, di rék-/ *adj.* —**directorially** /-ri əli/ *adv.* —**directorship** /di réktər ship, dī-/ *n.*

directorate /di réktərət, dī-/ *n.* a board of directors, e.g. of a company

director-general (*plural* **directors-general**) *n.* the title given to the head of some large public organizations, such as the BBC in Britain

Director of Public Prosecutions (*plural* **Directors of Public Prosecutions**) *n.* **1.** HEAD OF CROWN PROSECUTION SERVICE the head of the Crown Prosecution Service, which is responsible for the conduct of all criminal prosecutions in England and Wales **2.** PROSECUTING OFFICIAL in Australian states and at a federal level, the government official responsible for prosecutions on behalf of the Crown

director's chair *n.* **1.** CHAIR FOR FILM DIRECTOR the chair used by the director on the set of a film **2.** FOLDING CHAIR a light folding chair with a wooden or metal frame with arms, and a canvas back and seat

directory /di réktəri, dī-/ *n.* (*plural* **-ries**) **1.** BOOK OF NAMES a book containing the names of people and organizations, usually with telephone numbers, addresses, and other information about them, arranged alphabetically for reference **2.** LIST OF TENANTS a listing in the lobby of a building of the building's tenants and their floor or room numbers **3.** COMPUT INDEX OF COMPUTER FILES an index of files stored on a computer disk. A disk may have many separate directories containing different types of file. **4.** RULE BOOK a book of rules or instructions **5.** BUSINESS GROUP OF DIRECTORS a board of directors ■ *adj.* GIVING DIRECTION providing direction or advice

directory enquiries *n.* a service provided by a telephone company that provides the telephone number of anyone in the country who has agreed to have his or her number listed. US term **information, directory assistance**

direct primary *n.* a primary election in the United States, in which the candidates who will seek office as nominees of a political party are chosen directly by popular vote

direct question *n.* **1.** QUESTION THAT MUST BE ANSWERED a question directed to a specific person and requiring a response **2.** GRAM QUESTION IN DIRECT SPEECH a question repeated in the exact words that were spoken, placed inside quotation marks in writing

direct-reading *adj.* allowing the immediate reading of a measurement, without intervening calculations

directrix /di rékt riks, dī-/ (*plural* **-trixes** *or* **-trices** /-seez/) *n.* a fixed line used in constructing a curve or conic section, the distance from the line divided by the distance from a fixed point being identical for all points on the figure [Early 16thC. From medieval Latin, feminine form of late Latin *director*, from Latin *direct-*, past participle stem of *dirigere* (see DIRECT).]

direct selling *n.* = **direct marketing**

direct speech *n.* the repeating of speech by giving the exact words that were spoken, and in writing, conventionally shown inside quotation marks. US term **direct discourse**

direct tax *n.* a tax that is levied directly on the income or capital of a person or organization rather than as part of the price of goods or services

direful /dírf'l/ *adj.* being extremely threatening or ominous (*archaic*) —**direfully** *adv.* —**direfulness** *n.*

dire straits *npl.* a situation of emergency or desperate need

dire wolf *n.* a large extinct mammal similar to a wolf, found in North America during the Pleistocene Epoch. Latin name: *Canis dirus*. [*Dire*, a translation of *(Canis) dirus*, Latin name]

dirge /durj/ *n.* **1.** FUNERAL HYMN a song of mourning or lament, especially one about death or intended for a funeral **2.** MOURNFUL MUSIC a song or piece of music that sounds sad or depressing **3.** FUNERAL SERVICE a funeral service that is sung [Early 15thC. From Latin *dirige* (first word of the antiphon in the funeral service, Psalm 5:8), imperative singular of *dirigere* 'to guide' (see DIRECT).]

dirham /deer ram, deerrəm/ *n.* **1.** CURRENCY UNIT IN MOROCCO AND UAE a basic unit of currency in Morocco and the United Arab Emirates and a minor unit of currency in Libya. See table at **currency** **2.** NOTE WORTH A DIRHAM a note worth a dirham **3.** COIN WORTH A DIRHAM a coin worth a dirham, 100 of which are worth a riyal in Qatar and 1000 of which are worth a dinar in Libya [Late 18thC. From Arabic, from Greek *drachmē*, literally 'number of coins one hand can hold'.]

dirigible /dírrijəb'l/ *n.* AIR = **airship** ■ *adj.* STEERABLE able to be steered or navigated [Late 16thC. From Latin *dirigere* 'to direct, guide' (see DIRECT) + -IBLE; from the fact that an airship (in contrast to a balloon) can be steered.] —**dirigibility** /dírrijə bílləti/ *n.*

dirigisme /dírri zhizəm/ *n.* full and direct state control of a country's economy and social institutions [Mid-20thC. From French, where it was formed from *diriger* 'to direct', from Latin *dirigere* (see DIRECT).] —**dirigiste** /dírri zheest/ *adj.*

diriment /dírrimənt/ *adj.* invalidating a marriage in canon law [Mid-19thC. From The Latin stem *diriment-*, from *dirimere* 'to take apart'.]

dirk /durk/ *n.* DAGGER a dagger with a long straight blade, especially one that was formerly used by Scottish Highlanders ■ *vt.* (**dirks, dirking, dirked**) STAB to stab sb with a dagger [Mid-16thC. Origin unknown.]

Dirk Hartog Island /dúrk haar tog-/ uninhabited island off the western coast of Australia. It is the westernmost point on the continent, and in 1616, it was the site of the first landing by a European. Area: 613 sq. km/234 sq. mi.

Dirndl

dirndl /dúrnd'l/ *n.* **1.** **dirndl, dirndl skirt** FULL SKIRT a full skirt that is gathered at the waist **2.** TRADITIONAL DRESS a dress with a full gathered skirt and a tight, low bodice that is worn over a short-sleeved blouse and is part of German and Austrian national costume [Mid-20thC. From German *Dirndlkleid* 'dirndl dress': *Dirndl* from German dialect, literally 'little girl', from *Dirne* 'maid'.]

dirt /durt/ *n.* **1.** UNCLEAN SUBSTANCE a substance that spoils the cleanness of sb or sth ○ *There was a smear of dirt on his shirt.* **2.** EARTH earth, soil, or mud ○ *Children were playing in the dirt by the side of the road.* **3.** HARD-PACKED EARTH earth packed down to make a firm surface, especially mixed with gravel and cinders to make a racetrack for motor cycles or for horse racing ○ *dirt floors.* **4.** SCANDALOUS FACTS scandalous or damaging facts about sb ○ *The local paper may have some dirt on the candidates.* **5.** CORRUPTING INFLUENCE sth such as pornography or bad language that is considered to have a corrupting influence [13thC. By transposition of *r* and *i* from Old Norse *drit* 'excrement', from prehistoric Germanic.] —**dirtily** *adv.* —**dirtiness** *n.* ◇ **dig the dirt on sb** *or* **sth** to search for scandalous information about sb or sth in order to reveal it

dirt-cheap *adj., adv.* extremely cheap or cheaply (*informal*)

dirt track *n.* **1.** UNSURFACED TRACK a narrow road or path that is not surfaced, but consists of earth **2.** RACE TRACK a track of earth mixed with gravel and cinders that is used for horse racing or motorcycle racing

dirty /dúrti/ (**-ier, -iest**) **1.** *adj.* NOT CLEAN marked by dirt or covered in dirt ○ *dirty fingernails* **2.** CAUSING DIRT creating dirt or pollution ○ *a battered truck with a dirty engine* **3.** MAKING SB GRIMY likely to cause sb to be filthy or grimy ○ *Working on cars is a dirty job.* **4.** NOT KEPT UP lacking care and maintenance, especially of dwellings in a neighbourhood **5.** NOT HONEST OR LEGAL lacking honesty or moral integrity, especially if the rules of a game or law have been broken ○ *dirty tactics* **6.** *US* RELATING TO ILLEGAL DRUGS relating to the use or sale of illegal drugs by sb (*slang*) **7.** MALICIOUS characterized by extreme meanness and cruelty ○ *a dirty lie* **8.** RELATING TO SEX concerned with sex, especially in a way that is rude or suggestive **9.** ANGRY expressing anger, displeasure, or disapproval ○ *a dirty look* **10.** DESPICABLE immoral, or behaving in a despicable way (*informal*) **11.** LACKING BRIGHTNESS OR CLARITY characterized by a lack of lustre or clarity (*often used in combination*) ○ *The walls were a dirty green.* **12.** STORMY characterized by heavy rain and strong winds ○ *dirty weather* **13.** CREATING CONTAMINATION producing a lot of radioactive contamination ■ *adv.* (**-ier, -iest**) **1.** UNFAIRLY in an unfair or dishonest way ○ *You have to fight dirty if you want to win.* **2.** SUGGESTIVELY in a sexually suggestive or indecent way ■ *v.* (**-ies, -ying, -ied**) **1.** *vti.* MAKE DIRTY to make sth or sb dirty, or become dirty ○ *He wouldn't want to dirty his hands with that kind of work.* **2.** *vt.* DISHONOUR to make sth seem less honest or honourable ○ *to dirty sb's reputation* —**dirtily** *adv.* —**dirtiness** *n.* ◇ **get your hands dirty** to perform a degrading or unpleasant act, or to participate in such an act

WORD KEY: SYNONYMS

dirty, filthy, grubby, grimy, soiled, squalid, unclean

CORE MEANING: not clean

dirty the most general term, used to describe lack of cleanliness; **filthy** extremely dirty; **grubby** slightly unclean; **grimy** exhibiting ingrained or accumulated dirt;

soiled a fairly formal term, used to describe things such as bed linen and nappies that have become dirty in the course of normal use; **squalid** a term used to describe extremely dirty houses and living areas, usually with a suggestion of poor conditions; **unclean** a fairly formal term, frequently used in a moral or religious context.

WORD KEY: CULTURAL NOTE

Dirty Harry, a film by US director Don Siegel (1971). It is the story of San Francisco policeman Harry Callahan (Clint Eastwood), known as 'Dirty' because he always gets the worst jobs, and his attempts to apprehend a serial killer, Scorpio. This and subsequent films centring on the Callahan character resulted in *Dirty Harry* being used as an adjective meaning police who use unnecessary force, as in *Dirty Harry syndrome.* Famous lines spoken by the Callahan character also made their way into mainstream US English. An example is 'Go ahead, make my day!' from *Sudden Impact* (1983).

dirty dog *n.* sb who takes advantage of other people in small, dishonest, or unpleasant ways (*dated*)

dirty linen, dirty laundry *n.* personal matters that it would be embarrassing or disadvantageous to let other people know about ○ *Don't wash your dirty linen in public.*

dirty old man *n.* an older man who shows an interest in sex that is perceived as immoral, perverted, or generally unpleasant (*informal*)

dirty trick *n.* UNFAIR ACTION sth unfair or dishonest that is done to gain an advantage ■ **dirty tricks** *npl.* **1.** UNFAIR POLITICAL TACTICS tactics used in a political campaign to discredit an opponent in a way that is not completely fair or honest **2.** SPY TACTICS secret activities carried out by the spies of one government in order to disrupt or destroy the internal functioning of another nation (*informal*) **3.** COMMERCIAL ESPIONAGE the activity of stealing secret products or processes from one company and selling them to rival companies (*informal*)

dirty word *n.* **1.** OFFENSIVE WORD a swearword or offensive word **2.** UNPOPULAR THING sth that is disapproved of ○ *Delay seems to be a dirty word in this office!*

dirty work *n.* sth that sb wants to be done that is unpleasant, unfair, unkind, dishonest, or illegal

dis /diss/ (**disses, dissing, dissed**), **diss** *vt.* (*slang*) **1.** TREAT DISRESPECTFULLY to treat sb without respect, e.g. by talking back to sb in authority, or by being purposely rude or inconsiderate **2.** CRITICIZE to criticize sb or sth [Late 20thC. Origin uncertain: perhaps a shortening of DISRESPECT.]

Dis /diss/ *n.* in Roman mythology, the underworld, or region of the dead. Greek equivalent **Hades**

dis- *prefix.* **1.** to undo, do the opposite ○ *disapprove* **2.** opposite or absence of ○ *discourtesy* **3.** to deprive of, remove from ○ *dishonour* **4.** not ○ *disobedient* **5.** to free from ○ *disburden* **6.** completely ○ *dissever* [Directly and via Old French *des-* from Latin *dis-*, from *dis* 'apart', of unknown origin]

disability /díssə bílləti/ (*plural* **-ties**) *n.* **1.** RESTRICTED CAPABILITY TO PERFORM PARTICULAR ACTIVITIES an inability to perform some or all of the tasks of daily life **2.** MEDICAL CONDITION RESTRICTING ACTIVITIES a medically diagnosed condition that makes it difficult to engage in the activities of daily life **3.** LEGAL DISQUALIFIER sth that causes sb to be regarded in law as ineligible to perform a particular transaction

disability clause *n.* a clause in a life insurance policy, indicating the conditions that will apply if the holder becomes unable to work, including release from payment of further premiums

disable /di sáyb'l/ (**-bles, -bling, -bled**) *vt.* **1.** RESTRICT IN CERTAIN ACTIVITIES to make sb unable to perform the activities needed to earn a living or to carry out the basic tasks of daily life without difficulty **2.** STOP FROM WORKING to prevent a machine, weapon, system, or device from working by disconnecting a part of it **3.** DISQUALIFY LEGALLY to make sb ineligible in law to perform a particular transaction —**disablement** *n.*

disabled /di sáyb'ld/ *adj.* **1.** UNABLE TO PERFORM PARTICULAR ACTIVITIES used to describe sb with a condition that makes it difficult to perform some or all the basic tasks of daily life **2.** UNABLE TO OPERATE incapable of performing or functioning ■ *npl.* DISABLED PEOPLE people who are disabled

disabuse /díssə byóoz/ (**-buses, -busing, -bused**) *vt.* to tell sb or make sb realize that an idea is not true ○ *I was quickly disabused of my idealistic notions about the campaign.* ○ *She disabused him of many old prejudices.* [Early 17thC. Formed from ABUSE in the obsolete sense 'a delusion'.] —**disabusal** *n.*

disaccharide /dī sákə rīd/ *n.* a sugar formed from two single sugar molecules, e.g. the disaccharide sucrose, which is composed of glucose and fructose. Lactose and maltose are also disaccharides.

disaccord /díssə káwrd/ *n.* DISAGREEMENT lack of harmony or agreement (*formal*) ■ *vi.* (**-cords, -cording, -corded**) NOT AGREE to disagree or not be in accordance with one another (*formal*)

disaccredit /díssə kréddit/ (**-its, -iting, -ited**) *vt.* to take away sb's authorization or credentials

disaccustom /díssə kústəm/ (**-toms, -toming, -tomed**) *vt.* to make sb break a habit, or to make sb become unused to sth that was familiar

disadvantage /díssəd váantij/ *n.* **1.** BAD THING sth that makes a situation less good, or that makes sb or sth less effective or desirable **2.** BAD SITUATION a situation in which sb is weaker or less effective in relation to other people **3.** LOSS injury, loss, or damage (*formal*) ■ *vt.* (**-tages, -taging, -taged**) COUNT AGAINST to put sb or sth at a disadvantage

disadvantaged /díssəd váantijd/ *adj.* **1.** BADLY OFF in a worse position than someone else or other people **2.** LACKING COMPETITIVE ABILITY unable to perform well in a competitive or military endeavour

disadvantageous /díss advən táyjəss, diss ádvən-/ *adj.* not helpful or favourable —**disadvantageously** *adv.* —**disadvantageousness** *n.*

disaffect /díssə fékt/ (**-fects, -fecting, -fected**) *vt.* to make sb dissatisfied with sb or sth, especially sb to whom respect or loyalty is owed —**disaffected** *adj.* —**disaffectedly** *adv.* —**disaffectedness** *n.* —**disaffection** /-féksh'n/ *n.*

disaffiliate /díssə fílli ayt/ (**-ates, -ating, -ated**) *vti.* to end the connection or affiliation of one group with another, or to withdraw a personal association from a group or organization formally ○ *The group was formally disaffiliated from its parent body at the end of 1985.* —**disaffiliation** /díssə fílli áysh'n/ *n.*

disaffirm /díssə fúrm/ (**-firms, -firming, -firmed**) *vt.* **1.** DENY OR CONTRADICT to say that sth is not true or that the opposite is true (*formal*) **2.** CHANGE DECISION to alter a legal decision or to refuse to recognize or acknowledge sth formally —**disaffirmance** *n.* —**disaffirmation** /díss affər máysh'n/ *n.*

disaggregate /diss ággrəgət, -gayt/ (**-gates, -gating, -gated**) *vti.* to separate sth into its component parts or to break apart —**disaggregation** /díss agrə gáysh'n/ *n.*

disagree /díssə grée/ (**-grees, -greeing, -greed**) *v.* **1.** *vt.* NOT AGREE to have or put forward a different view or opinion from sb or from each other **2.** *vi.* NOT MATCH to fail to be in accordance with sth, or to show a different result **3.** *vi.* AFFECT BADLY to have an unpleasant effect on sb ○ *I love oysters, but they disagree with me.* **4.** *vi.* DISAPPROVE OF to be opposed to a rule, law, or idea [15thC. From French *désagréer*, from *agréer* 'to agree'.]

WORD KEY: SYNONYMS

disagree, differ, argue, dispute, take issue with, contradict, agree to differ, be at odds

CORE MEANING: to have or express a difference of opinion with sb

disagree the most general and wide-ranging term; **differ** a slightly more formal term for *disagree*; **argue** to give reasons for or against sth, usually in opposition to sb else; **dispute** to debate sth, often suggesting a heated argument; **take issue with** to disagree strongly with sb or sth; **contradict** to make a statement that shows or suggests that sth sb has just said is wrong; **agree to differ** to stop arguing and accept that the opposing viewpoints are irreconcilable; **be at odds** a term used to refer to people who are disagreeing or arguing with each other, especially over a period of time or about a particular issue.

disagreeable /díssə grée əb'l/ *adj.* **1.** UNPLEASANT causing feelings that are not enjoyable **2.** RUDE OR QUARRELSOME lacking courtesy or constantly finding a reason to disagree with sb —**disagreeability** /díssə gree ə bílləti/ *n.* —**disagreeableness** /díssə grée əb'lnəss/ *n.* —**disagreeably** /-əbli/ *adv.*

disagreement /díssə gréemənt/ *n.* **1.** FAILURE TO AGREE ABOUT STH the fact of having or expressing a different opinion and failing to agree about sth **2.** SLIGHT ARGUMENT a situation in which a number of people or groups argue **3.** DIFFERENCE failure to be in accordance with sth

disallow /díssə lów/ (**-lows, -lowing, -lowed**) *vt.* **1.** REJECT to refuse to accept sth because it is not true, valid, or correctly done **2.** CANCEL STH PREVIOUSLY ALLOWED to cancel a privilege or entitlement, or refuse to allow sth that was previously allowed —**disallowable** *adj.* —**disallowance** *n.*

disambiguate /díss am bíggyoo ayt/ (**-ates, -ating, -ated**) *vt.* to establish the true meaning of an expression, regulation, or ruling that is confusing or that could be interpreted in more than one way —**disambiguation** /díss am biggyoo áysh'n/ *n.*

disannul /díssə núl/ (**-nuls, -nulling, -nulled**) *vt.* to annul or cancel a law, rule, or privilege [15thC. Formed from DIS- in the sense 'completely' + ANNUL.] —**disannulment** *n.*

disappear *v.* /díssə péer/ (**-pears, -pearing, -peared**) **1.** *vi.* VANISH FROM SIGHT to cease to be seen, e.g. by moving away, or going behind or into sth **2.** *vi.* NOT BE FOUND to be gone from or no longer be seen in a place without any explanation **3.** *vi.* CEASE TO EXIST to no longer exist **4.** *vt.* CAUSE OPPONENT TO DISAPPEAR to make a political opponent disappear by arresting or killing the person without any process of law —**disappearance** *n.*

disappeared /díssə péerd/ *npl.* people who have been arrested by a regime that they opposed and whose fate is not known [Late 20thC. Translation of the Spanish past participle *desaparecido*. Originally 'those who disappeared' in Argentina during the military dictatorship (1976–83).]

disapplication /díss ápplí káysh'n/ *n.* a special exemption from the National Curriculum given to a school

disappoint /díssə póynt/ (**-points, -pointing, -pointed**) *v.* **1.** *vi.* BE NOT GOOD ENOUGH to be less good, attractive, or satisfactory than was hoped or expected **2.** *vt.* FAIL SB to let sb down by not doing sth, or by sth not happening as hoped or expected [15thC. From French *désappointer*, literally 'to deprive of an appointment'.]

disappointed /díssə póyntid/ *adj.* unhappy because sth was not as good, attractive, or satisfactory as expected, or because sth hoped for or expected did not happen —**disappointedly** *adv.*

disappointing /díssə póynting/ *adj.* not as good, attractive, or satisfactory as was expected or hoped —**disappointingly** *adv.*

disappointment /díssə póyntmənt/ *n.* **1.** FEELING OF BEING LET DOWN a feeling of sadness or frustration because sth was not as good, attractive, or satisfactory as expected, or because sth hoped for did not happen **2.** STH DISAPPOINTING sth or sb that disappoints sb, or an occasion when sb is disappointed **3.** FRUSTRATION the frustration of sb's hopes or wishes

Disappointment, Lake /díssə póyntmənt-/ dry salt lake in Western Australia, once thought to have incorporated a lagoon, hence its name. Area: 330 sq. km/130 sq. mi.

disapprobation /diss áppra báysh'n/ *n.* the expression of moral or social disapproval (*formal*)

disapproval /díssə proóv'l/ *n.* dislike or condemnation of sb or sth immoral or bad in some way

disapprove /díssə proóv/ (**-proves, -proving, -proved**) *v.* **1.** *vi.* NOT APPROVE to dislike, look down on, or condemn sb or sth as being immoral or bad in some way **2.** *vt.* REFUSE TO SANCTION to refuse to give approval or agree to sth (*formal*) —**disapproving** *adj.* —**disapprovingly** *adv.*

WORD KEY: SYNONYMS

disapprove, frown on, object to, criticize, condemn, deplore, denounce, censure

CORE MEANING: to have an unfavourable opinion of sth or sb

disapprove a general term meaning to judge sth negatively based on personal standards; **frown on** a term indicating mild disapproval; **object to** a somewhat stronger term, usually implying verbal expression of disapproval; **criticize** to identify specific flaws or faults in sth; **condemn** to express very strong disapproval of sth, usually publicly; **deplore** a fairly formal term expressing strong disapproval, often for moral reasons; **denounce** to issue a strong public criticism of sb or sth, usually formally or for the record; **censure** to condemn sb or sth strongly and publicly.

disarm /diss áarm/ (**-arms, -arming, -armed**) *v.* **1.** *vti.* MIL **GIVE UP WEAPONS** to give up a supply of weapons or reduce the strength of armed forces, or to force another nation to do this **2.** *vt.* MIL **DEFUSE BOMB** to make a bomb unable to explode, or to make a weapon incapable of being fired **3.** *vt.* **WIN OVER** to make sb less hostile or suspicious and more inclined to act in a friendly way ○ *They disarmed us with their confidence and skill.* —**disarmer** *n.*

disarmament /diss áarmәmәnt/ *n.* **1. REDUCTION IN ARMS** the process of reducing a nation's supply of weapons or the strength of its armed forces ○ *a believer in negotiated mutual disarmament* **2. GIVING UP ARMS** the condition of having given up weapons ○ *Disarmament brought peace to the troubled region.* [Late 18thC. Modelled on French *désarmement*.]

disarming /diss áarming/ *adj.* making sb feel more friendly or trusting —**disarmingly** *adv.*

disarrange /díssә ráynj/ (**-ranges, -ranging, -ranged**) *vt.* to disturb or spoil the order or arrangement of sth —**disarrangement** *n.*

disarray /díssә ráy/ *n.* **1. DISORGANIZED STATE** a disorganized and confused state ○ *The meeting was thrown into disarray by the surprise announcement.* **2. UNTIDINESS** a state of untidiness, especially in dress ■ *vt.* (**-rays, -raying, -rayed**) **1. MAKE DISORGANIZED** to make sth confused and disorganized **2. UNDRESS** to remove sb's clothes (*archaic*) [14thC. Probably modelled on Old French *disareer* 'to put in disorder'.]

disarticulate /díss aar tíkyoo layt/ (**-lates, -lating, -lated**) *vti.* to separate sth at the joints, or to become separated at the joints —**disarticulation** /díss aar tíkyoo láysh'n/ *n.* —**disarticulator** /díss aar tíkyoo laytәr/ *n.*

disassemble /díssә sémb'l/ (**-bles, -bling, -bled**) *vt.* to take sth apart, e.g. a piece of machinery —**disassembly** *n.*

disassociate /díssә sṓshi ayt, -sṓssi-/ (**-ates, -ating, -ated**) *vt.* **1. END ASSOCIATION WITH** to end an association or relationship with another person or group ○ *She had disassociated herself from that clique years ago.* **2. DISTANCE SELF** to deny any connection or involvement with sb or sth ○ *In a press conference, the MP attempted to disassociate himself from the scandal*

disassociation /díssә sṓshi áysh'n, -sṓssi-/ *n.* **1. ENDING OF RELATIONSHIP** the termination of an association or relationship with another person or group **2. DISTANCING OF SELF** the denial of any connection or involvement with sb or sth else

disaster /di záastәr/ *n.* **1. DAMAGING OR DESTRUCTIVE EVENT** an event that causes serious loss, destruction, hardship, unhappiness, or death **2. SB OR STH UNSUCCESSFUL** sb or sth that fails completely, especially in a way that is distressing, embarrassing, or laughable (*informal*) [Late 16thC. Via French *désastre* from Italian *disastro*, literally 'ill-starred', from Latin *astrum* 'star', from Greek *astron* (source of English *astronomy*).]

disaster area *n.* **1. PLACE NEEDING HELP** a place that is officially declared to be in a state of emergency and in need of special assistance after a natural disaster ○ *The southern half of the state has been declared a disaster area.* **2. MESS** a very messy, untidy, or disorganized place or situation (*informal*)

disaster movie *n.* a film that deals with a disaster such as an earthquake or plane crash in a dramatic and spectacular way

disastrous /di záastrәss/ *adj.* **1. CALAMITOUS** having seriously damaging results **2. COMPLETELY UNSUCCESSFUL** performed in an incompetent or awkward way [Late 16thC. Via French *désastreux* from, ultimately, Italian *disastro* (see DISASTER).] —**disastrously** *adv.* —**disastrousness** *n.*

disavow /díssә vów/ (**-vows, -vowing, -vowed**) *vt.* to deny any knowledge of or responsibility for sth, or any association with sb or sth (*formal*) —**disavowable** *adj.* —**disavowal** *n.* —**disavowedly** /díssә vówidli/ *adv.* —**disavower** *n.*

disband /diss bánd/ (**-bands, -banding, -banded**) *vti.* to break up as a group or organization, or to cause a group or organization to break up —**disbandment** *n.*

disbar /diss báar/ (**-bars, -barring, -barred**) *vt.* to take away officially the right of a barrister to practise law [Mid-17thC. Literally 'to remove from the bar', formed from BAR.] —**disbarment** *n.*

disbelief /díss bi léef/ *n.* the feeling of not believing or of not being able to believe sb or sth

disbelieve /díss bi léev/ (**-lieves, -lieving, -lieved**) *v.* **1.** *vt.* **NOT BELIEVE** to think that sth sb has said is untrue **2.** *vi.* **HAVE NO FAITH** to have no belief in sth, especially in God or religion —**disbeliever** *n.* —**disbelieving** *adj.* —**disbelievingly** *adv.*

disbud /diss búd/ (**-buds, -budding, -budded**) *vt.* **1.** GARDENING **REMOVE BUDS** to remove buds or shoots from a plant so that the remaining ones will be larger and stronger **2.** AGRIC **REMOVE ANIMAL'S HORNS** to remove the horns from a young animal

disburden /diss búrd'n/ (**-dens, -dening, -dened**) *v.* **1.** *vt.* **SHARE TROUBLES WITH SB** to gain relief by telling sb about sth that is causing anxiety or guilt **2.** *vt.* **TAKE OFF A LOAD** to relieve a person or animal of a load **3.** *vti.* **UNLOAD** to unload goods or luggage (*archaic*) —**disburdenment** *n.*

disburse /diss búrss/ (**-burses, -bursing, -bursed**) *vt.* to pay out money, especially from a fund [Mid-16thC. From Old French *desbourser*, literally 'to remove from the purse', from *bourse* 'purse'.] —**disbursable** *adj.* —**disbursement** *n.* —**disburser** *n.*

disc[1] /disk/, **disk** *n.* **1. ROUND FLAT OBJECT** object that is, or appears to be, thin, flat, and circular **2.** CARS **BRAKE PART** a circular piece of metal around the hub of a vehicle wheel, against which the pads of a disc brake press **3.** AGRIC **STEEL BLADE** a circular steel blade with a sharpened edge that is used on a disc harrow or plough **4.** ANAT, ZOOL **PART BETWEEN BONES OF SPINE** a flat round structure in the skeleton of a person or animal that separates the bones of the spine **5.** BOT **CENTRE OF FLOWERHEAD** the central part of the flowerhead of a composite plant, made up of tiny tubular flowers [Mid-17thC. Directly or via French *disque* from Latin *discus* 'dish, quoit', from Greek *diskos* (see DISH).]

disc[2] *n.* record

disc. *abbr.* **1.** discount **2.** discovered

disc- *prefix.* = **disco-** (*used before vowels*)

discalced /diss kálst/ *adj.* wearing sandals or going barefoot as part of the rules of some orders of monks, friars, or nuns [Mid-17thC. Shortening of obsolete *discalceated*, literally 'with shoes removed', ultimately from Latin *calceare* 'to shoe', from *calceus* 'shoe'.]

discant /díss kant/ *n.*, *vi.* (**-cants, -canting, -canted**) MUSIC = **descant** —**discanter** *n.*

discard /diss káard/ *v.* (**-cards, -carding, -carded**) **1.** *vt.* **THROW AWAY** to get rid of sth that is not wanted or needed **2.** *vt.* CARDS **REJECT CARD** to put down a card from a hand and not play it **3.** *vti.* CARDS **PLAY CARD** to play a card so that it has no value, because it is neither in the required suit nor a trump ■ *n.* **1.** CARDS **ACT OF DISCARDING** the act of discarding a card **2. STH DISCARDED** sb or sth that has been discarded [Mid-18thC. Literally 'to throw out a card (from a hand)', formed from CARD; hence 'to cast aside'.] —**discardable** /diss káardәb'l/ *adj.* —**discarder** /-káardәr/ *n.*

discarnate /diss káarnәt, -nayt/ *adj.* RELIG lacking a physical body [Mid-17thC. Coined from DIS- + the Latin stem *carn-* 'flesh' + -ATE.]

disc brake *n.* a brake that works by the friction of a caliper or pads against a rotating disc

disc camera *n.* a camera that uses film on a disc rather than a spool or cartridge

discern /di súrn, -zúrn/ (**-cerns, -cerning, -cerned**) *v.* **1.** *vt.* **SEE OR NOTICE STH UNCLEAR** to see sth that is not very clear or obvious **2.** *vt.* **UNDERSTAND** to understand sth that is not immediately obvious **3.** *vti.* **DISTINGUISH** to be able to tell the difference between two or more things [14thC. Directly or via French *discerner* from Latin *discernere*, literally 'to separate off', from *cernere* 'to separate, determine' (source of English *certain*).] —**discerner** *n.*

discernible /di súrnәb'l, -zúrnәb'l/, **discernable** *adj.* able to be seen, recognized, or understood

discernibly /di súrnәbli, -zúrnәbli/, **discernably** *adv.* in an obvious way or to a noticeable extent ○ *not discernibly different*

discerning /di súrning, -zúrning/ *adj.* showing good judgment and good taste —**discerningly** *adv.*

discernment /di súrnmәnt, -zúrnmәnt/ *n.* good taste and judgment

disc flower, **disc floret** *n.* a tiny tubular flower that is one of the group that forms the centre disc of the flowerhead of certain composite plants, e.g. the daisy

discharge *v.* /diss cháarj/ (**-charges, -charging, -charged**) **1.** *vti.* **EMIT OR DUMP LIQUID OR GAS** to emit, give off, or dispose of a gas or liquid **2.** *vt.* **DISMISS FROM INSTITUTIONAL SETTING** to allow or write the orders for sb to leave an institution, especially a hospital, or to make the decision yourself to leave such a place after being an inpatient **3.** *vt.* **CARRY OUT** to carry out a duty, responsibility, or promise (*formal*) **4.** *vt.* **FREE OR RELEASE FROM DUTY** to excuse or release sb from a duty or obligation **5.** *vt.* COMM **DISMISS EMPLOYEE** to dismiss sb from a job (*formal*) **6.** *vt.* FIN **PAY DEBT** to pay a debt in full (*formal*) **7.** *vti.* ARMS **SHOOT OR BE SHOT FROM** to fire a weapon or to be fired from a weapon (*formal*) **8.** *vt.* MIL **BE RELEASED FROM ARMED FORCES** to be formally released from service in the armed forces **9.** *vt.* LAW **RELEASE OR ACQUIT** to release a prisoner or acquit sb in a court of law **10.** *vt.* LAW **CANCEL COURT ORDER** to cancel or annul a court order **11.** *vti.* FREIGHT, SHIPPING **OFFLOAD SHIP'S CARGO** to unload cargo from a ship **12.** *vti.* ELEC **LOSE ELECTRIC CHARGE** to lose or release electric charge by the addition or loss of electrons from a stationary body, such as in static electricity **13.** *vi.* ELEC **SPARK** to give off electricity suddenly in the form of a spark or arc, such as occurs in the release of stored energy in a capacitator **14.** *vti.* ELEC **DRAIN ELECTRICITY** to drain slowly, or make the electricity in a battery drain slowly **15.** *vt.* ARCHIT **RELEASE PRESSURE ON BUILDING** to release the pressure on part of a building by spreading it over adjacent parts **16.** *vt.* TEXTILES **BLEACH FABRIC** to remove the colour from fabric by bleaching it **17.** *vi.* TEXTILES **RUN OR BLUR** to undergo a running or blurring of dyes ■ *n.* /diss chaarj/ **1. DISMISSAL FROM INSTITUTION** permission or orders to leave an institution, especially a hospital, after being a patient **2.** MIL **SEPARATION FROM ARMED FORCES** formal and official release of sb from the armed forces, or a document certifying this **3.** MED **MUCUS** a flow of fluid from the body, especially an unusual or large flow of mucus from the bodily orifices or pus from a wound **4. EMISSION OF SUBSTANCES** the emission, giving off, or dumping of gases, liquids, or chemicals **5. RATE OF EMISSION** the rate at which a gas or liquid is being emitted **6. PERFORMANCE OF DUTY** the carrying out of a duty, obligation, responsibility, or promise (*formal*) **7.** FIN **DEBT PAYMENT** the payment of a debt (*formal*) **8.** ARMS **FIRING** the firing of a gun (*formal*) **9.** LAW **PRISONER'S RELEASE** the release of a prisoner from custody **10.** ELEC ENG **PRODUCTION OF ELECTRICITY** the process of converting chemical energy into electrical energy, e.g. in a battery **11.** ELEC ENG **CONTINUOUS FLOW OF ELECTRICITY THROUGH AIR** the continuous flow of electric energy through air or a gas as a result of ionization, as occurs when a spark jumps a gap, or at a reduced pressure, as in a fluorescent lamp **12.** FREIGHT **CARGO OFFLOADING** the unloading of cargo **13.** GEOG **VOLUME OF RIVER WATER FLOW** the volume of water in a river flowing past a particular point during a specific time interval [14thC. Via Old French *descharger* from late Latin *discar(r)icare* 'to unload', from Latin *car(r)icare* 'to load'.] —**dischargeable** /diss cháarjәb'l/ *adj.* —**discharger** /diss cháarjәr/ *n.*

WORD KEY: SYNONYMS

See Synonyms at ***perform***.

discharged bankrupt *n.* a person whose period of bankruptcy has come to an end, and who is no longer bound by the restrictions that apply to bankrupts

discharge lamp *n.* an electric lamp that glows as a result of electricity passing through a gas

discharge tube *n.* a tube filled with low-pressure gas that glows when it conducts electricity at a given voltage. Discharge tubes are used in neon and fluorescent lights.

disc harrow *n.* a harrow with a series of discs set at an angle on one or more axles that loosen the soil when moved over ploughed land

disci plural of **discus**

disci- *prefix.* = **disco-** (*used before vowels*)

disciple *n.* **1.** FOLLOWER OF PERSON OR IDEA sb who strongly believes in the teachings of a leader, a philosophy, or a religion, and tries to act according to them **2. disciple, Disciple** ORIGINAL FOLLOWER OF JESUS CHRIST one of the 12 original followers of Jesus Christ, according to the Bible [Pre-12thC. From Latin *discipulus* 'learner', from *discere* 'to learn'. Ultimately from an Indo-European word that is also the ancestor of English *doctrine*.] —**discipleship** *n.* —**discipular** /di sípyŏolər/ *adj.*

Disciple *n.* a member of the Disciples of Christ

Disciples of Christ *n.* a Protestant denomination of the Christian Church, founded in the United States in 1809 by Thomas and Alexander Campbell. Its congregations regard the Bible as the sole rule of faith and living, and practise baptism by total immersion.

disciplinant /díssəplinənt/ *n.* sb who belonged to a now defunct Spanish Roman Catholic group whose members whipped themselves in public as a religious penance [Early 17thC. Via Spanish *disciplinantes* or Italian *disciplinanti*, both plural, from medieval Latin *disciplinare* 'to discipline', from Latin *disciplina* (see DISCIPLINE).]

disciplinarian /díssəpli náiri ən/ *n.* sb who insists that rules are obeyed strictly, and who punishes people who break them

disciplinary /díssəplinəri/ *adj.* **1.** RELATING TO ENFORCEMENT AND PUNISHMENT relating to the enforcing of rules and the punishing of people who break them **2.** EDUC RELATING TO ACADEMIC SUBJECT relating to an academic subject ○ *Teachers tried to cut across traditional disciplinary boundaries in their lessons.* —**disciplinarily** *adv.* —**disciplinarity** /-nárrəti/ *n.*

discipline /díssəplin/ *n.* **1.** MAKING PEOPLE OBEY RULES the practice or methods of ensuring that people obey rules by teaching them to do so and punishing them if they do not **2.** ORDER AND CONTROL a controlled orderly state, especially in a class of school children **3.** CALM CONTROLLED BEHAVIOUR the ability to behave in a controlled and calm way even in a difficult or stressful situation **4.** CONSCIOUS CONTROL OVER LIFESTYLE mental self-control used in directing or changing behaviour, learning sth, or training for sth **5.** EDUC ACTIVITY OR SUBJECT a subject or field of activity, e.g. an academic subject **6.** PUNISHMENT punishment designed to teach sb to obey rules **7.** CHR CHURCH RULES the system of rules and punishment used in a particular religious denomination ■ *v.* (**-plines, -plining, -plined**) **1.** *vr.* MAKE YOURSELF DO STH REGULARLY to make yourself act or work in a controlled or regular way **2.** *vt.* PUNISH to punish sb because he or she has broken the rules **3.** *vt.* TEACH OBEDIENCE OR ORDER TO to teach sb to obey rules or to behave in an ordered or controlled way [13thC. Directly or via French *descepline* from Latin *disciplina* 'instruction given to a disciple', from *discipulus* (see DISCIPLE).] —**disciplinable** *adj.* —**disciplinal** /díssə plín'l/ *adj.* —**discipliner** /díssəplinər/ *n.*

disciplined *adj.* showing orderliness and control in the way sth is done or sb behaves ○ *a well disciplined child* ○ *a disciplined organization*

disc jockey *n.* = **DJ**

disclaim /diss kláym/ (**-claims, -claiming, -claimed**) *v.* **1.** *vt.* DENY A CONNECTION WITH to deny that you know about sth or that you are responsible for sth **2.** *vt.* DENY VALIDITY OF to refuse to accept the validity or authority of sth **3.** *vti.* RENOUNCE LEGAL RIGHT to renounce a legal claim or right to sth [15thC. Via Anglo-Norman *disclaimer* from Old French *desclamer*, literally 'not to claim', from *clamer* 'to claim'.] —**disclamation** /dísklə máysh'n/ *n.*

disclaimer /diss kláymər/ *n.* **1.** REFUSAL TO ACCEPT RESPONSIBILITY a statement refusing to accept responsibility for sth, e.g. a written warning stating a possible hazard associated with a product or service and denying legal liability for any injury **2.** LAW STATEMENT RENOUNCING LEGAL RIGHT a statement saying that sb gives up a legal right or claim to sth, e.g. damages arising from an accident **3.** DENIAL OF KNOWLEDGE a statement denying knowledge of sth

disclose /diss klṓz/ (**-closes, -closing, -closed**) *vt.* **1.** TELL STH PREVIOUSLY SECRET to reveal sth that has been kept a secret **2.** SHOW STH PREVIOUSLY COVERED to reveal sth that has been covered or hidden [15thC. From Old French *desclos-*, present stem of *desclore*, from medieval Latin *disclaudere* 'to open', from Latin *claudere* 'to close'.] —**disclosable** *adj.* —**discloser** *n.*

disclosing agent *n.* a dye in liquid or tablet form that colours sth, especially the teeth to show plaque

disclosure /dis klṓzhər/ *n.* the revealing of information that was previously kept secret, or the information that is revealed

disco /dískō/ *n.* **1. disco, discotheque** CLUB OR PARTY WITH DANCING a club or party where people dance to recorded pop music, often introduced by a DJ **2.** STEADY-BEAT POP MUSIC FOR DANCING a style of pop music, popular in the 1970s for dancing, with a steady, pronounced beat. It developed from soul music, in response to the growing popularity of discos. **3.** STYLE OF DANCING TO DISCO MUSIC a style of popular dancing designed to accompany the steady repetitive beat of disco music, typified by free and flamboyant swinging movements with the hips and arms **4.** EQUIPMENT PLAYING RECORDED MUSIC FOR DANCERS the audio equipment used to play records for crowds of people to dance to, usually consisting of amplifiers, speakers, and a record, tape, or CD deck, often with lighting equipment ■ *vi.* (**-cos, -coing, -coed**) TAKE PART IN DISCO DANCING to dance to disco music (*informal*) [Mid-20thC. Shortening of DISCOTHEQUE.]

disco- *prefix.* **1.** disk ○ *discoid* **2.** phonograph record ○ *discography* [Via Latin from, ultimately, Greek *diskos* (see DISK)]

discobolus /diss kóbbələss/ (*plural* **-li** /-lī/), **discobolos** (*plural* **-li**) *n.* HIST a discus thrower in ancient Greece [Early 18thC. Via Latin from Greek *diskobolos*, literally 'disc-throwing', from *diskos* 'disc' + *-bolos* 'throwing', from *ballein* 'to throw'.]

discography /diss kóggrəfi/ (*plural* **-phies**) *n.* a list of the recordings made by a performer or a group, or of the recordings of a particular category of music —**discographer** *n.* —**discographic** /dískə gráffik/ *adj.*

discoid /dísk oyd/ *n.* FLAT ROUND OBJECT a disc-shaped object or part ■ *adj.* **discoid, discoidal** DISC-SHAPED shaped like a disc [Late 18thC. From Greek *diskoeidēs*, from *diskos* (see DISCUS).] —**discoid** *adj.*

discoloration /diss kúllə ráysh'n/, **discolouration** *n.* a change in the original or proper colour of sth that gives it an unpleasant, faded, darkened, or dirty appearance

discolour /dis kúllər/ (**-ours, -ouring, -oured**) *vti.* to change, or make sth change, from the original or proper colour and take on an unpleasant, faded, darkened, or dirty appearance [14thC. Directly or via Old French *descolorer* from medieval Latin *discolorare*, from Latin *colorare* 'to colour'.] —**discoloured** *adj.* —**discolourment** *n.*

discombobulate /dískəm bóbbyŏo layt/ (**-lates, -lating, -lated**) *vt.* *US, Can* to throw sb into a state of disconcerting confusion (*informal; often passive*) [Mid-19thC. Origin uncertain: probably an alteration of DISCOMPOSE or DISCOMFIT.] —**discombobulation** /dískəm bóbbyŏo láysh'n/ *n.*

discomfit /dis kúmfit/ (**-fits, -fiting, -fited**) *vt.* **1.** MAKE UNSETTLED OR CONFUSED to make sb feel confused, uneasy, or embarrassed **2.** THWART PLANS to frustrate sb's plans (*formal*) **3.** MIL DEFEAT ENEMY to defeat an enemy in battle (*archaic*) [13thC. From Old French *desconfit*, past participle of *desconfire* 'to destroy', literally 'not to make', from *confire* 'to make', from Latin *conficere* (see CONFECT).] —**discomfiter** *n.* —**discomfiture** /dis kúmfichər/ *n.*

discomfort /dis kúmfərt/ *n.* **1.** STATE OF PHYSICAL UNEASE very mild pain or a feeling of being physically uncomfortable **2.** EMBARRASSMENT feelings of awkwardness and embarrassment **3.** CAUSE OF UNEASE sth that causes physical or mental uneasiness **4.** CAUSE OF LACK OF COMFORT sth that makes sb feel physically uncomfortable or inconvenienced ■ *vt.* (**, -forts, -forting, -forted**) MAKE UNCOMFORTABLE to make sb feel physically or mentally uncomfortable [14thC. From Old French *desconfort*, from *desconforter*, literally 'to deprive of comfort', from *conforter* 'to comfort'.] —**discomfortable** *adj.* —**discomforting** *adj.* —**discomfortingly** *adv.*

discommode /dískə mṓd/ (**-modes, -moding, -moded**) *vt.* to cause problems or inconvenience to sb (*formal*) [Early 18thC. From obsolete French *discommoder*, literally 'to deprive of convenience', ultimately from Latin *commodus* 'suitable'.] —**discommodious** *adj.* —**discommodiously** *adv.*

discompose /dískəm pṓz/ (**-poses, -posing, -posed**) *vt.* to make sb lose his or her composure (*formal*) —**discomposedly** /dískəm pṓzidli/ *adv.*

discomposure /dískəm pṓzhər/ *n.* the state of being anxious, confused, or physically disordered

disconcert /dískən súrt/ (**-certs, -certing, -certed**) *vt.* **1.** CAUSE TO FEEL UNEASY to make sb feel ill at ease, slightly confused, or taken aback **2.** UPSET OR FRUSTRATE PLANS to prevent sb from carrying out plans or arrangements and therefore create confusion [Mid-17thC. From French *desconcerter*, literally 'to bring out of agreement', ultimately from Old Italian *concertare* 'to bring into agreement', of unknown origin (source of English *concert*).] —**disconcertion** /dískən súrsh'n/ *n.* —**disconcertment** /-súrtmənt/ *n.*

disconcerted /dískən súrtid/ *adj.* ill at ease, slightly confused, or taken aback

disconcerting /dískən súrting/ *adj.* making sb feel uneasy confusion and dismay —**disconcertingly** *adv.*

disconfirm /dískən fúrm/ (**-firms, -firming, -firmed**) *vt.* to show that sth such as a theory cannot be right (*formal*) —**disconfirmation** /díss konfər máysh'n/ *n.*

disconformity /dískən fáwrməti/ (*plural* **-ties**) *n.* **1.** NONCONFORMITY nonconformity (*archaic*) **2.** GEOL BREAK IN CONTINUITY IN SEDIMENTARY ROCKS a break in the sedimentary record in which the rock layers remain parallel

disconnect /dískə nékt/ *v.* (**-nects, -necting, -nected**) **1.** *vti.* DETACH POWER SOURCE FROM APPLIANCE to break the connection between an appliance and its source of power **2.** *vt.* SHUT OFF SUPPLY OF PUBLIC UTILITY to shut off the telephone line or the supply of water, gas, or electricity to a building **3.** *vt.* BREAK TELEPHONE CONNECTION to break or lose the connection between two people who were speaking on the telephone (*usually passive*) **4.** *vt.* DETACH ONE PART FROM ANOTHER to detach sth that was connected to sth else **5.** *vti.* BREAK OFF EMOTIONAL OR SPIRITUAL RELATIONSHIP to end, forget, or lose an emotional or spiritual connection with sth or sb ■ *n.* DISCONNECTION a disconnection of joined parts or things ○ *a disconnect between his words and his acts* —**disconnecter** *n.* —**disconnective** *adj.*

disconnected /dískə néktid/ *adj.* showing no logical connection or relationship ○ *rambling disconnected prose* —**disconnectedly** *adv.* —**disconnectedness** *n.*

disconnection /dískə néksh'n/, **disconnexion** *n.* **1.** BREAK IN UTILITIES OR POWER CONNECTION the disconnecting of a telephone line or a supply of gas, water, or electricity **2.** SEPARATION the separation of things that were formerly linked or connected

disconsolate /diss kónssələt/ *adj.* miserable or disappointed and unable to be cheered up [15thC. From medieval Latin *disconsolatus* 'comfortless', from Latin *consolatus*, past participle of *consolare* (see CONSOLE).] —**disconsolately** *adv.* —**disconsolateness** *n.* —**disconsolation** /diss kónssə láysh'n/ *n.*

discontent /dískən tént/ *n.* **1.** DISSATISFIED UNHAPPINESS unhappiness or dissatisfaction **2.** RESTLESS LONGING FOR BETTER THINGS a restless desire for sth better (*literary*) **3.** SB WHO IS DISCONTENTED sb who is dissatisfied and unhappy with a situation (*literary or formal*) ■ *adj.* = **discontented** —**discontentment** *n.*

discontented /dískən téntid/ *adj.* feeling unhappy or dissatisfied with a situation —**discontentedly** *adv.* —**discontentedness** *n.*

discontinue /dískən tínnyoo/ (**-ues, -uing, -ued**) *v.* **1.** *vti.* STOP to come to an end after happening regularly, or end sth that has been happening regularly **2.** *vt.* STOP MANUFACTURING to stop manufacturing sth, usually a particular model or type of product [15thC. Via French *discontinuer* from medieval Latin *discontinuare*, literally 'not to continue', from Latin *continuare* 'to continue'.] —**discontinuance** *n.* —**discontinuation** /dískən tínnyoo áysh'n/ *n.* —**discontinuer** /dískən tínnyooər/ *n.*

discontinued /dískən tínyood/ *adj.* no longer manufactured and distributed (*refers to a product*)

discontinuity /díss konti nyóo əti/ (*plural* **-ties**) *n.* **1.** BREAK IN OTHERWISE CONTINUOUS PROCESS a break or gap in a process that would normally be continuous **2.** MATH POINT OF CHANGE the point or value of a variable at which a curve or mathematical function shows an abrupt change as the variable smoothly increases or decreases **3.** MATH LACK OF MATHEMATICAL CONTINUITY the characteristic of being discontinuous **4.** MATH MATHEMATICAL VALUE a value of a variable for which a function is not continuous **5.** GEOL BOUNDARY BETWEEN ROCK TYPES a boundary between rock types deep within the Earth's crust that is detected as a change in the speed of seismic waves

discontinuous /dískən tínnyoo əss/ *adj.* **1.** PROCEEDING INTERMITTENTLY having breaks or gaps in an otherwise continuous process or line **2.** MATH HAVING MATHEMATICAL DISCONTINUITY with a mathematical discontinuity (*refers to variables and functions*) —**discontinuously** *adv.* —**discontinuousness** *n.*

discord /díss kawrd/ *n.* **1.** LACK OF AGREEMENT disagreement or strife between people, things, or situations **2.** MUSIC UNPLEASANT MUSICAL SOUNDS unpleasant or harsh sounds clashing with each other, usually musical notes that produce a disagreeable combination [13thC. Via Old French *discorde* from Latin *discordia*, from *discord-*, stem of *discors*, literally 'heart apart', from *cors* 'heart'.]

discordance /diss káwrd'nss/, **discordancy** /-d'nssi/ *n.* **1.** = **discord 2.** GENETICS GENETIC TRAIT IN ONE SIBLING the occurrence of a genetic trait in just one twin or sibling

discordant /diss káwrd'nt/ *adj.* **1.** DISAGREEING in disagreement **2.** MUSIC SOUNDING UNPLEASANT consisting of sounds, usually musical notes, that are harsh, unpleasant, or clashing —**discordantly** *adv.*

discotheque /dískə tek/ *n.* = **disco** *n.* 1 [Mid-20thC. From French *discothèque*, from *disque* 'disk, record' (via Latin from Greek *diskos*; see DISCUS) + *-thèque* 'library' (from *bibliothèque*).]

discount *n.* /díss kownt/ **1.** REDUCTION IN PRICE a reduction in the usual price of sth **2.** FIN = **discount rate 3.** FIN INTEREST DEDUCTED FROM FINANCIAL INSTRUMENT the interest deducted from the face value of a financial instrument or promissory note before a sale or loan is completed **4.** STOCK EXCH DEDUCTION FROM PAR VALUE OF SHARES the amount by which the (**par value**) of shares exceeds the market price actually paid by purchasers ■ *v.* /diss kównt/ (**-counts, -counting, -counted**) **1.** *vt.* DISMISS AS UNTRUE OR TRIVIAL to decide that sth can be disregarded as unimportant, irrelevant, or untrue ○ *We had already discounted the theory that they were involved.* **2.** *vt.* BUSINESS REDUCE IN PRICE to reduce the price of sth by a particular amount or percentage **3.** *vt.* ANTICIPATE THEN ADJUST to foresee sth and make adjustments to lessen or absorb its impact ○ *Tax cuts in the next budget have already been discounted by the City.* **4.** *vt.* FIN TRADE INVESTMENT AT REDUCED PRICE to buy or sell a financial instrument at a reduced price that is calculated according to the interest rate and risk on the investment **5.** *vti.* FIN MAKE SECURED LOAN AT REDUCED RATE to lend money on a negotiable long-term financial instrument at a reduced price that is calculated according to the instrument's risk and the interest due before its maturity ■ *adj.* /diss kównt/ WITH REDUCED PRICE less than the usual price, or selling goods for less than the usual price ○ *a discount warehouse* [Early 17thC. Partly from French *descompte*; partly from Italian *discontare*; both from, ultimately, medieval Latin *discomputare*, literally 'to count away', from Latin *computare* (see COMPUTE).] —**discountable** /diss kówntəb'l, díss kowntəb'l/ *adj.* —**discounter** /diss kówntər, díss kowntər/ *n.*

discounted cash flow *n.* a method of valuing an investment by calculating what future cash returns will be worth at the time they are received, based on estimates of future inflation and interest rates

discountenance /diss kówntinənss/ *vt.* (**-nances, -nancing, -nanced**) (*formal*) **1.** EMBARRASS to make sb embarrassed **2.** DISAPPROVE OF to discourage or disapprove of sb or sth ■ *n.* DISFAVOUR disapproval of sb or sth (*formal*)

discount house *n.* a financial institution that buys and sells negotiable bills of exchange at discounted rates

discount market *n.* the part of the financial market trading in discounted commercial bills, including banks, brokers, and discount houses

discount rate *n.* FIN the rate at which expected cash returns from a security are converted into the security's market price

discount store *n.* a shop that sells goods at prices that are reduced from those recommended by the manufacturers

discourage /dis kúrrij/ (**-ages, -aging, -aged**) *vt.* **1.** TRY TO STOP SB'S ACTIONS to try to stop sb from doing sth **2.** TEND TO STOP to tend to prevent sth from happening by making it more difficult or unpleasant ○ *dirty beaches that discourage sunbathing* **3.** MAKE LESS OPTIMISTIC to make sb feel less motivated, confident, or optimistic [15thC. From Old French *descoragier*, literally 'to deprive of courage', from *corage* 'courage'.] —**discourager** *n.*

discouragement /dis kúrrijmənt/ *n.* **1.** LOSS OF OPTIMISM feelings of lost motivation, confidence, or optimism **2.** ATTEMPTS TO STOP STH the process of attempting to stop sb from doing sth or to prevent sth happening **3.** STH THAT CAUSES LOSS OF OPTIMISM sth that makes sb lose motivation, confidence, or optimism

discouraging /dis kúrrijing/ *adj.* making sb feel less motivation, confidence, or optimism about sth —**discouragingly** *adv.*

discourse *n.* /díss kawrss/ **1.** SERIOUS SPEECH OR PIECE OF WRITING a serious and lengthy speech or piece of writing about a topic **2.** SERIOUS CONVERSATION serious discussion about sth between people or groups **3.** LING LANGUAGE language, especially the type of language used in a particular context or subject **4.** LING MAJOR UNIT OF LANGUAGE a unit of language, especially spoken language, that is longer than the sentence. The term is used by linguists when investigating features of language that extend beyond sentences. **5.** REASONING ABILITY reasoning or the ability to reason (*archaic*) ■ *vi.* /diss káwrs/ (**-courses, -coursing, -coursed**) **1.** SERIOUSLY SPEAK OR WRITE ON TOPIC to speak or write about a subject in a formal context and at length ○ *In the second part, the author discourses on ethics.* **2.** CONVERSE to have a conversation (*formal*) [15thC. From Latin *discursus* 'running to and fro', from *discurrere*, literally 'to run apart', from *currere* 'to run' (see CURRENT).] —**discourser** /diss káwrssər/ *n.*

discourteous /diss kúrti əss/ *adj.* lacking in politeness or good manners —**discourteously** *adv.* —**discourteousness** *n.*

discourtesy /diss kúrtəssi/ (*plural* **-sies**) *n.* behaviour or an action that is bad-mannered or impolite

discover /dis kúvvər/ (**-ers, -ering, -ered**) *vt.* **1.** FIND OUT ABOUT to find out information that was not previously known ○ *We discovered she'd known all along.* **2.** BE FIRST TO FIND OR LEARN to be the first person to find or learn sth previously unknown ○ *researchers discovered a new genetic link to the causes of the disease* **3.** FIND to find sb or sth unexpectedly or after a search ○ *The missing child was finally discovered in the town centre.* **4.** FIRST NOTICE INTEREST IN to realize for the first time that you enjoy or have a talent for a particular thing ○ *Having discovered painting in her 50s, she ended up making a living by it.* **5.** RECOGNIZE SB'S TALENT OR BEAUTY to realize that a musician, actor, performer, or everyday citizen has exceptional talent or unusual beauty, and help to bring him or her to prominence [14thC. Via Old French *descovrir* from late Latin *discooperire*, literally 'to uncover', from Latin *cooperire* 'to cover'.] —**discoverable** *adj.*

discovered check *n.* a move in chess that creates a check previously blocked by the piece moved

discoverer /di skúvvərər/ *n.* the person who is the first to find out sth new or to find a new place or thing ○ *Gay-Lussac was the discoverer of boron.*

discovery /di skúvvəri/ (*plural* **-ies**) *n.* **1.** STH LEARNED OR FOUND sth new that has been learnt or found ○ *These dinosaur remains were one of the most important discoveries of the century.* **2.** PROCESS OF LEARNING STH PREVIOUSLY UNKNOWN the fact or process of finding out about sth for the first time ○ *the discovery of DNA* ○ *a voyage of discovery* **3.** PROCESS OF FINDING STH the finding of sb or sth new or unexpected, or after a search **4.** RECOGNITION OF UNUSUAL TALENT OR BEAUTY the recognition of sb's exceptional talent or beauty, leading to that person's fame, or the person who is recognized in this way **5.** LAW MUTUAL DISCLOSING OF DATA OR DOCUMENTS the stage of a legal proceeding during which each side must provide data and documents to the other side **6.** LAW DISCLOSABLE DATA AND DOCUMENTS data or materials that a party in a legal proceeding must disclose to another party before or during the proceeding

Discovery Bay /di skúvvəri-/ bay on the southern New South Wales coast, Australia, southwest of Melbourne. It is 80 km/50 mi. wide.

disc plough *n.* an agricultural implement with a cutting disc fixed in a frame that is drawn by a tractor that cuts furrows in the soil and turns it up

discredit /dis kréddit/ *vt.* (**-its, -iting, -ited**) **1.** HARM REPUTATION OF to make sb or sth appear untrustworthy or wrong **2.** CAUSE TO SEEM DOUBTFUL to cast doubt on the validity or accuracy of sth **3.** NOT BELIEVE to not accept that sth is accurate or true ○ *Scientists generally discredit the theory of canals on Mars.* ■ *n.* **1.** LOSS OF REPUTATION the loss of sb's or sth's good name or reputation, or the person or thing that causes its loss ○ *Their conduct is regarded as a discredit to the whole industry.* **2.** DOUBT OR SUSPICION doubt about the validity or accuracy of sth

discreditable /dis krédditəb'l/ *adj.* bringing shame or dishonour to sb's good name or reputation —**discreditably** *adv.*

discreet /di skréet/ *adj.* **1.** CAREFUL TO AVOID OFFENDING PEOPLE careful to avoid embarrassing or upsetting others **2.** GOOD AT KEEPING SECRETS careful not to speak about anything that should be secret or confidential **3.** CIRCUMSPECTLY SUBTLE AND CAREFUL subtle and circumspect, ensuring that no undue attention is attracted **4.** MODEST modest, and not ostentatious or flashy [14thC. Via French *discret* from Latin *discretus* 'distinct', past participle of *discernere* 'to distinguish' (see DISCERN).] —**discreetness** *n.*

discreetly /di skréetli/ *adv.* taking care to avoid upsetting or embarrassing people, giving away anything confidential, or appearing immodest or flashy

discrepancy /di skréppənssi/ (*plural* **-cies**) *n.* a distinct difference between two things, e.g. sets of figures, that should match or correspond

discrepant /di skréppənt/ *adj.* differing where a match or correspondence is expected [15thC. From Latin *discrepant-*, present participle stem of *discrepare* 'to differ', literally 'to rattle apart', from *crepare* 'to rattle'.] —**discrepantly** *adv.*

discrete /diss kréet/ *adj.* **1.** COMPLETELY SEPARATE completely separate and unconnected **2.** MATH FINITE used to describe elements or variables that are distinct, unrelated, and have a finite number of values [14thC. From Latin *discretus* (see DISCREET).] —**discretely** *adv.*

discretion /di skrésh'n/ *n.* **1.** ABILITY TO AVOID OFFENCE the good judgment and sensitivity needed to avoid embarrassing or upsetting others **2.** FREEDOM TO DECIDE the freedom or authority to judge sth or make a decision about it ○ *Tipping is left to the customer's discretion.* **3.** CONFIDENTIALITY the ability to keep sensitive information secret [14thC. Via French *discrétion* from the Latin stem *discretion-* 'separation', later 'discernment', from *discret-*, past participle stem of *discernere* (see DISCERN).]

discretionary /di skrésh'nəri/ *adj.* **1.** GIVING SB AUTHORITY TO DECIDE giving sb the freedom to make a decision according to individual circumstances **2.** GIVEN OR REFUSED ACCORDING TO CIRCUMSTANCES given according to the merits of an individual case, rather than being provided or awarded automatically **3.** USABLE AS

WANTED able to be used as desired without any stipulations —**discretionarily** adv.

discretionary account n. a securities account in which the broker has been given the authority to make decisions about buying and selling without the customer's prior permission

discretionary trust n. a trust in which sb other than its founder, e.g. a trustee, determines the beneficiaries' shares

discriminable /di skrímminəb'l/ adj. able to be perceived as different or distinct [Mid-18thC. Coined from DISCRIMINATE + -ABLE.] —**discriminability** /di skrímminə bílləti/ n. —**discriminably** /di skrímminəbli/ adv.

discriminant /di skrímminənt/ n. MATH a relation between the coefficients a, b and c of a mathematical expression of the form $ax^2 + bx + c = 0$, used in the study of roots and other properties of the expression [Mid-19thC. From Latin discriminant-, present participle stem of discriminare (see DISCRIMINATE).]

discriminant function n. a statistical method used to place an item that could belong to any of two or more sets of variables in the correct set, with a minimal probability of error

discriminate /di skrímmi nayt/ v. (-nates, -nating, -nated) 1. vi. TREAT GROUP UNFAIRLY BECAUSE OF PREJUDICE to treat one person or group worse than others or better than others, usually because of a prejudice about race, ethnic group, age group, religion, or gender 2. vti. DISCERN DIFFERENCE to recognize or identify a difference ○ could not discriminate between red and green 3. vi. BE AWARE OF DIFFERENCES to pay attention to subtle differences and exercise judgment and taste ■ adj. SHOWING DISCRIMINATION showing the ability to appreciate quality or notice differences [Early 17thC. From Latin discriminat-, the past participle stem of discriminare 'to divide', from the stem discrimin- 'division', from discernere (see DISCERN).] —**discriminately** /-nətli/ adv.

discriminating /di skrímmi nayting/ adj. 1. RECOGNIZING DISTINCTIONS AND VALUING QUALITY able to identify subtle differences and appreciate good quality or taste ○ Discriminating customers prefer these handmade linens. 2. FIN DIFFERENTIAL used to describe tariffs that are set at different rates for different importers —**discriminatingly** adv.

discrimination /di skrímmi náysh'n/ n. 1. TREATING PEOPLE DIFFERENTLY THROUGH PREJUDICE unfair treatment of one person or group, usually because of prejudice about race, ethnic group, age group, religion, or gender 2. ABILITY TO NOTICE AND VALUE QUALITY the ability to appreciate good quality or taste 3. ATTUNEMENT TO SUBTLE DIFFERENTIATION the ability to notice subtle differences 4. ELECTRON ENG SIGNAL SELECTION the selection of a transmitted signal with a particular characteristic, such as frequency, by elimination of signals with other characteristics, using a discriminator —**discriminational** adj.

discriminative /di skrímminətiv/ adj. 1. = discriminatory adj. 1 2. RECOGNIZING DISTINCTIONS recognizing and acknowledging distinctions and differences —**discriminatively** adv.

discriminator /di skrímmi naytər/ n. ELECTRON ENG a device or circuit that translates phase or frequency variations into amplitude variations in a modulated signal, e.g. a radio signal, and is used to select signals with particular characteristics

discriminatory /di skrímminətəri/ adj. SOCIOL UNFAIRLY TREATING treating a person or group unfairly, especially because of prejudice about race, ethnicity, age, or gender 2. STATS STATISTICALLY UNBIASED used to describe a statistical test that is unbiased because the sampling procedure avoided the systematic distortion that could be introduced by an unrepresentative population —**discriminatorily** adv.

disc sander n. an electrically powered tool with a revolving abrasive disc, used for sanding, grinding, and polishing irregular surfaces

discursive /diss kúrssiv/ adj. 1. LENGTHY WITH DIGRESSIONS lengthy and including extra material that is not essential to what is being written or spoken about ○ One book is concise and snappy, while the other has a more relaxed, discursive style. 2. PHILOS RATIONAL using logic rather than intuition to reach a con-

clusion [Late 16thC. From medieval Latin discursivus, from discurs-, the past participle stem of discurrere (see DISCOURSE).] —**discursively** adv. —**discursiveness** n.

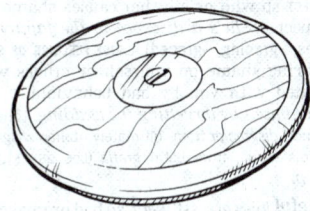

Discus

discus /dískəss/ (plural -cuses or -ci /-ī/) n. 1. ATHLETICS DISC THROWN IN ATHLETICS a weighted disc thrown in competitions by an athlete who spins with outstretched arms to launch it from the flat of his or her hand. The ancient Greek Olympic games included the throwing of a bronze discus. 2. ATHLETICS EVENT OF THROWING DISCUS the event or sport in which athletes compete to throw a discus as far as possible 3. ZOOL COLOURFUL AQUARIUM FISH a small colourful South American freshwater fish that has a compressed disc-shaped body and is popular as an aquarium fish. Latin name: Symphysodon discus. [Mid-17thC. Via Latin from Greek diskos 'disk, quoit, platter' (source of English disc and dish).]

discuss /di skúss/ (-cusses, -cussing, -cussed) vt. 1. TALK OVER to talk about a subject with others ○ need to discuss it with them first 2. WRITE OR SPEAK ABOUT TOPIC FORMALLY to consider a particular topic in speaking or writing ○ Chapter 3 discusses the events leading up to the War of Independence. [14thC. From Latin discuss-, past participle stem of discutere 'to dash to pieces', literally 'to shake apart', from quatere 'to shake'.] —**discussant** n. —**discusser** n. —**discussible** adj.

discussion /di skúsh'n/ n. 1. TALK BETWEEN PEOPLE talk or a talk between two or more people about a subject 2. SPOKEN OR WRITTEN EXAMINATION OF TOPIC a detailed consideration or examination of a topic in writing or speech —**discussional** adj.

disc wheel n. a car wheel with a continuous flat outer surface instead of spokes

disdain /diss dáyn/ n. INTENSE SCORN extreme contempt or disgust for sth or sb ■ vt. (-dains, -daining, -dained) LOOK DOWN ON to regard sb or sth as not worthy of respect [14thC. Origin uncertain: probably ultimately from Old French desdeignier, literally 'to treat as unworthy', from late Latin dedignare, from dignare 'to treat as worthy'.]

disdainful /diss dáynf'l/ adj. showing or feeling contempt or disrespect for sb or sth —**disdainfully** adv. —**disdainfulness** n.

disease /di zéez/ n. 1. MED MEDICAL CONDITION IN HUMANS a condition that results in medically significant symptoms in a human 2. BOT, VET MEDICAL CONDITION IN PLANTS OR ANIMALS a condition in plants or animals that causes medically significant symptoms 3. SPECIFIC DISORDER a disorder with recognizable signs and often having a known cause 4. PROBLEM IN SOCIETY a serious problem in society or with a particular group of people [14thC. From Old French desaise, literally 'lack of ease', from aise 'ease'.]

diseased /di zéezd/ adj. 1. MED, BOT, VET HAVING DISEASE affected by a disease 2. CORRUPT OR UNBALANCED affected, or seemingly affected by corruption or psychiatric disorder

diseconomy /díssi kónnəmi/ (plural -mies) n. ECON sth that contributes to increased costs

disembark /díssim báark/ (-barks, -barking, -barked) v. 1. vi. GET OFF PASSENGER VEHICLE to get off a passenger vehicle, especially a ship, aircraft, or train 2. vt. PUT PASSENGERS OR CARGO OFF VEHICLE to let passengers off a ship, bus, train, or aircraft, or to unload cargo (formal) [Late 16thC. From French désembarquer, Spanish desembarcar, or Italian disimbarcare, which were formed from French embarquer or the equivalent (see EMBARK).]

disembarkation /diss ém baar káysh'n, díss im-/ n. —**disembarkment** /díss im báarkmənt/ n.

disembarrass /díssim bárrəss/ (-rasses, -rassing, -rassed) vt. to free sb from sth embarrassing, unpleasant, or burdensome (formal) —**disembarrassment** n.

disembodied /díssim bóddid/ adj. coming from sb who cannot be seen, often regarded as eerie or frightening ○ a disembodied voice whispering in the darkness

disembody /díssim bóddi/ (-ies, -ying, -ied) vt. to free the soul or spirit from the body —**disembodiment** n.

disembowel /díssim bówəl/ (-els, -elling, -elled) vt. 1. REMOVE SB'S INTERNAL ORGANS to cut open the stomach of a person or animal and remove the internal organs, especially the intestines 2. CUT OUT SUBSTANCE to remove the internal substance, elements, or parts of sth (literary) —**disembowelment** n.

disembroil /díssim bróyl/ (-broils, -broiling, -broiled) vt. to free yourself or sb else from a difficult situation

disemploy /díssim plóy/ (-ploys, -ploying, -ployed) vt. to stop sb or sth from working (formal) —**disemployment** n.

disempower /díssim pówər/ (-ers, -ering, -ered) vt. to take power or influence away from sb or from yourself

disempowerment /díssim pówərmənt/ n. the loss of personal worth, self-esteem, or power, or the process of losing these

disenable /díssi náyb'l/ (-bles, -bling, -bled) vt. to prevent sth or make sth unable to operate or perform a function ○ disenabled the weapons system on the aircraft prior to landing —**disenablement** n.

disenchant /díssin cháant/ (-chants, -chanting, -chanted) vt. 1. CAUSE TO LOSE INTEREST to make sb stop believing that sth or sb is worthwhile, right, or deserving of support 2. FREE FROM MAGIC SPELL to free sb from an enchantment or magic spell [Late 16thC. From French désenchanter, literally 'to undo enchantment', from enchanter 'to enchant'.] —**disenchanter** n. —**disenchanting** adj. —**disenchantingly** adv.

disenchanted /díssin cháantid/ adj. no longer happy, supportive, or enthusiastic about sth or sb —**disenchantedly** adv.

disenchantment /díssin cháantmənt/ n. the loss of happiness about, satisfaction with, or enthusiasm for sth or sb ○ a growing disenchantment with the new government

disencumber /díssin kúmbər/ (-bers, -bering, -bered) vt. to relieve sb or sth of a burden or problem —**disencumberment** n.

disendow /díssin dów/ (-dows, -dowing, -dowed) vt. to withdraw an endowment, especially a gift of money —**disendower** n. —**disendowment** n.

disenfranchise /díssin fránch īz/ (-chises, -chising, -chised) vt. to deprive a person or organization of a privilege, immunity, or legal right, especially the right to vote —**disenfranchisement** /-fránchizmənt/ n.

disengage /díssin gáyj/ (-gages, -gaging, -gaged) v. 1. vti. PHYSICALLY DISCONNECT OR BECOME DISCONNECTED to disconnect one thing from another, or to become disconnected from sth 2. vt. MENTALLY DISCONNECT OR BECOME UNINVOLVED to mentally separate yourself or sb else from, or to become uninvolved in, a situation or difficulty 3. vti. MIL STOP FIGHTING IN WAR to bring troops out of, or end involvement in, a war or combat 4. vti. FENCING MOVE SWORD IN FENCING to move the point of your sword around an opponent's sword in order to open a new line of attack

disengagement /díssin gáyjmənt/ n. 1. RELEASE FROM STH the process or action in which sth or sb is released from a physical or mental attachment 2. MIL WITHDRAWAL OF ARMY the withdrawal of troops or an army from a war or combat

disentail /díssin táyl/ (-tails, -tailing, -tailed) vt. FIN, LAW to lift the restrictions on who may inherit a person's property —**disentailment** n.

disentangle /díssin táng g'l/ (-gles, -gling, -gled) vt. 1. UNTANGLE to untangle and free things that are muddled, tied, or knotted together 2. DISTINGUISH, ANALYSE, OR UNDERSTAND to clarify sth confusing, or to separate and analyse a confusion of ideas ○ *It was hard to disentangle fact from fiction in his account.* **3.** BREAK OFF RELATIONSHIP to free sb or yourself from a relationship or connection —**disentanglement** *n.*

disenthral /dissin thráwl/ (**-thrals, -thralling, -thralled**) *vt.* to set sb free from a situation of harsh control, or a condition resembling servitude (*formal*) —**disenthralment** *n.*

disentitle /dissin tít'l/ (**-tles, -tling, -tled**) *vt.* to take away sb's title or sb's right to sth (*formal*)

disentomb /dissin tóom/ (**-tombs, -tombing, -tombed**) *vt.* to take a body out of a tomb or from a place like a tomb. ◊ **exhume**

disentwine /dissin twín/ (**-twines, -twining, -twined**) *vti.* to become untangled or to untangle things that have become twisted or tangled together (*formal*)

disequilibrate /díssi kwílli brayt/ (**-brates, -brating, -brated**) *vt.* to put sth into a state of unbalance (*formal*) —**disequilibration** /díssi kwílli bráysh'n/ *n.*

disequilibrium /díss eekwi líbbri əm/ *n.* a state of instability or imbalance, usually in the economy

disestablish /díssi stáblish/ (**-lishes, -lishing, -lished**) *vt.* **1.** STOP LONG ESTABLISHED CUSTOM to undo or change sth that has been established for a long time **2.** END CONNECTION BETWEEN CHURCH AND STATE to end the official relationship between the state and a nation's official church or religion

disestablishment /díssi stáblishmənt/ *n.* the act or process of separation between the state and a nation's official church or religion

disestablishmentarian /díssi stáblishmən táiri ən/ *n.* sb who is opposed to having a church that is connected to and supported by the state

disesteem /díssi stéem/ *vt.* (**-teems, -teeming, -teemed**) THINK BADLY OF to have a low opinion of sb or sth (*formal*) ■ *n.* NO RESPECT lack of respect or esteem (*formal*) ○ *held in disesteem*

diseur /dee zúr/ *n.* ARTS a man, usually an actor, who is an accomplished reciter of dramatic monologues. Such recitals, often accompanied by music, were once a popular form of theatrical entertainment. [From French, literally 'talker', from *dire* 'to say', from Latin *dicere* (see DICTION)]

diseuse /dee z/ *n.* ARTS a woman, usually an actor, who is an accomplished reciter of dramatic monologues. Such recitals, often accompanied by music, were once a popular theatrical entertainment. [Late 19thC. From French, feminine of *diseur* (see DISEUR).]

disfavour /diss fáyvər/ *n.* **1.** CONDITION OF DISAPPROVAL the state of being disapproved of ○ *This fell into disfavour years ago.* **2.** NO RESPECT OR APPROVAL disapproval or lack of respect ○ *They were looked on with disfavour.* ■ *vt.* (**-ours, -ouring, -oured**) NOT LIKE OR APPROVE OF to dislike or disapprove of sth (*formal*)

disfiguration /diss fíggə ráysh'n/ *n.* = **disfigurement** *n.* 2

disfigure /diss fíggər/ (**-ures, -uring, -ured**) *vt.* to mar the appearance of sb or sth [14thC. From Old French *desfigurer*, literally 'to deprive sth of its figure', from Latin *figura* 'figure'.]

disfigurement /diss fíggərmənt/ *n.* **1.** STH THAT WORSENS SB'S APPEARANCE sth, e.g. a very bad haircut, that spoils the appearance of sb or sth **2.** ACT, PROCESS, OR STATE OF DISFIGURING the worsening of the appearance of sb or sth

disforest /diss fórrist/ (**-ests, -esting, -ested**) *vt.* **1.** = **deforest 2.** LAW, FORESTRY = **disafforest**

disfranchise /diss fránch īz/ (**-chises, -chising, -chised**) *vt.* POL = **disenfranchise** —**disfranchisement** /diss fránchizmənt/ *n.*

disfrock /dis frók/ (**-frocks, -frocking, -frocked**) *vt.* CHR = **defrock**

disgorge /dis gáwrj/ (**-gorges, -gorging, -gorged**) *vt.* **1.** POUR SUBSTANCES OUT to pour out liquid, gas, or other contents in a gushing stream **2.** LET PEOPLE OUT to let a large number of people come out of a building or vehicle at the same time ○ *a cruise ship disgorging thousands of passengers* **3.** REGURGITATE OR VOMIT to vomit or regurgitate food that has been eaten or partly eaten, as some birds and mammals do to feed their young [15thC. From Old French *desgorger*, literally 'to expel from the throat', from *gorge* 'throat' (source of English *gorge*).] —**disgorgement** *n.*

disgrace /diss gráyss/ *n.* **1.** STATE OF BEING DISAPPROVED OF shame or loss of respect arising from bad behaviour ○ *She was sent home in disgrace.* **2.** CAUSE OF SHAME OR DISRESPECT sb who or sth that causes shame or loss of respect ○ *She's a disgrace to the family.* ■ *vt.* (**-graces, -gracing, -graced**) CAUSE FEELINGS OF SHAME TO SB to bring shame on yourself or others who are associated with you by bad behaviour ○ *He disgraced himself by forgetting the wedding.* [Mid-16thC. Via French *disgracier* from, ultimately, Italian *disgrazia*, literally 'disfavour', from Latin *gratia* (see GRACE).] —**disgracer** *n.*

disgraceful /diss gráyssf'l/ *adj.* so bad or unacceptable that it is sth to be ashamed of ○ *The way they were treated was disgraceful.* —**disgracefully** *adv.* —**disgracefulness** *n.*

disgruntle /diss grúnt'l/ (**-tles, -tling, -tled**) *vt.* to make sb feel dissatisfied and irritated [Mid-17thC. Literally 'to grumble greatly', formed from obsolete *gruntle* 'to grumble, grunt', literally 'to grunt repeatedly', from GRUNT.] —**disgruntlement** *n.*

disgruntled /diss grúnt'ld/ *adj.* in a state of resentful dissatisfaction, anger, and irritation

disguise /diss gíz/ *vt.* (**-guises, -guising, -guised**) **1.** CHANGE SB'S APPEARANCE FOR CONCEALMENT to make changes in the appearance of sb or sth to avoid being recognized ○ *He fled the besieged city disguised as a woman.* **2.** HIDE STH TO PREVENT OTHERS KNOWING to hide feelings or facts from other people ○ *She couldn't disguise her horror.* **3.** CHANGE STH TO PREVENT RECOGNITION to change sth so that it cannot be recognized ○ *His voice has been disguised during the interview to conceal his identity.* ■ *n.* **1.** STH DONE TO PREVENT RECOGNITION sth worn or done in order to change sb's appearance and prevent recognition ○ *Anyone would have seen through such a flimsy disguise.* **2.** ALTERATION OR CONCEALMENT TO PREVENT RECOGNITION the alteration or concealment of sth in order to prevent it being seen or recognized by others ○ *a plot that relies on disguise* **3.** STATE OF ALTERED APPEARANCE an altered appearance intended to conceal sb's identity or make sb look like sb else ○ *The film star must be travelling in disguise.* [14thC. From Old French *desguis(i)er*, literally 'to remove your appearance', from *guise* 'appearance' (source of English *guise*).] —**disguisable** *adj.* —**disguiser** *n.*

disguised /diss gízd/ *adj.* **1.** CHANGED TO PREVENT RECOGNITION changed in appearance so as to prevent recognition **2.** CONCEALED concealed in an attempt to prevent recognition —**disguisedly** /diss gízidli/ *adv.*

disgust /diss gúst/ *n.* **1.** STRONG DISAPPROVAL OR REVULSION a feeling of horrified or sickened distaste for sth ○ *viewed the tawdry scandal with unconcealed disgust* **2.** IMPATIENT IRRITATION a feeling of impatient irritation ○ *Much to my disgust, I was compelled to hand over the documents.* ■ *vt.* (**-gusts, -gusting, -gusted**) MAKE SB FEEL REVOLTED to make sb feel sickened or revolted [Late 16thC. Via either French *desgoust* or Italian *disgusto*, literally 'to have a distaste for', from, ultimately, Latin *gustus* 'taste' (source of English *gusto*).] —**disgusted** *adj.* —**disgustedly** *adv.* —**disgustedness** *n.* —**disgustful** *adj.*

WORD KEY: SYNONYMS

See Synonyms at ***dislike***.

disgusting /diss gústing/ *adj.* **1.** REPELLENT AND SICKENING tending to repel and sicken people ○ *a disgusting smell* **2.** DISGRACEFUL completely unacceptable or disgraceful ○ *a disgusting waste of money* —**disgustingly** *adv.* —**disgustingness** *n.*

dish /dish/ *n.* **1.** HOUSEHOLD CONTAINER FOR SERVING FOOD a container for serving food **2.** FOOD SERVING OF FOOD a serving or plateful of food, especially one that forms only part of a larger meal **3.** FOOD FOOD PREPARED TO RECIPE OR STYLE food prepared to a particular recipe or in a particular style **4.** SCI SHALLOW OPEN CONTAINER a shallow open container used, e.g., in laboratories or hospitals **5.** ELECTRON ENG RADIO OR TELEVISION AERIAL a dish-shaped aerial transmitting and receiving radio or television signals, used, e.g. in radar and satellite broadcasting **6.** GEOL HOLLOW PLACE a shallow depression, e.g. in rock **7.** GOOD-LOOKING PERSON a good-looking person (*slang*) ■ **dishes** *npl.* HOUSEHOLD DIRTY PLATES, CUTLERY, AND PANS the plates, eating utensils, and pans that are dirtied during the cooking and eating of a meal ○ *my turn to wash the dishes* ■ *vt.* (**dishes, dishing, dished**) **1.** RUIN STH to ruin or thwart sth ○ *The rejection letter dished her hopes of a university place.* **2.** HOLLOW OUT to make or form a concave shape in sth [Pre-12thC. Via Latin *discus* 'dish, platter' from Greek *diskos* 'disc, platter', from *dikein* 'to throw' (source of English *discus*).]

dish out *vt.* **1.** HAND OUT FREELY to give sth out freely, especially criticism, money, punishment, or advice (*informal*) **2.** SERVE FOOD to serve food to people ○ *dishing out mashed potatoes*

dish aerial *n.* a transmitting and receiving aerial in the form of a dish-shaped reflector, used, e.g., in radar and in satellite broadcasting. US term **dish antenna**

dish antenna (*plural* **dish antennas** *or* **dish antennae**) *n.* *US* = **dish aerial**

disharmony /diss haármoni/ *n.* **1.** CONFLICT BETWEEN PEOPLE disagreement or conflict between people or groups who cannot get along with each other **2.** MUSIC LACK OF MUSICAL HARMONY lack of agreement in music or sounds, resulting in unpleasant sound combinations **3.** IMBALANCE lack of balance in sth such as the body or the environment —**disharmonious** /díss haar mōni əss/ *adj.* —**disharmoniously** /-əssli/ *adv.*

dishcloth /dísh kloth/ *n.* **1.** = **tea towel 2.** CLOTH FOR WASHING DISHES a cloth used for washing dishes

dishearten /diss haárt'n/ (**-ens, -ening, -ened**) *vt.* to make sb lose hope and enthusiasm —**disheartenment** *n.*

disheartening /diss haárt'ning/ *adj.* making sb lose hope or enthusiasm —**dishearteningly** *adv.*

dished /disht/ *adj.* **1.** CONCAVE hollowed out in a shape like a dish **2.** AUTOMOT POINTING IN TOWARDS EACH OTHER used to describe pairs of vehicle wheels that are set at an angle so that the bottoms are closer together than the tops **3.** DEFEATED completely exhausted, beaten, or thwarted

dishevel /di shévv'l/ (**-els, -eling** *or* **-elling, -eled** *or* **-elled**) *vt.* to disarrange sb's clothes or hair [Late 16thC. Origin uncertain: probably a back-formation from DISHEVELLED.] —**dishevelment** *n.*

disheveled *adj.* *US* = **dishevelled**

dishevelled *adj.* **1.** WITH UNTIDY HAIR OR CLOTHES with untidy hair or clothes **2.** UNTIDY disordered and untidy [14thC. From Old French *deschevelé*, past participle of *descheveler* 'to disarrange the hair', from *des-* 'apart' (from Latin *dis-*) + *chevel* 'hair' (from Latin *capillus*).]

dishonest /diss ónnist/ *adj.* meaning or meant to deceive, defraud, or trick people [14thC. Via Old French *deshoneste* from Latin *dehonestus*, from *honestus* 'honourable'.]

dishonestly /diss ónnistli/ *adv.* in a lying or deceitful way

dishonesty /diss ónnisti/ (*plural* **-ties**) *n.* **1.** DECEITFUL BEHAVIOUR the use of lies or deceit, or the tendency to be deceitful **2.** DISHONEST DEED a dishonest act or action

dishonor *n.*, *vt.* US = **dishonour**

dishonour *n.* **1.** LOSS OF OTHER PEOPLE'S RESPECT the loss of a good reputation **2.** CAUSE OF SHAME a cause of shame or loss of respect **3.** FIN FAILURE TO PAY CHEQUE failure or refusal by a bank or other financial institution to pay a cheque, bill of exchange, or other financial instrument ■ *vt.* (**-ours, -ouring, -oured**) **1.** BRING SHAME ON SB to do sth that brings shame on yourself or on people associated with you **2.** BREAK AGREEMENT to fail to keep a promise or agreement **3.** TREAT DISRESPECTFULLY to treat sb without any respect (*formal*) **4.** FIN FAIL TO PAY CHEQUE to fail to pay a cheque, bill of exchange, or other financial instrument (*formal*) **5.** DISGRACE WOMAN BY SEDUCTION OR RAPE to bring shame on a woman by seducing her before marriage, or by raping her (*archaic*) [14thC. Via Old French *deshonorer* from medieval Latin *dishonorare*, literally 'not to honour', from *honorare* 'honour'.] —**dishonourer** *n.*

dishonourable /diss ónnərəb'l/ *adj.* **1.** SHAMEFUL AND TO SB'S DISCREDIT morally unacceptable and liable to make sb lose the respect of others **2.** WITHOUT MORALS OR INTEGRITY behaving in a dishonest or morally unacceptable way —**dishonourableness** *n.* —**dishonourably** *adv.*

dishrag /dísh rag/ *n.* = dishcloth

dishtowel /dísh towəl/ *n. US, Can* = tea towel

dishwasher /dísh woshər/ *n.* **1.** MACHINE FOR WASHING DISHES an electrically operated machine that washes, rinses, and dries crockery and kitchen utensils **2.** SB WHO WASHES DISHES sb who washes dishes, especially in a restaurant

dishwashing liquid *n. US* = washing-up liquid

dishwater /dísh wawtər/ *n.* **1.** WATER USED FOR WASHING DISHES water that is or has been used for washing crockery or kitchen utensils **2.** WEAK DRINK a weak or tasteless drink

dishy /díshi/ (-ier, -iest) *adj.* good-looking (*informal*)

disillusion /díssi loozh'n/ *vt.* (-sions, -sioning, -sioned) DESTROY ILLUSION to destroy or undermine an ideal, illusion, or mistaken belief that is held by sb (*often passive*) ■ *n.* = disillusionment —**disillusive** /díssi loossiv/ *adj.*

disillusioned /díssi loozh'nd/ *adj.* disappointed by a frustrated ideal or belief

disillusionment /díssi loozh'nmənt/ *n.* disappointment caused by a frustrated ideal or belief

disincentive /dissin séntiv/ *n.* sth that deters sb from taking a particular action

disinclination /díssinkli náysh'n/ *n.* a reluctance to do sth

disincline /díssin klín/ (-clines, -clining, -clined) *vt.* to make sb reluctant or unwilling to do sth (*often passive*)

disinfect /díssin fékt/ (-fects, -fecting, -fected) *vt.* to clean sth so as to destroy disease-carrying microorganisms and prevent infection [Late 16thC. From French *désinfecter*, from *dés-* 'dis-' and *infecter* 'to infect'.] —**disinfection** /díssin féksh'n/ *n.* —**disinfector** /-féktər/ *n.*

disinfectant /díssin féktənt/ *n.* a chemical that destroys or inhibits the growth of microorganisms that cause disease

disinfest /díssin fést/ (-fests, -festing, -fested) *vt.* to free a place, person, or animal of small pests such as rodents or insects —**disinfestation** /díssin fe stáysh'n/ *n.*

disinflation /díssin fláysh'n/ *n.* a slowdown in the rate at which prices increase, e.g. during a recession —**disinflationary** *adj.*

disinformation /díssinfər máysh'n/ *n.* false or deliberately misleading information, often put out as propaganda [Mid-20thC. Modelled on Russian *dezinformatsiya*.]

disingenuous /díssin jénnyoo əss/ *adj.* **1.** WITHHOLDING INFORMATION withholding or not taking account of known information **2.** NOT GENUINELY SINCERE giving a false impression of sincerity or simplicity —**disingenuously** *adv.* —**disingenuousness** *n.*

disinherit /díssin hérrit/ (-its, -iting, -ited) *vt.* **1.** DEPRIVE OF INHERITANCE to change a will so as to deprive sb of an inheritance **2.** DEPRIVE OF RIGHT to deprive sb of a natural or established right or privilege —**disinheritance** *n.*

disinhibit /díssin híbbit/ (-its, -iting, -ited) *vt.* PSYCHOL to free sb from inhibitions (*technical*)

disinhibition /díssinhi bísh'n/ *n.* **1.** LOSS OF INHIBITION a loss of inhibition, e.g. through the influence of alcohol or drugs (*technical*) **2.** PSYCHOL TEMPORARY LOSS OF INHIBITION a temporary loss of inhibition caused by an outside stimulus, e.g. a loud noise **3.** CHEM REMOVAL OF INHIBITOR the removal of a substance that slows or stops a chemical reaction

disintegrate /diss ínti grayt/ (-grates, -grating, -grated) *v.* **1.** *vti.* BREAK INTO FRAGMENTS to break into components or fragments, or break sth into small pieces or constituent parts **2.** *vti.* LOSE WHOLENESS to destroy the cohesion, unity, or wholeness of sth, or undergo such destruction **3.** NUCLEAR PHYS SPLIT ATOMS to split the nuclei of atoms, or cause the nuclei of atoms to split —**disintegrable** /diss íntigrəb'l/ *adj.* —**disintegrative** /-grətiv/ *adj.*

disintegration /diss ínti gráysh'n/ *n.* **1.** BREAKING INTO PIECES irreversible breaking into components or fragments **2.** LOSS OF UNITY the loss of unity, cohesion, or integrity **3.** NUCLEAR PHYS BREAK-UP OF NUCLEUS the break-up of an atomic nucleus or an unstable elementary particle into smaller parts, either by radioactive decay or through bombardment with high-energy particles

disintegrator /diss ínti graytər/ *n.* **1.** NUCLEAR PHYS ATOM-SPLITTING MACHINE a machine in which atoms are split as a result of being hit by accelerated particles **2.** DISINTEGRATING AGENT a person, machine, or force that destroys or disintegrates sth

disinter /díssin túr/ (-ters, -terring, -terred) *vt.* **1.** DIG UP BODY to dig up or remove a dead body from a grave or tomb **2.** EXPOSE STH HIDDEN to expose sth that was hidden (*formal*) [Early 17thC. From French *désenterrer*, from *dés-* 'dis-' and *enterrer* 'to inter'.] —**disinterment** *n.*

disinterest /diss íntrəst/ *vt.* (-ests, -esting, -ested) FREE FROM INTEREST to cause sb to lose interest or partiality ■ *n.* IMPARTIALITY lack of bias or self-interest

disinterested /diss íntrəstid/ *adj.* **1.** IMPARTIAL free from bias or self-interest **2.** NOT INTERESTED indifferent, not interested, or no longer interested (*considered incorrect by many people*) —**disinterestedly** *adv.* —**disinterestedness** *n.*

disintermediation /díssintər méedi áysh'n/ *n.* COMM the elimination of intermediaries, e.g. wholesalers or retailers, in business transactions between producers and consumers

disintoxicate /dísin tóksi kayt/ (-cates, -cating, -cated) *vt.* = detoxify *v.* 2 —**disintoxication** /dísin tóksi káysh'n/ *n.*

disinvent /díssin vént/ (-vents, -venting, -vented) *vt.* to undo the invention of sth ○ *Nuclear weapons cannot be disinvented.*

disinvest /díssin vést/ (-vests, -vesting, -vested) *vti.* to withdraw an investment in sth

disinvestment /díssin véstmənt/ *n.* **1.** WITHDRAWING INVESTMENT the withdrawal of an investment **2.** REDUCTION OF INVESTMENT a reduction of investment caused by a selling of or deterioration in assets

disinvite /díssin vít/ (-vites, -viting, -vited) *vt.* to withdraw an invitation to sb (*humorous*)

disjoin /diss jóyn/ (-joins, -joining, -joined) *vti.* to disconnect parts, things, or ideas, or become separated [15thC. Via Old French *desjoign-*, the stem of *desjoindre*, from Latin *disjungere*, from *jungere* (see JOIN).] —**disjoinable** *adj.*

disjoint /diss jóynt/ (-joints, -jointing, -jointed) *v.* **1.** *vti.* SEPARATE AT JOINTS to separate sth at the joints, or be separated in this way **2.** *vti.* DISLOCATE to force or move sth out of its usual position, or undergo such a change **3.** *vt.* DESTROY UNITY to destroy the unity or coherence of sth **4.** *vt.* = disjoin [15thC. From Old French *desjoint*, the past participle of *desjoindre* (see DISJOIN).] —**disjoint** *adj.* —**disjointed** *adj.* —**disjointedness** *n.*

disjointedly /diss jóyntidli/ *adv.* in a way that makes connections or order unclear

disjunct /diss júngkt/ *adj.* **1.** SEPARATED discontinuous or separated in time or space **2.** MUSIC DESCRIBING NOTES A SECOND APART relating to two consecutive notes that are separated by an interval of a second **3.** MUSIC DESCRIBING A LEAPING MELODY relating to a melody in which leaps are the dominant feature rather than smooth progression ■ *n.* LOGIC CLAUSE either the p clause or the q clause in a logical proposition of the form 'p or q' [15thC. From Latin *disjunctus*, the past participle of *disjungere* (see DISJOIN).]

disjunction /diss júngksh'n/ *n.* **1.** DISCONNECTION a disconnection of joined parts or things **2.** LOGIC PROPOSITION WITH 'OR' a proposition of the form 'p or q' that is false if both p and q are false, but true if at least one of them is true **3.** LOGIC = disjunct *n.* **4.** GENETICS CHROMOSOME SEPARATION the separation of like chromosomes during cell division

disjunctive /diss júngktiv/ *adj.* **1.** DIVIDING serving to divide, or having the effect of dividing (*technical*) **2.** GRAM SHOWING CONTRAST used to describe a word, e.g. 'or', that establishes a contrast between two words or linguistic elements **3.** LOGIC CONTAINING OR RELATED TO A DISJUNCTION relating to or having the form of a proposition of the type 'p or q' ■ *n.* **1.** GRAM CONTRAST WORD a conjunction or other word that establishes a contrast **2.** LOGIC = disjunction *n.* 2 —**disjunctively** *adv.*

disjuncture /diss júngkchər/ *n.* = disjunction *n.* 1

disk *n.* **1.** COMPUT COMPUTER STORAGE DEVICE a device consisting of one or more magnetically or optically etched thin plates, used in a computer to store information **2.** *US* = disc

disk drive *n.* a device that a computer uses to read data from and write data to magnetic or optical disks

diskette /di skét/ *n.* = floppy disk

disk operating system *n.* an operating system for personal computers that uses disks and diskettes for storage of programs and data

disk pack *n.* a removable data storage device for use in minicomputers and mainframes, consisting of several magnetic or optical disks stacked one on top of another and handled as a unit

dislikable /diss líkəb'l/, **dislikeable** *adj.* hard to like because of being disagreeable or unpleasant

dislike /diss lík/ *vt.* (-likes, -liking, -liked) CONSIDER DISAGREEABLE to consider sth or sb disagreeable or unpleasant ■ *n.* **1.** DISAPPROVING FEELING an attitude or feeling of aversion, disapproval, or distaste **2.** STH PERSONALLY DISAGREEABLE sth that you do not like

────────── WORD KEY: SYNONYMS ──────────

dislike, distaste, hatred, hate, disgust, loathing, repugnance, abhorrence, animosity, antipathy, aversion

CORE MEANING: not liking sb or sth

dislike the most general term; **distaste** mild dislike, used especially of behaviour and activities; **hatred** extremely strong dislike; **hate** a more informal term for *hatred*; **disgust** very strong dislike and disapproval; **loathing** strong dislike and disgust, often referring to people; **repugnance** a fairly formal term for strong dislike and disgust, often referring to behaviour and activities; **abhorrence** a more formal term for repugnance; **animosity** intense dislike and hostility, usually used to refer to people; **antipathy** a deep-seated dislike that is often instinctive or intuitive; **aversion** strong, possibly unreasonable, dislike of a particular thing.

dislikeable *adj.* = dislikable

dislocate /dísslə kayt/ (-cates, -cating, -cated) *vt.* **1.** PUT OUT OF PLACE to put or force sth out of its usual place or position **2.** MED DISPLACE BODY PART to move or force a bone out of the joint into which it fits **3.** THROW INTO CONFUSION to disrupt, upset, or disturb the order of sth [Late 16thC. Origin uncertain: probably a back-formation from DISLOCATION.] —**dislocated** *adj.*

dislocation /dísslə káysh'n/ *n.* **1.** DISLOCATING OR BEING DISLOCATED the displacement of sth from its usual or proper position **2.** MED DISPLACEMENT OF BODY PART the displacement of a body part, especially of a bone, from its usual fitting in a joint **3.** CHEM IMPERFECTION IN CRYSTAL an irregularity in the fine structure (**lattice**) of an otherwise normal crystal [14thC. Via Old French from, ultimately, Latin *dislocare*, from *locare* (see LOCATE).]

dislodge /diss lój/ (-lodges, -lodging, -lodged) *vti.* to force sth or sb from a previously fixed or secure position, or leave such a position [15thC. From Old French *dislogier*, from *des-* 'dis-' and *logier* (see LODGE).] —**dislodgment** *n.*

disloyal /diss lóyəl/ *adj.* showing a lack of faith in or loyalty to sb or sth [15thC. From Old French *desloial*, from *des-* 'dis-' and *loial* (see LOYAL).] —**disloyally** *adv.*

disloyalty /diss lóyəlti/ (*plural* -ties) *n.* **1.** BEING DISLOYAL a lack of loyalty to a person, vow, organization, or state **2.** DISLOYAL ACT a disloyal or unfaithful act

dismal /dízzm'l/ *adj.* **1.** DEPRESSING depressing to the spirit or outlook **2.** HOPELESS showing a lack or failure of hope **3.** OF POOR QUALITY very poor or inadequate ○ *a dismal performance* [14thC. Via Anglo-Norman *dismal* 'unlucky days' from medieval Latin *dies mali*.] —**dismally** *adv.* —**dismalness** *n.*

dismal science *n.* political economy (*humorous*) [Coined by the Scottish essayist Thomas Carlyle (1795–1881).]

dismantle /diss mánt'l/ (-tles, -tling, -tled) *v.* **1.** *vt.* TAKE APART to take sth apart in a way that causes it to stop working **2.** *vi.* COME APART to be able to be separated into components **3.** *vt.* DESTROY STH BY REMOVING KEY ELEMENTS to destroy sth, e.g. an institution or system, by removing essential elements **4.** *vt.* REMOVE EQUIPMENT to strip a room or building of furniture or equipment [Late 16thC. From Old French *desmanteler* 'to tear down a fortress wall', from *des-* 'dis-' and *emmanteler* 'to shelter, fortify', from *mantel* 'cloak' (see MANTLE).] —**dismantlement** *n.* —**dismantler** *n.*

dismast /díss maást/ (**-masts, -masting, -masted**) *vt.* to break off or remove the mast or masts of a boat or ship —**dismastment** *n.*

dismay /diss máy/ *vt.* (**-mays, -maying, -mayed**) (*usually passive*) **1.** DISCOURAGE SB to cause sb to feel discouraged or disappointed **2.** ALARM SB to fill sb with alarm, apprehension, or distress ■ *n.* **1.** FEELING OF DISCOURAGEMENT a feeling of hopelessness, disappointment, or discouragement **2.** LOSS OF COURAGE a sudden loss of courage or confidence [14thC. From assumed Anglo-Norman *desmaiier*, of uncertain origin: ultimately a negative form of a prehistoric Germanic word meaning 'to be able', which is also the ancestor of English *may*.]

dismember /diss mémbər/ (**-bers, -bering, -bered**) *vt.* **1.** REMOVE LIMB FROM BODY to cut off or remove a limb or other part of a person or animal **2.** DIVIDE STH UP to cut or tear sth into pieces **3.** DESTROY STH BY TAKING IT APART to destroy sth by taking it apart so that its parts no longer work together ○ *dismembered the alliance* [14thC. Via Old French from assumed Vulgar Latin *dismembrare*, from Latin *membrum* (see MEMBER).] —**dismemberer** *n.* —**dismemberment** *n.*

dismiss /diss míss/ (**-misses, -missing, -missed**) *vt.* **1.** END EMPLOYMENT OF SB to stop employing sb, e.g. because of unsatisfactory work or wrongdoing **2.** SEND AWAY to send sb away, or give sb formal permission to leave **3.** REFUSE TO CONSIDER to refuse to give consideration to sth **4.** REJECT WITH REASON to consider sb or sth as unsuitable for a particular reason ○ *dismissed the idea as ridiculous* **5.** LAW REFUSE FURTHER HEARING IN COURT to refuse to give further hearing to a case in court **6.** CRICKET PUT PLAYER OR TEAM OUT to end the innings of a batsman or a team [15thC. From medieval Latin *dismiss-*, the past participle stem of *dismittere*, literally 'to send away', from Latin *mittere* (see MISSION).] —**dismissible** *adj.*

dismissal /diss míss'l/ *n.* **1.** ENDING OF SB'S EMPLOYMENT the removal of sb from employment **2.** NOTICE OF DISCHARGE an order or notice of discharge from employment or service **3.** SENDING AWAY the formal sending away of a person or group **4.** REJECTION the rejection of sth from consideration **5.** CRICKET PUTTING PLAYER OR TEAM OUT the ending of a batsman's or team's innings

dismissive /diss míssiv/ *adj.* indicating rejection, especially showing contempt or indifference —**dismissively** *adv.* —**dismissiveness** *n.*

dismount /diss mównt/ *v.* (**-mounts, -mounting, -mounted**) **1.** *vi.* GET OFF ANIMAL to get down from the back of an animal, e.g. a horse or camel **2.** *vi.* GET OFF CYCLE to get off a bicycle or motorcycle **3.** *vt.* REMOVE FROM FRAME to remove sth from a frame, mounting, stand, or support **4.** *vt.* THROW SB OFF to remove sb from a mounted position ○ *The horse dismounted its rider.* ■ *n.* ACT OF DISMOUNTING an act of dismounting or of being dismounted [Mid-16thC. Origin uncertain: probably modelled on obsolete French *désmonter*, literally 'to unseat', from *monter* (see MOUNT).] —**dismountable** *adj.*

Disney /dízni/, **Walt** (1901–66) US animator and producer. He created Mickey Mouse and Donald Duck, and originated the feature-length cartoon with *Snow White and the Seven Dwarfs* (1937). Full name **Walter Elias Disney**

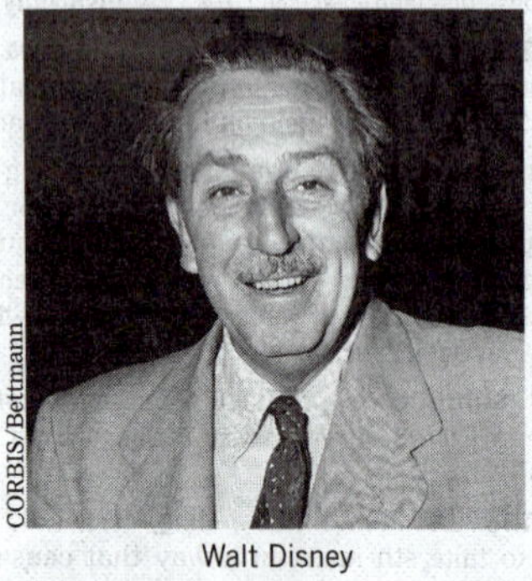
CORBIS/Bettmann
Walt Disney

Disneyesque /dízni ésk/ *adj.* reminiscent of, or in the style of, the sometimes whimsical films and cartoons created by Walt Disney or the Disney studios

disobedience /díssə beédi ənss/ *n.* refusal or failure to obey

disobedient /díssə beédi ənt/ *adj.* refusing or failing to obey, especially habitually [15thC. Via Old French from assumed Vulgar Latin *desobedient-*, from Latin *oboedient-*, the present participle stem of *oboedire* (see OBEY).] —**disobediently** *adv.*

disobey /díssə báy/ (**-beys, -beying, -beyed**) *vti.* to refuse or fail to obey a rule, instruction, or authority, or sb giving an instruction or in authority [14thC. Via French *désobéir* from assumed Vulgar Latin *desobedir*, from Latin *oboedire* (see OBEY).] —**disobeyer** *n.*

disoblige /díssə blíj/ (**-bliges, -bliging, -bliged**) *vt.* to be unwilling to help sb (*formal*) [Late 16thC. Via French *désobliger* from, ultimately, Latin *obligare* (see OBLIGE).]

disobliging /díssə blíjing/ *adj.* selfishly or rudely unwilling to help —**disobligingly** *adv.* —**disobligingness** *n.*

disomic /dī sṓmik/ *adj.* GENETICS with chromosomes occurring in pairs [Early 20thC. Coined from DI- + -SOME + -IC.] —**disomy** *n.*

disorder /diss áwrdər/ *n.* **1.** LACK OF ORDER a lack of systematic or orderly arrangement **2.** UNTIDINESS a state of untidiness ○ *found the room in complete disorder* **3.** LAW UNRULY BEHAVIOUR a public disturbance or breach of the peace **4.** MED ILLNESS a medical condition involving a disturbance to the normal functioning of the mind or body ■ *vt.* (**-ders, -dering, -dered**) UPSET ARRANGEMENT to disarrange or disturb the order of sth [15thC. Origin uncertain: possibly an alteration of obsolete *disordain*, under the influence of ORDER and French *désordre*.]

disordered /diss áwrdərd/ *adj.* **1.** UNTIDY OR CONFUSED marked by confusion or disarray **2.** NOT FUNCTIONING NORMALLY having lost normal physical functioning or thought processes ○ *disordered sleep*

disorderly /diss áwrdərli/ *adj.* **1.** LACKING ORDER lacking order or organization **2.** UNRULY unruly and resisting authority **3.** LAW DISTURBING THE PEACE disturbing the peace or violating public order —**disorderliness** *n.*

disorderly conduct *n.* any one of several minor offences likely to cause a breach of the peace

disorderly house *n.* an establishment such as a brothel or gaming club where activities take place that may become unruly or violate public order or decency

disorganisation *n.* = **disorganization**

disorganise *vt.* = **disorganize**

disorganization /diss áwrgə nī záysh'n/, **disorganisation** *n.* **1.** LACK OF ORGANIZATION a lack of organization or orderly arrangement **2.** DESTRUCTION OF ORDER the destruction of an order or system

disorganize /diss áwrgə nīz/ (**-izes, -izing, -ized**), **disorganise** (**-ises, -ising, -ised**) *vt.* to destroy or disrupt the organization, system, or unity of sth [Late 18thC. From French *désorganiser*, from *dés-* 'not' and *organiser* (see ORGANIZE).] —**disorganizer** *n.*

disorganized /diss áwrgə nīzd/, **disorganised** *adj.* lacking order and coherence

disorientate /-ən tayt/ (**-orientates, -orientating, -orientated**), **disorient** /diss áwri ənt/ (**-ents, -enting, -ented**) *vt.* **1.** MAKE SB LOSE BEARINGS to cause sb to feel lost or confused, especially with regard to direction or position **2.** CONFUSE SB to confuse sb by giving misleading information —**disorientation** /diss áwri ən táysh'n/ *n.*

disorientated /diss áwri ən taytid/, **disoriented** /-entid/ *adj.* **1.** HAVING LOST BEARINGS feeling lost or confused, especially with regard to direction or position **2.** CONFUSED not understanding clearly

disown /diss ṓn/ (**-owns, -owning, -owned**) *vt.* to refuse or no longer acknowledge a connection with sb or sth —**disowner** *n.* —**disownment** *n.*

disparage /dis spárrij/ (**-ages, -aging, -aged**) *vt.* to refer disapprovingly to sb or sth —**disparager** *n.*

disparagement /di spárrijmənt/ *n.* **1.** NEGATIVE CRITICISM negative or adverse criticism **2.** ACT OF DISPARAGING the act of criticizing or discrediting sb or sth **3.** LOWERING OF ESTEEM a lowering of esteem (*archaic*)

disparaging /di spárrijing/ *adj.* showing or expressing contempt or disapproval —**disparagingly** *adv.*

disparate /díspərət/ *adj.* used to describe things or people so completely unlike each other that they cannot be compared [15thC. From Latin *disparatus*, the past participle of *disparare* 'to separate', from *parare* 'to prepare' (see PARE).] —**disparately** *adv.* —**disparateness** *n.*

disparity /di spárrəti/ (*plural* **-ties**) *n.* **1.** LACK OF EQUALITY lack of equality between things or people **2.** UNLIKENESS dissimilarity or incongruity [Mid-16thC. Via French *disparité* from late Latin *disparitas*, from *paritas* (see PARITY).]

dispassion /diss pásh'n/ *n.* absence of prejudicial feeling ○ *viewed the chaos round her with dispassion*

dispassionate /dis pásh'nət/ *adj.* not influenced by emotion or personal feelings —**dispassionately** *adv.* —**dispassionateness** *n.*

dispatch /di spách/, **despatch** *vt.* (**-patches, -patching, -patched**) **1.** SEND STH to send off sth, e.g. a letter or parcel, to a particular destination **2.** SEND SB AWAY TO DO STH to instruct sb to go somewhere to carry out a task **3.** DEAL WITH STH QUICKLY to complete or deal with sth quickly or efficiently **4.** EAT UP to eat food quickly (*informal*) **5.** KILL SB to kill a person or animal ■ *n.* **1.** MAIL SENDING OFF the sending of sth or sb such as a letter or a messenger **2.** SPEED speed and efficiency ○ *carried out her duties with dispatch* **3.** OFFICIAL MESSAGE a message or report, especially an official communication from a diplomat or an officer in the armed forces **4.** PRESS NEWS REPORT a news item or report sent by a journalist or news agency ○ *dispatches from the scene of the fire* **5.** ACT OF KILLING the killing of a person or animal [Early 16thC. Via Italian *dispacciare* from, ultimately, a negative form of assumed Vulgar Latin *impactare* 'to impede', from Latin *impact-*, the past participle stem of *impingere* (see IMPINGE).]

dispatch box *n.* **1.** CASE FOR DOCUMENTS a case for carrying documents, especially a red case of the kind used by UK government ministers **2.** LECTERN either of two boxes in each side of the chamber in the House of Commons that are used as lecterns by ministers when they address Parliament

dispatch case *n.* a case for carrying papers or documents (*dated*)

dispel /di spél/ (**-pels, -pelling, -pelled**) *vt.* **1.** RID MIND OF STH to rid sb's mind of a particular thought or idea, especially an erroneous one **2.** DISPERSE STH to disperse or drive away sth ○ *clouds and mist that the sun soon dispelled* [15thC. From Latin *dispellere*, literally 'to drive away', from *pellere* (see PULSE).] —**dispeller** *n.*

dispensable /di spénssəb'l/ *adj.* able to be dispensed with or replaced —**dispensability** /di spénssə bílləti/ *n.* —**dispensableness** /-b'lnəss/ *n.*

dispensary /di spénssəri/ (*plural* **-ries**) *n.* **1.** DISTRIBUTION POINT FOR MEDICINES a place where medical supplies are stored and distributed to patients by a pharmacist **2.** TEMPORARY MEDICAL CENTRE a place where temporary or provisional medical treatment is provided

dispensation /díspən sáysh'n/ *n.* **1.** EXEMPTION exemption or release from a rule or obligation, especially a religious one **2.** DOCUMENT GIVING EXEMPTION an official document authorizing dispensation, especially religious dispensation **3.** RELIG RELIGIOUS SYSTEM in Christian belief, a divinely ordained religious system **4.** CHR DIVINE ORDERING in Christian belief, a divine ordering or management of affairs and events in the world **5.** RELIG RELIGIOUS EPOCH the time during which a religious doctrine or practice is believed to be in force **6.** DISPENSING the distribution or giving out of sth ○ *dispensation of emergency supplies* —**dispensational** *adj.*

dispensatory /di spénsətəri/ *adj.* relating to or granting dispensation, especially religious dispensation

dispense /di spénss/ (**-penses, -pensing, -pensed**) *v.* **1.** *vt.* PROVIDE STH to distribute sth to several recipients **2.** *vt.* SELL STH to sell sth at more than one location or to more than one customer **3.** *vt.* PHARM SUPPLY MEDICINES to supply medicine according to a prescription **4.** *vt.* LAW ADMINISTER JUSTICE to be an agent of the administration of justice **5.** *vi.* CHR GRANT DISPENSATION to grant a religious dispensation [14thC. Via Old French from Latin *dispensare*, from *dispendere*, literally 'to weigh out', from *pendere* 'to weigh' (see PENSIVE).]

dispense with *vt.* **1.** DO WITHOUT to manage without sth ○ *Since it's sunny, we can dispense with the rain gear.* **2.** GET RID OF to get rid of sth not wanted or needed ○ *Let's dispense with all these convoluted rules and regulations.*

dispenser /di spénssər/ *n.* **1.** DEVICE FOR DISPENSING GOODS a device that releases its contents in convenient or measured quantities when operated (*usually used in combination*) **2.** PROVIDER OF STH sb who or sth that distributes sth **3.** PHARM MEDICINE SUPPLIER sb who supplies medicine according to a prescription

dispensing optician *n.* = **optician** *n.* 1

dispersal /di spúrss'l/ *n.* **1.** DISTRIBUTION the distribution or scattering of people or things over an area **2.** BIOL NATURAL SPREAD OF SEED the natural distribution of plant seeds and the offspring of non-mobile organisms over a wide area by various methods **3.** BIOL MOVEMENT OF ORGANISMS the movement of organisms away from their place of birth or from centres of population density **4.** DISAPPEARANCE disappearance as a result of scattering or going away in different directions

dispersant /di spúrss'nt/ *n.* a liquid or gas that facilitates or improves the dispersion of small particles or droplets, e.g. in an aerosol —**dispersant** *adj.*

disperse /di spúrss/ (**-perses, -persing, -persed**) *vti.* **1.** SCATTER to cause sth to scatter, or go away in different directions **2.** DISTRIBUTE to distribute sth over a wide area, or become widespread **3.** CAUSE TO DISAPPEAR to cause sth to disappear, or disappear **4.** CHEM DISTRIBUTE EVENLY to distribute particles evenly throughout a medium, or become distributed in this way **5.** PHYS SEPARATE INTO COLOURS to separate white light into the component colours of the spectrum, or undergo this process [14thC. Via Old French from Latin *dispers-*, the past participle stem of *dispergere*, literally 'to scatter around', from *spargere* (see SPARSE).] —**disperser** *n.*

dispersion /di spúrsh'n/ *n.* **1.** DISPERSING the scattering or distribution of sth within an area or space **2.** BEING DISPERSED the fact or state of being spread, scattered, or distributed **3.** STATS DISTRIBUTION OF VALUES the distribution of a statistical frequency distribution about an average or median **4.** CHEM MEDIUM WITH DISPERSED PARTICLES a chemical system consisting of a gas, liquid, or colloid containing dispersed particles

Dispersion *n.* = **Diaspora**

dispersive /di spúrssiv/ *adj.* tending to cause dispersion —**dispersively** *adv.* —**dispersiveness** *n.*

dispirit /di spírrit/ (**-its, -iting, -ited**) *vt.* to discourage or dishearten sb

dispirited /di spírritid/ *adj.* affected by lack of energy and a loss of enthusiasm —**dispiritedly** *adv.* —**dispiritedness** *n.*

dispiriting /di spírriting/ *adj.* depressing or disheartening —**dispiritingly** *adv.*

displace /diss pláyss/ (**-places, -placing, -placed**) *vt.* **1.** MOVE FROM USUAL PLACE to move sth from its usual or correct place **2.** FORCE TO LEAVE HOME to force sb to leave his or her home or country, e.g. because of war **3.** REMOVE FROM POST to discharge or remove sb from an office, position, or job **4.** REPLACE to take the place of sb or sth **5.** CHEM TAKE PLACE OF ATOM to take the place of another atom or group in a compound **6.** PHYS REPLACE FLUID WITH OBJECT to replace a volume of fluid with a floating or submerged object, forcing the original fluid to move elsewhere —**displaceable** *adj.* —**displacer** *n.*

displaced person (*plural* **displaced persons** *or* **displaced people**) *n.* sb who has been forced to leave his or her home or country, especially because of war or political oppression

displacement /diss pláyssmənt/ *n.* **1.** DISPLACING OR BEING DISPLACED the moving or movement of sth from its usual or correct place **2.** PHYS, SHIPPING FLUID DISPLACED the fluid, e.g. water, that is forced to move by an object floating or submerged in it. It is often used as a measure of a ship's size. **3.** PHYS AMOUNT OF MOVEMENT IN PARTICULAR DIRECTION the amount of movement of an object measured in a particular direction **4.** CHEM CHEMICAL REPLACEMENT a chemical reaction in which one atom or chemical group takes the place of another in a compound **5.** PSYCHOL TRANSFER OF EMOTIONS OR BEHAVIOUR transfer of emotion from the original focus to another less threatening object or person, or the substitution of one response or piece of behaviour for another **6.** GEOL MOVEMENT OF GEOLOGICAL FAULT the distance that a point on one side of a geological fault has moved, relative to a corresponding point on the other side **7.** AUTOMOT ENGINE VOLUME the total volume displaced by the pistons in an internal combustion engine

displacement ton *n.* a unit of measure for the displacement of a floating ship, equivalent to 2240 lb

display /di spláy/ *v.* (**-plays, -playing, -played**) **1.** *vt.* MAKE VISIBLE to make sth visible or available for others to see **2.** *vt.* MAKE EVIDENT to reveal or make evident a quality or feeling **3.** *vti.* COMPUT SHOW DATA to show messages, data, or graphics on a monitor, or appear on a monitor **4.** *vti.* ZOOL SHOW STYLIZED BEHAVIOUR to show a particular pattern of animal behaviour, e.g. to attract a mate or defend a territory ■ *n.* **1.** VISUAL ARRANGEMENT a collection of things arranged or done for others to see, especially sth considered attractive, interesting, or entertaining (*often used in combination*) **2.** BEING VISIBLE OR ARRANGED FOR VIEWING the act of being clearly and easily visible or placed for people to view ○ *new work on display* **3.** EVIDENT FEELING OR QUALITY an evident feeling or quality ○ *a display of courage* **4.** PRINTING GRAPHIC ADVERTISING printed advertising that uses attractive pictures, typography, and other features **5.** COMPUT ELECTRONIC SCREEN an electronic device that presents visual information **6.** COMPUT INFORMATION ON A SCREEN the information shown on a computer monitor or other electronic device **7.** ZOOL STYLIZED BEHAVIOUR a particular pattern of animal behaviour used to produce a response in other animals, especially of the same species, e.g. when courting or defending territory ■ *adj.* PRINTING FOR ADVERTISING relating to typefaces that are designed for prominent use in advertising [Late 16thC. Via Old French *despleier* from Latin *displicare*, literally 'to unfold', from *plicare* (see PLY [2]).] —**displayer** *n.*

display cabinet, **display case** *n.* a case or stand with glass panels, used for showing items of interest

displease /diss pléez/ (**-pleases, -pleasing, -pleased**) *vti.* to annoy or dissatisfy sb [14thC. Via Old French *desplais-*, the stem of *desplaire*, from assumed Vulgar Latin *displacere*, from Latin *placere* (see PLACID).]

displeased /diss pléezd/ *adj.* annoyed or dissatisfied

displeasing /diss pléezing/ *adj.* causing annoyance or dissatisfaction —**displeasingly** *adv.*

displeasure /diss plézhər/ *n.* a feeling of annoyance or dissatisfaction [15thC. From Old French *desplaisir* 'to displease', used as a noun, from *des-* 'dis-' and *plaisir* 'pleasure' (see PLEASURE).]

displode /diss plṓd/ (**-plodes, -ploding, -ploded**) *vti.* to explode (*archaic*)

disport /di spáwrt/ *v.* (**-ports, -porting, -ported**) (*archaic or humorous*) **1.** *vr.* SHOW OFF to show off or try to draw attention to yourself **2.** *vi.* BEHAVE PLAYFULLY to behave in a playful manner ■ *n.* FORM OF ENTERTAINMENT a form of lively entertainment or diversion [14thC. From Old French *desporter* 'to divert', from *des-* 'apart' and *porter* 'to carry'.]

disposable /di spṓzəb'l/ *adj.* **1.** THROWAWAY designed to be thrown away after use **2.** AVAILABLE FOR USE used to describe money or assets that are available for use ■ *n.* STH TO BE USED ONLY ONCE sth that is designed to be thrown away after use, e.g. a paper cup (*often used in the plural*) —**disposability** /di spṓzə bíllәti/ *n.* —**disposableness** /-b'lnəss/ *n.*

disposable income *n.* **1.** INCOME AFTER TAX income that remains available for spending after deductions for taxes and other obligations **2.** FIN MONEY AVAILABLE FOR SPENDING the total amount of money that a country or community has available for spending

disposal /di spṓz'l/ *n.* **1.** PROCESS OF GETTING RID OF STH the process of throwing away or getting rid of sth **2.** ORDERLY ARRANGEMENT an orderly arrangement, distribution, or placement **3.** TRANSFERRING STH TO ANOTHER the transferring of sth valuable to another by sale or gift **4.** *US* GARBAGE DISPOSAL the disposing of domestic rubbish (*informal*)

dispose /di spṓz/ *v.* (**-poses, -posing, -posed**) **1.** *vt.* PUT IN PLACE to arrange or position sth for use or for a particular purpose (*formal; often passive*) **2.** *vti.* SETTLE to settle a matter by putting it into its correct or definitive form **3.** *vt.* INCLINE to make sb likely to experience sth **4.** *vt.* MAKE WILLING to make sb willing or receptive to sth (*often passive*) **5.** *vt.* BESTOW to bestow (*archaic*) ■ *n.* DISPOSAL disposal (*archaic*) [14thC. From French *disposer*, an alteration (under the influence of *poser* 'to place') of Latin *disponere*, literally 'to set out', from *ponere* (see POSITION).] —**disposer** *n.*

dispose of *vt.* **1.** GET RID OF STH to throw away or get rid of sth **2.** TRANSFER to transfer sth to another's ownership, by sale or other means **3.** ATTEND TO STH to deal with a matter in order to settle it (*formal*) **4.** KILL to kill a person or animal

disposition /díspə zísh'n/ *n.* **1.** PERSONALITY sb's usual mood or temperament **2.** BEHAVIOURAL TENDENCY an inclination or tendency to act in a particular way **3.** SETTLEMENT settlement of a business or legal matter **4.** = **disposal** *n.* 2, **disposal** *n.* 3 [14thC. Via French from, ultimately, Latin *disponere* (see DISPOSE).] —**dispositional** *adj.*

dispossess /díspə zéss/ (**-sesses, -sessing, -sessed**) *vt.* to take away possession or occupancy of sth, especially property (*archaic or formal*) [15thC. From Old French *despossesser*, from *des-* 'dis-' and *possesser* (see POSSESS).] —**dispossessor** *n.* —**dispossessory** *adj.*

dispossessed /díspə zést/ *adj.* DEPRIVED OF POSSESSION deprived of property or rights ■ *npl.* DISPOSSESSED PEOPLE people who have been deprived of their property or rights

dispraise /diss práyz/ *vt.* (**-praises, -praising, -praised**) EXPRESS DISAPPROVAL to express disapproval of sb (*archaic literary*) ■ *n.* DISAPPROVAL the expression of disapproval (*archaic*) —**dispraiser** *n.*

disprize /diss príz/ (**-prizes, -prizing, -prized**) *vt.* to be unwilling to appreciate the worth of sb or sth (*archaic*)

disproof /diss pró͞of/ *n.* **1.** PROVING WRONG the disproving of a legal argument or point **2.** EVIDENCE PROVING STH WRONG evidence that disproves sth

disproportion /díssprə páwrsh'n/ *n.* STH OUT OF PROPORTION sth that is out of proportion or unequal ■ *vt.* (**-tions, -tioning, -tioned**) MAKE STH DISPROPORTIONATE to make sth disproportionate —**disproportionable** *adj.* —**disproportionableness** *n.* —**disproportionably** *adv.*

disproportionate /díssprə páwrsh'nət/, **disproportional** /-sh'nəl/ *adj.* unequal or out of proportion in quantity, shape, or size —**disproportionately** *adv.* —**disproportionateness** *n.*

disproportionation /díssprə páwrsh'n áysh'n/ *n.* a chemical reaction in which a single substance acts as both oxidizing and reducing agent, resulting in the production of dissimilar substances

disprove /diss pró͞ov/ (**-proves, -proving, -proved**) *vt.* to show that sth is incorrect [14thC. From Old French *desprover*, from *des-* 'dis-' and *prover* (see PROVE).] —**disprovable** *adj.* —**disproval** *n.*

disputable /di spyó͞otəb'l/ *adj.* not definitely true or valid and therefore debatable or open to argument —**disputability** /di spyó͞otə bíllәti/ *n.* —**disputableness** /-b'lnəss/ *n.*

disputably /di spyó͞otəbli/ *adv.* used to suggest that the speaker or writer thinks sth is true and could defend that view against those who disagree

WORD KEY: USAGE

See Usage note at ***arguably.***

disputant /di spyó͞ot'nt/ *n.* PARTY TO CASE sb involved in an argument or a legal dispute ■ *adj.* IN A CASE engaged in an argument or a legal dispute

disputation /díspyo͞o táysh'n/ *n.* **1.** ARGUMENT arguing or disagreement (*formal*) **2.** EDUC FORMAL ACADEMIC DEBATE a formal academic debate in defence of a thesis

disputatious /díspyo͞o táyshəss/, **disputative** /dis pyóotativ/ *adj.* tending to argue or disagree without adequate cause (*formal*) —**disputatiously** *adv.* —**disputatiousness** *n.*

dispute /di spyóot/ *v.* (-putes, -puting, -puted) 1. *vti.* QUERY to question or doubt the truth or validity of sth 2. *vi.* DISAGREE to disagree or argue about sth 3. *vt.* CONTEST to fight for or strive to win sth (*formal*) 4. *vt.* OPPOSE to strive against or resist sth (*formal*) ■ *n.* 1. ARGUMENT serious argument or disagreement 2. INDUSTRIAL DISAGREEMENT a prolonged disagreement between management and workers or a trade union, often involving industrial action [Late 16thC. Via Old French from Latin *disputare*, literally 'to argue out', from *putare* 'to consider'.] —**disputer** *n.*

—————— **WORD KEY: USAGE** ——————
Pronunciation. The traditional pronunciation of both the noun and the verb is with the stress on the second syllable. More recently, it has been stressed on the first syllable, a practice common among trade union leaders (especially from northern England) and taken over by radio and television reporters. This pronunciation can sound awkward and is widely disliked.

—————— **WORD KEY: SYNONYMS** ——————
See Synonyms at *disagree*.

disqualification /diss kwóllifi káysh'n/ *n.* 1. INELIGIBILITY being or becoming ineligible to do or take part in sth 2. ACT OF BEING DISQUALIFIED an instance of being disqualified 3. STH THAT DISQUALIFIES sth that makes sb ineligible to do or take part in sth

disqualified /diss kwólli fīd/ *adj.* ineligible to compete or take part in sth, or deprived of the right to do sth

disqualify /diss kwólli fī/ (-fies, -fying, -fied) *vt.* 1. DECLARE UNFIT to make or declare sb unfit, unqualified, or ineligible to do or take part in sth 2. TAKE AWAY LEGAL RIGHT to deprive sb of a legal or other right or privilege —**disqualifiable** *adj.* —**disqualifier** *n.*

disquiet /diss kwī'ət/ *n.* LACK OF PEACE a lack of peace resulting from anxiety ■ *vt.* (-ets, -eting, -eted) MAKE ANXIOUS to make sb anxious or uneasy (*archaic or literary*) —**disquietly** *adv.* —**disquietness** *n.*

disquieted /diss kwī'ətid/ *adj.* anxious, worried, or uneasy (*archaic or literary*) —**disquietedly** *adv.* —**disquietedness** *n.*

disquieting /diss kwī'əting/ *adj.* causing discomfort, worry, or doubt to arise —**disquietingly** *adv.*

disquietude /diss kwī'ə tyo͞od/ *n.* = disquiet

disquisition /dískwi zísh'n/ *n.* a long formal essay or discussion on a subject (*formal*) [Early 17thC. Via French from, ultimately, Latin *disquirere* 'to inquire', from *quaerere* (see QUERY).] —**disquisitional** *adj.*

Benjamin Disraeli

Disraeli /diz ráyli/, **Benjamin, 1st Earl of Beaconsfield** (1804–81) British statesman and novelist. He was Conservative prime minister (1868, 1874–80), and author of *Coningsby* (1844) and *Sybil* (1845).

disrate /díss ráyt/ (-rates, -rating, -rated) *vt.* to demote sb in the military to a lower rank

disregard /dissri ga͝ard/ *vt.* (-gards, -garding, -garded) 1. IGNORE to ignore or pay no attention to sb or sth 2. TREAT WITHOUT RESPECT to treat sb or sth with contempt or without respect ■ *n.* NEGLECT lack of attention or respect —**disregarder** *n.* —**disregardful** *adj.* —**disregardfully** *adv.* —**disregardfulness** *n.*

disrelated /díss ri láytid/ *adj.* not related ○ *a series of disrelated arguments leading nowhere*

disrelish /diss réllish/ *vt.* (-ishes, -ishing, -ished) DISLIKE to dislike sth, or find sth distasteful (*archaic*) ■ *n.* AVERSION dislike or aversion (*archaic*)

disremember /díssri mémbər/ (-bers, -bering, -bered) *vti.* to forget or fail to remember sth (*informal*)

disrepair /díssri páir/ *n.* poor working order or condition as a result of neglect

disreputable /diss réppyo͞otəb'l/ *adj.* 1. NOT REPUTABLE lacking respectability on the basis of past or present actions 2. UNTIDY untidy, dirty, or worn in appearance (*humorous*) —**disreputability** /diss réppyo͞otə bíllati/ *n.* —**disreputableness** /-b'lnəss/ *n.* —**disreputably** /-bli/ *adv.*

disrepute /díssri pyo͝ot/ *n.* a lack or loss of good reputation or respect

disrespect /díssri spékt/ *n.* TOTAL CONTEMPT a lack of respect ■ *vt.* (-spects, -specting, -spected) SHOW NO RESPECT to show a lack of respect for sb or sth. ◊ dis

disrespectable /díssri spéktəb'l/ *adj.* not deserving or getting respect or social approval —**disrespectableness** *n.*

disrespectful /díssri spéktf'l/ *adj.* showing a lack of respect —**disrespectfully** *adv.* —**disrespectfulness** *n.*

disrobe /dis rṓb/ (-robes, -robing, -robed) *v.* 1. *vti.* UNDRESS to remove your own or sb else's clothing (*formal*) 2. *vt.* DIVEST OF AUTHORITY to strip sb of authority or office (*archaic*) [Late 16thC. From Old French *desrober*, from *des-* 'dis-' and *robe* 'ROBE'.] —**disrobement** *n.* —**disrober** *n.*

disrupt /dis rúpt/ (-rupts, -rupting, -rupted) *vt.* 1. INTERRUPT to interrupt the normal course of a process or activity 2. DESTROY ORDER to destroy the order or orderly progression of sth 3. SPLIT to break or burst sth (*archaic*) [15thC. From Latin *disrupt-*, the past participle stem of *disrumpere*, literally 'to break apart', from *rumpere* (see RUPTURE).] —**disrupter** *n.*

disruption /dis rúpsh'n/ *n.* 1. UNWANTED BREAK an unwelcome or unexpected break in a process or activity 2. SUSPENSION the interruption or suspension of normal activity or progress 3. STATE OF DISORDER a state of disorder caused by outside influence 4. **Disruption** *Scotland* CHR SPLIT IN CHURCH OF SCOTLAND a split in the Church of Scotland in 1843, leading to the formation of the Free Church. At issue was the question of patronage versus the choice of a minister by the congregation.

disruptive /dis rúptiv/ *adj.* interrupting normal order or progress —**disruptively** *adv.*

disruptive coloration *n.* a colouration pattern in an animal that confuses or disrupts the perception of its body outline, thus providing a means of protection

dissatisfaction /díss satiss fáksh'n, di sáttiss-/ *n.* a state or feeling of not being satisfied

dissatisfactory /díss satiss fáktəri/ *adj.* not satisfactory

dissatisfied /diss sáttiss fīd/ *adj.* not pleased or contented —**dissatisfiedly** *adv.*

dissatisfy /díss sáttiss fī/ (-fies, -fying, -fied) *vt.* to displease or fail to satisfy

dissect /dī sékt, di-/ (-sects, -secting, -sected) *v.* 1. *vti.* BIOL CUT AND EXAMINE to cut and separate the parts of animal or plant specimens for scientific study 2. *vt.* EXAMINE IN DETAIL to examine or analyse a person or subject in detail [Late 16thC. From Latin *dissect-*, the past participle stem of *dissecare*, literally 'to cut apart', from *secare* (see SECTION).] —**dissectible** *adj.* —**dissector** *n.*

dissected /dī séktid, di-/ *adj.* 1. BOT DIVIDED INTO PARTS used to describe a leaf that is divided into narrow lobes or segments 2. GEOL WITH HILLS AND VALLEYS used to describe a landscape that has been eroded into hills and valleys

dissection /dī séksh'n, di-/ *n.* 1. BIOL CUTTING AND EXAMINING the cutting and separating of the constituent parts of animal or plant specimens for scientific study 2. BIOL DISSECTED SPECIMEN sth that has been dissected, e.g. an anatomical specimen 3. EXAMINATION a thorough and detailed analysis or examination

disseise /diss seéz/ (-seises, -seising, -seised), **disseize** (-seizes, -seizing, -seized) *vi.* to deprive sb wrongfully of possession of land [14thC. From Anglo-Norman *disseisir*, a variant of Old French *dessaisir* 'to dispossess', from *des-* 'dis-' and *saisir* (see SEIZE).] —**disseisor** *n.*

disseisee /díss see zeé, diss seé zee/, **disseizee** *n.* wrongful deprivation of sb of his or her land

disseisin /diss seézin/, **disseizin** *n.* the act of wrongfully depriving sb of land [14thC. From Anglo-Norman *disseisine*, a variant of Old French *dessaisine*, from *dessaisir* (see DISSEISE).]

disseize *vt.* = disseise

disseizin *n.* = disseisin

dissemble /di sémb'l/ (-bles, -bling, -bled) *v.* 1. *vi.* PUT ON FALSE APPEARANCE to put on a false appearance in order to conceal facts, feelings, or intentions 2. *vt.* GIVE APPEARANCE to put on the appearance of sth not actually felt or true (*formal*) 3. *vt.* HIDE BY PRETENCE to hide real beliefs or intentions through misleading speech or behaviour (*formal*) [15thC. From Old French *dessembler* 'to be different', from *des-* 'dis-' and *sembler* 'to seem' (see SEMBLANCE).] —**dissemblance** *n.* —**dissembler** *n.*

dissembling /di sémbling/ *n.* ADOPTION OF FALSE APPEARANCE creation or adoption of a false appearance so as to elicit a false impression on the part of sb else ■ *adj.* FEIGNING feigning or pretending —**dissemblingly** *adv.*

disseminate /di sémmi nayt/ (-nates, -nating, -nated) *vti.* to distribute or spread sth, especially information, or become widespread [15thC. From Latin *disseminat-*, the past participle stem of *disseminare*, literally 'to sow abroad', from *semin-*, the stem of *semen* 'seed' (see SEMEN).] —**dissemination** /di sémmi náysh'n/ *n.* —**disseminative** /-nətiv/ *adj.* —**disseminator** /-naytər/ *n.*

—————— **WORD KEY: SYNONYMS** ——————
See Synonyms at *scatter*.

dissension /di sénsh'n/ *n.* disagreement or difference of opinion, especially when leading to open conflict [14thC. Via French from, ultimately, Latin *dissentire* (see DISSENT).]

dissensus /diss sénsəss/ *n.* a preponderance of disagreement [Mid-20thC. Blend of DISSENT and CONSENSUS.]

dissent /di sént/ *vi.* (-sents, -senting, -sented) 1. DISAGREE to disagree with a widely held or majority opinion 2. CHR NOT SUPPORT RELIGIOUS PRACTICES to refuse to conform to the authority, doctrines and practices of an established church 3. WITHHOLD ASSENT to withhold assent or approval ■ *n.* 1. DISAGREEMENT disagreement from a widely held or majority opinion 2. CHR RELIGIOUS NONCONFORMITY refusal to conform to the authority, doctrines, or practices of an established church 3. LAW MINORITY OPINION an opinion of a judge that is not in agreement with that of other judges 4. POL REFUSAL TO ACCEPT POLITICAL RULES opposition to the laws, norms, and structures of a political regime, especially on moral grounds [15thC. From Latin *dissentire*, literally 'to feel differently', from *sentire* (see SENTIENT).]

dissenter /di séntər/ *n.* sb who disagrees with the beliefs or opinions of a majority

Dissenter *n.* sb who refuses to accept the authority, doctrines, or practices of an established church, especially a Protestant who dissented from the Church of England in the 17th and 18th centuries

dissentient /di sénshi ənt/ *adj.* DISSENTING showing or expressing disagreement with the beliefs or opinions of a majority ■ *n.* DISSENTER sb who disagrees with the beliefs or opinions of a majority [Early 17thC. From Latin *dissentient-*, the present participle stem of *dissentire* (see DISSENT).] —**dissentience** *n.* —**dissentiency** *n.* —**dissentiently** *adv.*

dissenting /di sénting/ *adj.* 1. EXPRESSING OR SHOWING DISAGREEMENT disagreeing with the beliefs or opinions of a majority 2. **dissenting, Dissenting** CHR OF DISSENTERS relating or belonging to a group of religious nonconformists, especially an English Protestant denomination of the 17th or 18th centuries 3. LAW DISAGREEING WITH OTHER JUDGES disagreeing with the majority verdict or opinion of other judges —**dissentingly** *adv.*

dissepiment /di séppimənt/ *n.* BOT a dividing wall or membrane separating an organ, e.g. a plant ovary, into distinct chambers [Early 18thC. From Latin *dissaepimentum*, from *dissaepire* 'to make separate', from *saepire* 'to divide off', from *saepes* 'hedge' (source of English *septum*).] —**dissepimental** /di séppi mént'l/ *adj.*

dissertate /díssər tayt/ (**-tates, -tating, -tated**), **dissert** /di súrt/ (**-serts, -serting, -serted**) *vi.* to write or present a dissertation (*formal*) —**dissertator** *n.*

dissertation /díssər táysh'n/ *n.* **1.** LONG ESSAY a lengthy and formal written treatment of a subject, especially a long essay submitted as a requirement for a university degree **2.** FORMAL DISCOURSE a formal spoken or written discourse —**dissertational** *adj.* —**dissertationist** *n.*

disserve /diss súrv/ (**-serves, -serving, -served**) *vt.* to harm or to mistreat another (*formal*)

disservice /diss súrviss/ *n.* an action that causes harm or difficulty

dissever /di sévvər/ (**-ers, -ering, -ered**) *v.* (*formal*) **1.** *vt.* SEPARATE to separate or sever sth **2.** *vt.* BREAK UP to break up or divide sth **3.** *vi.* COME APART to come apart or become disunited [13thC. Via Anglo-Norman *desseverer* from, ultimately, late Latin *disseparare*, literally 'to split apart', from Latin *separare* (see SEPARATE).] —**disseverance** *n.* —**disseveration** /díss sevə ráysh'n/ *n.* —**disseverment** /di sévvərmənt/ *n.*

dissidence /díssidənss/ *n.* disagreement with authority or with prevailing opinion

dissident /díssidənt/ *n.* SB WHO DISAGREES sb who publicly disagrees with an established political or religious system or organization ■ *adj.* EXPRESSING DISAGREEMENT expressing or showing disagreement with authority or with prevailing opinion [Mid-16thC. From Latin *dissident-*, the present participle stem of *dissidere*, literally 'to sit apart', from *sedere* (see SEDENTARY).] —**dissidently** *adv.*

dissimilar /di símmilər/ *adj.* differing in one or more respects —**dissimilarly** *adv.*

dissimilarity /díssimi lárrəti/ (*plural* **-ties**) *n.* **1.** FACT OF DIFFERENCE the fact or state of being different in one or more respects **2.** POINT OF DIFFERENCE a point of difference or distinction

dissimilate /di símmi layt/ (**-lates, -lating, -lated**) *vti.* **1.** LOSE SIMILARITY to make sth dissimilar, or become dissimilar **2.** PHON CHANGE TO DIFFERENT CONSONANT SOUND to undergo linguistic dissimilation, or to change a consonant or consonants by this process [Mid-19thC. Formed from DIS- + ASSIMILATE.] —**dissimilative** /di símmilətiv/ *adj.* —**dissimilatory** /-təri/ *adj.*

dissimilation /di símmi láysh'n/ *n.* **1.** LOSS OF SIMILARITY the process of becoming dissimilar **2.** PHON SOUNDS BECOMING DISSIMILAR the development of a dissimilarity between two consonant sounds in a word that are originally identical

dissimilitude /díssi mílli tyood/ *n.* the condition or quality of differing or of being different to sth else or others (*formal*) [15thC. From Latin *dissimilitudo*, from *dissimilis*, literally 'unlike', from *similis* (see SIMILAR).]

dissimulate /di símmyoo layt/ (**-lates, -lating, -lated**) *vti.* to disguise or hide your true feelings, thoughts, or intentions (*formal*) [15thC. From Latin *dissimulat-*, the past participle stem of *dissimulare*, literally 'to disguise completely', from *simulare* (see SIMULATE).] —**dissimulation** /di símmyoo láysh'n/ *n.* —**dissimulative** /-yoolətiv/ *adj.* —**dissimulator** /-yoo laytər/ *n.*

dissipate /díssi payt/ (**-pates, -pating, -pated**) *v.* **1.** *vti.* CAUSE TO DIMINISH to cause sth to fade or disappear, or to undergo such a process **2.** *vt.* WASTE to spend or use sth wastefully **3.** *vi.* OVERINDULGE to indulge excessively or extravagantly in the pursuit of pleasure by physical methods [15thC. From Latin *dissipat-*, the past participle stem of *dissipare*, literally 'to scatter around'.] —**dissipater** *n.* —**dissipative** *adj.* —**dissipator** *n.*

dissipated /díssi paytid/ *adj.* overindulging in the pursuit of pleasure by physical methods —**dissipatedly** *adv.* —**dissipatedness** *n.*

dissipation /díssi páysh'n/ *n.* **1.** OVERINDULGENCE overindulgence in the pursuit of pleasure by physical methods **2.** WASTEFUL USE the use or squandering of resources, e.g. money or fuel (*formal*) **3.** DISAPPEARANCE disappearance through being scattered or dispersed **4.** REMOVAL the disappearing of a feeling or emotion, e.g. anger or anxiety

dissociable /di sóshəb'l/ *adj.* capable of being distinguished [Early 17thC. Via French from Latin *dissociabilis* 'separating, incompatible', from *dissociare* (see DISSOCIATE).] —**dissociability** /di sóshə bílləti/ *n.* —**dissociableness** /-əb'lnəss/ *n.* —**dissociably** /-əbli/ *adv.*

dissociate /di sóshi ayt, -sóssi-/ (**-ates, -ating, -ated**) *v.* **1.** *vt.* REGARD STH OR SB AS DISTINCT to treat sb or sth as distinct from or unconnected with sb or sth else **2.** *vt.* = **disassociate** *v.* 2 **3.** *vt.* = **disassociate** *v.* 1 **4.** *vti.* CHEM SPLIT STH INTO SIMPLER PARTS to cause the molecules of a compound to break down into simpler molecules, atoms, ions, or radicals, usually in a reversible reaction, or to break down in this way **5.** *vi.* PSYCHIAT SEPARATE OFF AREAS OF THE MIND to separate a group of mental processes from the rest of the mind, causing them to lose their normal relationship with it [Mid-16thC. From, ultimately, Latin *dissociare*, literally 'to separate from fellowship', from *sociare* 'to join together', from *socius* 'companion' (see SOCIAL).] —**dissociative** /di sóshi aytiv, -sóssi-, -ətiv/ *adj.*

dissociation /di sóshi áysh'n, -sóssi-/ *n.* **1.** TREATMENT OF STH AS UNCONNECTED the treatment of sb or sth as distinct or unconnected, or the fact of being regarded in this way **2.** = **disassociation** *n.* 2 **3.** = **disassociation** *n.* 1 **4.** CHEM DIVISION OF MOLECULE a breaking up of a molecule into simpler components **5.** PSYCHIAT SEPARATION OF EMOTIONS the separation of a group of normally connected mental processes, e.g. emotion and understanding, from the rest of the mind as a defence mechanism

dissoluble /di sóllyoob'l/ *adj.* = **soluble** [Mid-16thC. Directly or via French from Latin *dissolubilis*, from *dissolvere* (see DISSOLVE).] —**dissolubility** /di sóllyoo bílləti/ *n.* —**dissolubleness** /-yoob'lnəss/ *n.*

dissolute /díssə loot/ *adj.* overindulging in physical pleasures in a way or to an extent that is considered immoral or harmful [14thC. From Latin *dissolutus*, originally the past participle of *dissolvere* (see DISSOLVE). The underlying idea is of sth loosened or disconnected from accepted standards of behaviour.] —**dissolutely** *adv.* —**dissoluteness** *n.*

dissolution /díssə loósh'n/ *n.* **1.** BREAKING DOWN OF STH INTO PARTS the separating, decomposing, or disintegrating of sth into smaller or more basic constituents **2.** BREAKING UP OF STH the breaking up or destruction of an organization or institution ○ *the dissolution of parliament* **3.** FORMAL CLOSING the bringing to an end of a meeting or assembly, especially the formal ending of the current parliament's jurisdiction before a general election **4.** LAW ENDING OF LEGAL RELATIONSHIP the termination of a legal relationship, e.g. a business partnership or a marriage **5.** DEMISE sb's death (*formal*)

dissolve /di zólv/ *v.* (**-solves, -solving, -solved**) **1.** *vti.* BECOME ABSORBED IN LIQUID to become absorbed in a liquid solution, or cause this process to occur to a solid ○ *Dissolve two tablets in a glass of water.* **2.** *vti.* DISAPPEAR to fade away gradually and disappear, or make sth gradually fade away and disappear ○ *All his fears dissolved.* **3.** *vti.* BREAK UP to break up, or break sth up, into smaller or more basic parts **4.** *vi.* START LAUGHING OR CRYING to begin to laugh or cry uncontrollably **5.** *vt.* CLOSE FORMALLY to bring sth such as a meeting or a political assembly to a formal close, especially to end the jurisdiction of a current parliament before a general election **6.** *vt.* LAW END LEGAL RELATIONSHIP to bring a legal relationship, e.g. a business partnership or a marriage, formally to an end **7.** *vi.* CINEMA, TV, VIDEO SIMULTANEOUSLY FADE OUT AND IN to fade out slowly as a second image fades in, briefly merging one with the other ■ *n.* CINEMA, TV, VIDEO SIMULTANEOUS FADING OUT AND IN a change from one scene to another, with the first scene gradually fading out and the next one gradually fading in over it [14thC. From Latin *dissolvere*, literally 'to loosen asunder', from *solvere* 'to loosen'.] —**dissolvability** /di zólvə bílləti/ *n.* —**dissolvable** *adj.* —**dissolver** *n.*

dissolvent /di zólvənt/ *adj.* CAPABLE OF DISSOLVING STH able to dissolve another substance ■ *n.* = **solvent** *n.*

dissonance /díssənənss/ *n.* **1.** UNPLEASANT NOISE a combination of sounds that is unpleasant to listen to **2.** INCONSISTENCY lack of consistency or compatibility between actions or beliefs **3.** MUSIC UNSTABLE COMBINATION OF MUSICAL NOTES a combination of notes that, when played simultaneously, sounds displeasing and needs to be resolved to a consonance

dissonant /díssənənt/ *adj.* **1.** UNPLEASANT TO HEAR making or involving a combination of sounds that is unpleasant to listen to **2.** CONFLICTING incompatible or inconsistent (*formal*) **3.** MUSIC CONTAINING UNSTABLE CHORDS containing unstable chords or harmonies that need to be resolved to a consonance [15thC. From, ultimately, the Latin present participle stem *dissonant-* of *dissonare*, literally 'to be apart in sound', from *sonare* 'to sound'.] —**dissonantly** *adv.*

dissuade /di swáyd/ (**-suades, -suading, -suaded**) *vt.* to persuade sb not to do sth or not to believe, think, or feel sth [Early 16thC. From Latin *dissuadere*, literally 'to advise against', from *suadere* 'to advise, persuade'.] —**dissuadable** *adj.* —**dissuader** *n.*

dissuasion /di swáyzh'n/ *n.* persuasion not to do sth or not to believe, think, or feel sth [15thC. Directly or via French from the Latin stem *dissuasion-*, from the past participle stem *dissuas-* of *dissuadere* (see DISSUADE).]

dissuasive /di swáyssiv/ *adj.* convincing enough to persuade sb not to do sth or not to believe, think, or feel sth [Early 16thC. Formed from the Latin past participle stem *dissuas-* of *dissuadere* (see DISSUADE).] —**dissuasively** *adv.* —**dissuasiveness** *n.*

dissyllable *n.* = **disyllable**

dissymmetric /díss si méttrik, díssi-/, **dissymmetrical** /-méttrik'l/ *adj.* **1.** = **asymmetric 2.** FORMING MIRROR IMAGES showing the sort of symmetry possessed by things that are mirror images of each other [DISSYMMETRIC, mid-19thC; DISSYMMETRICAL, late 19thC] —**dissymmetrically** *adv.*

dissymmetry /diss símmitri, di-/ (*plural* **-tries**) *n.* **1.** = **asymmetry 2.** SYMMETRY OF OPPOSITES the kind of symmetry that exists between things that are mirror images of each other

dist. *abbr.* **1.** distance **2.** district

distaff /dí staaf/ (*plural* **-taffs** *or* **-taves** /-stayvz/) *n.* **1.** WOMEN'S CONCERNS women's work or any other matters traditionally considered to be the concern of women (*literary*) **2.** CRAFT ROD FOR UNSPUN THREAD a rod on which a fibre, e.g. wool or flax, is wound for sb to use when spinning by hand, or the corresponding rod on a spinning wheel [Old English *distæf*, from a prehistoric Germanic base meaning 'bunch of flax' (ancestor of English *dizen*) + an earlier form of STAFF]

distaff side *n.* a wife's or mother's side of a family

distal /díst'l/ *adj.* ANAT used to describe a body part situated away from a point of attachment or origin. For example, the elbow is distal to the shoulder. ◊ **proximal** [Early 19thC. Coined from DISTANT + -AL.] —**distally** *adv.*

distance /dístənss/ *n.* **1.** LENGTH BETWEEN TWO THINGS the length of the space separating two people, places, or things ○ *What's the distance between Paris and New York?* **2.** FAR-OFF PLACE a place or position far away, or not very close ○ *It's best seen from a distance.* **3.** CLOSENESS ALLOWING SOME ACTIVITY the space between two people, places, or things with regard to activity carried on between the two ○ *We can do nothing until they're within hailing distance.* **4.** AMOUNT OF SEPARATION the amount by which two places are separated, especially when thought of in terms of the time or inconvenience of a journey between the two ○ *She lives some distance away.* **5.** COOLNESS OR ALOOFNESS a cool or slightly aloof response to another person or group ○ *He suddenly felt the need to put some distance between himself and his friends.* **6.** INTERVAL OF TIME the interval between one point in time and another, especially a long interval ○ *You can't expect to remember all the details at a distance of more than 20 years.* **7.** AMOUNT OF PROGRESS the amount of progress that has been made or that is still to be made ○ *still some distance to go before we can reach an agreement* **8.** IDEOLOGICAL GULF difference of opinion or ideology ○ *There's still some distance between us with regard to the basic issues.* **9.** DIFFERENCE IN RANK difference in social status, or the extent of such a difference (*archaic*) **10.** HORSERACING SPACE GREATER THAN 20 LENGTHS a space of more than twenty lengths between two racehorses, usually the winner and the horse finishing second ○ *win by a distance* ■ *v.* **(-tances, -tancing, -tanced) 1.** *vr.* AVOID EMOTIONAL INVOLVEMENT to avoid becoming emotionally involved in sth, or encourage sb to feel less close emotionally to sth ○ *Try to distance yourself from past experiences.* **2.** *vt.* AVOID SUPPORTING to avoid giving any support to or having any involvement with sb or sth, or deny that you support or have any involvement with sb or sth ○ *He was trying to distance himself from the allegations.* **3.** *vt.* HORSERACING WIN BY A DISTANCE to beat another racehorse by more than twenty lengths [13thC. Directly or via French from Latin *distantia*, from *distant-* 'standing apart' (see DISTANT).] ◇ **go the distance** to continue until you have completed sth

distance learning *n.* education for students working at home, with little or no face-to-face with teachers and with material provided remotely, e.g. by e-mail, television, or post

distant /dístənt/ *adj.* **1.** FAR AWAY situated, living, or happening far away ○ *a distant galaxy* **2.** FAR AWAY IN TIME remote in time, either in the future or the past ○ *They hope to meet again in the distant future.* **3.** ALOOFLY RESERVED showing that sb does not want to be friendly or intimate **4.** FAINT so slight as to be hard to discern ○ *a distant resemblance* [14thC. Directly or via French from the Latin present participle stem *distant-* of *distare* 'to stand apart', from *stare* 'to stand'.] —**distantness** *n.*

distantly /dístəntli/ *adv.* **1.** FAR AWAY from far away and therefore usually not clear or loud ○ *We could distantly make out figures dancing in the village square.* **2.** FAR AWAY MENTALLY not concentrating on the immediate surroundings **3.** ALOOFLY in a detached, cold, or formal way ○ *He smiled at her distantly as she walked past.* **4.** NOT CLOSELY not closely in terms of family or blood relations ○ *distantly related*

distaste /diss táyst/ *n.* a feeling of dislike, disapproval, or mild disgust [Late 16thC. From DIS- + TASTE; modelled on Old French *desgoust*, literally 'distaste'.]

WORD KEY: SYNONYMS

See Synonyms at ***dislike***.

distasteful /diss táystf'l/ *adj.* **1.** UNPLEASANT provoking dislike, disapproval, or mild disgust **2.** DISAPPROVING showing that you dislike or disapprove of sth (*archaic*) —**distastefully** *adv.* —**distastefulness** *n.*

distemper[1] /dis témpər/ *n.* a viral disease that affects various animals, especially dogs and cats. ◊ **canine distemper, feline distemper** [Mid-16thC. Ultimately from late Latin *distemperare*, literally 'to combine awry' (referring to an imbalance of humours), from Latin *temperare* 'to combine' (see TEMPER).]

distemper[2] /dis témpər/ *n.* **1.** PAINT a type of paint in which the colouring material is mixed with water and a substance such as glue, size, rather than with oil. Distemper is often used for painting walls, theatrical scenery, and posters. **2.** PAINTING WITH DISTEMPER the use of distemper in painting posters and murals ■ *vt.* **(-pers, -pering, -pered)** PAINT STH WITH DISTEMPER to paint or cover sth, e.g. a wall, with distemper [14thC. Directly or via Old French *destremper* 'to soak, mix' from late Latin *distemperare*, literally 'to mix thoroughly', from Latin *temperare* 'to mix'.]

distend /di sténd/ **(-tends, -tending, -tended)** *vti.* to expand, swell, or inflate as if by pressure from within [14thC. From Latin *distendere*, literally 'to stretch apart', from *tendere* 'to stretch'.] —**distender** *n.* —**distensibility** /di sténssə bílləti/ *n.* —**distensible** /-ssəb'l/ *adj.* —**distension** /-ténsh'n/ *n.*

distich /dí stik/ *n.* two lines of poetry, sometimes rhyming, that form a complete unit in themselves [Early 16thC. Via Latin *distichon* from Greek *distikhon*, originally a form of *distikhos* 'of two rows or verses', from *stikhos* 'row, line of verse'.] —**distichal** *adj.*

distichous /dístikəss/ *adj.* used to describe leaves that grow in vertical rows on opposite sides of a stem —**distichously** *adv.*

distil /di stíl/ **(-tils, -tilling, -tilled)** *v.* **1.** *vti.* PURIFY LIQUID WITH HEAT to purify a liquid by heating it and then condensing its vapour, or to undergo purification in this way **2.** *vt.* MAKE ALCOHOLIC SPIRITS to produce alcoholic spirits using the process of heating liquid and condensing its vapour **3.** *vt.* CREATE FROM ESSENTIAL ELEMENTS to create sth from the essential or most important elements of sth larger or longer **4.** *vi.* EMERGE SLOWLY to be emitted slowly or in small quantities ○ *'Then slowly from the silence there distilled drops of music'* (John Buchan, *Greenmantle*; 1916) [14thC. From, ultimately, Latin *distillare*, alteration of *destillare*, literally 'to drip apart', from *stillare* 'to drip', from *stilla* 'drop'.] —**distillable** *adj.*

distill *vti.* US = **distil**

distillate /dístələt, -ayt/ *n.* **1.** CHEM LIQUID PRODUCED BY DISTILLATION a concentrated liquid produced by heating a liquid mixture and condensing the vapour **2.** ESSENCE the concentrated essence of sth

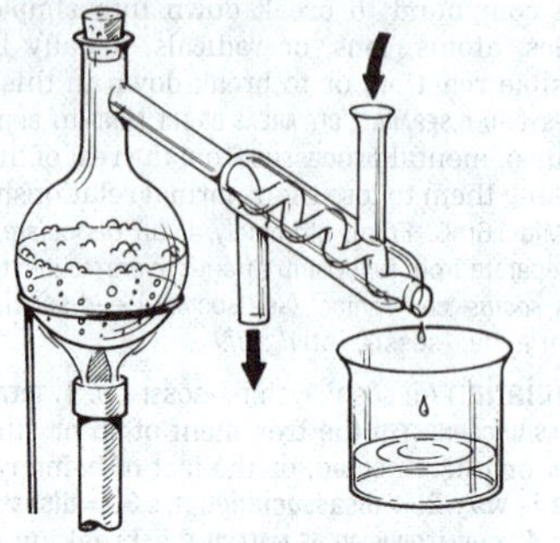

Distillation: Liquid is boiled (left) and the resulting vapour condensed (right)

distillation /dìstə láysh'n/ *n.* **1.** BOILING AND CONDENSING OF LIQUID the process of separating, concentrating, or purifying liquid by boiling it and condensing the resulting vapour. Alcoholic spirits, e.g. whisky and vodka, are made in this way. **2.** CONDENSED VERSION OF STH sth that consists of the essential points, aspects, or implications of sth larger or longer **3.** CHEM = **distillate** *n.* 1 —**distillatory** /di stíllətəri/ *adj.*

distillation column *n.* CHEM a hollow vertical column, fitted inside with perforated trays or packing material, in which liquid mixtures are separated into their components by heating the mixture and condensing the vapour produced

distilled /di stíld/ *adj.* **1.** SUMMING STH UP NEATLY derived from or encapsulating a wider experience or larger set of ideas **2.** CHEM RESULTING FROM DISTILLATION used to describe liquids that have been purified or concentrated by distillation

distiller /di stíllər/ *n.* a company that or person who produces alcoholic spirits such as whisky, vodka, and gin

distillery /di stílləri/ (*plural* **-ies**) *n.* a place where strong alcoholic drinks such as whisky, vodka, and gin are made by distilling

distinct /di stíngkt/ *adj.* **1.** SEPARATE clearly different and separate ○ *The word has two distinct senses.* **2.** APPARENT TO THE SENSES easy to hear, see, smell, or understand ○ *I have a very distinct memory of that day.* **3.** CERTAIN definite or undeniable ○ *I had the distinct impression they'd been arguing.* **4.** NOTICEABLE strong enough, large enough, or definite enough to be noticed ○ *There's a distinct smell of petrol in the car.* **5.** EMPHATIC very great in degree, e.g. as an honour felt or experienced ○ *a distinct privilege* [14thC. Directly or via French from the Latin past participle *distinctus* of *distinguere* 'to separate' (see DISTINGUISH).] —**distinctness** *n.*

distinction /di stíngksh'n/ *n.* **1.** DIFFERENCE a difference, or the recognition of a difference, between two or more things or people **2.** HIGH QUALITY excellence in quality or talent ○ *tailors of distinction* **3.** STH TO BE PROUD OF sth done or given as a mark of respect or honour ○ *I had the distinction of giving the opening address.* **4.** DISTINGUISHING FEATURE sth that characterizes or singles out sth or sb ○ *She has the dubious distinction of being the government's most slavish defender.* **5.** EDUC HIGH EXAMINATION GRADE a high mark in an examination

distinctive /di stíngktiv/ *adj.* **1.** DIFFERENT FROM OTHERS uniquely characteristic of a particular person, group, or thing **2.** PHON RELATING TO PHONEME'S DISTINGUISHING FEATURE relating to the features of a phoneme that distinguish it from other similar phonemes, e.g. the fact that it is labial, fricative, or nasal —**distinctively** *adv.* —**distinctiveness** *n.*

distinctly /di stíngktli/ *adv.* **1.** CLEARLY clearly or obviously enough to be easily seen, heard, remembered, identified, or understood ○ *I distinctly recall the incident.* ○ *I wasn't able to see what was going on very distinctly as I didn't have my glasses with me.* **2.** UNDENIABLY to a marked extent ○ *She was distinctly angry*

distingué /di stáng gay/ *adj.* having the confidence and dignity of sb who is used to being respected (*formal*) [Early 19thC. From French, the past participle of *distinguer* 'to distinguish' (see DISTINGUISH).]

distinguish /di stíng gwish/ **(-guishes, -guishing, -guished)** *v.* **1.** *vti.* RECOGNIZE DIFFERENCES to be aware of a difference between two or more people, groups, or things, or to show that they are different from each other ○ *to distinguish between fact and fiction* **2.** *vt.* BE THE IDENTIFYING DIFFERENCE to be the feature or characteristic that shows that one person, group, or thing is different from another ○ *What distinguishes dogs from wolves?* **3.** *vt.* MAKE STH OUT to be able to recognize or identify sth ○ *I could barely distinguish people's faces in the fog.* **4.** *vr.* DO STH WELL to attract attention and praise in a particular field ○ *He distinguished himself on the field of battle.* [Late 16thC. Formed from French *distinguer* or directly from Latin *distinguere*, literally 'to separate by pricking', from *stinguere* 'to quench' (presumed earlier 'to prick').] —**distinguisher** *n.*

distinguishable /di stíng gwishəb'l/ *adj.* **1.** DIFFERENT recognizably different **2.** DETECTABLE capable of being seen, heard, tasted, or detected in some way —**distinguishably** *adv.*

distinguished /di stíng gwisht/ *adj.* **1.** RECOGNIZED FOR EXCELLENCE well known and respected for a particular achievement, skill, knowledge, or talent ○ *a distinguished composer* **2.** CONFIDENT AND DIGNIFIED showing the confident and dignified appearance and manners of sb who is used to respect **3.** SUCCESSFUL showing or involving a great deal of skill, talent, or success

Distinguished Conduct Medal *n.* a medal awarded to noncommissioned officers, warrant officers, and ordinary soldiers and airmen and women in the British Army and Royal Air Force for distinguished conduct in action

Distinguished Flying Cross *n.* **1.** BRITISH AIR FORCE MEDAL a Royal Air Force medal awarded to noncommissioned and warrant officers for distinguished conduct when flying in action **2.** US FLYING MEDAL a US military medal awarded for extraordinary achievement or for heroism in air combat

Distinguished Service Cross *n.* **1.** BRITISH ARMED SERVICES MEDAL a British medal awarded in all branches of the armed forces for distinguished service in action **2.** US ARMY MEDAL a US Army medal awarded for extraordinary heroism against an enemy. It is the US Army's second highest award for bravery, the highest being the Congressional Medal of Honor.

Distinguished Service Medal *n.* a British medal awarded for distinguished conduct in action to noncommissioned officers and ordinary seamen and women in the Royal Navy and Royal Marines

Distinguished Service Order *n.* a British medal awarded to commissioned officers in all armed forces for distinguished service in action

distinguishing /di stíng gwishing/ *adj.* allowing one person, group, or thing to be told apart from another ○ *distinguishing characteristics*

distort /di stáwrt/ **(-torts, -torting, -torted)** *v.* **1.** *vt.* GIVE AN INACCURATE REPORT OF STH to describe or report sth in a way that is inaccurate or misleading **2.** *vti.* ALTER SHAPE to bend, twist, stretch, or change from a normal or natural shape, or make sth do this **3.** *vt.* MAKE STH UNNATURAL OR UNCLEAR to change sth such as an image in such a way that it becomes unclear or unrecognizable **4.** *vt.* ELECTRON ENG REPRODUCE INACCURATELY to amplify or reproduce sth, e.g. a radio signal, inaccurately [15thC. From the Latin past participle stem *distort-* of *distorquere*, literally 'to twist completely', from *torquere* 'to twist'.] —**distorter** *n.* —**distortive** *adj.*

distorted /di stáwrtid/ *adj.* **1. INACCURATELY REPORTED** described or reported in a way that is inaccurate or misleading ○ *a distorted version of events* **2. OUT OF SHAPE** bent or twisted out of shape **3. UNNATURAL OR UNCLEAR** changed in such a way as to become unclear or unrecognizable ○ *a distorted face in the mirror* —**distortedly** *adv.* —**distortedness** *n.*

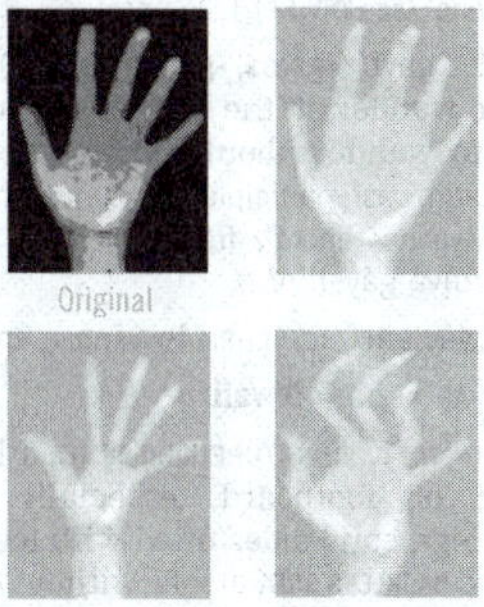

Distortion: Electronically manipulated images of a hand

distortion /di stáwrsh'n/ *n.* **1. MISLEADING ALTERATION** the altering of information in such a way that people are misinformed or misled **2. CHANGING FROM CORRECT SHAPE** the bending or twisting of sth out of its normal or natural shape **3. MISSHAPEN PART** a part of sth that has been bent, twisted, stretched, or forced out of its normal or natural shape **4. MAKING STH UNCLEAR** the altering of sth, e.g. a radio or television signal, to the extent that it becomes unclear or unrecognizable **5.** OPTICS **ALTERATION IN OPTICAL IMAGE** an alteration in an image in which the original proportions are changed, resulting from a defect in a lens or optical system —**distortional** *adj.* —**distortionary** *adj.*

distr. *abbr.* 1. distribution 2. distributor

distract /di strákt/ (**-tracts, -tracting, -tracted**) *vt.* **1. CATCH SB'S ATTENTION** to take sb's attention away from what he or she is doing or thinking, or from what is happening **2. AMUSE SB** to amuse or entertain sb, especially as a means of taking his or her mind off sth unpleasant **3. MAKE SB UNEASY** to unsettle sb's mind with disturbing, confusing, or conflicting emotions (*archaic*) ○ *'O Husband, Husband, my Heart long'd to see thee; but to see thee thus distracts me'.* (John Gay, *The Beggar's Opera*; 1728) [14thC. From the Latin past participle stem *distract-* of *distrahere*, literally 'to draw away', from *trahere* 'to draw, drag'.] —**distracter** *n.* —**distractibility** /di stráktə bílləti/ *n.* —**distractible** /-stráktəb'l/ *adj.* —**distractive** /-tiv/ *adj.* —**distractively** /-tivli/ *adv.*

distracted /di stráktid/ *adj.* **1. PREOCCUPIED** showing a lack of concentration **2. ANXIOUS** so worried or upset as to be unable to think clearly or act sensibly —**distractedly** *adv.* —**distractedness** *n.*

distracting /di strákting/ *adj.* **1. DIVERTING SB'S ATTENTION** taking sb's attention away from what he or she wants to do or ought to be doing **2. RELAXING** helping sb to relax and forget work or worries —**distractingly** *adv.*

distraction /di stráksh'n/ *n.* **1. STH THAT DIVERTS ATTENTION** sth that interferes with concentration or takes attention away from sth else **2. AMUSEMENT** sth providing entertainment or amusement, especially sth that takes the mind off work or worries and helps relaxation **3. EMOTIONAL UPSET** a state of great mental or emotional upset

distrain /di stráyn/ (**-trains, -training, -trained**) *vt.* to take and hold sb's property as a pledge for sth such as unpaid rent [14thC. From the Old French present stem *destreign-* of *destreindre*, from Latin *distringere* 'to draw asunder'.] —**distrainable** *adj.* —**distrainee** /di stray née/ *n.* —**distrainer** /di stráynər/ *n.* —**distrainment** /-mənt/ *n.*

distraint /di stráynt/ *n.* LAW the seizing of sb's movable property either in lieu of payment of a debt or in order to force the person to pay. US term **distress** *n.* 5 [Mid-18thC. Formed from DISTRAIN; modelled on CONSTRAINT.]

distrait /di stráy, dí stray/ *adj.* **1. INATTENTIVE** inattentive and slightly distracted or absent-minded (*literary*) **2. DISTRAUGHT** upset or perturbed (*archaic*) [14thC. Via French from the Old French past participle of *destraire* 'to distract', from Latin *distrahere* (see DISTRACT).]

distraught /di stráwt/ *adj.* **1. EXTREMELY UPSET** extremely upset and distressed **2. NOT IN MENTAL HEALTH** experiencing psychiatric disorder (*archaic*) [14thC. Alteration of archaic *distract* 'perplexed', from Latin *distractus*, past participle of *distrahere* (see DISTRACT); influenced by *straught*, former past participle of STRETCH.]

distress /di stréss/ *n.* **1. MENTAL SUFFERING** mental suffering, e.g. that caused by grief, anxiety, or unhappiness **2. HARDSHIP OR DIFFICULTY** difficulty or hardship caused by a lack of basic necessities **3. PHYSICAL PAIN** physical pain or discomfort **4. DANGER OR DIFFICULTY** great danger or difficulty, with a need for immediate assistance ○ *a ship in distress* **5.** LAW = **distraint** *n.* ■ *vt.* (**-tresses, -tressing, -tressed**) **1. UPSET SB** to make sb extremely upset, anxious, or alarmed **2. MAKE FURNITURE OR FABRIC LOOK OLD** to give a new piece of furniture or fabric an old or worn appearance [13thC. Via Old French *destresce* from assumed Vulgar Latin *districtia*, from the Latin past participle stem *district-* of *distringere*, literally 'to draw asunder' (see STRINGENT).]

distressed /di strést/ *adj.* **1. VERY UPSET** extremely upset, anxious, or unhappy **2. LACKING MONEY** not having enough money to live on **3. MADE TO LOOK OLDER** artificially given an old or worn appearance **4.** *US* LAW, FIN **REPOSSESSED FROM BAD DEBTOR** repossessed by a bank or other lender from the borrower and offered for sale at a reduced price ○ *a distressed loan*

distressing /di stréssing/, **distressful** /-stréssf'l/ *adj.* causing sb to feel extremely upset —**distressingly** *adv.*

distress signal *n.* a signal, e.g. a radio message or a flare, sent by a ship or aircraft in urgent need of assistance

distributary /di stríbbyootəri/ (*plural* **-ies**) *n.* a channel leading water away from a main single channel

distribute /di stríbbyoot/ (**-utes, -uting, -uted**) *v.* **1.** *vt.* **GIVE STH OUT** to deliver or share things out to people ○ *distribute prizes* **2.** *vt.* **SHARE STH OUT** to share sth out among a number of people **3.** *vt.* **SPREAD STH** to scatter sth about or spread it throughout a particular area or place **4.** *vt.* **DIVIDE INTO CLASSES** to divide sth up into different classes or categories **5.** *vt.* LOGIC **MAKE TERM APPLY TO ALL** to apply a term to all the members of the class it designates **6.** *vti.* MATH **MAKE OPERATION APPLY THROUGHOUT** to apply or make an operation, e.g. multiplication or division, apply to each part of a mathematical expression [15thC. From the Latin past participle stem *distribut-* of *distribuere*, literally 'to assign separately', from *tribuere* 'to assign' (see TRIBUTE).] —**distributable** *adj.*

WORD KEY: SYNONYMS

See Synonyms at ***scatter***.

distributed /di stríbbyootid/ *adj.* used to describe computer systems in which two or more computers have a telecommunications link to each other but can also operate independently

distributer *n.* = **distributor**

distribution /dìstri byóosh'n/ *n.* **1. GIVING OUT** the sharing out or delivery of things to a number of people **2. SHARING OUT** the process of dividing up and giving out sth, e.g. money, when it is shared by a number of people **3. SCATTERING** the scattering or spreading of sth over an area **4.** ECOL **ENTIRE AREA WHERE SPECIES IS FOUND** the area or areas taken together where sth is located or where a species lives and reproduces **5.** STATS **SPREAD OF STATISTICS** the spread of statistics within known or possible limits, especially in relation to the norm or to expectations **6.** LAW **SHARING OUT OF SB'S ESTATE** the dividing up of the estate of sb who has died intestate among people who are entitled to receive a share **7.** LOGIC **RECOMBINING OF TWO PROPOSITIONS** the recombining of two operations from one proposition in another equivalent proposition, e.g. 'p and (q or r)' is equivalent to '(p and q) or (p and r)' —**distributional** *adj.*

distributive /di stríbbyootiv/ *adj.* **1. INVOLVING DISTRIBUTION** relating to or involving the handing out, sharing out, or scattering about of things **2.** GRAM **REFERRING TO EACH MEMBER OF GROUP** referring to each member of a set or group individually and separately. 'Each', 'every', and 'either' are examples of distributive words in English. **3.** LOGIC **REFERRING TO INDIVIDUALS, NOT CLASSES** referring to an individual member of a class, or to each member individually **4.** MATH **PRODUCING EQUAL RESULTS** used to describe a mathematical expression with two operators whose expansion produces the same results whether operated on as a whole or as a sum of the parts ■ *n.* GRAM **DISTRIBUTIVE WORD** a word that refers to every member of a set or group individually and separately —**distributively** *adv.* —**distributiveness** *n.*

distributor /di stríbbyootər/, **distributer** *n.* **1. SB WHO DISTRIBUTES STH** a person who or an organization or thing that distributes sth **2.** COMM **WHOLESALER** a wholesaler who sells goods to retailers, usually within a specified geographic area **3.** AUTOMOT **DEVICE CONVEYING ELECTRICITY TO SPARK PLUGS** the device in a motor vehicle's engine that transfers electric current from the induction coil to the spark plugs **4.** CINEMA **ORGANIZATION ARRANGING SCREENING OF FILMS** an organization that advertises films and arranges with exhibitors, who own the cinemas, to have them shown

district /dístrikt/ *n.* **1. AREA** an area of a town or country, especially one with a particular distinguishing feature or one that is an administrative division ○ *a fruit-growing district* **2. SURROUNDING AREA** the area around a particular place, e.g. the area around sb's home or around a town [Early 17thC. Via French from medieval Latin *districtus* '(area of) jurisdiction', literally 'restraining (of offenders)', from the Latin stem *district-* (see DISTRESS).]

district attorney *n.* *US* in the United States, the prosecuting officer of a particular jurisdiction

district court *n.* **1. SCOTTISH MAGISTRATES' COURT** in Scotland, a magistrates' court dealing with minor offences, e.g. parking fines and nonpayment of debts **2. US DISTRICT TRIAL COURT** in the United States, the trial court in either a state or a federal district **3. AUSTRALIAN LOWER COURT** in some states of Australia, a court that deals with cases that are not important enough to be tried in a high court

district nurse *n.* a community nurse (*dated*)

District of Columbia federal district of the United States, situated on the Potomac and Anacostia rivers, coextensive with the city of Washington, D.C., the nation's capital. It was created in 1790–91. Area: 177 sq. km/68 sq. mi.

distringas /di stríng gəss, -gass/ *n.* in former times, a court order instructing a sheriff to repossess sb's property [15thC. From medieval Latin, 'you shall distrain' (the opening word of the writ), a form of *distringere* (see DISTRESS).]

distrust /diss trúst/ *n.* **LACK OF TRUST** a feeling that sb or sth is dishonest or unreliable and does not deserve to be trusted ■ *vt.* (**-trusts, -trusting, -trusted**) **HAVE NO CONFIDENCE IN SB** to have a feeling that sb or sth is dishonest or unreliable and does not deserve to be trusted —**distruster** *n.*

distrustful /diss trústf'l/ *adj.* showing lack of trust in sb or sth —**distrustfully** *adv.* —**distrustfulness** *n.*

disturb /di stúrb/ (**-turbs, -turbing, -turbed**) *vt.* **1. INTERRUPT SB** to interrupt or distract sb when he or she is busy **2. UPSET SB** to make sb feel anxious or slightly troubled **3. CHANGE SHAPE OR POSITION** to move sth so that it is not in its normal, expected, or correct shape or position ○ *Nothing had been disturbed.* **4. SPOIL PEACE AND QUIET** to spoil the quietness, stillness, or peacefulness of sth **5. AWAKEN** to waken sb or sth [12thC. Directly or via Old French *desto(u)rber* from Latin *disturbare*, literally 'to disturb completely', from *turbare* 'to disturb'.] —**disturber** *n.*

WORD KEY: SYNONYMS

See Synonyms at ***bother***.

disturbance /di stúrbənss/ *n.* **1. DISRUPTION OF PEACE** the disruption of a peaceful or ordered environment, or sth that causes such disruption **2. DISRUPTION OF CONCENTRATION** the disruption of sb's concentration, or sth that disrupts sb's ability to get on with a task in hand **3. COMMOTION** noisy and violent behaviour in a public place, or an incident involving such behaviour **4. MENTAL UPSET** psychological or emotional upset **5.** GEOL **EARTH TREMOR** a minor movement of the earth that falls short of an earthquake **6.** LAW

INTERFERENCE WITH SB'S RIGHTS any act that causes disruption to others or hinders them from pursuing normal legal activities **7.** METEOROL LOW-PRESSURE AREA a small area of low pressure

disturbance of the peace *n.* a violation of public order that disrupts or destroys public tranquillity

disturbed /di stúrbd/ *adj.* **1.** ANXIOUS worried or concerned **2.** TROUBLED unsettled and unhappy, with many troubles and upsets **3.** NOT IN MENTAL HEALTH affected by or displaying symptoms of psychiatric disorder

disturbing /di stúrbing/ *adj.* causing worry, or emotional or physical upset —**disturbingly** *adv.*

disulfide *n.* CHEM US = **disulphide**

disulfiram /dī súlfi ram/ *n.* a chemical compound used in the treatment of alcoholism for its deterrent effect. It causes nausea, vomiting, and other extreme effects when alcohol is consumed. Formula: $C_{10}H_{20}N_2S_4$. [Mid-20thC. From DISULFIDE + THIOUREA + AMYL.]

disulphide /dī súlfīd/ *n.* a chemical compound that has two atoms of sulphur combined with one or more other elements

disunion /diss yóonyən/ *n.* **1.** DISCORD disagreement or discord **2.** DIVISION INTO SMALLER PARTS the splitting up of sth into separate smaller parts or groups

disunite /díssyoō nít/ (**-nites, -niting, -nited**) *v.* **1.** *vt.* CAUSE DISAGREEMENT BETWEEN PEOPLE to create or be a source of disagreement between different people or factions within a group **2.** *vti.* DIVIDE STH to divide sth, or become divided, into smaller parts or groups —**disuniter** *n.* —**disunity** *n.*

disunited /díssyoō nítid/ *adj.* divided into separate groups or factions because of a disagreement or difference of opinion

disuse /diss yóoss/ *n.* the fact or condition of not being used, applied, or followed, especially for a long time

disused /diss yóozd/ *adj.* no longer in use, or no longer used for its original purpose ○ *a disused airfield*

disyllable /dī silləb'l, di-/, **dissyllable** *n.* **1.** LING TWO-SYLLABLE WORD a word composed of two syllables **2.** POETRY TWO-SYLLABLE POETIC UNIT a two-syllable unit of rhythm in poetry —**disyllabic** /dīssi lábbik, díssi-/ *adj.*

dit /dit/ *n.* the spoken form of the short sound used in Morse and other telegraphic codes. ◊ **dah** [Mid-20thC. An imitation of the sound.]

ditch /dich/ *n.* **1.** NARROW CHANNEL a long narrow channel dug in the ground, usually used for drainage or irrigation but sometimes used as a boundary marker **2.** SMALL BROOK a small natural stream or brook ■ *v.* (**ditches, ditching, ditched**) **1.** *vt.* ABANDON STH OR SB to abandon sth or sb as no longer wanted, liked, or needed (*informal*) **2.** *vti.* MAKE EMERGENCY LANDING ON WATER to land, or make an aircraft land, on water in an emergency (*informal*) **3.** *vti.* DIG DITCHES to enclose, drain, or irrigate an area with ditches, or dig ditches for this purpose [Old English *dīc*, from a prehistoric Germanic word meaning 'hole and mound produced by digging', which is also the ancestor of English *dig* and *dyke*] —**ditcher** *n.*

ditchwater /dích wawtər/ *n.* the dirty stagnant water found in ditches

ditheism /díthi izəm, dī thée-/ *n.* **1.** BELIEF IN TWO GODS belief in two equal gods **2.** BELIEF IN GOOD AND EVIL GODS the belief that the world is ruled by two equal and opposing forces or gods, one good and one evil —**ditheist** *n.* —**ditheistic** /díthi ístik/ *adj.*

dither /díthər/ *vi.* (**-ers, -ering, -ered**) **1.** BE AGITATED AND INDECISIVE to behave in a nervous and indecisive way **2.** *UKdial* TREMBLE to tremble or quiver, e.g. with cold ■ *n.* AGITATED OR INDECISIVE STATE a state of nervous agitation or indecisiveness [Mid-17thC. Alteration of obsolete *didder* 'to tremble, shake', of uncertain origin, but thought to suggest the action.] —**ditherer** *n.* —**dithery** *adj.*

dithering /díthəring/ *n.* **1.** NERVOUS INDECISIVENESS nervously confused indecisiveness in the face of alternative possible actions **2.** COMPUT SIMULATION OF COLOURS a technique of mixing pixels of several colours on a computer display to create the illusion of extra colours or shading

dithyramb /díthi ram, -ramb/ *n.* **1.** FERVENT SPEECH a passionately emotional speech or piece of writing (*formal*) **2.** IMPASSIONED GREEK CHORUS in ancient Greece, a wild and impassioned choral hymn, originally directed to the god Dionysus [Early 17thC. Via Latin *dithyrambus* from Greek *dithurambos*, of unknown origin.]

dithyrambic /díthi rámbik/ *adj.* (*formal*) **1.** FERVENT passionately emotional or wildly enthusiastic **2.** RELATING TO DITHYRAMB involving or relating to a dithyramb —**dithyrambically** *adv.*

ditsy /dítsi/ (**-sier, -siest**), **ditzy** (**-zier, -ziest**) *adj.* *US* silly or scatterbrained (*informal*) [Late 20thC. Origin uncertain: perhaps a blend of DOTTY and DIZZY.]

dittany /díttəni/ (*plural* **-nies** *or* **-ny**) *n.* **1.** PINK-FLOWERED PLANT OF S EUROPE an aromatic pink-flowered plant found in southern Europe and related to oregano and marjoram. It is cultivated as an ornamental and for its medicinal properties. Latin name: *Origanum dictamnus.* **2.** CULINARY HERB USED IN US an aromatic plant, cultivated in the United States as a kitchen herb. Latin name: *Cunila origanoides.* **3.** = **gas plant** [12thC. From Old French *ditain* and medieval Latin *ditaneum*, both ultimately from Greek *diktamnon*, of uncertain origin: perhaps named for *Diktē*, mountain on Crete where it grows.]

ditto /díttō/ *interj.* SAME HERE used instead of repeating sth that has just been said to indicate that the same thing applies to you (*informal*) ■ *adv.* THE SAME THING APPLIES ELSEWHERE indicating that whatever has just been said about one person or thing applies equally to sb or sth else ○ *The car will need to be cleaned; ditto the children* ■ *n.* (*plural* **-tos**) SYMBOLS REPRESENTING REPEATED MATTER a pair of symbols (") that together represent matter that is repeated directly from what appears above them but that is unstated ■ *vt.* (**-tos, -toing, -toed**) REPEAT STH to repeat or imitate sth that sb else has said or done [Early 17thC. Via a Tuscan dialect variant of Italian *detto* 'said', from the Latin past participle *dictus*. Originally used to avoid repeating the name of a month.]

ditty /dítti/ (*plural* **-ties**) *n.* a short simple popular song [14thC. Via Old French *dité* 'composition' from Latin *dictatum* 'thing dictated', from the past participle of *dictare* 'to dictate' (see DICTATE).]

ditty bag *n.* a small canvas or leather bag used by men for holding small personal belongings [*Ditty* of unknown origin]

ditzy *adj.* = **ditsy**

diuresis /dīyoō réesiss/ *n.* abnormally increased excretion of urine caused by excessive intake of fluids, a drug, or a disease [Late 17thC. From modern Latin, literally 'urination through', from Greek *ourēsis* 'urination'.]

diuretic /dīyoō réttik/ *adj.* CAUSING INCREASED URINE OUTPUT causing increased flow of urine ■ *n.* DRUG INCREASING URINE OUTPUT a medication or other agent that increases urine output [14thC. From, ultimately, late Latin *diureticus*, from Greek *diourētikos*, from *diourein*, literally 'to urinate through', from *ourein* 'to urinate'.] —**diuretically** *adv.*

diurnal /dī úrn'l/ *adj.* **1.** IN THE DAYTIME happening during the day as opposed to at night. ◊ **nocturnal 2.** EVERY DAY happening every day **3.** SCI VARYING WITHIN A DAY varying within the course of a single day **4.** BOT OPEN ONLY IN DAYTIME used to describe flowers that open during the day and close at night. ◊ **nocturnal 5.** ZOOL ACTIVE IN DAYTIME used to describe animals that are active during the day rather than at night. ◊ **nocturnal** ■ *n.* CHR WORSHIP BOOK in the Roman Catholic Church, a book containing the prayer and worship material for all the set daily services except matins [14thC. From late Latin *diurnalis*, from Latin *diurnus* 'daily', from *dies* 'day' (source of English *diary*).] —**diurnally** *adv.*

diurnal parallax *n.* the change in a celestial body's apparent position caused by the change in the observer's position because of the motion of the Earth in a day

diuron /dī́ ə ron/ *n.* a long-lasting agricultural herbicide used especially to kill annual weeds. Formula: $C_9H_{10}Cl_2N_2O$. [[Mid-20thC. Coined from DICHLOR- + UREA + -ON.]

div *n.* an unintelligent person (*slang insult*)

div. *abbr.* **1.** diversion **2.** divide **3.** dividend **4.** division **5.** divorced

diva /déevə/ (*plural* **-vas** *or* **-ve** /-vay/) *n.* **1.** WOMAN OPERA SINGER a distinguished woman singer, especially one who sings in operas **2.** TEMPERAMENTAL WOMAN an extremely arrogant or temperamental woman [Late 19thC. Via Italian from Latin, 'goddess', from the feminine of *divus* 'divine' (see DIVINE).]

divagate /dīvə gayt/ (**-gates, -gating, -gated**) *vi.* (*literary*) **1.** DIGRESS to wander off the subject under discussion **2.** WANDER to wander about somewhere [Mid-16thC. From the Latin past participle stem *divagat-* of *divagari*, literally 'to wander about', from *vagari* 'to wander'.] —**divagation** /dīvə gáysh'n/ *n.*

divalent /dī váylənt/ *adj.* CHEM having a valency of 2

Divali *n.* INDIAN RELIG = **Diwali**

divan /di ván/ *n.* **1.** FURNITURE KIND OF BED a bed with no headboard or footboard, especially one with, instead of legs, solid sides fitted with feet or castors **2.** FURNITURE BACKLESS SOFA a sofa without a back, and sometimes without arms **3.** ISLAMIC COURTROOM OR OTHER CHAMBER a courtroom, council chamber, or other official hall in some Islamic countries **4.** SMOKING ROOM in former times, a smoking room attached to a coffee shop or cigar shop **5.** POETRY ARABIC POEMS a collection of poems written in Persian or Arabic, often by a single poet [Late 16thC. Via French or Italian *divano* from Turkish *dīvān*, from Persian *dīvān*.]

divaricate /dī várri kayt, di-/ *vi.* (**-cates, -cating, -cated**) BRANCH OR FORK to branch or fork at a wide angle ■ *adj.* BIOL BRANCHING branching or forking at a wide angle [Early 17thC. From the Latin past participle stem *divaricat-* of *divaricare*, literally 'to stretch apart', from, ultimately, *varicus* 'straddling'.] —**divaricately** *adv.* —**divaricatingly** *adv.*

divarication /dī várri káysh'n, di-/ *n.* **1.** ANAT WIDE BRANCHING separation into widely spread parts or branches, or the point at which sth forks or branches **2.** DIFFERING IN OPINION a difference of opinion (*formal*)

dive /dīv/ *v.* (**dives, diving, dived**) **1.** *vi.* JUMP HEAD FIRST INTO WATER to jump or throw yourself into water head first, especially with your arms stretched out above your head **2.** *vi.* SWIM UNDER WATER to swim below the surface of a stretch of water, often with special breathing apparatus **3.** *vi.* GO TOWARDS BOTTOM OF WATER to go down steeply and quickly in the direction of the bottom of a body of water, sometimes in search of sth ○ *dive for treasure* **4.** *vi.* DESCEND STEEPLY AND RAPIDLY to fly or make an aircraft fly steeply and rapidly in the direction of the ground or the sea **5.** *vi.* THROW YOURSELF TO THE GROUND to jump quickly to one side or throw yourself forwards or sideways to the ground ○ *dive out of the way* **6.** *vi.* MOVE FAST to move quickly and in a rush in a particular direction ○ *dive for the door* **7.** *vti.* PUT HAND IN STH to put your hand or hands quickly into sth, e.g. a pocket, a bag, or a cupboard, in order to get sth out of it **8.** *vi.* BEGIN STH ENTHUSIASTICALLY to undertake or start on some activity with great enthusiasm ○ *He dived into the project.* **9.** *vi.* SWIMMING PERFORM JUMPS INTO WATER AS SPORT to perform a pattern of acrobatic movements in the air ending in a headfirst plunge into water, or do this regularly as a sport **10.** *vi.* NAVY GO UNDER WATER to cause sth such as a submarine to go below the surface of the sea **11.** *vi.* FIN DROP IN VALUE to fall sharply in value ■ *n.* **1.** HEADLONG JUMP INTO WATER a jump into water head first, especially with your arms stretched out above your head **2.** SWIMMING ACROBATIC PLUNGE an acrobatic plunge into water performed as a sport or in a competition **3.** SWIMMING ACT OF SWIMMING UNDER WATER a swim below the surface of a stretch of water, often with special breathing apparatus **4.** DESCENT TOWARDS BOTTOM OF WATER a steep and usually rapid descent in the direction of the bottom of a body of water **5.** NAVY SUBMARINE'S DESCENT a submarine's descent below the surface of the sea **6.** AIR STEEP DESCENT a bird's or aircraft's rapid and steep fall or flight in the direction of the ground or the sea **7.** QUICK MOVEMENT SIDEWAYS OR DOWN a quick jump or movement to one side, or forwards or sideways to the ground **8.** FAST MOVEMENT a rapid movement in a particular direction **9.** DISREPUTABLE ESTABLISHMENT a dirty, shabby, or disreputable place, e.g. a bar or club (*informal*) **10.** FIN SHARP FINANCIAL DROP a sharp fall in value **11.** SOCCER FOOTBALLER'S FALL a feigned dramatic

fall by a player to try to gain a free kick or penalty, or a goalkeeper's attempt to stretch horizontally to save a shot (*informal*) **12.** BOXING **BOXER'S FEIGNED FALL** a fall or injury feigned by a boxer in order to lose a fight dishonestly (*slang*) [Old English *dūfan* 'to sink' and *dȳfan* 'to dip', from a prehistoric Germanic base that is also the ancestor of English *deep* and *dip*]
dive in *vi.* to begin eating quickly and with gusto (*informal*)

dive-bomb (**dive-bombs, dive-bombing, dive-bombed**) *vt.* to descend steeply in a military aircraft and deliver bombs onto a target —**dive-bomber** *n.* —**dive-bombing** *n.*

dive brake *n.* AIR FORCE = **air brake** *n.* 2

Divehi /dívve i/ *n.* a dialect of Sinhalese spoken in the Republic of Maldives. Divehi is spoken by about 260,000 people. —**Divehi** *adj.*

diver /dívər/ *n.* **1. SB WHO DIVES IN WATER** sb who dives in water, e.g. sb trained to carry out underwater work or exploration, or a sportsperson performing acrobatic dives **2.** BIRDS **DIVING WATER BIRD** a water bird belonging to a family found in the northern hemisphere that is skilled in swimming and diving. Family: Gaviidae. US term **loon 3.** BIRDS **WATER BIRD** any water bird noted for its diving skills

diverge /dī vúrj, di-/ (**-verges, -verging, -verged**) *vi.* **1. SEPARATE** to separate and go in a different direction or different directions **2. DIFFER** to differ to some extent **3. NOT MATCH** to deviate from or not fit in with or conform to sth, e.g. a typical pattern or expressed wish [Mid-17thC. From medieval Latin *divergere*, literally 'to bend apart', from Latin *vergere* 'to bend' (see VERGE²).] —**diverging** *adj.*

divergence /dī vúrjənss/, **divergency** /-jənssi/ (*plural* **-cies**) *n.* **1. DIFFERENCE OR DISPARITY** a difference between two or more things, e.g. opinions or attitudes **2. FAILURE TO CONFORM OR MATCH** deviation from sth, e.g. a typical pattern or expressed wish **3. MOVING APART** the process of separating or moving apart to follow different paths or different courses **4. AMOUNT OF DIFFERENCE** the amount by which sth differs from sth else, especially where such a difference is not expected **5.** OPHTHALMOL **DEVIATION OF EYE FROM SIGHT LINE** a condition in which only one eye is directed at the object of interest and the other is directed outwards **6.** BIOL **DIFFERENT DEVELOPMENT** the development of different characteristics by organisms that come from the same ancestor, caused by the influence of different environments. ◊ **convergence 7.** MATH **SEQUENCE OF NUMBERS WITHOUT LIMIT** the characteristic of a series or sequence of numbers in which the value of the last term and the sum of the series are without limit. ◊ **convergence 8.** METEOROL **MOVEMENT OF AIR CURRENTS** a set of meteorological conditions in a given area in which the air expands and the net flow of air is out of the area, usually resulting in fair, dry conditions

divergent /dī vúrjənt/ *adj.* **1. MOVING APART** following paths or courses that become increasingly different or separate **2. DIFFERING** showing or having differences **3. NOT MATCHING STH** deviating from sth, e.g. a typical pattern or an expressed wish **4.** MATH **INCREASING WITHOUT LIMIT** used to describe a series or sequence of numbers in which each term is equal to or greater than the preceding term, and the value of the last term and the sum of the series are without limit **5.** GEOM **RADIATING FROM A POINT** used to describe lines radiating from a single point —**divergently** *adv.*

diverging lens *n.* a lens, usually concave, that causes a parallel beam of light to spread

divers /dívərz/ *adj.* more than one, and of various types (*formal*) [13thC. Via French from Latin *diversus*, the past participle of *divertere* 'to separate' (see DIVERT).]

diverse /dī vúrss, dí vurss/ *adj.* **1. CONSISTING OF DIFFERENT THINGS** made up of many different elements or kinds of things **2. DIFFERING FROM EACH OTHER** very different or distinct from one another [13thC. Variant of DIVERS.] —**diversely** *adv.* —**diverseness** *n.*

diversification /dī vúrssifi káysh'n/ *n.* **1. PROVISION OF VARIETY** the provision or development of greater variety **2.** COMM **DEVELOPMENT OF NEW BUSINESS** the expansion of a commercial organization or enterprise into new areas of business

diversiform /dī vúrssi fawrm/ *adj.* occurring in various forms (*formal*) [Early 18thC. From, ultimately, Latin *diversus* (see DIVERS) + -FORM.]

diversify /dī vúrssi fī/ (**-fies, -fying, -fied**) *vti.* **1. MAKE OR BECOME VARIED** to become more varied, or make sth more varied **2.** COMM **EXPAND INTO NEW AREAS OF BUSINESS** to expand, or expand a commercial organization, into new areas of business [15thC. Via Old French *diversifier* from medieval Latin *diversificare* 'to make unlike', from the Latin past participle *diversus* (see DIVERS).] —**diversifiability** /dī vúrssi fī ə bílləti/ *n.* —**diversifiable** /-fī əb'l/ *adj.* —**diversified** /-fīd/ *adj.* —**diversifier** *n.*

diversion /dī vúrsh'n/ *n.* **1. DISTRACTION** sth that takes sb's attention away from sth else, especially from more routine activities ○ *a welcome diversion from housework* **2.** TRANSP **ALTERNATIVE ROUTE** a route to be taken by traffic as an alternative to the normal route, when the normal route cannot be used. US term **detour 3. CHANGE OF PURPOSE OR USE** a change in the purpose or use of sth from what was intended or from what sth was previously **4. CHANGE OF DIRECTION OR PATH** a change in the direction or path of sth **5. PASTIME OR HOBBY** an activity or interest that takes sb's mind off more routine or serious things **6.** MIL **MOCK ATTACK** a mock attack aimed at drawing enemy attention and troops away from the place of the intended main attack [15thC. Directly or via French from the late Latin stem *diversion-* 'turning away', from the Latin past participle stem *divers-* (see DIVERS).] —**diversional** *adj.*

diversionary /dī vúrsh'nəri/ *adj.* designed or carried out to divert sb's attention away from sth

diversity /dī vúrssəti/ (*plural* **-ties**) *n.* **1. VARIETY** a variety of sth such as opinion, colour, or style ○ *a city of great cultural diversity* **2. DIFFERENCE OR DISCREPANCY** discrepancy, or a difference from what is normal or expected [14thC. Via French *diversité* from Latin *diversitas*, from *diversus* (see DIVERS).]

divert /dī vúrt/ (**-verts, -verting, -verted**) *vt.* **1. CHANGE STH'S PATH** to change the route or path taken by sth, e.g. traffic or a river **2. DRAW ATTENTION FROM STH** to take sb's mind off sth and draw attention to sth else **3. CHANGE PURPOSE OR USE** to change the purpose or use of sth from what it was previously **4. AMUSE SB** to amuse or entertain sb [15thC. Via French *divertir* from Latin *divertere*, literally 'to turn aside', from *vertere* 'to turn'.] —**diverter** *n.* —**divertible** *adj.* —**divertive** *adj.*

diverticula plural of **diverticulum**

diverticulitis /dívər tikyoo lítiss/ *n.* inflammation of abnormal protrusions (**diverticula**) of the lining of the large intestine, causing severe abdominal pain, often with fever and constipation

diverticulosis /dívər tikyoo lóssiss/ *n.* the presence of abnormal protrusions (**diverticula**) in the bowel, caused when the bowel muscles rupture the bowel wall

diverticulum /dívər tíkyooləm/ (*plural* **-la** /-lə/) *n.* a pouch or sac in the lining of the mucous membrane of a hollow organ, especially one produced in the bowel when the bowel muscle ruptures the bowel wall. ◊ **hernia** [Mid-17thC. From medieval Latin, 'byway', variant of Latin *deverticulum*, literally 'turning from', from, ultimately, *vertere* 'to turn'.] —**diverticular** *adj.*

divertimento /di vúrti méntō/ (*plural* **-ti** /-ti/) *n.* a piece of light classical instrumental music composed in several movements for an ensemble [Mid-18thC. From Italian, 'diversion', from *divirtire* 'to divert', from, ultimately, Latin *divertere* (see DIVERT).]

diverting /dī vúrting/ *adj.* amusing or entertaining, and acting as a temporary distraction from more routine or serious matters —**divertingly** *adv.*

divertissement /di vúrtiss moN/ *n.* **1.** BALLET **SERIES OF UNTHEMED DANCES** in ballet, a series of dances lacking a unifying theme **2.** DANCE **DANCE INTERLUDE** a dance interlude in a play or opera **3.** MUSIC **TUNES DERIVED FROM FAMOUS MELODIES** a set of tunes that are based on well-known melodies [Early 18thC. From French, from the stem *divertiss-* of *divertir* 'to divert', from Latin *divertere* (see DIVERT).]

divest /dī vést/ (**-vests, -vesting, -vested**) *vt.* **1. TAKE AWAY FROM SB** to take away sth, especially status or power, from sb or sth (*often passive*) **2. TAKE STH OFF** to remove sth, usually clothes (*formal or humorous*) **3. GIVE UP STH** to give up or get rid of sth, especially a belief or idea **4.** LAW **GIVE AWAY PROPERTY RIGHTS** to lose or give away rights to the possession of property, or deprive sb of them [Early 17thC. Alteration of obsolete *devest* 'deprive of sth', from Old French *de(s)vester*, literally 'to undress', from *vestir* 'to clothe', from Latin *vestire*.] —**divestible** *adj.* —**divestment** *n.* —**divesture** /dī véschər/ *n.*

divestiture /dī véstichər/ *n.* **1. DISPOSSESSION** the removal or deprivation of sth **2.** *US* **SALE OF PROPERTY** the sale of one or more of a company's subsidiaries, divisions, or holdings, or of its stock in those holdings

divi /dívvi/ (*plural* **-vis**) *n.* = **divvy**² *n.* (*informal*)

divide /di víd/ *v.* (**-vides, -viding, -vided**) **1.** *vti.* **SPLIT INTO PARTS** to split sth, or be separated or split, into two or more parts ○ *a dormitory divided into cubicles* **2.** *vti.* **SHARE STH** to share sth, or be shared, between two or more people or groups ○ *Her inheritance was divided equally among the children.* **3.** *vi.* **SEPARATE AND GO IN DIFFERENT DIRECTIONS** to split into two or more parts that go off in different directions **4.** *vti.* **SEPARATE TWO PLACES** to be a barrier or boundary between one place or thing and another ○ *The river divides the north of the island from the south.* **5.** *vt.* **CAUSE DISAGREEMENT BETWEEN PEOPLE** to be the cause or subject of disagreement between people **6.** *vti.* MATH **CALCULATE OCCURRENCE OF ONE NUMBER IN ANOTHER** to calculate how many times one number contains another **7.** *vt.* MEASURE **MARK STH OFF** to mark units or sections of a particular size on a measuring instrument, e.g. a ruler **8.** *vi.* POL **VOTE** to vote on an issue by separating into two groups, one for and one against, inside a legislative chamber such as Parliament ■ *n.* **1. BOUNDARY OR GAP** a boundary or gap that stands between two things, conditions, or groups **2.** *US* GEOG = **watershed** [14thC. From Latin *dividere*, literally 'to separate apart', from *-videre* 'to separate'. Ultimately from an Indo-European word that is also the ancestor of English *widow*.] —**dividable** *adj.*

divided /di vídid/ *adj.* **1. SEPARATED** separated into two or more parts or groups **2. IN TWO MINDS** drawn towards two or more different and often incompatible purposes or groups **3. IN DISAGREEMENT** in a state of internal discord, strife, or disagreement **4.** BOT **SEPARATED INTO SECTIONS** used to describe leaves that are divided into separate sections —**dividedly** *adv.* —**dividedness** *n.*

divided highway *n.* *US* = **dual carriageway**

divided skirt *n.* = **culottes**

dividend /dívvi dend/ *n.* **1. BONUS** sth good or desirable that is gained as a bonus along with sth else **2.** FIN **SHAREHOLDER'S SHARE OF PROFIT** company profits paid pro rata to shareholders, either in cash or in more shares **3.** FIN **PAYMENT TO COOPERATIVE'S CUSTOMER** a payment made periodically to the customer-members of a cooperative commercial organization, usually in proportion to the amount the member spends **4.** MATH **NUMBER DIVIDED BY ANOTHER** a number or quantity that is to be divided by another number or quantity. ◊ **divisor 5.** LAW **PROPORTION OF A BANKRUPT'S ESTATE** the proportion of a bankrupt party's estate that is to be divided among the creditors [15thC. Via Anglo-Norman *dividende* from Latin *dividendum* 'thing to be divided', a form of *dividere* (see DIVIDE).]

divider /di vídər/ *n.* a device that separates sth into sections, e.g. a screen that partitions a room or a sheet of card that separates the sections of a loose-leaf binder

dividers /di vídərz/ *npl.* an instrument with two

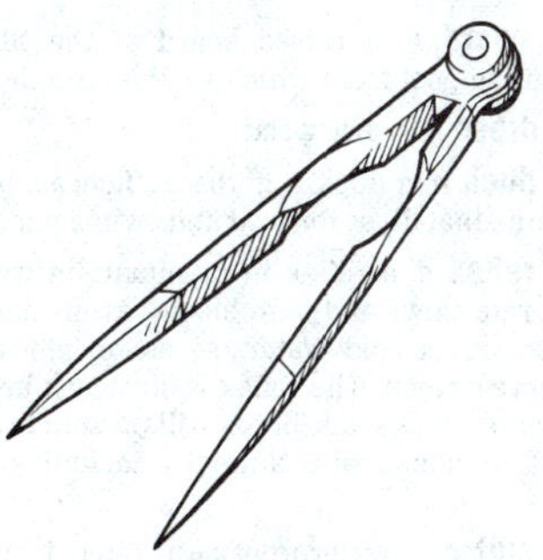

Dividers

movable pointed legs hinged at one end, used for measuring distances on maps and charts and for transferring measurements from one chart to another

dividing line *n.* sth that marks a change or distinction between two states or qualities

divination /dívvi náysh'n/ *n.* **1. SEEKING KNOWLEDGE BY SUPERNATURAL MEANS** the methods or practice of attempting to foretell the future or discovering the unknown through omens, oracles, or supernatural powers **2. PROPHECY** a prophecy or prediction **3. PREMONITION** a premonition or feeling of foreboding about sth that is going to happen —**divinatory** /di vínnətəri/ *adj.*

divine /di vín/ *adj.* **1.** RELIG **HAVING GODLIKE NATURE** being God or a god or goddess **2.** RELIG **RELATING TO GOD, GODS, OR GODDESSES** connected with, coming from, or caused by God or a god or goddess **3.** RELIG **CONNECTED WITH WORSHIP** connected with the worship or service of God or a god or goddess **4. LOVELY** pleasing or attractive (*informal or humorous*) ■ *v.* **(-vines, -vining, -vined) 1.** *vt.* **REALIZE STH** to come to understand or realize sth **2.** *vt.* **DISCOVER AS IF SUPERNATURALLY** to learn or discover sth by intuition, inspiration, or other apparently supernatural means **3.** *vt.* **PREDICT STH AS IF SUPERNATURALLY** to predict sth by apparently supernatural means **4.** *vti.* **SEARCH WITH DIVINING ROD** to search for underground water, metal, or minerals using sth such as a divining rod ■ *n.* RELIG **1. THEOLOGIAN** a member of the clergy, especially one who is knowledgeable about theology **2. Divine, divine GOD** God, or whatever else is believed to be the underlying creative and sustaining force in the universe [14thC. Via Old French *devin* from Latin *divinus*, from *divus* 'god' (source of English *diva*). Ultimately from an Indo-European word meaning 'shining'.] —**divinable** *adj.* —**divineness** /di vín niss/ *n.*

divinely /di vínli/ *adv.* **1. WONDERFULLY** well, pleasingly, or attractively (*informal or humorous*) **2.** RELIG **BY GOD, A GOD, OR GODDESS** by God or a god or goddess

diviner /di vínər/ *n.* sb who searches for underground water, metal, or minerals using sth such as a divining rod

divine right *n.* the belief that the monarch's authority comes directly from God rather than from the people

diving beetle *n.* a predatory water beetle adapted for swimming that has flattened hind legs and the capacity to breathe air trapped under its wings. Family: Dytiscidae.

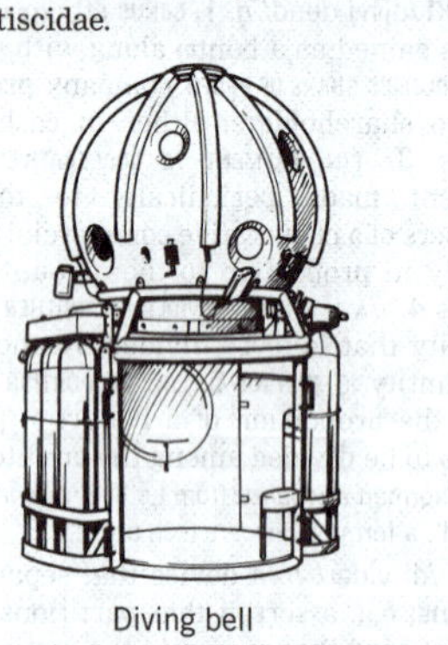

Diving bell

diving bell *n.* a metal bell-shaped device used for working underwater. It has an open bottom and is supplied with compressed air.

diving board *n.* a raised board at the edge of a swimming pool from which to dive into the water

diving dress *n.* = **diving suit**

diving duck *n.* a duck, e.g. the bufflehead, pochard, or scaup, that dives for food and swims under water

diving reflex *n.* a reflex in mammals in which the heart rate slows and skin blood vessels narrow on immersion in cold water, so as to help them to conserve oxygen. The reflex is strongest in aquatic animals such as seals, but is still present to a minor extent in nonaquatic animals, including human beings.

diving suit *n.* a waterproof suit, often including a helmet and an air supply, worn by divers

divining rod *n.* a forked stick used as a device for sensing underground water sources or minerals. The diviner holds an end of the rod in each hand, and the rod is said to dip sharply downwards when the diviner walks over a water source or minerals.

divinise *vt.* = **divinize**

divinity /di vínnəti/ (*plural* **-ties**) *n.* **1. THEOLOGY** the study of religion, especially the Christian religion **2. QUALITY OF BEING GOD, A GOD, OR GODDESS** the quality associated with being God, a god, or a goddess **3. divinity, Divinity GOD** God, a god or a goddess [13thC. From French *divinité*, from the Latin stem *divinitat-* 'godhead, divinity', from *divinus*, from *divus* 'god'.]

divinity school *n. US* a college for students training to be ministers

divinize /dívvi nīz/ **(-izes, -izing, -ized)**, **divinise (-ises, -ising, -ised)** *vt.* to regard a person, being, or object as a god or goddess (*formal*) —**divinization** /dívvi nī záysh'n/ *n.*

divisibility /di vízzə bílləti/ *n.* the capability of being divided exactly by a particular number

divisible /di vízzəb'l/ *adj.* **1. ABLE TO BE DIVIDED** able to be divided, especially without leaving a remainder **2. ABLE TO BE SEPARATED** capable of being separated into different parts [15thC. Directly or via French from late Latin *divisibilis*, from the Latin past participle stem *divis-* of *dividere* 'to separate apart'.] —**divisibleness** *n.* —**divisibly** *adv.*

division /di vízh'n/ *n.* **1. ACT OF SPLITTING INTO PARTS** the act of separating or splitting sth into parts, or an instance of this ○ *the division of the region into smaller administrative districts* **2. SHARING OUT OF STH** the separation of sth into parts to be shared out among people or groups ○ *The division of work between members of the group should be equal.* **3.** MATH **OPERATION OF DIVIDING ONE NUMBER BY ANOTHER** an operation used to calculate the number of times one number is contained in another **4. DISAGREEMENT** a disagreement or strong difference of opinion, especially when this leads to a split in a group ○ *Deep divisions exist within senior management itself as to the best way of dealing with the problem.* **5. STH SEPARATING** sth that separates things by forming a boundary between them **6. SEPARATE PART** one of the parts created when sth is split **7. SECTION OF ORGANIZATION** a section of a large organization that has a particular task or function ○ *the sales division of a large firm* **8.** SPORTS **GROUP OF TEAMS IN SPORTS LEAGUE** a group of teams of roughly similar standard in a sports league **9.** MIL **ARMY UNIT** a self-contained military unit in an army capable of sustained operations, including a headquarters and two or more brigades or, in the Marines, several regiments **10.** NAVY **NAVAL UNIT** a self-contained unit in a navy including a group of ships of the same class **11.** AIR FORCE **AIR FORCE UNIT** a self-contained unit in an air force including two or more fighter wings **12.** PUBLIC ADMIN **SMALL UNIT OF GOVERNMENT** a small unit of government, or an area administered by such a unit **13.** POL **PARLIAMENTARY VOTE** a vote in the British Parliament or a similar legislative body **14.** BOT **MAJOR CATEGORY IN PLANT CLASSIFICATION** a major category in the taxonomic classification of plants, comprising a group of classes. The corresponding category in animal classification is the phylum. **15.** GARDENING **SPLITTING PLANT ROOTS FOR PROPAGATION** the process of separating the root mass of a perennial plant into smaller pieces that are used to grow new plants **16.** LOGIC **LOGICAL FALLACY** a fallacy in which it is argued that what is true of a whole collectively is true of any of its parts. An example would be arguing that because a car is expensive so is its windscreen wiper. ◊ **composition 17.** MUSIC **GROUP OF ORGAN STOPS** a group of organ stops played on the same manual [14thC. Via Old French *devisiun* from the Latin stem *division-*, from the past participle stem *divis-* of *dividere* 'to separate apart'.] —**divisional** *adj.* —**divisionally** *adv.* —**divisionary** *adj.*

division bell *n.* a bell rung in the House of Commons when it is time for Members of Parliament to vote

division lobby *n.* = **lobby** *n.* 3

division of labour *n.* a system of organizing production by giving separate tasks to separate workers or groups of workers

division sign *n.* a sign (÷) placed between two numbers to show that the first number is divided by the second

divisive /di vísiv/ *adj.* causing disagreement or hostility within a group so that it is likely to split [Late 16thC. From late Latin *divisivus*, from the Latin past participle stem *divis-* of *dividere* 'to separate apart'.] —**divisively** *adv.* —**divisiveness** *n.*

divisor /di vízər/ *n.* a number divided into another number. ◊ **dividend** [15thC. Directly or via French *diviseur* from Latin *divisor*, from the past participle stem *divis-* of *dividere* 'to separate apart'.]

divorce /di váwrss/ *n.* **1.** LAW **OFFICIAL ENDING OF A MARRIAGE** the ending of a marriage by an official decision in a court of law **2. SEPARATION** a complete separation or split ■ *v.* **(-vorces, -vorcing, -vorced) 1.** *vti.* LAW **OFFICIALLY END A MARRIAGE** to end a marriage to sb by an official decision in a court of law **2.** *vt.* **SEPARATE STH** to separate or distinguish sth from sth else [14thC. Via French from Latin *divortium*, from *divortere*, variant of *divertere* 'to part, turn aside'.] —**divorceable** *adj.* —**divorcer** *n.* —**divorcive** *adj.*

divorcé /di váwr sée, -váwrss ay/ *n.* a man who is divorced [Late 19thC. From French, originally the past participle of *divorcer* 'to divorce', from, ultimately, Latin *divortium* (see DIVORCE).]

divorced /di váwrst/ *adj.* no longer married because the marriage has been ended by a divorce

divorcée /di váwr sée/ *n.* a woman who is divorced [Early 19thC. Partly from French, from the feminine of the past participle of *divorcer* 'to divorce', from, ultimately, Latin *divortium* (see DIVORCE); partly from DIVORCE + -EE.]

divot /dívvət/ *n.* a small lump of grass and earth accidentally dug out of the ground while playing a sport, especially golf [Early 16thC. Origin unknown. Originally Scots dialect 'piece of turf (especially for roofing cottages)'; the current sense dates from the late 19thC.]

divulgate /di vúl gayt/ **(-gates, -gating, -gated)** *vt.* to announce sth publicly (*archaic*) —**divulgater** *n.* —**divulgation** /dívv'l gáysh'n/ *n.*

divulge /dī vúlj/ **(-vulges, -vulging, -vulged)** *vt.* to reveal information, especially information that was previously secret [15thC. From, ultimately, Latin *divulgare*, literally 'to make widely known to the masses', from *vulgus* 'masses'.] —**divulgement** *n.* —**divulgence** *n.* —**divulger** *n.*

divulsion /dī vúlsh'n/ *n.* the act of tearing sth off or apart (*formal*) [Early 17thC. From, ultimately, the Latin stem *divulsion-*, from the past participle stem of *divellere*, literally 'to tear apart', from *vellere* 'to tear'.] —**divulsive** *adj.*

divvy[1] /dívvi/ (*plural* **-vies**) *n.* sb silly or unintelligent (*slang insult*) [Late 20thC. Origin unknown.]

divvy[2] /dívvi/ *vt.* **(-vies, -vying, -vied) DIVIDE STH UP** to divide sth up and share it out among a group of people (*informal*) ■ *n.* (*plural* **-vies**) **DIVIDEND** a dividend or share of the profits given to members of a co-operative (*informal*) [Late 19thC. Shortening of DIVIDEND.]

Diwali /di wáali/, **Divali** *n.* an important Hindu festival associated with Lakshmi, the goddess of prosperity, held in the autumn [Late 17thC. Via Hindi *diwālī* from Sanskrit *dīpāvalī* 'row of lights', from *dīpa* 'light, lamp'.]

Dix /diks/, **Otto** (1891–1969) German painter and etcher. His work depicts the horrors of World War I and the decadence of German society in its aftermath.

dixie /díksi/ *n.* a metal cooking pot used for making tea in the British army [Early 20thC. From Hindi *degcī*.]

Dixie *n.* **1.** *US* **SOUTHERN US STATES** the southern states that were members of the Confederacy during the American Civil War (*informal*) **2. AMERICAN CIVIL WAR SONG** the popular name for a song used as a Confederate marching tune during the American Civil War [Mid-19thC. Origin uncertain: perhaps an alteration of *Dixon*, from *Mason-Dixon Line*; or from assumed *Dixies* 'Louisiana banknotes', from French *dix* 'ten'.]

Dixieland /díksi land/, **dixieland** *n.* a style of jazz, originally from New Orleans, characterized by a fast two-beat rhythm and simultaneous improvisation [Early 20thC. From the *Original Dixieland Jazz Band*, the first jazz band to record commercially.]

Dixon /díks'n/, **Sir Owen** (1886–1972) Australian lawyer, Chief Justice of the High Court of Australia (1952–64), and an authority on constitutional law.

DIY, **d.i.y.** abbr. do-it-yourself

Diyarbakir /di yaàr bu keer/ city and capital of Diyarbakir Province in southeastern Turkey. Population: 375,800 (1990).

dizygotic /díˈzī góttik/, **dizygous** /dīˈzígəss/ adj. used to describe fraternal twins who developed from two separately fertilized eggs (zygotes). ◊ **monozygotic** [Mid-20thC. Coined from DI- + ZYGOTE + -IC.]

dizzy /dízzi/ adj. (-zier, -ziest) 1. UNSTEADY AND GIDDY unsteady, as if about to lose balance, and slightly giddy 2. CONFUSED AND BEWILDERED confused, overwhelmed, and unable to think clearly 3. FUN-LOVING BUT THOUGHTLESS fun-loving and rather silly or empty-headed (informal) 4. FAST extremely fast ○ dizzy speeds 5. EXTREME so high as to make sb giddy ○ the dizzy height of the tower ■ vt. (-zies, -zying, -zied) CAUSE SB TO FEEL DIZZY to cause sb to feel unsteady and slightly giddy, or confused and bewildered [Old English dysig 'foolish, stupid', from a prehistoric Germanic base that is also the ancestor of English doze] —**dizzily** adv. —**dizziness** n.

DJ n. 1. SB PLAYING RECORDED MUSIC sb who plays records or other recorded music for the entertainment of others, whether at a live dance or on the radio 2. DINNER JACKET a dinner jacket (informal)

djellaba /jə laábə/, **djellabah** n. a long loose-fitting robe with sleeves and a hood, worn especially in Islamic countries [Early 19thC. From Moroccan Arabic jellāb(a) or jellābiyya.]

Djerba /júrbə/ an island in southeastern Tunisia, on the Gulf of Gabes, in the Mediterranean Sea. Population: 92,269 (1984). Area: 510 sq. km/197 sq. mi.

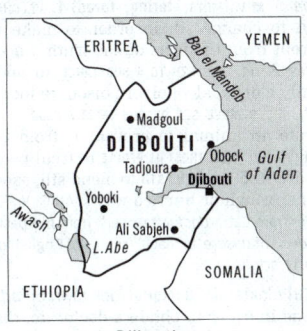

Djibouti

Djibouti /ji boóti/ 1. republic in the Horn of Africa, bounded by the Gulf of Aden, Somalia, Ethiopia, and Eritrea. Language: Arabic, French. Currency: Djibouti franc. Capital: Djibouti. Population: 434,116 (1997). Area: 23,200 sq. km/8,958 sq. mi. 2. the capital of the Republic of Djibouti. Population: 383,000 (1995).

djinn, **djinni** n. ♦ jinni

dk abbr. 1. dark 2. deck 3. dock

dl symbol. decilitre

D/L abbr. BANKING demand loan

D layer n. 1. = D region 2. LOWER LAYER OF EARTH'S MANTLE the lower layer of the Earth's mantle, from 720 km/450 mi. deep down to the boundary with the core

DLitt /dee lít/, **DLit** abbr. 1. Doctor of Letters 2. Doctor of Literature

DLO abbr. dead letter office

dlr abbr. dealer

dlvy abbr. delivery

dm symbol. decimetre

DM abbr. Deutschmark

DMAC n. a coding system used for broadcasting colour television programmes via satellite. Full form **duobinary multiplexed analogue component**

D-mark, **D-Mark** abbr. Deutschmark

DMD abbr. Doctor of Dental Medicine

DMK n. a political party in Tamil Nadu, India. Full form **Dravida Munnetra Kazgham**

DMS abbr. 1. Diploma in Management Studies 2. COMPUT data management system

DMSO n. a clear odourless liquid compound used as a solvent and in medicine to enable drugs applied to the skin to penetrate. Formula: $(CH_3)_2SO$. Full form **dimethylsulphoxide**

DMU abbr. decision-making unit

DMus /dee múz/ abbr. Doctor of Music

DMZ abbr. demilitarized zone

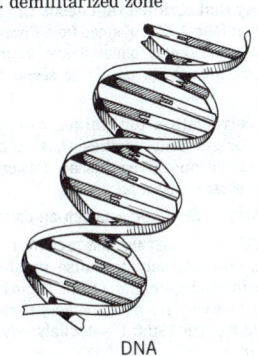

DNA

DNA n. a nucleic acid molecule in the form of a twisted double strand (**double helix**) that is the major component of chromosomes and carries genetic information. DNA, which is found in all living organisms except some viruses, is self-replicating and is responsible for passing along hereditary characteristics from one generation to the next. Full form **deoxyribonucleic acid**

DNAase /dee en áyz/, **DNase** n. an enzyme that aids the hydrolysis of DNA into smaller molecules. Full form **deoxyribonuclease**

DNA fingerprinting n. = **genetic fingerprinting**

DNA identification n. a forensic method of identifying sb on the basis of a DNA analysis

DNA polymerase n. an enzyme that uses single-stranded DNA to reproduce and repair DNA

DNase n. = DNAase

DNA virus n. a virus with a genome containing DNA

Dnieper /neépər, dneépər/, **Dnepr** the third longest river in Europe after the Volga and Danube. It rises west of Moscow and flows southwards and westwards through Russia, Belarus, and Ukraine, before emptying into the Black Sea. Length: 2,290 km/1,420 mi.

Dniester /neéstər, dneéstər/, **Dnestr** river that rises in the Carpathian Mountains and flows 1,400 km/870 mi. through Ukraine and Moldova before emptying into the Black Sea near Odessa

D-notice n. an official government communication to news editors advising them against publishing specified information for security reasons [D from its administrative classification letter]

do /doo/ (**does** (stressed) /duz/; (unstressed) /dəz/, **doing**, **did** /did/, **done** /dun/) CORE MEANING: a verb indicating that sb performs an action, an activity, or a task. It is often used as an informal equivalent of more specific and less frequent verbs, e.g. 'do your nails' instead of 'paint your nails'. ○ He usually did the cleaning on a Sunday morning. ○ Why won't you let me do your hair for you? ○ Assuming that your terminal is properly set, here is what you have to do to connect it.

1. vt. USE STH to use sth in a particular way ○ She's done absolutely nothing with the money she inherited. 2. vt. TAKE ACTION to take action in a particular situation in order to change it or solve a problem ○ Companies must decide what to do about their chemical waste. 3. vt. CAUSE STH to cause a particular effect or result ○ These disputes do little to help the peace process. ○ I could see what the divorce was doing to him. 4. vt. WORK AT STH to work at sth, particularly as a job or profession, or as a course of study ○ What does your mother do at the bank? 5. vt. BE OCCUPIED WITH STH to be occupied or busy with sth ○ Are you doing anything this evening? 6. vt. CONDUCT SELF to behave in a particular manner ○ Do what you want. 7. vi. FARE to be successful or unsuccessful to a particular extent ○ Automobile insurance firms are doing well this year. 8. vt. PROVIDE STH to prepare or provide sth ○ I'm sorry but we don't do a lunch menu. 9. vt. ACHIEVE A SPEED OR RATE to achieve a particular speed or rate ○ We were doing 55 down the motorway. ○ We did about 400 miles a day. 10. vt. STUDY STH to study or work at doing sth ○ Have you done Nabokov yet? ○ I've never been able to do algebra. 11. vt. PERFORM STH to perform or act a particular play, role, or accent ○ They're doing 'Macbeth' at the Hippodrome next month. ○ I'm not very good at doing accents. 12. vt. VISIT OR EXPLORE PLACE to visit or explore a country or city as a tourist (informal) ○ We're doing London tomorrow. 13. vti. BE ADEQUATE to be adequate in quantity or quality ○ A paper cup does just as well. ○ Just an orange juice will do me. 14. vt. SERVE TIME IN PRISON to serve a period of time in prison (slang) ○ He's doing time for cheating on his taxes. 15. vt. EXHAUST SB to wear sb out (informal) ○ After slaving in the garden for six hours, I'm done! 16. vt. ADAPT STH to translate or adapt a play, book, or other work ○ The novel was done into a feature film. 17. vt. CHEAT SB to cheat or trick sb (informal) ○ They did her out of her lunch money. 18. vt. ROB SB to rob a person or place (slang) ○ They got caught while they were doing the post office. 19. vt. ARREST SB to arrest sb (slang) ○ The police did her for possession. 20. vt. CONVICT SB to prosecute and convict sb of a crime (slang) ○ He got done for breaking and entering. 21. vt. Aus SPEND MONEY to spend or lose all your money (slang) ○ Have you done your money? 22. vt. TAKE DRUGS to take or use a narcotic drug (slang) 23. vt. HAVE SEX WITH SB to have sexual intercourse with sb (slang) 24. vt. MURDER SB to kill sb deliberately (slang) 25. vt. FORMS QUESTIONS AND NEGATIVES used with simple present and simple past tenses in the formation of questions and negative sentences. 'Do' and 'did' are often contracted to 'don't' and 'didn't' in negative structures. ○ What did he want? ○ Don't sit there! ○ It doesn't matter if you can't come. 26. vi. GIVES EMPHASIS used to emphasize a positive statement or command, often as a way of politely inviting or persuading sb to do sth ○ Yes, I do realize you can't finish the work today. ○ Please do be quiet! 27. vt. CHANGES THE EMPHASIS used to form inverted sentences in order to change the emphasis of a statement ○ I want to have a break just as much as you do. 28. vt. REPLACES ANOTHER VERB used to replace an earlier verb or verb phrase to avoid repetition, usually when comparing two things ○ She hopes to go to college, as do her brothers. 29. n. SOCIAL GATHERING a formal social gathering, e.g. a wedding reception (informal) 30. n. EXCREMENT excrement (informal) (used euphemistically) ○ a pile of doggy do [Old English dōn. Ultimately from an Indo-European word meaning 'to place'that is also the ancestor of English deed, theme, and fashion.] ◇ **could do with** be sure to benefit from sth ○ I could do with some help. ◇ **fair do's** used to call for fairness or justice, especially as a warning that an injustice may be occurring (informal) ◇ **have to do with sb or sth** 1. be connected with sb or sth 2. concern sb or sth 3. involve contact or a relationship with sth or sb ◇ **to do with** related to or about sth or sb ○ The lecture was to do with road safety.

pair to be more proper, perceiving *have got* as colloquial and even redundant, and pointing out that *have* alone is sufficient to signify possession. But *Have you change?* is not idiomatic, and *do have* has just as many syllables as *have got*. Therefore it is hard to see what reasonable basis exists for preferring *do have* to *have got*.

WORD KEY: SYNONYMS

See Synonyms at ***perform***.

do away with *vt.* **1.** ABOLISH STH to abolish sth so that it no longer happens or exists **2.** KILL SB to kill sb (*informal*)

do down *vt.* **1.** BELITTLE SB OR STH to suggest that sb or sth is insignificant or unimportant (*informal*) **2.** CHEAT SB to treat sb unfairly in order to gain an advantage

do for *vt.* **1.** CHARGE OR CONVICT SB OF OFFENCE to charge sb with an offence, or convict sb of a crime (*informal*) **2.** KILL SB to kill sb (*informal*) **3.** HARM SB OR STH to cause serious damage to sth or serious difficulties to sb (*dated informal*) **4.** EXHAUST SB to make sb feel so exhausted that he or she has no more energy or enthusiasm to continue (*dated informal*) **5.** WORK AS DOMESTIC CLEANER FOR SB to be employed to clean and tidy a house for sb (*dated informal*)

do in *vt.* (*informal*) **1.** KILL SB to kill or severely beat sb **2.** TIRE OUT to make sb feel exhausted

do out *vt.* to clean or tidy a place, e.g. a room or cupboard (*informal*)

do over *vt.* **1.** CLEAN OR REDECORATE PLACE to clean or redecorate a place, e.g. a house or room (*informal*) **2.** BEAT SB UP to subject sb to a violent beating (*slang*)

do up *vt.* **1.** FASTEN STH to fasten sth, e.g. with string or ribbons **2.** MAKE STH USABLE AGAIN to make sth fit to use again by repairing or decorating it **3.** GIVE STH DECORATIVE WRAPPING to wrap or cover sth in sth decorative (*often passive*) **4.** DRESS SMARTLY to dress sb or yourself in smart clothes (*informal*)

do without *vti.* to manage or survive without sth that you want, need, or normally have

DO *abbr.* **1.** Doctor of Optometry **2.** Doctor of Osteopathy

do. *abbr.* ditto

D/O *abbr.* COMM **1.** delivery order **2.** direct order

DOA *abbr.* dead on arrival

doable /dóo əb'l/ *adj.* able to be done or achieved

DOB, **d.o.b** *abbr.* date of birth

dobbin /dóbbin/, **Dobbin** *n.* a horse, especially a large heavy working horse [Late 16thC. From *Dobbin*, personal name, an alteration of *Robin*, literally 'little Robert', from *Robert*.]

dobby /dóbbi/ (*plural* **-bies**) *n.* a part of a loom that allows small figures to be woven on it [Late 17thC. Origin uncertain; perhaps from *Dobbie*, personal name, literally 'little Dob', from *Dob*, an alteration of *Rob*. Originally 'unintelligent person', later 'household spirit'.]

Dobell /dō bél/, **Sir William** (1899–1970) Australian painter. Noted for his portraits, he was an official war artist during World War II.

Doberman pinscher

Doberman pinscher /dṓbərmən pínshər/, **Dobermann pinscher, Doberman** *n.* a medium-sized to large powerful dog with a smooth black or dark brown coat, often used as a guard dog or for police work and belonging to a breed originating in Germany [Early 20thC. Named after Ludwig *Dobermann*, 19th-C German dog breeder who bred it; *pinscher* from German, breed name.]

dobra /dóbrə/ *n.* **1.** UNIT OF CURRENCY OF SÃO TOMÉ AND PRINCIPE the main unit of currency of São Tomé and Principe. See table at **currency** **2.** COIN WORTH A DOBRA a coin worth one dobra [Late 20thC. Via Portuguese from, ultimately, Latin *duplus* 'double' (source of English *double*).]

doc /dok/ *n.* a doctor (*informal*)

DOC *n.* a certification for Italian wine that guarantees its origin [From Italian *Denominazione di Origine Controllata*]

doc. *abbr.* document

Docetism /dō seétizəm, dṓsit-/ *n.* in Christianity, an early heresy that claimed that Jesus Christ was not a real person [Mid-19thC. Formed from *Docete* 'Docetist', via medieval Latin *Docetae* (plural) 'Docetists' from patristic Greek *Dokētai*, from Greek *dokein* 'to seem, appear'.] — **Docetist** *n.*

DOCG *n.* a certification for Italian wine that guarantees its origin and verifies that it meets production regulations [From Italian *Denominazione di Origine Controllata e Garantita*]

doch-an-doris *n. Scotland* = **deoch-an-doris**

docile /dṓ sīl/ *adj.* **1.** QUIET AND EASY TO CONTROL quiet, easy to control, and unlikely to cause trouble **2.** EASILY TAUGHT easy to teach (*archaic*) [15thC. From Latin *docilis*, from *docere* 'to teach' (see DOCTOR). 'Easy to control' is not attested until the late 18thC.] —**docilely** *adv.* —**docility** /dō sílləti/ *n.*

dock[1] /dok/ *n.* **1.** PLACE FOR SHIPS TO MOOR an area of water between two piers or next to a pier, where ships can be moored safely for loading and repair **2.** BUILDINGS AND WATER CONNECTED WITH SHIPPING all the offices, workshops, and other buildings associated with the loading and repair of ships, together with the nearby areas of water (*usually used in the plural*) US term **dockyard** **3.** *US* PIER OR WHARF a long narrow structure stretching out into a body of water, or a raised area of land alongside water where ships can load and unload **4.** ENCLOSED AREA OF WATER FOR SHIP an enclosed area of water for a ship in which the water level can be adjusted **5.** = **dry dock** ■ *vti.* (**docks, docking, docked**) **1.** MOOR to steer a ship into a dock and tie it up, or be steered in and tied up there **2.** SPACE TECH LINK UP WITH SPACECRAFT to link up with another spacecraft in space [14thC. From either Middle Low German *docke* or Middle Dutch *docke*, of uncertain origin: perhaps from Latin *ductio* 'leading', from Latin *ducere* 'to lead'.]

dock[2] /dok/ *n.* LAW the area in a lawcourt where the accused person stands during a trial [Late 16thC. Origin uncertain: probably originally thieves' slang, from Flemish *dok* 'fowl pen, rabbit hutch', of unknown origin.]

dock[3] /dok/ (*plural* **docks** *or* **dock**) *n.* **1.** PLANT IN BUCKWHEAT FAMILY a plant of the buckwheat family with greenish or reddish flowers, long broad leaves, and a long taproot. Genus: *Rumex*. **2.** BROAD-LEAFED WEED any broad-leafed weedy plant [Old English *docce*, from prehistoric Germanic]

dock[4] /dok/ *vt.* (**docks, docking, docked**) **1.** REMOVE TAIL to remove the tail of a dog, sheep, or other animal, leaving a short stump **2.** REDUCE WAGES to deduct a sum of money from sb's wages, especially as a punishment ■ *n.* **1.** SOLID PART OF TAIL the solid part of an animal's tail **2.** STUMP OF TAIL the stump left when an animal's tail has been docked [14thC. The verb came from the noun, of uncertain origin: perhaps from assumed Old English *docca* 'muscle', from a prehistoric Germanic base meaning 'round thing'.]

dockage /dókij/ *n.* **1.** MOORING CHARGE a charge payable for mooring at a dock **2.** FACILITIES FOR MOORED SHIPS the facilities for ships moored at a dock **3.** DOCKING PROCESS the process of docking a ship

docken /dókən/ (*plural* **-ens** *or* **-en**) *n. Scotland* **1.** DOCK PLANT a dock plant **2.** STH WORTHLESS sth worthless or unimportant [Old English *doccan*, a different grammatical form of *docce* (see DOCK[3])]

docker /dókər/ *n.* sb whose job is to load and unload ships. US term **longshoreman**

docket /dókit/ *n.* **1.** DOCUMENT LISTING CONTENTS OF PARCEL a short document listing the contents of a parcel or the goods being delivered, often also acting as a receipt **2.** SUMMARY OF COURT CASE a summary of the proceedings of a court case **3.** *US* LAW LIST OF FUTURE COURT CASES a list of pending cases in a court **4.** *US* LIST OF THINGS TO DO a list of things to do **5.** DOCUMENT SUMMARY a summary of a document **6.** CUSTOMS CERTIFICATE a customs certificate confirming payment of duty ■ *vt.* (**-ets, -eting, -eted**) **1.** *US* LAW PUT A LEGAL CASE IN THE CALENDAR to enter a legal case in the calendar of future cases **2.** LAW SUMMARIZE A COURT CASE to summarize a court case and enter the summary in the appropriate register **3.** LABEL A PACKAGE to label a package with a document giving the contents or delivery details **4.** SUMMARIZE STH to attach or give a summary of sth [15thC. Origin uncertain: perhaps formed from DOCK[4].]

dockland /dók land/ *n.* the area surrounding a city's docks or port (*often used in the plural*)

dockside /dók sīd/ *n.* the area of ground alongside the moorings in a dock or harbour

dockworker /dók wurkər/ *n. US* = **docker**

dockyard /dók yaard/ *n. US* = **dock**[1] *n.* 2

Doc Martens /dok maártənz/ *tdmk.* a trademark for a type of sturdy lace-up ankle-length boot

doco /dókō/ (*plural* **-cos**) *n. Aus* a documentary (*informal*) [Late 20thC. Shortening and alteration.]

doctor /dóktər/ *n.* **1.** MED SB MEDICALLY QUALIFIED sb qualified and licensed to give people medical treatment **2.** *US, Can* DENT, VET, MED DENTIST, VET, OR OSTEOPATH a title used before the names of health professionals such as dentists, vets, and osteopaths **3.** EDUC SB WITH THE HIGHEST UNIVERSITY DEGREE a title given to sb who has been awarded a doctorate, the highest level of degree awarded by a university **4.** CHR ROMAN CATHOLIC THEOLOGIAN in the earlier history of the Roman Catholic Church, an eminent and influential theologian **5.** SB WHO CAN MEND THINGS sb who is good at doing sth, especially mending or improving sth **6.** EDUC TEACHER OR SCHOLAR a teacher, or sb very knowledgeable (*archaic*) ■ *v.* (**-tors, -toring, -tored**) **1.** *vt.* CHANGE STH TO DECEIVE to change sth in order to make it appear different from the facts or the truth ○ *doctored the figures* **2.** *vt.* ADD STH TO A SUBSTANCE to add sth, especially a drug, alcohol, or poison, to food or drink **3.** *vt.* VET REMOVE SEX ORGANS FROM ANIMAL to spay or castrate an animal to prevent it from producing young **4.** *vti.* MED TREAT ILL PEOPLE to treat people when they are ill **5.** *vt.* MEND STH to mend sth, especially in a rather rough or hurried way [14thC. Via Old French *doctour* from Latin *doctor* 'teacher', from the past participle stem *doct-* of *docere* 'to teach' (source of English *docile*).] — **doctorly** *adj.*

doctoral /dóktərəl/, **doctorial** /dok táwri əl/ *adj.* written or done in order to obtain a doctorate, the highest degree awarded by a university

doctorate /dóktərət/ *n.* the highest level of university degree, usually awarded for a lengthy piece of original research but sometimes for other outstanding achievements

doctorial *adj.* = **doctoral**

Doctor of Philosophy *n.* **1.** HIGHEST UNIVERSITY DEGREE the highest level of university degree that can be studied for, awarded to sb who has successfully completed a lengthy piece of original research. A Doctor of Philosophy may be awarded in any subject except law, theology, or medicine. **2.** SB WITH DOCTOR OF PHILOSOPHY DEGREE sb who has been awarded the degree of Doctor of Philosophy

Doctor's Commons *npl.* the building in London that housed courts for the Church of England and the Admiralty between 1572 and 1867 [Commons from the common table or dining hall inside it]

doctrinaire /dóktri náir/ *adj.* DETERMINED TO USE A THEORY determined to use a particular theory or method and refusing to accept that there might be a better approach ■ *n.* SB WITH FIXED IDEAS sb who is determined to follow a particular theory or method and refuses to consider alternative approaches —**doctrinairism** *n.* —**doctrinarian** *n.*

doctrine /dóktrin/ *n.* **1.** RULE OR PRINCIPLE a rule or principle that forms the basis of a belief, theory, or policy **2.** IDEAS TAUGHT AS TRUTH a body of ideas, particularly in religion, taught to people as truthful or correct **3.** STH TAUGHT sth taught to people (*archaic*) [14thC. Directly or via French from Latin *doctrina* 'teaching, learning', from *doctor* (see DOCTOR).] —**doctrinal**

/dok trín'l/ *adj.* —**doctrinality** /dóktri nálləti/ *n.* —**doctrinally** /dok trín'li/ *adv.*

docudrama /dókyŏŏ draamə/ *n.* a dramatized film or television version of a true story [Mid-20thC. Blend of DOCUMENTARY and DRAMA.] —**docudramatic** /dókyŏŏdrə máttik/ *adj.*

document /dókyŏŏmənt/ *n.* **1.** FORMAL PIECE OF WRITING a formal piece of writing that provides information or that acts as a record of events **2.** OBJECT CONTAINING INFORMATION an object such as a film, photograph, or audio recording that contains information and can be used as evidence **3.** COMPUT COMPUTER FILE a computer file created using an applications program, e.g. a database, spreadsheet, illustration, or text file ■ *vt.* (**-ments, -menting, -mented**) **1.** RECORD INFORMATION IN OR ON MEDIA to make a record of sth by writing about it or by filming or photographing it **2.** SUPPORT A CLAIM WITH EVIDENCE to provide evidence for a statement or claim by supplying supporting information [15thC. Via French from Latin *documentum* 'lesson, example' (in medieval Latin 'instruction, official paper'), from *docere* 'to teach' (see DOCTOR).] —**documental** /dókyŏŏ mént'l/ *adj.* —**documenter** /dókyŏŏ mentər/ *n.*

documentable /dókyŏŏ méntəb'l/ *adj.* able to be verified or proved by evidence

documentalist /dókyŏŏ mént'list/ *n.* sb who specializes in documentation

documentary /dókyŏŏ méntəri/ *n.* (*plural* **-ries**) FACTUAL FILM OR TV PROGRAMME a film or TV programme presenting facts and information, especially about a political, historical, or social issue ■ *adj.* **1.** CONSISTING OF DOCUMENTS in the form of documents, or collected from documents **2.** GIVING FACTS giving facts and information rather than telling a fictional story —**documentarily** /dókyŏŏ méntərəli/ *adv.*

documentation /dókyŏŏ men táysh'n/ *n.* **1.** EVIDENTIAL OR REFERENCE DOCUMENTS documents provided or collected together as evidence or as reference material **2.** PROCESS OF PROVIDING WRITTEN INFORMATION the process of providing written details or information about sth **3.** COMPUT COMPUTER SOFTWARE INFORMATION the instructions, tutorials, and reference information provided to explain how to install and use software or a computer system

document feeder *n.* the part of a printer, scanner, or fax machine that holds a stack of papers and feeds them through the machine to be printed

document holder *n.* a stand that holds papers in a vertical position so that they can be read easily by sb working at a desk

docusoap /dókyŏŏ sōp/ (*unmarked inflection* **-soaps**) *n.* a television programme that combines documentary style with elements of soap opera, e.g. by showing the personal lives of people at their workplace [Combination of DOCUMENTARY + SOAP OPERA]

Dodd /dod/, **Charles Harold** (1884–1973) Welsh biblical scholar. He was a Congregational pastor and some-time lecturer at Oxford and Cambridge universities. From 1949 he directed the *New English Bible* project.

dodder[1] /dóddər/ (**-ders, -dering, -dered**) *vi.* **1.** SHAKE OR TREMBLE to tremble or shake slightly as a result of age **2.** WALK UNSTEADILY to walk slowly and unsteadily with shaking limbs as a result of age [Early 17thC. Alteration of or related to obsolete (except for dialect) *dadder* 'to quake, tremble', of unknown origin.] —**dodderer** *n.*

dodder[2] /dóddər/ (*plural* **-ders** *or* **-der**) *n.* a leafless rootless parasitic plant of the morning glory family that lacks chlorophyll and has a reddish twining stem and small white flowers. Genus: *Cuscuta*. [14thC. Origin uncertain: perhaps from prehistoric Germanic.]

doddered /dóddərd/ *adj.* having the top branches missing as a result of age or disease [Late 17thC. Origin uncertain: probably ultimately from *dod* 'to lop (a tree)', of unknown origin; influenced by DODDER[1].]

doddering /dóddəring/, **doddery** /-əri/ *adj.* walking unsteadily, especially as a result of age —**dodderingly** *adv.*

doddle /dódd'l/ *n.* sth very easy to do (*informal*) ○ *I'm sure I'll past the test – it'll be a doddle.* [Mid-20thC. Origin uncertain: perhaps an alteration of DAWDLE, or from *doddle* to toddle, totter.]

dodeca- *prefix.* phonograph record (*discography*) [From Greek *dōdeka*, from *duō* 'two' + *deka* 'ten']

dodecahedron /dố dekə heédrən/ (*plural* **-drons** *or* **-dra** /-drə/) *n.* a solid figure with 12 equal pentagonal faces meeting in threes at 20 vertices [Late 16thC. From Greek *dōdekaedron*, from *dōdeka* 'twelve' + *hedra* 'seat, face'.] —**dodecahedral** *adj.*

Dodecanese /dố dekə neéz/ group of islands in the southeastern Aegean Sea that form a department of Greece and an important tourist area. Capital: Rhodes. Population: 163,476 (1991). Area: 2,663 sq. km/1,028 sq. mi.

dodecanoic acid /dố dekə nố ik-/ = **lauric acid** [Mid-20thC. Formed from *dodecane* '(a kind of) paraffin', from DODECA- + -ANE.]

dodecaphonic /dố dekə fónnik/ *adj.* = **twelve-tone** —**dodecaphonism** *n.* —**dodecaphonist** *n.* —**dodecaphony** *n.*

dodecasyllable /dố dekə sílləb'l/ *n.* a line of verse of 12 syllables —**dodecasyllabic** *adj.*

dodge /doj/ *v.* (**dodges, dodging, dodged**) **1.** *vti.* MOVE QUICKLY TO AVOID STH to move quickly and suddenly to one side to avoid being caught or hit ○ *He dodged the punch.* **2.** *vt.* AVOID STH UNPLEASANT to avoid doing sth regarded as unpleasant **3.** *vt.* PHOTOGRAPHY MASK AREA OF PRINT to mask an area of a print during exposure to prevent light reaching it ■ *n.* **1.** TRICK TO AVOID DOING STH a clever trick or tactic to avoid doing sth ○ *a tax dodge* **2.** QUICK AVOIDING MOVEMENT a sudden quick movement to one side to avoid being caught or hit [Mid-16thC. Origin uncertain. Originally 'to go this way and that, haggle'.]

dodge ball *n.* a children's game in which opponents try to avoid being hit by a large rubber ball

Dodge City /dój-/ city in southern Kansas, on the northern bank of the Arkansas River, southwest of Great Bend. Population: 22,430 (1996).

Dodgem /dójjəm/ *tdmk.* a trademark for a bumper car

dodger /dójjər/ *n.* **1.** SB AVOIDING DUTY sb who avoids a duty or responsibility, especially by using dishonest or deceitful methods **2.** SB DISHONEST sb cunning and untrustworthy **3.** SHELTERING SCREEN ON SHIP a canvas screen on a ship or yacht to protect the person at the helm from spray **4.** *Aus* FOOD food, especially a sandwich or bread (*slang*)

dodgy /dójji/ (**-ier, -iest**) *adj.* (*informal*) **1.** SUSPECT OR DISHONEST suspect, dishonest, or untrustworthy **2.** RISKY dangerous or risky **3.** LIKELY TO BREAK DOWN unreliable and likely to break down or stop working —**dodgily** *adv.* —**dodginess** *n.*

Dodo

dodo /dốdō/ (*plural* **-dos** *or* **-does**) *n.* **1.** EXTINCT BIRD a large extinct flightless bird of the pigeon family that once inhabited Mauritius and neighbouring islands in the Indian Ocean. The dodo, which was heavy-set with short legs and a hooked bill, became extinct in the late 17th century. Latin name: *Raphus cucullatus*. **2.** SB THOUGHTLESS sb thoughtless or unintelligent (*informal insult*) **3.** OLD-FASHIONED PERSON sb who is regarded as old-fashioned, conservative, and out of date [Early 17thC. From Portuguese *doudo* 'fool, simpleton'.] —**dodoism** *n.* ◇ **(as) dead as a dodo** no longer existing, functioning, flourishing, or popular

Dodoma /dốdəmə/ official capital of Tanzania since 1983. It is situated in Dodoma Region about 402

km/250 mi. west of the former capital, Dar es Salaam. Population: 203,833 (1988).

doe /dō/ *n.* a mature female of several mammals, including the deer, kangaroo, rabbit, hare, and goat [Old English *dā*, of unknown origin]

DOE *abbr.* Department of Environment

doer /dŏŏ ər/ *n.* **1.** SB WHO DOES STH sb who does a particular thing (*often used in combination*) ○ *wrongdoer* **2.** SB ACTIVELY DOING THINGS sb who is active in doing things rather than just thinking or talking about them

doeskin /dố skin/ *n.* **1.** SKIN OF DEER the skin of various animals, including a doe, deer, and goat **2.** LEATHER light supple leather made from doeskin that is particularly suitable for gloves **3.** SMOOTH WOOLLEN CLOTH a densely woven smooth woollen cloth

doesn't /dúzz'nt/ *contr.* does not

doest /dŏŏ əst/ 2nd person present singular of **do** (*archaic*)

doeth /dŏŏ əth/ 3rd person present singular of **do** (*archaic*)

doff /dof/ (**doffs, doffing, doffed**) *vt.* **1.** TAKE OFF OR LIFT HAT to take off a hat, or lift and tilt it as a greeting or a mark of respect **2.** TAKE OFF CLOTHING to take off a coat or another piece of clothing [14thC. Contraction of archaic *do off* 'to take off'.] —**doffer** *n.*

dog /dog/ *n.* **1.** ZOOL DOMESTIC ANIMAL THAT BARKS a domestic carnivorous animal that typically has a long muzzle, pointed ears, a fur coat, and a long fur-covered tail, and whose characteristic call is a bark. Latin name: *Canis familiaris.* **2.** ZOOL WILD ANIMAL RESEMBLING DOMESTIC DOG any wild animal that resembles a domestic dog and belongs to the same family, e.g. a wolf, fox, dingo, or coyote. Family: Canidae. **3.** ZOOL MALE DOG a male dog, wolf, fox, or other member of the dog family **4.** CONTEMPTIBLE PERSON sb who is regarded as unpleasant or contemptible (*informal insult*) **5.** OFFENSIVE TERM sb who is regarded as not good to look at (*slang insult*) **6.** MAN a man of the particular type described (*informal*) ○ *You lucky dog!* **7.** US, Can STH USELESS OR INFERIOR sth useless or of a very poor standard (*informal*) **8.** Aus BETRAYER sb who betrays his or her associates (*informal*) **9.** HOUSEHOLD = **andiron 10.** METEOROL = **seadog 11.** MECH ENG GRIPPING TOOL a device for gripping or holding things ■ **dogs** *npl.* **1.** SPORTS DOG RACING greyhound racing in general, or a greyhound race meeting (*informal*) **2.** FEET sb's feet (*dated informal*) ■ *vt.* (**dogs, dogging, dogged**) **1.** BOTHER SB PERSISTENTLY to bother or trouble sb persistently (*often passive*) ○ *dogged by bad luck* **2.** FOLLOW SB CLOSELY to follow sb closely in a determined way ○ *dogging her footsteps* **3.** MECH ENG GRIP STH WITH MECHANICAL DEVICE to grip or hold sth firmly with a mechanical device [Old English *docga*, of uncertain origin: probably originally 'powerful breed of dog'. *Dog* did not supplant *hound* as the general English term for the animal until the 16thC.] ◇ **a dog in the manger** sb who cannot have or does not want sth, but who tries to prevent sb else from having or doing it ◇ **a dog's breakfast** *or* **dinner** sth that is messy, disorganized, or badly done (*informal*) ◇ **a dog's life** a wretched existence ◇ **dog eat dog** ruthlessly competitive ◇ **go to the dogs** in the final stages of a gradual decline in standards (*informal*) ◇ **let sleeping dogs lie** to take no action in a situation that is currently peaceful but potentially troublesome ◇ **put on the dog** US, Aus make a display of wealth or knowledge ostentatiously or pretentiously (*dated informal*)

dog-and-pony show *n.* US an elaborate business presentation or promotional event (*informal*)

dogbane /dóg bayn/ *n.* a plant with pungent milky juice, a bitter root, and small bell-shaped white or pink flowers. Genus: *Apocynum.*

dogberry[1] /dóg beri, -bəri/ (*plural* **-ries**) *n.* **1.** PLANT WITH BERRIES any one of various plants with berries, including dogwood **2.** BERRY OF DOGBERRY PLANT a berry of any dogberry plant

dogberry[2] /dóg beri, -bəri/ (*plural* **-ries**), **Dogberry** (*plural* **-ries**) *n.* an unintelligent but self-important official [Mid-19thC. Named after *Dogberry*, an unintelligent constable in *Much Ado About Nothing* by Shakespeare.] —**dogberryism** *n.*

dogcart /dóg kaart/ *n.* a two-wheeled vehicle drawn by a horse and seating two people back to back

dogcatcher /dóg kachər/ *n. US* = **dog warden**

dog chew *n.* a hard piece of leather or compressed edible material, given to a dog to chew on, either as a treat or to keep its teeth in good condition

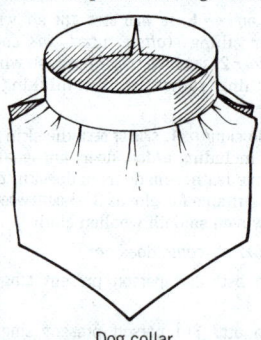

Dog collar

dog collar *n.* **1.** COLLAR FOR DOG a piece of leather or fabric worn around a dog's neck, often with the dog's name attached to it **2.** CHR CLERICAL COLLAR a clerical collar (*informal*) **3.** CLOSE-FITTING NECKLACE a necklace that fits closely round the neck

dog days *npl.* **1.** HOTTEST PERIOD OF THE SUMMER the hottest period of the summer. In ancient times the beginning of the dog days was heralded by the simultaneous rising of the Dog Star (**Sirius**) and the sun. **2.** LAZY PERIOD a lazy or inactive period of time [Mid-16thC. Translation of Latin *dies caniculares*, literally 'Dog Star days'.]

doge /dōj, dōzh/ *n.* the chief magistrate in Renaissance Venice and Genoa [Mid-16thC. Via French from, ultimately, Venetian Italian *doze*, ultimately from Latin stem *ducem* 'leader' (source of English *duke*).] —**dogeship** *n.*

dog-eared *adj.* **1.** HAVING WORN AND WELL-THUMBED PAGES having worn and well-thumbed pages that have been creased or folded over to mark the place reached in reading **2.** WORN OR SHABBY shabby or well-used

dog-end *n.* the discarded end of a cigarette after the rest of it has been smoked (*informal*)

dogey *n. US, Can* = **dogie**

dog fennel *n.* PLANTS = **mayweed** [So called from its fetid smell, and from its leaves being likened to those of fennel]

dogfight /dóg fīt/ *n.* **1.** AIR COMBAT BETWEEN FIGHTER PLANES an aerial combat involving two or more fighter planes **2.** FIERCE FIGHT a fierce violent fight **3.** FIGHT INVOLVING DOGS a fight between dogs —**dogfighting** *n.*

Dogfish

dogfish /dóg fish/ (*plural* **-fishes** *or* **-fish**) *n.* **1.** SMALL SHARK a small, long-tailed shark, either spiny or smooth-skinned, found in the Pacific, Atlantic, and Mediterranean. Families: Squalidae and Carcharhinidae and Scyliorhinidae. **2.** = **bowfin**

dogged /dóggid/ *adj.* determined to continue without giving up in spite of difficulties —**doggedly** *adv.* —**doggedness** *n.*

dogger[1] /dóggər/ *n.* a Dutch fishing vessel [14thC. From Middle Dutch.]

dogger[2] /dóggər/ *n.* GEOL a large mass of calcium-containing sandstone or ironstone occurring in sedimentary rock [Late 17thC. Origin uncertain: perhaps formed from DOG.]

doggerel /dóggərəl/, **doggrel** /dóggrəl/ *n.* **1.** POETRY POETRY WITH IRREGULAR RHYTHM poetry that does not scan well and is often not intended to be taken seriously **2.** POOR-QUALITY COMPOSITION sth that is badly written or makes no sense at all [14thC. Origin uncertain: probably formed from DOG (with its pejorative connotations).]

Doggett /dóggit/, **Thomas** (1660?–1721) Irish actor and playwright. Praised for performances in Congreve's plays, he also endowed 'Doggett's Coat and Badge', a trophy still annually contested by Thames oarsmen.

doggie *n.* = **doggy**

doggish /dóggish/ *adj.* **1.** RESEMBLING A DOG resembling a dog, or possessing the qualities of a dog **2.** BAD-TEMPERED bad-tempered and aggressive —**doggishly** *adv.* —**doggishness** *n.*

doggo /dóggō/ *adv.* not moving or making any sound in order not to be discovered ◊ *lying doggo* [Late 19thC. Formed from DOG, dogs having the capacity to lie in this manner.]

doggone /dóggon/, **doggoned** *adv., adj. US, Can* AN-NOYING used to emphasize how bad or annoying sth is (*informal*) ■ *interj. US* EXPRESSING ANNOYANCE used to express annoyance or irritation (*informal*) [Early 19thC. Origin uncertain: probably (perhaps via Scots dialect *dagone*) ultimately from GODDAMN.]

doggrel *n.* = **doggerel**

doggy /dóggi/, **doggie** *n.* (*plural* **-gies**) DOG a dog (*babytalk*) ■ *adj.* **1.** RESEMBLING A DOG resembling or typical of a dog's behaviour or appearance **2.** FOND OF DOGS fond of or interested in dogs (*informal*)

doggy bag, **doggie bag** *n.* a bag that can be used by a customer at a restaurant to take home any leftover food from his or her meal [*Doggy* from giving the food in it to a dog]

doggy paddle *n.* SWIMMING STROKE a swimming stroke in which the swimmer lies face down and makes rapid downward movements with the arms and legs underneath the body. This stroke is often used by children learning to swim and is not used in competitions. US term **dog paddle** ■ *vi.* (**doggy paddles, doggy paddling, doggy paddled**) SWIM USING DOGGY PADDLE to swim using the doggy paddle. US term **dog paddle**

dog handler *n.* a police officer or security guard who is in charge of a specially trained working dog

doghouse /dóg hows/ (*plural* **-houses** /-howziz/) *n. US, Can* = **kennel** ◇ **in the doghouse** in disgrace (*informal*)

dogie /dógi/, **dogy** (*plural* **-gies**), **dogey** (*plural* **-geys**) *n. US, Can* a calf with no mother [Late 19thC. Origin unknown.]

dog Latin *n.* Latin that is incorrect in some way, especially a word or phrase that is falsely made to look or sound like Latin for humorous or satiric effect

dogleg /dóg leg/ *n.* **1.** SHARP BEND a sharp bend or angle in sth, especially in a road **2.** GOLF GOLF HOLE WITH BEND a hole in golf in which the fairway contains a gentle or sharp bend ■ *vi.* (**-legs, -legging, -legged**) FORM A SHARP BEND to form a sharp bend or angle [From being likened to the bent form of a dog's hind leg] —**doglegged** /dóg léggid, dóg légd/ *adj.*

dogma /dógmə/ (*plural* **-mas** *or* **-mata** /-mətə/) *n.* **1.** RELIG RELIGIOUS BELIEF a belief or set of beliefs that a religion holds to be true **2.** GROUP BELIEF a belief or set of beliefs that a political, philosophical, or moral group holds to be true [Mid-16thC. Via late Latin from Greek *dogma* (stem *dogmat-*) 'opinion, tenet', from *dokein* 'to seem good, think' (source of English *orthodox* and *paradox*).]

dogmatic /dog máttik/, **dogmatical** /-ik'l/ *adj.* **1.** EXPRESSING RIGID OPINIONS prone to expressing strongly held beliefs and opinions **2.** RELATING TO DOGMA relating to or expressing a religious, political, philosophical, or moral dogma —**dogmatically** *adv.*

dogmatics /dog máttiks/, **dogmatic theology** *n.* RELIG the study of religious dogmas, especially Christian dogmas (*takes a singular verb*)

dogmatise *vti.* = **dogmatize**

dogmatism /dógmətizəm/ *n.* the tendency to express strongly held opinions in a way that suggests they should be accepted without question

dogmatist /dógmətist/ *n.* **1.** SB DOGMATIC sb who expresses strongly held opinions, expecting them to be accepted without question **2.** SB DEVISING DOGMA sb who devises a new religious, political, philosophical, or moral dogma

dogmatize /dógmə tīz/ (**-tizes, -tizing, -tized**), **dogmatise** (**-tises, -tising, -tised**) *vi.* to express strongly held opinions in a way that suggests they should be accepted without question —**dogmatization** /dógmə tī záysh'n/ *n.* —**dogmatizer** /dógmə tīzər/ *n.*

Dogon /dô gon/ (*plural* **-gon** *or* **-gons**) *n.* LANG a language of Mali and Burkina Faso, belonging to the Niger-Congo family and perhaps to the Gur group. Dogon is spoken by over 500,000 people. —**Dogon** *adj.*

do-gooder /-goodər/ *n.* sb who tries to help others, with the best intentions, but who can be perceived as unwelcome or even interfering (*informal*) —**do-goodery** *n.* —**do-gooding** *n., adj.*

dog paddle *n., vi.* (**dog paddles, dog paddling, dog paddled**) *US* = **doggy paddle**

dog racing *n.* the sport of greyhound racing in which dogs chase a mechanical hare round a track and spectators may bet on which dog will win

dog rose *n.* a European wild rose with delicate pink or white flowers. Latin name: *Rosa canina*. [Ultimately from an account in the ancient Roman Pliny's *Historia Naturalis* in which a soldier with rabies contracted from a dog-bite is cured with the root of this plant]

dogsbody /dógz bodi/ (*plural* **-ies**) *n.* sb who does all the boring menial jobs that others do not want to do (*informal*) [Early 19thC. First attested as British naval slang for a pudding made of peas.]

dogs' home *n.* a place where stray or abandoned dogs are cared for

dog show *n.* a competitive event in which dogs are judged on the qualities considered to be characteristic of the breed or type, e.g. appearance, obedience, and agility

dogsled /dóg sled/ *n.* a vehicle mounted on runners and pulled by dogs, designed to travel over snow and ice

dog's-tail *n.* a European grass that has flowers along a narrow spike. Genus: *Cynosurus*.

Dog Star *n.* ASTRON = **Sirius**

dog's-tooth check *n.* = **houndstooth check**

dog tag *n.* **1.** IDENTITY DISC FOR DOG a metal disc, attached to a dog's collar, that gives the name and address of the dog's owner and often the name of the dog **2.** *US* MIL IDENTIFICATION TAG FOR SOLDIERS a metal identification tag for a member of the military, worn on a chain around the neck (*informal*)

dogteeth /-teeth/ plural of **dogtooth**

dog-tired *adj.* completely exhausted (*informal*)

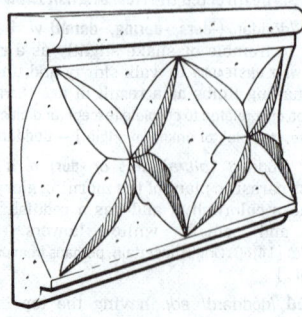

Dogtooth

dogtooth /dóg tooth/ (*plural* **-teeth**) *n.* **1.** DENT CANINE a canine tooth (*informal*) **2.** ARCHIT LATE MEDIEVAL ARCHITECTURAL FEATURE in 13th-century English architecture, a small raised ornamental feature on a building consisting of four leaf-shaped parts arranged to form an X-shape

dog-tooth check *n.* TEXTILES, CLOTHES = **houndstooth check**

dogtooth violet *n.* a small bulbous plant of the lily family that flowers in the spring and has red-speckled leaves and nodding yellow or purple flowers resembling lilies. Genus: *Erythronium*. [From the toothed inner segments of the perianth]

dogtrot /dóg trot/ *n.* a gentle trot at a steady pace

dog tucker *n. NZ* parts of a slaughtered sheep used as dog food

dog violet *n.* a Eurasian violet with blue and yellow flowers. Latin name: *Viola canina*.

dog warden *n.* sb employed to catch stray dogs. US term **dogcatcher**

dogwatch /dóg woch/ *n.* NAUT on a ship, the late afternoon watch from 4:00 P.M. to 6:00 P.M. or the early evening watch from 6:00 P.M. to 8:00 P.M.

dogwood /dóg wŏŏd/ (*plural* **-woods** *or* **-wood**) *n.* a tree or shrub that has clusters of small white flowers surrounded by four large white or reddish leaves (**bracts**). Genus: *Cornus*.

dogy *n. US, Can* = **dogie**

doh[1] /dō/ *n.* MUSIC a syllable that represents the first note in a scale when singing solfeggio. US term **doh**[2] [Mid-18thC. From Italian *do*, a replacement for the less singable medieval Latin syllable *ut* (source of English *gamut*.]

doh[2] /dō/ *n.* a syllable that represents the first note in a scale, used for singing solfeggio. In fixed solfeggio it represents the note C, while in solfeggio with movable doh it is used to represent the tonic of the key being sung. [Mid-18thC. From Italian *do*, a replacement for the less singable medieval Latin syllable *ut* (source of English *gamut*.)] ◇ **be up to high doh** *Scotland* to be extremely agitated or anxious (*informal*)

DoH, **DOH** *abbr.* Department of Health

Doha /dō haa, dō ə/ capital and largest city of Qatar, on the Persian Gulf. Population: 296,821 (1991).

Doily

doily /dóyli/ (*plural* **-lies**), **doyly** (*plural* **-lies**) *n.* a decorative lacy mat, usually made of lace, linen, or paper, that is put on plates under cakes or party food to display the food attractively [Late 18thC. Named after *Doiley* or *Doyley*, surname of a 17th-C London draper.]

doing[1] /dŏŏ ing/ present participle of **do**

doing[2] /dŏŏ ing/ *n.* **1.** CARRYING OUT OF STH the act of performing or carrying out sth ○ *It's all your doing.* **2.** BEATING OR REBUKE a beating or rebuke given as a punishment (*dated informal*) ■ **doings** *npl.* **1.** DEEDS OR ACHIEVEMENTS the things that sb has done **2.** SOCIAL ACTIVITIES social activities

doings /dŏŏ ingz/ *n.* sth whose name has been forgotten or is not known (*informal*)

doit /doyt/ *n.* **1.** MONEY OLD DUTCH UNIT OF CURRENCY a small low-value silver coin that was a Dutch unit of currency between the 15th and 17th centuries **2.** JOT sth that is very small and unimportant (*archaic*) [Late 16thC. From Middle Low German *doyt*.]

doited /dóytid/, **doitit** /-tit/ *adj. Scotland* behaving unreasonably or childishly, especially when the behaviour is thought to occur because of age [15thC. Origin uncertain: perhaps an alteration of the past participle *doted* of DOTE.]

do-it-yourself *n.* the activity of doing repairs and alterations in the home yourself, especially as a hobby, instead of employing tradespeople to do the work —**do-it-yourselfer** *n.*

dojo /dṓjō/ (*plural* **-jos**) *n.* a school or room for practising judo [Mid-20thC. From Japanese, literally 'way ground, pursuit place', from *dō* 'way, art' (source of English *kendo*) + *-jō* 'ground'.]

dol. *abbr.* dollar

dolabriform /dō lábbri fawrm/, **dolabrate** /-láb rayt/ *adj.* BOT having a shape like an axe head [Mid-18thC. Formed from Latin *dolabra* 'mattock, pickaxe'.]

Dolby /dólbi/ *tdmk.* a trademark for an electronic circuit that reduces noise on an audio tape recording

dolce /dólchi/ *adv.* sweetly and gently (*used as a musical direction*) [Early 19thC. Via Italian, 'sweet', from Latin *dulcis* (source of English *dulcet*).] —**dolce** *adj.*

dolce far niente /-faar nyén ti/ *n.* pleasant idleness and relaxation [Early 19thC. From Italian, literally 'sweet doing nothing'.]

Dolcelatte /dól chay látt ay/ *n.* a soft creamy Italian blue cheese with a mild flavour, made from cow's milk

dolce vita /-veetə/ *n.* a life of luxury and idle self-indulgence [Mid-20thC. From Italian, literally 'sweet life'.]

doldrums /dóldrəmz, dól-/ *npl.* **1.** STAGNATION a sluggish state in which sth fails to develop or improve **2.** GLOOMINESS a state of gloominess or very low energy **3.** METEOROL, SHIPPING AREA OF WINDS NORTH OF EQUATOR an area with no wind or light variable winds just north of the equator in the Atlantic and Pacific oceans, situated between the trade winds **4.** METEOROL, SHIPPING WEATHER CONDITIONS IN DOLDRUMS the weather conditions prevailing in the doldrums. These formerly caused problems for sailing ships, which could become becalmed there. [Late 18thC. Origin uncertain: perhaps formed (on the model of TANTRUM) from *dold* 'stupid, inactive', ultimately from Old English *dol* 'foolish'.]

dole[1] /dōl/ *n.* **1.** SOC WELFARE STATE UNEMPLOYMENT PAYMENT a regular sum of money paid by the state to people who are unemployed (*informal*) **2.** CHARITY the giving of clothes, money, or food to people who are in need **3.** SB'S FATE sb's fate in life (*archaic*) ■ *vt.* (**doles, doling, doled**) DISTRIBUTE STH AS CHARITY to distribute sth as charity to people who are in need [Old English *dāl* 'portion', from a prehistoric Germanic base that is also the ancestor of English *deal* and *ordeal*]

dole out *vt.* to give sth to each of a group of people (*informal*)

dole[2] /dōl/ *n.* grief, sadness, or misery (*archaic*) [13thC. Via Old French *dol* 'mourning' from popular Latin *dolus*, from Latin *dolere* 'to grieve, suffer pain' (source of English *condolence*).]

dole bludger *n. Aus* sb who lives off the dole and is thought to make no effort to find work (*informal*)

doleful /dólf'l/ *adj.* very sad and mournful —**dolefully** *adv.* —**dolefulness** *n.*

dolente /do lénti/ *adv.* in a sorrowful manner (*used as a musical direction*) [From Italian, present participle of *dolere* 'to feel grief', from Latin *dolere* (see DOLE[2])] —**dolente** *adj.*

dole queue *n.* the number of people who are unemployed and claiming money from the state

dolerite /dóllə rīt/ *n.* a medium-grained basic igneous rock typically forming a minor intrusion such as a sill or dyke. US term **diabase** [Mid-19thC. From French *dolérite*, from Greek *doleros* 'deceptive', from *dolos* 'deceit' (from its being difficult to distinguish from diorite).] —**doleritic** /dóllə ríttik/ *adj.*

dolichocephalic /dóllikō si fállik/, **dolichocephalous** /-séffələss/ *adj.* having a head disproportionately longer than it is wide, specifically one with a cephalic index of less than 75 [Mid-19thC. Coined from *dolicho-* 'narrow' (from Greek *dolikhos*) + -CEPHALIC.] —**dolichocephalism** /dóllikō séffəlizəm/ *n.*

dolichosaurus /dóllikō sáwrəss/ *n.* an extinct aquatic long-necked reptile that was common 65 million years ago [Coined from *dolicho-* 'narrow' (from Greek *dolikhos*) + -SAURUS, from their long necks and bodies]

Dolin /dóllin/, **Sir Anton** (1904–83) British dancer and choreographer. A soloist with Diaghilev (1923–25 and 1929) in the Ballets Russes dance company, he formed his own company (1927–28) with his principal partner, Alicia Markova. He later led the London Festival Ballet (1950–61). Pseudonym of **Sydney Francis Patrick Chippindall Healey Kay**

doline /də leenə/, **dolina** *n.* a large, often roughly circular basin of valley-sized proportions formed as a result of water dissolving surface limestone [Late 19thC. Via German from Slovene *dolina* 'valley'.]

do-little *n. US* sb who is lazy (*informal*)

D'Oliviera /dólli veerə/, **Basil Lewis** (b. 1931) South African-born British cricketer. He is a Cape Coloured all-rounder who played for England and Worcestershire. Controversy over his inclusion in the England team for the 1968–69 South African tour led to South Africa being excluded from international cricket from 1970 to 1992.

doll /dol/ *n.* **1.** CHILD'S TOY a child's toy in the shape of a person or baby **2.** WOMAN PLEASANT TO LOOK AT a woman or girl who is pleasant to look at and described in that sense (*informal; sometimes offensive*) [Mid-16thC. From the pet form of the female name *Dorothy* (compare the formation of *Moll* from *Mary*). Originally 'man's woman lover'.] —**dollish** *adj.* —**dollishly** *adv.* —**dollishness** *n.*

doll up *vt.* to make yourself or sb else, e.g. a child, look particularly smart and stylish, usually for a special occasion (*informal*)

dollar /dóllər/ *n.* **1.** COMMON UNIT OF CURRENCY a unit of currency used in the United States, Canada, Australia, and some other countries all around the world. See table at **currency 2. NOTE WORTH A DOLLAR** a note worth one dollar **3. FORMER FIVE-SHILLING COIN** formerly in the United Kingdom, a five-shilling coin (*informal*) [Mid-16thC. Via early Flemish *daler* or Low German from German *Taler*, shortening of *Joachimst(h)aler*, named after the silver mine of *Joachimsthal*, now Jáchymov, Czech Republic.]

dollarbird /dóllər burd/ *n.* a blue-grey bird with pale round patches on its wings the size of a dollar coin. It winters in Indonesia and New Guinea, migrating to Australia in summer. Latin name: *Eurystomus orientalis*.

dollar cost averaging *n.* STOCK EXCH the periodic and systematic purchase of a security regardless of the security price

dollar diplomacy *n. US* **1.** US POLICY PROTECTING OVERSEAS INVESTMENT in the United States, a policy aimed at encouraging and protecting American investment abroad **2.** USE OF FINANCIAL POWER IN DIPLOMACY the use of financial resources to facilitate foreign relations

dollars-and-cents *adj. US* considering finance as the determining factor

dollar sign *n.* the symbol ($) that represents a dollar

Dollfuss /dól fŏŏss/, **Engelbert** (1892–1934) Austrian statesman. A Christian Socialist leader who suppressed socialism, he was Chancellor of Austria (1932–34). He was murdered by Austrian Nazis.

dollhouse /dól howss/ (*plural* **-houses** /-howziz/) *n. US* = **doll's house**

dollop /dólləp/ *n.* SMALL AMOUNT OF STH a spoon-sized quantity of a thick liquid or a soft solid such as ice cream or cream (*informal*) ■ *vt.* (**-lops, -loping, -loped**) SPOON STH to spoon a quantity of a thick liquid or a soft solid (*informal*) [Late 16thC. Origin uncertain: perhaps from Scandinavian. Originally 'clump of grass or weeds'.]

doll's house *n.* a toy house containing miniature furniture. US term **dollhouse**

dolly /dólli/ *n.* (*plural* **-lies**) **1.** DOLL a toy doll (*babytalk*) **2.**

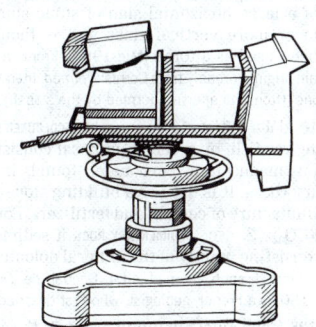

Dolly: Television camera on pedestal dolly

TV, CINEMA **MOVING PLATFORM FOR CAMERA OPERATOR** a platform with wheels on which a camera operator and camera are placed in order to film moving shots for a film or television programme **3.** MECH ENG **PLATFORM ON WHEELS FOR MOVING THINGS** a platform on wheels used to move heavy weights **4.** CIV ENG **WEIGHT DROPPED ON A PILE** a heavy weight dropped on a pile to force it into the ground **5.** CONSTR **TOOL FOR HOLDING RIVET** an anvil that holds one end of a rivet while the other end is being hammered **6.** METALL **HEAVY BLOCK HELD BEHIND HAMMERED METAL** a heavy block held behind sheet metal that is being hammered **7.** CRICKET **EASY CATCH** an easy catch ■ *vti.* **(-lies, -lying, -lied) MOVE CAMERA ON A DOLLY** to move a camera on a dolly

dolly bird *n.* a physically good-looking young woman (*dated informal; sometimes offensive*)

dolly drop *n.* in cricket, a ball bowled high and slowly that reaches the batsman without touching the ground

dolly mixture *n.* any of a variety of small coloured sweets sold as a mixture

dolly shot *n.* a shot filmed from a camera mounted on a wheeled platform

Dolly Varden /dólli va͡ard'n/ *n.* **1. LARGE-BRIMMED HAT** a woman's hat with a large brim, usually with one side turned down, and decorated with flowers **2.** (*plural* **Dolly Varden**) **RED-SPOTTED FISH** a trout or char with red spots found in lakes and streams of western North America and eastern Asia. Latin name: *Salvelinus malma.* [Late 19thC. Named after *Dolly Varden*, a woman of colourful dress in the novel *Barnaby Rudge* by Charles Dickens.]

dolma /dólmə/ (*plural* **-mas** *or* **-mades** /-ma͡a deez/) *n.* a vine or cabbage leaf with a savoury stuffing usually containing meat and rice, a speciality of Greek and Turkish cooking [Late 17thC. From Turkish, literally 'sth stuffed'.]

dolman /dólmən/ *n.* **1. WOMAN'S WIDE-SLEEVED COAT** a woman's coat with large sleeves cut in one piece with the body of the garment **2. LONG ROBE** a long Turkish robe [Late 16thC. Via French *dol(i)man* from, ultimately, Turkish *dolama(n)* 'robe'.]

dolman jacket *n.* a style of jacket worn by a horseman, usually worn like a cloak over the shoulders with the sleeves hanging loose

dolman sleeve *n.* a sleeve cut in one piece with the body of a garment such as a jacket or dress, particularly one fitting tightly at the wrist and wide at the armhole

Dolmen

dolmen /dólmən/ *n.* a prehistoric structure that consists of a large horizontal slab of stone supported by two or more vertical slabs and is thought to have been used as a tomb [Mid-19thC. From French, of uncertain origin: probably from Cornish *tolmen*, literally 'hole (of) stone' (from the aperture formed by the slabs).]

dolomite /dóllə mīt/ *n.* **1.** MINERALS **PALE-COLOURED MINERAL** a white, reddish, or greenish mineral consisting of calcium magnesium carbonate, found in sedimentary rocks. It is used as a building stone and in the manufacture of cement and fertilizers. Formula: $CaMg(CO_3)_2$. **2.** GEOL **SEDIMENTARY ROCK** a sedimentary rock consisting mainly of the mineral dolomite [Late 18thC. From French, named after Déodat de *Dolomieu* (1750–1801), a French geologist, who first described it.]

Dolomites /dóllə mīts/ mountain group in the eastern part of the northern Italian Alps. The highest peak is Marmolada, 3,342 km/10,964 ft.

dolor *n.* US = **dolour**

doloroso /dóllə rṓssō/ *adv.* to be played with sadness (*used as a musical direction.*) [Early 19thC. Via Italian from late Latin *dolorosus* (see DOLOUROUS).] —**doloroso** *adj.*

dolorous /dóllərəss/ *adj.* showing, causing, or involving sorrow or pain (*literary*) [14thC. Via Old French *doleros* from late Latin *dolorosus*, from Latin *dolor* (see DOLOUR).] —**dolorously** *adv.* —**dolorousness** *n.*

dolour /dóllər/ *n.* intense sadness (*literary*) [13thC. Via Old French *dolo(u)r* from Latin *dolor* 'pain, grief, sorrow', from *dolere* 'to feel pain'.]

Dolphin

dolphin /dólfin/ (*plural* **-phins** *or* **-phin**) *n.* ZOOL **1. SEA ANIMAL RELATED TO WHALES** an intelligent marine mammal (**cetacean**) that resembles a large fish and has teeth and a snout similar to a beak. Found almost worldwide, dolphins are related to whales but are smaller. Family: Delphinidae. **2. LARGE MARINE GAME FISH** a large sea fish of the perch family, popular as a game fish, that has a long dorsal fin, high blunt forehead, and a brilliant green, blue, and yellow body. Latin name: *Coryphaena hippurus* and *Coryphaena equisetis.* [14thC. Via Old French *daulphin* (source of English *dauphin*) from, ultimately, Greek *delphin* (source of English *delphinium*).]

dolphinarium /dólfi náiri əm/ (*plural* **-ums** *or* **-a** /-ri ə/) *n.* a large pool in which dolphins are kept, either for research or for public displays [Mid-20thC. Blend of DOLPHIN and AQUARIUM; modelled on OCEANARIUM.]

dolphinfish /dólfin fish/ (*plural* **-fish** *or* **-fishes**) *n.* = **dolphin** *n.* 2

dolphin striker *n.* a strut that helps to prevent upward movement of a spar extending from the front of a sailing vessel

dolt /dōlt/ *n.* sb thought of as being without intelligence (*informal insult*) [Mid-16thC. Origin uncertain: perhaps ultimately *dulled*, past participle of DULL.]

doltish /dṓltish/ *adj.* of low intelligence or showing lack of intelligence (*informal insult*) —**doltishly** *adv.* —**doltishness** *n.*

Dom /dom/, **dom** *n.* **1. ROMAN CATHOLIC TITLE** a title used before the name of some Roman Catholic monks, especially Benedictines **2. PORTUGUESE TITLE** a title formerly used before the names of certain members of the aristocracy and royalty in Portugal and Brazil [Late 17thC. Shortening of Latin *dominus* 'lord' (see DON[1]).]

DOM *abbr.* **1.** Deo Optimo Maximo **2.** dirty old man (*slang insult*)

dom. *abbr.* **1.** domestic **2.** MUSIC dominant

Dom. *abbr.* Dominican

-dom *suffix.* **1.** status, condition ○ *martyrdom* **2.** people associated with a particular status or rank ○ *fandom* **3.** office, rank, domain ○ *dukedom* [Old English *-dōm*. Ultimately from an Indo-European base meaning 'to put, place', which is also the ancestor of English *doom.*]

domain /dō máyn, də-/ *n.* **1. PURVIEW** the scope of a subject **2. SPHERE OF INFLUENCE** an area of activity over which sb has influence **3. TERRITORY GOVERNED** territory ruled by a government or a leader **4. LAND OWNED** an area of land owned and controlled by a person, family, or organization **5.** LAW **RIGHTS OF OWNERSHIP** rights relating to the ownership of land. ◊ **demesne** **6.** PHYS **REGION OF UNIFORM MAGNETISM** a region in a ferromagnetic material within which all the atoms are magnetically oriented in the same direction. Increasing the magnetic field increases the size and number of the domains. **7.** MATH **SET OF VALUES OF VARIABLE** the set of possible values specified for a given mathematical function **8.** *ANZ* **PUBLIC SPACE** a public recreation area **9.** COMPUT = **domain name** [15thC. From French *domaine*, an alteration of *demeine* 'demesne' (source of English *demesne*), from, ultimately, Latin *dominus* 'lord' (see DON[1]), the underlying sense being 'land belonging to a lord'.]

domain name *n.* the sequence of words, phrases, abbreviations, or characters that identifies a specific computer or network on the Internet and serves as its address

dome /dōm/ *n.* **1.** ARCHIT **HEMISPHERICAL ROOF** a hemispherical roof, e.g. on a palace or cathedral **2. HEMISPHERICAL TOP** sth that resembles a dome in shape and position, e.g. the cover of a furnace or the top of sb's head ○ *the dome of the sky* **3. HEMISPHERICAL BUILDING STRUCTURE** a hemispherical or convex structure, especially a building ○ *the Millennium Dome* **4. CRYSTAL FORMATION RESEMBLING A ROOF** a crystal form in which two inclined surfaces intersect to form an edge like a roof **5. LARGE STATELY BUILDING** a large grand building (*archaic*) **6.** GEOL **CURVED ROCK LAYER** a hemispherical topographic feature that slopes in all directions from a central point, formed by upward folding of sediments **7.** GEOL **LAVA MASS** a mass of solidified viscous lava formed above the vent of a volcano by the build-up of magma ■ *v.* **(domes, doming, domed)** **1.** *vti.* **FORM A HEMISPHERICAL SHAPE** to rise in a hemispherical shape, or form sth into this shape **2.** *vt.* **COVER WITH A DOME** to cover sth with a dome [Mid-17thC. Via French *dôme* from Italian *duomo* 'house, house of God, cathedral' (source of English *duomo*), from Latin *domus* 'house'.]

domed /dōmd/ *adj.* **1. HAVING A DOME** with a dome or many domes **2. LOOKING LIKE A DOME** with a shape or structure resembling a dome ○ *'His brow is deeply lined with thought, his head is highly domed'* (T. S. Eliot 'Macavity: The Mystery Cat'; 1939)

domesday /dóomz day/ *n.* doomsday (*archaic*)

Domesday Book, **Doomsday Book** *n.* a record of all the land in England, its value and its ownership, commissioned by William the Conqueror in 1085 [*Domesday* reflecting the book's status as the ultimate authority on matters within its compass]

domestic /də méstik/ *adj.* **1. RELATING TO HOME** relating to or used in the home or everyday life within a household **2.** DOMESTIC **RELATING TO FAMILY** relating to or involving the family or people living together within a household **3.** AGRIC **NOT WILD** kept as a farm animal or as a pet **4.** COMM **NOT FOREIGN** produced, distributed, sold, or occurring within a country ○ *domestic oil producers* **5.** POL **OF A NATION'S INTERNAL AFFAIRS** relating to the internal affairs of a nation or country ○ *domestic issues such as elections* **6. ENJOYING HOME** enjoying home and family life ■ *n.* **1. HOUSEHOLD SERVANT** sb employed to do housework in sb else's home or other duties in a large household **2.** COMM **PRODUCT NOT ORIGINATING ABROAD** a product manufactured within a country [15thC. Via French *domestique* from Latin *domesticus*, from *domus* 'house'.] —**domestically** *adv.*

domesticate /də mésti kayt/ **(-cates, -cating, -cated)** *vt.* **1.** AGRIC **TAME AN ANIMAL** to accustom an animal to living with or near people, usually as a farm animal or pet **2. ACCUSTOM TO HOUSEHOLD LIFE** to accustom sb to home life or housework (*humorous*) **3.** BIOL **ADAPT PLANTS AND ANIMALS FOR HUMANS** to cultivate plants or raise animals, selectively breeding them to increase their suitability for human requirements [Mid-17thC. From medieval Latin *domesticat-*, the past participle stem of *domesticare*, from Latin *domesticus* (see DOMESTIC).] —**domesticable** *adj.* —**domestication** /də mésti káysh'n/ *n.* —**domesticator** /də mésti kaytər/ *n.*

domesticated /də mésti kaytid/ *adj.* **1.** AGRIC **NOT WILD** accustomed to living near people, usually on a farm or in a home **2.** BIOL **RAISED FOR HUMANS** cultivated, raised, or bred for human requirements **3. ACCUSTOMED TO HOUSEWORK** accustomed to doing domestic chores in the home (*humorous*)

domesticity /dóm e stíssəti, dóm-/ *n.* **1. HOME LIFE** life as it is lived at home **2. FONDNESS FOR HOME LIFE** a liking for or familiarity with home life ■ **domesticities**

a at; aa father; aw all; ay day; air hair; ə about, edible, item, common, circus; e egg; ee eel; hw when; i it, happy; ī ice; 'l apple; 'm rhythm; 'n fashion; o odd; ō open; oo good; oo pool; ow owl; oy oil; th thin; th this; u up; ur urge;

INTERNET DOMAIN NAMES

The Domain Name System (DNS) is a method of translating Internet addresses from systematic alphabetical sequences to numeric codes so that messages can be transmitted from one computer or network to another. A DNS name appears in the form:

username@computer (or Internet provider).domain

Domains indicate the country — except for the United States, where no country code is used — or type of organization or both country and organization.

Selected Organization Domains

Domain	Organization
.ac	Educational Organization outside US
.co	Commercial Organization outside US
.com	Commercial Organization
.edu	Educational Organization
.gov	Government Organization
.int	International Organization
.mil	Military Organization
.net	Network Organization
.org	Private Organization

For countries other than the United States country domains can be combined with organization domains, e.g.:

.co.uk	UK Commercial Organization
.edu.au	Australian Educational Organization

Selected Country Domains

Domain	Country
.au	Australia
.bd	Bangladesh
.ca	Canada
.gh	Ghana
.hk	Hong Kong
.id	Indonesia
.ie	Ireland
.in	India
.ke	Kenya
.my	Malaysia
.nz	New Zealand
.ng	Nigeria
.pk	Pakistan
.sg	Singapore
.za	South Africa
.lk	Sri Lanka
.ug	Uganda
.uk	United Kingdom
.zm	Zambia
.zw	Zimbabwe

npl. **HOUSEHOLD MATTERS** the concerns of the home and family

domestic prelate *n.* a Roman Catholic priest with honorary membership of the papal household

Domett /dómmit/, **Alfred** (1811–87) English-born New Zealand statesman and poet. He was premier of New Zealand (1862–63). His poetical works include *Ranolf and Amohia* (1872).

domette /dō mét/ *n.* a soft fleecy fabric made from wool and acrylic fibres, used as lightweight interlining [Early 19thC. Origin unknown.]

domical /dómmik'l/ *adj.* **1.** **DOME-SHAPED** shaped like a dome **2.** **WITH A DOME** having a dome or domes

domicile /dómmi sīl/ *n.* **1.** **SB'S HOME** the house, flat, or other place where sb lives (*formal*) **2.** **LAW SB'S PLACE OF RESIDENCE** sb's true, fixed, and legally recognized place of residence, especially in cases of prolonged absence that require the person to prove a continuing and significant connection with the place **3.** **PLACE FOR PAYMENT** the place at which a bill of exchange is to be paid ■ *vt.* (**-ciles, -ciling, -ciled**) **GIVE A HOME** to establish sb in or provide sb with a place of residence [15thC. Directly or via French from Latin *domicilium*, from *domus* 'house'.]

domiciliary /dómmi sílli əri/ *adj.* **1.** **OF HOME** relating to a home or homes **2.** **FOR PEOPLE AT HOME** provided for or attending to people in their own homes ○ *domiciliary care* [Late 19thC. Via French *domiciliare* from medieval Latin *domiciliarius*, from *domicilium* (see DOMICILE).]

domiciliary care *n.* personal, domestic, or nursing care provided for people at home rather than in an institution

domiciliary services *npl.* services relating to care in the home, rather than in an institution

domiciliate /dómmi sílli ayt/ (**-ates, -ating, -ated**) *vt.* = **domicile** *v.* [Late 18thC. From Latin *domicilium* (see DOMICILE).]

dominance /dómminənss/ *n.* **1.** **POWER EXERTED OVER OTHERS** control or command wielded over others **2.** **FIRST**

IMPORTANCE prime importance, effectiveness, or prominence **3.** GENETICS **PRODUCTION OF GENETIC FEATURE** the property of a gene that causes a parental characteristic it controls to occur in any offspring **4.** ECOL **PREPONDERANCE OF ONE SPECIES** the preponderance of a single plant or animal species in a specific community or over a specific period

dominant /dómminənt/ *adj.* **1.** **IN CONTROL** in control or command over others **2.** **MORE IMPORTANT** more important, effective, or prominent than others **3.** GENETICS **PRODUCING SAME CHARACTERISTIC IN OFFSPRING** used to describe a gene that causes a parental characteristic it controls to occur in any offspring, or the characteristic itself **4.** ECOL **PREPONDERANT IN A COMMUNITY OR PERIOD** relating to a single plant or animal species that is preponderant within a specific community or over a specific period **5.** MUSIC **RELATING TO 5TH NOTE OF SCALE** relating to the fifth note of a musical scale or the harmony based around that note ■ *n.* MUSIC **1.** **5TH NOTE OF SCALE** the fifth note of a musical scale **2.** **CHORD BASED ON 5TH NOTE** a chord or key based on the fifth note of a musical scale [15thC. Via French from Latin *dominant-*, present participle stem of *dominari* (see DOMINATE).] —**dominantly** *adv.*

dominant estate *n. US* = **dominant tenement**

dominant hemisphere *n.* the half of the brain that tends to exercise greater control over certain functions, e.g. language or movement of the left or right side of the body

dominant tenement *n.* property that gives its owner certain rights over other property, e.g. the right to cross land belonging to sb else in order to reach your own house. US term **dominant estate**

dominate /dómmi nayt/ (**-nates, -nating, -nated**) *vti.* **1.** **CONTROL** to have control, power, or authority over sb or sth **2.** **BE PROMINENT** to be the most important aspect or element of sth **3.** **BE INFLUENTIAL** to have a prevailing influence on sb or sth **4.** **TOWER ABOVE** to overlook an area from a prominent and usually elevated position [Early 17thC. Partly from Latin *dominat-*, past participle stem of *dominari* 'to be lord, rule', from *dominus* 'lord' (see DON¹); partly as a back-formation from DOM-

INATION.] —**dominative** /dómminətiv/ *adj.* —**dominator** /-naytər/ *n.*

— **WORD KEY: ORIGIN** —

As well as giving rise to **dominate**, Latin *dominus* is also the source of English *danger, demesne, domain, domineer, domino, don,* and *dungeon.*

domination /dómmi náysh'n/ *n.* control, power, or authority over others or another [14thC. Via French from the Latin stem *domination-*, from *dominari* (see DOMINATE).]

dominatrix /dómmi náytriks/ (*plural* **-trices** /-tri seez/) *n.* a dominant woman partner in a sadomasochistic relationship [Mid-16thC. From Latin, 'woman ruler', the feminine of *dominator* 'ruler, lord', from, ultimately, *dominari* (see DOMINATE).]

domineer /dómmi neˊer/ (**-neers, -neering, -neered**) *vi.* to rule tyrannically, or behave in an overbearing way [Late 16thC. Via Dutch *domineren* from, ultimately, Latin *dominari* (see DOMINATE).]

domineering /dómmi neˊering/ *adj.* showing a desire or tendency to exercise excessive control or authority over others —**domineeringly** *adv.*

Domingo /də míng gō/, **Plácido** (*b.* 1941) Spanish opera singer. He is widely regarded as the greatest tenor voice of his time. Since 1990 he has often appeared with José Carreras and Luciano Pavarotti as one of the 'Three Tenors'.

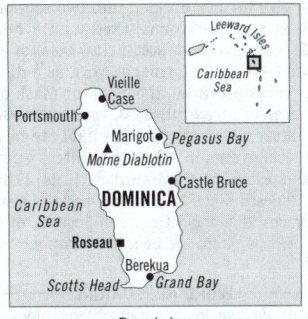

Dominica

Dominica /dómmi neˊekə, də mínnikə/ independent island republic in the West Indies, lying in the Caribbean Sea. Language: English. Currency: Eastern Caribbean dollar. Capital: Roseau. Population: 666,633 (1997). Area: 751 sq. km/290 sq. mi. Length: 47 km/29 mi. Official name **Commonwealth of Dominica**

dominical /də mínnik'l/ *adj.* CHR (*formal*) **1.** **OF JESUS CHRIST** relating to Jesus Christ as the Lord **2.** **RELATING TO SUNDAY** relating to Sunday as the day of the Lord [15thC. Directly or via French from late Latin *dominicalis*, from, ultimately, Latin *dominus* 'lord, master' (see DON¹).]

dominical letter *n.* any of the letters A to G used in the church calendar to denote all the Sundays of a given year. For example, if January 4 falls on a Sunday, the dominical letter for the year is D.

Dominican¹ /də mínnikən/ *n.* PEOPLES **1.** **SB FROM DOMINICAN REPUBLIC** sb who was born or brought up in the Dominican Republic, or who is a citizen of the Dominican Republic **2.** **SB FROM DOMINICA** sb who lives on or was born or brought up on the island of Dominica —**Dominican** *adj.*

Dominican² /də mínnikən/ *n.* CHR **MEMBER OF A RELIGIOUS ORDER** a member of the order of friars founded by St Dominic in 1215 ■ *adj.* **OF ST DOMINIC OR HIS ORDER** relating or belonging to St Dominic or his order of friars [Late 16thC. From medieval Latin *Dominicanus*, from the founder's name.]

Dominican Republic /də mínnikən-/ independent republic on Hispaniola Island, off the coast of Puerto Rica in the Caribbean Sea. It was proclaimed a republic in 1844. Language: Spanish. Currency: Dominican peso. Capital: Santo Domingo. Population: 7,868,731 (1997). Area: 48,734 sq. km/18,816 sq. mi. Length: 380 km/235 mi.

dominion /də mínnyən/ *n.* **1.** **RULING CONTROL** ruling power, authority, or control **2.** **SPHERE OF INFLUENCE** sb's area of influence or control **3.** **LAND RULED** the land

Dominican Republic

governed by a ruler (*often used in the plural*) ○ *the monarch's dominions beyond the sea* **4. dominion, Dominion** SELF-GOVERNING TERRITORY a self-governing part of the British Commonwealth or, formerly, the British Empire [15thC. Via Old French from the medieval Latin stem *dominion-*, from Latin *dominium* 'property, right of ownership', from *dominus* 'lord' (see DON[1]).]

dominium /də mínnyəm/ *n.* the right of ownership of property, especially land and buildings [Mid-18thC. From Latin (see DOMINION).]

domino /dómminō/ (*plural* **-noes**) *n.* **1.** BOARD GAMES SMALL OBLONG TILE any one of a set of small oblong blocks with its face divided into two sections, each section either blank or marked with a number of spots **2.** CLOTHES, LEISURE HOODED CLOAK AND MASK a hooded cloak and eye mask formerly worn as a disguise at a party (**masquerade**), the cloak or mask alone, or the wearer of any of these **3.** POL COUNTRY AFFECTED BY DOMINO THEORY a country thought likely to be affected by political events in another country, particularly by the spread of Communism [Late 17thC. From French, 'priest's winter hood', also 'masked cloak worn at masquerades' (the original sense in English), of uncertain origin: perhaps ultimately from Latin *dominus* 'lord' (see DON[1]).]

WORD KEY: ORIGIN

The use of **domino** for a small oblong block used in games (or **dominoes** for the game) is not found until the late 18th century, probably as an independent borrowing from French (certain French prisoners of war being thought to have brought the game to England). Why the game is so called is uncertain, but it might come from a likening of the gaming pieces (which often originally had white faces with ebony backs) to the pale faces of priests within dark **domino** hoods.

domino effect *n.* an inevitable succession of related and usually undesirable events, each caused by the preceding one. ◊ **domino theory** [So called because dominoes set up in a row fall in sequence once the first has fallen]

domino theory *n.* POL a theory that political events are interrelated and that one can trigger off a chain of others. The theory was developed by US President Dwight D. Eisenhower to warn of the spread of Communism in Southeast Asia. ◊ **domino effect**

dompass /dóm paass/ *n.* S Africa an identity document carried by Black people in South Africa during the apartheid era, used to restrict their movement within the country [Mid-20thC. From Afrikaans, from *dom* 'stupid' + *pas* 'pass'.]

don[1] /don/ *n.* **1.** UNIV UNIVERSITY OR COLLEGE TEACHER a university or college teacher, especially one at Oxford or Cambridge **2.** SPANISH MAN OF RANK a Spanish gentleman or aristocrat **3.** CRIMINOL LEADER OF ORGANIZED CRIME FAMILY a head of an organized crime family, especially in the Mafia **4.** PERSONAGE an important person (*archaic*) [Late 16thC. Via Spanish from Latin *dominus* 'lord' (source of English *domain*, *dominate*, *domino*, and *dungeon*).]

don[2] /don/ (**dons, donning, donned**) *vt.* to put on a garment (*formal*) [14thC. Contraction of *do on* 'to put on' (see DO). The word became largely obsolete in the 17thC, but was revived in the 19thC.]

Don[1] *n.* a title used before a man's name in Spain and other Spanish-speaking countries [Early 16thC. From Spanish (see DON[1]).]

Don[2] /don/ river rising southeast of Moscow, Russia, flowing through Volgograd and into the Sea of Azov. Length: 1,870 km/1,160 mi.

Dona /dónnə/ *n.* a title used before a married woman's name in Portugal and other Portuguese-speaking countries [Early 17thC. Via Portuguese from Latin *domina* 'lady', the feminine of *dominus* 'lord' (see DON[1]).]

Doña /dónnyə/ *n.* a title used before a married woman's name in Spain and other Spanish-speaking countries [Early 17thC. Via Spanish from Latin *domina* (see DONA).]

Donaldson /dónn'lds'n/, **Roger** (b. 1945) Australian-born New Zealand film maker. He directed *The Bounty* (1984) and *White Sands* (1992).

donate /dō náyt/ (**-nates, -nating, -nated**) *v.* **1.** *vt.* GIVE OR PRESENT to give or present sth, especially to a charitable organization or other good cause **2.** *vt.* MED GIVE BODY PART to give your own blood, tissue, organs, or reproductive material to be used in the treatment of another person, either while you are alive or after your death **3.** CHEM TRANSFER ELECTRONS to transfer electrons to another atom or molecule in a chemical reaction [Late 18thC. Back-formation from DONATION.]

WORD KEY: SYNONYMS

See Synonyms at *give*.

Donatello /dónnə tél ō/ (1386?–1466) Italian sculptor. In his bronze statue *David* (1430–35) and other works he revived the classical art of portraying independent functional human figures. Full name **Donato di Niccolò di Betto Bardi**

donation /dō náysh'n/ *n.* **1.** GIFT OR CONTRIBUTION a gift or contribution, especially a sum of money given to a charity ○ *All donations will be gratefully received.* **2.** ACT OF GIVING the act of giving sth, especially money to a charity [15thC. Via French from the Latin stem *donation-*, from, ultimately, Latin *donare* 'to give', from *donum* 'gift'.]

Donatism /dónətizəm/ *n.* the beliefs of the Donatists

Donatist /dónətist/ *n.* a member of a Christian group of the 4th and 5th centuries, originating in North Africa, that placed great emphasis on sanctity [Late 16thC. From late Latin *Donatista*, named after *Donatus*, the second Bishop of Carthage after Caecilian (whose consecration the Donatists did not recognize).]

donative /dónətiv/ *n.* **1.** OFFICIAL DONATION a donation, especially a formal or official one **2.** CHR CHURCH POSITION GIVEN AS GIFT a church office (**benefice**) that is or can be presented as a gift without reference to the bishop, as opposed to one received as a right ■ *adj.* MADE AS GIFT given or presented as a gift (*formal*) [15thC. Via Latin *donativum* from, ultimately, *donare* 'to give' (see DONATION).]

donator /dō náytər/ *n.* sb who gives or presents sth, especially money to a charity (*formal*) [15thC. Originally directly or via French *donateur* from Latin *donator*, from, ultimately, *donare* 'to give' (see DONATION); in modern use formed from *donate*.]

Doncaster /dóngkəstər/ town on the River Don in South Yorkshire, northern England. Population: 292,900 (1995).

done /dun/ past participle of *do* ■ *v.* Carib, Southern US ALREADY used as an auxiliary verb to express the sense of 'already' (*nonstandard*) ○ *He done leave.* ■ *adj.* **1.** CONCLUDED completed or finished **2.** COOK COOKED THROUGH cooked as thoroughly as required **3.** US PREORDAINED having been decided already, therefore permitting no alterations or changes (*slang*) ○ *It's a done deal, and you can't fight it.* **4.** SOCIALLY ACCEPTABLE acceptable to the established rules and expectations of a society **5.** CHEATED cheated or tricked (*informal*) ■ *interj.* AGREED used to confirm acceptance of a deal ◇ **have done with sth** to be finished with or have had enough of sth ○ *Why don't we just sell the house and have done with it?*

WORD KEY: USAGE

done or **finished**? It is sometimes maintained that **done** is the wrong word to indicate that one has completed sth. Certainly, *I have finished reading the newspaper* is more formal than *I'm done with the paper*. Not only does our one of these sentences use **finished** instead of **done** but also it uses **finished** as a past participle, whereas **done** in the example is being used as an adjective.

Finished, too, can be an adjective: *I'm finished with the paper.* Such adjectival uses are very common in casual speech and writing. For clarity's sake, the adjective **done** should not be used where it might be interpreted as the participle (*The work wasn't done well, but at least it was done before the deadline*). In formal contexts **finished** is preferable, and either it or **done** should modify what has been completed (*The job is finished*), rather than the one who has completed sth (*I am done*).

Done /dōn/, **Ken** (b. 1940) Australian painter and graphic designer. He is the creator of a widely marketed range of merchandise bearing his colourful designs. Full name **Kenneth Stephen Done**

donee /dō neé/ *n.* the recipient of a gift (*formal*) [Early 16thC. Formed from DONOR.]

done for *adj.* (*informal*) **1.** NEAR DEATH close to the point of dying **2.** EXHAUSTED extremely tired **3.** ABOUT TO BE RUINED facing defeat, ruin, or destruction

Donegal[1] /dónni gawl/ county in northwestern Ireland. The Atlantic Ocean lies to the west, Northern Ireland to the east. Population: 129,435 (1996). Area: 4830 sq. km/1865 sq. mi. Irish **Dœn Na nGall**

Donegal[2] /dónni gáwl, dónni gawl/ county in the northwestern region of the Republic of Ireland. The Atlantic Ocean lies to the west, and Northern Ireland to the east. Population: 129,435 (1996). Area: 4,830 sq. km/1,865 sq. mi.

Donegal tweed *n.* a rough tweed characterized by a white lumpy effect [Early 20thC. Named after County DONEGAL in Ireland, where it was first produced.]

doner kebab /dónnər-/, **donner kebab** *n.* pitta bread filled with slices cut from a block of spiced meat, usually lamb, grilled on a spit. Based on a Middle Eastern dish, it is usually eaten as a takeaway. US term **gyro** [From Turkish *döner kebap*, literally 'rotating kebab']

done thing *n.* the polite and proper thing to do in accordance with social etiquette (*informal*)

Donets /də néts/ river in Russia and Ukraine that flows into the River Don northeast of Rostov in southwestern Russia. Length: 1,020 km/631 mi.

Donets Basin major coalfield and industrial region in southeastern Ukraine. The basin extends across the Russian border into the Rostov region.

Donets'k /də nétsk/ industrial city in southeastern Ukraine, about 97 km/60 mi. northeast of the Black Sea. Population: 1,102,000 (1995).

done with *adj.* completely finished and no longer an issue of importance

dong[1] /dong/ *n.* **1.** DEEP TOLL a deep ringing sound **2.** ANZ PUNCH a heavy blow or punch (*informal*) ■ *vi.* (**dongs, donging, donged**) TOLL DEEPLY to make a deep ringing sound [Late 16thC. An imitation of the sound.]

dong[2] /dong/ *n.* a penis (*slang taboo*) [Mid-20thC. Origin uncertain.]

dong[3] /dong/ *n.* MONEY a Vietnamese coin. See table at **currency** [Early 19thC. From Vietnamese.]

donga /dóng gə/ *n.* S Africa a steep-sided gully formed by soil erosion [Late 19thC. From Nguni.]

dongle /dóng g'l/ *n.* a small hardware device that, when plugged into a computer, enables a specific copy-protected program to run, the program being disabled on that computer if the device is not present. The device is effective against software piracy. [Late 20thC. Origin uncertain: probably an arbitrary formation.]

Dongola /dóng gələ/ small town on the River Nile in northern Sudan, about 400 km/250 mi. northwest of Khartoum. Population: 5,626 (1973).

Dönitz /dónits/, **Doenitz, Karl** (1891–1980) German naval officer. He was commander of the German submarine arm (1936–43), naval commander-in-chief (1943–45), and Chancellor of Germany (April–May 1945) after Hitler's suicide.

Donizetti /dónni zétti/, **Gaetano** (1797–1848) Italian composer. He wrote 65 operas, ranging from dramas such as *Lucia di Lammermoor* (1835) to comic works such as *Don Pasquale* (1843).

donjon /dónjən, dúnj-/ *n.* a fortified central tower in a medieval castle [14thC. An early form of DUNGEON.]

Don Juan /dón jŏŏ ən, -waŕn/ n. a man who has a reputation for having casual sexual relationships with numerous women [Mid-19thC. Named after *Don Juan Tenorio*, a legendary Spanish nobleman known for his seduction of women.]

Donkey

donkey /dóngki/ (*plural* **-keys**) n. **1.** ANIMAL RESEMBLING A SMALL HORSE a small domesticated member of the horse family with a grey or brown coat, long ears, and a large head. Latin name: *Equus asinus.* **2.** UNINTELLIGENT PERSON sb thought of as lacking intelligence (*informal insult*) [Late 18thC. Origin uncertain: perhaps from DUN (the word originally rhymed with MONKEY); or perhaps a pet form of the name *Duncan*.]

donkey derby (*plural* **donkey derbies**) n. a race for people riding on donkeys, usually as a fundraising event or amusement, e.g. at a country fête

donkey engine n. a small auxiliary engine used either to start a larger engine or independently, e.g. for pumping water on steamships

donkey jacket n. UK a heavy jacket, usually made of dark blue woollen fabric, typically worn by people working outdoors

donkey's years npl. a very long time (*informal*) ○ *I haven't seen Jack for donkey's years.* [Origin uncertain: perhaps a pun on *donkey's ears*, or perhaps because the donkey is long-lived compared to most domestic animals]

donkey vote n. *Aus* at an election based on the preferential voting system, a vote in which the preferences are marked simply in the order that they appear on the ballot sheet. In Australia, where voting is compulsory, this is often a way of registering a protest vote or abstention.

donkeywork /dóngki wurk/ n. **1.** HARD WORK hard or boring work (*informal*) **2.** GROUNDWORK basic preparation or groundwork

Donleavy /don leévi/, **J. P.** (*b.* 1926) US-born Irish novelist, short-story writer, and playwright. His first novel, *The Ginger Man* (1955), was hailed as a comic masterpiece. Among his other novels are *A Singular Man* (1963) and *The Beastly Beatitudes of Balthazar B* (1968). Full name **James Patrick Donleavy**

Donna /dónnə/ n. a title used before a married woman's name in Italy [Early 17thC. Via Italian from Latin *domina* 'lady' (see DONA).]

Donne /dun/, **John** (1572–1631) English poet, prose writer, and clergyman, considered the greatest of the Metaphysical poets. An author of passionate love poetry, he was later ordained and appointed Dean of St Paul's (1621). His verse includes the love poems *Songs and Sonnets*, his *Satires* (both dating from the 1590s), *Divine Poems* (1607), and *Epithalamion* (1613).

donnée /dónnay/, **donné** n. **1.** BASIC ASSUMPTION a basic fact or assumption on which sth else, e.g. a literary or theatrical work, is based and from which it develops or moves forward **2.** THEME a theme or subject, e.g. of a literary or theatrical work [Late 19thC. From French, the feminine past participle, used as a noun, of *donner* 'to give'.]

donner kebab n. = doner kebab

donnert /dónnərt/ adj. *Scotland* **1.** UNINTELLIGENT lacking intelligence (*informal*) **2.** ASTONISHED very surprised [Early 18thC. From the past participle of Scots dialect *donner* 'to daze, stun', of uncertain origin: perhaps from Dutch *donderen* 'to thunder'.]

donnish /dónnish/ adj. resembling the stereotypical image of a university professor, e.g. in displaying erudition or being absent-minded —**donnishly** adv. —**donnishness** n.

donnybrook /dónni brŏŏk/ n. a riotous brawl [Mid-19thC. Named after *Donnybrook* Fair, an annual event known for its brawls, which was formerly held in Donnybrook, a suburb of Dublin in the Republic of Ireland.]

donor /dṓnər/ n. **1.** SB WHO GIVES STH sb who gives sth, especially money **2.** MED SB GIVING BLOOD OR BODY ORGAN sb who voluntarily gives part of his or her body for the treatment of another person, e.g. blood for transfusion, during life or after death, or an organ or tissue for transplantation **3.** ELECTRON ENG IMPURITY ADDED TO SEMICONDUCTOR an impurity (**dopant**), e.g. antimony, that is deliberately added to a pure semiconductor material, e.g. silicon, in order to increase its conductivity by increasing the number of free electrons, carriers of negative electrical charge **4.** CHEM ATOM PROVIDING ELECTRONS FOR A BOND an atom, molecule, or group that provides the pair of electrons necessary to form a chemical bond. ◊ **acceptor** [15thC. Via Anglo-Norman *donour* and Old French *doneur* from Latin *donator*, from, ultimately, *donare* 'to give' (see DONATION).] —**donorship** n.

donor card n. a card stating that specified organs, or sometimes the entire body, of the person carrying it may be used for the treatment of others after the donor's death

donor insemination n. the introduction into a woman's vagina of sperm from a man who is not the woman's sexual partner. The procedure is performed as a method of assisted conception with the intention of making the woman pregnant.

do-nothing n. a lazy or idle person (*informal*)

Don Quixote /dón kwíksət, -kee hṓti/ n. an impractical idealist who champions hopeless causes [Mid-17thC. Named after *Don Quixote*, the naively idealistic hero of the satirical romance *Don Quixote de la Mancha* (1605, 1615) by the Spanish author Cervantes.]

don't /dōnt/ contr. do not

don't know n. sb who has not made a decision one way or the other about a specific issue, e.g. before an election or in a market research survey (*informal*)

doo /dōō/ (*plural* **doos**) n. *Scotland* **1.** A DOVE a dove (*informal*) **2.** TERM OF ENDEARMENT used as a term of endearment [14thC. Variant of DOVE.]

doocot /dōōkit, dŏŏ-/, **dooket** n. *Scotland* a dovecote

doodad /dŏŏ dad/ n. *US* = doodah (*informal*) [Early 20thC. Origin unknown.]

doodah /dŏŏ daa/ n. a thing whose name sb cannot remember or does not know (*informal*) *US* term **doodad** [Early 20thC. Origin uncertain: probably from *dooda(h)* in the refrain to the song *Camptown Races*.]

doodle /dŏŏd'l/ vti. (**-dles, -dling, -dled**) SCRIBBLE DRAWINGS OR DESIGNS to draw aimlessly or absent-mindedly, usually while doing sth else such as having a telephone conversation or attending a meeting ■ n. DRAWING OR DESIGN a drawing or abstract design produced aimlessly or absent-mindedly while doing sth else [Early 17thC. From Low German *dudel-* in *dudeltopf* 'fool' (the original English sense). The senses 'idle drawing' and 'to draw aimlessly' date from the mid-20thC.] —**doodler** n.

doodlebug /dŏŏd'l bug/ n. **1.** FLYING BOMB the V-1 flying bomb (*informal*) **2.** US INSECTS INSECT LARVA the large-jawed larva of an antlion, or any similar insect larva

doo-doo /dŏŏ dŏŏ/ n. *US* human or animal excrement (*slang humorous*) [Mid-20thC. Origin uncertain: probably an alteration and repetition of DO.]

doofer /dŏŏfər/ n. an object or gadget whose name you cannot remember or do not know (*slang*) [Mid-20thC. Origin uncertain: probably from *do for* in phrases such as *that will do for now.*]

doohickey /dŏŏhiki/ (*plural* **-eys**) n. *US* an unspecified gadget (*informal*) [Early 20thC. Blend of DOODAD and HICKEY.]

dook /dŏŏk/ n. *Scotland* WOODEN PLUG TO SUPPORT NAIL a wooden plug that is forced into a wall to provide loadbearing support for a nail or screw ■ vt. (**dooks, dooking, dooked**) *Scotland* INSERT PLUG IN WALL to force a

wooden plug into a wall to support a nail or screw [Early 19thC. Origin unknown.]

dooket n. *Scotland* = doocot

doolally /dŏŏ lálli/ adj. used to describe sb with psychiatric disorder (*informal insult*) [Early 20thC. Alteration of *Deolali*, a town near Mumbai (Bombay) in India where British soldiers awaited their return home; sickness and boredom caused some to break down.]

doom /dŏŏm/ n. **1.** DISASTROUS DESTINY a dreadful fate, especially death or utter ruin **2.** OFFICIAL JUDGMENT an official judgment on sb (*formal*) **3.** doom, Doom RELIG LAST JUDGMENT the Last Judgment (*archaic*) ■ vt. (**dooms, dooming, doomed**) DESTINE TO DISASTER to condemn sb or sth to a dreadful fate [Old English *dōm* 'judgment, sentence, law'. Ultimately, from an Indo-European base meaning 'to set, put' that is also the ancestor of English *deed, deem, defeat,* and *do*.]

doomed /dŏŏmd/ adj. **1.** DESTINED TO DISASTER condemned to suffer a dreadful fate, especially one that is imminent and inescapable ○ *With our best player hurt, we were doomed to lose.* **2.** DESTINED TO FAILURE OR MISFORTUNE bound to fail or suffer sth unpleasant ○ *The partnership was doomed from the start.*

doom-laden adj. suggesting impending disaster or ruin

doom palm n. BOT = doum [Early 18thC. *Doum* from Arabic *dūm*.]

doomsayer /dŏŏm sayər/ n. sb who frequently prophesies disaster

doomsday /dŏŏmz day/ n. **1.** doomsday, Doomsday DAY OF FINAL JUDGMENT a day of final reckoning, especially, in Christian theology, the day of the Last Judgment **2.** END OF WORLD the final destruction or dissolution of the world

Doomsday Book n. = Domesday Book

doomster /dŏŏmstər/ n. sb who prophesies disaster (*informal*) [15thC. Alteration (modelled on DOOM) of DEEMSTER (in its original sense 'judge').]

doomwatch /dŏŏm woch/ n. expectation or prediction of imminent disaster [From *Doomwatch*, the name of a television series first broadcast by the BBC in 1970] —**doomwatcher** n.

doomy /dŏŏmi/ (**-ier, -iest**) adj. (*informal*) **1.** PESSIMISTIC not hopeful about the future **2.** OMINOUS instilling feelings of imminent disaster

Doona /dŏŏnə/ tdmk. *Aus* a trademark for a duvet or continental quilt

door /dawr/ n. **1.** MOVABLE PANEL AT AN ENTRANCE a movable barrier used to open and close the entrance to a building, room, cupboard, or vehicle. It is usually a solid panel, hinged to or sliding in a frame. **2.** GAP FORMING AN ENTRANCE the gap that forms the entrance to a building or room **3.** BUILDING OR ROOM a building or room considered in relation to those on either side ○ *Does she live two doors down the street or one?* [Old English *duru* 'door' and *dor* 'gate', both from, ultimately, an Indo-European word meaning 'entrance to the enclosure around the house' that is also the ancestor of English *thyroid*] ◊ **close** *or* **shut the door on sth** to disallow the possibility of sth happening ◊ **lay sth at sb's door** to blame sth on sb ◊ **out of doors** in the open air ◊ **show sb the door** to tell sb to leave

doorbell /dawr bel/ n. a bell placed on or beside a door, to be rung by visitors as a sign of their arrival

door bundle n. a bundle of equipment pushed out of an aircraft by hand before parachutists exit

doorcase /dawr kayss/ n. = doorframe

do-or-die adj. involving the determination to risk everything in an effort to succeed

doorframe /dawr fraym/ n. the frame constructed around the entrance to a building or room and into which a door is set

door furniture n. all the fittings used on doors, e.g. handles, locks, knockers, and letter boxes

doorjamb /dawr jam/ n. either of the vertical side pieces of a doorframe

doorkeeper /dawr keepər/ n. sb on duty at a door or gate, especially sb who guards the entrance

doorknob /dawr nob/ n. a round handle used to open or close a door

---

zh vision   In foreign words: kh German Bach; aN French vin; aaN French blanc; ö German schön, French feu; oN French bon; ŏN French un; ü French rue   Stress marks: ´ as in secret \séek rət\; academic \ákə démmik\

doorman /dáwrmən/ (*plural* **-men** /-mən/) n. sb on duty at the door of a building such as a nightclub or hotel, usually employed to assist customers, e.g. by calling cabs

doormat /dáwr mat/ n. **1.** MAT BY DOOR a mat to wipe your shoes on immediately before or after entering a building **2.** SB WHO DOES NOT RESIST sb who submits too easily to being treated without due consideration (*informal*)

doornail /dáwr nayl/ n. a nail with a large head formerly used to stud a door for decoration or reinforcement

doorpost /dáwr pōst/ n. = **doorjamb**

doorsill /dáwr sil/ n. = **threshold** n. 1

doorstep /dáwr step/ n. **1.** STEP IN FRONT OF DOOR a step at the entrance to a building **2.** THICK BREAD a very thick slice of bread, or a sandwich made from thickly cut bread (*informal*) ■ v. (**-steps, -stepping, -stepped**) **1.** vti. CANVASS ALL HOUSES IN AREA to make door-to-door visits to members of the public to ask for their support during an election campaign **2.** vt. WAIT AT DOOR OF FAMOUS PERSON to wait outside the home or workplace of politicians or celebrities in the hope of interviewing them —**doorstepping** n. ◇ **on your (own) doorstep** very near where you live

doorstop /dáwr stop/ n. **1.** STH USED TO KEEP DOOR OPEN a movable device such as a wedge or heavy object used to hold a door open **2.** DEVICE TO PROTECT WALL FROM DOOR a rubber stud or rubber-tipped projection on a wall, floor, or door that prevents damage to the wall when the door is opened

door to door adv. **1.** TO ALL HOUSES IN AREA going from one house to the next, usually in order to sell things, to collect money for charity, or to canvass support in an election **2.** OVER WHOLE JOURNEY from the place of departure to the place of arrival ○ *The trip took three hours door to door.*

door-to-door adj. (*not hyphenated after a verb*) **1.** COVERING ALL HOUSES IN AREA done or going from one house to the next **2.** COVERING WHOLE JOURNEY from the point of departure to the point of arrival

doorway /dáwr way/ n. **1.** ENTRANCE TO BUILDING an entrance to a building or room, especially one that has a door **2.** OPPORTUNITY a means of achieving or escaping from sth

doo-wop /dóo wop/ n. harmonized singing of nonsense syllables, with a rhythm-and-blues melody on top, popularized by street singers in the 1950s [Mid-20thC. An imitation of the sound.]

dop /dop/ n. S Africa a small drink (*slang*) [Late 19thC. Origin unknown.]

dopa /dópə/ n. a substance that occurs naturally in the body and is involved in the synthesis of adrenaline, dopamine, and the pigment melanin. It is also used in the form levodopa as a drug to treat Parkinson's disease. Formula: $C_9H_{11}NO_4$. [Early 20thC. Acronym formed from DI- + OXY- + PHENYL + ALANINE.]

dopamine /dópə meen/ n. a chemical compound, found in the brain, that transmits nerve impulses and is involved in the formation of adrenaline [Mid-20thC. Blend of DOPA and AMINE.]

dopant /dópənt/ n. a substance, e.g. arsenic or antimony, that is added in small quantities to a semiconductor material in order to change its electrical characteristics. Dopants are added during the manufacture of semiconducting diodes and transistors.

dope /dōp/ n. **1.** DRUGS ILLEGAL DRUG an illegal drug, especially cannabis (*slang*) **2.** DRUG AFFECTING PERFORMANCE a drug given illegally, e.g. to racehorses or athletes, to affect performance **3.** INSIDE INFORMATION confidential information about sb or sth (*slang*) **4.** CHEM VISCOUS LIQUID a viscous liquid used for lubrication, waterproofing and strengthening fabrics, coating aircraft wings, or improving the combustion of engine fuels **5.** CHEM ABSORBENT MATERIAL an absorbent material used in the manufacture of dynamite **6.** ELECTRON ENG = **dopant** ■ vt. (**dopes, doping, doped**) **1.** DRUGS ADD DRUG TO FOOD OR DRINK to add a drug to sb's food or drink secretly in order to affect the person's performance or consciousness adversely **2.** ELECTRON ENG ADD IMPURITY TO SEMICONDUCTOR to add a substance, e.g. arsenic or antimony to a

semiconductor material like silicon or germanium during the manufacturing process in order to increase its conductivity [Early 19thC. From Dutch *doop* 'thick dipping sauce', from *doopen* 'to dip, mix'.] —**doper** n.

dope up vt. to make sb drowsy or semiconscious by administering a drug such as an anaesthetic or an illegal narcotic (*slang*)

dope dog n. US a dog specially trained to locate by scent contraband narcotics hidden in luggage or packages, or concealed on sb's body (*informal*)

dope sheet n. a booklet that gives information about the horses entered for races (*slang*)

dopey /dópi/ (**-ier, -iest**), **dopy** (**-ier, -iest**) adj. showing a lack of good sense or intelligence (*informal insult*) —**dopily** adv. —**dopiness** n.

dopiaza /dópi azə/ n. in Indian cookery, a mildly spiced dish of meat or fish cooked with onions and tomatoes [From Hindi *do* 'two' + *pyāz* 'onion']

doping agent n. ELECTRON ENG = **dopant**

doppelgänger /dópp'l gangər, -geng-/ n. an apparition in the form of a double of a living person [Mid-19thC. From German, literally 'double-goer'.]

Doppler effect /dópplər-/, **Doppler shift** n. a perceived change in the frequency of a wave as the distance between the source and the observer changes. For example, the sound of a siren on a moving vehicle appears to change as it approaches and passes an observer. ◇ **blueshift, redshift** [Early 20thC. Named after Christian J. *Doppler* (1803–53), the Austrian mathematician and physicist who first explained it.]

Doppler radar n. a means of detecting a moving target that uses electromagnetic radiation and relies on a change in the frequency of microwave signals reflected from the target. [Mid-20thC. From its use of the DOPPLER EFFECT.]

Doppler shift n. = **Doppler effect**

dopy adj. = **dopey** (*informal*)

dor /dawr/ n. a European dung beetle that makes a droning sound as it flies. Latin name: *Geotrupes stercorarius*. [Old English *dora* 'bumblebee', of uncertain origin: probably an imitation of its buzzing sound]

Dor. abbr. Doric

dorado /də raádō/ (*plural* **-dos** or **-do**) n. **1.** = **dolphin** n. 2 **2.** S AMERICAN FISH a South American fish resembling a salmon. Genus: *Salminus*. [Early 17thC. Via Spanish, 'dolphinfish', literally 'gilded' (from its iridescent colours), from, ultimately, late Latin *deaurare* (see DORY[2]).]

Dorado /də raádō/ n. an inconspicuous constellation of the southern hemisphere between Reticulum and Pictor containing part of the Large Magellanic cloud at its southern end where it borders Mensa

Doráti /də raáti/, **Antal** (1906–88) Hungarian-born US conductor and composer. He was music director of several major orchestras and made over 500 recordings.

dorbeetle /dáwr beet'l/ n. = **dor**

Dorcas society /dáwrkəss-/ (*plural* **Dorcas societies**) n. a Christian women's charitable organization that gives clothes to the poor [Mid-19thC. Named after *Dorcas*, a Christian woman mentioned in the Bible (Acts 9:36, 39) who made clothes for the poor.]

Dorchester /dáwrchistər/ historic town in Dorset, England. Population: 15,037 (1991).

Dordogne /dawr dóyn, -dónnyə/ river in southwestern France. It rises in the Massif Central and flows generally westwards to join the Garonne north of Bordeaux. Length: 483 km/300 mi.

Dordrecht /dawr drekht/ city and port in Zuid-Holland Province, southwestern Netherlands. An ancient city with many medieval buildings, it is also an important industrial centre. Population: 113,394 (1994).

Doré /dáw ray/, **Gustave** (1833–83) French illustrator, painter, and sculptor. He is best known for his vivid wood engravings that were used as illustrations for the works of Dante, Poe, and Milton, among others. Full name **Paul Gustave Doré**

Dorian /dáwri ən/ n. MEMBER OF ANCIENT GREEK PEOPLE a member of a Greek-speaking people who overthrew

the Mycenaean civilization in mainland Greece about 1100 BC. They subsequently colonized the Peloponnese and other parts of the Mediterranean area. ■ adj. PEOPLES OF DORIANS relating to the Dorians or their culture [Mid-16thC. Via Latin *Dorius* 'of Doris' (a region of ancient Greece) from Greek *Dōrios*, from *Dōris* 'Doris'.]

Dorian mode n. a scale of notes originating in ancient Greek music and consisting of the eight notes of the diatonic scale rising from D to D

Doric /dórrik/ n. LANGUAGE **1.** ANCIENT GREEK DIALECT a dialect of ancient Greek spoken mainly in the area of the modern Peloponnese **2.** DIALECT OF ENGLISH a rural dialect of English, especially the dialect of Scots spoken in parts of northeastern Scotland ■ adj. **1.** ARCHIT IN SIMPLE CLASSICAL ARCHITECTURAL STYLE relating to or built in a style of architecture characterized by fluted columns with a rounded moulding at the top and no base **2.** PEOPLES OF DORIANS relating to or typical of the Dorians of ancient Greece or their culture **3.** LANGUAGE OF DORIC DIALECT relating to a Doric dialect [Mid-16thC. Via Latin *Doricus* 'of Doris' (a region of ancient Greece) from Greek *Dōrikos*, from *Dōris* 'Doris'.]

Doric order n. the first of the five classical orders of architecture, characterized by fluted columns with a rounded moulding at the top and no base. It was developed in Greece in the 7th century BC.

dork /dawrk/ n. an offensive term used to refer to sb who is seen as unattractive or socially inept (*slang insult*) [Mid-20thC. Origin uncertain: perhaps a variant of DIRK or an alteration of DICK. The original sense was 'penis'.]

Dorking[1] /dáwrking/ n. a heavy domestic fowl belonging to a breed originating in England and raised mostly for eating [Late 18thC. Named after DORKING[2].]

Dorking[2] /dáwrking/ town in northern Surrey, England. Population: 10,600 (1991).

dorky /dáwrki/ (**-ier, -iest**) adj. unintelligent or useless (*slang insult*)

dorm /dawrm/ n. a dormitory (*informal*) [Early 20thC. Shortening.]

dormant /dáwrmənt/ adj. **1.** BIOL NOT ACTIVELY GROWING in an inactive state, when growth and development slow or cease, in order to survive adverse environmental conditions **2.** TEMPORARILY INACTIVE temporarily inactive or not in use **3.** GEOL NOT ERUPTING used to describe a volcano that is not erupting, but not extinct **4.** LATENT latent and able to be aroused ○ *dormant feelings of uneasiness* **5.** HERALDRY SLEEPING in a heraldic device, portrayed in a sleeping posture [14thC. From French, literally 'sleeping', present participle of *dormir* 'to sleep', from Latin *dormire* (source of English *dormer* and *dormitory*).] —**dormancy** /-ənssi/ n.

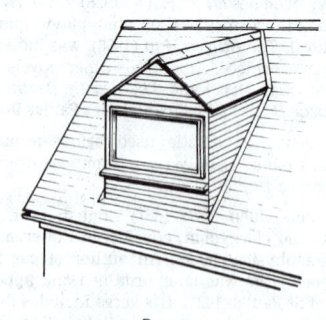

Dormer

dormer /dáwrmər/, **dormer window** n. a window for a room within the roof space that is built out at right angles to the main roof and has its own gable [Late 16thC. From Old French *dormēor* 'sleeping room', from *dormir* 'to sleep' (see DORMANT). The original English sense was 'dormitory or bedroom window'.]

dormice plural of **dormouse**

dormie /dáwrmi/ adj. in golf, as many holes up on an opponent as there are holes left to play ○ *dormie four* [Mid-19thC. Origin unknown.]

Dormition of the Blessed Virgin /dawr míshʹn-/ n. = **Assumption of the Virgin Mary** [*Dormition* via French from the Latin stem *dormition-* 'a sleeping', from, ultimately, *dormire* 'to sleep' (see DORMANT)]

dormitory /dáwrmitəri/ (*plural* **-ries**) *n.* **1.** ROOM WITH MANY BEDS a large room in which many people sleep, e.g. at a boarding school or in a hostel **2.** *US* = **hall of residence** [15thC. Via Latin *dormitorium* from, ultimately, *dormire* 'to sleep' (see DORMANT).]

dormitory town *n.* a small town whose residents commute to work in a nearby city. US term **bedroom community**

Dormobile /dáwrmō beel/ *tdmk.* a trademark for a motor vehicle equipped for living and sleeping in as well as travelling

Dormouse

dormouse /dáwr mowss/ (*plural* **-mice** /-mīss/) *n.* a small nocturnal rodent resembling a mouse with reddish-brown fur and a bushy tail. Dormice feed on nuts, berries, and seeds, and hibernate during the winter. Family: Gliridae. [15thC. Origin uncertain: perhaps an alteration, by association with MOUSE, of Anglo-Norman *dormeus* 'sleepy', from French *dormir* (see DORMANT).]

dornick /dáwrnik/ *n.* a heavy damask cloth [Named after *Doornik*, the Flemish name for the town of Tournai in Belgium, where it was first made]

Dornoch Firth /dáwr nok-, -nəkh-/ inlet of the North Sea in Highland District, Scotland. It is designated a National Scenic Area.

Dorothy bag /dórrəthi-/ *n.* a small handbag tied by drawstrings that are looped over the wrist to carry it (*dated*) [Early 20thC. From the name *Dorothy*.]

Dorothy Dixer /-díksər/, **dorothy dixer** *n. Aus* a question, usually asked in parliament, that allows a minister or other politician to give a previously prepared answer [Mid-20thC. Named after a popular advice column *Dear Dorothy Dix*, written by the US journalist E. M. Gilmer (1870–1951), who was suspected of making up many enquiries herself.]

dorp /dawrp/ *n. S Africa* a village or small country town in South Africa [Mid-19thC. From Dutch.]

Dors. *abbr.* Dorset

dors- *prefix.* = **dorso-**

dorsa plural of **dorsum**

dorsad /dáwr sad/ *adv., adj.* towards the back of the body [Early 19thC. From Latin *dorsum* (see DORSUM).]

dorsal /dáwrss'l/ *adj.* **1.** ANAT OF OR ON THE BACK relating to or situated on the back of the body **2.** BOT FACING AWAY FROM THE AXIS used to describe the underside of a leaf or other surface that faces away from the stem [15thC. Directly or via French from late Latin *dorsalis*, which was formed from Latin *dorsum* (see DORSUM).] —**dorsally** *adv.*

dorsal fin *n.* a single fin on the back of a fish or other aquatic animal e.g. a dolphin that gives it stability while swimming. ◊ **ventral fin**

Dorset /dáwrssit/ county on southern coast of England. Dorchester is the county town. Population: 673,000 (1994). Area: 2,654 sq. km/1,025 sq. mi.

Dorset Down *n.* a sheep belonging to a sturdy domestic breed with dense wool and a broad head, kept for lamb production [Named after DORSET, where it was bred]

Dorset Horn *n.* a sheep belonging to a domestic breed with large horns and dense fine-textured wool [Early 19thC. Named after DORSET, where it was bred.]

dorsiflexion /dáwrssi fléksh'n/ *n.* the bending back of a hand or foot, or of the fingers or toes

dorsiventral /dáwrssi véntrəl/ *adj.* **1.** BOT FLAT flat, with distinct upper and lower surfaces **2.** BIOL = **dorsoventral** *adj.* **1** —**dorsiventrality** /-ven trálləti/ *n.* —**dorsiventrally** /-véntrəli/ *adv.*

dorso- *prefix.* back, upper surface ◦ *dorsolateral* [From Latin *dorsum*]

dorsolateral /dáwrssō láttərəl/ *adj.* relating to or involving both the back and the side —**dorsolaterally** *adv.*

dorsoventral /dáwrssō véntrəl/ *adj.* **1.** BOT = **dorsiventral** *adj.* **1 2.** ANAT EXTENDING FROM BACK TO FRONT extending from the back of the body to the front

dorsum /dáwrssəm/ (*plural* **-sa** /-sə/) *n.* the back or upper surface of a part of the body, e.g. the hand or foot (*technical*) [Late 18thC. From Latin, 'the back' (source also of English *dorsal*, *dossier*, and *endorse*).]

Dortmund /dáwrtmənd, -moʻond/ city and inland port in North Rhine-Westphalia State in northwestern Germany. A major industrial centre, it is situated in the Ruhr district, about 32 km/20 mi. east of Essen. Population: 597,400 (1994).

dory[1] /dáwri/ (*plural* **-ries**) *n.* **1.** SMALL BOAT a small boat used for various purposes e.g. patrolling a harbour or transporting people from a larger vessel to the shore **2.** *US, Can* FISHING BOAT a narrow flat-bottomed fishing boat with high sides [Early 18thC. Origin uncertain: perhaps from Miskito *dóri*, literally 'dugout'.]

dory[2] /dáwri/ (*plural* **-ries**) *n.* a fish with a deep flattened body, spiny fins, and an extendable mouth, found near the ocean bottom. Family: Zeidae. [14thC. From French *dorée*, the feminine past participle, used as a noun, of *dorer* 'to gild', from late Latin *deaurare* 'to gild over', from *aurum* 'gold'.]

DOS /dos/ *n. abbr.* disk operating system

dos-à-dos /dō zaa dō, dóssi dō/ *n.* FURNITURE, CARS BACK-TO-BACK SEAT a seat on which two or more people can sit back to back, or a vehicle fitted with such a seat (*dated*) ■ *n., interj.* DANCE = **do-si-do** [Mid-19thC. From French, literally 'back to back' (the original English sense), from *dos* 'back' (source of English *dossier*), from, ultimately, Latin *dorsum* (see DORSUM).]

dosage /dóssij/ *n.* **1.** PHARM DOSE OF DRUG the amount of a drug to be taken at any one time and the intervals at which it should be taken ◦ *Do not exceed the recommended dosage.* **2.** MED ADMINISTRATION OR DETERMINATION OF DOSE the administration of a drug in measured amounts, or the determination of the correct or required amount **3.** ADDING EXTRA INGREDIENT the addition of an extra ingredient to sth, especially wine

dose /dōss/ *n.* **1.** PHARM, MED PRESCRIBED AMOUNT OF MEDICATION a measured quantity of medication, e.g. drugs or radiotherapy, administered at any one time or at stated intervals **2.** SHORT PERIOD OF STH UNPLEASANT a bout of sth unpleasant, especially a minor illness (*informal*) **3.** MED VENEREAL DISEASE an infection with a sexually transmitted disease (*slang*) **4.** MED, SCI EXPOSURE TO RADIATION the amount of radiation to which sb or sth is exposed during a specified time, either accidentally or as part of an experiment or medical treatment **5.** EXTRA INGREDIENT an additional ingredient, e.g. syrup added to wine to fortify it ■ *vt.* (**doses, dosing, dosed**) **1.** MED GIVE MEDICINE TO to administer medication to sb ◦ *I've been dosing myself up with flu remedies all week.* **2.** PHARM, MED MEASURE OUT MEDICATION to prescribe or administer the correct or required amount of medication **3.** ADD EXTRA INGREDIENT to add an extra ingredient to sth [15thC. Via French from, ultimately, Greek *dosis* 'prescribed portion' (literally 'a giving'), from *didonai* 'to give' (source of English *anecdote* and *antidote*).] ◊ **a dose of your own medicine** = **a taste of your own medicine** ◊ **go through sth like a dose of salts** to do and finish sth very quickly (*informal*)

dosemeter /dóss meetər/ *n.* = **dosimeter**

dosh /dosh/ *n.* money (*slang*) [Mid-20thC. Origin unknown.]

do-si-do /dóssi dō/ *n.* (*plural* **do-si-dos**) FIGURE IN SQUARE DANCING a movement in square dancing in which two dancers pass each other and circle back to back ■ *interj.* CIRCLE BACK TO BACK used to instruct dancers to

perform a do-si-do [Early 20thC. Alteration of DOS-À-DOS.] —**do-si-do** *vi.*

dosimeter /dō símmitər/ *n.* an instrument for measuring the amount of radiation absorbed by sb or sth, often fixed in a working area or worn by personnel who might be exposed to radiation [Late 19thC. Coined from DOSE + -METER.] —**dosimetric** /dóssi méttrik/ *adj.* —**dosimetrician** /-mə trísh'n/ *n.* —**dosimetrist** *n.* —**dosimetry** /-símmətri/ *n.*

doss /doss/ *vi.* (**dosses, dossing, dossed**) SLEEP ON MAKESHIFT BED to sleep or settle down to sleep, especially on an improvised bed (*slang*) ◦ *Can I doss down on your floor tonight?* ■ *n.* **1.** IMPROVISED OR BASIC BED a bed for the night or a place to sleep, especially a makeshift one or one in a dosshouse **2.** PERIOD OF SLEEP a period of sleep (*slang*) **3.** EASY TASK an easy job or activity (*slang*) [Late 18thC. Origin uncertain: perhaps via obsolete *dorse*, *doss* 'the back' from, ultimately, Latin *dorsum* (see DORSUM). If so, the underlying notion is probably 'to lie on your back'.]

dossal /dóss'l/, **dossel** *n.* a rich hanging for the back of an altar or the sides of a chancel in a church [Mid-17thC. Via medieval Latin *dossale* from, ultimately, Latin *dorsum* (see DORSUM).]

dosser /dóssər/ *n.* **1.** HOMELESS PERSON a homeless person who sleeps on the street or in a cheap lodging house (*slang*) **2.** *Ireland* LAZY PERSON a lazy or idle person

dosshouse /dóss hówss/ (*plural* **-houses** /-hówziz/) *n.* a cheap and very basic lodging house for homeless people (*slang*) US term **flophouse**

dossier /dóssi ay, -ər/ *n.* a collection of documents relating to a particular person or topic [Late 19thC. From French (originally 'bunch of papers with a label on the back'), from *dos* 'the back', from, ultimately, Latin *dorsum* (see DORSUM).]

dost /dust/ 2nd person present singular of **do** (*archaic*)

Fyodor Dostoyevsky

Dostoyevsky /dóst oy éfski/, **Fyodor** (1821–81) Russian novelist. He is author of *Crime and Punishment* (1866) and *The Brothers Karamazov* (1879–80). Full name **Fyodor Mikhaylovich Dostoyevsky**

dot[1] /dot/ *n.* **1.** WRITTEN OR PRINTED POINT a small round written or printed mark, e.g. that placed above the body of the lowercase letter 'i' or one of a set of three replacing missing text **2.** SPOT OR SPECK a small round mark, spot, or speck ◦ *The ship was just a dot on the horizon.* **3.** SMALL AMOUNT a very small amount, especially of butter used for basting **4.** COMPUT E-MAIL PUNCTUATION MARK a punctuation mark used to separate the various components of an internet address **5.** COMMUNICATION MARK USED IN MORSE CODE the shorter of the two signalling elements used in Morse code, represented as a small round mark **6.** MUSIC SYMBOL PLACED AFTER NOTE IN MUSIC in written or printed music, a small round mark placed after a note or rest to increase its value by half **7.** LOGIC MARK INDICATING LOGICAL CONJUNCTION a small round mark used in logic to join compound sentences when both elements are true ■ *v.* (**dots, dotting, dotted**) **1.** *vt.* MARK WITH DOT to mark sth with a dot ◦ *dot your i's* **2.** *vt.* SPRINKLE WITH DOTS to scatter or sprinkle sth with spots, specks, or small amounts of sth ◦ *Dot the surface with butter.* **3.** *vi.* MAKE SMALL ROUND MARK to make a small round mark [Old English *dott* 'head of a boil'. Probably from, ultimately, a prehistoric Germanic word meaning 'lump, plug'.] —**dotter** *n.* ◊ **dot the i's and cross the t's** to take care over the details of sth ◦ *We've drawn up the basis of the agreement but we have yet to dot the i's and cross the t's.* ◊ **on the dot (of)** exactly at the specified time ○ *arrived on the dot* ○ *was expected to get here on the dot of nine*

dot[2] /dot/ *n.* in law, a woman's dowry [Mid-19thC. Via Old French from Latin *dot-*, the stem of *dos* 'dowry' (see DOWER).] —**dotal** /dṓt'l/ *adj.*

dotage /dṓtij/ *n.* **1. WEAKNESS ASSOCIATED WITH AGE** the lack of strength or concentration sometimes believed to be characteristic of old age (*offensive*) **2. DANGEROUS INFATUATION** infatuation leading to folly (*archaic*) ○ *'Nay, but this dotage of our general's O'erflows the measure'* (William Shakespeare, *Anthony & Cleopatra*; 1606) [14thC. From DOTE.]

dotard /dṓtərd/ *n.* a person of advanced years, especially one considered to lack clear thought (*offensive insult*) [14thC. From DOTE.] —**dotardly** *adj.*

dotation /dō táysh'n/ *n.* in law, the giving of a dowry (*formal*) [14thC. From DOT[2].]

dote /dōt/ (**dotes, doting, doted**) *vi.* **1. SHOW EXTREME FONDNESS** to be excessively fond of sb or sth ○ *They dote on their grandchildren.* **2. LACK CLEAR THOUGHT** to lack clear thought in a way sometimes associated with old age (*archaic*) [12thC. Origin uncertain: perhaps from Middle Low German or Middle Dutch *doten* 'to be foolish' (the original English sense), of unknown origin.] —**doter** *n.*

doth /duth/ 3rd person present singular of **do** (*archaic*)

doting /dṓting/ *adj.* expressing and demonstrating great love and fondness for sb or sth ○ *doting parents of two new babies* —**dotingly** *adv.*

dot matrix *n.* a grid of dots selectively lighted or coloured to display or print letters, numbers, and other symbols

dot pitch *n.* a measure of the clarity or sharpness of an image on a computer screen, based on the amount of white space between the pixels or dots that form the image

dot product *n.* MATH = **scalar product**

dots per inch *n.* full form of **dpi**

dotted /dóttid/ *adj.* **1. WITH DOTS** marked or patterned with dots **2.** MUSIC **INCREASED IN VALUE BY HALF** used to describe a note or rest increased in value by half **3. COVERED WITH SPECKS** scattered or sprinkled with small things or larger things seen from a distance ○ *a sky dotted with stars* **4. RANDOMLY ARRAYED** spread randomly over a wide area ○ *a lawn dotted with hoop-skirted belles.*

dotted line *n.* a printed line formed from dots or dashes, especially one on which sb is to write sth such as a signature

dotted swiss *n.* a cotton fabric patterned with raised dots [Shortening of *Swiss muslin*]

dotterel /dóttrəl/ (*plural* **-els** *or* **-el**), **dottrel** (*plural* **-trels** *or* **-trel**) *n.* **1. EURASIAN BIRD** a reddish-brown Eurasian bird of the plover family with white markings on the head and neck. Latin name: *Eudromias morinellus.* **2. BIRD FOUND IN WETLANDS** a bird found throughout Australia, mainly in marshy areas or on seashores. Family: Charadriidae. **3.** (*plural* **-terels** *or* **-trels**) **GULLIBLE PERSON** sb who is easily deceived [15thC. Formed from DOTE + the suffix *-rel* (from Old French *-erel*), literally 'foolish little one', because the Eurasian plover is easy to catch.]

dottle /dótt'l/ *n.* the plug of tobacco that is left in a pipe after it has been smoked [15thC. From DOT[1]. The original sense was 'plug, stopper'.]

dottrel *n.* = **dotterel**

dotty /dótti/ (**-tier, -tiest**) *adj.* **1. SILLY** regarded as being silly, unreasonable, or lacking sense (*informal insult*) **2. UNCONVENTIONAL** behaving in a manner that seems amusingly strange to others (*informal*) **3. ABSURD** illogical, impractical, or absurd (*informal*) **4. INFATUATED** very fond of or passionately interested in sb or sth (*informal*) [Late 19thC. Origin uncertain: perhaps an alteration of Scots dialect *dottle* 'fool', from DOTE, or perhaps directly from DOTE. First recorded in the sense 'walking unsteadily'.] —**dottily** *adv.* —**dottiness** *n.*

Douai /doo áy/ city in Nord Department, Nord-Pas-de-Calais Region, northwestern France. A coal-mining and industrial centre, it is situated south of Lille. Population: 44,195 (1990).

Douala /doo áalə/, **Duala** leading port in Cameroon and chief city of Littoral province. It is situated about 193 km/120 mi. west of the capital Yaoundé. Population: 810,000 (1991).

Douay Bible /dóo ay-/, **Douay Version** *n.* **1. TRANSLATION OF LATIN BIBLE** a Roman Catholic translation of the Latin Vulgate version of the Bible into English, written in the early 17th century **2. COPY OF DOUAY BIBLE** a copy of the Douay Bible [Mid-19thC. Named after *Douay* (modern DOUAI), where it was completed in 1609.]

double /dúbb'l/ *adj.* **1. BEING TWICE AS MUCH OR MANY** being twice as much in size, number, or value **2. HAVING TWO LIKE PARTS** consisting of two identical, similar, or equal parts **3. MEANT FOR TWO PEOPLE** designed or intended for two people ○ *booked a double hotel room* **4. FITTING A DOUBLE BED** used to describe bedding of a size that will fit onto a double bed **5. TWO-LAYERED** consisting of two layers **6. FOLDED OVER ONCE** folded in two, or bent over **7. OF TWO ELEMENTS** consisting of two different elements **8. ACTING IN CONTRASTING OR OPPOSING WAYS** acting one way while feeling very differently, especially when this involves hypocrisy or deceit **9.** BOT **HAVING EXTRA PETALS** used to describe flowers that have more petals than normal, or plants that have flowers of this type **10.** MUSIC **SOUNDING AN OCTAVE BELOW** used to describe a musical instrument sounding an octave lower than the written music indicates ■ *adv.* **1. TWICE AS MUCH** twice as much as normal ○ *had to pay double to get in* **2. IN TWO LAYERS** so as to form two layers ■ *n.* **1. TWO TOGETHER** two viewed or regarded together **2. TWICE THE NORMAL AMOUNT** twice the normal or standard amount ○ *He offered me double.* **3.** BEVERAGES **TWO MEASURES OF DRINK** a drink containing two single measures, especially of spirits (*informal*) **4. DUPLICATE IN APPEARANCE** sb or sth that looks very like another, especially a living person bearing a strong resemblance to sb else **5. GHOST IDENTICAL TO LIVING PERSON** an apparition that closely resembles a living person **6.** CINEMA **STAND-IN FOR FILM STAR** sb who replaces a film actor in certain scenes, e.g. those that involve danger, special skill, or nudity **7.** HORSERACING **BET ON TWO RACES** a bet on two races, in which any winnings from the first become the stake for the second (*informal*) **8.** SPORTS **SUCCESS IN TWO EVENTS** success in two events or competitions in the same year or series, or against the same opponent **9.** DARTS **DART THAT LANDS IN OUTER RING** a throw of a dart that lands within the narrow outer ring of the dartboard, scoring twice the nominal value **10.** BRIDGE **CALL INCREASING SCORE OR BID** in an auction at bridge, a call that increases the score for succeeding or failing in a contract **11.** CUE GAMES **STROKE THAT MAKES BALL REBOUND** a stroke that makes the ball rebound against a cushion and land in the opposite pocket **12.** TENNIS **DOUBLE FAULT** a double fault (*informal*) **13.** MIL **FAST MARCHING PACE** a fast marching pace at twice the usual speed **14. ABRUPT DIRECTIONAL CHANGE** a sharp change of direction **15.** PRINTING = **doublet** *n.* 3 ■ **doubles** *npl.* RACKET GAMES **RACKET GAME BETWEEN PAIRS OF PLAYERS** a racket game played between two pairs of players ■ *v.* (**-bles, -bling, -bled**) **1.** *vti.* **INCREASE TWOFOLD** to make sth twice as large or numerous, or become twice as much or many ○ *We doubled our profits the following year.* **2.** *vt.* **FOLD IN TWO** to fold or bend sth in two **3.** *vt.* **MAKE A FIST** to clench the fist (*informal*) **4.** *vi.* **HAVE SECOND FUNCTION** to have a second or secondary function ○ *His felt hat doubles as a water pail.* **5.** *vi.* CINEMA **ACT AS STAND-IN** to replace a film actor in certain scenes **6.** *vi.* THEATRE **PLAY SECOND ROLE** to play an additional part in the same performance **7.** *vt.* MUSIC **DUPLICATE A MUSICAL PART** to duplicate a part, either at the same pitch or an octave above or below **8.** *vi.* MUSIC **PLAY MORE THAN ONE MUSICAL INSTRUMENT** to play one or more musical instruments, in addition to the principal one ○ *a violinist who doubles on cello* **9.** *vi.* BRIDGE **ANNOUNCE BRIDGE DOUBLE** to announce a double as a bid in an auction at bridge **10.** *vti.* CUE GAMES **REBOUND** to rebound, or make a ball rebound, off a cushion **11.** *vt.* CHESS **PLACE PIECES NEXT TO EACH OTHER** to place two chess pieces of the same type and colour together ○ *double your opponent's pawns* **12.** *vi.* BASEBALL **MAKE TWO-BASE HIT** to make a hit that gives the batter time to run to second base **13.** *vt.* NAUT **ROUND A HEADLAND** to sail around a headland [12thC. Via Old French *do(u)bler* from Latin *duplare*, from *duplus*, literally 'twofold' (source of English *duplicate*) from *duo* 'two'.] —**doubleness** /dúbbəlnəs, dúbb'lnəs/ *n.* ◇ **at the double, on the double** straight away and as quickly as possible ○ *told the children to get into lines at the double*

double back *vi.* to turn around and retrace your steps

double over *vi.* to bend from the waist in response to pain or laughter

double up *vi.* **1. SHARE WITH SB ELSE** to share sth with another person ○ *There weren't enough beds, so some of the children had to double up.* **2. BEND BODY SHARPLY** to bend the body over sharply

double act *n.* two entertainers who regularly perform together

double-acting *adj.* **1.** ENG **WITH PISTONS ACTING BOTH WAYS** with one or more pistons that move in both directions, giving two strokes per cycle **2.** CONSTR **ACTING IN OPPOSITE DIRECTIONS** acting in opposite directions from a central point

double agent *n.* sb who works as a spy for one government but supplies secret information about that government to another

double-bank (**double-banks, double-banking, double-banked**) *vti.* *ANZ* to ride with or carry a second person on a bicycle or horse (*informal*)

double bar *n.* a symbol, ‖, that marks the end of a piece of music or the end of its principal sections

double-barrelled *adj.* **1.** ARMS **WITH TWO BARRELS** used to describe a gun that has two barrels **2. WITH TWO NAMES TOGETHER** formed from two names, usually hyphenated **3. WITH TWO PURPOSES OR INTERPRETATIONS** serving two purposes, or open to two possible interpretations

double bass *n.* the largest and lowest in pitch of the instruments of the violin family, used in the modern symphony orchestra. It is also commonly found in jazz and dance bands, where it is usually plucked rather than bowed.

double-bass *adj.* used to describe an instrument that is larger and lower in pitch than others of its group

double bassoon *n.* = **contrabassoon**

double bed *n.* a bed intended for two people

double bill *n.* a programme of entertainment that has two main items, especially a cinema programme showing two full-length films

double bind *n.* **1. DILEMMA WITH NO GOOD ALTERNATIVES** an unresolvable situation from which there is no escape without undesirable consequences **2. DILEMMA CAUSED BY CONTRADICTORY DEMANDS** a situation in which conflicting demands make it impossible to do the right thing

double-blind *adj.* used to describe an experiment in which neither the experimenters nor the subjects know which of two similar treatments is genuine and which is a control procedure

double boiler *n.* a pair of cooking pots, one fitting on top of and partly inside the other. Food cooks gently in the upper pot while water simmers in the lower pot.

double bond *n.* a chemical bond in which two atoms share two pairs of electrons

double-breasted *adj.* used to describe a coat or jacket that has a large overlap at the front, usually with two sets of buttons

double bridle *n.* a bridle with four reins and a bit with two rings on each side

double check *n.* **1. SECOND CHECK OF STH** a second examination to make sure **2.** CHESS **CHECK FROM TWO PIECES SIMULTANEOUSLY** a situation in chess in which a king is in check from two pieces at once

double-check (**double-checks, double-checking, double-checked**) *vti.* to check sth twice or for a second time ○ *I double-checked that the windows were locked.*

double chin *n.* a fold of flesh or loose skin under the chin —**double-chinned** *adj.*

double-click (**double-clicks, double-clicking, double-clicked**) *vti.* to press and release a mouse button twice in rapid succession. Double-clicking is used in many programs to invoke specific commands.

double-clutch *vi.* *US* = **double-declutch**

double coconut *n.* = **coco-de-mer**

double concerto *n.* a concerto for two solo instruments

double cream *n.* *UK* cream with a high fat content that can be whipped to make it thicker

double cross *n.* a genetic cross in which a new hybrid is produced from parents each of which is a first-generation hybrid of pure strains

double-cross *vt.* (**double-crosses, double-crossing, double-crossed**) BETRAY ASSOCIATE to betray or cheat sb who believes that he or she is a partner or associate in the same, often criminal, enterprise ■ *n.* BETRAYAL OF ASSOCIATE an act of double-crossing a partner or associate —**double-crosser** *n.* —**double-crossing** *adj.*

double dagger *n.* the printed character (‡), used to mark a cross-reference, especially to a footnote

double date *n.* an arrangement for two couples to go out together socially as a foursome

double-date (**double-dates, double-dating, double-dated**) *vi.* to go out socially as a couple with another couple

double-dealing *n.* deliberately deceitful behaviour, especially involving the betrayal of a partner or associate —**double-dealer** *n.* —**double-dealing** *adj.*

Double-decker

double-decker *n.* **1.** TRANSP BUS WITH TWO DECKS a bus with an upper and a lower deck **2.** STH WITH TWO LAYERS sth that has two layers, levels, or tiers ○ *a double-decker sandwich*

double-declutch *vi.* to use the clutch twice when changing gear in a motor vehicle, first to put the gear lever into neutral and rev the engine, then to engage the new gear. US term **double-clutch**

double decomposition *n.* a chemical reaction in which two compounds exchange one or more of their components so that two new compounds are formed

double density *adj.* having double the normal storage capacity ○ *a double density disk*

double descent *n.* the use in some societies of sometimes mother's and sometimes father's ancestry in establishing different features of social identity or status

double digging *n.* AGRIC the process of digging a plot of ground to twice the normal depth and transferring soil from the lower level to the top in order to revitalize it before planting

double-digit *adj.* being between 10 and 99 ○ *double-digit inflation*

double dipping *n.* *US* the fraudulent receipt of two incomes from the government, e.g. by holding a government job and collecting a government pension at the same time (*informal*) —**double dipper** *n.*

double dissolution *n.* the dissolution of both houses of the Australian federal parliament by the Governor-General when the upper house repeatedly refuses to pass legislation already passed by the lower house

double doors *npl.* two full-length doors that meet in the middle of the doorway when closed

double-dotted *adj.* **1.** MUSIC HAVING TWO DOTS AFTER NOTE used to describe a musical note that has two dots following it to indicate that the length of the note is to be increased by three quarters **2.** USING DOUBLE-DOTTED NOTES characterized by the use of double-dotted notes

double dribble *n.* an illegal move in basketball, in which the player dribbles the ball with both hands simultaneously or, having stopped, starts to dribble again

double Dutch *n.* LANGUAGE speech or writing that cannot be understood at all (*informal*)

double-dyed *adj.* **1.** INVETERATE completely and permanently imbued with a particular characteristic or opinion (*literary*) **2.** TWICE-DYED dyed twice in order to fix the colour well

double-edged *adj.* **1.** AMBIGUOUS having two possible meanings or interpretations, especially one that is apparently innocuous and another that is intentionally cutting or malicious **2.** DOING TWO THINGS achieving two purposes or having two effects **3.** HAVING TWO CUTTING EDGES having a blade sharpened on both edges

double effect *n.* the ethical principle that intentionally doing wrong is impermissible, even if the action has good consequences, and that intentionally doing right is permissible, even if the action has bad consequences

double entendre /ˌdoob'l on tóndrə/ *n.* **1.** SEXUALLY AMBIGUOUS REMARK a remark that is ambiguous and sexually suggestive **2.** AMBIGUITY WITH SEXUALLY SUGGESTIVE MEANING ambiguity in which one meaning is sexually suggestive [Late 17thC. From obsolete French, literally 'double understanding'.]

double entry *n.* a bookkeeping system that records each transaction as a credit to one account and a debit from another (*hyphenated when used before a noun*)

double exposure *n.* **1.** SUPERIMPOSING OF PHOTOGRAPHIC IMAGES the exposure of two separate images on a single piece of photographic film **2.** PHOTOGRAPH WITH TWO SUPERIMPOSED IMAGES a photograph that contains one image superimposed on another

double-faced *adj.* **1.** FINISHED ON BOTH SIDES used to describe fabrics that are finished on both sides **2.** HAVING TWO USABLE SIDES having two faces or sides that can both be used ○ *a double-faced tape* **3.** TWO-FACED behaving insincerely or deceitfully

double fault *n.* in tennis, two consecutive serves that land outside the service box or in the net, with the result that the server loses a point

double-fault (**double-faults, double-faulting, double-faulted**) *vi.* in tennis, to make two consecutive faulty serves, and lose a point as a result

double feature *n.* *US* a programme consisting of two full-length films shown consecutively

double figures *npl.* the numbers with two digits, from 10 to 99 (*hyphenated when used before a noun*)

double first (*plural* **double firsts**) *n.* a first-class honours degree in two subjects studied simultaneously

double flat *n.* MUSIC **1.** SYMBOL LOWERING NOTE TWO SEMITONES a symbol, ♭♭, placed in front of a musical note to indicate that the pitch of the note is to be lowered by two semitones (*hyphenated when used before a noun*) **2.** NOTE WITH DOUBLE FLAT a musical note marked with a double flat

double glaze (**double glazes, double glazing, double glazed**) *vt.* to fit a window or building with double glazing

double glazing *n.* windows consisting of two layers of glass separated by a space, designed to provide improved heat and sound insulation (*hyphenated when used before a noun*)

Double Gloucester *n.* a hard English cheese that is slightly orange in colour [GLOUCESTER from the production of the cheese in Gloucestershire]

double-header *n.* a train pulled by two engines coupled together

double helix *n.* the molecular structure of DNA, consisting of a pair of polynucleotide strands connected by a series of hydrogen bonds and wound in opposing spirals

double-hung *adj.* used to describe a window that has two sashes, each sliding vertically in its own grooves

double indemnity *n.* *US, Can* the guaranteed payout of double the face value of a life insurance policy if the policyholder dies in an accident

double-jointed *adj.* used to describe a joint or limb that has unusual flexibility and can bend in the opposite direction to the normal one, or sb with such joints —**double-jointedness** *n.*

double knit *n.* a knitted fabric of double thickness (*hyphenated when used before a noun*)

double knitting *n.* knitting wool of medium thickness (*hyphenated when used before a noun*)

double life *n.* a situation in which sb is simultaneously involved in two sets of circumstances or relationships and keeps each completely separate, and usually secret, from the other

double magnum *n.* a wine bottle containing the equivalent of four standard bottles, used mainly for Bordeaux

double negation *n.* the principle that a proposition and the negation of its negation mean one and the same thing

double negative *n.* a phrase containing two negatives

— **WORD KEY: USAGE** —

Double negatives of the type *I don't know nothing*, in which two negatives close together are intended to reinforce each other, are considered illiterate in current standard English, acceptable though they were in earlier usage. These are to be distinguished from the acceptable, if somewhat uncommon, type *That's not a good idea, I don't think*, in which the reinforcing negatives appear in different clauses. The more usual type of acceptable double negative is seen in *It is not impossible* (= it is distinctly possible), in which the negatives are intended to cancel each other out. This is thought of as a figure of speech called litotes.

double obelisk *n.* PRINTING = **double dagger**

double occupancy *n.* the use of a hotel room or other accommodation by two people (*hyphenated when used before a noun*)

double or nothing *n.* US = **double or quits**

double or quits *n.* a bet in gambling where a player who owes money has the debt doubled or cancelled depending on the outcome of the next play

double-page spread *n.* a feature or article that fills two facing pages of a newspaper or magazine

double-park (**double-parks, double-parking, double-parked**) *vti.* to park a vehicle alongside another already parked and so cause an obstruction —**double-parker** *n.* —**double-parking** *n.*

double play *n.* a baseball play in which two players are put out

double pneumonia *n.* pneumonia affecting both lungs

double-quick *adj., adv.* extremely fast (*informal*)

double quote *n.* a quotation mark that consists of two marks ("), not one

doubler /dúbb'lər/ *n.* an electronic device that doubles an input frequency or voltage

double reed *n.* **1.** REED IN WOODWIND INSTRUMENTS a reed in the oboe, cor anglais, or bassoon consisting of two halves that vibrate against each other when air passes through them (*hyphenated when used before a noun*) **2.** WOODWIND INSTRUMENT WITH DOUBLE REED a woodwind instrument that has a double reed

double refraction *n.* the splitting of one ray of light into two in an anisotropic medium. US term **birefringence**

double rhyme *n.* a two-syllable rhyme e.g. 'cooking' and 'looking'

doubles /dúbb'lz/ (*plural* **-bles**) *n.* *Carib* a popular and cheap East Indian fast food consisting of a sandwich of curried chickpeas in two 'baras', or fried seasoned batter patties (*informal*)

double salt *n.* a salt such as alum that dissolves in solution as two substances but crystallizes as one

double saucepan *n.* = **double boiler**

double sculls *n.* a race between boats for two rowers who sit one behind the other and pull two oars each

double sharp *n.* MUSIC **1. SYMBOL RAISING NOTE TWO SEMITONES** a symbol, ♯ placed in front of a musical note to indicate that the pitch of the note is to be raised by two semitones (*hyphenated when used before a noun*) **2. NOTE WITH DOUBLE SHARP** a musical note marked with a double sharp

double-sided *adj.* used or usable on both sides

double-space (**double-spaces, double-spacing, double-spaced**) *vt.* to type or print text with a blank line between typed or printed lines

doublespeak /dúbb'l speek/ *n.* = **double talk** *n.* 1

double spread *n.* = **double-page spread**

double standard *n.* a principle, rule, or expectation that is applied unfairly to different groups, one group usually being condemned for the slightest offence while the other is treated far more leniently

double star *n.* **1.** = **binary star 2.** = **optical double star**

double-stop *vi.* (**double-stops, double-stopping, double-stopped**) **PLAY TWO STRINGS TOGETHER** to draw the bow of a stringed instrument simultaneously across two strings, producing two tones ■ *n.* **TWO-NOTE CHORD ON STRINGED INSTRUMENT** a musical chord of two notes played on a stringed instrument —**double-stopping** *n.*

doublet /dúbblət/ *n.* **1.** CLOTHES **MAN'S JACKET** a man's close-fitting jacket, with or without sleeves, popular in Europe between the 15th and 17th centuries **2.** LING **WORD WITH SAME ROOT AS ANOTHER** either of two similar words in a language that have the same historical root but have arrived at their current forms via different languages, e.g. 'mood' and 'mode' **3.** PRINTING **REPEATED PRINTED LETTER, WORD, OR LINE** a repeated letter, word, or line that is printed in error **4.** OPTICS **PAIR OF LENSES USED TOGETHER** a pair of lenses designed to be used together so that one lens cancels out the distortions in the other **5.** MINERALS **FAKE GEM** a fake gem made by sticking two pieces of glass together with a coloured layer between them or by sticking a thin layer of a gem on a base ■ **doublets** *npl.* **1.** GAMBLING **DICE WITH SAME NUMBER THROWN** a pair of dice thrown simultaneously each showing the same number of spots **2.** GAME **WORD GAME** a word game in which one word is transformed into another by substituting letters, the object being to achieve this in the minimum number of substitutions [14thC. From French, literally 'sth doubled'.]

double tackle *n.* a pair of double pulleys for lifting or pulling

double take *n.* a reaction of surprise or astonishment after an initial hesitation

double talk *n.* **1. TALK INTENDED TO CONFUSE OR DECEIVE** intentionally ambiguous or confusing talk **2. MIXTURE OF WORDS AND NONSENSE SYLLABLES** speech that includes a mixture of real words and nonsense syllables

double-team (**double-teams, double-teaming, double-teamed**) *vt.* *US* in various team games, to use two players to mark an opponent

doublethink /dúbb'l thingk/ *n.* the conscious or unconscious holding of two opposing beliefs at the same time [Coined by George Orwell in *1984* (1949)]

double time *n.* **1.** FIN **DOUBLE PAY** double the usual rate of pay **2.** MUSIC **DOUBLY FAST MUSICAL TEMPO** a tempo twice as fast as the basic tempo of a piece of music, or a passage played at that speed **3.** *US* MIL **FAST MARCHING PACE** a fast marching pace of 180 steps per minute

double-time (**double-times, double-timing, double-timed**) *vi.* *US* MIL to march at the fast pace of 180 steps per minute

doubleton /dúbb'ltən/ *n.* two cards of the same suit that are the only cards of that suit dealt to a player [Early 20thC. Modelled on SINGLETON.]

double-tonguing *n.* the production of a rapid series of staccato notes on a wind or brass instrument by using rapid movements of the tongue —**double-tongue** *vi.*

double top *n.* in darts, a score of double 20

doubletree /dúbb'l tree/ *n.* a bar used to harness two horses to a carriage or other vehicle [Modelled on SINGLETREE]

double vision *n.* a condition in which two images of the same object are seen simultaneously because the eyes are not focusing properly. Technical name **diplopia**

double whammy *n.* two setbacks or unpleasant experiences occurring very close together (*slang*)

double yellow line *n.* two lines painted in yellow at the edge of a road, indicating that parking is not permitted at most times of the day. ◊ **yellow line**

doubloon /du bloón/ *n.* a former Spanish gold coin [Early 17thC. From Spanish *doblón*, from *dobla* 'double', from, ultimately, Latin *duplus* 'double'.]

doublure /də bloór, doo-/ *n.* a lining, especially one made of leather or highly decorated, inside the cover of a book [Late 19thC. From French, literally 'lining'.]

doubly /dúbb li/ *adv.* **1. IN TWO WAYS** in two different ways **2. TO DOUBLE DEGREE** to twice the usual degree or extent

doubt /dowt/ *vt.* (**doubts, doubting, doubted**) **1. THINK STH UNLIKELY** to feel unconvinced or uncertain about sth, or think that sth is unlikely **2. NOT TRUST SB OR STH** to suspect that sth is not true, likely, or genuine, or that sb is not sincere or trustworthy **3.** *Scotland* **EXPECT STH** to tend to believe sth ■ *n.* **1. UNCERTAINTY OR MISTRUST** a feeling or state of uncertainty, especially as to whether sth is true, likely, or genuine, or as to whether sb is sincere or trustworthy **2.** PHILOS **METHOD OF PHILOSOPHICAL QUESTIONING** the method of questioning claims to knowledge, especially in the philosophy of Descartes **3. FEAR** fear (*archaic*) [13thC. Via Old French *doter* from Latin *dubitare* 'to be uncertain', from *dubius* 'uncertain' (source of English *dubious*). Earlier also 'to fear'.] —**doubtable** *adj.* —**doubtably** *adv.* —**doubtingly** *adv.* ◇ **beyond doubt** completely certain ◇ **no doubt** almost definitely ◇ **open to doubt, in doubt** not certain, settled, foreseeable with confidence, or finally proved

WORD KEY: USAGE

doubt whether, if, or **that?** The verb ***doubt*** is normally followed by *whether* or *if*, or by *that* if it is in the negative: *I doubt whether/if it's true* but *I don't doubt that it's true.* In recent usage, *that* has been used in positive contexts too: *I doubt that it's true.* This use remains disputed.

WORD KEY: SYNONYMS

See Synonyms at ***doubtful***.

doubter /dówtər/ *n.* sb who is sceptical or unsure about sth, especially a religion or a political system

doubtful /dówtf'l/ *adj.* **1. UNSURE** unsure or undecided about sth **2. UNLIKELY** not likely to happen or be successful **3. INVITING SUSPICION** probably not true, honest, reputable, or genuine —**doubtfulness** *n.*

WORD KEY: SYNONYMS

doubtful, uncertain, unsure, in doubt, have doubts, have reservations, dubious, sceptical

CORE MEANING: feeling doubt or uncertainty

doubtful a general term suggesting uncertainty or hesitancy; **uncertain** a less strong term than 'doubtful', suggesting that sb is hesitant or undecided; **unsure** another term for 'uncertain'; **in doubt** a term used to emphasize that sb or sth is in a state of uncertainty or indecision; **have doubts** a term suggesting uncertainty or lack of confidence; **dubious** a term suggesting strong doubt and, often, suspicion; **sceptical** a term used to suggest that sb doubts sth is true or that sth will happen.

doubtfully /dówtf'li/ *adv.* with or expressing doubt

doubting Thomas (*plural* **doubting Thomases**) *n.* sb who is generally doubtful or sceptical about things or refuses to believe sth until given proof [From Jesus Christ's apostle who doubted in the Bible (John 20:24–9)]

doubtless /dówtləss/ *adv.* **1. CERTAINLY** certainly or almost certainly ○ *That was doubtless their intention, as these documents show.* **2. PROBABLY** probably or presumably ○ *You would doubtless have been informed in due course.* ■ *adj.* (*formal*) **1. CERTAIN** impossible to doubt or deny **2. HAVING NO DOUBT** having no doubts or suspicions —**doubtlessly** *adv.* —**doubtlessness** *n.*

douc /dook/ *n.* a rare yellow-faced monkey of the langur family that lives in Southeast Asia. Latin name: *Pygathrix nemaeus.* [Late 18thC. From Vietnamese *douc.*]

douce /dooss/ *adj.* quiet, serious, and undemonstrative in character or expression (*regional*) [13thC. Via French *douce* 'sweet, gentle' from Latin *dulcis.*] —**doucely** *adv.* —**douceness** *n.*

douceur /doo súr/ *n.* sth given as a tip or a bribe [14thC. From French *douceur* 'sweetness favour', from *douce* 'sweet' (see DOUCE).]

douche /doosh/ *n.* **1. CLEANING BODY BY SQUIRTING WATER** a cleaning of part of the body, with a jet of water or air **2. EQUIPMENT PRODUCING CLEANSING WATER JET** a piece of equipment that produces a jet of water or air for a douche ■ *vti.* (**douches, douching, douched**) **CLEAN BODY WITH WATER JET** to clean a part of the body or body cavity with a jet of water or air [Mid-18thC. Via French from Italian *doccia* 'water pipe', from, ultimately, the Latin stem *duction-* 'leading (through a pipe)'.]

dough /dō/ *n.* **1.** COOK **MIXTURE OF FLOUR AND WATER** a soft elastic mixture of flour and water, often with other ingredients such as yeast, oil, butter, salt, and sugar, that becomes bread or pastry when baked **2. MONEY** cash and other financial assets (*slang*) **3. SOFT MASS** a soft elastic substance similar to baking dough, used, e.g., as children's modelling clay [Old English *dāg*. Ultimately from an Indo-European word meaning 'to form' that is also the ancestor of English *effigy, faint,* and *lady.*]

doughboy /dṓ boy/ *n.* **1.** FOOD **BREAD DUMPLING** a ball of bread dough boiled, steamed, or fried as a dumpling **2. dough boy, Dough boy** MIL **US SOLDIER** a US infantryman in World War I

doughface /dṓ fayss/ *n.* a Northerner who sided with the South during the American Civil War, especially a Northern congressman who refused to condemn slavery

doughnut /dṓ nut/ *n.* **1.** FOOD **ROUND CAKE WITH HOLE OR FILLING** a small sugar-coated cake of sweet dough, fried or baked, and either spherical with a filling of cream or jam, or ring-shaped with no filling **2.** MECH ENG **RING-SHAPED OBJECT** an object in the shape of an inflated ring, e.g. an accelerating tube in a nuclear reactor or a baby's floor cushion for sitting in ■ *vt.* (**-nuts, -nutting, -nutted**) **1. CROWD AROUND MP BEING FILMED** to surround a Member of Parliament who is speaking and being filmed for television in order to give the impression that the chamber is fuller than it really is **2. CROWD TELEVISION STUDIO AUDIENCE TOGETHER** to crowd members of a television studio audience together to give viewers the impression that the audience is much larger than it really is

WORD KEY: REGIONAL NOTE

The terms 'bun', 'cake', 'cookie', or 'gateau' are a good illustration of the fact that regions often have very different names for the same item of food. The ***doughnut*** seems to have had its origins in the United States in the early 19th century, but whilst ***doughnut*** is the commonest name for this delicacy, it is eaten – and enjoyed – under the name of 'gravy ring' in Northern Ireland.

doughty /dówti/ (**-tier, -tiest**) *adj.* brave and determined [Old English *dohtig*, from earlier *dyhtig* 'worthy, virtuous'. Ultimately from an Indo-European word meaning 'to be fit, prosper'.] —**doughtily** *adv.* —**doughtiness** *n.*

Doughty /dówti/, **Charles Montagu** (1843–1926) British travel writer and poet. His masterpiece is *Travels in Arabia Deserta* (1888).

doughy /dṓ i/ (**-ier, -iest**) *adj.* **1. RESEMBLING DOUGH IN CONSISTENCY** soft, sticky, and elastic, like dough **2. PALE AND FLABBY** unhealthily pale and a bit flabby —**doughiness** *n.*

Douglas /dúgglǝss/ capital of the Isle of Man. It is a popular holiday resort. Population: 22,214 (1991).

Douglas, Lord Alfred (1870–1945) British writer and poet. He was at the centre of the Oscar Wilde scandal. He wrote *The City of the Soul* (1899) and a verse collection *Sonnets and Lyrics* (1935).

Douglas, Gawin (1474?–1522) Scottish poet and bishop. His works include *The Palace of Honour* (1501?), and a translation of the *Aeneid* (1513?) , the first version of a Latin poet published in English.

Douglas, Sir James, 4th Earl of Morton (1516?–81) Scottish nobleman. As Lord High Chancellor of Scotland (1563) he secured the abdication of Mary, Queen of Scots. He was regent in 1572 but was ousted and finally executed.

Douglas, Kirk (*b.* 1916) US film actor. He has starred in over 70 Hollywood films, including *The Bad and the Beautiful* (1952). In 1995 he received a special Academy Award for his contribution to motion pictures. Real name **Issur Danielovitch**

Douglas, Michael (*b.* 1944) US television and film actor. He won an Academy Award for *Wall Street* (1987). His father is Kirk Douglas.

Douglas, Norman (1868–1952) British writer. His novels include *South Wind* (1917). His travel books *Siren Land* (1911) and *Old Calabria* (1928) were also popular. Full name **George Norman Douglas**

Douglas, William Orville (1898–1980) US associate justice of the Supreme Court. Of strongly held liberal views, he championed individual rights, especially free speech. He wrote a number of books, including *An Almanac of Liberty* (1954), and *Points of Rebellion* (1970).

Douglas fir *n.* **1.** TALL CONIFER a very tall pine tree that grows in northwestern North America and has distinctive rough bark and shaggy-looking cones. It is used for its timber and as a Christmas tree. Latin name: *Pseudotsuga menziesii.* **2.** WOOD OF DOUGLAS FIR TREE the strong durable wood of the Douglas fir tree [Named after Scottish botanist David *Douglas* (1798–1834)]

Douglas-Home /-hyoom/, **Sir Alec, 14th Earl of Home** (1903–95) British statesman and prime minister. He was foreign secretary (1960–63) and renounced his hereditary title to succeed Macmillan as Prime Minister (1963–64). He was made a life peer in 1974. Former name **Alexander Frederick Douglas-Home 14th Earl of Home**

Douglas spruce *n.* = **Douglas fir** *n.* 1

Doukhobor /dookō bawr/, **Dukhobor** *n.* a member of an 18th-century Russian Christian group that rejected state and church authority and emigrated to western Canada at the end of the century to escape persecution [Late 19thC. From Russian *Dukhobar,* from *dukh* 'spirit, Holy Ghost' + *-bor* 'fighter'.]

doula /doola/ *n.* a woman who is experienced in childbirth and who provides physical, emotional, and informational assistance and support to a mother before, during, or after childbirth [From Greek, 'most important woman servant' (who would have helped the woman of the house in childbearing)]

doum /doom/, **doum palm** *n.* = **doom palm**

douma *n.* = **duma**

dour /door/ *adj.* **1.** SEVERE OR UNFRIENDLY severe or gloomy, and unfriendly and unresponsive towards other people **2.** DETERMINED grimly and stubbornly determined ■ *Scotland* solemn, obstinate, unyielding [14thC. Origin uncertain: probably via Gaelic *dūr* 'obstinate', from Latin *durus* 'hard' (source also of English *endure*).] —**dourly** *adv.* —**dourness** *n.*

doura *n.* = **durra**

dourine /door een/ *n.* a sexually transmitted disease of horses and related animals that causes swollen genitals [Late 19thC. From French.]

Douro /doorō/, **Duero** river that rises in north-central Spain and flows westwards across Spain and northern Portugal, reaching the Atlantic Ocean near Oporto. Length: 895 km/556 mi.

douroucouli /doo roo kooli, doorə-/ (*plural* **-lis**) *n.* a fairly small, large-eyed, nocturnal South American monkey with an inflatable sac under its neck that amplifies its calls. Genus: *Aotus.* [Mid-19thC. Origin uncertain: probably from the language of the Rio Negro people in southern Venezuela.]

douse[1] /dowss/, **dowse** *vt.* (**douses, dousing, doused; dowses, dowsing, dowsed**) **1.** IMMERSE STH IN WATER to plunge or submerge sb or sth in water **2.** PUT LIQUID ON STH to put a lot of water or other liquid on sb or sth **3.** EXTINGUISH STH to put out a light, fire, or flame, especially with water ■ *n.* DRENCHING a thorough wetting or soaking [Early 17thC. Origin uncertain: perhaps from DOUSE[2] 'to strike'.] —**douser** *n.*

douse[2] /dowss/ *vt.* (**douses, dousing, doused**) **1.** LOWER SAIL to lower a sail, especially at speed **2.** TAKE OFF A HAT to take off a hat or other item of clothing (*archaic*) **3.** PUNCH OR STRIKE SB to punch or strike sb or sth (*archaic*) ■ *n.* A BLOW a punch or blow (*archaic*) [Mid-16thC. Origin uncertain.]

DOVAP /dō vap/ *n.* a system for measuring the speed and position of objects in flight that is based on the frequency of sound waves. Full form **Doppler velocity and position**

dove[1] /duv/ *n.* **1.** BIRDS BIRD OF PIGEON FAMILY a bird of the pigeon family that has a heavy body, a small head, and a cooing call. Family: Columbidae. **2.** POL SUPPORTER OF PEACE sb who supports peaceful measures and resists confrontation or war. ◊ **hawk 3.** TERM OF ENDEARMENT used as an affectionate name for a loved one ■ *adj., n.* = **dove-grey** [Assumed Old English *dūfe,* originally 'dark-coloured bird'. Ultimately from an Indo-European word meaning 'to darken'.]

dove[2] *US* past tense of **dive**

Dove /duv/ *n.* in Christianity, a manifestation or representation of the Holy Spirit

dovecote /dúvkōt/, **dovecot** /-kot/ *n.* a building or structure, e.g. mounted on a pole or set into a wall, with many separate entrances and compartments, used for housing domestic pigeons

dove-grey *adj.* of a mid-grey colour with a slight tinge of pink or blue —**dove -grey** *n.*

dovekie /dúvki/ (*plural* **dovekies**), **dovekey** (*plural* **dovekeys**) *n.* = **little auk** [Early 19thC. Literally 'small dove', formed from DOVE.]

dove prion *n.* a sea bird of the petrel family with a blueish grey back and black and white markings on its underparts, found in cool southern regions. Latin name: *Pachyptila desolata.*

Dover /dṓvər/ city and port on the southern coast of Kent, England. It is England's busiest resort and the one nearest to France. Population: 102,600 (1991).

Dover, Strait of the narrowest part of the English Channel, between Dover, England, and Calais, France. Length: 34 km/21 mi.

Dover sole *n.* **1.** EUROPEAN FLATFISH a flat-bodied European fish that is a popular food fish. Latin name: *Solea solea.* **2.** FLATFISH OF N AMERICAN PACIFIC a brownish mottled flat-bodied fish of the Pacific coast of North America that is a popular food fish. Latin name: *Microstomus pacificus.* [Early 20thC. Origin uncertain: probably named after *Dover,* England.]

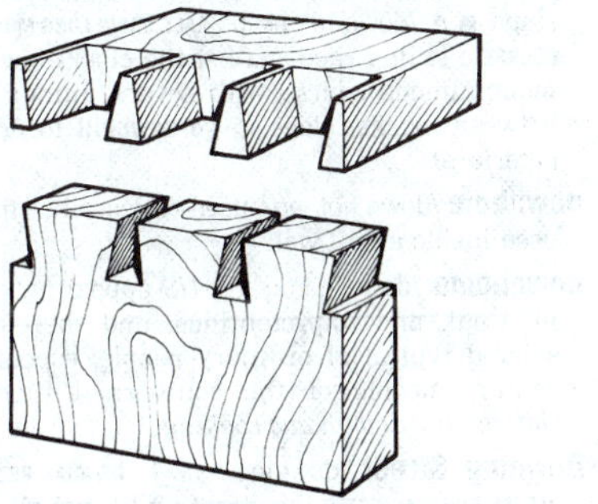

Dovetail

dovetail /dúv tayl/ *v.* (**-tails, -tailing, -tailed**) **1.** *vti.* FIT TOGETHER to fit neatly together or combine smoothly and efficiently, or to fit or combine things in this way **2.** *vt.* JOIN PIECES OF WOOD to join wooden boards with interlocking V-shaped tenons ■ *n.* **1.** V-SHAPED TENON a V-shaped projection on the end of a piece of wood that fits into a similarly shaped opening in another piece to form a strong joint **2. dovetail, dovetail joint** JOINT WITH DOVETAILS a joint made using dovetails [From its shape]

dovetail saw *n.* a small saw with a reinforced back, slightly smaller than a tenon saw and used for fine woodworking

dovish /dúvvish/ *adj.* advocating peaceful solutions and the avoidance of confrontation or war. ◊ **hawkish** —**dovishness** *n.*

Dovzhenko /dov zhéngkō/, **Aleksandr** (1894–1956) Ukrainian film director. His films include *Earth* (1930) and *Ivan* (1932).

dowager /dówəjər/ *n.* **1.** WIDOW WITH HUSBAND'S TITLE OR PROPERTY a woman who has inherited a title or property from her deceased husband **2.** WOMAN OF STATUS a rich-looking or respected woman of advanced years [Mid-16thC. From Old French *douagere,* from, ultimately, Latin *dos* 'dowry'.]

dowager's hump *n.* a marked abnormal curving of the spine around the area of the shoulder blades, caused by osteoporosis and found among women, often as the result of age

dowdy /dówdi/ (**-dier, -diest**) *adj.* **1.** PLAIN AND UNFASHIONABLE IN STYLE unattractively plain and unfashionable in style **2.** DRESSED PLAINLY wearing plain unfashionable clothes [Late 16thC. Origin uncertain: probably literally 'little poorly dressed woman', formed from *doue* 'poorly dressed woman'.] —**dowdily** *adv.* —**dowdiness** *n.*

dowel /dówəl/ *n.* **dowel, dowel pin** JOINING PEG a short wooden or metal peg used to join two pieces of wood or metal by fitting tightly at each end into specially drilled holes in the two pieces to be joined ■ *vt.* (**dowels, dowelling, dowelled**) JOIN WOOD OR METAL WITH DOWELS to join pieces of wood or metal using dowels [13thC. Origin uncertain.]

Dowell /dówəl/, **Anthony** (*b.* 1943) British dancer. He was a leading interpreter of classical and modern roles, notably in partnership with Antoinette Sibley. He became director of the Royal Ballet in 1986.

dower /dówər/ *n.* **1.** WIDOW'S INHERITANCE a dead man's estate, or part of his estate, inherited by his widow **2.** DOWRY a dowry (*archaic*) **3.** NATURAL GIFT sth, especially a skill or talent, with which sb is endowed (*literary*) ■ *vt.* (**-ers**) ENDOW to endow sb with sth (*literary*) [13thC. From Old French *douaire,* from Latin *dotare* 'to endow', from *dos* 'marriage portion'.]

dower house *n.* a house originally built by a rich landowner for his widow to live in after his death, especially a house on a country estate

Dow Jones Averages *tdmk.* a trademark for an index of the prices of selected industrial, transportation, and utilities stocks that is based on a formula developed and revised periodically by Dow Jones & Company, Inc.

Dowland /dówlənd/, **John** (1562–1626?) English composer and musician. A widely travelled lutenist, he influenced the development of Western vocal music through his *First Book of Songs, or Ayres* (1597).

down[1] /down/ (**downs, downing, downed**) CORE MEANING: a grammatical word used to indicate movement or position towards a lower level or the ground ○ (prep) *He ran down the stairs and opened the door.* ○ (prep) *The sheep was caught in brambles 50 ft down the hillside.* ○ (prep) *Tears were pouring down her cheeks.* ○ (adv) *I was numb from the waist down.* ○ (adv) *They all watched the sun go down.* ○ (adv) *She pressed a button and the window slid down.*

1. *prep.* TO LOWER LEVEL IN STH towards or at a lower level in sth ○ *I dropped my keys down a hole.* **2.** *prep.* ALONG towards or at a position further along the length of sth and usually at a somewhat lower level ○ *halfway down the street* **3.** *adv.* AT OR TO LOWER LEVEL at or to a physically lower level or position ○ *down in the basement* **4.** *adv.* ONTO SURFACE out of the hand and onto a surface ○ *She calmly put her fork down.* **5.** *adv.* AWAY FROM PRESENT LOCATION to another place away from your present location or base **6.** *adv.* TO MORE SOUTHERLY PLACE to a place in the south or to the south of your present location ○ *going down to Spain for the summer* **7.** *adv.* TO OR AT LOWER AMOUNT to or at a lower amount or price ○ *to get interest rates down* **8.** *adv.* SHORT BY SPECIFIED AMOUNT short of, having lost, or losing by a specified amount ○ *They were two goals down at half time.* **9.** *adv.* HAVING ONLY SPECIFIED AMOUNT LEFT having only a specified amount left ○ *I'm down to my last pound.* **10.** *adv.* IN PART PAYMENT in part payment for sth or as a deposit ○ *You put 5% down, and pay the rest in instalments.* **11.** *adv.* INCLUDING EVERYONE OR EVERYTHING including everyone or everything, from highest to lowest, within a specified group or hierarchy of people or things, or even including the particular person or thing mentioned ○ *everyone from the managing director down* ○ *account for everything down to the last farthing* **12.** *adv.* TO LATER PERIOD from an earlier to a later time or person ○ *The piano had been handed down to him by his grandmother.* **13.** *adv.* IN INFERIOR POSITION in or to an inferior, less free, or privileged position or condition ○ *holding political opponents down* **14.** *adv.* TO REDUCED CONDITION to a lower level of intensity or activity ○ *wind down after work* **15.** *adv.* INTO LESS SOLID STATE into a different and less solid state **16.** *adv.* ON PAPER in writing on paper, as a record **17.** *adv.* CHOSEN OR ARRANGED chosen or detailed for sth, or arranged or scheduled for a particular time or date ○ *We're down for two sessions next month.* **18.** *adv.* LEISURE VERTICALLY IN A CROSSWORD in a vertical position in a crossword ○ *still need the solution to 10 down.* ◊ **across 19.** *adv.* UNIV AWAY FROM UNIVERSITY away from, or no longer at, a university ○ *down from Cambridge* **20.** *adv.* NAUT TO WINDWARD having the rudder to windward **21.** *adj.* UNHAPPY unhappy and gloomy **22.** *adj.* COMPUT NOT IN OPERATION temporarily not in operation **23.** *adj.* MADE IN PART PAYMENT made or given in part payment for sth or as a deposit ○ *a down payment on the car* **24.** *adj.* AMERICAN FOOTBALL NOT IN PLAY no longer in play **25.** *adj.* BASEBALL PUT OUT eliminated from a game **26.** *adj.* ON THE GROUND lying on the ground ○ *a down tree* **27.** *interj.* INSTRUCTION TO DOG used as an instruction to a dog to stop jumping up, or to lie or sit ○ *Down boy!* **28.** *vt.* EAT OR DRINK to eat food or drink liquid, especially quickly or greedily **29.** *vt.* MAKE FALL TO THE GROUND to cause sb or sth to fall to the ground through being hurt or damaged **30.** *n.* AMERICAN FOOTBALL A MOVE MADE IN AMERICAN FOOTBALL one of four consecutive plays within which a team must either score or advance the ball at least ten yards **31.** *n.* AMERICAN FOOTBALL DECLARE BALL OUT OF PLAY to declare a ball as no longer in play in American football [Old English *dūn* 'hill', literally 'from the hill', of uncertain origin: perhaps ultimately from a Celtic word that is also the source of *dune*] ◇ **be down on sb, have a down on sb** to show dislike or hostility towards sb or sth, often giving him, her, or it unfair treatment (*informal*) ◇ **be down to sb** to be the responsibility of sb ◇ **be down to sth** to be the result of sth ◇ **be** *or* **go down with sth** to be or become ill with sth ◇ **down under** to or in Australia or New Zealand (*informal*) ◇ **down with sb** *or* **sth!** used to express disapproval of, opposition to, or a desire to get rid of sb or sth

down[2] /down/ *n.* **1.** SOFT FLUFFY FEATHERS the soft fluffy feathers that are a young bird's first plumage, or that lie beneath the outer feathers in some adult birds **2.** FEATHERS AS STUFFING the soft breast feathers of a duck or goose, especially the female eider duck, used to fill pillows and quilts. ◊ **eiderdown 3.** COVERING OF SOFT HAIRS a covering of fine fluffy hairs, e.g. on a child's skin or on the skin of some kinds of fruit [14thC. From Old Norse *dúnn* 'grassland', from Old English *dūn*, ultimately from an Indo-European word meaning 'to fly about like dust, whirl'.]

down[3] /down/ *n.* TREELESS HILL a grassy treeless hill or ridge (*often used in placenames*) ■ **downs** *npl.* ROLLING GRASSLAND an area of gently rolling, treeless, grassy upland, used mainly as pasture [Old English *dūn* (see DOWN[1])]

Down[1] /down/ *n.* a sheep belonging to a southern English breed, such as the South Down or Dorset Down [Named after the English *downs*, origin of the breeds]

Down[2] /down/ former county in southeast Northern Ireland. Population: 60,000 (1995). Area: 2,448 sq. km/945 sq. mi.

down-and-dirty *adj. US* crude and often unpleasant (*slang*) ○ *the down-and-dirty truth*

down-and-out *adj.* **1.** JOBLESS AND POOR having no money or job, often no home, and little hope of things getting better **2.** UNABLE TO CARRY ON completely incapacitated and unable to carry on ■ *n.* JOBLESS POOR PERSON sb who has no job, money, or hope, especially a homeless person

down-at-heel *adj.* shabbily dressed through poverty

downbeat /dówn beet/ *adj.* **1.** PESSIMISTIC showing or expressing pessimism and hopelessness **2.** CASUAL deliberately casual and relaxed (*informal*) **3.** UNDERSTATED carefully or deliberately understated or restrained ■ *n.* **1.** FIRST BEAT IN BAR the first beat in a bar of music **2.** CONDUCTOR'S DOWNWARD GESTURE INDICATING DOWNBEAT the downward movement made by a conductor to indicate the downbeat of a bar of music

down-bow *n.* the action of drawing a bow from its heel towards its point across a stringed instrument

downburst /dówn burst/ *n.* a powerful downward wind, often part of a thunderstorm system, that creates strong horizontal winds in all directions when it strikes the earth and is a danger to aircraft

downcast /dówn kaast/ *adj.* **1.** SAD sad and pessimistic **2.** LOOKING DOWN looking or directed towards the ground ○ *with downcast eyes*

downcourt /dówn kawrt/ *adj., adv.* SPORTS in, to, or towards the opposite end of a basketball or similar court

downdraft *n.* US = **downdraught**

downdraught /dówn draaft/ *n.* a downward movement of air, e.g. on the lee side of a mountain range or down a chimney

downer /dówner/ *n.* **1.** SEDATIVE DRUG a drug, especially a barbiturate, that induces calmness or sleepiness (*slang*) **2.** GLOOMY PERSON OR THING a gloomy person, situation, or experience (*informal*) **3.** GLOOMY MOOD a gloomy and pessimistic mood (*informal*) ○ *was on a real downer*

downfall /dówn fawl/ *n.* **1.** FAILURE OR RUIN the failure or ruin of a previously successful person, group, or organization **2.** CAUSE OF RUIN an action or situation responsible for the failure or ruin of a previously successful person, group, or organization **3.** METEOROL FALL OF RAIN OR SNOW a sudden heavy fall of rain or snow

downfallen /dówn fawlən/ *adj.* **1.** NEGLECTED in a seriously neglected or ruined condition **2.** *US* NO LONGER SUCCESSFUL fallen from a position of fame, power, or wealth

downgrade /dówn grayd/ *vt.* (**-grades, -grading, -graded**) **1.** LOWER STATUS to lower the status, value, or rating of sth ○ *The hurricane was downgraded to a tropical storm.* **2.** MOVE SB TO LESS IMPORTANT JOB to move sb from one post or job to another with less responsibility, status, or pay **3.** DISPARAGE to speak or write about sb or sth disparagingly ■ *n. US, Can* DOWNWARD SLOPE a downward slope on a road

downhaul /dówn hawl/ *n.* a rope for pulling down or holding down a sail or a spar

downhearted /dówn haártid/ *adj.* discouraged and unhappy —**downheartedly** *adv.* —**downheartedness** *n.*

downhill *adv.* /down híl/ TOWARDS BOTTOM OF HILL towards the bottom of a slope or hill ■ *adj.* /dówn hil/ SLOPING DOWN sloping down, or taking place on a downward slope ■ *n.* /dówn hil/ SKIING RACE DOWN LONG MOUNTAINSIDE COURSE a skiing race against the clock down a long mountainside course with several hundred yards between marker flags ◇ **go downhill** to decline or deteriorate

downhole /down hṓl/ *adj.* used to describe equipment used inside an oil well

downhome /down hṓm/ *adj. US* appealingly simple, informal, and unpretentious, and therefore considered typical of ordinary people, especially the country people of the southern United States (*informal*) ○ *downhome cooking*

Downing Street /dówning-/ *n.* **1.** OFFICIAL RESIDENCE OF BRITISH PRIME MINISTER the street off Whitehall in Westminster, central London, where the official residences of the British prime minister and chancellor of the Exchequer are located **2.** BRITISH GOVERNMENT the British prime minister or the British government ○ *Downing Street sources*

downland /dówn land/ *n.* undulating grass-covered hills in southern England or similar, but often flatter grassland in Australia and New Zealand

downlight /dówn līt/ *n.* a lamp or bulb whose light is directed straight downwards

downlink /dówn lingk/ *n.* a path for the transmission of signals and data between a vehicle or satellite in space and the Earth —**downlink** *vti.*

download /down lṓd/ *vti.* (**-loads, -loading, -loaded**) COMPUT TRANSFER DATA to transfer or copy data from one computer to another, or to a disk or peripheral device, or be transferred or copied in this way ■ *n.* COMPUT **1.** INSTANCE OF DOWNLOADING an instance or the process of downloading data **2.** DOWNLOADED DATA data that has been downloaded in a single operation

downmarket /dówn maarkit/ *adj.* cheap, appealing to mass taste, and regarded as being of low quality. = **downscale** ■ *adv.* TOWARDS LESS DISCRIMINATING SECTOR OF MARKET towards the part of the market that deals in cheaper, lower-quality goods for mass consumption

Downpatrick /down páttrik/ town in County Down, Northern Ireland. Its name comes from the 'dun' or large mound where St Patrick is reputedly buried. Population: 10,257 (1991).

down payment *n.* a part of the full price of sth paid at the time it is bought, with the remaining part to be paid later

downpipe /dówn pīp/ *n.* a pipe that carries rainwater from a roof gutter down to a drain or to the ground. US term **downspout**

downplay /down pláy/ (**-plays, -playing, -played**) *vt.* to make sth seem less important, significant, or serious than it really is

downpour /dówn pawr/ *n.* a heavy and sustained fall of rain

downrange /down ráynj/ *adj., adv.* away from where a missile was fired

downrigger /dówn riggər/ *n.* a fishing line attached to a weighted cable allowing the baited line to be trailed at or near the bottom of the water

downright /dówn rīt/ *adj.* **1.** ABSOLUTE complete and utter ○ *a downright lie* **2.** STRAIGHTFORWARD frank in expressing opinions **3.** POINTING DOWN pointing straight down (*archaic*) ■ *adv.* POSITIVELY positively and undeniably ○ *downright unfair* —**downrightly** *adv.* —**downrightness** *n.*

downriver /dówn rívvər/ *adv., adj.* towards or nearer the mouth of a river, or following the direction of its current

Downs /downz/ either of two chalk uplands in southern England, the North Downs in Surrey and Kent, and the South Downs in Hampshire and Sussex

downscale /down skáyl/ (**-scales, -scaling, -scaled**) *vti. US* to reduce the scale or extent of sth, especially a business

downshift /dówn shift/ (**-shifts, -shifting, -shifted**) *vi.* **1.** *US* CARS = **change down 2.** CHANGE LIFESTYLE to change a highly paid but stressful job for one that makes it possible to improve quality of life in other respects —**downshift** *n.*

downside /dówn sīd/ *n.* a negative side to sth that also has positive aspects

downsize /dówn sīz/ (**-sizes, -sizing, -sized**) *vti.* BUSINESS to reduce the size of a business or organization, especially by cutting the workforce

downslide /dówn slīd/ *n.* a downward trend or course

downspout /dówn spowt/ *n. US* = **downpipe**

Down's syndrome /dównz-/ *n.* a genetic disorder characterized by a broad skull, blunt facial features, short stature, and learning difficulties. It is caused by the presence of an extra copy of a particular chromosome. [Mid-20thC. Named after J. H. L. *Down* (1828–96), an English physician.]

downstage /dówn stáyj/ *adv., adj.* TO OR AT STAGE'S FRONT towards or at the front of a theatre stage ■ *n.* FRONT HALF OF STAGE the front half of a theatre stage

downstairs /dówn stáirz/ *adv.* TO LOWER FLOOR down the stairs or to a lower floor ■ *adj.* ON LOWER FLOOR on a lower or the lowest floor ○ *a downstairs bathroom* ■ *n.* **1.** LOWER FLOOR the lower floor of a building **2.** HOUSE'S SERVANTS all the servants of a household (*informal*) ◊ **upstairs** *n.* 2

downstate /dówn stáyt/ *adj., adv. US* **1.** IN OR TO SOUTH OF STATE in or to the southerly part of a US state **2.** AWAY FROM CITIES away from the big cities and in or into the more rural parts of a US state whose major metropolitan area is to the north ○ *downstate Illinois* ■ *n. US* SOUTHERLY OR RURAL PART OF STATE the southerly part of a US state, or the more rural part when the major metropolitan area is to the north —**downstater** *n.*

a at; aa father; aw all; ay day; air hair; ə about, edible, item, common, circus; e egg; ee eel; hw when; i it, happy; ī ice; 'l apple; 'm rhythm; 'n fashion; o odd; ō open; ŏŏ good; oo pool; ow owl; oy oil; th thin; th this; u up; ur urge;

downstream /dównstreem/ *adv., adj.* TOWARDS MOUTH OF RIVER towards or nearer the mouth of a river, or following the direction of the current ■ *adj.* INDUST OF LATER PRODUCTION STAGES relating to or occurring in the later stages of production ■ *adv.* GENETICS FURTHER FORWARD ON DNA MOLECULE further forward on a DNA molecule, in the direction in which the sequence is being read during replication. ◊ **upstream** ■ *n.* TRANSMISSION AWAY FROM CENTRAL NETWORK transmission of data on a network that is travelling away from a central distribution point. Downstream network capacity is generally greater than upstream capacity.

downswing /dównswing/ *n.* 1. DOWNWARD TREND a downward trend or course 2. GOLF DOWNWARD SWING OF GOLF CLUB the downward part of a golfer's swing

Down syndrome *n.* US = **Down's syndrome**

down-the-line *adj.* US unwavering in support of or adherence to rules or policy

downthrow /dówn thró/ *n.* the relative vertical displacement of rocks on one side of a fault

downtime /dówn tīm/ *n.* time during which work or production is stopped, e.g. because machinery is not working

down-to-earth *adj.* practical and realistic

downtown /dówn tówn/ *adj., adv.* US, Can, NZ IN OR TO TOWN'S CENTRE in or to the centre of a city, especially its business centre ■ *n.* US CITY CENTRE the centre of a city, especially its business centre —**downtowner** *n.*

downtrend /dówn trend/ *n.* a downward trend or tendency

downtrodden /-tród'n/, **downtrod** /-tród/ *adj.* made submissive by constant harsh treatment

downturn /dówn turn/ *n.* a period or trend in which business or economic activity is reduced or is less successful

downwardly mobile *adj.* moving to a lower status, social class, or income bracket

downward mobility *n.* movement to a lower status, social class, or income bracket

downwards /dównwərdz/, **downward** /dównwərd/ *adj.* 1. MOVING LOWER IN SPACE moving or directed to the ground or to a lower place 2. MOVING TO LOWER LEVEL moving to a lower level or condition 3. COMING FROM ORIGIN OR SOURCE descending from a source, origin, or beginning ■ *adv.* 1. TOWARDS LOWER PLACE towards the ground or a lower place 2. TO LOWER LEVEL to a lower level or condition 3. TO AND INCLUDING EVERYONE to and including all the members of an organization, even the most junior ■ *everyone from the managing director downwards* 4. TO LATER TIME to a later time or generation —**downwardly** *adv.* —**downwardness** *n.*

downwash /dówn wosh/ *n.* a downward wind, e.g. the wind created by an aircraft wing

downwind /dówn wínd/ *adv., adj.* 1. WITH THE WIND in the direction that the wind is blowing 2. FURTHER IN DIRECTION OF WIND in or into a position further along the line of the direction of the wind

downy /dówn i/ (**-ier, -iest**) *adj.* 1. SOFT soft and fluffy 2. COVERED WITH SOFT HAIRS covered with soft fine hairs 3. FEATHER-FILLED filled with feathers 4. SHARP-WITTED sharp-witted, alert, and aware (*archaic slang*) —**downiness** *n.*

downy mildew *n.* a disease of plants that produces grey velvety patches on lower leaf surfaces, caused by various fungi *Family* [Peronosporaceae]

downy woodpecker *n.* a small black and white North American woodpecker with a white back. The male also has a red head patch. Latin name: *Picoides pubescens.*

dowry /dówri/ (*plural* **-ries**) *n.* 1. BRIDE'S FAMILY'S GIFT TO BRIDEGROOM an amount of money or property given in some societies by a bride's family to her bridegroom or his family when she marries 2. MAN'S GIFT TO BRIDE an amount of money or property transferred by a man to his bride when they marry 3. CHR MONEY PAID TO ENTER NUNS' ORDER a sum of money required for a woman to enter some monastic orders 4. TALENT a natural talent (*literary*) [14thC. Via Anglo-Norman *dowarie* from Old French *douaire* (see DOWER).]

dowsabel /doóssə bel, dówssə-/ *n.* a woman or girl sweetheart (*archaic*) [Late 16thC. From French, an alteration of the name *Dulcibella*.]

dowse[1] /dowss/ (**dowses, dowsing, dowsed**) *vi.* to use a divining rod to search for underground water or minerals [Late 17thC. Origin unknown.]

dowse[2] *vt., n.* = **douse**[1]

dowse[3] /dows/ *vt., n.* = **douse**[2]

dowser /dówzər/ *n.* = **water diviner**

dowsing rod *n.* = **divining rod**

Dow theory /dów-/ *n.* a theory that states that stock-market prices can be forecast on the basis of the movements of a selected group of stocks

doxastic /dok sástik/ *n.* LOGIC OF BELIEF the branch of logic that deals with belief ■ *adj.* OF BELIEF relating to belief [Early 19thC. Coined from Greek *doxa* 'opinion' + -ASTIC.]

doxie *n.* RELIG = **doxy**[1]

doxology /dok sóllə ji/ (*plural* **-gies**) *n.* in Christian religious services, a hymn, prayer, or formula of worship in praise of God [Mid-17thC. From medieval Latin *doxologia*, literally 'science of opinion', from Greek *doxa* 'opinion'.] —**doxological** /dóksə lójjik'l/ *adj.* —**doxologically** /-lójjikli/ *adv.*

doxorubicin /dóksō roóbissin/ *n.* an antibiotic, obtained from a bacterium, that is used to treat many types of tumour [Late 20thC. Coined from DE + OXY + Latin *rubus* 'red' + MYCIN.]

doxy[1] /dóksi/ (*plural* **-ies**), **doxie** *n.* RELIG a set of beliefs, especially religious beliefs (*informal*) [Mid-18thC. From *-doxy*, in such words as ORTHODOXY and HETERODOXY.]

doxy[2] /dóksi/ (*plural* **-ies**) *n.* a man's woman lover, a woman who has many men lovers, or prostitute (*archaic slang*) [Mid-16thC. Origin unknown.]

doxycycline /dóksi sí kleen/ *n.* an antibiotic derived from tetracycline that is used to treat many diseases, especially diarrhoea in travellers and acne [Mid-20thC. Contraction of *deoxytetracycline*.]

doyen /dóyən/ *n.* a man who is the most experienced and respected member of a group or profession [15thC. Via French from Old French *deien*, from Latin *decanus* 'one set over ten persons' (see DEAN).]

doyenne /doy énn/ *n.* a woman who is the most experienced and respected member of a group or profession [Mid-19thC. From French, feminine form of *doyen* 'DOYEN'.]

Doyle /doyl/, **Sir Arthur Conan** (1859–1930) Scottish-born British writer and physician. He was author of the Sherlock Holmes detective novels, including *The Hound of the Baskervilles* (1902).

Doyle, Roddy (b. 1958) Irish novelist, playwright, and screenwriter. He won the 1993 Booker Prize with *Paddy Clarke Ha Ha Ha*, building on the success of his first two novels *The Commitments* (1987) and *The Snapper* (1990), both made into films.

D'Oyly Carte /dóyli kaárt/, **Richard** (1844–1901) British agent, manager, and producer. He founded an eponymous opera company in 1875 to perform the operettas of W. S. Gilbert and Arthur Sullivan. From 1881 these operettas were staged at his own Savoy Theatre, London.

doz. *abbr.* dozen

doze[1] /dōz/ *vi.* (**dozes, dozing, dozed**) 1. HAVE SHORT LIGHT SLEEP to sleep lightly for a short time, especially during the day 2. LAZE OR DAYDREAM to spend time lazily or in a daydream ■ *n.* LIGHT SLEEP a short light sleep [Mid-17thC. Origin uncertain: probably from Scandinavian.] —**dozer** *n.*

doze off *vi.* to fall into a light sleep, especially unintentionally

doze[2] /dōz/ (**dozes, dozing, dozed**) *vt.* = **bulldoze** (*slang*) [Mid-20thC. Back-formation from DOZER.]

dozed /dōzd/ *adj.* Ireland used to describe wood that is rotten or rubber that is perished [Late 18thC. Past participle of DOZE[1].]

dozen /dúzz'n/ *n.* (*plural* **-en**), *det.* GROUP OF 12 a group of 12 objects or people ■ *det.* (*informal*) 1. MANY a large number of *I've told you a dozen times already!* 2. **dozens** LOTS a large quantity or a great

many [13thC. Via Old French *dozeine* from Latin *duodecim* 'twelve', from *duo* 'two' + *decem* 'ten'.] —**dozenth** *adj.* ◊ **by the dozen** in large quantities ◊ **daily dozen** a regular regime of physical exercises

dozer /dózər/ *n.* a bulldozer (*slang*) [Mid-20thC. Shortening of BULLDOZER.]

doziness /dózinəss/ *n.* slowness in understanding sth or things in general (*informal*)

dozy /dózi/ (**-zier, -ziest**) *adj.* half asleep or tending to fall asleep or doze —**dozily** *adv.* —**doziness** *n.*

dp *abbr.* BASEBALL double play

DP *abbr.* 1. DP, dp COMPUT data processing 2. DP, dp PHYS dew point 3. displaced person

D/P *abbr.* 1. COMM documents against presentation 2. documents against payment

DPB *abbr.* NZ Domestic Purposes Benefit

DPhil /dee fíl/, **DPh** *abbr.* Doctor of Philosophy

dpi *n.* a measure of the density of the image produced by a computer screen or printer. Full form **dots per inch**

DPN *abbr.* diphosphopyridine nucleotide (*dated*)

DPP *abbr.* LAW Director of Public Prosecutions

DPS *abbr.* dividends per share

dpt *abbr.* 1. department 2. GRAM deponent

DPT *abbr.* diphtheria, pertussis, tetanus (vaccine)

dr *abbr.* 1. FIN debtor 2. MEASURE dram 3. dr, DR dining room (*used in advertisements*) 4. drawer

Dr *abbr.* 1. doctor 2. drachma 3. Drive (*used in addresses*)

DR *abbr.* 1. NAVIG dead reckoning 2. CONSTR dry riser

dr. *abbr.* 1. FIN debit 2. MONEY drachma 3. MEASURE dram

drab[1] /drab/ *adj.* (**drabber, drabbest**) 1. LACKING COLOUR OR BRIGHTNESS uninteresting to look at because of a lack of colour or brightness 2. BORING lacking interest, enthusiasm, or excitement 3. OF PALE GREYISH-BROWN COLOUR of a dull pale greyish-brown colour ■ *n.* 1. PALE GREYISH-BROWN COLOUR a dull pale greyish-brown colour 2. TEXTILES DULL-COLOURED FABRIC a grey or brown fabric [Early 16thC. From Old French *drap* 'cloth' (source of English *drape* and *trappings*). Originally 'cloth', then 'natural, undyed cloth', hence 'dull greyish-brown'.] —**drably** *adv.* —**drabness** *n.*

drab[2] /drab/ *n.* 1. OFFENSIVE TERM FOR DIRTY WOMAN a dirty, lazy, and untidy woman (*archaic insult*) 2. PROSTITUTE a prostitute (*archaic*) ■ *vi.* (**drabs, drabbing, drabbed**) USE PROSTITUTES to use prostitutes (*archaic*) [Early 16thC. Origin uncertain: perhaps from Dutch.]

drabbet /drábbit/ *n.* coarse undyed linen fabric [Early 19thC. Formed from DRAB[1].]

drabble /drább'l/ (**-bles, -bling, -bled**) *vti.* to become, or make sth, wet and dirty [14thC. From Low German *drabbeln* 'to splash in water', of uncertain origin: probably an imitation of the sound.]

Drabble /drább'l/, **Margaret** (b. 1939) British novelist, editor, and critic. Her novels explore the dilemmas of women in contemporary society and include *The Needle's Eye* (1972) and *The Radiant Way* (1987). She edited *The Oxford Companion to English Literature* (1985).

dracaena /drə séenə/, **dracena** *n.* 1. TROPICAL EVERGREEN PLANT a member of a genus of tropical evergreen plants that have long, strap-shaped, often variegated leaves and are popular as house plants. Genus: *Dracaena.* 2. PLANT LIKE DRACAENA a plant with long narrow leaves resembling a true dracaena. Genus: *Cordyline.* [Early 19thC. Via modern Latin from Greek *drakaina*, feminine of *drakōn* 'dragon', from the supposed resemblance of the juice of one of the species to dragon's blood.]

drachm /dram/ *n.* MONEY = **drachma** *n.* 2 [14thC. Via Old French *drachme* from, ultimately, Greek *drakhmē*, literally 'number of coins one hand can hold', from the assumed stem *drakh-* 'to grasp'.]

drachma /drákmə/ (*plural* **-mas** /-mi/ *or* **-mae**) *n.* 1. MONEY GREEK CURRENCY UNIT the main unit of currency of modern Greece. See table at **currency** 2. MONEY COIN WORTH ONE DRACHMA a coin worth one drachma 3. MONEY ANCIENT GREEK SILVER COIN a silver coin used in ancient Greece 4. MEASURE ANCIENT GREEK UNIT OF WEIGHT a unit of weight in ancient Greece [Early 16thC. Via Latin from Greek *drakhmē* (see DRACHM).]

Draco /dráykō/ *n.* an extensive but faint constellation of the northern hemisphere between Ursa Major and Hercules. It stretches part of the way around the celestial pole.

draco lizard *n.* = **flying lizard**

dracone /drá kōn/ *n.* a large flexible container for transporting liquids by towing them on the surface of the sea

Draconian /drə kṓni ən/, **draconian, Draconic** /-kónnik/, **draconic** *adj.* **1. TOO HARSH** unjustly harsh or severe **2. OF DRACO** relating to the Athenian statesman Draco of the 7th century BC, or to his wide-ranging and harsh code of laws [Late 19thC. From the Greek stem *Drakōn*- 'Draco'.] —**Draconianism** *n.* —**Draconically** *adv.*

draconic /drə kónnik/ *adj.* relating to or like a dragon or dragons —**draconically** *adv.*

draff /draf/ *n.* a residue left in brewing after the grain has been fermented, used as food for cattle [13thC. Origin uncertain.] —**draffy** *adj.*

draft /draaft/ *n.* **1. PRELIMINARY VERSION** a preliminary version of a piece of writing such as a speech, essay, or report **2. PRELIMINARY SKETCH** a preliminary sketch or plan **3.** *US* MIL = **call-up 4. LEVELLING LINE ON STONE** a line chiselled on the surface of a building stone as guide to laying it level ■ *n., adj.* US = **draught** ■ *vt.* **(drafts, drafting, drafted) 1. WRITE PRELIMINARY VERSION OF STH** to write a preliminary version of sth such as a speech or report **2. MAKE PLAN** to make a preliminary plan or sketch of sth, before all the required information is to hand **3. TRANSFER SB SOMEWHERE FOR DUTY** to move or send sb somewhere to carry out a particular task or general work and duties **4.** *US* = **call up 5.** *ANZ* **SORT LIVESTOCK INTO SMALLER GROUPS** to divide or sort livestock into smaller groups according to age, sex, or a particular characteristic [Mid-16thC. Form of DRAUGHT.] —**drafter** *n.*

draftee /draaf tée/ *n. US* sb who has been drafted for military service

draftsman *n.* US = **draughtsman**

draftsperson *n.* US = **draughtsperson**

draftswoman *n.* US = **draughtswoman**

drafty *adj.* US = **draughty**

drag /drag/ *v.* **(drags, dragging, dragged) 1.** *vt.* **PULL STH ALONG WITH EFFORT** to move sth, especially sth that is too large, heavy, or cumbersome to carry, by pulling it along the ground or across a surface **2.** *vt.* **PULL BY FORCE** to move or remove sb or sth that resists, usually by pulling at the person or object with considerable force or violence ○ *They dragged the fallen tree out of the road.* **3.** *vt.* **PERSUADE SB TO COME AWAY** to cause, persuade, or force sb to stop doing sth or to leave a place unwillingly ○ *I'm sorry to drag you away from your work.* **4.** *vti.* **TRAIL STH ALONG THE GROUND** to be in continuous contact with the ground while moving across it, or allow sth such as the foot or the bottom of a garment to do this ○ *He dragged his feet as he walked.* **5.** *vti.* **MOVE** to move, or move yourself or your feet, slowly and with difficulty or great reluctance ○ *I was so tired that I could scarcely drag myself up the stairs.* **6.** *vi.* **PASS OR PROCEED SLOWLY** to pass or proceed at a very slow and boring pace ○ *The afternoon was beginning to drag.* **7.** *vt.* COMPUT **MOVE ICON WITH MOUSE** to move an icon or other selected item on a computer screen by clicking on it with the mouse and pulling it to a new location **8.** *vt.* **SEARCH** to search a river bed, pond, or other area of water using a net or hook in an attempt to find sth that or sb who is missing **9.** *vi.* **PUFF ON SMOKING MATERIAL** to put a cigarette, pipe, or cigar to the mouth and suck in the smoke (*informal*) ■ *n.* **1. HINDRANCE** sb who or sth that slows down movement in any direction or progress in a particular area or activity ○ *These measures have been a drag on our economy.* **2.** AEROSP, PHYS **RESISTANCE TO MOTION** the resistance experienced by a body moving through a fluid medium, especially by an aircraft when travelling through the air. Symbol **D 3. SB OR STH BORING** a person, task, duty, or event that is held to be extremely boring and irritating (*informal*) ○ *It was such a drag having to take our heavy coats and hats with us.* **4. SLOW AND LABORIOUS MOVEMENT OR ACTION** an action or movement carried out slowly and with great effort or difficulty **5. DRAGGING MOVEMENT** a sound, movement, or act of dragging **6. CLOTHING OF OPPOSITE SEX** clothing characteristic of one sex worn by a member of the other, especially women's clothing when worn by men (*slang*) **7. PUFF** a puff on a cigarette, pipe, or cigar (*informal*) **8. LINE USED FOR DRAGGING RIVER** a line, chain, or hook that is used for searching or dredging the bottom of an area of water such as a river or pond **9.** TRANSP **MACHINE OR VEHICLE THAT IS DRAGGED** a vehicle such as a cart, sledge, or other vehicle that is pulled along the surface of the ground **10.** TRANSP **BRAKING DEVICE** a braking device, especially a horseshoe-shaped piece of metal fitted on the underside of the wheel of a horse-drawn vehicle **11.** HUNT **FOX SCENT** the scent left by a fox or other animal that is hunted by dogs **12.** HUNT **ARTIFICIAL SCENT** an artificial scent put on the ground for hunting dogs to follow **13.** HUNT = **drag hunt 14.** MOTOR SPORTS = **drag race 15.** TRANSP **HORSE-DRAWN COACH** a large coach, similar to a stagecoach but privately owned, with seats inside and on top and usually drawn by four horses [14thC. From either Old English *dragan*, an earlier form of DRAW, or Old Norse *draga*, both from a common prehistoric Germanic ancestor.] ◇ **drag your feet** *or* **heels** to be slow to act, usually because you would prefer to avoid doing anything if possible ○ *The Administration has been dragging its feet on the new budget proposals.*

WORD KEY: SYNONYMS

See Synonyms at *pull*.

drag down *vt.* **1. BRING TO LOWER LEVEL** to reduce sb or sth to a lower level or an inferior status by force or pressure of some kind ○ *Don't allow yourself to be dragged down by a timid banker.* **2. MAKE SB LISTLESS OR TIRED** to make sb feel listless, uninterested, or physically weak and tired ○ *Sitting at home all week really dragged me down.*

drag in *vt.* to involve sb or sth in sth when it is not necessary or appropriate to do so, especially to insist on mentioning sth that is not relevant in a conversation ○ *Mention music and he's bound to drag in a reference to the song he's just written.*

drag into *vt.* to involve sb in sth dishonest, disreputable, or otherwise undesirable ○ *What are you trying to drag me into?* ○ *They were dragged into the scandal.*

drag on *vi.* to continue for a very long time, especially past the expected or desired finishing time

drag out *vt.* to make sth last longer than is necessary or desirable

drag out of *vt.* to force sb to reveal or admit sth ○ *Are you going to tell me, or do I have to drag it out of you?*

drag up *vt.* **1. BRING UP THE PAST** to mention sth that sb does not want to be discussed or known because it is unpleasant, upsetting, or embarrassing, especially sth from that person's past **2. REAR WITHOUT MANNERS OR DISCIPLINE** to bring sb up in a lazy or undisciplined way (*informal humorous; usually passive*) ○ *Where were you dragged up?*

drag and drop *vt.* COMPUT to perform tasks on a computer by clicking onto items, moving them across the screen with the mouse, and releasing them on a particular icon

dragée /dra zháy/ *n.* **1. HARD-COATED SWEET** a sweet consisting of a nut, piece of fruit, or other centre covered in a hard sugar coating **2. TINY CONFECTIONERY BALL** a tiny silver-coated ball used for decorating cakes **3. SWEETENED PILL** a medicinal pill covered with a sugar coating to make it taste better [Late 17thC. From French, from Old French *dragie* (see DREDGE).]

draggle /drágg'l/ **(-gles, -gling, -gled)** *v.* **1.** *vti.* **MAKE OR BECOME WET AND DIRTY** to make sth wet and dirty by trailing it along the ground, or become wet and dirty by being trailed along the ground **2.** *vi.* **TRAIL ALONG BEHIND SB** to follow along behind sb else in a slow and usually undisciplined or slovenly fashion [Early 16thC. Origin uncertain: probably literally 'to drag repeatedly', formed from DRAG.]

draggy /drág gi/ **(-gier, -giest)** *adj.* (*informal*) **1. SLUGGISH** slow-moving ○ *a draggy musical* **2. TIRESOME** boring or otherwise annoying ○ *spent a draggy afternoon weeding the garden*

draghound /drág hownd/ *n.* a hound used in a drag hunt to follow an artificial scent trail

drag hunt *n.* a hunt in which a pack of hounds follows an artificial scent trail

drag-hunt (drag-hunts, drag-hunting, drag-hunted) *vti.* to hunt prey with a pack of hounds that follow an artificial scent trail

draglift /drág lift/ *n.* a ski lift with metal bars or ropes that people hold onto as they are pulled up to the top of a slope on their skis

dragline /drág līn/ *n.* **1. EXCAVATOR** an excavating machine with a digging bucket attached by cables to a long jib and operated by being dragged back towards the machine by another cable **2. LINE USED FOR DRAGGING** a line that is used for dragging, e.g. when hauling a load or dragging a river or pond

drag link *n.* a link that conveys motion from one point to another. In motor vehicles, it is used to connect the steering gear to the steering arm.

dragnet /drág net/ *n.* **1.** ANGLING **WEIGHTED NET** a net with weights on it used when trawling for fish at sea or when searching for sth at the bottom of a river or pond **2.** HUNT **GAME NET** a net that is drawn across the ground and used to trap small game **3.** CRIMINOL **POLICE HUNT FOR A CRIMINAL** a systematic and coordinated search for a wanted person made by police

dragoman /drággəmən/ (*plural* **-mans** *or* **-men** /-mən/) *n.* a guide or interpreter in certain Arabic-, Turkish-, or Persian-speaking countries (*archaic*) [16thC. Via French, Italian, and medieval Greek, from Arabic *targumān*, from Aramaic *tūrgemānā*, from Akkadian *targumānu* 'interpreter'.]

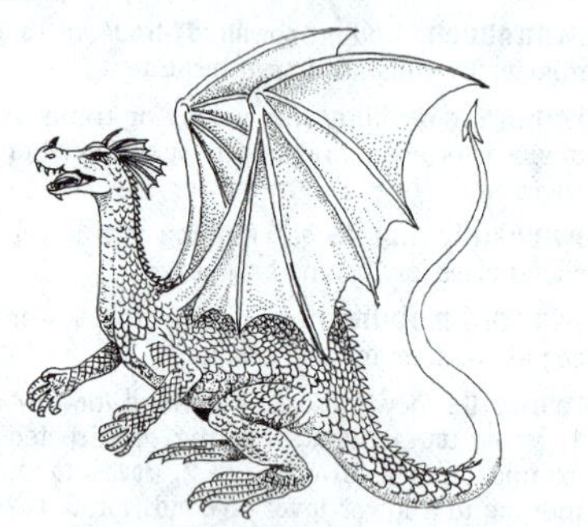

Dragon

dragon /drággən/ *n.* **1.** MYTHOL **SCALY GREEN MONSTER** a large and usually ferocious fire-breathing creature in myths, legends, and fairy tales that has green scaly skin, a long tail, and wings **2.** ZOOL **LARGE LIZARD** a large lizard, e.g. the Komodo dragon **3. INSULT FOR FORMIDABLE WOMAN** a woman who is regarded as fierce and formidable (*insult*) [13thC. Via Old French from Latin *draco*, from Greek *drákōn* 'snake', literally 'one with a deadly glance'. Ultimately from an Indo-European word meaning 'to look'.] ◇ **chase the dragon** to take heroin by heating it and breathing in the fumes (*slang*)

Dragon *n.* = **Draco**

dragon arum *n.* = **dragonroot** *n.* 1

dragon boat *n.* a long narrow boat decorated like a dragon, used especially by Chinese people when taking part in the boat races held during a particular festival. The festival is held every 5th May of the lunar year.

dragonet /drággənit/ (*plural* **-ets** *or* **-et**) *n.* a small brightly coloured spiny marine fish belonging to a family with flat heads, narrow bodies, and large pectoral fins, living near the bottom of warm shallow waters. Family: Callionymidae. [14thC. Formed from DRAGON.]

dragonfly /drággən flī/ (*plural* **-flies**) *n.* an insect with a large head and eyes, a long thin body, and two pairs of iridescent often blue wings that usually remain outstretched when the insect is at rest. Suborder: Anisoptera.

dragonroot /drággən root/ (*plural* **-roots** *or* **-root**) *n.* **1. LARGE FOUL-SMELLING ARUM** a tuberous, foul-smelling, and poisonous perennial plant belonging to the arum family. Latin name: *Dracunculus vulgaris*. **2.** = **green dragon**

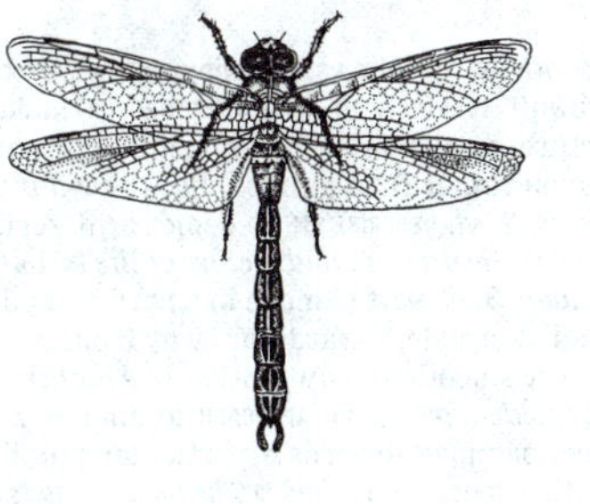

Dragonfly

dragon's blood *n.* a red resinous substance used to colour varnishes and lacquers. It comes from the fruit of various trees including the dragon tree.

dragon's teeth *npl.* rows of short wedge-shaped concrete posts fixed in the ground as an anti-tank barrier, especially in World War II (*slang*) ◇ **sow dragon's teeth** to take action that is, either deliberately or accidentally, the cause of future quarrelling and conflict (*literary*) ○ *a troublemaker known for her ability to sow dragon's teeth within the department*

dragon tree *n.* an evergreen tree native to the Canary Islands with a trunk that grows very thick clusters of spiky leaves and orange fruit. Its resin is a source of dragon's blood. Latin name: *Dracaena draco.*

dragoon /drə go͞on/ *n.* **1.** MOUNTED INFANTRYMAN in European armies of the 17th and 18th centuries, a mounted infantryman armed with a carbine **2.** CAVALRYMAN in armies of the late 18th and 19th centuries, a cavalryman, especially a heavily armed cavalryman. The word is retained in the names of some modern regiments that were originally cavalry regiments. ■ *vt.* **(-goons, -gooning, -gooned) 1.** FORCE SB to involve sb in an activity, or force sb to do sth, against his or her will ○ *He was dragooned into joining the chorus for the show.* **2.** SUBJUGATE SB to persecute or subjugate sb using military troops [Early 17thC. From French *dragon* 'carbine or musket', literally 'dragon' because the soldier carried a carbine or musket that 'breathed fire' like a dragon.]

drag queen *n.* a man who dresses as a woman, especially a performer who dresses in a flamboyant women's costume and traditionally affects feminine mannerisms for comic effect (*slang*)

drag race *n.* a race between cars with specially modified bodies and engines on a straight track over a distance of a quarter of a mile to discover which has the fastest acceleration —**drag racer** *n.* —**drag racing** *n.*

dragster /drágstər/ *n.* **1.** DRAG-RACING CAR a car that is specially designed for and used in drag racing **2.** DRIVER OF DRAG-RACING CAR a driver who takes part in a drag race

drag strip *n.* a short straight track, usually a quarter of a mile in length, used for drag racing

drain /drayn/ *n.* **1.** SEWAGE PIPE a pipe or channel that carries water or sewage away from a place **2.** STH THAT USES UP RESOURCES sth that diminishes or uses up resources or energy ○ *a serious drain on our financial resources* **3.** PROCESS OF LOSS OR DIMINISHING the gradual loss, withdrawal, or diminishing of sth regarded as an important resource ○ *the drain of trained personnel from the industry* **4.** MED DEVICE TO REMOVE FLUID FROM WOUND a tube or other device placed in a wound or incision to draw off fluids such as blood, pus, or water **5.** AGRIC ARTIFICIAL WATERWAY an artificial waterway that allows for land drainage ■ *v.* **(drains, draining, drained) 1.** *vti.* FLOW OR ALLOW TO FLOW OUT to flow out of sth, often leaving it empty or dry, or allow a liquid to do this **2.** *vti.* EMPTY OR DRY to empty or dry sth by allowing the water to flow out of or off it, or become empty or dry in this way ○ *The water drained slowly from the bath.* **3.** *vt.* AGRIC DRY OUT LAND to make marshy land drier by laying pipes, digging ditches or channels, or by any other means that removes the excess water **4.** *vt.* GEOG CHANNEL WATER AWAY FROM to be a channel for leading water off land ○ *The river Loire drains most of central France.* **5.** *vi.* GEOG DISCHARGE INTO STH to discharge water from its surface or channel into a river or lake (*refers to a geographical area or a smaller watercourse*) **6.** *vt.* DRINK STH UP to empty a cup, glass, or other container by drinking all its contents ○ *He drained his tea in one gulp and left.* **7.** *vt.* USE STH UP to use up or deplete sth gradually, especially sb's energy and resources, by making constant demands on it ○ *These payments are draining the country dry.* **8.** *vi.* WANE to disappear gradually, or become less strong or intense ○ *The colour drained from her cheeks.* **9.** *vt.* EXHAUST SB to leave sb feeling physically or emotionally exhausted ○ *It drains me to care for six active youngsters five days a week.* [Old English *drēahnian* 'to strain', literally 'to dry out', from a prehistoric Germanic word that is also the ancestor of English *drought* and *dry*] —**drainable** *adj.* ◇ **down the drain 1.** wasted or squandered with no hope of retrieval (*informal*) **2.** towards or in a state of total failure or ruin, especially financial failure (*informal*)

drainage /dráynij/ *n.* **1.** DRAINING PROCESS the process of draining liquid from sth **2.** SEWAGE SYSTEM a system of pipes or channels that carries water or sewage away from a place **3.** MED FLUID REMOVAL FROM BODY the removal of fluid such as water, blood, or pus from a wound or part of the body, usually by means of a tube **4.** FLUID REMOVED BY DRAINING water, sewage, or any other fluid removed by draining

drainage basin, drainage area *n.* = **catchment area**

drainage well *n.* a shaft sunk in waterlogged land, designed to draw water away from the surface soil layers

drainboard /dráyn bawrd/ *n. US* = **draining board**

drainer /dráynər/ *n.* a rack or container in which things are put so that liquid can drain off them

draining board *n.* a slightly sloping metal, wooden, or plastic surface next to a sink, with shallow grooves on it to allow water to drain off drying dishes into the sink. US term **drainboard**

drainpipe /dráyn pīp/ *n.* PIPE FOR RAINWATER a pipe that carries off rainwater, waste water, or sewage to or through the drains, especially a downpipe attached to the side of a house ■ **drainpipes, drainpipe trousers** *npl.* NARROW TROUSERS trousers with very narrow legs that were particularly popular in the 1950s, and again in the 1970s and 1980s in punk fashion

drain rod *n.* a flexible rod that can be attached end to end to a number of other similar rods and pushed up and down drainpipes to clear blockages

drake /drayk/ *n.* a male duck [13thC. Origin uncertain: probably ultimately from prehistoric Germanic.]

Drake /drayk/, **Sir Francis** (1540?–96) English navigator and admiral. He was the first Englishman to circumnavigate the globe, and he later helped to defeat the Spanish Armada (1588).

Drakensberg /draákənz burg/ mountain range extending through southeastern South Africa and Lesotho. The highest peaks, including Thabana-Ntlenya, 3,482 m/11,424 ft, are located around Lesotho's border with Kwazulu-Natal.

Drake Passage stretch of water in the Southern Ocean and the South Pacific Ocean, between South America and the Antarctic Peninsula. Length: 800 km/500 mi.

dram[1] /dram/ *n.* **1.** MEASURE UNIT OF WEIGHT a unit of mass in the avoirdupois system equal to 1/16 of an ounce (or approximately 1.77 grams) **2.** BEVERAGES SMALL ALCOHOLIC DRINK a small amount of an alcoholic drink, particularly whisky or brandy ○ *How about a wee dram before you go?* [15thC. Via Old French *drame* or medieval Latin *drama* from Greek *drakhmē* 'handful'.]

dram[2] *abbr.* dramatic

DRAM /dram/ *abbr.* dynamic random access memory

drama /draámə/ *n.* **1.** THEATRE PERFORMED PLAY a serious play written for performance on stage, television, or radio **2.** ARTS PLAYS AS GENRE works written for performance on the stage, radio, or television considered as a literary genre ○ *17th-century French drama* **3.** THEATRE PRODUCING OR PERFORMING PLAYS the performance, production, or writing of plays considered as a job, activity, or subject to be studied **4.** EXCITING EVENT a real-life event or situation that is particularly exciting or emotionally involving **5.** DRAMATIC EVENTS OR QUALITY exciting, tense, and gripping events and actions, or an exciting, tense, and gripping quality, either in a work of art or in a real-life situation ○ *an evening full of drama* [Early 16thC. Via late Latin from Greek, 'play, deed', from *dran* 'to do' (source of English *drastic*).]

drama college *n.* = **drama school**

drama documentary (*plural* **drama documentaries**) *n.* a documentary work, usually on television or radio, in which real events are re-enacted by actors, or in which real events and characters are mingled with fictional ones

drama queen *n.* sb who enjoys making the most out of any potentially dramatic situation, acting in an emotional and melodramatic way (*informal*)

drama school *n.* a college of higher education specifically devoted to the practical and theoretical study of acting, stage management, and direction, mainly for the theatre, but also for films and broadcasting

drama therapy *n.* a form of therapy that encourages people to use acting, role-playing, and improvisation to deal with psychological and emotional problems

dramatic /drə máttik/ *adj.* **1.** THEATRE FOR THE THEATRE written for the theatre, or relating to the theatre, plays, or acting **2.** EXCITING AND INTENSE characterized, in real life or in art, by the kind of intense and gripping excitement, startling suddenness, or larger-than-life impressiveness associated with drama and the theatre ○ *the dramatic sequence of events leading to his escape* **3.** SUDDEN AND MARKED large in degree or scale, and often occurring with surprising suddenness ○ *a dramatic jump in prices* **4.** STRIKING bold, vivid, or strikingly impressive in appearance, colour, or effect ○ *a dramatic view of the Alps* **5.** MUSIC HAVING POWERFUL EXPRESSIVE VOICE having a powerful singing voice especially suited to the expression of intense emotion, e.g. in tragic or villainous roles in opera [Late 16thC. Via Late Latin *dramaticus* from Greek *drāmatikos*, from *drama* (see DRAMA).]

dramatically /drə máttikli/ *adv.* **1.** IN A STARTLING AND ATTENTION-GRABBING WAY in a way that grabs the attention and causes an excited, shocked, or startled reaction **2.** MARKEDLY to a very noticeable degree and often with surprising suddenness ○ *Things have improved dramatically since your last visit.*

dramatic irony *n.* a situation, or the irony arising from a situation, in which the audience has a fuller knowledge of what is happening in a drama than a character does

dramatic monologue *n.* a poem or other literary work consisting of words supposedly spoken by a character, often in a specific situation, either directly to the reader or to a listener. Among the best-known dramatic monologues in English literature are those of Robert Browning, e.g. 'My Last Duchess' and 'Porphyria's Lover'.

dramatics /drə máttiks/ *n.* PRODUCTION OF PLAYS the performance and production of plays for the theatre, especially in a nonprofessional context (*takes a singular or plural verb*) ■ *npl.* MELODRAMATIC BEHAVIOUR theatrical and exaggerated behaviour (*takes a plural verb*) ○ *Spare us the dramatics, for goodness sake, and tell us what happened!*

dramatise *vt.* = **dramatize**

dramatis personae /draámətiss pər sṓ nī/ *n.* LIST OF CHARACTERS a list of the names of the characters that appear in a play, usually printed at the beginning of the text of a play or, sometimes, in a theatre programme ■ *npl.* CHARACTERS IN A DRAMA the characters who appear in a drama, or the people involved in a situation (*formal*) [From Latin, 'persons of the drama']

dramatist /drámmətist/ *n.* sb who writes plays for the stage, television, or radio

dramatization /drámmə tī záysh'n/, **dramatisation** *n.* **1.** THEATRE PLAY ADAPTED FROM FICTION an adaptation of a work of fiction or a presentation of a real event that is intended for performance on the stage, television, or radio **2.** THEATRE PROCESS OF ADAPTING the act, art, or process of turning a literary work or a real event into a drama for performance on the stage, television, or radio **3.** EXAGGERATION the act of making sth appear more dramatic or of exaggerating its importance

dramatize /drámmə tīz/ (**-tizes, -tizing, -tized**), **dramatise** (**-tises, -tising, -tised**) *v.* **1.** *vt.* THEATRE ADAPT STH FOR STAGE to turn a literary work or a real event into a drama for presentation on the stage, television, or radio **2.** *vti.* EXAGGERATE to make sth more dramatic, especially to exaggerate the importance or seriousness of a situation in an attention-seeking and theatrical way —**dramatizable** *adj.* —**dramatizer** *n.*

dramaturge /drámmə turj/ *n.* **1. dramaturge, dramaturgist** PLAYWRIGHT a playwright, particularly one who works with a specific theatre or company **2. dramaturge, dramaturg** LITERARY ADVISOR IN THEATRE a member of the staff of a theatre with mainly literary responsibilities such as choosing the plays for performance, editing and adapting texts where necessary, and writing programme notes [Mid-19thC. Via French from, ultimately, Greek *dramatourgos*, literally 'worker in drama', from *drama* (see DRAMA).]

dramaturgy /drámmə turji/ *n.* the art of the theatre, especially with regard to the techniques involved in writing plays —**dramaturgic** /drámmə túrjik/ *adj.* —**dramaturgical** /-túrjik'l/ *adj.* —**dramaturgically** /-túrjikli/ *adv.*

Drambuie /dram bóo i/ *tdmk.* a trademark for a sweet whisky-based liqueur made in Scotland

Drammen /drámmən/ city and seaport in southern Norway. It is situated about 48 km/30 mi. southwest of Oslo. Population: 52,143 (1993).

drank past tense of **drink**

drape /drayp/ *v.* (**drapes, draping, draped**) **1.** *vt.* PLACE FABRIC OVER STH to hang or place a piece of fabric over sth so that it falls in folds around it or covers it ○ *draped a scarf over her shoulders* **2.** *vt.* COVER OVER WITH FABRIC to cover sth over with a piece of fabric, usually so that the fabric hangs down around it in folds ○ *a chair draped in a dust sheet* **3.** *vi.* HANG IN FOLDS to hang or be able to hang in loose folds on or over sth ○ *a heavy fabric that will drape well* **4.** *vt.* LAY STH CASUALLY to place part of the body on or over sth, e.g. the back of a chair, in a relaxed and casual way ○ *She draped herself elegantly over the sofa.* ■ *n.* **1.** *US* = **curtain 2.** PIECE OF DRAPING FABRIC a piece of fabric used to drape over sth **3.** WAY FABRIC HANGS the way in which fabric hangs and forms folds, especially when made into a garment ○ *adjusting the drape of the dress* [15thC. From Old French *draper*, from *drap* 'cloth', from late Latin *drappus*, from, ultimately, a Celtic word (source of English *drab* and *trappings*).]

draper /dráypər/ *n.* sb who sells fabric and sewing materials in a shop (*dated*) [14thC. From Old French *drapier*, from *drap* (see DRAPE).]

Draper /dráypər/ city in northern Utah on the the Jordan River. It is a southern suburb of Salt Lake City. Population: 12,478 (1996).

drapery /dráypəri/ (*plural* **-ies**) *n.* **1.** CLOTH ARRANGED TO HANG IN FOLDS cloth or clothing that has been arranged to hang in elegant or decorative folds **2.** PIECE OF ELEGANTLY HANGING FABRIC a piece of fabric used as a decorative cover or garment and usually hanging in loose elegant folds **3.** *US* = **curtain 4.** FABRICS AND SEWING MATERIALS fabrics and sewing materials collectively, especially as goods sold in a shop ○ *the drapery department.* US term **dry goods 5.** DRAPER'S OCCUPATION the occupation of selling fabrics and sewing materials (*dated*) [14thC. From Old French *draperie*, from *drap* (see DRAPE).]

drastic /drástik/ *adj.* **1.** POWERFUL IN EFFECT having a powerful effect or far-reaching consequences ○ *a crisis calling for drastic remedies* **2.** VERY MARKED very noticeable, significant, and usually worrying because of its amount or degree [Late 17thC. From Greek *drastikos* 'effective, active', from *dran* 'to do' (source of English *drama*).]

drastically /drástikli/ *adv.* to a very great and usually very worrying degree

drat /drat/ *interj.* used to express annoyance or frustration (*informal*) [Early 19thC. Alteration of *od rot*, a shortening of *God rot*.]

dratted /dráttid/ *adj.* used to express annoyance or frustration with sth or sb (*informal*) ○ *Where is that dratted pen?*

draught /draaft/ *n.* **1.** CURRENT OF COLD AIR a current of uncomfortably cold air penetrating a room or other space **2.** CURRENT OF AIR IN ENCLOSED SPACE a current of air, especially one that is moving through an enclosed space such as a chimney or tunnel **3.** ENG REGULATING DEVICE a valve that regulates the flow of air to or from a pipe, e.g. a chimney **4.** PULLING ALONG OR DRAWING IN the act of pulling sth along, of drawing sth in, or of breathing or drinking sth **5.** MOUTHFUL OF AIR, LIQUID, OR SMOKE the amount of air, liquid, or smoke taken in in a single breath or swallow **6.** MED DOSE OF LIQUID MEDICINE a dose of medicine in liquid form (*dated*) **7.** BEVERAGES BEER IN BARRELS beer that is stored in and served from barrels or casks rather than bottles **8.** QUANTITY OF FISH FOUND IN NET the amount of fish found in a net when it is hauled in **9.** BOARD GAMES DRAUGHT PIECE any one of the 24 pieces used in a game of draughts. US term **checker 10.** SAILING DEPTH NEEDED BY SHIP TO FLOAT the distance between the waterline of a ship and the lowest part of its hull, which is the minimum depth of water it requires in order to float ■ *adj.* **1.** BEVERAGES SERVED FROM BARREL stored in and served from a barrel rather than a bottle **2.** AGRIC PULLING HEAVY LOADS used to pull heavy loads ○ *a draught animal* [12thC. From Old Norse *dráttr*, of prehistoric Germanic origin (related to English *draw*.)] —**draughter** *n.* ◇ **feel the draught** to be exposed to dangers or difficulties, especially through a shortage of money (*informal*) ◇ **on draught** available for serving from the barrel

draughtboard /dráaft bawrd/ *n.* a game board with eight rows of eight alternate black and white squares on it, used for playing draughts or chess. US term **checkerboard**

draughts /draafts/ *n.* a game that is played with 12 black and 12 white pieces on a chequered board. Pieces can only move diagonally, and are taken when enemy pieces 'jump' over them. US term **checkers** [12thC. From DRAUGHT in the obsolete sense 'act of drawing a piece across the board in chess and similar games'.]

draughtsman /dráaftsmən/ (*plural* **-men** /-mən/) *n.* **1.** TECHNICAL DESIGNER a man who makes detailed plans or drawings for buildings, ships, aircraft, or machines before they are built. This job is now done mainly by computer-aided design. **2.** MAN WHO DRAWS WELL a man who draws well or is considered from the point of view of his skill at drawing ○ *He's an excellent draughtsman.*

draughtsmanship /dráaftsmən ship/ *n.* skill in drawing or drafting shown by a person or in a piece of work

draughtsperson /dráafts purss'n/ *n.* sb who makes detailed drawings for buildings, ships, aircraft, or machines before they are built. This job is now done mainly by computer-aided design.

draughtswoman /dráafts wòomən/ (*plural* **-en** /-wimmin/) *n.* **1.** TECHNICAL DESIGNER a woman who makes detailed plans or drawings for buildings, ships, aircraft, or machines before they are built. This job is now done mainly by computer-aided design. **2.** WOMAN WHO DRAWS WELL a woman who draws well, or a woman considered from the point of view of her skill at drawing

draughty /dráafti/ (**draughtier, draughtiest**) *adj.* chilly and uncomfortable because of flowing currents of cold air —**draughtily** *adv.* —**draughtiness** *n.*

Drava /dráavə/ tributary of the River Danube, south-central Europe. It rises in the Carnic Alps, Italy, flows through Austria and Slovenia, and then forms part of Croatia's frontier with Hungary. Length: 719 km/447 mi. German **Drau**

Dravidian /drə víddi ən/ *n.* **1.** LANG FAMILY OF INDIAN LANGUAGES a family of over twenty languages spoken in southern India and northeastern Sri Lanka, including Tamil, Telugu, Kannada, and Malayalam. Over 200 million people speak a Dravidian language. **2.** PEOPLES MEMBER OF ABORIGINAL INDIAN PEOPLE a member of an ancient people who were the aboriginal inhabitants of India and who moved southwards during the influx of Indo-European peoples from the North [Mid-19thC. From Sanskrit *drāvida* 'relating to the Tamils', from *Dravida* 'Tamil'.] —**Dravidian** *adj.*

draw /draw/ *v.* (**draws, drawing, drew** /droo/, **drawn** /drawn/) **1.** *vti.* ARTS MAKE A PICTURE to make a line, picture, or plan on a surface using a pencil, pen, or crayon rather than paints ○ *She drew a picture of a flower.* **2.** *vt.* DESCRIBE STH to depict or describe sth in words ○ *He drew a vivid picture of life in 18th-century London.* **3.** *vi.* MOVE to move in a particular direction, often alongside, towards, or away from sth else, and with a smooth steady motion ○ *Another car drew alongside ours.* **4.** *vi.* APPROACH to approach through time, or move towards a particular point or stage in sth, especially its end ○ *The meeting was drawing to a close.* **5.** *vt.* PULL SB OR STH TOWARDS OR AWAY to pull sth or lead or pull sb in a particular direction, especially towards or away from sth ○ *She drew him towards the door.* **6.** *vt.* TRANSP PULL A VEHICLE to pull a vehicle along ○ *a carriage drawn by six white horses* **7.** *vt.* OPEN OR CLOSE A CURTAIN to pull a curtain or blind across a window so that it covers or uncovers it **8.** *vt.* PULL ON A STRING, ROPE, OR CORD to pull on a string, rope, or cord, usually in order to tighten it around sth **9.** *vt.* ARCHERY PULL BACK THE STRING OF A BOW to pull back the string of a bow prior to shooting an arrow **10.** *vt.* TAKE STH OUT to take or pull an object out of sth in which it has been enclosed or embedded ○ *He drew his hand from his pocket.* **11.** *vti.* PULL WEAPON FROM HOLSTER OR SHEATH to pull a weapon from a holster or sheath in order to use it **12.** *vt.* REMOVE LIQUID to remove liquid from a large container such as a barrel by means of a tap **13.** *vt.* MED DRAIN A WOUND to drain a liquid such as blood, pus, or water from a wound or incision **14.** *vt.* HAUL UP WATER to haul up water from a well or other source using a bucket on a rope **15.** *vt.* ELICIT A RESPONSE to cause sb or sth to make a particular type of response or sound ○ *The speech had drawn hoots of derision from the crowd.* **16.** *vt.* OBTAIN STH FROM SOURCE to obtain a physical or a moral resource from a particular place or thing ○ *They drew courage from our example.* **17.** *vt.* OBTAIN INFORMATION FROM SB to obtain information, a secret, or an opinion from sb by questioning or persuasion (*often passive*) ○ *She refused to be drawn on the subject.* **18.** *vt.* CAUSE TO BE DIRECTED TOWARDS STH to cause sb's attention, eye, or interest to be directed towards sb or sth **19.** *vt.* ATTRACT PEOPLE to attract sb or arouse people's interest or curiosity so that they come to see sth or sb ○ *The performance had drawn a huge crowd of onlookers.* **20.** *vt.* SUCK STH IN to suck sth in, especially air into the lungs ○ *I drew a long breath.* **21.** *vi.* ALLOW A CURRENT OF AIR THROUGH to allow a current of air to flow through, removing smoke or gases **22.** *vt.* FIN WITHDRAW MONEY to take money out of a bank or savings account, or a similar source ○ *You can draw up to £200 a day with this card.* **23.** *vt.* FIN RECEIVE MONEY to receive money regularly from a particular source **24.** *vt.* FIN WRITE A CHEQUE to write a cheque, bill of exchange, or promissory note on an account so that sb can receive money from that account **25.** *vt.* LAW WRITE OUT A LEGAL DOCUMENT to compose or write out a legal document in the proper form **26.** *vt.* ARRIVE AT A CONCLUSION OR INFERENCE to arrive at a particular conclusion or inference by examining the evidence for sth ○ *You'll have to draw your own conclusions.* **27.** *vt.* FORMULATE STH to formulate or state a distinction, comparison, or parallel between two or more different things ○ *There are certain parallels that may be drawn between the two cases.* **28.** *vt.* CHOOSE STH AT RANDOM to choose or be given sth at random, usually in order to ensure that all participants are treated fairly ○ *They drew lots to see who would have to go.* **29.** *vt.* CARDS TAKE A CARD to take a card from a stack, the pack, or the dealer during a card game **30.** *vt.* CARDS MAKE PLAYERS PLAY PARTICULAR SUIT to make the other players in a card game play the cards they have in a particular suit by repeatedly leading that suit ○ *drew all the trumps early in the hand* **31.** *vti.* SPORTS FINISH EQUAL to finish a game with the scores for the opposing sides level or with neither side having won ○ *Finland and Holland drew 1–1 in the semifinal.* **32.** *vt.* SHIPPING NEED PARTICULAR DEPTH OF WATER to need a particular depth of water in which to float **33.** *vti.* COOK STEEP IN BOILING WATER to steep tea leaves, or allow tea leaves to steep, in boiling water ○ *Let the tea draw for five minutes.* **34.** *vt.* INDUST MAKE WIRE to make wire by pulling a

a at; aa father; aw all; ay day; air hair; ə about, edible, item, common, circus; e egg; ee eel; hw when; i it, happy; ī ice; 'l apple; 'm rhythm; 'n fashion; o odd; ō open; ŏŏ good; oo pool; ow owl; oy oil; th thin; th this; u up; ur urge;

length of metal through a conical hole **35.** *vt.* REMOVE INNARDS FROM CARCASS to remove the innards from a carcass before cooking it **36.** *vt.* DISEMBOWEL SB to disembowel a hanged person, especially in former times **37.** *vt.* CUE GAMES GIVE BACKSPIN TO A BALL to give a backward spin to a ball when making a stroke, especially in billiards **38.** *vt.* GOLF MAKE THE BALL CURVE to hit the ball so that it curves in flight following the direction of the golfer's swing (to the left for a right-handed player) instead of travelling straight **39.** *vt.* BOWLING SEND BOWL IN A CURVE in bowling, to make the bowl travel along a curved path to the point aimed at ■ *n.* **1.** ACT OF DRAWING the act of pulling or sucking on sth or otherwise drawing sth **2.** GAMBLING LOTTERY a lottery, raffle, or other competition where the winner is decided by selecting a ticket at random **3.** GAMBLING CHOOSING LOTTERY WINNER the choosing of a winner in a lottery, raffle, or other competition by selecting a ticket at random ○ *The draw will be held next Wednesday.* **4.** SPORTS SELECTION OF OPPONENTS the act of selecting at random in which contestants are to play each other in a sporting contest, or the resulting list of matches to be played ○ *the draw for the third round of the competition* **5.** CARDS, GAMBLING STH CHOSEN AT RANDOM sth chosen at random, e.g. a ticket in a lottery or a card or cards taken from a stack or the dealer **6.** ATTRACTION sth or sb that interests a lot of people and attracts them as spectators, visitors, or customers ○ *The rock band will be a huge draw for the local fair.* **7.** SPORTS CONTEST THAT NEITHER SIDE WINS a contest that ends with both sides having the same score or with neither side having won **8.** DRAWING A GUN the action of pulling a gun from its holster in order to fire it, especially in a gunfight **9.** CARDS SECOND OR FURTHER DEAL in draw poker, the deal made to improve the players' hands after they have discarded [Old English *dragan*, from a prehistoric Germanic word meaning 'to carry', which is also the ancestor of English *drag*] —**drawable** *adj.*

—— WORD KEY: SYNONYMS ——
See Synonyms at *pull*.

draw back *vi.* to decide not to continue with some contemplated, planned, or agreed action ○ *They drew back from the deal at the last moment.*
draw in *v.* **1.** *vi.* BEGIN EARLIER to begin earlier, causing it to become darker sooner (*refers to nights or evenings in autumn*) **2.** *vi.* BECOME SHORTER to become shorter, so that it gets dark sooner (*refers to days in autumn*) **3.** *vt.* INVOLVE SB to get sb involved in sth unwillingly (*often passive*) ○ *I got drawn in before I realized what the argument was really about.*
draw off *vt.* to remove a small amount of liquid from a larger amount by means of a tube or pipe
draw on *v.* **1.** *vt.* USE STH to make use of a resource of some kind for personal benefit ○ *The novel draws on her experiences in Alaska.* **2.** *vi.* ENTER A LATER STAGE to enter a later stage or move towards its end ○ *As the day drew on I grew worried that they would not come.* **3.** *vt.* TAKE IN SMOKE to inhale the smoke from a cigarette or pipe ○ *He drew on his pipe.*
draw out *v.* **1.** *vt.* PROLONG STH to make sth continue longer than is usual, necessary, or desirable ○ *I drew the conversation out as long as I could.* **2.** *vi.* GROW LONGER to have more hours of daylight (*refers to days*) **3.** *vt.* GET SB TO TALK to encourage a shy, hostile, or reserved person to talk at length or in detail, or to become more forthcoming in a social or legal situation ○ *The prosecutor took great pains to draw the hostile witness out during cross-examination.*
draw up *v.* **1.** *vt.* WRITE STH OUT to prepare or write out a plan, list, or other document ○ *The lawyers are drawing up the terms of the contract as we speak.* **2.** *vti.* COME TO A STOP to arrive at a particular point or place in a vehicle or on a horse and stop, or bring a vehicle or horse to a halt ○ *A car drew up outside.* **3.** *vt.* BRING STH NEARER to place a chair or seat near sth or sb and sit down on it **4.** *vr.* STRAIGHTEN STH to straighten the body in order to reach full height and look as imposing or dignified as possible ○ *She drew herself up to her full height, then spoke.*

drawback /dráw bak/ *n.* sth that causes problems or is a disadvantage or hindrance ○ *The only drawback is the size of the machine.*

drawbar /dráw baar/ *n.* a strong metal bar fitted across the back of a tractor, locomotive, or other vehicle,

with a coupling on it to which machinery or a trailer can be hitched

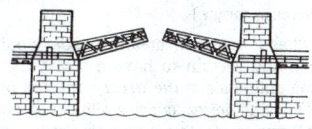

Drawbridge

drawbridge /dráw brij/ *n.* a bridge that is hinged at one end or in the middle and can be lifted up to cut off access to a place or allow sth to pass beneath it. Drawbridges are often built across water, either outside medieval castles that have a moat or along rivers or near harbours.
drawdown /dráw down/ *n.* a lowering of the level of the water in a reservoir
drawee /draw ée/ *n.* the person or organization from whose account money is taken when a cheque or other order for payment is drawn
drawer /drawr/ *n.* **1.** HOUSEHOLD PLACE TO STORE THINGS a storage compartment in a piece of furniture such as a desk, chest, or table that slides in and out and is usually shaped like a shallow rectangular box **2.** FIN SB WHO WRITES A CHEQUE sb who draws a cheque or money order **3.** SB OR STH THAT DRAWS sb or sth that draws, especially sb who draws pictures or plans **4.** SERVER IN AN INN sb who draws beer or serves customers in an inn (*archaic*)
drawers /drawrz/ *npl.* large old-fashioned underpants with short legs, worn by men or women (*dated*)
drawgate *n.* a barrier that can be raised or lowered to control the flow of water in a sluice
draw gear *n.* the couplings and other equipment used to couple railway carriages and trucks together
drawing /dráwing/ *n.* ARTS **1.** OUTLINE PICTURE a picture of sth made with a pencil, pen, or crayon, usually consisting of lines, often with shading, but generally without colour **2.** MAKING PICTURES the art, activity, or practice of making pictures using a pencil, crayon, or pen ○ *I never was very good at drawing.*
drawing board *n.* a large flat board used for drawing and design work, usually attached to a frame with legs and adjustable to different heights and angles ◇ **back to the drawing board** back to the beginning or the planning stage of a failed operation or project, ready to start all over again (*informal*) ○ *Since all else has failed, we're now back to the drawing board.*
drawing pin *n.* a short pin with a wide round top used for pinning paper or cardboard to a noticeboard, wall, or other surface. US term **thumbtack**
drawing room *n.* a large formal room in a house, in which guests are entertained [Mid-17thC. Shortening of *withdrawing-room*.]
drawknife /dráw nīf/ (*plural* **-knives** /-nīvz/) *n.* a tool for shaving the surface of wood, consisting of a narrow rectangular blade with a handle at either end fixed at right angles to it
drawl /drawl/ *vti.* (**drawls, drawling, drawled**) SPEAK SLOWLY to draw out the vowel sounds and pronounce words with a slow inflection when speaking ■ *n.* SLOW WAY OF SPEAKING a way of speaking in which the speaker draws out the vowel sounds and pronounces words slowly [Late 16thC. Origin uncertain: probably from Middle Dutch *dralen* 'to linger, delay', from *dragan* 'to draw'.] —**drawler** *n.* —**drawlingly** *adv.* —**drawly** *adj.*
drawn[1] /drawn/ *adj.* appearing tired and careworn, usually as a result of anxiety, grief, or illness ○ *He looked pale and drawn.*
drawn[2] past tense of **draw**
drawn butter *n.* melted butter that has had the solids

removed, served as a sauce, sometimes with herbs and seasoning

drawn-out *adj.* continuing longer than is intended or desired
drawn-thread work, **drawn work** *n.* a type of embroidery in which selected threads are pulled from the fabric and stitches are worked on the remaining threads to produce decorated open areas
drawplate /dráw playt/ *n.* a plate pierced by conical holes through which metal is drawn in wire-making
draw poker *n.* a form of poker in which each player is dealt five cards face down and after the first round of betting can draw replacements for any discards
drawshave /dráw shayv/ *n.* = **drawknife**
draw shot *n.* in cue games, a shot in which the cue ball is hit below centre so that the backspin makes it bounce back when it hits another ball
drawstring /dráw string/ *n.* a cord threaded through a hem, piping, or eyelets around the opening in a bag or a garment so that it can be drawn tight and the opening closed
drawtube /dráw tyoob/ *n.* a tube that slides inside another tube, e.g. one of the extending tubes in a telescope
dray /dray/ *n.* a large low horsedrawn cart with no fixed sides, designed for heavy loads, or a similar motorized vehicle, used especially by breweries [From Old English *dragan* 'to draw']
drayhorse /dráy hawrss/ *n.* a large horse used for pulling a dray
Drayton /dráyt'n/, **Michael** (1563–1631) English poet. His *England's Heroical Epistles* (1597) and *Polyolbion* (1612) sang the praises of England. His *Harmonie of the Church* (1591) offended the Archbishop of Canterbury, and was publicly burnt.
dread /dred/ *vti.* (**dreads, dreading, dreaded**) **1.** FEEL EXTREMELY FRIGHTENED to feel extremely frightened or worried about sth that may happen in the future **2.** BE RELUCTANT to be reluctant or frightened to do sth because it is unpleasant, upsetting, or annoying ■ *n.* **1.** TERROR a feeling of great fear or terror, especially at the thought of experiencing or encountering sth unpleasant **2.** SOURCE OF DREAD sth that is dreaded **3.** AWE a feeling of awe and reverence (*archaic*) ■ *adj.* (*literary*) **1.** FEARED causing fear and extreme anxiety ○ *The dread day arrived.* **2.** AWE-INSPIRING inspiring fear and respect or awe in equal measure [12thC. Shortening of *adreden*, from Old English *adrædan*, from *ondrædan* 'to counsel against', from *rædan* 'to counsel'.]
dread disease *n.* INSUR a serious and potentially fatal disease ○ *dread disease insurance*
dreaded /dréddid/ *adj.* inspiring great fear (*sometimes used humorously*)
dreadful /dréddf'l/ *adj.* **1.** EXTREMELY BAD extremely unpleasant, harmful, or serious in its effects ○ *a dreadful mistake* **2.** EXTREME extreme in character or degree ○ *a dreadful shame* **3.** AWE-INSPIRING inspiring awe (*literary*) —**dreadfulness** *n.*
dreadfully /dréddf'li/ *adv.* **1.** VERY to a very great extent **2.** BADLY in a very unsatisfactory or unpleasant way ○ *He behaved dreadfully.*

Dreadlocks: Bob Marley

dreadlocks /dréd loks/ *npl.* long strands of hair that have been twisted closely from the scalp down to the tips in a style made popular by Rastafarians [Mid-20thC. From DREAD + LOCK, because of the supposed fear on the part of non-Rastafarians of the power of faithful Rastafarians.]

dreadnought /dréd nawt/, **dreadnaught** *n.* a heavily armed battleship whose main guns are all of the same calibre [Early 20thC. Named after the British battleship *Dreadnought*, the first of its kind, from DREAD + NOUGHT, literally 'fear nothing'.]

dreads /dredz/ *npl.* = **dreadlocks** [Late 20thC. Contraction.]

dream /dreem/ *n.* **1.** IMAGININGS WHILE ASLEEP a sequence of images that appear involuntarily to the mind of a sleeping person, often a mixture of real and imaginary characters, places, and events **2.** WAKING IMAGININGS a series of images, usually pleasant ones, that pass through the mind of sb who is awake **3.** STH HOPED FOR sth that sb hopes, longs, or is ambitious for, usually sth difficult to attain or far removed from present circumstances **4.** IDLE HOPE an idea or hope that is impractical or unlikely ever to be realized **5.** VAGUE STATE a state of inattention owing to preoccupation with thoughts or fantasies **6.** STH BEAUTIFUL sb or sth that seems particularly good-looking or wonderful ■ *v.* (**dreams, dreaming, dreamt** /dremt/ *or* **dreamed, dreamt** *or* **dreamed**) **1.** *vti.* HAVE A DREAM WHILE SLEEPING to experience vivid mental images of events while sleeping **2.** *vi.* DAYDREAM to let the mind dwell on pleasant scenes and images while awake, often resulting in inattention **3.** *vi.* WISH to want sth very much and imagine having or doing it, though it may be unlikely ○ *For years I'd dreamed of living abroad.* **4.** *vi.* CONSIDER to think of or consider doing sth regarded as wrong or inappropriate ○ *How could you even dream of doing such a thing?* ■ *adj.* **1.** OCCURRING IN A DREAM occurring in or reminiscent of a dream ○ *a dream sequence* **2.** IDEAL perfect and wonderful in every way [13thC. Origin uncertain: perhaps from an assumed Old English word (influenced by Old Norse *draumr*). Ultimately from an Indo-European word meaning 'deception'.] —**dreamful** *adj.*

dream up *vt.* to devise or invent sth, especially a complicated, ingenious, or ridiculous plan

dreamboat /dreém bōt/ *n.* sb considered to be very good-looking (*dated informal*)

dreamer /dreémər/ *n.* **1.** SB WHO DREAMS sb who dreams or is dreaming **2.** SB WHO DAYDREAMS sb who is preoccupied with fantasies or unrealistic plans and is out of touch with reality

dreamily /dreémili/ *adv.* in a vague and absent-minded way that suggests a preoccupation with pleasant thoughts and fantasies ○ *He smiled dreamily.*

dreamland /dreém land/ *n.* **1.** FANTASY WORLD an imaginary, very pleasant or perfect sphere of existence that exists only in dreams **2.** SLEEP a state of sleep or unconsciousness (*informal*)

dreamless /dreémləss/ *adj.* deep, peaceful, and undisturbed by dreams ○ *a dreamless sleep* —**dreamlessly** *adv.* —**dreamlessness** *n.*

dreamlike /dreém līk/ *adj.* resembling a dream or the images in a dream, especially in seeming unreal and strange

dreamscape /dreém skayp/ *n.* a scene, setting, or picture that has the unreal or strange qualities usually associated with images in dreams

dreamt past tense, past participle of **dream**

dream team *n.* the best possible combination of people to perform a task (*informal*) [The nickname of the 1992 US Olympic basketball team that included Michael Jordan, Magic Johnson, and Larry Bird]

dream ticket *n.* *US* candidates standing as a team for associated political offices, especially those of President and Vice President, who seem to have between them all the qualities needed for electoral success (*informal*)

Dreamtime /dreém tīm/ *n.* in the mythology of Australian Aborigines, the period during which the earth was formed, the landscape shaped, and living things created

dream world *n.* a world that bears little resemblance to reality and exists only in the mind

dreamy /dreémi/ (**dreamier, dreamiest**) *adj.* **1.** VAGUE caused by dreaming or by thinking about sth very pleasant and absorbing **2.** GIVEN TO DAYDREAMING having a tendency to spend time daydreaming or lost in thought **3.** UNREAL strange, vague, or ethereal, like an image in a dream

drear /dreer/ *adj.* dark, foreboding, and gloomy (*literary*) ○ *It was a cold, drear day.* [Mid-16thC. Back formation from DREARY.]

dreary /dreéri/ (**drearier, dreariest**) *adj.* gloomy, unexciting, and certain to have a wearying and depressing influence ○ *the dreary routine of prison life* [Old English *drēorig* 'dripping with blood', from a prehistoric Germanic word that is probably also the ancestor of English *drowsy* and *drizzle*] —**drearily** *adv.* —**dreariness** *n.*

dreck /drek/ *n.* *US* worthless trashy stuff, especially low-quality merchandise [Early 20thC. From Yiddish *drek* 'filth, dung', from Middle High German *drec*.] —**drecky** *adj.*

dredge[1] /drej/ *n.* **1.** MACHINE FOR DIGGING UNDERWATER a machine equipped with a continuous revolving chain of buckets, a scoop, or a suction device for digging out and removing material from under water **2.** SHIPPING = **dredger**[1] *n.* 1 **3.** AGRIC SHELLFISH NET a net on a frame dragged along the bottom of the sea or a river to gather shellfish ■ *v.* **1.** *vt.* DIG STH UP WITH A DREDGE to remove or recover material from under water by means of a dredge **2.** *vti.* SHIPPING CLEAR A CHANNEL to clear, deepen, or widen a waterway, especially one intended for shipping, using a dredge **3.** *vti.* SEARCH WITH A DREDGE to search sth, or search for sth, using a dredge or a similar device [Early 16thC. Origin uncertain: perhaps formed from Old English *dragan* 'to draw' or Middle Dutch *dregghe* 'drag-net'.]

dredge up *vt.* to bring sth to light from an obscure source, e.g. to recall sth bad that happened long ago or unearth some scandalous information

dredge[2] /drej/ (**dredges, dredging, dredged**) *vt.* to sprinkle or cover food with a coating of icing sugar, flour, or sugar [Late 16thC. Via Old French *dragie* 'sugar-plum, sugar almond', from Latin *tragemata*, from Greek *tragēmata* 'spices, sweetmeats'.]

dredger[1] /dréjjər/ *n.* **1.** SHIPPING BOAT WITH DREDGE a boat or barge with a dredge on it, used mainly for clearing or deepening waterways **2.** = **dredge**[1] *n.* 1

dredger[2] /dréjjər/ *n.* a container with small holes in the top used for sprinkling icing sugar, flour, or sugar onto food

dree /dree/ (**drees, dreeing, dreed**) *vt.* *Scotland* to bear sth unpleasant [Old English *drēogan* 'to work, suffer', from a prehistoric Germanic word] ◇ **dree your (own) weird** *Scotland* to live your own life, accepting or making your own destiny

dreg /dreg/ *n.* a small amount, especially a small remainder of sth ○ *not a dreg of sympathy for them* [14thC. Origin uncertain: probably from Old Norse *dregg* 'sediment'.]

D region *n.* **1.** METEOROL LOWEST PART OF IONOSPHERE the lowest part of the ionosphere above the Earth's surface **2.** BIOCHEM SHORT SEQUENCE OF AMINO ACIDS a short sequence of amino acids at the end of an immunoglobulin chain that allows for variations and thus contributes to antibody diversity

dregs /dregz/ *npl.* **1.** GRITTY PARTICLES IN LIQUID small solid particles found in liquids such as coffee or wine that sink to the bottom of a container and are most in evidence when the container is nearly empty **2.** LEAST VALUABLE PART the least valuable or most unpleasant part of sth, especially a group of people ○ *the dregs of society* **3.** LAST REMAINING PART the last remaining, and often least attractive part of sth (*literary*) ○ *sat through the dregs of a long boring evening*

dreich /dreekh/ *adj.* *Scotland* used to describe weather that is dull and depressing [Old English *gedrēog* 'patient, serious', from a prehistoric Germanic word that is also the ancestor of English *dree*]

dreidel /dráyd'l/, **dreidl** *n.* a toy that looks like a spinning top used to play games during Hanukkah [Mid-20thC. From Yiddish *dreydl*, from Middle High German *dræhen* 'to turn'.]

drench /drench/ *vt.* (**drenches, drenching, drenched**) **1.** SOAK SB OR STH to make sb or sth completely wet ○ *I got absolutely drenched going out in the storm.* **2.** VET GIVE AN ANIMAL LIQUID MEDICINE to give an animal a large dose of medicine in liquid form by mouth ■ *n.* VET DOSE OF ANIMAL MEDICINE a large oral dose of medicine given to an animal in liquid form by mouth [Old English *drencan* 'to give to drink', from a prehistoric Germanic word that is also the ancestor of English *drink*. The underlying idea is of making sth drink.] —**drencher** *n.* —**drenching** *adj., n.*

Dresden /drézdən/ capital of the state of Saxony in east-central Germany. Almost completely destroyed during World War II, it has been largely rebuilt and restored. Population: 477,600 (1994).

Dresden china *n.* fine and delicate porcelain as made in Meissen near Dresden in Germany since the early 18th century. US term **Meissen**

dress /dress/ *v.* (**dresses, dressing, dressed**) **1.** *vti.* PUT CLOTHES ON to put clothes on sb **2.** *vi.* WEAR to wear clothes of a particular type, or wear them in a particular way ○ *She usually dresses in black.* **3.** *vi.* PUT ON APPROPRIATE CLOTHES to put on clothes appropriate to a particular occasion, especially formal clothes ○ *We need to dress for the theatre.* **4.** *vt.* DECORATE STH to make a place or thing look festive by putting special decorations on it ○ *They dressed the big house for the holidays.* **5.** *vt.* COMM ARRANGE GOODS IN A WINDOW DISPLAY to arrange goods in a shop window so that they look attractive ○ *windows that were dressed for spring* **6.** *vt.* MED COVER A WOUND to put a bandage or other protective covering on a wound **7.** *vt.* COOK PUT SAUCE ON SALAD to put mayonnaise, vinaigrette, or a similar type of sauce on a salad **8.** *vt.* COOK, HUNT CLEAN FISH AND GAME to clean and prepare fish, poultry, or meat for cooking or selling **9.** *vt.* ARRANGE HAIR to arrange hair, e.g. by combing, clipping, or oiling it **10.** *vti.* MIL COME INTO ALIGNMENT to come, or bring troops, into a correct alignment with one another for a parade formation **11.** *vt.* AGRIC SPREAD MANURE OR FERTILIZER ON SOIL to spread manure or fertilizer over the surface of an area of land **12.** *vt.* FINISH A MATERIAL to apply a finishing process to a material such as stone or timber, usually in order to give it a smooth and good-looking surface ■ *n.* **1.** WOMAN'S ONE-PIECE GARMENT a one-piece garment for women and girls combining a bodice, with or without sleeves, and a skirt and covering most of the body **2.** TYPE OF CLOTHES clothes of a particular type or style **3.** CLOTHES clothes and clothing in general, considered, e.g. as an item in a budget or from the point of view of sb's taste in them ○ *He has no interest in matters of dress.* **4.** CLOTHING REQUIRED FOR PARTICULAR OCCASION the clothing required for a particular occasion **5.** OUTWARD APPEARANCE the outward appearance or covering of a thing, especially a living thing, or the way in which sth is presented (*literary*) **6.** THEATRE DRESS REHEARSAL a dress rehearsal (*informal*) ■ *adj.* **1.** FORMAL worn on formal occasions ○ *dress uniform* **2.** REQUIRING FORMAL ATTIRE requiring formal clothes to be worn ○ *a dress banquet* [14thC. Via Old French *dresser* 'arrange, prepare' from Vulgar Latin *directiare*, from Latin *directus* 'straight' (source of English *direct*).] ◇ **dressed to kill** dressed in very glamorous clothes, especially when intending to impress sb (*informal*)

dress down *v.* **1.** *vi.* LOOK CASUAL to dress in a deliberately understated or casual way for an occasion (*informal*) **2.** *vt.* REPRIMAND SB to scold sb severely

dress up *v.* **1.** *vi.* DRESS FORMALLY to put on formal or especially elegant clothes, usually for a special occasion such as a party **2.** *vi.* PUT ON COSTUMES to put on a special costume or different clothes from those normally worn so as to look like or pretend to be sb else **3.** *vt.* DISGUISE STH to disguise sth unpleasant and try to make it look more pleasant

dressage /dréssaazh/ *n.* **1.** TRAINING A HORSE TO EXECUTE PRECISE MOVEMENTS the training of a horse to carry out a series of precise controlled movements in response to minimal signals from its rider **2.** DRESSAGE EVENT a competitive event in which horse and rider are judged on the elegance, precision, and discipline of the horse's movements [Mid-20thC. From French, literally 'training', from *dresser* (see DRESS).]

dress circle *n.* a separate raised section of the auditorium in a theatre, concert hall, or opera house, usually the first seating gallery above ground level

dress coat *n.* a coat, forming part of a man's full evening dress, that is usually black with a cutaway skirt and tails

dress code *n.* a set of requirements as to how people should dress when attending a function or visiting a place

dress-down day *n.* a day, typically a Friday, or days during the summer months, on which office workers wear casual clothing to work

dresser[1] /dréssər/ *n.* **1.** SHELVES AND A CHEST a piece of furniture consisting of a set of shelves on top of a chest containing cupboards and drawers, often used for storing crockery and cutlery in traditional kitchens ○ *a Welsh dresser* **2.** *US* BEDROOM CHEST OF DRAWERS a chest of drawers used in a bedroom for storing clothes sometimes with a mirror on top [Early 15thC. From Old French *dresseur*, from *dresser* (see DRESS).]

dresser[2] /dréssər/ *n.* **1.** SB WHO DRESSES IN PARTICULAR WAY sb who dresses in a particular way **2.** ACTOR'S ASSISTANT sb who helps an actor to put on or change a costume before and during a performance **3.** PERSONAL GROOMING ASSISTANT sb whose job it is to ensure that another person's wardrobe is in order **4.** SURGEON'S ASSISTANT sb who assists a surgeon during operations

dress form *n.* an adjustable tailor's dummy

dressing /dréssing/ *n.* **1.** MED WOUND COVERING a bandage, plaster, or other sterile covering that is put on a wound to protect it from infection or further damage **2.** SALAD SAUCE a sauce used on salads, usually with an oil and vinegar or mayonnaise base **3.** *US* STUFFING stuffing for poultry or meat **4.** AGRIC FERTILIZER natural or artificial fertilizer for spreading on the soil **5.** TEXTILES STIFFENING FOR FABRIC size used to stiffen fabrics

dressing-down *n.* a scolding or severe reprimand, often in public

dressing gown *n.* a coat made of soft light material that is worn over nightclothes, before or after taking a bath, or in the early stages of getting formally or smartly dressed

dressing room *n.* **1.** THEATRE ACTORS' ROOM TO PUT ON COSTUMES a room in a theatre where actors can prepare for a performance by putting on their make-up and costumes **2.** ROOM TO CHANGE CLOTHES IN a small room or alcove in a house, hotel suite, or other place that people can use when putting on or changing their clothes

dressing station *n.* a first-aid station near a combat area

dressing table *n.* a low table with drawers and a mirror on top, usually placed in a bedroom so that a woman can sit at it when putting on her make-up

dressmaker /dréss maykər/ *n.* sb who makes women's clothes, especially sb who makes a living by doing this —**dressmaking** *n.*

dress parade *n.* a military parade in which the soldiers wear formal dress uniform

dress rehearsal *n.* **1.** THEATRE FINAL REHEARSAL the final rehearsal of a play, in full costume and with lights, music, and effects, before it is given its first public performance **2.** FULL-SCALE PRACTICE BEFORE EVENT a full-scale practice before any important event

dress sense *n.* the ability to choose clothes well and coordinate colours and styles effectively

dress shield *n.* a small fabric pad worn around the armpits of a piece of clothing to prevent sweat from showing or staining it

dress shirt *n.* a man's shirt worn with formal evening wear, usually white and with either a stiff collar or a ruffle down the front

dress suit *n.* a man's suit worn as part of formal evening wear, especially with a tailcoat

dress uniform *n.* a ceremonial uniform worn by members of the armed forces for formal occasions

dressy /dréssi/ (-ier, -iest) *adj.* **1.** ELEGANT stylish and elegant **2.** AT WHICH GUESTS DRESS FORMALLY at which stylish and elegant clothes are worn ○ *a very dressy buffet luncheon* **3.** OVERDRESSED dressed in an inappropriately elaborate or showy way —**dressily** *adv.* —**dressiness** *n.*

drew past tense of **draw**

Drewe /droo/, **Robert Duncan** (*b.* 1943) Australian writer. He wrote the novel *The Savage Crows* (1976).

drey /dray/ (*plural* **dreys**) *n.* a squirrel's nest [Early 17thC. Origin unknown.]

Dreyer /dráyər/, **Carl Theodor** (1889–1968) Danish film director and screenwriter. His silent films include *The Passion of Joan of Arc* (1928).

Dreyfus /dráyfəss/, **Alfred** (1859–1935) French soldier. He was a Jewish army officer whose imprisonment for treason (1894–95) divided French public opinion. He was officially declared innocent in 1906.

drib /drib/ *n.* a very small amount, usually a tiny drop of liquid or a fragment of material ○ *just a drib of paint on the porch floor* [Early 18thC. Origin uncertain: perhaps from *drib* 'to drip', alteration of DRIP; or shortening of DRIBBLE or DRIBLET.] ◇ **in dribs and drabs** in very small amounts or stages, and usually in a rather haphazard way ○ *Wedding presents are beginning to arrive in dribs and drabs.*

dribble /dríbb'l/ *v.* (**-bles, -bling, -bled**) **1.** *vi.* PRODUCE SALIVA to let saliva spill out of the mouth **2.** *vti.* SPILL DROPS to flow, or allow a liquid to flow or spill out, in drops or a small stream **3.** *vti.* SPORTS MOVE BALL to move a ball along using small repeated movements of the foot, the hand, or a stick **4.** *vti.* BASKETBALL BOUNCE A BALL ON COURT to propel the ball in any direction on the court by bouncing it with the hands ■ *n.* **1.** TINY AMOUNT OF LIQUID a small amount of liquid that is falling or has fallen in drops or a thin stream **2.** SPORTS MOVEMENT WHILE DRIBBLING BALL a movement or run made while dribbling the ball, especially in basketball or football ○ *a hard, fast dribble to centre court* [Mid-16thC. Literally 'to drip frequently', formed from *drib* 'to drip', alteration of DRIP.] —**dribbler** *n.* —**dribbly** *adj.*

driblet /dríbblət/, **dribblet** *n.* a tiny amount of a liquid [Late 16thC. Coined from *drib* 'to drip', alteration of DRIP, + -LET.]

driest /drī́ist/, **dryest** superlative of **dry**

drift /drift/ *v.* (**drifts, drifting, drifted**) **1.** *vi.* BE CARRIED ALONG to be, or allow sth to be, carried along by the flow of water or air **2.** *vi.* MOVE AIMLESSLY to move in a slow, smooth, gentle, and unforced way, usually without any direction or purpose ○ *The crowd gradually drifted away.* **3.** *vi.* WANDER FROM PLACE TO PLACE AIMLESSLY to go from one place to another, never staying anywhere for very long and seemingly with little purpose **4.** *vi.* NAVIG WANDER FROM A SET COURSE OR POSITION to deviate from a set course, or move gradually away from a fixed position **5.** *vi.* CHANGE GRADUALLY to change or develop gradually, or move slowly from one point or position to another ○ *Prices have drifted downwards in recent weeks.* **6.** *vti.* FORM HEAPS to build up and form heaps as a result of the action of the wind or water currents, or cause sth such as snow, sand, or leaves to form heaps ■ *n.* **1.** PILED-UP DEPOSITS a heap, pile, or bank of sth such as snow, sand, or leaves created by the action of the wind or water currents **2.** DRIFTING MOVEMENT a slow gentle movement in which sth is, or seems to be, carried along on a current of air or water **3.** MATERIAL CARRIED ALONG an amount of sth carried along by the flow of air or water ○ *drifts of smoke coming from the chimneys* **4.** MOVEMENT OF PEOPLE a gradual movement over a period of time of groups of people or animals towards or away from a place ○ *the drift of young people away from rural areas* **5.** GRADUAL CHANGE a broad and gradual change or development, e.g. in people's opinions or behaviour ○ *a drift back to larger cars* ○ *a downward drift in prices* **6.** GENERAL MEANING the general meaning of an argument, opinion, or statement **7.** STATE OF INACTIVITY a state of inactivity or indecision in which a person or group is carried along by events **8.** NAVIG DEVIATION FROM COURSE the distance or extent to which a ship or aircraft deviates from its set course due to the action of wind or currents **9.** GEOL DEPOSIT OF GRAVEL a loose deposit of sand, gravel, or rock left by a glacier or ice sheet **10.** GEOG CURRENT the motion of a river or broad ocean current **11.** MINING HORIZONTAL MINESHAFT a horizontal or virtually horizontal mineshaft that follows a vein of ore **12.** MINING CONNECTING PASSAGE IN MINE a small passage in a mine connecting two main shafts or tunnels **13.** ELEC ENG UNCONTROLLED CHANGE IN A SETTING a slow uncontrolled change in a previously adjusted setting, e.g., in the frequency to which an electronic device has been set **14.** MECH ENG TAPERING STEEL TOOL FOR ENLARGING HOLES a tapering steel tool used to enlarge or align holes in pieces of metal before they are bolted or riveted **15.** SPORTS CONTROLLED SKID IN RACING CAR a controlled slide used by racing drivers as a method of cornering at high speed **16.** *S Africa* FORD a shallow part of a river, or a ford across it [14thC. From Old Norse *drift* 'snowdrift', from a prehistoric Germanic word that is also the ancestor of English *drive*. The underlying idea is of sth driven.] —**drifty** *adj.*

driftage /dríftij/ *n.* **1.** DRIFTED MATERIAL material that has drifted along on, and been deposited by, air or water currents **2.** NAVIG DEVIATION FROM SET COURSE the distance by which a ship or aircraft has deviated from its set course owing to winds or currents

drifter /dríftər/ *n.* **1.** WANDERER sb who does not stay in the same place or job for long but is always moving on, apparently aimlessly, from place to place **2.** SAILING, ANGLING FISHING BOAT WITH DRIFT NET a fishing vessel that fishes with a drift net

drift ice *n.* large areas of ice that float in the open sea

drift net *n.* a large fishing net supported by floats that is allowed to drift along with the current or is attached to a vessel

driftwood /drift wo͝od/ *n.* broken pieces of wood that are found washed up on a beach or riverbank or floating in the sea or a river

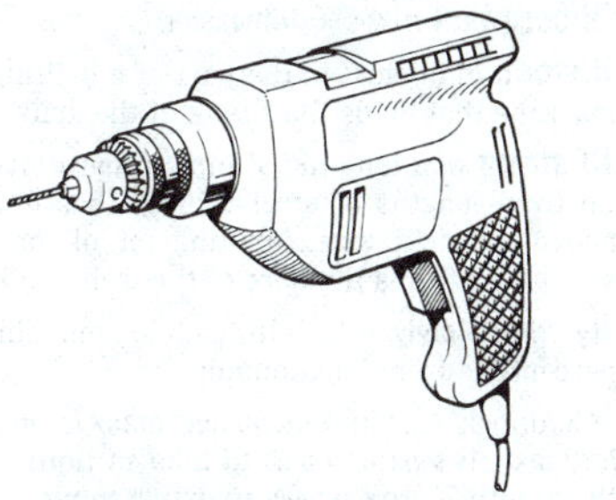

Drill

drill[1] /dril/ *n.* **1.** PART OF TOOL THAT BORES HOLES a long pointed piece of metal that is held in a machine and rotated at speed to bore holes in hard substances such as wood, metal, masonry, or rock **2.** BORING TOOL WITH DRILL a tool or machine that holds, drives, and bores holes with a drill **3.** MIL TRAINING BY REPETITION a type of military training, particularly in marching manoeuvres and weapons handling, that involves the constant repetition of a set pattern of movements or tasks **4.** EDUC REPEATED EXERCISE a sequence of tasks, exercises, or words repeated over and over until they can be performed faultlessly, as used in teaching military skills, languages, or basic arithmetic **5.** SAFETY ROUTINE a sequence of actions practised repeatedly so that people know what to do in an emergency to ensure their safety **6.** ROUTINE a set procedure or routine for doing sth (*informal*) **7.** ZOOL PREDATORY MOLLUSC a marine mollusc that preys on oysters by boring into their shells. Latin name: *Urosalpinx cinerea.* ■ *v.* (**drills, drilling, drilled**) **1.** *vti.* BORE A HOLE WITH A DRILL to bore a hole in sth with a drill **2.** *vti.* MIL PRACTISE MARCHING to practise marching manoeuvres repeatedly on a parade ground as a form of military training and discipline **3.** *vt.* EDUC TEACH A SUBJECT BY ROTE to make sb repeat a sequence of exercises or procedures over and over again in order to learn it **4.** *vt.* SHOOT SB OR STH to shoot sb with bullets, or shoot bullets into sth (*informal*) **5.** *vt.* SPORTS THROW OR HIT A BALL HARD to throw or hit a ball with great force in a straight line towards sb or sth (*informal*) [Early 16thC . From Middle Dutch *drillen* 'to make a hole, whirl'. Ultimately from an Indo-European word meaning 'to turn', which is also the ancestor of English *trite* and *threshold*.] —**drillable** *adj.*

WORD KEY: SYNONYMS

See Synonyms at ***teach***.

drill[2] /dril/ *n.* AGRIC **1. FURROW FOR SEEDS** a shallow furrow in which seeds are sown **2. SEED-PLANTING MACHINE** a machine for planting seeds in furrows **3. PLANTED ROW OF SEEDS** a row of seeds planted along a small furrow ■ *vt.* **(drills, drilling, drilled)** AGRIC **PLANT WITH DRILL** to plant seeds with a drill [Early 18thC. Origin uncertain: perhaps from DRILL[1].]

drill[3] /dril/ *n.* a tough cotton twill used especially for making working clothes and uniforms [Mid-18thC. From German *Drillich*, from Latin *trilix*, literally 'with three threads', from *licium* 'thread' (source of English *trellis*).]

drill[4] /dril/ *n.* a West African baboon with a black face and brown fur, similar to a mandrill though smaller in size. Latin name: *Papio leucophaeus*. [Mid-17thC. From a West African name for the baboon.]

drilling mud *n.* a mixture of clay, water, and chemicals pumped into a well as it is being bored to lubricate the drill, remove debris, and prevent gas or oil escaping

drilling platform *n.* a structure used in offshore oil drilling that supports drilling equipment and is either fixed to the seabed or floats independently

drill instructor *n.* *US* MIL = **drillmaster**

drillmaster /dríll maastər/ *n.* **1.** MIL **DRILLER OF TROOPS** a noncommissioned officer who trains soldiers in drill. US term **drill instructor 2. STRICT TRAINER** sb who trains people in a very strict and militaristic way

drill pipe *n.* = **drill string**

drill press *n.* a machine consisting of a powered drill on a vertical stand that is brought down onto the work automatically or by a hand lever

drill sergeant *n.* MIL = **drillmaster**

drillstock /dríll stok/ *n.* the part of a drilling tool or machine that holds the shank of the drill

drill string *n.* a long metal pipe, progressively built up from lengths of steel tubing, that is attached above the drill when drilling for oil or gas and eventually forms the bore of the well

drily /drīli/, **dryly** *adv.* with subtle and almost imperceptible irony or humour

drink /dringk/ *vti.* **(drinks, drinking, drank** /drangk/**, drunk** /drungk/**) 1. SWALLOW LIQUID** to take in liquid through the mouth **2. DRINK ALCOHOL** to drink an alcoholic beverage, especially habitually ○ *Don't drink and drive.* **3. TOAST SB BY RAISING A GLASS** to raise a glass and then drink from it as a sign that you wish sb or sth happiness, luck, success, or good health ■ *n.* **1. DRINKABLE LIQUID** liquid that can be drunk, usually in a container ○ *There isn't much food or drink in the house.* **2. AMOUNT OF LIQUID** an amount of liquid that sb drinks ○ *Could I have a drink of water?* **3. ALCOHOLIC BEVERAGE** alcoholic drink, especially an individual serving in a glass, bottle, or can **4. EXCESSIVE CONSUMPTION OF ALCOHOL** excessive consumption of alcohol **5. BODY OF WATER** the sea or a large body of water, e.g. a lake or swimming pool (*informal*) ○ *in the drink* ■ **drinks** *npl.* **INFORMAL PARTY WITH DRINKS SERVED** an informal party with alcoholic or other drinks served but not a meal [Old English *drincan*. Ultimately from a prehistoric Germanic word that is also the ancestor of English *drench* and *drown*.] ◇ **drink with the flies** *Aus* to drink alcohol by yourself (*informal*)

drink down *vt.* to consume a liquid quickly and completely ○ *Drink your coffee down before it gets cold.*

drink in *vt.* **1. ABSORB LIQUID** to absorb as much liquid as is available ○ *The plants drank in the welcome rain.* **2. ABSORB STH WITH MIND AND SENSES** to absorb eagerly every aspect of sth with the mind and senses ○ *She stood silently on the beach, drinking in the beauty.*

drink up *vt.* **1. FINISH A DRINK** to drink all of sth **2. ABSORB LIQUID COMPLETELY** to absorb a liquid completely ○ *The dry earth drank up the rain.*

drinkable /dríngkəb'l/ *adj.* **1. SAFE TO DRINK** safe for humans or animals to drink **2. NICE TO DRINK** pleasant or enjoyable to drink ○ *a very drinkable local fruit juice* —**drinkability** /dríngkə bílləti/ *n.* —**drinkableness** /dríngkəb'lnəss/ *n.*

drink-driving *n.* the offence of driving a vehicle while having a higher blood-alcohol content than the law allows. US term **drunk-driving** —**drink-driver** *n.*

drinker /dríngkər/ *n.* **1. SB WHO DRINKS STH PARTICULAR** sb who drinks a particular type of beverage (*used in combination*) ○ *I'm not a coffee drinker.* **2. SB WHO DRINKS ALCOHOLIC BEVERAGES** sb who drinks alcoholic beverages, especially to excess

drinking fountain *n.* a device attached to a wall that produces a jet of water that people can drink

drinking song *n.* a song, often rowdy or suggestive, sung by people drinking alcohol together

drinking-up time *n.* a period allowed in a public house after official closing time, when drinks already bought may be finished

drinking water *n.* water intended for people to drink, especially when free of harmful elements such as industrial waste, chemicals, or animal waste

drink problem *n.* = **drinking problem**

drinks machine *n.* a machine that dispenses various hot and cold drinks

Drinkwater /dríngk wawtər/, **John** (1882–1937) English playwright, poet, and actor. He was co-founder of Birmingham Repertory Theatre (1907), where he acted in his own verse dramas, including *Abraham Lincoln* (1918).

drip /drip/ *v.* **(drips, dripping, dripped) 1.** *vti.* **FALL OR LET FALL IN DROPS** to fall as drops of liquid, or let liquid fall as drops ○ *The tap is dripping.* **2.** *vt.* **LET STH OUT COPIOUSLY** to let out sth, particularly an emotion, in great quantity ○ *His voice positively dripped malice.* ■ *n.* **1. SMALL AMOUNT OF LIQUID** a drop of liquid or moisture ○ *a bucket to catch the drips* **2. DRIPPING OF LIQUID** an instance or the process of a liquid falling in drops ○ *Our ceiling has developed a drip.* **3. SOUND OF FALLING DROPS** the sound of drops of liquid falling onto sth ○ *the steady drip of a leaking tap* **4.** MED **MEDICAL PROCEDURE FOR INJECTING LIQUID** a medical procedure whereby considerable quantities of a therapeutic fluid, e.g. blood, plasma, saline, or glucose, are injected directly into sb's vein at an adjustable rate. A plastic bag containing the fluid is hung above the patient on a stand. US term **drip feed 5.** MED **FLUID USED IN A DRIP** the therapeutic fluid used in a drip (*informal*) ○ *Add 2 cc of morphine to the drip.* US term **drip feed 6.** MED **EQUIPMENT USED TO ADMINISTER A DRIP** the equipment used to administer a drip (*informal*) US term **drip feed 7. SOCIALLY INEPT PERSON** sb regarded by others as socially inept, inadequate, or uninteresting (*slang*) **8.** ARCHIT **PROTECTIVE GROOVE** a protective groove cut in a sill or other overhang of a wall or building to cause water to drip freely [Old English *dryppan*. Ultimately from an Indo-European base meaning 'to drop', which is also the ancestor of English *drop*, *droop*, and *drizzle*.]

drip with *vt.* **1. HAVE DROPS FALLING CONTINUOUSLY** to have liquid falling in a continuous stream of drops ○ *dripping with sweat* **2. HAVE TOO MUCH OF STH** to have too much of sth, especially some kind of adornment, usually in a way that is considered to be bad taste **3. GIVE VENT TO EMOTION** to give continuous expression to an emotion, especially a negative one such as spite, malice, or sarcasm ○ *Her voice dripped with sarcasm.*

drip coffee *n.* *US* = **filter coffee**

drip-dry *adj.* **REQUIRING NO IRONING** not wrinkling or creasing as it dries, and thus not needing ironing ○ *a drip-dry shirt* ■ *vti.* **(drip-dries, drip-drying, drip-dried) DRY WITHOUT CREASES** to dry without creases when hung up wet, or cause sth to dry in this way

drip feed *n.* MED **1.** = **drip** *n.* 4, **drip** *n.* 5, **drip** *n.* 6

drip-feed /dríp feed/ **(drip-feeds, drip-feeding, drip-fed)** *vt.* **1.** MED **ADMINISTER A DRIP TO** to pass a liquid, especially a sugar solution, directly into sb's vein using a drip **2.** GARDENING, AGRIC **PROVIDE PLANTS WITH A CONTINUOUS WATER SUPPLY** to provide water, and sometimes nutrients, to indoor plants or field crops continuously in small quantities **3.** FIN **PROVIDE MONEY IN INSTALMENTS** to give money to a new business in instalments at various stages of its development instead of giving the entire sum at the beginning (*informal*)

dripless /drípləss/ *adj.* *US* designed or made not to drip ○ *This teapot has a dripless spout.*

drip pan *n.* a shallow pan or baking sheet used in the oven to catch the juices of roasting meat

dripping /drípping/ *n.* FOOD **FAT FROM COOKING MEAT** the fat that melts off meat when it is being cooked and hardens when cold. It can be used for frying and basting, and as shortening when making pastry. ■ **drippings** *npl.* *US* FOOD **JUICES FROM COOKING MEAT** the juices, including fat, produced by roasting or frying meat ■ *adj.* **dripping wet THOROUGHLY WET** thoroughly wet ○ *She hurried in, cold and dripping wet from the storm.*

dripping wet *adj.* = **dripping**

drippy /drípi/ **(-pier, -piest)** *adj.* **1. WEAK AND INEFFECTUAL** weak and ineffectual (*slang insult*) **2. TOO SENTIMENTAL** silly and extremely sentimental (*slang*) [Early 19thC. From the notion of 'dripping with tears or sentiment'.] —**drippily** *adv.* —**drippiness** *n.*

dripstone /dríp stōn/ *n.* **1.** ARCHIT **PROTECTIVE STONE DRIP** a stone drip used to protect a projection over a door or window **2.** GEOL **FORM OF CALCIUM CARBONATE** calcium carbonate deposits in the form of stalactites or stalagmites

drissy /dríssi/ *adj.* *NZ* frantic (*informal*)

drivable /drívəb'l/, **driveable** *adj.* **1. NICE TO DRIVE** easy, comfortable, or pleasant to drive **2. IN A CONDITION TO BE DRIVEN** in good enough condition to be driven safely —**drivability** /drívə bílləti/ *n.*

drive /drīv/ *v.* **(drives, driving, drove** /drōv/**, driven** /drívv'n/**) 1.** *vti.* TRANSP **CONTROL MOVEMENT OF A VEHICLE** to operate a vehicle, controlling its speed and direction, or be operated so as to move in a particular direction ○ *He's learning to drive.* **2.** *vti.* TRANSP **TRAVEL OR CONVEY IN VEHICLE** to travel somewhere in a vehicle, or take sb somewhere in a vehicle ○ *I'll drive you to the airport.* **3.** *vt.* ENG **PROVIDE POWER FOR STH** to supply the power that makes sth work (*often passive*) ○ *The lawn mower is driven by a petrol engine.* **4.** *vt.* **STEER THE PROGRESS OF STH** to provide momentum towards the successful operation or functioning of sth ○ *This company is driven by a concern for quality.* **5.** *vt.* **FORCE INTO A CONDITION** to force sb or sth into a particular state or condition, often an extremely negative one ○ *Her son's behaviour drove her to despair.* **6.** *vt.* **COMPEL SB TO DO STH** to supply the emotional or physical energy that leads sb to act or behave in an extreme way ○ *Driven by fear, the elephants stampeded.* **7.** *vr.* **FORCE YOURSELF TO WORK TOO HARD** to force yourself to work too hard or too long hours at sth ○ *You drive yourself too hard.* **8.** *vt.* **FORCE PEOPLE OR ANIMALS TO MOVE** to force people or animals to go somewhere ○ *Rain drove them indoors.* **9.** *vt.* **FORCE STH IN OR OUT** to push, knock, or hammer sth forcefully into a particular position ○ *He drove the stakes into the ground.* **10.** *vti.* **MOVE OR PROPEL FORCEFULLY** to move or be blown or thrown with great force against sth, or provide the force that does this ○ *The wind drove the snow into huge drifts.* **11.** *vt.* **MAKE A HOLE** to make a hole or tunnel in sth using great force **12.** *vt.* SPORTS **HIT A BALL HARD** to kick or hit a ball forcefully when playing a sport **13.** *vti.* GOLF **HIT A LONG SHOT** to hit a long shot in golf, from either a tee or a fairway, when covering the principal distance between holes ○ *He drove into the rough.* **14.** *vti.* BASKETBALL **DRIBBLE DIRECTLY TOWARDS THE BASKET** in basketball, to dribble the ball through a particular area of the court towards the basket ○ *She's unstoppable when she drives the baseline.* **15.** *vt.* CRICKET **STRIKE BALL WITH FORCE** in cricket, to strike the ball very hard and straight with the bat held vertically **16.** *vt.* HUNT **CHASE GAME INTO THE OPEN** to chase a hunted animal into the open where it can be killed **17.** *vt.* *NZ* **FELL TREES BY CUTTING ONE DOWN** to cut down a tree in such a way that it falls on other trees and makes them fall ■ *n.* **1.** TRANSP **RIDE TAKEN IN A VEHICLE** a trip in a car or other vehicle ○ *go for a drive* **2.** TRANSP **ROAD LINKING HOUSE TO STREET** a paved area or private road that goes between a house or garage and the street. US term **driveaway 3.** TRANSP **WIDE ROAD** any street or road that can be used for vehicles, especially one that has pleasant views (*often used in placenames*) **4.** ENG **TRANSMISSION OF POWER** the means of converting power into motion in a machine, e.g. a motor vehicle (*often used in combination*) ○ *a car with four-wheel drive* **5.** COMPUT = **disk drive 6.** SPORTS **HARD HIT OF BALL** in some sports, a forceful shot or stroke in hitting a ball ○ *She has a good backhand drive.* **7.** GOLF **LONG SHOT** a long shot in golf, played from either a tee or fairway, when covering the main portion of the distance between the tee and green 8. BASKETBALL FAST MOVEMENT TOWARD BASKET in basketball, a fast direct run toward the basket while dribbling the ball ○ *Our players are having trouble scoring off drives.* 9. FOCUSED ENERGY energy and determination that helps sb achieve what he or she wants to do ○ *Do you have the drive to achieve your ambitions?* 10. PSYCHOL MOTIVATING NEED a powerful need or instinct, e.g. hunger or sex, that motivates behaviour 11. MAJOR PLANNED EFFORT an organized effort made by a lot of people working together to achieve a particular goal ○ *a recruitment drive* 12. LEISURE PARTY FOR PLAYING CARD GAME a social event for the purpose of playing a game, e.g. whist, often organized in order to raise funds (*used in combination*) ○ *a beetle drive* 13. MIL SUSTAINED MILITARY ATTACK a major sustained attack on an enemy, usually including armoured vehicles and large guns 14. ELECTRON ENG VOLTAGE voltage applied to the grid of a transmitting or amplifying valve or to the base of a transistor 15. AUTOMOT FORWARD POSITION IN AUTOMATIC TRANSMISSION in an automatic transmission, the principal shift position that moves the vehicle forwards [Old English *drīfan*. Ultimately from an Indo-European word that is also the ancestor of English *drift* and *drove*.]

driveable *adj.* = drivable

drive-by (*plural* **drive-bys**) *n.* a drive-by shooting (*informal*)

drive-by shooting *n.* an act of firing a firearm from a moving vehicle

drive chain *n.* an endless chain that transmits power from one toothed wheel to another in a mechanical system

drive-in *n.* a commercial establishment, e.g. a cinema, that provides services or products to customers while they remain in their cars (*often used before a noun*) —**drive-in** *n.*

drivel *n.* 1. SILLY TALK silly and irrelevant or inaccurate talk ○ *They're talking drivel.* 2. DROOLED SALIVA saliva dribbling from the mouth ■ *vi.* (-els, -elling, -elled) 1. TALK NONSENSE to talk silly and irrelevant or inaccurate nonsense 2. DROOL to let saliva dribble from the mouth [Old English *dreflian*, of uncertain origin] —**driveller** *n.* —**drivelling** *n.*

driven[1] past participle of **drive**

driven[2] *adj.* 1. COMPELLED BY PERSONAL NEED striving to achieve because of a strong need or inner compulsion ○ *Driven people are often overachievers.* 2. CAUSED BY having a particular thing as its principal cause (*used in combination*) ○ *a demand-driven economy*

driver /drívər/ *n.* 1. TRANSP SB WHO CAN DRIVE sb who operates a motor vehicle, or who is capable of operating one 2. TRANSP CHAUFFEUR sb who drives a car or limousine for other people 3. GOLF GOLF CLUB a golf club with a wide wooden head, deep face, and a long shaft, used to drive the ball from the tee down the fairway 4. ENG PART THAT TRANSMITS STH a part of a machine that causes another part to move 5. TECH TOOL THAT APPLIES PRESSURE a tool, e.g. a screwdriver or drill, that exerts heavy pressure on sth else 6. ELECTRON ENG ELECTRONIC CIRCUIT an electronic circuit that produces an output used to control another circuit 7. COMPUT CONTROLLING SOFTWARE computer software that controls the input and output of a particular device ○ *a printer driver* 8. STRONG FORCE sth that provides impetus or motivation, e.g. within an organization

driver ant *n.* = army ant [So called because they appear to herd other insects and small animals while on the march]

driverless /drívərləss/ *adj.* 1. LACKING A DRIVER WHILE MOVING moving out of control because the driver is missing 2. HAVING NO DRIVER not having a driver on a specific occasion ○ *Looks like we're driverless tonight.* 3. NEEDING NO DRIVER having no driver because of being automatically operated

driver's license *n.* US = driving licence

driver's seat *n.* US = driving seat

driver's side *n.* the side of a car on which the steering wheel is located, where the driver sits when operating a vehicle

drive shaft *n.* 1. MECH ENG ROTATING SHAFT TRANSMITTING ENGINE POWER a rotating shaft that transmits the power from a motor or engine to another part of the machine, e.g. from the engine to the propeller of an aircraft 2. AUTOMOT SHAFT TRANSFERRING POWER TO REAR WHEELS the shaft that transmits power from the transmission to the differential in a rear-wheel drive vehicle

drive-through *n.* US a business, e.g. a fast-food restaurant or bank, that provides goods or services through a special window to customers who remain in their cars (*often used before a noun*)

drive time *n.* a time during the morning or afternoon when commuters are driving to and from work in their cars and listening to the radio

drive train *n.* a mechanical part of a vehicle, including the drive shaft and universal joint, that connects the transmission with the axles and transmits power, torque, and motion

drive-up *n.* US a place in a commercial establishment such as a restaurant or bank where customers are served while remaining in their cars (*often used before a noun*)

driveway /drív way/ *n.* = drive

driving /dríving/ *adj.* 1. FALLING HARD falling or being blown very hard and forcefully ○ *driving rain* 2. ABLE TO MAKE STH HAPPEN having the ability or influence to make sth new or different happen ○ *She is the driving force behind the new development.* ○ *driving ambition* ■ *n.* TRANSP PROCESS OF OPERATING VEHICLE the act or process of operating a motor vehicle, especially with regard to how skilful sb is ○ *Your driving is even worse than usual today.* —**drivingly** *adv.*

driving chain *n.* = drive chain

driving examiner *n.* an official who conducts the test of sb's ability to drive, which people must pass to obtain a driving licence

driving gloves *npl.* gloves worn while driving a vehicle. They are usually made of leather or have leather palms and knitted fabric backs.

driving iron *n.* an iron golf club that can be used instead of a driver

driving licence *n.* a document obtained after sb has passed a test demonstrating that he or she knows how to drive safely and within the law

driving seat *n.* the seat in which the driver sits when operating a motor vehicle. US = **driver's seat** ◇ **in the driving seat** 1. in a position to determine the course or direction of sth 2. in charge of what is going on

driving test *n.* a test of driving skills and knowledge, usually consisting of both a written and a practical test that people must pass before driving without supervision on public roads

driving time *n.* = drive time *n.*

driving wheel *n.* a wheel that causes other wheels to rotate

drizzle /drízz'l/ *n.* METEOROL LIGHT RAIN light steady rain ■ *v.* (-zles, -zling, -zled) 1. *vi.* METEOROL RAIN LIGHTLY to rain lightly and steadily 2. *vt.* COOK DRIBBLE LIQUID OVER FOOD to pour very small quantities of a liquid in a thin stream over food ○ *Lightly drizzle the dressing over the vegetables.* [Mid-16thC. Origin uncertain: perhaps ultimately from Old English *drēosan* 'to fall', from a prehistoric Germanic word] —**drizzly** *adj.*

Drogheda /dróy idə/ historic city and seaport in the eastern Republic of Ireland. It is situated about 8 km/5 mi. from the Irish Sea. Population: 23,945 (1993).

drogue /drōg/ *n.* 1. NAUT = sea anchor 2. SPACE TECH, AIR = drogue parachute 3. MIL TARGET TOWED BY AN AIRCRAFT a cylindrical target towed behind an aircraft, used for firing practice 4. AIR RECEPTACLE ON A TANKER AIRCRAFT a funnel-shaped receptacle attached to the refuelling hose of a tanker aircraft that locates the probe of the receiving aircraft and fits over it, ensuring firm connection during refuelling 5. METEOROL WINDSOCK a windsock (*technical*) [Early 18thC. Origin uncertain.]

drogue parachute *n.* 1. SPACE TECH SMALL PARACHUTE FOR SPACECRAFT a small parachute, used on a spacecraft or

satellite re-entering the atmosphere, that is released before a larger one to slow the object and stabilize it 2. AIR SMALL PARACHUTE a small parachute used to release a larger one from its pack

droit /drwaa/ *n.* LAW a right or claim, either legal or moral, that is due to sb and must be acknowledged [15thC. Via French from late Latin *directum* 'rule', literally 'straight thing', from Latin *directus* (see DIRECT).]

droit de seigneur /drwáa də say nyúr/, **droit du seigneur** /-dyoo-/ *n.* the supposed former legal right of a feudal lord to have sexual intercourse with the bride or daughter of an inferior, usually a serf, on the night of her wedding [From French, literally 'lord's right']

droll /drōl/ *adj.* amusing in a wry or odd way ○ *Don't you enjoy his droll asides?* [Early 17thC. From French *drôle* 'buffoon, comical', of uncertain origin: perhaps ultimately from Middle Dutch *drol* 'imp, goblin'.] —**drolly** /drṓl li/ *adv.* —**drollness** *n.*

── WORD KEY: SYNONYMS ──
See Synonyms at *funny*.

drollery /drṓləri/ (*plural* -ies) *n.* 1. QUIRKY HUMOUR slightly odd or wry humour 2. TALKING OR BEHAVING AMUSINGLY talking or acting in a wryly or oddly amusing way ○ *Such drollery is inappropriate in a formal context.* 3. STH FUNNY an act or story that is wryly funny ○ *Whoever would have guessed that he was capable of such drolleries?*

-drome *suffix.* racecourse, field ○ *hippodrome* ○ *cosmodrome* [Via Latin from Greek *dromos* 'racecourse'. Ultimately from an Indo-European base meaning 'to walk, run', which is also the ancestor of English *tread*, *trip*, and *dromedary*.]

Dromedary

dromedary /drómmədəri, drúmm-/ (*plural* -ies) *n.* a camel with one hump, native to northern Africa and southwestern Asia where it is now domesticated and bred for working and racing. Latin name: *Camelus dromedarius*. [13thC. Via Old French *dromedaire* and late Latin *dromedarius* from, ultimately, Greek *dromad*, the stem of *dromas* 'running'.]

dromond /drómmənd, drúmm-/, **dromon** /-ən/ *n.* a sailing galley used during the Middle Ages [14thC. Via Anglo-Norman *dromund* from, ultimately, Greek *dromō* 'swift ship', from *dromos* 'running, race' (see -DROME).]

-dromous *suffix.* moving, migrating ○ *catadromous* [Formed from modern Latin -*dromus*, from Greek *dromos* 'running, race' (see -DROME)]

drone[1] /drōn/ *v.* (drones, droning, droned) 1. *vi.* MAKE A LOW HUMMING SOUND to make a continuous low humming sound 2. *vti.* TALK IN A BORING VOICE to talk for a long time in a boring voice ○ *I could hear his voice droning on in the background.* ■ *n.* 1. HUMMING SOUND a continuous low sound 2. MUSIC UNCHANGING NOTE HELD DURING MELODY a single note or chord that is held through a melodic part 3. MUSIC PIPE IN BAGPIPES PRODUCING CONTINUOUS NOTE one of the pipes in a bagpipe that produces a single continuous note [Early 16thC. From DRONE[2].] —**droningly** *adv.*

drone[2] /drōn/ *n.* 1. INSECTS NONWORKER MALE BEE a male bee that has no sting, does not gather pollen, and exists only to mate with the queen bee 2. LAZY PERSON sb who does not work or contribute anything, instead relying on the work or energy of other people 3. AIR PILOTLESS AIRCRAFT an aircraft whose flight is controlled from the ground [Old English *drān*. Ultimately from an Indo-European word meaning 'to buzz', which is also the ancestor of English *threnody*.] —**dronish** *adj.*

drone fly *n.* = **hoverfly**

drongo /dróng gō/ (*plural* **-gos**) *n.* **1. drongo** (*plural* **-gos** *or* **-go**), **drongo shrike** (*plural* **drongo shrikes** *or* **drongo shrike**) BIRDS TROPICAL BIRD a tropical bird found in Africa, Asia, and Australia that is usually black with a strong beak, glossy feathers, and a long forked tail. Family: Dicruridae. **2.** *ANZ* UNINTELLIGENT PERSON a thoughtless or unintelligent person (*informal insult*) [Mid-19thC. From Malagasy.]

droob /droob/ *n.* *ANZ* sb who is thought to be ineffectual (*informal insult*) [Mid-20thC. Origin uncertain: perhaps a blend of DRONE and BOOB.]

drool /drool/ *v.* (**drools, drooling, drooled**) **1.** *vi.* SHOW EXAGGERATED APPRECIATION to show excessive appreciation of sth or sb really liked or wanted **2.** *vi.* DRIBBLE SALIVA to let saliva dribble from the mouth ○ *The dog lay drooling at his feet.* **3.** *vti.* TALK NONSENSE to talk nonsense or foolishness ■ *n.* SALIVA DRIBBLING FROM THE MOUTH saliva dribbling from the mouth [Early 19thC. Origin uncertain: possibly an alteration of DRIVEL.] —**droolingly** *adv.*

droop /droop/ *v.* (**droops, drooping, drooped**) **1.** *vti.* HANG OR BEND DOWN LIMPLY to move lower, hang down, or sag limply, or make sth sag limply ○ *Her eyelids drooped with weariness.* **2.** *vi.* BE DISPIRITED to become discouraged or dejected ○ *His spirits drooped at the prospect of the long and arduous journey.* ■ *n.* SAGGING a lowered, sagging, or slumped position ○ *The droop of her shoulders suggested her disappointment.* [13thC. From Old Norse *drūpa*.] —**droopily** *adv.* —**droopiness** *n.* —**droopingly** *adv.* —**droopy** *adj.*

droop nose, droop snoot *n.* an aircraft nose section that can be tilted downward to increase the pilot's range of vision during landing and takeoff

drop /drop/ *v.* (**drops, dropping, dropped**) **1.** *vt.* LET GO OF STH to allow sth to fall, sometimes intentionally ○ *somebody had dropped a glove in the street.* **2.** *vi.* FALL to fall from a higher place to a lower place **3.** *vti.* MOVE TO A LOWER POSITION to move into a lower position, or move the body or part of the body lower ○ *He dropped into a chair.* **4.** *vti.* FALL IN DROPS to fall or make sth fall in drops of liquid ○ *We listened to the rain dropping on the roof.* **5.** *vti.* LESSEN to decrease, or reduce sth, to a lower level, rate, or number ○ *The temperature dropped sharply overnight.* **6.** *vi.* SLOPE DOWNWARDS to slope downwards, often in a particular way **7.** *vti.* LOWER THE VOICE to lower the voice to a quieter level, or become quieter ○ *She dropped her voice to a whisper.* **8.** *vt.* TAKE SB OR STH SOMEWHERE to take sb or sth to a place, usually by car, and leave the person or thing there ○ *Can you drop me at the bus station?* **9.** *vt.* WRITE TO SB to write and send a message or greeting to sb ○ *Drop me a line.* **10.** *vt.* STOP DOING OR PLANNING STH to abandon a plan or course of action ○ *The council have dropped plans to build a major new leisure centre.* **11.** *vti.* STOP TALKING ABOUT STH to stop talking about sth, or stop being talked about ○ *Can we drop the subject please?* **12.** *vt.* END RELATIONSHIP WITH SB to end a close or intimate relationship with sb (*informal*) **13.** *vt.* REMOVE SB to remove sb from a group of which she or he was formerly a member ○ *She may be dropped from the team.* **14.** *vt.* OMIT LETTER OR WORD to leave out a letter, word, or phrase ○ *You can drop the 'Sir': just call me Max.* **15.** *vi.* COLLAPSE FROM EXHAUSTION to collapse in a state of complete exhaustion ○ *I'm ready to drop.* **16.** *vi.* COLLAPSE to lose consciousness or die, especially suddenly or unexpectedly (*informal*) ○ *People were dropping like flies from the extreme heat.* **17.** *vt.* SPORTS LOSE A MATCH OR GAME to lose a match, game, or part of a game ○ *He got through to the finals without dropping a set.* **18.** *vt.* SAY STH CASUALLY to say sth with an air of pretended casualness ○ *She's dropping hints about what she wants for her birthday.* **19.** *vt.* *US* SPEND OR LOSE MONEY to spend or lose a particular amount of money on sth expensive or in gambling (*informal*) **20.** *vti.* SPORTS HIT A BALL INTO THE TARGET HOLE to make the ball go into a target, e.g. a hole or net, or go into a target hole or net **21.** *vt.* VET GIVE BIRTH TO to give birth to young, especially a foal **22.** *vt.* DRUGS TAKE ILLEGAL DRUGS to take an illegal drug by mouth, especially LSD or pills (*slang*) **23.** *vt.* SEW LOWER A HEM to lower the hem of sth, e.g. a garment or curtain **24.** *vt.* AIR DELIVER STH BY PARACHUTE to deliver sb or sth by parachute from an aircraft, e.g. soldiers or supplies **25.** *vt.* UNLOAD STH to unload sth from a ship or vehicle ■ *n.* **1.** SMALL ROUND PORTION OF LIQUID a very small amount of liquid that becomes a rounded or pear shape as it falls **2.** SMALL AMOUNT OF LIQUID any small amount of a liquid ○ *There's not a drop of milk in the house.* **3.** TINIEST AMOUNT the least amount of sympathy or other feeling (*used in negative statements*) ○ *I swear there isn't a drop of sympathy in that man.* **4.** DECREASE IN STH a decrease in quantity or amount ○ *a drop in salary* **5.** DISTANCE BETWEEN A HIGH POINT AND THE GROUND the distance between a higher level and a lower level or the ground **6.** DESCENT a slope or discontinuity in ground level, usually sharp or sudden **7.** FOOD SMALL ROUND SWEET a small round or oval sweet (*used in combination*) ○ *cough drops* **8.** ACCESSORIES ROUND EARRING OR PENDANT a roundish or pear-shaped earring or pendant **9.** MIL DESCENT BY PARACHUTE a descent from an aircraft by parachute **10.** DELIVERY a delivery ○ *make a drop every two weeks* **11.** GOODS DELIVERED BY PARACHUTE goods, e.g. equipment, that an aircraft delivers by parachute, or people dropped by parachute (*often used in combination*) **12.** SECRET REPOSITORY FOR DANGEROUS MESSAGES a secret place where sb leaves dangerous letters or messages to be picked up by sb else **13.** ACT OF LEAVING SECRET COMMUNICATION the act of leaving a dangerous letter, message, or goods at a prearranged location ○ *It's too dangerous to make the drop tonight.* **14.** THEATRE = **drop curtain** *n.* 1 **15.** ELECTRON ENG CONNECTION ON LINE a point on a transmission line where data can be put in or taken out **16.** TV SHORT SPUR a short line that feeds signals to an individual house from a cable television trunk line **17.** TRAP DOOR UNDER GALLOWS a trap door on which sb who is to be hanged stands under the gallows **18.** SEW CURTAIN LENGTH the measured length for a curtain, from the top of a window to its sill or to the floor ■ **drops** *npl.* PHARM LIQUID MEDICINE APPLIED IN SMALL QUANTITIES liquid medicine that is applied to the ear, nose, or eye using a device that produces a droplet each time it is squeezed [The noun is from Old English *dropa*, the verb from Old English *droppian*. Both ultimately from an Indo-European base that is also the ancestor of English *droop*, *drip*, and *drizzle*.] ◇ **a drop in the ocean** just a tiny part of the full quantity that is required, and thus insignificant ◇ **drop a clanger, drop a brick** to say sth tactless, inappropriate, or mistaken that will cause embarrassment (*informal*) ◇ **at the drop of a hat** without needing persuasion or prompting ◇ **let sth drop** to reveal information to sb, often casually or accidentally

drop away *vi.* **1.** = **drop** *v.* 6 **2.** LEAVE GRADUALLY to leave a group or formation gradually, either on purpose or not ○ *One by one, each jet banked and dropped away from the formation.* **3.** DISAPPEAR GRADUALLY to disappear gradually

drop back, drop behind *vi.* to move more slowly than other people and gradually fall farther behind them

drop by *v.* **1.** *vi.* VISIT SB CASUALLY to visit sb casually or without having agreed on a time **2.** *vt.* DELIVER STH OR SB SOMEWHERE to deliver sth or sb to a specific place ○ *Just drop the laundry by some time this afternoon.*

drop into *vt.* to go from a more active into a less active state of consciousness

drop off *v.* **1.** *vi.* DOZE OFF to fall asleep (*informal*) **2.** *vi.* DECREASE to decline or fall to a lower level (*informal*) ○ *Sales tend to drop off during the summer.* **3.** *vt.* TAKE SB OR STH SOMEWHERE to take sb or sth to a place, usually by car, and leave the person or thing there

drop out *vi.* **1.** LEAVE WITHOUT FINISHING STH to abandon a project or activity without finishing it ○ *He dropped out of college in his final year.* **2.** REJECT SOCIETY to reject conventional society and live in an alternative way (*informal*)

drop over, drop round *vi.* to visit sb casually and without agreeing on a time ○ *Drop round any time.*

drop cloth *n.* **1.** *US* = **dustsheet 2.** THEATRE = **drop curtain**

drop curtain *n.* **1.** UNFRAMED CURTAIN an unframed curtain that can be lowered to a theatre stage from the flies. It usually provides background scenery. **2.** LOWERABLE CURTAIN a theatre curtain that is raised or lowered on stage, rather than being opened or closed by moving sideways

drop forge *n.* a machine used to shape or stamp molten metal by placing it between two dies and dropping a weight on it —**drop-forge** *vt.*

drop front *n.* a part of a writing desk that can be lowered to provide a writing surface and then raised to conceal the inner part of the desk (*hyphenated before a noun*) ○ *a drop-front desk*

drop goal *n.* a goal in rugby scored by dropping the ball and then kicking it

drop hammer *n.* = **drop forge**

drop handlebars *npl.* on a racing bicycle, handlebars that curve downwards, enabling the rider to adopt a more aerodynamic posture

drop-in centre *n.* a place that people can visit without an appointment to get advice, information, or an opportunity to meet others

drop kick *n.* **1.** RUGBY, AMERICAN FOOTBALL METHOD OF KICKING A BALL a way of kicking a football by dropping it first and then kicking it just as it bounces up from the ground **2.** WRESTLING ILLEGAL WRESTLING MOVE in amateur wrestling, an illegal move in which one wrestler attacks another by leaping into the air and striking an opponent with both feet —**drop-kick** *vti.*

drop leaf *n.* an extension on the end of a table that can be folded down when not needed (*hyphenated before a noun*) ○ *a drop-leaf table*

droplet /dróppləṭ/ *n.* a very small drop of liquid

droplight /dróp līt/ *n.* an electric light that can be raised or lowered by using a rope, cord, or pulley

drop lock *n.* in international financial markets, a variable-rate bank loan that is automatically converted to a fixed-rate bond when long-term interest rates fall to a specified level

drop-off *n.* a fall in the level of sth

dropout /dróp owt/ *n.* **1.** EDUC SB WHO LEAVES WITHOUT COMPLETING A COURSE sb who fails to complete an educational course, usually at a college or university **2.** UNCONVENTIONAL PERSON sb who prefers to live an unconventional way of life (*informal*) **3.** RUGBY DROP KICK BY DEFENDERS TO RESTART a drop kick performed by a defending rugby team in order to restart a game, e.g. after a goal has been scored **4.** COMPUT SECTION WITHOUT DATA a small section on a magnetic tape or disk that is missing data

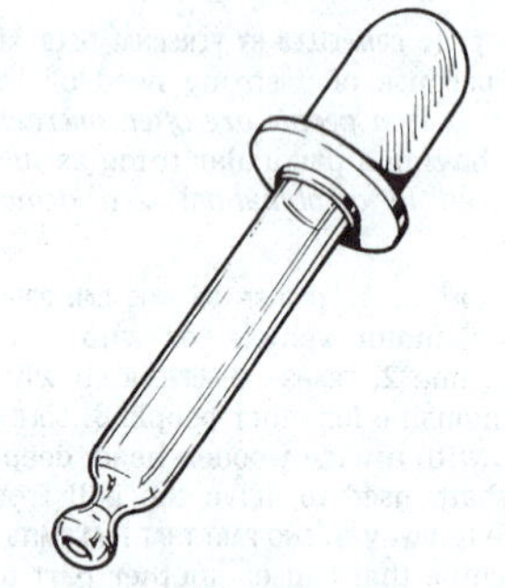

Dropper

dropper /dróppər/ *n.* **1.** TUBE FOR DISPENSING DROPS a small glass or plastic tube with a rubber bulb at one end that is used to suck up liquid and release it one drop at a time (*often used in combination*) ○ *an eye dropper* **2.** ANGLING PIECE OF MONOFILAMENT LINE a short piece of monofilament line, used by anglers to attach a fly above the tail fly

droppings /dróppingz/ *npl.* animal or bird excrement left on the ground or another surface

drop scone *n.* a small round flat cake made by dropping a spoonful of batter onto a heated pan or griddle

drop shipment *n.* a load of a product shipped directly from the manufacturer to the retailer but billed to a third party

drop shot *n.* a shot in a racket game in which the ball drops abruptly to the ground just after crossing over the net or hitting the wall

dropsided lorry /dróp sīdid-/ (*plural* **dropsided lorries**) *n.* an open lorry with hinged sides that can be lowered to allow loading or unloading

dropsied /drópsid/ *adj.* having a large accumulation of fluid between tissues or in a body cavity (*dated*)

dropsonde /dróp sond/ *n.* an instrument, dropped from an aircraft and carried down by a parachute, that transmits information about temperature, pressure, and humidity [Mid-20thC. Coined from DROP + RADIOSONDE.]

dropsy /drópsi/ *n.* oedema (*dated*) [13thC. Shortening of earlier *hydropsy*, via Old French *idropisie* from, ultimately, Greek *hudrōps*, 'sb with dropsy', from *hudōr* 'water' (see HYDRO-).]

drop tank *n.* on fighter and bomber planes, an extra tank of fuel that enables the aircraft to fly longer and farther. When the tank is empty or the plane enters combat it can be jettisoned.

dropwort /dróp wurt/ (*plural* **-worts** *or* **-wort**) *n.* **1.** EURASIAN PLANT a Eurasian plant that produces odourless clusters of small white or red flowers and has finely divided leaves. Latin name: *Filipendula vulgaris.* **2.** MARSH PLANT an umbelliferous marsh plant. Genus: *Oenanthe.* [Coined from DROP + WORT; so called because of the plant's tuberous root fibres]

drop zone *n.* an area where troops or goods such as military equipment or medical supplies are to be landed, usually by parachute

droshky /dróshki/ (*plural* **-kies**), **drosky** (*plural* **-kies**) *n.* an open four-wheeled carriage drawn by horses, formerly used in Russia and Poland [Early 19thC. From Russian *drozhki*, literally 'small wagon', from *drogi* 'wagon'. Ultimately from an Indo-European word that is also the ancestor of English *drag* and *draw.*]

drosometer /dro sómmitər/ *n.* a device for measuring dew deposits [Early 19thC. Coined from Greek *drosos* 'dew' + -METER.]

drosophila /dro sóffilə, drə-/ (*plural* **-las** *or* **-la** *or* **-lae** /-lee/) *n.* a small two-winged fruit fly that is frequently used in genetic research. Genus: *Drosophila.* [Early 19thC. From modern Latin, genus name, from Greek *drosos* 'dew' and *-philos* 'loving'.]

dross /dross/ *n.* **1.** STH WORTHLESS sth that is worthless or of a low standard or quality ○ *I considered her early fiction to be pure dross.* **2.** METALL SCUM ON METAL the scum formed on molten metals, usually caused by oxidation **3.** *Scotland* DOMESTIC SMALL COALS OR COAL DUST small coals or coal dust [Old English *drōs*. Ultimately from an Indo-European base denoting 'dark, muddy', which is also the ancestor of English *dregs* and *dark.*]

drossy /dróssi/ (**-ier, -iest**) *adj.* worthless, or very low in quality —**drossiness** *n.*

drought *n.* **1.** METEOROL PERIOD OF DRY WEATHER a long period of extremely dry weather when there is not enough rain for the successful growing of crops **2.** LACK OF STH a lengthy serious lack of sth ○ *She experienced a period of creative drought.* [Old English *drūgaþ*, literally 'dryness'. From a prehistoric Germanic base meaning 'dry', which is also the ancestor of English *dry* and *drain.*] —**droughty** *adj.*

drouth /drowth, drooth/ *n.* **1.** *Scotland, Ireland* DROUGHT a drought **2.** THIRST dryness or thirst (*regional informal*) —**drouthy** *adj.*

drove[1] past tense of **drive**

drove[2] /drōv/ *n.* **1.** AGRIC GROUP OF ANIMALS MOVING a large number of animals, especially cattle, moving in the same direction, especially when being driven **2.** BUILDING TYPE OF STONE CHISEL a broad-edged chisel used for dressing stone ■ **droves** *npl.* CROWDS OF PEOPLE very large numbers of people ○ *They came out of the football ground in droves.* ■ *vti.* (**droves, droving, droved**) AGRIC MOVE ANIMALS ALONG to move a herd or flock of animals from one place to another, usually over long distances, e.g. to new pastures or to market [Old English *drāf*, from *drīfan* (see DRIVE)]

drover /drōvər/ *n.* sb whose job is to move herds or flocks of animals from one place to another, e.g. to new pastures or to market

drove road *n. Scotland* a road or track along which cattle or sheep were formerly driven on foot to market

drown /drown/ (**drowns, drowning, drowned**) *v.* **1.** *vti.* PHYSIOL DIE BY IMMERSION IN WATER to die, or kill a person or animal, by immersion and usually suffocation in a liquid, normally water. Death occurs either from lack of oxygen or as a result of cardiac arrest from the lowered body temperature. ○ *death by drowning* **2.** *vt.* = **drown out 3.** *vt.* COVER WITH TOO MUCH LIQUID to cover or soak sth, usually an item of food, with too much liquid ○ *He served us pancakes drowned in syrup.* [13thC. Origin uncertain: probably from a Scandinavian source. Ultimately from a prehistoric Germanic base that is also the ancestor of English *drink* and *drench.*] —**drowner** *n.*

drown out *vt.* to make so much noise that it is impossible to hear another sound (*often passive*)

drowned /drownd/ *adj.* **1.** HAVING DIED BY IMMERSION having died by immersion in water **2.** THOROUGHLY SOAKED thoroughly soaked with water or another liquid

drowse /drowz/ *vi.* (**drowses, drowsing, drowsed**) BE HALF ASLEEP to be in a state partway between sleeping and waking ■ *n.* SLIGHTLY SLEEPY STATE a state partway between sleeping and waking [Late 16thC. Back-formation from DROWSY.]

drowsy /drówzi/ (**-ier, -iest**) *adj.* **1.** ALMOST ASLEEP almost asleep or very lightly asleep **2.** CAUSING SLEEPINESS tending to make sb feel sleepy ○ *a drowsy summer afternoon* **3.** SLUGGISH sluggish and dull [15thC. Origin uncertain: ultimately from Old English *drūsian* 'to be sluggish', from a prehistoric Germanic word that is also the ancestor of English *drop* and *droop.*] —**drowsily** *adv.* —**drowsiness** *n.*

drub /drub/ *vt.* (**drubs, drubbing, drubbed**) **1.** BEAT SB WITH A STICK to beat sb using a heavy stick or club **2.** DEFEAT AN OPPONENT to defeat an opponent comprehensively ○ *Their team really drubbed us last year.* **3.** STAMP YOUR FEET to stamp the feet hard on the ground ■ *n.* BLOW WITH A STICK a blow made using a heavy stick or club [Early 17thC. Origin uncertain: possibly from Arabic *ḍaraba* 'to beat'.] —**drubber** *n.*

drudge /druj/ *n.* SB WHO DOES MENIAL WORK sb who does work that is both boring and strenuous ■ *vi.* (**drudges, drudging, drudged**) DO MENIAL WORK to do boring or exhausting work [15thC. From an obsolete word meaning 'to work hard'.] —**drudger** *n.* —**drudgingly** *adv.*

drudgery /drújjəri/ *n.* exhausting, boring, unpleasant work

WORD KEY: SYNONYMS

See Synonyms at *work.*

drug /drug/ *n.* **1.** PHARM SUBSTANCE GIVEN AS MEDICINE a natural or artificial substance that is given to treat, prevent, or diagnose a disease or to lessen pain **2.** DRUGS ILLEGAL SUBSTANCE an often illegal and sometimes addictive substance that causes changes in behaviour and perception and is taken for the effects **3.** PHARM MEDICAL SUBSTANCE a substance given to treat or prevent illness that is officially listed in a medical pharmacopoeia ■ *vt.* (**drugs, drugging, drugged**) **1.** GIVE SB A DRUG to give a drug to sb **2.** ADD DRUG TO FOOD OR DRINK to mix a drug with food or a drink and give it to sb to make him or her fall asleep or become unconscious [14thC. From French *drogue*, of uncertain origin: possibly from Dutch *droog* 'dry', in a phrase meaning 'dry goods' or 'goods packed in barrels'.]

drug abuse *n.* deliberate use of an illegal drug or of too much of a prescribed drug

drug baron *n.* = **drug lord** (*informal*)

drugged /drugd/ *adj.* **1.** PHARM AFFECTED BY DRUGS heavily asleep, unconscious, or unable to function after being given drugs **2.** TIRED AND STUPEFIED extremely tired and unable to concentrate ○ *drugged with sleep*

drugget /drúggit/ *n.* **1.** TEXTILES CARPETING FABRIC a thick heavy fabric made of wool, or cotton and wool, used to cover floors **2.** HOUSEHOLD RUG a coarse rug made of wool or cotton and wool **3.** TEXTILES WOOLLEN FABRIC a woollen or woollen mix fabric formerly used to make clothing [Mid-16thC. From French *droguet*, of uncertain origin: perhaps from *drogue* 'drug, worthless stuff'.]

druggie /drúggi/, **druggy** (*plural* **-gies**) *n.* sb who regularly takes illegal drugs (*slang*)

druggist /drúggist/ *n. US, Can* a pharmaceutical chemist

druggy /drúggi/ *adj.* (**-gier, -giest**) TYPICAL OF HABITUAL DRUG-TAKER typical of sb who takes drugs regularly and often (*slang*) ○ *a druggy stupor.* ■ *n.* = **druggie** (*slang*)

drug lord *n.* sb who controls a large international network engaged in the production, processing, and sale of illegal drugs (*informal*)

drug pusher *n.* sb who sells illegal drugs

drug runner *n.* sb who transports illegal drugs, usually by ship or plane

drugs squad *n.* the department of a police force that investigates the use and sale of illegal drugs

drugstore /drúg stawr/ *n. US, Can* a shop where prescription and over-the-counter drugs are sold along with a wide variety of other goods and often including snacks

drug tsar *n.* in the UK, a senior official appointed to supervise the detection and suppression of illegal drug dealing (*informal*)

Druid /dróo id/ *n.* **1.** HIST PRIEST IN ANCIENT CELTIC RELIGION a priest in an ancient religion practised in Britain, Ireland, and Gaul until the people of those areas were converted to Christianity **2.** RELIG MODERN FOLLOWER OF ANCIENT CELTIC RELIGION sb who worships the forces of nature by means of meditation, prayer, and celebration of the Earth, seen as a modern-day representative of the ancient Celtic religion **3.** ARTS, POETRY OFFICER OF WELSH GORSEDD an officer of the Gorsedd, who administers eisteddfods in Wales [Mid-16thC. Directly or via French from Latin *druides* 'druids', of prehistoric Celtic origin. Probably from an Indo-European compound, 'tree, strength', (the ancestor of English *tree* and *true*) and 'seer'.] —**druidic** /droo íddik/ *adj.* —**druidical** /-íddik'l/ *adj.*

Druidess /dróo idəss/ *n.* **1.** PRIEST IN ANCIENT CELTIC RELIGION a woman priest in an ancient religion practised in Britain, Ireland, and Gaul until the people of those areas were converted to Christianity **2.** RELIG MODERN FOLLOWER OF ANCIENT CELTIC RELIGION sb who worships the forces of nature by meditation, prayer, and celebration of the earth, seen as a modern-day representative of the ancient Celtic religion

Druidism /dróo idizəm/ *n.* an ancient Celtic religion in which the forces of nature were worshipped, and the priests were also prophets and poets, or the modern religion said to derive from it

drum /drum/ *n.* **1.** MUSIC PERCUSSION INSTRUMENT a musical instrument usually consisting of a membrane stretched across a hollow frame and played by striking the stretched membrane. Other hollow objects are also used as drums. **2.** TAPPING SOUND a regular tapping sound made by sth striking a surface ○ *the drum of rain on the roof* **3.** LARGE CYLINDRICAL CONTAINER a large cylindrical container used for storing liquids, e.g. oil or chemicals **4.** SPOOL ON WHICH STH IS WOUND a large spool around which wire, cable, or rope is wound for storage **5.** PART IN A MACHINE a cylindrical hollow part in a machine, e.g. a washing machine **6.** ANAT = **eardrum 7.** ZOOL FISH THAT MAKES A RHYTHMIC SOUND a large bony saltwater or freshwater fish that emits a repeated rhythmic sound. Family: Sciaenidae. **8.** ARCHIT CYLINDRICAL STONE BLOCK one of the cylindrical stone blocks used to make a column **9.** ARCHIT SUPPORT FOR A DOME a band or other structure around the bottom of a dome or circular ceiling that supports it ■ *vi.* (**drums, drumming, drummed**) **1.** MUSIC PLAY A DRUM OR DRUMS to play a drum or drums **2.** TAP A SURFACE to tap repeatedly and rhythmically on a surface ○ *The rain was drumming on the roof.* **3.** BIRDS MAKE SOUND WITH THE BILL OR WINGS to make a repeated sound with the bill or wings (*refers to birds*) [Mid-16thC. Origin uncertain, probably from Middle Dutch *tromme*, literally 'instrument making a loud noise', ultimately of imitative origin.] —**drumming** *n.* ◇ **bang** *or* **beat the drum (for sb** *or* **sth)** to try to attract support and favourable attention for sb or sth that you favour (*informal*)

drum into *vt.* to tell sb sth repeatedly and persistently until the person has learned it or will always remember it (*often passive*)

drum out *vt.* (*usually passive*) **1.** EXPEL SB FROM A GROUP to force sb to leave a group or an organization, usually in disgrace **2.** MAKE SB STOP DOING STH to force sb to stop doing sth

drum up *vt.* **1.** TRY TO ELICIT to try actively to get more of sth such as business or support **2.** INVENT AN EXPLANATION to create or think up an explanation ○ *What excuse can I drum up this time?*

drum and bass *n.* a type of popular music originating in the UK in the 1990s that has a fast rhythm, complex percussion, and very low bass lines. It is influenced by hardcore and reggae.

drumbeat /drúm beet/ *n.* heavy unending criticism, typically public criticism ○ *a steady drumbeat of accusations*

drum brake *n.* a type of brake on vehicles that operates by applying pressure to the inner part of the wheel (**brake drum**)

drum corps *n.* a type of marching band whose instruments are limited to percussion and sometimes bugles or fifes that performs precisely choreographed field drills

drumfire /drúm fīr/ *n.* continuous heavy gunfire

drumfish /drúm fish/ (*plural* **-fish** *or* **-fishes**) *n.* = **drum** *n.* 7

drumhead /drúm hed/ *n.* **1.** MUSIC **MEMBRANE ON A DRUM** the membrane, usually made of calfskin or plastic, that is stretched over the frame of a drum **2.** NAUT **PART OF A CAPSTAN** the round topmost part of a capstan that holds the capstan bars in position for turning

drumhead court-martial *n.* an informal brief trial held during military operations to hear charges of serious offences committed by soldiers while in action [So called because an upturned drum serves as the magistrate's bench]

drum kit *n.* a set of percussion instruments used in bands, usually consisting of one or more snare drums, tom-toms, bass drums, and various cymbals. US term **drum set**

drumlin /drúmlin/ *n.* a long narrow ridge of gravel and rock deposited by a moving glacier, one end of which is blunt and the other end tapering [Mid-19thC. Formed from earlier *drum* 'ridge', from Irish *druim* 'back, ridge', of unknown origin.]

drum machine *n.* an electronic synthesizer that can reproduce drum and percussion sounds in various rhythms and combinations

drum major *n.* sb who leads a marching band and conducts it by moving a baton up and down and twirling it rhythmically

drum majorette *n. US* = **majorette**

drummer /drúmmər/ *n.* **1.** MUSIC **DRUM PLAYER** sb who plays the drums **2.** *US* **TRAVELLING SALESPERSON** a travelling salesperson **3.** (*plural* **-mers** *or* **-mer**) ZOOL **AUSTRALIAN FISH** an Australian fish that frequents rocky shores. Family: Kyphosidae.

Drummond /drúmmənd/, **William** (1585–1649) Scottish poet. As well as poetry, he wrote royalist pamphlets. *Poems* (1616) was his main publication. Known as **Drummond of Hawthornden**

drum roll *n.* a very fast regular beating on a drum that sounds like one long sound

drumstick /drúm stik/ *n.* **1.** MUSIC **STICK FOR BEATING A DRUM** the stick used to beat a drum **2.** FOOD **LOWER HALF OF A POULTRY LEG** the lower half of the leg of a bird such as a chicken when prepared for eating, so called because of its shape

drunk /drungk/ past participle of **drink** ■ *adj.* **1.** **INTOXICATED WITH ALCOHOL** having drunk too much alcohol and lost control over behaviour, movement, and speech **2.** **EMOTIONALLY INTOXICATED** overwhelmed with and judgmentally impaired by an intense emotion ○ *drunk with power* **3.** COOK **LONG-SOAKED** used to describe a meat dish in Chinese cooking in which the meat, usually chicken, has been immersed in a liquid and boiled or marinated overnight ○ *drunk chicken* ■ *n.* **1.** **SB WHO DRINKS ALL THE TIME** sb who habitually drinks too much alcohol or who is in a drunken state **2.** **DRINKING BOUT** a bout of drinking too much alcohol (*slang*) ○ *One more drunk, and I divorce you.*

drunkard /drúngkərd/ *n.* sb who habitually drinks too much alcohol

drunk-driver *n.* sb who drives a car after having drunk more than the legal limit of alcohol

drunk-driving *n. US* = **drink-driving**

drunken /drúngkən/ *adj.* **1.** **INVOLVING ALCOHOL** involving too much alcohol or occurring while people have had too much alcohol ○ *a drunken quarrel* **2.** **INTOXICATED** overly excited by or as if by having consumed too much alcohol **3.** **AFFECTED BY ALCOHOL** drunk or frequently drunk [Old English, old past participle of DRINK] —**drunkenly** *adv.* —**drunkenness** *n.*

drupe /droop/ *n.* a fruit with a thin outer skin, soft pulpy middle, and hard stony central part that encloses a seed. Apricots, plums, cherries, and almonds are drupes. [Mid-18thC. Via modern Latin from Latin *drupa* 'overripe olive', from Greek *druppa* 'olive', of uncertain origin.]

drupelet /dróoplət/, **drupel** /dróop'l/ *n.* a small fruit enclosing a single seed that with many other small sections makes up a compound fruit such as a blackberry or raspberry

Druze /drooz/ (*plural* **Druze** *or* **Druzes**), **Druse** (*plural* **Druse** *or* **Druses**) *n.* a member of a religion similar to Islam that is found mainly in Israel, Lebanon, and Syria [Late 18thC. Directly or via French from Arabic *durūz*, plural of *durzī*, from the name of the religion's founder, Muḥammad ibn Ismā'īl *ad-Darazī* (d. 1019).] —**Druzean** *adj.*

dry /drī/ *adj.* (**drier, driest**) **1.** **NOT WET** not wet, or no longer wet **2.** METEOROL **LACKING MOISTURE IN THE AIR** having very little or no rain or moisture in the air **3.** **NOT WET AND THUS COMFORTABLE** not wet and therefore comfortable to wear ○ *dry clothes* **4.** **LACKING IN APPROPRIATE MOISTURE** lacking in normal levels of natural oiliness or moisture ○ *dry skin* **5.** **DRAINED OF WATER** no longer having water because it has evaporated or been exhausted ○ *The spring has been dry for years.* **6.** **LACKING CUSTOMARY MOISTURE** not producing or accompanied by associated moisture, in the form of phlegm, tears, or vomit ○ *a dry cough* **7.** **NOT REQUIRING LIQUID FOR USE** manufactured so as to be usable without water ○ *dry shampoo* **8.** **WITHOUT FLESH ATTACHED** no longer having the meat attached ○ *dry bones* **9.** **THIRSTY** thirsty and dehydrated **10.** BEVERAGES **LACKING SWEETNESS** not sweet because the sugar has been broken down during the process of fermentation ○ *dry sherry* **11.** FOOD **SERVED WITHOUT FAT OR LIQUID** lacking the usual moist spread such as butter or jam ○ *dry toast* **12.** FOOD **UNAPPETIZINGLY LACKING MOISTNESS** lacking in appetizing moistness, e.g. because of being stale or overcooked **13.** **SHREWDLY AMUSING** witty in a shrewd, subtle, or sarcastic way **14.** **BORING AND ACADEMIC** dense and academic in style **15.** **MATTER-OF-FACT** plain and without unnecessary ornamentation ○ *a dry, matter-of-fact account of the incident* **16.** LAW **NOT ALLOWING ALCOHOL SALES** not allowing legal sale of alcoholic beverages **17.** ZOOL **NO LONGER GIVING MILK** used to describe a female animal that no longer produces milk **18.** **CONTAINING NO MOISTURE** from which the liquid or moisture has been removed ○ *dry weight* **19.** ELECTRON ENG **NOT CONDUCTING ELECTRICITY** used to describe a current-carrying path that cannot conduct electricity because the solder at the joint has not completely adhered to a surface ○ *a dry joint* ■ *v.* (**dries, drying, dried**) **1.** *vti.* **MAKE STH DRY** to make sth dry, or become dry ○ *It's your turn to dry the dishes.* **2.** *vi.* THEATRE **FORGET LINES IN PERFORMANCE** to forget lines during a performance or rehearsal **3.** *vt.* FOOD TECH **PRESERVE FOOD BY EXTRACTING MOISTURE** to preserve food, especially fruit, vegetables, and meat, by extracting most of the moisture from it ■ *n.* **1.** **DRY PLACE** a place that is dry or sheltered from the rain (*informal*) ○ *stay in the dry* **2.** *Aus* METEOROL **DRY SEASON** the dry season (*informal*) **3.** POL **RIGHT-WING POLITICIAN** a politician who is a member of the right wing of the British Conservative Party (*dated*) [Old English *drȳge*. Ultimately from a prehistoric Germanic word that is also the ancestor of English *drought* and *drain*.] —**dryable** *adj.* —**dryness** *n.*

WORD KEY: SYNONYMS

dry, dehydrated, desiccated, arid, parched, shrivelled, sere

CORE MEANING: lacking moisture

dry the most general term used to describe sth containing little or no moisture; **dehydrated** a term for sth from which water has been removed, also used to describe a person or animal whose body does not contain enough fluids; **desiccated** a formal term for *dehydrated.* It is not used to refer to people or animals; **arid** dry because of a lack of rain; **parched** dry because of excessive heat; **shrivelled** dry and shrunken; **sere** a rather literary term meaning withered and dry, used especially of plants.

dry off *vti.* to become drier, or make sth drier

dry out *vti.* **1.** **MAKE OR BECOME COMPLETELY DRY** to become completely dry, or make sth completely dry ○ *It will take a while for the plaster to dry out.* **2.** DRUGS **STOP USING ALCOHOL OR DRUGS** to purge alcohol or other drugs from the body, or put sb through such a process (*informal*)

dry up *v.* **1.** *vti.* **LOSE OR REMOVE MOISTURE** to lose water or moisture over a period, or make a river or pool lose its water over a period ○ *The river dried up centuries ago.* **2.** *vi.* **STOP BEING AVAILABLE** to stop being available as a resource ○ *Our project ended because our sources of funding dried up.* **3.** *vt.* **DRY DISHES** to dry plates, dishes, pans, and cutlery with a cloth after they have been washed **4.** *vi.* **STOP TALKING** to stop talking, or forget lines during a performance or rehearsal (*informal*) (*often used as a command*) ○ *Oh, just dry up, will you? I'm trying to think!* **5.** *vi.* **RUN OUT OF IDEAS** to be unable to perform as usual or as expected ○ *His ideas have dried up.*

dryad /drī ad, -əd/ (*plural* **-ads** *or* **-ades** /-ə deez/) *n.* in Greek mythology, a spiritual being believed to live in trees and forests [14thC. Via Latin from Greek *Druad-*, the stem of *Druas*, from *drus* 'tree'. Ultimately from an Indo-European word that is also the ancestor of English *tree.*] —**dryadic** /drī áddik/ *adj.*

dryasdust /drī əz dúst/ *n.* sb who bores audiences with tedious speeches (*dated*) [Late 19thC. From the name of the fictitious Dr Jonas *Dryasdust*, to whom Sir Walter Scott dedicated some of his novels.]

dry battery (*plural* **dry batteries**) *n.* an electric battery that has more than one dry cell

dry-bone ore *n.* a kind of smithsonite that has many holes, found near the surface of the Earth's crust

dry cell *n.* a current-generating electric cell that cannot be regenerated and contains an electrolyte in the form of a paste or within a porous material to keep it from spilling. ◊ **wet cell**

dry-clean (**dry-cleans, dry-cleaning, dry-cleaned**) *vt.* to clean clothes or other fabrics with a chemical solvent instead of water

dry-cleaner's (*plural* **dry-cleaner's**) *n.* a shop that takes clothes and household fabrics and cleans them using a chemical solvent

dry-cleaning *n.* **1.** **COMMERCIAL METHOD OF CLEANING CLOTHES** the professional cleaning of clothes and other fabrics using a chemical solvent rather than water **2.** **DRY-CLEANED ITEMS** clothes and other fabrics that require dry-cleaning or have just been dry-cleaned

dry cough *n.* a cough that does not produce phlegm

Dryden /drīd'n/, **John** (1631–1700) English poet, dramatist, and critic. His works include the play *Marriage à la Mode* (1672) and the verse satire *Absalom and Achitophel* (1681). He was made poet laureate by Charles II (1668), but having become a Catholic in 1685, was deprived of the office on the accession of William of Orange.

dry distillation *n.* = **destructive distillation**

dry dock *n.* an enclosed dock from which the water can be removed so that construction or repairs can be carried out below the waterline of a boat or ship —**dry-dock** *vti.*

dryer[1] comparative of **dry**

dryer[2], **drier** comparative of **dry** ■ *n.* **1.** **DRYING DEVICE** a machine or device for drying things **2.** **SUBSTANCE TO AID DRYING** a substance added to paint or ink to speed up the drying process

dry-eyed /-īd/ *adj.* unable or unwilling to shed tears ○ *He remained dry-eyed throughout the trial.*

dry farming *n.* a method of growing crops in dry areas by selecting plants that are drought-resistant and using mulch to retain moisture in the soil, so making irrigation unnecessary —**dry farmer** *n.*

dry fly *n.* a kind of artificial lure used in fly-fishing that remains on the surface of the water instead of sinking. ◊ **wet fly**

dry goods *npl. US* = **drapery** *n.* 4

dry hole *n.* an oil well that has been drilled but that produces no oil, or not enough to make it economically profitable

dry ice *n.* cold solid carbon dioxide at the temperature of –78.5°C/–110°F, used to keep other things very cold or to produce an artificial fog effect

drying oil *n.* an organic oil e.g. linseed or cottonseed oil, used as a base in paints and varnishes because it reduces drying time. Such oils form a tough thin film when exposed to air.

dry kiln *n.* a large oven used to season cut timber

dry land *n.* the land as distinct from the sea or a body of water

dryly *adv.* = **drily**

dry martini *n.* a cocktail that contains a little dry vermouth mixed with gin or vodka

dry measure *n.* a system of units used to measure dry products such as grains and fruits by volume, or a unit in such a system

dry nurse *n.* a nurse employed to look after sb's young baby but not to breastfeed it (*archaic*) ◊ **wet nurse** —**dry-nurse** *vt.*

dryopithecine /drī ō píthə seen/ (*plural* **-cines** *or* **-cine**) *n.* an extinct ape of the Miocene and Pliocene epochs, believed by some scientists to be the ancestor of modern apes and humans. Genus: *Dryopithecus.* [Mid-20thC. Formed from modern Latin *Dryopithecus*, genus name, from Greek *drus* 'tree' and *pithēkos* 'ape'.]

dry point *n.* 1. METHOD OF ENGRAVING a technique of engraving in intaglio on a metal, usually copper, plate that produces a feathery effect in the lines of the print 2. STEEL NEEDLE a hard steel needle used to engrave a metal plate 3. PRINT MADE BY DRY POINT an engraving or print made by using dry point

dry riser *n.* a waterless pipe that runs vertically, with connections on different levels of a building to which a firefighter's hose can be attached in case of fire

dry rot *n.* 1. BUILDING CRUMBLING DECAY IN WOOD dry crumbling decay in wood caused by various fungi. ◊ **wet rot** 2. BOT PLANT DISEASE a disease caused by various fungi that invade plant stems, bulbs, and fruits, causing them to dry out and decay 3. FUNGI DESTRUCTIVE FUNGUS a fungus that causes dry rot. Genus: *Merulius.*

dry run *n.* a rehearsal of a planned action or activity ○ *Let's have a dry run to make sure it's going to work.*

dry-salt (**dry-salts, dry-salting, dry-salted**) *vt.* to use salt to dry and preserve food

dry-salter *n.* sb who stocks and sells a variety of chemical products, e.g. dyes, and also salted, dried, and tinned foods (*archaic*) —**dry-saltery** *n.*

Drysdale /dríz dayl/ (*plural* **-dales** *or* **-dale**) *n. NZ* a sheep belonging to a breed raised commercially in New Zealand for its fleece, used in carpeting

Drysdale /dríz dayl/, **Sir Russell** (1912–81) English-born Australian landscape painter. Many of his best-known works portray the harshness of life in rural Australia. Full name **Sir George Russell Drysdale**

dry socket *n.* a painful condition caused when the blood left by an extracted tooth fails to clot or the clot is dislodged

dry-stone *adj.* built with pieces of stone that are fitted together without mortar ○ *a dry-stone wall*

Dry Tortugas National Park /-tawr tóogəz-/ national park in southwestern Florida that contains Fort Jefferson and Shark Island. Area: 262 sq. km/100 sq. mi.

DS, ds *abbr.* MUSIC dal segno

d.s. *abbr.* 1. days after sight 2. document signed

DSc *abbr.* Doctor of Science

DSC *abbr.* Distinguished Service Cross

DSL *abbr.* Digital Subscriber Line

DSM *abbr.* Distinguished Service Medal

DSO *abbr.* Distinguished Service Order

dsp *abbr.* died without issue [Latin *decessit sine prole*]

DSR *abbr.* debt service ration

DSS *abbr.* Department of Social Security

DSS *abbr.* Director of Social Services

DST *abbr.* daylight-saving time

DT *abbr.* Doctor Theologiae

DTI *abbr.* Department of Trade and Industry

DTP *abbr.* desktop publishing

dual /dyóo əl/ *adj.* 1. HAVING TWO SIMILAR ELEMENTS having two parts, functions, aspects, or items of a similar kind ○ *dual citizenship* 2. HAVING TWO DISTINCT ASPECTS made up of two distinct, often opposite, elements ○ *serve a dual purpose* 3. GRAM SPECIFYING TWO in various languages, used to describe or relating to a grammatical number category, in addition to singular and plural, that specifies two people or things ■ *n.* GRAM DUAL NUMBER OR INFLECTED FORM dual number, or, in various languages, the inflected form of a noun, pronoun, adjective, or verb that refers to dual number [Early 17thC. From Latin *dualis*, from *duo* 'two'. Ultimately from the Indo-European word for 'two', which is also the ancestor of English *two* and *binary*).] —**dually** *adv.*

Duala /dóo aálə, dóo aá laa/ (*plural* **-la** *or* **-las**) *n.* 1. PEOPLES MEMBER OF AN AFRICAN ETHNIC GROUP a member of an African ethnic group who live in Cameroon 2. LANG LANGUAGE OF THE DUALA the language of the Duala, belonging to the Bantu group of Niger-Congo languages. = **Douala** —**Duala** *adj.*

dual carriageway *n.* a road with two or more lanes of traffic in each direction divided by a central reservation or barrier. US term **divided highway**

dual in-line package *n.* a package consisting of a printed circuit board and a series of switches, used to control optional settings for electronic devices

dualism /dyóo əlizzəm/ *n.* 1. STATE OF HAVING TWO PARTS a state in which sth has two distinct parts or aspects, which are often opposites 2. PHILOS THEORY OF TWO OPPOSING CONCEPTS a philosophical theory based on the idea of opposing concepts, especially the theory that human beings are made up of two independent constituents, the body and the mind or soul 3. RELIG DOCTRINE OF OPPOSING PRINCIPLES the religious doctrine that two opposed and antagonistic forces of good and evil determine the course of events 4. RELIG DUAL NATURE OF PEOPLE the religious idea that people are inherently dual in nature, both spiritual and physical —**dualist** *n.* —**dualistic** /dyóo ə lístik/ *adj.* —**dualistically** /-lístikli/ *adv.*

duality /dyoo állәti/ (*plural* **-ties**) *n.* 1. STH CONSISTING OF TWO PARTS a situation or nature that has two states or parts that are complementary or opposed to each other 2. PHYS THEORY OF MATTER in microphysics, the theory that both wave and particle theory account for the behaviour of matter and energy under different conditions 3. GEOM MATHEMATICAL SYMMETRY OF OBJECTS OR OPERATIONS a mathematical symmetry in which certain objects or operations to be interchanged without invalidating a relationship, e.g. the interchange of points and lines in a plane in projective geometry

dual-purpose *adj.* capable of performing two functions satisfactorily ○ *a dual-purpose cleaner*

dub[1] /dub/ *vt.* (**dubs, dubbing, dubbed**) 1. GIVE DESCRIPTIVE NICKNAME to give a descriptive nickname to sb or sth ○ *The press dubbed him the King of Chess.* 2. POL CONFER A KNIGHTHOOD ON SB to give sb a knighthood by tapping the person on the shoulder with a sword as part of a formal ceremony 3. INDUST MAKE STH SMOOTH OR EVEN to dress a material, e.g. leather or timber, to make it smooth or even 4. ANGLING DECORATE AN ARTIFICIAL FLY to add material such as hair or fur to an artificial fly, to give body and a natural look ■ *n.* MUSIC SOUND OF A DRUM the sound a drum makes [Pre-12thC. From Anglo-Norman *duber*, a variant of Old French *adober* 'to equip with armour', of unknown origin.] —**dubber** *n.*

dub[2] /dub/ *vt.* (**dubs, dubbing, dubbed**) 1. CINEMA, TV ADD A SOUNDTRACK IN A DIFFERENT LANGUAGE to add a new soundtrack to a film or television show with the dialogue in a different language but synchronized as closely as possible with the actors' lips ○ *The film was dubbed into Italian.* 2. RECORDING COPY STH ONTO NEW MEDIUM to copy sth already recorded onto a different recording medium 3. RECORDING COPY to make a copy of a record or tape 4. RECORDING ADD SOUNDS TO A FILM to add sounds that have been recorded separately to a film soundtrack ■ *n.* 1. STH ADDED BY DUBBING new sounds added by dubbing 2. COPY OF RECORDING a copy made of a tape or recording 3. STYLE OF MUSIC a style of popular music, originating in reggae in the 1970s, involving remixing records to bring certain instruments into the foreground and causing others to echo (*informal*) [Early 20thC. Shortening of DOUBLE.] —**dubber** *n.*

dub[3] /dub/ *n.* a style of popular music, originating with reggae in the 1970s, that involves remixing records to bring some instruments into the foreground while causing some others to echo

dub[4] /dub/ *n. Scotland, N England* a puddle or small pool of water on the ground, especially in the road [15thC. Origin unknown.]

dub[5] /dub/ (**dubs, dubbing, dubbed**) *vi.* to make a contribution to the cost of sth (*archaic slang*) [Early 19thC. Origin unknown.]

Dubai /doo bī/, **Dubayy** city in the northeastern United Arab Emirates, and the capital city of Dubai state. Population: 674,100 (1995).

dubbin /dúbbin/ *n.* a mixture of oil and tallow rubbed into leather to soften it and make it waterproof [Early 19thC. Alteration of *dubbing*, present participle of DUB[1].]

dubbing /dúbbing/ *n.* 1. PROCESS OF ADDING NEW SOUNDTRACK the process of providing a new soundtrack for a film or television show with the dialogue in a different language but synchronized as closely as possible with the actors' lips 2. SOUNDTRACK a soundtrack recorded for a film or television show after the photography is finished 3. FINAL SOUNDTRACK a final mix of all the soundtracks for a film [Formed from DUB[2]]

dubbo /dúbbō/ *adj. ANZ* UNINTELLIGENT unintelligent (*slang insult*) ■ *n.* (*plural* **-bos**) *ANZ* UNINTELLIGENT PERSON an unintelligent person (*slang insult*) [Origin unknown]

Dubbo /dúbbō/ town in central New South Wales, Australia, located on the River Macquarie at the heart of an agricultural region. Population: 30,102 (1996).

Dubček /dóop chek, dóob-/, **Alexander** (1921–92) Czech statesman. His liberal reforms as leader of the Communist party led to Soviet invasion in 1968. Shortly afterwards, he was ousted from power. He re-emerged as a popular leader in 1989.

dubiety /dyoo bī əti/ (*plural* **-ties**) *n.* (*formal*) 1. UNCERTAINTY ABOUT STH a feeling of uncertainty about sth 2. STH DOUBTFUL sth about which you are unsure [Mid-18thC. From late Latin *dubietas*, from Latin *dubius* 'doubtful' (see DUBIOUS).]

dubious /dyóobi əss/ *adj.* 1. UNSURE ABOUT AN OUTCOME uncertain about an outcome or conclusion ○ *I was a little dubious about whether or not to trust him.* 2. POSSIBLY DISHONEST OR IMMORAL likely to be dishonest, untrustworthy, or morally worrying in some way ○ *It's a dubious proposition.* 3. OF UNCERTAIN QUALITY of uncertain quality, intention, or appropriateness ○ *The thesis is based on several dubious theories.* [Mid-16thC. Formed from Latin *dubius* 'doubtful'. The underlying meaning was 'split between two choices'.] —**dubiously** *adv.* —**dubiousness** *n.*

WORD KEY: SYNONYMS

See Synonyms at ***doubtful***.

dubitable /dyóobitəb'l/ *adj.* causing or leading to doubt or uncertainty (*formal*) [Early 17thC. From Latin *dubitabilis*, from *dubitare* 'to be uncertain'.] —**dubitably** *adv.*

Dublin /dúbblin/ city and capital of the Republic of Ireland. It is situated on the River Liffey in east-central Ireland, at the head of Dublin Bay on the Irish Sea. Population: 480,996 (1996). —**Dubliner** *n.*

dubnium /dúbni əm/ *n.* an extremely rare, unstable chemical element produced in high-energy atomic-ion collisions. Symbol **Db**

Du Bois /dóo bóyss/, **W. E. B.** (1868–1963) US historian, sociologist, and civil rights leader. He conducted the first research on the experience of Blacks in the United States and fought for racial equality, becoming the most influential African American intellectual of his time. Full name **William Edward Burghardt Du Bois**

Dubonnet /dóo bónnay, dyóo-/ *tdmk.* a trademark for a wine used as an apéritif

zh vision In foreign words: kh German Bach; aN French vin; aaN French blanc; ö German schön, French feu; oN French bon; öN French un; ü French rue Stress marks: ´ as in secret \séek rət\; academic \àkə démmik\

dub poetry *n.* a kind of performance poetry using the rhythms and speech styles of West Indian English [From disc jockeys dubbing their own words onto records]

Dubrovnik /do͞o brówník/ city, port, and holiday resort on the Dalmatian coast in southeastern Croatia. It suffered much damage during ethnic conflict in the 1990s. Population: 49,728 (1991).

Dubuffet /dyo͞o bo͞o fáy/, **Jean** (1901–85) French painter and sculptor. He was an avant-garde artist who rejected traditional techniques, often working with found objects and materials such as sand and plaster. Full name **Jean Philippe Arthur Dubuffet**

ducal /dyóok'l/ *adj.* belonging to, relating to, or like a duke or dukedom ○ *a ducal palace* [15thC. Via French from, ultimately, Latin *duc-*, the stem of *dux* 'leader'.] —**ducally** *adv.*

ducat /dúkət/ *n.* **OLD EUROPEAN COIN** a gold or silver coin formerly used in some European countries, e.g. Italy and the Netherlands ■ **ducats** *npl.* **CASH** money or cash (*dated informal*) [14thC. Via Old French from, ultimately, medieval Latin *ducatus* 'duchy' (see DUCHY); so called because the word appeared on early coins.]

duce /do͞o chay, do͞ochi/ *n.* an Italian term for 'leader'. The Italian Fascist leader Mussolini was called 'Il Duce'. [Early 20thC. Via Italian from, ultimately, Latin *dux* 'leader'.]

Duchamp /dyo͞o shaáN/, **Marcel** (1887–1968) French-born US artist. He displayed everyday objects as works of art, and helped to introduce Cubism to the United States. He became a citizen of the United States in 1954, and later his work became an inspiration for the pop art movement.

Duchenne muscular dystrophy /doo shén-/, **Duchenne's muscular dystrophy** /doo shénz-/, **Duchenne dystrophy, Duchenne's dystrophy** *n.* a form of muscular dystrophy that attacks the muscles of the upper respiratory and pelvic areas, usually affecting boys and causing death before maturity [Late 19thC. Named after the French neurologist G. B. A. *Duchenne* (1806–75), who first described it.]

duchess /dúchəss/ *n.* **1. HIGH-RANKING NOBLEWOMAN** a noblewoman of high rank. In the British Isles this is the highest hereditary title of nobility. **2. WIFE OR WIDOW OF A DUKE** the wife or widow of a duke ■ *vt.* **(-esses, -essing, -essed)** *Aus* **FLATTER SB** to treat sb like royalty, especially in an obsequious or fawning manner (*dated informal*) [14thC. Via Old French *duchesse* from medieval Latin *ducissa*, feminine form of *dux* 'leader'.]

duchesse potatoes /dyo͞o shéss-, duch éss-/ *npl.* a mixture of mashed potatoes, egg, and butter that is piped into the shape of a pyramid or nest and baked [*Duchesse* from French, 'duchess']

duchesse satin /dyoo shéss-/ *n.* a firm heavy satin with a glossy finish, used often for formal gowns

duchy /dúchi/ (*plural* **-ies**) *n.* the territory over which a duke or duchess has jurisdiction [14thC. Via Old French *duche* from medieval Latin *ducatus*, from Latin *duc-*, the stem of *dux* 'leader'.]

duck[1] /duk/ *n.* **1.** (*plural* **ducks** *or* **duck**) **BIRDS COMMON WATER BIRD** a common water bird with webbed feet, short legs, and a broad flat bill. It is found all over the world, with the exception of Antarctica. Order: Anseriformes. **2. FEMALE DUCK** a female duck. ◊ **drake 3.** FOOD **DUCK AS FOOD** the flesh of a duck when it is eaten as a food **4. duck, ducks DEAR** used when addressing sb in a friendly way (*regional informal*) ○ *Can I help you, ducks?* **5. ODD PERSON** sb who is mildly unconventional, especially appealingly so [Old English *dūce*, of uncertain origin: probably from assumed *dūcan* 'to dive' (see DUCK[2])] ◇ **take to sth like a duck to water** to have a natural talent for sth

duck[2] /duk/ *v.* **(ducks, ducking, ducked) 1.** *vti.* **BEND QUICKLY** to bend or move the head down quickly, especially to avoid being hit by sth **2.** *vi.* **MOVE QUICKLY** to move somewhere very quickly, often to avoid being seen ○ *I ducked behind a desk and kept as still as possible.* **3.** *vti.* **PLUNGE UNDER WATER** to push sb under water, or move quickly so as to go below the surface of the water ○ *No ducking.* **4.** *vt.* **AVOID STH** to avoid dealing with sth that ought to be dealt with ○ *The candidate ducked all the questions about her past* **5.** *vi.* BRIDGE **DELIBERATELY LOSE A TRICK** to play a card lower than an opponent's on purpose in order to lose a trick ■ *n.* **QUICK DOWNWARD MOVEMENT** a movement downwards with the head, especially to avoid being hit by sth [13thC. Origin uncertain: probably from assumed Old English *dūcan*, ultimately from a prehistoric West Germanic word meaning 'to dive, dip'.] —**ducker** *n.* ◇ **duck and run** to avoid meeting sb face to face

duck out *vi.* to avoid or dodge doing sth ○ *She's trying to duck out of paying her part of the bill.*

duck[3] /duk/ *n.* TEXTILES **STRONG CLOTH** strong, fairly stiff, closely-woven cloth, usually of cotton or canvas, used to make protective clothing and furnishings ■ **ducks** *npl.* CLOTHES **PAIR OF WHITE TROUSERS** a pair of trousers, usually white, or like those worn by sailors

duck[4] /duk/ *n.* a score of zero by a batsman or batswoman [Shortening of 'duck's egg', a zero] ◇ **break your duck** have your first success or victory after several failures

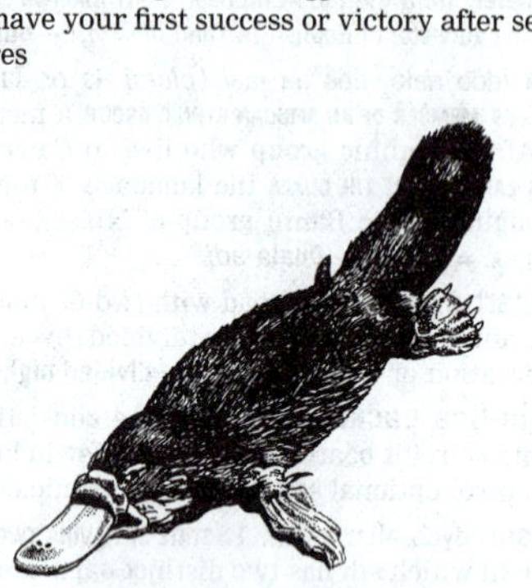

Duck-billed platypus

duck-billed platypus *n.* an Australian egg-laying aquatic mammal with a snout shaped like a duck's bill and webbed feet. Latin name: *Ornithorynchus anatinus.*

duckboard /dúk bawrd/ *n.* a temporary walkway made of wooden boards laid over a wet or muddy area to form a raised path

duck-egg blue *n.* a pale greenish-blue colour —**duck-egg blue** *adj.*

ducking stool *n.* formerly, in Europe and New England, a chair or stool in which an offender was tied and then immersed in water as a punishment

duckling /dúkling/ *n.* a duck that has not reached maturity

ducks *n.* ➧ **duck**[1] *n.* 4

ducks and drakes *n.* a game in which flat stones are bounced across water by throwing them almost parallel to its surface (*takes a singular verb*) [So called because of the game's similarity to a waterfowl's movements]

duck's arse *n.* full form of **DA** (*slang*)

duck soup *n. US* a task or feat done or accomplished easily (*slang*)

duckweed /dúk weed/ *n.* a stemless free-floating aquatic plant with small rounded leaves that is found on still temperate waters and eaten by waterfowl. Genus: *Lemna.*

ducky /dúki/, **duckie** *n.* (*plural* **-ies**) **DARLING** used as an affectionate way of addressing sb (*dated informal*) ■ *adj. US* **CHARMING** charmingly pretty (*dated informal*) ○ *a ducky little cottage*

duco /dyóokō/ *n. Aus* the paintwork on a motor vehicle [Originally a trade name]

duct /dukt/ *n.* **1. CHANNEL THROUGH WHICH STH FLOWS** a tube, pipe, or channel through which sth can flow or be carried, e.g. in air-conditioning equipment **2.** ANAT **TUBE IN A BODY ORGAN** a narrow tubular exit passageway in a gland or bladder through which fluid passes **3.** ELEC ENG **TUBE FOR CABLES** a tube or channel containing electrical cables ■ *vt.* **(ducts, ducting, ducted) 1. SUPPLY WITH DUCTING** to supply or equip sth such as a building with a duct or a system of ducts **2. CAUSE TO PASS THROUGH CHANNEL** to make a fluid or gas pass through a tube, pipe, or channel ○ *Exhaust fumes are ducted out of the workshop.* [Mid-17thC. From Latin *ductus*, from *ducere* 'to lead'.] —**ductal** *adj.* —**ductless** *adj.*

WORD KEY: ORIGIN

As well as giving rise to ***duct***, Latin *ducere* is also the source of English *aqueduct, conduct, deduce, deduct, douche, duke, educate, introduce, produce, reduce, seduce,* and *subdue.*

ductile /dúk tīl/ *adj.* **1. MALLEABLE ENOUGH TO BE WORKED** able to be drawn out into wire or hammered into very thin sheets ○ *ductile metal* **2. READILY SHAPED OR MOULDED** able to be moulded or shaped without breaking **3. READILY INFLUENCED** easily persuaded or influenced [14thC. Directly or via Old French *ductile* from Latin *ductilis* 'sth that may be led or conducted', from *ducere* 'to lead'.] —**ductilely** *adv.* —**ductileness** *n.* —**ductility** /duk tílləti/ *n.*

WORD KEY: SYNONYMS

See Synonyms at ***pliable***.

ducting /dúkting/ *n.* **1. SYSTEM OF DUCTS** a duct or system of ducts **2. MATERIAL FOR DUCTS** materials such as pipes and tubing that can be used as ducts

dud /dud/ *n.* **1. FAILURE AT STH** sb or sth considered ineffective or a failure (*informal*) **2. SHELL THAT DOES NOT EXPLODE** a munition that fails to fire or explode ■ *adj.* **(dudder, duddest) USELESS** useless for the intended purpose (*informal*) ○ *a dud cheque* [Early 19thC. Origin uncertain: perhaps from DUDS via 'sb in rags', hence 'useless thing', hence 'shell that failed to explode', hence 'failure'.]

dude /dyood, dood/ *n. US* (*slang*) **1. MAN** a man or boy ○ *He's one cool dude.* ○ *Hey, dude, what's up?* **2. CITY DWELLER ON HOLIDAY IN US WEST** an American who lives in a city or the Eastern United States and takes holidays on a dude ranch in the west, or who moves west to work or live ○ *'A new word has been coined. It is d-u-d-e ... It has sprung into popularity within the last two weeks'.* (*Brooklyn Daily Eagle*; 15 February, 1883) **3. FLASHILY DRESSED MAN** a man who wears flashy, highly stylish clothes [Late 19thC. Origin uncertain: perhaps from a German dialect word meaning 'fool'.]

dudeen /doo deén/ *n.* a clay tobacco pipe with a short stem [Mid-19thC. From Irish *dúidín*, literally 'small pipe', from *dúd* 'pipe'.]

dude ranch *n. US* a holiday resort offering outdoor activities that is or resembles a typical ranch of the Western United States

dudgeon /dújjən/ *n.* a fit of anger and irritation [Late 16thC. Origin unknown.] ◇ **in high dudgeon** in a very angry or irritated mood

Dudley /dúddli/ city and industrial centre near Birmingham in the West Midlands, England. Population: 192,171 (1991).

duds /duds/ *npl.* (*dated informal*) **1. CLOTHES** articles of clothing and accessories **2. SMALL BELONGINGS** small, portable personal possessions [15thC. Of uncertain origin.]

due /dyoo/ *adj.* **1. EXPECTED TO ARRIVE** expected to arrive imminently ○ *The baby is due in three weeks.* **2. READY FOR STH** awaiting an event, as part of a normal chain or progression of other events ○ *due for a long-awaited promotion* **3. PROPER AND APPROPRIATE** meeting all the necessary requirements and thus proper and appropriate to the situation ○ *after due consideration* **4. OWED** owed as a debt because of a right or an obligation ○ *Our deep gratitude is due to all those who have helped over the last few months.* **5.** FIN **PAYABLE** payable at once and on demand, or at a stipulated time ○ *Payment is due in 30 days.* **6. BECAUSE OF SB OR STH** caused by or attributable to sb or sth ○ *The delay was due to bad weather.* ■ *n.* **SB'S RIGHT** sth that sb has deserved or is owed ○ *I'll give you your due–you were absolutely right.* ■ **dues** *npl.* **MEMBERSHIP FEES** fees for membership of an organization or use of a facility ■ *adv.* **DIRECTLY AND EXACTLY** in a direct exact way or course ○ *due west* [13thC. Via Old French *deu* 'owed' from Latin *debitus*, from *debere* 'to owe' (source of English *debit* and *debt*.)]

duel /dyo͞o əl/ *n.* **1. FORMAL FIGHT OVER MATTER OF HONOUR** a prearranged combat, especially in former times, between two people with lethal weapons, usually to settle a disagreement over a matter of honour. The combatants were usually accompanied by seconds or supporters. **2. STRUGGLE BETWEEN TWO PARTIES** a struggle or conflict between two people or groups ■ *vi.* **(-els, -elling, -elled) 1. ENGAGE IN ONE-TO-ONE COMBAT** to fight sb one-to-one, typically with firearms or sabres and usually over a matter of honour **2. OPPOSE** to be involved in a conflict or struggle with sb [15thC. From medieval Latin *duellum* 'combat between two people', from (by folk etymology from Latin *duo* 'two') Latin *duellum*, an archaic form of *bellum* 'war'.] —**dueller** *n.* —**duellist** *n.*

duelling pistol *n.* a pistol specifically designed for fighting a duel, usually more finely manufactured than a normal pistol and often made in sets of two

duenna /dyoo énnə/ *n.* a woman acting as a chaperone or governess to a younger woman, especially in Spain and Portugal in former times [Mid-17thC. Via Spanish, 'married lady', from late Latin *domna*, from Latin *domina* 'lady' (source of English *dame*).]

due process of law *n.* legal procedures carried out in accordance with established rules and principles

duet /dyoo ét/ *n.* **1. COMPOSITION FOR TWO PERFORMERS** an instrumental or vocal composition written for two performers of equal importance **2. PAIR** a pair of people, animals, or things [Mid-18thC. Via Italian *duetto*, literally 'little duo' from *duo* 'two musicians', from Latin *duo* 'two' or perhaps via German *Duett*.] —**duettist** *n.*

duff[1] /duf/ *adj.* **USELESS** useless, broken, or of very low quality (*informal*) ■ *vt.* (**duffs, duffing, duffed**) **MISHIT A GOLF BALL** to play a bad shot in golf by hitting the ground behind the ball (*informal*) [Mid-19thC. Origin uncertain: perhaps a back-formation from DUFFER.]

duff up *vt.* to hit or kick sb repeatedly so as to cause injury (*slang*)

duff[2] /duf/ *n.* a heavy pudding, usually made with suet and dried fruit and steamed or boiled in a cloth ○ *plum duff* [Mid-19thC. Alteration of DOUGH (compare pronunciation of ENOUGH).]

duff[3] /duf/ *n.* the buttocks (*slang offensive*) [Late 19thC. Origin uncertain.] ◇ **up the duff** pregnant (*slang*)

Duff /duf/, **Alan** (*b.* 1950) New Zealand writer. He wrote *Once Were Warriors* (1990).

duffel /dúff'l/, **duffle** *n.* **1. TEXTILES WOOLLEN FABRIC** woollen material with a nap on both sides **2.** *US* **CAMPING GEAR** gear, including clothing and equipment, used by campers and hikers [Late 17thC. From Dutch *duffel*, named after *Duffel*, town in Belgium where the cloth was originally made.]

duffel bag *n.* a cylindrical bag for personal belongings that is fastened with a drawstring

Duffel coat

duffel coat *n.* **TEXTILES** a heavy medium-length coat with a hood and toggles for fastening it that is made from duffel

duffer /dúffər/ *n.* **1. UNINTELLIGENT PERSON** sb who is thought of as slow to learn or incompetent at sth (*dated informal insult*) **2. STH WORTHLESS** sth worthless or useless (*dated informal*) **3. PEDLAR** sb who peddles goods, especially cheap or worthless merchandise (*regional archaic*) [Mid-18thC. Origin uncertain: perhaps an alteration of Scottish *dowfart* 'dull, inactive fellow', or from Old Norse *daufr* 'deaf'.]

duffle *n.* = **duffel**

Dufy /dóofi/, **Raoul** (1877–1953) French painter, illustrator, and designer. Known for his paintings of the French Riviera in a popularized fauvist style, he also designed textiles and pottery.

dug[1] past participle, past tense of **dig**

dug[2] /dug/ *n.* **1. ANIMAL'S MAMMARY GLAND** an udder, teat, nipple, or breast of a female mammal **2. DISTASTEFUL TERM FOR HUMAN BREAST** the breast of a human being,

especially when regarded with distaste (*literary*) [Mid-16thC. Origin uncertain.]

Duggan /dúggən/, **Maurice** (1922–74) New Zealand writer. Noted for his short stories, his *Collected Short Stories* was published in 1981.

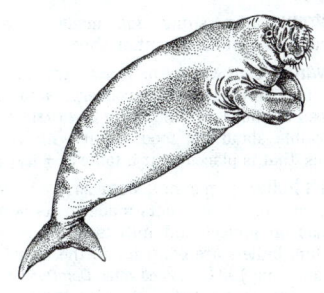

Dugong

dugong /dóo gong/ *n.* a large plant-eating mammal of shallow tropical coastal waters, related to the manatee. It has a two-lobed tail, cleft upper lip, forelimbs resembling flippers, and tusks in the male. Latin name: *Dugong dugon*. [Early 19thC. Ultimately from Malay *duyung*.]

dugout /dúg owt/ *n.* **1. MIL SOLDIERS' SHELTER** a hole dug in the ground that is covered and used as a shelter, especially by soldiers **2. SOCCER SOCCER SHELTER** either of two shelters beside a sports field, especially a soccer pitch, for team officials, e.g. the manager and trainer and team members who are not on the field **3. CANOE MADE FROM A HOLLOWED LOG** a canoe or boat hollowed out from a log or tree trunk

duh /də/ *interj.* *US* (*slang*) **1. RESPONSE TO STH ALREADY KNOWN** said as an ironic response to a simple question or statement to show that sb already knows the truth of sth that he or she has just been told ○ '*Billy asked me to the party, I think he really likes me!*' '*Duh!*' **2. HUMOROUS EXPRESSION OF STUPIDITY** said slowly in a humorous manner to suggest stupidity by imitating the hesitant noise sb might make to indicate that he or she does not know the answer to sth ○ '*What did you do with the keys?*' – '*Duh*'.

Duhamel /dyoo ə mel/, **Georges** (1884–1966) French writer and physician. His books include *Des légendes, des batailles* (1907), *La lumière* (1911), and *Civilisation* (1918).

Duigan /dígən/, **John** (*b.* 1949) English-born Australian film-maker. He was the writer and director of *The Year My Voice Broke* (1987) and *Flirting* (1989).

duiker /díkər/, **duyker** *n.* a small African antelope with short backward-pointing horns. Genera: *Cephalophus* and *Sylvicapra*. [Late 18thC. Via Afrikaans, 'diver', from, ultimately, Middle Dutch *dūken* 'to dive'.]

duikerbok /díkər bok/ *n.* a duiker that is the most widespread in Africa and is often found close to human settlements. Latin name: *Silvicapra grimma*. [Late 18thC. From Afrikaans, from *duiker* 'diver' + *bok* 'buck'.]

Duisburg /dyóoz burg, dyóoss-/ city in the state of North Rhine-Westphalia, northwestern Germany. It is a major inland port, at the junction of the Rhine and Ruhr rivers, about 16 km/10 mi. west of Essen. Population: 536,300 (1994).

Dukas /dyoo kaá/, **Paul Abraham** (1865–1935) French composer and teacher. His few works include the popular symphonic poem *The Sorcerer's Apprentice* (1897).

duke /dyook/ *n.* **1. HIGH-RANKING NOBLEMAN** a nobleman of very high rank. In the British Isles this is the highest hereditary title of the nobility. **2. RULER OF PRINCIPALITY** a prince who rules a duchy, principality, or other small state **3. FIST** a hand or fist, especially a fist clenched for fighting or a boxer's fist raised as an indication of victory (*slang*) (*often used in the plural*) [12thC. Via Old French *duc* from Latin *dux* 'leader', from *ducere* 'to lead'. 'Fist' from *Duke of Yorks*, rhyming slang for 'forks', that is, 'fingers, fists'.]

dukedom /dyóokdəm/ *n.* **1. RANK OF DUKE** the rank, position, or title of a duke **2.** = **duchy**

duke-the-beetle *n.* *Northern Ireland* sb who avoids sth such as an unpleasant task (*humorous*)

Dukhobor *n.* = **Doukhobor**

dulcet /dúlssit/ *adj.* pleasant to hear, especially by being soft or soothing [15thC. From Old French *doucet*, literally 'small sweet (thing)', from *doux* 'sweet', from Latin *dulcis*.]

dulciana /dúlssi aánə/ *n.* an organ stop or pipe of the diapason type, characterized by a soft sweet tone [Late 18thC. From medieval Latin, from Latin *dulcis* 'sweet'.]

dulcify /dúlssi fī/ (**-fies, -fying, -fied**) *vt.* to make sth agreeable, especially to the senses (*literary*) [Late 16thC. From Latin *dulcificare*, literally 'to make sweet', from *dulcis* 'sweet'.] —**dulcification** /dúlssifi káysh'n/ *n.*

dulcimer /dúlssimər/ *n.* a zither played with lightweight hammers or sometimes by plucking. ◊ **hammer dulcimer** [15thC. From French *doulcemer*, of uncertain origin: perhaps from Latin *dulcis* 'sweet' + *melos* 'song'.]

dulcinea /dúlssi neé ə/ *n.* a woman who is the object of sb's love, especially one who is idealized (*literary*) [Mid-17thC. From *Dulcinea*, the name of Don Quixote's love.]

dulfer /dúlfər/ *n.* in mountaineering, a classic method of abseiling using a rope wrapped around the body

dulia /dyoo lí ə, doó-, dyoo lí ə/ *n.* the veneration of saints and angels, as in the Roman Catholic and Eastern churches [Early 17thC. Via medieval Latin, 'service, work done', from Greek *douleia* 'slavery'.]

dull /dul/ *adj.* **1. BORING** arousing no interest or excitement **2. OVERCAST** not bright because of weather conditions such as thick clouds or mist **3. NOT VIVID** lacking vividness or brightness of hue **4. NOT INTENSELY FELT** not acutely or intensely felt or experienced, but prolonged ○ *a dull ache* **5. MUFFLED** muffled and not resonant ○ *a dull thud* **6. BLUNT** lacking sharpness or the ability to cut cleanly **7. UNINTELLIGENT** slow to understand or learn **8. SLOW TO RESPOND** lacking in alertness or speedy responsiveness ○ *dull reflexes* **9. NOT BRISK OR BUSY** without the usual or desirable number of transactions ○ *Trading was dull this morning.* **10. LISTLESS** lacking in energy or enthusiasm ○ *dull, scattered applause* ■ *vti.* (**dulls, dulling, dulled**) **1. BECOME OR MAKE LESS ACUTE** to become, or cause sth to become, less acute or intensely felt ○ *Sleepiness had dulled his hunger.* **2. REDUCE IN LOUDNESS** to become, or cause sth to become, quieter **3. BECOME OR MAKE BLUNT** to become, or cause sth to become, less sharp **4. BECOME OR MAKE LESS BRIGHT** to become, or cause sth to become, less bright or intense **5. BECOME OR MAKE LESS BUSY** to become, or cause sth to become, less brisk or busy [Old English *dol* 'slow-witted', from a prehistoric Germanic word that is also the ancestor of English *dolt* and *doldrums*] —**dullish** *adj.* —**dullness** *n.* —**dully** *adv.*

— **WORD KEY: SYNONYMS** —
See Synonyms at *boring*.

dullard /dúllərd/ *n.* sb regarded as unintelligent or slow to comprehend (*dated insult*) [15thC. Coined from DULL + -ARD.]

dullsville /dúlz vil/, **Dullsville** *n.* (*slang*) **1. STH BORING** a place, thing, or activity that is boring or unexciting ○ *This town is dullsville in the evening.* **2. BOREDOM** the condition of being bored or uninterested ○ *I sat there in dullsville during the entire eight-hour flight.* [Mid-20thC. Modelled on place names.]

dulse /dulss/ (*plural* **dulses** *or* **dulse**) *n.* a red alga with edible fronds that grows in the intertidal zone and near the low-water mark in northern temperate seas. Latin name: *Palmaria palmata*. [Early 17thC. From Irish and Gaelic *duileasg*.]

Duluth /də loóth/ major port and city in northeastern Minnesota, at the southern end of Lake Superior, northeast of Minneapolis. Population: 83,699 (1996).

duly /dyóoli/ *adv.* **1. PROPERLY AND SUITABLY** in a proper, correct, or suitable way ○ *duly grateful* **2. AS EXPECTED** at the proper or expected time ○ *A signal was given and our coach duly departed.* [14thC. Coined from DUE + -LY.]

duma /dóomə/, **douma** *n.* **1. MODERN RUSSIAN PARLIAMENT** the parliament of modern Russia, established in 1993 after the dissolution of the former Soviet Union **2. TSARIST RUSSIAN PARLIAMENT** a Russian council or parliament during the time of tsarist rule, set up around 1905 but quickly deprived of power [Late 19thC. From Russian, from Old Russian, 'council, thought', of uncertain origin: probably from a prehistoric Germanic word meaning 'to judge'.]

Dumas /dju maá/, **Alexandre** (1802–70) French novelist and dramatist. He wrote the celebrated novels *The Three Musketeers* (1844) and *The Count of Monte Cristo* (1844). Known as **Dumas père**

Dumas /dyóo maa/, **Alexandre** (1824–95) French playwright and novelist. He wrote *The Lady of the Camellias* (1848), on which Verdi based *La Traviata*. Known as **Dumas fils**

du Maurier, Daphne, Dame (1907–89) British novelist. Her books include *Jamaica Inn* (1936), *Rebecca* (1938), and *My Cousin Rachel* (1951).

du Maurier /dyoo mórri ay/, **Sir Gerald** (1873–1934) British actor-manager. He ran Wyndham's (1910–25) and the St James's (1926–34) theatres in London. Full name **Sir Gerald Hubert Edward Busson du Maurier**

dumb /dum/ *adj.* **1. UNABLE TO SPEAK** unable to speak, e.g. because of deafness or congenital physical impairment **2. TEMPORARILY SPEECHLESS** temporarily unable to speak because of shock, fear, surprise, or anger **3. DONE WITHOUT SPEECH** performed or expressed without using speech **4. INTENTIONALLY SILENT** deliberately not speaking or refusing to speak **5. LACKING HUMAN SPEECH** lacking the power of speech because not human **6. PRODUCING NO SOUND** designed or adapted to produce no sound **7. UNINTELLIGENT** having or characterized by a low level of intelligence (*informal insult*) **8.** COMPUT **NOT PROGRAMMABLE** able only to transmit information to or receive information from a computer, and not able to process data ○ *a dumb terminal* ■ *vt.* (**dumbs, dumbing, dumbed**) **MAKE TEMPORARILY SPEECHLESS** to make sb temporarily unable to speak, especially by using shock or surprise (*literary*) [Old English. Ultimately from an Indo-European word meaning 'sensory or mental impairment' that is also the ancestor of English *dull* and *doldrums*.] —**dumbly** *adv.* —**dumbness** *n.*

dumb down *vti.* to make sth less intellectually challenging (*informal*) ○ *parents and teachers who were adamantly opposed to dumbing down science courses*

Dumbarton /dum baárt'n/ town on the River Clyde in West Dunbartonshire, Scotland. Population: 21,962 (1991).

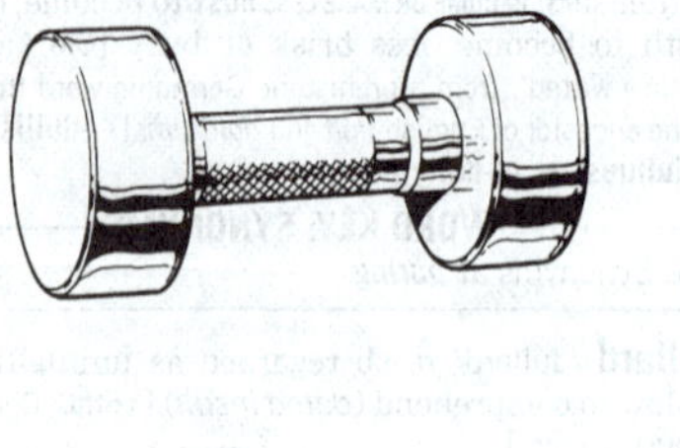

Dumbbell

dumbbell /dúm bel/ *n.* **1. WEIGHT FOR EXERCISING** an exercise weight in the form of a metal bar with a metal disc or ball at each end **2. UNINTELLIGENT PERSON** sb regarded as lacking in intelligence and common sense (*slang insult*)

dumb blonde *n.* a blonde woman stereotyped as being good-looking but unintelligent (*insult*)

dumb cane *n.* a poisonous tropical American plant that if chewed can lead to loss of speech in adults or death in children and small animals. Latin name: *Dieffenbachia seguine.*

dumb cluck *n.* sb regarded as very unintelligent or thoughtless (*dated insult*)

dumbfound /dum fównd/ (**-founds, -founding, -founded**), **dumfound** (**-founds, -founding, -founded**) *vti.* to make sb temporarily speechless with astonishment [Mid-17thC. From DUMB + CONFOUND.]

dumbo /dúmbō/ (*plural* **-bos**) *n.* sb unintelligent or very silly (*slang insult*) [Mid-20thC. Modelled on JUMBO.]

dumb show *n.* THEATRE **1. ACTORS' PANTOMIME** communication without words by actors using gesture or facial expressions **2. PLAY IN MIME** a play or part of a play presented in mime form

dumbstruck /dúm struk/ *adj.* made temporarily speechless by astonishment or shock

dumbwaiter /dúm wáytər/ *n.* **1. SMALL LIFT** a small lift used for moving food, crockery, and cutlery between the floors of a building **2. MOVABLE FOOD STAND** a movable stand for food, often with revolving shelves, that is placed near a table **3.** = **lazy Susan**

dumdum bullet /dúm dum-/, **dumdum** *n.* a bullet with a soft core or vertical cuts made in its point that expands on impact and inflicts a severe wound. Dumdum bullets are contrary to the Geneva Convention. [Late 19thC. Named after *DumDum*, town and arsenal near Calcutta, India, where the bullets were first produced.]

dumfound *vti.* = **dumbfound**

Dumfries /dum freéss/ market town in Dumfries and Galloway Region, Scotland, on the River Nith. The poet Robert Burns is buried there. Population: 38,000 (1996).

Dumfries and Galloway /-gállə way/ council area in southwestern Scotland. Population: 145,000 (1996). Area: 6,369 sq. km/2,459 sq. mi.

Dumfriesshire /dum freéss shər/ former county of Scotland until 1975, now part of Dumfries and Galloway

dummy /dúmmi/ *n.* (*plural* **-mies**) **1. MANNEQUIN IN A SHOP** a model of a human used for making or displaying clothes **2. MODEL USED BY A VENTRILOQUIST** a model of a human used, e.g. by a ventriloquist **3. IMITATION OF STH** an imitation of sth, especially one lacking a feature or function of the original and deceivingly substituted for it ○ *A lot of the system's switches are just dummies.* **4. SMALL OBJECT FOR BABY TO SUCK** a small rubber or plastic object with a teat that a baby is given to suck for comfort. US term **pacifier 5.** SPORTS **FEIGNED PASS IN BALL GAMES** a feigned pass or other move intended to deceive an opponent, especially a tackler, in football, rugby, or a similar game **6. PERSON OR ORGANIZATION ACTING AS FRONT** a person or organization serving as a front for another while pretending to be independent ○ *a dummy company* **7. UNINTELLIGENT PERSON** sb regarded as being unintelligent or silly (*informal insult*) **8. TACITURN PERSON** sb who says nothing or very little (*informal*) **9.** ARMS **NONEXPLOSIVE FORM OF MUNITION** a nonexplosive form of an explosive munition **10.** PUBL **MODEL PAGE** a page that looks like the final product but is a computer-generated or pasted-up facsimile showing general design specifications **11.** PUBL **MODEL BOOK** a set of model pages, often blank or containing only one signature, that have been bound and jacketed to give an idea of the final book. Dummies are used in preselling books. **12.** BRIDGE **EXPOSED HAND IN BRIDGE** an exposed hand of cards in bridge played by the player who is the first bidder of the suit in the final contract (**declarer**), or a player of this hand ■ *vt.* (**-mies, -mying, -mied**) PUBL **MAKE INTO PAGE OR BOOK FACSIMILE** to make up pages into page or book facsimiles ○ *dummied several pages for the sales conference* [Late 16thC. Coined from DUMB + -Y.] ◇ **spit the dummy** *Aus* to lose composure and throw a tantrum (*informal*)

dummy run *n.* a practice or tryout of a process or procedure

dummy variable *n.* a mathematical variable that can be replaced by another arbitrarily

dumortierite /dyoo máwrti ə rīt/ *n.* a hard fibrous bright blue, bluish-green, or pink mineral consisting of a silicate of aluminium and boron [Late 19thC. From French, named after Eugène *Dumortier*, a French palaeontologist.]

dump /dump/ *vt.* (**dumps, dumping, dumped**) **1. DROP OR PUT DOWN CARELESSLY** to deposit sth on a surface in a careless and usually noisy manner ○ *dumped the reports on my desk* **2. THROW OUT AS UNWANTED** to get rid of sth that is unwanted, especially by taking it and leaving it somewhere **3. DISPOSE OF WASTE** to dispose of waste by moving it to a prearranged site **4. TERMINATE RELATIONSHIP** to end a romantic or sexual relationship with sb, especially abruptly and hurtfully (*informal*) **5. REMOVE SB UNDESIRABLE** to remove sb deemed undesirable or a liability from a position such as leadership in a group, especially abruptly and unceremoniously (*informal*) **6. LEAVE SB TO BE CARED FOR** to entrust the care of sb, e.g. a child or a person of advanced years, to sb else or to an institution (*informal disapproving*) **7.** COMM **FLOOD MARKET WITH CHEAP MERCHANDISE** to flood a market with cheaply priced merchandise **8.** STOCK EXCH **GET RID OF STOCKS** to sell off large quantities of stock all at once, thereby driving the price down **9.** COUNSELLING **CONFIDE** to offload negative feelings by talking about them to sb, especially a friend or therapist ○ *I'm sorry to dump all this on you, but I've got no one else to talk to.* **10.** COMPUT **TRANSFER DATA WITHOUT PROCESSING** to transfer computer data from one site to another without processing it ■ *n.* **1. WASTE DISPOSAL SITE** a place where waste materials can be left **2. UNPLEASANT PLACE** an unpleasant or dirty place (*informal*) ○ *The hotel was a real dump.* **3.** MIL **MUNITIONS AND SUPPLY AREA** a place for the temporary storage of munitions, food, water, fuel, and other supplies for distribution to troops **4. ACT OF DEFECATING** an act of evacuating the bowels (*slang offensive*) **5. ACT OF THROWING STH AWAY** an act of discarding sth [14thC. Origin uncertain: perhaps from Scandinavian, from, ultimately, an Indo-European word meaning 'to hit', or from Dutch *dumpen* 'to immerse, topple'.]

dump on *vi.* *US* to insult, criticize, or otherwise denigrate sb else severely (*slang*)

dumpbin /dúmp bin/ *n.* a large open container used in a shop to display items casually, especially those offered at bargain prices

dumper /dúmpər/ *n.* **1. DISPOSER OF WASTE** a person who or machine that disposes of waste by taking it to a prearranged site **2.** TRANSP = **dumper truck**. US term **dump truck 3.** *ANZ* SWIMMING **POWERFUL OCEAN WAVE** a large wave able to fling a surfer onto the beach

dumper truck *n.* a heavy lorry with an open bed that can be tilted up and back to unload cargo such as gravel, dirt, or refuse from construction sites. US term **dump truck**

dumpling /dúmpling/ *n.* **1. SMALL BALL OF COOKED DOUGH** a small dough ball cooked and served with a stew or soup **2. PASTRY AND FRUIT DESSERT** a baked dessert consisting of pastry wrapped round fruit **3. SB SHORT AND PLUMP** sb who is endearingly short and plump (*informal insult*) [Early 17thC. Origin uncertain: perhaps formed from Low German *dump* 'damp, moist, heavy'.]

dump orbit *n.* an orbit that a communications satellite is moved into at the end of its useful life in which it will not collide with operational satellites

dumps /dumps/ *npl.* a state of sadness and hopelessness (*informal*) ○ *feeling down in the dumps* [Early 16thC. Plural of obsolete *dump*, of uncertain origin: perhaps from Dutch *domp* 'haze'.]

dump truck *n.* *US* = **tipper truck**

dumpy[1] /dúmpi/ (**-ier, -iest**) *adj.* having a short and plump build or shape (*insult*) [Mid-18thC. Origin uncertain: perhaps formed from Low German *dump* 'damp, heavy, lump' (possible source of English *dumpling*).] —**dumpily** *adv.* —**dumpiness** *n.*

dumpy[2] /dúmpi/ (**-ier, -iest**) *adj.* sad and gloomy (*dated*) [Early 17thC. Formed from obsolete *dump* 'fit of gloom' (see DUMPS).]

dumpy level *n.* a surveying instrument for taking levels with a short fixed horizontal telescope

dun[1] /dun/ *n.* **1.** COLOURS **BROWNISH-GREY COLOUR** a brownish-grey colour **2.** EQU **BROWNISH-GREY HORSE** a horse whose coat is brownish grey **3.** ANGLING **DARK FISHING FLY** a fishing fly of a grey to brown colour ■ *adj.* (**dunner, dunnest**) **1.** COLOURS **BROWNISH-GREY** of a brownish-grey colour **2. GLOOMY** gloomily and darkly bleak and depressing (*literary*) ○ *a dun and bare prairie* [Old English *dunn*. Ultimately from an Indo-European word that is also the ancestor of English *dusk*.]

dun[2] /dun/ *vt.* (**duns, dunning, dunned**) **HARASS FOR DEBT PAYMENT** to press or harass sb persistently for the settlement of a debt ■ *n.* **1. PAYMENT DEMAND** a pressing, usually written, demand for payment **2. DEBT COLLECTOR** sb whose job is to collect other people's debts [Early 17thC. Origin uncertain: perhaps a shortening of *dunkirk* 'privateer sailing from Dunkirk in France'; or named after Joe *Dun*, bailiff of Lincoln, famous for catching debtors.]

Dunant /dyoo naáN/, **Jean Henri** (1828–1910) Swiss philanthropist. He founded the International Red Cross (1862–64) and shared the first Nobel Peace Prize (1901).

Dunaway /dúnnə way/, **Faye** (b. 1941) US film actor. She has acted in various Hollywood films and won an Academy Award for *Network* (1976).

Dunbar, William (1460?–1520?) Scottish poet and priest. He was attached to the court of James IV, and his poetry includes *The Thistle and the Rose* (1503).

Dunbartonshire /dun baárt'nshər/ former county of central Scotland until 1975, now East Dunbartonshire and West Dunbartonshire

AKG London

Isadora Duncan

Duncan /dúngkən/, **Isadora** (1877–1927) US dancer. She laid the foundation for modern dance, basing her ideas on the dances of the ancient Greeks. Full name **Dora Angela Duncan**

dunce /dunss/ *n.* sb who is felt to be unintelligent or a slow learner, especially sb with no aptitude for a particular subject (*insult*) [Mid-16thC. From *Duns* in the name of John DUNS SCOTUS. Originally 'follower of Duns Scotus' (a contemptuous term).]

dunce's cap, **dunce cap** *n.* a conical paper hat formerly worn as a punishment by a pupil who was slow to learn or lazy at school

Dundalk /dún dawk/ town in County Louth in the Republic of Ireland. It is situated close to the border with Northern Ireland. Population: 25,843 (1991).

dunderhead /dúndər hed/ *n.* sb regarded as unintelligent or slow to learn (*informal insult*) [Early 17thC. Origin uncertain: perhaps from Dutch *dunderkop*, from *dunder* 'thunder' + *kop* 'head'.] —**dunderheaded** *adj.* —**dunderheadedness** *n.*

dune /dyoon/ *n.* a mound or ridge of sand formed by wind or water action, typically seen on coasts and in deserts [Late 18thC. Via French from Middle Dutch *dūne*.]

Dune buggy

dune buggy *n.* US a motorized beach vehicle, usually with no top and with oversized tyres to prevent it from getting mired in sand

Dunfermline /dun fúrmlin/ manufacturing town in Fife, Scotland. Population: 55,083 (1991).

dung /dung/ *n.* **1.** ANIMAL EXCREMENT the solid excrement of animals, especially large animals such as cattle or horses **2.** = **manure** ■ *vt.* (**dungs, dunging, dunged**) COVER WITH DUNG to cover land with dung or

manure [Old English, of uncertain origin: perhaps originally 'material for covering the earth', and ultimately from an Indo-European word meaning 'to cover', which may also be the ancestor of English *dingy*] —**dungy** *adj.*

Dungannon /dun gánnən/ town in County Tyrone, Northern Ireland. Population: 46,100 (1995).

dungaree /dúng gə reé/ *n.* a sturdy hard-wearing blue-denim fabric [Late 17thC. From Hindi *dungrī* 'kind of coarse cloth', named after the village near Mumbai (Bombay) where it was first made.]

dungarees /dúng gə reéz/ *npl.* **1.** WORK GARMENT OF TROUSERS AND BIB a garment made from strong material consisting of loose-fitting trousers with an attached bib and shoulder straps, intended to be worn over ordinary clothing for protection while working **2.** CASUAL GARMENT OF TROUSERS AND BIB a casual garment of trousers and bib front, usually made from denim and worn especially by women and children

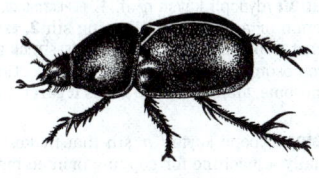

Dung beetle

dung beetle *n.* a scarab beetle that rolls large balls of dung into tunnels to feed the larvae that hatch from the eggs it lays there. Subfamily: Coprinae.

Dungeness /dúnjə néss/ shingle headland on the southern coast of Kent, England, with two nuclear power stations

dungeon /dúnjən/ *n.* **1.** PRISON CELL a prison cell, often underground, especially beneath a castle **2.** CASTLE KEEP the secure main tower of a castle (*archaic*) [14thC. Via Old French *donjon* 'castle keep' (later 'secure underground cell') from, ultimately, Latin *dominus* 'lord' (source of English *danger* and *dominion*).]

dunghill /dúng hil/, **dungheap** /-heep/ *n.* a pile of solid animal excrement

dunite /dúnīt/ *n.* a coarse-grained dark igneous rock consisting mainly of a magnesium-rich olivine. It is an important source of magnesium, chromium, and platinum. [Mid-19thC. Named after Mt *Dun* in New Zealand, where it is found.] —**dunitic** /də níttik/ *adj.*

dunk /dungk/ *vt.* (**dunks, dunking, dunked**) **1.** DIP FOOD IN LIQUID to dip food into a liquid before eating it **2.** QUICKLY SUBMERGE IN LIQUID to submerge sth in liquid, especially quickly and for a short time ■ *n.* US BASKETBALL = **dunk shot** [Early 20thC. Via Pennsylvanian German *dunke* 'to dip' from, ultimately, Old High German *dunkōn*.] —**dunker** *n.*

Dunker /dúngkər/, **Dunkard** /-ərd/ *n.* a member of a group of German-American Baptists, the German Baptist Brethren [Mid-18thC. From Pennsylvanian German, from *dunke* 'to dip'.]

Dunkirk /dun kúrk/ seaport and town in northern France, in the Nord Department, Nord-Pas-de-Calais Region, near Calais. In World War II over 330,000 Allied troops were evacuated from the town by sea, under constant enemy fire. Population: 71,071 (1990).

Dunk Island /dúngk-/ island in Australia, off the eastern coast of Queensland, south along the coast-line from Cairns

dunk shot *n.* US BASKETBALL a shot in basketball made by jamming or slamming the ball through the hoop from above

Dún Laoghaire /dun láirə, doon-, -leérə, -/ city and seaport on Dublin Bay on the eastern coast of the Republic of Ireland. Population: 55,540 (1991). Formerly **Kingston**

dunlin /dúnnlin/ (*plural* **-lins** *or* **-lin**) *n.* a small wading bird with a slightly downcurved bill and a black belly, found in North America, Europe, Africa, and Asia. Latin name: *Calidris alpina*. [Mid-16thC. Formed from DUN¹.]

Dunlop /dún lop/, **John Boyd** (1840–1921) British inventor. He invented the pneumatic tyre in about 1887, used at first for bicycles and later for the motor car.

Dunlop, Weary (1907–93) Australian distinguished surgeon and war hero. During World War II, he was taken prisoner in Java (1942). He kept a diary until the end of the war, revealing the frightful conditions that he and his companions endured on the Burma-Thailand Railway (1942–45). Real name **Sir Ernest Edward Dunlop**

dunnage /dúnnij/ *n.* packing material used to cushion cargo on a ship [14thC. Origin unknown.]

dunnakin /dúnnəkin/ *n.* a lavatory, especially an outside one without plumbing (*regional*) [Late 18thC. Origin uncertain: perhaps coined from DUNG.]

Dunnet Head /dúnnət-/ peninsula and northernmost point of mainland Scotland

dunnite /dúnnīt/ *n.* an explosive that contains ammonium picrate [Early 20thC. Named after its inventor US Army Col. B. W. *Dunn* (1860–1936).]

dunno /də nó, du-/ *contr.* (I) don't know (*nonstandard*) ○ '*Who broke the glass?*' '*Dunno*'.

dunnock /dúnnək/ *n.* a European woodland bird that resembles the house sparrow but is distinguished from it by its thin bill and grey head and breast. Latin name: *Prunella modularis*. [15thC. Origin uncertain: probably coined from DUN¹ + -OCK.]

dunny /dúnni/ (*plural* **-nies**) *n.* a lavatory (*regional informal*) [Early 19thC. Shortening and alteration of DUNNAKIN.]

Dunoon /də noón/ resort town on the western shore of the Firth of Clyde, Scotland. Population: 9,038 (1991).

Dunsinane /dun sínnən/ hill in central Scotland, near Perth. It figures in Shakespeare's play *Macbeth*. Height: 308 m/1,012 ft.

Duns Scotus /dúnz skótəss/, **John** (1266?–1308) Scottish philosopher and theologian. A deeply influential figure of the Middle Ages, he emphasized religious individuality and defended the theory of the Immaculate Conception. He founded the school of scholasticism known as Scotism.

Dunstable /dúnstəb'l/ industrial town in Bedfordshire, England. Population: 49,666 (1991).

Dunstable, Dunstaple, John (1390?–1453) English composer and mathematician. He wrote sacred and secular pieces that significantly advanced counterpoint and harmony. He also compiled tables of latitudes and longitudes (1438).

Dunstan /dúnstən/, **St** (909?–988) Anglo-Saxon prelate and reformer. As Abbot of Glastonbury (940), he insisted on the strict Benedictine Rule, which heralded the reform of English monasticism. He became Archbishop of Canterbury (960–88).

dunt /dunt/ *n.* (*regional*) **1.** INJURY FROM BLOW the injury or damage caused by a hit or a blow **2.** ACT OF HITTING a hit or a blow ■ *vt.* (**dunts, dunting, dunted**) HIT SB OR STH to strike sb or sth (*regional*) [15thC. Variant of DINT.]

Duntroon /dun troón/ suburb of North Canberra, Australian Capital Territory, Australia. Population: 1,906 (1996).

duo /dyoo ó/ (*plural* **-os**) *n.* **1.** DUET a duet, especially one for two instruments **2.** PLAYERS OF A DUET a pair of musicians who play together **3.** PAIR OF CLOSELY ASSOCIATED PEOPLE two people who are considered to be closely connected in some way **4.** SET OF TWO CLOSELY RELATED THINGS a set of two items considered as closely connected [Late 16thC. Via Italian *duo* 'two' from, ultimately, Latin.]

duo- *prefix.* two ○ *duopoly* [From Latin. Ultimately from the Indo-European word for 'two', which is also the ancestor of English *two* and *bi-*.]

duodecimal /dyoo ō déssim'l/ *adj.* BASED ON 12 using the number 12 as a base and counted or ordered in units of 12 or 12ths, or belonging to a system organized in this way. Although no longer commonly used, vestiges of a duodecimal system remain in such units as the foot being equal to 12 inches. ■ *n.* **1.** **DUODECIMAL NUMBER** a number in a counting system that uses units of 12 **2.** **12TH** a 12th part [Early 18thC. Formed from Latin *duodecimus* 'twelfth'.] —**duodecimally** *adv.*

duodecimo /dyoŏ ō déssi mō/ (*plural* **-mos**) *n.* a book size in which each leaf is formed by folding the printing sheet twelve times, or a book of this size [Mid-17thC. From Latin *in duodecimo* 'in twelfth'.]

duodenum /dyoŏ ō dée nəm/ (*plural* **-na** /-dée nə/ *or* **-nums**) *n.* the first short section of the small intestine immediately beyond the stomach [14thC. From medieval Latin *intestinum duodenum digitorum*, literally '12 finger-breadths long', from, ultimately, Latin *duodecim* 'twelve'.] —**duodenal** *adj.*

duologue /dyoŏ ə log/ *n.* **1.** **PIECE FOR TWO SPEAKING ACTORS** a play or part of a play in which only two actors speak **2.** **DIALOGUE BETWEEN TWO** a dialogue between two actors, or a conversation between two people [Mid-18thC. Blend of DUO and MONOLOGUE.]

duomo /dwṓmō/ (*plural* **-mos** *or* **-mi** /-mi/) *n.* a cathedral in Italy [Mid-16thC. Via Italian from Latin *domus* 'house'.]

duopoly /dyoo óppəli/ (*plural* **-lies**) *n.* an economic situation in which two powerful groups or organizations concentrate or dominate commerce in one business market or commodity [Early 20thC. Modelled on MONOPOLY.] —**duopolistic** /dyoo óppə lístik/ *adj.*

duopsony /dyoo ópsəni/ (*plural* **-nies**) *n.* a situation in which two competing buyers exert controlling influence over many sellers [Blend of DUO and *-opsony*, from Greek *opsōnía* 'purchasing of food']

dup. *abbr.* duplicate

Dupain /dyoo páyn/, **Max** (1911–92) Australian photographer. He is best known for his images of Australian beach culture, such as in his work *Sunbaker* (1937). Full name **Maxwell Spencer Dupain**

dupe /dyoop/ *vt.* (**dupes, duping, duped**) **TRICK SB** to persuade or induce sb to do sth by trickery or deception ○ *He was duped into thinking that they intended to pay.* ■ *n.* **VICTIM OF DECEIT** sb who is tricked or deceived, especially into doing sth [Late 17thC. From French, from Old French, of uncertain origin: perhaps an alteration of *huppe* 'hoopoe'; from the bird's supposedly stupid appearance.] —**dupability** /dyoŏpə bílləti/ *n.* —**dupable** /dyoŏpəb'l/ *adj.* —**duper** /dyoŏpər/ *n.* —**dupery** *n.*

dupion /dyoŏpi on/ *n.* a rough silk fabric woven from threads of a double cocoon [Early 19thC. Alteration of French *doupion* from Italian *doppione*, from *doppio* 'double'.]

duple /dyoŏp'l/ *adj.* MUSIC consisting of two beats to the bar or measure [Mid-16thC. From Latin *duplus* 'double'.]

Duplessis /dyoo pléssi/, **Maurice Le Noblet** (1890–1959) Canadian statesman. He was premier of Quebec (1936–39 and 1944–59) with the Union Nationale Party.

duplet /dyoŏplət/ *n.* **1.** CHEM **2 SHARED ELECTRONS** a pair of electrons shared between two atoms that are joined in a chemical bond **2.** MUSIC **GROUP OF 2 NOTES** a group of 2 notes played in the time usually required by three [Mid-17thC. Formed from DUPLE, modelled on DOUBLET.]

duple time *n.* a musical metre in which there are two beats to the bar, e.g. 2/4 or 6/8

duplex /dyoŏ pleks/ *n.* **1.** *Aus, Can, US* ARCHIT **2-FAMILY DWELLING WITH 2 ENTRANCES** a house that is divided into two halves and is inhabited by two separate families or tenants with separate entrances and exits **2.** ELECTRON ENG **SIMULTANEOUS TRANSMISSION IN BOTH DIRECTIONS** transmission of signals along a communications channel in both directions at the same time, e.g. over a telephone line ■ *adj.* **1.** **TWOFOLD** consisting of two parts, especially two identical or equivalent parts **2.** ENG **HAVING TWO PARTS PERFORMING ONE OPERATION** consisting of pairs of units or components that perform the same machine function but operate independently [Mid-16thC. From Latin *duplex*, literally 'twofold', from *plicare* 'to fold'.] —**duplexity** /dyoo pléksəti/ *n.*

duplicable /dyoŏplikəb'l/ *adj.* able to be copied exactly or repeated —**duplicability** /dyoŏplikə bílləti/ *n.*

duplicate /dyoŏpli kayt/ *vt.* (**-cates, -cating, -cated**) **1.** **COPY STH** to make an exact copy of sth **2.** **REPEAT STH** to do sth more than once, especially unknowingly or unnecessarily ■ *n.* **1.** **COPY OF STH** an exact copy, especially of a document **2.** **ANOTHER OF THE SAME** a spare of the same kind **3.** **REPEAT OF STH** a repeat of an earlier action or achievement ■ *adj.* **1.** **COPIED EXACTLY** being an exact copy of sth ○ *a duplicate key* **2.** **HAVING 2 CORRESPONDING PARTS** consisting of or existing in two corresponding parts [15thC. From Latin *duplicare* 'to make twofold, double', from *duplus* 'twofold'.] —**duplicately** /dyoŏpli kətli/ *adv.* —**duplicative** /-kətiv/ *adj.* ◇ **in duplicate** so as to create or consist of two exact copies

WORD KEY: SYNONYMS

See Synonyms at ***copy***.

duplicate bridge *n.* contract bridge in which the same hand is played by different consecutive players

duplication /dyoŏpli káysh'n/ *n.* **1.** **REPEATING OR COPYING** the action or an act of duplicating sth **2.** **EXACT COPY** an exact copy of sth **3.** GENETICS **REPETITION OF GENES** a chromosome mutation in which a section of a chromosome, along with the genes it carries, occurs twice

duplicator /dyoŏpli kaytər/ *n.* sth that makes copies, especially a machine for copying printed matter

duplicitous /dyoo plíssitəss/ *adj.* deceptive, dishonest, or misleading —**duplicitously** *adv.* —**duplicitousness** *n.*

duplicity /dyoo plíssəti/ *n.* **1.** **DECEITFULNESS** the fact of being deceptive, dishonest, or misleading **2.** **CONDITION OF BEING DOUBLE** the state of being double or in a pair (*formal*) ○ *the duplicity of the stars of the constellation* [15thC. Directly or via French *duplicité* from late Latin *duplicitas*, from Latin *duplic-*, stem of *duplex* (see DUPLEX).]

duppy /dúppi/ (*plural* **-pies**) *n.* *Carib* a ghost or spirit [Late 18thC. Origin uncertain: perhaps of West African origin.]

du Pré /dyoo práy/, **Jacqueline** (1945–87) British cellist and teacher. She is particularly famous for her interpretations of cello concertos. Her playing, though not her teaching, was halted in 1972 by multiple sclerosis.

Dupré /dyoo práy/, **Marcel** (1886–1971) French musician and composer. He was for many years the organist at Notre Dame Cathedral, Paris, and was director of the Paris Conservatoire (1954–56).

durable /dyoŏrəb'l/ *adj.* lasting for a long time, especially without sustaining damage or wear ○ *durable materials* ○ *a durable peace* [14thC. Via Old French *durable* from Latin *durabilis*, from *durare* 'to last, harden' (source of English *endure*).] —**durability** /dyoŏrə bílləti/ *n.* —**durableness** /dyoŏrəb'lnəss/ *n.* —**durably** /-əbli/ *adv.*

durable goods *npl.* long-lasting products, e.g. motor vehicles and large appliances such as cookers and refrigerators

durables /dyoŏrəb'lz/ *n.* = **durable goods**

Durack /dyoŏr ak/ river in northern Western Australia, which rises in the Kimberley Plateau and flows into the Timor Sea in the Cambridge Gulf. Length: 230 km/143 mi.

Durack, Dame Mary (1913–94) Australian writer. She wrote *Kings in Grass Castles* (1959), a historical account of her pioneering pastoralist forebears.

Durack Range mountain range in Western Australia, in the Kimberley region, west of Lake Argyle

dural /dyoŏrəl/ *adj.* relating to the dura mater, the outermost membrane around the brain and spinal cord [Late 19thC. Formed from *dura* (see DURA MATER).]

Duralumin /dyoŏ rállyoŏmin/ *tdmk.* a trademark for a strong low-density aluminium alloy, used especially in aircraft, that contains 3.5–4.5 per cent copper and small amounts of manganese

dura mater /dyoŏrə máytər/ *n.* the tough outermost membrane of the three that cover the brain and spinal cord [14thC. From medieval Latin, literally 'hard mother', translation of Arabic *al-'umm al-jāfiya* 'coarse mother'.]

duramen /dyoŏ ráymən/ *n.* heartwood (*technical*) [Mid-19thC. From Latin, 'hardness', from *durare* 'to last, harden'.]

durance /dyoŏrənss/ *n.* **1.** **DURATION** the period of duration of sth (*literary*) **2.** **IMPRISONMENT** forcible confinement or imprisonment (*archaic or literary*) [15thC. Via Old French from, ultimately, Latin *durare* 'to last, harden'.]

Duras /dyoŏ raa/, **Marguerite** (1914–96) Vietnamese-born French novelist, playwright, film director, and screenwriter. Her works include the screenplay for *Hiroshima, mon amour* (1959) and the novel *The Lover* (1985). Real name **Marguerite Donnadieu**

duration /dyoo ráysh'n/ *n.* the period of time that sth lasts or exists ○ *an interval of 15 minutes' duration* [14thC. Via Old French *duracioun* from, ultimately, Latin *durare* 'to last, harden'.] —**durational** *adj.* ◇ **for the duration** for the entire period of time that sth is going on or will continue to go on

durative /dyoŏrətiv/ *adj.* GRAM used to describe a verb in a continuous tense or aspect, or a verb indicating a continuous action

Durban /dúrbən/ city, seaport, and tourist resort in KwaZulu-Natal Province in eastern South Africa. Population: 715,699 (1991).

durbar /dúr baar/ *n.* formerly, an official reception held by a local prince or British governor in colonial India, or by a local chief or British official in colonial Africa [Early 17thC. Alteration of Urdu *darbār* from Persian *dar* 'door' + *bār* 'court'.]

Dürer /dyoŏrər/, **Albrecht** (1471–1528) German painter and engraver. The clarity of his paintings, e.g. in *Self Portrait* (1498), made him one of the most influential artists of the Reformation.

duress /dyoŏ réss/ *n.* **1.** **USE OF FORCE** the use of force or threats to make sb do sth **2.** LAW **ILLEGAL COERCION** illegal force or coercion used, e.g., against a criminal suspect or a prisoner in lawful custody before trial [14thC. Via Old French *duresse* from Latin *duritia*, literally 'hardness', from *durus* 'hard' (source of English *during*).]

Durex /dyoŏr eks/ *tdmk.* *UK* a trademark for a brand of condom

Durga /doŏrgə/ *n.* a goddess who is one of the most important Hindu deities, embodying for many the supreme manifest form of godhead

Durgapur /dúrgə poor/, **Durgāpur** city in eastern India in West Bengal State. It is a major steel-producing centre. Population: 425,836 (1991).

Durham[1] /dúrrəm/ historical cathedral city in northeastern England. It is the county town and cultural centre of County Durham. Population: 85,800 (1991).

Durham[2] *n.* a shorthorn beef or dairy cow belonging to a hardy breed originating in northeastern England [Named after the city of DURHAM]

Durham, County /dúrrəm/ county in northeastern England. The city of Durham is the administrative centre. Population: 507,100 (1995). Area: 2,435 sq. km/940 sq. mi.

durian /dyoŏri ən/ *n.* **1.** **TREE WITH FOUL-SMELLING FRUIT** a tree found in the tropical rain forests of Southeast Asia that has foul-smelling but deliciously flavoured fruits. Latin name: *Durio zibethinus*. **2.** **FRUIT OF DURIAN TREE** the fruit of the durian tree [Late 16thC. From Malay *durian*, from *duri* 'thorn, prickle'.]

duricrust /dyoŏri krust/ *n.* a hard crust formed on the surface of the soil by the precipitation of soluble minerals from mineral waters, particularly during the dry season in semiarid climates [Early 20thC. Coined from Latin *durus* 'hard' + CRUST.]

during /dyoŏring/ *prep.* **1.** **THROUGHOUT** throughout a particular period or event, either continuously or several times between the beginning and the end ○ *There was not even a whisper during the service.* **2.** **AT SOME POINT IN A PERIOD** at some point or moment within a particular period or event ○ *I can't remember the date, but it was during the winter.* [14thC. Present participle of obsolete *dure* 'to last', from Old French *durer*, from, ultimately, Latin *durus* 'hard', perhaps originally 'oak' (source of English *endure*).]

Durkheim /dúrk hīm/, **Émile** (1858–1917) French social theorist. His rigorous methodology, manifested in *Suicide* (1897) and other works, set the pattern for modern sociological studies.

durmast oak /dúr maast/, **durmast** *n.* an oak tree native to Europe and Asia Minor that has lobed leaves and yields a heavy flexible wood used in cabinetry. Latin name: *Quercus petraea.* [Late 18thC. Perhaps an error for *dunmast*, from DUN + MAST 'acorns'.]

durn /durn/ *interj., adj., adv., vt.* (**durns, durning, durned**) *Southern US* = **darn** (*informal*) [Variant of DARN]

duro (*plural* **-ros**) *n.* in some Latin American countries and formerly in Spain, a coin worth a peso or a dollar [Late 18thC. From Spanish *peso duro* 'hard or solid piastre'.]

durra /dŏŏrrə/, **dourra** *n.* a race of sorghum grown for its grain and as animal feed, especially in tropical and warm arid areas. Latin name: *Sorghum bicolor.* [Late 18thC. From Arabic *dura.*]

Durrell /dúrrəl/, **Gerald** (1925–95) British naturalist and writer, brother of Lawrence Durrell. His books include the autobiographical *My Family and Other Animals* (1956), about his childhood on Corfu, as well as such books as *The Stationary Ark* (1976), which concerns his zoo and wildlife conservation trust in Jersey.

Durrell, Lawrence (1912–90) British novelist, poet, and travel writer. The *Alexandria Quartet* novels (1957–60) established his reputation. Later works include *Tunc* (1968), *Nunquam* (1970), and the 'Avignon Quintet' (1974–85). Full name **Lawrence George Durrell**

Dürrenmatt /dyŏŏrrən mat/, **Friedrich** (1921–90) Swiss writer. He wrote plays, including *The Physicists* (1961), existentialist detective novels, and critical essays.

Durrës /dúrrəss/ city and seaport in western Albania, the capital of Durrës District, on the Adriatic Sea. It is situated about 32 km/20 mi. west of the capital Tirana. Population: 86,900 (1991).

durrie /dúrri/, **dhurrie** *n.* a flat-woven cotton rug made in India [Late 19thC. From Hindi *dari.*]

durrie /dúrri/ *n.* = **dhurrie**

durst /durst/ past tense of **dare** (*archaic*)

durum wheat /dyŏŏrəm/, **durum** *n.* a wheat that produces glutinous flour, used in making pasta. Latin name: *Triticum durum.* [Early 20thC. From Latin, a form of *durus* 'hard'.]

Duryea, Charles Edgar (1861–1938) US automaker and inventor. Together with his brother, he built one of the first cars in the United States (1893).

Duse /dŏŏze/, **Eleonora** (1859–1924) Italian actress. The emotional power of her acting, especially in dramas by her long-time lover Gabriele D'Annunzio, was equalled in her time only by that of Sarah Bernhardt.

Dushanbe /doo shaánbi/ capital city of Tajikistan, in the west of the country in the Gissar Valley. Population: 602,000 (1990).

dusk /dusk/ *n.* **1. PERIOD AFTER DAY BUT BEFORE NIGHT** the period of the day after the sun has gone below the horizon but before the sky has become dark **2. ABSENCE OF DAYLIGHT** partial or almost complete darkness (*literary*) ■ *adj.* **DIM** having little or insufficient light (*literary*) ■ *vti.* (**dusks, dusking, dusked**) **DARKEN** to become or make sth dark (*literary*) [Old English *dox* 'dark in colour'. Ultimately from an Indo-European word that is also the ancestor of English *obfuscate.*]

dusky /dúski/ (**-ier, -iest**) *adj.* **1. DARK-COLOURED** rather dark in colour **2. DIM** having little or insufficient light **3. OFFENSIVE TERM MEANING DARK-SKINNED** having a rather dark skin or complexion (*dated offensive*) —**duskily** *adv.* —**duskiness** *n.*

Dusky Sound coastal inlet in southwestern South Island, New Zealand. At 32 km/20 mi. long it is the country's largest fiord.

Düsseldorf /dŏŏss'l dawrf/ capital of North Rhine-Westphalia, west-central Germany. Situated on the River Rhine, about 32 km/20 mi. north of Cologne, it is the commercial and cultural centre of the greater Ruhr area. Population: 573,100 (1994).

dust /dust/ *n.* **1. SMALL DRY PARTICLES** very small dry particles of a substance such as sand or coal, either in the form of a deposit or a cloud **2. HOUSEHOLD DIRT** the small pieces of dirt that accumulate in a layer on horizontal surfaces in buildings **3. REMOVAL OF DUST** an act of removing small particles of dirt from sth, usually by wiping with a cloth **4. REMAINS FROM THE DECAY OF A BODY** the small particles that sth, especially a human body, is thought to be reduced to by decay after death **5. EARTH AS A BURIAL PLACE** dirt or soil, particularly that of sb's grave (*literary*) **6. RUBBISH** household rubbish **7.** MED **MINERS' DISEASE** silicosis or another respiratory disease affecting miners (*informal*) ■ *v.* (**dusts, dusting, dusted**) **1.** *vti.* **CLEAN OFF DIRT PARTICLES** to remove small particles of dirt from sth, usually by wiping with a cloth **2.** *vt.* **SPRINKLE** to sprinkle sth with a powdery substance, or sprinkle a powdery substance over sth ○ *Dust the board with flour to stop the dough sticking to it.* [Old English *dūst*, from a prehistoric Germanic word that is also the ancestor of English *fumigate* and *perfume*] —**dustless** *adj.* ◇ **(as) dry as dust** so scholarly and devoid of humour as to be arid in tone and content ◇ **bite the dust 1.** to die, especially in or as a result a fight (*informal*) **2.** to suffer total failure (*informal*) ◇ **gather dust** to remain unused over a period of time ◇ **kick up a dust, raise a dust** to cause a controversy or loud disturbance (*informal*) ◇ **shake the dust (of sth) from your feet** to leave somewhere for ever, especially when glad to do so ◇ **throw dust in sb's eyes** to attempt to deceive or mislead sb

dust down *vt.* **1. dust down, dust off RECYCLE STH OLD FOR NEW USE** to prepare sth for reuse or further consideration **2. WIPE OR BRUSH STH** to clean sth, especially by wiping or brushing it **3. REPRIMAND SB** to tell sb off severely (*dated*)

dust up *vt.* to attack sb either verbally or physically (*slang*)

dust-bath *n.* a form of grooming behaviour in animals, especially birds, that consists in rolling or making agitated movements in the dust on the ground in order to remove parasites

dustbin /dúst bin/ *n.* a large lidded usually cylindrical container for household rubbish, kept outdoors. US term **garbage can**

dustbin lorry, dustbin van *n. UK* = **dustcart**

dust bowl *n.* an area in a semiarid environment in which the topsoil is exposed and dust storms are likely to occur

Dust Bowl *n.* a large area in the southern part of the central United States that suffered badly from wind erosion during the 1930s

dustcart /dúst kaart/ *n. UK* a large motor vehicle used to collect and compact waste materials left bagged or in containers outside buildings

dust cloth *n. US* = **duster**

dust coat *n.* a woman's loose housecoat

dust cover *n.* **1. COVER FOR EQUIPMENT** a cover, often made from transparent plastic, for protecting a piece of equipment **2.** PUBL = **dust jacket 3.** = **dustsheet**

dust devil *n.* a rising or travelling funnel of dust, dirt, or sand that occurs on hot days, especially in desert or arid areas. Dust devils are smaller than tornadoes and are generally not dangerous.

duster /dústər/ *n.* **1. CLEANING CLOTH** a piece of cloth used for removing dust, especially from household objects and surfaces. US term **dust cloth 2. DUST REMOVER** a cloth or pad that removes household dust **3.** CLOTHES = **dust coat 4.** AGRIC **DEVICE FOR SPREADING AGROCHEMICALS** a machine or device for spreading powdered fungicide, insecticide, or fertilizer over crops or other plants **5.** CLOTHES **WOMAN'S LONG LOOSE COAT** a woman or girl's long loose coat, sometimes one without buttons or lapels

dustily /dústili/ *adv.* curtly and impolitely

dustiness /dústinəss/ *n.* **1. DUST-COVERED STATE** the state of being covered with or containing dust **2. CURTNESS** curtness and impoliteness

dusting /dústing/ *n.* **1. REMOVAL OF DUST** the act of removing small particles of dirt from sth, usually by wiping with a cloth **2. THIN POWDERY COVERING** a thin, sometimes patchy covering of a powdery substance ○ *a dusting of snow on the ground* **3. DEFEAT** a defeat or setback (*slang*) ○ *a candidate who took a real dusting at the polls*

dusting down *n.* a severe telling-off

dusting powder *n.* fine powder such as talcum powder, especially for use on the skin

dust jacket *n.* a paper book cover that protects the hardbound binding and that can be discarded

dustman /dústmən/ (*plural* **-men** /-mən/) *n. UK* sb employed to remove rubbish, especially from dustbins outside people's houses

dustpan /dúst pan/ *n.* a container with a flat base and an open front into which dirt and dust can be swept

dustsheet /dúst sheet/ *n.* a large piece of cloth placed over furniture or furnishings to protect them from dust, dirt, or paint. US term **drop cloth**

dust storm *n.* a strong hot dry wind laden with dust

dust-up *n.* a violent argument or physical altercation, often one that starts and stops quickly (*slang*)

dusty /dústi/ (**-ier, -iest**) *adj.* **1. FULL OF DUST** covered with or containing dust **2.** COLOURS **TINGED WITH GREY** containing tinges of grey with other colours ○ *dusty pink* **3. BORING** boring, especially because of being obscure or outdated ○ *dusty political slogans* **4. LIKE DUST** resembling dust ○ *a dusty gold powder* ◇ **not so dusty** all right, not so bad, in answer to a query as to how sb or sth is (*dated informal*)

Dusty /dústi/, **Slim** (*b.* 1927) Australian singer and songwriter. He was a country and western performer whose 1957 single 'The Pub with No Beer' became one of the best-selling records in the history of Australian popular music. Real name **David Gordon Kirkpatrick**

dusty answer *n.* a reply that is unhelpful and curt or impolite (*dated*)

dusty miller *n.* **1.** PLANTS **PLANT WITH DOWNY LEAVES** a plant with grey or white leaves covered with a down resembling dust. Latin name: *Senecio cineraria* and *Cerastium tomentosum.* **2.** = **rose campion**

dutch /duch/ *n. Cockney* sb's wife (*slang*) [Late 19thC. Shortening of DUCHESS.]

Dutch /duch/ *n.* **OFFICIAL LANGUAGE OF THE NETHERLANDS** the official language of the Netherlands and the Republic of Surinam, and one of the West Germanic group of Indo-European languages. Dutch is spoken by about 20 million people. ■ *npl.* **PEOPLE OF THE NETHERLANDS** the people of the Netherlands collectively ■ *adj.* **1. OF THE NETHERLANDS** relating to or typical of the Netherlands, or its people or culture **2. OF THE DUTCH LANGUAGE** relating to Dutch [14thC. From Middle Dutch *dutsch*, from a prehistoric Germanic word meaning 'people', which is also the ancestor of English *Deutschmark* and *Teuton*.] ◇ **go Dutch** to pay for your own part of the cost of a meal or entertainment

Dutch auction *n.* an auction in which the price is lowered gradually until sb makes a bid

Dutch barn *n.* a farm building with a curved roof and open sides and two levels. Hay, straw, and grain are stored on the upper level and animals are kept below. Dutch barns are usually built into a slope to provide easy access to the upper storey.

Dutch cap *n.* = **diaphragm** *n.* 2

Dutch clover *n.* = **white clover**

Dutch courage *n.* the temporary confidence supposedly obtained from drinking alcohol (*informal*) [Derogatory expressions containing *Dutch* stem from the rivalry between the Dutch and the English in the 17th and 18th centuries]

Dutch doll *n.* a wooden doll with jointed limbs and body

Dutch East Indies the islands of Indonesia from late 18th-century Dutch rule until Indonesian independence in 1949

Dutch elm *n.* a cultivated hybrid elm tree introduced to Great Britain from the Netherlands in the 17th century and now common in northeastern France and parts of western Great Britain and Ireland. Latin name: *Ulmus x hollandica.*

Dutch elm disease *n.* a disease of elm trees that killed many elms in Great Britain in the 1970s and 1980s. It is caused by a fungus *Ceratocystis ulmi*

carried by a bark beetle. [*Dutch* from the identification of the disease by Dutch scientists]

Dutch hoe *n.* a hoe used for weeding that is pushed instead of pulled

Dutchman /dúchmən/ (*plural* **-men** /-mən/) *n.* **1. MAN FROM THE NETHERLANDS** a man who was born in or is a citizen of the Netherlands **2.** CONSTR **PIECE USED TO REPAIR BUILDING** a piece of building material used to repair or conceal a fault in a construction ◇ **I'm a Dutchman** you may assert sth but even if you do, I do not believe you or it

Dutchman's breeches *n.* a woodland plant of the eastern United States that has creamy white flowers with two spurs. Latin name: *Dicentra cucullaria.* (*takes a singular or plural verb*)

Dutchman's pipe *n.* a woody climbing vine of the eastern United States that has mottled greenish-brown flowers shaped like the bowl and stem of an old-fashioned tobacco pipe. Latin name: *Aristolochia sipho.*

Dutch oven *n.* **1. HEAVY COOKING POT** an iron or earthenware container with a lid, used for cooking stews or casseroles **2. OUTDOOR OVEN** a metal box with an open front placed beside an open fire so that food can be cooked inside it

Dutch treat *n.* an outing, e.g. to a restaurant or theatre, at which each person pays for himself or herself (*informal*)

Dutch uncle *n.* sb, typically a mentor, who criticizes or advises in a frank, sometimes harsh manner (*informal*)

Dutch wife (*plural* **Dutch wives**) *n.* a firm bolster or framework used in bed to support the upper knee while sb is sleeping on his or her side

Dutchwoman /dúch wòomən/ (*plural* **-en** /-wimmin/) *n.* a woman who was born in or is a citizen of the Netherlands

duteous /dyóoti əss/ *adj.* obedient or submitting to duty (*literary*) —**duteously** *adv.* —**duteousness** *n.*

dutiable /dyóoti əb'l/ *adj.* subject to customs or other duties —**dutiability** /dyóoti ə bíllәti/ *n.*

dutiful /dyóotif'l/ *adj.* **1. MEETING OBLIGATIONS** done to fulfil obligations, often with little enthusiasm ○ *made a dutiful attempt at conversation* **2. OBEDIENT** acting according to obligations ○ *a dutiful and hard-working employee* —**dutifully** *adv.* —**dutifulness** *n.*

Dutton /dútt'n/, **Geoffrey Piers Henry** (*b.* 1922) Australian writer and editor. He wrote the poetry collection *Selective Affinities* (1985).

duty /dyóoti/ (*plural* **-ties**) *n.* **1. OBLIGATION** sth that sb is obliged to do for moral, legal, or religious reasons ○ *your duties as a parent* **2. ALLOCATED TASK** a task or service allocated to sb, especially in the course of work **3. NEED TO MEET OBLIGATIONS** the urge to meet moral or religious obligations ○ *a strong sense of duty* **4. RESPECT OWED TO OTHERS** the respect owed to people because of their age or status (*archaic*) **5.** ECON **TAX** a tax on goods, especially imports and exports **6. QUALITY** suitability for a particular grade of use (*usually used in combination*) ○ *heavy-duty shoes* ○ *medium-duty carpet* **7.** MECH ENG **MACHINE'S DESIGNATED WORKLOAD** the amount of work that a machine is designed to do, or a measure of a machine's efficiency **8.** AGRIC **VOLUME OF WATER NEEDED FOR IRRIGATION** the volume of water that is needed in order to irrigate an area of land so as to cultivate a crop from planting to harvest time [13thC. Via Anglo-Norman *dueté* from Old French *deu* 'owed', from Latin *debitus*, from *debere* 'to owe'.]

duty-free *adj.* **EXEMPTED FROM EXCISE DUTIES** on or at which no customs or excise duties have to be paid ■ *adv.* **WITHOUT CUSTOMS AND EXCISE DUTIES** without paying or charging customs or excise duties ■ *n.* **SHOP SELLING DUTY-FREE GOODS** a shop, especially at an airport or on board ship, that sells duty-free goods ■ **duty-frees** *npl.* **DUTY-FREE GOODS** duty-free goods, especially the allowance of duty-free goods that an individual is allowed to bring into his or her own country

Duty of Care *n.* the legal duty of everyone having control of waste to ensure that it is managed safely and transferred only to sb authorized to take it

duty officer *n.* an officer who is present in an office or headquarters and responsible for handling situations that may arise during a given period, especially a period when others are off duty

duumvir /dyoo úmvər/ (*plural* **-virs** *or* **-viri** /-və ree/) *n.* **1.** POL **ONE OF TWO PEOPLE SHARING AUTHORITY** either of two people who share a position of authority equally between them **2. ANCIENT ROMAN HOLDER OF JOINT OFFICE** a joint holder of any of the paired posts in the ancient Roman government or judiciary [Early 17thC. From Latin, from *duo* 'two' + *vir* 'man'.] —**duumvirate** /dyoo úmvirət/ *n.*

duvet /dóo vay, dyóo-/ *n.* **1. TYPE OF BED QUILT** a bed quilt made up of broad channels stuffed with down or synthetic material, usually used inside a removable washable cover in place of or together with sheets and blankets. US term **comforter 2. duvet, duvet jacket QUILTED DOWN-FILLED JACKET** a quilted jacket constructed from channels filled with down, intended for outdoor wear in severe weather conditions [Mid-18thC. Via French, 'down', from, ultimately, Old Norse *dūnn* (also the source of English *down*).]

duvetyn /dyóovə teen/, **duvetyne, duvetine** *n.* a soft velvety fabric with a nap, made of silk, cotton, wool, or rayon [Early 20thC. From French *duvetine*, from *duvet* 'down'.]

du Vigneaud, Vincent (1901–78) US biochemist. For his work on pituitary hormones, he won the Nobel Prize (1955).

dux /duks/ *n. Scotland* the student whose academic achievements are highest in a school, subject, or class [Mid-18thC. From Latin, 'leader'.]

duyker /díkər/ *n.* = **duiker**

DV *abbr.* Deo volente

dvandva /dvaán dvaa/ *n.* a compound word made up of two elements of equal status, which would make sense if joined by 'and' instead of being compounded, e.g. 'push-pull' and 'Marxist-Leninist' [Mid-19thC. From Sanskrit, formed from a doubling of *dva* 'two'.]

DVD a type of high-capacity optical compact disc that can store a much larger quantity of video, audio, or other information than can a conventional compact disc. Full form **digital video disc**

DVD-ROM a high-capacity digital video disc on which data can be stored but cannot be altered. Full form **digital versatile disc read only memory**

DVI *abbr.* digital video imaging

Dvina /dveénə/ river in northeastern Europe, comprising the Northern Dvina and the Western Dvina. Length: 1,768 km/1,090 mi.

DVLA *abbr.* Driving and Vehicle Licensing Agency

DVM *abbr.* Doctor of Veterinary Medicine

Dvořák /dváwr zhak/, **Antonín** (1841–1904) Bohemian Czech composer. An ardent nationalist, he based many themes on Czech or, e.g. his ninth symphony, *From the New World* (1893), US folk music.

DW *abbr.* distilled water

D/W *abbr.* LAW dock warrant

dwaal /dwaal/ *n. S Africa* a state of distractedness and inattention or confusion and bewilderment (*informal*) [From Afrikaans]

dwale /dwayl/ *n.* the poisonous deadly nightshade plant (*archaic*) [15thC. Origin uncertain: probably from Scandinavian.]

dwam /dwaam/ *n. Scotland* **INATTENTIVE STATE** a daydream or state of inattention ■ *vi.* (**dwams, dwamming, dwammed**) *Scotland* **FALL ILL OR FEEL FAINT** to become ill, especially suddenly, or feel faint [Early 16thC. Ultimately from a prehistoric Germanic base that is also the ancestor of English *dwell*.]

dwarf /dwawrf/ *n.* (*plural* **dwarves** /dwawrvz/ *or* **dwarfs**) **1.** LITERAT **SMALL HUMANOID CREATURE IN FOLKLORE** in fairy tales and folklore, a small creature with a mainly human appearance, associated with mountains, mines, and buried treasures. Fictional dwarves were often believed to have magic powers and to be sometimes malevolent. **2.** PHYSIOL **PERSON SMALL FOR MEDICAL REASONS** a person of small stature for medical reasons, usually sb with an average-sized body but unusually short limbs, or sb with growth hormone deficiency **3.** BIOL **SMALL PLANT OR ANIMAL** a plant or animal that is much smaller than others of its species, usually as a result of selective breeding (*often used before a noun*) ○ *a dwarf conifer* **4.** ASTRON = **dwarf star** ■ *vt.* (**dwarfs, dwarfing, dwarfed**) **1. MAKE SB OR STH SEEM SMALL** to make sb or sth else seem very small or very unimportant, by comparison ○ *The cathedral is dwarfed by the enormous tower blocks surrounding it.* **2. STUNT SB'S OR STH'S GROWTH** to stunt the growth of sb or sth [Old English *dweorg*, of prehistoric Germanic origin] —**dwarfish** *adj.* —**dwarfishly** *adv.* —**dwarfishness** *n.*

dwarf bean *n.* a short bushy type of French bean. Latin name: *Phaseolus vulgaris.* US term **bush bean**

dwarf chestnut *n.* = **chinquapin**

dwarfism /dwáwrfizəm/ *n.* BIOL, PHYSIOL the condition of being a dwarf

dwarf star, dwarf *n.* a star with relatively low mass, size, and luminosity. The Sun is a dwarf star. ◊ **giant star**

dwarves plural of **dwarf**

dweeb /dweeb/ *n. US* sb who is considered to be boring, silly, or socially inept (*slang insult*) [Late 20thC. Origin unknown.]

dwell /dwel/ *vi.* (**dwells, dwelling, dwelt** /dwelt/ *or* **dwelled**) **RESIDE** to live and have a home in a particular place (*literary*) ■ *n.* MECH ENG **REGULAR PAUSE** a regular pause in the operation of a machine [Old English *dwellan* 'to lead astray'. Ultimately from an Indo-European base meaning 'to rise in a cloud', which is also the ancestor of English *dust* and *typhus*.] —**dweller** *n.*
dwell on, dwell upon *vt.* to think, write, or talk about sth at considerable length

dwelling /dwélling/ *n.* **HOME** a house or other building or place in which sb lives (*formal*) ■ *adj.* **LIVING** living in a specified type of place or environment (*usually used in combination*)

dwelt past tense, past participle of **dwell**

DWEM /dwem/, **dwem** *abbr.* dead white European male (*slang offensive*)

dwindle /dwínd'l/ (**-dles, -dling, -dled**) *vti.* to decrease little by little in size, number, or intensity and approach zero, or reduce sth in this way ○ *Supplies were dwindling.* [Late 16thC. Formed from the obsolete verb *dwine* 'to waste away'. Ultimately from an Indo-European base meaning 'to become exhausted', which is also the ancestor of English *dead*.]

dwt *abbr.* deadweight tonnage

DX *symbol.* TELECOM long-distance

Dy *symbol.* dysprosium

dy. *abbr.* delivery

dyad /dí ad/ *n.* **1. COUPLE** two individual units, things, or people linked as a pair (*formal*) **2.** CHEM **ATOM WITH VALENCY OF TWO** an atom or chemical group with a valency of two **3.** MATH **VECTOR OPERATOR** a mathematical operator consisting of two vectors expressed without a multiplication sign between them **4.** MUSIC **TWO-NOTE CHORD** a musical chord consisting of two notes [Late 17thC. Via late Latin from the stem of Greek *duas*, from *duo* 'two'.] —**dyadic** /dī áddik/ *adj.* —**dyadically** /-áddikli/ *adv.*

Dyak /dí ak/ (*plural* **-aks** *or* **-ak**), **Dayak** (*plural* **-aks** *or* **-ak**) *n.* a member of a Malaysian people who live in the interior of Borneo and are noted for their communal long houses [Mid-19thC. From Malay, literally 'up-country'.]

dyarchy *n.* = **diarchy**

dybbuk /díbbək/ (*plural* **-buks** *or* **-bukim** /-kim/), **dibbuk** *n.* in Jewish folklore, a malevolent spirit of a dead person, believed able to take over a living person's body and control his or her behaviour unless exorcised [Early 20thC. Via Yiddish *dibek* from Hebrew *dibbūq*, from *dābaq* 'to cling'.]

dye /dī/ *v.* (**dyes, dyeing, dyed**) **1.** *vt.* **COLOUR STH BY SOAKING** to colour or stain sth, e.g. fabric or hair, by soaking it in a colouring solution so that it takes on the new colour permanently or semi-permanently **2.** *vi.* **COLOUR WELL OR BADLY** to respond to being treated with a colouring agent and take its colour in a particular way ■ *n.* **1. COLOURING AGENT** a natural or synthetic substance that can be used to colour sth such as a textile or hair and is most often applied in liquid form **2.** COLOURING SOLUTION a colouring solution containing a dye **3.** COLOUR PRODUCED BY A DYE the colour produced on sth by a dye [Old English *dēah* 'colour, a colour that hides'. The distinction in spelling between the verbs DIE and DYE is relatively recent.] —**dyable** *adj.* —**dyer** *n.*

dyed-in-the-wool *adj.* **1.** WHOLEHEARTEDLY AND STUBBORNLY ATTACHED TO STH wholeheartedly and stubbornly attached to a set of beliefs, political party, or philosophy and totally convinced of its merits **2.** TEXTILES DYED BEFORE WEAVING dyed before weaving into cloth

dyeline /dī līn/ *adj.* CHEM = **diazo**

dyer's-greenweed /dī ərz grēen weed/ *n.* a small Eurasian shrub similar to broom that produces clusters of flowers formerly used to produce a yellow dye. It is now naturalized in North America. Latin name: *Genista tinctoria*. [From the yellowish-green colour of the flowers]

dyer's rocket *n.* a Eurasian plant of the mignonette family that has spikes of pale yellowish-green flowers formerly used to produce a yellow dye. Latin name: *Reseda luteola*.

dyer's-weed *n.* any plant that yields a dye, especially dyer's greenweed and dyer's rocket

dyestuff /dī stuf/ *n.* = **dye** n. 1

dyewood /dī wŏŏd/ *n.* any wood that can be used as a dye

Dyfed /dúvvid/ former county in southwestern Wales. Carmarthen was its administrative centre. Population: 351,500 (1993). Area: 5,768 sq. km/2,227 sq. mi.

dying /dī̇ing/ *adj.* **1.** ABOUT TO DIE on the point of death **2.** OCCURRING JUST BEFORE DEATH carried out, spoken, or occurring at or just before the point of death **3.** FINAL occurring as sth is about to reach its end ○ *in the dying seconds of the game*

dyke[1] /dīk/, **dike** *n.* **1.** EMBANKMENT TO PREVENT FLOODS an embankment built along the shore of a sea or lake or beside a river to hold back the water and prevent flooding **2.** BARRIER a barrier or obstacle meant to keep sth out **3.** CAUSEWAY a raised roadway across a swamp or body of water **4.** US DITCH a drainage ditch or other artificial watercourse **5.** *Scotland* DRY-STONE WALL an enclosing or dividing wall, usually made of stone, often without mortar **6.** GEOL LONG MASS OF IGNEOUS ROCK a vertical or near-vertical mass of igneous rock that has forced its way upwards through overlying strata **7.** *ANZ* LAVATORY a lavatory (*informal*) ■ *vt.* (**dykes, dyking, dyked; dikes, diking, diked**) **1.** PROTECT WITH DIKES to enclose or protect an area of land with a dyke or series of dykes **2.** DRAIN WITH DITCHES to drain an area of land using ditches [13thC. Origin uncertain: probably from Old Norse *dík*, from a prehistoric Germanic word meaning 'hole and mound resulting from digging', which is also the ancestor of English *ditch*.] —**dyker** *n.*

dyke[2] /dīk/ *n.* a highly offensive term for a lesbian (*slang offensive*)

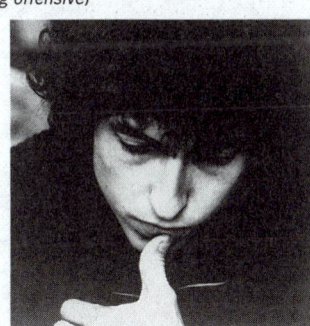

Bob Dylan

Dylan /díllən/, **Bob** (*b.* 1941) US folk singer. He wrote protest songs such as *'Blowin' in the Wind'* (1962) and *'The Times They Are A-Changin''* (1964). Real name **Robert Zimmerman**

dyn *symbol.* PHYS dyne

dynamic /dī námmik/ *adj.* **1.** VIGOROUS AND PURPOSEFUL full of energy, enthusiasm, and a sense of purpose and able both to get things going and to get things

done **2.** ACTIVE AND CHANGING characterized by vigorous activity and producing or undergoing change and development ○ *a dynamic economy* **3.** RELATING TO ENERGY involving or relating to energy and forces that produce motion **4.** RELATING TO DYNAMICS involved in or connected with the study of dynamics **5.** MUSIC RELATING TO LOUDNESS IN MUSIC relating to or indicating variations in the loudness of musical sounds **6.** PHYS CHANGING OVER TIME used to describe any system that changes over time ■ *n.* DRIVING FORCE a driving or energizing force, especially one involved in a process of social or psychological change [Early 19thC. Via French *dynamique* from, ultimately, Greek *dunamis* 'force', from *dunasthai* 'to be able'.] —**dynamical** *adj.* —**dynamically** *adv.*

dynamic markings, **dynamic marks** *npl.* MUSIC the symbols and words that indicate the degree of loudness or softness with which a piece, passage, or note of music should be played

dynamic range *n.* **1.** MUSIC VOLUME RANGE OF PIECE OF MUSIC the range of volume used within a single piece of music **2.** ELECTRON ENG RANGE OF REPRODUCIBLE SOUND the range over which an electronic audio system can operate to a set standard of performance based on given limits for noise and distortion

dynamics /dī námmiks/ *n.* **1.** CHANGE-PRODUCING FORCES the forces that tend to produce activity and change in any situation or sphere of existence (*takes a plural verb*) **2.** MUSIC LOUDNESS AND SOFTNESS IN MUSICAL PIECE the different levels of loudness and softness in a piece of music, and the way in which a performer reproduces them in performance (*takes a plural verb*) **3.** MUSIC DYNAMIC MARKINGS dynamic markings symbols and words (*takes a plural verb*) **4.** PHYS STUDY OF MOTION the study of motion and the way in which forces produce motion (*takes a singular verb*)

dynamism /dī́nimizəm/ *n.* **1.** VIGOROUSLY ACTIVE, FORCEFUL, AND ENERGIZING QUALITY a vigorously active, forceful, and energizing quality, especially as the hallmark of sb's personality or approach to a task **2.** THEORY OF FORCES a philosophical or scientific theory stressing the role of dynamic forces in explaining phenomena, especially by interpreting events as an expression of forces residing within the object or person involved —**dynamist** *n.* —**dynamistic** /dī́nə místik/ *adj.*

dynamite /dī́nə mīt/ *n.* **1.** POWERFUL EXPLOSIVE a powerful explosive used for blasting consisting of a porous material e.g. wood pulp or sawdust combined with ammonium or sodium nitrate, or nitroglycerine, and an antacid e.g. calcium carbonate **2.** VERY EXCITING OR POWERFUL THING sth that or sb who is exceptionally exciting or has an extremely powerful effect (*slang*) ○ *This music is absolute dynamite.* **3.** VERY DANGEROUS OR HARMFUL THING sth that or sb who is potentially very dangerous or harmful (*slang*) ○ *news stories that were political dynamite* ■ *vt.* (**-miting, -mited**) dynamites BLAST STH WITH DYNAMITE to blast or explode sth with dynamite [Mid-19thC. Coined from Greek *dunamis* 'force' + -ITE by its inventor, Swedish chemist Alfred NOBEL.] —**dynamiter** *n.*

dynamo /dī́nə mō/ (*plural* **-mos**) *n.* **1.** ELEC ENG GENERATOR OF ELECTRICITY FROM MECHANICAL ENERGY a machine that converts mechanical energy into electrical energy, usually in the form of direct current **2.** ENERGETIC PERSON a hard-working, tirelessly energetic person (*informal*) [Late 19thC. Shortening of *dynamo-electric machine*.]

dynamo- *prefix.* power, energy ○ *dynamometer* [From Greek *dunamis* (see DYNAMIC)]

dynamoelectric /dī́nəmō i léktrik/, **dynamoelectrical** /-trik'l/ *adj.* involved in or relating to the production of electrical energy from mechanical energy, and vice versa

dynamometer /dī́ni mómmitər/ *n.* an instrument used to measure mechanical force or power, e.g. the power output of an engine —**dynamometric** /dī́nəmō méttrik/ *adj.* —**dynamometry** /dī́nə mómmətri/ *n.*

dynamotor /dī́nə mōtər/ *n.* an electrical device combining a motor and generator and used to convert alternating current to direct current, and vice versa [Early 20thC. Coined from Greek *dunamis* 'force' (see DYNAMIC) + MOTOR.]

dynast /dínn ast, -əst/ *n.* **1.** RULER a ruler, especially a hereditary monarch (*literary*) **2.** MEMBER OR FOUNDER OF DYNASTY a member of a dynasty, or the founder of one [Mid-17thC. Via Latin from Greek *dunastēs* 'lord', from *dunasthai* 'to be able'.]

dynasty /dínnəsti/ (*plural* **-ties**) *n.* **1.** SUCCESSION OF HEREDITARY RULERS a succession of rulers from the same family **2.** PROMINENT AND POWERFUL FAMILY a prominent and powerful family or group of people whose members retain their power and influence through several generations [14thC. Via French *dynastie* or directly from late Latin *dynastia*, from, ultimately, Greek *dunastēs* 'lord' (see DYNAST).] —**dynastic** /di nástik/ *adj.* —**dynastically** /-kli/ *adv.*

dyne /dīn/ *n.* the unit of force in the cgs system equal to the force which will accelerate a mass of one gram one centimetre per second per second. 1 dyne is equivalent to 10^{-5} newton. [Late 19thC. Formed from Greek *dunamis* 'force' (see DYNAMIC).]

Dynel /dī nél/ *tdmk.* a trademark for a copolymer used in making fire- and insect-resistant textile fibre and derived from vinyl chloride and acrylonitrile

dys- *prefix.* bad, impaired, abnormal ○ *dysplasia* [Via Latin from Greek *dus-*]

dysarthria /diss aárthri ə/ *n.* difficulty in speech articulation due to lack of muscle control caused by damage to the central nervous system [Late 19thC. From modern Latin, formed from DYS- + Greek *arthron* 'joint'.]

dyscrasia /diss kráyzi ə/ *n.* any abnormal condition of blood cells [14thC. Via late Latin from Greek *dyskrasia*, literally 'bad mixture', from *krasis* 'mixing' (source of English *idiosyncrasy*).]

dysentery /díss'ntəri/ *n.* the disease of the lower intestine caused by infection with bacteria, protozoa, or parasites and marked by severe diarrhoea, inflammation, and the passage of blood and mucus [14thC. Via Old French *dissenterie* or directly from Latin *dysenteria*, from, ultimately, Greek *dusenteros*, literally 'bad intestines', from *enteron* 'intestine'.] —**dysenteric** /díss'n térrik/ *adj.*

dysfunction /diss fúngksh'n/ *n.* a medical abnormality in the functioning of an organ or other part or system of the body

dysfunctional /diss fúngksh'nəl/ *adj.* **1.** NOT PERFORMING ITS FUNCTION PROPERLY failing to perform the function that is normally expected ○ *counselling a dysfunctional family* **2.** SOCIOL RELATING BADLY unable to function emotionally as a social unit **3.** MED NOT FUNCTIONING NORMALLY unable to function normally as a result of disease or impairment

dysgenic /diss jénnik/ *adj.* involving or causing the inheriting of detrimental characteristics

dysgenics /diss jénniks/ *n.* the study of factors relating to or causing a decrease in the survival of the hereditarily well-adapted members of a line of descent (*takes a singular verb*)

dysgraphia /diss gráffi ə/ *n.* impairment of writing ability, arising from brain injury or disease

dyskinesia /díski neézi ə/ *n.* impairment of the control over ordinary muscle movement, often resulting in spasmodic movements or tics [Early 18thC. Via modern Latin from Greek *duskinēsia*, literally 'difficulty in moving', from *kinēsis* 'movement' (see -KINESIS).]

dyslexia /diss léksi ə/ *n.* a learning disorder marked by a severe difficulty in recognizing and understanding written language, leading to spelling and writing problems. It is not caused by low intelligence or brain damage. [Late 19thC. Coined from DYS- + Greek *lexis* 'speech', from *legein* 'to speak'.] —**dyslexic** *adj., n.*

dysmenorrhoea /díss menə reé ə/ *n.* severe pain or cramps in the lower abdomen during menstruation —**dysmenorrhoeal** *adj.* —**dysmenorrhoeic** *adj.*

dyspareunia /díspar yŏŏni ə/ *n.* pain occurring during sexual intercourse

dyspepsia /diss pépsi ə/ *n.* acid indigestion (*technical*) [Early 18thC. Via Latin from Greek *duspepsia*, literally 'difficult digestion', from *peptein* 'to cook, digest'.]

dyspeptic /diss péptik/ *adj.* **1.** HAVING INDIGESTION having acid indigestion **2.** BAD-TEMPERED in a bad temper, or having a bad-tempered disposition ■ *n.* BAD-TEMPERED PERSON an irritable bad-tempered person [Late 17thC. From Greek *duspeptos*, literally 'difficult of digestion', from *peptein* 'to cook, digest'.]

dysphagia /diss fáyji ə/ *n.* difficulty in swallowing, with a variety of possible causes —**dysphagic** /-fájjik/ *adj.*

dysphasia /dis fáyzi ə/ *n.* difficulty in speaking and understanding spoken or written language, caused by brain injury or disease —**dysphasic** *adj.*

dysphemism /dísfimizzəm/ *n.* **1.** SUBSTITUTION OF A COARSER WORD the deliberate substitution of an offensive expression for a neutral one **2.** OFFENSIVE SUBSTITUTE FOR NEUTRAL WORD an offensive expression deliberately substituted for a neutral one [Late 19thC. Formed from DYS- on the model of *euphemism*.] —**dysphemistic** /dísfi místik/ *adj.*

dysphonia /diss fóni ə/ *n.* hoarseness or difficulty in speaking as a result of dysfunction of the vocal cords caused by brain injury, brain disease, or chemical poisoning [Early 18thC. Via modern Latin from Greek *dusphōnia*, literally 'roughness of sound', from *phōnē* 'sound'.] —**dysphonic** /-fónnik/ *adj.*

dysphoria /diss fáwri ə/ *n.* a state of feeling acutely hopeless, uncomfortable, and unhappy [Mid-19thC. From Greek *dusphoria*, literally 'discomfort', from, ultimately, *pherein* 'to bear'.] —**dysphoric** /-fórrik/ *adj.*

dysplasia /diss pláyzi ə/ *n.* medically abnormal development or growth of a part of the body, e.g. an organ, bone, or cell, including the total absence of such a part —**dysplastic** /-plástik/ *adj.*

dyspnoea /disp née'ə/ *n.* difficulty in breathing caused, e.g., by heart disease or overexertion [Mid-17thC. Via Latin from Greek *duspnoia*, literally 'difficulty of breathing', from, ultimately, *pnein* 'to breathe'.] —**dyspnoeal** *adj.* —**dyspnoeic** *adj.*

dyspraxia /diss práksi ə/ *n.* **1.** POOR COORDINATION poor coordination displayed by some children, diagnosed by illegible handwriting and inability to catch a ball and clap while the ball is in the air. It sometimes accompanies dyslexia. **2.** IMPAIRMENT OF THE MOTOR SYSTEM an impairment in or partial loss of control of the body's motor system, resulting from brain damage. = **apraxia** [From Greek *duspraxia*, literally 'ill success', from *praxis* 'action' (see PRAXIS)] —**dyspraxic** *adj.*

dysprosium /diss prózi əm/ *n.* a soft silvery chemical element of the rare earth group that is paramagnetic, highly reactive, and used in laser materials and nuclear research. Symbol **Dy** [Late 19thC. Coined from Greek *dusprositos*, literally 'difficult to approach', from, ultimately, *ienai* 'to go' (source of English *ion*).]

dysrhythmia /diss ríthmi ə/ *n.* an irregularity in an otherwise normal rhythm, especially of heartbeats or brainwaves [Early 20thC. From modern Latin, literally 'bad rhythm', from, ultimately, Greek *rhuthmos* 'rhythm'.]

dystocia /diss tóshə/ *n.* abnormally difficult childbirth [Early 18thC. From Greek *dustokia*, literally 'difficult childbirth', from *tokos* 'childbirth'.] —**dystocial** *adj.*

dystopia /diss tópi ə/ *n.* an imaginary place where everything is as bad as it possibly can be, or a vision or description of such a place [Mid-20thC. Coined from DYS- + UTOPIA.] —**dystopian** *adj.*

dystrophic /diss tróffik/ *adj.* **1.** AFFECTED BY DYSTROPHY relating to or affected by dystrophy **2.** ECOL CONTAINING EXCESS HUMUS used to describe a pond or lake containing water that is brown in colour, abnormally acidic, and lacking in oxygen. Such water is unable to support much plant or animal life because of the amount of humus dissolved in it.

dystrophin /dístrəfin/ *n.* a protein found in normal muscle that is missing in muscle affected by some forms of muscular dystrophy

dystrophy /dístrəfi/ (*plural* **-phies**), **dystrophia** /diss trófi ə/ *n.* **1.** MED PROGRESSIVE DEGENERATION OF TISSUE progressive degeneration of a body tissue, e.g. muscle, as a result of inadequate nourishment of the affected part, due to some unknown cause **2.** ENVIRON EXCESSIVE HUMUS IN WATER a condition in which pond or lake water is unable to support thriving animal or plant life because of excessive humus content

dysuria /diss yóori ə/ *n.* pain or difficulty in urinating —**dysuric** *adj.*

dytiscid /di tíssid, dī-/ *n.* a carnivorous freshwater diving beetle. Family: Dytiscidae. [Mid-19thC. From modern Latin, formed from Greek *dutikos* 'able to dive', from *duein* 'to dive'.] —**dytiscid** *adj.*

Dyula /dee o'ola, dyoólə/ (*plural* **-la** *or* **-las**) *n.* **1.** PEOPLES MEMBER OF AN AFRICAN PEOPLE a member of an African people who live mainly in the rainforests of the Ivory Coast **2.** LANG MANDE LANGUAGE a Mande language spoken in parts of the Ivory Coast, Burkina Faso, and Ghana. Dyula is spoken by just over one million people. —**Dyula** *adj.*

dz. *abbr.* dozen

Dzerzhinsk /dur zhínsk/ city in central European Russia on the River Oka. It is a chemical-manufacturing centre. Population: 286,000 (1990).

dzo /zō/ (*plural* **dzos** *or* **dzo**), **zo** (*plural* **zos** *or* **zo**), **zho** (*plural* **zhos** *or* **zho**) *n.* an animal belonging to a breed developed from a hybrid between a cow and a yak [Mid-19thC. From Tibetan *mdso*.]

Dzongkha /zóngkə/, **Dzongka** *n.* the official language of Bhutan, a dialect of Tibetan. Dzongkha is spoken by just under one million people. [Early 20thC. From Tibetan, literally 'language of the fortress'.] —**Dzongkha** *adj.*

Dzungaria /dzoŏng gáiri ə, zoŏng-/ region in northwestern China, west of the Republic of Mongolia and east of Kazakhstan, in Xinjiang Uygur Autonomous Region

e¹ /ee/ (*plural* **e's**), **E** (*plural* **E's** *or* **Es**) *n.* **1.** 5TH LETTER OF THE ENGLISH ALPHABET the fifth letter of the modern English alphabet **2.** SPEECH SOUND CORRESPONDING TO THE LETTER 'E' the speech sound that corresponds to the letter 'E' **3.** LETTER 'E' WRITTEN a written representation of the letter 'E'

e² *symbol.* **1.** MATH the transcendental number 2.718 282... **2.** CHESS the fifth vertical row of squares from the left on a chessboard **3.** PHYS electron

E¹ *symbol.* **1.** PHYS energy **2.** PHYS electric field strength **3.** PHYS electromotive force (*usually written italicized*) **4.** LOGIC negative categorical proposition **5.** PHYS internal energy **6.** MEASURE exa- **7.** energy *n.* **5.**

E² /ee/ (*plural* **Es** *or* **E's**) *n.* **1.** MUSIC 3RD NOTE OF SCALE IN C the third note of a scale in C major **2.** MUSIC STH THAT PRODUCES AN E a string, key, or pipe tuned to produce the note E **3.** MUSIC SCALE BEGINNING ON E a scale or key that starts on the note E **4.** MUSIC WRITTEN SYMBOL OF E a graphic representation of the tone of E **5.** EDUC GRADE INDICATING VERY LOW QUALITY a grade or mark indicating that a student's work is of very low quality **6.** DRUGS ECSTASY the drug ecstasy or a tablet of the drug (*slang*) **7.** SOC SCI CASUAL WORKER a casual worker or sb who is dependent on the state

E³ *abbr.* **1.** east **2.** eastern **3.** ELEC earth **4.** English

e. *abbr.* **1.** engineer **2.** engineering

E. *abbr.* earl

e- *prefix.* **1.** electronic ○ *e-mail* **2.** electronic data transfer via the Internet ○ *e-commerce* [Shortening]

E111 *n.* a form that entitles EU citizens to free health care when visiting other EU countries

ea. *abbr.* each

EAC *abbr.* East African Community

each /eech/ *det., pron., adv.* used to refer to every member of a group of people or things, considered individually ○ *With each victory we get closer to the championship.* ○ *Is a VCR that can be connected to more than one TV better than buying one for each?* ○ *Environmental health officers were supervising an average of 40 cases each.* [Old English *ælc*. From a prehistoric Germanic compound meaning 'ever alike'.]

──────── **WORD KEY: USAGE** ────────

each or **every**? In some contexts these two words are nearly interchangeable, as in *I adore each puppy in the litter* and *I adore every puppy*. Here the only difference is a slight shift in perspective from considering the animals individually, with **each**, to considering them collectively, with **every**. Either of the words, placed before the noun, requires the noun and the verb to be singular: *each puppy is affectionate every puppy is affectionate.* **Each,** though not **every**, may also be placed after a plural noun, and then the plural governs the verb: *The puppies each have their own toys.* Also **each** can refer to two or more, whereas **every** must refer to three or more. **Each** can be an adjective or determiner (*each puppy*), a pronoun (*each of them*), and an adverb (*Give them a bowlful each*), whereas **every** is an adjective or determiner only.

each other *pron.* each one of two or more persons or things reciprocally

──────── **WORD KEY: USAGE** ────────

each other or **one another**? The traditional rule is that **each other** refers to two items and **one another** refers to more than two: *Joe and Lee respect each other deeply.*

All the people at the party knew one another already. However, this distinction is not supported by the weight of usage, and there is no good reason to reject the alternatives *Joe and Lee respect one another deeply* and *All the people at the party knew each other already,* although the last example sounds somewhat less natural than the others.

each way *adv.* on the same horse to come first or be placed second or third in a race ○ *had £5 each way on number 6* —**each-way** *adj.*

EACSO *abbr.* East African Common Services Organization

eager /eegər/ *adj.* **1.** ENTHUSIASTIC AND EXCITED ABOUT DOING STH enthusiastic and excited about sth and impatiently waiting to do or get it ○ *eager to help* ○ *eager for praise* **2.** FULL OF ENTHUSIASM AND IMPATIENCE expressing enthusiastic interest and expectation or an impatient desire to do sth ○ *eager face* [13thC. Via Anglo-Norman *egre* from, ultimately, Latin *acer* 'sharp' (source of English *acrid* and *vinegar*).] —**eagerly** *adv.* —**eagerness** *n.*

eager beaver *n.* sb who is exceptionally, or even excessively, ready and willing to work hard, carry out tasks, or volunteer (*informal*) [From the perceived industriousness of beavers. Originally a World War II expression in the United States for an over-zealous recruit.]

eagle /eeg'l/ *n.* **1.** BIRDS LARGE BIRD OF PREY a large and powerful bird of prey with a hooked bill and broad wing span that hunts by day and is noted for its keen eyesight and majestic soaring flight. Subfamily: Buteoninae. **2.** FIGURE OF AN EAGLE AS A SYMBOL the figure of an eagle used as a symbol of military or political power, e.g. on the standards carried by the Roman legions **3.** GOLF SCORE OF 2 UNDER PAR a score of two under par for a single hole in golf ■ *vti.* (**-gles, -gling, -gled**) GOLF SCORE 2 UNDER PAR to complete a hole in two strokes under par in golf [14thC. Via Anglo-Norman *egle* from Latin *aquila*.]

eagle eye *n.* extremely keen eyesight or the ability to notice what other people might miss —**eagle-eyed** *adj.*

eagle owl *n.* a large Eurasian owl, the largest species of owl in the world, with brownish plumage and tufts of feathers on its head that look like horns. Latin name: *Bubo bubo.*

eagle ray *n.* a large ray found in tropical and subtropical seas that has a projecting snout, massive jaws, and pectoral fins shaped like wings that propel it with a soaring motion. Family: Myliobatidae.

eaglet /eeglət/ *n.* a young eagle, especially before it leaves the nest

eagre /eegər/ *n.* GEOG = **bore**³ *n.* [Early 17thC. Origin unknown.]

ealdorman /áwldərmən/ (*plural* **-men** /-mən/) *n.* the principal magistrate and commander of the military forces of a shire in Anglo-Saxon England [Old English *ealdormann*, from *ealdor* 'an elder' + MAN]

Ealing /eeling/ borough in western London, England. Population: 275,257 (1991).

Ealing comedy *n.* any of the many British comedy films made at Ealing Studios from the 1930s to 1950s, especially those that have proved enduringly popular and are regarded as minor classics. Such films include *Kind Hearts and Coronets, The Lavender Hill Mob, The Man in the White Suit,* and *The*

Ladykillers, all starring Alec Guinness. [EALING from EALING STUDIOS]

Ealing Studios *n.* the film studios in Ealing, London, where a number of popular and highly regarded British comedy films were made from the 1930s to 1950s

Eames /eemz/ *tdmk.* a trademark for chairs, especially and originally ones of moulded plywood, whose seats and backs are shaped to accommodate human body contours

E & OE *abbr.* errors and omissions excepted (*used on invoices*)

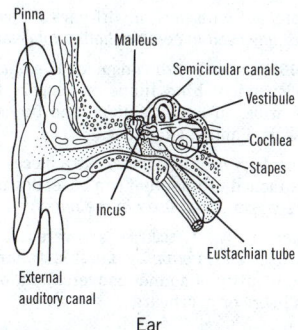

Ear

ear¹ /eer/ *n.* **1.** BIOL ORGAN OF HEARING the organ of hearing and balance in vertebrates that, in mammals, is divided into three parts, the external, middle, and inner ear. The external ear collects sound, the middle ear contains small bones that amplify and transmit it, while the inner ear maintains balance and contains sensory nerve endings for detecting sound. **2.** BIOL EXTERNAL PART OF HEARING ORGAN the external part of an ear, visible in humans and most mammals on each side of the head as a flap of cartilage with skin surrounding or covering it **3.** BIOL INVERTEBRATE SENSORY ORGAN SIMILAR TO AN EAR any sensory organ in invertebrates that is able to sense vibrations and perform a similar function to a vertebrate ear **4.** BIRDS = **ear tuft 5.** EAR SHAPE sth shaped like an ear, especially a handle on a jug or jar **6.** ABILITY TO TELL SOUNDS APART the ability to distinguish accurately between different sounds, e.g. in speech or music ○ *She has an ear for other languages.* **7.** ATTENTION sb's attention, especially sb's sympathetic or favourable attention [Old English *ēare.* Ultimately from an Indo-European word meaning 'ear', which is also the ancestor of English *aural.*] ◇ **all ears** listening, or ready to listen, attentively or enthusiastically to sth (*informal*) ◇ **go in one ear and out the other** to be forgotten as soon as heard and so have absolutely no effect on sb ◇ **have sb's ear** to be a trusted advisor to sb, especially sb powerful or influential ◇ **have or keep your ear to the ground** to remain continuously alert to discover new developments or information ◇ **out on your ear** unceremoniously thrown out or dismissed from a place or position you previously occupied (*informal*) ○ *You'll be out on your ear if you're late again.* ◇ **play it by ear** to improvise or adapt your response to a situation as it occurs rather than make plans in advance ◇ **set sth** *or* **sb by the ears** to cause conflict or disagreement among people or within an organization ◇ **set sth** *or* **sb on its** *or* **sb's ear** to send sth *or* sb into a state of excited agitation, shock, or confusion ◇ **wet behind the ears** very inexperienced or naive

ear[2] /eer/ *n.* BOT **PLANT PART CONTAINING GRAIN** the grain-bearing part at the top of the stalk of a cereal plant such as wheat or barley, or the grain-bearing part of maize or sweetcorn ■ *vi.* (**ears, earing, eared**) BOT **FORM EARS** to form the part of a cereal plant that contains the grains [Old English *ēar*. Ultimately from an Indo-European base meaning 'sharp' (see EAGER).]

earache /eer ayk/ *n.* pain in the middle or inner ear. Technical name **otalgia**

earbash /eer bash/ (**-bashes, -bashing, -bashed**) *v.* ANZ (*informal*) **1.** *vi.* **TALK NONSTOP** to talk nonstop ◇ *Will you two stop earbashing and give me a hand?* **2.** *vt.* **NAG SB** to nag or harangue sb ◇ *always earbashing me about the state of the garden*

earbashing /eer bashing/ *n.* ANZ a scolding or lecture from sb (*informal*) ◇ *copped a right earbashing for getting home late*

ear clip *n.* **1.** **ORNAMENT CLIPPED TO THE UPPER EAR** an ornament, e.g. a metal band, clipped to the upper part of the ear **2.** **CLIP-ON EARRING** a clip-on earring

eardrop /eer drop/ *n.* **PENDANT EARRING** a pendant earring ■ **eardrops** *npl.* **LIQUID EAR MEDICINE** liquid medicine for the ear, usually inserted with a dropper

eardrum /eer drum/ *n.* a membrane of thin skin and fibrous tissue that vibrates in response to sound waves, located between the external and the middle ear. Technical name **tympanic membrane**

eared /eerd/ *adj.* with ears, or with ears of a particular type (*usually used in combination*) ◇ *long-eared*

eared seal *n.* a seal with conspicuous external ears and independent hind limbs or flippers that are used to walk on land. Sealions and fur seals are eared seals. Family: Otariidae.

earflap /eer flap/ *n.* either of two extra pieces of fabric or fur attached to a hat that can be let down to keep the ears warm (*often used in the plural*)

earful /eer fool/ *n.* **1.** **SCOLDING** a severe scolding or lecture from sb (*informal*) **2.** **STH SB HEARS OR OVERHEARS** a large quantity of sound, conversation, or gossip that sb hears or overhears

Amelia Earhart

Earhart /air haart/, **Amelia** (1898–1937) US aviator. She was the first woman to fly solo over both the Atlantic (1932) and the Pacific (1935). She disappeared in the Pacific Ocean in 1937 while attempting a round-the-world flight.

earing /eering/ *n.* SAILING a small rope that attaches the upper corner of a sail to a yard [Early 17thC. Origin uncertain: perhaps from EAR[1].]

earl /url/ *n.* a British nobleman ranked above a viscount and below a marquess. The title corresponds to 'count' in continental Europe, which is not used in the United Kingdom, although a woman of equivalent rank is called a 'countess'. [Old English *eorl* 'warrior, nobleman', of unknown origin]

earldom /urldəm/ *n.* **1.** **RANK OF EARL** the rank or position of an earl or countess **2.** **TERRITORY** the territory belonging to or administered by an earl or countess

Earle /url/, **Augustus** (1793–1838) British painter. He is known for his vivid landscapes and paintings of early colonial life in Australia.

earless seal /eerless-/ *n.* a seal that does not have conspicuous external ears and has short front and hind flippers that are adapted for swimming rather than walking on land. Family: Phocidae.

Earl Grey *n.* a tea flavoured with bergamot to produce a lighter-coloured brew with a rather musky taste [Said to be named after Charles *Grey*, the second Earl Grey (1764–1845), British statesman and prime minister]

Earl Marshal *n.* an officer of the English peerage who presides over the College of Heralds and also organizes important ceremonial occasions

earlobe /eer lōb/ *n.* the soft fleshy lower part of the outer ear

early /url i/ *adv.* (**-lier, -liest**) **1.** **BEFORE THE EXPECTED TIME** before the expected or arranged time ◇ *they arrived early* **2.** **NEAR THE BEGINNING** at or near the beginning of a specified period, process, or event that is experienced over a period of time ◇ *early in the interview* **3.** **DURING THE FIRST STAGES** at a time when sth was not far advanced or developed or when sb was at a comparatively young age ◇ *She decided early that she wanted to become a teacher.* **4.** **SOON** promptly or soon ◇ *Post early for Christmas.* **5.** **BEFORE OTHER VARIETIES** before other varieties of the same plant or animal ■ *adj.* (**-lier, -liest**) **1.** **OCCURRING NEAR THE BEGINNING** occurring at or near the beginning of a period of time, process, or sequence of events ◇ *early reports indicate a high level of interest* **2.** **OCCURRING BEFORE THE EXPECTED TIME** occurring before the expected or arranged time ◇ *early retirement* **3.** **PRODUCED NEAR THE BEGINNING OF STH** produced at, characteristic of, or representing a not very advanced stage in the development of sth or sb ◇ *looking forward to an early end to the deadlock* **4.** **IN THE VERY NEAR FUTURE** due, expected, or requested to happen in the very near future **5.** BOT **RIPENING BEFORE OTHERS** ripening before other varieties of the same type ◇ *early peaches* [Old English *ǣrlīce*. Ultimately from an Indo-European word meaning 'day', which is also the ancestor of English *erst*.] ◇ **it's early days** things are at an early stage and it is uncertain how they will develop or turn out

WORD KEY: USAGE

The BBC recognised early *on that there was money to be made from selling archive programmes on video.* (*New Scientist*) *The expression* early on, *derived from* earlier on, *is a twentieth-century use.*

early bird *n.* (*informal*) **1.** **SB WHO GETS UP EARLY** sb who gets up early in the morning **2.** **SB WHO ARRIVES EARLY** sb who arrives earlier than the expected or arranged time [From the proverb *The early bird catches the worm*]

early closing *n.* the regular closing of most of the shops in a town or part of a town on one particular afternoon in the week

early day motion *n.* a motion tabled for discussion in Parliament on an unspecified day in the future when business finishes early, whose main purpose is to draw Parliament's attention to a particular topic

Early English *adj.* belonging to or typical of the style of early Gothic architecture used in the late 12th to late 13th century in England, characterized by sharply pointed arches and lancet windows —**Early English** *n.*

early mark *n.* Aus an occasion when permission is given to leave school before the normal time for the end of lessons ◇ **take an early mark** Aus to leave school, work, or a gathering or event early

early modern *adj.* designating, occurring during, or typical of the period in European and world history from 1485 to the late 18th century

early music *n.* MEDIEVAL AND RENAISSANCE MUSIC music written during the Medieval and Renaissance periods, sometimes also including the music of the Baroque and early Classical periods ■ *adj.* PERFORMED IN THE STYLE OF THE TIME typical of a way of performing early music that aims to be as authentic as possible, using period instruments, the contemporary performing style, and a carefully researched score

early retirement *n.* retirement from work before the usual age, often offered, with special inducements, by employers as a way of reducing staff numbers

early riser *n.* sb who gets up early in the morning, especially on a regular basis

early warning *n.* advance notice that sth, especially sth dangerous or threatening, is going to happen

early warning system *n.* a network of radar, satellites, or other sensing devices designed to give advance warning of an enemy attack, especially in time to take countermeasures

earmark /eer maark/ *vt.* (**-marks, -marking, -marked**) **1.** **DESIGNATE STH FOR PARTICULAR PURPOSE** to select and reserve sth to be used for a particular purpose ◇ *That money's already been earmarked for upgrading the computer system.* **2.** AGRIC **PUT AN IDENTIFICATION MARK ON AN ANIMAL'S EAR** to mark the ear of a farm animal with an identifying symbol, notch, or hole ■ *n.* **1.** **IDENTIFYING CHARACTERISTIC** sth enabling recognition of the nature or origins of sth (*often used in the plural*) ◇ *The crime seemed to have all the earmarks of an inside job.* **2.** AGRIC **IDENTIFICATION MARK ON AN ANIMAL'S EAR** an identifying symbol, hole, or notch in the ear of a farm animal [Early 16thC. The earliest meaning is that of marking an animal's ear.]

earmuffs /eer mufs/ *npl.* ear covers attached to an adjustable headband, worn in cold weather

earn /urn/ (**earns, earning, earned**) *v.* **1.** *vti.* **MAKE MONEY BY WORKING** to receive money or payment of some other kind in return for work done ◇ *earn enough to live on* **2.** *vt.* **DESERVE STH** to acquire sth as a reward for, or as a result of, your actions or behaviour ◇ *earn praise* ◇ *the remark earned him a stern rebuke* **3.** *vt.* FIN **PRODUCE INTEREST OR DIVIDENDS** to produce interest or dividends from money invested [Old English *earnian*. From a prehistoric Germanic base meaning 'to harvest', which is also the ancestor of German *Ernte* 'harvest'.]

Earn[1] /urn/ river in Tayside, central Scotland, that flows into the River Tay. Length: 74 km/46 mi.

Earn[2] river in Perth and Kinross, central Scotland, that flows ito the River Tay. Length: 74 km/46 mi.

earned income *n.* income from paid employment as opposed to income from investments

earnest[1] /urnist/ *adj.* **1.** **INTENSELY SERIOUS AND SINCERE** intensely, or even excessively, serious and sincere in manner or attitude **2.** **DONE IN A DEEPLY SINCERE WAY** undertaken or made in a spirit of deep seriousness and sincerity, or with deep feeling **3.** **DESERVING SERIOUS ATTENTION** of a serious nature or worthy of serious attention (*formal*) [Old English *eornost*, from a prehistoric Germanic base of uncertain origin] —**earnestly** *adv.* —**earnestness** *n.* ◇ **in earnest 1.** serious and sincere in your actions, words, or intentions **2.** more intensely, or in a determined and purposeful way

earnest[2] /urnist/ *n.* **1.** **earnest, earnest money** COMM **DOWN PAYMENT** a small advance payment that confirms a contract **2.** **TOKEN OF STH TO COME** a sign, foretaste, or pledge of sth to come (*literary*) [13thC. Origin uncertain: probably an alteration of Old French *erres* 'pledges', from Latin *arra* from, ultimately, Greek *arrabōn* 'pledge', from Hebrew *'ērābhôn*, from *'ārab* 'to pledge'.]

earnings /urningz/ *npl.* money earned, either through paid employment, as profit, or from investments

EAROM /ee rom/ *abbr.* COMPUT electrically alterable read-only memory

earphone /eer fōn/ *n.* a device that converts electric signals into audible sound and is worn on or held close to the ear (*often used in the plural*)

earpiece /eer peess/ *n.* **1.** **THE PART OF A DEVICE HEARD THROUGH** the part of a device such as a telephone, radio, or hearing aid that is held in, or close to, the ear **2.** **PART OF GLASSES FRAME AROUND THE EAR** the part of the frame of a pair of spectacles that fits over and round the ear

ear-piercing *n.* **MAKING HOLE FOR EARRING IN EARLOBE** the making of a hole through the earlobe with a sterilized needle, so that an earring can be attached through the hole ■ *adj.* **VERY LOUD AND SHRILL** extremely or painfully loud and shrill

earplug /eer plug/ *n.* a piece of sth soft such as wax or foam rubber that is placed in the ear to keep out noise, water, or cold (*often used in the plural*)

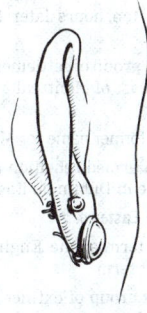
Earring

earring /ˈeer ring/ *n.* ACCESSORIES a piece of jewellery worn on the ear, usually either clipped to the earlobe or attached through a hole pierced in it (*often used in the plural*)

ear shell *n.* = abalone

earshot /ˈeer shot/ *n.* the distance within which sound is audible to sb ○ *within earshot* [Early 17thC. Modelled on words such as *bowshot* 'distance to which an arrow can be shot from a bow'.]

earsplitting /ˈeer spliting/ *adj.* extremely loud or shrill

earth /urth/ *n.* **1.** Earth, earth 3RD PLANET FROM SUN the third planet in order from the Sun with an orbital period of 365.26 days, a diameter of 12,756 km/7,926 mi., and an average distance from the sun of 149,600,000 km/93,000,000 mi. Surrounded by an atmosphere composed primarily of nitrogen and oxygen, it is the only planet in the universe known to support life. **2.** LAND the solid dry land surface of the Earth, as opposed to the sea or sky **3.** SOIL the soft, workable material in which plants grow **4.** HUMAN INHABITANTS OF EARTH all the human inhabitants of the Earth (*formal*) **5.** PURSUITS OF EVERYDAY LIFE the pursuits of everyday human life, especially as opposed to matters of the spirit **6.** ZOOL BURROW the hole or underground lair of a fox, or sometimes a badger **7.** ELEC ENG ELECTRICAL CONNECTION TO GROUND FOR SAFETY an electrical connection that is intended to carry current safely away from a circuit in the event of a fault, or a wire that makes such a connection. US term **ground 8.** ELEC ENG TERMINAL CONNECTED TO THE GROUND the terminal, e.g. in a plug or socket, from which an electrical connection is made to the ground. US term **ground 9.** COLOURS = earth colour **10.** PHILOS, HIST ONE OF THE FOUR ELEMENTS in ancient and medieval philosophy, one of the four elements, earth, air, fire, and water, from which it was believed everything was made ■ *vt.* (earths, earthing, earthed) ELEC ENG CONNECT APPLIANCE SAFELY TO GROUND to equip an electrical circuit or appliance with a connection to the ground so that current is carried away safely in the event of a fault. US term **ground** [Old English *eorpe*, from a prehistoric Germanic word] ◇ **come** *or* **be brought back (down) to earth** to become or be made aware of the usually unglamorous realities of your situation again ◇ **cost** *or* **charge the earth** to cost or charge a great deal of money ◇ **on earth** used to add intensity to a question, often indicating surprise or disbelief on the part of the questioner (*informal*) ○ *What on earth have you done to the computer now?* ◇ **run sb** *or* **sth to earth** to find sb or sth after a long and difficult search

earth up *vt.* to cover part of a plant, especially the lower stem, with soil, in order to protect it against frost or light, or to prevent it from turning green

earthborn /ˈurth bawrn/ *adj.* born on or originating from the Earth, and therefore human, mortal, or earthly (*literary*)

earthbound /ˈurth bownd/ *adj.* **1.** MUNDANE AND UNIMAGINATIVE exclusively concerned with or confined to ordinary everyday or worldly matters and lacking in imagination or spirituality **2.** HEADING TOWARDS EARTH heading or moving towards Earth

earth closet *n.* a toilet in which earth is used to cover the faeces, often consisting of a seat placed over a deep hole in the ground inside a small outdoor building

earth colour *n.* COLOURS any of a number of pigments,

e.g. umber or ochre, that are obtained from the earth

earthed /urtht/ *adj.* connected to the ground by an electrical earth

earthen /ˈurth'n/ *adj.* made of earth or baked clay

earthenware /ˈurth'n wair/ *n.* pottery made of fairly coarse-textured baked clay that is fired at a very low temperature

earthlight /ˈurth līt/ *n.* ASTRON = earthshine

earthling /ˈurthling/ *n.* especially in science fiction, a human being as contrasted with an extraterrestrial or supernatural being

earthly /ˈurthli/ (**-lier, -liest**) *adj.* **1.** CHARACTERISTIC OF THIS WORLD belonging to or characteristic of this world, especially as opposed to the spiritual realm or heaven **2.** POSSIBLE imaginable or possible

earthman /ˈurth man/ (*plural* **-men** /-men/) *n.* especially in science fiction, resident of Earth as referred to by an extraterrestrial

earth mother *n.* **1.** DEVOTEE OF NATURAL WAY OF LIFE a woman who is dedicated to nature and to natural, organic, and environmentally-friendly ways of doing things, often rejecting social conventions (*informal*) **2.** SENSUAL AND MOTHERLY WOMAN a woman who conveys a warm earthy combination of sensuality and motherliness **3.** THE EARTH PERSONIFIED AS MOTHER the Earth personified as a mother **4.** GODDESS SYMBOLIZING EARTH a goddess symbolizing earth and worshipped as a source of life and fertility

earthmover /ˈurth moovər/ *n.* a vehicle such as a bulldozer that is designed to move earth, especially in large quantities —**earthmoving** *adj.*

earthnut /ˈurth nut/ *n.* a plant, e.g. the peanut, that has underground pods

earth pillar *n.* a pillar of soft material capped by a boulder of more resistant rock that protects it from erosion

earthquake /ˈurth kwayk/ *n.* **1.** SHAKING OF THE EARTH'S CRUST a violent shaking of the Earth's crust that may cause destruction to buildings and installations and results from the sudden release of tectonic stress along a fault line or volcanic activity **2.** DISRUPTIVE EVENT an event that causes an upheaval in society, politics, or sb's life

earthrise /ˈurth rīz/ *n.* the rising of the Earth above the Moon's horizon, as seen from space or from the Moon itself

earth science *n.* a science that deals with the Earth's physical properties, structure, or development, e.g. geology

earthshattering /ˈurth shàttering/, **earthshaking** /ˈurth shayking/ *adj.* extremely great or important, or having an extremely powerful effect —**earthshatteringly** *adv.*

earthshine /ˈurth shīn/ *n.* sunlight reflected from the Earth that illuminates the part of the Moon not receiving light directly from the Sun

earth sign *n.* any of the three signs of the zodiac, Taurus, Virgo, or Capricorn, all associated with stability and consistency

earthstar /ˈurth staar/ *n.* a woodland fungus with a round outer surface that splits open in a star-shaped pattern to release spores. Genus: *Geastrum*.

earth station *n.* a system for relaying radio signals between one or more satellites and other communications networks. Earth stations may be on the ground, at sea, or in aircraft.

earth tone *n.* a colour that has an element of deep rich brown in it, e.g. gold or russet

earthward /ˈurthwərd/ *adj.* DIRECTED TOWARDS THE EARTH directed or facing towards the Earth ■ *adv.* **earthwards**, **earthward** TOWARDS THE EARTH in the direction of the Earth or the ground

earthwork /ˈurth wurk/ *n.* **1.** MIL EARTH FORTIFICATION a fortification made of earth **2.** CONSTR EXCAVATION AND EARTH-MOVING WORK construction work involving excavating, earth-moving, and building embankments

earthworm /ˈurth wurm/ *n.* a worm that burrows in the soil and helps to aerate and improve it. Family: Lumbricidae.

earthy /ˈurthi/ (**-ier, -iest**) *adj.* **1.** LIKE SOIL relating to or consisting of soil **2.** NOT SQUEAMISH OR PRETENTIOUS having or showing a hearty, cheerful, no-nonsense acceptance of the realities and facts of life **3.** CRUDE crude and coarse —**earthily** *adv.* —**earthiness** *n.*

ear trumpet *n.* an early type of hearing aid consisting of a trumpet-shaped device that was held to the ear

ear tuft /ˈeer tuft/ *n.* a tuft of feathers above the eyes of some owls and other birds, causing the bird to look larger or blend in with foliage but not used in hearing

earwax /ˈeer waks/ *n.* a yellowish waxy substance secreted by glands in the external ear to protect the delicate lining of the outer ear. Technical name **cerumen**

earwig /ˈeer wig/ *n.* SLENDER INSECT WITH PINCERS a common insect with a slender shiny body, small forewings, antennae, and pincers at the end of its abdomen. Order: Dermaptera. ■ *vi.* EAVESDROP to eavesdrop, or eavesdrop on sth (*dated slang*) [Old English *earwicga*. Literally 'ear-insect', from *eare* 'ear' + *wicga* 'insect'. The insect received its name from the belief that it creeps into people's ears.]

——— **WORD KEY: REGIONAL NOTE** ———
From the proliferation of existing forms, *earwigs* must have been very familiar in all parts of the British Isles, from Monmouth to Ayrshire, from Ireland and the Isle of Man to Sussex. Among the synonyms are *battle-twigs*, *cat-o'-two-tails*, *earlywigs*, *earywigs*, *harry-wiggles*, *skutchy-bells*, and *urrins*. Many of these names, like the insect, are no longer common.

ease /eez/ *n.* **1.** LACK OF DIFFICULTY lack of difficulty in doing or achieving sth ○ *defeated the challenger with ease* **2.** LACK OF AWKWARDNESS lack of awkwardness, stiffness, or self-consciousness in social situations ○ *He felt totally at ease with her.* **3.** COMFORT AND AFFLUENCE a comfortable and leisured state free from problems and restrictions, especially those caused by poverty ○ *a life of ease* **4.** RELAXATION a state of comfort and relaxation **5.** RELIEF FROM WORRY OR PAIN freedom or relief from worry or pain ■ *v.* (**eases, easing, eased**) **1.** *vt.* MAKE STH LESS UNPLEASANT to make sth less unpleasant, difficult, or restrictive **2.** *vt.* RELIEVE THE MIND OR BODY FROM PAIN to relieve sb's mind or body from pain or discomfort **3.** *vi.* ABATE to become less strong or intense ○ *The rain eased.* **4.** *vti.* MANOEUVRE GENTLY to manoeuvre gently and carefully, especially in a tight space, or manoeuvre sth in this way ○ *eased the truck into the space* **5.** *vt.* LOOSEN STH to slacken sth that is tied or fitted tightly **6.** *vt.* MAKE STH EASIER to enable sth to take place more easily [12thC. From Old French *aise* 'comfort', of uncertain origin: perhaps from Latin *adjacens* 'lying near'.]

easeful /ˈeezf'l/ *adj.* giving relief from pain, suffering, or distress (*literary*) —**easefully** *adv.* —**easefulness** *n.*

easel /ˈeez'l/ *n.* a freestanding upright support for a painter's canvas or a school blackboard, usually made of wood and having movable clamps [Late 16thC. Via Dutch *ezel* 'donkey', from, ultimately, Latin *asinus* 'ass' (source of English *ass*).]

easement /ˈeezmənt/ *n.* LAW a limited right to make use of a property owned by another, e.g. a right of way across the property [14thC. Via Old French *aisement* from, ultimately, *aise* 'comfort' (see EASE).]

easily /ˈeezili/ *adv.* **1.** WITHOUT DIFFICULTY in an easy manner and without difficulty or strain ○ *We can easily be there by lunchtime.* **2.** QUICKLY quickly and after comparatively little effort, stress, or provocation ○ *She doesn't give up easily.* **3.** BY FAR without doubt and by a large margin ○ *she's easily the best* **4.** PROBABLY used to show that sth might probably or could almost certainly happen ○ *He could easily have forgotten, so I'd better check.* **5.** AT LEAST certainly not less and probably far more than a particular number or amount ○ *There were easily 200 people at the meeting.* **6.** CALMLY in a relaxed and untroubled way

east /eest/ *n.* **1.** DIRECTION IN WHICH THE SUN RISES the direction that lies directly ahead of sb facing the rising sun or that is located towards the right-hand side of a conventional map of the world **2.** COMPASS POINT OPPOSITE WEST the compass point that lies directly opposite west **3.** east, East AREA IN THE EAST the part of an area, region, or country that is situated in or towards the east **4.** CHR **ALTAR END OF CHURCH** the end of a church where the altar is situated **5. east, East** GAMES **POSITION EQUIVALENT TO EAST** the position equivalent to east in any diagram consisting of four points at 90 degree intervals ■ *adj.* **1.** IN THE EAST situated in, facing, or coming from the east of a place, region, or country **2.** BLOWING FROM THE EAST blowing from the east ■ *adv.* TOWARDS THE EAST in or towards the east [Old English *ēast-*. Ultimately from an Indo-European word meaning 'to shine', which also produced English *aurora*. The underlying idea is of the point at which the sun rises.]

East Africa region in east-central Africa, usually taken to comprise Burundi, Kenya, Rwanda, Somalia, Tanzania, and Uganda —**East African** *n.*, *adj.*

East Anglia /-áng gli ə/ mainly agricultural region in eastern England. It covers most of Norfolk, Suffolk, and Cambridgeshire, and includes the Norfolk Broads and the Fens. —**East Anglian** *n.*, *adj.*

East Asia *n.* the countries of the Far East

East Ayrshire = **Ayrshire, East**

East Bengal former name for **Bangladesh** (1947–55)

East Berlin capital of East Germany from 1949 until 1990, when both Berlin and Germany were reunified —**East Berliner** *n.*

eastbound /éest bownd/ *adj.* going or leading towards the east

Eastbourne /éest bawrn/ seaside resort town and conference centre in East Sussex, England. Population: 88,600 (1995).

east by north *n.* the direction or compass point midway between east and east-northeast —**east by north** *adv.*, *adj.*

east by south *n.* the direction or compass point midway between east and east-southeast —**east by south** *adj.*, *adv.*

East Cape peninsular region in eastern North Island, New Zealand, that forms the easternmost part of the country. Most of the region is used for grazing sheep.

East Coast *n.* the easternmost part of the United States, consisting of the states along its eastern seaboard from Maine to Florida. The East Coast often refers to the oldest, most urban part of this area: New England, New York, New Jersey, Pennsylvania, Maryland, Virginia, and Washington, D.C.

East Dunbartonshire council area in central Scotland, formerly part of the Strathclyde Region. Population: 111,130 (1996). Area: 172 sq. km/66 sq. mi.

East End *n.* a densely populated area in the east of London —**East Ender** *n.*

Easter /éestər/ *n.* **1.** CHRISTIAN FESTIVAL the Christian festival commemorating the resurrection of Jesus Christ **2.** DAY OF THE EASTER FESTIVAL the day on which Easter is celebrated, the Sunday following the full moon on or after 21 March **3.** EASTER WEEKEND the period from Good Friday to Easter Monday [Old English *Ēastre*, from the name of a prehistoric Germanic dawn-goddess whose festival was celebrated at the vernal equinox. Ultimately from an Indo-European base meaning 'to shine' (see EAST).]

Easter bonnet *n.* a woman's hat, often elaborately decorated, traditionally worn for the first time at Easter

Easter Day *n.* = **Easter** *n.* 2

Easter egg *n.* **1.** CHOCOLATE EGG AS EASTER GIFT a chocolate egg, or, more traditionally, a hen's egg painted or dyed, given as a gift to children at Easter **2.** COMPUT HIDDEN ELEMENT OF A COMPUTER PROGRAM a secret message, graphic, animation, or sound effect hidden in a computer program and activated by a specific undocumented sequence of keystrokes. An Easter egg is typically intended as a harmless joke or as a way to display the credits of the program's development team.

Easter Island

Easter Island /éestər-/ island in the South Pacific Ocean belonging to Chile. It is noted for its huge carved stone heads and hieroglyphic tablets. Population: 2,095 (1989). Area: 117 sq. km/45 sq. mi. —**Easter Islander** *n.*

Easter lily *n.* a cultivated lily with large white flowers that bloom in the spring

easterly /éestərli/ *adj.* **1.** IN THE EAST situated in or towards the east **2.** BLOWING FROM THE EAST used to describe a wind that blows from the east ■ *n.* (*plural* **-lies**) WIND FROM THE EAST a wind blowing from the east —**easterly** *adv.*

Easter Monday *n.* the Monday after the Christian festival of Easter

eastern /éestərn/ *adj.* **1.** IN THE EAST situated in the east of a region or country **2.** FACING EAST situated in or facing the east **3.** EAST OF GREENWICH MERIDIAN lying east of the Greenwich meridian **4.** BLOWING FROM THE EAST used to describe a wind that blows from the east **5. eastern, Eastern** TYPICAL OF THE EAST typical of or native to the east of a geographical region

Eastern *adj.* **1.** RELIG OF THE EASTERN ORTHODOX CHURCH relating to the Eastern Orthodox Church **2.** OF THE COUNTRIES OF ASIA relating or belonging to the countries of Asia as viewed from Europe or North America

Eastern Cape /-káyp/ province in southeastern South Africa, created in 1994. Capital: Bisho. Population: 6,481,300 (1995). Area: 170,740 sq. km/65,925 sq. mi.

Eastern Empire *n.* = **Byzantine Empire**

easterner /éestərnər/ *n.* sb who comes from the eastern part of a country or region

Eastern European Time *n.* the standard time in the time zone centred on longitude 30° E, which includes Finland and Greece. It is two hours later than Universal Coordinated Time.

Eastern Ghats /-gáts/ mountain range in southeastern India, running parallel to the Bay of Bengal coast

eastern grey kangaroo *n.* a large silver-grey kangaroo that inhabits the forests and scrub of eastern Australia and Tasmania. Latin name: *Macropus giganteus.*

eastern hemisphere *n.* **1.** EASTERN HALF OF THE EARTH the half of the Earth that lies east of the Greenwich meridian and contains Asia, Australasia, and most of Europe and Africa **2.** COUNTRIES WITHIN EASTERN HEMISPHERE the countries within the eastern hemisphere, especially the countries of Asia

easternmost /éestərn mōst/ *adj.* **1.** FARTHEST TO THE EAST farthest to the east **2.** AT THE MOST EASTERN EXTREME located at the most eastern extreme of a county, state, or country

Eastern Orthodox Church *n.* the self-governing Orthodox Christian churches that originated in the Byzantine Empire and recognize the Patriarch of Constantinople as primate. They now comprise the churches of Eastern Europe, Russia, and Greece.

Eastern Standard Time *n.* **1.** STANDARD TIME IN E NORTH AMERICA the standard time in the time zone centred on longitude 75° W, which includes the eastern part of North America. It is five hours earlier than Universal Coordinated Time. **2.** STANDARD TIME IN E AUSTRALIA the standard time in the time zone centred on longitude 150° E, which includes the eastern part

of Australia. It is ten hours later than Universal Coordinated Time.

Eastern Townships group of settlements in southern Quebec province, east of Montreal and south of the St Lawrence River

Eastern Transvaal former name for **Mpumalanga**

Easter Rising *n.* an armed rebellion against British rule that took place in Dublin on Easter Day in 1916

Easter Sunday *n.* = **Easter** *n.* 2

Easter term *n.* the term at the English High Court that follows Hilary term

East Germanic *n.* a group of extinct languages that were formerly spoken in parts of eastern Europe. It is one of the three groups that form the Germanic branch of Indo-European. Gothic is the only language in this group that has any known written form. —**East Germanic** *adj.*

East Germany common name of a former republic of central Europe, reunited with the rest of Germany in 1990. It was founded under the influence of the Soviet Union in 1949 and recognized as an independent state in 1955. Area: 108,178 sq. km/41,768 sq. mi. —**East German** *n.*, *adj.*

East India Company *n.* a trading company established in England in 1600 to trade with the East Indies, and later with India, which it effectively governed for many years. Similar companies were also founded in the Netherlands and France.

East Indian *n.* Carib INDIAN LIVING IN WEST INDIES sb of Indian descent living in the West Indies ■ *adj.* RELATING TO THE EAST INDIES relating to or typical of the East Indies, or their peoples or cultures

East Indies /-ín deez/ collective name formerly applied to India, Southeast Asia, and the Malay Archipelago, especially Indonesia

easting /éesting/ *n.* **1.** DISTANCE TRAVELLED EAST the net distance eastwards that a vessel travels when making for the east **2.** PART OF A MAP REFERENCE the first part of a map reference that shows how far east a point lies from a reference line running from north to south **3.** NORTH-SOUTH GRID LINE ON MAP a grid line on a map running north to south

East Kilbride /-kil brîd/ manufacturing town in south-central Scotland near Glasgow, designated a New Town in 1947. Population: 81,400 (1991).

East London city in southeastern South Africa, a seaport and holiday resort. Population: 102,325 (1991).

East Lothian /-lôthi ən/ council area in southeastern Scotland, bordering the Firth of Forth and the North Sea. Population: 85,640 (1996). Area: 678 sq. km/262 sq. mi.

east-northeast *n.* COMPASS POINT BETWEEN E AND NE the direction or compass point midway between east and northeast ■ *adj.*, *adv.* IN THE EAST-NORTHEAST in, from, facing, or towards the east-northeast —**east-northeasterly** *adv.*

East Pakistan former name for **Bangladesh** (1955–71)

East Prussia former German province on the Baltic Sea that was divided between Poland and Russia in 1945 —**East Prussian** *n.*, *adj.*

East Renfrewshire council area in central Scotland, formerly part of the Strathclyde Region. Population: 89,417 (1996). Area: 173 sq. km/67 sq. mi.

East Riding of Yorkshire historic division of the county of Yorkshire in northeastern England, most of which was absorbed in 1974 into the now-abolished county of Humberside. Population: 308,400 (1995). ■ council area in northeastern England, established in 1996, covering largely the same area as the historic division

East River strait in southeastern New York State, separating Manhattan Island from Long Island. Length: 24 km/15 mi.

East Sea ♦ **Japan, Sea of**

east-southeast *n.* COMPASS POINT BETWEEN E AND SE the direction or compass point midway between east and southeast ■ *adj.*, *adv.* IN EAST-SOUTHEAST in, from, facing, or towards the east-southeast —**east-south-easterly** *adv.*

East Stewartry Coast /-styóō ərtri-/ designated National Scenic Area in southwestern Scotland

East Sussex county in southeastern England. The county seat is at Lewes. Population: 1,577,500 (1995). Area: 1,795 sq. km/693 sq. mi.

East Timor /-tēe mawr/ disputed territory on the island of Timor in southeast Asia. Its annexation by Indonesia in 1975 has led to continuing internal conflict. Population: 839,700 (1995). Area: 14,926 sq. km/5,763 sq. mi.

eastwards /éestwərdz/ adv. TOWARDS THE EAST in an easterly direction ■ n. POINT IN THE EAST a direction towards or a point in the east [Old English ēastwærde] —**eastward** adj. —**eastwardly** adj., adv.

Eastwood /éestwood/, **Clint** (b. 1930) US film actor and director. He is known for his action films such as *A Fistful of Dollars* (1964) and *Dirty Harry* (1971).

easy /éezi/ adj. (-ier, -iest) 1. NOT DIFFICULT not causing problems or difficulty or requiring much effort, work, or thought ○ *Answer the easy questions first.* ○ *It's easy to see why they chose him.* 2. INAPPROPRIATELY EFFORTLESS requiring less effort, thought, or emotional involvement than is appropriate or right ○ *always taking the easy way out* ○ *easy answers* 3. RELAXED AND INFORMAL relaxed, informal, and without awkwardness or self-consciousness, especially in social situations ○ *has an easy manner* 4. GOOD-NATURED good-natured and tolerant ○ *has an easy disposition* 5. FINANCIALLY PROSPEROUS characterized by financial prosperity and security and the comfort and peace of mind that goes with them 6. NOT HARSH not severe or harsh ○ *She's always claiming that easy discipline makes people soft.* 7. EASY TO TAKE ADVANTAGE OF not difficult to catch, acquire, take advantage of, or exploit ○ *unscrupulous sellers looking for easy targets* 8. LOOSE not tight or close-fitting ○ *jeans that are an easy fit* 9. UNHURRIED comfortable, unhurried, and not too fast ○ *took an easy pace up the trail* 10. NOT STEEP not steep or difficult to climb up or down ○ *It's an easy slope to the top.* 11. PLEASANT TO EXPERIENCE pleasant to experience through one of the senses, especially good to look at or soothing to listen to ○ *easy on the eyes* 12. LACKING PREFERENCES having no strong preferences (informal) ○ *We can do either; I'm easy.* 13. ECON READILY OBTAINABLE readily obtainable, because demand is lower than usual 14. ECON MARKED BY LOW DEMAND AND PRICES characterized by low demand or overproduction and hence low prices 15. PROMISCUOUS sexually promiscuous or too willing to become sexually involved (slang offensive) ■ adv. EASILY without difficulty or the need for hard work ○ *Everything comes easy to her.* ■ adj. (-ier, -iest) NOT ANXIOUS free from unpleasant feelings such as anxiety, guilt, or worry ○ *Rest easy; we'll be there soon.* ■ adv. WITHOUT PUNISHMENT without punishment or suffering ○ *Considering what they did, they got off easy.* ■ interj. USED TO CALM SB OR STH used to try to make a person or animal calm down or slow down (informal) [12thC. From Old French aisié, the past participle of aisier 'to put at ease', from aise 'comfort' (see EASE).] ◇ **easy on sth** an instruction or recommendation to sb not to use too much of sth (informal) ○ *Hey, easy on the whipped cream!* ◇ **go easy on sb** to treat or deal with sb gently, leniently, or without harsh criticism or reproaches (informal) ◇ **go easy on sth** to avoid using, eating, or drinking too much of sth (informal) ◇ **take it easy 1.** to relax, avoid effort, or not work too hard **2.** to calm down and avoid becoming upset or angry

──── **WORD KEY: SYNONYMS** ────

easy, *simple*, *straightforward*, *uncomplicated*
CORE MEANING: not difficult to do or achieve
easy a general word indicating the lack of effort required to do, achieve or understand sth; **simple** emphasizing sth that is not at all complicated and so can be done or understood quickly or with very little effort; **straightforward** used especially to suggest that a process or action is easy to carry out; **uncomplicated** used to suggest that sth is not especially difficult, but usually suggesting a greater degree of effort or thought than *easy* or *simple*.

easybeat /éezi beet/ n. Aus sb who is easily beaten in sport or any competitive endeavour

easy-care adj. easy to look after and keep clean, with simple washing instructions and needing minimal ironing

easy chair n. a comfortably upholstered chair, especially an armchair

easy game n. = easy meat (informal)

easygoing /éezi gṓ ing/ adj. **1.** RELAXED, INFORMAL, AND TOLERANT relaxed, informal, and tolerant in attitude and reluctant to make heavy demands or enforce strict discipline on people **2.** UNHURRIED unhurried and comfortable

easy listening n. popular music in an undemanding style, usually with a lyrical or romantic tune, gentle rhythms, and soft soothing orchestration

easy meat n. sb who or sth that is an easy prey for sb who has designs on him, her, or it (informal)

easy money n. **1.** MONEY MADE WITH LITTLE EFFORT money made with little effort, and often dishonestly **2.** MONEY BORROWED AT LOW INTEREST money that can be borrowed at a low rate of interest

easy-peasy /-péezi/ (easy-peasier, easy-peasiest) adj. extremely easy (informal) [A reduplicated form of EASY]

easy terms npl. payment by instalments

easy virtue n. lax sexual morals and promiscuous sexual habits (literary)

eat /eet/ (eats, eating, ate /et, ayt/, eaten /éet'n/) v. **1.** vti. CONSUME AS SUSTENANCE to take sth into the mouth as food and swallow it ○ *They hadn't eaten for three days.* **2.** vt. CONSUME USUALLY to include sth as a usual or fundamental part of a diet ○ *Do dogs eat fish?* **3.** vi. DINE to have a meal ○ *Are you ready to eat?* **4.** vt. BOTHER to bother or annoy sb (slang) ○ *What's eating her?* **5.** vt. USE A LOT OF STH to use or consume sth in large quantities (slang) ○ *a car that eats petrol* **6.** vti. PENETRATE to penetrate the surface of sth by corrosive or mechanical action ○ *Rust had eaten into the chrome.* **7.** vt. OFFENSIVE TERM to perform fellatio or cunnilingus on sb (taboo slang) [Old English etan. Ultimately from an Indo-European base that also produced English *edible*, *etch*, and *tooth*.]

eat away vt. to consume or destroy sth gradually ○ *eaten away in parts by acid rain*

eat away at vt. **1.** WORRY to worry or be a continual source of distress to sb ○ *Guilt had been eating away at him all day.* **2.** CONSUME GRADUALLY to deplete or use up sth gradually by taking small amounts regularly ○ *medical expenses eating away at our income*

eat in vi. to consume a meal at home ○ *Would you rather eat in or go to a restaurant?*

eat into vt. to use up part of sth, especially in a wasteful or nonproductive way

eat out vi. to consume a meal away from home, usually in a restaurant or similar establishment ○ *Let's eat out tonight.*

eat up v. **1.** vti. EAT COMPLETELY to consume food completely or with great appetite **2.** vt. OBSESS SB to absorb or obsess sb (usually passive) ○ *eaten up by envy* **3.** vt. RECEIVE ENTHUSIASTICALLY to receive sth with enthusiasm or pleasure (informal) ○ *The reading public eats up everything she writes.* **4.** vt. CONSUME QUICKLY to consume or deal with sth quickly (informal)

eatable /éetəb'l/ adj. FIT TO BE EATEN fit, suitable, or pleasant to eat ■ n. FOOD ITEM sth that is fit or suitable for eating (informal; usually used in the plural) ○ *buy some bread and other eatables*

──── **WORD KEY: USAGE** ────

eatable or **edible**? *Eatable* is used to refer to food that can be eaten with enjoyment, whereas *edible* refers to any substance in respect of its suitability as food. If sth is *eatable* it is also *edible*, but a substance can be *edible* without being *eatable* (for example, raw potatoes). Informally, however, *edible* is often used to mean *eatable* (though not usually the other way round): *The vegetables were overcooked but just about edible.* The same distinction applies to the negative forms of these words: *The meal was uneatable. Toadstools are inedible.*

eaten past participle of **eat**

eater /éetər/ n. a person who or animal that eats a particular food or eats in a particular way (often used in combination)

eatery /éetəri/ (plural -ies) n. a restaurant or other establishment where food is cooked and sold (informal)

eating /éeting/ n. FOOD food, especially of a particular quality ○ *These apples are good eating.* ■ adj. **1.**

SUITABLE FOR EATING suitable for human consumption, especially uncooked **2.** INVOLVING FOOD relating to or used for the consumption of food

eating disorder n. MED any emotional disorder, e.g. bulimia, that manifests itself in an irrational craving for or avoidance of food

eats /eets/ npl. food (slang) ○ *What do you do for eats around here?* [Late 19thC. Formed from the verb *eat*.]

EAU abbr. (East Africa) Uganda (international vehicle registration)

Eau Claire city in western Wisconsin, at the confluence of the Chippewa and Eau Claire rivers. Population: 56,856 (1990).

eau de cologne /ṓ də kə lṓn/ n. = cologne [Early 19thC. From French, literally 'water of Cologne'.]

eau de nil /ṓ də nέel/ adj. of a pale yellowish-green colour [Late 19thC. From French, literally 'water of the Nile'. The pale greenish colour supposedly resembles the colour of the Nile.] —**eau de nil** n.

eau de toilette /ṓ də twaa lét/ n. = toilet water [From French, literally 'toilet water']

eau de vie /ṓ də vée/ n. a strong alcoholic spirit, especially brandy [Mid-18thC. From French, literally 'water of life'.]

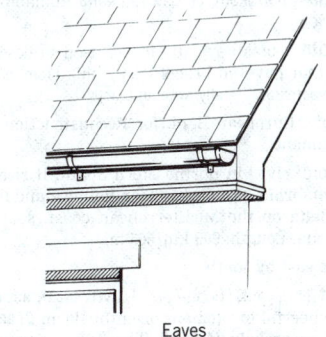

Eaves

eaves /eevz/ npl. the part of a roof that projects beyond the wall that supports it [Old English efes. Probably formed from the same prehistoric Germanic base as English over.]

eavesdrop /éevz drop/ (-drops, -dropping, -dropped) vi. to listen to a conversation without the speakers being aware of it [Early 17thC. Probably a back-formation from EAVESDROPPER.]

eavesdropper /éevz dropər/ n. sb who secretly listens to or overhears a conversation between others [15thC. From obsolete *eavesdrop* 'ground on which rainwater thrown off by eaves falls'; from the idea of sb standing in this area trying to hear private conversations.]

Eban /ée ban/, **Abba** (b. 1915) South African-born Israeli statesman. He worked for the United Nations in Palestine (1946) and later held diplomatic and ministerial posts in Israel. These include being Israel's ambassador to the UN (1948–59) and to the United States (1950–59), and deputy prime minister (1963–66). Born **Aubrey Solomon**

ebb /eb/ vi. (ebbs, ebbing, ebbed) **1.** RECEDE FROM THE SHORE to recede from the land, as the tide falls (refers to the sea or tidal water) **2.** DIMINISH to diminish or lessen in intensity ○ *the pain gradually ebbed away* ■ n. **1.** TIDAL MOVEMENT AWAY FROM LAND the movement of a receding tide away from the land **2.** DIMINUTION diminution or lessening ○ *the ebb and flow of the company's fortunes* [Old English ebbian. Formed from the prehistoric Germanic ancestor of English *off*; the underlying meaning is 'going away, departure'.] ◇ **at a low ebb** lacking hope and energy, or in a depleted condition

ebb tide n. a receding tide, or the time when this happens

Ebbw Vale /ébbōō-/ industrial town in Blaenau Gwent, southeastern Wales. Population: 24,100 (1996).

EBCDIC /éb see dik/ n. a binary computer character code, used to represent 256 standard letters, numbers, symbols, and control characters by means of eight binary digits. Full form **Extended Binary Coded Decimal Interchange Code**

EbN *abbr.* east by north

E-boat *n.* a fast torpedo boat used by the German navy in World War II [*E* a shortening of ENEMY]

Ebola /i bṓlə/, **Ebola virus** *n.* a contagious virus transmitted by blood and body fluids that causes the linings of bodily organs and vessels to leak blood and fluids, usually resulting in death [Late 20thC. Named after the River *Ebola* in Zaire, in the area of which the virus was first identified following an outbreak in 1976.]

ebon /ébbən/ *n.*, *adj.* ebony (*literary*) [14thC. Via Old French *eban* from, ultimately, Greek *ebenos*, of Semitic origin.]

ebonise *vt.* = ebonize

ebonite /ébbənīt/ *n.* MANUF = vulcanite

ebonize /ébbə nīz/ (-izes, -izing, -ized), **ebonise** (-ises, -ising, -ised) *vt.* to stain sth black so as to resemble ebony

ebony /ébbəni/ *n.* (*plural* -ies) **1.** ASIAN TREE a tree of tropical Asia that yields a hard wood. Genus: *Diospyros* **2.** DARK HARD WOOD the blackish hard wood of an ebony tree **3.** BROWNISH-BLACK COLOUR black with a tinge of olive or brown ■ *adj.* BROWNISH-BLACK of a black colour tinged with olive or brown [15thC. Formed from EBON, perhaps on the model of IVORY.]

Eboracum /i bórrəkəm, eë baw raá kəm/ Roman name for York

ebracteate /i brákti ayt, -ti ət/ *adj.* used to describe plants that have no bracts [Mid-19thC. From modern Latin *ebracteatus*, literally 'without bracts'.]

EBRD *abbr.* European Bank for Reconstruction and Development

Ebro /eëbrō/ river in northeastern Spain. It rises in the Cantabrian Mountains near Reinosa and flows to its delta on the Mediterranean coast, south of Tarragona. Length: 909 km/565 mi.

EbS *abbr.* east by south

ebullient /i búl yənt, i boōll-/ *adj.* **1.** LIVELY AND ENTHUSIASTIC full of cheerful excitement or enthusiasm **2.** BOILING boiling vigorously (*formal*) [Late 16thC. From Latin *ebullient-*, the present participle stem of *ebullire*, literally 'to bubble out', from *bullire* 'to bubble' (source of English *boil*).] —**ebullience** *n.*

ebullition /ébbə lísh'n/ *n.* **1.** BOILING a state of bubbling up or boiling (*formal*) **2.** OUTBURST a sudden outbreak of violent emotion (*literary*) [14thC. Via French from, ultimately, Latin *ebullire* (see EBULLIENT).]

eburnation /eëbər náysh'n, ébbər-/ *n.* an abnormal hardening of the surfaces of bones in a joint that have lost their cartilage covering, as occurs in such conditions as osteoarthritis [Mid-19thC. Formed from Latin *eburnus* 'made of ivory'.]

EBV *abbr.* Epstein-Barr virus

EB virus *n.* = Epstein-Barr virus

EC *abbr.* **1.** HIST European Community **2.** European Commission

écarté[1] /ay kaár tay/ *n.* a card game for two people played with 32 cards in which cards may be discarded in exchange for others [Early 19thC. From French, literally 'discarded'.]

écarté[2] /ay kaár tay/ *n.* a ballet position in which the arm and leg on one side of the body are extended [Early 20thC. From French, literally 'spread out'.]

ecce homo /ékay hṓmō, éksi-/ *n.* a portrayal of Jesus Christ crowned with thorns [From Latin, literally 'behold the man' (John 19: 5), the words spoken by Pontius Pilate to Jesus Christ's accusers after Jesus Christ had been crowned with thorns]

eccentric /ik séntrik, ek-/ *adj.* **1.** UNCONVENTIONAL unconventional, especially in a whimsical way ○ *an eccentric mode of dress* **2.** TECH AWAY FROM THE CENTRE away from the centre or axis **3.** GEOM HAVING DIFFERENT CENTRES used to describe circles with different centres **4.** ASTRON ELLIPTICAL used to describe an orbit that is elliptical rather than circular ■ *n.* **1.** UNCONVENTIONAL PERSON sb who is unconventional, especially in a whimsical way **2.** MECH ENG MECHANICAL DEVICE a mechanical device with an off-centre axis of revolution that converts the rotary motion of one component of a mechanism to reciprocating motion in another [Mid-16thC. Via late Latin *eccentricus* from

Greek *ekkentros*, literally 'out of centre', from *kentron* (see CENTRE).] —**eccentrically** *adv.*

eccentricity /ék sen tríssəti/ (*plural* -ties) *n.* **1.** ECCENTRIC QUALITY unconventionality, especially of a whimsical sort **2.** ECCENTRIC ACT an example or instance of unconventional, whimsical behaviour **3.** MECH ENG DISTANCE BETWEEN A MAIN AND SECONDARY AXIS the distance between the axis about which an object rotates and a secondary axis on the object at which a device such as a rod could be attached **4.** ASTRON DEVIATION the deviation of the path of an orbiting body from a true circle **5.** GEOM GEOMETRIC CONSTANT a constant that describes the shape of a conic section. It is equal to the ratio of the distance from a fixed point of any point on the curve to the distance of that point from the corresponding fixed straight line.

ecchymosis /éki mṓssiss/ (*plural* -moses /-seez/) *n.* bleeding into surrounding tissue caused by bruising (*technical*) [Mid-16thC. Via modern Latin from, ultimately, Greek *ekkhumonothai*, literally 'to pour out'.]

eccl., **eccles.** *abbr.* **1.** ecclesiastic **2.** ecclesiastical

Eccl., **Eccles.** *abbr.* BIBLE Ecclesiastes

Eccles /ék'lz/, **Sir John** (1903–97) Australian physiologist. He was joint winner of the 1963 Nobel Prize in physiology or medicine for his studies of the transmission of impulses between nerve cells. Full name **Sir John Carew Eccles**

Eccles cake *n.* a cake made from flaky pastry and filled with dried fruit [From Eccles, a town in northwestern England]

ecclesia /i kleézi ə/ (*plural* -ae /-zi ee/) *n.* **1.** CHR CONGREGATION OR CHURCH a church or congregation (*formal*) **2.** HIST ANCIENT GREEK ASSEMBLY in ancient Greece, an assembly of the citizens of a state [Late 16thC. Via Latin from Greek *ekklēsia* 'assembly', from *ekkalein* 'to call to come out, summon', from *kalein* 'to call'.]

Ecclesiastes /i kleézi ás teez/ *n.* a book in the Bible that discusses the futility of life and how to be a God-fearing person

ecclesiastic /-ástik/ *n.* a member of the clergy

ecclesiastical /i kleézi ástik'l/ *adj.* belonging to, involving, or typical of the Christian church or clergy —**ecclesiastically** *adv.*

ecclesiasticism /i kleézi ástisizəm/ *n.* **1.** ALL-ABSORBING REGARD FOR THE CHURCH all-absorbing regard for the principles and customary practices of the Christian Church **2.** CHURCH PRINCIPLES the principles or body of thought constituting organized Christianity

Ecclesiasticus /i kleézi ástikəss/ *n.* a book of teachings in the Jerusalem Version of the Bible

ecclesiology /i kleézi ólləji/ *n.* **1.** STUDY OF THE CHRISTIAN CHURCH the study of the history and theology of the Christian Church **2.** STUDY OF CHURCH ARCHITECTURE the study of the architecture and decoration of Christian churches

eccoccino /ékō cheénō/ (*plural* -nos) *n.* Aus in Australia, a drink similar to cappuccino made with a barley- and chicory-based powder (**Ecco**), instead of coffee

eccremocarpus /ékrəmə kaárpəss/ *n.* a climbing evergreen plant native to Chile and Peru that is widely cultivated for its decorative leaves and brightly-coloured tubular flowers. Genus: *Eccremocarpus*. [From modern Latin, genus name, formed from Greek *ekkremēs* 'suspended' + *karpos* 'fruit']

eccrine /ékrīn, ékrin/ *adj.* used to describe sweat glands that are distributed all over the body, especially on the hands and feet, that do not secrete organic matter, and that are important in regulating body temperature [Mid-20thC. From German *Ekkrin*, from Greek *ekkrinein* 'to secrete'.]

ecdysiast /ek dízzi ast/ *n.* a performer of striptease (*humorous*) [Mid-20thC. Coined by H. L. Mencken from ECDYSIS, on the model of *gymnast*.]

ecdysis /ékdississ, ek dī-/ *n.* ZOOL the regular moulting of an outer layer by arthropods, e.g. insects and crustaceans, and by reptiles [Mid-19thC. From Greek *ekdusis*, from *ekduein* 'to put off, shed'.]

ecdysone /ékdi sōn/ *n.* a hormone that promotes metamorphosis and ecdysis in insects and crustaceans

ecesis /i seéssiss/ *n.* the successful establishment of a plant or animal species in a new environment [Early 20thC. From Greek *oikēsis* 'an inhabiting', from *oikos* 'house'.]

Ecevit /échəvit/, **Bülent** (b. 1925) Turkish statesman. He was prime minister of Turkey in 1974 and again from 1978 to 1979.

ECG *abbr.* **1.** electrocardiogram **2.** electrocardiograph **3.** echocardiograph

ECGD *abbr.* Export Credits Guarantee Department

Echegaray y Eizaguirre /éch ay ga rí ee ay tha gírray/, **José** (1832–1916) Spanish playwright and politician. His poetic dramas won him a shared Nobel Prize in 1904, and he also held ministerial office (1868–74 and 1905).

echelon /éshə lon/ *n.* **1.** LEVEL IN A HIERARCHY a level of authority or rank in an organization or system ○ *the lower echelons of society* **2.** MIL FORMATION WITH OFFSET POSITIONS a formation in which individuals or units are positioned behind and to one side of those in front to give a stepped effect and allow each a clear view ahead **3.** AIR FORCE AIRCRAFT FORMATION WITH OFFSET POSITIONS a group of aircraft flying in positions behind and to one side of the aircraft in front **4.** PHYS DEVICE FOR STUDYING SPECTRA a series of glass plates of equal thickness arranged like steps, used in spectroscopy for studying the fine structure of spectral lines ■ *vti.* (-lons, -loning, -loned) FORM AN ECHELON to arrange sth in or form an echelon [Late 18thC. From French, 'rung', formed from *échelle* 'ladder', from Latin *scala* 'stair'.]

echeveria /échə veéri ə/ *n.* a usually stemless plant that is native to tropical America and cultivated for its rosettes of fleshy leaves and its tubular or bell-shaped flowers. Genus: *Echeveria*. [Mid-19thC. From modern Latin, genus name, named after Atanasio Echeverría, a Mexican botanical illustrator.]

echidna /i kídnə/ *n.* a spiny insect-eating mammal of Australia, Tasmania, and New Guinea, with a long snout and strong claws. Echidnas lay their eggs in burrows. Family: Tachyglossidae. [Mid-19thC. Via modern Latin, 'viper', from Greek, from *ekhis* 'viper'.]

echin- *prefix.* = echino- (*used before vowels*)

echinacea /éki náyssi ə/ *n.* **1.** BOT = coneflower **2.** HERBAL REMEDY a herbal remedy prepared from the pulverized leaves and stems of purple coneflowers, thought to bolster the immune system [Via modern Latin, genus name, from, ultimately, Greek *ekhinos* 'hedgehog, sea urchin']

echinate /éki nayt/, **echinated** /-naytid/ *adj.* used to describe plant and animal parts that have spines or similar outgrowths [Late 17thC. From Latin *echinatus*, from Greek *ekhinos* 'hedgehog, sea urchin'.]

echini plural of echinus

echino- *prefix.* **1.** spine ○ echinoderm **2.** echinoderm ○ echinoid [From Latin *echinus* 'sea urchin' (see ECHINUS)]

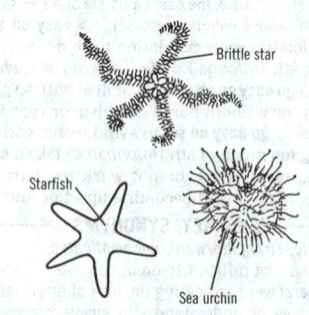

Echinoderm

echinoderm /i kínə durm/ *n.* a marine invertebrate animal that has a radially symmetrical body, tube feet, and a system of calcareous plates under the skin. Starfish, sea urchins, sea lilies, and sea cucumbers are echinoderms. Phylum: Echinodermata. [Mid-19thC. Coined from ECHINO- + Greek *derma* 'skin'.] —**echinodermal** /i kínə dúrm'l/ *adj.* —**echinodermatous** /-mətəss/ *adj.*

echinoid /i kí noyd, éka-/ *n.* a marine invertebrate animal with a hard ovoid body and movable spines.

Sea urchins and sand dollars are echinoids. Class: Echinoidea. —**echinoid** *adj.*

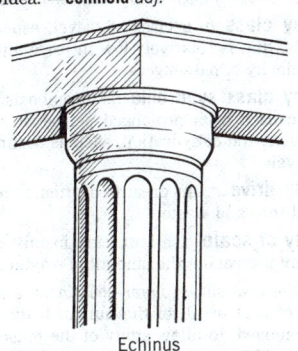

Echinus

echinus /i kínəss/ (*plural* **-ni** /-nī/) *n.* **1.** ARCHIT **ROUNDED MOULDING** a rounded moulding beneath the flat upper part (**abacus**) of a Doric or Tuscan column **2.** MARINE BIOL = **sea urchin** [14thC. Via Latin from Greek *ekhinos* 'hedgehog, sea urchin'.]

echium /éki əm/ *n.* a plant of the borage family, native to Europe, western Asia, and Africa, that has oblong or lance-shaped leaves and spikes of funnel-shaped flowers. Genus: *Echium.* [Late 19thC. From modern Latin, genus name, formed from Greek *ekhis* 'viper'; from the spotted markings on the plant's stem.]

echo /ékō/ *n.* (*plural* **-oes**) **1.** REPEATED SOUND the repetition of a sound caused by the reflection of sound waves from a surface **2.** SYMPATHETIC REACTION a reaction of agreement or sympathy ○ *Her songs found an echo in the hearts of thousands.* **3.** STH REPEATED sth repeated or imitated rather than original ○ *echoes of the boss's ideas* **4.** REMINDER sth that looks back to an earlier period or is reminiscent of it ○ *the current style with its echoes of the 1920s* **5.** EFFECT a lingering effect of an earlier event **6.** IMITATOR sb who imitates another, especially in slavish repetition of his or her opinions (*old*) **7.** PHYS RETURNED SIGNAL the signal reflected by an object struck by a radar transmission, or the image of this on a radar screen **8.** LITERAT REPETITION OF SOUNDS the repetition of sounds within a sequence of verse or prose **9.** MUSIC REPEATED MUSIC the repetition, usually quieter, of a phrase or note in music **10.** MUSIC ELECTRONIC SOUND REPETITION the repetition of sound created electronically for effect or by accident ○ *The echo on the guitar riff was added in the studio.* **11.** MUSIC ORGAN CONTROL a device on some organs that gives the effect of an echo coming from a distance ■ *v.* (**-oes, -oing, -oed**) **1.** *vt.* MAKE STH REPEAT to make a sound repeat by the reflection of sound waves ○ *The surrounding peaks echoed the eagle's cry.* **2.** *vt.* REPEAT to repeat a statement or opinion, especially in agreement or imitation ○ *The completed report echoed the initial assessment.* **3.** *vt.* IMITATE to imitate or incorporate elements of sth earlier ○ *The building's design echoes the surrounding Georgian terraces.* **4.** *vi.* RESOUND to resound by the reflection of sound waves ○ *Their footsteps echoed down the tunnel.* **5.** *vi.* BE FULL OF SOUND to be full of echoes of a sound ○ *The auditorium echoed with cheering.* **6.** *vt.* COMPUT DISPLAY AS A CHECK to return a character back to its source after a computer or communications device receives it, as an accuracy check. A common example is when a character is displayed on a computer monitor after it has been entered from a keyboard. [14thC. Via Old French or Latin from Greek *ēkhō* 'echo', also the mythological Echo, who faded away for love of Narcissus until only her voice remained.]

Echo /ékō/ *n.* the NATO phonetic alphabet code word for the letter 'E', used in international radio communications

echocardiogram /ékō kaàrdi ə gram/ *n.* the visual record produced by an echocardiograph

echocardiograph /ékō kaàrdi ə graaf, -graf/ *n.* an ultrasound device used to examine the working heart and display moving images of its action —**echocardiographic** /ékō kaàrdi ə gráffik/ *adj.* —**echocardiographically** *adv.* —**echocardiography** /ékō kaàrdi óggrəfi/ *n.*

echo chamber *n.* a room with sound-reflecting walls, used in making acoustic measurements or generating sound effects

echoencephalogram /ékō en séffələ gram/ *n.* the visual record produced by an echoencephalograph

echoencephalograph /ékō en séffələ graaf, -graf/ *n.* an ultrasound device used to examine the structures of the brain —**echoencephalographic** /ékō en séffələ gráffik/ *adj.* —**echoencephalographically** *adv.* —**echoencephalography** /ékō en séffə lóggrəfi/ *n.*

echography /e kóggrəfi/ *n.* PHYS = **ultrasonography**

echoic /e kố ik/ *adj.* **1.** OF OR LIKE AN ECHO resembling or relating to an echo **2.** POETRY = **onomatopoeic**

echoic memory *n.* the ability to remember and reproduce a sound in the two or three seconds after it is heard

echoism /ékō izəm/ *n.* **1.** POETRY = **onomatopoeia 2.** LING CHANGE OF VOWEL SOUND a process by which the sound of a vowel changes to imitate the sound of a preceding vowel

echolalia /ékō láyli ə/ *n.* the compulsive repetition of words spoken by sb else, often a sign of psychiatric disorder

echolocation /ékō lō káysh'n/ *n.* a means of locating an object using an emitted sound and the reflection back from it, used naturally by animals such as bats and electronically by humans

echo plate *n.* an electromechanical device used in broadcasting or recording to create the effect of reverberation or echo

echopraxia /ékō práksi ə/, **echopraxis** /-siss/ *n.* the compulsive imitation of the actions of others, often a sign of psychiatric disorder [Early 20thC. From modern Latin, formed from Greek *ēkhō* 'echo' + *praxis* 'action'.]

echo quilting *n.* a quilting stitch that follows the outlines of an appliquéd design

echo sounder *n.* a device used to ascertain water depth or to locate underwater objects by measuring the time taken for emitted sound waves to return from the bottom or from the object

echovirus /ékō vīrəss/ *n.* a virus found in the gastrointestinal tract that belongs to a group of retroviruses associated with intestinal and respiratory infections and meningitis [Mid-20thC. *Echos* an acronym formed from *entericcytopathogenichuman orphan.*]

Echuca /e choŏkə/ town in northern Victoria, Australia, located on the Murray River. Population: 12,483 (1996).

Eckhart /ék haart/, **Meister** (1260?–1328?) German philosopher and Christian theologian. His writings set him among the founders of German philosophical mysticism. He was influenced both by the teachings of Thomas Aquinas and by the doctrines of Neoplatonism. Real name **Johannes Eckhart**

éclair /ay kláir, i-/ *n.* **1.** FINGER-SHAPED CREAM CAKE a long thin cylinder of choux pastry usually filled with whipped cream and topped with chocolate icing **2.** HARD SWEET WITH SOFT FILLING a type of sweet consisting of a hard shell with a soft filling, usually toffee with chocolate inside [Mid-19thC. From French, literally 'lightning'.]

éclaircissement /ay kláir seess maáN/ *n.* a clearing up of sth puzzling (*literary*) [Mid-17thC. From French, literally 'clearing up'.]

eclampsia /i klámpsi ə/ *n.* an illness that sometimes occurs during the later stages of pregnancy and involves high blood pressure and convulsions sometimes followed by a coma [Mid-19thC. Via modern Latin from French *éclampsie*, from Greek *eklampsis* 'sudden development', from *eklampein* 'to shine out'.] —**eclamptic** /i klámptik/ *adj.*

éclat /ay klaá, áy klaa/ *n.* **1.** SUCCESS brilliant success ○ *The show came off with éclat.* **2.** DISPLAY ostentatious display **3.** RENOWN renown based on achievement [Late 17thC. From French, literally 'splinter, fragment'.]

eclectic /i kléktik/ *adj.* **1.** CHOOSING FROM VARIOUS SOURCES choosing what is best or preferred from a variety of sources or styles ○ *an eclectic taste in music* **2.** VARIED made up of elements from various sources

○ *an eclectic collection of paintings* ■ *n.* ECLECTIC PERSON sb who selects what is best or preferred from a variety of sources or styles [Late 17thC. From Greek *eklektikos*, literally 'picking out, selecting', from *eklegein* 'to pick out', from *legein* 'to choose'.] —**eclectically** *adv.*

eclecticism /i klékti sizəm/ *n.* the theory or use of an eclectic approach

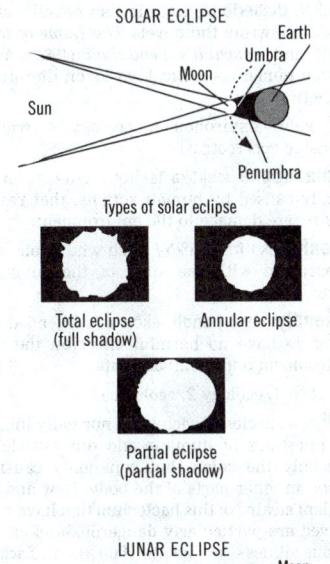

SOLAR ECLIPSE

Sun   Earth   Umbra   Moon   Penumbra

Types of solar eclipse

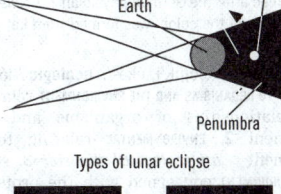

Total eclipse (full shadow)   Annular eclipse

Partial eclipse (partial shadow)

LUNAR ECLIPSE

Moon   Earth   Umbra   Penumbra

Types of lunar eclipse

Total eclipse (full shadow)   Partial eclipse (partial shadow)

Eclipse: Solar and lunar eclipses

eclipse /i klíps/ *n.* **1.** ASTRON OBSCURING OF A CELESTIAL BODY the partial or complete hiding from view of a celestial body, e.g. the Sun or Moon, when another celestial body comes between it and the observer **2.** LOSS OF LIGHT a loss or blocking of light **3.** DECLINE a loss of status, power, or favour ○ *the eclipse of the aristocracy* ■ *vt.* (**eclipses, eclipsing, eclipsed**) **1.** ASTRON OBSCURE CELESTIAL BODY to cause a total or partial obscuring of another celestial body **2.** SHADOW to block the light falling on sth, or cast a shadow on it **3.** OUTDO to outdo in achievement or become more powerful or popular than sth or sb ○ *a performance that eclipsed all the others* [13thC. Via Old French and Latin from Greek *ekleipsis*, from *ekleipein* 'no longer to appear or be present', from *leipein* 'to leave'.] —**eclipser** *n.*

eclipse plumage *n.* dull plumage grown for a short period by some birds, especially male ducks, after the brightly coloured breeding plumage has been shed

eclipsing binary, **eclipsing variable** *n.* a system in which one star's orbit periodically brings it between Earth and the other star of the pair

ecliptic /i klíptik/ *n.* PATH OF THE SUN'S ANNUAL MOTION the apparent path of the Sun's annual motion relative to the stars, shown as a circle passing through the centre of the imaginary sphere (**celestial sphere**) containing all the celestial bodies ■ *adj.* OF AN ECLIPSE relating to, involving, or typical of an eclipse [14thC. Via Latin from, ultimately, Greek *ekleipein* (see ECLIPSE); from the fact that eclipses of the Sun or Moon can occur only when the Moon crosses the ecliptic.]

eclogue /ék log/ *n.* a pastoral poem, usually in the form of a dialogue between shepherds [15thC. Via

Latin *ecloga* from Greek *eklogē* 'selection (of poems)', from *eklegein* (see ECLECTIC).]

eclosion /i klṓzh'n/ *n.* the emergence of an insect from its pupal case, or the hatching of a larva from an egg [Late 19thC. From French *éclosion*, from *éclore* 'to hatch, open', from, ultimately, Latin *excludere* 'to hatch' (source of English *exclude*).]

Eco /ékō/, **Umberto** (*b.* 1932) Italian novelist and academic. He wrote the novels *The Name of the Rose* (1981) and *Foucault's Pendulum* (1989), and has written numerous critical works on literature and aesthetics.

eco- *prefix.* environment, ecology ○ *ecofriendly* [Shortened from ECOLOGY]

ecocatastrophe /éekōkə tástrəfi, ékō-/ *n.* an event, usually caused by human actions, that results in very severe damage to the environment

ecofreak /éekō freek, ékō-/ *n.* sb who is obsessed or preoccupied with the state of the environment (*slang insult*)

ecofriendly /éekō frendli, ékō-/ *adj.* intended or perceived to have no harmful effect on the natural environment and its inhabitants

ecol. *abbr.* **1.** ecology **2.** ecological

E. coli *n.* a species of bacterium normally inhabiting the intestines of humans and other vertebrates, especially the colon, but commonly causing infection in other parts of the body. New and highly virulent strains of this bacterium that have recently evolved are particularly dangerous and can cause serious illness or death. Full form **Escherichia coli** [Late 20thC. Shortening of modern Latin *Escherichia coli*, named after the German physician T. *Escherich* (1857–1911). *Coli* 'of the colon' was formed from Latin *colon* (see COLON).]

ecological /éekə lójjik'l, ékə-/, **ecologic** /-lójjik/ *adj.* **1.** RELATING TO ORGANISMS AND THE ENVIRONMENT relating to the interrelationships of organisms and their environment **2.** ENVIRONMENTAL relating to the environment ○ *an ecological disaster* **3.** PROTECTIVE OF THE ENVIRONMENT concerned with the protection and preservation of the natural environment ○ *an ecological product* —**ecologically** *adv.*

ecology /i kólləji/ (*plural* **-gies**) *n.* **1.** STUDY OF ORGANISMS AND THE ENVIRONMENT the study of the relationships and interactions between living organisms and their natural or developed environment ○ *'A land ethic ... should be as honest as Thoreau's Walden, and as comprehensive as the sensitive science of ecology.'* (Stewart Udall, *The Quiet Crisis*; 1963) **2.** RELATIONSHIP BETWEEN AN ORGANISM AND THE ENVIRONMENT the relationships between individual organisms and between organisms and their environment **3.** = **human ecology** [Late 19thC. Coined from Greek *oikos* 'house, habitation' + -LOGY.] —**ecologist** *n.*

econ. *abbr.* **1.** economy **2.** economics **3.** economist

econometrics /i kónnə méttriks/ *n.* the application of mathematical and statistical techniques to economic data and problems (*takes a singular verb*) —**econometric** *adj.* —**econometrically** *adv.* —**econometrician** /i kónnə mə trísh'n/ *n.*

economic /ékə nómmik, éekə-/ *adj.* **1.** OF ECONOMY OR ECONOMICS relating to economics, the economy of a country, or money in general **2.** PROFITABLE producing or capable of producing a profit **3.** MATERIAL relating to or affecting material goods and resources **4.** = **economical** *adj.* 3 [Late 16thC. Directly or via French from Latin *oeconomicus* from Greek *oikonomikos* from *oikonomos* (see ECONOMY).]

WORD KEY: USAGE

economic or **economical**? The adjective ***economic*** denotes economics or the economy, and is concerned with 'aspects of the supply of goods and structure of wealth': *a Nobel Laureate's economic theories.* The adjective ***economical***, on the other hand, has to do with economy specifically in its senses 'making the best and most frugal use of resources' and 'inexpensiveness': *It is much more economical to buy in bulk. Public transport is economical, compared with hiring a limousine.* But the two adjectives can overlap in one sense, 'efficient in terms of contributing to thrift': *an economical [or economic] use of electricity.*

economical /ékə nómmik'l, éekə-/ *adj.* **1.** RESOURCEFULLY FRUGAL careful in making the best use of resources ○ *an economical cook* **2.** INEXPENSIVE costing relatively little in comparison with other things in the same class ○ *a home that's economical to run* **3.** EFFICIENT efficient in terms of avoiding unnecessary expenditure of time or energy ○ *an economical gesture*

WORD KEY: USAGE

See Usage note at ***economic.***

economically /ékə nómmikli, éekə-/ *adv.* **1.** WITH REGARD TO ECONOMY OR ECONOMICS with regard to economics, the economy of a country, or financial matters in general ○ *economically and socially developing societies* **2.** PROFITABLY in such a way as to produce a profit **3.** FRUGALLY in a thrifty, sparing, or careful manner

economic determinism *n.* the belief that the economic organization of a society determines the nature of all other aspects of its life

economic geography *n.* a branch of geography that deals with the distribution and use of an area's economic resources

economic geology *n.* the study of geological deposits from the viewpoint of their value as resources

economic indicator *n.* a quantity expressed statistically and taken as a measure of an economic variable

economic migrant *n.* sb who travels or migrates to an area where work or a better standard of living is available, especially when this involves entering another country

economic rent *n.* **1.** PAYMENT PRODUCING PROFIT a payment for use of a factor of production that is enough to make it profitable for the owner **2.** ACCOMMODATION PAYMENT a level of housing rent that is enough to make letting profitable for the owner

economics /ékə nómmiks, éekə-/ *n.* **1.** STUDY OF GOODS AND SERVICES the study of the production, distribution, and consumption of goods and services (*takes a singular verb*) **2.** FINANCIAL ASPECTS the financial element of sth (*takes a plural verb*) ○ *the economics of running a business* [Late 18thC. Probably from French *économique* + *-s*, based on the Latin plural *oeconomica*, translating Greek *ta oikonomika*, a treatise title on the duties of domestic life by Aristotle.]

economic union *n.* a merging of the economies of two or more states to function as a unit that shares a common financial policy and currency

economise *vi.* = **economize**

economism /i kónnə mizəm/ *n.* **1.** IMPORTANCE OF ECONOMICS the belief that economics is the most important element in a society **2.** IMPROVING OF LIVING STANDARDS the belief that bringing about an improvement in the living standards of its members is the chief goal of a political organization or trade union organization

economist /i kónnəmist/ *n.* **1.** SPECIALIST IN ECONOMICS sb who studies, works, or is an expert in the field of economics **2.** FRUGAL PERSON a frugal person (*archaic*)

economistic /i kónnə místik/ *adj.* showing bias towards economic factors

economize /i kónnə mīz/ (**-mizes, -mizing, -mized**), **economise** (**-mises, -mising, -mised**) *vi.* to reduce expenditure, or use resources less wastefully ○ *We had to economize on fuel.* —**economizer** *n.*

economy /i kónnəmi/ *n.* (*plural* **-mies**) **1.** ECON THRIFT the prudent managing of resources to avoid extravagant expenditure or waste **2.** SAVING a saving or attempt to reduce expenditure **3.** ECON, FIN SPARING USE a sparing, controlled, or efficient use of sth ○ *a graceful economy of effort* **4.** ECON FINANCIAL AFFAIRS the production and consumption of goods and services of a community regarded as a whole ○ *a gradual shift from an agricultural to an industrial economy* **5.** TRANSP = **economy class** **6.** SYSTEM a system of interacting elements, especially when seen as being harmonious ○ *the economy of the natural world* **7.** HOUSEHOLD MANAGEMENT the management of a household (*archaic*) ■ *adj.* ECON, FIN CHEAPER intended to be cheaper or give better value for money [15thC. Via French or Latin from Greek *oikonomiā*, from *oikonomos* 'steward of a household', from *oikos* 'house' + *nemein* 'to manage' (source of English *antinomian* and *nomad*).]

economy class *n.* a class of travel, especially on airlines, that is relatively low in price and carries the majority of passengers

economy class syndrome *n.* thrombosis believed to be caused by a prolonged period of restricted movement and dehydration, such as occurs during air travel

economy drive *n.* an organized attempt to reduce expenditure and waste

economy of scale *n.* a reduction in unit cost achieved by increasing the amount of production

écorché /é kawr shay/ (*plural* **-chés**) *n.* an anatomical model of part or all of the human body with the skin removed, to allow study of the muscle structure [Mid-19thC. From French, the past participle of *écorcher* 'to flay'.]

ecospecies /éekō spee sheez, ékō spee sheez/ (*plural* **-cies**) *n.* a species made up of several subgroups (**ecotypes**) and characterized by its ecological traits

ecosphere /éekō sfeer, ékō-/ *n.* = **biosphere**

écossaise /áy ko sáyz/ *n.* a lively folk dance in 2/4 time, or the music for this dance [Mid-19th C. French for 'Scottish'.]

ecosystem /éekō sistəm, ékō-/ *n.* a localized group of interdependent organisms together with the environment that they inhabit and depend on

ecoterrorism /éekō térrə rizzəm, ékō-/ *n.* the sabotage of the activities of individuals or corporations, e.g. industrial companies, considered to be polluting or destroying the natural environment —**ecoterrorist** *n.*

ecotone /éekə tōn, ékə tōn/ *n.* a zone of transition between two different ecosystems, e.g. where the sea meets the land [Early 20thC. Coined from ECO- + Greek *tonos* 'tension'.]

ecotourism /éekō tóorizəm, ékō-/ *n.* a form of tourism that strives to minimize ecological or other damage to areas visited for their natural or cultural interest

ecotoxicology /éekō tóksi kólləji, ékō-/ *n.* the study of how organisms are affected by chemicals released into the environment by human activities

ecotype /éekō tīp, ékō-/ *n.* a subgroup of a species of plant or other organism whose members show genetically determined adaptations to certain environmental conditions in their habitat

ecowarrior /éekō worri ər, ékō-/ *n.* an activist who takes direct, often unlawful action on an environmental issue

ecru /ékroo, áy-/ *adj.* of a pale brown colour, like unbleached linen [Mid-19thC. Via French, 'raw, unbleached', from, ultimately, Latin *crudus* 'raw' (source of English *crude*).] —**ecru** *n.*

ECS *abbr.* European Communications Satellite

ECSC *abbr.* European Coal and Steel Community

ecstasy /ékstəssi/ (*plural* **-sies**) *n.* **1.** INTENSE DELIGHT a feeling of intense delight **2.** INTENSE FEELING OR ACTIVITY a feeling or activity characterized by its extreme intensity ○ *an ecstasy of remorse* **3.** PSYCHOL LOSS OF SELF-CONTROL a mental state, usually caused by intense religious experience, sexual pleasure, or drugs, in which sb is so dominated by an emotion that self-control and sometimes consciousness are lost **4.** **ecstasy, Ecstasy** DRUGS ILLEGAL DRUG a drug used illicitly as a stimulant and relaxer of inhibitions. Formula: $C_{11}H_{15}NO_2$. [14thC. Via Old French from, ultimately, Greek *ekstasis*, from *existanai* 'to displace, drive out (of your mind)', from *histanai* 'to put'. The sense 'delight' developed in the 17thC.]

WORD KEY: CULTURAL NOTE

The Ecstasy of St Theresa, a sculpture by Italian artist Gianlorenzo Bernini (1645–52). An altarpiece in the Cornaro Chapel in the church of Santa Maria Della Vittoria in Rome, it depicts a vision experienced by the Spanish saint Theresa during which an angel pierced her heart with a golden arrow, causing pain but also intense religious rapture.

ecstatic /ik státtik, ek-/ *adj.* **1.** DELIGHTED showing or feeling great pleasure or delight **2.** DOMINATED BY

EMOTION completely dominated by an intense emotion ■ *n.* **SB SUBJECT TO A TRANCE** sb who undergoes spells of intense emotion —**ecstatically** *adv.*

ECT *abbr.* electroconvulsive therapy

ectasia /ek táyzi ə/, **ectasis** /éktəssiss/ *n.* a swelling or dilation of a part of the body (*technical*) [Late 19thC. From modern Latin, from Greek *ektasis*, from *ekteinein* 'to stretch out'.]

ecto- *prefix.* external, outside ○ *ectotherm* [From Greek *ektos*, from *ek* 'out' (see EXO-)]

ectocommensal /éktə kə méns'l/ *n.* a harmless parasitic plant or animal that lives on the outer surface or skin of another organism

ectoderm /éktə durm/ *n.* the outermost of three cell layers of an embryo, from which the epidermis, nervous tissue, and sense organs develop

ectogenesis /éktō jénnississ/ *n.* the development of an organism in an artificial environment, outside the body in which it would normally be found

ectogenous /ek tójjənəss/ *adj.* used to describe an organism, e.g. a parasitic bacterium, that grows or is able to grow outside the body of a host

ectomere /éktə meer/ *n.* a cell (**blastomere**) produced during the division of a fertilized egg that develops with others into the outer cell layer (**ectoderm**) of an embryo

ectomorph /éktə mawrf/ *n.* sb belonging to a physiological type that is tall with long lean limbs. ◊ **endomorph, mesomorph** —**ectomorphic** /éktə máwrfik/ *adj.*

-ectomy *suffix.* surgical removal of a part of the body ○ *iridectomy* [From modern Latin *-ectomia*, literally 'cutting out', from Greek *ek-* 'out' + *-tomia* '-tomy']

ectoparasite /éktə párrə sīt/ *n.* a parasite that lives on the outside of its host, e.g. on the skin or in the hair. Fleas are ectoparasites. —**ectoparasitic** /éktə párrə síttik/ *adj.* —**ectoparasitism** /éktə párrəsi tizəm/ *n.*

ectophyte /éktə fīt/ *n.* a parasitic plant that lives on the outer surface of its host —**ectophytic** /éktə fíttik/ *adj.*

ectopia /ek tōpi ə/ *n.* a change form the normal tpositioning of an organ or body part [Mid-19thC. From modern Latin, from Greek *ektopos* 'out of place', from *topos* 'place'.]

ectopic /ek tóppik/ *adj.* used to describe an organ or body part occurring in a position or form that is not usual or normal

ectopic pregnancy *n.* the development of a fertilized egg outside the womb, e.g. in a Fallopian tube

ectoplasm /éktə plazəm/ *n.* **1.** CELL BIOL **OUTER LAYER OF CELL CONTENTS** the dense outer layer of the substance (**cytoplasm**) that surrounds the nucleus of a cell **2.** PARANORMAL **GHOSTLY SUBSTANCE** the substance believed by spiritualists to issue from a medium who is communicating with spirits —**ectoplasmic** /éktə plázmik/ *adj.*

ectotherm /éktə thurm/ *n.* an animal that maintains its body temperature by absorbing heat from its environment. All animals other than birds and mammals are ectotherms. ◊ **poikilotherm** [Mid-20thC. Coined from ECTO- + Greek *thermē* 'heat'.] —**ectothermic** /éktə thúrmik/ *adj.*

ectotrophic /éktə tróffik, -trófik/ *adj.* used to describe an association (**mycorrhiza**) between a fungus and the roots of a plant, in which the fungus obtains its nourishment by enveloping the roots in a sheath. ◊ **endotrophic**

écu /áy kyoo/ *n.* any one of several former French silver or gold coins [Late 16thC. Via French from Latin *scutum* 'shield'; from the shield that was part of the design of such coins.]

ECU /áy kyoo/, **ecu** *n.* the former official monetary unit of the European Union, established in 1979. The currency ceased to exist at the end of 1999 when it was replaced by the Euro. Full form **European Currency Unit**

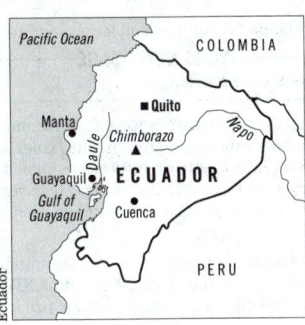

Ecuador /ékwə dawr/ equatorial republic in northwestern South America, bounded on the north by Colombia, on the south and east by Peru, and on the west by the Pacific Ocean. Language: Spanish. Currency: sucre. Capital: Quito. Population: 12,105,124 (1997). Area: 272,045 sq. km/107,037 sq. mi. Official name **Republic of Ecuador** —**Ecuadorian** /ékwə dáwri ən/ *n., adj.*

ecumenical /éekyoo ménnik'l/, **ecumenic** /-ménnik/ *adj.* **1.** CHR **CONCERNING CHURCH UNITY** relating to, involving, or promoting the unity of Christian Churches around the world **2.** UNIVERSAL involving all people or groups [Late 16thC. Formed from late Latin *oecumenicus* 'general, universal', from Greek *oikoumenikos*, from *oikoumenē* (*gē*) 'inhabited (world)', from *oikos* 'house, habitation'.] —**ecumenically** *adv.*

ecumenical council *n.* a gathering of leaders and representatives from the Christian Churches of the world

ecumenicalism *n.* = ecumenism

ecumenical patriarch *n.* the Archbishop of Constantinople, the most senior dignitary of the Eastern Church

ecumenicism *n.* = ecumenism

ecumenics /éekyoo ménniks/ *n.* the study of the aims and development of unity between different Christian denominations (*takes a singular verb*)

ecumenism /i kyoómə nizəm/, **ecumenicism** /éekyoo ménnisizəm/, **ecumenicalism** /éekyoo ménnik'lizəm/ *n.* a movement in the Christian Church aiming at unity between different denominations on basic issues

eczema /éksəmə/ *n.* an inflammation of the skin characterized by reddening and itching and the formation of scaly or crusty patches that may leak fluid [Mid-18thC. Via modern Latin from Greek *ekzema* 'eruption', from *zein* 'to boil', ultimately from an Indo-European word that is also the ancestor of English *yeast*.]

ed. *abbr.* **1.** edited **2.** edition **3.** editor **4.** education

-ed 1 *suffix.* **1.** used to form the past participle of regular verbs ○ *wasted* **2.** having, characterized by, like ○ *redheaded* ○ *bigoted* [Old English *-ed, -od*]

-ed 2 *suffix.* used to form the past tense of regular verbs ○ *nicked* ○ *landed* [Old English *-ede, -ode*]

edacious /i dáyshəss/ *adj.* voracious, or devoted to gluttony (*formal*) [Early 19thC. Formed from the Latin stem *edac-* 'voracious, gluttonous', from *edere* 'to eat'.] —**edacity** /i dássəti/ *n.*

Edam 1 /ee dam/ *n.* a mild cheese of Dutch origin with a slightly rubbery texture, typically formed into balls covered with red wax [Early 19thC. Named after EDAM[2], where it was originally made.]

Edam 2 /ee dam/ town in the western Netherlands, near Amsterdam, best known for the manufacture of the cheese to which it gives its name. Population: 25,603 (1994).

edaphic /i dáffik/ *adj.* ECOL used to describe the effect of soil characteristics, especially chemical or physical properties, on plants and animals [Late 19thC. Formed from Greek *edaphos* 'floor, ground, soil'.]

edaphic climax *n.* a stable ecological community (**climax**) that results from the content or properties of the soil rather than the climate

Edberg /éd burg/, **Stefan** (*b.* 1966) Swedish tennis player. He progressed from a junior grand slam in

1983 to winning both Wimbledon and the US Open singles championships (1988, 1990, 1991, and 1992).

EDC *abbr.* European Defence Community

Edda /éddə/ *n.* **1.** 12THC **NORSE POEM COLLECTION** a 12th-century collection of Old Norse poems **2.** 13THC **NORSE POEM COLLECTION** a 13th-century collection compiled by Snorri Sturluson containing Norse myths, poems, and a treatise on poetry [Late 17thC. Origin uncertain, probably from Old Norse *ōðr* 'spirit, mind, passion, song, poetry'.] —**Eddic** *adj.*

Eddington /éddingtən/, **Sir Arthur** (1882–1944) British astronomer. He confirmed Einstein's general theory of relativity and wrote the popular *The Expanding Universe* (1933). Full name **Sir Arthur Stanley Eddington**

eddo /éddō/ (*plural* **-does**) *n.* PLANTS = **taro** [Late 17thC. Of West African origin.]

eddy /éddi/ *n.* (*plural* **-dies**) **1.** SMALL WHIRL a movement in a flowing stream of liquid or gas in which the current doubles back to form a small whirl ○ *a pleasing pattern of eddies in the river* **2.** DIVERGENCE a relatively unimportant divergence from or movement contrary to the mainstream of sth ○ *negotiated a few political eddies* ■ *vti.* (**-dies, -dying, -died**) FLOW CONTRARY to flow or make sth flow contrary to the main current ○ *He waded out, the stream eddying around his legs.* [15thC. Origin uncertain, perhaps from Old Norse *iða* 'whirlpool', or from assumed Old English *edwæg*, literally 'back wave'.]

eddy current *n.* an electric current set up by an alternating magnetic field

Eddystone Rocks /édistən-/ dangerous rocks in the English Channel, near Plymouth, England. Four lighthouses have successively been built on or near the rocks since 1698.

Edelweiss

edelweiss /áyd'l vīss/ *n.* a small plant with white woolly leaves and small flowers, native to the Alps and mountains of Asia. Latin name: *Leontopodium alpinum*. [Mid-19thC. From German, literally 'noble white'.]

edema *n.* MED US = oedema

Eden 1 /eed'n/ *n.* **1.** ADAM AND EVE'S GARDEN in the Bible, the garden where Adam and Eve first lived **2.** PERFECT PLACE any place seen as being perfect, highly pleasing, or happy ○ *The first explorers saw America as an Eden.* —**Edenic** /ee dénnik/ *adj.*

Eden 2 /eed'n/ coastal town in southern New South Wales. Population: 3,106 (1996).

Eden, Anthony, 1st Earl of Avon (1897–1977) British statesman. Foreign secretary under Winston Churchill during World War II, he became prime minister in 1955 but resigned in 1957 after controversial military action against Egypt during the Suez Crisis of 1956. As foreign secretary in 1938, he had been an opponent of appeasement, and he served under Churchill in the War cabinet.

edentate /ee dén tayt/ *n.* any placental mammal found in tropical America that has few or no teeth. Sloths and armadillos are edentates. Order: Edentata. [Early 19thC. Via Latin *edentatus* from, ultimately, the stem *dent-* 'tooth'.]

edentulous /ee déntyŏŏləss/, **edentulate** /-lət, -layt/ *adj.* ZOOL, MED without any teeth [Early 18thC. From Latin *edentulus*, from the stem *dent-* 'tooth'.]

Edgar /édgər/, **King of the English** (944–975). His rule, from 959 to 975, was marked by clerical, judicial, and administrative reforms. Known as **The Peaceful**

Edgbaston /éj bastən/ district in Birmingham, England

edge /ej/ n. 1. BORDER a line or area that is the outermost part or the part farthest away from the centre of sth ○ a tablecloth with embroidered edges 2. PART ABOVE A DROP the area where land suddenly falls away steeply ○ the cliff edge 3. BRINK OR THRESHOLD the point or moment just before a marked change or event ○ on the edge of victory 4. MEETING SURFACES the line where two surfaces of sth solid meet ○ A cube has 6 faces and 12 edges. 5. SHARP SIDE the cutting side of a blade ○ a razor's edge 6. SHARPNESS sharpness of a blade ○ a knife with a fine edge 7. SHARP QUALITY a piercing, cutting, or wounding quality, e.g. of language or expression ○ There was an unmistakable edge to her remarks. 8. VIGOUR noticeable vigour and energy ○ After the time-out there was a new edge to the team's play. 9. ADVANTAGE an advantage over, e.g. a competitor (informal) 10. RIDGE a ridge, crest, or cliff (often used in place names) ■ v. (edges, edging, edged) 1. vt. ADD A BORDER to add a border to sth, especially a decorative one ○ a handkerchief edged with lace 2. vt. TRIM to cut, shape, or trim the border of sth ○ a tool for edging the lawn 3. vt. SHARPEN to sharpen or give a sharp edge to a blade 4. vi. MOVE GRADUALLY to move gradually sideways, or make sth move in this direction by pushing it ○ just room enough to edge through 5. vt. SPORTS STRIKE WITH SIDE to strike a ball or other object with the side of sth, e.g. a cricket bat or football boot ○ The batsman edged the first ball for four. 6. vt. SKIING LEAN A SKI to lean a ski over so that its edge cuts the snow [Old English ecg 'corner, edge, sword'. Ultimately from an Indo-European base meaning 'to be sharp or pointed', which also produced English acid, acute, alacrity, and oxygen.] ◇ **live on the edge** to be habitually in highly stressful and demanding situations, often involving physical risk and dange ◇ **on edge** in or into an irritated or nervous state ◇ **take the edge off sth 1.** to reduce the intensity or strength of sth ○ the snack took the edge off my hunger 2. to do sth that makes a tense situation less so

edge out vt. 1. MOVE OUT to move sb or sth gradually out of position ○ trying to edge him out of the presidency 2. DEFEAT to defeat a competitor by a narrow margin (informal) ○ She was edged out of the championship.

Edgehill /éj híl/ ridge in Warwickshire, England, where the first battle of the English Civil War was fought in 1642

edger /éjjər/ n. sb who or sth that edges sth, especially a gardening tool for edging

edge tool n. an implement that has at least one cutting edge

edgeways /éj wayz/ adv., adj. with the edge or side foremost ○ fit in edgeways ○ with an edgeways motion. US term **edgewise** ◇ **get a word in edgeways** to succeed in speaking when other people are talking nonstop (usually used in negative statements)

Edgewood /éjwŏŏd/ town in northeastern Maryland, northeast of Baltimore. Population: 23,903 (1990).

Edgeworth, Maria (1767–1849) British novelist. Her best-known work, Castle Rackrent, set in rural Ireland, influenced the development of the historical and regional novel in English.

edging /éjjing/ n. 1. BORDER sth used as a border or trim, usually for decoration or protection 2. FORMING OF AN EDGE the formation of an edge ■ adj. USED TO FORM EDGES used in forming an edge

edgy /éjji/ (-ier, -iest) adj. 1. ON EDGE nervous and irritable 2. INTENSE having an intense or energetic quality or atmosphere ○ an edgy district 3. STYLISH unusually smart or stylish ○ edgy clothes —**edgily** adv. —**edginess** n.

edh /eth/ (plural edhs), **eth** (plural eths) n. a printed or written character (ð) used in the runic alphabet and in modern phonetics to represent the 'th' sound in the English words 'this' and 'other' [Mid-19thC. From Danish, perhaps originally representing the sound of the letter.]

edible /éddəb'l/ adj. ABLE TO BE EATEN able to be eaten by human beings, or fit or suitable for eating ■ **edibles** npl. FOOD things to eat [Early 17thC. From Latin edibilis 'eatable', from edere 'to eat' (source of English obese).] —

edibility /éddə bílləti/ n. —**edibleness** /éddibəlnəss/ n.

─── **WORD KEY: USAGE** ───
See usage note at **eatable.**

edict /éedikt/ n. 1. DECREE a formal proclamation, especially one issued by a government, ruler, or other authority 2. AUTHORITATIVE COMMAND a formal or authoritative command [15thC. From Latin edictum, from the past participle of edicere 'to proclaim', from dicere 'to say'.]

Edict of Nantes /-naant/ n. a law promulgated by Henry IV in 1598 and revoked by Louis XIV in 1685 that allowed civil and religious tolerance to French Protestants

edification /éddifi káysh'n/ n. instruction or enlightenment, especially when it is morally or spiritually uplifting

edifice /éddifiss/ n. 1. BUILDING a building, especially a large or impressive one 2. STRUCTURE a large or complex structure or organization ○ the edifice of government [14thC. Via French from Latin aedificium, from aedificare 'to build' (see EDIFY).]

edify /éddifī/ (-fies, -fying, -fied) vt. to improve the morals or knowledge of sb [14thC. Via French édifier from Latin aedificare 'to build, construct', later 'to instruct', from aedis 'building, temple' + facere 'to make'.] —**edifier** n.

edifying /éddi fī ing/ adj. providing morally useful knowledge or information

Edinburgh /éddinbərə/ capital city of Scotland, situated on the southern shore of the Firth of Forth. It is home to a cathedral, a castle, the royal Palace of Holyrood House, three universities, and the headquarters of the Scottish Assembly. Population: 447,600 (1995).

Edinburgh, Duke of ♦ Prince Philip

Edinburgh rock n. a Scottish confectionery in the form of pastel-coloured sticks with a powdery texture, made of sugar, cream of tartar, and flavourings

Edirne /e déernə/ city of northwestern Turkey, northwest of Istanbul. Population: 102,300 (1990).

Thomas Alva Edison

Edison /éddiss'n/, **Thomas Alva** (1847–1931) US inventor. He invented the light bulb, the microphone (1877), the phonograph (1877), and many other devices.

edit /éddit/ vt. (-its, -iting, -ited) 1. PUBL PREPARE FOR PUBLICATION to prepare a text for publication by correcting errors and ensuring clarity and accuracy 2. PUBL DECIDE THE CONTENT OF A PUBLICATION to be in overall charge of the publication of a newspaper or magazine 3. BROADCAST DECIDE THE CONTENT OF A PROGRAMME to be in overall charge of the content of a broadcast programme 4. CINEMA CUT A FILM OR TAPE to cut and arrange a film or recording, deciding its final order and content ○ The show was edited down from hours of live recording. 5. PUBL, BROADCAST CUT MATERIAL to remove material from sth, such as a publication or broadcast item, e.g. because it is lengthy or offensive ■ n. PUBL EDITING the preparation of a text for publication or release, or a stage in this process ○ Look out for errors missed in the first edit. [Late 18thC. Back-formation from EDITOR.]

edit out vt. to delete or remove an unwanted part of a text, film, or recording ○ Her walk-on part was eventually edited out.

edit. abbr. 1. edited 2. edition 3. editor

edited /édditid/ adj. 1. READY TO PUBLISH prepared for publication, broadcast, or release by having errors corrected and other refinements made 2. WITH UNWANTED PARTS REMOVED used to describe sth such as a text or broadcast that has had unwanted material removed ○ an edited version of the original film

edition /i dísh'n/ n. 1. PUBL PRINTED VERSION one version of a publication issued serially, periodically, or in multiple formats ○ the morning edition of the newspaper 2. BROADCAST BROADCAST VERSION a version or instalment of a broadcast for a particular time or purpose ○ last week's edition of the show 3. PRINTING PRINTED BATCH a batch of identical copies of a publication all printed at the same time 4. BATCH OF ITEMS a batch or number of items all produced at the same time 5. SIMILAR THING a version or copy of sth [15thC. From Latin edition-, from edit-, the past participle stem of edere 'to give out', from dare 'to give'.]

editio princeps /i díshi ō prín seps/ (plural **editiones principes** /i díshi ō neez prínssi peez/) n. the first printed edition of a piece of writing (literary) [From modern Latin, literally 'first edition']

editor /édditər/ n. 1. PUBL PUBLISHING SUPERVISOR sb who is in overall charge of the publication of a book, newspaper, or magazine 2. PUBL CHIEF JOURNALIST sb who is in charge of a particular part of a newspaper or magazine 3. PUBL TEXT CORRECTOR sb who prepares a text for publication by correcting errors and improving accuracy and clarity 4. BROADCAST SB CONTROLLING PROGRAMME CONTENT sb who is in overall charge of the content of a broadcast programme 5. CINEMA SB WHO EDITS FILM sb who prepares the final version of a film, deciding its length and the order of shots and scenes 6. COMPUT = text editor [Mid-17thC. From late Latin, 'producer, publisher', from the Latin stem edit- (see EDITION).] —**editorship** n.

editorial /éddi táwri əl/ adj. PUBL, BROADCAST OF EDITING relating to, involving, or concerned with the editing of sth such as a text or broadcast ○ made lots of editorial comments in the margins ■ n. PUBL = leader —**editorialist** n. —**editorially** adv.

editorialize /éddi táwri ə līz/ (-izes, -izing, -ized), **editorialise** (-ises, -ising, -ised) vi. 1. PUBL WRITE EDITORIALS to express an opinion or view in an editorial 2. WRITE SUBJECTIVELY to introduce personal opinions or views, especially inappropriately ○ He couldn't resist the opportunity, when reporting on a burglary, to editorialize on security systems.

editor in chief (plural **editors in chief**) n. the executive editor of a publication, publishing house, or set of publications

EdM abbr. Master of Education [Latin, Educationis Magister]

Edmonton /édməntən/ capital city of Alberta, Canada, located in the centre of the province, on the North Saskatchewan River. Population: 862,597 (1996).

Edmund, St and King of East Anglia (841?–870). After defeat in battle by the Danes, he is said to have been martyred for refusing to deny Christianity.

Edmund I, King of the English (921–946). He made war on the Vikings, expelling them from England, and carried out legal reforms.

Edmund II, King of the English (981?–1016). He reigned for only a few months in 1016, until defeated in battle by Canute. He was allowed to keep control of the south of England, but died a month later. Known as **Edmund Ironside**

Edmund of Abingdon /édmənd/, **St** (1175?–1240) English priest and scholar. He was Archbishop of Canterbury from 1234 to 1240, and was canonized about 1249.

Edom /éedəm/ ancient country situated south of the Dead Sea, which according to the Bible was given to Esau

Edomite /éedə mīt/ n. 1. PEOPLES SB FROM EDOM a member of an ancient ethnic group who lived in the kingdom of Edom in pre-Christian times and who were noted for their long-standing hostility towards the Israelites 2. LANG EXTINCT LANGUAGE an extinct language formerly spoken in the ancient kingdom of Edom in the Middle East. It is one of the Semitic group of Afro-Asian languages and is related to Hebrew. — **Edomitic** /ēedə míttik/ adj.

EDP abbr. electronic data processing

EDT abbr. Eastern Daylight Time

EDTA n. a colourless compound that reacts with metals and is used in food preservation, as an anticoagulant, and to treat lead poisoning. Formula: $C_{10}H_{16}N_2O_8$. Full form **ethylene diamine tetra-acetate**

edu abbr. educational institution (used as an Internet suffix)

educ. abbr. 1. education 2. educational

educable /éddyŏŏkəb'l/, **educatable** /-kaytəb'l/ adj. able to learn or be taught [Mid-19thC. Formed from EDUCATE.] —**educability** /éddyŏŏkə bílləti/ n.

educate /éddyŏŏ kayt/ (-cates, -cating, -cated) v. 1. vti. TEACH to give knowledge to or develop the abilities of sb by teaching ○ educated at a state school 2. vt. ARRANGE SCHOOLING to arrange schooling for sb ○ They educated their daughters 3. vt. DEVELOP to develop or improve a faculty or sense 4. vt. TRAIN to train or instruct sb in a particular field [15thC. From Latin educat-, the past participle stem of educare 'to bring up, rear', related to educere 'to lead out', from ducere 'to lead'.]

— **WORD KEY: SYNONYMS** —
See Synonyms at **teach**.

educated /éddyŏŏ kaytid/ adj. 1. WELL-TAUGHT having had a good education ○ This is the writing of an educated person. 2. CULTURED showing good taste, expert knowledge, or cultivation ○ cast an educated eye over the antiques 3. KNOWLEDGEABLE having the benefit of experience or knowledge

educated guess n. a guess that is based on a degree of experience, knowledge, or information

education /éddyŏŏ káysh'n/ n. 1. EDUCATING the imparting and acquiring of knowledge through teaching and learning, especially at a school or similar institution ○ 'After all, what is education but a process by which a person begins to learn how to learn?' (Peter Ustinov, Dear Me; 1977) 2. KNOWLEDGE the knowledge or abilities gained through being educated 3. INSTRUCTION training and instruction in a particular subject, e.g. health matters 4. STUDY OF TEACHING the study of the theories and practices of teaching ○ a degree in education 5. SYSTEM FOR EDUCATING PEOPLE the system of educating people in a community or society ○ jobs in education 6. LEARNING EXPERIENCE an informative experience ○ Spending a weekend in their house was a real education.

education action zone n. a cluster of about 20 primary and secondary schools that work together to meet educational targets for improvement. They receive extra funding for three to five years and are run by a forum including businesses, parents and community organizations.

educational /éddyŏŏ káysh'nəl/ adj. 1. INSTRUCTIVE OR INFORMATIVE giving knowledge, instruction, or information 2. RELATING TO TEACHING AND LEARNING relating to, involving, or concerned with education —**educationally** adv.

educationalist /éddyŏŏ káysh'nəlist/, **educationist** /-káysh'nist/ n. an expert in the theories or administration of education

educational psychology n. a branch of applied psychology that studies children in an educational setting and is concerned with the assessment of ability and aptitude and the evaluation of teaching and learning methods. Educational psychologists also deal with problems experienced by some children at school and in other learning situations. — **educational psychologist** n.

Educational Welfare Officer n. sb employed by a local education authority to investigate the home background of children with difficulties at school, identify any problems there, and help to find solutions

educationist n. 1. = educationalist 2. EDUCATIONAL THEORIST sb who espouses and propounds educational theories (disapproving)

educative /éddyŏŏkətiv/ adj. giving or concerned with education

educator /éddyŏŏ kaytər/ n. 1. SB WHO EDUCATES a professional teacher 2. SPECIALIST IN EDUCATION an expert in the theories or administration of education

educatory /éddyŏŏkə tawri, éddyŏŏ káytəri/ adj. giving or concerned with education

educe /i dyŏóss/ (educes, educing, educed) vt. (formal) 1. ELICIT to elicit or derive sth, e.g. a conclusion 2. DEVELOP to make sth latent develop or appear [15thC. From Latin educere 'to lead out'.]

educt /ēe dukt/ n. a substance extracted from another substance without chemical alteration [Late 17thC. From Latin eductum, from the past participle of educere (see EDUCE).]

eduction /i dúksh'n/ n. 1. DERIVATION the derivation or development of sth, or sth derived or developed (formal) 2. TECH EXHAUST OF AN ENGINE the exhaust of an engine, especially an internal-combustion or steam engine (technical) [Mid-17thC. From the Latin stem eduction-, from educere (see EDUCE).]

edulcorate /i dúlkə rayt/ (-rates, -rating, -rated) vt. to remove soluble impurities from sth by washing (technical) [Mid-17thC. From medieval Latin edulcorat-, the past participle stem of edulcorare 'to sweeten', from Latin dulcis 'sweet'.]

edutainment /éddyŏŏ táynmənt/ n. television programmes, computer software, or other media content intended to entertain and educate the user at the same time [Late 20thC. A blend of EDUCATION and ENTERTAINMENT.]

Edward I /éddwərd-/, King of England (1239–1307). His reign (1272–1307) was marked by the development of parliamentary government and by conflicts with the Welsh, the Scots, and France. Known as **Edward Longshanks**

Edward II, King of England (1284–1327). Defeated by the Scots at the Battle of Bannockburn in 1314, his reign (1307–27) ended in his forced abdication and murder. He was the first future king to be styled Prince of Wales (1301). Known as **Edward of Caernarvon**

Edward III, King of England (1312–77). He ruled from 1327 until 1377. Through his mother, Isabella of France, he claimed the French throne, starting the Hundred Years War.

Edward IV, King of England (1442–83). As an outcome of the Wars of the Roses (1455–85), he became the first king of the House of York (1461–83). He was briefly deposed in 1470–71 by Lancastrian supporters of Henry VI.

Edward V, King of England (1470–83?). On his accession in 1483, he was imprisoned by the future Richard III in the Tower of London and is thought to have been assassinated. With his brother he is often referred to as one of the 'Princes in the Tower'.

Edward VI, King of England (1537–53). He was the son of Henry VIII and Jane Seymour. His reign (1547–53) saw rapid advancement of Protestantism in England.

Edward VII, King of the United Kingdom (1841–1910). Son of Queen Victoria, he was a keen sportsman and traveller, promoting good relations abroad. His reign (1901–10) is known as the Edwardian period.

Edward VIII, King of the United Kingdom (1894–1972). His brief reign (January-December 1936) ended in abdication after the British Government refused to agree to his marrying US divorcée Wallis Simpson.

Edward (the Confessor), St and King of the English (1002?–66). He was canonized in 1161, but his reign (1042–66) was troubled by political conflict between Norman and English groups.

Edward (the Martyr), St and King of the English (963?–978). He reigned from 975. His murder in 978 was possibly at the instigation of his stepmother Elfrida.

Edward, Lake lake in the Great African Rift Valley straddling the border between the Democratic Republic of Congo and Uganda. Area: 2,124 sq. km/820 sq. mi.

Edwardian /ed wáwrdi ən/ adj. OF THE REIGN OF EDWARD VII relating to, belonging to, or typical of British society

during the reign of Edward VII in the first decade of the 20th century ■ n. SB OF OR STUDYING THE EDWARDIAN ERA sb who was alive or active during the reign of Edward VII or who is a specialist in this period of history

Edwin /éddwin/, St and King of Northumbria (585?–633). He was converted to Christianity in 627. His reign (617–633) ended in death in battle against the pagan Penda of Mercia.

ee /ee/ (plural **een** /een/) n. Scotland an eye [Variant of EYE]

EE abbr. 1. electrical engineer 2. electrical engineering 3. Early English

e.e. abbr. errors excepted

-ee¹ suffix. 1. one who receives or benefits from an action ○ consignee 2. one who receives a thing ○ biographee 3. one who performs an action ○ attendee [Via Anglo-Norman from, ultimately, Latin -atus]

-ee² suffix. 1. one that resembles ○ coatee 2. a kind of, especially a small one ○ vestee 3. one connected with ○ bargee [Variant of -Y]

EE & MP abbr. Envoy Extraordinary and Minister Plenipotentiary

EEC abbr. HIST European Economic Community

EEG abbr. 1. echoencephalograph 2. electroencephalogram 3. electroencephalograph

eejit /ēe jit/ n. Ireland a thoughtless, unintelligent person (informal insult) [Late 19thC. Representing a pronunciation of IDIOT.]

eel /eel/ (plural **eels** or **eel**) n. 1. LONG THIN FISH a fish that has a long thin body resembling that of a snake, smooth skin without scales, and reduced fins. Most eels live in shallow marine waters. Order: Apodes. 2. FISH RESEMBLING AN EEL any fish similar to a true eel in appearance, e.g. an electric eel 3. DEVIOUS PERSON an untrustworthy or evasive person [Old English ǣl, from a prehistoric Germanic word of unknown origin]

eelgrass /ēel graass/ n. 1. MARINE PLANT RESEMBLING GRASS a perennial plant with long narrow dark-green leaves that grows submerged in shallow seawater. Genus: Zostera. 2. = tape grass

eelpout /ēel powt/ (plural **-pouts** or **-pout**) n. 1. ZOOL FISH RESEMBLING AN EEL a marine fish with a long thin body like an eel. Family: Zoarcidae. 2. = burbot

eelworm /ēel wurm/ (plural **-worms** or **-worm**) n. ZOOL = nematode

een Scotland plural of **ee**

e'en /een/ n. evening (literary) ■ adv. even (literary)

eeny /ēeni/ adj., n. the number one from old counting systems (regional)

— **WORD KEY: REGIONAL NOTE** —
Many children's rhymes are not as nonsensical as they might, at first, appear. It has been suggested that the four words '**eeny**, meeny, miney, mo' may be a recollection of an extremely old counting system. There is an Austrian rhyme beginning 'Eine, meine, mine, mu' and East Anglian shepherds are reputed to count one to four as 'Ina, mina, tethra, methera'. The 'Hickory, Dickory, Dock' rhyme may contain a relic of 8, 9, and 10, which are hevera, devera, dick in a Westmorland counting system.

EEO abbr. equal employment opportunity

e'er /air/ adv. ever (literary) [Late 16thC. Contraction.]

-eer suffix. a person engaged in or concerned with ○ auctioneer ○ charioteer [Via Old French -ier from, ultimately, Latin -arius]

eerie /ēeri/ (-rier, -riest) adj. unnerving or unusual in a way that suggests a connection with the supernatural ○ an eerie old house [13thC. Probably from, ultimately, Old English earg 'cowardly'. Originally in Scottish and northern English meaning 'fearful'; the sense 'causing fear' developed in the 18thC, becoming standard in the 19thC.] —**eerily** adv. —**eeriness** n.

EET abbr. Eastern European Time

eff /ef/ vti. used as a euphemism for 'fuck' (slang; offensive) [Mid-20thC. A spelling of the first letter of

FUCK.] ◇ **eff and blind** to swear or use offensive language (*slang*)

efface /i fáyss/ (**-faces, -facing, -faced**) *v.* **1.** *vt.* **RUB OUT** to remove or obliterate sth by or as if by wearing away or rubbing out **2.** *vr.* **BEHAVE HUMBLY** to act in an inconspicuous manner, especially because of shyness or modesty [15thC. From French *effacer* 'to wipe out, destroy', literally 'to remove the face', from *face* 'face, appearance'.] —**effaceable** *adj.* —**effacement** *n.* —**effacer** *n.*

effect /i fékt/ *n.* **1. RESULT** a change or changed state occurring as a direct result of action by sb or sth else ○ *showing the effects of prolonged malnutrition* **2. POWER TO INFLUENCE** success in bringing about a change in sb or sth, or the ability to achieve this ○ *I've told her again and again, but it has no effect on her.* **3. BEING IN FORCE OR OPERATION** the state of being in force, in operation, or the case, often from a particular point in time ○ *The new law doesn't come into effect until next month.* **4. IMPRESSION** an impression produced in the mind of sb who sees, hears, or reads sth, especially one that is deliberately intended or engineered **5. CAUSE OR PRODUCTION OF AN IMPRESSION** sth that produces an impression, or the actual process of causing a special feeling or impression ○ *a grand little speech made merely for effect* **6.** ARTS **SPECIAL SOUND, LIGHTING IN PLAY, FILM** sth done to produce a desired response or to add to the realism or theatricality of a film, play, or broadcast (*often used in the plural*) **7. MEANING OR INTENT** the intent or essential meaning conveyed, often in other words, by a statement, or words to that effect **8. SCIENTIFIC PHENOMENON** a scientifically observed and described phenomenon ■ **effects** *npl.* **BELONGINGS** sb's personal belongings, or the things that sb is carrying about him or her (*formal*) ○ *Her personal effects consisted of not much more than the clothes on her back.* ■ *vt.* (**-fects, -fecting, -fected**) **DO OR MAKE STH** to carry sth out, or succeed in making or doing sth (*formal*) ○ *They effected their escape through a rear window.* [14thC. Directly or via Old French from Latin *effectus*, from *efficere* 'to accomplish', literally 'to work out' (source of English *efficient*), from *facere* 'to make or do'.] —**effecter** *n.* —**effectible** *adj.* ◇ **in effect** used to indicate that what is being said represents the truth of the matter, even though the words used may not be those that other people would choose ○ *In effect, this means that the program is shut down.*

WORD KEY: USAGE

See Usage note at *affect.*

effective /i féktiv/ *adj.* **1. PRODUCING A RESULT** causing a result, especially the desired or intended result ○ *an effective remedy for headaches* **2. HAVING A STRIKING RESULT** successful, especially in producing a strong or favourable impression on people ○ *The painting had the characteristics of a winner, including effective colour use.* **3. ACTUAL** actual or in practice, even if not officially or theoretically so ○ *he was effective ruler during the monarch's last illness* **4. OFFICIALLY IN FORCE** officially in force, operative, or applicable ○ *a regulation effective as from next month* **5.** MIL **READY FOR ACTION** fully equipped and ready for action ■ *n.* MIL **MILITARY PERSONNEL OR EQUIPMENT** a soldier, military unit, or piece of military equipment that is ready for action —**effectiveness** *n.* —**effectivity** /éffek tívvəti/ *n.*

WORD KEY: USAGE

effective, **effectual**, **efficacious**, or **efficient**? All these words are about having some kind of *effect*. The main difficulty is in choosing between ***effective*** and ***effectual***. ***Effective*** means 'having or producing the desired effect' and refers to what actually happens or what (on the basis of experience, for example) might be expected to happen: *Exercise is an effective way of keeping healthy.* ***Effectual*** is a more formal word and refers to potential capability rather than known performance: *Publicizing stringent penalties is an effectual deterrent against illegal parking.* ***Efficacious*** is also a more formal word, is applied only to things or processes and not to people, and refers to the power sth has to produce a result: *Professional counselling proved more efficacious in the long term than medication.* ***Efficient*** has to do with the means or resources used in achieving a result in an economical manner: *efficient office communication procedures.* It also denotes the idea of being able to work directly to produce a given effect: *efficient causes of an early and highly successful space launch.*

WORD KEY: SYNONYMS

effective, efficient, effectual, efficacious

CORE MEANING: producing a result

effective suggesting the ability to produce the required result or the actual achievement of the result; **efficient** suggesting that sth or sb is capable of achieving the desired result with the minimum use of resources, time and effort; **effectual** a more formal word than 'efficient' suggesting the achievement of a desired result, especially when this has already taken place; **efficacious** a formal word, used especially to suggest that sth has the power to achieve the desired result.

effectively /i féktivli/ *adv.* **1. WELL** in a way that produces a desired result **2. ESSENTIALLY** in fact or in practical terms, though not usually directly or technically ○ *She was effectively barred from seeking another position with the firm.*

effector /i féktər/ *n.* **1.** PHYSIOL **RESPONDING ORGAN OR MUSCLE** a body part, e.g. a muscle or organ, that is activated by a stimulus, particularly a nerve impulse **2. AGENT CAUSING AN EFFECT** a substance, procedure, or agent that produces an effect, e.g. a nerve ending activating a muscle or a molecule affecting enzyme activity

effectual /i fékchoo əl/ *adj.* (*formal*) **1. POTENTIALLY EFFECTIVE** potentially successful in producing a desired or intended result **2. IN FORCE OR VALID** valid, or legally in force [14thC. From medieval Latin *effectualis*, from Latin *effectus* (see EFFECT).] —**effectuality** /i fékchoo álləti/ *n.* —**effectually** /-əli/ *adv.* —**effectualness** /i fékchoo əlnəss/ *n.*

WORD KEY: USAGE

See Usage note at *effective.*

effectuate /i fékchoo ayt/ (**-ates, -ating, -ated**) *vt.* to do, cause, or accomplish sth (*formal*) [Late 16thC. From medieval Latin *effectuat-*, past participle stem of *effectuare*, from Latin *effectus* (see EFFECT).] —**effectuation** /i fékchoo áysh'n/ *n.*

effeminate /i fémminət/ *adj.* (*disapproving*) **1. LIKE A GIRL OR WOMAN** similar to or imitating a woman or girl, or the behaviour, appearance, or speech traditionally associated with women and girls (*refers to men*) **2. OVERREFINED AND LACKING STRENGTH** weak through overrefinement or an absence of vigorous qualities [14thC. From Latin *effeminatus*, past participle of *effeminare* 'to make feminine', from *femina* 'woman' (source of English *feminine*).] —**effeminacy** *n.* —**effeminate** *n.* —**effeminately** *adv.* —**effeminateness** *n.*

effendi /e féndi/ (*plural* **-dis**) *n.* **1. IMPORTANT MAN** in Middle-Eastern countries, an important or well-educated man **2. TITLE OF RESPECT** a title of respect that is the Turkish equivalent of such terms as 'Mr' and 'Sir' [Early 17thC. Via Turkish *efendi* from modern Greek *aphentēs*, from Greek *authentēs* 'lord, master'.]

efferent /éffərənt/ *adj.* PHYSIOL conducting outwards or directing away from an organ, especially the brain or spinal cord. ◊ **afferent** [Mid-19thC. From Latin *efferent-*, present participle stem of *efferre* 'to bring out', from *ferre* 'to bring or carry'.] —**efferent** *n.*

efferent neuron *n.* ANAT = **motor neuron**

effervesce /éffər véss/ (**-vesces, -vescing, -vesced**) *vi.* **1. TO PRODUCE TINY GAS BUBBLES** to give off gas in small bubbles, often producing foam and a hissing sound (*refers to a liquid such as carbonated water or sparkling wine.*) **2. ESCAPE AS TINY BUBBLES** to be given off by a liquid in the form of small bubbles (*refers to gas*) **3. BE LIVELY OR EXCITED** to behave in a lively, high-spirited, or highly excited way [Early 18thC. From Latin *effervescere*, from *fervescere* 'to come to the boil', from *fervere* 'to be hot, to boil' (source of English *fervent*).] —**effervescence** *n.*

effervescent /éffə véss'nt/ *adj.* **1. BUBBLY** producing gas in the form of tiny bubbles **2. VIVACIOUS** lively and excited —**effervescently** *adv.*

effete /i féet/ *adj.* **1. DECADENT** characterized by decadence, overrefinement, or overindulgence **2. WEAK** lacking or having lost the strength or ability to get things done (*archaic*) **3. BARREN** no longer able to reproduce [Early 17thC. From Latin *effetus* 'worn out by bearing young', from *fetus* 'breeding' (source of English *foetus*).] —**effetely** *adv.* —**effeteness** *n.*

efficacious /éffi káyshəss/ *adj.* having the power to produce the desired result, especially a cure or an improvement in sb's physical condition (*formal*) [Early 16thC. From Latin *efficac-*, stem of *efficax*, from *efficere* (see EFFECT).] —**efficaciously** *adv.* —**efficaciousness** *n.*

WORD KEY: USAGE

See Usage note at *effective.*

efficacy /éffikəssi/, **efficacity** /éffi kássəti/ *n.* ability to produce the necessary or desired results [Early 16thC. From Latin *efficacia*, from *efficax* (see EFFICACIOUS).]

efficiency /i físh'nssi/ (*plural* **-cies**) *n.* **1. COMPETENCE** the ability to do sth well or achieve a desired result without wasted energy or effort, or the degree to which this ability is used **2.** TECH **MEASURE OF A MACHINE'S ENERGY EFFECTIVENESS** the ratio of the amount of energy used by a machine to the amount of work done by it. For example, the measurement of the amount of heat produced per unit of fuel when all of a fuel has been burned is a measure of a heating unit's efficiency. **3.** *US* = **efficiency apartment**

efficiency apartment *n.* *US* a small, usually furnished, flat consisting of one room that includes kitchen facilities, and a bathroom

efficient /i físh'nt/ *adj.* **1. WELL-ORGANIZED** performing tasks in an organized and capable way **2. ABLE TO FUNCTION WITHOUT WASTE** able to function well or achieve a desired result without waste ○ *an efficient use of fuel* **3.** PHILOSOPHY **ACTING DIRECTLY TO PRODUCE AN EFFECT** acting directly to bring sth into being or produce changes in it ○ *efficient cause* [14thC. From Latin *efficient-*, present participle stem of *efficere* (see EFFECT).] —**efficiently** *adv.*

WORD KEY: USAGE

See Usage note at *effective.*

effigy /éffiji/ (*plural* **-gies**) *n.* **1. DUMMY REPRESENTING SB DISLIKED** a dummy, often roughly made and intentionally amusing or insulting, representing sb or sth disliked or despised **2. CARVING** a carved representation of sb, used, e.g. as an architectural decoration or a monument [Mid-16thC. From Latin *effigies*, from *effingere* 'to portray or form', from *fingere* 'to fashion or shape'.]

effing /éffing/ *adj.* used as a euphemism for 'fucking', usually to express extreme annoyance, or inserted to add emphasis to what is being said (*slang offensive*)

effloresce /éfflə réss/ (**-resces, -rescing, -resced**) *vi.* **1.** CHEM **LOSE WATER FROM CRYSTAL** to lose water (**water of crystallization**) from a crystal **2. BLOOM** to bloom or develop, like a flower coming into blossom (*literary*) **3. PRODUCE FINE POWDER** to become covered with a layer of fine powder **4.** CHEM **BECOME ENCRUSTED WITH POWDERY DEPOSIT** to become encrusted with a powdery deposit or crystals as a result of a process of chemical change or the evaporation of a solution [Late 18thC. From Latin *efflorescere*, from *florescere* 'to come into flower', ultimately from *flos* 'flower'.]

efflorescence /éfflə réss'nss/ *n.* **1.** CHEM **LOSS OF WATER FROM CRYSTAL** the loss of water (**water of crystallization**) from a crystal **2. UNFOLDING AND FLOURISHING** a process or time of development and unfolding, or the culmination of this (*literary*) **3.** GEOL **POWDERY SUBSTANCE ON ROCK SURFACE** a powdery substance that forms on the surface of some rocks —**efflorescent** *adj.*

effluence /éffloo ənss/ *n.* **1. FLOWING OUT** the act or process of flowing out **2. STH THAT FLOWS OUT** sth, often an immaterial substance or intangible influence, that flows out from a source (*literary*)

effluent /éffloo ənt/ *n.* **1. LIQUID WASTE** liquid waste discharged from a sewage system, factory, nuclear power station, or other industrial plant **2. STREAM OR RIVER** a stream or river that flows out of a larger body of water such as a lake or a larger stream [15thC. From Latin *effluent-*, present participle stem of *effluere* 'to flow out', from *fluere* 'to flow' (source of English *fluent* and *fluid*).]

effluvium /i flóovi əm, e-/ (plural **-a** /-ə/) n. an unpleasant smell or harmful fumes given off by sth, usually waste or decaying matter (often used in the plural) [Mid-17thC. From Latin, formed from effluere (see EFFLUENT).] —**effluvial** adj.

efflux /éff luks/ n. **1.** INSTANCE OR ACT OF FLOWING OUT the act or process of flowing out **2.** STH THAT FLOWS OUT sth that flows out of sth else (formal) **3.** PASSING AWAY OF STH a passing away of sth, e.g. time (formal) [Mid-16thC. From medieval Latin effluxus, from Latin efflux-, past participle stem of effluere (see EFFLUENT).] —**effluxion** /i flúksh'n, e-/ n.

effort /éffərt/ n. **1.** ENERGY OR EXERTION mental or physical energy that is exerted in order to achieve a purpose ○ I wish they'd put a bit more effort into it. **2.** USE OF PHYSICAL OR MENTAL ENERGY the use of physical or mental energy, often in considerable quantities, in order to achieve a particular goal or overcome a particular difficulty ○ With an effort, he managed to get himself out of the bed. **3.** ATTEMPT an attempt to do sth, especially one that involves a considerable amount of exertion, work, or determination ○ He can at last make an effort to improve things. **4.** STH DONE sth that sb has made or done, especially for the first time ○ It's not bad for a first effort. **5.** PHYS APPLIED FORCE the force (**input force**) applied to a simple machine that produces an effect (**output force**) on the load [15thC. From French, formed from Old French esforcier 'to exert power', ultimately from Latin fortis 'strong'.] —**effortful** adj. —**effortfully** adv.

effortless /éffərtləss/ adj. involving or appearing to involve little or no effort —**effortlessly** adv. —**effortlessness** n.

effrontery /i frúntəri/ (plural **-ies**) n. behaviour or an attitude that is so bold or arrogant as to be insulting [Late 17thC. Via French effronterie from, ultimately, late Latin effrons 'barefaced', from frons 'forehead'.]

effulgence /i fúljənss, i fool-/ n. brightness or a brilliant light radiating from sth (literary) [Mid-17thC. From late Latin effulgentia, from Latin effulgere 'to shine brightly', from fulgere 'to shine'.] —**effulgent** adj.

effuse v. /i fyóoz/ (**-fuses, -fusing, -fused**) **1.** vti. POUR OUT to flow out, or produce a flow of sth such as a liquid, gas, or light (formal) **2.** vti. POUR OUT WORDS AND IDEAS to pour out words and ideas, or speak profusely about sth, generally in an excited way (formal) **3.** vi. RADIATE to spread out or radiate from sth ■ adj. /i fyóoss/ BOT IRREGULARLY SPREAD tending to spread loosely or irregularly ○ effuse lichens [15thC. From Latin effus-, past participle stem of effundere 'to pour out', from fundere 'to pour' (source of English futile).]

effusion /i fyóozh'n/ n. **1.** UNRESTRAINED OUTPOURING OF FEELINGS an extravagant and sometimes excessive expression of feelings in speech or writing **2.** ACT OF POURING OUT the pouring out of sth such as a liquid or light **3.** STH POURED OUT sth, e.g. a liquid, that is poured out **4.** MED MOVEMENT OF BODY FLUIDS the oozing of fluids from blood or lymph vessels into body cavities or intercellular tissue spaces as a result of inflammation, or the presence of excess blood or tissue fluid **5.** PHYS FLOW OF GAS THROUGH A SMALL APERTURE the flow of a gas through a small aperture under pressure, particularly when the aperture is so small that the distance between molecules is significant. The relative rates of effusion of gases are inversely proportional to the square roots of their densities in such a case.

effusive /i fyóossiv/ adj. giving or involving an extravagant and sometimes excessive expression of feelings in writing or speech ○ effusive thanks —**effusively** adv.

Efik /éffik/ (plural **-ik** or **-iks**) n. **1.** PEOPLES MEMBER OF A NIGERIAN PEOPLE a member of an Ibibio people who live in southeastern Nigeria **2.** LANG LANGUAGE SPOKEN IN PARTS OF NIGERIA a language spoken in parts of Nigeria that is one of the Niger-Congo family of African languages and is used by about four million people. Some linguists classify it with the Kwa branch of the Niger-Congo family, while others think of it as a non-Bantu language, forming part of the Benue-Congo branch. [Mid-19thC. From Efik.] —**Efik** adj.

EFL abbr. English as a Foreign Language

EFM abbr. electronic foetal monitor

eft /eft/ n. **1.** IMMATURE NEWT an immature newt in the terrestrial phase, usually reddish-orange in colour. Latin name: Notophthalmus viridescens. **2.** NEWT a newt (regional informal) [Old English efta, of unknown origin]

EFTA /éftə/ abbr. European Free Trade Association

EFTPOS /éft poss/ abbr. electronic funds transfer at point of sale

EFTS /efts/ n., abbr. electronic funds transfer system

e.g., **eg, eg.** abbr. for or as an example [From Latin 'for example']

EGA abbr. COMPUT enhanced graphics adapter

egad /i gád, ee-/ interj. used as an exclamation, generally to express surprise (archaic) [Late 17thC. From an alteration of AH + gad, a euphemism for GOD.]

egalitarian /i gálli táiri ən/ adj. maintaining, relating to, or based on a belief that all people are, in principle, equal and should enjoy equal social, political, and economic rights and opportunities [Late 19thC. From French égalitaire, from égal 'equal', from Latin aequalis (see EQUAL).] —**egalitarian** n. —**egalitarianism** /i gálli táiri ənizəm/ n.

Egeria /i jéeri ə/ n. a woman who acts as a trusted adviser or loyal companion (literary) [Early 17thC. From the Roman goddess who acted as adviser to the early Roman king Numa Pompilius.]

egest /i jést/ (**egests, egesting, egested**) vt. to excrete sth from a cell or organism (formal) [15thC. From Latin egest-, past participle stem of egerere, literally 'to carry out', from gerere 'to carry'.] —**egestion** /i jéss chən/ n. —**egestive** adj.

egesta /i jéstə/ npl. waste materials excreted from a cell or organism [Early 18thC. From Latin, neuter plural of egestus, past participle of egerere (see EGEST).]

egg[1] /eg/ n. **1.** BIOL ANIMAL REPRODUCTIVE STRUCTURE a large sex cell produced by birds, fish, insects, reptiles, or amphibians, enclosed in a protective covering that allows the fertilized embryo to continue developing outside the mother's body until it hatches **2.** BIRDS, FOOD HARD-SHELLED OBJECT LAID BY HEN the hard-shelled, oval, cream- or light-brown egg produced by a hen or similar fowl, used as food **3.** STH SHAPED LIKE A HEN'S EGG sth that resembles a hen's egg in shape, e.g. a carved or moulded ornament or chocolate made in an egg shape **4.** BIOL FEMALE REPRODUCTIVE CELL a female reproductive cell **5.** PERSON a person (dated informal) ○ All in all, he's not a bad egg. [14thC. From Old Norse. Ultimately from an Indo-European word that is also the ancestor of English ovary.] —**eggy** adj. ◇ **have egg on your face** to be left in an embarrassing or humiliating situation, especially because of having made an obvious mistake ◇ **put all your eggs in one basket** to rely entirely on one thing or person, or on the outcome of one plan or course of action

egg[2] /eg/ (**eggs, egging, egged**) vt. to encourage sb to do sth, especially sth wrong, foolish, or dangerous ○ She never would have done it herself, but the girls were egging her on. [12thC. From Old Norse eggja 'to urge', from a prehistoric Germanic word that is also the ancestor of English edge.]

Egg-and-dart

egg-and-dart n. an ornamental pattern, commonly used in mouldings on buildings or furniture, in which egg-shaped figures alternate with slightly tapered bars, arrows, or anchors

eggar n. ZOOL = egger

eggbeater /ég beetər/ n. **1.** HOUSEHOLD UTENSIL FOR BEATING EGGS a kitchen utensil used for beating or blending such ingredients as raw eggs or cream, especially one with two sets of spaced vertical blades rotated by turning a handle **2.** US AIR HELICOPTER a rotary-wing aircraft (slang)

egg bread n. US a soft cake of cornmeal and eggs, baked in a pan (regional)

eggcase n. a protective covering containing eggs, especially one produced by insects and molluscs

eggcup /ég kup/ n. a small bowl-shaped container, often with a short neck and wide base below the bowl, used for holding a boiled egg while it is being eaten

egg custard n. = custard n. 2

egger /éggər/, **eggar** n. a moth with a brown body and wings whose larvae spin egg-shaped cocoons in the branches of trees. Family: Lasiocampidae. [Early 18thC. Origin uncertain: probably from EGG, because of its egg-shaped cocoon.]

egg flip n. a drink made by mixing beaten egg, sugar, and an alcoholic beverage, usually sherry, brandy, or port

egg foo yung n. US = foo yung

egghead /ég hed/ n. sb who is very intelligent and whose interests are mainly intellectual and bookish (informal) [Early 20thC. From the idea that a high forehead indicates brains.] —**eggheaded** /ég héddid/ adj.

eggnog /égg nóg, ég nog/ n. a drink made of milk or cream, eggs, sugar, spice, and sometimes an alcoholic beverage such as brandy or rum, traditionally served in the winter, especially at Christmas [Early 19thC. Nog was a kind of strong beer (origin unknown).]

eggplant /ég plaant/ n. **1.** US, Can, ANZ PLANT WITH LARGE EDIBLE FRUIT a plant of the nightshade family that comes originally from southern and eastern Asia, and is closely related to the potato. Latin name: Solanum melongena. **2.** US, Can, ANZ FRUIT OF EGGPLANT the large, oval, fleshy, edible fruit of the eggplant, usually purple-skinned but also occurring in other colours, and widely used in dishes of Mediterranean origin **3.** US = aubergine

egg roll n. US a Chinese-American snack similar to a spring roll

egg sac n. the pouch or cocoon that a female spider spins to protect its eggs

eggs Benedict n. ham and a poached egg in hollandaise sauce on top of a slice of toast or a split toasted muffin, usually served for breakfast or brunch (takes a singular or plural verb) [Late 19thC. Origin uncertain: perhaps named after Samuel Benedict, a New York socialite, who together with a maître d'hôtel supposedly created the dish as a cure for his hangover.]

eggshell /ég shel/ n. **1.** BIOL HARD COVER OF AN EGG the hard brittle protective outer cover of the egg of a bird, or the similar tough outer covering of the eggs of animals such as crocodiles and turtles **2.** COLOURS PALE WHITISH COLOUR a pale yellowish-white colour ■ adj. **1.** COLOURS YELLOWISH-WHITE of a pale yellowish-white colour **2.** COLOURS SLIGHTLY GLOSSY having a slight sheen, giving a finish between that of gloss and matt paint **3.** FRAGILE, THIN, OR DELICATE as fragile, thin, or delicate as an eggshell ◇ **walk on eggshells** to proceed with extreme wariness, caution, and tact

eggshell blue adj. of a delicate pale blue colour —**eggshell blue** n.

egg slice n. a flat-bladed kitchen utensil for lifting fried eggs or omelettes out of a frying pan

egg timer n. a small hourglass or clockwork timing device used to time the boiling of an egg, usually capable of timing intervals of three to five minutes

egg tooth n. a small projection on the beak of a baby bird or the upper jaw of a baby reptile, used to cut through the eggshell when hatching and later shed

egg white n. the clear viscous liquid found between the yolk and the shell of an egg that turns solid and white when cooked

eglantine /égglən tīn/ (*plural* **-tines** *or* **-tine**) *n*. PLANTS = **sweetbrier** [14thC. Via French *églantine* from, ultimately, Latin *aculentus* 'spiny', ultimately from *acus* 'needle'.]

EGM *abbr*. extraordinary general meeting

Egmont, Mount /ég mont/ dormant volcano in Egmont National Park, southwestern North Island, New Zealand. Height: 2,518 m/8,261 ft.

ego /eégō, éggō/ (*plural* **egos**) *n*. **1.** APPROPRIATE SELF-ESTEEM sb's idea of his or her own importance or worth, usually of an appropriate level **2.** INFLATED OPINION OF YOURSELF an exaggerated sense of your own importance and a feeling of superiority to other people **3.** PSYCHOANAL PART OF THE MIND CONTAINING CONSCIOUSNESS in Freudian psychology, one of three main divisions of the mind, containing consciousness and memory and involved with control, planning, and conforming to reality ○ '*The poor ego has a still harder time of it; it has to serve three harsh masters, and has to do its best to reconcile the claims and demands of all three*'. (Sigmund Freud, *The Anatomy of the Mental Personality, Lecture 31*) ◊ **id**, **superego 2.** PHILOS THE SELF the individual self, as distinct from the outside world and other selves [Early 19thC. From Latin, 'I'.]

egocentric /eégō séntrik, éggō-/ *adj*. **1.** SELFISH interested only in the needs and wants of the self and not caring about other people **2.** LIMITED OR CONFINED IN OUTLOOK limited in outlook to things mainly relating to yourself, or confined to your own affairs or activities **3.** MORE CONCERNED WITH THE INDIVIDUAL THAN SOCIETY concerned with the individual rather than, or at the expense of, society as a whole **4.** PHILOS CENTRED ON THE SELF centred on the individual self, and considering it to be the hub of all experience — **egocentric** *n*. —**egocentrically** *adv*. —**egocentricity** /eégō sen tríssəti, éggō-/ *n*. —**egocentrism** /eégō séntrizəm, éggō-/ *n*.

ego ideal *n*. an ideal image of what you could or should be, built up from observation of parents or other admired people

egoism /eégō izəm, éggō-/ *n*. **1.** = **egotism** *n*. 1 **2.** PHILOS PURSUIT OF YOUR OWN WELFARE AND INTERESTS making personal welfare and interests your primary or only concern, sometimes at the expense of others **3.** ETHICS MORALITY DERIVED FROM SELF-INTEREST the belief that the correct basis for a moral code is every person's concern for his or her own best interests, or the doctrine supporting this belief

——— WORD KEY: USAGE ———

egoism or **egotism**? It is difficult to distinguish between these two words, which are equally common and are often used interchangeably, although there is a theoretical difference between them. *Egoism* refers, in terms of philosophy, to ethical and metaphysical theories in which self-interest is regarded as the principal motivating factor. And so an *egoist* believes an individual should seek as an end only his or her own welfare: *His conduct was characterised by ruthless egoism*. *Egotism* implies a vain and selfish absorption with the self as a matter of behaviour rather than an ethical principle, and an *egotist* is sb who behaves in a selfish or self-centred way: *Her egotism makes her oblivious to other people's concerns*.

egoist /eégō ist, éggō-/ *n*. **1.** ETHICS BELIEVER IN EGOISM sb who believes that the correct basis for a moral code is every person's concern for his or her own best interests **2.** = **egotist** —**egoistic** /eégō ístik, éggō-/ *adj*. —**egoistical** /eégō ístik'l/ *adj*. —**egoistically** /eégō ístikli/ *adv*.

egomania /eégō máyni ə, éggō-/ *n*. a dangerously obsessive preoccupation with the self —**egomaniac** *n*. —**egomaniacal** /eégō mə nī ək'l, éggō-/ *adj*. —**egomaniacally** /eégō mə nī əkli, éggō mə nī ákli/ *adv*.

egotism /eégōtizəm, éggō-/ *n*. **1.** INFLATED SENSE OF SELF-IMPORTANCE the possession of an exaggerated sense of self-importance and superiority to other people **2.** PREOCCUPATION WITH SELF the tendency to speak or write too much about the self **3.** SELFISHNESS selfishness or self-centredness [Early 18thC. Coined from EGO + 't' + -ISM.]

——— WORD KEY: USAGE ———

See Usage note at *egoism*.

egotist /eégōtist, éggō-/ *n*. **1.** CONCEITED PERSON sb with an exaggerated sense of his or her self-importance, especially sb who tends to speak or write about himself or herself all the time **2.** SELFISH PERSON sb who is selfish, self-absorbed, and self-centred — **egotistic** /eégō tístik, éggō-/ *adj*. —**egotistically** /-tístikli/ *adv*.

ego trip *n*. a course of action or an experience the main effect of which is to boost sb's own sense of self-importance (*slang*) —**ego-trip** *vi*. —**ego-tripper** *n*.

egregious /i greejəss, -ji əss/ *adj*. bad, blatant, or ridiculous to an extraordinary degree (*formal*) [Mid-16thC. Formed from Latin *egregius* 'illustrious' (literally 'outside the flock', from *greg-*, stem of *grex* 'flock'.) The original sense was 'remarkably good'.] —**egregiously** *adv*. —**egregiousness** *n*.

egress /eé gress/ *n*. **1.** ACT OF COMING OR GOING OUT the act of coming or going out from or of leaving a place (*formal*) **2.** RIGHT TO LEAVE the right to leave or go out from a place (*formal*) **3.** EXIT OR PATH OUT an exit from a place (*formal*) **4.** ASTRON = **emersion** *n*. 2 ■ *vi*. (**egresses**, **egressing**, **egressed**) COME OUT to come out from or leave a place (*formal*) [Mid-16thC. From Latin *egressus*, from *egredi* 'to go out', from *gradi* 'to proceed, to step'.]

egression /i grésh'n/ *n*. = **egress** *n*. 1

egret /eégrət/ *n*. a heron that produces long drooping ornamental feathers on the lower part of the back at the start of the breeding season. Egrets' feathers were once popular as decorations for women's hats, causing the birds to be hunted almost to extinction. Family: Ardeidae. [14thC. Via Anglo-Norman *egrette* from, ultimately, Provençal *aigreta*, from *aigron* 'heron', ultimately from a prehistoric Germanic word that is also the ancestor of English *heron*.]

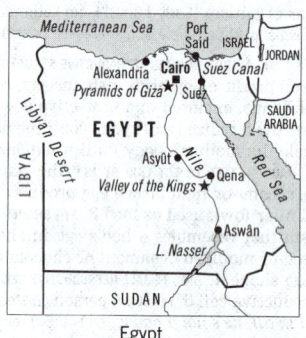

Egypt

Egypt /eéjipt/ country in northeastern Africa bordering the Mediterranean Sea and the Red Sea. It became a republic in 1952. Language: Arabic. Currency: Egyptian pound. Capital: Cairo. Population: 63,575,100 (1996). Area: 997,738 sq. km/385,229 sq. mi. Official name **Arab Republic of Egypt**

Egyptian /i jípsh'n/ *n*. **1.** NATIVE OR CITIZEN OF EGYPT sb who was born in or is a citizen of Egypt **2.** LANGUAGE OF ANCIENT EGYPT the language of ancient Egypt, a now extinct branch of the Afro-Asiatic family of African languages dating from roughly 3000 BC that developed into Coptic around AD 200 **3.** DIALECT OF ARABIC SPOKEN IN EGYPT the dialect of Arabic spoken in modern Egypt. Egyptian is spoken by about 65 million people. ■ *adj*. **1.** RELATING TO EGYPT AND THE EGYPTIANS relating to or typical of Egypt, its people, or their culture **2.** RELATING TO THE LANGUAGE OF ANCIENT EGYPT characteristic of or relating to the language of ancient Egypt **3.** RELATING TO THE ARABIC DIALECT OF EGYPT relating to the dialect of Arabic spoken in modern Egypt

Egyptology /eéjip tólləji/ *n*. the study of the history, archaeology, culture, and language of ancient Egypt —**Egyptologist** *n*.

eh /ay, e/ *interj*. (*informal*) **1.** PARDON? used to ask sb to repeat sth **2.** WHAT? used to express surprise at sth that has been said **3.** ISN'T THAT SO? used to invite sb to respond to sth that has been said, especially to agree with it or confirm that it is correct or accurately sums up a previous statement [Mid-16thC. Natural exclamation.]

EHF *abbr*. extremely high frequency

EHO *abbr*. Environmental Health Officer

Ehrlich /áirlik, -likh/, **Paul** (1854–1915) German bacteriologist and immunologist. His work on immunology won him a shared Nobel Prize in 1908. He also pioneered chemotherapy, developing Salvarsan as a treatment for syphilis.

EHV *abbr*. extra-high voltage

EIA *abbr*. environmental impact assessment

EIB *abbr*. European Investment Bank

Eichendorff /íkən dawrf, íkhən-/, **Joseph, Freiherr von** (1788–1857) German poet. His lyrical poems were set to music by Schumann, Mendelssohn, and others. He also wrote a popular novel, *Memoirs of a Good-for-Nothing* (1826). Full name **Joseph Karl Benedikt von Eichendorff**

Eichmann /íkmən, íkh-/, **Adolf** (1906–62) German Nazi official and war criminal. Nazi official, responsible for carrying out anti-Semitic policy during World War II. He was captured in Argentina in 1960 by Israeli agents, tried in Israel for 'crimes against humanity', and hanged two years later. Full name **Karl Adolf Eichmann**

Eid *n*. ISLAM **1.** = **Eid-ul-Adha 2.** = **Eid-ul-Fitr** [Late 17thC. From Arabic *'īd* 'festival', from Aramaic.]

eider /ídər/ (*plural* **-ders** *or* **-der**), **eider duck** *n*. a large sea duck of the northern hemisphere, the male of which has distinctive black-and-white plumage while the female, the source of eiderdown, has mottled brown plumage. Genus: *Somateria*. [Late 17thC. Via Icelandic *æður* from Old Norse *æðr*.]

eiderdown /ídər down/ *n*. **1.** BED COVERING a bed covering placed on top of sheets and blankets for extra warmth, consisting of a wide flat fabric container stuffed with a filling such as feathers or artificial fibres **2.** EIDER DUCK'S FEATHERS the soft fluffy breast feathers of the female eider duck, used to fill pillows and bed coverings

eidetic /ī déttik/ *adj*. PSYCHOL (*formal*) **1.** RECALLED WITH STARTLING ACCURACY recalled or reproduced with startling accuracy, clarity, and vividness ○ *eidetic images* **2.** ABLE TO RECALL WITH STARTLING ACCURACY able to recall or reproduce things previously seen with startling accuracy, clarity, and vividness ○ *an eidetic memory* [Early 20thC. From Greek *eidētikos*, from *eidos* 'form'.] —**eidetically** *adv*.

eidolon /ī dólən, ī dō lon/ (*plural* **-lons** *or* **-la** /-lə/) *n*. (*literary*) **1.** PHANTOM a ghostly figure or image **2.** AN IDEAL IMAGE an idealized image of sth or sb [Mid-17thC. From Greek *eidōlon* 'idol' (see IDOL).]

Eid-ul-Adha /eéd ool aadə/ *n*. a Muslim festival, the festival of the sacrifice, that marks the end of the annual pilgrimage to Mecca but is celebrated everywhere, especially by the sacrifice of sheep

Eid-ul-Fitr /eéd ool feetər/ *n*. a Muslim festival that marks the end of Ramadan, the period of fasting

Eiffel /íf'l/, **Gustave** (1832–1923) French engineer. A specialist in metal structures, he is best known as the designer of the Eiffel Tower (1889) and architect of the inner structure of the Statue of Liberty (1885). Full name **Alexandre Gustave Eiffel**

Eiffel Tower, Paris, France

AKG London

Eiffel Tower *n*. a 300 m-/984 ft-high iron tower in central Paris. It was designed by Gustave Eiffel for the 1889 Paris Exposition.

Eiger /ígər/ mountain peak in the Bernese Alps, southeast of Bern, Switzerland. The north face of the mountain is notorious for the number of mountaineers who have died attempting to climb it. Height: 3,970 m/13,025 ft.

Eigg /eg/ island of the Inner Hebrides, in north-western Scotland. Area: 67 sq. km/26 sq. mi. Population: 69 (1991).

eight /ayt/ n. **1.** NUMBER 8 the number 8, which is one more than 7 and one fewer than 9 **2.** STH WITH A VALUE OF 8 sth in a numbered series, e.g. a playing card, with a value of eight **3.** GROUP OF 8 a group of eight objects or people **4.** STH WITH 8 PARTS sth composed of eight parts or members, e.g. an eight-cylinder engine **5.** ROWING ROWING CREW a crew of eight rowers **6.** ROWING ROWING BOAT a long narrow rowing boat crewed by eight rowers [Old English e(a)hta. Ultimately from an Indo-European word that is also the ancestor of English *octave*, *October*, and *octo-*.] —**eight** adj., pron. ◇ **have one over the eight** to have too much to drink and get drunk (*informal*)

eight ball n. **1.** US, Can BLACK BALL IN POOL in pool, the black ball, because it has the number 8 on it **2.** FORM OF POOL a form of pool in which a player must pocket a given 7 of the 15 balls, and then pocket the eight ball, before his or her opponent does ◇ **behind the eight ball** US in a difficult or awkward position (*slang*)

eighteen /ay teen, áyt een/ n. **1.** NUMBER 18 the number 18, which is one more than 17 and one fewer than 19 **2.** STH WITH A VALUE OF 18 sth in a numbered series with a value of 18 **3.** GROUP OF 18 a group of 18 objects or people **4.** Aus AUSTRALIAN FOOTBALL TEAM a team of eighteen players in Australian Rules football [Old English e(a)hatēne, ultimately from prehistoric Germanic words that are also the ancestors of English *eight* and *ten*] —**eighteen** adj., pron.

18 certificate n. a certificate designating a film that has been classified as suitable only for people aged 18 or over because of the scenes of sex and violence it contains

eighteenmo /ay teen mō/ (*plural* **-mos**) n. PRINTING = **octodecimo**

eighteenth /ay teenth/ n. **1.** ONE OF 18 PARTS OF STH one of 18 equal parts of sth **2.** BIRTHDAY OF AN 18-YEAR-OLD the birthday of sb who has just reached 18 years of age —**eighteenth** adj., adv.

eightfold /áyt fōld/ adj. **1.** MULTIPLYING BY 8 multiplying the original figure by eight **2.** CONSISTING OF 8 PARTS consisting of eight parts ■ adv. BY A FACTOR OF 8 by eight, or to an amount eight times greater than the original

eighth n. one of eight equal parts of sth —**eighth** adj., adv.

eighth note n. US = **quaver**

eighth rest n. US = **quaver rest**

eightieth /áyti əth/ n. **1.** ONE OF 80 PARTS OF STH one of 80 equal parts of sth **2.** BIRTHDAY OF AN 80-YEAR-OLD the birthday of sb who has just reached 80 years of age —**eightieth** adj., adv.

eightsome reel /áytsəm-/ n. a Scottish social dance in reel time performed by sets of four couples in circles

eightvo /áyt vō/ (*plural* **-vos**) n. = **octavo** [From *8vo*, a written abbreviation for 'octavo']

eighty /áyti/ n. (*plural* **-ies**) **1.** NUMBER 80 the number 80, which is 8 times 10 **2.** GROUP OF 80 a group of 80 objects or people ■ **eighties** npl. **1.** NUMBERS 80 TO 89 the numbers 80 to 89, particularly as a range of temperature **2.** YEARS 1980 TO 1989 the years 1980 to 1989, or the years numbered 80 to 89 in any century **3.** PERIOD FROM AGE 80 TO 89 the period of sb's life from the age of 80 to 89 [13thC. Shortening of Old English *hundeahtatig*, from *hund-*, literally 'hundred' + e(a)hta 'eight' + *-tig* 'group of ten'.] —**eighty** adj., pron.

Eighty-Mile Beach beach in northwestern Western Australia, located 300 km/186 mi. northeast of Port Hedland. Length: 137 km/85 mi.

eighty-six (**eighty-sixes, eighty-sixing, eighty-sixed**), **86** (**86es, 86ing, 86ed**) vt. US (*slang*) **1.** GET RID OF SB to dispose of sb or sth **2.** REFUSE TO SERVE A CUSTOMER to refuse to serve sb in a restaurant or bar [Mid-20thC. Origin uncertain: perhaps rhyming slang for *nix* or from

---

Chumley's bar and grill, 86 Bedford Street, Greenwich Village, New York City.]

Eijkman /íkmən, íkh-/, **Christiaan** (1858–1930) Dutch physician. His research on diet-deficiency diseases, particularly beriberi, revealed the importance of vitamins in human physiology. He shared the Nobel Prize in 1929.

Eilat /ay laát/, **Elat** seaport, tourist resort, and leading oil port in southern Israel, situated at the head of the Gulf of Aqaba. Population: 33,300 (1993).

Eildon and Leaderfoot /eéldən ənd leédərfŏŏt/ designated National Scenic Area in the Scottish Borders district of southern Scotland

Eilean Siar, Comhairle nan /áylən sheer kóllri nən/ council area in the former Western Isles Region, the Outer Hebrides, Scotland

-ein suffix. a chemical compound related to one whose name ends in '-in' or '-ein' ◇ *fluorescein* [Alteration of -IN]

Albert Einstein

Library of Congress

Einstein /ínst īn/, **Albert** (1879–1955) German-born US physicist. His theory of general relativity revolutionized scientific thought and served as the theoretical foundation for later exploitation of atomic energy. He won a Nobel Prize in 1921 for his work explaining the photoelectric effect. He became a Swiss (1905) and later a US citizen (1940). He joined other physicists in writing to President Franklin Roosevelt to warn him that Germany could possibly make an atomic bomb.

einsteinium /ín stíni əm/ n. a synthetic radioactive chemical element, first identified in 1952. It is usually produced by irradiating plutonium and other elements. Symbol **Es** [Named after Albert EINSTEIN]

Einthoven /ínt hōv'n/, **Willem** (1860–1927) Dutch physiologist. His most important invention was the string galvanometer, which recorded precise measurements of electrical activity in the heart. He won the Nobel Prize in 1924.

eirenicon n. a proposal made in order to achieve peace or harmony

EISA abbr. COMPUT extended industry standard architecture

Dwight D. Eisenhower

US Military Academy

Eisenhower /íz'n howər/, **Dwight D.** (1890–1969) US soldier and statesman and 34th President of the United States. He was supreme commander of Allied forces in Europe during World War II. As president he adopted a policy of containing Communism throughout the world. Full name **Dwight David Eisenhower**. Known as **Ike**

Eisenstein, Sergey (1898–1948) Soviet film director. His innovative cinematographic techniques in films such as *The Battleship Potemkin* (1925) make him one of the great figures in the history of cinema.

eisteddfod /ī stédfəd, ī stéth vod/ (*plural* **-fods** or **-fodau** /áy steth vóddī, ī́-/) n. a traditional Welsh festival at which competitions are held for performers and composers of music and poetry [Early 19thC. From Welsh, literally 'session, sitting'.]

eiswein /íss vín/ n. a sweet white wine produced in Germany and Austria from grapes that have frozen on the vine, concentrating the sugar content

either /íthər, eéthər/ CORE MEANING: a grammatical word that introduces two situations, one of which may include or exclude the other ○ (det) *It won't make much difference either way.* ○ (pron) *I refuse to meet either of them.* ○ (conj) *Either there's a problem or there isn't.*

1. det., pron. ONE OR THE OTHER one or the other, when it does not matter which ○ (det) *You can execute commands on either machine.* ○ (pron) *If either fell behind, the other would help him to catch up.* ○ (pron) *You can get this information from either of the two addressees.* **2.** det., pron. INDICATES A NEGATIVE used to refer negatively to each of two situations where the negative includes them both ○ (det) *You cannot send e-mails to either address at the moment.* ○ (pron) *I'm not interested in either of them.* **3.** det. BOTH both of two things ○ *The red and yellow patches on either side of the sun are radiation from the dust ring.* **4.** conj. INDICATES ALTERNATIVES used to indicate that there is a choice between two or more options ○ *The only way to get round the city was either by the super freeways or by the canals and the gondolas.* ○ *Data sources may be either digital or analog.* **5.** adv. INDICATES CONNECTION used in a negative statement that indicates a connection or a partial agreement with a previous statement (*used at the end of a second statement*) ○ *You won't find really bad conditions, but you won't find luxury hotels either.* [Old English ǣgper, contraction of ǣg(e)hwæper, from a prehistoric Germanic phrase meaning 'always each of two', which contained the ancestors of English *aye* and *whether*]

--- **WORD KEY: USAGE** ---
Singular or plural after **either**? *Either* is normally used with a singular verb: *Has either of you been to Paris? Either Lee or David is responsible.* Informally, however, the plural is used when the choices are regarded collectively rather than individually, and it is quite natural to say *Have either of you been to Paris?*, which caters for the possibility that both the people addressed have done so. When **either ... or ...** occurs with a mixture of singular and plural subjects, the verb traditionally agrees with the one that is closer to it: *Either David or his parents are at home.*

either-or adj. offering a choice strictly limited to two options ○ *It's an either-or situation – either you accept or you refuse.*

ejaculate v. /i jákyŏŏ layt/ (**-lates, -lating, -lated**) **1.** vti. EJECT SEMEN DURING ORGASM to eject semen from the penis during an orgasm **2.** vt. EXCLAIM STH SUDDENLY to exclaim sth suddenly and usually forcefully (*literary*) ■ n. /i jákyoolət/ EJACULATED SEMEN semen that has been ejected from the penis during orgasm [Late 16thC. From Latin *ejaculat-*, past participle stem of *ejaculari* 'to throw out', ultimately from *jacere* 'to throw' (source of English *inject* and *project*).]

ejaculation /i jákyŏŏ láysh'n/ n. **1.** EJECTING OF SEMEN FROM PENIS the ejecting of semen from the penis during an orgasm **2.** SUDDEN EXCLAMATION a sudden, usually loud or forceful exclamation (*literary*)

ejaculatory /i jákyŏŏlətəri/ adj. **1.** RELATING TO EJACULATION involved in or related to the structures involved in ejaculation ○ *ejaculatory ducts* **2.** CHARACTERIZED BY SUDDEN BURSTS OF SPEECH spoken in or characterized by short bursts of loud or forceful speech (*formal*)

eject /i jékt/ (**ejects, ejecting, ejected**) v. **1.** vt. PUSH STH OUT WITH FORCE to cause sth to burst out from sth else with considerable force **2.** vt. REMOVE SB FROM A PLACE OR POSITION to force sb to leave a place or give up a position, e.g. a job or membership ○ *They were forcibly ejected from the meeting.* **3.** vi. AIR LEAVE AN AIRCRAFT IN AN ESCAPE DEVICE to escape from an aircraft in an emergency by means of an ejector seat or special capsule **4.** *vt.* LAW **EVICT SB** to remove sb, especially a tenant, from a property by taking legal action [15thC. From Latin *eject-*, past participle stem of *e(j)icere*, from *jacere* 'to throw'.] —**ejectable** *adj.* —**ejection** /i jéksh'n/ *n.* —**ejective** *adj.*

ejecta /i jéktə/ *n.* substances ejected from sth, especially the material thrown out by a volcanic eruption or from a star (*formal; takes a singular or plural verb*) [Late 19thC. From Latin, a plural form of the past participle of *e(j)icere* (see EJECT).]

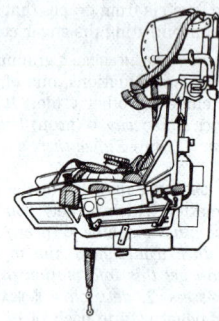
Ejection seat

ejection seat *n. US* AIR = **ejector seat**

ejectment /i jéktmənt/ *n.* **1.** EJECTING OR BEING EJECTED the process of ejecting sb or sth, or of being ejected from somewhere (*formal*) **2.** LAW RECOVERY OF REAL PROPERTY a legal action brought by sb to recover possession of land that is being held by sb else

ejector /i jéktər/ *n.* **1.** DEVICE FOR EJECTING STH a device for ejecting sth from sth else, especially a mechanism for ejecting an empty cartridge or shell from a gun **2.** PUMP USED TO WITHDRAW STH a jet pump device that uses water, steam, or air to remove a gas, fluid, or powder from a space

ejector seat *n.* a seat in the cockpit of an aircraft that in an emergency propels the occupant clear of the craft by means of a rocket or explosive device. US term **ejection seat**

eke out /eek-/ (**ekes out, eking out, eked out**) *vt.* **1.** MAKE STH LAST WITH SPARING USE to make a supply of sth last by using it as slowly and economically as possible **2.** SUPPLEMENT STH INSUFFICIENT OR INADEQUATE to supplement sth that is insufficient or inadequate, usually with difficulty and by hard work **3.** GET STH ONLY WITH EFFORT to manage to get or achieve sth but only on a small scale and with a great deal of effort ○ *eked out a bare existence* [Late 16thC. Later form of Old English *ēacan, ēacian,* from a prehistoric Germanic base related to Latin *augere* 'to increase'.]

ekistics /i kístiks/ *n.* the study of human settlements in all their aspects, including, e.g., the origin and development of towns and town planning (*takes a singular verb*) [Mid-20thC. From Greek *oikistikos,* from *oikizein* 'to settle', from *oikos* 'house' (source of English *economy* and *parish*).] —**ekistic** *adj.* —**ekistician** /éki stísh'n/ *n.*

el /el/ *n. US* an elevated railway in a city (*informal*)

elaborate *adj.* /i lábbərət/ **1.** COMPLEX having many different parts or a lot of detail and being organized in a complicated way **2.** FINELY OR RICHLY DECORATED made with a lot of intricate detail or extravagant ornamentation ○ *an elaborate headdress* **3.** DETAILED AND THOROUGH thought out or organized with thoroughness and careful attention to detail ■ *v.* /i lábbə rayt/ (**-rates, -rating, -rated**) **1.** *vi.* GIVE MORE DETAIL ABOUT STH to go into greater detail about sth that has already been spoken about or described in broad terms ○ *Would you care to elaborate on that?* **2.** *vt.* WORK STH OUT IN DETAIL to work out the details of sth **3.** *vti.* MAKE OR BECOME MORE COMPLEX to make sth more complex or ornate, or become more complex or ornate [15thC. From Latin *elaborat-,* past participle stem of *elaborare* 'to produce by effort or labour', from *labor* 'labour'.] —**elaborately** /i lábbərətli/ *adv.* —**elaborateness** /i lábbə ráysh'n/ *n.* —**elaboration** /i lábbə ráysh'n/ *n.* —**elaborator** /i lábbə raytər/ *n.*

Elam /éeləm/ ancient state in southwestern Iran, east of the River Tigris. It was established before 4000 BC and corresponds to the present-day Khuzistan Province, Iran.

Elamite /éeləm īt/ *n.* **1.** PEOPLES SB FROM ANCIENT ELAM sb who was born or who lived in the ancient Middle Eastern kingdom of Elam **2.** LANG ANCIENT LANGUAGE OF ELAM an extinct language formerly spoken in the ancient kingdom of Elam. Elamite has been attested by important discoveries of pictographic and cuneiform inscriptions dating from the third millennium BC through to the first millennium AD. ■ *adj.* RELATING TO ELAM relating to or typical of Elam, or its people, language, or culture —**Elamitic** /éelə míttik/ *adj.*

élan /ay lóN, ay lán/, **elan** *n.* vigour and enthusiasm, often combined with self-confidence and style (*literary*) [Mid-19thC. From French *élan,* formed from *élancer* 'to dart, throw', ultimately from *lance* 'LANCE'.]

Eland

eland /éeländ/ (*plural* **elands** *or* **eland**) *n.* the largest of living antelopes, found in central and southern Africa and distinguished by its humped shoulders, dewlap, and tightly spiralling horns. Genus: *Taurotragus.* [Late 18thC. Via Afrikaans from Dutch, 'elk', ultimately from Lithuanian *élnis.*]

élan vital /ay lóN vee taál, ay lán–/ *n.* in the philosophy of Henri Bergson, a creative life force present in all living things and responsible for evolution [From French]

elapid /élləpid/ *n.* a venomous snake that has its short fangs at the front of the upper jaw. Cobras, coral snakes, and mambas are elapids. Family: Elapidae. [Late 19thC. From modern Latin *Elapidae,* family name, ultimately from Greek *elaps,* variant of *el(l)ops,* a kind of fish, also a kind of sea serpent.] —**elapid** *adj.*

elapse /i láps/ *vi.* (**elapses, elapsing, elapsed**) GO BY to pass or go by, especially in a gradual, slow, or imperceptible way ○ *several hours elapsed* ■ *n.* PASSING OF A PERIOD OF TIME the passing of a certain period of time (*formal*) [Late 16thC. From Latin *elaps-,* past participle stem of *elabi* 'to slip away', from *labi* 'to glide, fall' (source of English *lapse*).]

Elara /éllərə/ *n.* a small natural satellite of Jupiter, discovered in 1905. It is approximately 80 km in diameter and occupies an intermediate orbit.

elasmobranch /i lássmə brangk, i lázmə–/ *n.* a fish with a cartilaginous skeleton. Sharks, rays, and skates are elasmobranchs. Subclass: Elasmobranchii. [Late 19thC. From modern Latin *Elasmobranchii,* subclass name, from Greek *elasmos* 'beaten metal' + *bragkhia* 'gills'.] —**elasmobranch** *adj.*

elastic /i lástik/ *n.* **1.** STRETCHY MATERIAL a strip or thread of rubber or similar stretchable material, or a fabric or tape with a stretchy material woven into it so that it can fit tightly round sth **2.** *US* = **rubber band** ■ *adj.* **1.** STRETCHY AND FLEXIBLE able to return quickly to its original shape and size after being bent, stretched, or squashed **2.** EASILY CHANGED able to incorporate changes or adapt to new circumstances easily **3.** MADE OF ELASTIC made of elastic **4.** SPRINGY having a light springy or bouncy quality, especially in movement **5.** PHYS RETURNING TO ITS ORIGINAL SHAPE AFTER STRESS used to describe a substance that is capable of returning to its original shape after undergoing stress or deformation [Mid-17thC. Via modern Latin *elasticus* from Greek *elastikos* 'driving, propelling', from *elaunein* 'to drive'. Originally used in describing the way gas expands.] —**elastically** *adv.*

elasticate /i lásti kayt/ (**-cates, -cating, -cated**) *vt.* to put strips or threads of rubber or some similar material into a fabric or item of clothing in order to make it stretchy and tight-fitting. US term **elasticize** *v.* 1

elastic band *n.* = **rubber band**

elastic collision *n.* a collision between two perfectly elastic bodies such that the final kinetic energy of the system is the same as the initial kinetic energy of the system

elastic fibre *n.* a smooth, long, thin, branching fibre in connective tissue, composed mainly of the fibrous protein elastin

elasticity /ée lass tíssəti/ *n.* **1.** ABILITY TO RETURN TO SHAPE the ability of an object or substance to return quickly to its original shape and size after being bent, stretched, or squashed **2.** FLEXIBILITY the ability to incorporate changes or adapt to new circumstances easily **3.** PHYS ABILITY TO REGAIN DIMENSIONS AFTER STRESS the property that makes a material return to its original dimensions after being stressed or deformed, or the degree to which this is exhibited **4.** ECON RELATIVE CHANGE IN AN ECONOMIC VARIABLE the relative change in an economic variable, e.g. demand, that occurs in reaction to changes in other variables, e.g. price or advertising input

elasticize /i lásti sīz/ (**-cizes, -cizing, -cized**) *vt.* **1.** *US* = **elasticate 2.** MAKE STH ELASTIC to make sth elastic or more elastic

elastic limit *n.* the maximum stress that can be applied to a material without the material becoming permanently deformed

elastin /i lástin/ *n.* a fibrous protein resembling collagen that is the main constituent of the elastic fibres of connective tissue [Late 19thC. Coined from ELASTIC + -IN.]

elastomer /i lástəmər/ *n.* a natural material, e.g. rubber, or a synthetic material, e.g. polyvinyl, that has elastic properties [Mid-20thC. Coined from ELASTIC + -MER.] —**elastomeric** /i lástə mérrik/ *adj.*

Elastoplast /i lástə plaast/ *tdmk.* a tradename for a range of plasters, bandages, and dressings

elate /i láyt/ (**elates, elating, elated**) *vt.* to make sb very happy and excited [Late 16thC. From Latin *elat-* (source of English *translate*), used as the past participle stem of *efferre* 'to carry up', from *ferre* 'to carry'.] —**elate** *adj.*

elated /i láytid/ *adj.* very happy and excited —**elatedly** *adv.* —**elatedness** *n.*

elater /éllətər/ *n.* a beetle that belongs to the click beetle family. Family: Elateridae. [Mid-17thC. From Greek *elatēr* 'driver', from *elaunein* 'to drive' (source of English *elastic*).]

elaterid /i láttərid/ *n.* = **elater** ■ *adj.* OF THE CLICK BEETLE FAMILY belonging or relating to the click beetle family

elation /i láysh'n/ *n.* a feeling of extraordinary happiness and excitement

Elba

Elba /élbə/ mountainous island off the western coast of Italy, the place of Napoleon's first period of exile (1814–15)

Elbe /elb/ river in central Europe that rises in the northern Czech Republic and flows about 1,167 km/725 mi. northwest to the North Sea

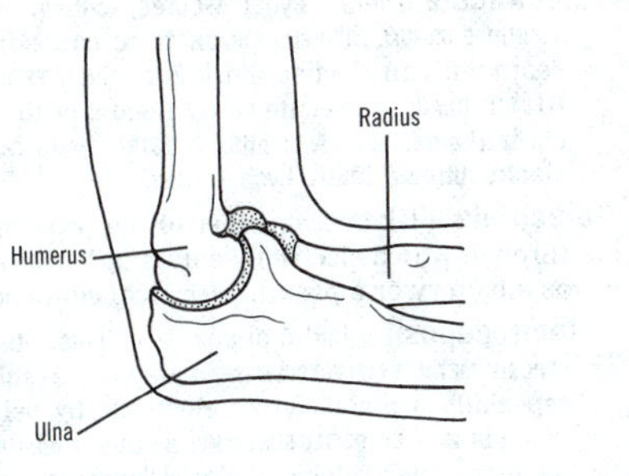

Elbow

elbow /élbō/ *n.* **1.** ANAT **JOINT IN THE ARM** the joint between the upper and lower parts of the human arm **2.** CLOTHES **PART OF A SLEEVE COVERING THE ELBOW** the part of a sleeve that covers the elbow **3.** ZOOL **JOINT IN AN ANIMAL LEG** the joint in an animal's forelimb corresponding to the elbow in humans **4.** CONSTR **BEND** a bend in sth such as a river, road, or pipe **5.** CONSTR **STH BENT** sth, especially a piece of pipe, made with a bend in it ■ *vti.* **(-bows, -bowing, -bowed) PUSH STH WITH THE ELBOW** to push or hit sb or sth with the elbow, or progress through a crowd by pushing with the elbow or elbows [Old English *el(n)boga*, literally 'arm bend', from the prehistoric Germanic ancestors of English *ell* and *bow*] ◇ **bend the** *or* **your elbow** to drink alcohol often (*informal*) ◇ **get the elbow, be given the elbow** to be dismissed or rejected (*informal*) ◇ **out at elbow, out at the elbows** poorly dressed, or short of money

elbow grease *n.* hard physical effort or work with the arms, especially scrubbing or polishing (*informal*)

elbowroom /élbō room, -rŏŏm/ *n.* (*informal*) **1. SPACE TO MOVE AROUND IN COMFORTABLY** space to move around or work in comfortably **2. FREEDOM TO TRY STH NEW** freedom from restriction for a time, especially to move or develop in a new area or direction

Elbrus, Mount /il brŏŏss/, **El'brus** the highest mountain in Europe, in the Caucasus Mountains in southern Russia, near the border with Georgia. Height: 5,642 m/18,510 ft.

Elburz Mountains /el bŏŏrz-/ mountain range in northern Iran, near the southern shore of the Caspian Sea. The highest peak is Damāvand, 5,604 m/18,386 ft.

elder[1] /éldər/ *adj.* **1. BORN EARLIER** born before others, especially within a family, or having more seniority. ➧ **Usage note below 2. SUPERIOR** superior to others, either by rank or experience ■ *n.* **1. PERSON BORN EARLIER** sb who was born before sb else ○ *She is five years my elder.* **2.** CHR **SENIOR MEMBER OF A CHURCH** a senior lay member in some Christian churches with responsibility for some aspects of church administration, the pastoral care of church members, and sometimes for teaching and preaching **3.** ANTHROP **SENIOR MEMBER OF A COMMUNITY** a member of a family, tribal group, or village who is respected for advanced years and has some influence and authority within the community **4.** *Can* **RESPECTED ADVISER** a respected senior member of a First Nations group who acts as an adviser [Old English *(i)eldra*, from a prehistoric Germanic word that is also the ancestor of English *eldest* and *old*] —**eldership** *n.*

WORD KEY: USAGE

elder or **older**? ***Elder*** and *eldest* are used only of people, and usually in the context of family relationships: *She is the elder of Ruth's daughters. Mark is my eldest son.* ***Older*** and *oldest* can apply to things as well as people and can be used in a wider range of grammatical constructions: *I am older than David. It is the oldest church in Paris.* When ***elder*** is used after a verb (for example *be*), it has to be preceded by *the*: *Who is the eldest?* not *Who is eldest?*

elder[2] /éldər/ *n.* a common shrub or small tree of the honeysuckle family that has flat clusters of white flowers and purplish-black berries. Latin name: *Sambucus nigra.* [Old English *ellærn*, of uncertain origin]

elderberry /éldər berri, -bəri/ (*plural* **-ries**) *n.* **1. FRUIT OF THE ELDER TREE** the purplish-black fruit of the elder tree, sometimes used to make wine **2.** BOT = **elder**[2]

elderly /éldərli/ *adj.* **1. PAST MIDDLE AGE** past middle age and approaching the rest of life (*sometimes considered offensive*) **2. CHARACTERISTIC OF OLDER PEOPLE** characteristic of or relating to older people **3. OLD-FASHIONED** old and somewhat old-fashioned ■ *npl.* **OLDER PEOPLE AS A GROUP** older people, considered as a group (*sometimes considered offensive*) —**elderliness** *n.*

elder statesman *n.* a person, advanced in years and experience, especially a politician or former politician, who is respected for his or her wisdom and whose advice is still valued and unofficially sought

eldest /éldist/ *adj.* first, either in age or seniority [Old English *(i)eldest*, from a prehistoric Germanic word that is also the ancestor of English *elder*[1] and *old*]

WORD KEY: USAGE

See Usage note at ***elder.***

ELDO /éldō/ *abbr.* SPACE TECH European Launch Development Organization

Eldon /éldən/, **1st Earl of** (1751–1838) British judge and statesman A judicially brilliant and strongly conservative lord chancellor (1801–06 and 1807–21), he was a leading opponent of the parliamentary Reform Bill (1832). Born **John Scott**

El Dorado /él də raádō/ *n.* **1. LEGENDARY PLACE OF FABULOUS WEALTH** a legendary place in South America where the streets were said to be paved with gold and wealth and riches were to be had in abundance **2. PLACE OF RICHES** a place that has great wealth or where great riches can be acquired [From Spanish, literally 'the gilded']

Eleatic /élli áttik/ *adj.* relating to an ancient Greek school of philosophy founded by Xenophanes or Parmenides that flourished in the 5th and 6th centuries BC. It advocated philosophical reflection over sensory observation. [Late 19thC. From Latin *Eliaticus*, from *Elea*, an ancient Greek city in southwestern Italy where the school flourished.] —**Eleatic** *n.* —**Eleaticism** /élli áttissizəm/ *n.*

elec. *abbr.* **1.** electric **2.** electrical **3.** electricity

elecampane /élli kam páyn/ (*plural* **-panes** *or* **-pane**) *n.* a tall perennial flowering plant that is related to daisies and dandelions and has yellow flowers and large toothed hairy leaves. It is a natural antibiotic and digestive stimulant, and the roots are used to make a herbal remedy that is effective in the treatment of coughs and fevers. Latin name: *Inula helenium.* [14thC. Ultimately a contraction of medieval Latin *enula campana*, literally 'elecampane of the fields', from *enula* 'elecampane', via Latin *inula* from Greek *helenion.*]

elect /i lékt/ *v.* **(elects, electing, elected) 1.** *vt.* **CHOOSE SB BY VOTE** to choose sb by a vote, e.g. for public office, an official role, or membership of some group ○ *She was elected leader of the commission.* **2.** *vt.* **DECIDE TO DO STH** to make a decision to do sth **3.** *vt.* RELIG **CHOOSE SB FOR SALVATION** to choose sb by divine will for salvation **4.** *vti. US* **CHOOSE STH** to choose or select sth, particularly a subject or course to study at university ○ *He elected French as his main subject.* ■ *adj.* **1. CHOSEN BUT NOT YET IN OFFICE** chosen by a vote but not yet formally installed in office (*used after a noun*) ○ *the president elect* **2.** RELIG **CHOSEN BY GOD** specially chosen by God for favour, salvation, or a task ○ *'Samson has assumed that, as an elect instrument, he must be always actively engaged in God's service'.* (John Spencer Hill, *John Milton: Poet, Priest and Prophet*; 1979) ■ *npl.* **1.** RELIG **PEOPLE CHOSEN BY GOD** people specially chosen or favoured by God, e.g. those chosen by God for salvation **2. SELECT GROUP** a specially privileged or gifted group (*literary*) ○ *World-class opera singers are among today's elect.* [15thC. From Latin *electus*, from *eligere* 'to choose', from *legere* (source of English *collect*, *neglect*, and *lecture*).]

electable /i léktəb'l/ *adj.* worthy to be elected, or having a good chance of being elected, especially to a public office —**electability** /i léktə bílləti/ *n.*

election /i léksh'n/ *n.* **1. EVENT FOR CHOOSING BY VOTE** an organized event at which sb is chosen for sth, especially a public office, by vote **2. CHOOSING OR BEING CHOSEN BY VOTE** the process of choosing sb or of being chosen by vote ○ *he stood for election* **3. SELECTION OF STH** the act or process of choosing sth, e.g. a course of action or subject (*formal*) **4.** RELIG **SELECTION BY GOD FOR STH** the fact of being chosen by God, or God's act of choosing sb for salvation, a task, or special favour

electioneer /i lékshə néer/ *vi.* **(-eers, -eering, -eered) 1. CAMPAIGN IN AN ELECTION** to take an active part in an election campaign, especially as, or on behalf of, a candidate for political office **2. DO STH JUST TO WIN VOTES** to attempt to win votes in an election by being insincere and unscrupulous (*disapproving*) ■ *n.* **electioneer, electioneerer CAMPAIGN WORKER** sb who works on behalf of a candidate or party in an election

elective /i léktiv/ *adj.* **1.** POL **REQUIRING ELECTION** chosen by a vote, or whose holder is chosen by a vote ○ *The monarchy at that time was elective not hereditary.* **2.** EDUC **NOT COMPULSORY** optional rather than essential or compulsory **3.** POL **RELATING TO VOTING** involving or concerned with voting **4. VOTING** empowered to vote ■ *n.* EDUC **OPTIONAL SUBJECT OF STUDY** an optional course that a student may select from among several alternatives —**electively** *adv.* —**electiveness** *n.*

elector /i léktər/ *n.* **1. SB WHO VOTES** sb who votes or is entitled to vote in an election **2. MEMBER OF AN ELECTORAL COLLEGE** a member of an electoral college or the Electoral College

Elector *n.* any one of the rulers of the German states within the Holy Roman Empire who was entitled to vote in the election of the emperor

electoral /i léktərəl/ *adj.* relating to or involving elections or electors —**electorally** *adv.*

electoral college *n.* a select body of people who elect sb to an office

Electoral college *n.* in the United States, the formal body elected by voters to choose the President and Vice President. Although US voters in effect choose a President and Vice President, they are formally voting for members of the Electoral College, who make the choice on their behalf.

electoral quota *n.* in Australia, the number of representatives of a state or territory that can be elected to the House of Representatives. The number is proportionate to the population of the state or territory, approximately one for every 70,000 inhabitants.

electoral roll, electoral register *n.* an official list of the names and addresses of the people in a given area who are entitled to vote in an election

electorate /i léktərət/ *n.* **1. GROUP OF VOTERS** all the officially qualified voters within a given country or area or for a given election **2.** *ANZ* **AREA REPRESENTED BY MP** an area represented by a Member of Parliament

electr- *prefix.* = **electro-** (*used before vowels*)

Electra /i léktrə/ *n.* in Greek mythology, the daughter of Agamemnon and Clytemnestra. She helped her brother Orestes to avenge their father's murder by killing their mother and Clytemnestra's lover. [From Greek *Ēlektra*, literally 'bright, beaming', from *ēlektōr* 'sun'; from her beauty]

Electra complex *n.* PSYCHOANAL a daughter's unconscious unresolved sexual attraction to her father. The term itself has now been rejected by most theorists.

Electra paradox *n.* a logical paradox arising from the possibility of sb knowing that sth is true when it is described in one way but not when it is described in another [From a Greek myth in which Electra is said to know her brother Orestes when he is described but not when she encounters him as a stranger]

electret /i léktrit/ *n.* a piece of insulating material that is permanently polarized and has a permanent electric field, used in microphones and telephones [Late 19thC. A blend of ELECTRICITY and MAGNET.]

electric /i léktrik/ *adj.* **1. INVOLVING OR CAUSED BY ELECTRICITY** involving, relating to, or caused by electricity. ➧ **Usage note below 2. FOR ELECTRICITY** carrying or conveying electricity **3. USING ELECTRICITY** powered or operated by electricity ○ *an electric guitar* **4. TENSE OR EXCITED** full of tension or excitement and anticipation **5. BRIGHT** extremely bright in colour ○ *electric blue* ■ *n.* **1. ELECTRICITY** electricity, or the electricity supply, e.g. to a house (*informal*) **2. STH OPERATED BY ELECTRICITY** a vehicle, machine, or other device that is powered by electricity ■ **electrics** *npl.* **ELECTRICAL EQUIPMENT OR PARTS** the parts of a device or system that are operated by, carry, or generate electricity, or electrically powered equipment [Mid-17thC. From modern Latin *electricus*, from *electrum* 'amber', from Greek *ēlektron*. The earliest manifestation of electricity was that produced by rubbing amber, hence the name.] —**electrically** *adv.*

WORD KEY: USAGE

electric or **electrical**? ***Electric*** is the word more commonly used to describe a device that works by electricity or is involved in producing or carrying electricity: *an electric oven; an electric socket.* ***Electrical*** is applied to more general things and to areas of study or activity that are concerned with electricity: *electrical appliances; electrical engineering.* ***Electric*** is more usual in the figurative meaning 'tense or excited': *The atmosphere at the meeting was electric.*

electrical /i léktrik'l/ *adj.* **1.** = **electric** *adj.* 1 **2.** = **electric** *adj.* 2 **3.** = **electric** *adj.* 3 ○ *electrical goods* **4. INVOLVING THE APPLICATION OF ELECTRICITY** involved in or involving the application of electricity in technology **5. RELATING TO ELECTRIC FUNCTIONING** involving or concerned with electric cables or circuits, or parts powered by electricity ○ *You'll need an electrician for the electrical work.* **6. CAUSED BY ELECTRICITY** caused by electricity or sth that uses or conveys electricity ■ **electricals** *npl.* FIN **ELECTRICITY COMPANY SHARES** shares in electricity companies

WORD KEY: USAGE

See Usage note at **electric.**

electrical engineering *n.* a branch of engineering that studies the practical applications of electricity in science and technology —**electrical engineer** *n.*

electric blanket *n.* a blanket containing an insulated electric heating element, used to warm a bed

electric chair *n.* **1. CHAIR FOR EXECUTING PEOPLE BY ELECTRICITY** a specially designed chair used especially in the United States to execute people sentenced to death by electrocuting them **2. SENTENCE OF DEATH BY ELECTROCUTION** a sentence of death by electrocution in an electric chair

electric eel *n.* a long air-breathing fish resembling a true eel that is found in South American rivers and can release a strong discharge of electricity from specialized organs in the tail region. Electric eels can produce a discharge of up to 650 volts, enough to stun a human being. Latin name: *Electrophorus electricus.*

electric eye *n.* a device that converts light into electrical energy or uses it to regulate a flow of current, often incorporated into automatic control systems for doors and lighting

electric fence *n.* a wire fence carrying an electric current that gives a mild electric shock to any person who or animal that touches it

electric field *n.* a field of force surrounding a charged body or associated with a fluctuating magnetic field, with which charged particles interact

electric fire *n.* a heater for a room with an element that is made hot by an electric current passing through it

electric guitar *n.* an electrically operated guitar, often with a solid body, that has a device for picking up sound fitted below the strings and connected to an amplifier and loudspeaker

electrician /i lek trísh'n, éllek-/ *n.* sb who installs, maintains, or repairs electrical wiring or electrical goods

electricity /i lek tríssəti, éllek-/ *n.* **1.** PHYS **ENERGY CREATED BY MOVING CHARGED PARTICLES** a fundamental form of kinetic or potential energy created by the free or controlled movement of charged particles such as electrons, positrons, and ions **2.** ELEC ENG **ELECTRIC CURRENT** electric current, especially when used as a source of power **3. ANTICIPATION OR TENSION** a feeling or atmosphere of excited anticipation or tension

electric jazz *n.* jazz produced using electronic instruments or other electronic devices

electric motor *n.* a machine that converts energy from electricity into mechanical energy

electric organ *n.* **1.** MUSIC **ORGAN POWERED BY ELECTRICITY** an organ whose sound is produced or amplified by means of electricity **2.** ZOOL **ELECTRICITY-PRODUCING MUSCLE IN FISH** specialized muscle tissue in some fish that creates an electric field used for finding enemies, obstacles, and food in murky water, and, in some species, for defence against attack

electric potential *n.* PHYS the work required to bring a unit of positive electric charge from infinity to a specified point in an electric field. Symbol *V*

electric ray *n.* a fish that lives in tropical or temperate seas and can emit a strong electric discharge from electric organs in its enlarged pectoral fins. Family: Torpedinidae.

electric razor *n.* a small electrically powered device used for shaving hair on the face or body

electric shock *n.* a sudden painful physical reaction consisting of nerve stimulation and muscle contraction caused by an electric current flowing through the body

electrify /i léktri fī/ (**-fies, -fying, -fied**) *vt.* **1. CONVERT TO USING ELECTRICITY** to convert sth, e.g. a railway line or a piece of machinery, so that it can operate on electric power **2.** PHYS **CHARGE ELECTRICALLY** to charge sth with electricity **3. THRILL SB** to cause sb to feel a sudden and surprising shock, thrill, or sense of excitement **4.** MUSIC **ELECTRICALLY AMPLIFY A MUSICAL INSTRUMENT** to amplify the sounds produced by a musical instrument by electrical means —**electrifiable** *adj.* —**electrification** /i léktrifi káysh'n/ *n.* —**electrifier** /i léktri fī ər/ *n.*

electrifyingly /i léktrə fī ingli/ *adv.* in an excitingly stimulating way

electro- *prefix.* **1.** electricity, electric, electronic ○ *electromyogram* **2.** electrolysis ○ *electrometallurgy* **3.** electron ○ *electropositive* [Via modern Latin from, ultimately, Greek *ēlektron* 'amber']

electroacoustic /i léktrō ə kóostik/ *adj.* used to describe a device that converts sound into electrical signals or vice versa

electroacoustics /i léktrō ə kóostiks/ *n.* a branch of electronics that is concerned with how electricity is converted into sound (*takes a singular verb*) —**electroacoustically** *adv.*

electroanalysis /i léktrō ə nálləssiss/ (*plural* **-ses** /-seez/) *n.* the use of electrolysis to perform chemical analysis —**electroanalytic** /i léktrō ànnə líttik/ *adj.* —**electroanalytical** /-líttik'l/ *adj.* —**electroanalytically** /-líttikli/ *adv.*

electrocardiogram /i léktrō kaárdi ə gram/ *n.* a visual record of the heart's electrical activity made using an electrocardiograph

electrocardiograph /i léktrō kaárdi ə graaf, -graf/ *n.* a device that records the electrical activity of the heart muscle via electrodes placed on the chest, and displays it as a visual record —**electrocardiographic** /i léktrō kaárdi ə gráffik/ *adj.* —**electrocardiographically** /-gráffikli/ *adv.* —**electrocardiography** /i léktrō kaárdi óggrəfi/ *n.*

electrocautery /i léktrō káwtəri/ *n.* the process of destroying unwanted tissue, e.g. warts and polyps, or sealing blood vessels, by means of an electrically heated needle

electrochemical series *n.* a series in which the chemical elements are arranged in order of decreasing tendency to lose electrons

electrochemistry /i léktrō kémmistri/ *n.* a branch of chemistry that studies chemical change associated with electrons and electricity —**electrochemical** /i léktrō kémmikl/ *adj.* —**electrochemically** /i léktrō kémmikli/ *adv.* —**electrochemist** *n.*

electrocoagulation /i léktrō kō ággyoo láysh'n/ *n.* the use of an electrical device that burns tissue to stop bleeding from small blood vessels during surgery or to destroy small tumours

electroconvulsive therapy /i léktrō kən vúlssiv-/ *n.* the passing of a small electric current through the brain to induce a seizure, used in the treatment of severe psychiatric disorders

electrocute /i léktrə kyoot/ (**-cutes, -cuting, -cuted**) *vt.* **1. INJURE OR KILL WITH ELECTRIC SHOCK** to cause injury or death with an electric shock **2.** CRIMINOL **EXECUTE IN THE ELECTRIC CHAIR** to execute sb by means of the electric chair [Late 19thC. A blend of ELECTRO- and EXECUTE.] —**electrocution** /i léktrə kyóosh'n/ *n.*

electrode /i lék trōd/ *n.* either of the two conductors through which electricity enters or leaves sth such as a battery or a piece of electrical equipment

electrodeposit /i léktrō di pózzit/ *vt.* (**-its, -iting, -ited**) **DEPOSIT METAL BY ELECTROLYSIS** to deposit a substance, especially a metal, on an electrode by using electrolysis ■ *n.* **DEPOSITED SUBSTANCE** a substance deposited by using electrolysis —**electrodeposition** /i lék trō déppə zísh'n/ *n.*

electrodynamics /i léktrō dī námmiks/ *n.* a branch of physics that studies how electric currents interact with magnetic and mechanical forces (*takes a singular verb*) —**electrodynamic** *adj.*

electrodynamometer /i léktrō dīnə mómmitər/ *n.* a device for measuring the strength of an electric current by the magnetic force it induces in a coil

electroencephalogram /i léktrō in séffələ gram/ *n.* the record of the electrical activity of the brain that is produced by an electroencephalograph

electroencephalograph /i léktrō in séffələ graaf, -graf/ *n.* a machine that uses electrodes placed on the scalp to monitor the electrical activity of different parts of the brain, recording these as complex tracings. Irregularities recorded in the tracings may help in the diagnosis of a range of organic brain disorders such as tumours and epilepsy and in establishing brain death. —**electroencephalographic** /i léktrō in séffələ gráffik/ *adj.* —**electroencephalography** /i léktrō in séffə lóggrəfi/ *n.*

electroform /i léktrə fawrm/ (**-forms, -forming, -formed**) *vt.* to form sth, e.g. a medal, by using electrolysis to coat the surface of the mould or matrix with a metal

electrograph /i léktrō graaf, -graf/ *n.* **1.** PHYS **ELECTROMETER** an electrometer that produces a graphical record of the measurements it makes, or the record it produces **2.** PHYS **GRAPH FROM AN ELECTROMETRE** the visual record produced by an electrometer **3. ELECTRICAL ENGRAVING DEVICE** an electrical device for engraving a design on a metal plate for use in printing patterns for fabrics or wallpaper **4.** TELECOM **ELECTRICAL PICTURE TRANSMISSION DEVICE** an apparatus used to transmit pictures by electrical means, e.g. by fax **5.** TELECOM **TRANSMITTED PICTURE** a printed picture produced by an electrograph

electrohydraulic /i léktrō hī drólik/ *adj.* using, or relating to the use of, electrical and hydraulic components —**electrohydraulically** *adv.*

electrokinetic /i léktrō ki néttik, -kī-/ *adj.* relating to or involving the motion of electrically charged particles and its effects —**electrokinetically** *adv.*

electrokinetics /i lék trōki néttiks, -kī-/ *n.* a branch of physics that deals with the motion of electrically charged particles (*takes a singular verb*) —**electrokineticist** /-néttissist/ *n.*

electroluminescence /i léktrō lóomi néss'nss/ *n.* the emission of light by sth such as a gas or phosphor resulting from a high-frequency electrical discharge —**electroluminescent** *adj.*

electrolyse /i léktrə līz/ (**-trolyses, -trolysing, -trolysed**) *vt.* to use electrolysis to decompose a chemical compound [Mid-19thC. A blend of ELECTROLYSIS and ANALYSE.]

electrolysis /i lek trólləssiss, éllek-/ *n.* **1.** CHEM **CHEMICAL SEPARATION BY ELECTRICITY** the conduction of electricity through sth melted or dissolved in order to induce decomposition of the melted or dissolved chemical into its components **2.** MED, COSMETICS **REMOVAL TECHNIQUE USING ELECTRICITY** the use of an electric current applied though a needle to remove body hair for cosmetic purposes, or to destroy warts, moles, or tumours for medical reasons

electrolyte /i léktrō līt/ *n.* **1.** CHEM **COMPOUND SEPARABLE INTO IONS IN SOLUTION** a chemical compound that separates into ions in a solution or when molten and is able to conduct electricity **2.** CHEM **ION** an ion in an electrolyte **3.** PHYSIOL **ION NEEDED BY CELL** any ion in

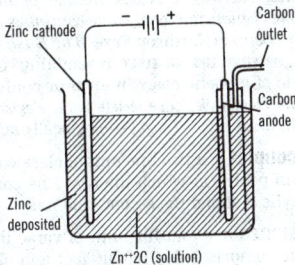

Electrolysis: Separation of zinc carbonate by electrolysis

cells, blood, or other organic material. Electrolytes help to control fluid levels in the body, maintain normal pH levels, and ensure the correct electric potential between nerve cells that enables the transmission of nerve signals.

electrolytic /i léktrŏ líttik/ *adj.* **1.** RELATING TO ELECTROLYSIS involved in or relating to electrolysis **2.** RELATING TO ELECTROLYTES relating to, containing, or consisting of electrolytes —**electrolytically** *adv.*

electrolytic cell *n.* **1.** DEVICE PRODUCING ELECTROLYSIS BY ELECTRICITY a device in which electrolysis can be produced, usually consisting of an electrolyte, its container, and electrodes **2.** DEVICE PRODUCING ELECTRICITY BY CHEMICAL REACTION a device consisting of an electrolyte, its container, and two electrodes, in which a chemical reaction between the electrolyte and the electrodes produces electricity

electrolyze *vt.* US = **electrolyse**

electromagnet /i léktrŏ mágnit/ *n.* a magnet consisting of a core, often made of soft iron, that is temporarily magnetized by an electric current in a coil that surrounds it

electromagnetic /i léktrŏ mag néttik/ *adj.* created by or relating to electromagnetism —**electromagnetically** *adv.*

electromagnetic field *n.* a field of force associated with a moving electric charge and consisting of electric and magnetic fields that are generated at right angles to each other

electromagnetic force *n.* the force resulting from the interaction of charged particles and their electric and magnetic fields

electromagnetic interference *n.* the interference in a circuit, e.g. disturbance on a television set, caused by the radiation of an electric or magnetic field or the operation of a nearby electric motor

electromagnetic radiation *n.* electromagnetic energy such as gamma rays, X-rays, ultraviolet light, visible light, infrared rays, microwaves, and radio waves. The radiation is characterized by having magnetic and electric fields that are perpendicular to one another and to the direction of propagation, and travels without a supporting medium.

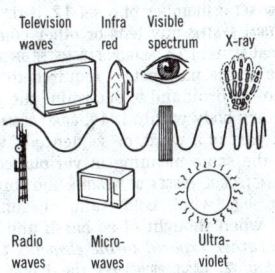

Electromagnetic spectrum: Some applications of electromagnetic radiation

electromagnetic spectrum *n.* the complete range of electromagnetic radiation from the shortest waves (**gamma rays**) to the longest (**radio waves**)

electromagnetic unit *n.* any unit in the centimetre-gram-second system of units for measuring electricity and magnetism that gives a value of 1 to the magnetic constant, e.g. the abampere or the abvolt

electromagnetic wave *n.* a wave of energy with a frequency within the electromagnetic spectrum, generated by the periodic fluctuation of an electromagnetic field resulting from the acceleration or oscillation of an electric charge. Electromagnetic waves can be reflected, refracted, and polarized, and exhibit interference and diffraction effects.

electromagnetism /i léktrŏ mágnə tizzəm/ *n.* **1.** MAGNETISM FROM ELECTRIC CURRENTS magnetism produced by an electric current **2.** INTERACTION OF ELECTROMAGNETIC FORCES the branch of physics concerned with the interaction of electric and magnetic fields and with electromagnetism

electromechanical /i léktrŏ mi kánnik'l/ *adj.* relating to or used to describe a mechanical device that is powered or controlled by electricity —**electromechanically** *adv.*

electrometallurgy /i léktrŏ mi tállərji, -métt'l urji/ *n.* the range of metallurgical processes in which electricity has a key role, e.g. electroplating and the use of arc furnaces

electrometer /i lek trómmitər, éllek-/ *n.* a sensitive device for measuring extremely low voltages by means of the forces of attraction and repulsion between charged bodies on plates or wires

electromotive /i léktrŏ mŏtiv/ *adj.* relating to or producing an electric current

electromotive force *n.* **1.** FORCE CAUSING ELECTRICITY FLOW a force that causes the flow of electricity from one point to another **2.** ENERGY CONVERTIBLE INTO ELECTRICITY the energy available in a source such as a battery for conversion into electricity from a chemical, mechanical, or other nonelectric form, measured in volts per unit of electric charge. Symbol E

electromyogram /i léktrŏ mí ə gram/ *n.* a graphical tracing of the electrical activity in a muscle at rest or during contraction, used to diagnose nerve and muscle disorders

electromyograph /i léktrŏ mí ə graaf, -graf/ *n.* a machine for producing an electromyogram from electrical activity picked up via electrodes inserted into muscle tissue. It consists of an amplifier, an electrically-activated trace-drawing pen, and a moving strip of paper.

electron /i lék tron/ *n.* a stable negatively charged elementary particle with a small mass that is a fundamental constituent of matter and orbits the nucleus of an atom

electronegative /i léktrŏ néggətiv/ *adj.* ◊ electropositive **1.** POSSESSING NEGATIVE ELECTRIC CHARGE with negative electric charge, and so tending to move towards a positive electric pole **2.** GAINING ELECTRONS IN CHEMICAL REACTION tending to gain electrons to form a bond in a chemical reaction

electronegativity /i léktrŏ neggə tívvəti/ *n.* a measure of the tendency of an atom in a molecule to attract the electrons in a chemical bond

electron gun *n.* a device such as one used in a cathode-ray tube, that directs a steady stream of electrons in a desired direction

electronic /i lek trónnik, éllek-/ *adj.* **1.** ELECTRON ENG INVOLVING A CONTROLLED FLOW OF ELECTRONS relating to, or produced or operated by, the controlled flow of electrons through a semiconductor, a gas, or free space **2.** ELECTRON ENG USING VALVES, TRANSISTORS, OR SILICON CHIPS relating to devices, systems, or circuits that employ components such as valves, integrated circuits, or transistors in their design **3.** COMPUT BY COMPUTER using or controlled by a computer or computer network, or relating to the use of computers in an activity ◦ *electronic banking* **4.** PHYS ELECTRONS relating to electrons ◦ *electronic spectrum* —**electronically** *adv.*

electronic data processing *n.* computer-based tasks that involve the input of data such as invoices or payrolls and its subsequent manipulation, usually using database programs

electronic flash *n.* a flash device used in high-speed photography that produces a very bright light by passing an electric charge through a gas-filled tube

electronic funds transfer at point of sale *n.* a system of paying for goods at the point of sale by the direct computerized transfer of money from the buyer's bank or building society account to the seller's

electronic journalism *n.* news coverage that is transmitted electronically, e.g. by television or over the Internet

electronic magazine *n.* a magazine that is distributed online over a computer network rather than being printed on paper

electronic mail *n.* full form of **e-mail**

electronic music *n.* music produced or modified by electronic means, often with the aid of a computer

electronic newsgathering *n.* television news coverage made at the time and place of the event or incident by means of video equipment

electronic office *n.* an office in which traditional office equipment such as typewriters, telephones, and fax machines are replaced by integrated programs running on computers (*dated*)

electronic organ *n.* an electric organ (*dated*)

electronic point of sale *n.* a computerized checkout system in shops that records sales by scanning bar codes, automatically updates the retailer's stock lists, and provides a printout of the customer's purchases

electronic publishing *n.* the production of documents in computer-readable form for distribution over a computer network or in other formats such as CD-ROMs

electronics /i lek trónniks, éllek-/ *n.* TECHNOLOGY OF ELECTRONIC DEVICES the branch of technology concerned with the design, manufacture, and maintenance of electronic devices (*takes a singular verb*) ■ *npl.* ELECTRONIC PARTS the electronic parts of a piece of equipment, or electronic devices and equipment generally

electronic shopping *n.* the ordering and purchase of goods and services over a computer network, especially over the Internet

electronic smog *n.* nonionizing radiation produced in the atmosphere by sources such as radar, radio and television broadcasting, considered by some people to pose a general health risk

electronic superhighway *n.* = information superhighway

electronic surveillance *n.* the gathering of information, especially in crime detection and prevention or in espionage, using electronic devices such as video cameras and wiretaps

electronic tagging *n.* the supervision of an offender by means of an electronic tracking device such as a bracelet, as an alternative to prison confinement

electronic transfer of funds *n.* the transfer of money from one account to another by computer

electron lens *n.* a device that creates an electric or magnetic field around the path of an electron beam so that the beam may be focussed

electron micrograph *n.* a photograph of a specimen taken using an electron microscope

electron microscope *n.* a high-powered microscope that uses beams of electrons focussed by an electron lens to create a magnified image on a fluorescent screen or photographic plate —**electron microscopy** *n.*

electron multiplier *n.* a device for amplifying a very small current using the effects of secondary emission. Electrons from the original current strike an anode, producing secondary electrons that are directed to the next anode in a multi-stage process until the desired level of current is obtained.

electron optics *n.* the science that deals with the direction, deflection, or focussing of beams of electrons by electric and magnetic fields, e.g. in electron lenses (*takes a singular verb*)

electron shell *n.* PHYS = **shell** *n.* **19**

electron transport *n.* the process in cells by which electrons are gradually transferred from compounds rich in energy to molecular oxygen by a series of chemical reactions, resulting in the release of energy subsequently used in the production of ATP

electron tube *n.* a device that consists of a sealed glass vessel containing a gas or a vacuum, within which electrons flow between electrodes

electron volt /i léktron vōlt/ *n.* **1. UNIT OF ENERGY** a unit of energy equal to the energy gained by an electron accelerated through a potential difference of one volt and equal to 1.602×10^{-19} joule. Symbol **eV** **2. UNIT OF MASS** the unit of mass of elementary particles, measured as a function of energy and usually expressed in terms of mega electron volts (**MeV**)

electro-osmosis *n.* the movement of a liquid through a membrane under the effect of an electric field

electrophile /i léktrō fīl/ *n.* an atom, molecule, or chemical group that is attracted to electrons or accepts them —**electrophilic** /i léktrō fíllik/ *adj.*

electrophonic /i léktrə fónnik/ *adj.* producing sound by means of electronic equipment

electrophoresis /i léktrō fə reéssiss/ *n.* the movement of charged particles in a colloid or suspension when an electric field is applied to them [Early 20thC. Coined from ELECTRO + Greek *phorēsis* 'being carried' (see -PHORE).] —**electrophoretic** /-fə réttik/ *adj.*

electrophorus /i lek tróffərəss, éllek-/ (*plural* **-ri** /-rī/) *n.* a device that produces electric charges from the friction between a disc and a metal plate [Late 18thC. Coined from ELECTRO + *-phorus*, a Latinization of -PHORE.]

electrophotography /i léktrōfə tóggrəfi/ *n.* any form of photography, e.g. xerography, that uses electricity to transfer an image onto paper —**electrophotographic** /i léktrō fōtə gráffik/ *adj.*

electrophysiology /i léktrō fízzi ólləji/ *n.* the branch of medicine or biology dealing with the study of electrical activity in human or animal bodies —**electrophysiologic** /-fízzi ə lójjik/ *adj.* —**electrophysiological** /-lójjik'l/ *adj.* —**electrophysiologically** /-lójjikli/ *adv.* —**electrophysiologist** /i léktrōfízzi ólləjist/ *n.*

electroplate /i léktrō playt/ *vt.* (**-plates, -plating, -plated**) **COAT A SURFACE WITH METAL BY ELECTROLYSIS** to use electrolysis to coat the surface of an object with metal ■ *n.* **ELECTROPLATED OBJECTS** objects coated with metal by means of electrolysis

electropositive /i léktrō pózzitiv/ *adj.* ◊ **electronegative** **1.** PHYS **POSSESSING POSITIVE ELECTRIC CHARGE** with a positive electric charge, and so tending to move towards a negative electric pole **2.** CHEM **RELEASING ELECTRONS TO FORM A CHEMICAL BOND** tending to release electrons to form a bond in a chemical reaction

electroreceptor /i léktrōri septər/ *n.* an organ in fish such as sharks, electric eels, and catfish that detects electrical charges

electroscope /i léktrō skōp/ *n.* a device that detects and measures an electric charge, usually consisting of a rod holding two strips of gold foil that separate when a like charge is applied to each —**electroscopic** /i léktrō skóppik/ *adj.*

electrosensitivity /i léktrō sénssə tívvəti/ *n.* the ability in an animal to detect naturally occurring electrical currents and use them to navigate or locate objects

electroshock /i léktrō shok/ *n. US* = **electroconvulsive therapy** ■ *vt.* (**-shocks, -shocking, -shocked**) *US* **GIVE ELECTROCONVULSIVE THERAPY TO SB** to administer electroconvulsive therapy to a patient

electroshock therapy *n.* PSYCHIAT = **electroconvulsive therapy**

electrostatic /i léktrō státtik/ *adj.* **1. RELATING TO STATIC ELECTRICITY** produced by or relating to static electricity **2. OF ELECTROSTATICS** relating to electrostatics —**electrostatically** *adv.*

electrostatic generator *n.* PHYS = **Van de Graaff generator**

electrostatic precipitator *n.* a device that removes small particles of smoke, dust, or oil from air by electrostatically charging them and then attracting them to an oppositely charged collector plate or surface —**electrostatic precipitation** *n.*

electrostatic printing *n.* a photocopying or printing process in which images are reproduced on a surface using electrostatic charges

electrostatics /i léktrō státtiks/ *n.* a branch of physics dealing with electric charges at rest (**static electricity**) (*takes a singular verb*)

electrostatic unit *n.* a unit for measuring the magnitude of forces of repulsion between static electrical charges in the centimetre-gram-second system, e.g. the statampere and the statvolt

electrosurgery /i léktrō súrjəri/ *n.* the use of an electrical device or current during surgery, e.g. to cut or cauterize tissue —**electrosurgical** *adj.* —**electrosurgically** *adv.*

electrotherapy /i léktrō thérrəpi/ *n.* any form of medical treatment that uses electricity as a cure or relief, e.g. as a way of stimulating nerves and the muscles they are connected to —**electrotherapeutic** /i léktrō thérrə pyoótik/ *adj.*

electrothermal /i léktrō thúrm'l/ *adj.* involving or relating to electricity and heat, or the production of heat by electricity ○ *electrothermal energy conversion*

electrotype /i léktrō tīp/ *n.* **1. DUPLICATE PRINTING PLATE MADE BY ELECTROPLATING** a duplicate of a block of type or engraving made by electroplating a wax, lead, or plastic mould of the original **2. PRINTED ITEM** sth printed from an electrotype ■ *vt.* (**-types, -typing, -typed**) **PRINT USING AN ELECTROTYPE** to print sth from an electrotype —**electrotyper** *n.* —**electrotypic** /i léktrō típpik/ *adj.*

electrovalency /i léktrō váylənss/, **electrovalence** (*plural* **-lencies** /-lənssi/) *n.* the combining power of an element, measured by the number of electrons one atom of it acquires from or transfers to another atom during the formation of a chemical compound —**electrovalent** *adj.*

electrovalent bond *n.* a chemical bond that is created during the formation of a compound by transfer of one or more electrons from one atom to another, the resulting oppositely charged ions being held together by attraction

electroweak /i léktrō week/ *adj.* PHYS used to describe a type of fundamental interaction uniting electromagnetic forces with the weak interaction

electrum /i léktrəm/ *n.* a pale-coloured alloy of silver and gold used in jewellery and ornaments [14thC. Via Latin, 'amber', from Greek *ēlektron*.]

electuary /i léktyoō əri/ (*plural* **-ies**) *n.* a sweet-tasting paste made by mixing a drug with syrup or honey, administered by being applied to the teeth, tongue, or gums [14thC. Via late Latin *electuarium*, of uncertain origin: probably from Greek *eleikton*, from *eleikhein* 'to lick up'.]

eleemosynary /élli ee móssinəri, -mózzinəri, éllee-/ *adj.* (*formal*) **1. OF CHARITY** relating to charity **2. SUPPORTED BY CHARITY** supported by or depending on charitable gifts [Late 16thC. Via medieval Latin *eleemosynarius*, from *eleemosyna* 'alms', from, ultimately, Greek *eleos* 'mercy'.]

elegance /élligənss/ *n.* **1. GRACE AND DIGNITY** a combination of graceful stylishness, distinction, and good taste in appearance, behaviour, or movement ○ *leaning in a pose of studied elegance against the mantelpiece* **2. CONCISENESS** a satisfying or admirable neatness, ingenious simplicity, or precision in sth ○ *the elegance of the solution* **3. STH ELEGANT** an elegant thing or quality [Early 16thC. Via French *élégance* from, ultimately, Latin *elegans* 'choice' (see ELEGANT).]

elegant /élligənt/ *adj.* **1. STYLISH AND GRACEFUL** stylishly graceful, and showing sophistication and good taste in appearance or behaviour ○ *A suit can be as expensive as you like; it's the wearer who makes it look elegant.* **2. SHOWING SKILL AND GRACE** executed or made with a combination of skill, ease, and grace ○ *an elegant forehand return* **3. CONCISE** satisfyingly and often ingeniously neat, simple, or concise ○ *an equation elegant in its simplicity* [15thC. Via French from Latin *elegans* 'choice', from, ultimately, *eligire* 'to pick out' (source of English *elect*).] —**elegantly** *adv.*

elegiac /élli jī ək/, **elegiacal** /-jī ək'l/ *adj.* **1. MOURNFUL** expressing sorrow or regret (*formal or literary*) ○ *'The same elegiac and lonely tone continues to haunt the later poetry'.* (Northrop Frye, *The Bush Garden*; 1972) **2.** LITERAT **LIKE AN ELEGY** resembling or characteristic of a poetic elegy in form or content [Late 16thC. Via French *élégiaque* or late Latin *elegiacus* from, ultimately, Greek *elegos* 'song'.] —**elegiacally** *adv.*

elegiac couplet *n.* a two-line unit of classical Greek and Latin poetry in which the first line comprises six dactylic feet and the second line five

elegiac stanza *n.* a four-line unit of verse in which each line comprises five iambic feet and alternate lines rhyme

elegist /éllijist/ *n.* sb who writes, reads, or recites an elegy

elegize /élli jīz/ (**-gizes, -gizing, -gized**), **elegise** (**-gises, -gising, -gised**) *v.* **1.** *vti.* **COMMEMORATE SB OR STH SORROWFULLY** to write or speak about sb or sth in a mournful, sorrowful way ○ *He elegized his lost comrade.* **2.** *vi.* **WRITE OR DELIVER AN ELEGY** to write, read, or recite an elegy

elegy /élliji/ (*plural* **-gies**) *n.* **1. MOURNFUL POEM** a mournful or reflective poem **2. POEM IN ELEGIAC COUPLETS OR STANZAS** a poem written in elegiac couplets or stanzas [Early 16thC. Via French *élégie* or directly from Latin *elegia* from, ultimately, Greek *elegos* 'song'.]

WORD KEY: CULTURAL NOTE

Elegy Written in a Country Churchyard, a poem by writer Thomas Gray (1750). Inspired by a churchyard at Stoke Poges, Buckinghamshire, England, it is a reflection on rural life, human ambitions, friendship, and mortality. It is considered the masterpiece of the 'graveyard' school of literature, which was popular in the 1740s and 1750s.

elem. *abbr.* elementary

element /éllimənt/ *n.* **1. SEPARATE PART OR GROUP** a separate, identifiable part of sth, or a distinct group within a larger group ○ *Landowners were the most stable element of society.* **2. LITTLE BIT** a small amount of sth ○ *There was an element of revenge in what she did.* **3. FACTOR** a cause or factor leading to sth ○ *Surprise was the key element in ensuring the success of the operation.* **4.** CHEM **BASIC UNIT OF MATTER** any substance that cannot be broken down into a simpler one by a chemical reaction. Elements consist of atoms with the same number of protons in their nuclei, and 92 occur naturally on Earth. **5.** HIST **SUPPOSED BASIC UNIT OF MATTER** any one of the four primary substances, earth, air, fire, and water, that were formerly thought to be the materials from which all matter is constructed **6. STH'S HABITAT** a natural habitat or environment **7.** ELEC, HOUSEHOLD **HEATING PART OF AN APPLIANCE** a part of an electric heater, cooker, or other appliance that heats up when an electric current is passed through it **8.** GEOM **CONSTITUENT OF GEOMETRICAL FIGURE** a point, line, plane, or other part of which a geometrical figure is composed **9.** ELEC **COMPONENT OF ELECTRIC CIRCUIT** any component of an electrical circuit **10.** MATH **PART OF MATHEMATICAL QUANTITY** a part of a given mathematical or geometric quantity, e.g. a number in an array or an angle in a triangle **11.** LOGIC, MATH **MEMBER OF SET** a member of a set **12.** OPTICS **COMPONENT OF AN OPTICAL SYSTEM** any lens or other component of an optical system **13.** ASTRON **PARAMETER DEFINING AN ORBIT** any one of the parameters required to define the nature of an orbit and to determine the position of a planetary body within it **14.** GRAM **GRAMMATICAL UNIT** a word, part of a word, or sequence of words that retains the same meaning in various contexts ■ *npl.* **1.** METEOROL **FORCES OF WEATHER** the forces of the weather, e.g. wind, cold, rain, or sunshine, especially when thought of as harsh and damaging ○ *We're rather exposed to the elements up here on the hilltop.* **2. BASIC PRINCIPLES** the basic and most important things to be learned when studying a subject ○ *She was endeavouring to teach us the elements of a good prose style.* **3.** CHR **BREAD AND WINE IN CHRISTIAN CEREMONY** the bread and wine used by Christians to celebrate the ceremony known as the Eucharist, Communion, or the Lord's Supper [14thC. Via Old French from Latin *elementum* 'rudiment', of uncertain origin.] ◇ **in your element** in the situation or environment to which you feel most suited or where you feel particularly happy

elemental /élli mént'l/ *adj.* **1.** FUNDAMENTAL basic and essential **2.** RELATING TO NATURAL FORCES relating to or caused by powerful natural forces ○ *elemental passions* **3.** reduced to, or reducing sth to, a stark simplicity ○ *classic, elemental sculptures* **4.** CHEM OF CHEMICAL OR ANCIENT ELEMENTS relating to the chemical elements, or to the elements of earth, air, fire, and water that were once supposed to be the basic units of matter

elementary /élli méntəri/ *adj.* **1.** RUDIMENTARY involving or encompassing only the most simple and basic facts or principles ○ *Anyone with an elementary knowledge of computing could have pointed that out to you.* **2.** SIMPLE TO DO OR UNDERSTAND requiring little skill or knowledge **3.** *US* EDUC OF AN ELEMENTARY SCHOOL relating to an elementary school or the education provided there —**elementarily** *adv.* —**elementariness** *n.*

elementary particle *n.* any one of the basic constituents of which matter and energy are composed, e.g. electrons, leptons, photons, or hadrons, held to be indivisible. They are elementary particles.

elementary school *n.* **1.** *US* SCHOOL FOR EARLY EDUCATION in the United States, a school that provides the first four to eight years of basic education **2.** FORMER TYPE OF SCHOOL a school of a type no longer in existence that was attended by children from the age of 5 until they left at 14

elemi /éllimi/ *n.* CHEM a fragrant resin obtained from various tropical trees and used in making varnishes, inks, ointments, and perfumes [Mid-16thC. Via modern Latin from Arabic *al-lāmī*.]

elenchus /i léngkəss/ (*plural* -**chi** /-kī/) *n.* an argument that refutes a proposition by proving the opposite of its conclusions [Mid-17thC. Via Latin from Greek *elegkhos* 'refutation'.] —**elenctic** *adj.*

Elephant

elephant /éllifənt/ (*plural* -**phants** or -**phant**) *n.* **1.** ZOOL LARGE GREYISH ANIMAL WITH LONG TRUNK a large grey or greyish-brown animal with a long flexible trunk, prominent ears, thick legs, and pointed tusks. Elephants are the largest living land animals. Three species of elephant remain in existence today: the African elephant, African forest elephant, and Asian or Indian elephant. Latin name: *Loxodonta africana* and *Loxodonta cyclotis* and *Elephas maximus*. **2.** STH VERY LARGE sb or sth that is extremely large or much larger than average **3.** PAPER LARGE SIZE OF SHEET OF PAPER a size of drawing or writing paper, 584 × 711 mm/23 × 28 in [13thC. Via Old French *olifant* from Latin *elephantus* from, ultimately, Greek *elephās* 'elephant, ivory'.]

Elephanta Island /élli fántə-/ island in Bombay harbour, western India, approximately 10 km/6 mi. east of Bombay. Area: 5 sq. km/2 sq. mi.

elephant folio *n.* a book size from 61 to 63.5 cm/24 to 25 in in height

elephant garlic *n.* a mild-flavoured variety of garlic with very large bulbs, often roasted as a vegetable. Latin name: *Allium ampeloprasum*.

elephant grass *n.* any of a number of tall coarse grasses or plants resembling grasses of tropical Africa and southern Asia. Genera: *Typha* and *Pennisetum*.

elephant gun *n.* a large-calibre gun, typically .410 or more, used in hunting big game.

elephantiasis /éllifən tí əssiss/ *n.* **1.** MED DISFIGURING ILLNESS CAUSING SWELLING a chronic disease in which parasitic worms obstruct the lymphatic system, causing enlargement of parts of the body such as the legs and scrotum and hardening of the surrounding skin. It is transmitted by mosquitoes. **2.** UNREASONABLE GROWTH excessive and unreasonable growth or development of sth [Mid-16thC. Via Latin from Greek, from *elephās* 'elephant'.]

elephantine /éllifán tīn/ *adj.* **1.** SLOW AND HEAVY moving in a slow, heavy, and often clumsy or awkward way ○ *the heavy, elephantine tread of his feet* **2.** ENORMOUS very large or very great **3.** LIKE AN ELEPHANT'S resembling that of an elephant [Early 16thC. Via Latin from Greek *elephantinos*, from *elephās* 'elephant'.]

elephant seal *n.* a large earless seal, the male of which has a long inflatable snout resembling an elephant's trunk. Elephant seals were hunted almost to extinction in the 19th century. Latin name: *Mirounga angustirostris* and *Mirounga leonina*.

elephant's ear *n.* **1.** PLANTS = taro **2.** BEGONIA OR BERGENIA a number of varieties of begonia or bergenia with large showy leaves

elephant's foot (*plural* **elephant's foots**) *n.* an ornamental southern African climbing or trailing plant of the yam family with a large above-ground tuber that is sometimes used for food. Latin name: *Dioscorea elephantipes*.

Eleusinian mysteries /éllyoō sínni ən-/ *npl.* an ancient Greek festival held annually at Eleusis and Athens that honoured and celebrated Persephone, Demeter, and Dionysus

elev. *abbr.* elevation

elevate /élli vayt/ (-**vates**, -**vating**, -**vated**) *vt.* **1.** RAISE STH UP to raise sth to a higher level or position **2.** RAISE SB TO HIGHER RANK to raise or promote sb or sth to a high or higher status, rank, or office ○ *elevated to the rank of bishop* **3.** INCREASE STH to increase the amount or intensity of sth ○ *This was one factor that elevated interest rates higher than they otherwise would have been.* **4.** RAISE SB'S MIND OR SPIRIT to lift sb's mind or spirit to a more enlightened or exalted level (*formal*) **5.** ARMS MAKE A GUN BARREL POINT HIGHER to make the barrel of a field gun point at a higher angle **6.** CHR LIFT UP HOST OR CHALICE to lift up the Host or the chalice in front of the congregation during a Mass [14thC. Via Latin *elevatus* from, ultimately, *levare* 'to lighten'.]

—— **WORD KEY: SYNONYMS** ——
See Synonyms at *raise*.

elevated /élli vaytid/ *adj.* **1.** AT A HIGH LEVEL OR POSITION raised above ground level, or situated at a higher level than sth else ○ *elevated track* **2.** HIGH OR HIGHER IN RANK high or higher in rank or status **3.** INCREASED increased in amount ○ *elevated levels of cholesterol* **4.** AT A HIGH MORAL OR INTELLECTUAL LEVEL set at a high moral or intellectual level ○ *Milton's elevated conception of the role of the poet*

elevated railway *n.* a rail system operating on a raised structure, usually above or over a street

elevation /élli váysh'n/ *n.* **1.** GEOG HEIGHT ABOVE A LOCATION the height above a specific reference point, especially sea level ○ *at an elevation of 1,000 metres above sea level* **2.** RAISING STH, OR BEING RAISED the act of raising sb or sth in height or status, or the process of being raised in height or status ○ *They congratulated him on his elevation to the cardinalship.* **3.** DEGREE OF BEING RAISED the degree or amount by which sb or sth is raised or elevated ○ *a figure skater who is able to get tremendous elevation in her triple jumps* **4.** INCREASE an increase in sth (*technical*) ○ *Among the effects was an elevation in the level of dopamine.* **5.** ARCHIT ARCHITECTURAL DRAWING OF A SIDE OF BUILDING a scale drawing of any side of a building or other structure ○ *the front elevation of the proposed new wing* **6.** CIV ENG ANGLE IN SURVEYING the angle between a horizontal line and the line from a surveying instrument to a point above the horizontal, e.g. between eye level and a line to a nearby rooftop **7.** ARMS ANGLE OF A GUN BARREL ABOVE HORIZONTAL the angle to which the barrel

of a large gun is raised above the horizontal **8.** CHR RAISING OF THE HOST AND CHALICE the raising and showing to the people of the Host or chalice by a priest immediately after their consecration in a Mass **9.** ASTRON = altitude *n.* 4 **10.** BALLET ABILITY TO JUMP, OR THE HEIGHT REACHED the ability of a ballet dancer to jump high and hold the position briefly, or the height a dancer can reach in jumping —**elevational** *adj.*

elevator /élli vaytər/ *n.* **1.** *US, Can, ANZ* TRANSP, BUILDING PLATFORM FOR TAKING UP OR DOWN a platform, cage, or enclosed compartment that is raised or lowered mechanically and used to take people or things to a higher or lower level in a building **2.** *Can, US* AGRIC GRAIN STOREHOUSE a storehouse for grain, equipped with a mechanism for taking in, lifting, and discharging the grain **3.** TECH HOISTING MACHINE a machine with scoops or similar devices for hoisting sth to a higher level **4.** AIR AIRCRAFT DEVICE CONTROLLING CLIMB AND DESCENT a hinged flap, either of a pair on the rear portion of the horizontal stabilizing surface or tail plane of an aircraft, used to control the aircraft's up and down movement **5.** AIR AIRCRAFT PLATFORM ON CARRIER on an aircraft carrier, a mechanized platform that transports aircraft from a below-the-deck hangar up to the flight deck and vice versa **6.** ANAT MUSCLE THAT LIFTS PART OF THE BODY a muscle that contracts to lift a part of the body

eleven /i lévv'n/ *n.* **1.** NUMBER 11 the number 11, which is one more than 10 and one fewer than 12 **2.** STH WITH A VALUE OF 11 sth in a numbered series with a value of 11 **3.** GROUP OF 11 a group of 11 objects or people **4.** SPORTS TEAM OF 11 a team of 11 players, e.g. a football team, a hockey team, or a cricket team [Old English *endleofan*, literally 'one over (ten)'] —**eleven** *adj.*, *pron.*

eleven-plus *n.* an examination formerly taken by all children in England and Wales in their last year of primary school, used to determine what sort of secondary education they would receive. A few education authorities still retain this exam.

elevenses /i lévv'nziz/ *n.* a snack, usually including a drink, taken in the middle of the morning, especially by children (*takes a singular or plural verb*)

eleventh /i lévv'nth/ *n.* one of 11 equal parts of sth [Old English *endleofeþa*. See ELEVEN.] —**eleventh** *adj.*, *adv.*

eleventh hour *n.* the last moment before sth happens ○ *'Time after time you'll find solutions are reached at the 59th minute of the eleventh hour'.* (John Major, *Guardian Weekly*; 3 April, 1994)

elevon /élli von/ *n.* a hinged flap on an aircraft, especially one with a delta wing or no tail, that functions both as an elevator and an aileron [Mid-20thC. A blend of ELEVATOR and AILERON.]

elf /elf/ (*plural* **elves** /elvz/) *n.* **1.** MYTHOL SMALL SUPERNATURAL MISCHIEF-MAKER a small lively creature resembling a human being, often considered to have a mischievous nature and magical powers **2.** SMALL MISCHIEVOUS PERSON any small person, especially a child, who plays pranks or tricks [Old English, of prehistoric Germanic origin]

ELF *abbr.* extremely low frequency

elfin /élfin/ *adj.* **1.** OF OR LIKE AN ELF like, characteristic of, or associated with elves **2.** BY ELVES caused or made by elves **3.** DELICATE small and delicate ○ *elfin features* **4.** SMALL AND LIVELY small, delicate, and charmingly sprightly, lively, or mischievous **5.** MAGICAL OR CHARMING having a magical or delicately charming quality

elfish /élfish/, **elvish** /élvish/, **elflike** /élf līk/ *adj.* **1.** OF OR LIKE AN ELF like or relating to an elf **2.** MISCHIEVOUS full of lively mischief —**elfishly** *adv.*

elflock /élf lok/ *n.* a tangled coil of hair (*often used in the plural*)

Elgar /él gaar/, **Sir Edward** (1857–1934) British composer. He was a major figure of late romanticism in music, writing both choral and orchestral works. His *Enigma Variations* (1899) and the patriotic *Pomp and Circumstance Marches* (1901–30) are among his most popular pieces.

Elgin /élgin/ city in northeastern Scotland and administrative centre of Moray district. Population: 19,027 (1991).

Sir Edward Elgar

George Eliot

Elgin Marbles *n.* Greek sculptures from the Parthenon in Athens, brought to Britain in 1806 by Thomas Bruce, seventh earl of Elgin, and now in the British Museum in London. The Greek government has requested their return.

elicit /i líssit/ (-its, -iting, -ited) *vt.* **1.** PROVOKE A REACTION to cause or produce sth as a reaction or response to a stimulus of some kind ○ *His jokes failed to elicit even the faintest of smiles from her.* **2.** DRAW OUT STH HIDDEN to bring to light, or cause sb to disclose, sth hidden or not immediately obvious, especially by a process of questioning or research ○ *What were their chances of eliciting any worthwhile information from such an obstinately uncooperative witness?* [Mid-17thC. Formed from Latin *elicitus* 'drawn out', from, ultimately, *lacere* 'to deceive'.] **—elicitation** /i líssi táysh'n/ *n.* **—elicitor** /i líssitər/ *n.*

elide /i lîd/ (elides, eliding, elided) *vt.* **1.** LANG OMIT ELEMENT OF WORD OR PHRASE to omit a vowel, consonant, or syllable of a word, or leave out part of a sentence or phrase **2.** OMIT STH to omit, delete, or ignore sth (*formal*) [Late 16thC. From Latin *elidere* 'to strike out', from *laedere* 'to strike'.]

eligible /éllijəb'l/ *adj.* **1.** QUALIFIED entitled or qualified to do, be, or get sth ○ *She is eligible to run for office.* **2.** MARRIAGEABLE considered a good candidate for marriage ○ *the most eligible bachelor in town* **3.** *US* FOOTBALL ALLOWED BY RULES TO CATCH A FOOTBALL permitted by the rules to catch a forward pass during a play in American football ■ *n.* SB OR STH ELIGIBLE sb who or sth that meets a set of requirements ○ *We've separated the eligibles from the nonstarters.* [15thC. Via middle French *éligible* 'fit to be chosen' from late Latin *eligibilis* 'that may be chosen', from Latin *eligere* 'to choose' (see ELECT).] **—eligibility** /éllijə bílləti/ *n.* **—eligibly** /éllijəbli/ *adv.*

eliminate /i límmi nayt/ (-nates, -nating, -nated) *vt.* **1.** TAKE SB OR STH AWAY to remove sth or sb from a list or group, or decide to disregard sb or sth as irrelevant or unimportant ○ *The police eliminated him from the list of suspects.* **2.** END STH to put an end to sth, usually sth undesirable ○ *They are pledged to eliminate poverty by the end of the century.* **3.** SPORTS PUT SB OUT OF A COMPETITION to defeat and put a player or team out of a competition ○ *The local team was eliminated in the first round.* **4.** DESTROY SB to kill sb, destroy sth, or make sb or sth ineffective ○ *The pills eliminated the dog's worms.* **5.** PHYSIOL DEFECATE OR URINATE to expel waste from the body (*technical*) **6.** MATH REMOVE A MATHEMATICAL VARIABLE to remove variables from two or more simultaneous mathematical equations by combining the equations [Mid-16thC. From Latin *eliminare*, literally 'to turn out of doors', from *limen* 'threshhold' (source of English *subliminal* and probably *sublime*).] **—elimination** /i límmi náysh'n/ *n.* **—eliminative** /i límminətiv/ *adj.* **—eliminatory** /i límminətəri/ *adj.*

eliminator /i límmi naytər/ *n.* a round in a competition or a question in a quiz, after which competitors who are defeated are removed

ELINT, **elint** *n.* the gathering of information by electronic means, e.g. from aircraft or ships, or the section of the military intelligence service involved in this [Mid-20thC. Shortening and blend of ELECTRONIC + INTELLIGENCE.]

Eliot /élli ət/, **George** (1819–80) British novelist. One of the greatest English novelists, she wrote works including *Adam Bede* (1854) and *Middlemarch* (1871–72). Real name **Mary Ann Evans**

Eliot, Sir John (1592–1632) English politician. He was active in the early stages of Parliament's struggle against King Charles I, who imprisoned him in the Tower of London in 1629, where he died.

T. S. Eliot

Eliot, T. S. (1888–1965) US-born British poet, critic, and dramatist. His poem *The Waste Land* (1922) represents a landmark in modern English poetry. He won a Nobel Prize in literature in 1948. Later works include *Four Quartets* (1935–42) and the verse drama *Murder in the Cathedral* (1935). Full name **Thomas Stearns Eliot**

ELISA /i lîzə/ *n.* a widely used technique for determining the presence or amount of protein in a biological sample, using an enzyme that bonds to an antibody or antigen and causes a colour change. Full form **enzyme-linked immunosorbent assay**

elision /i lízh'n/ *n.* **1.** LANGUAGE OMISSION OF ELEMENT OF WORD the omission of a vowel, consonant, or syllable while pronouncing or writing sth, sometimes as a natural shortening, as in 'He's', sometimes for literary or poetic effect, as in 't'is' **2.** ANY OMISSION OR DELETION the suppression, omission, or deletion of sth, or what has been suppressed, omitted, or deleted (*formal*) [Late 16thC. Via Latin *elisio* from, ultimately, *elidere* 'to strike out' (see ELIDE).]

elite /i léet, ay-/ *n.* **1.** PRIVILEGED MINORITY a small group of people within a larger group who have more power, social standing, wealth, or talent than the rest of the group (*takes a singular or plural verb*) ○ *They belonged to a privileged elite who were being groomed for the top posts in the administration.* **2.** PRINTING SIZE OF PRINTING TYPE a 10-point type that has about 12 characters to the inch, or just under 5 characters to the centimetre ■ *adj.* **1.** RICHEST, BEST, OR MOST POWERFUL belonging to an elite, especially in being more talented, privileged, or highly trained than the rest ○ *elite troops* **2.** FOR RICH OR PRIVILEGED PEOPLE with a membership that is restricted, especially to the rich or privileged [Late 18thC. Via French from, ultimately, Latin *eligere* 'to choose' (see ELECT).]

elitism /i léetizəm, ay-/ *n.* **1.** BELIEF IN CONCEPT OF SUPERIORITY the belief that some people or things are inherently superior to others and deserve preeminence, preferential treatment, or higher rewards because of their superiority **2.** POL, SOC SCI BELIEF IN CONTROL BY SMALL GROUP the belief that government or control should be in the hands of a small group of privileged, wealthy, or intelligent people, or the active promotion of such a system **3.** POL, SOC SCI CONTROL BY SMALL GROUP government or control by a small, specially qualified or privileged group **—elitist** *n.*, *adj.*

elixir /i líksər/ *n.* **1.** PHARM SWEETENED DRUG a sweetened flavoured solution of alcohol and water that acts as a medium for a drug and masks its taste **2.** HIST MIRACULOUS SUBSTANCE a substance once believed to prolong life indefinitely, or to transform base metals into gold **3.** CURE-ALL a panacea or a quick or magical cure [14thC. Via medieval Latin from Arabic *al-iksir*, from Greek *xērion* 'dry powder for treating wounds', from *xēros* 'dry'.]

Elizabeth /i lízzəbəth/, **Queen consort of the United Kingdom** (*b.* 1900). She married the second son of George V, who came to the throne as George VI in 1936, and is the mother of Queen Elizabeth II. Born **Lady Elizabeth Bowes-Lyon**

Elizabeth I /i lízzəbəth-/, **Queen of England and Ireland** (1533–1603). The daughter of Henry VIII and Anne Boleyn, she established the Protestant church in England and presided over a period of domestic political stability and global exploration.

Elizabeth II, **Queen of the United Kingdom** (*b.* 1926). Daughter of George VI and queen since 1952, she married Prince Philip in 1947 and has four children, Prince Charles, Princess Anne, Prince Andrew, and Prince Edward. Born **Princess Elizabeth Alexandra Mary**

Elizabethan /i lízzə beeth'n/ *adj.* **1.** HIST RELATING TO REIGN OF ELIZABETH I relating to or characteristic of the life and times of Elizabeth I, Queen of England and Ireland, who reigned from 1558 to 1603 **2.** ARCHIT DENOTING STYLE OF BUILDING AND DECORATION suggesting or embodying a style of English Renaissance building from the reign of Elizabeth I that emphasized symmetrical layouts and moulded or sculptured decoration with a German or Flemish influence

Elizabethan sonnet *n.* = **Shakespearean sonnet**

elk /elk/ (*plural* **elk** *or* **elks**) *n.* **1.** LARGE-ANTLERED N AMERICAN AND EURASIAN DEER a large thin-legged heavy-bodied deer of northern Europe, Asia, and North America with a long head and a bulbous pliable muzzle. The males have huge antlers. Latin name: *Alces alces.* US term **moose 2.** *US* = **wapitit** [Old English *eolh*]

Elk *n.* a member of a North American men's social and charitable organization, the Benevolent and Protective Order of Elks

elkhound /élk hownd/ *n.* a medium-sized sturdy dog belonging to a breed developed in Norway to hunt elk and other game. It has pointed ears, a broad head, and a thick grey coat. US term **Norwegian elkhound**

ell /el/ *n.* **1.** ARCHIT BUILDING EXTENSION an extension of a building, usually at right angles to the main part **2.** STH L-SHAPED sth L-shaped or with a right-angled bend [Late 18thC. Variant spelling of the letter *L*.]

Ella /éllə/, **Mark Gordon** (*b.* 1959) Australian rugby player. He was the first Aboriginal captain of Australia (1982).

ellagic acid /i lájjik-/ *n.* a crystalline compound obtained from oak galls and tannins. It has some capacity for reducing bleeding. Formula: $C_{14}H_6O_8$.

Ellef Ringnes Island /éllef ríng ness-/ one of the Canadian Sverdrup Islands, located in the Arctic Ocean, in the Northwest Territories. Area: 13,310 sq. km/5,139 sq. mi.

Ellesmere Island /élzmeer-/ island in Nunavut Territory, northern Canada, close to the northwestern coast of Greenland. Area: 212,690 sq. km/82,120 sq. mi.

Ellesmere Island National Park Reserve /élz meer-/ national park, established in 1980, in the northern part of Ellesmere Island situated in the Arctic Ocean, Nunavut, northeastern Canada. Area: 37,775 sq. km/14,585 sq. mi.

Ellesmere Port /élz meer-/ town in Cheshire, northwestern England, on the River Mersey. Population: 78,800 (1991).

Ellice Islands /éllis-/ former name for **Tuvalu** (until 1975)

Duke Ellington

Ellington /éllingtən/, **Duke** (1899–1974) US jazz pianist, composer, and band leader. He came to fame in the early 1930s and is known for compositions such as 'Sophisticated Lady' (1933). Real name **Edward Kennedy Ellington**

Elliott /élli ət/, **Herb** (*b.* 1938) Australian athlete. He was the winner of the gold medal for the 1,500 m at the 1960 Olympics. Between 1957 and 1961 he was never defeated over this distance. Full name **Herbert James Elliott**

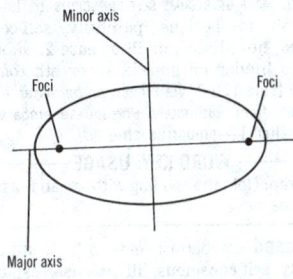
Ellipse

ellipse /i líps/ *n.* GEOM **1.** SHAPE RESEMBLING OVAL a shape like a stretched circle with slightly longer, flatter sides **2.** INTERSECTION OF CONE AND OBLIQUE PLANE the shape formed by the intersection of a right cone and an oblique plane that does not intersect the base of the cone [Mid-18thC. Via French from Latin *ellipsis*, from Greek *elleipsis* 'defect, omission', from *elleipein* 'to leave out, fall short'.]

ellipsis /i lípsiss/ (*plural* **-ses** /-seez/) *n.* **1.** GRAM OMISSION OF IMPLIED WORD the omission of one or more words from a sentence, especially when what is omitted can be understood from the context. The omission of 'go' in 'I went but my wife didn't' (= 'didn't go') is an example of ellipsis. **2.** PRINTING MARK INDICATING OMITTED TEXT a printed mark, usually three dots (...) or, less often, asterisks (***), used to indicate that sth has been omitted from a text [Early 17thC. From Latin (see ELLIPSE).]

ellipsoid /i líp soyd/ *n.* GEOM OVAL SHAPE a geometric surface or a solid figure shaped like a rugby ball. Any section through an ellipsoid is either an ellipse or a circle. ■ *adj.* OVAL-SHAPED in the shape of an ellipsoid —**ellipsoidal** /íllip sóyd'l, éllip-/ *adj.*

elliptical /i líptik'l/, **elliptic** /i líptik/ *adj.* **1.** GEOM LIKE ELLIPSE in the shape or pattern of a geometrical ellipse **2.** GRAM RELATING TO ELLIPSIS relating to ellipsis or containing an example of ellipsis **3.** HIGHLY ECONOMICAL IN SPEECH OR WRITING extremely concise in speech or writing, sometimes so concise as to be difficult or impossible to understand —**elliptically** *adv.*

ellipticity /íllip tíssəti, éllip-/ (*plural* **-ties**) *n.* the deviation or degree of deviation of an ellipse or ellipsoid from a perfect circle or sphere. Ellipticity is measured as the ratio of the major axis to the minor axis of the ellipse or ellipsoid.

Ellis /élliss/, **Havelock** (1859–1939) British psychologist. His *Studies in the Psychology of Sex* (1897–1928) was a landmark in the analysis of sexual behaviour. Full name **Henry Havelock Ellis**

Ellis Island /élliss-/ complex of one natural and two artificial islands in upper New York Bay, eastern New Jersey and southeastern New York State, near Manhattan. From 1892 to 1954 it served as a chief entry point for immigrants to the United States. Area: 11 hectares/27 acres.

Ellsworth Land /élz wurth-/ high plateau in western Antarctica, south of the Antarctic Peninsula. It rises at the Vinson Massif, the highest point in Antarctica, to 5,140 m/16,863 ft.

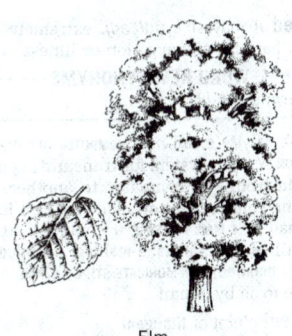
Elm

elm /elm/ *n.* **1.** LARGE DECIDUOUS TREE a large deciduous tree with serrated leaves and winged fruits, found throughout northern temperate regions. Genus: *Ulmus.* **2.** WOOD OF ELM TREE the hard heavy wood of the elm tree, used as fuel and in making furniture, boats, and buildings [Old English. Ultimately from an Indo-European word that also produced English *alder*.]

elm bark beetle *n.* the beetle that spreads the fungus causing Dutch elm disease. Family: Scolytidae.

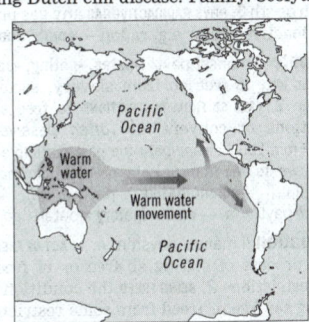
El Niño: Map showing movement of warm water currents across the Pacific Ocean

El Niño /el neényō/ *n.* METEOROL a periodic change occurring every 5 to 8 years in Pacific Ocean currents off South America, often bringing severe climate disruption to countries in and beside the Pacific [From Spanish, shortening of *El Niño de Navidad* 'the Christmas Child'; from the time of year when the currents change]

elodea /ə lṓdi ə/ *n.* a plant that grows submerged in ponds and ditches or is used in aquariums as an oxygenating plant. Canadian pondweed is a type of elodea. Genus: *Elodea.* [Late 19thC. From modern Latin, genus name, formed from Greek *helōdēs* 'marshy'.]

Elohim /e lṓ him, éllō heém/ *n.* in the Bible, a Hebrew word for God [Late 16thC. From Hebrew *elōhīm*, the plural of *elōah* 'God'.]

elongate /eé long gayt/ *vti.* (**-gates**, **-gating**, **-gated**) LENGTHEN to make sth longer, or become longer ■ *adj.* **1.** LONG long and narrow or slender (*technical*) **2.** MADE LONGER lengthened or stretched out (*formal*) [Mid-16thC. From late Latin *elongat-*, the past participle stem of *elongare* 'to lengthen', from Latin *longus* 'long'.] —**elongated** *adj.*

elongation /eé long gáysh'n/ *n.* **1.** LENGTHENING the act of lengthening sth, or the condition of being lengthened **2.** STH LENGTHENED sth that has become or been made longer **3.** ASTRON ANGLE BETWEEN SUN AND CELESTIAL OBJECT the angle between the Sun and either the Moon or a planet, as seen from Earth or a point in space

elope /i lṓp/ (**elopes**, **eloping**, **eloped**) *vi.* to go away suddenly without telling anyone, especially in order to get married without the knowledge or consent of parents or guardians, or to live with a lover [Late 16thC. From Anglo-Norman *aloper*, literally 'to run away', which was perhaps formed from a Middle English word meaning 'run'.] —**elopement** *n.* —**eloper** *n.*

eloquence /élləkwənss/ *n.* **1.** NOTABLE SPEAKING ABILITY the ability to speak forcefully, expressively, and persuasively **2.** EFFECTIVE LANGUAGE forceful, expressive, and persuasive language

eloquent /élləkwənt/ *adj.* **1.** SPEAKING OR SPOKEN BEAUTIFULLY AND FORCEFULLY said or saying sth in a forceful, expressive, and persuasive way **2.** EXPRESSING EMOTION CLEARLY expressing a feeling or thought clearly, memorably, or movingly [14thC. Via French from Latin *eloquent-*, the present participle stem of *eloqui* 'to speak out', from *loqui* 'to speak'.] —**eloquently** *adv.* —**eloquentness** *n.*

El Paso city in western Texas on the Rio Grande, a port of entry from Mexico. Population: 579,307 (1994).

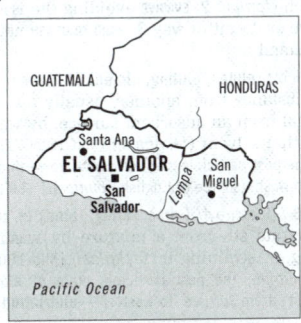
El Salvador

El Salvador /el sálvə dawr/ republic on the Pacific coast of Central America, bordered by Guatemala and Honduras. Language: Spanish. Currency: colón. Capital: San Salvador. Population: 5,661,827 (1997). Area: 21,041 sq. km/8,124 sq. mi. Official name **Republic of El Salvador** —**Salvadoran** *n.*, *adj.*

else /elss/ *adj.*, *adv.* **1.** IN ADDITION used to refer in a vague way to another person, place, or thing ○ (adj) *Something else I'd like to see is more jobs for skilled manual workers.* ○ (adj) *What else did she say?* ○ (adv) *Try to shop around and go somewhere else apart from your usual stores.* **2.** DIFFERENT used to refer in a vague way to sb or sth other or different ○ (adj) *Let's try something else.* ○ (adv) *He was unhappy and considered working somewhere else.* [Old English *elles.* Ultimately from an Indo-European word that also produced English *alter* and *alien.*]

elsewhere /élss wáir/ *adv.* at, in, or to another place ○ *If you're calling from elsewhere, please press 2 to contact reception.* ○ *They stock used books, and they have their own imprint that may be hard to find elsewhere.* [Old English *elles hwær*, literally 'other where']

ELT *n.* the teaching of English to people whose first language is not English. Full form **English Language Teaching**

eluant *n.* = eluent

Éluard /élloo aar/, **Paul** (1895–1952) French poet. He is one of France's greatest 20th-century lyric poets and co-author of the first surrealist manifesto (1924). He fought in the communist resistance in World War II. Pseudonym of **Eugène Grindel**

eluate /éllyoo ayt/ *n.* CHEM the liquid left after the process of elution, consisting of dissolved matter and the solvent used [Mid-20thC. Coined from Latin *eluere* (see ELUTE) + -ATE.]

elucidate /i loóssi dayt/ (**-dates**, **-dating**, **-dated**) *vti.* to explain or clarify sth (*formal*) [Mid-16thC. From late Latin *elucidat-*, the past participle stem of *elucidare* 'to make clear', from Latin *lucidus* 'clear' (source of English *lucid*).] —**elucidation** /i loóssi dáysh'n/ *n.* —**elucidative** /i loóssi daytiv, -dətiv/ *adj.* —**elucidator** /-daytər/ *n.*

elude /i loód/ (**eludes**, **eluding**, **eluded**) *vt.* **1.** ESCAPE OR AVOID to escape from or avoid sb or sth by cunning, skill, or resourcefulness **2.** ESCAPE SB'S UNDERSTANDING OR MEMORY to be beyond sb's understanding, or be unable to be recalled [Mid-16thC. From Latin *eludere* 'to deceive, escape from, win from sb at play', from *ludere* 'to play'.]

WORD KEY: USAGE

See Usage note at ***avoid.***

eluent /éllyoo ənt/, **eluant** *n.* a solvent used to remove sth from a substance [Mid-20thC. From Latin *eluent-*, the present participle stem of *eluere* (see ELUTE).]

Elul /e loól/ *n.* in the Jewish calendar, the 12th month of the civil year and the 6th month of the religious year. It is 29 days long. [Mid-16thC. From Hebrew *elūl.*]

elusion /i lóozh'n/ *n.* the act of avoiding or escaping from sb or sth (*formal*) [Mid-16thC. From the late Latin stem *elusion-*, from Latin *elus-*, the past participle stem of *eludere* (see ELUDE).]

elusive /i lóossiv/ *adj.* **1.** HARD TO FIND difficult to find or catch **2.** HARD TO PIN DOWN difficult to understand, define, or identify **3.** HARD TO REMEMBER not easily called to mind or memory —**elusively** *adv.* —**elusiveness** *n.*

elusory /i lóossəri/ *adj.* **1.** HARD TO FIND difficult to find or catch (*formal*) **2.** EVASIVE avoiding the issue in an evasive or deceitful way **3.** HARD TO GRASP not easy to understand

elute /i lóot/ (**elutes, eluting, eluted**) *vt.* CHEM to remove one substance from another, usually an adsorbed material from an adsorbent surface, by washing it out with a solvent (*technical*) [Mid-18thC. From Latin *elut-*, the past participle stem of *eluere* 'to wash out', from *luere* 'to wash' (source of English *ablution*).] —**elution** *n.*

elutriate /i lóotri ayt/ (**-ates, -ating, -ated**) *vt.* to purify or separate sth from a mixture by washing, decanting, or straining it (*technical*) [Mid-18thC. From Latin *elutriat-*, the past participle stem of *elutriare* 'to wash out', from *lutriare* 'to wash'.] —**elutriation** /i lóotri áysh'n/ *n.*

eluvia plural of **eluvium**

eluvial deposit *n.* a concentration of an ore deposit formed as a result of the removal of less dense host material

eluviation /i lóovi áysh'n/ *n.* GEOL a process by which material dissolved or suspended in water within soil moves down or sideways as rainwater moves through the soil

eluvium /i lóovi əm/ (*plural* **-a** /-ə/) *n.* GEOL an accumulated mass of soil, sand, silt, or rock debris resulting from weathering or drifting [Late 19thC. Coined from Latin *eluere* (see ELUTE) on the model of ALLUVIUM.] —**eluvial** *adj.*

elver /élvər/ *n.* a young freshwater eel, especially one that migrates from salt water [Mid-17thC. From English dialect *ellfare*, literally 'eel-journey', because they migrate into streams from the ocean.]

elves plural of **elf**

elvish *adj.* = **elfish**

Ely /éeli/ cathedral city in the fenland of Cambridgeshire, eastern England, on the River Ouse. It stands on a hill known as the Isle of Ely. Population: 11,760 (1994).

Elysian /i lízzi ən/ *adj.* **1.** RELATING TO ELYSIUM relating to or typical of Elysium **2.** BLISSFUL full of or giving great pleasure and delight (*literary*) [Mid-16thC. Formed from Latin *Elysium*, from Greek *Elusion pedion* 'Elysian field', of unknown origin.]

Elysian Fields *npl.* = **Elysium** *n.* 1

Elysium /i lízzi əm/ *n.* **1.** HEAVEN in Greek mythology, the home of the blessed after death **2.** IDEAL PLACE OR CONDITION any ideally delightful or blissful place or condition **3.** ASTRON BULGE ON SURFACE OF MARS an extensive low bulge on the surface of Mars in the northern hemisphere gently rising to a height of approximately 5 km/3 mi., supporting the volcanoes Hecate Tholus and Elysium Mons

elytron /élli tron/ (*plural* **-tra** /-trə/), **elytrum** /-trəm/ (*plural* **-tra**) *n.* a tough front wing, occurring in pairs on beetles and some other insects, that acts as a protective covering for the rear wings [Mid-18thC. From Greek *elutron* 'sheath'.]

em /em/ *n.* PRINTING **1.** VARIABLE MEASURE OF TYPE a unit of measurement of print size, equal to the point size of the typeface being used **2.** = **pica**² *n.*

'em /əm/ *contr.* them (*informal*) [14thC. Originally a variant of Old English *hem* 'them'; now regarded as a shortening of THEM.]

EM *abbr.* **1.** electromagnetic **2.** electron microscope

em- *prefix.* = **en-** (*used before m, b, or p*)

emaciate /i máyssi ayt/ (**-ates, -ating, -ated**) *vti.* to become, or make sb or sth become, extremely thin [Early 17thC. From Latin *emaciat-*, the past participle stem of *emaciare* 'to make lean, waste away', from *macer* 'lean' (source of English *meagre*).] —**emaciation** /i máyssi áysh'n/ *n.*

emaciated /i máyssi aytid/ *adj.* extremely thin, especially because of starvation or illness

WORD KEY: SYNONYMS

See Synonyms at ***thin.***

e-mail /ée mayl/, **email** *n.* **1.** COMPUTER-TO-COMPUTER COMMUNICATION SYSTEM a system for transmitting messages and data from one computer to another, using a telephone connection and modems. Full form **electronic mail 2.** E-MAIL MESSAGE a communication sent by e-mail ■ *vt.* (**e-mails, e-mailing, e-mailed; emails, emailing, emailed**) COMMUNICATE STH BY E-MAIL to send a message to sb by e-mail

emalangeni plural of **lilangeni**

emanate /émmə nayt/ (**-nates, -nating, -nated**) *v.* **1.** *vi.* COME FROM to come from or come out of sb, sth, or somewhere **2.** *vt.* SEND OUT to emit, send out, or give out sth such as rays or information (*formal*) [Mid-18thC. From Latin *emanat-*, the past participle stem of *emanare* 'to flow out, arise', from *manare* 'to flow'.] —**emanative** /émmənətiv/ *adj.*

emanation /émmə náysh'n/ *n.* **1.** ACT OF SENDING OUT the act of emitting, sending out, or giving out sth **2.** STH SENT OUT sth that issues or is sent out or given out from sb or sth **3.** PHYS RADIOACTIVE GAS any gas produced by radioactive decay, e.g. radon —**emanational** *adj.*

emancipate /i mánssi payt/ (**-pates, -pating, -pated**) *vt.* **1.** SET SB FREE to free sb from slavery, serfdom, or bondage **2.** FREE SB FROM RESTRICTIONS to free sb from restrictions or conventions (*often passive*) [Early 17thC. From Latin *emancipat-*, the past participle stem of *emancipare* 'to free from parental power', from *mancipium* 'ownership'.] —**emancipative** /-paytiv/ *adj.* —**emancipator** /-paytər/ *n.* —**emancipatory** /-pətəri/ *adj.*

emancipation /i mánssi páysh'n/ *n.* **1.** ACT OF FREEING the act or process of setting sb free or of freeing sb from restrictions **2.** BEING FREED the condition or fact of being set free or freed from some restriction

emarginate /i maárji nayt/ *adj.* BOT, BIOL with a notch at the tip [Late 18thC. From Latin *emarginatus*, the past participle of *emarginare* 'to remove the edges of'.] —**emargination** /i maárji náysh'n/ *n.*

EMAS /ée mass/ *n.* a voluntary scheme of the European Union in which commercial and other organizations are encouraged to assess their approach to environmental matters against certain criteria. Full form **Eco-Management and Audit Scheme**

emasculate /i máskyoo layt/ (**-lates, -lating, -lated**) *vt.* **1.** PHYSIOL CASTRATE to remove the testicles of a male human being or animal (*formal or literary*) **2.** WEAKEN SB OR STH to deprive sb or sth of effectiveness, spirit, or force (*formal*) (*sometimes considered offensive*) **3.** BOT REMOVE STAMENS FROM to remove the male reproductive organs (**stamens**) from a flower, e.g. to prevent self-pollination [Early 17thC. From Latin *emasculat-*, the past participle stem of *emasculare* 'to remove the male glands of, castrate', from *masculus* 'male'.] —**emasculation** /i máskyoo láysh'n/ *n.* —**emasculative** /i máskyoolətiv/ *adj.* —**emasculator** /-laytər/ *n.* —**emasculatory** /-lətəri, -laytəri/ *adj.*

embalm /im baám/ (**-balms, -balming, -balmed**) *vt.* **1.** PRESERVE DEAD BODY to treat a dead body with a preservative substance in order to stop it decaying **2.** KEEP STH INTACT to preserve sth from change or oblivion (*formal*) **3.** PERFUME STH to give a sweet scent to sth (*literary*) [14thC. From French *embaumer*, from *baume* 'balm'.] —**embalmer** *n.* —**embalmment** /im baám mənt, em-/ *n.*

embank /im bángk/ (**-banks, -banking, -banked**) *vt.* to surround or line a road, canal, or other area with an embankment

embankment /im bángkmənt/ *n.* a ridge or raised platform built of earth or stone to confine a waterway or support a road or railway line

embargo /em baárgō/ *n.* (*plural* **-goes**) **1.** POL ORDER STOPPING TRADE a government restriction or restraint on commerce, especially an order that prohibits trade in a given commodity or with a particular nation **2.** PROHIBITION any official restraint or prohibition **3.** POL ORDER HALTING MOVEMENT OF SHIPS a government order that prohibits commercial ships from entering or leaving its ports, often as a measure during war ■ *vt.* (**-goes, -going, -goed**) **1.** PROHIBIT OR FORBID STH to place an embargo on sth **2.** SEIZE STH to confiscate or seize sth for government use [Late 16thC. From Spanish, formed from *embargar* 'to restrain, seize, embargo', probably from assumed Vulgar Latin *imbarricare* 'to restrain, impede', from, ultimately, Latin *barra* 'bar'.]

embark /em baárk/ (**-barks, -barking, -barked**) *vti.* to go on board, or put or take sb or sth on board a ship or aircraft [Mid-16thC. From French *embarquer*, from *barque* 'ship' (source of English *barque*).] —**embarkation** /ém baar káysh'n/ *n.* —**embarkment** *n.*

embark on, embark upon *vti.* to start or engage in an undertaking

embarras de richesses /ómba raá də ree shéss/ *n.* an overabundance of desirable things that makes choice among them difficult [From French, literally 'embarrassment of wealth']

embarrass /im bárrəss, em-/ (**-rasses, -rassing, -rassed**) *v.* **1.** *vti.* MAKE OR BECOME SELF-CONSCIOUS to become or cause sb to become painfully self-conscious, ashamed, humiliated, or ill at ease **2.** *vt.* HOLD SB OR STH UP to hinder or impede sb or sth (*old*) (*often passive*) [Late 17thC. Via French *embarrasser* 'to impede, disconcert' from, ultimately, Portuguese *embaraçar*, from *baraço* 'halter'.] —**embarrassable** *adj.*

WORD KEY: USAGE

Spelling trap: Note the spelling with *-rr-* and *-ass*. ***Harass*** has only one *r*.

embarrassed /im bárrəst, em-/ *adj.* **1.** SELF-CONSCIOUS painfully self-conscious, ill at ease, ashamed, or humiliated **2.** SHORT OF MONEY in financial difficulties because of a lack of money —**embarrassedly** *adv.*

embarrassing /im bárrəssing, em-/ *adj.* causing painful self-consciousness, uncomfortableness, shame, or humiliation —**embarrassingly** *adv.*

embarrassment /im bárrəsmənt/ *n.* **1.** ACUTE SELF-CONSCIOUSNESS a feeling of painful self-consciousness, uncomfortableness, shame, or humiliation **2.** STH THAT CAUSES SELF-CONSCIOUSNESS sth that causes a feeling of painful self-consciousness, uncomfortableness, shame, or humiliation **3.** LACK OF MONEY a state of financial difficulty

embassy /émbəssi/ (*plural* **-sies**) *n.* **1.** AMBASSADOR'S HEADQUARTERS the residence and place of business of an ambassador **2.** EMBASSY STAFF an ambassador with his or her ambassadorial staff **3.** AMBASSADOR'S POSITION AND RESPONSIBILITIES the mission, rank, or function of an ambassador [Late 16thC. Via Old French *ambassé* from, ultimately, assumed Vulgar Latin *ambactiare* 'to go on a mission'.]

embattle /im bátt'l/ (**-tles, -tling, -tled**) *vt.* **1.** MIL POSITION FORCES to arrange forces in readiness for battle **2.** MIL FORTIFY STH to fortify sth such as a building, village, or position in battle (*archaic*) (*usually passive*) **3.** ARCHIT BUILD STH WITH BATTLEMENTS to provide a building with battlements (*archaic*) (*usually passive*) [14thC. From Old French *embataillier*, from *bataille* 'battle'.]

embattled /im bátt'ld/ *adj.* **1.** UNDER ASSAULT under attack or subject to controversy **2.** MIL FIGHTING OR READY TO FIGHT ready for or engaged in battle **3.** ARCHIT WITH BATTLEMENTS with battlements provided (*archaic*) **4.** HERALDRY LIKE BATTLEMENTS in heraldry, used to describe a design with an edge resembling battlements

embayment /im báymənt/ *n.* **1.** BAY a bay in a coastline (*technical*) **2.** BAY FORMATION the process by which a bay is formed in a coastline

embed /im béd/ (**-beds, -bedding, -bedded**), **imbed** (**-beds, -bedding, -bedded**) *v.* **1.** *vti.* PLACE OR BE PLACED SOLIDLY to fix sth or become fixed in a surrounding mass **2.** *vt.* SURROUND STH to surround or cover sth closely (*usually passive*) **3.** *vt.* FIX STH IN MIND to fix sth deeply in the mind or memory (*often passive*) **4.** *vi.* BECOME LODGED to become deeply and solidly lodged in sth

embellish /im béllish/ (-lishes, -lishing, -lished) vt. **1.** BEAUTIFY STH to increase the beauty of sth by adding ornaments or decorations **2.** ADD FICTITIOUS OR EXAGGERATED DETAILS TO to make an account or description more interesting by inventing or exaggerating details **3.** MUSIC ADD TO MELODY to add extra notes, accents, or trills to a melody to make it more beautiful or interesting [14thC. From Old French *embellir*, literally 'to make beautiful', from *bel* 'beautiful', from Latin *bellus* (source of English *beauty*).]

embellishment /im béllishmənt/ n. **1.** BEAUTIFICATION OF STH the act or process of adding ornaments or decorations to sth to make it more beautiful **2.** STH ADDED FOR BEAUTIFICATION sth added to increase beauty or interest **3.** MUSIC ADDITION TO MELODY the addition of notes, accents, or trills to a melody to make it more beautiful or interesting, or an added note, accent, or trill. ◊ **fioritura**

ember /émbər/ n. BURNING FRAGMENT a small piece of glowing or smouldering material from a dying fire ■ **embers** npl. **1.** REMAINS OF FIRE the glowing or smouldering remains of a dying fire **2.** REMAINS OF PASSION the dying but not yet extinguished remains of a great emotion, especially love (*literary*) [Old English *æmyrge*. Ultimately from an Indo-European word meaning 'to burn' that also produced English *combustion*.]

Ember Days npl. days of prayer and fasting in Roman Catholic and Anglican Churches, comprising the Wednesday, Friday, and Saturday following Pentecost, the first Sunday after Lent, September 14, and December 13 [*Ember* from Old English *ymbryne* 'circuit', literally 'running round', from *ryne* 'course, running'; from the fact that these days 'come round' four times a year]

embezzle /im bézz'l/ (-zles, -zling, -zled) vti. to take for personal use money or property that has been given on trust by others, without their knowledge or permission [15thC. From Anglo-Norman *embesiler* 'to steal', from Old French *besillier* 'to gouge, destroy', of unknown origin.] —**embezzlement** n. —**embezzler** n.

──────── **WORD KEY: SYNONYMS** ────────
See Synonyms at **steal**.

embitter /im bíttər/ (-ters, -tering, -tered) vt. **1.** MAKE SB BITTER to make sb feel bitter or aggrieved **2.** MAKE STH WORSE to make sth more bitter or acrimonious — **embitterment** n.

embittered /im bíttərd, em-/ adj. having become bitter, e.g. because of hardship, injustice, or neglect

emblaze[1] /im bláyz/ (-blazes, -blazing, -blazed) vt. (*archaic*) **1.** LIGHT STH UP to light up or illuminate sth **2.** SET STH ALIGHT to kindle sth or set it on fire [15thC. Formed from BLAZE[1].]

emblaze[2] /im bláyz/ (-blazes, -blazing, -blazed) vt. = **emblazon** (*archaic*) [Early 16thC. Formed from BLAZE[2].]

emblazon /im bláyz'n/ (-zons, -zoning, -zoned) vt. **1.** HERALDRY DECORATE FLAG OR SHIELD in heraldry, to decorate or adorn a shield or flag by depicting sth, especially a coat of arms **2.** ADD DESIGN TO STH to decorate or adorn sth such as clothing with bright colours or a symbol or picture **3.** MAKE SB OR STH FAMOUS to celebrate sb or sth, or make sb or sth famous (*literary*) (*often passive*) —**emblazoner** n. —**emblazonment** n.

emblazonry /im bláyz'nri/ (*plural* -ries) n. **1.** ACT OF EMBLAZONING the act or process of putting heraldic decorations on sth such as a shield or flag **2.** DECORATION heraldic decorations on such things as shields and flags

emblem /émbləm/ n. **1.** SYMBOL sth that visually symbolizes an object, idea, group, or quality **2.** BADGE A badge or sign that represents a person, group, or organization **3.** PAINTING ALLEGORICAL IMAGE an allegorical picture, often with a motto, used to illustrate a moral lesson [15thC. Via Latin *emblema* 'inlaid design' from, ultimately, Greek *emballein* 'to throw in, insert', from *ballein* 'to throw'.]

emblematic /émblə máttik/, **emblematical** /-máttik'l/ adj. relating to, consisting of, or acting as an emblem or symbol —**emblematically** adv.

emblematize /em blémmə tīz/ (-tizes, -tizing, -tized), **emblematise** (-tises, -tising, -tised) vt. to serve as a symbol of sth (*formal*)

embodiment /im bóddimənt/ n. **1.** CONCRETE EXPRESSION OF STH sb who or sth that is the tangible or visible expression of an idea or quality **2.** EMBODYING OF STH the act or process by which sth is made tangible or visible

embody /im bóddi/ (-ies, -ying, -ied) vt. **1.** MAKE STH TANGIBLE to give a tangible or visible form to sth abstract **2.** PERSONIFY STH to express or exemplify sth abstract in bodily form **3.** INCORPORATE THINGS INTO ORGANIZED WHOLE to gather and organize a number of things into a whole

embolden /im bóld'n/ (-ens, -ening, -ened) vt. to give sb courage or boldness

embolectomy /émbə léktəmi/ (*plural* -mies) n. the surgical removal of an embolus, usually a blood clot or other obstruction in a blood vessel

emboli plural of **embolus**

embolic /em bóllik/ adj. relating to or caused by an embolus or embolism

embolisation n. = **embolization**

embolism /émbəlizzəm/ n. **1.** MED BLOCKAGE OF ARTERY a condition in which an artery is blocked by an embolus, usually a blood clot formed at one place in the circulation and then lodging in another **2.** MED EMBOLUS an embolus (*informal*) **3.** CALENDAR INSERTION OF DAY OR DAYS the insertion of a day or days into a calendar **4.** CHR PRAYER DURING ROMAN CATHOLIC MASS in the Roman Catholic Church, a prayer for deliverance from evil inserted in a Mass after the Lord's Prayer [14thC. Via late Latin *embolismus* from Greek *embolismos*, from *emballein* 'to insert' (see EMBLEM).]

embolization /émbə lī záysh'n/, **embolisation** n. the process or condition in which a blood vessel is blocked by a blood clot or other obstruction (**embolus**)

embolus /émbələss/ (*plural* -li /-lī/) n. an abnormal mass, most commonly a blood clot, that becomes lodged in a blood vessel and obstructs it [Mid-17thC. Via Latin from Greek *embolos* 'peg, stopper, wedge', from *emballein* 'to insert' (see EMBLEM).]

embonpoint /om boN pwa′aN/ n. ABOVE-AVERAGE BODY WEIGHT a body weight that is above average and causes an impression of roundness (*humorous*) ○ 'She was slightly inclined to embonpoint'. (J. M. Barrie, *Peter Pan*; 1904) ■ adj. ABOVE AVERAGE BODY WEIGHT having a body weight that is above average and causes the impression of roundness (*humorous dated*) (*sometimes considered offensive*) [Late 17thC. From French, literally 'in good condition'.]

embosom /im bŏŏzəm/ (-oms, -oming, -omed) vt. (*archaic*) **1.** SURROUND SB OR STH PROTECTIVELY to surround or envelop sb or sth, especially in a protective way **2.** EMBRACE SB to take sb into your arms and hold him or her to your bosom **3.** CHERISH SB to cherish, foster, or care about sb

emboss /im bóss/ (-bosses, -bossing, -bossed) vt. **1.** DECORATE STH WITH RAISED PATTERN to decorate or mark a surface with a slightly raised design or lettering **2.** MAKE RAISED PATTERN OF STH to make sth as a raised pattern on a surface ○ *the title was embossed in gold lettering on the cover* [14thC. From Old French *embocer*, from *boce* 'protuberance, knoblike mass' (source of English *boss*[2]).] —**embosser** n.

embossment /im bóssmənt/ n. **1.** ACT OF EMBOSSING STH the act, process, or condition of making sth as or decorating sth with a slightly raised pattern **2.** RAISED DECORATION slightly raised decoration on a surface

embouchure /ómbŏŏ shŏŏr/ n. **1.** GEOG RIVER MOUTH the mouth of a river **2.** GEOG VALLEY MOUTH the mouth of a valley where it becomes a plain **3.** MUSIC POSITION OF LIPS AND TONGUE the adjustment of the lips and tongue in playing a wind instrument **4.** MUSIC MOUTHPIECE the mouthpiece of a wind instrument [Mid-18thC. From French, formed from *emboucher* 'to put to your mouth', from *bouche* 'mouth'.]

embourgeoisement /om boor zhwaaz ma′aN/ n. the process by which a social group becomes middle-class in manners and attitudes [Mid-20thC. From French, formed from *bourgeois* (see BOURGEOIS).]

embowed /im bŏd, em-/ adj. shaped like a vault or arch

embowel /im bówəl/ (-els, -eling, -eled) vt. (*archaic*) **1.** PUT DEEP IN STH to enclose, embed, or bury sth deeply **2.** = **disembowel**

embower /im bówər/ (-ers, -ering, -ered) vt. to shelter or enclose sb or sth in a bower or a place or structure resembling a bower (*archaic or literary*) [Late 16thC. Coined from EM- + BOWER.]

embrace /im bráyss/ v. (-braces, -bracing, -braced) **1.** vti. HUG SB to hug sb in your arms fondly, or hug each other fondly **2.** vt. MAKE USE OF STH to welcome and take advantage of sth eagerly or willingly **3.** vt. ADOPT STH to adopt or take up sth, especially a belief or way of life **4.** vt. COMPRISE STH to include sth as part of a whole **5.** vt. SURROUND STH to surround or enclose sth (*literary*) (*often passive*) ■ n. HUG GIVEN an affectionate or passionate hug [14thC. Via Old French *embracer*, literally 'to take into your arms', from, ultimately, Latin *bracchium* 'arm' (source of English *brace*, *bracelet*, and *bra*).] —**embraceable** adj. —**embracement** n. —**embracer** n.

embracery /im bráyssəri/ n. LAW, CRIMINOL the offence of trying to influence a judge or jury, e.g. by bribery, threats, or promises

embranchment /im bránchmənt/ n. **1.** BRANCHING OUT OF GEOGRAPHICAL FEATURE an act of branching out by a feature of the natural landscape, e.g. a river or mountain range **2.** BRANCH OF GEOGRAPHICAL FEATURE a branch of sth such as a river or mountain range [Mid-19thC. From French *embranchement*, from *branche* (source of English *branch*).]

embrangle /im bráng g'l/ (-gles, -gling, -gled) vt. to confuse, perplex, or entangle sb or sth (*archaic*) [Mid-17thC. Formed from obsolete *brangle* 'to shake, squabble', from French *branler* 'to shake'.] —**embranglement** n.

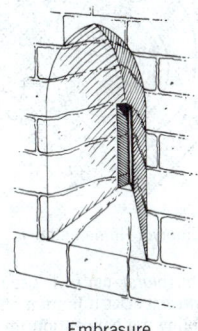

Embrasure

embrasure /im bráyzhər/ n. **1.** INDUST SLANTED OPENING IN FORTIFICATION a slanted opening in the wall or parapet of a fortification, designed so that a defender can fire through it on attackers **2.** ARCHIT TAPERED OPENING an opening in the wall of a building for a door or window, tapered so as to be wider on the inside than on the outside [Early 17thC. From French, formed from obsolete *embraser* 'to widen (a door or window)', of unknown origin.]

embrittle /im brítt'l/ (-tles, -tling, -tled) vti. to become or make sth become brittle

embrocate /émbrə kayt/ (-cates, -cating, -cated) vt. to rub lotion or liniment onto a part of the body [Early 17thC. From Latin *embrocat-*, the past participle stem of *embrocare* 'to treat with healing liquid', from late Latin *embroc(h)a*, from Greek *embrokhē* 'lotion'.]

embrocation /émbrə káysh'n/ n. a liniment or lotion for rubbing onto the body, usually to relieve muscle or joint pain

embroider /im bróydər/ (-ders, -dering, -dered) v. **1.** vti. CRAFT SEW PATTERN INTO STH to decorate sth with needlework **2.** vt. CRAFT MAKE STH BY SEWING to use needlework to make a decoration **3.** vti. EMBELLISH STORY to add exaggerated or fictitious details to an account of sth to make it more interesting [14thC. From Anglo-Norman *enbrouder*, from Old French *brouder* 'to embroider', of prehistoric Germanic origin.] —**embroiderer** n.

embroidery /im bróydəri/ (*plural* -ies) n. **1.** CRAFT ACT OF MAKING DECORATIVE NEEDLEWORK the craft of using needlework to make decorative designs **2.** CRAFT STH WITH DECORATIVE NEEDLEWORK sth produced by or ornamented with decorative needlework **3.** ADDITION OF FICTITIOUS DETAILS elaboration or embellishment in sb's account of sth to make it more interesting

Embroidery

embroil /im bróyl/ (-broils, -broiling, -broiled) vt. **1.** INVOLVE SB IN CONFLICT to involve sb or yourself in trouble, disagreement, or conflict **2.** MUDDLE OR MIX UP STH to make sth confused or over-complicated [Early 17thC. From French *embrouiller* 'to confuse, confound', from *brouiller* 'to mix confusedly', ultimately of prehistoric Germanic origin.]

embrown /im brówn/ (-browns, -browning, -browned) vt. to make sth darker, especially brown (*literary*)

embrue /im broó/ vt. = imbrue

Embryo: Human embryo

embryo /émbri ō/ (plural -os) n. **1.** MED HUMAN OFFSPRING IN INITIAL DEVELOPMENTAL STAGE a human offspring in the early stages following conception up to the end of the eighth week, after which it is classified as a foetus **2.** ZOOL ANIMAL IN INITIAL DEVELOPMENTAL STAGE the developing young of an animal from the earliest stages after conception up to birth or hatching **3.** BOT PLANT IN INITIAL DEVELOPMENTAL STAGE a plant in its earliest stages of development. In seed-bearing plants, the embryo is contained within the seed. **4.** EARLY FORM an early form or rudimentary stage of sth ○ *the embryo of an exciting new invention* [14thC. Via Latin from Greek *embruon*, from *bruein* 'to swell, grow'; the underlying idea is 'sth growing inside the body'.]

embryogenesis /émbri ō jénnəssiss/, **embryogeny** /-ójjini/ n. EMBRYOL the formation and growth of an embryo —**embryogenetic** /émbri ō jə néttik/ adj. —**embryogenic** adj.

embryology /émbri óllǝji/ n. **1.** STUDY OF EMBRYOS the scientific study of embryos and their development **2.** MED STUDY OF DEVELOPMENT OF HUMAN OFFSPRING the study of the growth and development of the human embryo and foetus from conception to birth —**embryologic** /émbri ə lójjik/ adj. —**embryologically** adv. —**embryologist** n.

embryonic /émbri ónnik/, **embryonal** /-ən'l/, **embryotic** adj. **1.** RELATING TO EMBRYO relating to or characteristic of an embryo **2.** embryonic, embryonic IN EARLY DEVELOPMENTAL STAGE in an initial or rudimentary stage of development —**embryonically** adv.

embryonic membrane n. any membranous structure, e.g. the amnion, chorion, or yolk sac, that comes from a fertilized ovum but does not become part of the embryo

embryo sac n. BOT a large oval cell found inside a female reproductive organ (**ovule**) of a flowering plant, that contains the egg cell, which gives rise to the embryo and the endosperm nuclei

embryotic /émbri óttik/ adj. = embryonic

embryo transfer n. EMBRYOL the transplanting of an embryo from one female animal into the womb of a surrogate mother

embus /im búss/ (-busses, -bussing, -bussed) vti. to put sb, especially troops, on a bus, or to get on a bus

emcee /ém seé/ n. MASTER OF CEREMONIES a master of ceremonies (*informal*) ■ vti. (-cees, -ceeing, -ceed) BE MASTER OF CEREMONIES to act as a master of ceremonies for an event (*informal*) [Mid-20thC. Represents the pronunciation of *MC*, shortening of *Master of Ceremonies*.]

em dash n. in printing, a dash that is one em long

-eme suffix. a distinctive unit of linguistic structure ○ *lexeme* [From French *-ème*, from *phonème* (see PHONEME)]

emend /i ménd/ (emends, emending, emended), **emendate** /-ates, -ating, -ated/ vt. to make corrections or alterations to improve a text [15thC. From Latin *emendare*, literally 'to take out a fault', from *menda* 'fault, blemish'.] —**emender** n.

——— **WORD KEY: USAGE** ———

See Usage note at **amend**.

emendation /eé men dáysh'n/ n. **1.** CORRECTION MADE a correction or alteration made to a text **2.** ACT OR PROCESS OF TEXT CORRECTION the act or process of correcting a text

emerald /émmərəld/ n. MINERALS GREEN GEMSTONE a form of beryl coloured green by chromium that is highly valued as a gemstone ■ adj., n. COLOURS = emerald green [13thC. Directly or via Old French *emeraude* from medieval Latin *esmeraldus*, alteration of Latin *smaragdus*, which came via Greek *smaragdos* 'green gem' from a Semitic word meaning 'to shine'.]

Emerald /émmərəld/ town in southeastern Queensland, Australia. It is an agricultural and mining centre. Population: 9,345 (1996).

emerald cut n. a rectangular multifaceted cut for gemstones, especially emeralds and diamonds

emerald green n. a bright green colour, like that of an emerald —**emerald-green** adj.

Emerald Isle n. Ireland, so called because of its vividly green countryside and because the wearing of green was associated with the struggle for national sovereignty (*literary*)

emerge /i múrj/ (emerges, emerging, emerged) v. **1.** vi. COME OUT to appear out of or from behind sth **2.** vi. SURVIVE to come out of an experience, condition, or situation, especially a difficult one **3.** vti. BECOME KNOWN to become known or apparent ○ *It emerged that I had been wrong all along.* **4.** vi. APPEAR OR HAPPEN to arise, appear, or occur [Late 16thC. From Latin *emergere* 'to rise out or up', from *mergere* 'to dive, plunge'.]

emergence /i múrjənss/ n. **1.** ACT OF EMERGING the act or process of coming out, appearing, or coming about **2.** INSECTS APPEARANCE IN ADULT FORM the appearance of the adult form (**imago**) of an insect on the completion of the change (**metamorphosis**) from the larval stage **3.** BOT OUTGROWTH FROM PLANT an outgrowth that lacks sap-conducting tissue, e.g. a thorn, coming from the body surface of a plant

emergency /i múrjənssi/ n. (plural -cies) **1.** SUDDEN CRISIS REQUIRING ACTION an unexpected and sudden event that must be dealt with urgently **2.** ANZ SPORTS RESERVE PLAYER a reserve player who replaces a member of a team who is injured or who has to pull out at the last minute ■ adj. **1.** USED IN EMERGENCY used or suitable for use in an emergency **2.** MED FOR IMMEDIATE TREATMENT requiring, providing, or given immediate medical attention (The underlying idea is of sth that suddenly 'emerges' or arises)

emergency brake n. US = handbrake

emergency cord n. US = communication cord

emergency exit n. an exit from a building or vehicle that is designed and designated as an escape route in an emergency such as a fire

emergency medicine n. a branch of medicine dealing with the treatment of patients whose condition requires urgent action

emergency powers npl. special powers given to a government or other authority to take extraordinary actions in order to cope with a crisis

emergency room n. US = casualty

emergency services npl. the fire brigade, the police, and the ambulance service collectively, especially when mobilized to deal with emergencies

emergency vehicle n. an ambulance, fire engine, police car, or other vehicle used by the emergency services

emergent /i múrjənt/ adj. **1.** POL NEWLY INDEPENDENT newly or recently independent as a nation. US term **emerging** adj. **2.** **2.** NEW appearing, arising, occurring, or developing, especially for the first time ■ n. **1.** PLANTS PLANT WITH UPPER PARTS ABOVE WATER a plant that has its roots under water but its upper part above the surface **2.** TREES TALL TREE a forest tree that stands taller than the trees around it

emergent evolution n. the theory of evolution in which new organisms and characteristics appear at crises not predictable from those already in existence

emerging /i múrjing/ adj. **1.** NEW starting to appear, arise, occur, or develop **2.** US POL = emergent

emerita /i mérritə/ adj. RETIRED BUT RETAINING PROFESSIONAL TITLE retired but retaining professional title, especially as a woman professor ○ *She's a professor emerita of biology.* ■ n. (plural -tae /-teé/) WOMAN RETAINING FORMER PROFESSIONAL TITLE a woman who has retired from a post but retains her former professional title, especially as a professor [Early 20thC. From Latin, the feminine form of *emeritus* (see EMERITUS).]

emeritus /i mérritəss/ adj. RETIRED BUT RETAINING PROFESSIONAL TITLE retired but retaining a professional title, especially as a professor ○ *He's a professor emeritus of chemistry.* ■ n. (plural -ti /-tī/) MAN RETAINING FORMER PROFESSIONAL TITLE a man who has retired from a post but retains his former professional title, especially as a professor [Early 17thC. From Latin, the past participle of *emerere* 'to serve out, earn, deserve', from *merere* 'to serve, earn' (source of English *merit*).]

emersed /i múrst/ adj. used to describe the stems, leaves, or other parts of an aquatic plant that stand above the water surface [Late 17thC. Formed from Latin *emersus*, the past participle of *emergere* (see EMERGE).]

emersion /i múrsh'n/ n. **1.** ACT OF EMERGING the act or process of emerging **2.** ASTRON REAPPEARANCE OF CELESTIAL BODY the reappearance of a celestial body after it has been eclipsed or occulted

emery /émməri/ n. a variety of the mineral corundum, that can be crushed and used as an abrasive for polishing hard surfaces [15thC. Via French *émeri* from Italian *smeriglio*, from, ultimately, Greek *smuris* 'abrasive powder'.]

emery board n. a small strip of card or thin wood coated with powdered emery and used for filing the fingernails

emery paper n. a strong paper coated with powdered emery and used as an abrasive and for polishing

emery wheel n. a wheel coated with powdered emery and used as an abrasive and for polishing

emesis /émmississ/ n. vomiting (*technical*) [Late 19thC. From Greek, formed from *emein* (see EMETIC).]

emetic /i méttik/ adj. CAUSING VOMITING causing a person or animal to vomit ■ n. STH CAUSING VOMITING a substance that causes vomiting [Mid-17thC. From Greek *emetikos*, from, ultimately, *emein* 'to vomit'. Ultimately an Indo-European word that also produced English *vomit*.] —**emetically** adv.

emetine /émmə teen, -tin/ n. an alkaloid extracted

Emetine

from a South American shrub (**ipecacuanha**) that was formerly used as an emetic. Formula: $C_{29}H_{40}O_4N_2$.

EMF, **emf** *abbr.* **1. EMF, emf** PHYS electromotive force **2.** ECON European Monetary Fund

EMG *abbr.* **1.** electromyogram **2.** electromyograph

-emia *suffix.* US = **-aemia**

emic /éemik/ *adj.* **1.** LING, SOC SCI **ANALYSING STRUCTURAL AND FUNCTIONAL ELEMENTS** relating to the analysis of structural and functional elements of language or behaviour **2.** ANTHROP **USING CATEGORIES OF PEOPLE STUDIED** relating to the organization and interpretation of data that makes use of the categories of the people being studied [Mid-20thC. Shortening of PHONEMIC.]

emigrant /émmigrənt/ *n.* **SB WHO MOVES TO ANOTHER COUNTRY** sb who leaves a place, especially his or her native country, to go and live in another country ■ *adj.* **MOVING TO ANOTHER COUNTRY** relating to those who have left a place, especially their native country, to go and live in another country

emigrate /émmi grayt/ (**-grates, -grating, -grated**) *vi.* to leave a place, especially a native country, to go and live in another country [Late 18thC. From Latin *emigrat-*, the past participle stem of *emigrare* 'to move away, depart from a place', from *migrare* (see MIGRATE).]

emigration /émmi gráysh'n/ *n.* the act of leaving a native country to live in another country

eminence /émminənss/ *n.* **1. HIGH POSITION** a position or rank of distinction or superiority **2. HILL** a high or raised area of ground (*formal*) **3.** ANAT **BODY PROJECTION** a projecting area of the body, especially a bone

Eminence /émminənss/ *n.* in the Roman Catholic Church, a title and form of address for a cardinal

éminence grise /áymi noNss gréez/ (*plural* **éminences grises** /áymi noNss gréez/) *n.* sb who exercises great power or influence secretly or unofficially [From French, literally 'grey eminence', originally the nickname of Père Joseph, secretary to Cardinal Richelieu, known as *Éminence Rouge* 'Red Eminence'; their respective habits were grey and red]

eminency /émminənsi/ *n., adj.* = **eminence** *n.* 1

eminent /émminənt/ *adj.* **1. OF HIGH STANDING** superior in position, fame, or achievement **2. CLEAR** easy to see or notice **3. HIGH** in a high or raised position [15thC. From Latin *eminent-*, the present participle of *eminere* 'to stand out, project', from *minere* 'to stand, project' (source also of English *imminent* and *prominent*).]

eminent domain *n.* the power of a government to take private property for public use, usually with compensation paid to the owner

eminently /émminəntli/ *adv.* **1. VERY** to a great degree ○ *is eminently qualified to be a corporate officer* **2. OBVIOUSLY** obviously or apparently (*archaic*)

emir /e méer/ *n.* **1. ISLAMIC RULER** an independent ruler, commander, or governor in some Islamic countries **2. DESCENDANT OF MUHAMMAD** a title for a descendant of the prophet Muhammad [Early 17thC. Via French from Arabic *amīr* 'commander'.]

emirate /émmirət, e méerət/ *n.* **1.** POL **STATUS OF EMIR** the rank or office of an emir **2.** POL, GEOG **PLACE UNDER EMIR'S RULE** an area ruled by an emir

emissary /émmissəri/ (*plural* **-ies**) *n.* **1. REPRESENTATIVE** an agent or representative sent on a particular mission **2. SPY** a secret agent or spy (*dated*) [Early 17thC. From Latin *emissarius*, literally 'sb who is sent out', from *emiss-*, the past participle stem of *emittere* (see EMIT).]

emission /i mísh'n/ *n.* **1. LETTING STH OUT** the act or process of letting sth out or giving sth out **2. STH GIVEN OUT** sth that is produced or given out **3.** PHYS **RELEASED ENERGY** energy released from a source, usually in the form of electromagnetic radiation **4.** PHYSIOL **STH RELEASED FROM BODY** a bodily discharge, especially of semen [15thC. From the Latin stem *emission-* 'a sending out', from *emiss-*, the past participle stem of *emittere* (see EMIT).]

emission nebula *n.* a cloud of interstellar gas and dust that emits light when electrons recombine with protons to form hydrogen atoms

emissivity /ímmi sívvəti, émmi-/ (*plural* **-ties**) *n.* the ability of a surface to emit radiation, measured as the ratio of the energy radiated by a surface to that radiated by a black body at the same temperature. Symbol *υ*

emit /i mít/ (**emits, emitting, emitted**) *vt.* **1. PRODUCE STH** to send or give out sth **2. UTTER STH** to utter sth as a sound **3.** FIN **PUT MONEY INTO CIRCULATION** to put currency in circulation [Early 17thC. From Latin *emittere* 'to send out', from *mittere* 'to send'.]

emitter /i míttər/ *n.* **1. SB OR STH THAT EMITS STH** sb who or sth that lets out or gives out sth **2.** ELECTRON ENG **SEMICONDUCTOR MATERIAL IN TRANSISTOR** a layer of semiconductor material in a transistor from which charge carriers, such as electrons, originate and control the current flow

Emmental /émmən taal/, **Emmenthal, Emmenthaler, Emmentaler** *n.* a hard cheese of Swiss origin with large holes and a mild nutty flavour [Early 20thC. From obsolete German, named after *Emmental*, a region in Switzerland.]

emmer /émmər/ *n.* a Eurasian wheat grown chiefly for fodder. Latin name: *Triticum dicoccum.* [Early 20thC. From German.]

emmet /émmit/ *n.* an ant (*regional archaic*) [Old English *æmete* (source also of English *ant*)]

Emmet /émmit/, **Robert** (1778–1803) Irish patriot. He was a member of the nationalist United Irishmen. With French encouragement, he launched an abortive uprising in Ireland in 1803, and was tried and hanged.

emmetropia /émmi trṓpi ə/ *n.* the normal condition of the eye in which vision is accurate [Mid-19thC. Coined from Greek *emmetros* 'in measure' + *ōps* 'eye' + -IA.] —**emmetropic** /-tróppik/ *adj.*

Emmy /émmi/ (*plural* **-mys**) *n.* a statuette awarded annually by the American Academy of Television Arts and Sciences for excellence in television programming, production, or performance [Mid-20thC. Origin uncertain: perhaps an alteration of *Immy*, engineering slang for 'image-orthicon camera', on the model of *Oscar* and other forenames used for awards.]

emollient /i mólli ənt/ *adj.* **1. SOOTHING TO SKIN** softening or soothing, especially to the skin **2. CALMING** trying to avoid anger and argument by using a calming manner ■ *n.* **SOOTHING SUBSTANCE** a substance that softens or soothes sth, especially the skin [Mid-17thC. From Latin *emollient-*, the present participle stem of *emollire* 'to soften', from *mollis* 'soft'.]

emolument /i móllyōōmənt/ *n.* any payment for work (*formal*) [15thC. From Latin *emolumentum* 'profit, gain', literally 'fee paid to a miller for grinding grain', from *emolere* 'to grind out'.]

WORD KEY: SYNONYMS

See Synonyms at ***wage***.

emote /i mṓt/ (**emotes, emoting, emoted**) *vi.* to make an exaggerated show of emotions, e.g. in the playing of a dramatic part (*literary or humorous*) [Early 20thC. Back-formation from EMOTION.]

:-) Happy
:-(Sad
|-| Asleep
;-) Winking
:-)) Very happy
:-~) User has a cold
:-* Blowing a kiss
:-& Tongue tied
(:+(Scared
(-D Laughing
:-() Talking
:-O Shocked
:-X Mute
~:-) Baby
|-O Yawning
@>- Rose
{:V Duck
3:-) Cow
<:3 Mouse
:8) Pig

Emoticon

emoticon /i mṓti kon/ *n.* a symbolic picture used in computer communications to convey emotions, constructed by arranging standard keyboard characters that are usually to be viewed sideways. A smile might be represented as :-). [Late 20thC. Blend of EMOTION and ICON.]

emotion /i mṓsh'n/ *n.* **1. HEIGHTENED FEELING** a strong feeling about sb or sth **2. AGITATION CAUSED BY STRONG FEELINGS** agitation or disturbance caused by strong feelings [Late 16thC. From French, formed from *émouvoir* 'to stir up the feelings of', from Latin *emovere*, literally 'to move out', from *movere* (see MOVE).]

emotional /i mṓsh'nəl/ *adj.* **1. EXPRESSING EMOTION** relating to or expressing emotion **2. EASILY AFFECTED BY EMOTIONS** being by nature easily affected by or quick to express emotions **3. AFFECTED BY EMOTION** openly affected by emotion, especially sadness **4. STIRRING EMOTIONS** arousing or affecting the emotions **5. INSPIRED BY EMOTION** inspired or governed by emotion rather than reason or will-power ○ *one of the more emotional issues before the public this decade* —**emotionality** /i mṓshə nálləti/ *n.* —**emotionally** *adv.*

emotionalise *vt.* = **emotionalize**

emotionalism /i mṓsh'nəlizəm/ *n.* **1. OPENNESS TO EMOTION** a tendency to be easily swayed by the emotions **2. DISPLAY OF EMOTION** an exaggerated or undue display of strong feelings

emotionalist /i mṓsh'nəlist/ *n.* **1. EMOTIONAL PERSON** sb whose thoughts or actions are greatly influenced by the emotions **2. OVERLY DEMONSTRATIVE PERSON** sb who is prone to undue displays of strong feelings

emotionalize /i mṓsh'nə līz/ (**-alizes, -alizing, -alized**), **emotionalise** (**-ises, -ising, -ised**) *vt.* to present or treat sth emotionally

emotionless /i mṓsh'n ləss/ *adj.* not having or showing emotions —**emotionlessly** *adv.* —**emotionlessness** *n.*

emotive /i mṓtiv/ *adj.* **1. CAUSING EMOTION** causing or intended to cause emotion ○ *emotive delivery of the last lines of the play* **2. INVOLVING EMOTION** showing or characterized by emotion ○ *an emotive plea for outlawing land mines* [Mid-18thC. Formed from Latin *emotus*, past participle of *emovere* 'to move out, remove'.] —**emotively** *adv.* —**emotiveness** *n.*

emotivism /i mṓtivizəm/ *n.* the theory that ethical terms are not statements but instead reflect the feelings of the user

EMP *abbr.* electromagnetic pulse

Emp. *abbr.* **1.** Emperor **2.** Empire **3.** Empress

empale (**-pales, -paling, -paled**) *vt.* = **impale**

empanada /émpə naádə/ *n.* a Spanish, Filipino, or Latin American turnover with a spicy savoury or sweet filling [Mid-20thC. From Spanish, from the past participle of *empanar* 'to bake or roll in pastry', literally 'to put into bread', from *pan* 'bread'.]

empanel *vt.* = **impanel**

empathize /émpəthīz/ (**-izes, -izing, -ized**), **empathise** (**-ises, -ising, -ised**) *vi.* **UNDERSTAND ANOTHER'S FEELINGS** to identify with and understand another person's feelings or difficulties

empathy /émpəthi/ *n.* **1. UNDERSTANDING OF ANOTHER'S FEELINGS** the ability to identify with and understand another person's feelings or difficulties **2. ATTRIBUTION OF FEELINGS TO AN OBJECT** the transfer of your own feelings and emotions to an object such as a painting —**empathetic** /émpə thétik/ *adj.* *n.*—**empathetically** *adv.*—**empathic** /empáthik/ *adj.*

Empedocles /em péddə kleez/ (490?–430BC) Sicilian-born Greek philosopher, poet, and statesman. He believed that matter was composed of four elements: earth, air, fire, and water. Known as **Empedocles of Akragas**

empennage /em pénnij, ómpə naázh/ *n.* the tail portion of an aircraft, including the stabilizer, elevator, vertical fin, and rudder [Early 20thC. From French, 'feathering (of an arrow)', from *empenner*, literally 'to feather in', from *penne* 'feather'.]

emperor /émpərər/ *n.* **1. RULER OF EMPIRE** a man who rules an empire **2.** = **emperor moth 3.** = **emperor butterfly** [12thC. From, ultimately, Latin *imperator* 'commander', from *imperare* 'to command', literally 'to prepare in relation to', from *parare* 'to prepare'.]

emperor butterfly *n.* a brightly coloured butterfly that typically has mottled purple and brownish markings. Family: Nymphalidae. [*Emperor* from the imperial associations of the colour purple]

emperor moth *n.* a large brightly coloured Eurasian moth with distinctive markings resembling eyes on its wings. It is the largest European moth. Latin name: *Saturnia pyri.* [*Emperor* from the large size of the moth]

emperor penguin *n.* an Antarctic penguin that has bluish-grey and black plumage, a white chest, and yellowish-orange neck markings. The largest of the penguins, the emperor penguin nurtures its eggs and young between its feet and a pouch-shaped fold in its abdomen. Latin name: *Aptenodytes forsteri.* [*Emperor* from the large size of the penguin]

emphasis /émfəssiss/ (*plural* **-ses**) *n.* **1.** IMPORTANCE special importance, significance, or stress **2.** FORCEFULNESS OF EXPRESSION forcefulness of expression to indicate the importance of sth **3.** GRAM EXTRA SPOKEN STRESS ON IMPORTANT WORD extra stress of voice put on a syllable, word, or phrase, usually to show its significance [Late 16thC. From, ultimately, Greek *emphasis* 'significance, appearance', from *emphainein* 'to show, indicate', literally 'to show in', from *phainein* 'to show'.]

emphasize /émfə sīz/ (**-sizes, -sizing, -sized**), **emphasise** (**-sises, -sising, -sised**) *vt.* to stress or give importance to sth

emphatic /im fáttik/ *adj.* **1.** WITH EMPHASIS expressed, thought, or done with emphasis **2.** DEFINITE forcible and definite **3.** GRAM SHOWING EMPHASIS GRAMMATICALLY used to describe a grammatical form that shows emphasis, e.g. the auxiliary 'do' in the statement 'I do like apples' [Early 18thC. From, ultimately, Greek *emphatikos*, from *emphasis* 'appearance' (see EMPHASIS).]

emphatically /im fáttikli, em-/ *adv.* **1.** FORCEFULLY with great force or definiteness **2.** USED FOR EMPHASIS used to reinforce the accuracy or appropriateness of a description ○ *It might be entertainment, but it is emphatically not education.*

emphysema /émfə séemə, -zéemə/ *n.* **1.** LUNG CONDITION CAUSING BREATHING IMPAIRMENT a chronic medical disorder of the lungs in which the air sacs are dilated or enlarged and lack flexibility, resulting in breathing impairment and sometimes infection **2.** ABNORMAL ENLARGEMENT CAUSED BY RETAINED GAS an abnormal enlargement of an organ or body tissue caused by retention of air or other gas [Mid-17thC. From, ultimately, Greek *emphusēma* 'swelling', from *emphusan* 'to inflate, blow in', from *phusan* 'to blow'.] —**emphysematous** /émfə sémmətəss, -séem-, -zémm-, -zéem-/ *adj.* —**emphysemic** /émfə séemik, -zéemik/ *adj.*

empire *n.* **1.** LANDS RULED BY SINGLE AUTHORITY a group of nations, territories, or peoples ruled by a single authority, especially an emperor or empress **2.** MONARCHY HEADED BY EMPEROR OR EMPRESS a monarchy that has an emperor or empress as its ruler **3.** PERIOD OF EMPIRE'S EXISTENCE the period during which an empire exists **4.** LARGE FAR-FLUNG BUSINESS a very large, powerful, and extensive industrial or commercial organization **5.** PART OF ORGANIZATION SB PERSONALLY CONTROLS a part of an organization controlled by a single person, especially sb who is keenly protective of personal power **6.** ABSOLUTE POWER supreme or absolute power (*formal* or *literary*) [13thC. Via Old French from Latin *imperium* 'command', from *imperare* (see EMPEROR).]

Empire *adj.* ARTS, ARCHIT FRENCH FIRST EMPIRE STYLE relating to a style of architecture, furniture, and clothing popular during the French First Empire (1804–15) during the reign of Napoleon I ■ *n.* BOT RED EATING APPLE a variety of red eating apple

empire-building *n.* the tendency to acquire power and authority within an organization, especially by adding extra staff or subordinates —**empire-builder** *n.*

Empire Day *n.* the former name for Commonwealth Day, used before 1958

Empire gown *n.* a woman's dress popular during the French First Empire, characterized by a low-cut neckline and a high waist from which the skirt hangs straight and loose

Empire State Building *n.* a skyscraper on Fifth Avenue in New York City built between 1930 and 1931. It has 102 storeys and was the tallest building in the world for several years.

empiric /em pírrik, im-/ *n.* **1.** SB GUIDED BY EXPERIENCE NOT THEORY sb who relies upon observation and experiment rather than theory to determine the truth about sth **2.** CHARLATAN OR IMPOSTOR a charlatan or quack, especially in medicine (*archaic*) [Mid-16thC. From, ultimately, Greek *empeirikos* 'experienced', from *empeiros* 'skilled', literally 'tried in', from *peira* 'try' (source of English *pirate*).]

empirical /em pírrik'l, im-/ *adj.* **1.** BASED ON OBSERVATION AND EXPERIMENT based on or characterized by observation and experiment rather than theory **2.** MED BASED ON PRACTICAL MEDICAL EXPERIENCE based on practical experience in the medical treatment of real cases rather than on applied theory or scientific proof **3.** PHILOS DERIVED SOLELY FROM EXPERIENCE derived as knowledge from experience, particularly from sensory observation, rather than from the application of logic —**empirically** *adv.*

empirical formula *n.* a chemical formula showing the relative proportion of elements in a compound instead of their structural arrangement or molecular weights, e.g. the formula H_2O

empiricism /em pírrissizəm/ *n.* **1.** PHILOS PHILOSOPHICAL BELIEF REGARDING SENSE-DERIVED KNOWLEDGE the philosophical belief that all knowledge is derived from the experience of the senses **2.** APPLICATION OF OBSERVATION AND EXPERIMENT the application of observation and experiment, rather than theory, in determining sth **3.** MED MEDICINE BASED SOLELY ON EXPERIENCE medicine that is based on practical experience rather than on theory and scientific proof —**empiricist** *n.*

emplace /im pláyss/ (**-places, -placing, -placed**) *vt.* to put sth into place or position [Mid-19thC. Back-formation from EMPLACEMENT.]

emplacement /im pláyssmənt/ *n.* **1.** MIL POSITION FOR LARGE WEAPONRY a position that is specially prepared for a large gun or group of guns **2.** POSITIONING OF STH the act of putting sth into place, or the condition of being in place [Early 19thC. From French, literally 'placing in', from *place* 'place'.]

emplane /im pláyn/ (**-planes, -planing, -planed**) *vti.* to board or allow sb to board an aircraft. US term **enplane**

employ /im plóy/ *vt.* (**-ploys, -ploying, -ployed**) **1.** GIVE PAID WORK TO SB to hire sb to work in exchange for money **2.** KEEP BUSY to keep sb occupied doing sth **3.** USE STH to make use of sth ■ *n.* **1.** EMPLOYED STATE the condition of working for pay (*formal*) ○ *I was in his employ.* **2.** JOB a job or occupation (*archaic*) [15thC. Via French *emploier* 'to apply' from Latin *implicare* 'to involve, enfold', from *plicare* 'to fold' (source of English *ply, pliant,* and *display*).] —**employability** /im plóyə bílləti/ *n.* —**employable** /im plóyəb'l/ *adj.*

WORD KEY: SYNONYMS

See Synonyms at ***use***.

employee /im plóy ee, ém ploy ée/ *n.* sb who is paid by sb else to do work

employee association *n.* a social or professional organization of employees who have the same employer

employer /im plóyər/ *n.* **1.** PERSON OR GROUP THAT ENGAGES WORKERS a person, business, or organization that engages and pays one or more workers **2.** SB WHO USES STH sb who uses or makes use of sth

employers' association *n.* an organization of employers, usually working in a similar area, that provides support for its members and negotiates in industrial disputes

employment /im plóymənt/ *n.* **1.** WORKING FOR PAY the condition of working for pay **2.** WORK OR JOB DONE BY SB the work, especially paid work, that sb does **3.** NUMBER OF PAID WORKERS IN POPULATION the total number or level of people that work for pay in a given population **4.** USE OF STH the use or practice of sth

empoison /im póyz'n/ (**-sons, -soning, -soned**) *vt.* to make sb resentful or bitter (*formal*) [14thC. From Old French *empoisoner*, literally 'to poison in', from *poison* 'POISON'.]

emporium /em páwri əm/ (*plural* **-ums** or **-a** /-ri ə/) *n.* a shop, usually a large shop, that offers a wide selection of goods (*formal* or *humorous*) [Late 16thC. From, ultimately, Greek *emporion*, from *emporos* 'merchant, traveller', literally 'journeyer in', from *poros* 'journey'.]

empower /im pówər/ (**-ers, -ering, -ered**) *vt.* **1.** GIVE AUTHORITY TO SB to give sb power or authority (*often passive*) **2.** INSPIRE SB WITH CONFIDENCE to give sb a sense of confidence or self-esteem —**empowerment** *n.*

empress /émprəss/ *n.* **1.** RULER OF EMPIRE a woman who rules an empire **2.** EMPEROR'S WIFE the wife or widow of an emperor

empressement /oN préss moN/ *n.* great attentiveness or cordiality (*formal*) [Early 18thC. From French, from *empresser* 'to urge, be eager', literally 'to press in', from *presser* 'to press' (see PRESS).]

emprise /em príz/ *n.* (*formal*) **1.** BOLD ADVENTURE a chivalrous, brave, or daring undertaking **2.** CHIVALROUS DARING chivalrous skill or daring [13thC. From French, from Old French *emprendre*, literally 'to seize into', from Latin *prendere* 'to seize'.]

empty /émpti/ *adj.* (**-tier, -tiest**) **1.** CONTAINING NOTHING not containing or holding anything ○ *a heap of empty packets* **2.** UNOCCUPIED unoccupied or uninhabited ○ *There's an empty office next door.* **3.** WITH NO PASSENGERS OR LOAD without passengers, a load, or cargo ○ *The bus goes back to the depot empty.* **4.** INSINCERE lacking sincerity or truthfulness ○ *another empty promise* **5.** MEANINGLESS without value, meaning, or purpose ○ *contemplating his empty existence* **6.** DULL devoid of vitality ○ *an empty look* **7.** UNFED hungry or lacking food ○ *can't work on an empty stomach* **8.** MATH, LOGIC WITHOUT MEMBERS OF SET used to describe a set that has no elements or members ■ *v.* (**-ties, -tying, -tied**) **1.** *vti.* REMOVE CONTENTS OF STH to remove or pour out the contents of sth **2.** *vti.* DISCHARGE OR TRANSFER to discharge or transfer sth, or be discharged and transferred **3.** *vr.* UNBURDEN YOURSELF to unburden or free yourself of sth ■ *n.* (*plural* **-ties**) CONTAINER WITHOUT CONTENTS a bottle or other container that has nothing in it [Old English *ǣmtig* 'unoccupied, at leisure', from *ǣmetta* 'rest, leisure', of uncertain origin; perhaps from *ǣ-* 'not' + METE. The underlying idea would be of not being assigned.] —**emptiable** *adj.* —**emptily** *adv.* —**emptiness** *n.*

WORD KEY: SYNONYMS

See Synonyms at ***vacant*** and ***vain***.

empty-handed *adj.* **1.** WITH NOTHING IN HANDS holding nothing in the hands **2.** HAVING GAINED NOTHING with nothing gained or achieved

empty-headed *adj.* silly or lacking in intelligence

empty nester *n.* a parent whose children have grown up and moved away from home (*informal*)

empty-nest syndrome *n.* distress, especially a lack of energy or an emotional letdown experienced by parents whose grown children have moved away from home [*Empty-nest* in reference to birds' nests]

empyema /ém pī éemə/ *n.* an accumulation of pus in a body cavity, e.g. the chest [Early 17thC. From, ultimately, Greek *empuēma*, from *empuein*, literally 'to put pus in', from *puon* 'pus'.] —**empyemic** *adj.*

empyreal /ém pī rée əl, em pírri əl/ *adj.* **1.** OF THE SKY relating to the sky, the celestial sphere, or heaven **2.** SUBLIME glorious and sublime (*literary*) [15thC. Formed from medieval Latin *empyreus* (see EMPYREAN).]

empyrean /ém pī rée ən, em pírri ən/ *n.* **1.** THE SKY OR HEAVENS the sky, heavens, or celestial sphere (*literary*) **2.** HIGHEST PART OF HEAVEN the highest part of heaven, believed in ancient Greek and Roman times to contain pure fire or light and believed by some Christians to be the dwelling place of God (*archaic*) ■ *adj.* = **empyreal** *adj.* 2 [15thC. Formed from medieval Latin *empyreus*, from Greek *empurios*, literally 'in fire', from, ultimately, *pur* 'fire'.]

EMS *abbr.* European Monetary System

emu[1] /ée myoo/ (*plural* **emus** or **emu**) *n.* a large flightless bird native to Australia that is related to the ostrich and has three-toed feet and loose shaggy feathers. Latin name: *Dromaius novaehollandiae.* [Early 17thC. Shortening of Portuguese *ema di gei* 'crane of the ground', of uncertain origin; probably from Moluccan *emeu*.]

emu[2], **EMU** *abbr.* electromagnetic unit

EMU /ée em yóo, ée myoo/ *abbr.* European Monetary Union

emu bush *n.* an inland Australian shrub whose fruit is eaten by emus. Genus: *Eremophila.*

emulate /émyoo layt/ (**-lates, -lating, -lated**) *vt.* **1.** TRY TO EQUAL SB OR STH to try hard to equal or surpass sb or sth, especially by imitation **2.** COMPETE SUCCESSFULLY

Emu

WITH SB OR STH to be successful in competing with or rival sb or sth **3.** COMPUT MAKE BEHAVE LIKE ANOTHER COMPUTER SYSTEM to modify a computer system so that it appears to behave like another computer system, and can thereby accept data and run programs that are designed for the system being emulated [Late 16thC. From, ultimately, Latin *aemulari* 'to rival', from *aemulus* 'rival'. Ultimately from a word that is also the ancestor of English *imitate* and *image*.] —**emulative** /émyoŏ laytiv, -lətiv/ *adj.* —**emulatively** *adv.*

—— **WORD KEY: SYNONYMS** ——
See Synonyms at *imitate*.

emulation /émyoŏ láysh'n/ *n.* **1.** RIVALRY BY IMITATION the attempt to equal or surpass sb or sth, usually by means of imitation **2.** COMPUT PROCESS OF IMITATING COMPUTER SYSTEM the process of successfully duplicating the performance of a computer device or program

emulator /émyoŏ laytər/ *n.* **1.** SB WHO EMULATES sb or sth that emulates another person or thing **2.** COMPUT HARDWARE OR SOFTWARE IMITATING ANOTHER SYSTEM hardware or software that permits a computer system to run programs written for and process data originating from a different type of computer system. ◊ **simulator** *n.* 1

emulous /émyoŏláss/ *adj.* **1.** KEEN TO RIVAL SB OR STH seeking to match or rival another's achievement or performance **2.** MOTIVATED BY RIVALRY motivated or characterized by rivalry or imitation [14thC. From Latin *aemulus* (see EMULATE).] —**emulously** *adv.* —**emulousness** *n.*

emulsifiable /i múlssi fī əb'l, i múlssi fī əb'l/, **emulsible** /i múlssəb'l/ *adj.* capable of forming an emulsion

emulsify /i múlssi fī/ (-fies, -fying, -fied) *vt.* to disperse sth in an emulsion, or convert two or more liquids into an emulsion —**emulsification** /i múlssifi káysh'n/ *n.*

emulsion /i múlsh'n/ *n.* **1.** SUSPENSION OF LIQUID WITHIN ANOTHER LIQUID a suspension of one liquid in another, e.g. oil in water or fat in milk **2.** PHOTOGRAPHY LIGHT-SENSITIVE PHOTOGRAPHIC COATING a thin light-sensitive coating of silver bromide or other silver halide in a medium such as gelatin on a photographic plate, paper, or film **3.** WATER-BASED PAINT WITH MATT FINISH a water-based paint that is mainly used for interior decorating and usually has a matt finish [Early 17thC. From, ultimately, Latin *emuls-*, the past participle stem of *emulgere* 'to milk out', from *mulgere* 'to milk'.] —**emulsive** /-siv/ *adj.*

emunctory /i múngktəri/ (*plural* -ries) *n.* a body part or organ that removes waste products from the body, e.g. the kidneys, lungs, or skin [14thC. From medieval Latin *emunctorius*, from, ultimately, Latin *emungere*, literally 'to blow the nose thoroughly', from *mungere* 'to blow the nose'.]

en /en/ *n.* a measure of printing width, half that of an em

EN *abbr.* enrolled nurse

en- *prefix.* **1.** to put or go into, cover with ○ *entomb* ○ *encamp* ○ *enfold* **2.** to provide with **3.** to cause to be ○ *enlarge* **4.** thoroughly ○ *enmesh* **5.** in, within, into ○ *enzootic* [Via Old French from, ultimately, Latin *in* 'in' (see IN)]

-en *suffix.* **1.** to cause to be or have ○ *brighten* ○ *strengthen* **2.** to come to be or have ○ *taughten* ○ *lengthen* **3.** made of or resembling ○ *wooden* [Via Latin from, ultimately, Greek *en*. Ultimately from an Indo-

European word that is also the ancestor of English *in*, *en-*, and *internal*.]

enable /in áyb'l/ (-bles, -bling, -bled) *vt.* **1.** PROVIDE SB WITH MEANS to provide sb with the resources, authority, or opportunity to do sth **2.** MAKE STH POSSIBLE to make sth possible or feasible [15thC. Coined from EN- + ABLE.] —**enabler** *n.*

enabling /in áybling/ *adj.* conferring new legal powers

enact /in ákt/ (-acts, -acting, -acted) *vt.* **1.** THEATRE ACT STH OUT to perform or relate sth using acting **2.** POL MAKE STH LAW to make proposed legislation into law [15thC. Coined from EN- + ACT, modelled on Anglo-Latin *inactitare*.] —**enactable** *adj.* —**enactive** *adj.* —**enactor** *n.* —**enactory** *adj.*

enactment /in áktmənt/ *n.* **1.** PROCESS OF ENACTING the act or process of enacting sth **2.** STH ENACTED sth that is enacted, especially a law

enamel /i námm'l/ *n.* **1.** INDUST GLASSY DECORATIVE OR PROTECTIVE COATING a glassy decorative or protective coating, usually coloured and opaque, that is fused onto metal, glass, or ceramics **2.** STH WITH ENAMEL COATING sth that is coated with enamel **3.** INDUST PAINT WITH A HARD SHINY FINISH a paint that gives a shiny smooth finish when dry **4.** SHINY SMOOTH TOUGH COATING any coating that is shiny, smooth, and durable ○ *nail enamel* **5.** DENT HARD LAYER ON TOOTH CROWN a hard thin calcium-containing layer that covers and protects the crown of a tooth ■ *vt.* (-els, -elling, -elled) **1.** COAT STH WITH ENAMEL to decorate or coat all or part of an object with enamel **2.** APPLY BRIGHT SHINY SURFACE TO STH to apply a shiny brightly coloured surface to sth [14thC. From Anglo-Norman *enamailler*, literally 'to enamel in', from, ultimately, Old French *esmail* 'enamel', from a prehistoric Germanic base meaning 'melting' that is also the ancestor of English *schmaltz*.] —**enameller** *n.*

enamelling /i námm'ling/ *n.* **1.** APPLICATION OF ENAMEL the process of applying enamel to sth **2.** SURFACE COATED WITH ENAMEL the surface of sth coated with enamel

enamelware /i námm'l wair/ *n.* household utensils coated with enamel

enamelwork /i námm'l wurk/ *n.* = enamelling *n.* 2

enamor *vt.* US = enamour

enamour /in ámmər/ (-ours, -ouring, -oured) *vt.* (*formal or literary*) **1.** INSPIRE SB WITH LOVE to inspire sb with love or passion **2.** CHARM SB to charm, fascinate, or captivate sb [13thC. From Old French *enamourer*, from *en-* 'to cause to' + *amour* 'love'.]

enantiomorph /i nánti ə mawrf/, **enantiomer** /-əmər/ *n.* either of a pair of molecules that are a mirror image of each other in structure but cannot be superimposed [Late 19thC. Coined from Greek *enantios* 'opposite' + -MORPH.] —**enantiomorphic** /i nánti ə máwrfik/ *adj.* —**enantiomorphism** /-máwrfizəm/ *n.* —**enantiomorphous** /-máwrfəss/ *adj.*

enate /ée nayt/ *adj.* MATERNALLY RELATED related through the mother ■ *n.* SB MATERNALLY RELATED sb related on the mother's side [Mid-17thC. From Latin *enatus*, past participle of *enasci* 'to issue out, be born'.]

enatic /ee náttik/ = enate *adj.*

enation /ee náysh'n/ *n.* a small outgrowth on an organ, especially on a leaf, caused by a virus infection [Mid-19thC. From the Latin stem *enation-*, from, ultimately, *enasci* 'to issue out, be born'.]

enc *abbr.* **1.** enclosed **2.** enclosure

encaenia /en séeni ə/ *n.* an event commemorating or dedicating an institution or community, e.g. a university, church, or city (*formal*) [14thC. Via Latin from Greek *egkainia* 'dedication festival', from *en* 'in' + *kainos* 'new'.]

encage /in káyj/ (-cages, -caging, -caged) *vt.* to confine sb or sth in or in sth resembling a cage (*formal*)

encamp /in kámp/ (-camps, -camping, -camped) *vti.* to lodge in a camp, or provide sb with a camp

encampment /in kámpmənt/ *n.* **1.** CAMPSITE a place occupied by a camp **2.** STAYING IN A CAMP residence in a camp, or the setting up of a camp

encapsulate /in kápsyoŏ layt/ (-lates, -lating, -lated), **incapsulate** (-lates, -lating, -lated) *v.* **1.** *vt.* CONDENSE STH to express sth in concise form **2.** *vti.* ENCLOSE to enclose sth or be enclosed completely [Late 19thC.

Coined from EN- + CAPSULE + -ATE.] —**encapsulation** /in kápsyoŏ láysh'n/ *n.* —**encapsulator** /in kápsyoŏ laytər/ *n.*

encapsulated /in kápsyoŏ laytid/ *adj.* used to describe an organ or tumour covered by a thin protective membrane

encapsule /in káp syool/ (-sules, -suling, -suled) *vt.* to encapsulate sth (*formal*) ○ *fruit encapsuled in a large, hard shell*

encase /in káyss/ (-cases, -casing, -cased), **incase** (-cases, -casing, -cased) *vt.* to surround sth completely with a case or cover —**encasement** *n.*

encash /in kásh/ (-cashes, -cashing, -cashed) *vt.* to convert a cheque or bond into cash (*formal*) —**encashable** *adj.* —**encashment** *n.*

encaustic /in káwstik, -kóstik/ *adj.* HAVING FUSED COLOURS having wax colours fused to a surface by heat ■ *n.* STH WITH FUSED COLOURS an object or work of art whose colours are fused to a surface by the application of heat, especially an earthenware tile decorated with an inlaid design in the style of medieval floor tiles [Late 16thC. Via Latin *encausticus* from Greek *egkaustikos*, from *egkaiein* 'to burn in'.]

enceinte[1] /on sánt/ *adj.* having a child developing in the womb (*formal*) (*used euphemistically*) [Early 17thC. Via French from medieval Latin *incincta* 'ungirded', from *cincta* 'girded'.]

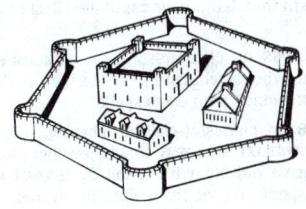

Enceinte

enceinte[2] /on sánt/ *n.* MIL **1.** DEFENSIVE ENCLOSURE a defensive wall or enclosure **2.** AREA ENCLOSED BY DEFENSIVE STRUCTURE a place protected by a defensive wall or enclosure [Early 18thC. Via French from Latin *incincta*, past participle of *incingere* 'to gird in'.]

Enceladus /en sélledaaə/ *n.* a small natural satellite of Saturn, discovered in 1789. It is 498 km in diameter and occupies an intermediate orbit.

encephal- *prefix.* = encephalo- (used before vowels)

encephalic /én si fállik, -ki-/ *adj.* related to the brain, or located within the cranium [Mid-19thC. Formed from Greek *egkephalos* 'brain'.]

encephalin /en séffəlin, -kéffə-/ *n.* MED = enkephalin

encephalitis /en séffə lítiss, -kéffə-/ *n.* inflammation of the brain, usually caused by a viral infection —**encephalitic** /-líttik/ *adj.*

encephalitis lethargica /-li thaárjikə/ *n.* sleeping sickness (*technical*) [From modern Latin: *lethargica* from Latin, a form of *lethargicus* 'sleepy'.]

encephalo- *prefix.* brain ○ *encephalogram* [Via modern Latin from Greek (*muelos*) *enkephalos* '(marrow) in the head', from *en* 'in' + *kephale* 'head' (see CEPHALIC)]

encephalogram /en séffələ gram, -kéffələ-/ *n.* **1.** BRAIN X-RAY an X-ray photograph of the brain **2.** = electroencephalogram

encephalograph /en séffələ graaf, -graf, -kéffə-, -graf/ *n.* **1.** = encephalogram *n.* 1 **2.** = electroencephalograph

encephalography /en séffə lóggrəfi, -kéffə-/ *n.* X-ray photography of the brain —**encephalographic** /en séffələ gráffik, -kéffələ-/ *adj.* —**encephalographically** /en séffələ gráffikli/ *adv.*

encephalomyelitis /en séffəlō mī ə lítiss, -kéffə-/ *n.* inflammation of the brain and spinal cord —**encephalomyelitic** /-mī ə líttik/ *adj.*

encephalon /en séffə lon, en kéffə-/ (*plural* -la /-lə/) *n.* the brain of a vertebrate [Mid-18thC. From Greek *egkephalon*, literally 'inside the head', from *kephalē* 'head'.] —**encephalous** *adj.*

encephalopathy /en séffə lóppəthi, -kéffə-/ *n.* any disease of the brain —**encephalopathic** /en séffələ páthik, -kéffələ-/ *adj.*

enchain /in cháyn, en-/ (**-chains, -chaining, -chained**) *vt.* **1. PUT SB OR STH IN CHAINS** to bind sb or sth with chains (*formal or literary*) **2. CAPTIVATE SB'S ATTENTION** to dominate sb's attention or thoughts (*literary*) [14thC. From French *enchainer*, from, ultimately, Latin *catenare* 'to chain'.] —**enchainment** *n.*

enchant /in chaánt/ (**-chants, -chanting, -chanted**) *vt.* **1. DELIGHT SB** to charm, delight, or captivate sb **2. PUT SB OR STH UNDER SPELL** to cast a spell on sb or sth [14thC. Via Old French *enchanter* from Latin *incantare*, literally 'to chant a magic formula upon', from *cantare* 'to sing'.]

enchanted /in chaántid/ *adj.* **1. DELIGHTED** charmed, delighted or captured by sb or sth **2. UNDER SPELL** put under a magic spell

enchanter /in chaántər/ *n.* **1. CHARMING OR DELIGHTFUL PERSON** sb who is charming or delightful **2. MAGICIAN** sb who casts spells

enchanter's nightshade *n.* a plant that is found in cool woodland regions and has small white flowers and bristly fruits. Genus: *Circaea.*

enchanting /in chaánting/ *adj.* captivating or delightful —**enchantingly** *adv.*

enchantment /in chaántmənt/ *n.* **1. STATE OF BEING ENCHANTED** the act or condition of being enchanted **2. CHARM** sth that delights or captivates **3. SPELL** a magic spell

enchantress /in chaántrəss/ *n.* **1. CHARMING WOMAN** a woman who is charming or delightful **2. WOMAN MAGICIAN** woman who casts spells

enchase /in cháyss/ (**-chases, -chasing, -chased**) *vt.* **1. SET JEWELLERY WITH GEMS** to set jewellery or other decorative objects with gems **2. DECORATE METAL** to emboss, engrave, or carve designs on metal [15thC. From French *enchasser* 'to set (gems), encase', from *chasse* 'case, box'.]

enchilada /én chi laádə/ *n.* a fried tortilla rolled around a savoury mixture of poultry, meat, or vegetables and served hot with a usually spicy sauce [Late 19thC. From Mexican Spanish, a form of the past participle of *enchilar* 'to season with chilli'.] ◇ **the whole enchilada** *US* the entirety of sth (*slang*)

enchiridion /én kī ríddi ən/ (*plural* **-ons** *or* **-a** /-di ə/) *n.* a manual or handbook (*archaic*) [Mid-16thC. Via late Latin from Greek *egkheiridion*, literally 'small thing in the hand', from *kheir* 'hand'.]

enchorial /en káwri əl/, **enchoric** /en káwrik/ *adj.* belonging to or used in a particular country, especially as a writing system [Early 19thC. Formed from Greek *egkōrios* 'in the country', from *khōra* 'country'.]

-enchyma *suffix.* cellular tissue ○ *aerenchyma* [From PARENCHYMA]

encipher /in sífər/ (**-phers, -phering, -phered**) *vt.* to convert a text into code or cipher —**encipherer** *n.* —**encipherment** *n.*

encircle /in súrk'l/ (**-cles, -cling, -cled**) *vt.* **1. SURROUND SB OR STH** to form a circle around sb or sth **2. MAKE CIRCUIT OF SB OR STH** to go in a circle around sb or sth —**encirclement** *n.* —**encircling** *adj.*

WORD KEY: USAGE

See Usage note at ***surround.***

Encke /éngkə/, **Johann Franz** (1791–1865) German astronomer. His significant research into the orbits of comets was rewarded posthumously when a comet was given his name.

encl. *abbr.* **1.** enclosed **2.** enclosure

enclasp /in klaásp/ (**-clasps, -clasping, -clasped**) *vt.* to embrace or hold sb or sth tightly (*literary*)

enclave /én klayv, ón-/ *n.* **1.** POL **REGION SURROUNDED BY FOREIGN TERRITORY** a small country or territory that is culturally or ethnically different from a surrounding larger and distinct political unit. ◊ **exclave 2. DISTINCT GROUP IN LARGER COMMUNITY** a distinct group that lives or operates together within a larger community [Mid-19thC. From French, from Old French *enclaver* 'to enclose', from Latin *in* 'in' + *clavis* 'key' (source of English *clavicle*).]

enclitic /in klíttik/ *adj.* depending on a preceding word for its formation or pronunciation [Mid-17thC. Via late Latin *encliticus* from Greek *egklitikos*, from *egklinein* 'to lean on'.]

enclose /in klṓz/ (**-closes, -closing, -closed**), **inclose** (**-closes, -closing, -closed**) *vt.* **1. SURROUND STH** to surround sth, or shut sth in **2. SURROUND LAND OR BUILDING WITH BOUNDARY** to surround land or a building with a fence, wall, or other boundary **3. INSERT STH IN ENVELOPE OR PACKAGE** to add sth to the contents of an envelope or package **4. HOLD STH** to hold or contain sth [14thC. From Old French *enclos*, the past participle of *enclore*, from Latin *includere* 'to shut in' (see INCLUDE).] —**enclosable** *adj.*

WORD KEY: USAGE

See Usage note at ***surround.***

enclosed order *n.* a Christian religious community whose members remain physically within it

enclosure /in klṓzhər/, **inclosure** *n.* **1. LAND SURROUNDED BY A BOUNDARY** an area of land surrounded by a fence, wall, or other boundary **2. BOUNDARY FENCE** a fence, wall, or other boundary surrounding sth **3. STH INSIDE A LETTER** sth added to a letter or package **4.** SPORTS **RESERVED AREA AT SPORTS EVENT** an area of ground at a sports event set aside for particular spectators or competitors **5. ACT OF ENCLOSING** the act or process of enclosing sth **6.** HIST **COMMON LAND TAKEN AS PRIVATE PROPERTY** between the twelfth and nineteenth centuries, the appropriation of land in England and Scotland, especially common land, so it could be fenced or hedged as private property **7.** CHR **RESTRICTED PART OF CONVENT OR MONASTERY** the part of a convent or monastery, especially the living quarters, that is restricted to members

encode /in kṓd/ (**-codes, -coding, -coded**) *vt.* **1. CONVERT TEXT TO CODE** to convert a message from plain text into code **2.** COMPUT **CONVERT COMPUTER CHARACTERS INTO DIGITAL FORM** to convert input data, e.g. analogue signals, characters, and commands, into a digital form recognizable by a computer **3.** GENETICS **PROVIDE GENETIC INFORMATION** to provide the genetic information that enables a polypeptide, RNA molecule, or one of their constituent groups to be produced (*refers to codons and genes*) —**encodement** *n.*

encomiast /en kṓmi ast/ *n.* sb who speaks or writes an encomium (*formal*) [Early 17thC. From Greek *egkōmiastēs*, from *egkōmiazein* 'to praise', from *egkōmion* 'eulogy'.]

encomium /en kṓmi əm/ (*plural* **-ums** *or* **-a** /-mi ə/) *n.* (*formal*) **1. TEXT EXPRESSING HIGH PRAISE** a formal text that expresses high praise for sb **2. HIGH PRAISE** an expression of high praise [Mid-16thC. Via Latin from Greek *egkōmion* 'eulogy', literally 'revel in', from *kōmos* 'revel' (source of English *comedy*).]

encompass /in kúmpəss/ (**-passes, -passing, -passed**) *vt.* **1. INCLUDE IN ENTIRETY** to include the entirety of sth **2. ENCIRCLE STH** to surround, envelop, or encircle sth **3. CAUSE STH TO OCCUR** to cause sth, or bring sth about (*formal*) —**encompassment** *n.*

encore /óng kawr/ *n.* **EXTRA OR REPEATED PERFORMANCE OF STH** an additional or repeated performance of sth in response to a demand from an audience ■ *interj.* **USED TO DEMAND REPEAT PERFORMANCE** used to demand an additional or repeated performance of sth ■ *vti.* (**-cores, -coring, -cored**) **ADD TO OR REPEAT PERFORMANCE OF** to give an additional or repeated performance of sth [Early 18thC. From French 'still, again'.]

encounter /in kówntər/ *vt.* (**-ters, -tering, -tered**) **1. MEET SB OR STH UNEXPECTEDLY** to meet sb or sth, usually unexpectedly **2. MEET SB OR STH IN CONFLICT** to confront sb or sth with hostility or aggression **3. COME UP AGAINST SB OR STH** to be faced with sb or sth, or come up against sb or sth ■ *n.* **1. UNEXPECTED MEETING** a meeting with sb or sth, usually unexpected and brief **2. CONFRONTATION** a hostile confrontation or contest [13thC. Via Old French *encontrer* 'to confront' from late Latin *incontra* 'in front of', from Latin *in-* 'in' + *contra* 'against'.]

encounter group *n.* a small group of people, often guided by a leader, who meet in order to achieve personal growth, self-awareness, and social skills by means of emotional expression and interaction

encourage /in kúrrij/ (**-ages, -aging, -aged**) *vt.* **1. GIVE SB HOPE OR COURAGE TO** to give sb hope, confidence, or courage **2. BE SUPPORTIVE OF SB** to urge sb in a helpful way to do or be sth **3. FOSTER STH** to assist sth to occur or increase [15thC. From French *encoragier*, from *en-* 'to cause' + *corage* 'courage'.] —**encourager** *n.*

encouragement /in kúrrijmənt/ *n.* **1. SUPPORT THAT INSPIRES CONFIDENCE** support of a kind that inspires confidence and a will to continue or develop **2. STH THAT ENCOURAGES** sb who or sth that encourages

encouraging /in kúrrijing/ *adj.* giving hope, confidence, or courage —**encouragingly** *adv.*

encroach /in krṓch/ (**-croaches, -croaching, -croached**) *vi.* **1. TRESPASS ON STH** to intrude gradually or stealthily, often taking away sb's authority, rights, or property **2. EXCEED PROPER LIMITS** to exceed the proper limits of sth [14thC. From Old French *encrochier* 'to seize', literally 'to hook in', from, ultimately, *croc* 'hook', from Old Norse *krókr* (source of English *crook*).] —**encroacher** *n.* —**encroachingly** *adv.* —**encroachment** *n.*

encrust /in krúst/ (**-crusts, -crusting, -crusted**), **incrust** (**-crusts, -crusting, -crusted**) *vt.* (*often passive*) **1. COVER STH WITH HARD COATING** to cover sth with a hard thick coating **2. DECORATE STH RICHLY** to embellish sth richly, especially with jewels [Early 17thC. Via French *incruster* from Latin *incrustare*, from *in-* 'upon' + *crusta* 'crust'.]

encrypt /in krípt/ (**-crypts, -crypting, -crypted**) *vt.* **1. CONVERT TEXT INTO CODE** to convert a text into code or cipher **2.** COMPUT **ENCODE COMPUTER DATA** to convert computer data and messages to sth incomprehensible by means of a key, so that it can be reconverted only by an authorized recipient holding the matching key —**encryption** /-krípsh'n/ *n.*

enculturation /en kúlchə ráysh'n/ *n.* = **socialization** [Mid-20thC. Coined from EN- + CULTURE + -ATION.] —**enculturative** /en kúlchərətiv/ *adj.*

encumber /in kúmbər/ (**-bers, -bering, -bered**), **incumber** (**-bers, -bering, -bered**) *vt.* **1. HINDER SB OR STH** to hamper or impede sb or sth **2. LOAD SB OR STH DOWN** to burden or weigh down sb or sth (*often passive*) **3. FILL STH WITH SUPERFLUOUS THINGS** to fill sth with superfluous matter or objects (*often passive*) [14thC. From Old French *encombrer* 'to obstruct', literally 'to put in a barrier', from *combre* 'barrier'.]

encumbrance /in kúmbrənss/ *n.* **1. BURDEN OR HINDRANCE** sb who or sth that hinders or burdens sb **2. BURDEN OR CLAIM ON PROPERTY** a lien, charge, or claim on property, especially a mortgage

encumbrancer /in kúmbrənssər/ *n.* sb who has a legal claim on property, especially a mortgage

ency., **encyc.**, **encycl.** *abbr.* encyclopedia

encyclical /en síklik'l/ *n.* CHR in the Roman Catholic Church, a formal statement issued by the Pope to bishops, often on matters of doctrine [Mid-17thC. From, ultimately, Greek *egkuklios* 'circular, general', literally 'in a circle', from *kuklos* 'circle' (see CYCLE).]

encyclopedia /in síklə péedi ə/, **encyclopaedia** *n.* a reference work offering comprehensive information on all or specialized areas of knowledge [Mid-16thC. From, ultimately, Greek *egkuklopaideia* 'general education', from *egkuklios* 'general' (see ENCYCLICAL) + *paideia* 'education', from *pais* 'boy, child' (source of English *paediatrician*).]

encyclopedic /in síklə péedik/, **encyclopaedic** *adj.* covering or including a broad range of detailed knowledge such as is found in an encyclopedia —**encyclopedically** *adv.*

encyclopedism /in síklə péedizəm/, **encyclopaedism** *n.* comprehensive learning or knowledge

encyclopedist /in síklə péedist/, **encyclopaedist** *n.* sb who compiles or contributes to an encyclopedia

Encyclopedist /in síklə péedist/ *n.* a writer or editor of the *Encyclopédie* (1751–72), a French reference work in which the advanced secular, technical, and political ideas of the period were articulated

encyst /en síst/ (**-cysts, -cysting, -cysted**) *vti.* to enclose or be enclosed in a cyst —**encystation** /énsiss táysh'n/ *n.* —**encysted** /en sístid, in sístid/ *adj.* —**encystment** *n.*

end[1] /end/ **(ends, ending, ended)** CORE MEANING: a noun indicating the last part of sth, either physically or in the abstract, and a verb indicating that sth finishes or stops ○ (n) *At the far end lay a vacant lot.* ○ (n) *bound with a red rubber band at one end* ○ (n) *shut at the end of 1991* ○ (n) *listened until the end* ○ (v) *We want to end discrimination.* ○ (v) *the weeks before school ends* ○ (v) *The reef ends in a perpendicular wall.*

1. *n.* **FINAL PART** the final part of a period of time, of an event, or of a book, film or other work ○ *The goal was to bring the information superhighway to even the most remote reaches of the globe by the end of the century.* ○ *His US mail address is at the end of the article.* **2.** *n.* **EXTREMITY OF OBJECT** the tip or extremity of a long narrow object ○ *I'm surprised he knows which end to hold the mike.* **3.** *n.* **LIMIT OR BOUNDARY** the limit, extent, or boundary of sth ○ *They walked the valley from end to end.* **4.** *n.* **STOPPING OF STH** the act or result of stopping sth ○ *call for an unconditional end to the pollution* **5.** *n.* **EXTREMITY OF A SCALE** either of the extreme points on a scale ○ *at both ends of the political spectrum* ○ *those at the high end of the income range* **6.** *n.* **GOAL** a goal, object, or purpose ○ *for purely political ends* **7.** *n.* **PART OF COMMUNICATIONS LINK** either of the places connected by a communications link ○ *Pick up the phone and find out who's on the other end.* **8.** *n.* **DEATH** the experience of death ○ *an untimely end* **9.** *n.* **LEFTOVER PIECE** a piece or part of sth that is left over **10.** *n.* **SHARE OF JOINT RESPONSIBILITY** a part or portion of shared responsibility ○ *Are you sure they'll honour their end of the deal?* **11.** *n.* SPORTS **AREA ON PLAYING FIELD** the area at either end of a playing field **12.** *n.* *US, Can* FOOTBALL **PLAYER POSITIONED AT END OF LINE** in American and Canadian football, a player positioned at either end of the offensive or defensive line **13.** *v. vti.* **STOP** to reach, or bring sth to, a close or a final point ○ *She abruptly ended the meeting.* ○ *The meeting ended without an agreement being made.* **14.** *vi.* **RESULT** to have an ultimate consequence or result ○ *The holiday ended in tragedy.* **15.** *vi.* **STOP AT A PLACE** to reach a particular place and stop there ○ *The road ends at a little village called Monkton.* **16.** *vi.* **HAVE A TIP** to have a particular kind of tip or extremity ○ *The dog's tail ends in a tuft of hair.* [Old English *ende.* Ultimately from an Indo-European word meaning 'front' that is also the ancestor of English *advance, antique,* and *until.*]
◇ **an end in itself** indicates that sth is worth having or doing although it may not lead to anything ○ *A friendship should be satisfying; it is an end in itself, and not a means to an end.* ◇ **at a loose end** having no purpose or occupation ○ *With all her work done, she found herself at a loose end.* US term **at loose ends** ◇ **at loose ends** *US* = **at a loose end** ◇ **at the end of the day** after everything has been taken into consideration ○ *You can give them as much advice as you like, but at the end of the day they'll have to decide for themselves.* ◇ **at your wit's end** totally perplexed and not knowing what to do ○ *I've tried everything to solve the problem; I'm at my wit's end.* ◇ **end for end** *US* reversed or inverted ○ *They turned the boxes end for end.* ◇ **end it all** commit suicide ◇ **end to end** in a row with the ends adjacent ○ *The beds of flowers were arranged end to end.* ◇ **in the end** finally ○ *In the end, I had to admit he was right.* ◇ **no end of sth** a great deal of sth (*informal*) ○ *The old photocopier gave us no end of trouble.* ◇ **on end 1.** for an uninterrupted period ○ *The rain continued for weeks on end.* **2.** in a vertical position ○ *We left the table standing on its end against the wall.* ◇ **the end of the line, the end of the road** the point beyond which sb or sth can no longer continue or survive ○ *The coming of the supermarkets was the end of the line for many small independent grocers.* ◇ **the (...) to end all (...)** sth that is so impressive or important that nothing else of the same kind will ever rival it ○ *the war to end all wars* ○ *the film to end all films* ◇ **to the bitter** *or* **to the very end** for as long as is possible, however unpleasant the situation becomes ○ *The company's policy was to fight to the bitter end all consequent damage suits.* ◇ **until the end of time** forever

end up *vi.* **1. TURN OUT TO BE** to become sth eventually **2. ARRIVE AT LAST** to arrive at a destination at long last

end[2] /end/ **(ends, ending, ended)** *vt.* to put hay or grain in a stack or barn (*regional*) [Early 17thC. Origin uncertain, perhaps a dialect variation or corruption of *in* 'to harvest', from Old English *innian* 'to lodge, put up', influenced by END[1].]

end- *suffix.* = **endo-** (*used before vowels*)

-end *suffix.* person or thing to be treated in a particular way ○ *adherend* [From Latin *-endus, -endum*]

endamage /en dámmij/ **(-ages, -aging, -aged)** *vt.* to cause injury or harm to sb or sth (*archaic*)

endamoeba /éndə meébə/ (*plural* **-moebae** *or* **-moebas** /-bee/ *or* **-mebas**) *n.* a parasitic protozoan found in the digestive tracts of some invertebrates, especially cockroaches and termites. Genus: *Endamoeba.*

endanger /in dáynjər/ **(-gers, -gering, -gered)** *vt.* to expose sb or sth to danger —**endangerment** *n.*

endangered /in dáynjərd/ *adj.* in danger or at risk, especially of ceasing to exist

endangered species *n.* a species of animal, plant or other organism, whose numbers are so few, or declining so quickly, that it may soon become extinct. Endangered species are sometimes protected under national or international law.

endarterectomy /én daartə réktəmi/ (*plural* **-mies**) *n.* the surgical removal of material that is wholly or partially obstructing blood flow in an artery [Mid-20thC. Coined from END- + ARTERY + -ECTOMY.]

en dash *n.* in printing, a dash that is one en in length

endear /in deér/ **(-dears, -dearing, -deared)** *vt.* to make sb or sth affectionately loved or greatly liked [Late 16thC. Coined from EN- + DEAR, modelled on French *enchérir.*]

endearing /in deéring/ *adj.* producing feelings of affection or fondness —**endearingly** *adv.*

endearment /in deérmənt/ *n.* **1. EXPRESSION OF AFFECTION** an expression of affection, especially if spoken **2. ACT OF BEING ENDEARED** the act or condition of being endeared

endeavor *vt.* US = **endeavour**

endeavour /in dévvər/ *vt.* **(-ours, -ouring, -oured) TRY TO DO STH** to make an effort to achieve sth ■ *n.* **1. EFFORT** an earnest exertion in order to achieve sth **2. ENTERPRISE** an enterprise or directed activity [15thC. From *put in dever,* partial translation of French *mettre en devoir,* literally 'to put in duty'; *devoir* from, ultimately, Latin *debere* 'to owe' (source of English *debt*).] —**endeavourer** *n.*

endemic /en démmik/ *adj.* **1.** MED **OCCURRING IN PARTICULAR PLACE** used to describe a disease occurring within a specific area, region, or locale **2.** ECOL **RESTRICTED TO PARTICULAR AREA** used to describe a species of organism that is confined to a particular geographical region, e.g. an island or river basin **3. CHARACTERISTIC OF AREA** characteristic of a particular place or among a particular group or area of interest or activity ■ *n.* MED **ENDEMIC DISEASE** an endemic disease [Mid-17thC. From, ultimately, Greek *endēmos* 'native', literally 'in the people', from *dēmos* 'people'.] —**endemically** *adv.* —**endemicity** /én de míssəti, éndə-/ *n.* —**endemism** /éndə mizəm/ *n.*

endergonic /éndər gónnik/ *adj.* used to describe a chemical or biochemical reaction in which energy is absorbed [Mid-20thC. Coined from END- + Greek *ergon* 'work' + -IC.]

endgame /énd gaym/ *n.* **1.** CHESS **LAST STAGE OF CHESS GAME** the final stage of a chess game in which only a few pieces are left on the board **2. ULTIMATE STAGE OF STH** the final stage of a process or contest ○ *As the trial neared its close, reporters watched closely to see what the prosecutors' endgame would be.*

ending /énding/ *n.* **1. FINAL PART OF STH** the final or concluding part of sth, e.g. a book or film **2. WAY STH IS FINISHED** the manner in which sth is ended **3.** LING **END PART OF WORD** the terminating part of a word, e.g. an inflection or suffix **4.** CHESS = **endgame** *n.* 1 **5.** PSYCHOL **PROCESS OF CONCLUDING A RELATIONSHIP** the process of concluding a relationship with another person, especially a therapist. An ending may offer sb an opportunity to explore feelings about separation and loss.

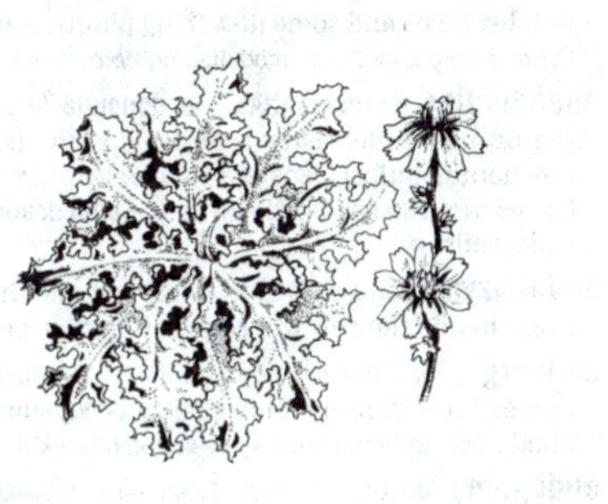
Endive

endive /én dīv, éndiv, óN deev/ (*plural* **-dives** *or* **-dive**) *n.* **1. LEAFY PLANT USED IN SALADS** a plant grown for its tightly packed curly leaves that are used in salads and as a garnish. Latin name: *Cichorium endivia.* **2.** *US* = **chicory** [14thC. From, ultimately, Latin *endivia* from medieval Greek *entubia,* of uncertain origin; perhaps ultimately from Semitic.]

endless /éndləss/ *adj.* **1. WITHOUT END** having no end or limit **2. CONTINUOUS** made continuous by joining the ends —**endlessly** *adv.* —**endlessness** *n.*

end line *n.* a line at the end of a court or field that marks the boundary of a playing area

end matter *n.* PUBL = **back matter**

endmost /énd mōst/ *adj.* **1. NEAREST END** nearest or at the end **2.** last or most distant

endnote /énd nōt/ *n.* a note of comment or reference placed at the end of a chapter, book, or essay

endo- *prefix.* in, within, inside ○ *endotracheal* [From Greek *endo.* Ultimately from an Indo-European base meaning 'in', which is also the ancestor of English *in, industry,* and *indigent.*]

endocardial /éndō kaárdi əl/ *adj.* **1. IN HEART** located within the heart **2. OF MEMBRANE OF HEART** concerned with the membranous lining of the heart's cavities (**endocardium**)

endocarditis /éndō kaar dítiss/ *n.* inflammation of the membranous lining of the heart's cavities (**endocardium**) —**endocarditic** /-díttik/ *adj.*

endocardium /éndō kaárdi əm/ (*plural* **-a** /-di ə/) *n.* the thin membranous lining of the heart's cavities

endocarp /éndə kaarp/ *n.* the innermost of the three layers of the wall (**pericarp**) of a fruit. It may be toughened or hardened, as in a cherry stone or peach stone. (*technical*) —**endocarpal** /éndə kaárp'l/ *adj.*

endocranium /éndō kráyni əm/ (*plural* **-a** /-ni ə/) *n.* = **dura mater** —**endocranial** *adj.*

endocrine /éndō krīn, -krin/ *adj.* relating to glands that secrete hormones internally directly into the lymph or bloodstream. ◊ **exocrine** [Early 20thC. Coined from ENDO- + Greek *krinein* 'to separate'.]

endocrine gland *n.* any gland of the body that secretes hormones directly into the blood or lymph, e.g. the thyroid, pituitary, pineal, and adrenal glands

endocrinologist /éndōkri nólləjist, -krī-/ *n.* a medical specialist who treats endocrine disorders

endocrinology /éndō kri nólləji, -krī-/ *n.* a branch of medicine dealing with disorders of the endocrine glands —**endocrinologic** /éndō krinə lójjik/ *adj.* —**endocrinological** *adj.*

endocytosis /éndō sī tóssiss/ *n.* the process by which a cell membrane folds inwards to take in substances bound to its surface [Mid-20thC. Coined from ENDO- + -CYTE + -OSIS.]

endoderm /éndō durm/ *n.* the innermost layer of an animal embryo that develops into the lining of the respiratory and digestive tracts [Mid-19thC. Coined from ENDO- + Greek *derma* 'skin'.] —**endodermal** /éndō dúrm'l/ *adj.*

endodermis /énd ō dúrmiss/ *n.* a layer of cells that marks the boundary between the inner core (**stele**) and outer surrounding tissue (**cortex**) of a plant root. It is also evident in the stems of certain plants, notably ferns and some flowering plants. [Late 19thC. Formed from ENDODERM, modelled on *epidermis*.]

endodontics /éndō dóntiks/, **endodontia** /-dónti ə/ *n.* the branch of dentistry that deals with diseases of the dental pulp (*takes a singular verb*) [Mid-20thC. Coined from ENDO- + ORTHODONTICS.] —**endodontic** *adj.* —**endodontist** *n.*

endoenzyme /énd ō én zīm/ *n.* an enzyme that functions inside the cell where it is found or produced

endoergic /énd ō úrjik/ *adj.* NUCLEAR PHYS relating to a nuclear reaction in which energy is consumed [Mid-20thC. Coined from ENDO- + Greek *ergon* 'work'.]

endogamy /en dóggəmi/ *n.* **1.** ANTHROP **MARRIAGE WITHIN GROUP** the social practice of marrying another member of the same clan, people, or other kinship group **2.** BOT **SELF-POLLINATION** pollination between the flowers of the same plant —**endogamous** *adj.*

endogenous /en dójjənəss/ *adj.* **1.** **WITHOUT EXTERNAL CAUSE** with no apparent external cause ○ *endogenous depression* **2.** BIOL **PRODUCED INSIDE ORGANISM** originating or growing within an organism or tissue ○ *endogenous secretions.* ◊ **exogenous** —**endogenously** *adv.* —**endogeny** *n.*

endolymph /éndō limf/ *n.* the fluid inside the membranous labyrinth of the ear —**endolymphatic** /éndō lim fáttik/ *adj.*

endometria plural of **endometrium**

endometriosis /éndō meétri óssiss/ *n.* a medical condition in which the mucous membrane (**endometrium**) that normally lines only the womb is present and functioning in the ovaries or elsewhere in the body

endometrium /éndō meétri əm/ (*plural* **-a** /-tri ə/) *n.* the mucous membrane that lines the womb and increases in thickness in the latter part of the menstrual cycle [Late 19thC. Coined from ENDO- + Greek *mētra* 'womb'.] —**endometrial** *adj.*

endomitosis /éndō mī tóssiss/ *n.* a process by which chromosomes divide within a cell but the nucleus does not, so that an increase in chromosome number results —**endomitotic** /-mī tóttik/ *adj.*

endomorph /éndō mawrf/ *n.* **1.** PHYSIOL **STOCKY PERSON** sb whose body has a stocky build and a prominent abdomen. ◊ **ectomorph, mesomorph 2.** MINERALS **MINERAL INSIDE ANOTHER** a mineral that is found within another mineral. An example of this is tourmaline, often found enclosed in quartz. ◊ **perimorph** —**endomorphic** /éndō máwrfik/ *adj.* —**endomorphy** /éndō mawrfi/ *n.*

endonuclease /éndō nyóokli ayz/ *n.* an enzyme that splits a DNA or RNA molecule by aiding the breakdown of bonds between nucleotides

endoparasite /éndō párrə sīt/ *n.* a parasite, e.g. a tapeworm, that lives inside its host —**endoparasitic** /éndō párrə síttik/ *adj.* —**endoparasitism** /éndō párrə sī tizəm/ *n.*

endopeptidase /éndō pépti dayz, -dayss/ *n.* an enzyme, e.g. pepsin that aids the breakdown of peptide bonds in proteins

endophyte /éndō fīt/ *n.* a plant or fungus that lives inside another plant. It may or may not be a parasite of its host plant. —**endophytic** /éndō fíttik/ *adj.*

endoplasm /éndō plazəm/ *n.* the inner, more fluid layer of cytoplasm in a cell —**endoplasmic** /éndō plázmik/ *adj.*

endoplasmic reticulum *n.* an intricate system of tubular membranes in the cytoplasm of a cell. It is responsible for the synthesis and transport of materials to and from cells.

end organ *n.* the specialized end of a sensory or motor nerve

endorphin /en dáwrfin/ *n.* a substance in the brain that attaches to the same cell receptors that morphine does. Endorphins are released when severe injury occurs, often abolishing all sensation of pain. [Late 20thC. Blend of ENDOGENOUS and MORPHINE.]

endorse /in dáwrss/ (**-dorses, -dorsing, -dorsed**), **indorse** (**-dorses, -dorsing, -dorsed**) *vt.* **1.** **APPROVE FORMALLY** to give formal approval or permission for sth ○ *This practice is not endorsed by head office.* **2.** **SUPPORT** to give public support to sb or sth, especially during an election ○ *decided to endorse the mayor as a candidate for higher office* **3.** COMM **PROMOTE** to give public approval of a product for advertising purposes ○ *a brand endorsed by a popular TV star* **4.** FIN **SIGN CHEQUE TO OBTAIN CASH** to sign the back of a cheque or postal order in order to cash it **5.** FIN **SIGN STH TO ASSIGN PAYMENT** to sign the back of a negotiable document in order to make it payable to a specified payee **6.** FIN **SIGN RECEIPT** to sign a document to acknowledge receipt of a payment **7.** **WRITE ON BACK OF DOCUMENT** to write a comment on the back of a document ○ *a fitness report that had been endorsed on the back by its recipient* **8.** **RECORD CONVICTIONS ON LICENCE** to record details of convictions for motoring offences on a driving licence ○ *You will pay a fine and have your licence endorsed with three penalty points.* [15thC. From medieval Latin *indorsare*, from Latin *dorsum* 'back' (source of English *dorsal* and *dossier*).] —**endorsable** *adj.* —**endorsee** /in dáwr seé/ *n.* —**endorser** /in dáwrssər/ *n.*

endorsement /in dáwrssmənt/, **indorsement** *n.* **1.** FIN **ACT OF ENDORSING** an act or instance of endorsing sth or sb ○ *make an endorsement of a cheque* **2.** **SIGNATURE OR WRITTEN COMMENT** sth, especially a signature, written on the back of a document to make it payable, approve it, or comment on it **3.** **OFFICIAL APPROVAL OR PERMISSION** official approval of or permission for sth **4.** **PUBLIC SUPPORT** public support for sb or sth **5.** COMM **ADVERTISING TESTIMONIAL** an instance of public approval of a product for advertising purposes **6.** **RECORD OF OFFENCE** details of a conviction for a motoring offence recorded on a driving licence **7.** INSUR **POLICY ALTERATION** a clause added to an insurance policy that changes the coverage

endoscope /éndə skōp/ *n.* a medical instrument consisting of a long tube inserted into the body, usually through a small incision. It is used for diagnostic examination and surgical procedures. —**endoscopic** /éndə skóppik/ *adj.* —**endoscopically** *adv.* —**endoscopy** /en dóskəpi/ *n.*

endoskeleton /éndō skéllitən/ *n.* the internal skeleton of an animal, especially of a vertebrate —**endoskeletal** *adj.*

endosmosis /énd oz móssiss/ *n.* osmosis in which fluid is absorbed from a surrounding fluid into a cell —**endosmotic** /-móttik/ *adj.* —**endosmotically** *adv.*

endosperm /éndō spurm/ *n.* the tissue that surrounds the embryo inside a plant seed and provides nourishment for it —**endospermic** /éndō spúrmik/ *adj.*

endospore /éndō spawr/ *n.* **1.** **ASEXUAL SPORE** an asexual spore that is formed inside the cells of certain bacteria and algae **2.** **INNER SPORE WALL** the inner layer of the wall of a spore —**endosporous** /en dóspərəss/ *adj.*

endosteum /en dósti əm/ (*plural* **-a** /-ti ə/) *n.* a layer of vascular tissue lining the inside of certain bones, e.g. the femur [Late 19thC. Coined from ENDO- + Greek *osteon* 'bone'.] —**endosteal** *adj.*

endosulfan /éndō súlfən/ *n.* an organochlorine insecticide and acaricide used to control insects, e.g. aphids and mites, on farm and garden crops. Its use is now restricted because of its toxic side effects. Formula: $C_9H_6Cl_6O_3S$. [Mid-20thC. Coined from ENDO- + SULFUR.]

endosymbiosis /éndō sím bi óssiss/ *n.* symbiosis in which one organism lives inside the body of another

endothecium /éndō theéshi əm, -theéssi əm/ (*plural* **-a** /-shi ə, -si ə/) *n.* **1.** **MOSS TISSUE** the inner tissue of the spore-producing capsule of a moss **2.** **ANTHER TISSUE** the tissue of the inner wall of an anther in a flower [Mid-19thC. Coined from ENDO- + Greek *thēkion* 'little case', a diminutive of *thēkē* 'chest'.]

endothelia plural of **endothelium**

endothelioma /éndō theeli ómə/ (*plural* **-mas** *or* **-mata** /-ómətə/) *n.* a tumour of cells that line internal body surfaces

endothelium /énd ō theéli əm/ (*plural* **-a** /-li ə/) *n.* a layer of cells that lines the inside of certain body cavities, e.g. blood vessels [Late 19thC. From modern Latin, formed from Greek *endon* 'within' + *thēlē* 'nipple'.] —**endothelial** *adj.* —**endothelioid** *adj.*

endotherm /éndō thurm/ *n.* an animal that is able to maintain a constant body temperature despite changes in the temperature of its environment [Mid-20thC. Coined from ENDO- + Greek *thermē* 'heat'.]

endothermic /éndō thúrmik/, **endothermal** /-thúrm'l/ *adj.* **1.** CHEM, PHYS **ABSORBING HEAT** used to describe a reaction that absorbs heat (*the preferred term in nuclear physics is 'endoergic'*) **2.** ZOOL **WARM-BLOODED** maintaining a constant body temperature despite changes in the temperature of the environment —**endothermy** /éndō thurmi/ *n.*

endotoxin /éndō tóksin/ *n.* a toxin produced within certain bacteria that is released only when the bacteria disintegrate —**endotoxic** *adj.*

endotracheal /éndōtrə keé əl/ *adj.* located in or passed through the windpipe ○ *an endotracheal tube*

endotrophic /éndō trőffik, -tróffik/ *adj.* used to describe an association (**mycorrhiza**) between a fungus and a plant in which the fungus obtains its nourishment from inside its plant host. ◊ **ectotrophic**

endow /in dów/ (**-dows, -dowing, -dowed**) *vt.* **1.** FIN **PROVIDE WITH MONEY** to provide a person or institution with income or property **2.** **PROVIDE WITH STH DESIRABLE** to provide sb or sth with desirable qualities, abilities, or characteristics ○ *Nature has endowed the area with a perfect climate.* **3.** **GIVE DOWER** to provide sb with a dower (*archaic*) [14thC. Via Anglo-Norman *endouer* from, ultimately, Latin *dotare* 'to provide with a dowry' (the original sense in English), from *dos* 'dowry'.]

endowment /in dówmənt/ *n.* **1.** FIN **FUNDS OR PROPERTY** an amount of income or property that has been provided to a person or institution, especially an educational institution **2.** FIN **GIVING OF ENDOWMENT** the giving of an endowment, or an instance of this **3.** **NATURAL QUALITY** a natural ability or quality ○ *A sharp mind was one of her many endowments.*

endowment assurance, **endowment insurance** *n.* life insurance that pays a set amount to the policyholder when the policy matures or to a beneficiary if the policyholder dies before maturity

endowment mortgage *n.* a mortgage in which the borrower pays the lender interest and repays the capital to a life assurance policy that repays the loan at maturity or when the borrower dies

endozoic /éndō zṓ ik/ *adj.* **1.** **LIVING IN ANIMAL** used to describe organisms that live inside an animal **2.** **DISPERSED THROUGH ANIMAL'S GUT** related to or being a method of seed dispersal in which the seeds are eaten by an animal and then passed out in the animal's faeces

endpaper /énd paypər/ *n.* a sturdy sheet of paper pasted to the inside of a book's front or back cover and to the spine edge of the first or last page

end pin *n.* the adjustable spike-shaped leg at the bottom of a cello or double bass that the instrument rests on while being played

endplay /énd play/ *n.* **BRIDGE TACTIC FORCING LOSS OF TRICK** a play in bridge in which an opponent is forced to lead near the end of the hand, with the result that he or she loses a trick that would otherwise have been won ■ *vt.* (**-plays, -playing, -played**) **FORCE BRIDGE OPPONENT TO LEAD** to force an opponent in bridge to lead near the end of a hand of bridge so that he or she will lose a trick

end point *n.* **1.** **COMPLETION** the point at which sth is complete or comes to an end **2.** CHEM **COMPLETION OF TITRATION** the point, marked by a colour change or other indicator, at which a titration is complete

endpoint /énd poynt/ *n.* MATH the point located at either end of a line segment or at the end of a ray

end product *n.* the final result of a process or series of events or operations

end rhyme *n.* the use of rhyme at the ends of lines of poetry, or an example of this

endrin /éndrin/ *n.* a poisonous white crystalline compound that is used as an insecticide. A chlorinated hydrocarbon, it is an isomer of dieldrin. Formula: $C_{12}H_8Cl_6O$. [Mid-20thC. Coined from ENDO- + DIELDRIN.]

end-stopped *adj.* used to describe poetry containing a pause in meaning at the end of a line or couplet, instead of continuing into the next line or couplet

endue /in dyóo/ (**-dues, -duing, -dued**), **indue** (**-dues, -duing, -dued**) *vt.* to endow sb or sth with an ability or quality ○ *His successes have endued him with an aura of invincibility.* [14thC. Via French *enduire* from, ultimately, Latin *ducere* 'to lead' (source of English *induce* and *duct*).]

endurable /in dyoórəb'l/ *adj.* able to be borne or tolerated ○ *The level of noise was barely endurable.* —**endurability** /in dyoórə bílləti/ *n.* —**endurably** /in dyoórəbli/ *adv.*

endurance /in dyoóranss/ *n.* **1.** ABILITY TO BEAR PROLONGED HARDSHIP the ability or power to bear prolonged exertion, pain, or hardship ○ *an endurance race* **2.** TOLERATION OF HARDSHIP an act or example of toleration of prolonged suffering or hardship ○ *an unflinching endurance of pain* **3.** PERSISTENCE OVER TIME the survival or persistence of sth despite the ravages of time ○ *the endurance of ancient traditions* [15thC. From French, formed from *endurer* (see ENDURE).]

endure /in dyoór/ (**-dures, -during, -dured**) *v.* **1.** *vti.* BEAR HARDSHIP to experience exertion, pain, or hardship without giving up ○ *The nation endured years of war to create a lasting peace.* **2.** *vt.* TOLERATE DISAGREEABLE THINGS to tolerate or accept sb or sth that is extremely disagreeable (*formal*) ○ *I cannot endure that song.* **3.** *vi.* SURVIVE to last or survive over a period of time, especially when faced with difficulties ○ *The philosophical ideas of the ancient Greeks endure to this day.* [14thC. Via French *endurer* from Latin *indurare* 'to harden', from *durus* 'hard'.]

enduring /in dyoóring/ *adj.* **1.** PERSISTING OR SURVIVING persisting or surviving in the face of difficulties **2.** LONG-SUFFERING patient or tolerant despite many difficulties —**enduringly** *adv.* —**enduringness** *n.*

end user *n.* a person or group that is one of the ultimate consumers or users that a product has been designed for ○ *a survey that is designed to assess what the end user really needs*

endways /énd wayz/, **endwise** *adv.* **1.** WITH END UP with an end up or forwards **2.** TOWARDS ENDS towards the ends **3.** WITH ENDS TOUCHING with one end next to another end

Endymion /en dímmi ən/ *n.* in Greek mythology, a handsome man loved by the moon goddess Selene

end zone *n.* either of the two areas at the ends of an American football field between the goal line and the end line where a touchdown is scored

ENE *abbr.* east-northeast

-ene *suffix.* an unsaturated organic compound ○ *butene* [From Greek *-ēnē*, feminine of *-ēnos*, an adjective suffix]

enema /énnəmə/ (*plural* **-mas** *or* **-mata** /-mətə/) *n.* **1.** INSERTION OF LIQUID INTO RECTUM the insertion of a liquid into the bowels via the rectum as a treatment, especially for constipation, or as an aid to diagnosis **2.** LIQUID USED IN ENEMA the liquid used in an enema ○ *a barium enema* [Late 17thC. Via late Latin from Greek, formed from *enienai* 'to send or put in', from *hienai* 'to send'.]

enemy /énnəmi/ (*plural* **-mies**) *n.* **1.** UNFRIENDLY OPPONENT sb who hates and seeks to harm or cause trouble for sb else **2.** MIL A MILITARY OPPONENT a person or group, especially a military force, that fights against another in combat or battle **3.** POL HOSTILE POWER a hostile nation or power **4.** HARMFUL THING sth that harms or opposes sth else ○ *In a case like this, time is the enemy.* [13thC. Via Old French *enemi* from Latin *inimicus* 'unfriendly', from *amicus* 'friend' (source of English *amicable*).]

energetic /énnər jéttik/ *adj.* **1.** FORCEFUL displaying great vigour or force **2.** REQUIRING STAMINA requiring great vigour or stamina [Mid-17thC. Via Greek *energētikos* 'active' from, ultimately, *ergon* 'work' (see ENERGY).] —**energetically** *adv.*

energetics /énnər jéttiks/ *n.* the branch of physics that studies energy and its transformations (*takes a singular verb*)

energize /énnər jīz/ (**-gizes, -gizing, -gized**), **energise** (**-gises, -gising, -gised**) *v.* **1.** *vt.* GIVE SB OR STH ENERGY to supply sb or sth with strength or power ○ *He felt energized by his nap.* **2.** *vti.* MAKE OR BECOME ACTIVE to become or cause sth to become vigorously active **3.** *vt.* ELEC SUPPLY WITH ELECTRICAL POWER to supply sth with a source of electrical power —**energization** /énnər jī záysh'n/ *n.* —**energizer** /énnər jīzər/ *n.*

energy /énnərji/ (*plural* **-gies**) *n.* **1.** VIGOUR liveliness and forcefulness ○ *She gave a speech that was full of energy.* **2.** ABILITY TO DO THINGS the ability or power to work or make an effort ○ *His illness left him feeling drained of energy.* **3.** FORCEFUL EFFORT a vigorous effort or action ○ *We must concentrate our energies on the task in hand.* **4.** PHYS POWER SUPPLY OR SOURCE a supply or source of electrical, mechanical, or other form of power **5.** PHYS CAPACITY TO DO WORK the capacity of a body or system to do work. Symbol *E* [Mid-16thC. Via French *énergie* from, ultimately, Greek *energeia*, from *ergon* 'work'.]

WORD KEY: ORIGIN

The Indo-European word from which ***energy*** ultimately comes is also the ancestor of English *irk*, *liturgy*, *organ*, *orgy*, *surgeon*, and *work*.

energy audit *n.* a survey of the use of energy in a building or organization, undertaken in order to make energy use as efficient as possible

energy balance *n.* a mathematical relationship, using the principle of the conservation of energy, that shows the energy inputs and outputs of a process or system

energy band *n.* PHYS = **band**[2] *n.* 9

energy-band theory *n.* PHYS = **band theory**

energy crisis *n.* a situation in which available sources of energy are not sufficient to meet the demand

energy efficient *adj.* using electrical or other energy in an economical way (*hyphenated when used before a noun*)

energy level *n.* one of the discrete stable energy values that can be assumed by a physical system, e.g. the electrons in an atom or an atomic nucleus

energy recovery *n.* the extraction of energy from synthetic materials, e.g. using the heat from incineration of solid waste to generate electricity

energy tax *n.* a tax on an energy source intended to discourage environmentally unfriendly sources and encourage energy conservation or use of alternative sources

enervate *vt.* /énnər vayt/ (**-vates, -vating, -vated**) WEAKEN to weaken sb's physical, mental, or moral vitality ○ *I was feeling quite enervated by the strain of moving house.* ■ *adj.* /i núrvit/ = **enervated** [Early 17thC. From Latin *enervare* 'to extract the sinews of, weaken', from *nervus* 'sinew' (source of English *nerve*).] —**enervation** /énnər váysh'n/ *n.*

enface /in fáyss/ (**-faces, -facing, -faced**) *vt.* to mark sth on the face of a document by writing, stamping, or printing [Mid-19thC. From EN- + FACE, modelled on ENDORSE.] —**enfacement** *n.*

en famille /oN fa meé/ *adv.* **1.** WITH THE FAMILY with the members of your family, especially at home **2.** INFORMALLY in an informal, relaxed, or casual way [Early 18thC. From French, literally 'in the family'.]

enfant terrible /óN foN te reéblə/ (*plural* **enfants terribles** /óN foN te reéblə/) *n.* **1.** SHOCKING PERSON sb whose unconventional behaviour, attitudes, or remarks are shocking to others **2.** AVANT-GARDE YOUNG ARTIST a young person, especially in the arts, who has become successful because of work that is radically innovative or extremely avant-garde [From French, literally 'terrible child']

enfeeble /in feéb'l/ (**-bles, -bling, -bled**) *vt.* to reduce the strength of sb or sth to the point of weakness [14thC. From Old French *enfiblir*, from *feble* (see FEEBLE).] —**enfeeblement** *n.*

enfeoff /in feéf/ (**-feoffs, -feoffing, -feoffed**) *vt.* **1.** GIVE SB LAND FREEHOLD to invest sb with the freehold possession of a piece of land **2.** MAKE SB VASSAL to make sb a feudal vassal by giving that person a fief or fee (*archaic*) [14thC. From Anglo-Norman *enfeoffer*, from Old French *fief* (see FIEF).] —**enfeoffment** *n.*

Enfield /én feeld/ *n.* = **Enfield rifle** *n.* 2

Enfield musket *n.* a muzzle-loading rifled musket used by British forces in the 19th century and by American troops in the American Civil War [Named after ENFIELD, where it was made]

Enfield rifle *n.* **1.** BRITISH RIFLE a .303-calibre bolt-action breech-loading rifle, used by British forces in World War I and until the 1930s. **2.** US RIFLE a .30-calibre bolt-action breech-loading rifle used by US forces in World War I. **3.** = **Enfield musket** [Named after ENFIELD, where the British rifle was made]

enfilade *n.* /énfi layd/ **1.** VULNERABLE POSITION a position in which troops are exposed to gunfire along the length of their formation **2.** RAKING FIRE gunfire that strikes a body of troops along its whole length ■ *vt.* /énfi láyd/ (**-lades, -lading, -laded**) **1.** FIRE AT STH ALONG ITS LENGTH to attack a position or body of troops with fire along its whole length **2.** FIRE ALONG WHOLE LENGTH OF ENEMY to place guns or troops in a position from which they can fire on the whole length of an enemy position or body of troops [Early 18thC. Via French, from, ultimately, *fil* 'thread', from Latin *filum* (source of English *filament* and *fillet*).]

enfleurage /óN flur raázh/ *n.* a process used in making perfume in which oils acquire fragrance by being exposed to the scent of flowers [Mid-19thC. From French, formed from *enfleurer* 'to saturate with the scent of flowers', from *fleur* 'flower'.]

enfold /in fṓld/ (**-folds, -folding, -folded**), **infold** (**-folds, -folding, -folded**) *vt.* **1.** ENVELOP to wrap, or wrap sth, completely around sb or sth **2.** EMBRACE to hold sb or sth in an embrace **3.** ENCLOSE OR SURROUND to enclose or surround sb or sth ○ *enfold a child in your love* —**enfolder** *n.*

enforce /in fáwrss/ (**-forces, -forcing, -forced**) *vt.* **1.** MAKE PEOPLE OBEY STH to compel obedience to a law, regulation, or command **2.** IMPOSE to impose sth by force **3.** STRENGTHEN to give strength or emphasis to sth ○ *enforce an argument* [13thC. Via French *enforcir* from, ultimately, Latin *fortis* 'strong' (source of English *fort* and *fortify*).] —**enforceability** /in fáwrssə bílləti/ *n.* —**enforceable** /in fáwrssəb'l/ *adj.* —**enforcement** /-fáwrssmənt/ *n.*

enforcer /in fáwrssər/ *n.* **1.** LAW SB WHO ENFORCES LAW sb who enforces a rule, law, or other order **2.** *US* CRIMINOL CRIMINAL WHO INTIMIDATES a member of a criminal gang who uses physical violence to intimidate and enforce compliance (*slang*)

enfranchise /in frán chīz/ (**-chises, -chising, -chised**) *vt.* **1.** GIVE SB RIGHT TO VOTE to give sb the right to vote in an election **2.** SET FREE to set sb free, especially from slavery **3.** ALLOW REPRESENTATION TO to grant political representation to a town or city [Early 16thC. From Old French *enfranchir*, from *franc* 'free' (source of English *frank*), from Latin *francus*.] —**enfranchisement** /-chiz-/ *n.*

ENG *abbr.* electronic newsgathering

eng. *abbr.* **1.** engine **2.** engineer **3.** engineering

Eng. *abbr.* **1.** England **2.** English

engage /in gáyj/ (**-gages, -gaging, -gaged**) *v.* **1.** *vti.* INVOLVE OR BECOME INVOLVED to involve sb in an activity, or become involved or take part in an activity **2.** *vt.* HIRE SB to hire sb for a job or to do some work **3.** *vt.* RESERVE STH to reserve or rent sth for personal use (*dated*) **4.** *vt.* REQUIRE USE OF STH to require the use or devotion of sth **5.** *vt.* HOLD SB'S ATTENTION to attract and hold sb's attention **6.** *vt.* ATTRACT SB BY PLEASING to attract or win the affection of sb by pleasing that person ○ *He was engaged by the child's charm.* **7.** *vti.* PROMISE TO DO STH to commit yourself or sth to an obligation ○ *She engaged to meet them tomorrow.* **8.** *vti.* MIL FIGHT SB to fight or begin a battle with an enemy **9.** *vti.* MECH ENG INTERLOCK to become interlocked, or bring sth together and cause sth to interlock **10.** *vti.* ACTIVATE OR BECOME ACTIVATED to activate sth or bring sth into operation, or become activated or operational [Early 16thC. From French *engagier*, from *gage* 'pledge'. Ultimately from a prehistoric Germanic word that is also the ancestor of English *wage*.] —**engager** *n.*

engagé /óng ga zháy/ *adj.* committed to a political cause or ideology, usually a left-wing one [Mid-20thC. From French, the past participle of *engager* (see ENGAGE).]

engaged /in gáyjd/ *adj.* **1.** HAVING AGREED TO MARRY having agreed to be married ○ *the newly engaged couple* **2.** OCCUPIED busy doing sth ○ *The Minister is otherwise engaged this afternoon.* **3.** MIL FIGHTING BATTLE fighting a military battle **4.** MECH ENG WITH PARTS INTERLOCKED with teeth or other parts interlocked and often in operation **5.** TELECOM CURRENTLY BEING USED FOR TELEPHONE

CALL used to describe a telephone line that is currently being used to make a telephone call. US term **busy** *adj.* 6 **6.** BUILDING BUILT INTO OR ATTACHED TO WALL used to describe a part of a building that is built into or attached to a wall

──── **WORD KEY: SYNONYMS** ────
See Synonyms at *busy*.

engaged tone *n.* a series of repeated short tones heard through a telephone when the line belonging to the number dialled is already being used. US term **busy signal**

engagée /óng ga zháy/ *adj.* used to describe a woman who is committed to a political cause or ideology, usually a left-wing one [Mid-20thC. From French, the feminine past participle of *engager* (see ENGAGE).]

engagement /in gáyjmənt/ *n.* **1.** AGREEMENT TO MARRY an agreement to get married ○ *announce our engagement* **2.** COMMITMENT TO ATTEND an arrangement to be present at an event, especially a business or social appointment **3.** PLEDGE FOR STH sth, e.g. a promise, that is freely made and that carries an obligation to do sth **4.** SHORT JOB a job that lasts for a short period of time, especially one for an entertainer in a club or theatre ○ *a week-long engagement in Las Vegas* **5.** MIL BATTLE a battle or other conflict involving military forces ○ *a minor engagement on the frontier* **6.** ACTIVE OR OPERATIONAL STATE an act or condition of being activated or becoming operational

──── **WORD KEY: SYNONYMS** ────
See Synonyms at *fight*.

engagement ring *n.* a ring given by a man to his fiancée to mark their engagement to marry. It is worn on the ring finger of the left hand.

engaging /in gáyjing/ *adj.* charming or pleasing in a way that attracts and holds the attention —**engagingly** *adv.*

en garde /oN gaárd/ *interj.* used to warn a fencer to assume the prescribed stance for the start of a match [From French, literally 'on guard']

Engelmann spruce /éng g'lmən-/ *n.* a large spruce tree found in western North America. Latin name: *Picea engelmannii*. [Mid-19thC. Named after the US botanist George *Engelmann* (1809–84).]

Popperfoto
Friedrich Engels

Engels /éng g'lz/, **Friedrich** (1820–95) German political thinker and revolutionary. He co-wrote the *Communist Manifesto* (1848) with Karl Marx and supported Marx financially. He lived mainly in England.

engender /in jéndər/ (**-ders, -dering, -dered**) *v.* **1.** *vti.* CREATE OR ARISE to arise or come into existence, or cause sth to do so ○ *Secrecy engenders suspicion.* **2.** *vt.* HAVE OFFSPRING to cause offspring to be conceived or born (*formal*) [14thC. Via French from Latin *ingenerare*, from *generare* 'to produce'.] —**engenderer** *n.*

engine /énjin/ *n.* **1.** MECH ENG MACHINE FOR POWERING EQUIPMENT a machine that converts energy into mechanical power or motion ○ *an oil-fired engine* **2.** RAIL RAILWAY LOCOMOTIVE a railway locomotive **3.** DRIVING FORCE OR ENERGY SOURCE sth that supplies the driving force or energy to a movement, system, or trend ○ *a political movement that was seen as a great engine of social change* **4.** MIL, HISTORY BATTLEFIELD MACHINE a battering ram, catapult, or other device used in warfare (*archaic*) ○ *a siege engine* [14thC. Via French

engin from Latin *ingenium* 'talent, clever device' (source of English *ingenious*).]

engine block *n.* = **cylinder block**

engined /énjind/ *adj.* powered by an engine or engines, often of a specified make or number (*usually used in combination*)

engine driver *n.* RAIL sb who operates a railway locomotive

engineer /énji néer/ *n.* **1.** ENG ENGINEERING PROFESSIONAL sb who is trained in a branch of professional engineering **2.** *US, Can* RAIL = **engine driver 3.** MECH ENG MECHANIC sb who operates or services machines **4.** SHIPPING, NAVY SHIP'S OFFICER an officer on a ship who is in charge of the engines **5.** MIL CONSTRUCTION SOLDIER a member of a unit of the armed forces that specializes in building and sometimes destroying bridges, fortifications, and other large structures **6.** PLANNER sb who plans, oversees, or brings about sth, especially sth that is achieved with ingenuity or secretiveness ○ *the engineer of the overthrow of the government* ■ *vt.* (**-neers, -neering, -neered**) **1.** CONTRIVE STH to plan sth or bring it about, especially in an ingenious or secretive manner **2.** ENG USE ENGINEERING SKILL TO DESIGN STH to use professional engineering skill to design or create sth ○ *This car was engineered in Italy.* **3.** GENETICS USE GENETIC ENGINEERING ON STH to use the techniques of genetic engineering on sth [14thC. Via Old French *engigneor* 'contriver' from, ultimately, Latin *ingenium* (see ENGINE).]

engineering /énji néering/ *n.* **1.** ENG APPLICATION OF SCIENCE TO DESIGNING THINGS the application of science in the design, planning, construction, and maintenance of buildings, machines, and other manufactured things ○ *leading the world in engineering* **2.** ENG PROFESSION INVOLVING TECHNICAL DESIGNING any one of various branches of engineering pursued as a profession, e.g. civil engineering or electronic engineering **3.** CONTRIVANCE the planning or bringing about of sth, especially when done with ingenuity or secretiveness

engine room *n.* the place on board a ship where the engines are housed

enginery /énjinri/ (*plural* **-ries**) *n.* a group of engines

engird /in gúrd/ (**-girds, -girding, -girded** *or* **-girt** /in gúrt/) *vt.* to encircle sth (*literary*)

engirdle /in gúrd'l/ (**-girdles, -girdling, -girdled**) *vt.* to surround or encircle sth (*literary*)

engirt past tense, past participle of **engird**

englacial /in gláysh'l/ *adj.* used to describe material or processes occurring within a glacier

England /íng glənd/ country forming the southern and largest part of Great Britain and of the United Kingdom. Capital: London. Population: 48,903,000 (1995). Area: 130,410 sq. km/50,351 sq. mi.

Englified /íng gli fīd/ *adj. Scotland* anglicized (*informal disapproving*)

English /íng glish/ *n.* **1.** LANG LANGUAGE OF US AND CANADA the official language of the United Kingdom of Great Britain and Northern Ireland, the Republic of Ireland, the United States, Canada, Australia, New Zealand, South Africa, and several other countries. There are about 350 million native speakers of English, and a further approximately 375 million people use it as a second language. **2.** PEOPLES PEOPLE FROM ENGLAND people who are born in England or are UK citizens living in England **3.** EDUC STUDY OF ENGLISH the English language, together with literature written in it, as a subject of scholarly or educational study ○ *study English* **4.** UNDERSTANDABLE ENGLISH clear, understandable spoken or written English, as distinct from technical jargon, dialect or nonstandard or incomprehensible speech or writing **5.** English, english *US* CUE GAMES = **side** ■ *adj.* **1.** OF THE LANGUAGE ENGLISH relating to, expressed in, or typical of the English language **2.** OF THE ENGLISH relating to, belonging to, or typical of the English or England ■ *vt.* (**-lishes, -lishing, -lished**) LANG (*archaic*) **1.** TRANSLATE STH INTO ENGLISH to translate sth into English **2.** ANGLICIZE STH to convert a word or phrase to an English spelling or pronunciation [Old English *Englisc*, from *Engle* 'the Angles'] —**Englishness** *n.*

──── **WORD KEY: WORLD ENGLISH** ────
English, a language originating in northwestern Europe, is the most widely used member of the Germanic language family. Anglo-Saxon settlers whose dialects were collectively known as 'Englisc' arrived in Britain in the 5th century and in due course their language became identified as the main one of the kingdom of England. This early English was a homogeneous tongue, and the characteristic hybrid vocabulary of the present-day language is the result, successively, of Scandinavian, Norman-French, and Greco-Latin influence. For convenience, English is usually divided into four historical phases: Old English (around 500–1150), Middle English (around 1150–around 1450), Early Modern English (around 1450–1700), and Modern English (around 1700 onwards). However, the distance and difference between Old and Modern English is as great as that between Latin and its descendant French. After 1707, English became the primary language of first the United Kingdom and Ireland, then the British Empire at large, from which the United States broke away in the 1770s. The world's primary English-speaking countries today are the United States, the United Kingdom, Canada, Australia, Ireland, South Africa, New Zealand, and Singapore, and the many other nations and territories using English include Bangladesh, Ghana, Guyana, India, Hong Kong, Kenya, Jamaica, Malta, Malaysia, Nigeria, Pakistan, and the Philippines. All territories using the language tend to have distinctive pronunciations, grammatical features, and items of vocabulary, and, increasingly, subvarieties of the standard international language. English is a primary working language of the United Nations and the European Union and the sole working language of the Commonwealth, NATO, Caricom, and ASEAN. It is also learned as a second language for purposes of education, employment, entertainment, electronic communication, and travel by a rapidly increasing number of people worldwide, approaching between one and two billion people. Since the 1960s the already immense literature of the language, primarily in the United States and United Kingdom, was markedly extended throughout the English-speaking world, with English becoming overwhelmingly the primary language of global communication and the media. See also the introductory essay on *World English*.

English bond *n.* an arrangement of bricks in a wall in which layers (**courses**) of bricks laid end to end (**stretchers**) alternate with layers of bricks laid side to side (**headers**). The stretchers of all layers are aligned vertically, and the headers are centred on the stretchers and the mortar joints between them.

English breakfast *n.* a breakfast usually consisting of cereal or fruit, followed by cooked bacon, eggs, sausages, and tomatoes, and then toast and marmalade or jam ○ *a choice of continental or full English breakfast*

English Canadian *n. Can* a Canadian whose first language is English or who is of English ancestry —**English-Canadian** *adj.*

English Channel area of water linking the North Sea with the Atlantic Ocean. It lies between England and France. Length: 560 km/350 mi. French **Manche**

English disease *n.* recurring industrial unrest marked by many strikes, formerly regarded by non-British commentators as endemic in and damaging to British industry

English Heritage *n.* a popular name for the Historic Buildings and Monuments Commission for England, a body partly funded by government and responsible for maintaining buildings and monuments of historical interest in England

English horn *n.* = **cor anglais**

Englishman /íng glishmən/ (*plural* **-men** /-mən/) *n.* a man who was born in England or is a British citizen living in England

English muffin *n. US* = **muffin**

English Nature *n.* the English division of the Nature Conservancy Council, a government agency responsible for various nature-conservation functions including national nature reserves, and for advising central government

English setter *n.* a hunting dog of a medium-sized breed of setter that has a silky white coat with brown or black markings

English springer spaniel *n.* a hunting dog of a medium-sized breed of spaniel that originated in England, with a silky coat that may be a mixture of white, black, liver, or tan

Englishwoman /ing glish wŏŏmən/ (*plural* **-en** /-wimmin/) *n.* a woman who was born in England or is a British citizen living in England

engobe /én gōb/ *n.* liquid clay used to decorate a ceramic piece before it has been fired and usually applied before the piece has dried [Mid-19thC. From French.]

engorge /in gáwrj/ (**-gorges, -gorging, -gorged**) *v.* **1.** *vti.* FILL WITH BLOOD to fill sth with blood until it is congested, or become filled with blood **2.** *vti.* EAT GREEDILY to eat sth greedily **3.** *vr.* GORGE YOURSELF to gorge or fill yourself with food [15thC. Via French *engorger* from, ultimately, Old French *gorge* 'throat'(see GORGE).] —**engorgement** *n.*

engr *abbr.* engineer

engr. *abbr.* **1.** engraved **2.** engraver **3.** engraving

engraft /in gráaft/ (**-grafts, -grafting, -grafted**), **ingraft** (**-grafts, -grafting, -grafted**) *vt.* **1.** GRAFT PLANT PART to graft a bud or other plant part from one plant onto another (*technical*) **2.** GRAFT ANIMAL TISSUE to graft animal tissue from one part of the body onto another part or onto another animal (*technical*) **3.** ATTACH STH PERMANENTLY to attach sth permanently to sth else by a process resembling grafting **4.** IMPLANT STH PERMANENTLY to implant sth permanently or deeply in sth else —**engraftment** *n.*

engrailed /in gráyld/ *adj.* **1.** EDGED WITH CONCAVE INDENTATIONS edged with a series of concave indentations **2.** EDGED WITH DOTS edged with a row of raised dots ○ *an engrailed gold coin* [14thC. From Old French *engresler* 'to make thin', from *gresle* 'thin', from Latin *gracilis* (source of English *gracile*).]

engrain (**-grains, -graining, -grained**) *vt.* = **ingrain**

engrave /in gráyv/ (**-graves, -graving, -graved**) *vt.* **1.** ARTS CARVE OR ETCH MATERIAL to carve or etch a hard surface with a design or lettering for decoration or printing ○ *engraved a silver cup* **2.** ARTS CARVE OR ETCH DESIGN to carve or etch a design or lettering into a hard surface for decoration or printing ○ *engraving a dedication on a watch* **3.** PRINTING PRINT IMAGE to print an image, especially a raised image, from an engraved printing plate **4.** IMPRESS STH to impress sth deeply, e.g. a memory on the mind —**engraver** *n.*

engraving /in gráyving/ *n.* **1.** PRINTING ENGRAVED PRINT a print of an image that was made using an engraved plate or block **2.** ARTS ENGRAVED DESIGN a design or lettering engraved into a hard surface for decoration or printing **3.** ARTS CUTTING OR ETCHING OF IMAGES the art or process of cutting or etching images into a hard surface **4.** PRINTING PRINTING SURFACE a plate, block, or other hard surface on which an image has been engraved for printing

engross[1] /in grṓss/ (**-grosses, -grossing, -grossed**) *vt.* **1.** OCCUPY SB'S ATTENTION to take up sb's whole attention ○ *The children were engrossed by the story.* **2.** STOCK EXCH BUY ALL OF STH to buy all of a commodity, or enough of it to control the market [14thC. Via Old French *en gros* or medieval Latin *in grosso*; literally 'in bulk, wholesale', both from late Latin *grossus* (see GROSS).] —**engrosser** *n.*

engross[2] /in grṓss/ (**-grosses, -grossing, -grossed**) *vt.* **1.** LAW MAKE FINAL COPY OF DOCUMENT to write or print the final version of a legal document **2.** COPY DOCUMENT to copy a document in large clear handwriting (*dated*) [14thC. Via Anglo-Norman *engrosser* or medieval Latin *ingrossare* from, ultimately, late Latin *grossus* 'bulky, coarse'.] —**engrosser** *n.*

engrossing /in grṓssing/ *adj.* engaging sb's whole attention —**engrossingly** *adv.*

engrossment /in grṓssmənt/ *n.* **1.** COMPLETELY ABSORBED STATE the complete absorption of sb's attention with sth **2.** LAW FINAL LEGAL COPY a formally prepared copy of a deed or other document for legal use **3.** LAW DOCUMENT PREPARATION the preparation of the final legal copy or a clean copy of a document (*dated*) **4.** STOCK EXCH CORNERING OF MARKET the purchasing of enough of a commodity to control the market in it

engulf /in gúlf/ (**-gulfs, -gulfing, -gulfed**), **ingulf** (**-gulfs, -gulfing, -gulfed**) *vt.* **1.** SWALLOW STH UP to surround, cover over, and swallow up sb or sth, as floodwaters do **2.** OVERWHELM to overwhelm sb or sth with a great amount or number of sth (*often passive*) ○ *The attacking hordes engulfed the undefended town.* —**engulfment** *n.*

enhance /in háanss/ (**-hances, -hancing, -hanced**) *vt.* **1.** IMPROVE to improve or add to the strength, worth, beauty, or other desirable quality of sth **2.** COMPUT INCREASE CLARITY OF IMAGE to increase the clarity, degree of detail, or another quality of an electronic image by using a computer program [13thC. Via Anglo-Norman *enhauncer* 'to raise up' (the original sense in English) from, ultimately, Latin *altus* 'high'.] —**enhancement** *n.* —**enhancer** *n.* —**enhancive** *adj.*

enharmonic /én haar mónnik/ *adj.* MUSIC used to describe notes, e.g. A♯ and B♭, that are spelt differently in a score but have the same pitch in a tempered scale, e.g. on the piano. In other scales or on other instruments, enharmonic notes may actually have different pitches. —**enharmonically** *adv.*

enigma /i nígmə/ *n.* sb or sth that is not easily explained or understood [Mid-16thC. Via Latin *aenigma* from Greek *ainigma*, from, ultimately, *ainos* 'fable'.]

WORD KEY: SYNONYMS

See Synonyms at ***problem***.

WORD KEY: CULTURAL NOTE

The Enigma Variations, an orchestral work by English composer Edward Elgar (1899). Elgar's most popular and widely performed work, it was originally entitled *Variations on an Original Theme*. Each of the variations is a musical portrait of a friend of Elgar, identified in the score only by his or her initials or nickname. The title of Elgar's piece influenced the Berlin engineer who built the now-famed German military cipher machine, a typewriter-like device capable of of producing an infinite number of ciphers: the engineer called the machine *Enigma* because he had been struck by Elgar's musical ciphers.

enigmatic /énnig máttik/, **enigmatical** /-máttik'l/ *adj.* difficult to interpret, understand, or explain —**enigmatically** *adv.*

WORD KEY: SYNONYMS

See Synonyms at ***obscure***.

enisle /in íl/ (**-isles, -isling, -isled**) *vt.* (*literary*) **1.** ISOLATE to isolate sb or sth from other people or things **2.** MAKE STH INTO ISLAND to make sth into an island

Eniwetok /énnə wée tok, ə neewi tok/ circular atoll in the northwestern Marshall Islands in the Northern Pacific Ocean, a former testing ground for nuclear weapons. Population: 715 (1988).

enjambment /in jám mənt/, **enjambement** *n.* the continuation of meaning, without pause or break, from one line of poetry to the next [Mid-19thC. Via French *enjambement* from, ultimately, *jambe* 'leg' (see JAMB).] —**enjambed** /in jámd/ *adj.*

enjoin /in jóyn/ (**-joins, -joining, -joined**) *vt.* **1.** COMMAND SB to command sb to do sth or behave in a certain way (*formal*) **2.** IMPOSE STH to urge or impose a condition or course of action upon others ○ *She enjoined secrecy upon all of us.* **3.** LAW FORBID OR COMMAND SB LEGALLY to forbid or command sb to do sth by means of a legal injunction —**enjoiner** *n.* —**enjoinment** *n.*

enjoy /in jóy/ (**-joys, -joying, -joyed**) *v.* **1.** *vt.* FIND STH PLEASING to take pleasure in sth ○ *She really enjoys ballet.* **2.** *vt.* HAVE USE OF STH to have the full and satisfying use or benefit of sth ○ *He enjoys sole possession of the estate.* **3.** *vt.* BENEFIT FROM DESIRABLE CONDITION OR SITUATION to benefit from a desirable condition or situation ○ *The resort enjoys months of uninterrupted sunshine.* **4.** *vr.* HAVE GOOD EXPERIENCE to have a pleasurable experience ○ *They all enjoyed themselves at the party.* **5.** *vt.* HAVE SEX WITH SB to have sexual intercourse with sb (*archaic*) [14thC. Via Old French *enjoir* from, ultimately, Latin *gaudere* 'to rejoice' (source of English *joy* and *gaudy*).] —**enjoyer** *n.*

enjoyable /in jóyəb'l/ *adj.* providing pleasure, or capable of providing pleasure ○ *The food is always enjoyable.* —**enjoyableness** *n.* —**enjoyably** *adv.*

enjoyment /in jóymənt/ *n.* **1.** PLEASURE pleasure that results from using or experiencing sth ○ *eating with great enjoyment* **2.** EXPERIENCING OF STH THAT PROVIDES PLEASURE the experiencing of sth that provides pleasure ○ *He wished his enjoyment of the concert would never end.* **3.** SOURCE OF PLEASURE sth that gives pleasure ○ *Fishing is one of her chief enjoyments.* **4.** USE OR BENEFIT the use or benefit of sth, especially as a legal right ○ *the enjoyment of his rights as a landowner*

enkephalin /en kéffəlin/, **encephalin** /-séffə-/ *n.* either of two chemicals with opiate qualities that are secreted in the brain and spinal cord and act to relieve pain [Mid-20thC. From Greek *enkephalos* 'brain', from *kephalē* 'head'.]

enkindle /in kínd'l/ (**-dles, -dling, -dled**) *v.* **1.** *vt.* AROUSE RESPONSE IN SB to spark an emotional or intellectual response in sb **2.** *vti.* BURN STH to set sth on fire, or start burning —**enkindler** *n.*

enl. *abbr.* **1.** enlarged **2.** enlisted

enlace /in láyss/ (**enlaces** *or* **inlaces, enlacing** *or* **inlacing, enlaced** *or* **inlaced**) *v.* **1.** *vt.* WRAP WITH LACES to wrap sth round with laces or sth similar **2.** *vti.* INTERTWINE WITH STH to intertwine with sth, or become intertwined —**enlacement** *n.*

enlarge /in láarj/ (**-larges, -larging, -larged**) *v.* **1.** *vti.* MAKE OR BECOME LARGER to increase the size, amount, or extent of sth, or become larger **2.** *vti.* BROADEN IN SCOPE to broaden the scope of sth, or become broader in scope ○ *the need for the investigation to be enlarged* **3.** *vi.* GIVE MORE DETAIL to speak or write at greater length or in more detail about sth **4.** *vt.* PHOTOGRAPHY MAKE LARGER PHOTOGRAPH to make a photographic print or image that is larger than the original negative, print, or slide

WORD KEY: SYNONYMS

See Synonyms at ***increase***.

enlargement /in láarjmənt/ *n.* **1.** PROCESS OF ENLARGING OR BEING ENLARGED the process of increasing, broadening, or enlarging sth, or of being increased, broadened, or enlarged **2.** ADDITION TO STH sth added to sth else to make it larger ○ *an enlargement to a house* **3.** ENLARGED CONDITION the increased, broadened, or enlarged state of sth **4.** PHOTOGRAPHY ENLARGED PHOTOGRAPH a photographic print or image that is larger than the negative, print, or slide from which it was made

enlarger /in láarjər/ *n.* **1.** PHOTOGRAPHY DEVICE THAT ENLARGES PHOTOGRAPHS a device for projecting an enlarged image of a photographic negative onto a sheet of sensitized paper **2.** SB OR STH THAT ENLARGES sb or sth that increases, broadens, or enlarges sth

enlighten /in lít'n/ (**-ens, -ening, -ened**) *vt.* **1.** GIVE INFORMATION TO SB to give clarifying information to sb ○ *Let me enlighten you about our problems.* **2.** FREE SB FROM IGNORANCE to free sb from ignorance, prejudice, or superstition ○ *an article written to enlighten his critics* **3.** RELIG TEACH SB RELIGION to teach religious beliefs to an unbeliever —**enlightener** *n.* —**enlightening** *adj.*

enlightened /in lít'nd/ *adj.* **1.** RATIONAL free of ignorance, prejudice, or superstition ○ *an enlightened age* **2.** WELL-INFORMED having a sound and open-minded understanding of all the facts, or based on such an understanding ○ *an enlightened piece of legislation* **3.** HAVING ACHIEVED GREAT SPIRITUALITY having achieved the realization of a spiritual or religious understanding, especially when it results in the transcendence of human suffering and desire

enlightenment /in lít'nmənt/ *n.* **1.** ENLIGHTENING OF SB the enlightening of sb or a cause of the enlightening of sb **2.** ENLIGHTENED STATE the condition of sb who has been enlightened **3.** BUDDHISM TRANSCENDENCE OF DESIRE AND SUFFERING a state attained when the cycle of reincarnation ends and desire and suffering are transcended, or the achievement of this state

Enlightenment *n.* an 18th-century intellectual movement in western Europe that emphasized reason and science in philosophy and in the study of human culture and the natural world

enlist /in líst/ (**-lists, -listing, -listed**) *vti.* **1.** MIL ENROL IN MILITARY to enrol sb in a branch of the armed forces, or join the armed forces **2.** GAIN SUPPORT to gain the cooperation or support of sb or sth, or become actively involved in an effort ○ *May I enlist your help in this?* [Mid-16thC. Formed from EN- + LIST, perhaps modelled on Dutch *inlijsten* 'to put on a list'.] —**enlistment** *n.*

enlisted person *n. US* a member of the US armed forces who is lower in rank than a commissioned or warrant officer

enliven /in lív'n/ (**-ens, -ening, -ened**) *vt.* **1.** INVIGORATE to make sb or sth more lively or interesting ○ *We felt enlivened after our walk in the fresh air.* **2.** MAKE BRIGHTER to make sth brighter or more cheerful ○ *A few more pictures on the wall would enliven this room.* —**enlivener** *n.* —**enlivenment** *n.*

en masse /óN máss/ *adv.* as a body or in a group ○ *people rising from their seats en masse, starting to cheer* [Late 18thC. From French, literally 'in a mass'.]

enmesh /in mésh/ (**-meshes, -meshing, -meshed**), **inmesh** (**-meshes, -meshing, -meshed**) *vt.* **1.** CATCH IN ENTANGLEMENT to entangle sb or sth in sth from which it is difficult to be extricated or separated ○ *a government enmeshed in scandal* **2.** CATCH IN NET to catch sb or sth in the mesh of a net —**enmeshment** *n.*

enmity /énmiti/ (*plural* **-ties**) *n.* the extreme ill will or hatred that exists between enemies ○ *trying to resolve age-old enmities* [Via Old French *enemistie* from, ultimately, Latin *inimicus* 'enemy' (see ENEMY)]

ennage /énnij/ *n.* in printing, the number of ens calculated as being in a piece of text for typesetting

ennead /énni ad/ *n.* a set of nine people or things (*formal*) [Mid-16thC. Via the Greek stem *ennead-* from *ennea* 'nine'.]

Ennerdale Water /énnər dayl-/ lake in western Cumbria, northwestern England, near Whitehaven, for which it provides water

Enniskillen /éniss kíllən/ town in the Fermanagh district, southwestern Northern Ireland. It stands on an island in the River Erne, which connects the two halves of Lough Erne. Population: 11,436 (1991).

Ennius /énni əss/, **Quintus** (239–169? BC) Roman poet and dramatist, called the founding father of Roman poetry. He introduced the hexameter into Roman verse, invented the literary miscellany, and wrote an epic of Roman history, of which only fragments survive.

ennoble /i nṓb'l/ (**-bles, -bling, -bled**) *vt.* **1.** MAKE SB OR STH NOBLE to make sb or sth noble or more dignified (*formal*) ○ *Your presence ennobles this gathering.* **2.** ELEVATE SB TO NOBILITY to confer a noble title on sb ○ *ennobled for his services to his country* —**ennoblement** *n.* —**ennobler** *n.*

ennui /ón wee/ *n.* weariness and dissatisfaction with life that results from a loss of interest or sense of excitement [Mid-18thC. Via French from, ultimately, Latin *in odio*, in the phrase *in odio est* 'it is hateful' (source of English *annoy*).]

ENO *abbr.* English National Opera

enoki /e nṓki/, **enoki mushroom** *n.* a white edible mushroom native to eastern Asia and North America that has a small cap and long thin stem. Latin name: *Flammulina velutipes.* [Late 20thC. From Japanese.]

enol /ée nol/ *n.* an organic compound that has a hydroxyl group bonded to a carbon atom that is attached to another carbon atom by a double bond [Mid-20thC. Coined from -ENE + -OL.] —**enolic** /ee nóllik/ *adj.*

enolase /éenō layz, -layss/ *n.* an enzyme that occurs in muscle tissue and in yeasts and is active in the metabolism of carbohydrates

enology /ee nólləji/ *n.* US = **oenology**

enormity /i náwrməti/ (*plural* **-ties**) *n.* **1.** WICKEDNESS extreme wickedness or moral offensiveness ○ *the enormity of his crimes against humanity* **2.** EXTREMELY WICKED DEED an extremely wicked or morally offensive deed **3.** IMMENSITY an extreme greatness of size, amount, or degree that is overwhelming ○ *the enormity of the budget deficit* **4.** GREAT SIGNIFICANCE great importance and consequence ○ *the enormity of the social change wrought by the Industrial Revolution* [15thC. Via French *énormité* from Latin *enormitas*, from *enormis* 'irregular' (see ENORMOUS).]

WORD KEY: USAGE

enormity or **enormousness**? ***Enormity*** is the older word, and after several changes in usage over several centuries it settled down in the 19th century in the meaning associated with wickedness or evil. It is used in this way both as a concept or attribute and as a concrete word with a plural form: *We were shocked by the enormity of the crime. The regime committed many enormities to suppress opposition.* ***Enormousness*** has the more neutral meaning in relation to size, so that *the enormousness of the task* implies a great or difficult task, whereas *the enormity of the task* implies a wicked or horrific task. Because ***enormousness*** is more awkward to use, ***enormity*** tends to encroach on it, but a better course is to find an alternative such as *immensity* or *vastness*.

enormous /i náwrməss/ *adj.* **1.** UNUSUALLY LARGE unusually large or great in size, amount, or degree **2.** WICKED extremely wicked or morally offensive (*archaic*) [Mid-16thC. From Latin *enormis* 'irregular', from *norma* 'rule' (source of English *normal*).] —**enormously** *adv.*

enormousness *n.* the quality of being huge in size, scope, or significance

WORD KEY: USAGE

See Usage note at ***enormity.***

enough /i núf/ *det.* **1.** ADEQUATE as much as is needed ○ *enough time to go shopping* **2.** AS MUCH AS BEARABLE as much or as many as can be tolerated ○ *in enough trouble already* ■ *adv.* **1.** IN THE RIGHT AMOUNT to an extent that is as much as is needed ○ *I couldn't run fast enough to catch the cat.* **2.** USED FOR EMPHASIS used to give emphasis to adverbs ○ *Oddly enough, our husbands had met each other just the day before.* **3.** SUFFICIENTLY to an extent that is as much as can be tolerated ○ *She was arrogant enough before the promotion.* **4.** PASSABLY to a moderate or satisfactory extent ○ *speaks the language well enough* ■ *pron.* NEEDED OR TOLERATED AMOUNT the amount that is needed or that can be tolerated ○ *take more cash because we never have enough* ■ *interj.* STOP THAT! used to tell sb firmly to stop doing sth (*informal*) ○ *Enough! There will be no more teasing in the car.* [Old English *genōg*, from prehistoric Germanic] ◇ **enough is enough** used by a speaker to indicate that he or she will tolerate no more of sth

WORD KEY: SYNONYMS

enough, sufficient, adequate, ample, plenty

CORE MEANING: equal in quantity to what is needed

enough a general word used to indicate that an amount or quantity is equal to what it needed; **sufficient** a fairly formal word used to indicate that there is enough of sth for a particular purpose; **adequate** a fairly formal word meaning the same as 'enough'. It is often used to indicate that there is only just enough of sth; **ample** used to indicate that there is more than enough of sth; **plenty** used to indicate that there is a large amount of sth and so there will be enough of it to meet requirements.

enounce /i nówns/ (**enounces, enouncing, enounced**) *vt.* **1.** SAY CLEARLY to pronounce a word clearly and definitely **2.** STATE FORMALLY to state sth in an official way (*formal*) [Early 19thC. Via French *énoncer* from Latin *enuntiare*, 'to tell' (see ENUNCIATE).] —**enouncement** *n.*

enow /i nów/ *adv., adj.* enough (*archaic*) ○ *'there are liars and swearers enow to beat the honest men and hang up them'* (William Shakespeare, *Macbeth*; 1606) [Old English. Via Middle English *inow* from Old English *genōge*, a plural form of *genōg*, (see ENOUGH).]

en passant /ón páss on, óN pa saánt/ *adv.* **1.** IN PASSING in passing rather than as the full focus of sb's attention (*formal*) ○ *He mentioned it en passant.* **2.** CHESS UNDER RULE FOR PAWN CAPTURE used when a pawn that has moved two squares is captured by an enemy pawn as if it had only moved one square ○ *capture a pawn en passant* [Mid-17thC. From French, literally 'in passing'.]

enplane /in pláyn/ *vti.* = **emplane**

enprint /én print/ *n.* a photographic print in standard size, usually 15 cm x 10 cm/6 in x 4 in, enlarged from a negative [Mid-20thC. From *enlarged print.*]

en prise /oN préez/ *adj.* used to describe a chess piece positioned in such a way that it could be captured if it is not moved [Early 19thC. From French, literally 'in (position for) capture'.]

enquire *vti.* = **inquire**

WORD KEY: USAGE

enquire or **inquire**? For many users, the two spellings are interchangeable, as with *enquiry* and *inquiry.* A useful distinction that many people maintain, however, is to use ***enquire*** and *enquiry* in contexts of casual requests for information, and to reserve ***inquire*** and *inquiry* for contexts of formal or official investigation: *He enquired after her health. Try directory enquiries. The police are inquiring into the circumstances that led up to his disappearance. There will have to be a public inquiry into the allegations.*

enquiry *n.* = **inquiry**

enrage /in ráyj/ (**-rages, -raging, -raged**) *vt.* to make sb furiously angry —**enragement** *n.*

en rapport /óN ra páwr/ *adv.* in harmony or sympathy with sb or sth (*formal*) [Early 19thC. From French, literally 'in agreement'.]

enrapt /in rápt/ *adj.* in a state of delight or ecstasy (*formal*)

enrapture /in rápchər/ (**-tures, -turing, -tured**) *vt.* to fill sb with delight (*formal*) —**enrapturement** *n.*

enrich /in rích/ (**-riches, -riching, -riched**) *vt.* **1.** IMPROVE to improve the quality of sth **2.** FOOD TECH IMPROVE NUTRITIONAL CONTENT OF FOOD to add substances such as vitamins or minerals to a food to improve its nutritional value ○ *calcium-enriched orange juice* **3.** MAKE WEALTHIER to increase the amount of wealth that sb or sth has **4.** PHYS ADD MORE OF CONSTITUENT TO SUBSTANCE to boost the amount of an active substance in a mixture, e.g. in a fuel **5.** AGRIC IMPROVE SOIL to improve the nutrient value of soil by adding natural or artificial fertilizers **6.** MAKE MORE BEAUTIFUL to add to the beauty of sth with decoration (*literary*) —**enricher** *n.*

enrichment /in ríchmənt/ *n.* **1.** STH THAT IMPROVES an added feature or quality that improves sth **2.** IMPROVING OF SB OR STH the addition of characteristics or elements that improve sb or sth ○ *the enrichment of the cultural experience* **3.** INCREASE IN WEALTH increase in a person's or organization's wealth

Enright /én rīt/, **D. J.** (*b.* 1920) British poet, author, and critic. He came to prominence as part of the so-called 'Movement' group of poets in the 1950s. Full name **Dennis Joseph Enright**

enrobe /in rṓb/ (**-robes, -robing, -robed**) *v.* **1.** *vti.* DRESS GRANDLY to put ceremonial robes on sb (*formal*) **2.** *vt.* MAKE SB GRAND OR NOBLE to invest sb with a grand or noble quality (*literary*)

enrol /in rṓl/ (**-rols, -rolling, -rolled**) *v.* **1.** *vti.* ENTER ON REGISTER to enter your own or sb else's name on an official register or list of members ○ *enrol the children in school* **2.** *vt.* MAKE SURE OF AVAILABILITY OF to make sure that sth, especially sb's help, will definitely be available **3.** *vt.* ROLL OR WRAP UP to form sth into a roll **4.** *vt.* WRITE OUT OFFICIAL COPY OF STH to produce the final version of sth, usually a formal document or record [14thC. From Old French *enroller*, literally 'to put on a roll', from *rolle* 'roll, register' (see ROLL).] —**enrollee** /in rō lée/ *n.*

enrolment /in rṓlmənt/ *n.* **1.** SIGNING UP FORMALLY the official act or process of entering your own or another person's name on a register or membership list **2.** NUMBER OF REGISTERED the number of people registered for sth, e.g. a class ○ *a sharp increase in student enrolments* **3.** LIST OF REGISTERED a list of people registered for or enrolled in sth

enroot /in ro͝ot/ (**-roots, -rooting, -rooted**) *vt.* to fix or establish sth firmly (*literary*)

en route /ón ro͝ot/ *adv.* during the journey to a destination [Late 18thC. From French, literally 'on (the) way'.]

ens /enz/ (*plural* **entia** /énshi ə, énti ə/) *n.* PHILOS an actual entity, as distinct from a quality or characteristic [Mid-16thC. From medieval Latin, present participle (on the model of Latin *absens* 'absent') of Latin *esse* 'to be'.]

Ens. *abbr.* NAVY ensign

ENSA /énssə/ *n.* a British organization formed to provide entertainment for Allied forces during World War II. Full form **Entertainments National Service Association**

ensanguine /in sáng gwin/ (**-guines, -guining, -guined**) *vt.* to stain, smear, or cover sth with blood (*archaic or literary; often passive*) ○ *'yet millions of men have supinely allowed the nerveless limbs of the posterity of such rapacious prowlers to rest quietly on their ensanguined thrones'* (Mary Wollstonecraft, *A Vindication of the Rights of Woman*; 1792)

ensconce /in skónss/ (**-sconces, -sconcing, -sconced**) *vt.* **1.** SETTLE IN COMFORTABLY to make sb or yourself comfortably established, as though ready to stay a long while (*often passive*) ○ *ensconced on the sofa* **2.** HIDE AWAY to hide sth somewhere, for safety or secrecy (*archaic or literary*) [Literally 'to put into a sconce']

ensemble /on sómb'l/ *n.* **1.** ARTS GROUP OF PERFORMERS a group of musicians, dancers, or actors who perform together with roughly equal contributions from all members (*takes a singular or plural verb*) **2.** FASHION OUTFIT OF CLOTHES a number of different items of clothing and accessories, put together to create an outfit **3.** STH FORMED BY SEVERAL ITEMS sth created from a number of individual parts put together deliberately **4.** MUSIC PART PERFORMED BY WHOLE GROUP a section of a larger work, e.g. a ballet or opera, that all the cast perform together ■ *adj.* ARTS COLLABORATIVE performed collaboratively, with no performer given prominence [Mid-18thC. From French, 'together', from Latin *insimul*, literally 'in at the same time', from *simul* 'at the same time' (source of English *simultaneous*).]

enshrine /in shrín/ (**-shrines, -shrining, -shrined**), **inshrine** (**-shrines, -shrining, -shrined**) *vt.* **1.** GIVE SPECIAL PROTECTION TO STH to protect sth from change, e.g. in a formal constitution ○ *principles enshrined in law* **2.** PUT STH INTO A SHRINE to keep or cherish sth in a shrine or other special place —**enshrinement** *n.*

enshroud /in shrówd/ (**-shrouds, -shrouding, -shrouded**) *vt.* **1.** OBSCURE to cover or obscure sth (*usually passive*) ○ *towers enshrouded in mist* **2.** WRAP IN SHROUD to cover sb in a shroud

ensiform /énssi fawrm/ *adj.* BIOL long and narrow with a pointed tip ○ *ensiform leaves* [Mid-16thC. Via French from modern Latin *ensiformis*, formed from *ensi-* 'sword' + *forma* 'FORM'.]

ensign /én sīn, énss'n/ *n.* **1.** FLAG INDICATING ALLEGIANCE a flag that shows the nationality of the ship or aircraft flying it or what military unit it belongs to **2.** FLAG WITH UNION FLAG IN CORNER a naval flag bearing a small Union Flag in the upper corner next to the staff (**canton**) **3.** NAVY US NAVY RANK a commissioned officer of the lowest rank in the United States Navy or Coast Guard **4.** BADGE OF OFFICE an emblem or sign that indicates an authority or command **5.** FLAG-BEARER sb who carries a standard or national emblem (*dated*) **6.** FORMER RANK IN BRITISH ARMY a commissioned officer of the lowest rank in the British infantry before 1871 [14thC. Via Old French *enseigne* from Latin *insignia* (plural) 'badges', literally 'marks on', ultimately from *signum* 'mark' (source of English *insignia*).]

ensilage /énssilij/ (**-lages, -laging, -laged**) *n.* **1.** MAKING OF SILAGE the harvesting and preservation of green fodder crops for future use by fermentation in a silo **2.** STORED FODDER green fodder preserved in a silo

ensile /en síl/ (**-siles, -siling, -siled**) *vt.* to preserve green fodder, e.g. grass, as silage by allowing it to ferment and become acidified in a silo [Late 19thC. Via French *ensiler* from Spanish *ensilar*, formed from *en* 'in' + *silo* 'SILO'.]

enslave /in sláyv/ (**-slaves, -slaving, -slaved**) *vt.* **1.** SUBJECT TO CONTROLLING INFLUENCE to subject sb to a dominating influence that takes away his or her freedom **2.** TO CLAIM OWNERSHIP OF SB to take sb prisoner and claim legal ownership of that person and his or her labour —**enslavement** *n.* —**enslaver** *n.*

ensnare /in snáir/ (**-snares, -snaring, -snared**), **insnare** (**-snares, -snaring, -snared**) *vt.* **1.** TRAP IN UNPLEASANT SITUATION to lure sb into a bad situation from which it is difficult to escape **2.** TRAP to catch an animal in a trap —**ensnarement** *n.* —**ensnarer** *n.*

ensnarl /in snaárl/ (**-snarls, -snarling, -snarled**) *vt.* to involve sb or sth in a situation that causes delay (*often passive*)

Ensor /én sawr, óN-/, **James Sydney, Baron** (1860–1949) Belgian painter and engraver. He was a forerunner of expressionism. His works, notably *Christ's Entry into Brussels* (1888), often incorporated masked figures and macabre medieval imagery.

ensoul /in sṓl/ (**-souls, -souling, -souled**), **insoul** (**-souls, -souling, -souled**) *vt.* (*literary*) **1.** GIVE A SOUL TO to endow sb with a soul **2.** KEEP DEEP WITHIN to cherish deeply sth such as a feeling or memory

ensphere /in sféer/ (**-spheres, -sphering, -sphered**), **insphere** (**-spheres, -sphering, -sphered**) *vt.* **1.** SURROUND to enclose sth in a sphere or in sth like a sphere (*literary*) **2.** MAKE SPHERICAL to make sth sphere-shaped (*formal*)

enstatite /énstə tīt/ *n.* a brown, grey, or yellowish form of the mineral pyroxene, consisting of magnesium silicate. It is often found in igneous rock and meteorites and may contain up to 10% ferrous iron silicate. [Mid-19thC. From German *Enstatit*, coined from the Greek stem *enstat* '-adversary' (from the refractoriness of the mineral).]

ensue /in syoó/ (**-sues, -suing, -sued**) *vi.* **1.** FOLLOW to follow closely after sth **2.** RESULT to be a consequence of sth [14thC. From Old French *ensu-*, stem of *ensuivre*, from assumed Vulgar Latin *insequere*, literally 'to follow in', from Latin *sequi* 'to follow' (see SUE).]

ensuing /in syoó ing/ *adj.* happening next or as a result

en suite /óN sweét/ *adj., adv.* LEADING OFF forming part of a larger unit or set of rooms ○ *an en suite bathroom* ■ *n.* (*informal*) **1.** ADJOINING BATHROOM a bathroom leading off the bedroom **2.** HOTEL ROOM WITH OWN BATHROOM a hotel bedroom with an en suite bathroom [Late 18thC. From French, literally 'in succession'.]

ensure /in shoór, in shawr/ (**-sures, -suring, -sured**), **insure** (**-sures, -suring, -sured**) *vt.* **1.** MAKE STH CERTAIN to make sure that sth will happen **2.** SAFEGUARD to protect sth or sb from harm

WORD KEY: USAGE

See Usage note at ***assure***.

enswathe /in swáyth/ (**-swathes, -swathing, -swathed**) *vt.* to wrap sb or sth in bandages or cloth (*literary*)

ENT *abbr.* MED ear, nose, and throat

-ent *suffix.* **1.** performing a particular action ○ *acquiescent* **2.** one that performs a particular action ○ *respondent* [From Latin *-ent-*, the stem of *-ens*, a present participle ending] —**-ence** *suffix.* —**-ency** *suffix.*

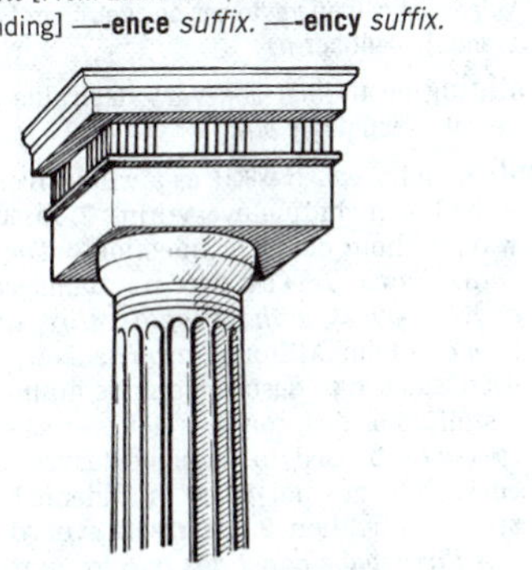

Entablature

entablature /en tábblәchәr/ *n.* in classical architecture, the section that lies between the columns and the roof. It comprises, from bottom to top, the architrave, frieze, and cornice. [Early 17thC. Via obsolete French from Italian *intavolatura* 'boarding', from *intavolare* 'to board up, put on a table', from *tavola* 'table'.]

entablement /in táyb'lmәnt/ *n.* a plinth (*technical*) [Mid-17thC. From French, from *table* 'table'.]

entail /in táyl/ *vt.* (**-tails, -tailing, -tailed**) **1.** HAVE AS CONSEQUENCE to involve or result in sth inevitably **2.** LAW RESTRICT OWNERSHIP OF BEQUEST to restrict the future ownership of property to particular descendants, through instructions written into a will ■ *n.* LAW **1.** = **entailment** *n.* 2 **2.** ENTAILED PROPERTY a property that has been entailed **3.** FUTURE OWNERS OF ENTAILED PROPERTY the line of descendants who own an entailed property [14thC. Literally 'to put under limitation', formed from Old French *taille* 'limitation', from *taillier* 'to cut' (see TAILOR).]

entailment /in táylmәnt/ *n.* **1.** LOGIC ONE PROPOSITION'S IMPLYING OF ANOTHER the relationship between one proposition and another that is a logically necessary consequence of it **2. entailment, entail** LAW RESTRICTION OF FUTURE OWNERSHIP the limiting of the future ownership of bequeathed property to particular descendants

entangle /in táng g'l/ (**-gles, -gling, -gled**) *vt.* **1.** TANGLE UP to make sth become twisted up in a mass of strands, e.g. netting or hair (*usually passive*) **2.** PUT INTO DIFFICULT SITUATION to involve sb or sth in a muddle that will be difficult to escape from (*usually passive*) ○ *entangled in corporate politics* **3.** COMPLICATE STH to make sth complicated

entanglement /in táng g'lmәnt/ *n.* **1.** COMPLICATED PERSONAL SITUATION a complicated situation involving two or more people **2.** CONFUSION confusion or a confused situation ○ *'He sat with his mouth full of toast and his eyes sparkling with mischief, watching my intellectual entanglement'.* (Arthur Conan Doyle, *The Valley of Fear*; 1915) **3.** TANGLED THING a mass of tangled objects

entasis /éntәssiss/ *n.* a slight bulge in the shaft of a column, designed to counter the visual impression of concavity that a perfectly straight column would give [Mid-18thC. From Greek, 'straining', literally 'stretching in', ultimately from *teinein* 'to stretch'.]

entelechy /in téllәki/ *n.* **1.** FULL EXISTENCE the real existence of a thing, not merely its theoretical existence **2.** LIFE-GIVING FORCE in some philosophies, a life-giving force believed to be responsible for the development of all living things [Early 17thC. Via late Latin from Greek *entelekheia*, literally 'having completeness', from *entelēs* 'complete', literally 'in the end', from *telos* 'end'.]

entente /on tónt/ *n.* **1.** FRIENDLY UNDERSTANDING BETWEEN COUNTRIES a state of friendly agreement or understanding that exists or is declared between two or more countries **2.** PARTIES IN AGREEMENT the parties involved in an entente [Mid-19thC. From French, literally 'understanding', from *entendre* (see INTEND).]

entente cordiale /-káwrdi aál/ (*plural* **ententes cordiales** /on tónt káwrdi aál/) *n.* amicable relations between countries or states, especially the agreement formed between France and Britain in 1904 [From French, literally 'friendly understanding']

enter /éntәr/ *v.* (**-ters, -tering, -tered**) **1.** *vti.* GO IN to go or come into a place **2.** *vt.* COMPUT WRITE OR TYPE IN to write or type sth in a book or on a computer ○ *The names and addresses are entered into a database.* **3.** *vt.* PUT IN FOR FORMAL CONSIDERATION to submit sth, e.g. a proposal, complaint, or bid, officially **4.** *vti.* BECOME COMPETITOR to take part in a competition **5.** *vt.* BECOME MEMBER OF to join or become officially involved in sth, especially a body such as a college or company **6.** *vi.* THEATRE WALK ON to come on stage during a play ○ *She enters stage right.* **7.** *vti.* MAKE HOLE IN STH to force a way into sth, or be pushed or inserted into sth, especially the human body ○ *The bullet entered through the anterior abdominal wall.* **8.** *vt.* LAW TAKE OWNERSHIP OF LAND LEGALLY to go onto land and take legal possession of it ■ *n.* COMPUT = **enter key** [13thC. Via Old French *entrer* from Latin *intrare* 'to go in, enter', formed from *intra* 'inside, within'.] —**enterable** *adj.*

enter into *v.* **1.** *vt.* TAKE PART ENTHUSIASTICALLY to get actively involved in sth ○ *Enter into the spirit of things.* **2.** *vt.* BE RELEVANT TO to be one of the factors that are relevant to sth ○ *Money doesn't enter into it.* **3.** *vt.* SIGN UP TO to become one of the parties bound by a contract **4.** *vi.* TAKE PART IN to become involved in sth **5.** *vt.* CONSIDER FORMALLY to go into a discussion or investigation about sth ○ *I do not propose to enter into the issue of who is responsible.*

enter on, enter upon *vt.* to start out on sth, e.g. an important task or a significant period

enter- *prefix* = **entero-** (*used before vowels*)

enteral feeding /énteral-/ *n.* direct infusion into the intestines of nutrients in liquid form [*Enteral* partly formed from ENTERIC and partly a back-formation from PARENTERAL]

enteric /en térrik/ *adj.* relating to or situated in the intestine [Mid-19thC. From Greek *enterikos*, from *enteron* 'intestine'.]

enteric fever *n.* = **typhoid**

enteritis /éntə ríːtiss/ *n.* inflammation of the intestine, most commonly of the small intestine

enter key *n.* a key on a computer keyboard that executes an instruction or begins a new line in text

entero- *prefix.* intestine ○ *enterotomy* [From Greek *enteron*. Ultimately from an Indo-European base meaning 'in, inside', which is also the ancestor of English *in, inter,* and *entrails*]

enterobiasis /éntərō bí əssiss/ *n.* infestation of the large intestine with pinworms, especially in children [Early 20thC]

enterocoele /éntərō seel/ *n.* a body cavity (**coelom**) formed from an outgrowth in the wall of an embryonic intestine, especially in invertebrate marine organisms such as starfish and sea urchins

enterocolitis /éntərō kə líːtiss/ *n.* inflammation of the small and large intestine as a result of infection

enterokinase /éntərō kí nayz/ *n.* an enzyme produced in the mucous membrane of the upper intestine that converts trypsinogen to trypsin

enteron /éntə ron/ *n.* ZOOL **1. DIGESTIVE SYSTEM** the alimentary canal, especially of an embryo **2. INTESTINE OF MARINE INVERTEBRATE** the intestine of marine invertebrates, e.g. sea anemones and jellyfish, with one opening that serves as both mouth and anus [Mid-19thC. From Greek, 'intestine'.]

enteropathy /éntə róppəthi/ (*plural* **-thies**) *n.* any disease of the intestines

enterostomy /éntə róstəmi/ (*plural* **-mies**) *n.* the surgical creation of a permanent opening into the intestine through the abdominal wall —**enterostomal** *adj.*

enterotomy /éntə róttəmi/ (*plural* **-mies**) *n.* a surgical incision into the intestine

enterotoxin /éntərō tóksin/ *n.* any toxin produced by bacteria that causes the vomiting and diarrhoea associated with food poisoning

enterprise /éntər prīz/ *n.* **1.** COMM **BUSINESS** a commercial company or firm **2. DARING PROJECT** a new, often risky venture that involves confidence and initiative **3. ENERGETIC CONFIDENCE** readiness to put effort into new, often risky, ventures or activities **4.** COMM **HIGHLY MOTIVATED INDUSTRY** organized business activities aimed specifically at growth and profit [15thC. From Old French *entreprise*, from the past participle of *entreprendre* 'to undertake', literally 'to take between', from *prendre* 'to take' (see PRIZE[2]).]

Enterprise Allowance Scheme *n.* formerly, a government scheme to help the unemployed set up in business by providing an allowance

enterprise zone *n.* an economically depressed urban area where the government encourages new business ventures by offering financial incentives

enterprising /éntər prīzing/ *adj.* showing initiative and a willingness to undertake new, often risky projects —**enterprisingly** *adv.*

entertain /éntər táyn/ (**-tains, -taining, -tained**) *v.* **1.** *vti.* **AMUSE OR INTEREST** to engage a person or audience by providing amusing or interesting material **2.** *vti.* **OFFER HOSPITALITY** to offer hospitality, especially by providing food and drink for people in your home **3.** *vt.* **CONSIDER** to turn sth over in your mind, looking at it from various points of view ○ *He would never entertain such an idea!* [15thC. From Old French *entretenir* 'to hold together, support', from assumed Vulgar Latin *intertenere* 'to hold between', from Latin *tenere* 'to hold'.]

entertainer /éntər táynər/ *n.* sb who amuses or interests others by telling jokes, singing, dancing, or acting, especially sb who does this for a living

entertaining /éntər táyning/ *adj.* enjoyable to watch, read, or listen to —**entertainingly** *adv.*

entertainment /éntər táynmənt/ *n.* **1.** ARTS **ART OF KEEPING PEOPLE ENTERTAINED** the various ways of amusing people, especially by performing for them **2. ENJOYMENT** the amount of pleasure or amusement you get from sth **3.** THEATRE **PERFORMANCE OR EXHIBITION** sth that is produced or performed for an audience ○ *chief among the evening's entertainments*

enthalpy /én thəlpi, en thálpi/ *n.* a thermodynamic property equal to the sum of the internal energy of a system and the product of its pressure and volume. Symbol **H** [Early 20thC. From Greek *enthalpein* 'to warm within', from *thalpein* 'to heat'.]

enthral /in thráwl/ (**-thrals, -thralling, -thralled**) *vt.* **1. DELIGHT** to delight or fascinate sb thoroughly, engaging that person's attention completely **2. ENSLAVE** to make sb a prisoner and claim legal ownership of that person (*literary*) [Late 16thC. Literally 'to enslave, make someone a thrall', formed from THRALL.] —**enthralment** *n.*

enthrall *vt.* US = **enthral**

enthralling /in thráwling/ *adj.* so interesting, delightful, or beautiful as to hold the attention completely —**enthrallingly** *adv.*

enthrone /in thrṓn/ (**-thrones, -throning, -throned**) *vt.* **1. PUT ON THRONE** to install a monarch or bishop, especially in a ceremony that involves seating the person on a throne (*formal*) **2. REGARD AS IMPORTANT** to regard sb as being worthy of adoration (*literary*) —**enthronement** *n.*

enthuse /in thyóoz/ (**-thuses, -thusing, -thused**) *vti.* to have, or make sb feel, great excitement or interest [Early 19thC. Back-formation from ENTHUSIASM.]

enthusiasm /in thyóozi azəm/ *n.* **1. EXCITED INTEREST** passionate interest in or eagerness to do sth **2. ENGROSSING INTEREST** sth that arouses a consuming interest [Late 16thC. Via late Latin from Greek *enthousiasmos* 'possession by (a) god', formed from *enthous* 'inspired', literally 'with (a) god in', from *theos* 'god'.]

enthusiast /in thyóozi ast/ *n.* sb who is very interested or involved in sth, especially sb with a particular hobby [Early 17thC. From Greek *enthousiastēs* 'one inspired (by a god)', from *enthous* (see ENTHUSIASM).]

enthusiastic /in thyóozi ástik/ *adj.* showing passionate interest in sth or eagerness about sth —**enthusiastically** *adv.*

enthymeme /énthə meem/ *n.* LOGIC an argument that assumes the truth of one or more premises and therefore omits them from the logical sequence [Late 16thC. Via Latin from Greek *enthumēma*, literally '(sth) in mind', ultimately from *thumos* 'mind'.]

entia PHILOS plural of **ens**

entice /in tīss/ (**-tices, -ticing, -ticed**) *vt.* to make a person or animal do sth by offering sth desirable [13thC. Via Old French *enticier* from assumed Vulgar Latin *intitiare* 'to set on fire', from Latin *titio* 'firebrand'.] —**enticer** *n.*

enticing /in tīssing/ *adj.* very desirable and hard to resist —**enticingly** *adv.*

entire /in tīr/ *adj.* **1. WHOLE** as a whole, from beginning to end or including everything **2. ABSOLUTE** in every way, without doubt or question ○ *The day was an entire fiasco.* **3. IN ONE PIECE** not damaged or broken up (*literary*) ○ *'with strength entire, and free Will arm'd'* (John Milton, *Paradise Lost*; 1667) **4.** VET **UNGELDED** used to describe a male animal, especially a stallion or dog, that has not been castrated **5.** BOT **SMOOTH-EDGED** used to describe leaves with smooth edges that are not lobed or indented ■ *n.* **1.** VET **STALLION** a stallion **2. EVERYTHING** everything (*formal*) ○ *A three-judge panel has rejected our appeal in its entire.* [14thC. Via Old French *entier* from Latin *integrum*, a form of *integer* 'whole, intact' (see INTEGER).] —**entireness** *n.*

entirely /in tīrli/ *adv.* **1. IN EVERY WAY** in every sense **2. ONLY** exclusively or individually

entirety /in tīrəti/ *n.* the whole extent of sth

entitle /in tīt'l/ (**-tles, -tling, -tled**) *vt.* **1. ALLOW TO CLAIM** to give sb the right to have or to do sth (*often passive*) **2. GIVE TITLE TO** to assign a title to sth such as a book (*usually passive*) **3. GIVE SPECIAL TITLE TO** to confer an official position or honour on sb that brings a particular title with it [14thC. Via Old French *entiteler* from late Latin *intitulare*, from *titulus* (see TITLE).]

entitlement /in tīt'lmənt/ *n.* **1. RIGHT TO STH** the right sb has to do or receive sth **2. STH YOU HAVE A RIGHT TO** a thing to which sb is entitled

entity /éntəti/ (*plural* **-ties**) *n.* **1. OBJECT** sth that exists as or is perceived as a single separate object **2.** PHILOSOPHY **EXISTENCE** the state of having existence **3.** PHILOSOPHY **ESSENTIAL NATURE OF STH** the essence or character of sth [Late 16thC. From medieval Latin *entitas*, from late Latin *ent-*, stem of *ens* (see ENS).]

entoderm /éntō durm/ *n.* = **endoderm**

entoil /in tóyl/ (**-toils, -toiling, -toiled**) *vt.* to capture or entangle sth or sb (*archaic*) [Late 16thC. Literally 'to place in a 'toil'', formed from *toil* 'net', from Old French *toile* 'cloth, web', from Latin *tela*.]

entom. *abbr.* entomology

entomb /in tóom/ (**-tombs, -tombing, -tombed**) *vt.* **1. PUT IN TOMB** to put a corpse into a tomb **2. PUT IN DEEP PLACE** to put sth in a place that is hidden or very deep ○ *the secret vaults where the treasures were entombed* **3. SERVE AS TOMB** to serve as a tomb for sb or sth ○ *the collapsed mine that entombed them*

entomo- *prefix.* insect ○ *entomophilous* [Via French from Greek *entomon* from *entomos* 'cut in two', from *en* 'in' + *temnein* 'to cut'; so called because of insects' distinctly segmented bodies]

entomol. *abbr.* entomology

entomology /éntə mólləji/ *n.* the branch of zoology that deals with the study of insects [Mid-18thC. From French *entomologie* or modern Latin *entomologia*, literally 'science of insects', formed from Greek *entomon* (see ENTOMO-).] —**entomological** /éntəmə lójjik'l/ *adj.* —**entomologically** /-lójjikli/ *adv.* —**entomologist** /éntə mólləjist/ *n.*

entomophagous /éntə móffəgəss/ *adj.* ZOOL feeding on insects

entomophilous /éntə móffiləss/ *adj.* BOT used to describe flowering plants that are pollinated by insects —**entomophily** *n.*

entourage /ón too raazh/ *n.* **1. PEOPLE ACCOMPANYING VIP** a group of special employees who go with a high-ranking or famous person on visits and engagements **2. ENVIRONMENT** the surroundings or environment (*literary*) [Mid-19thC. From French, where it was formed from *entourer* 'to surround', literally 'to make a circuit around', from *tour* 'circuit' (see TOUR).]

entr'acte /ón trakt/ (*plural* **-actes**) *n.* **1. BREAK BETWEEN ACTS OF PLAY** an interval between the acts of a play or opera **2. PERFORMANCE BETWEEN ACTS** an additional piece of entertainment during the break between the acts of a play or opera [Mid-18thC. From obsolete French, literally 'between the act(s)', from *acte* 'act'.]

entrails /én traylz/ *npl.* **1. INTERNAL ORGANS** an animal's or person's internal organs **2. STH'S INSIDES** the various working parts inside sth, especially sth complex **3.** HIST **ANIMAL'S INSIDES USED FOR ROMAN DIVINATION** the internal organs of a sacrificial animal, used by the ancient Romans to try to determine the will of the gods [13thC. Via Old French *entrailles* from medieval Latin *intralia*, alteration of Latin *interanea* 'intestines, guts', literally 'internal things', ultimately from *inter* 'between'.]

entrain[1] /in tráyn/ (**-trains, -training, -trained**) *vti.* TRANSP to board or to put sb or sth aboard a train —**entrainer** *n.* —**entrainment** *n.*

entrain[2] /in tráyn/ (**-trains, -training, -trained**) *v.* **1.** *vt.* **CAUSE TO HAPPEN** to cause sth to happen as a consequence of an action **2.** CHEM, PHYS **TRAP IN GAS OR LIQUID** to draw solid particles, air bubbles, or liquid drops into a moving fluid and carry them along in the flow [Mid-16thC. From Old French *entraîner*, literally 'to drag away', from *traîner* 'to drag' (see TRAIN).] —**entrainment** *n.*

entrance[1] /éntrənss/ *n.* **1. WAY IN** a door or gate that people enter through **2. COMING ONTO THE SCENE** the occasion or act of entering a place ○ *a highly theatrical entrance* **3. RIGHT OF ENTRY** the right to go into a place or to enter an institution [15thC. From Old French, where it was formed from *entrer* (see ENTER).]

entrance[2] /in traánss/ (**-trances, -trancing, -tranced**) *vt.* **1. FASCINATE** to hold sb's attention and produce a sense of wonder in that person **2. PUT SPELL ON** to make sb go into a trance

entrant /éntrənt/ *n.* sb who enters a competition or contest [Mid-17thC. From French, present participle of *entrer* (see ENTER).]

WORD KEY: SYNONYMS
See Synonyms at *candidate*.

entrap /in tráp/ (**-traps, -trapping, -trapped**) *vt.* **1.** TRICK INTO STH BAD to lead sb into doing sth wrong or into danger **2.** HUNT TRAP to catch sth such as an animal in a trap

entrapment /in trápmənt/ *n.* in the United States, the act of tricking sb into committing a crime in order to obtain a prosecution

entreat /in tréet/ (**-treats, -treating, -treated**) *vti.* to beg sb for sth, often repeatedly (*formal*) [14thC. From Old French *entraitier*, literally 'to treat in (a certain way)', from *traitier* 'to treat' (see TREAT).] —**entreatingly** *adv.*

entreaty /in tréeti/ (*plural* **-ies**) *n.* a serious and passionate request

entrechat /óntrə shaa/ *n.* in ballet, a leap in which the dancer's legs are crossed rapidly in the air and the heels are beaten together [Late 18thC. Via French from Italian *(capriola) intrecciata* 'intricate (caper)'.]

entrecôte /óntrə kōt/, **entrecôte steak** *n.* a piece of beef without any bone, cut from between the ribs [Mid-19thC. From French, literally 'between (the) rib(s)'.]

entrée /ón tray/ *n.* **1.** FOOD MAIN COURSE a dish served as the main part of a meal **2.** FOOD DISH BEFORE MAIN COURSE in a formal dinner, a light dish served before the main course **3.** RIGHT OF ENTRY sth that permits entry into sth, especially to an exclusive group or place [Late 18thC. From French (see ENTRY).]

entremets /óntrə may/ (*plural* **-mets**) *n.* **1.** DISH BETWEEN MAIN COURSE AND DESSERT in a formal dinner, a light dish served between the main course and the dessert **2.** DESSERT a sweet dish, especially one served after cheese in a multi-course dinner [15thC. From Old French, literally 'between the course(s)', from *mes* 'course'.]

entrench /in trénch/ (**-trenches, -trenching, -trenched**), **intrench** (**-trenches, -trenching, -trenched**) *v.* **1.** *vt.* DIG DITCH ROUND to defend sth by surrounding it with trenches **2.** *vt.* PROTECT to take action to protect an argument or position **3.** *vi.* ENCROACH to encroach upon or trespass on sb else's property or things (*archaic*) —**entrenchment** *n.*

entrenched /in trénch/ *adj.* **1.** FIRMLY HELD firmly held and hard to change ○ *deeply entrenched political views* **2.** FIRMLY ESTABLISHED firmly established and unlikely to change

entre nous /óntrə nóo/ *adv.* in confidence (*formal*) [Late 17thC. From French, literally 'between ourselves'.]

entrepôt /óntrə pō/ *n.* **1.** = **freeport** 2 **2.** WAREHOUSE a bonded warehouse [Early 18thC. From French, from *entreposer* 'to place in, store' from *poser* 'to place' (see POSE).]

entrepreneur /óntrəprə núr/ *n.* sb who sets up and finances new commercial enterprises to make a profit [Late 19thC. From French, literally 'one who undertakes', from *entreprendre* 'to undertake' (see ENTERPRISE).] —**entrepreneurial** *adj.* —**entrepreneurialism** *n.* —**entrepreneurism** *n.* —**entrepreneurship** *n.*

entresol /óntrə sol/ *n.* = **mezzanine** [Early 18thC. From Via French from Spanish *entresuelo*, literally 'between-level', from *suelo* 'level', ultimately from Latin *solea* 'sole' (see SOLE).]

entropy /éntrəpi/ (*plural* **-pies**) *n.* **1.** MEASURE OF DISORDER a measure of the disorder that exists in a system **2.** PHYS MEASURE OF UNAVAILABLE ENERGY a measure of the energy in a system or process that is unavailable to do work. In a reversible thermodynamic process, entropy is expressed as the heat absorbed or emitted divided by the absolute temperature. Symbol **S** **3.** COMMUNICATION MEASURE OF COMMUNICATIONS SYSTEM EFFICIENCY a measure of the random errors (**noise**) occurring in the transmission of signals, and from this a measure of the efficiency of transmission systems [Mid-19thC. Literally 'turning or change towards', formed from Greek *tropē* 'change', literally 'turning', on the model of ENERGY.] —**entropic** /en tróppik/ *adj.* —**entropically** /-tróppikli/ *adv.*

entrust /in trúst/ (**-trusts, -trusting, -trusted**), **intrust** (**-trusts, -trusting, -trusted**) *vt.* to give sth to another person to be responsible for

entry /éntri/ (*plural* **-tries**) *n.* **1.** GOING IN an act or instance of sb entering **2.** = **entrance**[1] *n.* 3 **3.** SINGLE WRITTEN ITEM an item or piece of data included in a list or a book **4.** COMPUT INCLUDING AN ITEM ON LIST the process of recording sth in writing or on a computer ○ *data entry* **5.** WAY IN a way into a place **6.** SB OR STH ENTERED IN CONTEST a person, animal, or item entered in a contest, or the total number entered ○ *the winning entry* **7.** THEATRE APPEARANCE ON STAGE the occasion when an actor comes on stage **8.** CARDS WINNING CARD in some games, a card that can win a trick and thus gain the lead for a player **9.** PASSAGE BETWEEN HOUSES a passage between the backs of two rows of houses, or leading into a block of flats, or to the backs of houses in a terrace (*regional*) [13thC. Via French *entrée* from Latin *intrata*, a form of the past participle of *intrare* 'to enter' (see ENTER).]

entryism /éntri izəm/ *n.* the tactic of joining an existing political party in large numbers with the purpose of changing its policies and direction —**entryist** *n.*

entry-level *adj.* at the lowest level and suitable for sb who is new to a job, field, or subject

Entryphone /éntri fōn/ *tdmk.* a trademark for an intercom system that links each flat in a building with the main door and allows the occupant to open the door remotely. *Entryphone* is also used in print with a lower-case 'e', to refer to a security intercom system at the door of a building.

entwine /in twín/ (**-twines, -twining, -twined**), **intwine** (**-twines, -twining, -twined**) *vti.* to twist things together, or to twist sth round sth else (*often passive*) —**entwinement** *n.*

entwist /in twíst/ (**-twists, -twisting, -twisted**), **intwist** (**-twists, -twisting, -twisted**) *vti.* = **entwine**

enucleate /i nyóokli ayt, -kli ət/ *vt.* (**-ates, -ating, -ated**) **1.** CELL BIOL TAKE OUT THE NUCLEUS to remove the nucleus of a cell **2.** SURG SURGICALLY REMOVE WITHOUT DAMAGE to remove sth surgically, such as a tumour, from its capsule while keeping it intact ■ *adj.* CELL BIOL WITHOUT A NUCLEUS used to describe a cell without a nucleus [Mid-16thC. From Latin *enucleat-*, past participle stem of *enucleare* 'to remove the pit from (olives, fruit)', from *nucleus* 'kernel' (see NUCLEUS).] —**enucleation** /i nyóokli áysh'n/ *n.*

E number *n.* **1.** IDENTIFICATION CODE FOR FOOD ADDITIVE a code by which a given additive is identified on food labels, in accordance with European law, consisting of the letter E followed by a number **2.** FOOD ADDITIVE a food additive (*informal*) [*E* is a shortening of EUROPEAN]

enumerable /i nyóomərəb'l/ *adj.* = **denumerable** [Late 19thC. Formed from ENUMERATE + -ABLE.]

enumerate /i nyóomə rayt/ (**-ates, -ating, -ated**) *vt.* **1.** LIST INDIVIDUALLY to name a number of things on a list one by one **2.** COUNT THE NUMBER OF to count how many things there are in sth [Mid-17thC. From Latin *enumerat-*, the past participle stem of *enumerare* 'to count out', from *numerus* 'number' (see NUMBER).] —**enumeration** /i nyóomə ráysh'n/ *n.* —**enumerative** /-ərətiv/ *adj.* —**enumerator** /-ə raytər/ *n.*

enunciate /i núnssi ayt/ (**-ates, -ating, -ated**) *v.* **1.** *vti.* SPEAK CLEARLY to pronounce sth distinctly **2.** *vt.* STATE CLEARLY to give a speech or statement that explains sth clearly [Early 17thC. From Latin *enuntiare* 'to announce', from *enuntiat-*, the past participle stem of *nuntius* 'message, messenger'.] —**enunciation** /i núnssi áysh'n/ *n.* —**enunciative** /-ssi ətiv, -ssi aytiv/ *adj.* —**enunciatively** *adv.* —**enunciator** /-ssi aytər/ *n.*

enure /i nyóor/ *vt.* = **inure**

enuresis /énnyoo réessiss/ *n.* involuntary discharge of urine, especially while asleep (*technical*) [Late 18thC. From modern Latin, from Greek *enourein* 'to urinate in', from *ouron* 'urine'.] —**enuretic** /énnyoo réttik/ *adj.*

envelop /in vélləp/ (**-ops, -oping, -oped**) *vt.* **1.** WRAP UP to enclose sb or sth completely (*often passive*) **2.** HIDE to conceal sth or sb (*often passive*) **3.** MIL SURROUND AN ENEMY to surround an enemy completely [14thC. From Old French *envoluper* 'to wrap in', of unknown origin.] —**enveloper** *n.* —**envelopment** *n.*

envelope /énvə lōp, ónv-/ *n.* **1.** PAPER COVER FOR A LETTER a flat pocket of paper with a sealable flap for holding letters **2.** ENCLOSING CASE sth that surrounds or encloses sth else ○ *seafood sauce in filo pastry envelopes* **3.** BIOL ENCLOSING STRUCTURE a covering that encloses and protects an animal's body or a biological structure, such as a shell or membrane **4.** MATH CURVE FORMING A TANGENT a curve or surface that forms a tangent to each of the members of a set of curves or surfaces, such as circles with a common centre but different radii **5.** AEROSP BALLOON the bag of an airship or balloon that contains the gas **6.** AEROSP PERFORMANCE LIMITS OF AN AIRCRAFT the performance limits of a piece of equipment, particularly of an aircraft [Early 18thC. From French *enveloppe*, from *envelopper* 'to wrap in' from Old French *envoluper* (see ENVELOP).] ◇ **push the envelope** to try to accomplish more than is theoretically possible (*informal*)

envenom /in vénnəm/ (**-oms, -oming, -omed**) *vt.* **1.** MAKE POISONOUS to make sth poisonous (*technical*) **2.** MAKE ANGRY AND BITTER to cause sb to become malicious or hostile (*formal*) —**envenomization** *n.*

Enver Pasha /énvər páshə/, **General** (1881–1922) Turkish soldier and statesman. He was elected leader of the revolutionary Young Turks in 1908 and became minister of war in 1914. After World War I he fled to Russia where he died in an anti-Bolshevik uprising.

enviable /énvi əb'l/ *adj.* likely to evoke feelings of envy ○ *in the enviable position of having two job offers to choose from* —**enviably** *adv.*

envious /énvi əss/ *adj.* wanting to have sb's else's success, good fortune, qualities, or possessions —**enviously** *adv.* —**enviousness** *n.*

environ /in vírən/ (**-rons, -roning, -roned**) *vt.* to surround sb or sth. ◊ **environs** [14thC. From Old French *environer*, literally 'to make a circle around', ultimately from *viron* 'circle', from *virer* 'to turn' (see VEER).]

environment /in vírənmənt/ *n.* **1.** ENVIRON NATURAL WORLD the natural world, within which people, animals, and plants live. It is regarded by many as being at risk from the harmful influences of industrialized societies. **2.** ENVIRON, ECOL SURROUNDING INFLUENCES all the external factors influencing the life of organisms, such as light or food supply **3.** SOC SCI SOCIAL AND PHYSICAL CONDITIONS the conditions that surround people and affect the way they live ○ *the nurturing environment a child needs*

Environment Agency *n.* the Government Agency responsible for environmental protection in England and Wales. It was formed by combining the National Rivers Authority, Her Majesty's Inspectorate of Pollution, and the waste regulation functions of local government.

environmental /in vírən mént'l/ *adj.* **1.** OF THE NATURAL WORLD relating to the natural world, especially to its conservation ○ *environmental groups* **2.** OF YOUR SURROUNDINGS relating to, or caused by, a person's or animal's surroundings

environmental art *n.* creative art, usually on a grand scale, that is meant to invite the viewer's participation by interacting with it

environmental assessment *n.* the identification of the likely environmental effects of a proposed development. US term **environmental impact statement**. ANZalternative **environmental impact statement**

environmental health *n.* the impact on human health of the environment, especially as safeguarded by government agencies dealing with areas such as water quality, food hygiene, and pest control

environmental impact *n.* the indirect and direct consequences of human actions on the natural environment

environmental impact statement *n. US, ANZ* = **environmental assessment**

environmentalism /in vírən mént'lizəm/ *n.* **1.** POL CONCERN FOR THE ENVIRONMENT the movement, especially in politics and consumer affairs, that works towards protecting the natural world from harmful human activities **2.** PSYCHOL THEORY OF ENVIRONMENTAL INFLUENCE a theory stating that a person's environment is more influential than heredity in determining his or her development

environmentalist /in vírən mént'list/ *n.* **1.** POL SB WORKING TO PROTECT THE ENVIRONMENT sb involved in issues relating to the protection of the natural world, especially a member of a political group campaigning against the perceived harmful effects of industrialized societies **2.** PSYCHOL BELIEVER IN THE DEVELOPMENTAL IMPORTANCE OF ENVIRONMENT a supporter of the theory that a person's environment is more influential than heredity in determining his or her development

environmentally /in vírən mént'li/ *adv.* with regard to the natural world and its vulnerability to destructive influences ○ *the environmentally aware consumer*

environmentally friendly, **environment-friendly** *adj.* designed to minimize harmful impact on the natural world, e.g. by using biodegradable ingredients

environmentally sensitive area *n.* a rural area designated by the government as in need of protection from certain modern farming practices. Farmers are compensated for adopting less damaging but less profitable methods.

environmental studies *n.* a course of academic study including a range of disciplines that relate to the environment (*takes a singular or plural verb*)

environs /in vírənz/ *npl.* the land or area surrounding a place [Mid-17thC. From French, plural of *environ* 'surroundings, around', literally 'in a circle', from *viron* (see ENVIRON).]

envisage /in vízzij/ (**-ages, -aging, -aged**) *vt.* (*formal*) **1.** FORESEE to conceive of and contemplate a future possibility ○ *Do you envisage being able to avert a crisis?* **2.** IMAGINE to form a mental picture of sth or sb **3.** CONSIDER to regard sth in a particular way [Early 19thC. From French *envisager*, literally '(to cause to be) in the face', from *visage* 'face' (see VISAGE).]

─────── **WORD KEY: USAGE** ───────
envisage or **envision**? In the sense of 'imagine', **envisage** is more common in British English, and **envision** in American English. **Envisage** should always carry the notion of a mental image and should not be used as an alternative for *expect*: *A further downward trend in share prices is envisaged* [use 'expected' instead] *during the coming weeks.*

envision /in vízh'n/ (**-sions, -sioning, -sioned**) *vt.* to form a mental picture of sth, typically sth that may occur or be possible in the future

─────── **WORD KEY: USAGE** ───────
See Usage Note at **envisage**.

envoi *n.* = envoy *n.* 3

envoy /én voy/ *n.* **1.** POL OFFICIAL REPRESENTATIVE sb acting as a diplomat on behalf of a national government or sent as an official messenger on behalf of a higher authority **2.** POL DIPLOMATIC MINISTER a minister in the Diplomatic Service, ranked immediately below ambassador **3. envoy, envoi** LITERAT CONCLUDING PART OF A POEM the final section of a book or play, or a short stanza at the end of a poem, used for summing up or as a dedication [Mid-17thC. From French *envoyé*, past participle of *envoyer*, 'to send', from assumed Vulgar Latin *inviare* 'to put on the way' from Latin *via* 'way'.]

envy /énvi/ *n.* WANTING WHAT SB ELSE HAS the resentful or unhappy feeling of wanting sb else's success, good fortune, qualities, or possessions ■ *vt.* (**-vies, -vying, -vied**) WANT WHAT SB ELSE HAS to desire sth possessed by sb else ○ *It would be churlish of me to envy them their success.* [13thC. Via Old French *envie* from Latin *invidia*, from *invidere* 'to look askance at', from *videre* 'to see' (see VIDEO).] —**envyingly** *adv.* ◇ **be the envy of sb** to be the object of sb's envy

enwind /in wínd/ (**-winds, -winding, -wound** /in wównd/, **-wound**) *vt.* to wind or coil sth around sb or sth (*literary*)

enwomb /in woóm/ (**-wombs, -wombing, -wombed**) *vt.* **1.** ENCLOSE WARMLY to hold sth or sb in a warm safe place (*literary*) **2.** CAUSE WOMAN TO BE PREGNANT to make a woman pregnant or be the child in a woman's womb (*archaic*) ○ *'I say, I am your mother; and put you in the catalogue of those that were enwombed mine'.* (William Shakespeare, *All's Well That Ends Well*; 1602)

enwound past participle, past tense of enwind

enwrap /in ráp/ (**-wraps, -wrapping, -wrapped**), **inwrap** (**-wraps, -wrapping, -wrapped**) *vt.* **1.** HOLD THE ATTENTION to

involve or engross sb or sth thoroughly (*formal*) (*often passive*) **2.** WRAP to wrap sth or sb up

enwreathe /in reéth/ (**-wreathes, -wreathing, -wreathed**), **inwreathe** (**-wreathes, -wreathing, -wreathed**) *vt.* to encircle sth, especially with decorations (*literary*)

Enzed /en zéd/ *n.* ANZ New Zealand (*informal*) [Early 20thC. Representing the initial letters of NEW ZEALAND.]

Enzedder /en zéddər/ *n.* ANZ a person from New Zealand (*informal*)

enzootic /én zō óttik/ *adj.* ZOOL AFFECTING ANIMALS IN A RESTRICTED AREA used to describe an animal disease that occurs only within a specific geographic area ■ *n.* ZOOL DISEASE OF ANIMALS a disease that affects animals in a specific area, locale, or region [Late 19thC]

enzyme /én zīm/ *n.* a complex protein produced by living cells that promotes a specific biochemical reaction by acting as a catalyst [Late 19thC. Via German *Enzym* from modern Greek *enzumos* 'leavened', literally 'with leaven in', from Greek *zumē* 'leaven'.] —**enzymatic** /én zī máttik, énzi-/ *adj.* —**enzymic** /en zímik, -zímmik/ *adj.* —**enzymically** /en zímikli, en zímm-/ *adv.*

enzymology /énzi móllǝji/ *n.* the branch of biochemistry that deals with enzymes

e.o. *abbr.* ex officio

eo- *prefix.* oldest, earliest ○ *eolithic* [From Greek *ēōs* 'dawn'. Ultimately from an Indo-European word that is also the ancestor of English *aurora*.]

EOC *abbr.* Equal Opportunities Commission

Eocene /eé ō seen/ *n.* the epoch of geological time when mammals first appeared, 56.5 to 35.4 million years ago —**Eocene** *adj.*

EOE *abbr.* equal opportunity employer (*used in job advertisements*)

EOF *abbr.* COMPUT end of file

eohippus /eé ō híppǝss/ (*plural* **-puses**) *n.* a small prehistoric horse that lived in North America. It was dog-sized and had four toes on the forefeet and three on the hind. [Late 19thC. From modern Latin, literally 'dawn horse', from Greek *hippos* 'horse'.]

eolian *adj.* US = aeolian

Eolian *n., adj.* = Aeolian

Eolic *adj., n.* = Aeolic

eolith /eé ō lith/ *n.* one of the oldest stone tools used by humans, believed by some scientists to have formed naturally

eolithic /eé ō líthik/ *adj.* relating to the earliest part of the Stone Age, during which time simple stone tools began to be used

e.o.m. *abbr.* COMM end of the month

eon *n.* = aeon

eosin /eé ōssin/ *n.* a red crystalline solid used as a biological stain and as a dye in cosmetics. Formula: $C_{20}H_6Br_4O_5K_2$. [Mid-19thC. Coined from Greek *ēōs* 'dawn' + -IN; so called because of its colour.]

eosinophil /eé ō sínnōfil/ *n.* a granular white blood cell that stains with the dye eosin and is thought to play a part in allergic reactions and the body's response to parasitic diseases [Late 19thC. Coined from EOSIN + -PHIL.] —**eosinophilic** /eé ō sínnǝ fíllik/ *adj.* —**eosinophilous** /eé ōsi nóffilǝss/ *adj.*

eosinophilia /eé ō sínnǝ fílli ǝ/ *n.* an increase in the number of granular white blood cells that stain with the dye eosin, occurring in some allergies and parasitic diseases

-eous *suffix.* ♦ **-ous** [Formed from Latin *-eus*, a suffix forming adjectives of material, such as *aureus*, 'golden', from *aurum*, 'gold']

EP *n.* a phonograph record that is the size of a single but contains a longer recording on it and is designed to be played at 33 1/3 revolutions per minute rather than 45 [Mid-20thC. Shortening of EXTENDED PLAY.]

Ep. *abbr.* BIBLE Epistle

e.p. *abbr.* CHESS en passant

ep- *prefix.* = epi- (used before vowels or h)

EPA *n.* a cholesterol-reducing fatty acid found in some types of fish oil. Abbr of eicosapentaenoic acid

EPAC *n.* the Economic Planning and Advisory Committee, an independent body made up of leading politicians and business figures that advises the Australian federal government on economic policy

epact /eé pakt/ *n.* a period of about 11 days that represents the difference between the lunar year and the solar year [Mid-16thC. Via Old French from late Latin, from Greek *epaktē (hēmera)*, 'added (day)', literally '(day) led in', from *agein* 'to lead'.]

epanalepsis /i pánnǝ lépsiss/ (*plural* **-ses** /-seez/) *n.* a phrase or words repeated later on in a speech or text as a rhetorical device [Late 16thC. From Greek 'repetition', literally 'taking up again', from *epana-* 'again' + *lēpsis* 'taking'.] —**epanaleptic** *adj.*

epanorthosis /i pán awr thóssiss/ (*plural* **-orthoses** /-seez/) *n.* the immediate rephrasing of sth said or written in order to emphasize or correct it [Late 16thC. From Greek 'correction', literally 'setting straight again', from *epana-* 'again' + *orthōsis* 'making straight', ultimately from *orthos* 'straight'.] —**epanorthotic** /i pánnawr thóttik/ *adj.*

eparch /éppaark/ *n.* **1.** CHR BISHOP a bishop in the Greek Orthodox Church **2.** POL GREEK GOVERNOR the governor of a modern Greek province [Mid-17thC. From Greek *eparkhos*, literally 'ruler over', from *arkhos* 'ruler' (see -ARCH).]

eparchy /éppaarki/ (*plural* **-chies**) *n.* **1.** CHR DIOCESE a bishop's diocese in the Greek Orthodox Church **2.** POL PART OF A GREEK PROVINCE a political subdivision of a province in modern Greece [Late 18thC. From Greek *eparkhia* 'prefecture, province', from *eparkhos* (see EPARCH).]

epaulet *n.* US = epaulette

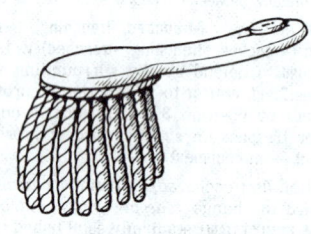

Epaulet

epaulette /éppǝ lét/ *n.* a decoration on the shoulder of a jacket, especially on a military uniform. Epaulettes are worn on the shoulders of a uniform jacket or coat, and in officers' dress are usually made of gold or silver braid. [Late 18thC. From French, literally 'small shoulder', from *épaule* 'shoulder', from, ultimately, Latin *spatula* 'broad piece, shoulder blade' (see SPATULA).]

épée /éppay/ (*plural* **épées**) *n.* **1.** FENCING SWORD a fencing sword that has a narrow triangular blade with a blunted end and a large handguard, heavier than a foil. It derives from the type of sword formerly used in duelling. **2.** FENCING WITH ÉPÉES the sport of fencing using épées [Late 19thC. From French, literally 'sword', from Latin *spatha* 'broad double-edged sword' (see SPATHE).] —**épéeist** /éppay ist/ *n.*

epeirogeny /éppī rójjǝni/, **epeirogenesis** /e pírō jénnǝssiss/ *n.* the slow movements of the Earth's crust that lead to the formation of features such as continents [Late 19thC. Coined from Greek *ēpeiros* 'mainland, continent' + -GENY.] —**epeirogenic** /e pírō jénnik/ *adj.* —**epeirogenically** /-jénnikli/ *adv.*

epenthesis /i pénthǝssiss/ *n.* insertion of an extra sound into a word, as happens in some dialect pronunciations or in a word's development over time. The 'b' in 'crumble' is an example of epenthesis. [Mid-17thC. Via modern Latin from Greek, where it was formed from *epentithenai*, literally 'to put in also', ultimately from *tithenai* 'to place'.] —**epenthetic** /éppen théttik/ *adj.*

epergne /i púrn/ *n.* a large elaborate centrepiece for a table with containers for fruit or confectionery [Mid-18thC. Origin uncertain: probably from French *épergne* 'savings, treasury', from Old French *espargnier*, from a prehistoric Germanic word that is also the ancestor of English *spare*.]

epexegesis /e péksi jéessiss/ (*plural* **-ses** /-jéess eez/) *n.* **1.** ADDITIONAL WORDS EXPLAINING A TEXT the addition of words or phrases to a text to clarify its meaning **2.** WORD ADDED FOR CLARIFICATION a word or phrase added to help explain the sense of a text [Early 17thC. From, literally 'explaining in addition', from *exēgēsis* (see EXEGESIS).] —**epexegetic** /e péksi jéttik/ *adj.* —**epexegetical** /-jéttik'l/ *adj.* —**epexegetically** /-jéttikli/ *adv.*

Eph. *abbr.* BIBLE Ephesians

eph- *prefix.* = **epi-**

ephah /éefə/, **epha** *n.* an ancient Hebrew unit of dry measure, roughly equivalent to a bushel or 33 litres [14thC. From Hebrew *ēpāh*.]

ephebe /i féeb, éffeeb/, **ephebus** /i féebəss/ (*plural* **-bi** /i féebī/), **ephebos** (*plural* **ephebi** /i féebī/) *n.* in ancient Greece, a young man aged between 18 and 20 who had just reached manhood or full citizenship and was undergoing military training [Mid-19thC. Via Latin *ephebus* from Greek *ephēbos*, literally 'one approaching manhood', from *hēbē* 'early manhood'.] —**ephebic** *adj.*

ephedrine /éffi dreen/, **ephedrin** /-drin/ *n.* a white odourless alkaloid that is used to enlarge air passages in asthma attacks, relieve allergic nasal congestion, and dilate the pupils, and as a central nervous system stimulant. It can be manufactured synthetically or obtained from a shrub. [Late 19thC. Formed from modern Latin *Ephedra*, from Latin *ephedra* 'horsetail', from the Greek name of a genus of plants, some of which contain this substance.]

ephemera[1] plural of **ephemeron**

ephemera[2] /i fémmərə, i féemərə/ *n.* (*plural* **-ae** /i fémmə ree, i féemə ree/ *or* **-as**) **1.** STH SHORT-LIVED sth that is transitory and without lasting significance **2.** INSECTS = **mayfly** *n.* 1 ■ *npl.* COLLECTABLE ITEMS a range of collectable items that were originally designed to be short-lived ○ *He's a collector of ticket stubs, theatre programmes, and other ephemera.* [14thC. From medieval Latin, feminine of late Latin *ephemerus* 'lasting only a day', from Greek *ephēmeros*, from *hēmera* 'day'.]

ephemeral /i fémmərəl, i fée-/ *adj.* SHORT-LIVED lasting for only a short period of time ○ *the ephemeral nature of slang* ■ *n.* SHORT-LIVED ORGANISM a plant or insect that lives for only a short period of time. Groundsel and mayflies are ephemerals. —**ephemerality** /i fémmə rálləti, i féemə-/ *n.* —**ephemerally** /i fémmərəli, i fée-/ *adv.* —**ephemeralness** /-rəlnəss/ *n.*

ephemerid /i fémmərid, i fée-/ *n.* an insect of the mayfly family that emerges in the summer from a long aquatic larval stage and lives only a matter of hours as an adult. Family: Ephemeridae. [Late 19thC. From modern Latin *Ephemeridae*, family name, from, ultimately, Greek *ephēmeros* (see EPHEMERA[2]).]

ephemeris /i fémməriss, i fée-/ (*plural* **ephemerides** /éffi mérrideez/) *n.* a table listing the future positions of the Sun, Moon, and planets over a given period of time [Early 16thC. Via Latin from Greek, where it was formed from *ephēmeros* (see EPHEMERA[2]).]

ephemeris time *n.* a system of time measurement based on the Earth's orbit round the Sun and therefore independent of the irregularities of the Earth's rotation

ephemeron /i fémməron, i féemərən/ (*plural* **-a** /-mərə/ *or* **-ons**) *n.* a short-lived thing (*usually used in the plural*) [Late 16thC. From Greek *ephēmeron*, a form of *ephēmeros* (see EPHEMERA[2]).]

Ephes. *abbr.* BIBLE Ephesians

Ephesians /i féezh'nz/ *n.* one of the books of the Bible, consisting of a letter from the Apostle Paul to the early Christians (*used with a singular verb*) [15thC. Formed from Latin *ephesius* 'of Ephesus', from Greek *ephesios*, from *Ephesos* 'Ephesus', a Greek city in Asia Minor.]

Ephesus /éffəssəs/ ancient Greek city on the western coast of Asia Minor, in present-day Turkey. An important centre for early Christianity, it was the site of the temple of Artemis, one of the Seven Wonders of the World.

ephod /ée fod, éffod/ *n.* an embroidered garment, believed to be like an apron with shoulder straps, worn by Hebrew priests in ancient Israel [14thC. From Hebrew *ēpōd*.]

ephor /ée fawr, éffawr/ (*plural* **-ors** *or* **-ori** /éefə rī/) *n.* in ancient Greece, one of five magistrates elected in any of various Dorian states, especially Sparta, to supervise the king [Late 16thC. Directly or via Latin *ephorus* from Greek *ephoros* 'overseer', from *horan* 'to see'.] —**ephoral** /éefərəl, éffərəl/ *adj.* —**ephorate** /ée fawrət, éffawrət/ *n.*

Ephraimite /éefrayim īt/ *n.* **1.** MEMBER OF THE TRIBE OF EPHRAIM a member of the Hebrew tribe of Ephraim **2.** SB FROM THE KINGDOM OF ISRAEL sb born in the northern kingdom of Israel

epi- *prefix.* **1.** on, over, above ○ *epiphyte* ○ *epipelagic* **2.** around, near ○ *epicalyx* **3.** after, in addition ○ *epiphenomenon* [From Greek *epi* 'upon']

epiblast /éppi blast/ *n.* the outer layer of cells in an early embryo (**blastula**). It develops into ectoderm. —**epiblastic** /éppi blástik/ *adj.*

epiboly /i píbbəli/ *n.* the growth of a layer of rapidly dividing cells over a layer of more slowly dividing cells during embryo development. This process occurs in the eggs of birds and reptiles. [Late 19thC. From Greek *epibolē* 'throwing on', from *epiballein* 'to throw on', from *ballein* 'to throw' (see BALLISTIC).] —**epibolic** /éppi bóllik/ *adj.*

epic /éppik/ *n.* **1.** POETRY LONG NARRATIVE POEM a lengthy narrative poem in elevated language celebrating the adventures and achievements of a legendary or traditional hero, e.g. Homer's *Odyssey* **2.** POETRY EPIC POETRY epic poetry as a genre ○ *This term we'll cover epic, romance, and allegory.* **3.** ARTS LARGE-SCALE PRODUCTION a work of literature, cinema, television, or theatre that is large-scale and expensively produced and often deals with a historical theme **4.** LONG SERIES OF EVENTS a long series of events characterized by adventures or struggle ○ *Our trek across town turned out to be an epic.* ■ *adj.* **1.** POETRY ABOUT AN EPIC relating to or being an epic ○ *Milton's 'Paradise Lost' is an epic poem.* **2.** LIKE AN EPIC having some of the characteristics of an epic ○ *an epic story of true love and adventure* **3.** VERY LARGE OR HEROIC impressive by virtue of greatness of size, scope, or heroism ○ *a scandal of epic proportions* [Late 16thC. Via Latin *epicus* from Greek *epikos*, from *epos* (see EPOS).] —**epical** *adj.* —**epically** *adv.*

epicalyx /éppi káyliks, -kálliks/ (*plural* **-lyxes** *or* **-lyces** /-li seez/) *n.* a ring of modified leaves (**bracts**) at the base of a flower that resemble an extra calyx, found in the carnation, hibiscus, and mallow

epicanthic fold /éppi kánthik-/ *n.* a fold of skin from the eyelid that partially covers the part of the eye nearest the nose

epicanthus /éppi kánthəss/ (*plural* **-thi** /-thī/) *n.* = **epicanthic fold** [Mid-19thC. Coined from EPI- + CANTHUS.]

epicarp /éppi kaarp/ *n.* = **exocarp**

epicene /éppi seen/ *adj.* **1.** HAVING CHARACTERISTICS OF BOTH SEXES having both male and female characteristics **2.** NEITHER MALE NOR FEMALE of neither male nor female sex **3.** WITH FEMALE CHARACTERISTICS having typically female characteristics (*literary*) (*used of a male*) **4.** WEAK lacking vigour and strength **5.** GRAM SAME FOR MASCULINE AND FEMININE having only one grammatical form for both masculine and feminine, in languages where nouns have genders ■ *n.* **1.** SB OR STH EPICENE an epicene person or thing (*literary*) **2.** GRAM NOUN WITH SAME MASCULINE AND FEMININE FORM a noun with the same grammatical form for both masculine and feminine in languages where nouns have genders [15thC. Via late Latin *epicoenus* from Greek *epikoinos*, literally 'in common', from *koinos* 'common'.] —**epicenism** /éppi séenizəm/ *n.*

epicenter /éppi sentər/ *n.* US = **epicentre**

epicentre /éppi sentər/ *n.* **1.** GEOL EARTH'S SURFACE ABOVE THE FOCUS OF AN EARTHQUAKE the exact location on the Earth's surface directly above the focus of an earthquake or underground nuclear explosion **2.** FOCAL POINT the very centre or focal point ○ *Paris is the epicentre of the fashion world.* [Mid-19thC. From Greek *epikentron*, neuter of *epikentos* 'situated on a centre', from *kentros* 'centre' (see CENTRE).] —**epicentral** /éppi séntrəl/ *adj.*

epicotyl /éppi kóttil/ *n.* the tip of a plant embryo above the embryonic leaves (**cotyledons**) that gives rise to the stem of the new plant [Late 19thC. Coined from EPI- + Greek *kotulē* (see COTYLEDON).]

epic simile *n.* a lengthy simile developed over a number of lines of verse in narrative poetry

epicure /éppi kyoor/ *n.* **1.** GOURMET sb who has developed a refined taste for food **2.** SENSUAL PERSON sb who is dedicated to sensual pleasure and luxury [14thC. From medieval Latin *epicurus*, from EPICURUS. Originally 'follower of Epicurus'.] —**epicurism** *n.*

epicurean /éppi kyŏŏ rée ən/ *adj.* **1.** DEVOTED TO SENSUAL PLEASURE devoted to sensual pleasures and luxury, especially good food **2.** PLEASING TO AN EPICURE suitable for or pleasing to an epicure ○ *led an epicurean life* ■ *n.* = **epicure** *n.* 2 [14thC. Directly or via French *épicurien* from Latin *epicureus*, from EPICURUS.] —**epicureanism** *n.*

Epicurean /éppi kyŏŏ rée ən/ *adj.* OF EPICURUS relating to the philosophy of Epicureanism ■ *n.* ADHERENT OF EPICUREANISM a follower of Epicureanism

Epicureanism /éppi kyŏŏrée ənizəm/ *n.* the school of philosophy founded by Epicurus and its teachings

Epicurus /éppi kyŏŏrəss/ (341–270 BC) Greek philosopher. His philosophy, Epicureanism, taught that the greatest good is freedom from pain and emotional disturbance.

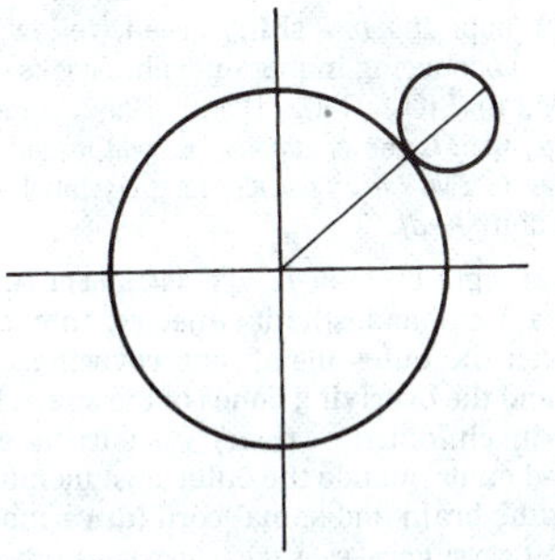

Epicycle

epicycle /éppi sīk'l/ *n.* **1.** PLANET'S CIRCULAR MOTION in the Ptolemaic theory of the solar system, a circle that is followed by a planet, the circle itself being centred on a larger circle within which is the Earth. The epicycle accounts for irregularities of planetary motion in geocentric astronomy. **2.** GEOM CIRCLE THAT ROLLS AROUND ANOTHER a circle that rolls around the circumference of another circle, either inside or outside [14thC. Via French *épicycle* or late Latin *epicyclus* from Greek *epikuklos*, literally 'on a circle', from *kuklos* 'circle' (see CYCLE).] —**epicyclic** /éppi sīklik, -síklik/ *adj.* —**epicyclical** /-sīklik'l, -síklik'l/ *adj.*

epicyclic train *n.* a system of gears arranged such that one or more gears engage with and revolve around a fixed or moving part

epicycloid /éppi sī kloyd/ *n.* a mathematical curve traced by a point on the circumference of a circle that rolls around the outside of the circumference of another circle —**epicycloidal** /éppi sī klóyd'l/ *adj.*

epidemic /éppi démmik/ *n.* **1.** MED FAST-SPREADING DISEASE an outbreak of a disease that spreads more quickly and more extensively among a group of people than would normally be expected **2.** RAPID DEVELOPMENT a rapid and extensive development or growth, usually of sth unpleasant ○ *an epidemic of civil unrest and rioting* ■ *adj.* SPREADING UNUSUALLY QUICKLY AND EXTENSIVELY spreading more quickly and more extensively among a group of people at the same time than would normally be expected ○ *Influenza was epidemic.* [Early 17thC. From French *épidémique*, from *épidémie* 'an epidemic', from, ultimately, Greek *epidēmia* 'disease prevalent among the people', from *dēmos* 'people'.] —**epidemically** *adv.* —**epidemicity** /éppidə míssəti/ *n.*

WORD KEY: SYNONYMS

See Synonyms at ***widespread***.

epidemiology /éppi dèemi óllәji/ *n.* **1.** STUDY OF DISEASE ORIGIN AND SPREAD the scientific and medical study of the causes and transmission of disease within a population **2.** PATTERN OF DISEASE DEVELOPMENT the origin and development characteristics of a particular disease [Late 19thC. Coined from Greek *epidēmia* (see EPIDEMIC) + -OLOGY.] —**epidemiological** /éppi dèemi ә lójjik'l/ *adj.* —**epidemiologically** /-lójjikli/ *adv.* —**epidemiologist** /éppi dèemi óllәjist/ *n.*

epidermis /éppi dúrmiss/ *n.* **1.** ANAT OUTER LAYER OF THE SKIN the thin outermost layer of the skin, itself made up of several layers, that covers and protects the underlying dermis **2.** BIOL OUTER LAYER OF INVERTEBRATES' CELLS the outer layer of cells of invertebrates that secretes the protective waxy cuticle **3.** BOT OUTER CELL LAYER OF A PLANT the outermost layer of cells on a plant. In woody plants the epidermis is usually replaced by corky protective tissue (**periderm**). [Early 17thC. Via late Latin from Greek, literally 'above skin', from *derma* 'skin' (see DERMATO-).] —**epidermal** *adj.* —**epidermic** *adj.* —**epidermoid** *adj.*

epidiascope /éppi dí әskōp/ *n.* a device for projecting an enlarged image of an opaque or transparent object onto a screen [Early 20thC. Coined from EPI- + DIA- + -SCOPE.]

epididymis /éppi díddimiss/ (*plural* **-mides** /éppidi dímmәdeez/) *n.* a coiled tube attached to the back and upper side of the testicle that stores sperm and is connected to the vas deferens [Early 17thC. From Greek *epididumis*, from *didumis* 'testicle, twin', from *duo* 'two'.] —**epididymal** /éppi díddim'l/ *adj.*

epidote /éppi dōt/ *n.* a shiny green, yellow, or black mineral occurring in metamorphic rocks. Formula: $Ca_2(Al,Fe)_3(SiO_4)_3(OH)$. [Early 19thC. From French *épidote*, from Greek *epididonai* 'to give in addition', from *didonai* 'to give'; from its very long crystals.] —**epidotic** /éppi dóttik/ *adj.*

epidural /éppi dyóorәl/ *n.* MED ANAESTHETIC INJECTION INTO SPINE a local anaesthetic injected into the space between the outer membrane covering the spinal cord and the overlying bones of the spine. It is often used in childbirth. ■ *adj.* ANAT ON THE DURA MATER located on or outside the outermost membrane covering the brain and spinal cord (**dura mater**) [Late 19thC. Coined from EPI- + *dura*, from DURA MATER + -AL.]

epifauna /éppi fawnә/ *npl.* ECOL animals that live on the sea floor, or attached to other animals or objects under water —**epifaunal** /éppi fáwn'l/ *adj.*

epifocal /éppi fók'l/ *adj.* located or occurring at the point on the Earth's surface directly above the focus (**epicentre**) of an earthquake or underground nuclear explosion

epigamic /éppi gámmik/ *adj.* ZOOL used to describe a trait or behaviour that attracts a mate, such as large antlers or bright colours [Late 19thC. Formed from EPI- + Greek *gamos* 'marriage'.]

epigastrium /éppi gástri әm/ (*plural* **-a** /-tri ә/) *n.* ANAT the upper middle part of the abdomen [Late 17thC. Via late Latin from Greek *epigastrion*, a form of *epigastrios* 'over the belly', from *gaster* 'belly' (see GASTRIC).]

epigeal /éppi jèe әl/ *adj.* **1.** BIOL, BOT LIVING ON SURFACE OF GROUND living or growing on or right above the surface of the ground. ◊ **hypogeal 2.** BOT GERMINATING WITH SEED LEAVES HELD ALOFT used to describe seed germination in which the embryo elongates so that the seed leaves (**cotyledons**) are carried above the soil to form the first leaves of the new plant [Mid-19thC. Formed from Greek *epigeios* 'on the earth', from *gē* 'earth'.]

epigene /éppi jeen/ *adj.* GEOL formed or occurring at the Earth's surface, especially with reference to weathering, erosion, and deposition [Early 19thC. Via French *épigène* from Greek *epigenēs* 'born on or after', from *-genes* (see -GEN).]

epigenesis /éppi jénnәssiss/ *n.* **1.** EMBRYOL EMBRYONIC DEVELOPMENT BY GRADUAL CHANGE the theory that the development of tissues and organs during embryonic development proceeds by successive gradual change **2.** GEOL CHANGE IN THE MINERAL CONTENT OF ROCK change in the mineral content or structure of a rock through external influences, such as the injection of a vein of ore into existing rock —**epigenesist** *n.* —**epigenetic** /éppijә néttik/ *adj.* —**epigenetically** /-néttikli/ *adv.* —**epigenist** /i píjjәnist/ *n.*

epigenous /i píjjәnәss/ *adj.* BOT growing on the upper surface of an organism

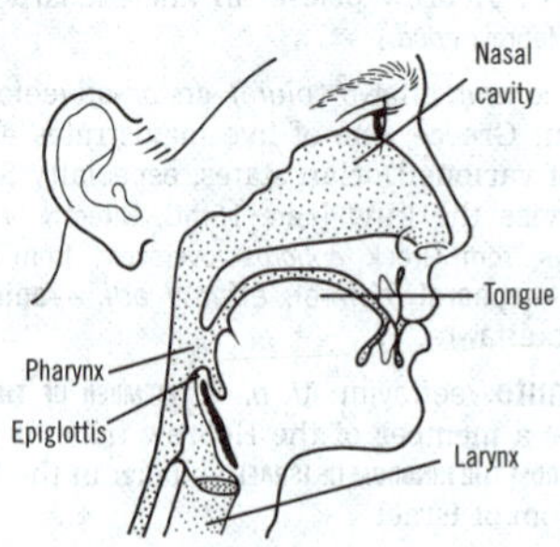

Epiglottis

epiglottis /éppi glóttiss/ (*plural* **-tises** *or* **-tides** /-glóttideez/) *n.* a flap of cartilage situated at the base of the tongue that covers the opening to the air passages when swallowing, preventing food or liquids from entering the windpipe (**trachea**) [Early 16thC. From Greek *epiglōttis*, literally 'on the tongue', from *glōtta* 'tongue'.] —**epiglottal** *adj.* —**epiglottic** *adj.*

epigone /éppi gōn/, **epigon** /-gon/ *n.* a follower, especially of an important artist or philosopher, who is a mediocre imitator (*formal or literary*) [Mid-18thC. Singular of *epigones* 'epigones', which came via French from, ultimately, Greek *epigonoi*, plural of *epigonos* 'offspring', literally 'one born after', from *gignesthai* 'to be born'.] —**epigonic** /éppi gónnik/ *adj.* —**epigonous** /e píggәnәss/ *adj.* —**epigonism** /i píggәnizәm/ *n.*

epigram /éppi gram/ *n.* **1.** WITTY SAYING a concise, witty, and often paradoxical remark or saying **2.** POETRY SHORT POEM a short poem, often expressing a single idea, that is usually satirical and has a witty ending **3.** WITTY EXPRESSION a written or spoken mode of expression that is witty or concise like an epigram [15thC. Directly or via French *épigramme* from Latin *epigramma*, from Greek, literally 'writing upon', from *graphein* 'to write'.] —**epigrammatism** /éppi grám mәtizәm/ *n.* —**epigrammatist** /-grámmәtist/ *n.*

epigrammatic /éppigrә máttik/, **epigrammatical** /-máttik'l/ *adj.* **1.** LIKE AN EPIGRAM containing or in the form of an epigram **2.** USING EPIGRAMS tending to use epigrams —**epigrammatically** *adv.*

epigrammatize /éppi grámmә tīz/ (**-matizes, -matizing, -matized**), **epigrammatise** (**-ises, -ising, -ised**) *vti.* to create a short and witty poem or saying about sth

epigraph /éppi graaf, -graf/ *n.* **1.** LITERAT INTRODUCTORY QUOTATION a quotation at the beginning of a book, chapter, or section of a book, usually related to its theme **2.** SCULPTURE, ARCHIT INSCRIPTION ON A MONUMENT an inscription on sth, e.g. a statue or building [Late 16thC. From Greek *epigraphē*, from *epigraphein* 'to write on', from *graphein* 'to write'.] —**epigraphic** /éppi gráffik/ *adj.* —**epigraphical** /-gráffik'l/ *adj.* —**epigraphically** /-gráffikli/ *adv.*

epigraphy /e píggrәfi/ *n.* **1.** INSCRIPTIONS inscriptions or introductory quotations as a whole **2.** STUDY OF INSCRIPTIONS the study and deciphering of ancient inscriptions —**epigrapher** *n.* —**epigraphist** *n.*

epigynous /e píjjәnәss/ *adj.* BOT used to describe a flower in which the sepals, petals, and stamens arise from the enlarged tip of the flower axis (**receptacle**) above the ovary [Mid-19thC. From modern Latin *epigynus*, from Greek *gunē* 'woman' (used to mean 'pistil').] —**epigyny** *n.*

epilation /éppi láysh'n/ *n.* = **depilation** [Late 19thC. From French *épilation*, from *épiler* 'to remove hair', from Latin *pilus* 'hair'.]

epilepsy /éppi lepsi/ (*plural* **-sies**) *n.* a medical disorder involving episodes of abnormal electrical discharge in the brain and characterized by periodic sudden loss or impairment of consciousness, often accompanied by convulsions [Mid-16thC. Via French *épilepsie* from, ultimately, Greek *epilēpsia*, literally 'seizure', from *epilambanein* 'to seize', from *lambanein* 'to grasp'.]

epileptic /éppi léptik/ *adj.* CONCERNING EPILEPSY relating to or affected by epilepsy ■ *n.* SB WITH EPILEPSY sb who has epilepsy (*offensive*) [Early 17thC. Via French *épileptique* from, ultimately, Greek *epilēptikos*, from *epilēpsia* (see EPILEPSY).] —**epileptically** *adv.*

epileptiform /éppi lépti fawrm/ *adj.* resembling epilepsy

epileptogenic /éppi léptә jénnik/ *adj.* causing or able to cause an epileptic episode

epileptoid /éppi lép toyd/ *adj.* **1.** = **epileptiform 2.** SHOWING SYMPTOMS LIKE EPILEPSY showing symptoms similar to those of epilepsy

epilimnion /éppi límni әn/ *n.* the uppermost circulating layer of warm water in a lake with different temperatures at different levels in summer [Early 20thC. Coined from EPI- + Greek *limnion*, literally 'small lake', from *limnē* 'lake'.]

epilogue /éppi log/ *n.* **1.** THEATRE CONCLUDING SPEECH a short speech, usually in verse, that an actor addresses directly to the audience at the end of a play **2.** THEATRE ACTOR GIVING A SHORT SPEECH the actor who addresses a short speech, usually in verse, directly to the audience at the end of a play **3.** LITERAT SHORT SECTION AT THE END OF A BOOK a short chapter or section at the end of a literary work, sometimes detailing the fate of its characters **4.** FINAL PROGRAMME a short programme, usually of religious content, that used to be broadcast at the end of the day [15thC. Via French *épilogue* from, ultimately, Greek *epilogos*, literally 'additional speech', from *logos* 'speech'.] —**epilogist** /e píllәjist/ *n.*

epimysium /éppi mízzi әm/ (*plural* **-a** /-zi ә/) *n.* the covering of connective tissue surrounding a muscle [Early 20thC. From modern Latin, from Greek *mus* 'muscle' (see MUSCLE).]

epinasty /éppi nasti/ (*plural* **-ties**) *n.* the outward and downward bending of a plant part resulting from different growth rates on the upper and lower sides [Late 19thC. Coined from EPI- + Greek *nastos* 'pressed together'.] —**epinastic** /éppi nástik/ *adj.*

epinephrine /éppi néf reen/, **epinephrin** /-frin/ *n.* a synthetic form of adrenaline that relaxes the airways and constricts blood vessels, used to treat asthma and to reduce blood loss. Formula: $C_9H_{13}NO_3$. = **adrenaline** [Late 19thC. Coined from EPI- + -INE + Greek *nephros* 'kidney'.]

epineurium /éppi nyóor ri әm/ (*plural* **-a** /-ri ә/) *n.* a sheath of connective tissue around a nerve [Late 19thC. From modern Latin, from Greek *neuron* 'nerve'.] —**epineurial** *adj.*

epipelagic /éppipә lájjik/ *adj.* relating to or living in the upper zone of the ocean, from the surface to a depth of about 200 m

Epiph. *abbr.* Epiphany

epiphany /i píffәni/ (*plural* **-nies**) *n.* **1.** APPEARANCE OF A GOD the manifestation of a divine being **2.** SUDDEN REALIZATION a sudden intuitive leap of understanding, especially through an ordinary but striking occurrence ○ *It came to him in an epiphany what his life's work was to be.* [17thC. Via French *épiphanie* from, ultimately, Greek *epiphaneia* 'manifestation', from *epiphanein* 'to manifest', from *phanein* 'to show'.] —**epiphanic** /éppi fánnik/ *adj.* —**epiphanous** /i píffәnәss/ *adj.*

Epiphany *n.* CHR a Christian festival observed on 6 January, celebrating the divine manifestation of Jesus Christ through the Three Wise Men's visit, or, in the Eastern Orthodox Church, the baptism of Jesus Christ

epiphenomenalism /éppifi nómminәlizәm/ *n.* the view that consciousness is merely an aftereffect of physical processes in the brain and nervous system —**epiphenomenalist** /-nómminәlist/ *n.*

epiphenomenon /éppifi nómminәn/ (*plural* **-ena** /-ә/) *n.* **1.** SECONDARY PHENOMENON a secondary phenomenon resulting from another **2.** MED ADDITIONAL SYMPTOM a secondary incidental condition or symptom that appears during the course of an illness —**epiphenomenal** /-nómmin'l/ *adj.* —**epiphenomenally** *adv.*

epiphysis /e píffәssiss/ (*plural* **-ses** /-seez/) *n.* **1.** END OF A LONG BONE the end of a long bone that fuses with the shaft of the bone at the point where it was previously separated by cartilage. This is to allow bone growth during development. Once the epiphyses fuse, no further growth of long bones is possible. **2.**

PINEAL GLAND a pineal gland (*archaic*) [Mid-17thC. Via modern Latin from Greek *epiphusis*, literally 'growing on', from *phusis* 'growth'.] —**epiphyseal** /éppi fízzi əl/ *adj.*

epiphyte /éppi fīt/ *n.* a plant that grows on top of or is supported by another plant but does not depend on it for nutrition. Mosses, tropical orchids, and many ferns are epiphytes. —**epiphytic** /éppi fíttik/ *adj.* —**epiphytically** /-fíttikli/ *adv.*

epiphytotic /éppi fī tóttik/ *adj.* **RELATING TO EPIDEMIC OF PLANT DISEASE** used to describe an outbreak of disease that rapidly affects many plants in a given area ■ *n.* **SUDDEN PLANT DISEASE OUTBREAK** a plant disease that suddenly and rapidly affects many plants in a given area

Epis. *abbr.* **1. Epis., Episc.** CHR Episcopal **2. Epis., Episc.** CHR Episcopalian **3.** BIBLE Epistle

episcopacy /i pískəpəssi/ (*plural* **-cies**) *n.* **1. CHURCH GOVERNMENT BY BISHOPS** church government by bishops, as in the Roman Catholic, Eastern and Anglican Churches **2.** = **episcopate** *n.* 3 [Mid-17thC. Formed from ecclesiastical Latin *episcopatus* (see EPISCOPATE), modelled on PRELACY.]

episcopal *adj.* **1. OF BISHOPS** relating to a bishop or bishops **2. GOVERNED BY BISHOPS** involving or recognizing church government by bishops [15thC. From French *épiscopal* or ecclesiastical Latin *episcopalis*, from *episcopus* (see BISHOP).] —**episcopally** *adv.*

Episcopal /i pískəp'l/ *adj.* relating to or being the Protestant Episcopal Church

Episcopal Church *n.* an independent branch of the Anglican Church in North America and Scotland

episcopalian /i pískə páyli ən/ *adj.* **BELIEVING IN CHURCH GOVERNMENT BY BISHOPS** adhering to or practising church government by bishops ■ *n.* **BELIEVER IN GOVERNMENT BY BISHOPS** a supporter of church government by bishops —**episcopalianism** *n.*

Episcopalian *adj.* **BELONGING TO THE EPISCOPAL CHURCH** relating to or belonging to the Episcopal Church ■ *n.* **MEMBER OF THE EPISCOPAL CHURCH** a member of the Episcopal Church of North America or Scotland —**Episcopalianism** *n.*

episcopalism /i pískəpəlizzəm/ *n.* the belief that authority in a church government should lie in a group of bishops

episcopate /i pískəpət/ *n.* **1. OFFICE OR POSITION OF BISHOP** the office, position, or term of office of a bishop **2. DIOCESE** a bishop's diocese or jurisdiction **3. BISHOPS** bishops as a group [Mid-17thC. From ecclesiastical Latin *episcopatus*, from *episcopus* (see BISHOP).]

episcope /éppi skōp/ *n.* a device for projecting an enlarged image of an opaque object such as a printed page or a photograph onto a screen using reflected light

episiotomy /i pízzi óttəmi/ (*plural* **-mies**) *n.* an incision sometimes made to enlarge the vaginal opening in the late stages of labour to prevent tearing and facilitate the birth [Late 19thC. Coined from Greek *epision* 'pubic region' + -TOMY.]

episode /éppi sōd/ *n.* **1. SIGNIFICANT INCIDENT** an event that is a part of but distinct from a greater whole and that often has some kind of significance ○ *Let's try to put this unfortunate episode behind us, shall we?* **2.** LITERAT, TV, RADIO **PART OF SERIALIZED WORK** a part of a serialized work that is published or broadcast separately ○ *Find out what happens in next week's thrilling episode.* **3.** LITERAT **EVENT IN A NARRATIVE** an incident, description, or series of events in a narrative that is part of the whole but may digress from the main plot ○ *The episode in the library reveals a lot about the main character.* **4.** MED an occurrence of a particular illness or symptom of an illness, usually one of a connected series, often repeated over a period of time ○ *episodes of breathlessness and chest pain* **5.** THEATRE **SECTION OF GREEK TRAGEDY** a section of an ancient Greek tragedy between two choruses **6.** MUSIC **DIGRESSIVE MUSICAL PASSAGE** a digressive passage between two musical themes, e.g. in a rondo or fugue [Late 17thC. From Greek *epeisodion* 'addition', a form of *epeisodios* 'coming in besides', from *eisodos* 'coming in', from *hodos* 'road'.]

episodic /éppi sóddik/, **episodical** /-sóddik'l/ *adj.* **1. OF AN EPISODE** in the form of an episode, or resembling an episode in nature **2. DIVIDED INTO EPISODES** divided into or composed of closely connected but independent sections **3. SPORADIC** happening at irregular intervals ○ *episodic pain in the lower back* **4. TEMPORARY** of a limited duration ○ *episodic wind squalls* —**episodically** /-sóddikli/ *adv.*

episome /éppi sōm/ *n.* a genetic unit that can multiply independently in host cells or when integrated with a chromosome. Bacterial plasmids are examples of episomes. [Mid-20thC. Coined from EPI- + Greek *sōma* 'body'.] —**episomal** /éppi sōm'l/ *adj.* —**episomally** /-sōm'li/ *adv.*

Epist. *abbr.* BIBLE Epistle

epistasis /i pístəssiss/ (*plural* **-ses** /-seez/) *n.* the nonappearance of a characteristic determined by one gene because it has been suppressed or masked by the activity of another gene [Early 19thC. From Greek, literally 'stoppage', from *ephistanai* 'to stop', literally 'to put on', from *histanai* 'to put'.] —**epistatic** /éppi státtik/ *adj.*

epistaxis /éppi stáksiss/ (*plural* **-staxes** /-seez/) *n.* a bleeding from the nose (*technical*) [Late 18thC. Via modern Latin from Greek, where it was formed from *epistazein*, literally 'to drip at (the nose)', from *stazein* 'to drip'.]

epistemic /éppi stéemik/ *adj.* involving or relating to knowledge (*formal*) [Early 20thC. Formed from Greek *epistēmē* 'knowledge', from *epistasthai* 'to know', literally 'to stand over', from *histasthai* 'to stand'.] —**epistemically** /-stéemikli, -stémmikli/ *adv.*

epistemics /éppi stéemiks/ *n.* the use of logic, philosophy, psychology, and linguistics to study knowledge and how it is processed by humans (*takes a singular verb*)

epistemology /i písti mólləji/ *n.* the branch of philosophy that studies the nature of knowledge, in particular its foundations, scope, and validity [Mid-19thC. Coined from Greek *epistēmē* (see EPISTEMIC) + -OLOGY.] —**epistemological** /i pístimə lójjik'l/ *adj.* —**epistemologically** /-lójjikli/ *adv.* —**epistemologist** /i písti mólləjist/ *n.*

epistle /i píss'l/ *n.* **1. LETTER** a long formal letter that often serves to instruct (*formal*) **2.** LITERAT **BOOK IN LETTER FORM** a literary work in the form of a letter [12thC. Directly or via Old French from Latin *epistola*, from Greek *epistolē*, literally 'sth sent', from *stellein* 'to send'.]

Epistle *n.* **1.** BIBLE **LETTER FROM THE APOSTLE PAUL OR OTHERS** any of the letters written by the apostle Paul or other early Christian writers and included as books of the Bible **2.** CHR **EXCERPT FROM EPISTLE** an excerpt from one of the Epistles read as part of the service in a Christian church

epistle side, Epistle Side *n.* the right side of a Christian church, as you face the altar [So called because it is the side from which an extract from one of the Epistles is traditionally read as part of the Communion service]

epistolary /i pístələri/, **epistolatory** /-tələtəri, i pístə láytəri/ *adj.* **1. ASSOCIATED WITH CORRESPONDENCE BY LETTER** associated with, conducted by, or suitable for letters (*formal*) **2.** LITERAT **IN THE FORM OF A LETTER OR LETTERS** taking the form of a letter or a series of letters [Mid-17thC. *Epistolary* directly or via French *épistolaire* from Latin *epistolaris*, from *epistola* (see EPISTLE).]

epistoler *n.* = **epistler**

epistrophe /i pístrəfi/ *n.* repetition of a word, phrase, or other expression at the end of consecutive clauses or sentences for rhetorical effect, as occurs in the expression 'of the people, by the people, for the people' [Late 16thC. From Greek, from *epistrephein* 'to turn about', from *strephein* 'to turn'.]

epistyle /éppi stīl/ *n.* ARCHIT = **architrave** [Mid-16thC. Directly or via French *épistyle* from Latin *epistylium*, from Greek *epistulion*, literally 'on a column', from *stulos* 'column'.]

epitaph /éppi taaf, -taf/ *n.* LITERAT **1. INSCRIPTION ON A TOMBSTONE** an inscription on a tombstone or monument commemorating the person buried there **2. SPEECH OR WRITING COMMEMORATING A DEAD PERSON** a short speech or piece of writing celebrating the life of a recently deceased person [14thC. Via French *épitaphe* from, ultimately, Greek *epitaphion* 'sth above a tomb or burial', from *taphos* 'funeral ceremonies, tomb'.]

epitasis /i píttəssiss/ (*plural* **-ses** /-seez/) *n.* in classical drama, the middle part of a play that develops the main action [Late 16thC. Via modern Latin from Greek, where it was formed from *epiteinein* 'to intensify, stretch upon', from *teinein* 'to stretch'.]

epitaxy /éppi taksi/, **epitaxis** /éppi táksiss/ *n.* growth of a layer of crystal on a single crystal of another substance [Mid-20thC. From French *épitaxie*, literally 'growth on', from Greek *taxis* 'growth'.] —**epitaxial** /-táksi əl/ *adj.*

epithalamium /éppithə láymi əm/ (*plural* **-a** /-mi ə/), **epithalamion** (*plural* **-a** /-mi ə/) *n.* a poem or song written or performed in celebration of a wedding [Late 16thC. From, ultimately, Greek *epithalamion*, literally '(song sung) at the bridal chamber', a form of *epithalamios*, literally 'at the bridal chamber', from *thalamos* 'bridal chamber'.] —**epithalamic** /éppithə lámmik/ *adj.*

epithelia plural of **epithelium**

epithelial /éppi théeli əl/ *adj.* used to describe tissue that forms a thin protective layer on exposed bodily surfaces and forms the lining of internal cavities, ducts, and organs

epithelialise *vti.* = **epithelialize**

epithelialization /éppi théeli ə lī záysh'n/, **epithelialisation** *n.* the covering of a surface by the development of epithelial tissue, as in the healing of a wound

epithelialize /éppi théeli ə līz/ (**-izes, -izing, -ized**), **epithelialise** (**-ises, -ising, -ised**), **epithelize** /éppi théelīz/ (**-izes, -izing, -ized**), **epithelise** (**-ises, -ising, -ised**) *vti.* to become or cause to become covered with epithelial tissue, as in the healing of a wound

epithelise *vti.* = **epithelialize**

epithelium /éppi théeli əm/ (*plural* **-a** /-li ə/ *or* **-ums**) *n.* a thin layer of tightly packed cells lining internal cavities, ducts, and organs of animals and covering exposed bodily surfaces, especially in healing wounds [Mid-18thC. From modern Latin, where it was formed from Greek *thēlē* 'teat, nipple'; from its originally being applied to tissue with a nipple-like surface.]

epithelize /éppi théelīz/ *vti.* = **epithelialize** —**epithelization** /éppi théeli záysh'n/ *n.*

epithermal /éppi thúrm'l/ *adj.* used to describe veins of gold or silver originally formed deep within the Earth's crust from ascending hot solutions

epithet /éppi thet/ *n.* **1.** LING **DESCRIPTIVE WORD ADDED TO SB'S NAME** a descriptive word or phrase added to or substituted for the name of a person or thing, highlighting a characteristic feature or quality ○ *easy to see how she earned herself the epithet 'The All-Knowing'* **2.** LANG **OFFENSIVE TERM** an abusive insulting word or phrase **3.** BIOL **PART OF A TAXONOMIC NAME** in biological classification, the specific name that follows the generic name, e.g. 'sapiens' in 'Homo sapiens' [Late 16thC. Directly or via French *épithète* from Latin *epitheton* 'sth added', from Greek *epitheto*, past participle of *epitithenai* 'to put on', from *tithenai* 'to place'.] —**epithetic** /-théttik/ *adj.* —**epithetical** /-théttik'l/ *adj.*

epitome /i píttəmi/ *n.* **1. TYPICAL EXAMPLE** a highly representative example of a type, class, or characteristic ○ *Isn't she just the epitome of elegance?* **2.** LITERAT **SUMMARY OF A WRITTEN WORK** a brief summary of a piece of written work (*formal*) [Early 16thC. Via Latin from Greek, from *epitemnein* 'to cut short', from *temnein* 'to cut'.]

epitomize /i píttə mīz/ (**-omizes, -omizing, -omized**), **epitomise** (**-ises, -ising, -ised**) *vt.* **1. EXEMPLIFY** to be a highly representative example of sth ○ *This incident epitomizes all that is wrong with modern society.* **2.** LITERAT **SUMMARIZE** to write a brief summary of a piece of writing (*formal*) —**epitomization** /i píttə mī záysh'n/ *n.* —**epitomist** /-mist/ *n.*

epizoic /éppi zō ik/ *adj.* **1.** BIOL **LIVING ON THE EXTERIOR OF ANIMAL** used to describe a nonparasitic animal or plant that lives on the external surface of a living animal **2.** BOT **DISPERSED BY ANIMALS** used to describe plants whose seeds or spores are dispersed by being attached to the coats of animals —**epizoism** /-zō izzəm/ *n.*

epizoon /éppi zṓ on/ (*plural* **-a** /-ə/), **epizoite** /-zṓ īt/ *n.* an organism that lives on the external surface of a living animal [Mid-19thC. From modern Latin, literally 'on an animal', from Greek *zōion* 'animal'.] —**epizoan** *adj.*

epizootic /éppi zō óttik/ *adj.* **RELATING TO AN EPIDEMIC OF ANIMAL DISEASE** used to describe an outbreak of disease that rapidly affects many animals in a given area at the same time ■ *n.* **DISEASE SIMULTANEOUSLY AFFECTING MANY ANIMALS** a disease that rapidly affects a large number of animals in a given area at the same time [Late 18thC. From French *épizootique*, literally 'at animals', ultimately from Greek *zōion* 'animal'.] —**epizootically** /-óttikli/ *adv.*

e pluribus unum /áy plóor ribəss óonəm, -yóonəm/ one out of many (*used as the motto of the United States*) [Latin]

EPNS *abbr.* electroplated nickel silver

epoch /ée pok/ *n.* **1.** HISTORY, TIME **SIGNIFICANT PERIOD** a significant period in history or in sb's life ○ *The invention of the telephone marked an epoch in the development of international communication.* **2. START OF A HISTORICALLY SIGNIFICANT PERIOD** the beginning of a long period of history considered particularly significant ○ *His accession to the throne marked the beginning of a new epoch.* **3.** GEOL **UNIT OF GEOLOGICAL TIME** a unit of geological time that is a division of a period and is characterized by rock formation ○ *the Holocene and Pleistocene epochs of the Quaternary period* **4.** ASTRON **MOMENT IN TIME AS A REFERENCE POINT** a precise moment in time arbitrarily chosen as a reference point for defining the position of celestial bodies [Early 17thC. Via modern Latin *epocha* from Greek *epokhē* 'pause (in time)', literally 'holding back', from, ultimately, *ekhein* 'to hold'.]

epochal /éppok'l, ée pok'l/ *adj.* **1. VERY SIGNIFICANT** highly significant or momentous ○ *Her resignation had an epochal impact on the company.* **2. CHARACTERISTIC OF AN EPOCH** characteristic of or relating to a long period of history considered particularly significant (*formal*)

epoch-making *adj.* having great importance or momentous significance ○ *Galileo's epoch-making discoveries*

epode /éppōd/ *n.* **1.** THEATRE **PART OF A LYRIC ODE** the part of a lyric ode in classical Greek drama that follows the strophe and the antistrophe **2.** POETRY **TYPE OF LYRIC ODE** a type of lyric ode characterized by couplets made up of a long line followed by a shorter one [Early 17thC. Directly or via French *épode* from Latin *epodos*, from Greek *epōidos* 'sung after', from *ōidē* 'song'.]

eponym /éppə nim/ *n.* **1. PERSON AFTER WHOM STH IS NAMED** the name of a person or mythical character from which another name or term is derived **2.** MED **MEDICAL NAME FROM A PERSON** a medical name, e.g. of a disease, coming from the name of a person **3.** LANGUAGE **NAME DERIVED FROM A PERSON** a name derived from the name of a person or mythical character. For example, 'Rome' is an eponym coming from 'Romulus'. [Mid-19thC. From Greek *epōnumos* 'given as a name', literally 'name on', from *onuma* 'name'.] —**eponymic** /éppə nímmik/ *adj.*

eponymous /i pónniməss/ *adj.* having the name that is used as the title or name of sth else, especially the title of a book, play, or film ○ *the eponymous hero* —**eponymously** *adv.*

EPOS /ée poss/ *abbr.* electronic point of sale

epoxide /i póksīd/ *n.* a chemical compound containing a three-membered ring consisting of an oxygen atom bonded to each of two carbon atoms [Mid-20thC. Coined from EPI- + OXIDE.]

epoxy /i póksi/ *adj.* **RELATING TO EPOXIDE** relating to an epoxide or epoxy resin ■ *n.* (*plural* **-ies**) = **epoxy resin** ■ *vt.* (**-ies, -ying, -ied**) **STICK WITH EPOXY RESIN** to stick one thing to another using epoxy resin [Mid-20thC. Coined from EPI- + OXY-.]

epoxy resin, epoxide resin *n.* a tough synthetic resin that sets after the application of heat or pressure, contains epoxy groups, and is used in adhesives and surface coatings

Epping Forest /épping-/ area of ancient woodland in Essex, southeastern England

EPROM /ée prom/ *n.* an integrated circuit that can be programmed by a manufacturer and subsequently erased and reprogrammed by a user to correct an error in the original program or to add a function. Full form **erasable-programmable read-only memory**

eps *abbr.* earnings per share

epsilon /ep sílən, épsilon/ *n.* the fifth letter of the Greek alphabet, represented in the English alphabet as 'e'. See table at **alphabet** [Early 18thC. From Greek *e psilon* 'short e' (literally 'bare e').]

Epsom /épsəm/ town in Surrey, southeastern England. There is a racecourse on Epsom Downs, where the Derby horse race is run. Population: 69,200 (1995).

Epsom salts *n.* a bitter-tasting medicinal preparation of hydrated magnesium sulphate formerly widely used as a purgative or to help reduce swelling. Formula: $MgSO_4.7H_2O$. (*takes a singular verb*) [Mid-18thC. Named after EPSOM: the salts were originally obtained from the water of a mineral spring there.]

Epstein /ép stīn/, **Sir Jacob** (1880–1959) US-born British sculptor. His massively powerful, usually nude figures, including *Genesis* (1930), caused an uproar. His later portrait bronzes and monumental works were more immediately popular and less controversial.

Epstein-Barr virus /ép stīn báar-/ *n.* a virus believed to cause glandular fever and associated with Burkitt's lymphoma and some carcinomas [Mid-20thC. Named after the British virologists M.A. *Epstein* (born 1921) and Y.M. *Barr* (born 1932), who discovered it.]

EQ *n.* the ratio of educational attainment to chronological age. Full form **educational quotient**

eq. *abbr.* **1.** equal **2.** equation **3.** equivalent

equable /ékwəb'l/ *adj.* **1. CALM** calm and not easily disturbed ○ *She maintained the most equable of temperaments despite her financial problems.* **2. NOT EXTREME** free from variation and marked extremes [Mid-16thC. From Latin *aequabilis*, from *aequare* (see EQUATE).] —**equability** /ékwə bílləti/ *n.* —**equableness** /ékwəb'lnəss/ *n.* —**equably** *adv.*

equal /éekwəl/ *adj.* **1. IDENTICAL** identical in size, quantity, value, or standard ○ *equal quantities of flour and sugar* **2. WITH THE SAME RIGHTS** having the same privileges, rights, status, and opportunities as others ○ *with all citizens equal before the law* **3. WITH AN EVEN BALANCE** evenly balanced between opposing sides ○ *hoping for a more equal match in the second game* **4. EQUIPPED WITH THE NECESSARY QUALITIES** equipped with the necessary qualities or means to accomplish sth ○ *didn't think he would be equal to the task* **5. EQUIVALENT** having the same effect, value, or meaning as another ■ *n.* **SB OR STH EQUAL** sb or sth equal in quality to another ○ *As a defender he has no equal in the Premiership.* ■ *v.* (**equals, equalling, equalled**) **1.** *vt.* MATH **HAVE SAME VALUE AS** to be equal to, usually in value ○ *Two plus two equals four.* **2.** *vt.* **DO STH EQUAL TO STH ELSE** to do, produce, or achieve sth to the same standard or of the same value as sth else ○ *And with that jump, she has equalled the world record.* **3.** *vi.* **BECOME EQUAL** to become identical or the same ○ *It will all equal out in the end.* [14thC. From Latin *aequalis*, from *aequus* (see EQUATE).] ◇ **first among equals** the most powerful or influential person in a group whose members are supposed to have equal status

equal-area *adj.* on a map projection, accurately representing the relative sizes of regions that are of equal area, although distorting shape and direction

equalise *vti.* = **equalize**

equalitarian /i kwólli táiri ən/ *n.*, *adj.* = **egalitarian** —**equalitarianism** *n.*

equality /i kwólləti/ (*plural* **-ties**) *n.* **1. STATE OF BEING EQUAL** rights, treatment, quantity, or value equal to all others in a given group ○ *full equality under the law* **2.** MATH **EQUATION WITH EQUAL QUANTITIES** an equation in which the quantities on either side of an equal sign are the same

equalize /éekwə līz/ (**-izes, -izing, -ized**), **equalise** (**-ises, -ising, -ised**) *v.* **1.** *vt.* **MAKE EQUAL** to make things uniform or equal ○ *You must equalize the liquid levels in each bottle.* **2.** *vi.* SPORTS **ACHIEVE SAME SCORE** to score a point or goal that brings a score level with that of an opponent ○ *They equalized just before half-time.* —**equalization** /éekwə lī záysh'n/ *n.*

equalizer /éekwə līzər/, **equaliser** *n.* **1. SB OR STH THAT EQUALIZES** sb or sth that makes things uniform or equal **2.** ELECTRON ENG **ELECTRONIC SOUND ADJUSTER** an electronic device used to reduce distortion in a sound system by internally adjusting the system's response to different audio frequencies **3.** SPORTS **GOAL OR POINT THAT LEVELS SCORES** a goal or point that brings a person or team's score level with that of an opponent **4.** *US* ARMS **WEAPON** a dangerous weapon, e.g. a knife or gun (*slang*)

equally /éekwəli/ *adv.* **1. IN SAME WAY** in an identical or uniform way ○ *treat people equally* **2. TO SAME EXTENT** to the same degree or extent ○ *This issue is equally important.* **3. IN SAME-SIZED AMOUNTS** in parts or amounts of the same size ○ *Divide it equally between four people.* **4. AT THE SAME TIME** used to introduce a second statement that is of equal importance to the first but may contrast or balance it ○ *I want the business to succeed, but equally, I don't want to be working all the time.*

WORD KEY: USAGE

equally or **as** You can say *She is a brilliant pianist, and her brother is equally talented* or *She is a brilliant pianist, and her brother is as talented*, but not *She is a brilliant pianist, and her brother is equally as talented.*

equal opportunity *n.* the availability of the same rights, position, and status to all people, regardless of gender, sexual preference, age, race, ethnicity, or religion (*often used in the plural*) ○ *the implementation of an equal opportunities policy*

equal sign, equals sign *n.* a mathematical symbol (=) used to indicate that two or more numbers, symbols, or terms have the same value as each other

equal temperament *n.* MUSIC the division of a musical octave into 12 equal half steps in the tuning of an instrument

equanimity /ékwə nímməti, éekwə-/ *n.* evenness of temper even under stress ○ *faced his critical constituents with equanimity* [Early 17thC. From Latin *aequanimitas*, from *aequus* 'even' (see EQUATE) + *animus* 'mind' (source of English *magnanimous*).] —**equanimous** /i kwánniməss, i kwónni-/ *adj.*

equate /i kwáyt, ee-/ (**equates, equating, equated**) *v.* **1.** *vt.* **CONSIDER AS EQUIVALENT** to treat, show, or consider sth as equivalent to sth else ○ *equating money with happiness* **2.** *vt.* MATH **FORM AN EQUATION** to form an equation involving an equality **3.** *vi.* **APPEAR TO BE EQUAL** to be or appear to be the same (*formal*) ○ *Their two accounts of the incident seem to equate.* [15thC. From Latin *aequat-*, the past participle stem of *aequare* 'to make equal', from *aequus* 'equal, even' (source of English *egalitarian, adequate*, and *iniquity*).] —**equatability** /i kwáytə bílləti, ee-/ *n.* —**equatable** /i kwáytəb'l, ee-/ *adj.*

equation /i kwáyzh'n/ *n.* **1.** MATH **STATEMENT OF EQUALITY** a mathematical statement that two expressions, usually divided by an equals sign, are of the same value **2. ACT OF REGARDING AS EQUAL** the act or process of making things equal or considering them to be equal **3. STATE OF BEING EQUAL** the state of being the same or equivalent ○ *bring the balance of power into equation* **4. SITUATION INVOLVING MANY VARIABLE FACTORS** a situation that has two or more variable elements to be considered ○ *The selling option just does not enter into the equation.* **5.** CHEM **REPRESENTATION OF A CHEMICAL REACTION** a written representation of the reactants and products in a chemical reaction —**equational** *adj.* —**equationally** *adv.*

equation of state *n.* CHEM an equation that states the relationship between the pressure, temperature, and volume of a gas or liquid

equation of time *n.* the difference between apparent solar time and mean solar time, usually expressed as a correction to the apparent time, and varying in a complex annual pattern between maxima of about fifteen minutes in February and November

equator /i kwáytər/ *n.* **1.** GEOG **IMAGINARY CIRCLE AROUND EARTH** the imaginary great circle around the Earth that is the same distance from the North and South Poles and divides the Earth into the northern and southern hemispheres **2.** ASTRON **IMAGINARY CIRCLE AROUND A CELESTIAL BODY** the imaginary great circle around a celestial body that is everywhere the same distance from the poles **3.** GEOM CIRCLE DIVIDING A SPHERE INTO TWO a circle that divides a sphere or other surface into two equal parts **4.** ASTRON = **celestial equator** [14thC. Directly or via French *équator* from medieval Latin *aequator*, in the phrase *aequator diei et noctis* 'equalizer of day and night', from *aequare* (see EQUATE).]

equatorial /ékwə táwri əl, eékwə-/ *adj.* **1.** OF EQUATOR relating to or present near the equator **2.** IN EQUATOR'S PLANE situated in the plane of an equator —**equatorially** /ékwə táwri əli, eékwə-/ *adv.*

equatorial current *n.* a current that moves in a westerly direction near the surface of an ocean at the equator

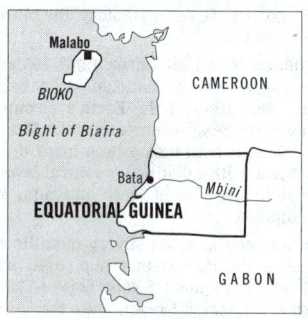

Equatorial Guinea

Equatorial Guinea independent republic in western Africa comprising a mainland section, Río Muni, and several islands. Language: Spanish. Currency: CFA franc. Capital: Malabo. Population: 442,516 (1997). Area: 28,051 sq. km/10,831 sq. mi. Official name **Republic of Equatorial Guinea**

equatorial plate *n.* the plane midway between the poles of the spindle of a dividing cell, where chromosomes are aligned

equatorial telescope *n.* an astronomical telescope mounted so that it allows a celestial body to be kept in view without adjustment as the Earth rotates. This is accomplished by mounting it on two axes at right angles to each other, the one about which it rotates being parallel to the Earth's axis.

equerry /i kwérri, ékwəri/ (*plural* -**ries**) *n.* **1.** MIL PERSONAL ATTENDANT OF BRITISH SOVEREIGN an officer who is the personal attendant of the British monarch or a member of the royal family **2.** MIL, EQU OFFICER RESPONSIBLE FOR ROYAL HORSES in the past, an officer in an aristocratic or royal household who was responsible for the supervision of the horses [Early 16thC. Via obsolete French *escurie* (source of French *écurie* 'stable') from Old French *esquierie* 'company of squires, prince's stables', from *esquier* 'squire' (see ESQUIRE), perhaps influenced by Latin *equus* 'horse'.]

equestrian /i kwéstri ən/ *adj.* **1.** OF HORSES relating to horses or riding **2.** DEPICTING SB ON HORSEBACK depicting sb mounted on a horse ○ *an equestrian statue* **3.** OF MOUNTED SOLDIERS composed of soldiers on horseback ■ *n.* SKILLED RIDER sb who is skilled at riding horses or performing on horseback [Mid-17thC. Formed from Latin *equester* 'belonging to a horseman', from *eques* 'horseman, knight', from *equus* 'horse'.] —**equestrianism** *n.*

equestrienne /i kwéstri én/ *n.* a woman who is skilled at riding horses or performing on horseback [Mid-19thC. Formed from EQUESTRIAN on the model of French feminine nouns ending in -*enne*.]

equi- *prefix.* equal ○ *equimolar* [From Latin *aequus* (source of English *equal*)]

equiangular /eékwi áng gyŏŏlər, ékwi-/ *adj.* used to describe a geometric figure in which all the angles are equal [Mid-17thC. Formed from late Latin *equiangulus*, from Latin *angulus* 'corner' (see ANGLE).]

equidistant /eékwi dístənt, ékwi dístənt/ *adj.* situated at the same distance from two or more places or points ○ *Birmingham is equidistant from Leeds and London.* [Late 16thC. From French *équidistant* or the medieval Latin stem *equidistant-*, from the Latin stem *distant-* (see DISTANT).] —**equidistance** *n.* —**equidistantly** *adv.*

equilateral /eékwi láttərəl, ékwi-/ *adj.* WITH EQUAL SIDES used to describe a geometric figure in which all the sides are of equal length ■ *n.* **1.** EQUILATERAL FIGURE a geometric figure with all of its sides of equal length

2. SIDE OF AN EQUILATERAL FIGURE any side of a geometric figure that is the same length as the other sides [Late 16thC. Directly or via French *équilateral* from late Latin *aequilateralis*, from Latin *lateralis* (see LATERAL).] —**equilaterally** *adv.*

equilibrant /i kwíllibrənt/ *n.* a force able to balance out another force and produce an equilibrium [Late 19thC. Via French *équilibrant* from, ultimately, *équilibre* 'balance', from Latin *aequilibrium* (see EQUILIBRIUM).]

equilibrate /eékwi lí brayt, i kwílli brayt/ (-**brates**, -**brating**, -**brated**) *vti.* to be evenly balanced, or counterbalance sth, or bring sth into a state of balance [Mid-17thC. From late Latin *aequilibrare*, from *libra* (see EQUILIBRIUM).] —**equilibration** /eékwi lí bráysh'n, i kwílli-/ *n.* —**equilibrator** /i kwílli braytər/ *n.* —**equilibratory** /i kwílli bráytəri/ *adj.*

equilibrist /i kwíllibrist/ *n.* a performer skilled in the art of balancing, especially tightrope walking (*dated or formal*)

equilibrium /eékwi líbbri əm, ékwi-/ (*plural* -**ums** or -**a** /-ri ə/) *n.* **1.** SITUATION OF BALANCE a state or situation in which opposing forces or factors balance each other out and stability is attained **2.** EMOTIONAL STABILITY a mental state of calmness and composure **3.** PHYS, CHEM BALANCE BETWEEN FORCES a static or dynamic state in which all forces or processes are in balance and there is no resultant change **4.** BODILY BALANCE a physical state or sense of being able to maintain bodily balance [Early 17thC. From Latin *aequilibrium* 'equal balance', from *libra* 'balance' (source of English *deliberate*, and of the symbol £ and the abbreviation *lb*).]

equimolar /eékwi mốlər, ékwi-/ *adj.* CHEM with an equal concentration of moles in one litre of solution

equimolecular /eékwimə lékyŏŏlər, ékwimə-/ *adj.* CHEM used to describe a substance or mixture that has the same number of molecules as another

equine /é kwīn, eé kwīn/ *adj.* **1.** ZOOL OF HORSES relating to, belonging to, or affecting horses **2.** RESEMBLING A HORSE characteristic of or similar to a horse in appearance or behaviour **3.** ZOOL BELONGING TO THE HORSE FAMILY belonging to or characteristic of the family of mammals that includes horses, zebras, and donkeys ■ *n.* ZOOL HORSE OR THEIR RELATIVES a horse or other member of the horse family [Late 18thC. From Latin *equinus*, from *equus* 'horse'.]

equinoctial /eékwi nóksh'l, ékwi nóksh'l/ *adj.* **1.** TIME OCCURRING AT AN EQUINOX happening at or near either of the two equinoxes **2.** BOT WITH FLOWERS OPEN AT DEFINITE TIMES used to describe a plant whose flowers open and close at specific times of day **3.** ASTRON OF THE CELESTIAL EQUATOR relating to the celestial equator ■ *n.* **1.** METEOROL STORM AT AN EQUINOX a storm or strong wind that occurs at a time when day and night are the same length (**equinox**) **2.** ASTRON = **celestial equator** [14thC. From French *équinoctial* from, ultimately, Latin *aequinoctium* (see EQUINOX).]

equinoctial circle *n.* ASTRON = **celestial equator**

equinoctial point *n.* either of the two points on the celestial sphere where the Sun crosses the celestial equator. The points are called respectively the First Point of Aries and the First Point of Libra.

equinoctial year *n.* = **solar year**

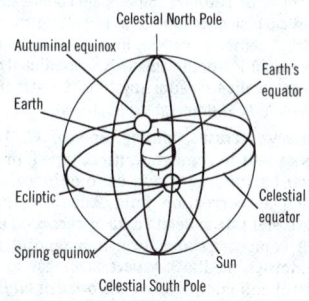

Equinox: Diagram showing positions of Sun and Earth at spring and autumnal equinoxes

equinox /eékwi noks, ékwi-/ *n.* **1.** TIME OF EQUAL DAY AND NIGHT either of the two annual crossings of the equator by the Sun, once in each direction, when

the length of day and night are approximately equal everywhere on Earth. The equinoxes occur around March 21 and September 23. **2.** = **equinoctial point** [14thC. Directly or via French *équinoxe* from Latin *aequinoctium*, literally 'equal night', from *nox* 'night'.]

equip /i kwíp/ (**equips**, **equipping**, **equipped**) *vt.* **1.** PROVIDE WITH NECESSITIES to provide sb or sth with what is needed for a particular activity or purpose, e.g. with the appropriate tools, supplies, parts, or clothing ○ *a computer equipped with a modem and a CD-ROM drive* **2.** PREPARE TO ACCOMPLISH STH to prepare sb with the necessary education, training, or experience to succeed at a task or role in life (*often passive*) ○ *I'm sorry, but I don't feel equipped to answer that question.* [Early 16thC. From French *équiper*, probably formed from Old Norse *skipa* 'to fit out a ship', from *skip* 'ship'.] —**equipper** *n.*

equip. *abbr.* equipment

equipage /ékwipij/ *n.* **1.** TRANSP, EQU WELL-EQUIPPED CARRIAGE a horse-drawn carriage, especially a luxurious one, or a carriage together its with horses and attendants **2.** EQUIPMENT AND SUPPLIES FOR EXPEDITIONS the necessary equipment and supplies for an undertaking, especially a military expedition or ship's journey **3.** EMPLOYEES AND ATTENDANTS the retinue of a person of high rank in society (*archaic*) [Mid-16thC. Originally denoting the crew, later the equipping of a ship, hence the equipment provided.]

equipartition /eékwi paar tísh'n, ékwi-/ *n.* the equal distribution of energy among the components of motion, such as linear movement and rotation, of the gas molecules in a system

equipment /i kwípmənt/ *n.* **1.** NECESSARY ITEMS the tools, clothing, or other items needed for a particular purpose or activity ○ *camping equipment* **2.** PROVIDING SB WITH EQUIPMENT the equipping of sb or sth with what is necessary for a particular purpose or activity **3.** PERSONAL RESOURCES FOR SUCCESS the intellectual and emotional resources that enable a person to succeed at a task or role in life

equipoise /ékwi poyz, eékwi-/ *n.* (*formal*) **1.** BALANCED STATE a condition where weights are in balance or there is a balance between different social, emotional, or intellectual influences **2.** STH CAUSING BALANCE sth that creates a balanced state, usually by counterbalancing some other force or thing ■ *vt.* (-**poises**, -**poising**, -**poised**) COUNTERBALANCE to counterbalance a weight or influence

equipollent /eékwi póllənt, ékwi-/ *adj.* having the same weight, influence, validity, or effect as another, or as each other (*formal*) [14thC. From Old French *equipolent*, from, ultimately, Latin *pollere* 'to be strong'.] —**equipollence** *n.* —**equipollency** *n.* —**equipollently** *adv.*

equiponderant /eékwi póndərənt, ékwi-/ *adj.* equal, or evenly balanced, in weight, influence, or effect (*formal*) [Mid-17thC. From medieval Latin *aequiponderant-*, the present participle stem of *aequiponderare* 'to weigh the same', from *ponderare* 'to weigh' (source of English *ponder*).] —**equiponderance** *n.* —**equiponderancy** *n.*

equiponderate /eékwi póndə rayt, ékwi-/ (-**ates**, -**ating**, -**ated**) *vt.* to equal the strength, power, or effect of sth, creating a state of balance (*formal*) [Mid-17thC. From medieval Latin *aequiponderare* (see EQUIPONDERANT), or an alteration of *preponderate* by substitution of *equi*- for *pre*-.]

equipotential /eékwipə ténsh'l, ékwi-/ *adj.* used to describe a surface that has the same electric or gravitational potential at all points —**equipotentiality** /eékwipə ténshi álləti, ékwi-/ *n.*

equiprobable /eékwi próbbəb'l, ékwi-/ *adj.* equally likely to be true or to occur according to logic or mathematics

equitable /ékwitəb'l/ *adj.* **1.** FAIR characterized by justice or fairness and impartiality towards those involved (*formal*) **2.** LAW RELATING TO THE LAW OF EQUITY applicable under the law of equity as distinguished from common or statute law [Mid-16thC. From French *équitable*, from *équité* (see EQUITY).] —**equitableness** *n.* —**equitably** *adv.*

equitation /ékwi táysh'n/ *n.* the skill and theory of riding horses (*formal*) [Mid-16thC. Directly or via French *équitation* from the Latin stem *equitation-*, from *equitare* 'to ride on horseback', from, ultimately, *equus* 'horse'.]

equites /ékwi teez/ *npl.* **1. ANCIENT ROMAN CAVALRY** the cavalry of ancient Rome **2. PRIVILEGED ROMANS** the privileged class of ancient Romans, ranking just below the senators, whose members served as cavalry [Early 17thC. From Latin, plural of *eques* 'horse-rider', from *equus* 'horse'.]

equity /ékwiti/ *n.* (*plural* **-ties**) **1. FAIRNESS** actions, treatment of others, or a general condition characterized by justice, fairness, and impartiality (*formal*) **2.** LAW **MODIFICATION OF COMMON LAW** the system of jurisprudence that supplements common and statutory law, when those bodies of law are inadequate in the attainment of justice **3.** LAW **JUSTICE TEMPERED BY ETHICS** justice applied in conformity with the law, but influenced at the same time by principles of ethics and fair play **4.** LAW **FAIR CLAIM** a claim that is judged to be just and fair **5.** FIN **PART OF THE VALUE PAID FOR** the value of a piece of property over and above any mortgage or other liabilities relating to it ■ **equities** *npl.* STOCK EXCH **SHARES ENTITLING HOLDER TO PROFITS** shares of stock in a corporation that pay the holder some of the company's profits [14thC. Via French *équité* from, ultimately, Latin *aequus* 'fair' (see EQUATE).]

Equity /ékwiti/ *n.* the trade union for actors

equity capital *n.* funds for a business raised by selling shares or by retaining earnings

equity of redemption *n.* the right of a mortgagor to redeem mortgaged property by paying the sum owed within a reasonable time after the date on which payment was due

equiv. *abbr.* equivalent

equivalence /i kwívvələnss/, **equivalency** /-lənssi/ *n.* **1. BEING THE SAME OR SIMILAR** the fact of being the same, effectively the same, or interchangeable with sth else **2.** MATH, LOGIC **RELATIONSHIP BETWEEN STATEMENTS** the relationship between two statements, both of which are either true or false, and each of which can be proved from the other

equivalence relation *n.* the relation between members of a set that is reflexive, symmetrical, and transitive, e.g. if 'a' equals 'b' and 'b' equals 'c', then 'a' equals 'c'

equivalency *n.* = **equivalence**

equivalent /i kwívvələnt/ *adj.* **1. EQUAL** being the same, or effectively the same, in effect, value, or meaning as sth and usually interchangeable with it ○ *That's equivalent to the amount of energy needed to power a single light bulb.* **2.** GEOM **OF THE SAME SIZE BUT DIFFERENT SHAPE** used to describe geometric figures that have different shapes but equal areas, e.g. a circle and a square, or equal volumes, e.g. a cylinder and a cube **3.** MATH **WITH THE SAME SOLUTION** used to describe equations that share a common solution or solutions, e.g. for both 2x-3 = x+2 and x-5 = 0 the solution is x = 5 **4.** MATH, LOGIC **IN AN EQUIVALENCE RELATION** used to describe members of a set that are in a reflexive, symmetrical, and transitive relation with each other ■ *n.* **1. STH CONSIDERED THE SAME** sth that is considered to be equal to or have the same effect, value, or meaning as sth else ○ *He's the Italian equivalent of the Chancellor of the Exchequer.* **2.** CHEM = **equivalent weight** [15thC. From French *équivalent*, from, ultimately, late Latin *aequivalere* 'to be of equal value', from Latin *valere* 'to be strong' (see VALENCY).] —**equivalently** *adv.*

equivalent weight *n.* CHEM the mass of a substance that will combine with or replace 8 parts by weight of oxygen or 1.008 parts of hydrogen

equivocal /i kwívvək'l/ *adj.* **1. AMBIGUOUS** open to more than one interpretation, especially in being deliberately expressed in an ambiguous way in an attempt to mislead sb ○ *an equivocal reply to a tough question* **2. DIFFICULT TO INTERPRET** difficult to interpret, understand, or respond to ○ *Their stance on this issue is equivocal and nobody knows how they are likely to react.* **3. RAISING DOUBTS** arousing doubts and suspicions, especially about sb's honesty or sincerity ○ *To arrive at the peace talks with an armed guard was an equivocal gesture.* [Mid-16thC. Formed from late Latin *aequivocus* (see EQUIVOCATE).] —**equivocality** /i kwívvə kállәti/ *n.* —**equivocalness** /i kwívvək'lnəss/ *n.* —**equivocally** /-kli/ *adv.*

equivocate /i kwívvə kayt/ (**-cates, -cating, -cated**) *vi.* to speak vaguely or ambiguously, especially in order to mislead ○ *When pressed for a firm answer, she equivocated.* [15thC. From late Latin *aequivocare*, from *aequivocus* 'ambiguous', literally 'equal-voiced', from Latin *vox* 'voice' (see VOICE).] —**equivocatingly** *adv.* —**equivocator** *n.* —**equivocatory** *adj.*

equivocation /i kwívvə káysh'n/ *n.* **1. USE OF AMBIGUITY** the use of vague or ambiguous and sometimes misleading language ○ *What we ask for is facts: what we get is equivocation or downright lies.* **2. AMBIGUOUS STATEMENT** an expression or statement that is vague or ambiguous and often deliberately misleading ○ *Their equivocations could not disguise the fact that corruption was rife in the committee.* **3.** LOGIC **WRONG LOGICAL CONCLUSION** an invalid conclusion based on statements in which one term has two different meanings

equivoque /ékwi vōk, ēkwi-/, **equivoke** *n.* (*formal*) **1. PLAY ON WORDS** an amusing use of an ambiguous word **2. AMBIGUOUS WORD OR PHRASE** a word or phrase with a double meaning **3. AMBIGUITY** ambiguity, double meaning, or misleading words and expressions [Early 17thC. Directly or via French *équivoque* from late Latin *aequivocus* (see EQUIVOCATE).]

Equuleus /e kwо́oli əss/ *n.* the second-smallest constellation, situated in the northern hemisphere between Pegasus and Aquarius

er /ur/ *interj.* used to express hesitation [Mid-19thC. An imitation of the sound.]

Er *symbol.* erbium

ER *abbr.* **1.** *US* emergency room **2.** Elizabetha Regina **3.** Eduardus Rex

-er[1] *suffix.* **1.** one that performs or undergoes a particular action ○ *adjuster* ○ *fryer* **2.** a person connected with, often as an occupation ○ *trucker* **3.** a person from a particular place ○ *Londoner* ○ *foreigner* [Partly Old English *-ere*, partly via Anglo-Norman from, ultimately, Latin *-arius*, and partly from Old French *-eor* (see OR[1])]

-er[2] *suffix.* more ○ *greener* ○ *slower* [Old English *-re*, *-ra*]

era /éerə/ *n.* **1. TIME DISTINCTIVE PERIOD OF HISTORY** a period of time made distinctive by a significant development, feature, event, or personality ○ *during the postwar era* **2.** TIME **PERIOD WITH OWN CHRONOLOGICAL SYSTEM** a time period within which years are consecutively numbered from a particular significant event that provides its starting point ○ *the Christian era* **3.** TIME **DATE THAT BEGINS PERIOD** a significant date or event that is regarded as the beginning of a new period of time ○ *The agreement marked an era in US-Soviet relations.* **4.** PREHIST **DIVISION OF EARTH'S HISTORY** a division of geological time composed of several periods [Mid-17thC. From late Latin *aera* 'number used as a basis for counting'.]

ERA *abbr.* **1.** *US* Equal Rights Amendment ■ **2.** a law passed by Parliament in 1988, covering the publication of information on schools, open enrolment, and grant-maintained schools. Abbr of **Education Reform Act**

eradicate /i ráddi kayt/ (**-cates, -cating, -cated**) *vt.* to destroy or get rid of sth completely, so that it can never recur or return [15thC. From Latin *eradicat-*, the past participle stem of *eradicare* 'to pull up by the roots' (the original sense in English), from *radix* 'root' (source of English *radish*).] —**eradicable** *adj.* —**eradicably** /-kəbli/ *adv.* —**eradication** /i ráddi káysh'n/ *n.* —**eradicative** /i ráddikətiv/ *adj.* —**eradicator** /-kaytər/ *n.*

erase /i ráyz/ (**erases, erasing, erased**) *vt.* **1. REMOVE WRITTEN MATERIAL** to remove written, typed, or printed material by rubbing it out, or to obliterate it with sth such as correction fluid **2.** COMPUT, RECORDING **DELETE RECORDED DATA** to delete data or recorded material from a computer's memory, a magnetic tape, or other storage media **3. REMOVE OR DESTROY** to remove or destroy sth completely ○ *an ancient civilization, all traces of which had been erased over time* [Late 16thC. From Latin *eras-*, the past participle stem of *eradere* 'to scrape out', from *radere* 'to scrape' (see RAZE).] —**erasability** /i ráyzə bílləti/ *n.* —**erasable** /i ráyzəb'l/ *adj.*

eraser /i ráyzər/ *n.* = **rubber**

Erasmus /i rázməss/, **Desiderius** (1466?–1536) Dutch scholar and writer. His works, combining a Christian outlook with Renaissance humanism, influenced both sides during the Reformation. Among his many other works was a new edition of the Greek New Testament (1516).

Erastianism /i rásti ə nizəm/ *n.* the theory that the state not a church should have the ultimate authority in ecclesiastical matters [Late 17thC. Named after *Erastus*, 1524–83, a Swiss Protestant theologian, attributed with the theory.] —**Erastian** *n.*, *adj.*

erasure /i ráyzhər/ *n.* **1. REMOVAL** the complete removal or destruction of sth ○ *an erasure of data from a hard drive* **2. ERASED PLACE OR MARK** the place where sth has been rubbed out, or the mark left behind

Erato /érrətō/ *n.* in Greek mythology, the muse of lyric poetry. ◊ **Muse**

Eratosthenes /érrə tósthə neez/ (276?–196?BC) Greek astronomer and mathematician. He is best known for his calculation of the Earth's circumference, which was the most accurate until the 17th century. ■ *n.* ASTRON **CRATER ON MOON** a prominent deep crater on the Moon with a distinctive central peak, located at the southern edge of Mare Imbrium, 58 km/36 mi. in diameter

erbium /úrbi əm/ *n.* a soft silvery metallic chemical element of the rare-earth group, used in certain alloys and as a pigment. Symbol **Er** [Mid-19thC. Named after *Ytterby*, a town in Sweden, where the first rare-earth mineral was discovered.]

ere /air/ *prep.*, *conj.* before or earlier in time than (*literary or archaic*) [Old English *ǣr*]

Erebus, Mount /érribəss/ active volcano on the eastern coast of Ross Island, Antarctica. Height: 3,794 m/12,448 ft.

erect /i rékt/ *adj.* **1. STRAIGHT AND VERTICAL** in an upright position ○ *an erect plant stem* **2.** PHYSIOL **FIRM AND RIGID** stiff and swollen as a result of being filled with blood, e.g. when sexually aroused **3.** OPTICS **RIGHT SIDE UP** used to describe an optically produced image that is the correct way up and not inverted **4. ALERT** in an alert state (*archaic*) ■ *v.* (**erects, erecting, erected**) **1.** *vt.* **CONSTRUCT** to build a structure from basic parts and materials ○ *The building was erected in 1885.* **2.** *vt.* **PUT TOGETHER** to fit sth together and put it into position so that it is ready for use **3.** *vt.* **SET UPRIGHT** to fix sth in an upright position **4.** *vt.* **ESTABLISH** to bring an organization, system, or theory into being ○ *The corporation erected a new legal department just to deal with mergers and acquistions.* **5.** *vt.* GEOM **DRAW FIGURE ON BASE** to draw or construct a line or figure on a given base **6.** *vti.* PHYSIOL **BECOME OR MAKE RIGID** to become, or cause an organ to become, stiff and swollen by being filled with blood [14thC. From Latin *erectus*, past participle of *erigere* 'to set up', from *regere* 'to direct or rule' (see REGENT).] —**erectable** *adj.* —**erectly** *adv.* —**erectness** *n.*

WORD KEY: SYNONYMS

See Synonyms at ***build***.

erecter *n.* = **erector**

erectile /i rék tīl/ *adj.* capable of filling with blood under pressure, swelling, and becoming stiff —**erectility** /irek tílləti/ *n.*

erection /i réksh'n/ *n.* **1. PUTTING STH UP** the construction or setting up of sth **2.** PHYSIOL **SWELLING OF TISSUE** the swollen and stiffened state of erectile tissue, especially that of the penis, usually as a result of sexual arousal **3. STRUCTURE** sth that has been built or constructed (*formal*)

erector /i réktər/, **erecter** *n.* **1. MUSCLE** a muscle that is capable of raising or holding up a body part **2. SB WHO ERECTS THINGS** sb or sth that erects things, generally things made elsewhere

E region *n.* the middle part of the ionosphere, lying approximately 80 to 110 km/50 to 70 mi. above the Earth's surface, that reflects medium-length radio waves

erelong /air lóng/ *adv.* soon or in a short time (*archaic or literary*)

eremite /érrə mīt/ *n.* sb who lives in solitude, especially for religious reasons (*literary*) [13thC. From Old French *eremite* or late Latin *eremita* (see HERMIT).] —**eremitic** /érrə míttik/ *adj.* —**eremitical** /-míttik'l/ *adj.* —**eremitism** /érrə mī tizəm/ *n.*

erenow /air nów/ adv. previously (archaic or literary)

erethism /érrithizəm/ n. excessive sensitivity of a body part to stimuli (technical) [Early 19thC. From French éréthisme, from, ultimately, Greek erethizein 'to irritate'.] —**erethismic** /érri thízmik/ adj. —**erethistic** /-thístik/ adj. —**erethitic** /-thíttik/ adj.

erewhile /air wîl/, **erewhiles** /-wîlz/ adv. some time ago (archaic or literary)

erf /urf/ (plural **erfs** or **erven** /úrvən/) n. S Africa a small plot of land on which to build, usually in urban areas [Late 17thC. From Dutch, 'land, yard'.]

erg[1] /urg/ n. the unit of energy or work in the cgs system equal to the work done by a force of one dyne acting through a distance of one centimetre. 1 erg is equivalent to 10^7 joule. [Late 19thC. From Greek ergon 'work'.]

erg[2] /urg/ (plural **ergs** or **areg** /ə rég/) n. a large, relatively flat area of desert covered with shifting windswept sand, especially in the Sahara [Late 19thC. Via French from Arabic 'irk, 'erg.]

ergative /úrgətiv/ adj. GRAM **1.** ALLOWING OBJECT TO BE SUBJECT used to describe a class of verbs in which the object of the transitive form can be used as the subject of the intransitive form with an equivalent meaning. 'Open' is an example of an ergative verb, in that 'I opened the door' and 'The door opened' have equivalent meanings. **2.** WITH DOER OF ACTION AS OBJECT used to describe a case of nouns in languages such as Inuit and Basque in which the object of the verb acts, while the subject is affected by the action ■ n. GRAM **ERGATIVE WORD** an ergative verb or a noun in the ergative case [Mid-20thC. Formed from Greek ergatēs 'worker'.]

ergo /úrgō/ adv., conj. therefore (formal) [14thC. From Latin.]

ergocalciferol /úrgō kal síffə rol/ n. = **vitamin D**$_2$ [Mid-20thC. Coined from ERGOSTEROL + CALCIFEROL.]

ergometer /ur gómmitər/ n. an instrument for measuring muscle power or work done by muscles, e.g. when exercising [Late 19thC. Coined from Greek ergon 'work' + -METER.] —**ergometric** /úrgə méttrik/ adj.

ergonomic /úrgə nómmik/ adj. designed for maximum comfort, efficiency, safety, and ease of use, especially in the workplace —**ergonomically** adv.

ergonomics /úrgə nómmiks/ n. STUDY OF WORKPLACE DESIGN the study of how a workplace and the equipment used there can best be designed for comfort, safety, efficiency, and productivity (takes a singular verb) ■ npl. DESIGN OF WORKPLACE OR EQUIPMENT those factors or qualities in the design of sth, especially a workplace or equipment used by people at work, that contribute to comfort, safety, efficiency, and ease of use [Mid-20thC. Coined from Greek ergon 'work' on the model of ECONOMICS.] —**ergonomist** /ur gónnəmist/ n.

ergosterol /ur góstə rol/ n. a crystalline steroid alcohol that is found mainly in yeast and moulds and is converted to vitamin D$_2$ by ultraviolet light. Formula: $C_{28}H_{44}O$. [Early 20thC. Coined from ERGOT + STEROL.]

ergot /úrgət, úrgot/ n. **1.** FUNGUS ATTACKING CEREALS a disease of cereals caused by a parasitic fungus that grows in dense black masses (**sclerotia**) in the grains of the ear. Latin name: Claviceps purpurea. **2.** FUNGAL BODIES USED IN MEDICINE the dried sclerotia of an ergot fungus that yield substances used in drugs to treat migraine and to induce uterine contractions in childbirth [Late 17thC. From French, literally 'cock's spur' (of unknown origin), because the diseased grain resembles a cock's claw.] —**ergotic** /ur góttik/ adj.

ergotamine /ur góttə meen/ n. an alkaloid drug derived from ergot that causes constriction of blood vessels and is used to treat migraine. Formula: $C_{35}H_{39}N_5O_5$.

ergotism /úrgətizəm/ n. a severe toxic reaction to food containing ergot-contaminated grain or excessive amounts of drugs containing ergot derivatives. The toxin produces neurological and gastrointestinal symptoms and, if not properly treated, gangrene.

Erhard /áir haard/, **Ludwig** (1897–1977) German statesman. As finance minister, he achieved West Germany's postwar economic revival and was the Christian Democratic Chancellor from 1963 until 1966.

erica /érrikə/ (plural **-cas** or **-ca**) n. an evergreen shrub or small tree of the heath family with small leathery leaves and bell-shaped flowers. All the heaths and several heathers are types of erica. Genus: Erica. [Early 17thC. Via modern Latin, genus name, from Greek ereikē 'heath'.]

ericaceous /érri káyshəss/ adj. **1.** BELONGING TO HEATH FAMILY belonging or relating to the heath family, a group of evergreen shrubs and small trees that includes the heath, heather, rhododendron, azalea, and arbutus **2.** FOR LIME-HATING PLANTS used to describe potting compost that is suitable for ericaceous and other acid-loving or lime-hating plants

Eric the Red /érrik-/ (950?–1000?) Norwegian explorer. He was the father of Leif Ericson. Banished from Scandinavia for manslaughter, he explored Greenland (982–86), where he established the first European settlement. Real name **Eric Thorvaldson**

Eridanus /e ríddənəss/ n. an extensive but faint constellation of the southern hemisphere meandering from Orion in the north to Hydrus in the south. The bright star (**Achernar**) is located at its southern end.

Erie /éeri/ n. an extinct language formerly spoken in an area along the southern shores of Lake Erie. It was one of the Iroquoian group of the Hokan-Siouan family of North American languages. —**Erie** adj.

Erie, Lake /éeri/ lake in the United States and Canada. It is one of the five Great Lakes of North America. Area: 25,667 sq. km/9,910 sq. mi.

Erie Canal artificial inland waterway between Buffalo, on Lake Erie, and Albany, New York, where it links with the River Hudson. Length: 584 km/363 mi.

Erigena /érri jéenə, -gáynə/, **Johannes Scotus** (815?–877?) Irish-born scholar. In his fusion of traditional Christianity with neoplatonism, he was a pioneer of medieval scholasticism.

erigeron /i ríjjə ron/ (plural **-ons** or **-on**) n. a plant of the daisy family, many species of which are cultivated as ornamentals. Fleabane is a type of erigeron. Genus: Erigeron. [Early 17thC. Via Latin from Greek, literally 'early old man', from its former application to the groundsel, an early-flowering plant with fluffy white seed heads.]

Erin /érrin/ n. the country of Ireland (literary)

Erin go bragh /érrin gō braá/ interj. Ireland an expression meaning 'Ireland forever' [From ERIN + Irish go brách, go bráth, literally 'till doomsday']

Erinyes /i rínni eez/ npl. = **Furies**

eristic /e rístik/ adj. eristic, eristical ARGUMENTATIVE fond of or characterized by argument or controversy (formal) ■ n. (formal) **1.** ART OF DISPUTING the skill or practice of debating, especially in a manner involving subtle logic and specious argument **2.** DEBATER sb who is an expert or delights in argument and controversy [Mid-17thC. From Greek eristikos, from, ultimately, eris 'strife'.] —**eristically** adv.

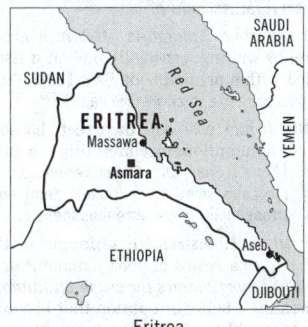

Eritrea

Eritrea /érri tráy ə/ republic on the Red Sea coast in northeastern Africa. A former Italian colony, it became part of Ethiopia in 1952 and fully independent in 1993. Language: Tigrinya, Tigre, Arabic. Currency: nakfa. Capital: Asmara. Population: 3,714,963 (1997). Area: 121,144 sq. km/46,774 sq. mi. Official name **State of Eritrea** —**Eritrean** n., adj.

erk /urk/ n. **1.** LOWLY MEMBER OF RAF an aircraftman or woman or other low-ranking member of the Royal Air Force (slang) **2.** SEAMAN a non commissioned sailor in the Royal Navy (slang) **3.** UNPLEASANT PERSON sb who is disliked or despised (dated slang) [Early 20thC. Origin uncertain: perhaps an alteration of airc (a shortening of AIRCRAFTMAN.)]

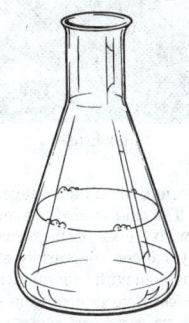

Erlenmeyer flask

Erlenmeyer flask /úrlən mï ər-/ n. a cone-shaped laboratory flask with a narrow neck and broad flat bottom [Late 19thC. Named after the German chemist Emil Erlenmeyer 1825–1909.]

ERM abbr. Exchange Rate Mechanism

Ermine

ermine /úrmin/ (plural **-mines** or **-mine**) n. **1.** SMALL NORTHERN STOAT a small northern stoat, a member of the weasel family, with dark fur whose silky winter coat is white except for a black-tipped tail. Latin name: Mustela erminea. **2.** WHITE FUR OF ERMINE the white fur of an ermine, once valued as a symbol of wealth, nobility, or high rank **3.** OFFICE REPRESENTED BY ERMINE FUR the rank or office of a dignitary whose robe is trimmed in ermine fur [12thC. From Old French (h)ermine, probably from medieval Latin (mus) Armenius 'Armenian (mouse)'.]

erne /urn/ (plural **ernes** or **erne**), **ern** (plural **erns** or **ern**) n. a long-winged European sea eagle. Latin name: Haliaetus albicilla. [Old English earn. Ultimately from an Indo-European word that is also the ancestor of Greek ornis 'bird' (source of English ornithology).]

Erne /urn/ name of two lakes in County Fermanagh, Northern Ireland, called Upper and Lower Lough Erne, and of the river that connects them

Ernie /úrni/, **ERNIE** the machine used for drawing winning premium bond numbers [Mid-20thC. Acronym formed from electronic random number indicating equipment.]

Ernst /airnst, urnst/, **Max** (1891–1976) German-born French artist. A co-founder of Dada and surrealism, he is known for the startling and violent imagery of his works.

erode /i rōd/ (**erodes, eroding, eroded**) v. **1.** vti. GEOL WEAR AWAY LAND to wear away outer layers of rock or soil, or to be gradually worn away by the action of wind or water **2.** vt. GEOL FORM BY WEATHERING to form a land feature such as a valley or gully by the action of wind or water ○ The runoff from the rain eroded a gully. **3.** vti. BREAK DOWN GRADUALLY to diminish or destroy sth such as a relationship or feeling gradually over time, or to be gradually diminished or destroyed ○ Deceit will erode any friendship. **4.** vti. CHEM EAT AWAY to eat into or destroy sth by corrosion

Max Ernst

or chemical action, or to be damaged or destroyed in this way ○ *The acid eroded the copper.* **5.** *vt.* MED **WEAR TISSUE AWAY** to cause tissue to wear away as a result of decay, cancer, ulceration, or the chemical processes associated with inflammation [Early 17thC. Directly or via French *éroder* from Latin *erodere* 'to gnaw off', from *rodere* 'to gnaw' (see RODENT).] —**erodent** *n., adj.* —**erodibility** /i rṓdə bílləti/ *n.* —**erodible** /i rṓdəb'l/ *adj.*

erogenous /i rójjənəss/, **erogenic** /érrə jénnik/, **erotogenic** /i róttə jénnik/ *adj.* **1. SEXUALLY SENSITIVE** sensitive and arousing sexual feelings when touched or stroked **2. SEXUALLY AROUSING** stimulating sexual desire [Late 19thC. Coined from EROS + -GENOUS.]

erogenous zone *n.* an area of the body that is sensitive to sexual stimulation

Eros /éer oss/ *n.* **1. GREEK GOD OF LOVE** the god of love in ancient Greece **2. Eros, eros SEXUAL LOVE** sexual love or desire **3.** PSYCHOL **INSTINCT FOR SELF-PRESERVATION** in psychoanalytic theory, the instincts for self-preservation, pleasure, and procreation considered as a group [Late 17thC. Via Latin from Greek, 'sexual love'.]

erosion /i rṓzh'n/ *n.* **1.** GEOL **WEARING AWAY OF ROCK** the gradual wearing away of rock or soil by physical breakdown, chemical solution, and transportation of material, as caused, e.g. by water, wind, or ice **2. GRADUAL BREAKING DOWN** the gradual destruction or reduction and weakening of sth such as a relationship or sb's power ○ *The erosion of profits was due to careless management.* **3.** MED **WEARING AWAY OF TISSUE** the wearing away of surface tissue by disease, ulceration, cancer, or the chemical processes associated with inflammation **4.** DENT **LOSS OF TOOTH ENAMEL** loss of tooth enamel caused by excessive intake of acidic citrus juices or through repeated contact with stomach acid, as in bulimia [Mid-16thC. From French *érosion*, from, ultimately, Latin *eros-*, the past participle stem of *erodere* (see ERODE).] —**erosional** *adj.* —**erosionally** *adv.*

erosive /i rṓssiv/ *adj.* causing the gradual breaking down or wearing away of sth, especially rock or soil —**erosiveness** *n.* —**erosivity** /erō sívvəti/ *n.*

erotic /i róttik/ *adj.* **1. AROUSING SEXUAL FEELINGS** arousing, or designed to arouse, feelings of sexual desire **2. MARKED BY SEXUAL DESIRE** characterized by or arising out of sexual desire [Mid-17thC. Via French *érotique* from Greek *erōtikos*, from *erōs* 'sexual love'.] —**erotically** *adv.*

erotica /i róttikə/ *n.* art or literature intended to arouse sexual desire by portraying sex in an explicit way. ◊ **pornography** [Mid-19thC. From Greek *erōtika*, neuter plural of *erōtikos* (see EROTIC).]

eroticise *vt.* = **eroticize**

eroticism /i rótti sizzəm/, **erotism** /érrə tizzəm/ *n.* **1. EROTIC QUALITY** an erotic quality in sth, especially an erotic style or subject in literature or art ○ *the eroticism of her poetry* **2. SEXUAL DESIRE** feelings of sexual desire **3. EXCESSIVE SEXUAL EXCITEMENT** unusually persistent or frequent sexual interest or desire —**eroticist** *n.*

eroticize /i rótti sīz/ (**-cizes, -cizing, -cized**), **eroticise** (**-cises, -cising, -cised**) *vt.* to make sth erotic, especially by giving a sexual quality to sth not usually regarded in that way ○ *The paintings were thought to eroticize flowers.* —**eroticization** /i rótti sī záysh'n/ *n.*

erotism *n.* = **eroticism**

erotogenic *adj.* = **erogenous**

erotology /érrə tólləji/ *n.* the study of erotic material and the stimulation of sexual desire —**erotological** /érrətə lójjik'l/ *adj.* —**erotologist** /érrə tólləjist/ *n.*

erotomania /i róttō máyni ə/ *n.* **1. EXCESSIVE SEXUAL DESIRE** excessive and insatiable feelings of sexual desire **2.** PSYCHIAT **BELIEF IN NONEXISTENT RELATIONSHIP** the delusion of being loved by and romantically involved in a relationship with a person, especially sb famous or of high social position —**erotomaniac** /-máyni ak/ *n.*

err /ur, air/ (**errs, erring, erred**) *vi.* (*formal*) **1. MAKE MISTAKE** to make a mistake or do an incorrect thing ○ *The committee erred in interpreting the contract in this way.* **2. BEHAVE BADLY** to behave badly and do sth that is morally wrong ○ *'To err is human, to forgive, divine'.* (Alexander Pope, *Essay On Criticism*; 1711) [13thC. Via Old French *errer* from Latin *errare* 'to wander'. The underlying sense is of wandering from the right path.] ◇ **err on the side of sth** to show a particular quality, e.g. caution or generosity, to a greater extent than is strictly necessary in order to avoid the risks involved in its opposite

errancy /érrənssi/ *n.* (*formal*) **1. INCORRECT BEHAVIOUR** incorrect or morally wrong behaviour **2. TENDENCY TO DO WRONG** the propensity for making mistakes or acting improperly

errand /érrənd/ *n.* **1. SHORT TRIP FOR SB ELSE** a short trip somewhere to do sth on behalf of sb else, e.g. to buy sth or deliver a message ○ *She sometimes runs errands for me if I'm not well enough to go out.* **2. PURPOSE OF ERRAND** the task that sb goes on an errand to carry out ○ *My errand was to collect her suit from the dry cleaners.* [Old English *ǣrende* 'message, mission', of unknown origin]

errant /érrənt/ *adj.* **1. BEHAVING BADLY** behaving in an unacceptable manner **2. GOING ASTRAY** wandering from an intended course or not reaching an intended destination **3. LOOKING FOR ADVENTURE** wandering in search of adventure and romance (*literary*) **4. MOVING IRREGULARLY** with no regular or purposeful pattern of motion [14thC. From Latin *errant-*, the present participle stem of *errare* (see ERR).] —**errantly** *adv.*

errantry /érrəntri/ *n.* the wandering, romantic, and adventurous life of a knight errant

errata /e ráatə/ plural of **erratum** ■ *npl.* **LIST OF PRINTING ERRORS** a list of mistakes noticed after a book was printed, often included as a separate sheet in the book

erratic /i ráttik/ *adj.* **1. INCONSISTENT** not predictable, regular, or consistent, especially in being likely to depart from or fall below expected standards at any time ○ *His driving tends to be rather erratic.* **2. OFTEN CHANGING DIRECTION** often changing direction and not following any definite course **3.** GEOL **CARRIED AND DEPOSITED BY ICE** used to describe a rock or boulder that was carried from its source by ice and deposited when the ice melted ■ *n.* **1. SB BEHAVING UNPREDICTABLY** sb who does not behave predictably **2.** GEOL **ROCK MOVED BY ICE** a piece of rock that was carried from its source by ice and deposited when the ice melted [14thC. From Old French *erratique*, from, ultimately, Latin *errare* (see ERR).] —**erratically** *adv.* —**erraticism** /i ráttissizəm/ *n.*

erratum /e ráatəm/ (*plural* **-ta** /-tə/) *n.* a mistake in printing or writing, especially one on a list that is included with a printed book [Mid-16thC. From Latin, neuter past participle of *errare* (see ERR).]

erroneous /i rṓni əss/ *adj.* incorrect, based on an incorrect assumption, or containing sth that is incorrect [14thC. From Old French *erroneus*, from, ultimately, the Latin stem *erron-* 'truant', from *errare* (see ERR).] —**erroneously** *adv.* —**erroneousness** *n.*

error /érrər/ *n.* **1. MISTAKE** sth unintentionally done wrong, e.g. as a result of poor judgment or lack of care ○ *The report blames the crash on human error.* **2. WRONG BELIEF** a belief or opinion that is contrary to fact or to established doctrine ○ *Errors and superstitions were to be banished by the pure light of science.* **3. STATE OF BELIEVING OR ACTING WRONGLY** a state in which sb holds incorrect beliefs or opinions or acts wrongly or misguidedly **4. BEING WRONG** incorrectness, inappropriateness, or unacceptability ○ *He's seen the error of his ways and has decided to apologize.* **5.** COMPUT **PROBLEM DETECTED BY PROGRAM** the failure of a computer program, subroutine, or system to produce an anticipated result, such as the result of a calculation not falling within an expected range **6.** MATH **MATHEMATICAL DIFFERENCE** a variation between the true value of a mathematical quantity and a calculated or measured value [13thC. From Old French *err(o)ur*, from, ultimately, Latin *errare* (see ERR).] —**errorless** *adj.* ◇ **in error 1.** by mistake **2.** mistaken or acting on the basis of a false assumption or belief

WORD KEY: SYNONYMS

See Synonyms at ***mistake***.

error code *n.* a unique combination of characters printed or displayed by a computer or communicated between parts of a program indicating an error or specific problem in software or hardware operation

error message *n.* a message indicating that a computer has encountered a problem and often suggesting alternative action. The message may take the form of a display on a monitor, text on a printer, a computer-generated voice, or a sequence of audio signals.

ersatz /áir zats/ *adj.* imitating or presented as a substitute for sth of superior quality (*disapproving*) [Late 19thC. From German, literally 'replacement'.]

Erse /urss/ *n.* LANG = **Gaelic** *n.* ■ *adj.* **OF GAELIC LANGUAGE** relating or belonging to the Gaelic language, especially Irish Gaelic [14thC. Early Scots variant of IRISH.]

Ershad /úrsh ad, ur shád/, **Hussain Mohammad** (*b.* 1930) Indian-born Bangladeshi soldier and statesman. He seized power in 1982, declared himself president in 1983, and retained office in a controversial election (1986). He resigned in 1990 and was sentenced to long imprisonment.

Erskine /úrskin/, **Ralph** (*b.* 1914) British architect. An appreciation of the needs of the community informs his large public housing projects, such as the Byker Wall estate (1968–80) in Newcastle upon Tyne.

Erskine, Thomas, 1st Baron Erskine (1750–1823) British advocate and politician. His forensic skill, often exercised in defending political radicals such as Thomas Paine, was considered matchless in his time. He was briefly lord chancellor (1806–07).

erst /urst/ *adv.* in the past or a long time ago (*archaic*) [Old English *ǣrest* 'first']

erstwhile /úrst wīl/ *adj.* **FORMER** who in the past was sth, e.g. a friend or supporter, but now no longer is ○ *Since leaving the bank, she has been ostracized by her erstwhile colleagues.* ■ *adv.* **FORMERLY** at a time in the past (*archaic*) ◊ **erewhile**

erub *n.* = **eruv**

erucic acid /i róossik-/ *n.* a soft, colourless, solid fatty acid derived from rape seeds. It is used primarily in the manufacture of plastics. [*Erucic* formed from Latin *eruca* 'rape plant']

eruct /i rúkt/ (**eructs, eructing, eructed**), **eructate** /i rúk tayt/ (**-tates, -tating, -tated**) *vti.* to expel stomach gases through the mouth (*technical*) [Mid-17thC. From Latin *eructare* 'to belch or vomit up', from *ructare* 'to belch'.] —**eructation** /i rúk táysh'n, ée ruk táysh'n/ *n.*

erudite /érrōo dīt/ *adj.* having or showing great knowledge gained from study and reading ○ *scholars erudite in Sanskrit* [15thC. From Latin *eruditus*, past participle of *erudire* 'to instruct', from *rudis* 'untrained' (source of English *rude*).] —**eruditely** *adv.* —**eruditeness** *n.*

erudition /érrōo dísh'n/ *n.* knowledge acquired through study and reading ○ *a work of great erudition*

WORD KEY: SYNONYMS

See Synonyms at ***knowledge***.

erupt /i rúpt/ (**erupts, erupting, erupted**) *v.* **1.** *vti.* **VIOLENTLY RELEASE MATERIAL** to eject material such as gas, steam, ash, or lava, usually violently, from within ○ *The volcano last erupted in 1935.* **2.** *vi.* **BURST OUT** to burst out suddenly or violently ○ *Tired of her comments, he suddenly erupted into a fit of temper.* **3.** *vi.* MED **APPEAR ON SKIN** to appear as a rash or blemish on the skin or a mucous membrane **4.** *vi.* DENT **COME THROUGH GUM** to break through and emerge from a gum (*technical*) (*refers to growing teeth*) [Mid-17thC. From

Latin *erupt-*, past participle stem of *erumpere*, literally 'to break out', from *rumpere* 'to break' (source of English *rupture*).] —**eruptible** *adj.* —**eruptive** *adj.* —**eruptively** *adv.*

eruption /i rúpsh'n/ *n.* **1.** VIOLENT RELEASE OF MATERIAL the violent ejection of material, such as gas, steam, ash, or lava from a volcano **2.** OUTBURST a sudden outburst or occurrence of sth **3.** MED RASH OR BLEMISH ON SKIN a rash or blemish, or the appearance of a rash or blemish on the skin or a mucous membrane **4.** DENT EMERGENCE OF TOOTH an emergence of a growing tooth from a gum

eruv /érrōŏv/, **erub** *n.* the physical boundary within which certain relaxations of the rules concerning the Jewish Sabbath are allowed. It may be the walls of a town, a natural barrier, or a special construction. [Early 18thC. From Hebrew *'ērūbh*, literally 'mixture'.]

erven plural of **erf**

Erving /úrving/, **Julius** (b. 1950) US basketball player He is widely regarded as one of the greatest and most exciting scorers in basketball history. Full name **Julius Winfred Erving II**. Known as **Dr J**

-ery, **-ry** *suffix.* **1.** place for ○ *brewery* **2.** activity or behaviour ○ *trickery* **3.** collection of ○ *crockery* **4.** qualities or character of ○ *buffoonery* **5.** state, condition ○ *drudgery* [From Old French *-erie*, from *-er* '-er, -or' + *-ie* '-y']

erysipelas /érri síppələss/ *n.* a severe skin rash accompanied by fever and vomiting and caused by a streptococcal bacterium [14thC. Via Latin from Greek *erusipelas*, literally 'red skin'.] —**erysipelatous** /érrissi péllətəss/ *adj.*

erythema /érri theémə/ *n.* redness of the skin as a result of a widening of the small blood vessels near its surface. It has various causes, including fever and inflammation. [Late 18thC. From Greek *eruthēma*, from, ultimately, *eruthros* 'red'.] —**erythematous** /érri theémətəss, érri thémmətəss/ *adj.* —**erythemic** /-theémik/ *adj.*

erythr- *prefix.* = **erythro-** (used before vowels)

erythrism /érri thrizəm, i ríth rizəm/ *n.* unusual redness of plumage or hair, often accompanied by a ruddy complexion in humans [Late 19thC. Coined from Greek *eruthros* 'red' + -ISM.] —**erythrismal** /érri thrízm'l/ *adj.*

erythrite /érri thrīt, i ríth rīt/ *n.* pale red cobalt arsenate that occurs as crystals on cobalt minerals and is used as a glass pigment [Mid-19thC. Coined from Greek *eruthros* 'red' + -ITE.]

erythro- *prefix.* **1.** red ○ *erythrocyte* **2.** erythrocyte ○ *erythroblast* [From Greek *eruthros* 'red'. Ultimately from an Indo-European base that is also the ancestor of English *red* and *ruddy*.]

erythroblast /i ríthrə blast/ *n.* ANAT an immature red blood cell that is found in bone marrow and eventually develops into a mature red blood cell. Unlike a mature red blood cell, an erythroblast has a nucleus. —**erythroblastic** /i ríthrə blástik/ *adj.*

erythroblastosis /i ríthrō bla stóssiss/ *n.* the abnormal presence of immature red blood cells in the bloodstream that occurs especially in erythroblastosis fetalis

erythroblastosis fetalis /-fi tálliss/ *n.* a serious blood disease of foetuses and newborn babies, in which the antibodies produced by a rhesus-negative mother destroy the red blood cells of a rhesus-positive foetus [*Fetalis* from modern Latin, 'foetal']

erythrocyte /i ríthrō sīt/ *n.* = **red blood cell** —**erythrocytic** /i ríthrō síttik/ *adj.*

erythromycin /i ríthrō míssin/ *n.* an antibiotic used in treating a broad range of bacterial infections. It is derived from cultures of a bacterium *Streptomyces erythreus*.

erythropoiesis /i ríthrō poy éessiss/ *n.* the formation of red blood cells, a process that begins with stem cells in the bone marrow and ends with the release of mature red blood cells (**erythrocytes**) into circulation [Early 20thC. Coined from ERYTHROCYTE + Greek *poiēsis* 'creation' (see POESY).] —**erythropoietic** /-éttik/ *adj.*

erythropoietin /i ríthrō poy éetin, -éttin/ *n.* a hormone produced in the kidneys that stimulates increased development of red blood cells in the bone marrow. The kidneys produce erythropoietin in response to lowered oxygen levels in body tissues. [Mid-20thC. Coined from ERYTHROPOIESIS + -IN.]

Es *symbol.* einsteinium

ES *abbr.* **1.** El Salvador (*international vehicle registration*) **2.** Eastern States

-es *suffix.* = **-s**

ESA *abbr.* **1.** environmentally sensitive area **2.** European Space Agency

Esc *abbr.* COMPUT escape (key)

escadrille /éskədril, éskə dríl/ *n.* a squadron of usually six aircraft, especially a French air squadron of World War I [Early 20thC. Via French from Spanish *escuadrilla*, literally 'little squadron', from *escuadra* 'squadron'.]

escalade /éskə láyd/ *n.* CLIMBING WALL WITH LADDERS an attack involving the use of ladders to scale the walls of a fortified place ■ *vt.* (**-lades, -lading, -laded**) CLIMB WALL WITH LADDERS to scale the walls of a fortification using ladders [Late 16thC. Directly or via French from Spanish *escalada*. Ultimately from medieval Latin *scalare* 'to climb' (source of English *scale*).] —**escalader** /éskə láydər/ *n.*

escalate /éskə layt/ (**-lates, -lating, -lated**) *vti.* to become or cause sth to become greater, more serious, or more intense [Early 20thC. Back-formation from ESCALATOR. Originally, 'to travel on an escalator'.] —**escalation** /éskə láysh'n/ *n.* —**escalatory** /éskə láytəri/ *adj.*

WORD KEY: USAGE

His claims are certain to escalate into a big political scandal. No one uses **escalate** now to mean 'ride on an escalator', and the figurative meaning has taken over completely. Its earliest and still most common uses are in connection with military activity and conflicts: *Officials killed by mine as terrorist attacks escalate.* It is used most effectively when it describes a development that proceeds in stages, rather than as a simple synonym for *increase* or *mount*.

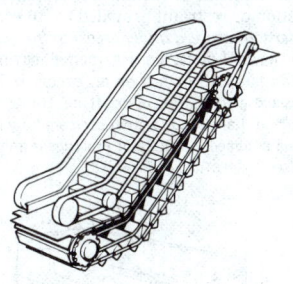

Escalator

escalator /éskə laytər/ *n.* a set of moving steps attached to a continuously circulating belt, that carries people up or down between different levels in a building [Early 20thC. From ESCALADE, modelled on ELEVATOR.]

escalator, **escalator clause** *n.* a stipulation in a contract that makes an increase or decrease in sth conditional on a change in sth else. It might, e.g. relate compensation to cost of living or prices to sales.

escallop /éskə lop, e skólləp/ *n.* SEW = **scallop** *n.* 6 [15thC. From Old French *escalope* 'shell' (see SCALLOP).]

escalope /éskə lop, e skólləp/ *n.* FOOD a slice of boneless lean meat, especially veal or poultry, that is beaten flat for cooking quickly or rolling around a stuffing. US term **scallop** *n.* 7 [Early 19thC. Via French from Old French, 'shell' (see ESCALLOP); probably from its curling into a shell shape in cooking.]

escapade /éskə payd/ *n.* sth exciting or adventurous that sb does or is involved in, especially sth showing recklessness or disregard for authority [Mid-17thC. Via French from Spanish *escapada* 'an escape', from, ultimately, assumed Vulgar Latin *excappare* (see ESCAPE).]

escape /i skáyp/ *v.* (**-capes, -caping, -caped**) **1.** *vti.* BREAK FREE FROM CAPTIVITY to free yourself and get away from captivity or confinement ○ *prisoners who attempted to escape* **2.** *vt.* AVOID BAD SITUATION to avoid danger, harm, or involvement in an unpleasant situation ○ *There's no escaping the fact that the house needs painting.* **3.** *vi.* LEAK OUT to leak out from a container **4.** *vt.* BE TEMPORARILY UNKNOWN TO to fail to be noticed, remembered, or understood by sb ○ *a little village whose name escapes me for the moment* **5.** *vti.* BE UTTERED to be uttered by sb unintentionally ○ *A muffled curse escaped his lips.* **6.** *vi.* BOT SPREAD FROM GARDEN INTO THE WILD to spread from a garden or other cultivated area and become established in the wild (*refers to cultivated plants*) **7.** *vi.* COMPUT EXIT COMPUTER PROCEDURE to exit from a computer program or file, cancel a command or operation, or return from the currently active menu to a previous one ■ *n.* **1.** BREAKING FREE FROM CAPTIVITY an act of getting free from captivity or confinement ○ *He made his escape while the guard was asleep.* **2.** AVOIDANCE OF BAD SITUATION the avoidance of a dangerous, harmful, or unpleasant situation ○ *an escape from danger* **3.** MEANS OF GETTING AWAY a method, means, or route by which sb can escape from a place or situation **4.** GAS OR LIQUID LEAK a leak of gas or liquid from a container **5.** BOT WILD PLANT ONCE CULTIVATED a plant that has spread from a garden or other cultivated area and is growing wild **6.** COMPUT COMPUTER KEY the key on a computer keyboard that allows a user to exit a program, cancel a command, or return to a previous menu ○ *Press escape to exit the program.* **7.** COMPUT = **escape code** [13thC. Via Old Northern French *escaper* from, ultimately, assumed Vulgar Latin *excappare*, literally 'to throw off your cloak', from *cappa* 'cloak' (source of English *cape*).] —**escapable** *adj.* —**escaper** *n.*

escape artist *n.* **1.** PERFORMER SKILLED AT ESCAPING a performer who is skilled at escaping from restraints or confinement **2.** SB ADEPT AT ESCAPING DIFFICULTIES sb who is skilled at getting out of difficulties or apparently very dangerous or compromising situations

escape clause *n.* a clause in a contract that sets out the conditions under which a party to the contract can be released from his or her obligations under it

escape code *n.* a sequence of one or more characters instructing a device that what follows is not part of the regular data but rather a command. For example an escape code might instruct a printer to print in italics the text that follows the code.

escapee /i skáy peé, éskay peé/ *n.* sb who has escaped from captivity (*literary*)

escape hatch *n.* a small opening providing a way out of an enclosed space, such as a submarine, through which people can escape in an emergency

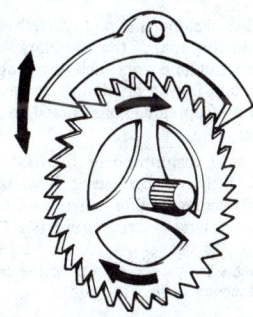

Escapement: Pallets on arm (top)
engage teeth on wheel, driving gears
in the movement

escapement /i skáypmənt/ *n.* **1.** CLOCK MECHANISM a mechanism in a clock or watch that allows power from a spring or falling weight to turn gears connected to the hands **2.** PIANO MECHANISM a mechanism in a piano that allows the hammer to rebound from a string after striking it **3.** TYPEWRITER MECHANISM a mechanism in a typewriter or printer that regulates the relative movement between the paper carrier and the typing or printing position on a line [Late 18thC. From its allowing a cogwheel to 'escape' or be released repeatedly.]

escape road (*unmarked inflection* **escape roads**) *n.* a road branching off from a steep hill or sharp bend into which a vehicle can turn if it gets into difficulties

escape velocity *n.* the minimum speed at which an object must travel to escape a planet's or moon's gravitational field in order to orbit around it or move off into space. At or near the Earth's surface, the escape velocity is about 40,000 kph/25,000 mph.

escape wheel *n.* a toothed wheel in the mechanism of a watch or clock, designed to regulate the movement of the pendulum or balance wheel and so move the hands at regular intervals

escapism /i skáypizəm/ *n.* **1.** ESCAPE FROM EVERYDAY REALITY sth such as fantasy or entertainment that makes it possible to forget about the ordinary or unpleasant realities of life for a while **2.** INDULGENCE IN FANTASIES TO ESCAPE REALITY the act of indulging in daydreams or fantasies to escape from everyday reality

escapist /i skáypist/ *adj.* HELPING TO FORGET providing a means of forgetting about everyday or unpleasant realities for a while ■ *n.* SB AVOIDING REALITY sb who tries to avoid reality by indulging in daydreams or fantasies

escapologist /éskə póllǝjist/ *n.* = **escape artist**

escapology /éskə póllǝji/ *n.* the skill of escaping from restraints or confinement as a form of entertainment

escargot /e skaárgō/ *n.* a snail that is cooked and eaten, especially served in its shell with melted garlic butter [Late 19thC. Via French from, ultimately, Old Provençal *escaragol*, of unknown origin.]

escarole /éskərōl/ *n. US* = **endive** *n.* 1 [Early 20thC. Via French from Italian *scariola*, from, ultimately, Latin *esca* 'food' (see ESCULENT).]

escarp /i skaárp/ *n.* the inner side of a ditch dug as a fortification [Late 17thC. Via French *escarpe* from Italian *scarpa* 'slope' (see SCARP).]

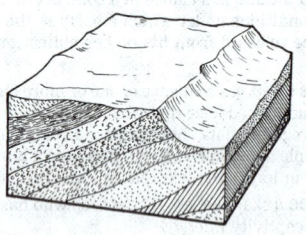
Escarpment

escarpment /i skaárpmənt/ *n.* **1.** STEEP RIDGE a steep slope or cliff that marks the boundary of a flat or gently sloping upland area such as a plateau, often formed by faulting or erosion. ◊ **scarp 2.** SLOPE IN FORTIFICATION a steep slope constructed in front of a fortification

-escent *suffix.* **1.** beginning or inclined to be, becoming, slightly ○ *acquiescent* ○ *alkalescent* **2.** having a particular kind of lustre ○ *adularescent* **3.** resembling, having ○ *arborescent* [Via French from Latin *-escent-*, the stem of *-escens*, the present participle ending of verbs in *-escere*, expressing the beginning of action] —**-escence** *suffix.*

eschar /és kaar/ *n.* a dry scab formed on skin that has been burned or cauterized [15thC. Directly or via Old French *escare* from late Latin *eschara* 'scab' (see SCAR[1]).]

eschatology /éskə tóllǝji/ *n.* the body of religious doctrines concerning the human soul in its relation to death, judgment, heaven, and hell [Mid-19thC. Coined from Greek *eskhatos* 'last' + -LOGY.] —**eschatological** /éskətə lójjikl/ *adj.* —**eschatologically** /-lójjikli/ *adv.* —**eschatologist** /éskə tóllǝjist/ *n.*

escheat /iss cheét/ *n.* **1.** REVERSION OF PROPERTY TO STATE the reversion of the property of a deceased person to the state in the United States, or to the Crown in England before 1926, when there are no legal heirs **2.** HIST REVERSION OF PROPERTY TO FEUDAL LORD in medieval

England, the reversion to a feudal overlord of the property of a deceased person when there was no legal heir or when a tenant was outlawed **3.** PROPERTY AFFECTED BY ESCHEAT property that reverts by escheat [13thC. From Old French *eschete* and Anglo-Latin *escheta*, from assumed Vulgar Latin *excadere*, literally 'to fall away', from Latin *cadere* (see CADENCE).] —**escheatable** *adj.*

Escher /éshər/, **M. C.** (1898–1972) Dutch graphic artist. He is known for his distinctive prints depicting intricate interlocking patterns and optical illusions based on mathematical concepts. Full name **Maurits Cornelis Escher**

eschew /iss choó/ (**-chews, -chewing, -chewed**) *vt.* to avoid doing or using sth on principle or as a matter of course [14thC. From Old French *eschiver*. Ultimately from a prehistoric Germanic word that is also the ancestor of English *shy*.] —**eschewal** *n.*

eschscholzia /e shóltsi ə/, **eschscholtzia** *n.* = **California poppy** [Late 19thC. From modern Latin, named in honour of the Russian naturalist J. F. *Eschscholtz* (1793–1831).]

Escoffier /i skóffi ay/, **Auguste** (1846–1935) French chef and cookery author. Master of the haute cuisine style of French cookery, he gained an international reputation while working in London at the Savoy (1890–99) and Carlton (1899–1919) hotels. Full name **Georges Auguste Escoffier**

escolar /éskə laár/ *n.* a deepwater fish of tropical and temperate seas with a slim bony body, jutting lower jaw, and sharp teeth. Family: Gempylidae. [Late 19thC. Via Spanish, 'student' (because of the rings around its eyes resembling spectacles), from late Latin *scholaris* (see SCHOLAR).]

escort *n.* /éss kawrt/ **1.** SB ACCOMPANYING SB OR STH one or more persons accompanying sb or sth as a guard or guide, or as a mark of honour **2.** MIL ACCOMPANYING MILITARY VESSEL OR AIRCRAFT one or more warships or fighter aircraft accompanying a larger, more vulnerable ship or aircraft as protection ○ *The bombers were joined by their fighter escort when they reached the coast.* **3.** MAN AS SOCIAL PARTNER a man accompanying a woman on a social occasion **4.** HIRED SOCIAL PARTNER a man or woman who is hired to accompany another person as a companion, especially to a social event or entertainment **5.** PROTECTION OR SECURITY FOR JOURNEY protection or restraint provided by an escort ○ *The prisoner will proceed under escort to the guardhouse.* ■ *vt.* /i skáwrt/ (**-corts, -corting, -corted**) GO WITH AS ESCORT to accompany sb or sth as an escort ○ *The butler will escort you to the door.* [Late 16thC. Via French *escorte* from Italian *scorta*, from *scorgere* 'to guide', which came via assumed Vulgar Latin *excorrigere* from Latin *corrigere* (see CORRECT).]

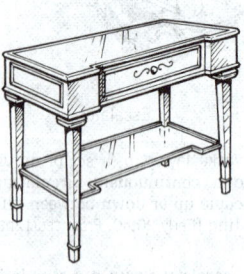
Escritoire

escritoire /éskri twaár/ *n.* a writing desk, often with a hinged flap that conceals drawers and pigeonholes [Late 16thC. Via Old French, 'writing box', from medieval Latin *scriptorium* (see SCRIPTORIUM).]

escrow /éskrō, e skrō/ *n.* **1.** STH HELD INDEPENDENTLY UNTIL CONDITION MET an amount of money or property granted to sb but held by a third party and only released after a condition has been met **2.** STATE OF BEING AN ESCROW the condition of being held as an escrow ■ *vt.* (**-crows, -crowing, -crowed**) PUT IN ESCROW to place sth in escrow [Mid-17thC. From Anglo-Norman *escrowe* 'scroll', a variant of Old French *escroe* (see SCROLL).]

escudo /i skoódō/ (*plural* **-dos**) *n.* **1.** UNIT OF PORTUGUESE CURRENCY a unit of currency used in Portugal. See table at **currency 2.** OLD UNIT OF CURRENCY any one of

various units of currency that were formerly used in Spain and countries of South America **3.** COIN WORTH ONE ESCUDO a coin worth one escudo [Early 19thC. Via Spanish and Portugese from Latin *scutum* 'shield' (see SCUTUM), because early coins resembled heraldic shields.]

esculent /éskyoŏlənt/ *adj.* EDIBLE fit to be eaten (*formal*) ■ *n.* EDIBLE SUBSTANCE sth edible, especially a plant (*formal*) [Early 17thC. From Latin *esculentus*, from *esca* 'food', from *edere* 'to eat' (see EDIBLE).]

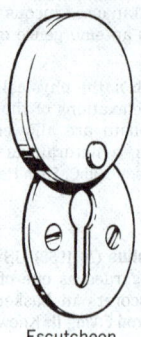
Escutcheon

escutcheon /i skúchən/ *n.* **1.** HERALDRY HERALDIC SHIELD a shield, especially one used in heraldry to display a coat of arms **2.** PROTECTIVE SHIELD a plate or shield fixed around sth, e.g. a light switch or keyhole, as an ornament or to protect the surrounding surface **3.** NAUT NAME PLATE ON VESSEL a panel on the stern of a vessel on which the vessel's name is shown [15thC. Via Anglo-Norman *escuchon* from, ultimately, Latin *scutum* 'shield' (see SCUTUM).] —**escutcheoned** *adj.*

Esd. *abbr.* BIBLE Esdras

Esdraelon, Plain of /éss dray eé lon/ plain in northern Israel between the Sea of Galilee and the River Jordan on the east and the Mediterranean Sea on the west. It is approximately 58 km/36 mi. long and has an average width of 24 km/15 mi.

Esdras /éz drass/ *n.* **1.** BOOK OF APOCRYPHA either of two books in the Apocrypha **2.** BOOK OF ROMAN CATHOLIC BIBLE either of two books of the Roman Catholic version of the Bible (**Douay Bible**), equivalent to the books of Ezra and Nehemiah in the Authorized Version

ESE *abbr.* east-southeast

-ese *suffix.* **1.** from, of, native to, or inhabiting a particular place ○ *Taiwanese* **2.** the language of a particular place ○ *Faeroese* **3.** style or jargon ○ *officialese* [Via Old French *-eis* and Italian *-ese* from Latin *-ensis* 'originating in']

eserine /éssə reen, -rin/ *n.* = **physostigmine** [Mid-19thC. From French *ésérine*, from Efik *esere* 'Calabar bean'.]

esker /éskər/, **eskar** /és kaar, éskər/ *n.* a long narrow winding ridge of sand or gravel, deposited by a stream flowing under a glacier [Mid-19thC. From Irish *eiscir*, from Old Irish *escir*, of unknown origin.]

Eskimo /éski mō/ *adj., n.* (*plural* **-mos** *or* **-mo**) = **Inuit** [Late 16thC. From French *Esquimaux*, ultimately of Algonquian origin.]

─── WORD KEY: USAGE ───
Sensitivity trap: The Inuit Circumpolar Conference, held in 1977 in Barrow, Alaska, chose officially to replace the term *Eskimo* with *Inuit* (which means 'the real people'). *Eskimo* nonetheless remains in common use, appearing even in academic contexts. Because some may find it offensive, care should be exercised in using this word.

Eskimo-Aleut *n.* a family of languages spoken in Greenland, Alaska, Canada, Siberia, and the Aleutian Islands

Eskimo dog *n.* a large powerful thick-coated dog with erect ears that is used to pull sleds in Arctic regions

Eskimo roll *n.* a process or procedure by which a capsized kayak is rolled over underwater in order to come up righted

Eskişehir /ess keé she heer/ city in western Turkey, west of Ankara. Population: 413,300 (1990).

Esky /éski/ *tdmk. Aus* a trademark for an insulated portable container for keeping food and beverages cool

Eskimo dog

ESL *abbr.* English as a second language

ESOL /éē sol/ *abbr.* English for speakers of other languages

ESOP /ēē sop/ *n.* a scheme in which employees acquire stock of the company they work for by making tax-deductible contributions [Late 20thC. Acronym formed from *employee stock ownership plan.*]

esophagus *n.* US = oesophagus

esoteric /éssō térrik, eēssō-/ *adj.* **1. RESTRICTED TO INITIATES** intended for or understood by only an initiated few **2. ABSTRUSE** difficult to understand **3. SECRET** secret or highly confidential [Mid-17thC. From Greek *esōterikos* 'belonging to an inner circle', from *esōterō* 'inner', from *esō* 'within'.] —**esoterically** *adv.*

esoterica /éssō térrikə, eēssō-/ *npl.* things that are for initiates only, or are difficult or secret [Early 20thC. From Greek *esōterika*, from *esōterikos* (see ESOTERIC).]

esotericism /éssō térrissizəm, eēssō-/ *n.* **1. ESOTERIC BELIEFS OR PRACTICES** beliefs or practices that are arcane, mysterious, or secret **2. STATE OF BEING ESOTERIC** the condition or quality of being esoteric

ESP *abbr.* **1.** English for special purposes **2.** extra-sensory perception

esp. *abbr.* especially

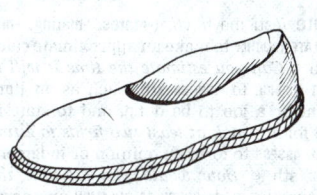

Espadrille

espadrille /éspə dríl, éspədríl/ *n.* a light shoe with a fabric or canvas upper and a sole made of twisted cord, sometimes tied with lacing around the ankle [Late 19thC. Via French from Provençal *espardilho*, from *espart* 'esparto' (from which it was originally made), from Latin *spartum* (see ESPARTO).]

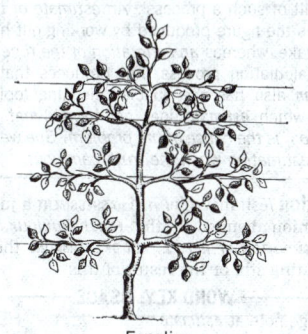

Espalier

espalier /i spálli ay, -li ər/ *n.* a plant, especially a fruit tree, trained to grow flat against an upright surface, e.g. a wall or fence, or on wires [Mid-17thC. Via

French from Italian *spalliera* 'shoulder support', from *spalla* 'shoulder', from Latin *spatula* (see SPATULA).]

esparto /e spaár tō/ (*plural* **-tos**), **esparto grass** *n.* a long coarse grass found in southern Europe and North Africa whose fibres are used in making paper, ropes, and mats. Latin name: *Stipa tenacissima*. [Mid-19thC. Via Spanish from Latin *spartum*, from Greek *sparton* 'rope'.]

especial /i spésh'l/ *adj.* (*formal*) **1. NOTABLE** unusual or exceptional **2. PARTICULAR** particular or specific [13thC. Via Old French from Latin *specialis*, literally 'of a specific kind', from *species* (see SPECIES).]

especially /i spésh'li/ *adv.* **1. EXCEPTIONALLY** to an unusual or exceptional degree **2. PARTICULARLY** used to single out one among a range **3. CHIEFLY** in most cases **4. EXPRESSLY** for a particular or specific purpose

———— **WORD KEY: USAGE** ————

especially or **specially**? Although there is a clear difference in meaning, both words are used surprisingly often when the other is intended: *The car is designed especially for handicapped people.* (**Specially** is wanted here because the car is designed 'for a special purpose'.) *The buildings are not specially large.* (**Especially** is wanted because the buildings are not 'more than usually' large.) In rapid conversation, the first syllable of **especially** tends to be slurred or omitted so that it sounds no different from **specially**, and this practice can affect the correct choice when the words are written.

Esperance /éspərənss/ port on the southwestern coast of Western Australia, located in a farming region. Population: 8,647 (1996).

Esperanto /éspə rántō/ *n.* an artificial language invented in 1887 as a means of making international communication easier. It is based on the root forms of certain words common to the major European languages. In general, the word order is similar to that of English, although the grammar is more highly inflected. [Late 19thC. Named after Doctor *Esperanto*, literally 'one who hopes', the Esperanto pseudonym of the Polish philologist Ludwik Zamenhof 1859–1917, who invented the language.] —**Esperantist** *n.*

espial /i spí əl/ *n.* (*archaic*) **1. ACT OF SIGHTING STH** the action of sighting or discovering sth **2. ACT OF NOTICING STH** the action of noticing or detecting sth **3. ACT OF SPYING** the action of secretly watching sb or sth [14thC. From Old French *espialle*, from *espier* (see SPY).]

espionage /éspi ə naazh, éspi ə naázh/ *n.* the use of spying or spies to gather secret information [Late 18thC. From French *espionnage*, from *espionner* 'to spy', from *espion* 'spy'. Ultimately of prehistoric Germanic origin.]

esplanade /ésplə náyd, ésplə naád, ésplə nayd/ *n.* **1.** TRANSP **OPEN WALKWAY** a long level area, especially by the sea, for walking or driving along **2.** MIL **LEVEL AREA OUTSIDE FORTIFICATION** a wide level area outside a fortification, where attackers will be exposed to fire from defenders [Late 17thC. From French, from, ultimately, Latin *explanare*, literally 'to flatten out' (see EXPLAIN).]

espousal /i spówz'l/ *n.* **1. ADOPTION AS BELIEF** the adoption of sth as a belief or cause **2. MARRIAGE** a betrothal or wedding (*formal; often used in the plural*)

espouse /i spówz/ (**-pouses, -pousing, -poused**) *vt.* **1. ADOPT** to adopt or support sth as a belief or cause **2. MARRY OR GIVE IN MARRIAGE** to marry sb or give sb in marriage (*archaic*) [15thC. Via Old French *espouser* from Latin *sponsare*, from *spons-*, the stem of *spondere* (see SPONSOR).] —**espouser** *n.*

espressivo /éspre seē vō/ *adv.* played in an expressive way (*used as a musical direction*) [Late 19thC. From Italian, 'expressively'.]

espresso /e spréssō/ *n.* **1. STRONG COFFEE MADE IN A SPECIAL MACHINE** dark strong-tasting coffee made by using a special machine to pass steam under pressure or boiling water through finely ground coffee beans **2. CUP OF ESPRESSO** a serving of espresso coffee, usually in a small cup ○ *Two espressos and a cappuccino.* **3. MACHINE FOR MAKING ESPRESSO** a machine for making espresso coffee ○ *the hiss of the espresso* [Mid-20thC. From Italian (*caffè*) *espresso*, literally 'pressed-out (coffee)', from the past participle of *esprimere* 'to press out', from Latin *exprimere* (see EXPRESS).]

esprit /e sprée/ *n.* lively intelligence or wit [Late 16thC. From French (see SPIRIT).]

esprit de corps /-də káwr/ *n.* a feeling of pride in belonging to a group and a sense of identification with it [From French, literally 'group spirit']

espy /i spí/ (**-pies, -pying, -pied**) *vt.* to catch sight of or detect sth (*formal*) [14thC. From Old French *espier* (see SPY).]

Esq. *abbr.* Esquire (*in correspondence*)

-esque *suffix.* in the style of, like ○ *Pythonesque* [Via French from, ultimately, assumed Vulgar Latin *-iscus*, of Germanic origin (ultimately related to English *-ish*)]

Esquimalt /éski mawlt/ seaport and naval station on southeastern Vancouver Island, British Columbia, Canada. It is a suburb of the city of Victoria. Population: 16,192 (1991).

esquire /i skwír/ *n.* a youth serving as an attendant or shield-bearer to a medieval knight, especially as a stage in his own training for knighthood [14thC. Via Old French *escuier* from late Latin *scutarius* 'shield bearer', from Latin *scutum* 'shield' (see SCUTUM).]

Esquire /i skwír/ *n.* a courtesy title placed after a man's full name, especially in correspondence

ESR *abbr.* **1.** PHYS electron spin resonance **2.** MED erythrocyte sedimentation rate

ESRC *abbr.* Economic and Social Research Council

ESRO /ézrō/ *abbr.* European Space Research Organization

ess /ess/ *n.* **1. s** the letter s or S **2. STH S-SHAPED** sth shaped like an S [Mid-16thC. From Latin *es*.]

-ess *suffix.* woman or girl ○ *heiress* [Via Old French and Latin from, ultimately, Greek *-issa*]

essay /éssay/ *n.* **1. SHORT NONFICTION PROSE PIECE** a short analytical, descriptive, or interpretive piece of literary or journalistic prose dealing with a particular topic, especially from a personal and unsystematic viewpoint **2. SET WRITTEN PIECE** a short piece of written work set as an assignment for a student **3. WORK RESEMBLING A WRITTEN ESSAY** an artistic or journalistic work resembling a written essay but in another medium ○ *not so much a short film as a cinematographic essay* **4. ATTEMPT AT STH** an attempt to accomplish sth (*formal*) **5. TEST OF STH** a test or trial of sth (*formal*) ■ *vt.* (**-says, -saying, -sayed**) **1. ATTEMPT** to try out or attempt sth (*formal*) ○ *Shall we essay a walk on the promenade?* **2. TEST** to make a test of sth ○ *essay his theory* [15thC. Via Old French *essaier* 'to try' from assumed Vulgar Latin *exagiare*, literally 'to weigh out', from *agere* (see ACT).]

essayist /éssayist/ *n.* a writer of literary or journalistic essays

essayistic /éssay ístik/ *adj.* resembling or styled like a literary or journalistic essay

essay question *n.* a question in an examination that must be answered in a prose piece of a specified length

Essen /éss'n/ industrial city in the Ruhr valley, North Rhine-Westphalia State, west-central Germany. Population: 626,100 (1990).

essence /éss'nss/ *n.* **1. IDENTIFYING NATURE** the quality or nature of sth that identifies it or makes it what it is **2. BASIC FEATURE** the most basic element or feature of sth ○ *Lack of time is the essence of the problem.* **3. PERFECT FORM** the perfect or idealized form of sth, especially when embodied in a person ○ *She is the essence of tact.* **4.** PHILOS **IDEAL NATURE OF STH** the ideal nature of sth, independent of and prior to its existence **5.** RELIG **SPIRITUAL ENTITY** a spiritual entity **6.** BIOCHEM **CHEMICAL CONSTITUENT OF PLANT** an extract or derivative of a plant that contains its characteristic or special chemical constituents **7.** COOK, COSMETICS **CONCENTRATED PLANT EXTRACT** a concentrated substance extracted from a plant that retains the plant's essential properties, such as flavour and fragrance ○ *peppermint essence* [14thC. Via French from Latin *essentia*, from *essent-*, the present participle stem of *esse* 'to be' (source of English *entity*). Ultimately from an Indo-European word meaning 'to be'.] ◊ **in essence** fundamentally or intrinsically ◊ **of the essence** of the highest importance for achieving sth

essential /i sénsh'l/ *adj.* **1.** NECESSARY of the highest importance for achieving sth ○ *It is essential that we arrive on time.* **2.** BASIC being the most basic element or feature of sth or sb ○ *We wanted the biography to tell us the essential nature of the man.* **3.** PERFECT being the pure or perfect form or embodiment of sth **4.** BIOCHEM REQUIRED IN DIET used to describe a nutrient such as a fatty acid that is required in the diet for the health and growth of an organism but not synthesized in the body **5.** DEFINING constituting the property or characteristic of sth that makes it what it is ○ *Being three-sided is essential to being a triangle.* **6.** MED WITHOUT KNOWN CAUSE used to describe a disease that has no known cause ■ *n.* STH ESSENTIAL sth that is necessary or fundamental ○ *Having your own computer is an essential for this kind of work.* ○ *She soon picked up the essentials of the subject.* [14thC. From late Latin *essentialis*, from Latin *essentia* (see ESSENCE).] —**essentiality** /i sénshi állәti/ *n.* —**essentially** /i sénsh'li/ *adv.* —**essentialness** /-nәss/ *n.*

WORD KEY: SYNONYMS

See Synonyms at ***necessary***.

essential amino acid *n.* any amino acid needed by the body to maintain growth but not synthesized by the body and usually obtained from food

essential element *n.* a chemical element that is necessary to the healthy growth of an organism

essentialism /i sénsh'lizәm/ *n.* the doctrine that things have an essence or ideal nature that is independent of and prior to their existence —**essentialist** *n.*

essential oil *n.* an oil made from an extract of a plant or substance that preserves its fundamental properties such as flavour and fragrance

Essex /éssiks/ county in eastern England. Chelmsford is the county town. Population: 1,577,500 (1995). Area: 3,674 sq. km/1,419 sq. mi.

Essex, David (*b.* 1947) British singer, songwriter, and actor. His successful stage appearances, notably in *Evita* (1978) and his own *Mutiny* (1985), enabled him to progress from pop idol to all-round entertainer. Pseudonym of **David Albert Cook**

Essex, Robert Devereux, 2nd Earl of (1566–1601) English soldier and court favourite Reputedly the lover of Elizabeth I. Following military failure in Ireland in 1599, he led an abortive insurrection in London and was beheaded.

Essex girl *n.* a stereotype of a young woman from the Essex area as brash, lower-class, unintelligent, materialistic, and sexually promiscuous (*slang informal insult*)

Essex man *n.* a stereotype of a man from the Essex area as suburban, having disposable income but no taste, vulgar in appearance and habits, and predominantly conservative politically (*slang informal insult*)

essonite /éssә nīt/ *n.* a type of garnet ranging in colour from yellow to brown [Early 19thC. Coined from Greek *hēssōn* 'inferior' (because it is less hard than other garnets) + -ITE.]

EST *abbr.* Eastern Standard Time

est. *abbr.* **1.** established **2.** estimated **3.** estuary

Est. *abbr.* BIBLE Esther

-est *suffix.* most ○ *hardest* ○ *sloppiest* [Old English]

establish /i stábblish/ (**-lishes, -lishing, -lished**) *v.* **1.** *vt.* FIX PERMANENTLY to place sth securely and permanently in a position, situation, or condition ○ *A settlement was established here two hundred years ago.* **2.** *vt.* INAUGURATE to start or set up sth that is intended to continue or be permanent ○ *The firm was established in 1954.* **3.** *vt.* PROVE to investigate sth and prove or confirm its truth or validity ○ *Have we established who gave the instruction?* **4.** *vt.* CAUSE TO BE RECOGNIZED to cause sth or sb to become generally accepted or recognized ○ *The victory established his superiority.* ○ *Her first novel established her on the literary scene.* **5.** *vt.* RELIG MAKE A CHURCH NATIONAL AND OFFICIAL to make a church an official national institution **6.** *vti.* GARDENING CAUSE A PLANT TO GROW SUCCESSFULLY to grow, or cause a plant to grow, successfully in a new place ○ *The new owners established an avenue of poplars.* ○ *Keep the area well weeded to allow the seedlings to establish.* [14thC. From Old French *establiss-*, the stem of *establir*, from Latin *stabilire*, literally 'to make stable', from *stabilis* (see STABLE).] —**establisher** *n.*

established *adj.* **1.** ACCEPTED AS TRUE generally recognized as being true or valid ○ *an established fact* **2.** SUCCESSFUL having gained public recognition in a particular sphere of activity ○ *an established author* **3.** GROWING SUCCESSFULLY growing strongly ○ *an established garden* **4.** LEGALLY RECOGNIZED legally recognized and sometimes financially supported as an official national institution, especially the Church of England ○ *an established church*

establishing shot *n.* a shot in a film that introduces a new scene

establishment /i stábblishmәnt/ *n.* **1.** ESTABLISHING STH the act of establishing sth or the condition of being established ○ *the establishment of new guidelines for users* **2.** COMM STH ESTABLISHED sth that is established as a business, institution, or successful undertaking ○ *The establishment hired several new managers.* **3.** COMM BUSINESS PREMISES a place of business ○ *The restaurant manager told them they were now barred from the establishment.* **4. establishment, Establishment** PEOPLE IN POWER a group of people who hold power in a society or social group and dominate its institutions ○ *One period's avant-garde becomes the next's artistic establishment.* **5.** PERMANENT STAFF the staff of a permanent organization, institution, or department, especially in the military or government. Used particularly in relation to the size and deployment of staff. **6.** HOUSEHOLD a place of residence, or the household that occupies it

establishmentarian /i stábblishmәn táiri әn/ *n.* **1.** MEMBER OF THE SOCIAL ESTABLISHMENT a supporter or member of the establishment in a society or social group **2.** MEMBER OF ESTABLISHED CHURCH a supporter or member of an established church —**establishmentarianism** *n.*

estaminet /e stámmi náy/ *n.* a small and simple café, bar, or bistro, especially in France [Early 19thC. From French, of uncertain origin: possibly from Walloon *staminé* 'cowshed', from *stamo* 'hitching post', probably of prehistoric Germanic origin.]

estancia /e stánssi ә/ *n.* a large landed estate, especially a cattle ranch, in South America [Mid-17thC. Via Spanish, literally 'station', from medieval Latin *stantia*, from Latin *stant-*, the present participle stem of *stare* 'to stand' (see STATION).]

estate /i stáyt/ *n.* **1.** RURAL PROPERTY WITH A RESIDENCE an area of rural, privately owned property that includes a large residence **2.** COMMERCIAL OR INDUSTRIAL AREA a large area set aside for industrial or commercial use **3.** ALL OF SB'S PROPERTY the whole of sb's property, possessions, and capital **4.** PROPERTY OF A DEAD OR BANKRUPT PERSON the assets and liabilities of sb who is dead or bankrupt **5.** ESTATE CAR estate car (*informal*) **6.** SB'S OVERALL SITUATION the circumstances, period, or condition in which sb lives **7.** POL, HIST ONE OF 3 TRADITIONAL RANKS especially formerly in Europe, any of three traditional ranks or sectors of society with some political power, broadly the clergy, the nobility, and the middle class **8.** POL, HIST DIVISION OF PARLIAMENT any of three divisions of parliament or constitutional government, either the Lords Temporal, Lords Spiritual, and the Commons, or the Crown, the House of Lords, and the House of Commons. The Scottish parliament before the Union was composed of the three estates of the high-ranking clergy, the barons, and the representatives of the royal burghs. **9.** = **plantation** [13thC. From Old French *estat* (see STATE). The underlying meaning is 'condition in which sb lives'.]

estate agent *n.* **1.** SB WHO SELLS HOUSES FOR CLIENTS a person or business that sells or leases houses and other buildings and land on behalf of the owners. US term **real estate agent 2.** MANAGER OF LANDED PROPERTY sb who manages a landed property on behalf of its owner — **estate agency** *n.*

estate-bottled *adj.* bottled by the same vineyard at which the wine was made

estate car *n. UK* a car with extra carrying space behind the seats, a rear seat that folds down, and a hinged rear door [From its ability to hold the owner's possessions]

estd, est'd *abbr.* established

esteem /i stéem/ *vt.* (**-teems, -teeming, -teemed**) **1.** VALUE HIGHLY to value sb or sth highly **2.** REGARD AS STH to consider or regard sth or sb as being in a particular category ○ *I esteem him a friend.* ■ *n.* **1.** HIGH REGARD high valuation of sb or sth ○ *It was a relationship founded on mutual esteem.* **2.** VALUATION judgment or estimation of the worth of sb or sth [Early 16thC. Via Old French *estimer* 'to value' from Latin *aestimare* (see ESTIMATE).]

WORD KEY: SYNONYMS

See Synonyms at ***regard***.

ester /éstәr/ *n.* an organic often fragrant compound formed in a reaction between an acid and an alcohol with the elimination of water [Mid-19thC. From German, a contraction of *Essigäther* 'acetic ether'.]

esterase /éstә rayz, éstә rayss/ *n.* any enzyme that acts as a catalyst in the hydrolysis of an ester

esterify /e stérri fī/ (**-fies, -fying, -fied**) *vti.* to change or make a substance change into an ester —**esterification** /e stérrifi káysh'n/ *n.*

Esth. *abbr.* BIBLE Esther

Esther /éstәr/ *n.* **1.** JEWISH QUEEN IN THE BIBLE in the Bible, the Jewish Queen of Persia who is described as having rescued her Jewish subjects from massacre **2.** BOOK OF BIBLE a book in the Bible that tells the story of Esther

esthesia *n.* US = **aesthesia**

esthete *n.* US = **aesthete**

esthetic *adj., n.* US = **aesthetic**

estheticize *vt.* US = **aestheticize**

esthetics *n.* US = **aesthetics**

estimable /éstimәb'l/ *adj.* **1.** ADMIRABLE deserving respect or admiration **2.** ABLE TO BE ESTIMATED able to be estimated (*archaic*) [15thC. From Old French, from, ultimately, Latin *aestimare* (see ESTEEM).] —**estimableness** *n.* —**estimably** *adv.*

estimate /ésti mayt/ *vti.* (**-mates, -mating, -mated**) **1.** CALCULATE ROUGHLY to make an approximate calculation of sth ○ *Can you estimate the time it will take?* **2.** SUBMIT A PRICE to assess sth, such as an item to be bought or a job to be done, and to state a likely price for it ○ *Ask at least two firms to estimate the job.* **3.** ASSESS to form an opinion or judgment about sb or sth ○ *How would you estimate that performance?* ■ *n.* **1.** ROUGH CALCULATION an approximate calculation ○ *At least a thousand people attended, at my estimate.* ○ *Here are the estimates for next month's sales figures.* **2.** APPROXIMATE PRICE an assessment of the likely price of sth, such as an item to be bought or a job to be done ○ *Their estimate is the lowest.* [Late 16thC. From Latin *aestimare* 'to value' (source also of English *esteem*), of unknown origin.] —**estimative** /éstimәtiv, -maytiv/ *adj.* —**estimator** /-maytәr/ *n.*

WORD KEY: USAGE

estimate or **estimation**? Broadly speaking, ***estimation*** refers to 'a thinking or valuing process' and ***estimate*** to 'the result of such a process'. *An estimate of the time needed* is the figure produced by working out how long sth will take, whereas *an estimation of the time needed* is the calculation process that produces that figure. ***Estimation*** also has the special meaning 'opinion or regard', which ***estimate*** does not have: *What, in your estimation, is the cause of the problem? She went down in their estimation when the truth came out.*

estimation /ésti máysh'n/ *n.* **1.** ASSESSMENT a judgment or opinion about sb or sth ○ *Her behaviour bore out his estimation of her.* **2.** ACT OF ESTIMATING the act of estimating sth, or the result of this

WORD KEY: USAGE

See Usage note at ***estimate***.

estival *adj.* US = **aestival**

estivate *vi.* US = **aestivate**

estivation *n.* US = **aestivation**

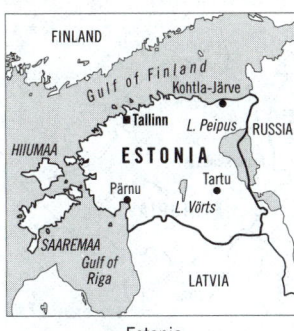

Estonia

Estonia /e stōnia/ republic on the Gulf of Finland in northeastern Europe, north of Latvia and west of Russia. The smallest of the Baltic States, it gained its independence from the Soviet Union in 1991. Language: Estonian. Currency: kroon. Capital: Tallinn. Population: 1,437,000 (1997). Area: 45,227 sq. km/17,462 sq. mi. Official name **Republic of Estonia**

Estonian /e stōni ən/ *n*. **1.** SB FROM ESTONIA sb who was born or brought up in Estonia, or who has Estonian citizenship **2.** LANGUAGE OF ESTONIA the official language of Estonia. It is one of the Finnic group of the Finno-Ugric branch of the Uralic family of languages. About 1.7 million people speak Estonian. ■ *adj.* OF ESTONIA relating to or typical of Estonia or its people, language, or culture

estop /i stóp/ (**-tops**, **-topping**, **-topped**) *vt.* **1.** PREVENT BY LEGAL RULE to use the legal rule of estoppel to prevent sth **2.** PREVENT to stop or prevent sth (*archaic*) [15thC. From Anglo-Norman and Old French *estopper*, literally 'to plug up', from, ultimately, Latin *stuppa* 'tow, broken flax', used for plugging gaps.] —**estoppage** *n.*

estoppel /i stópp'l/ *n.* a legal rule that prevents sb from stating a position inconsistent with one previously stated, especially when the earlier representation has been relied upon by others [Mid-16thC. From Old French *estouppail* 'stopper', from *estopper* (see ESTOP).]

estradiol *n.* US = oestradiol

estrange /i stráynj/ (**-tranges**, **-tranging**, **-tranged**) *vt.* to cause sb to stop feeling friendly or affectionate towards sb else or sympathetic towards a tradition or belief (*usually passive*) ○ *He managed to become estranged from all of his friends.* [15thC. Via Old French *estrangier* 'to alienate' from Latin *extraneare* 'to treat as a stranger', from *extraneus* (see STRANGE).] —**estranger** *n.* — **estrangement** *n.*

estranged /i stráynjd/ *adj.* no longer living with a husband or wife

estray /i stráy/ *n.* in law, a domestic animal that has strayed and has no obvious owner (*formal*) [Early 16thC. Via Anglo-Norman from Old French *estraier* (see STRAY).]

estreat /i street/ *n.* COPY OR TRANSCRIPT OF LEGAL RECORD a true extract from or copy of a legal record ■ *vt.* (**-treats**, **-treating**, **-treated**) COPY TO AID IN PROSECUTION to make a copy from a legal record in order to prosecute sb [15thC. From Anglo-Norman *estrete*, the past participle of *estraire* 'to extract', from Latin *extrahere* (see EXTRACT).]

estriol /éstri ol, éess-/ *n.* US = oestriol

estrogen *n.* US = oestrogen

estrogen-replacement therapy *n.* US = hormone replacement therapy

estrone *n.* US = oestrone

estrous *adj.* US = oestrous

estrus *n.* US = oestrus

estuarine /éstyoō rīn, éstyoō rin/ *adj.* relating to, formed in, or found in an estuary

estuary /éstyoō ri/ (*plural* **-ies**) *n.* the wide lower course of a river where the tide flows in, causing fresh and salt water to mix [Mid-16thC. From Latin *aestuarium*, from *aestus* 'heat, surge, tide'.] —**estuarial** /éstyoō áiri əl/ *adj.*

estuary English *n.* a variety of standard English influenced by Cockney, spoken by people in London and southeastern England along the Thames Estuary (*informal*)

—WORD KEY: WORLD ENGLISH—

Estuary English, or Estuary, is a variety spoken in and around Greater London, especially among younger people, and so named because it was first noticed in the early 1980s in Essex and Kent, counties north and south of the Thames Estuary. For some people, Estuary is a positive development, for others it is a deplorable departure from tradition and good taste. Generally perceived as a compromise between popular London usage (especially Cockney) and Received Pronunciation (RP), it is largely the province of the young, used by both the upwardly mobile and pupils of the public (that is, private) schools, who adapt away from RP, a form of speech traditionally identifying higher social class. Estuary appears to be spreading north and west, partly encouraged by postwar emigration from London, partly by egalitarianism, and partly by popular culture and the media. Among its features are: (1) The use of /w/ rather than /l/ at or near the end of syllables: taw 'tall', miwk 'milk', and St. Paw's Cathedraw 'St Paul's Cathedral'; in Estuary, forty and faulty have the same pronunciation 'fowty'; (2) Use of glottal stops instead of the consonants /k, p, t/ at the ends of syllables, as in 'a pa'er on a te'nicaw ma'er' for a paper on a technical matter. (3) The use of /i/ instead of /I/ in word-final position: 'citee' for city, 'lovelee' for lovely, 'reallee' for really. See COCKNEY, RECEIVED PRONUNCIATION.

e.s.u., **ESU** *abbr.* electrostatic unit

esurient /i syóori ənt/ *adj.* very hungry or greedy (*archaic or formal*) [Late 17thC. From Latin *esurient-*, the present participle stem of *esurire* 'to be hungry', literally 'to want to eat', from *edere* (see EDIBLE).] —**esurience** *n.* — **esuriency** *n.*

ET *abbr.* extraterrestrial

-et *suffix.* **1.** small one ○ *falconet* **2.** sth worn on ○ *anklet* [Via Old French from assumed Vulgar Latin *-ittum*, of unknown origin]

eta¹ /éetə/ *n.* the seventh letter of the Greek alphabet, represented in the English alphabet as 'e' or 'ē' [15thC. From Greek *ēta*.]

eta² /áytə/ (*plural* **etas** *or* **eta**) *n.* in former times, a member of a Japanese class that was restricted to doing menial and disagreeable tasks [Late 19thC. From Japanese.]

ETA¹ *abbr.* estimated time of arrival

ETA², **Eta** *n.* a Basque nationalist guerrilla group that seeks separation and independence from Spain for the Basque region [Mid-20thC. From Basque, an acronym for *Euzkadi ta Askatsuna* 'Basque Nation and Liberty'.]

Étagère

étagère /áy taa zháir/ *n.* a piece of furniture made up of open shelves, used to hold small objects [Mid-19thC. Via French from Old French *estagiere* 'scaffold', from *estage* (see STAGE).]

et al. /et ál/ *adv.* and elsewhere [Shortening of Latin *et alibi* 'and elsewhere']

etalon /étta lon/ *n.* a spectroscopic device that has two flat parallel reflecting surfaces and is used to measure wavelengths [Early 20thC. From French *étalon* 'standard', from Old French *estal* 'standing place' (see STALE).]

etamine /étta meen/ *n.* a light, loosely woven cotton or worsted fabric [Early 18thC. Via French from, ultimately, Latin *stamineus* 'made of threads', from *stamen* 'thread' (see STAMEN).]

etc. *abbr.* et cetera

et cetera /it séttərə/, **etcetera** *adv.* AND SO ON used to indicate that a list contains other unspecified items ○ *an urgent request for clothes, food, medicines, etc* ■ *n.* STH OR SB UNSPECIFIED one of several or many unspecified things or people [From Latin, literally 'and the rest']

etch /ech/ (**etches**, **etching**, **etched**) *v.* **1.** *vti.* DESIGN CUT A DESIGN INTO STH WITH ACID to create a design or drawing on the surface of sth, especially a printing plate, by the action of an acid **2.** *vti.* CUT MARKS WITH STH SHARP to cut a design or mark into the surface of sth using a sharp point or laser beam **3.** *vt.* MAKE CLEARLY VISIBLE to leave a clear and distinct impression of sth (*usually passive*) ○ *His sorrow was etched on his face.* [Mid-17thC. Via Dutch *etsen* from, ultimately, Old High German *ezzen* 'to eat away'. Ultimately from an Indo-European word that is also the ancestor of English *eat* and *edible*.] —**etcher** *n.*

etching /éching/ *n.* **1.** CREATION OF CUT DESIGNS the art or process of creating etched designs or making prints from etched surfaces **2.** PRINT FROM AN ETCHED PLATE a print made from an etched plate **3.** PRINTING PLATE FOR ETCHING a printing plate with an etched design

ETD *abbr.* estimated time of departure

eternal /i túrn'l/ *adj.* **1.** EXISTING THROUGH ALL TIME lasting for all time without beginning or end ○ *eternal life* **2.** UNCHANGING unaffected by the passage of time ○ *eternal truths* **3.** SEEMINGLY EVERLASTING seeming to go on for ever or recur incessantly (*informal*) ○ *an eternal student* ■ *n.* WHAT LASTS FOR EVER sth that exists everlastingly [14thC. From Old French, from, ultimately, Latin *aeternus*.] —**eternality** /éetər nálləti/ *n.* —**eternally** /i túrn'li/ *adv.*

Eternal /i túrn'l/ *n.* God as a universal spirit

Eternal City *n.* Rome, the capital of Italy (*literary*)

eternalize /i túrn'l īz/ (**-izes**, **-izing**, **-ized**), **eternalise** (**-ises**, **-ising**, **-ised**) *vt.* **1.** MAKE ETERNAL to make sth eternal **2.** MAKE IMMORTAL to make sth so famous as to become immortal

eternal triangle *n.* a sexual or romantic relationship among three persons that involves jealousy or other emotional conflicts [From the notion that such relationships have been known throughout history]

eternise *vt.* = eternize

eternity /i túrnəti/ *n.* **1.** INFINITE TIME time without beginning or end ○ *lost for all eternity* **2.** TIMELESSNESS the condition, quality, or fact of being without beginning or end **3.** RELIG TIMELESSNESS AFTER DEATH a timeless state conceived as being experienced after death **4.** VERY LONG TIME a very long or seemingly very long period of time ○ *It will take an eternity to put it together again.* ■ **eternities** *npl.* TRUTHS SAID TO BE ETERNAL beliefs or ideas about life that are conceived as being timeless [14thC. Via Old French *eternite* from Latin *aeternitas*, from *aeternus* (see ETERNAL).]

—WORD KEY: CULTURAL NOTE—

From Here to Eternity, a film by US director Fred Zinnemann (1953). Based on James Jones's 1951 novel of the same name, it depicts the lives of US military personnel in Hawaii immediately prior to the attack on Pearl Harbor. It is perhaps best remembered for a scene in which Burt Lancaster and Deborah Kerr embrace in the surf.

eternity ring *n.* a ring with gemstones set round its whole circumference, intended to symbolize everlasting love

eternize /i túr nīz/ (**-nizes**, **-nizing**, **-nized**), **eternise** (**-nises**, **-nising**, **-nised**) *vt.* = eternalize [Mid-16thC. From French *éterniser*, from, ultimately, Latin *aeternus* (see ETERNAL).]

etesian wind /i téezhi ən-/ *adj.* an annual summer wind that blows from the northwest in the Aegean Sea and other parts of the eastern Mediterranean [Early 17thC. *Etesian* formed from Latin *etesius* 'annual', from Greek *etēsios*, from *etos* 'year'. Ultimately from an Indo-European word meaning 'year'.]

ETF *n.*, *abbr.* electronic transfer of funds

eth *n.* = edh

ethambutol /e thámbyoō tol/ *n.* an antimicrobial substance used in combination with other drugs in the treatment of tuberculosis. Formula: $C_{10}H_{24}N_2O_2$. [Mid-20thC. Coined from ETHYL + AMINE + BUTANOL.]

ethanal /eéthə nal, éthə-/ *n.* = **acetaldehyde**

ethanamide /i thánnə mīd/ *n.* = **acetamide**

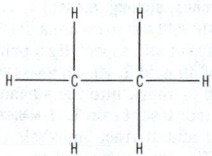

Ethane

ethane /eé thayn, é thayn/ *n.* a colourless odourless gas that is highly flammable and occurs naturally in petroleum and natural gas. It is used as a fuel and in refrigeration. Formula: C_2H_6. [Late 19thC. Coineded from ETHYL + -ANE.]

ethanedioic acid /eé thayn dī ō ik, é thayn-/ *n.* CHEM = **oxalic acid**

ethanoic acid /eéthənō ik-, éthə-/ *n.* = **acetic acid**

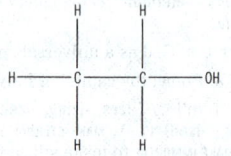

Ethanol

ethanol /eéthə nol, éthə nol/ *n.* a colourless liquid with a pleasant smell that is produced naturally from fermentation by yeasts and other micro-organisms. It is used in alcoholic beverages, as a solvent, and in the manufacture of other chemicals. Formula: C_2H_5OH. [Early 20thC. Coined from ETHANE + -OL.]

ethanolamine /eéthə nóllə meen, éthə-/ *n.* any of three colourless solid or viscous substances. They are used widely in industry, e.g. in manufacturing antibiotics, cosmetics, detergents, and herbicides.

Ethelbert /éth'l burt/, **King of Kent** (552?–616). He dominated southern England during his reign (560–616) and was the first Christian Anglo-Saxon monarch, being baptized in 597 by St Augustine of Canterbury.

Ethelred I /éth'l red/, **King of the West Saxons and Kentishmen** (830?–871). His reign (866–71) saw continual struggle with Danish invaders, whom he defeated at Ashdown in 871.

Ethelred II, **King of the English** (968–1016). His reign was marked by bitter military struggles. Known as **Ethelred the Unready**

ethene /é theen/ *n.* ethylene (*technical*) [Mid-19thC. Coined from ETHYL + -ENE.]

ether /eéthər/ *n.* **1.** CHEM LIQUID SOLVENT AND ANAESTHETIC a volatile colourless liquid with a pleasant smell. It is used as a solvent and was formerly used as an anaesthetic. Formula: $C_2H_5OC_2H_5$. **2.** CHEM ORGANIC COMPOUND WITH LINKED HYDROCARBON GROUPS any organic compound containing two hydrocarbon groups linked by an oxygen atom **3.** ether, aether PHYS HYPOTHETICAL ELECTRO-MAGNETIC MEDIUM a medium formerly believed to fill the atmosphere and outer space and to carry electromagnetic waves ○ *send a message across the ether* **4.** ether, aether SKY the sky or upper reaches of the atmosphere (*literary*) **5.** ether, aether AIR air (*literary*) [14thC. Via Latin *aether* from Greek *aither*

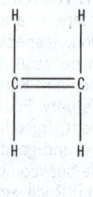

Ethene

'upper air'. Ultimately from an Indo-European word meaning 'to burn', which is also the ancestor of English *aestival*, *edifice*, and *estuary*.] —**etheric** /ee thérrik, i thérrik/ *adj.*

ethereal /i theéri əl/ *adj.* **1.** EXQUISITE very delicate or highly refined ○ *ethereal beauty* **2.** AIRY very light, airy, or insubstantial ○ *Her fragrance lingered in the room, an ethereal reminder of her presence.* **3.** HEAVENLY belonging to the heavens or the celestial sphere **4.** CHEM OF ETHER consisting of, containing, or relating to ether [Early 16thC. Via Latin *aetherius* from, ultimately, Greek *aithēr* (see ETHER).] —**ethereality** /i theéri álləti/ *n.* —**ethereally** /i theéri əli/ *adv.* —**etherealness** /-əlnəss/ *n.*

etherealize /i theéri ə līz/ (**-izes, -izing, -ized**), **etherealise** (**-ises, -ising, -ised**) *vt.* **1.** MAKE ETHEREAL to make sth very delicate or refined **2.** CHEM MAKE INTO ETHER to turn sth into ether —**etherealization** /i theéri ə IT záysh'n/ *n.*

Etherege /éthərij/, **Sir George** (1635?–91) English playwright. His witty and mildly risqué plays, such as *The Man of Mode* (1676), established the style for what is now called Restoration comedy.

etherify /eéthəri fī, i thérri fī/ (**-fies, -fying, -fied**) *vt.* CHEM to convert a substance, especially an alcohol, into ether (*technical*) —**etherification** /i thérrifi káysh'n/ *n.*

etherize /eéthə rīz/ (**-izes, -izing, -ized**), **etherise** (**-ises, -ising, -ised**) *vt.* = etherify —**etherization** /eéthə rī záysh'n/ *n.* —**etherizer** /eéthə rīzər/ *n.*

Ethernet /eéthər net/ *tdmk.* a trademark for a system for exchanging messages between computers on a local area network using coaxial, fibre-optic, or twisted-pair cables

ethic /éthik/ *n.* SET OF PRINCIPLES a system of moral standards or principles ○ *the Protestant work ethic.* ○ **ethics** ■ *adj.* = ethical *adj.* 2 [Late 19thC. Via French *éthique* from, ultimately, Greek *ēthikē*, from *ēthikos* 'ethical', from *ēthos* 'character, nature' (see ETHOS).]

ethical /éthik'l/ *adj.* **1.** CONFORMING TO ACCEPTED STANDARDS consistent with agreed principles of correct moral conduct ○ *While such activities are not strictly illegal, they are certainly not ethical.* **2.** ethical, ethic OF ETHICS relating to or involving ethics **3.** PHARM AVAILABLE BY PRESCRIPTION ONLY used to describe a drug that is available only through a doctor's prescription —**ethicality** /éthi kálləti/ *n.* —**ethically** /éthikli/ *adv.* —**ethicalness** /éthik'lnəss/ *n.*

ethicist /éthissist/ *n.* sb who studies ethics or is devoted to ethical ideals

ethics /éthiks/ *n.* **1.** STUDY OF MORALITY'S EFFECT ON CONDUCT the study of moral standards and how they affect conduct (*takes a singular verb*) **2.** CODE OF MORALITY a system of moral principles governing the appropriate conduct for an individual or group (*takes a plural verb*) [15thC. Via Old French *ethiques* from, ultimately, Greek *ēthika*, from *ēthikos* 'ethical' (see ETHIC).]

Ethiopia /eéthi ópi ə/ landlocked country in north-eastern Africa, separated from the Red Sea by Eritrea and Djibouti, and from the Gulf of Aden by Somalia. It is the oldest independent country in Africa. Language: Amharic. Currency: birr. Capital: Addis Ababa. Population: 57,098,762 (1997). Area: 1,133,380 sq. km/437,600 sq. mi. Official name **Federal Democratic Republic of Ethiopia**

Ethiopian /eéthi ópi ən/ *n.* **1.** SB FROM ETHIOPIA sb who was born or brought up in Ethiopia, or who has Ethiopian citizenship **2.** OLD TERM FOR BLACK PERSON a term, now considered offensive, for a Black person

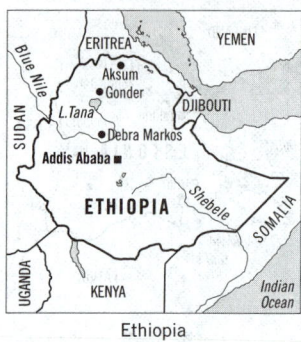

Ethiopia

(*archaic*) ■ *adj.* **1.** OF ETHIOPIA relating to or typical of Ethiopia or its people or culture **2.** ZOOL OF AFRICA SOUTH OF THE SAHARA used to describe Africa south of the Sahara as a biogeographical area

Ethiopic /eéthi óppik, -ópik/ *n.* LANG = **Ge'ez** [Mid-17thC. Via Latin from Greek *aithiopikos*, from the stem *Aithiop-* 'Ethiopian', from *aithein* 'to burn' + *ōps* 'face'.]

ethmoid bone /éth moyd/ *n.* a perforated bone in the skull whose outer surfaces form part of the outer wall of the nasal cavity and the inner wall of the eye socket [Mid-18thC. From Greek *ēthmoeidēs* 'sievelike', from *ēthmos* 'sieve'.] —**ethmoidal** /eth móyd'l/ *adj.*

ethnic /éthnik/ *adj.* **1.** SHARING CULTURAL CHARACTERISTICS sharing distinctive cultural traits as a group in society ○ *ethnic minorities* **2.** OF A GROUP SHARING CULTURAL CHARACTERISTICS relating to a group or groups in society with distinctive cultural traits ○ *ethnic origins* **3.** OF SPECIFIED ORIGIN OR CULTURE belonging to a particular group by descent or culture rather than by nationality **4.** CULTURALLY TRADITIONAL belonging to or typical of the traditional culture of a social group ○ *ethnic clothing* **5.** IDENTIFIED BY CULTURE belonging to or typical of a specified culture, often used about cultures originating elsewhere than the location of the item described ○ *various ethnic restaurants* ○ *ethnic jewellery* ■ *n.* US, Can MEMBER OF AN ETHNIC GROUP a member of an ethnic group within a society [14thC. Via late Latin *ethnicus* 'heathen' from Greek *ethnikos*, from *ethnos* 'people, nation'. Ultimately from an Indo-European base denoting 'self'.] —**ethnically** *adv.*

ethnic cleansing *n.* the violent elimination or removal from an area of people attacked because of their ethnic backgrounds, by means of genocide or forced expulsion

ethnicity /eth níssəti/ (*plural* **-ties**) *n.* ethnic affiliation or distinctiveness

ethnic minority *n.* an ethnic group that is a minority within a nation or society

ethno- *prefix.* people, culture ○ *ethnohistory* [From Greek *ethnos* 'people, nation' (see ETHNIC)]

ethnobotany /éthnō bóttəni/ *n.* the scientific study of the traditional classification and uses of plants in different human societies —**ethnobotanical** /éthnōbə tánnik'l/ *adj.* —**ethnobotanically** /-tánnikli/ *adv.* —**ethnobotanist** /éthnō bóttənist/ *n.*

ethnocentrism /éthnō séntrizəm/ *n.* a belief in or assumption of the superiority of your own social or cultural group (*disapproving*) —**ethnocentric** *adj.* —**ethnocentrically** *adv.* —**ethnocentricity** /éthnō sen tríssəti/ *n.*

ethnogenesis /éthnō jénnəssiss/ *n.* the creation of a new ethnic group identity

ethnography /eth nóggrəfi/ *n.* a branch of anthropology concerned with the description of ethnic groups —**ethnographer** *n.* —**ethnographic** /éthnə gráffik/ *adj.* —**ethnographically** /-gráffikli/ *adv.*

ethnohistory /éthnō hístəri/ *n.* the scientific study of how cultures have developed through history —**ethnohistorian** /éthnō hi stáwri ən/ *n.* —**ethnohistoric** /-hi stórrik/ *adj.*

ethnolinguistics /éthnō ling gwístiks/ *n.* the scientific study of the relationship between language and culture (*takes a singular verb*) —**ethnolinguist** /éthnō líng gwist/ *n.* —**ethnolinguistic** /éthnō ling gwístik/ *adj.* —**ethnolinguistically** /-gwístikli/ *adv.*

---

ethnology /eth nólləji/ n. **1. STUDY OF ETHNIC GROUPS** the comparison of different cultures, or the study of how and why cultures differ. Ethnology can focus on one culture through time, or several cultures at the same time. **2. = cultural anthropology —ethnologic** /éthnə lójjik/ adj. **—ethnologically** /éthnə lójjikli/ adv. **—ethnologist** /eth nólləjist/ n.

ethnomethodology /éthnō méthə dólləji/ n. the study of how people interact in ways that maintain the social structure of the situations in which they find themselves **—ethnomethodologist** n.

ethnomusicology /éthnō myoozi kólləji/ n. the study of the music of non-Western cultures **—ethnomusicological** /éthnō myoozikə lójjik'l/ adj. **—ethnomusicologist** /éthnō myoozi kóllәjist/ n.

ethology /i thólləji/ n. **1. STUDY OF ANIMAL BEHAVIOURAL PATTERNS** the study of the behaviour of animals in their natural habitat, usually proposing evolutionary explanations **2. = human ethology** [Mid-17thC. From Latin ethologia, from, ultimately, Greek ēthos (see ETHOS).] **—ethological** /éethə lójjik'l/ adj. **—ethologist** /i thólləjist/ n.

ethos /ée thoss/ n. the fundamental and distinctive character of a group, social context, or period of time, typically expressed in attitudes, habits, and beliefs [Mid-19thC. From Greek ēthos 'custom, disposition'. Ultimately from an Indo-European base denoting 'self', which is also the ancestor of English self, suicide, idiom, and custom.]

ethoxy /ee thóksi/ adj. forming or containing a chemical group composed of ethyl and oxygen. Formula: CH_3CH_2O. [Late 19thC. Coined from ETHYL + OXY-.]

ethoxyethane /ee thóksi ée thayn/ n. ether (technical)

ethoxyl /ee thóksil/ adj. = ethoxy

ethyl /ée thīl, éth'l/ n. a chemical group containing carbon and hydrogen, deriving from ethane. Formula: CH_3CH_2. [Mid-19thC. Coined from ETHER + -YL.]

ethyl acetate n. a volatile colourless liquid with a pleasant fruity smell. It is used in making perfumes and as a solvent. Formula: $C_4H_8O_2$.

ethyl alcohol n. = ethanol

ethylamine /éthilə méen/ n. a colourless liquid used in oil refining and detergents. Formula: $C_2H_5NH_2$.

ethylate /éthi layt/ (-ates, -ating, -ated) vt. to attach an ethyl group to a molecule or to one of the molecules of a compound **—ethylation** /éthi láysh'n/ n.

ethyl carbamate n. CHEM = urethane

ethylene /éthi leen/ n. a colourless flammable gas occurring in petroleum and natural gas and produced by ripening fruit. It is used in the manufacture of polymers and other chemicals, in metallurgy, and to ripen and colour harvested fruit. Formula: C_2H_4. **—ethylenic** /éthi léenik/ adj.

ethylene glycol n. a viscous colourless liquid with a sweet taste. It is used as an antifreeze and in the manufacture of polyester. Formula: $C_2H_6O_2$.

ethyl mercaptan n. a strong-smelling colourless liquid that is added to odourless fuels to give them an odour so that leaks can be detected. Formula: C_2H_5SH.

ethyne /ée thīn, éth īn/ n. = acetylene

etic /éttik/ adj. ANTHROP making use of preestablished categories for organizing and interpreting anthropological data, rather than categories recognized within the culture being studied. ◊ **-emic** [Mid-20thC. From PHONETIC.]

-etic suffix. used to form adjectives from nouns ending in -esis ◊ geodetic [Via Latin from Greek -ētikos, from -etos]

etiolated /ée ti ə laytid/ adj. used to describe a plant that is abnormally tall and spindly and deficient in green pigment chlorophyll owing to lack of light [Late 18thC. Formed from etiolate, from French étioler, of uncertain origin: perhaps from Norman French étieuler 'to grow into stalks', ultimately from Latin stipula 'straw'.] **—etiolation** /ée ti ə láysh'n/ n.

etiology n. = aetiology

etiquette /étti ket/ n. the rules and conventions governing correct or polite behaviour in society in general or in a particular social or professional group or situation ◊ *Etiquette dictates that wedding invitations should be acknowledged in writing.* [Mid-18thC. From French, 'ticket', also 'etiquette' (probably from the custom of giving rules for behaviour either on a soldier's lodging ticket or on cards given out at court).]

Etna, Mount /étnə/ volcano in eastern Sicily. It is the highest active volcano in Europe and has had over ninety recorded eruptions. Height: 3,323 m/10,902 ft.

Eton /ée t'n/ town in Buckinghamshire, England, on the River Thames opposite Windsor. Eton College is a leading independent school. Population: 3,523 (1991).

Eton collar n. a broad stiff white collar turned down over the collar and lapels of a coat or jacket, especially one worn as part of the Eton College uniform

Eton College /ée t'n-/, **Eton** n. a public school in the town of Eton, in Buckinghamshire, southeastern England. It was founded in 1440 by Henry VI. **—Etonian** /ee tóni ən/ n., adj.

Eton crop n. a hairstyle in which the hair is cut short and lies flat, fashionable among women in the 1920s [From its resemblance to a schoolboy's short haircut]

Eton jacket n. a short black jacket with wide lapels and an open front, formerly worn by the pupils of Eton College

Etosha National Park /e tóshə-/ national park in Namibia, southwestern Africa. Established in 1958, it contains the Etosha Pan, a salt desert that was once a lake. Area: 20,700 sq. km/8,000 sq. mi.

étrier /áytri ay/ n. a short rope ladder using in mountain climbing [Mid-20thC. From French, 'stirrup, rope ladder'.]

Etruria /e troóri ə/ ancient region on the northwestern coast of peninsular Italy, where the Etruscan civilization flourished in the first millennium BC. The region occupied roughly the same area as present-day Tuscany and part of Umbria, and at its greatest extent stretched from the Alps to the River Tiber. **—Etrurian** n., adj.

Etruscan: Gable end from Villa Giulia, Rome, Italy (4th century BC)

Etruscan /i trúskən/ n. **1. MEMBER OF AN ANCIENT PEOPLE FROM ETRURIA** a member of an ancient people who lived in Etruria. Their civilization flourished during the period from the eighth to the sixth centuries BC, although they survived until overcome by the Romans during the second century BC. **2. ANCIENT LANGUAGE OF ETRURIA** an extinct language spoken in ancient Etruria that has no relation to the languages of the Indo-European family [Early 18thC. Formed from Latin Etruscus 'of Etruria'.] **—Etruscan** adj.

et seq. 1. AND THE FOLLOWING ONE and another following, especially the next page in a book. Full form **et sequens, et sequentia 2. et seq., et seqq. AND THOSE THAT FOLLOW** and others following, especially the next pages in a book. Full form **et sequentia** [Shortening of Latin et sequens (or sequentia) 'and the following one (or ones)']

-ette suffix. **1.** small ◊ diskette **2.** female ◊ usherette **3.** imitation ◊ leatherette [From Old French, feminine of -et]

étude /áy tyood/ n. a short musical composition for a solo instrument intended to develop a point of technique or to display the performer's skill, but often played for its artistic merit [Mid-19thC. From

French, 'study', via Old French estudie (source of English study) from Latin studium.]

étui /ay twée/ n. a small ornamental case for needles or other small items [Early 17thC. From French, from Old French estui 'prison', from estuier 'to keep'.]

ety., etym. abbr. **1.** etymology **2.** etymological

etyma plural of etymon

etymol. abbr. **1.** etymological **2.** etymology

etymologize /étti mólla jīz/ (-gizes, -gizing, -gized), **etymologise** (-gises, -gising, -gised) vti. to study, trace, or describe the origin and development of a word, or make a suggestion as to its possible origin and development

etymology /étti mólləji/ (plural -gies) n. **1. STUDY OF WORD ORIGINS** the study of the origins of words or parts of words and how they have arrived at their current form and meaning **2. HISTORY OF A WORD** the origin of a word or part of a word, or a statement of this and how it has arrived at its current form and meaning. An etymology often shows the different forms the word has taken in passing from one language to another, and sometimes shows related words in other languages. ◊ *The words have the same spelling but different etymologies.* [14thC. Via Old French ethimologie from, ultimately, Greek etumologia, from etumon (see ETYMON).] **—etymological** /éttimə lójjik'l/ adj. **—etymologically** /éttimə lójjikli, éttimə lójjikəli/ adv. **—etymologist** /étti mólləjist/ n.

etymon /étti mon/ (plural -mons or -ma /-mə/) n. **1. ORIGIN OF A WORD** an earlier form of a word or part of a word, especially the first recorded form in any language **2. ROOT OF A WORD** a word or part of a word from which another word is derived [Late 16thC. Via Latin from Greek etumon 'true sense of a word', from etumos 'true', hence 'original'.]

Eu symbol. europium

EU abbr. European Union

eu- prefix. good, well, true, easily ◊ euphonious ◊ euplastic [Via Latin from Greek eus]

eubacteria /yoó bak teéri ə/ npl. in modern biological classification, all those bacteria considered to be the true bacteria, characterized by their rigid cell walls

eucalypt n. = eucalyptus [Late 19thC. Shortening.]

eucalyptol /yoókə líp tol/, **eucalyptole** /-tōl/ n. a colourless oily liquid obtained from eucalyptus oil, used in pharmaceuticals, perfumes and flavourings. Formula: $C_{10}H_{18}O$.

Eucalyptus

eucalyptus /yoókə líptəss/ (plural -tuses or -ti /-tī/), **eucalypt** /yoókə lipt/ n. a tall evergreen tree mainly native to Australia that has tough aromatic leaves and flowers in clusters and provides good timber, resin, and an oil with medicinal properties. There are more than 600 species. Genus: *Eucalyptus.* [Early 19thC. From modern Latin, genus name, from Greek eu- 'well' + kaluptos 'covered', from the covering on the tree's buds.]

eucaryote n. BIOL = eukaryote

Eucharist /yoókərist/ n. **1. CEREMONY WITH SYMBOLIC BREAD AND WINE** a ceremony in many Christian churches during which symbolic or consecrated bread and wine are consumed, to commemorate the last meal of Jesus Christ with his disciples before his death **2. SYMBOLIC BREAD AND WINE** the symbolic or consecrated bread and wine eaten and drunk during the ceremony of the Eucharist [14thC. Via Old French *eucariste* from, ultimately, Greek *eukharistia* 'giving of thanks', from *eukharistos* 'grateful', from *kharizesthai* 'to show favour' (source of English *charisma*).] —**Eucharistic** /yoókə rístik/ *adj.*

euchre /yoókər/ *n.* **1.** CARD GAME OF WINNING TRICKS a card game played with the highest 32 cards in the pack in which each player receives five cards and must take at least three tricks to win. It is played mainly in North America. **2.** THWARTING OF AN OPPONENT AT EUCHRE an instance of preventing another player from making the three tricks needed to win a game of euchre ■ *vt.* (**-chres, -chring, -chred**) **1.** THWART AN OPPONENT AT EUCHRE to prevent another player from taking the three tricks needed to win a game of euchre **2.** *ANZ, Can, US* TRICK to cheat, trick, or deceive sb [Early 19thC. Origin uncertain: perhaps from German dialect *Jucker(spiel)*.]

euchromatin /yoo krómətin/ *n.* an expanded form of the material of which chromosomes are composed, occurring when DNA is being actively copied. It stains lightly only with basic dyes. —**euchromatic** /yoókrə máttik/ *adj.*

Euclid /yoóklid/ (*fl.* 300 BC) Greek mathematician. He taught in Alexandria and compiled the 13-volume *Elements* (300? BC), the standard text on geometry until the 19th century.

Euclidean /yoo klíddi ən/, **Euclidian** *adj.* relating to Euclid or his system of geometry

Euclidean geometry *n.* geometry according to the principles of Euclid, as described in his *Elements*, in which only one line parallel to another given line may pass through a given point

eudemon /yoo deémən/, **eudaemon** *n.* a benevolent supernatural being [Early 17thC. From Greek *eudaimōn* 'having a guardian spirit', hence 'fortunate, happy', from *daimōn* 'spiritual being, guardian' (source of English *demon*).]

eudemonism /yoo deémənizəm/, **eudaemonism** *n.* an ethical doctrine that characterizes the value of life in terms of happiness —**eudemonist** *n.* —**eudemonistic** /yoo deémə nístik/ *adj.*

eudiometer /yoódi ómmitər/ *n.* an instrument used to measure the volume changes that take place in chemical gas reactions [Late 18thC. Formed from Greek *eudios* 'fine (weather)' (from *eu-* 'good' + *Zeus* 'god of the sky'), because an increase in the oxygen content of air supposedly forecast good weather.] —**eudiometric** /yoódi ə méttrik/ *adj.* —**eudiometrically** /-méttrikli/ *adv.* —**eudiometry** /yoódi ómmətri/ *n.*

Eudoxus of Cnidus /yoo dóksəss əv knídəss/ (408?–355?BC) Greek astronomer and mathematician. He developed a mathematical model for predicting planetary motion. His geometrical discoveries are thought to be behind much of Euclid's *Elements*.

eugenicist /yoo jénnissist/, **eugenist** /yoójənist/ *n.* sb who studies proposed ways of improving the human species, especially by selective breeding, or who advocates the principles or practice of eugenics

eugenics /yoo jénniks/ *n.* the proposed improvement of the human species by encouraging or permitting reproduction of only those individuals with genetic characteristics judged desirable. It has been regarded with disfavour since the Nazi period. (*takes a singular verb*) [Late 19thC] —**eugenic** *adj.* —**eugenically** *adv.*

eugenist *n.* = eugenicist

eugenol /yoóji nol/ *n.* a colourless oily liquid obtained

Eugenol

from cloves and used in dentistry to reduce pain and in perfumes. Formula: $C_{10}H_{12}O_2$. [Late 19thC. Formed from *eugenia*, genus name of the clove tree, ultimately named after Prince *Eugene* of Savoy (1663–1736), Austrian general.]

euglena /yoo gleénə/ *n.* a single-celled freshwater organism that has appendages (**flagella**) for locomotion and produces its food by photosynthesis. Genus: *Euglena*. [Mid-19thC. From modern Latin, genus name, from Greek *eu-* 'well' + *glēnē* 'eyeball', perhaps from its reddish eyespot.] —**euglenoid** /yoo gleén oyd/ *adj.*

euhemerism /yoo heémərizəm/ *n.* the theory that mythology has its origins in history, the gods being deified heroes of the past [Mid-19thC. Formed from Latin *Euhemerus*, from Greek *Euēmeros* (4thC BC), name of a Greek writer who maintained that the deities of Greek mythology were deified men and women.] —**euhemerist** *n.* —**euhemeristic** /yoo heémə rístik/ *adj.* —**euhemeristically** /-rístikli/ *adv.*

eukaryote /yoo kárri ot/, **eucaryote** *n.* any organism with one or more cells that have visible nuclei and organelles. The group contains all living and fossil cellular organisms except bacteria and blue-green algae. [Mid-20thC. Coined from EU- + Greek *karuōtos* 'having nuts', from *karuon* 'nut', from, ultimately, an Indo-European word that is also the ancestor of English *cancer*.] —**eukaryotic** /yoo kárri óttik/ *adj.*

eulachon /yoólə kon/ (*plural* **-chons** or **-chon**) *n.* = **candlefish** [Mid-19thC. From Lower Chinook *úłxan*.]

Euler /óylər, yoólər/, **Leonhard** (1707–83) Swiss mathematician. With Joseph Lagrange, he was the foremost mathematician of his century. In some 800 publications he laid the foundations of modern analytical mathematics.

eulogia[1] /yoo lóji ə/ *n.* bread blessed and given after the liturgy in the Eastern Orthodox Church to those not present at the Eucharist [Mid-18thC. Via late Latin, 'consecrated bread', from, ultimately, Greek (see EULOGIUM).]

eulogia[2] *plural of* eulogium

eulogise *vt.* = eulogize

eulogistic /yoólə jístik/ *adj.* full of praise for sb or sth (*formal*) —**eulogistically** *adv.*

eulogium /yoo lóji əm/ (*plural* **-a** /-ji ə/ *or* **-ums**) *n.* a eulogy (*formal*) [Early 17thC. From medieval Latin, probably a blend of *eulogia* 'praise' (from Greek, formed from *eu-* 'well' + *-logia* 'speaking') and Latin *elogium* 'epitaph'.]

eulogize /yoólə jīz/ (**-gizes, -gizing, -gized**), **eulogise** (**-gises, -gising, -gised**) *vti.* to praise sb or sth very highly (*formal*) —**eulogizer** *n.*

eulogy /yoólə ji/ (*plural* **-gies**) *n.* **1.** SPOKEN OR WRITTEN TRIBUTE a speech or piece of writing that praises sb or sth very highly, especially a tribute to sb who has recently died **2.** HIGH PRAISE great praise (*formal*) [15thC. From medieval Latin *eulogium* (see EULOGIUM).] —**eulogist** *n.*

Eumenides /yoo ménni deez/ *n.* three sister goddesses in Greek mythology. They were originally fertility goddesses, but were later identified with the Furies. [Late 17thC. Via Latin from Greek, from *eumenēs* 'kindly, friendly', from *menos* 'spirit'.]

eunuch /yoónək/ *n.* **1.** CASTRATED HUMAN MALE a man or boy whose testicles have been removed or do not function. Eunuchs were formerly employed in Islamic countries to guard the women of a harem or as court officials. **2.** INEFFECTUAL MAN a man who lacks power or effectiveness (*informal insult*) [15thC. Via Latin *eunuchus* from Greek *eunoukhos* 'attendant of a bedroom or harem', from *eunē* 'bed' + *ekhein* 'to keep'.] —**eunuchism** *n.*

eunuchoid /yoónə koyd/ *adj.* lacking fully developed male sexual organs or characteristics

euonymus /yoo ónniməss/ *n.* a tree or shrub of northern temperate regions cultivated for its decorative evergreen foliage and clusters of orange or red fruits. The spindle tree is a type of euonymus. Genus: *Euonymus*. [Mid-19thC. Via modern Latin, genus name, from, ultimately, Greek *euōnumos*, literally 'of good name', hence 'lucky' (perhaps euphemistic, since the flowering of the tree was taken to be an omen of disease).]

eupatrid /yoo páttrid/ (*plural* **-ridae** /-dee/ *or* **-rids**) *n.* sb belonging to the hereditary class of nobles and

landowners in ancient Athens [Mid-19thC. From Greek *eupatridēs* 'sb of noble ancestry', literally 'having a good father', from *patēr* 'father'.]

eupepsia /yoo pépsi ə/ *n.* good or efficient digestion [Early 18thC. From Greek, 'digestibility', from *eupeptos* 'easy to digest' (see EUPEPTIC).]

eupeptic /yoo péptik/ *adj.* **1.** PHYSIOL RELATING TO GOOD DIGESTION relating to or producing good digestion **2.** CHEERFUL with a cheerful manner or disposition [Late 17thC. Formed from Greek *eupeptos* 'easy to digest, having good digestion', from *peptein* 'to digest'.] —**eupeptically** *adv.*

euphemise *vti.* = euphemize

euphemism /yoófəmizəm/ *n.* **1.** LESS OFFENSIVE SYNONYM a word or phrase used in place of a term that might be considered too direct, harsh, unpleasant, or offensive. A wide range of euphemisms is used in connection with death, sex, and excretion. ○ *The phrase 'collateral damage' is a euphemism for injury to civilians during a military operation.* **2.** USE OF INOFFENSIVE WORDS the use of a word or phrase that is more neutral, vague, or indirect to replace a direct, harsh, unpleasant, or offensive term [Late 16thC. From Greek *euphēmismos*, from *euphēmizein* 'to speak with pleasing words', from, ultimately, *phēmē* 'speech'.] —**euphemist** *n.* —**euphemistic** /yoófə místik/ *adj.*

euphemize /yoófə mīz/ (**-mizes, -mizing, -mized**), **euphemise** (**-mises, -mising, -mised**) *vti.* to avoid saying or writing sth direct, harsh, unpleasant, or offensive by using milder or more indirect language —**euphemizer** *n.*

euphonious /yoo fóni əss/ *adj.* **1.** PLEASANT-SOUNDING having a pleasant sound **2.** EASIER TO PRONOUNCE made easier to pronounce by a change in speech sounds —**euphoniously** *adv.* —**euphoniousness** *n.*

euphonise *vt.* = euphonize

Euphonium

euphonium /yoo fóni əm/ *n.* a brass instrument similar to, but smaller than, a tuba, used mainly in military and brass bands [Mid-19thC. Coined from Greek *euphōnos* 'well-sounding' (see EUPHONY) + -IUM.]

euphonize /yoófə nīz/ (**-nizes, -nizing, -nized**), **euphonise** (**-ises, -ising, -ised**) *vt.* **1.** MAKE PLEASANT-SOUNDING to make sth sound pleasant **2.** PHON FACILITATE PRONUNCIATION to change speech sounds to make sth easier to pronounce

euphony /yoófəni/ (*plural* **-nies**) *n.* **1.** PLEASANT SOUND a pleasant sound, especially in speech or pronunciation **2.** PHON CHANGING OF SPEECH SOUNDS changing of speech sounds to make sth easier to pronounce [15thC. From French *euphonie*, from, ultimately, Greek *euphōnos* 'sweet-voiced', from *phōnē* 'sound'.] —**euphonic** /yoo fónnik/ *adj.* —**euphonically** /-fónnikli/ *adv.*

euphorbia /yoo fáwrbi ə/ *n.* a plant with milky juice and green flowers. Spurges and poinsettia are euphorbias. Genus: *Euphorbia*. [12thC. Alteration of Latin *euphorbea*, from *Euphorbus* (1stC BC), a physician to Juba, king of Mauretania, who supposedly discovered the plant.] —**euphorbiaceous** /yoo fáwrbi áyshəss/ *adj.*

euphoria /yoo fáwri ə/ *n.* a feeling of great joy, excitement, or well-being ○ *She was in a state of euphoria after her win.* [Late 17thC. Via modern Latin from, ultimately, Greek *euphoros*, literally 'borne well', hence 'healthy'. Originally in the meaning 'happiness brought about by relief from pain'.]

euphoriant /yoo fáwri ənt/ *n.* a drug or other substance that induces euphoria —**euphoriant** *adj.*

euphoric /yoo fórrik/ *adj.* extremely happy or excited ○ *She'll be euphoric when she hears these results.* —**euphorically** *adv.*

euphotic /yoo fótik, -fóttik/ *adj.* used to describe the upper layer of a body of water that allows the penetration of enough light to support photosynthetic, or green, plants [Early 20thC. Coined from EU- + the Greek stem *phōt-* 'light' + -IC.]

Euphrates /yoo fráyteez/ river in southwestern Asia, rising in Turkey and flowing through Syria and Iraq before joining the River Tigris near the Persian Gulf. Length: 2,700 km/1,700 mi.

Euphrosyne /yoo frózzi nee/ *n.* MYTHOL in Greek mythology, one of the three Graces who lived on Mount Olympus and were attendants of the goddess Aphrodite

euphuism /yoo fyoo izəm/ *n.* **1.** LITERAT **AFFECTED LITERARY STYLE** a literary style of the 16th and 17th centuries characterized by excessive use of devices such as alliteration, antithesis, and simile **2.** LANG **AFFECTED LANGUAGE OR EXPRESSION** an affected or pompous expression or use of language (*formal*) [Late 16thC. Named after *Euphues*, a fictional character in the works of John LYLY. The name itself was based on Greek *euphuēs* 'shapely'.] —**euphuist** *n.* —**euphuistic** /yoo fyoo ístik/ *adj.* —**euphuistically** /-ístikli/ *adv.*

euplastic /yoo plástik/ *adj.* healing readily

euploid /yoo ployd/ *adj.* WITH AN EVEN CHROMOSOME NUMBER with a chromosome number that is an even multiple of the basic chromosome set for the species ■ *n.* A EUPLOID CELL OR ORGANISM a euploid cell or organism —**euploidy** /yoop loydi/ *n.*

Eur. *abbr.* **1.** Europe **2.** European

Eur- *prefix.* = **Euro-** (*used before vowels*)

Eurasian /yoor áyzh'n, yoor áysh'n/ *n.* sb of both European and Asian descent [Mid-19thC] —**Eurasian** *adj.*

Euratom /yoor áttəm/ *n.* a body formed in 1957 to coordinate the development and use of atomic energy in Europe, later incorporated into the European Community [Mid-20thC. Contraction of the first two words of its full name, European Atomic Energy Commission.]

eureka /yoo reekə/ *interj.*, *n.* used to express delight on finding, discovering, or solving sth or finally succeeding in doing sth ○ *I rolled back the carpet and eureka – there it was!* [Early 17thC. From Greek *heurēka*, literally 'I have found (it)', from *heuriskein* 'to find', supposedly exclaimed by Archimedes when he discovered the principle of water displacement.]

eurhythmic /yoo ríthmik/, **eurythmic, eurythmical** /-ríthmik'l/, **eurythmical** *adj.* **1.** HARMONIOUS having an aesthetically pleasing rhythm or structure **2.** OF EURHYTHMICS relating to eurhythmics or eurhythmy

eurhythmics /yoo ríthmiks/, **eurythmics** *n.* a system of physical exercise, therapy, and musical training in which the body moves rhythmically and gracefully in interpretation of a piece of music (*takes a singular or plural verb*) [Early 20thC. Coined from EU- + RHYTHM + -ICS.]

eurhythmy /yoo ríthmi/, **eurythmy** *n.* **1.** STRUCTURAL HARMONY harmony of proportion or structure **2.** RHYTHMICAL MOVEMENT TO VERSE OR MUSIC a system of rhythmical movement performed to verse or music for artistic or therapeutic purposes. It was invented by Rudolf Steiner. [Late 16thC. Via Latin from Greek *euruthmia* 'good proportion', from *rhuthmos* 'proportion, rhythm' (source of English *rhythm*).]

Euripides /yoo ríppi deez/ (480?–406? BC) Greek dramatist. After Aeschylus and Sophocles, he was the third of the great dramatists of the classical period in Athens. His works have been revived through the centuries and have influenced many writers, from Milton and Racine to those of the present day.

euro /yoorō/ (*plural* **-ros** *or* **-ro**) *n.* Aus = **wallaroo** [Mid-19thC. From an Australian Aboriginal language.]

Euro /yoorō/ (*plural* **-ros**) *n.* the currency unit of 11 countries in the European Union, introduced in 1999 as part of economic and monetary union, which by 2002 will have replaced local currency in the

participating member states. ◊ **Ecu** [Late 20thC. Shortening of EUROPEAN.]

Euro- *prefix.* Europe, European ○ *Eurocurrency* [From EUROPE]

euro-ad *n.* an advertisement that is designed or suitable for use in all countries of the European Union

Eurobeach /yoorō beech/ *n.* a bathing beach in any of the countries of the European Union that meets the EU regulations for safe levels of bacteria in the water

Eurobond /yoorō bond/ *n.* a bond measured in dollars or other currency and sold to investors from a country other than that whose currency is specified in the bond

Eurocentric /yoorō séntrik/ *adj.* focusing on Europe or its people, institutions, and cultures, sometimes in an arrogant way (*disapproving*) —**Eurocentrism** /yoorō séntrizəm/ *n.*

Eurocheque /yoorō chek/ *n.* a cheque that can be written in the currency of any European and some other countries, drawing on the writer's personal bank account in any of the participating countries

Eurocrat /yoorə krat/, **eurocrat** *n.* an administrative official of the European Union, especially one in a senior post [Mid-20thC. Blend of EURO- and BUREAUCRAT.]

Eurocurrency /yoorō kurənssi/ (*plural* **-cies**) *n.* money deposited by companies and governments in banks outside the home country

Eurodollar /yoorō dolər/ *n.* a United States dollar on deposit in a bank outside the United States, especially a European bank (*usually used in the plural*)

Euroland /yoorō land/, **euroland** *n.* the countries in the European Union committed to adopting the common European currency, the euro

Euromarket /yoorō maarkit/ *n.* **1.** EUROPE AS A MARKET the European Union considered as a single market **2.** EUROPEAN FINANCIAL MARKETS the European financial markets collectively, especially when considered as a finance source for international trade

Euro-MP *n.* a member of the European Parliament

Europa /yoo rōpə/ *n.* a large natural satellite of Jupiter, discovered in 1610 by Galileo. It is 3130 km in diameter and thought to have a thin icy crust.

Europe the second smallest continent after Australia, lying west of Asia, north of Africa, and east of the Atlantic Ocean. Population: 728 million. Area: 10,525,000 sq. km/4,065,000 sq. mi.

European /yoorə pée ən/ *adj.* **1.** OF EUROPE relating to or typical of Europe or its peoples, languages, or cultures **2.** OF THE EUROPEAN UNION belonging to, relating to, or connected with the European Union ■ *n.* **1.** SB FROM EUROPE sb who was born or brought up in a European country, is a citizen of a European country, or is of European descent **2.** ADVOCATE OF EUROPEAN UNION sb who supports the principles and ideals of the European Union

European Commission *n.* the executive arm of the European Union, which formulates community policy and drafts most community legislation

European Community *n.* an economic and political union of 12 European countries that developed from the European Economic Community and was itself replaced in 1993 by the European Union

European Currency Unit *n.* full form of **ECU**

European Economic Community *n.* the alliance of six European countries begun in 1957 to promote free trade in Europe, and subsequently expanded in both numbers and areas of interest, and called the European Union

European Free Trade Association *n.* a union of western European countries, established in 1960 to eliminate trade tariffs between member states. The original members were Austria, Denmark, Great Britain, Norway, Portugal, Sweden, and Switzerland. Abbr of **EFTA**

Europeanise *vt.* = **Europeanize**

Europeanism /yoorə pée ənizəm/ *n.* support for the European Union, and for its further development

Europeanize /yoorə pée ə nīz/ (**-izes, -izing, -ized**), **Europeanise** (**-ises, -ising, -ised, -ised**) *vt.* **1.** MAKE EUROPEAN to make sb or sth part of European culture, or change sb or sth to fit in with European life, customs, or ideas **2.** MAKE PART OF EUROPEAN UNION to make a country part of the European Union, or make sth conform to the regulations or specifications of the European Union —**Europeanization** /yoorə pée ə nī záysh'n/ *n.*

European Monetary System *n.* a system for stabilizing currency exchange rates within the European Union, using the ERM. The introduction of a single European currency is its ultimate goal.

European Parliament *n.* the primarily advisory legislature of the European Union. It consists of directly elected representatives from each Member State.

European Union: Map showing
member states

European Union *n.* the economic and political alliance of 15 European nations, including the United Kingdom. Its goals include a single economic community and social and political cooperation.

europium /yoo rōpi əm/ *n.* a soft silvery-white metallic chemical element of the rare-earth group that is used in lasers. Symbol **Eu** [Early 20thC. From modern Latin, from Latin *Europa* 'Europe'.]

Eurosceptic /yoorō skeptik/ *n.* a British person, especially a politician, who is not in favour of closer links between Britain and the European Union —**Euroscepticism** /yoorō sképti sizəm/ *n.*

Eurostar /yoorō staar/ *tdmk.* a trademark for the high-speed passenger train and train service designed specifically to use the Channel Tunnel. It can run on both British and Continental railway systems.

Eurovision /yoorō vizh'n/ *tdmk.* a trademark for an organization of primarily European television broadcasters that shares news and programmes amongst its members

Eurovision song contest *n.* an annual competition, broadcast on television, in which singers from primarily European countries perform a specially composed song, and the participating nations vote for their favourite. The contest has been criticized for the blandness of the winning entries and the political nature of the voting.

eury- *prefix.* wide, broad ○ *euryphagous* [From Greek *eurus* (source of English *aneurysm*)]

eurybathic /yoori báthik/ *adj.* used to describe aquatic organisms that tolerate a wide range of depths [Early 20thC. Coined from EURY- + Greek *bathos* 'depth' + -IC.] —**eurybath** /yoori baath/ *n.*

Eurydice /yoo ríddissi/ in Greek mythology, the wife of Orpheus. When she died, Orpheus pursued her to Hades. His lyre-playing won her release, but his failure to observe its conditions resulted in her irrevocable loss.

euryhaline /yoori háy leen, -háy līn/ *adj.* used to describe aquatic organisms that tolerate a wide range of salinity [Late 19thC. Coined from EURY- + Greek *halinos* 'of salt'.]

euryphagous /yoo ríffəgəss/ *adj.* used to describe organisms that feed on a variety of different things

eurypterid /yoo ríptərid/ *n.* an extinct invertebrate animal, some types of which were very large, that was common in fresh or brackish water during the Palaeozoic era. It was related to the ancestors of the horseshoe crab. Order: Eurypterida. [Late 19thC. Formed from modern Latin *Eurypterida*, order name, from Greek *eury-* 'wide' + *pteron* 'wing'.]

eurythermal /yoŏri thúrm'l/, **eurythermic** /-thúrmik/, **eurythermous** /-thúrməss/ *adj.* used to describe organisms that tolerate a wide range of temperatures —**eurytherm** /yoŏri thurm/ *n.*

eurythmic, eurythmical *adj.* = eurhythmic

eurythmics *n.* = eurhythmics

eurythmy *n.* = eurhythmy

eurytopic /yoŏri tóppik/ *adj.* used to describe organisms that tolerate a wide range of environmental conditions [Mid-20thC. Coined from EURY- + Greek *topos* 'place' + -IC.]

Eusebius of Nicomedia /yoo seébi əss əv níkə meédi ə/ (*d.* 342?) Syrian bishop and Christian theologian. He helped to spread Arianism, which denies Jesus Christ's divinity. He was patriarch of Constantinople (339–42).

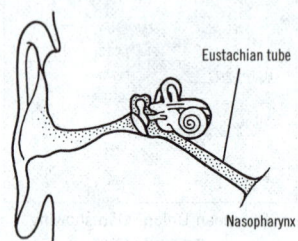

Eustachian tube

Eustachian tube /yoo stáysh'n-/ *n.* a bony passage extending from the middle ear to the nasopharynx that has a role in equalizing air pressure on both sides of the eardrum [Mid-18thC. Named after Bartolomeo *Eustachio* (1520–74), an Italian anatomist known for his descriptions of the human ear and heart.]

eustasy /yoŏstəssi/ (*plural* **-sies**) *n.* a worldwide change in sea level, as a result of melting glaciers or earth movements [Mid-20thC. Back-formation from EUSTATIC (from German, from Greek *eu* 'well' + *statikos* 'static'), as if an anglicization of hypothetical modern Latin *eustasis*.] —**eustatic** /yoo státtik/ *adj.*

eutectic /yoo téktik/ *adj.* FORMED AT THE LOWEST FREEZING POINT used to describe a mixture, especially an alloy, that has the lowest freezing point of all combinations or constituents, or to refer to the temperature at which this occurs ■ *n.* EUTECTIC SUBSTANCE a substance or mixture that is eutectic [Late 19thC. Formed from Greek *eutēktos* 'easily melting', from *tēkein* 'to melt'.]

Euterpe /yoo túrpi/ *n.* MYTHOL in Greek mythology, the muse of lyric poetry and music. ◊ **Muse**

euthanasia /yoŏthə náyzi ə, -náyzhə/ *n.* the act or practice of killing sb who has an incurable illness or injury, or allowing or assisting that person to die. Euthanasia is illegal in most countries. [Early 17thC. From Greek, 'easy death', from *thanatos* 'death'.]

euthenics /yoo thénniks/ *n.* the study of ways of improving people's environment and living standards in order to improve their health and wellbeing (*takes a singular verb*) [Early 20thC. Coined from Greek *euthēnein* 'to thrive' + -ICS.] —**euthenist** /yoŏthənist/ *n.*

eutherian /yoo theéri ən/ *adj.* HAVING A PLACENTA used to describe a mammal whose young develop to an advanced stage within the womb surrounded by a placenta ■ *n.* PLACENTAL MAMMAL a mammal whose young develop within the womb surrounded by a placenta. Subclass: Eutheria. (*technical*) [Late 19thC. Formed from modern Latin *Eutheria*, subclass name, from, ultimately, Greek *thērion* 'wild animal'.]

eutrophic /yoo trófik, -tróffik/ *adj.* ECOL used to describe a body of water whose oxygen content is depleted by organic nutrients (**eutrophication**) [Mid-20thC. Formed from Greek *eutrophia*, literally 'good nutrition', from *trephein* 'to nourish'. Applied earlier to medicine that promotes good nutrition.] —**eutrophy** /yoŏtrəfi/ *n.*

eutrophication /yoo trófi káysh'n, -tróffi-/ *n.* the process by which a body of water becomes rich in dissolved nutrients, thereby encouraging the growth and decomposition of oxygen-depleting plant life and resulting in harm to other organisms. The problem occurs in freshwater lakes or shallow seas when human sewage or nitrates and phosphates from fertilizers drain into them.

eV *symbol.* electronvolt

EV *abbr.* BIBLE English Version

EVA *abbr.* extravehicular activity

evacuant /i vákyoo ənt/ *adj.* CAUSING DISCHARGE FROM BODY used to describe a drug or treatment that causes a discharge, especially an emptying of the bowels ■ *n.* DRUG CAUSING DISCHARGE a drug or other substance that brings about a discharge, especially an emptying of the bowels

evacuate /i vákyoo ayt/ (**-ates, -ating, -ated**) *v.* 1. *vt.* MAKE EVERYONE LEAVE A PLACE to empty a dangerous or potentially dangerous place of people ○ *Towns near the nuclear plant were evacuated as a precautionary measure.* 2. *vti.* MOVE TO SAFETY to leave or cause people to leave a place of danger and go somewhere safer ○ *The government has evacuated all its embassy officials from the city.* 3. *vti.* PHYSIOL EMPTY BOWELS OR BLADDER to discharge faeces or urine from the body (*technical*) 4. *vt.* EMPTY to empty sth by removing all its contents (*formal*) 5. *vt.* PHYS CREATE VACUUM IN to remove a gas from sth, leaving a vacuum [14thC. From Latin *evacuat-*, the past participle stem of *evacuare* 'to empty (the bowels)' and, in late Latin, 'to clear out', from *vacuus* 'empty' (source of English *vacuum*).] —**evacuative** *adj.* —**evacuator** *n.*

evacuation /i vákyoo áysh'n/ *n.* 1. CLEARING OF A DANGEROUS PLACE an emptying of a dangerous or potentially dangerous place 2. MOVING PEOPLE TO SAFETY a removal of people from a dangerous or potentially dangerous place 3. PHYSIOL DISCHARGE OF BODILY WASTE elimination of faeces or urine from the body (*technical*) 4. PHYSIOL BODILY WASTE faeces or urine eliminated from the body (*technical*) 5. PHYS CREATION OF A VACUUM the making of a vacuum by the removal of gas from sth

evacuee /i vákyoo eé/ *n.* sb who is removed from a place of danger and sent somewhere safer, especially during a war [Early 20thC. Anglicization of French *évacué*, from the past participle of *évacuer* 'to cease to occupy', from Latin *evacuare* (see EVACUATE).]

evade /i váyd/ (**evades, evading, evaded**) *v.* 1. *vt.* CLEVERLY ESCAPE to escape or avoid sb or sth, usually by ingenuity or guile 2. *vt.* AVOID STH UNPLEASANT to avoid doing sth unpleasant, especially sth that is a moral or legal obligation 3. *vti.* GIVE INDIRECT RESPONSE TO to avoid dealing with or responding directly to sth 4. *vt.* BE UNATTAINABLE to be difficult or impossible for sb to find, obtain, or achieve (*formal*) [Early 16thC. Via French *évader* from Latin *evadere* 'to escape', literally 'to go away', from *vadere* 'to go, walk' (source of English *invade*).] —**evadable** *adj.* —**evader** *n.*

— WORD KEY: USAGE —
See Usage note at *avoid.*

evaginate /i vájji nayt/ (**-nates, -nating, -nated**) *vt.* to turn a hollow structure or bodily organ inside out [Mid-17thC. From Latin *evaginat-* the past participle stem of *evaginare* 'to unsheathe', from *vagina* 'sheath' (source of English *vagina*).] —**evagination** /i vájji náy sh'n/ *n.*

evaluate /i vállyoo ayt/ (**-ates, -ating, -ated**) *vt.* 1. EXAMINE AND JUDGE to consider or examine sth in order to judge its value, quality, importance, extent, or condition ○ *We evaluated the situation carefully.* 2. PUT A VALUE ON to estimate the monetary value of sth ○ *The appraiser evaluated the property at £100,000* 3. MATH FIND NUMERICAL VALUE to calculate a numerical value for a mathematical expression ○ *evaluate an expression* [Mid-19thC. Back-formation from EVALUATION.] —**evaluator** *n.*

evaluation /i vállyoo áysh'n/ *n.* 1. ASSESSMENT OF VALUE the act of considering or examining sth in order to judge its value, quality, importance, extent, or condition 2. STATEMENT OF VALUE a spoken or written statement of the value, quality, importance, extent, or condition of sth [Mid-18thC. From French *évaluation*, from *évaluer* 'to find the value of', from *value* 'VALUE'.]

evaluative /i vállyoo ətiv/ *adj.* 1. DETERMINED BY ASSESSMENT relating to or based on examination and judgment of the value, quality, or importance of sth 2. PHILOS NORMATIVE expressing a judgment about sth, or assigning a value to it, as opposed to describing a fact

evan. *abbr.* 1. evangelical 2. evangelist

evanesce /évvə néss/ (**-nesces, -nescing, -nesced**) *vi.* to grow less until completely gone (*literary*) ○ *His cares evanesced.* [Mid-19thC. From Latin *evanescere* 'to vanish' ultimately from *vanus* 'empty', from, ultimately, an Indo-European word that is also the ancestor of English *want*.]

evanescent /évvə néss'nt/ *adj.* disappearing after only a short time ○ *an evanescent moment* —**evanescence** *n.* —**evanescently** *adv.*

evang. *abbr.* 1. evangelical 2. evangelist

evangel /i vánjəl/ *n.* 1. CHR CHRISTIAN GOSPEL the Christian gospel (*archaic*) 2. **evangel, Evangel** CHR ANY OF FOUR CHRISTIAN GOSPELS any of the four Christian Gospels: Matthew, Mark, Luke, or John (*archaic*) 3. BASIC DOCTRINE a basic doctrine or set of moral or political principles or teachings (*formal*) [14thC. Via Old French *evangile* from, ultimately, Greek *euaggelion* 'good news', from *euaggelos* 'bringing good news', from *eu* 'good' + *aggelein* 'to announce'.]

evangelic, Evangelic *adj.* = evangelical

evangelical /eé van jéllik'l/ *adj.* 1. **evangelical, Evangelical, evangelic, Evangelic** CHR OF PARTICULAR PROTESTANT CHURCHES relating or belonging to any Protestant Christian church whose members believe in the authority of the Bible and salvation through the personal acceptance of Jesus Christ 2. **evangelical, evangelic** WITH STRONG BELIEFS enthusiastic or zealous in support of a particular cause and very eager to make other people share its beliefs or ideals 3. **evangelical, evangelic** CHR RELATING TO THE CHRISTIAN GOSPELS relating to or based on the Christian Gospels: Matthew, Mark, Luke, or John ■ *n.* **evangelical, Evangelical** MEMBER OF EVANGELICAL CHRISTIAN CHURCH a member of an evangelical Christian church or movement —**evangelically** *adv.*

evangelicalism /eé van jéllik'lizəm/, **Evangelicalism** *n.* a Protestant movement of the Christian church whose members believe in the authority of the Bible and salvation through the personal acceptance of Jesus Christ

evangelise *vti.* = evangelize

evangelism /i vánjəlizəm/ *n.* 1. CHR SPREADING OF CHRISTIANITY the spreading of Christianity, especially through the activities of evangelists 2. CRUSADING ZEAL great enthusiasm, fervour, or zeal for a particular cause

evangelist /i vánjə list/ *n.* 1. CHRISTIAN WHO CONVERTS OTHERS sb who tries to persuade other people to become Christians, especially one who travels around speaking at public meetings or making radio or television broadcasts 2. **evangelist, Evangelist** WRITER OF CHRISTIAN GOSPEL any of the writers of the first four Christian Gospels: Matthew, Mark, Luke, or John —**evangelistic** /i vánjə lístik/ *adj.* —**evangelistically** /-lístikli/ *adv.*

evangelize /i vánjə līz/ (**-izes, -izing, -ized**), **evangelise** (**-ises, -ising, -ised**) *vti.* 1. CHR CONVERT TO CHRISTIANITY to convert sb or the people of an area to Christianity, especially by preaching or missionary work 2. BE ADVOCATE FOR A CAUSE to try to persuade other people to share enthusiasm for particular beliefs and ideals —**evangelization** /i vánjə līzáysh'n/ *n.* —**evangelizer** /i vánjə līzər/ *n.*

Evans, Mount mountain in north-central Colorado, site of a high-altitude laboratory. Height: 4,348 m/14,264 ft.

Evans /évvənz/, **Sir Arthur John** (1851–1941) British archaeologist. His excavations on Crete (1899–1935), notably at Knossos, uncovered a Bronze Age culture he termed Minoan. His restoration techniques remain controversial.

Evans /évv'nz/, **Dame Edith** (1888–1976) British actor. She is remembered for her Shakespearean roles and also for her performance as Lady Bracknell in the 1951 film of *The Importance of Being Earnest.* Full name **Dame Edith Mary Evans**

Evans, Sir Geraint (1922–92) Welsh singer and teacher. He was an operatic baritone of outgoing personality. His long career (1948–84) embraced some 70 roles, notably Verdi's *Falstaff.* Full name **Sir Geraint Llewellyn Evans**

Evans-Pritchard, E.E., Sir (1902–73) British anthropologist Often living with the traditional peoples he studied, he pioneered the view that sees their beliefs as forming a coherent, functional system. Full name **sir Edward Evan Evans-Pritchard,**

Evansville /évənz vil/ city in southwestern Indiana, on the northern bank of the Ohio River, southwest of Bloomington. Population: 123,456 (1996).

evaporable /i váppərəb'l/ *adj.* able to evaporate —**evaporability** /i váppərə bílliti/ *n.*

evaporate /i váppə rayt/ (**-rates, -rating, -rated**) *v.* **1.** *vti.* CHANGE LIQUID TO VAPOUR to change a liquid into a vapour, usually by heating to below its boiling point, or to change from a liquid to vapour in this way ○ *The water evaporates, increasing the moisture in the air.* **2.** *vt.* REMOVE LIQUID FROM to remove liquid from sth, usually by heating, to produce a more concentrated or solid substance **3.** *vi.* VANISH to disappear gradually or fade away to nothing **4.** *vt.* PHYS TO DEPOSIT A FILM to deposit sth such as a metal film on a surface through the condensation of a vaporized substance [15thC. From Latin *evaporat-*, the past participle stem of *evaporare*, literally 'to go out in vapour', from *vapor* 'VAPOUR'.] —**evaporative** /i váppərətiv/ *adj.*

evaporated milk *n.* milk that has been thickened by removing some of the water by evaporation

evaporation /i váppə ráysh'n/ *n.* a process in which sth is changed from a liquid to a vapour without its temperature reaching the boiling point

evaporator /i váppə raytər/ *n.* **1.** PART OF REFRIGERATION SYSTEM the vaporization portion of a refrigeration system **2.** WATER-REMOVING DEVICE a vaporizing device that removes water or other solvents to obtain the dried or concentrated residue, as in the preparation of powdered milk from milk

evaporite /i váppə rīt/ *n.* a sedimentary rock or deposit that results from the evaporation of salt water in lagoons and saline lakes. Gypsum and rock salt are evaporites. [Early 20thC. Coined from EVAPORATION + -ITE.]

evapotranspiration /i váppō tránspə ráysh'n/ *n.* the return of moisture to the air through both evaporation from the soil and transpiration by plants [Mid-20thC. Coined from EVAPORATION.]

evasion /i váyzh'n/ *n.* **1.** AVOIDANCE OF STH avoidance of sth unpleasant, especially a moral or legal obligation **2.** MEANS OF AVOIDANCE a means of escaping or avoiding sth, especially one that involves cunning or deceit **3.** AVOIDING AN ISSUE not giving a direct answer to a direct question, usually in order to conceal the truth [15thC. Via Old French *évasion* from, ultimately Latin *evadere* (see EVADE).]

WORD KEY: USAGE

See Usage note at ***avoidance.***

evasive /i váyssiv/ *adj.* **1.** AVOIDING AN ISSUE not giving a direct answer to a direct question **2.** AVOIDING TROUBLE intended to avoid sth unpleasant, e.g. trouble or an attack ○ *took evasive action* [Early 18thC] —**evasively** *adv.* —**evasiveness** *n.*

Evatt /évvət/, **Herbert Vere** (1894–1965) Australian judge and politician. He was deputy prime minister (1946–49) and leader of the Australian Labor Party (1951–60). He was also first president of the General Assembly of the United Nations (1948–49).

eve /eev/ *n.* **1. eve, Eve** DAY BEFORE FESTIVAL the day, evening, or night before a religious festival or public holiday **2.** PERIOD BEFORE EVENT the day or days immediately before an important event or special occasion ○ *He died on the eve of his 100th birthday.* **3.** EVENING an evening (*literary*) ○ *on a cold winter's eve* [12thC. Originally a variant of EVEN².]

Eve /eev/ *n.* in the Bible, the first woman created by God, and Adam's companion in the Garden of Eden

evection /i véksh'n/ *n.* a periodic irregularity in the motion of the Moon caused by the variation in the gravitational attraction of the Sun as the Moon orbits the Earth [Mid-17thC. From the Latin stem *evection-*, from *evect-*, the past participle stem of *evehere* 'to carry out, elevate', from *vehere* 'to carry' (source of English *inveigh, vehicle,* and *vex*).] —**evectional** *adj.*

Evelyn /eévlin/, **John** (1620–1706) English writer and government official. His *Diary* (1640–1704), which gives a vivid picture of his contemporaries, was first published in 1818.

even¹ /eév'n/ *adj.* **1.** NOT SLOPING, ROUGH, OR IRREGULAR having no slope, roughness, or irregularities **2.** AT THE SAME HEIGHT at the same distance above the ground or other point of reference **3.** ALIGNED lining up along the same horizontal or vertical line and usually with equal spaces between **4.** NOT CHANGING OR FLUCTUATING not changing or fluctuating in level or strength **5.** THE SAME THROUGHOUT the same all over or throughout ○ *an even consistency* **6.** EQUAL IN AMOUNT equal in amount, number, or extent ○ *At the end of the first round, the score was even.* **7.** WELL-BALANCED between competitors of equal strength or skill, and therefore fair or well-balanced **8.** NOT OWING ANYTHING not or no longer owing anything to each other (*informal*) ○ *Give me five pounds, and we'll call it even.* **9.** MATH EXACTLY DIVISIBLE BY TWO used to describe a number or quantity that can be exactly divided by two with nothing left over, e.g. 2, 6, 30, or 518. ◊ **odd 10.** WITH AN EVEN NUMBER having a number that can be exactly divided by two ○ *on the even pages* **11.** CALM AND STEADY calm and controlled **12.** EXACT IN AMOUNT exact in amount, number, or extent ○ *an even dozen* ■ *vti.* (**evens, evening** /eévəning/, **evened**) LEVEL OR EQUALIZE to make sth more level or equal, or become more level or equal ○ *Atlanta scored three quick runs to even the score.* [Old English *efen*, from a prehistoric Germanic word meaning either 'flat, level' or 'equal, alike'] —**evener** *n.* —**evenness** *n.* ◇ **get even (with sb)** to take revenge on sb ○ *They took advantage of me, and I was determined to get even.*

even out *vti.* **1.** FLATTEN OR LEVEL STH to become or make sth more flat, smooth, or level **2.** EQUALIZE THINGS to make two or more different things more equal, or become more equal

even up *vti.* to become or make sth more equal, fair, or well-balanced

even² /eév'n/ *n.* evening (*literary*) ○ *at even, when the sun was set* [Old English *æfen* (see EVENING)]

even³ /eév'n/ CORE MEANING: used for emphasis to indicate sth surprising, unlikely, or extreme ○ *Even I know how to repair a puncture!*

adv. **1.** SO MUCH AS used after a negative for emphasis to indicate sth unexpected and usually annoying or disappointing ○ *She couldn't even remember my name.* **2.** TO A GREATER EXTENT used for emphasis in comparisons to indicate the degree to which sth exists ○ *His writing is even more untidy than hers, and hers is barely legible.* **3.** FURTHERMORE used to indicate that the description that follows applies in addition to and more strongly or precisely than the preceding one ○ *She is careful with her money, even miserly.* **4.** THAT IS TO SAY used to emphasize a statement (*archaic*) **5.** ALL THE WAY used to emphasize that sth is true completely and fully (*archaic*) ○ *I will follow thee even unto the ends of the earth.* [Old English *efne*, from a prehistoric Germanic base that also produced English *even¹*]

even break *n.* an equal opportunity for winning or losing

even chance *n.* an equal likelihood that sth will or will not happen

evenfall /eév'nfawl/ *n.* the beginning of evening (*archaic*)

evenhanded /eév'n hándid/ *adj.* treating everyone fairly, without favouritism or discrimination ○ *an evenhanded distribution of the profits* —**evenhandedly** *adv.* —**evenhandedness** *n.*

evening /eévning/ *n.* **1.** LATE PART OF DAY the part of the day between afternoon and night, as daylight begins to fade **2.** TIME BEFORE BEDTIME the part of the day between sunset or the last main meal of the day and bedtime ○ *We went out for the evening.* **3.** EVENING'S ACTIVITY a social gathering, meeting, or entertainment held in the evening ○ *Thank you for the enjoyable evening.* **4.** PERIOD AT END the final part of a period of time, e.g. sb's life or a historical era (*literary*) ○ *the evening of the British Empire* **5.** AFTERNOON the afternoon (*regional*) ■ *interj.* GOOD EVENING good evening (*informal*) [Old English *æfnung*, from *æfen* (source of English *even²*), from, ultimately, an Indo-European word meaning 'lateness']

evening class *n.* a course or session of adult education held between approximately 7pm and 10pm, usually once a week throughout the school year

evening dress *n.* **1.** FORMAL CLOTHING clothing worn by men or women for formal social events held in the evening. A man in evening dress usually wears a dinner jacket and black tie, and a woman usually wears a full-length dress of elegant design. **2.** WOMAN'S FORMAL DRESS a woman's dress suitable for formal social events held in the evening, usually a full-length dress of elegant design. US term **evening gown**

evening gown *n.* = **evening dress** *n.* 2

evening prayer, Evening Prayer *n.* = **evensong** *n.* 1

Evening primrose

evening primrose *n.* a biennial plant with hairy leaves and yellow flowers that open in the evening. Its seeds yield an oil used especially in treatments for menstrual problems. Genus: *Oenothera.*

evenings /eévningz/ *adv.* *US* in the evening, especially regularly

evening star *n.* a bright planet that can be seen in the western sky around sunset, usually Venus but occasionally Mercury

Evenki /i véngki/ (*plural* **-ki** *or* **-kis**), **Ewenki** (*plural* **-ki** *or* **-kis**) *n.* **1.** PEOPLES MEMBER OF ASIAN ETHNIC GROUP a member of an ethnic group that lives mainly in eastern parts of Asiatic Russia and the northwest of China **2.** LANG LANGUAGE SPOKEN IN ASIATIC RUSSIA a language spoken in eastern parts of Asiatic Russia and the northwest of China that belongs to the Manchu-Tungus group of the Mongolian branch of Altaic. Evenki is spoken by about 30,000 people. [Via Russian, 'Evenki people', from Evenki] —**Evenki** *adj.*

evenly /eévənli/ *adv.* **1.** EQUALLY in equal amounts, numbers, parts, or shares **2.** UNIFORMLY with the same thickness, consistency, amount, or degree over or throughout sth **3.** WITH EQUAL SPACING with gaps of the same size between each item **4.** IN BALANCE having the same weight, strength, or skill as another **5.** STEADILY in an unchanging, regular, or rhythmical way **6.** CALMLY AND UNEMOTIONALLY in a calm unemotional way

even money *n.* EQUAL ODDS a betting situation in which the odds of winning or losing are equal and the winnings equal the stake ■ *adj.* AS LIKELY AS NOT equally likely or unlikely ○ *It's even money she'll forget.*

evens /eévənz/ *adj., adv.* with equal odds of winning or losing a bet

evensong /eév'n song/ *n.* **1.** EVENING SERVICE IN ANGLICAN CHURCH the daily evening worship service of the Anglican Church **2.** VESPERS vespers (*archaic*) **3.** EVENING evening (*archaic*)

even-steven /steévən/, **even Stevens** /steévənz/ *adj.* (*informal*) **1.** SETTLED EQUALLY AND FAIRLY with all debts or grievances mutually settled **2.** EQUAL IN SCORE with equal scores or chances of winning ○ *At the end of the first round the two teams were even-steven.* [Origin uncertain: probably an arbitrary rhyming formation, although *Steven* is obsolete slang for 'money']

event /i vént/ *n.* **1.** IMPORTANT INCIDENT an occurrence, especially one that is particularly significant, interesting, exciting, or unusual ○ *the events leading up to the strike* **2.** ORGANIZED OCCASION an organized occasion such as a social function or sporting competition

○ *She has competed in many international events.* **3.** SPORTS **INDIVIDUAL SPORTING CONTEST** any of the races or other competitions that form part of a larger sporting occasion, e.g. the Olympic Games ○ *The 100 metres is his best event.* **4.** PHILOS **OCCURRENCE** a happening or occurrence **5.** PHYS **SINGLE POINT IN SPACE-TIME** an occurrence defined in the theory of relativity as a single point in space-time **6.** COMPUT **OCCURRENCE AFFECTING COMPUTER PROGRAM** an occurrence or happening of significance to a computer program, e.g. the clicking of a mouse button or the completion of a write operation to a disk ■ *vi.* (**events, eventing, evented**) EQU **COMPETE IN EVENTING** to compete in equestrian competitions, especially eventing [Late 16thC. From Latin *eventus*, from the past participle of *evenire* 'to happen', literally 'to come out' from *venire* 'to come' (see VENTURE).] ◇ **be wise after the event** to know with hindsight what should have been done or said in a situation ◇ **in the event** contrary to what was expected ◇ **in the event of sth** if sth should happen

event-driven *adj.* used to describe a computer program with a main loop that waits for an event, e.g. the pressing of a mouse button, and then passes the details of it along

even-tempered *adj.* not easily angered or upset

eventer /i véntər/ *n.* a horse that or rider who regularly competes at eventing

eventful /i véntf'l/ *adj.* **1.** **INTERESTING OR EXCITING** full of important, interesting, or exciting occurrences **2.** **MEANINGFUL** having a major effect on a sb's life —**eventfully** *adv.* —**eventfulness** *n.*

event horizon *n.* the theoretical boundary surrounding a black hole, within which gravitational attraction is so great that nothing, not even radiation, can escape because the escape velocity is greater than the speed of light

eventide *n.* evening (*literary*)

eventide home *n.* a home for elderly people

eventing /i vénting/ *n.* an equestrian competition that includes dressage, cross-country riding, and stadium jumping, usually over three days

eventless /i véntləss/ *adj.* having no significant events

eventual /i vénchoo əl/ *adj.* **1.** **ULTIMATE** happening in the course of time or events, usually much later ○ *her eventual fall from power* **2.** **CONTINGENT** depending on circumstances or unknown future events (*archaic*) [Early 17thC. From French *éventuel*, from, ultimately, Latin *eventus* 'outcome' (see EVENT).]

eventuality /i vénchoo álləti/ (*plural* **-ties**) *n.* a possible occurrence or result, especially sth undesirable or unexpected (*formal*) ○ *We must be prepared for all eventualities.*

eventually /i vénchoo əli/ *adv.* **1.** **IN THE END** after a long time, especially after many problems or setbacks ○ *We eventually managed to open the door.* **2.** **ULTIMATELY** at some later time after a series of events ○ *She hopes eventually to study.*

eventuate /i vénchoo ayt/ (**-ates, -ating, -ated**) *vi.* to happen as a final result (*formal*) ○ **eventuate in** *vt.* to cause or result in sth, especially after an extended period of time (*formal*) ○ *The oil spill eventuated in the destruction of wildlife habitats along the coast.*

evenweave /eevən weev/ *n.* a fabric with warp and weft threads of the same thickness and tension, and with an equal number of warp and weft threads in any square measurement

ever /évvər/ *adv.* **1.** **AT ANY TIME** used for emphasis in indicating any time in the past or future ○ *This is the most fascinating book I've ever read.* ○ *Have you ever been skiing?* ○ *Rarely if ever does he phone when he's late.* **2.** **USED TO INDICATE SURPRISE** used for emphasis to indicate surprise, shock, or incomprehension at sth ○ *Where ever can it be?* **3.** **INCREASINGLY** to an increasing degree (*formal*) ○ *The questions were becoming ever more technical.* **4.** **USED AS INTENSIFIER** used to emphasize a particular quality, especially to express enthusiasm (*informal*) ○ *It'll be ever such fun!* **5.** **ALWAYS** showing at all times a particular quality ○ *He is ever anxious to please.* [Old English *æfre*. Ultimately from an Indo-European word meaning 'eternity' that is also the ancestor of English *age*.] ◇ **for ever**

for a very long time (*informal*) ○ *He's been in the bathroom for ever!*

WORD KEY: USAGE
---

*The best dictionary **ever**:* Some people object to this use of **ever** because they maintain that **ever** should include the future as well as the past. However, the future can rarely be accounted for, and the idiom is well established in conversational use, although it would not normally be used in more formal spoken or in written English.

Mount Everest: West shoulder of the mountain

Everest, Mount /évvərist/ mountain in the Himalayas on the border between Nepal and the Tibet Autonomous Region of China. It is the highest mountain in the world. Height: 8,848 m/29,028 ft.

everglade /évvər glayd/ *n. US* a stretch of marshy grassland usually covered with water for at least part of the year [Early 19thC. Back-formation from EVERGLADES.]

Everglades National Park

Everglades National Park /évvər glaydz-/ national park in southern Florida, established in 1947. It contains the largest subtropical wilderness in the United States. Area: 6,102 sq. km/2,356 sq. mi.

evergreen /évvər green/ *adj.* **1.** BOT **WITH LEAVES THROUGHOUT THE YEAR** used to describe a tree or shrub that retains its foliage throughout the year **2.** **REMAINING FRESH OR POPULAR** used to describe people or things that always seem fresh, lively, or interesting, and that remain popular despite their age ■ *n.* **1.** BOT **EVERGREEN TREE** a tree or shrub that keeps its foliage throughout the year **2.** **EVERGREEN PERSON OR THING** sb or sth that remains fresh, lively, interesting, or popular

everlasting /évvər láasting/ *adj.* **1.** **LASTING FOR EVER** never failing or coming to an end **2.** **LASTING A LONG TIME** continuing indefinitely or for a long time **3.** **INCESSANT** going on for too long and becoming tedious or annoying ○ *everlasting grumbling* ■ *n.* **1.** **INFINITY** infinite time **2.** **everlasting, everlasting flower** PLANTS **FLOWER THAT LOOKS FRESH WHEN DRIED** a plant with flowers that keep their shape and colour when dried, e.g. helichrysum —**everlastingly** *adv.* —**everlastingness** *n.*

Everlasting *n.* God (*literary*)

evermore /évvər máwr/ *adv.* from now until the end of time or the end of sb's life (*literary*) ○ *I will be evermore in your debt.*

eversion /i vúrsh'n/ *n.* MED, BIOL **1.** **TURNING INSIDE OUT** the process or condition of being turned inside out ○ *eversion of the bladder* **2.** **TURNING OUTWARDS** a condition of being turned outwards ○ *an eversion of the feet* [Mid-18thC. Directly or via French from the Latin stem

eversion-, from *evers-*, the past participle stem of *evertere* (see EVERT).] —**eversible** /i vúrssib'l/ *adj.*

evert /i vúrt/ (**everts, everting, everted**) *vt.* to turn an organ or other body part outwards or inside out [Mid-16thC. From Latin *evertere*, literally 'to turn out', from *vertere* 'to turn' (see VERSE).]

Chris Evert

Evert /évvərt/**, Chris** (*b.* 1954) US tennis player. She won 16 grand slam singles championships during her career (1972–89). Full name **Christine Marie Evert**

every /évvri/ CORE MEANING: used to indicate each member of a group without exception ○ *dangers to health with which every citizen is familiar* ○ *Every life has value.* ○ *The press have been scrutinizing his every decision.*

det. **1.** **THE UTMOST** used to emphasize that there is all there could be of a particular quality ○ *The government has every intention of exploring this issue.* **2.** **EACH, OCCURRING INTERMITTENTLY OR PROPORTIONATELY** used to indicate each occurrence in recurrent or intermittent groups of things, or to indicate a ratio ○ *We intend to meet every two weeks.* ○ *Take this medicine every three hours.* [13thC. From the Old English phrase *æfre ælc* 'ever each'.]

WORD KEY: USAGE

See Usage note at *each*.

everybody *pron.* = everyone

everyday /évvree day/ *adj.* **1.** **ORDINARY AND UNREMARKABLE** having no remarkable feature to set it apart ○ *an everyday story of city life* **2.** **HAPPENING OR DONE EACH DAY** happening or done each day ○ *an everyday occurrence* **3.** **USED ON ORDINARY OCCASIONS** suitable for use on ordinary days or for routine tasks, rather than on special occasions ■ *n.* **ORDINARY OCCASIONS** routine or daily life —**everydayness** *n.*

WORD KEY: USAGE
---

everyday or **every day**? When you intend either an adjective (for the most part this will come before a noun, as in *everyday life* or a noun that means 'ordinary occasions' *part of the everyday*, the one-word version is correct. Adverbial uses *We should eat fruit every day* and the noun use that means 'each day' *Every day is different* call for the two-word version. Thus *everyday in every way* means 'ordinary in all respects', whereas *every day in every way* means 'daily and completely'.

Everyman /évvri man/ *n.* **1.** **Everyman, everyman ORDINARY PERSON** sb, usually a man, considered to be typical or representative of all human beings **2.** **HERO OF MORALITY PLAY** the hero of a medieval morality play who represents the whole of the human race

every man jack, **every man Jack** *n.* every single member of a group of people, without exception (*informal*) ○ *They ran away, every man jack of them.*

everyone /évvri wun/**, everybody** /évvri bodi/ *pron.* every person, whether of a defined group or in general ○ *Everyone is going to come to the office party.* ○ *This is not just for one area; it will affect everyone around the country.*

everything /évvri thing/ *pron.* **1.** **THE ENTIRETY** all the items, actions, or facts in a given situation ○ *We used to sit in front of his mother's house and talk about everything.* ○ *Everything I do is for my family.* ○ *Is everything all right?* **2.** **STH ALL-IMPORTANT** used to emphasize that sb or sth is the most important person or thing there is ○ *To them, family is everything.*

everywhere /évvri wair/ *adv.* in or to all conceivable places ○ *Children everywhere play these games.* ○ *Her cat followed her everywhere she went.*

Everywoman /évvri wŏŏmən/, **everywoman** *n.* a woman considered to be typical or representative of woman generally [Mid-20thC. Modelled on EVERYMAN.]

Eve's pudding *n.* a baked pudding of apples topped with sponge [From the apple eaten by Eve in the Garden of Eden]

eve-teasing *n. South Asia* the harassment of young women —**eve-teaser** *n.*

evg *abbr.* evening

Evian /évvi oN, évvi an/ *tdmk.* a trademark for a bottled mineral water from Evian, France

evict /i víkt/ (**evicts, evicting, evicted**) *vt.* **1.** EJECT SB FROM A PROPERTY to force a tenant to leave a property, especially the tenant's residence, usually because he or she has failed to comply with the terms of the letting contract **2.** THROW OUT OF A PLACE to force sb to leave a place, usually because of bad behaviour ○ *She was evicted from the game for insulting the referee* **3.** GET BACK PROPERTY to recover property or title to property from sb by legal means [(see EVINCE)] —**eviction** /i víksh'n/ *n.* —**evictor** /i víktər/ *n.*

evictee /i vík tée/ *n.* sb who is evicted from a property

evidence /évvidənss/ *n.* **1.** SIGN OR PROOF sth that gives a sign or proof of the existence or truth of sth, or that helps sb to come to a particular conclusion ○ *There is no evidence that the disease is related to diet.* **2.** PROOF OF GUILT the objects or information used to prove or suggest the guilt of sb accused of a crime ○ *The police have no evidence.* **3.** STATEMENTS OF WITNESSES the oral or written statements of witnesses and other people involved in a trial or official inquiry ■ *vt.* (**-dences, -dencing, -denced**) DEMONSTRATE OR PROVE to demonstrate or prove sth (*usually passive*) ○ *Their unwillingness to participate is evidenced by their failure to contact us.* ◇ **turn King's** *or* **Queen's evidence** to give evidence against a partner in crime so as to receive a less severe sentence

evident /évvidənt/ *adj.* easy or clear to see or understand ○ *The full extent of her injuries did not become evident until they tried to move her.* [See VISION]

evidential /évvi dénsh'l/ *adj.* relating to, consisting of, or based on evidence ○ *statements with no evidential value.* US term **evidentiary** —**evidentially** *adv.*

evidentiary /évvi dénshəri/ *adj. US* = **evidential**

evidently /évvidəntli/ *adv.* **1.** CLEARLY used to indicate that sth is undoubtedly true, often because it is there to be seen ○ *Evidently, you have not grasped all the ramifications of this proposal.* **2.** APPARENTLY used to indicate that sth may be true based on available evidence ○ *He then completely ignored her, evidently intent on hurting her feelings even more.*

evil /éev'l/ *adj.* **1.** MORALLY BAD profoundly immoral or wrong **2.** HARMFUL deliberately causing great harm, pain, or upset ○ *This evil act is clearly the work of terrorists.* **3.** DEVILISH connected with the Devil or other powerful destructive forces ○ *evil spirits* **4.** CAUSING MISFORTUNE characterized by, bringing, or signifying bad luck ○ *an evil omen* **5.** MALICIOUS characterized by a desire to cause hurt or harm ○ *an evil mood* **6.** DISAGREEABLE very unpleasant ○ *What an evil smell!* ■ *n.* **1.** WICKEDNESS the quality of being profoundly immoral or wrong **2. evil, Evil** FORCE CAUSING HARMFUL EFFECTS the force held to bring about harmful, painful, or unpleasant events ○ *a struggle between good and evil* **3.** STH EVIL a situation or thing that is very unpleasant, harmful, or morally wrong [Old English *yfel*. Ultimately from an Indo-European word meaning 'exceeding due limits'.] —**evilly** *adv.* —**evilness** *n.*

evildoer /éev'l doo ər, éev'l dŏŏ ər/ *n.* sb who does evil things —**evildoing** *n.*

evil eye *n.* **1.** LOOK OF STRONG DISLIKE a piercing look that conveys strong feelings of hatred, disapproval, jealousy, or malice, or that supposedly can cause harm **2.** SUPPOSED HARMFUL MAGICAL POWER a supernatural or magical power that some people believe can bring harm or cause bad luck ○ *an amulet to protect children from the evil eye*

Evil One *n.* the Devil

evince /i vínss/ (**evinces, evincing, evinced**) *vt.* **1.** SHOW CLEARLY to show a feeling or a quality clearly ○ *She evinced her disapproval of the production by leaving the auditorium.* **2.** REVEAL to indicate sth by action or implication [Late 16thC. From Latin *evincere*, literally 'to win out' (source also of English *evict*), from *vincere* 'to conquer' (see VICTOR).] —**evincible** *adj.* —**evincive** *adj.*

eviscerate /i víssə rayt/ (**-ates, -ating, -ated**) *vt.* **1.** DISEMBOWEL to remove the internal organs or entrails of a person or an animal **2.** REMOVE IMPORTANT PART OF to remove an essential part of sth and so weaken it **3.** SURG REMOVE THE CONTENTS OF AN ORGAN to remove the contents of the eyeball or another organ or body cavity [Late 16thC. From Latin *eviscerare*, from *viscera* (see VISCERA).] —**evisceration** /i víssə ráysh'n/ *n.* —**eviscerator** /i víssə raytər/ *n.*

evocation /éevō káysh'n, évvō-/ *n.* **1.** EVOKING a recreation of sth not present, especially an event or feeling from the past ○ *an accurate evocation of that period* **2.** LAW TRANSFER OF COURT CASE the transfer of a case from a lower to a higher court for review

evocative /i vókətiv/ *adj.* prompting vivid memories or images of things not present, especially things from the past ○ *an outfit evocative of the 1960s* —**evocatively** *adv.* —**evocativeness** *n.*

evoke /i vṓk/ (**evokes, evoking, evoked**) *vt.* **1.** STIMULATE MEMORIES FROM PAST to bring to mind a memory or feeling, especially from the past ○ *evoke childhood memories* **2.** CAUSE REACTION OR FEELING to provoke a particular reaction or feeling ○ *Her question evoked a bitter retort.* **3.** CAUSE TO APPEAR to make beings appear who are normally invisible ○ *evoke a spirit* [Early 17thC. From Latin *evocare*, literally 'to call out', from *vocare* 'to call' (see VOCAL).] —**evocable** /évvəkəb'l, i vṓkəb'l/ *adj.* —**evocator** /évvə kaytər/ *n.* —**evoker** *n.*

evolute /éevə loot, évvə-/ *n.* MATH the curve formed by the set of points that are the centres of curvature of another geometric curve (**involute**) [Mid-18thC. From Latin *evolutus*, the past participle of *evolvere* (see EVOLVE).]

evolution /éevə lóosh'n, évvə-/ *n.* **1.** BIOL THEORY OF DEVELOPMENT FROM EARLIER FORMS the theoretical process by which all species develop from earlier forms of life. On this theory, natural variation in the genetic material of a population favours reproduction by some individuals more than others, so that over the generations all members of the population come to possess the favourable traits. **2.** BIOL DEVELOPMENTAL PROCESS the natural or artificially induced process by which new and different organisms develop as a result of changes in genetic material **3.** GRADUAL DEVELOPMENT the gradual development of sth into a more complex or better form ○ *the evolution of democracy in Western Europe* **4.** PHYS GIVING OFF HEAT OR GAS the emission of heat, gas, or vapour **5.** PATTERN CAUSED BY MOVEMENT a pattern formed by a series of movements **6.** MATH FINDING ROOT OF NUMBER an algebraic operation in which the root, e.g. the square root or cube root, of a number is found. ◊ **involution 7.** MIL MILITARY EXERCISE a military exercise or manoeuvre carried out according to a plan [Early 17thC. Formed from Latin *evolut-*, the past participle stem of *evolvere* (see EVOLVE).] —**evolutional** *adj.* —**evolutionally** *adv.*

evolutionary /éevə lóosh'nəri, évvə-/ *adj.* **1.** BIOL OF EVOLUTION relating to the theory of evolution **2.** FROM EVOLUTION resulting from or conferred by evolution ○ *evolutionary advantage* **3.** GRADUAL developing in small increments that accumulate to bring about significant change ○ *an evolutionary process* —**evolutionarily** *adv.*

evolutionism /éevə lóosh'nizəm, évvə-/ *n.* **1.** BIOL EVOLUTIONARY THEORY the theory of biological evolution **2.** BELIEF IN EVOLUTION belief in the theory of biological evolution —**evolutionist** *n.*

evolve /i vólv/ (**evolves, evolving, evolved**) *v.* **1.** *vti.* DEVELOP GRADUALLY to develop sth gradually, often into sth more complex or advanced, or undergo such development **2.** *vti.* BIOL DEVELOP VIA EVOLUTIONARY CHANGE in evolutionary theory to develop from an earlier biological form, or to develop a characteristic in this way **3.** *vt.* PHYS EMIT HEAT OR GAS to give off heat, gas, or vapour [Early 17thC. From Latin *evolvere*, literally 'to roll out', from *volvere* 'to roll' (source of English *volume* and *revolver*; see VOLUTE).] —**evolvable** *adj.* —**evolvement** *n.* —**evolver** *n.*

ewe /yoo/ *n.* a female sheep, especially when fully grown [Old English *ēowu*. Ultimately from an Indo-European word meaning 'sheep', which is also the ancestor of English *ovine*.]

Ewe /é way, áy-/ (*plural* **Ewe** *or* **Ewes**) *n.* **1.** MEMBER OF A W AFRICAN PEOPLE a member of a West African people living in coastal regions of Ghana, Togo, and Benin **2.** LANGUAGE OF THE EWE the language of the Ewe, belonging to the Kwa branch of the Niger-Congo family. Ewe is spoken by about three million people. [Mid-19thC. From *Ewe*.] —**Ewe** *adj.*

ewe-neck *n.* a thin concave neck in a horse or dog, considered to be a defect —**ewe-necked** *adj.*

Ewer

ewer /yóo ər/ *n.* a large jug or pitcher with a wide spout [15thC. Via Anglo-Norman from Old French *aiguière*, from, ultimately, Latin *aquarius* 'of water', from *aqua* 'water' (see AQUA).]

EWO (*plural* **EWOs**) *abbr.* Educational Welfare Officer

ewt /yoot/ *n. S England* ZOOL a newt (*informal*) [14thC. Variant of EFT.]

ex[1] /eks/ *n.* the letter X [Late 19thC. From the pronunciation of the letter X.]

ex[2] /eks/ *n.* a former spouse, boyfriend, or girlfriend (*informal*) [Early 19thC. From EX-[1].]

ex[3] /eks/ *prep.* **1.** FIN EXCLUDING not including or participating in ○ *ex dividend* **2.** COMM SOLD FROM sold directly from with no charge before collection ○ *ex works* [Mid-19thC. From Latin (see EX-[1]).]

ex. *abbr.* **1.** example **2. ex., exc.** except **3. ex., exch.** exchange **4.** examination **5.** executive **6.** express **7.** extra

Ex. *abbr.* BIBLE Exodus

ex-[1] *prefix.* **1.** out, outside, away ○ *exclave* ○ *explant* **2.** not, without ○ *exstipulate* **3.** former ○ *ex-convict* [From Latin 'out of'. Ultimately from an Indo-European word meaning 'out', which is also the ancestor of English *external*.]

ex-[2] *prefix.* = **exo-** (*used before vowels*)

exa- one million million million (10^{18}). Symbol **E** [From HEXA-]

exacerbate /ig zássər bayt/ (**-bates, -bating, -bated**) *vt.* to make an already bad or problematic situation worse ○ *Her silence merely exacerbated the problem.* [Mid-17thC. From Latin *exacerbat-*, the past participle stem of *exacerbare*, literally 'to make thoroughly harsh', from *acerbare* 'to make harsh', from *acerbus* 'bitter' (see ACERBIC).] —**exacerbation** /ig zássər báysh'n/ *n.*

exact /ig zákt/ *adj.* **1.** CORRECT accurate and correct in all important details ○ *an exact account* **2.** PRECISE precise and not allowing for any variation ○ *a cheque for the exact amount* **3.** THIS AND NO OTHER used to emphasize that what is being referred to is one precise and often significant thing and not any other ○ *on this exact spot* **4.** STRICT rigorous and thorough ○ *an exact argument* **5.** FUNCTIONING ACCURATELY characterized by precise measurements ○ *exact instruments* ■ *vt.* (**-acts, -acting, -acted**) **1.** GET to demand and obtain sth, especially payment ○ *exacted a heavy tribute from their defeated enemies* **2.** INFLICT AS SUFFERING to make sb endure sth unpleasant (*formal*) ○ *I was already thinking how I could exact revenge for what he had done.* **3.** REQUIRE to call for sth as a matter of necessity or urgency [15thC. From Latin *exactus*, the past participle of *exigere* 'to demand', literally 'to drive out' (source of English *essay*), from *agere* 'to drive' (see AGENT).] —**exactable** *adj.* —**exactness** *n.* —**exactor** *n.*

exacting /ig záktiŋ/ *adj.* **1.** DEMANDING demanding hard work and great effort ○ *an exacting boss* **2.** DEMANDING ATTENTION requiring concentration and strict attention to detail ○ *an exacting job* —**exactingly** *adv.* —**exactingness** *n.*

exaction /ig záksh'n/ *n.* **1.** ACT OF DEMANDING AND OBTAINING STH the act of forcing sb to give sth, especially payment **2.** UNFAIR DEMAND an unfair or excessive demand for sth, especially money (*formal*) **3.** PAYMENT OBTAINED BY FORCE a sum of money or a payment that has been forcibly demanded and obtained (*formal*)

exactitude /ig zákti tyood/ *n.* the quality or state of being exact, precise, or accurate ○ *'The children were drilled in their parts with a military exactitude; obedience and punctuality became cardinal virtues'.* (Frank Norris, *McTeague – A Story of San Francisco*; 1899)

exactly /ig záktli/ *adv.* **1.** PRECISELY used to emphasize that a particular quality or quantity is stated precisely ○ *One circuit of the park is exactly two miles.* **2.** FULLY used to emphasize that what is stated is true in all details or to the fullest extent ○ *He did exactly what I said he would.* **3.** SHOWING AGREEMENT used to indicate agreement that what has just been said is true or correct ○ *'We need to give this more thought'. 'Exactly'.* **4.** SHOWING DISAPPROVAL used in questions to ask for precise information, often implying suspicion or disapproval ○ *So exactly what are you doing?*

exact science *n.* a science such as physics that deals with precise quantifiable measurements

exaggerate /ig zájjə rayt/ (**-ates, -ating, -ated**) *v.* **1.** *vti.* OVERSTATE STH to state that sth is better, worse, larger, more common, or more important than is true or usual **2.** *vt.* MAKE MORE NOTICEABLE to make sth appear more noticeable or prominent than is usual or desirable [Mid-16thC. From Latin *exaggerat-*, the past participle stem of *exaggerare*, 'to heap up', from *agger* 'heap', from, *gerere* 'to carry' (see GESTURE).] —**exaggeratedly** *adv.* —**exaggeratingly** *adv.* —**exaggerative** /ig zájjərətiv, -raytiv/ *adj.* —**exaggerator** /-raytər/ *n.*

exaggeration /ig zájjə ráysh'n/ *n.* **1.** EXAGGERATING the act or activity of exaggerating sth ○ *a personality given to exaggeration* **2.** EXAGGERATED STATEMENT behaviour or a statement that exaggerates sth

exalt /ig záwlt, -zólt/ (**-alts, -alting, -alted**) *vt.* **1.** PROMOTE to raise sb or sth in rank, position, or esteem (*formal*) ○ *exalted to the rank of major* **2.** PRAISE to praise or worship sb or sth (*formal*) **3.** INTENSIFY to increase the intensity or effect of sth (*formal*) **4.** STIMULATE to stimulate a mental quality or faculty (*archaic*) ○ *'Of Lorna, of my lifelong darling, of my more and more loved wife, I will not talk; for it is not seemly that a man should exalt his pride'.* (R. D. Blackmore, *Lorna Doone, A Romance of Exmoor*; 1869) **5.** RAISE to raise sb or sth physically (*archaic*) [15thC. From Latin *exaltare*, literally 'to put up high', from *altus* 'high' (see ALTO).] —**exalter** *n.*

exaltation /ég zawl táysh'n, ég zol-/ *n.* **1.** FEELING OF EXTREME HAPPINESS a feeling of intense or excessive happiness or exhilaration (*formal*) ○ *the miseries and exaltations of romance* **2.** RAISING UP the act of raising or holding sth up (*formal*) **3.** FLOCK a flock of larks (*literary*)

exalted /ig záwltid, -zóltid/ *adj.* (*formal*) **1.** ELEVATED high in rank, position, or esteem **2.** NOBLE grand or noble in character **3.** HIGH-SPIRITED in very high spirits —**exaltedly** *adv.* —**exaltedness** *n.*

exam /ig zám/ *n.* **1.** TEST OF KNOWLEDGE OR ABILITY a test designed to assess sb's ability or knowledge in a particular subject or field ○ *a chemistry exam* **2.** *US* MED = **examination** *n.* 3 [Mid-19thC. Shortening of EXAMINATION.]

examen /ig záymən/ *n.* in the Roman Catholic Church, an examination of conscience [Early 17thC. From Latin (see EXAMINE).]

examination /ig zámmi náysh'n/ *n.* **1.** INSPECTION the process of looking at and considering sth carefully with the aim of learning sth ○ *Their applications are currently under examination.* **2.** EDUC full form of **exam** *n.* 1 **3.** MED MEDICAL INSPECTION OF PATIENT a medical inspection carried out on a patient. US term **exam** **4.** MED STUDY OF SAMPLES FOR MEDICAL DIAGNOSIS the study of laboratory samples from a patient in order to diagnose an illness **5.** LAW INTERROGATION IN LAW COURT an interrogation of a witness or party to a case in a court of law

examination paper *n.* = **exam paper**

examine /ig zámmin/ (**-ines, -ining, -ined**) *vt.* **1.** STUDY to inspect or study sb or sth in detail ○ *examine the scene for fingerprints* **2.** INVESTIGATE to analyse sth in order to understand or expose it ○ *examine your conscience* **3.** EDUC TEST to test the knowledge or ability of sb by setting written, oral, or practical examinations **4.** MED INSPECT CONDITION OF A PATIENT to inspect a patient in order to determine his or her condition or health ○ *examined by a doctor* **5.** LAW INTERROGATE A WITNESS to ask questions of a witness or other party to a case in a court of law [14thC. Via French from Latin *examinare* 'to weigh', from *examen* 'weighing out', from *exigere* (see EXACT).] —**examinable** *adj.* —**examinee** /ig zámmi neé/ *n.* —**examiner** /ig zámmi nər/ *n.*

examine-in-chief (**examines-in-chief, examining-in-chief, examined-in-chief**) *vt.* to ask questions of a witness or other party in a court of law who is giving primary evidence in support of the case being presented by the questioner. ◊ **cross-examine** —**examination-in-chief** *n.*

exam paper, **examination paper** *n.* the printed set of questions used to test sb's knowledge in an exam

example /ig zaámp'l/ *n.* **1.** SAMPLE sth that is representative by virtue of having typical features of the thing it represents ○ *a fine example of baroque carving* **2.** MODEL a person, action, or thing taken as a model to be copied or avoided by others ○ *Her achievement is an example to us all.* **3.** ILLUSTRATION SUPPORTING STH an illustration that supports or provides more information on an opinion, theory, or principle ○ *The prosecutor then listed several examples of the accused's mismanagement of funds.* **4.** LEARNING AID an exercise or description that illustrates a principle, method, or problem ○ *Each chapter contains easy-to-follow examples.* **5.** PERSON PUNISHED sb punished as a warning to others who may be inclined to offend in the same way ■ *vt.* (**-ples, -pling, -pled**) EXEMPLIFY to exemplify (*archaic*) (*usually passive*) [14thC. Via Old French from Latin *exemplum*, originally 'sth taken out, sample', from *eximere* 'to take out', from *emere* 'to take'.] ◇ **for example** used to introduce a typical instance of sb or sth ◇ **make an example of sb** to punish sb as a warning to others who might be inclined to offend in the same way

exanthema /ék san theémə/ (*plural* **-themata** /-mətə/ *or* **-themas**), **exanthem** /ek sánthəm/ *n.* **1.** SKIN RASH a skin rash appearing as a sign of some infectious diseases, such as measles **2.** DISEASE WITH RASH a disease characterized by the appearance of a skin rash, e.g. measles or scarlet fever [Mid-17thC. Via late Latin from Greek *exanthēma* 'eruption', literally 'blossoming out', from *anthein* 'to blossom', from *anthos* 'flower'.] —**exanthematic** /ek sánthi máttik/ *adj.* —**exanthematous** /ék san thémmətəss/ *adj.*

exarch /éks aark/ *n.* **1.** CHR EASTERN ORTHODOX BISHOP a bishop in the Eastern Orthodox Church, ranked above a metropolitan and below a patriarch **2.** HIST PROVINCIAL BYZANTINE RULER the ruler of a province in the Byzantine Empire [Late 16thC. Via ecclesiastical Latin *exarchus* from Greek *exarkhos* 'leader', from *exarkhein* 'to lead', from *arkhein* 'to rule'.] —**exarchal** /ek saárk'l/ *adj.*

exarchate /éks aar kayt, ek saárk-/, **exarchy** /éks aarki/ (*plural* **-chies**) *n.* the office, domain, or term of an exarch

exasperate /ig záspə rayt, -zaásp-/ (**-ates, -ating, -ated**) *vt.* **1.** MAKE ANGRY to make sb very angry or frustrated, often by repeatedly doing sth annoying (*usually passive*) ○ *Guests were exasperated by their hosts' constant bickering.* **2.** WORSEN to make an unpleasant condition or feeling worse (*literary*) [Mid-16thC. From Latin *exasperat-*, the past participle stem of *exasperare* 'to irritate, roughen', literally 'to make thoroughly rough', from *asper* 'rough'.] —**exasperatedly** *adv.* —**exasperating** *adj.* —**exasperatingly** *adv.*

WORD KEY: SYNONYMS

See Synonyms at *annoy*.

exasperation /ig záspə ráysh'n, -zaáspə-/ *n.* annoyance and frustration, often caused by an irritation that cannot be overcome or stopped

exc. *abbr.* **1.** excellent **2.** except **3.** **exc., ex.** excepted **4.** **exc., ex.** exception **5.** excursion

Exc. *abbr.* Excellency

Excalibur /ek skállibər/ *n.* in Arthurian legend, King Arthur's magic sword that was given to him by the mysterious Lady of the Lake [15thC. Alteration of medieval Latin *Caliburnus*, from Middle Welsh *Caletuwlch* or Middle Irish *Caladbolg*, the name of a sword of Irish legend.]

ex cathedra /éks kə theédrə/ *adj., adv.* with the authority of status or rank (*formal*) ○ *imposed the decisions ex cathedra* [From Latin, literally 'from the (teacher's) chair']

excavate /ékskə vayt/ (**-vates, -vating, -vated**) *v.* **1.** *vti.* REMOVE EARTH to remove earth or soil by digging or scooping out ○ *Before the foundations can be laid, they will have to excavate about two metres of soil.* **2.** *vti.* HOLLOW STH OUT to make a hole or cavity in sth by removing the material inside ○ *excavate a tooth* **3.** *vt.* FORM BY HOLLOWING to form a shape or cavity by hollowing ○ *excavates a hollow in the sand as its nest* **4.** *vti.* ARCHAEOL DIG FOR ARTEFACTS to dig in a place carefully and methodically, taking notes about procedures, conditions, and finds, with a view to uncovering objects of archaeological interest **5.** *vti.* UNCOVER STH WITH DIFFICULTY to discover or uncover sth valuable by effort [Late 16thC. From Latin *excavat-*, the past participle stem of *excavare* 'to hollow out', from *cavare* 'to hollow', from *cavus* 'hollow' (see CAVE).]

excavation /ékskə váysh'n/ *n.* **1.** EXCAVATING the act or process of digging, removing earth, hollowing sth out, or excavating an archaeological site ○ *recent excavations in Sumatra* **2.** HOLE MADE BY DIGGING a hole that has been made by digging or hollowing sth out, or part of an archaeological site that has been excavated

excavator /ékskə vaytər/ *n.* **1.** MECHANICAL DIGGER a large machine with a hinged metal bucket attached to a hydraulic arm, used to move large quantities of earth or soil or for lifting **2.** DIGGER a person or animal that digs or hollows sth out, especially sb engaged in archaeological excavation

exceed /ik seéd/ (**-ceeds, -ceeding, -ceeded**) *vt.* **1.** BE GREATER THAN to be greater than sth in quantity, degree, or scope ○ *The cost of the film is reported to exceed 20 million dollars.* **2.** GO BEYOND LIMITS to go beyond the limits of sth in quantity, degree, or scope ○ *He was fined for exceeding the speed limit.* ○ *You've exceeded your authority.* **3.** OUTDO to be better than sth or sb ○ *descriptions of nature that far exceed in merit anything else we've heard* [14thC. Via Old French *exceder* from Latin *excedere* 'to go beyond, depart', literally 'to go out', from *cedere* 'to go' (see CEDE).]

exceeding /ik seéding/ *adj.* ENORMOUS very great (*literary*) ○ *exceeding joy* ■ *adv.* EXCEEDINGLY to an unusually high degree (*archaic*)

exceedingly /ik seédingli/ *adv.* to an unusually high degree ○ *You've been exceedingly generous.*

excel /ik sél/ (**-cels, -celling, -celled**) *v.* **1.** *vti.* DO WELL OR BETTER to do very well, or do better than all others or than a given standard **2.** *vi.* BE VERY GOOD to be outstanding or have a particular talent in sth ○ *excels in marketing* [15thC. From Latin *excellere*, literally 'to rise above', from assumed *cellere* 'to rise'. Ultimately from an Indo-European word meaning 'hill', which is also the ancestor of English *hill* and *culminate*.]

excellence /éksələnss/ *n.* **1.** SUPERIORITY the quality or state of being outstanding and superior ○ *an award for excellence in photography* **2.** OUTSTANDING FEATURE a feature or respect in which sb or sth is superior and outstanding

Excellency /éksələnssi/ (*plural* **-cies**), **Excellence** /-lənss/ *n.* a title and form of address for some high officials, e.g. governors, ambassadors, and high-ranking Roman Catholic clergy

excellent /éksələnt/ *adj.* EXTREMELY GOOD of a very high quality or standard ■ *interj.* AGREED used to show wholehearted approval or agreement —**excellently** *adv.*

excelsior /ek sélssi awr, ik-/ *n. US* packing material made from wood shavings [Late 18thC. From Latin, literally 'higher', from *excelsus* 'high', from the past participle of *excellere* (see EXCEL); in the noun usage, from a proprietary name.]

except /ik sépt/ (**-cepts, -cepting, -cepted**) CORE MEANING: a grammatical word indicating the only person or thing that does not apply to a statement just made, or a fact that modifies the truth of that statement ○ (prep) *Every house in the street except ours is painted white.* ○ (prep) *I like all vegetables except cabbage.* ○ (conj) *The fires that annually sweep over the prairies prevent the growth of timber, except along the river courses.* ○ (conj) *He dislikes the game except when he wins.*

1. *vt.* OMIT to leave out or exclude sb or sth (*formal*) (*usually passive*) ○ *'Hazel eyes excepted, two years more might make her all that he wished'.* (Jane Austen, *Emma*; 1816) **2.** *conj.* unless (*archaic*) [14thC. From Latin *exceptus*, the past participle of *excipere* 'to take out', from *capere* 'to take' (see CAPTURE).] ◇ **except for** apart from ○ *He had always been healthy except for an irregular heartbeat.*

WORD KEY: USAGE

except, except for, or **excepting** Often whether to use ***except*** or ***except for*** is a matter of indifference: *We'd all seen the film except [or except for] Sally.* Where the exception is closely paired with what it is an exception to, **except** is more usual: *All of us except Sally had seen the film.* **Except for** is used where the connection to what is being excepted is indirect, and is also more common at the beginning of a sentence: *Except for that, we were bored the whole time.* ***Excepting*** is the correct choice after *not*: *We'd all seen the film, not excepting Sally.*

excepted /ik séptid/ *adj.* with the exception of a particular person or thing ○ *present company excepted*

excepting /ik sépting/ *prep., conj.* used to indicate the only person or thing excluded from statement just made (*formal*)

WORD KEY: USAGE

See Usage note at ***except.***

exception /ik sépsh'n/ *n.* **1.** SB OR STH EXCLUDED sb or sth that is not included in or does not fit into a general rule, pattern, or judgment ○ *make an exception for family members* **2.** EXCLUSION the act or condition of being excluded **3.** CRITICISM a criticism, usually a negative one (*formal*) **4.** LAW LEGAL CLAUSE a clause in a legal document that limits the effect of a part or the whole of it ○ *read through and approved all the exceptions* ◇ **the exception that proves the rule** sth that, by being an exception, shows that a general rule exists

exceptionable /ik sépsh'nəb'l/ *adj.* causing or liable to cause objection or offence (*formal*)

WORD KEY: USAGE

See Usage note at ***exceptional.***

exceptional /ik sépsh'nəl/ *adj.* **1.** UNUSUAL not conforming to a general rule or pattern ○ *exceptional circumstances* **2.** OUTSTANDING having or showing intelligence or ability well above average ○ *an exceptional talent* —**exceptionality** /ik sépshə nálləti/ *n.* —**exceptionally** /ik sépsh'nəli/ *adv.* —**exceptionalness** /-nəss/ *n.*

WORD KEY: USAGE

exceptional or **exceptionable?** ***Exceptional*** is the more common word and refers, often favourably, to 'sth or sb unusual in some way': *She has exceptional powers of concentration.* Occasionally, ***exceptional*** is used in a factual or neutral way that is not meant to be a compliment: *Expenses can only be reimbursed in exceptional cases.* ***Exceptionable***, despite its similar sound, has a quite different meaning, 'sth to which exception can be taken': *There was sth in his manner that we found exceptionable.* More often, it is used in the negative form *unexceptionable*, meaning 'acceptable, satisfactory, adequate'.

exceptive /ik séptiv/ *adj.* relating to or of the nature of an exception

excerpt *n.* /éks urpt/ EXTRACTED PART a section or passage taken from a longer work, e.g. a book, film, musical composition, or document ■ *vt.* /ek súrpt/ (**-cerpts, -cerpting, -cerpted**) TAKE A PART FROM LONGER WORK to select a section or passage from a longer work (*usually passive*) [Mid-16thC. From Latin *excerptus*, the past participle of *excerpere*, literally 'to pluck out', from *carpere* 'to pluck' (source of English *carpet*).] —**excerptible** /ik súrptəb'l/ *adj.* —**excerption** /ik súrpsh'n/ *n.* —**excerptor** /ik súrptər/ *n.*

excess *n.* /ik séss, éks ess/ **1.** SURPLUS an amount or quantity beyond what is considered normal or sufficient ○ *leaped up in an excess of enthusiasm* **2.** EXTRA the amount by which one quantity exceeds another **3.** UNRESTRAINED BEHAVIOUR behaviour or activity that goes beyond what is socially or morally acceptable, or beyond what is good for sb's health or well-being ○ *led a life of excess* **4.** *UK, Carib* INSUR MONEY PAID TOWARDS INSURANCE CLAIM a particular amount of money that a policy-holder must pay towards the cost of any insurance claim made ○ *an insurance policy with a £50 excess.* US term **deductible** ■ *adj.* /éks ess, ek séss/ **1.** MORE THAN ENOUGH more than is usual, required, or allowed ○ *excess capacity* **2.** REQUIRED IN ADDITION that constitutes or is required as an additional payment ○ *excess postage* ■ *vt.* (**-cesses, -cessing, -cessed**) *US* DISMISS FROM EMPLOYMENT to dismiss an employee as part of a programme of redundancies ○ *excessed in the most recent downsizing* [14thC. Via French *excès* from Latin *excessus*, from the past participle of *excedere* (see EXCEED).]

excess baggage *n.* luggage that is heavier than the amount a passenger is allowed to take on a flight without an extra charge

excess demand *n.* demand for a product or service that outstrips the supply and so pushes the price up

excessive /ik séssiv/ *adj.* beyond what is considered acceptable, proper, usual, or necessary (*disapproving*) ○ *excessive hilarity* —**excessively** *adv.* —**excessiveness** *n.*

excess luggage *n.* = **excess baggage**

excess supply *n.* supply of a product or service that outstrips the demand and so pushes the price down

exch. *abbr.* **1. exch., ex.** exchange **2. exch., Exch.** exchequer

exchange /iks cháynj/ *v.* (**-changes, -changing, -changed**) **1.** *vt.* GIVE STH AND GET STH to give sth and receive sth different in return ○ *exchange land for peace* ○ *exchange tokens for cash* **2.** *vti.* SWAP to give sth and receive another of the same or an equivalent in return ○ *exchange glances* **3.** *vt.* REPLACE STH to hand sth over and receive as a replacement sth more suitable or more satisfactory ○ *exchanged her coat for one a size smaller* **4.** *vt.* CHESS TAKE A PIECE OF SIMILAR VALUE in chess, to take a piece in return for a piece of your own, usually of similar value, that your opponent has just taken or will soon take ■ *n.* **1.** GIVING AND RECEIVING the action or process or an instance of exchanging sth for sth else or for sth the same ○ *an exchange of compliments* **2.** ARGUMENT a short conversation, usually between two people or groups who are angry ○ *a bitter exchange* **3.** STH GIVEN OR RECEIVED sth given or received in place of another **4.** EDUC ARRANGEMENT TO VISIT ANOTHER COUNTRY an arrangement between families, schools, or organizations in different countries for stays in each other's country **5.** COMM BUILDING USED FOR COMMERCIAL ACTIVITIES a building formerly or still used as a centre for the trading of commodities, securities, or other assets **6.** UTIL = **telephone exchange 7.** FIN MONEY TRANSFER BETWEEN TWO CURRENCIES the transferring or a transfer of equal amounts of money between two currencies **8.** FIN SYSTEM OF PAYMENTS a system of payments in which commercial documents, e.g. bills of exchange, are used instead of money **9.** COMM FEE FOR PAYMENT the percentage or fee that is charged when paying in commercial documents instead of money **10.** CHESS TAKING OF CHESS PIECES the taking of chess pieces of similar value by each player in consecutive or nearly consecutive moves **11.** CHESS TRADE OF A ROOK FOR A MINOR PIECE taking a rook just before or after your opponent takes your knight or bishop, or vice-versa. The player taking the rook wins the exchange. **12.** TRANSFER OF PARTICLE the transfer of a particle between two others [14thC. Via Old French *eschangier* from assumed Vulgar Latin *excambiare*, from late Latin *cambiare* 'to barter' (see CHANGE).] —**exchangeability** /iks cháynjə bílləti/ *n.* —**exchangeable** /iks cháynjəb'l/ *adj.* —**exchanger** /-jər/ *n.*

exchange force *n.* a force existing between particles due to the transfer of another particle

exchange rate *n.* the rate at which a unit of the currency of one country can be exchanged for a unit of the currency of another

Exchange Rate Mechanism *n.* a system of controlling the exchange rate between some countries in the European Union

exchequer /iks chékər/ *n.* **1. exchequer, Exchequer** GOVERNMENT DEPARTMENT COLLECTING TAXES formerly in the United Kingdom, and in some other countries, the government department responsible for collecting taxes and managing public spending **2. exchequer, Exchequer** GOVERNMENT FUNDS a national treasury or account, especially the UK government's account at the Bank of England, or the assets in it **3.** PERSONAL FUNDS private funds or finances (*archaic*) **4. Exchequer** = **Court of Exchequer** [13thC. From Old French *eschequier* 'counting table, chessboard', from *eschec* 'check', from the custom of counting royal revenue on a checked tablecloth.]

excimer /ék sīmər/ *n.* CHEM a stable atomic pair (**dimer**) in which one of the two bound atoms is in a higher energy state [Mid-20thC. Blend of EXCITED and DIMER.]

excipient /ik síppi ənt/ *n.* an inert substance, e.g. starch or gum arabic, that is combined with a drug to make it easier to administer [Early 18thC. From Latin *excipient-*, the present participle stem of *excipere* 'to receive, take out' (see EXCEPT).]

excise[1] *n.* /ék sīz/ **1.** TAX ON GOODS FOR THE HOME MARKET taxation of or a tax imposed on goods for a domestic market only **2.** LICENSING CHARGE a tax paid for a licence, e.g. one required to use a vehicle on public roads or to engage in certain commercial activities ■ *vt.* /ik sīz/ (**-cises, -cising, -cised**) TAX to impose an excise on sb or sth [15thC. Via Middle Dutch *excijs* from Old French *acceis*, partly from assumed Vulgar Latin *accensum*, from Latin *census* (see CENSUS), and partly from Old French *assise* (see ASSIZE).] —**excisable** /ik sīzəb'l/ *adj.*

excise[2] /ik síz/ (**-cises, -cising, -cised**) *vt.* **1.** DELETE to edit or delete a part of sth, e.g. a text (*formal*) **2.** REMOVE SURGICALLY to remove sth by cutting, especially in surgery [Late 16thC. From Latin *excis-*, the past participle stem of *excidere* 'to cut out', from *caedere* 'to cut' (see CAESURA).] —**excision** /ik sízh'n/ *n.*

excise duty *n.* tax imposed on goods intended for a domestic market only

exciseman /ék sīz man/ (*plural* **-men** /-men/) *n.* formerly, sb hired by the government to collect excise duty and prevent smuggling

excitable /ik sītəb'l/ *adj.* **1.** EASILY STIMULATED nervous and liable to become quickly excited **2.** PHYSIOL ABLE TO RESPOND TO STIMULUS used to describe a nerve or tissue that is able to respond to a stimulus —**excitability** /ik sītə bílləti/ *n.* —**excitableness** /ik sītəb'lnəss/ *n.* —**excitably** /-əbli/ *adv.*

excitant /ik sītənt, éksitənt/ *adj.* STIMULATING tending to excite or stimulate sth ■ *n.* (*plural* **-tants**) STIMULANT a drug or other agent that stimulates or augments a response

excitation /éksi táysh'n, éks ī-/ *n.* **1.** EXCITING the act or process of exciting sth (*formal*) **2.** BEING EXCITED the state of being excited **3.** PHYSIOL ACTIVITY CAUSED BY STIMULATION the activity or altered condition produced in a cell, tissue, or organ as a result of stimulation **4.** ELEC ENG PRODUCTION OF MAGNETIC FIELD the production of a magnetic field in a generator or motor by passing electricity through the coil **5.** PHYS RAISING ENERGY OF ATOM FROM LOWEST the addition of sufficient energy to an electron, atom, atomic nucleus, or molecule, to raise it from its lowest energy level (**ground state**) to a higher energy level **6.** ELECTRON ENG APPLICATION OF SIGNAL MAKING TRANSISTOR OPERATE the application of an electrical signal to a device such as a transistor causing it to operate

excite /ik sít/ (**-cites, -citing, -cited**) *v.* **1.** *vti.* STIMULATE FAVOURABLY to cause sb to feel enjoyment or pleasurable anticipation ○ *an exciting story* **2.** *vt.* STIMULATE UNFAVOURABLY to make a person or animal feel nervous apprehension or an unpleasant state of heightened emotion ○ *Don't excite the dog or he'll bite.* **3.** *vt.* AROUSE AN EMOTION to cause sb to feel a particular emotion or reaction ○ *excite suspicion* **4.** *vt.* EVOKE to cause a memory, thought, or other response to form in the mind ○ *an image that excited a memory* **5.** *vt.* AROUSE PHYSICALLY to cause sb to feel physical desire **6.** *vt.* PHYSIOL INCREASE STH'S ACTIVITY to stimulate or increase the rate of activity of an organ, tissue, or other body part **7.** *vt.* PHYS RAISE A PARTICLE TO A HIGHER ENERGY LEVEL to raise a particle or system of particles, e.g. an electron, atom, atomic nucleus, or molecule, above its lowest energy level (**ground state**) to a higher energy level **8.** *vt.* ELEC ENG PRODUCE MAGNETIC FIELD IN ELECTRIC MACHINE to produce a magnetic field in a generator or motor by supplying electricity to the coil **9.** *vt.* ELECTRON ENG APPLY SIGNAL CAUSING DEVICE TO OPERATE to apply an electrical signal that will cause a device, such as a transistor, to operate [14thC. Directly or via French from Latin *excitare* 'to rouse', literally 'to call forth repeatedly', from, ultimately, *ciere* 'to call, set in motion' (see CITE).]

excited /ik sítid/ *adj.* **1.** HAPPY AND ENTHUSIASTIC happy and enthusiastic about sth pleasant that is happening or is about to happen **2.** AGITATED nervous, agitated, and unable to relax **3.** PHYSICALLY AROUSED in a state of physical arousal —**excitedly** *adv.* —**excitedness** *n.*

excited state *n.* PHYS the condition of a physical system, especially of atoms and atomic nuclei, that has an energy level higher than the lowest possible level (**ground state**)

excitement /ik sítmənt/ *n.* **1.** BEING EXCITED the feeling or condition of lively enjoyment or pleasant anticipation ○ *finding it difficult to contain her excitement* **2.** EXCITING EVENT sth that engages people's attention or emotions in a lively and compelling way ○ *Going in a helicopter was a great excitement for the children.* **3.** EXCITING STH the act or process of exciting sth ○ *excitement of electrons*

exciter /ik sítər/ *n.* **1.** CAUSE OF EXCITEMENT sb or sth that causes excitement **2.** ELEC ENG SMALL AUXILIARY GENERATOR a small generator or transmitter that provides the necessary energy to run a larger device or amplifier **3.** RADIO ELECTRICAL OSCILLATOR an oscillator for supplying a radio transmitter with the basic wave that is modified to carry a radio signal

exciting /ik síting/ *adj.* causing feelings of happiness and enthusiasm or nervousness and tension —**excitingly** *adv.*

exciton /éksi ton, ék sī ton/ *n.* PHYS a mobile neutral combination of an electron in an excited state and a hole in a crystal. Exciton activity is important in semiconductors. [Mid-20thC. Coined from EXCITATION + -ON.]

excl. *abbr.* **1.** exclamation **2.** exclusive

exclaim /ik skláym/ (**-claims, -claiming, -claimed**) *vti.* to speak or cry out loudly and suddenly, often through surprise, anger, or excitement [Late 16thC. Directly or via French *exclamer* from Latin *exclamare*, literally 'to call out', from *clamare* 'to call' (see CLAIM).] —**exclaimer** *n.*

exclamation /ékskla máysh'n/ *n.* **1.** SUDDEN CRY a word, phrase, or sentence that is shouted out suddenly, often through surprise, anger, or excitement ○ *an exclamation of horror* **2.** EXCLAIMING the act of crying out suddenly —**exclamational** *adj.*

exclamation mark *n.* **1.** PUNCTUATION FOR EXCLAMATION a punctuation mark (!) used after an exclamation or interjection, and sometimes after a command **2.** MARK INDICATING HAZARD OR MISTAKE a mark (!) used to indicate a road hazard or a mistake or point of note in a text, or as a mathematical or logical symbol

exclamation point *n.* US = **exclamation mark**

exclamatory /ik sklámmətəri/ *adj.* using, of the nature of, or relating to an exclamation or exclamations (*formal*) —**exclamatorily** *adv.*

exclaustration /éks klaw stráysh'n/ *n.* a monk's or nun's return to lay life after relinquishing vows [Mid-20thC. From the modern Latin stem *exclaustration-*, literally 'putting out of the enclosed space', from Latin *claustrum* 'enclosed space' (see CLOISTER).]

exclave /éks klayv/ *n.* a part of a country that is isolated from the main body of the country, being surrounded by foreign territory [Late 19thC. Coined from EX- + ENCLAVE.]

exclosure /eks klṓzhər/ *n.* an area fenced in to keep out animals or intruders [Early 20thC. Coined from EX- + CLOSURE on the model of ENCLOSURE.]

exclude /ik skloòd/ (**-cludes, -cluding, -cluded**) *vt.* **1.** KEEP OUT to prevent sb or sth from entering or participating ○ *I felt excluded from the family celebrations.* **2.** REJECT to prevent sb or sth from being considered or accepted ○ *cannot exclude the possibility of treason* **3.** OMIT to fail to include sth or sb ○ *Three names were inadvertently excluded from the list.* **4.** EDUC BAN SCHOOLCHILD to ban a child from attending school on disciplinary grounds for a temporary, indefinite, or permanent period [14thC. From Latin *excludere*, literally 'to shut out', from *claudere* 'to shut' (see CLOSE).] —**excludability** /ik skloòdə bíllәti/ *n.* —**excludable** /ik skloòdəb'l/ *adj.* —**excluder** /-dər/ *n.*

exclusion /ik skloòzh'n/ *n.* **1.** EXCLUDING the act of excluding sth or sb **2.** BEING EXCLUDED the state of being excluded, especially from mainstream society and its advantages ○ *addressing the issue of social exclusion* **3.** EXCLUDED PERSON OR THING sb or sth that has been excluded [15thC. From the Latin stem *exclusion-*, from *exclus-*, the past participle stem of *excludere* (see EXCLUDE).] —**exclusionary** /ik skloòzh'nəri/ *adj.*

exclusionary rule *n.* a law that prevents illegally obtained evidence from being used in a criminal trial

exclusionist /ik skloòzh'nist/ *adj.* US **1.** DISCRIMINATORY used to describe a policy that excludes individuals or groups from areas or rights and privileges **2.** PROTECTIONIST used to describe a policy that excludes specific imports or forms of commerce ■ *n.* US EXCLUSION ADVOCATE sb who supports exclusionist policies —**exclusionism** *n.* —**exclusionistic** /ik skloòzh'n ístik/ *adj.*

exclusion principle *n.* QUANTUM PHYS = **Pauli exclusion principle**

exclusion zone *n.* **1.** AREA OF BAN an area where an authority has banned a particular activity **2.** HAZARDOUS AREA an area that is out of bounds to people because a hazardous substance has been released ○ *the Chernobyl exclusion zone*

exclusive /ik skloòssiv/ *adj.* **1.** HIGH-CLASS limited to a group of people, especially one considered fashionable or wealthy ○ *an exclusive club* **2.** SELECTIVE excluding or intending to exclude many from participation or consideration **3.** RESTRICTED IN USE only available to or used by one person, group, or organization ○ *Members have exclusive use of the pool.* **4.** APPEARING IN ONE PLACE published or broadcast in only one place ○ *exclusive coverage* **5.** SOLE being the only one **6.** CONFINED TO ONE THING limited to one thing and excluding everything else ○ *exclusive attention* **7.** NOT INCLUDING THE STATED NUMBERS not including the numbers, dates, or other series members mentioned immediately before ○ *from 8 July to 10 July exclusive* **8.** COMM RESTRICTING TRADE restricting trade in certain goods or services only to those who have signed the contract or agreement **9.** LOGIC WHERE BOTH CANNOT BE TRUE used to describe a proposition (**disjunction**) where one alternative rules out the other, e.g. being an odd number rules out the possibility of being an even number. ◊ **inclusive** ■ *n.* REPORT IN ONE PUBLICATION OR PROGRAMME a news report or article that is printed in only one publication or broadcast on only one channel ○ *an exclusive on the wedding* [15thC. From medieval Latin *exclusivus*, from Latin *exclus-*, the past participle stem of *excludere* (see EXCLUDE).] —**exclusively** *adv.* —**exclusiveness** *n.* —**exclusivity** /ék skloo sívvəti/ *n.* ◇ **exclusive of** not including ○ *The price covers all your vacation costs, exclusive of travel insurance.*

exclusivism /ik skloòssivizzəm/ *n.* the practice or policy of being exclusive or excluding others —**exclusivist** *n., adj.*

excogitate /eks kójji tayt/ (**-tates, -tating, -tated**) *vt.* to consider or think about sth carefully and thoroughly (*formal*) [Early 16thC. From Latin *excogitat-*, the past participle stem of *excogitare*, literally 'to think out', from *cogitare* 'to think' (see COGITATE).] —**excogitable** *adj.*

excommunicate *vt.* /ékskə myoòni kayt/ (**-cates, -cating, -cated**) EXCLUDE SB FROM THE CHRISTIAN COMMUNITY to exclude a baptized Christian from taking part in Communion because of doctrine or moral behaviour that is adjudged to offend against God or the Christian community ■ *adj.* /ékskə myoònikət, -kayt/ EXCOMMUNICATED having been officially excluded from taking part in the Eucharist ■ *n.* /ékskə myoònikət, -kayt/ EXCOMMUNICATED PERSON sb who has been officially excluded from taking part in the Eucharist [15thC. From late Latin *excommunicare*, literally 'to put out of the community', from Latin *communis* 'common'.] —**excommunicable** /ékskə myoònikəb'l/ *adj.* —**excommunicative** /-kətiv/ *adj.* —**excommunicator** /-kaytər/ *n.*

excommunication /ékskə myoòni káysh'n/ *n.* **1.** EXCLUSION FROM THE CHRISTIAN COMMUNITY the act of excommunicating a baptized member of the Christian church **2.** BEING EXCOMMUNICATED the condition of being excommunicated

ex-convict, **ex-con** *informal n.* sb who has served time in prison, having been convicted of a crime

excoriate /ik skáwri ayt, -skórri-/ (**-ates, -ating, -ated**) *vt.* **1.** DENOUNCE to criticize sb or sth very strongly (*formal*) ○ *The paper excoriated the government's conduct in this case.* **2.** TEAR SB'S SKIN OFF to tear the skin off a person or animal (*formal*) **3.** MED REMOVE SKIN LAYER to destroy or remove an area of skin, often through abrasion or chemical action [15thC. From Latin *excoriat-*, the past participle stem of *excoriare* 'to strip off the hide', from *corium* 'hide, skin'.] —**excoriation** /ik skáwri áysh'n, -skórri-/ *n.* —**excoriator** /ik skáwri aytər, -skórri-/ *n.*

excrement /ékskrimənt/ *n.* waste material, particularly faeces, discharged from the body (*technical*) [Mid-16thC. From Latin *excrementum*, from *excretus*, the past participle of *excernere* 'to discharge' (see EXCRETE).] —**excremental** /ékskri mént'l/ *adj.* —**excrementitious** /ékskri men tíshəss/ *adj.*

excrescence /ik skréss'nss/ *n.* **1.** BIOL OUTGROWTH a growth that sticks out from the body of a human, animal, or plant, especially an abnormal or diseased one **2.** UNSIGHTLY ADDITION an ugly addition or extension to sth, e.g. a building

excrescent /ik skréss'nt/ *adj.* **1.** SUPERFLUOUS added or growing out unnecessarily (*formal*) **2.** BIOL RELATING TO AN OUTGROWTH relating to or like an outgrowth on an organism **3.** LING ADDED IN SPEAKING used to describe a speech sound that occurs in a word to allow ease of pronunciation [15thC. From Latin *excrescent-*, the present participle stem of *excrescere* 'to grow out', from *crescere* 'to grow' (see CRESCENT).] —**excrescently** *adv.*

excreta /ik skreétə/ *npl.* any waste matter discharged from the body, e.g. faeces, or urine (*technical*) [Mid-19thC. From Latin, literally 'things excreted', from a form of the past participle of *excernere* (see EXCRETE).] —**excretal** *adj.*

excrete /ik skreét/ (**-cretes, -creting, -creted**) *vt.* **1.** PHYSIOL EXPEL WASTE FROM THE BODY to isolate and discharge waste matter generated during metabolism, e.g. through urinating or defecating (*formal*) ◊ **secrete 2.** PHYSIOL, BOT EXPEL WASTE FROM TISSUES to eliminate waste matter from leaves and roots [Early 17thC. From Latin *excret-*, the past participle stem of *excernere*, literally 'to separate out', from *cernere* 'to separate' (source of English *discern*).] —**excreter** *n.* —**excretory** *adj.*

excretion /ik skreésh'n/ *n.* **1.** EXCRETING OF WASTE MATTER the act or process of discharging waste matter from the tissues or organs **2.** WASTE MATTER waste matter that has been discharged from an animal or a plant

excruciate /ik skroòshi ayt/ (**-ates, -ating, -ated**) *vt.* (*formal*) **1.** TORMENT SB to inflict severe mental and emotional distress on sb **2.** TORTURE SB to inflict physical pain on sb [Late 16thC. From, ultimately, Latin *excruciare*, literally 'to torture thoroughly', from *cruciare* 'to torture, crucify', from the stem *cruc-* 'cross' (see CROSS).] —**excruciation** /ik skroòshi áysh'n/ *n.*

excruciating /ik skroòshi ayting/ *adj.* **1.** EXTREMELY PAINFUL extremely painful, physically or emotionally **2.** HARD TO BEAR intolerably embarrassing, tedious or irritating ○ *The first act was bad enough, but the second was just excruciating.* —**excruciatingly** *adv.*

exculpate /éks kul payt, iks kúl payt/ (**-pates, -pating, -pated**) *vt.* to free sb from blame or accusation of guilt (*formal*) [Mid-17thC. From medieval Latin *exculpare*, literally 'to remove from blame', from Latin *culpa* 'blame' (see CULPABLE).] —**exculpable** /ik skúlpəb'l/ *adj.* —**exculpation** /éks kul páysh'n/ *n.*

exculpatory /ik skúlpətəri/ *adj.* tending to prove that sb is free from guilt or blame (*formal*) ○ *exculpatory evidence*

excursion /ik skúrsh'n, -skúrzh'n/ *n.* **1.** SHORT TRIP a short trip to a place and back, for pleasure or a purpose **2.** GROUP ON A SHORT TRIP a group of people who are on an excursion **3.** DIGRESSION a temporary change of direction ○ *After an unsuccessful excursion into banking, he returned to public life.* **4.** MIL SORTIE a military raid or attack (*archaic*) **5.** PHYS ALTERNATING MOTION an oscillating or alternating motion away from a point of equilibrium and back **6.** PHYS DISTANCE COVERED the distance traversed by an oscillating excursion away from a point of equilibrium and back **7.** PHYSIOL MOVEMENT OF A BODY PART the movement of a part or organ of the body, e.g. the lungs, from the resting position to another position [Late 16thC. From the Latin stem *excursion-*, from *excurs-*, the past participle stem of *excurrere* 'to run out', from *currere* (see CURRENT).]

WORD KEY: CULTURAL NOTE

The Excursion, a poem by the English poet William Wordsworth (1814). Originally intended to be part of a philosophical work called *The Recluse*, it describes the poet's travels with a character called The Wanderer. On their way they meet Solitary, who has lost faith in human nature, and the Pastor, who describes the rewards of virtue.

excursionist /ik skúrsh'nist, -skúrzh'n-/ *n.* sb who goes on an excursion, especially for pleasure (*dated*)

excursive /ik skúrssiv/ *adj.* tending to digress from the main topic, often in a rambling and wordy manner (*formal*) [Late 17thC. Formed from obsolete *excurse* 'to digress', from the Latin stem *excurs-* (see EXCURSION); perhaps modelled on DISCURSIVE.] —**excursively** *adv.* —**excursiveness** *n.*

excursus /ek skúrssəss/ (*plural* **-suses** *or* **-sus**) *n.* a lengthy digression from the main topic (*formal*) [Early 19thC. From Latin, 'excursion', from the past participle of *excurrere* 'to run out', from *currere* 'to run' (see CURRENT).]

excusatory /ik skyóozətəri/ *adj.* tending or serving to excuse sb or sth (*formal*)

excuse *v.* /ik skyóoz/ (**-cuses, -cusing, -cused**) **1.** *vt.* FORGIVE STH to release sb from blame or criticism for a mistake or wrongdoing ○ *excuse their tardiness* **2.** *vt.* OVERLOOK STH to make allowances for sb or sth ○ *Please excuse my spelling.* **3.** *vt.* RELEASE SB FROM AN OBLIGATION to release sb from an obligation or responsibility ○ *excused from games because of a sprained ankle* **4.** *vt.* JUSTIFY STH to provide a reason or explanation for sb's behaviour that makes it appear more acceptable or less offensive ○ *That doesn't excuse the way he acted last night.* **5.** *vt.* ALLOW SB TO LEAVE to allow sb to leave, or say politely that sb should leave ○ *asked if he could be excused* **6.** *vr.* APOLOGIZE FOR LEAVING to leave with a polite apology or explanation ○ *excused herself and left the room* ■ *n.* /ik skyóoss/ **1.** JUSTIFICATION a reason or explanation, not necessarily true, given in order to make sth appear more acceptable or less offensive ○ *There can be no excuse for laziness.* **2.** FALSE REASON a false reason that enables sb to do sth he or she wants to do or avoid sth he or she does not want to do ○ *the perfect excuse to do nothing* **3.** BAD EXAMPLE sb who is not very good at what he or she does (*informal*) ○ *a poor excuse for a cook* **4.** *US* = **sick note** [15thC. Via Old French *escuser* from Latin *excusare*, literally 'to remove from accusation', from *causa* 'accusation' (see CAUSE).] —**excusable** *adj.* —**excusableness** *n.* —**excusably** /-əbli/ *adv.* —**excuser** *n.*

excuse-me, **excuse-me dance** *n.* a dance in which participants interrupt other pairs to invite a change of partner

ex-directory *adj. UK* TELECOM not listed in the telephone directory by request. ◊ **unlisted**

ex dividend *adv., adj.* without the right to the current dividend on purchase

exe /eks/ *suffix.* COMPUT used after the dot in a computer file name to show that the file is a program

exeat /éksi at/ *n.* **1.** LEAVE OF ABSENCE a short leave of absence from a boarding school or institution, usually lasting a day or a weekend **2.** PERMISSION FOR PRIEST TO MOVE formal leave to move to a new diocese granted by a bishop to a priest [Early 18thC. From Latin, 'let him or her go out', 3rd person singular present subjunctive of *exire* 'to go out'.]

exec /ig zék/ *n.* an executive or executive officer (*informal*) [Late 19thC. Shortening.]

exec. *abbr.* executor

execrable /éksikrəb'l/ *adj.* **1.** VERY BAD extremely bad or of very low quality ○ *has execrable taste* **2.** DETESTABLE deserving to be detested ○ *execrable behaviour* [14thC. Via Old French from Latin *execrabilis*, from *execrari* (see EXECRATE).] —**execrableness** *n.* —**execrably** *adv.*

execrate /éksi krayt/ (**-crates, -crating, -crated**) *v.* (*literary or formal*) **1.** *vt.* DETEST SB OR STH to feel loathing for sb or sth **2.** *vt.* DENOUNCE SB OR STH to declare sb or sth to be loathsome **3.** *vti.* CURSE SB OR STH to curse or put a curse on sb or sth [Mid-16thC. From Latin *execrari*, literally 'to unconsecrate', from *sacrare* (see CONSECRATE).] —**execrative** /éksikrətiv/ *adj.* —**execrator** /-kraytər/ *n.*

execration /éksi kráysh'n/ *n.* (*literary or formal*) **1.** CURSE a curse ○ *'With an execration the thoroughly terrified robber threw down the pocketbook, and the relieved owner hastened forward to pick it up'.* (Horatio Alger, Jr., *Struggling Upward*; 1868) **2.** STH CURSED sth that is cursed or detested **3.** EXECRATING the act of execrating sb or sth, or the state of being execrated

executable /éksi kyootəb'l/ *adj.* ABLE TO BE RUN AS A PROGRAM used to describe a file that is capable of being run as a program on a computer ■ *n.* EXECUTABLE FILE a computer file that can be run as a program and that often carries the extension .exe

executant /ig zékyootənt/ *n.* sb who performs a piece of music, dance, or theatre, usually to a very high standard (*formal*)

execute /éksikyoot/ (**-cutes, -cuting, -cuted**) *v.* **1.** *vt.* CARRY STH OUT to put an instruction or plan into effect **2.** *vt.* PERFORM STH to complete or perform an action or movement, especially one requiring skill **3.** *vt.* CREATE STH to produce or create sth, usually a work of art, to a specific design ○ *execute a drawing* **4.** *vt.* LAW KILL SB to put sb to death as part of a judicial or extrajudicial process **5.** *vti.* COMPUT RUN ON COMPUTER to run a computer file or program in response to a command or instruction **6.** *vt.* LAW SIGN A LEGAL DOCUMENT BEFORE WITNESSES to sign a will or other legal document in the presence of witnesses in order to make it binding **7.** *vt.* LAW CARRY OUT TERMS OF A LEGAL DOCUMENT to carry out the terms laid out in a will, legal document, or legal decision ○ *execute a sentence* [14thC. From, ultimately, Latin *exsecut-*, the past participle stem of *exsequi*, literally 'to follow out', from *sequi* 'to follow' (see SEQUENCE).] —**executer** *n.*

WORD KEY: SYNONYMS

See Synonyms at ***kill*** and ***perform***.

execution /éksi kyóosh'n/ *n.* **1.** LAW KILLING the killing of sb as part of a judicial or extrajudicial process **2.** PERFORMING OF STH the carrying out of an action, instruction, command, or movement ○ *a plan that failed in execution* **3.** MANNER OF PERFORMANCE the style or manner in which sth is carried out or accomplished **4.** LAW ENFORCEMENT OF A COURT JUDGMENT the carrying out or enforcing of a judgment made in court **5.** LAW CARRYING OUT OF LEGAL PROVISIONS the carrying out of the provisions of a legal document such as a will or contract **6.** LAW WRIT a legal writ that orders the carrying out of a judgment or decision

executioner /éksi kyóosh'nər/ *n.* **1.** LAW OFFICIAL WHO CARRIES OUT AN EXECUTION sb who puts to death sb who has been sentenced to capital punishment **2.** CRIMINOL ASSASSIN a hired assassin

execution time *n.* the amount of time needed for a complete run of a computer program

executive /ig zékyootiv/ *n.* **1.** MANAGEMT SENIOR MANAGER a senior manager in a company or organization, whose job it is to make and implement major decisions **2.** POL GOVERNMENT SECTION RESPONSIBLE FOR DECISIONS the section of a country's government responsible for implementing legislative decisions **3.** POL COMMITTEE THAT MAKES DECISIONS a committee or group in a political organization that makes decisions and has the authority to implement them ○ *the executive of the Transport Union* ■ *adj.* **1.** MANAGEMT, POL OF POLICYMAKING responsible for or relating to the making and implementing of general decisions in a company, organization, or government ○ *a meeting of the executive committee* **2.** BUSINESS FOR BUSINESSPEOPLE restricted to or designed to be used by businessmen and businesswomen ○ *an executive toy* **3.** VERY EXPENSIVE very expensive and so only affordable by those who earn high salaries ○ *executive homes* [15thC. From Old French *executif*, from *executer* 'to carry out', ultimately from Latin *execut-* (see EXECUTE).] —**executively** *adv.*

executive agreement *n.* an agreement between a US president and a foreign head of state that has not been given approval by the Senate

Executive Council *n.* **1.** CANADIAN PROVINCIAL CABINET in Canada, the cabinet of a provincial government **2.** AUSTRALIAN AND NEW ZEALAND GOVERNMENT BODY in Australia and New Zealand, a body made up of the Governor-General or Governor and government ministers. It meets in order to brief the Governor-General or Governor on policies and formally approve government appointments and legislation.

executive director *n.* a director of a company who is employed by the company in a senior management position

executive jet *n.* a small jet aircraft designed for private use, especially one used to transport corporate executives

executive officer *n.* **1.** MIL SECOND-IN-COMMAND an officer who is second in command of a military or naval unit **2.** MANAGEMT SENIOR MANAGER sb in a senior management position in an organization

executive privilege *n.* in the United States, the right of the President and other government officials in the executive branch to refuse to reveal confidential material if this would interfere with the administration's ability to govern

executive producer *n.* **1.** CINEMA, TV HEAD PRODUCER AT A STUDIO the head producer in charge of other producers at a film or television studio **2.** CINEMA A PRODUCER CONTROLLING FINANCES FOR FILM the producer who handles the finances for a film

executive secretary *n.* **1.** SB RUNNING BUSINESS AFFAIRS a senior official who handles an organization's business affairs **2.** TOP-LEVEL SECRETARY a secretary who reports to a senior manager or executive in a company

executive session *n.* a meeting of the US Senate, closed to the public, to discuss confidential government business such as judicial appointments or the ratification of treaties

executive toy *n.* a small but usually sophisticated and expensively produced toy, e.g. a Newton's cradle, marketed as suitable for an executive's desk where it may aid concentration or relieve stress

executor /ig zékyootər/ *n.* **1.** LAW SB IMPLEMENTING A WILL sb named in a will or appointed by a court to carry out the instructions contained in a will **2.** SB WHO DOES STH sb who carries sth out, e.g. an order [13thC. Via Anglo-Norman *execut(o)ur* from Latin *executor*, from *execut-* (see EXECUTE).] —**executorial** /ig zékyoo táwri əl/ *adj.* —**executorship** /ig zékyootərship/ *n.*

executory /ig zékyootəri/ *adj.* **1.** LAW COMING INTO EFFECT LATER coming into effect at a future time or in accordance with circumstances **2.** ADMINISTRATIVE relating to the task or process of carrying out laws, policies, or instructions [15thC. From late Latin *executorius*, from Latin *executor* (see EXECUTOR). First recorded in the sense 'operative, in force (of a law)'.]

exedra /éksidrə, ek séedrə/ *n.* **1.** ARCHIT, HIST CONVERSATION ROOM a room for relaxation or conversation in ancient Greece and Rome, especially a semicircular recess in a larger hall with a continuous bench along the wall **2.** FURNITURE LONG CURVED OUTDOOR BENCH a long curved or semicircular outdoor bench, usually with a high back **3.** ARCHIT RECESS any kind of recess or niche (*technical*) [Early 18thC. Via Latin from Greek, literally 'outside seat', from *hedra* 'seat' (source of English *-hedron*).]

exegesis /éksi jéessiss/ (*plural* **-ses** /-seez/) *n.* the explanation or interpretation of texts, especially from the Bible, or an explanation or interpretation of a particular text [Early 17thC. From Greek *exēgēsis*, from *exēgeisthai* 'to interpret', literally 'to lead or guide out', from *hēgeisthai* 'to guide'.]

exegete /éksi jeet/ *n.* sb who studies and interprets texts, especially religious writings [Mid-18thC. From Greek *exēgētes*, from *exēgeisthai* (see EXEGESIS).]

exegetic /éksi jéttik/, **exegetical** /-jéttik'l/ *adj.* **1.** OF TEXTUAL STUDY relating to the study and interpretation of texts, especially religious writings **2.** EXPLANATORY intended to explain or interpret sth, especially a written text (*formal*) [Early 17thC. From Greek *exēgētikos*, from *exēgeisthai* (see EXEGESIS).] —**exegetically** *adv.*

exegetics /éksi jéttiks/ *n.* the branch of theology dealing with the study and interpretation of scripture (*takes a singular verb*)

exegetist /éksi jéetist/ *n.* = **exegete**

exempla plural of **exemplum**

exemplar /ig zémplaar, -lər/ *n.* **1.** IDEAL an ideal example of sth, worthy of being copied or imitated (*literary*) ○ *Michelangelo's David is an exemplar of Renaissance sculpture.* **2.** TYPICAL EXAMPLE a typical example or instance of sth (*literary*) **3.** PUBL COPY OF A BOOK a copy of a book or text, especially one from which further copies have originated [15thC. Directly or via French *exemplaire* from late Latin *exemplarium*, from Latin *exemplum* (see EXAMPLE).]

exemplary /ig zémpləri/ *adj.* **1.** SETTING AN EXAMPLE so good or admirable that others would do well to copy it ○ *the child's exemplary conduct* **2.** SERVING AS AN EXAMPLE designed to serve as a warning to others ○ *exemplary punishment* **3.** GIVING AN EXAMPLE serving as an illustration or example of sth (*formal*) [Late 16thC. From late Latin *exemplaris*, from Latin *exemplum* (see EXAMPLE).] —**exemplarily** *adv.* —**exemplariness** *n.* —**exemplarity** /égz em plárrəti/ *n.*

exemplary damages *npl.* damages well above the value of the loss suffered, awarded to punish the offender and deter others

exemplification /ig zémplifi káysh'n/ *n.* **1.** EXAMPLE a thing that acts as an example or illustration of sth **2.** GIVING EXAMPLES the process of giving examples to illustrate or explain sth **3.** LAW OFFICIAL COPY an official copy of a legal document [Directly or via Anglo-Norman from the medieval Latin stem *exemplification-*, from *exemplificare* (see EXEMPLIFY)]

exemplify /ig zémpli fī/ (**-fies, -fying, -fied**) *vt.* **1.** BE AN EXAMPLE OF STH to show or illustrate sth by being a typical or model example of it ○ *He exemplified all the qualities of a natural leader.* **2.** GIVE AN EXAMPLE OF STH to give an example or examples in order to make sth clearer or more convincing ○ *Perhaps you could exemplify your point with a few statistics.* **3.** LAW MAKE A COPY OF DOCUMENT to make an official copy of a legal document [15thC. From medieval Latin *exemplificare*, from Latin *exemplum* (see EXAMPLE).] —**exemplifiable** *adj.* —**exemplifier** *n.*

exempli gratia /eg zém plī gráati aa/ *adv.* full form of **e.g.** (*literary*) [Mid-17thC. From Latin, literally 'for example's sake'.]

exemplum /ig zémpləm/ (*plural* **-pla** /-plə/) *n.* **1.** ILLUSTRATIVE STORY a brief story told to illustrate a moral point or support an argument **2.** EXAMPLE an example or illustration (*literary*) [Late 19thC. From Latin (see EXAMPLE).]

exempt /ig zémpt/ *adj.* NOT SUBJECT TO STH freed from or not subject to sth such as a duty, tax, or military service that others have to do or pay ○ *tax-exempt savings accounts* ■ *vt.* (**-empts, -empting, -empted**) **1.** FREE SB FROM AN OBLIGATION to allow or entitle sb not to do sth that others are obliged to do **2.** RELEASE STH FROM A RULE to release sth from a rule that applies to others ○ *a law that exempts certain capital gains from taxes* ■ *n.* EXEMPT PERSON OR THING sb or sth that is exempt from sth [14thC. Directly or via French from Latin *exemptus*, past participle of *eximere* (see EXAMPLE).] —**exemptible** *adj.*

exemption /ig zémpsh'n/ *n.* **1.** FREEDOM FROM AN OBLIGATION permission or entitlement not to do sth that others are obliged to do **2.** EXEMPT PERSON OR THING sb who or sth that is exempt from sth, especially an amount of money that is not subject to taxation ○ *a range of tax exemptions*

exenterate /ig zéntə rayt/ (**-ates, -ating, -ated**) *vt.* to remove surgically all the organs and other contents of a body cavity, usually to minimize the spread of cancer [Early 17thC. From the Latin *exenterat-*, past participle stem of *exenterare*, which was modelled on Greek *exenterizein*, literally 'to remove the intestine', from *enteron* 'intestine'.] —**exenteration** /ig zéntə ráysh'n/ *n.*

exequies /éksikwiz/ *npl.* a funeral ceremony (*literary*) [14thC. Via Old French from Latin *exsequias* 'funeral procession, obsequies', from *exsequi* (see EXECUTE) in the sense 'to accompany to the grave'.]

exercise /éksər sīz/ *n.* **1.** FITNESS, VET PHYSICAL ACTIVITY physical activity and movement, especially when intended to keep a person or animal fit and healthy ○ *regular exercise is important* **2.** FITNESS, GYMNASTICS PHYSICAL MOVEMENT a physical movement or action, or a series of them, designed to make the body stronger and fitter or to show off gymnastic skill (*often used in the plural*) ○ *warmup exercises* **3.** PRACTICE OF A SKILL OR PROCEDURE a series of actions, movements, or tasks performed repeatedly or regularly as a way of practising and improving a skill or procedure (*often used in the plural*) ○ *voice exercises for singers* **4.** EDUC PIECE OF WORK a piece of work intended to test sb's knowledge or skill ○ *Test yourself by doing the exercises at the back of the book.* **5.** MIL MILITARY TRAINING OPERATIONS OR MANOEUVRES a set of extensive operations or manoeuvres, usually under simulated combat conditions, intended to train military personnel, test their equipment, and assess their capabilities **6.** ACTIVITY INTENDED TO ACHIEVE A PARTICULAR PURPOSE an action, activity, or undertaking intended to achieve a particular purpose ○ *The object of the exercise is to make money fast.* **7.** CARRYING OUT OR USING STH the carrying out or making use of sth such as a choice, duty, responsibility, or right (*formal*) ○ *We urge the exercise of patience and restraint.* ■ *v.* (**-cises, -cising, -cised**) **1.** *vi.* FITNESS TAKE EXERCISE to undertake physical exercise in order to keep fit and healthy **2.** *vt.* FITNESS SUBJECT TO PHYSICAL EXERTION to subject the body, or part of it, to repetitive physical exertion or energetic movement in order to strengthen it or improve its condition ○ *a routine designed to exercise your back and thigh muscles* **3.** *vt.* VET EXERT AN ANIMAL PHYSICALLY to make an animal exert itself physically in order to keep it healthy and fit **4.** *vt.* DO EXERCISES TO DEVELOP A SKILL to develop a particular faculty or skill by carrying out specific tasks or procedures repeatedly or systematically **5.** *vt.* PUT STH TO PRACTICAL USE to make use of a right or responsibility ○ *They have the power to prevent the merger, if they choose to exercise it.* **6.** *vt.* SHOW A TYPE OF BEHAVIOUR to adopt a type of behaviour or quality of character when dealing with a situation ○ *Exercise extreme care in your dealings with them.* **7.** *vt.* OCCUPY OR WORRY SB to be a cause for serious thought, worry, or anxiety to sb (*formal*) ○ *It is not a question that has exercised me greatly in the past.* **8.** *vti.* MIL TAKE PART IN MILITARY TRAINING OPERATIONS to take part in, or make troops take part in, large-scale operations or manoeuvres as part of combat training [14thC. Via French *exercice* from Latin *exercitium*, from *exercere* 'to keep busy', literally 'to drive on or out, let loose', from *arcere* 'to restrain' (source of English *arcane*).] —**exercisable** *adj.*

exercise bike, **exercise bicycle** *n.* a fitness machine in the form of a stationary bicycle that is pedalled vigorously for exercise

exercise book *n.* **1.** BOOK CONTAINING EXERCISES a book containing exercises in a particular subject for students to complete **2.** BOOK FOR WRITING IN a book containing blank pages for school students to write or draw on

exercise price *n.* STOCK EXCH the price at which the holder of stock options or warrants has the right to buy or sell. US term **striking price**

exerciser /éksər sīzər/ *n.* **1.** APPARATUS FOR KEEPING FIT a piece of equipment used to exercise all or part of the body **2.** SB WHO EXERCISES sb who does physical exercises or who exercises sth, especially sb employed to exercise racehorses

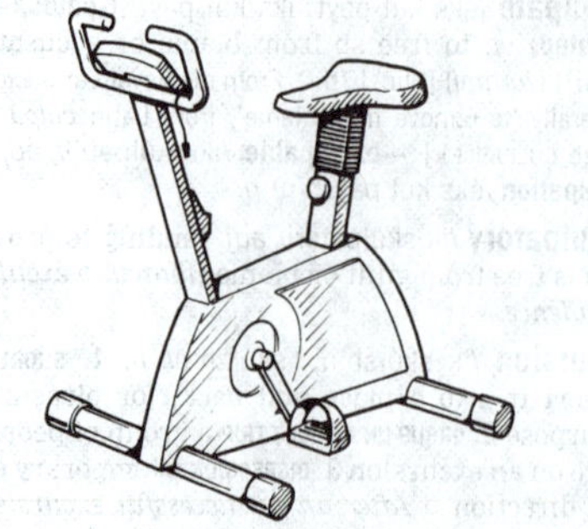

Exercise bike

exergonic /éksər gónnik/ *adj.* used to describe a biochemical reaction in which energy is released and that can therefore take place spontaneously, without being started by energy from another source [Mid-20thC. Coined from EX- + Greek *ergon* 'work' (source of English *energy*) + -IC.]

exergue /ek súrg, éks urg/ *n.* the part of a coin or medal that carries details such as the date and place of minting [Late 17thC. Via French from medieval Latin *exergum*, from Greek *ex-* 'outside' + *ergon* 'work'. The underlying sense is 'sth outside the (main) work'.]

exert /ig zúrt/ (**-erts, -erting, -erted**) *v.* **1.** *vt.* BRING STH TO BEAR to apply influence, pressure, or authority in an attempt to have a powerful effect on a situation **2.** *vr.* MAKE AN EFFORT to make a strenuous physical or mental effort [Mid-17thC. From Latin *ex(s)ert-*, past participle stem of *ex(s)erere* 'to thrust out, put forth', from *serere* 'to join, plait, entwine' (source of English *series*).]

exertion /ig zúrsh'n/ *n.* **1.** STRENUOUS EFFORT strenuous physical exercise or effort **2.** STRENUOUS ACTION an action that involves strenuous physical effort (*often used in the plural*) ○ *After his exertions in the garden, he felt he deserved a rest.* **3.** BRINGING STH TO BEAR the application of pressure or influence (*formal*) ○ *the exertion of pressure on unsuspecting clients*

Exeter /éksitər/ historic cathedral city on the River Exe in Devon, southwestern England. Population: 106,600 (1995).

exeunt /éksi unt, -ay ənt/ *vi.* used as a stage direction in a text in place of 'exit' when more than one person is to leave the stage. ◊ **exit** [15thC. From Latin, literally 'they go out', 3rd person plural of *exire* (see EXIT).]

exfoliate /eks fṓli ayt/ (**-ates, -ating, -ated**) *v.* **1.** *vi.* SCI FALL OFF IN FLAKES to come off the outer surface of sth in thin flakes, scales, or layers **2.** *vti.* SCI REMOVE THIN OUTER LAYER to remove or shed a thin outer layer from sth, e.g. skin, a mineral, or a bone in surgery **3.** *vti.* COSMETICS, DERMAT SCRUB SKIN to scrub skin with a gritty substance to remove the dead surface layer **4.** *vti.* MINERALS SPLIT INTO THIN LAYERS to split, or split a mineral, into thin layers [Mid-17thC. From late Latin *exfoliat-*, past participle stem of *exfoliare*, literally 'to take leaves from', from Latin *folium* 'leaf' (source of English *foliage*).] —**exfoliation** /eks fṓli áysh'n/ *n.* —**exfoliative** /eks fṓli ətiv/ *adj.* —**exfoliator** /-aytər/ *n.*

ex gratia /eks gráyshə/ *adj., adv.* given as a gift, favour, or gesture of goodwill, rather than because it is owed ○ *an ex gratia payment* [Mid-18thC. From Latin, literally 'out of kindness'.]

exhalation /éks hə láysh'n/ *n.* **1.** PHYSIOL BREATH FROM THE LUNGS a breath exhaled from the lungs **2.** PHYSIOL BREATHING OUT the act of breathing out **3.** SCENT OR VAPOUR GIVEN OFF a scent, a vapour, or fumes given off by sth (*literary*)

exhale /eks háyl, eg záyl/ (**-hales, -haling, -haled**) *vti.* **1.** PHYSIOL BREATHE OUT to breathe out, or breathe sth out **2.** GIVE OFF OR BE GIVEN OFF to give off sth such as a smell or a vapour, or be given off (*literary*) [14thC. Via French *exhaler* from Latin *exhalare*, from *halare* 'to breathe'.]

exhaust /ig záwst/ *v.* (**-hausts, -hausting, -hausted**) **1.** *vt.* TIRE SB OUT to make sb feel very tired or weak **2.** *vt.* USE STH UP to use up all that is available of sth ○ *our supplies of fuel were now exhausted* **3.** *vt.* TRY OUT ALL POSSIBILITIES to try out or consider every one of a number of possibilities 4. *vt.* SAY EVERYTHING ABOUT STH to say or write everything about sth, so that nothing is left to be discussed 5. *vt.* DRAIN STH OF ITS RESOURCES to draw off or use up all the resources contained within sth ○ *over-grazing that has exhausted the pasture* 6. *vti.* TECH LET OUT WASTE GASES to escape, or allow steam or waste gases to escape, at the end of an industrial process ○ *Waste gases are exhausted through the flue.* 7. *vt.* SCI REMOVE GAS TO CREATE A VACUUM to remove all of the air or gas from a container in order to create a vacuum inside it ■ *n.* TECH 1. DISCHARGE OF WASTE GASES the discharge of waste gases, vapour, and fumes created by and released at the end of a process, especially from the working of an internal-combustion engine 2. ESCAPE SYSTEM FOR WASTE GASES a pipe or other piece of apparatus through which waste gases escape [Mid-16thC. From Latin *ex-haust-*, past participle stem of *exhaurire* 'to draw out', from *haurire* 'to draw (water) out or up, to drain'.] —**exhauster** *n.* —**exhaustibility** /ig záwstə bílləti/ *n.* —**exhaustible** /ig záwstəb'l/ *adj.*

exhausted /ig záwstid/ *adj.* 1. WORN OUT extremely tired or weak 2. USED UP completely used up —**exhaustedly** *adv.*

exhaustion /ig záwsch'n/ *n.* 1. MED EXTREMELY TIRED OR WEAK STATE a state of extreme physical or mental tiredness or collapse ○ *he was close to exhaustion* 2. ACT OF EXHAUSTING STH the process of using up the entire stock or contents of sth (*formal*) [Early 17thC. From the Latin stem *exhaustion-*, from the past participle stem *exhaust-* of *exhaurire* 'to draw out, exhaust' (see EXHAUST).]

exhaustive /ig záwstiv/ *adj.* involving or dealing with everything relevant to the matter in hand ○ *an exhaustive account of the author's life* —**exhaustively** *adv.* —**exhaustiveness** *n.* —**exhaustivity** /ig záwss tívvəti/ *n.*

exhaust pipe *n.* a pipe that allows waste gases to escape from a vehicle's engine. US term **tailpipe**

exhibit /ig zíbbit/ *v.* (**-its, -iting, -ited**) 1. *vti.* DISPLAY ART to display sth, especially a work of art, in a public place such as a museum or gallery 2. *vt.* SHOW STH TO OTHERS to show sth off for others to look at or admire ○ *She decided it was a good time to exhibit her skills as a solver of business disputes.* 3. *vt.* REVEAL A QUALITY to show the outward signs of sth, especially an emotion or a physical or mental condition (*formal*) ○ *The wings exhibited signs of metal fatigue.* 4. *vt.* LAW GIVE STH AS EVIDENCE to present sth to be used as evidence in a court of law ■ *n.* 1. OBJECT ON DISPLAY an object displayed in public, especially in a gallery or museum or for a show or competition 2. = **exhibition** *n.* 1 3. LAW PIECE OF EVIDENCE an object or document presented or identified as evidence in a court of law [15thC. Partly from Latin *exhibere* 'to hold out, display', from *habere* 'to hold'; partly a back-formation from EXHIBITION.] —**exhibitory** *adj.*

exhibiter *n.* = **exhibitor**

exhibition /éksi bísh'n/ *n.* 1. PUBLIC DISPLAY OF WORKS OF ART a public display, usually for a limited period, of a collection of works of art or objects of special interest 2. DISPLAYING OF STH the displaying of sth in public ○ *one or two of the works on exhibition* 3. DEMONSTRATION OF SKILL a demonstration of a particular skill or craft ○ *a karate exhibition* 4. DISPLAY OF BEHAVIOUR a display of a particular type of behaviour, usually bad behaviour ○ *What did she mean by that little exhibition, I wonder?* 5. SCHOOL'S GRANT TO STUDENT a sum of money, usually of lower value than a scholarship, that a school or university awards a student to help with the cost of his or her studies [14thC. Directly or via French from the late Latin stem *exhibition-* 'handing over, display', from Latin *exhibere* (see EXHIBIT). Originally in the sense 'maintenance, support'.] ◇ **make an exhibition of yourself** to behave embarrassingly in public and attract attention to yourself

WORD KEY: CULTURAL NOTE

Pictures at an Exhibition, a suite of piano pieces by the Russian composer Modest Mussorgsky (1874). The compositions were written in memory of the architect and painter Victor Alexandrovich Hartmann and inspired by paintings and drawings displayed at a memorial exhibition of the artist's work.

exhibitioner /éksi bísh'nər/ *n.* a student who has been awarded an exhibition by a school or university

exhibition game *n.* a sports contest played purely as a display of skill and an entertainment for spectators, with no prizes or competition points at stake

exhibitionism /éksi bísh'nizəm/ *n.* 1. ATTENTION-SEEKING loud, exaggerated, or boastful behaviour designed to attract attention 2. PSYCHIAT EXPOSING OF THE GENITALS a psychological disorder causing a compulsion to show the genitals in public —**exhibitionist** *n.* —**exhibitionistic** /éksi bíshə nístik/ *adj.*

exhibition match *n.* = **exhibition game**

exhibitive /ig zíbbitiv/ *adj.* displaying or demonstrating sth (*formal*) —**exhibitively** *adv.*

exhibitor /ig zíbbitər/, **exhibiter** *n.* 1. SB WITH WORK ON DISPLAY sb who exhibits sth, especially sb whose artistic work is included in an exhibition 2. CINEMA SB WHO SCREENS A FILM a person who or company that screens a film

exhilarate /ig zíllə rayt/ (**-rates, -rating, -rated**) *vt.* to make sb feel happy, excited, and more than usually vigorous and alive [Mid-16thC. From Latin *exhilarat-*, past participle stem of *exhilarare*, literally 'to gladden thoroughly', from *hilarare* 'to gladden', ultimately from Greek *hilaros* 'cheerful, glad' (source of English *hilarious*).] —**exhilarating** *adj.* —**exhilaratingly** *adv.* —**exhilarative** /ig zíllərətiv/ *adj.* —**exhilarator** /ig zíllə raytər/ *n.*

exhilaration /ig zíllə ráysh'n/ *n.* a feeling of happiness and excitement combined with renewed vigour and a heightened sense of being alive

exhort /ig záwrt/ (**-horts, -horting, -horted**) *v.* (*formal*) 1. *vt.* URGE TO DO STH to urge sb strongly and earnestly to do sth 2. *vi.* GIVE EARNEST ADVICE to give sb urgent or earnest advice [14thC. Directly or via French *exhorter* from Latin *exhortari*, literally 'to encourage thoroughly', from *hortari* 'to encourage, urge'.] —**exhorter** *n.*

exhortation /égz awr táysh'n/ *n.* (*formal*) 1. STH INTENDED TO URGE OR PERSUADE sth said or written in order to urge sb strongly to do sth 2. GIVING OF ADVICE the giving of earnest advice or encouragement

exhortative /ig záwrtətiv/, **exhortatory** /-tətəri/ *adj.* intended to urge or inspire sb to do sth (*formal*)

exhume /eks hyoóm, ig zyoóm/ (**-humes, -huming, -humed**) *vt.* 1. DIG UP A BODY to dig up a corpse from a grave 2. RE-INTRODUCE STH to reveal, re-establish, or refer again to sth long forgotten or neglected ○ *Cultures are re-invented, and dead traditions exhumed for the tourists.* [15thC. From medieval Latin *exhumare*, from *humare* 'to bury', from *humus* 'ground, earth' (source of English *humus*, *humiliate*, and *humble*).] —**exhumation** /éks hyoo máysh'n/ *n.* —**exhumer** /eks hyoómər, ig zyoómər/ *n.*

exigency /éksijənsi, ig zíjjənssi/ (*plural* **-cies**), **exigence** /éksijənss/ *n.* (*formal*) 1. URGENT NEED sth that a situation demands or makes urgently necessary and that puts pressure on the people involved (*often used in the plural*) ○ *unable to cope with the exigencies of political life* 2. STH NEEDING IMMEDIATE ACTION a difficult situation requiring urgent action [Late 16thC. From late Latin *exigentia*, from the Latin present participle stem *exigent-* of *exigere* 'to demand, require' (see EXACT).]

exigent /éksijənt/ *adj.* (*formal*) 1. REQUIRING ACTION needing immediate action 2. DEMANDING making heavy demands on sb ○ *suffered at the hands of an exigent schoolmaster* [Early 17thC. From Latin *exigent-* (see EXIGENCY).] —**exigently** *adv.*

exiguous /ig zíggyoo əss, ik sígg-/ *adj.* scanty or meagre (*formal*) ○ *eking out their exiguous supplies* [Mid-17thC. Formed from Latin *exiguus*, from *exigere* 'to weigh precisely, measure' (see EXACT).] —**exiguity** /éksi gyoó əti/ *n.* —**exiguously** /ig zíggyoo əssli, ik síggyoo-/ *adv.* —**exiguousness** /-əssnəss/ *n.*

exile /égz īl, éks-/ *n.* 1. ABSENCE FROM YOUR OWN COUNTRY unwilling absence from your own country or home, whether enforced by a government or court as a punishment, or imposed for political or religious reasons 2. SB LIVING OUTSIDE HIS OR HER OWN COUNTRY sb who is forced to live in another country, either for personal or political reasons or after being ordered to leave as a punishment 3. BANISHMENT FROM HOME OR COUNTRY official expulsion from a home country or area, sometimes to a specified place, as a punishment ■ *vt.* (**-iles, -iling, -iled**) BANISH SB FROM HOME OR COUNTRY to order sb to leave and stay away from his or her own country or home as a punishment [14thC. Via French *exil* from Latin *exilium* 'banishment', from *exul* 'banished person'.] —**exilic** /eg zíllik, ek síllik/ *adj.*

exine /éksin, ék sīn/ *n.* the outer layer of a pollen grain or other spore. The surface patterns vary among different plant groups, allowing the makeup of former plant populations to be deduced from preserved pollen samples. [Late 19thC. Origin uncertain; perhaps formed from EX- + modern Latin *in-* 'fibrous tissue' (from Greek *in-*, *is* 'fibre, sinew').]

exist /ig zíst/ (**-ists, -isting, -isted**) *vi.* 1. BE to be, especially to be a real, actual, or current thing, not merely sth imagined or written about ○ *Does life exist on other planets?* 2. LIVE to be alive or continue to live ○ *Humans need water and food to exist.* 3. OCCUR to be present or found in a particular place or situation ○ *Shortages on products in high demand exist.* 4. SURVIVE to manage to survive or stay alive ○ *The lost hikers existed for two days on berries.* 5. LIVE AN UNSATISFACTORY LIFE to live an unsatisfactory, joyless, or humdrum life, as opposed to an exciting or meaningful one [Early 17thC. Origin uncertain; probably a back-formation from EXISTENCE.]

existence /ig zístənss/ *n.* 1. BEING REAL the state of being real, actual, or current, rather than imagined, invented, or obsolete ○ *evidence for the existence of other worlds* 2. PRESENCE IN A PLACE OR SITUATION the presence or occurrence of sth in a particular place or situation ○ *discovered the existence of the bacterium in sheep* 3. WAY OF LIVING a way of living, especially a life of severe hardship ○ *scratch out a pitiable existence* 4. EVERYTHING all living things (*literary*) ○ *hymns that celebrate the wonder of existence* 5. SINGLE LIVING THING sth that lives or exists (*literary or archaic*) [14thC. Directly or via French from late Latin *existentia*, from Latin *ex(s)istere* 'to emerge, come into being', from *sistere* 'to cause to stand firm'.]

existent /ig zístənt/ *adj.* (*formal*) 1. REAL real or actual, not imagined or invented 2. CURRENT currently existing or in operation ■ *n.* REAL THING a real or living thing (*formal*)

existential /égzi sténsh'l, éksi-/ *adj.* 1. RELATING TO HUMAN EXISTENCE concerned with or relating to existence, especially human existence 2. PHILOS CRUCIAL IN SHAPING INDIVIDUAL DESTINY in the context of existentialism, involved in or vital to the shaping of an individual's self-chosen mode of existence and moral stance with respect to the rest of the world 3. LOGIC GOVERNED BY THE EXISTENTIAL QUANTIFIER governed by the existential quantifier and thus asserting the existence of sth by saying that there is at least one object that possesses the properties specified ■ *n.* LOGIC EXISTENTIAL PROPOSITION a proposition governed by the existential quantifier —**existentially** *adv.*

existentialism /égzi sténsh'l izəm, ékzi-/ *n.* a 20th-century philosophical movement that denies that the universe has any in-built meaning or purpose and requires individuals to take responsibility for their own actions and shape their own destinies [Mid-20thC. From German *Existentialismus*, a translation of Danish *existents-forhold* 'condition of existence'.] —**existentialist** *adj., n.*

existential quantifier *n.* the logical constant, frequently symbolized as 'Ex', that is a prefix to another clause and that is read as saying 'there is at least one object such that'. ◊ **universal quantifier**

existing /ig zísting/ *adj.* currently present, in operation, or available ○ *Existing legislation is inadequate to cover these cases.*

exit /éksit, égzit/ *n.* 1. MEANS OF LEAVING A PLACE a door or other means of leaving a room or building 2. DEPARTURE an act of leaving a room, building, or gathering 3. DEATH departure from life (*formal*) 4. THEATRE ACTOR'S LEAVING OF THE STAGE an actor's departure from the stage 5. TRANSP PLACE FOR LEAVING AN MOTORWAY any of the slip roads by which a vehicle can leave a motorway or other main road with limited access 6. COMPUT TERMINATION OF A COMPUTER OPERATION an act of terminating a computer operation ■ *v.* (**-its, -iting, -ited**) 1. *vti.* LEAVE to leave sth such as a room, building, or gathering ○ *In the event of a fire, exit the building at the rear.* 2. *vi.* DIE to cease to live (*literary*) 3. *vi.* THEATRE GO OFFSTAGE to leave the stage during a performance of a play (*refers to an actor*) ◊ **exeunt 4.** *vti.* COMPUT **TERMINATE A COMPUTER PROGRAM** to terminate the running of a computer operating system, program, or routine in a program [Mid-16thC. From Latin *exitus* 'a departure', past participle, used as a noun, of *exire* 'to go out', from *ire* 'to go'.]

exit permit *n.* a permit granted to a banned person in South Africa during apartheid rule, allowing the person to leave the country without right of return

exit poll *n.* a poll designed to give an early indication of the result of an election, conducted by asking people how they voted as they leave the place of voting

ex libris /éks leébriss/ (*plural* **ex libris**) *adv.* from the library of the person whose name follows (*used on bookplates*) [From Latin, literally 'from the books (of)', in reference to the owner's library]

Exmoor /éks moor, -mawr/ *n.* an Exmoor sheep or Exmoor pony

Exmoor Horn *n.* = **Exmoor sheep**

Exmoor National Park national park in a moorland area of Somerset and northern Devon, southwestern England. Area: 692 sq. km/267 sq. mi.

Exmoor pony *n.* a small sturdy pony with a long thick mane and a light brown muzzle, belonging to a breed originating on Exmoor

Exmoor sheep (*plural* **Exmoor sheep**) *n.* a sheep with horns and short wool, belonging to a breed originating on Exmoor

Exmouth /éksməth/ **1.** port and seaside resort at the mouth of the River Exe, in Devon, southwestern England. Population: 31,770 (1994). **2.** town overlooking Exmouth Gulf on the coast of Western Australia, site of the US-Australian Naval Communications Station. Population: 3,128 (1991).

Exmouth Gulf inlet of the sea in northwestern Western Australia. A major satellite communications station is situated nearby.

ex nihilo /eks nī́hilō/ *adv., adj.* from or out of nothing (*formal*) [Late 16thC. From Latin.]

exo- *prefix.* outside, external ○ *exothermic* [From Greek *exō*, from *ex* 'out'. Ultimately from an Indo-European base that is also the ancestor of English *ex-*, *extra-*, and *extreme*.]

exobiology /éksō bī ólləji/ *n.* a branch of biology concerned with the possibility that life forms exist on other planets and with the problems of adapting the Earth's life forms to alien environments — **exobiological** /éksō bī́ ə lójjik'l/ *adj.* —**exobiologist** /éksō bī ólləjist/ *n.*

exocarp /éksō kaarp/ *n.* the outer layer of the fruit wall (**pericarp**)

Exocet /éksō set/ *tdmk.* a trademark for a French-manufactured surface-to-surface guided missile with a high-explosive warhead, used by Argentine forces against the British task force in the Falklands War of 1982

exocrine /éksō krīn, -krin/ *adj.* used to describe or relating to glands such as sweat glands or salivary glands that release a secretion through a duct to the surface of an organ. ◊ **endocrine** [Early 20thC. Coined from *exo-* + Greek *krinein* 'to separate' (source of English *crisis* and *hypocrite*).]

exocyclic /éksō sī́klik, -síklik/ *adj.* situated outside a chemical ring structure ○ *an exocyclic bond*

exocytosis /éksō sī tṓssiss/ *n.* the release of substances contained in a sac (**vesicle**) within a cell by a process in which the membrane surrounding the sac unites with the membrane forming the outer wall of the cell —**exocytotic** /éksō sī tóttik/ *adj.*

Exod. *abbr.* BIBLE Exodus

exodontics /éksō dóntiks/, **exodontia** /éksō dónshə/ *n.* the branch of dentistry concerned with extracting teeth (*takes a singular verb*) [Early 20thC. Coined from EXO- + Greek *odont-*, stem of *odous* 'tooth'.] —**exodontist** *n.*

exodus /éksədəss/ *n.* a departure or going out or away from a place that involves large numbers of people [Pre-12thC. Via ecclesiastical Latin '(biblical Book of) Exodus' from Greek, literally 'way out', from *hodos* 'way, road'.]

Exodus *n.* **1. 2ND BOOK OF THE BIBLE** the second book of the Bible, which describes the flight of the Israelites from Egypt and Moses receiving the Ten Commandments on Mount Sinai **2. FLIGHT OF ISRAELITES FROM EGYPT** the flight of Moses and the Israelites from Egypt, as described in the second book of the Bible [Pre-12thC. See EXODUS.]

exoenzyme /éksō én zīm/ *n.* an enzyme that operates outside the cell in which it was produced, e.g. a digestive enzyme

exoergic /éksō úrjik/ *adj.* NUCLEAR PHYS = **exothermic** [Mid-20thC. Coined from EXO- + Greek *ergon* 'work' (source of English *energy*) + -IC.]

ex off. *abbr.* ex officio

ex officio /éks ə físhi ō/ *adv., adj.* as a result of the official position sb holds ○ *Heads of state are often ex officio heads of the armed forces* [Mid-16thC. From Latin, literally 'out of duty, on account of office'.]

exogamy /ek sóggəmi/ *n.* **1.** ANTHROP **MARRIAGE TRADITION** the custom in some societies of marrying outside their people's own tribe, clan, or social group **2.** BIOL **FUSION OF UNRELATED CELLS** the fusion of sex cells (**gametes**) of organisms not closely related, as occurs in cross pollination and outbreeding —**exogamous** *adj.*

exogenous /ek sójjənəss/ *adj.* originating outside an organism or system. ◊ **endogenous** [Mid-19thC. Formed from modern Latin *exogena* 'growing on the outside', from Greek *genēs* 'born'.] —**exogenously** *adv.*

exon[1] /éks on/ *n.* a discontinuous sequence of DNA that codes for protein synthesis and carries the genetic code for the final messenger RNA molecule. ◊ **intron** [Late 20thC. Coined from *expressed* (past participle of EXPRESS) + -ON.]

exon[2] /éks on/ *n.* any of the four officers who command the Yeomen of the Guard in London [Mid-18thC. Representing the pronunciation of French *exempt* 'exempt', used to denote a cavalry officer in the French army who was exempt from ordinary military duties.]

exonerate /ig zónnə rayt/ (**-ates, -ating, -ated**) *vt.* **1. FREE SB FROM BLAME OR GUILT** to declare officially that sb is not to blame, or is not guilty of a crime **2. FREE SB FROM AN OBLIGATION** to relieve sb from an obligation or responsibility [15thC. From Latin *exonerat-*, past participle stem of *exonerare*, literally 'to take off a burden', from *onus* 'burden' (source of English *onerous* and *onus*).] — **exoneration** /ig zónnə ráysh'n/ *n.* —**exonerative** /ig zónnərətiv/ *adj.*

exophthalmos /éks of thálməss/, **exophthalmus, exophthalmia** /-thálmi ə/ *n.* abnormal protrusion of the eyeball resulting, e.g., from an aneurysm [Early 17thC. Directly or via modern Latin *exophthalmus* from Greek *exophthalmos*, literally '(condition of) the eye being outside', from *ophthalmos* 'eye' (source of English *ophthalmic*).] —**exophthalmic** *adj.*

exor. *abbr.* executor

exorbitant /ig záwrbitənt/ *adj.* **1. UNREASONABLY HIGH OR LARGE** far greater or higher than is reasonable ○ *exorbitant* **2. EXTREME** going beyond what is reasonable, proper, or manageable [15thC. Ultimately from Christian Latin *exorbitare* 'to go out of the track', from Latin *orbita* 'track', from *orbis* 'circle'. Originally 'not within the intended scope of a law'.] —**exorbitance** *n.* —**exorbitantly** *adv.*

exorcism /éks awr sizəm/ *n.* **1.** RELIG **DRIVING OUT OF EVIL SPIRITS** the use of prayer or religious ritual to drive out evil spirits **2.** RELIG **CEREMONY TO DRIVE OUT EVIL SPIRITS** a religious ceremony in which sb endeavours to drive out an evil spirit believed to be possessing a person or place **3.** RELIG **THING DONE TO EXPEL EVIL** a special ritual or spoken formula used with the intention of driving out evil spirits **4. CLEARING THE MIND OF OPPRESSIVE FEELINGS** the act of ridding the mind of oppressive feelings or memories [14thC. Via ecclesiastical Latin *exorcismus* from ecclesiastical Greek *exorkismos*, from *exorkizein* (see EXORCIZE).] —**exorcist** *n.*

exorcize /éks awr sīz, éksər-/ (**-cizes, -cizing, -cized**), **exorcise** (**-cises, -cising, -cised**) *vt.* **1.** RELIG **FREE A PERSON OR PLACE FROM EVIL** to use prayers and religious rituals with the intention of ridding a person or place of the presence or influence of evil spirits **2.** RELIG **SEND EVIL AWAY** to use prayers and religious rituals with the intention of driving away an evil spirit believed to have been possessing a person or place **3. GET RID OF AN OPPRESSIVE FEELING** to clear the mind of a painful or oppressive feeling or memory [15thC. Directly or via French *exorciser* from ecclesiastical Latin *exorcizare*, from Greek *exorkizein*, literally 'to swear out (an evil spirit)', from *orkos* 'oath'.] —**exorcizer** *n.*

exordium /ek sáwrdi əm/ (*plural* **-ums** *or* **-a** /-di ə/) *n.* an opening section, especially of a lecture or a piece of scholarly writing (*formal*) [Late 16thC. From Latin, formed from *exordiri* 'to begin'.] —**exordial** *adj.*

exoskeleton /éksō skéllitən/ *n.* a hard covering on the outside of many organisms such as crustaceans, insects, turtles, and armadillos that provides support and protection —**exoskeletal** *adj.*

exosmosis /éks oz mṓssiss/ *n.* movement of fluid towards a solution of lower concentration, as is the case when water percolates through a cell membrane into the medium surrounding the cell [Mid-19thC. An alteration of obsolete *exosmose*, from French, literally 'a pushing out', from Greek *ōsmos* 'act of pushing' (source of English *osmosis*).] —**exosmotic** /éks oz mṓtik/ *adj.*

exosphere /éksō sfeer/ *n.* the outermost region of the atmosphere of the Earth or another planet — **exospheric** /éksō sférrik/ *adj.*

exospore /éksō spawr/ *n.* a spore that is formed outside a parent cell, e.g. by partitioning of parental material, or outside a spore-bearing organ

exostosis /éksō stṓssiss/ (*plural* **-ses** /-seez/) *n.* an abnormal benign bony growth on the surface of a bone or a tooth root, caused by inflammation or repeated trauma [Late 16thC. From Greek, 'bony outgrowth', formed from *osteon* 'bone' (source of English *osteo-*).]

exoteric /éksō térrik/ *adj.* capable of being understood by most people, not just an informed or select minority (*formal*) [Mid-17thC. Via Latin *exotericus* from Greek *exōterikos*, from *exōterō* 'outer', from *exō* 'outside'.] — **exoterically** *adv.*

exothermic /éksō thúrmik/, **exothermal** /-thúrm'l/ *adj.* CHEM, PHYS used to describe a reaction that produces heat (*preferred term in nuclear physics is 'exoergic'*) [Late 19thC. From French *exothermique*, from Greek *thermē* 'heat' (source of *thermometer*).] —**exothermically** *adv.*

exotic /ig zóttik/ *adj.* **1. STRIKINGLY DIFFERENT** strikingly unusual and often very colourful and exciting or suggesting distant countries and unfamiliar cultures **2. FROM DISTANT COUNTRY** from or relating to distant, especially tropical, places ○ *exotic fruits* **3.** ECOL **FROM ELSEWHERE** introduced from another place or region ○ *an exotic species* ■ *n.* **EXOTIC PERSON OR THING** sb who or sth that is exotic, especially a plant or animal [Late 16thC. Via Latin *exoticus* from Greek *exōtikos*, from *exō* 'out, outside', the underlying notion being 'foreign, out of the ordinary'.] —**exotically** *adv.* —**exoticism** /ig zóttissizəm/ *n.* —**exoticness** *n.*

exotica /ig zóttikə/ *npl.* exotic or extraordinary things, especially when forming a collection [Late 19thC. From Latin, neuter plural of *exoticus* (see EXOTIC).]

exotic dancer *n.* a striptease artist

exotoxin /éksō tóksin/ *n.* a highly potent soluble toxin produced by a bacterium and released into its infected host, often affecting the central nervous system. Exotoxins are produced in diphtheria, botulism, and tetanus and are among the most potent known toxins.

exp *symbol.* MATH exponential function

exp. *abbr.* **1.** experiment **2.** experimental **3.** expired **4.** expires **5.** export **6.** exported **7.** express

expand /ik spánd/ (**-pands, -panding, -panded**) *v.* **1.** *vti.* **MAKE OR BECOME LARGER** to become or cause sth to become larger in size, scope, or extent, or greater in number or amount ○ *We need to expand our client base.* **2.** *vti.* PHYS **INCREASE IN SIZE OR VOLUME** to increase or cause sth to increase in size or volume as a result of a rise in temperature or decrease in pressure **3.** *vti.* **OPEN OUT** to open out or open sth out wider after being kept folded in **4.** *vti.* **DESCRIBE STH MORE FULLY** to explain or describe sth more fully, usually by giving more detail ○ *If you expanded that argument a little, it would fill another chapter.* **5.** *vt.* **GIVE THE FULL FORM OF STH** to give the full form of sth such as the abbreviation of a word **6.** *vi.* **RELAX** to relax and become friendlier and more talkative (*formal*) **7.** *vt.* MATH **REWRITE A MATHEMATICAL EXPRESSION** to rewrite a mathematical expression as the sum or product of its terms, e.g. $(x+1)(x-1)+2x$ expands to x^2+2x-1 [15thC. Directly or via Anglo-Norman *espaundre* from Latin *expandere* 'to spread out', from *pandere* 'to spread'.] —**expandability** /ik spándə bílləti/ *n.* —**expandable** /ik spándəb'l/ *adj.* —**expander** /ik spándər/ *n.*

------ **WORD KEY: SYNONYMS** ------
See Synonyms at *increase*.

expanded /ik spándid/ *adj.* **1.** **MADE LARGER** extended, unfolded, or outstretched **2.** INDUST **MADE INTO FOAM** used to describe plastics made into a lightweight solid foam by the introduction of gas during the manufacturing process ○ *expanded polyurethane* **3.** PRINTING **WIDER THAN USUAL** used to describe typefaces or printed characters that are wider than usual in relation to their height

expanded metal *n.* strong metal mesh made by cutting slits in sheet metal and stretching it out of shape, used as a reinforcing material in construction

expanse /ik spánss/ *n.* a wide area or surface, especially of sea, land, or sky [Mid-17thC. From modern Latin *expansum* 'firmament', neuter past participle (used as a noun) of Latin *expandere* (see EXPAND).]

expansible /ik spánssəb'l/ *adj.* able to expand or be expanded —**expansibility** /ik spánssə bílləti/ *n.*

expansile /ik spán sīl/ *adj.* **1.** **RELATING TO EXPANSION** relating to expansion or the ability to expand **2.** **EXPANSIBLE** able to expand or be expanded

expansion /ik spánsh'n/ *n.* **1.** **PROCESS OF BECOMING ENLARGED** the process of increasing, or increasing sth, in size, extent, scope, or number ○ *This site does not give us enough room for expansion.* **2.** **INCREASE** an increase, or the amount by which sth increases, in size, extent, or scope ○ *Geologists measured the expansion of the volcanic island.* **3.** PHYS **INCREASE IN DIMENSIONS** an increase in the dimensions of sth as a result of a rise in temperature or decrease in pressure **4.** **GROWTH BY ACQUISITION** the increase of a country's size by the acquisition of new territory ○ *westward expansion* **5.** **FULLER TREATMENT** a fuller or more detailed treatment or version of sth ○ *The expansion of 'Dr' is 'Doctor'.* **6.** ENG **COMBUSTION STAGE IN AN ENGINE** a stage in an engine cycle during which the fuel and air mixture explodes, thereby increasing in volume and providing power **7.** MATH **EXPANDED MATHEMATICAL EXPRESSION** the result of expanding a mathematical expression

expansionary /ik spánsh'nəri/ *adj.* bringing about expansion, especially economic or territorial expansion

expansion board *n.* COMPUT = expansion card

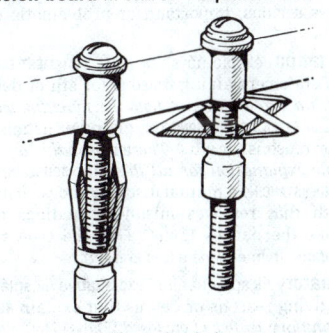

Expansion bolt

expansion bolt *n.* a bolt with an attachment on the screw end that expands as the bolt is tightened, thereby securing it

expansion card *n.* a printed circuit board inserted into a computer to add features or capability

expansionism /ik spánsh'nizəm/ *n.* a policy of expanding a country's economy or territory —**expansionist** *n., adj.* —**expansionistic** /ik spánshə nístik/ *adj.*

expansion joint *n.* a gap between adjacent parts or surfaces, e.g. between the concrete sections that form the road surface of a bridge, to prevent buckling when they expand under heat

expansion slot *n.* a receptacle connected to and interfacing with a computer's internal circuitry and designed to hold an expansion card

expansive /ik spánssiv/ *adj.* **1.** **COMMUNICATIVE** willing to talk openly and at some length, usually in a relaxed and jovial way ○ *He gradually became more expansive once he got to know us.* **2.** **EXTENSIVE** covering a wide area or broad in scope (*formal*) ○ *a large house with expansive grounds* **3.** **EXPANDING** capable of, having a tendency to, or typically undergoing expansion ○ *polymers with expansive capability* **4.** **WITH OUTSTRETCHED ARMS** with the arms stretched out and open wide ○ *an expansive gesture* **5.** **LAVISH** generous, lavish, or extravagant in scale ○ *an expansive lifestyle* **6.** PSYCHIAT **HAVING EXAGGERATED FEELINGS OF SELF-WORTH** characterized by extreme feelings of euphoria and delusions of grandeur or self-importance —**expansively** *adv.* —**expansiveness** *n.* —**expansivity** /ék span sívvəti/ *n.*

ex parte /eks paárti/ *adj., adv.* made or undertaken on behalf of only one of the parties involved in a court case [Early 17thC. From Latin, literally 'from a (or the) side'.]

expat /éks pát/ *n.* an expatriate (*informal*) [Mid-20thC. Shortening.]

expatiate /ek spáyshi ayt/ (*-ates, -ating, -ated*) *vi.* **1.** **SPEAK OR WRITE AT LENGTH** to speak or write about sth at length ○ *We had to listen to him expatiating on the shortcomings of our system.* **2.** **WANDER** to wander or roam at will (*archaic*) [Mid-16thC. From Latin *ex(s)patiat-*, past participle stem of *ex(s)patiari*, literally 'to walk out', from *spatiari* 'to walk', from *spatium* 'space' (source of English *space*). Originally 'to roam freely'.] —**expatiation** /ek spáyshi áysh'n/ *n.*

expatriate *n.* /eks páttri ət, -páytri-, -ayt/ **1.** **SB WHO HAS MOVED ABROAD** sb who has left his or her home country to live or work abroad, usually for a long period of time **2.** **SB WITHOUT CITIZENSHIP** sb who has renounced his or her citizenship or whose citizenship has been repealed ■ *adj.* /eks páttri ət, -páytri-, -ayt/ **RELATING TO THOSE LIVING ABROAD** relating to or typical of people who live abroad ■ *v.* /eks páttri ayt, -páytri-/ (*-ates, -ating, -ated*) **1.** *vi.* **SETTLE ABROAD** to settle in another country **2.** *vti.* **TAKE AWAY SB'S CITIZENSHIP** to deprive sb of native citizenship, or renounce native citizenship voluntarily **3.** *vt.* **EXPEL SB FROM HIS OR HER OWN COUNTRY** to send sb away from his or her own country as a punishment [Mid-18thC. From Latin *expatriat-*, past participle stem of *expatriare*, literally 'to leave your native land', from *patria* 'native land', from *pater* 'father'.] —**expatriation** /eks páttri áysh'n, -páytri-/ *n.*

expect /ik spékt/ (*-pects, -pecting, -pected*) *v.* **1.** *vti.* **CONFIDENTLY BELIEVE** to believe with confidence, or think it likely, that an event will happen in the future ○ *A few setbacks along the way were only to be expected.* **2.** *vt.* **WAIT FOR AN ANTICIPATED THING** to wait for, or look forward to, sth that you believe is going to happen or arrive ○ *We'll expect you late morning, then.* ○ *I'm expecting a visit from them any day now.* **3.** *vt.* **DEMAND STH AS A RIGHT OR DUTY** to demand or anticipate receiving sth because of a perceived right to it or because it is sb's duty to give it ○ *They expect you to abide by their rules.* **4.** *vti.* **BE GOING TO HAVE A BABY** to be pregnant with or look forward to the birth of a child (*informal*) (*used only in progressive tenses*) ○ *She is expecting her third in July.* [Mid-16thC. From Latin *ex(s)pectare* 'to look out for', from *spectare* 'to look at', from *specere* 'to look, look at'.] —**expectable** *adj.* —**expectably** *adv.* —**expectedly** *adv.* —**expectedness** *n.*

------ **WORD KEY: USAGE** ------
See Usage note at *envisage*.

expectancy /ik spéktənssi/ (*plural* *-cies*), **expectance** /ik spéktənss/ *n.* **1.** **EXCITED ANTICIPATION** excited awareness that sth is about to happen ○ *An air of expectancy hung over the crowd.* **2.** STATS **STH EXPECTED** sth expected, especially an amount or length of time expected on the basis of statistical calculations

expectant /ik spéktənt/ *adj.* **1.** **EXCITEDLY ANTICIPATING STH** excitedly aware that sth is about to happen **2.** **EXPECTING A BABY** expecting the birth of a baby **3.** **EXPECTING STH FAVOURABLE** expecting sth, especially sth that will bring success or wealth (*formal*) [14thC. Directly or via

French from Latin *ex(s)pectant-*, present participle stem of *ex(s)pectare* (see EXPECT).]

expectation /éks pek táysh'n/ *n.* **1.** **ANTICIPATION OF STH HAPPENING** a confident belief or strong hope that a particular event will happen **2.** **NOTION OF STH** a mental image of sth expected, often compared to its reality (*often used in the plural*) ○ *All our expectations of a quiet evening at home were dashed by the arrival of guests.* **3.** **EXPECTED STANDARD** a standard of conduct or performance expected by or of sb (*often used in the plural*) ○ *Her work wasn't up to expectations so she was dismissed.* **4.** = **expectancy** *n.* **1** ■ **expectations** *npl.* **PROSPECTS FOR THE FUTURE** sb's likely prospects of wealth or success in the future

expected value *n.* the value of a random variable that is most likely to occur, calculated by taking the sum of every possible value multiplied by a factor representing the probability of its occurrence

expectorant /ik spéktərənt/ *adj.* **PRODUCING AND GETTING RID OF PHLEGM** causing phlegm to be produced or liquefied and coughed up ■ *n.* **MEDICINE FOR COUGHS** a medicine that stimulates the production and secretion of phlegm, used to treat coughs

expectorate /ik spéktə rayt/ (*-rates, -rating, -rated*) *vti.* to cough up and spit out phlegm, thus clearing the bronchial passages [Early 17thC. From Latin *expectorat-*, past participle stem of *expectorare*, literally 'to get out of the chest', from *pectus* 'chest, breast' (source of English *pectoral*).] —**expectoration** /ik spéktə ráysh'n/ *n.*

expediency /ik speédi ənssi/ (*plural* *-cies*), **expedience** /-ənss/ *n.* **1.** **USE OF SHORT-TERM EFFECTIVE METHODS** the use of methods that bring the most immediate benefits, based on practical rather than moral considerations (*disapproving*) **2.** **APPROPRIATENESS** the usefulness, appropriateness, or advisability of sth, especially of a particular action or type of behaviour in a particular situation ○ *doubts about the expediency of such a course in the present crisis* **3.** = **expedient** *n.*

expedient /ik speédi ənt/ *adj.* **1.** **APPROPRIATE** appropriate, advisable, or useful in a situation that requires action **2.** **ADVANTAGEOUS** advantageous for practical rather than moral reasons (*disapproving*) ○ *She changed her vote because it was expedient for her to do so.* ■ *n.* **STH ACHIEVING AIMS QUICKLY** sth done or a method used to achieve an aim quickly, regardless of whether it is fair, right, or wise in the long term [14thC. Directly or via French from Latin *expedient-*, present participle stem of *expedire* (see EXPEDITE).] —**expediently** *adv.*

expedite /ékspə dīt/ (*-dites, -diting, -dited*) *vt.* (*formal*) **1.** **SPEED UP THE PROGRESS OF STH** to ensure that sth takes place or is dealt with more quickly than usual **2.** **DEAL WITH QUICKLY AND EFFICIENTLY** to deal with sth, especially a business transaction, swiftly and efficiently [15thC. From Latin *expedit-*, past participle stem of *expedire* 'to set free', literally 'to free the feet', from ultimately, *pes* 'foot' (source of English *pedal*).] —**expediter** *n.*

expedition /ékspə dísh'n/ *n.* **1.** **ORGANIZED JOURNEY BY A GROUP** a journey made by a group of people for a specific purpose, e.g. to explore unknown territory, to do scientific study, or to achieve a military objective ○ *a scientific expedition to the ocean floor* **2.** **PEOPLE MAKING EXPEDITION** a group of people who go on an expedition together ○ *The expedition returned at the end of the month.* **3.** **OUTING** a short journey, usually for a pleasurable purpose **4.** **PROMPTNESS** speed, promptness, or efficiency in doing sth ○ *carried out our errand with expedition* [15thC. Directly or via French from the Latin stem *expedition-*, from *expedire* (see EXPEDITE).]

expeditionary /ékspə dísh'nəri/ *adj.* sent to fight or do military service in another country ○ *an expeditionary force*

expeditious /ékspə díshəss/ *adj.* speedy or carried out promptly and efficiently —**expeditiously** *adv.* —**expeditiousness** *n.*

expel /ik spél/ (*-pels, -pelling, -pelled*) *vt.* **1.** **DISMISS SB FROM AN ORGANIZATION** to compel sb to leave or give up membership of an institution such as a school, political party, or club ○ *expel a child from school* **2.** **DRIVE OUT** to push or drive sth out with force ○ *Air is expelled under pressure from outlets under the hovercraft's apron.* [14thC. From Latin *expellere*, literally 'to drive out', from *pellere* 'to beat, drive' (source of English *appeal* and *pulse*).] —**expellable** *adj.* —**expeller** *n.*

expellant /ik spéllənt/, **expellent** *adj.* MED **ABLE TO EXPEL STH** capable of expelling sth, especially from the body ■ *n.* MED **MEDICINE TO REMOVE WORMS** a medicine that causes the body to get rid of sth undesirable, especially intestinal worms

expellee /ik spél ée, éks pel ée/ *n.* sb who has been expelled from an organization

expellent *adj., n.* MED = **expellant**

expend /ik spénd/ (**-pends, -pending, -pended**) *vt.* **1. USE UP** to use up time, energy, effort, or some other resource **2. SPEND MONEY** to spend money or an amount of money (*formal*) [15thC. From Latin *expendere* 'to weigh out (especially money in payment)', from *pendere* 'to weigh, weigh out' (source of English *dispense, pendant, pendulum,* and *spend*).] —**expender** *n.*

expendable /ik spéndəb'l/ *adj.* **1. NOT WORTH PRESERVING** not worth preserving or saving for reuse **2. DISPENSABLE** easily sacrificed or dispensed with if the need arises or in order to achieve an aim ■ *n.* **EXPENDABLE ITEM** an expendable person or thing —**expendability** /ik spéndə bílləti/ *n.*

expenditure /ik spéndichər/ *n.* **1. MONEY SPENT** an amount of money spent, as a whole or on a particular thing ○ *when income exceeds expenditure* **2. USING UP** the consuming or using up of sth ○ *the huge expenditure of time and human resources on this scheme* [Mid-18thC. From EXPEND; modelled on *expenditor* 'sb in charge of expenditure'.]

expense /ik spénss/ *n.* **1. MONEY SPENT ON STH** the amount of money spent in order to buy or do sth **2.** ACCT **VALUE OF RESOURCE USED** the value of a resource that has been used during the current accounting period and can be charged against revenues for that period **3. STH EXPENSIVE TO BUY** sth that costs money, usually a lot of money, to buy, keep, or run **4. USING UP** the using up or loss of sth ○ *preserved his integrity at the expense of his job* ■ **expenses** *npl.* **BUSINESS EXPENDITURES** an amount of money that sb spends for business purposes that is reimbursable by an employer or deductible from income tax [14thC. Via Anglo-Norman from, ultimately, Latin *expendere* (see EXPEND).]

expense account *n.* **1. AGREEMENT TO REPAY AN EMPLOYEE'S WORK COSTS** a facility given by an employer that entitles an employee to be repaid for some or all of the expenses incurred in the course of his or her employment **2. AMOUNT OR RECORD OF EXPENSES** the amount or a record of an employee's expenses during a particular period

expensive /ik spénssiv/ *adj.* **1. COSTING A LOT** costing a lot of money **2. CHARGING A LOT** charging high prices **3. VERY DISADVANTAGEOUS** involving serious losses or disadvantage to a particular person or group ○ *an expensive first half for the home team* —**expensively** *adv.* —**expensiveness** *n.*

experience /ik spéeri ənss/ *n.* **1. INVOLVEMENT IN STH OVER TIME** active involvement in an activity or exposure to events or people over a period of time, leading to an increase in knowledge and skill **2. KNOWLEDGE AND SKILL ACQUIRED** the knowledge of and skill in sth gained through being involved in it or exposed to it over a period of time ○ *Paper qualifications are no substitute for real-life experience.* **3. STH THAT HAPPENS TO SB** sth that happens to sb, or an event that sb is involved in ○ *an experience that changed his life* **4. DIRECT PERSONAL AWARENESS OF STH** direct personal awareness of or contact with a particular thing ○ *Very few of us remember our first experience of pain.* **5. SUM TOTAL OF AN INDIVIDUAL'S EXPERIENCES** the sum total of the things that have happened to an individual and of his or her past thoughts and feelings ○ *Nothing quite like this has ever been done before, at least not in my experience.* **6.** PHILOS **KNOWLEDGE FROM OBSERVATION** knowledge acquired through the senses rather than through abstract reasoning ■ *vt.* (**-ences, -encing, -enced**) **1. HAVE EXPERIENCE OF STH** to be exposed to, involved in, or affected by sth ○ *the most thrilling ride I've ever experienced* **2. FEEL STH** to feel a particular sensation or emotion ○ *You might experience a tingling sensation in your face.* [14thC. Via French from Latin *experientia*, from *experiri* 'to try out' (source of English *experiment*). Ultimately from an Indo-European word that also produced English *fear* and *pirate*. Originally 'testing'.]

WORD KEY: CULTURAL NOTE

Songs of Experience, a collection of poems by the English writer William Blake (1794). Blake's *Songs of Innocence* (1789) described the world from the optimistic viewpoint of an innocent child. In this, its adult counterpart, he portrays a world of disease, poverty, and irredeemable corruption. The collection includes perhaps his best-known poem, 'The Tyger'.

experienced /ik spéeri ənst/ *adj.* possessing knowledge and skill acquired through involvement in or exposure to sth over a period of time ○ *an experienced pilot*

experiential /ik spéeri énsh'l/ *adj.* derived from or relating to experience as opposed to other methods of acquiring knowledge [Mid-17thC. From EXPERIENCE; modelled on a word such as INFERENTIAL.] —**experientially** *adv.*

experiment *n.* /ik spérrimənt/ **1.** SCI **SCIENTIFIC TEST** a test, especially a scientific one, carried out in order to discover whether a theory is correct or what the results of a particular course of action would be ○ *experiments in parapsychology* **2. DOING STH NEW** an attempt to do sth new, or a trying out of sth to see what will happen ○ *We switched to decaffeinated coffee as an experiment.* **3. USING OF REPEATED TRIALS AND TESTS** the use of tests and trials in order to make discoveries ○ *The most efficient way of working was developed by experiment.* ■ *vi.* /ik spérrimənt, -ment/ (**-ments, -menting, -mented**) **1. TRY NEW THINGS** to try out new methods of doing or using things ○ *a reluctance to experiment with new ingredients* **2.** SCI **CARRY OUT A SCIENTIFIC TEST** to carry out a scientific test of a theory or process [14thC. Directly or via Old French from Latin *experimentum* 'trial, test', from *experiri* (see EXPERIENCE).] —**experimenter** *n.*

experimental /ik spérriméntʼl/ *adj.* **1. RELATING TO STH NEW AND UNTRIED** employing ideas, methods, or materials that have not been tried before ○ *a new, experimental form of treatment* **2.** SCI **RELATING TO SCIENTIFIC EXPERIMENTS** relating to, involving, or based on scientific experiments **3. BASED ON EXPERIENCE AND EVIDENCE** based on experience and practical evidence rather than on ideas —**experimentally** *adv.*

experimentalism /ik spérri mént'lizəm/ *n.* the use of new techniques in artistic, literary, and musical works —**experimentalist** *n.*

experimental psychology *n.* the branch of psychology that studies the basic mechanisms of the mind, e.g. perception, thinking, learning, and memory, often using experiments with individuals in controlled situations

experimentation /ik spérri men táysh'n/ *n.* **1. USING SCIENTIFIC TESTS** the conducting or use of scientific tests **2. USING NEW METHODS** the use of new and untried methods

expert /éks purt/ *n.* **SKILLED OR KNOWLEDGEABLE PERSON** sb with a great deal of knowledge about, or skill, training, or experience in, a particular field or activity ○ *a medical expert* ■ *adj.* **1. SKILFUL OR KNOWLEDGEABLE** having a great deal of knowledge about, or skill, training, or experience in, a particular field or activity ○ *an expert pizza maker* **2. GIVEN OR DONE BY AN EXPERT** given or done by sb who is very knowledgeable or highly skilled, trained, or experienced [14thC. Via French from Latin *expertus*, the past participle of *experiri* (see EXPERIENCE). The underlying meaning is 'sb who knows from experience'.] —**expertly** *adv.* —**expertness** *n.*

expertise /éks pur téez/ *n.* the skill, knowledge, or opinion of sb who is an expert [Mid-19thC. From French, formed from *expert* (see EXPERT).]

expert system *n.* a computer program that applies artificial-intelligence methods to the task of problem-solving by using detailed knowledge and attempting to simulate the reasoning processes of an expert

expert witness *n.* an expert called to answer questions on the stand in a court of law in order to provide specialized information relevant to the case being tried

expiate /ékspi ayt/ (**-ates, -ating, -ated**) *vt.* to make amends, show remorse, or suffer punishment for having done sth wrong [Late 16thC. From Latin *expiat-*, the past participle stem of *expiare*, literally 'to atone completely', from *pius* (see PIOUS).] —**expiator** *n.* —**expiatory** /ékspi ətəri, ékspi áytəri/ *adj.*

expiation /ékspi áysh'n/ *n.* **1. ATONING OR SUFFERING PUNISHMENT FOR WRONGDOING** making amends, showing remorse, or suffering punishment for a wrongdoing **2. STH DONE OR GIVEN AS ATONEMENT** sth done or given to make up for a wrongdoing

expiration /ékspi ráysh'n/ *n.* **1. ENDING** the act of coming to an end, or the fact of having come to an end **2.** PHYSIOL **EXHALATION** the act or process of breathing out (*technical*) **3. DYING** the act or fact of dying (*literary*)

expiration date *n.* *US* = **expiry date**

expiratory /ik spírətəri/ *adj.* relating to the process of breathing out, or used in breathing out

expire /ik spír/ (**-pires, -piring, -pired**) *vi.* **1. END OR BE NO LONGER VALID** to come to an end, or be no longer valid or in operation ○ *my visa has expired* **2.** PHYSIOL **BREATHE OUT** exhale (*technical*) **3. DIE** to die or release a last breath (*formal or literary*) [14thC. Via French from Latin *exspirare*, literally 'to breathe out', from *spirare* 'to breathe' (source of English *spirit*). The underlying meaning is 'to breathe your last, die'.]

expiry /ik spíri/ (*plural* **-ries**) *n.* **1. ENDING OR CEASING TO BE VALID** the fact of coming to an end and being no longer valid after a certain period of time ○ *two weeks before the date of expiry* **2. DEATH** death, especially the death of a person (*formal or literary*)

expiry date *n.* US term **expiration date 1. DATE STH SHOULD BE USED BY** a date printed on the packaging of food and medicines that indicates the time after which they should not be used **2. DATE A CREDIT CARD EXPIRES** the date after which a credit card is no longer valid

explain /ik spláyn/ (**-plains, -plaining, -plained**) *v.* **1.** *vti.* **GIVE DETAILS ABOUT STH** to give an account of sth with enough clarity and detail to be understood by sb else ○ *I explained to him that we had no option.* **2.** *vt.* **CLARIFY STH'S MEANING** to make the meaning of sth clear to sb ○ *can you explain this sentence to me?* **3.** *vti.* **GIVE REASON FOR STH** to give the reason for sth, often as justification for sth that has happened **4.** *vr.* **OFFER JUSTIFICATION** to give reasons to justify personal behaviour or actions ○ *You'll have to explain yourself to the head teacher.* **5.** *vr.* **CLARIFY IDEAS** to express ideas or thoughts in a way that is easily understood ○ *I'm sorry, I'm not explaining myself very well.* [Early 16thC. From Latin *explanare*, literally 'to flatten out, unfold', from *planus* 'flat, clear' (see PLANE).] —**explainable** *adj.* —**explainer** *n.*

explain away *vt.* to give excuses, reasons, or explanations for sth in an attempt to show that it is less serious, important, or problematic than it seems

explanation /éksplə náysh'n/ *n.* **1. STATEMENT EXPLAINING STH** a statement giving reasons for sth or details of sth ○ *an explanation of how the machine works* **2. GIVING OF DETAILS OR REASONS** the giving of details about sth or reasons for sth ○ *There's probably a perfectly simple explanation for all this.* **3. DISCUSSION TO END A MISUNDERSTANDING** a mutual discussion or clarification of sth that removes misunderstandings or reconciles the parties [14thC. From the Latin stem *explanation-*, from *explanare* (see EXPLAIN).]

explanatory /ik splánnətəri/, **explanative** /ik splánnətiv/ *adj.* giving reasons or details that explain sth ○ *an explanatory leaflet is enclosed* [Early 17thC. From late Latin *explanatorius*, from Latin *explanare* (see EXPLAIN).] —**explanatorily** *adv.*

explant /ek splaánt/ *vt.* (**-plants, -planting, -planted**) **REMOVE TISSUE FROM AN ORGANISM FOR CULTURING** to remove living tissue from an organism and place it in a culture medium ■ *n.* **TISSUE REMOVED FOR CULTURING** tissue removed from an organism and placed in a culture medium [Early 20thC. Modelled on IMPLANT.] —**explantation** /éks plaan táysh'n/ *n.*

expletive /ik spléetiv/ *n.* **1.** LING **SWEARWORD** an exclamation, especially a swearword **2.** GRAM **WORD WITH NO MEANING** a word that carries no meaning but has a grammatical function in a sentence. In the sentence 'There are three books on the table', 'there' is an expletive. **3.** POETRY **MEANINGLESS WORD IN A LINE OF POETRY**

a word added to a line of verse in order to fill it out, usually for the sake of the metre. In the line from a folksong 'When and that I was a little tiny lad', the words 'and that' are expletives. ■ *adj.* GRAM, POETRY **USED AS AN EXPLETIVE** functioning as an expletive in a sentence or poem [Early 17thC. From late Latin *expletivus*, from *explet-*, the past participle stem of *explere*, literally 'to fill up', from *plere* 'to fill' (see COMPLETE).]

expletory /ik spleétəri/ *adj.* GRAM, POETRY = **expletive** [Late 17thC. Formed from Latin *explet-*, the past participle stem of *explere* (see EXPLETIVE).]

explicable /ik splíkəb'l, éksplik-/ *adj.* able to be explained —**explicably** *adv.*

explicate /ékspli kayt/ (**-cates, -cating, -cated**) *vt.* **1.** **EXPLAIN STH** to explain sth, especially a literary text, in a detailed and formal way **2.** **DEVELOP A THEORY** to explain and develop an idea or theory and show its implications [Early 16thC. From Latin *explicat-*, the past participle stem of *explicare*, literally 'to unfold', from *plicare* 'to fold' (see PLY[2]).] —**explication** /ékspli káysh'n/ *n.* —**explicative** *adj.* —**explicatively** *adv.* —**explicator** /ékspli kaytər/ *n.*

explicit /ik splíssit/ *adj.* **1.** **CLEAR AND OBVIOUS** expressing all details in a clear and obvious way, leaving no doubt as to the intended meaning ○ *explicit instructions* **2.** **DEFINITE** definite and unqualified rather than implied or guessed at ○ *I didn't have explicit knowledge of what was going on, but I knew that something was happening.* **3.** **SEX** portraying nudity or sexual activity in an open and direct way **4.** MATH **WITH ONLY INDEPENDENT VARIABLES** used to describe a mathematical function that contains only variables whose value is independent of the value of the other variables in the function [Early 17thC. Directly or via French, from Latin *explicitus*, the past participle of *explicare* (see EXPLICATE).] —**explicitly** *adv.* —**explicitness** *n.*

explode /ik splód/ (**-plodes, -ploding, -ploded**) *v.* **1.** *vti.* **BLOW UP OR BURST** to blow up or burst with a sudden release of chemical or nuclear energy and a loud noise, or cause sth to blow up or burst explosively **2.** *vti.* **BURST OR SHATTER** to burst like a bomb or shatter into many pieces, or cause sth to burst or shatter **3.** *vi.* **EXPRESS EMOTION** to give vent to an emotion, suddenly or violently ○ *He exploded into roars of laughter.* **4.** *vi.* **INCREASE DRAMATICALLY** to increase suddenly in extent or severity in an uncontrolled way ○ *The growth rate in home ownership exploded.* **5.** *vi.* **PRODUCE A VIVID DISPLAY** to produce a vivid, often sudden display of light or colour ○ *Her late paintings explode with intense reds and oranges.* **6.** *vi.* **COME SUDDENLY** to appear or start as suddenly and forcefully as an explosion ○ *The band exploded onto the pop scene late last year.* **7.** *vt.* **DISPROVE A THEORY** to show that a belief or theory is completely wrong [Mid-16thC. From Latin *explodere* 'to drive off the stage by clapping', from *plaudere* 'to clap' (source of English *applaud* and *plaudit*). The modern meaning developed from 'drive off noisily'.] —**exploder** *n.*

exploded /ik splódid/ *adj.* showing the parts of sth as separate items in a diagram, but with their relative positions maintained ○ *an exploded diagram*

exploit *vt.* /ik splóyt/ (**-ploits, -ploiting, -ploited**) **1.** **TAKE ADVANTAGE OF SB** to take selfish or unfair advantage of a person or situation, usually for personal gain **2.** **USE STH FOR BENEFIT** to use or develop sth in order to gain a benefit ■ *n.* /éks ployt/ **NOTABLE ACT** an interesting or daring action or achievement [Mid-16thC. Via Old French *esploit* 'accomplishment', from Latin *explicitum*, the past participle of *explicare* 'to unfold' (see EXPLICATE). The underlying meaning is 'to make progress, be successful'.] —**exploitable** *adj.* —**exploiter** *n.*

exploitation /éks ploy táysh'n/ *n.* **1.** **UNFAIR TREATMENT OR USE** unfair treatment or use of sb or sth, usually for personal gain **2.** **DEVELOPMENT OF STH FOR BENEFIT** the use or development of sth to produce a benefit

exploitive /ik splóytiv/, **exploitative** /-tətiv/ *adj.* making use of sb or sth unfairly —**exploitively** *adv.* —**exploitiveness** *n.*

exploration /éksplə ráysh'n/ *n.* **1.** **TRAVEL FOR DISCOVERY** travelling to discover what a place is like or where it is ○ *polar exploration* **2.** **STUDY OR CONSIDERATION OF STH** an investigation or the study of sth such as data, or the consideration and testing of sth such as possible courses of action **3.** **SEARCHING FOR NATURAL RESOURCES** the testing of a number of places for natural resources, e.g. drilling or boring for samples that will be examined for possible mineral deposits **4.** MED **EXAMINATION FOR DIAGNOSIS** the examination of a part of the body for the purpose of diagnosis

exploratory /ik splórrətəri, -spláwrə-/ *adj.* involving exploration ○ *an exploratory mission* ○ *exploratory surgery*

explore /ik spláwr/ (**-plores, -ploring, -plored**) *v.* **1.** *vti.* **TRAVEL FOR DISCOVERY** to travel to a place to discover what it is like or what is there **2.** *vti.* **INVESTIGATE OR STUDY STH** to make a careful investigation or study of sth ○ *the committee is exploring all possible avenues of research* **3.** *vti.* **SEARCH A PLACE FOR NATURAL RESOURCES** to make a search of an area for natural resources such as mineral deposits **4.** *vt.* MED **EXAMINE STH FOR DIAGNOSIS** to examine a part of the body in order to make a diagnosis [Mid-16thC. Via French, from Latin *explorare* 'to search out', from *plorare* 'to cry out', perhaps as in hunting for game.]

explorer /ik spláwrər/ *n.* sb who travels to places that were previously unknown or unnavigated

explosion /ik splózh'n/ *n.* **1.** **SUDDEN NOISY RELEASE OF ENERGY** the sudden loud release of energy and a rapidly expanding volume of gas that occurs when a bomb detonates or gas explodes **2.** **BURSTING OR SHATTERING OF STH** a bursting with a loud noise, or a shattering of sth into many pieces **3.** **SUDDEN BURST OF EMOTION** a sudden release of intense feeling such as anger ○ *an explosion of rage* **4.** **DRAMATIC INCREASE** a sudden and dramatic increase in the extent or severity of sth, e.g. a population or an activity ○ *the explosion in e-mail subscriptions* **5.** **SUDDEN APPEARANCE** the sudden and forceful appearance of sb or sth, or sudden and forceful beginning of sth **6.** **INTENSE DISPLAY** a vivid, often sudden display of light or colour **7.** PHON = **plosion** [Early 17thC. From the Latin stem *explosion-*, from *explos-*, the past participle stem of *explodere* (see EXPLODE).]

explosive /ik splóssiv, -splóz-/ *adj.* **1.** **LIABLE TO EXPLODE** capable of exploding, or likely to explode **2.** **OPERATED BY EXPLODING** designed to explode, or operated by means of sth that explodes **3.** **LIKELY TO GENERATE VIOLENT ANGER** likely to cause or erupt suddenly into angry disagreement or violence ○ *an explosive temperament* **4.** **SUDDEN AND DRAMATIC** happening or appearing suddenly and dramatically ○ *The company capitalized on the explosive increase in the popularity of their new game.* **5.** PHON = **plosive** *n.* ■ *n.* **1.** **STH THAT EXPLODES** any substance or device that suddenly produces a volume of rapidly expanding gas **2.** PHON = **plosive** —**explosively** *adv.* —**explosiveness** *n.*

expo /ékspō/ *n.* a large exhibition or internationally sanctioned exposition [Mid-20thC. Shortening of EXPOSITION.]

exponent /ik spónənt/ *n.* **1.** **ADVOCATE** sb who supports a cause and speaks in favour of it **2.** **EXPLAINER OF STH** sb who explains or interprets sth ○ *an exponent of Kant's philosophy* **3.** **PRACTITIONER OF AN ART OR SKILL** a performer or practitioner of some art or skill, especially sb who is regarded as an excellent example of how sth should be done **4.** MATH **INDICATOR OF THE TIMES TO MULTIPLY A NUMBER** a number or variable placed to the upper right of a number or mathematical expression that indicates the number of times the number or expression is to be multiplied by itself, as in 2^3, which equals 8 [Late 16thC. From Latin *exponent-*, the present participle stem of *exponere* (see EXPOUND).]

exponential /ékspə nénsh'l, ékspō-/ *adj.* **1.** MATH **RELATING TO EXPONENT** used to describe a mathematical entity such as a curve, function, equation, or series that contains, is expressed as, or involves numbers or quantities raised to an exponent **2.** MATH **USING A BASE OF NATURAL LOGARITHMS** used to describe a mathematical entity that involves the transcendental number *e*, the base of natural logarithms, raised to an exponent **3.** **RAPIDLY DEVELOPING** rapidly becoming greater in size ○ *an exponential increase in sales* —**exponentially** *adv.*

exponential function *n.* a mathematical expression with the formula e^x, in which *e* is the base of natural logarithms. Symbol **exp**

exponential notation *n.* = **scientific notation**

exponentiation /ékspə nénshi áysh'n, ékspō-/ *n.* the multiplication of a number or quantity by itself a given number of times, the number of times being the power to which the number or quantity is to be raised

export *v.* /ik spáwrt, éks pawrt/ (**-ports, -porting, -ported**) **1.** *vti.* COMM **SEND GOODS ABROAD** to send goods for sale or exchange to other countries **2.** *vt.* SOC SCI **SPREAD A SOCIETY'S CULTURE TO ANOTHER SOCIETY** to cause the spread of ideas, values, or a way of life from one society, culture, or nation to another **3.** *vt.* COMPUT **ALTER THE FORMAT OF COMPUTER DATA** to convert data from a computer program into a form suitable for use by a different program ■ *n.* /éks pawrt/ **1.** COMM **SELLING OF GOODS ABROAD** the selling of goods to other countries **2.** COMM **PRODUCT SOLD ABROAD** a product sold and transported to another country **3.** BEVERAGES **TYPE OF SCOTTISH BEER** a type of strong brown beer brewed in Scotland [15thC. From Latin *exportare*, literally 'to carry away', from *portare* (see PORT[1]).] —**exportability** /ik spáwrtə bílləti, éks pawrtə-/ *n.* —**exportable** *adj.* —**exportation** /éks pawr táysh'n/ *n.* —**exporter** *n.*

expose /ik spóz/ (**-poses, -posing, -posed**) *v.* **1.** *vt.* **LET STH BE SEEN** to uncover sth or turn it over in order for it to be seen or with the result that it can be seen ○ *expose the wound to the air* **2.** *vt.* **PUT SB IN AN UNPROTECTED SITUATION** to put sb or sth in a vulnerable or potentially dangerous situation ○ *financially exposed* **3.** *vt.* **MAKE SB EXPERIENCE STH** to cause sb to have a personal and often enlightening experience of sth **4.** *vt.* **REVEAL SB'S WRONGDOINGS** to reveal that sb has done sth wrong, especially by publishing or broadcasting the information **5.** *vr.* **REVEAL THE BODY INDECENTLY** to uncover a part of the body, especially the genitals, in public in an indecent way **6.** *vt.* PHOTOGRAPHY **ALLOW LIGHT ONTO A FILM** to allow light to fall on light-sensitive material such as photographic film **7.** *vt.* ANTHROP **LEAVE A BABY TO DIE OUTSIDE** especially in earlier societies, to abandon a baby to die in the open air, e.g. because it was not healthy **8.** *vt.* CHR **SHOW STH TO BE REVERED** to display sth for religious veneration, e.g. the Eucharist in a Roman Catholic service [15thC. Via French (influenced by *poser* 'to place') from Latin *exponere*, literally 'to set out' (see EXPOUND).] —**exposal** *n.* —**exposer** *n.*

exposé /ek spóz ay/ (*plural* **-sés**) *n.* **1.** **PUBLICATION OF WRONGDOING** a book or article that reveals details of a scandal or crime **2.** **DECLARATION OF FACTS** a formal and systematic statement giving facts about sth [Early 19thC. From French, the past participle of *exposer* (see EXPOSE).]

exposed /ik spózd/ *adj.* **1.** **VISIBLE OR UNPROTECTED** uncovered and therefore visible or without protection ○ *Cover any exposed areas of skin liberally with sunscreen.* **2.** **WITH NO SHELTER** unprotected from wind and weather by shelter from trees or higher ground **3.** **UNPROTECTED FROM HARM** vulnerable to danger or harm **4.** MOUNTAINEERING **CARRIED OUT ON OPEN ROCK FACE** carried out on a high, sheer, and open rock face ○ *an exposed ascent* —**exposedness** /ik spózidnəss, -spózd-/ *n.*

exposition /ékspə zísh'n/ *n.* **1.** **DETAILED DESCRIPTION OR DISCUSSION** a detailed description of a theory, problem, or proposal discussing the issues involved, or a commentary on a written text discussing its meaning and implications **2.** **ACT OF DESCRIBING OR DISCUSSING STH** the act of describing and discussing a theory, problem, or proposal or commenting on a written text **3.** **EXHIBITION OR FAIR** a large exhibition, e.g. of industrial achievements, sometimes international in scope **4.** MUSIC **OPENING SECTION OF A PIECE OF MUSIC** the opening section of a piece of music, especially of a sonata or fugue, in which the principal themes are introduced **5.** CHR **DISPLAYING STH TO THE PUBLIC** the act of showing or displaying sth such as a relic or the host for veneration **6.** LITERAT, THEATRE **FACTUAL BACKGROUND OF NOVEL OR PLAY** the basic facts of setting, period, character, or other relevant parts of a literary work, usually fictional or meant for the theatre [14thC. Directly or via French, from the Latin stem *exposition-*, from *exposit-*, the past participle stem of *exponere* (see EXPOUND).] —**expositive** /ik spózzitiv/ *adj.* —**expositor** /-tər/ *n.* —**expository** /-təri/ *adj.*

ex post facto /éks pōst fáktō/ *adj., adv.* applying to events that have already occurred as well as to subsequent events [Mid-17thC. From Latin *ex postfacto*, literally 'from what is done afterwards'.]

expostulate /ik spóstyŏŏ layt/ (**-lates, -lating, -lated**) *vi.* to express disagreement or disapproval, or attempt to dissuade sb from doing sth [Late 16thC. From Latin *expostulat-*, the past participle stem of *expostulare*, literally 'to demand from', from *postulare* (see POSTULATE).] —**expostulation** /ik spóstyŏŏ láysh'n/ *n.* —**expostulator** /ik spóstyŏŏ laytər/ *n.* —**expostulatory** /-lətəri/ *adj.*

WORD KEY: SYNONYMS

See Synonyms at ***object***.

exposure /ik spṓzhər/ *n.* **1. CONTACT WITH OR EXPERIENCE OF STH** the experience of coming into contact with some environmental condition or social influence that has an effect, either harmful or beneficial **2.** MED **HARMFUL EFFECTS OF WEATHER** the harmful effects of cold or other extreme weather conditions **3.** BROADCAST, PRESS **PUBLICITY** reporting of events by the broadcast or print media **4. REVELATION OF A SCANDAL OR IDENTITY** the revelation of a scandal or of sb's secrets or private information **5.** PHOTOGRAPHY **TIME AND INTENSITY OF LIGHT** an amount of light permitted to fall on light-sensitive material such as film or paper coated with emulsion **6.** PHOTOGRAPHY **TAKING OF A PHOTOGRAPH** the act or process of taking a photograph **7.** PHOTOGRAPHY **FILM OR PLATE EXPOSED FOR PHOTOGRAPH** a section of film or a photographic plate exposed to light in taking a photograph **8.** BUILDING **POSITION OF A ROOM OR BUILDING** the direction sth faces or the way it is sited relative to sunlight or wind direction ○ *This room has a southern exposure.* **9.** FIN **RISK OF FINANCIAL LOSS** the state of being at risk of financial loss or the amount of possible financial loss involved **10.** MOUNTAINEERING **DEGREE EXPOSED TO THE WEATHER** the extent to which a rock face is exposed to the weather **11.** ANTHROP **LEAVING OF A BABY TO DIE OUTDOORS** the former practice in some societies of leaving a baby in the open to die, e.g. because it was not healthy **12.** GEOL **ROCKY OUTCROPPING** the outcropping of bare rock in a landscape, enabling mapping of the underlying geology

exposure meter *n.* a device for measuring the intensity of light for photography, often giving the value as a combination of shutter speed and lens aperture

expound /ik spównd/ (**-pounds, -pounding, -pounded**) *vti.* to give a detailed description and explanation of a theory or viewpoint or an explanation of the meaning and implications of a written text [13thC. Via Old French *espondre*, from Latin *exponere* 'to explain', literally 'to set forth', from *ponere* 'to place' (see POSITION).] —**expounder** *n.*

express /ik spréss/ *v.* (**-presses, -pressing, -pressed**) **1.** *vt.* **SAY STH** to state thoughts or feelings in words ○ *I'd like to express my gratitude to everyone* **2.** *vt.* **SHOW MEANING SYMBOLICALLY** to convey meaning by gesture, behaviour, representation in art or drama, or in some other symbolic way **3.** *vr.* **REVEAL THOUGHTS** to make thoughts and feelings known to others ○ *able to express herself through her music* **4.** *vt.* **REPRESENT STH AS A SYMBOL** to use a symbol, figure, or formula to represent sth such as a quantity in a different way ○ *Express the fractions as decimal numbers.* **5.** *vt.* **SQUEEZE STH OUT** to force a liquid out of sth by squeezing or pressing (*formal*) ○ *to express juice from lemons and limes* **6.** *vt.* MAIL **SEND STH BY SPECIAL FAST DELIVERY** to send a package or message using a special rapid-delivery service **7.** *vt.* GENETICS **PRODUCE AN INHERITED CHARACTERISTIC** to produce an observable inherited characteristic (*refers to genes*) ○ *Some genes are only expressed in adults.* ■ *adj.* **1.** TRANSP, MAIL **DONE OR TRAVELLING VERY QUICKLY** travelling, moving, or delivered quickly and directly to the destination ○ *Take the express train.* **2.** COMM **OF BRIEF TRANSACTIONS** relating to purchases or other transactions that can be completed quickly and easily because, e.g., only one item or cash is involved **3. EXPLICIT** stated in a clear, unambiguous way ○ *it was his express wish* **4. SPECIFIC** definitely, and usually exclusively, intended or specified ○ *formed for the express purpose of making a profit* ■ *adv.* MAIL, TRANSP **BY EXPRESS DELIVERY OR TRANSPORT** by a special high-speed delivery service or an express train, bus, or similar mode of transport ■ *n.* **1.** TRANSP **FAST TRAIN OR BUS** a fast train or bus that travels to its destination directly, making few or no stops on the way **2.** MAIL **FAST DELIVERY SERVICE** a special fast delivery service or the organization providing it [14thC. Ultimately from medieval Latin *expressare*, literally 'to press out' (verb) and Latin *expressus* 'clearly evident' (adjective), both from, ultimately, Latin *exprimere*, literally 'to press out', from *premere* (see PRESS).] —**expresser** *n.* —**expressible** *adj.*

expression /ik sprésh'n/ *n.* **1. LOOK ON SB'S FACE** a look on sb's face, conveying a thought or feeling ○ *She listened with a puzzled expression.* **2.** LANG **WORD OR PHRASE** a word or group of words that communicates an idea **3. CONVEYING OF THOUGHTS OR FEELINGS** the communication of thoughts or feelings, e.g. directly to another person ○ *a heart-rending expression of sorrow* **4. WAY OF COMMUNICATING STH** sth done or given as a means of communicating a feeling or thought to sb else **5. INFLECTION IN THE VOICE** sb's intonation or tone of voice **6.** MUSIC **INTERPRETIVE ELEMENT OF MUSIC** the interpretive element of music, including tempo, dynamics, articulation, and phrasing, by which a player or singer draws out its emotional content, or its emotion stirs the feelings **7.** MATH **MATHEMATICAL REPRESENTATION** any combination of constants, operators, and variables representing numbers or quantities, e.g. (5 + x) **8. EXTRACTION OF LIQUID** the pressing out of a liquid from a substance using pressure **9.** GENETICS **EFFECT OR ACTION OF A GENE** the effect or action produced by a particular gene —**expressional** *adj.*

expressionism /ik sprésh'nizəm/ *n.* **1.** PAINTING **ART MOVEMENT CONCENTRATING ON EXPRESSING EMOTION** an artistic movement that flourished in Germany between 1905 and 1925 whose adherents sought to represent feelings and moods rather than objective reality, often distorting colour and form. The term is also used more loosely to apply to the work of Matisse and the Fauves. **2.** THEATRE, LITERAT **LITERARY MOVEMENT PRESENTING STYLIZED REALITY** a literary movement of the early 20th century, especially in the theatre, that represented external reality in a highly stylized and subjective manner, attempting to convey a psychological or spiritual reality rather than a record of actual events. Typical expressionists are the playwrights August Strindberg, Georg Wedekind, and Eugene O'Neill. —**expressionist** *n., adj.* —**expressionistic** /ik spréshə nístik/ *adj.* —**expressionistically** /-nístikli/ *adv.*

expressionless /ik sprésh'nləss/ *adj.* showing no emotion or interest by the tone of voice or by the look on the face —**expressionlessly** *adv.*

expression mark (*plural* **expression marks** *or* **expression markings**) *n.* a symbol or written direction, often in Italian, that indicates the expression to be used in performing a piece of music

expressive /ik spréssiv/ *adj.* **1. FULL OF EXPRESSION** expressing a great deal of feeling and meaning ○ *an expressive face* **2. CONVEYING STH** communicating a particular meaning ○ *a gesture expressive of the utmost contempt* **3. OF SPEAKING AND WRITING** relating to disorders involving the expression of ideas in speech and writing as opposed to the interpretation of what is heard or read —**expressively** *adv.*

expressivity /éks pre sívvəti/ (*plural* **-ties**) *n.* **1. ABILITY TO EXPRESS FEELING OR THOUGHT** the ability or the extent to which sb has the ability to communicate emotion or meaning **2.** GENETICS **GENE'S EFFECT ON AN ORGANISM** the extent to which a gene affects the observable characteristics (**phenotype**) of an organism

express lane *n. US* = **fast lane**

expressly /ik spréssli/ *adv.* **1. SPECIFICALLY** having a deliberate and specific intention or purpose or sb specific in mind **2. UNAMBIGUOUSLY** in a clear and unambiguous way ○ *He expressly rejected my offer.*

Express Mail *tdmk.* a trademark for the overnight delivery service of the United States Postal Service

expresso *n.* = **espresso**

expressway /ik spréss way/ *n. US* a limited-access road with several lanes in each direction, designed for fast direct travel especially through or round a city

expropriate /ik sprṓpri ayt/ (**-ates, -ating, -ated**) *vti.* to take property or money from sb, either legally for the public good or illegally by theft or fraud [Late 16thC. From medieval Latin *expropriat-*, the past participle stem of *expropriare*, literally 'to take away and make your own', from Latin *proprius* 'your own' (see PROPER).] —**expropriation** /ik sprṓpri áysh'n/ *n.* —**expropriator** /ik sprṓpri aytər/ *n.* —**expropriatory** /-ətəri/ *adj.*

expt *abbr.* experiment

exptl *abbr.* experimental

expulsion /ik spúlsh'n/ *n.* **1. DISMISSAL FROM A PLACE OR MEMBERSHIP** the act of compelling sb to give up membership in or leave an institution such as a school, political party, or club, usually as a punishment **2. FORCING SB OR STH OUT** the forcing out of sth or sb from sth ○ *expulsion of air from the lungs* [15thC. From the Latin stem *expulsion-*, from *expuls-*, the past participle stem of *expellere* (see EXPEL).] —**expulsive** *adj.*

expunge /ik spúnj/ (**-punges, -punging, -punged**) *vt.* **1. GET RID OF STH COMPLETELY** to delete sth unwanted from a written record, or blot out sth unpleasant from the memory **2. DO AWAY WITH STH** to destroy or put an end to sth [Early 17thC. From Latin *expungere*, literally 'to prick out', from *pungere* 'to mark with a point' (see PUNGENT); from the placing of points next to the text to be deleted.] —**expunction** /ik spúngksh'n/ *n.* —**expunger** /ik spúnjər/ *n.*

expurgate /ékspər gayt/ (**-gates, -gating, -gated**) *vt.* to remove words or passages considered offensive or unsuitable from a book before publication [Late 17thC. From the Latin *expurgat-*, the past participle stem of *expurgare*, literally 'to cleanse out', from *purgare* (see PURGE).] —**expurgation** /ékspər gáysh'n/ *n.* —**expurgator** /ékspər gaytər/ *n.* —**expurgatorial** /ik spúrgə táwri əl/ *adj.* —**expurgatory** /ek spúrgətəri/ *adj.*

exquisite /ik skwízzit, ékskwizit/ *adj.* **1. FINELY BEAUTIFUL** very beautiful and delicate or intricate ○ *exquisite workmanship* **2. EXCELLENT** perfect and delightful **3. SENSITIVE AND DISCRIMINATING** sensitive and capable of detecting subtle differences ○ *exquisite taste in dress* **4. INTENSE** felt with a sharp intensity ○ *exquisite pain* [Mid-16thC. From Latin *exquisitus*, the past participle of *exquirere*, literally 'to seek out', from *quaerere* (see QUERY). The underlying meaning is 'sought after, choice, perfect'.] —**exquisitely** *adv.* —**exquisiteness** *n.*

exsert /ek súrt/ *vt.* (**-serts, -serting, -serted**) BIOL **EXTEND STH OUT** to thrust out or project sth ○ *A bee exserts its sting.* ■ *adj.* **exsert, exserted** BIOL **PROJECTING** projecting beyond an enclosing or adjoining part ○ *an exsert stamen* [Early 19thC. From Latin *exsert-*, the past participle stem of *exserere* (see EXERT).] —**exsertion** /ek súrsh'n/ *n.*

ex-service *adj.* **1. HAVING SERVED IN ARMED FORCES** having served in the armed forces in the past **2. RELATING TO FORMER ARMED FORCES PERSONNEL** provided for or concerned with people who have served in the armed forces

ex-serviceman *n.* a man formerly in the armed forces

ex-servicewoman *n.* a woman formerly in the armed forces

ex silentio /éks si lénshō/ *adv.* from or based on a lack of evidence to the contrary [Early 20thC. From Latin, literally 'from silence'.]

ext. *abbr.* **1.** extension **2.** exterior **3.** external **4.** PHARM extract

extant /ek stánt, ékstənt/ *adj.* still in existence ○ *Three copies of the document are extant.* [Mid-16thC. From Latin *extant-*, the present participle stem of *exstare*, 'to exist', literally 'to stand out', from *stare* 'to stand' (see STATION).]

WORD KEY: SYNONYMS

See Synonyms at ***living***.

extemporaneous /ik stémpə ráyni əss/, **extemporary** /ik stémpərəri/, **extemporal** /ik stémpərəl/ *adj.* **1. DONE UNREHEARSED** performed without any preparation **2. PREPARED BUT SAID WITHOUT NOTES** prepared in advance but delivered without notes **3. SPEAKING UNREHEARSED** speaking without preparation or notes **4. MAKESHIFT** done as a temporary measure [Mid-17thC. Formed from late Latin *extemporaneus*, from *ex tempore*, literally 'out of the moment'.] —**extemporaneity** /ik stémpərə née əti, -náy əti/ *n.* —**extemporaneously** /ik stémpə ráyni əssli/ *adv.* —**extemporaneousness** /-əssnəss/ *n.*

extempore /ik stémpəri/ *adj., adv.* with little or no preparation [Mid-16thC. From Latin *ex tempore*, literally 'out of the moment', from *tempor-*, the stem of *tempus* 'time' (source of English *tempo* and *temporary*).]

extemporize /ik stémpə rīz/ (**-rizes, -rizing, -rized**), **extemporise** (**-rises, -rising, -rised**) *vti.* **1. PERFORM STH WITHOUT PREPARATION** to perform or speak without having made any preparation **2.** MUSIC **IMPROVISE MUSIC** to compose or perform a piece of music by improvising **3. HANDLE IN A MAKESHIFT WAY** to do or devise sth in a makeshift fashion [Mid-17thC. Formed from EXTEMPORE.] —**extemporization** /ik stémpə rī záysh'n/ *n.* —**extemporizer** /ik stémpə rīzər/ *n.*

extend /ik sténd/ (**-tends, -tending, -tended**) *v.* **1.** *vi.* **OCCUPY DISTANCE OR SPACE** to continue for a distance or occupy a space, often within a particular range ○ *the city centre extends for another mile in both directions* **2.** *vi.* **CONTINUE FOR A TIME** to last or continue for a period of time, usually a particular one **3.** *vti.* **APPLY TO SB OR STH** to affect or apply to sb or sth, or make sth affect or apply ○ *the offer extends to new readers too* **4.** *vt.* **INCREASE STH'S SIZE** to make sth larger or longer ○ *extend the driveway* **5.** *vt.* **INCREASE TIME SPAN** to increase the length of time sth lasts or the length of time before sth applies or ceases to apply **6.** *vt.* **INCREASE LIMITS** to broaden or expand the range, influence, or scope of sth ○ *a vital research project that will extend our knowledge of the disease* **7.** *vt.* **INCREASE AN AMOUNT BY ADDING STH** to increase the amount of sth by adding sth else to it ○ *There's not much stew left, but we could always extend it by adding more potatoes and vegetables.* **8.** *vti.* **OPEN OUT INTO SPACE** to stretch out into space, or stretch sth out **9.** *vt.* **OFFER OR GIVE STH** to offer or provide sth to sb ○ *to extend the hand of friendship* **10.** *vt.* **MAKE AN EXTRA EFFORT TO DO STH** to work or make sb or sth work as hard as possible to achieve the best possible result ○ *They had to extend themselves to finish on time* **11.** *vt.* FIN **CALCULATE THE LINE TOTAL ON INVOICE** to calculate the total on the line of an invoice by multiplying quantity by price [14thC. From Latin *extendere*, literally 'to stretch out', from *tendere* (see TENDER[2]).] —**extendability** /ik sténdə bílləti/ *n.* —**extendable** /ik sténdəb'l/ *adj.*

WORD KEY: SYNONYMS

See Synonyms at ***increase***.

extended /ik sténdid/ *adj.* **1. LENGTHIER THAN USUAL** lasting longer than expected or planned **2. MADE LONGER OR LARGER** stretched or pulled out, lengthened, enlarged, or expanded **3. HAVING A WIDER RANGE** having wider influence, effect, or application **4.** PRINTING = **expanded** —**extendedly** *adv.*

Extended Binary Coded Decimal Interchange Code *n.* COMPUT full form of **EBCDIC**

extended family *n.* the family as a unit embracing parents and children together with grandparents, aunts, uncles, cousins, and sometimes more distant relatives. ◊ **nuclear family**

extended-play *adj.* **1. RECORDING FOR A LONGER TIME** used to describe a videotape format that can record four or six hours of material on a two-hour tape (*not hyphenated after a verb*) **2. WITH A LONGER RECORDING ON EACH SIDE** used to describe a vinyl record of the same size as a single but with two tracks on each side rather than one (*not hyphenated when used after a verb*)

extender /ik sténdər/ *n.* **1.** INDUST **SUBSTANCE ADDED TO MODIFY A PRODUCT** a substance that is added to a product to dilute it, add body to it, or modify it in other ways **2.** PRINTING **PROJECTING PART OF LETTER** the part of a lower-case letter such as 'p' or 'h' that projects above or below the body of the letter

extensible /ik sténssəb'l/, **extensile** /ik stén sīl/ *adj.* having the capability of being extended [Early 17thC. Directly or via French, from medieval Latin *extensibilis*.] —**extensibility** /ik sténssə bílləti/ *n.* —**extensibly** /ik sténssəbli/ *adv.*

extensimeter *n.* = **extensometer**

extension /ik sténsh'n/ *n.* **1.** BUILDING **ADDITION TO A BUILDING** a room or area added to an existing building ○ *We're having an extension built onto the kitchen.* **2. ADDITIONAL PIECE** a piece that has been or can be added, or that can be pulled out, to enlarge or lengthen sth **3.** UTIL **ADDITIONAL TELEPHONE LINE** an additional telephone line or telephone connected to the main line in a building or organization, often having its own number **4.** UTIL **TELEPHONE NUMBER OF AN EXTENSION** the number used to contact a telephone extension within a building or organization **5.** ELEC = **extension lead 6. ADDITIONAL PERIOD OF TIME** an additional period of time allowed for completion of work or payment of a debt ○ *You'll never finish that essay on time; why don't you ask for an extension?* **7.** PUBLIC ADMIN, LAW **EXTENDED DRINKS LICENCE** permission to serve alcoholic drinks until a later time than usual **8. EXTENDING OR BEING EXTENDED** the act or process of increasing the size, scope, range, or application of sth, or the fact of being increased in size, scope, range, or application **9. RANGE** the range or sphere over which sth extends **10.** EDUC **OFF-CAMPUS UNIVERSITY TEACHING PROGRAM** courses or facilities provided by a college or university for people who are unable to attend classes on the campus or during scheduled class periods **11.** MED = **traction 12.** ANAT **STRAIGHTENING OF A LIMB** the stretching out of a limb after it has been bent, or the position attained by a limb after stretching it **13.** LOGIC **BROADER SENSE OF AN EXPRESSION** the broad range of meaning of an expression, as opposed to its precise meaning. The extension of the term 'man' is the set comprising all men, whereas the meaning of the word 'man' is 'an adult male human being'. **14.** MATH **SET INCLUDING TWO SIMILAR SETS** a mathematical set that includes as subsets all the members of a given set and of another similar set **15.** COMPUT = **file extension** ■ **extensions** *npl.* HAIR **EXTRA HAIR ATTACHED TO YOUR OWN HAIR** lengths of real or synthetic hair attached to the hair to create longer hairstyle [Early 16thC. From the late Latin stem *extension-*, from Latin *extens-*, the past participle stem of *extendere* (see EXTEND).] —**extensional** *adj.* —**extensionally** *adv.*

extension cable *n.* a cable that can be used to attach an extension lead to an electric supply when the lead itself is too short to reach it

extension lead *n.* a length of electrical lead with a plug at one end and a socket at the other, used to connect an appliance when the electrical supply is some distance away

extensive /ik sténssiv/ *adj.* **1. VAST** covering a large area ○ *a hotel set in extensive grounds* **2. BROAD IN SCOPE** great in extent, range, or application ○ *extensive research into a subject* **3. LARGE IN AMOUNT** great in amount or number **4.** AGRIC **USING LOW TECHNOLOGICAL INPUT** relating to a farming practice in which a large area of land is cultivated using little labour and expense, resulting in a relatively small crop. ◊ **intensive** [Early 17thC. Directly or via French from late Latin *extensivus*, from the Latin *extens-*, the past participle stem of *extendere* (see EXTEND).] —**extensively** *adv.* —**extensiveness** *n.*

extensometer /ék sten sómmitər/, **extensimeter** /-símmitər/ *n.* a device for measuring small changes of length in a sample, especially those caused by stress or thermal expansion in a metal [Late 19thC. Coined from Latin *extens-*, the past participle stem of *extendere* (see EXTEND) + -METER.]

extensor /ik sténssər, ik stén sawr/ *n.* a muscle that straightens or extends a part of the body such as an arm or leg [Early 18thC. From modern Latin, formed from Latin *extens-*, the past participle stem of *extendere* (see EXTEND).]

extent /ik stént/ *n.* **1. RANGE OR SCOPE** the area or range covered or affected by sth ○ *a technique for determining the location and extent of brain damage* **2. DEGREE** the degree to which sth applies ○ *To what extent should we allow newspaper reporters into people's private lives?* **3. REGION** an area of land or water ○ *a vast extent of fertile land* **4.** LAW **WRIT ALLOWING SEIZURE OF PROPERTY** a writ that authorizes sb to take possession of the property of sb who owes him or her money [Late 16thC. Via Anglo-Norman *extente* 'valuation of land' from, ultimately, Latin *extendere* (see EXTEND).]

extenuate /ik sténnyoo ayt/ (**-ates, -ating, -ated**) *vt.* to make a mistake or wrongdoing seem less serious than it first appeared, or to provide a mitigating excuse for sth that has happened [Early 16thC. From Latin *extenuat-*, the past participle stem of *extenuare*, literally 'to thin out', from *tenuis* 'thin' (see TENUOUS).] —**extenuating** *adj.* —**extenuatingly** *adv.* —**extenuation** *n.* —**extenuative** /ik sténnyoo ətiv/ *adj.* —**extenuator** /-aytər/ *n.* —**extenuatory** /-ətəri/ *adj.*

exterior /ik steéri ər/ *adj.* **1. ON THE OUTSIDE** on or for the outside of sth ○ *added protection for the exterior walls of the building* **2. COMING FROM OUTSIDE** coming from outside or beyond sth or sb ○ *There must be some exterior cause for this.* **3.** CINEMA **OUTDOOR** taken out of doors or depicting an outdoor scene ○ *an exterior shot* ■ *n.* **1. OUTSIDE** the outside surface, appearance, or coating of sth **2. OUTWARD APPEARANCE** sb's outward appearance as distinct from his or her inner thoughts **3.** CINEMA, ARTS **SCENE OUTSIDE** an outdoor scene, especially as represented in the visual arts [Early 16thC. From Latin, literally 'more outward', from *exter* (see EXTERNAL).] —**exteriority** /ik steéri órrəti, éks teeri órrəti/ *n.*

exterior angle *n.* **1. ANGLE ON THE OUTSIDE OF A POLYGON** an angle on the outside of a polygon, formed between a side and an extension of an adjacent side **2. ANGLE FORMED BY A LINE CROSSING LINES** any of the four angles formed on the outside of a pair of lines that are crossed by a third line

exteriorize /ik steéri ə rīz/ (**-izes, -izing, -ized**), **exteriorise** (**-ises, -ising, -ised**) *vt.* **1.** = **externalize 2.** SURG **REMOVE AN INTERNAL ORGAN** to remove an internal organ from the body, e.g. to perform surgery on it —**exteriorization** /ik steéri ə rī záysh'n/ *n.*

exterminate /ik stúrmi nayt/ (**-nates, -nating, -nated**) *vt.* to kill or destroy sb or sth completely ○ *a species nearly exterminated by hunting* [Late 16thC. From Latin *exterminat-*, the past participle stem of *exterminare*, literally 'to drive beyond the boundaries', from *termen* 'boundary', a variant of *terminus* (see TERMINUS).] —**extermination** /ik stúrmi náysh'n/ *n.* —**exterminatory** /-nətəri/ *adj.*

exterminator /ik stúrmi naytər/ *n.* **1. SB PAID TO KILL VERMIN** sb who kills insects, rodents, and other vermin **2. EXTERMINATING PERSON OR THING** sb or sth that kills or destroys sb or sth else [14thC]

extern /ék sturn/, **externe** *n.* *US* a nonresident doctor or other staff member attached to a hospital [Early 17thC. Via French *externe* from Latin *externus* (see EXTERNAL).] —**externship** *n.*

external /ik stúrn'l/ *adj.* **1. OUTSIDE** situated on, happening on, or coming from the outside ○ *The sudden collapse of the empire should not be put down to external forces alone.* **2. FOR USE ON THE OUTSIDE** suitable or designed for use only on the outside or surface of sth, especially the body **3. OUTSIDE STH'S SCOPE** existing outside the body or mind, or the limits of sth ○ *What real evidence is there for the existence of the external world?* **4. VISIBLE FROM OUTWARD APPEARANCE** conveyed by sb's or sth's outward appearance, as opposed to what is inside or underneath **5. OUTSIDE AN ORGANIZATION** relating to, forming, or from a separate or independent organization ○ *The investigation must be carried out by members of an external body.* **6.** POL **RELATING TO FOREIGN COUNTRIES** dealing with or involving relations with foreign countries ■ *n.* **1. STH'S EXTERIOR** the outer surface of sth **2.** *Aus* EDUC **EXTRAMURAL STUDENT** an extramural student ■ **externals** *npl.* **1. OUTWARD APPEARANCES** the outward appearance of sb or sth, especially when it is not considered to be a true indication of the person's or thing's real nature **2. SURROUNDINGS** sb or sth's circumstances or environment [Late 16thC. Partly formed from French *externe* and partly from Latin *externus*, both ultimately from *exter* 'outward, on the outside'.] —**externally** *adv.*

external-combustion engine *n.* an engine that converts into power heat generated from fuel consumed outside the engine. A steam engine is a type of external-combustion engine. ◊ **internal-combustion engine**

external degree *n.* a degree for which the candidate does not follow a formal course of study within a university, but sits the required examinations to gain the qualification

external ear *n.* the outside part of the ear, consisting of the auricle and auditory canal

external examination *n.* an examination set and marked by an authority outside a candidate's own school, college, or university —**external examiner** *n.*

externalism /ik stúrn'lizəm/ *n.* **1. EXCESSIVE CONCERN ABOUT OUTWARD APPEARANCES** excessive concern about outward forms and appearances, especially in religious matters **2.** PHILOSOPHY **VIEW THAT THOUGHTS DEPEND ON EXTERNALS** the view that the content of thoughts depends at least partly on relationships with objects outside the mind —**externalist** *n.*

externality /ékstur nálləti/ (*plural* **-ties**) *n.* **1. QUALITY OF BEING EXTERNAL** the fact or quality of being external **2. STH OUTSIDE OR EXTERNAL** an outward form or appearance, or anything that is outside or external to sb or sth **3.** ECON **CONSEQUENCE OF PRODUCTION IGNORED IN PRICING** a factor, e.g. environmental damage, that results from the way sth is produced but is not taken into account in establishing the market price of the goods or materials concerned **4.** PHILOSOPHY **EXISTENCE INDEPENDENT OF THE MIND** the quality sth has of existing independently of the mind that perceives it

externalize /ik stúrnə līz/ (**-izes, -izing, -ized**), **externalise** (**-ises, -ising, -ised**) *vt.* **1. GIVE OUTWARD EXPRESSION TO STH** to express ideas or feelings in some visible or perceptible way in order to communicate them to others **2. PERCEIVE STH AS EXTERNAL** to attribute sth to causes in the outside world **3.** PSYCHOL **ATTRIBUTE FEELINGS TO OUTSIDE CAUSES** to attribute emotions or inner conflicts to outside causes, sources, or surroundings —**externalization** /ik stúrnə lī záysh'n/ *n.*

external respiration *n.* the exchange of gases between an organism's respiratory system, e.g. the lungs in vertebrates, and the outside environment

externe /ék sturn/ *n.* = **extern**

exteroceptor /ékstərō septər/ *n.* a body part or sensory organ such as the eye, ear, or any of the nerve endings in the skin that is able to receive outside stimuli [Early 20thC. Coined from Latin *exter* (see EXTERNAL) + RECEPTOR.] —**exteroceptive** *adj.*

exterritorial *adj.* = **extraterritorial**

extinct /ik stíngkt/ *adj.* **1.** BIOL **HAVING NO LIVING MEMBERS** having no members of the species or family in existence, as is the case with many organisms known only from fossils **2. NO LONGER IN EXISTENCE** having died out or ceased to exist ○ *relics of extinct and forgotten civilizations* **3.** GEOL **NO LONGER ERUPTING** no longer active or likely to erupt ○ *an extinct volcano* **4.** SOC SCI, LAW **NOT NOW VALID** no longer valid or practised ○ *This custom has for many years been almost extinct.* **5. EXTINGUISHED** extinguished, quenched, or no longer burning [15thC. From Latin *exstinctus*, the past participle of *exstinguere* (see EXTINGUISH).]

WORD KEY: SYNONYMS

See Synonyms at ***dead***.

extinction /ik stíngksh'n/ *n.* **1.** BIOL **THE FACT OF BECOMING EXTINCT** the death or ceasing to exist of all members of a species or family of organisms **2. OBSOLESCENCE** the process or fact of disappearing completely from use ○ *'Dominant languages and dialects spread widely, and lead to the gradual extinction of other tongues'.* (Charles Darwin, *The Descent of Man*; 1871) **3.** GEOL **PROCESS OF BECOMING INACTIVE** the permanent ceasing of eruptions in a volcano **4.** SOC SCI, LAW **BEING NO LONGER USED** the state of no longer being valid or practised, or the process of ceasing to be valid or practised **5. DESTRUCTION** the destruction or killing off of sb or sth ○ *the extinction of self and ego through meditation* **6.** PHYS, ASTRON **LOWERING OF RADIATION INTENSITY** reduction of radiation intensity because of absorption or scattering as it passes through matter. This effect is observed in the reduction in the intensity of electromagnetic radiation reaching Earth from celestial bodies because of the interference of interstellar gas and dust. **7.** PSYCHOL **REDUCTION IN RESPONSE** the decreasing or dying out of a behavioural response created by conditioning because of lack of reinforcement —**extinctive** *adj.*

extinguish /ik stíng gwish/ (**-guishes, -guishing, -guished**) *vt.* **1. PUT OUT A FIRE OR LIGHT** to put out sth that is burning or giving off light ○ *The lamps along the terrace had not been extinguished.* **2. END STH** to take away or bring to an end sth such as a hope, feeling, custom, or practice ○ *As the days went by, hope for more survivors was extinguished.* **3. DESTROY SB OR STH** to kill or destroy sb or sth completely (*literary*) ○ *They came with a large army in order to be certain of extinguishing the enemy by force of numbers.* **4. OUTSHINE** to outshine or eclipse sth or sb by having greater brilliance ○ *Beauty that extinguishes all others by comparison.* **5.** LAW **PAY DEBT** to pay off a debt **6.** LAW **MAKE STH INVALID** to make sth no longer valid or applicable **7.** PSYCHOL **DECREASE RESPONSE** to cause a decrease in a conditioned response through lack of reinforcement [Early 16thC. Formed from Latin *exstinguere*, literally 'to quench completely', from *stinguere* 'to quench, prick' (source of English *distinguish* and *instinct*).] —**extinguishable** *adj.* —**extinguishment** *n.*

extinguisher /ik stíng gwishər/ *n.* **1.** = **fire extinguisher 2. STH THAT ENDS OR REMOVES STH** sb or sth that puts an end to sth else or eliminates its effects

extirpate /ék stur payt/ (**-pates, -pating, -pated**) *vt.* **1. COMPLETELY REMOVE STH UNDESIRABLE** to completely get rid of, kill off, or destroy sth or sb considered undesirable (*formal*) **2.** SURG **REMOVE BY SURGERY** to remove sth surgically [Mid-16thC. From Latin *exstirpat-*, the past participle stem of *exstirpare*, literally 'to root out', from *stirps* 'stem, root', of unknown origin.] —**extirpation** /ék stur páysh'n/ *n.* —**extirpative** /éks tur paytiv/ *adj.* —**extirpator** /ék stur paytər/ *n.*

extn *abbr.* extension

extol /ik stṓl/ (**-tols, -tolling, -tolled**) *vt.* to praise sb or sth with great enthusiasm and admiration (*formal or literary*) [Early 16thC. From Latin *extollere*, literally 'to raise up', from *tollere* 'to raise'. Ultimately from an Indo-European word that also produced English *elate* and *toll*.] —**extoller** *n.* —**extolment** *n.*

extort /ik stáwrt/ (**-torts, -torting, -torted**) *vt.* to obtain sth such as money or information, from sb by using force, threats, or other unacceptable methods ○ *I wouldn't want to speculate about what means were used to extort the confessions.* [15thC. From Latin *extort-*, the past participle stem of *extorquere*, literally 'to twist out', from *torquere* 'to twist' (see TORQUE[1]).] —**extorter** *n.* —**extortive** *adj.*

extortion /ik stáwrsh'n/ *n.* **1.** LAW **OBTAINING STH BY ILLEGAL THREATS** the crime of obtaining sth such as money from sb using illegal methods of persuasion **2. EXCESSIVE CHARGING** the charging of an excessive amount of money for sth (*informal*) **3. GETTING STH BY FORCE** the acquiring of anything through the use of force or threats —**extortionary** *adj.* —**extortioner** *n.* —**extortionist** *n.*

extortionate /ik stáwrsh'nət/ *adj.* **1. EXCESSIVE** highly excessive, especially in price **2. INVOLVING EXTORTION** involving or using extortion —**extortionately** *adv.*

extra /ékstrə/ *adj.* **1. MORE THAN USUAL** added to, or over and above, the usual, original, or necessary amount ○ *Take extra precautions when travelling in bad weather.* **2. MORE AND BETTER** greater in degree and of better quality than is normal **3. CHARGED FOR IN ADDITION** charged for in addition to the basic cost ○ *You get one free drink with the meal; further drinks are extra.* ■ *adv.* **EXCEPTIONALLY** to a greater extent than is usual or expected ○ *Be extra careful at that crossing.* ■ *pron.* **MORE** more than the usual amount or price ○ *The hotel charges extra for satellite television.* ■ *n.* **1. STH ADDITIONAL** sth additional or unexpected ○ *The books at the end of the list are optional extras that you can read if you have time.* **2. STH CHARGED IN ADDITION** sth for which an additional charge is made, or the additional charge itself ○ *This is the guaranteed full price and there are no hidden extras.* **3.** CINEMA **NONSPEAKING FILM ACTOR** sb employed in a minor, usually nonspeaking, part in a film, e.g. in a crowd scene **4.** PRESS **SPECIAL EDITION OF A NEWSPAPER** a special edition of a newspaper or magazine, often reporting later news or concentrating on a particular subject ○ *a sports extra* **5. RUN SCORED WITHOUT BAT** a run added to a team's score but not credited to an individual batsman, e.g. as a result of the bowler bowling a no-ball or a wide [Mid-17thC. Origin uncertain: probably shortening of EXTRAORDINARY, whose prefix comes from Latin *extra* (see EXTRA-).]

extra-, **extro-** *prefix.* beyond or outside sth ○ *extraterrestrial* ○ *extracurricular* [From Latin *extra* 'outside, beyond', from *exter* 'outer' (source of English *exterior*)]

extracellular /ékstrə séllyōōlər/ *adj.* situated or happening outside a cell or cells —**extracellularly** *adv.*

extrachromosomal /ékstrə krṓmə sṓm'l/ *adj.* used to describe an inheritance of characteristics that is controlled by factors that are not carried on chromosomes

extracorporeal /ékstrə kawr páwri əl/ *adj.* situated or happening outside the body —**extracorporeally** *adv.*

extra cover *n.* **1.** CRICKET **FIELDING POSITION** a fielding position that lies between (**cover**) and (**mid-off**) **2. FIELDER** a player fielding in the position of extra cover

extracranial /ékstrə kráyni əl/ *adj.* situated or happening outside the skull

extract /ik strákt/ *vt.* (**-tracts, -tracting, -tracted**) **1. PULL STH OUT** to pull sth out, often using force ○ *have a tooth extracted* **2. OBTAIN STH FROM SOURCE** to obtain sth from a source, usually by separating it out from other material ○ *a few snippets of information that I managed to extract from the conversation* **3. GET STH BY FORCE** to obtain sth from sb who is unwilling to give it, often by using force or threats ○ *After a lengthy interrogation the police extracted a confession from him.* **4. COPY STH OUT FROM STH** to copy or remove a passage from a text ○ *This passage is extracted from the author's memoirs.* **5. DERIVE PLEASURE FROM** to obtain pleasure or enjoyment from sth **6.** CHEM, INDUST **TAKE STH OUT OF COMPOUND** to obtain a substance from a compound, in solid, liquid, or gas form, by using an industrial or chemical process **7.** MATH **FIND THE ROOT OF NUMBER** to calculate the value of the root, e.g. the square root or cube root, of a number ■ *n.* **1. PASSAGE** a passage taken from a publication, film, or play ○ *The novelist read a few extracts from her forthcoming book.* **2.** CHEM, INDUST **STH SEPARATED FROM A COMPOUND** a substance obtained from a compound by an industrial or chemical process ○ *mineral extracts* **3. PURIFIED SUBSTANCE** a concentrated or purified substance obtained by first using a solvent to dissolve this substance when present in a mixture and then evaporating the solvent ○ *vanilla extract* **4. CONCENTRATED SOLUTION** a preparation, usually in alcohol, containing the pharmaceutically active components of a natural product such as a plant [15thC. From Latin *extract-*, the past participle stem of *extrahere* 'to pull out', from *trahere* 'to pull'.] —**extractable** *adj.*

extraction /ik stráksh'n/ *n.* **1. TAKING OUT OF STH** the process of extracting sth or of being extracted, or a thing that has been extracted **2. REMOVAL OF A TOOTH** the removal of a tooth or teeth **3. SEPARATION OF SUBSTANCES** the separation of a substance from a mixture by dissolving one or more of the components in a solvent

extractive /ik stráktiv/ *adj.* **1. EXTRACTABLE** capable of being extracted **2. USED IN AN EXTRACTION PROCESS** used in the process of extraction **3. OBTAINED BY EXTRACTION** obtained as a result of extraction ■ *n.* **1. STH EXTRACTABLE** sth that can be extracted **2.** CHEM **PART OF A CHEMICAL EXTRACT** the insoluble part of a chemical extract —**extractively** *adv.*

extractor /ik stráktər/ *n.* **1. SB OR STH THAT EXTRACTS** sb who or sth that extracts sth **2. DEVICE FOR TAKING OUT LIQUID** a device that removes a liquid from a solid, e.g. the juice out of a fruit **3.** = **extractor fan 4.** ARMS **PART OF GUN** a part of a firearm that removes spent cartridges from the chamber

extractor fan *n.* an electric fan, often set into a window, used to remove steam, fumes, or stale air from a room or building

extracurricular /ékstrə kə ríkyōōlər/ *adj.* **1.** EDUC **OUTSIDE CURRICULUM** done or happening outside the normal curriculum of a school, college, or university **2. OUTSIDE NORMAL DUTIES** not part of the normal duties of a job or profession **3. WITH SB OTHER THAN A PARTNER** involving sb other than a spouse or partner (*informal*)

extraditable /ékstrə dītəb'l/ *adj.* **1. WITHIN THE TERMS OF AN EXTRADITION AGREEMENT** used to describe a crime for which sb may be extradited, or a person who has committed such a crime **2. ABLE TO BE EXTRADITED** able to be extradited

extradite /ékstrə dīt/ (**-dites, -diting, -dited**) *vt.* to return sb accused of a crime by a different legal authority to that authority for trial or punishment [Mid-19thC. Back-formation from EXTRADITION, probably on the model of *expedition* and *expedite*.]

extradition /ékstrə dísh'n/ *n.* the handing over by a government of sb accused of a crime in a different country for trial or punishment there [Mid-19thC. From French, formed from Latin *ex-* 'out' + the stem *tradition-* 'deliverance' (see TRADITION).]

extrados /ek stráy doss/ (*plural* **-dos** *or* **-doses**) *n.* the outer curve of an arch [Late 18thC. From French, formed from Latin *extra* 'outside' + French *dos* 'back'.]

extragalactic /ékstrəgə láktik/ *adj.* existing, originating, or happening outside the Milky Way, the galaxy that contains the solar system

extrajudicial /ékstrə joo dísh'l/ *adj.* **1.** OUTSIDE NORMAL LEGAL PROCEEDINGS happening or originating outside the normal course of legal proceedings **2.** OUTSIDE A COURT'S JURISDICTION outside the jurisdiction of a court —**extrajudicially** *adv.*

extralegal /ékstrə leeg'l/ *adj.* not permitted by or subject to the law —**extralegally** *adv.*

extralimital /ékstrə límmit'l/ *adj.* used to describe a species or group of organisms found outside a given area, e.g. a population of lions outside a national park

extramarital /ékstrə márrit'l/ *adj.* involving sexual relations with sb other than a marriage partner

extramundane /ékstrə mun dáyn/ *adj.* not belonging to the physical world [Mid-17thC. From late Latin *extramundanus*, from *extra mundum* 'outside the world or universe'.]

extramural /ékstrə myóorəl/ *adj.* **1.** EDUC OUTSIDE USUAL STUDY COURSES outside or additional to the usual courses of study at a university, college, or other educational institution, though usually connected with them **2.** OUTSIDE WALLS outside the walls or boundaries of sth, e.g. a castle, town, or organization [Mid-19thC. Formed from Latin *extra muros* 'outside the walls'.]

extraneous /ik stráyni əss/ *adj.* **1.** NOT RELEVANT not relevant or applicable **2.** NOT ESSENTIAL not essential or important **3.** COMING FROM OUTSIDE existing or coming from outside [Mid-17thC. Formed from Latin *extraneus* 'foreign, strange' (source of English *strange*), from *extra* 'outside' (see EXTRA-).] —**extraneously** *adv.* —**extraneousness** *n.*

extranet /ékstrə net/ *n.* an extension of the intranet of a company or organization. An extranet gives authorized outsiders, e.g. customers, suppliers, or business partners, controlled access to parts of the intranet.

extranuclear /ékstrə nyóokli ər/ *adj.* **1.** BIOL OUTSIDE CELL NUCLEUS existing in or affecting parts of a cell outside the nucleus **2.** PHYS OUTSIDE ATOM NUCLEUS existing, happening, or originating outside the nucleus of an atom

extraordinaire /ik stráwdi náir/ *adj.* excellent or outstanding ○ *a piano player extraordinaire* [Mid-20thC. Via French from Latin *extraordinarius* (see EXTRAORDINARY).]

extraordinary /ik stráwrd'nəri, ékstrə áwrd'nəri/ *adj.* **1.** VERY UNUSUAL very unusual and deserving attention and comment because of being wonderful, excellent, strange, or shocking ○ *For a ten-year-old, her mathematical abilities are quite extraordinary.* **2.** ADDITIONAL additional and having a special purpose ○ *an extraordinary general meeting* **3.** EMPLOYED FOR SPECIAL PURPOSE employed for a special purpose or to do additional work ○ *ambassador extraordinary* **4.** ADDITIONAL AND GREATER additional to and going beyond the scope of sth in ordinary or established use ○ *Extraordinary measures are necessary in these highly unusual circumstances.* [15thC. From Latin *extraordinarius*, from *extra ordinem* 'out of order, exceptionally'.] —**extraordinarily** *adv.* —**extraordinariness** *n.*

extra point *n.* FOOTBALL in US football, a point scored by kicking the field goal awarded after a touchdown

extrapolate /ik stráppə layt/ (**-lates, -lating, -lated**) *v.* **1.** *vti.* INFER to use known facts as the starting point from which to draw inferences or draw conclusions about sth unknown ○ *If we extrapolate from the data, we can come up with a reasonable prediction.* **2.** *vt.* MATH ESTIMATE A VALUE to estimate a value that falls outside a range of known values, e.g. by extending a curve on a graph [Mid-19thC. Coined from EXTRA- + INTERPOLATE. In early use, it denoted the insertion of intermediate terms in a mathematical series.] —**extrapolation** /ik stráppə láysh'n/ *n.* —**extrapolative** /ik stráppələtiv/ *adj.* —**extrapolator** /-laytər/ *n.*

extrasensory /ékstrə sénssəri/ *adj.* relating to or involving powers of perception other than the normal five senses

extrasensory perception *n.* the apparent ability of some people to become aware of things by means other than the normal senses, e.g. through clairvoyance or telepathy

extraterrestrial /ékstrətə réstri əl/ *adj.* OUTSIDE THE EARTH existing or coming from somewhere outside the Earth and its atmosphere ■ *n.* ALIEN a supposed living creature that comes from outside the Earth

extraterritorial /ékstrə térri táwri əl/, **exterritorial** /éks térri-/ *adj.* **1.** POL OUTSIDE TERRITORIAL BOUNDARY situated or coming from outside a country's territorial boundary **2.** INTERNAT LAW RELATING TO EXTRATERRITORIALITY relating to or involving exemption from the legal jurisdiction of a country of residence —**extraterritorially** *adv.*

extraterritoriality /ékstrə térri táwri álləti/ *n.* exemption from the legal jurisdiction of a country of residence, as granted e.g. to foreign diplomats

extra time *n.* an additional fixed period played at the end of a match if the scores are equal at full time and a decisive result is needed. US term **overtime** *n.* 3

extrauterine /ékstrə yóotə rīn, -rin/ *adj.* occurring or situated outside the womb ○ *extrauterine pregnancy*

extravagance /ik strávvəgənss/, **extravagancy** /-gənssi/ (*plural* **-cies**) *n.* **1.** WASTEFUL SPENDING excessive or wasteful spending of money ○ *condemned to poverty by their father's extravagance* **2.** EXPENSIVE THING sth that is expensive or wasteful ○ *A car like that is an extravagance in today's economic climate.* **3.** EXTRAVAGANT NATURE the exaggerated, excessive, or extremely flamboyant nature of sth, e.g. a wild unreasonableness in sb's speech or behaviour

extravagant /ik strávvəgənt/ *adj.* **1.** SPENDING TOO MUCH characterized by spending excessively or wastefully ○ *I think it's extravagant to spend £250 on a shirt.* **2.** BEYOND WHAT IS REASONABLE exaggerated or unreasonable ○ *The scientific community has dismissed these claims as wildly extravagant.* **3.** UNREASONABLY HIGH IN PRICE unreasonably high in price or cost ○ *can't afford their extravagant asking price* **4.** FLAMBOYANT profusely or exaggeratedly decorated, decorative, or showy ○ *hair dyed pink and done in the most extravagant coiffure* **5.** ABUNDANT extremely abundant ○ *The fire produced extravagant quantities of smoke and very little heat.* [14thC. From medieval Latin, from Latin *extra* 'outside' + *vagari* 'to wander' (source of English *vagabond* and *vagrant*). An early meaning is 'uncodified', referring to papal decrees.] —**extravagantly** *adv.* —**extravagantness** *n.*

extravaganza /ik strávvə gánzə/ *n.* **1.** LAVISH ENTERTAINMENT a lavish and spectacular entertainment **2.** SPECTACULAR DISPLAY any spectacular or fanciful display [Mid-18thC. From Italian *estravaganza* 'peculiar behaviour', from *estravagante* 'extravagant'. The English spelling with 'x' was influenced by *extravagance*.]

extravasate /ik strávvə sayt/ (**-sates, -sating, -sated**) *vti.* to leak, or cause blood or other fluid to leak, from a vessel into the surrounding tissue, following injury, burns, or inflammation [Mid-17thC. Coined from EXTRA- + Latin *vas* 'vessel' + -ATE.] —**extravasation** /ik strávvə sáysh'n/ *n.*

extravascular /ékstrə váskyoolər/ *adj.* not contained in the body's blood vessels or lymph vessels

extravehicular activity /ékstrə vi híkyoolər-/ *n.* an activity undertaken by an astronaut outside the spacecraft during a mission, e.g. a repair to the craft, or an experiment on the surface of the Moon

extraversion *n.* = **extroversion**

extravert *n., adj.* = **extrovert**

extra virgin olive oil *n.* the highest quality of olive oil, made from the first cold pressing of ripe olives

extreme /ik streem/ *adj.* **1.** HIGH IN DEGREE OR INTENSITY highest in intensity or degree ○ *will withstand extreme pressure* **2.** NOT REASONABLE going far beyond what is reasonable or normal ○ *an extreme reaction* **3.** FARTHEST OUT farthest out, especially from the centre ○ *They live in the extreme north of the country.* **4.** SEVERE very strict or severe ○ *A government must take extreme measures during wartime.* **5.** LEISURE SENSATION-SEEKING denoting an activity in which participants actively seek out dangerous or even life-threatening experiences ■ *n.* **1.** FURTHEST LIMIT the furthest limit or highest degree of sth ○ *the extreme of bad taste* **2.** END OF SCALE sth or sb that represents either of the two ends of a scale or range, e.g. the highest or lowest degree of sth, or a quality and its polar opposite ○ *Between these two extremes there must be a middle way.* **3.** MATH FIRST OR LAST TERM the first or last term in a mathematical proportion or series ■ **extremes** *npl.* DRASTIC MEASURES drastic or unreasonable measures ○ *The authorities have been driven to extremes by the widespread popular unrest.* [15thC. Via French *extrême* from Latin *extremus* 'farthest, last', literally 'most out', a superlative form of *ex* 'out'.] —**extremeness** *n.*

extremely /ik streemli/ *adv.* to a very high degree ○ *She plays the violin extremely well.*

extremely high frequency *n.* a radio frequency in the range between 30,000 and 300,000 megahertz

extremely low frequency *n.* a radio frequency below 30 hertz

extreme unction *n.* the sacrament of anointing the sick in the Roman Catholic Church (*dated*)

extremist /ik streemist/ *n.* SB WITH EXTREME OPINIONS sb who holds extreme or radical political or religious beliefs ■ *adj.* BEYOND THE MODERATE involving, typical of, or motivated by extreme opinions, especially in politics or religion

extremity /ik strémməti/ *n.* (*plural* **-ties**) **1.** FARTHEST POINT a point that is the farthest out, especially from the centre ○ *the southernmost extremity of the continent* **2.** HIGHEST DEGREE the highest degree or greatest intensity of sth ○ *in the extremity of her grief* **3.** DANGER a situation of great danger or distress ○ *They prayed for help in their extremity.* **4.** LIMB a limb of a person or animal, or the part of a limb that is farthest from the body, especially sb's hand or foot ○ *Frostbite attacks the extremities first.* **5.** STATE OF BEING EXTREME the state of being extreme, especially extremely dangerous or severe ○ *You don't seem to understand the extremity of the situation.* ■ **extremities** *npl.* DRASTIC MEASURES drastic or unreasonable measures (*formal*) ○ *There was no need for such extremities.*

extricate /ékstri kayt/ (**-cates, -cating, -cated**) *vt.* to release sb or sth with difficulty from a physical constraint or an unpleasant or complicated situation ○ *It took an hour to extricate the vehicle from the mud.* ○ *He hoped their intervention might extricate him from his embarrassing predicament.* [Early 17thC. From Latin *extricat-*, past participle stem of *extricare*, literally 'to remove from perplexities', from *tricae* (plural) 'perplexities'.] —**extricable** /ik strikəb'l, ékstrik-/ *adj.* —**extrication** /ékstri káysh'n/ *n.*

extrinsic /ek strínssik, -zik/ *adj.* **1.** INESSENTIAL that is not an essential part of sth ○ *It's a good point, but extrinsic to the argument.* **2.** COMING FROM OUTSIDE coming or operating from outside sth ○ *the importance of extrinsic influences on a nation's literature* [Mid-16thC. From late Latin *extrinsecus* 'outer', from Latin *exter* 'external' + adverb-forming ending *-im* + *secus* 'alongside of'.] —**extrinsically** *adv.*

extro- *prefix.* = **extra-** [Alteration of EXTRA-, on the model of its antonym *intro-*]

extrorse /ik stráwrss/, **extrorsal** /ik stráwrss'l/ *adj.* facing or turning outwards or away from a centre [Mid-19thC. From late Latin *extrorsus* 'in an outward direction', from Latin *extra* 'outside' + *versus* 'towards', past participle of *vertere* 'to turn'.]

extroversion /ékstrə vúrsh'n/, **extraversion** *n.* **1.** PSYCHOL INTEREST IN THINGS OUTSIDE THE SELF interest in and involvement with people and things outside the self **2.** MED TURNING INSIDE OUT the turning inside out of an organ or other body part, especially the womb [Mid-17thC. Coined from EXTRO- + the Latin stem *version* 'turning', from *vertere* 'to turn'.] —**extroversive** *adj.* —**extroversively** *adv.*

extrovert /ékstrə vurt/, **extravert** *n.* **1.** OUTGOING PERSON sb who is sociable, self-confident, and uninhibited when with other people **2.** SB WITH INTEREST OUTSIDE SELF sb who goes beyond self-interest and is involved with other people and things ■ *adj.* **1. OUTGOING** typical of a sociable or outgoing person **2. TYPICAL OF SB WITH OUTWARD INTEREST** characteristic of sb who is interested in and involved with people and things outside the self [Early 20thC. Coined from EXTRO- + Latin *vertere* 'to turn'.] —**extroverted** *adj.*

───── **WORD KEY: USAGE** ─────
Spelling trap The original spelling is **extravert**, which is still more common in American usage. In British English, however, the form **extrovert**, influenced by *intro-vert*, is now standard.

extrude /ik strood/ (**-trudes, -truding, -truded**) *v.* **1.** *vt.* **FORCE STH OUT** to force or squeeze sth out **2.** *vt.* **INDUST MAKE BY FORCING THROUGH MOULD** to make sth by forcing a semi-soft material such as plastic or molten metal through a specially shaped mould or nozzle **3.** *vi.* = **protrude** [Mid-16thC. From Latin *extrudere* , literally 'to thrust out', from *trudere* 'to thrust'.]

extrusion /ik stroozh'n/ *n.* **1.** **INDUST STH FORMED BY BEING EXTRUDED** sth formed by forcing semi-soft material through a specially shaped mould or nozzle **2.** **INDUST PROCESS OF EXTRUDING** the process or an instance of making sth by forcing semi-soft material through a specially shaped mould or nozzle **3.** **GEOL IGNEOUS ROCK** an igneous rock formed by the emission of molten material (**magma**) through cracks in the earth's surface where it forms a lava flow **4.** **GEOL MOVEMENT OF MOLTEN ROCK** the movement of molten material (**magma**) from a volcano or through cracks in the earth's surface to form solidified igneous rock [Mid-16thC. From the medieval Latin stem *extrusion-*, from Latin *extrudere* (see EXTRUDE).]

extrusive /ik stroossiv/ *adj.* used to describe rock formed from molten material (**magma**) that has flowed out of cracks in the Earth's surface

exuberant /ig zyoob'rənt/ *adj.* **1. FULL OF ENTHUSIASM** full of happy high spirits and vitality **2. ABUNDANT** growing in great abundance or profusion **3. LAVISH** lavish or elaborate, often to the point of being excessive [15thC. Via French from Latin *exuberant-*, the present participle stem of *exuberare* 'to be very fruitful', from *uberare* 'to be fruitful', from *uber* 'fertile'.] —**ex-uberance** *n.* —**exuberantly** *adv.*

exudate /éksyoo dayt, égz-/ *n.* a substance such as sweat or a cellular waste product that is exuded from a cell or organ

exudation /éksyoo dáysh'n, égz-/ *n.* **1. RELEASE THROUGH PORES OR CUT** the release of a substance through pores or a surface cut, e.g. the release of sweat from the body or resin from a tree **2.** = **exudate** —**exudative** /éksyoo daytiv, égz-/ *adj.*

exude /ig zyood/ (**-udes, -uding, -uded**) *v.* **1.** *vt.* **SHOW A PARTICULAR QUALITY CLEARLY** to communicate a particular quality or feeling in abundance and very clearly, usually through general behaviour and body language ○ *a voice that exuded confidence* **2.** *vti.* **RELEASE SLOWLY** to release sth such as a liquid or an odour slowly from a gland, pore, membrane, or cut, or ooze out slowly [Late 16thC. From Latin *exudare, exsudare*, literally 'to ooze out like sweat', from *sudare* 'to sweat'.]

exult /ig zúlt/ (**-ults, -ulting, -ulted**) *vi.* **1. BE VERY HAPPY** to be extremely happy or joyful about sth ○ *exulted in his new-found freedom* **2. BE TRIUMPHANT** to be very happy or triumphant about sth unpleasant that happens to sb else ○ *The victors exulted over their enemies' annihilation.* [Late 16thC. Via French *exulter* from Latin *exsultare*, literally 'to keep leaping up', from *exsalire*, literally 'to leap out', from *salire* 'to leap' (source of English *salient*).] —**exultance** *n.* —**exultingly** *adv.*

exultant /ig zúltənt/ *adj.* extremely happy, joyful, or triumphant ○ *an exultant roar from the crowd* —**exultantly** *adv.*

exultation /ég zul táysh'n, ék sul-/ *n.* a feeling or the expression of great happiness, triumph, or joy ○ *jumping in exultation at the news*

exurb /éks urb/ *n.* *US* a prosperous residential area outside a city, beyond the suburbs [Mid-20thC. Back-formation from EXURBAN (from Latin *ex* 'out of' + *urbs* 'city') on the model of *suburb*.] —**exurban** /eks úrbən/ *adj.* —**exurbanite** /ek súrbənīt/ *n.*

exurbia /eks úrbi ə/ *n.* *US* the prosperous residential area beyond the suburbs of a city [Mid-20thC. Coined from EX- + *-urbia*, on the model of *suburbia*.]

exuviae /ig zyoóvi ee/ *npl.* a skin, shell, or other body covering cast off by an animal [Mid-17thC. From Latin, 'things cast off', formed from *exuere* 'to divest oneself of'.] —**exuvial** *adj.*

ex works *adv., adj.* excluding any costs incurred after an item leaves the factory, such as delivery charges and retailer's profit (*hyphenated when used before a noun*) ○ *I know where I can buy one ex works.* ○ *They quoted me an ex-works price.*

-ey *suffix.* = **-y** [Variant]

eyas /í əss/ *n.* a young hawk or falcon, especially one bred for falconry [15thC. Alteration of obsolete *nias*, from French *niais* 'bird taken from the nest', from Latin *nidus* 'nest'. Initial 'n' lost by misdivision ('an ias'), as in ADDER.]

AKG London

Jan van Eyck: Portrait engraving by Joachim von Sandrart

Eyck /īk/**, Jan van** (1390?–1441) Flemish painter. He painted in vivid oil colours in a naturalistic style and is regarded as the greatest Flemish artist of the 15th century.

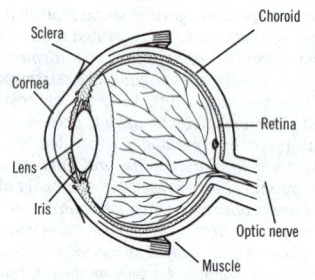

Cross-section of a human eye

eye /í/ *n.* **1.** **ANAT ORGAN OF VISION** the organ of sight or light sensitivity in vertebrates, usually occurring in pairs. The eye is an approximately spherical organ with light-sensitive rod and cone cells in the retina, which is responsible for converting light into impulses that are transmitted to the brain for interpretation. **2.** **VISIBLE AREA OF THE EYE** the externally visible part of the eye, and the area of face around it, including the orbit, eyelid, and eyelashes **3.** **POWER OF SIGHT** the ability to see (*often used in the plural*) ○ *If my eyes get any worse I'll have to wear glasses.* **4.** **ATTENTION** sb's attention or gaze ○ *He took his eye off the prisoners at the wrong moment.* **5.** **EXPRESSION** a look, or the facial expression of a person looking ○ *She looked me over with a cold eye.* **6.** **APPRECIATION OF STH** an ability to recognize and appreciate sth ○ *He's got a good eye for spotting a talent.* **7.** **OPINION** a point of view or way of thinking ○ *He can do no wrong in her eyes.* **8.** **ZOOL** = **eyespot** *n.* 2 **9.** **BOT NEW SHOOT ON POTATO** a dark round patch on a potato tuber, from which a new shoot grows **10.** **SEW HOLE IN NEEDLE** a hole in the top of a needle for passing a thread through **11.** **CLOTHES LOOP PART OF FASTENER** a loop, usually metal, into which a small hook fits, used as a means of fastening two parts of a garment together **12.** **METEOROL CENTRE OF A STORM** a calm area at the centre of a storm ■ *vt.* (**eyes, eyeing** *or* **eying, eyed**) **1.** **LOOK AT STH** to look at sth or sb inquisitively ○ *She quickly eyed the building up and down.* **2.** **OGLE** to give sb a look that signals sexual interest (*informal*) ○ *A man*

was eyeing her from across the room. [Old English *eage*. Ultimately from an Indo-European base that produced the word for 'eye' in all Indo-European languages and is also the ancestor of English *atrocious, inoculate*, and *window*.]

◇ **close** *or* **shut your eyes to sth** to ignore or overlook sth obvious ◇ **cry your eyes out** to cry bitterly ◇ **give sb the (glad) eye** to look at sb in a way that signals sexual interest ◇ **have eyes in the back of your head** to be aware of what is happening when unable to see it (*informal*) (*usually in negative context*) ◇ **keep your eye on the ball 1.** to watch sb or sth closely **2.** to take care of sb or sth, especially for a short time ◇ **turn a blind eye to sth** *ANZ* to take the best parts of sth for yourself ◇ **turn a blind eye to sth** to pretend not to be aware of sth ◇ **with an eye to sth** having sth as a purpose or objective ◇ **with your eyes (wide) open** fully aware of all that is involved in what you are doing

eyeball /í bawl/ *n.* **ROUND MASS OF THE EYE** the round mass of the eye within its bony socket ■ *vt.* (**-balls, -balling, -balled**) **STARE AT SB** to stare at sb or sth intently (*informal*)

eye bank *n.* a place where human corneas taken from people who have recently died are stored for use in corneal transplants

eyebolt /í bōlt/ *n.* a bolt with an eye or ring at the end instead of the usual head, used for pulling, lifting, or fastening

eyebright /í brīt/ *n.* a plant of the snapdragon family with small white and purple flowers, used in the past for treating eye diseases. Genus: *Euphrasia*.

eyebrow /í brow/ *n.* **1.** **HAIR ABOVE EYE SOCKET** the arched line of hair above each eye socket **2.** **BONY RIDGE ABOVE THE EYE** the upper bony ridge of the eye socket. Technical name **supraorbital ridge**

eyebrow pencil *n.* a soft cosmetic pencil used to darken the eyebrows

eye candy *n.* sth visually pleasing but intellectually undemanding (*slang*)

eye-catcher *n.* sb who or sth that tends to attract people's attention

eye-catching *adj.* that attracts people's attention easily

eye chart *n.* a sheet printed with different sizes of letters, used to test eyesight

eye contact *n.* the act of looking directly into the eyes of another person

eyecup /í kup/ *n.* *US* = **eyebath**

eyed /īd/ *adj.* having an eye or eyes, usually of a specified kind (*usually used in combination*) ○ *a sharp-eyed observer* ○ *a wide-eyed stare*

eye dialect *n.* the use of spellings that represent the sound of dialectal or nonstandard forms, e.g. 'enuff' or 'wimmin'

eye drops *npl.* liquid medication for the eyes, usually applied with a dropper

eyeful /í fool/ *n.* **1.** **GOOD LOOK** a long steady look at sth or sb (*informal*) ○ *Get an eyeful of this!* **2. SB OR STH BEAUTIFUL** sb who or sth that is very beautiful, especially an attractive woman (*slang offensive*)

eyeglass /í glaass/ *n.* **1.** **SINGLE LENS FOR CORRECTING VISION** a single framed lens for correcting defective vision, e.g. a monocle **2.** = **eyepiece** ■ **eyeglasses** *npl. US* **GLASSES** a pair of glasses (*formal*)

eyehole /í hōl/ *n.* **1.** = **eyelet** *n.* 1 **2.** = **peephole** *n.* 2

eyehook /í hŏok/ *n.* a hook that is fixed to a ring at the end of a rope or chain

eyelash /í lash/ *n.* **1.** **HAIR AT EDGE OF EYELID** any of the short hairs that grow out of the edge of the eyelid **2.** **ROW OF HAIRS EDGING EYELID** the row of short hairs that grow out of the edge of the eyelid

eyelet /í lət/ *n.* **1.** **HOLE FOR CORD** a small hole, especially in fabric, for a lace or cord to be passed through **2.** **METAL REINFORCEMENT FOR EYELET** a small ring of metal or stiff fabric fixed to an eyelet to strengthen its edges **3.** **ORNAMENTED HOLE IN EMBROIDERY** a small hole with ornamental stitched edges in embroidered fabric **4.** = **peephole** *n.* 2 [14thC. Anglicization of Old French *oillet*, literally 'little eye', from *oil* 'eye', from Latin *oculus*.]

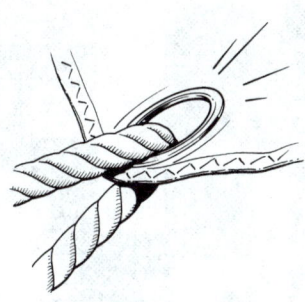

Eyelet

eyelevel /ˈlevv'l/ *adj.* positioned approximately at the same height as a person's eyes ○ *a cooker with an eyelevel grill*

eyelid /ˈlid/ *n.* a protective fold of skin and muscle that can be closed to cover the front of the eyeball ◇ **not bat an eyelid** to show no sign of emotion, especially of surprise

eyelift /ˈlift/ *n.* a surgical operation to improve the appearance of the area around the eyes, e.g. by removing wrinkles

eyeliner /ˈlīnər/ *n.* a cosmetic worn along the edges of the eyelids to emphasize the eyes

eye opener *n.* a surprising or revealing experience or piece of information —**eye-opening** *adj.*

eye patch *n.* a covering worn over one eye to protect it or as concealment

eyepiece /ˈpeess/ *n.* the lens or group of lenses in an optical instrument on the side that the user looks through

eye-popping *adj.* so striking or unusual that eyes widen in amazement (*informal*) ○ *an eye-popping crimson dress* —**eye-popper** *n.*

eye rhyme *n.* the use of rhymes as words that, because they are similarly spelt, look as if they rhyme but are in fact pronounced differently, e.g. 'bough' and 'enough'

eyeshade /ˈshayd/ *n.* a tinted or opaque visor worn round the head above the eyes to protect them from glare

eye shadow *n.* a coloured cosmetic for the area around the eyes, especially the eyelids

eyeshot /ˈshot/ *n.* the range over which the eye can see

eyesight /ˈsīt/ *n.* the power of sight

eye socket *n.* either of the two bony recesses in the skull that contain the eyeballs

eyes-only *adj.* intended to be seen only by the person to whom it is addressed ○ *an eyes-only memo from the chief*

eyesore /ˈsawr/ *n.* an offensively ugly building or place ○ *That old office block is a real eyesore and ought to be pulled down.*

eyespot /ˈspot/ *n.* **1.** BIOL **LIGHT-SENSITIVE PART** a small pigmented area or organelle that is sensitive to light, found in some algae and simple multicellular organisms, including some flatworms, and jellyfish **2.** ZOOL **EYE-SHAPED MARKING** a marking shaped like an eye, e.g. on the wings of some butterflies or on a peacock's tail

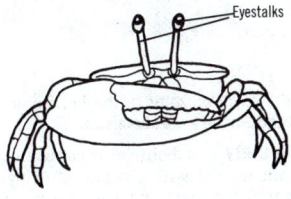

Eyestalks

Eyestalk

eyestalk /ˈstawk/ *n.* a flexible stalk with a compound eye at the tip found in crustaceans and some molluscs

eyestrain /ˈstrayn/ *n.* tiredness or irritation in the eyes caused e.g. by an uncorrected visual defect or by prolonged close work. It is not recognized as a medical condition by ophthalmologists.

Eyetie /ˈīt ī/ *n.* offensive term for an Italian person (*slang offensive*) ■ *adj.* offensive term meaning Italian (*slang offensive*) [Early 20thC. Formed from *Eye-talian*, representing a nonstandard pronunciation of ITALIAN.]

eyetooth /ˈtooth/ (*plural* **-teeth** /-teeth/) *n.* a canine tooth found on each side of the upper jaw [From its being directly below the eye] ◇ **give your eyeteeth for sth** to be prepared to do anything to be able to do or have sth

eyewash /ˈwosh/ *n.* **1.** CLEANSING LIQUID a liquid used to cleanse or soothe the eyes **2.** NONSENSE pretentious nonsense that is intended to flatter or deceive (*informal*) ○ *The official version is just so much eyewash.*

eyewear /ˈwair/ *n.* sth worn over the eyes to protect them or correct sight, e.g. glasses, goggles, or contact lenses

eyewitness /ˈwitnəss, ˈwitnəss/ *n.* sb who sees sth happen and can give evidence about it

eyot *n.* = **ait**

eyra /ˈāirə/ *n.* a jaguarundi in its reddish-brown seasonal colour phase. Latin name: *Felis yagouaroundi*. [Early 17thC. Via Spanish from Tupi-Guarani *(e)irára*.]

Eyre, Lake /air/ the largest salt lake in Australia, located in central South Australia. Area: 9,475 sq. km/3,658 sq. mi.

Eyre, Edward John (1815–1901) British explorer and colonial official. He completed the first overland trip from Sydney to Adelaide and led further expeditions into central and southwestern Australia.

Eyre Peninsula peninsula in southern South Australia that separates the Great Australian Bight from the Spencer Gulf

eyrie /ˈeêri, ˈáiri, ˈīri/ *n.* **1.** EAGLE'S NEST the nest of a bird of prey, especially an eagle, in a high and inaccessible place **2.** HIGH INACCESSIBLE PLACE any high and inaccessible place, often a fortified one **3.** BROOD OF BIRD OF PREY the brood of a bird of prey [15thC. From medieval Latin *aeria*, which probably came via Old French *aire* from Latin *area* 'level ground, garden bed', later 'bird of prey's nest' (source of English *area*). The spelling 'eyrie' was introduced in the 17thC in the mistaken belief that the word was derived from Middle English *eye(e)* 'egg'.]

eyrir /ˈáy reer/ (*plural* **aurar** /ˈó raar/) *n.* **1.** MINOR UNIT OF ICELANDIC CURRENCY a minor unit of currency in Iceland, 100 of which are worth a krona. See table at **currency 2.** COIN WORTH AN EYRIR a coin with a value of one eyrir [Early 20thC. From Icelandic, probably ultimately from Latin *aureus* 'gold coin'.]

Eysenck /ˈzengk/, **H. J.** (1916–97) German-born British psychologist. He was an authority on personality studies and contributed to the controversial area of the links between genetics and intelligence.

Ez. *abbr.* BIBLE Ezra

Ezek. *abbr.* BIBLE Ezekiel

Ezekiel /i zeêki əl/ *n.* **1.** HEBREW PROPHET a Hebrew priest and prophet who lived in the 6th century BC. As the Jews' spiritual leader during the Babylonian captivity, he foretold the creation of a Jewish nation. **2.** BOOK OF BIBLE the book of the Bible that tells the story of the Jews' exile in Babylon in the 6th century BC. It is traditionally attributed to Ezekiel and contains his prophecies of the destruction and subsequent rebuilding of Jerusalem and Judah. See table at **Bible**

e-zine /ˈee zeen/ *n.* a web site with contents and layout modelled on those of a print magazine. Some more ambitious e-zines charge a subscription fee but many are devoted to a specific topic or field and are distributed free to their readership. [From e(lectronic) (maga)zine]

Ezr. *abbr.* BIBLE Ezra

Ezra /ˈézzrə/ *n.* **1.** HEBREW PRIEST a Hebrew high priest who lived in the 5th century BC. He led the Jews back to Jerusalem from their exile in Babylon and founded a Jewish nation. **2.** BOOK OF BIBLE the book of the Bible that tells the story of the rebuilding of the Jewish state in Palestine 536–432 BC after the Babylonian captivity. It is traditionally attributed to the prophet Ezra. See table at **Bible**

Ff

f¹ /ef/ (*plural* **f's**), **F** (*plural* **F's**) *n.* **1. 6TH LETTER OF ENGLISH ALPHABET** the sixth letter of the modern English alphabet **2. SPEECH SOUND CORRESPONDING TO LETTER 'F'** the speech sound that corresponds to the letter 'F' **3. LETTER 'F' WRITTEN** a written representation of the letter 'F'

f² *symbol.* **1. OPTICS** f-number **2. PHYS** focal length **3. PHYS** frequency *n.* 4. **4. MATH** function **5.** femto- **6. CHESS** the sixth vertical row of squares from the left on a chessboard **7. PHYS** force

f³ *abbr.* **1.** Fahrenheit **2.** fluorine **3.** franc **4. MUSIC** forte

F /ef/ (*plural* **Fs** *or* **F's**) *n.* **1. 4TH NOTE OF SCALE IN C** the 4th note of a scale in C major **2. STH THAT PRODUCES F** a string, key, or pipe tuned to produce the note F **3. SCALE BEGINNING ON F** a scale or key that starts on the note F **4. WRITTEN SYMBOL FOR F** a graphic representation of the tone of F

f. *abbr.* **1.** following (page) **2.** folio **3. SPORTS** foul

F. *abbr.* **1.** fathom **2.** February **3.** female **4. GRAM** feminine **5. METALL** fine **6.** folio **7.** Friday

F- *abbr.* fighter (plane)

f/ *symbol.* **PHOTOGRAPHY** f-number

F2F *abbr.* face-to-face (*used in e-mail messages*)

fa *n.* **MUSIC** = **fah**

FA *abbr.* **1.** Football Association **2.** field artillery **3.** financial adviser **4.** freight agent

f.a. *abbr.* fire alarm

faa, f.a.a. *abbr.* **INSUR, SHIPPING** free of all average

FAA *abbr.* **1. US** Federal Aviation Administration **2.** Fleet Air Arm

fab /fab/ *adj.* fabulous (*dated informal*) ○ *It was a fab party!* [Mid-20thC. Shortening.]

Peter Carl Fabergé: Decorative jewelled egg (1901)

AKG London

Fabergé /fábbər zhay/, **Peter Carl** (1846–1920) Russian goldsmith and jeweller. He designed and produced highly decorative gifts, notably gold-and-enamel Easter eggs, for European royalty. Born **Karl Gustavovich Fabergé**

Fabian /fáybi ən/ *adj.* **1. RELATING TO FABIAN SOCIETY** relating to, belonging to, or typical of the Fabian Society **2. CAUTIOUS** cautious, using delay, or avoiding direct confrontation ■ *n.* **MEMBER OF FABIAN SOCIETY** a member of the Fabian Society, or sb who sympathizes with its political principles [Late 16thC. From Latin *Fabianus* 'of Fabius'; from the cautious tactics of the Roman general Quintus Fabius Maximus.]

Fabianism /fáybi ənizəm/ *n.* the beliefs or tactics of the Fabian Society **—Fabianist** *n.*

Fabian Society *n.* a political organization founded in Britain in 1884 with the aim of bringing about socialism by gradual and lawful means rather than by revolution

Fabius Maximus /fáybi əss máksiməss/, **Quintus** (?–203BC) Roman commander and statesman. As a result of his delaying tactics, Rome countered the invasion of Hannibal during the Second Punic War. Full name **Quintus Fabius Maximus Verrucosus**. Known as **Fabius Cunctator (the 'Delayer')**

fable /fáyb'l/ *n.* **1. STORY THAT TEACHES A LESSON** a short story with a moral, especially one in which the characters are animals **2. FALSE ACCOUNT** a false or improbable account of sth ○ *His version of events turned out to be a complete fable.* **3. LEGEND** a story about supernatural, mythological, or legendary characters and events **4. MYTHS AND LEGENDS** myths and legends collectively ○ *a character out of fable* ■ *vt.* (**-bles, -bling, -bled**) **TELL IN FABLE** to tell the story of or describe sth in a fable or similar type of fictional work (*usually passive*) ○ *Cerberus, the three-headed dog fabled to guard the entrance to the underworld* [13thC. Via Old French from Latin *fabula* 'story', from *fari* 'to speak'. Ultimately from an Indo-European base that also produced English *affable*, *fairy*, and *profess*. Originally 'falsehood, pretence'.] **—fabler** *n.*

── WORD KEY: CULTURAL NOTE ──
Fables, a collection of stories attributed to Greek writer Aesop (?6th century BC). Many of the tales feature animals as characters and each one illustrates a specific moral. Traditionally said to be the origin of the literary fable (although earlier examples have been found), they were used by the ancient Greeks for both educational and rhetorical purposes.

fabled /fáyb'ld/ *adj.* **1. LEGENDARY** famous from being described or recounted in legends **2. FICTITIOUS** made-up or fictitious

fabliau /fábbli ō/ (*plural* **-aux** /-ōz/) *n.* a comic and often bawdy story in verse, especially of a kind popular in 12th- and 13th-century France [Early 19thC. From French, from the plural of Old French *fablel*, literally 'little story', from *fable* (see FABLE).]

Fablon /fáb lon/ *tdmk.* a trademark for an adhesive-backed plastic material supplied in sheet form and used especially to cover shelves and other surfaces

Fabre /fábbrə/, **Jean Henri** (1823–1915) French entomologist. Renowned for his close observations, he highlighted the role of inherited instinct in insects.

fabric /fábbrik/ *n.* **1. CLOTH** cloth of any type made from thread or fibres, whether woven, knitted, or felted **2. TEXTURE** the particular texture or quality of a kind of cloth **3. SUBSTANCE** the fundamental structure or make-up of sth ○ *the fabric of her being* **4. BUILDING STRUCTURAL MATERIAL** the material from which sth is constructed, especially a building, or the physical structure of sth ○ *Has there been any damage to the actual fabric of the church?* **5. GEOL ROCK COMPOSITION** the texture of a rock with respect to its macroscopic and microscopic arrangement of minerals and particles [15thC. Via Old French *fabrique* from Latin *fabrica* 'trade, manufactured object, workshop', from *faber* 'worker in metal or stone, artisan'. The meaning '(manufactured) cloth' developed in the late 18thC.]

fabricate /fábbri kayt/ (**-cates, -cating, -cated**) *vt.* **1. INVENT** to make up sth that is not true ○ *The evidence against him has been fabricated.* **2. CONSTRUCT** to make sth from different parts **3. FORGE** to make a fraudulent imitation of a signature or document [15thC. From Latin *fabricat-*, the past participle of *fabricare* 'to make' (source also of English *forge*), from *fabrica* (see FABRIC).] **—fabricator** *n.*

fabrication /fábbri káysh'n/ *n.* **1. UNTRUTH** sth that is not true but has been made up ○ *This story is a mere fabrication.* **2. CONCOCTING LIES** the invention of sth that is not true ○ *engaged in the fabrication of stories to discredit him* **3. ACT OF MAKING** the construction of sth, or sth that has been constructed or made **4. COUNTERFEIT** a fraudulent imitation of a signature or document

── WORD KEY: SYNONYMS ──
See Synonyms at **lie**.

fabulist /fábbyoōlist/ *n.* **1. FABLE WRITER** sb who composes or recites fables **2. LIAR** sb who tells fanciful lies

fabulous /fábbyoōləss/ *adj.* **1. EXCELLENT** extremely good, pleasant, or enjoyable (*informal*) **2. AMAZING** amazingly or almost unbelievably great or wonderful **3. TYPICAL OF A FABLE** existing only in, described in, or typical of myths and legends [15thC. Directly or via French *fabuleux* from Latin *fabulosus* 'celebrated in fable', from *fabula* (see FABLE). The meaning 'extremely good' developed in the mid-20thC.] **—fabulously** *adv.* **—fabulousness** *n.*

fac. *abbr.* **1.** facsimile **2. MATH** factor **3.** factory

Fac. *abbr.* Faculty

façade /fə saád/, **facade** *n.* **1. ARCHIT VISIBLE SURFACE** the face of a building, especially the principal or front face showing its most prominent architectural features **2. DECEPTIVE APPEARANCE** the way sth or sb appears on the surface, especially when that appearance is false or meant to deceive ○ *Her geniality is just a façade.* [Mid-17thC. From French, formed from *face* (source of English *face*) on the model of Italian *facciata*.]

face /fayss/ *n.* **1. FRONT OF HEAD** the front of the human head, where the eyes, nose, mouth, chin, cheeks, and forehead are **2. PERSON** a person being looked at (*informal*) ○ *It's nice to see so many familiar faces here today.* **3. COUNTENANCE** a facial expression or look of a specified kind ○ *Why the long face?* **4. UNPLEASANT FACIAL EXPRESSION** an expression in which the face is distorted, e.g. to show distaste or as a way of being rude to sb ○ *The children made faces at him behind his back.* **5. WAY STH LOOKS** the general or outward appearance of sth ○ *The arrival of the motor car changed the face of the modern city.* **6. FALSE APPEARANCE** an outward appearance that does not show the true nature of sb's feelings or situation or is intended to deceive ○ *Even after a third defeat he was still putting on a brave face.* **7. REPUTATION** personal prestige, or the respect accorded to sb by others ○ *a way of enabling her to back down without losing face* **8. BOLDNESS** impudence or self-assurance (*informal*) ○ *How can he have the face to come back here after what he said?* **9. FACE MAKE-UP** make-up for the face (*informal*) **10. GEOM SURFACE OF OBJECT** a plane surface or side of a three-dimensional object, e.g. a geometric figure, or gem, that is presented towards a particular direction ○ *A cube has six faces.* **11. OUTSIDE OF BUILDING** the exterior of the front or side of a large building ○ *the evening sun shining on the west face*

12. GEOG **SIDE OF CLIFF** the steep exposed side of a cliff **13.** GEOG **SIDE OF MOUNTAIN** any of the steep sides of a mountain, usually specified according to its orientation ○ *the north face of the Eiger* **14.** MINING **WORKING AREA IN A MINE** an area in a mine from which a mineral such as coal is being extracted **15.** PRINTING **TYPEFACE** a typeface, or the area of a printing character that actually prints **16. DIAL ON CLOCK OR INSTRUMENT** the surface of a timepiece or similar instrument that displays the time or other data **17.** CARDS **SIDE OF CARD SHOWING VALUE** the side of a playing card that is marked with numbers and symbols **18. FUNCTIONAL SIDE OF AN IMPLEMENT** the side of sth such as a tool or golf club that is most important in carrying out its function **19.** COINS **SIDE OF COIN** either surface of a coin, especially one with sb's head on it **20. CELEBRITY** a well-known or important person (*informal*) ○ *We get a few faces in the club at the weekend.* ■ *v.* **(faces, facing, faced) 1.** *vti.* **TURN TOWARDS SB OR STH** to be positioned or turn so that the face or front side is directed a particular way or towards sth or sb ○ *The largest bedroom faces south.* **2.** *vt.* **BE LOOKING AT SB OR STH** to be in a position opposite sb or sth ○ *The boys faced each other.* **3.** *vt.* **COME UP AGAINST SB OR STH** to meet or confront sb or sth directly and bravely ○ *Their retreat was cut off and they had no choice but to stand and face the enemy.* **4.** *vt.* **ACCEPT THE FACTS** to accept the reality of a difficult or unpleasant situation ○ *Let's face it, our chances of being on time are slim.* **5.** *vt.* **HAVE TO CONTEND WITH STH** to have to deal with or undergo sth unpleasant or difficult ○ *She was faced with the task of breaking the news to her family.* **6.** *vt.* **BE ENCOUNTERED BY SB** to be met and overcome by sb ○ *the difficulties facing the new administration* **7.** *vt.* **EXPECT STH BAD** to have the prospect of experiencing sth unpleasant, usually within a short period of time ○ *They face ruin if the bank calls in the loan.* **8.** *vt.* **LINE OR DECORATE STH** to line or trim the edge of sth with a contrasting material ○ *The cuffs were faced with velvet.* **9.** *vt.* **SMOOTH** to put a smooth surface on a piece of stone [13thC. Via French (source also of English *façade* and *facet*) from Latin *facies* 'appearance, aspect, form', hence 'face'.] **—faceable** *adj.* ◇ **face to face 1.** in the actual presence of another person **2.** in direct contact with, or having first-hand knowledge of, an unpleasant fact or situation ◇ **fly in the face of** to defy sth deliberately or recklessly ◇ **have a long face** to look miserable or disappointed ◇ **in (the) face of sth** when confronted by or in spite of sth (*slang*) ◇ **not just a pretty face** having more to offer than an attractive appearance ◇ **set your face against sth** to oppose sth with determination ○ *He won't dare show his face at her house again after her brother threw him out.* ◇ **show your face somewhere or at sth** to put in an appearance somewhere

WORD KEY: ORIGIN

The Latin word *facies* from which ***face*** is derived is also the source of English *façade*, *facet*, *superficial*, and *surface*.

face about *vti.* to turn to face the other way, or turn sb or sth to face the other way
face down *vt.* to prevail against sb in a direct confrontation
face off *v.* **1.** *vti.* SPORTS **BEGIN PLAY** to start or restart play in ice hockey, lacrosse, and other sports by dropping the puck or ball between two opposing players **2.** *vi.* **CONFRONT SB** to confront each other, or confront sb (*informal*)
face out *vt.* to endure sth such as criticism or misfortune bravely
face up to *vt.* **1. ACCEPT** to accept having to deal with sth unpleasant **2. CONFRONT** to confront sb or sth bravely

faceache /fáyss ayk/ *n.* used as a way of addressing or referring to sb who is ugly or looks miserable (*slang insult*)

face angle *n.* an angle between two flat surfaces on a polyhedron

face card *n.* US = **court card**

face-centred *adj.* used to describe a crystal lattice with an atom in the centre of each unit cell face as well as at the corners

facecloth /fáyss kloth/ *n.* a small cloth used in washing the face and hands. US term **washcloth**

-faced *suffix.* **1. WITH SO MANY FACES** having a specified number of faces **2. WITH A CERTAIN KIND OF FACE** having a face of a specified kind

facedown /fáyss down/ *n.* a determined confrontation between two adversaries

face flannel *n.* = **facecloth**

faceless /fáyssləss/ *adj.* lacking character or distinction as an individual **—facelessly** *adv.* **—facelessness** *n.*

facelift /fáyss lift/ *n.* **1.** SURG **COSMETIC SURGERY OF THE FACE** a surgical operation in which the skin of the face is pulled back and up to tighten it and remove wrinkles **2. SMARTENING UP** a renovation or refurbishment of sth e.g. an area or a building ○ *The whole dockside area could do with a facelift.*

face mask *n.* **1.** = **face pack 2. COVERING FOR FACE** a covering for the whole head or the face alone, used either to protect or to disguise the face

face-off *n.* **1.** SPORTS **BEGINNING OF PLAY** a start or restart of play in ice hockey, lacrosse, and other sports in which the referee drops the puck or ball between two opposing players **2. CONFRONTATION** a direct conflict

face pack *n.* a cosmetic preparation that cleanses the pores of the face and removes dead layers of skin

faceplate /fáyss playt/ *n.* **1.** ENG **PART OF A LATHE** a perforated metal disc at the end of the spindle or headstock of a lathe for holding a workpiece in place **2. SEE-THROUGH PART OF HEADGEAR** the transparent part of a piece of protective headgear that protects the face while allowing the wearer to see **3. FRONT OF A CATHODE-RAY TUBE** the front of a cathode-ray tube, on which an image is seen

face powder *n.* a flesh-coloured cosmetic powder applied to the face to make it look smoother or less shiny

facer /fáyssər/ *n.* **1. LATHE TOOL** a lathe tool used to smooth a surface **2. STH ASTONISHING** sth that is astonishing or very difficult to deal with (*dated informal*) ○ *This latest development is a facer, and no mistake!*

face-saving *adj.* intended to preserve sb's reputation and dignity ○ *find a face-saving compromise* **—face-saver** *n.*

facet /fássit/ *n.* **1. AN ASPECT OF STH** any one of the several parts or possible aspects of sth **2. FACE OF A GEMSTONE** any of the faces of a cut gemstone **3.** ZOOL, INSECTS **PART OF INSECT EYE** any of the separate lens segments in the compound eye of an insect or other arthropod **4.** ANAT **FLAT AREA** any smooth flat area on a hard surface such as a bone or a tooth ■ *vt.* **(facets, faceting *or* facetting, faceted *or* facetted) CUT FACETS IN STH** to cut facets in sth, especially a precious stone such as a diamond [Early 17thC. From French *facette*, literally 'little face', from *face* (see FACE).]

facetiae /fə séeshi ee/ *npl.* (*literary*) **1. WITTY REMARKS** witty or humorous remarks **2. COARSE BOOKS** coarsely humorous books [Early 16thC. From Latin *facetiae* 'jokes', the plural of *facetia* (see FACETIOUS).]

face time *n.* **1.** US COMPUT **TIME SPENT FACE-TO-FACE** time spent dealing face-to-face with other people (*informal*) ○ *The schedule calls for the weekly e-mail reports as well as some actual face time between team members.* **2. TIME SPENT ON TELEVISION** the amount of time that sb spends appearing on television ○ *We need more face time to sway public opinion on this issue.* **3. EXTRA TIME AT PLACE OF EMPLOYMENT** the amount of time sb spends at his or her place of employment, especially beyond normal working hours ○ *What is she trying to prove with all this face time?*

facetious /fə séeshəss/ *adj.* **1. SUPPOSED TO BE FUNNY** intended to be humorous but often silly or inappropriate **2. NOT IN EARNEST** not to be taken seriously ○ *a facetious suggestion* [Late 16thC. From French *facétieux*, from *facétie* 'joke', from Latin *facetia*, from *facetus* 'graceful, witty'.] **—facetiously** *adv.* **—facetiousness** *n.*

WORD KEY: SYNONYMS

See Synonyms at ***funny***.

face-to-face *adj.*, *adv.* **1. IN EACH OTHER'S PRESENCE** in the physical presence of sb else (*not hyphenated when used after a verb*) **2. HEAD-ON** in direct contact or confrontation ○ *We came face-to-face with the situation.*

face value *n.* **1. STATED VALUE** the value that is stated on sth, especially a note, coin, or stamp **2. SEEMING WORTH** what sth seems to mean or be worth, which may be better than its true worth or meaning ○ *We'd be unwise to accept his promises at face value.*

Facey /fáyssi/, **Albert Barnett** (1894–1982) Australian writer. He is the author of *A Fortunate Life* (1981), his autobiography.

facia *n.* = **fascia**

facial /fáysh'l/ *adj.* **ON THE FACE** relating to the face ○ *an unhappy facial expression* ■ *n.* **BEAUTY TREATMENT FOR FACE** a beauty treatment for the face, usually consisting of a facial massage followed by cleansing and makeup **—facially** *adv.*

facial nerve *n.* a nerve of the seventh cranial pair that controls the muscles of the face and jaw, and the sensory abilities of the palate, front of the tongue, and nose

facial scrub *n.* a slightly abrasive cream or lotion used on the face to remove a layer of dead skin and improve the complexion

-facient[1] *suffix.* causing or making sth [From Latin *facient-*, the present participle stem of *facere* 'to do, make']

-facient[2] *suffix.* causing, making ○ *febrifacient* [From Latin *facient-*, the present participle stem of *facere* 'to do, make' (see FACT)]

facies /fáyshi eez, -shiz/ (*plural* **-es**) *n.* **1.** BIOL **GENERAL APPEARANCE** the general characteristic appearance of sth e.g. a plant or animal species **2.** GEOL **ROCK FEATURES INDICATING FORMATION** the combined physical and chemical features of a rock that indicate the manner of its formation or deposition **3.** MED **FACIAL APPEARANCE LINKED TO DISEASE** the appearance of sb's face as a characteristic of a particular disease or condition [Early 18thC. From Latin, 'face' (see FACE).]

facile /fáss īl/ *adj.* **1. SUPERFICIAL** made or arrived at without any serious thought or depth of feeling and therefore of little value or significance **2. FLUENT BUT INSINCERE** produced, spoken, or speaking so fluently and easily as to seem insincere or superficial **3. EASY TO DO** requiring little effort **4. WORKING EASILY** working or acting smoothly and easily [15thC. Via French, 'easy', from Latin *facilis* 'easy to do, pliant, courteous', from *facere* 'to do, make'.] **—facilely** *adv.* **—facileness** *n.*

facile princeps /fássili prínseps/ *n.* sb who is the obvious leader of a group (*literary*) [From Latin, literally 'easily first']

facilitate /fə sílli tayt/ **(-tates, -tating, -tated)** *vt.* to make sth easy or easier to do [Early 17thC. Via French *faciliter* from Italian *facilitare* 'to make easy', from *facile* 'easy', from Latin *facilis* (see FACILE).] **—facilitative** /-tətiv/ *adj.*

facilitation /fə sílli táysh'n/ *n.* **1. SIMPLIFICATION** the process of making sth easy or easier **2.** MED **EASING OF NERVE TRANSMISSION** a decrease in the resistance to a nerve impulse in a neural pathway, brought about by prior or repeated stimulation

facilitator /fə sílli taytər/ *n.* **1. SB ENABLING STH TO HAPPEN** sb who aids or assists in a process, especially by encouraging people to find their own solutions to problems or tasks **2. MEETING ORGANIZER** sb who organizes and provides the services for a meeting, seminar, or other event

facility /fə sílləti/ *n.* (*plural* **-ties**) **1. SKILL** an ability to do sth easily **2. EFFORTLESSNESS** ease in doing sth or in being done **3. STH WITH A FUNCTION** sth designed or created to provide a service or fulfill a need (*often used in the plural*) ○ *A wide range of facilities is available at the sports centre.* ■ **facilities** *npl.* **TOILET** a toilet

facing /fáyssing/ *n.* **1.** CLOTHES **LINING THAT FINISHES EDGE** a lining that finishes the edge of sth, especially a piece of fabric sewn and turned in on a garment to finish the edges neatly **2.** BUILDING **WALL SURFACE** a layer of material that covers the outer surface of a wall, applied for decoration or protection ■ **facings** *npl.*

CLOTHES **CUFFS AND COLLAR OF JACKET** contrasting coverings on the cuffs and collar of a jacket, especially a military jacket

-facing *suffix.* pointing in the specified direction

façonné /fássə nay/, **faconne** *n.* **1. FABRIC WITH WOVEN PATTERN** a fabric with a pattern or design woven into it **2. PATTERN** the woven pattern on a façonné fabric [Late 19thC. From French, literally 'fashioned'.]

facsimile /fak símməli/ *n.* **1. COPY OF STH** an exact copy of sth, e.g. a document, a coin, or sb's handwriting **2. FAX** a fax ■ *vt.* **(-iles, -iling, -iled) MAKE COPY OF STH** to make an exact copy or reproduction of sth [Late 16thC. From modern Latin, from Latin *facere* 'to do, make' + *simile*, 'similar'.]

facsimile edition *n.* a book or print that is reprinted in exactly the same style as an earlier edition, often being a photographic reproduction of the original

fact /fakt/ *n.* **1. STH KNOWN TO BE TRUE** sth that can be shown to be true, to exist, or to have happened **2. TRUTH OR REALITY OF STH** the truth or actual existence of sth, as opposed to the supposition of sth or a belief about sth **3. PIECE OF INFORMATION** a piece of information such as a statistic or a statement of the truth **4.** LAW **ACTUAL COURSE OF EVENTS** the circumstances of an event, motion, occurrence, or state of affairs, rather than an interpretation of its significance ○ *Matters of fact are issues for a jury, while matters of law are issues for the court.* **5.** LAW **STH BASED ON EVIDENCE** sth that is based on or concerned with the evidence presented in a legal case [15thC. From Latin *factum* 'deed', from the past participle of *facere* 'to do'.] ◇ **after the fact** after sth, especially a criminal act, has been done ◇ **before the fact** before sth, especially a criminal act, has been done ◇ **in (point of) fact** in truth or reality

WORD KEY: ORIGIN

The Latin word *facere* from which ***fact*** is derived is also the source of English *difficult, effect, factor, fashion, feasible, feat, feature,* and *fetish.*

fact-finding *adj.* **FOR GATHERING INFORMATION** intended to find out information about sth ■ *n.* **GATHERING INFORMATION** activity that is intended to find out information about sth —**fact-finder** *n.*

facticity /fak tíssəti/ *n.* the reality, truth, or truthfulness of sth (*formal*) [Mid-20thC. Formed from FACT.]

faction[1] /fáksh'n/ *n.* **1. DISSENTING MINORITY WITHIN LARGER GROUP** a group that is a minority within a larger group and has specific interests or beliefs that are not always in harmony with the larger group **2. CONFLICT WITHIN GROUP** conflict or dissension within a group [15thC. Via French from Latin *faction-*, literally 'act of making', from *fact-*, past participle stem of *facere* (see FACT).] —**factional** *adj.* —**factionally** *adv.*

faction[2] /fáksh'n/ *n.* **1. TECHNIQUE OF DRAMATIZING HISTORY** a type of writing or film-making that portrays real people or events by dramatizing the facts using the techniques of fiction **2. DRAMATIZED WORK BASED ON REAL LIFE** a piece of writing, a film, or a television programme that portrays real people or events in a dramatized way [Mid-20thC. Blend of FACT and FICTION.] —**factional** *adj.*

-faction[1] *suffix.* the making or production of sth ○ *liquefaction*

-faction[2] *suffix.* making, producing ○ *rarefaction* [Via Old French from, ultimately, Latin *facere* 'to do, make' (see FACT)]

factionalism /fáksh'nəlizəm/ *n.* the existence of or conflict between groups within a larger group —**factionalist** *n.*

factionalize[1] /fáksh'nə līz/ **(-izes, -izing, -ized), factionalise (-ises, -ising, -ised)** *vti.* to split, or cause sth to split, into factions

factionalize[2] *vt.* to dramatize actual events

factious /fákshəss/ *adj.* liable to cause, taking part in, or typical of conflict within a group [Mid-16thC. Directly or via French *factieux* from Latin *factiosus*, from *faction-* (see FACTION[1]).] —**factiously** *adv.* —**factiousness** *n.*

factitious /fak tíshəss/ *adj.* **1. INSINCERE** contrived and insincere rather than genuine **2. ARTIFICIAL** not real or natural but artificial or invented (*formal*) [Mid-17thC. From Latin, from *faction-* (see FACTION[1]).] —**factitiously** *adv.* —**factitiousness** *n.*

factitive /fáktətiv/ *adj.* used to describe a verb that takes a direct object and a complement. An example is 'appoint' in 'They appointed her Head of Department' where 'her' is the direct object and 'Head of Department' is a noun complement. [Mid-19thC. From Latin *factitivus*, from *factitare* 'to frequent'.] —**factitively** *adv.*

fact of life *n.* **UNAVOIDABLE TRUTH** an unavoidable truth, especially an unpleasant one ■ **facts of life** *npl.* **SEX EDUCATION** basic information on sexual matters and reproduction

factoid /fákt oyd/ *n.* **1. UNRELIABLE INFORMATION** sth that may not be true but is widely accepted as true because it is repeatedly quoted, especially in the media **2. SINGLE FACT** a small and often unimportant bit of information

factor /fáktər/ *n.* **1. INFLUENCE** sth that contributes to or has an influence on the result of sth ○ *Access to emergency exits is an important factor when planning the layout of a public building.* **2. LEVEL** a quantity or level of sth **3. AMOUNT BY WHICH STH IS MULTIPLIED** an amount by which sth is multiplied to give a specific result ○ *The number of visitors to the museum has increased by a factor of three.* **4.** MATH **QUANTITY MULTIPLIED WITH OTHERS** one of two or more numbers or quantities that can be multiplied together to give a specified number or quantity ○ *3 and 5 are factors of 15.* **5.** BUSINESS **SB TRADING FOR COMMISSION** a person who or organization that buys and sells goods for a commission **6.** BUSINESS **BUSINESS AGENT** sb who or an organization that carries out business for another **7.** *Scotland* BUSINESS **MANAGER OF ESTATE** a person who or firm that manages an estate or property on behalf of the owner **8.** BIOCHEM **BIOLOGICAL SUBSTANCE** a biological substance that promotes a physiological process, e.g. blood coagulation. ◊ **factor VIII** ■ *v.* **(-tors, -toring, -tored) 1.** *vi.* BUSINESS **ACT AS FACTOR** to work as a factor **2.** *vt.* MATH **WORK OUT FACTORS** to calculate the factors of a given number or expression **3.** *vt. Scotland* **MANAGE ESTATE** to manage an estate or property on behalf of the owner [15thC. Via French from Latin, from *fact-*, past participle stem of *facere* (see FACT).] —**factorability** /fáktərə bílləti/ *n.* —**factorable** /-tərəb'l/ *adj.*

factor in *vt.* to include or consider sth as contributing to or influencing sth else, e.g. when making a decision

factorage /fáktərij/ *n.* **1. MONEY CHARGED BY FACTOR** the fees or commission charged by a factor **2. WORK OF A FACTOR** the business of working as a factor

factor analysis *n.* a statistical technique used to determine the relative strength of various influences on an outcome

factorial /fak táwriəl/ *n.* **PRODUCT OF MULTIPLICATION** the number resulting from multiplying a whole number by every whole number between itself and 1 inclusive. 6 factorial, or 6!, is 6 x 5 x 4 x 3 x 2 x 1 = 720. Symbol ! ■ *adj.* **1. RELATING TO FACTORIAL** relating to or involving a factorial **2.** BUSINESS **INVOLVING FACTOR** involving or typical of a commercial factor or the work of such a factor —**factorially** *adv.*

factoring /fáktəring/ *n.* **1. WORK OF A FACTOR** the work of a commercial factor **2. BUYING OF DEBTS** the business of buying debts at a discount so as to make a profit from collecting them

factorize /fáktə rīz/ **(-izes, -izing, -ized), factorise (-ises, -ising, -ised)** *vti.* to find out or calculate the factors of a given integer or equation. US term **factor** —**factorization** /-záysh'n/ *n.*

factorship /fáktərship/ *n.* the position or business of being a factor for another person or business

factor VIII *n.* a protein substance, one of a number that promote clotting of blood. Its inherited absence causes haemophilia.

factory /fáktəri/ (*plural* **-ries**) *n.* **1. BUILDING WHERE GOODS ARE MANUFACTURED** a building or complex of buildings where goods are manufactured on a large scale (*often used before a noun*) ○ *a factory worker* **2. PRODUCTIVE PLACE** a place where a lot of things of a particular kind are produced (*informal*) ○ *As far as popular music was concerned, it was a hit factory.* **3.** COMM **PLACE ABROAD WHERE AGENTS DID BUSINESS** in the past, a place where business was carried out abroad by commercial agents (**factors**), especially a trading station

factory farm *n.* a farm where animals are reared by intensive methods and on a large scale using modern industrial equipment —**factory farming** *n.*

factory floor *n.* = **shop floor** *n.* 1

factory ship *n.* a large fishing vessel equipped to process and freeze its own catch, or a whole fleet's catch, of fish or whales

factotum /fak tṓtəm/ *n.* sb employed to do a variety of jobs for sb else [Mid-16thC. From Latin, literally 'do everything!', from *fac* 'do!', imperative of *facere* (see FACT), + *totum* 'all' (source of English *total*).]

factsheet /fákt sheet/ *n.* a printed sheet or booklet giving information about sth, especially a broadcast programme

factual /fákchoo əl/ *adj.* **1. CONTAINING FACTS** involving, containing, or based on facts **2. TRUTHFUL** consisting of the truth, or including only those things that are real or actual [Mid-19thC. Modelled on ACTUAL.] —**factuality** /fákchoo álləti/ *n.* —**factually** /fákchoo əli/ *adv.* —**factualness** /-choo əlnəss/ *n.*

factualism /fákchoo əlizəm/ *n.* a strict devotion to or adherence to facts —**factualist** *n.*

facula /fákyŏŏlə/ (*plural* **-lae** /-lee/) *n.* a large bright extremely hot region on the Sun's surface, usually occurring near a sunspot [Early 18thC. From Latin, literally 'little torch'.] —**facular** *adj.*

facultative /fák'ltətiv/ *adj.* **1. NOT REQUIRED** optional rather than obligatory **2. ALLOWING STH TO HAPPEN** enabling or capable of permitting sth to happen or be done, but not able to force its occurrence **3.** BIOL **ASSOCIATED WITH A VARIETY OF CONDITIONS** able to live or take place under a range of external conditions ○ *a facultative parasite.* ◊ **obligate** —**facultatively** *adv.*

faculty /fák'lti/ (*plural* **-ties**) *n.* **1. MENTAL ABILITY** a mental power or ability that sb has, e.g. reason or memory **2. ABILITY** any capacity or ability that sb is born with or learns ○ *have a great faculty for learning languages* **3. DIVISION OF UNIVERSITY** a department or group of departments dealing with a particular subject in a university or college **4. TEACHING STAFF FOR PARTICULAR UNIVERSITY DIVISION** the teaching staff of a particular faculty in a university or college **5.** *US, Can* **ENTIRE TEACHING STAFF** the entire teaching staff of a university, college, or school, including any administrators holding academic rank **6. ALL MEMBERS OF PROFESSION** all of the people who practise a particular profession, especially medicine **7. POWER GRANTED BY AUTHORITY** a power or right given by an authority [14thC. Via French *faculté* from Latin *facultas*, from *facilis*, 'easy' (source of English *facility*).]

Faculty of Advocates *n. Scotland* the professional association for advocates in the Scottish legal system

FA Cup *n.* a yearly knockout competition open to football teams that belong to the Football Association of England, or the trophy awarded to the winning team

fad /fad/ *n.* **1. SHORT-LIVED FASHION** sth that is very popular but only for a short time **2. PERSONAL IDIOSYNCRASY** sth that is important only to a particular person [Mid-19thC. Origin uncertain: perhaps a shortening of *fidfad*, a shortening of FIDDLE-FADDLE.]

Fadden /fádd'n/, **Sir Arthur William** (1895–1973) Australian statesman. He was leader of the Country Party (1941–58) and was briefly prime minister of Australia in 1941.

faddish /fáddish/ *adj. US* = **faddy** —**faddishly** *adv.* —**faddishness** *n.*

faddism /fáddizəm/ *n.* the existence of or participation in briefly popular fashions —**faddist** *n.*

faddy /fáddi/ **(-dier, -diest)** *adj.* tending to have strongly held, but brief, enthusiasms. US term **faddish** *adj.* —**faddiness** *n.*

fade /fayd/ *v.* **(fades, fading, faded) 1.** *vti.* **GRADUALLY BECOME LESS** to lose or make sth lose brightness, colour, or loudness gradually ○ *The clothes had faded from months of washing.* **2.** *vi.* **BECOME TIRED** to lose strength, freshness, and vigour ○ *His concentration faded after about an hour.* **3.** *vi.* **DISAPPEAR SLOWLY** to die away or vanish gradually ○ *The film ends with a close-up that gradually fades to black.* **4.** *vi.* **LOSE EFFECTIVENESS** to become less effective temporarily **5.** *vti.* **GOLF STRIKE GOLF BALL SO IT CURVES** to hit a golf ball deliberately so that, in a right-handed shot, it curves slightly from left to right ■ *n.* **1. GRADUAL LESSENING** an instance of sth gradually becoming quieter, less bright, or less distinct **2. GRADUAL DISAPPEARANCE OF IMAGE** a gradual disappearance of an image in a film or television show **3.** *US* **OFFENSIVE TERM** an offensive term for a Black person who has adopted white friends and attitudes (*slang offensive*) **4.** **GOLF GOLF SLICE** a golf shot in which the ball spins slightly from left to right in the air [14thC. From French *fade* 'weak, pale', of uncertain origin: probably from a Vulgar Latin blend of Latin *fatuus* 'insipid' and *vapidus* 'flat'.] —**fadable** *adj.* —**fadedness** *n.*

fade away *vi.* **1. GRADUALLY DISAPPEAR** to become gradually fainter or weaker and finally disappear **2. WASTE AWAY** to become thin and unhealthy

fade in *vti.* to gradually make a sound audible or an image visible, or become gradually audible or visible

fade out *vti.* to gradually make an image or sound fainter until it disappears, or become gradually fainter before disappearing

fade up *vti.* = **fade in**

fade-in *n.* the gradual introduction of a sound until it is audible, or of an image until it is visible and clear

fadeless /fáydləss/ *adj.* not affected by fading from sunlight or washing —**fadelessly** *adv.*

fade-out *n.* **1. GRADUAL DECREASE IN LOUDNESS OR BRIGHTNESS** a gradual decrease in loudness or brightness as a sound or image becomes fainter and less distinct, and eventually disappears **2. BROADCAST WEAKENING OF TV OR RADIO SIGNAL** a gradual reduction in the strength of a broadcast television or radio signal, especially with temporary loss of reception, often because of interference in transmission

fader /fáydər/ *n.* a control on technical equipment that makes a sound or picture fade in or out

fade-up *n.* = **fade-in**

fado /fáá doo/ (*plural* -**dos**) *n.* a type of sad Portuguese folk song [Early 20thC. From Portuguese, literally 'fate'.]

faecal /féek'l/ *adj.* relating to or consisting of faeces

faeces /féeseez/ *npl.* the body's solid waste matter, composed of undigested food, bacteria, water, and bile pigments and discharged from the bowel through the anus [14thC. From Latin, plural of *faex* 'sediment, dregs'.] —**faecal** /féek'l/ *adj.*

faena /fa áynə/ *n.* a series of manoeuvres in the final stages of a bullfight, leading up to the killing of the bull by the matador [Early 20thC. From Spanish, literally 'task'.]

Faer. *abbr.* Faeroe Islands

faerie /fáyəri, faíri/, **faery** (*plural* -**ies**) *n.* (*literary*) **1. FAIRYLAND** the world of the fairies, or fairyland **2. FAIRY** a fairy [Late 16thC. A mock-medieval word based on French (source of English *fairy*) introduced by the author Edmund Spenser.]

Faeroe Islands /fáyrō íləndz/ = **Faroe Islands**

Faeroese *n.*, *adj.* = **Faroese**

faff about /fáff-/ (**faffs about, faffing about, faffed about**), **faff around** (**faffs around, faffing around, faffed around**) *vi.* to waste time by being indecisive or fussing unnecessarily (*informal*) [Faff: thought to suggest the action of the breeze. Originally 'to blow as a light blustery wind'.]

fag[1] /fag/ *n.* **1. STH BORING** sth that is tedious or that makes sb weary (*informal*) **2.** *UK* **ERRAND BOY** a schoolboy at a public school who in the past had to do menial jobs and run errands for an older schoolboy (*dated*) ■ *v.* (**fags, fagging, fagged**) **1.** *vti.* *US* **EXHAUST THROUGH WORK** to tire out, or cause to become exhausted, through drudgery or hard labour **2.** *vi.* *UK* **ACT AS ERRAND BOY** to do menial jobs and run errands for an older schoolboy (*dated*) [Mid-16thC. Originally the verb, of uncertain origin: perhaps an alteration of FLAG. Current senses evolved from 'to droop, decline' through 'bent over by weariness'.]

fag[2] /fag/ *n.* a cigarette (*informal*) [Late 19thC. Shortening of FAG END.]

fag[3] /fag/ *n.* *US* an offensive term for a homosexual man (*slang offensive*) [Early 20thC. Shortening of FAGGOT.] —**faggy** *adj.*

fag end *n.* **1. CIGARETTE STUB** the end of a cigarette that has been smoked (*informal*) **2. LAST AND WORST PART OF STH** the last part of sth after the best of it has been used ○ *the fag end of the day* **3. REMNANT OF CLOTH** the remaining part of a piece of cloth, most of which has been used [Fag of unknown origin. Originally 'flap, sth hanging down'.]

fagged, **fagged out** *adj.* very tired or exhausted (*informal*)

faggot[1] /fággət/ *n.* **1. BUNDLE OF STICKS FOR FIREWOOD** a bundle of sticks or twigs, especially wood to be burnt as fuel **2. METALL BUNDLE OF PIECES OF METAL** a bundle of pieces of metal, especially pieces of iron or steel for welding **3. FOOD OFFAL MEATBALL** a ball of chopped meat, usually pork offal, mixed with bread and herbs that is baked in the oven ■ *vt.* (**-gots, -goted**) **1. COLLECT STH AND TIE INTO BUNDLE** to collect things, especially sticks, and tie them into a bundle or bundles **2. SEW STITCH WITH FAGGOTING** to sew sth using faggoting [13thC. Via Old French from Italian *faggotto*, ultimately from Greek *phakelos* 'bundle'.]

faggot[2] /fággət/ *n.* *US* an offensive term for a homosexual man (*slang offensive*) [Early 20thC. From an earlier use of FAGGOT[1], 'bundle of sticks', as an offensive term for a woman. Compare BAGGAGE.] —**faggoty** *adj.*

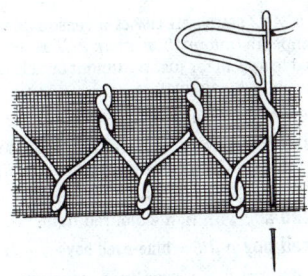

Faggoting

faggoting /fággəting/ *n.* **1. SEW DECORATIVE WAY OF JOINING FABRIC** a decorative way of sewing two hemmed pieces of fabric together, leaving a gap between them that is filled with an insertion stitch **2. CRAFT EMBROIDERY TECHNIQUE** a technique of embroidery in which sections of lengthwise threads are pulled out and the cross threads tied into bundles, producing a decorative openwork effect [Mid-19thC]

fag hag *n.* *US* an offensive term for a woman who enjoys socializing with homosexual men (*slang offensive*)

fagot *n.* *US* = **faggot**

fagoting *n.* *US* = **faggoting**

fah[1] /faa/ *n.* = **fa**

fah[2], **fa** *n.* a syllable that represents the fourth note in a scale, used for singing solfege. In fixed solfege it represents the note C, while in solfege with movable doh it is used to represent the tonic of the key being sung.

Fah. *abbr.* Fahrenheit

fahlband /fáál band/ *n.* a thin bed of rock that contains metal sulphide minerals, although not in sufficient quantity to be used as an ore [Late 19thC. From German, literally 'pale (ash-coloured) band'.]

Fahr. *abbr.* Fahrenheit

Fahrenheit /fárrən hīt/ *adj.* using or measured on a temperature scale on which water freezes at 32°F and boils at 212°F under normal atmospheric conditions. In scientific and technical contexts temperatures are now usually measured in degrees (**Celsius**) rather than Fahrenheit. ◊ **Celsius, kelvin**. Symbol **F** [Mid-18thC. Named after Gabriel *Fahrenheit* (1686–1736), the German physicist who invented the thermometric Fahrenheit scale.]

faience /fī óNss, -aáNss/, **faïence** *n.* earthenware decorated with opaque metallic glazes (*often used before a noun*) ○ *a faience bowl* [Late 17thC. From French, named for *Faïence* 'Faenza', town in northern Italy where this type of pottery was first made.]

fail /fayl/ *v.* (**fails, failing, failed**) **1.** *vi.* **BE UNSUCCESSFUL** to be unsuccessful in trying to do sth ○ *This plan can't fail.* **2.** *vi.* **BE UNABLE TO DO STH** to be incapable of doing sth, or choose not to do sth ○ *She failed to see what the problem was.* **3.** *vti.* **EDUC NOT PASS EXAM OR COURSE** to fall short of the standard required to pass an examination or course ○ *He failed English.* **4.** *vt.* **EDUC JUDGE STUDENT NOT GOOD ENOUGH** to judge a student not good enough to pass an examination or a course **5.** *vi.* **STOP FUNCTIONING OR GROWING** to stop working, or not perform or grow as expected ○ *The brakes on the car failed.* **6.** *vi.* **COMM COLLAPSE FINANCIALLY** to collapse financially, becoming insolvent or bankrupt ○ *The business failed after six years.* **7.** *vt.* **LET SB DOWN** to let sb down by not doing what is expected or needed, or abandon or forsake sb ○ *My courage failed me.* **8.** *vi.* **BECOME WEAKER** to lose strength, loudness, or brightness ○ *The light began to fail.* ■ *n.* **EDUC FAILURE** an instance of falling short of the standard required to pass an examination or course, especially if given as an essay or examination grade [13thC. Via Old French *faillir* from Latin *fallere*, 'to deceive sb's hopes, disappoint'.] ◊ **without fail** for certain, or without any possibility of sth specified not happening

failing /fáyling/ *n.* **SHORTCOMING** a fault or weakness ■ *prep.* **WITHOUT** if sth does not happen ○ *Failing a resolution of the dispute by this afternoon, we will suspend you.*

failing school *n.* in the UK, a school judged by the Secretary of State for Education, on the advice of inspectors, to be in need of special attention and help to bring it up to the required standard

faille /fayl/ *n.* a closely woven silk, cotton, or rayon fabric that is slightly ribbed [Mid-16thC. From French, of uncertain origin: probably via Old Northern French from Middle Dutch *falie* 'scarf'.]

fail-safe *adj.* **1. SWITCHING TO SAFE CONDITION** designed to switch equipment or a system to a safe condition if there is a fault or failure, e.g. as a thermostat turns sth off if it overheats **2. SURE TO SUCCEED** not capable of failing ■ *n.* **STH THAT SAFEGUARDS** a fail-safe device or procedure

failure /fáylyər/ *n.* **1. LACK OF SUCCESS** a lack of success in sth, or an unsuccessful attempt at doing sth **2. STH LESS THAN THAT REQUIRED** sth that falls short of what is required or expected ○ *Failure will not be tolerated.* **3. STH THAT FAILS** sb who or sth that is unsuccessful **4. BREAKDOWN OF STH** a breakdown or decline in the performance of sth, or an occasion when sth stops working or stops working adequately ○ *engine failure* **5. LACK OF DEVELOPMENT OR PRODUCTION** inadequate growth, development, or production of sth ○ *crop failure* **6. BUSINESS BANKRUPTCY** a financial collapse, usually leading to bankruptcy

failure to thrive *n.* pronounced lack of growth in a child due to inadequate absorption of nutrients or a serious heart or kidney condition, resulting in below-average height and weight

fain /fayn/ *adv.* (*archaic*) **1. HAPPILY** with gladness or eagerness **2. PREFERABLY** in preference ■ *adj.* (*archaic*) **1. EAGER** willing or eager **2. COMPELLED** forced by an obligation or circumstances [Old English *faegen* 'glad', from a prehistoric Germanic word that is also the ancestor of English *fawn* 'to act slavishly']

fainéant /fáyni ənt/ *adj.* **IDLE** tending to do nothing, or unwilling to do anything (*literary*) ■ *n.* **SB LAZY** sb who is idle or unwilling to do anything (*literary*) [Early 17thC. From French, alteration of *fait-nient*, literally 'does nothing', by folk etymology from *faignant* 'shirker'.]

fainites *interj.* = **fains** (*regional archaic*) [Early 19thC. Alteration of *fains* I.]

fáinne /faán jə/ (*plural* **-nes**) *n.* in Ireland, a ring worn on a pin by people to show that they are willing and able to speak Gaelic [From Irish Gaelic, literally 'ring']

fains /faynz/ *interj.* used to call for a truce or claim exemption from sth (*regional archaic*) [Early 19thC. Origin uncertain: perhaps an alteration of FEND, or from French *se feindre*, 'to make excuses, hang back (in battle)'.]

faint /faynt/ *adj.* **1.** DIM not bright, clear, or loud **2.** UNENTHUSIASTIC feeble and done without conviction ○ *damned him with faint praise* **3.** DIZZY dizzy or weak, as if about to become unconscious ○ *All of a sudden he felt faint.* **4.** SLIGHT remote or slight ■ *vi.* (**faints, fainting, fainted**) **1.** MED LOSE CONSCIOUSNESS BRIEFLY to become unconscious, especially for a short time, because of a reduction in the flow of blood to the brain **2.** WEAKEN to become weak or lose courage (*archaic*) ■ *n.* MED SUDDEN LOSS OF CONSCIOUSNESS a sudden, usually brief, loss of consciousness, caused by a reduction in the flow of blood to the brain. Technical name **syncope** [13thC. From Old French, from *faindre* 'to pretend, shirk'. The meaning 'not bright' evolved from 'cowardly, lazy' through 'feeble'.] —**fainter** *n.* —**faintish** *adj.* —**faintly** *adv.* —**faintness** *n.*

faint-hearted *adj.* lacking courage, boldness, or enthusiasm —**faint-heartedly** *adv.* —**faint-heartedness** *n.*

WORD KEY: SYNONYMS

See Synonyms at ***cowardly***.

fainting fit *n.* an attack of dizziness, often leading to unconsciousness

fair[1] /fair/ *adj.* **1.** REASONABLE OR UNBIASED not exhibiting any bias, and therefore reasonable or impartial **2.** DONE PROPERLY according to the rules ○ *fair and free elections* **3.** LIGHT-COLOURED light-coloured, or with light-coloured hair or skin **4.** SIZEABLE reasonably large in size or quantity ○ *They had a fair number of responses to the advertisement.* **5.** BETTER THAN ACCEPTABLE quite good, or very reasonable ○ *a fair understanding* **6.** ACCEPTABLE no more than acceptable or average ○ *Your performance this year has only been fair.* **7.** PLEASING TO LOOK AT beautiful or pleasing to the eye **8.** VERY GREAT utter or extreme (*informal*) ○ *We had a fair old struggle to get the piano into the house.* **9.** METEOROL NOT STORMY OR CLOUDY sunny or clear, and without much wind **10.** NOT BLOCKED clear and unobstructed ○ *a fair view of the enemy's forces* **11.** UNSULLIED not marred by any blemish or stain **12.** FALSE DESPITE APPEARANCES seemingly good or true, but actually false or insincere **13.** SAILING GOOD FOR SAILING favourable for sailing or travel by ship ○ *a fair wind* ■ *adv.* **1.** PROPERLY in accordance with the rules or what is expected ○ *He's always played fair with me.* **2.** DIRECTLY in a direct or straight way, and squarely ○ *hit fair in the centre of the board* **3.** QUITE quite or rather (*regional informal*) ○ *I'm getting fair sick of this.* ■ *v.* (**fairs, fairing, faired**) **1.** *vi. Scotland* METEOROL IMPROVE to become bright after cloud or rain (*refers to the weather or sky*) **2.** *vt.* MAKE SMOOTH AND EVEN to smooth or streamline the surface of sth, e.g. of an airplane wing or tabletop [Old English *faeger* 'beautiful', from a prehistoric Germanic word meaning 'suitable', which is also the ancestor of English *fake*] ◇ **a fair crack of the whip** a reasonable chance to attempt sth ◇ **fair and square** justly, or according to the rules ◇ **fair enough 1.** used to say that you accept sth, though you would probably have been happier with sth better (*informal*) **2.** acceptable and understandable, but not ideal ◇ **fair's fair** used to urge or appeal for just or even treatment (*informal*) ◇ **fair to middling** reasonably good or reasonably well (*informal*) (*hyphenated when used before a noun*) ◇ **no fair** *US* sth that is unfair or against the rules (*informal*)

fair[2] /fair/ *n.* **1.** LEISURE OUTDOOR EVENT WITH AMUSEMENTS a temporary outdoor entertainment with amusements such as machines to ride on, sideshows, and food stands, usually set up on open ground and moving from place to place. US term **carnival 2.** LIVESTOCK MARKET a large market selling a wide range of goods including livestock, sometimes with amusements and sideshows **3.** COMMERCIAL EXHIBITION an exhibition, often held annually, at which companies show their products to potential buyers ○ *a book fair* **4.** SALE TO RAISE MONEY a sale of goods to raise money for sth, especially a charity **5.** *US* = **show 6.** *Scotland* TRADES HOLIDAY an annual two-week trades holiday observed in summer at different times in various towns, especially the Glasgow Fair, which occupies the last two weeks in July [13thC. Via Old French *feire* from late Latin *feria* 'holiday', from Latin *feriae* (plural) 'holiday, religious festival'.]

Fairbanks /fáir bangks/ city in eastern Alaska, on the northern bank of the Tanana River, northeast of Anchorage. Population: 32,960 (1996).

Fairbanks, Douglas (1883–1939) US silent film actor. He is best known for his swashbuckling performances in films such as *The Mark of Zorro* (1920). Real name **Douglas Elton Ulman**

Fairburn /fáir burn/, **A. R. D.** (1904–57) New Zealand journalist and writer. His works include *Strange Rendezvous* (1952). Full name **Arthur Rex Dugant Fairburn**

fair copy *n.* an unmarked version of a document that has been corrected and retyped or printed out again

Fairfax /fáir faks/, **John** (1804–77) English-born Australian newspaper proprietor. He was the owner of the *Sydney Morning Herald* and founder of the Fairfax media dynasty.

Fairfax, Thomas, 3rd Baron Fairfax of Cameron (1612–71) English general. He was commander of the Parliamentary army during the Civil War.

fair game *n.* **1.** LEGITIMATE TARGET sb who or sth that it is considered permissible to pursue, ridicule, or attack **2.** HUNT LEGITIMATELY HUNTED ANIMAL an animal that the rules of a particular sport allow people to hunt (*archaic*)

fair go *n. ANZ* REASONABLE CHANCE a reasonable chance to attempt sth (*informal*) ■ *interj. ANZ* BE FAIR, OR THAT'S FAIR used to appeal for just treatment or acknowledge that sth is just (*informal*)

fair green *n.* GOLF = **fairway** *n.* 1

fairground /fáir grownd/ *n.* a large open outdoor space where fairs or exhibitions may be held ○ *fairground attractions*

fair-haired *adj.* with light-coloured hair

fair-haired boy *n. US* = **blue-eyed boy**

fairing[1] /fáiring/ *n.* a streamlined structure added to an aircraft, car, or other vehicle to reduce drag. ◊ **cowling**

fairing[2] /fáiring/ *n.* **1.** SWEET BISCUIT a sweet buttery biscuit **2.** GIFT a gift, especially one brought back from, or given at, a fair (*archaic*)

fairish /fáirish/ *adj.* **1.** REASONABLE reasonably good or large ○ *a fairish amount* **2.** LIGHT IN COLOUR quite light in colour —**fairishly** *adv.*

Fair Isle[1] /fáyr īl/ *n.* **1.** KNITTING DESIGN any traditional Shetland Islands knitting design, used especially for sweaters, that incorporates bands of repeated multicoloured geometrical motifs **2.** KNITTING TECHNIQUE FOR MULTI-COLOURED DESIGNS a technique of knitting designs with two or more colours in which any colours not actually being knitted are woven into the back of the work [Mid-19thC. Named after *Fair Isle*, one of the Shetland Islands off the Scottish coast, where garments in this pattern were first knitted.]

Fair Isle[2] /fáir īl/ the southernmost of the Shetland Islands, off the northern coast of Scotland. It is situated approximately mid way between the main Shetland Islands and the Orkney Islands.

fairlead /fáir leed/, **fairleader** /-leedər/ *n.* a ring, hole, or other device through which a rope is guided in order to reduce friction and prevent chafing, or to keep it in place

fairly /fáirli/ *adv.* **1.** HONESTLY in a just and honest, proper, or legitimate way **2.** MODERATELY to a reasonable or moderate degree ○ *a fairly easy decision* **3.** COMPLETELY in a complete, full, or utter way ○ *The ground fairly shook with the impact.*

fair-minded *adj.* able to make impartial and just judgments, or resulting from such a judgment —**fair-mindedness** *n.*

fairness /fáirnəss/ *n.* **1.** QUALITY OF BEING FAIR the condition of being just or impartial **2.** BEAUTY beauty, or the condition of being pleasing to look at ◇ **in (all) fairness** being just and impartial

fair play *n.* **1.** PLAYING GAME BY RULES the playing of a game without cheating or breaking the rules **2.** PROPER CONDUCT conduct that is just and equitable ◇ **fair play to sb** *Ireland* used to express general good wishes to sb (*informal*)

fair sex *n.* women and girls (*dated*)

fair shake *n.* just treatment, or a reasonable chance to attempt sth (*informal*)

fair-skinned *adj.* having pale skin of a type that is easily burned by the sun

fair-spoken *adj.* speaking in a pleasant and polite way —**fair-spokenness** *n.*

fairway /fáir way/ *n.* **1.** GOLF GRASS BETWEEN GOLF TEE AND GREEN the closely mown area on a golf hole that forms the main avenue between a tee and a green **2.** SHIPPING NAVIGABLE CHANNEL FOR BOATS a navigable channel or the usual course followed by vessels in a river, harbour, or other body of water

Fairweather, Mount /fáir wethər/ mountain in the St Elias Mountains between Alaska and British Columbia, Canada. Part of Glacier Bay National Park and Preserve, it is the highest peak in southern Alaska. Height: 4,663 m/15,300 ft.

Fairweather, Ian (1891–1974) Scottish-born Australian painter. His works show strong Asian and Aboriginal influences. Among his best known paintings is *Monastery* (1960–61).

fair-weather *adj.* **1.** FOR OR IN GOOD WEATHER suitable, done, or taking part only when the weather is fine **2.** NOT STEADFAST able to be relied upon only when things are going well

Fairweather Cape cape on the southeastern coast of Alaska, approximately 55 km/35 mi. south of Mount Fairweather

fairy /fáiri/ *n.* (*plural* **-ies**) **1.** SMALL SUPERNATURAL CREATURE an imaginary supernatural being, usually resembling a small person, with magic powers. In folklore, fairies may be kindly or malicious. **2.** OFFENSIVE TERM an offensive term for a homosexual man (*slang offensive*) ■ *adj.* OF FAIRIES relating to, belonging to, or typical of fairies ○ *the fairy folk* [14thC. From Old French *faerie* 'enchantment', from *fae* 'fairy', from Latin *fata* 'the Fates', plural of *fatum* 'fate'.]

fairy bread *n. Aus* bread and butter sprinkled with hundreds and thousands (*informal*)

fairy cycle *n.* a small children's bicycle or tricycle

fairy godmother *n.* **1.** KIND FAIRY in some fairy stories, a kind fairy in the form of a woman who gives vital help to sb, especially to the hero or heroine. Perhaps the most famous fairy godmother is the one who appears to Cinderella and enables her to attend the prince's ball. **2.** SB VERY HELPFUL sb, especially a woman, who gives generous help, often anonymously

fairyland /fáiri land/ *n.* **1.** LAND OF FAIRIES the imaginary country where fairies live **2.** ENCHANTING PLACE any enchanting place, e.g. a fantasy world existing in sb's imagination

fairy lights *npl.* a long string of small, often coloured, electric lights, used on Christmas trees and for other types of decoration

fairy ring *n.* a ring of grass darker than the surrounding grass, traditionally thought to be associated with dancing fairies but actually marking the outer edge of growth of various underground perennial fungi

fairy ring champignon *n.* a buff-coloured edible fungus, often growing in a ring-shaped cluster. Latin name: *Marasmius oreades.*

fairy shrimp *n.* a tiny soft-bodied crustacean found in fresh or brackish water, with an elongated body and eleven pairs of appendages. Order: Anostraca.

fairy tale, **fairy story** *n.* **1.** STORY ABOUT FAIRIES a story for children about fairies or other imaginary beings and events, often containing a moral message **2.** UNLIKELY EXPLANATION an improbable invented account of sth, often a false excuse

fairy-tale *adj.* **1.** FROM FAIRY TALE derived from or typical of a fairy tale **2.** FORTUNATE AND HAPPY like sth from a fairy tale, especially in being fortunate, happy, or extravagantly beautiful

Grimm's Fairy Tales, a collection of folk tales compiled and edited by German scholars Jacob and Wilhelm Grimm (1812–15). Based on written sources dating back to the 16th century and on German folk tales, it includes many stories now famous worldwide, including 'Cinderella', 'Hansel and Gretel', and 'Rumpelstiltskin'. With their universal themes the tales were seen by the Grimms as repositories of the hopes, passions, and fears of humankind.

fairy thorn *n.* in Northern Ireland, a hawthorn bush left growing in the middle of a field through fear that misfortune would befall whoever chopped it down

fairy wren *n.* an Australian wren, the male of which has colourful breeding plumage each year. Genus: *Malurus*.

Faisalabad /fízələ bad/, **Faisalābād** city situated in the Punjab, northeastern Pakistan, 121 km/75 mi. west of Lahore. Population: 1,104,209 (1981).

fait accompli /fáyt ə kóm plee/ (*plural* **faits accomplis** /fáyt ə kóm plee/) *n.* sth that is already done or decided and seems unalterable [Mid-19thC. From French, literally 'accomplished fact'.]

faites vos jeux /fáyt vō zhö/ *v.* used by a croupier in roulette and other gambling games to ask people to place their bets [From French]

faith /fayth/ *n.* **1. BELIEF OR TRUST** belief, devotion to, or trust in sb or sth, especially without logical proof **2. RELIG RELIGION OR RELIGIOUS GROUP** a system of religious belief, or the group of people who adhere to it **3. RELIG TRUST IN GOD** belief in and devotion to God ○ *Her faith is unwavering*. **4. SET OF BELIEFS** a strongly held set of beliefs or principles ○ *people of different political faiths* **5. LOYALTY** allegiance or loyalty to sb or sth [13thC. Via Old French *feid* from Latin *fides* 'trust, belief' (source of English *confide* and *fealty*). Ultimately from an Indo-European word that is also the ancestor of English *federal*.] ◇ **keep faith with** be loyal or true to a person or promise ◇ **on faith** without demanding proof

faithful /fáythf'l/ *adj.* **1. CONSISTENTLY LOYAL** consistently trustworthy and loyal, especially to a person, a promise, or duty **2. NOT PROMISCUOUS** not having sexual relations with sb other than a spouse or partner **3. CONSCIENTIOUS** displaying or resulting from a sense of responsibility or devotion to duty **4. CORRECT** accurate and true ○ *a faithful account of the events* **5. WITH UNWAVERING BELIEF** believing firmly in sth or sb, especially a religion ■ *n.* **SB OR STH RELIABLE** sb who or sth that can be trusted or depended on ■ *npl.* **1. faithful, Faithful RELIG RELIGIOUS BELIEVERS** the believers in a religion considered as a group, especially Muslims or Christians **2. LOYAL SUPPORTERS** people who believe in or follow sb or sth, especially the loyal members of a political party ○ *the party faithful* —**faithfulness** *n.*

faithfully /fáythf'li/ *adv.* in a loyal, true, or accurate way ◇ **yours faithfully** used immediately before the signature to end a letter that is not addressed to sb by name

faith healer *n.* sb who treats illness or disorders in other people through prayer, sometimes also laying his or her hands on the person being treated —**faith healing** *n.*

faithless /fáythləss/ *adj.* **1. DISHONEST** dishonest, or disloyal to sb or sth, e.g. in not keeping a promise or performing a duty **2. UNTRUSTWORTHY** not to be trusted or relied on **3. RELIG NOT RELIGIOUS** not believing in a religious faith —**faithlessly** *adv.* —**faithlessness** *n.*

fajita /fə héetə/ *n.* a Mexican dish consisting of beef or other meat that has been marinated, grilled, cut into strips, and served in a soft flour tortilla [Late 20thC. From Mexican Spanish, literally 'little strip, belt'.]

fake[1] /fayk/ *n.* **STH NOT GENUINE** sb or sth that is not genuine but is presented as, or appears to be, genuine ■ *adj.* **NOT GENUINE** not genuine, but meant to be taken for genuine ■ *v.* (**fakes, faking, faked**) **1.** *vt.* **FALSELY PRESENT STH AS GENUINE** to make or produce sth and claim it is genuine when it is not **2.** *vti.* **PRETEND FEELING OR KNOWLEDGE** to pretend to have, feel, or know sth ○ *faked a knowledge of Italian* **3.** *vt.* **ARTS IMPROVISE WHILE PERFORMING** to improvise or ad-lib a

piece of music or lines in a play during a performance [Late 18thC. From *feague*, 16th-century criminal slang for 'to rob, tamper with', of uncertain origin; probably from German *fegen* 'to polish, refurbish'.]

fake out *vt.* *US* to deceive or surprise sb, especially by bluffing (*informal*)

fake[2] /fayk/ *vt.* (**fakes, faking, faked**) **COIL ROPE** to coil or loop a rope so that it will not tangle when used ■ *n.* **COIL OF ROPE** a single coil or loop of a rope that has been faked [15thC. Origin unknown.]

fakeer *n.* = **fakir**

faker /fáykər/ *n.* sb who pretends that sth such as an emotion is genuine when it is not —**fakery** *n.*

fakir /fáy keer, fə kéer/, **faqir, fakeer** *n.* **1. ISLAM MENDICANT MUSLIM** a religious Muslim, especially a Sufi, who lives by begging **2. INDIAN RELIG HINDU MENDICANT** a Hindu ascetic who lives by begging and whose religious practice often includes the performance of extraordinary feats of physical endurance [Early 17thC. Directly or via French from Arabic, literally 'poor man'.]

fa-la /faa laa/, **fal la** *n.* a refrain in 16th and 17th century English songs, using the meaningless syllables 'fa-la-la'

falafel /fə laáf'l/, **felafel** *n.* a deep-fried ball of ground chickpeas seasoned with onions and spices, often eaten in pitta bread with salad and yogurt or tahini sauce. It was originally a Middle Eastern dish. [Mid-20thC. Via Egyptian Arabic *falāfil* from Arabic *fulful* 'pepper'.]

Falange /fə lánj/ *n.* a Spanish fascist movement founded in 1933 and dissolved in 1977. It was the official ruling party of Spain under Francisco Franco. [Mid-20thC. From Spanish, 'phalanx'.] —**Falangist** *n.*

Falasha /fə láshə/ (*plural* **-shas** or **-sha**) *n.* a member of an Ethiopian Jewish religious group now largely living in Israel [Early 18thC. From Amharic, 'exile'.]

falbala /fálbələ/ *n.* a gathered trimming or ruffle used as decoration [Early 18thC. From French, of ultimately unknown origin.]

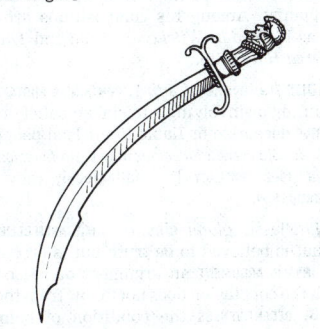

Falchion

falchion /fáwlchən/ *n.* **1. SHORT MEDIEVAL SWORD** a short sword with a broad slightly curved blade, used in medieval times **2. SWORD** a sword (*archaic*) [14thC. Via Old French *fauchon* from, ultimately, Latin *falc-*.]

falcon /fáwlkən/ *n.* **1. BIRDS FAST-FLYING BIRD OF PREY** a bird of prey related to the hawk that is fast and powerful and often catches birds as they fly. Family: Falconidae. **2. HUNT HAWK TRAINED TO HUNT** a hawk that is trained to hunt small birds and animals. In falconry the term is used only for female hawks. [13thC. Via Old French *fau(l)con* from the late Latin stem *falcon-*, of uncertain origin: perhaps formed from Latin *falc-*, stem of *falx* 'sickle', because its talons resemble sickles.]

The Maltese Falcon, a film by US director John Huston (1941). Based on Dashiell Hammett's 1930 detective novel, this is regarded as one of the finest examples of film noir. Private investigator Sam Spade's attempts to track down the murderer of his partner lead to a group of people who share a common interest in a priceless statuette of a falcon.

falconer /fáwlkənər/ *n.* sb who breeds falcons or trains them to use them to hunt small birds and animals

falconet /fáwlkə net/ *n.* a small falcon, originally from Asia. Genus: *Microhierax*.

falconiform /fawl kóni fawrm/ *adj.* relating to or resembling birds of prey with strong and sharply hooked beaks, strong feet and sharp claws for grasping prey, and large wings

falconine /fáwlkə nīn/ *adj.* relating to, involving, or typical of a falcon

falconry /fáwlkənri/ *n.* the breeding, training, and use of falcons or other hawks to hunt small prey and return from flight at a falconer's direction

falcula /fálkyoölə/ (*plural* **-culae** /-lee/) *n.* a curved claw, especially of a bird [From Latin, literally 'small sickle', from *falc-* (see FALCATE)] —**falculate** /fálkyoö layt/ *adj.*

falderal /fáaldə raal/, **folderol** /fóldə rol/ *n.* **1.** silly nonsense (*dated*) **2. TRINKET** an attractive but valueless object or trinket **3. MUSIC SONG REFRAIN** a meaningless chorus or refrain in a song (*archaic*) [Early 19thC. From *fol de rol*, a nonsense refrain in songs.]

Faldo /fáldō/, **Nick** (b. 1957) British golfer. A British Ryder Cup team member, he has twice won the British Open (1987 and 1990) and is a three-time US Masters champion (1989, 1990, and 1996). Full name **Nicholas Alexander Faldo**

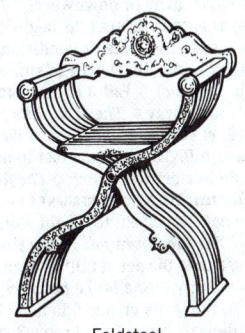

Faldstool

faldstool /fáwld stool/ *n.* **1. FOLDING SEAT FOR BISHOP** a folding seat, especially one used by a bishop when officiating away from his throne or at another church **2. FOLDING STOOL FOR WORSHIPPER** a small folding stool with a raised desklike attachment at which a worshipper kneels to pray **3. CORONATION STOOL FOR BRITISH SOVEREIGN** a stool on which the British sovereign kneels at his or her coronation [Old English *fældstōl*, from FOLD 'to be collapsible' + STOOL 'seat'; partly from medieval Latin *faldistolium*, ultimately from prehistoric Germanic]

Faliscan /fə lískən/ *n.* an ancient language spoken in Italy before Latin, which was related to and replaced it [Late 17thC. Formed from Latin *Faliscus* 'of Falerii', important city of Etruria.]

Falkirk /fáwl kurk/ **1.** industrial town in central Scotland between Edinburgh and Glasgow. Population: 35,610 (1991). **2.** council area in central Scotland, formerly part of the Central Region. Population: 142,610 (1996). Area: 299 sq. km/115 sq. mi.

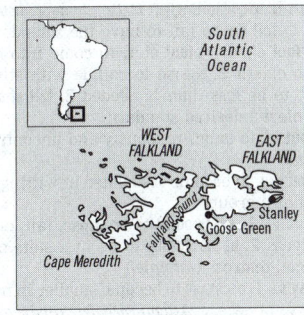

Falkland Islands

Falkland Islands /fáwlklənd-/ group of islands and British dependency in the South Atlantic Ocean, 483 km/300 mi. east of the Strait of Magellan. Population: 2,100 (1993). Area: 12,173 sq. km/4,700 sq. mi.

fall /fawl/ *vi.* (**falls, falling, fell** /fel/, **fallen** /fáwlən/) **1. MOVE DOWNWARDS** to come down freely from a higher to a lower position, moved by the force of gravity ○ *The vase fell to the ground and shattered*. **2. DROP**

OR BE LOWERED to drop or be dropped or lowered ○ *The curtain fell at the end of the performance.* **3.** COME DOWN SUDDENLY FROM UPRIGHT POSITION to drop or come down suddenly from an upright position, especially by accident ○ *The horse fell at the first fence.* **4.** BECOME LOWER to become lower or be reduced in amount, value, or quality ○ *Prices have fallen in the last year.* **5.** ACOUSTICS BECOME LOWER IN PITCH to become lower in pitch or volume **6.** MIL BE TAKEN BY FORCE to be conquered or captured by a military force ○ *The city fell despite the best efforts of the army.* **7.** MIL DROP TO GROUND IN BATTLE to drop to the ground in battle after being wounded or having died ○ *He fell at the Battle of Waterloo.* **8.** POL COLLAPSE POLITICALLY to lose political power or be defeated ○ *The government fell after 18 months in office.* **9.** BE DRAPED to hang down ○ *When her hair is down it falls across her shoulders.* **10.** TAKE PLACE to happen or occur as if falling on sth and enveloping it ○ *Night fell suddenly.* **11.** DISPLAY DISAPPOINTMENT to show an expression of disappointment ○ *Their faces fell when they heard the result.* **12.** GROW SAD to become sad and gloomy or to lose hope ○ *Our hearts fell.* **13.** STOP TO LOOK to settle or come to rest ○ *His gaze fell on an open book.* **14.** BE AVERTED to look away or downwards ○ *Her eyes fell.* **15.** BEGIN TO BE IN SPECIFIED STATE to begin to be in, or enter into, a specified state or condition ○ *The class eventually fell silent.* **16.** CHR SIN to sin, or give in to temptation (*archaic*) ◊ **Fall 17.** GEOG SLOPE to slope downwards and away ○ *The land falls gradually to the lake.* **18.** BE DUE to become due ○ *When does the next payment fall?* **19.** CRICKET BE LOST to be lost to the bowling side in a cricket match ○ *The fourth wicket fell just after tea.* **20.** BECOME PREGNANT to become pregnant (*regional*) **21.** START to begin doing sth vigourously ○ *The labourers fell to work on the ditch.* ■ *n.* **1.** ACT OF FALLING the act of falling or moving down freely or suddenly ○ *She broke her arm in a fall.* **2.** STH FALLEN sth that falls or has fallen, or the amount that has fallen ○ *a heavy fall of snow* **3.** DISTANCE DOWN the distance that sth drops or could fall ○ *a ten-foot fall* **4.** LOWERING OF STH a decrease in the amount, size, quantity, or quality of sth ○ *Even a slight fall in prices is welcome.* **5.** GEOG SLOPE a slope that heads downwards and away **6.** fall, Fall US, Can = autumn **7.** GEOG WATERFALL a waterfall or steep rapids (*often used in the plural; often used in placenames*) ○ *Niagara Falls* **8.** MIL MILITARY LOSS a military defeat or collapse, or the loss of sth to an enemy ○ *the fall of Leningrad* **9.** POL POLITICAL COLLAPSE a loss of political power or control ○ *the fall of the government* **10.** RELIG SINNING a giving in to temptation, or the committing of a sin **11.** END OF HOISTING ROPE the end of a rope or chain to which power is applied when hoisting sth **12.** WRESTLING WRESTLING MOVE a scoring move in wrestling in which one wrestler forces his or her opponent's shoulders to the floor for a specified period **13.** HAIR HAIRPIECE a hairpiece of long hair, usually attached to the top of the head and covered over in front by the wearer's own hair **14.** PLANTS DOWNWARD FACING PART OF IRIS BLOSSOM the outer part of an iris flower, resembling a petal that hangs down in front [Old English *feallan*, from prehistoric Germanic] ◊ **fall flat** to fail to have the intended effect ◊ **fall foul of, fall afoul of 1.** to come into conflict with sb or sth **2.** SAILING to collide with sth ◊ **fall short 1.** to be less than is needed **2. fall short of** to fail to meet a desired standard

fall about *vi.* to laugh raucously and uncontrollably (*informal*)

fall among *vt.* to become associated unwittingly with sb, sth, or a group

fall apart *vi.* **1.** BREAK DOWN to collapse, fail, or break into pieces **2.** BE DISTRESSED to be in a state of great emotional distress (*informal*)

fall away *vi.* **1.** DECREASE to become smaller in number, quantity, or size ○ *Attendance fell away after the third week of the course.* **2.** SLOPE to slope downwards **3.** STOP ASSOCIATING WITH SB to withdraw friendship, devotion, or support

fall back *vi.* **1.** RETREAT to retreat or move back, e.g. during a battle **2.** BE OVERTAKEN to be overtaken by others in a race or contest

fall back on, fall back upon *vt.* to resort to sth, especially sth familiar, if other plans do not work out

fall behind *v.* **1.** *vti.* FAIL TO KEEP UP to fail to keep up

with sb or sth **2.** *vi.* BE LATE to be late in doing sth, e.g. making a regular payment or completing a task ○ *He fell behind with the car payments.*

fall below *vt.* to fail to reach a desired standard or amount

fall down *vi.* **1.** COLLAPSE to collapse or drop to the ground **2.** FAIL to be invalid or unsuccessful

fall down on *vt.* to be unsuccessful or negligent in sth

fall for *vt.* **1.** FALL IN LOVE WITH to become infatuated with sb or sth, or fall in love **2.** BE DUPED BY STH to be deceived by sth

fall in *v.* **1.** *vti.* ARMY FORM RANKS to join or form an organized rank ○ *The whistle blew and the soldiers fell in.* **2.** *vi.* CAVE IN to collapse inwards

fall in with *vt.* **1.** MEET AND JOIN to meet and start associating with sb or a group **2.** AGREE WITH to agree or comply with sth or sb

fall off *v.* **1.** *vi.* DECLINE to decrease in size, number, or quality ○ *Share prices have fallen off in the last couple of days.* **2.** *vti.* SAILING SAIL DOWNWIND to deviate from a course to sail downwind, or make a vessel sail downwind

fall on *vt.* **1.** ATTACK to attack sb vigorously, especially by surprise (*literary*) **2.** BEGIN STH EAGERLY to begin eating or doing sth eagerly **3.** = fall to v. 1

fall out *v.* **1.** *vi.* QUARREL to have a quarrel with sb, especially one that leads to strained relations **2.** *vi.* OCCUR to happen **3.** *vti.* BREAK RANKS to leave or break up an organized rank or position

fall through *vi.* to fail to work out successfully

fall to *v.* **1.** *vt.* BE DUTY OF SB to be the responsibility, obligation, or duty of sb or a group ○ *It falls to the council to decide the matter.* **2.** *vti.* START to begin doing sth **3.** *vt.* BE GIVEN to be given by right or inheritance to sb

fall upon *vt.* **1.** = fall on **2.** = fall to

Fall *n.* in Judaism and Christianity, the lapse of humankind into a sinful state as a result of Adam and Eve's sin in disobeying God

fal la *n.* = fa-la

Falla /fí ə/, **Manuel de** (1876–1946) Spanish composer and pianist. Among his compositions are ballets such as *Wedded by Witchcraft* (1915) and *The Three-Cornered Hat* (1919).

fallacious /fə láyshəss/ *adj.* **1.** CONTAINING MISTAKEN BELIEF containing or involving a mistaken belief or idea **2.** DECEPTIVE deceptive or liable to mislead people [Early 16thC. Via Old French *fallacieux* from Latin *fallaciosus*, from *fallacia* (see FALLACY).] —**fallaciously** *adv.* —**fallaciousness** *n.*

fallacy /fálləssi/ (*plural* -cies) *n.* **1.** MISTAKEN BELIEF OR IDEA sth that is believed to be truth but is erroneous **2.** LOGIC INVALID ARGUMENT an argument or reasoning in which the conclusion does not follow from the premises **3.** DECEPTIVENESS the condition of being misleading or deceptive **4.** LOGIC LOGICAL ERROR IN ARGUMENT a mistake made in a line of reasoning that invalidates it [15thC. Via Old French *fallace* from Latin *fallacia* 'deception', from *fallere* 'to deceive'.]

fallal /fal lál/ *n.* a fancy ornament or piece of clothing [Early 18thC. Origin uncertain: said to be suggested by FALBALA.] —**fallalery** *n.*

fallback /fáwl bak/ *n.* **1.** REPLACEMENT OR ALTERNATIVE sth that can be used as a replacement or substitute if sth else does not or would not work **2.** MIL RETREAT a retreat or withdrawal

fallen *adj.* **1.** KILLED killed in battle **2.** ON THE GROUND on the ground after dropping down ○ *freshly fallen snow* ■ *n.* PEOPLE WHO DIED IN WAR those people killed in war, especially while fighting

fallen angel *n.* in Christianity, one of the angels led by Satan who rebelled against God and were cast out of heaven

fallen arch *n.* a flattening of the arches of the foot (*usually used in the plural*)

fallen woman *n.* a woman who is seen as sinful or dishonoured because she has had sexual relations outside marriage (*dated disapproving*)

faller /fáwler/ *n.* **1.** SB OR STH THAT FALLS a person, animal, or thing that falls **2.** *Australian* FELLER OF TREES sb who cuts down trees

fallfish /fáwl fish/ (*plural* -fish *or* -fishes) *n.* a large minnow native to eastern North America that is known for its substantial nests, made by piling up small pebbles. Latin name: *Semotilus corporalis.*

fall guy *n.* (*informal*) **1.** SB WHO CAN BE FOOLED sb who is easily tricked or deceived **2.** SCAPEGOAT sb who takes the blame for sth that sb else has done

fallible /fálləb'l/ *adj.* **1.** TENDING TO ERR liable to make mistakes **2.** NOT TRUE liable to be wrong or misleading [15thC. From medieval Latin *fallibilis*, from *fallere* 'to deceive'.] —**fallibility** /fállə bílləti/ *n.* —**fallibleness** /fálləb'lnəss/ *n.* —**fallibly** /-bli/ *adv.*

falling band *n.* a large collar, often trimmed with lace, turned down flat onto the shoulders and worn by men in the 17th century

falling-off *n.* a decline in quality or quantity

falling-out (*plural* **fallings-out**) *n.* a quarrel or disagreement, especially one that leads to strained relations with sb

falling sickness *n.* epilepsy (*archaic*)

falling star *n.* = meteor

fall line *n.* **1.** GEOG LINE ALONG TOP OF SLOPE an imaginary line along the edge of higher land, marked by rapids and waterfalls, that indicates where rivers begin to descend more steeply from a highland region to a lowland one **2.** SKIING, GEOG NATURAL ROUTE OF DESCENT OF HILL the natural route of descent on a hill between two given points **3.** MOUNTAINEERING LINE CONNECTING HIGH AND LOW POINT vertical line connecting a high and low point on a mountain or cliff

falloff /fáwl of/ *n.* a decrease or decline, especially in prices of sth or demand for sth

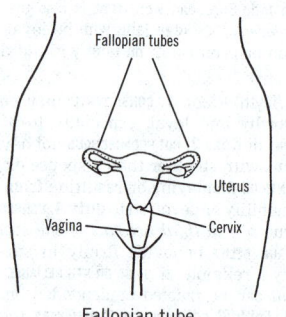

Fallopian tubes · Uterus · Vagina · Cervix

Fallopian tube

fallopian tube /fə lṓpi ən-/, **Fallopian tube** *n.* either of two narrow tubes through which a female mammal's eggs pass from either of the ovaries to the womb [Early 18thC. Named after Gabriele *Fallopio* (1523–62), the Italian anatomist who is reputed to have discovered the structures.]

fallout /fáwl owt/ *n.* **1.** PHYS RADIOACTIVE PARTICLES a cloud of radioactive dust that is created by a nuclear explosion and settles back down to the earth **2.** PHYS, METEOROL DESCENT OF RADIOACTIVE DUST the descent to the earth of particles from a cloud of radioactive dust **3.** INCIDENTAL CONSEQUENCES consequences, especially undesirable ones, that result incidentally from a situation or event

fallout shelter *n.* a place of refuge built to protect people from the effects of a nuclear weapon

fallow[1] /fállō/ *adj.* **1.** AGRIC LEFT UNSEEDED AFTER PLOUGHING left unseeded after ploughing for a period of time in order to recover natural fertility **2.** CURRENTLY INACTIVE currently inactive but with the possibility of activity or use in the future ■ *n.* AGRIC FALLOW LAND land that has been left fallow [13thC. From Old English *fealh*, from *fealgian* 'to break up land by ploughing'.] —**fallowness** *n.*

fallow[2] /fállō/ *adj.* of a light yellowish-brown colour [Old English *fealu*. Ultimately from an Indo-European word that is also the ancestor of English *appal*, *pale*, and *pallid*.] —**fallow** *n.*

Fallow deer

fallow deer *n.* a deer that lives in Europe and Asia, the male of which has broad flattened antlers and a variably coloured coat spotted with white in summer. Latin name: *Dama dama*.

Falmouth /fálməth/ seaside resort on the estuary of the River Fal, Cornwall, southeastern England. Population: 20,297 (1991).

false /fawlss, folss/ *adj.* (**falser, falsest**) **1.** INCORRECT not conforming to facts or truth **2.** MISTAKEN resulting from a mistaken belief or misunderstanding **3.** ARTIFICIAL imitating, copying, or having the same function as the other thing named and replacing or used alongside it **4.** DELIBERATELY DECEPTIVE done with or having the intention of deceiving sb **5.** NOT GENUINE intentionally made or adopted to deceive sb **6.** TREACHEROUS disloyal and untrustworthy **7.** BIOL CONFUSABLE WITH NAMED PLANT OR ANIMAL superficially resembling and often mistaken for the plant or animal named ○ *false acacia* ■ *adv.* (**falser, falsest**) DISHONESTLY in a dishonest and disloyal way (*literary*) [Pre-12thC. Directly or via Old French from Latin *falsus*, from *fallere* 'to deceive' (source of English *fail* and *fault*).] —**falsely** *adv.* —**falseness** *n.*

false acacia *n.* a North American deciduous tree of the pea family, with hanging clusters of fragrant flowers, compound leaves, thorns, and long seed pods. Genus: *Robinia*. US term **locust**

false alarm *n.* **1.** NEEDLESS ALARM a situation in which an alarm goes off unnecessarily **2.** STH CAUSING NEEDLESS WORRY sth that appears to be a problem but is not ○ *The company's impending bankruptcy proved to be a false alarm.*

false bedding *n.* = **cross-bedding**

false-card (**false-cards, false-carding, false-carded**) *vi.* to play a card in bridge to mislead an opponent about the cards held in the suit led

false dawn *n.* **1.** LIGHT OCCURRING BEFORE SUNRISE light that appears in the east just before dawn **2.** FAVOURABLE SIGN HAVING EXPECTATIONS UNFULFILLED a sign that promises but does not deliver good results

false friend *n.* **1.** DECEPTIVE FOREIGN WORD a word in a second language that looks as if it could be translated by the corresponding word in the first language but actually has a different meaning **2.** TREACHEROUS FRIEND a friend proved to be disloyal and untrustworthy

false fruit *n.* = **pseudocarp**

falsehood /fáwlss hood, fólss-/ *n.* **1.** LIE a lying or erroneous statement **2.** UNTRUTH sth that is untrue **3.** TELLING OF LIES the telling of untruths

—————— **WORD KEY: SYNONYMS** ——————
See Synonyms at *lie*.

false imprisonment *n.* the unlawful confinement of sb

false keel *n.* an extension to a boat's keel, added to protect the main keel or to increase stability

false memory syndrome *n.* a situation in which examination, therapy or hypnosis has elicited apparent memories, especially of childhood abuse, that are disputed by family members and often traumatic to the patient

false move *n.* an action showing an error of timing or judgment

false note *n.* sth that seems inappropriate, inconsistent, and badly timed

false position *n.* a situation in which sb is forced to act in an inconsistent or uncharacteristic way

false pregnancy *n.* = **phantom pregnancy**

false pretences *npl.* deception or misrepresentation in order to gain sth from sb ○ *He gained her trust under false pretences and didn't tell her he was wanted by the police.*

false rib *n.* any of the lower ribs, the bottom five pairs in humans, not connected directly to the sternum

false start *n.* **1.** ABANDONED START OF RACE a situation in which a competitor in a race breaks a regulation governing the starting procedure and the race has to be restarted **2.** UNSUCCESSFUL START a failed attempt to begin sth

false step *n.* **1.** CARELESS ACT an action showing an error of judgment **2.** STUMBLE an act of stumbling

false topaz *n.* = **citrine**

falsetto /fawl séttō, fol-/ *n.* (*plural* **-tos**) **1.** HIGH SINGING METHOD a method used by male singers to sing at a very high pitch by using more air and a combination of vocal chord vibration and head resonance. It is used by countertenors in classical music and has been applied to pop music by groups such as the Beach Boys. **2.** FALSETTO SINGER a male singer who sings in a very high voice **3.** FALSETTO VOICE a very high voice used by a male singer ■ *adv.* IN FALSETTO VOICE in an artificially or unusually high voice [Late 18thC. From Italian, literally 'little false (one)', from *falso* 'false', from Latin *falsus* (see FALSE).]

false vampire *n.* a bat that hunts and feeds on smaller bats, and is therefore falsely believed to feed on blood. There are five species of false vampires in Europe and Asia and one in Central and South America. Families: Megadermatidae and Phyllostomatidae.

falsework /fáwlss wurk, fólss-/ *n.* a structure or frame that supports sth that is being built

falsie /fáwlssi, fólssi/ *n.* either of two pads worn inside a bra to make the breasts look larger or more shapely (*informal*)

falsification /fáwlssifi káysh'n, fólss-/ *n.* **1.** FRAUDULENT ALTERATION the alteration of documents or evidence for the purposes of deception **2.** LIE a deliberate misrepresentation of the truth or facts

falsify /fáwlssi fī, fólss-/ (**-fies, -fying, -fied**) *vt.* **1.** ALTER FRAUDULENTLY to alter sth in order to deceive sb **2.** DISPROVE to prove that sth is incorrect **3.** MISREPRESENT to misrepresent the facts in order to mislead ○ *They falsified every detail of their story.* [15thC. Directly or via French *falsifier* from medieval Latin *falsificare* 'to act dishonestly', from, ultimately, Latin *falsus* (see FALSE) + Latin *facere* 'to make, do' (source of FACT).] —**falsifiability** /fáwlssi fī ə bílləti, fólss-/ *n.* —**falsifiable** /fáwlssi fī əb'l, fólss-/ *adj.* —**falsifier** /-fī ər, -/ *n.*

falsity /fáwlssəti, fólss-/ *n.* (*plural* **-ties**) **1.** BEING UNTRUE the fact or condition of being untrue **2.** STH UNTRUE sth that is incorrect or untrue [13thC. Directly or via French from Latin *falsitas*, from *falsus* (see FALSE).]

Falstaffian /fawl stáafi ən/ *adj.* typical of the Shakespearean character Sir John Falstaff in being bawdy, pleasure-loving, given to outlandish bragging, and of great size

faltboat /fált bōt/ *n.* a boat like a kayak consisting of a waterproof fabric that covers a collapsible frame. US term **foldboat** [Early 20thC. From German *Faltboot*, literally 'folding boat', from *falten* 'to fold' + *Boot* 'boat'.]

falter /fáwltər, fól-/ (**-ters, -tering, -tered**) *v.* **1.** *vi.* LOSE CONFIDENCE to become unsure and hesitant **2.** *vi.* BEGIN TO FAIL to lose strength, power, or vitality **3.** *vi.* STUMBLE to move unsteadily **4.** *vti.* HESITATE IN SPEECH to speak or say sth hesitatingly ○ *Trembling with shame, she faltered an apology.* [14thC. Origin uncertain: possibly from Scandinavian.] —**falterer** *n.* —**falteringly** *adv.*

—————— **WORD KEY: SYNONYMS** ——————
See Synonyms at *hesitate*.

FAM *abbr.* Free and Accepted Masons

fam. *abbr.* **1.** familiar **2.** family

Famagusta /fámmə gōóstə/ seaport and resort on the eastern coast of Cyprus, near Nicosia. It was a wealthy Venetian colony in the 15th and 16th centuries. Population: 38,960 (1996).

fame /faym/ *n.* **1.** RENOWN the condition of being very well known **2.** REPUTATION sb's reputation (*archaic*) **3.** RUMOUR rumour or report (*archaic*) [12thC. Via French from Latin *fama* 'talk, report, reputation' (source of English *famous*, *infamous*, and *defame*).]

famed /faymd/ *adj.* very well known ○ *The restaurant was famed for its steaks.*

familial /fə mílli əl/ *adj.* relating to or involving a family

familiar /fə mílli ər/ *adj.* **1.** OFTEN ENCOUNTERED well known, commonly seen or heard, and easily recognized **2.** ACQUAINTED WITH STH with a thorough knowledge and good understanding of sth ○ *Are you familiar with the theory?* **3.** FRIENDLY in or characteristic of a close personal relationship with sb **4.** IMPERTINENTLY INTIMATE unduly friendly or intimate in a way that is seen as presumptuous or impertinent (*dated*) **5.** FAMILIAL relating to or involving a family (*archaic*) ■ *n.* **1.** RELIG SPIRIT HELPING WITCH the supposed aid or helper of a witch, usually supposed to be a spirit with supernatural powers that takes the form of an animal, e.g. a cat **2.** INTIMATE FRIEND a close friend and companion (*formal*) **3.** CHR LAY MEMBER OF MONASTERY sb who lives and works in a monastic community but has not taken a vow **4.** CHR HOUSEHOLD ATTENDANT OF POPE OR BISHOP sb who undertakes domestic duties in the household of a pope or Roman Catholic bishop [13thC. Via French *familier* from Latin *familiaris*, from *familia* (see FAMILY).] —**familiarly** *adv.* —**familiarness** *n.*

familiarise *vt.* = **familiarize**

familiarity /fə mílli árrəti/ *n.* **1.** GOOD KNOWLEDGE thorough knowledge and understanding of sth ○ *Familiarity with database systems would be an advantage.* **2.** INTIMACY closeness and friendliness in a personal relationship **3.** FAMILIAR QUALITY the quality of being familiar ○ *The place had a strange familiarity about it.* **4.** UNWELCOME INTIMACY an intimacy that is improper and presumptuous (*dated*)

familiarize /fə mílli ə rīz/ (**-izes, -izing, -ized**), **familiarise** (**-ises, -ising, -ised**) *vt.* to acquire or provide sb with information or experience necessary for understanding or doing sth ○ *You should familiarize yourself with the emergency procedure.* —**familiarization** /fə mílli ə rī záysh'n/ *n.* —**familiarizer** /fə mílli ə rīzər/ *n.*

familiar spirit *n.* = **familiar** *n.* 1

family /fámmli/ *n.* (*plural* **-lies**) **1.** GROUP OF RELATIVES a group of people who are closely related by birth, marriage, or adoption. ◊ **extended family, nuclear family 2.** PEOPLE LIVING TOGETHER a group of people living together and functioning as a single household, usually consisting of parents and their children **3.** OTHERS IN SB'S FAMILY the other members of the family to which sb belongs ○ *He always spends Sunday afternoon with his family.* **4.** OFFSPRING a child or set of children born to sb ○ *They're not ready to start a family.* **5.** LINEAGE all the people who are descended from a common ancestor **6.** GROUP WITH STH IN COMMON a group whose members are related in origin, characteristics, or occupation **7.** LING RELATED LANGUAGES a group of languages that have a common origin **8.** BIOL SET OF RELATED ORGANISMS a category in the taxonomic classification of related organisms, comprising one or more genera **9.** MATH RELATED MATHEMATICAL SHAPES OR EXPRESSIONS a set of related mathematical curves, surfaces, or functions, usually expressed as a single equation containing one or more parameters or arbitrary constants ○ *a family of concentric circles* **10.** PHYS RELATED ISOTOPES a group of radioactive isotopes that collectively constitute a decay series or chain **11.** US BRANCH OF MAFIA a branch of the Mafia or of a similar large criminal group (*informal*) **12.** *South Asia* WIFE sb's wife ■ *adj.* **1.** USED BY FAMILY used, owned, or employed by a family, or suitable for one **2.** APPROPRIATE FOR CHILDREN suitable to be experienced by families with children **3.** SERVING FAMILIES serving families not just businesses or institutions [15thC. From Latin *familia* 'servants of a household, household, family', from *famulus* 'servant'.] ◇ **in the family way** pregnant (*dated informal*)

family allowance *n.* a former allowance paid by the government in the United Kingdom and Canada to parents or guardians of children below a specified age. Now called **child benefit**

family benefit *n.* an allowance paid by a government to parents or guardians of dependent children, e.g. in New Zealand

family Bible *n.* a large Bible handed down in a family from one generation to another. A family Bible usually contains records of births, marriages, and deaths.

family circle *n.* the members of a family who are closely related and usually who live together

family court *n.* in the United States, a court that rules on domestic disputes, especially those involving the care and custody of children

family credit *n.* a regular payment made by the UK government to families on a low income with at least one dependent child

Family Division *n.* a branch of the High Court of Justice in the United Kingdom, handling divorce and cases concerning the custody of children

family doctor *n.* a GP

family man *n.* a married man who enjoys family life and spends a lot of time with his wife and children

family name *n.* = **surname**

family planning *n.* the use of birth control methods to choose the number and timing of children born into a family

family room *n.* a room reserved for the use of people with children, especially in a pub

family tree *n.* a chart that shows the relationships of members of a family over time, including dates of marriages, births, and deaths

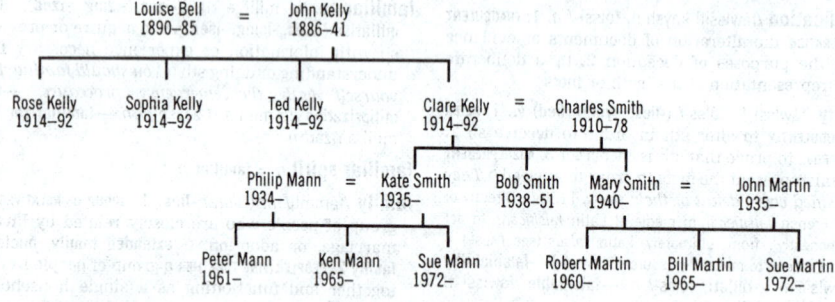

Family tree

famine /fámmin/ *n.* **1.** ᴇxᴛʀᴇᴍᴇ ꜰᴏᴏᴅ sᴄᴀʀᴄɪᴛʏ a severe shortage of food resulting in widespread hunger **2.** ᴅᴇꜰɪᴄɪᴇɴᴄʏ ᴏꜰ sᴛʜ a severe shortage of sth **3.** ᴇxᴛʀᴇᴍᴇ ʜᴜɴɢᴇʀ extreme hunger and starvation [14thC. From French, from *faim* 'hunger', from, ultimately, Latin *fames* (source of English *famish*).]

famish /fámmish/ (**-ishes, -ishing, -ished**) *vti.* **1.** sᴛᴀʀᴠᴇ to be extremely hungry, or make sb extremely hungry (*often passive*) **2.** ᴅɪᴇ ᴏꜰ ʜᴜɴɢᴇʀ to die or kill sb by starvation (*archaic*) [14thC. Formed from earlier *fame*, from Old French *afamer*, from assumed Vulgar Latin *affamare*, literally 'to hunger towards', from Latin *fames*.] —**famishment** *n.*

famous /fáymᴇss/ *adj.* **1.** ᴠᴇʀʏ ᴡᴇʟʟ ᴋɴᴏᴡɴ known and recognized by many people **2.** ᴇxᴄᴇʟʟᴇɴᴛ excellent and satisfying (*dated*) [14thC. Via Old French *fameus* from Latin *famosus*, from *fama* (see FAME).] —**famously** *adv.* **famousness** *n.*

famulus /fámmyooᴌᴇss/ (*plural* **-li** /-lī/) *n.* a personal secretary or attendant, especially to a scholar or magician (*literary*) [Mid-19thC. From Latin, 'servant' (see FAMILY).]

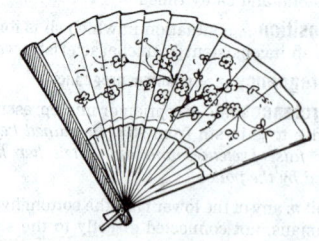

Fan

fan[1] /fan/ *n.* **1.** ᴅᴇᴠɪᴄᴇ ꜰᴏʀ ᴍᴏᴠɪɴɢ ᴀɪʀ a device to cool or circulate currents of air, especially one with rotating blades **2.** ᴘᴇʀsᴏɴᴀʟ ᴄᴏᴏʟɪɴɢ ᴅᴇᴠɪᴄᴇ a flat disc on a handle or a semicircular device of folding struts of paper, silk, or plastic for waving to and fro in order to cool the face **3.** sᴛʜ ꜰᴀɴ-sʜᴀᴘᴇᴅ sth in the shape of an open handheld fan, e.g. the tail of a peacock **4.** ᴀɢʀɪᴄ ᴡɪɴɴᴏᴡɪɴɢ ᴍᴀᴄʜɪɴᴇ a series of revolving blades used to winnow or clean grain ■ *v.* (**fans, fanning, fanned**) **1.** ʙʟᴏᴡ ᴏɴ sᴛʜ to blow a current of air steadily and lightly across or around sth, either cooling or agitating it ○ *A cool breeze fanned the shore.* **2.** *vt.* ᴍᴏᴠᴇ ᴀɪʀ ᴜsɪɴɢ ꜰᴀɴ to move air about using a fan **3.** *vt.* sᴛɪʀ ᴜᴘ to cause emotions to become more intense or a situation to become more volatile **4.** *vt.* ᴀɢʀɪᴄ sᴇᴘᴀʀᴀᴛᴇ ɢʀᴀɪɴ ꜰʀᴏᴍ ᴄʜᴀꜰꜰ to winnow grain by blowing away the chaff **5.** *vt.* ᴀʀᴍs ꜰɪʀᴇ ɢᴜɴ ᴡɪᴛʜ ʀᴇᴘᴇᴀᴛᴇᴅ ᴄʜᴏᴘᴘɪɴɢ ᴍᴏᴠᴇᴍᴇɴᴛ to fire a gun repeatedly by holding the trigger back and chopping at the hammer with the open hand **6.** *vti.* sᴘʀᴇᴀᴅ ᴀᴄʀᴏss sᴛʜ to spread or spread sth out in the shape of an open handheld fan [Pre-12thC. From Latin *vannus* 'device for winnowing grain'. The sense of cooling device developed in the 16thC as a metaphorical extension.] —**fanner** *n.*

fan out *vti.* to spread or spread sth out in the shape of an open handheld fan

fan[2] /fan/ *n.* **1.** ᴋᴇᴇɴ ᴀᴅᴍɪʀᴇʀ an enthusiastic admirer of a celebrity or public performer **2.** = **fanatic** *n.* **2** [Late 19thC. Shortening of FANATIC. The word is first recorded from the 17thC, but it was not used regularly until the 19thC (referring to sports supporters).]

Fanagalo /fánnᴇgalō/, **Fanakalo** /-kᴇlō/ *n.* a pidgin spoken in parts of South Africa. It is based on Zulu and English and developed mainly in the mining communities of Namibia and Zimbabwe, and around Johannesburg. [Mid-20thC. From the common phrase *fana ga lo* 'like this' in the lingua franca of southern African mines: probably from Zulu (*kuluma*) *fana ka lo*, literally 'speak like this'.] —**Fanagalo** *adj.*

fanatic /fᴇ náttik/ *n.* **1.** ᴇxᴛʀᴇᴍɪsᴛ sb who has extreme and sometimes irrational enthusiasms or beliefs, especially in religion or politics **2.** ꜰᴀɴ ᴏꜰ sᴛʜ sb who is very enthusiastic about a pastime or hobby ■ *adj.* = **fanatical** [Mid-16thC. Directly or via French from Latin *fanaticus* 'inspired by a god, frenzied', from *fanum* 'temple' (source of English *profane*).]

fanatical /fᴇ náttik'l/ *adj.* excessively enthusiastic about a particular belief, cause, or activity —**fanatically** *adv.* —**fanaticalness** *n.*

fanaticise *vti.* = **fanaticize**

fanaticism /fᴇ náttisizᴇm/ *n.* an extreme and often irrational enthusiasm or belief

fanaticize /fᴇ nátti sīz/ (**-cizes, -cizing, -cized**), **fanaticise** (**-cises, -cising, -cised**) *vti.* to make sb fanatical about sth, or become fanatical

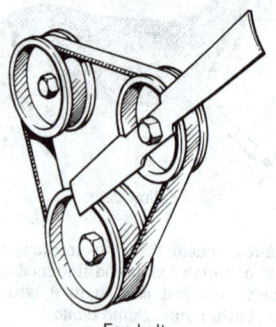

Fan belt

fan belt *n.* a continuous belt that turns a fan, especially one turning the cooling fan in the engine of a motor vehicle

fanciable /fánssi ᴇb'l/ *adj.* sexually desirable (*informal*)

fancier /fánssi ᴇr/ *n.* **1.** ᴇɴᴛʜᴜsɪᴀsᴛ sb especially interested in or enthusiastic about sth **2.** ʙʀᴇᴇᴅᴇʀ ᴏꜰ ᴘʟᴀɴᴛ ᴏʀ ᴀɴɪᴍᴀʟ sb with a special interest in the breeding of a particular animal or plant

fanciful /fánssif'l/ *adj.* **1.** ɪᴍᴀɢɪɴᴀʀʏ based on imagination or dreams **2.** ɪᴍᴀɢɪɴᴀᴛɪᴠᴇ ᴀɴᴅ ɪᴍᴘʀᴀᴄᴛɪᴄᴀʟ led by imagination rather than realism and practicality **3.** ᴄᴜʀɪᴏᴜsʟʏ ᴍᴀᴅᴇ strangely and imaginatively designed or made —**fancifully** *adv.* —**fancifulness** *n.*

fan club *n.* an organization whose members are devoted to a celebrity or public performer, providing information and sometimes organizing special events

fancy /fánssi/ *adj.* (**-cier, -ciest**) **1.** ɴᴏᴛ ᴘʟᴀɪɴ elaborately and ornately decorated **2.** ɪɴᴛʀɪᴄᴀᴛᴇ intricately and skilfully performed **3.** ᴀɪᴍɪɴɢ ᴛᴏ ɪᴍᴘʀᴇss attempting or expected to impress **4.** ᴇxᴘᴇɴsɪᴠᴇ excessively priced or valued ○ *fancy prices* ○ *fancy restaurants charging high prices* **5.** sᴇʟᴇᴄᴛɪᴠᴇʟʏ ʙʀᴇᴅ used to describe animals that have been bred for specific features and qualities ■ *v.* (**-cies, -cying, -cied**) **1.** ᴡɪsʜ ꜰᴏʀ sᴛʜ to want to do or have sth ○ *I fancy a walk this afternoon.* ○ *Do you fancy a coffee?* **2.** *vt.* ᴅᴇsɪʀᴇ sʙ to find sb sexually desirable (*informal*) ○ *I'm sure he fancies you!* **3.** *vr.* ꜰʟᴀᴛᴛᴇʀ ʏᴏᴜʀsᴇʟꜰ to have too high an opinion of yourself ○ *He rather fancies himself as a musician.* **4.** *vt.* sᴜᴘᴘᴏsᴇ to be inclined to think that sth is the case ○ *I fancy that it will be bright and sunny tomorrow.* **5.** *vt.* ɪᴍᴀɢɪɴᴇ to form the idea of sth in the imagination **6.** *vt.* sᴇʟᴇᴄᴛ ᴀs ᴡɪɴɴᴇʀ to think that sb will succeed ○ *Who do you fancy for the title?* ■ *interj.* ᴇxᴘʀᴇssɪɴɢ sᴜʀᴘʀɪsᴇ used to express surprise (*informal*) ○ *Fancy! All that money!* ○ *Fancy that! I would never have believed it!* ○ *Fancy them splitting up after all these years!* ■ *n.* (*plural* **-cies**) **1.** sᴜᴅᴅᴇɴ ʟɪᴋɪɴɢ an impulsive desire for sth ○ *The hat caught my fancy.* **2.** ɴᴏᴛɪᴏɴ an unfounded belief about sth **3.** sᴛʜ ɪᴍᴀɢɪɴᴀʀʏ sth created by the imagination, especially sth of a playful or superficial nature **4.** ʟɪᴋᴇʟʏ ᴡɪɴɴᴇʀ sth or sb thought likely to succeed or win **5.** ᴘʟᴀʏꜰᴜʟ ɪᴍᴀɢɪɴᴀᴛɪᴠᴇɴᴇss the faculty of using the imagination playfully or inventively **6.** ɢᴏᴏᴅ ᴛᴀsᴛᴇ good critical taste and judgment (*formal*) **7.** ʙᴏxɪɴɢ ᴇɴᴛʜᴜsɪᴀsᴛs enthusiasts of a sport or pastime, especially boxing (*archaic*) [15thC. A contraction of FANTASY. The adjective arose from the idea of sth varied according to the fancy.] —**fancily** *adv.* —**fanciness** *n.*

fancy dress *n.* unusual clothing worn to a social gathering, often depicting a famous person, fictional character, or historical period [Because it is a costume arranged according to the wearer's fancy]

fancy-free *adj.* free to go anywhere and do anything ○ *footloose and fancy-free* [Literally 'free from the power of love', from FANCY in an obsolete sense of the word, 'love, amorous inclination']

fancy goods *npl.* small items sold as gifts or novelties

fancy man *n.* (*dated informal*) **1.** WOMAN'S LOVER the lover or boyfriend of a woman, especially a married woman **2.** PIMP a man who finds customers for prostitutes in return for part or all of their earnings

fancy woman *n.* (*dated informal*) **1.** MAN'S LOVER the lover or girlfriend of a man, especially a married man **2.** PROSTITUTE a prostitute

fancywork /fánssi wurk/ *n.* embroidery and other decorative needlework

fan dance *n.* an erotic dance in which large fans are used to mask and reveal parts of the dancer's nude body

fandangle /fan dáng g'l/ *n.* a gaudy ornament or piece of jewellery of little value [Mid-19thC. Origin uncertain: perhaps an alteration of FANDANGO, modelled on the obsolete *newfangle* 'new thing or fashion, novelty'.]

fandango /fan dáng gō/ (*plural* **-gos**) *n.* **1.** DANCE SPANISH DANCE a vigorous Spanish or Latin American dance in triple time, traditionally performed by a man and woman as a courtship ritual **2.** MUSIC DANCE MUSIC a piece of music for the fandango, in triple time [Mid-18thC. From Spanish, of uncertain origin: perhaps African.]

fane /fayn/ *n.* a temple or shrine to a god or gods (*archaic*) [14thC. From Latin *fanum* 'temple' (source of English *fanatic*).]

fanfare /fán fair/ *n.* **1.** TRUMPET FLOURISH a short dramatic series of notes played on trumpets or other brass instruments, especially to mark the arrival of sb important **2.** SHOWY DISPLAY any dramatic and ostentatious event, especially an announcement or publicity stunt [Mid-18thC. From French, of uncertain origin: perhaps from, ultimately, Arabic *farfār* 'chatterer'; or perhaps an imitation of the sound.]

fanfold /fán fōld/ *adj.* folded into pleats by making alternate folds in opposite directions ○ *fanfold computer paper*

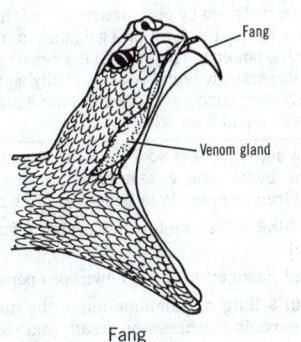

Fang

fang /fang/ *n.* **1.** CANINE TOOTH a long pointed tooth of a mammal on each side of the mouth towards the front **2.** SNAKE'S TOOTH a tooth of a venomous snake, with a hollow or grooves through which venom is injected **3.** SPIDER'S MOUTHPART either of the pair of mouthparts of a spider, from which poison is emitted **4.** *Aus* FAST DRIVE a high-speed drive in a motor vehicle (*slang*) ○ *Let's go for a fang down to the beach.* ■ **fangs** *npl.* TEETH the teeth (*informal*) ■ *vti.* (**fangs, fanging, fanged**) *Aus* DRIVE FAST to drive a motor vehicle at high speed (*slang*) [Old English, 'plunder, booty'. In Middle English, the word also had the sense of 'grasp' or 'embrace', from which the meaning of 'animal's tooth' presumably derives.]

Fang /fang/ (*plural* **Fang** *or* **Fangs**) *n.* **1.** PEOPLES MEMBER OF W AFRICAN PEOPLE a member of a people who live mainly in the rain forests of Gabon, Equatorial Guinea, and Cameroon **2.** LANG W AFRICAN LANGUAGE the language spoken by the Fang. It is a Bantu language of the Benue-Congo branch of the Niger-Congo family of African languages. About two million people speak Fang. [Mid-19thC. From French *Fan*, of uncertain origin: probably from Fan *Pangwe*.] —**Fang** *adj.*

fanged /fangd/ *adj.* having fangs

fangy /fánggi/ *adj. Aus* able to move or function at high speed (*slang*)

fanheater /fán heetar/ *n.* an electric heater that blows out a current of warm air using a fan

fanjet /fán jet/ *n.* = **turbofan**

fan letter *n.* a letter written to a celebrity by a fan

fanlight /fán līt/ *n.* **1.** FAN-SHAPED WINDOW a semicircular window above a door or another window, often with struts forming the shape of an open handheld fan **2.** WINDOW ABOVE DOOR a small rectangular window above a door. US term **transom 3.** = **skylight**

fan mail *n.* letters sent to celebrities by their fans

fanny /fánni/ (*plural* **-nies**) *n.* **1.** TABOO TERM a taboo term for the female genitals (*taboo slang*) **2.** *US, Can* BUTTOCKS the buttocks (*informal*) [Early 20thC. Origin uncertain: perhaps from *Fanny*, the nickname of *Frances*.]

Fanny Adams /fánni áddəmz/ *n.* tinned meat or stew, especially as fed to sailors (*archaic slang*) [Late 19thC. The name of a young girl who was murdered and dismembered c. 1867.]

fanny pack *n. US* = **bum bag**

fan palm *n.* a palm tree such as the palmetto that has divided fan-shaped leaves

fantabulous /fan tábbyŏŏlass/ *adj.* extremely good (*humorous*) [Mid-20thC. A blend of FANTASTIC and FABULOUS.]

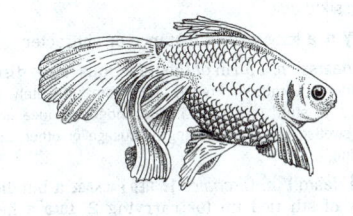

Fantail

fantail /fán tayl/ *n.* **1.** FAN-SHAPED TAIL OR END a tail or the end of sth shaped like an open handheld fan **2.** BIRDS PIGEON WITH FAN-SHAPED TAIL a breed of domestic pigeon with a broad fan-shaped tail **3.** BIRDS BIRD WITH BROAD TAIL a small flycatcher of Australia, New Zealand, and Asia with a fan-shaped tail. Genus: *Rhipidura.* **4.** ZOOL GOLDFISH WITH BROAD TAIL a goldfish with a broad double tail fin **5.** WINDMILL SAIL a secondary sail on a windmill that keeps the main sails facing into the wind **6.** *US* SHIPPING ROUNDED PART OF STERN a rounded overhanging part of a ship's stern

fan-tan /fán tan/ *n.* **1.** GAMBLING GAMBLING GAME a Chinese gambling game in which players bet on how many items that have been concealed under a bowl remain after being counted off in fours **2.** CARDS CARD GAME a card game in which players seek to discard all their cards in a sequence based on the same suit as a seven that has been led [Late 19thC. From Chinese, from *fān* 'turn, chance' + *tān* 'to spread out'.]

fantasia /fan táyzi ə, fántə zee ə/ *n.* an instrumental composition in a free and improvisatory style, sometimes based on well-known melodies [Early 18thC. From Italian, literally 'fantasy, imagination', from Latin *phantasia* (see FANTASY).]

— **WORD KEY: CULTURAL NOTE** —

Fantasia, a film produced by Walt Disney (1940). This ambitious attempt to popularize classical music consists of cartoon animation matched to eight famous musical compositions. Its best-known sequences include hippos dancing to Ponchielli's 'Dance of the Hours' and Mickey Mouse as the protagonist of Dukas' 'The Sorcerer's Apprentice'.

fantasise *vti.* = **fantasize**

fantasist /fántəssist/ *n.* sb who imagines fantasies

fantasize /fántə sīz/ (**-sizes, -sizing, -sized**), **fantasise** (**-sises, -sising, -sised**) *vti.* to form or indulge in fantasies of the imagination

fantast /fán tast/ *n.* sb who has impractical daydreams [Late 16thC. Via German *Phantast* from Greek *phantastēs* 'boaster', from *phantazein* or *phantazesthai* (see FANTASY).]

fantastic /fan tástik/, **fantastical** /fan tástik'l/ *adj.* **1.** EXCELLENT extraordinarily good **2.** BIZARRE extremely strange or weird in appearance **3.** INCREDIBLE apparently impossible but real or true **4.** UNLIKELY unusual and unlikely to be successful **5.** ENORMOUS much larger than is usual, expected, or desirable **6.** IMAGINARY existing only in the imagination ■ *interj.* EXPRESSING PLEASURE used to express amazement at and approval of some event or piece of information (*informal*) ○ *You won the game? Fantastic!* [14thC. Via French from, ultimately, Greek *phantastikos*, from *phantazein* or *phantazesthai* (see FANTASY).] —**fantasticality** /fan tásti kálləti/ *n.* —**fantasticalness** /fan tástik'lnəss/ *n.*

fantastically /fan tástikli/ *adv.* **1.** VERY extremely **2.** VERY WELL in a superb way **3.** STRANGELY in a weird and strange way

fantasy /fántəssi/, **phantasy** *archaic n.* (*plural* **-sies**) **1.** MENTAL IMAGE OR DREAM an image or dream created by the imagination **2.** PSYCHOL CREATION OF MENTAL IMAGES the creation of exaggerated mental images in response to an ungratified need **3.** IMPRACTICAL IDEA an unrealistic and impractical idea **4.** IMAGINATIVE POWER the creative power of the imagination **5.** LITERAT GENRE OF FICTION a type of fiction featuring imaginary worlds and magical or supernatural events **6.** MUSIC = **fantasia** ■ *vti.* (**-sies, -sying, -sied**) = **fantasize** [14thC. Via Old French from Greek *phantasia*, 'appearance, imagination', from, ultimately, *phainein* 'to show' (source of English *phantom* and *phenomenon*).]

fantasy football *n.* a competition in which players create their own football team from among real footballers in a number of teams and score points according to the real footballers' performances

Fanti /fánti/ (*plural* **-ti** *or* **-tis**), **Fante** (*plural* **-te** *or* **-tes**) *n.* **1.** PEOPLES MEMBER OF AFRICAN PEOPLE a member of an African people living in the rain forests of Ghana and the Côte d'Ivoire **2.** LANG W AFRICAN LANGUAGE a dialect of Akan spoken in parts of Ghana and the Côte d'Ivoire [Early 19thC. From Fanti.] —**Fanti** *adj.*

Fantin-Latour /fóN taN la tŏŏr/, **Henri** (1836–1904) French painter and lithographer. He is famed for his group portraits and still lifes, especially those of flowers. Full name **Ignace Henri Jean Théodore Fantin-Latour**

fantod /fánt od/ *n.* nervous anxiety (*informal*) ○ *He had a fit of the fantods.* [Mid-19thC. Origin unknown.]

fan vaulting *n.* a form of vaulting in which ribs fan out from the four corners of a bay, like a fan

fanwort /fán wurt/ *n.* an aquatic plant of the lily family that has fan-shaped submerged and floating leaves. Genus: *Cambomba.*

fanzine /fán zeen/ *n.* an amateur magazine produced for fans of a pastime or celebrity [Mid-20thC. Coined from FAN² + MAGAZINE.]

FAO *abbr.* Food and Agricultural Organization (of the UN)

f.a.o. *abbr.* for the attention of

FAQ /fak, éf ay kyŏŏ/ *abbr.* **1.** FAQ, FAQs COMPUT frequently asked questions **2.** SHIPPING free alongside quay

f.a.q. *abbr.* COMM fair average quality

faqir *n.* = **fakir**

far /faar/ (**farther** /faárthər/ *or* **further** /fúrthər/, **farthest** /faárthist/ *or* **furthest** /fúrthist/) CORE MEANING: an adverb and adjective indicating that sth is a long way away in distance or time ○ *These vessels had been venturing as far as Iceland for cod.* ○ *They have been fishing in the area as far back as 1980.*

1. *adv.* A LONG WAY OFF at, to, or from a great distance ○ *We saw the first outline of the shore far away.* **2.** *adv.* A LONG TIME OFF at or to a long time distant from the point of reference ○ *The well was contaminated as far back as 1986.* **3.** *adv.* MUCH OR MANY to or by a considerable degree ○ *Keeping a dog healthy is far more complicated than it seems.* ○ *There are far fewer factory jobs available these days.* **4.** *adj.* DISTANT remote in space or time ○ *He stood there, gazing into the far distance.* **5.** *adj.* MORE DISTANT more distant from sb or sth ○ *Becky cowered in a far corner of the room.* **6.** *adj.* EXTREME having an extreme position in a particular direction ○ *His politics are far left of centre.* [Old English *feor(r)*, from the comparative of the assumed Germanic word for 'beyond'. Ultimately from an Indo-European word that is also the ancestor of English *forth* and *prow*.] —**farness** *n.* ◇ **far and away** without a doubt and by a large margin ○ *She is far and away the best player that we have.* ◇ **far and near** everywhere

○ *Doctors from far and near flocked to his bedside.* ◇ **far and wide** covering a great distance ○ *The church bells will be heard far and wide.* ◇ **far from** indicates that sth is not the case ○ *Such warm weather is far from typical of this time of year.* ◇ **far from it** on the contrary ○ *He was not the tallest boy in the class – far from it.* ◇ **far gone 1.** in a state of deterioration and unable to function ○ *These shoes can't be repaired – they're too far gone.* **2.** very drunk (*informal*) ○ *there's nothing pleasant about someone that far gone.* ◇ **go far 1.** to be very successful ○ *He is very talented and I am sure he will go far in his chosen career.* **2.** to last or be sufficient ○ *Three loaves of bread won't go far once my family gets going.* ◇ **go too far** to do or say sth that is unacceptable or that exceeds reasonable limits ○ *Harriet paused, and realized that she had gone too far.* ◇ **in so far as** to the extent that ◇ **so far 1.** up to this moment ○ *So far, 150 people have shown an interest in the product.* **2.** up to a certain point, extent, or degree ○ *Freedom of information can only go so far.* ◇ **so far so good** indicates satisfaction with progress made up to this point ○ *So far so good, but the last part of the climb is the hardest.* ◇ **thus far** up to this point ○ *The evidence thus far pointed clearly and conclusively against him.*

farad /fárrəd, fá rad/ *n.* the SI unit of capacitance equal to that of a capacitor carrying one coulomb of charge when a potential difference of one volt is applied. Symbol **F** [Mid-19thC. Named after Michael FARADAY.]

faradaic *adj.* = faradic

faraday /fárrə day/ *n.* a unit of electricity equal to that needed to deposit a unit amount of singly charged substance during electrolysis, equivalent to 96,485 coulombs. Symbol **F** [Early 20thC. Named after Michael FARADAY.]

Michael Faraday

Faraday /fárrə day/, **Michael** (1791–1867) British physicist and chemist. He is best known for his discoveries of electromagnetic induction and of the laws of electrolysis. He also showed how electromagnetic induction could be used in generators and transformers.

faradic /fə ráddik/, **faradaic** /fárrə dáy ik/ *adj.* relating to an intermittent alternating current produced in the secondary winding of an induction coil [Late 19thC. From French *faradique*, named after Michael FARADAY.]

faradise *vt.* = faradize

faradism /fárrədizəm/ *n.* the therapeutic application of an alternating electric current to stimulate nerve and muscle function [Late 19thC. Named after Michael FARADAY. See -ISM.]

faradize /fárrə díz/ (**-dizes, -dizing, -dized**), **faradise** (**-dises, -dising, -dised**) *vt.* to use an alternating electric current to stimulate nerve and muscle function [Mid-19thC. Named after Michael FARADAY.] —**faradization** /fárrə dī záysh'n/ *n.* —**faradizer** /fárrə dīzər/ *n.*

farandole /fárrəndōl/ *n.* **1.** DANCE **PROVENÇAL DANCE** a lively dance from the Provence region of France in which dancers link hands to form a weaving line following the leader **2.** MUSIC **MUSIC FOR FARANDOLE DANCE** a piece of music for the farandole, in six-eight or four-four time [Mid-19thC. Via French from modern Provençal *farandoulo*, of unknown origin.]

faraway /fáarə wáy/ *adj.* **1.** REMOTE a great distance away **2.** SOUNDING DISTANT heard from a distance **3.** DREAMY having a dreamy, absent-minded expression or appearance —**farawayness** *n.*

farce /faarss/ *n.* **1.** COMIC PLAY a comic play in which authority, order, and morality are at risk and ordinary people are caught up in extraordinary goings on **2.** ABSURD SITUATION a ridiculous situation in which everything goes wrong or becomes a sham ○ *It was a complete farce – the bride changed her mind at the last minute and the two families ended up having a public slanging match.* **3.** STYLE OF COMIC DRAMA the style of comic drama in which authority, order, and morality are at risk and ordinary people are caught up in extraordinary goings on [Early 16thC. Via French, literally 'stuffing', from, ultimately, Latin *farcire*. In the Middle Ages comical interludes were often inserted into religious plays.]

farceur /faar súr/ *n.* **1.** SB INVOLVED WITH FARCES an actor in or writer of farces **2.** JOKER sb who is intentionally comical [Late 17thC. From French, from *farce* (see FARCE).]

farcical /fáarssik'l/ *adj.* **1.** ABSURD AND MIXED UP resembling a farce in being ridiculous and confused **2.** IN STYLE OF FARCE performed or written in the style of a farce —**farcicality** /fáarssi kálləti/ *n.* —**farcically** /fáarsikli/ *adv.*

far cry *n.* a long way in distance or character

farcy /fáarssi/ *n.* a form of the infectious horse disease glanders [14thC. Via French *farcin* from, ultimately, Latin *farcire* 'to stuff' (see FARCE). The underlying idea is that of a swollen gland resembling a sausage or other stuffed pudding.]

fardel /faard'l/ *n.* (*archaic*) **1.** TIED PACKAGE a bundle or pack of sth tied up for carrying **2.** LOAD a heavy load [14thC. From Old French, 'bundle, load', the diminutive of *farde* 'bundle', of uncertain origin; perhaps ultimately from Arabic *fardah*, *farde* 'load'.]

fare /fair/ *n.* **1.** COST OF TRAVEL the amount charged for a journey **2.** PASSENGER a paying passenger in a taxi **3.** FOOD food that is provided, especially when simple and substantial **4.** ENTERTAINMENT the range of entertainment provided ■ *vi.* (**fares, faring, fared**) **1.** MANAGE IN DOING STH to get on in a specified way in doing or experiencing sth ○ *How did she fare in the exam?* **2.** HAPPEN to turn out in a specified way for sb **3.** TRAVEL to go on a journey **4.** EAT to dine or be given food (*old*) [Old English *fær* or *faru* 'journey', from prehistoric Germanic. The sense 'food' seems to derive from the notion of 'how well sb is faring, how sb is provided for'.]

Fareham /fáirəm/ market town between Portsmouth and Southampton in Hampshire, southern England. Population: 54,866 (1991).

fare stage *n.* **1.** SECTION OF BUS ROUTE one of the divisions of a bus route used for calculating the fare **2.** BUS STOP a bus stop marking the boundary of a division in a bus route on which the fare is calculated

farewell /fair wél/ *n.* EXPRESSION OF PARTING GOOD WISHES an expression of good wishes at parting ■ *adj.* SAYING GOODBYE marking an end, conclusion, or leavetaking ■ *interj.* GOODBYE used to express good wishes at parting (*dated*) ○ *Farewell, my friend!* [14thC. From the phrase *fare well*, originally addressed to sb setting out on a journey.]

Farewell, Cape /fáir wel/ cape on the northern coast of the South Island, New Zealand. It is the northernmost point of the South Island.

farfel /fáarf'l/, **farfal** *n.* pasta in the shape of small grains [Late 19thC. From Yiddish *farfl*, from Middle High German *varveln* 'noodle, noodle soup'.]

far-fetched *adj.* exaggerated and unconvincing [The first meaning of the word was 'brought from far']

far-flung *adj.* **1.** WIDESPREAD distributed over a wide area **2.** REMOTE at a great distance

Fargo /fáargō/ city in southeastern North Dakota, on the Minnesota border, south of Grand Forks. Population: 83,788 (1996).

Faridabad /fə reèdə bad/, **Farīdābād** industrial city in northern India, 30 km/19 mi. south of Delhi, in the state of Haryana. Population: 617,717 (1991).

farina /fə reènə/ *n.* **1.** FLOUR flour or meal made from wheat, nuts, or vegetables **2.** STARCH starch, es-

pecially that made from potatoes [14thC. From Latin *farina* 'ground corn, flour, meal', from *far* (see FARRAGO).]

farinaceous /fárri náyshəss/ *adj.* containing or consisting of starch [Mid-17thC. From late Latin *farinaceus*, from Latin *farina* 'flour'.]

farinose /fárrinōss, -nōz/ *adj.* **1.** FOOD TECH YIELDING STARCH consisting of or yielding starch **2.** BOT FLOURY IN APPEARANCE with a powdery or floury appearance, especially because of a covering of fine whitish hairs [Early 18thC. From late Latin *farinosus*, from Latin *farina* 'flour'.]

farl /faarl/ *n. Scotland* a triangular oatcake, scone, or piece of shortbread, made by cutting a round cake into four [Late 17thC. A contraction of *fardel* 'fragment, piece, quarter', itself a contraction of FOURTH + DEAL (noun). The original meaning was 'quarter of a thin cake'.]

farm /faarm/ *n.* **1.** AGRICULTURAL LAND AND BUILDINGS an area of land where crops are grown or animals are reared for sale, for commercial purposes, together with appropriate buildings **2.** PLACE PRODUCING PARTICULAR ANIMALS OR CROPS an area of land or water where particular animals, birds, fish, or crops are raised for commercial purposes (*usually used in combination*) ○ *a trout farm* **3.** FARM BUILDINGS a farmhouse or group of farm buildings **4.** LAND USED BY INDUSTRY a piece of land on which sth is stored, produced or processed, especially on an industrial scale (*usually used in combination*) ○ *a sewage farm* ■ *v.* (**farms, farming, farmed**) **1.** *vti.* USE LAND FOR AGRICULTURE to use land for growing crops and rearing animals for sale **2.** *vt.* REAR STH COMMERCIALLY to rear animals, birds, or fish commercially **3.** *vt.* = farm out [14thC. Via French *ferme* 'lease' from medieval Latin *firma* 'fixed payment', from Latin *firmare* 'to fix, settle, confirm', from *firmus* 'firm'.] —**farmable** *adj.* —**farming** *n.*

WORD KEY: CULTURAL NOTE

Animal Farm, a novel by George Orwell (1945). A satirical allegory of Stalinist Russia, it describes how a group of farm animals, led by pigs, overthrow their human owner and try to run the farm on egalitarian principles. Corrupted by power, the pigs distort their ideology to support their increasingly brutal tyranny, justifying their actions with slogans such as 'All animals are equal, but some are more equal than others'.

farm out *vt.* **1.** SEND WORK OUT to send work out to be done by sb else **2.** SEND ELSEWHERE FOR CARE to send children or animals to be looked after by sb else

farm bike *n. NZ* a motorcycle designed for use off the road

farmer /fáarmər/ *n.* sb who owns or operates a farm

farmer's lung *n.* inflammation of the lungs marked by chronic shortness of breath and caused by an allergic reaction to fungal spores from mouldy hay

farm hand *n.* = farmworker

farmhouse /fáarm howss/ *n.* (*plural* **-houses**) **1.** FARMER'S HOUSE a house on a farm, especially the main dwelling place of the farmer **2.** = farmhouse loaf ■ *adj.* MADE ON FARM produced on a farm or of a similar style or quality to that produced on a farm

farmhouse loaf *n.* a large rectangular white loaf with a rounded top that is baked in a tin

farmland /fáarm land/ *n.* land that is suitable for farming or used by farmers

farmstay /fáarm stay/ *n. ANZ, Can* a stay on a farm as a paying guest, providing some experience of rural life

farmstead /fáarm sted/ *n.* a farm and all its buildings, regarded as a unit

farm team *n. US, Can* a sports team in a minor league that is owned by or affiliated to a major league team

farmworker /fáarm wurkər/ *n.* sb hired to work on a farm

farmyard /fáarm yaard/ *n.* an enclosed or surfaced area beside farm buildings

Farnborough /fáarnbərə/ town in Hampshire, southern England, the site of an annual air show. Population: 52,535 (1991).

Farnham /fáarnəm/, **John Peter** (*b.* 1949) English-born Australian recording artist. His *Whispering Jack* (1986) was the best-selling Australian album of the 1980s.

faro /fáirō/ *n.* a card game in which players bet against the dealer on the order in which cards are turned up [Mid-18thC. Origin uncertain: probably an alteration of earlier *pharaoh*, modelled on Italian *faraone*.]

Faro /fáarō/ seaport on the southern coast of Portugal and capital of the Algarve District. It is the country's southernmost city. Population: 31,966 (1991).

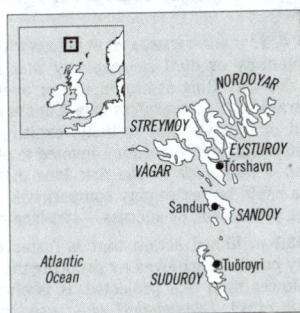

Faroe Islands

Faroe Islands /fáyrō íləndz/, **Faeroe Islands** group of islands in the North Atlantic Ocean, almost midway between Iceland and the Shetland Islands. The islands have been Danish territory since 1814. Capital: Tórshavn. Population: 43,382 (1995). Area: 1,399 sq. km/540 sq. mi.

Faroese /fáirō éez/ (*plural* -ese), **Faeroese** (*plural* -ese) *n.* **1.** LANG LANGUAGE OF FAROE ISLANDS the language spoken on the Faroe Islands. It is a member of the North Germanic group of the Germanic branch of Indo-European. About 45,000 people speak Faroese. **2.** SB FROM FAROE ISLANDS sb who was born in, brought-up, or who lives in the Faroe Islands —**Faroese** *adj.*

far-off *adj.* distant in location or time

farouche /fə róosh/ *adj.* **1.** LACKING SOCIAL SKILLS unsociable and lacking grace because of fierceness, sullenness, or shyness **2.** MENACING menacing in appearance or behaviour [Mid-18thC. Via French from medieval Latin *forasticus*, from Latin *foras* 'out-of-doors' (source of English *foreign*).]

Farouk I /fə róok/, King of Egypt (1920–65). He was the last king of Egypt (1936–52), and after a coup lived in exile in Monaco.

far-out *adj.* (*slang*) **1.** UNUSUAL strange and unconventional **2.** EXCELLENT extremely good or enjoyable —**far-outness** *n.* ◇ **far out!** used to express amazement and approval (*slang*)

Farquhar /fáarkər/, **George** (1678–1707) Irish dramatist. His best known works are *The Recruiting Officer* (1706) and *The Beaux' Stratagem* (1707).

farraginous /fə rájjinəss/ *adj.* consisting of many things mixed together (*formal*)

farrago /fə ráagō/ (*plural* -gos *or* -goes) *n.* a confused mixture of things [Mid-17thC. From Latin, 'mixed fodder for cattle, medley', from *far* 'spelt, grain' (source of English *farina*).]

far-reaching *adj.* with widespread implications, influences, or effects

Farrelly /fárrəli/, **Midget** (*b.* 1944) Australian surfer. He was the winner of the first official surfing world championship, held in Sydney, Australia, in 1964. Real name **Bernard Farrelly**

Farrer /fárrər/, **William James** (1845–1906) English-born Australian agricultural scientist, who was a pioneer of wheat breeding in Australia. He developed domestic strains of wheat that produced greater yields than overseas strains.

farrier /fárri ər/ *n.* sb who makes and fits horseshoes [Mid-16thC. Via French *ferrier* from Latin *ferrarius*, from *ferrum* 'horseshoe, iron'.] —**farriery** *n.*

farrow[1] /fárrō/ *vi.* (-rows, -rowing, -rowed) PRODUCE PIGLETS to give birth to a litter of piglets ■ *n.* LITTER OF PIGS a litter of young pigs [Old English *fearh* 'young pig'. Ultimately from an Indo-European word that is also the ancestor of Latin *porcus* 'pig' (source of English *pork*, *porcelain*, and *porcupine*).]

farrow[2] /fárrō/ *adj.* not pregnant with a calf [15thC. Origin uncertain; probably from Flemish *verwe-*, *varwe-*, in *verwekoe*, *varwekoe*, *verrekoe* 'cow that has become barren'.]

farruca /fə róoka/ *n.* a form of flamenco dance [Early 20thC. From Spanish, 'Galician or Asturian', from *Farruco*, a pet-name of *Francisco* 'Francis'.]

farseeing *adj.* = farsighted *adj.* 1, farsighted *adj.* 3

Farsi /fáarssi/ *n.* the official language of Iran, also spoken in parts of Afghanistan, Bahrain, Tadzhikistan, and the United Arab Emirates. It belongs to the Indo-Iranian branch of Indo-European languages. Farsi is spoken by about 30 million native speakers and by around a further 55 million people who use it as a second language. [Late 19thC. Via Arabic, 'Persia', modern-day Iran, from Persian *Pars*.] —**Farsi** *adj.*

farsighted /fáar síitid/ *adj.* **1.** farsighted, farseeing HAVING SOUND JUDGMENT wise and able to anticipate the future **2.** *US* = long-sighted **3.** farsighted, farseeing SEEING FAR able to see a long way —**farsightedly** *adv.* —**farsightedness** *n.*

fart /faart/ *vti.* (**farts**, **farting**, **farted**) OFFENSIVE TERM an offensive term meaning to release intestinal gases through the anus, usually with an accompanying sound (*slang offensive*) ■ *n.* **1.** OFFENSIVE TERM an offensive term used to refer to a release of intestinal gases through the anus (*slang offensive*) **2.** OFFENSIVE TERM a highly offensive term for sb who is unpleasant, boring, or irritating (*taboo insult*) [Old English *feortan*. Ultimately from an Indo-European word that is also the ancestor of Greek *perdix* 'partridge' (named for the sharp whirring sound it makes when suddenly flushed).] ◇ **fart about** *vi.* offensive term meaning to waste time by behaving foolishly (*slang offensive*)

farther /fáarthər/ *adv.* ◇ **further 1.** TO GREATER DISTANCE to or at a point that is more distant in space or time **2.** TO GREATER EXTENT to a greater degree or extent ■ *adj.* **1.** MORE DISTANT more distant in space or time **2.** ADDITIONAL that is more than or adds to the quantity or extent of sth (*archaic*) ◇ **further** [13thC. From earlier *ferther*, a variant of FURTHER, probably modelled on *ferthren* 'to further'.] —**farthermost** *adj.*

farthest /fáarthist/ *adv.* ◇ **furthest 1.** TO GREATEST DISTANCE to a more distant point in space or time than anything else **2.** TO GREATEST EXTENT to a greater degree or extent than anything else ■ *adj.* MOST DISTANT more distant in space or time than anything else. ◇ **furthest**

farthing /fáarthing/ *n.* **1.** FORMER BRITISH COIN a former British coin worth a quarter of the old penny **2.** THE LEAST the lowest value or smallest amount [Old English *fēorthung* 'quarter of a penny', from *fēortha* 'fourth' + *-ing* 'fractional part'. Ultimately from an Indo-European word that is also the ancestor of English *four* and *tessera*.]

farthingale /fáarthing gayl/ *n.* a structure worn under the skirt by women in the late 16th and early 17th centuries to give it the shape of a cone, bell, or drum [Early 16thC. Via Old French *verdugale* from Spanish *verdugado*, from *verdugo* 'rod, stick' (from the wooden hoops used to sustain the structure).]

fartlek /fáart lek/ *n.* = interval training [Mid-20thC. From Swedish, literally 'speed-play', formed from *fart* 'speed' + *lek* 'play'.]

Far West *n. US* the area of the continental United States west of the Great Plains

FAS *abbr.* **1.** foetal alcohol syndrome **2.** SHIPPING free alongside ship

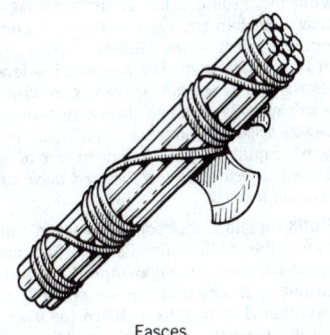

Fasces

fasces /fáss eez/ *npl.* a bundle of rods containing an axe with a projecting blade, carried in front of magistrates in ancient Rome [Late 16thC. From Latin, plural of *fascis* (see FASCIST).]

fascia /fáyshə, fáyshi ə, fáshə, fáyssi ə/ (*plural* **-ciae** /-shi ee/ *or* **-cias**) *n.* **1.** ARCHIT FLAT SURFACE ON BUILDING the flat horizontal surface immediately below the edge of a roof **2.** fascia, facia NAMEPLATE OVER SHOP the flat surface that is above a shop window and usually carries the name of the shop **3.** fascia, facia = dashboard *n.* 1 **4.** ANAT CONNECTIVE TISSUE a sheet or band of connective tissue covering or binding together parts of the body, e.g. muscles or organs **5.** BAND OF COLOUR a broad band of colour, e.g. on an insect [Mid-16thC. From Latin, 'band, fillet, casing of a door' (source of English *fess*).] —**fascial** /fáysh'l/ *adj.*

fasciate /fáshi ayt/, **fasciated** /-aytid/ *adj.* used to describe plant stems or branches that have grown together and become abnormally flattened [Mid-17thC. From Latin *fasciare* 'to swathe', from *fascia* (see FASCIA).] —**fasciately** *adv.*

fasciation /fáshi áysh'n/ *n.* abnormal fusion and flattening of several plant stems

fascicle /fássik'l/ *n.* **1.** BUNDLE a small bunch or bundle of sth **2.** BOT PLANT PARTS BUNCHED TOGETHER a cluster of plant parts such as branches, leaves, or stems **3.** ANAT BUNDLE OF FIBRES a bundle of nerve, muscle, or tendon fibres **4.** PUBL PART OF BOOK PUBLISHED AS INSTALMENT a section of a book published in instalments as a volume or pamphlet [15thC. From Latin *fasciculus* 'small bundle', from *fascis* (see FASCIST).] —**fascicled** *adj.*

fascicular /fə síkyoólər/ *adj.* forming a bundle or cluster

fasciculate /fə síkyoo layt, -lət/ *adj.* = fascicular —**fasiculately** *adv.* —**fasciculation** /fə síkyoo láysh'n/ *n.*

fascicule /fássi kyool/ *n.* PUBL = fascicle *n.* 4 [Late 19thC. From Latin *fasciculus* (see FASCICLE).]

fascinate /fássi nayt/ *v.* (-nates, -nating, -nated) *v.* **1.** *vti.* CAPTIVATE to hold sb's attention completely or irresistibly **2.** *vt.* IMMOBILIZE SB OR STH to make sb or sth unable to move, especially out of fear [Late 16thC. From Latin *fascinare* 'to cast an evil eye on, bewitch', from *fascinum* 'spell, witchcraft'.] —**fascinatedly** *adv.* —**fascinator** *n.*

fascinating /fássi nayting/ *adj.* inspiring a great interest or attraction —**fascinatingly** *adv.*

fascination /fássi náysh'n/ *n.* **1.** POWER TO CAPTURE ATTENTION the power to hold sb's attention completely or irresistibly **2.** STH FASCINATING sth that inspires great interest **3.** INTEREST IN STH complete absorption in sth interesting ○ *I can't understand his fascination with tarantulas.*

fascine /fə séen/ *n.* a long piece or bundle of wood used for engineering purposes to line or fill a trench [Late 17thC. Via French from Latin *fascina*, from *fascis* 'bundle' (see FASCIST).]

fascioliasis /fə see ə líf əssiss, fássi ə-/ *n.* a disease caused by an infestation of parasitic liver flukes [Late 19thC. From modern Latin *Fasciola hepatica* 'liver fluke', from Latin *fasciola* 'small bandage', from *fascia* (see FASCIA).]

Fascism /fáshizəm/ *n.* **1.** DICTATORIAL GOVERNMENT OF MUSSOLINI a system of government practised by Benito Mussolini in Italy between 1922 and 1943 that was characterized by dictatorship, centralized control of private enterprise, repression of opposition, and extreme nationalism **2.** fascism, Fascism DICTATORIAL MOVEMENT any movement, tendency, or ideology that favours dictatorial government, centralized control of private enterprise, repression of all opposition, and extreme nationalism [Early 20thC. From Italian *fascismo*, from *fascio* (see FASCIST).]

Fascist /fáshist/ *n.* **1.** SUPPORTER OF FASCISM IN ITALY sb who belonged to Benito Mussolini's party or who supported Fascism in Italy between 1922 and 1943 **2.** fascist, Fascist SUPPORTER OF FASCISM sb who supports or advocates a system of government characterized by dictatorship, centralized control of private enterprise, repression of all opposition, and extreme nationalism [Early 20thC. Via Italian *Fascista*, from *fascio* 'group, bundle', from, ultimately, Latin *fascis* (see FASCES).] —**fascistic** /fə shístik/ *adj.*

fash[1] /fash/ (**fashes**, **fashing**, **fashed**) *v.* Scotland, N England **1.** *vti.* ANNOY to annoy sb, or be annoyed **2.** *vi.* BOTHER TO DO STH to take the trouble to do sth [Mid-16thC. From Middle French *fascher* 'to annoy', from assumed Vulgar Latin *fastidiare* 'to disgust', from Latin *fastidium* 'disgust'.]

fash[2] /fash/ *n.* US **FASHION** fashion (*slang*) ■ *adj.* US **FASHIONABLE** fashionable (*slang*) [Late 19thC. Shortening.]

fashion /fásh'n/ *n.* **1.** **CLOTHING STYLES** style in clothing, hair, and personal appearance generally, or the business of creating, promoting, or studying the latest styles ○ *the latest in men's fashions* **2.** **CURRENT STYLE** the style of dress, behaviour, way of living, or other expression that is popular at present ○ *a way of speaking that is no longer in fashion* **3.** **MANNER** a particular way of behaving or doing sth **4.** **SHAPE** the form or shape of sth **5.** **TYPE** a type or variety ■ *vt.* (**-ions, -ioning, -ioned**) **1.** **MAKE STH** to give shape or form to sth ○ *fashion a chair from some leftover pieces of wood* **2.** **INFLUENCE STH** to change sb's character or beliefs by influence or training ○ *attitudes fashioned by his grandparents* **3.** **ADAPT STH** to adapt sth or make sth suitable ○ *fashion it to fit over the bump in the middle* **4.** **CONTRIVE STH** to contrive or manage sth (*archaic*) [14thC. Via French *façon* 'shape' from the Latin stem *faction-* 'making', from the past participle of *facere* 'to make' (source of English *facile*).] —**fashioner** *n.* ◇ **after a fashion** in some way but not very well

――― **WORD KEY: SYNONYMS** ―――
See Synonyms at **make**.

-fashion *suffix.* in the manner of

fashionable /fásh'nəb'l/ *adj.* **1.** **CURRENTLY POPULAR** following a style or fashion that is currently popular ○ *fashionable ideas* **2.** **TRENDY** popular with or frequented by rich, famous, or otherwise glamorous people ○ *a fashionable nightspot* —**fashionableness** *n.* —**fashionably** *adv.*

fashion house *n.* a business that designs, makes, and sells fashionable clothes, typically associated with a named designer

fashionista /fásh'n éestə/ *npl.* sb who is a devoted enthusiast of the fashion industry (*informal*) [Coined from FASHION + Latin *-ista*]

fashion model *n.* sb who models clothes as a profession

fashionmonger /fásh'n mung gər/ *n.* sb who follows, sets, or studies fashion (*archaic*) —**fashionmongering** *adj.*

fashion photography *n.* the art or practice of taking photographs of models wearing clothes or clothing accessories, especially for fashion magazines

fashion plate *n.* **1.** **PICTURE SHOWING FASHION** an illustration showing a style of clothing, especially a current or new fashion **2.** **FASHIONABLE PERSON** sb who wears the latest fashions or who is fashionably dressed

fashion victim *n.* sb whose taste for fashionable clothes is sth of an obsession (*informal*)

Fassbinder /fáss bindər/, **Rainer Werner** (1946–82) German film director. He is renowned for politically controversial plays and films, such as *The Marriage of Maria Braun* (1979), that often criticize social institutions.

fast[1] /faast/ *adj.* **1.** **ACTING OR MOVING RAPIDLY** acting, functioning, or moving quickly, or capable of doing this ○ *a fast car* **2.** **DONE QUICKLY** lasting or taking a relatively short time ○ *a fast trip* **3.** **RUNNING AHEAD OF TIME** indicating a time that is later than the correct time **4.** **CONDUCIVE TO RAPID SPEED** adapted to or allowing rapid movement ○ *driving in the fast lane* **5.** **REQUIRING SPEEDY MOVEMENT** requiring agility and quickness of movement and reaction **6.** **PHOTOGRAPHY WITH SHORT EXPOSURE** used to describe photographic equipment that requires or permits a relatively short exposure time **7.** **DEBAUCHED** energetically pursuing excitement and enjoyment (*informal*) ○ *a fast crowd* **8.** **PROMISCUOUS** wanting or tending to start sexual relationships with people very soon after meeting them (*informal*) **9.** **TRICKY** using quick-wittedness to trick or cheat people (*informal*) ○ *a fast bargainer* **10.** **MADE EASILY** acquired very easily and sometimes dishonestly (*informal*) ○ *fast money* **11.** **UNFADING** not liable to fade or change colour **12.** **STRONG AND CLOSE** strong, close, and steadfast, as in a relationship ○ *fast friends* **13.** **FASTENED** firmly attached, fastened, or fixed **14.** **SHUT** firmly closed ■ *adv.* **1.** **RAPIDLY** at

great speed ○ *You drive too fast.* **2.** **IMMEDIATELY** in quick succession **3.** **AT INCORRECT TIME** ahead of the correct time ○ *The clock is running a little fast.* **4.** **SOUNDLY** deeply in a state of sleep **5.** **FIRMLY** allowing no movement or no chance of slipping or escaping ○ *held fast by ice* **6.** **RECKLESSLY** without regard to consequences (*informal*) ○ *live fast and die young* **7.** **CLOSE** so as to be nearby (*archaic*) [Old English *fæst* 'firm', from a prehistoric Germanic word that is also the ancestor of English *avast*.] ◇ **pull a fast one** to trick or cheat sb (*informal*)

fast[2] /faast/ *v.* (**fasts, fasting, fasted**) **1.** *vi.* **ABSTAIN FROM FOOD** to abstain from all or certain types of food, especially as an act of religious observance **2.** *vt.* **DEPRIVE OF FOOD** to deprive a person or animal of food ■ *n.* **PERIOD OF FASTING** a period of time spent abstaining from food [Old English *fæstan*, from a prehistoric Germanic word meaning 'firm' (see FAST[1]). The underlying sense is of 'holding fast' to an observance.] —**faster** *n.*

fast-acting *adj.* beginning to take effect soon after being used ○ *a fast-acting analgesic*

fastback /fáast bak/ *n.* **1.** **CAR DESIGN FEATURE** a back of a car that forms a continuous curve downwards from the rear edge of the roof **2.** **CAR** a car with a fastback

fast bowler *n.* in cricket, a bowler who specializes in bowling the ball quickly —**fast bowling** *n.*

fast break *n.* in team sports, a swift counterattack made in an attempt to score before the opposing players have the chance to recover their defensive positions —**fast-break** *vi.*

fast-breeder reactor *n.* a nuclear reactor in which the chain reaction is maintained mainly by fast neutrons. It is capable of producing more fissionable material than it consumes.

fasten /fáass'n/ *v.* (**-tens, -tening, -tened**) *v.* **1.** *vti.* **SECURE STH** to attach sth firmly, usually using parts or devices made to achieve this, or become firmly attached in this way ○ *These snaps won't fasten.* **2.** *vti.* **SHUT TIGHTLY** to close sth firmly or securely, or become firmly or securely closed ○ *fasten the door shut* **3.** *vt.* **HOLD STH FIRMLY** to use a tool, device, or body part to hold sb or sth firmly **4.** *vti.* **CONCENTRATE ATTENTION** to focus the mind or eyes concentratedly on sth, or become focused in this way ○ *His suspicions fastened upon the woman sitting opposite him.* **5.** *vi.* **BECOME A NUISANCE** to become associated closely with sb in a persistent and usually unwelcome manner ○ *just some bloke who fastened onto me in the street* [Old English *fæstnian*, literally 'to make firm or fast', ultimately from a prehistoric Germanic word meaning 'firm' (see FAST[1])]

fastener /fáass'nər/ *n.* a device, e.g. a button, hook, or zip, used to close sth, especially a piece of clothing

fastening /fáass'ning/ *n.* a device that fastens sth, e.g. a clasp, hook, or lock

fast food *n.* highly processed restaurant foods, e.g. burgers, that are prepared quickly or are available on demand (*hyphenated when used before a noun*) ○ *a fast-food diet*

fast-forward *n.* **1.** **FUNCTION FOR WINDING TAPE FORWARDS** a function on an electronic recording device, e.g. a tape or videocassette recorder, that causes the tape to wind forwards quickly **2.** **BUTTON FOR FAST-FORWARD FUNCTION** a mechanism, e.g. a button or switch, used to control the fast-forward function on an electronic recording device ■ *vti.* (**fast-forwards, fast-forwarding, fast-forwarded**) **1.** **ADVANCE TAPE RAPIDLY** to wind a tape forwards quickly on an electronic recording device **2.** **ADVANCE QUICKLY** to advance rapidly, or move sth forwards rapidly, e.g. in time or in rate of progress (*informal*) ○ *decided to fast-forward negotiations so as to avoid a strike*

fastidious /fa stíddi əss/ *adj.* **1.** **DEMANDING** concerned that even the smallest details should be just right ○ *fastidious about his appearance* **2.** **DELICATE** easily disgusted by things that are not perfectly clean **3.** **SCORNFUL** showing disdain or scorn (*archaic*) [15thC. From Latin *fastidiosus*, from *fastidium* 'disgust'.] —**fastidiously** *adv.* —**fastidiousness** *n.*

fastigia plural of **fastigium**

fastigiate /fa stíjji ət, -ayt/, **fastigiated** /-aytid/ *adj.* used to describe a tree or other plant with upright

clustering branches that taper towards the top, e.g. a Lombardy poplar —**fastigiately** *adv.*

fastigium /fa stíjji əm/ (*plural* **-ums** or **-a** /fa-ə/) *n.* a period during which an illness, often a fever, is at its most severe [Late 17thC. From Latin.]

fasting /fáasting/ *n.* abstention from all or certain types of food, especially as an act of religious observance

fast lane *n.* **1.** **TRANSP PASSING LANE OF MOTORWAY** the lane of a motorway or dual carriageway that is used by vehicles travelling at high speed or overtaking slower traffic. US term **express lane** **2.** **HECTIC LIFESTYLE** the kind of lifestyle that is busy, exciting, often highly stressful, and sometimes devoted to pleasure (*informal*) ○ *living life in the fast lane* **3.** **ROUTE TO SUCCESS** a rapid but extremely competitive route to progress, promotion, or success —**fast-lane** *adj.*

fast motion *n.* filmed action that is faster than is naturally possible, achieved by shooting the film at a rate slower than that projected. It is often used for comic effect. (*hyphenated when used before a noun*) ○ *a fast-motion sequence*

fastness /fáastnəss/ *n.* **1.** **FIXEDNESS** the state or quality of being firm, fixed, or secure ○ *deceived about the fastness of their friendship* **2.** **UNFADING QUALITY** the ability of a dye to retain its colour and not to fade **3.** **FORTRESS** a fortress, stronghold, or other secure place (*archaic or literary*) **4.** **REMOTE PLACE** a remote and secluded or secret place (*archaic or literary*) **5.** **RAPIDITY** swiftness of movement or progress (*archaic*)

fast neutron *n.* a neutron that has energy in excess of 1.5 MeV, sufficient to produce fission in Uranium-238

fast stream *n.* a group of employees selected for rapid promotion within an organization

fast-talk *vt.* to influence or deceive sb with false but appealing arguments (*informal*) ○ *fast-talked them into parting with the car keys* —**fast-talker** *n.*

fast track *n.* **1.** **RAIL RAILWAY TRACK FOR FAST TRAINS** a railway track for fast trains alongside one for slower trains **2.** **RAPID ROUTE TO PROGRESS** a rapid and sometimes highly competitive route to progress or advancement that exists alongside the slower conventional one (*informal*) ○ *a fast track to promotion for the brightest recruits* —**fast-track** *adj.*

fast-track *v.* **1.** *vti.* **GO QUICKLY** to advance, develop, or process sth rapidly, or be handled rapidly ○ *fast-tracking the best of the new recruits* **2.** *vt.* **DEAL WITH FIRST** to give priority to sb or sth ○ *fast-track an application* —**fast-tracker** *n.*

fastuous /fástyoo əss/ *adj.* (*archaic*) **1.** **CONCEITED** excessively self-satisfied and disdainful of others **2.** **OSTENTATIOUS** designed to impress others [Mid-17thC. From Latin *fastuosus*, from Latin *fastus* (see FASH).]

fat /fat/ *n.* **1.** **BIOCHEM NUTRITIONAL COMPONENT OF FOOD** a greasy water-insoluble solid or semisolid chemical compound that is among the chief nutritional components of food. Fats are esters of glycerol and fatty acids. ○ *a diet that is lower in fat* **2.** **ANAT TISSUE CONTAINING FAT** animal or vegetable tissue made up of cells that contain fat, especially the layer of cells under the skin that in excess make sb overweight **3.** **COOK COOKING MEDIUM** a solid or liquid substance such as butter or sunflower oil that is derived from animals or plants and is used as a cooking medium or ingredient ○ *rub the fat into the flour* **4.** **EXCESS** amounts that are surplus to what is needed or wanted (*informal*) ○ *a budget with little fat* **5.** **Aus OFFENSIVE TERM** an offensive term for erect penis (*slang offensive*) ■ *adj.* (**fatter, fattest**) **1.** **OVERWEIGHT** having a bodyweight greater than is considered desirable or advisable **2.** **CONTAINING FAT** containing a lot of fat or too much fat ○ *pork that was rather fat* **3.** **THICK** very wide or large ○ *a fat book* **4.** **PROFITABLE** bringing large profits or financial rewards ○ *a fat defence contract* **5.** **REWARDING** providing good opportunities ○ *offered a fat part in a film* **6.** **RICH** owning great wealth ○ *grown fat on the profits of illegal arms deals* **7.** **PLENTIFUL** with abundant contents, stocks, or supplies ○ *a fat savings account* **8.** **AGRIC FERTILE** land that is very productive for agricultural purposes (*archaic*) **9.** **CHEM RICH IN CONTENT** with a high content of a particular material or substance, e.g. resin in wood or volatile hydrocarbons in coal **10.** **MINIMAL**

very little (*informal*) ○ *A fat lot of help you are!* ■ *vti.* (**fats, fatting, fatted**) AGRIC **FATTEN AN ANIMAL** to fatten an animal, usually before slaughtering it [Old English *fǣt(t)*. Ultimately from an Indo-European word meaning 'fat', which is probably also the ancestor of English *pine* and *pituitary*.] —**fatly** *adv.* —**fatness** *n.* ◇ **chew the fat** to have a leisurely conversation (*informal*) ◇ **the fat is in the fire** sth irreversible has happened that will cause trouble

FAT /fat/ *n.* in the MS-DOS disk-operating system on a computer, an internal store of information about the structure of stored files on a disk (*often used before a noun*) Full form **file allocation table**

fatal /fáyt'l/ *adj.* **1. LEADING TO DEATH** causing death, or capable of causing death ○ *a fatal car crash* **2. RUINOUS** causing destruction, disaster, or ruin ○ *a fatal mistake in calculations* **3. DECISIVE** at which time important decisions or choices are made ○ *the fatal day of his first treasonous act* **4. PREDESTINED** arranged or controlled by fate ■ *n. US* **INSTANCE OF DEATH** an instance of death, especially one caused by a car, plane, train, or bus crash (*informal*) ○ *a fatal on the turnpike during rush hour* [14thC. Directly or via French from Latin *fatalis*, from *fatum* (see FATE).] —**fatalness** *n.*

WORD KEY: SYNONYMS

See Synonyms at *deadly*.

WORD KEY: CULTURAL NOTE

Fatal Attraction, a film by Adrian Lyne (1987). It portrays a married man's brief but passionate involvement with a single woman and her violent reaction when he attempts to end their relationship.The spurned lover attacks the man's family, and, having apparently been finally drowned by the husband, suddenly returns to life before being shot dead. This movie title quickly came to be used in the United States to indicate the wrath of a scorned woman: 'There was no such attack rape, the defense will counter vehemently. The woman ... will be proved to be a *Fatal Attraction* psychotic'. *Washington Post* (1 December, 1991).

WORD KEY: CULTURAL NOTE

The Fatal Shore, a book by Australian writer Robert Hughes (1987). A detailed history of the early years of Australia, focusing on the convict transportation system and the lives of those affected by it. It argues that the system was designed to rid Britain of an entire criminal underclass.

fatalism /fáyt'lizəm/ *n.* **1.** PHILOSOPHY **DOCTRINE OF FATE** the philosophical doctrine holding that all events are fated to happen and that human beings cannot therefore change their destinies **2. BELIEF IN FATE** the belief that people are powerless against fate, or the attitude of resignation and passivity that sometimes results from this belief

fatalist /fáyt'list/ *n.* sb who believes in the philosophical doctrine of fatalism

fatalistic /fáyt'l ístik/ *adj.* **1. SUBMITTING TO FATE** feeling or demonstrating resignation in the face of events regarded as controlled by fate ○ *a fatalistic attitude* **2.** PHILOS **OF FATALISM** relating to the philosophical doctrine of fatalism —**fatalistically** *adv.*

fatality /fə tálləti, fay-/ (*plural* **-ties**) *n.* **1. UNEXPECTED DEATH** a death resulting from accident or disaster ○ *The traffic accident resulted in three fatalities.* **2. DEADLINESS** the ability to cause death, disaster, or destruction ○ *fatality associated with toxic waste exposure* **3. PREDETERMINATION BY FATE** the quality or state of being predetermined by fate **4. EVENTS THOUGHT FATED** an event or train of events thought to be determined by fate

fatality rate *n.* = **death rate**

fatally /fáyt'li/ *adv.* **1. SO AS TO CAUSE DEATH** in a manner that results in death ○ *fatally wounded* **2. SO AS TO CAUSE RUIN** in a manner resulting in disaster or ruin ○ *fatally mistaken* **3. INEVITABLY** as a result of unalterable fate

fata morgana /faàtə mawr gaánə/, **Fata Morgana** *n.* a mirage or an illusion (*literary*) [From Italian, literally 'fairy Morgan', in reference to the legendary magician MORGAN LE FAY; from the belief that a fairy caused the mirage frequently seen near the Strait of Messina]

fatback /fát bak/ *n. US* fatty meat from the upper part of a side of pork, usually dried and cured by salt

WORD KEY: REGIONAL NOTE

The upper part of a side of bacon, usually without lean, is also called *fat meat, fat pork, boiling meat, dry salt meat, salt bacon, salt meat, seasoning meat, side meat, sowbelly*, and *white bacon*. The meat is used in the South and West primarily to season boiled and steamed vegetables. Because the substance so closely approximates ordinary bacon, in both its location on the hog and its applications in cooking, ***fatback*** often merges with *middling meat, streak of lean*, and other bacon synonyms, all of which invariably include lean.

fat body *n.* **1. FATTY TISSUE IN INSECTS** a fatty tissue in the bodies of insects, especially larvae, used as a source of energy during metamorphosis and hibernation **2. FATTY TISSUE IN AMPHIBIANS AND REPTILES** a fatty tissue found near the genital glands of certain amphibians and reptiles

fat camp *n. US* a residential camp that helps children to lose undesired weight (*slang*)

fat cat *n.* an extremely wealthy and privileged person, often sb whose wealth is regarded as undeserved (*slang*) (*hyphenated when used before a noun*) ○ *fees charged by fat-cat lawyers*

fat cell *n.* any cell that is specialized for the synthesis and storage of fat

fate /fayt/ *n.* **1. FORCE PREDETERMINING EVENTS** the force or principle believed to predetermine events ○ *little knew what fate had in store for him* **2. OUTCOME** a consequence or final result ○ *What was the fate of the mission?* **3. DESTINY** sth consequential that inevitably happens to sb or sth ○ *felt it was her fate to marry him* **4. UNHAPPY CONSEQUENCE** a disastrous or ruinous outcome ■ *vt.* (**fates, fating, fated**) **MAKE STH INEVITABLE** to predetermine sth, usually with negative results (*usually passive*) [14thC. From, ultimately, Latin *fatum*, literally 'sth spoken (by the gods)', from the past participle of *fari* 'to speak' (source of English *fable* and *fairy*).] ◇ **tempt fate** to do sth risky that might end in misfortune or disaster, and depend too much on luck

fated /fáytid/ *adj.* believed to be controlled or predetermined by fate ○ *fated mishaps*

fateful /fáytf'l/ *adj.* **1. CRITICALLY IMPORTANT** after which an important, often dire consequence seems to have been made inevitable ○ *a fateful decision* **2. DECIDED BY FATE** predetermined or controlled by fate **3. OMINOUS** prefiguring what is to come, especially when it is sth disastrous ○ *a fateful sign* —**fatefully** *adv.* —**fatefulness** *n.*

Fates /fayts/ *npl.* in Greek mythology, the three goddesses, Clotho, Lachesis, and Atropos, often depicted as women of advanced years spinning, who were believed to decree the events in and duration of sb's life. The Greeks believed that Clotho spun the thread that represented sb's life, Lachesis decided the extent of it, and Atropos was responsible for cutting it. Roman equivalent **Parcae**

fat face *n.* any typeface with wide main strokes and prominent serifs, producing a relatively heavy and dark image when set as text

fat farm *n.* a health farm dedicated to helping people lose weight (*slang*)

fath. *abbr.* fathom

fathead /fát hed/ *n.* an unintelligent or thoughtless person who is extremely slow to understand things or makes very bad decisions (*slang insult*) —**fatheaded** /fát héddid/ *adj.* —**fatheadedly** *adv.* —**fatheadedness** *n.*

fat hen *n.* a common weed of the goosefoot family, with a mealy white covering over the whole plant and small pale green flowers. Latin name: *Chenopodium album.* US term **pigweed** [Origin uncertain; perhaps from a fanciful likening of its seeds to hen's eggs because they contain fat and albumen and were formerly eaten as food]

father /faáthər/ *n.* **1. MALE PARENT** a male parent of a human being or animal ○ *been like a father to me* **2. MAN ACTING AS PARENT** a man who brings up and looks after a child as if he were its male parent **3. MAN ANCESTOR** a man who is an ancestor, especially the founder of a family or people ○ *the land of our fathers and mothers* **4. FOUNDER** a man who establishes, founds, or originates sth ○ *the father of modern linguistics* **5. PRECURSOR** a precursor, prototype, or early version of sth **6. MAN LEADER** a man who is a community or civic leader ○ *the town fathers* **7. OLDEST MEMBER** the oldest or most senior member of an institution ■ *v.* (**-thers, -thering, -thered**) **1.** *vt.* **HAVE OFFSPRING** to beget offspring as a male parent **2.** *vti.* **ACT AS FATHER** to act as a father to sb, especially giving advice, comfort, and protection **3.** *vt.* **ORIGINATE STH** to create, found, or establish sth ○ *father a plan* [Old English *fæder*. Ultimately from an Indo-European word that is also the ancestor of English *patriarch, paternal*, and *perpetrate*.]

WORD KEY: CULTURAL NOTE

Fathers and Sons, a novel by Russian writer Ivan Turgenev (1862). It deals with the conflicting attitudes towards social change (particularly the emancipation of serfs) among Russia's younger radical intelligentsia, represented by the novel's nihilistic protagonist, Bazarov, and the older liberal gentry, to which Turgenev himself belonged. The novel was seen as Turgenev's acknowledgment that Russia's future was now in the hands of a new generation.

Father *n.* **1. GOD** in the Christian religion, God, especially when considered as the first person of the Holy Trinity **2.** = **Church Father 3. TITLE FOR CHRISTIAN CLERGYMAN** a title and form of address used for Christian clergymen, especially in the Roman Catholic, Eastern Orthodox, and Episcopal churches **4. RESPECTFUL TITLE FOR MAN** a respectful term of address for a man who is past middle age **5. PERSONIFICATION** sth personified as man of advanced years

Father Christmas *n.* the patron saint of children, commonly identified with Saint Nicholas, usually depicted as a jolly old man with a white beard who brings presents at Christmas. US term **Santa Claus**

father confessor *n.* (*literary*) **1. PRIEST** a Roman Catholic priest who hears confessions and gives advice **2. ADVISER** any man in whom sb confides and whose advice is sought

father figure *n.* a man whom other people look up to for advice, inspiration, or protection

fatherhood /faáthər hòod/ *n.* the status of a man who is sb's father, or the fact that he is a father

father-in-law (*plural* **fathers-in-law**) *n.* **1. SPOUSE'S FATHER** the father of sb's husband or wife **2. STEPFATHER** a stepfather (*archaic*)

fatherland /faáthər land/ *n.* **1. HOMELAND** sb's native land or country **2. ANCESTRAL COUNTRY** the native land of sb's ancestors

father-lasher *n.* a large sea scorpion with short spines, found in European and North Atlantic coastal waters. Latin name: *Myoxocephalus scorpius* and *Myoxocephalus bubalis.*

fatherless /faátharləss/ *adj.* having no father, or no one identified as father —**fatherlessness** *n.*

fatherly /faátharli/ *adj.* having or showing the qualities associated with a father, usually love, support, and protection ○ *fatherly affection* —**fatherliness** *n.*

father of the chapel (*plural* **fathers of the chapel**) *n.* a shop steward representing members of a trade union in a printing office

Father's Day *n.* the third Sunday in June, observed as a celebration of fatherhood in Britain, the United States, Canada, Australia, and some other Commonwealth countries

Father Time *n.* the personification of time as a bearded man of advanced years, usually wearing a robe and carrying a scythe and an hourglass

fathom /fáthəm/ *n.* **MEASURE OF WATER DEPTH** a unit of length equal to 1.83 m/6 ft, used mainly in nautical contexts for measuring the depth of water ■ *vt.* (**-oms, -oming, -omed**) **1. MEASURE WATER DEPTH USING SOUNDING LINE** to measure the depth of water, especially using a sounding line **2. COMPREHEND** to understand sth, usually sth profound or mystifying ○ *couldn't fathom why he came back* [Old English *fæþm*, of uncertain origin: probably 'length spanned by outstretched arms', ultimately from an Indo-European word meaning 'to spread', which is also the ancestor of English *petal* and *patent*] —**fathomable** *adj.* —**fathomer** *n.*

fathomless /fáthəmləss/ *adj.* **1.** ENDLESSLY DEEP too deep to be measured **2.** MYSTIFYING impossible to understand —**fathomlessly** *adv.* —**fathomlessness** *n.*

fatidic /fay tíddik/, **fatidical** /-tíddik'l/ *adj.* seeming to foretell the future (*archaic*) [Early 17thC. From Latin *fatidicus*, from *fatum* 'fate' (see FATE) + *dicere* 'to say' (source of English *diction*).] —**fatidically** *adv.*

fatigable /fáttigəb'l/ *adj.* able or tending to become exhausted —**fatigability** /fáttigə bílləti/ *n.* —**fatigableness** /fáttigəb'lnəss/ *n.*

fatigue /fə teeg/ *n.* **1.** MENTAL OR PHYSICAL EXHAUSTION extreme tiredness or weariness resulting from physical or mental activity ○ *The soldiers were weak with fatigue after the long march.* **2.** PHYSIOL INABILITY TO RESPOND TO STIMULUS temporary inability of an organ or part such as a muscle or nerve cell to respond to a stimulus and function normally, following continuous activity or stimulation **3.** INABILITY TO RESPOND TO SITUATION temporary inability of sb to respond to a situation as a result of overexposure or excessive activity (*often used in combination*) ○ *compassion fatigue* **4.** WEAKENING OF MATERIAL UNDER STRESS the weakening or breakdown of a material subjected to prolonged or repeated stress **5.** MIL NONMILITARY WORK manual or menial work done by soldiers, often as a punishment (*often used before a noun*) ■ **fatigues** *npl.* MIL BATTLEDRESS informal military uniforms worn day to day and in battle, as distinct from formal uniforms ■ *vti.* (**-tigues, -tiguing, -tigued**) **1.** MAKE OR BECOME TIRED to tire sb out, or become tired out, as a result of physical or mental activity **2.** WEAKEN UNDER STRESS to weaken or break sth, or become weakened or broken, when subjected to prolonged or repeated stress [Mid-17thC. Via French *fatiguer*, from Latin *fatigare*, of uncertain origin: probably 'to drive to the breaking point', from *ad fatim* 'to bursting' + *agere* 'to drive'.]

fatigued /fə teegd/ *adj.* **1.** EXHAUSTED exhausted or weary as a result of physical or mental activity **2.** WEAKENED UNDER STRESS weakened or broken as a result of being subjected to prolonged or repeated stress

Fátima /fáttimə/ village in west-central Portugal, and place of pilgrimage for Roman Catholics, about 105 km/65 mi. northeast of Lisbon. It has been a shrine since 1917. Population: 5,445 (1991).

Fatimid /fátti mid/, **Fatimite** /fátti mīt/ *n.* **1.** MEMBER OF MUSLIM DYNASTY a member of a Muslim dynasty, descended from Muhammad's daughter Fatima and her husband Ali, that ruled North Africa and parts of Egypt and Syria from 909 to 1171 AD **2.** FATIMA'S DESCENDANT any descendant of Fatima and Ali [Mid-19thC. Formed from Arabic *Fāṭima* 'Fatima'.]

fat lip *n.* a lip swollen from having been hit in a fist fight (*informal*) ○ *gave him a fat lip*

fat mouse *n.* a nocturnal short-tailed mouse found in dry regions of Africa and eaten as a delicacy because of its high stored fat content. Genus: *Steatomys.*

fatshedera /fáts héddərə/ *n.* a hybrid ornamental plant with glossy leaves and pale green flowers. Latin name: *Fatsia japonica × Hedera helix.* [Mid-20thC. From modern Latin *Fatsia* (genus of shrubs) + *Hedera* (genus of climbing plants, from Latin, 'ivy').]

fatsia /fátsi ə/ *n.* a shrub with leaves divided like the fingers on a hand and clusters of white flowers, commonly grown as a houseplant. Latin name: *Fatsia japonica.* [From modern Latin, genus name]

fatso /fát sō/ (*plural* **-sos** *or* **-soes**) *n.* an offensive term used to refer to or address sb who is overweight (*slang insult*) [Mid-20thC. Origin uncertain: probably formed from *fats*, offensive term for an overweight person.]

fat stock *n.* livestock that has been fattened and is ready for sale or slaughter

fat-tailed sheep *n.* a sheep, found mostly in North Africa and the Middle East, that has coarse wool and large quantities of fat stored in the tail and rump, and is raised for meat and milk

fatten /fátt'n/ (**-tens, -tening, -tened**) *v.* **1.** *vti.* MAKE OR BECOME FAT to become fat or fatter, or make sb fat or fatter **2.** *vti.* FEED ANIMAL to make an animal fat by feeding it plentifully, usually for slaughter **3.** *vt.* ENLARGE to make sth larger, richer, or fuller ○ *fatten*

your *wallet* **4.** *vt.* FERTILIZE to make land or soil more fertile ○ *fatten the soil with manure* —**fattenable** *adj.* —**fattener** *n.*

fattening /fátt'ning/ *adj.* **1.** HIGH IN FAT high in fat or calorie content, and so likely to make some people gain weight **2.** GROWING FAT becoming fat in readiness for slaughter —**fatteningly** *adv.*

fatty /fátti/ (**-tier, -tiest**) *adj.* **1.** CONTAINING FAT containing fat or grease, especially in large or distasteful amounts **2.** DERIVED FROM FAT derived from fat, or chemically related to fat ○ *fatty alcohol* **3.** WITH ACCUMULATED FAT containing accumulated fat, sometimes in undesirable amounts ○ *fatty tissue* ■ *n.* (*plural* **-ties**) OFFENSIVE TERM an offensive term used to refer to or address sb who is overweight (*informal insult*) —**fattiness** *n.*

fatty acid *n.* an organic acid belonging to a group that may occur naturally as waxes, fats, and essential oils, and are found in animal and plant materials. Fatty acids consist of a straight chain of carbon atoms linked by single bonds and end in a carboxyl group. Formula: $C_nH_{n+1}COOH$.

fatty degeneration *n.* deterioration in the function of an organ, e.g. the liver or heart, caused by the accumulation of abnormally high levels of fats in its cells

fatty oil *n.* = **fixed oil**

fatuity /fə tyoo əti/ (*plural* **-ties**) *n.* (*formal*) **1.** SELF-SATISFIED UNINTELLIGENCE complacency combined with lack of intelligence or thought **2.** UNINTELLIGENT ACTION an action or remark that is unintelligent or thoughtless —**fatuitous** *adj.*

fatuous /fáttyoo əss/ *adj.* showing lack of intelligence coupled with a lack of awareness ○ *a fatuous joke* [Early 17thC. Formed from Latin *fatuus* (source of English *infatuate*. Originally 'tasteless, vapid'.] —**fatuously** *adv.* —**fatuousness** *n.*

fatwa /fát waa/, **fatwah** *n.* a formal legal opinion or religious decree issued by an Islamic leader [Early 17thC. From Arabic, from *aftā* 'to decide a point of law' (source of English *mufti*).]

fatware /fát wair/ *n.* COMPUT = **bloatware**

fatwitted /fát witid/ *adj.* tending to act in a thoughtless or unintelligent way (*dated insult*)

faubourg /fó boorg/ *n.* an inner suburb or quarter of a city, especially in France [15thC. From French, an alteration (influenced by *faux* 'false') of Old French *forsborc*, from Latin *foris* 'outside' and late Latin *burgus* 'fat' (of prehistoric Germanic origin).]

faucal /fáwk'l/, **faucial** /fáwsh'l/ *adj.* **1.** ANAT OF FAUCES relating to the fauces **2.** PHON FROM PHARYNX used to describe speech sounds that originate in the pharynx [Early 19thC. Formed from Latin *fauces* 'throat' (see FAUCES).]

fauces /fáw seez/ *npl.* the passage between the back of the mouth and the pharynx [15thC. From Latin, 'throat' (source of English *suffocate*), of unknown origin.]

faucet /fáwssit/ *n.* US = **tap** [14thC. Via Old French *fausset* or Provençal *falset* from *falser* 'to bore in', from late Latin *fausser falsare* 'to corrupt', from Latin *falsus* 'false'.]

faucial *adj.* = **faucal**

Library of Congress
William Faulkner

Faulkner /fáwknər/, **William** (1897–1962) US writer. He is regarded as one of the greatest American novelists whose stream-of-consciousness works about Southern life, including *The Sound and the Fury*

(1929). He won the 1949 Nobel Prize in literature. Full name **William Cuthbert Faulkner** —**Faulknerian** /fawk neèri ən/ *adj.*

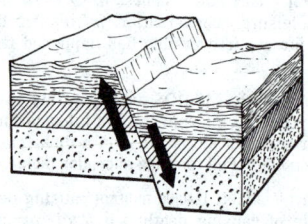
Fault: Displacement of rock layers in Earth's crust

fault /fawlt, folt/ *n.* **1.** RESPONSIBILITY responsibility for a mistake, failure, or act of wrongdoing **2.** PERSONAL SHORTCOMING a failing or character weakness in sb ○ *My main fault is laziness.* **3.** DEFECT sth that detracts from the integrity, functioning, or perfection of a thing **4.** MISTAKE an error, especially in calculation **5.** MISDEMEANOUR a wrongful action **6.** GEOL DISPLACEMENT IN EARTH'S CRUST a displacement of rock layers in the Earth's crust in response to stress, accompanied by a break in the continuity of the rocks on each side of the fault line **7.** RACKET GAMES INVALID SERVE IN RACKET GAMES a serve in certain racket games, e.g. tennis, that is invalid because it fails to land within a prescribed area **8.** SHOWJUMPING PENALTY MARK IN SHOW-JUMPING a penalty mark awarded in showjumping for various errors such as a failure or refusal to clear a fence **9.** HUNT LOSING SCENT OF ANIMAL an occasion on which the hounds in a hunt lose the scent of the animal they are chasing ■ *v.* (**faults, faulting, faulted**) **1.** *vt.* BLAME SB OR STH to blame, criticize, or find a defect in sb or sth ○ *He gave an excellent performance that could not be faulted.* **2.** *vi.* MAKE MISTAKE to commit a fault or make a mistake (*archaic*) **3.** *vi.* GEOL DISPLACE to respond to stress by becoming displaced and developing as a geological fault (*refers to rock layers*) [13thC. Via Old French *faut(e)* 'lack' from assumed Vulgar Latin *fallitum* 'failing', from Latin *fallere* 'to fail' (source of English *fail*).] ◇ **find fault with sb** *or* **sth** to criticize sb or sth, often unfairly ○ *She's always finding fault with the children's work.* ◇ **to a fault** excessively ○ *She was rather naive, and generous to a fault.*

―― WORD KEY: SYNONYMS ――
See Synonyms at *flaw.*

faultfinder /fáwlt fīndər, fólt-/ *n.* sb who constantly complains or is given to petty criticism

faultfinding /fáwlt fīnding, fólt-/ *n.* **1.** CRITICISM constant and often petty complaining or criticism **2.** TRACING FAULTS the process of locating and diagnosing faults within an electrical, electronic, or mechanical system (*often used before a noun*) ○ *faultfinding procedures* ■ *adj.* CRITICAL given to complaining or finding fault

faultless /fáwltləss, fólt-/ *adj.* having no faults or defects ○ *a faultless performance* —**faultlessly** *adv.* —**faultlessness** *n.*

fault line *n.* a linear feature on the Earth's surface, occurring where displaced rock layers have broken through the Earth's surface

fault plane *n.* the surface along which displacement of rock layers has taken place in a geological fault

fault tolerance *n.* the ability of an individual computer or computer network to preserve the integrity of data and continue operating when one or more components are malfunctioning

faulty /fáwlti, fólti/ (**-ier, -iest**) *adj.* **1.** WITH FAULTS containing defects, especially ones that cause malfunctions ○ *faulty wiring* **2.** BLAMEWORTHY guilty or deserving blame (*archaic*) —**faultily** *adv.* —**faultiness** *n.*

faun /fawn/ *n.* in Roman mythology, a rural god, often depicted as a creature with the body of a man and the legs and horns of a goat. Greek equivalent

satyr [14thC. Directly or via French *faune* from Latin *Faunus* FAUNUS.]

fauna /fáwnə/ (*plural* **-nas** *or* **-nae** /-ee/) *n.* **1. ANIMAL LIFE IN GENERAL** the animal life of a particular region or period, considered as a whole. ◊ **flora 2. LIST OF ANIMALS** a catalogue or list describing the animals of a particular region or period [Late 18thC. Via modern Latin from late Latin *Fauna* 'Fauna', an ancient Italian rural goddess, the sister of FAUNUS.] —**faunal** *adj.* —**faunally** *adv.*

Faunus /fáwnəss/ *n.* in Roman mythology, the god of nature, farming, and fertility. He was the grandson of Saturn. Greek equivalent **Pan**

Fauré /fáwr ay/, **Gabriel** (1845–1924) French composer and organist. His best-known work is the *Requiem* (1887) for solo voices, choir, and orchestra. Full name **Gabriel Urbain Fauré**

Faust /fowst/ (1480?–1540?) German fortune-teller and magician. Reputed to have sold his soul to the devil, he is most noted for the legends concerning him that formed the basis for numerous literary and musical works. —**Faustian** *adj.*

faute de mieux /fōt də myő/ *adv.* in the absence of sth better (*literary*) ○ *the feeling that she had married him faute de mieux* [From French, literally 'lack of better']

fauteuil /fō tő i/ *n.* an upholstered armchair, usually with open sides (*literary or technical*) [Mid-18thC. Via French from Old French *faudestuel* 'folding chair', from a prehistoric Germanic compound word formed from the ancestors of English *fold* + *stool*.]

fautor /fáwtər/ *n.* (*archaic*) **1. SUPPORTER** sb who supports a person or cause **2. PATRON** sb who gives protection or material support, e.g. in the form of funding [14thC. From Latin *fautor*, from *favere* (see FAVOUR).]

Fauve /fōv/, **fauve** *n.* an artist belonging to a 20th-century movement in French painting (**Fauvism**) characterized by the use of simple forms and bright colours (*often used before a noun*) [Early 20thC. From French, literally 'wild animal', via Old French *falve* 'tawny' from prehistoric Germanic; from the vivid colours the painters used.]

fauvette /fō vét/ *n.* a small bird belonging to the family of warblers, especially a garden warbler [Late 18thC. From French, literally 'little wild or tawny one', from *fauve* 'wild, tawny' (see FAUVE).]

Fauvism /fóvizəm/, **fauvism** *n.* an early 20th-century movement in painting, begun in about 1905 by a group of French artists, including Matisse, and characterized by the use of simple forms and vivid colours

Fauvist /fóvist/ *n.* = **Fauve** —**Fauvist** *adj.*

faux /fō/ *adj.* made in imitation of a natural material, e.g. leather or fur [Late 20thC. Via French from, ultimately, Latin *falsus* (see FALSE).]

faux ami /fó a meé/ (*plural* **faux amis**) *n.* LING = **false friend** *n.* 1 [From French, literally 'false friend']

faux-naïf /fó nī éef/ *adj.* **FALSELY UNSOPHISTICATED** pretending to be simple or without sophistication (*literary*) ■ *n.* **FAUX-NAÏF PERSON** sb who affects innocence or lack of sophistication (*literary*) [From French, literally 'falsely naive']

faux pas /fó paá/ (*plural* **faux pas** /fó paáz/) *n.* an embarrassing blunder that breaks a social convention of some kind (*literary*) [From French, literally 'false step']

WORD KEY: SYNONYMS

See Synonyms at ***mistake***.

fava bean /faávə-/ *n.* US = **broad bean** [Early 20thC. *Fava* via Italian from Latin *faba*.]

fave /fayv/ *n., adj.* favourite (*dated slang*) [Mid-20thC. Shortening.]

favela /fə véllə, faa-/ *n.* a shantytown or slum area, especially in Brazil [Mid-20thC. From Brazilian Portuguese, of uncertain origin; perhaps named after *Favela*, a hill near Rio de Janeiro where such towns were built.]

faveolate /fə veé ələt, -ə layt/ *adj.* with a honeycomb or pitted pattern (*formal*) [Mid-19thC. Formed from modern Latin *faveolus*, literally 'little honeycomb', from Latin *favus* 'honeycomb'.]

fave rave *n.* a favourite person, thing, or experience, e.g. a favourite film, song, or food (*slang*)

Faverin /fáyvə reen, -rin/ *tdmk.* a trademark for fluvoxamine, a drug that is used to treat depression and obsessive-compulsive disorders

favism /faávizəm/ *n.* acute anaemia caused by an allergic reaction to broad beans or the plant's pollen, usually as a result of a hereditary enzyme deficiency [Early 20thC. From Italian *favismo*, from *fava* 'broad bean' (see FAVA BEAN).]

favonian /fə vṓni ən/ *adj.* LITERAT **1. WESTERLY** blowing from the west, or relating to the west wind (*literary*) **2. FAVOURABLE** benign or kind [Mid-17thC. From Latin *favonianus*, from *Favonius* 'west wind' (source of English *foehn*.]

favor *n., v.* US = **favour**

favorite *adj., n.* US = **favourite**

favour /fáyvər/ *n.* **1. KIND ACT** an act of kindness performed or granted out of good will ○ *lent me the car as a favour* **2. ATTITUDE OR APPROVAL** an approving, friendly, or supportive attitude ○ *They seem to be out of favour with the judges.* **3. PREFERENCE** preferential treatment shown to sb **4. TOKEN OF LOYALTY** sth given or worn as a token of love, allegiance, or good will **5. SMALL GIFT** a small gift given to each guest at a party **6. MESSAGE** a communication, especially a formal letter (*archaic*) **7. APPEARANCE** the way sth or sb looks to others (*archaic*) **8. FACE** a facial expression or feature (*archaic*) ■ **favours** *npl.* **SEX** sexual intimacy, especially when consented to by a woman (*dated*) ■ *vt.* (**-vours, -vouring, -voured**) **1. PREFER SB OR STH** to show a preference for or to sb or sth ○ *He favoured loud suits and colourful ties.* **2. TREAT SB OR STH WELL** to treat sb or sth with particular approval or kindness ○ *She has been favouring him since he got a new car.* **3. SUPPORT SB OR STH** to express support for sb or sth ○ *voters who favoured reform* **4. ASSIST SB OR STH** to be advantageous to sb or sth ○ *tax measures that favour the rich* **5. SHOW SB PREFERENTIAL TREATMENT** to distinguish sb by giving him or her sth valuable ○ *favoured him with a seat next to her* **6. BE CAREFUL WITH STH** to treat or use sth gently ○ *favouring a bad knee* **7. RESEMBLE SB** to resemble sb, usually a parent, in appearance ○ *favours his uncle* [14thC. Via Old French 'friendly regard', from Latin *favor*, from *favere* 'to be well disposed towards'.] —**favourer** *n.* ◇ **curry favour with sb** to try to gain favour with a superior by flattery and obsequiousness ○ *They put more energy into currying favour with the principal than they ever put into their work.*

favourable /fáyvərəb'l/ *adj.* **1. ADVANTAGEOUS** acting in a beneficial way ○ *favourable winds* **2. PROMISING** suggesting future improvement or good results ○ *a favourable outlook* **3. APPROVING** expressing approval or admiration ○ *a favourable reaction* **4. GAINING APPROVAL** winning approval or favour **5. CONSENTING** expressing agreement or consent ○ *a favourable response* —**favourableness** *n.* —**favourably** *adv.*

favoured /fáyvərd/ *adj.* **1. CHOSEN** preferred to any other ○ *The favoured plan is unfortunately the costliest.* **2. DISTINGUISHED** enjoying the advantages of a particular thing ○ *a child favoured with his mother's looks and father's good nature* **3. PRIVILEGED** enjoying advantages or privileges denied to others —**favouredness** *n.*

favourite /fáyvərit/ *adj.* **MOST LIKED** most liked, or preferred above all others ■ *n.* **1. MOST LIKED PERSON OR THING** sb who or sth that is especially liked or preferred above others ○ *Which author is your favourite?* **2. SB FAVOURED BY SUPERIOR** sb who is treated with special favour by a superior ○ *a cherished position as one of the King's favourites* **3. ONE MOST LIKELY TO WIN** a competitor considered to be the most likely to win, especially in a horse race [Late 16thC. Via obsolete French *favorit* from, ultimately, Italian *favorito*, the past participle of *favorire* 'to favour', from *favore* 'favour', from Latin *favor* (see FAVOUR).]

favouritism /fáyvəritizəm/ *n.* **1. UNFAIRLY FAVOURING PERSON OR GROUP** the practice of giving special treatment or unfair advantages to a person or group ○ *The teacher was accused of showing favouritism towards certain pupils.* **2. STATUS AS PREFERRED PERSON** the state of being a favourite person ○ *basking in your favouritism*

Favrile glass /fə vreél-/ *tdmk.* a trademark for a type of iridescent glass that was used in the early 20th century to make lampshades, vases, and other objects in the Art Nouveau style. It was developed in the United States by L. C. Tiffany.

favus /fáyvəss/ *n.* an infectious skin disease that affects people, especially on the scalp, and some domestic animals, causing the formation of dry yellowish incrustations. It is caused by a fungus, *Trichophyton schoenleinii*. [Mid-16thC. From Latin, 'honeycomb'; from the appearance of the skin lesions.]

Fawcett /fáwssit/, **Dame Millicent** (1847–1929) British suffragist. She headed the National Union of Women's Suffrage Societies (1897–1919). Born **Millicent Garrett**

Fawkes /fawks/, **Guy** (1570–1606) English conspirator. He was executed for his role in the Gunpowder Plot against James I on 5 November, 1605.

Fawkner /fáwknər/, **John Pascoe** (1792–1869) English-born Australian pioneer. He was one of the first Europeans to explore and settle in the Port Phillip Bay region. He and John Batman are considered the cofounders of the city of Melbourne.

fawn[1] /fawn/ *n.* **1. YOUNG DEER** a young deer, especially one that is unweaned or less than a year old **2. YELLOWISH-BROWN COLOUR** a pale yellowish-brown colour ■ *adj.* **OF YELLOWISH-BROWN COLOUR** of a pale yellowish-brown colour ○ *wearing a fawn jacket* ■ *vi.* (**fawns, fawning, fawned**) **HAVE YOUNG** to give birth to a fawn [14thC. Via French *faon* 'young animal', from the assumed vulgar Latin stem *feton-*, from Latin *fetus* 'offspring' (source of English *foetus*).]

fawn[2] /fawn/ *vi.* (**fawns, fawning, fawned**) **1. SEEK FAVOUR BY FLATTERY** to seek attention or curry favour by flattery and obsequious behaviour ○ *admirers fawning at his feet* **2. TRY TO PLEASE** to attempt to please sb by showing enthusiastic affection ○ *started fawning all over me as soon as I walked in* [Old English *fagnian* 'to rejoice', from *fægen* 'glad', source also of English *fain*] —**fawner** *n.* —**fawningly** *adv.* —**fawningness** *n.*

fax /faks/ *n.* **1. MESSAGE SENT ELECTRONICALLY** an image or document that is transmitted in digitized electronic form over telephone lines and reproduced in its original form on the receiving end **2. SYSTEM FOR TRANSMITTING DOCUMENTS** a system of transmitting documents and images electronically over telephone lines (*often used before a noun*) ○ *sent by fax* **3. TRANSMITTING MACHINE** a machine incorporating a telephone that sends and receives documents or images via fax ■ *vt.* (**faxes, faxing, faxed**) **SEND ELECTRONICALLY** to send a message or document electronically using a fax machine [Mid-20thC. Shortening of FACSIMILE.]

fax-modem *n.* a modem that enables a computer to send and receive faxes

fax-on-demand *n.* TECH, TELECOM technology that will send a facsimile automatically to sb who telephones a particular number for information

fay[1] /fay/ *n.* a fairy, elf, or other small supernatural being from folklore (*literary*) ○ *'You are, upon the whole, a sort of fay, or sprite – not a woman!'* (Thomas Hardy, *Jude the Obscure*; 1895) [14thC. Via Old French *fa(i)e* 'fairy' from Latin *Fata*, the goddess of fate, from *fatum* (source also of English *fairy*; see FATE).]

fay[2] /fay/ *n.* faith, religious or personal (*archaic*) ○ *'Ah, sirrah, by my fay, it waxes late: I'll to my rest'.* (Shakespeare, *Romeo and Juliet*; 1594) [14thC. From Old French *fei*, earlier *feid* (see FAITH).]

fay[3] /fay/ (**fays, faying, fayed**) *vti.* to join pieces of wood together tightly, or fit tightly inside another piece of wood [Old English *fēgan*. Ultimately from an Indo-European base meaning 'to fasten', which is also the ancestor of English *impale, compact*, and *peace*.]

faze /fayz/ (**fazes, fazing, fazed**) *v.* **1.** *vt.* **FLUSTER SB** to disconcert or disturb sb ○ *News of the disaster didn't seem to faze her.* **2.** *vi. Ireland* **HAVE EFFECT** to have a visible effect on sb ○ *The cold didn't faze on him.* [Mid-19thC. Variant of dialectal *feeze* 'to frighten', from Old English *fēsian* 'to drive away', from prehistoric Germanic.]

fazenda /fə zéndə/ *n.* a large estate, farm, plantation, or cattle ranch, especially in Brazil or Portugal [Early 19thC. Via Portuguese, originally 'place with things to be done', from Latin *facienda* 'things to be done', from *facere* 'to do' (source also of English *hacienda*; see FACT).]

FBA *abbr.* Fellow of the British Academy

fbd *abbr.* SHIPPING freeboard

FBI *n.* a bureau of the US Department of Justice that deals with matters of national security, interstate crime, and crimes against the government. Full form **Federal Bureau of Investigation**

FBR *abbr.* fast-breeder reactor

fc *abbr.* PRINTING follow copy

FC *abbr.* **1.** Football Club **2.** Forestry Commission

FCA *abbr.* Fellow of the Institute of Chartered Accountants (in England and Wales)

fcap *abbr.* foolscap

FCCA *abbr.* Fellow of the Chartered Association of Certified Accountants

FCII *abbr.* Fellow of the Chartered Insurance Institute

F clef *n.* = **bass clef**

FCO *abbr.* Foreign and Commonwealth Office

fcp *abbr.* foolscap

FD *abbr.* Fidei Defensor

FDA *n.* the United States federal agency that oversees trade in and the safety of food and drugs. Full form **Food and Drug Administration**

F distribution *n.* a statistical measure of the spread or scattering of members of two observed random samples as a test of whether the samples have the same variability. The F-distribution is obtained by taking the ratio of the chi-square distributions of the samples divided by the number of their degrees of freedom. [Mid-20thC. Named after Sir Ronald Fisher (*d.* 1962), an English geneticist and statistician.]

FDR *abbr.* Franklin Delano Roosevelt

Fe *symbol.* iron [From Latin *ferrum* 'iron']

feague /feeg/ (**feagues, feaguing, feagued**), **feak** /feek/ (**feaks, feaking, feaked**) *vt.* (*archaic*) **1. BEAT SB** to beat, whip, or punish sb or sth **2. MYSTIFY SB** to confound or perplex sb [Late 16thC. Origin uncertain; perhaps from German *fegen* 'to sweep'.]

feal /feel/ *adj.* showing loyalty or faithfulness (*archaic*)

fealty /fée əlti/ (*plural* **-ties**) *n.* **1. ALLEGIANCE TO FEUDAL LORD** the loyalty sworn to a feudal lord by a vassal or tenant **2. FAITHFULNESS** loyalty or allegiance shown to anyone (*archaic or literary*) [13thC. Via Old French *feau(l)te* from Latin *fidelitas* (see FIDELITY).]

fear /feer/ *n.* **1. FEELING OF ANXIETY** an unpleasant feeling of apprehension or distress caused by the presence or anticipation of danger ○ *showed no signs of fear* **2. FRIGHTENING THOUGHT** an idea, thought, or other entity that causes feelings of fear ○ *irrational fears* **3. REVERENCE** awe or reverence, especially towards God **4. WORRY** a concern about sth that threatens to bring bad news or results (*often used in the plural*) ○ *fears for their safe return* **5. CHANCE** chance or likelihood of an undesirable thing happening ○ *There's no fear that he'll misunderstand.* ■ *v.* (**fears, fearing, feared**) **1.** *vti.* **BE AFRAID** to be frightened of sb or sth, or frightened about doing sth ○ *She fears going to the dentist.* **2.** *vt.* **EXPRESS REGRETFULLY** to be sorry to say sth (*formal*) ○ *I fear that you have not been successful on this occasion.* **3.** *vt.* **REVERE** to show respect for or be in awe of sb or sth ○ *fear God* **4.** *vt.* **FRIGHTEN** to make sb afraid (*archaic*) [Old English *fǣr* 'calamity, danger' and *fǣran* 'to frighten'. Ultimately from an Indo-European base meaning 'to try', which is also the ancestor of English *peril* and *experience*.]

fear for *vt.* to be worried or apprehensive about sb who or sth that appears to be at risk or in danger

fearful /féerf'l/ *adj.* **1. FRIGHTENING** causing or likely to cause fear ○ *a fearful storm* **2. WORRIED** feeling anxiety or apprehension ○ *fearful for the safety of her investment* **3. TIMID** nervous and easily frightened ○ *a fearful kitten* **4. SHOWING FEAR** arising from or expressing fear ○ *a fearful expression* **5. REVERENTIAL** feeling awe or reverence for sb or sth ○ *gazed in fearful wonder* **6. VERY BAD** extreme in degree, intensity, or badness (*informal*) ○ *had a fearful headache* —**fearfully** *adv.* —**fearfulness** *n.*

fearless /féerləss/ *adj.* courageous in the face of dangers or challenges —**fearlessly** *adv.* —**fearlessness** *n.*

fearnought /féer nawt/, **fearnaught** *n.* (*archaic*) **1. CLOTH** a thick woollen cloth used for jackets and overcoats (*often used before a noun*) **2. GARMENT** a jacket or overcoat made of fearnought [From the protection from the weather it affords, as a result of which you need 'fear nothing']

fearsome /féerssəm/ *adj.* **1. FRIGHTENING** inspiring fear ○ *a fearsome howling* **2. IMPRESSIVE** evoking awe and respect **3. TIMID** easily frightened ■ *adv.* **VERY** used to emphasize how severe sth is (*regional dated*) ○ *It was fearsome cold.* —**fearsomely** *adv.* —**fearsomeness** *n.*

feart /feert/ *adj. Scotland* feeling or showing fear [Variant of AFRAID]

feasibility /feezə bílləti/ (*plural* **-ties**) *n.* **1. FEASIBLE QUALITY** the degree to which sth can be carried out or achieved (*often used before a noun*) ○ *examining the feasibility of the proposed merger* **2. STH FEASIBLE** sth that can be carried out or achieved ○ *That idea is not even a feasibility.*

feasibility study *n.* a preliminary study undertaken to assess whether a planned project is likely to be practical and successful, and also estimating its cost

feasible /féezəb'l/ *adj.* **1. POSSIBLE** capable of being accomplished or put into effect **2. PLAUSIBLE** reasonable enough to be believed or accepted ○ *a feasible plan* [15thC. From French *faisable*, from *fais-*, the stem of *faire* 'to do', from Latin *facere* (see FACT).] —**feasibleness** *n.* —**feasibly** *adv.*

feast /feest/ *n.* **1. CELEBRATORY MEAL** an elaborate meal for many people that celebrates an occasion ○ *a wedding feast* **2. LARGE MEAL** any large and elaborate meal **3. STH VERY AGREEABLE** sth that provides a great deal of pleasure ○ *a feast for the eyes* **4.** RELIG **RELIGIOUS CELEBRATION** a periodic religious celebration, often marked by a special meal ■ *v.* (**feasts, feasting, feasted**) **1.** *vi.* **ATTEND CELEBRATORY MEAL** to be present at a celebratory meal **2.** *vi.* **ENJOY EATING** to eat heartily or with enjoyment ○ *feasting on strawberries and cream* **3.** *vt.* **PROVIDE FEAST FOR** to entertain sb with a feast **4.** *vi.* **TAKE DELIGHT** to derive great pleasure from sth, or enjoy sth at length ○ *feast on the magnificent scenery* [12thC. Via Old French *feste* from, ultimately, Latin *festum* (source of English *festival* and *festoon*).] —**feaster** *n.*

feast day *n.* **1.** RELIG **DAY OF RELIGIOUS FESTIVAL** a day on which a religious festival takes place **2. DAY OF EATING** a day on which an elaborate celebratory meal is enjoyed

Feast of Dedication, **Feast of Lights** *n.* JUDAISM = **Hanukkah**

Feast of Lots *n.* JUDAISM = **Purim**

Feast of St Michael and All Angels *n.* CHR = **Michaelmas**

Feast of Tabernacles *n.* JUDAISM = **Sukkoth**

Feast of the Assumption *n.* CHR = **Assumption of the Virgin Mary**

Feast of the Holy Innocents *n.* CHR = **Holy Innocents' Day**

Feast of Weeks *n.* JUDAISM = **Shavuoth**

feat[1] /feet/ *n.* **1. NOTABLE ACT** a remarkable act or achievement involving courage, skill, or strength ○ *She achieved the impressive feat of winning three gold medals.* **2. ACTIVITY** an art, skill, or profession (*archaic*) [14thC. Via Old French *fait* 'deed' from Latin *factum* (see FACT).]

feat[2] /feet/ *adj.* (*archaic*) **1. SKILFUL** possessing or demonstrating great skill **2. STYLISHLY ELEGANT** elegant or neat in appearance [Via Old French *fet* from Latin *factus*, literally 'made (for sth)', the past participle of *facere* (see FACT)] —**featly** *adv.*

feather /féthər/ *n.* **1. PART OF BIRD'S PLUMAGE** an individual part of a bird's plumage, consisting of a hollow central shaft with numerous interlocking fine strands on either side **2. STH RESEMBLING FEATHER** sth, e.g. the leaf of a plant, with light or wispy strands that give it a superficial resemblance to a feather **3. FLAW IN PRECIOUS STONE** a feather-shaped flaw, especially one found in a precious stone **4. UNIMPORTANT THING** sth small, trivial, or of minimal value **5.** ARCHERY **ARROW ATTACHMENT** a piece of a feather attached to the end of an arrow or dart to make it fly straight **6.** ARCHERY **BLUNT END OF ARROW** the end of an arrow that has a feather fitted on it, as distinct from its head **7.** JOINERY **PART OF WOOD JOINT** a projecting strip of wood fitted into a groove in the edge of a board to form a joint **8.** NAVY **TRACK MADE BY PERISCOPE** the track made on the surface of the sea by a submarine's periscope **9.** ROWING **HORIZONTAL OAR POSITION** the horizontal position of an oar, after raising it from the water between strokes, that reduces wind resistance ■ **feathers** *npl.* **1.** ZOOL **LONG HAIR ON ANIMAL'S LEGS** fringes of hair on the legs or tails of certain dogs and horses **2. ATTIRE** the clothes that sb is wearing (*dated*) ■ *v.* (**-ers, -ering, -ered**) **1.** *vt.* **FIT STH WITH FEATHERS** to fit sth, e.g. an arrow, with a feather or feathers **2.** *vt.* **COVER STH WITH FEATHERS** to cover or decorate sb or sth with feathers **3.** *vi.* **GROW FEATHERS** to grow or form feathers (*refers to birds*) **4.** *vti.* **FRAY** to fray a surface or end by cutting it or wearing it away, or become frayed in this way **5.** *vi.* **SPREAD** to grow or move out at an angle from a central line, in a pattern resembling the structure of a feather **6.** *vti.* ROWING **TURN OAR BLADE HORIZONTAL** to turn an oar with the blade face parallel to the water, after raising it from the water between strokes, in order to reduce wind resistance **7.** *vt.* AIR **ALTER PROPELLER BLADES** to change the angle of an aircraft's propeller so that the line of the blades is roughly parallel to the line of flight and air resistance is minimized **8.** *vt.* HAIR **CUT HAIR TO FORM LAYERS** to style hair by cutting and thinning, giving a layered texture **9.** *vt.* JOINERY **CONNECT BOARDS WITH TONGUE-AND-GROOVE** to join two boards or pieces of wood by using a tongue-and-groove joint [Old English *feþer*. Ultimately from an Indo-European word meaning 'to fly', which is also the ancestor of English *pen*, *pterodactyl*, and *appetite*.] —**feathery** *adj.* ◇ **a feather in sb's cap** an act or achievement that gives sb cause to be proud ○ *Being asked to give the after-dinner speech was a feather in my cap.*

featherbed /féthər bed/ (**-beds, -bedding, -bedded**) *vt.* to pamper sb, or protect sb from unpleasantness

feather boa *n.* a long thin scarf made of feathers

featherbone /féthər bōn/ *n.* a substitute for whalebone, originally made from the quills of domestic fowl, used as a corset bone [Modelled on WHALEBONE]

featherbrain /féthər brayn/ *n.* a forgetful, thoughtless, or inattentive person (*informal insult*) —**featherbrained** *adj.*

feather duster *n.* a brush used for dusting, made of long feathers attached to a stick

feathered /féthərd/ *adj.* **1. WITH FEATHERS** covered or decorated with feathers **2. LIKE A FEATHER** with many fine parallel strands ○ *a feathered lace border*

featheredge /féthər ej/ *n.* **1.** JOINERY **TAPERED BOARD** a board or plank with a thin tapering edge **2.** JOINERY **TAPERING EDGE OF BOARD** the thinner tapering edge of a wedge-shaped board or plank **3.** PAPER = **deckle edge** ■ *vt.* (**-edges, -edging, -edged**) JOINERY **HONE TO AN EDGE** to taper a side or end of a board to a very thin edge

feather grass *n.* a perennial grass plant that has feathery clusters of spikelets. Genus: *Stipa.*

featherhead /féthər hed/ *n.* = **featherbrain** (*informal insult*) —**featherheaded** /féthər héddid/ *adj.*

feathering /féthəring/ *n.* **1. PLUMAGE** the feathers on a bird **2. FEATHERS ATTACHED TO ARROW** the feathers attached to an arrow or dart, or their arrangement **3.** ZOOL **LONG HAIR ON ANIMAL'S LEGS** fringes of hair on the legs or tails of certain dogs and horses **4.** PRINTING **PRINTING DEFECT** the spreading of ink in veiny lines through printed paper that is too absorbent

feather palm *n.* a palm tree with leaves that resemble feathers, e.g. a date palm

feather star *n.* a free-swimming marine invertebrate animal related to the starfish, with between five and ten feathery arms radiating from a central disc. Order: Comatulida.

featherstitch /féthər stich/ *n.* **EMBROIDERY STITCH** ornamental embroidery stitching with a zigzag pattern ■ *vt.* (**-stitches, -stitching, -stitched**) **SEW STH WITH FEATHERSTITCH** to sew or decorate sth with featherstitch

featherweight /féthər wayt/ *n.* **1. LIGHT BOXER** a professional boxer weighing not more than 57 kg/126 pounds, between bantamweight and lightweight **2.** SPORTSPERSON a competitor of light weight in other sports, e.g. wrestling **3.** STH LIGHT sb or sth that is very light, small, or insignificant

feathery /féthəri/ *adj.* **1.** RESEMBLING FEATHERS similar to a feather or feathers, especially in lightness or softness **2.** CONSISTING OF FEATHERS made of or covered in feathers —**featheriness** *n.*

feature /féechər/ *n.* **1.** PART OF FACE a part of a face that contributes to its distinctiveness, especially the eyes, nose, or mouth **2.** DISTINCTIVE PART a part of sth that distinguishes it **3.** CINEMA FULL-LENGTH FILM a full-length film or, formerly, the main film in a cinema programme **4.** PUBL REGULAR ARTICLE a regular item in a newspaper or magazine **5.** PUBL MAIN STORY a story or article that is given particular prominence in a newspaper or magazine **6.** BROADCAST MAIN PROGRAMME a television or radio programme that is considered highly important or popular **7.** SPECIAL ATTRACTION sth offered as a special attraction, e.g. a particular aspect of sth ○ *a refrigerator with several energy-saving features* **8.** LING PROPERTY OF LINGUISTIC UNIT a distinctive property of a linguistic unit. Voicing is a feature of the consonants *b, d,* and *g.* **9.** APPEARANCE the general appearance of sb or sth (*archaic*) ■ *v.* (**-tures, -turing, -tured**) **1.** *vt.* CONTAIN STH AS IMPORTANT ELEMENT to have or present sb or sth as an important element of sth ○ *This week's activities will feature pony-trekking and golf.* **2.** *vti.* GIVE PROMINENCE TO IN PERFORMANCE to give prominence to sb taking part in a performance or to sth performed or portrayed in a performance, or be given prominence in this way ○ *a movie featuring two of the most popular actors* **3.** *vi.* FIGURE IN STH to figure in or be a part of sth ○ *Marriage doesn't feature in his plans.* **4.** *vt.* RESEMBLE SB to resemble sb physically, especially facially (*regional*) ○ *She features her mother.* [14thC. Via Old French *faiture*, from, ultimately, Latin *facere* 'to do, make' (see FACT). Originally in English, 'shape or proportions', especially of the body.]

featured /féechərd/ *adj.* **1.** GIVEN PROMINENCE given prominence or treated as a special attraction **2.** HAVING SPECIFIED FACIAL FEATURES having facial features of a particular kind (*often used in combination*) ○ *a sharp-featured man*

feature film *n.* a full-length film for the cinema

feature-length *adj.* being as long as a feature film ○ *a feature-length episode of a TV show*

featureless /féechərləss/ *adj.* lacking any characteristics or properties that can be considered distinctive

Feb. *abbr.* February

febrific /fi bríffik/, **febriferous** /fi bríffərəss/ *adj.* **1.** CAUSING FEVER capable of causing sb to have a fever **2.** HAVING FEVER affected by a fever [Early 18thC. From French *fébrifique* (now obsolete), from Latin *febris* 'fever' (see FEVER).]

febrifuge /fébbri fyooj/ *n.* DRUG THAT REDUCES FEVER a drug or treatment that is capable of reducing a fever ■ *adj.* REDUCING FEVER capable of reducing a fever [Late 17thC. From French *fébrifuge*, from Latin *febris* 'fever' (see FEVER).] —**febrifugal** /fi bríffyoōg'l/ *adj.*

febrile /féeb rīl/ *adj.* relating to, involving, or typical of fever [Mid-17thC. From French *fébrile* or medieval Latin *febrilis*, both formed from Latin *febris* 'fever'.]

February /fébbroo əri, fébbyoo-/ (*plural* **Februaries**) *n.* the second month of the year in the Gregorian calendar, between January and March. It has 28 days, except in every fourth year, when it has 29. [14thC. Via Old French *feverier* from, ultimately, Latin *februarius (mensis)* '(month) of purification', from a Roman festival of purification held in this month.]

fec. *abbr.* fecit

fecal *adj.* US = **faecal**

feces *npl.* US = **faeces**

feckless /fékləss/ *adj.* **1.** GOOD-FOR-NOTHING unable or unwilling to do anything useful **2.** UNLIKELY TO BE SUCCESSFUL lacking the thought or organization necessary to succeed ○ *feckless attempts at starting a business* [Late 16thC. From obsolete *feck* 'value, efficacy', a shortening of EFFECT.] —**fecklessly** *adv.* —**fecklessness** *n.*

fecula /fékyoōlə/ (*plural* **-lae** /-lee/) *n.* **1.** STARCH a starch extracted as sediment from a mixture of water and crushed plants **2.** INSECT DROPPING a piece of excrement, especially an insect dropping [Late 17thC. From Latin *faecula* 'crust of wine', from *faex* 'dregs, sediment' (source of English *faeces*).]

feculent /fékyoōlənt/ *adj.* very dirty or foul, especially when polluted by excrement (*formal*) [15thC. Directly or via French *féculent* from Latin *faeculentus*, from *faeces* (see FAECES).] —**feculence** *n.*

fecund /fékənd, féek-/ *adj.* **1.** FERTILE capable of producing much vegetation or many offspring (*formal*) **2.** HIGHLY PRODUCTIVE capable of producing many different works or works that are highly imaginative ○ *a fecund liar* [14thC. Directly or via French *fécond* from Latin *fecundus*.]

fecundate /fékən dayt, féek-/ (**-dates, -dating, -dated**) *vt.* (*formal*) **1.** MAKE SB OR STH PRODUCTIVE to make sb or sth fruitful or productive **2.** MAKE SB PREGNANT to fertilize sth, or make sb pregnant —**fecundation** /fékən dáysh'n, féek-/ *n.*

fecundity /fi kúndəti/ *n.* **1.** ABILITY TO PRODUCE OFFSPRING the ability to produce offspring, especially in large numbers **2.** CREATIVE PRODUCTIVITY the ability to produce many different and original ideas (*formal*)

fed past participle, past tense of **feed**

Fed /fed/, **fed** *n.* US in the United States, a Federal agent or official, especially an agent of one of the watchdog agencies such as the Federal Bureau of Investigation or the Environmental Protection Agency (*informal*)

Fed., **fed.** *abbr.* **1.** Federal **2.** Federated **3.** Federation

fedayee /fə daá yee/ (*plural* **fedayeen** /-yeen/) *n.* an Arab commando or guerrilla, especially one who fights against Israel [Mid-20thC. From Arabic and Persian *fidā'i* 'sb who sacrifices himself or herself'.]

federacy /féddərəssi/ (*plural* **-cies**) *n.* an alliance of people or countries formed to achieve a shared purpose (*archaic*) [Mid-17thC. From FEDERATE, or a shortening of CONFEDERACY.]

federal /féddərəl/ *adj.* **1.** MADE UP OF ALLIES relating to a form of government in which several states or regions defer certain powers, e.g. in foreign affairs, to a central government while retaining some measure of self-government **2.** CENTRAL relating to a political unit established on a federal basis, especially its central government **3.** ASSOCIATED relating to or characteristic of a unified body with constituent elements that retain a measure of autonomy ■ *n.* SUPPORTER OF ALLIANCE sb who supports joining an alliance [Mid-17thC. From Latin *foeder-*, the stem of *foedus* 'treaty'. Ultimately from an Indo-European base meaning 'to trust', which is also the ancestor of English *confide, faith,* and *abide*).]

Federal Bureau of Investigation *n.* full form of **FBI**

Federal Court *n.* in Australia, a national court that has jurisdiction in matters relating to corruption, bankruptcy, industrial relations, corporations law, taxation, and trade. It can overrule decisions made by Supreme Courts of the Australian territories and certain decisions made by state Supreme Courts.

federal district *n.* an area in which the seat of the national government of a federation, e.g. the United States, is located

federal government *n.* **1.** CENTRAL GOVERNMENT the central government of a federation **2.** AUSTRALIAN NATIONAL GOVERNMENT in Australia, the national government based in Canberra

federalise *vt.* = **federalize**

federalism /féddərəlizəm/ *n.* **1.** POLITICAL SYSTEM a political system in which several states or regions defer certain powers, e.g. in foreign affairs, to a central government while retaining a limited measure of self-government **2.** POLITICAL PRINCIPLE the principle of a federal system of government, or support for such a system

Federalism *n.* the political doctrine of the former Federalist Party of the United States

federalist /féddərəlist/ *n.* sb who supports a federal system of government

Federalist *n.* sb who supported the former Federalist Party of the United States

Federalist Party *n.* a former political party of the United States advocating a strong centralized government within the federal system. Founded in 1787, it declined in influence after 1800.

federalize /féddərə līz/ (**-izes, -izing, -ized**), **federalise** (**-ises, -ising, -ised**) *vt.* **1.** JOIN STATES IN FEDERAL UNION to bring various states together in a federal union **2.** PUT STH UNDER FEDERAL CONTROL to place sth under the control of a federal government —**federalization** *n.*

federate /féddə rayt/ (**-ates, -ating, -ated**) *vti.* to join, or cause various bodies to join together, in a federation [Late 17thC. From Latin *foederare*, from *foedus* (see FEDERAL).]

federation /féddə ráysh'n/ *n.* **1.** JOINING IN FEDERAL UNION an act of joining in a federal union or a federal system of government **2.** POLITICAL UNIT a political unit formed from smaller units on a federal basis **3.** ALLIANCE a group of various bodies or parties that have united to achieve a common goal

Federation *n.* **1.** AUSTRALIAN UNION the uniting of the Australian colonies on the first day of 1901 to form the Commonwealth of Australia, ruled by a single federal government **2.** AUSTRALIAN ARCHITECTURAL STYLE an Australian architectural style, typical of the period during which Federation took place, that is characterized by redbrick walls, terracotta roof tiles, ornate window frames, and stained-glass windows

fedora /fi dáwrə/ *n.* a soft felt hat with a brim and a crease along the length of its crown [Late 19thC. From *Fédora*, title of a drama by Victorien Sardou (1831–1908).]

fed up *adj.* having reached the limits of tolerance or patience with sb or sth (*informal*) ○ *I know she's fed up with working all the time.*

fee /fee/ *n.* **1.** PAYMENT FOR SERVICES a payment for professional services **2.** CHARGE MADE BY INSTITUTION a charge made by an institution, e.g. for membership, entrance, or the administering of an examination **3.** TIP an extra sum of money given to sb, e.g. sb waiting in a restaurant, for good service (*archaic*) **4.** LAW HERITABLE INTEREST IN LAND a right to land that can be passed on by inheritance **5.** = **fief** *n.* 1 **6.** *Scotland* TEMPORARY FARM WORK a six-month engagement as a farm worker (*archaic*) ■ *vti.* (**fees, feeing, feed**) *Scotland* (*archaic*) **1.** HIRE SB to employ sb, or accept employment **2.** DO FARM WORK FOR SIX MONTHS to hire sb as a farm worker for a fixed term of six months, or accept a six-month's engagement as a farm worker [14thC. Via Anglo-Norman from medieval Latin *feudum* (see FEUD[2]).]

WORD KEY: SYNONYMS

See Synonyms at ***wage***.

WORD KEY: ORIGIN

The word ***fee*** and its close relatives *feudal* and *fief* take us back to the very beginnings of feudal society in Europe, when the ownership of cattle was symbolic of wealth. The Indo-European source of ***fee***, denoting 'livestock', is also the source of the German word *Vieh*, meaning 'cattle'.

feeble /féeb'l/ (**-bler, -blest**) *adj.* **1.** PHYSICALLY OR MENTALLY WEAK lacking physical or mental strength or health **2.** UNCONVINCING unlikely to convince ○ *a feeble excuse* [12thC. Via Old French *fe(i)ble* from, ultimately, Latin *flebilis* 'lamentable', later 'weak', from *flere* 'to weep'.] —**feebleness** *n.* —**feebly** *adv.*

WORD KEY: SYNONYMS

See Synonyms at ***weak***.

feeble-minded *adj.* **1.** OFFENSIVE TERM an offensive term for mentally challenged (*offensive*) **2.** UNINTELLIGENT unintelligent or thoughtless (*insult*) **3.** NOT WELL-THOUGHT-OUT done without forethought, or lacking a well-thought-out plan **4.** IRRESOLUTE lacking in will or resolution (*archaic*) —**feeble-mindedly** *adv.* —**feeble-mindedness** *n.*

feed /feed/ *v.* (**feeds, feeding, fed, fed**) **1.** *vt.* GIVE FOOD TO SB to give food to a person or an animal **2.** *vt.* GIVE STH AS FOOD to give sth as food to a person or an animal **3.** *vt.* SERVE AS FOOD FOR SB to serve as or be enough food for a person or an animal **4.** *vi.* EAT to eat food, or take in nourishment **5.** *vt.* **SUPPORT STH** to sustain or encourage a specific belief or behaviour ○ *Compliments merely feed vanity.* **6.** *vt.* **PROVIDE STH WITH NECESSARY MATERIAL** to provide the necessary materials for sth to operate **7.** *vti.* **MOVE GRADUALLY** to move sth gradually into, through, or out of sth, or be moved in this way **8.** *vt.* ARTS **GIVE PERFORMER CUE** to deliver a line or cue to a fellow performer **9.** *vti.* SPORTS **PASS BALL TO FELLOW PLAYER** to pass a ball to a teammate (*informal*) **10.** *vt.* UTIL **SUPPLY STH WITH POWER** to supply power or an electrical signal to a system, component, or station **11.** *vt.* RUGBY **PUT BALL IN SCRUMMAGE ILLEGALLY** in rugby, to put the ball into the scrummage illegally by putting it at the feet of teammates ■ *n.* **1. ACT OF FEEDING** an act or occasion of feeding **2. FOOD** food, especially for animals or babies **3. LARGE MEAL** a meal, especially a large and satisfying one (*dated informal*) **4. MATERIAL PROVIDER** a device that supplies material to a machine, as does the paper tray on a printer **5.** ARTS **SB WHO PROVIDES CUES** sb who delivers a line or cue to a fellow performer [Old English *fēdan*; related to *foda* (see FOOD)]

feed into *vt.* **1. CONTRIBUTE TO STH** to add weight and impetus to sth **2. JOIN WITH STH LARGER** to connect with and contribute to sth larger, e.g. a road or river

feed up *vt.* to give a person or an animal plenty of food to eat in order to build up that person's or animal's weight

feedback /fēed bak/ *n.* **1. RETURN OF OUTPUT** the return of part of the output of a machine, system, or circuit to the input in a way that affects its performance **2. NOISE IN LOUDSPEAKER** the high whistling or howling noise caused by feedback in a loudspeaker **3. RESPONSE** comments in the form of opinions about and reactions to sth, intended to provide useful information for future decisions and development

feedback circuit *n.* a circuit in which a portion of the output signal is returned to the input, often in order to control or stabilize the circuit

feedback control loop *n.* the connection or path that forms an electrical loop from the output to the input of a feedback circuit

feedback factor *n.* a portion of an output signal that is returned to and combined with the input signal

feedback inhibition *n.* an internal control on a hormone or enzyme that causes a reduction in activity once the end product reaches a certain concentration

feedback loop *n.* a cycle in which two agents each act to reinforce the other's action

feedbag /fēed bag/ *n.* **1. BAG FOR ANIMAL FEED** a bag or sack containing food for livestock **2.** *US* = **nosebag**

feeder /fēedər/ *n.* **1. EATER** sb who or sth that eats, gives food to others, or is fed **2. CONTAINER FOR ANIMAL'S FOOD** a device that supplies food for animals and birds ○ *a bird feeder in the garden* **3. BIB** a baby's bib or bottle (*dated*) **4. MACHINE PART** a part of a machine that accepts or controls the input of material to be processed ○ *a document feeder* **5.** GEOG **TRIBUTARY** a stream or river that joins the flow of a larger one **6.** TRANSP **CONNECTING CARRIER** a road, railway, or airline that carries traffic from a relatively small place to a city in order to connect with a larger carrier **7.** UTIL **POWER LINE** a power line that carries power from a generating station to a substation or network **8.** RADIO **CONNECTION** a line that connects an aerial to a receiver or transmitter **9.** EDUC **PRIMARY SCHOOL** a primary school from which a secondary school receives an annual intake of pupils **10.** GARDENING **PLANT REQUIRING FERTILIZER** a plant that requires a large amount of fertilizer to grow, and especially flower, well ○ *Fuchsias are gross feeders.*

feeding bottle *n.* a bottle with a plastic or rubber teat used to give milk or other liquids to a baby or young animal

feeding frenzy *n.* **1.** ZOOL **VIOLENT FEEDING BY MANY ANIMALS** an intense violent period of eating that occurs when a large number of animals of the same or related species, e.g. sharks or piranhas, converge on a food source **2. INSTANCE OF FRANTIC ACTIVITY** an instance of frantic activity centred on a person or organization that occurs when other people, especially journalists, sense an opportunity they can exploit (*informal*)

feeding ground *n.* an area where animals, birds, or fish regularly come to feed

feedlot /fēed lot/ *n.* *US* an area or building in which livestock are kept while being fattened for slaughter

feedstock /fēed stok/ *n.* a raw material used in the industrial manufacture of a product

feedstuff /fēed stuf/ *n.* feed for livestock, especially consisting of processed and balanced ingredients

feedthrough /fēed throo/ *n.* an electrical conductor that connects two sides of a circuit board

feel /feel/ *v.* (**feels, feeling, felt** /felt/) **1.** *vt.* **TOUCH STH** to perceive sth using the sense of touch **2.** *vt.* **TOUCH SB SEXUALLY** to touch sb or a part of sb's body for the purpose of sexual gratification **3.** *vt.* **EXAMINE STH** to test or examine sth by touching it **4.** *vt.* **ADVANCE HESITANTLY** to make your way forward slowly, guided by the sense of touch or tentatively, because what is ahead is dark or uncertain **5.** *vi.* **USE TOUCH IN SEARCHING** to use the sense of touch to try to find sth ○ *feel around for my keys* **6.** *vt.* **HAVE SENSATION IN BODY PART** to have physical sensation in a particular part of the body **7.** *vt.* **EXPERIENCE STH** to experience an emotion or physical sensation ○ *I feel no regret.* **8.** *vi.* **SEEM TO YOURSELF** to seem to yourself to be in a particular physical or emotional state ○ *Don't feel sad.* **9.** *vi.* **CAUSE PARTICULAR SENSATION** to cause a particular physical or emotional sensation ○ *The water feels cold.* **10.** *vt.* **BE AWARE OF STH** to be instinctively aware of sth, usually an emotion, that is not visible or apparent **11.** *vt.* **BE AFFECTED BY STH** to be deeply affected emotionally by sth painful **12.** *vt.* **THINK STH IS TRUE** to be convinced about sth by instinct or intuition rather than concrete evidence ○ *I feel you're lying to me.* **13.** *vt.* **BELIEVE STH** to have the opinion or belief that sth is the case ○ *She felt she could no longer carry on.* ■ *n.* **1. ACT OF TOUCHING** an act of touching sth **2. IMPRESSION GAINED FROM TOUCH** an impression of sth gained through touching or being touched by it ○ *the feel of wool against the skin* **3. IMPRESSION SENSED FROM STH** a particular impression, appearance, effect, or atmosphere sensed from sth ○ *a hotel with a more traditional feel* **4. SENSE OF TOUCH** the sensation felt on touching sth ○ *hot to the feel* **5. INSTINCT FOR STH** an instinctive understanding of, or talent for, sth ○ *He has a feel for these things.* **6. GROPE** an uninvited sexual touch (*informal*) [Old English *fēlan*. Ultimately from an Indo-European base that is also the ancestor of English *palpable*.] ◇ **feel like 1.** to have an inclination or desire for sth **2.** to have or acknowledge a physical or emotional condition that is considered comparable to sth else

feel for *vt.* to experience sympathy or compassion for sb

feel out *vt.* to try to establish, often in an indirect way, the nature of a situation or sb's attitude or opinion about sth

feel up *vt.* to touch sb sexually, especially without permission (*informal*)

feel up to *vt.* to consider yourself ready for sth or able to do sth

feeler /fēelər/ *n.* **1. SB WHO FEELS** sb who or sth that feels sth **2.** ZOOL **TOUCHING ORGAN** an organ of touch in various animals, e.g. an insect's antenna **3. ATTEMPT TO TEST OTHERS' REACTION** sth said or done to test the reaction of others to an idea, plan, or project

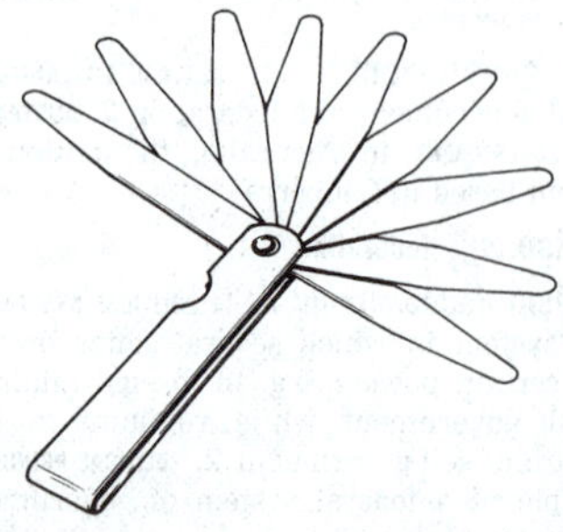

Feeler gauge

feeler gauge *n.* a thin strip of metal of a specific size used to measure or set a gap between parts of a mechanism

feel-good *adj.* causing, involving, or typical of a sense of wellbeing or satisfaction

feeling /fēeling/ *n.* **1. SENSE OF TOUCH** the sensation felt on touching sth **2. ABILITY TO HAVE PHYSICAL SENSATION** the ability to perceive physical sensation in a part of the body ○ *Slowly the feeling returned to his fingers.* **3. STH FELT PHYSICALLY OR MENTALLY** a perceived physical or mental sensation **4. STH FELT EMOTIONALLY** a perceived emotion **5. AFFECTION** the emotional response of love, sympathy, or tenderness towards sb **6. ABILITY TO EXPRESS EMOTION** the capacity to experience strong emotions **7. IMPRESSION SENSED FROM STH** a particular impression, appearance, effect, or atmosphere sensed from sth ○ *There was a feeling of abandonment about the old house.* **8. INSTINCTIVE AWARENESS** an instinctive awareness or presentiment of sth ○ *I have a feeling you're going to be disappointed.* **9. INSTINCTIVE UNDERSTANDING OR TALENT** an instinctive understanding of, or talent for, sth ○ *has a real feeling for this kind of work* **10. EXPRESSIVENESS** the ability to express strong emotion, especially in performance ○ *Play the piece again with more feeling.* ■ **feelings** *npl.* **SENSIBILITIES** sb's emotional susceptibilities ○ *I didn't want to hurt their feelings.* ■ *adj.* **1. SENSITIVE TO TOUCH** able to experience the sensation of touch **2. EXPRESSIVE** expressing or full of strong emotion **3. HAVING STRONG EMOTIONS** easily or strongly affected by emotion —**feelingly** *adv.*

fee simple (*plural* **fees simple**) *n.* a form of property ownership in which the owner has outright and unconditional disposal rights. ◊ **fee tail**

feet plural of **foot** ◇ **drag your feet (on sth)** to delay doing sth

fee tail (*plural* **fees tail**) *n.* a form of property ownership in which the property may be inherited only by a specified line of heirs. ◊ **fee simple** [From TAIL]

Fehling's solution /fáylingz-/ *n.* a solution of copper sulphate, sodium potassium tartrate, and sodium hydroxide used to detect the presence of aldehydes, including sugars [Late 19thC. Named after the German chemist Hermann von *Fehling* (1812–85).]

feign /fayn/ (**feigns, feigning, feigned**) *vt.* **1. PRETEND STH** to make a show or pretence of sth ○ *She feigned ignorance.* **2. INVENT STH** to make up or fabricate sth **3. COPY** to imitate or copy sb or sth [13thC. From French *feign-*, the present stem of *feindre* 'to pretend, shirk' (source of English *faint*), from Latin *fingere* 'to fabricate, form' (source of English *fiction*, *figure*, and *figment*).]

feijoa /fay yṓ ə/ *n.* **1. AMERICAN TREE** a South American tree related to myrtle and cultivated for its edible fruit. Latin name: *Acca sellowiana.* **2. FRUIT TASTING LIKE PINEAPPLE** an edible green fruit of the feijoa tree that has a flavour similar to pineapple and is eaten raw or used in cooking or making jams and preserves [Late 19thC. From modern Latin, genus name, named after the Brazilian naturalist J. da Silva *Feijó* (1760–1824).]

feijoada /fáy zhoo áad aa/ *n.* a Brazilian party dish consisting of meat with rice, black beans, green vegetables such as kale, sliced oranges, and a hot pepper sauce, all served on platters [Mid-20thC. From Portuguese, formed from *feijão*, any of various edible beans, from Latin *phaseolus*.]

feint[1] /faynt/ *n.* **1.** MIL **MOCK ATTACK** a mock attack by a military force, intended to draw the enemy's attention away from the true attack **2.** SPORTS **DECEPTIVE MOVE** a deceptive move in a competitive sport **3. DECEPTIVE ACTION** a deceptive action made to disguise what is really intended ■ *vti.* (**feints, feinting, feinted**) **MAKE FEINT** to carry out a feint [Late 17thC. From French *feinte* 'sham, pretence', from the past participle of *feindre* (see FEIGN).]

feint[2] /faynt/ *adj.* used to describe paper with faint horizontal lines across it as a guide for writing [Late 17thC. Via French *feinte*, use as a noun of the feminine past participle of *feindre* (see FEIGN).]

feisty /fīsti/ (**-ier, -iest**) *adj.* (*informal*) **1. SPIRITED** characterized by spirited, sometimes aggressive, behaviour **2.** *US, Can* **IRRITABLE** likely to respond in an irritable or touchy way [Late 19thC. From FEIST 'small dog' (from the temperament of a spoilt pet dog).]

felafel *n.* = **falafel**

feldspar /féld spaar/, **felspar** /fél-/ *n.* an extremely common aluminosilicate mineral found in most igneous and metamorphic rocks and many sediments. It contains varying proportions of calcium, sodium, potassium, and other minerals. Feldspar minerals are subdivided into two groups, alkali feldspars and plagioclase feldspars. [Late 18thC. Alteration of German *Feldspath*, literally 'field mineral'. Spelling variation *fels-* comes from a mistaken association with German *Fels* 'rock'.] —**feldspathic** /feld spáthik/ *adj.*

feldspathoid /féld spath oyd/ *n.* a rock-forming mineral found in silica-deficient alkaline igneous rocks [Literally 'similar to feldspar']

felicific /feélə síffik/ *adj.* creating or intended to cause happiness (*formal*) [Mid-19thC. From Latin *felicificus*, from *felix* 'happy' (see FELICITY).]

felicitate /fə líssi tayt/ (**-tates, -tating, -tated**) *vt.* to congratulate sb, or wish sb happiness (*formal*) [Early 17thC. From late Latin *felicitare* 'to make happy', from Latin *felix* 'happy' (see FELICITY).] —**felicitator** *n.*

felicitation /fə líssi táysh'n/ *n.* **ACT OF CONGRATULATING** an act of congratulating or wishing sb happiness (*formal*) ■ **felicitations** *npl.* **FRIENDLY GREETING** used as a greeting or to wish sb happiness (*formal*)

felicitous /fə líssitəss/ *adj.* **1. APPROPRIATE** appropriate or highly suitable ○ *a felicitous choice of words* **2. PLEASANT** pleasing or agreeable **3. FORTUNATE** happy or fortunate [Mid-16thC. Formed from FELICITY.] —**felicitously** *adv.* —**felicitousness** *n.*

felicity /fə líssəti/ (*plural* **-ties**) *n.* **1. HAPPINESS** happiness or contentment **2. STH PRODUCING HAPPINESS** sth that creates happiness **3. APPROPRIATENESS** an appropriate or pleasing manner **4. STH APPROPRIATE** sth appropriate or pleasing [14thC. Via Old French *félicité* from, ultimately, Latin *felix* 'fruitful, happy'. Ultimately from an Indo-European base meaning 'to suck, suckle', which is also the ancestor of English *female, foetus, fellatio,* and *fecund.*]

felid /feélid/ (*plural* **-lids** *or* **-lid**) *n.* an animal belonging to the cat family. Lions, tigers, and domestic cats are felids. Family: Felidae. (*technical*) [Late 19thC. Via modern Latin *Felidae*, family name, from, ultimately, Latin *feles* 'cat'.]

feline /fée līn/ *adj.* **1. OF CAT FAMILY** belonging to or typical of animals of the cat family, including lions, tigers, and domestic cats **2. RESEMBLING CAT** similar to a cat, especially in graceful movement or stealthiness ○ *feline suppleness* ■ *n.* **MEMBER OF CAT FAMILY** an animal belonging to the cat family. Domestic cats, lions, and tigers are felines. Family: Felidae. [Late 17thC. From Latin *felinus*, from *feles* 'cat'.] —**felinely** *adv.* —**felineness** *n.*

feline distemper *n.* an infectious viral disease of cats that causes vomiting and diarrhoea and is often fatal

fell[1] past tense of **fall** [13thC. Via Old Norse *fjall* 'hill' from, ultimately, an Indo-European base that is also the ancestor of German *Fels* 'rock'.]

fell[2] /fel/ *vt.* (**fells, felling, felled**) **1. CHOP TREE DOWN** to cut down a tree **2. KNOCK SB DOWN** to knock sb down, or cause sb to fall **3.** SEW **SEW SEAM FLAT** to sew a seam by turning an edge over and sewing it down on the inside ■ *n.* **1.** FORESTRY **NUMBER OF TREES CUT DOWN** an amount of timber cut down at one time or over one period **2.** SEW **SEWN SEAM** a seam sewn by turning an edge over and sewing it down on the inside [Old English *fel(l)* 'to cause to fall' from, ultimately, prehistoric Germanic] —**fellable** *adj.*

fell[3] /fel/ *adj.* (*archaic or literary*) **1. FIERCE** having an extremely cruel or vicious character **2. LETHAL** capable of killing sb or destroying sth **3. INAUSPICIOUS** having a bad or malign outcome [13thC. From Old French *fel*, a form of *felon* (see FELON[1]).]

fell[4] /fel/ *n.* a hillside or mountainside without trees

fell[5] /fel/ *n.* **1. ANIMAL HIDE** the hide of an animal **2. THIN MEMBRANE** the thin membrane between an animal's hide and its flesh [Old English. Ultimately from an Indo-European base that is also the ancestor of English *pelt* and *film*.]

fella /féllə/ *n.* a man or boy (*informal*) [Mid-19thC. Alteration of FELLOW.]

fellah /féllə/ (*plural* **-lahin** /féllə heén/ *or* **-laheen** *or* **-lahs**) *n.* a member of the labouring class in an Arab country who lives off the land [Mid-18thC. From Arabic *fallah* 'tiller of the soil', from *falahah* 'to split, till the soil'.]

fellate /fe láyt/ (**-lates, -lating, -lated**) *vti.* to perform oral sex for a man (*formal*) [Late 19thC. From Latin *fellare* 'to suck'. Ultimately from an Indo-European base meaning 'to suck', which is also the ancestor of English *foetus, female,* and *felicity*.] —**fellation** /fe láysh'n/ *n.* —**fellator** /fe láytər/ *n.*

fellatio /fe láyshi ō/ *n.* the act or practice of sucking or licking a man's penis to provide sexual stimulation (*formal*) [Late 19thC. From modern Latin, from Latin *fellat-* the past participle stem of *fellare* (see FELLATE).]

feller[1] /féllər/ *n.* **1.** FORESTRY **TREE CUTTER** sb who cuts down trees **2.** SEW **SB WHO FELLS SEAMS** a person who or a machine attachment that fells seams

feller[2] /féllər/ *n.* a man or boy (*informal*) [Early 19thC. Representing a nonstandard pronunciation of FELLOW.]

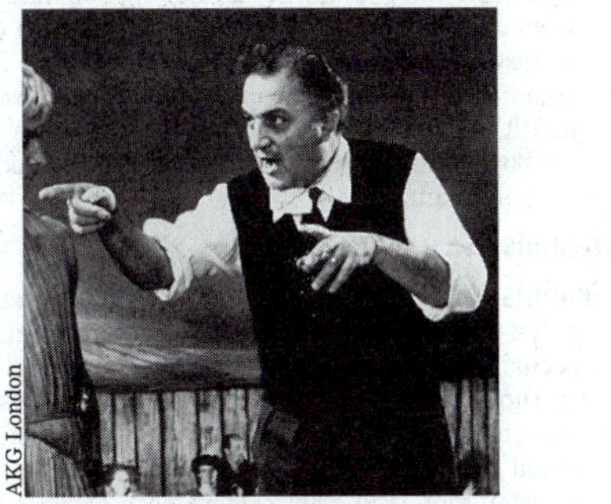

Federico Fellini: Directing his *Satyricon* (1969)

Fellini /fe leéni/, **Federico** (1920–93) Italian film director. He was known for his use of fantasy and satire, and won Academy Awards for *La Strada* (1954), *Nights of Cabiria* (1957), *8½* (1963), and *Amarcord* (1974).

fellmonger /fél mung gər/ *n.* sb who prepares and sells animal skins —**fellmongering** *n.*

felloe /félli/, **felly** (*plural* **-lies**) *n.* an outer rim of a wooden wheel, or a segment of this, with a metal tyre shrunk around it [Old English]

fellow /féllō/ *n.* **1. MAN OR BOY** a man or boy (*dated*) **2. BOYFRIEND** sb's boyfriend (*dated informal*) **3. ONE OF PAIR** either one of a pair of objects **4. COMPANION** a companion or colleague (*dated*) **5. EQUAL** sb or sth of the same rank or quality **6. LOW-CLASS PERSON** sb considered to be socially inferior, especially in belonging to the working class or not having money (*archaic*) **7. fellow, Fellow** UNIV **MEMBER OF UNIVERSITY STAFF** sb on the governing board of a university or college, usually also a member of the teaching staff ○ *a Cambridge Fellow* **8.** UNIV **GRADUATE STUDENT** a graduate student who is supported by a university department to teach or do research ○ *a research fellow* ■ *adj.* **BEING IN SAME GROUP** belonging to the same group, occupation, rank, or location [Old English *feolaga* 'partner', from Old Norse *félagi*, from *fé* 'money' and a prehistoric Germanic base meaning 'to lay down'. The underlying idea is 'sb laying down money in a joint venture'.]

WORD KEY: CULTURAL NOTE

Poor Fellow My Country, a novel by Australian writer Xavier Herbert (1975). Set in northern Australia between 1936 and 1942, it depicts the disastrous effects of white settlement on Aboriginal peoples through the interwoven stories of pastoralists, government representatives, and local Aboriginals. Running to 850,000 words, it is the longest novel ever published in Australia.

Fellow /féllō/ *n.* a member of a learned or scientific society ○ *Fellow of the Royal College of Surgeons*

fellow feeling *n.* an awareness of having interests in common with other people and feeling sympathy for them

fellow servant *n.* an employee whose employer is not legally responsible for harm or injury done to him or her by another employee

fellowship /féllō ship/ *n.* **1. COMMUNION** a sharing of common interests, goals, experiences, or views **2. SOCIETY** a group of people who share common interests, goals, experiences, or views **3. COMPANIONSHIP** companionship or friendly association **4. SIMILARITY** membership in a group, or the sharing of characteristics with others **5.** UNIV **MEMBERSHIP OF UNIVERSITY STAFF** membership of the governing board of a university or college usually also involving teaching duties **6.** UNIV **GRADUATE POST** a university post awarded to a graduate student who is supported by a university department to teach or undertake research **7.** UNIV **FINANCIAL ENDOWMENT** a financial endowment set up to support graduate students

Fellowship *n.* the fellows of a university or college considered as a body

fellow traveller *n.* **1. SB ON SAME JOURNEY** sb who is making the same journey as another at the same time **2. COMMUNIST SYMPATHIZER** sb who sympathizes with the cause of an organized group, especially the Communist Party, without becoming a member

fell-running /fél runing/ *n.* the sport of competitive running over fells

fell-walking /fél wawking/ *n.* the pastime of walking on fells

felly *n.* = **felloe**

felo de se /feélō di seé/ (*plural* **felones de se** /fee lṓ neez di seé/ *or* **felos de se**) *n.* **1. SB WHO KILLS SELF** sb who commits suicide **2. KILLING SELF** an act of committing suicide [Early 17thC. From Anglo-Latin, 'crime against yourself'.]

felon[1] /féllən/ *n.* **1. CRIMINAL** formerly in England and Wales, sb guilty of a felony **2. SB EVIL** sb whose behaviour and actions are evil or depraved (*archaic*) ■ *adj.* **EVIL** characterized by evil or depravity (*archaic*) [13thC. Via Old French from medieval Latin *fello* 'evildoer' (source of English *fell*[3]), of uncertain origin.]

felon[2] /féllən/ *n.* = **whitlow** [14thC. Origin uncertain: perhaps from Latin *fel* 'gall, bile'.]

felonious /fə lṓni əss/ *adj.* **1. RELATING TO FELONY** relating to felonies, or constituting a felony **2. EVIL** characterized by evil or depravity (*archaic*) —**feloniously** *adv.* —**feloniousness** *n.*

felonry /féllənri/ (*plural* **-ries**) *n.* a group of felons, especially the criminals in a penal colony (*dated*)

felony /félləni/ (*plural* **-nies**) *n.* formerly in England and Wales, and still in the United States, a serious crime such as murder that is punished more severely than a misdemeanour [13thC. From Old French *felonie*.]

felsic /félssik/ *adj.* used to describe igneous rocks or minerals that are light in colour, indicating relatively high levels of quartz and feldspars [Early 20thC. Coined from FELDSPAR + SILICA.]

felsite /fél sīt/ *n.* a light-coloured igneous rock consisting chiefly of feldspar and quartz, that can only be precisely classified by microscopic examination [Late 18thC. Formed from FELSPAR.] —**felsitic** /fel síttik/ *adj.*

felspar *n.* = **feldspar**

felt[1] past tense, past participle of **feel**

felt[2] /felt/ *n.* **1. WOOL OR ANIMAL-HAIR FABRIC** a fabric made from wool or animal hair by compressing, heating, or treating the natural fibres with chemicals **2. SYNTHETIC FABRIC** a synthetic fabric made by the process of matting, especially a heavy paper permeated with asphalt, used to seal roofs ○ *roofing felt* ■ *v.* (**felts, felting, felted**) **1.** *vt.* **MAKE INTO FELT** to make sth into felt **2.** *vt.* **COVER WITH FELT** to cover sth with felt ○ *felting the roof* **3.** *vi.* **BECOME MATTED** to become matted, or come to resemble felt [Old English. Ultimately from an Indo-European base meaning 'to strike, beat, pound', which is also the ancestor of English *anvil, push, pelt*[2], and *polish*.] —**felty** *adj.*

felting /félting/ *n.* **1. FELT FABRIC** felt, or any material made in a similar way **2. MAKING OF FELT** the process of making felt

felt pen *n.* = **felt-tipped pen**

felt tip *n.* **1. FELT PEN POINT** a pen point made from felt or a similar compressed fibre **2.** = **felt-tipped pen**

felt-tipped pen *n.* a pen with a point made from felt or a similar compressed fibre

Felucca

felucca /fə lúkə/ n. a small sailing boat with curving triangular sails (**lateen-rigged**), used in the Mediterranean and on the Nile [Early 17thC. Via Italian from, ultimately, Mediterranean Arabic *fluka*.]

felwort /fél wurt/ n. a plant of the gentian family that is native to Europe and China and has purple flowers. Latin name: *Gentianella amarella*. [Old English *feldwyrt*, literally 'field plant']

fem. abbr. **1.** GRAM feminine **2.** BIOL female

female /fée mayl/ adj. **1.** BIOL OF SEX CAPABLE OF CHILDBEARING relating to, belonging to, or characteristic of the sex that produces eggs or young **2.** RELATING TO WOMEN relating to, belonging to, or considered typical of women or girls **3.** BOT PRODUCING SEEDS used to describe the part of a plant, e.g. a carpel, that produces the female sex cells **4.** BOT HAVING CARPELS used to describe flowers that have carpels but no stamens **5.** ENG MADE WITH A RECESS used to describe a component or part of a component, e.g. an electric socket, that has a recess designed to receive a corresponding projecting part ■ n. **1.** BIOL FEMALE PERSON a female person or animal **2.** GIRL OR WOMAN a girl or woman (*offensive*) **3.** BOT PLANT WITH FEMALE FLOWERS a plant that has only female flowers [14thC. Alteration (under the influence of MALE) of Old French *femelle* from Latin *femella*, from *femina* 'woman' (see FEMININE).] —**femaleness** n.

female circumcision, female genital mutilation n. the practice of circumcision of adolescent women in some cultures that generally involves the surgical removal of the clitoris or the sewing up of the vaginal opening

female impersonator n. a man, often appearing as a solo theatrical performer, who dresses as and imitates a woman

feme /fem/ n. in law, a woman or wife [Mid-16thC. Via Anglo-Norman from Latin *femina* (see FEMININE).]

feme covert (*plural* **femes covert**) n. in law, a married woman [From Anglo-Norman, literally 'covered woman']

feme sole (*plural* **femes sole**) n. in law, a single woman, including women not married, widows, divorcées, and married women living independently and separately from their husbands [From Anglo-Norman]

Femidom /fémmi dom/ tdmk. a trademark for a contraceptive device consisting of a sheath of thin rubber that is inserted into a vagina before insertion of a penis

femineity /fémmə née i tee/ n. the quality of looking and behaving in ways conventionally thought to be appropriate for a woman [Early 19thC. Formed from Latin *femineus* 'womanish', from *femina* (see FEMININE).]

feminine /fémmənin/ adj. **1.** CONVENTIONALLY CHARACTERISTIC OF WOMEN conventionally believed to be typical of or appropriate for a woman or girl **2.** ATTRIBUTED TO WOMEN considered to be specific to women **3.** EFFEMINATE used to describe qualities, actions, or types of behaviour in a man or boy that are conventionally associated with women or girls **4.** GRAM CLASSIFIED GRAMMATICALLY AS FEMALE IN GENDER used to describe or relating to a class of words or forms in various languages that includes the majority of words referring to females ■ n. GRAM FEMININE WORD OR FORM a word or form that in a particular language is classified grammatically as feminine [14thC. Via Old French from Latin *femininus*, from *femina* 'woman', literally 'she who suckles'. Ultimately from an Indo-European base meaning 'to suck', which is

also the ancestor of English *foetus*, *fecund*, and *felicity*.] —**femininely** adv. —**feminineness** n.

feminine caesura n. a pause in a line of scanned verse that does not come immediately after a stressed syllable

feminine ending n. **1.** GRAM GRAMMATICALLY FEMININE LAST PART OF WORD an inflectional morpheme attached to the end of a word that marks it as belonging to the feminine gender **2.** POETRY UNSTRESSED LAST SYLLABLE OF LINE an ending of a line of verse that ends with an extra unstressed syllable

feminine rhyme n. a rhyme scheme in which the lines containing rhyming words end in unstressed syllables

femininity /fémmə nínnəti/ n. **1.** CONVENTIONALLY FEMININE QUALITY the quality of looking and behaving in ways conventionally thought to be appropriate for a woman or girl **2.** WOMEN women as a group (*dated*) **3.** CONVENTIONAL IDEA ABOUT WOMEN a manner or feature commonly attributed to women **4.** EFFEMINACY the qualities, actions, or types of behaviour in a man or boy that are conventionally associated with women or girls

feminise vt. = feminize

feminism /fémmənizəm/ n. **1.** BELIEF IN WOMEN'S RIGHTS belief in the need to secure, or a commitment to securing, rights and opportunities for women equal to those of men **2.** MOVEMENT FOR WOMEN'S RIGHTS the movement committed to securing and defending equal rights and opportunities for women equal to those of men [Mid-19thC. From French *féminisme*.]

feminist /fémmənist/ n. BELIEVER IN WOMEN'S RIGHTS sb who believes in the need to secure rights and opportunities for women equal to those of men, or sb who works to secure these rights and opportunities ■ adj. RELATING TO WOMEN'S RIGHTS relating to, believing in, or working for rights and opportunities for women equal to those of men [Late 19thC. From French *féministe*.]

feminize /fémmə nīz/ (**-nizes, -nizing, -nized**), **feminise** (**-nises, -nising, -nised**) vt. **1.** MAKE STH SUITABLE FOR WOMEN to cause sb or sth to acquire characteristics considered suitable for women **2.** MAKE SB CONVENTIONALLY LIKE WOMAN to make sb behave in ways conventionally associated with women (*often passive*) **3.** MED MAKE MALE DEVELOP FEMALE SEXUAL CHARACTERISTICS to cause a man to develop secondary female sexual characteristics as a result of a hormone imbalance —**feminization** n.

femme /fem/ n. **1.** WOMAN a woman or girl (*dated informal*) **2.** PERSON BEHAVING IN CONVENTIONALLY FEMININE WAY a person who behaves in a conventionally feminine way (*slang*) ■ adj. BEHAVING IN FEMININE WAY used to describe a person, originally usually a lesbian, who behaves in a conventionally feminine way (*slang*) [Early 19thC. Originally borrowed from the French 'woman', by Lord Byron (1788–1824), for inclusion in his *Journals*.]

femme fatale /fám fə taál/ (*plural* **femmes fatales** /-taál/) n. a woman who is considered to be highly attractive and to have a destructive effect on those who succumb to her charms (*disapproving*) [Borrowed from the French (literally 'deadly woman'), by George Bernard Shaw (1856–1950), who used the term in his letters]

femora plural of femur

femoral /fémmərəl/ adj. relating to, in, or involving the thigh or femur [Late 18thC. Formed from Latin *femor-*, the stem of *femur* 'thigh'.]

femto- prefix. a thousand million millionth (10^{-15}) o *femtometre*. Symbol **f** [Formed from Danish or Norwegian *femten* 'fifteen']

femur /fée mər/ n. **1.** ANAT MAIN BONE IN HUMAN THIGH the main bone in the human thigh, the strongest bone in the body **2.** ZOOL LARGE BONE IN VERTEBRATE LEG a bone equivalent to the human thighbone in other vertebrates **3.** INSECTS INSECT LEG PART the third and largest segment of an insect's leg, between the trochanter and the tibia [Mid-16thC. Originally an architectural term from Latin *femor-, femur* 'thigh', of unknown origin. The anatomical sense was first used in the late 18thC.]

fen /fen/ n. low-lying, inland marshy area, now often drained and cultivated because of its nutrient-rich soil. ◊ **Fens** [Old English *fen(n)*, of prehistoric Germanic origin]

fence /fenss/ n. **1.** ENCLOSING STRUCTURE a structure erected to enclose an area and act as a barrier, especially one made of wood or with posts and wire **2.** HORSERACING, SHOWJUMPING OBSTACLE a specially constructed obstacle that horses must jump over in a race or as part of a showjumping circuit **3.** CRIMINOL BUYER OF STOLEN GOODS sb who buys stolen goods from thieves and then sells the goods (*slang*) **4.** FENCING FENCING the art or practice of fencing (*archaic*) ■ v. (**fences, fencing, fenced**) **1.** vt. ENCLOSE AREA WITH FENCE to enclose an area or bar a gap by erecting a fence **2.** vti. CRIMINOL DEAL IN STOLEN GOODS to buy or sell stolen goods (*slang*) **3.** vi. FENCING FIGHT WITH SWORD to fight using a slender sword, formerly in combat, now as a competitive sport **4.** vi. EVADE QUESTIONING to avoid answering a question o *a candidate fencing with the press* **5.** vi. ARGUE to engage in repartee or witty argument with sb [14thC. Originally a shortening of DEFENCE.] —**fenceless** adj. —**fencer** n. ◊ **mend fences** to restore good relations with a friend or neighbour after a dispute or quarrel ◊ **sit** or **be on the fence** to refuse to make a choice between sides in a dispute or contest

fence in vt. **1.** ENCLOSE STH WITH FENCE to enclose sb or sth inside a fence **2.** RESTRICT SB to limit or restrain sb's freedom of movement or action

fence off vt. to enclose or separate sth with a fence

fence sitter n. sb who will not or cannot make a choice between sides in a dispute or contest

Fencing: As one fencer lunges forwards the other prepares to parry

fencing /fénssing/ n. **1.** SWORD FIGHTING the art or practice of fighting with slender swords, formerly in combat, now as a competitive sport **2.** FENCE MATERIALS materials used in making fences, e.g. posts and wire **3.** FENCES fences considered collectively **4.** EVASIVENESS evasiveness in responding to questioning **5.** REPARTEE repartee or witty argument **6.** CRIMINOL DEALING IN STOLEN GOODS the business of buying and selling stolen goods (*slang*)

fend /fend/ v. (**fends, fending, fended**) **1.** vt. PROTECT SB OR STH to defend sb or sth from harm (*archaic*) **2.** vi. STRIVE to strive or make an effort (*regional*) ■ n. EFFORT an effort, especially one sb makes for himself or herself (*regional*) [13thC. Shortening of DEFEND.]

fend for vt. to support or provide for sb, especially yourself o *He's used to fending for himself.*

fend off vt. **1.** REPULSE SB OR STH to push sb or sth away, or turn sb or sth aside **2.** NAUT PUSH OFF FROM to push against an approaching vessel or object in order to prevent a collision

fender /féndər/ n. **1.** FIRE GUARD a metal guard built onto the front of an open fire to prevent coals from falling out **2.** US RAIL METAL GUARD AT FRONT OF LOCOMOTIVE a metal guard built onto the front of a locomotive to push away any obstruction and lessen injury to people or animals struck by the locomotive **3.** NAUT PROTECTIVE CUSHION an inflatable cylinder, rubber tyre, or sth similar, hung over the side of the vessel to protect it from rubbing against a pier or another ship **4.** US AUTOMOT = wing **5.** US = mudguard

fender-bender n. US a collision between vehicles in which only minor damage occurs (*informal*)

fender pile n. a pile driven into the bottom of a body

of water near a berth to protect the pier or wharf against damage by incoming vessels

Fenech /fénnək/, **Jeff** (*b.* 1964) Australian boxer. He was winner of three world titles, including the IBC world bantamweight championship (1985), and the WBC super-bantamweight (1987) and featherweight (1988) championships. Full name **Jeffrey Fenech**

fenestella /fénnə stéllə/ (*plural* **-lae** /-lee/) *n.* **1.** PART OF ALTAR a small opening for holding relics at the south side of an altar in a Roman Catholic church **2.** NICHE IN CHANCEL WALL a niche in the wall of a chancel that houses the piscina and credence table **3.** ARCHIT WINDOW a small window or similar opening in a wall [Late 18thC. From Latin, diminutive of *fenestra* 'window'.]

fenestra /fi néstrə/ (*plural* **-trae** /-tree/) *n.* **1.** ANAT SMALL ANATOMICAL OPENING a small anatomical opening covered by a membrane, e.g. either of two cavities (**fenestra rotunda; fenestra ovalis**), inside the ear **2.** ZOOL TRANSPARENT MARKING a transparent marking on a moth's wing **3.** ARCHIT WINDOW a window or similar opening on the outer wall of a building [Early 19thC. From Latin, 'window'.] —**fenestral** *adj.*

fenestrated /fə néss traytid, fénnə-/, **fenestrate** /fə néss trayt, fénnə-/ *adj.* **1.** ARCHIT HAVING WINDOWS made with windows or similar openings **2.** BIOL WITH OPENINGS with openings or perforations **3.** ZOOL WITH TRANSPARENT MARKINGS used to describe a moth's wing that has transparent markings

fenestration /fénni stráysh'n/ *n.* **1.** ARCHIT WINDOW DESIGN the design and placing of windows in a building **2.** SURG EAR OPERATION the surgical cutting of an opening in the labyrinth of the inner ear to restore sb's hearing

feng shui /fúng shwáy/ *n.* the Chinese system that studies people's relationships to the environment in which they live, especially their dwelling or workspace, in order to achieve maximum harmony with the spiritual forces perceived to influence all places [Late 18thC. From Chinese, literally 'wind water'.]

Fenian /féeni ən/ *n.* **1.** POL IRISH REVOLUTIONARY a member of an Irish revolutionary republican organization founded in the United States in 1857 to fight for Irish independence **2.** MYTHOL LEGENDARY IRISH WARRIOR a member of the legendary Irish warriors, the Fianna **3.** OFFENSIVE TERM FOR IRISH ROMAN CATHOLIC an offensive term for an Irish Roman Catholic, especially one with nationalist tendencies (*regional offensive*) [Early 19thC. From Old Irish *féne*, a name for the ancient population of Ireland.] —**Fenianism** *n.*

fenland /fén land/ *n.* a wide inland area of low-lying marshy land, especially in East Anglia

fennec /fén ek/ *n.* a small large-eared fox that lives in the deserts of North Africa and has light tan fur and big pointed ears. Latin name: *Vulpes zerda*. [Late 18thC. Via Arabic *fanak* from Persian.]

Fennel

fennel /fénn'l/ *n.* **1.** AROMATIC PLANT an aromatic plant of European origin, the seeds and feathery leaves of which have a light aniseed flavour and are used in cooking. Genus: *Foeniculum*. **2.** EDIBLE PLANT a type of fennel that produces a bulb and clump of short edible stalks resembling celery but with an aniseed flavour. It can be eaten raw or cooked. Latin name: *Foeniculum vulgare* var. *azoricum*. [Old English *finugle*, from Vulgar Latin *fenuculum*, diminutive of *faenum* 'hay', said to be so called because of its appearance and sweet odour]

Fens /fenz/ region of reclaimed marshland in eastern England, surrounding the Wash and covering parts of the counties of Cambridgeshire, Lincolnshire, and Norfolk. Area: 2,000 sq. km/772 sq. mi.

fentanyl /féntənil/ *n.* a narcotic drug used medicinally as a painkiller [An alteration of the drug's chemical name]

Fenugreek

fenugreek /fénnyoo greek/ *n.* **1.** EURASIAN PLANT a Eurasian plant with white flowers and aromatic seeds. Latin name: *Trigonella foenum-graecum*. **2.** AROMATIC SEEDS the aromatic seeds of the fenugreek plant, used medicinally and to flavour food ○ *add a pinch of fenugreek* [Old English *fenogrecum*, superseded in Middle English by forms via Old French *fenugrec* from Latin *faenugraecum*, literally 'Greek hay', dried and used by the Romans for fodder]

fenuron /fénnyoo ron/ *n.* a compound used as a herbicide. Formula: $C_9H_{12}N_2O$. [Formed from fen-, an alteration of PHEN- + UREA + -ON]

feoff /feef/ *n.* = **fief 1** ■ *vt.* (**feoffs, feoffing, feoffed**) GRANT SB FIEF to grant a fief to sb [13thC. Via Anglo-Norman *feoffer* from Old French *feu, fieu* 'fee', from late Latin *feudum* (see FEUD²)]

feoffee /fe feé/ *n.* a vassal holding a fief granted by a feudal lord

feoffment /féfmənt, feéf-/ *n.* an act or the process of granting a fief to sb

FEP *abbr.* front-end processor

-fer *suffix.* one that bears ○ *conifer* [From Latin, from *ferre* 'to carry' (see FERTILE)]

ferae naturae /fé rī nə tyóō rī/ *adj.* living in the wild (*technical*) [Mid-17thC. From Latin, literally 'of wild nature'.]

feral /férrəl, feérəl/, **ferine** /fé rīn, feér īn/ *adj.* **1.** GONE WILD used to describe animals that live or grow in the wild after having been domestically reared or cultivated **2.** SAVAGE similar to or typical of a wild animal [Early 17thC. From Latin *ferus* 'wild animal'.]

fer-de-lance /fáir də láanss/ (*plural* **fer-de-lance** *or* **fer-de-lances** *or* **fers-de-lance** /fáir də láanss/) *n.* a large, highly venomous tropical American snake that belongs to the pit viper family. It is mottled brown and grey. Latin name: *Bothops atrox*. [Late 19thC. From French, 'spear head'.]

Ferdinand I /fúrdi nand/, **King of Spain** (1005?–65). He was king of Castile (1035–65) and León (1037–65), and reconquered much of Portugal from the Moors. Known as **Ferdinand the Great**

Ferdinand III, **King of Hungary** (1608–57). King of Bohemia (1627–57) and Holy Roman Emperor (1637–57), he commanded the imperial armies fighting the Thirty Years' War.

fere *n.* (*archaic*) **1.** FRIEND a friend or companion **2.** SPOUSE a husband or wife [Old English *gefēra*, literally 'fellow traveller']

feretory /férrətəri/ (*plural* **-ries**) *n.* a container or an area in a church where relics are kept [14thC. Literally '(object or place) for the purpose of carrying'. Via Old French *fiertre*, from, ultimately, Greek *pheretron* 'bier', from *pherein* 'to carry' (see -PHORE).]

Fergana /fər gaánə/ city in eastern Uzbekistan, about 420 km/260 mi. east of the capital, Tashkent. Population: 226,500 (1991). Also known as **Farghona**. Formerly **Skobelev**

feria /feéri ə/ (*plural* **-as** *or* **-ae** /feéri ee/) *n.* in the Roman Catholic Church, any weekday on which

there is no feast [14thC. From Latin, 'holiday'.] —**ferial** *adj.*

ferly /fúrli/, **ferlie** /férli/ *n.* (*plural* **-lies**) *Scotland* STH STRANGE a curious object or occurrence ■ *adj.* (**-lier, -liest**) *Scotland* UNUSUAL not usually seen or experienced [Old English *færlic* 'dangerous, alarming, awesome']

Fermanagh /fər mánnə/ former county in Ulster Province, northeastern Northern Ireland. The main town is Enniskillen.

Fermat /fər mát, fúr maa/, **Pierre de** (1601–65) French mathematician. One of the greatest 17th-century mathematical theorists, he was a pioneer in the fields of probability theory, analytic geometry, and differential calculus.

fermata /fər maátə/ (*plural* **-matas** *or* **-mate** /-tay/) *n.* **1.** TIME EXTENSION IN MUSIC an act of holding a note, chord, or pause longer than the indicated time value **2.** = **pause** *n.* 4 [Late 19thC. From Italian.]

ferment *vti.* /fər mént/ (**-ments, -menting, -mented**) **1.** SUBJECT TO FERMENTATION to subject sth to fermentation, or be subjected to fermentation **2.** STIR UP to stir up sb or sth, or be stirred up **3.** DEVELOP to cause, develop or evolve sth, or be developed or evolved ○ *Her brain was continually fermenting new schemes.* ■ *n.* /fúr ment/ **1.** COMMOTION a state or situation of extreme agitation or commotion about sth **2.** SUBSTANCE CAUSING FERMENTATION an agent, an enzyme or cell that causes fermentation [14thC. Via Old French *fermenter*, from, ultimately, Latin *fermentum* 'yeast'.] —**fermentability** /fər méntə bílləti/ *n.* —**fermentable** /fər méntəb'l/ *adj.*

fermentation /fúr men táysh'n/ *n.* the biochemical process in which a microorganism breaks down a substance into simpler ones, especially the creation of alcohol by the action of yeast on sugar. Many pharmaceuticals are produced by fermentation.

fermentation lock *n.* a valve used in winemaking to seal a container of fermenting wine, allowing gas to escape but no air to enter

fermentative /fər méntətiv/ *adj.* relating to or causing fermentation

fermenter /fər méntər/ *n.* **1.** = **ferment** *n.* **2 2. fermenter, fermentor** FERMENTATION APPARATUS an apparatus that maintains the ideal conditions for fermentation, e.g. the growing of microorganisms

fermi /fúrmi/ *n.* a unit of length used mainly for nuclear distances, equivalent to 10^{-15} metre [Early 20thC. Named after Enrico FERMI.]

Fermi /fúrmi/, **Enrico** (1901–54) Italian-born US physicist. He received the 1938 Nobel Prize for his work on particle physics and nuclear fission. He constructed the first atomic pile at the University of Chicago (1942).

fermion /fúrmi on/ *n.* an elementary particle with a half-integral spin that obeys the Pauli exclusion principle. Electrons, protons, and neutrons are types of fermion. [From the name of Enrico FERMI + -ON]

fermium /fúrmi əm/ *n.* a radioactive element produced artificially by the bombardment of plutonium with neutrons. Symbol **Fm** [From the name of Enrico FERMI + -IUM]

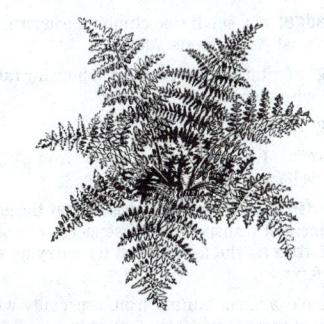

Fern

fern /furn/ (*plural* **ferns** *or* **fern**) *n.* a plant that has roots, stems, and fronds, but no flowers, and reproduces by means of spores. Order: Filicales. [Old English *fearn* from Indo-European] —**ferny** *adj.*

Fernando de Noronha /fur nándō də no rónyə/ island group in the Atlantic Ocean off the coast of Brazil, approximately 400 km/250 mi. northeast of Cape São Roque. Population: 1,266 (1980). Area: 26 sq. km/10 sq. mi.

fern bar *n.* a bar or restaurant with ferns for decoration

fernbird /fúrn burd/ (*plural* **-birds** *or* **-bird**) *n.* a small brown and white bird that lives in swampy areas in New Zealand and has tail feathers that resemble ferns. Latin name: *Bowdleria punctata*.

fernery /fúrnəri/ (*plural* **-ies**) *n.* **1.** PLACE FOR GROWING FERNS a container or cultivated area in which ferns are grown **2.** FERN COLLECTION a collection of growing ferns

fern seed *n.* a tiny spore by which a fern reproduces. Because their smallness makes them difficult to see, at one time it was believed that carrying fern seeds made sb invisible. ○ '*We have the receipt of fern seed, we walk invisible*' (William Shakespeare, *Henry IV Pt I*; 1597)

ferntickles /fúrntik'lz/, **ferny-tickles** /fúrni-/ *npl.* freckles (*regional*) [15th C. Of unknown origin.]

ferocious /fə róshəss/ *adj.* **1.** FIERCE very fierce or savage **2.** EXTREME very intense [Mid-17thC. From Latin *ferox*, literally 'wild-looking'.] —**ferociously** *adv.* —**ferociousness** *n.* —**ferocity** /fə róssəti/ *n.*

-ferous *suffix.* bearing, containing, producing ○ *diamondiferous* [Coined from -FER + -OUS]

ferr- *prefix.* = **ferro-**

Ferrara /fə raárə/ city on the River Po near Bologna in Emilia-Romagna Region, northern Italy. Population: 137,099 (1992).

Ferrari /fə raári/, **Enzo** (1898–1988) Italian racing car driver and automobile manufacturer. He designed and produced racing cars that have achieved success in Grand Prix competitions since the 1950s.

ferredoxin /férrə dóksin/ *n.* an iron-containing protein that occurs in plants and certain bacteria and is active in the process of photosynthesis [Mid-20thC. Coined from Latin *ferrum* 'iron' + REDOX + -IN.]

ferreous /férri əss/ *adj.* relating to or containing iron [Mid-17thC. Formed from Latin *ferreus* 'of iron'.]

ferret[1] /férrit/ *n.* (*plural* **-rets** *or* **-ret**) DOMESTICATED POLECAT a typically albino polecat bred for use in hunting rabbits or rats and kept as a pet. Latin name: *Mustela eversmanni*. ■ *vti.* (**-rets, -reting, -reted**) HUNT USING FERRET to hunt rabbits or rats using a ferret [14thC. Via Old French *furet* from assumed Vulgar Latin *furittus*, literally 'little thief', from Latin *fur* 'thief' (see FURTIVE).] —**ferreter** *n.* —**ferrety** *adj.*
ferret about, **ferret around** *vi.* to search in an area persistently ○ *ferreting about in a drawer*
ferret out *vt.* **1.** LOCATE STH BY PERSISTENT SEARCHING to force sb or sth out of a hiding place by persistent searching **2.** DISCOVER STH SECRET to discover sth hidden by persistent searching

ferret[2] /férrit/ *n.* a narrow silk tape used for edging or binding fabric [Mid-17thC. Origin uncertain: probably an alteration of Italian *fioretti* 'floss silk' (the original sense in English), literally 'little flowers', from *fiore* 'flower' (see FLORIN).]

ferret badger *n.* a small tree-climbing badger native to Southeast Asia. Genus: *Melogale*.

ferreting[1] /férriting/ *n.* the practice of hunting rabbits or rats with ferrets

ferreting[2] /férriting/ *n.* = **ferret**[2] *n.*

ferri- *prefix.* **1.** = **ferro-** **2.** ferric iron ○ *ferricyanide* [From Latin *ferrum* 'iron']

ferriage /férri ij/ *n.* **1.** TRANSPORTATION BY FERRY the action or business of transporting passengers or cargo by ferry **2.** FERRY FEE the fee charged for carrying sb or sth by ferry

ferric /férrik/ *adj.* containing iron, especially with a valency of three [Late 18thC. Formed from Latin *ferrum* 'iron'.]

ferric ammonium citrate *n.* a nontoxic iron-containing salt of iron used in low doses to treat the iron-deficiency condition anaemia. Formula: $Fe(NH_4)_3(C_6H_5O_7)_2$.

ferric oxide *n.* a reddish-brown solid containing iron and oxygen. It occurs in rust and the mineral haematite and is used as a pigment, in jeweller's rouge for polishing, and on magnetic recording tape. Formula: Fe_2O_3.

ferric sulphate *n.* a pale yellow solid chemical containing iron, oxygen, and sulphur. It is used in pigments, water purification, dyeing, and in medicine. Formula: $Fe_2(SO_4)_3$.

ferricyanide /férri sí ə nīd/ *n.* any salt containing iron and six cyanide groups. They are used to make pigments.

Ferrier /férri ər/, **Kathleen** (1912–53) British contralto. She studied music seriously from 1940 and is particularly famous for her performance in 1947 of Mahler's song cycle *Das Lied von der Erde*. She died of cancer at the peak of her career.

ferriferous /fe rífferəss/ *adj.* used to describe a rock or mineral deposit that contains iron, often at a level high enough to make extraction economically worthwhile [Early 19thC. Coined from Latin *ferrum* 'iron' + -FEROUS.]

ferrimagnetism /férri mágnətizəm/ *n.* a property of some substances, e.g. ferrites, in which two different types of iron having unequal magnetic moments occur aligned in antiparallel, giving an appreciable bulk magnetization —**ferrimagnet** *n.* —**ferrimagnetic** /férri mag néttik/ *adj.*, *n.* —**ferrimagnetically** *adv.*

Ferris wheel

Ferris wheel /férriss-/, **ferris wheel** *n.* a fairground ride consisting of a giant revolving wheel with seats that hang down from its rim and stay horizontal as the wheel rotates [Late 19thC. Named after the American engineer G. W. G. Ferris (1859–96), its inventor.]

ferrite /férrīt/ *n.* **1.** MAGNETIC IRON OXIDE a mixed oxide of iron and another metal such as cobalt or nickel. They are ceramic materials with magnetic properties and are used in the electronics industry and in magnets. **2.** FORM OF IRON OCCURRING IN STEEL a form of iron occurring in steel, cast iron, and pig iron **3.** IRON MINERAL iron oxide containing mineral, e.g. magnetite, found as small grains in various types of rock [Mid-19thC. Formed from Latin *ferrum* 'iron'.]

ferritin /férritin/ *n.* a spherical complex of iron and protein mainly found in the liver and spleen that is one of the forms in which iron is stored in the body. When required, iron is released and used in the production of haemoglobin in red blood cells. [Mid-20thC. Coined from FERRI- + -*t*- + -IN.]

ferro- *prefix.* **1.** iron ○ *ferroalloy* **2.** CHEM ferrous iron ○ *ferrocyanide* [From Latin *ferrum* 'iron']

ferroalloy /férrō álloy/ *n.* an iron alloy, containing a large proportion of one or more other elements, that is added to molten metal during iron and steel production to give the required composition

ferrocene /férrō seen/ *n.* an orange-red crystalline solid in which an atom of iron is situated between two rings that are composed of five carbon and five hydrogen atoms. Formula: $Fe(C_5H_5)_2$. [Mid-20thC. Coined from FERRO- + -*cene*, a contraction of *cyclopentadiene*, a hydrocarbon obtained in the cracking of petroleum hydrocarbons.]

ferroconcrete /férrō kóng kreet/ *n.* = **reinforced concrete**

ferrocyanide /férrō sí ə nīd/ *n.* any salt containing

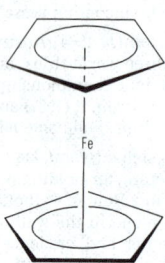

Ferrocene

iron and six cyanide groups. They are used to make blue pigments.

ferroelectric /férrō i léktrik/ *adj.* WITH SPONTANEOUS ELECTRIC POLARIZATION used to describe a crystalline compound that has a natural spontaneous electric polarization that can be reversed by the application of an electric field ■ *n.* FERROELECTRIC SUBSTANCE a substance that is ferroelectric —**ferroelectrically** *adv.* —**ferroelectricity** /férrō i lek tríssəti, -éllek-/ *n.*

ferromagnesian /férrō mag neézh'n/ *adj.* used to describe silicate minerals that contain high levels of iron and magnesium, e.g. olivines

ferromagnetic /férrō mag néttik/ *adj.* with the property of ferromagnetism. Iron, cobalt, and nickel are ferromagnetic metals.

ferromagnetism /férrō mágnətizəm/ *n.* a property of some substances, including iron and some alloys, in which application of a weak magnetic field within a certain temperature range induces high magnetism. Small discrete regions within the substance (**domains**) align with the direction of an applied magnetic field and produce the bulk magnetization. —**ferromagnet** *n.* —**ferromagnetic** *adj.*, *n.* —**ferromagnetically** *adv.*

ferromanganese /férrō mang gə neéz, férrō máng gə neez/ *n.* an alloy of iron and manganese used to add manganese during the making of steel and cast iron

ferronneries /fe rónnəriz/ *n.* a variety of ceramics that copies forms from metalwork, e.g. candlesticks (*takes a singular verb*) [Early 20thC. From French, 'iron work, wrought iron'.]

ferrosilicon /férrō síllikən/ *n.* an alloy of iron and silicon, used in the production of steel and cast iron

ferrotype /férrō tīp/ *n.* a positive photograph made on a plate of sensitized iron

ferrous /férrəss/ *adj.* containing iron with a valency of two [Mid-19thC. Formed from Latin *ferrum* 'iron'.]

ferrous oxide *n.* a black solid containing iron and oxygen. It is used in the manufacture of steel and enamels. Formula: FeO.

ferrous sulphate *n.* a white or pale green salt containing iron, oxygen, and sulphur. It occurs naturally as the mineral copperas, and is used in inks, tanning, and in the treatment of iron-deficient anaemia. Formula: $FeSO_4.7H_2O$.

ferrous sulphide *n.* a black solid containing iron and sulphur. It occurs naturally in pyrites and marcasite, and is used in making hydrogen sulphide. Formula: FeS.

ferruginous /fe roójinəss/ *adj.* **1.** CONTAINING IRON containing or resembling iron **2.** RUST-COLOURED of a reddish-brown colour, like rust [Mid-17thC. Formed from Latin *ferrugin*, the stem of *ferrugo* 'iron rust', from *ferrum* 'iron'.]

ferruginous duck *n.* a common European diving duck with reddish-brown plumage that lives in fresh or blackish water. Latin name: *Aythya nyroca*.

ferrule /férrool, férrəl/, **ferule** *n.* **1.** PROTECTIVE CAP ON SHAFT a usually metal cap or ring attached to the end of sth long and thick, e.g. a walking stick, in order to strengthen it **2.** CYLINDRICAL JOINT a metal cylinder used to make a pipe joint **3.** ANGLING CONNECTION FOR FISHING ROD PIECES a connection that joins the pieces of a fishing rod, consisting of male and female couplings that fit together ■ *vt.* FIT WITH FERRULE to provide sth with a ferrule [Early 17thC. Alteration of earlier *virolle* (influenced by Latin *ferrum* 'iron'), from, ultimately, Latin *viriae* 'bracelets'.]

ferry /férri/ *n.* (*plural* **-ries**) **1. BOAT MAKING REGULAR SHORT CROSSING** a boat used to transport passengers, vehicles, or goods across water, especially one operating regularly across a river or narrow channel **2. COMMERCIAL TRANSPORT SERVICE** a commercial service transporting passengers, vehicles, or goods across water **3. PLACE WHERE FERRY BERTHS** a place where passengers, vehicles, or goods are transported across water by ferry **4. RIGHT TO OPERATE FERRY** a legal right to operate and charge for a ferry service ■ *v.* (**-ries, -rying, -ried**) **1.** *vt.* **TRANSPORT SB OR STH BY FERRY** to transport sb or sth across water by ferry **2.** *vi.* **GO BY FERRY** to travel by ferry **3.** *vt.* **TRANSPORT PASSENGERS** to transport passengers or goods back and forth by any vehicle ○ *He had to ferry his children to school every morning.* **4.** *vt.* AIR **DELIVER AIRCRAFT** to deliver an aircraft by flying it to its operator [14thC. From Old Norse *ferja*, or from *ferju-*, the stem of *ferjuskip* and *ferjukarl* 'ferryman'. Ultimately from a prehistoric Germanic word.]

ferryboat /férri bōt/ *n.* = **ferry** *n.* 1

ferryman /férri man, -mən/ (*plural* **-men** /-mən/) *n.* sb who owns, operates, or works on a ferry

fertile /fúr tīl/ *adj.* **1.** BIOL **ABLE TO PRODUCE OFFSPRING** capable of breeding or reproducing **2.** BOT **ABLE TO PRODUCE FRUITS OR SEEDS** able to produce sex cells, seeds, spores, or fruit **3.** BIOL **ABLE TO DEVELOP** used to describe an egg or seed that has the capacity to grow and develop **4. REPRODUCING OFTEN** producing many offspring **5.** AGRIC **PRODUCING GOOD CROPS** used to describe an area that produces many plants, fruit, or crops **6.** AGRIC, GARDENING **RICH IN PLANT NUTRIENTS** used to describe soil or land that is rich in the nutrients needed to sustain the growth of healthy plants **7. CREATIVE** readily able to produce new ideas ○ *a fertile imagination* **8.** NUCLEAR PHYS **CAPABLE OF BECOMING FISSILE** capable of being converted into fissile or fissionable material, typically in a nuclear reactor [15thC. Directly or via French from Latin *fertilis*, from *ferre* 'to bear'. Ultimately from an Indo-European base meaning 'to carry' which is also the ancestor of English *bear, bier, burden,* and *-phore*.] — **fertilely** *adv.* —**fertileness** *n.* —**fertility** /fur tíllәti/ *n.*

Fertile Crescent /fúr tīl-/ *n.* an area of fertile land in the Middle East reaching from Israel to the Persian Gulf and incorporating the Tigris and Euphrates rivers in modern Iraq. The ancient Babylonian, Sumerian, Assyrian, Phoenician, and Hebrew civilizations arose here.

fertilisation *n.* = **fertilization**

fertilise *vt.* = **fertilize**

fertiliser *n.* = **fertilizer**

fertility /fur tíllәti/ *n.* **1. BEING FERTILE** the quality or condition of being fertile **2. BIRTHRATE** the birthrate of a population [15thC. Via French *fertilité* from Latin *fertilitas*, from *fertilis* (see FERTILE).]

fertility cult *n.* a form of religion using ceremonies meant to ensure the fertility of the people and agriculture of a community

fertility drug *n.* a synthetic chemical that enhances female fertility by stimulating the release of ova from the ovaries. Some fertility drugs are also used in in vitro fertilization programmes.

fertilization /fúrti lī záysh'n/, **fertilisation** *n.* **1.** BIOL **STARTING REPRODUCTION** the act or process of enabling reproduction by insemination or pollination **2.** BIOL **UNION OF MALE AND FEMALE GAMETES** the union of male and female reproductive cells (**gametes**) to produce a fertilized reproductive cell (**zygote**) **3.** AGRIC, GARDENING **APPLYING FERTILIZER** the act or process of applying fertilizer to soil

fertilize /fúrti līz/ (**-lizes, -lizing, -lized**), **fertilise** (**-lises, -lising, -lised**) *vt.* **1.** BIOL **UNITE FEMALE AND MALE REPRODUCTIVE CELLS** to unite a female gamete with a male gamete, thus enabling the development of a new individual to take place. Fertilization can take place inside the female's body, as in humans, or outside the body, as in fish. **2.** AGRIC, GARDENING **APPLY FERTILIZER** to apply fertilizer to soil or plants [Mid-17thC. Formed from FERTILE.] —**fertilizable** *adj.*

fertilizer /fúrtilīzәr/, **fertiliser** *n.* **1.** AGRIC, GARDENING **SUBSTANCE AIDING PLANT GROWTH** a substance usually added to or spread onto soil to increase its ability to support plant growth. Fertilizers include organic materials, e.g. manure, and synthetic chemicals, e.g. nitrates. **2.** BIOL **FERTILIZING AGENT** an agent that fertilizes plants or animals, e.g. an insect fertilizing a plant

ferula /férryŏŏlә, férrŏŏlә/ (*plural* **-las** *or* **-lae** /-lee, -/) *n.* PLANTS a Mediterranean plant of the parsley family with thick stems and finely divided leaves from which strong-smelling resinous gums are extracted that can be used medicinally. Genus: *Ferula.* [14thC. From Latin, 'fennel stalk, rod'.] —**ferulaceous** /férroo láyshәss, férryoo-/ *adj.*

ferule[1] /férrool, férrәl/ *n.* a cane, rod, or flat piece of wood used to punish children by striking them, usually on the hand [15thC. From Latin *ferula* 'fennel stalk', formerly used by schoolmasters to punish children.]

ferule[2] *n., vt.* = **ferrule**

ferulic acid /fe ryŏŏlik-/ *n.* a compound similar to the aromatic chemical vanillin that is obtained from some plants. Ferulic acid is a component of asafoetida, a bitter resin derived from a plant of the parsley family. Formula: $C_{10}H_{10}O_4$. [*Ferulic* formed from FERULA]

fervency /fúrvәnssi/ *n.* = **fervour**

fervent /fúrvәnt/ *adj.* **1. SHOWING PASSIONATE ENTHUSIASM** showing ardent or extremely passionate enthusiasm **2. GLOWINGLY HOT** so hot as to glow (*archaic or literary*) [14thC. Via Old French from, ultimately, Latin *fervere* 'to boil'. Ultimately from an Indo-European word meaning 'to bubble' which is also the ancestor of English *barm*.] —**fervently** *adv.* —**ferventness** *n.*

fervid /fúrvid/ *adj.* = **fervent** [Late 16thC. From Latin *fervidus*, from *fervere* 'to boil' (see FERVENT).] —**fervidly** *adv.* —**fervidness** *n.*

fervor *n. US* = **fervour**

fervour /fúrvәr/ *n.* **1. INTENSITY** extreme intensity of emotion or belief **2. GREAT HEAT** intense heat (*archaic or literary*) [14thC. Via Old French from Latin *fervor*, from *fervere* 'to boil' (see FERVENT).]

fescennine /féssi nīn/, **Fescennine** *adj.* indecent, especially using coarse or vulgar language (*archaic or literary*) [Early 17thC. From Latin *Fescenninus*, 'of Fescennia', a town in ancient Etruria known for its scurrilous verse.]

fescue /fés kyoo/, **fescue grass** *n.* a perennial grass that has narrow spiky leaves and is often grown for lawns or pasture. Several varieties have been developed that can be grown on soils contaminated with heavy metals. Genus: *Festuca.* [14thC. Alteration of earlier *festu*, from Old French, 'straw', from Latin *festuca*.]

fesse /fess/, **fess** *n.* a broad horizontal band crossing the middle section of a heraldic shield [15thC. Via Old French *fesse* from, ultimately, Latin *fascia* 'band, sash'.]

fesse point *n.* the central point of a heraldic shield

fess up /fess-/ (**fesses up, fessing up, fessed up**) *vi. US* to admit to sth (*informal*) ○ *Come on, fess up, was it you?* [Early 19thC. Shortening of CONFESS.]

fest /fest/ *n.* a gathering of people for a specific activity, or an event where a lot of a particular activity goes on (*informal; usually used in combination*) ○ *a music fest* [Mid-19thC. Via German *Fest* from Latin *festum* 'feast'.]

-fest *suffix.* used in compounds such as 'gore-fest' and 'horror-fest' by fans to denote films filled with horrific gory detail ○ *'Night of the Living Dead' is a real gore-fest.*

festal /fést'l/ *adj.* festive (*dated or literary*) [15thC. Via Old French from, ultimately, Latin *festum* 'festival'.] — **festally** *adv.*

fester /féstәr/ *v.* (**-ters, -tering, -tered**) **1.** *vi.* **PRODUCE PUS** to produce pus because of an infection or ulceration, usually of the skin **2.** *vi.* **BECOME ROTTEN** to decay or rot **3.** *vi.* **DETERIORATE** to be in or enter a state of decline **4.** *vti.* **RANKLE** to become, or make sb become, increasingly bitter, irritated, or resentful ■ *n.* MED **SORE DISCHARGING PUS** a small sore or ulcer containing or discharging pus [14thC. Via Old French *festre* 'pipe-like ulcer', from Latin *fistula*.]

festination /fésti náysh'n/ *n.* a style of tottering walk that is characteristic of people with Parkinson's disease [Mid-16thC. Formed from Latin *festinare* 'to hurry'.]

festival /féstiv'l/ *n.* **1. TIME OF CELEBRATION** a day or period of celebration, often one of religious significance **2. PROGRAMME OF CULTURAL EVENTS** a programme or series of performances or other cultural events, usually held at regular intervals, often in one place ■ *adj.* **APPROPRIATE TO FESTIVAL** typical of or appropriate to a festival [14thC. Via Old French from, ultimately, Latin *festivus* 'festive', from *festum* 'feast'.]

festive /féstiv/ *adj.* **1. RELATING TO CELEBRATION** relating to, suitable for, or typical of a feast, festival, or holiday **2. CHEERFUL** marked by cheerfulness and joy [Mid-17thC. From Latin *festivus* 'festive', from *festum* 'feast'.] — **festively** *adv.* —**festiveness** *n.*

festive season *n.* the period leading up to and including Christmas and the New Year

festivity /fe stívvәti/ *n.* (*plural* **-ties**) **1. ENJOYMENT** the enjoyment or merrymaking typical of a celebration **2. CELEBRATION** a celebration, feast, or party ■ **festivities** *npl.* **CELEBRATIONS** celebrations or merrymaking [14thC. Directly or via French from Latin *festivitas*, from, ultimately, *festum* 'feast'.]

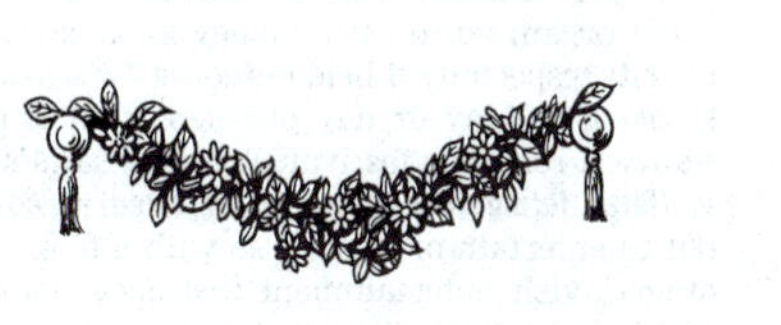

Festoon

festoon /fe stóon/ *n.* **1. GARLAND** an ornamental chain of flowers, leaves, or ribbons hanging in a loop or curve between two points **2. ARTISTIC REPRESENTATION OF FESTOON** a carved or painted representation of a festoon, e.g. on a building, in a painting, or in pottery ■ *vt.* (**-toons, -tooning, -tooned**) **1. HANG FESTOONS ON STH** to decorate sth with festoons **2. JOIN WITH FESTOONS** to join things together with festoons **3. SHAPE STH INTO FESTOONS** to make sth into festoons [Mid-17thC. Via French *feston* from Italian *festone*, originally 'ornament for festivities', from assumed vulgate Latin *festa* 'festivities' which was formed from Latin *festum* (see FESTIVE).]

festoon blind *n.* a blind for a window, made of cloth gathered into rows that can be drawn up to hang in curves

festooned /fe stóond/ *adj.* covered with festoons or other things used as decorations ○ *The whole room was festooned with roses.*

festschrift /fést shrift/, **Festschrift** (*plural* **-schrifts** *or* **-schriften** /-shriftәn/) *n.* a volume of writings by various people collected in honour of sb, e.g. a writer or scholar [Early 20thC. From German, literally 'celebration-writing'.]

FET *abbr.* field-effect transistor

feta /féttә/ *n.* a firm crumbly salty cheese, originally from Greece, made from sheep's or goat's milk and preserved in brine. It is now produced in other countries, though still most often used as an ingredient in Greek dishes. [Mid-20thC. From modern Greek *pheta*.]

fetal *adj.* = **foetal**

fetch[1] /fech/ *v.* (**fetches, fetching, fetched**) **1.** *vt.* **GO AND GET STH** to go after and bring back sb or sth ○ *She went upstairs to fetch her car keys.* **2.** *vt.* **CAUSE TO COME** to make sb or sth appear or come **3.** *vt.* **SELL FOR** to sell for a certain price ○ *The painting fetched £600 at an auction.* **4.** *vti.* **RETRIEVE STH** to retrieve animals that have been shot or sth that has been thrown, e.g. a stick or ball ○ *The boy threw the ball and told the dog to fetch it.* **5.** *vt.* **UTTER** to utter a sigh or groan with a deep breath **6.** *vt.* **HIT SB A BLOW** to hit sb with a blow (*informal*) ○ *fetched the bully a slap on the face* **7.** *vt.* **DRAW IN BREATH** to draw in a breath **8.** *vt.* **PLEASE** to attract or charm sb (*often passive*) ○ *fetched* *by the notion of going to London* **9.** *vt.* NAUT **ARRIVE SOMEWHERE BY BOAT** to reach or arrive at a place by sailing ○ *fetched port at nightfall* ■ *n.* **1. ACT OF FETCHING** the act or an instance of fetching sth or sb **2. STRATAGEM** a dodge, trick, or stratagem ○ *They used cunning fetches to swindle money out of the gullible.* **3.** METEOROL **DISTANCE WIND TRAVELS UNOBSTRUCTED** the distance wind or waves can travel without obstruction [Old English *feccean*] —**fetcher** *n.* ◇ **fetch and carry (for sb)** to do menial tasks for sb

fetch up *v.* **1.** *vi.* **ARRIVE** to arrive at or come to a halt somewhere (*informal*) ○ *After a week on the road, we fetched up at a small coastal town.* **2.** *vi.* NAUT **HALT SUDDENLY** to come to a sudden halt ○ *The boat fetched up on a sandbar.* **3.** *vt.* **CAUSE TO STOP** to make sb or sth come to a stop ○ *His abrupt tone fetched me up short.* **4.** *vt.* **VOMIT** to vomit sth (*informal*) **5.** *vt.* **BRING SB UP** to bring up children or rear animals (*regional dated*)

fetch[2] /fech/ *n.* a vision, apparition, or ghost appearing as the doppelgänger of a living person [Late 17thC. Origin uncertain: possibly from the verb, as sb sent to fetch souls.]

fetching /féching/ *adj.* **1. GOOD-LOOKING** pleasant, stylish, or becoming in appearance **2. CHARMING** having a charming or captivating quality —**fetchingly** *adv.*

fête /fayt/, **fete** *n.* **1. BAZAAR** a bazaar, sale, or other event organized to raise money for a cause or for charity, especially if held outdoors ○ *a school fête* **2. HOLIDAY** a holiday or day of celebration **3. RELIGIOUS FESTIVAL** a religious festival such as a saint's day ■ *vt.* (**fêtes, fêting, fêted; fetes, feting, feted**) **HONOUR SB WITH FÊTE** to entertain or honour sb with a fête, feast, or other lavish entertainment (*usually passive*) [Mid-18thC. French from, ultimately, Latin *festum*.]

fête champêtre /fáyt shaaN péttrə/ (*plural* **fêtes champêtres** /fáyt shaaN péttrə/) *n.* an outdoor party or festival [From French, literally 'rural festival']

fetich *n.* = **fetish**

fetid /féttid, féetid/, **foetid** *adj.* with a rotten or offensive smell ○ *fetid odour of rotten meat* [15thC. From Latin *fetidus*, from *fetere* 'to stink'.] —**fetidly** *adv.* —**fetidness** *n.*

fetish /féttish/, **fetich** *n.* **1. OBJECT OF OBSESSION** an object, idea, or activity that sb is irrationally obsessed with or attached to ○ *make a fetish of neatness* **2.** PSYCHIAT **OBJECT AROUSING SEXUAL DESIRE** sth, e.g. an inanimate object or nonsexual part of the body that arouses sexual excitement in some people **3. MAGICAL OBJECT** sth, especially an inanimate object, that some people revere or worship because they believe it has magical powers or is animated by a spirit [Early 17thC. Via French *fétiche* 'charm, sorcery' from, ultimately, Latin *factitius* 'made by art, artificial' (see FACTITIOUS).]

fetishise *vt.* = **fetishize**

fetishism /féttishizəm/ *n.* **1. OBSESSION WITH STH** excessive or obsessive attachment or devotion to sth **2.** PSYCHIAT **SEXUAL AROUSAL WITH FETISH** the use of a fetish to produce sexual arousal **3. BELIEF IN FETISH** belief in, use of, or worship of a magical fetish

fetishist /féttishist/ *n.* sb who uses a fetish for sexual arousal —**fetishistic** /fétti shístik/ *adj.* —**fetishistically** /-shístikli/ *adv.*

fetishize /féttishīz/ (**-izes, -izing, -ized**), **fetishise** (**-ises, -ising, -ised**) *vt.* to make a fetish of sth

fetlock /fét lok/ *n.* **1. PROJECTION ON HORSE'S LEG** a part of the lower leg of a horse or related animal situated above and behind the hoof and projecting down from the associated joint **2. HAIR ON FETLOCK** the tuft of hair growing on a fetlock **3. fetlock, fetlock joint LEG JOINT** the joint at the fetlock [14thC. Believed to be formed from an earlier form of FOOT + LOCK 'hair'.]

fetor /féetər/, **foetor** *n.* a strong offensive smell [15thC. From Latin, from *fetere* 'to stink' (source of English *fetid*).]

fetoscope *n.* = **foetoscope**

fetter /féttər/ *n.* (*often used in the plural*) **1. SHACKLE FOR ANKLES** a chain or shackle fastened to sb's ankles or feet **2. RESTRAINT** a means of confinement or restraint ○ *These harsh rules keep us in fetters.* ■ *vt.* (**-ters, -tering, -tered**) **1. PUT FETTERS ON SB** to shackle sb with fetters **2. RESTRAIN SB OR STH** to confine, restrict, or restrain sb or sth ○ *fettered by her own inhibitions* [Old English *feter*. Ultimately from a prehistoric Germanic word.]

fettle /fétt'l/ *n.* METALL = **fettling** ■ *vt.* (**-tles, -tling, -tled**) **1. MAKE STH READY** to put sth in order or readiness, especially by adding a finishing touch (*regional*) **2.** MANUF **TRIM CASTING** to remove moulding or excess material from a ceramic or metal casting **3.** METALL **LINE OR REPAIR FURNACE** to line the hearth of a furnace with fettling, or repair the lining of a furnace [Old English *fetel* 'girdle, strap'] —**fettler** *n.* ◇ **in fine** *or* **good fettle** in good health, condition, or spirits

fettling /fétt'ling/ *n.* loose refractory material, typically sand or ore, used to line the hearths of some types of furnace before adding the molten metal

fettuccine /féttə chéeni/, **fettuccini** *n.* **1. NARROW FLAT PASTA** a type of pasta made in narrow flat strips, slightly narrower and thicker than tagliatelle (*takes a singular or plural verb*) **2. DISH MADE WITH FETTUCCINE** a pasta dish made with fettuccine [Early 20thC. From Italian, literally 'little ribbons'.]

fetus *n.* a foetus (*technical*)

feu /fyoo/ *n.* **1. RIGHT OF USE** in Scotland, a right to use land or property in return for an annual payment (**feu duty**) **2. TENURE FOR MONEY** a form of land tenure in feudal times in Scotland, on the basis of paying rent in money or grain and not in military service **3. LAND HELD BY FEU** a piece of land held by feu [15thC. From Old French (source of English *fee*).]

feuar /fyoó ər/ *n.* sb who is a tenant of a feu

feud[1] /fyood/ *n.* **1. LONG VIOLENT DISPUTE** a bitter prolonged violent quarrel or state of hostility between families, clans, or other groups **2. CONTINUOUS HOSTILITY** any prolonged dispute or quarrel ■ *vi.* (**feuds, feuding, feuded**) **PARTICIPATE IN FEUD** to take part in or perpetuate a feud [13thC. From Old French *fe(i)de* 'vendetta' (originally, 'hostility'). Ultimately from a prehistoric Germanic word that is also the ancestor of English *foe*.]

feud[2] /fyood/ *n.* = **fief** *n.* 1 [Early 17thC. From medieval Latin *feudum*, 'land or other property used as a reward for service'. Ultimately from an Indo-European word denoting 'wealth' or 'cattle', which is also the ancestor of English *fee*, *pecuniary*, and *peculiar*.]

feud. *abbr.* **1.** feudal **2.** feudalism

feudal /fyoód'l/ *adj.* **1. RELATING TO FEUDALISM** relating to, typical of, or resembling feudalism **2. RELATING TO FIEF** relating to a fief [Early 17thC. From medieval Latin *feudalis*, from *feudum* (see FEUD[2]).] —**feudally** *adv.*

feudalise *vt.* = **feudalize**

feudalism /fyoód'lizəm/ *n.* **1. MEDIEVAL SOCIAL SYSTEM** the legal and social system that existed in medieval Europe, in which vassals held land from lords in exchange for military service **2. SYSTEM LIKE FEUDALISM** a system of economic, political, or social organization resembling European feudalism, e.g. in medieval Japan —**feudalist** *n.* —**feudalistic** /fyoód'l ístik/ *adj.*

feudality /fyoo dálləti/ (*plural* **-ties**) *n.* **1. BEING FEUDAL** the quality or condition of being feudal **2. FEUDAL REGIME** a feudal holding or system

feudalize /fyoód'l īz/ (**-izes, -izing, -ized**), **feudalise** (**-ises, -ising, -ised**) *vt.* to make sth feudal in nature —**feudalization** /fyoód'l ī záysh'n/ *n.*

feudatory /fyoódə təri/ *n.* (*plural* **-ries**) **TENANT OF FEUDAL LAND** sb holding land by feudal tenure ■ *adj.* **1. INVOLVING FEUDAL RELATIONSHIP** relating to or typical of the relationship between a feudal lord and vassal **2. SUBJECT TO OVERLORDSHIP** owing feudal allegiance to an overlord or another state [Late 16thC. From medieval Latin *feudatorius*, from the past participle of *feudare* 'to invest with feudal property'.]

feu duty *n.* an annual payment made by the owner of a building in Scotland to the nominal feudal superior for the right to use the land or property

feuilleton /fö́ i ton, fö́ i toN/ *n.* **1. PART OF EUROPEAN NEWSPAPER** a section of a European newspaper containing reviews, serial fiction, and articles of general interest **2. STH IN FEUILLETON** an article, review, or other piece published in a feuilleton [Mid-19thC. Via French *feuillet*, literally 'little leaf' from, ultimately, Latin *folium* (see FOLIO).]

fever /féevər/ *n.* **1. ABNORMALLY HIGH BODY TEMPERATURE** a body temperature that is abnormally high, usually caused by bacterial or viral infections and commonly accompanied by shivering, headache, and an increased pulse rate. Technical name **pyrexia** **2. DISEASE WITH FEVER** a disease in which people typically have an abnormally high body temperature, e.g. typhoid fever, yellow fever, and scarlet fever **3. STATE OF EXCITEMENT** a state of intense agitation, excitement, or emotion (*often used in combination*) ○ *On the morning of the wedding, everyone was in a fever of excitement.* **4. CRAZE** an intense and often brief enthusiasm or craze ■ *vt.* (**-vers, -vering, -vered**) **1. AFFECT WITH FEVER** to affect sb or sth with fever (*archaic*) (*usually passive*) **2. AGITATE SB** to throw sb into a state of agitation or excitement [Pre-12thC. From Latin *febris*.]

fevered /féevərd/ *adj.* **1. AFFECTED BY FEVER** affected by fever **2. EXCITED** showing great activity, agitation, or excitement

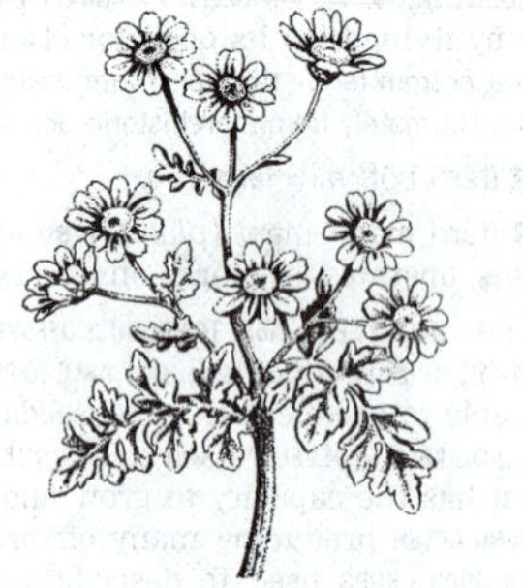

Feverfew

feverfew /féevər fyoo/ *n.* a perennial European plant with small white flowers, whose leaves are a popular remedy for headaches and migraine. Latin name: *Tanacetum parthenium*. [Pre-12thC. From Latin *febris* 'fever' + -FUGE.]

feverish /féevərish/ *adj.* **1. HAVING FEVER** affected by or having the symptoms of a fever **2. RELATING TO FEVER** relating to, causing, or caused by fever ○ *a feverish cold* **3. AGITATED** showing agitation, excitement, or restlessness —**feverishly** *adv.* —**feverishness** *n.*

feverous /féevərəss/ *adj.* feverish (*archaic*) —**feverously** *adv.*

fever pitch *n.* a state of intense activity, agitation, or excitement

fever tree *n.* a tree whose leaves or bark have been used to treat fevers, especially a tree of the southeastern United States that was used to treat malaria. Latin name: *Pinckneya pubens*.

few /fyoo/ CORE MEANING: a grammatical word used to indicate that there are not many or hardly any people or things ○ (det) *There were few books on the shelves.* ○ (det) *spending her few free hours relaxing in front of the television* ○ (pron) *Many people have entered the contest, but few will be successful.* ○ (pron) *Few of the gardens had been cared for.*

1. *npl., pron.* **LIMITED NUMBER** a limited or exclusive number, e.g. an elite or minority of people ○ (n) *the fortunate few who managed to escape sickness this winter* ○ (n) *The needs of the many outweigh the needs of the few.* ○ (pron) *Few would have thought it.* **2.** *det., pron.* **a few SOME, THOUGH NOT MANY** not very many people or things, but more than two, and sometimes more than might be expected ○ (det) *We had a few meetings before signing the contract.* ○ (pron) *Only a few ever achieve real artistic success.* ○ (pron) *A few of the kids wanted to watch a video.* [Old English *fēawa*. Ultimately from an Indo-European base denoting smallness, which is also the ancestor of Latin *paucus* 'little' (source of English *poor*).] —**fewness** *n.* ◇ **a good few** several, or a fairly large number (*informal*) ◇ **few and far between** scarce or infrequent (*informal*) ◇ **quite a few** a fairly large number (*informal*)

fey /fay/ *adj.* **1. OTHERWORLDLY** with a manner or appearance giving an impression of otherworldliness or unworldliness **2. SUPERNATURAL** relating to or typical of magic or the supernatural **3. CLAIRVOYANT** supposedly able to see into the future **4.** *Scotland* **DOOMED TO DIE** doomed or destined to die, especially as indicated by peculiar, usually elated, behaviour [Old English *fǣge* 'fated to die', of prehistoric Germanic origin] —**feyly** *adv.* —**feyness** *n.*

Feynman diagram /fīnmən-/ *n.* a diagrammatic representation of interactions between elementary particles [Named after US physicist Richard *Feynman* (1918–88)]

fez /fez/ (*plural* **fezzes**) *n.* a brimless felt hat shaped like a cone with a flat top, usually red with a black tassel, worn by men in eastern Mediterranean and North African countries. In the past it was the national headdress of Turkish men. [Early 19thC. Via French from Turkish *fes*. Probably named after FEZ, where they were originally made.]

Fez /fez/, **Fès** city in northern Morocco, northeast of Casablanca. The oldest of the country's four imperial cities, it is about 161 km/100 mi. east of Rabat. Population: 564,000 (1993).

Fezzan /fə zán/ desert region and former province in southwestern Libya that was part of the Ottoman Empire from the 16th to the 19th centuries

FF, ff. *symbol.* MUSIC fortissimo

ff. *abbr.* **1.** following (*used of lines or pages*) **2.** folios

ffa *abbr.* SHIPPING free from alongside

FGS *abbr.* Fellow of the Geological Society

FH *abbr.* fire hydrant

fhp *abbr.* friction horsepower

FHSA *abbr.* Family Health Services Authority

FIA *abbr.* Fellow of the Institute of Actuaries

fiacre /fee áakrə/ *n.* a small horse-drawn carriage with four wheels, used in the past for hire like a taxi [Late 17thC. From French, named after the Hôtel de St *Fiacre*, where it was first hired out.]

fiancé /fi ón say/ *n.* the man to whom a woman is engaged to be married [Mid-19thC. From French, the past participle of *fiancer* 'to betroth', from, ultimately, Old French *fiance* 'a promise'.]

fiancée /fi ón say/ *n.* the woman to whom a man is engaged to be married [Mid-19thC. From French, the feminine form of *fiancé* (see FIANCÉ).]

fianchetto /fi ən chéttō, -kéttō/ *n.* (*plural* **-tos** *or* **-ti**) CHESS MOVE OF BISHOP in chess, the development of a bishop by moving it from its original position to the second square of the adjacent knight's file ■ *vt.* (**-tos, -toing, -toed**) MOVE BISHOP to move a bishop using a fianchetto [Mid-19thC. From Italian, literally 'little flank', from *fianco* 'flank'.]

Fianna /fée ənə/ *npl.* in Irish mythology, a band of warriors led by the legendary Finn MacCool and celebrated for feats of heroism [Late 18thC. From Irish, 'band of warriors and hunters'.]

Fianna Fáil /fée ənə fóyl, -fáal/ *n.* an important Irish political party founded in 1926 [From Irish, literally 'warriors of Ireland']

fiasco /fi áskō/ (*plural* **-cos**) *n.* a total failure, especially a humiliating or ludicrous one [Mid-19thC. Via Italian, 'bottle' from medieval Latin *flasco* 'flask'. The sense from *far fiasco*, literally 'to make a bottle', used in theatrical slang for 'to fail in a performance'.]

fiat /fée at, fī at/ *n.* **1.** OFFICIAL SANCTION a formal or official authorization of sth **2.** ARBITRARY ORDER an authoritative and often arbitrary command [14thC. From Latin, literally 'let it be done'.]

fiat money *n.* money that a government declares to be legal tender although it is not based on or convertible into coin and therefore depends on government decree to determine its value

fib /fib/ *n.* WHITE LIE an insignificant, harmless, or small lie (*informal*) ■ *vi.* (**fibs, fibbing, fibbed**) TELL WHITE LIES to tell an insignificant, harmless, or small lie (*informal*) [Early 17thC. Origin uncertain: perhaps a shortening of earlier *fible-fable* 'nonsense' (an alteration of FABLE).] —**fibber** *n.*

WORD KEY: SYNONYMS

See Synonyms at ***lie***.

fiber *n.* *US* = **fibre**

Fibonacci number /feebə náachi-/ *n.* a number in the unending Fibonacci sequence

Fibonacci sequence *n.* the unending series of numbers 0,1,1,2,3,5,8 … in which each number except for the first two is the sum of the preceding two. This sequence frequently occurs with applications in botany, psychology, and astronomy, e.g. providing a better correspondence for the distances between the Sun and the planets than does Bode's law. [Named after Leonardo *Fibonacci*, the 13thC Italian mathematician who first described it]

fibr- *prefix.* = **fibro-** (*used before vowels*)

fibre /fībər/ *n.* **1.** THIN THREAD a long slender thread or filament **2.** INDUST THREAD FOR YARN a fine thread or filament of a natural or synthetic material, e.g. cotton or nylon, that can be spun into yarn **3.** TEXTILES CLOTH cloth or material made of fibres **4.** FIBROUS STRUCTURE the texture or structure of a material made of fibres **5.** ESSENTIAL CHARACTER the fundamental character, quality, or makeup of sth **6.** STRENGTH OF CHARACTER sb's strength of character or sense of right and wrong ○ *the moral fibre of this nation* **7.** HEALTH COARSE FIBROUS SUBSTANCES IN FOOD the coarse fibrous substances in grains, fruits, and vegetables that aid digestion and clean out the intestines. Primarily composed of cellulose, this largely indigestible plant matter is considered to play a role in the prevention of many diseases of the digestive tract. ○ *Whole grain bread and brown rice are rich in fibre.* **8.** BOT LONG THICK-WALLED PLANT CELL a long narrow plant cell that has walls thickened with lignin and is a major component of the plant's supporting and strengthening tissue. Fibre cells are frequently found in the outer walls of plant stems. **9.** MANUF PLANT CELLS MAKING ROPE AND TEXTILES strands of fibre cells removed from the stems or leaves of some plants, e.g. flax, that can be separated and woven **10.** BOT THIN ROOT a thin narrow root of a plant **11.** ANAT THREAD-SHAPED BODY STRUCTURE a long thin structure of the body tissues, e.g. muscle cells and nerve cells [Mid-16thC. Via French from Latin *fibra* 'filament', of uncertain origin.] —**fibred** *adj.*

fibreboard /fībər bawrd/ *n.* building material made by compressing wood fibres into sheets

fibre bundle *n.* a flexible group of parallel optical fibres held in a fixed arrangement with respect to each other

fibrefill /fībər fil/ *n.* synthetic material used for stuffing or insulation, e.g. in cushions, duvets, or clothing

fibreglass /fībər glaass/ *n.* **1.** GLASS FIBRES glass fibres compressed to make materials such as insulation **2.** MATERIAL MADE FROM FIBREGLASS a material made from fibreglass and used in the construction of many things including boat hulls and car bodies

fibre optics *n.* the technology of transferring information, e.g. in communications or computer technology, through a number of thin flexible glass or plastic tubes (**optical fibres**) using modulated light waves. Information is transmitted in the form of coded pulses. (*takes a singular verb*) —**fibre-optic** *adj.*

fibrescope /fībər skōp/ *n.* an instrument that uses fibre optics to transmit images from inaccessible places such as the interior of the body. Thin flexible fibres can be introduced into blood vessels, e.g. as a diagnostic tool or to assist in microsurgery.

fibri- *prefix.* = **fibro-**

fibriform /fíbbri fawrm, fībri-/ *adj.* in the form of a fibre or fibres

fibril /fībrəl/, **fibrilla** /-fī brĭllə, -/ (*plural* **-lae**) *n.* a small or delicate fibre or part of a fibre [Mid-17thC. From modern Latin *fibrilla*, literally 'little fibre', from *fibra* 'fibre'.] —**fibrillar** /fī brĭllər, fi-/ *adj.* —**fibrillary** /-əri/ *adj.* —**fibrilliform** /-i fawrm/ *adj.* —**fibrillose** /-brĭllōss/ *adj.* —**fibrillous** /-brĭləss/ *adj.*

fibrillate /fī bri layt, fíbbri-/ (**-lates, -lating, -lated**) *vti.* to undergo, or make the heart or muscles undergo, rapid irregular beating or uncontrolled contraction (**fibrillation**) [Mid-19thC. Formed from modern Latin *fibrilla* (see FIBRIL).] —**fibrillative** *adj.*

fibrillation /fībri láysh'n, fíbbri-/ *n.* **1.** RAPID IRREGULAR HEARTBEAT rapid chaotic beating of the heart muscles in a nonsynchronous way such that normal heartbeat is not maintained and the affected part of the heart may stop pumping blood **2.** RAPID CONTRACTION OF MUSCLE FIBRE rapid uncontrolled contraction of individual muscle fibres with little or no movement of the muscle as a whole **3.** FORMATION OF FIBRES the formation of fibres or fibrils

fibrin /fíbrin, fíbb-/ *n.* an insoluble fibrous protein produced in the liver from the soluble protein fibrinogen during the blood clotting process. It forms a network of fibres in which blood cells become trapped, thus producing a clot. [Early 19thC. Coined from FIBRE + -IN.]

fibrinogen /fī brínnəjən, fi-/ *n.* a soluble protein in the blood that is made in the liver and is converted to insoluble fibrin by the action of the enzyme thrombin in response to tissue damage. Fibrinogen is a clotting factor and is required to prevent major blood loss. —**fibrinogenic** /fíbrinō jénnik/ *adj.* —**fibrinogenically** /-jénnikəli/ *adv.* —**fibrinogenous** /fíbri nójənəss/ *adj.*

fibrinoid /fíbri noyd, fíbb-/ *adj.* RESEMBLING FIBRIN relating to or resembling the protein fibrin ■ *n.* MATERIAL RESEMBLING FIBRIN a naturally occurring material resembling the protein fibrin, normally found in the placenta and formed in connective tissue and blood vessel walls in some diseases

fibrinolysin /fíbrə nóllissin/ *n.* any enzyme found in the blood that breaks down the protein fibrin found in blood clots and disperses them. Plasmin is a fibrinolysin.

fibrinolysis /fíbrə nóllississ/ *n.* the destruction of fibrin, especially its enzymatic breakdown by a fibrinolysin such as plasmin —**fibrinolytic** /fíbrinō líttik/ *adj.*

fibrinous /fíbbrinəss/ *adj.* relating to or containing fibrin

fibro /fíbrō/ (*plural* **-bros**) *n.* *Aus* **1.** INDUST FIBROCEMENT the material fibrocement (*informal*) **2.** BUILDING BUILDING MADE OF FIBROCEMENT a house made of fibrocement [Mid-20thC. Shortening.] —**fibro** *adj.*

fibro- *prefix.* **1.** FIBRE used to mean fibre **2.** FIBROUS TISSUE used to mean fibrous tissue [From Latin *fibra* 'fibre']

fibroblast /fíbrō blast/ *n.* a large flat cell that secretes the proteins that form collagen and elastic fibres and the substance between the cells of connective tissue

fibrocartilage /fíbrō kaártilij, -tlij/ *n.* a type of strong, relatively inelastic cartilage containing bundles of collagen fibres

fibrocement /fíbrō si mént/ *n.* a building material made of cement bound with asbestos fibres into sheets

fibrocystic /fíbrō sístik/ *adj.* being an unusual growth of fibrous tissue that contains cystic spaces, occurring particularly in glandular tissue such as the breast. Fibrocystic disease of the pancreas is called cystic fibrosis.

fibroid /fī broyd/ *adj.* LIKE FIBRES resembling or consisting of fibres or fibrous tissue ■ *n.* FIBROUS TISSUE GROWTH a benign growth composed of fibrous and muscle tissue, especially one that develops in the wall of the womb and is associated with painful and excessive menstrual flow. Fibroids can be removed surgically and are not life-threatening, but fibroids in the womb reduce the chance of pregnancy.

fibroin /fíbrō in/ *n.* a tough insoluble white protein secreted by spiders and silkworms that quickly solidifies into a strong thread, used to form cocoons and webs

fibroma /fī brómə/ (*plural* **-mas** *or* **-mata** /-mətə/) *n.* a nonmalignant tumour of fibrous connective tissue such as cartilage [Mid-19thC. Coined from Latin *fibra* 'fibre' + -OMA.] —**fibromatous** *adj.*

fibrose[1] /fíbrōss/ (**-broses, -brosing, -brosed**) *vi.* to form tissue consisting of or resembling fibres [Late 19thC. Back-formation from FIBROSIS.]

fibrose[2] /fíbrōss/ *adj.* containing or resembling fibres (*technical*)

fibrosis /fī brṓssiss/ *n.* an abnormal thickening and scarring of connective tissue most often following injury, infection, lack of oxygen, or surgery —**fibrotic** /fī bróttik/ *adj.*

fibrositis /fíbrə sítiss/ *n.* pain and stiffness, especially in the back muscles

fibrous /fíbrəss/ *adj.* **1.** CONSISTING OF FIBRES consisting of or resembling fibres **2.** GEOL IN ELONGATED THREADS used to describe a mineral that crystallizes in thin elongated threads, e.g. asbestos —**fibrously** *adv.* —**fibrousness** *n.*

fibrous root *n.* any of the fine roots of some plants, e.g. grasses, that are roughly the same length and branch in all directions

fibrovascular /fíbrō váskyōōlər/ *adj.* used to describe plant tissue that provides structural support and conducts sap

fibrovascular bundle *n.* = **vascular bundle**

fibula /fíbbyōōlə/ (*plural* **-lae** /-lee/ *or* **-las**) *n.* **1.** HUMAN LEG BONE the outer and narrower of the two bones in the human lower leg, between the knee and the ankle **2.** ANIMAL LEG BONE the thinner outermost bone of the two bones that form the lower leg of terrestrial vertebrates between the knee and ankle, or the hind leg of a four-legged animal **3.** BROOCH a brooch or clasp shaped like a modern safety pin, worn by the ancient Greeks and Romans to fasten cloaks [Late 16thC. From Latin, 'brooch, clasp', perhaps formed from *figere* 'to fasten'. The sense 'bone in the leg' comes from the two bones' similarity in shape to a Roman *fibula*.] —**fibular** *adj.*

-fic *suffix.* making, causing ○ *sudorific* [From Latin *-ficus*, from *facere* 'to make, do' (see FACT)]

-fication *suffix.* production, process ○ *versification* ○ *unification* [From the Latin stem *-fication-*, from *-ficatus*, the past participle stem of verbs ending in *-ficare* 'to make', from, ultimately, *facere* 'to make, to do']

fiche /feesh/ *n.* (*informal*) **1.** MICROFICHE a microfiche **2.** ULTRAFICHE an ultrafiche [Mid-20thC. Shortening.]

fichu /fée shoo/ *n.* a woman's triangular scarf made of a lightweight material such as muslin or lace, worn around the neck and shoulders, especially in the 18th and early 19th centuries [Mid-18thC. Via French, 'knotted', from, ultimately, Latin *figere* 'to fasten' (see FIX).]

fickle /fík'l/ (**-ler, -lest**) *adj.* likely to change, especially in affections, intentions, loyalties, or preferences [Old English *ficol* 'deceitful'. Ultimately from an Indo-European word meaning 'hostile'.] —**fickleness** *n.*

fictile /fík tīl/ *adj.* **1.** MALLEABLE moulded or capable of being moulded, as, e.g. clay can be for making pottery **2.** MADE OF CLAY moulded in earth or clay by a potter **3.** RELATING TO POTTERY-MAKING relating to the making of earthenware or pottery [Early 17thC. Via Latin *fictilis* from, ultimately, *fingere* 'to make, shape'.]

fiction /fíksh'n/ *n.* **1.** LITERARY WORKS OF IMAGINATION novels and stories that describe imaginary people and events **2.** WORK OF FICTION a novel, story, or other work of fiction **3.** UNTRUE STATEMENT sth that is untrue and has been made up to deceive people ○ *The account she gave was pure fiction.* **4.** ACT OF PRETENDING the act of pretending or inventing sth such as a story or explanation **5.** LAW STH ASSUMED TO BE TRUE sth that is assumed in law to be true regardless of whether or not it is really true [14thC. Via Old French from Latin *fictio*, from *fingere* 'to make, shape'.]

— WORD KEY: ORIGIN —
The Latin word *fingere*, from which *fiction* is derived, is also the source of English *effigy*, *faint*, *feign*, *figment*, and *figure*.

fictional /fíksh'nəl/ *adj.* **1.** NOT TRUE not real or true but made up by sb **2.** RELATING TO FICTION occurring in, invented for, or relating to novels or stories —**fictionality** /fíkshə nálləti/ *n.* —**fictionally** /fíksh'nəli/ *adv.*

fictionalize /fíksh'nə līz/ (**-izes, -izing, -ized**), **fictionalise** /fíkshənə līz/ (**-ises, -ising, -ised**) *vt.* to make sth into fiction, or make a fictional version of sth ○ *a fictionalized life of Shakespeare* —**fictionalization** /fíksh'nə līzáysh'n/ *n.*

fictitious /fik tíshəss/ *adj.* **1.** FALSE not true or genuine, and intended to deceive ○ *He gave a fictitious name when confronted.* **2.** FICTIONAL invented by sb's imagination, especially as part of a work of fiction **3.** LAW ASSUMED TO BE SO assumed to be true for legal purposes, regardless of whether or not it really is [Early 17thC. Formed from Latin *ficticius* from, ul-

timately, *fingere* 'to make, shape'.] —**fictitiously** *adv.* —**fictitiousness** *n.*

fictive /fíktiv/ *adj.* **1.** RELATING TO FICTION relating to fiction or imaginative invention **2.** NOT REAL not genuine or true [Late 15thC. Directly or via French from medieval Latin *fictivus*, from *fingere* 'to make, shape'.] —**fictively** *adv.*

fid /fid/ *n.* **1.** TOPMAST SUPPORT a bar used to support a topmast on a ship **2.** TAPERED TOOL FOR SPLICING a tapered wooden implement used to separate the strands of a rope in splicing [Early 17thC. Origin unknown.]

FID *abbr.* Aus Financial Institutions Duty

-fid *suffix.* divided in parts ○ *multifid* [From Latin *-fidus*, from *fid-*, the stem of *findere* 'to split' (see FISSI-)]

FID DEF, **Fid. Def.** *abbr.* Fidei Defensor

fiddle /fídd'l/ *n.* **1.** MUSIC VIOLIN a musical instrument of the viol or violin family, especially the violin. Violins are often called fiddles in folk, bluegrass, or country music, but in classical music this can sometimes be disparaging. **2.** FRAUDULENT ACTIVITY a fraudulent or illegal way of getting money (*informal*) **3.** DELICATE OPERATION a difficult activity or operation requiring intricate work with the hands (*informal*) ○ *It can be a bit of a fiddle trying to change the battery in this watch.* **4.** TRIVIAL MATTERS nonsensical or trivial matters or behaviour **5.** NAUT GUARDRAIL ON SHIP'S TABLE a small guardrail on top of a table or stove on a ship, used to prevent things from sliding off in rough weather ■ *v.* (**-dles, -dling, -dled**) **1.** *vi.* MUSIC PLAY VIOLIN to play the fiddle **2.** *vi.* MOVE HANDS NERVOUSLY to move the hands or fingers nervously or restlessly, or play with sth in the hands in this way ○ *The schoolboy fiddled nervously with his tie.* **3.** *vi.* TAMPER WITH STH to interfere, meddle, or tamper with sth (*informal*) ○ *Who's been fiddling with my computer?* **4.** *vi.* TINKER WITH STH TO FIX IT to manipulate or tinker with sth to try to make it work properly ○ *She fiddled with the controls on the video recorder.* **5.** *vt.* SWINDLE to cheat or swindle sb (*informal*) **6.** *vt.* FALSIFY STH to falsify sth, e.g. financial accounts, especially for dishonest personal gain (*informal*) **7.** *vt.* GET STH BY CHEATING to get or achieve sth by cheating or deceiving (*informal*) ○ *She fiddled her way into that job.* **8.** *vti.* WASTE TIME to waste time doing unimportant things ○ *fiddle the day away* [Pre-12thC. From medieval Latin *vitula* 'instrument played at festivals', from *vitulari* 'to hold celebrations' (source of English *violin*).] ◇ **be on the fiddle** to be involved in making money by fraudulent or illegal means (*informal*)

fiddle about, **fiddle around** *vi.* to waste time doing unimportant things (*informal*)

fiddleback /fídd'l bak/, **fiddleback chair** *n.* a chair with a back shaped like the body of a fiddle

fiddle-de-dee /fídd'l dee deé/ *interj.* used to express mild annoyance, disagreement, or impatience (*dated informal*) [From FIDDLE and a nonsensical ending]

fiddle-faddle /fídd'l fad'l/ *n.* NONSENSE nonsense or trifling matters (*informal*) ■ *interj.* NONSENSE! used to express the view that sth is nonsense (*dated informal*) ■ *vi.* (**fiddle-faddles, fiddle-faddling, fiddle-faddled**) WASTE TIME to fuss, mess about, or waste time with unimportant matters (*informal*) [Late 16thC. From FIDDLE and earlier *faddle* 'nonsense'.] —**fiddle-faddler** *n.*

Fiddlehead

fiddlehead /fídd'l hed/, **fiddleneck** /-nek/ *n.* **1.** NAUT CARVING ON SHIP'S BOW an ornamental carving on a ship's bow, shaped like the scroll at the end of the fingerboard of a violin **2.** US, Can PLANTS EDIBLE FERN

SHOOT the coiled frond of a young fern often cooked and eaten as a delicacy

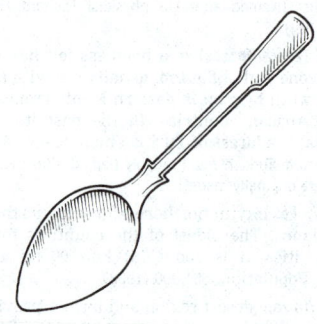
Fiddle pattern

fiddle pattern *n.* the design of a fork or spoon with a handle that has a tapering wide end —**fiddle-pattern** *adj.*

fiddler /fídd'lər/ *n.* **1.** MUSIC VIOLIN PLAYER sb who plays the violin **2.** SB WHO TOYS WITH STH sb who plays or fiddles with sth aimlessly **3.** SWINDLER sb who cheats or swindles others (*informal*) **4.** ZOOL = **fiddler crab**

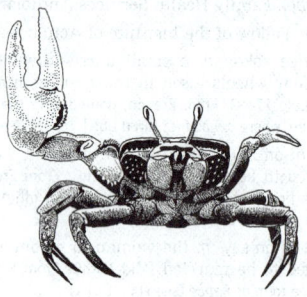
Fiddler crab

fiddler crab *n.* a small marine burrowing crab. Males have one enlarged claw that they move like a violinist's arm as a signal during courtship. Genus: *Uca*.

fiddlestick /fídd'l stik/ *n.* (*informal*) **1.** VIOLIN BOW a bow for playing a violin **2.** THING OF LITTLE VALUE sth that is unimportant or worthless ○ *I don't care a fiddlestick what you think.*

fiddlesticks /fídd'l stiks/ *interj.* used to express mild annoyance, disagreement, or impatience (*dated informal*)

fiddlewood /fídd'l wŏŏd/ *n.* **1.** TREES TROPICAL TREE a tropical American tree that yields a hard wood. Genus: *Citharexylum*. **2.** INDUST WOOD OF FIDDLEWOOD TREE the hard wood of the fiddlewood tree

fiddling /fídd'ling/ *adj.* petty or unimportant

fiddly /fíddli/ (**-dlier, -dliest**) *adj.* difficult to do, handle, or use, usually because it involves small objects or intricate work with the hands (*informal*) ○ *Changing the battery in this type of watch can be quite a fiddly job.*

FIDE *abbr.* International Chess Federation [From French, an acronym formed from *Fédération Internationale des Échecs*]

Fidei Defensor /fi dáy ee də fén sawr, fídi ī-/ *n.* defender of the faith, a title of English sovereigns first given by Pope Leo X to Henry VIII and shown in abbreviation on pre-decimal British coins [From Latin]

fideism /fée day izəm, ffdi-/ *n.* the view that religious knowledge depends on faith and revelation [Late 19thC. Formed from Latin *fides* 'faith' (see FAITH).] —**fideist** *n.* —**fideistic** /fée day ístik, ffdi-/ *adj.*

Fidelism /fee dél|izəm/ *n.* the practice or policies of Castroism [Mid-20thC. Named after Fidel CASTRO.]

fidelity /fi délləti/ *n.* **1.** LOYALTY loyalty to an allegiance, promise, or vow **2.** SEXUAL FAITHFULNESS faithfulness to a sexual partner, especially a husband or wife **3.** FACTUAL ACCURACY accuracy in describing or reporting facts or details **4.** ELECTRON ENG PRECISION OF REPRODUCTION the extent to which an electronic device, e.g. a

a at; aa father; aw all; ay day; air hair; ə about, edible, item, common, circus; e egg; ee eel; hw when; i it, happy; ī ice; 'l apple; 'm rhythm; 'n fashion; o odd; ō open; ŏŏ good; oo pool; ow owl; oy oil; th thin; th this; u up; ur urge;

stereo system or television, accurately reproduces sound or images [15thC. Directly or via French from Latin *fidelitas* 'faithfulness' from, ultimately, *fides* 'faith' (see FAITH).]

fidget /fíjjit/ *vi.* (**-ets, -eting, -eted**) **1. MOVE ABOUT NERVOUSLY** to move about in a restless, absent-minded, or uneasy manner ○ *The lecture was so boring we couldn't stop fidgeting.* **2. FIDDLE NERVOUSLY** to fiddle or play with sth in a restless, absent-minded, or uneasy manner ○ *He kept fidgeting with his glasses as he spoke to her.* ■ *n.* **SB WHO FIDGETS** sb who fidgets in a restless, absent-minded, or uneasy manner ■ **fidgets** *npl.* **UNEASINESS** a state of restlessness or unease expressed by continual nervous movements [Late 17thC. Alteration of earlier *fidge* 'to twitch, fidget'.] — **fidgetingly** *adv.*

fidgety /fíjjəti/ *adj.* **1. INCLINED TO FIDGET** tending to fidget **2. UNEASY** restless or ill at ease —**fidgetiness** *n.*

fiducial /fi dyóoshi əl/ *adj.* **1. FOUNDED ON TRUST** founded on or relating to faith or trust (*formal*) **2. USED AS BASIS OF REFERENCE** accepted or used as a standard of comparison, measurement, or reference **3.** LAW RESEMBLING LEGAL TRUST resembling a legal trust [Late 16thC. Via late Latin *fiducialis* from, ultimately, Latin *fidere* 'to trust'.] —**fiducially** *adv.*

fiduciary /fi dyóoshi əri/ *adj.* **1. RELATING TO A TRUST RELATIONSHIP** relating to the relationship between a trustee and the person or body for whom the trustee acts **2. RELATING TO A TRUST** relating to or based on a trust ■ *n.* (*plural* **-ies**) **TRUSTEE** sb who is entrusted with the management of property or with the power to act on behalf of and for the benefit of another [Late 16thC. Via Latin *fiduciarius* '(holding) in a trust' from, ultimately, *fides* 'trust' (see FAITH).] —**fiduciarily** *adv.*

fie /fī/ *interj.* used to express disapproval, annoyance, or disgust with sb or sth (*archaic*) [14thC. Via French *fi* from Latin, an exclamation of disgust at a stench.]

fief /feef/ *n.* **1. PIECE OF LAND GRANTED BY LORD** a piece of land, rather than money, formerly granted by a feudal lord to sb in return for service **2.** = **fiefdom** [Early 17thC. Via French from Old French *fieu*, from medieval Latin *feudum* (see FEUD[2]).]

fiefdom /féefdəm/ *n.* **1. LANDS OF FEUDAL LORD** the lands controlled by a feudal lord **2. STH UNDER SB'S INFLUENCE OR AUTHORITY** sth such as territory or a sphere of activity that is controlled or dominated by a particular person or group

field /feeld/ *n.* **1.** AGRIC **AREA OF AGRICULTURAL LAND** an area of open ground, especially an area used to grow crops or graze livestock **2.** SPORTS **PLAYING AREA** an open expanse of ground kept or marked out as a playing area for a particular sport **3.** GEOL **AREA RICH IN RESOURCES** an area of land or seabed that is rich in an exploitable natural resource **4.** GEOG **BROAD AREA OF STH** an expanse of sth such as ice, snow, or lava **5. AREA OF ACTIVITY** an activity or subject, especially one that is sb's particular responsibility, speciality, or interest **6. PLACE OUTSIDE INSTITUTION** the setting outside a workplace, office, school, or laboratory in which sb has direct contact with clients, the public, or the phenomena being studied **7.** MIL **AREA OF MILITARY OPERATIONS** the scene or location of military operations or manoeuvres **8.** MIL **BATTLEFIELD** an area where a battle is fought **9.** MIL **BATTLE** a battle (*archaic literary*) **10.** SPORTS **GROUP OF CONTESTANTS** all the participants in a race or other competitive event **11.** SPORTS **ALL PARTICIPANTS EXCEPT FAVOURITE** all the participants in a race or competitive event except the favourite, winner, or leader ○ *five lengths ahead of the field* **12.** CRICKET **ARRANGEMENT OF FIELDERS** a particular arrangement of cricket fielders around the wicket ○ *five lengths ahead of the field* **13.** MATH **SET OF MATHEMATICAL ELEMENTS** a set of mathematical elements having two properties that are like addition and multiplication for ordinary numbers **14.** PHYS **AREA OF FORCE** an area or region within which a force exerts an influence at every point **15.** = **field of view 16.** COMPUT **STORAGE AREA FOR INFORMATION** an area in a computer memory or program, or on a monitor screen, where information can be entered and manipulated **17.** HERALDRY **BACKGROUND FOR DESIGN** the background surface or colour on which a design is displayed, e.g. on a flag, coin, or coat of arms ■ *v.* (**fields, fielding, fielded**) **1.** *vt.* SPORTS **RETRIEVE BALL** to retrieve, pick up, or catch a ball in play, usually after it has been struck by a

batter in baseball or rounders or a batsman in cricket **2.** *vi.* SPORTS **BE A FIELDER** to act as a fielder in cricket, baseball, or rounders **3.** *vt.* **SELECT SB FOR A COMPETITION** to select a person, group, or team to participate in an event, especially a competitive event ○ *We did not have enough players to field a team* **4.** *vt.* **DEPLOY A GROUP** to send out a large number of people or things to accomplish a task, especially to deploy military forces for action **5.** *vt.* **DEAL WITH QUESTION OR COMPLAINT** to handle sth such as a question or complaint [Old English *feld*. Ultimately from an Indo-European base meaning 'flat', which also produced English *flat*, *plate*, and *place*.] ◇ **play the field** to avoid a romantic relationship with one person by dating many people

field ambulance *n.* a team of medical workers who give first aid to wounded soldiers in the front line of a battle

field artillery *n.* large guns mobile enough to be brought close to the front line of a battle

field battery *n.* a small unit of field guns

field boot *n.* a knee-length close-fitting boot

field coil *n.* the coil of wire that, when carrying current, produces the magnetization inside an electrical motor or generator needed for it to operate

field cornet *n.* a civilian invested with the authority of a military officer and empowered to act as a magistrate

fieldcraft /féeld kraaft/ *n.* knowledge and experience of nature combined with the skills necessary for living outdoors or in the wild

field day *n.* **1. TIME OF UNRESTRAINED ACTIVITY** an opportunity for unrestrained or rewarding activity ○ *If the slightest hint of this gets out, the press will have a field day.* **2.** US **DAY FOR AMATEUR COMPETITIONS** a day devoted to amateur outdoor sports and competitions, especially at a school **3. DAY FOR OUTDOOR ACTIVITIES** a day spent in outdoor activities or study

field-effect transistor *n.* a transistor, with three or more electrodes, in which the output current is controlled by a variable electric field

field emission *n.* the liberation of electrons from the surface of a metallic conductor subjected to a strong electric field

fielder /féeldər/ *n.* a player in cricket, baseball, or rounders who is positioned on the field of play to catch or retrieve the ball when it is struck by the batsman or batter

field event *n.* an athletics event, e.g. the discus, javelin, long jump, or high jump, that takes place on an open area not on a track

fieldfare /féeld fair/ (*plural* **-fares** *or* **-fare**) *n.* a migratory Eurasian thrush with reddish-brown plumage and a grey head and rump and a noisy call. Latin name: *Turdus pilaris*. [Assumed Old English *feldefare* 'field dweller']

field glasses *npl.* a pair of binoculars

field goal *n.* **1.** FOOTBALL **GOAL MADE WITH A KICK** in American football, a score worth three points, made by kicking the ball over the crossbar from a point about ten yards behind the line of scrimmage **2.** BASKETBALL **GOAL IN NORMAL PLAY** in basketball, a goal made during normal play by throwing the ball through the basket. It is worth two points, or three points if scored from beyond a specified distance.

field-grade officer *n.* = **field officer**

field guide *n.* an illustrated manual that is used to identify plants, animals, or birds in their natural habitats

field hand *n.* US sb who works on a farm cultivating or harvesting crops

field hockey *n.* US = **hockey**

field hospital *n.* a centre for medical treatment on a battlefield or in an isolated place

Fielding /féelding/**, Henry** (1707–54) British novelist and dramatist. Of his 25 plays, the most popular was the farce *Tom Thumb* (1730). He is also considered to be a founder of the English novel.

field lens *n.* the lens that is farthest from the eye in the compound eyepiece of an optical instrument

field magnet *n.* an electromagnet or permanent magnet that supplies the magnetic field in an electric machine

field marshal *n.* an officer holding the highest rank in the British army or in the armies of some other countries

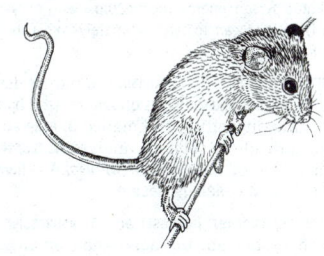

Fieldmouse

fieldmouse /féeld mowss/ *n.* **1. SMALL EURASIAN MOUSE** a small Eurasian mouse with large eyes and ears and a long tail that lives in fields and gardens. Genus: *Apodemus.* **2.** US **N AMERICAN VOLE** the most common North American vole. Genus: *Microtus.*

field officer *n.* a military officer of the middle rank, e.g. a major or colonel

field of fire *n.* an area exposed to fire from a weapon or group of weapons

field of honour *n.* a battlefield, or the site of a duel (*archaic*)

field of vision *n.* the whole area that can be seen by the eyes when they are kept fixed in one direction

field poppy *n.* = **corn poppy**

W. C. Fields

Fields /feeldz/**, W. C.** (1880–1946) US actor and comedian. He is best known for his portrayal of irascible irresponsible characters struggling to keep one step ahead of the law. One of his most popular films is *My Little Chickadee* (1940). Real name **William Claude Dukenfield**

fieldsman /féeldzmən/ (*plural* **-men** /féeldzmən/) *n.* a fielder in cricket

field sports *npl.* outdoor country sports that involve killing or capturing animals, especially hunting, shooting, and fishing

field study *n.* a piece of research undertaken outside the laboratory or place of learning, usually in a natural environment or among the general public

field test *n.* a test carried out on a product under normal conditions of use

field-test *vt.* to test a device or product by using it under normal conditions

field trial *n.* **1.** = **field test 2. CONTEST FOR HUNTING DOGS** a competition to determine how well hunting dogs perform

field trip *n.* a trip made by students or researchers to study sth firsthand

field winding *n.* = **field coil**

fieldwork /féeld wurk/ *n.* **1. WORK DONE OUTSIDE NORMAL PLACE OF WORK** work undertaken outside the school, office, or laboratory in order to gain knowledge through direct contact and observation **2.** MIL **TEM-**

PORARY FORTIFICATION a temporary defensive earthwork or fortification —**field worker** n.

fiend /feend/ n. **1.** DEVIL an evil supernatural being, especially a devil from hell **2.** SB EVIL sb who is extremely wicked or cruel **3.** PERSON WITH STRONG INTEREST sb who is keen and devotedly interested in a particular topic, occupation, or activity [Old English *fēond* 'hated person, enemy' (hence 'the enemy of everyone', the Devil), from *fēogan* 'to hate'; ultimately from a prehistoric Germanic word]

fiendish /feendish/ adj. **1.** DIABOLICAL like a devil or demon **2.** CUNNING AND MALICIOUS characterized by devilish cunning, ingenuity, and malice **3.** PERPLEXING extremely difficult to solve or analyse **4.** DISAGREEABLE extremely bad or unpleasant (informal) —**fiendishly** /feendishli/ adv. —**fiendishness** n.

fierce /feerss/ (**fiercer, fiercest**) adj. **1.** AGGRESSIVE characterized by or showing aggression or anger ○ *a fierce guard dog* **2.** VIOLENT OR INTENSE characterized by the violence or intensity of the forces, activity, or participants involved ○ *It was a fierce battle.* ○ *a fierce storm* **3.** PROFOUND deeply and intensely felt and often aggressively expressed ○ *He felt a fierce loyalty to his family.* [13thC. Via Anglo-Norman *fers* 'brave, proud, hostile', from, ultimately, Latin *ferus* 'wild, untamed' (source of English *feral*).] —**fiercely** adv. —**fierceness** n.

fieri facias /fī ə rī fáyshi əss/ n. a legal document that authorizes a sheriff to seize a debtor's property to settle the claim of a creditor [From Latin, literally 'you should cause to be done']

fiery /fīri/ (**-ier, -iest**) adj. **1.** GLOWING HOT burning or full of fire **2.** RED bright red in colour **3.** SHOWING INTENSE EMOTION full of or prone to sudden extremes of emotions **4.** SPICY extremely hot or spicy to the taste —**fierily** adv. —**fieriness** n.

fiery cross n. a burning wooden cross, originally carried by runners in the Scottish Highlands to call men to arms and later adopted by the Ku Klux Klan in the United States

fiesta /fi éstə/ n. **1.** RELIGIOUS FESTIVAL a celebration or festival linked to a religious holiday and held especially in Spanish-speaking countries **2.** FESTIVAL any festival or celebration [Mid-19thC. Via Spanish from, ultimately, Latin *festum*.]

FIFA /feefə/ abbr. the governing organization of international football [From French, an acronym formed from *Fédération Internationale de Football Association*]

fife /fīf/ n. a small high-pitched flute without keys, often used in military and marching bands [Mid-16thC. Origin uncertain; via German *Pfeife*, or French *fifre* 'fife, fife player' from, ultimately, assumed Vulgar Latin *pipa*, from Latin *pipare* 'to peep, chirp' (source of English *pipe*).] —**fifer** n.

Fife /fīf/ council area in east-central Scotland. It is often called the Kingdom of Fife. Population: 351,600 (1995). Area: 1,323 sq. km/511 sq. mi.

fife rail n. a low rail round the lower part of the mast of a sailing ship, with belaying pins to which running rigging is attached [Origin unknown]

FIFO /fífō/ abbr. first in, first out

fifteen /fif teen/ n. **1.** NUMBER 15 the number 15 **2.** STH WITH VALUE OF 15 sth in a numbered series with a value of 15 **3.** GROUP OF 15 a group of 15 objects or people **4.** TEAM OF 15 PLAYERS a team of 15 players, especially a rugby union team [Old English *fīftēne*, from *fīf* 'five' + *-tēne* (from a prehistoric German word meaning 'ten')] —**fifteen** adj., pron.

fifteenth /fif teenth/ n. **1.** ONE OF 15 PARTS OF STH one of 15 equal parts of sth **2.** 15 IN A SERIES the ordinal number assigned to item number 15 in a series —**fifteenth** adj., adv.

fifth /fifth/ n. **1.** ONE OF 5 PARTS OF STH one of five equal parts of sth **2.** 5 IN A SERIES the ordinal number assigned to item number five in a series **3.** MUSIC 5-NOTE INTERVAL in a diatonic scale, an interval stretching from one note to another five notes higher, or the sound made when both these notes are played simultaneously **4.** AUTOMOT 5TH GEAR in some cars or motor vehicles, the fifth gear **5.** BALLET = **fifth position** [Old English *fīfta*, from *fīf* (see FIVE)] —**fifth** adj., adv.

Fifth n. US the Fifth Amendment (informal) ◇ **take the Fifth** US refuse to answer an awkward or self-incriminating question (informal)

Fifth Amendment n. an amendment to the US Constitution stating, among other things, that defendants or witnesses in criminal trials need not testify against or incriminate themselves and may not be retried for an offence a second time

fifth column n. a secret or subversive group that seeks to undermine the efforts of others and promote its own ends [Originally denoting the supporters that General Mola claimed to have inside Madrid during the Spanish Civil War, in addition to the four columns of his army besieging the city] —**fifth columnist** n.

fifth-generation adj. used to describe a highly advanced and as yet undeveloped level of computer technology, incorporating artificial intelligence

fifthly /fifthli/ adv. used to introduce the fifth point in an argument or discussion

fifth position n. a position in ballet in which the feet are turned outwards with the heel of the front foot level with and touching the base of the big toe of the back foot

fifth wheel n. **1.** SB OR STH UNNECESSARY sb or sth whose presence is superfluous or unwanted **2.** SPARE WHEEL a spare wheel for a four-wheeled vehicle **3.** ARTICULATED BEARING OR COUPLING a horizontal bearing that allows a vehicle's front axle to swivel left or right relative to its body, or that allows a trailer attached to a tractor vehicle to pivot

fiftieth /fifti əth/ n. **1.** ONE OF 50 PARTS one of 50 equal parts of sth **2.** 50 IN A SERIES the ordinal number assigned to item number 50 in a series **3.** 50TH BIRTHDAY sb's 50th birthday —**fiftieth** adj., adv.

fifty /fífti/ n. (plural **-ties**) **1.** NUMBER 50 the number 50, equal to 5 times 10 **2.** GROUP OF 50 a group of 50 objects or people **3.** £50 NOTE a banknote worth 50 pounds ■ npl. **1.** NUMBERS 50 TO 59 the numbers 50 to 59, particularly as a range of temperature ○ *in the low fifties* **2.** YEARS 1950 TO 1959 the years 1950 to 1959 **3.** PERIOD FROM AGE 50 TO 59 the period of sb's life from the age of 50 to 59 [Old English *fīftig*, from *fīf* (see FIVE)] —**fifty** adj., pron.

fifty-fifty adj., adv. IN EXACTLY EQUAL SHARES in two equally divided parts or shares ○ *We'll split the profits fifty-fifty.* ■ adj. EQUAL equally likely that either of two possibilities may come about ○ *a fifty-fifty chance*

Fig

fig[1] /fig/ n. **1.** SWEET-TASTING FRUIT a pear-shaped fruit with sweet-tasting flesh and many seeds that is eaten fresh, preserved, or dried **2.** TREE a small tropical or subtropical tree of the mulberry family that bears figs. Latin name: *Ficus carica*. [13thC. Via Old French *figue* from, ultimately, Latin *ficus*.] ◇ **not give** or **care a fig for** sb or sth not to care about sb or sth at all

fig[2] /fig/ n. the way sb is dressed, usually in particularly grand or formal clothing (archaic) [Mid-19thC. From obsolete *feague* 'to beat, to work at briskly', of uncertain origin; probably from German *fegen* 'to polish'.]

fig. abbr. **1.** figurative **2.** figure

fight /fīt/ v. (**fights, fighting, fought** /fawt/) **1.** vti. USE VIOLENCE to use violent physical means such as blows with fists or a weapon to try to overpower sb **2.** vti. GO TO WAR to go to war, or engage in armed conflict with another country, force, or group **3.** vi. TAKE PART IN WAR to take part in a war or battle, e.g. as a

member or unit of the armed forces involved in it **4.** vt. CARRY ON BATTLE OR CONTEST to enter into or carry on a battle or other contest such as an election or court case **5.** vi. STRUGGLE DETERMINEDLY to make a strenuous effort to do, obtain, achieve, or defend sth **6.** vti. OPPOSE STH to make vigorous efforts to oppose, resist, or overcome sth or sb ○ *fight injustice* **7.** vi. QUARREL to argue or quarrel with sb or with each other **8.** vti. BOX AGAINST SB to take part in a boxing match against sb ■ n. **1.** VIOLENT ENCOUNTER a conflict between individuals or groups in which each tries to do physical harm to, or defeat, the other **2.** STRUGGLE a determined effort to achieve or gain sth, or to resist or oppose sth or sb **3.** VERBAL CONFRONTATION a verbal dispute or quarrel **4.** ABILITY OR WILLINGNESS TO FIGHT the ability or willingness to continue a battle or struggle ○ *We've still got a lot of fight left in us.* **5.** BOXING MATCH a boxing match or similar contest [Old English *feohtan* 'to fight', ultimately from a prehistoric West Germanic word] —**fightable** adj. ◇ **fight it out** to fight or argue until a decisive result is obtained ◇ **fight shy of** sth to try to avoid sth

—— WORD KEY: SYNONYMS ——

fight, battle, war, conflict, engagement, skirmish, clash

CORE MEANING: a struggle between opposing forces
fight a general word used to talk about a physical struggle between opponents. It can be used both of individuals or groups of people, such as battalions or armies; **battle** a fight between large organized opposing forces that is part of an ongoing war or campaign; **war** a state of hostilities between nations, states, or factions involving the use of arms and the occurrence of a series of fights or battles; **conflict** a situation in which opposing forces struggle for supremacy. It is often used to talk about a prolonged and bitter struggle; **engagement** a formal word used to describe a hostile encounter that is part of a continuing struggle such as a war and that suggests that the encounter has been anticipated and planned; **skirmish** a brief minor fight, usually one that is part of an ongoing conflict; **clash** a short, fierce encounter, usually involving physical combat and often forming part of an ongoing conflict.

fight back v. **1.** vi. GET BACK AT SB to resist or retaliate when attacked **2.** vi. COUNTERATTACK to counterattack or make a determined effort to recover after initial defeat or difficulty **3.** vt. RESTRAIN TEARS OR EMOTION to suppress sth such as tears or the outward expression of an emotion or impulse

fight off vt. **1.** FEND OFF AN ATTACKER to drive away or resist an attacker **2.** AVOID CATCHING STH to make an effort not to succumb to sth such as an illness or an unpleasant feeling

fighter /fītər/ n. **1.** ATTACKING AIRCRAFT a fast armed military aircraft designed principally to attack enemy aircraft **2.** VERY DETERMINED PERSON sb who is very determined and struggles hard to achieve or resist sth **3.** BOXER sb who takes part in boxing matches

fighter-bomber n. an aircraft designed to combine the roles of fighter and bomber

fighting chance n. a possibility of success, but only with sustained effort

fighting cock n. a male domestic fowl that has been bred and trained for fighting. US term **gamecock**

Fighting fish

fighting fish n. a small brightly coloured, highly aggressive freshwater fish with long flowing fins that is found in Southeast Asia and elsewhere and is also kept in aquariums. Genus: *Betta*.

fight-or-flight reaction *n.* a set of physiological changes, including an increase in heart rate, blood pressure, and the flow of epinephrine, that constitutes the body's instinctive response to impending danger or other stress

fig leaf *n.* **1.** ARTS **COVERING FOR GENITALS IN ART** a stylized representation of a leaf of the fig tree, formerly used as a covering for the genitals in painting or sculpture **2. STH MEANT TO HIDE STH ELSE** an unconvincing or inadequate attempt to conceal sth considered shameful or wrong

figment /fígmənt/ *n.* sth produced by or only existing in sb's imagination ○ *a figment of her imagination* [15thC. From Latin *figmentum* 'formation, figure, creation', from *fingere* 'to form or shape'.]

figural /fíggərəl/ *adj.* = **figurative** *adj.* 2

figurant /fíggyŏŏrənt/ *n.* a ballet dancer who performs in group numbers but does not dance solo [Late 18thC. From French present participle of *figurer* 'to represent', from, ultimately, Latin *figura* 'FIGURE'.]

figurante /fíggyŏŏ rónt/ *n.* a woman ballet dancer who performs in group numbers but does not dance solo [Late 18thC. From French feminine form of *figurant* 'FIGURANT'.]

figuration /fíggə ráysh'n/ *n.* **1.** MUSIC **USE OF MUSICAL FIGURES AS EMBELLISHMENT** the use of musical figures or other ornaments to embellish or vary a theme **2.** ARTS **GIVING STH FIGURATIVE FORM** the process of giving allegorical or emblematic form to sth abstract, especially by representing it using human or animal figures **3. FIGURATIVE REPRESENTATION OF STH** a depiction of sth in emblematic or allegorical form

figurative /fíggərətiv/ *adj.* **1. NOT LITERAL** using or containing a nonliteral sense of a word or words **2. REPRESENTATIONAL** relating to or representing form in art by means of human or animal figures **3. REPRESENTING BY ALLEGORICAL FIGURES** using an allegorical or emblematic human or animal figure to represent an abstract idea or quality —**figuratively** *adv.* —**figurativeness** *n.*

figure /fíggər/ *n.* **1. SYMBOL REPRESENTING NUMBER** a symbol representing sth other than a letter of the alphabet, especially a number **2. AMOUNT EXPRESSED NUMERICALLY** an amount or value expressed as a number **3. SB'S BODY SHAPE** the shape of an individual human body, especially with regard to its slimness or attractiveness **4.** ARTS **REPRESENTATION** a representation of a human being in a picture or sculpture **5. HUMAN SHAPE SEEN INDISTINCTLY** a human shape seen in outline or indistinctly or that is unidentified **6. SB WITHIN PARTICULAR CONTEXT** an individual, especially with regard to status within a particular context, e.g. in history or in a community or profession ○ *She was a prominent figure in her community.* **7. SB SERVING AS EXAMPLE** sb regarded as having qualities that exemplify a particular role in life (*usually used in combination*) ○ *father figure* **8. WAY SB APPEARS TO OTHERS** the general impression sb makes on other people ○ *He cut a dashing figure on the morning of his wedding.* **9.** PUBL **ILLUSTRATIVE DRAWING OR DIAGRAM** an illustrative drawing or diagram in a book or article **10. SHAPE OR OUTLINE OF STH** sth represented by a shape or outline **11.** GEOM **GEOMETRICAL FORM** any two- or three-dimensional geometrical form consisting of points, lines, curves, or planes **12.** CRAFT **PATTERN OR DESIGN** a pattern or design, especially on cloth or wood **13.** DANCE, ICE SKATING **DANCE OR SKATING ROUTINE** a particular sequence of movements carried out by dancers or ice skaters as part of a dance or routine **14.** MUSIC **GROUP OF MUSICAL NOTES** a short progression of musical notes that produces a single and distinct impression **15.** LOGIC **FORM OF SYLLOGISM** the form of an Aristotelian syllogism as determined by the position of the middle term ■ **figures** *npl.* **MATHEMATICAL CALCULATIONS** calculations involving numbers (*informal*) ■ *v.* **(-ures, -uring, -ured) 1.** *vi.* **BE INCLUDED IN STH** to appear, take part, or be included in sth ○ *did not figure in the outcome* **2.** *vt.* **IMAGINE STH** to form an idea about or envision sth **3.** *vti.* *US* **BE UNSURPRISING** to be or happen as expected ○ *It just figures she'd show up late.* [13thC. Via French from Latin *figura* 'form, shape, figure', from *fingere* 'to make or shape' (source of English *effigy, faint,* and *fiction*).]

figure out *vt.* **1. WORK STH OUT** to find a solution or explanation for sth **2. DECIDE** to reach a decision or conclusion about sth

WORD KEY: SYNONYMS

See Synonyms at ***deduce.***

figured /fíggərd/ *adj.* decorated with a design or pattern

figured bass *n.* a bass part of a musical composition, typically baroque or classical, in which the notes have numbers written above them to indicate which chords to play

figure eight, figure of eight *n.* an outline of the number eight formed with two loops and one continuous line, e.g. in figure skating or aerobatics

figurehead /fíggər hed/ *n.* **1.** SHIPPING **CARVED FIGURE ON BOW OF SHIP** a carving, usually of a full or half-length human figure, built into the bow of a sailing ship **2. SB NOMINALLY IN CHARGE** sb who appears to be the head of an organization or institution but has no real responsibility or authority

figure-hugging *adj.* fitting closely around the body and revealing its shape

figure of merit *n.* a parameter or characteristic of a machine, component, or instrument that is used as a measure of its performance

figure of speech *n.* an expression or use of language in a nonliteral sense in order to achieve a particular effect. Metaphors, similes, and hyperbole are all common figures of speech.

figure skating *n.* a form of competitive skating in which skaters trace patterns on the ice and perform spins, jumps, and other manoeuvres —**figure skater** *n.*

figurine /fíggə reen/ *n.* a small ornamental figure, often of pottery or metal [Mid-19thC. Via French from Italian *figurina* 'small figure', from, ultimately, Latin *figura* (see FIGURE).]

fig wasp *n.* a wasp native to Europe that breeds in caprifigs and pollinates the flowers of wild fig trees. Each species of fig is believed to be pollinated by a different species of wasp. Genus: *Blastophaga.*

figwort /fíg wurt/ (*plural* **-worts** *or* **-wort**) *n.* a tall woodland plant of the snapdragon family that has clusters of small greenish flowers. Genus: *Scrophularia.* [Mid-16thC. From FIG[1], used as a dialect term for haemorrhoids, which it was used to treat.]

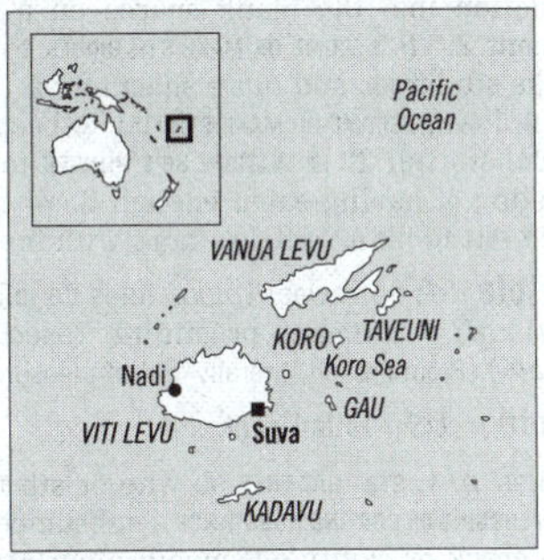

Fiji

Fiji /fééji/ island nation in the southern Pacific Ocean north of New Zealand and east of northern Australia. A British colony from 1874, it gained its independence in 1970. Language: English. Currency: Fijian dollar. Capital: Suva. Population: 792,441 (1997). Area: 18,376 sq. km/7,095 sq. mi. Official name **Republic of Fiji**

Fijian /fee jée ən/ *n.* **1.** LANG **LANGUAGE SPOKEN IN FIJI** a language spoken on the islands of Fiji, belonging to the eastern branch of the Austronesian family of languages. About 400,000 people speak Fijian. **2.** PEOPLES **SB FROM FIJI** sb who was born or brought up on the islands of Fiji, or who has Fijian citizenship —**Fijian** *adj.*

filament /fílləmənt/ *n.* **1. SLENDER STRAND OR FIBRE** a slender strand or fibre of a material **2.** ELEC ENG **WIRE CONDUCTOR IN LIGHT BULB** a thin wire or ribbon that, when an electric current passes through it, acts as the light-producing element in an incandescent bulb or the electron-emitting element in a valve **3.** BOT **FLOWER PART** the stalk that supports the pollen-bearing anther in the male reproductive organ (**stamen**) of a flower. ◊ **anther 4.** BIOL **LONG STRAND OF CELLS** a long strand consisting of similar cells joined end to end, as found, e.g. in certain bacteria and algae [Late 16thC. Via French, or modern Latin *filamentum*, from, ultimately, Latin *filum* 'thread'.] —**filamentary** /fíllə méntəri/ *adj.* —**filamentous** /-téss/ *adj.*

filaria /fi láiri ə/ (*plural* **-ae** /fi láiri ee/ *or* **-a**) *n.* a parasitic nematode worm that is carried as a larva by biting insects and lives as an adult in the blood or tissues of vertebrates, causing filariasis. Family: Filaridae. [Mid-19thC. From modern Latin *Filaria*, former genus name, from Latin *filum* 'thread'.] —**filarial** *adj.* —**filarian** *adj.*

filariasis /fíllə rí əssiss/ *n.* a disease caused by parasitic worms (**filaria**) that inflames and obstructs the lymphatic glands, sometimes resulting in elephantiasis

filature /fílləchər/ *n.* **1. REELING OF SILK FROM COCOONS** the process of reeling silk fibres from cocoons **2. SILK REEL** a reel used in reeling silk fibres **3. SILK FACTORY** a factory for reeling silk fibres [Mid-18thC. Via French from Italian *filatura*, from *filare* 'to spin', from, ultimately, Latin *filum* 'thread'.]

filbert /fílbərt/ (*plural* **-berts** *or* **-bert**) *n.* **1.** FOOD = **hazelnut 2.** = **hazel** [14thC. From Anglo-Norman *philbert*, named after St *Philibert*, whose feast day falls on the 22nd of August, the month hazelnuts begin to ripen.]

filch /filch/ (**filches, filching, filched**) *vt.* to steal sth furtively, usually a small item or amount of little value (*informal*) [13thC. Origin uncertain, perhaps from Old English *fylcian* 'to marshal troops', later changing meaning to 'to attack, to take as booty'.] —**filcher** *n.*

WORD KEY: SYNONYMS

See Synonyms at ***steal.***

file[1] /fīl/ *n.* **1. STORAGE FOR PAPERS** a folder, cabinet, or other container that holds papers for convenient storage and reference **2. ORDERED COLLECTION** a collection of related documents or papers arranged so they can be consulted easily **3.** COMPUT **COMPUTER INFORMATION** a uniquely named collection of program instructions or data stored on a hard drive, disk, or other storage medium and treated as a single entity **4. LINE** a line of people or things standing or moving one behind the other ■ *v.* (**files, filing, filed**) **1.** *vt.* **STORE STH IN ORDER** to arrange and store sth in a file for future reference **2.** *vt.* LAW **SUBMIT STH** to submit sth such as a claim or complaint to the appropriate authority so that it can be put on record **3.** *vi.* LAW **BRING A LAWSUIT** to make a formal application for sth such as a divorce **4.** *vt.* PRESS **SEND IN A NEWS REPORT** to send in a report or story to a newspaper or news agency **5.** *vi.* **MOVE IN LINE** to move in line one behind the other [15thC. Via French *filer* 'to thread on a string' (the original sense in English) from, ultimately, Latin *filum* 'thread' (because documents were hung on pieces of string for easy reference).] —**filer** *n.*

file away *vt.* **1. PUT STH AWAY** to store sth in a file for future reference **2. KEEP STH IN MIND** to take careful note of sth in order to remember it

file[2] /fīl/ *n.* ENG **METAL TOOL** a metal tool, usually long and narrow and with sharpened ridges on one or more of its surfaces, that is used to smooth down or wear away wood or metal ■ *vti.* (**files, filing, filed**) **MAKE STH SMOOTH USING A FILE** to smooth or wear away the surface of sth using a file [Old English *fēol*. Ultimately via a prehistoric Germanic word from an Indo-European base meaning 'to cut or carve', which also produced English *depict* and *pigment.*]

file extension *n.* a combination of characters following the dot after the name of a file created with DOS-based software, certain combinations identifying the file as being of a standardized type

file manager *n.* a computer program that helps to arrange and manipulate files and directories of files

filename /fīl naym/ *n.* a set of characters, sometimes restricted in number, serving as an identifying title for a computer file and often including a file extension

file server *n.* a computer in a network that stores application programs and data files accessed by the other computers in the network

filet *n.* COOK = **fillet** *n.* 1 ■ *vt.* COOK = **fillet** *v.* 1 [Mid-19thC. French form of FILLET.]

filet mignon /fíllay meen yon/ *n.* a small round boneless piece of beef cut from the inside of the loin and usually grilled or fried

filial /fílli əl/ *adj.* **1.** OF CHILDREN TO PARENTS relating or appropriate to a child's relationship with, or feelings towards, his or her parents ○ *filial duty* **2.** GENETICS DESCRIBING FIRST HYBRID GENERATION used to describe the first generation that results from crossing two parental lines [15thC. Directly or via Old French from late Latin *filialis* 'of a son or daughter', from Latin *filius* 'son' and *filia* 'daughter'.] —**filially** *adv.* —**filialness** *n.*

filiate /fílli ayt/ (**-ates, -ating, -ated**) *vt.* to affiliate sb or sth (*formal*)

filiation /fílli áysh'n/ *n.* **1.** PROCESS OF ESTABLISHING PATERNITY the process of determining legally who is the father of a child whose paternity is in dispute **2.** BEING SB'S CHILD the condition of being the child of particular parents (*formal*) **3.** AFFILIATION affiliation (*formal*)

filibeg /fílli beg/, **philibeg** *n. Scotland* a kilt (*literary*) [Mid-18thC. From Scottish Gaelic *feileadh-beag*, literally 'little kilt'.]

filibuster /fílli bustər/ *n.* POL POLITICAL DELAYING TACTIC a tactic such as a long irrelevant speech or several such speeches used to delay or prevent the passage of legislation ■ *vti.* (**-ters, -tering, -tered**) TRY TO BLOCK LEGISLATION WITH A FILIBUSTER to try to stop legislation being passed by making long speeches [Mid-19thC. Via Spanish *filibustero* from, ultimately, Dutch *vrijbuiter* 'pirate' (source of English *freebooter*).] —**filibusterer** *n.* —**filibusterism** *n.* —**filibusterous** *adj.*

filicide /fílli sīd/ *n.* (*formal*) **1.** KILLING OF OWN CHILD the killing by a parent of a son or daughter **2.** KILLER OF OWN CHILD a parent who kills his or her own son or daughter [Mid-17thC. From Latin *filius* 'son' or *filia* 'daughter'.] —**filicidal** /fílli sīd'l/ *adj.*

filiform /fílli fawrm/ *adj.* BIOL long, thin, and fine like a thread [Mid-18thC. From Latin *filum* 'thread' + FORM.]

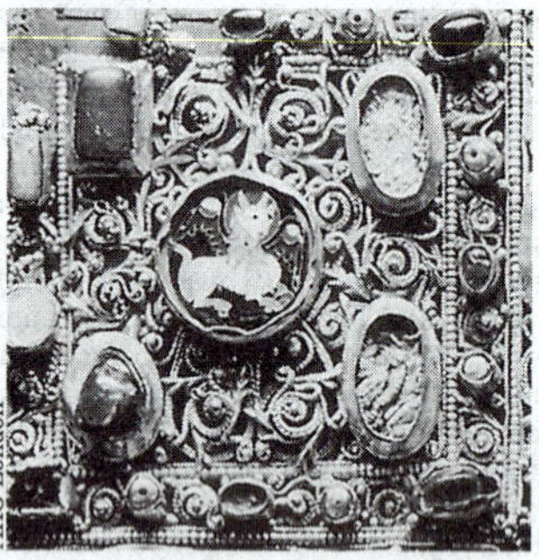

AKG London

Filigree: Detail of decorative filigree and jewelled medieval book cover (1225–30)

filigree /fílli gree/ *n.* **1.** LACY METAL ORNAMENTATION delicate decorative openwork made from thin twisted wire in silver, gold, or another metal **2.** DELICATE WORK a delicate ornamental tracery ■ *adj.* IN A DELICATE PATTERN made in a delicate ornamental openwork design ■ *vt.* (**-grees, -greeing, -greed**) FORM STH INTO A DELICATE PATTERN to form sth into a delicate ornamental openwork design [Late 17thC. An alteration of French *filigrane* 'filigree' from Italian *filigrana*, from Latin *filum* 'thread' + *granum* 'grain'.]

filing /fíling/ *n.* a tiny particle or shaving of metal, such as might have been removed with a file (*often used in the plural*) ○ *iron filings*

filing cabinet *n.* a piece of office furniture containing drawers for storing files

Filipino /fílli peenō/, **Pilipino** *adj.* **Filipino, Philippine** OF THE PHILIPPINES relating to or typical of the Philippines or their people or culture ■ *n.* (*plural* **-nos**) **1.** LANG OFFICIAL LANGUAGE OF THE PHILIPPINES the official language of the Philippines, an Austronesian language based on Tagalog. Over 15,000,000 people speak Filipino. **2.** PEOPLES SB FROM THE PHILIPPINES sb who was born or brought up in the Philippines, or who has Philippine citizenship

fill /fil/ *v.* (**fills, filling, filled**) **1.** *vti.* MAKE STH FULL OR BECOME FULL to make a container full, or become full ○ *The bath filled rapidly.* **2.** *vt.* TAKE UP ALL THE SPACE to take up all or most of the space inside or cover the whole or most of the surface area of sth ○ *the room was filled with light* **3.** *vt.* COVER A BLANK AREA to cover a page or a blank space on a page with writing or drawing **4.** *vt.* BECOME ABUNDANT to become present and very noticeable throughout sth ○ *The scent of spring filled the air.* **5.** *vt.* MAKE SB FEEL STH POWERFULLY to cause sb to experience a strong emotion, usually to the exclusion of all others ○ *The news filled me with dread.* **6.** *vt.* CLOSE UP A HOLE to plug a hole, crack, or cavity in sth **7.** *vt.* MEET A NEED to satisfy a need or requirement ○ *The retreat filled her need for solitude.* **8.** *vt.* OCCUPY FREE TIME to occupy a period of time with an activity ○ *They filled their days with DIY and gardening until she returned.* **9.** *vt.* POL HOLD OFFICE to hold a job or office and carry out the duties associated with it **10.** *vt.* CHOOSE SB to elect or appoint sb to a job or position **11.** *vt.* COOK PUT A FILLING INTO STH to put a type of food into sth such as a cake or sandwich as its filling **12.** *vt.* CONSTR ADD STH TO RAISE A SURFACE LEVEL to build up the surface of sth with earth, stones, or other materials until it reaches a desired level **13.** *vti.* NAUT POWER A SAIL WITH WIND to stretch a sail and make it bulge out, or bulge out under the pressure of the wind ■ *n.* **1.** PLENTY OF STH a sufficient or excessive quantity of sth ○ *I've had my fill of his complaints.* **2.** ENOUGH TO MAKE A CONTAINER FULL enough of sth to fill a container, or the act of filling a container **3.** CONSTR MATERIAL TO RAISE A SURFACE material, e.g. earth or stones, used to build up the surface of sth to a desired level **4.** MUSIC IMPROVISED MUSIC music improvised to fill designated spaces in a jazz or other musical score [Old English *fyllan*, ultimately from a prehistoric Germanic word]

fill in *v.* **1.** *vt.* COMPLETE THE BLANK SPACES IN STH to write information into the blank spaces on a form or document. US term **fill out** *v.* 1 **2.** *vt.* COLOUR A BLANK SPACE ON STH to cover a blank space on sth with colouring or shading **3.** *vt.* PLUG A CAVITY AND MAKE THE SURFACE LEVEL to put material into a cavity in a surface to make the surface level **4.** *vt.* OCCUPY TIME to spend a period of time that would otherwise be unoccupied in an activity **5.** *vi.* SUBSTITUTE FOR SB to act as a substitute for sb **6.** *vt.* GIVE SB INFORMATION to supply sb with information about sth **7.** *vt.* BEAT SB UP to subject sb to a beating (*slang*)

fill out *v.* **1.** *vt.* COMPLETE THE BLANK SPACES IN STH to write information into the blank spaces on a form or document **2.** *vti.* BECOME OR MAKE STH BIGGER to become or make sth larger and more substantial

fill up *v.* **1.** *vti.* BECOME OR MAKE STH FULL to become full, or make sth full **2.** *vt.* SATISFY SB'S HUNGER to give sb the feeling of having eaten enough **3.** *vi.* CARS MAKE FUEL TANK FULL to fill a vehicle's tank with fuel

fille de joie /fee də zhwaa/ (*plural* **filles de joie** /fee də zhwaa/) *n.* a woman prostitute (*used euphemistically*) [From French, literally 'girl of pleasure']

filled gold *n.* US = **rolled gold**

filler /fíllər/ *n.* **1.** STH THAT FILLS sb who or sth that fills sth **2.** PLUGGING OR COATING SUBSTANCE a substance used to plug a crack or cavity or smooth a surface before painting or varnishing **3.** SUBSTANCE ADDED FOR BULK a substance such as sizing that is used to fill spaces or add bulk or strength to a material **4.** PRESS, BROADCAST LESS IMPORTANT MATERIAL sth, often relatively unimportant, added to fill space, e.g. in a newspaper or between items in a broadcast or performance **5.** TOBACCO FILLING the tobacco inside a cigar or cigarette **6.** INDUST PADDING a material such as cotton or down that is used to stuff sth such as a quilt or toy

fillér /fíllair/ *n.* **1.** HUNGARIAN CURRENCY UNIT a subunit of currency in Hungary one hundred of which make a forint. See table at **currency 2.** MONEY COIN WORTH A FILLÉR a coin worth one fillér [Early 20thC. From Hungarian.]

filler cap *n.* = **petrol cap**

fillet /fíllit/ *n.* **1.** COOK BONELESS PORTION OF FISH OR MEAT a boneless portion cut from a fish, a poultry breast, or the rib area of beef, lamb, or pork **2.** ACCESSORIES RIBBON WORN AROUND THE HEAD a ribbon or narrow band of fabric worn around the head across the forehead, as an ornament or to hold back the hair **3.** ARCHIT FLAT NARROW MOULDING a raised or sunken ornamental surface set between larger surfaces **4.** PRINTING DECORATIVE LINE ON THE COVER OF BOOK a thin decorative line impressed onto the cover of a book, or the tool used to make it ■ *vt.* (**-lets, -leting, -leted**) **1.** FOOD CUT A FILLET FROM STH to cut and prepare boneless portions of fish, poultry, or meat **2.** USE A FILLET AS BINDING OR DECORATION to bind hair or decorate a surface with a fillet [14thC. Via Old French *filet*, from, ultimately, Latin *filum* 'thread'.]

fill-in *n.* a temporary replacement or substitute for sb

filling /fílling/ *n.* **1.** DENT PLUG FOR A DECAYED TOOTH a plug made of metal or composite material, used to fill a cavity in a decayed tooth **2.** GETTING STH FILLED the process or an instance of having sth such as a cavity in a tooth filled **3.** STH USED TO FILL STH a substance or material used to fill the space inside sth, pad it, or add bulk to it **4.** FOOD FOOD MIXTURE PUT INSIDE STH a food mixture that is put inside sth else such as a pie, pastry case, or sandwich **5.** TEXTILES THREADS GOING ACROSS FABRIC the horizontal threads or yarn in a woven fabric ■ *adj.* SATISFYING HUNGER leaving sb with the feeling of having eaten enough

filling station *n.* a petrol station

fillip /fíllip/ *n.* **1.** FEELING OF ENCOURAGEMENT sth that stimulates or encourages sth or sb **2.** SNAPPING MOVEMENT OF THE FINGERTIP AGAINST THE THUMB a snapping of the tip of one of the fingers against the ball of the thumb in order to make a sound or to propel a small object ■ *vt.* (**-lips, -liping, -liped**) **1.** PROPEL STH WITH A FILLIP to strike or propel sth by snapping the fingertip against the ball of the thumb **2.** GIVE SB OR STH AN INCENTIVE to provide a stimulus or encouragement to sb or sth [15thC. An imitation of the sound of flicking or snapping the fingers.]

fill light *n.* in photography and film-making, a secondary source of light used to eliminate, reduce, or soften shadows

Fillmore /fíl mawr/, **Millard** (1800–74) US statesman and 13th president of the United States. A member of the Whig Party, he served as vice president (1849–50) before assuming the presidency (1850–53) upon the death of Zachary Taylor.

fill-up *n.* a filling of sth, especially a vehicle's fuel tank

filly /fílli/ (*plural* **-lies**) *n.* **1.** ZOOL YOUNG FEMALE HORSE a female horse under four years of age **2.** OFFENSIVE TERM an offensive term for a young woman or girl (*dated informal offensive*) [15thC. From Old Norse *fylja*. Ultimately from a prehistoric Germanic word that is also the ancestor of English *foal*.]

film /film/ *n.* **1.** CINEMA SERIES OF MOVING PICTURES ON SCREEN a series of real or fictional events recorded by a camera and projected onto a screen as a sequence of moving pictures, usually with an accompanying soundtrack. US term **movie 2.** CINEMA MOTION PICTURES COLLECTIVELY films collectively, considered as a medium for recording events, a form of entertainment, or an art form **3.** PHOTOGRAPHY COATED STRIP FOR TAKING PICTURES a thin translucent strip or sheet of cellulose coated with an emulsion sensitive to light, used in a camera to take still or moving pictures **4.** INDUST VERY THIN SHEET OF STH material, especially a plastic, in the form of a very thin, flexible, and usually translucent or transparent sheet, often used for wrapping things **5.** THIN LAYER a thin coating of a substance such as dust, liquid, or ice covering the surface of sth **6.** STH MAKING A VIEW HAZY a thin haze or mist, or sth similar that blurs sb's view ■ **films** *npl.* CINEMA FILM INDUSTRY the motion-picture industry (*informal*) ■ *v.* (**films, filming, filmed**) **1.** *vt.* PHOTOGRAPHY TAKE PICTURES OF STH to record sb or sth on film **2.** *vti.* CINEMA MAKE A MOTION PICTURE to make or be involved in the making of a motion picture **3.** *vt.* CINEMA MAKE FILM OF STH to make a motion picture of a book, story, or event **4.** *vi.* CINEMA BE GOOD FOR FILMING to be a suitable subject for cinematic treatment ○ *a story that would film well* **5.** *vt.* COVER WITH A THIN LAYER to cover the surface of sth with a thin coating of a substance [Old English *filmen* 'membrane, skin', ultimately via a prehistoric Germanic word from an Indo-European base that also produced English *pelt*]

film over *vi.* to become covered with a thin or misty layer of sth

film badge *n.* a piece of photographic film incorporated into a badge and used to register the wearer's exposure to nuclear radiation

filmgoer /fílm gō ər/ *n.* sb who goes to a cinema to see films, especially on a regular basis. US term **moviegoer**

filmic /fílmik/ *adj.* characteristic or reminiscent of a cinema film, especially in the techniques used to tell a story or describe a scene —**filmically** *adv.*

film library *n.* a large collection of cinema films or newsreels used as an archive or for hire

filmmaker /fílm maykər/ *n.* sb who produces or directs cinema films —**filmmaking** *n.*

film noir /fílm nwaár/ (*plural* **films noirs** /fílm nwaár/) *n.* a motion picture of a type popular in the 1940s and 1950s, often filmed in urban settings with extensive use of shadows, cynical in outlook, and featuring antiheroes [Mid-20thC. From French, literally 'black film'.]

filmography /film óggrəfi/ (*plural* **-phies**) *n.* a list of the motion pictures made by a particular actor or director, or on a particular subject [Mid-20thC. A blend of FILM and BIBLIOGRAPHY.]

filmsetting /fílm setting/ *n.* a typesetting process that involves projecting the characters that are to be printed onto photographic film and then making printing plates from the film. US term **photocomposition** —**filmset** *vt.* —**filmsetter** *n.*

film star *n.* a well-known film actor or actress. US term **movie star**

filmstrip /fílm strip/ *n.* a length of developed photographic film containing a series of still images to be projected on a screen

filmy /fílmi/ (**-ier, -iest**) *adj.* **1.** LIGHT AND AIRY consisting or made of very thin translucent material **2.** COVERED WITH A FILM covered or misted over with a thin layer of sth —**filmily** *adv.* —**filminess** *n.*

filmy fern *n.* a small fern that grows in humid regions, has translucent leaves, and forms sheets on moist rocks. Genus: *Hymenophyllum.*

filo /feélō/, **filo pastry** *n.* very thin sheets of pastry dough used to make papery crisp small pastries or large dishes, used especially in Greek cooking. US term **phyllo** [Mid-20thC. From Greek *phullo* 'leaf'.]

FILO /fī lō/ *abbr.* ACCT first in, last out

fils[1] /filss/ (*plural* **filses** *or* **fils**) *n.* MONEY **1.** ARAB CURRENCY UNIT a subunit of currency in Iraq, Bahrain, Jordan, Kuwait, and Yemen, one hundred of which are equivalent to one riyal. See table at **currency 2.** COIN WORTH A FILS a coin worth one fils [Late 19thC. From Arabic *fals*, a small copper coin.]

fils[2] /feess/ *n.* in France and French-speaking countries, a word used after a man's or boy's surname to distinguish him from his father of the same name ○ *Henri Dupont fils.* ◊ **père** [Late 19thC. From French, 'son'.]

filter /fíltər/ *n.* **1.** STRAINING DEVICE a device made of or containing a porous material used to collect particles from a liquid or gas passing through it **2.** POROUS MATERIAL USED FOR STRAINING any porous layer or material such as sand, paper, or cloth, used in or as a filter **3.** PHOTOGRAPHY TINTED SCREEN a tinted glass or dyed gelatine screen placed on a camera lens to reduce light intensity, exclude some types of light, control the rendering of colour, or distort an image **4.** ELECTRON ENG DEVICE RESTRICTING THE PASSAGE OF FREQUENCIES an acoustic, electric, electronic, or optical device, instrument, or computer program that allows the passage of some frequencies or digital elements and blocks others **5.** = **filter tip** *n.* 1 **6.** TRANSP DIRECTIONAL TRAFFIC SIGNAL an additional traffic signal at a junction, in the form of a green arrow, to indicate that vehicles may turn left or right while traffic going straight ahead is halted ■ *v.* (**-ters, -tering, -tered**) **1.** *vt.* PASS STH THROUGH A FILTER to put sth such as a fluid, light, or electrical impulses through a filter to remove or recover sth **2.** *vi.* PASS THROUGH STH to seep or pass through a filter or sth that is intended to act as a barrier ○ *The sunlight filtered in through the shutters.* **3.** *vi.* TRICKLE to move or pass slowly and gradually ○ *People filtered into the auditorium.* **4.** *vti.* TRANSP TURN WHILE TRAFFIC AHEAD HALTED to turn, or allow traffic to turn, right or left at a junction while the traffic going straight ahead is halted [14thC. Via Old French *filtre* 'felt' (used for filtering liquids, the original sense in English), from medieval Latin *filtrum*. Ultimately, from a prehistoric Germanic word that also produced English *felt*.] —**filterer** *n.* —**filterless** *adj.*

filterable /fíltərəb'l/, **filtrable** /fíltrəb'l/ *adj.* capable of being passed through a filter —**filterability** /fíltərə bíllәti/ *n.*

filter bed *n.* a thick layer of sand, gravel, clinker, or other filtering material in a tank, used to remove sewage or other impurities from liquids

filter cake *n.* a deposit of semisolids or solids that are separated out and deposited between layers of filtering material after a fluid has been passed through them

filter coffee *n.* **1.** COFFEE PASSED THROUGH FILTER coffee made by passing hot water through finely ground coffee held in a filter made of paper, cloth, or wire mesh. US term **drip coffee 2.** GROUND COFFEE BEANS coffee beans ground to the right consistency for making filter coffee

filter-feeder *n.* an aquatic animal such as a clam, sponge, or baleen whale that feeds on particles or small organisms that it filters from the water —**filter-feeding** *n.*

filter paper *n.* a type of porous paper used as or in a filter

filter tip *n.* **1.** FILTERING DEVICE ON A CIGARETTE a small cylindrical mouthpiece made of a dense porous material attached to the end of a cigarette to remove tar and other impurities from the smoke **2.** FILTERED CIGARETTE a cigarette with a filter tip —**filter-tipped** *adj.*

filth /filth/ *n.* **1.** FOUL DIRT dirt or refuse that is disgusting or excessive **2.** MORALLY OBJECTIONABLE MATERIAL sth considered extremely morally objectionable or obscene, e.g. coarse language or explicit descriptions or depictions of sexual activity **3.** POLICE an offensive term for the police (*slang insult*) [Old English *fȳð*, ultimately from a prehistoric Germanic word that is also the ancestor of English *foul*]

filthy /fílthi/ (**-ier, -iest**) *adj.* **1.** EXTREMELY DIRTY extremely or disgustingly dirty ○ *Your hands are filthy!* **2.** MORALLY OBJECTIONABLE considered extremely morally objectionable or obscene **3.** DESPICABLE used to express contempt or strong disapproval (*informal*) ○ *a filthy liar* **4.** UNPLEASANT extremely unpleasant (*informal*) ■ *adv.* VERY to an extreme degree (*informal*) ○ *filthy rich* —**filthily** *adv.* —**filthiness** *n.*

WORD KEY: SYNONYMS

See Synonyms at ***dirty.***

filtrable *adj.* = **filterable**

filtrate /fíl trayt/ *n.* FILTERED MATERIAL the material that emerges from a filtering process, usually a liquid or gas from which impurities have been removed ■ *vti.* (**-trates, -trating, -trated**) PASS THROUGH A FILTER to pass through or put sth through a filter [Early 17thC. From modern Latin *filtrat-*, past participle stem of *filtrare* 'to filter', from medieval Latin *filtrum* (see FILTER).]

filtration /fil tráysh'n/ *n.* the process of passing through or putting sth through a filter

filum /fíləm/ (*plural* **-la** /-lə/) *n.* a fine part or structure of a living organism that is long and thin like a thread [Mid-19thC. From Latin, 'thread, filament, fibre'.]

FIMBRA /fímbrə/ *abbr.* Financial Intermediaries, Managers, and Brokers Regulatory Association

fimbria /fímbri ə/ (*plural* **-ae** /-ee/) *n.* ANAT a fringed border or part in the body, e.g. that found at the entrance to the Fallopian tubes [Mid-18thC. From Latin, 'border, fringe'.] —**fimbrial** *adj.*

fimbriate /fímbri ət/, **fimbriated** /-aytid/ *adj.* used to describe parts of organisms having a fringed border [15thC. From Latin *fimbriatus* 'fringed', from *fimbria* 'border, fringe'.] —**fimbriation** /fímbri áysh'n/ *n.*

fin /fin/ *n.* **1.** ZOOL PART OF A FISH USED FOR MOTION a flexible organ, sometimes paddle-shaped, fan-shaped, or triangular, extending from the body of a fish or aquatic animal and helping to balance it or propel it through the water **2.** SHIPPING PART ATTACHED TO THE HULL OF SUBMARINE a wing-shaped often movable blade attached low on the hull of a vessel such as a submarine that helps to control and stabilize it **3.** AIR UPRIGHT PART OF AIRCRAFT'S TAIL a fixed vertical surface at the tail of an aircraft giving stability and to which the rudder is attached **4.** AIR, AEROSP STABILIZING STRUCTURE ON ROCKET OR MISSILE any small flat fixed structure extending from the body of a rocket, missile, or aircraft, often near the tail, to give stability in flight **5.** RIB ON A HEATING DEVICE a flat metal part projecting from a heating mechanism such as a radiator that helps to increase the transfer of heat to the surrounding air **6.** SWIMMING = **flipper 7.** CARS DECORATIVE EXTENSION ON A CAR BODY an ornamental extension on the body of a motor vehicle, especially on the rear wing ■ *vi.* (**fins, finning, finned**) SWIM USING FINS to swim or beat the water with fins, or show a fin above water [Old English *fin(n)*. Ultimately from a prehistoric Germanic word that probably came from Latin *pinna* 'feather, wing' (source of English *pin, pinion,* and *pinnacle*).] —**finned** *adj.*

FIN *abbr.* Finland

fin. *abbr.* **1.** finance **2.** financial **3.** finish

Fin. *abbr.* **1.** Finland **2.** Finnish

finable /fínəb'l/ *adj.* subject to or punishable by a fine

finagle /fi náyg'l/ (**-gles, -gling, -gled**) *vti.* to trick, cheat, or manipulate sb in order to obtain or achieve sth (*informal*) ○ *He finagled his way out of the difficulty.* [Early 20thC. Probably from dialectal *fainaigue*, of unknown origin.] —**finagler** *n.*

final /fín'l/ *adj.* **1.** LAST last of a number or series of similar things ○ *a final reminder* **2.** ALLOWING NO CHANGE conclusive and allowing no further discussion ○ *the editor's decision is final* **3.** ENDING occurring at the end of sth ○ *the final curtain* ■ *n.* END OF A SERIES the last and most important in a series of sporting or other contests that decides the winner of a tournament or competition ■ **finals** *npl.* **1.** SPORTS LAST DECISIVE ROUNDS OF A TOURNAMENT the last decisive rounds of a knockout tournament or competition during which the winners of previous rounds play each other **2.** EDUC EXAMINATIONS AT THE END OF A UNIVERSITY COURSE the examinations that take place at the end of a course of study at university or studies for a professional qualification [14thC. Directly or via French from Latin *finalis* 'last', from *finis* 'final moment, end' (source of English *finance* and *finish*).]

final accounts *npl.* the set of accounts produced by a business at the end of its accounting year

final approach *n.* the last stage of an aircraft's descent before landing, from its turning into line with the runway to the procedures immediately preceding touchdown

final cause *n.* the ultimate goal towards which a process is directed

final cut *n.* the approved and edited version of a film prior to its being released for viewing by the public

finale /fi naáli/ *n.* **1.** THEATRE FINAL THEATRICAL NUMBER a scene or number that brings a stage performance or an act of a performance to an end **2.** MUSIC FINAL MOVEMENT a final movement or section of a musical composition **3.** FINAL EVENT IN A SERIES an event that is the last or climactic event in a series [Mid-18thC. Via Italian from Latin *finalis* (see FINAL).]

finalise *vt.* = **finalize**

finalism /fín'lizəm/ *n.* the belief or proposition that all events are determined by their final causes —**finalistic** /fínə lístik/ *adj.*

finalist /fín'list/ *n.* sb who has qualified to take part in the finals of a tournament or competition

finality /fī nálləti/ (*plural* **-ties**) *n.* **1.** QUALITY OF BEING FINAL the quality, state, or condition of being concluded or decided, permitting no further progress or development ○ *he spoke with an air of finality* **2.** FINAL ACTION an act, belief, or statement that is final

finalize /fínə līz/ (**-izes, -izing, -ized**), **finalise** (**-ises, -ising, -ised**) *v.* **1.** *vti.* PUT STH INTO FINAL FORM to bring sth to a point at which everything has been agreed upon and arranged **2.** *vt.* COMPLETE STH to complete an agreement, sale, or other transaction —**finalization** /fínə lī záysh'n/ *n.* —**finalizer** /fínə līzər/ *n.*

finally /fīn'li/ *adv.* 1. AT LAST after a long period of time or a long delay and often after previous unsuccessful attempts ○ *So you've finally decided to ask her out, have you?* 2. DEFINITIVELY in a way that rules out further continuance, change, or discussion ○ *The venue won't be finally decided until the next meeting.* 3. AS LAST IN THE SERIES as the last in a series of things or actions ○ *We visited Belgium, Holland, Germany, and finally Switzerland.* 4. AS THE LAST THING TO BE SAID used to introduce the last in a series of things said by sb ○ *Finally, I'd like to thank all of you for coming here tonight.*

Final Solution, final solution *n.* the plan to murder systematically all the Jews of Europe, conceived and put into action by the Nazis during World War II [Translation of German *Endlösung*]

finance /fī nanss, fi nánss/ *n.* 1. CONTROL OF MONEY the business or art of managing the monetary resources of an organization, country, or individual ○ *high finance* 2. MONEY NECESSARY TO DO STH the money necessary to do sth, especially to fund a project ■ **finances** *npl.* THE MONEY SB HAS the money at the disposal of a person, organization, or country ○ *It'll depend on the state of my finances at the end of the month.* ■ *vt.* **(-nances, -nancing, -nanced)** PROVIDE MONEY FOR STH to raise or provide the money required for sth or by sb [14thC. From French, from *finer* 'to end, settle' (the original sense in English), from, ultimately, Latin *finis* 'end'. Its present-day monetary connotation derived from the notion of settling a debt.] —**financeable** /fī nánssəb'l/ *adj.*

finance bill *n.* an act passed by a legislature to raise or provide money for public expenditure

finance company, finance house *n.* a business enterprise that loans money to individuals or companies against collateral, especially to buy items on hire purchase

financial /fī nánsh'l, fi-/ *adj.* 1. CONNECTED WITH MONEY relating to or involving money or finance 2. *ANZ* WELL OFF having enough or plenty of money to dispose of (*informal*) ○ *We're both working, so we're financial at the moment.* —**financially** *adv.*

Financial Times Industrial Ordinary Share Index *n.* an index of prices on the London Stock Exchange based on the average price of thirty shares. It is produced by the *Financial Times.*

Financial Times Stock Exchange 100 Index *n.* full form of **FTSE 100 Index**

financial year *n.* a 12-month period at the end of which all accounts are completed in order to furnish a statement of a company's, organization's, or government's financial condition. A financial year does not necessarily correspond to a calendar year, e.g. for tax purposes a year runs from 6 April to 5 April the following year. US term **fiscal year**

financier /fī nánssi ər, fi-/ *n.* sb who is practised or skilled in financial matters and has considerable personal wealth [Early 17thC. From French, formed from *finance* (see FINANCE).]

finback /fín bak/ *n.* a large baleen whale that has a prominent dorsal fin. Latin name: *Balaenoptera physalus.* ◊ **rorqual**

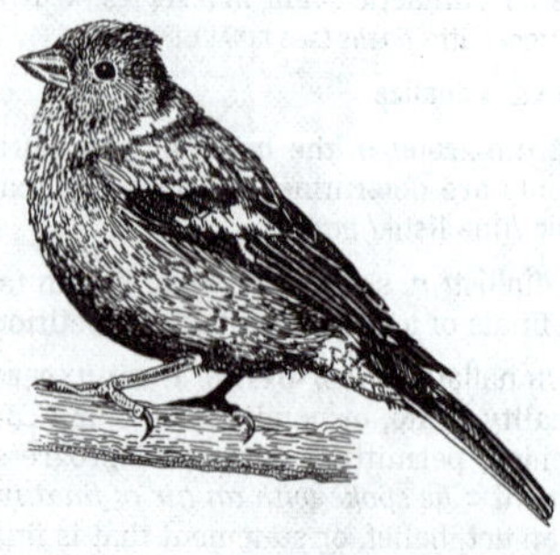

Finch

finch /finch/ *n.* a small songbird that has a short broad seed-eating bill and colourful plumage in males. Family: Fringillidae. [Old English *finc*, from prehistoric Germanic]

Finch /finch/, **Peter** (1916–77) British actor. A stage and screen performer, he received a posthumous Academy Award for his role in *Network* (1976). Full name **Peter George Frederick Ingle Finch**

find /fīnd/ *v.* **(finds, finding, found** /fownd/) 1. *vt.* DISCOVER STH to discover sth or sb after a search ○ *He was found wandering a mile from his home.* 2. *vt.* GET STH BACK to recover sth after losing it ○ *I can't find my car keys.* 3. *vt.* DISCOVER STH FOR FIRST TIME to realize, understand, or locate sth for the first time, especially by studying or observing ○ *We have to find answers to the problem of global warming.* 4. *vt.* DISCOVER STH ACCIDENTALLY to notice or come across sb or sth by chance ○ *I found my glasses under the table.* 5. *vt.* EXPERIENCE STH to notice or experience sth personally ○ *They found great comfort in their work.* ○ *I think you'll find them easy to get along with.* 6. *vt.* MANAGE TO GET STH to make a special effort to gather sth together or summon sth up ○ *I don't know where we'll find the money.* 7. *vt.* REACH GOAL to succeed in reaching sth aimed for ○ *He has finally found his true form as a world-class tennis player.* 8. *vt.* SCI RECORD AS OCCURRING to observe sth such as a natural species as existing or occurring (*often passive*) ○ *This species is found all across the continent.* 9. *vti.* LAW REACH A VERDICT to decide about sth or sb at the end of a legal procedure, or announce the decision reached ○ *The jury found for the plaintiff.* 10. *vt.* SUPPLY NEED to bring or provide sth that is necessary for a process to occur ○ *You will need to find your own transport and equipment for the job.* 11. *vr.* BECOME CONSCIOUS OF YOUR OWN CONDITION to become aware of being in a particular place or state ○ *He found himself in an empty street.* 12. *vr.* MAKE DECISIONS ABOUT YOUR OWN LIFE to become more self-aware and self-motivated (*informal*) ○ *She finally found herself and became a successful artist.* ■ *n.* NEW DISCOVERY sth noteworthy or valuable that has been found, or sb who is talented and is brought to public attention ○ *a real find* [Old English *findan*. Ultimately from an Indo-European word meaning 'to tread or go', which is also the ancestor of English *path*, *peripatetic*, and *pontiff*.] —**findable** *adj.*

find out *v.* 1. *vti.* DISCOVER DETAILS to get to know sth, especially by asking sb or searching in an appropriate source, or just by chance ○ *I don't know how they found out about the proposed merger.* 2. *vt.* DETECT WRONGDOING to detect and expose an offence ○ *He was quickly found out and his lies exposed.*

finder /fīndər/ *n.* 1. SB FINDING THINGS sb who or sth that locates things 2. ASTRON SMALL TELESCOPE ATTACHED TO LARGER TELESCOPE a small wide-angle telescope attached parallel to the optical axis of a larger telescope to help locate celestial objects

fin de siècle /fáN də syéklə/ *n.* the final years of the 19th century, characterized as being a time of decadence and self-doubt (*hyphenated before a noun*) [From French, literally 'end of the century']

finding /fīnding/ *n.* 1. RESEARCH RESULT a piece of information obtained from an investigation, especially scientific research 2. LAW VERDICT a conclusion that is reached and recorded at the end of a judicial or other formal inquiry ■ *npl.* *US* MATERIALS FOR CRAFTWORK small articles or tools used in making craftwork, e.g. metal clips used on earrings

fine[1] /fīn/ *adj.* 1. QUITE WELL OR SATISFACTORY in a good, acceptable, or comfortable condition (*informal*) ○ *The patient is doing fine.* 2. NOT COARSE made up of tiny particles ○ *fine sand* 3. SUNNY with sunny and clear skies ○ *a fine morning* 4. THIN very thin, sharp, or delicate ○ *fine features* ○ *fine hair* 5. GOOD-LOOKING very good to look at ○ *a fine view of the valley* 6. OUTSTANDING far better than the average ○ *a fine wine* 7. UNPLEASANT extremely unsuitable or undesirable (*informal; used ironically*) ○ *This is a fine mess!* 8. SPURIOUSLY IMPRESSIVE sounding or looking good, but probably just for show (*used ironically*) ○ *nothing but fine gestures* 9. DELICATELY FORMED showing special skill, detail, or intricacy, especially in artistic work ○ *fine detail* 10. SMALL AND DELICATE set very closely and carefully together ○ *fine stitching* 11. VERY SUBTLE so particular or small that it may hardly be noticeable ○ *a maze of fine legal detail* ○ *a fine distinction* 12. EXTREMELY PURE with any or most impurities removed, especially in a precious metal ■ *adv.* 1. WELL very well (*informal*) ○ *It works just fine.* 2. INTO SMALL PIECES into tiny or delicate bits ○ *Chop the onions very fine.* ■ *v.* **(fines, fining, fined)** 1. *vt.* SHARPEN to make sth thinner or sharper (*technical*) 2. *vti.* PURIFY to purify beer or wine [13thC. From French *fin*, from, ultimately, Latin *finire* 'to finish' (see FINISH). The underlying sense is of sth finished.] —**fineness** *n.*

WORD KEY: ORIGIN

The Latin word *finire* from which **fine** is derived is also the source of English *affinity, confine, define, final, finance, finesse, finish, finite, paraffin,* and *refine.*

fine[2] /fīn/ *n.* LAW CASH PAID AS PUNISHMENT a sum of money that sb is ordered to pay for breaking a law or rule ■ *vt.* **(fines, fining, fined)** LAW PUNISH BY IMPOSING A PAYMENT to take a fixed amount of money from sb who has broken a rule or a law [13thC. Via French *fin* from Latin *finis* 'end', used in medieval Latin to denote a sum to be paid on completion of legal proceedings.]

fine[3] /feen/ *n.* = **fine champagne**

fine[4] /féé nay/ *n.* the place on a music score that shows where the piece finishes after a repeated section, or the symbol that marks the place [Late 18thC. From Italian, from Latin *finis* 'end'.]

fine art *n.* 1. ARTS CREATION OF BEAUTIFUL OBJECTS artistic work that is meant to be appreciated for its own sake, rather than to serve some useful function 2. EDUC COLLEGE COURSE IN ART a course of study designed to teach students practical artistic skills as well as the theory and history of art 3. ARTS PURE ART any art form, e.g. painting, sculpture, architecture, drawing, or engraving, that is considered to have purely aesthetic value (*often used in the plural*) 4. IMPRESSIVELY DETAILED TECHNIQUE sth that requires great skill, talent, or precision (*informal*) ○ *the fine art of public speaking*

fine champagne *n.* a liqueur brandy made in the Champagne region of France [Mid-19thC. From French *fine champagne* 'fine (brandy from) Champagne'.]

fine chemical *n.* a chemical product that is made in relatively small quantities and is typically high in cost, e.g. a flavouring or vitamin

fine-grained, fine-grain *adj.* formed with a smooth, even, or closely-patterned grain

fine leg *n.* 1. POSITION ON CRICKET PITCH in cricket, a fielding position behind the batsman and close to the ball's line of flight, on the side opposite to the way the batsman's body is facing 2. FIELDER AT FINE LEG a fielder in cricket who has been positioned at fine leg

finely /fīnli/ *adv.* 1. INTO SMALL PIECES into small, thin, or delicate pieces 2. SKILFULLY in a careful, delicate, or sensitive way ○ *an actor finely tuned to her audience's reactions* ○ *finely wrought*

fine print *n.* BUSINESS = **small print**

finery[1] /fīnəri/ *n.* clothing, jewellery, or accessories that are especially dressy and smart, usually worn on special occasions [Late 17thC. Formed from FINE, modelled on BRAVERY.]

finery[2] /fīnəri/ (*plural* **-ies**) *n.* a furnace that converts cast iron into wrought iron [Late 16thC. From French *finerie*, from Old French *finer* 'to refine'.]

fines herbes /feénz airb/ *npl.* a mixture of finely chopped herbs used to flavour a dish [From French, literally 'fine herbs']

finespun /fīn spún/ *adj.* spun or stretched out thinly

finesse /fi néss/ *n.* 1. PHYSICAL SKILL elegant ability and dexterity ○ *As a top-flight tennis star, she made up in finesse what she lacked in power.* 2. TACTFUL TREATMENT a delicate and skilful approach in dealing with a troublesome situation 3. BRIDGE TACTIC IN BRIDGE in bridge, an attempt to win a trick with a lower-value card while holding a higher card not in sequence, hoping that an opponent cannot play an intervening card ■ *vti.* **(-nesses, -nessing, -nessed)** 1. BRIDGE TRY WINNING A TRICK WITH A LOWER CARD in bridge, to attempt to win a trick with a lower-value card while holding a higher card not in sequence, hoping that an opponent does not have an intervening card 2. BE TACTFUL to use a delicate and skilful approach, or achieve sth by delicate handling (*literary*) [Mid-16thC. From French, literally 'fineness', from *fin* (see FINE[1]). The word originally denoted purity, especially of metals, or delicacy.]

fine structure *n.* the separation of light of particular wavelengths produced by atoms or molecules into two or more very similar wavelengths, caused by the interaction of particular quantum mechanical properties

fine-tooth comb, **fine-toothed comb** *n.* **1.** TOOL FOR COMBING THOROUGHLY a comb with very narrow tightly-set teeth **2.** DETAILED APPROACH a thorough approach to an investigation or search, examining every detail ○ *went over the figures with a fine-tooth comb but failed to find the error*

fine-tune (**fine-tunes**, **fine-tuning**, **fine-tuned**) *v.* **1.** *vt.* IMPROVE ENGINE PERFORMANCE OF to adjust the engine of a motor vehicle to improve its performance **2.** *vti.* GET STH JUST RIGHT to make tiny adjustments to sth in order to achieve the best possible performance or appearance —**fine-tuning** *n.*

finfoot /fín fŏŏt/ (*plural* -**foots** *or* -**foot**) *n.* BIRDS = **sungrebe**

Barnaby's
Fingal's Cave

Fingal's Cave /fíng gəlz-/ cave on Staffa Island in the Inner Hebrides, off the western coast of Scotland. Height: 18 m/60 ft. Length: 70 m/228 ft.

finger /fíng gər/ *n.* **1.** ANAT DIGIT OF THE HAND any of the digits of the hand, sometimes excluding the thumb (*often used before a noun*) **2.** CLOTHES PART OF GLOVE any of the long narrow parts of a glove that fits the finger **3.** NARROW STRIP sth that resembles a finger in shape ○ *a finger of sand* **4.** FOOD LONG NARROW PORTION OF FOOD a small portion of food about as long and thick as a finger **5.** BEVERAGES APPROXIMATE QUANTITY OF ALCOHOL an approximate measure of alcoholic beverage in a glass, equal in depth to the width of a finger **6.** MEASURE APPROXIMATE UNIT OF LENGTH an approximate unit of measurement, equal to the width or length of a finger. Also called **digit** ■ *v.* (-**gers**, -**gering**, -**gered**) **1.** *vt.* TOUCH to feel or move the fingers across sth, often in a gentle, affectionate, or thoughtful way ○ *she fingered the fabric lovingly* **2.** *vt.* CRIMINOL GIVE UP TO POLICE to tell the police about the whereabouts or illegal activities of sb (*slang*) **3.** *vti.* MUSIC PLAY INSTRUMENT USING THE FINGERS to handle the strings or keys of a musical instrument with the fingers **4.** *vt.* MUSIC MARK WITH INSTRUCTIONS FOR FINGERING to show on a musical score which fingers the musician should use **5.** *vt.* COMPUT LOCATE COMPUTER USERS to run a computer program that obtains and displays information about other users on the same computer or on other computers connected through a network or the Internet [Old English. Ultimately from an Indo-European word meaning 'five', which is also the ancestor of English *five*, *fist*, *pentagon*, and *quintet*.] —**fingerer** *n.* ◇ **cross your fingers** used to express a hope that things will turn out well ◇ **have a finger in every pie** to be involved in many advantageous or lucrative projects ◇ **have a finger in the pie** to be involved in a particular project, especially an advantageous or lucrative one ◇ **let sth slip through your fingers** to fail to take advantage of sth that would have been of benefit to you ◇ **put your finger on sth** to identify sth, especially sth difficult or elusive ◇ **twist sb round your little finger** to succeed in getting sb to do exactly as you wish

fingerboard /fíng gər bawrd/ *n.* a long strip of wood fixed on the neck of string instruments against which strings are pressed in order to vary the pitch

finger bowl *n.* a small bowl of water set beside a place at a table so that fingers can be cleaned, e.g. after picking up food with the hands

finger buffet *n.* a selection of food prepared for guests at a party to help themselves to and eat with their fingers, usually while standing up

finger food *n.* small items of food made to be eaten with the fingers

fingerfuck /fíng gər fuk/ (-**fucks**, -**fucking**, -**fucked**) *vt.* an offensive term meaning to use the fingers to stimulate a woman's genitals (*offensive taboo*)

finger hole *n.* any one of a series of holes on a woodwind instrument that a player covers with the fingers in order to register a pitch

fingering /fíng gəring/ *n.* **1.** USE OF FINGERS the use of the fingers to do sth **2.** MUSIC USE OF FINGERS ON MUSICAL INSTRUMENT the action or technique of using the fingers in playing a musical instrument

Finger Lakes /fíng gər-/ group of eleven glacial lakes in western New York, the centre of the state's wine region

fingerling /fíng gərling/ *n.* a small fish less than one year old, especially a salmon or trout

fingermark /fíng gər maark/ *n.* a smear or greasy mark left after sb has touched sth

finger millet *n.* a short-stemmed millet with an ear divided into five parts, cultivated widely in southern India, Sri Lanka, and parts of Africa. Latin name: *Eleusine coracana*. [From its ears that resemble the fingers of a hand]

fingernail /fíng gər nayl/ *n.* a flat protective layer of keratin that covers the end part of a finger's upper surface

finger pick *n.* a musician's pick with a curved handle for attaching it to the finger

finger post *n.* a notice shaped like a pointing hand, indicating the direction, and usually the distance, to a particular place

fingerprint /fíng gər print/ *n.* **1.** PATTERN ON A FINGERTIP an impression of the curved lines of skin at the end of a finger that is left on a surface or made by pressing an inked finger on to paper **2.** DISTINGUISHING CHARACTERISTIC a unique characteristic, mark, or pattern that can be used to identify sb or sth ■ *vt.* (-**prints**, -**printing**, -**printed**) RECORD THE FINGERPRINTS OF to press each of sb's fingertips in ink and then on to paper to make a set of marks that can be used to identify the person

finger roll *n.* a small narrow soft bread roll

fingerspelling /fíng gər spelling/ *n.* a form of sign language communication using the fingers to gesture the spelling of words

fingerstall /fíng gər stawl/ *n.* a sheath-shaped protective covering worn over an injured finger

fingertip /fíng gər tip/ *n.* FINGER'S END the tip of a finger ■ *adj.* USING THE FINGERTIPS involving the use of the fingertips and so very sensitive or delicate ○ *fingertip controls* ◇ **have sth at your fingertips 1.** to know all the details of sth thoroughly **2.** to have sth available and nearby

finger wave *n.* a wave made by shaping damp hair with the fingers and a comb

Fingo /fíng gō/ (*plural* -**go** *or* -**gos**) *n.* a member of an African people who live among the Xhosa in the Eastern Cape province of South Africa [Early 19thC. From Xhosa *mfengu* 'destitute wanderer'.]

finial /fíni əl, fínni əl/ *n.* **1.** ARCHIT ARCHITECTURAL DECORATION a carved decoration at the top of a gable, spire, or arched structure **2.** FURNITURE FURNITURE DECORATION an ornamental feature, e.g. a carved knob, on the top or end of a part of a piece of furniture **3.** PRINTING CURVE IN A TYPEFACE a curve that ends a main stroke in some italic typefaces [15thC. Via assumed Anglo-Norman or Anglo-Latin, literally 'final', from, ultimately, Latin *finis* 'end'.] —**finialled** *adj.*

finicky /fínniki/ (-**ier**, -**iest**), **finicking**, **finical** /-k'l/ *adj.* **1.** FUSSY concentrating too much on small unimportant details **2.** TOO DETAILED complicated by trivial details [Late 16thC. Earliest occurrence as *finical*, probably coined from FINE + -ICAL. *Finicking* is recorded from the mid-17thC and *finicky* from the early 19thC.] —**finickiness** *n.*

— WORD KEY: SYNONYMS —
See Synonyms at *careful*.

fining /fíning/ *n.* **1.** CLARIFICATION OF LIQUID the process of clarifying a liquid, especially wine or beer **2.** INDUST REMOVING GAS FROM MOLTEN GLASS the process of removing undissolved gas from molten glass

finis /fínniss/ *interj.* used to indicate that sth has or must come to an end completely [14thC. From Latin, literally 'end'.]

finish /fínnish/ *v.* (-**ishes**, -**ishing**, -**ished**) **1.** *vti.* NO LONGER CONTINUE to come to an end, or bring sth to an end ○ *we finished eating* **2.** *vt.* CONSUME to eat, drink, or use all of sth ○ *Who finished the cake?* **3.** *vt.* DESTROY to kill, ruin, or exhaust sb or sth (*informal*) ○ *His dishonesty finished him in business.* **4.** *vt.* COMPLETE THE SURFACE EFFECT OF to treat sth, especially wood or metal, in order to achieve a desired surface effect **5.** *vt.* MAKE JUST RIGHT to give sth or sb the final touches, qualities, or skills that are required to create a desired effect ■ *n.* **1.** END PART the terminating part of sth **2.** SPECIAL TOP LAYER a surface texture or final coat applied to sth, especially wood or metal ○ *a mirror with a gilt finish* **3.** SPORTS SPURT OF SPEED AT END a final part of a race, especially a sprint, acceleration, or challenge near the finishing line **4.** CONSTR, MANUF QUALITY OF WORKMANSHIP the degree of care with which a product has been manufactured or a job of work has been carried out, judged by its final appearance ○ *The finish on the woodwork is poor.* [14thC. Via Old French *fenir* from Latin *finire*, from *finis* 'end'.]

finish off *vt.* **1.** COMPLETE to bring sth to an end, e.g. by making it as complete as is wished or needed **2.** USE UP to eat, drink, or use up all of sth **3.** DESTROY to kill, ruin, or exhaust sb or sth (*informal*)

finish up *v.* **1.** *vt.* USE UP to eat, drink, or use up all of sth **2.** *vi.* ARRIVE FINALLY to be in a particular place or condition in the end, often not the planned one

finish up with *vt.* to be left with sth ○ *We finished up with nothing.*

finish with *vt.* **1.** NO LONGER WANT TO SEE to end a relationship or partnership with sb (*informal*) **2.** NOT NEED ANY MORE to stop using, wanting, or being interested in sth

finished /fínnisht/ *adj.* **1.** DONE WELL produced and completed with skill and professionalism **2.** OF NO FURTHER USE with no further prospect of success or development

— WORD KEY: USAGE —
See Usage note at *done*.

finisher /fínnishər/ *n.* **1.** SB WHO COMPLETES STH sb who completes sth, e.g. a task or a race **2.** SB WHO ADDS FINISHING TOUCHES sb who completes the final stage of a process in manufacturing or restoration

finishing /fínnishing/ *n.* the tasks that complete the production process of a garment, fabric, or material

finishing line *n.* a real or imaginary line that marks the end of a race. US term **finish line**

finishing school *n.* a fee-paying school for girls close to school-leaving age in which social skills, the arts, and academic courses are taught

finishing touch *n.* a final small change or addition made to sth

finish line *n.* US = **finishing line**

Finisterre, Cape /fínni stáir/ promontory in the autonomous region of Galicia, northwestern Spain, extending into the Atlantic Ocean and forming the westernmost part of the mainland

finite /fín ìt/ *adj.* **1.** LIMITED with an end or limit ○ *we have only a finite amount of resources* **2.** MATH COUNTABLE having a countable number of elements **3.** MEASURABLE subject to measurable limitations **4.** GRAM USING VERB appearing in a verb form that limits person, number, and tense [14thC. From Latin *finitus*, past participle of *finire* (see FINISH).] —**finitely** *adv.* —**finiteness** *n.*

finitude /fínni tyood/ *n.* the condition of being finite (*formal*)

fink /fingk/ *n.* US **1.** SB LOATHSOME sb who is thought to be obnoxious or loathsome (*dated slang insult*) **2.** CRIMINOL INFORMER sb who gives an authority such as a police officer information about another's criminal or bad behaviour (*dated slang disapproving*) **3.** **STRIKEBREAKER** sb who continues to work when fellow workers are on strike (*dated slang*) ■ *vi.* (**finks, finking, finked**) US **1.** **INFORM ON OTHERS** to give an authority information about another's criminal or bad behaviour (*dated slang disapproving*) ○ *He finked on his buddies after the police questioned him.* **2.** **BE A STRIKEBREAKER** to continue to work in defiance of a strike (*dated slang*) ■ *vi.*

fink out *vi.* US to fail to do sth after previously agreeing or volunteering to do it (*dated slang*)

fin keel *n.* a fin-shaped part that extends downwards from the underside of a sailing boat to give extra stability

Finland

Finland /fínlənd/ republic in northern Europe on the Baltic Sea. Approximately a third of the country lies within the Arctic Circle. Language: Finnish, Swedish. Currency: markka. Capital: Helsinki. Population: 5,137,269 (1997). Area: 338,145 sq. km/130,559 sq. mi. Official name **Republic of Finland**

Finland, Gulf of arm of the Baltic Sea, extending about 400 km/250 mi. east between Finland and Estonia. Area: 30,044 sq. km/11,600 sq. mi.

Finlandize /fínlən dīz/ (**-izes, -izing, -ized**), **Finlandise** (**-ises, -ising, -ised**) *vt.* to make a small country or power act in an accommodating way towards a superpower rather than confronting it [Mid-20thC. So called because Finland was compelled to behave in this way towards the Soviet Union after World War II.] — **Finlandization** /fínlən dī záysh'n/ *n.*

Finlay /fín lay/ river in north-central British Columbia, Canada, that flows southeast into Williston Lake. Length: 400 km/250 mi.

Finn /fin/ *n.* **1.** **SB FROM FINLAND** sb who was born or brought up in Finland, or who has Finnish citizenship **2.** **SPEAKER OF A FINNIC LANGUAGE** sb who speaks a Finnic language [Old English *Finnas*]

Finn /fin/, **Neil** (b. 1956) New Zealand singer and songwriter. A former member of the groups Split Enz and Crowded House, he began his solo career in 1998.

finnan haddock /fínnən-/, **finnan haddie** /-háddi/ *Scotland n.* haddock split and smoked on the bone over oak or peat, giving the flesh a pale yellow colour [*Finnan* is an alteration of *Findon*, a fishing village near Aberdeen, where the product was first made]

finner /fínnər/ *n.* = finback

Finnic /fínnik/ *n.* **N EUROPEAN LANGUAGE GROUP** a group of languages that includes Finnish, Estonian, Lapp, and some other northeastern European languages. The group is from the Finno-Ugric branch of the Uralic family of languages and has about seven million speakers. ■ *adj.* **1.** **OF FINNIC** relating to the Finnic group of languages **2.** = Finnish *adj.* 1

Finnish /fínnish/ *n.* **OFFICIAL LANGUAGE OF FINLAND** the official language of Finland, also spoken in parts of Estonia and European Russia. It is from the Finnic group of the Finno-Ugric branch of the Uralic family of languages. About six million people speak Finnish. ■ *adj.* **1.** **OF FINLAND** relating to or typical of Finland, or its people or culture **2.** **OF THE FINNISH LANGUAGE** relating to the language Finnish

Finn MacCool /fín mə koól/ *n.* a legendary Irish hero, chief of the band of warriors known as the Fianna

Finno-Ugric /fínnō yoógrik/, **Finno-Ugrian** /-yoógri ən/ *n.* a group of languages that includes Finnish, Estonian, Lapp, Hungarian, and some other northeastern European languages. It is one of the two major branches of the Uralic family of languages. About 22 million people speak one of the languages classified as Finno-Ugric. ◊ **Samoyed** —**Finno-Ugric** *adj.*

fino /feénō/ (*plural* **-nos**) *n.* a very pale dry sherry [Mid-19thC. From Spanish, literally 'fine', from Latin *finire* (see FINISH).]

finocchio /fi nóki ō/ (*plural* **-o** or **-os**) *n.* = fennel *n.* 2 [Early 18thC. Via Italian from Vulgar Latin *feniculum* (see FENNEL).]

fin whale *n.* = finback

FIO *abbr.* for information only

f.i.o. *abbr.* for information only

fiord *n.* = fjord

Fiordland National Park /fyáwrdlənd-/ national park on the southwestern coast of the South Island, New Zealand, established in 1952. It was designated a World Heritage Site in 1986. Area: 12,116 sq. km/4,678 sq. mi.

fioritura /fi áwri tyoórə/ (*plural* **-re** /-ray/) *n.* an embellished vocal figure in opera of the 17th and 18th centuries, similar to a cadenza and often improvised. It was later applied to keyboard and violin music. ◊ **embellishment** [Mid-19thC. From Italian, from *fiorire* 'to flower', from, ultimately, Latin *florere* (see FLOURISH).]

fipple /fípp'l/ *n.* a small wooden plug in a woodwind instrument or organ pipe that redirects air and creates vibrations [Early 17thC. Origin uncertain.]

fipple flute *n.* an end-blown flute containing a fipple

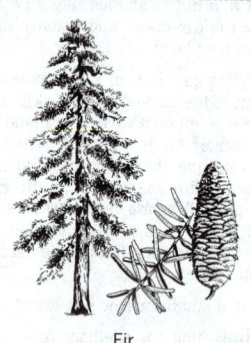

Fir

fir /fur/ (*plural* **firs** or **fir**) *n.* **1.** **EVERGREEN TREE WITH NEEDLE-SHAPED LEAVES** an evergreen tree with single flat needle-shaped leaves and erect female cones. Genus: *Abies*. **2.** **EVERGREEN RESEMBLING A FIR** an evergreen tree that resembles the true fir, e.g. the Douglas fir **3.** **WOOD OF THE FIR** the wood of the fir or a related tree [14thC. Origin uncertain.]

Firbank /fúr bangk/, **Ronald** (1886–1926) British novelist. He is the author of humorous novels such as *Caprice* (1917) and *The Flower Beneath the Foot* (1923). Full name **Arthur Annesley Ronald Firbank**

fire /fīr/ *n.* **1.** **PROCESS OF BURNING** the rapid production of light, heat, and flames from sth that is burning, e.g. in the combustion of wood, coal, or petroleum **2.** **BLAZE** the light, heat, and flames caused by sth that is burning ○ *sat at a roaring fire* **3.** **PILE OF BURNING FUEL** a collection of material such as logs or coal that is set alight and used as fuel for heating, cooking, or burning sth ○ *a forest fire* **4.** **HOUSEHOLD HEATING DEVICE** an electric or gas-fuelled appliance that can be used to produce heat in a building **5.** **DESTRUCTIVE BURNING OF STH** a situation in which sth is destroyed or damaged by burning, e.g. a building or an area of land (*often used before a noun*) ○ *destroyed by fire* ○ *fire damage* **6.** **ARMS DISCHARGE FROM GUNS** a discharge of ammunition from one or more guns ○ *The troops advanced under heavy fire.* **7.** **CONTINUOUS ATTACK** a series of things that follow each other quickly and relentlessly, especially if hostile or intimidating ○ *She took heavy fire from her political opponents.* **8.** **ARMS LAUNCH OF A PROJECTILE** the process or timing of sending off a missile or rocket **9.** **GEM'S BRILLIANCE** the shine and

sparkle of a diamond or similar gemstone **10.** **PASSION** energy, spirit, or intensity of feeling ○ *the composer's creative fire* **11.** PHILOS, HIST **ONE OF ELEMENTS OF ANCIENTS** in ancient and medieval philosophy, one of the four elements, the active principle of fire, also considered important in astrology ■ *v.* (**fires, firing, fired**) **1.** *vti.* **DISCHARGE AMMUNITION** to discharge ammunition or a projectile **2.** *vti.* **LAUNCH STH FORCEFULLY** to launch sth powerfully through the air **3.** *vt.* **DISMISS SB FROM WORK** to dismiss sb from employment (*informal*) **4.** *vi.* **START UP** to begin to burn fuel and start working ○ *The engine fired and the racing car took off.* **5.** *vt.* **STOKE OR FILL WITH FUEL** to keep supplying fuel to sth, e.g. a furnace, engine, or oven **6.** *vt.* CERAMICS **BAKE IN A KILN** to put pottery into a kiln to be baked hard **7.** *vt.* **STRIKE WITH FORCE** to hit or throw sth forcefully **8.** *vt.* **EXCITE** to arouse strong emotion in sb (*often passive*) ○ *She was fired with enthusiasm.* **9.** *vt.* **DESTROY WITH FIRE** to cause sth to burn, especially in order to destroy it (*formal or dated*) ○ *Crossing the border, the invaders fired the first town they encountered.* ■ *interj.* **1.** **WARNING CRY** used to tell others that a dangerous fire has started **2.** ARMS **COMMAND TO SHOOT** used to command that guns or other weapons, missiles, or projectiles are to be discharged at sb or sth ○ *Ready, aim, and fire!* [Old English *fȳr.* Ultimately from an Indo-European word that is also the ancestor of English *pyre, pyrites,* and *empyreal.*] — **firer** *n.* ◊ **on fire 1.** in a condition of combustion in which flames, heat, and usually smoke are being produced **2.** full of eagerness or passion ◊ **play with fire** to do sth dangerous or risky ◊ **set fire to sth** to make sth start burning ◊ **set the world on fire** to do sth remarkable or very successful ◊ **under fire 1.** MIL shot at by weapons **2.** subject to severe criticism

—— **WORD KEY: SYNONYMS** ——

fire, blaze, conflagration, inferno
CORE MEANING: referring to burning and flames
fire a general word, used to describe flames that were started deliberately and are under control, for example a bonfire. It can also be used to describe uncontrolled flames, whether caused accidentally or on purpose; **blaze** used like **fire** but suggesting a greater degree of intensity and brightness, and more rapid burning; **conflagration** a fairly formal word, used to describe a fierce, destructive fire, especially one that affects a large building or area; **inferno** used especially in journalism to describe a fierce, destructive fire.

—— **WORD KEY: CULTURAL NOTE** ——

Pale Fire, a novel by Russian-born US writer Vladimir Nabokov (1962). Partly an attack on parasitic critics, it is presented as a long poem by John Shade, with introduction, notes, and index by Charles Kinbote. Kinbote's commentary gradually reveals him to be an unscrupulous critic, ready to use the work of others to further his own career.

fire away *vi.* **1.** ARMS **BEGIN SHOOTING** to begin or keep on shooting **2.** **BEGIN** to begin doing sth, especially asking questions (*informal*)

fire off *vt.* **1.** **DIRECT IN SHARP BURSTS** to deliver a series of things, especially questions or demands **2.** ARMS **SHOOT** to discharge a bullet or some other projectile

fire up *v.* **1.** *vt.* **GET GOING** to initiate the operation of sth **2.** *vti.* **START TO BURN** to begin to burn, or set sth burning **3.** *vi.* **BECOME ENTHUSIASTIC** suddenly to become very enthusiastic

fire alarm *n.* a bell or siren that is sounded if a fire starts

fire and brimstone *n.* eternal punishment [From the use of fire and brimstone in the Bible (Genesis 19:24, Revelation 19:20) as instruments of God's punishment]

fire ant *n.* a predatory ant of tropical or temperate regions that inflicts a painful sting. Genus: *Solenopsis*. [So called because of the burning sensation its sting causes]

firearm /fír aarm/ *n.* a portable weapon such as a pistol or rifle that fires ammunition

fireback /fír bak/ *n.* a metal lining placed behind a fireplace, or the area of wall where it is placed

fireball /fír bawl/ *n.* **1.** **NUCLEAR PHYS CENTRE OF A NUCLEAR EXPLOSION** the highly ionized spherical region of bright hot gas and dust at the centre of a nuclear explosion **2.** ASTRON, METEOROL **BRIGHT METEOR** an exceptionally bright meteor **3. BALL LIGHTNING** a discharge of ball lightning **4. = ball of fire** (*informal*)

fire blight *n.* an infectious disease of apples, pears, and other fruit trees that blackens leaves and kills branches and is caused by the bacterium *Erwinia amylovora*

firebomb /fír bom/ *n.* **BOMB STARTING A FIRE** a bomb designed to start a fire ■ *vti.* (**-bombs, -bombing, -bombed**) **PLACE A DEVICE TO START FIRE** to attack a target with a device designed to start a fire —**firebomber** *n.* —**firebombing** *n.*

firebox /fír boks/ *n.* an enclosure for a fire in a stove, furnace, or the engine of a steam locomotive

firebrand /fír brand/ *n.* **1. BURNING STICK** a burning stick carried by sb as a torch or a weapon **2. AGITATOR** sb with a strong or aggressive personality who encourages unrest

firebrat /fír brat/ *n.* a small wingless insect related to silverfish, found in warm moist places. Latin name: *Thermobia domestica.*

firebreak /fír brayk/ *n.* a strip of land that has been cleared of trees, bushes, and any other combustible material in order to prevent a fire from spreading

firebrick /fír brik/ *n.* a type of brick that can withstand very high temperatures, used to make fireplaces and furnaces

fire brigade *n.* an organization of people trained to prevent, control, and extinguish fires and to rescue people from fires and other dangerous situations. US term **fire department**

firebug /fír bug/ *n.* sb who causes deliberate damage or destruction by starting fires, especially repeatedly and for pleasure (*slang*)

fireclay /fír klay/ *n.* a durable clay that can withstand great heat, used to make firebricks, crucibles, and furnace linings

fire control *n.* the control of naval or artillery fire directed at a target

firecracker /fír krakər/ *n.* a small paper or cardboard cylinder filled with an explosive that makes one or several loud bangs when it is lit

firecrest /fír krest/ *n.* a small European bird of the warbler family. The top of the head is bright orange in the male and bright yellow in the female. Latin name: *Regulus ignicapillus.*

fired /fírd/ *adj.* **1. KILN-BAKED** baked hard in a kiln **2. FUELLED** using a particular fuel to provide the heat or power (*used in combination*) ○ *a gas-fired boiler*

firedamp /fír damp/ *n.* a mixture of methane and other hydrocarbon gases that forms in coalmines. It becomes explosive when it mixes with air. [From an earlier sense of DAMP 'noxious gas']

fire department *n.* US = **fire brigade**

firedog /fír dog/ *n.* Southern US = **andiron**

fire door *n.* **1. DOOR CONFINING A FIRE** a fireproof door that is normally kept closed or locked, ensuring that any fire is confined to one area **2. EMERGENCY EXIT** an emergency exit opened from inside

firedrake /fír drayk/, **firedragon** /-dragən/ *n.* a dragon that breathes fire (*archaic or literary*) [**Drake** from *draca* 'dragon', ultimately from Greek *drakōn* 'serpent' (source of English *dragon*)]

fire drill *n.* a rehearsal for evacuating a building quickly and safely in the event of a fire or other emergency

fire-eater *n.* **1. ENTERTAINER USING FIRE** sb who entertains by appearing to swallow flames from a burning stick **2. SB EASILY PROVOKED** sb who is aggressive, angry, or argumentative (*informal*) —**fire-eating** *n.*

fire engine *n.* a large road vehicle equipped with ladders, hoses, and other equipment to fight fires and rescue people

fire escape *n.* a specially designed means of getting clear of a building if it catches fire, especially an exterior metal stairway attached to the building

fire extinguisher *n.* a cylindrical metal container holding a substance such as foam or vaporizing liquid that can be sprayed onto a fire

firefight /fír fīt/ *n.* MIL a fierce battle involving a heavy exchange of gunfire

firefighter /fír fītər/ *n.* sb who helps to control and extinguish fires and rescue people trapped by fire or in other dangerous situations —**firefighting** *n.*

firefly /fír flī/ (*plural* **-flies**) *n.* a winged nocturnal beetle that, during courtship, produces an intermittent light from luminescent chemicals in its abdominal organs. Family: Lampyridae.

fireguard /fír gaard/ *n.* **1. SCREEN PROTECTING FROM FIRE** a metal, usually meshed, screen that is put around the front of an open fire, mainly to stop sparks from flying out and to prevent people from going too close **2. = firebreak**

firehouse /fír howss/ *n.* US = **fire station**

fire hydrant *n.* an upright pipe, usually in a street, connected to a water main with a valve to which a hose can be attached, e.g. by firefighters

fire insurance *n.* insurance that offers coverage against damage or loss due to fire

fire irons *npl.* a collection of implements used for tending a fire in a fireplace, especially a shovel, tongs, poker, and brush

firelight /fír līt/ *n.* the flickering light given off by an open fire

firelighter /fír lītər/ *n.* a small piece of an inflammable substance that helps fuel to catch fire quickly

firelock /fír lok/ *n.* in early firearms, a mechanism that struck a spark from flint or steel and caused a charge to explode

fireman /fírmən/ (*plural* **-men** /-mən/) *n.* **1. MAN WHO IS FIREFIGHTER** a man who is firefighter, especially one who works for a fire brigade **2. RAIL, SHIPPING STOKER** a man who stokes a furnace, especially on a steam locomotive or steamboat **3. DRIVER'S ASSISTANT** an assistant to the driver of an electric or diesel train

Firenze /fi réntsay/ Italian **Florence**

fire opal *n.* a translucent reddish opal

fireplace /fír playss/ *n.* a recess, usually with a mantelpiece above it, built into the wall of a room as a place to light an open fire

firepower /fír powər/ *n.* MIL the capability of a military unit or weapon to direct effective fire at an enemy

fire practice *n.* = **fire drill**

fireproof /fír proof/ *adj.* **UNBURNABLE OR VERY RESISTANT TO FIRE** treated or manufactured so as to be impossible or very difficult to burn and therefore destroy by fire ■ *vt.* (**-proofs, -proofing, -proofed**) **MAKE FIREPROOF** to make sth such as a fabric fireproof

fire raiser *n.* = **arsonist**

fire-resistant *adj.* treated or made so that it is very slow to catch fire and burn

fire-retardant *adj.* tending not to catch fire easily and therefore checking the spread of fire

fire sale *n.* a sale of goods or property damaged in a fire

fire screen *n.* **1. = fireguard** 1 **2. SCREEN TO COVER FIREPLACE** a free-standing screen placed in front of a fireplace to act as a heat shield or as a decorative screen when a fire is not lit

fire ship *n.* HIST in former times, a ship loaded with explosives or combustibles that was set on fire and allowed to drift as a weapon among enemy ships

fireside /fír sīd/ *n.* **PLACE BY A FIRE** the space around a fireplace or hearth ■ *adj.* **SAFE AND COMFORTABLE** of a cosy, familiar, or homely nature

fire sign *n.* ZODIAC one of the three signs of the zodiac Aries, Leo, or Sagittarius, traditionally associated with a fiery, assertive, and dynamic temperament

fire station *n.* a building where professional firefighters are stationed and their vehicles and equipment are kept

firestone /fír stōn/ *n.* a form of sandstone that can withstand great heat, used to line kilns and furnaces

firestorm /fír stawrm/ *n.* **1. LARGE UNCONTROLLABLE BLAZE** a large extremely intense fire sustained by strong inwardly rushing winds that feed a rising column of hot air **2. US INTENSE DISTURBANCE** a strong, sometimes violent, upheaval or outburst ○ *a firestorm of protest*

fire thorn *n.* PLANTS = **pyracantha**

fire trail *n.* Aus a road through forest or bush land that enables firefighters to reach wildfires in remote areas

firetrap /fír trap/ *n.* any building or structure regarded as a fire hazard, either because it is built of combustible materials or lacks adequate means of escape

firetruck *n.* US = **fire engine**

firewalking /fír wawking/ *n.* the rite or practice of walking barefoot over hot coals, ashes, or stones —**firewalker** *n.*

firewall /fír wawl/ (**-walls, -walling, -walled**) *n.* **1. BUILDING WALL PREVENTING THE SPREAD OF FIRE** a fireproof wall put in place to ensure that if a fire occurs it is confined to one area **2. COMPUT SECURITY SOFTWARE** a piece of computer software intended to prevent unauthorized access to system software or data

fire watcher *n.* sb who watches for fires, especially a member of an air-raid patrol during World War II

firewater /fír wawtər/ *n.* strong and harsh-tasting alcoholic spirits (*dated slang*)

fireweed /fír weed/ (*plural* **-weed** *or* **-weeds**) *n.* = **rosebay willowherb** [So called because the plants are often the first to grow on land that has been burned]

firewood /fír wŏod/ *n.* wood that is burned as fuel

firework /fír wurk/ *n.* **BRIGHT EXPLODING OBJECT** a package of manufactured chemicals designed to make a loud and brilliant explosion when lit (*often used before a noun*) ○ *a firework party* ■ **fireworks** *npl.* **1. SHOW USING FIREWORKS** a display of many brilliant fireworks **2. ANGRY OUTBURST** a display of violent temper (*informal*) **3. SPECTACULAR DISPLAY** any impressive display of talent (*informal*)

firing /fíring/ *n.* the application of great heat to a ceramic object in a kiln, to harden it or to fix an applied substance such as a glaze

firing line *n.* **1. MIL FRONT POSITION IN BATTLE** an exposed position from which guns are fired at an enemy, or the troops who occupy it **2. VANGUARD OF ACTION** the forefront of a movement, operation, or activity, especially one that is controversial

firing order *n.* the sequence of ignition of the cylinders in an internal-combustion engine

firing party *n.* = **firing squad**

firing pin *n.* a pin behind the barrel of a firearm that strikes the container of explosive (**primer**) to make the cartridge fire

firing squad *n.* a group of soldiers with the task of carrying out an execution by gunfire or delivering a ceremonial volley over a grave

firkin /fúrkin/ *n.* **1. BREWING MEASURE** a British unit of capacity used especially in the brewing industry, equal to nine gallons **2. WOODEN TUB** a small wooden tub (*archaic*) [14thC. Origin uncertain: probably from assumed Middle Dutch *verdelkijn*, literally 'small fourth', from *veerde* 'fourth'.]

firm[1] /furm/ *adj.* **1. NOT YIELDING TO THE TOUCH** compact and solid when pressed ○ *a firm mattress* **2. SECURE** fixed securely and unlikely to give way ○ *a firm hold* **3. DETERMINED** showing certainty or determination ○ *You must be more firm with them.* **4. TRUSTWORTHY** reliable and able to be trusted **5. STEADY** showing no or few fluctuations ■ *adv.* **WITH DETERMINATION** in a determined and unshakable way ○ *They stood firm despite a wave of criticism.* ■ *vti.* (**firms, firming, firmed**) **MAKE OR BECOME FIRM** to become firm or firmer, or make sth firm or firmer [14thC. Via Old French from Latin *firmus.*] —**firmly** *adv.* —**firmness** *n.*

firm up *vt.* **1. SETTLE** to make sth more definite, clear, or less liable to change ○ *Let's firm up the date of the meeting.* **2.** *vi.* **STABILIZE** to become less liable to fluctuation

firm[2] /furm/ *n.* a group of people who form a commercial organization selling goods or services [14thC. From Italian *firma*, late Latin *firmare* 'to confirm by signing', from Latin, 'to strengthen', from *firmus* 'strong'.]

firmament /fúrməmənt/ *n.* the sky, considered as an

arch (*literary*) [13thC. Via French from Latin *firmamentum*, from, ultimately, *firmus* 'firm, strong'.]

firmware /fúrm wair/ *n.* a set of computer instructions used so frequently that it is stored on a memory chip in a computer rather than being part of a program. ◊ **software, hardware** [*Firm* from the fact that the instructions will not be lost when the power is shut off]

firn /furn/ *n.* GEOG = **névé** [Mid-19thC. Via German, literally 'of last year', from Old High German *firni* 'old'.]

firn wind *n.* a summer wind that blows downhill off a glacier during the day

first /furst/ *adj.* **1.** BEFORE THE REST preceding or ahead of any others in order **2.** EARLIER THAN THE REST occurring before any others in a series **3.** MOST IMPORTANT with a higher rank, significance, or authority than others in the same category **4.** FUNDAMENTAL forming a basis or foundation for sth **5.** BEST best in quality or achievement ■ *n.* **1.** NEW THING sth that has not been done before or has not occurred before (*informal*) **2.** CARS FIRST GEAR the lowest gear in a motor vehicle (*informal*) **3.** EDUC HIGH ACADEMIC QUALIFICATION an undergraduate university degree awarded for the highest level of academic achievement (*informal*) ◊ **second, third 4.** AUTOMOT ALTERNATIVE FOR FIRST GEAR the lowest forward gear in a motor vehicle **5.** BALLET = **first position** ■ *pron.* ONE AHEAD OF ANY OTHER sb who or sth that is positioned before any other in achievement, rank, quality, or time ■ *adv.* **1.** BEFORE OTHERS earlier than sth or sb else **2.** ORIGINALLY for the first time **3.** INITIALLY at the start **4.** MORE WILLINGLY used to indicate a preference [Old English *fyr(e)st*. Ultimately from an Indo-European word that is also the ancestor of English *fore*, *principal*, and *priest*.] ◊ **first cab off the rank** *Aus* sb who or sth that is the first to act (*informal*)

first aid *n.* emergency medical treatment for sb who is ill or injured, given before more thorough medical attention can be obtained

First Amendment *n. US* an amendment to the US Constitution that forbids Congress from interfering with a citizen's freedom of religion, speech, assembly, or petition

first base *n.* the initial base that a player attempts to reach in baseball ◊ **get to first base** *US* to succeed in the initial phase of an activity, especially in making advances to a prospective girlfriend (*informal*)

first-born *n.* ELDEST OFFSPRING the first offspring to be born to a set of parents ■ *adj.* BORN FIRST born first of all

First Cause *n.* in Christianity, God as the originator of everything

first class *n.* **1.** BEST CLASS the highest rank, standard, or quality **2.** BEST ACCOMMODATION the best accommodation offered on an aeroplane, ship, or train

first-class *adj.* **1.** BEST of the highest standard of excellence **2.** MOST LUXURIOUS most exclusive and expensive **3.** MAIL GIVEN PRIORITY IN THE POSTAL SERVICE costing more to post and given priority in delivery ■ *adv.* **1.** IN FIRST CLASS expensively and exclusively **2.** MAIL WITH POSTAL PRIORITY more expensively and with higher priority as post

first course *n.* a dish or selection of dishes served at the beginning of a meal

first cousin *n.* = **cousin** *n.* 1

first-day cover *n.* an envelope, often specially designed, that bears a newly issued stamp and a postmark for the day of issue

first-degree burn *n.* a burn marked by pain and reddening of the skin but without blistering or charring of tissue

first-degree murder *n. US* murder that is carried out with the planned and deliberate intention of killing sb

first edition *n.* **1.** ORIGINAL COPY OF A BOOK a copy of a book in its original printed and published format **2.** ORIGINAL PRINTING OF A PUBLICATION the total number of copies of a book issued by the original publisher in the first instance **3.** FIRST NEWSPAPER OF DAY the first batch or copy of a newspaper on a day of publication

first eleven *n.* in football, cricket, and other team sports with eleven players per team, the best of

several teams competing for the same club at different levels

first estate *n.* in societies that date from feudal times, the social and political class that consists of senior members of the clergy

first fifteen *n.* in rugby, the best of several teams competing for the same club at different levels

first finger *n.* ANAT = **index finger**

First Fleet *n. Aus* a fleet of ships that transported the first group of convicts and immigrants to Australia in 1788

first floor *n.* **1.** ONE LEVEL ABOVE GROUND the floor of a building immediately above the ground level floor. US term **second floor 2.** *US, Can* = **ground floor**

first-foot *n. Scotland* FIRST VISITOR IN NEW YEAR the first person to visit a household in the New Year ■ *vti.* (**first-foots, first-footing, first-footed**) *Scotland* ACT AS FIRST-FOOT to be the first visitor to a household in the New Year

first-footer *n. Scotland* = **first-foot** *n.*

first-footing *n. Scotland* the traditional practice of going to the house of a friend or neighbour soon after midnight on 31 December, with good wishes and gifts of food, drink, and fuel

first fruits *npl.* **1.** FIRST CROP HARVESTED the first harvest of the season or year **2.** FIRST BENEFITS the first results of an activity

first-generation *adj.* **1.** SOC SCI WITH IMMIGRANT PARENTS relating to or being the children of parents who have left one country to settle in another **2.** COMPUT OF THE EARLIEST KIND used to describe the earliest computers, which were based on vacuum tubes

firsthand /fúrst hánd/ *adj., adv.* obtained directly from an original source rather than via sb else

first lady *n.* **1.** first lady, First Lady *US* US LEADER'S SPOUSE OR WOMAN PARTNER the wife or female partner of the President of the United States or of a US state governor, or the woman appointed by him to act as his official hostess **2.** GOVERNMENT LEADER'S PARTNER the wife or woman partner of a high government official, especially of a country's leader **3.** WOMAN AT THE TOP the most important or respected woman member of a profession or field of activity

first language *n.* **1.** NATIVE LANGUAGE the language that sb learned in infancy **2.** MAIN LANGUAGE the principal language in a neighbourhood, district, region, or country

first lieutenant *n.* **1.** *US* MIL RANK IN THE US FORCES a commissioned officer in the US Army, Marine Corps, and Air Force ranking immediately below captain and above second lieutenant **2.** NAVY NAVAL OFFICER MAINTAINING A SHIP a naval officer in charge of the upkeep and maintenance of a ship

first light *n.* the earliest part or time of the day, when the Sun begins to rise

firstling /fúrstling/ *n.* the first of sth, e.g. an offspring, product, or result (*archaic or literary*)

first love *n.* **1.** FIRST EXPERIENCE OF LOVE the experience of being in love for the first time **2.** FIRST RECIPIENT OF LOVE the first object of sb's romantic love or affectionate admiration

firstly /fúrstli/ *adv.* used to introduce the first point in an argument or discussion

first mate *n.* an officer on a merchant ship or any nonnaval vessel who ranks immediately below the captain

First Minister *n.* the title of the leader of the National Assembly of Northern Ireland, Scotland, or Wales

first name *n.* a personal name that accompanies a family name to identify sb fully

First Nation, **first nation** *n. Can* in Canada, a community of indigenous people who are bound by treaty to the federal government

first night *n.* the first public performance of a new production of a play or show, or the day on which this takes place (*hyphenated when used before a noun*) ◊ *first-night nerves*

first nighter /-nîtər/ *n.* sb who regularly attends the first night of new plays or shows

first offender *n.* sb with no previous criminal record who breaks the law and is convicted for the first time

first officer *n.* **1.** = **first mate 2.** AIRCRAFT COMMANDER the aircraft commander, or captain, of a commercial aircraft

first-past-the-post *adj. UK, Can* used to describe a voting system in which the winning candidate needs to receive more votes than any other candidate but does not need to get an absolute majority of the votes cast

first person *n.* the style of verb and accompanying pronoun that is used when referring to the speaker or writer, or a group including the speaker or writer

1st person plural *n.* LING the form of a verb used with 'we'

1st person singular *n.* LING the form of a verb used with 'I'

first position *n.* a position in ballet in which the feet are turned outwards with the heels touching

first post *n.* the first of two bugle calls at the end of the day, signalling to military personnel that it is time to retire to barracks before lights out

first principle *n.* a fundamental rule underlying a theory, faith, or procedure

first quarter *n.* one of four phases of the Moon, during which one half of the Moon's visible surface is illuminated by the Sun

first-rate *adj.* of the best quality or the highest standard

first reading *n.* the introduction of a bill in a legislature prior to debate and a vote

first refusal *n.* the right to decide whether or not to buy sth before it is offered to other potential buyers

first school *n.* in some localities, a school for pupils from five to eight years of age

first strike *n.* the use of nuclear weapons against an enemy that is similarly armed, intended to destroy its military capacity and prevent it from attacking first (*hyphenated before a noun*) ◊ *first-strike capability*

first water *n.* the highest grade in gemstones

First World *n.* the principal industrialized countries of the world, including the United States, the United Kingdom, the nations of Western Europe, Japan, Canada, Australia, and New Zealand

First World War *n.* = **World War I**

firth /furth/ *n. Scotland* a river estuary, or a wide inlet of the sea (*often used in placenames*) [14thC. From Old Norse *fjörðr* (see FJORD).]

fisc /fisk/ *n.* **1.** *US* TREASURY a public treasury **2.** ROYAL TREASURY royal funds, especially those belonging to a Roman emperor (*archaic*) [Late 16thC. Directly or via French from Latin *fiscus*, literally 'rush basket', later 'purse, treasury'.]

fiscal /físk'l/ *adj.* **1.** OF THE PUBLIC TREASURY relating to public revenues, especially those raised from taxation ◊ *fiscal prudence* **2.** FINANCIAL relating to financial matters in general ■ *n. Scotland* = **procurator fiscal** [Mid-16thC. Directly or via French from Latin *fiscalis*, from *fiscus* (see FISC).]

fiscal year *n. US* = **financial year**

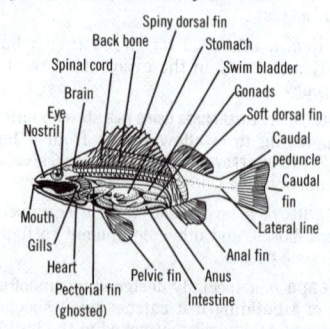

Fish: Anatomy of a fish

Labels: Spiny dorsal fin · Stomach · Swim bladder · Gonads · Back bone · Spinal cord · Soft dorsal fin · Brain · Caudal peduncle · Eye · Caudal fin · Nostril · Lateral line · Mouth · Anal fin · Gills · Anus · Heart · Intestine · Pectoral fin (ghosted) · Pelvic fin

fish /fish/ *n.* (*plural* **fish** *or* **fishes**) **1.** ZOOL AQUATIC VERTEBRATE WITH GILLS any cold-blooded aquatic vertebrate animal that typically has jaws, fins, scales, a slender body, a two-chambered heart, and gills for providing oxygen to the blood (*often used before a noun*) ○ *a fish tank* **2.** FOOD FISH CONSUMED AS FOOD the flesh of any edible fish consumed as food, either cooked or raw (*often used before a noun*) ○ *fish soup* **3.** SB UNUSUAL sb who is unusual or regarded as strange (*informal*) ○ *an odd fish* ■ v. (**fishes, fishing, fished**) **1.** vi. CATCH FISH to use a rod, net, or some other method to bring fish out of the water **2.** vt. CATCH FISH IN A PLACE to try to get fish from a particular river, lake, or stream **3.** vi. SEARCH to feel around with the hands in order to find sth (*informal*) [Old English *fisc*. Ultimately from an Indo-European word that is also the ancestor of English *Pisces* and *porpoise*.] ◇ **drink like a fish** to habitually drink a lot of alcoholic liquor (*informal*) ◇ **have other fish to fry** to have sth else to do, usually sth more interesting (*informal*) ◇ **like a fish out of water** ill at ease in a situation

fish for vt. to search, especially in an indirect way or in difficult circumstances

fish out vt. to find sth or take sth out, especially after searching with the hands (*informal*) ○ *He fished out a coin from his pocket.*

Fish n. ZODIAC = **Pisces**

fish and chips n. a fillet of fish deep-fried in batter, served with chips (*takes a singular or plural verb*)

fishbowl /físh bōl/ n. **1.** ROUND GLASS BOWL a round clear open-topped container of water in which a pet goldfish is kept **2.** PUBLIC LIFESTYLE a place or condition of high public visibility and little or no personal privacy

fish cake n. a round flat individual savoury cake made from cooked fish mixed with potato and other ingredients, coated with breadcrumbs, and fried, baked, or grilled

fish duck n. BIRDS = **merganser**

fish eagle n. BIRDS = **osprey**

fisher /físhər/ n. a carnivorous mammal of northern North America, a species of marten, with dense dark brown fur. Latin name: *Martes pennanti*. [Old English]

Fisher /físhər/, **Andrew** (1862–1928) Scottish-born Australian statesman. He was leader of the Australian Labor Party (1907–15) and prime minister of Australia (1908–09, 1910–13, and 1914–15).

fisherman /físhərmən/ (*plural* **-men** /-mən/) n. sb who fishes as a sport or occupation

fisherman's bend n. a knot used to tie the end of a line to a ring or spar

fisherman's knot n. a knot for joining the ends of two ropes, consisting of one or two overhand knots that tighten with tension on the line

fishery /físhəri/ (*plural* **-ies**) n. **1.** REGION OF WATER FOR FISHING a region of water where industrial fishing is practised **2.** FISHING INDUSTRY the catching, processing, or selling of fish, including the industries and occupations involved in these activities **3.** FISH BUSINESS a business that harvests, processes, or sells fish **4.** PLACE FOR REARING FISH a region of water or a tank in which fish are reared **5.** LAW RIGHT TO FISH the right to fish in an area

Fishes /físhiz/ n. ZODIAC = **Pisces**

Fisheye lens: View from a fisheye lens of Wall Street, New York City

fisheye lens /físh ī-/ n. a wide-angle lens that gives an extremely wide field of view, up to 180 degrees.

Straight lines are curved and distorted by this type of lens.

fish farm n. a place with facilities for rearing fish commercially —**fish farmer** n. —**fish farming** n.

fish finger n. a rectangular piece of filleted or minced fish covered in breadcrumbs or batter, usually bought frozen in packs. US term **fish stick**

fishgig /físh gig/ n. ANGLING a pole with barbs, used for spearing fish [Mid-16thC. By folk etymology from earlier FIZGIG, by association with FISH.]

fish hawk n. = **osprey**

fishhook /físh hŏŏk/ n. **1.** HOOK FOR CATCHING FISH a sharp metal hook used for catching fish **2.** LOGIC SYMBOL IN LOGIC a symbol used in logic to represent a conditional such as 'if' or 'then'

fishing /físhing/ n. the sport, industry, or occupation of catching fish

fishing ground n. an area of the sea where a country has the right to fish

fishing rod n. a long flexible pole to which a fishing line and usually a reel are attached for catching fish

fish joint n. a connection in which two rails or beams are joined together by one or more fishplates [*Fish* of uncertain origin: probably from French *fiche* (see FISHPLATE)]

fish kettle n. an oblong pan, often with a rack inside, for cooking a whole fish

fish knife n. a broad-bladed knife with blunt edges, used for eating fish

fish ladder n. a series of pools on an incline separated by short increments so as to enable fish to swim up past a dam or other obstruction

fish louse n. a small flat rounded crustacean with sucking mouth parts that lives as a parasite on fish. Class: Branchiura.

fishmeal /físh meel/ n. a substance prepared from ground dried fish, used as an animal feed and a fertilizer

fishmonger /físh mungər/ n. sb who sells fish to eat

fishnet /físh net/ n. **1.** TEXTILES FABRIC SIMILAR TO NETTING an open mesh fabric that looks like netting and is often used to make stockings and tights **2.** US, Can NET FOR FISHING a net used to catch fish

fish owl n. a large southern Asian owl with sharp curved claws that lives in wooded country near water. It feeds mainly on fish, but also eats snakes, other small vertebrates, insects, and occasionally carrion, hunting by day. Genus: *Ketupa*.

fishplate /físh playt/ n. a flat piece of metal bolted between two abutting rails or beams to join them, especially on a railway track [Mid-19thC. *Fish* of uncertain origin: probably from French *fiche* 'peg', from *fichier* 'to drive in, fasten', from, ultimately, Latin *figere* (source of English *fix*).]

fishpond /físh pond/ n. a pond where fish are found or kept

fishskin disease /físhskin-/ n. ichthyosis (*informal*)

fish slice n. a kitchen utensil with a flat slotted blade, used for turning over food during cooking

fish stick n. US = **fish finger**

fishtail /físh tayl/ vi. (**-tails, -tailing, -tailed**) AIR SWING AEROPLANE'S TAIL TO REDUCE SPEED to move the tail of an aeroplane from side to side in order to reduce speed ■ adj. CLOTHES GATHERED AND FLARED used to describe the back of a skirt or dress that has a section that is closely gathered or pleated and then flares out

fishwife /físh wīf/ n. **1.** COARSE AND LOUD WOMAN a woman who is seen as coarse and loud-voiced (*insult*) **2.** WOMAN FISH SELLER a woman selling fish in former times (*archaic*)

fishy /físhi/ (**-ier, -iest**) adj. **1.** LIKE FISH like fish, especially in taste, smell, or coldness or sliminess to the touch **2.** DUBIOUS arousing suspicion (*informal*) **3.** EXPRESSIONLESS cold and expressionless, like the eye of a fish —**fishily** adv. —**fishiness** n.

Fisk /fisk/, **Sir Ernest Thomas** (1886–1965) English-born Australian telecommunications engineer. In 1918 he received the first wireless transmission sent from the United Kingdom to Australia.

fissi- prefix. **1.** cleft, separated ○ *fissipedal* **2.** biological fission ○ *fissiparous* [From Latin *fissus*, past participle of *findere* 'to split'. Ultimately from an Indo-European base that is also the ancestor of English *bite* and *boat*.]

fissile /físsīl/ adj. **1.** NUCLEAR PHYS = **fissionable 2.** GEOL ABLE TO BE SPLIT used to describe a rock that can be split along a grain or a plane of cleavage, e.g. slate or schist [Mid-17thC. Formed from Latin *fiss-*, the past participle stem of *findere* (see FISSION).] —**fissility** /fi sílləti/ n.

fission /físhən/ n. **1.** BREAKING UP the act or process of separating into parts **2.** NUCLEAR PHYS SPLITTING OF ATOMIC NUCLEUS RELEASING ENERGY the spontaneous or induced splitting of an atomic nucleus into smaller nuclei, usually accompanied by a significant release of energy **3.** BIOL DIVISION OF AN ORGANISM the division of a single-celled organism into two equal parts, each part growing into a complete organism [Early 17thC. From the Latin stem *fission-*, from *fiss-*, the past participle stem of *findere* 'to split' (source of English *fissure*).]

fissionable /físh'nəb'l/ adj. able to undergo nuclear fission —**fissionability** /físh'nə bílləti/ n.

fission bomb n. an atom bomb (*technical*)

fission-track dating n. a method of determining the age of a mineral by observing the tracks made in it by fission products of the uranium atoms it contains

fissiparous /fi síppərəss/ adj. BIOL used to describe an organism that reproduces by dividing into two equal parts, each of which grows into a complete organism —**fissiparously** adv.

fissiped /físsə ped/ adj. fissiped, fissipedal ZOOL WITH SEPARATED TOES used to describe animals that have toes separated from each other, e.g. dogs and cats ■ n. SEPARATE-TOED ANIMAL an animal with separate toes. Suborder: Fissipedia. [Mid-17thC. From late Latin *fissiped-*, from, ultimately, Latin *findere* 'to split' + *ped-*, *pes* 'foot'.]

fissure /físhər/ n. **1.** CRACK a long narrow crack or opening, especially in rock **2.** PROCESS OF SPLITTING the process of dividing along a line **3.** ANAT SPLIT IN BODY PART a natural or pathological division in a body part **4.** SCHISM IN GROUP a division in a group or party ■ vti. (**-sures, -suring, -sured**) SPLIT OR CAUSE TO SPLIT to split sth along fairly regular lines, or undergo this process [14thC. Directly or via French from Latin *fissura*, from the stem *fiss-* (see FISSION).]

fist /fist/ n. **1.** CLENCHED HAND a hand with the fingers closed in the palm **2.** HAND a hand (*informal*) **3.** = **fistful 4.** PRINTING = **index** n. ☞ ■ v. (**fists, fisting, fisted**) **1.** vt. HIT SB WITH THE FIST to hit sb or sth with a fist **2.** vti. = **fistfuck** (*offensive taboo*) [Old English *fȳst*, from a prehistoric Germanic word of uncertain origin: probably ultimately from an Indo-European word meaning 'five', which is also the ancestor of English *five*]

fistfight /físt fīt/ n. a fight in which bare fists are used

fistfuck /físt fuk/ (**-fucks, -fucking, -fucked**) vti. an offensive term meaning to insert a fist into sb's vagina or anus for sexual pleasure (*offensive taboo*)

fistful /fístfŏŏl/ n. the amount that can be held within a fist

fistic /fístik/ adj. relating to boxing (*informal*)

fisticuffs /físti kufs/ npl. fighting using the fists (*archaic or humorous*) [Early 17thC. Origin uncertain: probably from *fisty* 'with the fists' + CUFF 'blow'.]

fistula /fístyŏŏlə/ (*plural* **-las** *or* **-lae** /-lee/) n. an abnormal opening or passage between two organs or between an organ and the skin, caused by disease, injury, or congenital malformation [14thC. Directly or via French from Latin *fistula* 'pipe, flute' (source of English *fester*).]

fistulous /fístyŏŏləss/, **fistular** /-lər/, **fistulate** /-lət/ adj. **1.** MED WITH A FISTULA having or resembling a fistula **2.** ANAT TUBULAR tubular **3.** ANAT MADE UP OF TUBES composed of or containing tubes

fit[1] /fit/ v. (**fits, fitting, fitted**) **1.** vti. BE THE RIGHT SIZE OR SHAPE to be of a suitable size or shape for sth or sb ○ *See if this jacket fits.* **2.** vti. BE APPROPRIATE to be appropriate or suitable for sth ○ *make the punishment fit the crime* **3.** vti. BE COMPATIBLE to agree or be in accordance with sth ○ *no one fitting that description* **4.** vt. CLOTHES TRY CLOTHING ON to try clothing on sb to determine if changes are necessary **5.** vt. EQUIP SB OR STH to provide sb or sth with equipment of a particular kind ○ *fitted with extra security features* **6.** *vt.* MAKE STH READY to make sb or sth ready or suitable for a task, function, or purpose ○ *an education that will fit her for a career in business* **7.** *vt.* INSTALL STH to install sth, or put sth in place ■ *adj.* (**fitter, fittest**) **1.** APPROPRIATE suitable, acceptable, or appropriate for a purpose ○ *dishes fit for everyday use* **2.** WORTHY worthy or deserving of sth ○ *not fit to serve as an officer* **3.** WELL IN HEALTH in good health **4.** STRONG AND HEALTHY physically strong and healthy, especially because of taking regular exercise ○ *getting fit* **5.** APPEARING LIKELY TO DO STH appearing likely to do sth because of being in an extreme condition (*informal*) ○ *looked fit to burst in a shirt too small for him* **6.** SEXUALLY DESIRABLE sexually desirable (*regional slang*) ■ *n.* **1.** WAY THAT STH FITS the way in which sth conforms to standards of proper length, tightness, and shape ○ *These shoes are a better fit than the other pair.* **2.** RELATIONSHIP FOR BEST FUNCTION a relationship between corresponding parts or related things that enables proper functioning ○ *check the replacement chassis for fit* **3.** MECH ENG CLOSENESS OF SURFACES the closeness of contact between adjacent surfaces in a mechanical assembly **4.** *Ireland* STANZA a verse in poetry (*formal*) [14thC. Origin uncertain: probably originally in the sense 'to marshal troops', later 'to be suitable'.]

fit in *v.* **1.** *vi.* CONFORM WELL to conform harmoniously to other members of a group or other things in a setting ○ *She's been able to fit in well at her new school.* **2.** *vt.* FIND TIME FOR to find a time or place for sb or sth that does not disturb other arrangements ○ *The dentist can fit you in at three.* ○ *I love the theatre but can't fit it into my schedule.*

fit out *vt.* to equip or provide sth or sb with required items, e.g. supplies or clothes

fit up *vt.* **1.** EQUIP SB OR STH to provide or equip sb or sth with sth **2.** MAKE SB APPEAR GUILTY to make sb who is innocent appear guilty (*slang*)

fit² /fit/ *n.* **1.** SUDDEN OUTBURST a sudden occurrence of a physical activity or an emotional mood ○ *a fit of laughing* ○ *a coughing fit* **2.** CONVULSIONS sudden violent convulsions, e.g. in a child with a high fever or sb experiencing a seizure [14thC. Origin uncertain: perhaps from Old English *fitt* 'conflict'. The meaning 'sudden attack' evolved from 'experience of hardship'.] ◊ **by fits and starts** starting and stopping repeatedly ◊ **throw a fit** to show strong emotion, especially anger (*informal*)

fitch /fich/, **fitchet** /fíchət/ *n.* = **polecat** [15thC. From Middle Dutch *fisse*.]

fitful /fítf'l/ *adj.* starting and stopping irregularly ○ *a fitful sleep* —**fitfully** *adv.* —**fitfulness** *n.*

fitly /fítli/ *adv.* in an appropriate way or place (*archaic*)

fitment /fítmənt/ *n.* sth that can be detached or taken down

fitness /fítnəs/ *n.* **1.** BEING PHYSICALLY FIT the state of being physically fit **2.** SUITABILITY suitability of sb or sth to a particular purpose **3.** GENETICS ABILITY TO REPRODUCE SUCCESSFULLY the ability of an individual to produce offspring that survive and reproduce

fitness centre *n.* a place with facilities and equipment for people to maintain or improve their physical fitness

fitted /fítid/ *adj.* **1.** MADE TO FIT tailored to fit closely to the body **2.** BUILT FOR A SPACE built for and fixed into a designated space **3.** WITH FITTED FURNITURE with fitted furniture **4.** CUT TO COVER FLOOR cut to cover a floor area exactly. US term **wall-to-wall**

fitted sheet *n.* a sheet with elastic at the corners that makes it fit snugly over a mattress

fitter /fítər/ *n.* **1.** INDUST SB WHO MAINTAINS MACHINERY sb who maintains, repairs, or assembles mechanical equipment **2.** CLOTHES SB WHO ALTERS CLOTHES sb who alters clothes to make them fit

fitting /fítting/ *adj.* SUITABLE appropriate for the circumstances ○ *a fitting end to her career* ■ *n.* **1.** DETACHABLE PART a detachable part, especially for a device or machine **2.** TRYING ON OF CLOTHES the trying on of a piece of clothing to see if it requires alteration **3.** FITTER'S WORK the work performed by a fitter **4.** CLOTHES SIZE a size of clothes or shoes ■ **fittings** *npl.* FURNITURE AND ACCESSORIES furniture and accessories not per-

manently fixed to a building —**fittingly** *adv.* —**fittingness** *n.*

fitting room *n.* a room for trying on or fitting clothes in a shop

fit-up *n.* (*slang*) **1.** FALSIFICATION OF EVIDENCE an act of falsifying evidence so as to make sb appear guilty of a crime. Also called **frame-up**. ▪ **2.** THEATRE PORTABLE SET a set and its props that are easily erected

Ella Fitzgerald

AKG London

Fitzgerald /fits jérrəld/, **Ella** (1917–96) US jazz singer. She was known for her scat singing and extensive song repertoire.

F. Scott Fitzgerald

Library of Congress

Fitzgerald, F. Scott (1890–1940) US writer. He penned novels and short stories that chronicled the mood and manners of the 1920s. Among his works is *The Great Gatsby* (1925). Full name **Francis Scott Key Fitzgerald**

Fitzroy /fits roy/ river in northern Western Australia that rises in the Durack Range and empties into the Indian Ocean near Derby. Length: 620 km/385 mi.

Fitzsimmons /fits símmənz/, **Bob** (1862–1917) British-born New Zealand boxer. In 1897 he became world heavyweight champion, a title he held until 1899. Full name **Robert Prometheus Fitzsimmons**

five /fiv/ *n.* **1.** NUMBER 5 the number 5 **2.** GROUP OF 5 a group of five objects or people **3.** STH WITH VALUE OF 5 sth in a numbered series, e.g. a playing card, with a value of 5 ○ *the five of clubs* ○ *to throw a five* [Old English *fíf*. Ultimately from an Indo-European word meaning 'five', which is also the ancestor of English *pentagon*, *punch* 'beverage', and *Pentecost*.] —**five** *adj.*, *pron.*

five-and-dime *n.* US a shop in the United States of a type, now obsolete, that sold household goods, toys, sweets, small pets, and other assorted items at reasonable prices (*dated*)

five-a-side *n.* a type of soccer with five players in each team

Five Civilized Nations, **Five Civilized Tribes** *npl.* five Native North American tribes, the Choctaw, Cherokee, Chickasaw, Creek, and Seminole, who were briefly self-governing in the Indian Territory after being displaced from their land in the southeastern United States

five-eighth *n.* ANZ a rugby player positioned between the half-backs and three-quarters

five-finger *n.* a plant, e.g. cinquefoil, that has leaves or flowers with five segments

fivefold /fív fōld/ *adj.* **1.** TIMES 5 with or equal to five times as much or as many **2.** WITH 5 PARTS composed

of five parts or sections ■ *adv.* BY FIVE TIMES AS MUCH by five times as much or as many

five hundred *n.* euchre or rummy in which the winner is the first to reach 500 points

five Ks *n.* the five distinctive features of dress worn by members of a Sikh order (**Khalsa**). ◊ **kesh, kangha, kirpan, kuccha, kara**

five o'clock shadow *n.* beard growth noticeable late in the day on a man who shaved in the morning

five of a kind *n.* a poker hand consisting of four cards of the same denomination plus a wild card

fivepenny /fífpəni/ *adj.* costing or worth five pence

fivepins /fívpinz/ *n.* a bowling game played in Canada in which five skittles are used (*takes a singular verb*)

fiver /fívər/ *n.* **1.** 5-POUND NOTE a note worth five pounds **2.** US 5-DOLLAR NOTE a banknote worth five dollars

fives /fívz/ *n.* a game like squash but in which the ball is hit with the hand or a bat (*takes a singular verb*) [Mid-17thC. Origin uncertain: probably plural of FIVE.]

five-spice powder *n.* a Chinese mixed spice consisting of star anise, anise or Szechuan pepper, cinnamon, fennel, and cloves

fivespot *n.* US a banknote worth five dollars (*slang*)

five-star *adj.* first-class, or offering the highest standards and quality

five-star general *n.* a general of the highest rank, with an insignia of five stars

five stones *n.* the game of jacks when five small stones are used as the throwing pieces (*takes a singular verb*)

fix /fiks/ *v.* (**fixes, fixing, fixed**) **1.** *vt.* MEND OR CORRECT STH to repair, mend, or correct sth **2.** *vt.* AGREE STH to agree, arrange, or settle sth, especially a time or a price **3.** *vt.* FASTEN STH to fasten sth in place **4.** *vt.* ATTRIBUTE STH to attribute sth, especially blame ○ *to fix the blame on other people* **5.** *vti.* MAKE OR BECOME SECURE to make sth stable, firm, or secure, or become so **6.** *vt.* DIRECT STH to direct or concentrate the eyes, attention, or mind ○ *She fixed her eyes on the path ahead.* **7.** *vt.* HOLD SB'S ATTENTION to hold or capture the attention or interest of sb ○ *fixed us with a baleful smile* **8.** *vt.* INFLUENCE STH DISHONESTLY to influence a person or outcome dishonestly (*informal*) ○ *The trial was fixed.* **9.** *vt.* TAKE REVENGE ON to take revenge on or punish sb (*informal*) **10.** *vt.* US PREPARE STH AS FOOD to prepare sth, especially a meal or a drink (*informal*) **11.** *vt.* US ARRANGE OR ORDER STH to arrange sth, or put sth in order (*informal*) **12.** *vt.* US VET STERILIZE AN ANIMAL to spay or castrate an animal (*informal*) **13.** *vi.* DRUGS INJECT A DRUG to inject an illegal drug (*slang*) **14.** *vt.* BIOCHEM CONVERT NITROGEN TO A STABLE FORM to convert atmospheric nitrogen to a stable or biologically available form (*refers to soil bacteria*) **15.** *vti.* CHEM MAKE OR BECOME STABLE to make a chemical or compound stable and nonvolatile, or undergo this process **16.** *vt.* PHOTOGRAPHY, PAINTING MAKE PERMANENT to treat sth such as a photographic film or plate with chemicals in order to make a permanent image **17.** *vt.* BIOL PRESERVE STH FOR EXAMINATION to prevent change and decay in a specimen by preserving it in a chemical solution, especially for study under the microscope ■ *n.* **1.** PREDICAMENT a predicament or difficult situation (*informal*) ○ *in a fix* **2.** SUPERFICIAL SOLUTION an immediate and often temporary solution (*informal*) ○ *a quick fix* **3.** NAVIG CALCULATION OF POSITION a calculation of the position of an object using radar or other forms of observation **4.** UNDERSTANDING an understanding or identification of sth (*informal*) ○ *Do you have a fix on what the problem is?* **5.** INFLUENCING DISHONESTLY an instance of influencing an outcome or person dishonestly (*informal*) **6.** DRUGS ILLEGAL DRUG INJECTION an injection of an illegal drug (*slang*) **7.** STIMULATING DOSE a dose of or exposure to sth pleasurable and stimulating (*humorous*) ○ *a chocolate fix* [15thC. Immediate origin uncertain: ultimately from Latin *fix-*, the past participle stem of *figere* 'to fix'.] —**fixable** *adj.*

fix on *vt.* to select sth

fix up *vt.* **1.** ARRANGE STH to arrange sth, e.g. a meeting or a date **2.** ARRANGE A CONTACT FOR SB to arrange a business or social contact, or a romantic or sexual partner, for sb **3.** **REPAIR STH** to restore sth to working order or proper order

fixate /fíks ayt/ **(-ates, -ating, -ated)** *v.* **1.** *vti.* **FOCUS ON STH** to focus exclusively on sth **2.** *vt.* **OBSESS SB** to obsess or preoccupy sb or sth totally **3.** *vti.* PSYCHOL **FORM A FIXATION** to form or have a psychological fixation to a person or object **4.** *vti.* **BECOME OR MAKE FIXED** to make sth stable or secure, or become so [Late 19thC. Formed from the Latin stem *fix-* (see FIX).]

fixation /fik sáysh'n/ *n.* **1.** **OBSESSION** an obsession or preoccupation **2.** PSYCHOL **IMMATURE PSYCHOSEXUAL BEHAVIOUR** a theoretical abnormally strong libidinal attachment to a person or object, formed during early childhood, that results in neurotic or arrested psychosexual behaviour in adulthood **3.** BIOCHEM **CONVERSION OF NITROGEN** the conversion by soil bacteria of atmospheric nitrogen to a stable and biologically available form ○ *nitrogen fixation* **4.** CHEM **STABILIZATION OF CHEMICAL** the process of stabilizing a chemical or compound **5.** BIOL **PRESERVING FOR EXAMINATION** the process of preserving a biological specimen with a chemical

fixative /fíksətiv/ *n.* **1.** **LIQUID SPRAYED FOR PROTECTION** a liquid sprayed onto a drawing, photograph, or other surface to protect it **2.** **GLUE** a substance used to hold sth in place **3.** COSMETICS **PERFUME ADDITIVE** a substance added to a perfume to make it evaporate less rapidly **4.** BIOL **CHEMICAL PRESERVATIVE** a chemical solution that preserves a biological specimen for microscopic study **5.** TEXTILES **FABRIC ADDITIVE** a substance applied to dyed fabrics to make the dye colourfast ■ *adj.* **TENDING TO FIX** acting or tending to fix sth

fixed /fikst/ *adj.* **1.** **SECURE** immovable or securely in position **2.** **NOT SUBJECT TO CHANGE** not subject to change in amount or time **3.** **NOT CHANGING** unchanging in expression **4.** **AGREED ON** arranged or agreed upon **5.** **HELD IN MIND** firmly or dogmatically held in the mind **6.** **PROVIDED WITH STH** in the position of having sth at your disposal (*informal*) ○ *How are you fixed for money?* **7.** **DISHONESTLY ARRANGED** unfairly or illegally arranged (*slang*) **8.** CHEM **CHEMICALLY STABLE** combined in stable form ○ *fixed nitrogen* **9.** ZODIAC **STABLE IN ZODIACAL TERMS** used to describe Taurus, Leo, Scorpio, and Aquarius, signs of the zodiac associated with stability —**fixedly** /fíksidli/ *adv.* —**fixedness** /fíksidnəss/ *n.*

fixed asset *n.* an asset of a business that is central to its operation and is not traded (*usually used in the plural*)

fixed cost *n.* a business expense that does not vary according to the amount of business (*usually used in the plural*)

fixed-head coupé *n.* a car with four seats, two doors, and a fixed roof

fixed idea *n.* = **idée fixe**

fixed line *adj.* used to describe a telephone that is connected to a network via underground or overground lines ○ *'The card is free and can be used from any mobile or fixed line phone'.* (*Marketing Week*; December 1998)

fixed oil *n.* a nonvolatile oil composed of fatty acids, usually of animal or vegetable origin

fixed penalty *n.* a fine for a specific amount given for a particular offence

fixed penalty notice *n.* a ticket that the police can issue on the spot for minor motoring offences

fixed point *n.* a temperature, e.g. boiling or freezing point, that has a fixed value under specific conditions and can be used to calibrate instruments

fixed-point *adj.* used to describe or relating to a mathematical notation system, e.g. the decimal system, in which the point separating whole numbers from fractional values is in a fixed position

fixed-wing *adj.* used to describe an aircraft that has stationary wings, especially as distinct from rotor blades

fixer /fíksər/ *n.* **1.** **SB OR STH THAT FIXES** a person who or an object that fixes sth **2.** **SB WHO ARRANGES STH DISHONEST** sb who arranges sth, especially using dishonest or illegal means (*slang*) **3.** PHOTOGRAPHY **CHEMICAL IN PHOTOGRAPHY** a chemical that halts the development of a photographic image on film or paper

fixing /fíksing/ *n.* **HOLDING DEVICE** a means for holding an item in place ■ **fixings** *npl. US, Can* COOK **INGREDIENTS** the ingredients required for a dish

fixity /fíksəti/ (*plural* **-ties**) *n.* **1.** **STATE OF BEING FIXED** the quality or state of being fixed and unchanging **2.** **STH NOT CHANGING** sth that is unchanging (*formal*)

fixture /fíkschər/ *n.* **1.** **OBJECT IN FIXED POSITION** an object with a fixed position and function **2.** **ESTABLISHED PERSON** sb considered to be permanently established in a place or position **3.** **SPORTS EVENT** a sports event or its date **4.** **SOCIAL EVENT** a select social event or its date [Late 16thC. Origin uncertain: probably an alteration, on the model of MIXTURE, of *fixure*, from late Latin *fixura*, from Latin *fix-* (see FIX).]

fizgig /fízgig/ *n.* **1.** **FLIRTATIOUS GIRL** a flippant or flirtatious girl (*dated*) **2.** **FIZZING FIREWORK** a firework that fizzes when in motion **3.** ANGLING = **fishgig** [Early 16thC. Origin uncertain: probably from FIZZ + *gig* 'giddy girl'; 'fishgig' sense probably ultimately from Spanish *fisga* 'harpoon'.]

fizz /fiz/ *vi.* **(fizzes, fizzing, fizzed)** **1.** **PRODUCE GAS BUBBLES** to produce bubbles of gas **2.** **HISS** to make a hissing or continuous soft crackling sound ■ *n.* **1.** **EFFERVESCENCE** the sparkling quality of a drink caused by bubbles of gas **2.** **HISSING SOUND** a hissing or continuous soft crackling sound **3.** **LIVELINESS** a quality of liveliness or excitement ○ *All the fizz has gone out of the election campaign.* **4.** BEVERAGES **SPARKLING DRINK** a sparkling drink, especially champagne [Mid-17thC. An imitation of the sound.]

fizzer /fízzər/ *n. Aus* an event that fails to live up to expectations (*informal*)

fizzle /fízz'l/ *vi.* **(-zles, -zling, -zled)** **1.** **MAKE HISSING SOUND** to make a gentle hissing sound **2.** **FAIL AFTER GOOD START** to fail or peter out, especially after a good start ■ *n.* **1.** **HISSING SOUND** a gentle hissing sound **2.** **FAILURE** a fiasco or total failure (*informal*) [Mid-16thC. Origin uncertain: probably from obsolete *fist* 'to break wind' (source also of English *feist*), from prehistoric Germanic.]

fizzy /fízzi/ **(-ier, -iest)** *adj.* producing or containing gas bubbles —**fizzily** *adv.* —**fizziness** *n.*

Barnaby's

Fjord: Geiranger Fjord, Norway

fjord /fée awrd/, **fiord** *n.* a long narrow coastal inlet with steep sides, often formed by glacial action, especially along the west coast of Norway [Late 17thC. Via Norwegian from Old Norse *fjǫ̈rðr*. Ultimately from an Indo-European word that is the ancestor of English *fare*, *firth*, and *ford*.]

Fkr *symbol.* Faroese krona

FL *abbr.* **1.** Florida **2.** Liechtenstein (*international vehicle registration*) **3.** Flight Lieutenant

fl. *abbr.* **1.** floor **2.** MONEY florin **3.** floruit **4.** MUSIC flute

Fl. *abbr.* **1.** Flanders **2.** Flemish

Fla. *abbr.* Florida

flab /flab/ *n.* excess or unwanted fat on sb's body (*informal disapproving*) [Early 20thC. Back-formation from FLABBY.]

flabbergast /flábbər gaast/ **(-gasts, -gasting, -gasted)** *vt.* to amaze or astonish sb completely (*informal; usually passive*) [Late 18thC. Origin uncertain: perhaps from FLABBY or FLAPPER + AGHAST.]

flabby /flábbi/ **(-bier, -biest)** *adj.* **1.** **HAVING EXCESS FAT** having excess body fat or sagging flesh (*informal disapproving*) **2.** **WEAK** done without vitality or force (*informal*) [Late 17thC. Alteration of FLAPPY.] —**flabbily** *adv.* —**flabbiness** *n.*

flabella plural of **flabellum**

flabellate /flə béllit/, **flabelliform** /flə bélli fawrm/ *adj.* shaped like an open handheld fan [Late 18thC. Formed from Latin *flabellum* (see FLABELLUM).]

flabellum /flə bélləm/ (*plural* **-la** /-lə/) *n.* **1.** BIOL **FAN-SHAPED BODY PART** fan-shaped organ or body part **2.** CHR **FAN USED IN ROMAN CATHOLIC CHURCH** a fan with a long handle, used in the past in the Roman Catholic Church to keep away insects during the Communion service [Mid-19thC. From Latin *flabellum* 'fan', from *flabrum* 'gust', from *flare* 'to blow' (source of English *flatulent*).]

flaccid /fláksid/ *adj.* **1.** **LIMP** soft, limp, or lacking firmness **2.** **LACKING VITALITY** lacking energy, enthusiasm, or competence [Early 17thC. Directly or via French from Latin *flaccidus*, from *flaccus* 'flabby'.] —**flaccidity** /flak síddəti/ *n.* —**flaccidly** /fláksidli/ *adv.*

flack[1] /flak/ *n. US, Can* **PRESS AGENT** a press agent or publicist (*slang*) ■ *vti.* **(flacks, flacking, flacked)** *US, Can* **BE PRESS AGENT** to act as a press agent or publicity agent for sb (*slang*) [Mid-20thC. Origin uncertain: possibly a variant of FLAK, from the supposed similarity between antiaircraft fire and the noisy babbling of press agents.] —**flacker** *n.* —**flackery** *n.*

flack[2] *n.* = **flak**

flacon /flákon/ *n.* a small, often decorated, stoppered bottle used especially for perfume [Early 19thC. From French *fla(s)con* (see FLAGON).]

flag[1] /flag/ *n.* **1.** **CLOTH FLOWN AS EMBLEM** a piece of cloth, often rectangular and flown from a pole, carrying a distinctive design and used as an emblem or for signalling **2.** **DECORATION** a small ornament, emblem, or badge showing the colours and design of a flag **3.** POL **NATIONAL IDENTITY SYMBOLIZED BY FLAG** national or group identity symbolized by a flag **4.** **MARKING DEVICE** a marking device, e.g. a tab, attached to sth to make it easier to identify or more conspicuous **5.** PRESS = **masthead** *n.* 2 **6.** NAVY = **flagship** *n.* 1 **7.** ZOOL **HAIR FRINGE BENEATH DOG'S TAIL** a fringe of hair that grows on the lower part of the tail in some dog breeds, e.g. setters **8.** ZOOL **DEER'S TAIL** the tail of a deer **9.** AMERICAN FOOTBALL **PENALTY MARKER** a coloured cloth thrown to the ground by a football official in American football to indicate illegal play **10.** TRANSP **MARKER SHOWING A TAXI FOR HIRE** formerly, a small marker on a taximeter, raised to show a taxi's availability for hire **11.** COMPUT **COMPUTER PROGRAM MARKER** an indicator generated by a computer program to indicate a certain condition, e.g. an error **12.** MUSIC **NOTE MARKER** an angled line on the stem of a musical note, indicating its value ■ *vt.* **(flags, flagging, flagged)** **1.** **MARK STH** to mark sth, e.g. a page or a place, in order to draw attention to it ○ *I've flagged the passages that need rewriting.* **2.** **INDICATE** to draw sb's attention to sth ○ *'The...service is quick to flag up offers and discounts to new members.'* (*Internet Magazine*; November 1998) **3.** COMMUNICATION **SEND INFORMATION BY FLAG** to send information using a flag or flags **4.** **STOP VEHICLE BY WAVING AT DRIVER** to make a vehicle or its driver stop by making signs to the driver **5.** AMERICAN FOOTBALL **INDICATE PENALTY** to indicate a penalty by throwing down a flag **6.** **DECORATE STH WITH FLAGS** to decorate sth with flags **7.** HUNT **ATTRACT ANIMAL'S ATTENTION** to attract the attention or curiosity of wild game by waving sth [Mid-16thC. Origin unknown. The English word is perhaps the source of the related forms found in all modern Germanic languages.] —**flagger** *n.* ◇ **show the flag** to attend a gathering just to show loyalty or support towards a country, company, or family

WORD KEY: CULTURAL NOTE

Flag, a painting by US artist Jasper Johns (1945). The first of many such variations that Johns created on this theme, it consists of a US flag painted on canvas using encaustic. Its apparent banality infuriated many commentators; others responded positively to its playful ambiguity (is it a flag or a painting?) and saw it as Johns' reaction to the emotionalism of Abstract Expressionism.

flag[2] /flag/ **(flags, flagging, flagged)** *vi.* **1.** **BECOME WEAK OR TIRED** to become weak, tired, or less attentive **2.** **HANG LIMPLY** to hang down limply or droop [Mid-16thC. Origin uncertain: perhaps a variant of earlier *flakken*, *flakeren* 'to flutter', both from a Scandinavian word.]

flag[3] /flag/ n. = **flagstone** n. 1 ▪ vt. (**flags, flagging, flagged**) **PAVE AREA WITH FLAGSTONES** to pave a surface with flagstones [15thC. Origin uncertain: probably of Scandinavian origin.]

flag[4] /flag/ n. 1. **PLANTS IRIS PLANT** a plant of the iris family, usually one with large flowers and leaves 2. **BOT LONG NARROW PLANT LEAF** a long narrow leaf of a plant such as an iris [14thC. Origin uncertain: perhaps originally 'flutterer', from Scandinavian.]

flag captain n. the captain of the flagship of a fleet

flag day n. a day on which people collect money for a charity, and those who contribute are given a small sticker. US term **tag day**

Flag Day n. 14 June, a holiday in the United States commemorating the official adoption of the design of the United States flag in 1777. It is marked by flying the flag in public places and by special activities in schools.

flagella plural of **flagellum**

flagellant /flájjələnt/, **flagellator** /flájjə laytər/ n. 1. **RELIG SELF-PUNISHING PENITENT** sb who whips himself or herself as a form of penance 2. **PSYCHOL SB SEXUALLY STIMULATED BY WHIPPING** sb who finds sexual gratification in whipping another or in being whipped [Late 16thC. From Latin *flagellant-*, present participle stem of *flagellare* 'to whip', from *flagellum* (see FLAGELLUM).] —**flagellantism** n.

flagellar /flə jéllər/ adj. relating to a flagellum

flagellate[1] /flájjə layt/ (**-lates, -lating, -lated**) vt. to whip sb, especially for sexual or religious purposes [Early 17thC. From Latin *flagellat-*, the past participle stem of *flagellare* 'to whip', from *flagellum* (see FLAGELLUM).]

flagellate[2] /flájjəlayt, -layt/ adj. **flagellate, flagellated** **BIOL** 1. **RESEMBLING A LONG THREAD** similar to a long thin cellular appendage (**flagellum**) 2. **WITH APPENDAGES RESEMBLING THREADS** used to describe an organism or cell that has long thin cellular appendages (**flagella**) ▪ n. **MICROORGANISM WITH FLAGELLA** a microorganism with tiny cellular appendages (**flagella**). Some flagellates are pathogenic parasites that cause diseases such as giardiasis in humans.

flagellation[1] /flájjə láysh'n/ n. the act of whipping yourself or sb else, especially for sexual or religious purposes

flagellation[2] /flájjə láysh'n/ n. the formation or arrangement of flagella on an organism

flagellator n. = **flagellant**

flagelliform /flə jéllə fawrm/ adj. **BIOL** long, tapering, and very narrow [Early 19thC. Coined from FLAGELLUM + -FORM.]

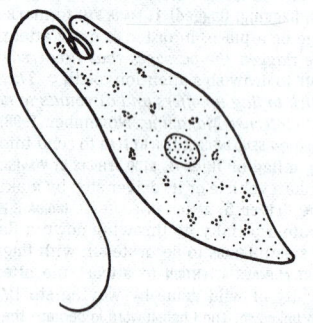

Flagellum

flagellum /flə jélləm/ (plural **flagella** /-lə/ or **flagellums**) n. 1. **BIOL SLENDER CELLULAR APPENDAGE** a slender tapering narrow outgrowth of the cells of many micro-organisms, e.g. protozoa, that is by itself or in groups, a means of locomotion 2. **INSECTS ANTENNA PART** the very narrow terminal part of an insect's antenna [Early 19thC. From Latin *flagellum*, literally 'little scourge', from *flagrum* 'scourge' (probably the source of English *flail*).]

flageolet[1] /flájjə lét/ n. **PLANTS** a slender-podded variety of French bean that can be eaten either fresh or dried [Late 19thC. Via French from, ultimately, Latin *phaseolus* 'bean'.]

flageolet[2] /flájjə lét/ n. **MUSIC** a musical instrument of the 16th and 17th centuries similar to the flute [Mid-17thC. From French, literally 'little flute', from Old French

flageol 'flute', of uncertain origin: probably ultimately from Latin *flare* 'to blow'.]

flag fall n. the minimum amount charged for the hire of a taxi

flagged /flagd/ adj. paved with flagstones

flagging[1] /flágging/ adj. 1. **WEAKENING** decreasing in strength, power, or ability 2. **HANGING LIMPLY** hanging down limply or drooping (archaic) —**flaggingly** adv.

flagging[2] /flágging/ n. an area paved with flagstones

flagitious /flə jíshəss/ adj. (formal) 1. **CRUEL OR WICKED** extremely cruel, wicked, or vicious 2. **NOTORIOUS** notorious or infamous [14thC. From Latin *flagitiosus*, from *flagitium* 'shameful crime', from *flagitare* 'to demand vehemently'.] —**flagitiously** adv. —**flagitiousness** n.

flagman /flágmən/ (plural **-men** /-mən/) n. sb who carries a flag, usually to make signals

flag of convenience n. a flag of a country under which a ship is registered chosen for its favourable regulations, not for any real connection with the ship's owners or business

flag officer n. a naval officer of admiral level who is entitled to fly the flag or pennant of the Royal Navy

flag of truce n. a white flag flown to indicate surrender, a request or offer of conference, or other peaceful intent

flagon /flággən/ n. 1. **JUG** a jug with a handle, narrow neck, spout, and sometimes a lid 2. **LARGE BOTTLE FOR ALCOHOLIC DRINK** a large bottle with a short or narrow neck for an alcoholic drink, especially cider 3. **FLAGON'S CONTENTS** the amount that a flagon will hold [14thC. Via French from the late Latin *flascon-* 'flask' (source of English *flask*).]

flagpole /flág pōl/ n. a pole on which a flag is flown

flag rank n. a rank at admiral level that gives entitlement to fly a Royal Navy flag or pennant

flagrant /fláygrənt/ adj. 1. **SCANDALOUS** very obvious and contrary to standards of conduct or morality ○ *a flagrant violation of the suspect's civil rights* 2. **ON FIRE** on fire or blazing (archaic) [15thC. Directly or via French from Latin *flagrant-*, the present participle stem of *flagrare* 'to burn' (source of English *conflagration*).] —**flagrance** n. —**flagrantly** adv.

flagrante ♦ **in flagrante delicto**

flagship /flág ship/ n. 1. **NAVY COMMANDING SHIP** the ship from which the admiral or unit commander controls the operation of a fleet 2. **SHIPPING MAIN COMMERCIAL SHIP** the main ship in a commercial fleet 3. **MOST IMPORTANT OF GROUP** the most important or prestigious among a group of similar and related things ○ *the flagship of the hotel chain*

flagstaff /flág staaf/ n. = **flagpole**

flagstick /flág stik/ n. **GOLF** the flag pole that marks the position of the hole on a putting green

flagstone /flág stōn/ n. 1. **PAVING STONE** a slab of stone or concrete used for making floors or paving 2. **GEOL ROCK THAT SPLITS INTO SLABS** fine-textured rock that can be split into slabs suitable for use in paving [Flag from FLAG[3]]

flag-waving n. an excessive and emotional display of patriotism —**flag-waver** n.

flail /flayl/ v. (**flails, flailing, flailed**) 1. vti. **THRASH AROUND** to thrash or swing sth around violently or uncontrollably, or move in this way 2. vt. **HIT STH** to strike or hit sth ▪ n. 1. **AGRIC MANUAL THRESHING IMPLEMENT** a manual threshing implement consisting of a wooden handle attached to a free-swinging wooden or metal bar 2. **ARMS WEAPON SHAPED LIKE FLAIL** a weapon shaped like a threshing flail, used especially in the Middle Ages [Pre-12thC. Origin uncertain: probably from an assumed Old English word (influenced by Old French *flaiel*), from, ultimately, Latin *flagellum* 'whip' (see FLAGELLUM).]

flair /flair/ n. 1. **TALENT** a natural ability or aptitude 2. **ELEGANCE** obvious elegance or stylishness [Late 19thC. From French *flair* 'sense of smell', from Old French *flairier* 'to smell', from late Latin *flagrare*, alteration of Latin *fragrare* 'to emit an odour'.]

— **WORD KEY: SYNONYMS** —
See Synonyms at *talent*.

flak /flak/, **flack** n. 1. **ARMS GROUND-BASED ANTI-AIRCRAFT FIRE** anti-aircraft fire directed from the ground 2. **CRITICISM** strong adverse criticism (informal) [Mid-20thC. From German, an acronym from *Flieger* 'aeroplane' + *Abwehr* 'defence' + *Kanone* 'canon'.]

flake[1] /flayk/ n. 1. **SMALL FLAT PIECE** a small flat piece or small part of a layer broken or detached from a larger object 2. **SMALL MANUFACTURED ITEM** a small flat object that is manufactured, sold, and used or consumed in quantity 3. **US ODD PERSON** sb with unconventional and irrational behaviour and ideas (insult) 4. **Aus FISH AS FOOD** the flesh of various types of shark and similar fish, sold as food and often used for fish and chips ▪ v. (**flakes, flaking, flaked**) 1. vi. **FORM INTO FLAKES AND FALL OFF** to form into flakes and fall or peel off 2. vt. **BREAK STH INTO FLAKES** to break sth into flakes, or break flakes from sth 3. vt. **COVER STH WITH FLAKES** to cover or coat sth with flakes [14thC. Origin uncertain; probably from Scandinavian.] —**flaker** n.

flake out vi. to collapse or fall asleep because of exhaustion

flake[2] /flayk/ n. a platform or frame for drying fish or other food [14thC. Origin uncertain: perhaps from Old Norse *flaki* 'wicker shield'.]

flake[3] /flayk/ n., vt. (**flakes, flaking, flaked**) **NAUT** = **fake**[2] [Early 17thC. Related to FAKE.]

flake white n. a pigment made from flakes of white lead

flak jacket n. a reinforced vest or jacket for protection against gunfire or shrapnel

flaky /fláyki/ (**-ier, -iest**) adj. 1. **LIKE FLAKES** made of or similar to flakes 2. **TENDING TO BREAK OFF IN FLAKES** forming or tending to break off in flakes 3. **US UNCONVENTIONAL** unconventional or irrational (informal) —**flakily** adv. —**flakiness** n.

flaky pastry n. a type of pastry made from layers of pastry dough dotted with fat. It puffs up and forms light layers when baked.

flam[1] /flam/ n. (regional) 1. **DECEPTION** a lie or deception 2. **DRIVEL** nonsense or trivial talk ▪ vt. (**flams, flamming, flammed**) **DECEIVE SB** to cheat or deceive sb (regional) [Early 17thC. Origin uncertain: perhaps a shortening of FLIMFLAM or *flamfew* 'bauble'.]

flam[2] /flam/ n. a drumbeat of two nearly simultaneous strokes [Late 18thC. Origin uncertain: probably an imitation of the sound.]

flambé /flóm bay/, **flambée** vt. (**-bées, -béeing, -béed**) **POUR ALCOHOLIC DRINK ON FOOD AND IGNITE** to pour an alcoholic spirit over food and light it in order to burn off the alcohol and impart the flavour of the spirit to the food ▪ adj. **SERVED IN IGNITED SPIRIT** served with an alcoholic spirit, usually brandy, that has been poured over the food and burnt off or left burning ○ *bananas flambée* [Late 19thC. From French, the past participle of *flamber* 'to singe, pass through flame', ultimately from Latin *flamma* 'flame'.]

flambeau /flámbō/ (plural **-beaux** /-bō/ or **-beaus**) n. 1. **TORCH** a lighted torch made of wicks dipped in wax 2. **CANDLESTICK** a large decorative candlestick 3. *Carib* **TORCH LIT WITH KEROSENE** a torch made by stuffing cloth into a bottle or sometimes a bamboo joint containing kerosene [Mid-17thC. From French, 'torch, flame', from *flambe* 'flame', from, ultimately, Latin *flamma* 'flame'.]

Flamborough Head /flámbərə-/ headland on the eastern coast of Yorkshire, northern England. It has steep limestone cliffs and a lighthouse.

flamboyant /flam bóyənt/ adj. 1. **SHOWY** showy and dashing in a self-satisfied way 2. **BRIGHTLY-COLOURED** brightly-coloured and striking 3. **HIGHLY DECORATED** elaborate or richly decorated 4. **AUDACIOUS** unrestrained by prevailing standards of propriety 5. **ARCHIT OF FRENCH GOTHIC ARCHITECTURE** used to refer to the final stage of French Gothic architecture from the 14th to the 16th centuries that is noted for its fine detailing and pointed decoration ▪ n. **TREES** = **royal poinciana** [Mid-19thC. From French, the present participle of *flamboyer* 'to blaze', from *flambe* 'flame', ultimately from Latin *flamma* 'flame'.] —**flamboyance** n. —**flamboyantly** adv.

flame /flaym/ n. 1. **HOT GLOWING BODY OF BURNING GAS** a hot glowing body of burning gas, often carrying fine incandescent particles 2. **STRONG FEELING** an intense feeling or emotion **3.** LOVER a sweetheart or lover (*informal*) ○ *an old flame* **4.** REDDISH-ORANGE COLOUR a brilliant reddish-orange colour ■ *adj.* REDDISH-ORANGE COLOUR of a brilliant reddish-orange colour ■ *v.* (**flames, flaming, flamed**) **1.** *vi.* PRODUCE FLAME to burn producing flame **2.** *vi.* HAVE FIERY GLOW to have or develop a fiery glow, especially suddenly ○ *Her cheeks flamed as she spoke.* **3.** *vi.* FEEL STRONG EMOTION to display or feel intense emotion **4.** *vt.* SET FIRE TO STH to set fire to sth **5.** *vt.* MAKE STH BURN to make sth burn (*archaic*) **6.** *vti.* COMPUT CRITICIZE SB ELECTRONICALLY to deluge sb with offensive and disparaging e-mail ■ *n.* COMPUT ANGRY E-MAIL MESSAGE a rude, abusive, or threatening e-mail message or newsgroup posting [14thC. Via Anglo-Norman from French *flamme*, from Latin *flammula* 'little flame', from *flamma* 'flame'.] — **flamer** *n.* —**flamy** *adj.* ◇ **fan the flames** to make a tense or difficult situation worse ◇ **shoot sb** or **sth down in flames** to reject or refute an idea or suggestion emphatically

flame-arc lamp *n.* a lamp that uses an electric arc maintained between carbon electrodes that are infused with metallic salts to provide colour to the flame

flame carbon *n.* a carbon electrode containing metallic salts that, with other similar carbon electrodes, has the effect of colouring the arc produced between the electrodes

flame cell *n.* a hollow excretory cell in certain invertebrates, e.g. flatworms, that has a tuft of projections (**cilia**) resembling hairs whose movement serves to force out waste products [*Flame* from the movement of the cilia, which resemble tongues of flame]

flame gun *n.* a type of flame-thrower used to burn weeds

flamen /fláymən/ (*plural* **flamens** or **flamines** /flámmi neez/) *n.* a priest in ancient Rome belonging to a group of 15, each of whom oversaw the rituals connected with a particular deity [14thC. From Latin.]

Flamenco

flamenco /flə méngkō/ (*plural* **-cos**) *n.* **1.** DANCE VIGOROUS SPANISH DANCE WITH HAND CLAPPING a dance originating in Spain that features hand clapping and stamping of the feet **2.** MUSIC MUSIC FOR SPANISH DANCE the strongly rhythmic music that accompanies flamenco dancing [Late 19thC. Via Spanish, 'Flemish person', from Middle Dutch *Vlaming* (see FLAMINGO).]

flame of the forest *n.* a tree that is native to tropical West Africa and is cultivated as an ornamental for its large bright red sepals. Latin name: *Mussaenda erythrophylla.*

flameout /fláym owt/ *n.* the unintentional extinguishing of the flame of a jet engine in flight, e.g. through a failure of combustion or the fuel supply

flameproof /fláym proof/ *adj.* **1.** RESISTANT TO FIRE resistant to catching fire (*often used of textiles and clothing*) **2.** ELEC ENG NOT EXPLOSIVE used to describe electrical apparatus that is designed so that an explosion of inflammable gas inside will not ignite inflammable gas outside **3.** COOK FOR COOKING WITH DIRECT HEAT used to describe containers that can be used when cooking on a hob or under a grill ■ *vt.* (**-proofs, -proofing, -proofed**) MAKE STH FLAME RESISTANT to make sth resistant to flames or combustion — **flameproofer** *n.*

flame-retardant *adj.* made or chemically treated to resist catching fire

flame test *n.* a test for the presence of various metals in a substance by noting the colours produced when a small amount is placed in a flame and vapourized

flame-thrower *n.* a weapon that projects a stream of burning liquid

flame tree *n.* **1.** TREE WITH REDDISH FLOWERS a tropical tree that is cultivated for its bright orange, yellow, or red flowers. Royal poinciana is a flame tree. **2.** FLOWERING AUSTRALIAN TREE an Australian tree noted for its bright red flowers that bloom in spring when the tree is leafless. Latin name: *Brachychiton acerifolius.*

flame war *n.* COMPUT a period of repeated exchanges of abusive and insulting e-mail between individuals or groups

flamines *npl.* plural of **flamen** *n.*

flaming /fláyming/ *adj.* **1.** PRODUCING FLAMES burning and producing flames **2.** INTENSE very angry, intense, or passionate ○ *flaming indignation* **3.** GLOWING brightly glowing ○ *flaming cheeks* **4.** VIVID IN COLOUR quite vivid in colour **5.** USED TO EXPRESS ANGER used to emphasize the following word or phrase and especially to express anger or annoyance (*informal*) ○ *I wish they wouldn't play their flaming music so loud!* ■ *n.* COMPUT DELUGE OF CRITICAL E-MAIL the directing of a large volume of abusive and insulting e-mail at sb, often as part of a flame war

Flamingo

flamingo /flə míng gō/ *n.* (*plural* **-gos** or **-goes** or **-go**) **1.** BIRDS LARGE PINK WADING BIRD a large wading bird native to tropical brackish waters that has a long neck and legs, downward-curving bill, webbed feet, and pinkish-white feathers with black wing quills. Family: Phoenicopteridae. **2.** COLOURS DEEP PINK COLOUR a deep pink colour tinged with orange ■ *adj.* COLOURS OF DEEP PINK COLOUR of a deep pink colour tinged with orange [Mid-16thC. Via Portuguese from obsolete Spanish *flamengo*, of uncertain origin: perhaps from Dutch *Vlaming* 'Flemish person', or ultimately from Latin *flamma* (see FLAME).]

──── **WORD KEY: ORIGIN** ────

Whether its ultimate source is Dutch or Latin, the motivation behind the bird's name is its bright appearance. The Latin derivation would make it the 'flame'-coloured bird; the Dutch derivation would depend on the reputation the people of Flanders had in the Middle Ages for bright flamboyant dress (whence the Spanish dance, the *flamenco*).

flaming sword *n.* a bromeliad, or subshrub, with yellow flowers and reddish bract pigmentation, native to French Guiana and cultivated elsewhere. Latin name: *Vriesea splendens.*

flammable /flámməb'l/ *adj.* readily capable of catching fire —**flammability** /flámmə bílləti/ *n.*

flan /flan/ *n.* **1.** FOOD, COOK OPEN FILLED PASTRY CASE an open, usually round, pastry or sponge case with a savoury or fruit filling **2.** METALL METAL DISC FOR STAMPING AS COIN a circular metal blank ready to be stamped as a coin [Mid-19thC. Via French from the medieval Latin stem *fladon-*, from a prehistoric Germanic base that is also the ancestor of English *flat*.]

Flanders /fláandərz/ former region in northwestern Europe that was a powerful independent state between the 11th and 14th centuries. It is equivalent to the present-day provinces of Flanders in Belgium, Nord Department in France, and part of Zeeland Province in the Netherlands.

Flanders poppy *n.* = **corn poppy** [*Flanders* from the use of the flower as the emblem of the Allied soldiers who died on the battlefields of FLANDERS in World War I]

flânerie /fláanə ree/ *n.* aimless idling or strolling (*literary*) [Late 19thC. From French, from *flâner* 'to stroll, lounge about'.]

flâneur /flaa núr/ *n.* sb who is idling or loafing about (*literary*) [Mid-19thC. From French, from *flâner* (see FLÂNERIE).]

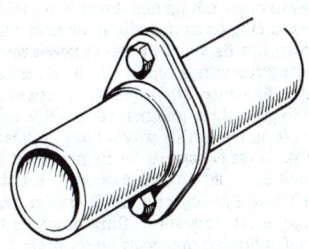

Flange

flange /flanj/ *n.* a projecting collar, rim, or rib on an object for fixing it to another object, holding it in place, or strengthening it. Flanges are often found on pipes and shafts. [Late 17thC. Origin uncertain: perhaps a variant of *flanch* 'device at the side of an escutcheon'. The current meaning evolved via 'protruding rim' from 'part that widens out'.] —**flanged** *adj.*

flanged rail *n.* an early form of rail with a raised edge (**flange**) on one side to stabilize wheels travelling on it. On modern trains the flange is on the wheel.

flank /flangk/ *n.* **1.** ANAT SIDE OF LOWER TORSO either side of the body of a human or an animal between the last rib and the hip **2.** COOK CUT OF MEAT FROM ANIMAL'S FLANK a cut of meat, especially beef, from an animal's flank, that is typically tough and requires slow cooking in liquid **3.** SIDE OF STH the side of any object **4.** MIL SIDE OF MILITARY FORMATION the left or right side of a military formation **5.** SPORTS SIDE OF SPORTS FIELD either of the sides of a sports field ○ *not used to playing on the left flank* ■ *vt.* (**flanks, flanking, flanked**) BE BY SIDE OF to be on or at the side of sth or sb ○ *He was flanked by secret service officers.* [Pre-12thC. From French *flanc*, of uncertain origin: probably from assumed Old Frankish *hlanca* 'side', from a prehistoric Germanic base that is also the ancestor of English *flinch*.]

flanker /flángkər/ *n.* **1.** MIL SOLDIER IN PROTECTIVE UNIT one of the soldiers in a unit that protects the flank of a military column on the march **2.** RUGBY WING FORWARD a wing forward who plays on either of the flanks **3.** AMERICAN FOOTBALL = **flankerback 4.** AMERICAN FOOTBALL = **split end** *n.* **2**

flankerback /flánkər bak/ *n.* AMERICAN FOOTBALL in American football, an offensive back positioned outside the play formation

flannel /flánn'l/ *n.* **1.** SOFT COTTON CLOTH a soft cotton cloth with a nap on one side, used for warm clothing, sleepwear, and sheets **2.** SOFT WOOLLEN CLOTH a soft closely woven woollen or wool-blend cloth used for clothing **3.** = **facecloth 4.** INSINCERE OR EVASIVE TALK indirect, empty, deceptive, or flattering talk (*informal*) ■ *v.* (**flannels, flannelling, flannelled, flanneled**) **1.** *vt.* WRAP SB IN FLANNEL to wrap or clothe sb in flannel **2.** *vt.* CLEAN STH WITH FLANNEL to wash, clean, or rub sb or sth with a flannel **3.** *vti.* TALK IN EVASIVE OR INSINCERE WAY to talk, or talk to sb, in an evasive or flattering way, especially to deceive ■ **flannels** *npl.* **1.** TROUSERS MADE OF FLANNEL clothing, especially trousers, made from flannel **2.** WHITE TROUSERS WORN FOR CRICKET white long trousers worn when playing particular sports, especially cricket [14thC. Origin uncertain: ultimately from either Welsh *gwlanen* 'woollen article' (from *gwlân* 'wool') or French *flaine*, a kind of coarse wool.] — **flannelly** *adj.*

flannelboard /flánn'l bawrd/ *n.* a board covered with flannel to which pictures and cloth cutouts will stick that is used in primary education

flannelette /flánnə lét/ *n.* a light cotton cloth with a soft brushed surface on one side

flannelflower /flánn'l flowər/ *n.* a plant that grows in eastern Australia and has white flowers covered with soft white hairs. Latin name: *Actinotus helianthi.*

Flannery /flánnəri/, **Tim** (*b.* 1956) Australian biologist. He is the author of *The Future Eaters* (1994). Full name Timothy Flannery

flan ring *n.* a round tin with a removable base, for cooking a flan or quiche

flap /flap/ *v.* (**flaps, flapping, flapped**) **1.** *vti.* MOVE WINGS UP AND DOWN to move sth up and down, especially wings or arms during or as if in flight, or to be moved up and down in this way **2.** *vi.* FLY BY MOVING WINGS to fly by moving the wings repeatedly **3.** *vti.* MOVE OR SWAY REPEATEDLY to cause sth to move or sway in one direction and then another repeatedly and often noisily, or move in this way ○ *flags flapping in the breeze* **4.** *vi.* BE PANICKY to be flustered or panicky (*informal*) **5.** *vt.* HIT WITH BROAD OBJECT to hit sb or sth with a broad flat object ○ *He flapped his hand on the table.* **6.** *vt.* TOSS STH to fling down or toss sth (*informal*) ○ *flapped the report on the table* **7.** *vt.* PHON MAKE AN 'R' SOUND to make an 'r' sound by briefly striking the roof of the mouth with the tongue, as in 'parrot' ■ *n.* **1.** FLAT THIN PIECE USED AS COVER a flat thin piece attached along one edge, usually used as a cover for an opening ○ *the flap of an envelope* **2.** PUBL DUST JACKET PART either of the two parts of a dust jacket that fold inside a book's cover and are usually printed with information about the book or author **3.** ACT OR SOUND OF FLAPPING an act of or the sound made by flapping ○ *The bird disappeared with a flap of its wings.* **4.** A PANICKED STATE a state of panic or upset (*informal*) ○ *Don't get into a flap about it.* **5.** BLOW FROM BROAD OBJECT a blow or slap from a broad object **6.** AIR AIRCRAFT WING CONTROL SURFACE a narrow movable surface attached to the rear edge of an aircraft wing that is used to create lift or drag **7.** SURG MASS OF TISSUE FOR GRAFTING a mass of tissue, used for surgical grafting, that remains partially attached and retains its blood supply **8.** PHON 'R' SOUND an 'r' sound made by briefly striking the roof of the mouth with the tongue, as in 'parrot' [14thC. Origin uncertain: the noun first meant 'blow, slap', and so is probably imitative of the sound.]

flapdoodle /fláp dood'l/ *n.* silly talk or nonsense (*dated slang*) [Mid-19thC. Origin unknown: perhaps thought to suggest foolishness.]

flapjack /fláp jak/ *n.* **1.** CHEWY CAKE MADE WITH OATS a cake made of oats, syrup, and butter and cut into squares before eating **2.** *US* = **pancake** *n.* 1

flappable /fláppəb'l/ *adj.* tending to get flustered or panicky (*informal*)

flapper /fláppər/ *n.* **1.** YOUNG UNCONVENTIONAL WOMAN OF THE 1920s a young woman of the 1920s who disdained prior conventions of decorum and fashion. Flappers were associated with the Charleston dance, bobbed hair, heavy make-up, and drop-waisted very short dresses. **2.** YOUNG BIRD a bird that is learning to fly **3.** STH FLAPPING AROUND an object that flaps around **4.** BROAD FLAT OBJECT a broad flat object used for striking sth [Late 16thC. 'Young unconventional woman' of uncertain origin: either from *flapper* 'young wild duck' (from FLAP), or dialectal *flap* 'woman of loose character'.]

flappy /fláppi/ (**-pier, -piest**) *adj.* flapping about, or likely to flap about

flare /flair/ *v.* (**flares, flaring, flared**) **1.** *vti.* BURN SUDDENLY AND BRIGHTLY to burn, or cause sth to burn, suddenly and brightly **2.** *vi.* START UP AGAIN to recur, worsen, or intensify suddenly **3.** *vi.* BECOME ANGRY to become suddenly angry **4.** *vti.* WIDEN OUT to widen out, or to cause sth to widen out ○ *Her nostrils flared.* **5.** *vt.* SIGNAL SB FOR HELP to signal sb for help by means of a device used to produce a light signal **6.** *vt.* INDUST BURN OFF GAS to ignite and burn off unwanted waste gas in open air ■ *n.* **1.** SUDDEN BLAZE OF LIGHT a sudden blaze of light or fire, especially one used to signal distress or location or used for illumination ○ *the flare of naval signal lights* **2.** DEVICE FOR PRODUCING FLARE a device used to produce a light signal calling for help ○ *a distress flare* **3.** FLAME a sudden or unsteady flame ○ *the flare of distant oil wells* **4.** WIDENING SHAPE a shape that widens out ○ *a long skirt with a flare* **5.** OUTBURST OF EMOTION a sudden outburst, especially of a negative emotion ○ *a flare of anger* **6.** AMERICAN

FOOTBALL SHORT AND WIDE PASS in American football, a pass to a back running laterally **7.** OPTICS, PHOTOGRAPHY UNWANTED LIGHT IN AN OPTICAL DEVICE unwanted light reaching a photographic image, especially when reflected from an internal lens **8.** INDUST FLAME FOR BURNING OFF WASTE GAS a flame that burns off unwanted waste gas in the open air **9.** MED INFLAMMATION an area of inflammation on the skin ■ **flares** *npl.* TROUSERS WITH WIDE LEGS BELOW KNEE trousers with legs that widen significantly below the knee, first popular in the late 1960s [Mid-16thC. Origin uncertain.]

flareback /fláir bak/ *n.* **1.** ARMS FLAME INSIDE GUN'S BREECH a flame inside a gun's breech caused by the ignition of gases remaining after the weapon has been fired **2.** REACTION DIRECTED BACK TOWARDS ORIGIN a reaction or effect directed back towards a point of origin

flared /flaird/ *adj.* widening out

flare stack *n.* a large open-air burner used to dispose of excess flammable gas at an oil refinery, well, or platform

flare-up *n.* **1.** SUDDEN OUTBURST OF AGGRESSION a sudden occurrence of emotion or violence (*informal*) **2.** RECURRENCE OF STH a recurrence of sth, especially a disease **3.** SUDDEN OCCURRENCE OF FIRE OR LIGHT a sudden occurrence or increase of fire or light

flaring /fláiring/ *adj.* **1.** BURNING DIMLY burning dimly or unsteadily **2.** SHOWY bright and showy **3.** BECOMING WIDER widening out —**flaringly** *adv.*

flash /flash/ *v.* (**flashes, flashing, flashed**) **1.** *vti.* EMIT LIGHT SUDDENLY to cause light to appear suddenly or in brief bursts from sth, or to appear in this way ○ *We could see the lights of police cars flashing in the distance.* **2.** *vti.* REFLECT LIGHT FROM ANOTHER SOURCE to reflect light suddenly or briefly, or make sth such as a lamp reflect from a surface ○ *sunlight flashing on the water* **3.** *vti.* CATCH FIRE SUDDENLY to burst into flame suddenly, or cause sth to burst into flame **4.** *vti.* COMMUNICATION SIGNAL TO SB WITH LIGHTS to signal to sb or communicate sth by quickly turning lights on and off ○ *The driver flashed us to indicate that we could cross the street.* **5.** *vi.* MOVE QUICKLY to move or pass very quickly in a particular direction **6.** *vti.* APPEAR MOMENTARILY to appear briefly, or show sth briefly ○ *flash a message onto the screen* **7.** *vi.* EXPOSE BODY INDECENTLY IN PUBLIC to expose the genitals briefly and intentionally in public (*informal*) **8.** *vt.* DISPLAY STH OSTENTATIOUSLY to show off or display sth in order to impress people (*informal*) ○ *She's always flashing her money around.* **9.** *vt.* FILL STH WITH RUSH OF WATER to fill sth suddenly with a great flow of water **10.** *vt.* COAT STH FOR PROTECTION to cover the surface of an object with a thin coating, usually for protection or as a stage in processing **11.** *vt.* BUILDING PROTECT ROOF FROM LEAKING to install flashing on a roof joint or window joint to make it waterproof ■ *n.* **1.** SUDDEN BURST OF LIGHT a sudden bright display of light, fire, or sth bright ○ *flashes of lightning* **2.** SUDDEN BURST OF MOOD OR THOUGHT a sudden occurrence of an emotional mood or intellectual activity ○ *a flash of inspiration* **3.** BRIEF MOMENT a brief moment or instant ○ *I'll be there in a flash.* **4.** LIGHT PATCH a patch of light or bright colour on a dark background, e.g. on an animal's coat **5.** PHOTOGRAPHY BRIGHT LIGHTING USED IN PHOTOGRAPHY the brief illumination of a subject for photographic purposes **6.** PHOTOGRAPHY DEVICE USED TO LIGHT PHOTOGRAPHIC SUBJECT a device used in flash photography to produce a short, bright light (*informal*) **7.** RUSH OF WATER a sudden rush of water down a watercourse, or a device that produces this **8.** BROADCAST NEWS FLASH a sudden important news story requiring immediate broadcast (*informal*) **9.** MIL BADGE ON UNIFORM OR VEHICLE a badge or insignia on a uniform or vehicle **10.** CLOTHES COLOURED STRIP WORN ON SOCKS in Highland dress, a short strip of coloured material folded over the garter and protruding below the folded-over top of the socks (*usually used in the plural*) **11.** LANGUAGE USED IN UNDERWORLD the language used by criminals, thieves, and their associates (*archaic slang*) ■ *adj.* **1.** SHOWY expensive or expensive-looking, especially in a showy and vulgar way (*informal*) ○ *with his big car and his flash clothes* **2.** INSINCERE insincere, false, or counterfeit ○ *an outpouring of flash sentiment* **3.** sudden and brief ○ *flash thunderstorms* [13thC. Originally in the sense 'to splash'; probably an imitation of the sound. Later senses probably evolved from the idea of

light suddenly and briefly reflected from disturbed water.] ◇ **flash in the pan** a sudden brief success that is not, or not likely to be, repeated ◇ **in a flash 1.** very rapidly **2.** suddenly

flash back *vi.* **1.** PSYCHOL RECALL PAINFUL MEMORY to recall an intensely vivid memory of a traumatic experience **2.** CINEMA, LITERAT RETURN TO EARLIER EVENT to go back to a scene at an earlier point in a narrative, out of chronological order, to fill in information or explain sth in the present

flash forward *vi.* to jump forward in time to a scene at a later point in a narrative, out of chronological order, usually for dramatic effect or irony

flashback /flásh bak/ *n.* **1.** PSYCHOL PAINFUL MEMORY an intensely vivid memory of a traumatic experience that returns repeatedly **2.** CINEMA, LITERAT EARLIER EVENT OR SCENE a scene or event from the past that appears in a narrative out of chronological order, to fill in information or explain sth in the present ○ *Much of the film's exposition is handled through flashbacks.* **3.** DRUGS DRUG AFTER-EFFECT the later experiencing of the effects of a hallucinogenic drug such as LSD long after discontinuing use of the drug

flash blindness *n.* temporary blindness after the flash of a gun discharge or other explosion, particularly at night

flashboard /flásh bawrd/ *n.* a structure made of boards fitted at the top of a dam to add to its height and increase the amount of water that can be held back

flashbulb /flásh bulb/ *n.* a small glass bulb filled with shredded metallic foil that produces a brief intense flash of light for taking photographs

flash burn *n.* a burn caused by brief exposure to a source of intense heat

flashcard /flásh kaard/ (*plural* **flashcards** *or* **flash cards**) *n.* a card with words or numbers printed on it that is briefly displayed as a learning device

flasher /fláshər/ *n.* **1.** SB WHO EXPOSES PRIVATE PARTS sb who gains sexual pleasure from publicly exposing the genitals (*informal*) **2.** AUTOMOT FLASHING LIGHT a light that flashes as a signal, especially one on a road vehicle used to indicate the direction in which the driver intends to turn **3.** TECH DEVICE MAKING LIGHT FLASH a device that switches a light on and off automatically to make it flash

flash flood *n.* a sudden and often destructive surge of water down a narrow channel or sloping ground, usually caused by heavy rainfall

flash-forward *n.* a scene or event from the future that appears in a narrative out of chronological order, usually for dramatic effect or irony

flashgun /flásh gun/ *n.* a device that holds a flashtube or flashbulb and automatically discharges it as the attached camera's shutter opens

flashing /fláshing/ *n.* pieces of sheet metal attached around the joints and angles of a roof to protect against leakage

flashlight /flásh līt/ *n.* **1.** *US* = **torch 2.** PHOTOGRAPHY BURST OF BRIGHT LIGHT FOR PHOTOGRAPHY a brief intense flash of light produced by a photographic lamp **3.** BRIGHT FLASHING LIGHT any bright light that flashes, e.g. a beacon

flash memory *n.* a programmable read-only computer memory chip that can be erased and reprogrammed in blocks rather than one byte at a time

flashover /flásh ōvər/ *n.* an unintended electric arc around or over the surface of an insulator

flash photography *n.* photography that illuminates its subject with a brief flash of artificial light

flash photolysis (*plural* **flash photolyses**) *n.* a method of studying photochemical reactions in gases. The gas is exposed to very brief intense flashes of light and the results are analysed with a spectroscope.

flashpoint /flásh poynt/ *n.* **1.** CHEM TEMPERATURE OF VAPOUR IGNITION the lowest temperature at which a flammable liquid will give off enough vapour to ignite briefly when exposed to a flame **2.** CRITICAL STAGE the critical stage in some process, event, or situation at which action, change, or violence occurs **3.** TROUBLE SPOT a place where violence is likely to break out suddenly, usually as a result of social or political tension

a at; aa father; aw all; ay day; air hair; ə about, edible, item, common, circus; e egg; ee eel; hw when; i it, happy; ī ice; 'l apple; 'm rhythm; 'n fashion; o odd; ō open; oo good; oo pool; ow owl; oy oil; th thin; th this; u up; ur urge;

flashtube /flásh tyoob/ *n.* a glass or quartz tube filled with xenon gas that emits a short intense burst of light for flash photography when electric current is passed through it

flash unit *n.* PHOTOGRAPHY a flashgun, or a unit comprising a flashgun and reflector

flashy /fláshi/ (**-ier, -iest**) *adj.* **1.** OSTENTATIOUSLY SMART smart and expensive-looking in an obvious or ostentatious way **2.** MOMENTARILY BRILLIANT showing momentary or superficial brilliance —**flashily** *adv.* —**flashiness** *n.*

flask /flaask/ *n.* **1.** SCI SMALL BOTTLE a small glass bottle, often with a long neck, of the type used in laboratory work **2.** HOUSEHOLD = **hip flask 3.** VACUUM FLASK a vacuum flask **4.** ARMS = **powder horn 5.** METALL MOULD USED IN FOUNDRY a frame packed full of sand, used in a foundry to make a mould **6.** ENERGY CONTAINER FOR SPENT NUCLEAR FUEL a very strong container in which irradiated nuclear fuel is transported [14thC. Immediate origin uncertain: from medieval Latin *flasca*, ultimately, perhaps, from prehistoric Germanic.]

flat[1] /flat/ *adj.* (**flatter, flattest**) **1.** LEVEL AND HORIZONTAL level and horizontal, without any slope ○ *The flat plains stretch for miles.* **2.** EVEN AND SMOOTH even and smooth, without any bumps or hollows ○ *back on the flat road* **3.** NOT CURVED not curved inwards or outwards ○ *a wok with a flat bottom* **4.** WITH LITTLE CURVATURE with relatively little depth or curvature ○ *a vase with flat sides* **5.** LYING HORIZONTAL in a horizontal position, parallel with or stretched out on the ground ○ *plants lying flat after the heavy rain* **6.** TOUCHING STH ELSE with whole extent touching another surface at all points ○ *Stand it flat against the wall.* **7.** BEVERAGES NO LONGER FIZZY having lost effervescence ○ *flat champagne* **8.** WITHOUT ELECTRICAL CHARGE used to describe a battery that has lost its electrical charge **9.** NOT FULL OF AIR no longer full of air ○ *a flat tyre* **10.** MUSIC BELOW CORRECT PITCH sounded or sounding a little lower than the intended pitch level ○ *Your E string is flat.* **11.** MUSIC ONE SEMITONE BELOW NATURAL pitched one semitone below the specified note ○ *in the key of B flat minor* **12.** LACKING EXCITEMENT without any interest or excitement ○ *Some days life just seems flat.* **13.** COOK FLAVOURLESS without flavour or seasoning ○ *This soup tastes rather flat.* **14.** MONOTONOUS IN SOUND with no variation in pitch or intonation ○ *expressed her displeasure in a flat voice* **15.** COMM COMMERCIALLY INACTIVE not commercially active ○ *The market is fairly flat at the moment.* **16.** FIN NOT VARYING not varying in amount or level ○ *They charge a flat fee of £50.* **17.** EMPHATICALLY ABSOLUTE categorical and without any qualification ○ *a flat denial of the charges* **18.** CLOTHES LOW-HEELED with low heels or no heels at all ○ *flat shoes* **19.** NOT SHINY not shiny or glossy ○ *a flat white paint* **20.** SAILING TIGHT stretched so as to be tight **21.** MED INDICATING CESSATION OF PHYSIOLOGICAL ACTIVITY showing no variation on a monitoring machine, and thereby indicating that physiological activity has stopped ○ *a flat EKG* **22.** PHON RESEMBLING VOWEL SOUND IN 'FAT' used to describe the vowel 'a' as it is pronounced in 'fat' or 'badge' ■ *adv.* (**flatter, flattest**) **1.** MUSIC BELOW PITCH below the intended pitch ○ *She tends to sing flat.* **2.** VERY used to add emphasis (*informal*) ○ *flat broke* **3.** EXACTLY no more and no less ○ *He ran the mile in four minutes flat.* **4.** FIN WITHOUT INTEREST not accruing any interest ○ *The bonds were trading flat.* ■ *n.* **1.** LEVEL SURFACE a flat part or surface ○ *the flat of a knife blade* **2.** MUSIC NOTE LOWERED BY SEMITONE a sign (♭) placed next to a note to show that it is to be lowered by a semitone, or a note that is lowered a semitone ○ *a key with four flats* **3.** GEOG LARGE STRETCH OF LEVEL GROUND a large level stretch of, e.g. mud, exposed at low tide or of salt deposits (*usually used in the plural*) ○ *the great salt flats* **4.** TRANSP DEFLATED TYRE a tyre that has become deflated (*informal*) **5.** THEATRE MOVABLE SCENERY theatrical scenery mounted on a movable wooden frame **6.** SHIPPING = **flatboat 7.** MAIL BIG FLAT ENVELOPE a large flat piece of mail **8.** HORSERACING HORSERACING OVER LEVEL GROUND horseracing over level ground with no fences to be jumped, or the season in which this takes place ■ **flats** *npl.* CLOTHES LOW-HEELED SHOES shoes with low heels ■ *vt.* (**flats, flatting, flatted**) *US* MUSIC **1.** = **flatten** *v.* 5 **2.** = **flatten** *v.* 6 [14thC. From Old Norse *flatr.* Ultimately from an Indo-European word that is also the ancestor of English *flounder, flan,* and *plate.*] —**flatness** *n.*

flat[2] /flat/ *n.* **1.** SET OF ROOMS ON ONE FLOOR living quarters in part of a building, usually on one floor. US term **apartment 2.** *NZ* SHARED HOUSE a house that is shared with people who are not relatives ■ *vi. ANZ* SHARE A FLAT to share a flat with sb (*informal*) ○ *We used to flat together at uni.* [Early 19thC. Alteration, influenced by FLAT[1], of Scots *flet* 'interior of a house', from Old English *flet(t)* 'house', earlier 'floor'. Ultimately from the same Indo-European word as English *flat*[1].]

flatbed /flát bed/ *n.* **1.** = **flatbed trailer 2.** = **flatbed truck**

flatbed lorry *n.* = **flatbed truck**

flatbed press *n.* = **cylinder press**

flatbed trailer *n.* a trailer consisting of a completely open platform with no sides or railings

flatbed truck, flatbed lorry (*plural* **flatbed lorries**) *n.* a truck that has a completely open platform at the rear with no sides or railings

flatboat /flát bōt/ *n.* a large boat with a flat bottom used for transporting goods on shallow waterways

flatbread /flát bred/ *n.* bread baked in round flat loaves and usually made with unleavened dough. Examples are pitta, nan, chapatis, and tortillas.

flat cap *n.* **1.** CLOTH CAP a cloth cap with a brim at the front and a flat soft top **2.** HIST ELIZABETHAN MAN'S HAT WITH LOW CROWN a hat with a low crown and a narrow brim worn in the 16th and 17th centuries by men, especially Londoners

flatcar /flát kaar/ *n. US* a railway freight wagon that has no roof or sides

flat chat *adv. Aus* AS FAST AS POSSIBLE as fast and energetically as possible (*informal*) ○ *We've got a deadline next week so we're all working flat chat.* ■ *adj. Aus* BUSY extremely busy (*informal*) ○ *Sorry, mate, I can't help you – I'm flat chat.*

flat-chested /-chéstid/ *adj.* having small breasts

flat-coated retriever *n.* a large dog with a thick, smooth, black or reddish-brown coat, belonging to a breed originally developed in England for retrieving game

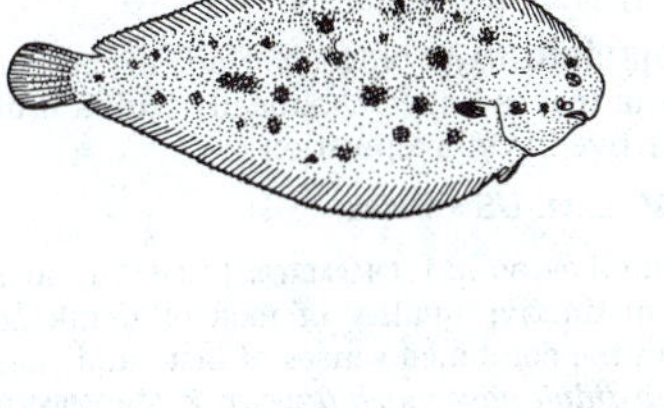

Flatfish

flatfish /flát fish/ (*plural* **-fish** *or* **-fishes**) *n.* any fish with a flat body and both eyes on the upper side. Flounder, sole, and halibut are types of flatfish. Order: Pleuronectiformes.

flatfoot /flát fŏŏt/ *n.* **1.** ANAT FOOT PROBLEM an abnormal condition of the feet in which the arches are so low that all of the sole makes contact with the ground. ◊ **splayfoot 2.** (*plural* **-foots** *or* **-feet**) OFFENSIVE TERM an offensive term for a police officer, typically one on foot patrol (*dated slang offensive*)

flat-footed /flát fŏŏtid/, **flatfooted** *adj.* **1.** ANAT HAVING FLAT FEET used to describe sb with flat feet **2.** AWKWARD awkward or clumsy (*informal*) **3.** UNPREPARED unable to react or respond quickly ○ *Her question caught me flat-footed.* ■ *adv.* UNEQUIVOCALLY without beating about the bush (*informal*) ○ *'a good many come out flatfooted and said it was scandalous'* (Mark Twain, *The Adventures of Huckleberry Finn*; 1884) —**flat-footedly** *adv.* —**flat-footedness** *n.*

flathead /flát hed/ (*plural* **-heads** *or* **-head**) *n. ANZ* flat-skulled fish found in the Indian and Pacific oceans and eaten as food in Australia and New Zealand. Family: Platycephalidae.

Flathead /flát hed/ (*plural* **-head** *or* **-heads**) *n.* a member of a Native North American people who originally lived in western Montana and northern Idaho

flathead catfish *n.* a large catfish that has a yellowish body with brown markings. It is found in the streams of the Mississippi Valley and the southeastern United States. Latin name: *Pylodictis olivaris.*

flatiron /flát ī ərn/ *n.* an iron used to press clothes, especially one that has to be heated on a hearth or stove

flatland /flát land/ *n.* an expanse of land that does not vary in height above sea level

flatlet /flátlət/ *n.* a small flat that has only a few rooms

flatline /flát līn/ (**-lines, -lining, -lined**) *vi. US* to show none of the electrical currents associated with heart activity on a cardiac monitor (*slang*) —**flatliner** *n.*

flatly /flátli/ *adv.* **1.** FIRMLY firmly and without qualification ○ *They flatly rejected our offer.* **2.** IN FLAT VOICE in a voice that shows no emotion

flatmate /flát mayt/ *n.* sb with whom a person shares a flat ○ *We're advertising for a new flatmate.*

flat out *adv.* (*informal*) **1.** AS QUICKLY AS POSSIBLE as fast and energetically as possible ○ *The factory staff are working flat out to finish the order.* **2.** FAST at top speed **3.** BLUNTLY in a blunt manner ○ *told me flat out he didn't trust me*

flatpack /flát pak/ *n.* an item of furniture that is sold as a set of pieces packed flat, for ease of storage and transportation, and assembled by the buyer

flat race *n.* **1.** HORSERACE WITHOUT JUMPS a horserace that is run over level ground, without fences to be jumped. ◊ **steeplechase 2.** ORDINARY RACE in children's sports competitions, an ordinary race without obstacles or special features, e.g. sacks or eggs and spoons (*dated*) —**flat racing** *n.*

flatten /flátt'n/ (**-tens, -tening, -tened**) *v.* **1.** *vti.* MAKE OR BECOME FLAT to make sth flat or flatter, or become flat or flatter **2.** *vr.* STAND FLAT AGAINST STH to press the body against a flat surface **3.** *vt.* DEFEAT SB to defeat sb convincingly (*informal*) **4.** *vt.* CRUSH OR HUMILIATE SB to make sb feel crushed or humiliated **5.** *vt.* MUSIC TAKE NOTE DOWN ONE SEMITONE to lower a note one semitone. US term **flat 6.** *vt.* MUSIC SING OR PLAY STH FLAT to sing or play a note below the intended pitch. US term **flat** —**flattener** *n.*

flatten out *v.* **1.** *vi.* BECOME STABLE AND LOWER to become lower and relatively stable ○ *Stock prices have flattened out over the year.* **2.** *vti.* SPREAD OUT to spread out, or spread sth out, over an area

flatter[1] /fláttər/ (**-ters, -tering, -tered**) *v.* **1.** *vt.* COMPLIMENT SB TO WIN FAVOUR to compliment sb too much, often without sincerity, especially in order to gain an advantage **2.** *vt.* APPEAL TO SB'S VANITY to please sb by paying him or her particular attention, especially with a request to take some prominent role ○ *I was flattered to be asked to judge the competition.* **3.** *vt.* MAKE SB OR STH LOOK GOOD to show sb or sth to advantage, or make sb or sth seem better looking than in reality ○ *a studio portrait that really flatters her* **4.** *vr.* CONGRATULATE YOURSELF EXCESSIVELY to feel satisfied with some aspect of yourself or with sth you have done, especially when the perception is false ○ *He flatters himself on being a good judge of character.* [12thC. Origin unknown; perhaps a back-formation from FLATTERY.] —**flatterer** *n.* —**flattering** *adj.* —**flatteringly** *adv.*

flatter[2] /fláttər/ *n.* INDUST any tool used to make sth flat, as used, e.g. by a blacksmith [From Old Norse *flatr* (see FLAT[1])]

flattery /fláttəri/ *n.* **1.** PAYING OF COMPLIMENTS TO WIN FAVOUR an act or instance of complimenting sb, often excessively or insincerely, especially in order to get sth **2.** COMPLIMENTS complimentary remarks, especially when excessive or insincere [14thC. From Old French *flaterie*, from *flater* 'to flatter'. Probably ultimately from a prehistoric Germanic word that is also the ancestor of English *flat* 'made smooth'.]

flatties /fláttiz/ *npl.* shoes with a low heel or no heel at all (*informal*)

flattish /fláttish/ *adj.* somewhat or relatively flat ○ *a flattish hairdo*

flattop /flát top/ *n.* a hairstyle in which the hair is brushed up and then cut short and flat across the top

flat tuning *n.* the tuning of a musical instrument, or of a number of instruments playing together, such that the pitch of all the notes is lower than normal. This is sometimes done by early-music groups.

flatulence /fláttyŏŏlənss/, **flatulency** /-lənssi/ *n.* **1.** MED WIND IN DIGESTIVE SYSTEM excessive gas in the stomach and intestines that causes discomfort **2.** LANGUAGE BOMBASTIC STYLE pretentiousness or pomposity in speech or writing

flatulent /fláttyŏŏlənt/ *adj.* **1.** MED CAUSING WIND IN DIGESTIVE SYSTEM causing excessive gas to be created in the stomach and intestines **2.** MED FULL OF DIGESTIVE GAS having excessive gas in the digestive system **3.** POMPOUS OR SELF-IMPORTANT having or showing excessive self-importance [Late 16thC. Via French from modern Latin *flatulentus*, from Latin *flatus* 'blowing, blast', from *flare* 'to blow' (source of English *flare*).] —**flatulently** *adv.*

flatus /fláytəss/ (*plural* **-tus** *or* **-tuses**) *n.* gas produced in the digestive system by bacterial fermentation and containing high amounts of hydrogen sulphide and methane, usually expelled from the body through the anus (*technical*) [Mid-17thC. From Latin (see FLATULENT).]

flatware /flát wair/ *n.* US, Can **1.** = cutlery **2.** FLAT OR SHALLOW TABLEWARE dishes used for eating that are flat or relatively shallow, e.g. plates and saucers, as opposed to deeper pieces such as cups and bowls (**hollowware**)

flat-water *adj.* done on a calm or slow-moving body of water

flatways /flát wīz/ *adv.* with the flat side down or foremost

flatweave /flát weev/, **flat-woven** *adj.* woven without a pile ○ *flatweave carpet*

flat white *n.* ANZ a cup of white coffee, usually made with espresso coffee and hot milk [Because it is not frothy]

flatwise /flát wīz/ *adv.* US = flatways

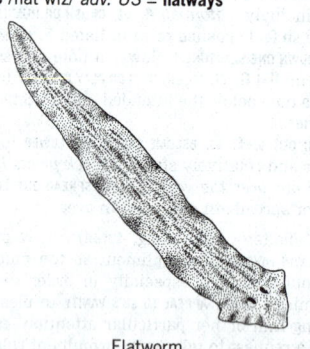

Flatworm

flatworm /flát wurm/ *n.* a worm with a soft, flattened body. Some flatworms, e.g. tapeworms, are parasites. Phylum: Platyhelminthes.

flat-woven *adj.* = flatweave

Flaubert /flṓ bair/, **Gustave** (1821–80) French novelist. A dominant figure in the realist school, he achieved fame with his first published novel, *Madame Bovary* (1856). —**Flaubertian** /flṓ báirti ən/ *adj.*

flaunching /fláwnching/ *n.* a cement or mortar fillet at the junction where a masonry chimney stack comes through a roof that is designed to throw off water [Early 19thC. Variant of FLANCHING.]

flaunt /flawnt/ *v.* (**flaunts, flaunting, flaunted**) **1.** *vt.* SHOW STH OFF to display sth ostentatiously ○ *She flaunts her wealth every chance she gets.* **2.** *vr.* PARADE YOURSELF to parade yourself without shame or modesty **3.** *vti.* WAVE OR MAKE STH WAVE to wave or flutter in the wind, or make sth wave or flutter by moving it around (*dated*) ■ *n.* DISPLAY an ostentatious display [Mid-16thC. Origin unknown: perhaps a blend of FLOUT and VAUNT.] —**flaunter** *n.* —**flauntingly** *adv.*

WORD KEY: USAGE

Flaunt or *flout* a rule? In terms of ignoring or showing gross contempt for a rule, for a convention, or for a law, only *flout* is the correct choice: *The motorist flouted the law when he double-parked.* When expressing the idea of vulgar or ostentatious display, the writer's only choice

is *flaunt*: *She flaunted her ill-gotten riches by purchasing a vulgar mansion and seven luxury cars.*

flautist /fláwtist/, **flutist** /flṓŏtist/ *n.* sb who plays the flute [Mid-19thC. From Italian *flautisto*, from *flauto* 'flute', from Provençal *flaut* (see FLUTE).]

flav- *prefix.* = flavo- (used before vowels)

flavanone /fláyvənōn/ *n.* a colourless crystalline compound derived from flavone, or any plant substance derived from flavone. Formula: $C_{15}H_{12}O_2$. [Mid-20thC. Coined from FLAVO- + -ANE + -ONE.]

flavin /fláyvin/ *n.* a yellow pigment such as riboflavin that is soluble in water and occurs in organic tissues [Mid-19thC. Coined from Latin *flavus* 'yellow' + -IN.]

flavine /flá veen/ *n.* flavin (*dated*) [Mid-19thC. Coined from Latin *flavus* 'yellow' + -INE.]

flavo- *prefix.* **1.** yellow ○ *flavin* **2.** flavin ○ *flavoprotein* [From Latin *flavus* 'yellow'. Ultimately from an Indo-European word denoting a bright colour, which is also the ancestor of English *blue* and *bleach*.]

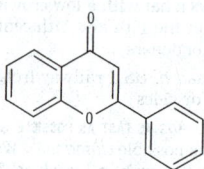

Flavone

flavone /flá vōn/ *n.* a crystalline compound from which yellow pigments are derived, found on the leaves or in the stems and seed capsules of primroses and some other plants. Formula: $C_{15}H_{10}O_2$. [Late 19thC. Coined from FLAVO- + -ONE.]

flavonoid /fláyvə noyd/ *n.* a naturally occurring phenolic compound belonging to a group that includes many plant pigments

flavoprotein /fláyvō prṓ teen/ *n.* an enzyme containing flavin that is linked chemically with a protein and is active in cell respiration

flavor *n., vt.* US = flavour

flavour /fláyvər/ *n.* **1.** CHARACTERISTIC TASTE an identifiable or distinctive quality of food or drink perceived with the combined senses of taste and smell ○ *The soup didn't have much flavour.* **2.** STH ADDING FLAVOUR TO FOOD a substance used to give food or drink an identifiable or distinctive taste **3.** UNIQUE CHARACTERISTIC the unique individual characteristic of an artistic work, especially a work of literature **4.** TYPE a type or kind of sth (*informal*) '*any flavor of mainframe you like*' (*The LOD/H Technical Journal, Issue 3*; 1988) **5.** PHYS PROPERTY OF ELEMENTARY PARTICLES a physical property that distinguishes types of quarks and some types of lepton **6.** ODOUR OR FRAGRANCE a quality perceived with the sense of smell alone (*archaic*) ■ *vt.* (**-vours, -vouring, -voured**) **1.** GIVE FLAVOUR TO FOOD to give food or drink an identifiable or distinctive taste, usually by adding sth ○ *Flavour the stew with rosemary.* **2.** GIVE STH UNIQUENESS to give a unique characteristic to an artistic work, especially a work of literature ○ *A certain terseness flavours her prose.* [14thC. Alteration, influenced by *savour*, of Old French *flaor* 'aroma' (the original sense in English), ultimately from a blend of Latin *flatus* 'blowing' (see FLATULENT), and *foetor* 'stench'.] —**flavourer** *n.*

flavour enhancer *n.* a substance, especially monosodium glutamate, added to processed food or drink to improve or intensify its flavour

flavourful /fláyvərf'l/ *adj.* with a strong pleasant taste —**flavourfully** *adv.* —**flavourfulness** *n.*

flavouring /fláyvəring/ *n.* a natural or artificial substance added to food or drink to give it an identifiable or distinctive taste

flavourless /fláyvərləss/ *adj.* without an identifiable or distinctive taste

flavoursome *adj.* = flavourful

flaw[1] /flaw/ (**flaws, flawing, flawed**) *n.* **1.** BLEMISH MAKING STH IMPERFECT a defect in an object that makes it imperfect or less valuable **2.** ABSTRACT IMPERFECTION an imperfection, shortcoming, or weakness in sth abstract ○ *There's a flaw in your argument.* **3.** LAW INVALIDATING DEFECT IN DOCUMENT in a legal document, a defect that can make it invalid [14thC. Origin uncertain: perhaps from Old Norse *flaga* 'stone slab', ultimately from prehistoric Germanic. The original meaning was 'flake'; the sense 'defect' probably originated in WHITLOW, literally 'white fissure'.]

WORD KEY: SYNONYMS

flaw, imperfection, fault, defect, failing, blemish
CORE MEANING: sth that detracts from perfection
flaw used to describe sth such as an unintended mark or crack that prevents sth from being totally perfect and detracts from its value. It can also be used to describe a weakness in sb's character or in a plan, theory, or system; **imperfection** a more formal word for 'flaw'; **fault** used to describe sth that prevents sth or sb from being perfect or from functioning correctly. It is usually used to talk about more serious problems than 'flaw'; **defect** used to describe a fault in a machine, system, or plan, especially one that prevents it from functioning correctly; **failing** used to describe sth that mars sb or sth in some way, often used to describe an unfortunate feature of sb's personality or character; **blemish** used to describe a mark of some kind that detracts from sth's appearance, often used of the complexion or skin. It can also be used to describe sth that detracts from sb's otherwise undamaged reputation or record.

flaw[2] /flaw/ *n.* **1.** METEOROL GUST OF WIND a brief gust of wind **2.** METEOROL SQUALL a short storm or spell of bad weather **3.** SUDDEN STRONG FEELING a sudden show of strong feeling (*archaic*) [Early 16thC. Probably from Middle Low German *vlāge*, or from Scandinavian. Ultimately from an Indo-European word meaning 'to strike' that is also the ancestor of English *plague*.] —**flawy** *adj.*

flawed /flawd/ *adj.* imperfect or defective ○ *The interpretation is seriously flawed.*

flawless /fláwləss/ *adj.* without any blemish or imperfection ○ *a flawless performance* —**flawlessly** *adv.* —**flawlessness** *n.*

Flax

flax /flaks/ *n.* **1.** PLANTS PLANT YIELDING LINEN FIBRE AND OIL a plant with blue flowers that is widely cultivated for its seeds, which produce linseed oil, and its stems, from which the fibre to make linen is obtained. Latin name: *Linum usitatissimum.* **2.** TEXTILES FIBRE USED TO MAKE LINEN a fine light-coloured textile fibre obtained from flax [Old English *flæx*. Ultimately from an Indo-European word meaning 'to plait' that was also the ancestor of English *plait*, *ply*, *complicate*, and *perplexed*.]

flaxen /fláks'n/ *adj.* **1.** COLOURS PALE GREYISH-YELLOW having the pale greyish-yellow colour of flax **2.** TEXTILES MADE FROM FLAX made from flax fibres

flaxy /fláksi/ (**-ier, -iest**) *adj.* resembling flax in appearance or texture

flay /flay/ (**flays, flaying, flayed**) *vt.* **1.** LASH OR FLOG to whip or beat a person or animal severely **2.** STRIP SKIN OFF to remove the skin or outer covering from sb or sth **3.** CRITICIZE HARSHLY to criticize sb or sth harshly and severely, and sometimes unfairly **4.** STRIP OF BELONGINGS to take all the money or valuables from sb, especially by the use of deceit, intimidation, or similar means (*dated*) [Old English *flēan*. Ultimately from an Indo-European word meaning 'to strike' that was also the ancestor of English *flaw*[2].] —**flayer** *n.*

F layer *n.* GEOL the transition zone between the solid inner core of the Earth and its more fluid outer layer, at a depth of approximately 5,100 km/3,200 mi [*F* following the system of naming the three layers, beginning with *D*]

fld *abbr.* field

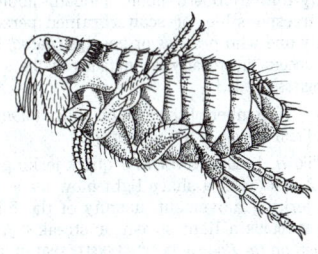

Flea (life size x50)

flea /flee/ *n.* **1.** INSECTS SMALL LEAPING BLOODSUCKING INSECT a small wingless insect with legs adapted for jumping that sucks blood and lives as a parasite on warm-blooded animals. Order: Siphonaptera. **2.** ZOOL ANIMAL RESEMBLING FLEA a small beetle or crustacean that resembles or jumps like a flea, e.g. a water flea, flea beetle, or sand flea [Old English *flēa(h)*. Ultimately from an Indo-European word that was also the ancestor of English *puce*.] ◇ **a flea in sb's ear** a sharp reprimand

fleabag /flee bag/ *n.* a dirty or scruffy living being, especially one that is infested with fleas (*informal*)

fleabane /flee bayn/ *n.* a wild plant with yellow flowers that was once believed to repel fleas. Cultivated varieties of fleabane have flowers of different colours. Genus: *Erigeron*.

flea beetle *n.* a very small beetle with large hind legs adapted for jumping. The beetle and its larvae are pests of vegetable crops. Subfamily: Halticinae.

fleabite /flee bīt/ *n.* **1.** BITE OF FLEA the bite of a flea or the small red mark caused by this **2.** SMALL ANNOYANCE a small loss or petty annoyance (*informal*)

flea-bitten *adj.* **1.** COVERED WITH FLEAS OR FLEABITES covered with fleabites or infested with fleas **2.** CHEAP AND SHABBY cheap, shabby, or run-down (*informal*) **3.** ZOOL WITH PALE FLECKED COAT used to describe a horse that has a pale coat with reddish-brown flecks

flea collar *n.* a collar, usually for dogs or cats, containing a chemical that repels or kills fleas

fleam /fleem/ *n.* **1.** WOODWORK EDGE OF TOOTH ON SAW a bevelled cutting edge on the teeth of a saw **2.** SURG KNIFE USED IN BLOODLETTING a surgical knife formerly used to open a vein in bloodletting [15thC. Via Old French *flieme* from, ultimately, Greek *phlebotomon*, literally 'vein-cutter' (see PHLEBOTOMY), from *phlebos* 'vein'.]

flea market *n.* a market, usually outdoors, with individual stalls selling various kinds of merchandise, e.g. antiques, used household items, and cut-price goods

fleapit /flee pit/ *n.* a cheap run-down cinema or theatre

fleawort /flee wurt/ (*plural* **-wort** *or* **-worts**) *n.* **1.** PLANT WITH YELLOW FLOWERS a European plant with yellow flowers and furry leaves arranged in clusters, once reputed to repel fleas. Genus: *Senecio*. **2.** = plough-man's spikenard [Because the seeds look like fleas]

flèche /flaysh, flesh/, **fleche** *n.* **1.** ARCHIT SLENDER CHURCH SPIRE a slender spire, especially one that emerges from the roof of a church at the point where the ridges intersect **2.** ARCHIT BUTTRESS FEATURE a joint at the top of a buttress, designed to add weight and assist in transferring load from roof to ground **3.** MIL POINTED FORTIFICATION a fortification with two faces that form a jutting angle [Early 18thC. From French, literally 'arrow', from Old French *fleche* (see FLETCHER). Sense 2 of FLÈCHE, the earliest modern sense, dates from the early 18thC.]

Flèche

fléchette /flay shét/, **flechette** *n.* a small arrow or dart used in various kinds of missiles or projectiles intended to kill or injure people [Early 20thC. From French, literally 'little arrow', from *flèche* (see FLÈCHE).]

fleck /flek/ *n.* SMALL MARK any one of a number of very small marks, streaks, or pieces scattered on a surface or throughout a block of sth ○ *flecks of mica in granite* ■ *vt.* (**flecks, flecking, flecked**) STREAK OR SPOT to mark sth with small streaks or spots ○ *Sunlight flecked the path ahead.* [14thC. Origin uncertain.]

Flecker /flékər/, **James Elroy** (1884–1915) British poet. He was author of the collection *The Golden Journey to Samarkand* (1913) and the verse drama *Hassan*, produced posthumously in 1922.

flection *n.* = flexion

fled past participle, past tense of **flee**

fledge /flej/ (**fledges, fledging, fledged**) *v.* **1.** *vt.* BIRDS RAISE YOUNG BIRD to raise a young bird until it can fly **2.** *vi.* BIRDS GROW FLIGHT FEATHERS to grow the wing and tail feathers necessary for flying **3.** *vt.* ARCHERY EQUIP ARROW WITH FEATHERS to put feathers on an arrow **4.** *vt.* PROVIDE WITH FEATHERS to provide or cover sth with feathers or sth similar [Mid-16thC. From the obsolete adjective *fledge* 'fledged, ready to fly'. Ultimately from a prehistoric Germanic word that is also the ancestor of English *fly*.]

fledgling /fléjling/, **fledgeling** *n.* **1.** BIRDS YOUNG BIRD WITH NEW FLIGHT FEATHERS a young bird that has recently grown the feathers necessary for flying **2.** SB INEXPERIENCED a young or inexperienced person ■ *adj.* INEXPERIENCED inexperienced because still learning or just starting ○ *a fledgling business*

flee /flee/ (**flees, fleeing, fled** /fled/) *v.* **1.** *vti.* RUN AWAY to run away from sth ○ *fled the burning building* **2.** *vi.* DISAPPEAR QUICKLY to pass or disappear quickly (*literary*) [Old English *flēon*. Ultimately from an Indo-European word also the ancestor of English *pneumonia*.] —**fleer** *n.*

fleece /fleess/ *n.* **1.** ZOOL WOOLLY COAT OF SHEEP the coat of wool on a sheep or similar animal **2.** AGRIC WOOL SHORN FROM SHEEP the wool shorn at one time from a sheep or similar animal **3.** SOFT COVERING a soft woolly covering or mass ○ *rocks with a fleece of moss* **4.** TEXTILES SOFT FABRIC WITH NAP OR PILE a soft warm fabric with a brushed nap or woolly pile, especially one used to make or line outer garments **5.** CLOTHES WARM JACKET a jacket made from a soft warm fabric with a brushed nap ■ *vt.* (**fleeces, fleecing, fleeced**) **1.** SWINDLE OUT OF MONEY to take too much money from sb by cheating or overcharging (*informal*) ○ *They make their living by fleecing tourists.* **2.** AGRIC SHEAR SHEEP to shear wool from a sheep **3.** COVER WITH STH RESEMBLING FLEECE to cover sth with sth soft and woolly in texture or appearance (*literary*) ○ *Clouds fleeced the summer sky.* [Old English *flēos*. Probably ultimately from an Indo-European word that is also the ancestor of English *plume*.] —**fleecer** *n.*

fleecy /flee'ssi/ (**-ier, -iest**) *adj.* **1.** MADE OF FLEECE consisting of fleece or sth similar **2.** RESEMBLING FLEECE soft and woolly in appearance or texture —**fleecily** /flee'ssili/ *adv.* —**fleeciness** *n.*

fleet[1] /fleet/ *n.* **1.** NAVY GROUP OF NAVAL SHIPS a number of warships functioning as a single unit under one command, or all the ships of a nation's navy **2.** COMM, TRANSP VEHICLES OR CRAFT UNDER SINGLE OWNERSHIP a number of road vehicles, boats, or aircraft owned, working, or managed as a unit, usually by a com-

mercial enterprise ○ *The company has a large fleet of service vehicles.* [Old English *flēot* 'ships', from *flēotan* 'to float, swim'. Ultimately from a prehistoric Germanic word that is the ancestor also of English *float* and probably of *fleet*[2] and *fleet*[3].]

fleet[2] /fleet/ (**fleets, fleeting, fleeted**) *adj.* (*literary*) **1.** MOVING QUICKLY moving quickly or nimbly **2.** QUICKLY PASSING passing or fading quickly [Early 16thC. Origin uncertain: probably from Old Norse *fljótr*, and ultimately from prehistoric Germanic (see FLEET[1]).] —**fleetly** *adv.* —**fleetness** *n.*

fleet[3] /fleet/ *n.* a creek or inlet (*regional*) [Old English *flēot*. Ultimately from prehistoric Germanic (see FLEET[1]).]

fleet admiral, **Fleet Admiral** *n.* an officer in the United States Navy of the highest rank, with an insignia of five stars

Fleet Air Arm *n.* the branch of the Royal Navy concerned with air operations

fleet chief petty officer *n.* a noncommissioned officer or rank in the Royal Navy

fleeting /flee'ting/ *adj.* passing or fading quickly [Old English, from *flēotan* (see FLEET[1]). The original sense was 'floating', later 'flowing'; hence 'flowing or gliding quickly away'.] —**fleetingly** *adv.* —**fleetingness** *n.*

— WORD KEY: SYNONYMS —
See Synonyms at *temporary*.

Fleet Street *n.* the people and practices involved in the British newspaper industry [Because most British national newspapers were formerly produced in *Fleet Street*, central London]

fleishig /fláyshik, flī'-/, **fleishik** *adj.* under Jewish dietary laws, relating to, containing, or used as meat or meat products. ◊ **milchig, parev** [Mid-20thC. From Yiddish *fleyshik*, from *fleysh* 'meat'. Ultimately from a prehistoric Germanic word that is also the ancestor of English *flesh*.]

Flem. *abbr.* Flemish

Fleming /flémming/ *n.* **1.** SB FROM FLANDERS sb who lives in or was born or brought up in Flanders **2.** FLEMISH SPEAKER a Belgian who speaks Flemish. ◊ **Walloon** [Old English *Flǣming*. Directly and via Old Norse from Middle Dutch *Vlaminc*.]

Fleming /flémming/, **Sir Alexander** (1881–1955) British microbiologist. He shared a Nobel Prize in medicine in 1945 for his discovery of the world's first antibiotic, penicillin.

Fleming, Ian (1908–64) British writer. His fictional hero James Bond, secret agent 007, appeared in twelve novels and seven short stories, beginning with *Casino Royale* (1953).

Flemish /flémmish/ *adj.* OF FLANDERS relating to or typical of Flanders, the Flemings, or their language or culture ■ *n.* LANG BELGIAN LANGUAGE one of the official languages of Belgium. It is from the West Germanic group of the Germanic branch of Indo-European and is very similar to Dutch. About five million people speak Flemish. ■ *npl.* PEOPLES PEOPLE OF FLANDERS the people of Flanders, or Flemish-speaking people [14thC. From Middle Dutch *Vlāmisch*, from *Vlām-land* 'Flanders'.]

Flemish bond *n.* a style of brickwork in which bricks laid with the end facing out (**headers**) alternate with those laid lengthwise (**stretchers**), horizontally and vertically

Flemish school *n.* art and artists of the 15th and 16th centuries in The Netherlands. Artists of the Flemish school, e.g. Van Eyck and Rogier van der Weyden, combined carefully observed subjects with complex religious iconography.

flense /flenss/ (**flenses, flensing, flensed**), **flench** /flench/ (**flenches, flenching, flenched**) *vt.* to strip the skin or blubber from a whale or seal [Early 19thC. From Danish *flensa*.] —**flenser** *n.*

flesh /flesh/ *n.* **1.** PHYSIOL SOFT TISSUE OF BODY the soft tissues, primarily muscle and fat, that cover the bones of people and other animals **2.** PHYSIOL HUMAN SKIN AS OUTER SURFACE the outer surface of the human body **3.** UNWANTED WEIGHT unwanted weight or fatty tissue (*informal*) ○ *could afford to lose some flesh* **4.** COOK MEAT OF ANIMALS the flesh of animals, including birds and fish, regarded as food **5.** COOK MEAT EXCLUDING

BIRDS AND FISH the flesh of mammals, as opposed to birds or fish, regarded as food (*archaic*) **6.** FOOD, PLANTS **PULP OF FRUITS AND VEGETABLES** the soft pulpy edible parts of fruits and vegetables, as opposed to the skin, core, stone, and other parts that are not usually eaten **7.** = **flesh and blood** *n.* 1 ○ *so cruel to their own flesh* **8. PEOPLE** people in general (*literary*) ○ *the way of all flesh* **9. PHYSICAL ASPECT OF HUMANITY** the physical body along with its needs and limitations, as opposed to the soul, mind, or spirit **10. SUBSTANCE** substance as distinct from form or style ○ *Actions give flesh to theory.* **11.** COLOURS = **flesh-colour** ■ *vt.* **(fleshes, fleshing, fleshed) 1.** HUNT **INSTRUCT ANIMAL BY FEEDING** to teach a dog or bird to hunt by feeding it the meat of a freshly killed animal **2. ACCUSTOM TO KILLING** to accustom sb to bloodshed and the killing of other people (*literary*) **3. GET BLOOD ON WEAPON** to thrust a pointed weapon into sb's flesh, especially when using it for the first time (*literary*) **4. CLEAN INSIDE OF ANIMAL SKIN** in tanning, to scrape away the soft tissue adhering to a hide [Old English *flǣsc* 'soft tissue, meat'] ◇ **in the flesh** in person ◇ **press the flesh** to greet and shake the hands of many people in public, as a political or promotional exercise (*informal*)

flesh out *v.* **1.** *vt.* **AMPLIFY** to add substance and detail to sth ○ *flesh out a business proposal* **2.** *vi.* **PUT ON WEIGHT** to put on weight or become overweight (*informal*)

flesh and blood *n.* **1. RELATIVES** people, or a person, related to sb by birth **2.** = **flesh** *n.* 9 ■ *adj.* **flesh-and-blood** ARTS **REALISTICALLY REPRESENTING PEOPLE** representing life, people, and events in a way perceived as believable or realistic

flesh-colour *n.* a pink colour with tinges of yellow or grey, like that of a white person's skin —**flesh-coloured** *adj.*

flesher /fléshər/ *n.* **1. SB OR STH THAT CLEANS HIDES** in tanning, a person or a device that removes any flesh adhering to the inside of an animal hide **2.** *Scotland* **BUTCHER** sb who sells meat (*dated; still found on shop fronts*)

flesh fly *n.* a fly whose larvae feed on the flesh of living or dead animals. Family: Sarcophagidae.

fleshings /fléshingz/ *npl.* flesh scraped from an animal's hide

fleshly /fléshli/ (**-lier, -liest**) *adj.* **1. BODILY** relating to the human body ○ *the fleshly concerns of daily living* **2. RELATING TO PHYSICAL PLEASURE** enjoying or concerned with the pleasures of the body **3. NOT SPIRITUAL** not focused on spiritual matters **4. PLUMP** plump or fat (*archaic*) —**fleshliness** *n.*

fleshpot /flésh pot/ *n.* a place known to provide sexual or sensual entertainment (*usually used in the plural*) ○ *Police keep an eye on the local fleshpots.* [Mid-16thC. Allusion to the Bible, *Exodus* 16:3, where the Israelites remember past feasting. Originally 'cooking-pot'; the underlying idea is of physical or sensual gratification.]

flesh wound *n.* a wound that penetrates the flesh but does not damage bones or vital organs

fleshy /fléshi/ (**-ier, -iest**) *adj.* **1. PLUMP** plump or fat **2. WITH MORE FLESH** with thicker or softer flesh than other parts of the body ○ *the fleshy part of the hand at the base of the thumb* **3. SOFT AND JUICY** with thick soft juicy pulp ○ *the fleshiest peaches of the season* —**fleshiness** *n.*

fletch /flech/ (**fletches, fletching, fletched**) *vt.* ARCHERY = **fledge** *v.* 3 [Mid-17thC. Alteration of FLEDGE, influenced by FLETCHER.]

fletcher /fléchər/ *n.* sb who makes arrows [13thC. From Old French *flech(i)er*, from *flèche* 'arrow'. Ultimately from a prehistoric Germanic word that is also the ancestor of English *fly, fledge,* and *flow*.]

Fletcher /fléchər/, **John** (1579–1625) English dramatist. A writer of Jacobean tragicomedies, he collaborated with Francis Beaumont on many plays, including *The Maid's Tragedy* (1610–11).

fletchings /fléchingz/ *npl.* the feathered part of an arrow

Fleur-de-lis

fleur-de-lis /flúr də lée/ (*plural* **fleurs-de-lis** /flúr də léez/), **fleur-de-lys** (*plural* **fleurs-de-lys**) *n.* **1.** HERALDRY **HERALDIC DEVICE RESEMBLING LILY OR IRIS** a heraldic symbol or design in the form of three tapering petals tied by a surrounding band, formerly used by the kings of France **2.** PLANTS = **iris** [From Old French *flour de lys*, literally 'flower of the lily']

fleuret /flur rét, floor-/, **fleurette** *n.* a decorative motif in the form of a small flower [Early 19thC. From French, literally 'little flower', from *fleur* 'flower', from Old French *flour* (see FLOWER).]

flew past tense of **fly**[1]

flex[1] /fleks/ *v.* (**flexes, flexing, flexed**) **1.** *vt.* **BEND A BODY PART** to bend sth, especially a joint of the body **2.** *vi.* **BEND** to bend or be able to be bent ○ *The board flexes as you step on it.* **3.** *vti.* **PRODUCE MUSCULAR CONTRACTION** to move or tense a muscle, or become tense or contracted ■ *n.* **BENDING ABILITY** bending or ability to bend [Early 16thC. From Latin *flex-* (see FLEXIBLE).]

flex[2] /fleks/ *n.* flexible insulated electric cable, especially that attached to an electrical appliance [Early 20thC. Shortening of FLEXIBLE.]

flexatone /fléksə tōn/ *n.* a musical percussion instrument consisting of a handle with a narrow metal sheet attached that is struck to produce a tunable sound

flexibility /fléksə bíllәti/ (*plural* **-ties**) *n.* **1. BEING ABLE TO BEND WITHOUT BREAKING** the ability to bend or be bent repeatedly without damage or injury **2. ABILITY TO ADAPT TO NEW SITUATION** the ability to change or be changed according to circumstances ○ *The proposed system lacks flexibility.* **3. BEING SUBJECT TO INFLUENCE** the capacity to be persuaded or influenced

flexible /fléksəb'l/ *adj.* **1. ABLE TO BEND WITHOUT BREAKING** able to bend or be bent repeatedly without damage or injury **2. ABLE TO ADAPT TO NEW SITUATION** able to change or be changed according to circumstances **3. SUBJECT TO INFLUENCE** able to be persuaded or influenced [15thC. Directly or via French from Latin *flexibilis*, from *flex-*, past participle stem of *flectere* 'to bend' (source of English *deflect, reflect,* and *genuflect*).] —**flexibly** *adv.* —**flexibleness** *n.*

flexile /fléksil, flék sīl/ *adj.* = **flexible** *adj.* 1 [Mid-17thC. From Latin *flexilis*, from *flex-* (see FLEXIBLE).]

flexion /fléksh'n/, **flection** *n.* **1. BENDING OF LIMB** the bending of a limb or joint **2. POSITION OF BENT PART** the position of a bent limb or joint **3. BENDING OF STH** the bending of sth or its bent state **4.** GRAM **INFLECTION** an inflection (*archaic*) [Early 17thC. From the Latin stem *flexion-*, from *flex-* (see FLEXIBLE).] —**flexional** *adj.*

flexitime /fléks tīm/ *n.* a system that allows employees to set their own daily times of starting and finishing work, within certain limits [Late 20thC. Blend of FLEXIBLE and TIME.]

flexography /flek sóggrəfi/ *n.* a relief printing technique that uses a rotary press, a flexible plate, and a water-based ink [Mid-20thC. Coined from Latin *flexus* (see FLEXOR) + -GRAPHY.] —**flexographer** *n.* —**flexographic** /fléksə gráffik/ *adj.* —**flexographically** /-gráffikli/ *adv.*

flexor /fléksər/ *n.* a muscle that bends a joint or limb when it is contracted [Early 17thC. From modern Latin, from Latin *flexus*, past participle of *flectere* (see FLEXIBLE).]

flextime /fléks tīm/ *n.* US = **flexitime**

flexuous /fléksyoo əss/, **flexuose** /-ōss/ *adj.* curving, winding, or turning (*formal*) [Early 17thC. From Latin *flexuosus*, from, ultimately, *flectere* (see FLEXIBLE).] —**flexuosity** /fléksyoō óssəti/ *n.* —**flexuously** /fléksyoō əssli/ *adv.*

flexural /flékshərəl/ *adj.* **1. BENDING** turning, curving, or bending **2. SITUATED IN BODILY CREASE** occurring at a crease or bend in part of the body, e.g. behind the knee

flexure /flékshər/ *n.* **1. BENDING** a bending or being flexed **2.** ANAT **BEND OR CURVE** a bend or curve, e.g. in a body part or organ [Late 16thC. From Latin *flexura*, from *flex-* (see FLEXIBLE).]

flibbertigibbet /flíbbərti jibbit, flíbbərti jibbit/ *n.* a silly, irresponsible, or scatterbrained person, especially one who prattles or gossips (*dated*) [15thC. Origin uncertain: probably an imitation of the sound of meaningless prattle.]

flic /flik/ *n.* a member of the French police (*slang*) [Late 19thC. From French, of unknown origin.]

flick[1] /flik/ *n.* **1. QUICK MOVEMENT** a quick jerking movement **2. QUICK BLOW** a sharp light blow made with a quick jerking movement, usually of the finger **3. SPLASH OF COLOUR** a light splash or streak ○ *flicks of paint left on the floor* **4.** HOCKEY **PENALTY SHOT** in hockey, a penalty shot taken from the penalty spot ■ *v.* (**flicks, flicking, flicked**) **1.** *vti.* **HIT WITH QUICK BLOW** to hit sth sharply or lightly with the end of sth, usually in a quick jerking movement ○ *He flicked me with his towel.* **2.** *vti.* **MOVE JERKILY** to move or make sth move with a quick sharp jerk ○ *The cow's tail flicked back and forth.* **3.** *vt.* **MOVE WITH QUICK BLOW** to move, propel, or remove sth with a sharp light blow or a quick movement of the finger or hand ○ *Would you flick that bug off me?* **4.** *vt.* SOCCER **GUIDE THE BALL GENTLY** to guide the ball gently and deftly with your foot or head into the goal or to a team-mate **5.** *vti.* HOCKEY **TAKE PENALTY SHOT** to take a penalty flick [15thC. An imitation of the sound of a light blow.]

flick through *vt.* to turn the pages of a book or magazine quickly ○ *flicked through a couple of magazines while I waited*

flick[2] /flik/ *n.* **FILM** a film (*dated slang*) ■ **flicks** *npl.* **THE CINEMA** the cinema (*dated informal*) [Early 20thC. Shortening of FLICKER; from the flickering appearance of early films.]

flick[3] /flik/ *n.* (*informal*) **1.** *Wales, S England* **ANIMAL FAT** animal fat found round kidneys and other offal **2.** *N England* **SIDE OF BACON** a side of bacon [Late 16thC. Origin uncertain: probably a variant of FLITCH.]

flicker /flíkər/ *vi.* (**-ers, -ering, -ered**) **1. SHINE UNSTEADILY** to burn or shine unsteadily **2. FLUTTER OR MOVE JERKILY** to move with a fluttering or fast jerky motion **3. APPEAR BRIEFLY** to appear or exist only briefly ○ *A smile flickered across her face.* ■ *n.* **1. FLUCTUATING LIGHT** an unsteady or wavering light ○ *the flicker of candles in the dark* **2. QUICK MOVEMENT** a quick fluttering movement **3. TRANSIENT FEELING OR EXPRESSION** a brief feeling that quickly passes, or an indication of this on sb's face ○ *A flicker of joy briefly lit her eyes.* [Old English *flicorian* 'to flutter'. The underlying sense is of wavering unsteady movement.] —**flickeringly** *adv.*

flick knife *n.* a pocketknife with a concealed blade that opens as soon as a button on the handle is pressed. US term **switchblade**

flier /flī ər/, **flyer** *n.* **1.** AIR **AIRCRAFT PILOT** the pilot of an aircraft **2.** AIR **AIRCRAFT PASSENGER** a passenger on an aircraft ○ *frequent fliers* **3.** PRESS **PRINTED SHEET WIDELY DISTRIBUTED** a short piece of printed matter, usually an advertisement, that is widely distributed **4.** BUILDING **STEP IN STRAIGHT STAIRCASE** a rectangular step in a straight flight of stairs **5.** *US* **RISKY UNDERTAKING** a daring or risky financial undertaking (*informal*) **6.** ATHLETICS, SWIMMING **FLYING START** a flying start (*informal*) [13thC. Originally in the general sense 'sth that flies'.]

flies 3rd person present singular of **fly**[1]. plural of **fly**[2]

flight[1] /flīt/ *n.* **1. PROCESS OR ACT OF FLYING** the process or act of moving through the air or through space **2. AIR JOURNEY** a journey through air or space in a form of transport ○ *daily flights of a thousand miles or more* **3. SCHEDULED FLIGHT** a scheduled flight with a commercial airline, usually designated by letters and numbers ○ *flight TC546 to Vancouver* **4. ABILITY TO FLY** the ability to travel through the air with wings ○ *an experimental ultralight tested for flight* ○ *an ancient bird incapable of flight* **5.** BUILDING **SERIES OF**

STEPS BETWEEN FLOORS a group of stairs that go from one level of a building to another ○ *We live three flights up.* **6.** GROUP FLYING TOGETHER a group of aircraft or birds flying together, sometimes in a set pattern **7.** AIR FORCE GROUP OF AIRCRAFT a group of aircraft operating together as a separate unit, e.g. those available for the monarch's personal use ○ *the Queen's flight* **8.** RAPID MOVEMENT swift passage, progress, or motion, especially through the air **9.** EXTRAORDINARY MENTAL FEAT an act or the process of imagining extraordinary things ○ *flights of the imagination* **10.** TAIL OF ARROW OR DART the feathers on an arrow or dart **11.** SPORTS HURDLES ON RACETRACK a line of hurdles across a racetrack ■ *v.* (**flights, flighting, flighted**) **1.** *vi.* FLY TOGETHER to fly or migrate together **2.** *vt.* SHOOT FLYING BIRD in hunting, to shoot a bird as it flies **3.** *vt.* PUT TAIL ON ARROW OR DART to put feathers on an arrow or dart **4.** *vt.* SPORTS CAUSE TO FLOAT TOWARDS TARGET to make a ball or dart seem to float inexorably towards its target [Old English *flyht*. Ultimately from a prehistoric Germanic word that was also the ancestor of English *fly*[1].]

flight[2] /flīt/ *n.* the act of running away from sth or sb [12thC. Ultimately from a prehistoric Germanic word that was also the ancestor of English *flee*.]

flight arrow *n.* a light arrow used for long-distance shooting

flight attendant *n.* sb employed by an airline to attend to the needs, comfort, and safety of passengers during flights

flight bag *n.* a soft suitcase of a size that can be carried on an aircraft

flight deck *n.* **1.** NAVY RUNWAY ON AIRCRAFT CARRIER the upper deck of an aircraft carrier that is used as a runway **2.** AIR PART OF AEROPLANE WITH THE CONTROLS the compartment at the front of an aeroplane where the pilot, copilot, and flight engineer sit

flight engineer *n.* the crew member of an aeroplane who monitors the performance of its systems including the engines

flight envelope *n.* a set of limits to performance, such as speed, altitude, range, payload, and manoeuvrability, that exist in the design of an aircraft

flight feather *n.* any feather in a bird's wing or tail that is necessary for flight. These feathers are usually large and stiff.

flightless /flītləs/ *adj.* used to describe birds that are incapable of flight. Ostriches, penguins, and kiwis are flightless.

flight level *n.* the height at which a particular aircraft is allowed to fly at a particular time

flight lieutenant *n.* a junior commissioned rank in the Royal Air Force , or the person holding this rank

flight line *n.* the area of an airfield, especially a military airfield, where aeroplanes are parked, serviced, and loaded or unloaded

flight of fancy *n.* an idea or thought that is very imaginative but completely impractical or even ridiculous

flight path *n.* the course taken by an aircraft, space vehicle, or projectile

flight plan *n.* a record outlining the details of a proposed flight

flight recorder *n.* an electronic instrument installed on an aircraft that records details of its performance in flight. The details recorded can be used to discover the cause of a crash.

flight sergeant *n.* a senior noncommissioned rank in the Royal Air Force, or a person holding this rank

flight simulator *n.* a computerized device that exactly reproduces the conditions that occur on the flight deck of an aircraft and that can be used to train pilots

flight surgeon *n.* a medical officer in the US Air Force who practises aviation medicine and looks after the health of flight crews

flight-test (**flight-tests, flight-testing, flight-tested**) *vt.* to test the performance of an aircraft, spacecraft, missile, or component in flight —**flight test** *n.*

flighty /flīti/ (**-ier, -iest**) *adj.* unreliable, capricious, and constantly changing opinions, especially in choice of sexual partners —**flightily** *adv.* —**flightiness** *n.*

flimflam /flīm flam/ *n.* (*slang*) **1.** TRICK OR SWINDLE a trick or attempt to cheat or swindle sb **2.** DECEPTIVE TALK talk that confuses or deceives ■ *vt.* (**-flams, -flamming, -flammed**) CHEAT OR TRICK to swindle or cheat sb (*slang*) [Mid-16thC. Origin uncertain.] —**flimflammer** *n.*—**flimflammery** *n.*

flimsy /flīmzi/ *adj.* (**-sier, -siest**) **1.** FRAGILE weak and easily broken **2.** EASILY TORN light, thin, and easily torn **3.** UNCONVINCINGLY WEAK unconvincing and difficult to believe ○ *The grounds for an appeal are flimsy at best.* ■ *n.* COMM CARBON COPY a thin piece of carbon paper or a copy made with it [Early 18thC. Origin uncertain: probably formed from an alteration of FILM on the model of, e.g. CLUMSY.] —**flimsily** *adv.* —**flimsiness** *n.*

—————— **WORD KEY: SYNONYMS** ——————
See Synonyms at *fragile*.

flinch[1] /flinch/ (**flinches, flinching, flinched**) *vi.* **1.** REACT PHYSICALLY TO PAIN OR FEAR to make an involuntary small backward movement in response to pain or sth frightening or shocking **2.** AVOID CONFRONTING to avoid thinking about sth, confronting sth, or doing sth ○ *We will not flinch from danger.* [Mid-16thC. From Old French *flenchir* 'to turn aside'. Ultimately from a prehistoric Germanic word meaning 'to bend', which is also the ancestor of English *link*.] —**flincher** *n.* —**flinchingly** *adv.*

—————— **WORD KEY: SYNONYMS** ——————
See Synonyms at *recoil*.

flinch[2] /flinch/ (**flinches, flinching, flinched**) *vt.* = **flense** *v.*

flinders /flīndərz/ *npl.* tiny fragments of sth [15thC. Origin uncertain: perhaps of Scandinavian origin.]

Flinders /flīndərz/ river in northern Queensland, Australia that rises near Hughenden in the Great Dividing Range and flows northwest to the Gulf of Carpentaria. Length: 840 km/520 mi.

Flinders, Matthew (1774–1814) British explorer. He was the first sailor to circumnavigate Tasmania (1798) and Australia (1802–03).

Flinders bar /flīndərz-/ *n.* a bar of soft iron mounted under a compass to compensate for local magnetism and prevent it affecting the reading of the compass [Named after Matthew FLINDERS]

Flinders Island island off the northeastern coast of Tasmania, Australia. Local industries include fishing, farming, and tourism. Population: 924 (1996). Area: 1,359 sq. km/525 sq. mi.

Flinders Range mountain chain in eastern South Australia. More than 500 km/310 mi. long, its highest point is St Mary's Peak, 1,166 m/3,825 ft.

fling /fling/ *v.* (**flings** /flung/, **flinging, flung**) **1.** *vt.* THROW VIOLENTLY to throw sth or sb fast using a lot of force **2.** *vr.* JUMP QUICKLY to jump forcefully in a way that seems impressive or dramatic, or to jump on sb or sth in the same way ○ *She flung herself onto the chair and began to sob.* **3.** *vt.* MOVE YOUR HEAD OR ARMS to move your head or arms in a particular direction suddenly and dramatically **4.** *vr.* WORK ENTHUSIASTICALLY AND ENERGETICALLY to start doing sth with great enthusiasm and energy ○ *You can depend on the fact that she will fling herself into every project she undertakes.* ■ *n.* (*informal*) **1.** SHORT AFFAIR a brief sexual relationship **2.** TIME FOR PLEASURE a period of carefree enjoyment, especially before a more serious or worried period [13thC. Of Scandinavian origin. Ultimately from an Indo-European word meaning 'to strike', which is also the ancestor of English *complain*, *plague*, and *apoplexy*.] —**flinger** *n.*

—————— **WORD KEY: SYNONYMS** ——————
See Synonyms at *throw*.

fling off *vt.* to take off a piece of clothing quickly or to remove forcefully sth that is covering you

flint /flint/ *n.* **1.** GEOL VERY HARD QUARTZ THAT MAKES SPARKS a very hard greyish-black fine-grained form of quartz that occurs widely as nodules and bands in chalk. It produces a spark when struck with steel and was used in prehistoric times to make tools. **2.** ARCHAEOL TOOL MADE OF FINE-GRAINED QUARTZ a piece of fine-grained

quartz shaped into a tool by prehistoric people **3.** SPARK-MAKING ROCK a piece of flint used to make a spark **4.** PART OF CIGARETTE LIGHTER the part of a cigarette lighter, consisting of a small iron alloy cylinder, that makes a spark ○ *My lighter's not working, I think I need a flint.* [Old English. Ultimately from a prehistoric Germanic word meaning 'to split', which is also the ancestor of English *split*, *splinter*, *splint*, and *splice*.]

flint corn *n.* a type of maize with kernels that contain hard starch. Popcorn is a type of flint corn. Latin name: *Zea mays.*

flint glass *n.* high-quality glass containing lead oxide that has a high refractive index and is used to make lenses, cut glass, and costume jewellery

flinthead /flint hed/ *n.* = **wood stork** [Late 18thC. From its black head; originally used for 'flint arrow-head'.]

flint-hearted /-haärtid/ *adj.* pitilessly lacking in feeling, caring, and compassion (*literary*)

flint-knapping *n.* the activity, largely carried out by prehistoric people, of chipping and splitting flint to make tools —**flint-knapper** *n.*

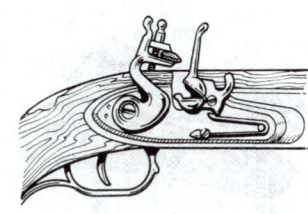

Flintlock

flintlock /flint lok/ *n.* **1.** TYPE OF FIREARM a firearm with a firing mechanism (**gunlock**) where a flint embedded in the hammer ignites a gunpowder charge **2.** EARLY FIRING MECHANISM a firing mechanism (**gunlock**) that has a flint embedded in the hammer to produce the spark [Late 17thC]

Flintshire /flintshər/ county in northeastern Wales, on the border with England. Population: 145,700 (1995). Area: 437 sq. km/169 sq. mi.

flinty /flīnti/ (**-ier, -iest**) *adj.* **1.** STERN AND UNEMOTIONAL hard, inflexible, and showing no emotion **2.** GEOL CONTAINING FLINT containing or related to flint —**flintily** *adv.* —**flintiness** *n.*

flip /flip/ *v.* (**flips, flipping, flipped**) **1.** *vti.* TURN STH OVER to turn sth over from one side to the other with a quick movement of the wrist, hand, or fingers **2.** *vt.* MOVE WITH QUICK LIGHT MOTION to move or flick sth with a small sharp quick motion ○ *She flipped the light on and walked in.* **3.** *vt.* TOSS CARELESSLY to throw or toss sth carelessly and lightly ○ *flip a pen across the table* **4.** *vti.* TURN PAGES OF READING MATERIAL to turn the pages of a magazine or book quickly ○ *flipping through a magazine* ○ *She was standing at her desk flipping the pages of her diary.* **5.** *vti.* SPIN COIN to flick the edge of a coin with your thumb so that it spins in the air, using the random nature of which side of the coin is uppermost when it lands to help make a decision **6.** *vi.* GET SUDDENLY ANGRY to become very angry or upset suddenly (*slang*) ○ *When I told her I wouldn't help her, she just flipped.* **7.** *vi.* GET EXCITED AT STH NICE to become excited over sth that is pleasurable or attractive (*slang*) ■ *adj.* FLIPPANT showing a lack of seriousness that is considered inappropriate (*informal*) ○ *a flip remark* ■ *n.* **1.** COIN'S SPIN the spin of a coin or other object as it is tossed or thrown ○ *decided by the flip of a coin* **2.** GYMNASTICS TURNING OF BODY a turning of the body through 360 degrees by springing on the ground or in diving **3.** BEVERAGES ALCOHOL AND EGG DRINK an alcoholic drink containing beaten egg [Mid-16thC. Origin uncertain: probably an imitation of the sound.] ◇ **flip your lid** to react to sth or sb in the strongest, most emotionally uncontrolled manner possible (*slang*)

flipbook /flip book/ *n.* a small book containing a series of images of the same thing in different positions that create the illusion of movement when the pages are turned quickly

flip chart *n.* a visual aid consisting of a large pad of paper mounted on an easel, used to present information

flip-flop *n.* **1.** CLOTHES **BACKLESS SANDAL** a backless foam-rubber sandal with a V-shaped strap secured between the toes and at the sides of the foot (*informal*) **2.** GYMNASTICS **BACKWARDS FLIP** a backwards flip of the body **3.** *US* **CHANGE OF MIND** a change of opinion, especially by a politician (*informal*) **4.** ELECTRON ENG **CIRCUIT WITH TWO STABLE STATES** an electronic circuit or mechanical device that has two stable states and can be switched between the two. Early computers used flip-flops as their memory storage units. ■ *vi.* **(flip-flops, flip-flopping, flip-flopped)** *US* **CHANGE OPINION** to change your opinion, especially when this leads to a change of policy (*informal*)

flippant /flíppənt/ *adj.* showing a lack of seriousness that is thought inappropriate [Early 17thC. Formed from FLIP, on the model of heraldic adjectives such as RAMPANT.] —**flippancy** *n.* —**flippantly** *adv.*

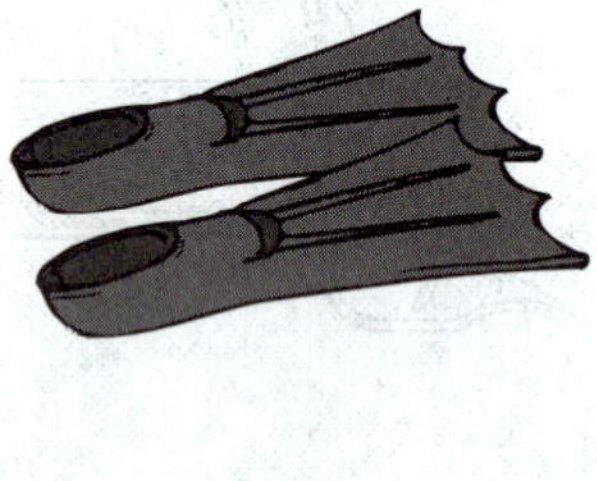

Flippers

flipper /flíppər/ *n.* **1.** ZOOL **AQUATIC ANIMAL'S LIMB** a broad flat limb that an aquatic animal, such as a penguin, seal, or whale, uses for swimming **2.** SWIMMING **DIVER'S FOOTWEAR** a broad flat rubber extension worn on each of the feet to aid in swimming **3.** LEISURE **PINBALL FEATURE** a small button-operated bat in a pinball machine that is used to keep the ball in play

flipping /flípping/ *adj., adv.* used to emphasize annoyance or displeasure with sth (*slang*) ○ *Will you turn that flipping music down?*

flip side *n.* **1. THE DISADVANTAGES** the disadvantages involved in doing sth as opposed to the advantages that have previously been mentioned (*slang*) **2. LESS POPULAR SONG ON RECORD** the song on a single record that the record company thinks will be less popular with record buyers, or the side of the record with that song on it (*dated*)

flirt /flurt/ *v.* **(flirts, flirting, flirted) 1.** *vi.* **BEHAVE IN PLAYFULLY AND ALLURING WAY** to behave in a playfully alluring way **2.** *vt.* **FLICK STH** to flick or jerk sth ■ *n.* **SB BEHAVING IN A PLAYFULLY ALLURING WAY** sb who behaves in a playfully alluring way [Mid-16thC. Origin uncertain.] —**flirter** *n.* —**flirtingly** *adv.*

flirt with *vt.* to consider an idea without doing anything serious about it or letting it have an effect ○ *flirted with the idea of going to college, but decided not to*

flirtation /flur táysh'n/ *n.* **1. PLAYFUL ROMANTIC INVOLVEMENT** a short playful interaction based on lighthearted feeling or behaviour **2. PERIOD OF CASUAL INTEREST IN STH** a period of considering or participating in sth in a superficial way ○ *a flirtation with vegetarianism*

flirtatious /flur táyshəss/ *adj.* behaving playfully and in a way that gives the impression of sexual interest —**flirtatiously** *n.* —**flirtatiousness** *adv.*

flirty /flúrti/ **(-ier, -iest)** *adj.* **1.** = **flirtatious** (*informal*) **2. SUITABLE FOR A FLIRT** suitable for a flirtatious person or a person in a flirtatious mood —**flirtily** *adv.* —**flirtiness** *n.*

flit /flit/ **(flits, flitting, flitted)** *vi.* **1. MOVE FROM PLACE TO PLACE** to move quickly from one place to another without stopping for long **2. BE BRIEFLY PRESENT** to be briefly present or visible **3.** *Scotland* **MOVE HOUSE** to move to a different residence [12thC. From Old Norse *flytja* 'to carry about'. Ultimately from a prehistoric Germanic base meaning 'to float', which is also the ancestor of English *float* and *flutter*.] —**flitter** *n.*

flitch /flich/ *n.* **1.** FORESTRY **TIMBER CUT LENGTHWAYS** a log cut lengthways from a tree, ready for further processing at a mill **2.** FOOD **SIDE OF BACON** a side of bacon or one side of a pork carcass without the leg or shoulder [Old English *flicce*. Ultimately from a prehistoric Germanic word meaning 'to tear', which is also the source of English *fleck, flay*, and *flesh*.]

flite (flites, fliting, flited) *vi.* = **flyte** (*regional*)

flitter /flíttər/ *vi.* **(-ters, -tering, -tered) MOVE RESTLESSLY** to move about in a restless or nervous way ■ *n.* **QUICK MOVEMENT** a rapid, repetitive, or back-and-forth movement in sth small [14thC. Formed from FLIT.]

flittermouse /flíttər mowss/ (*plural* **-mice** /flíttər mīss/) *n.* a bat (*regional*) [Mid-16thC. Translation of German *Fledermaus*.]

flitting /flítting/ *n. Scotland* an act of moving house

flivver /flívvər/ *n.* a small, cheap, and usually old car (*archaic informal*) [Early 20thC. Origin unknown.]

float /flōt/ *v.* **(floats, floating, floated) 1.** *vi.* **REST ON SURFACE OF LIQUID** to move or rest on the surface of a liquid without sinking **2.** *vt.* **MOVE ON LIQUID** to place sth or make sth move on the surface of a liquid **3.** *vi.* **STAY UP IN AIR** to move slowly and lightly through the air **4.** *vi.* **BE HEARD OR SMELT FAINTLY** to carry across a distance, especially as a sound or smell ○ *The sound of laughter floated across the water.* **5.** *vi.* **MOVE GRACEFULLY** to move lightly and gracefully (*literary*) ○ *They floated across the dance floor.* **6.** *vt.* **PROPOSE PLAN** to propose a plan for consideration in order to see what response it receives (*informal*) **7.** *vi.* **LIVE AIMLESSLY** to live without a fixed purpose or plan **8.** *vt.* FIN **SELL SHARES IN COMPANY** to finance a company by selling shares in it to the public on the stock exchange **9.** *vt.* FIN **SELL SHARES OR BONDS** to offer shares or bonds for sale on a stock exchange **10.** *vti.* ECON **ALLOW CURRENCY VALUE TO CHANGE** to allow the exchange rate value of a currency to fluctuate freely in an open market **11.** *vt.* AGRIC **IRRIGATE LAND** to flood or irrigate land ■ *n.* **1. FLOATING OBJECT** an object or device that floats or is used to keep another object buoyant **2.** SWIMMING **SWIMMING AID** a buoyant rectangular board that supports the arms and top of the body of a swimmer. US term **flutterboard 3.** COMM **MONEY KEPT FOR CHANGE** a small amount of money in coins and notes that shopkeepers keep in the till so that they can give customers change **4. VEHICLE IN CARNIVAL PARADE** a truck or other large vehicle that has been disguised with elaborate decorations, typically with a single theme, and then is driven as part of a carnival parade **5.** ANGLING = **bobber 6.** *UK* TRANSP **DELIVERY VEHICLE** a small, usually electrically-powered, delivery vehicle **7.** *US* BEVERAGES **CARBONATED DRINK WITH ICE CREAM** a carbonated drink with a scoop of ice cream floating in it **8.** SHIPPING **PADDLE WHEEL BLADE** a blade in a paddle wheel **9.** BUILDING **A PLASTERER'S TROWEL** a tool with a handle and flat rectangular blade for applying plaster to a wall **10.** BANKING **PERIOD BETWEEN DEPOSIT AND WITHDRAWAL** the period between the deposit of funds by a customer and the availability of the funds to the customer **11.** MECH ENG **BALL IN FLOW-REGULATING DEVICE** the hollow ball that rests on the water level in a tank as part of the device (**ballcock**) that regulates the flow of water into the tank **12.** BIOL = **air bladder** [Old English *flotian*. Ultimately from a prehistoric Germanic base that is also the ancestor of English *fleet*[1].] —**floatability** /flōtə bílləti/ *n.* —**floatable** /flōtəb'l/ *adj.*

float around *vi.* to be the subject of frequent discussion or attention ○ *a rumour floating around about a pending engagement*

float chamber *n.* a chamber in a carburettor that has a floating valve to control the entry and level of petrol

floater /flōtər/ *n.* **1. STH FLOATING** sb or sth that is floating **2.** HR **WORKER SHIFTING TO VARIOUS TASKS** an employee who is switched from job to job as needed **3.** *US* HR **CASUAL WORKER** a casual labourer who goes from job to job (*informal*) **4. DEAD BODY** a dead body found floating in the water (*slang*) **5.** *Aus* FOOD **MEAT PIE IN GRAVY** a meat pie served in pea soup or gravy **6.** OPHTHALMOL **SPOT INTERFERING WITH VISION** a shadow of opaque debris in the vitreous humour of the eye seen as a moving dark spot, or as a group of them, by the person affected. Technical name **muscae volitantes**

float glass *n.* flat polished transparent glass made by solidifying molten glass as it floats on liquid of higher density, such as tin

floating /flṓting/ *adj.* **1. NOT FIXED INTO POSITION** not fixed but moving around **2.** MED **OUT OF NORMAL POSITION** not in the normal place in the body, having moved out of position ○ *a floating kidney* **3.** FIN **FLUCTUATING IN MONETARY VALUE** free to fluctuate in exchange rate value in relation to other currencies ○ *the floating euro*

floating assets *npl.* = **current assets**

floating charge *n.* an unsecured charge on the assets of a company that allows them to be commercially used until the company ceases operations or the creditor demands collateral

floating debt *n.* short-term government borrowing

floating dock *n.* **1. SUBMERSIBLE DOCK** a large structure that can be submerged to let a ship enter and then raised with the ship inside to be used as a dry dock **2. MOVABLE SMALL DOCK** a small dock supported by pilings on which it can move up and down with the flow and ebb of the tide or changing water level caused by other means

floating island *n.* a dessert consisting of custard on which are placed pieces of meringue that appear to float

floating-point *adj.* relating to the handling of large numbers, in a computer with limited memory, by moving the decimal point and calculating with each number expressed as a factor of 10

floating policy *n.* a marine insurance policy that covers loss of or damage to goods during transport, regardless of the ship carrying them

floating rib *n.* a rib not attached to the breastbone. In humans the two lower ribs, the eleventh and twelfth, on each side are floating ribs.

floating voter *n.* sb who does not consistently vote for the same political party in elections. US term **swing voter**

floatplane /flṓt playn/ *n.* a seaplane that has one or more floats that enable it to land on water

float tank *n.* = **flotation tank**

floaty /flṓti/ **(-ier, -iest)** *adj.* **1. VERY LIGHT** seeming to move slowly through the air **2. ABLE TO FLOAT** capable of floating easily

floc /flok/ *n.* a woolly (**flocculent**) mass that forms in a liquid as a result of precipitation or the aggregation of suspended particles [Early 20thC. Shortening of FLOCCULUS.]

floccillation /flóksə láysh'n/ *n.* aimless plucking at the bedclothes, a sign that a person is approaching death [Mid-19thC. Formed from modern Latin *floccillus* 'little tuft of wool', from Latin *floccus* (see FLOCCUS).]

floccose /flókōss/ *adj.* BOT used to describe plant parts that are covered with tufts of soft hair [Mid-18thC. From late Latin *floccosus*, from Latin *floccus* (see FLOCCUS).]

flocculate /flókyŏŏ layt/ **(-lates, -lating, -lated)** *vti.* **1. FORM MASSES** to cause particles suspended in water to aggregate into clumps or masses that then sink or can be removed by filtering **2. FORM FLUFFY MASSES** to form or cause to form fluffy masses (*refers to clouds*) —**flocculation** /flókyŏŏ láysh'n/ *n.*

floccule /flók yool/ *n.* a small mass of woolly or cloudy particles [Mid-19thC. From modern Latin *flocculus* (see FLOCCULUS).]

flocculent /flókyŏŏlənt/ *adj.* **1. WITH FLUFFY APPEARANCE** having a fluffy or woolly appearance **2. WITH WOOLLY MASSES** used to describe the woolly mass of solids (**precipitate**) produced in a liquid by a chemical reaction **3.** INSECTS **COVERED WITH TUFTS** covered with soft waxy tufts or flakes [Early 19thC. Formed from Latin *floccus* (See FLOCCUS).] —**flocculence** *n.* —**flocculency** *n.* —**flocculently** *adv.*

flocculus /flókyŏŏləss/ (*plural* **-li** /-lī/) *n.* ASTRON a mass of gas that appears as either a dark or a bright spot on the surface of the Sun, often near to a sunspot [Late 18thC. From modern Latin, literally 'small tuft of wool', from Latin *floccus* (see FLOCCUS).]

floccus /flókəss/ (*plural* **-ci** /flók sī/) *n.* BOT, ZOOL a tuft of woolly hair or a fluffy or downy covering [Mid-19thC. From Latin, 'tuft of wool', of unknown origin.]

flock /flok/ *n.* **1.** GROUP OF BIRDS OR SHEEP a group of birds, sheep, or goats that travel, live, or feed together **2.** CROWD OF PEOPLE a large group of people of the same type **3.** CHR CONGREGATION the members of a church congregation under the leadership of a priest or minister ■ *vi.* (**flocks, flocking, flocked**) GO IN LARGE NUMBERS TO STH to go to a place or event in large numbers [Old English *flocc*]

flock paper *n.* a type of wallpaper with a raised pattern [*Flock* 'powdered wool' (with which this sort of paper was originally made), from Latin *floccus* (see FLOCCUS)]

Flodden Field /flódd'n-/ hill in Northumberland, England, near the Scottish border. It was the site of a battle in 1513 in which King James IV of Scotland was defeated and killed.

floe /flō/ *n.* = **ice floe** [Early 19thC. Origin uncertain: probably from Norwegian *flo* 'layer'. Ultimately from an Indo-European base meaning 'to be flat', which is also the ancestor of English *flake, flag, fluke,* and *plank.*]

flog /flog/ (**flogs, flogging, flogged**) *vt.* **1.** BEAT A PERSON OR ANIMAL VERY HARD to hit very hard using sth such as a whip, strap, or stick **2.** COMM SELL to sell sth (*informal*) [Late 17thC. Origin uncertain: perhaps a shortening and alteration of Latin *flagellare* (see FLAGELLATE), originally in school slang.] —**flogger** *n.* ◇ **flog sth to death** to repeat sth, such as a story or idea, so often that people become bored with it (*informal*)

flokati /flə kaáti/ (*plural* **-tis**) *n.* a handwoven woollen Greek rug with a shaggy pile [Mid-20thC. From modern Greek *phlokatē*, from, ultimately, Latin *floccus* (see FLOCCUS).]

flong /flong/ *n.* a sheet of papier-mâché used to make a mould for the metal plate used to print a page of newspaper [Late 19thC. Anglicization of French *flan* 'mould' (see FLAN).]

flood /flud/ *n.* **1.** WATER COVERING PREVIOUSLY DRY AREA a very large amount of water that has overflowed from a source such as a river or a broken pipe onto a previously dry area **2.** HIGH TIDE the flowing in to land of water, associated with a rising tide **3.** HUGE NUMBER a very large number of people or things ○ *a flood of complaints* **4.** = **floodlight** *n.* 1 ■ *v.* (**floods, flooding, flooded**) **1.** *vti.* COVER AREA WITH WATER to cover a previously dry area with large amounts of water, or to be covered with large amounts of water **2.** *vti.* OVERFLOW to undergo conditions in which water overflows banks or barriers **3.** *vi.* ARRIVE IN LARGE NUMBERS to arrive somewhere in very large numbers ○ *Messages of support are still flooding in.* **4.** *vt.* SEND LOTS OF CALLS OR LETTERS TO to send a very large number of calls, letters, or complaints to an organization (*usually used in the passive*) ○ *We have been flooded with offers of help.* **5.** *vi.* FEEL EMOTION SUDDENLY AND INTENSELY to feel a particular emotion, sensation, or memory suddenly and intensely **6.** *vt.* ECON FILL MARKET TO EXCESS to supply too much of a product to a market, pushing prices down and keeping them low **7.** *vti.* CARS SUPPLY TOO MUCH PETROL TO CARBURETTOR to send too much petrol to a carburettor in a car engine, or be supplied with too much, so that the car fails to start **8.** *vti.* FILL WITH LIGHT to shine strongly so that a place becomes filled with a bright or glowing light (*literary*) **9.** *vi.* MED BLEED A LOT FROM THE WOMB to bleed profusely from the womb, e.g. after childbirth (*technical*) **10.** *vi.* GYN BLEED A LOT IN MENSTRUATION to bleed profusely during a menstrual period (*technical*) [Old English *flōd*. Ultimately from a prehistoric Germanic word that is also the ancestor of English *flow.*] —**floodable** *adj.* —**flooder** *n.* ◇ **be in flood** to be very full of water, so that it overflows banks or barriers ◇ **be in floods of tears** to cry a lot

flood out *vt.* to force sb to leave a place or stop using sth because flooding makes it impossible to stay or continue

Flood *n.* in the Bible (Genesis 7–8), a devastating flood covering the earth, a sign of God's anger at humanity's wickedness. The Flood was survived only by Noah, his family, and pairs of all the animal species who took refuge in the ship (**ark**) that Noah built at God's command.

flooded /flúddid/ *adj.* **1.** UNDER WATER covered with water as a result of a river overflowing or a pipe bursting **2.** CARS FAILING TO SUSTAIN IGNITION failing to start after having been supplied with too much fuel

floodgate /flúd gayt/ *n.* a gate in a sluice that is used to control the flow of water

floodlight /flúd līt/ *n.* **1.** POWERFUL LAMP USED AT NIGHT a large powerful lamp that produces a strong broad beam of artificial light and is used to illuminate the outside of public buildings or sports events at night **2.** POWERFUL BEAM OF LIGHT a broad powerful beam of intense bright light produced artificially ■ *vti.* (**-lights, -lighting, -lit, -lit** /flúd lit/) LIGHT STH WITH FLOODLIGHTS to illuminate sth with floodlights

floodmark /flúd maark/ *n.* the highest level reached by a tide or flood water, or a mark that indicates this level

flood meadow *n. Wales, Ireland, W Country* AGRIC low-lying land likely to be waterlogged in wet weather

floodplain /flúd playn/, **flood plain** *n.* an area of low-lying land across which a river flows that is covered with sediment as a result of frequent flooding

flood tide *n.* **1.** RISING TIDE the incoming tide or the period of time between low water and the following high water **2.** IRRESISTIBLE FORCE an irresistible or overwhelming force of feeling, such as strong public outrage or enthusiasm

floodwall /flúd wawl/ *n.* a wall built along the seashore or the bank of a river to prevent flooding of adjacent land

floodwater /flúd wawtər/ *n.* the water of a flood that is carried over river and stream banks to inundate previously dry land

floor /flawr/ *n.* **1.** BUILDING PART OF ROOM TO WALK ON the flat horizontal part of a room on which people walk **2.** BUILDING STOREY all the rooms on one level of a building ○ *an office on the fourth floor* **3.** GEOG NATURAL GROUND LEVEL the ground at the bottom of an ocean, lake, cave, valley or forest **4.** LEVEL AREA a flat open space for an activity or seating ○ *Are your seats in the stands or on the floor?* **5.** POL PART OF LEGISLATURE WHERE MEMBERS SIT the part of the building housing a legislative body where the members sit and where official debates and discussions take place ○ *the floor of the House* **6.** STOCK EXCH PLACE WHERE SECURITIES ARE TRADED the part of a stock exchange where securities, futures, or options contracts are traded **7.** MANUF MANUFACTURING AREA OF FACTORY the area of a factory where workers manufacture or assemble products ○ *the factory floor* **8.** COMM PART OF STORE FOR MERCHANDISE DISPLAY the part of a shop where merchandise is displayed and sold **9.** DANCE DANCE FLOOR a dance floor (*informal*) **10.** PEOPLE PRESENT AT MEETING all the people present in the audience at a meeting as opposed to the main speakers ○ *I'll take questions from the floor later.* **11.** FIN LOWEST LIMIT a lower limit on an interest rate or the value of an asset ○ *The floating rate loan has a floor of 6%.* **12.** CARS PART OF CAR INTERIOR the flat lower part of a motor vehicle's interior where the accelerator, clutch, and brake pedals are found and where the driver and passengers put their feet ■ *vt.* (**floors, flooring, floored**) **1.** ASTONISH to leave sb astonished and unable to react ○ *He was floored by the announcement of the changes.* **2.** BOXING KNOCK DOWN to knock sb down with a punch **3.** *US* CARS PRESS ACCELERATOR DOWN HARD to depress a motor vehicle's accelerator down as far as it will go in order to increase speed to the maximum (*slang*) [Old English *flōr*. Ultimately from an Indo-European word meaning 'flat', which is also the ancestor of English *field, plain, plane,* and *palm.*] —**floorer** *n.* ◇ **have the floor** to address a meeting or to have the right to address a meeting ◇ **take the floor 1.** to rise to speak to a group of people **2.** to begin to dance, e.g. in a ballroom or nightclub ◇ **take to the floor** to begin to dance, e.g. in a ballroom or nightclub ◇ **wipe the floor with sb** to defeat sb completely and decisively (*informal*)

floorage /fláwrij/ *n.* the floor area of a building

floorboard /fláwr bawrd/ *n.* BUILDING one of the strips of wood that are used to make a wood floor

floor exercise *n.* an event in a gymnastics competition that consists of a series of tumbling exercises in a timed routine performed on a mat

floor hockey *n. US, Can* a version of hockey played using hockey sticks and a plastic puck or ball in a gymnasium. It is occasionally played with bladeless sticks and a rubber ring.

flooring /fláwring/ *n.* the materials from which a floor is made

floor lamp *n. US* = **standard lamp**

floor leader *n.* a member of an American legislative body chosen by fellow party members to organize their activities and strategy on the floor of the legislature

floor manager *n.* **1.** SUPERVISOR IN STORE an employee of a department store or large shop who is in charge of one floor or department, supervising staff and dealing with customers' complaints **2.** TV STAGE MANAGER the stage manager of a television programme

floor plan *n.* a plan of a room or floor of a building drawn to scale as if viewed from above

floorshow /fláwr shō/ *n.* a series of shows featuring dancers, singers, comedians, or magicians at a nightclub [Early 20thC. Because it is presented on the floor.]

floozy /flóozi/ (*plural* **-zies**) *n.* an insulting term for a woman who wears vulgar gaudy clothes and frequents places considered to be disreputable (*slang insult*) [Early 20thC. Origin uncertain.]

flop /flop/ *vi.* (**flops, flopping, flopped**) **1.** SIT OR LIE DOWN HEAVILY to sit or lie down heavily by relaxing the muscles and letting the body fall **2.** MOVE LIMPLY to move limply or heavily **3.** FAIL COMPLETELY to be completely unsuccessful (*informal*) ■ *n.* **1.** TOTAL FAILURE a complete failure (*informal*) **2.** HEAVY DULL SOUND the sound made by sth falling heavily [Early 17thC. Alteration of FLAP.] —**flopper** *n.*

flophouse /flóp howss/ (*plural* **-houses** /flóp howziz/) *n. US* a cheap hotel or rooming house (*informal*) [Early 20thC. From FLOP 'to lie down, sleep'.]

floppy /flóppi/ *adj.* (**-pier, -piest**) HANGING LIMPLY soft and tending to hang down limply or loosely ■ *n.* (*plural* **-pies**) COMPUT = **floppy disk** (*informal*) —**floppily** *adv.* —**floppiness** *n.*

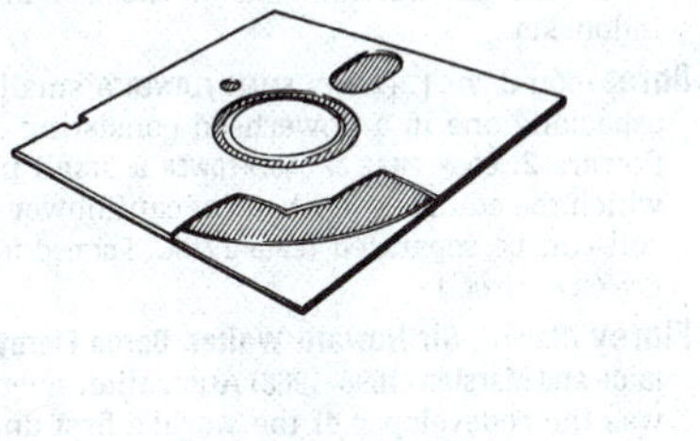

Floppy disk

floppy disk *n.* a small flexible magnetically coated disk on which data can be stored or retrieved by a computer, or the disk and the rigid protective plastic case in which it is contained [Late 20thC. From its flexibility, as opposed to a HARD DISK.]

flops /flops/, **FLOPS** *abbr.* floating-point operations per second (*used to indicate the speed of a computer*)

floptical /flóptik'l/ *adj.* relating to or being a system for storing computer data on a disk that combines magnetic and optical technology [Late 20thC. Blend of FLOPPY and OPTICAL.]

flor., **fl.** *abbr.* floruit

flora /fláwrə/ (*plural* **-ras** *or* **-rae** /-ree/) *n.* **1.** BOT PLANTS plant life, especially all the plants found in a particular country, region, or time regarded as a group (*formal*) ○ *the flora of Australia.* ◊ **fauna 2.** BOT DESCRIPTION OF PLANTS a systematic set of descriptions of all the plants of a particular place or time **3.** MICROBIOL BACTERIA THAT INHABIT BODY ORGANS all the usually harmless bacteria inhabiting an area or part of the body, regarded as a group or population [Early 16thC. From Latin *Flora*, the Roman goddess of flowers, from *flor-*, the stem of *flos* 'flower' (source of English *flower.*)]

floral /fláwrəl/ *adj.* **1.** PLANTS **CONSISTING OF FLOWERS** containing or made up of flowers **2. DECORATED WITH FLOWERS** ornamented or decorated with flowers or with representations of them **3.** BOT **RELATING TO FLOWERS** relating to or being a part of a flower [Mid-17thC. From Latin *Floralis* 'pertaining to the goddess Flora' (the original English meaning), or formed from *flor-* (see FLORA).] —**florally** *adv.*

floral envelope *n.* = **perianth**

Floreal /fláwriəl/ *n.* CALENDAR the eighth month of the year in the French Revolutionary calendar, corresponding to 21 April to 20 May in the Gregorian calendar [Early 19thC. From French *Floréal*, from Latin *floreus* 'flowery', from *flor-* (see FLORA).]

Florence /flórrənss/ capital of Firenze Province and Tuscany Region, central Italy. Situated on the River Arno, about 233 km/145 mi. northwest of Rome, it is one of the world's leading artistic and cultural centres. Population: 397,434 (1992). Italian **Firenze**

Florence fennel *n.* = **fennel** *n.* **2** [Named after the city of FLORENCE, Italy]

Florentine /flórrən tīn/ *adj.* **1.** PEOPLES **OF FLORENCE** relating to or typical of the Italian city of Florence, or its people or culture **2.** ARTS **TYPICAL OF ART OF RENAISSANCE FLORENCE** relating to or characteristic of the style of art or architecture that flourished in Florence during the Renaissance **3.** COOK **WITH SPINACH** cooked or served with spinach ○ *eggs Florentine* ■ *n.* **1.** PEOPLES **SB FROM FLORENCE** sb who lives in or was born or brought up in the Italian city of Florence **2.** FOOD **TYPE OF BISCUIT** a biscuit containing candied peel, fruit, and nuts and covered in a thick layer of chocolate [13thC. From Latin *Florentinus*, from *Florentia* 'Florence'.]

Florentine stitch *n.* = **bargello stitch**

Flores /flórress/ **1.** mountainous island in southeastern Indonesia, one of the Lesser Sunda Islands. The chief towns are Ende and Ruteng. Population: 272,750 (1989). Area: 14,200 sq. km/5,480 sq. mi. **2.** island in the northwestern Azores, in the Atlantic Ocean. Santa Cruz is the chief town. Population: 4,435 (1991). Area: 150 sq. km/58 sq. mi.

florescence /flaw réss'nss/ *n.* flowering (*formal*) [Late 18thC. From modern Latin *florescentia*, from Latin *florescent-*, the present participle stem of *florescere* (see FLOURISH).] —**florescent** *adj.*

Flores Sea sea situated between the eastern end of Java and the western end of the Banda Sea in Indonesia

floret /flórrət/ *n.* **1.** PLANTS **SMALL FLOWER** a small flower, especially one in a flowerhead consisting of many flowers **2.** COOK **PIECE OF CAULIFLOWER** a small part into which the edible flower head of cauliflower or broccoli can be separated [Late 17thC. Formed from Latin *flor-* (see FLORA).]

Florey /fláwri/, **Sir Howard Walter, Baron Florey of Adelaide and Marston** (1898–1968) Australian scientist. He was the codeveloper of the world's first antibiotic, penicillin. He shared the Nobel Prize in medicine in 1945.

Florianópolis /flórri ə nóppəliss/ city and capital of Santa Catarina State, southern Brazil, situated on Santa Catarina Island. Population: 254,944 (1991).

floriated /fláwri aytid/ *adj.* ARCHIT decorated with designs based on flowers and leaves [Mid-19thC. Formed from Latin *flor-* (see FLORA).]

floribunda /flórri búndə/ *n.* a hybrid type of cultivated rose that has small flowers growing in large sprays [Late 19thC. From modern Latin, feminine of *floribundus*, literally 'flowering profusely', from Latin *flor-* (see FLORA).]

floricane /fláwri kayn/ *n.* a plant stem that flowers and bears fruit in its second year, e.g. in raspberries [Coined from Latin *flor-* (see FLORA + CANE)]

floriculture /fláwri kulchər/ *n.* the growing of flowers as a crop [Early 19thC. Coined from Latin *flor-* (see FLORA) on the model of HORTICULTURE.] —**floricultural** /fláwri kúlchərəl/ *adj.* —**floriculturally** /-rəli/ *adv.* —**floriculturist** /-rist/ *n.*

florid /flórrid/ *adj.* **1. OF RUDDY COMPLEXION** having an unhealthily glowing pink or red complexion **2. ORNATE IN WORDING AND STYLE** ornate and overly complicated in wording and general style **3. HEALTHY** in a state of good health (*archaic*) [Mid-17thC. Via French from Latin *floridus* 'flowery', from *flor-* (see FLORA).] —**floridity** /flo ríddəti/ *n.* —**floridly** /flórridli/ *adv.* —**floridness** /-nəss/ *n.*

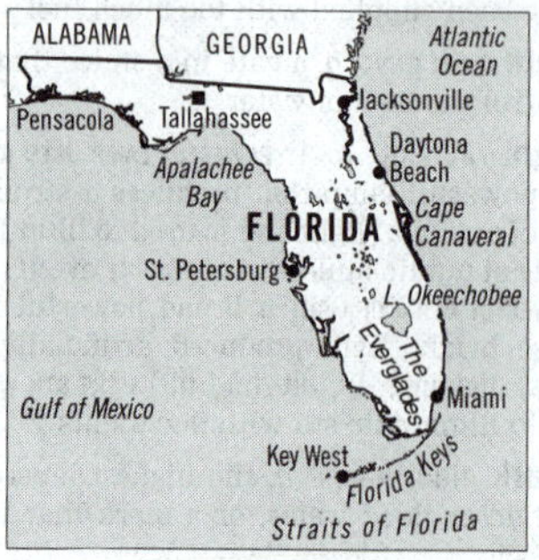

Florida

Florida /flórridə/ state in the southeastern United States bordered by Alabama, Georgia, the Atlantic Ocean, and the Gulf of Mexico. Capital: Tallahassee. Population: 14,653,945 (1997). Area: 155,213 sq. km/59,928 sq. mi. —**Floridian** /flə ríddi ən/ *adj., n.*

Florida Keys /-keez/ chain of islands and reefs in southern Florida, extending southwestwards in an arc from the southern end of Biscayne Bay into the Gulf of Mexico. The islands, which include Key Largo and Key West, are connected by bridges and causeways and are a popular vacation destination. Length: 360 km/225 mi.

floriferous /flaw ríffərəss/ *adj.* bearing or able to bear many flowers [Mid-17thC. Formed from Latin *florifer*, from *flor-* (see FLORA).] —**floriferously** *adv.* —**floriferousness** *n.*

florilegium /fláwri leeji əm/ (*plural* **-a** /-ji ə/) *n.* an anthology of literary extracts (*archaic*) [Early 17thC. From modern Latin, literally 'a gathering of flowers', a translation of Greek *anthologion*.]

florin /flórrin/ *n.* **1. OLD BRITISH COIN** a unit of currency used in Britain between 1849 and 1968, equivalent to two shillings **2. GOLD OR SILVER COIN** a gold or silver coin, especially a Dutch guilder **3. FLORENTINE COIN** a gold coin first minted in Florence in 1252, or any similar coin used elsewhere in Europe [14thC. Via Old French from, ultimately, Italian *fiore* 'flower' (because the name was first used for a coin bearing the figure of a fleur-de-lis), from Latin *flor-* (see FLORA).]

Florio /fláwri ō/, **John** (1553–1625) English lexicographer and translator. He published an Italian-English dictionary (1598) and a translation of Montaigne's *Essays* (1603).

florist /flórrist/ *n.* **1. SB WHO SELLS FLOWERS** sb who owns or works in a shop that sells flowers and ornamental plants **2. florist, florist's SHOP SELLING FLOWERS** a shop that sells flowers and other ornamental plants [Early 17thC. Formed from Latin *flor-* (see FLORA).]

floristics /flo rístiks/ *n.* a branch of botany dealing with the types, numbers, distribution, and relationships of plant species in a particular area or areas (*takes a singular verb*) [Late 19thC. Coined from FLORA + -ISTICS.]

-florous *suffix.* bearing flowers ○ *multiflorous* [Formed from Latin *flor-*, the stem of *flos* (see FLOWER)]

floruit /flórroo it/ *v.* used, especially abbreviated as 'fl'., before the name or numeric designator of the period in the past when a specified person or movement was most active. (*literary formal*) [Mid-19thC. From Latin, literally 'flourished'.]

flory /fláwri/ *adj.* HERALDRY containing a fleur-de-lis [14thC. Anglicization of Old French *floré*, from *flor* (see FLOWER).]

floss /floss/ *vti.* (**flosses, flossing, flossed**) DENT **CLEAN BETWEEN TEETH** to clean between individual teeth using dental floss ■ *n.* **1.** DENT = **dental floss 2.** TEXTILES **SILKWORM FIBRES** short or waste fibres prepared from the the outer surface of the cocoon of a silkworm **3.** PLANTS **PLANT FIBRES** the mass of fine silk fibres that covers the seeds of the ceiba tree or of a cotton plant **4.** SEW **EMBROIDERY THREAD** an embroidery thread made up of six strands loosely twisted together but which can be separated for fine work [Mid-18thC. Origin uncertain: possibly an alteration of French *floche* 'down, velvet pile', from Latin *floccus* (see FLOCCUS).] — **flosser** *n.*

flossy /flóssi/ (**-ier, -iest**) *adj.* **1.** *US* **FLASHILY ORNATE** ornate or showy in a flashy, often almost vulgar way **2. OF OR LIKE FLOSS** consisting of or looking like floss — **flossily** *adv.* —**flossiness** *n.*

flotage /flṓtij/ *n.* **1.** = **flotation** *n.* **1 2.** = **flotsam** *n.* **1**

flotation /flō táysh'n/ *n.* **1.** FIN **SELLING OF SHARES IN COMPANY** the financing of a company by selling shares in it or a new debt issue, or the offering of shares and bonds for sale on the stock exchange **2. FLOATING** the act, process, or condition of floating **3. CAPABILITY OF FLOATING** the ability to float on a liquid or remain on top of a soft surface (*technical*) **4.** TRANSP **ADHERENCE OF TYRE TO SURFACE** the ability of a tyre tread to adhere to and remain on top of a soft surface such as wet ground or snow **5.** CHEM **SEPARATION PROCESS** a process for separating materials, such as a mixture of minerals in an ore, according to their different abilities to float in a given liquid, such as water [Early 19thC. Formed from FLOAT.]

flotation bags *npl.* large bags that inflate when a helicopter or spacecraft lands in the sea and keep it afloat and upright

flotation tank *n.* a sealed tank filled with salt water and minerals that sb can float in to relieve stress

flotation therapy *n.* a method of relieving stress that involves floating in salt water in a sealed tank while listening to music

flotel /flō tél/ *n.* a moored boat or an oil rig that provides accommodation by workers on offshore oil rigs [Late 20thC. Contraction of *floating hotel*.]

flotilla /flō tíllə/ *n.* **1.** SAILING **FLEET OF VESSELS** a fleet of usually small vessels **2. GROUP OF THINGS** a group of things operating or moving together [Early 18thC. From Spanish, literally 'small fleet', from *flota* 'fleet', which came via Old French *flote* from Old Norse *floti*.]

flotsam /flótsəm/ *n.* **1.** SHIPPING **WRECKAGE FLOATING IN SEA** wreckage, debris, or refuse from a ship, found floating in the water. In maritime law flotsam is what is found floating after a ship has sunk and jetsam is what is thrown from a ship while it was in trouble. **2. MARGINALIZED PEOPLE** people who live on the margins of society, such as vagrants, the homeless, or the destitute (*considered offensive in some contexts*) [Early 17thC. From Anglo-Norman *floteson*, from *floter* 'to float', of prehistoric Germanic origin.] ◇ **flotsam and jetsam** discarded objects or odds and ends

flounce[1] /flownss/ *vi.* (**flounces, flouncing, flounced**) **MOVE WITH ANGRY SWAGGER** to move with exaggerated angry swaggering motions showing displeasure or indignation ■ *n.* **JERKY MOVEMENT** an exaggerated movement of the body that shows displeasure or indignance [Mid-16thC. Origin uncertain: perhaps from a Scandinavian source.]

flounce[2] /flownss/ *n.* SEW a strip of cloth that has been gathered into pleats on one side and then stitched onto a garment or onto a set of curtains as a decoration [Early 18thC. Alteration of Old French *fronce* 'pleat' (probably influenced by FLOUNCE[1]), of prehistoric Germanic origin.]

flouncing /flównssing/ *n.* material used to make flounces

flounder[1] /flówndər/ (**-ders, -dering, -dered**) *vi.* **1. MAKE UNCONTROLLED MOVEMENTS** to make clumsy uncontrolled movements while trying to regain balance or move forward **2. HESITATE IN CONFUSION** to act in a way that shows confusion or a lack of purpose **3. BE IN SERIOUS DIFFICULTY** to have serious problems and be close to failing [Late 16thC. Origin uncertain: possibly a blend of FOUNDER and BLUNDER.]

flounder[2] /flówndər/ (*plural* **-der** *or* **-ders**) *n.* **1. EDIBLE FLATFISH** a flatfish that lives at the bottom of shallow coastal waters and is an important food fish. Families: Pleuronectidae and Bothidae. **2. EDIBLE EUROPEAN FLATFISH** a European flatfish that has a greyish-brown mottled skin with orange spots, is covered with prickly scales, and is edible. Latin name: *Platichthys flesus.* [15thC. Via Anglo-Norman *floundre* from a Scandinavian source related to Old Swedish *flundra*. Ultimately from an Indo-European word meaning 'to be flat', the ancestor of English *flat, plate,* and *plant*.]

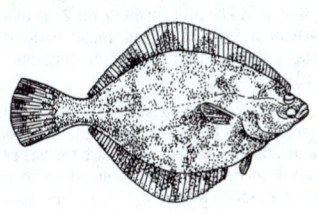

Flounder

flour /flówər/ *n.* FOOD **1.** FINELY GROUND CEREAL GRAINS a powder made by grinding the edible parts of cereal grains and used to make bread, cakes, or pastry and to thicken sauces **2.** GROUND FOODSTUFF a finely ground powder made from any dried vegetable such as chickpea, banana, cassava, or potato ■ *vt.* (**flours, flouring, floured**) COOK COVER WITH FLOUR to cover or coat food, food preparation utensils, or a work surface with flour [13thC. Variant of FLOWER, in the sense 'finest quality' (i.e. ground meal).]

flourish /flúrrish/ *v.* (**-ishes, -ishing, -ished**) **1.** *vi.* BE HEALTHY OR GROW WELL to be strong and healthy or to grow well, especially because conditions are right **2.** *vi.* DO WELL to sustain continuous steady strong growth **3.** *vt.* WAVE to wave sth in a dramatic way that draws attention to it ■ *n.* **1.** HAND MOVEMENT a dramatic body movement, such as a sweep of the hand, that attracts attention **2.** LOOP OR CURL an embellishment to sth handwritten, such as a loop or curly line **3.** MUSIC ORNAMENTAL TRUMPET CALL a fanfare heralding the arrival of an important person **4.** MUSIC SHORT PRELUDE OR POSTLUDE a short, often improvised, passage at the beginning or end of a piece of music **5.** MUSIC SHOWY MUSICAL INTERLUDE brief, often showy, technical passage within a piece of music [13thC. From Old French *floriss-*, the stem of *florir* 'to bloom', from, ultimately, Latin *florere*, from *flor-* (see FLORA).] —**flourisher** *n.*

flour moth *n.* a grey moth with larvae that infest stored grain. Latin name: *Ephestia kuhniella.*

floury /flów əri/ (**-ier, -iest**) *adj.* FOOD **1.** COVERED WITH FLOUR covered or coated with flour or tasting of flour **2.** SLIGHTLY CRUMBLY easily crumbling when cooked ○ *floury potatoes*

flout /flowt/ (**flouts, flouting, flouted**) *vt.* to show contempt for a law or convention by openly disobeying or defying it [Mid-16thC. Origin uncertain: perhaps from an earlier word meaning 'to play the flute', as if in mockery.] —**flouter** *n.* —**floutingly** *adv.*

───── **WORD KEY: USAGE** ─────

See Usage note at **flaunt**.

flow /flō/ *vi.* (**flows, flowing, flowed**) **1.** MOVE FREELY FROM PLACE TO PLACE to move or be moved freely from one place to another in large numbers or amounts in a steady unbroken stream ○ *measures to allow traffic to flow freely* **2.** PHYSIOL CIRCULATE IN BODY to move through the veins and arteries of the body (*refers especially to blood*) **3.** COMMUNICATION BE SAID FLUENTLY to be expressed uninhibitedly and eloquently ○ *The conversation began to flow.* **4.** BE AVAILABLE IN QUANTITY to be readily available and consumed in large amounts ○ *The lemonade flowed freely.* **5.** BE EXPERIENCED INTENSELY to be experienced very intensely, often in a way that is visible to other people ○ *A wave of love flowed across her face.* **6.** EMANATE AS RESULT to derive from sth as a result or series of results (*literary*) ○ *The consequences that flowed from the decision were worrying.* **7.** HANG LOOSELY to fall or hang loosely and gracefully ○ *Her long hair flowed over her shoulders.* **8.** OCEANOG MOVE TOWARDS LAND to move towards the land as the tide rises (*refers to the sea or tidal water*) **9.** GEOL CHANGE SHAPE UNDER PRESSURE to change shape gradually in response to pressure without the development of cracks or fissures ■ *n.* **1.** MOVEMENT OF FLUID OR ELECTRICAL CHARGE the movement of liquid, gas, or electrical charge **2.** MASS OR QUANTITY FLOWING a mass or quantity of material that is flowing or has flowed ○ *a giant lava flow pouring down into the valley* **3.**

MENSTRUAL FLOW the flow or quantity of blood during menstruation **4.** UNHINDERED STEADY MOVEMENT the steady unbroken stream of people, goods, vehicles, money, or information from one place to another ○ *the unending flow of refugees* **5.** OCEANOG TIDAL MOVEMENT TOWARDS LAND the movement of a rising tide towards the land **6.** COMMUNICATION ELOQUENT EXPRESSION OF THOUGHTS the continuous eloquent expression of thoughts or ideas in speech or writing **7.** *Scotland* GEOG BOGGY EXPANSE an expanse of wet peat bog ○ *the flow country* **8.** *US* PSYCHOL EXPERIENCE OF HEIGHTENED AWARENESS psychological and physical experience in which challenges presented are perfectly matched by the participants' skills, often resulting in heightened states of awareness, confidence, and performance [Old English *flōwan.* Ultimately from an Indo-European word that is also the ancestor of English *flood* and *pluvial.*] ◇ **go with the flow** to follow the lead of other people and react to their opinions or actions rather passively

flowage /flṓ ij/ *n.* **1.** FLOWING the act of flowing or overflowing **2.** OVERFLOWING WATER the water resulting from overflow **3.** CIV ENG GRADUAL DEFORMATION the gradual change in shape that occurs in certain solids, e.g. asphalt, that can flow without breaking when, e.g. heat is applied

flow chart *n.* a diagram that represents the sequence of operations in a process

flow-charting *n.* the designing of a flow chart or charts

flow cytometry *n.* a diagnostic test revealing the arrangement and amount of DNA in a cell, used to distinguish benign cells from malignant ones or to monitor the effect of anticancer treatment

flow diagram *n.* = flow chart

flower /flówər/ *n.* **1.** COLOURED PART OF PLANT a coloured, sometimes scented, part of a plant that contains its reproductive organs. It consists of a leafy shoot with modified leaves, petals, and sepals surrounding male or female organs, stamens, and pistils. **2.** STEM WITH FLOWER a plant stem with one or more flowers that has been picked from the plant on which it grew **3.** PLANT WITH FLOWERS a small plant grown for the attractiveness of its flowers **4.** BEST the best part of or most perfect example of sth ○ *the flower of the nation's youth* **5.** *N England* USED TO ADDRESS SB AFFECTIONATELY used as a way of addressing sb you like or love (*informal*) ■ **flowers** *npl.* CHEM FINE CHEMICAL POWDER a fine powder produced by sublimation or condensation ■ *vi.* (**-ers, -ering, -ered**) **1.** BOT PRODUCE BLOOMS to begin to produce blooms **2.** DEVELOP TO MATURITY to develop and reach maturity [12thC. From Anglo-Norman *flur* and Old French *flour*, both from Latin *flor-* (see FLORA).]

flowerbed /flówər bed/ *n.* a clearly delineated area of a garden or park planted with flowering plants

flower bug *n.* an insect that feeds on other small insects found in flowers. Family: Anthorcoridae.

flower child *n.* a young person in the 1960s-1970s who rejected materialism and war, especially the Vietnam War, and preached universal peace and love as the solution to the world's problems (*informal*) [From their custom of wearing or carrying flowers as a symbol of peace]

flower clock *n.* a seed head comprising a mass of seeds, each bearing a hair and dispersed by the wind, such as that of a dandelion

flowered /flówərd/ *adj.* **1.** ORNAMENTED WITH FLOWERS decorated with flowers or having a floral pattern **2.** WITH BLOOMS having flowers (*usually used in combination*) ○ *a large-flowered variety*

flowerer /flówərər/ *n.* a plant that flowers, usually at a particular time or in a particular manner ○ *a late flowerer*

floweret /flówərət/ *n.* COOK = floret *n.* 2

flower fly *n.* = hoverfly

flower girl *n.* **1.** GIRL WHO IS BRIDAL ATTENDANT a young girl who carries flowers in the procession at a wedding **2.** WOMAN OR GIRL FLOWER SELLER a girl or woman who sells flowers in the street

flower head *n.* **1.** CLUSTER OF SMALL FLOWERS a cluster of small flowers on a single stem **2.** CLUSTER OF FLOWER BUDS a dense arrangement of flower buds, such as in cauliflower or broccoli

flowering /flówering/ *adj.* ABLE TO PRODUCE BLOOMS capable of producing noticeable flowers ■ *n.* PERIOD OF SUCCESS the moment in the development of an idea, style, or movement when it gains recognition and becomes successful

flowering currant *n.* an ornamental deciduous shrub that has dark green aromatic leaves in spring and small tubular red or pink flowers that are sometimes followed by round black fruits. Latin name: *Ribes sanguineum.*

flowering dogwood *n.* a spreading deciduous tree with green oval leaves that turn red or purple in autumn and small greenish flowers surrounded by four white or pink bracts resembling petals. Latin name: *Cornus florida.*

Corolla

Petal

Stigma

Style

Stamen — Anther
Filament

Ovules

Ovary

Sepal

Flower: Cross-section of a flower

flowering maple *n.* *US* = abutilon

flowering rush *n.* a deciduous water plant similar to a rush that has narrow twisted leaves and is grown for its pink flowers. Latin name: *Butomus umbellatus.*

flower-of-an-hour, **flower-of-the-hour** (*plural* **flowers-of-the-hour**) *n.* a European herbaceous annual plant that has oval serrated leaves and is grown for its trumpet-shaped creamy-white or pale yellow flowers. Latin name: *Hibiscus trionum.* [Because its petals are short-lived]

flower-pecker *n.* a small songbird found in Australia and southeast Asia that has a long tongue and feeds on nectar, berries, and insects. Family: Dicaeidae.

flower people *npl.* young 1960s-1970s peace activists, the flower children, regarded as a group (*informal*)

flowerpot /flówər pot/ *n.* a clay or plastic container in which plants are grown

flower power *n.* the idea advocated by some young people in the 1960s and 1970s that universal peace and love should replace the materialism and militarism of Western society [From its adherents' custom of wearing flowers as a symbol of peace and love]

flower pressing *n.* the process of preserving cut flowers by laying them on a flat surface and pressing them with a heavy object

flowery /flówəri/ (**-ier, -iest**) *adj.* **1.** LITERAT, COMMUNICATION POMPOUSLY LITERARY full of ornate, overly elaborate expressions **2.** ORNAMENTED WITH FLOWERS decorated or patterned with flowers **3.** LIKE FLOWERS relating to flowers —**floweriness** *n.*

flowmeter /flṓ meetər/ *n.* an instrument for measuring the rate of flow of liquids or gases, especially in a pipe

flown past participle of **fly**[1]

flow-on *n.* ANZ an increase in wages awarded to one union or group of workers as a result of a pay rise awarded to another union or group working in the same field, or the process by which this is done

flow sheet *n.* 1. = flow chart 2. CHEM ENG DIAGRAM OF PIPEWORK a schematic diagram showing the equipment and connecting pipes that make up a process plant and sometimes showing flow rates and quantities of material

flowstone /flṓ stōn/ *n.* a layered deposit of calcium carbonate (**calcite**) on rock where water has flowed or dripped, e.g. on the walls or floor of a cave. ◊ **dripstone**

fl oz, **fl. oz.** *abbr.* fluid ounce

FLQ *n.* a terrorist organization seeking the secession of Quebec from Canada. It was particularly active during the 1960s and 1970s. Full form **Front de Libération du Québec**

Flt Lt, **F/Lt, F. Lt** *abbr.* AIR FORCE Flight Lieutenant

Flt Sgt *abbr.* AIR FORCE Flight Sergeant

flu /floo/ *n.* a viral illness producing a high temperature, sore throat, running nose, headache, dry cough, and muscle pain. The illness is widespread, especially during winter months, and can sometimes be fatal. [Mid-19thC. Shortening of INFLUENZA.]

flucloxacillin *n.* a penicillin drug used to treat streptococcal infections in wounds or sometimes pneumonia. This form of penicillin is effective against bacteria resistant to earlier forms of the drug.

fluconazole *n.* a drug that is prescribed to combat and control fungi

fluctuate /flúkchoo ayt/ (**-ates, -ating, -ated**) *vi.* to change often from high to low levels or from one thing to another in an unpredictable way [Mid-17thC. From Latin *fluctuat-*, the past participle stem of *fluctuare*, the past participle of *fluere* 'to flow' (see FLUENT).] —**fluctuant** *adj.*

fluctuation /flúkchoo áysh'n/ *n.* constant unpredictable change in the level, degree, or intensity of sth

flue[1] /floo/ *n.* 1. SMOKE OR HEAT OUTLET a shaft, tube, or pipe used as an outlet to carry smoke, gas, or heat from a chimney or furnace 2. **flue, flue pipe** MUSIC TYPE OF ORGAN PIPE an organ pipe in which the sound is produced by passing air across a lipped opening 3. MUSIC OPENING ON ORGAN PIPE the lipped opening on an organ pipe that initiates vibrations and sound when air passes across it [15thC. Origin unknown.]

flue[2] /floo/ (*plural* **flues** or **flews**) *n.* a type of fishing net, especially a dragnet [15thC. From Middle Dutch *vluwe* 'fishing net'.]

flue-cure (**flue-cures, flue-curing, flue-cured**) *vt.* to cure tobacco with radiant heat supplied through flues from a furnace —**flue-cured** *adj.*

flue gas *n.* the smoke in the uptake of a boiler fire that consists mainly of carbon dioxide, carbon monoxide, and nitrogen

fluellin /floo éllən/, **fluellen** *n.* an annual wild plant related to the toadflax, foxglove, and snapdragon. Genus: *Kickxia*. [Mid-16thC. Alteration of Welsh *llysiau Llywelyn*, literally 'Llewelyn's herbs', named after LLEWELYN AP GRUFFUDD or LLEWELYN AP IORWERTH.]

fluency /floo ənssi/ *n.* 1. ABILITY TO SPEAK LANGUAGE the ability to speak a language effortlessly and correctly 2. EFFORTLESS CLEAR EXPRESSION the ability to express sth effortlessly and clearly

fluent /floo ənt/ *adj.* 1. ABLE TO SPEAK WITH EASE able to speak a language effortlessly and correctly 2. EFFORTLESSLY EXPRESSED spoken or expressed effortlessly and clearly 3. SMOOTHLY FLOWING flowing in a smooth graceful way (*literary*) [Late 16thC. From Latin *fluent-*, the present participle stem of *fluere* 'to flow'.] —**fluently** *adv.*

The Latin word *fluere*, from which **fluent** is derived, is also the source of English *affluent, effluent, flu, fluctuate, fluid, fluorides, flush, fluvial, flux, influence, mellifluous*, and *superfluous*.

flue stop *n.* an organ stop that controls a set of flue pipes

fluey /floo i/ (**-ier, -iest**) *adj.* having the symptoms of flu

fluff /fluf/ *n.* 1. LIGHT BALLS OF THREAD soft light balls of thread or fibre that collect together on material such as wool or cotton 2. BIRDS, PLANTS DOWNY FUZZ the soft downy fuzz found on young birds or some seeds 3. NONSENSE sth that is of no importance or consequence (*slang*) ■ *vt.* (**fluffs, fluffing, fluffed**) 1. DO BADLY to do sth badly because of loss of concentration or forgetfulness (*informal*) 2. SHAKE SO AS TO INSERT AIR to shake, pat, or brush sth in order to get air into it 3. BIRDS RAISE FEATHERS to raise the feathers in a way that makes the body appear bigger [Late 18thC. Origin uncertain.]

fluffy /flúffi/ (**-ier, -iest**) *adj.* 1. SOFT AND LIGHT consisting of sth soft and light to the touch such as wool or feathers 2. DOWNY OR FEATHERY covered in sth soft and light to the touch such as down or feathers 3. COOK SOFT AND LIGHT IN TEXTURE soft and light in texture because air has been beaten or whisked in —**fluffily** *adv.* —**fluffiness** *n.*

flügelhorn /floog'l hawrn/, **flugelhorn** *n.* a brass instrument with valves, similar to a cornet but with a larger bell [Mid-19thC. From German *Flügelhorn*, literally 'wing horn'; from its use to signal to beaters on the flanks in a shoot.] —**flügelhornist** *n.*

fluid /floo id/ *n.* 1. LIQUID anything liquid (*not used in technical contexts*) 2. PHYS, CHEM LIQUID OR GAS a substance such as a liquid or gas whose molecules flow freely, so that it has no fixed shape and little resistance to outside stress ■ *adj.* 1. PHYS FLOWING capable of flowing like a liquid or gas (*technical*) 2. MOVING OR SMOOTHLY CARRIED OUT smooth and graceful in a way that seems relaxed ○ *a series of fluid arm movements* 3. UNSTABLE likely to change ○ *The situation in the western sector is fluid.* [15thC. Via Old French from Latin *fluidus* 'flowing', from *fluere* 'to flow'.] —**fluidal** *adj.* —**fluidally** *adv.* —**fluidity** /floo íddəti/ *n.* —**fluidly** /floo idli/ *adv.* —**fluidness** /-nəss/ *n.*

fluid clutch *n.* = fluid drive

fluid drive *n.* a device for transmitting rotation between two shafts by means of the acceleration and deceleration of a hydraulic fluid by bladed turbines, used in automatic transmissions in motor vehicles

fluid dynamics *n.* the scientific study of the forces acting on liquids and gases and the resulting movements of these fluids (*takes a singular verb*)

fluidextract /floo id éks trakt/ *n.* a solution of a vegetable drug in alcohol with one millilitre of the solution having an equivalent activity of one gram of the powdered drug

fluidic /floo íddik/ *adj.* 1. OF FLUIDS relating to fluids 2. OPERATED BY FLUIDICS relating to or operated by fluidics

fluidics /floo íddiks/ *n.* the use of systems based on the movements and pressure of fluids to control operations, instruments, and industrial processes (*takes a singular verb*)

fluidize /floo i dīz/ (**-izes, -izing, -ized**), **fluidise** (**-ises, -ising, -ised**) *vt.* 1. CAUSE TO BE FLUID to make sth fluid 2. MAKE SOLID BEHAVE LIKE FLUID to make a solid move as a fluid, e.g. by pulverizing it into fine powder and passing a gas through it to induce flow —**fluidization** /floo i dī záysh'n/ *n.* —**fluidizer** /floo i dīzər/ *n.*

fluidized bed *n.* a powder or other solid particulate material suspended in an upward flow of air or other gas. The material behaves like a fluid and is an effective way to transfer heat or moisture between a gas and a solid or to operate certain chemical reactions.

fluid mechanics *n.* the branch of mechanics that deals with the properties of gases and liquids and their application in practical engineering (*takes a singular verb*)

---

fluid ounce *n.* 1. US UNIT OF LIQUID MEASUREMENT a unit of volume measurement in the US Customary system equal to $\frac{1}{16}$ of a US pint or 29.57 ml 2. UK UNIT OF LIQUID MEASUREMENT a unit of liquid measurement in the Imperial system equal to $\frac{1}{20}$ of an Imperial pint or 28.41 ml

fluke[1] /flook/ *n.* ACCIDENTAL SUCCESS sth surprising or unexpected that happens by accident (*informal*) ■ *vti.* (**flukes, fluking, fluked**) CUE GAMES POT BALL BY ACCIDENT to make a successful shot by accident in pool, billiards, or snooker [Mid-19thC. Origin unknown.]

fluke[2] /flook/ *n.* ZOOL 1. = trematode 2. = flounder[2] [Old English *flōc*. Ultimately from an Indo-European base meaning 'to be flat', which is also the ancestor of English *flake, flag*, and *plank*.]

fluke[3] /flook/ *n.* 1. SHIPPING PART OF ANCHOR either of the triangular blades at the end of each arm of an anchor 2. ANGLING, ARCHERY BARB ON HARPOON a barb on the head of a harpoon or an arrow, or the barbed head itself 3. ZOOL PART OF WHALE'S TAIL either of the two horizontal lobes of the tail of a whale or other similar sea animal, used in propelling the animal through the water [Mid-16thC. Origin uncertain: perhaps from FLUKE[2], because of its shape.]

fluky /floo ki/ (**-ier, -iest**), **flukey** (**-ier, -iest**) *adj.* accidentally and unexpectedly successful (*informal*) —**flukily** *adv.* —**flukiness** *n.*

flume /floom/ *n.* 1. GEOG NARROW GORGE a narrow gorge with a stream running through it 2. ARTIFICIAL CHANNEL an artificial water channel or chute used, e.g., to transport logs, for studying water and sediment movement, or as part of a fairground ride 3. ARTIFICIAL CHANNEL TO MEASURE RIVER'S FLOW an artificial channel constructed in a river in order to measure water flow and movement of sediment 4. ENG STRUCTURE FOR MEASURING WATER DISCHARGE a structure in a river that is used to measure water discharge [12thC. Via Old French *flum* from Latin *flumen* 'river', from *fluere* 'to flow' (see FLUENT).]

flummery /flúmməri/ *n.* 1. MEANINGLESS WORDS meaningless words, statements, or language, especially when intended as flattery (*literary*) 2. FOOD CREAM OR CUSTARD DESSERT a cream, milk, or custard dessert set with gelatine and sometimes flavoured with Madeira and lemon. It was originally made with liquid from boiled oatmeal set with gelatine or isinglass. [Early 17thC. Anglicization of Welsh *llymru*.]

flummox /flúmməks/ (**-moxes, -moxing, -moxed**) *vt.* to leave sb confused or perplexed and unable to react (*informal*) [Mid-19thC. Origin uncertain.]

flung past participle, past tense of **fling**

flunk /flungk/ (**flunks, flunking, flunked**) *v.* (*informal*) 1. *vti.* FAIL ACADEMICALLY to fail an exam or subject 2. *vt.* US GIVE FAILING GRADE to give a student a failing grade [Early 19thC. Origin unknown.] —**flunker** *n.*

flunk out *vi.* US to be expelled from a school, college, or course because of poor academic performance (*informal*)

flunky /flúngki/ (*plural* **-kies**), **flunkey** (*plural* **-keys**) *n.* 1. SERVILE ASSISTANT an assistant who carries out unimportant jobs for sb and who behaves obsequiously to that person (*informal*) 2. MANSERVANT IN LIVERY a man who is a servant in livery, e.g. a footman [Mid-18thC. From Scots, of uncertain origin: perhaps an alteration of FLANKER 'sb who stands at your flank'.] —**flunkyism** *n.*

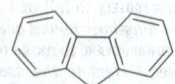

Fluorene

---

fluor /floo áwr/ *n.* = **fluorite** [Early 17thC. From modern Latin, 'mineral used as a flux' (see FLUORIC).]

fluor- *prefix.* = **fluoro-** (*used before vowels*)

fluorapatite /floor ráppǝ tīt/ *n.* a common form of the mineral apatite consisting of calcium fluorophosphate

fluorene /floor een/ *n.* a white insoluble crystalline solid obtained from coal tar and used in making dyes. Formula: $C_{13}H_{10}$. [Late 19thC. Coined from FLUORO- (because the compound fluoresces + -ENE).]

fluoresce /floor réss/ (-resces, -rescing, -resced) *vi.* PHYS to exhibit or undergo the phenomenon of fluorescence [Late 19thC. Back-formation from FLUORESCENT.] —**fluorescer** *n.*

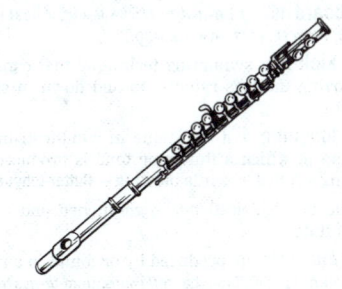
Fluorescein

fluorescein /floor réssi in, floórǝ seen/, **fluoresceine** *n.* an orange-red crystalline compound that fluoresces green in blue light, used to detect defects in the cornea in the eye. Formula: $C_{20}H_{12}O_5$. [Late 19thC. Coined from FLUORESCE + -EIN.]

fluorescence /floor réss'nss/ *n.* **1.** EMISSION OF LIGHT the emission of electromagnetic radiation, especially light, by an object exposed to radiation or bombarding particles **2.** LIGHT EMITTED the radiation emitted as a result of fluorescence

fluorescent /floor réss'nt/ *adj.* **1.** PHYS CAPABLE OF FLUORESCING exhibiting or able to undergo fluorescence ○ *a fluorescent dye* **2.** DAZZLING IN COLOUR very bright and dazzling in colour ○ *fluorescent pink* [Mid-19thC. Coined from FLUORSPAR (because fluorspar has this property) + -ESCENT.]

fluorescent lamp, **fluorescent light** *n.* an electric lamp containing a low pressure vapour, usually mercury, in a glass tube. When an electric current is passed, ultraviolet radiation is produced and is converted into visible light by an internal coating on the tube.

fluorescent tube *n.* the tube of a fluorescent lamp

fluoric /floo órrik/ *adj.* relating to or produced from fluorine or fluorspar [Late 18thC. From obsolete French *fluorique*, from modern Latin *fluor* 'mineral used as a flux', from Latin, 'flow', from *fluere* 'to flow' (see FLUENT).]

fluoridate /floóri dayt/ (-dates, -dating, -dated) *vt.* to treat water by adding small quantities of fluoride salts to the water supply in order to prevent tooth decay in a local population

fluoridation /floóri dáysh'n/ *n.* the addition of small quantities of fluoride salts to the water supply as a public health measure to help prevent tooth decay

fluoride /floor īd/ *n.* any chemical compound consisting of fluorine and another element or group [Early 19thC. Coined from FLUORINE + -IDE.]

fluorimeter *n.* = **fluorometer**

fluorimetric /floóri méttrik/ *adj.* = **fluorometric**

fluorimetry /floor rímmitri/ *n.* the scientific measurement of fluorescence

fluorinate /floóri nayt/ (-nates, -nating, -nated) *vt.* to treat sth, or cause sth to combine with fluorine or a fluorine compound —**fluorination** /floóri náysh'n/ *n.*

fluorine /floor een/ *n.* a toxic pale yellow gaseous chemical element of the halogen group that is the most reactive and oxidizing agent known and occurs principally in fluorspar and cryolite. Symbol **F** [Early 19thC. Coined from modern Latin *fluor* (see FLUORIC) + -INE.]

fluorite /floor īt/ *n.* a mineral form of calcium fluoride, occurring in veins with other minerals as well-formed crystals of various colours, including a banded purple variety, known as Blue John, used as a flux. Formula: CaF_2. [Mid-19thC. Coined from modern Latin *fluor* (see FLUORIC) + -ITE.]

fluoro- *prefix.* **1.** fluorine ○ *fluoride* **2.** fluorescence ○ *fluoroscope* [From FLUORINE and FLUOR]

fluorocarbon /floórō kaárbǝn/ *n.* a chemically inert compound containing carbon and fluorine. Fluorocarbons are used as nonstick coatings, lubricants, refrigerants, and solvents.

fluorochemical /floórō kémmik'l/ *n.* any chemical compound containing fluorine

fluorochrome /floórō krōm/ *n.* a molecule or part of a molecule that exhibits fluorescence, used as a marker in biological specimens

fluorography /floo róggrǝfi/ *n.* = **photofluorography**

fluorometer /floor rómmitǝr/ (*plural* -rometers or -rimeters) *n.* an instrument used to detect and measure fluorescence —**fluorometric** /floórō méttrik/ *adj.* —**fluorometry** /floor rómmǝtri, floor rómmitri/ *n.*

fluoroscope /floórǝ skōp/ *n.* an instrument with which X-ray images of the body can be viewed directly on a screen —**fluoroscopic** /floórǝ skóppik/ *adj.* —**fluoroscopically** /-skóppikli/ *adv.*

fluoroscopy /floor róskǝpi/ *n.* the examination of a person using a fluoroscope —**fluoroscopist** *n.*

fluorosis /floor róssiss/ *n.* a condition caused by excessive exposure to fluorine and marked by mottling of the teeth and damage to the bones —**fluorotic** /floor róttik/ *adj.*

fluorspar /floor spaar/ *n.* = **fluorite** [Late 18thC. From modern Latin *fluor*, 'mineral used as a flux' (see FLUORIC) + SPAR.]

fluphenazine /floo fénnǝ zeen/ *n.* an antipsychotic drug used as a tranquillizer in the treatment of schizophrenia [Mid-20thC. Contraction of *fluorophenothiazine*, its chemical name.]

flurry /flúrri/ *n.* (*plural* -ries) **1.** BURST OF ACTIVITY a short period when a lot of things happen **2.** METEOROL BURST OF WEATHER a short period of snowfall or rainfall, or a gust of wind ■ *v.* (-ries, -rying, -ried) **1.** *vt.* UNCERTAIN to make sb feel agitated and confused **2.** *vi.* METEOROL SNOW LIGHTLY to snow lightly and intermittently ○ *It flurried for an hour or so, then it stopped.* [Late 17thC. Origin uncertain: probably a blend of obsolete *flurr* 'to flutter' and HURRY.]

flush[1] /flush/ *v.* (**flushes, flushing, flushed**) **1.** *vti.* GO RED to become or cause sb to become red in the face or on the skin **2.** *vti.* HAVE ROSY COLOUR to glow or cause sth to glow with a reddish colour **3.** *vti.* MAKE WATER FLOW THROUGH TOILET to clean a toilet by causing water to flow into the bowl, or undergo this process **4.** *vt.* DISPOSE OF IN TOILET to put sth into the toilet and flush it **5.** *vt.* CLEAN WITH WATER to clean or clear sth by liberally pouring water or another liquid into, on, or through it ■ *n.* **1.** SUDDEN FEELING a sudden intense feeling **2.** BEGINNING OF GOOD TIME the beginning of an exciting or pleasurable period **3.** SUDDEN RUSH OF THINGS a sudden increased number of things **4.** REDDISHNESS an appearance of reddish colour **5.** SURGE OF HEAT a sudden surge of heat **6.** GARDENING NEW GROWTH a burst of new growth appearing rapidly on a plant [13thC. Origin uncertain: perhaps from FLUSH[3].] —**flusher** *n.*

flush[2] /flush/ *adj.* **1.** LEVEL completely level so as to form an even surface **2.** BESIDE OR AGAINST directly next to or closely against sth ○ *The chairs were flush against the wall.* **3.** TEMPORARILY RICH having plenty of money temporarily (*informal*) **4.** ABUNDANT abundant or overflowing ○ *a party flush with celebrities* **5.** PRINTING WITH EVEN MARGIN with an even margin on a printed page, without any indentations ■ *adv.* **1.** COMPLETELY LEVEL so as to be completely level and form an even surface without sticking out **2.** DIRECTLY directly or squarely ○ *was hit flush on the jaw* ■ *vt.* (**flushes, flushing, flushed**) FIT THINGS COMPLETELY LEVEL to fit two things so that they are completely level and form an even surface [Mid-16thC. Origin uncertain: probably from FLUSH[1].] —**flushness** *n.*

flush[3] /flush/ *vt.* (**flushes, flushing, flushed**) DRIVE OUT OF HIDING to force a person or animal out of hiding ■

n. HUNT FRIGHTENED BIRDS a bird or birds frightened out of hiding [13thC. Origin unknown.] —**flusher** *n.*

flush[4] /flush/ *n.* in poker and other games, a hand consisting of cards all in the same suit [Early 16thC. Via obsolete French *flus* from, ultimately, Latin *fluxus* (see FLUX).]

flushable /flúshǝb'l/ *adj.* that can be disposed of by flushing it down the toilet

flushed /flusht/ *adj.* **1.** RED-FACED red in the face **2.** EXCITED feeling excited or happy

fluster /flústǝr/ *vti.* (-ters, -tering, -tered) MAKE OR BECOME NERVOUS to make sb nervous or agitated, or become so ■ *n.* CONFUSED STATE a nervous or agitated state [Early 17thC. Origin uncertain.] —**flustered** *adj.*

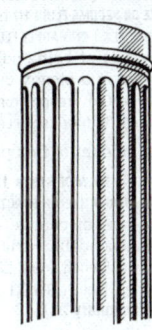
Flute

flute /floot/ *n.* **1.** MUSIC WIND INSTRUMENT WITH HIGH SOUND a woodwind instrument with a cylindrical metal body usually held out to the right of the player, who blows across a hole in the mouthpiece to generate a high-pitched sound. The flute family includes the piccolo, the alto flute, and the bass flute. **2.** MUSIC REEDLESS INSTRUMENT any wind instrument without a reed **3.** MUSIC ORGAN STOP an organ stop with a tone like a flute **4.** ARCHIT GROOVE IN COLUMN a groove running down an architectural column **5.** DECORATIVE GROOVE a decorative groove or pleat **6.** HOUSEHOLD, WINE TALL GLASS FOR SPARKLING WINE a tall narrow glass used for sparkling wines ■ *v.* (**flutes, fluting, fluted**) **1.** *vi.* MAKE SOUND LIKE FLUTE to whistle, sing, or speak in a way that suggests the sound of a flute **2.** *vt.* MAKE FURROWS IN to make rounded grooves in sth [14thC. Via Old French *flaute* and Middle Dutch *flute* from Old Provençal *flaut*, of uncertain origin: possibly a blend of *flaujol* 'flageolet' and *laut* 'lute'.]

fluted /flootid/ *adj.* **1.** DECORATIVELY FURROWED decorated with parallel grooves **2.** SOUNDING LIKE FLUTE similar in sound to a flute

fluter /flootǝr/ *n.* **1.** FLUTING MAKER sb who makes fluting in sth **2.** MUSIC FLUTE-PLAYER a flautist

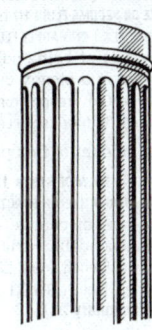
Fluting

fluting /flooting/ *n.* **1.** DECORATIVE FURROWS decoration with parallel grooves **2.** MAKING DECORATIVE FURROWS the forming of decorative grooves **3.** MAKING FLUTE SOUND playing the flute, or making sounds like those of the flute

flutist /flootist/ *n.* = **flautist**

flutter /flúttǝr/ *v.* (-ters, -tering, -tered) **1.** *vi.* WAVE GENTLY to move gently but with quick changes in direction or wavy motion **2.** *vti.* MOVE STH LIGHT to move sth light or small in quick back-and-forth motions **3.** *vti.* FLAP WINGS to flap the wings rapidly **4.** *vi.* FLY to move by flapping the wings rapidly **5.** *vi.* BEAT RAPIDLY to beat rapidly, either as a disorder of the heart or because of nervousness or excitement **6.** *vi.* **QUIVER** to have a quivering feeling because of nervousness or excitement **7.** *vt.* **MAKE NERVOUS** to make sb feel agitated or nervous (*usually used in the passive*) **8.** *vi.* **MOVE RESTLESSLY** to move about in a restless or nervous way ■ *n.* **1.** **QUICK MOVEMENT** a rapid, repetitive, or back-and-forth movement in sth small **2.** **AGITATION** a state of nervous excitement or agitation **3.** **MED RAPID HEARTBEAT** a condition marked by rapid, but regular, heartbeat **4.** **RECORDING SOUND DISTORTION** a high frequency distortion in the pitch of recorded sound **5.** **BETTING SMALL BET** a small bet on sth (*informal*) [Old English *floterian*. Ultimately from a prehistoric Germanic word that is also the ancestor of English *flit* and *fleet*.] —**flutterer** *n.* —**flutteringly** *adv.* —**fluttery** *adj.*

flutterboard /flútter bawrd/ *n. US* **SWIMMING** = **float** [Mid-20thC. From FLUTTER KICK + BOARD.]

flutter kick *n.* a swimming technique that consists of moving the legs rapidly up and down in short strokes

flutter tonguing *n.* a technique in wind-instrument playing in which a fluttering tone is produced by making a rolled 'r' while blowing —**flutter-tongue** *vti.*

fluty /flóoti/ (**-ier, -iest**) *adj.* high-pitched and clear, like a flute

fluvial /flóovi əl/ *adj.* produced by or found in a river or stream [14thC. From Latin *fluvialis*, from *fluvius* 'river', from *fluere* 'to flow' (see FLUENT).]

fluviomarine /flóovi ō mə reén/ *adj.* **1.** **OF RIVERS AND SEAS** relating to water and sediment deposits of rivers in a marine environment **2.** **BIOL** = **diadromous** [Mid-19thC. Coined from Latin *fluvius* 'river' (see FLUVIAL) + MARINE.]

flux /fluks/ *n.* **1.** **CONSTANT CHANGE** constant change and instability **2.** **SOLDERING AID** a substance that promotes the fusion of two substances or surfaces, as in soldering or welding **3.** **PHYS RATE OF FLOW ACROSS AREA** the rate of flow of sth, such as energy, particles, or fluid volume, across or onto a given area **4.** **PHYS STRENGTH OF FIELD IN PARTICULAR AREA** the strength of a field acting on a particular area, equal to the area size multiplied by the component of the field acting at right angles to the area **5.** **MED ABNORMAL BODILY DISCHARGE** an abnormal discharge or flow from the body, especially the bowels (*dated*) **6.** **METALL SMELTING AID** a substance added to molten ore that combines with impurities to form slag which can be extracted **7.** **CERAMICS GLAZE COMPONENT** a substance added to a ceramic glaze to make it flow more readily **8.** **PHILOS THEORY OF CHANGE** the notion that change is the fundamental nature of reality, as described by Heraclitus **9.** **OCEANOG QUANTITY OF MOVEMENT** the quantity of water or other material moved in a given direction during a given time period ■ *v.* (**fluxes, fluxing, fluxed**) **1.** *vti.* **MAKE OR BECOME FLUID** to make sth fluid, or become fluid **2.** *vt.* **MECH ENG APPLY FLUX TO** to apply flux to sth, especially a joint being soldered **3.** *vi.* **FLOW ALONG OR OUT** to move in a steady current or stream (*archaic*) [14thC. Via Old French from Latin *fluxus*, the past participle of *fluere* 'to flow' (see FLUENT).]

flux density *n.* the amount of flux per unit area

fluxion /flúksh'n/ *n.* **1.** **FLOW OF STH** a flow or discharge of liquid **2.** **MATH DERIVATIVE OF FUNCTION** a derivative, representing the rate of change of a function in relation to an independent variable (*dated*) [Mid-16thC. Directly or via French from Latin *flux-*, the past participle stem of *fluere* (see FLUENT).] —**fluxional** *adj.* —**fluxionally** *adv.* —**fluxionary** *adj.*

fly[1] /flī/ *v.* (**flies, flying, flew** /floo/, **flown** /flōn/) **1.** *vi.* **BIRDS, AIR MOVE THROUGH AIR** to travel through the air using wings or an engine **2.** *vi.* **AIR TRAVEL IN AIRCRAFT** to travel in an aircraft **3.** *vt.* **AIR TAKE OR SEND BY AIR** to take or send goods or passengers in an aircraft **4.** *vti.* **AIR BE PILOT** to pilot an aircraft or spacecraft **5.** *vt.* **AIR TRAVEL OVER AREA BY AIR** to travel over a particular area in an aircraft **6.** *vi.* **AIR TRAVEL WITH AIRLINE OR IN CLASS** to travel with a particular airline or in a particular class in an aircraft ○ *She always flies with the same airline.* **7.** *vti.* **FLOAT THROUGH AIR** to make sth such as a kite move through the air, or move in this way **8.** *vti.* **DISPLAY FLAG ON POLE** to display a flag by attaching it to a pole, building, or mast, or be displayed in this way **9.** *vt.* **SHIPPING SHOW COUNTRY OF REGISTRATION** to display a

flag that indicates the country of registration **10.** *vi.* **MOVE FREELY IN AIR** to move freely because of the speed of the air ○ *She ran down the street, her hair flying.* **11.** *vi.* **GO VERY FAST** to go somewhere or leave somewhere at top speed **12.** *vi.* **MOVE QUICKLY AND FORCEFULLY** to move with speed and explosive force **13.** *vi.* **PASS QUICKLY** to pass very fast ○ *The weekend had simply flown.* **14.** *vi.* **BE DISCUSSED INCREASINGLY** to be passed on or gossiped about by a swiftly increasing number of people ○ *Bad news flies.* **15.** *vi.* **BE QUICK TO DO STH** to rush to do sth quickly **16.** *vi.* **US BE ACCEPTABLE** to be acceptable, successful, or useful (*informal*) ○ *come up with a proposal that will fly* **17.** *vi.* **DISAPPEAR** to disappear or be used up quickly ○ *Money just flies out of her hands.* **18.** *vt.* **THEATRE HANG ABOVE STAGE** to suspend lights or set components above a stage **19.** *vt.* **HUNT USE HUNTING HAWK** to cause a hawk to fly after prey ■ *n.* (*plural* **flies**) **1.** **CLOTHES FRONT OPENING OF TROUSERS** an opening at the front of a pair of trousers with a fold of fabric that covers a zip or row of buttons (*usually plural*) **2.** **ENTRANCE FLAP OF TENT** a flap at the entrance of a tent **3.** *US* = **flysheet** **4.** **WIDTH OF FLAG** the distance between the outer edge of a flag and the staff it is attached to **5.** **EDGE OF FLAG** the outer edge of a flag **6.** **TRANSP HORSE-DRAWN CARRIAGE** in former times, a carriage for hire, drawn by one horse ■ **flies** *npl.* **THEATRE AREA ABOVE STAGE** the space above a stage in a theatre, where lights, scenery, etc. are hung. [Old English *fleogan*. Ultimately from an Indo-European word that is also the ancestor of English *fly*[2], *flee*, *flight*, and *fledgling*.] —**flyable** *adj.* ◇ **fly high** to enjoy a period of great success or happiness ◇ **let fly (at sb)** **1.** to speak angrily to sb **2.** to throw sth ◇ **on the fly** **COMPUT** while a computer program is running (*informal*) ◇ **send sb** or **sth flying** to cause sb or sth to go through the air by force of impact

fly at *vt.* to attack sb by rushing towards and hitting him or her, or with angry words. US term **fly into**

fly in *vi.* to arrive by aircraft

fly into *vt.* to suddenly start feeling and expressing a strong emotion ○ *fly into a rage*

fly out *vi.* **AIR** to travel by plane to a particular destination or from a particular airport

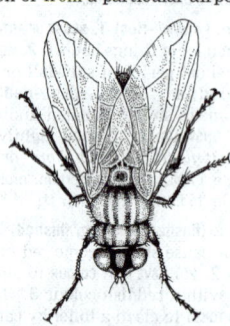
Fly (life size x10)

fly[2] /flī/ (*plural* **flies**) *n.* **1.** **INSECTS SMALL TWO-WINGED INSECT** a two-winged insect. Many flies, e.g. houseflies, are pests. Order: Diptera. **2.** **INSECTS FLYING INSECT** any flying insect, e.g. a caddis fly or dragonfly (*usually used in combination*) **3.** **ANGLING FLY-FISHING LURE** a fishhook with feathers or other attachments to make it resemble a flying insect, used in fly-fishing [Old English *fleoge*. Ultimately from the same prehistoric Germanic base as FLY[1].] ◇ **a fly in the ointment** a problem that spoils a good situation ◇ **there are no flies on sb** used to say that sb is not lacking in intelligence or understanding

fly[3] /flī/ *adj.* **1.** **CLEVER AND SHARP** smart and aware of everything that is happening (*informal*) **2.** *US* **HIP** stylish and fashionable (*slang*) [Early 19thC. Origin unknown.]

fly[4] /flī/ (*plural* **flies**) *adj.* **1.** **CRAFTY** shrewd and clever, in a crafty way (*informal*) **2.** *US* **STYLISH** attractive and stylish (*slang*)

fly agaric *n.* a poisonous mushroom with a bright red or orange cap and white spots. Latin name: *Amanita muscaria.* [From its former use as an insecticide]

fly ash *n.* fine particles of ash resulting from the combustion of a solid fuel

Fly agaric

flyaway /flī ə way/ *adj.* easily made airborne or affected by a breeze ○ *flyaway hair*

flyback /flī bak/ *n.* in a television tube, the rapid return of the electron beam in the direction opposite to scanning

flyblow /flī blō/ *n.* **MAGGOT OR MAGGOTS** the egg or larva of a blowfly or flesh fly, or an infestation with such eggs or larvae ■ *vt.* (**-blows, -blowing, -blew** /-bloo/, **-blown** /-blōn/) **CONTAMINATE** to contaminate sth such as the eggs or larvae of a blowfly

flyblown /flī blōn/ *adj.* **1.** **WITH MAGGOTS** containing maggots and therefore not fit to eat **2.** **DIRTY** dirty and in bad condition **3.** **TAINTED** contaminated with sth undesirable

flyboat /flī bōt/ *n.* a small fast boat [Late 16thC. By folk etymology from Dutch *vlieboot*, from *Vlie*, the name of a channel off the northern coast of the Netherlands.]

fly bridge *n.* = **flying bridge**

flyby /flī bī/ *n.* a flight close to a particular position or object, usually by a space vehicle to a planet, usually for observation purposes

fly-by-night *adj.* **1.** **UNSCRUPULOUS IN BUSINESS** unscrupulous or not creditworthy in business or commerce **2.** **EPHEMERAL** not lasting long ■ *n.* **fly-by-night, fly-by-nighter 1.** **ABSCONDING DEBTOR** sb who leaves without paying debts **2.** **DUBIOUS OR SHAKY BUSINESS** a business with financial problems or a bad reputation [From the tactic of sneaking away at night in order to avoid paying debts]

fly-by-wire *n.* an aircraft flight control system that has electronic rather than mechanical controls

Flycatcher

flycatcher /flī kachər/ *n.* **1.** **INSECT-EATING SONGBIRD** a songbird that has a slender bill and feeds on insects caught in flight. Families: Muscicapidae and Tyrannidae. **2.** **AMERICAN BIRD** any similar American bird of the Tyrannidae family

fly-drive *adj.* including a flight and a hired car at the destination

flyer *n.* = **flier**

fly-fish *vi.* to fish using a rod, reel, and line and a fishhook lure meant to resemble a fly —**fly-fisher** *n.* —**fly-fishing** *n.*

flyfisherman (*plural* **-men**) *n.* sb who fishes using a rod, reel, line, and fishhook lure meant to resemble a fly

fly front *n.* an opening at the front of a garment, with a fold of fabric that covers a zip or row of buttons

fly gallery *n.* a hidden platform above a stage from

where objects suspended from the flies are controlled

fly half *n.* RUGBY = **stand-off half**

flying /flɪˈ ing/ *adj.* **1.** AIR, BIRDS **ABLE TO FLY** capable of flight **2.** MOVING FAST moving very quickly **3.** PASSING QUICKLY happening or passing very quickly **4.** SAILING NOT HELD AT EDGE held at the corners only, not the edge (*refers to a sail*) ■ *n.* AIR AIR TRAVEL travel by aircraft, or the piloting of aircraft

─────── **WORD KEY: CULTURAL NOTE** ───────

The Flying Dutchman, an opera by German composer Richard Wagner (1843). The protagonist of this three-act composition is a Dutch seaman who, as a result of an act of blasphemy, has been condemned to roam the oceans until he is saved by the love of a woman. In Norway, he meets Senta, who commits a desperate act of faith that results in his redemption.

flying boat *n.* a seaplane with a fuselage that acts like a boat's hull and provides buoyancy on water

flying bomb *n.* any explosive robot plane, guided missile, or rocket bomb (*informal*)

flying bridge *n.* an open deck of a boat or ship with a secondary set of navigational devices

Flying buttress

flying buttress *n.* an exterior support for a wall (**buttress**) that sticks out from the wall and is typically arch-shaped, often used in Gothic cathedrals to withstand the outward thrust of the very high walls

flying colours ◇ **with flying colours** very successfully

flying doctor *n.* ANZ a doctor who visits patients by aircraft

flying dragon *n.* = **flying lizard**

flying field *n.* a small airfield from which aircraft, usually light aircraft, can operate

Flying fish

flying fish *n.* a fish found in warm or tropical seas with fins that can be held out like wings, enabling it to glide short distances above the water. Family: Exocoetidae.

flying fox *n.* a large Australasian fruit bat with a wingspan up to 152 cm/5 ft. Genus: *Pteropus*.

flying frog *n.* an Asian frog that uses its webbed feet to glide between the trees in which it lives. Latin name: *Racophorus reinwardii*.

flying gurnard *n.* a tropical marine fish that resembles the gurnard but has large fins enabling it to glide short distances above the water. Family: Dactylopteridae.

Flying fox

flying jib *n.* on a boat or ship with more than one sail at the front, the foremost triangular sail projecting from the vessel

flying leap *n.* a jump or leap taken while running

flying lemur *n.* a mammal of Southeast Asia with a flap of skin between its front and back limbs that it uses to glide between the trees in which it lives. Family: Dermoptera.

flying lizard *n.* a small tropical lizard with a flap of skin between its front and back limbs that it uses to glide through the air. Genus: *Draco*.

flying machine *n.* an aircraft, especially a very early one (*dated*)

flying mare *n.* a wrestling manoeuvre in which the attacker grasps the opponent's arm and then turns to throw the opponent over the shoulder

flying officer *n.* an officer in the Royal Air Force who ranks above a pilot officer and below a flight lieutenant

flying phalanger *n.* a small Australasian marsupial that uses a flap of skin between its front and back limbs to glide between trees. Family: Phalangeridae.

flying picket *n.* a picketing striker who travels to various workplaces to support local strikes

flying saucer *n.* a disc-shaped flying object believed to be an extraterrestrial spacecraft

flying squad *n.* a group of police officers who can be quickly deployed

flying squirrel *n.* a nocturnal squirrel of northern Europe, North America, and Asia that uses a flap of skin between its front and back limbs to glide between trees. Family: Petauristinae.

flying start *n.* a start of a race in which competitors cross the starting line at racing speed ◇ **off to a flying start** begun or beginning very successfully

fly-kick *n.* in certain martial arts, a kick executed in mid-air with one leg straight and the other flexed at the knee and hip

flyleaf /flɪˈ leef/ (*plural* -**leaves** /-leevz/) *n.* the first page in a hardback book, which forms a continuous sheet with the page stuck inside the front cover [From FLY¹]

flyman /flɪˈ mən/ (*plural* -**men**) *n.* sb whose job is to operate scene elements from the flies in a theatre

Flymo /flɪˈ mō/ *tdmk.* a trademark for a light lawnmower that rides on a cushion of air

Flynn /flin/, **Errol** (1909–59) Australian-born US actor.

Errol Flynn: As the Earl of Essex in *The Private Lives of Elizabeth and Essex* (1939)

AKG London

He played the swashbuckling hero in romantic costume dramas in films such as *Captain Blood* (1935) and *The Adventures of Robin Hood* (1938). Real name **Leslie Thomas Flynn**.

Flynn, John (1880–1951) Australian missionary. He was the founder of the Australian Inland Mission Aerial Medical Service (1928), which became the Royal Flying Doctor Service.

fly-on-the-wall *adj.* showing people in their normal daily lives (*refers to a television programme*)

fly orchid *n.* a European orchid in which the lower part of the flower resembles an insect. Latin name: *Ophrys insectifera*.

flyover /flɪˈ ōvər/ *n.* **1.** TRANSP ROAD ON BRIDGE a bridge with a main road on it crossing another main road. ◇ **overpass 2.** US AIR = **fly-past**

flypaper /flɪˈ paypər/ *n.* paper coated with a sticky and poisonous substance that attracts and kills flies

fly-past *n.* AIR the flight of an aircraft or formation of aircraft over a place as a spectacle for people on the ground. US term **flyover** *n.* 2 [Modelled on FLYOVER]

flyposting /flɪˈ pōsting/ *n.* putting up posters in places where they are not legally permitted

fly rod *n.* a long flexible fishing rod for use in fly-fishing

flysch /flish/, **Flysch** *n.* a thick deposit of sedimentary rock formed in marine environments by erosion of adjacent steep mountains [Early 19thC. From Swiss German.]

flyscreen /flɪˈ skreen/ *n.* a screen made of wire mesh that fits over a window to exclude insects

flysheet /flɪˈ sheet/ *n.* printed information or advertising on a sheet or pamphlet

fly sheet *n.* a light tarpaulin secured over the top of a tent. US term **fly¹** *n.* 3

flyspeck /flɪˈ spek/ *n.* **1.** FLY'S FAECES a tiny mark made by a fly's faeces **2.** TINY MARK any tiny mark or stain ■ *vt.* (-**specks, -specking, -specked**) MARK WITH FLYSPECKS to mark sth with the tiny spots of flies' faeces or similar stains (*usually used in the passive*)

fly spray *n.* a poisonous liquid that kills insects, sprayed from an aerosol

fly swatter *n.* a tool used to strike and kill insects, consisting of a long flexible handle with a flat piece of plastic net attached

Flytaal /flɪˈ taal/ *n.* S Africa an urban South African speech form originating in township slang, based on Afrikaans and African languages and used among men and boys [From Afrikaans, from FLY³ + Afrikaans *taal* 'language']

flyte /flīt/ (**flytes, flyting, flyted**), **flite** (**flites, fliting, flited**) *vti.* Scotland to give sb a severe but eloquent scolding [Old English *flītan*]

flyting /flɪˈ ting/ *n.* Scotland **1.** ANGRY EXCHANGE an angry but eloquent scolding or verbal exchange **2.** POET'S COMPETITION a competition between poets consisting of the exchange of insults

fly-tipping *n.* the illegal deposit of rubbish in unauthorized places

flytrap /flɪˈ trap/ *n.* **1.** PLANTS = **Venus flytrap 2.** FLY-CATCHING DEVICE a device for catching flies

fly-tying *n.* the making of artificial flies that can be used to catch fish —**fly-tier** *n.*

flyway /flɪˈ way/ *n.* a route taken by migrating birds

flyweight /flɪˈ wayt/ *n.* a boxer of the lightest weight in professional competition, up to 51 kg/112 lbs

flywheel /flɪˈ weel/ *n.* a heavy wheel or disc that

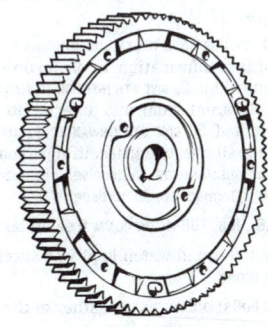

Flywheel

helps to maintain a constant speed of rotation in a machine or to store energy

flywhisk /flíˈwisk/ n. a tool for brushing away flies, traditionally a bunch of horsehair attached to a handle

fm abbr. **1.** fathom **2.** from

Fm symbol. fermium

FM abbr. **1.** (plural **FMs**) field manual **2.** AERON figure of merit **3.** RADIO frequency modulation

FMCG abbr. fast-moving consumer goods

Fmk, **FMk** abbr. Finnish markka

fml abbr. formal

FMS abbr. **1.** AIR flight management system **2.** PSYCHOL false memory syndrome

fn. abbr. footnote

fndr abbr. founder

FNQ abbr. Aus Far North Queensland

f-number n. PHOTOGRAPHY the ratio of the focal length to the effective diameter of a camera lens. Symbol **f**, **f/** [f shortening of FOCAL]

FO abbr. **1.** field-grade officer **2.** field order **3.** finance officer **4.** flight officer **5.** flying officer **6.** Foreign Office

fo. abbr. folio

foal /fṓl/ n. YOUNG HORSE an unweaned horse or related animal ■ vti. (**foals, foaling, foaled**) GIVE BIRTH to give birth to a foal [Old English fola. Ultimately from an Indo-European word meaning 'small', also the ancestor of English few, poor, and filly.]

foam /fṓm/ n. **1.** MASS OF BUBBLES a mass of bubbles of gas or air on the surface of a liquid **2.** THICK FROTHY SUBSTANCE a thick but light mixture that contains a lot of tiny bubbles ○ Beat the egg whites into a foam. **3.** FIRE-EXTINGUISHING SUBSTANCE a thick chemical froth used to extinguish flames **4.** MATERIAL CONTAINING BUBBLES rubber, plastic, or other material filled with many small bubbles of air to make it soft or light **5.** FROTHY SALIVA frothy saliva produced as a result of exertion or disease **6.** SEA the sea (literary) ■ v. (**foams, foaming, foamed**) **1.** vi. PRODUCE BUBBLES to produce a mass of bubbles **2.** vi. PRODUCE FROTHY SALIVA to produce foam from the mouth **3.** vi. BE ANGRY to express great anger (informal) **4.** vt. FILL WITH BUBBLES to transform a material into foam by aerating it in liquid form and then solidifying it [Old English fām. Ultimately from an Indo-European word that is also the ancestor of English spume and pumice.] ◇ **foam at the mouth** to produce foam from the mouth as a result of exertion, illness, or anger

foamed slag n. slag from a blast furnace that is aerated while it is still molten, used as a building or insulation material

foam rubber n. rubber that has been aerated to form a spongy material, used for mattresses, padding, and insulation

foamy /fṓmi/ (**-ier, -iest**) adj. covered with, full of, or consisting of foam —**foamily** adv. —**foaminess** n.

fob /fob/ n. **1.** CHAIN FOR POCKET WATCH a chain or ribbon used to attach a pocket watch to a waistcoat **2.** ORNAMENT ON KEY RING an ornament attached to a key ring **3.** ORNAMENT ON CHAIN a watch or ornament worn on the end of a chain or ribbon attached to clothing **4.** POCKET FOR WATCH a small pocket for a watch on a waistcoat [Mid-17thC. Origin uncertain: perhaps from German dialect.]

fob off vt. **1.** MISLEAD SO AS TO STALL QUESTIONING to give false or inadequate information to sb in order to stop further questions **2.** GIVE STH INFERIOR TO to provide sb with sth different from and inferior to what the person wanted **3.** GIVE STH UNWANTED TO to pass sth unwanted to sb else, using deceitful persuasion [Late 16thC. From obsolete FOB 'to deceive', of uncertain origin: perhaps from German foppen 'to deceive'.]

f.o.b., **F.O.B.**, **fob**, **FOB** abbr. COMM free on board

fob watch n. a round watch kept in a special pocket on a waistcoat

FoC (plural **FoCs**) abbr. PRINTING father of the chapel

f.o.c., **F.O.C.**, **foc**, **FOC** abbr. COMM free of charge

focaccia /fə káchə/ n. a type of flat Italian bread, sprinkled with a topping before baking, and served hot or cold [Mid-20thC. From Italian, from assumed Vulgar Latin focacia, from, ultimately, Latin focus (see FOCUS). The underlying idea is of sth baked in the hearth.]

focal /fṓkˈl/ adj. **1.** PRINCIPAL main and most important **2.** RELATING TO FOCUSING IMAGE relating to bringing an image into focus **3.** AT OR FROM FOCAL POINT located at, passing through, or measured from, a focal point —**focally** adv.

focal distance n. = focal length

focal infection n. a bacterial infection in one part of the body that may cause symptoms elsewhere in the body

focalize /fṓkə līz/ (**-izes, -izing, -ized**) **focalise** (**-ises, -ising, -ised**) v. **1.** vti. FOCUS to focus sth or bring sth into focus **2.** vt. LOCALIZE STH to limit sth to a local area —**focalization** /fṓk lī záysh'n/ n.

focal length n. the distance from the centre of a lens or the surface of a mirror to the point at which light passing through the lens or reflected from the mirror is focused. Symbol **f**

focal-plane shutter n. a camera shutter positioned just in front of the film, as opposed to one built into the lens

focal point n. **1.** POINT WHERE RAYS FROM LENS CONVERGE the point at which parallel rays meeting a lens, curved mirror, or other optical system converge or appear to diverge **2.** CENTRE OF ATTENTION sb or sth receiving concentrated attention, or to which attention is drawn

focal ratio n. = f-number

fo'c's'le n. = forecastle

focus /fṓkəss/ n. **1.** MAIN EMPHASIS concentrated effort or attention on a particular thing ○ The committee's focus must be on finding solutions to the problem. **2.** AREA OF CONCERN an area of concern, responsibility, or investigation ○ an inquiry with a narrow focus **3.** CONCENTRATED QUALITY a concentrated and unified quality ○ to bring focus to the problem **4.** SHARPNESS OF IMAGE the quality of being sharply defined with clear edges and contrast **5.** SEEING SHARPLY the condition of seeing sharply and clearly **6.** (plural **-ci**) = focal point **7.** (plural **-ci**) MED DISEASE ORIGIN the point from which a disease spreads, or where it localizes **8.** (plural **-ci**) GEOG, NUCLEAR PHYS EARTHQUAKE ORIGIN the point of origin within the earth of an earthquake or underground nuclear explosion **9.** (plural **-ci**) MATH POINT ON CONE a fixed point in a plane that in combination with a particular straight line specifies a conic section. For any point on the conic section the ratio of the distance from the focus to the nearest point on the line is constant. ■ vti. (**-cuses or -cusses, -cusing or -cussing, -cused or -cussed**) **1.** CONCENTRATE MAINLY ON STH to give your main attention to one thing or one aspect of a thing **2.** ADJUST VISION TO SEE CLEARLY to adjust your vision so that you see clearly and sharply, or to become adjusted for clear vision **3.** ADJUST LENS to adjust a lens so that the image viewed is clear and sharp [Mid-17thC. From Latin focus 'hearth, fireplace' (source also of English foyer and fuel), perhaps because it was the 'centre' of the home.] —**focusable** adj. —**focuser** n.

focused /fṓkəst/ **focussed** adj. **1.** CONCENTRATED concentrated on a single thing **2.** SINGLE-MINDED single-minded and determined

focus group n. a small group of representative people who are questioned about their opinions as part of political or market research

FOD abbr. TECH, TELECOM abbr for fax-on-demand

fodder /fódder/ n. **1.** ANIMAL FOOD hay, straw, and similar food for livestock **2.** MATERIAL FOR STIMULATING RESPONSE people, ideas, or images that are useful in stimulating a creative or critical response **3.** EXPENDABLE PEOPLE OR THINGS people or things regarded as the necessary but expendable ingredient that makes a system or scheme work (usually used in combination) ○ case studies seized upon as thesis fodder ■ vt. (**-ders, -dering, -dered**) FEED LIVESTOCK to give food to livestock [Old English fōdor. Ultimately from an Indo-European base meaning 'to feed', which is also the ancestor of English food, foster, repast, and companion.] —**fodderer** n.

foe /fṓ/ n. an enemy or opponent of sb or sth (literary) [Old English gefā. Ultimately from an Indo-European base meaning 'hostile', which is also the ancestor of English fey, feud, and fickle.]

FOE, **FoE** abbr. Friends of the Earth

foehn /fön/, **föhn** n. a warm dry wind blowing down the lee slope of a mountain range, originally and especially the Alps [Mid-19thC. Via German from, ultimately, Latin favonius 'west wind', from favere 'to favour, be well disposed towards'.]

foetal /féetˈl/, **fetal** adj. relating to or characteristic of a foetus [Early 19thC. Formed from FOETUS.]

foetal alcohol syndrome n. a condition affecting babies born to women who drank excessive amounts of alcohol during pregnancy, characterized by a range of effects including facial abnormalities and learning difficulties

foetal haemoglobin n. a type of haemoglobin that is most common in the foetus and newborn, normally present only in small amounts in adults except in certain forms of anaemia

foetal position n. a body position in which the body lies curled up on one side with the head bowed and the legs and arms drawn in towards the chest. As well as being a comfortable position for relaxation, the foetal position is often assumed by people during intense emotional trauma.

foeticide /féeti sīd/, **feticide** n. **1.** DESTRUCTION OF FOETUS the act of destroying a foetus **2.** AGENT FOR DESTROYING FOETUS an agent or drug used to destroy a foetus —**foeticidal** /féeti sīd'l/ adj.

foetid adj. = fetid

foetiparous /fi típpərəss/, **fetiparous** adj. used to describe animals that give birth to incompletely developed young. Kangaroos and other marsupials are foetiparous. [Late 19thC. Coined from FOETUS + -PAROUS.]

foetor n. = fetor

foetoscope /féetō skōp/, **fetoscope** n. a fibre-optic device that is passed through a woman's abdomen to view a foetus in the uterus, and sometimes also to remove material for examination —**foetoscopy** /fee tóskəpi/ n.

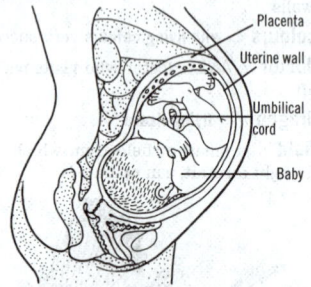

Placenta
Uterine wall
Umbilical cord
Baby

Foetus: Human foetus

foetus /féetəss/, **fetus** n. an unborn vertebrate at a stage when all the structural features of the adult are recognizable, especially an unborn human offspring after eight weeks of development [14thC. From Latin, 'offspring' (source of English fawn 'young deer').]

fog /fog/ n. **1.** THICK MIST condensed water vapour in the air at or near ground level **2.** CLOUD OF STH a cloud of sth in the air, e.g. smoke, that reduces visibility **3.** HAZY MUDDLE a state of confusion or lack of clarity **4.** OBSCURING AGENT sth that serves to obscure or conceal ○ a fog of excuses **5.** PHOTOGRAPHY BLURRED AREA an area on a photograph that is unclear or obscured by stray light **6.** CHEM SUSPENDED PARTICLES a cloud or suspension of liquid particles ■ v. (**fogs, fogging, fogged**) **1.** vti. MAKE OR BECOME OBSCURED to cause condensation to form on a transparent surface, or to become covered with condensation **2.** vt. MAKE UNCLEAR to make sth unclear or confused **3.** vti. PHOTOGRAPHY EXPOSE STH TO LIGHT to contaminate film or a developing image with light, usually accidentally, or to undergo this process [Mid-16thC. Origin uncertain: perhaps of Scandinavian origin.] —**fogged** adj.

fog bank n. a mass of thick fog, especially at sea

fogbound /fóg bownd/ *adj.* **1.** STOPPED BY FOG unable to move or operate because of visibility diminished by fog **2.** SHROUDED IN FOG enveloped in fog

fogbow /fóg bō/ *n.* a faint arc of light seen in fog opposite the sun [Mid-19thC. Modelled on RAINBOW.]

fogdog /fóg dog/ *n.* a bright white spot seen in breaking fog near the horizon [Mid-19thC. Modelled on SUN DOG.]

fogey *n.* = **fogy**

Foggia /fójji ə/ capital of Foggia Province in the Apulia Region, southeastern Italy. It is about 124 km/77 mi. northeast of Naples. Population: 155,674 (1992).

foggy /fóggi/ (**-gier, -giest**) *adj.* **1.** CHARACTERIZED BY FOG filled with or obscured by fog **2.** VAGUE very unclear or hazy ○ *We only had a foggy idea of the visitor's name.* **3.** VISUALLY UNCLEAR obscured or translucent because of a covering of condensation or sth similar —**foggily** *adv.* —**fogginess** *n.*

foghorn /fóg hawrn/ *n.* a horn sounded on a ship or boat when fog reduces visibility, as a warning to other vessels

foglamp /fóg lamp/ *n.* = **fog light**

fog light *n.* a front or rear light on a car with a beam designed to penetrate fog

fogy /fṓgi/ (*plural* **-gies**), **fogey** *n.* an old-fashioned person who resists change or novelty [Late 18thC. From Scots, of uncertain origin.] —**fogyish** *adj.* —**fogyism** *n.*

FOH *abbr.* THEATRE front of house

föhn *n.* = **foehn**

FOIA *abbr.* Freedom of Information Act

foible /fóyb'l/ *n.* **1.** WEAKNESS OR QUIRK an idiosyncrasy or small weakness (*usually used in the plural*) **2.** FENCING BLADE PART the weakest part of a sword blade from the middle to the point [Mid-17thC. Via obsolete French *foible* from Old French *feble* (see FEEBLE).]

foie gras /fwaá graá/ *n.* goose liver swollen by force-feeding the bird on maize before slaughter. It is usually eaten in the form of pâté. [Early 19thC. From French, literally 'fatted liver'.]

foil[1] /foyl/ *n.* **1.** METAL IN THIN SHEETS metal in a thin flexible sheet **2.** METAL COATING ON MIRROR the thin reflective metal coating on the back of a mirror **3.** GOOD CONTRAST a useful or interesting contrast to sth **4.** SHIPPING = **hydrofoil** *n.* 2 **5.** AIR = **aerofoil 6.** ARCHIT ARC IN GOTHIC WINDOW an arc at the top of a Gothic window ■ *vt.* (**foils, foiling, foiled**) COVER WITH FOIL to cover or coat sth with foil [14thC. Via Old French from Latin *folium* 'leaf' and *folia* 'leaves'.]

foil[2] /foyl/ (**foils, foiling, foiled**) *vt.* **1.** THWART SB'S SUCCESS to prevent sb from succeeding in sth **2.** HUNT OBSCURE TRAIL to obscure the trail of prey in order to hinder pursuers [14thC. Origin uncertain: perhaps partly from French *fouler* 'to full cloth', and partly from an early variant of DEFILE.]

foil[3] /foyl/ *n.* a long thin sword with a small disc on the end, used in fencing [Late 16thC. Origin unknown.]

foils *n.* the art or sport of fencing with foils (*takes a singular verb*) —**foilsman** *n.*

foist /foyst/ (**foists, foisting, foisted**) *vt.* **1.** IMPOSE ON SB to force sb to accept sth undesirable **2.** INSERT SURREPTITIOUSLY to introduce or insert sth surreptitiously **3.** GIVE SB STH INFERIOR to give sb sth inferior on the pretence that it is genuine, valuable, or desirable [Mid-16thC. Origin uncertain: probably from Dutch dialect *vuisten* 'to hold in one's hand' (as when hiding dice), from Middle Dutch *vuist* 'fist'.]

FOL *abbr. ANZ* Federation of Labour

fol. *abbr.* **1.** folio **2. fol., foll.** followed **3. fol., foll.** following

folacin /fṓlləssin/ *n.* = **folic acid** [Mid-20thC. Coined from FOLIC ACID + -IN.]

folate /fṓ layt/ *n.* **1.** = **folic acid 2.** FOLIC ACID DERIVATIVE a salt or ester of folic acid [Mid-20thC. Coined from FOLIC ACID + -ATE.]

fold[1] /fōld/ *v.* (**folds, folding, folded**) **1.** *vt.* BEND FLAT to bend sth thin and flat over on itself **2.** *vt.* MAKE SMALLER BY FOLDING to bend sth over on itself more than once **3.** *vti.* BEND TO MAKE COMPACT to bend part of sth so as to make it more streamlined or more compact ○ *a bicycle that folds to fit into the car* **4.** *vt.* BEND LIMBS TOGETHER to draw in the arms, legs, or hands towards the body or place them together with the joints bent **5.** *vt.* BRING WINGS TOGETHER to bring the wings together or next to the body **6.** *vt.* COVER to wrap or cover sth ○ *folded the note inside a magazine* **7.** *vt.* PUT ARMS ROUND to put your arms round sb **8.** *vi.* GO OUT OF BUSINESS to fail and stop operating as a business **9.** *vi.* CARDS GIVE UP HAND in poker and other games, to stop playing your hand in the belief that it cannot win **10.** *vti.* GEOL BEND ROCK to cause a layer of rock to bend, or to undergo this process ■ *n.* **1.** BENT PART a part of sth folded **2.** CREASE a line, crease, or raised part made when sth has been folded **3.** HANGING FOLDED PART a part of sth that hangs in a folded shape ○ *the folds of his cassock* **4.** COIL a single coil in a rope or a snake lying in coils **5.** GEOL BEND IN ROCK a bend formed in a rock layer in response to forces in the rock **6.** SMALL VALLEY a small valley in a hilly area [Old English *fealdan*. Ultimately from an Indo-European base meaning 'to fold', which is also the ancestor of the *-ple* of English *triple, quadruple*, etc.] —**foldable** *adj.*

fold in *vt.* to add a food ingredient to a mixture carefully and lightly

fold up *v.* **1.** *vti.* FOLD COMPLETELY to fold sth completely, or to become folded completely **2.** *vi.* COLLAPSE to collapse from laughter, pain, or strong emotion

fold[2] /fōld/ *n.* **1.** GROUP WITH THINGS IN COMMON a group to which sth or sb naturally belongs because of shared interests or traits **2.** ENCLOSED AREA FOR SHEEP an enclosed area where sheep or other livestock can be kept **3.** ENCLOSED ANIMALS sheep or other livestock in a fold **4.** FLOCK a flock of sheep ■ *vt.* (**folds, folding, folded**) ENCLOSE LIVESTOCK to enclose livestock safely [Old English *fald*, of unknown origin]

-fold *suffix.* **1.** divided into parts ○ *manifold* **2.** times ○ *tenfold* [Old English *-feald*; related to *fealdan* (see FOLD)]

foldaway /fṓld ə way/ *adj.* designed to be folded for compact storage

foldboat /fṓld bōt/ *n.* = **faltboat**

folder /fṓldər/ *n.* **1.** FOLDED CARD TO HOLD PAPERS a piece of card folded to make a file in which papers can be held **2.** COMPUT FILE CONTAINER a conceptual container for computer files in some operating systems, corresponding to a directory or subdirectory **3.** FOLDED PAMPHLET a circular printed on folded paper

folderol *n.* = **falderal**

folding /fṓlding/ *adj.* designed to be folded for compact storage

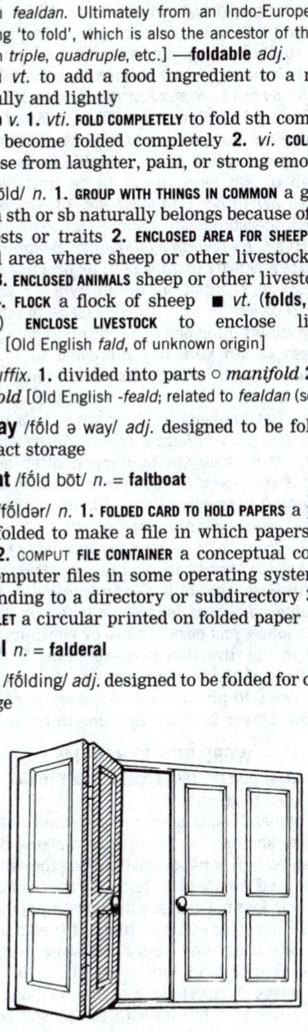

Folding door

folding door *n.* a door consisting of hinged panels that fold against each other

folding money *n.* money in the form of notes rather than coins (*informal*)

folding press *n.* a wrestling manoeuvre in which the opponent is pressed into a foetal position and held down

foldout /fṓld owt/ *n.* = **gatefold**

foldup /fṓld up/ *adj.* designed to be folded for compact storage

foliaceous /fṓli áyshəss/ *adj.* **1.** OF OR RESEMBLING A LEAF relating to or resembling a plant leaf or leaves **2.** BEARING LEAVES bearing leaves or similar structures [Mid-17thC. Formed from Latin *foliaceus*, from *folium* 'leaf'.]

foliage /fṓli ij/ *n.* **1.** LEAVES the leaves of a plant or tree **2.** LEAFY DECORATION decoration consisting of, or like, plant leaves **3.** ARCHIT BUILDING ORNAMENTATION architectural ornamentation based on leaves and stems [Mid-15thC. Alteration (influenced by Latin *folium*) of Old French *foillage*, from *foille* 'leaf', from Latin *folium* 'leaf'.] —**foliaged** *adj.*

foliage plant *n.* GARDENING a plant cultivated for its good-looking leaves

foliar /fṓli ər/ *adj.* relating to, producing, or being the leaves of a plant [Late 19thC. From modern Latin *foliaris*, from Latin *folium* 'leaf'.]

foliate *adj.* /fṓli ət, fṓli ayt/ **1.** OF OR LIKE LEAVES relating to or resembling leaves **2.** GEOL = **foliated** *adj.* 1 **3.** LEAF-SHAPED in the shape of a leaf ■ *v.* /fṓli ayt/ (**-ates, -ating, -ated**) **1.** *vt.* DECORATE WITH LEAVES to decorate sth with leaves or very thin layers **2.** *vt.* MAKE METAL INTO FOIL to form metal into a thin sheet or foil **3.** *vt.* PUBL NUMBER A BOOK'S PAGES to number the leaves of a book or manuscript **4.** *vi.* DEVELOP FOLIAGE to develop foliage **5.** *vti.* LAYER to separate sth into very thin layers, or to undergo this process [Early 17thC. The adjective is from Latin *foliatus*, from *folium* 'leaf'; the verb is formed directly from Latin *folium*.]

-foliate *suffix.* having leaves ○ *bifoliate* [From FOLIATE]

foliated /fṓli aytid/ *adj.* **1.** GEOL LAYERED formed in or composed of separable layers **2.** ARCHIT DECORATED WITH LEAVES OR FOLIAGE decorated with stylized architectural leaves or foliage

foliation /fṓli áysh'n/ *n.* **1.** LEAF FORMATION the formation of leaves **2.** LEAF BEARING the state of being in leaf **3.** ARCHIT ORNAMENTATION architectural ornamentation consisting of stylized foliage **4.** ARCHIT GOTHIC WINDOW DECORATION architectural decoration consisting of carving between two arches (**cusps**) and arcs (**foils**) at the top of Gothic windows **5.** PUBL NUMBERING OF SHEETS the numbering of consecutive leaves in a book or manuscript **6.** GEOL ROCK TEXTURE a characteristic of metamorphosed rocks in which minerals are aligned in one direction so that the rock can readily be split into thin layers **7.** LEAF DECORATION decoration with a design based on leaves

folic acid /fṓlik-, fóllik-/ *n.* a vitamin of the B complex, found in green vegetables, fruit, and liver [*Folic* formed from Latin *folium* 'leaf' , because the vitamin is found in leafy green vegetables]

folie à deux /fólli a dő/ (*plural* **folies à deux**) *n.* a psychiatric disorder with symptoms common to two people who are very close. Often only one person actually has a disorder, the other choosing to share the symptoms or delusions of the first. [Late 19thC. From French, literally 'dual delusion'.]

folio /fṓli ō/ *n.* (*plural* **-os**) **1.** LARGE BOOK OR MANUSCRIPT a book or manuscript in the largest size usual for books **2.** LARGE SHEET FOR BOOK a large sheet of paper that folds to give four pages **3.** PAGE NUMBERED ON FRONT a paper or parchment page that is numbered on the front but not the back **4.** PAGE NUMBER a page number (*technical*) **5.** LAW MEASUREMENT FOR LEGAL DOCUMENTS a unit for measuring the length of legal documents, usually 72 or 90 words in Britain and 100 in the US **6.** ACCT LEDGER PAGE a page, or two facing pages, of a ledger ■ *vt.* (**-os, -oing, -oed**) NUMBER PAGES to number the pages in a book ■ *adj.* LARGE-FORMAT printed in folio size [Mid-15thC. From late Latin *folio*, literally 'at the page', from Latin *folium* 'leaf, page'.]

foliose /fṓli ōss, fṓli ōz/ *adj.* used to describe the body (**thallus**) of a lichen or similar plant that is thin, flattened, and lobed like a leaf [Early 18thC. From Latin *foliosus*, from *folium* 'leaf'.]

folk /fōk/ *npl.* **1. folk, folks** PEOPLE IN GENERAL people, especially people of the same type (*both forms take a plural verb*) **2. folks** USED TO ADDRESS PEOPLE used to address a group of people informally (*informal*) ○ *Folks, we're ready to start now.* **3. folks** PARENTS OR RELATIVES parents or close family ■ *n.* MUSIC = **folk music** ■ *adj.* **1.** TRADITIONAL IN COMMUNITY traditional or passed down in a community or country **2.** RELATING TO IDEAS OF ORDINARY PEOPLE coming from the traditional beliefs or ideas of ordinary people [Old English *folc*. Ultimately from an Indo-European base meaning 'to fill', which is also the ancestor of English *fill, full*, and possibly *plebeian*.]

folk art *n.* paintings and decorative objects made in a naive style

folk dance *n.* 1. TRADITIONAL DANCE a dance that is traditional to a culture, community, or country 2. MUSIC FOR TRADITIONAL DANCE a piece of music that accompanies a traditional folk dance

Folkestone /fṓkstən/ port and resort in Kent, southeastern England. A major ferry port, it is the British terminal for the Channel Tunnel. Population: 45,587 (1991).

Folketing /fṓlkə ting/ *n.* the parliament of Denmark [From Danish, literally 'people's assembly']

folk etymology *n.* 1. REPLACEMENT OF UNKNOWN WORD the replacement of an unfamiliar word or form by a more familiar one. An example is the replacement of *girasole* with *Jerusalem* in *Jerusalem artichoke.* 2. INCORRECT ORIGIN FOR WORD an idea about the origin of a word that is generally believed but is wrong

folk hero *n.* sb who attains legendary status among the public

folkie /fṓki/ *n.* (*informal*) 1. FOLK SINGER a folk singer or musician 2. FOLK MUSIC ENTHUSIAST a fan of folk music

folklore /fṓk lawr/ *n.* 1. TRADITIONAL LOCAL STORIES traditional stories and explanations passed down in a community or country 2. LOCAL LEGENDS stories and gossip that become traditional within a group of people 3. ETHNOL STUDY OF TRADITIONS the study of traditional stories, music, and customs [Mid-19thC] —**folkloric** *adj.*

folklorist /fṓk lawrist/ *n.* sb who studies the traditional stories, music, and customs of a particular culture or community, or these phenomena generally —**folkloristic** /fṓk law rístik/ *adj.*

folk mass *n.* a Christian mass in which folk music replaces some or all of the traditional music

folk medicine *n.* medicine based on traditional customs and belief. It often uses herbal remedies and is usually practised by healers not trained in conventional medicine.

folk memory *n.* a memory kept alive by a community and passed from one generation to the next

folk music *n.* 1. TRADITIONAL SONGS AND MUSIC traditional songs and music, passed from one generation to the next 2. MODERN MUSIC IN TRADITIONAL STYLE modern music composed in imitation of traditional music

folk-rock *n.* popular music that combines the melodies of folk music with the rhythms of rock music

folk singer *n.* sb who sings traditional or modern folk songs —**folk singing** *n.*

folk song *n.* 1. TRADITIONAL SONG a traditional song that has been passed down orally 2. MODERN SONG IN TRADITIONAL STYLE a modern song composed in the style of traditional folk music. Modern folk songs are often performed by a solo singer.

folksy /fṓksi/ (-sier, -siest) *adj.* 1. IN STYLE OF FOLK TRADITIONS simple and unsophisticated in the tradition of folk crafts or folklore 2. *US* FRIENDLY friendly and informal 3. AFFECTEDLY TRADITIONAL artificially or affectedly traditional and homy —**folksily** *adv.* —**folksiness** *n.*

foll. *abbr.* **foll., fol.** followed

follicle /fóllik'l/ *n.* 1. ANAT SMALL SAC a small anatomical sac, cavity, or gland, involved in secretion or excretion 2. BOT DRY SEED POD a dry case formed from a single fruit that splits along one side to release seeds [Early 15thC. From Latin *folliculus* 'small sack', from *follis* 'bellows'. Ultimately from an Indo-European word meaning 'to swell', which is also the ancestor of English *belly, billow,* and *bulge.*] —**follicular** /fo líkyŏŏlər/ *adj.*

follicle-stimulating hormone *n.* a hormone that stimulates the growth of egg follicles in the ovaries and the making of sperm in the testes

folliculitis /fo líkyŏŏ lítiss/ *n.* inflammation of one or more follicles, especially of the hair, producing small boils

follies /fólliz/ *n.* a somewhat old-fashioned theatrical revue with elaborate costumes, music, and dancing (*takes a singular or plural verb*)

follow /fóllō/ (-lows, -lowing, -lowed) *v.* 1. *vti.* COME AFTER STH OR SB to come after sth or sb in position, time, or sequence ○ *We had steak and chips followed by strawberries.* 2. *vt.* ADD TO STH ALREADY DONE to add to sth already done by doing sth else, usually a related thing ○ *She followed her lecture with a demonstration.* 3. *vti.* GO AFTER to go after or behind sb or sth, moving in the same direction, especially to find out where he, she, or it is going, or go to the same place ○ *The dog followed them home.* 4. *vt.* KEEP UNDER SURVEILLANCE to have sb's movements under constant surveillance ○ *We've had the suspect followed for the past week.* 5. *vt.* WATCH CLOSELY to watch, observe, or pay close attention to sb or sth ○ *Her eyes followed me around the room.* 6. *vt.* GO ALONG to go along sth such as a road or path ○ *Follow the footpath to the edge of the forest.* 7. *vt.* GO IN SAME DIRECTION AS to take the same course or go in the same direction as sth else ○ *The road follows the river along the bottom of the valley.* 8. *vt.* GO AS DIRECTED BY to go in the direction indicated by sth such as a signpost 9. *vt.* OBEY to act in accordance with sth, especially with instructions or directions given by sb else ○ *If you follow my instructions, nothing can go wrong.* 10. *vt.* DEVELOP IN ACCORDANCE WITH to be or develop in accordance with sth, usually already known about or established ○ *The behaviour of such children usually follows the same pattern.* 11. *vt.* BE INFLUENCED BY to be led, guided, or influenced by sb or sth ○ *They followed Plato in believing the material world to be essentially unreal.* 12. *vti.* DO THE SAME AS to do the same as sb or sth, or take sb or sth as a model to be imitated ○ *She followed her father into medicine.* 13. *vti.* UNDERSTAND STH to understand sth such as an explanation or narrative ○ *He couldn't follow her explanation.* 14. *vt.* ENGAGE IN ACTIVITY to engage in or practise sth such as a career, occupation, or lifestyle ○ *I decided to follow a career in law.* 15. *vt.* KEEP UP TO DATE WITH to keep yourself informed about or up to date with the progress of sth you are interested in ○ *Are you following the television series about twins?* 16. *vt.* BE ABOUT to be about sb or sth, especially to describe or depict what happens to sb or sth over a period of time ○ *The story follows a typical American family.* 17. *vti.* RESULT FROM STH to happen after and as a result of sth else ○ *Issue too many instructions and confusion invariably follows.* 18. *vti.* BE LOGICAL RESULT to be a logical consequence of sth ○ *That follows logically from their decision to cancel the project.* 19. *vt.* READ WORDS OR MUSIC to read the words or music of sth while listening to it [Old English *folgian, fylgan*] —**followable** *adj.* ◇ **as follows** as listed or described next ◇ **follow your nose** 1. to go or continue straight ahead in the direction you are facing 2. to act in accordance with your instincts or intuition ◇ **follow suit** 1. CARDS to play a card of the same suit as the previous player 2. to do the same thing as sb else

WORD KEY: SYNONYMS

follow, chase, pursue, tail, shadow, stalk, trail

CORE MEANING: to go after

follow a general word used to talk about one person going after another, for example by walking down the street behind him or her or driving along the same route. It can be used whether this is deliberate or happens by chance, and does not necessarily suggest that the person going after the other wants or intends to catch up; **chase** used to talk about one person following another and trying to reach or catch him or her. It usually suggests speed; **pursue** suggesting a determination and an ongoing effort to catch up with the person being followed; **tail** an informal word suggesting that sb is following someone else secretly for purposes of surveillance; **shadow** similar to 'tail', used especially to talk about the activities of spies and detectives; **stalk** used to talk about the stealthy following of an animal, often by a hunter in search of prey. It is now also used to talk about the obsessive following of sb and the harassment of that person, especially when this constitutes a criminal offence; **trail** used to talk about following tracks or traces left by a person or animal, usually because the person or animal is no longer in sight.

follow on *vi.* 1. CONTINUE to continue or resume a course of action, narrative, etc ○ *I'll follow on from where you left off.* 2. CRICKET BAT AGAIN AFTER FINISHING FIRST INNINGS to begin a team's second innings immediately after finishing its first because its first-innings score is a specified number of runs less than that of the other team. In test cricket, a first-innings deficit of 200 runs is required for a follow-on, in county cricket, one of 150 runs.

follow out *vt.* to carry sth out in full, or to the end

follow through *vti.* 1. FINISH DOING STH to take further action as a consequence or extension of a previous action, especially to continue sth through to completion 2. CONTINUE MOTION OF SWING OR THROW to continue the movement of the arm or leg past the point of contact or release after hitting, throwing, or kicking a ball or other object in a sport

follow up *vt.* 1. ACT ON INFORMATION to act or make further investigations on the basis of information received ○ *Police are following up a new lead.* 2. DO STH EXTRA to continue or add to sth already done by doing some related thing ○ *I followed up my phone call with a letter of confirmation.*

follower /fóllō ər/ *n.* 1. SB LED BY ANOTHER sb who is led, guided, or influenced by sb, especially by a political or religious leader 2. SUPPORTER a fan, supporter, or admirer of sb or sth, especially of a sports team 3. MEMBER OF ENTOURAGE a servant, attendant, or subordinate, usually one of a number of people accompanying an important person 4. IMITATOR sb or sth that copies or imitates sth else 5. MOURNER sb who mourns another's death (*regional*) ○ *The followers couldn't all get into the church.*

following /fóllō ing/ *adj.* 1. NEXT coming after in time or sequence 2. ABOUT TO BE MENTIONED about to be mentioned or listed ○ *He has visited the following countries: Canada, France, and Australia.* 3. MOVING THE SAME WAY blowing or flowing in the same direction as sb or sth, especially a boat or aircraft, is travelling ○ *a following wind* ■ *n.* 1. GROUP OF FOLLOWERS a group of people who admire or support sb or sth over a period of time ○ *The band has a large following in this country.* 2. STH TO BE SPECIFIED the people or things about to be mentioned or listed (*takes a plural verb*) ○ *You will need the following: a piece of wood, a saw, a hammer, and some nails.* ■ *prep.* AFTER after sth, or after sth and as a result of it ○ *Following the accident it was months before he felt safe in a car.*

follow-my-leader *n.* a game in which the players, usually children, move along in a line, all copying the actions of the person at the front. US term **follow-the-leader**

follow-on *adj.* CONTINUING OR RESULTING coming after as a continuation or consequence ■ *n.* 1. CONTINUATION OR CONSEQUENCE OF PREVIOUS EVENT an action or event that is a continuation or consequence of a previous one 2. CRICKET ACT OF FOLLOWING ON the immediate beginning of a second innings by a team that has been asked to follow on

follow shot *n.* 1. **follow shot, follow** TYPE OF SHOT IN BILLIARDS in billiards and similar games, a shot that makes the cue ball continue to move in the same direction as the target ball after striking it 2. CINEMA SHOT MADE WITH MOVING CAMERA a camera shot in which the camera moves with the subject following alongside or behind

follow-through *n.* 1. CONTINUATION AND COMPLETION further action continuing or completing sth previously done or begun ○ *Your follow-through on the project was less than satisfactory.* 2. CONCLUDING PART OF STROKE the continuation of the movement of the arm or leg past the point of contact or release after hitting, throwing, or kicking a ball or other object in a sport

follow-up *n.* 1. CONTINUATION further action or investigation or a subsequent event that results from and is intended to supplement sth done before ○ *The conference was intended as a follow-up to the summit meeting in Vienna.* 2. STH GIVING MORE INFORMATION a book, film, article, or report that continues a story or provides further information —**follow-up** *adj.*

folly /fólli/ (*plural* -lies) *n.* 1. UNREASON thoughtlessness, recklessness, or thoughtless or reckless behaviour ○ *She realized, too late, the folly of her course of action.* ○ *It would be folly to continue.* 2. IRRATIONAL THING a thoughtless or reckless act or idea (*often used in the plural*) 3. ARCHIT ECCENTRIC BUILDING a building of eccentric or overelaborate design, usually built for decorative rather than practical purposes 4. *US* MISGUIDED UNDERTAKING an undertaking that is excessively costly or extravagant, especially one that leads to financial loss or ruin [13thC. From Old French *folie*, from *fol* 'foolish' (see FOOL).]

Folsom /fólsəm, fólsəm/ *adj.* belonging to or typical of a prehistoric culture of the southern plains of North America that made leaf-shaped flint projectile points with a concave base [Early 20thC. Named after *Folsom*, a village in northeast New Mexico, where remains typical of the culture were found.]

foment /fō mént, fə mént/ (**-ments, -menting, -mented**) *vt.* to cause or stir up trouble or rebellion (*formal*) [14thC. From late Latin *fomentare*, from Latin *fomentum*, 'warm soothing application', from *fovere*, 'to warm, keep warm'.] —**fomentation** /fó men táysh'n, fómən-/ *n.*

fomites /fómi teez/ *npl.* inanimate objects capable of carrying germs from an infected person to another person, e.g. clothes or bedding [Mid-19thC. From Latin, plural of *fomes* 'kindling wood'.]

fond[1] /fond/ *adj.* **1.** FEELING AFFECTION feeling love, affection, or a strong liking for sb or sth ○ *I've grown fond of this old house.* **2.** LIKING STH liking sth, or finding enjoyment in doing it ○ *She's too fond of the sound of her own voice.* ○ *His dog is fond of chasing rabbits.* **3.** AFFECTIONATE showing or characterized by affection, love, or pleasant feelings ○ *fond memories of the time we spent there* **4.** OVERLY DOTING feeling or showing excessive affection, often to the point of being overindulgent with sb ○ *Her fond parents could deny her nothing.* **5.** OVER-OPTIMISTIC unrealistic, though often dearly wished for ○ *fond hopes* **6.** UNCRITICALLY GULLIBLE gullible or easily led to believe sth that is not true (*regional or archaic*) [14thC. Origin uncertain: probably from the past participle of obsolete *fonnen* 'to be foolish', from *fonne* 'fool', of unknown origin.] —**fondly** *adv.* —**fondness** *n.*

fond[2] /fond, foN/ *n.* a background, especially of a piece of decorated lace [Mid-17thC. Via French from Latin *fundus* 'bottom' (see FUND).]

fondant /fóndənt/ *n.* **1.** SUGAR PASTE a smooth paste made from boiled sugar syrup, often coloured or flavoured, used as a filling for chocolates or as a coating for cakes, nuts, or fruit **2.** SOFT SWEET a sweet made from or filled with fondant [Late 19thC. From French, present participle of *fondre* (see FONDUE).]

fondle /fónd'l/ (**-dles, -dling, -dled**) *v.* **1.** *vt.* STROKE LOVINGLY to stroke, handle, or touch sth or sb gently, in a loving or affectionate way ○ *idly fondling the cat's ears* **2.** TOUCH IN AN AGGRESSIVE WAY to touch or caress sb in an aggressive or unwelcome way [Late 17thC. Back-formation from obsolete *fondling* 'foolish person', from FOND[1].] —**fondler** *n.*

fondue /fón dyoo, fón doo/ *n.* any of various dishes eaten by dipping small pieces of food into the contents of a pot, usually melted cheese, hot oil, or a sauce, placed on the table [Late 19thC. From French, a form of the past participle of *fondre* 'to melt', from Latin *fundere* (source of English *funnel*, *fusion*, and *confuse*).]

Fongafale /fóngə pa'ali/ capital of Tuvalu, located on Funafuti Atoll in the western Pacific Ocean. It is the country's only port of entry. Population: 3,839 (1996).

font[1] /font/ *n.* **1.** RECEPTACLE FOR BAPTISMAL WATER a large container in a church for the water used in baptisms. A font is usually made of stone, sometimes ornately carved, and mounted on a stand. **2.** RECEPTACLE FOR HOLY WATER a container for holy water, usually found at the entrance to a Roman Catholic church **3.** HOLDER FOR LIQUID any holder for liquid, e.g. the part of an oil-burning lamp that contains the oil **4.** ABUNDANT SOURCE OF STH sb or sth seen as a source or inexhaustible supply of sth (*literary*) **5.** FOUNTAIN a fountain, spring, or well (*literary*) [Pre-12thC. From the *font-* Latin stem of *fons* 'spring'.] —**fontal** *adj.*

font[2] /font/, **fount** /fownt, font/ *n.* a full set of printing type or of printed or screen characters of the same design and size [Late 16thC. From Old French *fonte* 'casting', from *fondre* (see FONDUE).]

Fontainebleau /fóntinblō/ town in the Ile-de-France Region on the River Seine, about 64 km/40 mi. southeast of Paris, France, the site of a magnificent 16th-century chateau. Population: 18,037 (1990).

fontanel *n.* US = fontanelle

Cap line
X line — Ascender
Base line — X-height
Descender line — Descender

Examples of type

Times   Courier   Gill
Font

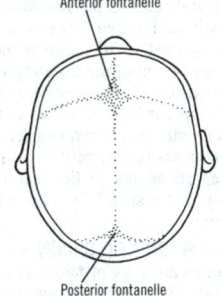

Anterior fontanelle

Posterior fontanelle
Fontanelle

fontanelle /fóntə nél/ *n.* a soft, membrane-covered space between bones at the front and the back of a young baby's skull [15thC. From Old French *fontenel*, literally 'little spring', from *fontaine* (see FOUNTAIN); originally applied to an outlet for bodily secretions.]

Dame Margot Fonteyn

Fonteyn /fon táyn/, **Dame Margot** (1919–91) British ballet dancer She was known for her role as Aurora in *The Sleeping Beauty* and her partnership with Rudolf Nureyev during the 1960s and 1970s. Born **Margaret Hookham**

fontina /fon teenə/ *n.* a semihard mild Italian cheese made from cows' milk [Mid-20thC. From Italian dialect, of unknown origin.]

food /food/ *n.* **1.** SOURCE OF NUTRIENTS FOR LIVING THINGS material that provides living things with the nutrients they need for energy and growth **2.** SOLID NOURISHMENT substances, or a particular substance, providing nourishment for people or animals, especially in solid as opposed to liquid form **3.** MENTAL OR SPIRITUAL STIMULUS sth that sustains or stimulates the mind or soul ○ *food for thought* [Old English *fōda*. Ultimately from an Indo-European word that is also the ancestor of English *feed*, *fodder*, and *pastor*.] —**foodless** *adj.*

food additive *n.* a natural or artificial substance that is added to food during processing to make it look or taste better or last longer

food bank *n.* US a place where food is collected before being distributed to people who have no money

food chain *n.* a hierarchy of different living things, each of which feeds on the one below

food court *n.* the part of a shopping centre where snacks and light meals can be bought from a number of different outlets, often with a communal eating area

food fish *n.* any fish that people eat

foodie /foódi/, **foody** (*plural* **-ies**) *n.* sb who takes an enthusiastic interest in cooking or eating good food (*informal*)

food mixer *n.* an electrical kitchen appliance used to beat eggs or cream or to mix together the ingredients for cakes and batters. It usually has two detachable beaters that are rotated electrically at varying speeds, and it may be hand-held or fixed to a stand over a bowl.

food poisoning *n.* acute inflammation of the mucous membrane of the stomach and intestines caused by eating food contaminated with toxic substances or with microorganisms that generate toxins

food processor *n.* an electrical kitchen appliance consisting of a container in which food is cut, sliced, shredded, grated, blended, beaten, or liquidized automatically by a variety of removable revolving blades

foodstuff /food stuf/ *n.* sth that can be eaten, especially one of the basic elements of the human diet (*usually used in the plural*)

food web *n.* the interlocking food chains within an ecological community

foody *n.* = foodie

fool /fool/ *n.* **1.** UNINTELLIGENT OR THOUGHTLESS PERSON sb who lacks good sense or judgment ○ *Only a fool would invest in a scheme like this.* **2.** RIDICULOUS PERSON sb who looks or is made to appear ridiculous, or who behaves in a ridiculous way ○ *I feel such a fool dressed like this.* **3.** US ENTHUSIAST sb who is particularly talented at, interested in, or fond of sth specified ○ *an absolute fool for the finer things in life* **4.** COURT ENTERTAINER sb employed in the past to amuse a monarch or noble, usually by telling jokes, singing comical songs, or performing tricks **5.** FOOD CREAMY FRUIT DESSERT a cold dessert made from puréed fruit mixed with cream or custard **6.** OFFENSIVE TERM an offensive term for sb who has below average intelligence or a psychiatric disorder (*archaic offensive*) ■ *adj.* US UNINTELLIGENT AND NOT SENSIBLE showing a lack of good sense or judgment (*informal*) ○ *That fool salesman said it would fit.* ■ *v.* (**fools, fooling, fooled**) **1.** *vt.* TRICK to trick or deceive sb ○ *Don't be fooled by her promises.* **2.** *vi.* SPEAK IN JEST to say sth jokingly or not seriously, or pretend, jokingly, that sth false is true ○ *I was only fooling – of course you can come.* **3.** *vi.* BEHAVE COMICALLY to behave in a comical, playful, or silly way [13thC. Via Old French *fol* from Latin *follis* 'bellows, windbag' (used by St. Augustine of Hippo in reference to a person).] ◇ **be nobody's fool** to be wise enough not to be easily deceived ◇ **make a fool (out) of sb** to deceive or trick sb, or make sb look ridiculous

fool around, fool about *vi.* **1.** BEHAVE IRRESPONSIBLY to behave in a thoughtless or irresponsible way ○ *Don't fool around with those tools.* **2.** CLOWN AROUND to behave in a silly or comical way **3.** WASTE TIME to waste time by doing silly or unimportant things **4.** HAVE CASUAL SEX to participate in casual or illicit sexual relationships

fool with *vt.* to treat or handle sb or sth without due care or respect ○ *Who's been fooling with the TV?*

foolery /foóləri/ (*plural* **-ies**) *n.* (*dated*) **1.** IRRESPONSIBLE BEHAVIOUR irresponsible or playful behaviour **2.** IRRESPONSIBLE ACT an irresponsible or playful act

foolhardy /fool haardi/ *adj.* showing boldness or courage but not wisdom or good sense —**foolhardily** *adv.* —**foolhardiness** *n.*

foolish /foólish/ *adj.* **1.** NOT SENSIBLE showing, or resulting from, a lack of good sense or judgment **2.** SEEMING RIDICULOUS feeling or appearing ridiculous ○ *Wipe that foolish grin off your face!* **3.** UNIMPORTANT lacking importance or substance ○ *a foolish little worry* —**foolishly** *adv.* —**foolishness** *n.*

foolproof /fool proof/ *adj.* **1.** DESIGNED TO FUNCTION DESPITE HUMAN ERROR designed to continue working properly in the face of any kind of human error, incompetence, or misuse **2.** INFALLIBLE so well thought out that failure is thought to be impossible

foolscap /fool skap, foólz kap/ *n.* **1.** LARGE PAPER SIZE a large size of paper, approximately 13.5 in by 17 in, mostly used for writing and printing **2.** US = **fool's**

cap [Late 17thC. So called from the watermark of a fool's cap originally on this paper.]

fool's cap *n.* a brightly coloured cap with points ending in bells or tassels, worn in the past by court jesters

fool's errand *n.* a task that is performed for no good reason or that fails to accomplish anything useful

fool's gold *n.* pyrite or any other iron or copper sulphide mineral that has a golden metallic lustre

fool's mate *n.* the quickest checkmate in chess, achieved on the second move by the player with the black pieces

fool's paradise *n.* a state of happiness that is temporary and insubstantial because it is based on illusions or unrealistic hopes ○ *living in a fool's paradise*

fool's-parsley *n.* a poisonous European weed, naturalized in North America, with white flowers and finely divided leaves that resemble parsley. Latin name: *Aethusa cynapium.*

foosball /fŏŏz bawl/ *n. US* = **table football**

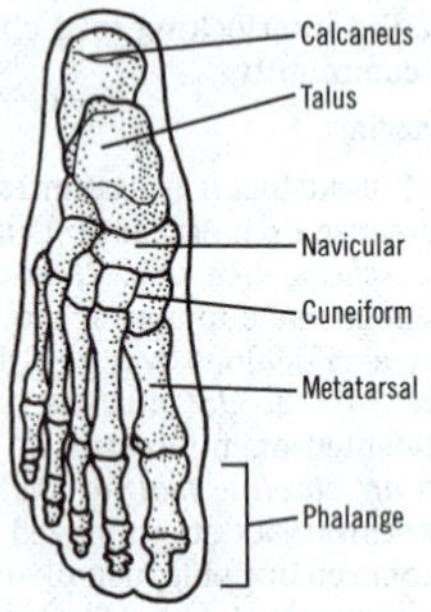
Calcaneus
Talus
Navicular
Cuneiform
Metatarsal
Phalange
Foot: Bone structure of a human foot

foot /fŏŏt/ *n.* (*plural* **feet**) **1.** ANAT **PART AT END OF LEG** the part of the leg of a vertebrate below the ankle joint that supports the rest of the body and maintains balance when standing and walking ○ *The wave knocked me off my feet.* **2.** ZOOL **ORGAN OF ATTACHMENT** an organ or muscle surface that an invertebrate, such as a mollusc, uses to grip or move itself along **3.** MEASURE **UNIT OF LENGTH** a unit of length in the Imperial and US Customary systems equal to .3048 m/12 inches. There are three feet in a yard. ○ *The aircraft is cruising at 30,000 feet* **4. LOWEST PART** the bottom or lowest part of sth ○ *a note scribbled at the foot of the page* **5. PART OF SOCK** the part of a sock, stocking, or boot that is shaped to cover the foot **6. PART RESEMBLING FOOT** sth that is shaped like or acts like a human or animal foot, e.g. a shaped part at the end of the leg of a chair **7.** BOT **LOWER PART OF PLANT** the lower part of the stem of a plant, or the base of the spore-producing body (**sporophyte**) of mosses and liverworts **8.** SEW **PART OF SEWING MACHINE** the part of a sewing machine, close to the needle, that is lowered onto the material to hold it in position. Most sewing machines have detachable and interchangeable feet for different functions. **9. WAY OF WALKING** a particular way of walking **10.** ARMY **SOLDIERS WHO FIGHT ON FOOT** soldiers who fight principally on foot, rather than on horses or in vehicles (*takes a plural verb*) ○ *an officer commanding a company of foot* **11.** POETRY **UNIT OF POETIC METRE** a basic unit of rhythm in poetry, made up of a fixed combination of stressed and unstressed or long and short syllables ■ **foots** *npl.* **1.** FOOD TECH **SEDIMENT DEPOSITED IN LIQUID** the solid material that gradually falls to the bottom of various liquids, such as vegetable oil **2.** THEATRE **FOOTLIGHTS** footlights (*informal*) ■ *vt.* (**foots, footing, footed**) **1. PAY FULL COST OF** to pay the full amount of sth ○ *We had to foot the bill for the party.* **2. ADD UP FIGURES** to add up the figures in a column ○ *footed the columns of the budget* **3. MAKE FOOT OF SOCK** in knitting or sewing, to add the part that will cover the foot to a sock or stocking [Old English *fōt*] ◇ **drag your feet** to move or do sth slowly and reluctantly on purpose (*informal*) ◇ **fall** *or* **land on your feet** to end up in a good position, especially after having been in a difficult situation ◇ **find your feet 1.** to become accustomed to a new situation and able to cope with it **2.** to manage to stand up, especially after having fallen ◇ **a foot in the door** the first stage towards a goal, especially when this is difficult to achieve ◇ **foot it 1.** to walk rather than ride in a vehicle or on a horse ○ *We had to foot it all the way home.* **2.** to dance (*dated*) ◇ **get off on the wrong foot** to begin sth badly, such as a new relationship or job ◇ **get on** *or* **to your feet 1.** to rise from a reclining or sitting position **2.** to return to a healthy or financially stable condition after a period of illness or financial difficulty ◇ **have sb** *or* **sth at your feet** to be the object of enormous admiration and devotion from sb or sth ◇ **have feet of clay** to have a weakness or flaw that is not obvious at first ◇ **have** *or* **keep both** *or* **your feet on the ground** to act and think sensibly and realistically ◇ **on foot** walking, as opposed to riding on horseback or in a vehicle ◇ **put your best foot forward** to try as hard as you can to impress or please sb ◇ **put your feet up** to stop working and relax ◇ **put your foot down 1.** to be firm about sth and make sure your wishes are obeyed or respected **2.** to make a motor vehicle travel faster by pressing the accelerator ◇ **put your foot in it** to make an embarrassing mistake, especially by being tactless (*informal*) ◇ **shoot yourself in the foot** to do sth that unexpectedly turns out to be disadvantageous or harmful to your own interests ◇ **sweep sb off his** *or* **her feet** to charm sb completely or make sb fall in love with you in a very short time

WORD KEY: ORIGIN

The Indo-European ancestor of ***foot*** is also the ultimate source of English *antipodes, impede, octopus, pawn,* meaning 'chess piece', *pedal, pedestal, pedestrian, pedigree, pioneer, podium, pyjamas, quadruped, tripod,* and *vamp,* meaning 'shoe part'.

Foot /fŏŏt/, **Michael** (*b.* 1913) British statesman and writer. A fiery orator and leader of the Labour Party (1980–83), his books include a two-volume biography of *Aneurin Bevan* (1962–73). He was editor of *Tribune* and a political columnist on the *Daily Herald.*

footage /fŏŏtij/ *n.* **1.** CINEMA **FILMED SEQUENCE SHOWING EVENT** a shot or sequence of shots on film or videotape, usually of a particular scene or event, or the length of film or videotape that contains these shots ○ *They had some good footage of the president's visit to the island.* **2.** BUILDING **SIZE IN FEET** the size or amount of sth measured in feet **3.** CINEMA **LENGTH OF PIECE OF FILM** the length of a piece of film in feet **4. PAYMENT BY SIZE** payment by the foot for work **5. AMOUNT PAID** the amount paid for work measured by the foot

foot-and-mouth disease *n.* a highly contagious viral disease affecting animals with divided hooves, especially cattle, sheep, and pigs, in which the animal develops ulcers in the mouth and near the hooves

football /fŏŏt bawl/ *n.* **1. GAME WITH ROUND BALL** a game in which two teams of 11 players try to kick or head a round ball into the goal defended by the opposing team. US term **soccer 2.** *US* = **American football 3.** FOOTBALL **BALL GAME** any of various games in which two teams kick or carry a ball into a goal or over a line, such as rugby, Australian rules, or Gaelic football **4. BALL USED IN FOOTBALL** the large round ball used in the game of football **5. PROBLEM PASSED AROUND** a point or problem that is used as an excuse for argument by opposing groups, without any real attempt at finding a solution —**footballer** *n.*

footbath /fŏŏt baath/ (*plural* **-baths** /-baathz/) *n.* **1. CONTAINER FOR WASHING FEET** a bowl used when bathing the feet, or a shallow pool where people can disinfect their feet before entering a swimming pool **2. BATHING OF FEET** the action of bathing the feet

footboard /fŏŏt bawrd/ *n.* **1. BOARD AT BOTTOM OF BED** a vertical part across the bottom end of a bedstead **2. SUPPORT FOR FEET** a board or small platform used to support the feet in a vehicle

footboy /fŏŏt boy/ *n.* a boy employed as a servant or page

foot brake *n.* a brake operated by pressing a pedal with the foot, especially in a motor vehicle

footbridge /fŏŏt brij/ *n.* a narrow bridge suitable for people walking and not for vehicles

footcloth /fŏŏt kloth/ *n.* a decorative cloth that is placed over the back of a horse and reaches the ground on both sides (*archaic*)

foot-dragger *n.* sb who is slow or reluctant to do what is necessary (*informal*) —**foot-dragging** *n.*

footed /fŏŏtid/ *adj.* having feet, a foot, or a walk of a specified kind, or a specified number of feet (*usually used in combination*) ○ *leaden-footed dancing*

footer[1] /fŏŏtər/ *n.* **1. TEXT AT BOTTOM OF PAGE** a piece of text, such as a title or date, below the main text on a page, especially one that is automatically inserted on each page by word-processing software **2. SB OR STH MEASURED IN FEET** sb or sth of a specified height or length in feet (*usually used in combination*) ○ *Both of her sons were six-footers.* **3.** ARCHIT, BUILDING = **footing** *n.* **5**

footer[2] /fŏŏtər/, **fouter** *vi.* (**-ers, -ering, -ered**) *Scotland* **POTTER** to spend time doing trivial or useless things, or to play idly with sth ○ *Can you not do something useful instead of footering about?* ■ *n. Scotland* **1. SB DOING TRIVIAL THINGS** sb who spends time doing trivial or useless things, or who plays idly with sth **2. AWKWARD JOB** a job that is awkward or involves working with small parts ○ *It was a bit of a footer putting it back together again.* [Mid-18thC. From Old French *foutre* 'to have sex with', from Latin *futuere.*]

footfall /fŏŏt fawl/ *n.* the sound made by sb's foot striking the ground as he or she walks

foot fault *n.* a fault committed in tennis by a server whose foot touches any part of the baseline or court before the ball has been hit —**foot-fault** *vi.*

footgear /fŏŏt geer/ *n.* coverings worn on the feet, especially shoes and boots

foothill /fŏŏt hil/ *n.* a hill at the bottom of a higher mountain or mountain range and forming part of the approaches to it (*often used in the plural*)

foothold /fŏŏt hōld/ *n.* **1. PLACE FOR CLIMBER'S FOOT** a place or thing that will support the foot of a climber, especially a crack, hollow, or ledge in a rock face **2. FIRM BASE FOR PROGRESS** a secure starting position from which further advances can be made ○ *The company has gained a foothold in the multimedia industry.*

footie /fŏŏti/ *n.* football (*informal*)

footing /fŏŏting/ *n.* **1. STABILITY OF FEET** a stable secure position for or placement of the feet when standing or walking ○ *He missed his footing on the icy slope.* **2. BASE FOR PROGRESS** a foundation or basis for further advancement or development ○ *The project began on a firm financial footing.* **3. STATUS OF STH** the status or condition of sth, often in relation to sth else ○ *The government moved swiftly to place the armed forces on a war footing.* **4. STATUS OF SB** the position or status of people in relation to one another ○ *I'm glad to be back on a friendly footing with her.* **5.** ARCHIT, BUILDING **FOUNDATION** the foundation or base of a structure, such as a wall or column

footle /fŏŏt'l/ *vi.* (**-tles, -tling, -tled**) (*informal*) **1. ACT AIMLESSLY** to waste time doing unnecessary or unimportant things **2. ACT OR TALK POINTLESSLY** to talk nonsense or behave in a pointless way ■ *n.* **NONSENSE** silly nonsense [Late 19thC. Origin uncertain: perhaps from FOOTER[2].] —**footler** *n.*

footless /fŏŏtləss/ *adj.* lacking a foot or feet

footlights /fŏŏt līts/ *npl.* **1. LIGHTS ALONG FRONT OF STAGE** a row of lights along the front of the stage in a theatre, directed away from the audience and towards the performers **2. THEATRICAL PROFESSION** the theatre as a profession

footling /fŏŏtling/ *adj.* (*informal*) **1. UNIMPORTANT** having no importance or serious usefulness **2. LACKING SKILL** lacking skill or competence [Late 19thC. Formed from FOOTLE.]

footloose /fŏŏt looss/ *adj.* free to go anywhere and do anything because not limited by personal ties or responsibilities

footman /fŏŏtmən/ (*plural* **-men**) *n.* **1. LIVERIED SERVANT OF ARISTOCRACY** a man employed as a servant, especially a servant in uniform in a mansion or palace **2.** HOUSEHOLD **FIRESIDE STAND** a low metal stand, usually with four legs, for utensils in a fireplace **3.** ARMY **SOLDIER** a soldier who fights on foot (*archaic*) **4. WALKER** sb who travels by walking (*archaic*)

footmark /fo͝ot maark/ *n.* = **footprint** *n.* 1

footnote /fo͝ot nōt/ *n.* **1. INFORMATION AT FOOT OF PAGE** a note at the bottom of a page, giving further information about sth mentioned in the text above. A reference number or symbol is usually printed after the relevant word in the text and before the corresponding footnote. **2. ADDITIONAL DETAIL** an extra comment or information added to what has just been said ○ *As a footnote, let me say that I only found this out yesterday.* **3. MINOR DETAIL** a relatively unimportant part of a larger issue or event ○ *His career, considered glorious at the time, is now but a footnote in history.* ■ *vt.* (**-notes, -noting, -noted**) **SUPPLY WITH FOOTNOTES** to provide a text with footnotes, or to provide a footnote for a particular reference within the text

footpad[1] /fo͝ot pad/ *n.* a robber or highwayman who operated on foot rather than on a horse (*archaic*) [Late 17thC. *Pad*, from obsolete *pad* 'path, highway robbery, highwayman', from Dutch.]

footpad[2] /fo͝ot pad/ *n.* a flat structure at the end of a leg of a spacecraft, designed to prevent the craft sinking into the surface it has landed on

foot passenger *n.* a passenger on a car ferry who is not travelling with a motor vehicle

footpath /fo͝ot paath/ (*plural* **-paths** /fo͝ot paathz/) *n.* a narrow path for people on foot ○ *Please keep to the footpath.*

footplate /fo͝ot playt/ *n.* the part of a railway locomotive from which the driver operates the controls

foot-pound *n.* a unit of work equal to the work done by lifting a mass of one pound vertically against gravity through a distance of one foot

foot-pound-second *adj.* relating or belonging to a system of measurements based on the foot, pound, and second as base units of length, mass, and time

footprint /fo͝ot print/ *n.* **1. OUTLINE OF FOOT** a mark made by the foot of a person or animal or a shoe, especially an indentation on sth soft like snow or a dirty mark on a floor ○ *footprints in the ground below the window* **2. SPACE OCCUPIED BY MACHINE** the area covered by sth, especially the amount of space a piece of computer hardware occupies on a desk, floor, or other surface **3. BROADCAST RANGE** the area over which sth occurs or is effective, such as the area where a signal from a communications satellite can be received

footrace /fo͝ot rayss/, **foot race** *n.* a race run by people on foot

footrest /fo͝ot rest/ *n.* a support for both feet when sitting down, e.g. beneath a desk, or for one foot while standing, e.g. a low rail at a bar

footrope /fo͝ot rōp/ *n.* **1. ROPE AT LOWER EDGE OF SAIL** a rope to which the lower edge of a sail is stitched **2. ROPE FOR STANDING ON** a rope fixed beneath a ship's yard for sailors to stand on as they furl a sail

foot rot /fo͝ot rot/, **footrot** *n.* **1.** VET, AGRIC **INFECTION OF SHEEP AND CATTLE** a bacterial infection of sheep and cattle that causes inflammation of the hooves **2.** BOT **PLANT DISEASE** a fungal disease that causes the roots and base of a plant to rot

foot rule *n.* a strip of wood, metal, or plastic, used for measuring and drawing straight lines, that is one foot long or is marked in feet

footsie /fo͝otsi/ *n.* a form of flirtation in which people use their feet to touch the feet and legs of sb else, especially done secretly while sitting at a table (*informal*) [Mid-20thC. A humorous formation from FOOT.] ◇ **play footsie 1.** to touch another person's foot or leg with your own, often secretly under a table, as a form of flirtation (*informal*) **2.** *US* to collaborate with another person or organization, often in an underhand way (*informal*)

footslog /fo͝ot slog/ (**-slogs, -slogging, -slogged**) *vi.* to march, tramp, or trudge on foot, especially over difficult ground, such as thick mud —**footslogger** *n.* —**footslogging** *n.*

foot soldier *n.* a soldier who fights principally on foot, not on horseback or in a vehicle

footsore /fo͝ot sawr/ *adj.* with feet that are painful or tired, usually from too much walking —**footsoreness** *n.*

footstall /fo͝ot stawl/ *n.* **1. BASE OF PILLAR** the pedestal or base of a structure, especially a pillar or statue **2. STIRRUP** a stirrup on a sidesaddle

footstep /fo͝ot step/ *n.* **1. SOUND OF FEET** the sound made when sb's foot hits the ground in walking ○ *I heard footsteps on the stairs.* **2. MOVEMENT OF FOOT** the action of raising a foot and putting it down somewhere else while walking **3. DISTANCE COVERED BY STEP** the distance covered by a single step in walking **4. MARK MADE BY FOOT** a mark left by the sole of a foot or shoe **5. STEP OR STAIR** a single step or stair on which to put a foot while moving up or down ◇ **follow in sb's footsteps** to take the same course in life or work as another person has done in the past

footstone /fo͝ot stōn/ *n.* a memorial stone at the foot of a grave

footstool /fo͝ot stool/ *n.* a low stool, often with a padded top, on which to rest the feet while sitting down

footwall /fo͝ot wawl/ *n.* the rock layer that lies immediately beneath a vein of ore or other mineral deposit or a fault plane

footway /fo͝ot way/ *n.* a narrow path or walk for people on foot, e.g. beside a road or railway line

footwear /fo͝ot wair/ *n.* coverings worn on the feet, especially shoes, boots, sandals, or slippers, but often including socks or stockings

footwell /fo͝ot wel/ *n.* the hollow space below a motor vehicle's dashboard where people in the front seats can put their feet

footwork /fo͝ot wurk/ *n.* **1. MOTION OF FEET** the movement of sb's feet in sport or dancing, especially when this is done with skill **2. SKILFUL MANOEUVRING** skilful or devious manoeuvring in order to achieve or avoid sth (*informal*) ○ *Their fancy footwork helped get them out of the problem.* **3.** *US* **WORK THAT INVOLVES WALKING** work that involves a lot of moving around, especially on foot

footworn /fo͝ot wawrn/ *adj.* **1. WORN DOWN BY FEET** worn down or made thin by being walked on by many people for a long time **2.** = **footsore**

foo yung /foo yúng, -yóng, -yo͝ong/, **foo young, fu yung** *n.* a Chinese-style dish, similar to an omelette, in which the eggs are combined with beansprouts, onions, and meat or seafood. US term **egg foo yung** [Mid-20thC. From Cantonese *foo yung*, literally 'hibiscus'.]

foozle /fooz'l/ *vti.* (**-zles, -zling, -zled**) **BUNGLE STH** to do sth badly or clumsily, especially to bungle a shot in golf ■ *n.* **STH DONE BADLY** sth done badly or clumsily, especially a bungled shot in golf [Mid-19thC. Origin uncertain: perhaps from German dialect *fuseln* 'to do bad work'.] —**foozler** *n.*

fop /fop/ *n.* a man who is so obsessed by fashion and vain about his own appearance that he becomes ridiculous [15thC. Origin uncertain.] —**foppish** *adj.* —**foppishly** *adv.* —**foppishness** *n.*

foppery /fóppəri/ (*plural* **-ies**) *n.* any or all of the characteristics of a fop, such as his extravagant style of dress or affected manners

for[1] (*stressed*) /fawr/; (*unstressed*) /fər/ CORE MEANING: a preposition indicating that sth is directed at sb, done to benefit sb, or done on sb's behalf ○ *Look – there's a letter for you.* ○ *I'd do anything for you.* ○ *The lawyer acted for some of the heirs.*

1. *prep.* **AIMED AT** intended to be received or used by, or aimed at sb ○ *It's for you – it's a present.* ○ *advice for first-time buyers* **2.** *prep.* **TO THE BENEFIT OF** intending or intended to benefit sb or sth ○ *She would make any sacrifice for the cause.* **3.** *prep.* **ON BEHALF OF** on behalf of or instead of sb or sth ○ *Would you mind making my apologies for me?* **4.** *prep.* **IN THE SERVICE OF** in the service or employment of sb or sth ○ *She works for a large company.* **5.** *prep.* **TOWARDS** in the direction of ○ *The following day, we headed for Paris.* **6.** *prep.* **LASTING** indicating how long sth lasts, continues, or extends ○ *The interview only lasted for a few minutes.* ○ *There was fog for the next mile or so.* **7.** *prep.* **BECAUSE OF** indicating a reason why sth happens or is done ○ *I did it for love.* **8.** *prep.* **DESIGNED WITH A PURPOSE** indicating the purpose of an object, action, or activity ○ *That towel is for drying your hands on.* **9.** *prep.* **LINKS CONCEPTS** used to link two concepts, one of which is the object of the other ○ *a cause for concern* ○ *a passion for opera* **10.** *prep.* **IN EXCHANGE FOR** at a cost of, or giving or receiving sth in exchange ○ *I got this hat in the market for next to nothing* **11.** *prep.* **INSTEAD OF** instead of or in place of sth, sometimes mistakenly ○ *You'll have to find a stand-in for him while he's away.* ○ *I took her for the boss.* **12.** *prep.* **GIVEN WHAT IS USUAL** with reference to the normal characteristics of sth ○ *It's very warm for April.* **13.** *prep.* **INDICATING OCCASION** at, or planned to be at, a particular time, or on a particular occasion ○ *The meeting was scheduled for four o'clock.* ○ *Will you be home for Christmas?* **14.** *prep.* **INDICATES COMPARISON** indicating a comparison or equivalence between two things ○ *Pound for pound, the elephant's energy consumption is the lowest of all land animals.* **15.** *prep.* **IN ORDER TO GET** in order to get, achieve, have, keep, or become sth ○ *Lee's hoping for promotion.* ○ *He was searching for a place to sit.* **16.** *prep.* **DESPITE** in spite of or notwithstanding sth ○ *He enjoyed himself very much, for all his complaining.* **17.** *prep.* **INDICATES RESPONSIBILITY** indicating that sb has the right or responsibility to do sth ○ *I can't help you – it's for you to decide.* **18.** *prep.* **HAVING THE SAME MEANING** having the same meaning as another word or phrase ○ *The everyday term for rubella is German measles.* **19.** *prep.* **INDICATES CROSS-REFERENCE** indicating that information can be found elsewhere ○ *For further details, consult the owner's manual.* **20.** *adv., prep.* **IN SUPPORT OF STH** in favour of, or in support of sth ○ (prep) *Who's for the motion and who's against?* ○ (adv) *Ten voted for, and eleven against.* **21.** *conj.* **BECAUSE** because, seeing that (*formal*) ○ *I left in haste, for I was already late for the appointment.* [Old English. Ultimately from an Indo-European word meaning 'forward', which is also the ancestor of English *forth, hausfrau,* and *paramount.*] ◇ **for it, in for it** certain or likely to be punished (*informal*)

for[2] *prefix.* **1.** away, down, falsely ○ *forfend* ○ *forswear* **2.** completely, extremely ○ *forgather* [Old English; related to *for* 'before, in place of' (see FOR)]

for. *abbr.* **1.** foreign **2.** forestry

f.o.r. *abbr.* COMM free on rail

for- *prefix.* **1. FORMS NEGATIVE WORDS** used to form words with a strong negative content, e.g. rejecting or prohibiting sth ○ *forbid* ○ *forsake* **2. FORMS INTENSE WORDS** used to form words that suggest intensity or extremeness ○ *forlorn* [Old English]

fora *npl.* plural of **forum**

forage /fórrij/ *n.* **1. FOOD FOR ANIMALS** food for animals, especially crops grown to feed horses, cattle, and other livestock **2. SEARCH** a search or the process of searching for sth, especially a search for food and supplies or a search among a varied collection of things **3. RAID BY SOLDIERS** a raid carried out by soldiers, especially to seize food or supplies ■ *v.* (**-ages, -aging, -aged**) **1.** *vi.* **WANDER AROUND SEARCHING** to go from place to place looking for food and supplies **2.** *vti.* **RAID FOR FOOD** to raid a place, especially for food or supplies **3.** *vi.* **SEARCH FOR STH** to search or try to find sth ○ *He foraged around in the drawer and pulled out a faded photograph.* **4.** *vt.* **FIND BY SEARCHING** to obtain sth, especially food, from a place by searching or rummaging ○ *She foraged a half-eaten cake from the bin.* **5.** *vt.* **FEED ANIMALS** to give fodder to horses, cattle, or other animals [14thC. From Old French *fourrage*, from *fuerre* 'fodder, straw', from, ultimately, a prehistoric Germanic word that is also the ancestor of English *fodder.*]

forage cap *n.* US term **service cap**

forager /fórrijər/ *n.* a person or animal that forages for sth, especially food

foram /fáwrəm/ *n.* a foraminifer [Early 20thC. Shortening.]

foramen /fə ráy men, fo-/ (*plural* **-ramina** /fə rámminə/ *or* **-ramens**) *n.* a natural opening or cavity in a human or animal body, usually one through which blood vessels and nerves pass through bone [Late 17thC. From Latin, from *forare* 'to bore a hole'.] —**foraminal** /fə rámminəl, fo-/ *adj.* —**foraminous** /-minəss, -/ *adj.*

foramen magnum /-mágnəm/ *n.* the opening at the base of the skull through which the spinal cord passes to become the medulla oblongata of the brain [Late 19thC. From Latin, literally 'large opening'.]

foramen ovale /-ō váali/ *n.* an opening in the wall between the two sides of the foetal heart that allows blood to pass from right to left. Sometimes it fails to close after birth and persists into adulthood. [Mid-19thC. From Latin, literally 'oval opening'.]

foramina plural of **foramen**

foraminifer /fórrə mínnifər/ (*plural* **-fers,** *unmarked inflection* **-fera**) *n.* a large, mainly marine protozoan that has a shell perforated with many small holes through which temporary cytoplasmic protrusions (**pseudopodia**) project. The calcium-containing shells of foraminifera are the main component of chalk and certain limestone deposits. Order: Foraminifera. [Mid-19thC. From modern Latin *Foraminifera* (plural), order name, from Latin *foramen* (see FORAMEN) + *-fer* 'bearing'.] —**foraminiferal** /fo rámmi nífførəl, fórrəmi-/ *adj.* —**foraminiferous** /fo rámmi nífførəss, fórrəmi-/ *adj.*

forasmuch as /fərəz múch əz/ *conj.* since, or in view of the fact that (*formal*)

foray /fóray/ *n.* **1.** SUDDEN RAID a sudden attack or raid by a military force **2.** EXPLORATION OF STH UNFAMILIAR an attempt at some new occupation or activity ○ *the ex-player's first foray into management* **3.** BRIEF JOURNEY a short trip or visit to a place, usually for a particular purpose ■ *v.* (**-ays, -aying, -ayed**) **1.** *vi.* MAKE INCURSION to make a sudden attack or raid **2.** *vt.* RAID to raid or loot a place [14thC. Back-formation from *forayer* 'plunderer', from Old French *fourrier*, from *fuerre* (see FORAGE). The underlying idea is of a search for food.] —**forayer** *n.*

forb /fawrb/ *n.* any broad-leaved herbaceous plant that is not a grass, especially one that grows in a prairie or meadow [Early 20thC. From Greek *phorbē* 'food', from *pherbein* 'to feed'.]

forbade, **forbad** *vt.* past tense of **forbid**

forbear[1] /fawr báir/ (**-bears, -bearing, -bore** /-báwr/, **-borne** /-báwrn/) *v.* **1.** *vi.* HOLD BACK FROM STH to not do or say sth that you could do or say, especially when this shows self-control or consideration for the feelings of others (*formal*) ○ *I forbore to criticize their efforts, though criticism was well deserved.* **2.** *vti.* BE TOLERANT to tolerate sth with patience or endurance (*formal*) ○ *patiently forbore their failures* **3.** *vt.* AVOID to give up or avoid sth (*archaic*) ○ *I must forbear jealousy.* [Old English *forberan*, literally 'to bear against'] —**forbearer** *n.* —**forbearing** *adj.* —**forbearingly** *adv.*

forbear[2] *n.* = **forebear**

forbearance /fawr báirənss/ *n.* **1.** PATIENCE patience, tolerance, or self-control, especially in not responding to provocation **2.** REFRAINING FROM DOING STH the fact of deliberately not doing or saying sth when you could do or say it (*formal*) **3.** REFRAINING FROM LEGAL RIGHT the fact of not exercising a legal right, especially of not insisting on payment of a debt at the due date and giving the debtor more time to pay

Forbes /fawrbz/ town and agricultural centre in central New South Wales, Australia. Population: 7,467 (1996).

Forbes, George William (1869–1947) New Zealand statesman. He was prime minister of New Zealand (1930–35).

forbid /fər bíd/ (**-bids, -bidding, -bade** /-bád, -báyd/ *or* **-bad** /fər bád/, **-bidden** /fər bídd'n/ *or* **-bid**) *vt.* **1.** ORDER NOT TO DO STH to tell sb, especially forcefully, not to do or have sth ○ *I forbid you to mention his name.* **2.** NOT ALLOW to state authoritatively that sth must not be done ○ *The rules of the game strictly forbid the use of a dictionary.* **3.** MAKE STH IMPOSSIBLE to make sth impossible or prevent it from happening (*formal*) ○ *Discretion forbids me to mention any names.* [Old English *forbēodan*, literally 'to command against'] —**forbiddance** *n.* —**forbidder** *n.* ◇ **God** *or* **heaven(s)** *or* **Lord forbid** used to express the hope that sth will not happen or be done

forbidden /fər bídd'n/ *adj.* **1.** NOT PERMITTED not allowed by order of sb or by law ○ *That's a forbidden subject in this company.* **2.** OUT OF BOUNDS to which entry is not allowed or allowed only to a certain person or group of people ○ *This part of the temple was forbidden to everybody except the high priest.* **3.** IMPROBABLE OR DISALLOWED LEVEL OR TRANSITION used to describe an energy level or transition in a quantum mechanical system that is either highly improbable or disobeys selection rules and is therefore not allowed

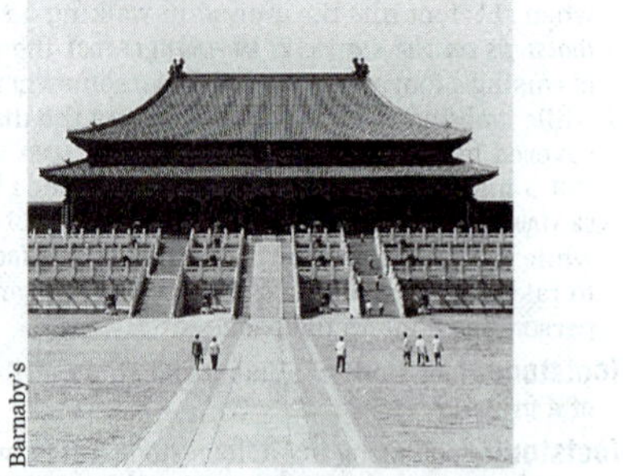

Forbidden City: Hall of Supreme Harmony

Forbidden City *n.* a walled complex of buildings (1421–1911) in Beijing, China, that includes the former Imperial Palace. It was closed to ordinary citizens until 1912 and is now a museum.

forbidden fruit (*plural* **forbidden fruits** *or* **forbidden fruit**) *n.* sth desired or pleasurable that sb is not allowed to have or do, especially some form of sexual indulgence that is illegal or considered immoral [From the passage in the Bible (Genesis 2:17) that tells of the fruit, forbidden to Adam and Eve, of the tree of knowledge of good and evil]

forbidding /fər bídding/ *adj.* **1.** HOSTILE presenting an appearance that seems hostile or stern ○ *The mountains looked distant and forbidding.* **2.** UNINVITING appearing to involve a great deal of unpleasantness or difficulty ○ *the forbidding prospect of further difficulties ahead* **3.** DANGEROUS OR THREATENING appearing to present a danger or threat ○ *a rocky and forbidding shore* —**forbiddingly** *adv.* —**forbiddingness** *n.*

forbore past tense of **forbear**

forborne past participle of **forbear**

force[1] /fawrss/ *n.* **1.** POWER OR STRENGTH the power, strength, or energy that sb or sth possesses ○ *Trees were blown down by the force of the storm.* **2.** PHYSICAL POWER physical power, effort, or violence used against sb or sth that resists ○ *The use of force should be a last resort.* **3.** EFFECTIVENESS OR VALIDITY the condition of being effective, valid, or applicable ○ *The new regulations come into force next week.* **4.** NONPHYSICAL POWER power or strength that is intellectual or moral rather than physical ○ *swayed by the force of your argument* **5.** SB OR STH WITH GREAT INFLUENCE sb or sth that has great power or influence, especially in a particular field ○ *She remained a force in local politics until her death.* **6.** MIL GROUP ORGANIZED TO FIGHT a body of military personnel, ships, or aircraft brought together to fight in a battle or a war ○ *A naval task force has been sent to the area.* **7.** POLICE OFFICERS a professional body of police officers ○ *He left the force in 1985.* **8.** PEOPLE WORKING TOGETHER a group of people who work together for a particular purpose **9.** PHYS INFLUENCE THAT MOVES STH a physical influence that tends to change the position of an object with mass, equal to the rate of change in momentum of the object. Symbol *F* **10.** METEOROL WIND STRENGTH the strength of the wind, especially as measured on the Beaufort scale, from 0 to 12 (*often used in combination*) ○ *a force nine gale* ■ **forces** *npl.* ORGANIZED MILITARY SERVICE the professional military organizations belonging to a particular country ○ *Were you in the forces?* ■ *vt.* (**forces, forcing, forced**) **1.** COMPEL to use superior strength, violence, or any kind of physical or mental power to make sb or yourself do sth against his, her, or your own will or inclination ○ *The weather forced us to turn back.* ○ *She forced herself to be polite to him.* **2.** MOVE WITH STRENGTH to use physical strength or violence to move sth or sb that puts up resistance ○ *If the key won't turn easily, don't force it.* ○ *She forced the dog back into the house.* **3.** CREATE BY STRENGTH to create sth, such as a way through sth, using physical strength or another kind of power ○ *They forced a path through the jungle.* **4.** OBTAIN BY PRESSURE to obtain sth or make sth happen by using physical or mental pressure ○ *She's been trying to force a confrontation all week.* **5.** BREAK OPEN to open sth that is locked or jammed by using power or effort, often breaking or damaging it in the process ○ *This door has been forced.* **6.** STRAIN to produce or use sth in a strained or unnatural way ○ *Just agree with whatever she says and try to force a smile.* **7.** GARDENING MAKE PLANT MATURE to cause a plant to flower or mature before its normal time **8.** RAPE to subject sb to rape (*dated*) **9.** CARDS, GAME MAKE PLAYER PLAY CERTAIN WAY to give a player in a game no choice but to play a particular card or make a particular bid or move [13thC. Via Old French from Latin *fortis* 'strong' (source of English *fortress*, *effort*, and *fortitude*).] —**forceable** *adj.* —**forceless** *adj.* —**forcer** *n.* ◇ **in force 1.** in a large or strong group **2.** effective or valid ◇ **join forces** to combine together or combine with sb else for a joint effort

force down *vt.* **1.** SWALLOW WITH DIFFICULTY to eat or drink sth very reluctantly, often because pressured to do so or to avoid offending sb **2.** MAKE AIRCRAFT LAND to compel an aircraft to land, usually because of lack of fuel, damage, or bad weather

force on, force upon *vt.* to make sb or a group of people accept sth unwillingly ○ *This method was forced upon us by head office.*

force[2] /fawrss/ *n. N England* a waterfall [Early 17thC. From Old Norse *fors* 'waterfall'.]

forced /fawrst/ *adj.* **1.** NOT NATURAL not natural or spontaneous, but produced by an act of will ○ *The courtiers greeted the king's witticism with forced laughter.* **2.** NECESSARY not done voluntarily but out of necessity **3.** COMPELLED done because sb who has power requires it —**forcedly** /fáwrssidli/ *adv.* —**forcedness** /-sidnəss/ *n.*

forced labour *n.* work that sb is made to do against his or her will, often as a punishment or to repay a debt

forced landing *n.* an unscheduled landing that a pilot is compelled to make, usually because of an emergency

forced march *n.* a march made as quickly as possible and without the normal amounts of rest

force-feed (**force-feeds, force-feeding, force-fed**) *vt.* **1.** COMPEL TO TAKE IN NOURISHMENT to make people or animals swallow food, against their will, e.g. by putting it directly down their throat through a funnel or tube. Animals may be force-fed to fatten them up, and people who refuse to eat because of a protest or a psychiatric disorder may be force-fed to keep them alive. **2.** FORCE TO LEARN to make people study or learn things, often without fully understanding or appreciating them, that they might reject if given the choice

force field *n.* in science fiction, an invisible protective barrier around sth

forceful /fáwrssf'l/ *adj.* **1.** POWERFUL possessing or characterized by strength and power **2.** IMPRESSIVE OR PERSUASIVE tending to make a powerful impression on people or to persuade people ○ *a forceful argument for merging our businesses* —**forcefully** *adv.* —**forcefulness** *n.*

force-land (**force-lands, force-landing, force-landed**) *vti.* to land an aircraft before it gets to its destination because of an emergency ○ *The pilot had to force-land in a field.*

force majeure /fáwrss ma zhúr/ *n.* **1.** LAW EVENT THAT MAKES SB DO STH an unexpected event that crucially affects sb's ability to do sth and can be put forward in law as an excuse for not having carried out the terms of an agreement (*formal*) **2.** SUPERIOR POWER a force that is superior in power or impossible to resist [Late 19thC. From French, literally 'superior force'.]

force-march (**force-marches, force-marching, force-marched**) *vti.* to make soldiers or prisoners march somewhere in the shortest possible time and without the normal amounts of rest ○ *The infantry escaped by force-marching back to the river crossing.* ○ *The captured personnel were force-marched north.*

forcemeat /fáwrss meet/ *n.* finely chopped meat, fish, or vegetables mixed with spices or other ingredients and used as a stuffing or garnish [Late 17thC. *Force*, variant of FARCE.]

force of habit *n.* the ability of a pattern of behaviour that has become habitual to reassert itself automatically even in situations where it is no longer appropriate ○ *Even after she retired, she woke at six every morning by force of habit.*

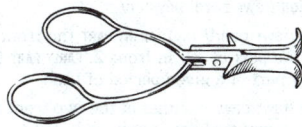

Forceps

forceps /fáwr seps, -səps/ (*plural* **-ceps** *or* **-cipes**) *npl.* **1.** SURG SURGICAL INSTRUMENT a specialized surgical instrument resembling tongs or tweezers, used for grasping or moving tissues or organs or for applying materials such as gauze pads during operations **2.** BIOL BODY PART SIMILAR TO PINCER a body part that is shaped or works like pincers, such as the grasping parts of some insects [Mid-16thC. From Latin, 'pincers', of uncertain origin: perhaps from assumed *formiceps*, from *formus* 'warm' + *capere* 'to take'.]

force pump *n.* a pump that uses pressure to move a liquid

forcible /fáwrssəb'l/ *adj.* **1.** USING STRENGTH using physical power against sb or sth that resists ○ *the forcible removal of the lock* **2.** PERSUASIVE powerful or tending to persuade people ○ *It was a forcible reminder that we must be on our guard.* —**forcibility** /fáwrssə bílləti/ *n.* —**forcibleness** /fáwrssəb'lnəss/ *n.* —**forcibly** /-əbli/ *adv.*

ford /fawrd/ *n.* CROSSING PLACE THROUGH SHALLOW WATER a shallow part of a river or stream where people, animals, or vehicles can cross it ■ *vt.* (**fords, fording, forded**) CROSS IN SHALLOW WATER to walk, ride, or drive across a river or stream at a place where the water is shallow [Old English, from a prehistoric Germanic word that is also the ancestor of English *fjord*] —**fordable** *adj.*

Ford /fawrd/, **Ford Madox** (1873–1939) British novelist. His masterpiece was *The Good Soldier* (1915). He also founded *The English Review* (1908). Real name **Ford Hermann Hueffer**

Gerald R. Ford

Ford /fawrd/, **Gerald R.** (*b.* 1913) US statesman and 38th president of the United States. He was the only president (1974–77) elected neither president nor vice president, having attained those posts following the resignations of Richard Nixon and Spiro Agnew, respectively. Full name **Gerald Rudolph Ford**

Ford /fawrd/, **Henry** (1863–1947) US industrialist, best known for his pioneering achievements in the automobile industry. In 1903 he founded a major motor company, introducing assembly-line production on a massive scale.

Forde /fawrd/, **Frank** (1890–1983) Australian politician. He was briefly caretaker prime minister of Australia in July 1945 after the death of John Curtin. Full name **Francis Michael Forde**

Henry Ford

fore /fawr/ *n.* FRONT the front of sth, or sth at the front (*literary*) ■ *adj.* AT FRONT OF SHIP OR AIRCRAFT having a position at or near the front of sth, especially a ship, an aircraft, or an animal ■ *adv.* TOWARDS THE FRONT at or towards the front, especially of a ship or aircraft ■ *interj.* GOLF WARNING ABOUT GOLF BALL shouted to warn people that you are hitting a golf ball in their direction [Old English, 'before, previously'] ◇ **to the fore** to a position of prominence or importance

fore- *prefix.* **1.** before, earlier ○ *forejudge* **2.** front, in front ○ *forebrain* [Old English, from *fore* (see FORE)]

fore-and-aft *adj.* parallel to or running along the length of sth, especially a ship

fore-and-after *n.* a ship with a fore-and-aft rig ['After', from AFT + -ER]

fore-and-aft rig *n.* an arrangement of a ship's sails such that, when set, they are parallel to the length of the vessel

fore-and-aft sail *n.* US = **gaffsail**

forearm[1] /fáwr aarm/ *n.* the part of the human arm between the elbow and the wrist, or the corresponding part of an animal's foreleg

forearm[2] /fawr aárm/ (**-arms, -arming, -armed**) *vt.* to prepare or arm sb in advance

forearm smash *n.* a blow struck with the forearm in wrestling

forebear /fáwr bair/, **forbear** *n.* ancestor, especially one who died a long time ago (*often used in the plural*) [15thC. From FORE- + *bear*, variant of obsolete *beer* 'someone who is', from BE.]

forebode /fawr bốd/ (**-bodes, -boding, -boded**) *vti.* (*formal*) **1.** PORTEND OR PREDICT to be or give an advance warning of sth that may happen, especially sth undesirable ○ *The gathering clouds foreboded a terrible storm.* **2.** HAVE PREMONITION to have a feeling that sth bad is going to happen before it does —**foreboder** *n.*

foreboding /fawr bốding/ *n.* **1.** PREMONITION a feeling that sth bad is going to happen **2.** BAD OMEN a sign or warning that sth bad is going to happen ■ *adj.* OMINOUS indicating, warning, or suggesting that sth undesirable is likely to happen —**forebodingly** *adv.* —**forebodingness** *n.*

forebrain /fáwr brayn/ *n.* the front section of the brain in adults or the frontmost of the three parts of the brain in an embryo

forecaddie /fáwr kadi/ *n.* a caddie on a golf course who watches from the fairway to see where the balls land

forecast *vt.* /fáwr kaast/ (**-casts, -casting, -casted, -cast** *or* **-casted**) **1.** SUGGEST WHAT WILL HAPPEN to predict or work out sth that is likely to happen, e.g. the weather conditions for the days ahead **2.** BE EARLY SIGN OF STH to be an advance indication of sth that is likely or certain to happen ■ *n.* **1.** WEATHER PREDICTION a prediction of weather conditions for the near future, usually broadcast on television or radio or printed in a newspaper ○ *Have you heard the forecast for tomorrow?* **2.** PREDICTION OF FUTURE DEVELOPMENTS an estimation or calculation of what is likely to happen in the future, especially in business or finance [15thC. Originally 'to contrive in advance'.] —**forecastable** *adj.* —**forecaster** *n.*

forecastle /fốks'l/, **fo'c's'le** *n.* **1.** FRONT PART OF SHIP the space at the front end of a ship below the main deck, traditionally where the crew's quarters were

located **2.** RAISED DECK AT BOW a raised section of deck at the bow of a ship

fore-check (**fore-checks, fore-checking, fore-checked**) *vi.* to check a player of an opposing ice hockey team in the opposition's defensive zone —**fore-checker** *n.*

foreclose /fawr klốz/ (**-closes, -closing, -closed**) *v.* **1.** *vti.* LAW, FIN END A MORTGAGE to take away a mortgagee's right to redeem a mortgage, usually because payments have not been made ○ *The bank foreclosed on the property.* **2.** *vt.* SHUT OUT to bar or exclude sb or sth (*formal*) **3.** *vt.* SETTLE BEFOREHAND to settle or resolve sth in advance (*formal*) **4.** *vt.* PREVENT to prevent or hinder sth (*formal*) **5.** *vt.* HOLD EXCLUSIVELY to have an exclusive right or claim to sth (*formal*) [13thC. From Old French *forclos*, past participle of *forclore*, ultimately from Latin *foris* 'outside' + *claudere* 'to close' (see CLOSE 'to shut').] —**foreclosable** *adj.*

foreclosure /fawr klốzhər/ *n.* a legal process by which a mortgagee's right to redeem a mortgage is taken away, usually because of failing to make payments

forecourse /fáwr kawrss/ *n.* a foresail, especially the lowest of a ship's foresails

forecourt /fáwr kawrt/ *n.* **1.** SPACE IN FRONT OF BUILDING an open area at the front of a building, especially one in front of a petrol station, hotel, or railway station **2.** SPORTS FRONT SECTION OF COURT the part of the court nearest the net or front wall in games such as tennis, badminton, and handball

foredeck /fáwr dek/ *n.* the part of a ship's deck between the bridge and the forecastle

foredoom /fawr dốom/ (**-dooms, -dooming, -doomed**) *vt.* to condemn sth or sb in advance to failure or destruction (*literary; usually passive*)

fore-edge *n.* the outer edge of a printed page

forefather /fáwr faathər/ (*plural* **-thers**) *n.* (*often used in the plural*) **1.** MALE ANCESTOR a male ancestor, usually one who died long ago (*literary*) ○ *in the proud tradition of our forefathers* **2.** PRECURSOR a member of an earlier generation from whom traditions, values, or ideas have been inherited

forefend /fawr fénd/ (**-fends, -fending, -fended**) *vt.* = **forfend** (*literary*)

forefinger /fáwr fing gər/ *n.* ANAT = **index finger**

forefoot /fáwr fốot/ (*plural* **-feet** /-feet/) *n.* **1.** ZOOL ANIMAL'S FRONT FOOT either of the front feet of a four-legged animal **2.** NAUT FRONT OF KEEL the front end of a ship's keel

forefront /fáwr frunt/ *n.* **1.** LEADING POSITION the most prominent, important, active, or responsible position in sth **2.** FOREMOST PART the part at or nearest the front of sth

foregather (**-ers, -ering, -ered**) *vi.* = **forgather**

forego[1] /fawr gố/ (**-goes, -going, -went** /-wént/, **-gone** /-gón/) *vti.* to go or come before sth in position, time, or sequence (*formal*) [Old English *foregan*] —**foregoer** *n.*

forego[2] *vt.* = **forgo**

foregoing /fawr gố ing, fáwr gō ing/ *adj.* PREVIOUSLY MENTIONED going or coming before sth, especially in speech or writing ■ *n.* PRECEDING ITEM in speech or writing, the thing that has just been mentioned ○ *As is evident from the foregoing, much remains to be done.*

foregone /fáwr gon/ *adj.* **1.** DONE ALREADY previously completed or determined **2.** PAST previous or former (*archaic*)

foregone conclusion *n.* sth that will inevitably happen as a result of sth else

foreground /fáwr grownd/ *n.* **1.** PART THAT APPEARS NEAREST the part of a picture or scene that appears nearest the viewer **2.** = **forefront** 1 ■ *adj.* COMPUT CURRENTLY RECEIVING COMMANDS currently receiving commands, usually through the keyboard, at the same time as one or more other programs or tasks are operating independently ○ *foreground processing* ■ *vt.* (**-grounds, -grounding, -grounded**) HIGHLIGHT to put sth in an important position and so draw attention to it

foregut /fáwr gut/ *n.* the front end of the embryonic gut in animals. In vertebrates it develops into the pharynx, oesophagus, stomach, and top part of the intestines.

forehand /fáwr hand/ *n.* **1.** SPORTS **STROKE IN RACKET GAMES** in racket games, a basic stroke played with the palm of the racket hand facing forwards **2.** EQU **FRONT PART OF HORSE** the part of a horse in front of the rider and saddle ■ *adj.* SPORTS **PLAYED AS FOREHAND** in racket games, played with the palm of the racket hand facing forwards, or relating to a stroke played in this way ■ *adv.* **WITH FOREHAND STROKE** in racket games, with a forehand stroke or action ■ *vt.* (**-hands, -handing, -handed**) SPORTS **PLAY WITH FOREHAND STROKE** in racket games, to hit the ball with a forehand stroke —**forehanded** /fáwr hándid/ *adj., adv.* —**forehandedly** *adv.* —**forehandedness** *n.*

forehead /fórrid, fáwr hed/ *n.* the part of the face above the eyebrows, below the hairline and between the temples [Old English *foreheafod*, literally 'front head', from *heafod*, an earlier form of HEAD]

forehock /fáwr hok/ *n.* a cut of bacon taken from the front leg, including the hock and knuckle and the part up to the collar

forehoof /fáwr hoof/ (*plural* **-hooves** /-hoovz/ *or* **-hoofs**) *n.* the hoof of either of the two front legs of a four-legged animal **(quadruped)**

foreign /fórrin/ *adj.* **1. OF ANOTHER COUNTRY** relating to, from, or located in a country or countries other than your own ○ *She speaks three foreign languages.* **2. DEALING WITH ANOTHER COUNTRY** dealing with or involved with a country or countries other than your own ○ *foreign policy* **3. COMING FROM OUTSIDE** introduced from outside into a place where it does not belong, often in the human body ○ *a foreign body in her eye* **4. UNCHARACTERISTIC** not usually associated with a particular person or thing ○ *Such outbursts are quite foreign to her nature.* **5. IRRELEVANT** not related or relevant (*formal*) ○ *observations that are foreign to the matter in hand* **6.** LAW **BEYOND JURISDICTION** being beyond the jurisdiction of a particular area or country [13thC. Via Old French *forein* from, ultimately, Latin *foras foris* 'out of doors, abroad', from *fores* 'door' (source of English *forest*).] —**foreignly** *adv.* —**foreignness** *n.*

Foreign and Commonwealth Office *n.* the official name of the Foreign Office in the United Kingdom

foreign bill *n.* a bill of exchange that is issued in one country but payable in another

foreign correspondent *n.* a journalist who sends news reports from other countries for broadcast or publication in his or her own country

foreign draft *n.* = **foreign bill**

foreigner /fórrinər/ *n.* **1. SB FROM ANOTHER COUNTRY** sb who was born in or comes from a country other than your own **2. OUTSIDER** sb who does not feel or is not considered to be part of a particular group

foreign exchange *n.* **1. FOREIGN MONEY** the currencies of countries other than your own, or international currencies generally **2. DEALINGS IN FOREIGN MONEY** the conversion of one currency into another or the buying and selling of different currencies

foreignism /fórrinizəm/ *n.* sth that is characteristically foreign, especially a custom or idiom (*formal*)

foreign legion *n.* a section of an army consisting of foreign volunteers, especially that of the French army

foreign minister *n.* a minister in a government who is responsible for relations with other countries

foreign ministry *n.* in many countries, the department of government responsible for relations with other countries

foreign mission *n.* **1.** INTERNAT REL **DIPLOMATIC PERSONNEL** diplomatic personnel sent to represent their country abroad **2.** CHR **MISSIONARIES** missionaries who try to convert the inhabitants of another country to Christianity or another religion

foreign office *n.* in the United Kingdom and some other countries, the department of the government that is responsible for relations with other countries. ◊ **Foreign and Commonwealth Office**

foreign secretary *n.* the cabinet minister in the United Kingdom government responsible for relations with other countries and head of the Foreign and Commonwealth Office

foreign service *n.* a country's diplomatic and consular staff, especially that of the United States

forejudge /fawr júj/ (**-judges, -judging, -judged**) *vti.* to judge a matter before knowing all the facts or evidence (*formal*) —**forejudgment** *n.*

foreknow /fawr nṓ/ (**-knows, -knowing, -knew** /-nyóō/, **-known** /-nṓn/) *vt.* to have knowledge or awareness that sth is going to happen, either from information that has been acquired, or by paranormal means (*formal*) —**foreknowable** *adj.* —**foreknowingly** *adv.*

foreknowledge /fawr nóllij/ *n.* knowledge or awareness that sth is going to happen, either from information that has been acquired, or by paranormal means (*formal*)

forelady /fáwr laydi/ (*plural* **-dies**) *n.* *US* = **forewoman** *n.* 1

foreland /fáwrlənd/ *n.* **1.** GEOG **HEADLAND** a stretch of land that juts out into the sea or an estuary **2.** GEOG **LAND IN FRONT** land described in relation to what lies behind it, especially a plain in front of mountains **3. ROCK IN FRONT OF MOUNTAINS** a stable undeformed mass of rock that juts out in front of a mountain belt

Foreland /fáwrlənd/ either of two headlands, North Foreland and South Foreland, both of which have lighthouses, on the eastern coast of Kent, southeastern England

foreleg /fáwr leg/ *n.* either of the two front legs of a four-legged animal **(quadruped)**

forelimb /fáwr lim/ *n.* either of the two front limbs of a four-limbed vertebrate, e.g. a flipper, arm, wing, or fin

forelock[1] /fáwr lok/ *n.* **1. LOCK OF HAIR ON FOREHEAD** a lock of hair that grows or falls over the forehead **2.** ZOOL **FRONT OF HORSE'S MANE** the part of a horse's mane that falls forward between its ears ◇ **tug your forelock** to show too much respect or deference for sb in authority (*dated*)

forelock[2] /fáwr lok/ *n.* a pin or wedge inserted through the end of a bolt to stop it being removed

foreman /fáwrmən/ (*plural* **-men** /-mən/) *n.* **1. MAN IN CHARGE OF OTHER WORKERS** a man who is in charge of a group of other workers, e.g. on a building site or in a factory **2.** LAW **LEADER OF JURY** sb chosen by the other members of a jury to be their leader [13thC. Because he is the most important man.] —**foremanship** *n.*

foremast /fáwr maast/; *nautical usage* /fáwrməst/ *n.* the mast nearest the front or bow of a vessel with two or more masts

foremilk /fáwr milk/ *n.* the relatively low-fat milk with a high sugar content that is produced by a woman's breast at the beginning of a breast feed

foremost /fáwr mōst/ *adj.* **1. CHIEF** most important or notable **2. FURTHEST FORWARD** nearest to the front ○ *the foremost section of the aircraft* ■ *adv.* **1. IN FIRST POSITION** most importantly, or in the most important position ○ *a partner who will put your interests foremost* **2. TO THE FRONT** at or towards the front [Old English *formest*, from *forma* 'first' + -EST, but later understood as if from FORE and -MOST]

foremother /fáwr muthər/ *n.* a woman ancestor, usually one who died long ago

forename /fáwr naym/ *n.* = **first name**

forenamed /fáwr naymd/ *adj.* previously named or mentioned (*formal*)

forenoon /fáwr noon/ *n.* the period of time between dawn and noon or immediately before noon

forensic /fə rénssik, -rénzik/ *adj.* **1. CRIME-SOLVING** relating to the application of science to decide questions arising from crime or litigation ○ *forensic evidence* **2. OF DEBATING** relating to debate and formal argumentation ○ *forensic oratory* [Mid-17thC. From Latin *forensis* 'of legal proceedings', originally 'of the forum (as a place of discussion)', from *forum* (see FORUM).] —**forensicality** /fə rénssi kálləti, -rénzi-/ *n.* —**forensically** /fə rénssikli, -rénzik-/ *adv.*

forensic medicine *n.* the branch of medicine that has a specifically legal purpose, e.g. establishing the cause of a death

forensics /fə rénssiks, -rénziks/ *npl.* the practice or study of formal debate (*takes a singular or plural verb*)

foreordain /fáwr awr dáyn/ (**-dains, -daining, -dained**) *vt.* to arrange or determine an event in advance of its happening (*formal*) —**foreordainment** *n.* —**foreordination** /fáwr awrdi náysh'n/ *n.*

forepart /fáwr paart/ *n.* **1. FRONT PART** the front part of sth or the part of sth in front **2. EARLY PART** the first or early part of a given period of time

forepaw /fáwr paw/ *n.* either of the two front feet of a land mammal that does not have hooves

forepeak /fáwr peek/ *n.* the interior part of a vessel nearest the bow

foreperson /fáwr purss'n/ (*plural* **-persons** *or* **-people** /-peep'l/) *n.* **1. WORKER IN CHARGE OF OTHERS** a skilled worker who is in charge of a group of other workers, e.g. on a building site or in a factory **2.** LAW **JURY LEADER** sb chosen by the other members of a jury to be their leader

fore plane *n.* a plane used in carpentry or joinery for preliminary smoothing, intermediate in size between a jack plane and a jointer plane

foreplay /fáwr play/ *n.* mutual sexual stimulation that takes place before intercourse

forequarter /fáwr kwawrtər/ *n.* **CARCASS PORTION** half of the front half of a pork, lamb, or beef carcass ■ **forequarters** *npl.* **FRONT PART OF ANIMAL** the front legs, shoulders, and adjoining parts of a horse or similar animal

forereach /fawr réech/ (**-reaches, -reaching, -reached**) *v.* **1.** *vti.* **SAIL AHEAD** to gain on or pass another sailing vessel, especially when sailing into the wind **2.** *vi.* **MOVE ON WATER WITHOUT POWER** to continue moving in a ship after the sails have been taken down or the engine switched off

forerun /fawr rún/ (**-runs, -running, -ran** /-rán/, **-run**) *vt.* **1. HERALD** to serve as an indication of or anticipate sth that is to happen (*formal*) **2. GO BEFORE** to go before sth (*archaic*) **3. PREVENT** to prevent or forestall sth (*archaic*)

forerunner /fáwr runnər/ *n.* **1. PREDECESSOR** an earlier person or thing that had a role or function similar to sb or sth coming later ○ *the forerunner of the modern food processor* **2. SB OR STH SHOWING FUTURE** sb or sth that brings news of or is an indication of what is to happen ○ *a forerunner of unsettled weather* **3. ONE AHEAD OF OTHERS** sb or sth that goes ahead of others, e.g. a skier who skis down a course just before the beginning of a race

foresaid /fáwr sed/ *adj.* aforesaid (*archaic*)

foresail /fáwr sayl/; *nautical usage* /fáwrss'l/ *n.* **1. MAIN SQUARE SAIL** the main square sail on the front mast of a square-rigged vessel **2. MAIN TRIANGULAR SAIL** the main or lowest triangular sail on a fore-and-aft-rigged vessel

foresee /fawr sée/ (**-sees, -seeing, -saw** /-sáw/, **-seen** /-séen/) *vti.* to know or expect that sth is going to happen before it does ○ *He couldn't have foreseen the consequences of his scheme.* [Old English *foresēon*, literally 'to see before'] —**foreseeable** *adj.* —**foreseer** *n.*

foreshadow /fawr sháddō/ (**-ows, -owing, -owed**) *vt.* to indicate or suggest sth, usually sth unpleasant, that is going to happen —**foreshadower** *n.*

foreshank /fáwr shangk/ *n.* **1. TOP PART OF ANIMAL'S FRONT LEG** the upper part of either of the two front legs of a four-legged animal **2. CUT OF MEAT** a cut of meat taken from the foreshank of a lamb or sheep

foresheet /fáwr sheet/ *n.* **ROPE FOR FORESAIL** a rope used to keep a corner of a foresail in place ■ **foresheets** *npl.* **PART OF BOAT** the part of an open boat that lies forward of the structural member used as the foremost rower's seat

foreshock /fáwr shok/ *n.* a slight tremor or minor earthquake, often one of many and usually preceding a larger earthquake or volcanic eruption

foreshore /fáwr shawr/ *n.* **1. SHORE BETWEEN HIGH AND LOW WATERMARKS** the part of a shore that lies between the highest and lowest watermarks **2.** DRY SHORE the part of a shore between the high watermark and cultivated or economically exploited land

foreshorten /fawr sháwrt'n/ (**-ens, -ening, -ened**) *vt.* **1.** DRAWING SHOW STH SHORTER THAN IT IS in drawing, to make sth appear shorter than it actually is in order to create a three-dimensional effect on the basis of the laws of perspective **2.** ABRIDGE to make a text shorter (*formal*)

foreshow /fawr shṓ/ (**-shows, -showing, -showed, -shown** /-shṓn/) *vt.* to indicate sth that is going to happen (*archaic*)

foresight /fáwr sīt/ *n.* **1.** ABILITY TO THINK AHEAD the ability to envisage possible future problems or obstacles **2.** PREMONITION an act or instance of knowing sth beforehand **3.** LOOKING FORWARDS the act of looking forwards **4.** READING TAKEN IN SURVEYING in surveying, an observation or measurement made looking forwards **5.** ARMS FRONT GUNSIGHT the front sight on a gun —**foresighted** /fawr sītid/ *adj.*

foreskin /fáwr skin/ *n.* a fold of skin that covers the end of the penis

forest /fórrist/ *n.* **1.** LARGE DENSE GROWTH OF TREES a large area of land covered in trees and other plants growing close together, or the trees growing on it **2.** WOODLAND FOR HUNTING especially in former times, an area of woodland owned by a monarch and set aside for hunting **3.** LARGE NUMBER OF UPRIGHT OBJECTS a collection of often tall upright objects, densely packed and so resembling a forest of trees ○ *a forest of microphones* ■ *vt.* (**-ests, -esting, -ested**) CREATE FOREST ON LAND to plant an area with a large number of trees [13thC. Via Old French from late Latin *forestis (silva)*, literally 'outside (woods)', from *foris* 'out of doors' (see FOREIGN).] —**forestal** *adj.* —**forested** *adj.* —**forestial** /fə résti əl/ *adj.*

forestall /fawr stáwl/ (**-stalls, -stalling, -stalled**) *vt.* **1.** PREVENT OR HINDER to prevent or hinder sb from doing sth or sth from happening by acting in advance **2.** ANTICIPATE to think of or do sth beforehand (*archaic*) **3.** COMM HINDER SALE OF to stop or slow down sales of a product at a one-off event or market by buying that product in large quantities beforehand [14thC. From Old English *foresteall* 'ambush', literally 'position in front', from *steall* 'standing position'.] —**forestaller** *n.* —**forestalment** *n.*

forestation /fórri stáysh'n/ *n.* the planting or incidence of trees over a large area

forestay /fáwr stay/ *n.* a rope or cable (**stay**) extending from the head of the foremast to the deck of a ship and used for supporting the mast

forester /fórristər/ *n.* **1.** MANAGER OF FOREST sb engaged in forest management and conservation **2.** FOREST DWELLER a person or animal living in a forest (*archaic*) **3.** INSECTS WOODLAND MOTH a woodland moth that flies by day. Family: Zyglaenidae.

forest floor *n.* the layer of organic matter on the ground in a forest

forest green *adj.* of a dark green colour, like the foliage on a pine tree ○ *forest-green uniforms* —**forest green** *n.*

forestland /fórrist land/ *n.* a piece of land covered with trees or set aside for the cultivation of trees

forest oriole *n.* = **oriole**

forest park /fórrist paárk/ *n.* in New Zealand, a large forested area that is open to the public and has certain recreational facilities

forestry /fórristri/ *n.* **1.** PLANTING AND GROWING TREES the science or skill of planting and growing trees or managing forests **2.** FOREST MANAGEMENT the management of forests for profitable ends such as timber production **3.** COMMERCIAL FORESTLAND forestland, especially that planted and commercially managed rather than growing naturally

foretaste *n.* /fáwr tayst/ SAMPLE OF FUTURE a sample or indication of what is to come ■ *vt.* (**-tastes, -tasting, -tasted**) HAVE FORETASTE OF to have a sample or indication of what is to come

foretell /fawr tél/ (**-tells, -telling, -told**) *vt.* to predict what is going to happen, especially by means of supposed magic or supernatural powers (*literary*) —**foreteller** *n.*

forethought /fáwr thawt/ *n.* careful thought in order to be prepared for the future —**forethoughtful** /fawr tháwtf'l/ *adj.* —**forethoughtfully** /-tháwt fəli/ *adv.* —**forethoughtfulness** /-tháwtf'lnəss/ *n.*

foretime /fáwr tīm/ *n.* time before the present (*archaic*)

foretoken *n.* /fáwr tōk'n/ WARNING SIGN a warning sign of what is to come (*literary*) ■ *vt.* /fawr tṓk'n/ (**-kens, -kening, -kened**) WARN OF to be or give a warning sign of what is to come (*literary*)

foretold past participle, past tense of **foretell**

foretop /fáwr top/; *nautical usage* /fáwrtəp/ *n.* a platform at the top of a ship's foremast

fore-topgallant *adj.* relating to the section of a mast directly above the foremast

fore-topmast *n.* the mast above the platform at the top of a ship's foremast

fore-topsail *n.* a sail attached to the mast above the platform at the top of a ship's foremast

forever /fər évvər/ *adv.* **1. forever, for ever** FOR ALL TIME for all future time **2. forever, for ever** FOR VERY LONG TIME for a very long time, or what seems to be a very long time (*informal*) ○ *It's going to take me forever to finish this.* **3.** CONSTANTLY regularly or constantly, and often annoyingly (*informal*) **4.** AT ALL TIMES at all times or on every occasion (*literary*) ○ *From that moment on, she was forever careful.* [13thC. From *for ever*, not used as one word until the late 17thC.]

forevermore /fər évvər máwr/, **for evermore** *adv.* from now on and for all time (*literary*)

forewarn /fawr wáwrn/ (**-warns, -warning, -warned**) *vt.* to warn sb about sth that is going to happen (*often passive*) —**forewarner** *n.* —**forewarningly** *adv.*

forewing /fáwr wing/ *n.* either of the pair of front wings on a four-winged insect

forewoman /fáwr wòomən/ (*plural* **-en** /-wimmən/) *n.* **1.** WOMAN IN CHARGE OF OTHER WORKERS a woman who is in charge of a group of workers, e.g. on a building site or in a factory **2.** LAW WOMAN JURY LEADER a woman chosen by the other members of a jury to be their leader

foreword /fáwr wurd/ *n.* an introductory note, essay, or chapter in a book, often written by sb other than the author

foreyard /fáwr yaard/ *n.* the lowest spar for supporting a sail on a foremast

Forfar /fáwrfər/ market town and administrative centre in Angus council area, eastern Scotland. Population: 12,961 (1991).

forfeit /fáwrfit/ *n.* **1.** PENALTY FOR WRONGDOING sth that is taken away as a punishment or has to be given up to make up for a mistake or wrongdoing **2.** LAW PENALTY FOR BREAKING LAW sth that is taken away as a penalty for breaking a law or contract **3.** GIVING STH UP the act or an instance of giving sth up or being deprived of sth as a punishment **4.** LEISURE PENALTY IN GAME an object that a player must give up or a task that a player must perform as a penalty in a game ■ *adj.* TAKEN AWAY AS PUNISHMENT taken away or given up as a punishment for a mistake or wrongdoing ■ *vt.* (**-feits, -feiting, -feited**) **1.** LOSE to lose sth or have sth taken away as punishment for a mistake or wrongdoing ○ *forfeit the right to your inheritance* **2.** GIVE UP to give sth up willingly in order to pursue or obtain sth else ○ *forfeited his peerage for a seat in the House of Commons* **3.** LAW TAKE AWAY AS PENALTY to take sth away as a penalty for breaking a law or contract [13thC. From Old French *forfet*, past participle of *forfaire* 'to commit a crime', literally 'to do beyond', from *fors* 'beyond', from Latin *foris* (see FOREIGN).] —**forfeitable** *adj.* —**forfeiter** *n.*

forfeits /fáwrfits/ *n.* LEISURE a game in which a player must give sth up or perform a task each time he or she commits a fault or loses a round (*takes a singular verb*)

forfeiture /fáwrfichər/ *n.* LAW **1.** STH FORFEITED sth that has been taken away or has had to be given up as a penalty for breaking a law or contract **2.** GIVING STH UP the act of forfeiting sth

forfend /fawr fénd/ (**-fends, -fending, -fended**), **forefend** (**-fends, -fending, -fended**) *v.* (*archaic*) **1.** *vti.* PREVENT STH HAPPENING to protect or secure against sth happening ○ *Heaven forfend that I should end up like that!* **2.** *vt.* FORBID to forbid or prohibit sth [14thC. Literally 'to fend before', formed from FEND.]

forgather /fawr gáthər/ (**-ers, -ering, -ered**), **foregather** (**-ers, -ering, -ered**) *vi.* (*formal*) **1.** ASSEMBLE AS GROUP to come together as a group **2.** MEET BY CHANCE to meet, usually by chance **3.** ASSOCIATE WITH to spend time socially with sb [15thC. By folk etymology (by association with GATHER) from Dutch *vorgaderen* 'to meet, assemble'.]

forgave past tense of **forgive**

forge[1] /fawrj/ *n.* **1.** METAL WORKSHOP a workshop where metal is heated and shaped into objects by hammering **2.** FURNACE FOR HEATING METAL a furnace used to heat metal to a very high temperature **3.** MACHINE FOR HAMMERING METAL a machine with two tool faces that are brought together to hammer pieces of metal into specific shapes ■ *v.* (**forges, forging, forged**) **1.** *vti.* MAKE ILLEGAL COPY OF STH to make or produce an illegal copy of sth so that it looks genuine, usually for financial gain **2.** *vt.* ESTABLISH WITH EFFORT to establish and strive to develop sth with great effort ○ *forge a durable relationship with the community* **3.** *vt.* SHAPE METAL to shape or form metal by heating and hammering it [13thC. From French *forger* 'to make', from Latin *fabricare* (source of English *fabricate*).] —**forgeability** /fáwrjə bíllәti/ *n.* —**forgeable** /fáwrjəb'l/ *adj.*

forge[2] /fawrj/ (**forges, forging, forged**) *vi.* **1.** MOVE FORWARD to move forward with a sudden increase of speed ○ *forging past the runner on the inside* **2.** MAKE PROGRESS to move slowly and steadily ○ *'We were forging through a narrow passage, rock-lined, and tube-like'.* (Edgar Rice Burroughs, *The Gods of Mars*; 1913) [Mid-18thC. Origin uncertain: perhaps an alteration of FORCE[1].]

forge ahead *vi.* to move forward rapidly or steadily and persistently

forger /fáwrjər/ *n.* sb who makes or produces illegal copies, e.g. of documents or signatures, usually for financial gain

forgery /fáwrjəri/ (*plural* **-ies**) *n.* **1.** COPYING STH ILLEGALLY the act of making or producing an illegal copy of sth so that it looks genuine, usually for financial gain **2.** ILLEGAL COPY an illegal copy of sth, e.g. a document or painting, that has been made to look genuine

forget /fər gét/ (**-gets, -getting, -got** /-gót/, **-gotten** /-gótt'n/) *v.* **1.** *vti.* NOT REMEMBER to fail or be unable to remember sth ○ *I'll never forget my first day at school.* **2.** *vt.* LEAVE BEHIND to leave sth behind accidentally ○ *I've forgotten my keys.* **3.** *vti.* NEGLECT SB OR STH to fail to give due attention to sb or sth ○ *Don't just disappear and forget about us all.* **4.** *vt.* STOP WORRYING to stop thinking or worrying about sb or sth ○ *I'd just forget about it if I were you.* **5.** *vti.* NOT MENTION to fail to mention sb or sth **6.** *vr.* LOSE CONTROL OF to lose control of your manners, emotions, or behaviour ○ *Oh dear, I'm forgetting myself! Let me take your coat.* [Old English *forgietan*, literally 'to miss your hold on', from a prehistoric Germanic word that is also the ancestor of English *get*] —**forgetter** *n.* ◇ **forget it 1.** used to let sb know that sth is not really very important and so not worth worrying about (*informal*) **2.** used to tell sb that you are definitely not going to do sth that has been suggested, proposed, or asked of you (*informal*)

WORD KEY: SYNONYMS

See Synonyms at ***neglect***.

forgetful /fər gétf'l/ *adj.* **1.** ABSENT-MINDED tending to forget things **2.** NEGLECTFUL not giving due attention to sb or sth (*formal*) ○ *forgetful of his contractual obligations* **3.** CAUSING FORGETFULNESS causing sb to forget sth (*archaic literary*) —**forgetfully** *adv.* —**forgetfulness** *n.*

forget-me-not *n.* a small herbaceous plant of the borage family that has small delicate pale blue flowers. Genus: *Myosotis.* [A translation of Old French *ne m'oubliez mie*, because the flower was worn by lovers]

forgettable /fər géttəb'l/ *adj.* not easily remembered or not worthy of being remembered

forgive /fər gív/ (**-gives, -giving, -gave** /fər gáyv/, **-given** /fər gívv'n/) *v.* **1.** *vti.* STOP BEING ANGRY ABOUT STH to stop being angry about or resenting sb or sb's behaviour **2.** *vt.* PARDON to excuse sb for a mistake, mis-

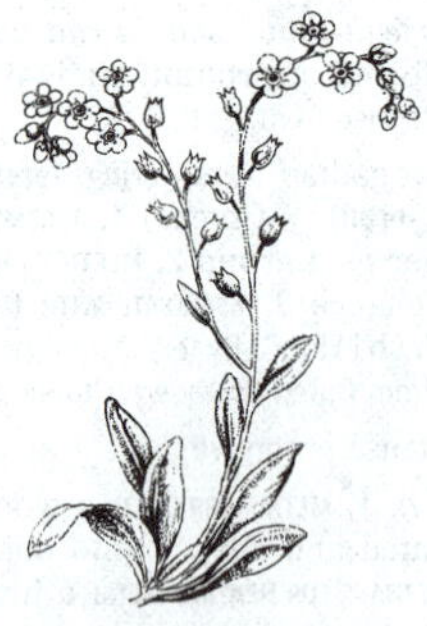

Forget-me-not

understanding, wrongdoing, or an inappropriateness **3.** *vt.* **CANCEL OBLIGATION** to cancel an obligation, such as a debt [Old English *forgiefan*, literally 'to abstain from giving'. The underlying idea is of giving up resentment or a claim.] —**forgivable** *adj.* —**forgivably** *adv.* —**forgiver** *n.*

forgiveness /fər gívnəss/ *n.* **1. ACT OF PARDONING SB** the act of pardoning sb for a mistake or wrongdoing **2. FORGIVING QUALITY** the tendency to forgive offences readily and easily ○ *She had little forgiveness in her nature.* [Old English *forgiefenes*, formed from the past participle of *forgiefan* (see FORGIVE). Etymologically 'for-given-ness'.]

forgiving /fər gívving/ *adj.* **1. INCLINED TO FORGIVE** willing to forgive, especially in most circumstances **2. ALLOWING FOR DEGREE OF IMPERFECTION** allowing for or coping well with a degree of imprecision, lack of skill, or other imperfection ○ *You'll have to improve your technique or get a more forgiving fishing rod.* —**forgivingly** *adv.* —**forgivingness** *n.*

forgo /fawr gṓ/ (**-goes, -going, -went** /-wént/, **-gone** /-gón/), **forego** (**-goes, -going, -went, -gone**) *vt.* to do without sth, especially voluntarily ○ *forgo the comforts of home while travelling* [Old English *forgan*, literally 'to go away from, pass by']

forgot past tense of **forget**

forgotten past participle of **forget**

for instance *n.* an example of sth (*informal*) ○ *Give me a for instance.*

forint /fórrint/ *n.* **1. UNIT OF HUNGARIAN CURRENCY** the basic unit of Hungarian currency, a coin equivalent to 100 fillér. See table at **currency 2. FORINT COIN** a coin worth one forint [Mid-20thC. From Hungarian, from Italian *fiorino* 'florin' (see FLORIN).]

fork /fawrk/ *n.* **1. UTENSIL FOR EATING** a small, usually metal utensil with a handle and two, three, or four prongs, used for picking up food for eating or turning food in cooking **2. GARDEN OR AGRICULTURAL TOOL** a garden or agricultural tool with a handle and usually three or four prongs. It is used for digging, lifting, and turning over. **3. DIVIDING POINT IN ROAD OR RIVER** the point where a road or river divides into two or more parts **4. BRANCH OF ROAD OR RIVER** one of the branches that a road or river divides into **5.** TECH **PART OF MACHINE** a part of a machine or device that has prongs or is fork-shaped **6.** CHESS **CHESS POSITION** a chess position in which two pieces are under attack from one of the opponent's pieces, usually the knight **7.** METEOROL **FLASH OF LIGHTNING** a branch or flash of forked lightning ■ *v.* (**forks, forking, forked**) **1.** *vti.* **MOVE WITH FORK** to carry, pick up, dig, or turn sth over using a fork **2.** *vi.* **DIVIDE INTO TWO** to split into two or more branches (*refers to roads and rivers*) **3.** *vi.* **GO ALONG FORK** to take one of the branches that a road or river has divided into **4.** *vt.* **CAUSE TO BRANCH** to make sth into a shape that branches in two **5.** *vt.* CHESS **MOVE PIECE IN CHESS** to position a piece so that it is threatening two of the opponent's pieces at the same time [Old English *forca*, via prehistoric Germanic from Latin *furca* 'pitchfork' (source of English *bifurcate*] —**forker** *n.* —**forkful** /fáwrkfòol/ *n.*

fork out, fork up *vti.* to pay the money required for sth or spend a lot of money, often grudgingly (*informal*)

forked /fawrkt/ *adj.* divided into two or more branches —**forkedly** /fáwrkidli/ *adv.* —**forkedness** /-kidəss/ *n.*

forked lightning *n.* lightning that appears as a jagged line of light splitting into two or more branches near the ground. US term **chain lightning**

forked tongue *n.* a tongue that speaks lies or words that are insincere or misleading (*literary or humorous*)

forklift /fáwrk lift/ *n.* **1. LIFTING DEVICE** a lifting device with two long rigid steel bars that can be raised and lowered, used especially to move pallets loaded with boxes or other goods **2.** = **forklift truck** ■ *vt.* (**-lifts, -lifting, -lifted**) **LIFT HEAVY GOODS** to lift or move heavy loads using a forklift

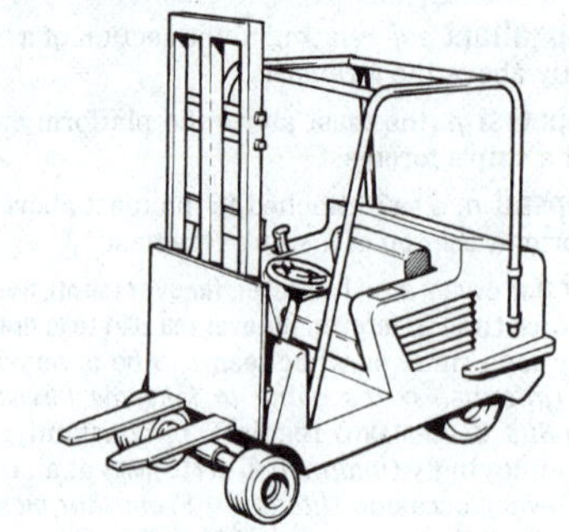

Forklift truck

forklift truck *n.* a small motor-driven vehicle equipped with a forklift, used especially in factories for moving goods on pallets

forlorn /fər láwrn, fawr-/ *adj.* **1. LONELY AND MISERABLE** lonely and miserable, as though deserted or abandoned **2. DESOLATE** deserted or abandoned and showing signs of neglect **3. HOPELESS** desperate and doomed to failure (*literary*) **4. DEPRIVED** deprived of sth (*archaic literary*) ○ *'My only strength and stay: forlorn of thee, Whither shall I betake me, where subsist?'* (John Milton, *Paradise Lost*; 1667) [Old English *forloren*, originally the past participle of *forlēosan*, literally 'to lose completely'] —**forlornly** *adv.* —**forlornness** *n.*

forlorn hope *n.* **1. FUTILE HOPE** a desperate or futile hope **2. DESPERATE UNDERTAKING** a desperate or doomed undertaking **3.** MIL **SOLDIERS ON DESPERATE MISSION** a group of soldiers sent on a very dangerous if not hopeless mission [By folk etymology from Dutch *forloren hoop*, literally 'lost troop']

form /fawrm/ *n.* **1. BASIC STRUCTURE** the nature, structure, or essence of a thing, considered apart from its content, colour, texture, or composition **2. MANIFESTATION** the particular way that sth is or appears to be ○ *bonuses in the form of extra days off or cash payments* **3. VARIETY OF STH** a type or kind of sth that has various different types or kinds ○ *Friction is a form of energy.* **4. SHAPE OF STH** the shape or appearance of a thing that makes it identifiable ○ *a constellation in the form of a diamond* **5. INDISTINCT SHAPE** a shape like a person or other living thing that cannot be clearly made out ○ *a shadowy form in the distance* **6. DOCUMENT** a document, usually with blank spaces for answers or information to be supplied ○ *fill out the form* **7. CONDITION OF SB OR STH** the condition of an organization, team, performer, athlete, or animal, with regard to fitness, health, and ability to perform well ○ *a violinist at the top of her form* **8.** SPORTS **TRACK RECORD** the previous record of a horse, athlete, or team **9.** ARTS **OUTLINE STRUCTURE** the structure, design, or arrangement of a work of art or piece of writing, as opposed to its content **10.** ARTS **MODE OF EXPRESSION** a fixed mode of literary or musical expression ○ *a strict adherence to sonata form* **11. MOULD OR FRAME** a mould, frame, or model within which or around which sth can be shaped ○ *concrete forms* **12.** EDUC **SCHOOL CLASS** a class or year in a school, especially in Britain until the 1990s, when 'forms' were replaced by 'years' **13. BEHAVIOUR** behaviour or manners with reference to propriety ○ *It's considered bad form to cheat at games.* **14. FORMULA** a fixed set of words or procedures, e.g. in a religious ceremony or a legal document **15.** CLOTHES **HUMAN SHAPE** a model of a human body or torso, used for fitting or displaying clothes **16.** FURNITURE **BENCH** a long low wooden seat or bench with no back rest **17.** *US* PRINTING = **forme 18.** ZOOL **HARE'S LAIR** the lair or nest in which a hare lives **19.** LING **WORD IN RELATION TO ITS ROOT** a word considered in relation to its root or the word it is derived from **20.** LING **LOOK OR SOUND OF WORD** the way a word is written or how it sounds, as opposed to its meaning **21.** BIOL **SUBDIVISION OF VARIETY** a subdivision of a classification of organisms, usually indicating a minor difference among members, e.g. in colour **22. CRIMINAL RECORD** recorded past criminal activity (*slang*) ■ *v.* (**forms, forming, formed**) **1.** *vti.* **GIVE SHAPE TO STH** to give a shape or arrangement to sth, or take shape ○ *A circle of onlookers formed around the injured man.* **2.** *vti.* **START TO EXIST** to cause sth to develop or exist, or begin to develop or exist, especially as part of a natural process ○ *Crystals began to form at the bottom of the jar.* **3.** *vt.* **MAKE** to make or construct sth, often by arranging or combining component parts ○ *The plural is formed by adding an 's'.* **4.** *vt.* **CONCEIVE OF** to develop an opinion, impression, or idea in the mind ○ *not enough information to form an opinion* **5.** *vt.* **CAUSE TO DEVELOP** to influence sb strongly through teaching, discipline, or example, and cause a particular personal development ○ *an early life in the country that formed his quiet nature* **6.** *vt.* **CREATE** to acquire or establish and develop sth intangible, such as a habit or relationship ○ *considered forming an alliance* **7.** *vt.* **SERVE AS** to constitute or be a basic element or characteristic of sth ○ *a mountain range forming a natural boundary between the two countries* **8.** *vt.* **SET UP** to establish sth, e.g. a structure ○ *form a fan club* [13thC. Via French *forme* from Latin *forma* 'mould, shape, beauty' (source of English *formal*, *formula* and *uniform*).] —**formable** *adj.* ◇ **take form** to become visible, distinct, or discernible ○ *A plan started to take form in his mind.* ◇ **true to form** as could be expected judging from sb's past behaviour ○ *True to form, she was exactly twenty minutes late.*

-form *suffix.* having a particular form ○ *fibriform* [From Latin *forma* 'form']

formal /fáwrm'l/ *adj.* **1. CONVENTIONALLY CORRECT** characterized by or organized in accordance with conventions governing ceremony, behaviour, or dress ○ *He's terribly formal.* **2. OFFICIAL** done or carried out in accordance with established or prescribed rules ○ *We made a formal protest.* **3. METHODICAL** done in an organized and precise manner ○ *We don't have the skills in this lab to do formal research in artificial intelligence.* **4. NOT FAMILIAR IN STYLE** used in serious, official, or public communication but not appropriate in everyday contexts ○ *a formal word* **5.** CLOTHES **ELEGANT TO WEAR** suitable for wearing for an important occasion, e.g. a jacket and tie for men and a long dress or gown for women ○ *formal dress required* **6.** EDUC **ACQUIRED IN SCHOOL OR COLLEGE** undertaken or acquired by study in an educational institution, e.g. a school, college, or university ○ *no formal training as a journalist* **7. ORDERED** arranged or laid out in a regular, ordered, or symmetrical way ○ *a formal garden* **8. OF FORM OF STH** relating to the form of sth **9. OFFICIALLY CONSTITUTED** officially constituted or organized as opposed to spontaneously developed ○ *a formal organization* **10.** LOGIC, MATH **SYMBOLIC** relating to or using symbols and abstract structures rather than natural language **11.** PHILOS **OF ESSENCE RATHER THAN CONTENT** relating to the structure or essence of sth rather than its content ■ *n.* *US* **CLOTHES** an outfit of clothing for an important social occasion, especially a woman's full-length dress ○ *a new formal for the prom* [14thC. From Latin *formalis*, from *forma* (see FORM).] —**formally** *adv.* —**formalness** *n.*

formaldehyde /fawr máldi hīd/ *n.* a colourless gas with a distinctive smell that is used in making resins and fertilizers and that, when dissolved in water, gives a solution in which organic specimens are preserved. Formula: HCHO. [Late 19thC. Coined from FORMIC + ALDEHYDE.]

formalin /fáwrməlin/ *n.* a solution of formaldehyde in water, used as a disinfectant and for preserving organic specimens [Late 19thC. Coined from FORMALDEHYDE + -IN.]

formalise *vti.* = **formalize**

formalism /fáwrm'lizəm/ *n.* **1.** RELIG, ARTS **EMPHASIS ON OUTWARD APPEARANCE** a strong or excessive emphasis on outward appearance or form instead of content or meaning **2.** PHILOS, MATH THEORY OF SYMBOLS the view that mathematical symbols are meaningless, though mathematical concepts and structures can be valuable **3.** THEATRE STYLIZATION stylization and emphasis on symbolism in theatrical productions — **formalist** n. —**formalistic** /fáwrmə lístik/ adj. —**formalistically** /-lístikli/ adv.

formality /fawr málləti/ (plural **-ties**) n. **1.** FORMALNESS the quality or condition of being formal, or the degree to which sth is formal ○ dress to suit the formality of the occasion **2.** OFFICIAL PROCEDURE an official procedure that must be followed as part of a longer procedure or event (often used in the plural) ○ several formalities to complete at customs **3.** NECESSARY BUT INSIGNIFICANT PROCEDURE a procedure that must be followed because it is a rule or custom, but has little significance or effect in itself ○ just a formality **4.** ATTENTION TO PROPRIETY strict or excessive attention to propriety or ceremony

formalize /fáwrmə līz/ (**-izes, -izing, -ized**), **formalise** (**-ises, -ising, -ised**) v. **1.** vt. MAKE OFFICIAL to make sth official or valid, often by deciding on the details and then signing a document **2.** vt. GIVE SHAPE TO to give a particular shape or form to sth **3.** vti. MAKE STH FORMAL to make sth formal or more formal ○ a formalized version of his earlier account —**formalizable** adj. —**formalization** /fáwrmə līzáysh'n/ n. —**formalizer** /-līzər/ n.

formal logic n. PHILOS the branch of logic concerned with the formal methods of deducing conclusions from propositions

formal methods npl. methods of specifying and evaluating computer systems that draw on techniques from mathematics and logic

formant /fáwrmənt/ n. a frequency range where vowel sounds are at their most distinctive and characteristic pitch [Early 20thC. Via German from Latin formant-, present participle stem of formare, from forma (see FORM).]

format /fáwr mat/ n. **1.** STRUCTURE the way in which sth is presented, organized, or arranged ○ change the format of the conference to accommodate more speakers **2.** PUBL LAYOUT the layout and presentation of a publication, including its size, and the type of paper and type used ○ a small-format reference work **3.** COMPUT DATA ORGANIZATION the structure or organization of digital data for storing, printing, or displaying ○ files in ASCII format ■ vt. (**-mats, -matting, -matted**) **1.** ARRANGE LAYOUT OF to arrange the layout or organization of sth **2.** COMPUT ORGANIZE DISK FOR DATA STORAGE to organize a disk in such a way that data can be stored on it [Mid-19thC. Via French and German from Latin formatus (liber) '(book) shaped (in a special way)', from formare (see FORMANT).]

formate /fáwr mayt/ n. any salt or ester of formic acid [Early 19thC. Coined from FORMIC + -ATE.]

formation /fawr máysh'n/ n. **1.** DEVELOPMENT the process by which sth develops or takes a particular shape ○ a strong influence on the formation of her character **2.** CREATION the process of creating sth or coming into existence ○ the formation of a bipartisan legislative committee **3.** SHAPE OF STH the shape or structure that sth develops into ○ interesting cloud formations **4.** FORMAL PATTERN the pattern into which a number of people or things are arranged ○ Twelve planes flew past in formation. **5.** GEOL ROCK UNIT a unit of rock consisting of a succession of strata or an igneous intrusion —**formational** adj.

formation dance n. a dance in which a line or circle of couples moves through a choreographed sequence of steps. Formation dance teams often compete against one another. —**formation dancing** n.

formative /fáwrmətiv/ adj. **1.** INFLUENTIAL important and influential, particularly in the shaping or development of character ○ during their formative years **2.** LING USED TO FORM WORDS relating to or used in the formation of derived words or inflected forms of words ■ n. LING WORD-FORMING ELEMENT an element such as a suffix or prefix used in the formation of derived words or inflected forms of words — **formatively** adv.

formative assessment n. EDUC the assessment at regular intervals of a student's progress with ac-

companying feedback in order to help to improve the student's performance

form class n. **1.** LING PART OF SPEECH a part of speech **2.** SET OF WORDS a group of words with one or more grammatical characteristics in common

form criticism n. **1.** LITERAT LITERARY CRITICISM textual criticism that examines the literary conventions used in order to discover the origin and history of a text or its creators **2.** BIBLE BIBLE SCHOLARSHIP a method of analysing the Bible to determine the presumed original oral form of the written text by removing known historical conventions that emerged at a later period —**form critic** n. —**form critical** adj.

forme /fawrm/ n. a body of typographic elements assembled in a metal frame (**chase**) in preparation for printing. US term **form** n. **17** [15thC. Variant of FORM.]

Formentera /fáwrmən táirə/ the fourth largest of the Spanish Balearic Islands in the western Mediterranean Sea. Population: 5,435 (1998). Area: 77 sq. km/30 sq. mi.

former[1] /fáwrmər/ adj. **1.** PREVIOUS occurring at or existing in an earlier time or period ○ met her on a former occasion **2.** HAVING BEEN STH having had the name or status specified during an earlier period ○ the former Soviet Union **3.** FIRST OF TWO being the first of two things or people mentioned **4.** PRECEDING earlier or near the beginning of a text or list ○ a conclusion inconsistent with the argument in the former part of the paper ■ n. THE FIRST OF TWO the first of two things or people mentioned ○ Smith and Brown both work here, the former is an accountant and the latter is an engineer. [12thC. Literally 'more first', formed from Old English forma 'first', literally 'most before', from a prehistoric Germanic word that is also the ancestor of English fore.]

former[2] /fáwrmər/ n. **1.** SCHOOL STUDENT a member of a form or class in a school, especially in Britain until the 1990s, when 'forms' were replaced by 'years' (always used in combination) ○ a sixth former **2.** SHAPER OF STH sb or sth that forms, creates, or shapes sth **3.** ELEC ENG SHAPING TOOL a tool used for giving the correct shape to an electrical coil or winding

formerly /fáwrmərli/ adv. during or at an earlier period, but no longer

formestane n. a drug used to treat certain breast cancers that works by blocking the formation of the oestrogen needed for the growth of the tumour

formfitting /fáwrm fitting/ adj. fitting tightly around the contours of the body ○ formfitting sportswear

form genus n. an artificial taxonomic category based on similarities that may be superficial. Imperfect fungi and fragmented plant fossils are grouped in form genera.

formic /fáwrmik/ adj. **1.** ZOOL OF ANTS relating to ants **2.** CHEM OF FORMIC ACID relating to or containing formic acid [Late 18thC. Formed from Latin formica 'ant'.]

Formica /fawr míkə/ tdmk. a trademark for a strong plastic laminate sheeting that is durable and easy to clean, and is often used to cover work surfaces, e.g. in kitchens

formic acid n. a colourless corrosive liquid that occurs naturally in ants and some plants. It is commonly used in the paper and textile industries and in the manufacture of insecticides and refrigerants. Formula: $HCOOH$.

formicary /fáwrmikəri/ (plural **-ies**), **formicarium** /fáwrmi káiri əm/ (plural **-a** /-ri ə/) n. an ant hill, including its subterranean passages (technical) [Early 19thC. From medieval Latin formicarium, from Latin formica 'ant'.]

formication /fáwrmi káysh'n/ n. a neurologically based hallucination in which sb feels as if insects are crawling on his or her skin. It is found in some cases of chemical toxicity and among drug and alcohol abusers. [Early 18thC. From the Latin stem formication-, from formicare 'to crawl like an ant', from formica 'ant'.]

formidable /fáwrmidəb'l, fər míddəb'l/ adj. **1.** DIFFICULT TO DEAL WITH difficult to deal with or overcome ○ a formidable task **2.** AWE-INSPIRING inspiring respect or wonder because of size, strength, or ability ○ a

formidable display of skill **3.** FRIGHTENING causing fear, dread, or alarm [14thC. Directly or via French from Latin formidabilis, from formidare 'to fear', from formido 'terror'.] —**formidability** /fáwrmidə bílləti, fər míddə bílləti/ n. —**formidableness** /fáwrmidəb'lnəss, fər míddəb'lnəss/ n. —**formidably** /fáwrmidəbli, fər míddəbli/ adv.

formless /fáwrmləss/ adj. **1.** SHAPELESS lacking a clear shape or structure ○ a formless figure in the mist **2.** DISORGANIZED lacking apparent organization or structure **3.** NOT MATERIAL existing without a physical form ○ formless beings —**formlessly** adv. —**formlessness** n.

form letter n. a printed letter that is sent out to a large number of people, e.g. one dealing with a frequently arising complaint, or one used in advertising

formula /fáwrmyŏolə/ (plural **-las** or **-lae** /fáwrmyŏo lee/) n. **1.** PLAN OR METHOD a plan for or method of doing sth ○ draw up a peace formula between two countries **2.** METHOD OF DOING STH a prescribed and more or less invariable way of doing sth to achieve a particular end **3.** ESTABLISHED FORM OF WORDS an established and recognized form of words, e.g. in a ceremony or legal document **4.** CHEM SET OF SYMBOLS REPRESENTING CHEMICAL COMPOSITION a representation of the chemical composition of a chemical compound using symbols to represent the types of atom involved **5.** MATH, PHYS RULE EXPRESSED IN SYMBOLS a rule or principle represented in symbols, numbers, or letters, often in the form of an equation ○ a formula for calculating the distance between planets **6.** formula, Formula MOTOR SPORTS CATEGORY OF RACING CAR a category of racing car according to technical specifications such as engine capacity, size, and weight, used as a basis for professional competition (usually used in combination) ○ formula one racing **7.** FOOD MILK FOR BABIES a preparation used as an alternative to human breast milk and intended to provide all the nutrients an infant requires [Early 17thC. From Latin, literally 'little form', from forma (see FORM).]

formulaic /fáwrmyŏo láy ik/ adj. **1.** EXPRESSED AS FORMULA having the nature of or expressed in terms of a formula **2.** UNORIGINAL unoriginal and reliant on previous models or ideas ○ His writing is stilted and formulaic. —**formulaically** adv.

formularize /fáwrmyŏolə rīz/ (**-rizes, -rizing, -rized**), **formularise** (**-rises, -rising, -rised**) vt. = formulate v. **3** —**formularization** /fáwrm yŏolə rī záysh'n/ n. —**formularizer** /fáwrmyŏolə rīzər/ n.

formulary /fáwrmyŏoləri/ n. (plural **-ies**) **1.** PHARM PHARMACEUTICAL REFERENCE BOOK a reference book containing a list of pharmaceutical products with details of their use, preparation, properties, and formulas **2.** RELIG RELIGIOUS WRITINGS a book or collection of writings or procedures, especially ones connected with a Church **3.** FIXED FORMULA a fixed formula for doing sth or dealing with sth (archaic or technical) ■ adj. OF FORMULA relating to or having the nature of a formula

formulate /fáwrmyŏo layt/ (**-lates, -lating, -lated**) vt. **1.** DEVISE to draw sth up carefully and in detail ○ formulated his plan **2.** EXPRESS to express or communicate sth carefully or in specific words ○ formulate an opinion **3.** MATH, PHYS EXPRESS IN FORMULA to express sth by means of or as a formula —**formulation** /fáwrmyŏo láysh'n/ n. —**formulator** /fáwrm yŏo laytər/ n.

formula weight n. = molecular weight

formulise vt. = formulize

formulism /fáwrmyŏo lizzəm/ n. a belief in or reliance on formulas, especially inadequate or obsolete ones —**formulist** n., adj. —**formulistic** /fáwrmyŏo lístik/ adj.

formulize /fáwrmyŏo līz/ (**-lizes, -lizing, -lized**), **formulise** (**-lises, -lising, -lised**) vt. = formulate v. **3** —**formulization** /fáwrm yŏo līzáysh'n/, fáwrmyə-/ n.

form word n. = function word

formwork /fáwrm wurk/ n. a structure generally made of timber in which liquid concrete is placed, compacted, and allowed to harden

formyl /fáwr mīl/ n. a chemical group containing carbon, hydrogen, and oxygen. Formula: HCO. [Mid-19thC. Coined from FORMIC + -YL.]

Fornax /fáwr naks/ *n.* a small inconspicuous constellation of the southern hemisphere between Eridanus and Sculptor

fornicate[1] /fáwrni kayt/ (**-cates, -cating, -cated**) *vi.* to have sexual intercourse outside marriage [Mid-16thC. Ultimately from ecclesiastical Latin *fornicari*, from the Latin stem *fornic-* 'arch' (see FORNIX), later 'brothel' because prostitutes in Rome solicited under building arches.] —**fornicator** *n.*

fornicate[2] /fáwrnikət/, **fornicated** /fáwrni kaytid/ *adj.* with an arched, vaulted, or bending form [Early 19thC. From Latin *fornicatus*, from the stem *fornic-* (see FORNIX).]

fornication /fáwrni káysh'n/ *n.* **1.** LAW **CONSENTING SEX INVOLVING SB UNMARRIED** sexual intercourse between two consenting adults, who are not married to each other **2.** BIBLE **SEXUAL BEHAVIOUR CONSIDERED IMMORAL** in the Bible, sexual intercourse between a man and woman who are not married, or any form of sexual behaviour considered to be immoral

fornix /fáwrniks/ (*plural* **-nices** /fáwrni seez/) *n.* ANAT a structure or fold in the shape of an arch, especially either of two bands of white fibres that meet at the base of the brain [Late 17thC. From Latin (stem *fornic-*), 'arch, vault', of uncertain origin: probably from *furnus* 'oven with an arched shape' (source of English *furnace*).]

Forrest /fórrist/, **Sir John, 1st Baron Forrest of Bunbury** (1847–1918) Australian explorer and politician. He was the leader of the first expedition to cross Australia from west to east. He subsequently became the first premier of Western Australia.

forsake /fər sáyk/ (**-sakes, -saking, -sook** /-sŏŏk/, **-saken** /-sáykən/) *vt.* **1. ABANDON** to withdraw companionship, protection, or support from sb **2. GIVE UP** to give up, renounce, or sacrifice sth that gives pleasure [Old English *forsacan*, literally 'to abstain from disputing', later 'to give up', hence 'to abandon', from *sacan* 'to dispute'] —**forsaken** *adj.* —**forsakenly** *adv.* —**forsakenness** *n.* —**forsaker** *n.*

forsooth /fər sŏŏth/ *adv.* in truth (*archaic*) [Old English *forsoþ*, literally 'for the truth']

forspent /fawr spént/ *adj.* exhausted or tired out (*archaic*) [Late 16thC. From the past participle of Old English *forspendan* 'to spend completely, exhaust'.]

Forster /fáwrstər/, **E. M.** (1879–1970) British novelist. He was the author of *A Room with a View* (1908), *Howards End* (1910), and *A Passage to India* (1924). Full name **Edward Morgan Forster**

forsterite /fáwrstə rīt/ *n.* a magnesium silicate mineral of the olivine group [Early 19thC. Named after the German naturalist J.R. *Forster* (1729–98).]

Forster-Tuncurry /fáwrstər tun kúrri/ port and tourist centre on the northern coast of New South Wales, Australia, consisting of the twin towns of Forster and Tuncurry. Population: 15,943 (1996).

forswear /fawr swáir/ (**-swears, -swearing, -swore** /-swáwr/, **-sworn** /-swáwrn/) *v.* (*archaic or literary*) **1.** *vt.* **REJECT STRONGLY** to vow to stop doing, having, or using sth ○ *forswear political violence* **2.** *vt.* **DENY** to deny sth under oath or completely ○ *foreswore all knowledge of the crime* **3.** *vi.* **PERJURE YOURSELF** to be guilty of giving false evidence under oath [Old English *forswerian*, literally 'to renounce by swearing']

forsythia /fawr sīthi ə/ *n.* a shrub grown for its small bell-shaped bright yellow flowers that come out in early spring before the leaves. Genus: *Forsythia*. [Mid-19thC. Named in honour of the Scottish horticulturalist William *Forsyth* (1737–1804).]

fort /fawrt/ *n.* **1. FORTIFIED POSITION** a building or group of buildings with strong defences, usually strategically located and guarded by troops **2.** *US* **MILITARY COMPOUND** a permanent military post consisting of several buildings ○ *Fort Bragg* [15thC. Directly or via French from Italian *forte* 'strong (place)', from Latin *fortis* 'strong'.] ◇ **hold the fort** to take charge of sth in the absence of the person usually responsible

WORD KEY: ORIGIN

The Latin word *fortis* from which **fort** is derived is also the source of English *forte*, *fortitude*, *fortress*, and *pianoforte*.

fort. *abbr.* fortification

fortalice /fáwrtəliss/ *n.* a small fort or part of the fortifications of a larger fort (*archaic*) [15thC. From medieval Latin *fortalitia*, from Latin *fortis* 'strong'.]

forte[1] /fáwr tay, fawrt/ *n.* **1. STRONG POINT** sth that sb is particularly good at ○ *Cooking is not really my forte.* **2.** FENCING **STRONG PART OF SWORD** the strongest section of a sword's blade, between the middle and the hilt [Mid-17thC. Via French *fort* 'strong' from Latin *fortis*; later influenced by FORTE[2].]

forte[2] /fáwr tay, fáwrti/ *adv.* **LOUDLY** to be played or sung loudly (*used as a musical direction*) Symbol **f** ■ *n.* **LOUD NOTE OR PASSAGE** a note or passage of music played or sung, or to be played or sung, loudly [Early 18thC. Via Italian, 'strong, loud', from Latin *fortis*.] —**forte** *adj.*

fortepiano /fáwrti pi ánn ō/ (*plural* **-os**) *n.* an early form of the piano, especially the piano of the 18th century [Mid-18thC. From Italian, from *forte* 'loud' + *piano* 'soft'.]

forte-piano *adv.* starting loud and then becoming suddenly soft (*used as a musical direction*) Symbol **fp** —**forte-piano** *adj.*

forth /fawrth/ *adv.* **1. ONWARD** forward in time, place, degree, or order (*formal*) ○ *from this day forth* **2. INTO VIEW** out into view (*formal*) ○ *brought forth the prisoner* **3. ABROAD** away from a particular place, e.g. a country or region (*archaic*) ■ *prep.* **AWAY FROM** out of or away from (*archaic*) [Old English *forþ*. Ultimately from an Indo-European word that is also the ancestor of English *fore*.] ◇ **and so forth** used to indicate that there are more things of the kind just mentioned, without having to name them ○ *bottles, cans, jars, and so forth*

Forth /fawrth/ river in southern Scotland that flows eastwards from Aberfoyle, in Perthshire, to Alloa, where it widens to form the Firth of Forth. Length: 104 km/65 mi.

Forth, Firth of estuary of the River Forth in south-eastern Scotland. It extends about 77 km/48 mi. eastwards from Alloa to the North Sea.

forthcoming /fawrth kúmming/ *adj.* **1. FUTURE** about to appear or happen ○ *plans for the forthcoming celebration* **2. READY WHEN WANTED** available when required or requested ○ *We were assured that the money would be forthcoming.* **3. INFORMATIVE** willing to talk or give information ○ *not very forthcoming about his personal life*

forthright /fáwrth rīt/ *adj.* **OUTSPOKEN** direct in speech or manner and very honest ■ *adv.* **1. OUTSPOKENLY** in a direct and very honest way **2. IMMEDIATELY** at once (*archaic*) [Old English, from FORTH + RIGHT in the sense 'directly'] —**forthrightly** *adv.* —**forthrightness** *n.*

forthwith /fáwrth wíth, -wíth/ *adv.* without delay (*formal*) [13thC. From *forth with* 'along with'.]

fortieth /fáwrti əth/ *n.* **1. ONE OF 40 PARTS OF STH** one of 40 equal parts of sth **2. 40TH BIRTHDAY** sb's 40th birthday —**fortieth** *adj.*, *adv.*

fortification /fàwrtifi káysh'n/ *n.* **1. STRUCTURE FOR DEFENCE** a structure or structures, e.g. a wall, ditch, or rampart, built in order to strengthen a place's defences (*often used in the plural*) **2. BUILDING OF DEFENCES** the art or practice of strengthening or creating defences, e.g. by building walls or digging ditches **3. PLACE THAT CAN BE DEFENDED** a position or place that can be defended

fortified wine /fáwrti fīd-/ *n.* a drink such as sherry, port, or Marsala, that is made from wine to which a strong alcohol, such as grape brandy, has been added. Fortified wines are usually drunk as aperitifs, digestifs, or liqueurs.

fortify /fáwrti fī/ (**-fies, -fying, -fied**) *vt.* **1. MAKE PLACE SAFER** to make a place less susceptible to attack by building or creating defensive structures such as walls, ditches, or ramparts **2. MAKE STRUCTURE STRONGER** to strengthen or reinforce the structure of sth ○ *fortify a seawall* **3. ADD INGREDIENTS TO FOOD OR DRINK** to add further ingredients to food or drink in order to improve its flavour or add nutrients (*usually passive*) ○ *breakfast cereal fortified with vitamins* **4. STRENGTHEN OR ENCOURAGE** to give sb physical, mental, or moral strength or encouragement **5. MAKE MORE POWERFUL** to make sth more powerful or persuasive ○ *fortify an argument* [15thC. From French *fortifier*, from late Latin *fortificare*, literally 'to make strong', from Latin *fortis* 'strong'.] —**fortifiable** *adj.* —**fortifier** *n.* —**fortifyingly** *adv.*

fortis /fáwrtiss/ *adj.* **PRONOUNCED FORCEFULLY** denoting a consonant, e.g. 'p' or 't', that is produced with great muscular tension and pressure of breath ■ *n.* (*plural* **-tes**) **FORCEFULLY PRONOUNCED CONSONANT** a fortis consonant, such as 'p' or 't' [Early 20thC. From Latin, 'strong'.]

fortissimo /fawr tíssimō/ *adv.* **VERY LOUDLY** extremely loudly (*used as a musical direction*) Symbol **ff** ■ *n.* (*plural* **-mos** *or* **-mi**) **FORTISSIMO PIECE OF MUSIC** a passage of music, or an individual note or chord, played fortissimo [Early 18thC. From Italian, 'loudest', from *forte* 'loud, strong' (see FORTE[2]).] —**fortissimo** *adj.*

fortitude /fáwrti tyood/ *n.* strength and endurance in a difficult or painful situation [14thC. Via French from Latin *fortitudo* 'strength, courage', from *fortis* 'strong'.] —**fortitudinous** /fáwrti tyóodinəss/ *adj.*

Fort Knox /fawrt nóks/ a military reservation in northern Hardin County, central Kentucky. It has been the location of the US Gold Depository since 1936. Area: 13,350 hectares/33,000 acres.

Fort Lauderdale /-láwdər dayl/ city and county seat of Broward County, southeastern Florida, situated on the Atlantic Ocean 40 km/25 mi. north of Miami. Population: 162,842 (1994).

fortnight /fáwrt nīt/ *n.* a period of 14 days [Old English *feowertine niht* 'fourteen nights']

fortnightly /fáwrt nītli/ *adj.*, *adv.* **EVERY TWO WEEKS** occurring once every 14 days ■ *n.* (*plural* **-lies**) **PUBLICATION APPEARING EVERY OTHER WEEK** a publication that appears once every two weeks

Fortral /fáwr tral/ *tdmk.* a trademark for a narcotic pain reliever used for severe injury, cancer, or chronic pain

FORTRAN /fáwr tran/ *n.* the earliest high-level computer programming language [Mid-20thC. Contraction of FORMULA + TRANSLATION.]

fortress /fáwrtrəss/ *n.* **1. MILITARY INSTALLATION** a fortified place with a long-term military presence, often including a town **2. STH IMPOSSIBLE TO GET INTO** sth that is impenetrable or acts as protection [14thC. From Old French *forteresse* 'strong place', from, ultimately, Latin *fortis* 'strong'.]

fortuitous /fawr tyóo itəss/ *adj.* **1. ACCIDENTAL OR UNPLANNED** happening by chance **2. HAPPENING BY LUCKY CHANCE** happening as a result of a lucky accident **3. LUCKY** bringing or indicating good fortune [Mid-17thC. From Latin *fortuitus*, from, ultimately, *fors* 'chance, luck'.] —**fortuitously** *adv.* —**fortuitousness** *n.*

fortuity /fawr tyóo əti/ (*plural* **-ties**) *n.* **1. CHANCE OCCURRENCE** sth that happens by chance or accident **2. LUCKY CHANCE** lucky chance or accident

fortunate /fáwrchənət/ *adj.* **1. LUCKY** enjoying good luck **2. RESULTING FROM LUCK** happening as a result of good luck **3. BRINGING LUCK** bringing good luck [14thC. From Latin *fortunatus*, from *fortuna* 'Fate, luck'.] —**fortunateness** *n.*

WORD KEY: SYNONYMS

See Synonyms at ***lucky***.

WORD KEY: CULTURAL NOTE

A Fortunate Life, an autobiography by Australian writer Albert Facey (1981).This working man's account of his deprived childhood and subsequent involvement in many of the country's major events (World War I, the Depression, post-war unionism) is regarded as a classic story of an Australian everyman.

fortunately /fáwrchənətli/ *adv.* **1. LUCKILY** by lucky chance **2. HAPPILY** used to show that the speaker or writer is happy to be able to report sth ○ *Fortunately, we've been given more time to finish the job.*

fortune /fáwrchən/ *n.* **1. GREAT WEALTH OR PROPERTY** a large amount of financial wealth or material possessions **2. LARGE SUM OF MONEY** an extremely large amount of money **3. fortune, Fortune FATE** chance, or the personification of chance, regarded as affecting human activities **4. LUCK** luck, especially good luck **5. DESTINY** an individual's destiny ■ **fortunes** *npl.* **LIFE'S UPS AND DOWNS** chance happenings throughout life that may turn out well or badly [13thC. Via French from Latin *fortuna* 'Fate, luck' (especially good luck).]

fortune cookie *n.* a Chinese biscuit folded and baked around a piece of paper on which a saying or a prediction of sb's fortune is written. Fortune cookies are served in Chinese restaurants in the United States.

fortune hunter *n.* sb who wants to become rich quickly and easily, especially by making a deliberate attempt to marry a wealthy partner — **fortune hunting** *n.* —**fortune-hunting** *adj.*

fortune-teller *n.* sb who makes predictions about sb's future by such methods as reading palms, looking into a crystal ball, using tarot cards, or examining tea leaves —**fortune-telling** *n., adj.*

Fort William /-wíllyəm/ town at the foot of Ben Nevis on the shore of Loch Eil, in the Great Glen, western Scotland. Population: 10,391 (1991).

forty /fáwrti/ *n.* (*plural* **-ties**) **1.** NUMBER 40 the number 40 **2.** GROUP OF 40 a group of 40 objects or people **3.** TENNIS TENNIS POINT in a game of tennis, the score awarded to a player with a score of thirty on winning a further point ■ **forties** *npl.* **1.** NUMBERS 40 TO 49 the numbers 40 to 49 ○ *in the low forties* **2.** 1940 TO 1949 the years 1940 to 1949 **3.** PERIOD FROM AGE 40 TO 49 the period of sb's life from the age of 40 to 49 [Old English *feowertig,* literally 'four tens', from *feower* 'four'] —**forty** *adj., pron.*

forty-five *n.* **1.** SMALL GRAMOPHONE RECORD a record smaller than an LP that is played at 45 revolutions per minute **2.** *US, Can* .45-CALIBRE PISTOL a pistol with a .45 calibre.

Forty-Five *n.* the Jacobite Rebellion of 1745–46

fortyish /fáwrti ish/ *adj.* **1.** APPROXIMATELY 40 approximately 40 in number **2.** AGED ABOUT 40 about the age of 40

forty-niner /-nínər/ *n.* a prospector in the gold rush of 1849 in California

forty-ninth parallel *n. Can* the border between the United States and Canada, that runs at 49° latitude along most of its length

fortysomething /fáwrti sumthing/ *n.* SB IN FORTIES sb between 40 and 49 years of age (*informal*) ■ *adj.* BETWEEN 40 AND 49 between 40 and 49 years of age

forty winks *n.* a short sleep (*informal; takes a singular or plural verb*)

forum /fáwrəm/ (*plural* **forums** *or* **fora** /-rə/) *n.* **1.** PLACE TO EXPRESS YOURSELF a medium, e.g. a magazine or newspaper, in which the public may debate an issue or express opinions **2.** MEETING FOR DISCUSSION a meeting to discuss matters of general interest **3.** HIST PUBLIC SQUARE IN ROMAN CITIES a public square or marketplace in ancient Roman cities where business was conducted and the law courts were situated **4.** LAW LAW COURT a law court or tribunal **5.** COMPUT INTERNET DISCUSSION GROUP an Internet discussion group for participants with common interests [15thC. From Latin, literally 'outdoor place', denoting an enclosed space around a house, later a marketplace. Ultimately from an Indo-European word that was the ancestor of English *door* and *foreign.*]

forward /fáwrwərd/ CORE MEANING: to or towards a front position or direction ○ (adv) *Conover pushed his cup forward, but Johnny ignored it.* ○ (adj) *Most of the energy in petrol makes engines hot; less than half gets converted to forward motion.*

1. *adv.* **forward, forwards** AHEAD to or towards what is ahead in space or time ○ (adv) *He sprang forward and embraced his grandmother.* **2.** *adv.* PROGRESSING towards a goal ○ *The company has taken a step forward in employee safety.* **3.** *adv.* INDICATES IMPROVEMENT indicates that sth progresses or improves ○ *The EU is moving forward on monetary union.* **4.** *adv.* NAUT TO FRONT OF VESSEL towards the front of a boat or ship ○ *I was ordered forward to swab the deck.* **5.** *adv.* TOWARDS THE FRONT towards the front of sth such as an aircraft or a building ○ *I'd like to be seated further forward.* **6.** *adv.* TO PUBLIC ATTENTION from obscurity into public view ○ *The unknown actor came forward and accepted the lead role.* **7.** *adj.* AHEAD directed towards what is ahead in space and time ○ *The magnetic field exerts a forward force on charged particles.* **8.** *adj.* RELATING TO THE FUTURE directed towards a future goal ○ *forward planning* **9.** *adj.* NAUT AT FRONT OF VESSEL situated at or near the front of a boat or ship ○ *the forward deck* **10.** *adj.* AT THE FRONT situated at or near the front of sth such as an aircraft or a building ○ *The forward seats are the most popular.* **11.** *adj.* UNRESTRAINED IN BEHAVIOUR behaving boldly in defiance of moral or social restraints ○ *I'm not sure I approve of her behaviour – she's very forward.* **12.** *adj. NZ* WELL in good condition (*refers to an animal*) **13.** *n.* SPORTS ATTACKING PLAYER an attacking player in some team sports, such as football, rugby, hockey, or basketball **14.** *vt.* **forward** (*3rd person present singular* **-wards,** *present participle* **-warding,** *past participle* **-warded**) REDIRECT MAIL to send on mail from the address to which it was originally sent ○ *She was anxious to know if any letters might have come that had not been forwarded to her.* **15.** *vt.* ADVANCE OR PROMOTE to assist the progress of sth ○ *I will do anything you like if it means we can forward your cause.* [Old English *forweard,* literally 'in the direction of the front', from *fore* (see FORE)]

forward bias *n.* a voltage applied to a semiconductor or a junction in such a device, in the direction that carries a higher current

forwarder /fáwrwərdər/ *n.* an individual or company whose business is the collection, shipment, and delivery of goods

forwarding /fáwrwərding/ *n.* the collection, shipment, and delivery of goods

forwarding address *n.* a new address to which mail is to be redirected

forward-looking *adj.* planning for or looking ahead to the future

forwardly /fáwrwərdli/ *adv.* in a bold manner, defying moral or social restraints

forward market *n.* a financial market in which contracts are entered for the purchase and sale of commodities and stocks that are to be delivered at a future date

forwardness /fáwrwərdnəss/ *n.* bold behaviour in defiance of moral or social restraints

forward pass *n.* **1.** RUGBY ILLEGAL RUGBY PASS in rugby, an illegal pass in which the ball goes forward **2.** AMERICAN FOOTBALL AMERICAN FOOTBALL PASS TOWARDS OPPONENTS' GOAL in American football, a pass thrown from a position behind the line of scrimmage in the direction of the opposing team's goal

forward roll *n.* a move in gymnastics in which the back of the neck is first placed on the ground and the body is rolled forward

forwards *adv.* = **forward**

Fosbury flop /fózbəri-/ *n.* a technique used in the high jump in which the contestant clears the bar with the back of the shoulders followed by the arched body [Mid-20thC. Named after the US athlete Richard (Dick) *Fosbury* (born 1947), who developed the technique.]

foscarnet *n.* a drug used to treat a type of herpes virus that is often associated with AIDS

fossa[1] /fóssə/ (*plural* **-sae** /-see/) *n.* a hollow, pit, or groove in a part of the body, e.g. a bone [Mid-17thC. From Latin, literally 'ditch' (see FOSSE).]

fossa[2] (*plural* **-sas** *or* **-sa** /-see/) *n.* a slender reddish-brown carnivorous mammal from Madagascar that resembles a cat, has sharp retractile claws, and feeds on small animals, birds, and insects. Species: *Cryptoprocta ferox.* [Mid-19thC. From Malagasy *fosa.*]

fosse /foss/ *n.* a wide ditch, usually filled with water and used for defence [Pre-12thC. Via French from Latin *fossa,* from *fodere* 'to dig' (source of English *fossil*).]

Fosse Way /fóss-/ Roman road in England that starts in Axminster, Devon, and runs northeastwards to Lincoln. Length: 300 km/200 mi.

fossick /fóssik/ (**-sicks, -sicking, -sicked**) *vi. ANZ* **1.** RUMMAGE to rummage or look for sth ○ *She fossicked around in the drawer for the key.* **2.** LOOK FOR GOLD to search for gold or gems in mines or streams that have already been worked [Mid-19thC. From English dialect *fossick* 'to ferret out, to get by asking', of unknown origin.] —**fossicker** *n.*

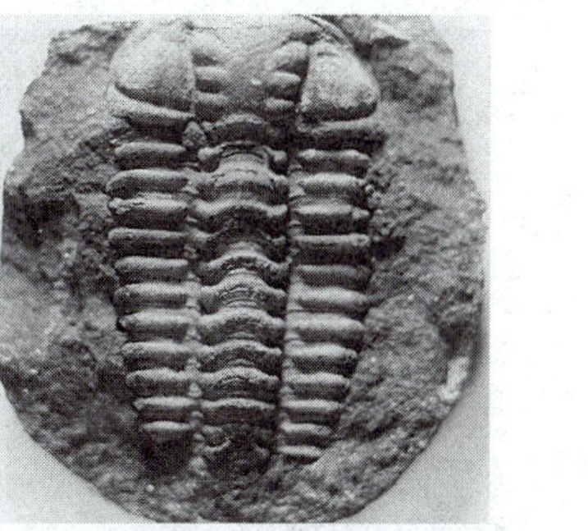

Barnaby's

Fossil: Trilobite

fossil /fóss'l/ *n.* **1.** PRESERVED REMAINS OF ANIMAL OR PLANT the remains of an animal or plant preserved from an earlier era inside a rock or other geological deposit, often as an impression or in a petrified state **2.** SB WHO WILL NOT CHANGE sb who is hopelessly out of date or unwilling to accept change (*informal insult*) **3.** STH OUTDATED sth that has outlived its usefulness, e.g. a discredited theory **4.** LING OLD WORD NOW USED SPECIFICALLY a word or part of a word that was once used generally but now survives only in a few contexts, such as *couth* in *uncouth* [Mid-16thC. Via French *fossile* from Latin *fossilis* 'dug up', from *fodere* 'to dig'. Originally denoting a fossilized fish that was believed to have lived underground.]

fossil fuel *n.* any carbon-containing fuel, e.g. coal, peat, petroleum, and natural gas, derived from the decomposed remains of prehistoric plants and animals

fossiliferous /fóssi líffərəss/ *adj.* having fossils within it (*refers to rocks or other geological deposits*)

fossilize /fóssə līz/ (**-izes, -izing, -ized**), **fossilise** (**-ises, -ising, -ised**) *vti.* **1.** MAKE OR BECOME FOSSIL to convert sth into a fossil, to preserve sth as a fossil, or to become a fossil **2.** BE UNABLE TO CHANGE to become outdated, fixed, or unchanging, or to make sb or sth incapable of change —**fossilizable** *adj.* —**fossilization** /fóssə lī záysh'n/ *n.* —**fossilized** /fóssə līzd/ *adj.*

fossil water *n.* water in underground strata that has accumulated over millions of years and is therefore not a renewable resource, unlike other ground water

fossorial /fo sáwri əl/ *adj.* used to describe animals that have large forelimbs or other adaptations for digging and burrowing, or to describe the parts of the body used for this purpose [Mid-19thC. Formed from medieval Latin *fossorius,* from Latin *fossor* 'digger', from *fodere* (see FOSSIL).]

foster /fóstər/ *v.* (**-ters, -tering, -tered**) **1.** *vti.* REAR CHILD WHO IS NOT YOURS to look after or bring up in your home a child who is not your own, often on a short-term basis and in exchange for payment by a local authority **2.** *vt.* ARRANGE CARE FOR CHILD to put a child temporarily in the care of adults who are not its parents **3.** *vt.* NURTURE A CHILD to provide a child with care and upbringing **4.** *vt.* DEVELOP to encourage the development of sth **5.** *vt.* KEEP ALIVE FEELING OR THOUGHT to keep a feeling or thought alive ■ *adj.* PROVIDING OR RECEIVING PARENTAL CARE giving or receiving a home and parental care and upbringing, usually on a short-term basis, although unrelated by blood or adoption. Foster care is provided for children whose natural parents are dead, absent, or unfit or unable to look after them. [Old English *fostrian* 'to nourish', later 'to raise a child', from *foster* 'food'. Ultimately from a prehistoric Germanic word that was also the ancestor of English *food* and *forage.*] —**fosterer** *n.*

Foster /fóstər/, **David** (*b.* 1944) Australian novelist. His works include *Moonlite* (1981) and *The Glade Within the Grove* (1996).

Foster, Sir Norman (*b.* 1935) British architect. His designs such as the terminal building (1991) for Stansted Airport, Essex combine elegant forms with complex engineering and technologically advanced materials. He won the Pritzker Architecture Prize in 1999. Full name **Sir Norman Robert Foster**

fosterage /fóstərij/ *n.* **1.** CARING FOR ANOTHER'S CHILD the act of looking after or bringing up a child who is not one's own, often on a short-term basis and in

Andrew Ward

Sir Norman Foster

exchange for payment by a local authority **2. BEING A FOSTER CHILD** the process of being looked after or brought up in a home by parents who are not one's own **3. ENCOURAGING DEVELOPMENT** the process of encouraging the development of sth beneficial

fosterling /fóstərling/ *n.* a child who is fostered (*dated or literary*) [Old English *fostorling*, literally 'little nourished one' (see FOSTER)]

fou /foo/ *adj. Scotland* extremely drunk (*informal*) [Mid-16thC. Alteration of FULL.]

Foucault /foókō/, **Michel** (1926–84) French philosopher. He showed how ideas of truth about human nature change in the course of history. His chief works were *Madness and Civilization* (1960), *The Order of Things* (1966), and *Discipline and Punish* (1975).

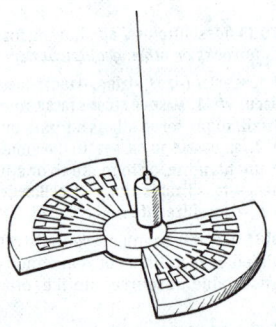

Foucault's pendulum

Foucault('s) pendulum /foókōz-/ *n.* a heavy free-swinging pendulum suspended by a long thin wire, whose plane of motion appears to change as the earth rotates [Mid-19thC. Named after the French physicist Jean-Bernard Léon *Foucault* (1819–68), who first used such a pendulum to demonstrate the rotation of the earth.]

fouetté /fwéttay, foo ə tay/ *n.* a ballet step in which the dancer stands on one foot and moves the other leg quickly out and in again, often while doing a pirouette [Mid-19thC. From French, past participle of *fouetter* 'to whip'.]

fought past tense, past participle of **fight**

foul /fowl/ *adj.* **1. DISGUSTING** disgusting to the senses **2. FILLED WITH DIRT** clogged with dirt or so obstructed as to be unusable **3. DIRTY** covered in dirt **4. CONTAMINATED** contaminated by impurities **5. UNPLEASANT** extremely unpleasant or disagreeable in nature (*informal*) **6. VULGAR** obscene or otherwise offensive in expression or behaviour **7. SPORTS ILLEGAL IN SPORT** contrary to the rules of a sport **8. DISHONEST** behaving in an unfair and unacceptable way **9. INCLEMENT** stormy or wet and unpleasant for outdoor activities (*refers to weather*) **10. ROTTEN** decaying and rotten **11. EVIL** spiritually or morally vicious **12. ENSNARLED** entangled with sth and unable to move **13. UNENJOYABLE** extremely low in quality ■ *n.* **1. SPORTS ILLEGAL ACTION IN SPORT** an illegal action against an opposing player or an action that breaks the rules of a sport **2. NAUT ENTANGLEMENT PREVENTING MOVEMENT** in sailing, an entanglement or collision that prevents movement ■ *v.* **(fouls, fouling, fouled) 1.** *vti.* **SPORTS ACT ILLEGALLY IN SPORT** to act illegally against an opposing player or to violate a rule of a sport **2.** *vti.* **ENSNARL AND PREVENT MOVEMENT** to entangle or catch sth so that it cannot move, or become entangled or caught and unable

to move **3.** *vti.* **OBSTRUCT OR BECOME OBSTRUCTED** to clog or block sth, or to become clogged or blocked **4.** *vt.* **MAKE DIRTY** to make sth dirty, especially by defecation **5.** *vt.* **BRING DISGRACE ON** to bring disgrace to a person or to sb's reputation [Old English *ful* 'filthy, decaying'. Ultimately from a prehistoric Germanic word that was also the ancestor of English *defile* and *filth*.] —**fouler** *n.* — **foully** /fówl li/ *adv.* —**foulness** *n.*

foul up *vti.* **1. HANDLE STH POORLY** to do sth badly or incompetently, or to be bungled or mismanaged (*informal*) **2. OBSTRUCT OR BECOME OBSTRUCTED** to choke, clog, or entangle sth, or to become choked, clogged, or entangled

foulard /foo laar, -laard/ *n.* **1. SOFT PATTERNED CLOTH** a soft silk or rayon fabric, usually patterned **2. ARTICLE MADE OF SOFT PATTERNED FABRIC** sth made of foulard, especially a scarf or handkerchief [Mid-19thC. From French, of unknown origin.]

foul-mouthed *adj.* using obscene or otherwise offensive language, especially habitually

foul play *n.* **1. UNFAIRNESS** unfair action or behaviour **2. CRIME** treachery or criminal violence **3. SPORTS ACTION AGAINST RULES** action that is contrary to the rules of a sport

foul-up *n.* a blunder or the confusion or failure that results from error (*informal*)

foumart /foo maart, fóomət/ *n.* a polecat (*archaic*) [Assumed Old English *fulmearþ*, from an earlier form of FOUL (from its unpleasant smell) + *mearþ* 'marten']

found[1] /fownd/ **(founds, founding, founded)** *vt.* **1. SET UP INSTITUTION** to establish and organize sth for the future, e.g. an institution or business **2. PROVIDE WITH BASIS** to support sth, e.g. a conclusion, with evidence or reasoning [13thC. Via French *fonder* from Latin *fundare*, from *fundus* 'bottom, base' (source of English *fund*, *fundamental*, and *profound*).]

found[2] /fownd/ **(founds, founding, founded)** *vt.* **1. CAST METAL OR GLASS** to cast sth, especially metal or glass, by melting it and pouring it into a mould **2. CAST FROM MOULD** to produce objects, e.g. machine parts, by melting metal or glass and pouring it into moulds [14thC. Via French *fondre* 'to dissolve and blend' (the original sense in English) from Latin *fundere* 'to pour or melt' (source of English *fuse*, *diffuse*, and *confound*).]

found[3] past tense, past participle of **find**

foundation /fown dáysh'n/ *n.* **1. SUPPORT FOR A BUILDING** a part of a building, usually below the ground, that transfers and distributes the weight of the building onto the ground (*often used in the plural*) **2. SUPPORT FOR IDEA** the basis of sth, e.g. a theory or an idea **3. COSMETICS BASE LAYER OF MAKE-UP** a type of cosmetic in liquid, cream, or cake form, usually coloured, that is applied as a base for make-up **4. ESTABLISHING OF INSTITUTION OR ORGANIZATION** the setting up of an institution or organization **5. CHARITABLE OR EDUCATIONAL ORGANIZATION** an institution, e.g. a school, research establishment, charitable trust, or hospital, that has been formally set up with an endowment fund **6. FUND SUPPORTING INSTITUTION** an endowment fund that supports an institution **7. RULES OF AN INSTITUTION** the charter setting up an institution and the statutes and rules by which it is governed **8. = foundation garment** —**foundational** *adj.* —**foundationally** *adv.*

foundation course *n.* an introductory course, usually taken as a first level in more extended studies

foundation garment *n.* a piece of women's underwear intended to control and shape the figure, e.g. a corset

foundation school *n.* a state primary or secondary school that owns its own land and has responsibility for staffing and for admissions arrangements. ◊ **community school**

foundation stone *n.* **1. STONE BEGINNING CONSTRUCTION** a stone laid during a ceremony to mark the start of construction of a building or institution **2. BASIS FOR STH** the basis on which sth is founded

foundation stop *n.* an organ stop with a strong fundamental tone

foundation subject *n.* any of ten subjects specified in the 1988 National Curriculum that must be studied in schools in England and Wales, three of which have priority as core subjects

founder[1] /fówndər/ *n.* a person who establishes an institution, business, or organization

founder[2] /fówndər/ *v.* **(-ders, -dering, -dered) 1.** *vti.* **SINK OR CAUSE TO SINK** to become filled with water and sink, or to make sth sink **2.** *vi.* **BREAK DOWN** to collapse and fail ○ *Negotiations foundered on a single issue.* **3.** *vi.* **CRUMPLE** to give way and fall to the ground **4.** *vi.* **BE BOGGED DOWN** to become stuck in soft ground or snow **5.** *vi.* **STUMBLE** to stumble or injure a leg **6.** *vti.* **MAKE OR BECOME ILL BY OVERFEEDING** to make livestock ill by overfeeding or to become ill by overfeeding ■ *n.* **VET = laminitis** [14thC. From Old French *fondrer* 'to send or sink to the bottom, fall in ruins', from, ultimately, Latin *fundus* 'bottom' (source of English *found*[2]).]

founder member *n.* a member of an organization who also helped to found it

founding father *n.* sb who creates an important institution, movement, or organization

Founding Father *n.* one of the members of the convention that drafted the US Constitution

foundling /fówndling/ *n.* an abandoned baby of unknown parentage (*dated*) [13thC. Formed from the past participle of FIND, possibly influenced by Dutch *vondeling*.]

found object *n.* ARTS **= objet trouvé**

foundry /fówndri/ *n.* (*plural* **-ries**) *n.* **1. WORKPLACE FOR CASTING METAL OR GLASS** a building equipped for the casting of metal or glass **2. MAKING CASTINGS** the skill or practice of casting metal or glass

fount[1] /fownt/ *n.* (*literary*) **1. SOURCE** a source of sth **2. FOUNTAIN** a fountain or spring of water [16thC. Shortening of FOUNTAIN.]

fount[2] /fownt/ *n.* = **font**[2]

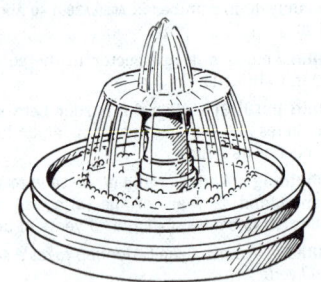

Fountain

fountain /fówntin/ *n.* **1. ORNAMENTAL WATER FEATURE** an ornamental structure featuring a jet or jets of water, often emerging from a statue into a pool **2. NATURAL SPRING** a natural source of water **3. DRINKING FOUNTAIN** a small jet of drinking water, especially one in a public place that can be activated by a button or handle **4. SPRAY OF LIQUID** a jet of water or some other liquid **5. SPRAY OF SUBSTANCE** a sudden discharge of sth into the air, e.g. sparks, lava, or steam **6. SOURCE** the source of sth abstract **7. RESERVOIR OF LIQUID** a reservoir of liquid for use as needed, e.g. in an oil lamp or for printing ink [14thC. Via French *fontaine* from Latin *fontanus* 'of a spring', from *fons* 'spring' (also the original sense in English).]

fountainhead /fówntin hed/ *n.* **1. SOURCE OF STREAM** a spring that is the source of a stream **2. PRIMARY SOURCE** the primary source of sth abstract

fountain pen *n.* a pen with a pointed metal tip (**nib**) that is supplied with ink from a refillable reservoir in the body of the pen or from an inserted cartridge

four /fawr/ *n.* **1. NUMBER 4** the number 4 **2. STH WITH VALUE OF 4** sth in a numbered series, e.g. a playing card, with a value of 4 ○ *the four of spades* ○ *throw a four* **3. GROUP OF 4** a group of 4 objects or people ○ *a four for bridge* **4. CRICKET CRICKET SHOT SCORING 4 RUNS** in cricket, a shot that hits the ground and then bounces out of bounds. It scores four runs. **5. ROWING 4-OARED RACING BOAT** a light narrow racing boat with four oars **6. ROWING 4-MEMBER ROWING CREW** a rowing crew with four members **7. BOWLS BOWLING TEAM** a team of four bowls players ■ **fours** *npl.* ROWING **BOAT RACES** races for boats with a crew of four [Old English *fēower*. Ultimately from an Indo-European word that was also the ancestor of English *square*, *quadrant*, *trapezium*, and *tetra-*.] —**four** *adj.*, *pron.*

four-ball *n.* GOLF a match between two pairs of golfers in which the better score of each side at each hole is counted [So called because four balls are used in this type of game]

four-by-four *n.* a four-wheel-drive motor vehicle

four-by-two *n.* a commonly used size of timber with a cross section measuring approximately 10 cm/4 in by approximately 5 cm/2 in. US term **two-by-four**

fourchette /foor shét/ *n.* a small band that joins the folds of skin at the back of the opening to the vagina, sometimes torn in childbirth [Mid-18thC. From French, literally 'small fork', from *fourche*, from Latin *furca* 'pitchfork, forked stick' (source of English *fork*).]

four-colour *adj.* used to describe a process by which full-colour printing is achieved by superimposing images in cyan, magenta, yellow, and black

four-cycle *adj.* US = **four-stroke**

four-dimensional *adj.* having or determined by four dimensions, especially as in some formulations of relativity theory which use three spatial dimensions and a mathematically modified form of time as the fourth

Fourdrinier /foor drínni ər, -ni ay/ *n.* a type of paper-making machine that produces a continuous web or roll of paper [Mid-19thC. Named after the 19th-century British papermakers, Henry and Sealy *Fourdrinier*, who patented such a machine.]

four-eyed fish *n.* a fish from Central America whose eyes are divided into two lobes so that the upper part can see above the water and the lower part can see below. Latin name: *Anableps anableps*.

four-eyes (*plural* **four-eyes**) *n.* an insulting term for sb who wears spectacles (*informal insult*)

four flush *n.* a bad hand in poker, containing four cards of the same suit and one odd card

four-flush (**four-flushes, four-flushing, four-flushed**) *vi.* **1.** CARDS BET BOLDLY WITH LOSING HAND to bet coolly and boldly in poker despite holding a bad hand, e.g. a four flush **2.** US BRAZENLY MISLEAD to try to mislead sb in a bold way (*informal*) —**four-flusher** *n.*

fourfold /fáwr fōld/ *adj.*, *adv.* MULTIPLIED BY 4 four times as great in size or amount ■ *adj.* **1.** WITH 4 ELEMENTS with four elements or members **2.** CONSISTING OF 4 PARTS consisting of four parts or made up of four parts

four-four-two *n.* one of the most common outfield team formations in soccer, comprising four defenders, four midfielders, and two attackers

4GL *abbr.* COMPUT fourth-generation language

four-handed /fáwr handid/ *adj.* **1.** GAME HAVING 4 PLAYERS played by four people (*refers to a game, especially a card game*) **2.** MUSIC FOR 2 PIANO PLAYERS composed or arranged for two people to play at the piano

Fourier /fóò rri ay/, **Charles** (1772–1837) French social scientist. His *Theory of Four Movements and of General Destinies* (1808) advocated a socialist reorganization of society. Full name **François Marie Charles Fourier**

Fourier analysis /fóò ri ər-, fòò ri ay-/ *n.* the analysis of a periodic function using the terms of a Fourier series as an approximation [Early 20thC. Named after J. B. J. *Fourier* (see FOURIER SERIES).]

Fourier series *n.* an infinite trigonometric series of terms consisting of constants multiplied by sines or cosines, used in the approximation of periodic functions [Late 19thC. Named after the French mathematician Jean Baptiste Joseph *Fourier* (1768–1830), who devised the series.]

four-in-hand *n.* **1.** 4-HORSE CARRIAGE a carriage drawn by four horses with one driver **2.** 4 HORSES DRAWING CARRIAGE a team of four horses drawing a carriage

four-leaf clover, **four-leaved clover, four-leafed clover** *n.* a clover leaf divided into four leaflets instead of the usual three, believed to bring good luck to the person who finds it

four-letter word *n.* any short English word relating to sex or excretion that is often used as a swearword and is generally regarded as offensive or taboo [From

the fact that the most common words of this kind consist of four letters]

four-o'clock (*plural* **four-o'clock** *or* **four-o'clocks**) *n.* a tropical American plant with tubular red, white, or yellow flowers that open in the late afternoon. Latin name: *Mirabilis jalapa*.

fourpenny one /fáwrpəni-/ *n.* a punch with the fist (*dated informal*) [Possibly from rhyming slang *fourpenny bit* 'hit']

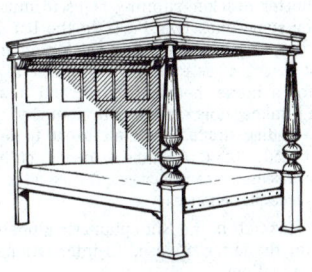

Four-poster

four-poster, **four-poster bed** *n.* a bed with a tall post at each corner, from which a canopy and curtains are sometimes hung

fourragère /foorə zhair/ *n.* a braided cord awarded as a military decoration to a unit or individual, and usually worn on the left shoulder of a uniform [Early 20thC. From French, from *fourrage* (see FORAGE).]

fourscore /fawr skáwr/ *adj.* the number 80 or a quantity of 80 (*archaic*) ○ *fourscore years and ten* [13thC]

foursome /fáwrsəm/ *n.* **1.** GROUP OF 4 PEOPLE a group of four people, usually taking part in some activity together **2.** GOLF GOLF GAME WITH PARTNERS a game of golf between two pairs of players, especially when each pair has one ball that the partners hit alternately

foursquare /fawr skwáir/ *adv.*, *adj.* SHOWING DETERMINATION showing certainty and determination ■ *adj.* SOLID solidly built and strong [14thC. The main modern meanings all derive from the original sense 'having four equal sides', and hence, 'stable and firm'.]

four-star *adj.* HIGH-OCTANE having a high octane number (*refers to petrol*) ■ *n.* HIGH-OCTANE PETROL high-octane petrol, once the most commonly used in vehicles with petrol engines

four-stroke *adj.* having a piston that makes four strokes to complete a cycle (*refers to an internal-combustion engine*). US term **four-cycle**

fourteen /fawr teen/ *n.* **1.** NUMBER 14 the number 14 **2.** STH WITH VALUE OF 14 sth in a numbered series with a value of 14 **3.** GROUP OF 14 a group of 14 objects or people —**fourteen** *adj.*, *pron.*

fourteenth /fawr teenth/ *n.* **1.** ONE OF 14 PARTS OF STH one of 14 equal parts of sth **2.** 14 IN A SERIES the ordinal number assigned to item number 14 in a series —**fourteenth** *adj.*

fourth /fawrth/ *n.* **1.** ONE OF 4 PARTS OF STH one of four equal parts of sth **2.** BALLET = **fourth position 3.** MUSIC INTERVAL OF 4 NOTES in a standard musical scale, the interval between one note and another that lies three notes above or below it. In the scale of C major, C and F form a fourth. **4.** MUSIC NOTE A 4TH AWAY FROM ANOTHER in a standard musical scale, a note that is a fourth away from another note —**fourth** *adj.*, *adv.*

fourth dimension *n.* time in relativity theory modified mathematically and used in combination with the usual three spatial dimensions to specify the location in space and time of events —**fourth-dimensional** *adj.*

Fourth Estate, **Fourth Estate** *n.* journalists, the press, or the media in general [Originally, any significant power other than the three estates (the Lords Spiritual, the Lords Temporal, and the House of Commons); Edmund BURKE supposedly first applied it to the press]

fourth-generation language *n.* an advanced computer programming language that is more like human language than are the standard high-level programming languages

fourthly /fáwrthli/ *adv.* used to introduce the fourth point in an argument or discussion

fourth position *n.* a position in ballet in which the feet are turned outwards with the right leg extended so that the right foot is one step in front of the left foot

fourth-rate *adj.* so bad that it is worse than second-rate and third-rate

Fourth World *n.* the poorest or least developed countries in the Third World

4WD *abbr.* four-wheel drive

four-wheel drive *n.* a system of transmitting power from the driving mechanism to all four wheels of a motor vehicle to provide better traction under difficult conditions

Fouta Djallon /foòttə yaá lon/, **Futa Djallon** plateau region in north-central Guinea. Its highest point is the Massif du Tamgué, 1,537 m/5,043 ft. Area: 77,700 sq. km/30,000 sq. mi.

fouter /fóòər/ *n.* Scotland = **footer**[2] [Late 16thC. Via Old French *foutre* from Latin *futuere* 'to have sexual intercourse with'. Apparently originally used like FUCK in phrases such as 'fuck all' or 'not give a fuck'.]

fovea /fóvi ə/ (*plural* **-ae** /-vi ee/) *n.* **1.** TINY CAVITY a small hollow in the surface of a part of the body **2.** = **fovea centralis** [Late 17thC. From Latin, literally 'small pit'.] —**foveal** *adj.* —**foveate** /fóvi ayt, -ət/ *adj.*

fovea centralis /-sen traáliss/ *n.* a shallow pit in the centre of the retina that is free of blood vessels and has the highest concentration of cells sensitive to colour and bright light (**cones**). The fovea centralis is the area of most acute vision. [From Latin, 'centra foveal']

Foveaux Strait /fóvō-/ stretch of the South Pacific Ocean between the South Island and Stewart Island, New Zealand. At its narrowest, it is 18 km/11 mi. wide.

foveola /fō vée ələ/ (*plural* **-lae** /-lee/) *n.* a small fovea [Mid-19thC. From Latin, 'small fovea', from *fovea* (see FOVEA).] —**foveolar** *adj.* —**foveolate** /fóvi ə layt, -lət/ *adj.* —**foveolated** /-laytid/ *adj.*

Fowey /foy/ small seaport and resort in Cornwall, southwestern England. Population: 1,939 (1991).

fowl /fowl/ (*plural* **fowls** *or* **fowl**) *n.* **1.** CHICKEN a common domesticated chicken **2.** BIRD RELATED TO CHICKEN a bird related to the chicken, e.g. a turkey, grouse, pheasant, or partridge. Order: Galliformes. **3.** EDIBLE OR GAME BIRD any bird that is used as food or hunted for sport, e.g. a goose or duck **4.** BIRD'S FLESH the flesh of an edible bird, traditionally chicken, especially an old or male bird **5.** BIRD any bird at all (*archaic*) [Old English *fugol* 'bird'. Ultimately from a prehistoric Germanic word that was also the ancestor of English *fly*.]

fowler /fówlər/ *n.* sb who shoots or traps wild birds as a livelihood or for sport

Fowles /fowlz/, **John** (b. 1926) British novelist. His works include *The Collector* (1963), *The Magus* (1966), and *The French Lieutenant's Woman* (1969). Full name **John Robert Fowles**

fowling /fówling/ *n.* the shooting or trapping of wild birds as a livelihood or for sport

fowling piece *n.* a light gun that fires small shot, used in hunting game birds

fox /foks/ *n.* **1.** WILD ANIMAL WITH BUSHY TAIL a carnivorous

Fox

mammal of the dog family that has a pointed muzzle, large ears, a long bushy tail, and usually reddish-brown or grey fur. Foxes are found throughout most of the world and hunt alone, mainly at night, relying on cunning and an acute sense of hearing and smell. Genus: *Vulpes.* **2. FOX FUR** the fur of the fox **3. TRICKSTER** a sly and cunning person (*informal*) **4.** *US* **GOOD-LOOKING PERSON** a good-looking young person (*informal*) ■ *vt.* (**foxes, foxing, foxed**) **1. BAFFLE** to confuse or baffle sb (*often passive*) **2. DECEIVE OR OUTWIT** to deceive or outwit sb by means of sly trickery [Old English. Ultimately from an Indo-European word probably meaning 'tail'.]

Fox /foks/ *n.* **1.** PEOPLES **MEMBER OF NATIVE N AMERICAN PEOPLE** a member of a Native North American people that lived in Michigan, Wisconsin, Illinois, and Iowa, and whose members now live mainly in Oklahoma and Iowa. Following US attempts under a spurious treaty to move the Fox from their lands in Illinois, they joined with the Sauk in the Black Hawk War of 1832. **2.** LANG **ALGONQUIAN LANGUAGE** a language spoken in parts of Iowa and Oklahoma. It is one of the Algonquian group of the Algonquian-Wakashan family of North American languages. About 2,000 people speak Fox. ■ *adj.* **RELATING TO FOX** relating or belonging to the Fox people, or their language or culture

Fox /foks/, **Charles James** (1749–1806) British statesman. He was twice foreign secretary (1782, 1806) and one of the principal leaders of the Whig Party in the period of the US and French revolutions.

Fox, George (1624–91) English religious leader. The founder of the Quakers, he was frequently imprisoned for his beliefs. He wrote the *Journal* (1674).

Fox, Sir William (1812–93) English-born New Zealand explorer, statesman, and painter. He was premier of New Zealand (1856, 1861–62, 1869–72, 1873).

FOX /foks/ *abbr.* Futures and Options Exchange

foxed /fokst/ *adj.* stained with yellowish-brown spots from having been kept in damp conditions (*refers to books or paper*)

foxfire /fóks fīr/ *n.* a luminescent glow produced by some fungi when in contact with rotting wood

Fox Glacier glacier in Westland National Park, on the southwestern coast of the South Island, New Zealand. Length: 11 km/7 mi.

Foxglove

foxglove /fóks gluv/ (*plural* **-glove** *or* **-gloves**) *n.* a tall plant that has numerous thimble-shaped purple or white flowers and is the source of the drug digitalis. Latin name: *Digitalis purpurea.*

fox grape *n.* a wild grape of the eastern United States that has purplish fruit and is the source of many cultivated grape varieties. Latin name: *Vitis labrusca.*

foxhole /fóks hōl/ *n.* a small hole dug in the ground to protect a sniper or other soldier from enemy fire

foxhound /fóks hownd/ *n.* a small short-haired dog that has great speed and stamina, belonging to either of two breeds that are used to hunt foxes

fox hunter *n.* **1. HUNTER OF FOXES** sb who regularly hunts foxes for sport **2. FOXHUNTING HORSE** a horse used for foxhunting

foxhunting /fóks hunting/ *n.* a sport in which mounted hunters pursue a fox through open countryside with a pack of foxhounds

foxie /fóksi/ *n. Aus* = **fox terrier** (*informal*) [Early 20thC. Shortening.]

foxtail /fóks tayl/, **foxtail grass** *n.* a grass with soft cylindrical spikes resembling the tail of a fox. Genera: *Alopecurus Setaria* and *Hordeum.*

fox terrier *n.* a small wire-haired or smooth-haired dog belonging to a breed that has a white coat with dark markings

foxtrot /fóks trot/ *n.* **1.** DANCE **BALLROOM DANCE** a ballroom dance that alternates longer slower walking steps and shorter quicker running steps to music with four, or sometimes two, beats to the bar **2.** MUSIC **MUSIC FOR FOXTROT** a piece of music for dancing the foxtrot **3.** EQU **A HORSE'S SLOW TROTTING PACE** a slowish pace for a horse, between a trot and a walk, in which it takes short steps in a broken rhythm ■ *vi.* (**-trots, -trotting, -trotted**) **DANCE THE FOXTROT** to dance the foxtrot [Early 20th C. From the short steps of the fox; in the dance sense perhaps reinforced by the name of Harry *Fox*, a vaudeville performer.]

Foxtrot /fóks trot/ *n.* the Nato phonetic alphabet code word for the letter 'F', used in international radio communications

foxy /fóksi/ (**-ier, -iest**) *adj.* **1. LIKE A FOX** like a fox, especially in appearance or through having a strong pungent smell **2.** COLOURS **REDDISH-BROWN** of a reddish-brown colour, like the fur of the fox **3. CRAFTY** clever in a cunning or deceitful way **4.** *US* **ALLURING** sensually alluring (*informal*) **5.** PAPER **WITH DAMP SPOTS** discoloured with yellowish-brown spots of damp or mildew. US term **foxed 6.** WINE **SHARP OR MUSKY** having the rather sharp, pungent, or musky flavour of fox grapes

foyer /fóy ay, fwī ay/ *n.* **1. PUBLIC RECEPTION AREA** the reception area in a public building such as a hotel or theatre **2.** *US* **ENTRANCE HALL** the entrance hall or vestibule in a private house [Mid-19thC. Via French from medieval Latin *focarius*, from Latin *focus* 'fireplace, hearth' (see FOCUS).]

fpm *abbr.* feet per minute

FPO *abbr.* field post office

fps *abbr.* **1.** MEASURE feet per second **2. fps, f.p.s.** MEASURE foot-pound-second **3.** PHOTOGRAPHY frames per second

fps units, fps system of units *n.* a system of units based on the foot, second, and pound mass that is now almost wholly superseded by SI units

Fr *symbol.* francium

fr. *abbr.* **1.** fragment **2.** from

Fr. *abbr.* RELIG Father ■ *abbr.* France ■ *abbr.* **1.** French **2.** Friday **3.** Friar **4.** Frau **5.** franc

Fra /fraa/, **fra** *n.* used as a title for an Italian monk or friar, the equivalent of the English title 'Brother' [Late 19thC. From Italian, shortening of *frate* 'brother, friar', from Latin *frater* (source of English *fraternal*).]

fracas /frák aa/ (*plural* **-cas**) *n.* a noisy quarrel or fight [Early 18thC. From French, 'crash, roar', from, ultimately, Italian *fracassare* 'to cause an uproar'.]

fractal /frákt'l/ *n.* **REPEATING GEOMETRICAL PATTERN** an irregular or fragmented geometrical shape that can be repeatedly subdivided into parts, each of which is a smaller copy of the whole. Fractals are used in computer modelling of natural structures that do not have simple geometric shapes, e.g. clouds, mountainous landscapes, and coastlines. ■ *adj.* **OF FRACTALS** involving or relating to fractals [Late 20thC. From French, coined by the mathematician Benoît Mandelbrot from Latin *fract-*, the past participle stem of *frangere* (see FRACTION).]

fraction /fráksh'n/ *n.* **1.** MATH **NUMBER THAT IS NOT A WHOLE** a number that is not a whole number, such as $\frac{1}{2}$ (**vulgar fraction**) or 0.5 (**decimal fraction**), formed by dividing one quantity into another **2. SMALL AMOUNT** a small part, amount, or proportion of sth ○ *a fraction of the cost* **3. PART** a part or element of a larger whole or group **4.** CHEM **SEPARATED COMPONENT** an individual component or portion of a mixture, separated by differences in chemical or physical properties **5.** CHR **BREAKING OF BREAD BY PRIEST** during Holy Communion in the Roman Catholic tradition, the breaking off of a piece of bread by the priest who places it in the chalice [14thC. Via Old French from the late Latin stem *fraction-*, from Latin *fract-*, past participle stem of *frangere* 'to break'. Ultimately from an Indo-European base that is also the ancestor of English *break*.] ◇ **a fraction** by or over a very small amount or distance

WORD KEY: ORIGIN

The Latin *frangere*, from which ***fraction*** is derived, is also the source of English *fracture, fragile, fragment, frail,* and *saxifrage.*

fractional /frákshənəl/ *adj.* **1.** MATH **OF FRACTIONS** involving or relating to fractions **2. SLIGHT** very small or slight ○ *a fractional increase in temperature* **3.** CHEM **RELATING TO COMPONENT SEPARATION** relating to the process of separating individual components from a mixture on the basis of the chemical or physical properties that make them different from other components

fractional distillation *n.* the process of separating components that have different boiling points from a volatile liquid, by first heating the liquid and then condensing and collecting the components as they vaporize

fractionalize /fráksh'nə līz/ (**-izes, -izing, -ized**), **fractionalise** (**-alises, -alising, -alised**) *vt.* to divide sth into parts or sections —**fractionalization** /fráksh'nə lī záysh'n/ *n.*

fractionally /fráksh'nəli/ *adv.* very slightly, or to a very slight degree

fractionate /frákshə nayt/ (**-ates, -ating, -ated**) *v.* **1.** *vti.* **DIVIDE OR BREAK INTO PARTS** to divide or break, or to divide or break sth, into parts (*formal*) **2.** *vt.* CHEM **SEPARATE MIXTURE INTO ITS COMPONENTS** to separate a mixture into its components, e.g. by crystallization or distillation —**fractionation** /frákshə náysh'n/ *n.* —**fractionator** /frákshə naytər/ *n.*

fractious /frákshəss/ *adj.* irritable and likely to complain or misbehave [Late 17thC. Formed from FRACTION, originally perhaps in the sense 'disposed to break up relationships'.] —**fractiously** /frákshəssli/ *adv.* —**fractiousness** *n.*

fracture /frákchər/ *n.* **1. BREAK OF BONE** a break in a bone **2. ACT OF BREAKING STH** the act of breaking sth, especially a bone **3. BREAK OR CRACK** a break, split, or crack in an object or a material **4. SPLIT IN SYSTEM OR ORGANIZATION** a split or division in sth such as a system, organization, or agreement ○ *the fractures that are already starting to appear in the peace treaty* **5.** GEOL **ROCK BREAK** a break in a rock or mineral, across which there is a separation ■ *vti.* (**-tures, -turing, -tured**) **1. BREAK** to break or crack sth, especially a particular bone or a bone in a particular part of the body **2. CAUSE OR UNDERGO DAMAGE** to cause damage or disruption to sth or destroy it, or to be damaged, disrupted, or destroyed [Mid-16thC. Directly or via French from Latin *fractura*, from, ultimately, *frangere* 'to break' (see FRACTION).] —**fracturable** *adj.*

frae /fray/ *prep. Scotland* from [13thC. Variant of FRO.]

fraenum /fréenəm/ (*plural* **-nums** *or* **-na** /-nə/) *n.* a small fold of skin or membrane that limits the movement of an organ, especially the band of tissue connecting the tongue to the floor of the mouth [Mid-18thC. From Latin *frenum* 'bridle', from *frendere* 'to grind'.]

fragile /frájj īl/ *adj.* **1. EASILY BROKEN** easy to break, damage, or harm, usually because delicate or brittle ○ *The models were too fragile to be used as toys.* **2. EASILY DESTROYED** not strong, sound, or secure and unlikely to withstand any severe stresses and strains that may be put on it ○ *a fragile peace* **3. PHYSICALLY WEAK** in a weak or delicate bodily state, usually as a result of illness [15thC. Directly or via French from Latin *fragilis* (source also of English *frail*), from, ultimately, the same base as *frangere* 'to break' (see FRACTION).] —**fragilely** *adv.* —**fragility** /frə jílləti/ *n.*

WORD KEY: SYNONYMS

fragile, delicate, frail, flimsy, frangible, friable

CORE MEANING: easily broken or damaged

fragile used to describe things that do not have a strong structure or are not made of robust materials, and are therefore easily broken or damaged; **delicate** similar to 'fragile', used especially to talk about things that are beautiful or remarkable because of their fragility; **frail** used especially in written English to talk about sth easily broken or damaged. It is also used to talk about people who are so physically weak that they seem very vulnerable to injury; **flimsy** used showing disapproval to describe sth that is easily broken, torn, or damaged because it is badly or cheaply made. It can also be used to describe clothing that is light and insubstantial; **frangible** a formal or technical word meaning brittle or easily broken; **friable** a formal or technical word meaning likely or easy to crumble.

fragile-X syndrome *n.* a genetic condition caused by an abnormal X chromosome with an apparently almost detached part near the end of the long arm, that causes learning difficulties in boys and men

fragment *n.* /frágmənt/ **1.** BROKEN PIECE a piece, usually a small piece, broken off sth or left when sth is shattered **2.** INCOMPLETE PIECE an incomplete or isolated piece of sth ○ *I noted down fragments of the conversation.* ■ *vti.* /frag mént/ **(-ments, -menting, -mented) 1.** BREAK INTO SMALL PIECES to break, or break sth, into small pieces ○ *The metal is designed to fragment on impact.* **2.** BREAK UP to lose, or to cause sth to lose, a sense of unity or cohesion, with the result that sth splits into isolated and often conflicting elements ○ *Society is starting to fragment.* [Mid-16thC. Directly or via French from Latin *fragmentum*, from, ultimately, the same base as produced *frangere* 'to break' (see FRACTION).]

fragmental /frag mént'l/ *adj.* **1.** = **fragmentary 2.** GEOL MADE UP OF ROCK FRAGMENTS used to describe rocks that are made up of fragments of preexisting rocks

fragmentary /frágməntəri/ *adj.* consisting of the physical fragments of sth, or of small disconnected items that are usually insufficient to form a whole or serve a satisfactory purpose —**fragmentarily** *adv.*

fragmentation /frágmən táysh'n, -men-/ *n.* **1.** BREAKING UP OF STH the process of shattering or breaking up into fragments **2.** LOSS OF UNITY AND COHESION the loss of unity and cohesion and the breakup of sth into isolated and often conflicting elements ○ *The result, inevitably, would be social fragmentation.* **3.** SHATTERING OF EXPLOSIVE DEVICE the scattering of the shattered parts of a grenade or other explosive device **4.** COMPUT BREAKING UP OF DATA PACKET a process in which packets of computer data are broken up into smaller pieces for more efficient storage and transmission. The danger inherent in this process is that the relationship between the pieces may be lost.

fragmentation bomb *n.* a bomb or shell with a thick casing that is designed to shatter on detonation into many destructive fragments in order to cause maximum damage or injury

fragmentation grenade *n.* a grenade with a thick casing that is designed to shatter on detonation into many destructive fragments, causing maximum damage or injury

fragmented /frag méntid/ *adj.* made up of disconnected parts or elements and lacking overall coherence

fragmentize /frágmən tīz/ **(-tizes, -tizing, -tized)** *vti.* *US* = **fragment**

fragrance /fráygrənss/ *n.* **1.** NICE ODOUR a pleasant smell **2.** SWEETNESS OF SMELL the characteristic of being sweet-smelling **3.** PERFUME sth such as a perfume or cologne, which has a distinctive smell ○ *a great new fragrance for men*

WORD KEY: SYNONYMS

See Synonyms at ***smell***.

fragrance strip *n.* a sealed strip of card or paper included with sth such as a magazine advertisement and impregnated with a fragrance that is released when the cover is peeled off

fragrancy /fráygrənssi/ *n.* = **fragrance** *n.* 2

fragrant /fráygrənt/ *adj.* having a pleasant or sweet smell [15thC. Directly or via French from Latin *fragrant-*, the present participle stem of *fragrare* 'to emit a (good or bad) odour'.] —**fragrantly** *adv.*

fraidy-cat /fráydi-/ *n.* *US* = **scaredy-cat** [*Fraidy* formed from a shortening of AFRAID. *Cat* perhaps from that animal's generally skittish nature.]

frail /frayl/ **(frailer, frailest)** *adj.* **1.** WEAK in a weakened state or in bad health **2.** EASY TO BREAK OR DAMAGE made of weak or delicate materials and easy, or apparently easy, to break or damage **3.** INSUBSTANTIAL lacking any substantial foundation in fact or reality and unlikely to be realized or be successful ○ *frail hopes of success* **4.** MORALLY WEAK easily tempted and led into sin or wrongdoing [14thC. Via Old French *fraile* from Latin *fragilis* (see FRAGILE).] —**frailly** *adv.*

WORD KEY: SYNONYMS

See Synonyms at ***fragile*** and ***weak***.

frailty /fráylti/ (*plural* **-ties**) *n.* **1.** WEAKNESS physical weakness or weakness of materials and construction **2.** MORAL WEAKNESS inherent moral weakness in humanity or in an individual leading to difficulty in resisting temptation or avoiding wrongdoing **3.** CHARACTER FLAW a character flaw arising out of moral weakness (*often used in the plural*) ○ *ordinary human frailties*

fraise /frayz/ *n.* a cone-shaped grooved drill bit used for enlarging a previously drilled hole [Early 17thC. From French, literally 'abdominal lining of a calf'; from the numerous folds of this lining.]

Fraktur /frak to͝or/, **fraktur** *n.* a thick ornate style of printed letter, the standard typeface for all printing in German until around the middle of the 20th century [Late 19thC. Via German from, ultimately, Latin *fractura* (see FRACTURE). The underlying sense is that the elaborate shape of the letters seems to break up the words.]

Fra Mauro /fraá máwrō/ *n.* an eroded crater on the Moon north of Mare Nubium, approximately 95 km/59 mi. in diameter. Apollo 14 landed close to Fra Mauro in 1971.

framboesia /fram beézi ə/ *n.* MED = **yaws** [Early 19thC. From modern Latin, coined from French *framboise* 'raspberry'; from the shape and colour of the sores produced by the disease.]

frame /fraym/ *n.* **1.** SUPPORTING STRUCTURE an underlying or supporting structure that consists of solid parts such as beams or struts with spaces between them and that has sth built around or on top of it ○ *a bike with a steel frame* **2.** SURROUNDING STRUCTURE a structure that surrounds or encloses a particular space ○ *a picture frame* ○ *a door frame* **3. frame, frames** OPHTHALMOL LENS-HOLDING PART OF SPECTACLES the part of a pair of spectacles that holds the lenses and fits around the wearer's face **4.** PIECE OF EQUIPMENT a piece of equipment made of bars fitted together with spaces between, e.g. for children to climb on or to help a person to walk ○ *a child's climbing frame* **5.** CRAFT HOLLOW SHAPE FOR NEEDLECRAFTS AND PAINTING an open structure across which a piece of material can be stretched to be painted or embroidered, or across which threads can be stretched for weaving **6.** CONTEXT the general background or context against or within which sth takes place ○ *the story's historical frame* **7.** HUMAN BODY a person's body, especially with reference to its size and shape ○ *He eased his enormous frame into the chair.* **8.** CINEMA, PHOTOGRAPHY SINGLE PICTURE ON STRIP OF FILM any one of the individual pictures that make up a strip of cinema film, or a single exposure on a strip of photographic negative or slide images **9.** TV TV PICTURE the picture that appears on a television screen **10.** CINEMA, TV VISIBLE PART OF FILMED ACTION in film, video, or TV, the particular area of action that is captured by the camera and forms the rectangular image that appears on the screen ○ *characters moving out of the frame to the left* **11.** PHOTOGRAPHY IMAGE BORDER the border or set of borders of a projected image **12.** PUBL SINGLE PICTURE IN COMIC STRIP any one of the individual pictures that make up a comic strip **13.** GARDENING = **cold frame 14.** *US* BOWLS ROUND OF TEN-PIN BOWLING one of the 10 rounds in a ten-pin bowling game **15.** CUE GAMES GAME IN SNOOKER any one of the individual games that make up a match in snooker, billiards, and pool. US term **rack 16.** CUE GAMES TRIANGULAR TEMPLATE FOR SNOOKER BALLS a wooden triangle used to arrange the target balls into their required positions at the beginning of a game of snooker or pool. US term **rack 17.** CUE GAMES BALLS POSITIONED BY FRAME the target balls when in position for the start of a game of snooker or pool. US term **rack 18.** TELECOM, COMPUT SINGLE CYCLE OF PULSES a single cycle of pulses in a string of repeated pulses ■ *vt.* **(frames, framing, framed) 1.** MOUNT IN A FRAME to mount a picture in a frame **2.** FORM SURROUNDING FRAMEWORK FOR to form a surrounding border or a framework, especially a decorative or contrasting one, around sth (*often passive*) ○ *a delicate face framed by abundant black hair* **3.** CONSTRUCT IDEA OR STATEMENT to construct or compose sth that is to be written or spoken ○ *She framed her words carefully.* **4.** EXPRESS IN PARTICULAR WAY to express sth in a particular type of language ○ *framed the argument in legal language* **5.** MOUTH WORDS to mouth words silently **6.** CAUSE TO APPEAR GUILTY to make an innocent person appear guilty, e.g. by forging incriminating evidence (*slang*) **7.** ARRANGE RESULT IN ADVANCE to use dishonest or illegal methods to arrange the result of a contest in advance, e.g. by paying a player to lose deliberately (*slang*) ■ *adj.* CONSTR, ARCHIT WITH WOODEN FRAMEWORK constructed on a framework of wooden beams, then covered with boards or shingles ○ *a white frame house with black shutters* [Old English *framian* 'to make progress, be helpful', hence 'to prepare, shape'. Formed from *fram* 'forward' (related to modern English *from*). The noun developed from the verb, originally in the sense 'structure'.] —**frameable** *adj.* —**framer** *n.* ◇ **in the frame** among those who are involved in sth or under consideration for sth (*informal*)

Janet Frame

Frame /fraym/, **Janet** (*b.* 1924) New Zealand writer. Her novels, short stories, and autobiographical works include *To the Island* (1983) and *An Angel at My Table* (1984). Real name **Janet Paterson Frame Clutha**

frame of mind *n.* a person's psychological state, attitude, or mood at a particular time

frame of reference *n.* **1.** STANDARDS USED FOR JUDGING OR DECIDING the set of norms, values, or ideas that affect the way sb interacts with others, either in everyday life or in particular situations **2.** GEOM SET OF GEOMETRIC AXES a set of geometric axes used to determine the location of a point in space

frame story *n.* a narrative that provides the framework within which a number of different stories, which may or may not be connected, can be told. An example of a frame story is the pilgrims' ride to Canterbury, which provides the starting point for Chaucer's *Canterbury Tales.*

frame-up *n.* (*slang*) **1.** PLOT MAKING SB INNOCENT APPEAR GUILTY a conspiracy to make an innocent person appear guilty, e.g. by forging incriminating evidence **2.** DISHONEST PREARRANGING OF CONTEST RESULT a situation in which the result of a contest is dishonestly or illegally arranged in advance

framework /fráym wurk/ *n.* **1.** SYSTEM OF INTERCONNECTING BARS a structure of connected horizontal and vertical bars with spaces between them, especially one that forms the skeleton of another structure **2.** UNDERLYING SET OF IDEAS a set of ideas, principles, agreements, or rules that provides the basis or the outline for sth that is more fully developed at a later stage ○ *The purpose of this meeting is to provide a framework for the discussions at next week's conference.* **3.** CONTEXT the general background or context to a particular action or event ○ *within the framework of Jewish religious tradition* **4.** CRAFT ARTICLES WOVEN OR EMBROIDERED ON FRAME articles produced by weaving or embroidering cloth on a frame

framing /fráyming/ *n.* **1.** FRAMES frames or frameworks collectively **2.** WAY STH IS FRAMED the way that sth is framed **3.** CINEMA COMPOSITION OF FILM SCENE the composition of a scene within the visual field of the camera for shooting in a film **4.** CINEMA ADJUSTMENT OF FILM PROJECTOR SETTINGS adjustment of the settings on a film projector so that the image is in the correct position on the screen

franc /frangk/ n. **1.** UNIT OF FRENCH CURRENCY the basic unit of French currency, worth 100 centimes. See table at **currency 2.** FRANC COIN a coin worth a franc. Symbol **F** [14thC. From French, of uncertain origin: probably from the Latin phrase *Francorum rex* 'King of the Franks', imprinted on a type of gold coin first minted in 1360.]

France

France /fraanss/ republic and the largest country in western Europe. Its present constitution was established in 1958 with the proclamation of the Fifth Republic. Language: French. Currency: franc. Capital: Paris. Population: 58,609,285 (1997). Area: 543,965 sq. km/210,026 sq. mi. Official name **French Republic**

France /fraaNss/, **Anatole** (1844–1924) French writer. He produced a large body of writings, including novels, drama, verse, critical and philosophical essays, and historical works. He won the Nobel Prize in literature in 1921. Pseudonym of **Jacques Anatole François Thibault**

franchise /frán chīz/ n. **1.** COMM LICENCE TO SELL COMPANY'S PRODUCTS an agreement or licence to sell a company's products exclusively in a particular area, or to operate a business that carries that company's name **2.** RIGHT TO VOTE the right to vote, especially to elect representatives to a national legislature or a parliament **3.** PRIVILEGE GRANTED BY AUTHORITY a right or privilege, or an exemption from a duty or obligation, granted by a government or other authority **4.** COMM AREA OF COMMERCIAL OPERATION the area in which sb has a commercial franchise **5.** US SPORTS PROFESSIONAL TEAM a professional sports team that is a member of an organized league **6. franchise, franchise player** SPORTS VALUABLE PLAYER a player who is valuable and important to the team ■ vt. **(-chises, -chising, -chised)** GRANT TRADING FRANCHISE TO to grant a commercial franchise to a person or small company [14thC. From French, formed from *franc* 'free' (see FRANK).] —**franchisement** /-chiz-/ n.

franchisee /frán chī zeé/ n. a person or small company granted a licence to sell a company's products or operate under a company's name exclusively within a stated area

franchiser /frán chīzər/, **franchisor** /frán chīzər, -chī záwr/ n. a company that grants sb an exclusive licence to sell its products or operate under its name in a stated area

Francis I /fráanssiss/, **King of France** (1494–1547) French monarch. His reign (1515–47) was dominated by conflict with Charles V, Holy Roman Emperor.

Franciscan /fran sískən/ n. MEMBER OF RELIGIOUS ORDER a member of an order of friars and nuns, founded by St Francis of Assisi, that now has three separate branches and is largely devoted to missionary and charitable work ■ adj. RELATING TO ST FRANCIS OR FRANCISCANS relating to St Francis of Assisi, or to the religious order he founded [Late 16thC. Via French *franciscain* from modern Latin *Franciscanus*, from *Franciscus* 'Francis'.]

Francis of Sales /fráanss əv saál/, **St** (1567–1622) French churchman and writer. A leader of the Counter-Reformation, he became bishop of Geneva (1602).

francium /fránss i əm/ n. an unstable radioactive chemical element of the alkali-metal group, found in uranium ore and made artificially from actinium and thorium. Symbol **Fr** [Mid-20thC. Named after *France*, home of the element's discoverer.]

Francisco Franco

Franco /frángkō/, **Francisco** (1892–1975) Spanish general and authoritarian leader. He defeated the Republican army during the Spanish Civil War (1936–39) and established a dictatorship in Spain in 1939, ruling until his death in 1975.

Franco- prefix. France, French ○ *Francophile* [From late Latin *Francus* 'Frank', of Germanic origin]

Franconian /frang kốni ən/ n. GROUP OF MEDIEVAL GERMAN DIALECTS a group of medieval dialects of German that were spoken in an area stretching from present-day Bavaria and Alsace, and up the Rhine valley ■ adj. OF FRANCONIAN relating to the Franconian group of dialects

Francophile /frángkō fīl/, **Francophil** /-fil/ n. PERSON WHO LIKES FRANCE a person who likes France, the French people, and the French way of life ■ adj. LIKING FRANCE AND FRENCH liking or admiring France, the French, or the French way of life

Francophobe /frángkō fōb/ n. a person who dislikes France and the French people —**Francophobia** /frángkō fốbi ə/ n.

Francophobic /frángkō fốbik/ adj. having an intense dislike of France, French people, or the French way of life

Francophone /frángkō fōn/ n. SPEAKER OF FRENCH a person who speaks French, especially as his or her native language ■ adj. **1.** FRENCH-SPEAKING having French as his or her native or main language **2.** OF FRENCH-SPEAKING AREA relating to a place where French is used as the main language, the official language, or a lingua franca ○ *Francophone Africa* —**Francophonic** /frángkō fónnik/ adj.

frangible /fránjəb'l/ adj. capable of being broken or damaged [15thC. Directly or via Old French from medieval Latin *frangibilis*, from *frangere* 'to break' (see FRACTION).] —**frangibility** /fránjə bílləti/ n.

——— **WORD KEY: SYNONYMS** ———
See Synonyms at **fragile**.

frangipane /fránji payn/ n. an almond-flavoured cream or paste used in pastries, cakes, and other sweet foods [Mid-19thC. From French, 'frangipani'; from the bitter almonds used in making the perfume frangipani.]

Frangipani

frangipani /fránji pánni, -paáni/ (plural **-is**) n. **1.** TREES TREE WITH PERFUMED FLOWERS a tropical American deciduous tree with white, yellow, or pink flowers that have an extremely strong sweet perfume. Genus: *Plumeria*. **2.** PERFUME perfume made from the flowers of the frangipani tree, or in imitation of their scent **3.** COOK = **frangipane 4.** TREES AUSTRALIAN EVERGREEN TREE a small or medium-sized native Australian evergreen

tree found in eastern coastal forests, which has large fragrant cream or yellow flowers. Latin name: *Hymenosporum flavum*. [Mid-19thC. Named after Muzio *Frangipani*, an Italian marquis of the 16thC, who created a perfume for scenting gloves.]

Franglais /fróng glay/, **franglais** n. MIXTURE OF FRENCH AND ENGLISH an informal form of French that includes a liberal sprinkling of English loan words and phrases. For French traditionalists, it is a pejorative term, the concept seen as tangible evidence of the extent to which British and American cultural imperialism has permeated French and French-Canadian life. ■ adj. OF FRANGLAIS relating to Franglais [Mid-20thC. From French, blend of *français* 'French' and *anglais* 'English'.]

frank /frangk/ adj. **1.** EXPRESSING TRUE OPINION open, honest, and sometimes forceful in expressing true feelings and opinions **2.** OPEN AND BLUNT allowing people's true feelings and opinions to be openly and often bluntly stated **3.** PLEASINGLY HONEST having or showing an appealingly open and honest nature ○ *a frank manner that won her many friends* **4.** UNDISGUISED openly expressed, and so not concealed or disguised ○ *regarded him with frank loathing* ■ vt. **(franks, franking, franked)** MAIL **1.** PRINT MARK OVER STAMP to print an official mark over the stamp on a letter or parcel to show that payment has been formally accepted **2.** PRINT MARK TO SHOW POSTAGE PAID to print a mark on a piece of mail, instead of using a postage stamp, to show that postage has been paid or that there is no postage charge ■ n. MAIL **1.** OFFICIAL MARK ON PIECE OF MAIL an official mark printed on a piece of mail to show that postage has been paid or that postage is free of charge **2.** RIGHT TO FREE MAIL DELIVERY the right to have mailed items delivered free of charge [14thC. Via French, 'free, generous, candid' from medieval Latin *francus* 'Frank, free' (see FRANK); from the granting of full political freedom in Gaul only to the Franks.] —**frankness** n.

Frank n. a member of any of several Germanic peoples who originally lived along the Rhine valley, and spread westwards during the decline of the Roman Empire in the 4th century AD. They conquered vast areas of western Europe, taking over Gaul and becoming the dominant people in an area covering most of present-day western Germany. [Old English *Franca*. Later reinforced by French *Franc* and medieval Latin *Francus* (source of English *franc* and *frank*), from the same prehistoric Germanic ancestor.]

Anne Frank

Frank /frangk/, **Anne** (1929–45) German-born Dutch writer. She kept a diary during her years in hiding during the German occupation of the Netherlands (1942–44). She and her family were captured in 1944, and she died in a concentration camp.

Frankenstein /frángkən stīn/ n. **1.** CREATOR OF DESTRUCTIVE THING sb who creates sth that causes widespread ruin or destruction, or that brings about the creator's own downfall **2. Frankenstein, Frankenstein's monster** OUT-OF-CONTROL INVENTION a creation or invention that may get beyond its maker's control and cause problems ○ *Frankenstein food* **3.** MONSTER a monster in the shape of a very large coarse-featured person, often with features such as bolts in the neck and a shambling walk [Early 19thC. From the title of Mary Shelley's 1818 novel in which the hero creates a living man.]

Frankfurt[1] /frángk furt/, **Frankfurt am Main** /-am mín/ city in the state of Hessen, west-central Germany. Situated on the River Main, it is a major commercial and financial centre. Population: 656,200 (1994).

a at; aa father; aw all; ay day; air hair; ə about, edible, item, common, circus; e egg; ee eel; hw when; i it, happy; ī ice; 'l apple; 'm rhythm; 'n fashion; o odd; ō open; oo good; oo pool; ow owl; oy oil; th thin; th this; u up; ur urge;

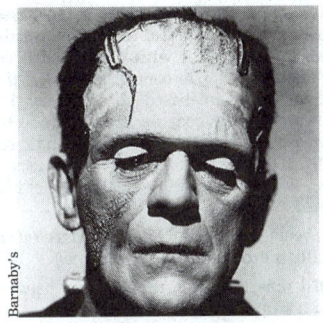

Frankenstein

Frankfurt[2], **Frankfurt an der Oder** /-an der ṓdər/ city east of Berlin on the River Oder, in Brandenburg State, northeastern Germany. Population: 87,863 (1989).

frankfurter /fráŋk furtər/, **frankfurt** /-furt/ *n.* a thin-skinned sausage, originally from Germany, that is made of finely minced smoked pork or beef and is often grilled, fried, or boiled [Late 19thC. From German *Frankfurter Wurst*, a smoked sausage first produced at Frankfurt am Main.]

frankincense /fráŋkin senss/ *n.* an aromatic gum or resin, often burned as an incense, especially in religious ceremonies, and also used in perfumes. It is obtained from an African tree. Latin name: *Boswellia sacra*. [14thC. From Old French *franc encens*, literally 'superior-quality incense'.]

Frankish /fráŋkish/ *n.* EXTINCT GERMANIC LANGUAGE an extinct ancient language spoken by the Franks, one of the West Germanic group of the Germanic branch of Indo-European languages. The French vocabulary shows a huge Frankish influence. ■ *adj.* **1.** OF FRANKS relating to or typical of the Franks, or their culture or language **2.** OF FRANKISH LANGUAGE relating to the Frankish language

Franklin /fráŋklin/ river in southwestern Tasmania, Australia. A popular whitewater rafting river, it rises on Mount Huge near Lake St Clair and flows southwards into the Gordon River. Length: 120 km/75 mi.

Aretha Franklin

Franklin, Aretha (b. 1942) US soul singer. Known as 'The Queen of Soul', she began her recording career in 1960. Her most famous recordings include 'Respect' (1967) and 'I Never' (1967). Full name **Aretha Louise Franklin**

Franklin, Sir John (1786–1847) British naval officer and explorer. He died during his fourth Arctic expedition, in which the Northwest Passage was discovered (1845).

franklinite /fráŋkli nīt/ *n.* a black weakly magnetic mineral of the spinel group, consisting of an oxide of iron, manganese, and zinc. Formula: $ZnFe_2O_4$. [Early 19thC. Named after *Franklin*, New Jersey, where it is found.]

frankly /fráŋkli/ *adv.* **1.** HONESTLY in an honest and sincere, and often in a blunt and forthright way, without trying to hide true feelings or opinions ○ *a number of personal questions that he answered remarkably frankly* **2.** INTRODUCING HONEST OPINION used to indicate that you are expressing an honest personal opinion, often a negative one ○ *Most of what she said was, frankly, a pack of lies.*

frantic /frántik/ *adj.* **1.** OUT OF CONTROL EMOTIONALLY in a state in which it is impossible to keep feelings or behaviour under control, usually through fear, worry, or frustration **2.** EXCITED, HURRIED, AND CONFUSED characterized by great haste and excitement and a lot of usually disorganized activity [Early 16thC. Via French *frénétique* from Latin *phreneticus* (see FRENETIC).] —**frantically** *adv.* —**franticness** *n.*

Franz-Josef Glacier /fránts jṓzəf-/ glacier in Westland National Park on the western coast of the South Island, New Zealand. Length: 11 km/7 mi.

Franz Josef Land /fránts jṓzəf-/ archipelago of about 100 small ice-covered islands in the Arctic Ocean, northwestern Russia, including Alexandra Land, George Land, Wilczek Land, and Graham Bell Island. Area: 20,700 sq. km/8,000 sq. mi.

frap /frap/ (**fraps, frapping, frapped**) *vt.* to tie sth down, or tie things together, with ropes [Mid-16thC. From Old French *fraper* 'to hit'.]

frappé /fráppay/ *adj.* BEVERAGES **CHILLED** chilled, or poured over crushed ice ■ *n.* **1.** BEVERAGES **ICED ALCOHOLIC DRINK** an alcoholic drink, especially a liqueur, served poured over crushed ice **2.** FOOD **COLD DESSERT** a dish consisting of fruit-flavoured water ice, served before a meal or as a dessert [Mid-19thC. From French, the past participle of *frapper* 'to hit, chill'.]

Fraser /fráyzər/ river in south-central British Columbia, Canada. It rises in the Rocky Mountains and empties into the Strait of Georgia, near Vancouver. Length: 1,370 km/850 mi.

Fraser, Dawn (b. 1937) Australian swimmer. She was the first woman to swim the 100 metres freestyle in under one minute, and the first swimmer to win three consecutive Olympic Golds in that event (1956, 1960, and 1964). Full name **Dawn Lorraine Fraser**

Fraser, Malcolm (b. 1930) Australian statesman. Elected as a member of Parliament for the Liberal Party in 1955, he served as prime minister of Australia from 1975 to 1983. Full name **John Malcolm Fraser**

Fraser, Neale Andrew (b. 1933) Australian tennis player. The winner of the 1960 Wimbledon men's singles title, he was the Australian Davis Cup team coach from 1970 to 1993.

Fraser, Peter (1884–1950) Scottish-born New Zealand statesman. A Labour Party politician, he served as prime minister of New Zealand from 1940 to 1949.

Fraser Island island off the coast of southern Queensland, Australia. It is the largest sand island in the world. Area: 1,662 sq. km/642 sq. mi.

frass /frass/ *n.* insect excrement or debris left behind by an insect or insect larva [Mid-19thC. From German, formed from *fressen* 'to eat, devour'.]

frat /frat/ *n.* US a fraternity at a college or university (*informal*) [Late 19thC. Shortening.]

fraternal /frə túrn'l/ *adj.* **1.** OF BROTHERS existing between brothers, or felt by one brother for another **2.** SHOWING FRIENDSHIP AND MUTUAL SUPPORT showing friendship and mutual support between people or groups that share the same interests or aims ○ *fraternal greetings* **3.** OF FRATERNITIES relating to or organized as a fraternity **4.** EMBRYOL FROM TWO SEPARATE OVA used to describe twins that have developed from two separate ova, rather than a single ovum [15thC. From medieval Latin *fraternalis*, from, ultimately, Latin *frater* 'brother'. Ultimately from the same Indo-European word as English *brother*.] —**fraternalism** *n.* —**fraternally** *adv.*

fraternity /frə túrnəti/ (*plural* **-ties**) *n.* **1.** PEOPLE WITH STH IN COMMON a group of people with sth in common, e.g. being in the same job or sharing the same pastime ○ *the banking fraternity* **2.** BROTHERLY LOVE brotherly love, or feelings of friendship and mutual support between people ○ *liberty, equality, and fraternity* **3.** SOCIETY FORMED FOR COMMON PURPOSE a group or society formed by people who share the same interests **4.** US SOCIETY FOR COLLEGE MEN a social society for men who are students at an American college or university, with a name consisting of individually pronounced Greek letters. ◊ **sorority** [14thC. Via French *fraternité* from Latin *fraternitas* from, ultimately, *frater* (see FRATERNAL).]

fraternize /fráttər nīz/ (**-nizes, -nizing, -nized**), **fraternise** (**-nises, -nising, -nised**) *vi.* to spend time with other people socially, especially people with whom you should not be friendly ○ *fraternizing with the enemy* [Early 17thC. Via French *fraterniser* from medieval Latin *fraternizare*, from, ultimately, Latin *frater* (see FRATERNAL).] —**fraternization** /fráttər nī záysh'n/ *n.* —**fraternizer** /fráttər nīzər/ *n.*

fratricide /fráttri sīd, fráytri-/ *n.* **1.** KILLING A BROTHER the crime in which sb kills his or her own brother **2.** KILLER OF BROTHER sb who kills his or her own brother [15thC. Via French from Latin *fratricida* 'brother-killer'.] —**fratricidal** /fráttri sīd'l, fráytri-/ *adj.*

Frau /frow/ *n.* used as a title, equivalent to 'Mrs' or 'Ms', before the name or professional title of a girl or an unmarried woman in German-speaking countries. Frau is also used as a courtesy title for some unmarried women, especially of senior status

fraud /frawd/ *n.* **1.** CRIME OF CHEATING PEOPLE the crime of obtaining money or some other benefit by deliberate deception **2.** SB WHO DECEIVES BY PRETENDING sb who deliberately deceives people by imitation or impersonation **3.** STH INTENDED TO DECEIVE sth that is intended to deceive people ○ *a story that was subsequently exposed as a fraud* [14thC. Via Old French *fraude* from the Latin stem *fraud-* 'cheating, fraud'.]

fraud squad *n.* the branches of the British police force that have special responsibility for investigating crimes of fraud

fraudster /fráwdstər/ *n.* sb who commits fraud

fraudulent /fráwdyoolənt/ *adj.* not honest, true, or fair, and intended to deceive people —**fraudulence** *n.* —**fraudulently** *adv.*

fraught /frawt/ *adj.* **1.** FULL OF full of or accompanied by problems, dangers, or difficulties ○ *an evening fraught with embarrassment* **2.** TENSE AND ANXIOUS full of, or expressing, nervous tension and anxiety ○ *looking fraught and close to tears* [14thC. From the past participle of obsolete English *fraught* 'to load with cargo', from Middle Dutch or Middle Low German *vrachten*.]

Fräulein /fróy līn, frów-/ *n.* used as a title, equivalent to 'Miss' or 'Ms', before the name or professional title of a girl or an unmarried woman in German-speaking countries, and also as a form of address

Fraunhofer lines /frównhófər-/ *npl.* narrow dark lines in the Sun's spectrum, caused mainly by absorption in the cooler outer layers of the Sun's atmosphere [Mid-19thC. Named after the German scientist, Joseph von *Fraunhofer* (1787–1826).]

fraxinella /fráksi néllə/ *n.* PLANTS = **gas plant** [Mid-17thC. From modern Latin, literally 'small ash tree', from Latin *fraxinus* 'ash'; from the shape of the leaves.]

fray[1] /fray/ *vti.* (**frays, fraying, frayed**) **1.** WEAR AWAY AND HANG IN THREADS to wear away the edge or surface of cloth or rope by friction, or to be worn away, causing threads to hang loose ○ *The jacket had frayed at the cuffs.* **2.** BECOME STRAINED OR STRAIN to become strained, causing irritability or anger, or to cause sb's nerves, temper, or patience to become strained ○ *Soon tempers would start to fray.* ■ *n.* WORN PART WITH LOOSE THREADS a worn area on cloth or rope, with loose threads showing [15thC. Via French *frayer* from Latin *fricare* 'to rub' (see FRICTION).]

fray[2] /fray/ *n.* **1.** ARGUMENT OR FIGHT an argument, quarrel, or fight ○ *Local newspapers were not slow to join the fray.* **2.** LIVELY ACTIVITY OR SITUATION an exciting, energetic, or stressful activity or situation ○ *back to the fray* [14thC. Shortening of AFFRAY.]

Fray Bentos /fray bén toss/ port and capital of Río Negro Department, western Uruguay, on the River Uruguay, approximately 282 km/175 mi. northwest of Montevideo. Population: 20,135 (1985).

frazil /fráyzil, frázzil/ *n.* ice that forms as small plates drifting in rapidly flowing water where it is too turbulent for pack ice to form [Late 19thC. From Canadian French *frasil*.]

frazzle /frázz'l/ *n.* **1.** EXHAUSTED STATE a state of complete emotional and physical exhaustion **2.** US FRAYED STATE a frayed or tattered condition ■ *vt.* (**-zles, -zling, -zled**) EXHAUST to tire sb out emotionally and physically [Early 19thC. Origin uncertain: probably a blend of FRAY[1] and FRIZZLE[1] or obsolete *fazle* 'to ravel'.] ◊ **to a frazzle 1.** into a state of complete emotional and physical exhaustion **2.** completely, especially until sth is thoroughly scorched, blackened, or charred

frazzled /frázz'ld/ *adj.* exhausted and in a very confused or irritable state (*informal*)

FRCM *abbr.* Fellow of the Royal College of Music

FRCO *abbr.* Fellow of the Royal College of Organists

FRCP *abbr.* Fellow of the Royal College of Physicians

FRCS *abbr.* Fellow of the Royal College of Surgeons

FRCVS *abbr.* Fellow of the Royal College of Veterinary Surgeons

freak[1] /freek/ *n.* **1.** STRIKINGLY UNUSUAL PERSON, ANIMAL, PLANT a person, animal, or plant that is strikingly unusual, and appears to be unique or occurs very rarely (*offensive in some contexts*) **2.** UNUSUAL OCCURRENCE a highly unusual or unlikely occurrence, often brought about by a unique or very rare combination of circumstances **3.** SB UNCONVENTIONAL sb who behaves unusually or has unusual tastes or habits (*informal insult*) **4.** FANATIC sb who is fanatical about sth (*informal*) ○ *a club for fitness freaks* **5.** DRUG USER an addict or user of a particular drug (*slang*) **6.** IMPULSE sth sb suddenly does or decides for no real reason ■ *adj.* HIGHLY UNUSUAL OR UNLIKELY highly unusual or unlikely, and often brought about by a unique or very rare combination of circumstances ■ *vti.* **(freaks, freaking, freaked) 1.** BECOME OR MAKE OVER-EMOTIONAL to become, or make sb, very nervous, upset, or angry (*informal*) ○ *She'll freak when she hears what she missed by not going with us.* **2.** DRUGS BEHAVE STRANGELY ON DRUGS to experience, or cause sb to experience, wild or irrational behaviour, sometimes accompanied by hallucinations or feelings of paranoia, often as a result of taking drugs (*slang*) [Mid-16thC. Origin uncertain: perhaps originally a dialect word, from Old English *frician* 'to dance'.]

freak[2] /freek/ **(freaks, freaking, freaked)** *vt.* to streak or spot sth with colour (*literary*) [Mid-17thC. Origin uncertain: perhaps an alteration of obsolete *freck* 'to dapple' (probably a shortening of FRECKLE), by association with STREAK.]

freaking /fréeking/ *adj.* *US* used euphemistically in place of *frigging* or *fucking* to indicate the intensity of the user's feelings towards sb or sth (*slang offensive*) [Late 20thC. Formed from FREAK[1].]

freakish /fréekish/ *adj.* **1.** VERY UNUSUAL extremely, disconcertingly, or ridiculously unusual (*offensive in some contexts*) ○ *a freakish accident* **2.** SUDDENLY VARIABLE tending to change suddenly and unpredictably ○ *freakish weather* —**freakishly** *adv.*

freak-out /fréek owt/, **freakout** *n.* **1.** EMOTIONAL OUTBURST an outburst of emotion or wild behaviour (*informal*) **2.** DRUG-INDUCED ATTACK OF PARANOIA a drug-induced bout of hallucination or paranoia, especially a frightening one (*slang*)

freaky /fréeki/ **(-ier, -iest)** *adj.* unusual, strange, or bizarre (*slang*) —**freakily** *adv.* —**freakiness** *n.*

freckle /frék'l/ *n.* BROWN SKIN SPOT a harmless small brownish patch on sb's skin, usually one of a cluster, that becomes larger and deeper in colour when the skin is exposed to the sun. Freckles are caused by the presence of larger melanin-containing cells in the basal layer of the skin. ■ *vti.* **(-les, -ling, -led)** MARK WITH FRECKLES to become marked with, or mark sth with, freckles [15thC. Alteration of obsolete *frecken* 'freckle', from Old Norse *freknur* 'freckles'.] —**freckly** *adj.*

Frederick II /frédrik/, **King of Prussia** (1712–86). Under his political and military leadership (1740–86), Prussia doubled in size and became a major European power. He gathered a circle of writers and musicians about him at his palace of Sans Souci. Known as **Frederick the Great**

Fredericton /frédriktən/ capital of New Brunswick Province, eastern Canada, situated in the south-central part of the province, on the St John River. Population: 46,500 (1996).

free /free/ *adj.* **(freer, freest) 1.** NOT REGULATED not controlled, restricted, or regulated by any external thing ○ *You are free to choose.* **2.** NOT A PRISONER not, or no longer, physically bound or restrained, e.g. as a prisoner or in slavery ○ *Once outside the prison walls he would be a free man.* **3.** NOT RESTRICTED IN RIGHTS not subject to censorship or control by a ruler, government, or other authority, and enjoying civil liberties ○ *It's a free country.* **4.** SELF-RULING not ruled by a foreign country or power **5.** DISREGARDING TRADITIONAL LIMITATIONS performed or written without being subjected to traditional conventions or restraints ○ *free verse* **6.** NOT AFFECTED BY STH STATED not subject to or affected by sth specified, especially sth undesirable ○ *drinking water that is free of contamination* ○ *free of charge* **7.** NOT CONTAINING STH not containing sth specified (*often used in combination*) ○ *a salt-free diet* **8.** COSTING NOTHING requiring no money to be paid ○ *Win a free meal for two.* **9.** NOT BUSY not busy or working, or time during which sb is not busy or working ○ *She'll be free in a moment.* **10.** NOT BEING USED not being used, or not already reserved or taken by sb else ○ *no free seats left* **11.** NOT ATTACHED not tied or attached to sth ○ *grabbed the free end of the rope* **12.** NOT BLOCKED not blocked or obstructed by anything ○ *allowing the free flow of electricity* **13.** NOT PHYSICALLY RESTRICTED not restricted by sth such as tight clothing, stiffness, or lack of space ○ *a layer of dirt interfering with the free movement of the mechanism* **14.** GIVING STH READILY giving or expending sth generously, or too readily ○ *They're very free with their advice.* **15.** NOT EXACT not following the original version of sth word for word or very precisely ○ *a free translation* **16.** OPEN AND HONEST spontaneous, open, and without awkwardness or reserve in speaking to or dealing with other people ○ *an appealingly free manner* **17.** CHEM NOT CHEMICALLY COMBINED not chemically combined with another substance **18.** PHYS NOT ATTACHED TO LARGER BODY not permanently attached to a larger body such as an atom or molecule, and thus having a relatively wide range of movement **19.** NAUT FAVOURABLE favourable to sailing ○ *a free wind* **20.** LING ABLE TO BE USED ALONE used to describe a unit of meaning (**morpheme**) that can be used on its own as a word, rather than needing to be part of another word. ◊ **bound**[4] ■ *adv.* WITHOUT COST without paying any money ○ *They let you in free if you show your student card.* ■ *vt.* **(frees, freeing, freed) 1.** RELEASE FROM CAPTIVITY to release sb from physical bonds or restrictions, captivity, or slavery ○ *The defendants were freed after having been found not guilty.* **2.** RID OF STH to remove a restriction, a burden, or an unwanted or undesirable thing from sb or sth ○ *freed from the responsibilities of high public office* **3.** MAKE AVAILABLE OR ENABLE to make sb or sth available for use or able to do sth ○ *This should free you to do more of your own research.* **4.** UNCLOG STH OBSTRUCTED to clear sth of an obstruction [Old English *freo*. Ultimately from an Indo-European word meaning 'dear, beloved', which is also the ancestor of English *friend*.] —**freeness** *n.* ◇ **for free** without paying ◇ **make free with sb** to behave in too familiar and informal a way towards sb ◇ **make free with sth** to use sth in an overfamiliar or overindulgent way, without showing respect or restraint

WORD KEY: USAGE

See Usage note at ***gift***.

free up *vt.* **1.** MAKE AVAILABLE to make available for use sth that is currently occupied, otherwise employed, or subject to a restriction ○ *I need to free up some space on my hard disk.* **2.** LOOSEN OR UNJAM to enable sth that is tightly fastened, jammed, or blocked to move freely (*informal*)

free agent *n.* **1.** SB ABLE TO ACT FREELY sb who is not responsible to or for anyone else and can do as he or she pleases **2.** *US* UNATTACHED PROFESSIONAL PLAYER a professional athlete who is in a position to sign a contract to play for any team

free alongside ship *adj., adv.* COMM with the cost of delivery to the quayside included, but not the cost of loading onto a ship

free association *n.* **1.** SPONTANEOUS EXPRESSION OF THOUGHTS the spontaneous and uncensored expression of thoughts or ideas, allowing each one to lead to or suggest the next **2.** PSYCHOANAL TECHNIQUE FOR EXPLORING THE UNCONSCIOUS in psychoanalysis, a technique for exploring a patient's unconscious by stimulating the spontaneous and uncensored expression of thoughts or feelings through the use of stimuli such as key words —**free-associate** *vi.*

freebase /frée bayss/ *v.* **(-basing, -based, -based) 1.** *vt.* PREPARE COCAINE FOR SMOKING to prepare cocaine for smoking by heating it with water and a volatile liquid such as ether to concentrate it **2.** *vti.* SMOKE COCAINE to smoke freebased cocaine (*slang*) ■ *n.* CONCENTRATED COCAINE cocaine that has been concentrated using water and a volatile liquid such as ether [From the idea that the concentrated cocaine base of the original mixture is 'freed' in the process of treatment with ether]

freebie /fréebi/ *n.* sth given or obtained free of charge, especially a promotional gift (*informal*)

freeboard /frée bawrd/ *n.* the distance between the deck of a ship and the level of the water

freeboot /frée boot/ **(-boots, -booting, -booted)** *vi.* to live off things stolen or plundered [Late 16thC. Back-formation from FREEBOOTER.]

freebooter /frée bootər/ *n.* sb who lives by plundering others, especially a pirate [Late 16thC. From Dutch *vrijbuiter*, literally 'sb who takes booty freely' (source also of English *filibuster*).]

freeborn /frée bawrn/ *adj.* **1.** BORN AS FREE CITIZEN born as a free citizen, rather than in slavery or serfdom **2.** RELATING TO FREE CITIZENS relating to or intended for people who are freeborn

Free Church *n.* a Protestant church free from state control in running its affairs, having separated from the church established as the official church of the state

free climbing *n.* mountain or rock climbing without aids such as spikes and ladders, though usually with ropes and other safety equipment

freedman /-mən, -men/ (*plural* **-men**) *n.* a man who has been freed from slavery

freedom /fréedəm/ *n.* **1.** ABILITY TO ACT FREELY a state in which sb is able to act and live as he or she chooses, without being subject to any, or to any undue, restraints and restrictions ○ *live in freedom* **2.** RELEASE FROM CAPTIVITY OR SLAVERY release or rescue from being physically bound, or from being confined, enslaved, captured, or imprisoned ○ *hostages enjoying their first taste of freedom for months* **3.** COUNTRY'S RIGHT TO SELF-RULE a country's right to rule itself, without interference from or domination by another country or power **4.** RIGHT TO ACT OR SPEAK FREELY the right to speak or act without restriction, interference, or fear ○ *were given the freedom to take photographs and interview workers* **5.** ABSENCE OF STH UNPLEASANT the state of being unaffected by, or not subject to, sth unpleasant or unwanted ○ *Freedom from want or fear is one of society's four principal freedoms.* **6.** EASE OF MOVEMENT the ability to move easily without being limited by sth such as tight clothing or lack of space ○ *Releasing the catch allows complete freedom of movement in all directions.* **7.** RIGHT TO TREAT PLACE AS OWN the right to use or occupy a place and treat it as your own ○ *In the closed season, we had the freedom of the whole house and the beach.* **8.** HONORARY CITIZENSHIP citizenship of a town or city, together with special privileges, formally awarded to sb as an honour **9.** FRANKNESS openness and friendliness in speech or behaviour **10.** EXCESSIVE CONFIDENCE OR FAMILIARITY overconfidence, overfamiliarity, or a lack of proper restraint or decorum **11.** PHILOS FREE WILL the ability to exercise free will and make choices independently of any external determining force

Freedom Charter *n.* *S Africa* a document setting out the basic rights of all South Africans, composed in 1955 in opposition to the Nationalist government, and constituting the manifesto of the African National Congress

freedom fighter *n.* sb who participates in an armed revolution against a government or political system regarded as unjust

freedom march *n.* an organized march by people campaigning for civil rights, e.g. any of the marches that took place in the United States in the 1960s aimed at ending racial segregation —**freedom marcher** *n.*

freedom rider *n.* a civil rights activist who, during the early 1960s, joined one of the interracial groups riding on buses through parts of the southern United States to protest against racial segregation

freedwoman /freed woomən/ (plural -en /-wimin/) n. HIST a woman who has been freed from slavery

free electron n. an electron that is not bonded to an atom or molecule and so is free to move under external electric or magnetic fields

free energy n. a measure of the capacity of a system to do work, or a measure of the likelihood of a particular chemical reaction to form products. Symbol *G*

free enterprise n. the doctrine or practice of giving business the freedom to trade and make a profit without government control

free fall, free-fall n. 1. DESCENT WITH UNOPENED PARACHUTE a descent through the air with an unopened parachute as the first part of a parachute jump 2. RAPID DECLINE a sudden, rapid, and uncontrollable decline or descent in a particular system ○ *The news sent the stock market into a free fall.* 3. PHYS UNRESTRICTED MOVEMENT IN GRAVITATIONAL FIELD an ideal state in which the only force to which sth is subjected is the earth's gravitational attraction. A craft in space, e.g., is subject only to a diminished gravitational force and is not restricted by buoyancy or air resistance, producing near weightlessness.

free-fall (free-falls, free-falling, free-fell, free-fallen) vi. 1. DESCEND WITH UNOPENED PARACHUTE to descend towards the ground with an unopened parachute during the first part of a parachute jump 2. DROP SUDDENLY to undergo a sudden sharp drop in value, popularity, or credibility

free flight n. the movement of a rocket or missile through the air after its engine has stopped

free-floating adj. not committed or dedicated to one particular thing, especially a political party or cause

free-floating anxiety n. PSYCHOANAL a state of anxiety that is not associated with any specific event or external condition

Freefone /free fon/ tdmk. a trademark for a phone system in which the holder of the phone number pays the cost of the call, rather than the caller

free-for-all n. a disorganized argument, contest, or fight, usually with everybody present joining in (*informal*)

free form n. a shape, especially a piece of sculpture, that is asymmetrical and irregular though usually with a flowing outline

freeform /free fawrm/ adj. 1. WITH FLOWING SHAPES OR OUTLINES unconventional in shape or design, especially flowing and curving as opposed to regular or geometrical 2. ORIGINAL, NOT STANDARD spontaneously or individually created, rather than being produced in accordance with accepted or prescribed standards

free hand n. complete freedom to take action or make decisions

freehand /free hand/ adj., adv. done by hand and without using drawing instruments such as rulers or compasses

freehold /free hold/ n. 1. LEGAL OWNERSHIP OF PROPERTY legal ownership of a property giving the owner unconditional rights, including the right to grant leases and take out mortgages 2. FREEHOLD PROPERTY a property that has freehold status

freeholder /free holdər/ n. a property owner who has a freehold

free house n. a pub that is not owned by a particular brewery and so is free to sell whatever beers and other products it chooses

free jazz n. a style of jazz, developed in the 1960s, that has no set harmonies or melodic patterns

free kick n. in football, a kick of a stationary ball for an infringement by opponents, who must stand at least 10 yards from where the kick is taken. A goal can be scored by a player taking a direct free kick, whereas an indirect free kick requires that the ball touch another player before entering the goal.

free labour n. workers who do not belong to any trade union

freelance /free laanss/ n. 1. freelance, freelancer sb WORKING FOR DIFFERENT COMPANIES a self-employed person working, or available to work, for a number of employers, rather than being committed to one, and usually hired for a limited period 2. MAVERICK sb, especially a politician, who is not committed to any group and takes action or forms alliances independently 3. freelance, free lance HIST MEDIEVAL MERCENARY a mercenary soldier in medieval Europe ■ adj. WORKING AS A FREELANCE working or earning a living as a freelance ■ adv. AS A FREELANCE independently, as a freelance ○ *worked freelance as a journalist* ■ vi. (-lances, -lancing, -lanced) WORK AS A FREELANCE to work independently as a freelance [Early 19thC. From the idea of a medieval knight with a lance offering his services to whoever was willing to pay.]

free-living adj. BIOL able to live or move independently, rather than being parasitic, symbiotic, or sessile ○ *free-living organisms*

freeload /free lod/, free lod/ (-loads, -loading, -loaded) vi. to live shamelessly on sb else's generosity or hospitality, never sharing costs or responsibilities (*informal*) [Mid-20thC. Back-formation from FREELOADER.] —**freeloading** /free loding/ n.

freeloader /free lodər/ n. sb who lives on sb else's generosity or hospitality without sharing costs or responsibilities (*informal*) [Mid-20thC. Originally US truckers' slang for sb who had goods carried along with sb else's cargo at no charge.]

free love n. sexual relationships without marriage or any commitment to a single partner, especially as practised by the 19th- and early-20th-century avant garde and in the 1960s

free lunch n. sth given free and with nothing expected in return (*informal*) [From the expression 'There's no such thing as a free lunch', implying that recompense is always eventually exacted for an apparent act of selfless generosity]

freely /free li/ adv. 1. WITHOUT RESTRICTIONS without restrictions, controls, or limits ○ *able to move freely from country to country* 2. IN LARGE AMOUNTS in large or generous quantities ○ *Conversation flowed freely all night.* 3. OPENLY honestly and openly ○ *felt able to speak freely about his ordeal for the first time* 4. WITHOUT TIGHTNESS OR STIFFNESS without being restricted by sth such as tight clothing, stiffness, or lack of space ○ *clothes that allowed him to move more freely* 5. USED TO EMPHASIZE HONESTY used to persuade others that sb is being open and honest by accepting criticism ○ *I freely admit that mistakes were made.*

freeman /free mən/ (plural -men /-mən/) n. 1. HIST MAN NOT ENSLAVED a man who is not enslaved or not in serfdom 2. MAN GIVEN FREEDOM OF A PLACE a man who has been formally given citizenship of a place, together with various special privileges, as an honour ○ *a freeman of the city*

Freeman /free mən/, **Cathy** (b. 1973) Australian sprinter. The first Aboriginal sprinter to win a gold medal at the Commonwealth Games (1994), she went on to win a silver medal in the 400 metres at the 1996 Olympic Games. Full name **Catherine Astrid Salome Freeman**

free market n. an economic system in which businesses operate without government control in matters such as pricing and wage levels —**free-market** adj. —**free-marketeer** n.

freemartin /free martin/ n. a sterile female twin born with a male calf [Late 17thC. Origin uncertain: perhaps from FREE + Irish *mart* 'cow'.]

freemason /free mayssən/ n. a member of an organization of skilled stonemasons travelling from place to place in medieval Europe [14thC. Origin uncertain: perhaps from the fact that such masons worked without restriction by guilds.]

Freemason n. a member of a worldwide society of men, the Free and Accepted Masons, that is known particularly for its charitable work and for its secret rites

Freemasonry /free mayss'nri/ n. 1. PRACTICES OF FREEMASONS the institutions, beliefs, and practices of the Freemasons 2. Freemasonry, freemasonry INSTINCTIVE UNDERSTANDING AND COMRADESHIP an instinctive understanding and comradeship amongst people with sth in common

freenet /free net/ n. an online computer information network or service that charges low or no access fees and is often run by volunteers as a public service

free on board adj., adv. with the cost of delivery to a port and loading onto a ship included

free on rail adj., adv. with the cost of delivery to a railway station and loading onto a train included

free port n. 1. PORT OPEN TO ALL SHIPPING a port open to commercial ships from all countries on equal terms 2. DUTY-FREE ZONE a zone, connected to a port or airport, that allows the duty-free import of goods that are to be re-exported

free radical n. a highly reactive atom or group of atoms with an unpaired electron

free-range adj. 1. NOT CAGED free to move about and feed at will, rather than being confined in a battery or pen ○ *free-range chickens* 2. FROM FREE-RANGE ANIMALS produced by free-range poultry or livestock ○ *free-range eggs*

free rein n. complete freedom to make decisions and take action without consulting anyone else

free ride n. sth obtained at no cost or with no effort

free settler n. Aus a settler who emigrated to Australia through choice, rather than being transported as a convict

freesheet /free sheet/ n. a free newspaper or news sheet, especially one delivered to all the households in a particular area and funded by advertising

Freesia

freesia /free zhə, free zi ə/ n. a plant native to southern Africa, popular for its clusters of fragrant flowers in a variety of bright colours. Genus: *Freesia*. [Late 19thC. Named after Friedrich H. T. *Freese*, German physician.]

free skating n. competitive ice skating in which the skater makes up his or her own programme from a list of approved moves

free soil n. US those states in the United States in which slavery was prohibited before the American Civil War. ◊ **Free State**

free-soil adj. US HIST that prohibited slavery or opposed its extension to other states in the time before the American Civil War (*refers to states in the United States*)

free space n. a region in which there is no matter and no gravitational or electromagnetic fields

free speech n. the right to express any opinion publicly

free spirit n. sb who lives the way he or she wants to, regardless of what convention dictates or what others expect

free-spoken adj. expressing opinions frankly, without worrying about embarrassing or offending others

freestanding /free standing/ adj. 1. NOT FIXED TO A SUPPORT standing alone, and not fixed to a wall, floor, or other structure for support 2. GRAM GRAMMATICALLY INDEPENDENT grammatically independent and able to function as a main clause

Free State n. 1. US NONSLAVE STATE OF PRE-CIVIL WAR UNITED STATES any one of the US states that prohibited slavery before the American Civil War. ◊ **free soil** 2. S Africa S AFRICAN PROVINCE a province of South Africa, in the centre of the country, north of the Orange River. Former name **Orange Free State** 3. HIST IRISH FREE STATE the Irish Free State

freestone /frée stōn/ *n.* **1.** BUILDING **STONE THAT CUTS WITHOUT BREAKING** a variety of masonry stone that has a uniform texture and can be chiselled without breaking or splitting, e.g. limestone or fine sandstone **2.** FOOD **FRUIT STONE** a stone to which the flesh of a fruit does not cling, or any fruit that has such a stone

freestyle /frée stīl/ *adj.* **1.** SPORTS **WITH FREE CHOICE OF STYLE** in which each competitor may use a style of his or her own choosing (*refers to a sporting event*) **2.** SWIMMING **USING FRONT CRAWL** in which the competitors use the fastest swimming stroke, the front crawl stroke (*refers to a swimming contest*) **3.** WRESTLING **NO-HOLDS-BARRED** in which all legal holds and tactics are allowed (*refers to a wrestling style*) ■ *n.* SPORTS **FREESTYLE CONTEST** a freestyle race or event —**freestyler** *n.*

free-swimming *adj.* able to swim about freely, as opposed to living attached to sth or in one position ○ *free-swimming larvae*

freet /freét/ *n. Ireland* a superstition [Mid-16thC. From Old Norse *frett* 'news, inquiry, augury'.]

freethinker /free thíngkər/ *n.* sb who refuses to accept established views or teachings, especially on religion, and forms opinions as a result of independent inquiry —**freethinking** *adj., n.*

free thought *n.* thinking that does not recognize the authority of, and is unrestricted by, established views or teachings, especially in religious matters

free throw *n.* in basketball, an opportunity to shoot at the basket unhindered by the opposing players, awarded to a player who has been fouled

Freetown /frée town/ capital, largest city, and chief port of Sierra Leone, on the western coast of Africa. Founded in 1787 as a settlement for freed slaves, it became the capital when Sierra Leone gained independence in 1961. Population: 470,000 (1994).

free trade *n.* international trade that is not subject to protective regulations or tariffs intended to restrict foreign imports —**free-trader** *n.*

free verse *n.* verse without a fixed metrical pattern, usually having unrhymed lines of varying length

free vote *n.* a vote in the British parliament or any similar body, in which members may vote according to their consciences and personal opinions rather than as instructed by their party leaders

freeware /frée wair/ *n.* any computer programme or application that is available at no cost to the user

freeway /frée way/ *n.* **1.** *US, Can, Aus* **SUPERHIGHWAY** a limited-access road usually consisting of three lanes for vehicles moving in both directions, intended for travelling relatively fast over long distances **2.** *US* **TOLL-FREE ROAD** a road that can be used without paying a toll

free-weight *n.* a weight such as a dumbbell or barbell that is used for lifting exercises and is not attached to any other piece of apparatus

freewheel /free weél/ *vi.* (**-wheels, -wheeling, -wheeled**) **1. TRAVEL WITHOUT USING POWER** to continue moving on a bicycle or in a vehicle without using power to drive the wheels ○ *Once you get to the top, you can freewheel all the way down the other side.* **2. LIVE IN CAREFREE WAY** to live or act without conventional constraints, purpose, or regard for responsibilities ■ *n.* **1. DEVICE ON BICYCLE** a mechanism in the hub of the rear wheel of a bicycle that enables the rear wheel to continue to rotate when the rider stops pedalling **2.** AUTOMOT **DEVICE IN MOTOR VEHICLE TRANSMISSION** a mechanism in the transmission of a motor vehicle that disengages the drive shaft and allows it to rotate freely when revolving at a higher speed than the engine shaft

freewheeling /free weéling/ *adj.* **1. TRAVELLING WITHOUT POWER** continuing to move without the use of power **2.** *US, Can* **CAREFREE** without conventional constraints, purpose, or regard for responsibilities ○ *led a freewheeling life of travel and adventure* **3.** *US, Can* **UNSTRUCTURED** not restricted by rules, formal structure, or established procedures ○ *a freewheeling discussion that touched on many topics* **4.** TRANSP **WITH A FREEWHEEL** relating to, having, or using a freewheel mechanism on a bicycle or vehicle

free will *n.* the ability to act or make choices as a free and autonomous being and not solely as a result of compulsion or predestination ◇ **of your own free will** without being forced by sb or sth else

freewill /frée wil/ *adj.* done willingly rather than by compulsion

free world *n.* the countries of the world with democratic governments and capitalist or moderately socialistic economic systems, as opposed to those with totalitarian or Communist governments or economic systems

freeze /freez/ *v.* (**freezes, freezing, froze** /frōz/, **frozen** /frṓz'n/) **1.** *vti.* CHEM **TURN LIQUID TO SOLID THROUGH COLD** to be changed, or cause liquid to change, into a solid by the loss of heat, especially to change water into ice ○ *Salt water freezes at a lower temperature than fresh water.* **2.** *vti.* **COVER OR BECOME COVERED WITH ICE** to become covered, or cause the surface of sth to be covered, with ice ○ *The lake froze for only the second time in living memory.* **3.** *vti.* **BLOCK OR BECOME BLOCKED WITH ICE** to become blocked, or cause sth to become blocked, with ice ○ *Do you think it's cold enough to freeze the pipes in the attic?* **4.** *vti.* **BECOME HARD** to harden, or cause sth to harden, through the effects of cold or frost ○ *We couldn't play because the ground was frozen solid.* **5.** *vti.* **STICK TO STH BECAUSE OF COLD** to become, or cause sth to become, fixed or stuck to sth else as a result of cold ○ *The wipers were frozen to the windscreen.* **6.** *vt.* **PRESERVE WITH EXTREME COLD** to preserve sth, especially food, by subjecting it to and storing it at a temperature well below freezing point ○ *Store airtight up to two weeks or freeze.* **7.** *vti.* **FEEL VERY COLD** to feel, or cause sb to feel, extremely cold ○ *They left us to freeze outside, while they went into the house.* **8.** *vti.* **BE HARMED OR KILLED BY COLD** to be harmed or killed, or harm or kill sb or sth, with cold or frost **9.** *vi.* **DROP TO FREEZING POINT** to be at or fall to a temperature at or below freezing point ○ *The forecast says it's likely to freeze again tonight.* **10.** *vti.* **STOP MOVING** to stop, or cause sb to stop and remain still, e.g. as a result of fear or surprise or as part of a game ○ *A loose floorboard creaked in the passage; Jenny froze.* **11.** *vi.* **COME TO A STANDSTILL THROUGH SHOCK** to become unable to act, react, or speak in a normal way, usually through fear or shock ○ *I was OK in rehearsals, but in front of an audience, I simply froze.* **12.** *vt.* **TREAT ICILY** to discourage or intimidate sb by behaving in an unfriendly or hostile way ○ *She froze him with an icy glare.* **13.** *vt.* **HALT STH BEFORE COMPLETION** to halt or limit the development or production of sth ○ *The talks remain frozen at the procedural stage.* **14.** *vt.* **KEEP AT PRESENT LEVEL** to fix sth such as prices, rents, or wages at a particular level, usually by government action to prevent an increase ○ *Interest rates were frozen at their 1996 level.* **15.** *vt.* **KEEP ASSET FROM DISAPPEARING** to prevent a financial asset from being sold or liquidated ○ *They froze her bank account* **16.** *vt.* **PROHIBIT** to stop the manufacture, sale, or use of sth **17.** *vi.* **BECOME UNFRIENDLY** to become suddenly unfriendly and uncommunicative ○ *When I asked him about campaign contributions, he simply froze, and I couldn't get anything out of him for the rest of the interview.* **18.** *vt.* MED **ANAESTHETIZE BODY PART** to anaesthetize part of sb's body with a local anaesthetic (*informal*) **19.** *vt.* CINEMA, VIDEO **STOP FILM AT PARTICULAR FRAME** to stop a moving film at a particular frame and show that frame as a still image **20.** *vt.* **CAPTURE INSTANT OF MOVEMENT** to produce a still photographic image of sb or sth in movement or action ○ *He pressed the Pause button, freezing her delighted expression.* ■ *n.* **1.** METEOROL **VERY COLD WEATHER** a period when the temperature drops and stays below freezing point especially for a long time **2. RESTRICTION ON STH** a restrictive measure that prevents sth such as prices, wages, or production from rising above a particular level ○ *a temporary freeze on imports* ■ *vi.* (**freezes, freezing, froze** /frōz/, **frozen** /frṓz'n/) to stop responding (*refers to computers*) ○ *The screen freezes whenever I attempt to save a document.* [Old English *frēosan*. Ultimately from an Indo-European word meaning 'to freeze, burn', which was also the ancestor of English *frost* and *prurient*.]

freeze out *vt.* to exclude sb from participation in sth by cold or unfriendly treatment ○ *We feel we are being frozen out of the negotiations.*

freeze up *v.* **1.** *vi.* **BECOME FROZEN AND BLOCKED** to become blocked with ice **2.** *vt.* **PREVENT FROM MOVING BECAUSE OF ICE** to hold sth fast in ice so that it cannot move (*usually passive*) ○ *The ship was frozen up in the Arctic for three months.*

freeze-dry *vt.* to preserve sth, especially food, by first freezing it, then placing it in a vacuum to remove moisture before returning it to room temperature. The low processing temperature and absence of liquid water help to retain colour, flavour, and texture. —**freeze-dried** *adj.* —**freeze-drying** *n.*

freeze-etching *n.* SCI the preparation of a specimen for examination by an electron microscope by freezing and fracturing it so that its internal structure can be seen and a replica made of it

freeze-frame *n.* **1. FRAME OF FILM VIEWED SINGLY** a single frame of a film or video recording viewed as a static image **2.** VIDEO **DEVICE ALLOWING VIEWING OF SINGLE FRAME** a device on a video recorder that enables a single static image to be viewed ■ *vt.* **PRESENT AS STATIC IMAGE** to present sth contained in a single frame from a film or video recording as a static image

freezer /freézər/ *n.* a storage cabinet, compartment, or room, where food or other perishable goods can be frozen and preserved at a very low temperature

freezer burn *n.* the pale dry spots that form when moisture evaporates from frozen food that is inadequately wrapped

freeze-up *n.* a period of extremely cold weather

freezing /freézing/ *adj.* **VERY COLD** extremely cold ■ *n.* **FREEZING POINT** the freezing point of water

freezing mixture *n.* a mixture of substances, usually ice and salt, used in laboratories to produce a temperature below the freezing point of water

freezing point *n.* the temperature at which a liquid solidifies, e.g. the temperature at which water turns to ice

free zone *n.* an area at a port or in a city where goods may be received or stored without payment of customs duties

F region *n.* the highest part of the ionosphere that reflects high-frequency radio waves. It is divided into two layers, the F_1 that extends upwards from 180 km/112 mi. and is present only during the day, and the F_2 extending upwards from 300km/186 mi.

Freiburg /frī burg/ city and tourist centre in Baden-Württemberg State, southwestern Germany. It is the cultural and economic centre of the Black Forest. Population: 197,800 (1994).

freight /frayt/ *n.* **1. GOODS FOR TRANSPORT** goods or cargo carried by a commercial means of transport **2. COMMON CLASS OF TRANSPORT** the ordinary method or class of commercial transport for goods, slower and cheaper than express **3. CHARGE FOR CARRYING GOODS** a charge paid for the transport of goods **4.** *US* = **freight train 5. BURDEN** a load or burden (*literary*) ■ *vt.* (**freights, freighting, freighted**) **1. TRANSPORT GOODS** to send or transport goods or cargo by commercial carrier **2. LOAD TRANSPORT WITH CARGO** to load a ship, train, aircraft, or vehicle with goods or cargo to be transported **3.** SHIPPING **HIRE OR HIRE OUT SHIP** to hire or hire out a ship to transport goods and passengers **4. FILL OR BURDEN** to load sth said or done with sth such as significance or emotion, or to burden sb or sth with a feeling or emotion (*literary; usually passive*) [15thC. From Middle Low German or Middle Dutch *vrecht*, a variant of *vracht* (source of English *fraught*).]

freightage /fráytij/ *n.* **1. TRANSPORT CHARGE** a charge paid for the transport of goods or cargo **2. COMMERCIAL CARRIAGE OF GOODS** the commercial transport of goods or cargo **3. GOODS CARRIED** the goods that are carried by a particular ship or vehicle

freight car *n.* a railway wagon that carries freight, usually one that is enclosed

freighter /fráytər/ *n.* **1. FREIGHT CARRIER** a ship or aircraft designed to carry freight **2. SHIPPER OR CHARTERER** sb who is responsible for sending, forwarding, or receiving freight, or who charters a ship to carry freight

freight ton *n.* a unit used in measuring and pricing freight in maritime shipping, varying according to the type of goods carried but usually corresponding to 1000 kilograms or 40 cubic feet

freight train *n.* a railway train that carries only freight

Frei Ruiz-Tagle /fráy roo éess taá glay/, **Eduardo** (*b.* 1942) Chilean government leader. He became president in 1994 and attempted to curb military power by constitutional reform.

Fremantle /frée mant'l/ city and port in southwestern Western Australia, now part of the metropolitan area of Perth. Population: 23,407 (1996).

fremitus /frémmitəss/ (*plural* **-tus**) *n.* a vibration or tremor, resulting from a physical action such as speaking or coughing, felt by hand and used to assess whether the chest is affected by disease [Early 19thC. From Latin, literally 'roaring', from *fremere* 'to roar'.]

frena plural of **frenum**

French /french/ *n.* **1.** LANG LANGUAGE OF FRANCE the official language of France and many countries worldwide. It belongs to the Romance group of Indo-European languages that developed from Latin. French is spoken by about 70 million native speakers, with about a further 220 million people using it as a second language. **2.** BEVERAGES **FRENCH VERMOUTH** French vermouth ■ *npl.* PEOPLES **FRENCH PEOPLE** the people of France collectively ■ *adj.* **1.** OF FRANCE relating to or typical of France, or its people or culture **2.** OF FRENCH LANGUAGE belonging or relating to the French language [Old English *frencisc*. Ultimately from a prehistoric Germanic word that was also the ancestor of English *Frank*.]

─── **WORD KEY: CULTURAL NOTE** ───

The French Connection, a film by US director William Friedkin (1971). Set in New York, it depicts the attempts of an uncompromising policeman, Popeye Doyle, to break up an international drug ring originating in Marseille, France. It is memorable for Gene Hackman's intense performance and a dramatic chase along elevated railway tracks. '*French Connection*-style drug enforcement operations' and other such expressions soon came to be used regularly in the United States as a result of the film's fame.

French bean *n.* **1.** BEAN PLANT a small bushy or tall climbing bean plant with slim green pods and white or purplish flowers. Latin name: *Phaseolus vulgaris.* US = **string bean 2.** EDIBLE POD OF BEAN PLANT the pod of a French bean plant eaten whole as a vegetable

French bread *n.* white bread in the form of a long slim cylindrical loaf with a crisp crust and soft inside

French Cameroons /-kámmə roónz/ former region in west-central Africa, administered by France from 1919 to 1960, and now part of Cameroon

French Canada *n.* the parts of Canada where French is spoken

French-Canadian *n.* **1.** French-Canadian, French Canadian PEOPLES **FRENCH-SPEAKING CANADIAN** sb who was born in or who lives in any of the French-speaking parts of Canada **2.** LANG CANADIAN FORM OF FRENCH the form of the French language spoken in Canada ■ *adj.* CONCERNING FRENCH-SPEAKING CANADA OR CANADIAN FRENCH relating to the French-speaking part of Canada or to the form of French spoken there

French chalk *n.* a soft white variety of talc used by tailors to make marks on cloth and by dry cleaners to remove grease stains from clothes

French Community /-kə myoónəti/ an association linking France and several former French colonies. It was created in 1958 to replace the French Union.

French Creole *n.* sb of European and African descent whose ancestors were French immigrants to Trinidad

French cricket *n.* an informal form of cricket that is played with bats and a soft ball, and with the batter's legs acting as the wicket

French cuff *n.* a wide cuff, usually for a shirtsleeve, that is designed to be folded back upon itself and fastened with a cufflink

French curve *n.* ARCHIT, TECH a thin piece of plastic or other material with curved edges and a number of curved shapes cut out of it, designed to help designers and engineers draw curves

French door *n.* US = **French window**

French dressing *n.* **1.** MIXTURE OF OIL, VINEGAR, AND SEASONING a salad dressing made of oil and vinegar with seasoning, whisked or shaken until emulsified or mixed **2.** US MIXTURE OF MAYONNAISE AND TOMATO a creamy salad dressing, usually made commercially, consisting of mayonnaise with tomato flavouring

French Equatorial Africa former French territory in west-central Africa between 1910 and 1958. It consisted of the present countries of the Central African Republic, Chad, the Republic of Congo, and Gabon.

French Foreign Legion *n.* = **Foreign Legion**

French fried potatoes *npl.* chips, especially when cut long and thin (*formal*)

French fries *npl.* thin strips of potato fried in deep fat

French Guinea former name for **Guinea**

French heel *n.* a curved heel of medium height for women's shoes

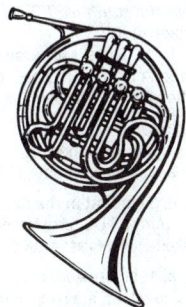

French horn

French horn *n.* a brass musical instrument consisting of a long looped pipe ending in a wide round bell, with additional straight or curved pipes and valves attached to it within the loop

Frenchify /frénchi fī/ (**-fies, -fying, -fied**) *vt.* to give a French appearance or character to sth or sb, especially in a way considered overrefined and decadent —**Frenchification** /frénchifi káysh'n/ *n.*

French India former territory comprising four French colonies in India that was ceded to India in 1956

French kiss *n.* a kiss in which one partner's tongue is inserted in the other partner's mouth

French knickers *npl.* women's wide-legged knickers

French knot *n.* an ornamental embroidery stitch made by looping the thread three or four times around the needle before inserting the needle in the fabric

French leave *n.* a quick departure or absence, without explanation or permission [From a supposed French custom of leaving a party without saying goodbye to the host or hostess. The French equivalent, however, *filer à l'anglaise*, translates as 'to leave in the English way'.]

French letter *n.* a condom (*dated informal*) [Origin uncertain: *letter* perhaps in the sense 'hinderer', from obsolete *let* 'to hinder']

Frenchman /frénchmən/ (*plural* **-men**) *n.* a man who was born in or is a citizen of France

Frenchmans Cap /frénchmənz káp/ mountain in southwestern Tasmania, Australia, at the heart of the Franklin-Lower Gordon Wild Rivers National Park. Height: 1,443 m/4,734 ft.

French marigold *n.* a flower, originally from Central America, that is widely cultivated in gardens for its flower heads of yellowish-orange and red petals. Latin name: *Tagetes patula.*

French mustard *n.* a mild-tasting mustard made with wine or unripe grape juice

French pleat *n.* a woman's hairstyle in which the hair is formed into a vertical roll at the back of the head

French polish *n.* shellac dissolved in alcohol, used as a varnish for wood

French-polish *vt.* to varnish sth with French polish

French press pot *n.* US = **cafetiere**

French Republican Calendar, French Revolutionary Calendar *n.* the calendar adopted by the French during and briefly after the French Revolution. It had 12 months of 30 days, each made up of three ten-day weeks. The months were given the names Vendémiaire, Brumaire, Frimaire, Nivôse, Pluviôse, Ventôse, Germinal, Floréal, Prairial, Messidor, Thermidor, and Fructidor, alluding to nature and seasonal weather.

French roll *n.* = **French pleat**

French roof *n.* a mansard roof

French seam *n.* a seam stitched twice, completely enclosing the raw or cut edges of the fabric

French stick *n.* a thin loaf of French bread

French Sudan former name for **Mali** (1898–1959)

French toast *n.* **1.** BREAD AND BEATEN EGG FRIED sliced bread dipped in egg beaten with milk and lightly fried or grilled. It may be served dusted with sugar, as a sweet, but can be eaten as a savoury snack with seasoning added to the egg and milk. **2.** BREAD TOASTED ON ONE SIDE bread toasted on one side only and buttered on the other (*regional*)

French twist *n.* = **French pleat**

French vermouth *n.* unsweetened vermouth

French West Africa former French colonial territory in western Africa between 1895 and 1958. It consisted of the present countries of Benin, Burkina Faso, Côte d'Ivoire, Guinea, Mali, Mauritania, Niger, and Senegal.

French window *n.* either of a pair of doors in an outside wall made of glass panels and opening in the middle (*usually used in the plural*)

Frenchwoman /frénch woomən/ (*plural* **-en** /-wimin/) *n.* a woman who was born in or is a citizen of France

frenetic /frə néttik/ *adj.* characterized by feverish activity, confusion, and hurry ○ *frenetic activity* [14thC. Via French *frénétique* from, ultimately, Greek *phrenitis* 'delirium', literally 'brain disease', from *phrēn* 'mind'.] —**frenetically** *adv.* —**freneticism** /-ssizzəm/ *n.*

frenulum /frénnyooləm/ (*plural* **-la** /-lə/) *n.* **1.** BRISTLE ON HIND WING OF MOTHS a small stiff bristle on the hind wing of moths that keeps the forewings and hind wings together during flight **2.** ANAT SMALL MEMBRANE a small fold of skin or membrane that limits the movement of an organ, typically smaller than a frenum [Early 18thC. From modern Latin, literally 'small', from Latin *frenum* (see FRAENUM).]

frenzied /frénzid/ *adj.* characterized by uncontrolled activity, agitation, or emotion such as excitement or rage

frenzy /frénzi/ *n.* **1.** OUT-OF-CONTROL BEHAVIOUR a state of uncontrolled activity, agitation, or emotion such as excitement or rage **2.** BURST OF ACTIVITY a burst of energetic activity [14thC. Via Old French *frenesie* from, ultimately, Greek *phrenitis* (see FRENETIC).]

Freon /frée on/, **freon** *tdmk.* a trademark for any of a number of chemical compounds containing fluorine, and often chlorine or bromine, used, e.g. as solvents, as aerosol propellants, and in refrigeration

freq. *abbr.* **1.** frequency **2.** GRAM frequentative **3.** frequently

frequency /frée kwənssi/ (*plural* **-cies**) *n.* **1.** frequency, frequence FREQUENT OCCURRENCE the fact of happening often or regularly at short intervals ○ *quite good friends, judging by the frequency of his visits* **2.** RATE OF OCCURRENCE the number of times that sth happens during a particular period of time ○ *We're trying to establish the frequency of his visits. Did he come once a month?* **3.** BROADCAST BROADCASTING WAVELENGTH a wavelength on which a radio or television signal is broadcast and to which a receiving set can be tuned **4.** PHYS RATE OF RECURRENCE the number of times that sth such as an oscillation, a waveform, or a cycle is repeated within a particular length of time, usually one second. Symbol *v*, *f* **5.** STATS NUMBER OF OCCURRENCES OF STATISTICAL RESULT the number of times a particular result occurs in a statistical survey

(absolute frequency), or the ratio of that number to the total results obtained in the survey (**relative frequency**)

frequency distribution *n.* a way of classifying statistical data that allows comparisons of the results in each category

frequency modulation *n.* a method of radio transmission in which the frequency of the wave carrying the signal is varied in accordance with the particularities of the sound being broadcast

frequent *adj.* /freˈkwənt/ **1.** OCCURRING OFTEN happening often or regularly at short intervals ○ *Her frequent appearances on television suggested she was moving up the party hierarchy.* **2.** HABITUAL belonging to the class specified on a regular basis ○ *a frequent visitor to the museum* ■ *vt.* /fri kwént/ (**-quents, -quenting, -quented**) GO OFTEN TO PLACE to go to or be in a place often [15thC. Via French *fréquent* from Latin *frequent-*, the stem of *frequens* 'crowded, numerous'.] —**frequentation** /frêe kwen táysh'n/ *n.* —**frequenter** /fri kwéntər/ *n.* —**frequentness** /freˈkwəntnəss/ *n.*

frequentative /fri kwéntətiv/ *adj.* LING EXPRESSING REPETITION OF ACTION that expresses repeated action (*refers to a verb, verb form, or affix*) ■ *n.* FREQUENTATIVE WORD a frequentative verb, verb form, or affix

frequently /freˈkwəntli/ *adv.* on many occasions with little time between them ○ *They change their address so frequently, it's difficult to know where to send the letter.*

Fresco: Detail of 16th-century wall painting at Sigirya, Sri Lanka

fresco /fréskō/ *n.* (*plural* **-coes** *or* **-cos**) **1.** PAINTING DONE ON FRESH PLASTER a painting on a wall or ceiling made by brushing watercolours onto fresh damp plaster, or onto partly dry plaster **2.** TECHNIQUE OF PAINTING ON FRESH PLASTER the technique or method of painting on fresh plaster ■ *vt.* (**-coes, -coing, -coed**) PAINT WALL OR CEILING WITH FRESCO to paint a fresco on a wall or ceiling [Late 16thC. From Italian, 'fresh' (referring to plaster). Ultimately of prehistoric Germanic origin.] —**frescoer** *n.* —**frescoist** *n.*

fresh /fresh/ *adj.* **1.** NOT OLD OR STALE recently harvested or made and showing no sign of staleness or decay ○ *Peas fresh from the pod.* **2.** NOT PRESERVED, PROCESSED, OR MATURED that has not been preserved, matured, or processed, e.g. by canning or freezing ○ *You can't get fresh peas here, only canned or frozen.* **3.** ADDITIONAL OR AS REPLACEMENT additional to or replacing sth that existed, was used before, or is past its best ○ *I took out the old ink cartridge and put in a fresh one.* **4.** NEW OR GOOD AS NEW new or clean and showing no signs of previous use ○ *The hotel provides fresh towels.* **5.** NOT AFFECTED BY TIME PASSING not changed, diminished, or spoiled by the passage of time ○ *Write it down while it's still fresh in your memory.* **6.** PURE AND WHOLESOME natural, pure, and wholesome, especially in smell ○ *the fresh smell of clean linen* **7.** EXCITINGLY DIFFERENT excitingly or refreshingly different from what sb is used to or what has been done previously ○ *fresh ideas.* **8.** NOT TIRED alert and full of energy ○ *I'd better get this done while my mind is still fresh.* **9.** NOT SALT not salty (*refers to water*) **10.** BLOWING STRONGLY blowing quite strongly (*refers to a breeze or wind*) ◊ **fresh breeze, fresh gale 11.** COOL cool or colder than usual **12.** BRIGHT pleasantly bright, light, and pure or clear **13.** YOUTHFUL young and healthy-looking **14.** MAKING UNWANTED SEXUAL ADVANCES making inappropriate sexual overtures to sb (*informal*) **15.** OVERFAMILIAR bold and overfamiliar towards sb, especially towards sb

considered a superior (*informal*) ○ *Don't you get fresh with me, young man.* **16.** RECENTLY ARRIVED having recently come from a place, activity, or production ○ *Fresh from his trip to the Antarctic, Sir Ronald is in the studio to tell us about his experiences.* **17.** WITHOUT EXPERIENCE lacking experience **18.** AGRIC HAVING RECENTLY CALVED having recently calved and able to give milk ■ *adv.* RECENTLY quite recently ■ *n.* COOL PERIOD the cool early part of the day [Partly Old English *fersc* 'pure, not salty', and partly from Old French *freis* 'new, recent', both ultimately of the same prehistoric Germanic origin] —**freshness** *n.*

WORD KEY: SYNONYMS
See Synonyms at *new*.

fresh breeze *n.* a force-five wind on the Beaufort Scale, blowing at between 30 and 38 km/h/19 and 24 mph

freshen /frésh'n/ *v.* (**-ens, -ening, -ened**) *v.* **1.** *vti.* MAKE OR BECOME FRESHER to make sth fresh or fresher or to become fresh or fresher **2.** *vi.* INCREASE IN STRENGTH to blow more strongly (*refers to wind*) ○ *wind force three, freshening from the south-west* **3.** *vt.* REFILL A DRINK to refill sb's glass or drink

freshen up *v.* **1.** *vi.* WASH AND IMPROVE APPEARANCE to become and feel clean and neat by washing or changing clothes **2.** *vt.* = **freshen** *v.* 3

freshener /frésh'nər/ *n.* a substance, or a device releasing a substance, designed to remove or cover odours, e.g. in a carpet or room

fresher /fréshər/ *n.* a student in the first year at college or university (*informal*) US term **freshman** [Late 19thC. Formed from a shortening of FRESHMAN.]

freshet /fréshət/ *n.* **1.** SUDDEN FLOOD a small sudden flood or rise in the level of a river, caused by heavy rainfall or a rapid thaw, especially after a period of dry weather **2.** STREAM OF FRESH WATER a stream of fresh water emptying into a body of salt water [Late 16thC. Origin uncertain: probably from Old French *freschete*, from *freis* (see FRESH).]

fresh gale *n.* a force-eight wind on the Beaufort Scale, blowing at between 62 and 74 km/h/39 and 46 mph

freshly /fréshli/ *adv.* done recently

freshman /fréshmən/ *n.* (*plural* **-men**) **1.** = **fresher 2.** US BEGINNER sb who is new in a particular post or position or is a beginner at sth

freshwater /frésh wawtər/ *adj.* **1.** GEOG NOT MARINE relating to, consisting of, or living in fresh water **2.** SAILING INLAND used on or accustomed to only inland waters, not the sea

fresh-water Yankee *n.* *Carib* an offensive term for sb who returns to the Caribbean after a visit abroad, usually to the United States, behaving and speaking like sb from the place visited (*slang offensive*)

Fresnel lens /fráy nel-/ *n.* a thin lens of short focal length with a surface comprised of concentric rings, each having a curvature corresponding to a similar ring of a plain convex lens [Mid-19thC. Named after the French physicist, Augustin-Jean FRESNEL who invented it.]

Fresno /fréznō/ city and county seat of Fresno County, central California, 249 km/155 mi. southeast of San Francisco. Population: 386,551 (1994).

fret[1] /fret/ *v.* (**frets, fretting, fretted**) **1.** *vti.* WORRY OR MAKE SB WORRY to be or to cause sb to be worried, irritated, or agitated about sth **2.** *vti.* WEAR AWAY to wear away or corrode the surface of sth or to become worn away or corroded **3.** *vt.* MAKE BY CONSTANT RUBBING to create a hole or groove in sth by constant wear or rubbing **4.** *vti.* FLOW IN RIPPLES OR SMALL WAVES to flow, or to cause water to flow, with a constant busy rippling motion or with small choppy waves (*literary*) ○ '*I love the brooks that down their channels fret*' (Wordsworth, *Ode on Intimations of Immortality*, 1807) ■ *n.* **1.** FRETTING STATE a restless complaining state brought on by anxiety or irritation ○ *The baby's in a fret.* **2.** HOLE MADE BY FRETTING a hole, groove, or mark made by constant wear or rubbing [Old English *fretan* 'to devour'. Ultimately from a prehistoric Germanic word meaning 'to eat up', formed from the ancestor of English *eat* and *etch*.]

fret[2] /fret/ *n.* MUSIC a small ridge across the fingerboard of a stringed instrument such as a guitar or sitar, indicating the position in which to place the fingers to produce a particular note [Early 16thC. Origin unknown.] —**fretted** *adj.*

fret[3] /fret/ *n.* ORNAMENT OR BORDER WITH GEOMETRICAL PATTERN a pattern of repeated geometrical figures, usually consisting of straight lines, used as an ornament or in an ornamental border ■ *vt.* (**frets, fretting, fretted**) DECORATE WITH A FRET to decorate sth with a fret or with fretwork [14thC. From Old French *frete* 'trellis', of unknown origin.]

fretful /frétf'l/ *adj.* easily worried, irritated, or agitated by sth —**fretfully** *adv.* —**fretfulness** *n.*

fretman (*plural* **fretmen**) *n.* MUSIC a musician who plays guitar, especially in jazz or pop music (*slang*)

fretsaw /frét saw/ *n.* a saw with a thin narrow fine-toothed blade usually mounted across a U-shaped frame and used for cutting curved shapes in wood [Mid-19thC. From FRET[3].]

fretwork /frét wurk/ *n.* **1.** ORNAMENTAL WOODWORK WITH OPEN PATTERN ornamental woodwork made by cutting many holes in a piece of wood with a fretsaw to create an intricate pattern of wood and spaces **2.** FRET PATTERNS decorative designs consisting of frets [Early 17thC. From FRET[3].]

AKG London

Sigmund Freud

Freud /froyd/, **Sigmund** (1856–1939) Austrian physician and founder of psychoanalysis. He developed many theories central to psychoanalysis, the psychology of human sexuality, and dream interpretation. His works include *The Interpretation of Dreams* (1899) and *Totem and Taboo* (1913).

Freudian /fróydi ən/ *adj.* **1.** RELATING TO FREUD relating to Sigmund Freud, his writings, or his psychoanalytical theories and methods **2.** CONCERNING ROLE OF SEXUALITY IN BEHAVIOUR demonstrating or understandable in terms of Freud's theories, especially with regard to sexuality and its role in human relations ■ *n.* FOLLOWER OF FREUD sb who follows Freud or is influenced by Freud's theories or methods of psychoanalysis —**Freudianism** *n.*

Freudian slip *n.* an accidental mistake, usually the use of the wrong word in a sentence, that is thought to betray sb's subconscious preoccupations

Freyberg /frí burg/, **Bernard Cyril, 1st Baron of Wellington and Munstead** (1889–1963) English-born New Zealand soldier and statesman. He was winner of a Victoria Cross (1916), commander of the New Zealand forces in the Middle East during World War II, and governor-general of New Zealand (1946–52).

Freycinet Peninsula /fráysinət-/ peninsula in eastern Tasmania, Australia, part of which is in Freycinet National Park. Length: 30 km/19 mi.

FRG *abbr.* Federal Republic of Germany

FRGS *abbr.* Fellow of the Royal Geographical Society

Fri. *abbr.* Friday

friable /frí əb'l/ *adj.* easily reduced to tiny particles ○ *sand incorporated to make the soil more friable* [Mid-16thC. Directly or via French from Latin *friabilis*, from *friare* 'to crumble.'] —**friability** /frí ə bílləti/ *n.* —**friableness** *n.*

WORD KEY: SYNONYMS
See Synonyms at *fragile*.

friar /frí ər/ *n.* a man belonging to any of several Roman Catholic religious orders [13thC. Via French *frère* from Latin *frater* 'brother' (see FRATERNAL).] —**friarly** *adj.*

friar's balsam *n.* a compound whose main ingredient is benzoin, used as an inhalant for colds and sore throats

friar's lantern *n.* SCI = will-o'-the-wisp

friary /frí əri/ (*plural* -**ies**) *n.* a community of friars or the buildings in which they live

fricassee /fríkə say, -sáy, -see, -seé/ *n.* (*plural* -**sees**) MEAT STEWED IN WHITE SAUCE fish or meat such as chicken or veal cooked in white stock, or a wine and stock mixture, that is thickened with cream ■ *vt.* (-**sees**, -**seeing**, -**seed**) COOK AS FRICASSEE to cook fish or meat as a fricassee [Mid-16thC. From French *fricassée*, the feminine past participle of *fricasser* 'to cut up and cook in sauce', possibly a blend of *frire* 'to fry' and *casser* 'to break'.]

fricative /fríkətiv/ *adj.* PHON MADE BY BREATH FRICTION made by forcing the breath through a narrow opening ■ *n.* FRICATIVE CONSONANT a fricative consonant, e.g. 'f' or 'z' [Mid-19thC. From modern Latin *fricativus*, from Latin *fricare* (see FRICTION).]

FRICS *abbr.* Fellow of the Royal Institute of Chartered Surveyors

friction /fríksh'n/ *n.* **1.** RUBBING the rubbing of two objects against each other when one or both are moving **2.** DISAGREEMENT disagreement or conflict, stopping short of violence, between individuals, groups, or nations with differing aims or views **3.** MED DELIBERATE RUBBING deliberate rubbing of a body part as a way of stimulating blood circulation, warming, or relieving pain **4.** PHYS RESISTANCE ENCOUNTERED BY MOVING OBJECT the resistance encountered by an object moving relative to another object with which it is in contact [Mid-16thC. Via French from the Latin stem *friction-*, from *fricare* 'to rub' (source of English *dentifrice* and *fray*).] —**frictional** *adj.*

friction clutch *n.* a clutch in a vehicle or machine that transmits power through surface friction between two plates covered with a layer of a fibrous material, e.g. asbestos

friction match *n.* a match that lights when rubbed against an abrasive surface

friction tape *n.* US = insulating tape

Friday /frí day, -di/ *n.* the fifth day of the week, coming after Thursday and before Saturday [Old English *Frīgedæg* 'day of the goddess Frigg', whose name comes ultimately from a prehistoric Germanic verb meaning 'to love' that was also the ancestor of English *friend* and *free*.]

Fridays /frídayz, -diz/ *adv.* on every Friday

fridge /frij/ *n.* a refrigerator [Early 20thC. Shortening.]

fridge-freezer *n.* a refrigerator and a freezer contained as two separate cabinets in a single upright unit

fried /frīd/ *adj.* **1.** COOKED BY FRYING having been cooked by frying **2.** US INTOXICATED incapacitated by alcohol or drugs (*informal*) **3.** US EXHAUSTED incoherent from fatigue (*slang*)

Betty Friedan

Friedan /free dán/, **Betty** (*b.* 1921) US feminist leader, author, and founder in 1966 of the National Organization for Women (NOW). Her landmark book *The Feminine Mystique* (1963) challenged the idealization of women's traditional roles. Born **Betty Naomi Goldstein**

Friedman /freedmən/, **Milton** (*b.* 1912) US economist and Nobel laureate (1976). He is considered a leading protagonist of the theory that a free market, rather than government intervention, can best produce a balanced rate of economic growth.

friend /frend/ *n.* **1.** SB EMOTIONALLY CLOSE TO ANOTHER sb who has a close personal relationship of mutual affection and trust with another ○ *I know her, in fact she's a friend of mine.* **2.** ACQUAINTANCE sb who has a casual relationship with another, e.g. a business acquaintance ○ *I've got a friend at the office who might be able to help out.* **3.** ALLY sb who is not an enemy ○ *You can say what you like about the government, you're among friends here.* **4.** ADVOCATE OF A CAUSE sb who defends or supports a cause, group, or principle ○ *She's no friend of tax-and-spend policies.* **5.** PATRON OF INSTITUTION OR ORGANIZATION sb who supports a charity or institution by donating time or money ○ *a friend of the Bournemouth Symphony Orchestra* [Old English *frēond*. Ultimately from the present participle of a prehistoric Germanic verb meaning 'to love' that was also the ancestor of English *free*, *affray*, and *Friday*.] ◇ **fair-weather friend** sb whose friendship with another is conditional upon the other's good fortune ◇ **friends (with)** a friend of or on friendly terms with sb ◇ **make friends (with)** to begin a friendship or get on friendly terms with sb

Friend *n.* a member of the Religious Society of Friends, called Quakers

Friend /frend/, **Donald Stuart Leslie** (1915–89) Australian artist. He is noted for his decorative, sensual paintings and drawings, particularly those produced in Bali (1967–80).

friendless /fréndləss/ *adj.* without a friend —**friendlessness** *n.*

friendly /fréndli/ *adj.* (-**lier**, -**liest**) **1.** AFFECTIONATE AND TRUSTING characteristic of or suitable to a relationship between friends ○ *She's been friendly to us since we moved in.* **2.** HELPFUL tending to be beneficial or favourable towards sb or sth ○ *They're on quite friendly terms with one another, but I wouldn't say they were close.* **3.** ON THE SAME SIDE not antagonistic towards or in conflict with another ○ *All the aircraft we saw were friendly.* **4.** PLEASANT AND WELCOMING with a pleasant welcoming atmosphere **5.** NOT FIERCELY COMPETITIVE not played or undertaken in a fiercely competitive mood **6.** SPORTS NOT PART OF A COMPETITION played mainly for practice or entertainment and not as a fixture in a competition or league **7.** EASY TO USE safe or easy to use or operate or easy to understand (*usually used in combination*) ○ *made of child-friendly materials* **8.** MAKING SEXUAL OVERTURES behaving in a way that reveals a sexual desire for sb or a desire to start a sexual relationship with sb (*used euphemistically*) ■ *adv.* (-**lier**, -**liest**) LIKE A FRIEND in a manner that befits friends ■ *n.* (*plural* -**ies**) SPORTS GAME NOT FORMING PART OF COMPETITION a game that is played mainly for practice or entertainment and not as a fixture in a competition or league ○ *a series of friendlies* —**friendlily** *adv.* —**friendliness** *n.* ◇ **friendly with** being a friend of or on friendly terms with sb

friendly fire *n.* gunfire or artillery fire coming from your own or your allies' forces, not the enemy, and sometimes causing accidental death or injury

Friendly Islands /fréndli-/ = Tonga

friendly society *n.* an association of people who contribute regularly to a fund in order to provide themselves with sickness benefits, life assurance, and retirement pensions when required

friendship /frénd ship/ *n.* **1.** RELATIONSHIP BETWEEN FRIENDS a relationship between two or more people who are friends ○ *a friendship that has lasted more than 40 years* **2.** MUTUALLY FRIENDLY FEELINGS the mutual feelings of trust and affection and the behaviour that typify relationships between friends ○ *Any feeling of friendship towards him had long since disappeared.* **3.** FRIENDLY RELATIONS a relationship between individuals, organizations, or countries that is characterized by mutual assistance, approval, and support ○ *Anglo-American friendship*

Friends of the Earth *n.* an international organization that lobbies and campaigns on environmental matters (*takes a singular or plural verb*)

frier *n.* = fryer

fries *npl.* = French fries

Friesian /freézh'n, freézi ən/ *n.* LARGE BLACK AND WHITE COW an animal belonging to a breed of large black and white dairy cattle. US term **Holstein** ■ *n.*, *adj.* = **Frisian** [Early 20thC. Variant of FRISIAN.]

Friesland /freézlənd/ coastal province in northern Netherlands, that includes four of the West Frisian Islands. Population: 609,579 (1995). Area: 3,353 sq. km/1,295 sq. mi.

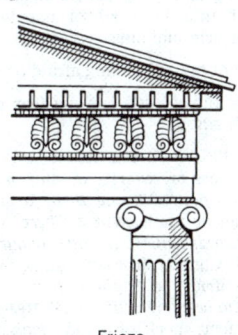

Frieze

frieze[1] /freez/ *n.* **1.** DECORATIVE BAND ALONG WALL a band of decoration running along the wall of a room, usually just below the ceiling **2.** HORIZONTAL BAND ON CLASSICAL BUILDING a horizontal band forming part of the entablature of a classical building, situated between the architrave and the cornice, and often decorated with sculpted ornaments or figures [Mid-16thC. Via French *frise* from, ultimately, Latin *Phrygium* (*opus*) 'Phrygian (work)' (the Phrygians being famous for their craftmanship).]

frieze[2] /freez/ *n.* coarse woollen cloth with a long shaggy nap [15thC. Via French *frise* from medieval Latin *frisia*, literally 'Frisian (cloth)'.]

frig /frig/ (**frigs**, **frigging**, **frigged**) *vti.* (*taboo*) **1.** TABOO WORD MEANING TO HAVE SEX a taboo term that means to have sexual intercourse with sb **2.** TABOO WORD MEANING TO MASTURBATE a taboo term that means to masturbate, or to masturbate sb [Late 16thC. Origin uncertain: perhaps via Old French *friquer* 'to rub' from Latin *fricare* (see **frig about**).]

frig about, **frig around** *vi.* to waste time or act in an aimless unproductive way (*taboo offensive*)

Frigate

frigate /fríggət/ *n.* **1.** WARSHIP BETWEEN CORVETTE AND DESTROYER a British warship next in size below a destroyer and with a similar armament and function **2.** US MEDIUM-SIZED WARSHIP a US warship of medium size, larger than a destroyer but smaller than a cruiser, and used mainly for escort duty **3.** SAILING SHIP EQUIPPED FOR WAR a fast square-rigged fighting ship in the 18th and early 19th centuries, next in size below a ship of the line [Late 16thC. Via French *frégate* from Italian *fregata*, of unknown origin. The word originally denoted a light, fast rowing or sailing boat.]

frigate bird *n.* a large tropical seabird with large powerful wings, dark-coloured plumage, a forked tail, and a down-turned beak. Latin name: *Family Fregatidae*. [Said to be so named because of its swift flight]

frigging /frígging/ *adj.*, *adv.* used as a swearword or to add emphasis (*taboo offensive*)

fright /frīt/ *n.* **1. SUDDEN FEAR** a sudden intense feeling of being threatened or in danger **2. EXPERIENCE OF BEING AFRAID** an experience of fright **3. STH VERY UNPLEASANT LOOKING** sb or sth that looks grotesque, ludicrous, or extremely unattractive (*informal*) ○ *My hair's a fright this morning.* [Old English *fryhto*]

frighten /frīt'n/ (**-ens, -ening, -ened**) *v.* **1.** *vti.* **MAKE OR BECOME AFRAID** to make sb feel fear or to be made to feel fear **2.** *vt.* **SCARE INTO LEAVING** to force or drive sb or sth away through fear [Mid-17thC. Formed from FRIGHT.] —**frightener** *n.* ◇ **put the frighteners on sb** to frighten sb into doing sth or not doing sth, especially for criminal purposes (*slang*)

frightened /frīt'nd/ *adj.* feeling afraid or alarmed

frightening /frītning/ *adj.* causing fear or alarm —**frighteningly** *adv.*

frightful /frītf'l/ *adj.* **1. VERY SERIOUS** used to indicate the seriousness or severity of sth ○ *now faced the frightful prospect of losing their farm* **2. FOUL** extremely bad or unpleasant ○ *There is a frightful smell in the bedroom.* ○ *a frightful odour* **3. VERY GREAT** used to indicate that sb or sth is an extreme example of sth specified ○ *a frightful liar* ○ *The speaker turned out to be a frightful bore.* **4. TERRIFYING** capable of causing fear, shock, or dread ○ *looked down from a frightful height* —**frightfulness** *n.*

frightfully /frītfəli/ *adv.* extremely or excessively ○ *I'm frightfully sorry, but you'll have to go.*

frigid /fríjjid/ *adj.* **1. SEXUALLY UNRESPONSIVE** unable or unwilling to respond sexually, to enjoy sexual intercourse, or to have orgasm during intercourse **2. LACKING EMOTIONAL WARMTH** without or behaving without warmth, friendliness, or enthusiasm **3. VERY COLD** with a very cold temperature ○ *I was kept waiting in a frigid little room.* [15thC. From Latin *frigidus*, from *frigus* 'cold' (source of English *refrigerate*).] —**frigidity** /fri jíddəti/ *n.* —**frigidly** /fríjjidli/ *adv.* —**frigidness** *n.*

Frigid Zone *n.* either of two areas of the Earth's surface, one lying between the Arctic Circle and the North Pole, the other lying between the Antarctic Circle and the South Pole

frigorific /fríggə ríffik/ *adj.* producing extreme cold (*archaic*) [Mid-17thC. From Latin *frigorificus*, from *frigus* (see FRIGID).]

frijol /fri hṓl/ (*plural* **-joles**), **frijole** /fri hṓli, -hṓ lay/; *or with Spanish pronunciation* /fri khṓl ay/ *n.* in the cooking of Mexico and the southwestern United States, a bean such as the pinto, kidney, or black bean [Late 16thC. Via Spanish, Catalan *fesol*, and Latin *phaseolus* from, ultimately, Greek *phasēlos* 'legume', of unknown origin.]

WORD KEY: REGIONAL NOTE

This name marks the Mexican American territory of South and West Texas, New Mexico, Arizona, and Southern California. ***Frijoles*** are sometimes called *Mexican beans*.

frill /fril/ *n.* **1. DECORATIVE BAND WITH MANY FOLDS** a strip of material gathered into many tight folds and sewn along one edge, and usually attached as a decoration to sth **2.** COOK **PAPER BAND WITH FRINGED EDGE** a paper band with one edge cut into a decorative fringe, placed on bone ends as decoration and to allow the meat to be picked up by the bone end **3.** COOK **DECORATIVE PAPER BAND ROUND CAKE** a band of paper with both edges cut into a fringe, wrapped around the side of a cake, a savoury pudding, or a pie as a decorative finish **4.** ZOOL **RUFF OF FEATHERS, FUR, OR SKIN** a ring of fur or feathers or a fold of skin around the neck of a bird or animal that looks like a decorative frill **5. UNNECESSARY ADDITION** an addition to sth that is unnecessary, though it may enhance its appearance, interest, or value (*usually used in the plural*) ○ *I just want a basic, simple, no-frills stereo.* ■ *vt.* (**frills, frilling, frilled**) **1. MAKE INTO FRILL** to make a strip of fabric or paper into a frill **2. ADD FRILL TO** to decorate sth with a frill [Late 16thC. Origin uncertain: perhaps from Flemish *frul*.] —**frilled** *adj.* —**frilly** *adj.*

frilled lizard *n.* a large Australian lizard, with a broad membrane of skin around its neck that it can spread out like a ruff. Latin name: *Chlamydosaurus kingii*.

Frimaire /fri máir/ *n.* the third month of the French Revolutionary Calendar, corresponding to the period from about 21 November to 20 December [Early 19thC. From French, from *frimas* 'hoar-frost', of prehistoric Germanic origin.]

fringe /frinj/ *n.* **1. DECORATIVE EDGING OF STRANDS** a decorative border of short parallel strands or ravelled threads held closely together at one end by stitching or a band of fabric and hanging loosely at the other end **2. HAIR HANGING OVER FOREHEAD** a border of hair cut to fall over the forehead. US term **bangs 3. ANY BORDER OR EDGING** sth that serves as or resembles a border **4. OUTER LIMIT** the outer edge or sth considered to be on the outer edge and not central to an activity, interest, or issue (*often used in the plural*) ○ *outposts on the fringes of civilization* **5. LESS IMPORTANT AREA** an area of action that is far away from the centre of activity or interest in a particular field (*usually used in the plural*) ○ *on the fringes of political life* **6.** GOLF **AREA BORDERING PUTTING GREEN** the area surrounding a putting green on a golf course where the grass is allowed to grow slightly longer than it is on the green itself **7.** POL **FACTION WITHIN A GROUP** members of a group or organization such as a political party who hold views not representative of the group and usually more extreme than those of the group **8.** ARTS **PART OF ARTS FESTIVAL** part of an arts festival or similar event devoted to experimental or low-budget work **9.** OPTICS **BAND PRODUCED BY DIFFRACTION OF LIGHT** a light, dark, or coloured band of light produced by diffraction or interference **10.** US = **fringe benefit** (*informal*) ■ *adj.* **1. OUTLYING** situated on the edge or away from the centre of sth **2.** LITERAT, THEATRE **MINOR** playing a minor role in a play or story **3. UNCONVENTIONAL** not part of the established or conventional mainstream of sth such as the cinema, theatre, or medicine **4. NOT IN MAIN PART** not in the main part of sth such as a conference or organization, especially if putting forward or discussing radical or unconventional ideas ■ *vt.* (**fringes, fringing, fringed**) **1. FORM FRINGE AROUND** to form a fringe or border around sth ○ *A thin moustache and beard fringed his lips.* **2. DECORATE WITH FRINGE** to decorate sth with a fringe [14thC. Via Old French from, ultimately, Latin *fimbriae* 'threads', of unknown origin.] —**fringed** *adj.* —**fringy** *adj.*

WORD KEY: CULTURAL NOTE

The Fringe Dwellers, a novel by Australian writer Nene Gare (1961). Set on the west coast of Australia, it tells the story of a mixed-race Aboriginal family, the Comeaways, who find themselves shunned and mistreated by white society and cut off from their Aboriginal traditions. It was made into a film by Bruce Beresford in 1986.

fringe area *n.* BROADCAST an area at or just beyond the edge of a radio or television transmitter's range where signals are likely to be weak or distorted

fringe benefit *n.* **1. ADDITIONAL EMPLOYEE BENEFIT** an additional benefit provided to an employee, e.g. a company car or health insurance **2. ADDITIONAL ADVANTAGE** any additional or incidental advantage derived from a particular activity

fringed orchis *n.* an orchid with a fringed lip. Different species have yellow, white, purple, or greenish flowers. Genus: *Habenaria*.

fringe dweller *n.* *Aus* sb who lives at the edge of a town or city, usually in an impoverished area

fringe tree *n.* either of two ornamental small trees, one native to the eastern United States and the other to China, that have hanging clusters of white flowers with narrow petals. Genus: *Chionanthus*.

fringing reef *n.* a coral reef that borders or is directly attached to the shore of an island or a continent

frippery /fríppəri/ *n.* (*plural* **-ies**) **1. ARTICLE OF ADORNMENT WORN FOR SHOW** a showy article of clothing or an adornment worn for display or effect **2. OSTENTATION** pretentious display or showiness **3. STH TRIFLING** sth of little value or importance ■ *adj.* **UNNECESSARY AND WITHOUT VALUE** unnecessary, essentially valueless, and worn or used simply for display or effect [Mid-16thC. Via French *friperie* from, ultimately, Old French *frepe* 'rag, old clothes', of uncertain origin.]

Fris. *abbr.* Frisian

Frisbee /frízbi/ *tdmk.* a trademark for a plastic disc thrown from person to person in a game

Frisch /frish/, **Max** (1911–91) Swiss dramatist and novelist. His plays include *The Firebugs* (1958) and *Andorra* (1961). Among his novels are *I'm Not Stiller* (1954), *Homo Faber* (1957), and *Man in the Holocene* (1979). Full name **Max Rudolf Frisch**

frisé /freé zay/ *n.* a fabric with long nap, usually of uncut loops, used for upholstery and rugs [Late 19thC. From French, from the past participle of *friser* (see FRIZZ).]

frisée /freé zay/ *n.* = **endive** *n.* 1 [Late 20thC. From French, literally 'curly', the feminine past participle of *friser* (see FRIZZ).]

Frisian /frízh'n, frízzi ən/, **Friesian** *n.* **1.** LANG **GERMANIC LANGUAGE** a language spoken in parts of the Netherlands and Germany. It belongs to the West Germanic group of the Germanic branch of Indo-European languages. **2.** PEOPLES **SB FROM FRIESLAND OR FRISIAN ISLANDS** sb who was born in or is a citizen of Friesland or the Frisian Islands [Late 16thC. Formed from Latin *Frisii* 'the Frisians', from Old Frisian *Frīsa*.] —**Frisian** *adj.*

Frisian Islands /freézian íləndz/ ISLANDS group of islands in the North Sea off the coasts of the Netherlands, northwestern Germany, and southwestern Denmark. They include the Dutch West Frisian Islands, the German East Frisian Islands, and the North Frisian Islands, divided between Germany and Denmark.

frisk /frisk/ *v.* (**frisks, frisking, frisked**) **1.** *vi.* **LEAP OR DANCE ABOUT PLAYFULLY** to leap, skip, or dance around in a carefree way **2.** *vt.* **SEARCH QUICKLY** to search sb with a quick pass of the hands over clothes and into pockets ■ *n.* **1. PLAYFUL LEAP** a playful leap, skip, or dance **2. QUICK SEARCH** a quick search of sb's clothes and pockets [Early 16thC. From Old French *frisque* 'lively', of uncertain origin: probably from prehistoric Germanic.] —**frisker** *n.* —**frisking** *n.*

frisket /frískit/ *n.* a thin frame that keeps a sheet of paper in position and masks any portions not to be printed while the sheet is being printed on a hand-operated press [Late 17thC. From French *frisquette*, from Old French *frisque* (see FRISK).]

frisky /fríski/ (**-ier, -iest**) *adj.* behaving or tending to behave in a lively, playful way —**friskily** *adv.* —**friskiness** *n.*

frisson /freésson, frísson, freesóN/ *n.* a brief intense reaction, usually a feeling of excitement, recognition, or terror, accompanied by a physical shudder or thrill [Late 18thC. Via French, literally 'shiver', from, ultimately, an assumed Vulgar Latin stem *friction-*, from Latin *frigere* 'to be cold'.]

frit[1] /frit/ *n.* CERAMICS **1. BASIC MATERIALS FOR GLASS OR GLAZE** the basic materials from which glass, pottery glazes, or enamels are made, when they are in a partially bonded state at the beginning of the manufacturing process **2. GROUND FLUX** a flux that is stabilized by melting it with silica and regrinding it into a fine powder ■ *vt.* (**frits, fritting, fritted**) **MAKE INTO FRIT** to fuse or partially fuse materials in order to make frit [Mid-17thC. From Italian *fritta*, the feminine past participle of *friggere* 'to fry', from Latin *frigere* (source of English *fry*[1]).]

frit[2] /frit/ *adj.* frightened (*regional*) [Early 19thC. Past participle of obsolete *fright* 'to frighten', from Old English *fryhtan*, from the noun FRIGHT.]

frit fly *n.* a small black fly whose larvae are destructive to cereal crops. Latin name: *Oscinella frit*. [From Latin *frit*, 'speck on an ear of corn']

fritillary /fri tílləri/ (*plural* **-ies**) *n.* **1.** PLANTS **FLOWER WITH SPOTTED PETALS** a plant of the lily family with long narrow leaves and one or two bell-shaped flowers whose petals are marked with a spotted or chequered pattern. Genus: *Fritillaria*. **2.** ZOOL **SPOTTED BUTTERFLY** a brownish butterfly with black spots or narrow bands on its wings and usually silver spots on the underside of its hind wings. Family: Nymphalidae. [Mid-17thC. From modern Latin *Fritillaria*, genus name, from Latin *fritillus* 'dice box'; probably because the flower of some varieties resembles a small chequered box.]

frittata /fri taátə/ *n.* a firm thick Italian omelette that may contain any of a variety of chopped ingredients, including meat or vegetables [Mid-20thC.

From Italian, from *fritto*, the past participle of *friggere* (see FRIT[1]).]

fritter[1] /fríttər/ *n.* a piece of meat, fish, vegetable, or fruit dipped in batter and fried [14thC. From French *friture*, from, ultimately, Latin *frict-*, the past participle stem of *frigere* 'to fry' (source of English *fry*[1]).]

fritter[2] /fríttər/ (**-ters, -tering, -tered**) *vt.* to break, cut, or tear sth into small pieces or shreds (*old*) [Early 18thC. From obsolete *fritters* 'fragments, scraps', of unknown origin.]

fritter away *vt.* to waste sth by expending it in small quantities over a period of time on things that are not worthwhile

fritto misto /frítto místo/ (*plural* **fritto mistos** *or* **fritti misti** /frítti místi/) *n.* an Italian dish consisting of a mixture of bite-sized pieces of various foods such as seafood, meat, or vegetables, and sometimes sweet things such as cake, deep-fried in light batter [From Italian, literally 'mixed fry']

Friulian /fri óoli ən/, **Friulan** /-óolən/ *n.* **1.** LANG **DIALECT SPOKEN IN NORTHERN ITALY** a dialect of Rhaetian spoken in northwestern parts of Italy. ◊ **Ladin, Romansch 2.** PEOPLES **SB FROM FRIULI OR SPEAKING FRIULIAN** sb who was born in or is a citizen of Friuli or a speaker of the Friulian dialect —**Friulian** *adj.*

frivol /frívv'l/ (**-ols, -olling, -olled**) *v.* **1.** *vi.* BEHAVE FRIVO-LOUSLY to behave or spend time in a frivolous way **2.** *vt.* WASTE FOOLISHLY to spend or waste sth such as time or money foolishly or frivolously [Mid-19thC. Back-formation from FRIVOLOUS.] —**frivoller** *n.*

frivolity /fri vólləti/ (*plural* **-ties**) *n.* **1.** FRIVOLOUS BEHAVIOUR silly and trivial behaviour or activities **2.** STH FRIVO-LOUS a frivolous action or thing **3.** TRIVIALITY the state of being trivial and unimportant [Late 18thC. Via French *frivolité* from, ultimately, Latin *frivolus* (see FRIVOLOUS).]

frivolous /frívvələss/ *adj.* **1.** NOT WORTH TAKING SERIOUSLY lacking in intellectual substance and not worth serious consideration **2.** SILLY silly and trivial [15thC. Formed from Latin *frivolus* 'silly, unimportant', of uncertain origin.] —**frivolously** *adv.* —**frivolousness** *n.*

frizz /friz/ *vti.* (**frizzes, frizzing, frizzed**) FORM INTO TIGHT CURLS to form or to cause the hair to form a mass of tight curls or tufts ■ *n.* **1.** FRIZZED HAIR a mass of tightly curled or tufted hair **2.** FRIZZING the frizzing of hair [Late 16thC. From French *friser* 'to curl', of uncertain origin: perhaps formed from *fris-*, the stem of *frire* (see FRY[1]).]

frizzle[1] /frízz'l/ (**-zles, -zling, -zled**) *vti.* **1.** BURN OR SHRIVEL to burn or shrivel, or to cause to burn or shrivel, especially while cooking **2.** FRY AND SIZZLE to sizzle while frying or cooking or to fry and cook sth so that it sizzles [Mid-18thC. Origin uncertain: probably a blend of FRY and FIZZLE or SIZZLE.]

frizzle[2] /frízz'l/ *vti.* (**-zles, -zling, -zled**) FRIZZ to frizz hair or to become frizzed ■ *n.* CURL a short tight curl [Mid-16thC. Origin uncertain: possibly formed from FRIZZ.]

frizzy /frízzi/ (**-zier, -ziest**), **frizzly** (**frizzlier, frizzliest**) *adj.* forming or styled in tight curls —**frizzily** *adv.* —**frizziness** *n.* —**frizzliness** *n.*

Frl. *abbr.* Fräulein

frm *abbr.* from

fro /frō/ *adv.* ♦ **to and fro** [13thC. From Old Norse *frá* 'from'. Ultimately from a prehistoric Germanic word that was also the ancestor of English *from*.]

Frobisher /frṓbishər/, **Sir Martin** (1535?–94) English navigator. He led an unsuccessful expedition in search of the Northwest Passage (1576), and played a prominent part in the defeat of the Spanish Armada.

frock /frok/ *n.* **1.** DRESS a woman's or girl's dress (*dated*) ○ *I'll put on my posh frock if the mayor's going to be there.* **2.** LOOSE OUTER GARMENT a loose baggy outer garment with sleeves that covers the top half of the body to below the waist, traditionally worn by artists and farm workers **3.** CHR MONK'S GOWN the loose full-length gown with wide sleeves worn by the monks, friars, or clerics of some religious orders **4.** CLOTHES, HIST **18TH-CENTURY MAN'S COAT** an informal coat with narrow skirts and collar worn by men in the 18th century ■ *vt.* (**frocks, frocking, frocked**) **1.** CHR INDUCT AS MEMBER OF CLERGY to invest sb as a member of

the clergy **2.** MIL ASSUME HIGHER RANK WITHOUT COR-RESPONDING PAY to assume the title, uniform, and authority, but not the salary, of the next highest military rank before being officially promoted to it. This practice is more common in the Navy than in the other services. [14thC. From French *froc*, ultimately of prehistoric Germanic origin.]

Frock coat

frock coat *n.* in the 19th century, a man's knee-length coat for formal day wear

froe /frō/, **frow** *n.* a cutting tool with one end of its blade fastened at right angles to a short handle, used to split wood along the grain to make shingles or barrel staves [Late 16thC. Origin uncertain: possibly from FROWARD, in the sense 'turned away'.]

Froebelian /frō béeli ən/ *adj.* relating to Friedrich Wilhelm August Froebel, the German educator who established the first kindergarten, or to the system of education through kindergartens (**the Froebel system**) that he advocated

Frog

frog[1] /frog/ *n.* **1.** AMPHIB **SMALL WEB-FOOTED WATER ANIMAL** a small tailless amphibious animal with smooth moist skin, webbed feet, and long back legs used for jumping. Family: Ranidae. **2.** MUSIC NUT ON BOW a nut used to secure and tighten the strings of a violin bow and hold them away from the bow stick **3.** CRAFT SUPPORT FOR FLOWERS IN ARRANGEMENT an object, usually with spikes or perforations, used to support the stems of flowers when making a flower ar-rangement [Old English *frogga*] ◇ **have a frog in the** *or* **your throat** to be hoarse and unable to speak clearly

frog[2] /frog/ *n.* a decorative fastening for the front of a garment, consisting of a loop of braid or cord and a button, knot, or toggle that fits into the loop [Early 18thC. Origin unknown.] —**frogged** *adj.*

frog[3] /frog/ *n.* a tough flexible pad in the middle of the sole of a horse's hoof [Early 17thC. Origin uncertain: possibly an alteration (influenced by FROG[1]) of Italian *forchetta* or French *fourchette* of the same meaning, both literally 'little fork'.]

frog[4] /frog/ *n.* a steel plate used to guide the wheels of a train over a place where two rails cross one another [Mid-19thC. Origin uncertain: possibly from FROG[1], because the shape of the rails resembles a frog's legs.]

Frog /frog/, **frog** *n.* an offensive term for a French person (*slang offensive*) [Late 18thC. From the supposed prominence of frogs' legs in the French diet.]

frogbit /frog bit/ *n.* a floating plant that grows in stagnant water and has heart-shaped leaves and white flowers. Latin name: *Hydrocharis morsus-ranae*. US term **frog's bit** [Late 16thC. *Bit* in the obsolete sense 'sth bitten, food'.]

frogeye /frog ī/ *n.* a fungal disease of plants that causes rounded spots to appear on the leaves

frogfish /frog fish/ (*plural* **-fish** *or* **-fishes**) *n.* a fish living at the bottom of the sea that has a globe-shaped warty or prickly body and fins adapted for catching its prey. Family: Antennariidae.

frogging /frógging/ *n.* ornamental braid fastenings on the front of a jacket [Late 19thC. Formed from FROG[2].]

froghopper /frog hopər/ *n.* a jumping plant-sucking insect with larvae that produce cuckoo spit. US term **spittlebug** [Early 18thC. Because of their shape and because they leap.]

frog kick *n.* a kick used especially in swimming the breaststroke, in which the legs are first simul-taneously bent, then straightened, to push the swimmer along

frogman /frógmən/ (*plural* **-men** /-mən/) *n.* an under-water swimmer equipped with breathing ap-paratus, a wetsuit, flippers, and other underwater gear, especially sb engaged in military, police, or rescue work

frogmarch /frog maarch/ *vt.* (**-marches, -marching, -marched**) **1.** FORCE FORWARD to force sb to walk with arms pinned behind the back **2.** CARRY FACE DOWN to carry a drunken or uncooperative person face down between four people, each of whom is holding him or her by a leg or an arm (*archaic*) ■ *n.* ACT OF FROGMARCHING SB the act or process of frogmarching sb

frogmouth /frog mowth/ *n.* an Australian or Asian nocturnal bird that has grey or brown plumage and a wide mouth with a hooked bill. Frogmouths prey on insects and other small creeping animals by swooping down on them with the mouth wide open. Family: Podargidae.

frog's-bit *n.* US PLANTS = **frogbit**

frogspawn /frog spawn/ *n.* a floating mass of fertilized frog's eggs in a transparent jelly

frog spit *n.* **1.** MASS OF AQUATIC PLANTS a foamy green mass of small aquatic plants or algae floating on the surface of a pond **2.** INSECTS = **cuckoo spit** [From its resemblance to spittle]

frolic /fróllik/ *vi.* (**-ics, -icking, -icked**) PLAY LIGHTHEARTEDLY to frisk about, behave, or play in a carefree, un-inhibited way ○ *children frolicking on the sands* ■ *n.* **1.** STH LIVELY AND CAREFREE a lively carefree game, action, or amusement **2.** CAREFREE PLAY lively carefree play or behaviour ○ *'As a result, Anne had the golden summer of her life as far as freedom and frolic went'.* (Lucy Maud Montgomery, *Anne of Green Gables*; 1908) [Early 16thC. From Dutch *vrolijk* 'glad, joyous', from *vro* 'happy'.] —**frolicker** *n.*

frolicsome /frólliksəm/ *adj.* frisky and full of fun and high spirits

from (*stressed*) /from/; (*unstressed*) /frəm/ CORE MEANING: a preposition used to indicate the source or be-ginning of sth, in terms of location, situation, or time ○ *The condition can manifest itself anytime from adolescence onward.* ○ *Most funding comes from government and private grants and loans.* ○ *high-lights from her latest novel* ○ *You can connect to our computer network from home.*

prep. **1.** RANGE used to indicate a range, either of time, amount, or things ○ *We are open from 2 to 4.30.* ○ *They sell everything, from washing machines to magazines.* **2.** DISTANCE used to indicate the dis-tance between two things or places ○ *The nearest town is not far from here.* **3.** USING indicating the materials or substances used in order to make sth ○ *built from native pine* **4.** CAUSE used to indicate the cause of or reason for sth ○ *low morale resulting from staff cuts* **5.** RESTRAINT used to indicate that an action does not happen or should not happen ○ *prevented from seeing her* [Old English. Ultimately from an Indo-European word meaning 'forward, toward' that was also the ancestor of English *forth, before, primary*, and *private*.]

fromage frais /frómmaazh fráy/ *n.* a fresh cheese that has a light creamy taste, a texture like thick cream, and a variable fat content [From French, literally 'fresh cheese']

Frome, Lake /frōm/ salt lake in northeastern South Australia. Normally dry, it measures approximately 98 km/60 mi. by 48 km/30 mi.

fromenty *n.* = **frumenty**

frond /frond/ *n.* **1.** LARGE DIVIDED LEAF a large leaf divided into many thin sections that is found on many flowerless plants, especially ferns and palms **2.** SEAWEED RESEMBLING FERN LEAVES any growth that resembles the leaf of a fern or palm tree, especially a growth of seaweed that resembles leaves [Late 18thC. From Latin *frond-*, the stem of *frons* 'leaf', of unknown origin.] —**fronded** *adj.*

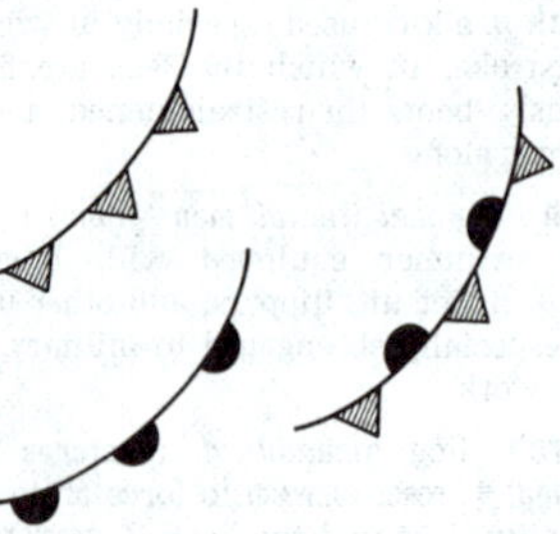

Front: Meteorological symbols indicating warm and cold weather fronts

front /frunt/ *n.* **1.** PART OR SURFACE FACING FORWARD the part or surface that faces forward, is intended to be seen first, has the main entrance, or is facing the direction of motion or the direction people face ○ *You can only see the front of the house from here.* **2.** FORWARD AREA, SECTION, OR POSITION the area, section, or position just ahead of, close to, or at the forward part of sth ○ *You sit in the front and I'll ride in the back.* **3.** FRONT DOOR OR GARDEN the front door or the area beyond it ○ *I'll go out the front, and you go out the back.* **4.** BEGINNING OR FIRST PAGES the beginning or first pages of a book or magazine **5.** FAÇADE OF BUILDING a façade of a building, especially the one that faces the street, or a part of it ○ *bring the car around to the front* **6.** SIDE OF PROPERTY ADJOINING STH the side of a property that borders sth else, e.g. a street, lake, or river **7.** FORWARD DIRECTION the direction straight ahead ○ *face the front* **8.** POSITION AHEAD OF SB a place or position approximately ahead of sb ○ *Just up to our front was a clump of trees.* **9.** LEADING POSITION a prominent or leading position in any field of activity ○ *companies at the front of genetic research* **10.** NOTICEABLE POSITION a conspicuous position ○ *a disturbing aspect that came to the front* **11.** ASPECT OF STH a way of viewing a situation ○ *Things looked desperate on all fronts.* **12.** SEASIDE PROMENADE a street, area of land, or promenade running along beside the beach or shore at a seaside or lakeside resort **13.** MIL BATTLE ZONE an area where armies are facing one another or where fighting between armies is taking place ○ *soldiers returning from the front* **14.** MIL SPACE DEFENDED BY ARMY UNIT the width of territory occupied or defended by an army or a military unit facing an enemy ○ *Each section was defending a front of some two miles.* **15.** MIL DIRECTION IN WHICH TROOPS ARE FACING the direction in which troops are facing when formed up in line **16.** AREA OF ACTIVITY a stated area of activity or operations ○ *There have been a lot of changes on the domestic front since we last got together.* **17.** METEOROL INTERFACE BETWEEN DIFFERING AIR MASSES a line along which one mass of air meets another that is different in temperature or density **18.** POL GROUP WITH COMMON PURPOSES a group of people or organizations with a common purpose, especially a broad political coalition ○ *a national liberation front* **19.** CLOTHES FRONT PART OF GARMENT the part of a garment, or the clothing, that covers the front part of the body, especially the chest ○ *You've got gravy all down your front.* **20.** CLOTHES DETACHABLE SHIRT FRONT a detachable shirt front, especially part of a man's formal dress shirt **21.** DELIBERATELY ASSUMED BEHAVIOUR a manner or type of behaviour adopted by sb in order to deal with a situation or disguise the person's true feelings ○ *put on a brave front* **22.** COVER FOR ILLEGAL ACTIVITIES an apparently respectable person, organization, or business acting as a cover for illegal or secret activities **23.** FIGUREHEAD a nominal leader or head who has no real authority **24.** IMPERTINENCE cheek or cockiness ○ *That took a bit of front!* **25.** FACE the face or forehead (*archaic*) ■ *adj.* **1.** AT OR NEAR THE FRONT situated at, on, or near the front of sth, or placed further forward than others **2.** LING PRODUCED WITH TONGUE FORWARD IN MOUTH produced with the back of the tongue close to the forward part of the roof of the mouth ■ *v.* (**fronts, fronting, fronted**) **1.** *vti.* FACE STH to have a front that faces towards sth ○ *a hotel fronting the ocean* **2.** *vt.* GIVE FRONT COVERING OR APPEARANCE TO to give sth a front or visible surface of a particular kind ○ *The building is fronted with red brick.* **3.** *vt.* BE THE HEAD OF to be the head, leader, or spokesperson of a group or organization such as a band ○ *a group fronted by a young lawyer from London* **4.** *vt.* HOST A SHOW to act as the presenter or host of a television or radio programme **5.** *vi.* ACT AS RESPECTABLE COVER FOR to act as a respectable cover for sth secret or illegal or for sb doing sth secret or illegal **6.** *vt.* CONFRONT to confront sb or sth (*archaic*) [13thC. Via French from Latin *front-*, the stem of *frons* 'forehead, front', of unknown origin.] ◇ **in front 1.** leading or ahead of sb or sth else **2.** close to or in the front of sth or further forward than sb else **3.** in the lead in a race or competition ○ *Polls show the current mayor far in front as the election nears.* ◇ **in front of 1.** ahead of sb or in the direction in which sb is facing **2.** close to the front of sth **3.** in the presence, sight, or hearing of sb ◇ **out front 1.** THEATRE in front of the curtain or in the auditorium, as opposed to on the stage **2.** at or to the front of a building ○ *I'll go out front and talk to them.* ◇ **up front 1.** close to the front of sth, or further forward than others **2.** in advance, e.g. before any work is done or any goods are delivered

WORD KEY: CULTURAL NOTE

All Quiet on the Western Front, a novel by German writer Erich Maria Remarque (1929). This classic anti war novel, which was based on the author's own experiences as an 18-year-old soldier in the German army during World War I, is a grimly realistic account of trench warfare. It was made into a film by Lewis Milestone in 1930.

front up *vi.* ANZ to arrive or appear somewhere ○ *You can't just front up here and expect me to help you.*

front. *abbr.* frontispiece

frontage /frúntij/ *n.* **1.** FRONT OF BUILDING the front side of a building or piece of property **2.** LAND BETWEEN BUILDING AND STREET the land between a building and a street or road **3.** LENGTH OF FRONT the length of the front of a building or piece of land next to a street, river, or lake **4.** PIECE OF LAND ADJOINING STH a piece of land situated next to a street, river, or lake **5.** OUTLOOK the direction in which a building faces or its outlook

frontal[1] /frúnt'l/ *adj.* **1.** AT OR IN THE FRONT situated at or in the front of sth **2.** SHOWING THE FRONT OF STH showing or depicting the front of sb or of sth, especially the full view of a naked body **3.** MIL TOWARDS ENEMY FRONT directed against an enemy's front, usually across open ground ○ *a frontal attack* **4.** DIRECT AND FORCEFUL direct, forceful, and intended to be overwhelming **5.** ANAT RELATING TO FOREHEAD relating to the forehead or the front part of the skull **6.** METEOROL RELATING TO WEATHER FRONTS involving or relating to weather fronts —**frontally** *adv.*

frontal[2] /frúnt'l/ *n.* **1.** ALTAR CLOTH a cloth covering for the front of an altar **2.** FAÇADE OF BUILDING the façade of a building or tomb [14thC. Via Old French *frontel* 'ornament for the forehead' from Latin *frontale*, from *front-* (see FRONT).]

frontal bone *n.* the bone forming the front part of the skull that shapes the forehead and part of the eye sockets and nasal cavity

frontal lobe *n.* the front part of each hemisphere of the brain

frontal lobotomy *n.* a prefrontal lobotomy (*dated*)

front bench *n.* **1.** BENCH FOR POLITICAL LEADERS in Parliament, the bench on each side nearest the floor of the House, reserved for Government ministers on one side and their Opposition counterparts on the other **2.** MOST IMPORTANT POLITICIANS the most important members of the Government or Opposition, who sit on the front bench in Parliament —**frontbencher** *n.*

front burner *n.* a position of importance or priority (*informal*) ○ *a scheme which seems to be no longer on the front burner* [From the part of a hob which is used for rapid cooking]

frontcourt /frúnt kawrt/ *n.* **1.** TARGET HALF OF BASKETBALL COURT in basketball, the half of a court containing the basket in which a team attempts to score **2.** FRONT-PLAYING BASKETBALL PLAYERS the forwards and centre of a basketball team

front door *n.* **1.** CHIEF ENTRANCE the main entrance to a house or other building, closed by a door **2.** CHIEF MEANS the usual and unsuspicious way of achieving a position

front end *n.* **1.** COMPUT USER INTERFACE the user interface of a computer system **2.** = **front-end processor**

front-end *adj.* **1.** FIN OF START OF PROCESS relating to the start of a process or project, especially a commercial or financial one ○ *heavy front-end costs* **2.** COMPUT OF USER INTERFACE relating to the user interface of a computer system

front-end load *n.* an amount, making up a large part of the initial payments, paid by an investor in an insurance scheme or long-term investment, intended to cover commission and other expenses

front-end processor *n.* a computer used to receive data and carry out preliminary processing on it before passing it on to another computer for further processing

frontier /frun teer/ *n.* **1.** BORDERLAND a border between two countries, or the land immediately adjacent to this ○ *cross the frontier into Spain* **2.** EDGE OF SETTLEMENT the part of a country with expanding settlement that is being opened up by hunters, herders, and other pioneers in advance of full urban settlement **3.** LIMIT OF KNOWLEDGE the furthest limit of knowledge in a particular field ○ *pushing back the frontiers of science* [14thC. From Anglo-Norman *frounter*, French *frontière* 'front part (of an army)', from *front* 'forehead' (see FRONT). The original English sense was 'front side, forepart'.]

frontiersman /frún teerzmən, frun teerzmən/ (*plural* **-men** /-mən, -/) *n.* a man living in a frontier area, especially an area newly opened up for settlement

frontierswoman /frún teerz wŏŏmən, frun teerz wŏŏmən/ (*plural* **-en** /-wimin, -/) *n.* a woman living in a frontier area, especially an area newly opened up for settlement

frontispiece /frúntiss peess/ *n.* **1.** PUBL BOOK ILLUSTRATION an illustration at the beginning of a book, usually facing the title page **2.** ARCHIT BUILDING FAÇADE the principal façade of a building, treated as a separate element **3.** ARCHIT PEDIMENT a pediment, usually ornamental, above a window or door [Late 16thC. By folk etymology from French *frontispice* (by association with PIECE), from late Latin *frontispicium* 'façade' (literally 'viewing the forehead'), from, ultimately, Latin *frons* 'forehead' + *specere* 'to look at'.]

frontlet /frúntlət/ *n.* **1.** HIST DECORATIVE BAND a decorative band worn on the forehead **2.** ZOOL ANIMAL'S FOREHEAD an animal's forehead, especially when, as in certain birds, it has a different colour from the rest of the head **3.** CHR ALTAR-CLOTH BORDER a decorated border on the frontal of an altar [15thC. From Old French *frontelet* 'little forehead band', from *frontel* (see FRONTAL[2]).]

front line, frontline *n.* **1.** MIL FORWARD LINE the forward line of a battle, position, or formation (*hyphenated when used before a noun*) **2.** ADVANCED POSITION the most advanced, important, or conspicuous position in any situation **3.** BASKETBALL = **frontcourt** *n.* 2 ■ *adj.* **frontline, front-line 1.** AT LIMITS OF ATTAINMENT that is the most advanced or important of its kind ○ *a frontline technological development* **2.** BORDERING A TROUBLE SPOT relating to countries that border another country in which an armed conflict is taking place

front-load *vt.* to assign the bulk of the costs of an insurance scheme or long-term investment to an early stage

front loader *n.* a washing machine in which clothes are loaded through a door at the front rather than the top

front man *n.* (*informal*) **1.** FIGUREHEAD sb who is presented as being in charge of an organization or activity while the real authority is, for reasons of illegality or secrecy, kept hidden **2.** MUSIC LEAD SINGER the lead singer of a band or other musical group

front matter *n.* the material that appears in a book before the main text, e.g. the title page, the cataloguing-in-publication data, the table of contents, and the preface

front of house *n.* **1.** AREA FOR AUDIENCE the parts of a theatre, cinema, concert hall, or other performance venue where members of the audience are normally admitted (*hyphenated when used before a noun*) **2.** AREA FOR DINERS the parts of a restaurant where customers sit and are served, as opposed to the kitchens

frontogenesis /frúntō jénnississ/ *n.* the formation or development of a weather front [Mid-20thC. Coined from FRONT + -GENESIS.]

frontolysis /frun tóllississ/ *n.* the weakening or disappearance of a weather front [Mid-20thC. Coined from FRONT + -LYSIS.]

fronton /frón ton, fron tón/ *n.* a court used for the game of pelota or jai alai [Late 19thC. From Spanish 'gable, wall of a frontón', from *fronte* 'forehead', from the Latin stem *front-* (see FRONT).]

front-page *adj.* important or interesting enough to appear on the front page of a newspaper

front room *n.* a sitting room in a house, often one reserved for more formal entertaining

frontrunner /frunt rúnnər, frúnt runər/ *n.* sb in a leading position in a race or contest (*informal*) ○ *the new frontrunner in the party leadership contest*

frontwards /frúntwərd(z)/, **frontward** /-wərd/ *adv.* towards or in the direction of the front —**frontwards** *adv.*

front-wheel drive *n.* a system of powering motor vehicles that uses the engine to drive the front wheels only

frost /frost/ *n.* **1.** FROZEN WATER crystals of frozen water deposited on a cold surface **2.** FREEZING TEMPERATURE an outdoor temperature below freezing point, resulting in the deposit of ice crystals ○ *had a hard frost as late as May* **3.** CHILLY MANNER a coldness of manner **4.** FAILURE OR FLOP sth, e.g. an artistic performance or a new book, that meets with an unenthusiastic reception (*informal*) ○ *The opening night was a true frost.* **5.** FREEZING the act or process of freezing ■ *v.* (**frosts, frosting, frosted**) **1.** *vti.* METEOROL COVER WITH FROST to cover sth with frost, especially hoarfrost, or become covered with frost **2.** *vt.* MAKE OPAQUE to make sth, especially glass or a window, unable to be seen through by giving its surface a rough or fine-grained texture **3.** *vt.* US FOOD PUT ICING ON to cover a cake or other pastry with icing or frosting **4.** *vt.* AGRIC, GARDENING KILL BY FREEZING to damage or kill crops or garden plants by frost [Old English *forst, frost,* from a prehistoric Germanic base that also produced English *freeze*]

frost up *vi.* to become covered in frost or ice, especially in a way that hinders a function ○ *The freezer has frosted up so much that the door won't close.*

Robert Frost

Frost /frost/, **Robert** (1874–1963) US poet, best known for his spare poems about New England life, including 'Stopping by Woods on a Snowy Evening' and 'The Road Not Taken'. The unofficial poet laureate of the United States, he won the Pulitzer Prize four times (1924, 1931, 1937, and 1943). Full name **Robert Lee Frost**

frostbite /frost bīt/ *n.* INJURY BY FREEZING damage to body extremities caused by prolonged exposure to freezing conditions, characterized by numbness, tissue death, and gangrene ■ *vt.* (**-bites, -biting, -bit, -bitten**) INJURE BY FREEZING to damage sth by prolonged exposure to freezing conditions (*usually passive*)

frostbound /frost bownd/ *adj.* confined to one place because of frost ○ *We were frostbound in our cabin for three days.*

frost-free *adj.* used to describe an appliance such as a refrigerator or freezer that does not need to be defrosted

frosting /frósting/ *n.* **1.** SOFT ICING a variety of soft icing for cakes made by whisking egg whites and sugar over hot water or incorporating hot syrup into whisked egg whites **2.** US RICH ICING icing that is typically thick and rich from the addition of milk, eggs, butter, or cream **3.** ROUGH SURFACE a roughened or dull surface produced on sth, especially glass or metal

frost line *n.* **1.** GEOG DEPTH LIMIT OF FROST the point below the surface of the ground beyond which frost will not penetrate **2.** METEOROL LINE ON MAP SHOWING FROST a line on a map joining places subject to the same number of frosts a year or to the same degree of frost

frost weathering *n.* the shattering of rock caused by the freezing of water in surface cracks and hollows, and in the pore spaces

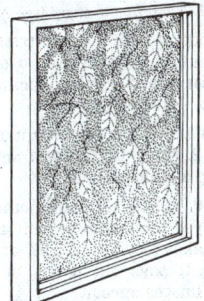

Frostwork

frostwork /frost wurk/ *n.* **1.** ARTS PATTERNS MADE BY FROST the patterns made by frost on various surfaces, especially windows, that often resemble tracery or the fronds of ferns **2.** IMITATION OF FROST PATTERNS decoration on metal or glass imitating the patterns made naturally by frost

frosty /frósti/ (**-ier, -iest**) *adj.* **1.** VERY COLD cold enough for the formation of frost **2.** COVERED IN FROST covered in frost, especially hoarfrost **3.** COLD IN MANNER cold and unwelcoming in manner **4.** WHITE LIKE FROST looking like hoarfrost, especially in whiteness ○ *a shock of matted frosty hair* —**frostily** *adv.* —**frostiness** *n.*

froth /froth/ *n.* **1.** FOAM a mass of bubbles in or on the surface of a liquid **2.** FOAMY SALIVA a foamy mixture of saliva and air bubbles produced at the mouth in some diseases or by exhaustion **3.** TRIVIA anything seen as being insubstantial or trivial ○ *The conversation at the party was mostly froth and posturing.* ■ *v.* (**froths, frothing, frothed**) **1.** *vt.* CAUSE TO FOAM to make sth produce foam, or cover sth with foam **2.** *vi.* CREATE FOAM to produce foam or emerge as foam ○ *froth at the mouth* [14thC. From Old Norse *froða* or *frauð*.]

froth flotation *n.* = flotation *n.* 5

frothy /fróthi/ (**-ier, -iest**) *adj.* **1.** FULL OF FOAM characterized by, covered in, or producing foam **2.** TRIVIAL with no serious content or purpose ○ *a frothy sitcom* —**frothily** *adv.* —**frothiness** *n.*

frottage /frottaazh, fro taázh/ *n.* **1.** ARTS RUBBING IN ART an art technique in which a rubbing is taken of a surface to create a design **2.** PSYCHOL SEXUAL RUBBING the obtaining of sexual pleasure by rubbing the clothed body against that of others, usually strangers in crowded places [Mid-20thC. From French, 'rubbing, friction', from *frotter* 'to rub', of unknown origin.]

Froude /frood/, **J. A.** (1818–94) British historian. Strongly influenced by Thomas Carlyle, he is best known for his 12-volume *History of England from the Fall of Wolsey to the Defeat of the Spanish Armada* (1856–70). Full name **James Anthony Froude**

froufrou /fróo froo/ *n.* **1.** RUSTLING OF SILK the sound made by the rustling of silk, especially women's dresses **2.** FANCY TRIMMINGS fancy trimmings or elaborate decoration, especially on women's clothes [Late 19thC. From French, an imitation of the sound.]

froward /fró ərd/ *adj.* stubbornly disobedient or contrary (*old*) ○ *always a froward child* [Old English *frāward* 'in a direction leading away from', formed from Old Norse *frá* 'from' (see FRO) + -WARD] —**frowardly** *adv.* —**frowardness** *n.*

frown /frown/ *v.* (**frowns, frowning, frowned**) **1.** *vi.* MAKE DISPLEASED EXPRESSION to show a facial expression of displeasure or concentration by wrinkling the brow **2.** *vt.* EXPRESS BY FROWNING to communicate sth by frowning ■ *n.* DISPLEASED EXPRESSION a facial expression of displeasure or concentration made by wrinkling the brow [14thC. From Old French *froignier* 'to frown, snort', from *froigne* 'scowl'.] —**frowner** *n.* —**frowningly** *adv.*

frown on, frown upon *vt.* to dislike or disapprove of sth

— **WORD KEY: SYNONYMS** —
See Synonyms at *disapprove.*

frowsty /frówsti/ (**-ier, -iest**) *adj.* unpleasant to be in because of mustiness, staleness, or a bad smell ○ *a frowsty atmosphere in the room.* US term **frowzy** *adj.* 2 [Mid-19thC. Originally a dialect word, of uncertain origin: perhaps an alteration of FROWZY.] —**frowstiness** *n.*

frowzy /frówzi/ (**-ier, -iest**), **frowsy** (**-ier, -iest**) *adj.* **1.** UNTIDY untidy or shabby in personal appearance or manner of dress ○ *a frowzy layabout* ○ *frowzy curtains at a tenement window* **2.** STUFFY unpleasant to be in because of mustiness, staleness, or a bad smell. US = **frowsty** [Late 17thC. Origin unknown.] —**frowziness** *n.*

froze past tense of **freeze**

frozen /fróz'n/ past participle of **freeze** ■ *adj.* **1.** WITH ICE covered by or made into ice ○ *a frozen lake* **2.** AFFECTED BY ICE made inoperable, damaged, or obstructed by ice or freezing temperatures ○ *All trains are delayed because of frozen points.* ○ *no running water in the house because of frozen pipes* **3.** EXTREMELY COLD characterized by extreme cold ○ *the frozen north* **4.** PRESERVED BY FREEZING preserved by freezing for eating at a later time ○ *frozen pizza* **5.** IMMOBILE immobile or unable to move ○ *She stood there, frozen in terror.* **6.** FIN FIXED deliberately fixed at a given level to avoid undesirable economic or social consequences **7.** FIN NOT TO BE SOLD that cannot be sold or otherwise liquidated (*refers to assets*) ○ *the country's frozen assets* —**frozenly** *adv.* —**frozenness** *n.*

frozen shoulder *n.* a condition in which a shoulder joint becomes stiff and painful, especially after having been kept in one position for a time

FRPS *abbr.* Fellow of the Royal Photographic Society

FRS *abbr.* Fellow of the Royal Society

frt *abbr.* freight

fructan /frúktən/ *n.* a natural polymer, composed of units of fructose arranged in a chain, that is an important source of stored energy for some plants [Mid-20thC. Coined from FRUCTOSE + -AN.]

Fructidor /frúkti dawr/ *n.* the 12th month of the year in the French Revolutionary calendar, corresponding to 18 August to 16 September in the Gregorian calendar [Late 18thC. From French, formed from Latin *fructus* 'fruit' (see FRUIT) + Greek *dōron* 'gift'; from its being the time when fruit is ripe for gathering.]

fructiferous /fruk tíffərəss, frook-/ *adj.* used to describe a tree or other plant that bears fruit [Mid-17thC. Formed from Latin *fructifer* 'fruit-bearing', from *fructus* 'fruit' (see FRUIT).]

fructification /frúktifi káysh'n, frook-/ *n.* **1.** PRODUCTION OF FRUIT the production of fruit or fruits by a tree or other plant **2.** FRUIT OF SEED-BEARING PLANT the fruit produced by a seed-bearing plant **3.** SEED-BEARING PART a seed-bearing or spore-bearing part of a plant, alga, or fungus

fructify /frúkti fī, fróok-/ (**-fies, -fying, -fied**) *vti.* to become, or cause to become, productive or fruitful [14thC. Via French *fructifier* from Latin *fructificare*, from *fructus* 'fruit' (see FRUIT).]

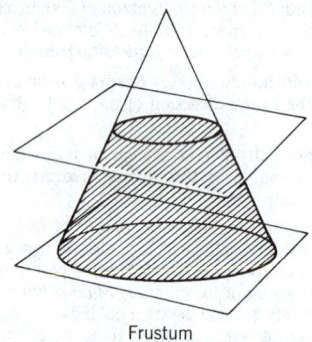

Fructose

fructose /frúk tōz, -tōss, fróok tōz, -tōss/ *n.* a sugar found in certain fruits and honey. Formula: $C_6H_{12}O_6$. [Mid-19thC. Coined from Latin *fructus* 'fruit' (see FRUIT) + -OSE.]

fructuous /frúk tyoo əss/ *adj.* productive of much fruit, or full of fruit (*literary*) [14thC. Directly or via Old French from Latin *fructuosus*, from *fructus* 'fruit' (see FRUIT).]

frugal /fróog'l/ *adj.* **1.** THRIFTY characterized by thriftiness and avoidance of waste **2.** MEAGRE involving very little expense [Early 16thC. Directly or via French from Latin *frugalis*, from *frugi* 'economical, useful', from *frug*, the stem of *frux* 'fruit, value'.] —**frugality** /froo gálləti/ *n.* —**frugally** /fróog'li/ *adv.* —**frugalness** /-g'lnəss/ *n.*

frugivore /fróoji vawr/ *n.* an animal that eats mainly fruit [Mid-20thC. Coined from the Latin stem *frug-* 'fruit' + *-vore* 'eating' (via French from Latin -*vorus*; see -VOROUS).]

frugivorous /froo jívvərəss/ *adj.* used to describe an animal that eats mainly fruit [Early 18thC. Coined from the Latin stem *frug-* 'fruit' (source of English *frugal*) + -VOROUS.]

fruit /froot/ *n.* **1.** EDIBLE PART OF PLANT an edible part of a plant, usually fleshy and containing seeds **2.** OVARY OF PLANT the ripened seed-bearing ovary of a plant. It is usually considered to be sweet and fleshy, as in plums, but may be dry, as in poppies, or be a simple edible supporting structure, as in strawberries. **3.** SPORE-PRODUCING PART a spore-producing part of a plant **4.** PRODUCE the produce of any plant grown or harvested by humans ○ *the fruits of the field* **5.** PRODUCT OF STH the product or consequence of sth done ○ *We are now seeing the fruits of our efforts.* **6.** WINE FRUITY TASTE a fruity taste in wine ○ *a big red with lots of fruit* **7.** OFFSPRING the offspring of humans or animals (*dated*) **8.** US OFFENSIVE TERM an offensive term for a gay man (*offensive insult*) ■ *vti.* (**fruits, fruiting, fruited**) PRODUCE FRUIT to bear fruit, or cause a plant or tree to bear fruit ○ *This variety fruits in August.* [12thC. Via French from Latin *fructus* 'enjoyment, produce, fruit', from the past participle of *frui* 'to enjoy, have the use of'.] ◇ **bear fruit** to be successful in the end, typically after planning and effort have been expended ◇ **old fruit** a term of address for a man, especially a friend (*dated informal*)

fruitage /fróotij/ *n.* **1.** FRUIT PRODUCTION the production of fruit, the condition of a plant or tree when bearing fruit, or the time when this happens **2.** FRUITS fruits as a group **3.** RESULT OR EFFECT the results or cumulative set of effects deriving from a usually long-term process (*formal*)

fruitarian /froo taíri ən/ *n.* sb who follows a rare vegetarian diet consisting only of fruit, including nuts, seeds, and any other form of plant fruit [Late 19thC. Modelled on VEGETARIAN.]

fruit bat *n.* a large bat found in Europe, Asia, and Africa. Most fruit bats eat fruit but others eat pollen or nectar. Suborder: Megachiroptera.

fruitcake /fróot kayk/ *n.* **1.** FOOD CAKE WITH DRIED FRUIT IN IT a dense cake containing dried fruit such as raisins, currants, and sultanas. Rich fruitcakes with a high proportion of fruit have a long shelf life, as the high sugar content acts as a preservative. **2.** SB IRRATIONAL sb considered to be irrational or out of touch with reality (*informal insult*)

fruit cocktail *n.* a fruit salad made up of small or diced fruits such as pears, peaches, and pineapple, typically sold canned in syrup and usually served as a dessert

fruit drop *n.* **1.** PREMATURE FALLING OF FRUIT the falling from the tree of fruit that is not fully ripe **2.** BOILED SWEET a fruit-flavoured boiled sweet

fruiterer /fróotərər/ *n.* sb who deals in fruit [15thC. Formed from obsolete *fruiter* 'sb who deals in or has care of fruit'.]

fruit fly *n.* **1.** PLANT-EATING FLY a small insect that eats plant tissue. Order: Trypetidae. **2.** FRUIT-EATING FLY a small insect that eats decaying fruit. Genus: *Drosophila.*

fruitful /fróotf'l/ *adj.* **1.** BEARING MUCH FRUIT bearing fruit, especially in abundance **2.** PROLIFIC producing many offspring ○ *a fruitful marriage* **3.** CAUSING FERTILITY causing or promoting fertility or productivity ○ *fruitful soil* **4.** CREATIVE highly productive or creative **5.** SUCCESSFUL OR BENEFICIAL producing useful results or benefits —**fruitfully** *adv.* —**fruitfulness** *n.*

fruiting body *n.* a part of certain fungi from which spores are released

fruition /froo ísh'n/ *n.* **1.** COMPLETION a state or point in which sth has come to maturity or had a desired outcome ○ *Our plans have come to fruition.* **2.** ENJOYMENT OF INTENDED OUTCOME the enjoyment of a desired outcome when it happens **3.** BOT PLANT'S FRUIT PRODUCTION the production of fruit by a tree or other plant [15thC. Via French from the late Latin stem *fruition-*, from, ultimately, Latin *frui* 'to enjoy' (see FRUIT).]

fruitless /fróotləss/ *adj.* **1.** UNSUCCESSFUL producing nothing or nothing worthwhile ○ *a fruitless discussion* **2.** NOT BEARING FRUIT producing no fruit —**fruitlessly** *adv.* —**fruitlessness** *n.*

fruitlet /fróotlət/ *n.* **1.** SMALL FRUIT a fruit of smaller than normal size **2.** PART OF MULTIPLE FRUIT any of the parts that make up a multiple fruit

fruit machine *n.* UK a coin-operated gambling machine played by pushing a button or pulling a lever that makes pictures of fruit or other objects spin briefly. It pays out if any of certain combinations of images appear.

fruit salad *n.* a mixture of pieces of fruit, usually in fruit juice or syrup, served as a dessert. The fruit may be fresh, canned, dried, or a mixture of these. Canned fruit salad usually contains popular canned fruits such as peaches, pears, and pineapple.

fruit sugar *n.* = fructose

fruit tree *n.* a tree that produces edible fruit and is cultivated for that reason

fruitwood /fróot wŏŏd/ *n.* the wood of a fruit tree, especially when used in cabinet-making

fruity /fróoti/ (**-ier, -iest**) *adj.* **1.** OF FRUIT relating to, resembling, or reminiscent of fruit **2.** RICH IN TONE rich and resonant in voice tone **3.** SEXUALLY SUGGESTIVE salacious or indecent in content (*informal*) —**fruitily** *adv.* —**fruitiness** *n.*

frumentaceous /froomən táyshəss/ *adj.* made from, containing, or like wheat or any similar grain [Mid-17thC. Formed from late Latin *frumentaceus*, from *frumentum* 'corn, grain' (see FRUMENTY).]

frumenty /fróomənti/, **fromenty** /frómənti/, **furmenty** /fúrmənti/, **furmety** /fúrməti/, **furmity** *n.* an old-fashioned pudding of wheat cooked to a porridge, usually with milk added. Regional variations add fruit or enrich the porridge with eggs. [14thC. From Old French *frumentee, fourmentee,* from *frument, fourment* 'grain', from Latin *frumentum,* perhaps from *frui* 'to enjoy' (see FRUIT).]

frump /frump/ *n.* a term used to insult a woman considered by the speaker not to be good looking or to dress well (*informal insult*) [Mid-16thC. Origin uncertain: probably a shortening of earlier *frumple* 'wrinkle', from, ultimately, Middle Dutch *verrompelen* 'to rumple completely'. The original English meaning was 'sneering speech'.]

frumpy /frúmpi/ (**-ier, -iest**), **frumpish** *adj.* unattractive, drab, or dowdy —**frumpily** *adv.* —**frumpiness** *n.*

frusemide /frússə mīd/ *n.* a diuretic drug used in treating hypertension and oedema. US term **fu-**

rosemide [Mid-20thC. Coined from *fru-* (alteration of the first syllable of *furyl* 'chemical derived from furan') + *-sem-* (of unknown origin) + -IDE.]

frustrate /fru stráyt/ *vt.* (**-trates, -trating, -trated**) **1.** THWART to prevent sb or sth from succeeding or sth from coming to fruition ○ *All attempts to put to sea were frustrated by high winds.* **2.** DISCOURAGE to make sb feel discouraged, exasperated, or weary ■ *adj.* THWARTED thwarted or blocked (*archaic*) ○ *All their schemes for their new house were frustrated.* [15thC. From Latin *frustrari* 'to deceive, frustrate, render useless', from *frustra* 'in vain, without effect'.] —**frustrater** *n.* —**frustrating** *adj.* —**frustratingly** *adv.*

frustrated /fru stráytid/ *adj.* feeling unfulfilled or unsatisfied

frustration /fru stráysh'n/ *n.* **1.** FRUSTRATING OF SB OR STH an act or instance of causing sb or sth to be dissatisfied or unfulfilled **2.** STH THAT THWARTS sth that blocks, thwarts, and upsets sb all at the same time ○ *His lack of ambition was a frustration to his father.* **3.** DISSATISFACTION a feeling of disappointment, exasperation, or weariness caused by aims being thwarted or desires unsatisfied

frustule /frúss tyool/ *n.* the hard cell wall of a microscopic organism (**diatom**) [Mid-19thC. From Latin *frustulum* 'small piece', from *frustum* 'bit (cut off), piece (of a whole)'.]

Frustum

frustum /frústəm/ *n.* the part of a solid between its base and a plane that cuts it parallel to the base [Mid-17thC. From Latin 'bit (cut off), piece (of a whole)' (source of English *frustule*).]

frutescent /froo téss'nt/ *adj.* looking or growing like a shrub [Early 18thC. Coined from Latin *frutex* 'shrub' + -ESCENT.] —**frutescence** *n.*

fruticose /fróoti kōz, -kōss/ *adj.* = frutescent [Mid-17thC. From Latin *fruticosus*, from *frutic-*, the stem of *frutex* 'shrub'.]

fry[1] /frī/ *v.* (**fries, frying, fried**) **1.** *vti.* COOK QUICKLY IN FAT to cook sth in fat over high heat, or be cooked in this way **2.** *vi.* BECOME HOT OR OVERHEATED to become extremely hot as a result of the surrounding environment or temperature (*informal*) ○ *We'll fry in this heat!* **3.** *vti.* US EXECUTE OR BE EXECUTED to execute sb or be executed in an electric chair (*slang*) (*offensive in some contexts*) ■ *n.* (*plural* **fries**) OFFAL offal or a dish made from offal, especially as eaten fried [13thC. Via French *frire* from Latin *frigere* 'to roast, fry' (source of English *fritter*[1]).]

fry[2] /frī/ *npl.* **1.** YOUNG FISHES the young of various fish **2.** YOUNG ANIMALS the young of various animals that breed or hatch in large numbers **3.** CHILDREN small offspring of human parents (*humorous*) ○ *Will the young fry like this picture book?* [13thC. Origin uncertain: probably from Anglo-Norman *frei*, Old French *frai* 'spawn', from *froier* 'to rub, spawn', from Latin *fricare* 'to rub' (source of English *friction*).]

Fry /frī/, **Christopher** (*b.* 1907) British dramatist. His verse drama *The Lady's Not for Burning* (1948) brought him considerable popularity. Other plays include *Venus Observed* (1951), and *Curtmantle* (1962). Born **Christopher Harris**

Fry, Elizabeth (1780–1845) British prison reformer. A Quaker, she campaigned for improvements in prison conditions throughout Europe. Born **Elizabeth Gurney**

FRY *abbr.* Federal Republic of Yugoslavia

fryer /frí ər/, **frier** *n.* **1.** VESSEL FOR FRYING a vessel in which food is fried (*usually used in combination*) **2.** US CHICKEN a young chicken suitable for frying

frying pan *n.* a shallow metal pan with a long handle, used for frying food ◇ **out of the frying pan (and) into the fire** from one difficult or dangerous situation to an even worse one

fry-up *n.* (*informal*) **1.** FRYING A MEAL an act or occasion of frying several types of food together for a meal **2.** FRIED MEAL a mixture of fried food

FSA *abbr.* Fellow of the Society of Antiquaries

FSH *abbr.* **1.** follicle-stimulating hormone **2.** CARS full service history

f-stop *n.* any of the settings for a lens aperture that correspond with an f-number

ft *abbr.* **1.** foot *or* feet **2.** fortification

FT *abbr.* Financial Times

fth., fthm. *abbr.* fathom

FT index *n.* any of the share indexes compiled by the Financial Times

FTP *n.* STANDARD PROCEDURE FOR TRANSFERRING FILES a set of rules or standard procedure that allows a user on one computer to transfer files to and from another computer over a network, e.g. the Internet. Full form **file-transfer protocol** ■ *vt.* (**FTPs, FTPing, FTPed**) TRANSFER USING FTP to transfer data using FTP

FTSE 100 Index /fóotsi wun húndrəd-/ an average of the London stock exchange prices of the stocks of the 100 largest British companies, published daily. Full form **Financial Times Stock Exchange 100 Index**

fubsy /fúbsi/ (**-sier, -siest**) *adj.* of short stature and wide girth (*archaic*) [Late 18thC. Formed from obsolete *fub(s)* 'small plump person' (of uncertain origin: perhaps a blend of FAT and CHUB).]

Fuchs /fóoks/, **Sir Vivian Ernest** (*b.* 1908) British geologist and explorer. He led the first journey across Antarctica (1957–58).

Fuchsia

fuchsia /fyóoshə/ *n.* **1.** PLANTS FLOWERING PLANT a plant or shrub widely grown for its drooping purplish, reddish, or white flowers. Genus: *Fuchsia.* **2.** COLOURS DEEP PINK COLOUR a brilliant deep pink colour tinged with purple ■ *adj.* COLOURS OF DEEP PINK COLOUR of a brilliant deep pink colour tinged with purple [Late 18thC. From modern Latin, genus name, named after Leonhard *Fuchs* (1501–66), a German botanist.]

fuchsin /fóoksin/, **fuchsine** /fóok seen, -sin/ *n.* a darkgreen crystalline solid that when dissolved in water makes a bluish-red solution. It is used to dye textiles, to stain bacteria, and as a disinfectant. Formula: $C_{20}H_{19}N_3 \cdot HCl$. [Mid-19thC. Either from French *fuchsine*, or formed from its source, German *Fuchs* 'fox' (a translation of French *Renard*, name of the company that first produced the dye).]

fuci plural of **fucus**

fuck /fuk/ *v.* (**fucks, fucking, fucked**) (*taboo offensive*) **1.** *vti.* OFFENSIVE TERM an offensive term meaning to have sexual intercourse, or have sexual intercourse with a specified person **2.** *vt.* OFFENSIVE TERM an offensive term used like a command, often followed by you, it, or another word to express anger, contempt, or rejection **3.** *vt.* OFFENSIVE TERM an offensive term meaning to ruin, botch, or destroy sth ■ *n.* (*taboo offensive*) **1.** OFFENSIVE TERM an offensive term meaning an act of sexual intercourse **2.** OFFENSIVE TERM an

offensive term meaning sb considered as a sexual partner of a specified quality **3.** OFFENSIVE TERM an offensive term meaning sth of little or no value ■ *interj.* OFFENSIVE TERM an offensive term used without a following word to express anger, disgust, fear, or surprise (*taboo offensive*) [Early 16thC. Origin uncertain: perhaps from a Scandinavian source, in which case the underlying sense might be 'to beat, bang'.]

fuck about, fuck around *vt.* (*taboo offensive*) **1.** OFFENSIVE TERM an offensive term meaning to behave stupidly or carelessly **2.** OFFENSIVE TERM an offensive term meaning to treat sb in a careless, insincere, or inconsiderate way

fuck off *vi.* (*taboo offensive*) **1.** OFFENSIVE TERM an offensive term used as a command dismissing sb in an angry or contemptuous way **2.** OFFENSIVE TERM an offensive term meaning to go away

fuck up *v.* (*taboo offensive*) **1.** *vt.* OFFENSIVE TERM an offensive term meaning to damage or botch sth **2.** *vt.* OFFENSIVE TERM an offensive term meaning to make sb confused or inflict emotional or mental damage on sb **3.** *vi.* OFFENSIVE TERM an offensive term meaning to make a bad mistake or bungle sth

fuck with *vt.* US an offensive term meaning to treat sb in a careless or disrespectful way (*taboo offensive*)

fucker /fúkər/ *n.* **1.** OFFENSIVE TERM a highly offensive term expressing extreme dislike for the person so addressed (*taboo insult*) **2.** OFFENSIVE TERM an offensive term meaning any unnamed person, an obscene equivalent of guy or fellow (*taboo offensive*) **3.** OFFENSIVE TERM an offensive term meaning sb, especially a man, who has sexual intercourse (*taboo offensive*)

fuckface /fúk fayss/ *n.* a highly offensive term for a despicable person (*taboo insult*)

fucking /fúking/ *adj.* an offensive term used to intensify or emphasize a word or statement (*taboo offensive*)

fuckup /fúk up/ *n.* (*taboo offensive*) **1.** OFFENSIVE TERM an offensive term meaning a bad mistake or sth bungled **2.** OFFENSIVE TERM an offensive term meaning an incompetent or bungling person

fuckwit /fúk wit/ *n.* a highly offensive term for an unintelligent person (*taboo offensive*)

fucoid /fyóo koyd/, **fucoidal** /-koyd'l/ *adj.* relating to, typical of, or resembling the seaweed fucus

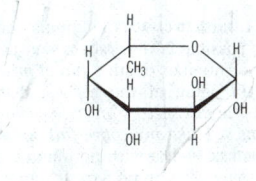

Fucose

fucose /fyóo kōz, -kōss/ *n.* a sugar found in glycosides and polysaccharides associated with certain blood groups [Early 20thC. Coined from FUCUS + -OSE; from its presence in brown algae.]

fucoxanthin /fyóo kō zánthin/ *n.* a brown carotenoid pigment found in some algae [Late 19thC. Coined from FUCUS + XANTHO- + IN; from its presence in brown algae.]

fucus /fyóokəss/ *n.* (*plural* **-ci** /fyóossī/ *or* **-cuses**) *n.* a greenish-brown seaweed. Genus: *Fucus.* [Early 17thC. Via modern Latin, genus name, from Latin, 'rock lichen, red or purple colour', from Greek *phukos* 'seaweed'.]

fuddle /fúdd'l/ *v.* (**-dles, -dling, -dled**) **1.** *vt.* CONFUSE AS IF WITH DRINK to make a person or mental faculty confused, often through intoxication **2.** *vi.* DRINK TOO MUCH to drink too much alcohol regularly (*archaic*) ■ *n.* FUDDLED STATE a state of confusion or drunkenness [Late 16thC. Origin uncertain: perhaps related to Low German *fuddeln* 'to work carelessly as if drunk'.]

fuddy-duddy /fúddi dudi/ (*plural* **fuddy-duddies**) *n.* an old-fashioned or dull person, especially one past middle age (*informal*) (*offensive in some contexts*) ○ *This is for kids, not fuddy-duddies like us.* [Early

20thC. Origin uncertain: perhaps an alteration of FUSSY+DAD.]

fudge /fuj/ *n.* **1.** SWEET a type of soft toffee made by boiling milk and sugar and then beating the liquid until it crystallizes and becomes slightly grainy in texture. Many flavourings and other ingredients can be added. **2.** NONSENSE nonsensical talk (*informal*) ■ *vti.* (**fudges, fudging, fudged**) ALTER TO DECEIVE to fiddle with or otherwise alter sth in order to deceive or remain noncommittal (*informal*) ○ *fudged the figures to make the bottom line look better* [Early 17thC. Origin uncertain: perhaps an alteration of earlier *fadge* 'to make fit, adjust'; the underlying meaning of the confectionery sense is perhaps 'bodged up toffee'.]

Fuegian /fyoo éeji ən, fwáyji-/ *adj.* OF TIERRA DEL FUEGO relating to or typical of Tierra del Fuego, or its people or culture ■ *n.* S AMERICAN FROM TIERRA DEL FUEGO a Native South American who was born on or lives on any of the islands of Tierra del Fuego

fuel /fyóo əl/ *n.* **1.** SOURCE OF ENERGY sth that is burned to provide power or heat **2.** SOURCE OF NUCLEAR ENERGY the fissionable material used to create power in a nuclear generator **3.** SOURCE OF STIMULATION sth that stimulates or maintains sth else, especially an emotion ○ *Her refusal to answer questions added fuel to his curiosity.* ■ *v.* (**-els, -elling, -elled**) **1.** *vt.* SUPPLY WITH FUEL to supply sth with material to burn for power or heat **2.** *vt.* STIMULATE to stimulate or maintain sth, especially an emotion **3.** *vi.* OBTAIN FUEL to take on supplies of fuel for running a vehicle [12thC. Via Anglo-Norman *fuaille*, Old French *fouaille* from assumed Vulgar Latin *focalia*, literally '(things) for the fire', from Latin *focus* 'fireplace, hearth' (see FOCUS).] —**fueller** *n.*

fuel cell *n.* a device that generates electricity by converting the chemical energy of a fuel and an oxidant to electrical energy

fuel efficiency *n.* the ability to make the best use of the fuel being used —**fuel-efficient** *adj.*

fuel injection *n.* a system for running an internal-combustion engine without using a carburettor, forcing vaporized fuel under pressure directly into the combustion chamber —**fuel-injected** *adj.*

fuel oil *n.* a product of liquid petroleum, burned chiefly to power ships and locomotives and to provide domestic heating

fuel rod *n.* a metal tube containing nuclear fuel that is used in some types of nuclear reactor

fug /fug/ *n.* a stale or airless atmosphere [Late 19thC. Origin uncertain: probably an alteration of FOG.]

fugacious /fyoo gáyshəss/ *adj.* **1.** BRIEF fleeting or passing away quickly (*formal*) **2.** BOT QUICKLY WITHERING lasting only briefly before withering or dropping [Early 17thC. Formed from the Latin stem *fugac-* 'fleeing swiftly', from *fugere* (see FUGITIVE).] —**fugaciously** *adv.* —**fugaciousness** *n.* —**fugacity** /fyoo gássəti/ *n.*

fugal /fyóog'l/ *adj.* relating to or resembling a fugue —**fugally** *adv.*

fugato /fyoo gaatō/ *adv., adj.* IN FUGUE STYLE in the style of a fugue ■ *n.* (*plural* **-tos**) PIECE IN FUGUE STYLE a piece of music in the style of a fugue [Mid-19thC. From Italian, literally 'fugued', from the past participle of *fugare* 'to compose as a fugue', from *fuga* 'fugue' (see FUGUE).]

-fuge *suffix.* one that drives out ○ *febrifuge* [Via French from, ultimately, Latin *fugere* 'to flee' (see FUGITIVE) and *fugare* 'to drive out' (from *fuga* 'flight').]

fugitive /fyóojitiv/ *n.* **1.** SB WHO RUNS AWAY sb who is running away, e.g. from justice, enemies, or brutal treatment **2.** STH ELUSIVE an elusive or ephemeral thing ■ *adj.* **1.** RUNNING AWAY FROM STH fleeing, especially fleeing arrest or punishment **2.** BRIEF lasting only briefly ○ *the fugitive hours* **3.** ITINERANT moving around from place to place **4.** WRITTEN FOR PARTICULAR OCCASION written or composed for a particular occasion or on a subject of only passing interest ○ *a collection of essays, letters, and fugitive pieces* **5.** DIFFICULT TO UNDERSTAND difficult to understand or retain ○ *the fugitive nature of higher mathematics* [14thC. Directly or via French from Latin *fugitivus*, from *fugit-*, the past participle stem of *fugere* 'to flee' (source of English *fugacious*, *refuge*, and *refugee*).] —**fugitively** *adv.* —**fugitiveness** *n.*

fugle /fyōˈg'l/ (-les, -gling, -gled) vi. to act as or like a fugleman in training or leading others [Mid-19thC. Back-formation from FUGLEMAN.]

fugleman /fyōˈg'lmən/ n. 1. MIL SOLDIER TRAINING OTHERS a soldier formerly used to teach drill movements by performing them in front of trainees 2. LEADER sb acting as a leader or example to others [Early 19thC. Alteration of German *Flügelmann*, literally 'wing man, man on the flank'.]

fugu /fyoō ɡoō/ n. a poisonous pufferfish that is eaten, especially in Japan, after the poisonous parts are removed [Mid-20thC. From Japanese.]

fugue /fyoog/ n. 1. MUSIC MUSICAL FORM a musical form in which a theme is first stated, then repeated and varied with accompanying contrapuntal lines 2. **fugue, fugue state** PSYCHIAT SELECTIVE MEMORY LOSS a disordered state of mind, in which sb typically wanders from home and experiences a loss of memory relating only to the previous, rejected, environment [Late 16thC. Directly or via French from Italian *fuga*, from Latin, 'flight'.]

Mount Fuji

Fuji, Mount /foōˈji, mownt/, **Fujiyama** /foōji aˈamə/ the highest mountain in Japan, on central Honshu Island, southwest of Tokyo. A dormant volcano in the shape of an almost perfect cone, it is considered to be sacred by many Japanese people. Height: 3,776 m/12,387 ft.

Fujian /foō jyén/, **Fukien** /foō kyén/ province of southeastern China, on the coast opposite the island of Taiwan. Capital: Fuzhou. Population: 31,830,000 (1994). Area: 121,000 sq. km/46,720 sq. mi.

Fujimori /foōji máwri/, **Alberto** (b. 1938) Peruvian political leader. He became president of Peru in 1990 and is the first person of Japanese descent to lead a Latin American country.

Fujiyama /foōji yaˈamə/ = Fuji [Mount]

Fukushima /foōkoō sheemə/ capital city of Fukushima Prefecture, on the Abukuma River in north-central Honshu, Japan. Population: 280,958 (1990).

Fukuyama /foōkoō yaˈamə/ city on the Inland Sea in Hiroshima Prefecture, Honshu Island, Japan. Population: 365,612 (1990).

-ful suffix. 1. full of ○ *hateful* 2. having the nature of ○ *rightful* 3. tending to ○ *forgetful* 4. an amount that fills ○ *capful* 5. full to ○ *brimful* [Old English, from *full* (see FULL)]

Fula /foōlə/ (plural -la or -las), **Fulah** (plural -lah or -lahs) n. 1. PEOPLES MEMBER OF AFRICAN NOMADIC PEOPLE a member of an ethnically diverse nomadic people living in various parts of western and central Africa 2. LANG = **Fulani** n. 1 [Late 18thC. From Fulani *pulo* 'person'.]

Fulani /foō laˈani/ (plural -ni or -nis) n. 1. LANG W AFRICAN LANGUAGE a language spoken over a large area of West Africa, especially in Nigeria, Guinea-Bissau, Burkina-Faso, Gambia, Benin, Guinea, and Senegal. It is one of the Niger-Congo family of African languages. About 15 million people speak Fulani. 2. PEOPLES = **Fula** n. 1 [Mid-19thC. From Hausa.]

Fulbright /foōl brīt/, **J. William** (1905–95) US educator and statesman. As a US Democratic senator from Arkansas (1945–74) and chair of the influential Senate Foreign Relations Committee (1959–74), he was a leading critic of the Vietnam War. He sponsored the Fulbright Act (1946), which enacted a major US programme of international educational exchanges. Full name **James William Fulbright**

fulcrum /foōlkrəm/ (plural -crums or -cra /-krə/) n. 1. PIVOT the point or support about which a lever turns 2. PROP sth that supports sth else revolving about it or depending on it ○ *The fulcrum of the building plan is the major retail tenant.* 3. ZOOL SUPPORT IN ANIMAL part of an animal that acts as a hinge or support, especially scales on the fins of some fish [Late 17thC. From Latin, 'post or foot of a couch, bedpost', formed from the base of *fulcire* 'to prop up, support'.]

fulfil /foōl fíl/ (-fils, -filling, -filled) v. 1. vt. ACHIEVE STH DESIRED to do what is necessary to bring about or achieve sth expected, desired, or promised ○ *went on to fulfil her early promise of greatness* 2. vt. CARRY OUT to do what is necessary to carry out a request or command ○ *The instructions have been fulfilled to the letter.* 3. vt. SATISFY REQUIREMENT to be good enough or of the type necessary to meet a standard or requirement 4. vt. COMPLETE to do what is necessary to complete or bring sth to an end 5. vt. SUPPLY AMOUNT OF ORDER to supply the full amount of sth ordered 6. vr. REALIZE AMBITIONS to feel satisfied with what you are doing, or realize your expectations or ambitions [Old English *fullfyllan* 'to fill up, make full', from earlier forms of FULL + FILL] —**fulfiller** n. —**fulfilment** n.

fulfill vt. US = fulfil

fulfilling /foōl fílling/ adj. giving satisfaction to sb as an activity or goal in life ○ *a fulfilling job opportunity*

fulgent /fúljənt/ adj. shining or gleaming brilliantly (*literary*) [15thC. From Latin *fulgere* 'to flash, shine' (source of English *effulgent* and *refulgent*).] —**fulgently** n. —**fulgently** adv.

fulgurate /fúlgyoō rayt/ (-rates, -rating, -rated) v. 1. vt. MED DESTROY BY ELECTRICITY to destroy unwanted tissue, such as warts, using a high-frequency electric current 2. vi. FLASH to flash with or like lightning (*formal*) [Mid-17thC. From Latin *fulgurat-*, the past participle stem of *fulgurare* 'to lighten, flash', from, ultimately, *fulgere* (see FULGENT).] —**fulguration** /fúlgyoō ráysh'n/ n.

fulgurite /fúlgyoō rīt/ n. a tube of hard, glassy material formed by lightning striking sand [Mid-19thC. Coined from Latin *fulgur* 'lightning' + -ITE.]

fuliginous /fyoō líjinəss/ adj. (*formal*) 1. SOOTY having the colour or consistency of soot or smoke 2. OBSCURE like soot in cloudiness or obscurity [Late 16thC. Directly or via French *fuligineux* from late Latin *fuliginosus*, from Latin *fuligin-*, the stem of *fuligo* 'soot'.] —**fuliginously** adv.

full[1] /foōl/ adj. 1. FILLED TO CAPACITY holding as much or as many as is possible 2. WITH MUCH OR MANY having a large amount or number of sth ○ *full of mischief* 3. GREATEST IN EXTENT being at the highest degree or largest extent ○ *at full speed* ○ *an engine running at full revolutions* ○ *I like my coffee full strength.* 4. COMPLETE WITH NOTHING MISSING with nothing or nobody left out or missing, or with no part uncompleted or used ○ *the full complement of staff* 5. COMPLETELY DEVELOPED at the end or peak of development ○ *roses in full bloom* 6. COMPLETELY SO having reached or fulfilled all requirements for a position, rank, or description ○ *a full colonel* 7. HAVING EATEN ENOUGH satisfied by an amount eaten or drunk 8. BUSY WITH ACTIVITY filled with activity or achievement ○ *live a full life* 9. PLUMP fleshy and with a rounded shape 10. WITH SAME PARENTS sharing both natural parents ○ *my full brother* 11. CHARGED WITH EMOTION affected by strong deep emotion ○ *We left the place with full hearts and shining eyes.* 12. PREOCCUPIED deeply preoccupied with a large filled agenda, or with some fact or idea to the extent of being unable to think or talk about anything else ○ *She's always full of her latest schemes.* 13. SONOROUS with depth or power, e.g. of sound 14. WINE RICHLY FLAVOURED with a rich strong flavour and substantial quality 15. CLOTHES WITH MUCH FABRIC made with a lot of fabric and not close-fitting 16. DRUNK drunk (*slang*) ■ adv. 1. COMPLETELY to the greatest or complete extent ○ *turn full round* 2. DIRECTLY OR EXACTLY in a precise or exact position ○ *He took a punch full on the mouth.* 3. VERY to a high degree ○ *What happened next we know full well.* ■ n. FULLEST STATE the greatest or highest degree ○ *We enjoyed ourselves to the full.* ■ v. (fulls, fulling, fulled) vt. SEW GATHERS AND TUCKS to make a garment full by sewing gathers or tucks in it 2.

vi. BECOME FULL to wax and become full (*refers to the moon*) [Old English. From a prehistoric Germanic word that is also the ancestor of English *fill*; ultimately from an Indo-European base that is also the ancestor of English *complete*.]
◇ **be full of yourself** to be very conceited and arrogant
◇ **full up** completely full ◇ **in full** to the complete amount or extent, omitting nothing ○ *The opera has never been performed in full.*

full[2] /foōl/ (fulls, fulling, fulled) vti. TEXTILES to make cloth bulkier by dampening and beating it, or become bulkier by being dampened and beaten [14thC. Origin uncertain: probably a back-formation from *fuller*, perhaps influenced by French *fouler* 'to press'.]

fullback n. a player in a defensive position in sports such as football, rugby or hockey

full-blooded adj. 1. VIGOROUS healthily vigorous, or forceful 2. THOROUGHBRED of unmixed breed —**full-bloodedly** adv. —**full-bloodedness** n.

full-blown adj. 1. COMPLETE in its most complete, extreme, strongest, or developed form ○ *full-blown malaria* 2. FULLY IN BLOOM blooming and fully open

full board n. board at a hotel or guest house that includes accommodation and all meals. US term **American plan**

full-bodied adj. 1. WINE RICHLY FLAVOURED with a rich strong flavour and substantial quality 2. RICHLY SOUNDING rich in tone and strong in volume

full-bottomed adj. long and full at the back (*refers to a wig*)

full circle adv. back to the starting point, usually after passing through various stages

full count n. in baseball, the situation in which the batter has three balls and two strikes

full-court press n. in basketball, the practice of putting pressure on opposing players in all parts of the court as opposed to merely defending the backcourt

full dress n. clothes suitable or prescribed for a ceremony or formal occasion (*hyphenated when used before a noun*)

full-dress adj. of considerable importance and often complete or exhaustive ○ *a full-dress investigation*

fuller[1] /foōlər/ n. TEXTILES sb who makes cloth bulkier by dampening and beating it [Pre-12thC. Formed from Latin *fullo*, of unknown origin.]

fuller[2] /foōlər/ n. METALL a hammer used by a blacksmith for forging grooves and spreading hot iron [Mid-19thC. Origin uncertain: perhaps from FULL[1] in the sense 'to make full'.]

Fuller /foōlər/, **Roy** (1912–92) British poet and novelist He is noted for his *New and Collected Poems, 1934–84* (1985). He also wrote several novels, including *Image of a Society* (1956) and three volumes of memoirs.

Fuller, Thomas (1608–61) English clergyman, author, and historian. He was the author of the *History of the Worthies of England* (1662), a biographical dictionary.

fullerene /foōllə reen/ n. a form of carbon comprising up to 500 carbon atoms arranged in a sphere or tube. Fullerenes are very heat resistant and have unique electrical properties, with potential uses in electronics and as lubricants. [Late 20thC. Shortening.]

fuller's earth n. an absorbent clay used in fulling cloth and in filtering liquids

fuller's teasel n. a plant of Europe and Asia with prickly flower heads, formerly used to raise the nap on cloth. Latin name: *Dipsacus sativus*.

full-faced, **full face** adj. with the whole of the face visible, facing the viewer ○ *a full face portrait*

full-fashioned adj. US = fully-fashioned

full-fledged adj. US = fully-fledged

full-frontal adj. 1. EXPOSING GENITALS showing the whole front of the body including the genitals 2. UNRESTRAINED whole-hearted and uninhibited (*informal*) ○ *She made a full-frontal attack on her opponents.*

full house n. a poker hand containing three cards of the same value and a pair of a different value

full-length *adj.* **1.** FALLING TO ANKLES extending to the ankles or floor (*refers to a garment, e.g. a coat or skirt*) **2.** SHOWING WHOLE BODY showing the whole length of the body (*refers to a portrait mirror, or the like*) **3.** NOT SHORTENED consisting of the whole or usual amount or duration of sth

full marks *npl.* **1.** PERFECT SCORE a perfect score in an assessment or examination **2.** HIGH PRAISE high praise or commendation (*informal*) ○ *Full marks to the driver for managing to find the place.*

full monty /-mónti/ *n.* everything that is needed or appropriate or makes up a full set or the whole of sth (*slang*) [*Monty* of uncertain origin: perhaps a shortening of *Montague*, from *Montague Burton*, name of a British firm of gentleman's outfitters, with reference to a full suit of clothes]

full moon *n.* **1.** MOON APPEARING AS COMPLETE CIRCLE the phase of the Moon when its surface as seen from the Earth is fully illuminated by the Sun **2.** TIME OF FULL MOON the period of time during which the Moon appears fully illuminated as a circle [Origin uncertain]

full-mouthed *adj.* **1.** VET WITH ALL TEETH having the complete set of adult teeth **2.** LOUD said loudly or vigorously

full nelson *n.* a wrestling hold in which one wrestler puts both arms beneath an opponent's arms from behind and then exerts pressure by clasping the hands at the back of the opponent's neck

fullness /fo͝olnəss/ *n.* the quality or condition of being full or complete ○ *the fullness of her explanation*

full-on *adj. ANZ* **1.** ALL-OUT taken to the limits ○ *The wedding was a full-on display of pomp and ceremony.* **2.** EXCESSIVE excessive to the extent of being overbearing ○ *She's a bit full-on, isn't she?*

full point *n.* = **full stop**

full-rigged *adj.* having at least three square-rigged masts

full-scale *adj.* **1.** LIFE-SIZE having exactly the same dimensions and proportions as the original **2.** TOTAL done with total commitment of effort and resources ○ *a full-scale manhunt*

full-size, **full-sized** *adj.* being the normal size for its kind

full stop *n.* **1.** GRAM PUNCTUATION MARK the punctuation mark '.' that is used at the end of a sentence or in abbreviations. US term **period 2.** COMPLETE STOP a complete halt or an end ○ *This delay has brought production to a full stop.*

full time *n.* END OF MATCH the end of a match in football and other sports ■ *adj., adv.* **full-time, full time** FOR THE WHOLE USUAL TIME during all of the time considered standard or appropriate for the activity in question —**full-timer** *n.*

full-wave rectifier *n.* a circuit used in the design of electronic equipment such as radios, computers, and televisions that operates on both the positive and negative cycles of an alternating current

fully /fo͝olli/ *adv.* **1.** COMPLETELY to the greatest extent possible or required ○ *The flight is fully booked.* **2.** FOR WHAT IS SPECIFIED to the full extent of the time, quantity, or number specified ○ *We waited fully 40 minutes.*

fully featured *adj.* used to describe an electronic device or piece of software that has all the features that a user would hope for or expect ○ *'Manufacturers can offer high speed, fully featured modems, suitable for existing or new computers'.* (*Internet Magazine*; November 1998)

fully-fledged *adj.* **1.** BIRDS WITH ADULT FEATHERS having grown adult feathers and so being able to fly **2.** COMPLETELY DEVELOPED at a point of complete development or maturity ○ *a fully-fledged microelectronics industry* **3.** FULLY QUALIFIED with full status or rank ○ *a fully-fledged helicopter pilot*

fulmar /fo͝olmər/ *n.* a heavy short-tailed seabird living in polar regions. Genus: *Fulmarus.* [Late 17thC. Originally a Hebridean Norn dialect word, from Old Norse *fúll* 'foul' (from the bird's habit of regurgitating its stomach's contents when disturbed) + *már* 'gull'.]

fulminant /fo͝olminənt/ *adj.* **1.** EXPLODING exploding violently **2.** MED SUDDEN AND SEVERE coming on suddenly and with severe symptoms of short duration [Early 17thC. Directly or via French from, ultimately, Latin *fulminare.*]

fulminate /fo͝olmi nayt, fúl-/ *vti.* (**-nates, -nating, -nated**) **1.** SPEAK SCATHINGLY to express forcible criticism ○ *an article fulminating against the arms trade* **2.** EXPLODE to detonate or explode violently, or cause sth to detonate or explode violently ■ *n.* CHEM EXPLOSIVE SALT OR ESTER any explosive salt or ester of fulminic acid, especially fulminate of mercury [15thC. From Latin *fulminare* 'to lighten, strike with lightning', from *fulmen* 'lightning'.] —**fulmination** /fo͝olmi náysh'n, fúl-/ *n.* —**fulminator** /fo͝olmi naytər, fúl-/ *n.* —**fulminatory** /-naytəri, -/ *adj.*

fulminate of mercury *n.* the mercury salt of fulminic acid, often used in explosives and detonators. Formula: $HgC_2N_2O_2$.

fulminating /fo͝olmi nayting, fúl-/ *adj.* **1.** EXPLOSIVE able or likely to explode or detonate **2.** MED = **fulminant** *adj.* 2

fulminic acid /fo͞ol minnik-, ful-/ *n.* an unstable compound that smells of bitter almonds. It is used in the manufacture of explosives. Formula: HONC. [Formed from the Latin stem *fulmin-* the stem of *fulmen* 'lightning that strikes' (see FULMINATE)]

fulsome /fo͝olsəm/ *adj.* **1.** EXCESSIVELY COMPLIMENTARY effusive or fawning to the point of being offensive ○ *embarrassed by their fulsome praise* **2.** LAVISH great in amount or intensity [13thC. From FULL + -SOME.] —**fulsomely** *adv.* —**fulsomeness** *n.*

fulvous /fo͝olvəss, fúl-/ *adj.* of an orange-brown colour (*literary*) [Mid-17thC. Formed from Latin *fulvus* 'reddish-yellow'.]

Fu Manchu moustache /fo͞o manchóo-/ *n.* a moustache with long drooping ends [Named after *Fu Manchu*, a character with such a moustache in the novels of Sax Rohmer, pen name of British writer Arthur Sarsfield Ward (1886–1959)]

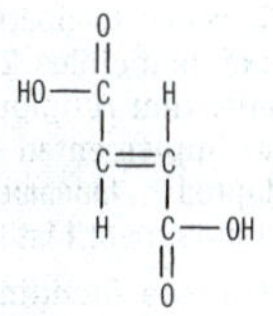

Fumaric acid

fumaric acid /fyoo márrik-/ *n.* a colourless crystalline solid that occurs naturally in certain plants and moulds and is synthesized from benzene. It is used in making resins. Formula: $C_4H_4O_4$. [Formed from modern Latin *Fumaria*, genus name or fumitory, from late Latin, 'fumitory', from Latin *fumus* 'smoke']

fumarole /fyóomərōl/ *n.* a vent in a volcanic area from which steam and hot gases such as sulphur dioxide are emitted [Early 19thC. Via Italian *fumaruolo* from late Latin *fumariolum* 'vent, smoke-hole', from, ultimately, Latin *fumus* 'smoke'.] —**fumarolic** /fyóomə róllik/ *adj.*

fumatory /fyóomətəri/ (*plural* **-ries**) *adj.* relating to, involving, or typical of fumigation or smoking [Mid-19thC. From assumed Latin *fumatorius*, from *fumare.*]

fumble /fúmb'l/ *v.* (**-bles, -bling, -bled**) **1.** *vti.* GROPE CLUMSILY to grope clumsily in searching for sth ○ *He fumbled in his pockets for his keys.* **2.** *vi.* HESITATE to act clumsily, hesitantly, or unsuccessfully ○ *She fumbled through the introductions.* **3.** *vt.* BUNGLE to do sth clumsily or inefficiently ○ *This is your last chance, so don't fumble it.* **4.** *vti.* SPORTS DROP OR MISHANDLE BALL in sports, to drop or fail to catch a ball ■ *n.* FUMBLED ACTION an act or instance of fumbling [Mid-16thC. Origin uncertain: possibly from a Scandinavian source.] —**fumbler** *n.* —**fumblingly** *adv.*

fume /fyoom/ *v.* (**fumes, fuming, fumed**) **1.** *vi.* BE ANGRY to feel great anger, especially anger that is not fully expressed **2.** *vi.* EMIT GAS to emit gas, smoke, or vapour, or be emitted in this form **3.** *vt.* FUMIGATE to treat sth with a gas, smoke, or other fumigant **4.** *vt.* DARKEN to expose wood, especially oak, to vapour or gas given off by ammonia in order to darken it (*usually passive*) ■ *n.* **1.** SMOKE smoke, gas, or vapour, especially when unpleasant or harmful (*often used in the plural*) ○ *a chemical that emits noxious fumes when exposed to air* **2.** ACRID SMELL an acrid or nauseating smell (*often used in the plural*) **3.** FIT OF ANGER a state of great anger [14thC. Via Old French *fum* from Latin *fumus* 'smoke' (source of English *perfume*).] —**fumingly** *adv.* —**fumy** *adj.*

fume cupboard *n.* an enclosed ventilated chamber in which to conduct experiments involving harmful vapours

fumet /fyoo mét/ *n.* a strongly-flavoured stock obtained from cooking fish, meat, or vegetables [Early 18thC. From French, from *fumer* 'to smoke', ultimately from Latin *fumus* (see FUME).]

fumigant /fyóomigənt/ *n.* a substance that gives off fumes, especially one used as a disinfectant or to kill pests [Late 19thC. From Latin *fumigare* (see FUMIGATE).]

fumigate /fyóomi gayt/ (**-gates, -gating, -gated**) *vti.* to treat sth with fumes, especially to disinfect it or to kill pests [Mid-16thC. From *fumigare* 'to smoke', from *fumus* 'smoke'.] —**fumigation** /fyóomi gáysh'n/ *n.* —**fumigator** /fyóomi gaytər/ *n.*

fuming sulphuric acid *n.* a very concentrated solution of sulphuric acid that gives off fumes

fun /fun/ *n.* **1.** AMUSEMENT a time or feeling of enjoyment or amusement ○ *Just for fun, we wore silly hats.* **2.** STH AMUSING sth such as an activity that provides enjoyment or amusement ○ *Skiing is fun for the whole family.* **3.** MOCKERY playful joking, often at the expense of another ○ *What's said in fun can still hurt.* ■ *adj.* **1.** AMUSING providing enjoyment or amusement (*informal*) ○ *We'll have a fun time tonight.* **2.** CHEAP AND FLAMBOYANT flamboyant in style and often made of cheap synthetic materials, designed to be used or worn for fun ○ *fun jewellery* ■ *vi.* (**funs, funning, funned**) BEHAVE PLAYFULLY to behave in a playful or joking way (*informal*) ○ *Don't pay any attention to him; he's just funning.* [Late 17thC. From earlier English *fon* 'fool', the probable source of *fond.*] ◇ **fun and games** activity, difficulty, or trouble (*informal*) (*used ironically*) ○ *A broken sprinkler in the stockroom overnight gave us some fun and games in the morning.* ◇ **like fun 1.** with great speed or effort (*informal*) ○ *We'll have to work like fun to finish this order on time.* **2.** certainly not (*informal*) ○ *Like fun I am!* ◇ **make fun of sb** *or* **sth** to make sb or sth appear ridiculous ◇ **poke fun at sb** *or* **sth** to mock or ridicule sb or sth

funambulist /fyoo námbyo͝olist/ *n.* an acrobat who walks while balancing on a suspended rope [Late 18thC. Formed from French *funambule* or its source, Latin *funambulus*, from *funis* 'rope' + *ambulare* 'to walk' (source of English *amble*).] —**funambulism** *n.* —**funambulate** *vi.*

Funchal /fo͞on shaál/ capital of the Madeira Islands, an autonomous region of Portugal, in the North Atlantic Ocean. Situated on the southern coast of Madeira, it is a major resort. Population: 109,960 (1991).

function /fúngksh'n/ *n.* **1.** PURPOSE an action or use for which sth is suited or designed ○ *a watch with an alarm function* **2.** ROLE an activity or role assigned to sb or sth **3.** EVENT a social gathering or ceremony, especially a formal or official occasion ○ *a black-tie function* **4.** MATH VARIABLE QUANTITY DETERMINED BY OTHERS' VALUES a variable quantity whose value depends upon the varying values of other quantities **5.** DEPENDENT FACTOR a quality or characteristic that depends upon and varies with another ○ *Success is a function of determination and ability.* **6.** MATH CORRESPONDENCE BETWEEN MEMBERS OF DIFFERENT SETS a relationship between two mathematical sets, in which each member of one set corresponds uniquely to a member of the other set. Symbol **f 7.** COMPUT SINGLE COMPUTER OPERATION a named and stored basic operation of a computer yielding a single result when invoked **8.** COMPUT COMPUTER PROGRAM'S MAIN PURPOSE the purpose of a computer program or piece of computer equipment, e.g. database management or printing **9.** LING ROLE OF WORD OR PHRASE a grammatical role performed by a word or phrase in a particular construction ○ *Noun phrases can fulfil many functions.* **10.** UTILITY practical usefulness, as distinct from, e.g. aesthetic appeal ○ *the relationship between form and function* ■ *vi.* (**-tions, -tioning, -tioned**) **1.** SERVE PURPOSE to serve a particular purpose or perform a particular role ○ *hats functioning both as fashion statements and as protection against the sun* **2.** BE IN WORKING ORDER to operate normally, fulfilling a purpose or role ○ *When the heart ceases to function, the patient is clinically dead.* [Mid-16thC. From the Latin stem *function-*, from *funct-*, the past participle stem of *fungi* 'to perform' (source of English *defunct*).] —**functionless** *adj.*

functional /fúngksh'nəl/ *adj.* **1.** PRACTICAL having a practical application or serving a useful purpose ○ *designs that are functional yet fun* **2.** OPERATIONAL in good working order or working at the moment ○ *The lift will not be functional for several hours.* **3.** MED HAVING NO ORGANIC CAUSE without apparent organic or structural cause ○ *a functional disorder* **4.** LING RELATING TO LANGUAGE AS COMMUNICATION relating to the function of language as a communicating tool, rather than to its form ○ *functional linguistics* —**functionality** /fúngkshə nálləti/ *n.* —**functionally** /fúngksh'nəli/ *adv.*

functional food *n.* food containing nutritional additives that is promoted as being beneficial to health and able to prevent or reduce certain diseases such as tooth decay and cancer ○ *'the first spread formulated to act against cholesterol in a market for so-called functional foods'* (*The Guardian*; April 1999)

functional group *n.* a group of atoms that reacts as a single unit and determines the properties and structure of a particular class of compounds, e.g. a hydroxyl group in alcohols

functional illiterate *n.* sb whose reading and writing abilities are inadequately developed to meet everyday needs —**functionally illiterate** *adj.*

functionalism /fúngkshə'nəlizəm/ *n.* **1.** BELIEF IN FUNCTION OVER FORM belief that the intended function of sth should determine its design, construction, and choice of materials, or a 20th-century design movement based on this **2.** PHILOSOPHY PHILOSOPHY EMPHASIZING THE PRACTICAL any philosophy or system that gives practical and utilitarian concerns priority over aesthetic concerns **3.** SOC SCI ASSESSMENT OF SOCIAL INSTITUTIONS BY ROLE the analysis and explanation of social institutions according to the function they perform in society, e.g. the family seen as an institution for social stability and cohesion —**functionalist** /fúngksh'nəlist/ *n., adj.*

functional literacy *n.* the level of skill in reading and writing that an individual needs to cope with everyday adult life

functional shift *n.* a change in the grammatical function of a word, e.g. from noun to verb, as happens when the noun 'wallpaper' is used as the verb 'to wallpaper'

functionary /fúngksh'nəri/ (*plural* **-ies**) *n.* sb who performs official duties, especially sb whose duties are regarded as trivial

function change *n.* = **functional shift**

function key *n.* a button on a computer keyboard or terminal that instructs the computer to perform a specific task. The same key may be programmed to perform different tasks in different programs.

function shift *n.* = **functional shift**

function word *n.* a word that has little meaning on its own but serves a particular syntactic or semantic function in a phrase or sentence, e.g. conjunctions 'such as' and 'but'

functor /fúngktər/ *n.* **1.** STH PERFORMING FUNCTION sb or sth that performs a function (*formal*) **2.** LING = **function word** [Mid-20thC. Formed from FUNCTION, on the model of such words as *factor*.]

fund /fund/ *n.* **1.** SUPPLY a source or stock of sth **2.** RESERVE OF MONEY a sum of money saved or invested for a particular purpose **3.** ORGANIZATION ADMINISTERING RESERVE OF MONEY an organization that manages a sum of money for a particular purpose ■ **funds** *npl.* **1.** MONEY money, especially money that is available to spend ○ *I'm a bit short of funds at the moment.* **2.** UK GOVERNMENT SECURITIES British government securities that finance the national debt and pay a fixed rate of interest ■ *vt.* (**funds, funding, funded**) **1.** PROVIDE MONEY FOR to provide money needed to finance a project or keep it running (*often passive*) ○ *environmental projects funded by local government* **2.** PROVIDE MONEY TO PAY DEBT to provide a sum of money to pay off a debt or its interest **3.** MAKE DEBT LONG-TERM to convert a short-term debt into a long-term debt with a fixed rate of interest **4.** PUT IN RESERVE to store sth up for future use ○ *a notebook in which snippets of overheard conversations are funded* [Mid-17thC. From Latin *fundus* 'bottom' (source of English *found*[1]). The word was first borrowed in the Latin senses 'bottom, basis'; the modern meanings developed from the sense 'source of supply'.]

fundament /fúndəmənt/ *n.* **1.** FOUNDING PRINCIPLE an underlying principle or theory on which sth is founded (*formal*) (*often used in the plural*) **2.** ANAT BUTTOCKS the buttocks or the anus (*archaic or humorous*) [13thC. Via Old French *fondement* from, ultimately, Latin *fundus* 'bottom'.]

fundamental /fúndə mént'l/ *adj.* **1.** BASIC relating to or affecting the underlying principles or structure of sth ○ *We need to make fundamental changes in our business.* **2.** CENTRAL serving as an essential part of sth ○ *Free speech is one of the fundamental rights guaranteed by the US constitution.* **3.** MUSIC OF A CHORD'S LOWEST NOTE relating to the lowest note of a chord in root position, the note that gives the chord its basic harmony **4.** PHYS OF LOWEST FREQUENCY relating to or produced by the lowest frequency component in a complex vibration ■ *n.* **1.** BASIC PRINCIPLE OR ELEMENT a basic and necessary component of sth, especially an underlying rule or principle (*often used in the plural*) ○ *The class teaches the fundamentals of karate.* **2.** MUSIC PRINCIPAL TONE the principal tone in a chord, from which other harmonics are generated **3.** PHYS LOWEST FREQUENCY the lowest frequency in a vibration or periodic wave

fundamental interaction *n.* PHYS = **interaction** *n.* 3

fundamentalism /fúndə mént'lizəm/ *n.* **1.** MOVEMENT ADVOCATING RETURN TO TRADITIONAL PRINCIPLES a religious or political movement based on a literal interpretation of and strict adherence to doctrine, especially as a return to former principles **2.** SUPPORT FOR LITERAL EXPLANATION the belief that religious or political doctrine should be implemented literally, not interpreted or adapted —**fundamentalist** *n., adj.* —**fundamentalistic** /fúndə ment'l ístik/ *adj.*

fundamental law *n.* the founding rules and principles or constitution on which a government is based, as distinct from its legislative acts

fundamentally /fúndə mént'li/ *adv.* in a way that relates to or affects sth at its most basic level ○ *Your argument is fundamentally flawed.*

fundamental particle *n.* = **elementary particle**

fundamental unit *n.* = **base unit**

funded debt *n.* that part of the British national debt that has no deadline for repayment

fundholder /fúnd hōldər/ *n.* a general practition that has opted to manage its own budget and liaise directly with hospitals, rather than leave these administrative tasks to the area health authority

fundholding /fúnd hōlding/ *adj.* with direct responsibility for budget management and liaison with hospitals for specialist treatment of patients, rather than dealing with administration via the local health authority

fundi[1] /fún di/ (*plural* **-dis**) *n. S Africa* a learned person or an expert on a topic ○ *The political fundis got together to work out a compromise.* [Mid-20thC. Origin uncertain: probably from Ndebele, Xhosa, or Zulu *umfundi* 'disciple, learner'.]

fundi[2] plural of **fundus**

fundie /fúndi/, **fundy** (*plural* **-ies**) *n.* a member of any fundamentalist political or religious group, or a radical member of a generally liberal or mainstream group (*informal; often considered offensive*) [Late 20thC. Formed from FUNDAMENTALIST.]

funding /fúnding/ *n.* financial support

fundraiser /fúnd rayzər/ *n.* **1.** SB WHO RAISES MONEY sb who solicits money for a non-profit-making organization, especially sb whose job is to organize campaigns to raise money **2.** MONEY-RAISING ACTIVITY an activity or event that is intended to generate money to support a non-profit-making organization

fundraising /fúnd rayzing/ *n.* the organized activity of soliciting and collecting funds for a non-profit-making organization

fundus /fúndəss/ (*plural* **-di** /-dī/) *n.* the part of a hollow organ farthest from its opening, e.g. the part of the eye's retina opposite the pupil [Mid-18thC. From Latin, 'bottom'.] —**fundic** *adj.*

fundy *n.* = **fundie**

Fundy, Bay of /fúndi/ inlet of the Atlantic Ocean off Canada, separating New Brunswick and Nova Scotia, Canada. Its rapid tides are among the highest in the world, reaching 18 m/60 ft. Depth: 200 m/650 ft. Length: 150 km/94 mi.

funeral /fyo͞onərəl/ *n.* **1.** CEREMONY FOR SB WHO HAS DIED a rite held to mark the burial or cremation of a corpse, especially a ceremony held immediately before burial or cremation **2.** END an end to sth's existence ○ *We have witnessed the funeral of the amateur game.* **3.** FUNERAL PROCESSION a procession of mourners following a body to its place of burial or cremation [14thC. Via Old French *funerailles* 'funeral rites' from medieval Latin *funeralia*, from late Latin *funeralis* 'of death rituals', from Latin *funer-*, the stem of *funus* 'death ritual'.] ◇ **be sb's funeral** to be sb else's problem or worry (*informal*) ○ *If he wants to work extra hours, that's his funeral.*

funeral director *n.* = **undertaker**

funeral home *n.* = **funeral parlour**

funeral parlour *n.* a business establishment where corpses are prepared for burial or cremation and where a funeral service may also be performed and the body viewed by mourners. US term **funeral home**

funerary /fyo͞onərəri/ *adj.* relating to or suitable for a burial or funeral ○ *a funerary procession* [Late 17thC. From late Latin *funerarius*, from Latin *funer-*, the stem of *funus* 'funeral'.]

funereal /fyoo nééri əl/ *adj.* **1.** OF OR LIKE A FUNERAL relating to or suitable for a funeral **2.** GLOOMY very slow, solemn, mournful, or dismal [Early 18thC. Formed from Latin *funereus*, from *funer-*, the stem of *funus* 'funeral'.] —**funereally** *adv.*

funfair /fún fair/ *n.* = **fair**[2] *n.* 1

funfest /fún fest/ *n. US* a party, especially one at which amusing activities are organized (*informal*)

fungal /fúng g'l/, **fungous** /-gəss/ *adj.* **1.** FROM A FUNGUS caused by a fungus ○ *a fungal infection* **2.** OF OR LIKE FUNGUS in the form of a fungus or similar to a fungus in appearance or texture

fungi plural of **fungus**

fungible /fúnjib'l/ *adj.* **1.** DESCRIBING PERISHABLE GOODS perishable and traded or exchanged in measurable quantities or numbers (*refers to goods such as grain or wine*) **2.** SUBSTITUTABLE capable of being interchanged ■ *n.* STH TRADED OR SUBSTITUTED a commodity that is fungible (*often used in the plural*) [Late 17thC. From medieval Latin *fungibilis*, from Latin *fungi* 'to perform' (see FUNCTION).] —**fungibility** /fúnji bílləti/ *n.*

fungicide /fúnji sīd, fúng gi-/ *n.* a substance used to destroy or inhibit the growth of fungi —**fungicidal** /fúnji sīd'l, fúng gi-/ *adj.* —**fungicidally** /-sīdəli/ *adv.*

fungiform /fúnji fawrm, fúng gi-/ *adj.* shaped like a mushroom

fungistat /fúnji stat, fúng gi-/ *n.* a substance that inhibits the growth of fungi without killing them —**fungistatic** /fúnji státtik, fúng gi-/ *adj.*

fungo /fúng gō/ (*plural* **-goes**) *n.* BASEBALL in baseball, an act of hitting the ball high into the air using a special lightweight bat, usually to give fielders catching practice [Mid-19thC. Origin unknown.]

fungoid /fúng goyd/ *adj.* OF OR LIKE FUNGUS resembling, characteristic of, or caused by a fungus ○ *a fungoid growth* ■ *n.* FUNGUS a fungus, or a growth resembling a fungus

fungous *adj.* = **fungal**

fungus /fúng gəss/ (*plural* **-gi** /-gī/ *or* **-guses**) *n.* a single-celled or multicellular organism without chloro-

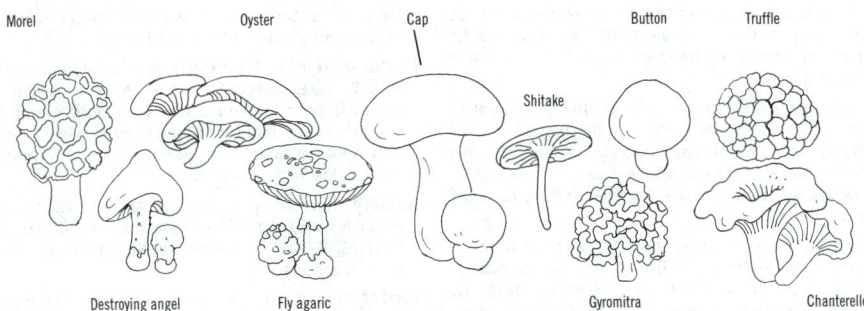

Morel | Oyster | Cap | Button | Truffle

Shitake

Destroying angel | Fly agaric | Gyromitra | Chanterelle

Fungus: Varieties of mushroom

phyll that reproduces by spores and lives by absorbing nutrients from organic matter. Fungi include mildews, moulds, mushrooms, rusts, smuts, and yeasts. [Early 16thC. From Latin, of unknown origin.]

funicle /fyoónik'l/ n. = **funiculus** [Mid-17thC. An anglicization of Latin *funiculus* (see FUNICULUS).]

funicular /fyoo níkyŏŏlər/ adj. 1. OF ROPE'S TENSION relating to a rope, especially its tension 2. MECH ENG ROPE-OPERATED operated by a rope or cable, especially one wound or pulled by a machine 3. ANAT, BOT OF A FUNICULUS relating to a funiculus ■ n. RAIL CABLE-OPERATED RAILWAY a funicular railway or railway car [Mid-17thC. Formed from FUNICULUS.]

Funicular railway

funicular railway n. a railway used on short steep inclines in which cars that counterbalance each other run on parallel tracks linked to a cable

funiculus /fyoo níkyŏŏləss/ (plural **-li** /-li/) n. 1. ANAT CORD-SHAPED BODY PART a cord-shaped part of the body such as the umbilical cord or a bundle of nerve fibres in the spinal cord 2. BOT OVULE STALK a stalk of a plant ovule that connects it or a seed to the placenta [Mid-17thC. From Latin, literally 'little rope', from *funis* 'rope'.]

funk[1] /fungk/ n. MUSIC 1. MUSICAL STYLE a type of popular music that derives from jazz, blues, and soul and is characterized by a heavy rhythmic bass and backbeat 2. EARTHY MUSICAL QUALITY a rhythmic earthy quality in music (slang) [Mid-20thC. Back-formation from FUNKY[1].]

funk[2] /fungk/ n. (dated informal) 1. FEAR a state of intense fear or panic ○ in a funk about his exam tomorrow 2. COWARD sb who is easily frightened or who has behaved in a cowardly way ■ vti. (**funks**, **funking**, **funked**) NOT DO STH OUT OF FEAR to fail to do sth, or to avoid doing it, because of fear (dated informal) ○ I meant to tell her but funked at the last moment. [Mid-18thC. Origin unknown.]

funk[3] /fungk/ n. US a strong unpleasant odour (slang) ○ get the funk out of my clothes [Early 17thC. Origin uncertain: possibly via dialectal French *funquer* 'to smoke' from, ultimately, Latin *fumigare* (see FUMIGATE).]

funk hole n. 1. REFUGE a place where sb hides from danger 2. TRENCH a soldier's trench or dugout (archaic slang)

funky[1] /fúngki/ (**-ier**, **-iest**) adj. (slang) 1. MUSIC SYNCOPATED AND RHYTHMIC with the beat and the syncopated rhythmic bass typical of funk music 2. FASHION HIP unconventional and individualistic in behaviour or style ○ a return to the funky styles of the 1970s

[Mid-20thC. Formed from FUNK[3].] —**funkily** adv. —**funkiness** n.

funky[2] (**-ier**, **-iest**) adj. US having a strong unpleasant odour (slang) [Late 18thC. Formed from FUNK[3].] —**funkiness** n.

funky[3] /fúngki/ (**-ier**, **-iest**) adj. in a state of fear or panic (dated informal) [Mid-19thC. Formed from FUNK[2].] —**funkily** adv. —**funkiness** n.

funnel /fúnn'l/ n. 1. UTENSIL USED IN POURING LIQUIDS a cone-shaped utensil with a large opening at the top and a small opening or tube at the bottom, used to guide liquids and other substances into containers 2. CHIMNEY a vertical pipe from which smoke and exhaust gases escape, especially one on a steamship or steam train ■ v. (**-nels**, **-nelling**, **-nelled**) 1. vti. MOVE INTO NARROW SPACE to move or direct sth into and through a narrow space ○ an efficient system for funnelling crowds through the turnstiles 2. vt. CONCENTRATE RESOURCES SOMEWHERE to direct or channel all of sth from one place or use to another ○ Funds were funnelled away from domestic projects. 3. vt. MAKE FUNNEL-SHAPED to form sth into the shape of a funnel [15thC. Via Provençal *fonilh* from, ultimately, Latin *infundibulum*, from *infundere* 'to pour in', from *fundere* 'to pour' (source of English *found*, *fuse*, and *confuse*).]

funnel cloud n. a funnel-shaped cloud that projects from the base of a thundercloud and often develops into a tornado

funnelform /fúnn'l fawrm/ adj. used to describe a flower or other plant part that is shaped like a funnel or cone

Funnel-web spider

funnel-web spider, **funnel-web** n. a large black highly venomous spider that is native to Australia and makes funnel-shaped webs. Family: Dipluridae.

funnily /fúnnili/ adv. 1. INTRODUCING COMMENT ON STH STRANGE used to introduce a comment on sth considered strange or odd ○ Funnily enough, nobody seemed to notice. 2. STRANGELY in a way that seems strange or odd ○ She has been acting funnily ever since the operation. 3. COMICALLY in an amusing or humorous way

funny /fúnni/ adj. (**-nier**, **-niest**) 1. COMICAL causing amusement, especially enough to provoke laughter 2. STRANGE odd or perplexing ○ That's funny, I can't find my keys. 3. UNCONVENTIONAL out of the ordinary in a quaint or comical way ○ a funny little doorway through an arch 4. UNWELL slightly ill, e.g. nauseated or faint (informal) 5. TRICKY sly, deceitful, or dishonest (informal) ○ Don't try anything funny, or I'll call the police. ■ n. (plural **-nies**) JOKE an amusing remark

or joke (informal) [Mid-18thC. Formed from FUN.] —**funniness** n.

funny bone n. 1. ELBOW POINT the point at the outside of the elbow where a nerve is so close to the longer arm bone that a blow often causes a tingling sensation (informal) 2. SENSE OF HUMOUR sb's perception of what is amusing [From the tingling feeling when the nerve is hit, probably also with some punning reference to HUMERUS 'arm bone' and HUMOROUS]

funny business n. dealings or goings-on that involve trickery, deceit, or dishonesty (informal)

funny farm n. an offensive term, once considered humorous, referring to a psychiatric hospital (slang offensive)

funny man /fúnni man/ (plural **funny men** /-mən/) n. a man who is a comedian, clown, or humorist

funny money n. (informal) 1. CRIMINOL COUNTERFEIT MONEY counterfeit or forged currency 2. CRIMINOL ILLICITLY GAINED MONEY money obtained from a legally or morally suspect source 3. FIN CURRENCY WITH LITTLE VALUE currency, especially an unfamiliar one, with an inflated value

fun park n. an area with amusement facilities, especially water slides and rides

fun run n. a non-competitive run over a moderately long course, organized to promote health and fitness or to raise money for charity

funster /fúnstər/ n. sb who enjoys telling or playing jokes or who simply likes to have fun (informal)

fur /fur/ n. 1. ZOOL MAMMAL'S COAT the soft dense coat of hair on a hairy mammal 2. ZOOL ANIMAL HAIR hairs from an animal's coat 3. INDUST DRESSED PELT a dressed pelt from an animal such as a mink or seal that includes the animal's soft coat of hair and is used for garments and decoration 4. CLOTHES FUR COAT a garment made from fur pelts, especially a coat, jacket, or stole 5. STH HAIRY sth with a fuzzy or hairy texture or appearance 6. MED COATING ON THE TONGUE a whitish coating of dead cells on the tongue that sometimes accompanies an illness (informal) 7. LIME DEPOSIT FROM HARD WATER mineral deposits from hard water that cling to the insides of plumbing fixtures 8. HERALDRY PELT ON COAT OF ARMS a representation of an animal skin on a coat of arms [14thC. From Old French *forrer* 'to line' (the original sense in English), from *forre* 'lining'. The noun came from the verb. Ultimately from a prehistoric Germanic word meaning 'protector, feeder' (ancestor also of English *fodder*).] —**furred** /furd/ adj. ◇ **make the fur fly** to cause trouble or a disturbance (informal)

fur up vti. to become coated, or to coat the insides of plumbing fixtures and water containers, with mineral deposits from hard water

Fur /fur/ n. a language spoken in parts of Chad and in western Sudan. It belongs to the Nilo-Saharan family of African languages. Fur is spoken by about 400,000 people. —**Fur** adj.

fur. abbr. furlong

furan /fyŏŏ ran, fyoo rán/ *n.* a colourless flammable liquid. It is used as a solvent and in the manufacture of polymers, especially. Formula: C_4H_4O. [Late 19thC. Contraction of FURFURAN.]

furanose /fyŏŏrə nōz/ *n.* a sugar with a chemical structure that contains a ring of four carbon atoms and one oxygen atom

furbearer /fúr bairər/ *n.* an animal with fur, especially fur with a high commercial value such as that of a fox or mink —**furbearing** *adj.*

furbelow /fúrbelō/ *n.* **1.** FASHION **RUFFLE** a gathered or pleated piece of material, especially as an ornament on a woman's garment ○ *Her dress was decorated with furbelows.* **2. FLAMBOYANT BEHAVIOUR** a showy or pretentious way of behaving (*literary; often used in the plural*) ■ *vt.* (**-lows, -lowing, -lowed**) FASHION **DECORATE STH WITH RUFFLE** to add a furbelow to a garment for ornamentation [Late 17thC. Origin uncertain: possibly an alteration of French dialect *farbella* or Provençal *farbello* 'fringe', from Italian *faldella*, literally 'small fold', from *falda* 'fold'.]

furbish /fúrbish/ (**-bishes, -bishing, -bished**) *vt.* **1. POLISH** to brighten sth by polishing ○ *stone steps scrubbed and brasses furbished* **2. REFURBISH** to refurbish sth (*literary*) [14thC. From the Old French verb stem *fourbiss-*, which was ultimately of prehistoric Germanic origin.] —**furbisher** *n.*

furcate /fúr kayt/ *vi.* (**-cates, -cating, -cated**) **TO FORK** to divide into two separate strands or branches ■ *adj.* **FORKED** divided into separate strands or branches ○ *furcate leaves* [Early 19thC. From late Latin *furcatus* 'forked', from Latin *furca* 'fork' (source of English *fork*).] —**furcately** /fúrkətli/ *adv.* —**furcation** /fur káysh'n/ *n.*

furcula /fúrkyŏŏlə/ (*plural* **-lae** /-lee/) *n.* the wishbone of a bird (*technical*) [Mid-19thC. From Latin, literally 'small fork', from *furca* 'fork'.] —**furcular** *adj.*

furfur /fúr fur/ (*plural* **-fures** /-fyŏŏ reez, fúrfə-/) *n.* DERMAT a tiny piece of scaly or flaky skin, e.g. a particle of dandruff (*technical*) [From Latin, 'bran, scales']

furfuraceous /fúrfə ráyshəss/ *adj.* **1.** DERMAT **SCALY** covered with or resembling particles of dandruff **2.** BOT **LIKE BRAN** relating to or resembling bran

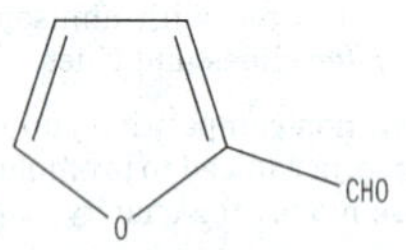

Furfural

furfural /fúrfərəl/ *n.* a colourless liquid with a distinctive smell. It occurs widely in plants and is used in making plastics, in oil refining, and in agriculture. Formula: $C_5H_4O_2$.

furfuran /fúrfə ran/ *n.* = **furan**

Furies /fyŏŏreez/, **furies** *npl.* in Greek mythology, three terrifying snake-haired winged goddesses who mercilessly punished wrongdoing, especially when committed within families. There were three Furies, named Alecto, Megaera, and Tisiphone. ◊ **Eumenides**

furioso /fyŏŏri ṓssō/ *adv.* to be played with vigour and passion (*used as a musical direction*) [Mid-17thC. Via Italian from Latin *furiosus* (see FURIOUS).] —**furioso** *adj.*

furious /fyŏŏri əss/ *adj.* **1. INFURIATED** extremely or violently angry ○ *I was furious with him for spreading such lies.* **2. VERY ENERGETIC** involving a great deal of energy, violence, or speed ○ *the pianist's furious assault on the keys* [14thC. Via Old French *furieus* from Latin *furiosus*, from *furia* 'rage' (see FURY).] —**furiously** *adv.* —**furiousness** *n.*

furl /furl/ *vti.* (**furls, furling, furled**) **ROLL OR BECOME ROLLED UP** to roll up and secure sth made of fabric, e.g. an umbrella, a flag, or a sail, or be rolled up and secured ■ *n.* **FURLED SECTION** a rolled-up section of sth such as a flag or sail [Late 16thC. From French *ferler*, from *ferm* 'firm, firmly' (see FIRM[1]) + *lier* 'to tie' (source of English *liable*).]

furlong /fúr long/ *n.* a measure of distance equal to 220 yards (approximately 201 metres), now used mainly on racecourses [Old English *furlang*, from *furh* 'furrow' (see FURROW) + *lang* 'long' (see LONG). The original meaning was 'the length of a single furrow ploughed across a field'.]

furlough /fúr lō/ *n.* **LEAVE FROM DUTY** leave of absence from duty, especially military duty, or an official paper authorizing leave ■ *vt.* (**-loughs, -loughing, -loughed**) **GIVE LEAVE TO** to grant leave of absence to sb, especially a member of the armed forces [Early 17thC. From Dutch *verlo* 'leave'. Ultimately from a prehistoric Germanic word that is also the ancestor of English *leave*.]

furmenty *n.* = **frumenty**

furmety *n.* = **frumenty**

furmity *n.* = **frumenty**

furn. *abbr.* furnished

furnace /fúrniss/ *n.* **1.** TECH **ENCLOSURE PRODUCING GREAT HEAT** an enclosure in which heat is produced by burning fuel, e.g. to warm a building or smelt metal ○ *an oil furnace* **2. SOMEWHERE HOT** an intensely hot place (*informal*) ○ *This kitchen is a furnace!* **3. TERRIBLE EXPERIENCE** a testing or demanding experience [13thC. Via Old French *fornais* from Latin *fornax*. Ultimately from an Indo-European base meaning 'to warm, heat' that is also the ancestor of English *burn*, *brandy*, and *brimstone*.]

Furneaux Group /fúrnō-/ group of islands situated off the coast of northeastern Tasmania, Australia. The largest islands are Flinders and Cape Barren Island. Population: 1,010. Area: 2,330 sq. km/900 sq. mi.

furnish /fúrnish/ (**-nishes, -nishing, -nished**) *vt.* **1. PUT FURNITURE IN A PLACE** to provide and install furniture and other fittings, e.g. carpets and curtains, in a place ○ *The lobby is furnished in an Art Deco style.* **2. SUPPLY** to supply sth or to provide sb with sth (*formal*) ○ *Could you furnish us with the names and addresses of clients?* [15thC. From Old French *furniss-*, the stem of *furnir* (source also of English *veneer*). Ultimately from a prehistoric Germanic base denoting 'furtherance, advance' that is also the ancestor of English *from*.] —**furnisher** *n.*

furnishings /fúrnishing/ *npl.* articles of furniture and other useful or decorative items for a room, such as carpets and curtains

furniture /fúrnichər/ *n.* **1. TABLES AND CHAIRS** the movable items such as chairs, desks, or cabinets in an area such as a room or patio **2.** PRINTING **TYPE SEPARATORS** strips of wood, metal, or plastic that are placed between type in order to make spaces and hold the type in place in the frame (**chase**) in which they are arranged **3. EQUIPMENT** the equipment or accessories used for an activity, e.g. a ship's tackle or a horse's saddle and harnesses (*archaic*) **4.** JOINERY **FITTINGS ON WOODEN ARTICLES** the metal or plastic accessories fitted to an item of joinery or cabinetwork, e.g. door hinges and drawer handles [Early 16thC. From Old French *fourniture*, from *furnir* 'to furnish' (see FURNISH).]

furniture beetle *n.* a borer beetle with larvae that are destructive to furniture and other wood. Latin name: *Anobium punctatum.*

furor /fyŏŏrawr, fyŏŏrə/ *n.* US = **furore**

furore *n.* **1. UPROAR** an angry or indignant public reaction to sth ○ *The verdict of not guilty created a furore in the courtroom.* **2. EXCITEMENT** a state of intense excitement or activity ○ *the furore surrounding the release of their latest album* **3. CRAZE** an enthusiastically embraced fad **4. ANGRY OUTBURST** a violent outburst of anger (*archaic*) [15thC. From Latin, from *furere* 'to rage'.]

furosemide /fyŏŏrōssə mīd/ *n.* *US* = **frusemide** [Mid-20thC]

furphy /fúrfi/ (*plural* **-phies**) *n.* *Aus* a piece of rumour or gossip (*slang*) [Early 20thC. Named after the *Furphy* family, who manufactured water carts in Australia during World War I, such carts being a place where troops gathered and swapped gossip.]

Furphy /fúrfi/, **Joseph** (1843–1912) Australian writer. He is the author of *Such is Life* (1903), an account of Australian rural life in the 1880s.

furrier /fúrri ər/ *n.* **1. FUR DEALER** sb who buys and sells furs **2. MAKER OR SELLER OF FUR GARMENTS** a person or establishment that makes or sells clothes and accessories of animal fur [14thC. Alteration (on the model of CLOTHIER) of earlier *furrer*, from Old French *forreor*, from *forrer* 'to line with fur' (see FUR).]

furriery /fúrri əri/ *n.* **1.** CLOTHES **FUR GARMENTS** fur accessories and articles of clothing considered collectively **2.** BUSINESS **FURRIER'S BUSINESS** the business or craft of a furrier

furring /fúring/ *n.* **1.** CLOTHES **FUR PART OF CLOTHING** fur trim or lining for a garment **2. WHITE COVERING** a whitish coating, e.g. on the tongue of sb who is ill **3.** CONSTR **MAKING A SURFACE OF STRIPS** the placing of strips of wood, metal, or brick across the studs or joists in a building to create a firm and level foundation for plaster, plasterboard, flooring, or another surface **4.** INDUST **STRIPS USED UNDER SURFACE** strips used in a building for furring (*often used before a noun*) ○ *furring strips*

furrow /fúrrō/ *n.* **1.** AGRIC **PLOUGH TRENCH** a narrow trench in soil made by a plough **2. GROOVE** a rut or groove in a surface **3. FOREHEAD WRINKLE** a wrinkle on the skin of the forehead **4.** *S Africa* AGRIC **IRRIGATION TRENCH** in South Africa, a narrow trench dug to deliver water to a field or garden ■ *vti.* (**-rows, -rowing, -rowed**) **MAKE FURROWS IN STH** to make furrows in sth such as land or the forehead, or become marked with furrows ○ *He furrowed his brow.* [Old English *furh*] —**furrowed** *adj.*

furry /fúri/ (**-rier, -riest**) *adj.* **1. COVERED IN FUR** covered in or with a coat that is covered in fur ○ *furry animals* **2. LOOKING OR FEELING LIKE FUR** resembling fur in texture or appearance **3.** MED **COVERED IN WHITISH COATING** covered with a whitish coating of dead cells (*refers to the tongue or the inside of the mouth*)

fur seal *n.* a seal with a double coat of fur, including a dense soft underfur that is highly valued for making garments. Many fur seal populations have been severely decreased by commercial hunting. Genera: *Arctocephalus* and *Callorhinus.*

Fur Seal Islands /fúr seel-/ = **Pribilof Islands**

Fürth city in the state of Bavaria, southern Germany, situated just northwest of Nuremberg. Population: 108,000 (1993).

further /fúrthər/ *adj.* **ADDITIONAL** that is more than or adds to the quantity or extent of sth ○ *until further notice* ○ *Do you have anything further to add?* ■ *adv.* **1. TO GREATER DISTANCE** to or at a point that is more distant in place or time ○ *We pushed further into the woods.* ○ *further into the future.* ◊ **farther 2. TO GREATER EXTENT** to a greater degree or extent ○ *Let's not pursue the matter any further.* ◊ **farther 3. IN ADDITION** used to introduce an additional statement or point ○ *She said further that she would not accept any excuses.* ■ *vt.* (**-thers, -thering, -thered**) **ADVANCE** to help or give a boost to the progress of sth ○ *All this media attention will further our cause.* [Old English *furþor, furþur* 'more forward'. Ultimately from a prehistoric Germanic base that is also the ancestor of English *forth*.] —**furtherer** *n.* ◇ **further to** following on from sth that has been written or discussed ○ *Further to our phone conversation, I would like to confirm the order.*

furtherance /fúrthərənss/ *n.* the aiding or advancing of the progress of sth ○ *In furtherance of our campaign, we ask that everyone make a contribution.*

further education *n.* post-school education or training for adults that does not lead to a university degree

furthermore /fúrthər mawr, fúrthər máwr/ *adv.* used to introduce an additional statement or point ○ *She claimed furthermore that he did not own the business but only worked there.*

furthermost /fúrthər mōst/ *adj.* most distant or remote

furthest /fúrthist/ *adj.* **MOST DISTANT** more distant in place or time than anything else ○ *In our solar system, Pluto is the furthest planet from the sun.* ◊ **farthest** ■ *adv.* ◊ **farthest 1. TO GREATEST DISTANCE** to or at a more distant point in space or time than anything else ○ *Whoever gets the furthest wins the prize.* **2. TO GREATEST EXTENT** to a greater degree or extent than anything else ○ *The dollar has fallen furthest against the pound for the last year.*

furtive /fúrtiv/ *adj.* **1.** SECRETIVE done in a way that is intended to escape notice ○ *conspirators exchanging furtive glances* **2.** SHIFTY with the appearance, or giving the impression, of sb who has sth to hide [Early 17thC. Via Old French *furtif* from Latin *furtivus* 'hidden, stolen', from *furtum* 'theft', from *fur* 'thief' (source of English *ferret*). Ultimately from an Indo-European word meaning 'to carry'.] —**furtively** *adv.* —**furtiveness** *n.*

WORD KEY: SYNONYMS

See Synonyms at ***secret***.

furuncle /fyŏŏr ungk'l/ *n.* a boil on the skin (*technical*) [Late 17thC. From Latin *furunculus*, literally 'small thief', hence 'knob on a vine' (because it 'steals' the sap), from *fur* (see FURTIVE).] —**furuncular** /fyŏŏ rúngkyŏŏlər/ *adj.* —**furunculous** /-ləss/ *adj.*

furunculosis /fyŏŏ rúngkyŏŏ lóssiss/ *n.* **1.** DERMAT SKIN DISORDER WITH MULTIPLE BOILS a condition in which large areas of the skin are covered in persistent boils **2.** BIOL FISH DISEASE a virulent bacterial disease that affects salmon and trout and can be devastating in densely populated waters, e.g. in fish farms

fury /fyŏŏri/ (*plural* **-ries**) *n.* **1.** RAGE violent anger ○ *She could not contain her fury any longer.* **2.** BURST OF ANGER a state or outburst of violent anger ○ *He stormed off in a fury.* **3.** WILDFORCE a state of excited or frenetic activity ○ *debris scattered in the wake of the tornado's fury* **4.** OFFENSIVE TERM FOR ANGRY WOMAN an offensive term for a woman who is considered by the speaker to be malevolent and spiteful (*offensive*) **5. fury, Fury** ➧ **Furies** [14thC. Via Old French *furie* from Latin *furia*, from *furere* 'to rage'.] ◇ **like fury** with great speed or energy

WORD KEY: SYNONYMS

See Synonyms at ***anger***.

WORD KEY: CULTURAL NOTE

The Sound and the Fury, a novel by US writer William Faulkner (1929). Set in the American South, it recounts the financial and moral decline of a wealthy family. The story, which centres on the daughter Caddy, is told in four parts, three of which are narrated by family members, one of them a mentally disabled son, Benjy.

furze /furz/ *n.* = **gorse** [Old English *fyrs*, of uncertain origin]

fusain /fyoo záyn, fyŏŏ zayn/ *n.* **1.** DRAWING CHARCOAL STICK a fine stick of charcoal for drawing, made from wood from the spindle tree **2.** DRAWING CHARCOAL DRAWING a drawing or sketch done with fusain charcoal **3.** MINERALS GREY COAL dark grey bituminous carbon found in some kinds of coal [Late 19thC. Via French, 'spindle tree, charcoal made from its wood' from, ultimately, Latin *fusus* 'spindle'.]

fuscous /fúskəss/ *adj.* of a dark brown colour tinged with grey [Mid-17thC. Formed from Latin *fuscus* 'dusky'. Ultimately from an Indo-European word that is also the ancestor of English *dusk*.]

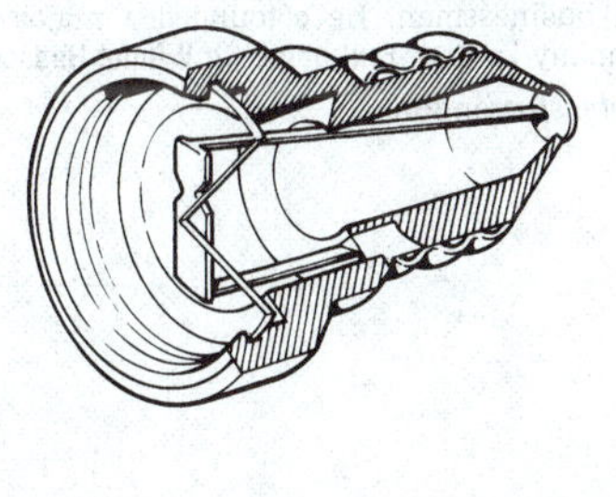

Fuse

fuse[1] /fyooz/ *n.* ELEC ENG ELECTRICAL CIRCUIT BREAKER an electrical safety device containing a piece of a metal that melts if the current running through it exceeds a certain level, thereby breaking the circuit ■ *vti.* (**fuses, fusing, fused**) **1.** STOP WORKING BECAUSE OF DAMAGED FUSE to stop functioning, or to cause an electrical circuit or appliance to stop functioning, because of a damaged electrical fuse ○ *In trying to find the fault, he managed to fuse all the other lights too.* **2.** COMBINE to unite or blend things, or become united or blended into a whole ○ *sensations and ideas fusing intimately together* **3.** LIQUEFY to melt sth such as metal or plastic, or become melted at a very high temperature [Late 16thC. From Latin *fus-*, the past participle stem of *fundere* 'to melt, pour' (source of English *foundry* and *fusion*).] ◇ **blow a fuse 1.** ELEC ENG to overload an electric circuit causing the fuse to melt, thereby breaking the circuit **2.** to fly into a temper (*informal*) ○ *She'll blow a fuse when you tell her.*

fuse[2] /fyooz/ *n.* **1.** EXPLOSIVE LEAD a cord or trail of a combustible substance that is ignited at one end to carry a flame to an explosive device further away **2.** DETONATOR a mechanical or electrical detonator that triggers an exploding device such as a bomb or grenade ■ *vt.* (**fuses, fusing, fused**) EQUIP DEVICE WITH DETONATOR to equip an exploding device such as a bomb or grenade with a mechanical or electrical detonator [Mid-17thC. Via Italian *fuso* 'spindle' from Latin *fusus* (source of English *fuselage*). So called because early bomb fuses were spindle-shaped hollow tubes filled with gunpowder.]

fuse box *n.* a box, often a cupboard fitted to a wall, that contains the fuses that protect all the electrical circuits in a building or part of a building

fused /fyoozd/ *adj.* fitted with a fuse for safety purposes (*refers to an electrical appliance*)

fused quartz, fused silica *n.* = **quartz glass**

fusee /fyoo zée/, **fuzee** *n.* **1.** WINDPROOF MATCH a large-headed match that is not easily extinguished in the wind **2.** MECH ENG CLOCK PULLEY a conical pulley with a spiral groove, used in clock and watch mechanisms [Late 16thC. Via French *fusée* 'spindle, fuse, flare' from, ultimately, Latin *fusus* 'spindle' (source also of English *fuse*[2]).]

fuselage /fyŏŏzə laazh, fyŏŏzəlij/ *n.* an aeroplane's body, containing the cockpit, passenger seating, and cargo hold but excluding the wings [Early 20thC. From French, from, ultimately, Latin *fusus* 'spindle' (source of English *fuse*[2]). The underlying meaning is 'spindle-shaped'.]

Fuseli /fyŏŏz'li/, **Henry** (1741–1825) Swiss painter and art critic. His imaginative paintings, emphasizing melodrama, fantasy, and horror, influenced key figures of the Romantic movement, such as William Blake. Real name **F**

fusel oil /fyŏŏz'l-/ *n.* an oily liquid mixture that occurs in insufficiently distilled alcoholic liquors. It is used as a solvent and in chemical manufacturing. [Mid-19thC. *Fusel* from German, 'bad liquor'.]

Fushun /fŏŏ shŏŏn/ city and industrial centre in Liaoning Province, northeastern China. Population: 1,202,388 (1991).

fusible /fyŏŏzəb'l/ *adj.* easily melted or liquefied (*refers to metals and other materials*) ○ *fusible alloys* —**fusibility** /fyŏŏzə bílləti/ *n.*

fusiform /fyŏŏzi fawrm/ *adj.* tapering at both ends, like a spindle ○ *fusiform bacteria* [Mid-18thC. Formed from Latin *fusus* 'spindle'.]

fusil /fyŏŏzil/ *n.* a lightweight musket with a flintlock firing mechanism [Late 16thC. From French, 'steel in a flintlock, musket', from, ultimately, late Latin *focus* 'fire'.]

fusile /fyoo zīl/, **fusil** /-zil/ *adj.* (*archaic*) **1.** MADE BY CASTING made by melting or casting metal **2.** MELTABLE easily melted or liquefied **3.** MADE LIQUID in a molten state [14thC. From Latin *fusilis* 'melted', from the stem *fus-* (see FUSE[1]).]

fusilier /fyŏŏzi léer/, **fusileer** *n.* **1.** BRITISH SOLDIER IN SOME REGIMENTS a soldier in any of several British army regiments that were formerly armed with lightweight muskets (**fusils**) **2.** SOLDIER WITH MUSKET in former times, a soldier armed with a lightweight musket (**fusil**) [Late 17thC. From French, formed from *fusil* 'musket' (see FUSIL).]

fusillade /fyŏŏzi layd, fyŏŏzi laad/ *n.* **1.** ARMS BLAST OF GUNFIRE a firing of several guns at once or in quick succession **2.** ONSLAUGHT a sustained attack or barrage, e.g. of missiles or words ■ *vt.* (**-lades, -lading, -laded**) FIRE AT ENEMY to subject an enemy to a sustained burst of gunfire [Early 19thC. From French, formed from *fusiller* 'to shoot', from *fusil* 'musket' (see FUSIL).]

fusilli /fyoo zílli/ *npl.* pasta in the form of short spiral shapes [Late 20thC. From Italian, literally 'little spindles', from, ultimately, Latin *fusus* 'spindle'.]

fusion /fyŏŏzh'n/ *n.* **1.** HEATING AND LIQUEFYING STH the molten state of a substance, or the change it undergoes to become molten **2.** BLENDING OF THINGS the merging or blending of two or more things, e.g. materials or ideas ○ *a fusion of vegetarianism and pacifism* **3.** PHYS = **nuclear fusion 4.** MUSIC COMBINATION OF MUSICAL STYLES the blending or resulting blend of musical styles or elements from more than one tradition, e.g. jazz and rock [Mid-16thC. Directly or via French from the Latin stem *fusion-*, from *fundere* 'to melt' (see FUSE[1]).]

fusion bomb *n.* a nuclear bomb, especially a hydrogen bomb, whose explosion is caused by the energy released by a nuclear fusion reaction

fusion food *n.* a style of cooking that uses different ingredients and techniques from around the world, especially one that combines both Eastern and Western influences

fusionism /fyŏŏzh'nizəm/ *n.* the formation of political coalitions, support for their formation, or belief in their effectiveness —**fusionist** *n., adj.*

fuss /fuss/ *n.* **1.** COMMOTION needlessly or excessively busy or excited activity **2.** NEEDLESS WORRY excessive concern over details or trivial matters **3.** PROTEST a complaint or protestation, often over sth insignificant ○ *The kids made a fuss about going to bed early.* **4.** ARGUMENT a noisy disagreement or dispute ○ *There'll be a fuss if he gets home late again.* **5.** DISPLAY OF AFFECTION OR CONCERN an excited or abundant display of affection or affectionate concern ○ *irritated by the fuss they make of her little brother* **6.** decoration or ornamentation regarded as excessive ○ *I want a dress without so much fuss around the neckline.* ■ *vi.* (**fusses, fussing, fussed**) **1.** WORRY TOO MUCH to be too concerned about details or trivial matters **2.** FIDDLE WITH STH to keep moving or touching sth busily, nervously, or aimlessly ○ *He fussed with the dials, hoping he'd look like he knew what he was doing.* [Early 18thC. Origin unknown.] —**fusser** /fússər/ *n.* ◇ **be fussed** to have a strong preference for sth (*informal*) ○ *I'm not fussed where we sit.*

fussbudget /fús bujit/ *n.* US = **fusspot** (*informal*) [Early 20thC. From BUDGET 'bundle'.]

fussock /fússək/ *n.* a donkey (*regional*) [Origin uncertain: perhaps from earlier FUSSOCK 'unweildily fat woman']

WORD KEY: REGIONAL NOTE

We do not know how long donkeys have been bred in the British Isles, but they were popularized by itinerant friars and have a variety of names including *cuddy, dicky, fussock, jason, jerusalem two-stroke, moke, neddy,* and *jinny.*

fusspot /fús pot/ *n.* sb who worries a lot about unimportant things (*informal*) US term **fussbudget**

fussy /fússi/ (**-ier, -iest**) *adj.* **1.** CONCERNED WITH MINOR THINGS tending to worry over details or trivial things **2.** CHOOSY very dogmatic about likes and dislikes ○ *a very fussy eater* **3.** ELABORATE made or decorated with excessive detail ○ *a dress with a fussy lace collar*

WORD KEY: SYNONYMS

See Synonyms at ***careful***.

fustian /fústi ən/ *n.* **1.** TEXTILES COTTON-LINEN CLOTH a coarse sturdy cloth of a cotton-linen blend **2.** TEXTILES COTTON FABRIC WITH NAP any hardwearing fabric with a raised nap made mainly from cotton, e.g. corduroy or moleskin **3.** BOMBAST pompous or pretentious speech or writing ■ *adj.* BOMBASTIC written or spoken with pretentiousness or pomposity [13thC. Via Old French from medieval Latin *fustaneum*, perhaps from Latin *fustis* 'wooden club', translation of Greek *xulina (lina)* 'linen from wood'. The underlying idea is 'heavy, used as padding'.]

fustic /fústik/ *n.* **1.** TREES DYE-YIELDING TREE a tropical American tree that belongs to the mulberry family. Its wood yields a yellow dye. Latin name: *Chlorophora tinctoria*. **2.** INDUST WOOD YIELDING YELLOW DYE the wood of the fustic tree **3.** INDUST YELLOW DYE a yellow dye obtained from the wood of the fustic tree **4.** TREES TREE OF EUROPE YIELDING DYE a European sumac tree whose wood is a source of yellow dye. Latin name:

Cotinus coggyria. [15thC. Via Old French *fustoc* from Arabic *fustuk*, from Greek *pistakē* 'pistachio tree'.]

fustigate /fústi gayt/ (**-gates, -gating, -gated**) *vt.* **1.** CLUB to beat sb with a club (*archaic*) **2.** CHASTISE to criticize sb or sth severely (*literary*) [Mid-17thC. From late Latin *fustigare,* from Latin *fustis* 'club' (see FUSTY) + *agere* 'to do' (source of English *act*).] —**fustigation** /fústi gáysh'n/ *n.*

fusty /fústi/ (**-tier, -tiest**) *adj.* **1.** STALE-SMELLING smelling of damp, dust, mildew, or age **2.** OUTDATED old-fashioned and conservative in style, appearance, habits, or attitudes (*disapproving*) ○ *transform a rather fusty image* [Late 15thC. Formed from obsolete *fust* 'wine cask', which came via Old French from Latin *fustis* 'wood, club'. The underlying meaning is 'having the musty smell of old wood'.] —**fustily** *adv.* —**fustiness** *n.*

fut. *abbr.* **1.** future **2.** FIN futures

futhark /fóo thaark/, **futhorc** /fóo thawrk/, **futhork** *n.* the common runic alphabet of 24 letters, used in northwestern Europe from the 3rd to 17th centuries [Mid-19thC. From the first six letters: *f, u, þ, a* or *o, r,* and *k*.]

futile /fyóo tīl/ *adj.* **1.** IN VAIN with no practical effect or useful result **2.** FRIVOLOUS lacking serious value, substance, or a sense of responsibility [Mid-16thC. From Latin *futilis* 'leaky, worthless'. Ultimately from an Indo-European base meaning 'to pour', which is also the ancestor of English *fuse*[1] and *gush*.] —**futilely** *adv.* —**futileness** *n.*

futilitarian /fyoo tílli táiri ən/ *n.* BELIEVER IN FUTILITY OF HUMAN EFFORT sb who believes that human efforts are wasted and futile ▪ *adj.* BELIEVING IN HUMAN FUTILITY holding or expressing the belief that all human effort is futile [Early 19thC. Formed from FUTILITY, on the model of UTILITARIAN.] —**futilitarianism** *n.*

futility /fyoo tílləti/ (*plural* **-ties**) *n.* **1.** POINTLESSNESS lack of usefulness or effectiveness **2.** POINTLESS ACTION an action that has no use, purpose, or effect

futon /fóo ton/ *n.* **1.** JAPANESE-STYLE MATTRESS a firm Japanese-style cotton-covered mattress used as a seat or bed, either on the floor or on a wooden frame **2.** FUTON WITH WOODEN FRAME a futon together with the wooden frame it sits on, especially a frame designed to convert from a sofa to a bed [Late 19thC. From Japanese.]

futtock /fúttək/ *n.* any of the curved middle timbers that form the frame of a traditional wooden boat or ship [13thC. Origin uncertain: possibly an alteration of assumed *fothok*, literally 'foot-hook'.]

futtock plate *n.* any of the circular metal plates fitted to the tops of a ship's shorter masts. Ropes or rods supporting a taller mast are secured to them.

futtock shroud *n.* a rope or rod stretching from the top of a taller mast to the top of a lower mast, to support the taller mast

future /fyóochər/ *n.* **1.** TIME TO COME time that has yet to come ○ *saving money for the future* **2.** HAPPENINGS TO COME events that have not yet happened ○ *The future will be shaped by our advancing technology.* **3.** FUTURE CONDITION an expected or projected state ○ *Her future is bleak.* **4.** GRAM TENSE REFERRING TO THINGS TO COME the tense or form of a verb used to refer to events that are going to happen or have not yet happened ▪ **futures** *npl.* FIN COMMODITIES TRADED FOR LATER DELIVERY goods or stocks sold for future delivery, or the contracts for them ▪ *adj.* **1.** YET TO OCCUR expected to be or happen at a time still to come ○ *my future sister-in-law* **2.** GRAM OF OR IN TENSE EXPRESSING FUTURE in or relating to the form of a verb that expresses actions or states that are going to happen or have not yet happened [14thC. Via Old French from Latin *futurus* 'going to be'. Ultimately from an Indo-European verb meaning 'to grow, become, be', which is also the ancestor of English *be* and *build*.]

futureless /fyóochərləss/ *adj.* seeming to have no chance of developing or being successful ○ *ploughed money into futureless schemes* —**futurelessness** *n.*

future perfect *n.* the form of a verb expressing a completed action in the future, as 'will have finished' does in the sentence 'They will have finished by tomorrow'

future shock *n.* difficulty in and stress from coping with rapid changes in society, especially with technological changes [From the title of a book by Alvin Toffler (b. 1928)]

future tense *n.* = future *n.* 4

futurism /fyóochərizəm/ *n.* **1.** futurism, Futurism ARTS ARTISTIC MOVEMENT VALUING TECHNOLOGY'S BEAUTY an early 20th-century artistic movement that attempted to express the dynamic nature of the modern age using technology as its subject **2.** BELIEF IN NEED TO LOOK FORWARD belief in the need to look to the future rather than reflect on the past, coupled with an optimism that personal and social fulfilment lies in the future [Early 20thC. Modelled on Italian *futurismo* and French *futurisme*.] —**futurist** *n., adj.*

futuristic /fyóochə rístik/ *adj.* **1.** AHEAD OF THE TIMES suggesting some future time in its design or technology, or using designs and technology thought likely to become popular or commonplace in the future **2.** SHOWING FUTURE LIFE depicting life in some future time —**futuristically** /fyóochə rístikli/ *adv.*

futurity /fyoo tyóorəti, -chóorəti/ (*plural* **-ties**) *n.* **1.** FUTURE the future as a concept or state ○ *a grammatical construction expressing futurity* **2.** FUTURE EVENT an event that is going to happen or has not happened yet (*formal*) ○ *We'll have to await those futurities before we can make a decision.*

futurology /fyoochə rólləji/ *n.* the study and forecasting of the future, with predictions based on the likely outcomes of current trends —**futurological** /fyóochərə lójjik'l/ *adj.* —**futurologist** /fyóochə rólləjist/ *n.*

fu yung, fu yong *n.* = foo yung

fuzee *n.* = fusee

Fuzhou /fóo zhó/ city and capital of Fujian Province, southeastern China, near the mouth of the Min River, northeast of Taiwan. Population: 874,809 (1990).

fuzz[1] /fuz/ *n.* FLUFF a mass of short fine hairs or fibres ▪ *vti.* (**fuzzes, fuzzing, fuzzed**) **1.** COVER STH WITH FUZZ to become covered or cover sth with fuzz ○ *sweaters that fuzz after the first wash* **2.** BLUR OR BECOME BLURRED to make sth, e.g. an image or explanation, blurred or unclear, or become blurred or unclear ○ *All this talk has fuzzed my brain.* [Late 16thC. Origin uncertain: probably from Dutch or Low German.]

fuzz[2] /fuz/ *n.* the police (*slang dated*) [Early 20thC. Origin unknown.]

fuzzbox /fúz boks/ *n.* an electrical device that distorts the sound that passes through it, especially a pedal-operated device wired to an electric guitar

fuzzy /fúzzi/ (**-ier, -iest**) *adj.* **1.** COVERED WITH FUZZ covered with a mass of short fine hairs or fibres **2.** CONSISTING OF FUZZ in the form of a mass of short fine hairs or fibres **3.** FRIZZY growing in a very tight curly mass (*refers to hair*) **4.** BLURRED not sharp enough to be seen or heard clearly ○ *a fuzzy picture* **5.** INCOHERENT not clearly thought out or set out ○ *The initial plan was fairly fuzzy.* [Early 17thC. Origin uncertain: possibly from Low German *fussig* 'spongy'. The earliest meaning in English was 'spongy, not firm'.] —**fuzzily** *adv.* —**fuzziness** *n.*

fuzzyheaded /fúzzi héddid/ *adj.* not thinking clearly, or not expressing thoughts or ideas clearly (*informal*) ○ *a fuzzyheaded notion* —**fuzzyheadedness** *n.*

fuzzy logic *n.* logic that allows for imprecise or ambiguous answers to questions. It forms the basis of the kind of computer programming designed to allow computers to mimic human intelligence.

fuzzy-wuzzy /-wúzi/ (*plural* **fuzzy-wuzzies** or **fuzzy-wuzzy**) *n.* **1.** OFFENSIVE TERM FOR SUDANESE SOLDIER a highly offensive name that British soldiers gave to their Sudanese enemies during the North African campaigns of the late 19th century (*archaic taboo offensive*) **2.** OFFENSIVE TERM FOR BLACK PERSON a highly offensive word used by some Caucasian people to refer to the dark-skinned inhabitants of any country (*dated taboo offensive*) [Late 19thC. *Wuzzy* an alteration of FUZZY. The word originally referred to any Black person, especially one with tightly curly hair.]

fv *abbr.* folio verso [Latin, 'on the reverse (i.e. left-hand) page']

fwd *abbr.* forward

f.w.d. *abbr.* **1.** four-wheel drive **2.** front-wheel drive

FWIW *abbr.* for what it's worth (*used in e-mail messages*)

FX *abbr.* **1.** FIN foreign exchange **2.** CINEMA (special) effects [Late 20thC. Representing a pronunciation of EFFECTS.]

-fy *suffix.* to make, cause to become ○ *gasify* ○ *ladify* [Via Old French *-fier* from, ultimately, Latin *facere* 'to do, make' (see FACT)]

FYI *abbr.* for your information

fyke /fīk/, **fyke-net** *n.* a bag-shaped fishing net, held open by hoops [Mid-19thC. Via Dutch *fuik* from Middle Dutch *fuke*.]

fylfot /fíl fot/ *n.* an old decorative or religious symbol in the form of a swastika [15thC. Origin unknown.]

Fyn /fün/ the second-largest island in Denmark, between southern Jutland and the island of Sjælland. Capital: Odense. Population: 470,528 (1996). Area: 2, 980 sq. km/1,150 sq. mi.

fynbos /fín boss/ *n.* S Africa the scrubland that is characteristic of the western Cape area of South Africa, consisting of shrubs resembling heaths with hard leaves [Late 19thC. From Afrikaans, 'small shrubs', literally 'fine bush'.]

Fysh /fish/, **Sir Hudson** (1895–1974) Australian aviator and businessman. He cofounded a major airline company in 1920. Full name **Sir Wilmot Hudson Fysh**

fz. *abbr.* sforzando

g[1] /jee/ (*plural* **g's**), **G** (*plural* **G's** *or* **Gs**) *n.* **1.** 7TH LETTER OF ENGLISH ALPHABET the seventh letter of the modern English alphabet **2.** SPEECH SOUND CORRESPONDING TO LETTER 'G' the speech sound that corresponds to the letter 'G' **3.** LETTER 'G' WRITTEN a written representation of the letter 'G'

g[2] *symbol.* **1.** PHYS acceleration of free fall as a result of gravity **2.** CHESS the seventh row of vertical squares from the left on a chessboard

g[3] *abbr.* MEASURE gram

G[1] /jee/ (*plural* **G's** *or* **Gs**) *n.* **1.** CINEMA GENERAL-AUDIENCE FILM RATING in Australia and the United States, a cinema censorship classification meaning that a film or video is suitable for anyone to watch **2.** *US* MONEY $1000 one thousand dollars (*slang*) **3.** MUSIC 5TH NOTE OF SCALE IN C the fifth note of a scale in C major **4.** MUSIC STH THAT PRODUCES A G a string, key, or pipe tuned to produce the note G **5.** MUSIC SCALE BEGINNING ON G a scale or key that starts on the note G **6.** MUSIC WRITTEN SYMBOL OF G a graphic representation of the tone of G

G[2] *symbol.* **1.** ELEC conductance **2.** PHYS Gibb's function **3.** PHYS gravitational constant **4.** BIOCHEM guanine

G[3] *abbr.* **1.** MEASURE giga- **2.** EDU good (*used as a grade*)

g. *abbr.* **1.** gauge **2.** GRAM gender **3.** MONEY guilder **4.** MONEY guinea

G. *abbr.* **1.** Gulf (*used in place names*) **2.** MONEY guilder **3.** MONEY guinea

G8 /jee áyt/ *n.* the group of the eight most industrialized nations in the world, comprising Canada, France, Germany, Italy, Japan, Russia, the United Kingdom, and the United States. Representatives from these countries meet regularly to discuss and draw up global economic policies. Full form **Group of Eight** [*G*, a shortening of GROUP]

Ga *symbol.* gallium

GA *abbr.* **1.** general agent **2.** General Assembly (of the United Nations) **3.** SHIPPING, INSUR general average **4.** Georgia

ga. *abbr.* gauge

Ga. *abbr.* Georgia

GAA *abbr.* Gaelic Athletic Association

gab /gab/ *vi.* (**gabs, gabbing, gabbed**) CHAT IDLY to talk at length about trivial matters (*informal*) ○ *We just sat there gabbing all afternoon.* ■ *n.* CHITCHAT light conversation about nothing in particular (*informal*) [Early 18thC. Origin uncertain, possibly shortening of GABBLE.] —**gabber** *n.*

GABA *abbr.* gamma-aminobutyric acid

gabardine /gábbər déen/ *n.* **1.** TEXTILES SMOOTH TWILL FABRIC a smooth hardwearing cotton, wool, or synthetic fabric woven with a pattern of parallel diagonal ridges (**twill**) ○ *a gabardine jacket* **2.** CLOTHES GABARDINE GARMENT a garment made of gabardine **3.** CLOTHES = **gaberdine** *n.* 1 [Early 20thC. Alteration of GABERDINE.]

gabble /gább'l/ *v.* (**-bles, -bling, -bled**) **1.** *vti.* SPEAK UNINTELLIGIBLY to speak or say sth rapidly and incoherently **2.** *vi.* BIRDS MAKE THROATY GOOSE SOUND to make the high throaty sounds that geese and some other birds make ■ *n.* **1.** FAST UNINTELLIGIBLE TALK rapid incoherent talking **2.** BIRDS SOUND GEESE MAKE the high throaty sounds that geese and some other birds make [Late 16thC. Origin uncertain, possibly from Middle Dutch *gabbelen*, an imitation of the sound.] —**gabbler** *n.*

gabbro /gábbrō/ *n.* a dark coarse-grained basic igneous rock containing calcium-rich plagioclase feldspar and pyroxene [Mid-19thC. Via Italian dialect from, possibly, Latin *glaber* 'smooth, bald'.] —**gabbroic** /gə brṓ ik/ *adj.*

gabby /gábbi/ (**-bier, -biest**) *adj.* talking or inclined to talk to an excessive, irritating degree (*informal*)

gabelle /gə bél/ *n.* **1.** HIST SALT TAX a French tax on salt imposed until 1790 **2.** TAX IN ANOTHER COUNTRY any tax, especially a tax imposed in a foreign country (*literary*) [15thC. Via Old French *gabel* from, ultimately, Arabic *ḳabāla* 'tax, duty'.]

gaberdine /gábbər déen/ *n.* **1.** CLOTHES MEDIEVAL GARMENT a long loose coat or smock made of coarse cloth, worn by men, especially Jewish men, during the Middle Ages **2.** TEXTILES = **gabardine** *n.* 1 **3.** CLOTHES = **gabardine** *n.* 2 [Early 16thC. Via Old French *gauvardine* from, ultimately, perhaps, Middle High German *wallevart* 'pilgrimage', from *wallōn* 'to wander' + *vart* 'journey'. The underlying meaning is thus 'pilgrim's garb'.]

gabion /gáybi ən/ *n.* **1.** MIL ROCK-FILLED BASKET AS FORTIFICATION a wickerwork basket filled with rocks, used as a temporary fortification **2.** CIV ENG STONE-FILLED DRUM IN WATERWAY CONSTRUCTION a cylindrical metal container filled with earth and stones, used in the construction and rerouting of waterways and in flood control [Mid-16thC. Via French from Italian *gabbione*, literally 'large cage', from *gabbia* 'cage', from Latin *cavea* (source of English *cage*).]

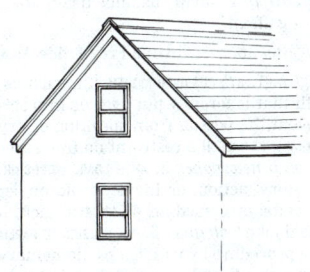

Gable

gable /gáyb'l/ *n.* **1.** PEAK OF BUILDING'S SIDE WALL the triangular top section of a side wall on a building with a pitched roof that fills the space beneath where the roof slopes meet **2.** = **gable end 3.** TRIANGULAR BUILDING DECORATION a triangular structure, e.g. a canopy over a door or window, added to a building for decoration [14thC. Directly or via Old French from Old Norse *gafl*. Possibly, ultimately, from an Indo-European word meaning 'head', the underlying idea being 'sth at the top'.] —**gabled** *adj.*

──── **WORD KEY: CULTURAL NOTE** ────

Anne of Green Gables, a children's story by Canadian writer Lucy Maud Montgomery (1908). Set on Prince Edward Island in Canada, it is the story of a vivacious 11-year-old orphan, Anne Shirley, who is sent to live with farmers Matthew and Marilla Cuthbert. Having expected a boy, the Cuthberts cannot hide their disappointment, but Anne's courage, spirit, and vivid imagination soon win them over.

Clark Gable

Gable /gáyb'l/, **Clark** (1901–60) US film actor. He won an Academy Award for his performance in the romantic comedy *It Happened One Night* (1934), but he is best known for his role as Rhett Butler in *Gone With the Wind* (1939). Full name **William Clark Gable**

gable end *n.* a side wall that comes to a peak where the slopes of a pitched roof meet

gable roof *n.* a roof with two slopes and a gable at each end

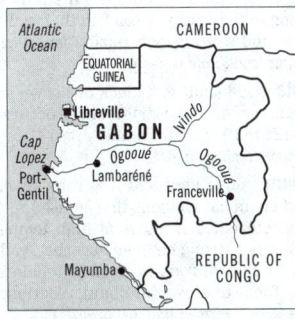

Gabon

Gabon /ga bón, gə bóN/ republic in west-central Africa on the Atlantic coast. It became independent from France in 1960. Language: French. Currency: CFA franc. Capital: Libreville. Population: 1,190,159 (1997). Area: 267,667 sq. km/103,347 sq. mi. Official name **Gabonese Republic**. Former name **French Equatorial Africa** —**Gabonese** /gággə neéz/ *n., adj.*

Gaborone /gábbə rṓni/ capital of Botswana, situated in the southeast of the country, about 19 km/12 mi. from the border with South Africa. Population: 133,791 (1991).

gad[1] /gad/ *vi.* (**gads, gadding, gadded**) BE OUT HAVING FUN to go around having fun in a carefree and aimless manner (*dated*) ○ *gadding about* ■ *n.* WANDERING carefree or aimless wandering (*dated*) [15thC. Origin uncertain: probably a back-formation from obsolete *gadling* 'wanderer', from Old English *gædeling* 'companion', ultimately from a prehistoric Germanic word that is also the ancestor of English *gather*.] —**gadder** *n.*

gad[2] /gad/ *n.* **1.** MINING HEAVY TOOL USED IN MINING a heavy steel or iron wedge with a pointed or chisel-shaped edge used in mining to break coal, rock, or ore from the rock face **2.** AGRIC CATTLE PROD a sharp pointed tool used to drive cattle ■ *vt.* (**gads, gadding, gadded**)

MINING **SEPARATE MINERALS FROM ROCK** to break up coal or ore using a gad [13thC. From a prehistoric Germanic word meaning 'pointed stick' that is also the ancestor of English *yard* ('three feet').]

Gad /gad/ *interj.* used to express surprise or to add emphasis (*archaic*) [15thC. Alteration of GOD.]

gadabout /gádə bowt/ *n.* sb who goes about looking for pleasure in an aimless and restless way (*dated informal*)

Gadaffi /gə dáffi/, **Qadaffi, Muammar al-** (*b.* 1942) Libyan military and political leader. He seized power in a coup against the monarchy (1969). He imposed Islamic and socialist policies and supported revolutionary and terrorist movements abroad.

gadarene /gáddə reén/ *adj.* rushing headlong en masse (*literary*) [Early 19thC. Via Latin from Greek *Gadarēnos* 'inhabitant of Gadara', the town that was the site of the herd of swine's headlong rush into the sea in Matthew 8:28 in the Bible.]

gadfly /gád flī/ (*plural* **-flies**) *n.* **1.** INSECTS **FLY THAT BITES LIVESTOCK** a fly that irritates livestock by biting them and sucking their blood. Horseflies are a type of gadfly. Family: Tabanidae. **2. SB ANNOYING** sb who persistently irritates or torments another person (*dated*) [*Gad* from GAD[2]]

gadget /gájjit/ *n.* **1. INGENIOUS DEVICE** a small device that performs or aids a simple task **2. TRIVIAL DEVICE** a small object or device that appears useful but is often unnecessary or superfluous [Late 19thC. Origin unknown. Said to have started as a sailors' slang term for some unspecified tool.] —**gadgety** *adj.*

gadgeteer /gájji teér/ *n.* sb who invents or enjoys using gadgets

gadgetry /gájjitri/ *n.* gadgets collectively, especially when perceived as impressively complicated

Gadhelic /gad héllik/ *n.* LANG = **Goidelic** [Early 16thC. Via medieval Latin *gathelicus*, from *Gathelus*, from Irish *Gaedheal*, plural of *Gaedhil*, which evolved from Old Irish *Goídel* (see GAEL).]

gadid /gáydid/, **gadoid** /gáy doyd/ *n.* **FISH OF COD FAMILY** a sea fish of the family that includes cod, haddock, and whiting. Family: Gadidae. ■ *adj.* **OF COD FAMILY** belonging to the family of sea fish that includes cod, haddock, and whiting [Mid-19thC. Formed from modern Latin *gadus* 'cod', from Greek *gados*.]

gadolinite /gáddəlinīt/ *n.* a black or brown silicate of beryllium, iron, and yttrium that occurs in pegmatite [Early 19thC. Named after Johan *Gadolin* (1760–1852), Finnish mineralogist.]

gadolinium /gáddə línni əm/ *n.* a rare silvery-white metallic chemical element that is used to improve the characteristics of alloys at high temperatures. Because it is a strong neutron absorber, gadolinium is used in control rods in nuclear reactors and in nuclear fuels to slow the chain reaction. Symbol **Gd** [Late 19thC. Formed from GADOLINITE.]

gadroon /gə dróon/, **godroon** *n.* an ornamental feature that consists of a series of convex curves or inverted fluting. It is often applied as an edging to a curved surface, especially on silver. [Late 17thC. Formed from French *godron* 'pucker, crease'.] —**gadrooned** *adj.* —**gadrooning** *n.*

gadwall /gád wawl/ *n.* a freshwater duck with grey or brown plumage that is common in Europe and North America. Latin name: *Anas strepera.* [Mid-17thC. Origin unknown.]

gadzooks /gad zóoks/ *interj.* used to express surprise or as a mild oath (*archaic or humorous*) [Late 17thC. From GAD + *zooks*, of unknown origin.]

Gael /gayl/ *n.* **1. SB WHO SPEAKS GAELIC** sb from Scotland, Ireland, or the Isle of Man who speaks Gaelic **2. SCOTTISH HIGHLANDER** sb from the Scottish Highlands [Mid-18thC. From Scots Gaelic *Gael* and *Gàidheal*, from Old Irish *Goídel* plural of Gáidl.]

Gaelic /gáylik/ *n.* LANG **CELTIC LANGUAGE OF BRITISH ISLES** any of the Celtic languages used in parts of Ireland, Scotland, and the Isle of Man ■ *adj.* **1. OF GAELIC** belonging to or using any of the Celtic languages of Ireland, Scotland, or the Isle of Man **2. OF GAELIC-SPEAKING PEOPLE** relating to or typical of Gaelic-speaking people or their culture

Gaelic coffee *n.* = **Irish coffee**

Gaelic football *n.* a game played in Ireland with 15 players on each side, the aim of which is to punch or kick a ball into or over a goal

Gaeltacht /gáyl takht/ *n.* the parts of Ireland or Scotland where Gaelic is spoken by a large proportion of the population [Early 20thC. From Irish.]

gaff[1] /gaf/ *n.* **1.** ANGLING **HOOKED FISH POLE** a pole with a large hook on the end that is used to hold and land a large fish **2.** SAILING **POLE AT TOP OF SAIL** a pole attached at the back of a mast and used to support the upper edge of a gaffsail **3.** GAMBLING **METAL SPUR ON FIGHTING COCK** a metal spur that is fixed to the leg of a fighting cock **4.** UTIL **HOOK FOR SB MAINTAINING OVERHEAD LINE** a climbing hook used by sb erecting or repairing a telephone or power line ■ *vt.* (**gaffs, gaffing, gaffed**) **1.** ANGLING **CATCH FISH WITH HOOKED POLE** to catch and hold a fish with a gaff **2. ARM WITH A GAFF** to provide or arm sth, e.g. a fighting cock, with a gaff [14thC. From Old French *gaffe* 'boat hook' (see GAFFE).]

gaff[2] /gaf/ *n.* worthless nonsense (*informal*) [Early 19thC. Origin unknown.] ◇ **blow the gaff** to reveal a secret (*slang*)

gaff[3] *n.* **1. HOUSE** the place where sb lives (*dated slang*) ○ *Nice gaff you've got yourself here!* **2. PLACE OF ENTERTAINMENT** a music hall or theatre (*dated informal*) [Early 19thC. Origin unknown.]

gaffe /gaf/ *n.* a clumsy social mistake or breach of etiquette, e.g. an undiplomatic remark [Early 20thC. From French, originally 'boat hook', from Old French, from Old Provençal *gaf*, of uncertain origin: perhaps from prehistoric Germanic.]

gaffer /gáffər/ *n.* **1.** *UK* **BOSS** the boss, owner, or supervisor of a workplace (*informal*) **2.** CINEMA **CHIEF LIGHTING ELECTRICIAN ON FILM SET** the chief electrician in charge of lighting on a film or television set (*informal*) **3.** *UK* **MAN** man of advanced years, especially a man from the country (*informal*) **4. HUSBAND** sb's husband (*regional*) [Late 16thC. Origin uncertain: probably a contraction of GODFATHER, with 'ga-' by association with GRANDFATHER.]

gaff-rig *n.* a sailing vessel rigged with gaffsail —**gaff-rigged** *adj.*

gaffsail /gáf sayl/ *n.* a quadrilateral sail that extends behind the mast rather than across the boat. The upper edge is supported by a pole (**gaff**) attached to the mast. US term **fore-and-aft sail**

gaff-topsail *n.* a small, usually triangular sail set above a gaffsail

GAFTA /gáftə/ *abbr.* Grain and Free Trade Association

gag /gag/ *n.* **1. STH PUT OVER MOUTH** sth, such as a piece of cloth that is forcibly put over or into sb's mouth to prevent the person from speaking or crying out **2. RESTRAINT OF SPEECH** a restraint on free speech ○ *put a gag on a newspaper* **3.** ARTS **COMIC WORDS OR ACTION** a comic story, action, or incident told or performed by an actor or comedian **4. TRICK** a trick, hoax, or practical joke (*informal*) **5.** POL **CLOSURE OF PARLIAMENTARY DEBATE** a procedure by which a parliamentary debate can be stopped and a vote taken immediately **6.** SURG **MOUTH PROP** a device that is placed in a patient's mouth to keep it open during surgical work on the mouth or throat **7. CHOKING** an instance or the action of choking or retching (*informal*) ■ *v.* (**gags, gagging, gagged**) **1.** *vt.* **PUT STH OVER SB'S MOUTH** to put sth over or into sb's mouth to prevent the person from speaking or crying out **2.** *vt.* **RESTRAIN SPEECH** to prevent or restrain the free speech of sb or sth **3.** *vti.* **CHOKE OR RETCH** to make sb nearly choke or retch, or to choke or retch because of sth stuck in the throat or because of a very unpleasant sight or smell **4.** *vi.* ARTS **TELL JOKES** to tell jokes or perform as a comedian (*informal*) **5.** *vt.* SURG **PROP SB'S MOUTH OPEN** to hold sb's mouth open during surgery by means of a gag **6.** *vt.* EQU **PUT STRONG BIT ON HORSE** to put a strong bit (**gag-bit**) on a horse **7.** *vt.* **OBSTRUCT PIPE OR VALVE** to stop up, block, or obstruct sth such as a pipe or valve [15thC. Origin uncertain: probably an imitation of the sound of choking.]

gaga /gáa gaa/ *adj.* **1. OFFENSIVE TERM MEANING IRRATIONAL** an offensive term that deliberately insults sb's mental abilities, especially those of a senior citizen (*informal offensive*) **2. VERY ENTHUSIASTIC** completely infatuated or very enthusiastic (*informal*) ○ *totally gaga about that boyfriend of hers* [Early 20thC. From French, an imitation of the sound of mumbling.]

gagaku /gágga koo/ *n.* an ancient form of Japanese classical music used at the imperial court and on ceremonial occasions [Early 20thC. From Japanese, from *ga* 'elegance' + *gaku* 'court music'.]

Yuri Gagarin

Gagarin /gə gaárin/, **Yuri** (1934–68) Soviet cosmonaut. He became the first person to be launched into space when he orbited the earth in *Vostok I* on 12 April 1961. Full name **Yuri Alekseyevich Gagarin**

Gagauz /gə gáwz/ (*plural* **-gauz** /-zi/ *or* **-gauzi**) *n.* **1.** LANG **TURKIC LANGUAGE** a Turkic language spoken in an area to the north of the Black Sea, especially in southern parts of Moldova, Ukraine, and Romania. About 150,000 people speak Gagauz. **2. Gagauz** (*plural* **-gauz** *or* **-gauzi**), **Gagauzian** PEOPLES **MEMBER OF TURKIC PEOPLE** a member of a Turkic people who live in the south-western region of Moldova —**Gagauz** *adj.*

gag-bit *n.* a strong bit sometimes used to help control an unruly horse

gage[1] /gayj/ *n.* (*archaic*) **1. PLEDGE** sth that is given or left as security until a debt is paid or an obligation is fulfilled **2. TOKEN OF CHALLENGE** a glove or other object that is thrown down or offered as a challenge to fight **3. CHALLENGE** a challenge to fight ■ *vt.* (**gages, gaging, gaged**) (*archaic*) **1. OFFER STH AS PLEDGE** to offer sth as security against a debt or other obligation **2.** BETTING **OFFER AS STAKE IN BET** to offer sth as a stake in a bet [13thC. From Old French, ultimately from a prehistoric Germanic word that is also the ancestor of English *wed*.]

gage[2] *n.*, *vt.* = **gauge**

gagger /gággər/ *n.* a piece of metal used to wedge the core of a casting mould in position

gaggle /gágg'l/ *n.* **1.** BIRDS **GROUP OF GEESE** a flock of geese **2. GROUP OF PEOPLE** a group of people, especially a noisy or disorderly group ○ *a gaggle of children* [14thC. Origin uncertain: perhaps literally 'to cry like a goose repeatedly', an imitation of the sound.]

gahnite /gaá nīt/ *n.* a dark green mineral consisting of zinc aluminium oxide [Early 19thC. Named after J. G. *Gahn* (1745–1818), Swedish chemist.]

gaiety /gáy əti/ (*plural* **-ties**) *n.* **1. JOYFULNESS** a light-hearted and lively feeling or way of behaving **2. SPIRITED ACTIVITY** joyful and lively activity or festivity **3. BRIGHT OR FANCY APPEARANCE** the showiness or bright colourful appearance of sth such as clothing (*dated*) [Mid-17thC. From Old French *gaieté*, from *gai* (see GAY).]

gaijin /gī jin/ (*plural* **-jin**) *n.* a foreigner in Japan or among Japanese [Mid-20thC. From Japanese, contraction of *gaikoku-jin*, literally 'sb from a foreign country'.]

gaily /gáyli/ *adv.* **1. JOYFULLY OR LIGHTHEARTEDLY** in a happy, cheerful, or carefree manner **2. SHOWING LACK OF CONCERN** showing a lack of concern or awareness **3. IN BRIGHT COLOURS** brightly or colourfully (*dated*)

gain[1] /gayn/ *v.* (**gains, gaining, gained**) **1.** *vt.* **ACQUIRE STH EARNED** to obtain sth through effort, skill, or merit ○ *gain recognition as an actor* **2.** *vt.* **WIN STH BY COMPETING** to win sth in competition or conflict ○ *gained second place in the dash* **3.** *vt.* **EARN STH** to earn or obtain sth by work ○ *gain a living* **4.** *vi.* **PROFIT** derive advantage from sth ○ *No one stands to gain from the deal.* **5.** *vti.* **BECOME GREATER** to grow or increase, or acquire more of sth ○ *She was steadily gaining in confidence.* **6.** *vt.* **PERSUADE TO SUPPORT** to acquire the support of sb through persuasion ○ *The movement quickly gained followers.* **7.** *vt.* **MAKE ARISE** to cause sth to arise or become operative ○ *gain his confidence* **8.** *vt.* **ESTABLISH RELATIONSHIP** to begin to have or establish a particular relationship with sb ○ *gain a mentor and a friend* **9.** *vi.* **GET BETTER** to improve or become better in some respect ○ *gaining in proficiency* **10.** *vi.* **GET CLOSER OR FARTHER AWAY** to come closer to sb or sth pursued, or increase the distance from a pursuer ○ *They are behind but they're gaining on us.* **11.** *vti.* **INCREASE IN OR BY STH** to come to have more of sth, or increase by a specified amount ○ *The pound had gained two points* **12.** *vti.* **TIME** **RUN AHEAD OF CORRECT TIME** to run fast so as to record a time ahead, or a specified amount of time ahead, of the correct one ○ *My watch gains at least 10 minutes every day.* **13.** *vt.* **REACH** to arrive at a place that it was intended or hoped to reach (*literary*) ○ *once we had finally gained the shore* ■ *n.* **1.** **ACHIEVEMENT** an advantage or improvement that has been earned or acquired through effort ○ *despite the political gains of recent years* **2.** **AMOUNT INCREASED** an increase or profit of a specified amount ○ *a small weight gain* **3.** **BENEFIT** financial profit or personal advantage **4.** **ELEC ENG** **MEASURE OF INCREASE IN SIGNAL STRENGTH** a ratio of the output power to the input power of an amplifier that is more than one and indicates an increase in signal strength **5.** **ELEC ENG** = **antenna gain** ■ **gains** *npl.* **EARNINGS AND ACQUISITIONS** sth acquired, earned, or won, especially money [15thC. Via Old French from a prehistoric Germanic word meaning 'to graze, hunt'.] —**gainable** *adj.*

—— WORD KEY: SYNONYMS ——
See Synonyms at **get**.

gain² /gayn/ *n.* **NOTCH TO FIT STH INTO** a notch or groove cut into a board so that another part can be fitted into it ■ *vt.* (**gains, gaining, gained**) **1.** **CUT NOTCH IN STH** to cut a notch or groove into a board so that another part can be fitted into it **2.** **FIT PART IN NOTCH** to fit a part into a gain or connect parts using a gain [Mid-19thC. Origin unknown.]

gainer /gáynər/ *n.* **1.** **SB GAINING** sb who or sth that gains **2.** **SWIMMING** **DIVE WITH BACK SOMERSAULT** a dive in which the diver jumps forwards, does a back somersault in the air, and enters the water feet first, facing away from the board

gainful /gáynf'l/ *adj.* bringing profit or advantage — **gainfulness** *n.*

gainfully /gáynf'li/ *adv.* in an activity that brings profit or advantage ○ *gainfully employed*

gainsay /gáyn sáy/ (**-says, -saying, -said** /-séd/, **-said** /gáyn séd/) *vt.* (*formal*) **1.** **DENY STH** to say that sth is false **2.** **CONTRADICT SB OR STH** to deny the truth of sth or of what sb says ○ *I won't gainsay you.* [14thC. Coined from *gain-*, from Old English *gegn* 'against' (source of English *again*), + **SAY.**] —**gainsayer** *n.*

Gainsborough /gáynzbərə/, **Thomas** (1727–88) British painter. He painted society portraits and English landscapes including *The Watering Place* (1777).

'gainst /genst, gaynst/, **gainst** *prep.* against (*literary*) [Late 16thC. Shortening.]

Gairdner, Lake /gáirdnər/ dry salt lake in south-central South Australia, about 385 km/240 mi. northwest of Adelaide. Area: 4,766 sq. km/1,840 sq. mi.

gait /gayt/ *n.* **1.** **MANNER OF WALKING** a way of walking, running, or moving along on foot ○ *his familiar shambling gait* **2.** **RIDING** **PATTERN OF HORSE'S STEPS** any one of the four paces of a horse, walk, trot, canter, and gallop, each having a specific pattern of leg movements [15thC. Variant of **GATE** 'way, street'.]

-gaited *suffix.* with a particular way of walking ○ *slow-gaited*

gaiter /gáytər/ *n.* a strip of fabric, leather, or lightweight waterproof material covering the leg from the instep to either the ankle or the knee. Modern gaiters are usually made of waterproof fabric and worn by climbers, walkers, or skiers. (*usually used in the plural*) [Early 18thC. Via French from a prehistoric Germanic base meaning 'twist', later, 'ankle'.] —**gaitered** *adj.*

Gaitskell /gáytskəl/, **Hugh** (1906–63) British politician. He was a member of parliament from 1945 and

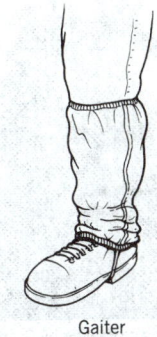
Gaiter

Labour Party leader (1955–63). Full name **Hugh Todd Naylor Gaitskell**

gal /gal/ *n.* a girl or woman (*slang*) (*sometimes considered offensive*) [Late 18thC. Reproducing a certain pronunciation of GIRL.]

gal. *abbr.* gallon

Gal. *abbr.* BIBLE Galatians

gala /gáalə/ *n.* **1.** **PARTY** a special festive occasion that typically includes food and entertainment **2.** **SPORTING COMPETITION** a sporting event, especially a swimming contest with a variety of different races and competitions [Early 17thC. Via Old French *gale* 'merrymaking' from, ultimately, Arabic *khil'a* 'fine garment given as a present', hence 'festive attire', 'festive occasion'.]

galact- *prefix.* = **galacto-**

galactagogue /gə láktə gog/ *adj.* BIOL **INDUCING MILK FLOW** causing the production and secretion of milk ■ *n.* MED **MILK STIMULATOR** an agent that stimulates the production and flow of breast milk [Coined from GALACT- + Greek *agōgos* 'leading', from *agein* 'to lead']

galactic /gə láktik/ *adj.* relating or belonging to a galaxy, especially the Milky Way [Mid-19thC. Formed from *galakt-*, the stem of *gala* 'milk' (see GALAXY).] —**galactically** *adv.*

galactic equator, **galactic circle** *n.* the imaginary circle on the sky formed by extending the plane that passes through the centre of the Galaxy. It is inclined at approximately 62° to the celestial equator.

galactopoiesis /gə láktō poy éssiss/ *n.* the production of milk by the cells of the glandular structure of the breast

galactopoietic /gə láktō poy éttik/ *adj.* **OF MILK PRODUCTION BY BODY** relating to or stimulating milk production in the mammary glands ■ *n.* **AGENT STIMULATING MILK FLOW** a substance that stimulates the secretion of milk

galactorrhea *n.* US = **galactorrhoea**

galactorrhoea /gə láktō rée ə/ *n.* excessive milk flow during lactation, or spontaneous milk flow in the absence of childbirth and nursing

galactosaemia /gə láktō séemi ə/ *n.* a genetic disorder causing the absence of an enzyme necessary for the breakdown of galactose in milk to glucose

galactosamine /gə lák tóssə meen/ *n.* a crystalline amino acid derived from the sugar galactose and found in cartilage and bacterial cell walls. Formula: $C_6H_{13}O_5N$.

galactose /gə láktōss/ *n.* a white crystalline sugar

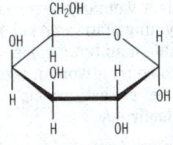
Galactose

found in certain plant gums and mucilages and one of the principal constituents of lactose, which is the main sugar of milk. Formula: $C_6H_{12}O_6$.

galactosemia *n.* US = **galactosaemia**

galago /gə láagō/ (*plural* **-gos**) *n.* = **bushbaby** [Mid-19thC. From modern Latin, genus name.]

galah /gə láa/ *n.* **1.** **AUSTRALIAN COCKATOO** an Australian cockatoo with a grey back and wings, a pink breast and head, and a pale pink crest. It is the most common parrot in Australia. Latin name: *Eulophus roseicapillus.* **2.** *Aus* **SILLY PERSON** a silly or thoughtless person (*informal insult*) [Mid-19thC. From an Aboriginal language.]

Galahad /gállə had/ *n.* **1.** **KNIGHT OF THE ROUND TABLE** the purest knight of the Round Table in Arthurian legend, who succeeded in his quest for the Holy Grail **2.** **SB WHO ACTS NOBLY** a man considered to be chivalrous, noble, or pure in actions or attitudes

galangal /gə láng g'l/ *n.* **1.** **PLANTS** **PLANT OF GINGER FAMILY** a plant of the ginger family grown in eastern Asia for its pungent underground stem. Latin name: *Alpinia officinarum.* **2.** **FOOD** **SPICE RESEMBLING GINGER** the underground stem of a galangal plant, sold fresh, or dried and ground, and used in cookery and medicine **3.** **PLANTS** = **galingale** [Pre-12thC. Via Old French *galingal* from Arabic *kálanjān*, of uncertain origin: perhaps from Chinese *gāoliángjiāng*, from *gāoliáng*, district in Guangdong Province + *jiāng* 'ginger'.]

galantine /gállən teen/ *n.* a dish of boned and cooked white meat, poultry, or fish, usually stuffed, that is moulded into shape and served cold in its own jelly or coated with aspic [14thC. Via Old French from medieval Latin *galatina*.]

galanty show /gə lánti-/ *n.* a play performed by manipulating paper figures and casting their shadows on a screen ['Galanty' of uncertain origin: perhaps from Italian *galanti*, plural of *galante*]

Galapagos giant tortoise /gə láppəgəss-, -goss-/, **Galapagos tortoise** *n.* a giant tortoise that is native to the Galápagos Islands. It grows up to 1.2 m/4 ft long and weighs up to 225 kg/500 lb. Latin name: *Geochelone elephantopus.*

Galápagos Islands

Galápagos Islands /gə láppəgəss-/ group of islands in the Pacific Ocean approximately 1,050 km/650 mi. west of Ecuador. They are known for harbouring unique species of wildlife, especially the giant tortoise. Area: 7,844 sq. km/3,029 sq. mi.

galatea /gállə tée ə/ *n.* a strong cotton fabric with a twill weave that is often striped and is used to make clothes [Late 19thC. Named after HMS *Galatea*; the fabric was originally used for children's sailor suits.]

Galatea /gállə tée ə/ *n.* a small inner natural satellite of Neptune, discovered in 1989 by the spacecraft Voyager 2. It is approximately 150 km/95 mi. in diameter.

Galati /ga látsi/ inland port in Romania, on the River Danube, about 177 km/110 mi. northeast of Bucharest. Population: 326,728 (1994).

Galatians /gə láysh'nz/ *n.* a book of the Bible believed to be a letter from St Paul to the people of Galatia (*takes a singular verb*) [Early 17thC. Formed from *Galatia*, an ancient country of central Asia Minor.]

galavant /gálli vant/ *vi.* = **gallivant**

galaxy /gálləksi/ (*plural* **-ies**) *n.* **1.** **ASSEMBLY OF STARS, GAS, AND DUST** a group of billions of stars and their planets, gas, and dust that extends over many thousands of light-years and forms a unit within the universe. Held together by gravitational forces, most of the estimated 50 billion galaxies are shaped as spirals and ellipses, with the remainder being asymmetric. **2. DISTINGUISHED ASSEMBLY** a gathering of famous, brilliant, or distinguished people or things [14thC. Via Old French from, ultimately, Greek *galaxias (kuklos)*, literally 'milky (circle)', from *galakt-*, the stem of *gala* 'milk'.]

Galaxy *n.* = Milky Way

galbanum /gálbənəm/ *n.* a yellowish to green or brown aromatic bitter gum resin derived from several related Asian plants and used in incense or medicinally as a counterirritant. Genus: *Ferula.* [12thC. Via Latin from Greek *khalbanē*, from Semitic.]

gale /gayl/ *n.* **1. WIND OF FORCE 8 OR 9** an extremely strong wind that measures 8 or 9 on the Beaufort scale and has a speed of between 63 km/39 mi. and 87 km/54 mi. per hour **2. STRONG WIND** a very strong wind **3. BREEZE** a light breeze (*archaic*) [Mid-16thC. Origin uncertain: perhaps from Norwegian *galen* 'bad' (referring to wind).]

galea /gáy li ə/ (*plural* **-ae** /-ee/) *n.* a part or organ shaped like a helmet, e.g. the upper petal of some flowers or one of the mouthparts of an insect [Mid-19thC. From Latin, 'helmet'.] —**galeate** /gáyli ət/ *adj.*

Galen /gáylən/ (129–199?) Greek physician and scholar. His anatomical studies formed the basis of European medical practice for 1,400 years.

galena /gə leénə/ *n.* a lustrous blue-grey crystalline mineral that consists mainly of lead sulphide and is the main source of lead. Galena crystals were once used as rectifiers in crystal radio sets. [Late 17thC. From Latin, 'lead at a certain stage of smelting'.]

galenical /gay lénnik'l/ *n.* **NATURAL DRUG** any medicinal preparation that is made from plant or animal tissue, especially vegetable matter, rather than being created synthetically ■ *adj.* **NOT SYNTHETIC** made from plant or animal tissue rather than synthesized [Mid-17thC. Formed from GALEN, because he prescribed such remedies.]

galenite /gáylə nīt/ *n.* = galena

galère /ga láir/ *n.* **1. GROUP OF PEOPLE WITH COMMON FEATURE** a group of people with a particular attribute or interest, especially sth undesirable, in common **2. UNPLEASANT SITUATION** an unpleasant predicament [Mid-18thC. Via French, 'galley', from Catalan *galera*, from Middle Greek *galea*.]

Galibi /gaa leébi/ (*plural* **-bi** *or* **-bis**) *n.* **1. PEOPLES MEMBER OF NATIVE S AMERICAN PEOPLE** a member of an indigenous South American people who live in French Guiana **2. LANG CARIB LANGUAGE** a language spoken in French Guiana, one of the Carib group of American languages. Galibi is spoken by fewer than a thousand people. [Late 19thC. From Carib, literally 'strong man'.] —**Galibi** *adj.*

Galilean[1] /gálli leé ən/ *n.* **1. PEOPLES SB FROM GALILEE** sb who lives or was born or brought up in Galilee **2. CHR CHRISTIAN** a Christian (*archaic*) **3. CHR JESUS CHRIST** Jesus Christ (*archaic or literary*) ■ *adj.* **RELATING TO GALILEE** relating to or typical of Galilee, or its people or culture [Mid-16thC. Formed from Latin *Galilea* 'GALILEE'.]

Galilean[2] /gálli leé ən/ *adj.* relating to the Italian scientist Galileo, his theories, or his inventions

galilee /gálli lee/ *n.* a small porch or chapel found at the western end of some medieval churches or cathedrals [15thC. Via Old French from medieval Latin *galilea*, named after Latin *Galilea* 'GALILEE', said to be from the position of Galilee as the province most distant from Jerusalem.]

Galilee /gálli lee/ region of ancient Palestine, now part of northern Israel, situated between the River Jordan and the Sea of Galilee. It was the scene of Jesus Christ's ministry.

Galilee, Sea of freshwater lake on the River Jordan in northeastern Israel. It is 209 m/686 ft below sea level. Area: 166 sq. km/64 sq. mi.

Galileo: Portrait drawing by Guido Reni

AKG London

Galileo /gálli láy ō/ (1564–1642) Italian physicist and astronomer. One of the founders of Europe's scientific revolution, his main contributions include the application of the telescope to astronomy and the discovery of the laws of falling bodies and the motions of projectiles. Born **Galileo Galilei**

galingale /gálling gayl/ *n.* a plant of the sedge family with reddish flowers growing in a cluster directly from the stem and aromatic roots that were used medicinally in the past. Latin name: *Cyperus longus.* [See GALANGAL]

galiot /gálli ət/, **galliot** *n.* **1. LIGHT FAST GALLEY** a light fast ship propelled by sails and oars that was used in the past in the Mediterranean **2. SINGLE-MASTED SHIP** a light shallow single-masted Dutch merchant ship used in the past [15thC. Via Old French (literally 'little galley') from, ultimately, medieval Latin *galea* 'galley'.]

galipot /gálli pot/ *n.* crude turpentine in resin form that is obtained from several species of pine found in southern Europe [Late 18thC. Via French from Provençal *garapot* 'pine resin'.]

gall[1] /gawl/ *n.* **1. AUDACITY** impudent boldness ○ *And then he had the gall to tell us to leave!* **2. BITTER FEELING OR EXPERIENCE** a feeling of bitterness or resentment (*literary*) ○ *Her betrayal turned his love to gall.* **3. PHYSIOL BILE** bile (*archaic*) [12thC. From Old Norse *gall* 'bile', from a prehistoric Germanic word meaning 'yellow'.]

gall[2] /gawl/ *n.* **1. VET SORE CAUSED BY RUBBING** a sore on the skin of an animal that is caused by friction **2. CAUSE OF ANGER** sth that angers or irritates sb (*dated*) **3. ANGER** a feeling of annoyance or anger (*dated*) ■ *vt.* (**galls, galling, galled**) **1. ANGER SB** to make sb extremely angry **2. BREAK THE SURFACE DUE TO FRICTION** to break or damage a surface, especially the skin, by friction or rubbing [14thC. From Middle Low German *galle* 'sore', of uncertain origin: perhaps originally 'astringent substance'.]

gall[3] /gawl/ *n.* a swelling on a tree or plant caused by insects, fungi, bacteria, or animal damage [14thC. Via Old French from Latin *galla* 'oak apple'.]

gall. *abbr.* gallon

Galla /gállə/ *n.*, *adj.* **LANG, PEOPLES** = Oromo [Late 19thC. Origin uncertain: perhaps from Arabic *galīz* 'rough'.]

gallamine /gállə meen/ *n.* a short-acting but powerful muscle relaxant used by anaesthetists during the induction of general anesthesia [Late 19thC. From *gallic* (from GALLIUM) + AMINE.]

gallant /gállənt, gə lánt/ *adj.* **1. COURTEOUS** courteous and thoughtful, especially towards women **2. BRAVE** brave, spirited, and honourable (*literary*) **3. MAJESTIC** grand and majestic (*archaic*) **4. STYLISH** stylish or showy in dress (*archaic*) ■ *n.* **1. MAN COURTEOUS TO WOMEN** a man who is courteous and thoughtful in his behaviour towards women (*archaic*) **2. MALE LOVER** a man who is a woman's lover (*archaic*) **3. DANDY** a fashionable young man (*archaic*) **4. BRAVE MAN** a brave and honourable man (*archaic*) ■ *vti.* (**-lants, -lanting, -lanted**) **WOO** to court a woman (*archaic*) [14thC. From Old French, the present participle of *galer* 'to make merry'.] —**gallantly** *adv.*

gallantry /gálləntri/ (*plural* **-ries**) *n.* **1. COURAGE** bravery, especially in war or in a situation of great danger **2. COURTESY** courteous and thoughtful behaviour, especially towards women **3. STH GALLANT SAID OR DONE** a courageous or chivalrous action or remark (*dated*)

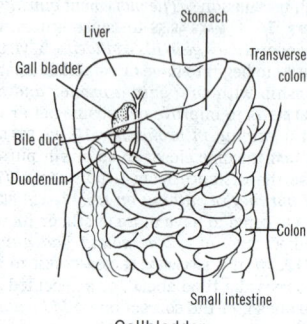
Gallbladder

gallbladder /gáwl bladər/ *n.* a small muscular sac on the right underside of the liver, in which bile secreted by the liver is stored and concentrated until needed for the digestive process

Galle /gállə, gawl/ port on the southwestern coast of Sri Lanka. Population: 84,000 (1990).

galleass /gálli ass/, **galliass** *n.* a large fast warship with three masts, used in the Mediterranean in the 16th and 17th centuries [Mid-16thC. Via Old French from Old Italian *galeaza* 'large galley'.]

Galleon

galleon /gálli ən/ *n.* a large three-masted sailing ship used especially by the Spanish between the 15th and 18th centuries [Early 16thC. Either via Middle Dutch *galjoen* from Old French *galion* 'large galley', or from Spanish *galeón*.]

galleria /gállə reé ə/ *n.* a roofed court with shops or businesses opening onto it, usually at several levels [Late 19thC. From Italian.]

gallery /gálləri/ (*plural* **-ies**) *n.* **1. ARTS PLACE FOR ART EXHIBITIONS** a place where artwork is exhibited and sometimes sold **2. ARCHIT COVERED WALKWAY** a long covered passageway that is open on one or both sides **3. ARCHIT ENCLOSED WALKWAY** a corridor, hall, or other enclosed passageway inside a building **4. ARCHIT LONG NARROW ROOM** a long narrow space or room used for a particular purpose **5. ARCHIT BALCONY** a balcony or passage running along the wall of a large building, often used for viewing an activity **6. UNDERGROUND TUNNEL OR PASSAGE** an underground tunnel or passage, especially one made by an animal or one that is part of a mine or a military site **7. PHOTOGRAPHY STUDIO** a photographer's studio **8. THEATRE PART OF THEATRE** a seating area projecting from the back and sides out over the main floor of a theatre, especially the highest section of this area containing the cheapest seats **9. THEATRE SEATS IN THE GALLERY** the seats located in the gallery of a theatre **10. THEATRE AUDIENCE IN CHEAPEST SEATS** the people who sit in the gallery of a theatre **11. OFFENSIVE TERM** an offensive term applied to the general public, viewed as having no discrimination or sophistication (*offensive*) **12. THEATRE STAGE RIG** a narrow platform above a stage from which technicians can adjust lights, move props, or operate machinery **13. SPORTS SPECTATORS AT A COMPETITION** a group of spectators, especially at a tennis or golf match **14. ASSORTED COLLECTION** a varied collection of people or things ○ *a gallery of famous names* **15. TV SOUNDPROOF ROOM IN STUDIO** a soundproof room with a glass front in a television studio, from which the director or technical staff can oversee the studio floor **16. NAUT SHIP'S**

BALCONY a platform or balcony at the rear of a ship **17. FURNITURE DECORATIVE RAIL** a decorative metal or wooden rail on a table top, shelf, or tray [15thC. Via Old French *galerie* 'portico' from, ultimately, medieval Latin *galeria*, of uncertain origin: perhaps an alteration of *galilea* (see GALILEE).] —**galleried** *adj.* ◇ **play to the gallery** to do or say sth that will appeal to those regarded as less educated, discriminating, or sophisticated

gallery forest *n.* a strip of forest that grows along a river in an area where there are no other trees

galley /gálli/ (*plural* **-leys**) *n.* **1. SHIPPING LARGE SHIP USING OARS OR SAILS** a large ship propelled by oars or sails or both, that was used in ancient and medieval times, especially in the Mediterranean **2. SHIPPING ROWING BOAT** a long boat propelled by oars **3. TRANSP BOAT, TRAIN, OR AIRCRAFT KITCHEN** a kitchen on a boat, train, or aircraft **4. PRINTING PRINT TRAY** a long metal tray used for holding type that is ready for printing **5. PRINTING** = **galley proof** [13thC. Via Old French and medieval Latin from medieval Greek *galea*, of unknown origin.]

galley proof *n.* PRINTING a first test copy of printed material, usually not divided into pages, on which corrections are marked

galley slave *n.* **1. HIST ENSLAVED OARSMAN** one of a team of criminals or enslaved men forced in the past to row a galley **2. DRUDGE OR DOGSBODY** sb who is given menial tasks to do (*dated humorous*)

gallfly /gáwl flī/ (*plural* **-flies**) *n.* an insect such as the gall midge or gall wasp that causes swellings (**galls**) on plants when it deposits its eggs on them [*Gall* from GALL³]

galliard /gálli aard/ *n.* **1. DANCE SPIRITED DANCE** a lively dance popular in England, France, Spain, and Italy in the 16th and 17th centuries **2. MUSIC FOR GALLIARD** the music for a galliard, written in triple time, part of the baroque dance suite ■ *adj.* **LIVELY** lively or spirited (*archaic*) [14thC. From Old French, of uncertain origin: perhaps from a Celtic word.]

galliass *n.* SHIPPING = **galleass**

Gallic /gállik/ *adj.* **1. FRENCH** relating to or typical of France, or its people or culture **2. GAULISH** relating or belonging to ancient Gaul or the Gauls [Late 17thC. Formed from Latin *Gallia* 'Gaul'.]

Gallic acid

gallic acid /gállik-/ *n.* a colourless crystalline solid that occurs in plants and is obtained from tannin. It is used as a tanning agent, in making inks and paper, and in photography. Formula: $C_7H_6O_5$. [*Gallic*, formed from Latin *galla* 'oakgall' (because the acid is made from the oakapple and other vegetable products)]

Gallican /gállikən/ *n.* **SUPPORTER OF GALLICANISM** a supporter of Gallicanism in the Roman Catholic Church ■ *adj.* **RELATING TO GALLICANISM** relating to or advocating Gallicanism

Gallicanism /gállikənizəm/ *n.* CHR a French movement in favour of giving the Roman Catholic Church in individual countries more autonomy and reducing the authority of the pope

Gallicise *vt.* = **Gallicize**

Gallicism /gállisizəm/ *n.* a word or phrase of French origin used in another language

Gallicize /gálli sīz/ (**-cizes**, **-cizing**, **-cized**), **Gallicise** (**-cises**, **-cising**, **-cised**) *vti.* to become French or like sth French, or make sth, e.g. a word, custom, or characteristic French —**Gallicization** /gálli sī záysh'n/ *n.*

galligaskins /gálli gáskinz/ *npl.* CLOTHES **1. BREECHES OR STOCKINGS** loose-fitting breeches or stockings that were worn by men in the 16th and 17th centuries **2. LOOSE TROUSERS** very loose-fitting trousers **3. LEATHER LEGGINGS** leather leggings worn in the 19th century [Late 16thC. Origin uncertain: perhaps an alteration of French *garguesques*, which is, ultimately, from Latin *Graecus* 'Greek'.]

gallimaufry /gálli máwfri/ (*plural* **-fries**) *n.* a jumble of various things or people (*dated*) [Mid-16thC. From French *galimafrée*, of unknown origin.]

galling /gáwling/ *adj.* with the effect of frustrating and annoying sb —**gallingly** *adv.*

gallinule /gálli nyool/ *n.* an aquatic bird of swampy regions that both wades and swims and typically has dark plumage and a yellow-tipped red bill with a red shield above it. Family: Rallidae. [Late 18thC. From modern Latin *gallinula* 'little hen'.]

galliot *n.* = **galiot**

Gallipoli /gə líppəli/ peninsula in European Turkey, extending into the Dardanelles, and including an important seaport of the same name. It has historically been of great strategic importance to Istanbul. The peninsula was the site of a major World War I campaign in 1915, when Allied troops including many from Australia and New Zealand, failed to take control of the Dardanelles.

gallipot /gálli pot/ *n.* a small pot used by chemists as a container for medicaments. In the past these were earthenware, but modern gallipots are made of foil, stainless steel, or polypropylene. [15thC. Origin uncertain: probably coined from GALLEY + POT, with the idea that such pots were brought in galleys from the Mediterranean.]

gallium /gálli əm/ *n.* a rare metallic chemical element, blue-grey when solid and silver when liquid, that is found in coal and ores. Symbol **Ga** [Late 19thC. Formed from Latin *Gallia* 'France'.]

gallium arsenide *n.* a dark-grey crystalline solid containing gallium and arsenic. It is used in making semiconductors, solar cells, and lasers. Formula: GaAs.

gallivant /gálli vant/ (**-vants**, **-vanting**, **-vanted**), **galavant** (**-vants**, **-vanting**, **-vanted**) *vi.* (*informal*) **1. TRAVEL AROUND FOR PLEASURE** to travel around with no purpose except enjoyment **2. PLAY AROUND AMOROUSLY** to flirt or play romantically [Early 19thC. Origin uncertain; perhaps an alteration of GALLANT.]

galliwasp /gálli wosp/ *n.* a lizard with a long body that is related to the slowworm and is found in marshes of Central America and the West Indies. Family: Anguidae. [Late 17thC. Origin unknown.]

gall midge *n.* a small fly resembling a mosquito whose larvae cause swellings (**galls**) on plants. Family: Cecidomyiidae.

gall mite *n.* a mite that causes swellings (**galls**) on the fruits, leaves, or buds of plants. Family: Phytoptidae.

gallnut /gáwl nut/ *n.* a small round swelling (**gall**) on a plant

galloglass /gálló glaass/, **gallowglass** *n.* a medieval mercenary soldier or armed servant of a Celtic chieftain, especially in Ireland [15thC. From Irish *gallóglach*, literally 'young foreign servant, warrior'.]

gallon /gállən/ *n.* **1. BRITISH UNIT OF VOLUME** a unit of capacity in the imperial system equal to eight imperial pints (approximately 4.55 litres) **2. US US UNIT OF VOLUME** a unit of capacity in the US Customary system equal to eight US pints (approximately 3.79 litres) ■ *adj.* **HOLDING A GALLON** with a capacity of one gallon ○ *a gallon jar* [13thC. Via Old French from medieval Latin *galleta* 'jug', of uncertain origin: perhaps from Celtic.]

gallonage /gállənij/ *n.* **1. CAPACITY IN GALLONS** a capacity or amount measured in gallons **2. RATE OF LIQUID TRANSFER** the rate at which a liquid is used, pumped, or transmitted, measured in gallons per second, minute, or hour

galloon /gə loon/ *n.* a narrow band of embroidery, lace, braid, or silver or gold thread, used as a trimming on clothes or upholstery [Early 17thC. From French *galon*, from *galonner* 'to trim with braid', of unknown origin.] —**gallooned** *adj.*

galloot *n.* = **galoot**

gallop /gálləp/ *n.* **1. FASTEST PACE OF HORSE** the fastest pace of a horse, in which all four feet are off the ground at the same time **2. FAST PACE OF FOUR-LEGGED ANIMAL** a fast movement similar to a horse's gallop made by any four-legged animal **3. FAST RIDE ON HORSE** a ride on a horse at a gallop ■ *v.* (**-lops**, **-loping**, **-loped**) **1.** *vti.* **RIDE HORSE FAST** to ride a horse at a gallop **2.** *vt.* **MOVE STH QUICKLY** to move or transport sth at a gallop or at a very fast pace **3.** *vi.* **DO STH VERY FAST** to do sth in a great hurry ○ *gallop through lunch* [Early 16thC. From Old French *galoper*, a variant of *waloper*, of prehistoric Germanic origin.] —**galloper** *n.*

gallopade /gállə payd, -paad, gállə paád/ *n.* DANCE, MUSIC = **galop** [Mid-18thC. From French *galopade*, from *galoper* (see GALLOP).]

galloping /gálləping/ *adj.* **1. FAST-DEVELOPING** proceeding or developing at a very fast rate ○ *galloping pneumonia* **2. LIKE GALLOP** relating to or resembling a gallop, in speed or rhythm

Gallo-Romance /gálló-/, **Gallo-Roman** *n.* a group of dialects spoken in France between the 7th and the 10th centuries AD. It constitutes an intermediate developmental stage between the end of Vulgar Latin and the appearance of Old French. —**Gallo-Romance** *adj.*

Gallovidian /gállə víddi ən/ *n.* **SB FROM GALLOWAY** sb who lives or who was born or brought up in Galloway ■ *adj.* **FROM GALLOWAY** relating to or coming from Galloway [Mid-17thC. Formed from medieval Latin *Gallovidia* GALLOWAY.]

Galloway /gállə way/ area on the Solway Firth in southwestern Scotland, part of Dumfries and Galloway council area

gallowglass *n.* HIST = **galloglass**

gallows /gállóz/ (*plural* **-lows**) *n.* **1. FRAME FOR HANGING CRIMINALS** a wooden frame, usually made of two upright posts and a crossbeam with a noose attached, used to execute people by hanging **2. STRUCTURE RESEMBLING GALLOWS** a structure that resembles a gallows, e.g. one used to suspend slaughtered animals **3. EXECUTION BY HANGING** death by hanging as capital punishment for a criminal offence [13thC. Via Old Norse *gálgi* from a prehistoric Germanic word meaning 'pole'. The use of the plural form developed because the structure has two upright posts.]

gallows bird *n.* sb who deserves to be hanged (*archaic informal*)

gallows humour *n.* macabre humour that finds irony or comedy in serious matters such as death

gallows tree *n.* = **gallows** *n.* 1

gallstone /gáwl stōn/ *n.* a small hard mass that forms in the gallbladder, sometimes as a result of infection or blockage

Gallup /gálləp/, **George** (1901–84) US public opinion analyst and statistician. A pioneer in the use of statistical methods for determining public opinion on social, economic, and political issues, he is best known for founding the Gallup Poll (1935). Full name **George Horace Gallup**

Gallup poll /gálləp-/ *n.* a survey in which a sample of people taken as a representative cross section of society are asked their opinions on a given subject [Mid-20thC. Named after George H. GALLUP.]

gallus /gálləss/ *adj.* Scotland daring in a cocky or foolhardy way (*informal*) [Late 16thC. Alteration of GALLOWS, originally with the sense 'fit to be hanged, wicked'.]

galluses /gálləssiz/ *npl.* US, Scotland braces for trousers [Mid-19thC. Plural of *gallus*, alteration of GALLOWS; from the two supports.]

gall wasp *n.* a wasp that lays its eggs in plant tissue, causing swellings (**galls**). Family: Cynipidae.

galoot /gə loot/, **galloot** *n.* sb who is clumsy or thoughtless (*slang insult*) [Early 19thC. Origin unknown.]

galop /gálləp, gə lóp/ *n.* **1. DANCE LIVELY DANCE** a lively dance that was popular in the 19th century **2. MUSIC MUSIC FOR DANCE** the music for a galop, in double time [Mid-19thC. From French.]

galore /gə láwr/ *adj.* in large quantities or numbers ○ *There'll be food galore at the party.* [Early 17thC. From Irish *go leor*, literally 'to sufficiency'.]

galoshes /gə lóshiz/ *npl.* a pair of waterproof shoes, often made of rubber, worn over other shoes as protection against rain or snow [14thC. Via Old French *galoche* 'little sandal' from Latin *gallicula*, from *gallica (solea)* 'sandal (from Gaul)'.]

Galtieri /gálti áiri/, **Leopoldo** (*b.* 1926) Argentine soldier and politician. As president of Argentina's military junta (1981–82), he ordered the invasion of the Falkland Islands that provoked a war with Great Britain (1982). Full name **Leopoldo Fortunato Galtieri**

galumph /gə lúmf/ (**-lumphs, -lumphing, -lumphed**) *vi.* (*informal*) **1.** MOVE BOISTEROUSLY OR CLUMSILY to walk or run in a boisterous or clumsy way **2.** MOVE EXULTANTLY to stride or march in a prancing triumphant way [Late 19thC. Blend of GALLOP and TRIUMPH, coined by Lewis Carroll in *Through the Looking Glass* (1872).]

galuth /ga lóoth/ *n.* the Jewish Diaspora [Late 20thC. From Hebrew *gālūth*, literally 'exile'.]

galv. *abbr.* **1.** galvanic **2.** galvanized

galvanic /gal vánnik/ *adj.* **1.** ELEC ENG RELATING TO CHEMICALLY PRODUCED DIRECT CURRENT relating to or involving the direct-current electricity that is chemically generated between dissimilar metals, e.g. in a battery **2.** LIKE ELECTRIC SHOCK sudden, startling, or convulsive, like an electric shock or its effects [Late 18thC. (See GALVANISM).] —**galvanically** *adv.*

galvanic skin response *n.* a change in the electrical conductivity of the skin caused by sweating and increased blood flow and linked to a strong emotion such as fear. Lie detector tests use this change as a way of measuring whether sb is telling the truth.

galvanism /gálvənìzəm/ *n.* **1.** ELEC ENG PRODUCTION OF ELECTRICITY BY CHEMICAL REACTION the production of direct-current electricity from a chemical reaction, e.g. between dissimilar metals in a battery **2.** MED ELECTRICITY AS MEDICAL THERAPY the application of electricity to the human body to stimulate nerves and muscles as part of a medical treatment [Late 18thC. From French, named after Luigi GALVANI whose research led to the discovery that electricity can result from chemical action.]

galvanize /gálvə nīz/ (**-nizes, -nizing, -nized**), **galvanise** (**-nises, -nising, -nised**) *vt.* **1.** STIMULATE TO ACT to stimulate sb or sth into great activity **2.** ELEC ENG COAT METAL WITH ZINC to coat a metal, usually iron or steel, with zinc to prevent corrosion **3.** MED STIMULATE ELECTRICALLY to stimulate the nerves or muscles of sb's body using an electric current [Early 19thC. From French (see GALVANISM).] —**galvanization** /gálvə nī záysh'n/ *n.* —**galvanizer** /gálvə nīzər/ *n.*

galvanometer /gálvə nómmitər/ *n.* an instrument used to detect or measure the strength and direction of small electric currents by means of a coil in a magnetic field that moves a pointer or light —**galvanometric** /gálvənə méttrik/ *adj.* —**galvanometry** /gálvə nómmətri/ *n.*

Galway /gáwl way/ **1.** seaport on Galway Bay and capital of County Galway, on the western coast of the Republic of Ireland. Population: 50,853 (1991). **2.** county in Connacht Province, western Republic of Ireland. Population: 131,503 (1996). Area: 5,939 sq. km/2,293 sq. mi.

Galway Bay inlet of the Atlantic Ocean on the western coast of Ireland

Galwegian /gal wéejən/ *n., adj.* = **Gallovidian** [Late 18thC. From GALLOWAY, modelled on NORWEGIAN.]

gam[1] /gam/ *n.* **1.** ZOOL MIGRATING WHALES a group of migrating whales **2.** SHIPPING SOCIAL VISIT BETWEEN WHALERS a social visit between whalers or other sailors, especially while at sea (*informal*) **3.** *New Zealand* SEA BIRDS a flock of sea birds ■ *vi.* (**gams, gamming, gammed**) SHIPPING MEET AT SEA to meet socially, especially at sea (*informal*) [Mid-19thC. Origin unknown.]

gam[2] /gam/ *n.* sb's leg, especially a woman's (*old slang*) (*sometimes considered offensive*) [Late 18thC. Origin uncertain: probably an alteration of *gamb*, a heraldic term for a device on a shield, resembling an animal's leg.]

gama grass /gáamə-/ *n.* a tall coarse grass that is grown in North America for fodder. Latin name: *Tripsacum dactyloides*. [Mid-19thC. *Gama* of uncertain origin: perhaps an alteration of GRAMA.]

gamay /gámmay/ *n.* a red grape used in making wine, especially Beaujolais [Mid-19thC. Named after *Gamay*, the village in Burgundy, eastern France, where this grape is a native variety.]

gamba /gámbə/ *n.* MUSIC = **viola da gamba**

gambade *n.* = **gambado**[2] [Early 16thC. From French, of uncertain origin: possibly from Italian *gambata*, from *gamba* 'leg', or via late Latin *gamba* 'horse's leg', from Greek *kampē* 'bend'.]

gambado[1] /gam báydō/ (*plural* **-dos** *or* **-does**) *n.* **1.** LEATHER FOOT PROTECTOR either of a pair of protective leather holders for a rider's feet attached to a horse's saddle **2.** LEG COVERING either of a pair of rider's leggings [Mid-17thC. Formed from Italian *gamba* 'leg' + *-ado*.]

gambado[2] /gam báy dō/ (*plural* **-dos** *or* **-does**), **gambade** *n.* **1.** DRESSAGE LOW JUMP BY HORSE in dressage, a low leap in which the horse has all four feet off the ground **2.** LEAP a leap or caper **3.** PRANK a prank or escapade [Early 19thC. From Spanish *gambada*, from *gamba* 'leg'.]

gambeer *n.* = **gambier**

Gambia /gámbi ə/ river in western Africa that rises in Guinea, flows westwards through the Gambia, and empties into the Atlantic Ocean near Banjul. Length: 1,100 km/700 mi.

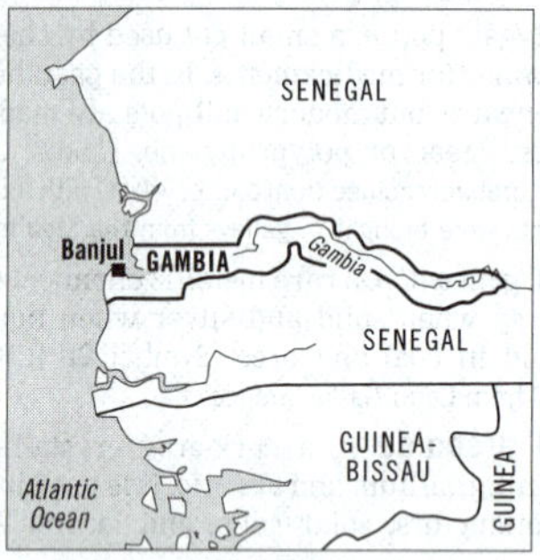

The Gambia

Gambia, The republic on the western coast of Africa, bordered on the north, east, and south by Senegal. Language: English. Currency: dalasi. Capital: Banjul. Population: 1,248,085 (1997). Area: 11,295 sq. km/4,361 sq. mi. —**Gambian** *n., adj.*

gambier /gám beer/, **gambir, gambeer** *n.* a resinous astringent substance obtained from the leaves of a tropical Asian woody vine and used medicinally as an astringent or tonic and also in tanning and dyeing. Latin name: *Uncaria gambir*. [Early 19thC. From Malay *gambir*, the name of the plant.]

gambit /gámbit/ *n.* **1.** STRATAGEM a manoeuvre or stratagem used to secure an advantage **2.** CONVERSATIONAL OPENER a remark used to open a conversation **3.** CHESS OPENING MOVE IN CHESS in chess, an opening move in which a player sacrifices a pawn or other minor piece in order to gain a strategic advantage [Mid-17thC. From Italian *gambetto* 'act of tripping someone up (in wrestling)' (modelled on French *gambit*), from *gamba* 'leg'.]

gamble /gámb'l/ *v.* (**-bles, -bling, -bled**) **1.** *vi.* PLAY GAMES OF CHANCE to play games such as poker or roulette that involve risking money, or bet on horse races or other events, in the hope of winning money **2.** *vt.* BET MONEY to bet a sum of money on the outcome of an event or competition **3.** *vi.* TAKE A CHANCE ON STH to take a risk in the hope and expectation of a desired result ○ *gambling on nice weather* **4.** *vi.* ENDANGER STH to behave in a way that risks harming sb or sth ○ *gambled with the success of the show* **5.** *vt.* PUT STH DANGEROUSLY AT RISK to lose or risk losing sth, especially money, by betting or doing sth dangerous or rash ○ *She gambled her inheritance away.* ■ *n.* **1.** BET a bet made in the hope of winning money **2.** STH DONE THAT IS RISKY an action whose outcome is uncertain and very possibly undesirable [Early 18thC. Coined from GAME + *-le*, literally 'to keep on playing'.] —**gambler** *n.*

gambling /gámbling/ *n.* playing games of chance or betting in the hope of winning money

gamboge /gam bṓj, -bṓzh/ *n.* **1.** RESIN a resin obtained from an Asian tree that is the main constituent of a yellow pigment **2.** PIGMENT a yellow pigment made from gamboge resin **3.** COLOURS YELLOW COLOUR a strong yellow colour [Mid-17thC. Coined from modern Latin *gambaugium*, from *Cambodia*, CAMBODIA, where the tree is native.]

gambol /gámb'l/ *vi.* (**-bols, -bolling, -bolled**) LEAP PLAYFULLY to leap or skip about playfully ■ *n.* PLAYFUL LEAPING an instance of leaping about playfully [Mid-16thC. Alteration of GAMBADE.]

gambrel /gámbrəl/ *n.* **1.** ZOOL JOINT ABOVE HORSE'S FOOT the joint of a leg of an animal, especially a horse, that corresponds to the human ankle **2.** BUTCHER'S FRAME a frame in the shape of a horse's hind leg used by butchers for hanging animal carcasses **3.** ARCHIT = **gambrel roof** [Mid-16thC. From Old Northern French *gamberel*, from *gambier* 'forked stick', from *gambe*, a variant of *jambe* 'leg'.]

gambrel roof *n.* ARCHIT **1.** ROOF WITH SLOPING ENDS AND SIDES a roof with sloping ends and sides and a small gable at both ends **2.** *US, Can* ROOF WITH TWO SLOPES a roof that has two slopes on each side, the lower slope being steeper than the upper

game[1] /gaym/ *n.* **1.** STH PLAYED FOR FUN an activity that people participate in, together or on their own, for fun ○ *It's only a game!* **2.** COMPETITIVE ACTIVITY WITH RULES a sporting or other activity in which players compete against one another by following a fixed set of rules ○ *How many people do you need to play this game?* **3.** MATCH a particular occasion when a competitive game is played ○ *Saturday's game has been cancelled.* **4.** SPORTS PART OF MATCH in sports such as tennis, a specific subsection of play that goes towards making up a set or match **5.** ASPECT OF GAME a particular aspect of a competition ○ *They lost because their offensive game was terrible.* **6.** STYLE OF PLAYING the style or level of skill with which sb plays a particular sport ○ *raise your game* **7.** NUMBER NEEDED TO WIN the total number of points needed to win a contest **8.** RULES GOVERNING SPORT the rules governing a particular competition or sport **9.** EQUIPMENT an item or set of items such as a board, dice, counters, a pack of cards, or a piece of computer software that is needed to play a particular game ○ *'Did you bring any games with you'? – 'Yes, we brought Scrabble'.* **10.** ACTIVITY RESEMBLING GAME any activity that resembles a game, e.g. one that involves intense interest and competitiveness and is carried out by its own specific and often unspoken rules **11.** STRATAGEM OR TACTIC a way of behaving that is aimed at manipulating people or trying to deceive them ○ *So that's your game?* **12.** ILLEGAL ACTIVITY OR RACKET a strategy, activity, or behaviour that is questionable, and often illegal (*informal*) **13.** OCCUPATION a business or occupation (*informal*) ○ *the advertising game* **14.** STH NOT TAKEN SERIOUSLY an activity or situation that sb does not treat seriously ○ *Life's a game as far as he's concerned.* **15.** HUNT ANIMALS FOR HUNTING wild animals, birds, or fish that are hunted for sport **16.** FOOD MEAT OF HUNTED ANIMALS the meat of wild animals, birds, or fish that have been killed for sport **17.** RIDICULE OR THE OBJECT OF IT the act of ridiculing sb for fun, or the target of ridicule, criticism or trickery ○ *She's easy game for a trickster like him.* **18.** MATH MATHEMATICAL MODEL OF CONTEST a mathematical model describing a contest played under specified rules in which each participant has only partial control ■ **games** *npl.* EVENT WITH MANY SPORTING CONTESTS an event that consists of many different sporting activities and usually lasts for several days ■ *adj.* **1.** READY AND WILLING ready and willing to do sth, especially sth new or unusual **2.** BRAVE brave in spirit or character ■ *vi.* (**games, gaming, gamed**) GAMBLE to play games of chance for money [Old English, from a prehistoric Germanic compound meaning 'people participating together'] —**gamely** *adv.* —**gameness** *n.* ◇ **a game of two halves** a game that might change later in the match, with the current loser starting to win ◇ **ahead of the game** anticipating and reacting more promptly than others to new developments ◇ **give the game away** to reveal a secret, usually without intending to ◇ **on the game** working as a prostitute (*informal*) ◇ **play the game** to follow the rules of a given situation, even if they are unspoken ◇ **the game's up** the plan or trick has failed or been discovered (*informal*)

game[2] /gaym/ adj. an offensive term meaning injured or with impaired mobility, formerly applied to limbs ◇ *a game left foot* [Late 18thC. Origin uncertain, perhaps from Old French *gambi* 'crooked'.]

game bird n. a bird such as a pheasant or grouse that is hunted for sport.

Gameboy /gaym boy/ tdmk. a trademark for a hand-held video-game machine with a very small monochrome LCD screen, graphics capability, and an extensive selection of games.

game chips npl. thin round slices of fried potato served with game.

gamecock /gaym kok/ n. = fighting cock

game fish n. 1. FISH GOOD FOR ANGLING AND EATING freshwater fish that is highly prized for angling and eating. Trout, salmon, and char are game fish. ◊ coarse fish 2. FISH CAUGHT FOR SPORT any fish, particularly any sea fish, that is caught for sport, especially any one favoured for its fighting ability. Sharks are popular game fish. —**game fishing** n.

game fowl n. a domestic fowl bred and trained for fighting.

gamekeeper /gaym keeper/ n. sb employed to look after birds or animals hunted for sport, e.g. on an estate or game reserve —**gamekeeping** n.

gamelan /gaym lan/ n. an Indonesian orchestra that consists mainly of percussion instruments that chimes, gongs, and wooden xylophones [Early 19thC. From Javanese.]

game law n. a law that controls the catching and killing of fish, birds, or other animals for sport, e.g. one that specifies the extent of a hunting or shooting season

game of chance n. a game, usually played for money, in which the outcome depends to some degree on chance, e.g. on the throw of dice

game of skill n. a game such as chess or bridge, in which the outcome depends entirely or principally on the skill of the players

game plan n. 1. SPORTS STRATEGY TO WIN COMPETITION the strategy that a team or player devises beforehand to use during a game 2. STRATEGY TO ACHIEVE OBJECTIVE a strategy that sb devises to achieve a particular goal

game point n. 1. SITUATION WITH POTENTIAL TO WIN in games such as tennis and badminton, a situation in which one player or side has only to win the next point to win the game 2. WINNING POINT the point that will decide the final outcome of a game

game reserve, game preserve n. a large area of land where birds or animals are kept in protected conditions in the wild, for conservation purposes or to be hunted for sport

games /gaymz/ n. gymnastics, athletics, team sports and other forms of physical exercise taught to children at school (*takes a singular verb*)

game show n. a television programme in which people compete for money or prizes

gamesmanship /gaymzmanship/ n. 1. STRATEGIC BEHAVIOUR the use of tactics or strategems to gain an advantage in business, politics, or life ◊ *political gamesmanship* 2. PLAY OF QUESTIONABLE FAIRNESS the use of unconventional but not strictly illegal tactics to gain an advantage in a competitive game —**gamesman** n.

gamesome /gaymssm/ adj. eager to play or have fun (archaic) —**gamesomely** adv. —**gamesomeness** n.

games room n. a room in a house or public building that is set aside and equipped for games such as billiards or table tennis

gamester /gaymster/ n. sb who plays gambling games (archaic)

gamet- prefix. = gameto-

gametangium /gamm tanji am/ (plural **-a** -a/) n. BOT the part of a plant, especially an organ or cell in algae and fungi, where gametes are produced [Late 19thC. Coined from modern Latin *gameta* (see GAMETE) + Greek *aggeion* 'vessel' + -IUM.]

gamete /gammeet/ n. GENETICS a specialized male or female cell with half the normal number of chromosomes that unites with another cell of the opposite sex in the process of sexual reproduction. Ova and spermatozoa are gametes that unite to produce a cell (zygote) that may develop into an embryo. [Late 19thC. From modern Latin, *gameta* /-meetə/ 'marriage'.] —**gametic** /gə mettik/ adj. —**gametically** /-mettikli/ adv.

game theory n. a mathematical theory primarily concerned with determining an optimal strategy for situations in which there is competition or conflict, such as in business activities or military operations —**game theoretic** adj.

game warden n. sb who looks after wild animals such as fish or birds, e.g. on a game reserve

gamey adj. = gamy

gameto- , **gamet-** prefix. relating to a gamete [From GAMETE.]

gametocyte /gə meetō sīt/ n. 1. GENETICS CELL PRODUCING MALE OR FEMALE CELLS a cell that divides to produce two specialized male or female cells (gametes) 2. MICROBIOL MALARIA ORGANISM the malaria organism in the stage in its life cycle during which it reproduces in the blood of a mosquito

gametogenesis /gə meetō jénnessis/ n. GENETICS the production of gametes from gametocytes by cell division (meiosis) —**gametogenic** adj. —**gametogenous** /-jénniss/ adj.

gametophore /gə meetō fawr/ n. an upright branch in plants such as mosses that bears the reproductive organs —**gametophoric** /gə meetō fórrik/ adj.

gametophyte /gə meetō fīt/ n. the phase in the life cycle of a plant in which sex organs and gametes are produced —**gametophytic** /gə meetō fíttik/ adj.

gamin /gámin/ n. a young child, usually a boy, often homeless, who roams the streets (archaic) [Mid-19thC. From French, of uncertain origin: perhaps from French dialect *gamer* 'to steal'.]

gamine /gámeen/ n. 1. BOYISH GIRL a girl or young woman who is boyish in appearance 2. GIRL STREET URCHIN a young girl, often homeless, who roams the streets ■ adj. APPEALINGLY BOYISH boyish in appearance [Late 19thC. From French, feminine of *gamin* (see GAMIN).]

gaming /gáyming/ n. GAMBLING playing games such as poker or roulette for money or involving gambling games ■ adj. RELATING TO GAMBLING

gamma /gámmə/ n. 1. 3RD LETTER OF GREEK ALPHABET the third letter of the Greek alphabet, represented in the English alphabet as 'g'. See table at alphabet 2. EDUC SCHOOL MARK the Greek letter gamma given as a mark to a student for a piece of work or in an examination 3. THIRD ITEM the third item in a classification system or in a series of things 4. PHOTOGRAPHY MEASURE OF CONTRAST OF IMAGE a measure of the degree of contrast in a developed photograph or a television picture 5. CHEM 3RD ITEM IN POSITION IN CARBON CHAIN the third position in a carbon chain or ring, starting from a particular group or atom. Symbol γ ■ adj. CHEM 3RD NEAREST TO DESIGNATED ATOM used to describe the third nearest atom to a designated atom or group of atoms in an organic molecule. [15thC. From late Greek.]

gamma-amino butyric acid n. an amino acid that inhibits the transmission of nerve impulses

gamma camera n. an instrument used in medicine to produce images of internal organs after the injection of a radioactive drug into the body, where the drug releases gamma rays

gammadion /ga mäydi an/ n. a pattern consisting of four capital Greek gammas, especially when joined to form a swastika [Mid-19thC. From late Greek, from *gamma* (see GAMMA).]

gamma globulin n. a protein component of blood serum that contains the antibodies, the body's main defence against infection. It is also produced commercially from human plasma and used in the treatment and prevention of diseases such as measles, hepatitis, and poliomyelitis.

gammahydroxybutyrate /gámmə hī dróksi byóot rayt/ n. a colourless chemical compound that occurs naturally in animals, used for treating anxiety and as an anaesthetic. Formula: $C_4H_8O_3$.

gamma radiation n. electromagnetic waves of higher frequency and shorter wavelength than X-rays that is emitted by some radioactive isotopes or in some nuclear reactions

gamma ray n. a high-energy photon emitted after nuclear reactions or spontaneously from the nucleus of a radioactive atom that lowers the energy level of the nucleus. Gamma rays do not carry any electric charge or mass and share the high-frequency end of the electromagnetic spectrum with X-rays, which have similar properties.

—— WORD KEY: REGIONAL NOTE ——
See Regional note at *gaffer*.

gammer /gámmər/ n. a woman of advanced years, especially a woman from the country (dated informal) [Late 16thC. Origin uncertain: probably a contraction of GODMOTHER, with 'ga-' by association with GRANDMOTHER.]

gammon[1] /gámmən/ n. 1. BACON the lower part of a side of bacon, cooked whole or cut into slices 2. HAM cured or smoked ham [15thC. From Old Northern French *gambon* 'ham', from *gambe* 'leg'.]

gammon[2] /gámmən/ n. WIN AT BACKGAMMON a win in backgammon when the losing player has not succeeded in removing any pieces from the board ■ vt. (**-mons, -moning, -moned**) BEAT SB AT BACKGAMMON to beat sb in backgammon before the person has managed to remove any pieces from the board [Mid-18thC. Formed from Middle English *gamen*, earlier form of GAME.]

gammon[3] /gámmən/ n. NONSENSE false or meaningless talk that is intended to deceive (dated informal) ■ vti. (**-mons, -moning, -moned**) DECEIVE SB to trick or deceive sb, especially by talking nonsense (dated informal) [Early 18thC. From GAMMON[2].]

gammon[4] /gámmən/ vt. to fasten a bowsprit to the front of a ship [Late 17thC. Origin uncertain: perhaps from GAMMON[1].]

gammy /gámmi/ adj. (**-mier, -miest**) stiff or painful unable to move as before, usually because of injury or some medical disorder (informal) ◇ *a gammy leg* [Mid-19thC. From GAMMON[1], probably with reference to the tying up of a ham.]

gamo- prefix. 1. joined together ◇ gamopetalous 2. sexual ◇ gamogenesis [From Greek *gamos* 'marriage']

gamogenesis /gámmō jénnessis/ n. sexual reproduction (technical) —**gamogenetic** /-jə néttik/ adj. —**gamogenetically** /-néttikli/ adv.

gamopetalous /gámmō séppeləss/ adj. used to describe a large old one (archaic)

gamp /gamp/ n. an umbrella, especially a large old one (archaic informal) [Mid-19thC. Named after Sarah Gamp, a character in the Charles Dickens novel *Martin Chuzzlewit*, who carries an umbrella.]

gamut /gámmət/ n. 1. FULL RANGE OF MUSICAL NOTES the entire range of sth 2. COMPLETE RANGE OF MUSICAL NOTES the whole series of recognized musical notes, from lowest to highest 3. LOWEST MEDIEVAL MUSICAL NOTE the lowest note of medieval musical theory, two Gs below middle C 4. MEDIEVAL MUSICAL SCALE SYSTEM the medieval scale system based around a repeated series of six notes (hexachord) [15thC. Contraction of medieval Latin *gamma ut*, from Greek *gamma*, the letter representing the lowest note below the top note in the medieval scale.]

gamy /gáymi/ adj. (**-ier, -iest**) 1. FOOD TASTING OF OR LIKE GAME having a strong flavour like that of a wild bird or animal that is hunted for food 2. RANK-SMELLING having a strong bad smell 3. LEWD sexually suggestive or obscene —**gamily** adv. —**gaminess** n.

-gamy suffix. 1. marriage ◇ polygamy 2. reproductive union ◇ syngamy 3. reproductive organs, method of fertilization ◇ karyogamy [Formed from Greek *gamos* 'marriage'] —**-gamic** suffix. —**-gamous** suffix.

ganache /gə nash, ga-/ n. a sweet creamy chocolate filling or icing for cakes and pastries [Late 20thC. Via French, literally 'jaw', and Italian *ganascia* from, ultimately, Greek *gnathos* (see GNATHIC).]

Ganapati /gánna pátti/ *n.* EASTERN RELIG = **Ganesha**

Ganda /gánda/ *n.* a language spoken in parts of Uganda that is a member of the Bantu group of the Benue-Congo branch of the Niger-Congo family of African languages. About four million people speak Ganda. [Mid-20thC. From Bantu.]

gander /gándar/ *n.* **1. MALE GOOSE** an adult male goose **2. OFFENSIVE TERM** an offensive term used about or to sb who is thought to be unserious and frivolous **3.** **LOOK** a look or glance at sb or sth (*informal*) [Old English *gandra*. Ultimately from an Indo-European word meaning 'goose' that is also the ancestor of English *goose* and *gannet*.]

Gander /gándar/ town on Canada's Island of Newfoundland that is home to the region's air traffic control centre. Population: 10,364 (1996).

Indira Gandhi
United Nations

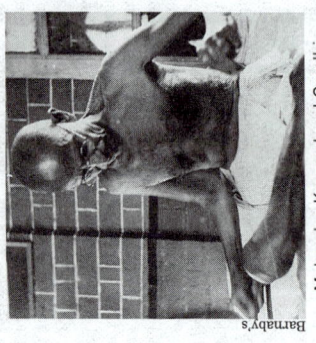
Mohandas Karamchand Gandhi
Barnaby's

Gandhi (gándi/, **Indira** (1917-84) Indian national leader. The daughter of Jawaharlal Nehru, she was twice prime minister of India (1966-77, 1980-84) and was assassinated by members of her Sikh bodyguard. Born **Indira Priyadarshini Nehru**

Gandhi, Mohandas Karamchand (1869-1948) Indian national leader. His campaign of nonviolent civil resistance to British rule led to India's independence (1947). He was assassinated by a Hindu extremist. Known as **Mahatma 'Great Soul' Gandhi**

G & S *abbr.* Gilbert and Sullivan

G & T, g and t *abbr.* gin and tonic

gandy dancer /gándi-/ *n. US* a labourer who lays or maintains railway tracks (*slang*) [Origin unknown]

ganef /gáanef/, **ganev** /gáanev/, **ganof** /gónnef/, **gonif**, **gonof** *n.* a thief, cheater, or sb who is unscrupulous (*informal insult*) [Early 20thC. Via Yiddish from Hebrew *gannāb*.]

Ganesha /ge néesha/, **Ganesa** /-néessa/, **Ganesh** /-nésh/ *n.* in Hinduism, the god of wisdom and problem-solving who is the son of Shiva and Parvati and is represented as a pot-bellied man with an elephant's head

ganev *n.* = ganef

gang[1] /gang/ *n.* **1. GROUP OF TROUBLE-MAKING YOUNG PEOPLE** a group of young people who spend time together for social reasons and may engage in delinquent behaviour **2. GROUP OF CRIMINALS** a group of people *who work together for some criminal or antisocial purpose* **3.** GROUP OF WORKERS a group of people working together, especially a group of labourers **4. PEOPLE WHO ENJOY EACH OTHER'S COMPANY** a group of people with similar interests who like to spend time together **5. SET OF TOOLS** a set of tools or devices arranged to be

used or operated together ■ *vt.* (**gangs, ganging, ganged**) **1. PUT OBJECTS IN GROUP** to group similar objects in a set **2.** ELECTRON ENG **COMBINE SWITCHES** to combine several switches or devices on a single shaft so as to switch multiple connections at one time [12thC. From Old Norse *gangr* 'journey'. Ultimately from a prehistoric Germanic word meaning 'to go'. The underlying idea is of a group of people going about together.]

gang up *vi.* **1. JOIN TOGETHER FOR ATTACK** to join together to attack a person or group **2. ACT TOGETHER** to join together to exert pressure or accomplish sth

gang[2] /gang/ (**gangs, ganging, ganged**) *vi. Scotland* to go (*nonstandard*) [Old English *gangan*. Ultimately from a prehistoric Germanic word that is also the ancestor of GANG[1].]

gang[3] /gang/ *n.* = **gangue**

Ganga /gáng ga/ *n. S Asia* the River Ganges

gangbang /gáng bang/ *n.* (*slang; considered offensive by some people*) **1. SERIAL INTERCOURSE WITH ONE PERSON** sexual intercourse between one consenting person and several others in succession **2. GANG RAPE** a multiple rape by a gang of people ■ *v.* (*slang; considered offensive by some people*) **1.** *vti.* **HAVE MULTIPLE INTERCOURSE WITH ONE PERSON** to participate in an occasion where several people in succession have intercourse with the same person **2.** *vti.* **GANG-RAPE** to gangrape sb **3.** *vi. US* **BE MEMBER OF VIOLENT GANG** to participate in the activities of a criminal or violent gang — **gangbanger** *n.*

gangbusters /gáng busterz/, **gangbuster** *adj. US* usually successful or effective (*slang*) ◊ *It's a gangbusters promotion that brings the customers in.*

ganger /gángar/ *n.* the foreman of a group of workmen

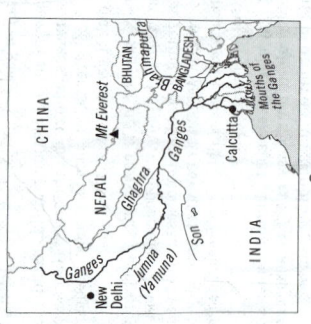
Ganges
CHINA / Mt Everest / NEPAL / Brahmaputra / BHUTAN / BANGLADESH / Ghaghra / Ganges / Son / Jumna (Yamuna) / INDIA / Ganges / New Delhi / Calcutta / Mouths of the Ganges

Ganges /gán jeez/ river in northern India, regarded as sacred by Hindus. It rises in the Indian Himalayas, flows southeastwards through Bangladesh, and empties into the Bay of Bengal, forming one of the world's largest deltas. Length: 2,511 km/1,560 mi.

gangland /gáng land, -land/ *n.* the world of organized crime — **gangland** *adj.*

ganglia plural of **ganglion**

gangling /gáng gling/, **gangly** /gáng glee/ (**-glier, -gliest**) *adj.* tall and thin, with a loose awkward gait [Early 19thC. Origin uncertain: perhaps formed from GANG[3]]

ganglion /gáng gli ən/ (*plural* **-a** /-ə/ *or* **-ons**) *n.* **1.** ANAT **CLUSTER OF NERVE CELLS** a structure that contains a dense cluster of nerve cells **2.** MED **SWELLING ON JOINT OR TENDON** a harmless swelling similar to a cyst that forms on a joint or tendon [Late 17thC. From Greek *gagglion* 'tumour, nerve bundle'.] — **ganglionated** /gáng gli ənaytid/ *adj.* — **ganglionic** /gáng gli ónnik/ *adj.*

gangly *adj.* = **gangling** [Late 19thC. Alteration of GANGLING.]

gangplank /gáng plangk/ *n.* a movable structure such as a bridge or plank used when boarding or disembarking from a ship [Mid-19thC. Literally 'plank for going' (see GANG[1]).]

gang rape *n.* a rape of one person by several people in succession — **gang-rape** *vti.*

gangrene /gáng green/ *n.* **DEATH OF TISSUE** local death and decay of soft tissues of the body as a result of lack of blood to the area. It has various causes, including extreme heat or cold, obstruction of blood vessels by disease or a blood clot, or a neurological disorder. ■ *vti.* (**-grenes, -grening, -grened**) **GET GANGRENE** to affect body tissue with gangrene, or become affected, with gangrene [Mid-16thC. Via French from,

ultimately, Greek *gaggraina*.] — **gangrenous** /gáng grinas/ *adj.*

gangsta rap /gángsta-/ *n.* a type of rap music in which the lyrics tend to deal with gangs and killings [*Gangsta*, alteration of GANGSTER]

gangster /gángstar/ *n.* a member of an organized gang of criminals, especially a racketeer — **gangsterish** *adj.* — **gangsterism** *n.*

gangue /gang/, **gang** *n.* worthless rock or other matter occurring in a vein or deposit within or alongside a valuable mineral. ◊ **matrix** [Early 19thC. Via French from German *Gang* 'way, lode'.]

gangway /gáng way/ *n.* **1. NARROW WALKWAY** a narrow passageway, especially a temporary walkway **2.** **ENTRANCE IN SHIP'S SIDE** an opening in the side of a ship through which it is boarded by means of a gangplank **3.** = **gangplank 4.** **AISLE BETWEEN SEATS** an aisle between seating, especially the one separating two blocks of seating in the House of Commons ■ *interj.* **MAKE WAY** used to indicate to people in a crowd that they should make way because sb is coming through [Late 17thC. Literally 'way for going' (see GANG[1]).]

ganister /gánnistar/ *n.* a hard silica-containing rock that can endure high temperatures and is used to line furnaces [Early 19thC. Origin unknown.]

ganja /gánja, gáan-/ *n.* a potent form of marijuana used for smoking [Early 19thC. From Hindi *gãjā*.]

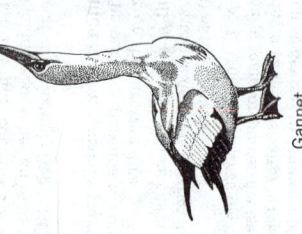
Gannet

gannet /gánnit/ *n.* **1. FISH-EATING SEABIRD** a large fish-eating seabird, typically white with black-tipped wings, that lives in offshore colonies in oceanic regions. Genus: *Morus*. **2.** GLUTTON a gluttonous person (*informal*) [Old English *ganot*. Ultimately from an Indo-European word meaning 'goose' (see GANDER).]

Gannett Peak /gánnit-/ mountain in the Central Rocky Mountains, western Wyoming. It forms part of the Wind River Range and is the highest peak in the state. Height: 4,207 m/13,804 ft.

gannister *n.* = ganister

ganof *n.* = ganef

ganoid /gánnoyd/ *adj.* BONY AND DIAMOND-SHAPED used to describe a type of scale found on gars and other primitive fish, consisting of dentine-covered bone with a thick outer layer of a substance (ganoine) similar to enamel ■ *n.* FISH WITH GANOID SCALES a primitive fish that has ganoid scales [Mid-19thC. Via French from, ultimately, Greek *ganos* 'brightness'. From its shiny surface.]

gansey /gánzi/ (*plural* **-seys**) *n.* CLOTHES a heavy jumper, especially one worn by a fisherman (*regional*) [Late 19thC. Alteration of GUERNSEY.]

Gansu /gán sóo/ province of northern China dominated by semiarid plateaus and basins. It is a major agricultural region, producing wheat, millet, kaoling, and soya beans. Industry has also developed there from the 1950s. Capital: Lanzhou. Population: 23,780,000 (1994). Area: 454,000 sq. km/175,300 sq. mi.

gantline /gánt līn, -lin/ *n.* a rope run through a pulley on a mast and used to hoist people or things [Mid-18thC. Origin uncertain: perhaps an alteration of *girtline*, from a variant of GIRTH.]

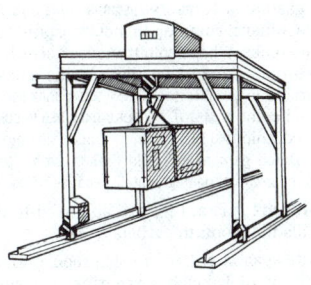

Gantry

gantry /gántri/ (*plural* **-tries**) *n.* **1.** RAIL SUPPORT FRAMEWORK FOR RAILWAY SIGNALS a frame spanning railway tracks and used to display signals **2.** ENG SUPPORT FRAMEWORK FOR MACHINERY a spanning framework used to support machinery, e.g. the platform that supports a crane or the structure used to erect and service rockets [Late 16thC. Origin uncertain: perhaps an alteration of Old Northern French *gantier* 'trellis' (via Latin *cantherius* from, ultimately, Greek *kanthēlia* 'carrying-baskets'), or from *gawn* 'bucket' (alteration of GALLON) + TREE.]

Ganymede /gánni meed/ *n.* **1.** MYTHOL CUPBEARER OF GREEK GODS in Greek mythology, a beautiful young Trojan prince whom Zeus carried off to Mount Olympus to be cupbearer to the gods. In later times he symbolized homosexual love, or the spirit's ascent to heaven. **2.** ASTRON MOON OF JUPITER the largest of Jupiter's moons

Gao /gaá ō, gow/ town and ancient trading centre on the southern edge of the Sahara, in eastern Mali. It is situated on the River Niger, about 322 km/200 mi. east of Timbuktu. Population: 54,874 (1987).

gaol *n.*, *vt.* = **jail** [13thC. From Old Northern French *gaiole*, a variant of Old French *jaiole* (see JAIL).]

───── **WORD KEY: CULTURAL NOTE** ─────

The Ballad of Reading Gaol, a poem by writer Oscar Wilde (1898). Wilde's last work, written while he was incarcerated for 'homosexual activities', it is the story of the trial and execution of murderer Charles Thomas Wooldridge, a fellow inmate at the jail. It deals with the harshness of prison conditions and the idea of forgiveness.

gaoler /jáylər/ *n.* = **jailer**

gap /gap/ *n.* **1.** BREAK IN STRUCTURE a break or opening in a structure or arrangement, e.g. a fence or military defence line **2.** STH MISSING an area where there is a complete or partial absence of sth, such as data ○ *gaps in his employment record* **3.** INTERVAL OF TIME an interval of time during which some action or event stops occurring ○ *a gap of three years* **4.** DISPARITY a significant difference between two things, attitudes, or perceptions ○ *the gap between rich and poor* **5.** PROBLEM CAUSED BY DISPARITY a problem caused by a difference between things, attitudes, or perceptions ○ *technology gap* ○ *generation gap* **6.** GEOG OPENING BETWEEN MOUNTAINS a ravine or pass in a mountain range **7.** ELEC ENG = **spark gap** ■ *v.* (**gaps, gapping, gapped**) **1.** *vti.* PRODUCE OR DEVELOP GAP to create a gap or opening in a barrier, or become open or separated by a gap **2.** *vt.* ELEC ENG ADJUST SPARK PLUG GAP to adjust the gap between the electrodes of a spark plug **3.** *vt.* N England AGRIC THIN OUT PLANTS to thin out plants to allow others more room to grow (*informal*) ○ *I hate having to gap the carrots.* [14thC. From Old Norse, 'chasm'.] —**gappy** *adj.*

gape /gayp/ *vi.* (**gapes, gaping, gaped**) **1.** STARE WITH MOUTH OPEN to stare in open-mouthed surprise or wonder **2.** OPEN THE MOUTH to open the mouth wide **3.** OPEN A GAP to open or split apart with a gap ■ *n.* **1.** OPEN-MOUTHED STARE a stare of wonder or surprise in which the mouth is wide open **2.** OPENING OF MOUTH an opening of the mouth wide, e.g. when surprised **3.** YAWN an opening of the mouth to yawn **4.** ZOOL WIDTH OF OPEN MOUTH the width of the open mouth of an animal **5.** BIG GAP a wide opening in sth [13thC. From Old Norse *gapa* 'to open the mouth'.]

───── **WORD KEY: SYNONYMS** ─────
See Synonyms at *gaze*.

gaping /gáyping/ *adj.* wide open and deep —**gapingly** *adv.*

gap-toothed *adj.* with wide spaces between the teeth

gap year *n.* a period of time taken off by a student after the completion of secondary education and before starting higher or further education

gar[1] /gaar/ (*plural* **gar** *or* **gars**) *n.* a large primitive freshwater fish found in North and Central America that has a heavy armour of bony scales and a long toothy jaw. Family: Lepisosteidae. [Mid-18thC. Shortening of GARFISH.]

gar[2] /gaar/ (**gars, garring, garred**) *vt. Scotland* to make sb do sth (*nonstandard*) [13thC. From Old Norse *gera* 'to make'.]

garage /gárraazh, -rij/ *n.* **1.** BUILDING FOR MOTOR VEHICLES a building for parking or storing one or more motor vehicles **2.** ESTABLISHMENT REPAIRING MOTOR VEHICLES an establishment that repairs and often sells motor vehicles, and that sometimes sells oil, diesel, and petrol ■ *vt.* (**-rages, -raging, -raged**) PUT VEHICLE IN GARAGE to park or store a motor vehicle in a garage [Early 20thC. From French, formed from *garer* 'to shelter'. Ultimately from a prehistoric Germanic word meaning 'to protect' (see GARRET).]

garage sale *n. US, ANZ* a sale of used or unwanted household items that is held in the garage or driveway of the seller's home

Garagum Desert /gárrə gum-/ desert occupying a large proportion of Turkmenistan. Consisting mainly of sand dunes and areas of hard-packed clay, it supports very little vegetation. Area: 285,000 sq. km/110,000 sq. mi.

garam masala /gaárəm mə saálə/ *n.* a mixture of spices used in Indian cooking to impart a hot pungent flavour to a dish [Mid-20thC. From Hindi *garam masālā*, literally 'hot spices'.]

Garamond /gárrə mond/, **Garamond type** *n.* a Roman typeface often used in books [Mid-19thC. Named after the French type founder Claude *Garamond* (1499–1561).]

garb /gaarb/ *n.* **1.** CLOTHES TYPICAL OUTFIT a particular type of clothing, especially the uniform or typical outfit worn by a profession **2.** APPEARANCE the outward appearance that sb or sth has ○ *The garb of compromise concealed their war plans.* ■ *vt.* (**garbs, garbing, garbed**) DRESS SB to clothe sb or yourself in a particular type of clothing [Late 16thC. Via obsolete French *garbe* 'elegance' from Italian *garbo*. Ultimately from a prehistoric Germanic word meaning 'to make ready' that is also the ancestor of English *gear*.]

garbage /gaárbij/ *n.* **1.** NONSENSE talk or writing that is worthless nonsense or lies **2.** SB OR STH WORTHLESS sb who or sth that is considered totally worthless **3.** *US* DISCARDED WASTE OR USELESS MATERIAL discarded food waste, or any other unwanted or useless material **4.** COMPUT WORTHLESS DATA inaccurate, useless, or meaningless data in a computer [15thC. From Anglo-Norman, of unknown origin.] —**garbagy** *adj.*

garbage can *n.* = **dustbin**

garbage man /gaárbij man/ *n. US, Can, Aus* sb employed to remove rubbish

garbage truck *n. US, Can, Aus* a large motor vehicle used to collect and compact waste materials left bagged or in containers outside buildings

garbanzo /gaar bánzō/ (*plural* **-zos**), **garbanzo bean** *n.* = **chickpea** [Mid-18thC. From Spanish.]

garble /gaárb'l/ *vt.* (**-bles, -bling, -bled**) **1.** JUMBLE MEANING OF STH to confuse sth unintentionally or through ignorance and thereby give the wrong impression **2.** COMMUNICATION SCRAMBLE TRANSMISSION OF STH to cause the corruption of a transmitted message or signal ○ *The announcement was completely garbled.* **3.** TAKE BEST PART OF STH to cull the best parts from sth (*archaic*) ■ *n.* COMMUNICATION CONFUSING MESSAGE a confused or jumbled message, piece of information, or signal, or the confusing or jumbling of information [15thC. Via Italian *garbellare* 'to sift' and Arabic *garbala*, from ultimately, late Latin *cribellum* 'small sieve', from Latin *cribrum* 'sieve'.] —**garbled** *adj.*

garbo /gaárbō/ (*plural* **-bos**) *n. Aus* a garbage collector (*slang*) [Mid-20thC. Formed from GARBAGE.]

garboard /gaár bawrd/ *n.* the continuous band of planking on a ship's hull next to its keel [Early 17thC. From obsolete Dutch *gaarboord*, of uncertain origin: perhaps from *garen* 'to gather' + *boord* 'board'.]

garbology /gaar bólləji/ *n. US* the study of a cultural group by an examination of what it discards —**garbologist** *n.*

garçon /gaár son, -soN/ *n.* a waiter in a French restaurant or café [Early 17thC. From French.]

garda /gaárdə/ (*plural* **-daí** /gaar deé/) *n.* a police officer in the Republic of Ireland and a member of the Garda [See GARDA]

Garda /gaárdə/ *n.* the police force of the Republic of Ireland [Early 20thC. From Irish, shortening of *Garda Síochána*, literally 'civic guard'.]

Garda, Lake /gaárdə/ the largest lake in Italy and a major resort region. It is situated in northern Italy, between Brescia and Verona. Area: 370 sq. km/143 sq. mi.

gardaí *plural of* **garda**

garden /gaárd'n/ *n.* **1.** CULTIVATED AREA AROUND HOUSE an area of cultivated land, often with a lawn, situated around, in front of, or behind a house. US term **yard 2.** PLANTED AREA OF GROUND a plot of ground where plants such as fruits, vegetables, and flowers are grown **3.** PARK a park or recreational area for the public, generally planted with flowers, shrubs, and trees (*often used in the plural*) **4.** FARMING REGION a fertile, well-cultivated region **5.** OUTDOOR EATING AND DRINKING ESTABLISHMENT an eating or drinking establishment that serves its patrons outdoors ■ *adj.* **1.** RELATING TO GARDENS produced in, frequenting, or used in a garden **2.** COMMON of the common or ordinary kind. US term **garden-variety** ■ *vi.* (**-dens, -dening, -dened**) LOOK AFTER GARDEN to plan or tend a garden [14thC. Via Old Northern French *gardin* from Vulgar Latin (*hortus*) *gardinus* 'enclosed (garden)'. Ultimately from a prehistoric Germanic word that is also the ancestor of English *yard*.] ◇ **everything in the garden is lovely** everything is fine ◇ **lead sb up the garden path** to mislead or deceive sb, often gradually over a period of time

───── **WORD KEY: CULTURAL NOTE** ─────

The Secret Garden, a children's story by English writer Frances Hodgson Burnett (1911). It is the tale of a lonely orphan, Mary Lennox, who is sent to live with her uncle Archibald, a widower whose wife died as a result of a fall from a tree in her beloved garden. In restoring the garden, Mary finds happiness and helps the family recover from its misfortune.

garden apartment *n. US* **1.** = **garden flat 2.** BLOCK OF FLATS WITH GARDEN a block of flats that has a garden or lawn

garden centre *n.* a retail establishment that sells plants and gardening equipment

garden city *n.* a planned residential community with landscaped gardens and parks. ◊ **garden suburb**

gardener /gaárd'nər/ *n.* sb who tends a garden or lawn, either as a profession or a hobby

garden flat *n.* a flat on the ground floor or in the basement of a building with access to a lawn or garden. US term **garden apartment**

garden gnome *n.* a small statue representing a gnome, used as an ornament in gardens

gardenia /gaar deéni ə/ *n.* **1.** EVERGREEN TREE BEARING WHITE FLOWERS an evergreen tree or shrub native to warm regions of Africa and Asia and widely cultivated for its shiny leaves and fragrant white flowers. Genus: *Gardenia.* **2.** GARDENIA FLOWER the flower of a gardenia tree or shrub [Mid-18thC. From modern Latin, genus name. Named after the Scottish-American naturalist Alexander *Garden* (1730–91).]

garden party *n.* a large formal party held in a garden, especially in the grounds of a large house

Gardens /gaárd'nz/ *n.* used in street names (*takes a singular or plural verb*)

garden suburb *n.* a planned residential community with landscaped gardens and parks on the outskirts of a city. ◊ **garden city**

─────────────────────────────
zh vision   In foreign words: kh German Bach; aN French vin; aaN French blanc; ö German schön, French feu; oN French bon; üN French un; ü French rue   Stress marks: ´ as in secret \seék rət\; academic \ákə démmik\

garden-variety *adj. US* = **garden** *adj.* 2

garderobe /gáard rōb/ *n.* (*archaic*) **1.** WARDROBE a wardrobe or room where clothes may be kept **2.** CLOTHING the clothing in a wardrobe or room for clothes **3.** BEDROOM a bedroom **4.** OUTDOOR TOILET a small building housing a toilet consisting of a bench with holes made above a pit [14thC. From Old French, from *garder* 'to keep' + *rote* 'robe'.]

Gardner /gáardnər/, **Wayne Michael** (*b.* 1959) Australian motorcycle racer. He was winner of the 1987 World Road Racing Championship.

James A. Garfield

Library of Congress

Garfield /gáar feeld/, **James A.** (1831–81) US statesman and 20th president of the United States. A Republican member of the US House of Representatives (1863–80), he was president for only four months before he was assassinated. Full name **James Abram Garfield**

garfish /gáar fish/ (*plural* **-fishes** *or* **-fish**) *n.* **1.** EUROPEAN MARINE FISH a European fish of northern temperate seas that is greenish to dark blue with silvery sides. Its elongated jaws with sharp teeth resemble a beak. Latin name: *Belone belone.* **2.** = **gar**[1] [15thC. *Gar* from Old English *gār* 'spear'. From the shape of its jaw.]

gargantuan /gaar gántyoo ən/ *adj.* tremendously large in amount, number, or size [Late 16thC. Formed from *Gargantua*, the name of the giant hero of *Gargantua* by Rabelais.]

gargle /gáarg'l/ *v.* (**-gles, -gling, -gled**) **1.** *vti.* CLEANSE MOUTH AND THROAT to rinse or disinfect the mouth and throat by holding liquid in the back of the mouth and stirring it up with air breathed out from the lungs **2.** *vi.* MAKE GUTTURAL SOUND to make a sound like that made when rinsing the mouth with liquid ■ *n.* **1.** MOUTHWASH a liquid used to rinse the mouth **2.** GUTTURAL SOUND a sound like that made when rinsing the mouth with liquid [Early 16thC. From French *gargouiller*, from Old French *gargouille* 'throat' (source of English *gargoyle*), from Latin *gurgulio* 'gullet' (source of English *gurgle*).]

Gargoyle

gargoyle /gáar goyl/ *n.* **1.** GROTESQUE DRAINAGE SPOUT ON BUILDING a spout in the form of a grotesque animal or human figure that projects from the gutter of a building and is designed to cast rainwater clear of the building **2.** STATUE OF GROTESQUE FIGURE a grotesque carved figure **3.** SB LIKE CARVED FIGURE sb who is said to resemble a carved gargoyle (*insult*) [15thC. From Old French *gargouille* (see GARGLE), because the water seems to come out of its throat.]

garibaldi /gárri báwldi/ *n.* **1.** WOMAN'S LOOSE-FITTING BLOUSE a woman's loose-fitting blouse that imitates the red shirt worn by Giuseppe Garibaldi **2. garibaldi,**

garibaldi biscuit CURRANT BISCUIT a type of flat square biscuit with a central layer of currants [Mid-19thC. Named after GARIBALDI.]

Garibaldi /gárri báwldi/, **Giuseppe** (1807–82) French-born Italian patriot. He played a leading role in the unification of Italy (1859–61), defeating the rulers of Sicily and Naples at the head of his army, the so-called 'Red Shirts'.

garish /gáirish/ *adj.* **1.** GAUDY crudely showy ○ *a garish outfit* **2.** OVERLY ORNAMENTED excessively ornate or elaborate ○ *a garish balcony and staircase* **3.** DRESSED TOO BRIGHTLY wearing clothing or make-up that is extremely brightly coloured **4.** TOO BRIGHT excessively bright ○ *a hideous garish yellow* [Mid-16thC. Origin unknown.] —**garishly** *adv.* —**garishness** *n.*

garland /gáarlənd/ *n.* **1.** FLOWER WREATH a wreath of intertwined flowers or leaves worn as ornament or as a sign of honour **2.** HANGING FLOWER DECORATION a festoon of flowers or paper hung as decoration **3.** LITERAT LITERARY COLLECTION a collection of short pieces of literature ■ *vt.* (**-lands, -landing, -landed**) DECORATE WITH GARLAND to decorate or adorn sb or sth with garlands [14thC. From Old French *garlande*, of unknown origin.]

Garlic

garlic /gáarlik/ (*plural* **-lic** *or* **-lics**) *n.* **1.** PLANTS STRONG-TASTING PLANT USED IN COOKING a plant grown for its strongly flavoured bulbs that are used in cooking and medicine. Latin name: *Allium sativum.* **2.** COOK BULB OF GARLIC a bulb or clove of garlic with a pungent odour and flavour that is commonly used in cooking **3.** PLANTS PLANT SIMILAR TO GARLIC any plant related to or resembling true garlic [Old English *gārlēac.* From Old English *gār* 'spear' + an earlier form of LEEK. From its spear-like leaves.] —**garlicky** *adj.*

garlic bread *n.* bread seasoned with butter and garlic and baked or toasted

garlic mustard *n.* a hedgerow plant of Europe and Asia with heart-shaped leaves, small white flowers, and a pungent garlicky smell. Latin name: *Alliaria petiolata.*

garlic press *n.* a small kitchen tool, usually metal or plastic, that minces a clove of garlic by squeezing it through small holes

garlic salt *n.* a preparation of salt and powdered garlic used as a food seasoning

garlic sausage *n.* a type of salami that contains garlic as its main seasoning

garment /gáarmənt/ *n.* CLOTHING ITEM a piece of clothing ■ *vt.* (**-ments, -menting, -mented**) DRESS SB to put clothing on sb (*literary*) (*often passive*) [14thC. From French *garnement*, literally 'equipment', from *garnir* (see GARNISH).]

garment bag *n.* a piece of soft-sided luggage specifically shaped for carrying dresses, suits, or other clothing on hangers

garner /gáarnər/ *vt.* (**-ners, -nering, -nered**) **1.** GATHER IN STH to gather sth into storage or into a granary **2.** WIN OR GAIN STH to earn or acquire sth by effort **3.** GATHER INFORMATION to collect or accumulate sth such as information or facts ■ *n.* GRANARY a storage place for grain (*archaic*) [12thC. Via Anglo-Norman *gerner* 'storehouse' from, ultimately, Latin *granarium* (see GRANARY).]

Garner /gáarnər/, **Helen** (*b.* 1942) Australian writer. Her works include the novel *Monkey Grip* (1977) and the nonfiction work *The First Stone* (1995).

garnet /gáarnit/ *n.* **1.** RED SEMIPRECIOUS STONE a crystalline silicate mineral common in metamorphic and some igneous rocks, whose colour varies according to its composition. Some deep red garnets are used as semiprecious gemstones. **2.** COLOURS DARK RED COLOUR a dark red colour ■ *adj.* COLOURS DARK RED IN COLOUR of a dark red colour [13thC. Origin uncertain: probably via Middle Dutch *garnate* from Old French *grenat* 'dark red', from *pome grenate* 'pomegranate', because of its colour.]

garnetiferous /gáarni tíffərəss/ *adj.* used to describe minerals that contain garnets

garnierite /gáarni ərīt/ *n.* a soft green mineral that consists of nickel-rich serpentine, a form of hydrated nickel magnesium silicate, and is an important source of nickel [Late 19thC. Named after the French geologist Jules *Garnier* (1839?–1904), who discovered it.]

garnish /gáarnish/ *vt.* (**-nishes, -nishing, -nished**) **1.** ENHANCE FOOD OR DRINK to add sth as an accompaniment to food or drink that enhances its flavour or appearance **2.** EMBELLISH STH to decorate sth with an ornament **3.** LAW = **garnishee** *v.* 1, **garnishee** *v.* 2 ■ *n.* **1.** ENHANCEMENT FOR FOOD OR DRINK sth added as an accompaniment to food or drink to enhance its flavour or appearance **2.** STH DECORATIVE an ornament or decoration for sth **3.** EXTORTED MONEY a fee extorted from a new convict or worker (*archaic slang*) [14thC. From French *garniss-*, the stem of *garnir* 'to equip, adorn, warn', of prehistoric Germanic origin.] —**garnishing** *n.*

garnishee /gáarni sheé/ *vt.* (**-ees, -eeing, -eed**) **1.** CONFISCATE DEBTOR'S MONEY to take the money or property of a debtor by legal authority **2.** SUMMONS DEBTOR to serve sb with a legal summons concerning the taking of wages or property to satisfy a debt ■ *n.* SUMMONSED DEBTOR sb who is served with a legal summons concerning the taking of wages or property to satisfy a debt

garnishment /gáarnishmənt/ *n.* **1.** LAW SUMMONS FOR DEBTOR a legal summons or warning concerning the taking of property or wages of a debtor to satisfy a debt **2.** DECORATION an ornamentation or embellishment on or of sth

garniture /gáarnichər/ *n.* sth that decorates or embellishes sth [15thC. From French, formed from *garnir* (see GARNISH).]

Garonne /ga rón/ river in southwestern France. Rising in the Spanish Pyrenees, it flows through Toulouse and Bordeaux before joining the Dordogne at the Gironde estuary. Length: 645 km/400 mi.

garpike /gáar pīk/ (*plural* **-pikes** *or* **-pike**) *n.* **1.** = **gar**[1] *n.* **2.** = **garfish** *n.* 1 [Late 18thC. From GAR[1].]

garret /gárrət/ *n.* a room at the top of a house, immediately below the roof [15thC. From Old French *garite* 'watchtower', from *garir* 'to defend'. Ultimately from a prehistoric Germanic word meaning 'to protect' that also produced English *warn*.]

Garrett /gárrət/, **Peter** (*b.* 1953) Australian singer and political activist. He was a founding member of the rock group Midnight Oil (1977) and president of the Australian Conservation Foundation (1989–93). Full name **Peter Robert Garrett**

Garrick /gárrik/, **David** (1717–79) British actor, theatrical manager, and playwright. He brought a new naturalism to the stage in legendary performances, and managed London's Drury Lane Theatre (1747–76).

garrison /gárrissən/ *n.* **1.** STATIONED TROOPS a body of troops stationed at a military post **2.** PLACE FOR STATIONING TROOPS a military post where troops are stationed ■ *vt.* (**-sons, -soning, -soned**) **1.** SUPPLY PLACE WITH TROOPS to provide a fort or town with a military post and troops **2.** STATION TROOPS AT PLACE to station troops at a military post [13thC. From Old French, 'fortification', formed from *garir* (see GARRET).]

garrotte /gə rót/, **garrote** *n.* **1.** METHOD OF EXECUTION BY STRANGULATION a method of execution in which an iron band is tightened around the neck of the condemned person until death occurs **2.** METAL BAND USED TO EXECUTE SB a band of metal placed around the neck in order to execute sb by strangulation **3.** WEAPON FOR STRANGULATION a weapon consisting of a wire or cord with handles at either end, used in strangulation ■ *vt.* (**-rottes, -rotting, -rotted; -rotes, -roting, -roted**) STRANGLE

SB to execute or kill sb by strangling with a garrote [Early 17thC. From Spanish *garrote* 'cudgel, stick for tightening a cord', perhaps of Celtic origin.]

garrulity /gə roólətí, ga-/ *n.* excessive or pointless talkativeness

garrulous /gárrələss, gárr yoŏ-/ *adj.* **1.** TALKING TOO MUCH excessively or pointlessly talkative **2.** WORDY using many or too many words [Early 17thC. Formed from Latin *garrulus*, from *garrire* 'to chatter'.] —**garrulously** *adv.* —**garrulousness** *n.*

—————— WORD KEY: SYNONYMS ——————
See Synonyms at *talkative*.

garryowen /gárri ŏ in/ *n.* RUGBY = up-and-under [Mid-20thC. Named after the Irish rugby club *Garryowen*.]

garter /gaártər/ *n.* **1.** RETAINING BAND an elastic band used to hold up a stocking, sock, or shirt sleeve **2.** *US* = suspender ■ *vt.* (**-ters, -tering, -tered**) SUPPORT BY ELASTIC BAND to hold up a stocking, sock, or sleeve with an elastic band [14thC. From Old French *gartier*, from *garet* 'bend of the knee', of Celtic origin.]

Garter *n.* **1.** = Order of the Garter **2.** BADGE OF GARTER the badge that signifies membership of the Order of the Garter **3.** MEMBERSHIP IN GARTER membership in the Order of the Garter

garter belt *n. US* = suspender belt

garter snake *n.* a small nonpoisonous snake of North and Central America whose back is typically marked with yellow or red stripes running the length of the body. If disturbed, it may emit a pungent odour. Genus: *Thamnophis*.

garter stitch *n.* knitting done in the same stitch, whether knit or purl, for every row [From its original use in making garters]

garth /gaarth/ *n.* a small courtyard or enclosed space [14thC. From Old Norse *garðr*.]

Marcus Garvey
Popperfoto

Garvey /gaárvi/, **Marcus** (1887–1940) Jamaican-born US civil rights advocate. He founded the Universal Negro Improvement Association (1914) and created a 'Back to Africa' movement in the United States. Full name **Marcus Moziah Garvey**

Gary /gárri/ steel-producing city in northwestern Indiana, on the southern shore of Lake Michigan, west of Portage. Population: 110,975 (1996).

gas /gass/ *n.* (*plural* **gases** or **gasses**) **1.** CHEM SUBSTANCE SUCH AS AIR a substance such as air that is neither a solid nor a liquid at ordinary temperatures and that has the ability to expand indefinitely **2.** UTIL, GEOL FOSSIL FUEL a combustible gaseous substance such as natural gas or coal gas, used as a fuel **3.** MIL, CRIMINOL GAS FOR POISONING OR ASPHYXIATING a gaseous mixture used as a poison, irritant, or asphyxiating agent **4.** PHARM ANAESTHETIC a gaseous substance used as an anaesthetic **5.** *US* AUTOMOT GASOLINE gasoline for internal-combustion engines **6.** *US* AUTOMOT CAR ACCELERATOR the pedal used for accelerating a motor vehicle (*informal*) ○ *step on the gas* **7.** *US* PHYSIOL FLATULENCE gaseous product of digestion (*informal*) **8.** MINING METHANE AND AIR the highly explosive product of methane combined with air **9.** SB OR STH ENTERTAINING sb or sth such as an experience that is very thrilling or entertaining (*informal*) **10.** NONSENSE meaningless empty talk (*informal*) ■ *v.* (**gases** or **gasses, gassing, gassed**) **1.** *vt.* TO HARM SB WITH GAS to attack, injure, or kill a person or animal with a poisonous, irritating, or asphyxiating gas **2.** *vi.* RELEASE GAS to give off gas or a gas **3.** *vi.* TALK IDLY to talk too much, especially

about unimportant matters (*informal*) [Mid-17thC. From Dutch, coined by the Flemish chemist J. B. van Helmont (1577–1644), based on Greek *khaos* 'empty space' (source of English *chaos*).] —**gassing** *n.*

gasbag /gáss bag/ *n.* sb who talks too much, especially about unimportant matters (*informal*)

gas burner *n.* the nozzle or opening from which gas issues and burns, e.g. on a cooker

gas chamber *n.* a room in which people are killed by means of poisonous gas (*technical*) = gas oven

gas chromatograph *n.* a device used in gas chromatography for separating the volatile constituents of a substance

gas chromatography *n.* a method of separating the volatile constituents of a substance by means of gas, for the purpose of analysis

gascon /gásskən/ *n.* sb who is very boastful [Late 18thC. From the legendary boastfulness of the people of Gascony.]

Gascon /gásskən/ *n.* **1.** PEOPLES SB FROM GASCONY sb who lives in or was born or brought up in Gascony, formerly a province in southwestern France **2.** LANGUAGE FRENCH DIALECT a dialect of French spoken in Gascony [14thC. Via French from, ultimately, Latin *Vasco* (source of English *Basque*).] —**Gascon** *adj.*

gas constant *n.* the constant in an equation that describes the relation of the pressure and volume of a gas to its absolute temperature. It equals 8.314 joules per kelvin. Symbol **R**

gas-cooled reactor *n.* a nuclear reactor that uses carbon dioxide or helium as a coolant

Gascoyne /gás koyn/ river in northern Western Australia, that rises between the Collier and Robinson ranges and empties into the Indian Ocean at Shark Bay. Length: 760 km/472 mi.

gas-discharge tube *n.* a tube containing gas from which light is emitted when an electric current is passed through the gas atoms and excites them

gaseous /gássi əss, gáyssi-/ *adj.* **1.** RESEMBLING GAS neither solid nor liquid and with a tendency to expand infinitely **2.** VERBOSE having or using too many words, especially in a meaningless way (*informal*) **3.** CONTAINING GAS full of gas, or containing a gas such as carbon dioxide [Late 18thC. Formed from GAS, on the model of AQUEOUS.] —**gaseousness** *n.*

gas fitter *n.* a worker who fits and repairs gas pipes, fittings, and appliances

gas gangrene *n.* a form of gangrene, caused by aerobic clostridia bacteria, in which gas forms in injured body tissue

gas-guzzler *n. US* a motor vehicle that burns comparatively large amounts of fuel (*informal*)

gash /gash/ *n.* DEEP CUT a long deep narrow slash or cut ■ *vt.* (**gashes, gashing, gashed**) MAKE CUT IN to make a long deep narrow slash or cut in flesh or a surface [Mid-16thC. Alteration of Old Northern French *garser* 'to cut', via late Latin *charaxare* 'to sharpen' from Greek *kharassein* (source of English *character*).]

gasholder /gáss hōldər/ *n.* a very large tank used to store gas that is used as combustible fuel

gasiform /gássi fawrm/ *adj.* = gaseous *adj.* 1

gasify /gássifī/ (**-fies, -fying, -fied**) *vti.* to convert a solid or liquid into a gas, or become a gas —**gasification** /gássifi káysh'n/ *n.*

gas jet *n.* **1.** = gas burner **2.** GAS FLAME a flame of burning gas

Gaskell /gásk'l/, **Elizabeth** (1810–65) British novelist. Her novels document social conditions in newly industrialized Britain, and include *Mary Barton* (1848), *Cranford* (1853), and *North and South* (1855). Born **Elizabeth Cleghorn Stevenson**

gasket /gáskit/ *n.* **1.** TECH RUBBER SEAL a piece of material such as rubber, used to render a joint impermeable to gas or liquid **2.** SAILING ROPE FOR SAIL a light line for securing a furled sail [Early 17thC. Origin uncertain: perhaps an alteration of French *garcette* 'thin cord', literally 'little girl', (perhaps in allusion to a girl's pigtail).] ◇ **blow a gasket** to explode in anger or rage (*informal*)

gaskin /gáskin/ *n.* ZOOL PART OF HORSE'S REAR LEG the part of the back leg of a four-legged hoofed animal,

especially a horse, that is equivalent to the lower thigh in humans ■ **gaskins** *npl.* CLOTHES GALLIGASKINS galligaskins (*archaic*) [Late 16thC. Origin uncertain: perhaps a shortening of GALLIGASKINS, or an alteration of GASCON.]

gaslight /gáss līt/ *n.* **1.** ILLUMINATION FROM BURNING GAS light produced by burning coal gas or natural gas **2.** LAMP FUELLED BY GAS a lamp or fixture that produces light by burning gas

gas-liquid chromatography *n.* = gas chromatography

gaslit /gásslit/ *adj.* illuminated by light from lamps or fixtures that burn gas

gasman /gáss man/ (*plural* **-men** /-men/) *n.* a worker who checks gas meters in order to note the amount of gas used in a specific period

gas mark *n.* a mark on the temperature regulator of the oven of a gas cooker, indicating a gradation of heat

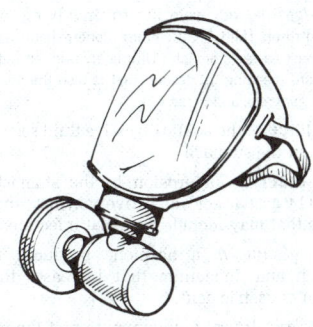
Gas mask

gas mask *n.* a mask provided with a filter and worn to protect the wearer's face and lungs from harmful gases

gas meter *n.* a device installed inside or outside a residential or commercial building to measure the amount of gas consumed in a specific period

gasohol /gássəhol/ *n. US* a fuel used in motor vehicles that consists of 90 per cent petrol blended with 10 per cent alcohol. The alcohol is produced by the fermentation of an agricultural product high in sugar, e.g. corn. [Late 20thC. A blend of GASOLINE and ALCOHOL.]

gasoline /gássəleen/ *n. US* = petrol [Mid-19thC. Coined from GAS + -OL + -INE.]

gasometer /ga sómmitər/ *n.* **1.** GAS-MEASURING APPARATUS an apparatus for measuring and storing gas in a laboratory **2.** = gasholder

gas oven *n.* **1.** OVEN IN HOUSE OR FACTORY a household or commercial oven that uses natural or coal gas to create heat **2.** SPACE FOR GASSING PEOPLE a space, e.g. a room or building, for executing people by means of poisonous gas, especially as used by Nazi Germany during World War II

gasp /gaasp/ *n.* **1.** SUDDEN BREATH a sudden short audible intake of breath, e.g. in surprise or pain **2.** DIFFICULT BREATHING a laborious effort to breathe ■ *v.* (**gasps, gasping, gasped**) **1.** *vi.* LABOUR TO BREATHE to breathe with difficulty **2.** *vi.* BREATHE IN SHARPLY draw in breath loudly and spasmodically **3.** *vt.* SAY STH WITH GASP to say sth with a sudden intake of breath [14thC. From Old Norse *geispa* 'to yawn'.] ◇ **be gasping (for sth)** to feel a desperate need for a drink or cigarette (*informal*) ◇ **the last gasp** sb's final attempt or action, or the final phase of sth

Gaspé Peninsula /ga spáy-/ peninsula in southeastern Quebec Province, Canada, bounded by the St Lawrence River, Chaleur Bay, and New Brunswick. Area: 29,500 sq. km/11,390 sq. mi.

gasper /gaáspər/ *n.* a cigarette, especially a cheap one (*dated slang*)

gas plant *n.* a Eurasian perennial plant of the rue family with white flowers and strong-smelling leaves that give off a flammable gas. Latin name: *Dictamnus albus*.

gasser /gássər/ *n.* **1.** UTIL GAS WELL a well that produces natural gas **2.** = gasbag (*informal*)

gas station *n.* US = **petrol station.** ◊ **service station**

gassy /gássi/ (**-sier, -siest**) *adj.* **1. FULL OF GAS** full of or containing gas such as carbon dioxide **2. LIKE GAS** resembling gas **3. VERBOSE** having or using too many words, especially in a meaningless way (*informal*) —**gassily** *adv.* —**gassiness** *n.*

gastarbeiter /gást aarbītər/ (*plural* **-ter** *or* **-ters**), **Gastarbeiter** (*plural* **-ter** *or* **-ters**) *n.* an immigrant worker, especially one who came to the former West Germany in the 1960s and 1970s [Mid-20thC. From German, literally 'guest worker'.]

gastight /gáss tīt/ *adj.* preventing any gas from passing through

gastr- *prefix.* = **gastro**

gastrectomy /gass tréktəmi/ (*plural* **-mies**) *n.* surgical removal of all or part of the stomach. It is usually performed in the treatment of stomach cancer or severe stomach ulcers.

gastric /gástrik/ *adj.* relating to, involving, or near the stomach [Mid-17thC. From modern Latin *gastricus*, from Greek *gastēr* 'stomach'. Ultimately from an Indo-European word meaning 'to devour' that is also the ancestor of English *gangrene* and *cress*.]

gastric juice *n.* the acidic digestive fluid secreted by glands in the stomach

gastric ulcer *n.* an erosion in the stomach wall caused by gastric acid, digestive enzymes, and other factors that may include bacterial infection

gastrin /gástrin/ *n.* a hormone produced in the stomach and duodenum that increases the production of gastric acid

gastritis /gass trítiss/ *n.* inflammation of the mucous membrane that lines the stomach. It may be acute or chronic, and it is often associated with excessive intake of alcohol.

gastro- *prefix.* stomach, belly ○ *gastrectomy* [From Greek *gastr-*, the stem of *gastēr* 'belly' (see GASTRIC)]

gastrocnemius /gástrok neémi əss, -trək-/ (*plural* **-i** /-mi/) *n.* the largest muscle in the calf of the leg, extending from the thigh bone to the Achilles tendon. When it contracts it causes the foot to point downwards. [Late 17thC. Via modern Latin from Greek *gastroknēmia* 'calf of the leg', literally 'stomach of the leg' (from its bulging form).]

gastroduodenostomy /gástrō dyoŏ ō dee nóstəmi/ (*plural* **-mies**) *n.* a surgical operation in which the duodenum is joined to an opening made in the stomach wall. It is performed, e.g., to bypass an obstruction or narrowing in the stomach outlet.

gastroenteritis /gástrō éntə rítiss/ *n.* inflammation of the stomach and the intestines, usually as a result of bacterial or viral infection. The symptoms include vomiting and diarrhoea, and the illness typically lasts three to five days.

gastroenterology /gástrō éntə róllǝji/ *n.* the branch of medicine concerned with the study and treatment of diseases of the stomach and intestines and their associated organs —**gastroenterologic** /-éntərə lójjik/ *adj.* —**gastroenterologist** /gástrō éntə róllǝjist/ *n.*

gastrointestinal /gástrō in téstinəl/ *adj.* relating to the stomach and intestines

gastrolith /gástrō lith/ *n.* **1. ZOOL STONE SWALLOWED TO AID DIGESTION** a stone swallowed by an animal such as a bird or dinosaur, as an aid to the digestion of food **2. MED STONE FORMED IN STOMACH** a stone that has formed in the stomach

gastronome /gástrənōm/, **gastronomist** /gass trónn əmist/ *n.* a connoisseur of good food [Early 19thC. From French, back-formation from *gastronomie* (see GASTRONOMY).]

gastronomy /gass trónnəmi/ (*plural* **-mies**) *n.* **1. GOURMET EATING** the art and appreciation of preparing and eating good food **2. PARTICULAR CUISINE** a particular style of cooking or dining, e.g. one that is typical of a country or region [Early 19thC. Via French *gastronomie* from Greek *gastronomia*, an alteration of *gastrologia*, literally 'study of the stomach'.] —**gastronomic** /gástrə nómmik/ *adj.* —**gastronomically** /-nómmikli/ *adv.*

gastroplasty /gas tróppləsti/ (*plural* **-ties**) *n.* a surgical operation to repair a malformation of the stomach

gastropod /gástrə pod/ *n.* a mollusc that has a head with eyes, and a large flattened foot, and often a single shell. Limpets, snails, and slugs are types of gastropod. Class: Gastropoda. [Early 19thC. From modern Latin *Gastropoda*, class name, literally 'stomach-foot'.] —**gastropod** *adj.* —**gastropodous** /-tróppədəs/ *adj.*

gastroscope /gástrə skōp/ *n.* an instrument passed through the mouth and used to examine the stomach, consisting of a flexible tube that contains optical fibres coupled to an eyepiece and light source —**gastroscopic** /-skóppik/ *adj.* —**gastroscopy** /gas tróskəpi/ *n.*

gastrostomy /gas tróstəmi/ (*plural* **-mies**) *n.* a surgical operation in which an opening is made through the wall of the stomach and is joined to an opening in the adjacent abdominal wall. It is performed to allow food and liquids to be placed directly into the stomach via a tube when the oesophagus is affected by disease or recovering from surgery.

gastrotomy /gass tróttəmi/ (*plural* **-mies**) *n.* a surgical incision into the stomach, for examination of the cavity or to remove a foreign object

gastrovascular /gástrō váskyoŏlər/ *adj.* used to describe a part of the body involved in both digestion and circulation, e.g. the central body cavity of certain jellyfish

gastrula /gástroŏlə/ (*plural* **-las** *or* **-lae** /-leə/) *n.* the stage in embryonic development after the blastula during which the embryo develops two layers [Late 19thC. From modern Latin, literally 'little stomach', formed from Greek *gastēr* 'stomach' (see GASTRIC).] —**gastrular** /gástroŏlər/ *adj.*

gastrulation /gástroŏ láysh'n/ *n.* the process of cell movements by which a developing embryo forms distinct layers that later grow into particular organs —**gastrulate** *vi.*

gas turbine *n.* an internal-combustion engine in which a turbine is turned by hot gases consisting of compressed air and the products of the fuel's combustion

gasworks /gás wurks/ *n.* a factory where gas for heating and illuminating is produced, especially from coal (*takes a singular or plural verb*)

gat[1] /gat/ *n.* a passage or channel of water that extends inland from a shore [Late 16thC. Origin uncertain: probably from Old Norse *gat* 'hole'.]

gat[2] /gat/ *n.* a handgun (*dated slang*) [Early 20thC. Shortening of GATLING GUN.]

gat[3] /gat/ past tense of **get** (*archaic*)

gate /gayt/ *n.* **1. HINGED BARRIER ACROSS GAP** a movable barrier, usually on hinges, that closes a gap in a fence or wall **2. OPENING IN WALL** an opening in a wall or fence **3. OPENING IN DEFENSIVE STRUCTURE** an opening in a castle or city wall or other defensive structure **4. POINT OF ACCESS** a means of access or entrance **5. BARRIER AT TOLLBOOTH** a movable barrier restricting access, e.g. at a tollbooth **6. STARTING GATE** a starting gate (*informal*) **7. TRANSP ARRIVAL OR DEPARTURE POINT FOR PASSENGERS** the area at an airport where passengers arrive and depart **8. BARRIER FOR FLUID** a sliding barrier, valve, or other mechanism for regulating the passage of a fluid **9. SPECTATORS ADMITTED TO EVENT** the total number of persons who pay for admission to an entertainment or sporting event **10. TOTAL MONEY FROM TICKETS** the total amount of money paid for tickets of admission to an entertainment or sports event **11. SKIING PATH BETWEEN POLES IN SLALOM** the space between two markers through which a skier passes in a slalom race **12. COMPUT LOGIC CIRCUIT** a logical device in a computer, with one output channel and one or more input channels, that emits a signal only when certain input conditions are met **13. ELECTRON ENG REGULATING SWITCH** an electronic switch that regulates the flow of current in a circuit **14. ROWING HINGED FASTENING FOR OAR** a fastening with a hinge that serves to keep an oar in its rowlock **15. *N England, Scotland* WAY** a path or road **16. *N England, Scotland* HABIT** a habitual method or style of doing sth ■ *vt.* (**gates, gating, gated**) **1. CONFINE TO SCHOOL GROUNDS** to punish a student by confining him or her to the school or college grounds **2. CONTROL USING GATE** to control or regulate sb or sth with a gate **3. PUT GATE IN STH** to install a gate in sth, e.g. in a fence [Old English *geat*.]

Partly from, and influenced by, Old Norse *gata* 'path' (source also of English *gait*). Ultimately from a prehistoric Germanic word meaning 'opening in a wall'.]

── **WORD KEY: REGIONAL NOTE** ──

Gate used to mean 'a way, road, path', a fact illustrated by the many streets in the north of England with names such as *Broadgate*, *Cannongate*, *Stonegate*, and *Swinegate*. The /g/ pronunciation is due to Viking influence. The poet W. B. Yeats would have been called 'Gates' if his ancestors had been northerners.

gateau /gáttō/ (*plural* **-teaux** /-tōz/), **gâteau** (*plural* **-teaux**) *n.* **1. RICH CAKE** a rich cake, usually consisting of several layers held together with a cream filling **2. BAKED SAVOURY FOOD** savoury food baked and served in a form resembling a cake [Mid-19thC. From French, 'cake'.]

gatecrasher /gáyt krashər/ *n.* sb who attends a party, entertainment, or sporting event without an invitation or ticket —**gatecrash** *vti.*

gatefold /gáyt fōld/ *n.* a page in a publication that is larger than the other pages and is folded to fit

gatehouse /gáyt howss/ (*plural* **-houses** /-howziz/) *n.* a building or house above or beside a gate

gatekeeper /gáyt keepər/ *n.* **1. GUARD AT GATE** a supervisor or guard who tends a gate **2. ACCESS CONTROLLER** an individual or group that controls access to sb or sth

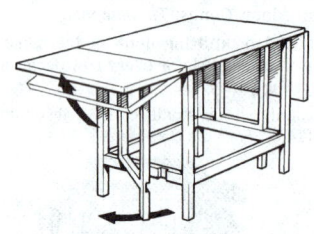

Gateleg table

gateleg table /gáyt leg-/ *n.* a drop-leaf table with movable legs that swing out to support the leaves

gate money *n.* = **gate** *n.* 10

gatepost /gáyt pōst/ *n.* one of the posts on either side of a gate. One post supports the gate and the gate closes against and is fastened to the other.

gater, 'gater *n.* = **gator**

Popperfoto

Bill Gates

Gates /gayts/, **Bill** (*b.* 1955) US entrepreneur. He co-founded Microsoft™ Corporation to develop the DOS operating system, and developed a major international telecommunications corporation. He wrote *The Road Ahead* (1995) about his vision of society and technology. Full name **William Henry Gates III**

Gateshead /gáyts hed/ industrial town in Durham, northeastern England. Population: 201,800 (1995).

Gates of the Arctic National Park and Preserve national park consisting mainly of tundra in northern Alaska, north of the Arctic Circle. Area: 30,448 sq. km/11,756 sq. mi.

gateway /gáyt way/ *n.* **1. OPENING FITTED WITH GATE** an opening that may be closed by a gate **2. ACCESS POINT**

a means of entrance or access to sb or sth **3.** COMPUT **COMPUTER-NETWORK CONNECTION** software or hardware that links two computer networks

gateway drug *n.* a drug that does not cause physical dependence but may lead to the use of addictive drugs

gather /gáthər/ *v.* **(-ers, -ering, -ered) 1.** *vti.* **FORM INTO GROUP** to bring people or things together, or come together, to form a group **2.** *vt.* **HARVEST STH** to pick or harvest a crop **3.** *vt.* **COLLECT IDEAS OR DATA** to compile sth such as information or ideas from various sources **4.** *vt.* **ATTRACT FOLLOWING** to attract a group of people as supporters, followers, or an audience ○ *The street players have gathered quite a crowd.* **5.** *vti.* **ACCUMULATE STH** to accumulate a gradually increasing mass or quantity of sth, or to be accumulated gradually ○ *clouds gathered on the horizon* **6.** *vt.* **DRAW ON STH** to summon up energies, courage, or strength from within **7.** *vt.* **SURMISE STH** to conclude sth from intuition or observation **8.** *vt.* **BRING CLOSE** to draw sb or sth close **9.** *vt.* **LIFT SB OR STH UP** to pick or scoop sb or sth up **10.** *vti.* **WRINKLE BROW** to draw the brow into wrinkles, or be drawn into wrinkles **11.** *vt.* SEW **PULL FABRIC TOGETHER** to draw fabric together in a series of folds along a line of stitching **12.** *vt.* PRINTING **PUT PAGES IN ORDER** to assemble the printed sections of a book in the correct order for binding **13.** *vt.* CRAFT **PREPARE MOLTEN GLASS FOR BLOWING** to collect molten glass at the end of a tube for blowing and shaping **14.** *vi.* MED **FORM PUS-FILLED HEAD** to form and fill with pus ■ *n.* **1.** SEW **FOLD IN FABRIC** one in a series of folds in fabric **2.** CRAFT **MOLTEN GLASS BALL** a ball of molten glass collected on a tube for blowing and shaping [Old English *gaderian.* Ultimately from an Indo-European word meaning 'to bring together' that is also the ancestor of English *together* and *good.*] —**gatherer** *n.*

WORD KEY: SYNONYMS

See Synonyms at ***collect.***

gathering /gáthəring/ *n.* **1.** **ASSEMBLY** a meeting or crowd of people **2.** **CLUSTER OF THINGS** a collection of objects **3.** **COLLECTING OF STH** the collecting of people or objects into a group **4.** MED **BOIL** a pus-filled swelling **5.** SEW **FOLDS IN CLOTH** a series of folds in fabric

gathering stitch *n.* a line of running stitches sewn with a single length of thread. One end of the thread is secured while the other is pulled up to form gathers in the fabric.

Gatling gun /gátling-/ *n.* an early machine gun with multiple barrels firing in rotation [Mid-19thC. Named after the US inventor R. J. *Gatling* (1818–1903), who developed it.]

gator /gáytər/, **'gator, gater, 'gater** *n. US* an alligator (*informal*) [Mid-19thC. Shortening.]

GATT /gat/, **Gatt** *abbr.* HIST General Agreement on Tariffs and Trade

Gatwick /gáttwik/ London's second largest international airport, located to the south of the city on the border between the counties of Surrey and Sussex. It is on the site of an old racecourse.

gauche /gōsh/ *adj.* lacking grace or tact in social situations [Mid-18thC. From French, literally 'left-handed'.] —**gauchely** *adv.* —**gaucheness** *n.*

gaucherie /gṓshəri, -reé/ *n.* **1.** **SOCIAL AWKWARDNESS** a lack of grace or tact in social situations **2.** **SOCIALLY AWKWARD ACT** an act that is graceless or tactless [Late 18thC. From French, formed from *gauche* (see GAUCHE).]

gaucho /gówchō/ (*plural* **-chos**) *n.* a cowboy of the South American pampas or prairie [Early 19thC. From American Spanish, of uncertain origin: probably from Araucanian *kauču.*]

gaud /gawd/ *n.* a showy trinket or ornament [14thC. Origin uncertain: perhaps via Old French *gaudir* 'to rejoice' from Latin *gaudere* (source of English *joy* and *rejoice*).]

gaudery /gáwdəri/ (*plural* **-ies**) *n.* showy and ostentatious clothing or jewellery, or its display

gaudy[1] /gáwdi/ **(-ier, -iest)** *adj.* brightly coloured or showily decorated to an unpleasant or vulgar degree [15thC. From GAUD.] —**gaudily** *adv.* —**gaudiness** *n.*

gaudy[2] /gáwdi/ (*plural* **-ies**) *n.* an annual celebration or dinner held at certain universities and university colleges [Mid-16thC. From Latin *gaudium* 'joy' (source of English *joy*), from *gaudere* 'to rejoice'.]

gauge /gayj/, **gage** *vt.* **(gauges, gauging, gauged; gages, gaging, gaged) 1.** **CALCULATE** to determine the amount, quantity, size, or extent of sth ○ *It's quite difficult to gauge the distance accurately.* **2.** **EVALUATE** to form a judgment of sth uncertain or variable, especially sb's behaviour, feelings, or abilities ○ *Try to gauge his mood before launching the proposal.* **3.** **ENSURE CONFORMITY TO STANDARD** to ensure that sth conforms to a standard of measurement ■ *n.* **1.** **MEASUREMENT** a standard measurement or scale of measurement **2.** **MEASURING DEVICE** a device or instrument for measuring an amount or quantity or for testing accuracy **3.** **CRITERION** a standard or system of measurement for assessing sb or sth ○ *a gauge of the applicant's ability* **4.** RAIL **DISTANCE BETWEEN RAILS** the distance between the two rails of a railway track or tramway **5.** AUTOMOT **DISTANCE BETWEEN WHEELS** the distance between two wheels on an axle of a vehicle **6.** **THICKNESS OF WIRE** the diameter of sth, especially of wire or a needle **7.** **THICKNESS OF A MATERIAL** the thickness of a thin material such as sheet metal or plastic film **8.** ARMS **DIAMETER INSIDE GUN BARREL** the diameter of the inside of a gun barrel, especially a shotgun barrel **9.** NAUT **RELATIVE POSITION** the position of a ship in relation to another vessel and the wind **10.** TEXTILES **FINENESS OF A KNIT** the fineness of knitted fabric expressed in terms of the number of loops for each unit of width **11.** CONSTR **ADDED PROPORTION OF PLASTER OF PARIS** the proportion of plaster of Paris that is added to mortar to speed up the setting of the mixture [14thC. From Old Northern French, a variant of French *jauge,* of uncertain origin: probably ultimately from a prehistoric Germanic word.] —**gaugeable** *adj.*

gauger /gáyjər/ *n.* **1.** **CUSTOMS OFFICER INSPECTING BULK GOODS** a customs officer whose job is to inspect bulk goods on which duty is supposed to be paid **2.** **STH FOR GAUGING** a person who or instrument that gauges sth

Gauguin /gṓ gaN/, **Paul** (1848–1903) French painter. One of the most influential postimpressionist painters, he is known for his use of flat fields of deep colour. After 1891 he lived mostly in Polynesia, the inspiration of many for his most powerful works. Full name **Eugène Henri Paul Gauguin**

Gauhati /gow haáti/ industrial city and port on the River Brahmaputra in Assam State, northeastern India. Population: 584,342 (1991).

Gaul /gawl/ *n.* **1.** HIST **ANCIENT FRANCE** in ancient times, a region of western Europe that covered roughly what is now France, Belgium, and neighbouring parts of Italy, the Netherlands, and Germany. It was invaded and conquered by the Romans first before 100 BC and then again in the Gallic Wars (58–51 BC) under Julius Caesar. **2.** HIST, PEOPLES **SB FROM GAUL** sb who was born in or lived in ancient Gaul **3.** PEOPLES **FRENCH PERSON** sb who is French [15thC. From Latin *Gallus,* of uncertain origin: probably from Celtic.]

gauleiter /gów lītər/, **Gauleiter** *n.* **1.** HIST **PROVINCIAL HEAD** a political head of a district in Nazi Germany **2.** **TYRANNICAL OFFICIAL** a tyrannical local official [Mid-20thC. From German, formed from *Gau* 'administrative district' + *Leiter* 'leader'.]

Gaulish /gáwlish/ *n.* **EXTINCT CELTIC LANGUAGE** an extinct language spoken in Gaul before the Roman conquest and belonging to the Celtic branch of the Indo-European languages ■ *adj.* **OF GAUL OR GAULISH** relating to or typical of ancient Gaul, or its people, language, or culture

Gaullism /gṓl izəm/ *n.* **1.** **BELIEFS OF CHARLES DE GAULLE** the nationalist and conservative principles and policies of General Charles de Gaulle, leader of France after World War II, and his followers **2.** **FRENCH POLITICAL MOVEMENT** the political movement founded on the principles of Charles de Gaulle

Gaullist /gṓlist/ *n.* **SUPPORTER OF GAULLISM OR DE GAULLE** a supporter of Gaullism or de Gaulle ■ *adj.* **RELATING TO GAULLISM** relating to, typical of, or supporting Gaullism or de Gaulle

gault /gawlt/ *n.* a heavy dense clay or soil high in clay content, especially that of a series of clay and marl beds in southern England [Late 16thC. Origin unknown.]

gaunt /gawnt/ *adj.* **1.** **THIN** extremely thin and bony in appearance **2.** **STARK** stark in outline or appearance [15thC. Origin unknown.] —**gauntly** *adv.* —**gauntness** *n.*

gauntlet[1] /gáwntlət/ *n.* a glove with a long wide cuff that covers part of the forearm, usually made of fabric, leather, or, in the past, metal, when worn as part of armour [15thC. From French *gantelet* 'little glove', ultimately from a prehistoric Germanic word.] ◇ **throw down the gauntlet** to issue a challenge

gauntlet[2] /gáwntlət/ *n.* a punishment formerly used in the military in which sb was forced to run between two lines of men armed with weapons who beat him as he passed [Mid-17thC. Alteration, influenced by GAUNTLET[1], of *gantlop,* from Swedish *gatlopp* 'passageway'.] ◇ **run the gauntlet** to have to endure attack or criticism from all sides

gaur /gów ər/ *n.* a large wild ox with a dark coat that lives in the mountains of southeastern Asia. Latin name: *Bos gaurus.* [Early 19thC. From Sanskrit *gaura;* ultimately from an Indo-European word that is also the ancestor of English *cow.*]

Gause's principle /gáwziz-/, **Gause principle** *n.* ECOL = **competitive exclusion** [Named after the Russian biologist G. F. *Gause* (born 1910) , who established the principle.]

gauss /gows/ (*plural* **gauss**) *n.* the cgs unit of magnetic flux density, equivalent to 10^{-4} tesla [Late 19thC. Named after the German mathematician Karl Friedrich *Gauss* (1777–1855), who applied mathematical principles to magnetism.]

Gaussian /gówssi ən/ *adj.* with the characteristics or shape of a normal curve or normal statistical distribution [Late 19thC. Named after K. F. *Gauss* (see GAUSS).]

Gauteng /khow téng/ province created in 1994 in northern South Africa, containing Johannesburg, the province's capital, Soweto and Pretoria. Population: 7,048,300 (1995). Area: 18,810 sq. km/7,260 sq. mi.

Gautier /gṓ tyay/, **Théophile** (1811–72) French writer. His works include the novel *Mademoiselle de Maupin* (1835) and the verse collection *Émaux et camées* (1852).

gauze /gawz/ *n.* **1.** TEXTILES **FINELY-WOVEN FABRIC** a thin loosely-woven cloth, usually cotton or silk, that is almost transparent and is used for curtains and clothes **2.** MED **SURGICAL DRESSING** a dressing made of loosely woven material such as cotton that is applied in many layers to wounds **3.** INDUST **WIRE MESH** a thin mesh made of wire or other material **4.** **PIECE OF WIRE GAUZE** a piece of wire gauze used as a screen or filter in sth such as a smoker's pipe **5.** **HAZE** a fine haze or mist [Mid-16thC. From French *gaze,* of uncertain origin: perhaps named after the town of *Gaza* in Palestine, where fine fabrics were made, or perhaps ultimately from Arabic *qazz* 'raw silk'.] —**gauzily** *adv.* —**gauzy** *adj.*

gavage /gáv aazh/ *n.* the feeding of an animal or a person through a tube passed into the stomach [Late 19thC. From French, formed from *gaver* 'to stuff down the throat'.]

gave past tense of **give**

gavel /gávv'l/ *n.* **AUCTIONEER'S HAMMER** a small hammer used by an auctioneer, a judge, or chair of a meeting to draw people's attention or to mark the conclusion of a transaction ■ *vti.* **(-els, -elling, -elled) USE GAVEL** to use a gavel to bring an end to sth or to stop discussion [Early 19thC. Origin unknown.]

gavial /gáyvi əl/ *n.* = **gharial** [Early 19thC. Via French (possibly as a scribal error) from Hindi *ghaṛiyāl* GHARIAL.]

Gävle /yévvlə/ port and capital of the county of Gävleborg, eastern Sweden, about 161 km/100 mi. north of Stockholm. Population: 90,587 (1995).

gavotte /gə vót/ *n.* **1.** DANCE **FRENCH COUNTRY DANCE** a French country dance popular in the 18th century and similar to the minuet but slightly faster in pace **2.** MUSIC **MUSIC FOR GAVOTTE** a piece of music for the gavotte, written in 4/4 time [Late 19thC. Via French from, ultimately, Provençal *Gavot* 'an inhabitant of the Alps'.]

Gawain /gaáwayn/ *n.* in Arthurian legend, a knight who was the enemy of Sir Lancelot and who fought a mysterious green knight

Gawd /gawd/, **gawd** *interj.*, *n.* God (*slang; used to suggest irony in oaths*)

gawk /gawk/ *vi.* (**gawks, gawking, gawked**) STARE to stare stupidly (*informal*) ■ *n.* CLUMSY PERSON sb who is awkward or clumsy (*dated insult*) [Late 17thC. Origin uncertain: perhaps from, ultimately, Old Norse *gá* 'to heed'.]

— **WORD KEY: SYNONYMS** —
See Synonyms at **gaze**.

gawky /gáwki/ (**-ier, -iest**) *adj.* awkward and clumsy, often because of being tall and not well coordinated (*informal*) —**gawkily** *adv.* —**gawkiness** *n.*

Gawler /gáwlər/ town in southern South Australia. It is an agricultural centre and dormitory suburb of Adelaide. Population: 15,484 (1996).

gawp /gawp/ (**gawps, gawping, gawped**) *vi.* to stare stupidly or rudely (*informal*) ○ *Don't just stand there gawping, help her!* [Late 17thC. Origin uncertain: perhaps an alteration of GAPE.]

— **WORD KEY: SYNONYMS** —
See Synonyms at **gaze**.

gay /gay/ *adj.* **1.** HOMOSEXUAL homosexual in sexual orientation **2.** MERRY full of light-heartedness and merriment (*dated*) **3.** BRIGHT IN COLOUR brightly coloured (*dated*) **4.** CAREFREE having or showing a carefree spirit (*dated*) **5.** DEBAUCHED leading a debauched or dissolute life (*dated*) ■ *n.* SB HOMOSEXUAL a homosexual, especially a male homosexual [13thC. From Old French *gai* 'happy', of uncertain origin: probably from Frankish.] —**gayness** *n.*

Gay /gay/, **John** (1685–1732) English poet and dramatist. He is best known for *The Beggar's Opera* (1728), a ballad opera combining burlesque and political satire.

gayal /gə yál/ (*plural* **-yal** *or* **-yals**) *n.* a wild or semidomesticated ox of India and Myanmar (Burma) with a dark coat and white leg markings. Latin name: *Bos frontalis.* [Late 18thC. From Bengali.]

Marvin Gaye

Gaye /gay/, **Marvin** (1939–84) US singer and songwriter. He was one of the most successful soul singers from the 1960s and had an international bestselling hit with 'I Heard It Through the Grapevine' (1968).

gayety *n.* US = **gaiety**

gayly *adv.* US = **gaily**

gay pride *n.* a movement in the gay community that encourages gays to be open about their homosexuality and to be proud of being gay (*informal*)

gaz. *abbr.* **1.** gazette **2.** gazetteer

Gaza /gáːzə/ seaport and principal city of the Gaza Strip, on the Mediterranean coast. An important city in biblical times, it has both historical and current political significance. Population: 293,000 (1990).

gazar /gə zaár/ *n.* a stiff loosely-woven kind of silk [Mid-20thC. Origin uncertain: perhaps from, ultimately, Arabic *qazz* 'raw silk'.]

Gaza Strip region on the eastern Mediterranean coast bordered on the south by Egypt and on the east and north by Israel. Administered by Egypt from 1949 and Israel from 1967, it became an autonomous zone under the control of the Palestinian National Authority in 1994. The city of Gaza is the region's administrative centre. Population: 731,296 (1994). Area: 360 sq. km/139 sq. mi.

gaze /gayz/ *vi.* (**gazes, gazing, gazed**) LOOK FIXEDLY to look for a long time with a fixed stare ○ *He gazed longingly at the yacht.* ■ *n.* STEADY LOOK a long steady look or stare [14thC. Origin uncertain: perhaps from a Scandinavian language.] —**gazer** *n.*

— **WORD KEY: SYNONYMS** —
gaze, stare, gape, gawk, gawp, ogle, rubberneck
CORE MEANING: to look at sb or sth steadily or at length
gaze to look at sb or sth steadily and for a long time, especially with great attention, admiration, or fascination; **stare** to look at sb or sth fixedly and intently, often with wide-open eyes, in amazement, fear, or admiration. It can also be used to mean to look fixedly at sb or sth in a rude way or in a way that makes the person being looked at feel uncomfortable; **gape** to look at sb or sth in amazement or wonder, usually with an open mouth; **gawk** an informal word meaning to look at sb or sth fixedly and often rather rudely, especially with a stupid expression; **gawp** an informal word used in British English with the same meaning as 'gawk'; **ogle** to look steadily at sb in a lecherous, suggestive way; **rubberneck** an informal word, usually used showing disapproval, meaning to look fixedly at sb or sth with great curiosity.

gazebo /gə zeéb ō/ (*plural* **-bos** *or* **-boes** /-ōz/) *n.* a small, usually open-sided and slightly elevated building, situated in a spot that commands a good view [Mid-18thC. Origin uncertain: perhaps from GAZE on the model of Latin future tenses in *-ebo*, intended to mean 'I shall gaze'.]

gazehound /gáyz hownd/ *n.* a dog e.g. a greyhound or Afghan hound that hunts by sight rather than by smell

Gazelle

gazelle /gə zél/ (*plural* **-zelles** *or* **-zelle**) *n.* a small graceful swift antelope, native to the arid plains of Africa and Asia, that has long ringed horns and black face markings. Genera: *Gazella* and *Procapra.* [Early 17thC. From Old French *gazel*, of uncertain origin: probably via Spanish from Arabic *ghazāl*.]

gazette /gə zét/ *n.* **1.** NEWSPAPER a newspaper, especially the official paper of an organization ○ *the South London Gazette* **2.** PUBLICATION WITH OFFICIAL NEWS an official publication in which government appointments, public notices, lists of bankruptcies, and other items appear ○ *the Court Gazette* ■ *vt.* (**-zettes, -zetting, -zetted**) PUBLISH IN GAZETTE to publish or announce sth or name sb in a gazette (*often passive*) [Early 17thC. Directly or via French from Italian *gazzetta*, from Venetian dialect *gazeta de la novità* 'a pennyworth of news'.]

gazetteer /gázzə teér/ *n.* **1.** GEOGRAPHICAL REFERENCE BOOK a dictionary or index of places, usually with descriptive or statistical information **2.** JOURNALIST a journalist (*archaic*)

gazpacho /gaz pách ō, gəs paách-/ (*plural* **-chos**) *n.* a chilled Mexican or Spanish soup based on stock or tomato juice and containing chopped raw vegetables and seasoning [Early 19thC. From Spanish.]

gazump /gə zúmp/ *vt.* (**-zumps, -zumping, -zumped**) (*informal*) **1.** CHARGE SB MORE FOR HOUSE to charge the buyer of a house more than the originally agreed price, usually after receiving a better offer for the property ○ *We've been gazumped.* **2.** SWINDLE SB to swindle sb ■ *n.* ACT OF GAZUMPING an act of gazumping sb (*informal*) [Early 20thC. Origin unknown.] —**gazumper** *n.*

gazunder /gə zúndər/ (**-ers, -ering, -ered**) *vt.* to lower the amount of money that is being offered to the seller of a property after a price has already been

agreed (*informal*) [Late 20thC. A blend of GAZUMP and UNDER.] —**gazunderer** *n.*

GB *abbr.* **1.** PHYS gilbert **2.** Great Britain

GBE *abbr.* Knight or Dame Grand Cross of the Order of the British Empire

GBH *abbr.* grievous bodily harm

Gbyte *abbr.* COMPUT gigabyte

GC *abbr.* **1.** George Cross **2.** gigacycle

GCB *abbr.* Knight or Dame Grand Cross of the Order of the Bath

GCD *abbr.* greatest common divisor

GCE *n.* an examination for secondary-school pupils in England and Wales at Advanced level (**A level**) and formerly at Ordinary level (**O level**), set and marked by various independent examination boards. At Ordinary level it has been replaced by the GCSE. Full form **General Certificate of Education**

GCF, gcf *abbr.* MATH greatest common factor

GCH *abbr.* gas central heating

GCHQ *abbr.* Government Communications Headquarters

G clef *n.* = **treble clef**

GCMG *abbr.* Grand Cross of the Order of St Michael and St George

GCSE *n.* an examination for 16-year-olds in England and Wales that includes coursework assessment by individual schools as well as examination by independent boards. It was formed from a combination of the General Certificate of Education O level and the Certificate of Secondary Education. Full form **General Certificate of Secondary Education**

GCVO *abbr.* Grand Cross of the Victorian Order

Gd *symbol.* gadolinium

Gdansk /gə dánsk/ city, seaport, and shipbuilding centre in northern Poland. It is situated at the mouth of the River Vistula, on the Baltic Sea. Population: 462,800 (1995). German **Danzig**

g'day /gə dáy/ *interj. Australian* hello or good day (*informal*) [Contraction]

Gdns *abbr.* Gardens (*used in addresses*)

GDP *abbr.* gross domestic product

GDR *abbr.* German Democratic Republic

gds *abbr.* goods

Gdynia /gə dínnyə/ seaport and city on the Gulf of Gdansk, northern Poland, about 16 km/10 mi. northwest of Gdansk. Population: 251,400 (1995).

Ge *symbol.* germanium

ge- *prefix.* = **geo-** (*used before vowels*)

gean /geen/ *n.* a tree native to Europe, West Asia, and North Africa,. from which the sweet cherry was developed. Latin name: *Prunus avium.* [Mid-16thC. From Old French *guine*, of unknown origin.]

geanticline /jee ánti klīn/ *n.* a large region of rock raised up from the earth's surface [Late 19thC. Coined from Greek *gē* 'earth' + ANTICLINE.] —**geanticlinal** /jee ánti klīn'l/ *adj.*

gear /geer/ *n.* **1.** ENG PART THAT TRANSMITS MOTION a toothed mechanical part, e.g. a wheel or cylinder that engages with a similar toothed part to transmit motion from one rotating body to another **2.** ENG DEVICE TO TRANSMIT MOTION a mechanism that transmits motion from one part to another part for performing a specific function ○ *steering gear* **3.** ENG FIXED TRANSMISSION SETTING one of several fixed transmission settings in a vehicle that determine power or direction **4.** LEVEL OF EFFICIENCY the particular speed or efficiency with which sb works (*informal*) ○ *I feel as if I'm still in first gear.* **5.** AUTOMOT ENGAGED STATE the state of a vehicle when one of its gears is engaged ○ *The car won't start when it's in gear.* **6.** MACHINERY a piece or system of machinery with a particular function **7.** EQUIPMENT the equipment that is needed for a specific activity (*informal*) ○ *hiking gear* **8.** FASHION CLOTHES clothes and accessories of a particular kind (*informal*) ○ *You've got to have the right gear.* **9.** NAUT SAILING EQUIPMENT the equipment, rigging, and other objects that belong to a particular boat or sailor **10.** ILLEGAL DRUGS illegal drugs (*slang*) **11.** RIDING HARNESS a horse's harness ■ *vt.* (**gears, gearing, geared**) **1.** ENG

PUT GEARS IN STH to equip sth with gears **2.** AUTOMOT **ENGAGE GEAR** to put a vehicle into gear [13thC. From Old Norse *gervi* 'to make ready'.]

gear to/gear towards *vt.* to adapt or adjust sth so that it fits in or works effectively with sth else (*usually passive*) ○ *We've tried to gear ourselves to the younger market.*

gear up *vti.* to prepare sb or take action in preparation for sth or to do sth (*usually passive or continuous*) ○ *We're all geared up for the next round of talks.*

gearbox /géer boks/ *n.* **1.** CASING ROUND GEARS the protective casing surrounding a set of gears **2.** SET OF GEARS a set of gears and the protective casing that covers it in a vehicle or engine ○ *A horrible clunking noise came from the gearbox.* US term **transmission**

gearing /géering/ *n.* **1.** ENG SET OF GEARS a set of mechanical gears, or the power that it provides ○ *complaints about the gearing on the older model* **2.** ENG PROVIDING STH WITH GEARS the process or act of providing a system with gears **3.** FIN PROPORTION OF CAPITAL AS DEBT the ratio of a company's debt capital to the value of its ordinary shares. US term **leverage**

gear lever *n.* a lever in a car or other vehicle or machine that is used to change or engage gears. US term **gearshift**

gearshift /géer shift/ *n.* US, Can = **gear lever**

gear stick *n.* = **gear lever**

gear train *n.* a collection of gears used to transmit power

gearwheel /géer weel/ *n.* = **gear** *n.* 1

geasa *n.* Ireland an inescapable bond supposedly imposed on sb by supernatural power (*formal*)

Gecko

gecko /gék ō/ (*plural* **-os** *or* **-oes**) *n.* a small tropical or subterranean nocturnal insect-eating lizard with hooked ridges on the pads of its feet that permit it to climb smooth · vertical surfaces. Family: Gekkonidae. [Late 18thC. From Malay dialect *geko(k)*.]

geddit /géddit/ *interj.* do you understand? (*slang*) ○ *We're goin' now, geddit?* [Late 20thC. Fast speech pronunciation of *get it.*]

gee /jee/ (**gees, geeing, geed**) *vt.* to encourage sb to continue doing sth or to do sth faster (*informal*) [Mid-18thC. From *gee*, a command to a horse to move or go faster, of unknown origin.]

gee up *interj.* HURRY UP! used to urge a horse, cow, or similar animal to move faster, to go straight ahead, or to turn right ■ *vt.* HURRY ANIMAL UP to urge a horse, cow, or similar animal to move faster, to go straight ahead, or to turn right

Gee /jee/, **Maurice Gough** (b. 1931) New Zealand novelist. His novels include *Plumb* (1978).

gee-gee *n.* a horse (*informal; usually used by or to children*) [Mid-19thC. Childish repetition of GEE.]

geek /geek/ *n.* US **1.** SB AWKWARD sb who is considered unattractive and socially awkward (*insult*) **2.** ARTS OUTRAGEOUS SIDESHOW PERFORMER a sideshow performer whose act consists of outrageous feats such as biting the heads off live animals **3.** COMPUT OBSESSIVE COMPUTER USER sb who enjoys or takes pride in using computers or other technology, often to what others consider an excessive degree (*informal disapproving*) [Late 19thC. Origin uncertain: perhaps from, ultimately, Low German *gek* 'fool'.] **—geeky** *adj.*

Geelong /ji lóng/ industrial city and seaport in Victoria, southeastern Australia. Population: 125,382 (1996).

geese plural of **goose**

gee whiz *interj.* US = **gee**

gee-whiz *adj.* US causing or characterized by wonderment (*informal*) ○ *a gee-whiz new electronic gadget*

Ge'ez /gée ez/ *n.* an ancient language formerly spoken in Ethiopia and still the liturgical language in the Ethiopian Christian Church [Late 18thC. From Ethiopic.]

geezer /géezər/ *n.* an offensive term for a man past middle age (*informal offensive*) [Late 19thC. Representing a dialect pronunciation of guiser (from GUISE), literally 'sb in disguise', later used to denote an odd-looking person.]

gefilte fish /gə fíltə-/ *n.* a Jewish dish consisting of finely chopped fish mixed with crumbs, eggs, and seasoning and served as balls or cakes. Gefilte fish was originally a dish of finely chopped or minced fish stuffed in a fish's body cavity before boiling or poaching. [Late 19thC. From Yiddish, 'stuffed fish'.]

gegenschein /gáygən shīn/ *n.* a faint elliptical glow in the night sky opposite the setting sun, caused by the reflection of sunlight by dust in space [Late 19thC. From German, literally 'opposite glow'.]

Geiger counter /gígər-/, **Geiger-Müller counter** /-moollər-/ *n.* an instrument used to detect and measure the intensity of ionizing radiation, e.g. particles from a radioactive substance [Early 20thC. Named after the German physicist Hans Geiger (1882–1945), its inventor along with Walter M. Müller.]

geisha /gáyshə/ (*plural* **-sha** *or* **-shas**), **geisha girl** *n.* **1.** JAPANESE HOSTESS a Japanese woman educated to accompany men as a hostess, with skills such as dancing, conversation, and music **2.** JAPANESE PROSTITUTE a Japanese prostitute [Late 19thC. From Japanese *geisha* 'entertainer'.]

gel[1] /jel/ *n.* **1.** CHEM SEMISOLID a semisolid mixture of small particles of a solid in a liquid (**colloid**) **2.** THEATRE LIGHT FILTER a sheet of coloured acetate used in theatre, television, and film lighting to create different lighting effects **3.** HAIR HAIR STYLING CREAM a substance with the consistency of jelly that is used for styling hair ■ *vi.* (**gels, gelling, gelled**) **1.** BECOME GEL to become semisolid, having been in a liquid state **2.** TAKE FORM to take on a definite form (*informal*) ○ *The idea didn't begin to gel until I got home.* **3.** GET ON to get on well together (*informal*) [Late 19thC. Shortening of GELATIN.] **—gelable** *adj.*

gel[2] /jel/ *n.* a girl (*dated; usually associated with the upper classes*) ○ *She's a fine gel!* [Representing a British upper-class pronunciation of GIRL]

gelada /jéllədə/ (*plural* **-das** *or* **-da**), **gelada baboon** *n.* a large baboon with brown hair and a bare red patch on its chest, native to northeastern Africa. Latin name: *Theropithecus gelada.* [Mid-19thC. From Amharic *č'ällada.*]

gelate /jé láyt/ (**-ates, -ating, -ated**) *vi.* to become or form a gel [Early 20thC. Back-formation from GELATION.]

gelati plural of **gelato**

gelatin /jéllətin/, **gelatine** /-teen/ *n.* **1.** SEMISOLID PROTEIN a transparent protein material made from boiling animal hides, bone, and cartilage that forms a firm gel when mixed with water. It is used in foods, medicine, glue, and photography. **2.** SUBSTANCE WITH CONSISTENCY OF JELLY a substance, e.g. agar, that resembles gelatin **3.** FOOD JELLY-LIKE FOOD a sweet food made of flavoured gelatin **4.** THEATRE = **gel** *n.* 2 [Early 19thC. Via French *gélatine* from Italian *gelatina* from, ultimately, Latin *gelata* 'frozen'.]

gelatinize /ji látti nīz/ (**-nizes, -nizing, -nized**), **gelatinise** (**-nises, -nising, -nised**) *v.* **1.** VTI CHANGE TO THE CONSISTENCY OF GELATIN to make sth gelatinous, or become gelatinous **2.** *vt.* PHOTOGRAPHY COAT STH WITH GELATIN to coat a photographic medium with gelatin **—gelatinization** /ji látti nī záysh'n/ *n.* **—gelatinizer** /-nīzər/ *n.*

gelatinous /ji láttinəss/ *adj.* **1.** SEMISOLID having a semisolid form resembling gelatin **2.** RELATING TO GELATIN relating to or containing gelatin **—gelatinously** *adv.* **—gelatinousness** *n.*

gelation[1] /jə láysh'n/ *n.* the solidification of a liquid by freezing [Mid-19thC. From the Latin stem *gelation-*, from *gelare* 'to freeze'.]

gelation[2] /jə láysh'n/ *n.* the process of becoming a gel [Early 20thC. From GEL.]

gelato /jə laátō/ (*plural* **-ti** /-ti/ *or* **-tos**) *n.* an Italian ice cream made from milk, gelatin, sugar, and fruit [Early 20thC. From Italian, literally 'frozen', from, ultimately, Latin *gelare* 'to freeze'.]

geld[1] /geld/ (**gelds, gelding, gelded** *or* **gelt** /gelt/), *vt.* **1.** VET CASTRATE ANIMAL to castrate an animal, especially a horse **2.** REMOVE SB'S STRENGTH to take away the strength or virility of sb or sth [13thC. From Old Norse *gelda*, from *geldr* 'barren'.]

geld[2] /geld/ *n.* a land tax paid by landholders to the crown in late Anglo-Saxon and Norman times [15thC. Via medieval Latin *geldum* from Old English *gield* 'payment'. Ultimately from a prehistoric Germanic word that is also the ancestor of English *yield*.]

gelding /gélding/ *n.* a castrated horse or other animal. ◊ **stallion** [14thC. From GELD[1].]

Geldof /gél dof/, **Bob** (b. 1954) Irish musician and philanthropist. He was the leader of the rock group the Boomtown Rats (1975–86), founded the charity Band Aid for famine relief (1984), and received an honorary knighthood (1986). Full name **Robert Frederick Xenon Geldof**

gelid /jéllid/ *adj.* exceedingly cold (*literary*) [Early 17thC. From Latin *gelidus*, from *gelu* 'frost, intense cold' (source of English *jelly*).] **—gelidity** /je líddəti/ *n.* **—gelidly** /jéllidli/ *adv.*

gelignite /jéllig nīt/ *n.* dynamite consisting of gelled nitroglycerin, potassium nitrate, and wood pulp or guncotton. It is often used under water. [Late 19thC. Coined from GELATIN + Latin *ignis* 'fire'.]

Martha Gellhorn

Gellhorn /géll hawrn/, **Martha** (1908–98) US journalist and novelist. She became a war correspondent in 1937 and reported on the Spanish Civil War (1936–39) and World War II. Her novels include *Stricken Field* (1940) and *Liana* (1948).

gelt past participle, past tense of **geld**

gem /jem/ *n.* **1.** JEWEL a precious stone that has been cut and polished for use as jewellery or decoration **2.** SB OR STH EXCELLENT sb or sth considered to be valuable, useful, or beautiful (*informal*) ○ *Our babysitter is such a gem!* ■ *vt.* (**gems, gemming, gemmed**) DECORATE STH WITH GEMS to decorate sth with gems or with sth resembling gems (*literary; usually passive*) [Pre-12thC. From Latin *gemma* 'bud, jewel'.]

Gemara /gə maárə/ *n.* JUDAISM the second part of the Talmud, forming a set of commentaries on the first part of the Talmud, the Mishnah [Early 17thC. From Aramaic *gĕmārā* 'completion'.]

gemfish /jém fish/ (*plural* **-fishes** *or* **-fish**) *n.* an Australian food fish found in southeastern waters, prized for its delicate flesh. Latin name: *Rexea solandri.*

geminate /jémmi nayt/ *adj.* **geminate, geminated** IN PAIRS growing or arranged in pairs ○ *a geminate leaf* ■ *vti.* (**-nates, -nating, -nated**) DOUBLE to make sth paired, or become paired or doubled [Late 16thC. From Latin *geminat-*, the past participle stem of *geminare*, from *geminus* 'twin'.] **—gemination** /jémmi náysh'n/ *n.*

Gemini /jémmi nī/ *n.* **1.** ASTRON THE TWINS CONSTELLATION a constellation in the northern hemisphere, also known as the Twins or Castor and Pollux, after its two brightest stars **2.** ZODIAC **THIRD ZODIAC SIGN** in astrology, the third sign of the zodiac, falling between Taurus and Cancer, roughly between the dates 21 May and 20 June ■ *n., v.* **Gemini, Geminian** ZODIAC **SB BORN UNDER GEMINI** sb whose birthday falls between 21 May and 20 June [Pre-12thC. From Latin, plural of *geminus* 'twin'.] —**Gemini** *adj.*

gemma /jémmə/ (*plural* **-mae** /-m ee/) *n.* an asexual bud-shaped structure that can detach from the parent plant and form a new individual. Liverworts and mosses produce gemmae. [Late 18thC. From Latin, literally 'bud, jewel'.] —**gemmaceous** /je máyshəss/ *adj.*

gemmate /jémmayt/ *adj.* **REPRODUCING BY GEMMAE** forming gemmae or reproducing by means of gemmae ■ *vi.* (**-mates, -mating, -mated**) **REPRODUCE BY GEMMAE** to form gemmae or reproduce by means of gemmae [Early 17thC. From Latin *gemmat-*, the past participle stem of *gemmare* 'to produce buds', from *gemma* 'bud, jewel'.] —**gemmation** /je máysh'n/ *n.*

gemmiferous /je míffərəs/ *adj.* **1.** GEOL **PRODUCING GEMS** producing precious stones **2.** BIOL **WITH GEMMAE** bearing gemmae

gemmiparous /je míppərəs/ *adj.* = **gemmate** *adj.*

gemmology /je mólləji/, **gemology** *n.* the study of gems and gemstones —**gemmological** /jémmə lójjik'l/ *adj.* —**gemmologist** /je mólləjist/ *n.*

gemmulation /jémmyoŏ láysh'n/ *n.* production of gemmules, or reproduction by means of gemmules

gemmule /jém yool/ *n.* BIOL a reproductive structure produced by asexual reproduction in freshwater and marine sponges

gemology *n.* = **gemmology**

gemot /gi mṓt/, **gemote** *n.* an assembly for judicial or legislative purposes in pre-Norman England [Old English *gemōt*. Formed from *mōt* (see MOOT).]

gemsbok /gémz bok/ (*plural* **-boks** *or* **-bok**) *n.* a large antelope with long straight horns and broad black markings on its head and upper legs, found in southwestern and eastern Africa. Latin name: *Oryx gazella*. [Late 18thC. Via Afrikaans from Dutch, literally 'wild antelope buck'.]

gemstone /jém stōn/ *n.* a mineral or stone suitable for use in jewellery after cutting and polishing

gemütlich *German* /gə mū́tli*kh* kīt/ *adj.* warm and friendly (*literary*) [Mid-19thC. From German, formed from *Gemüt* 'heart, spirit'.]

gemütlichkeit /gə mū́tli*kh* kīt/ *n.* warmth and friendliness (*literary*) [Mid-19thC. From German *Gemütlichkeit*, from *gemütlich* 'GEMUTLICH'.]

gen /jen/ *n.* information (*informal*) [Mid-20thC. Origin uncertain: perhaps a shortening of *general information*.] **gen up** /jén-/ (**gens up, genning up, genned up**) *v.* (*informal*) **1.** *vi.* **FIND INFORMATION** to find out all the information on a subject **2.** *vt.* **GIVE SB INFORMATION** to give sb all the information on a subject (*usually passive*)

gen. *abbr.* **1.** gender **2.** general **3.** GRAM genitive **4.** genus

Gen. *abbr.* **1.** General **2.** BIBLE Genesis

-gen *suffix.* **1.** one that produces ○ *hallucinogen* **2.** one that is produced ○ *cultigen* [Via French *-gène* from Greek *-genēs* 'born'. Ultimately from an Indo-European base meaning 'to beget', which is also the ancestor of English *kin*, *generic*, and *gene*.] —**-genic** *suffix.* —**-genous** *suffix.* —**-geny** *suffix.*

gendarme /zhónd aarm, zhaaNd-/ *n.* **1.** **FRENCH POLICE OFFICER** a police officer in France and French-speaking countries. In France gendarmes are part of the armed forces, their responsibility being that of general law enforcement. **2.** **POLICE OFFICER** a police officer (*slang*) [Mid-16thC. From French, a singular formed from *gens d'armes*, literally 'men of arms'.]

gendarmerie /zhond áarməri, zhaaNd-/ *n.* **1.** **GENDARMES COLLECTIVELY** gendarmes considered as a body **2.** **FRENCH POLICE STATION** in France and French-speaking countries, a police station or police barracks [Mid-16thC. From French, formed from *gendarme* 'GENDARME'.]

gender /jéndər/ *n.* **1.** **SB'S SEX** the sex of a person or organism, or of a whole category of people or organisms (*often used euphemistically to avoid the word 'sex'*) **2.** **FACT OF PEOPLE HAVING DIFFERENT GENDERS** the fact of people having different genders, or of people feeling different or being treated differently because of their gender ○ *Gender is not an issue when we take on new staff.* **3.** LING **CATEGORIZATION OF NOUNS** the classification of nouns and pronouns in certain languages according to the forms taken by adjectives, modifiers, and other grammatical items associated syntactically with them **4.** LING **CATEGORY OF NOUN** any one of the categories, e.g. masculine, feminine, neuter, or common into which nouns and pronouns are divided in languages that have gender [14thC. Via Old French *gendre* from, ultimately, Latin *gener-*, the stem of *genus* 'birth, kind' (source of English *genus*).]

WORD KEY: USAGE

gender or **sex**? Traditionally, ***gender*** has referred to grammatical classifications in languages that have masculine, feminine, and neuter nouns; and ***sex*** has referred to the biological classifications to which gender is analogous. For some time, however, anthropologists have used ***gender*** to distinguish cultural categories from biological ones (*Gender roles are indistinct among the young of this society; the two sexes play together frequently*). Cultural and biological categories are interrelated, of course, and thus at times it can be difficult to decide which word is more appropriate. ***Sex*** is for the most part to be preferred, except where the word may be ambiguous (*When you're looking at CVs, does sex matter to you?*) and in idiomatic expressions such as *gender gap* ('difference between the sexes') and *gender-bending* ('the blurring of distinctions between the sexes').

gender bender *n.* an offensive term for sb who dresses or acts in a way that is intended to blur the traditional distinctions between men and women (*slang offensive*) —**gender bending** *n.*

gendered /jéndərd/ *adj.* relating to or appropriate to one gender rather than the other ○ *gendered clothing*

gender gap *n.* a noticeable difference in behaviour or attitudes between men and women or boys and girls

gender-neutral *adj.* avoiding references to masculinity and femininity and their cultural associations

gene /jeen/ *n.* the basic unit capable of transmitting characteristics from one generation to the next. It consists of a specific sequence of DNA or RNA that occupies a fixed position (**locus**) on a chromosome. [Early 20thC. Via German *Gen* from Greek *genos* 'birth, race'.]

WORD KEY: ORIGIN

The Indo-European ancestor of ***gene*** is also the ultimate source of English *gender, genealogy, generate, generous, genesis, genie, genital, genius, genocide, gingerly, gonorrhoea, indigenous, ingenuous, jaunty, kin, kind, nation*, and *nature*.

-gene *suffix.* = **-gen**

genealogy /jeéni álləji/ (*plural* **-gies**) *n.* **1.** **STUDY OF THE HISTORY OF FAMILIES** the study of the history of families and the line of descent from their ancestors **2.** **FAMILY HISTORY** a pedigree or line of descent that can be traced directly from an ancestor or earlier form, especially that of an individual or family **3.** **FAMILY TREE** a chart or table that shows the line of descent from an ancestor or earlier form, especially that of an individual or family **4.** BIOL **STUDY OF PLANT OR ANIMAL DEVELOPMENT** the study of the line of development of a plant or animal from earlier forms [14thC. Via French *généalogie* from, ultimately, Greek *genealogia*, from *genea* 'race, generation'.] —**genealogical** /jeéni ə lójjik'l/ *adj.* —**genealogically** /-kli/ *adv.* —**genealogist** /jeéni álləjist/ *n.*

gene amplification *n.* the production of many copies of a section of DNA, naturally or by technological means

gene flow *n.* the natural transfer of genes from one population into the genetic make-up of another population through hybridization and interbreeding

gene frequency *n.* the ratio of a specific variation of a gene (**allele**) to the total number of variations in a particular population

gene gun *n.* a device that inserts DNA directly into cells

gene pool *n.* **1.** **ALL GENES OF POPULATION** the total of all genes carried by all individuals in an interbreeding population **2.** **ALL GENES OF SPECIES** the total of all genes existing among all individuals of a species

gene probe *n.* a fragment of DNA or RNA marked by a chemical or radioactive substance that will bind to a given gene, used as a tag in order to identify or isolate that gene

genera plural of **genus**

generable /jénnərəb'l/ *adj.* capable of being generated [15thC. From Latin *generabilis*, from *generare* (see GENERATE).]

general /jénnərəl/ *adj.* **1.** **OVERALL** relating to or including all or nearly all of the members of a category or group, or all or nearly all parts of a whole ○ *a general increase in demand* **2.** **USUAL** applying or happening in most cases ○ *as a general rule* **3.** **WIDESPREAD** shared or participated in by many ○ *a general sense that something ought to be done* **4.** **MISCELLANEOUS** having a varied content or wide scope ○ *a general store* **5.** **NOT SPECIALIZED** not specialized, or lacking specialized knowledge ○ *a book that was intended for the general reader* **6.** **NOT SPECIFIC** not specific, detailed, or clearly defined ○ *She spoke in the most general terms.* **7.** **HIGH-RANKING** with overall authority or of superior rank ○ *a general manager* ■ *n.* **1.** (*plural* **generals** *or* **Generals**) MIL **HIGH MILITARY RANK** a military rank below field marshal and above a lieutenant general, or an officer who holds this rank **2.** MIL = **general officer 3.** MED **GENERAL ANAESTHETIC** a general anaesthetic (*informal*) **4.** **GENERAL HOSPITAL** a general hospital (*informal*) **5.** **PRINCIPLE** a general principle or fact (*archaic; usually plural*) **6.** **THE PUBLIC** the public as a whole (*archaic*) [12thC. Via French from Latin *generalis* 'of the whole class', from, ultimately, *genus* 'race, kind' (source of English *genus*).] —**generalness** *n.* ◇ **in general 1.** as a whole **2.** in most cases or circumstances

WORD KEY: CULTURAL NOTE

The General, a film by US director Buster Keaton (1926). Regarded as one of the greatest silent comedies, it is set during the American Civil War and based on a historical incident: the hijack of a Confederate train by Union soldiers. Keaton plays railroad man Johnnie Gray, whose attempts to recapture the train involve superb visual gags, gripping drama, and brilliantly timed stunts.

general anaesthetic *n.* an anaesthetic that produces loss of sensation in the whole body together with unconsciousness

general assembly, **General Assembly** *n.* **1.** **HIGHEST CHURCH LEGISLATIVE BODY** the highest governing body of various Presbyterian churches, especially the Church of Scotland, or the meeting of such a body **2.** INTERNAT REL **UN ASSEMBLY** the assembly of the United Nations **3.** *NZ* POL **NEW ZEALAND PARLIAMENT** the parliament of New Zealand

general average *n.* liability for loss or damage to an insured ship or its cargo that is shared among all those with an interest in the venture

General Certificate of Education *n.* full form of **GCE**

General Certificate of Secondary Education *n.* full form of **GCSE**

generalcy /jénnərəlsi, jénnrəlsi/ *n.* the office of general, or the period during which this office is held

general delivery *n. US* **1.** MAIL = **poste restante** *n.* 1 **2.** = **poste restante** *n.* 2

general election *n.* an election in which the citizens of a country or state vote to elect representatives of all constituencies to a legislative body, e.g. the Houses of Parliament

General Headquarters *n.* MIL full form of **GHQ**

general hospital *n.* a hospital that does not specialize in any one particular kind of medicine

generalisation *n.* = **generalization**

generalise *vti.* = **generalize**

generalissimo /jénnərə líssimō/ (*plural* **-mos**) *n.* in some countries, the supreme commander of a combined military force consisting of the air force, navy, and army [Early 17thC. From Italian, literally 'great general', from, ultimately, Latin *generalis* (see GENERAL).]

generalist /jénnərəlist/ *n.* sb who has knowledge, skills, or interests in a variety of fields but no specialist knowledge in any one field

generality /jénnə rálləti/ (*plural* **-ties**) *n.* **1.** STATE OF BEING GENERAL the quality or state of being general **2.** GENERAL STATEMENT a statement or remark that concerns the main aspects of sth rather than the details **3.** GENERAL PRINCIPLE a statement or principle that is true or applies in most cases **4.** UNIMPORTANT REMARK a remark about sth that is not important in itself but is useful to open or keep up a conversation **5.** MAJORITY the majority (*archaic*)

generalization /jénnərə lī záysh'n/, **generalisation** *n.* **1.** GENERAL STATEMENT a statement or conclusion that is derived from and applies equally to a number of cases ○ *not enough data to permit a generalization* **2.** SWEEPING STATEMENT a statement presented as a general truth but based on limited or incomplete evidence **3.** MAKING OF GENERALIZATIONS the making of general or sweeping statements **4.** LOGIC INFERENCE FROM INSTANCE the application of the rules of inference that go from an instance to a universal or to an existential statement **5.** PSYCHOL USE OF LEARNED RESPONSE the act of responding to a new stimulus in a similar way as to a conditioned stimulus

generalize /jénnərə līz/ (**-izes, -izing, -ized**), **generalise** (**-ises, -ising, -ised**) *v.* **1.** *vti.* EXPRESS STH GENERAL to express sth general on the basis of particulars **2.** *vi.* MAKE SWEEPING STATEMENT to state a supposed general truth about sth on the basis of limited or incomplete evidence **3.** *vti.* GIVE WIDER USE TO to use sth or be used in a wider or different range of circumstances **4.** *vt.* MAKE GENERALLY KNOWN to bring sth into general use or to general knowledge (*usually passive*) **5.** *vi.* MED SPREAD to spread to other parts of the body **6.** *vti.* LOGIC MAKE INFERENCE to infer a general conclusion from particulars, or a universal statement from an instance —**generalizable** *adj.*

generally /jénnərəli/ *adv.* **1.** USUALLY in most cases or circumstances **2.** AS A WHOLE as a whole or without exception ○ *not meant for the public generally* **3.** VAGUELY without being specific, detailed, or clearly defined ○ *spoke generally about his life* **4.** WIDESPREAD so as to be widespread

general meeting *n.* a meeting to which all members of a group or organization are invited

general officer *n.* an officer of the army, navy, or air force who ranks above a colonel

general paralysis of the insane full form of **GPI**

general practice *n.* the work of a doctor who treats patients' general medical problems, referring them to hospitals for more specialized care

general practitioner *n.* full form of **GP**

general purpose *adj.* useful for a wide variety of purposes

general relativity *n.* PHYS = **relativity** *n.* 2

generalship /jénnərəl ship/ *n.* **1.** MIL MILITARY COMMAND the art or practice of exercising military leadership in a war **2.** MIL GENERAL'S RANK the rank or period of tenure of a general **3.** LEADERSHIP skilful leadership or management of people or an organization

general staff *n.* a group of military officers whose job is to assist senior officers in the planning and coordination of military operations

general studies *n.* a course of study at school or university that covers a broad range of general topics rather than specializing in one specific area

general theory of relativity *n.* = **relativity** *n.* 2

generate /jénnə rayt/ (**-ates, -ating, -ated**) *vt.* **1.** CREATE to bring sth into existence or effect ○ *measures to generate more income* **2.** PRODUCE ELECTRICITY to produce electricity from a power station or generator **3.** ENERGY PRODUCE ENERGY to produce or originate a form of energy through a chemical or physical process **4.** MATH, LING PRODUCE SET to produce a set or sequence by the application of defined rules or the performance of defined operations **5.** GEOM PRODUCE FORM to create a curve with a moving point or a surface with a moving curve [Early 16thC. From Latin *generat-*, the past participle stem of *generare* 'to beget', from, ultimately, *genus* 'race, birth'.]

generation /jénnə ráysh'n/ *n.* **1.** GROUP OF CONTEMPORARIES all of the people who were born at approximately the same time, considered as a group, and especially when considered as having shared interests and attitudes ○ *a generation that grew up with rationing* **2.** STAGE IN DESCENT a single stage in the descent of a family or a group of people or animals or plants, or the individuals belonging to the same stage ○ *three generations down the line* **3.** TIME TAKEN TO PRODUCE NEW GENERATION the period of time that it takes for people, animals or plants to grow up and produce their own offspring, in humans held to be between 30 and 35 years ○ *after three generations of war and conflict* **4.** SPECIFIC GENERATION a specified numbered stage in the sequence of generations born or living in a country into which a family came as immigrants (*usually used in combination*) ○ *first-generation immigrants* **5.** TECH NEW TYPE a particular stage in the development of a product or technology, especially one marking a significant advance ○ *one of the new generation of computers* **6.** BIOL PHASE IN LIFE CYCLE one of the successive phases that make up the life cycle of certain organisms ○ *the gametophyte generation* **7.** ENERGY PRODUCTION OF POWER the production of electricity, heat, or some other form of energy **8.** BIOL PRODUCTION OF YOUNG the act or process of bringing offspring into being **9.** MATH, GEOM GENERATING OF GROUP OR SHAPE the act or process of generating a set, sequence, curve, or surface **10.** PHYS NUCLEI IN CHAIN REACTION in a chain reaction, a group of nuclei that come from a previous group —**generational** *adj.*

generation gap *n.* the difference in attitudes, behaviour, and interests between people of different generations, especially between parents and their children

generation X, **Generation X** *n.* the generation of people born roughly during the years 1965 to 1980 in Western countries, especially the United States, often regarded as disillusioned, cynical, or apathetic [From the novel by Douglas Coupland, *Generation X: Tales for an Accelerated Culture*] —**generation Xer** *n.*

generation Y, **Generation Y** *n.* *US* the generation of people born approximately in or after 1980 in Western countries, especially the United States (*informal*) [From GENERATION X]

generative /jénnərətiv/ *adj.* **1.** BIOL RELATING TO REPRODUCTION relating to the production of young **2.** WITH PRODUCTIVE CAPABILITY involving the ability to produce or originate sth ○ *generative linguistic theory* —**generatively** *adv.* —**generativeness** *n.*

generative cell *n.* BIOL = **gamete**

generative grammar *n.* the rules from which all the grammatical sentences, and only the grammatical sentences, of a language can be generated

generator /jénnə raytər/ *n.* **1.** ELEC ENG DEVICE FOR PRODUCING ELECTRICITY a machine or device that is used to convert mechanical energy, e.g. that provided by the combustion of fuel, into electricity **2.** CHEM DEVICE FOR PRODUCING GAS a device in which a gas is formed **3.** ORIGINATOR sb or sth responsible for generating sth such as an idea, plan, or strategy

generatrix /jénnə raytriks/ (*plural* **-trices** /-tri seez/) *n.* an element such as a point or line that is used in the production of a geometric figure such as a curve or surface

generic /jə nérrik/ *adj.* **1.** SUITABLE FOR A BROAD RANGE usable or suitable in a variety of contexts ○ *generic software that can run on a variety of machines* **2.** BIOL OF A GENUS relating to or characteristic of a genus **3.** PHARM WITH GENERAL NAME used to describe a pharmaceutical product that does not have a brand name or trademark [Late 17thC. Via French *générique* from, ultimately, Latin *genus* 'race, kind'.] —**generically** *adv.*

generosity /jénnə róssəti/ (*plural* **-ties**) *n.* **1.** KINDNESS willingness to give money, help, or time freely **2.** NOBILITY nobility of character **3.** SUBSTANTIAL SIZE pleasingly large size or quantity ○ *He ate everything, despite the generosity of the portions.* **4.** GENEROUS ACT a generous, kind, or noble act [15thC. From Latin *generositas*, from *generosus* (see GENEROUS).]

generous /jénnərəss/ *adj.* **1.** KIND having or showing a willingness to give money, help, or time freely ○ *a very generous offer* **2.** NOBLE having or showing nobility of character ○ *a generous gesture of forgiveness* **3.** SUBSTANTIAL pleasingly large in size or quantity ○ *a generous slice of cake* **4.** WINE FULL-FLAVOURED used to describe wine that is rich and full-flavoured [Late 16thC. Via French *généreux* from Latin *generosus* 'of noble birth', from, ultimately, *genus* 'race, birth'.] —**generously** *adv.* —**generousness** *n.*

WORD KEY: SYNONYMS

generous, magnanimous, munificent, bountiful, liberal

CORE MEANING: giving readily to others

generous used of sb to suggest a warm-hearted desire to give and to help others. It is also used of sth given, when the thing or amount given is considerably more than might have been anticipated; **magnanimous** a formal word suggesting more a general generosity of mind and spirit than a desire to give generously to an individual. It is sometimes used to suggest paternalism or a tendency to patronize or condescend; **munificent** more formal than 'magnanimous' and used both of sb giving and sth given, to indicate generosity on a very grand scale, often indicating great wealth on the part of the giver; **bountiful** a formal and literary word, not commonly used in modern English. It describes sb who is exceptionally generous, particularly to less fortunate people; **liberal** used to describe sb who is exceptionally generous. It can be used of sth given to indicate that it is substantial and freely given.

Genesee /jénnə sée/ river in the northeastern United States, rising in Pennsylvania and flowing northwards past Rochester, New York, before emptying into Lake Ontario. Length: 232 km/144 mi.

gene sequence *n.* the order of nucleotides in a gene

gene sequencing, **genetic sequencing** *n.* the process of determining the individual arrangement of nucleotides that compose a given gene, used especially in studying genetic changes in a virus

genesis /jénnəssiss/ (*plural* **-ses** /-seez/) *n.* the time or circumstances of sth's coming into being ○ *the genesis of this new project* [Early 17thC. From GENESIS.]

Genesis *n.* the first book of the Bible, in which the story of the creation of the world is told [Pre-12thC. Via Latin from Greek.]

-genesis *suffix.* production, origin ○ *sporogenesis* [Via Latin from Greek, 'birth' (see GENESIS)]

gene-splicing *n.* a technique in which segments of DNA or RNA, often from different organisms, are combined, in order to be introduced into an organism

genet[1] /jénnit/ *n.* **1.** ZOOL SMALL CARNIVORE a small carnivorous mammal related to the civet that inhabits wooded regions of southern Europe and Africa and has a ringed tail, spotted sides, and retractable claws. Genus: *Genetta.* **2.** GENET FUR the fur of the genet [14thC. From Old French *genette*, of uncertain origin: probably from Arabic *jarnait.*]

genet[2] *n.* = **jennet**

gene therapy *n.* the treatment of a genetic disease through the insertion of normal or genetically altered genes into cells in order to replace or make up for the nonfunctional or missing genes

genetic /jə néttik/, **genetical** /-tik'l/ *adj.* involving, resulting from, or relating to genes or genetics [Mid-19thC. From GENESIS, modelled on words such as *antithesis, antithetic.*] —**genetically** *adv.*

genetically modified *adj.* used to describe an organism that has received genetic material from another, resulting in a permanent change in one or more of its characteristics

genetically modified organism *n.* a plant, animal, or microorganism produced by genetic engineering (*usually plural*)

genetic code *n.* the specific order of the nucleotide sequences in DNA or RNA that form the basis of heredity through their role in protein synthesis

genetic counselling *n.* counselling that concerns the risks, treatments, and management of inherited genetic disorders for people with some likelihood of being affected by them, either personally or as parents —**genetic counsellor** *n.*

genetic drift *n.* the random changes that occur in the gene frequency of small, isolated populations, resulting in the loss or preservation of certain genes over the generations

genetic engineering *n.* = **genetic modification** —**genetic engineer** *n.*

genetic fingerprint *n.* a DNA sequence taken from a region of a chromosome that is known to be highly variable, used as an accurate means of identifying an individual

genetic fingerprinting *n.* the analysis and use of DNA patterns from body tissues such as blood, saliva, or semen in order to establish sb's identity

geneticist /jə néttissist/ *n.* sb who studies or is an expert in genetics

genetic load *n.* the average number of unfavourable recessive mutations per individual in a population

genetic manipulation *n.* = **genetic modification**

genetic map *n.* a graphic representation of the specific arrangement of genes on a chromosome

genetic mapping *n.* the technique or process of identifying genes on a chromosome

genetic marker *n.* a known, usually dominant, gene that is used to identify specific genes, chromosomes, and traits known to be associated with that gene

genetic modification *n.* the alteration and recombination of genetic material by technological means, with applications in treating disease, enhancing desired plant and animal characteristics, and manufacturing biological products such as insulin

genetics /jə néttiks/ *n.* **1. STUDY OF HEREDITY** a branch of biology dealing with heredity and genetic variations (*takes a singular verb*) **2. ORGANISM'S GENETIC MAKE-UP** the genetic make-up of an organism or group of organisms (*takes a singular or plural verb*)

gene transfer *n.* the insertion of genetic material from one organism into another in a laboratory procedure, to produce a specific effect, e.g. resistance to disease

genetrix /jénnə triks/ (*plural* **-rices** /-tri seez/) *n.* ANTHROP a biological mother (*technical*) ◊ **genitor** [15thC. Via Old French *genetris* or directly from Latin *genetrix*, from *gignere* 'to beget'.]

geneva *n.* = **genever**

Geneva /jə neévə/ city in western Switzerland, capital of Geneva Canton, situated at the western end of Lake Geneva. It is the headquarters of many international organizations, including the International Red Cross and The World Health Organization. Population: 174,363 (1994). French **Genève**

Geneva, Lake the largest lake in central Europe. It straddles the border between Switzerland and the Haut-Savoie Department in southeastern France. Area: 583 sq. km/225 sq. mi.

Genevan /jə neévən/ *n.* PEOPLES **SB FROM GENEVA** sb who lives in or who was born or brought up in Geneva ■ *adj.* **1.** PEOPLES **OF GENEVA** relating to or typical of the city of Geneva, Switzerland or its inhabitants or culture **2. Genevan, Genevese** RELIG **OF CALVINISM** relating to the teachings of Protestant reformer John Calvin or to Calvinism

genever /jə neévər/, **geneva** *literary n.* a type of Dutch gin [Early 18thC. Via Dutch *genever* from Old French *genevre* from, ultimately, Latin *juniperus* 'juniper'.]

Genevese /jénnə veéz/ *npl.* **PEOPLE OF GENEVA** the people of Geneva ■ *adj.* = **Genevan**

genial /jeéni əl/ *adj.* **1. KIND** having a kind and good-natured disposition or manner **2. MILD** pleasantly mild and warm so as to be conducive to life and growth ○ *a genial climate* [Mid-16thC. From Latin *genialis* 'nuptial', from *genius* (see GENIUS).] —**geniality** /jeéni álləti/ *n.* —**genially** /jeéni əli/ *adv.* —**genialness** /-nəss/ *n.*

genic /jénnik/ *adj.* relating to or produced by a gene or genes —**genically** *adv.*

geniculate /jə níkyŏŏlət/ *adj.* **1. BENT LIKE A KNEE** bent at an angle like a knee ○ *geniculate antennae* **2. WITH JOINT THAT BENDS** with a joint or joints that can be bent like a knee [Early 17thC. From Latin *geniculatus* 'knotted', from, ultimately, *genu* 'knee'.] —**geniculately** *adv.* —**geniculation** /jə níkyŏŏ láysh'n/ *n.*

genie /jeéni/ (*plural* **-nies** *or* **-nii** /-ni ī/) *n.* a magical spirit in Arabian folklore that has supernatural powers and will obey the commands of the person who summons it. ◊ **jinni** [Mid-17thC. Via French *génie* from Latin *genius* (see GENIUS).]

genii[1] plural of **genius**

genii[2] plural of **genie**

genipap /jénni pap/ *n.* **1.** TREES **TROPICAL EVERGREEN TREE** a tropical American evergreen tree of the madder family that has an edible fruit. Latin name: *Genipa americana.* **2.** FOOD **FRUIT OF THE GENIPAP** the edible reddish-brown fruit of the genipap tree, resembling an orange and used in preserves and drinks [Early 17thC. Via Portuguese *jenipapo* from Tupi *ianipaba*.]

genital /jénnit'l/ *adj.* relating to the external sexual organs or to reproduction [14thC. Directly or via French from Latin *genitalis*, from, ultimately, *gignere* 'to beget'.] —**genitally** *adv.*

genital herpes *n.* a sexually transmitted disease caused by the herpes simplex virus and affecting the genital and anal regions with painful blisters

genitals /jénnit'lz/, **genitalia** /-táyli ə/ *npl.* the reproductive organs, especially the external sex organs

genital wart *n.* a wart of the genital or anal area caused by a sexually transmitted virus

genitive /jénnətiv/ *n.* **1. POSSESSIVE GRAMMATICAL CASE** a grammatical case in some languages that affects nouns, pronouns, and adjectives and that usually indicates possession **2. INSTANCE OF GENITIVE** a word, phrase, or form in the genitive ■ *adj.* **OF THE GENITIVE** belonging or relating to the genitive [14thC. Directly or via French *génitif* from Latin *genitivus*, from, ultimately, *gignere* 'to beget'.]

genitor /jénnitər/ *n.* ANTHROP a natural or biological father (*technical*) ◊ **genetrix** [15thC. Directly or via French *géniteur* from Latin *genitor*, from, ultimately, *gignere* 'to beget'.]

genitourinary /jénnitō yŏŏrinəri/ *adj.* relating to or affecting the genital and urinary organs

geniture /jénnichər/ *n.* sb's birth (*literary or archaic*) [Mid-16thC. Directly or via French from Latin *genitura*, from *gignere* 'to beget'.]

genius /jeéni əss/ *n.* **1. SB WITH OUTSTANDING TALENT** sb with exceptional ability, especially sb whose intellectual or creative achievements gain worldwide recognition **2. OUTSTANDING TALENT** exceptional talent of a particular kind **3. SB WITH PARTICULAR SKILL** sb who has a particular skill ○ *a genius with computers* **4.** (*plural* **genii**) **QUALITY** a special quality that characterizes a place, period, or people **5.** (*plural* **genii**) **GUARDIAN SPIRIT** in Roman mythology, a guardian spirit of a person, place, or institution **6.** (*plural* **genii**) **DEMON** a demon or supernatural being **7. INFLUENCE** a strong influence, or sb who exerts a strong influence ○ *an evil genius* [14thC. From Latin, 'guardian spirit', from *gignere* 'to beget'.]

WORD KEY: SYNONYMS

See Synonyms at ***talent***.

genius loci /-lō sī/ *n.* **1. CHARACTERISTIC ATMOSPHERE OF A PLACE** the atmosphere that characterizes a place **2. GUARDIAN OF A PLACE** the guardian spirit of a place [From Latin, literally 'spirit of the place']

genizah /ge neézə/ (*plural* **-zoth**) *n.* a repository for Hebrew documents and sacred books that are no longer in use, e.g. because they are old and worn, but must not be destroyed [Late 19thC. From Hebrew, literally 'hiding place', from *gānaz* 'hide'.]

genned-up /jénd-/ *adj.* having acquired the necessary knowledge or information about sb or sth (*informal*)

genoa /jénnō ə, jə nő ə/, **genoa jib** *n.* a particularly large triangular front sail on a sailing boat, especially a racing yacht [Mid-20thC. Named after GENOA.]

Genoa /jénnō ə/, **Genova** /-və/ seaport and industrial city on the Gulf of Genoa, northwestern Italy, the capital of Genoa Province, Liguria Region. Population: 659,754 (1993). —**Genoese** /jénnō eéz/ *n., adj.*

genocide /jénnə sīd/ *n.* the systematic killing of all the people from a national, ethnic, or religious group, or an attempt to do this [Mid-20thC. Coined from Greek *genos* 'race' + -CIDE.] —**genocidal** /jénnə sīd'l/ *adj.* —**genocidally** /-sīd'li/ *adv.*

genome /jeén ōm/ *n.* the full complement of genetic information that an individual organism inherits from its parents, especially the set of chromosomes and the genes they carry [Mid-20thC. Coined from Greek *genos* 'offspring, race' + CHROMOSOME.] —**genomic** /ji nőmik/ *adj.*

genomics /ji nőmiks/ *n.* the study of the relationships between gene structure and biological function in organisms (*takes a singular verb*)

genotype /jénnə tīp/ *n.* **1. GENETIC MAKE-UP** the genetic makeup of an organism, as opposed to its physical characteristics **(phenotype) 2. GENETIC GROUP** a group of organisms that share a similar genetic make-up [Early 20thC. From German *Genotypus*, from Greek *genos* 'offspring, race' + Latin *typus* (see TYPE).] —**genotypic** /jénnə típpik/ *adj.* —**genotypically** /-típpikli/ *adv.*

-genous *suffix.* a suffix that forms adjectives from nouns ending in -gen and -geny

genre /zhónrə, zhóNrə/ *n.* **1. CATEGORY OF ARTISTIC WORKS** one of the categories that artistic works of all kinds can be divided into on the basis of form, style, or subject matter. For example, detective novels are a genre of fiction. **2.** PAINTING **PAINTINGS OF HOUSEHOLD SCENES** a type of painting depicting household scenes [Early 19thC. Via French, 'type', from, ultimately, Latin *genus* (see GENDER).]

WORD KEY: SYNONYMS

See Synonyms at ***type***.

genro /gén rő/ (*plural* **-ro**) *n.* **1. JAPANESE EMPEROR'S ADVISERS** in Japan in the 19th and early 20th centuries, a group of elder statesmen who advised the emperor (*takes a singular or plural verb*) **2. MEMBER OF THE GENRO** a member of the genro advising the Japanese emperor [Late 19thC. From Japanese, literally 'first elders'.]

gens /jenz/ (*plural* **gentes** /jén teez/) *n.* **1. ROMAN CLAN** in ancient Rome, a group of aristocratic families with the same name, descended from a common ancestor on the male side (*takes a singular or plural verb*) **2.** ANTHROP **CLAN** a clan, especially one that traces its descent on the male side (*dated*) [Mid-19thC. From Latin, 'race, clan'.]

gent /jent/ *n.* a gentleman (*dated informal*) ◊ **gents**

gentamicin /jéntə mīssin/ *n.* an antibiotic used to treat many infections and usually administered by injection. It can cause serious side effects. [Mid-20thC. From *genta-*, of uncertain origin, perhaps from GENTIAN VIOLET, + an alteration of -MYCIN.]

genteel /jen teél/ *adj.* **1. WELL-MANNERED** having or displaying refinement and good manners, especially manners that suggest, or are thought typical of, an upper-class background **2. PRETENTIOUS** overdoing the refinement, delicacy of behaviour, or snobbishness thought typical of the upper classes in order to create an impression of higher social status [Late 16thC. From French *gentil* (see GENTLE).] —**genteelly** *adv.* —**genteelness** *n.*

genteelism /jen teélizəm/ *n.* a word or phrase used in place of another one considered vulgar

gentes plural of **gens**

gentian /jénsh'n/ *n.* **1. SHOWY FLOWERING PLANT** a plant with bright blue, yellow, white, or red trumpet-shaped flowers that belongs to either of two genera, one alpine and arctic, the other temperate. Genera: *Gentiana* and *Gentianella.* **2. ROOT OF THE GENTIAN** the dried roots and rhizome of a yellow-flowered gentian, used as a digestive stimulant in herbal medicine [14thC. From Latin *gentiana*, named after *Gentius*, the 2ndC BC king of Illyria.]

gentian blue *adj.* of a purplish-blue colour —**gentian blue** *n.*

gentian violet *n.* a green dye derived from rosaniline that forms a violet solution in water and is used as a biological stain. It was formerly used in antiseptic lotions.

gentile /jént īl/ *n.* **1.** NON-JEWISH PERSON sb who is not Jewish **2.** SB CHRISTIAN sb who is Christian, as distinguished from sb who is Jewish **3.** NON-MORMON in the Church of Latter Day Saints, sb who is not Mormon **4.** HEATHEN sb who does not believe in God (*disapproving*) ■ *adj.* **1.** NOT JEWISH not belonging to the Jewish people or faith **2.** CHRISTIAN Christian, as distinguished from Jewish **3.** GRAM DENOTING PLACE OR PEOPLE used to describe a noun such as 'Welsh' or 'Texan' that gives the name of a place or a people [14thC. From Latin *gentilis*, literally 'of the same clan' (see GENTILE). The meaning 'non-Jewish' evolved from its use in translations of biblical Hebrew *goy* '(non-Jewish) nation'.]

gentility /jen tílləti/ *n.* **1.** REFINEMENT courteous and well-mannered behaviour, especially when it suggests an upper-class background **2.** UPPER-CLASS STATUS the status or way of life of sb from the upper classes **3.** PRETENTIOUSNESS exaggeratedly refined, delicate, or snobbish behaviour, affected in order to create an impression of higher social status **4.** MEMBERS OF THE UPPER CLASS people from the upper classes (*takes a singular or plural verb*) [From French *gentilité*, from *gentil* (see GENTILE)]

gentle /jént'l/ *adj.* (**-tler, -tlest**) **1.** KIND having a mild and kind nature or manner **2.** MILD OR MODERATE being moderate in force or degree so that the effects are not severe ○ *a gentle reprimand* **3.** USING LITTLE FORCE using little force or violence ○ *a gentle tap on the shoulder* **4.** NOT STEEP not very steep ○ *a gentle slope* **5.** CHIVALROUS having a gracious and honourable manner (*archaic*) **6.** UPPER-CLASS relating to or having a high social status or class ■ *vt.* (**-tles, -tling, -tled**) **1.** SOOTHE SB to cause sb to become less agitated by means of words or actions (*literary*) **2.** TAME AN ANIMAL to calm an animal and make it domesticated (*formal*) **3.** RAISE TO THE NOBILITY to raise sb to the nobility (*archaic*) ■ *n.* SB FROM UPPER CLASS sb of high social class (*archaic*) [Pre-12thC. Via French *gentil* 'well-born' from Latin *gentilis*, literally 'of the same clan', from *gens* (see GENS). The underlying sense is of befitting a well-bred person.] —**gentleness** *n.*

gentle breeze *n.* a wind with a speed of between 13 and 19 km/8 and 12 mi. per hour

gentlefolk /jént'l fōk/, **gentlefolks** *npl.* upper class people (*archaic*)

gentleman /jént'lmən/ (*plural* **-men** /-mən/) *n.* **1.** POLITE AND CULTURED MAN a cultured man who behaves with courtesy and thoughtfulness **2.** MAN used as a polite term to refer to a man, regardless of social position or behaviour ○ *Good morning, ladies and gentlemen.* **3.** UPPER-CLASS MAN a man from a high social class, especially a man with an independent income **4.** HIST MAN WITH A COAT OF ARMS in English history, a man who was not strictly of noble birth but was entitled to a coat of arms. He ranked above a yeoman in the social order. **5.** SMUGGLER a smuggler (*archaic*) —**gentlemanliness** *n.* —**gentlemanly** *adj.*

gentleman-at-arms *n.* a member of a troop of forty men who act as a ceremonial guard for the British sovereign on state occasions

gentleman-farmer *n.* **1.** FARMER WITH INDEPENDENT MEANS a farmer with an independent source of income who farms for pleasure rather than for money **2.** FARM OWNER a man who owns a farm but employs a manager and staff to work it

gentleman's agreement, **gentlemen's agreement** *n.* an agreement based on trust, not written down, and not enforceable by law

gentleman's gentleman *n.* the manservant of an upper-class man (*dated*)

gentlewoman /jént'l woomən/ (*plural* **-en** /-wimin/) *n.* **1.** POLITE AND CULTURED WOMAN a polite and cultured woman who behaves with courtesy and thoughtfulness **2.** UPPER-CLASS WOMAN a woman from a high social class, especially a woman with an independent income **3.** HIST LADY'S PERSONAL ATTENDANT a woman acting as a personal attendant to a lady of high social rank

gently /jéntli/ *adv.* **1.** SOFTLY softly, using little pressure ○ *touched him gently on the shoulder* **2.** MILDLY mildly or moderately ○ *gently falling rain* **3.** NOT STEEPLY not steeply or sharply ○ *a gently sloping gradient*

gentrification /jéntrifi káysh'n/ *n.* the transformation that takes place when middle-class people move into a working-class area and impose their own tastes, usually banishing local character and making property unaffordable for locals (*disapproving*)

gentrify /jéntri fī/ (**-fies, -fying, -fied**) *vt.* to transform a traditionally working-class area into a middle-class neighbourhood, usually at the expense of local character and with the result that property becomes unaffordable for local people —**gentrification** /jéntrifi káysh'n/ *n.*

gentry /jéntri/ *n.* **1.** THE UPPER CLASSES the group of people who make up the upper social classes (*takes a singular or plural verb*) **2.** ENGLISH SOCIAL CLASS the English social class that ranks just below the aristocracy and consists of families who are not of noble birth but are entitled to have a coat of arms (*takes a singular or plural verb*) **3.** PEOPLE people of a particular kind [14thC. From Old French *genterie* 'nobility', from *gentil* (see GENTILE).]

gents /jents/ *n.* a public toilet for men. US term **men's room**

genuflect /jénnyoo flekt/ (**-flects, -flecting, -flected**) *vi.* **1.** KNEEL to bend the right knee to the floor and rise again as a gesture of religious respect, particularly in a Roman Catholic or Anglican church **2.** SHOW EXCESSIVE RESPECT to show undeserved or unnecessarily deferential respect for sb or sth [Mid-19thC. From ecclesiastical Latin *genuflectere*, literally 'to bend the knee', from *genu* 'knee' + *flectere* 'to bend'.] —**genuflection** /jénnyoo fléksh'n/ *n.* —**genuflector** /jénnyoo flektər/ *n.*

genuine /jénnyoo in/ *adj.* **1.** REAL, NOT ARTIFICIAL having the qualities or value claimed ○ *a genuine Cézanne* **2.** SINCERELY FELT not affected or pretended ○ *a look of genuine surprise* **3.** CANDID honest and open in relationships with others ○ *a very genuine person* **4.** OF UNMIXED BREEDING being of unmixed breeding ○ *of genuine stock* [Late 16thC. From Latin *genuinus*, of uncertain origin: perhaps an alteration of *ingenuus* 'native'.] —**genuinely** *adv.* —**genuineness** *n.*

genus /jéenəs, jénn-/ (*plural* **genera** /jénnərə/) *n.* **1.** SET OF CLOSELY RELATED SPECIES a category in the taxonomic classification of related organisms, comprising one or more species. Similar genera are grouped into families. **2.** LOGIC BROADER TERM FOR STH the more general class or kind in which sth is included, e.g. the species 'dog' is included in the genus 'animal' **3.** GROUP a class or group of any kind [Mid-16thC. From Latin, 'birth, race, kind' (source of English *general*).]

geo- *prefix.* **1.** earth, soil ○ *geomagnetic* ○ *geophyte* **2.** geography, global ○ *geostrategy* [From Greek *gē* 'earth' (source of English *geode* and *apogee*)]

geobotany /jēe ō bóttəni/ *n.* = phytogeography —**geobotanical** /jēe ō bə tánnik'l/ *adj.* —**geobotanist** /-bóttənist/ *n.*

geocentric /jēe ō séntrik/ *adj.* **1.** HAVING EARTH AT ITS CENTRE used to describe the solar system when it is regarded as having the Earth as its centre **2.** CONSIDERED FROM EARTH'S CENTRE measured from, or considered as if viewed from, the centre of the Earth **3.** WITH EARTH AS THE CENTRE OF FOCUS having the Earth and its inhabitants as the centre of a theory or belief —**geocentrically** *adv.*

geochemistry /jēe ō kémmistri/ *n.* the study of the chemical composition of the Earth's solid matter, as well as the solid matter of other planets, meteors, and asteroids —**geochemical** /jēe ō kémmik'l/ *adj.* —**geochemically** /-kémmikli/ *adv.* —**geochemist** /-kémmist/ *n.*

geochronology /jēe ō krə nólləji/ *n.* the study of the ages and relative ages of geological events and rock formations —**geochronological** /jēe ō krónnə lójjik'l/ *adj.* —**geochronologically** /-lójjikli/ *adv.* —**geochronologist** /-krə nólləjist/ *n.*

geochronometry /jēe ō krə nómmətri/ *n.* the measurement of the age of a rock, mineral, or sequence of rocks, or of an event such as a volcanic eruption —**geochronometric** /jēe ō krónnə méttrik/ *adj.*

geocorona /jēe ō kə rốnə/ *n.* the outermost region of the Earth's atmosphere reaching to approximately

15 Earth radii in height and consisting mainly of hydrogen

geode /jēe ōd/ *n.* **1.** HOLLOW ROCK WITH CRYSTALS a roughly spherical rock mass containing a cavity lined or filled with crystals that have grown unimpeded and so are frequently perfectly formed **2.** CAVITY IN HOLLOW ROCK the crystal-lined cavity within a geode [Late 17thC. Via Latin *geodes* from Greek *geōdēs* 'earthy', from *gē* 'earth'.]

geodesic /jēe ō déessik/ *adj.* **1.** GEOM RELATING TO THE GEOMETRY OF CURVES relating to the geometry of curved surfaces **2.** GEOL = geodetic ■ *n.* GEOM SHORTEST LINE the shortest line between two points on a curved or flat surface

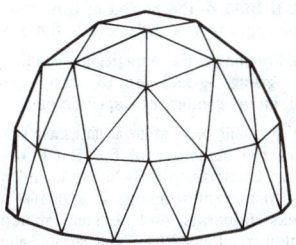

Geodesic dome

geodesic dome *n.* a dome that has many flat straight-sided faces formed by a framework of bars that intersect to form equilateral triangles or polygons

geodesic line *n.* = geodesic *n.*

geodesy /jēe óddəssi/ *n.* the branch of science that deals with the precise measurement of the size and shape of the Earth, the mapping of points on its surface, and the study of its gravitational field [Late 16thC. Via modern Latin from Greek *geōdaisia*, from *daiein* 'to divide'.] —**geodesist** *n.*

geodetic /jēe ō déttik/, **geodetical** /-déttik'l/ *adj.* relating to the precise measurement of the Earth's surface or of points on its surface [Late 17thC. From Greek *geōdaitēs* 'land surveyor', from *daiein* 'to divide'.] —**geodetically** *adv.*

geodetic survey *n.* a survey of a very large area of land, with the curvature of the Earth's surface taken into account

geoduck /goo i duk/, **gweduc** *n.* a very large edible clam found on the northwestern Pacific coast of North America. Latin name: *Panope generosa*. [Late 19thC. From a Salishan language.]

geoeconomics /jēe ō éekənómmiks, -ék-/ *n.* the study of how the economies of the world's nations relate to and affect one another (*takes a singular verb*) —**geoeconomic** /jēe ō éekənómmik, -ék-/ *adj.* —**geoeconomically** *adv.* —**geoeconomist** /jēe ō i kónnə mist/ *n.*

geog. *abbr.* **1.** geographic **2.** geographical **3.** geography

geographer /ji óggrəfər/ *n.* sb who studies geography or is an expert in geography [Mid-16thC. Via late Latin from Greek *geōgraphos*, literally 'writer about the Earth'.]

geographical /-gráffik'l/, **geographic** /jēe ə gráffik/ *adj.* relating to geography in general, or to the geography of a specific region [Mid-16thC. Via French *géographique* or late Latin *geographicus* from Greek *geōgraphikos*, from *geōgraphos* (see GEOGRAPHER).] —**geographically** *adv.*

geographical mile *n.* = nautical mile

geography /ji óggrəfi/ (*plural* **-phies**) *n.* **1.** STUDY OF EARTH'S PHYSICAL FEATURES the study of all the physical features of the Earth's surface, including its climate and the distribution of plant, animal, and human life **2.** PHYSICAL FEATURES the physical features of a place or region, e.g. mountains and rivers **3.** LAYOUT OF A PLACE the arrangement of the different parts of a building, city, or other place **4.** ARRANGEMENT the way that sth is arranged and the relationships between its different elements ○ *the geography of the criminal* *mind* [15thC. Via Latin *geographia* from Greek *geōgraphia*, literally 'writing about the Earth'.]

geohydrology /jeé ō hī drólləji/ *n.* = **hydrogeology** —**geohydrologic** /jeé ō hīdrə lójjik/ *adj.* —**geohydrologist** /-hī drólləjist/ *n.*

geoid /jeé oyd/ *n.* **1. EARTH'S SHAPE** the slightly flattened sphere that is the shape of the Earth, used in calculating the precise measurements of points on the Earth's surface. ◊ **geodesy 2. HYPOTHETICAL SURFACE OF EARTH** a hypothetical surface of the Earth that would exist if a cross-section were taken at sea level. It is perpendicular to the force of gravity at every point. [Late 19thC. From Greek *geoeidēs* 'earthlike', from *gē* 'Earth'.] —**geoidal** *adj.*

geol. *abbr.* **1.** geologic **2.** geological **3.** geology

geological time *n.* the period of time that extends from the beginning of the world to the present day

geologize /ji ólla jīz/ (**-gizes, -gizing, -gized**), **geologise** (**-gises, -gising, -gised**) *vti.* to study geology in general, or the geology of a specific place

geology /ji ólləji/ *n.* **1. STUDY OF ROCKS AND MINERALS** the study of the structure of the Earth or another planet, in particular its rocks, soil, and minerals, and its history and origins **2. STRUCTURE OF AN AREA** the rocks, minerals, and physical structure of a particular area [Mid-18thC. From modern Latin *geologia*, literally 'description of the Earth'.] —**geologic** /jeé ə lójjik/ *adj.* —**geological** /-lójjik'l/ *adj.* —**geologically** /-lójjikli/ *adv.* —**geologist** /jeé ólləjist/ *n.*

geom. *abbr.* **1.** geometric **2.** geometrical **3.** geometry

geomagnetic pole *n.* = **magnetic pole** *n.* 2

geomagnetic storm *n.* = **magnetic storm**

geomagnetism /jeé ō mágnətizəm/ *n.* **1. EARTH'S MAGNETISM** the magnetic properties of the Earth **2. STUDY OF EARTH'S MAGNETISM** the study of the magnetic properties of the Earth —**geomagnetic** /jeé ō mag néttik/ *adj.* —**geomagnetically** /-néttikli/ *adv.*

geomancy /jeé ō manssi/ *n.* the art or practice of making predictions based on patterns made by a handful of earth thrown on the ground or by lines connecting randomly placed dots [14thC. Via medieval Latin from Greek *geōmanteia*, literally 'divination from the Earth', from *manteia* 'divination'.] —**geomancer** *n.* —**geomantic** /jeé ō mántik/ *adj.*

geometer /ji ómmitər/ *n.* sb who studies, or is an expert in, geometry [15thC. Via late Latin from Greek *geōmetrēs*, literally 'land measurer', from, ultimately, *gē* 'Earth' + *metrēs* 'measurer'.]

geometric /jeé ə métrik/, **geometrical** *adj.* **1. RELATING TO GEOMETRY** conforming to the laws and methods of geometry **2. USING SIMPLE LINES** using straight lines and simple shapes, e.g. circles or squares **3. INCREASING FAST** increasing or decreasing very rapidly ○ *geometric growth* [Mid-17thC. Via French *géométrique* from, ultimately, Greek *geōmetrikos*, from *geōmetrēs* (see GEOMETER).] —**geometrically** *adv.*

Geometric *adj.* relating to a period of ancient Greek culture, between about 900 and 700 BC, noted for its decorative use of simple lines and shapes, especially on pottery

geometric mean *n.* the average of a set of *n* values, described mathematically as the *n*th root of their product

geometric progression *n.* a series of numbers in which each number is separated by a numerical step. In the series 1, 4, 16, 64, the numerical step is 4.

geometrics /jeé ə métriks/ *npl.* straight lines and simple shapes, e.g. circles or squares, used in design and decoration

geometric series *n.* a series of numbers (**geometric progression**) separated by a constant numerical step expressed as a sum, e.g. 1+4+16+64

geometrid /ji ómmətrid/ *n.* a moth with a slender body and broad wings and larvae that crawl with a characteristic looping movement. Family: Geometridae. [Late 19thC. From modern Latin *Geometridae*, genus name, literally 'land measurers' (see GEOMETER). So called because the caterpillar moves as though measuring the ground.] —**geometrid** *adj.*

geometrize /ji ómmə trīz/ (**-trizes, -trizing, -trized**), **geometrise** (**-trises, -trising, -trised**) *v.* **1.** *vt.* **REPRESENT IN GEOMETRIC FORM** to represent sth in geometric form **2.** *vti.* **APPLY RULES OF GEOMETRY** to apply the principles of geometry to sth —**geometrization** /ji ómmə trī záysh'n/ *n.*

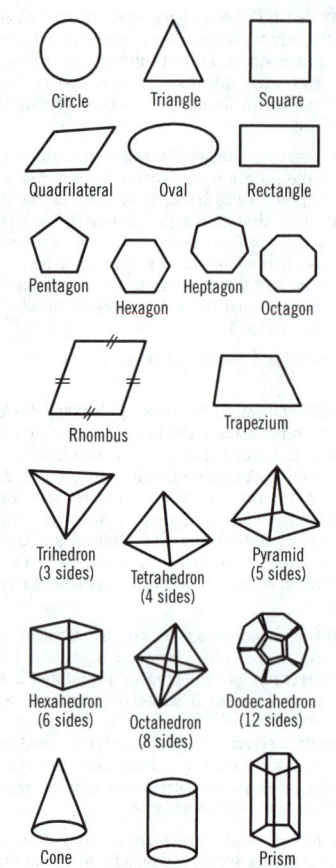

Geometry: Shapes and solids

geometry /ji ómmətri/ *n.* **1. MATHEMATICS OF SHAPES** the branch of mathematics that is concerned with the properties and relationships of points, lines, angles, curves, surfaces, and solids **2. KIND OF GEOMETRY** any subclass of geometry, e.g. a set of distinct theories or its application to a particular type of problem or object **3. ARRANGEMENT OF STH** the way the different parts of sth fit together in relation to each other [14thC. Via French *géométrie* from, ultimately, Greek *geōmetria*, literally 'measuring of the Earth', from *gē* 'Earth' + *metron* 'measure'.]

geomorphic /jeé ō máwrfik/ *adj.* relating to the surface features of the Earth or another planet

geomorphology /jeé ō mawr fólləji/ *n.* the branch of geology that examines the formation and structure of the features of the surface of the Earth or another planet's surface —**geomorphologic** /jeé ō mawrfə lójjik/ *adj.* —**geomorphologically** /-lójjikli/ *adv.* —**geomorphologist** /jeé ō mawr fólləjist/ *n.* —**geomorphological** *adj.*

geophagy /ji óffəji/ *n.* the eating of soil, clay, or chalk

geophone /jeé ə fōn/ *n.* an electronic instrument that picks up vibrations in the Earth

geophysics /jeé ō fízziks/ *n.* the branch of earth science that deals with the physics and physical processes of the Earth, especially using noninvasive techniques, e.g. acoustic surveys of the structure of rocks —**geophysical** *adj.* —**geophysically** *adv.* —**geophysicist** *n.*

geophyte /jeé ə fīt/ *n.* a perennial plant that propagates from organs that are below ground, e.g. bulbs, tubers, or rhizomes

geopolitics /jeé ō póllətiks/ *n.* **STUDY OF GEOGRAPHY'S RELATION TO POLITICS** the study of the relationship between a country's politics and its geography and population distribution, or of the effect that geography and population distribution have on political relations between countries (*takes a singular verb*) ■ *npl.* **INFLUENCES OF GEOGRAPHY ON POLITICS** the relationships that exist between a country's politics and its geography and population distribution, or the influences that geography and population distribution have on political relations between countries (*takes a singular verb*) [Early 20thC. Blend of GEOGRAPHY and POLITICS.] —**geopolitical** /jeé ō pə líttik'l/ *adj.* —**geopolitically** /-líttikli/ *adv.* —**geopolitician** /jeé ō pólla tísh'n/ *n.*

geoponics /jeé ō pónniks/ *n.* the scientific study of agriculture (*takes a singular verb*) —**geoponic** *adj.*

Geordie /jáwrdi/ *n.* **1. SB FROM TYNESIDE** sb who was born on or lives on Tyneside in northeastern England, especially sb who speaks the local dialect of English **2. DIALECT SPOKEN IN TYNESIDE** the dialect of English spoken in Tyneside in northeastern England [Mid-19thC. From the local pronunciation of *Georgie*, diminutive of the name *George*.] —**Geordie** *adj.*

WORD KEY: WORLD ENGLISH

A spoken variety among the general population in and around the city of Newcastle-upon-Tyne in northeastern England. The term is an informal variation of George, formerly a common man's name among the miners and sailors of the area, and is often used for sb from Tyneside, a common nickname for which is 'Geordieland'. The dialect derives ultimately from Northumbrian, the northernmost division of Old English, and is the only vernacular in England in which initial h is pronounced. Typically, a glottal stop replaces /k, p, t/ at the ends of syllables (as in *Ah can? kee? 'em ou?* 'I can't keep them out'), and the closing vowel in such words as *bonnie* ('pretty') is long: 'bonnee'.

George I /jawrj/, King of Great Britain and Ireland (1660–1727) German-born British monarch. The great-grandson of James I, he was the first of Britain's Hanoverian kings (1714–27).

George II, King of Great Britain and Ireland (1683–1760) German-born British monarch. As king (1727–60), he was a field commander in the War of the Austrian Succession (1740–48).

George III, King of the United Kingdom (1738–1820). He was the first British-born Hanoverian king. His reign (1760–1820) was marked by the American War of Independence. In later years, he was increasingly affected by a psychiatric disorder that led finally to the establishment of a regency (1811) under his son, later George IV.

George IV, King of the United Kingdom (1762–1830). Notorious for his extravagant habits, he was regent for George III (1811–20) and king (1820–30).

George V, King of the United Kingdom (1865–1936). Notable for his naval career, he reigned from 1910 to 1936, and renounced the family's German titles during World War I.

George VI, King of the United Kingdom (1895–1952). He succeeded to the throne after the abdication of his brother Edward VIII (1936). He was greatly admired for his national leadership during World War II.

George, Lake lake in the foothills of the Adirondack Mountains, eastern New York State. Noted for its beauty, it has long been a resort centre and was of military importance during the French and Indian War and the American War of Independence. Area: 114 sq. km/44 sq. mi.

George Cross *n.* a British medal awarded, especially to civilians, for gallantry

Georgetown /jáwrj town/ **1.** town and capital of the Cayman Islands, West Indies, situated on Grand Cayman Island. Population: 12,000 (1988). **2.** affluent residential and commercial district of northwestern Washington, D.C. and the home of Georgetown University. Originally a Potomac River port, it was incorporated into the District of Columbia in 1871.

George Town /jáwrj town/ **1.** town in northern Tasmania, Australia. It is one of Australia's oldest settlements. Population: 6,929 (1996). **2.** seaport and capital city of Penang state, Malaysia. It was the site of the first British settlement in Malaysia. Population: 219,380 (1991).

Georgia

Georgia /jáwrjə/ **1.** US state bordered by South Carolina, the Atlantic Ocean, Florida, Alabama, North Carolina, and Tennessee. Capital: Atlanta. Population: 7,486,242 (1997). Area: 152,750 sq. km/58,977 sq. mi. **2.** republic on the eastern coast of the Black Sea bordered on the north by Russia and on the south by Turkey, Armenia, and Azerbaijan. The country is dominated by the Greater Caucasus to the north and the Lesser Caucasus to the south. Language: Georgian. Currency: lari. Capital: Tbilisi. Population: 5,160,042 (1997). Area: 69,700 sq. km/26,900 sq. mi. Official name **Republic of Georgia**

Georgian[1] /jáwrjən/ adj. **1.** HIST OF 1714 TO 1830 IN BRITAIN relating to the time of Kings George I, II, III, and IV of Great Britain and Ireland, who reigned consecutively from 1714 to 1830 **2.** ARCHIT OF 18THC ARCHITECTURAL STYLE built in or imitating a style of architecture or furniture that flourished in Great Britain and the United States in the 18th and early 19th centuries **3.** LITERAT RELATING TO 20THC LITERARY MOVEMENT relating to a movement in early 20th-century poetry that favoured traditional styles ■ n. **1.** HIST SB FROM GEORGIAN TIMES sb who lived during the Georgian era **2.** LITERAT GEORGIAN WRITER a writer whose works belong to the Georgian literary movement

Georgian[2] /jáwrjən/ n. **1.** LANG OFFICIAL LANGUAGE OF GEORGIA the official language of the Republic of Georgia. It belongs to the Kartvelian family of languages. **2.** PEOPLES SB FROM GEORGIA sb who was born or lives in or is a citizen of the Republic of Georgia **3.** SB FROM US STATE OF GEORGIA sb who was born in or lives in the state of Georgia in the United States [15thC. Formed from *Georgia*, a region in the Caucasus and a state of the United States.] —**Georgian** adj.

Georgian Bay /jáwrjən-/ northeastern arm of Lake Huron, in southeastern Ontario, Canada. Area: 15,000 sq. km/5,800 sq. mi.

georgic /jáwrjik/ adj. RURAL relating to or depicting rural life (literary) ■ n. POETRY POEM ABOUT RURAL LIFE a poem about rural life [Early 16thC. Via Latin from Greek geōrgikos, from geōrgos 'farmer', from gē 'Earth'.]

geoscience /jeé ō sī əns/ n. a science such as geology or geophysics that deals with the Earth —**geoscientist** /jeé ō sī əntist/ n.

geosphere /jeé ō sfeer/ n. the solid matter of the Earth, as distinct from the seas, plants, animals, and surrounding atmosphere —**geospheric** /jeé ō sférrik/ adj.

geostationary /jeé ō stáysh'nəri/ adj. used to describe the orbit of satellite that circles the Earth above the equator at a speed matching the Earth's rotation, thus appearing to remain stationary, or the satellite itself. Most communications satellites are in geostationary orbit.

geostrategy /jeé ō stráttəji/ (plural -gies) n. **1.** STRATEGY IN RELATION TO GEOPOLITICS the study of strategy in relation to the geopolitical situation of a country or region **2.** POLICY BASED ON GEOPOLITICS the policy of a nation based on a combination of geographical and political factors —**geostrategic** /jeé ō strə teéjik/ adj. —**geostrategist** /jeé ō stráttəjist/ n.

geostrophic /jeé ō stróffik/ adj. arising from the rotation of the Earth —**geostrophically** adv.

geosynchronous /jeé ō sing krənəss/ adj. = **geostationary**

geosyncline /jeé ō sing klīn/ n. a long broad depression in the Earth's crust where it has sunk over time as it has accumulated a thick layer of sedimentary deposits —**geosynclinal** /jeé ō sing klīn'l/ adj.

geotaxis /jeé ō táksiss/ n. movement by an organism or cell in response to the force of gravity —**geotactic** /jeé ō táktik/ adj. —**geotactically** /-táktikli/ adv.

geotectonic /jeé ō tek tónnik/ adj. relating to the large-scale structure of the Earth's crust —**geotectonically** adv.

geothermal /jeé ō thúrm'l/, **geothermic** adj. relating to or produced by the heat in the interior of the Earth —**geothermally** adv.

geotropism /ji ótrəpizəm/ n. plant growth or movement in response to gravity. Upward growth of plant parts, against gravity, is called negative geotropism, and downward growth of roots, positive geotropism. —**geotropic** /jeé ō tróppik/ adj. —**geotropically** /-tróppikli/ adv.

ger. abbr. gerund

Ger. abbr. **1.** German **2.** Germany

gerah /geerə/ n. an ancient Hebrew coin worth one twentieth of a shekel [Mid-16thC. From Hebrew gērāh.]

Geraldton /jérrəldtən/ port on Champion Bay, Western Australia, about 375 km/233 mi. north of Perth. Population: 25,243 (1996).

geraniol /ji ráyni ol/ n. a pale yellow or colourless alcohol that is found in many essential oils. It smells like geraniums and is used in making perfumes and flavourings. Formula: $C_{10}H_{18}O$. [Late 19thC. Coined from GERANIUM + -OL.]

Geranium

geranium /jə ráyni əm/ n. **1.** PLANTS PLANT WITH BRIGHTLY COLOURED FLOWERS a popular garden plant with large rounded leaves and bright red, pink, or white flowers on tall stalks. Genus: *Pelargonium*. (not used technically) **2.** PLANTS PLANT WITH SAUCER-SHAPED FLOWERS a plant with divided leaves and pink, blue, white, or red saucer-shaped flowers. Cranesbill and herb Robert are types of geranium. Genus: *Geranium*. **3.** COLOURS BRIGHT RED COLOUR a bright red colour tinged with orange, similar to that of a scarlet geranium ■ adj. BRIGHT RED of a bright red colour tinged with orange [Mid-16thC. Via Latin from Greek *geranion*, from *geranos* 'crane', from the resemblance of the spur on some species' fruit to a crane's bill.]

Gerbil

gerbil /júrb'l/ n. a small rodent resembling a mouse with long back legs that is native to hot dry parts of Africa and Asia. Some species are popular as pets. Subfamily: Gerbillinae. [Mid-19thC. Via French *gerbille* from modern Latin *gerbillus*, diminutive of *gerboa* (see JERBOA).]

gerent /jérrənt/ n. a ruler or leader (literary) [Late 16thC. From, ultimately, Latin *gerere* 'to carry on'.]

gerenuk /gérrinook/ (plural -nuks or -nuk) n. a slender East African antelope, the male of which has long horns that curve backwards. Latin name: *Litocranius walleri*. [Late 19thC. From Somali.]

gerfalcon /jur fáwlkən/ n. BIRDS = **gyrfalcon**

geriatric /jérri átrik/ adj. **1.** MED RELATING TO ELDERLY PEOPLE relating to the diagnosis, treatment, and prevention of illness in elderly people **2.** OFFENSIVE TERM REFERRING TO AGE an offensive term meaning very old, especially when sb is considered too old to be useful or taken seriously (offensive) ■ n. MED ELDERLY PERSON an elderly person, in a medical context (technical) [Early 20thC. Coined from Greek gēras 'old age' + -IATRIC on the model of PAEDIATRIC.]

geriatrician /jérri ə trísh'n/ n. a doctor who specializes in medical care for the elderly

geriatrics /jérri átriks/ n. the branch of medicine that deals with the illnesses and medical care of elderly people (takes a singular verb) ◊ **gerontology**

geriatrist /jérri áttrist/ n. = **geriatrician**

germ /jurm/ n. **1.** BIOL MICROORGANISM a microorganism, especially one that can cause disease **2.** BIOL CELL the smallest element in an organism, e.g. a spore or a fertilized egg, that is capable of growing into a complete adult or part **3.** BEGINNING the first sign of sth that will develop ◊ the germ of an idea [Mid-15thC. Via French germe from Latin germen 'seed, sprout', from gignere 'to beget'.]

german /júrmən/ adj. having the same parents, or closely related ◊ brothers-german [Via French germain from Latin germanus 'having the same parents', from germen (see GERM)]

German n. **1.** PEOPLES SB FROM GERMANY sb who was born or brought up in Germany, or who has German citizenship **2.** LANG OFFICIAL LANGUAGE OF GERMANY the official language of Germany, Austria, and Liechtenstein and one of the official languages of Switzerland. It belongs to the Germanic branch of Indo-European languages and is spoken in many parts of the world by about 100 million native speakers, with approximately a further 100 million using it as a second language. **3.** SB WHO SPEAKS GERMAN sb whose first language is German ■ adj. **1.** RELATING TO GERMANY relating to or typical of Germany, or its people or culture **2.** RELATING TO GERMAN relating to the German language [14thC. From Latin *Germanus*, applied to a group of related peoples of northern and central Europe.]

German cockroach n. a small brown cockroach that is a common pest throughout the world. Latin name: *Blattella germanica*.

germander /jur mándər/ (plural -ders or -der) n. a flowering plant that has small pink, white, or pale purple flowers with a small upper lip. Genus: *Teucrium*. [15thC. Via medieval Latin germandr(e)a from, ultimately, Greek khamaidrus, literally 'ground oak'.]

germane /jur máyn/ adj. suitably related to sth, especially sth being discussed (formal) [Early 17thC. Variant of GERMAN.] —**germanely** adv. —**germaneness** n.

German East Africa former German territory comprising present-day Burundi, Rwanda, and Tanzania. Following World War I, Belgium took over Ruanda-Urundi, now Burundi and Rwanda, while Britain took over Tanganyika, or Tanzania.

Germanic /jur mánnik/ n. EUROPEAN LANGUAGE GROUP a group of languages spoken across northwestern Europe that forms a branch of Indo-European and is conventionally divided into the three sub-groups West, North, and East Germanic. About 500 million people use one of the languages classified as Germanic as their first language. ■ adj. **1.** OF GERMANIC relating to the group of languages classified as Germanic **2.** OF GERMANY of Germany, or its people or culture [Mid-17thC. From Latin Germanicus, from Germanus (see GERMAN).]

Germanism /júrmənizəm/ n. **1.** GERMAN WORD a word or phrase borrowed or adapted from the German language **2.** GERMAN QUALITY a custom or trait regarded as typically German **3.** LIKING FOR GERMANY fondness for Germany and all things German

Germanist /júrmənist/ *n.* a student of or specialist in German language, literature, and culture

germanium /jur máyni əm/ *n.* a brittle grey crystalline chemical element that is a metalloid that is used as a semiconductor and in alloys. Symbol **Ge** [Late 19thC. Coined from Latin *Germanus* 'German' by Clemens Winkler, the German chemist who discovered it (see GERMAN).]

German measles *n.* a highly contagious viral disease that causes swelling of the lymph glands and a reddish-pink rash on the skin. It affects children particularly. and can be harmful to the unborn baby of a pregnant woman who contracts it.

Germanophile /jur mánnə fīl/ *n.* an admirer of Germany and the Germans

Germanophobe /jur mánnə fōb/ *n.* sb who dislikes Germany and the Germans

German shepherd *n.* = Alsatian

German silver *n.* = nickel silver

Germany

Germany /júrməni/ federal republic in central Europe. Divided into East and West Germany following World War II, it became a unified country again in 1990. Language: German. Currency: Deutschmark. Capital: Berlin. Population: 82,071,765 (1997). Area: 356,959 sq. km/137,823 sq. mi. Official name **Federal Republic of Germany**

germ cell *n.* BIOL = germ *n.* 2

germicide /júrmi sīd/ *n.* a preparation that kills germs —**germicidal** /júrmi sīd'l/ *adj.*

germinal /júrmin'l/ *adj.* **1.** OF REPRODUCTIVE CELLS relating to reproductive cells **2.** OF THE EARLY STAGES relating to or belonging to the earliest stage in the development of sth (*formal*) [Early 19thC. From Latin *germen* (see GERM).] —**germinally** *adv.*

Germinal /zháirminal/ *n.* the seventh month of the year in the French Revolutionary calendar, corresponding to 22 March to 20 April in the Gregorian calendar [Early 19thC. Via French from Latin *germen* (see GERM).]

germinal vesicle *n.* the enlarged nucleus of an egg before it develops into an ovum

germinate /júrmi nayt/ (-nates, -nating, -nated) *v.* **1.** *vti.* START GROWING FROM SEED to start to grow from a seed or spore into a new individual **2.** *vi.* DEVELOP to be created and start to develop [Late 16thC. From Latin *germinare*, from *germen* (see GERM).] —**germination** /júrmi náysh'n/ *n.* —**germinative** /júrminətiv/ *adj.* —**germinator** /júrmi naytər/ *n.*

Germiston /júrmistən/ gold-mining city in Gauteng Province, northeastern South Africa, about 13 km/8 mi. southeast of Johannesburg. Population: 134,005 (1991).

germ layer *n.* any of the three distinct layers of cells formed during an embryo's early stages of development (**gastrulation**)

germ line *n.* a group of cells in a developing embryo from which reproductive cells (**gametes**) develop, regarded as the line of descent from one generation to another

germplasm *n.* the hereditary material that is transmitted from one generation to another

germ theory *n.* **1.** THEORY THAT GERMS CAUSE INFECTIONS the theory that all infectious and contagious diseases are caused by microorganisms **2.** THEORY OF BIOLOGICAL DEVELOPMENT the theory that organisms develop from

previous generations through the growth of germ cells

germ tube *n.* a hollow tube that grows from a germinating spore

germ warfare *n.* = biological warfare

germy /júrmi/ (-ier, -iest) *adj.* full of harmful microorganisms (*informal*) —**germiness** *n.*

gerodontics /jérrō dóntiks/ *n.* the branch of dentistry focusing on the needs of elderly people (*takes a singular verb*) [Late 20thC. Coined from Greek *gēras* 'old age' + ODONTO- + -ICS.] —**gerodontic** *adj.*

Gerona /jə rṓnə/ city and capital of Gerona Province, in the autonomous region of Catalonia, northeastern Spain. It is situated about 89 km/55 mi. northeast of Barcelona. Population: 70,576 (1996).

AKG London
Geronimo

Geronimo /jə rónnimō/ (1829–1909) US Chiricahua Apache leader. He was a legendary warrior who led his people in raids on settlers and US troops before being captured in 1886. Born **Goyathlay**

geront-, **geronto-** *prefix.* aging, old age ○ *gerontology* [Via French from, ultimately, Greek *geront-*, the stem of *gerōn* 'old man'; related to *gēras* 'old age' (source of English *geriatrics*)]

gerontocracy /jérr on tókrəssi/ (*plural* -cies) *n.* **1.** GOVERNMENT BY ELDERS a system of government in which the elders are chosen as rulers **2.** GOVERNING ELDERS a group of elders who make up a government (*takes a singular or plural verb*) —**gerontocrat** /jə róntə krat/ *n.* —**gerontocratic** /-kráttik/ *adj.*

gerontology /jérr on tólləji/ *n.* the scientific study of ageing and its effects. ◊ **geriatrics** —**gerontologic** /jə róntə lójjik/ *adj.* —**gerontological** *adj.* —**gerontologist** /jérr on tólləjist/ *n.*

Gerry /gérri/, **Elbridge** (1744–1814) US statesman and vice president of the United States. He signed the Declaration of Independence and the Articles of Confederation, and as governor of Massachusetts (1810–12) reorganized electoral districts in a process that came to be called 'gerrymandering'.

gerrymander /jérri mandər/ *vti.* (-ders, -dering, -dered) TRY TO GET EXTRA VOTES UNFAIRLY to manipulate an electoral area, usually by altering its boundaries, in order to gain an unfair political advantage in an election ■ *n.* ACT OF GERRYMANDERING an unfair manipulation of an electoral area for political advantage [Early 19thC. A blend of Elbridge GERRY and SALAMANDER, from the shape of an electoral district he created to favour his own party.]

AKG London
George Gershwin

Gershwin /gúrshwin/, **George** (1898–1937) US composer. Jazz, classical, and popular influences com-

bined in his outstandingly inventive works, many of which became American classics. He wrote *Rhapsody in Blue* (1924), the opera *Porgy and Bess* (1935), and, with his brother Ira Gershwin, songs including 'Someone to Watch Over Me'. Born **Jacob Gershvin**

Gershwin, Ira (1896–1983) US lyricist and dramatist. A collaborator with his brother George Gershwin and other leading composers, he wrote lyrics for 20 Broadway musicals, and shared a Pulitzer Prize for *Of Thee I Sing* (1931). Born **Israel Gershwin**

gerund /jérrənd/ *n.* **1.** NOUN FROM A VERB a noun formed from a verb, describing an action, state, or process. In English, it is formed from the verb's *-ing* form, as 'smoking' is in the phrase 'No smoking'. **2.** LATIN NOUN a Latin noun ending in '-ndum', formed from a verb and describing an action, state, or process [Early 16thC. From late Latin *gerundium*, from, ultimately, Latin *gerere* 'to carry on'.] —**gerundial** /jə rúndi əl/ *adj.*

gerundive /jə rúndiv/ *n.* a Latin adjective ending in '-ndus', formed from a verb and meaning 'that must or ought to be done' [15thC. From late Latin *gerundivus modus* 'gerundive mood', from *gerundium* (see GERUND).] —**gerundival** /jérrən dīv'l/ *adj.*

gesso /jéssō/ (*plural* -soes) *n.* **1.** PLASTER USED IN ART a mixture of plaster and glue or size, used in sculpture and as a background for paintings **2.** PIECE OF ART USING GESSO a painting done on gesso, or a sculpture done in gesso [Late 16thC. Via Italian from Latin *gypsum* (see GYPSUM).] —**gessoed** *adj.*

gest /jest/, **geste** /zhest/ *n.* (*archaic*) **1.** ADVENTURE a heroic exploit or adventure **2.** TALE OF ADVENTURE a story or romance, especially one written in verse [12thC. Via Old French from Latin *gesta* 'actions', from *gerere* 'to carry, act'.]

Gestalt /gə shtált/ (*plural* -stalts *or* -stalten), **gestalt** *n.* a set of elements such as a person's thoughts and experiences considered as a whole and regarded as amounting to more than the sum of its parts [Early 20thC. From German, 'shape'.] —**gestaltist** *n.*

Gestalt psychology, **gestalt psychology** *n.* a branch of psychology that treats behaviour and perception as an integrated whole and not simply the sum of individual stimuli and responses

Gestalt therapy, **gestalt therapy** *n.* a form of psychotherapy in which emphasis is placed on feelings and on the influence on personality development of unresolved personal issues from the past

Gestapo /ge staápō/ *n.* the secret state police under the Nazi regime in Germany, noted for its brutality [Mid-20thC. A German acronym, formed from *Geheime Staatspolizei* 'Secret State Police'.]

gestate /jestáyt/ (-tates, -tating, -tated) *vti.* **1.** MED CARRY OFFSPRING IN THE WOMB to carry offspring in the womb, or develop as offspring in the womb **2.** DEVELOP IDEAS IN THE MIND to develop in the mind, or allow an idea or plan to develop in the mind [Mid-19thC. From Latin *gestare* (see GESTATION).]

gestation /je stáysh'n/ *n.* **1.** MED CARRYING OF OFFSPRING IN THE WOMB the process of carrying offspring in the womb during pregnancy **2.** MED PERIOD OF DEVELOPMENT OF THE FOETUS the period of development of the offspring during pregnancy **3.** DEVELOPMENT the development of an idea or plan in the mind, or the time it takes to develop [Mid-16thC. From the Latin stem *gestation-*, from *gestare* 'to carry in the womb', from *gerere* 'to carry'.] —**gestational** *adj.* —**gestatory** *adj.*

geste *n.* = gest

gesticulate /je stíkyoō layt/ (-lates, -lating, -lated) *vti.* to move the arms or hands when speaking, or express sth with movements of the arms or hands [Early 17thC. From Latin *gesticulari*, from, ultimately, *gestus* 'action, gesture', from *gerere* 'to carry, act'.] —**gesticulative** /je stíkyoō lətiv/ *adj.* —**gesticulator** *n.* —**gesticulatory** /-lətəri/ *adj.*

gesticulation /je stíkyoō láysh'n/ *n.* movement with the hands or arms, usually accompanying speech [15thC. From the Latin stem *gesticulation-*, from *gesticulari* (see GESTICULATE).]

gesture /jéschər/ *n.* **1.** BODY MOVEMENT a movement made with a part of the body in order to express meaning or emotion, or to communicate an instruction **2.** ACTION COMMUNICATING STH an action intended to communicate feelings or intentions **3.** USE OF GESTURES the use of body movements to communicate ■ *vti.* **(-tures, -turing, -tured)** MAKE A BODY MOVEMENT to make a movement with a part of the body in order to express meaning or emotion, or to communicate an instruction [15thC. From medieval Latin *gestura* 'deportment', from Latin *gerere* 'to carry, act' (source of English *digest* and *suggest*).] —**gestural** *adj.* —**gesturally** *adv.*

WORD KEY: ORIGIN

The Latin word *gerere* from which **gesture** is derived is also the source of English *congest, digest, gestation, gesticulate, ingest, jest, jester,* and *suggest.*

gesundheit /gə zóont hīt/ *interj.* used as an expression of good health to sb who has just sneezed (*humorous*) [Early 20thC. From German, literally 'health'.]

get[1] /get/ **(gets, getting, got, got** /got/) CORE MEANING: a verb indicating that sb obtains, receives, earns, or is given sth. It is often used instead of more formal terms such as 'obtain' or 'acquire'. ○ *We're trying to ensure that our child gets a good education* ○ *Where will they get the money to buy the land?*

1. *vi.* BECOME to become, or begin to have a particular quality ○ *When I get nervous, I get scared.* **2.** *vt.* CAUSE STH TO BE DONE to cause sth to happen or be done ○ *I must get the car cleaned.* **3.** *vt.* BRING STH to fetch or bring sth ○ *I'm going back to my apartment to get my watch.* ○ *I'll get your coat for you.* **4.** *vt.* CATCH AN ILLNESS to be affected by an illness or medical condition ○ *He got chicken-pox last year.* **5.** *vi.* BE IN A PARTICULAR STATE to enter or leave a particular state or condition ○ *Get ready to leave in five minutes.* **6.** *vi.* MOVE SOMEWHERE to succeed in moving somewhere, or arrive somewhere ○ *It was already midnight when we got home.* **7.** *vt.* BEGIN STH to begin doing sth (*informal*) ○ *Let's get going – we have to be there by eight.* **8.** *v.* FORMS PASSIVES used instead of 'be' as an auxiliary verb to form passives ○ *If you play with matches you will get burned.* **9.** *vt.* ARREST SB to arrest or capture sb (*informal*) ○ *They got him just as he was running out of the bank.* **10.** *vt.* MANAGE STH to manage or contrive sth (*informal*) ○ *How did they get to be so successful?* **11.** *vt.* PREPARE FOOD to prepare a meal ○ *I'll get dinner tonight.* **12.** *vt.* PERSUADE SB to persuade sb to do sth ○ *Colleagues had tried to get her to take a vacation.* **13.** *vt.* UNDERSTAND STH to hear or understand sth, e.g. a joke or sb's point (*informal*) ○ *What's that? I didn't get what you said.* **14.** *vt.* USE A FORM OF TRANSPORTATION to take a particular form of transportation ○ *I don't want to drive – I'd rather get a plane.* **15.** *vt.* OBTAIN A RESULT to obtain a result, e.g. by experiment or calculation ○ *What's the answer? I get nine.* **16.** *vt.* RECEIVE A SIGNAL to receive a broadcast signal, e.g. a radio or television broadcast ○ *I can't get Channel 5 with that aerial.* **17.** *vt.* IRRITATE SB to annoy or irritate sb (*informal*) ○ *That high whining noise really gets me.* **18.** *vt.* HAVE THE TIME to have the time or opportunity to do sth ○ *I'll fix it as soon as I get the time.* **19.** *vt.* HAVE AN IDEA to have or receive an idea, impression, feeling, or benefit ○ *You've got the wrong impression – I'm not like that at all.* ○ *I get a lot of pleasure from his stories.* **20.** *vt.* MANAGE TO SEE STH to succeed in seeing sth ○ *get a close-up look* **21.** *vt.* HIT SB to hit sb (*informal*) ○ *The blow got him in the face.* **22.** *vt.* HAVE REVENGE ON SB to have revenge on sb, especially by killing the person (*informal*) ○ *The heroes get Dracula in the end.* **23.** *vi.* GAIN ACCESS TO SB to gain access to sb with intent to bribe him or her (*informal*) ○ *I thought he was incorruptible, but they finally got to him.* **24.** *vi.* TO LEAVE to leave (*informal*) (*often used in commands*) ○ *Now get!* **25.** *vt.* CONCEIVE SB to beget or conceive sb (*archaic*) [13thC. Via Old Norse *geta* from, ultimately, an Indo-European base meaning 'to seize', which is also the ancestor of English *guess*.] —**getable** *adj.* ◇ **get with it** become fashionable and responsive to new styles and ideas (*informal*)

WORD KEY: SYNONYMS

get, acquire, obtain, gain, procure, secure

CORE MEANING: to come into possession of sth

get a general word, meaning to become the owner of sth or to succeed in finding and possessing it, that can be substituted for any of the other words in this group; **acquire** a more formal word than ***get***, sometimes used to suggest that getting sth took a lot of time or effort; **obtain** a more formal word than ***get***, sometimes used to emphasize the active seeking out of or striving to get sth; **gain** used to suggest greater effort than *obtain* and possibly that merit or expertise was involved in getting sth, and is often used to emphasize that the thing gained is advantageous or profitable; **procure** used to emphasize a great degree of effort that has gone into coming into possession of sth; **secure** used to suggest that sth was difficult to get but that the ownership of it is now certain.

get about *vi.* **1.** MOVE ABOUT to be able to move with a medical condition **2.** BECOME KNOWN to become known, especially contrary to sb's wishes **3.** TRAVEL to travel, especially contrary to expectations **4.** = **get around** *v.* 1

get across *v.* **1.** *vti.* MAKE STH UNDERSTOOD to make sth understood or to communicate clearly ○ *I don't seem to be getting across to you.* **2.** *vt.* ANNOY SB to annoy or irritate sb ○ *She's really managed to get across him, somehow.*

get after *vt.* to keep telling sb to do sth in an annoying way (*informal*) ○ *You'll have to get after him if you want it finished by the weekend.*

get ahead *vi.* to become successful, especially when compared to others ○ *He's a good worker, but he hasn't got what it takes to get ahead in this line of business.*

get along *vi.* **1.** *US* BE FRIENDLY WITH SB to be on good terms with sb socially **2.** MANAGE to make progress in a situation ○ *How's he getting along in the new job?* **3.** LEAVE to leave a place (*often used in commands*)

get around *vi.* **1.** HAVE A SOCIAL LIFE to be socially active and aware of what is happening ○ *I have the feeling you don't get around much.* **2.** BECOME KNOWN to become widely known ○ *If news of this gets around, I may have to leave town.* ◗ **get round 3.** SAY OR DO STH AT LAST finally to say or do sth after delay, hesitation, or being involved with other things ○ *I wondered when you'd get around to telling me that.*

get at *vt.* **1.** REACH SB OR STH to succeed in reaching, finding, or making contact with sb or sth ○ *I'm determined to get at the truth if it takes all night.* **2.** MEAN STH to imply, suggest, or be trying to say sth ○ *What exactly are you getting at?* **3.** CRITICIZE SB REPEATEDLY to criticize sb continually and unreasonably ○ *You're always getting at me, and I'm sick of it.* **4.** BRIBE SB to bribe or influence sb ○ *It was obvious that some of the committee had been got at by our rivals.*

get away *vi.* **1.** ESCAPE to escape from sb or sth ○ *They caught one man, but the rest got away.* **2.** LEAVE A PLACE to succeed in leaving or spending time away from a place ○ *We hope to get away for a few days next month.* ■ *interj.* EXPRESSING DISBELIEF used as an expression of disbelief ○ *Get away! He never said that – did he?*

get away with *vt.* to manage to do sth without being blamed or penalized, or without experiencing some other bad result that should have been expected ○ *You could get away with a phone call, but it would be better to write.*

get back to recover sth that has been given away, lent to sb or lost ◇ **get back at** to take your revenge on sb

get by *vi.* to manage to survive or just make ends meet ○ *It's hard to get by on £50 a week.*

get down *v.* **1.** *vt.* DEMORALIZE SB to make sb demoralized or discouraged ○ *This job is beginning to get me down.* **2.** *vt.* WRITE STH to write sth down, especially immediately **3.** *vt.* SWALLOW STH to swallow sth, especially unwillingly or with difficulty ○ *The medicine smelled so bad I just couldn't get it down.* **4.** *vi. US* HAVE FUN to relax and enjoy yourself in an unrestrained way (*informal*) ○ *It's time to get down and party.*

get down to *vt.* to start concentrating seriously on sth or getting sth done

get in *v.* **1.** *vi.* TO ARRIVE to arrive somewhere, especially home ○ *When does your plane get in?* **2.** *vi.* BE CHOSEN to succeed in being admitted to a group or organization, e.g. by election or interview ○ *You know if they get in they'll change some of the old laws.* **3.** *vti.* GET INVOLVED WITH SB OR STH to become involved, or let sb become involved, with a group or in an activity ○ *She got in with the golf club crowd.* **4.** *vt.* MANAGE TO DO STH to succeed in finding or making an opportunity to do sth ○ *I don't think we can get four interviews in before lunch.*

get into *vt.* **1.** START TO BE IN A BAD SITUATION to begin to experience difficulties, or make sb experience difficulties ○ *You got us into this mess, you sort it out.* ○ *You'll get into all kinds of trouble if you do that.* **2.** GET INVOLVED OR INTERESTED IN STH to become involved or absorbed in sth ○ *She's starting to get into programming.*

get off *v.* **1.** *vi.* LEAVE to leave a place or position ○ *We have to get off at crack of dawn tomorrow.* **2.** *vti.* BE ABLE TO LEAVE WORK to be allowed to leave work, especially at the end of the working day ○ *What time do you get off this afternoon?* **3.** *vt.* SEND A COMMUNICATION OR PARCEL to send a written communication or parcel ○ *I need to get these letters off tonight.* **4.** *vi.* HAVE A LUCKY ESCAPE to experience only minor consequences of a mistake, misguided action, or accident ○ *Considering what might have happened, I think you got off very lightly.* **5.** *vti.* GAIN AN ACQUITTAL to be acquitted in a court of law, or successfully defend sb in a court of law (*informal*) ○ *A good lawyer could get him off with no trouble.* **6.** *vi. US* BE SO BOLD to be bold enough to say or do sth (*informal*) (*usually disapproving*) ○ *Where does he get off thinking he can speak to me that way?* **7.** *vi.* BE AROUSED OR EXCITED to experience excitement, physical arousal, or the effects of a drug (*slang*)

get off with *vt.* to start a flirtation or sexual relationship with sb (*informal*)

get on *vi.* **1.** DEAL WITH A SITUATION to deal with a situation and make reasonable progress of a particular kind ○ *How's Ben getting on at school?* **2.** BE FRIENDLY to have a reasonably friendly social relationship with sb ○ *She gets on well with the neighbours.* **3.** KEEP GOING to continue doing sth ○ *I'd better get on – I've got a lot more to do.* **4.** BECOME OLDER to become more advanced in years ○ *She's getting on, you know, you can't expect her to do everything she used to.* **5.** BE ALMOST STH to be approaching a particular age, time, number, or amount ○ *We collected getting on for 200 signatures.*

get out *v.* **1.** *vti.* LEAVE OR MAKE SB LEAVE to leave a place or situation, or enable sb to leave one **2.** *vi.* BECOME KNOWN to become widely known, especially contrary to sb's wishes ○ *If this ever gets out, I'll be so embarrassed!* **3.** *vt.* PRODUCE OR PUBLISH STH to produce or publish sth, especially a newspaper or magazine ■ *interj. US* EXPRESSING DISBELIEF used as an expression of disbelief (*informal*) ○ *Get out! You actually said that?*

get out of *vt.* to avoid doing or having to experience sth, or enable sb to avoid sth ○ *He got out of paying for the meal.*

get over *vt.* **1.** RECOVER FROM STH to recover from an illness or bad experience ○ *He's upset, but he'll get over it.* **2.** DEAL WITH A DIFFICULTY to overcome or cope with a difficulty ○ *Once she'd got over her lack of confidence, she enjoyed the meeting.* **3.** MAKE PEOPLE UNDERSTAND OR ACCEPT STH to succeed in making sth clear or persuasive ○ *He's very good at getting his ideas over to an audience.* **4.** GET STH FINISHED to finish dealing with sth boring, annoying, or unpleasant ○ *I just want to get the whole thing over with as soon as possible.*

get round *v.* US term **get around 1.** *vt.* DEAL SUCCESSFULLY WITH OBSTRUCTION to manage to operate in spite of a regulation, prohibition, or difficulty ○ *There must be some way of getting round the regulations.* **2.** *vt.* PERSUADE SB to talk or charm sb into doing what you want ○ *could rely on Sheila to get round him* **3.** *vi.* SAY OR DO STH AT LAST finally to say or do sth after delay, hesitation, or being involved with other things ○ *She somehow never gets round to cleaning the house.*

get through *v.* **1.** *vt.* SURVIVE DIFFICULT TIME to endure to the end of a difficult time or situation ○ *How I got through those weeks I just don't know.* **2.** *vt.* USE OR SPEND STH to use, eat, or spend sth, especially a large amount in a short time ○ *We seem to be getting through the copier paper at an alarming rate.* **3.** *vti.* MAKE SB UNDERSTAND to make sb understand sth that is being communicated ○ *How can I get it through to you that this is our only hope?* **4.** *vi.* SUCCEED IN CONTACTING SB to contact sb, especially by telephone ○ *I finally got through to her.*

get to *vt.* to start to annoy sb ○ *His whining was beginning to get to me.*

get together *v.* **1.** *vi.* MEET to meet for social or business purposes ○ *The project team needs to get together once a week or so.* **2.** *vi.* FORM AN ALLIANCE to form an alliance or relationship ○ *They may be getting* together to corner the market. **3.** *vt.* **GATHER STH** to bring together or accumulate sth, especially money ○ *They managed to get together enough capital to start a business.* **4.** *vt.* **GET STH ORGANIZED** to organize your personal affairs or focus your approach to an activity (*informal*) ○ *took some time off to get her life together* ○ *better get it together before his boss loses patience*

get up *v.* **1.** *vti.* **GET OUT OF BED** to get out of bed, or make sb get out of bed **2.** *vi.* **STAND UP** to rise to your feet from a seated position **3.** *vt.* **ROUSE ENERGY** to rouse your energy, strength, courage, or similar qualities ○ *I'm trying to get up the enthusiasm to go back to work.* **4.** *vt.* **ORGANIZE STH** to organize sth by persuading other people to take part ○ *She got up a collection to help homeless people.* **5.** *vt.* **DRESS SB** to dress sb in a particular way (*informal*) ○ *She was got up as Cleopatra.* **6.** *vi.* **GET STRONGER** to become stronger or more turbulent (*refers to wind or the sea*)

get up to *vt.* to do sth bad or annoying (*informal*) ○ *I have no idea what they've been getting up to while we've been away.*

get² /get/ *n.* **1.** Scotland, N England **BRAT** an unpleasant child (*often used as an insult, implying illegitimacy*) **2.** **MALE ANIMAL'S OFFSPRING** the progeny sired by an animal, especially a racehorse **3.** **RACKET GAMES DIFFICULT TENNIS RETURN** in tennis and some other racket games, a shot that makes a difficult return

geta /gétta/ (*plural* **-ta** *or* **-tas**) *n.* a Japanese shoe with a wooden sole [Late 19thC. From Japanese.]

getaway /gétta way/ *n.* **1.** **ACT OF LEAVING** an act of leaving a place, especially a quick exit made by sb who has just committed a crime **2.** **START OF MOVEMENT** an act of starting to move, e.g. in a race

get back to *v.* **1.** *vt.* **RETURN TO STH** to return to a place, topic, or activity ○ *Let's get back to what Steve was saying earlier.* **2.** *vt.* **REPLY TO SB** to give sb an answer or continue a discussion, especially by letter, e-mail, or telephone ○ *Leave it with me, and I'll get back to you as soon as possible.*

Gethsemane, Garden of /geth sémməni/ in a book of the Bible, the olive grove just outside Jerusalem where Jesus Christ was betrayed after the Last Supper (Matthew 26: 36)

getter /géttər/ *n.* a substance added to absorb the unwanted product of a chemical process, e.g. the excess gas in a light bulb

get-together *n.* a meeting or social gathering (*informal*)

get-tough *adj.* taking a firm and decisive approach to social or political problems

getup /gét up/, **get-up** *n.* the costume or clothes that sb is wearing (*informal*)

get-up-and-go *n.* energy and enthusiasm (*informal*)

get-well *adj.* expressing the hope that sb will soon recover from an illness ○ *a get-well card*

geullah /gə óóllə/ *n.* a Jewish prayer of thanks to God for the deliverance of the Jews from Egypt

GeV *abbr.* giga-electron volt

gewgaw /gyóó gaw/ *n.* a showy but inexpensive object, especially an ornament [12thC. Origin uncertain: perhaps a doubled form of Old French *gogue* 'joke' (source of English *agog*).]

Gewürztraminer /gə vóórts trə meenər/ *n.* **1.** **WHITE GRAPE** a white grape used in winemaking, grown especially in Alsace and in Germany **2.** **WHITE WINE** a medium-dry, slightly spicy, white wine made from the Gewürztraminer grape [Mid-20thC. From German, from *Gewürz* 'spice' + *Traminer*, name of a type of grape, from *Termeno*, a village in northern Italy where it was originally identified.]

gey /gī/ *adv.* Scotland (*nonstandard*) **1.** **RATHER** rather **2.** **VERY** very [Early 18thC. Scots dialect variant of GAY.]

geyser /géezə, gízə/ *n.* **1.** **GEOG SPRING GUSHING HOT WATER AND STEAM** a spring that throws a jet of hot water or steam into the air at regular or irregular intervals **2.** **HOUSEHOLD WATER HEATER** a boiler that heats water for use in the home, gas-fired and activated by turning on a tap [Late 18thC. Named after *Geysir*, a hot spring in Iceland, from Old Norse *geysa* 'to gush'.]

Geyser: Rotorua, New Zealand

geyserite /gízə rīt/ *n.* a grey or white mineral deposited by geysers and hot springs. It looks like opal and, like opal, is a form of hydrated silica.

G-force *n.* the force of gravity [Mid-20thC. *G* a shortening of *gravity*.]

GG *abbr.* **1.** Governor General **2.** Girl Guides

gge *abbr.* garage (*used in advertisements*)

GH *abbr.* **1.** Ghana (*international vehicle registration*) **2.** growth hormone

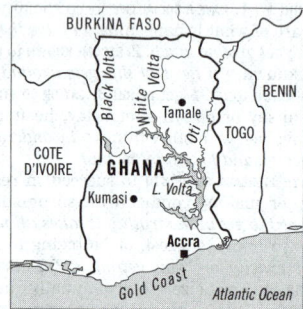

Ghana

Ghana /gaánə/ republic on the northern coast of the Gulf of Guinea in western Africa, bordered by Burkina Faso, Togo, and Côte d'Ivoire. It became independent from Britain in 1957. Language: English. Currency: cedi. Capital: Accra. Population: 18,100,703 (1997). Area: 238,537 sq. km/92,100 sq. mi. Former name **Gold Coast** (until 1957) —**Ghanaian** /gaa náy ən/ *n., adj.*

Ghanaian English *n.* a variety of English spoken in Ghana

———WORD KEY: WORLD ENGLISH———

The English language as used in Ghana (population 17m), the largest English-speaking nation in West Africa after Nigeria. Local contact with the language dates from 1631. Standard English is official, West African Pidgin English is widespread, and indigenous languages include Ashanti, Ewe, Fanti, and Ga, all of which have an influence on English usage, especially in vocabulary. Ghanaians strongly resist the idea of a distinctive Ghanaian English, and although standard and pidgin shade into one another, many seek to maintain a sharp line between them. Local usage is non-rhotic, i.e., *r* is not pronounced in such words as *art*, *door*, *worker*. Usage includes expressions adopted from local languages, often as the first element in compounds, as in the terms *bodom beads*, *kente cloth*, and in localisms such as an *airtight* 'a metal box', an *outdooring* 'a christening ceremony', and to *enskin* 'to enthrone a chief by draping him in an animal skin'. See AFRICAN ENGLISH.

gharial /gáiri əl, gárri-/ *n.* a large Indian fish-eating crocodile. US term **gavial** [Early 19thC. From Hindi *ghariyāl*.]

gharry /gárri/ (*plural* **-ries**) *n.* S Asia a horse-drawn carriage in the Indian subcontinent, especially one for hire [Early 19thC. From Hindi *gārī*.]

ghastly /gaástli/ *adj.* (**-lier, -liest**) **1.** **HORRIFYING** horrifying, shocking, or very upsetting ○ *She had a ghastly experience with the last dentist she went to.* **2.** **TERRIBLE** very bad or unpleasant ○ *There's a ghastly smell coming from somewhere in this room.* **3.** **NOT**

WELL very unwell (*informal*) ○ *If I drink too much, I always wake up feeling ghastly in the morning.* **4.** **VERY PALE** very pale or white, reminiscent of a ghost or a corpse (*literary*) ■ *adv.* **EXTREMELY** used to emphasize paleness or whiteness ○ *'Her eyes grew large, her face ghastly pale'.* (Charlotte Gilman, *Herland*; 1915) [14thC. Formed from obsolete *gast* 'to frighten'. The *gh-* spelling was first used in the late 16thC, under the influence of GHOST.] —**ghastliness** *n.*

ghat /gaat, gawt/ *n.* in the Indian subcontinent, a place on a river bank with steps down to the water, especially one where people bathe as a sacred rite or one near which the dead are cremated [Early 17thC. From Hindi *ghāt*.]

Ghats /gaats, gawts, guts/ ♦ **Eastern Ghats, Western Ghats**

ghazal /gaáz'l/ *n.* **1.** **LYRIC POEM** an Arabic, Persian, or Urdu lyric poem consisting of five or more couplets that may each have a different theme **2.** **POEM SET TO MUSIC** a lyric poem in Urdu, set to music and sung in a distinctive style. Ghazals are popular in Indian films. [Late 18thC. Via Persian from Arabic *gazal*.]

ghazi /gaázi/ *n.* a warrior who has fought for Islam against non-Muslims [Mid-18thC. From Arabic *al-ğāzī*, active participle of *ğazā* 'to invade'.]

GHB *abbr.* gamma hydroxybutyrate

ghee /gee/, **ghi** *n.* clarified butter, especially as used in Indian cooking. Traditionally a mark of generous hospitality, ghee is also used in Hindu religious observances. [Mid-17thC. Via Hindi *ghī* from Sanskrit *ghrtam*, of uncertain origin: perhaps formed from *gharati* 'to sprinkle'.]

Ghent /gent/ capital of East Flanders Province, north-western Belgium. One of Belgium's oldest cities, it is situated about 56 km/35 mi. northwest of Brussels. Population: 226,464 (1996).

gherao /gə rów/ *vt.* (**gheraos, gheraoing, gheraoed**) S Asia **SURROUND SB AS PROTEST** to surround and virtually imprison an official, employer, or manager, typically at the workplace, as a form of political or industrial protest ■ *n.* **ACT OF SURROUNDING SB AS PROTEST** the surrounding and virtual imprisonment of an official, employer, or manager as a political or industrial protest [Mid-20thC. Formed from Hindi *ghernā* 'to surround'.]

gherkin /gúrkin/ *n.* **1.** **FOOD SMALL CUCUMBER** a small cucumber used for pickling **2.** **FOOD PRICKLY FRUIT** a prickly hard-skinned fruit from a West Indian climbing plant, used for pickling when it is unripe **3.** **PLANTS TROPICAL CLIMBING PLANT** a West Indian climbing plant of the cucumber family that produces gherkins. Latin name: *Cucumis anguria*. [Early 17thC. From assumed obsolete Dutch *gurkkijn*, literally 'small cucumber', from *gurk* 'cucumber', of uncertain origin: perhaps from, ultimately, late Greek *aggourion* 'watermelon'.]

ghetto /géttō/ (*plural* **-tos** *or* **-toes**) *n.* **1.** **MINORITY'S AREA OF A CITY** an area of a city lived in by a minority group, especially a run-down and densely populated area lived in by a group that experiences discrimination **2.** **JEWISH QUARTER** in former times, an area in European towns in which the Jewish population was required to live **3.** **STATE OF SOCIAL EXCLUSION** the social situation of any group of people who are segregated in some way from the mainstream of a society or culture, resulting in discrimination or restriction of opportunity [Early 17thC. From Italian, of uncertain origin: possibly an alteration of *getto* 'foundry', after the site of a 16thC Venetian ghetto.]

ghetto blaster *n.* a large radio and cassette or CD

Ghetto blaster

player with a built-in speaker at each end, carried by a handle at the top (*informal*) (*often considered offensive*) [From its popularity among inner-city youth]

ghettoize /géttō īz/ (-izes, -izing, -ized), **ghettoise** (-ises, -ising, -ised) vt. **1.** SEGREGATE A MINORITY GROUP to restrict a minority group to a specific area of a city **2.** LIMIT OPPORTUNITIES to limit the opportunities of a group of people (*sometimes considered offensive*) —**ghetto-ization** /géttō ī záysh'n/ n.

ghi n. COOK = **ghee**

ghillie n. CLOTHES = **gillie**

ghost /gōst/ n. **1.** SUPPOSED SPIRIT REMAINING AFTER DEATH the spirit of sb who has died, supposed to appear as a shadowy form or to cause sounds, the movement of objects, or a frightening atmosphere in a place **2.** TRACE a faint, weak, or greatly reduced appearance, trace, or possibility of sth ○ *The ghost of a smile hovered around her lips.* **3.** SECONDARY IMAGE a faint duplicate image of sth seen on a screen or through a telescope, and caused by the reception of a double signal or by a mechanical defect **4.** NONEXISTENT PERSON OR THING sb who or sth that seems to exist but does not, e.g. a name entered on a list by mistake **5.** RELIG SOUL sb's soul or spirit (*archaic*) **6.** = **ghostwriter** ■ vt. (**ghosts, ghosting, ghosted**) = **ghostwrite** [Old English *gāst*. The *gh*- spelling appeared in the 15thC, probably under the influence of Middle Dutch *gheest*.] ◇ **give up the ghost 1.** to die (*literary*) **2.** to stop working or functioning for good (*informal*)

—————— WORD KEY: CULTURAL NOTE ——————
Ghosts, a play by Norwegian dramatist Henrik Ibsen (1881). Ibsen's penetrating study of hereditary determinism tells the story of Osvald Alving, who discovers that his recently deceased father led a debauched life and that the girl he loves is actually his illegitimate half-sister. These revelations also confirm Osvald's fears that he has inherited a degenerative venereal disease from his father.

ghostbuster /gōst bustər/ n. (*informal*) **1.** SB CLAIMING TO DRIVE AWAY GHOSTS sb who is supposed to be able to drive away ghosts, poltergeists, and other apparitions from the places they haunt **2.** TAX OFFICIAL an employee of the Inland Revenue whose job is to track down people who have not declared their income for tax purposes

ghost crab n. a white burrowing crab that inhabits sandy shorelines in many parts of the world. Genus: *Ocypoda*. [From its pale appearance]

ghost dance n. **1.** NATIVE N AMERICAN DANCE a religious dance of western Native North Americans, performed with the spirits of all the Native Americans murdered by the European immigrants **2. ghost dance, Ghost Dance** NATIVE N AMERICAN RELIGIOUS MOVEMENT a religious movement, widely spread among Plains Native American peoples in North America in the late 19th century, that promised the revival of traditional Native North American culture

ghosting /gōsting/ n. the appearance of faint duplicate images on a screen or monitor, or through a telescope

ghostly /gōstli/ (-lier, -liest) adj. **1.** LIKE A GHOST like a ghost in being insubstantial, pale, or apparently not of this world **2.** REMINISCENT OF GHOSTS having an atmosphere or quality that suggests ghosts or the presence of ghosts ○ *the ghostly music that opens the symphony* **3.** RELIG OF THE SOUL spiritual, or connected with the soul (*archaic*) —**ghostliness** n.

ghost moth n. a large pale moth found throughout Europe. The male is white and the female is pale yellow with orange markings. Latin name: *Hepialis humuli*.

ghost site n. a Web site that is obsolete and no longer updated but that is still available for viewing

ghost story n. a story about a ghost or ghosts, or a haunted place or person, intended to make the reader or hearer feel frightened or uneasy

ghost town n. **1.** DESERTED TOWN a town with no inhabitants, or very few, especially one that was formerly a busy prosperous place, e.g. an abandoned mining town in the western United States **2.** DESERTED PLACE a formerly or normally inhabited place

that is deserted (*informal*) ○ *The business district is a ghost town on weekends.*

ghost train n. a small open-topped train at a fairground that takes passengers through a dark space filled with amusingly frightening sights and sounds

ghost word n. LING a word created through a mistake that may be copied afterwards into other texts and eventually enter a language

ghostwrite /gōst rīt/ (-writes, -writing, -wrote /-rōt/, -written /-rit'n/) vti. to write sth as a ghostwriter

ghostwriter /gōst rītər/ n. sb who writes sth for or with another person on the understanding that the other person will receive sole credit as the author

ghoul /gool/ n. **1.** SB MORBIDLY INTERESTED IN REPULSIVE THINGS sb who has a morbid fascination with death, disaster, or repulsive things in general **2.** MYTHOL EVIL SPIRIT an evil and terrifying spirit **3.** ISLAM BODY-SNATCHING DEMON an evil demon in Islamic folklore that eats freshly buried bodies, and often abducts children or attacks unwary travellers [Late 18thC. From Arabic *gūl*.]

ghoulish /goolish/ adj. **1.** MORBID showing an unpleasant or unhealthy fascination with death and destruction **2.** HIDEOUS terrifyingly hideous or cruel —**ghoulishly** adv. —**ghoulishness** n.

GHQ n. the headquarters of an organization, especially a military headquarters commanded by a general. Full form **General Headquarters**

ghyll n. = **gill**[3]

GHz abbr. gigahertz

GI[1] /gee í/ n. US SOLDIER a soldier in the United States armed forces ■ adj. US **1.** FOR SOLDIERS provided or issued by the armed forces for the use of its members ○ *a GI hat* **2.** FOR VETERANS for veterans of the armed forces ○ *GI benefits* [Mid-20thC. Shortening of *government issue*, a reinterpretation of *GI* 'galvanized iron' written on various items of US Army equipment (e.g. *GI can* 'galvanized iron dustbin').]

GI[2], **g.i.** abbr. **1.** galvanized iron **2.** gastrointestinal

giant /jí ənt/ n. **1.** MYTHOL VERY TALL OR LARGE CREATURE in fairytales and legends, a being who is usually similar to a human in shape but is much taller, larger, and stronger **2.** MYTHOL MYTHOLOGICAL CREATURE in Greek mythology, a being of immense size and strength who fought against Zeus and the other gods of Mount Olympus **3.** STH LARGER THAN THE NORM a person, animal, plant, or organization that is much larger than the norm **4.** SB EXTRAORDINARILY ACCOMPLISHED sb whose talents or achievements are particularly outstanding ○ *one of the giants of the silent-movie era* **5.** MINING = **monitor** n. **10 6.** ASTRON = **giant star** ■ adj. **1.** VERY BIG taller, larger, or more powerful than the norm ○ *a giant tidal wave* **2.** LARGER THAN USUAL greater than the usual number or amount ○ *a giant saving* [13thC. Via Old French *geant* from, ultimately, Greek *gigas* (source of English *giga-*).]

giant anteater n. a large bushy-tailed anteater, now rare, of the pampas regions of South America. Latin name: *Myrmecophaga tridactyla*.

giant clam n. an extremely large clam of the Pacific and Indian oceans, weighing as much as 230kg/500 lbs. Latin name: *Tridacna gigas*.

giantism /jí əntizəm/ n. MED = **gigantism**

giant-killer n. sb who or sth that defeats a supposedly superior or much better known opponent, especially in sport, business, or politics —**giant-killing** n.

giant panda n. = **panda** n. **1**

giant peacock moth n. the largest European moth, mottled brown in colour, with an oval like an eye on each wing and a wingspan that can reach 15 cm/6 in. Latin name: *Saturnia pyri*.

giant planet n. any of the four largest planets in the solar system, Jupiter, Saturn, Uranus, and Neptune

Giant's Causeway /jí ənts káwz way/ headland on the northern coast of Northern Ireland, consisting of thousands of polygonal columns of basalt, thought to be ancient lava formations

giant sequoia, **giant redwood** n. a very tall coniferous evergreen tree of California that can reach a height

of 80 m/260 ft and can measure 30 m/100 ft around the base. Latin name: *Sequoiadendron giganteum*.

giant star n. a low-density star with a diameter up to 100 times greater than that of the Sun

giant tortoise n. any very large tortoise of the Galapagos and Seychelles islands. Their shells can grow to be 1.2 m/4 ft long. Genus: *Geochelone*.

giaour /jów ər/ n. a non-Muslim, especially a Christian (*archaic insult*) [Mid-16thC. Via Turkish *gâvur* from, ultimately, Arabic *kafir* 'unbeliever'.]

giardia /jee aárdi ə/ n. **1.** MICROBIOL PARASITIC ORGANISM a single-celled protozoan, some forms of which live as parasites in the gut of humans and other vertebrates, causing an infection (**giardiasis**). Genus: *Giardia*. **2.** MED = **giardiasis** [Early 20thC. From modern Latin, genus name, named after A. *Giard* (1846–1908), the French biologist who discovered it.]

giardiasis /jee aar dí əssiss/ n. infection of the gut by a water-borne microscopic protozoan giardia. It is usually caused by drinking contaminated water and results in severe diarrhoea and vomiting.

gib /gib/ n. METAL WEDGE sth such as a wedge, pin, bolt, or plate that is made of metal and holds another piece of metal or a machine part in place ■ vt. (**gibs, gibbing, gibbed**) SECURE STH WITH GIB to hold sth in place with a gib [Late 18thC. Origin unknown.]

Gib /jib/ n. Gibraltar (*informal*)

gibber /jíbbər/ vi. (-bers, -bering, -bered) BE INCOHERENT to make sounds or speak words unintelligibly ○ *Stop gibbering and tell me what's gone wrong.* ■ n. GIBBERING SPEECH rapid incoherent or unintelligible speech [Early 17thC. Supposedly imitative of the sound.]

gibberellic acid /jíbbə réllik-/ n. a plant growth hormone involved in stem elongation. Formula: $C_{19}H_{22}O_6$.

gibberellin /jíbbə réllin/ n. a hormone that occurs in fungi and plants that stimulates cell elongation and the growth of stems and leaves [Mid-20thC. Formed from modern Latin *Gibbera*, genus of fungi, from Latin *gibbus* 'hump'.]

gibberish /jíbbərish/ n. spoken or written language perceived as incomprehensible, and probably not worth comprehending [Early 16thC. Origin uncertain: probably formed from GIBBER on the model of SPANISH, POLISH, etc.]

gibbet /jíbbit/ n. **1.** HANGING POST an upright post with a beam projecting horizontally from its top, from which the bodies of executed criminals were hung on public display **2.** = **gallows** ■ vt. (-bets, -beting, -beted) **1.** HANG SB to execute sb by hanging (*archaic*) **2.** DISPLAY SB'S BODY AFTER EXECUTION to display the body of a criminal on a gibbet after execution **3.** ATTACK SB'S REPUTATION to expose sb to ridicule or contempt, especially in popular publications (*archaic*) [12thC. From Old French *gibet* 'staff, gallows', literally 'small staff', from *gibe* 'staff', of uncertain origin: possibly from prehistoric Germanic.]

Gibbon

gibbon /gíbbən/ n. a small tree-dwelling ape of Southeast Asia with a slender body and long arms that allow it to swing rapidly and agilely from branch to branch. Genus: *Hylobates*. [Late 18thC. From French, of unknown origin.]

Gibbon, Edward (1737–94) British historian. His major work, *The History of the Decline and Fall of the Roman Empire* (1776–88), is a classic of British historiography.

gibbous /gíbbəss/ *adj.* **1.** ASTRON MORE THAN HALF ILLUMINATED used to describe the moon or a planet before and after it is full, when it has more than half its disc illuminated **2.** BIOL BULGING bulging outwards, or swollen [14thC. From late Latin *gibbosus* 'hunchbacked', from Latin *gibbus* 'hump'.] —**gibbosity** *n.* —**gibbously** *adv.* —**gibbousness** *n.*

Gibbs /gibz/, **May** (1876–1969) English-born Australian writer and illustrator. She wrote children's books, including *Snugglepot and Cuddlepie* (1918).

gibbsite /gíbzīt/ *n.* a grey-white mineral that is a hydrated aluminium oxide, found in deposits of laterite and bauxite. It is used as a source of aluminium. [Early 19thC. Named after George Gibbs (1776–1833), the US mineralogist who discovered it.]

gibe /jīb/, **jibe** *n.* MOCKING REMARK a comment that is intended to hurt or provoke sb or to show derision or contempt ■ *vti.* (**gibes, gibing, gibed; jibes, jibing, jibed**) MAKE INSULTING REMARKS to make deliberately provocative or mocking remarks about sb or sth [Mid-16thC. Origin uncertain: perhaps from Old French *giber* 'to handle roughly'.] —**gibingly** *adv.*

giblets /jíbbləts/ *n.* the liver, heart, gizzard, and neck of a bird that has been prepared for cooking. Giblets are often boiled to make stock for gravy. [14thC. From Old French *gibelet* 'game stew', of uncertain origin: perhaps formed from *gibier* 'game'.]

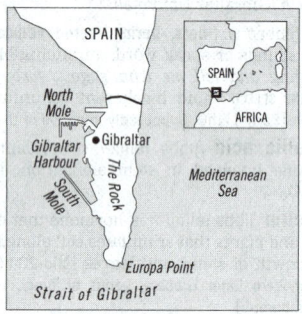

Gibraltar

Gibraltar /ji bráwltər, -brólt-/ British dependency on a narrow promontory that is the southernmost point of the Iberian Peninsula. It occupies a strategic position at the western entrance to the Mediterranean Sea. Population: 27,170 (1995). Area: 5.8 sq. km/2.3 sq. mi. —**Gibraltarian** /ji brawl táiri ən, -brol-/ *n., adj.*

Gibraltar, Rock of limestone and shale ridge at the southern tip of the Iberian Peninsula, overlooking the Strait of Gibraltar. Height: 426 m/1,396 ft.

Gibraltar, Strait of channel connecting the Mediterranean Sea to the Atlantic Ocean and separating North Africa from the Rock of Gibraltar. Length: approximately 65 km/40 mi.

Gibran /ji braàn/, **Kahlil** (1883–1931) Lebanese-born US mystic, painter, and poet. His mystical works inspired a new school of Arab American poetry, and *The Prophet* (1923) reached a wide popular audience.

Gibson /gíbs'n/, **Mel** (b. 1956) US-born Australian actor. Best known for his action roles in *Mad Max* (1979) and the *Lethal Weapon* series (1987–98), he also directed and starred in the Academy Award-winning *Braveheart* (1995). Real name **Columcille Gerard Gibson**

Gibson Desert desert in central Western Australia, consisting mainly of sand ridges and plains. Area: 156,000 sq. km/60,200 sq. mi.

gid /gid/ *n.* a disease affecting livestock, especially sheep that makes them walk and stand unsteadily. It is caused by an infestation of the brain by the larva of a tapeworm. [Early 17thC. Back-formation from GIDDY.]

giddap /gi dáp, -dúp/ *interj.* = giddyup

giddy /gíddi/ *adj.* (**-dier, -diest**) *adj.* **1.** DIZZY feeling unsteady and as if about to fall down **2.** CAUSING DIZZINESS causing dizziness or a feeling of unsteadiness **3.** NOT SENSIBLE not level-headed and sensible, and liable to act impulsively or behave foolishly (*dated*) [Old English

gidig 'severely mentally ill'. Ultimately from a prehistoric Germanic base that is also the ancestor of English *God*.] —**giddily** *adv.* —**giddiness** *n.*

giddyup /gíddi úp/ *interj.* used to make horses go faster [Early 20thC. Alteration of GET UP.]

Gide /zheed/, **André** (1869–1951) French writer. His many works of fiction and nonfiction frequently explore the theme of moral responsibility, and include his celebrated *Journal* (1939–51). He won the Nobel Prize in literature (1947). Full name **André Paul Guillaume Gide**

gie *n.* = GI²

Gielgud /geel good/, **Sir John** (b. 1904) English actor. He was one of the leading Shakespearian interpreters of his generation. Full name **Sir Arthur John Gielgud**

GIF *abbr.* graphic interchange format

gift /gift/ *n.* **1.** STH GIVEN TO SB sth that is given to sb, usually to give pleasure or to show gratitude ○ *a birthday gift* **2.** SPECIAL TALENT a talent or skill that sb appears to have been born with ○ *a gift for making people feel at ease* **3.** STH EASILY GAINED sth that is obtained or achieved easily, thus allowing an advantage (*informal*) ○ *The final goal was a gift from the Uruguay defence.* **4.** ACT OF GIVING the act of giving sth to sb ○ *her gift of £500,000 to build a new school* ■ *vt.* (**gifts, gifting, gifted**) GIVE STH to give or concede sth to sb as a gift [13thC. From Old Norse *gipt*. Ultimately from a prehistoric Germanic base that is also the ancestor of English *give*.] ◇ **be in the gift of sb** to be sth that sb has the right or power to give

—————— WORD KEY: USAGE ——————

Marketing people are fond of the expression *free gift*, if the frequency with which they use it is any indication. But because any *gift* worthy of its name is free, the result of using the two words together is both illogical and exaggerated. The phrase *free gift* should be avoided.

—————— WORD KEY: SYNONYMS ——————
See Synonyms at *talent*.

GIFT *n.* a method designed to aid conception in which eggs are removed from a woman's ovary, mixed with sperm, and placed in one of her fallopian tubes. Full form **gamete intrafallopian transfer**

gift certificate *n. US* = gift token

gifted /gíftid/ *adj.* **1.** TALENTED having great natural talent or intelligence **2.** SHOWING TALENT showing that sb has great natural talent ○ *a gifted performance* **3.** EDUC EXCEPTIONAL requiring special education because of exceptional talent or intelligence ○ *a gifted student* —**giftedness** *n.*

—————— WORD KEY: SYNONYMS ——————
See Synonyms at *intelligent*.

gift of the gab *n.* a natural ability to talk fluently, eloquently, or persuasively (*informal*)

gift of tongues *n.* a form of speech produced in a state of religious ecstasy or trance, usually unintelligible and thought by some to manifest the influence of the Holy Spirit. ◇ speaking in tongues

gift shop *n.* a shop selling small decorative or amusing items that are intended to be bought as gifts or souvenirs

gift token, gift voucher *n.* a slip of paper issued by a shop that can be exchanged for goods worth its purchase price, usually given to sb in an attractive card as a gift. US term **gift certificate**

giftwrap /gíft rap/ *n.* giftwrap, giftwrapping DECORATED WRAPPING PAPER specially decorated paper used to wrap gifts ■ *vt.* (**-wraps, -wrapping, -wrapped**) WRAP STH IN GIFTWRAP to wrap sth in specially decorated paper

Gifu /gee foo/ city and capital of the Gifu Prefecture, central Honshu, Japan, 105 km/65 mi. northwest of Nagoya. Population: 410,324 (1990).

gig¹ /gig/ *n.* **1.** ONE-HORSE CARRIAGE a light open two-wheeled carriage pulled by a single horse. It was a popular form of private transport in 19th-century Europe and the United States. **2.** ONE-HORSE CART a light one-horse open two-wheeled passenger cart, driven for recreation or as a sport **3.** ROWING BOAT a small light rowing boat carried on board a sailing ship **4.** RACING BOAT a light rowing boat used for

racing [Late 18thC. Origin uncertain: perhaps from obsolete *gig* 'rotary machine for raising nap on fabric, whirling thing' (now only in WHIRLIGIG).]

gig² /gig/ *n.* MUSICAL PERFORMANCE a performance by a musician or group of musicians at a venue where they are booked to play but do not regularly perform (*informal*) ■ *vi.* (**gigs, gigging, gigged**) PLAY A GIG to give a musical performance to an audience in exchange for payment (*informal*) [Early 20thC. Origin unknown.]

gig³ /gig/ *n.* a gigabyte (*informal*)

giga- *prefix.* **1.** A THOUSAND MILLION a thousand million (10⁹) ○ *gigaton* **2.** a binary billion ○ *gigabyte* [From Greek *gigas* (see GIANT)]

gigabit /gíggəbit/ *n.* a unit of capacity of a computer local area network, equal to one megabyte of computer information, or 1,073,741,824 bits

gigabyte /gíggə bīt/ *n.* a unit of computer data or storage space equivalent to 1,024 megabytes

gigacycle /gíggə sīk'l/ *n.* a unit of electrical oscillation equal to 1000 million cycles

gigaflop /gíggə flop/ *n.* a unit of measure of computer processing speed equal to 1000 million floating-point operations per second [Late 20thC. Coined from GIGA- + an acronym formed from *floating-point operations per second*.]

gigahertz /gíggə hurts/ (*plural* **-hertz**) *n.* a unit of frequency equal to 1000 million hertz, or cycles, per second

gigantesque /jígan tésk/ *adj.* as big as, or big enough for, a giant (*literary*)

gigantic /jī gántik/ *adj.* **1.** VERY BIG very large, tall, or bulky **2.** GREAT very great ○ *Clearing the site is a gigantic task in itself.* [Early 17thC. Formed from the Latin stem *gigant-* 'giant', from Greek *gigas* (source of English *giant*).] —**gigantically** *adv.*

gigantism /jī gántizəm, jī gan-/ *n.* excessive growth due to over-production of growth hormone by the pituitary gland before the end of adolescence

gigaton /gíggə tun, jíggə-/ *n.* a unit of explosive force equal to 1000 million tons of TNT

gigawatt /gíggə wot, jíggə-/ *n.* a unit of electrical power equal to 1000 million watts. Symbol **GW**

giggle /gíg'l/ *vti.* (**-gles, -gling, -gled**) LAUGH LIGHTLY to laugh audibly but not loudly, sometimes without meaning to, in a way that is typical of children ■ *n.* **1.** NERVOUS LAUGH a quiet laugh that is often nervous or half-suppressed **2.** STH FUN sth that is fun or that makes sb laugh (*informal*) ■ **giggles** *npl.* FIT OF LAUGHTER an uncontrollable and recurring urge to laugh (*informal*) [Early 16thC. Imitative of the sound.] —**giggler** *n.* —**giggling** *adj.* —**giggly** *adj.*

GIGO /gígō/ *n.* COMPUT the principle in computer technology that a program or process is only as good as the ideas and data put into it. Full form **garbage in, garbage out**

gigolo /jíggəlō/ (*plural* **-los** /zhígga loz/) *n.* **1.** PAID MAN COMPANION a man who receives payments or gifts from a woman in exchange for being her sexual or social partner **2.** PROFESSIONAL DANCING PARTNER a man whose job is to be a dancing partner or escort for a woman [Early 20thC. From French, formed as the masculine of *gigole* 'professional woman dance partner'.]

gigot /jíggət, zhígg-, zhiggō/ *n.* **1.** LAMB OR MUTTON a French and Scottish cut of lamb or mutton taken from the leg **2.** LEG OF MUTTON a leg of mutton [Early 16thC. From French, literally 'small leg', formed from French dialect *gigue* 'leg', from *giguer* 'to hop'.]

gigot sleeve *n.* a sleeve that is close-fitting on the lower arm and full and loose on the upper arm [From its shape]

Gijón /gi hón/ seaport on the Bay of Biscay in Asturias Province in northwestern Spain, 26 km/16 mi. northeast of Oviedo. Population: 270,867 (1995).

Gila monster

Gila monster /heĕlə-, geĕlə-/ n. a large brightly coloured venomous lizard that lives in the desert areas of the southwestern United States and Mexico and feeds on eggs and small mammals. Latin name: *Heloderma suspectum*. [Late 19thC. Named after the GILA RIVER where the lizards are found.]

Gila River /heĕlə-, geĕlə-/ river that rises in southwestern New Mexico and flows westwards, crossing Arizona to join the River Coloradonear Yuma. It is an important source of irrigation water. Length: 1,014 km/630 mi.

gilbert /gĭlbərt/ n. a unit of magnetomotive force in the centimetre-gram-second system, equal to 0.7958 ampere-turns in the SI system [Late 19thC. Named after William *Gilbert* (1544–1603), English physician and scientist.]

Gilbert /gĭlbərt/, **Sir W. S.** (1836–1911) British librettist and dramatist. He is best known for his long collaboration with Sir Arthur Sullivan writing light operas including *The Pirates of Penzance* (1879). Full name **Sir William Schwenck Gilbert**

Gilbert and Ellice Islands /-élliss-/ former British colony situated in the western Pacific Ocean. The group consisted of the Gilbert Islands, now part of Kiribati, and the Ellice Islands, now Tuvalu. Area: 733 sq. km/283 sq. mi.

gild /gĭld/ (**gilds, gilding, gilded**) vt. **1.** COVER STH WITH GOLD to cover sth with a thin layer of gold leaf or of a substance that looks like gold **2.** COLOUR STH GOLD to give a golden colouring or tinge to sth (*literary*) [Old English *gyldan*. Ultimately from a prehistoric Germanic base that is also the ancestor of English *gold*.] —**gilder** n.

gilded /gĭldĭd/ adj. **1.** ARTS = gilt[1] adj. **2.** WEALTHY wealthy and privileged ◊ *gilded youth*

gilding /gĭldĭng/ n. **1.** COVERING STH WITH GOLD the process of applying a thin layer of gold leaf, or sth that looks like gold, to a surface **2.** = gilt[1] n. 1

Gilead, Mount /-gĭlli ad/ mountain in northwestern Jordan that also gives its name to an area east of the River Jordan, the Dead Sea, and the Sea of Galilee. Height: 1,096 m/3,597 ft.

Giles /jīlz/, **Ernest** (1835–97) British-born Australian explorer. He was the leader of five expeditions to central and western Australia between 1872 and 1876. Full name **William Ernest Powell Giles**

gilet /zhee láy/ n. **1.** WAISTCOAT-TYPE BODICE a bodice to a dress or a ballet-dancer's costume that is shaped like a waistcoat **2.** WAIST- OR HIP-LENGTH JACKET a light sleeveless jacket, similar to a waistcoat but often longer, and sometimes made of padded or quilted material [Late 19thC. From French.]

gill[1] /gĭl/ n. **1.** BREATHING ORGAN OF FISH the organ that fish and some other aquatic animals use to breathe, consisting of a membrane containing many blood vessels through which oxygen passes. They are internal in most fish and external in tadpoles and some molluscs. **2.** SPORE-PRODUCING ORGAN OF MUSHROOM any of the thin radiating plates on the underside of the cap of a mushroom or other fungus where its spores are produced [14thC. From Old Norse.] —**gilled** adj. ◊ **green around the gills** looking on the point of being sick (*informal*) ◊ **to the gills** to the fullest possible extent

gill[2] /jĭl/ n. a unit of liquid measure equal to a quarter of a pint (142 ml in Britain and 118 ml in the US [The UK pint is 1.201 times the volume of a US

pint] [14thC. Via Old French *gille* from, ultimately, late Latin *gillo* 'water pot'.]

gill[3] /gĭl/, **ghyll** n. (*regional*) **1.** FAST-FLOWING STREAM a small fast-flowing stream, usually on a hill or mountain **2.** WOODED RAVINE a ravine with tree-covered sides [14thC. From Old Norse *gil*.]

gill[4] /jĭl/, **jill** n. **1.** FERRET a female ferret (*regional*) **2.** YOUNG WOMAN a young woman (*archaic; sometimes considered offensive*) [15thC. Shortening of the female forename *Gillian* from, ultimately, Latin *Juliana*, from *Julius*, name of a Roman gens.]

gill arch /gĭl-/ n. the bony or cartilaginous arch supporting the filaments that make up the gill of a fish

Gilles de la Tourette syndrome /jeĕl-/ n. MED full form of **Tourette's syndrome**

gill fungus /gĭl-/ n. a fungus that produces its spores from gills underneath a cap

gillie /gĭlli/, **ghillie** n. **1.** Scotland HUNTER'S ATTENDANT OR GUIDE sb whose job is to assist or guide people who go angling or deer-stalking in Scotland **2.** LIGHT SHOE WITH LONG LACES a low-cut tongueless shoe that laces across the foot and sometimes up the ankle [Late 17thC. From Gaelic *gille*.]

Gillies /gĭlliss/, **Sir Harold** (1882–1960) New Zealand surgeon. He pioneered plastic surgery and wrote the standard text, *The Principles and Art of Plastic Surgery* (1957). Full name **Sir Harold Delf Gillies**

Gillingham /jĭllingəm/ town on the River Medway in Kent, southeastern England. Population: 95,800 (1995).

gillion /jĭllyən/ n. 1,000 million (*dated technical*) ◊ **billion** [Mid-20thC. A blend of GIGA- and MILLION.]

gill net /gĭl-/ n. a net that is suspended vertically in the water like a curtain in order to catch fish by their gills —**gillnetter** n.

gill slit /gĭl-/ n. one of the openings on either side of the head of a fish or amphibian that contain its gills

gillyflower /jĭlli flowər/ n. **1.** SWEET-SCENTED FLOWER a scented flower, such as a stock or wallflower (*archaic*) **2.** CLOVE-SCENTED PINK a clove-scented pink or carnation [14thC. By folk etymology (by association with FLOWER) from French *girofle*, via medieval Latin *caryophyllum* 'clove' (its original English meaning) from Greek *karuophullon*, literally 'nut leaf'.]

Gilmore /gĭl mawr/, **Dame Mary Jean** (1865–1962) Australian poet and journalist. She campaigned for Aboriginal rights and radical social causes, and wrote nine collections of verse. Born **Mary Jean Cameron**

Gilsonite /gĭlsə nīt/ tdmk. a trademark for a pure bitumen, used in manufacturing waterproof coatings

gilt[1] /gĭlt/ n. **1.** ARTS THIN LAYER OF GOLD a thin layer of gold, or a substance that looks like gold, applied to a surface **2.** FIN GOVERNMENT BOND a bond issued by the government (*often used in the plural*) ■ adj. COVERED WITH GILT covered with a thin layer of gold, or a substance that looks like gold [15thC. From the past participle of GILD.] ◊ **take the gilt off the gingerbread** to spoil sth that sb was enjoying or looking forward to having or doing

gilt[2] /gĭlt/ n. a young female pig, especially one that has not yet had a litter [14thC. From Old Norse *gyltr*.]

gilt-edged adj. **1.** FIN VERY SAFE FINANCIALLY very safe as an investment **2.** ARTS WITH A GOLD EDGE having a gilded edge **3.** EXCELLENT very good, especially because of being free of risk and advantageous (*informal*) ◊ *This is a gilt-edged opportunity to recoup our losses.*

gimbal /jĭmb'l/ n. **1.** NAVIG RING FOR HOLDING A COMPASS STEADY a pivoted ring mounted at right angles to one or two others to ensure that sth such as a ship's compass always remains horizontal **2.** MECH ENG CONNECTION OF THE REVOLVING PARTS OF A MACHINE an interconnection that allows one part of a mechanism such as a clock's works to revolve independently of another revolving part that contains it ■ vt. (**-bals, -balling, -balled**) PUT ON GIMBALS to support sth on gimbals [Late 16thC. Variant of GIMMAL.]

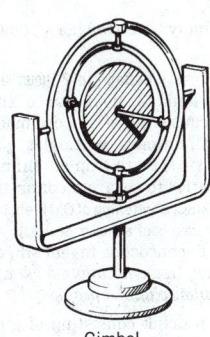

Gimbal

gimcrack /jĭm krak/ adj. SHOWY BUT SHODDILY MADE showy or superficially appealing, but badly made and worthless ■ n. STH SUPERFICIALLY APPEALING BUT SHODDY sth that is showy but cheap and badly made [14thC. Origin unknown.] —**gimcrackery** n.

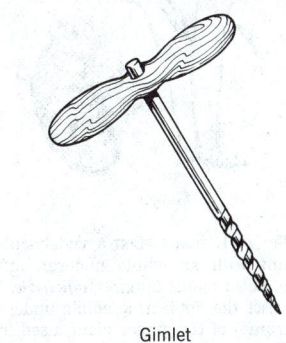

Gimlet

gimlet /gĭmlət/ n. **1.** JOINERY TOOL FOR BORING HOLES IN WOOD a small tool for boring holes in wood consisting of a slim metal rod with a sharp corkscrew end, fitted in a handle at a right angle **2.** BEVERAGES COCKTAIL WITH LIME JUICE a cocktail made of vodka or gin with lime juice ■ adj. PIERCING seeming to penetrate or pierce sb or sth ◊ *'to meet anew the gimlet glances'* (Thomas Hardy, *Jude the Obscure*; 1895) [14thC. From Old French *guimble*, literally 'small auger', from *guimble* 'auger', of prehistoric Germanic origin.]

gimlet-eyed adj. having eyes that seem to pierce and penetrate or to notice everything

gimmal /gĭmmal, jĭm-/ n. = gimbal [Late 16thC. Alteration of obsolete *gemel* 'double ring', via Old French from Latin *gemellus*, literally 'little twin', from *geminus* 'twin'.]

gimme /gĭmmi/ contr. give me (*nonstandard*)

gimmick /gĭmmik/ n. **1.** DISHONEST TRICK a piece of trickery or manipulation intended to achieve a result dishonestly ◊ *It's not a genuine offer, just a sales gimmick.* **2.** US HIDDEN DISADVANTAGE a piece of concealed information that, if known, would make an offer or opportunity less attractive ◊ *It sounds great, but what's the gimmick?* **3.** STH ATTENTION-GRABBING sth such as a new technique or device that attracts attention or publicity **4.** GADGET an ingenious device, mechanism, or ploy, especially one that works in a concealed way [Early 20thC. Origin unknown.] —**gimmicky** adj.

gimmickry /gĭmmikri/ n. **1.** GIMMICKS gimmicks in general **2.** USE OF GIMMICKS the use of a gimmick or gimmicks to deceive or attract attention

gimp[1] /gĭmp/, **guimpe** n. a silk or cotton trimming that has a wire or cord running through it [Mid-17thC. From Dutch, of unknown origin.]

gimp[2] /gĭmp/ n. US **1.** DIFFICULTY IN WALKING difficulty in walking, caused by injury, or stiffness (*informal*) **2.** OFFENSIVE TERM FOR PHYSICALLY CHALLENGED a highly offensive term for a physically challenged person, especially sb who has difficulty walking or who uses a wheelchair (*slang offensive*) **3.** CLUMSY PERSON sb who is clumsy or ineffectual (*slang insult*) (*often considered offensive*) [Early 20thC. Origin uncertain: perhaps an alteration of GAMMY.] —**gimpy** adj.

gin[1] /jĭn/ n. **1.** BEVERAGES COLOURLESS ALCOHOLIC DRINK a strong colourless alcoholic spirit distilled from grain and flavoured with juniper berries **2.** CARDS GIN

RUMMY gin rummy (*informal*) [Early 18thC. Shortening of GENEVER.]

gin² /jin/ *n.* **1.** HIST = **cotton gin 2.** HOIST a simple hoist operated by hand **3.** HUNT **TRAP** a snare or trap, usually one consisting of a noose made of wire for catching small animals ■ *vt.* **(gins, ginning, ginned) 1.** HUNT **CATCH STH IN GIN** to trap an animal with a gin **2.** CLEAN RAW COTTON to separate cotton from its seeds with a gin [13thC. Shortening of Old French *engin* 'engine'. The underlying idea is of a clever device.]

gin up *vt.* US to concoct or invent sth, or exaggerate its importance (*regional informal*) ○ *a story ginned up by the public relations people*

gin and it *n.* a drink consisting of gin and Italian vermouth (*informal*) [*It* is a shortening of ITALIAN]

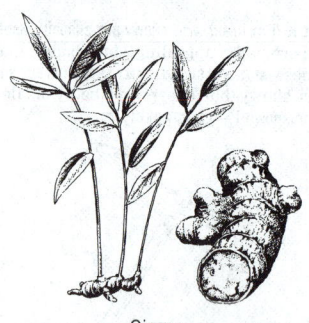

Ginger

ginger /jínjər/ *n.* **1.** PLANTS **PLANT** a widely-cultivated Asian plant with an edible underground stem **(rhizome)**. Latin name: *Zingiber officinale*. **2.** FOOD **HOT-TASTING SPICE** the hot-tasting edible underground stem **(rhizome)** of the ginger plant, used fresh in Asian cookery and as a spice in powdered form **3.** COLOURS **ORANGE- OR BROWNISH-YELLOW COLOUR** a yellow colour with an orange or brownish tinge ■ *adj.* **HAVING GINGER COLOUR** of an orange- or brownish-yellow colour ■ *vt.* **(-gers, -gering, -gered)** COOK **ADD GINGER TO STH** to add ginger as a spice to sth [Pre-12thC. From Old English *gingifer* and Old French *gingi(m)bre*, via Latin and Greek from Pali *singivera*.] —**gingery** *adj.* ◇ **ginger up** to liven or add excitement to sth (*informal*)

───── **WORD KEY: ORIGIN** ─────

The source of the Pali word from which *ginger* derives was a Sanskrit compound meaning literally 'horn-body' – a reference to the shape of the edible ginger root. By the time it had passed through Greek *ziggiberis* into Latin, it had become *zinziberi*. In post-classical times this developed to *gingiber* or *gingiver*, which Old English borrowed as *gingifer*. English acquired the word again in the 13th century from Old French, and this combined with the descendant of the Old English form to produce Middle English *gingivere*, from which modern English 'ginger' is derived.

ginger ale *n.* an effervescent nonalcoholic drink, flavoured with ginger

ginger beer *n.* a mildly alcoholic cloudy effervescent drink made by fermenting a mixture of syrup and ginger

gingerbread /jínjər bred/ *n.* **1.** GINGER-FLAVOURED CAKE a moist dark cake made with syrup or treacle and flavoured with ginger **2.** GINGER-FLAVOURED BISCUIT a ginger-flavoured biscuit, often cut into the stylized shape of a person, animal, or Christmas tree **3.** ARCHIT **ELABORATE DECORATION** showy and elaborate decoration, especially on the outside of a building (*often used before a noun*) ○ *a Victorian gingerbread style of cottage* [13thC. By folk etymology (by association with BREAD) from Old French *gingembrat* 'preserved ginger' from, ultimately, medieval Latin *gingiber* 'ginger'.]

gingerbread man *n.* a biscuit in the stylized shape of a person, made from gingerbread and often decorated with icing

ginger group *n.* UK, Can a group, often within a party or association, whose aim is to stimulate debate and press for more radical or decisive action on sth

gingerly /jínjərli/ *adv.* VERY CAUTIOUSLY in a very cautious, wary, or tentative way ○ *He gingerly unscrewed the radiator cap.* ■ *adj.* VERY CAUTIOUS very cautious,

wary, or tentative ○ *Not for her the gingerly approach – she came straight out with the question.* [Early 16thC. Origin uncertain: perhaps formed from Old French *gensor* 'pretty'.] —**gingerliness** *n.*

ginger nut, **ginger snap** *n.* a small round crisp ginger-flavoured biscuit

ginger wine *n.* wine made by fermenting bruised ginger with sugar and water. Ginger wine is traditionally regarded as a warming drink for winter.

gingham /gíngəm/ *n.* a light plain-weave fabric with checks, stripes, or plaids in white and coloured cotton (*often used before a noun*) ○ *a gingham dress* [Early 17thC. Via Dutch *gingang* from Malay *genggang* 'striped'.]

gingiva /jin jǐvə, jínjivə/ (*plural* **-vae** /-veə/) *n.* gum around the roots of the teeth (*technical*) [Late 19thC. From Latin.]

gingival /jin jǐv'l, jínjiv'l/ *adj.* relating to or affecting the gums (*technical*)

gingivectomy /jínji véktəmi/ (*plural* **-mies**) *n.* a surgical operation to remove tissue from the gums

gingivitis /jínji vítiss/ *n.* inflammation of the gums around the roots of the teeth

gingko /gíngkō/ *n.* = **ginkgo**

ginglymus /jíng gliməss/ (*plural* **-mi** /-mī/) *n.* ANAT a hinge joint of the human body (*technical*)

gink /gink/ *n.* sb, especially a man, who is considered strange, unintelligent, or clumsy (*informal insult*) [Early 20thC. Origin unknown.]

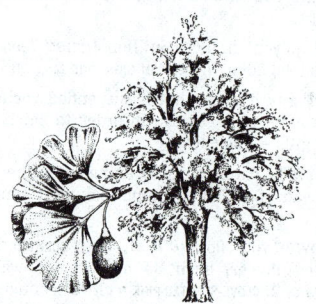

Ginkgo

ginkgo /gíngkō/ (*plural* **-goes**), **gingko** (*plural* **-koes**) *n.* a tall deciduous tree with small fan-shaped leaves and edible seeds. Native to China and widely cultivated elsewhere, it is the only remaining member of a primitive order of trees. Latin name: *Ginkgo biloba*. [Late 18thC. Via Japanese *ginkyō* from Chinese *yínxing* 'silver apricot'.]

ginkgo biloba *n.* a herbal preparation made from the pulverized leaves of the ginkgo tree and used to treat a variety of disorders [From the Modern Latin genus name]

ginnel /gínn'l/ *n.* N England a narrow alley or passageway between two walls or buildings [Early 17thC. Origin uncertain: perhaps from French *chenel* 'channel'.]

ginormous /jī náwrməss/ *adj.* extremely big (*informal*) [Mid-20thC. Blend of GIGANTIC and ENORMOUS.]

gin palace *n.* a large bar or public house furnished or decorated in a gaudy and pretentious style (*archaic*)

gin rummy *n.* a card game similar to rummy in which two players collect sets and sequences of cards. A hand can be won if cards totalling ten or fewer points are uncombined. [From GIN¹; a pun on RUMMY, as if it were formed from RUM the alcoholic drink]

ginseng /jín seng/ (*plural* **-sengs** *or* **-seng**) *n.* **1.** TONIC MEDICINE a forked aromatic root used in traditional Chinese medicine. Ginseng is now widely used as a tonic, and is credited with stimulative and restorative powers. **2.** MEDICINAL PLANT a plant that produces the ginseng root, found in Asia and in North America. Genus: *Panax*. [Mid-17thC. From Chinese *rénshēn*, from *rén* 'man' + *shēn* a type of herb. Perhaps from the shape of the root.]

gin sling *n.* an iced drink consisting of gin, water, and lemon or lime juice [*Sling* of uncertain origin: possibly influenced by German *schlingen* 'to swallow']

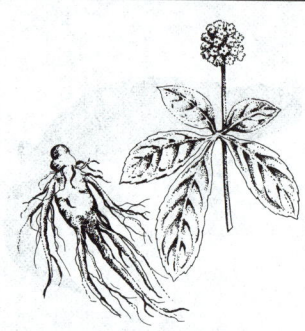

Ginseng

Giotto /jóttō/ (1266?–1337) Italian painter. One of the first European painters to portray human forms naturalistically, he exerted a profound influence on artists of the Renaissance. Full name **Giotto di Bondone**

gip *vt.*, *n.* = **gyp**

gippo /jíppō/ (*plural* **gippos**) *n.* an offensive term for a Romany person (*regional offensive*)

Gippsland /gíps land/ fertile region in southeastern Victoria, Australia, stretching from Western Port to the New South Wales border and bounded in the north by the Australian Alps

gippy tummy /jíppi-/ *n.* diarrhoea or similar stomach trouble, especially if brought on by travel to a hot country (*dated informal*) [From offensive British slang *Gippy* 'Egyptian'; from its affecting travellers to Egypt]

Gipsy *n.*, *adj.* = **Gypsy**

Giraffe

giraffe /jə raáf/ (*plural* **-raffes** *or* **-raffe**) *n.* an African ruminant mammal with an extremely long neck, long legs, and a yellowish coat mottled with brown patches that lives in open grassland. The giraffe is the tallest living animal. Latin name: *Giraffa camelopardalis*. [Late 16thC. Via French *girafe* or Italian *giraffa*, both from Arabic *zarāfa*.]

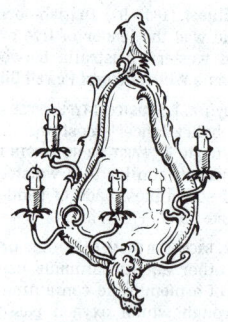

Girandole

girandole /jírrəndōl/, **girandola** /ji rándələ/ *n.* **1.** WALL-MOUNTED CANDLEHOLDER a wall-mounted branched candleholder that often incorporates a mirror between the candlestick branches **2.** STARBURST JEWELLERY an earring or pendant with a large central stone surrounded by several smaller ones **3.** ROTATING FIREWORK an elaborate rotating firework **4.** WATER JET a revolving water jet [Mid-17thC. Via French from Italian *girandola* from, ultimately, late Latin *gyrare* 'to gyrate'.]

girasol /jírrə sol/ (*plural* **-sols**), **girosol** *n.* MINERALS = **fire opal** [Late 16thC. From Italian *girasole* 'sunflower', from *girare* 'to turn' + *sole* 'sun'.]

Giraudoux /zheér ō doo/, **Jean** (1882–1944) French writer. He is remembered for witty novels and plays including *The Madwoman of Chaillot* (1945). Full name **Hyppolyte Jean Giraudoux**

gird[1] /gurd/ (**girds, girding, girded** *or* **girt** /gurt/, **girded** *or* **girt**) *v.* **1.** *vr.* GET READY to prepare yourself for conflict or vigorous activity **2.** *vt.* PUT BELT AROUND SB to put a girdle or belt around yourself or another person (*literary*) **3.** *vt.* FASTEN STH ON to secure sth to yourself with a belt, straps, or a girdle (*literary*) **4.** *vt.* SURROUND STH to surround or encompass sth (*literary*) ○ *a castle girded with a moat* **5.** *vt.* INVEST SB to provide sb with or dress sb in sth that is a sign of rank or honour (*literary*) [Old English *gyrdan*. Ultimately from a prehistoric Germanic base that is also the ancestor of English *girth*.]

gird[2] /gurd/ *vti.* (**girds, girding, girded**) *N England* JEER AT SB to jeer or gibe at sb ■ *n. N England* GIBE a gibe or taunt [12thC. Origin unknown. The original meaning was 'to move roughly, strike', hence the idea of a wounding remark.]

girder /gúrdər/ *n.* a large strong beam, often of steel, forming a main spanning and supporting element in a framework [Early 17thC. Formed from GIRD[1]. Originally applied to a wooden beam in a floor; from the idea that it 'girds' or supports the joists.]

girdle[1] /gúrd'l/ *n.* **1.** CLOTHES WOMAN'S FOUNDATION GARMENT a woman's elasticated foundation garment or corset extending from the waist to the thigh **2.** ACCESSORIES NARROW BELT a cord worn round the waist to hold in a large loose-fitting garment such as a kaftan or a monk's habit **3.** STH THAT SURROUNDS anything that surrounds or encircles sth (*literary*) **4.** ANAT RING OF BONE a ring-shaped structure of bone, especially the pelvic girdle and pectoral girdle that support the upper and lower limbs **5.** PART OF CUT GEMSTONE the outer edge of a gem, by which it is held in its setting **6.** FORESTRY RING ROUND TREE TRUNK a ring round a tree trunk made by removing the bark and a layer of the underlying cellular tissue (**cambium**) in order to kill the tree ■ *vt.* (**-dles, -dling, -dled**) **1.** SURROUND STH to surround or encircle sth (*literary*) **2.** CUT RING OF BARK FROM TREE to remove a ring of bark and a layer of the underlying cellular tissue (**cambium**) from a tree trunk in order to kill the tree [Old English *gyrdel*, of prehistoric Germanic origin]

girdle[2] /gúrd'l/ *n. Scotland, N England* a griddle (*nonstandard*) [15thC. Scots dialect alteration of GRIDDLE.]

girdler /gúrdlər/ *n.* an insect that makes a groove round a branch or twig in which to lay its eggs, thereby killing the branch

giri /gírri/ *n.* a social obligation or debt (*informal*) [From Japanese]

girl /gurl/ *n.* **1.** FEMALE CHILD a human female from birth until the age at which she is considered an adult **2.** YOUNG WOMAN a young woman (*often considered offensive*) **3.** ANY WOMAN a woman of any age, especially one who is a friend, a contemporary, or younger than the speaker (*informal; often considered offensive*) ○ *a night out with the girls* **4.** DAUGHTER sb's daughter, especially when a child (*informal*) **5.** GIRLFRIEND a man's or boy's girlfriend **6.** WAY OF ADDRESSING WOMAN used as a friendly, intimate, or patronizing form of address to a woman (*offensive in some contexts*) **7.** OFFENSIVE TERM an offensive term referring to a young woman servant or employee (*dated*) (*offensive*) **8.** *S Africa* OFFENSIVE TERM an offensive term referring to a Black female servant (*offensive*) **9.** FEMALE CREATURE a female animal or other creature, especially a young one (*informal; often used before a noun*) ○ *a girl kitten* [13thC. Origin unknown. Originally denoting a child of either sex.] — **girlhood** *n.* ◇ **a big girl's blouse** a man who is weak, sentimental, or ineffectual (*insult*)

WORD KEY: USAGE

girl or **woman**? ***Girl*** is used more often as an alternative for ***woman***, especially in reference to a young woman, than *boy* is for *man*. (*Boy* in reference to an adult is normally found only in the plural or in meanings associated with the word *boyfriend*.) The use of ***girl*** for an adult is sometimes regarded as patronizing or disrespectful, especially when it comes from a man.

girl Friday *n.* a young woman whose job is to be sb's personal assistant and to do general office work (*sometimes considered offensive*) [Modelled on 'Man Friday', the hero's all-round helper in *Robinson Crusoe* (1719) by the English writer Daniel Defoe]

girlfriend /gúrl frend/ *n.* **1.** WOMAN OR GIRL SWEETHEART OR LOVER a girl or woman with whom sb has a romantic or sexual relationship **2.** WOMAN FRIEND a woman who is the friend of another woman

Girl Guide *n.* a member of the Guide's Association (*dated*)

girlie /gúrli/ *adj.* SHOWING NUDE WOMEN showing or involving naked or scantily dressed women (*often considered offensive*) ■ *n.* **1.** OFFENSIVE TERM an offensive term of address when used by a man to a woman (*offensive*) **2.** LITTLE GIRL a little girl (*dated informal*) ■ *adj.* (*comparative* **girlier**, *superlative* **girliest**) = **girly**

girlish /gúrlish/ *adj.* **1.** OF GIRLS typical or characteristic of girls **2.** IMMATURE more suitable for a girl than for an adult woman —**girlishly** *adv.* —**girlishness** *n.*

Girl Scout *n.* a member of the girls' branch of the worldwide Scout movement in the United States

girly /gúrli/ (**-ier, -iest** *or* **-iest**) *adj.* extremely or deliberately feminine ○ *a girly lace collar*

girn /gurn/ (**girns, girning, girned**), **gurn** (**gurns, gurning, gurned**) *vi.* **1.** *Scotland, N England* COMPLAIN to complain, whine, or grumble **2.** *Scotland, N England* GRIMACE to make a bad-tempered or discontented face **3.** PULL WEIRD FACES to use the facial muscles to pull and twist the face into an absurdly grotesque expression, especially in a competition [14thC. Alteration of GRIN by changing the central sounds around. Originally meaning 'to snarl', the present senses became current in the 18thC.]

giro /jīrō/ *n.* (*plural* **-ros**) **1.** BANK TRANSFER SYSTEM a system that enables money to be transferred quickly and cheaply between accounts or between the financial institutions of a country **2.** BENEFIT CHEQUE a cheque, cashable at a post office, for the payment of a state benefit such as unemployment benefit (*informal*) ■ *vt.* (**-ros, -roing, -roed**) PAY MONEY BY GIRO SYSTEM to pay or transfer money by the giro system [Late 19thC. Via German from Italian, 'circulation (of money)'.]

giron *n.* = **gyron**

Gironde /zhi rónd, zhi róNd/ navigable river estuary in southwestern France, formed where the Dordogne and Garonne rivers meet. Length: 72 km/45 mi.

girosol *n.* = **girasol**

girt[1] past tense, past participle of **gird**

girt[2] /gurt/ (**girts, girting, girted**) *vt.* **1.** ENCIRCLE STH to encircle or surround sth (*literary*) **2.** MEASURE GIRTH OF BODY to take the measurement round the body (*archaic*)

girth /gurth/ *n.* **1.** DISTANCE ROUND the distance round sth thick and cylindrical, e.g. a tree trunk, sb's waist or sb ○ *a man of ample girth* **2.** RIDING SADDLE BAND a broad band fastened around the belly of a horse to keep a saddle in place ■ *vt.* (**girths, girthing, girthed**) **1.** SADDLE A HORSE to put or fasten a girth on a horse **2.** SURROUND STH to surround or encircle sth (*literary*) [14thC. From Old Norse *gjörð* 'girdle'.]

gisarme /gi zaárm/ *n.* a medieval foot soldier's weapon that had a long shaft and a head with an axe blade on one side and a sharp point on the other [13thC. From Old French *guisarme*, of uncertain origin: probably from prehistoric Germanic.]

Gisborne /gízbərn/ administrative region and important wine area on the North Island, New Zealand, that includes the city of the same name. Population: (1996). Area: 13,703 sq. km/5,291 sq. mi.

gismo *n.* = **gizmo**

gist /jist/ *n.* **1.** MAIN POINT the essential point or meaning of sth **2.** GROUNDS FOR LEGAL ACTION the essential grounds for a legal action [Early 18thC. From the Old French phrase *cest action gist* 'this action lies', from the idea of the 'basis' of a legal action, third person singular of *gesir* 'to lie'.]

git /git/ *n.* an annoying, troublesome, unpleasant, or thoughtless person (*informal insult*) [Mid-20thC. Variant of GET[2].]

gite /zheet/ *n.* a house, cottage, or apartment in France offering fairly simple accommodation that can be rented for a self-catering holiday [Late 18thC. From French *gîte* 'stopping place'.]

gittern /gíttərn/ *n.* a medieval stringed instrument that was a forerunner of the guitar [14thC. Via Old French *guiterne* from, ultimately, Latin *cithara* (see CITHARA).]

give /giv/ (**gives, giving, gave** /gayv/, **given** /gívv'n/) CORE MEANING: a verb used to indicate that sb presents or delivers sth that he or she owns to another person to keep or use it ○ *He gave Brian £800 with the understanding he would pay the rest at a later date.* ○ *The programme would give education grants to people who do community service.* ○ *My mother gave me this cardigan for Christmas.* ○ *What will you give me for the car?* ○ *When we arrived they gave us badges with our names on.*

1. *vt.* PASS STH TO SB to place sth that you are holding in the temporary possession of another person ○ *Could you give me the phone?* ○ *He gave her the umbrella while he searched in his pockets for some loose change.* **2.** *vt.* GRANT STH TO SB to allow sb to have sth such as power or a right ○ *Opponents of the bill claimed it gave too much power to the mine owners.* **3.** *vt.* COMMUNICATE STH to impart or convey sth such as information, advice, or opinions **4.** *vt.* CONVEY STH to cause sb to have an idea or impression ○ *Whatever gave you that idea?* **5.** *vt.* IMPART STH to make sb experience a particular physical or emotional feeling ○ *She said the steady paycheck gave her a sense of security.* **6.** *vt.* PERFORM STH to carry out or perform sth in public ○ *Not one of these actors gave a performance that was worthy of the prize.* **7.** *vt.* MAKE OR DO STH used with nouns referring to physical actions to indicate that the action is being made or done ○ *She gave Paul a quick, accusing glance.* **8.** *vt.* PROVIDE SERVICE to perform an action or service for sb ○ *He gave her a foot massage to relax her.* ○ *The guide gave us a tour of the ruins.* **9.** *vt.* DEVOTE STH to devote sth such as time or effort, or sacrifice sth for sb ○ *He gave his whole life to helping children in need.* **10.** *vt.* ORGANIZE STH to spend time organizing a social event ○ *They gave her a great send off when she retired last year.* **11.** *vt.* CAUSE SB TO BELIEVE STH to lead sb to have a particular understanding about sth ○ *I was given to understand that they would be coming to us for one weekend.* **12.** *vt.* VALUE STH to estimate sth at a particular amount or value ○ *What do you give for his chances of getting her back?* **13.** *vi.* YIELD to collapse or break under pressure ○ *The wheel gave under the heavy load.* ○ *When people are under constant pressure from work and home, something has to give.* **14.** *vt.* CONCEDE STH to yield to sb, or admit that sb has an advantage or a particular characteristic or ability **15.** *vt.* TOAST SB to propose a toast to sb ○ *I give you the bride and groom!* **16.** *n.* RESILIENCE the ability or tendency to yield under pressure [Old English *giefan*. Ultimately from an Indo-European base meaning 'to give', which is also the ancestor of English *habit*.] ◇ **give it up for sb** *or* **sth** to applaud sb or sth enthusiastically (*slang*) ◇ **give me** I'd rather do or have (*informal*) ○ *Give me a quiet evening with a book any time.* ◇ **give or take** used to indicate that a figure given is fairly accurate, within the stated range ○ *worth about half a million, give or take a few thousand pounds*

WORD KEY: SYNONYMS

give, present, confer, bestow, donate, grant

CORE MEANING: to hand over sth to sb

give a general word used to talk about the handing over of sth to sb else, often without compensation; **present** used especially to talk about giving sth in a formal or ceremonial way; **confer** a fairly formal word used to talk about giving sb an honour, privilege, or award, often at a formal ceremony; **bestow** a formal word used, like 'confer', to talk about giving sb an honour, privilege, or award. It can also be used to talk about giving a gift and is often used to suggest that this is an act of great generosity, or to suggest condescension on the part of the giver; **donate** used to talk about giving a contribution to some kind of good cause. It is used specifically in a medical context to talk about the giving of blood for blood transfusions or of organs for purposes of transplant; **grant** used to talk about giving sth abstract such as permission or approval, especially at the discretion of a person in authority. It can also be used to talk about giving concrete gifts such as money.

give away *vt.* **1.** GIVE STH AS A PRESENT to give or offer sth without charging for it **2.** DISCLOSE BY MISTAKE to reveal information or a secret, often without meaning to **3.** BETRAY to betray sb by providing information **4.** PRESENT BRIDE TO HUSBAND AT WEDDING to accompany a bride to her future husband's side and formally present her to him just before the words of the wedding ceremony are spoken **5.** SPORTS LET OPPONENT SCORE POINT to allow an opponent to get an advantage, especially inadvertently, through poor or illegal play **6.** *ANZ* ABANDON STH to abandon or give up on sth

give back *vt.* to return sth, especially to its rightful or original owner

give in *v.* **1.** *vi.* LOSE to admit defeat **2.** *vi.* ACCEPT CONDITIONS to accept demands or conditions **3.** *vt.* HAND OVER to hand over or deliver sth, especially a piece of school work, to sb who is expecting it ○ *He gave his essay in a week late.* **4.** *vi. US* BREAK to collapse or break under pressure

give of *vr.* to devote or dedicate your time or energy to sth

give off *v.* **1.** *vt.* EMIT STH to send out or emit sth **2.** *vi. N Ireland* SAY STH ANGRILY to speak one's mind angrily (*informal*)

give on to *vt.* to overlook or lead to sth ○ *The French windows give on to a small paved area.*

give out *v.* **1.** *vt.* HAND OVER to hand over or distribute sth **2.** *vt.* MAKE STH KNOWN to declare sth or make sth known, especially publicly ○ *She gave out the exam marks in reverse order.* **3.** *vt.* EMIT to send out or emit sth **4.** *vi.* BE USED UP to run out or be finished ○ *My courage gave out, and I couldn't face her after all.* **5.** *vi.* STOP WORKING to fail, or stop working **6.** *vt.* CRICKET DISMISS A BATSMAN in cricket, to declare that a batsman is dismissed

give over *vi.* to stop doing sth, especially sth that is annoying to others (*informal; usually a command*)

give over to *v.* **1.** *vt.* RESERVE STH FOR A PURPOSE to dedicate or assign sth to a particular purpose or use ○ *This area will be given over to a children's playground.* **2.** *vr.* ABANDON YOURSELF TO STH to abandon yourself to an emotion or experience (*literary*) ○ *She gave herself over to despair.*

give up *v.* **1.** *vi.* SURRENDER to surrender or admit defeat **2.** *vt.* HAND OVER SB OR STH to hand over or part with sb or sth ○ *She gave up her seat to the man with a baby.* **3.** *vt.* STOP USING OR DOING STH to stop or renounce using or doing sth ○ *give up chocolate for a week* **4.** *vt.* STOP TRYING to abandon a pursuit that has a goal ○ *Darkness fell, but they didn't give up trying to finish the game or match.* **5.** *vt.* LOSE HOPE FOR GOOD OUTCOME to stop hoping for a good outcome with regard to sb or sth ○ *Where have you been? We'd given you up as lost.* **6.** *vt.* DEVOTE YOURSELF TO STH to devote or dedicate yourself to an emotion, experience, or activity, especially exclusively ○ *He gave himself up to working for the cause.* **7.** *vt.* REVEAL INFORMATION to reveal information or a secret

give up on *vt.* **1.** ABANDON PLAN to abandon sth, especially a plan **2.** DESPAIR OF SB OR STH to lose hope about sb or sth

give way *vi.* **1.** to become useless, break, or otherwise fail, especially under weight or pressure or from age or wear **2.** TRANSP to slow down or stop in order to let another vehicle pass

give way to *vt.* **1.** to allow sb or sth to have priority or to take precedence **2.** to be replaced or superseded by sb or sth ○ *The rain gave way to patchy sunshine.* **3.** to allow sth, especially an emotion, to be expressed

give-and-take *n.* (*informal*) **1.** COOPERATION AND COMPROMISE mutual cooperation and understanding between people or groups, often involving concessions on all sides **2.** MUTUALLY BENEFICIAL EXCHANGE OF IDEAS a useful exchange of ideas or information in which everyone involved benefits

giveaway /gív əway/ *n.* **1.** STH THAT REVEALS sth that serves to reveal, betray, or expose sth ○ *Her accent's a dead giveaway.* **2.** GIFT sth that is offered free of charge or at very little cost, often as a publicity gimmick or incentive to buy (*informal*) **3.** = **freesheet** **4.** *US* GAME SHOW a radio or TV game show that offers contestants the chance to win prizes, especially cash prizes (*informal*) ■ *adj.* (*informal*) **1.** VERY INEXPENSIVE extremely low in price **2.** FREE free of charge ○ *a giveaway sample of a new shampoo*

giveback /gív bak/ *n.* sth that is or has been returned (*informal*)

given /gív'n/ past participle of **give** ■ *adj.* **1.** PARTICULAR relating to a specific person, thing, or concept **2.** ARRANGED EARLIER previously arranged or specified **3.** VALIDATED validated or executed on the date mentioned (*formal*) ○ *this last will and testament given by my hand this 13th day of February 1898* ■ *prep.* **1.** GRANTED assuming that sb has the opportunity or ability to do or have sth ○ *Given time, I'm sure we can find a solution.* **2.** IN VIEW OF taking into consideration ○ *given the uncertainty of the situation* ■ *n.* ACCEPTED FACT a fact or event that is accepted as true or definite at the outset and that affects following or subsequent reasoning ◇ **be given to** to be inclined to sth or likely to do or be sth

given name *n.* the name or names that sb is given at birth or baptism in addition to the family name

giver /gívvər/ *n.* sb who gives sth (*often used in combination*)

Giza /géezə/ city in northern Egypt on the western bank of the River Nile, southwest of Cairo. It is the site of the Sphinx and Egypt's three most famous pyramids. Population: 2,144,000 (1992).

gizmo /gízmō/ (*plural* **-mos**), **gismo** (*plural* **-mos**) *n.* a gadget, especially a mechanical or electrical device considered to be more complicated than necessary or one whose name is not known or forgotten (*informal*) ○ *a new video recorder with all the latest gizmos* [Mid-20thC. Origin unknown.]

gizzard /gízzərd/ *n.* **1.** BIRDS PART OF BIRD'S DIGESTIVE TRACT a thick-walled muscular sac in the alimentary tract of birds, situated immediately behind the first chamber of the stomach, where food is broken down by muscular action. The food is also ground against small stones ingested for that purpose. **2.** ZOOL DIGESTIVE STRUCTURE a structure in invertebrates and fish where digestion takes place **3.** ANAT STOMACH the stomach or alimentary canal generally (*informal*) [14thC. Via Old French *giser* from, ultimately, Latin *gigeria* 'cooked poultry entrails'.]

Gk *abbr.* Greek

glabella /glə béllə/ (*plural* **-lae** /-lee/) *n.* the part of the human forehead that lies just above the nose and between the eyebrows. It is one of the crucial points used in measuring and classifying skull types in physical anthropology and craniometry. [Early 19thC. Via modern Latin from, ultimately, Latin *glaber* (see GLABROUS).] —**glabellar** *adj.*

glabrate /gláybrayt, -brət/ *adj.* **1.** = **glabrous** *adj.* **2.** ALMOST HAIRLESS almost completely smooth and hairless [Mid-19thC. Formed from Latin *glabrare* 'to make bald', from *glaber* (see GLABROUS).]

glabrescent /glay bréssənt/ *adj.* becoming hairless over time

glabrous /gláybrəss/ *adj.* smooth and lacking hairs or bristles ○ *glabrous leaves* [Mid-17thC. Formed from Latin *glaber* 'bald'.] —**glabrousness** *n.*

glacé /glássay/ *adj.* **1.** GLAZED WITH SUGAR SOLUTION coated with a sugar solution that results in a glazed finish ○ *glacé cherries* **2.** MADE FROM ICING SUGAR AND LIQUID made by mixing icing sugar and a liquid, usually water **3.** SMOOTHLY GLOSSY having a smooth glossy finish [Mid-19thC. From French, the past participle of *glacer* 'to glaze', from *glace* (see GLACIER).]

Glace Bay /gláyss-/ town on the Atlantic coast in Cape Breton County, northeastern Nova Scotia, Canada, situated on the Atlantic Ocean 19 km/12 mi. east of Sydney. Population: 19,501 (1991).

glacial /gláysh'l/ *adj.* **1.** RELATING TO GLACIER relating to or caused by a glacier or glaciers ○ *glacial movements and deposits* **2.** CONTAINING EXPANSES OF ICE characterized by the presence of ice masses **3.** GEOL ICE-AGE used to describe any geological time when a large part of the earth was covered in ice **4.** FRIGID icily cold ○ *a glacial wind* **5.** COLDLY HOSTILE unfriendly or hostile ○ *a glacial look* **6.** DETACHED characterized by detachment and an absence of emotion ○ *glacial determination* **7.** SLOW moving or advancing extremely slowly ○ *the glacial pace of the negotiations* ■ *n.* **glacial, Glacial** = **glacial period** [Mid-17thC. Via Old French from Latin *glacialis* 'icy', from *glacies* (see GLACIER).] —**glacially** *adv.*

glacial acetic acid *n.* acetic acid that is 99.8% or more pure [Because it forms crystals that resemble ice]

glacial period, **glacial epoch** *n.* any period of geological time when most of the earth was covered in ice

glaciate /gláyssi ayt/ (**-ates, -ating, -ated**) *v.* **1.** *vti.* ICE OVER to cover sth, or become covered, with the action of a glacier **2.** *vt.* AFFECT BY GLACIER to affect sth by the action of a glacier, especially by erosion [Early 17thC. From Latin *glaciare* 'to freeze', from *glacies* (see GLACIER).] —**glaciation** /gláyssi áysh'n/ *n.*

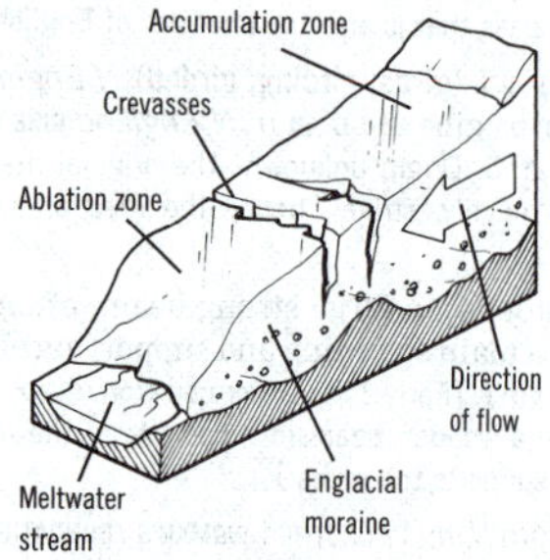

Glacier: Composition of a glacier

glacier /glássi ər/ *n.* a large body of continuously accumulating ice and compacted snow, formed in mountain valleys or at the poles, that deforms under its own weight and slowly moves [Mid-18thC. From French, formed from *glace* 'ice', from, ultimately, Latin *glacies*.] —**glaciered** *adj.*

glacier cream *n.* a sunblock designed to combat the effects of ultraviolet radiation that climbers experience above the snow line, where the sun reflects strongly off the snow

glacier meal *n.* = **rock flour**

glacier milk *n.* water cloudy with particles of rock that flows from a melting glacier

glaciologist /gláyssi óllәjist/ *n.* sb who studies the formation, movement, and effects of glaciers

glaciology /gláyssi ólləji/ *n.* the branch of scientific study concerned with the formation, movement, and effects of glaciers and ice in general —**glaciologic** /gláyssi ə lójjik/ *adj.* —**glaciological** /-lójjik'l/ *adj.*

glacis /gláyssis/ (*plural* **-cises** /-si seez/ *or* **-cis** /-siz/) *n.* **1.** GENTLE INCLINE a slope, especially one that is not very long or steep **2.** DEFENSIVE SLOPE a slope in front of a fortification designed to make it easier to fire on attacking forces **3.** NEUTRAL TERRITORY a stretch of neutral ground between two opposing or warring forces **4.** = **glacis plate** [Late 17thC. From French, formed from Old French *glacier* (see GLANCE).]

glacis plate *n.* the armoured plate at the front of a military tank [From its slant]

glad[1] /glad/ *adj.* (**gladder, gladdest**) **1.** DELIGHTED happy and pleased ○ *I'm so glad you came.* **2.** CHEERFULLY WILLING willing or ready to do sth ○ *always glad to help* **3.** GRATEFUL appreciative of or grateful for sth ○ *glad of the chance to relax* **4.** PLEASING giving pleasure, delight, or happiness ○ *on this glad occasion* **5.** BRIGHT bright and cheerful (*literary*) ○ *this glad June day* ■ *vti.* (**glads, gladding, gladded**) GLADDEN to gladden sb (*archaic*) [Old English *glæd*. Ultimately from a prehistoric Germanic word. Originally in the meaning 'bright, shining'.] —**gladness** *n.*

glad[2] /glad/ *n.* PLANTS a gladiolus (*informal*) [Early 20thC. Shortening.]

gladden /gládd'n/ (**-dens, -dening, -dened**) *vti.* to feel or cause sb to feel cheerful and hopeful ○ *It gladdens my heart to hear that.*

glade /glayd/ *n.* an area in a wood or forest without trees or bushes [Early 16thC. Origin uncertain.] —**glady** *adj.*

glad hand *n.* **1.** WARM BUT INSINCERE HANDSHAKE a hand extended in welcome or greeting, especially one offered insincerely or for motives of self-advancement **2.** CONVIVIAL HELLO a friendly welcome

glad-hand (**glad-hands, glad-handing, glad-handed**) *vti.* to offer sb a friendly greeting or handshake, often insincerely or for motives of self-advancement —**glad-hander** *n.*

gladiate /gláddi ət/ *adj.* shaped like a sword ○ *the gladiate leaves of an iris* [Late 18thC. Formed from Latin *gladius* (see GLADIATOR).]

gladiator /gláddi aytər/ *n.* **1.** FIGHTER IN ROMAN ARENA a professional fighter in ancient Rome who fought another combatant or a wild animal in public entertainments set in an arena. Often gladiators were criminals or enslaved men who were equipped variously with nets, nooses, swords, or other weapons. **2.** KEEN SUPPORTER OR CAMPAIGNER sb who vigorously fights for or against a cause or actively campaigns for or against sth **3.** *US* BOXER a professional boxer (*informal*) [Mid-16thC. From Latin, formed from *gladius* 'sword'.] —**gladiatorial** /gláddi ə táwri əl/ *adj.*

gladiolus /gláddi óləss/ (*plural* **-lus** *or* **-li** /-lī/ *or* **-luses**), **gladiola** /-ólə/ (*plural* **-las** *or* **-la**) *n.* **1.** PLANTS TALL FLOWERING GARDEN PLANT a tropical and southern African plant with long sword-shaped leaves and large funnel-shaped flowers arranged in tall spikes that is widely grown as a garden flower. Genus: *Gladiolus.* **2.** ANAT CENTRE OF BREASTBONE the large central part of the breastbone (**sternum**) [16thC. From Latin, literally 'little sword', from *gladius* (see GLADIATOR).]

gladly /gládli/ *adv.* **1.** WITH GREAT WILLINGNESS more than willingly ○ *I'll gladly help.* **2.** HAPPILY in a pleased, cheerful, or happy way

glad rags *npl.* sb's best clothes, reserved for special occasions (*informal*)

gladsome /gládssəm/ *adj.* feeling, showing, or bringing happiness (*literary*) ○ *gladsome tidings* —**gladsomely** *adv.* —**gladsomeness** *n.*

Gladstone[1] /gládstən/ *n.* a small four-wheeled horse-drawn carriage with a collapsible roof [Mid-19thC (see GLADSTONE BAG)]

Gladstone[2] /gládstən/ coastal city in southeastern Queensland, Australia, an industrial centre and tourist resort. It is the gateway to the southern Great Barrier Reef. Population: 26,415 (1996).

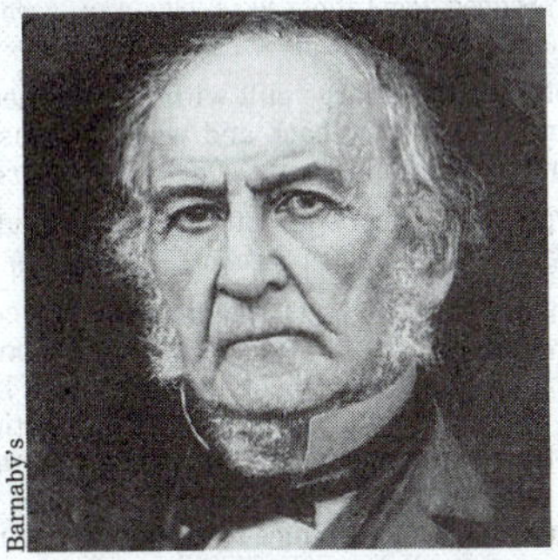

W. E. Gladstone

Gladstone, W. E. (1809–98) British statesman. The leader of the Liberal Party after 1867, he was four times prime minister between 1868 and 1894. He introduced national education in Britain (1870). Full name **William Ewart Gladstone**

Gladstone bag *n.* a small suitcase or portmanteau consisting of a rigid frame on which two compartments of the same size are hinged together [Late 19thC. Named after William Ewart GLADSTONE, who was noted for the unusual amount of travelling he undertook in the course of his public life.]

Glagolitic /glággō líttik/ *adj.* **1.** LANG OF OR IN SLAVONIC ALPHABET belonging or relating to or written in the ancient Slavonic alphabet that was replaced by the Cyrillic alphabet and survives only in certain Roman Catholic liturgical books **2.** CHR OF CROATIAN CATHOLIC COMMUNITY belonging or relating to a Roman Catholic community of southwestern Croatia, whose liturgical books continue to be written in the Glagolitic alphabet [Early 19thC. Via modern Latin

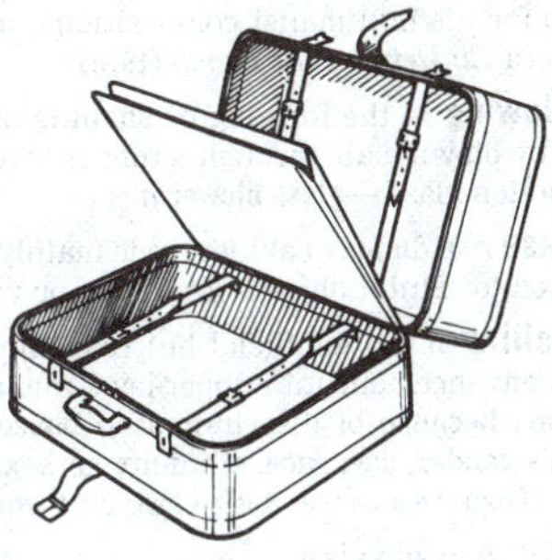
Gladstone bag

glagoliticus and Serbo-Croatian *glagoljica* from, ultimately, Old Church Slavonic *glagolŭ* 'word'.]

glair, glaire *n.* **1.** EGG WHITE a sizing, glazing, or adhesive substance made from egg white and used especially in bookbinding **2.** SUBSTANCE SIMILAR TO EGG-WHITE SIZING a substance that resembles glair in appearance or function ■ *vt.* (**glairs, glairing, glaired; glaires, glairing, glaired**) PUT GLAIR ON STH to apply glair to sth [14thC. Via French from, ultimately, Latin *clarus* 'clear'.]

glam /glam/ *adj.* EXTREMELY GLAMOROUS glamorous, especially in an overstated or ironic way (*slang*) ○ *a really glam dress* ■ *n.* **1.** EXTREME GLAMOUR glamour, especially when it is overstated or ironic (*slang*) **2.** MUSIC GLAM ROCK glam rock (*informal*) ■ *vt.* (**glams, glamming, glammed**) **glam, glam up** GLAMORIZE EXCESSIVELY to make sb or sth glamorous, especially in an overstated or camp way (*slang*) [Mid-20thC. Shortening.]

Glamorgan /glə máwrgən/ former county in southern Wales that included the present-day counties of Cardiff and Swansea

glamorize /glámmə rīz/ (**-izes, -izing, -ized**), **glamorise** (**-ises, -ising, -ised**) *vt.* **1.** MAKE GLAMOROUS to make sb or sth glamorous **2.** ROMANTICIZE to make sth seem more interesting, romantic, or glamorous than it really is —**glamorization** /glámmə rī záysh'n/ *n.* —**glamorizer** /-rīzər/ *n.*

glamorous /glámmərəss/, **glamourous** *adj.* **1.** EXCITING AND DESIRABLE desirable, especially in an exciting, stylish, or opulent way ○ *a glamorous life-style* **2.** ARTIFICIALLY GOOD-LOOKING dressed or made up to be good-looking, especially in a high-fashion manner ○ *glamorous models strutting along the catwalk* —**glamorously** *adv.* —**glamorousness** *n.*

glamour /glámmər/ *n.* **1.** EXCITING ALLURE an irresistible alluring quality that sb or sth possesses by virtue of seeming much more exciting, romantic, or fashionable than ordinary people or things ○ *the glamour of a career in the movies* **2.** HIGH-FASHION AND EXPENSIVE GOOD LOOKS striking physical good looks or sexual impact, especially when it is enhanced with highly fashionable clothes or make-up **3.** SPELL a magical spell or charm (*archaic*) ■ *adj.* HAVING STYLISH GOOD LOOKS OR DESIRABLE EXCITEMENT characterized by glamour ○ *a glamour job in advertising* [Early 18thC. Originally a Scottish English alteration of GRAMMAR, meaning 'enchantment, spell'.]

glamourous *adj.* = **glamorous** *adj.* 1, **glamorous** *adj.* 2

glam rock *n.* a style of pop music in the UK in the 1970s performed by singers and musicians wearing outrageous clothes, make-up, hairstyles, and huge platform-soled boots. Its most famous exponents were the singers Gary Glitter and Marc Bolan and the band Sweet.

glance /glaanss/ *v.* (**glances, glancing, glanced**) **1.** *vi.* LOOK QUICKLY to look at sth quickly, especially for only a second or two ○ *He glanced in our direction.* **2.** *vi.* MAKE A CURSORY EXAMINATION to look over or through sth without really studying it **3.** *vi.* TOUCH ON BRIEFLY to make a brief or passing allusion to sth ○ *an introductory course that merely glances at the wider historical issues* **4.** *vi.* GLINT OR SHINE to reflect or shine, especially intermittently or for only a short time ○ *green feathers glancing in the sunlight* **5.** *vt.* STRIKE AT ANGLE to strike sth briefly or lightly at an angle ○ *The stone glanced his shoulder.* **6.** *vt.* CRICKET DEFLECT CRICKET BALL in cricket, to hit a bowled ball with the bat held at an angle so that the ball is deflected to the leg side ■ *n.* **1.** QUICK LOOK a quick look at sb or sth ○ *a glance in our direction* **2.** PASSING MENTION a brief mention of sth ○ *The book takes only a brief glance at contemporary music.* **3.** CURSORY EXAMINATION a cursory quick examination of sth ○ *I haven't even had a glance at the report yet.* **4.** OBLIQUE STRIKE an act or instance of sth striking another thing briefly or lightly at an angle **5.** GLINT OF LIGHT a sudden or quick flash or gleam of light ○ *glances of sunlight through the trees* **6.** CRICKET DEFLECTION OF CRICKET BALL in cricket, a stroke in which the bat is held at an angle so that the ball is deflected to the leg side [15thC. Alteration (influenced by *glent* 'to shine') of earlier glace, from Old French *glacier* 'to slide' (see GLACIER.] ◇ **at a glance** immediately and without having to make a close study ◇ **at first glance** initially or on first examination

glance off *vt.* to come into quick light contact with sth and then deflect at an angle ○ *The stone glanced off the windscreen.*

glancing /glaanssing/ *adj.* **1.** STRIKING OBLIQUELY coming into contact with another object and then deflecting at an angle ○ *a glancing blow* **2.** FLICKERING OR FLASHING giving off light in a flickering or flashing manner **3.** TEMPORARY lasting only a short time —**glancingly** *adv.*

gland[1] /gland/ *n.* **1.** ANAT SECRETING CELL MASS a mass of cells or an organ that removes substances from the bloodstream and excretes them, or secretes them back into the blood in concentrated or altered form with a specific physiological purpose. Endocrine glands are ductless and secrete directly into the bloodstream, while exocrine glands, e.g. the salivary glands, the pancreas, and the liver, secrete via ducts to a surface. **2.** ANAT ORGANIC STRUCTURE RESEMBLING GLAND an organ or other anatomical structure that resembles a gland, especially, in popular usage, a lymph node **3.** BOT PLANT ORGAN a secreting organ or structure of a plant, e.g. a nectary gland [Late 17thC. Via French from, ultimately, Latin *glandula*, literally 'little acorn', 'tonsil' (from its shape), from *glans* 'acorn'.] —**glandless** *adj.*

gland[2] /gland/ *n.* a metal sleeve fitted round a rotating shaft or rod to prevent leakage, e.g. round a shaft emerging from a ship's hull [Early 19thC. Origin uncertain: probably from, ultimately, Old Norse *glam* 'noise'.]

glanders /glándərz/ *n.* an infectious, often fatal disease of horses, characterized by ulcers of the skin, lungs, or upper respiratory tract and heavy discharge of mucus from the nose. It is caused by a bacterium *Pseudomonas mallei.* (*takes a singular verb*) [15thC. Via Old French *glandres* 'swelling of the glands' from, ultimately, Latin *glandula* (see GLAND[1]).] —**glandered** *adj.* —**glanderous** *adj.*

glandes plural of **glans**

glandular /glándyōōlər/, **glandulous** /glándyōōləss/ *adj.* **1.** ANAT RELATING TO GLANDS relating to, functioning as, or affecting a gland or glands **2.** MED RESULTING FROM GLAND DYSFUNCTION used to describe a condition caused by a malfunctioning gland or glands **3.** HAVING GLAND characterized by the presence of a gland or glands **4.** BODILY natural to the body, especially hormonally or sexually (*informal*) [Mid-18thC. Via French *glandulaire* from, ultimately, Latin *glandula* (see GLAND[1]).]

glandular fever *n.* an acute infectious disease caused by the Epstein-Barr virus and marked by fever, swelling of the lymph nodes, sore throat, and an increased amount of lymphocytes in the blood. Technical name **infectious mononucleosis**

glandule /glándyool/ *n.* a small gland or a part resembling a small gland [14thC. Directly or via French from Latin *glandula* (see GLAND[1]).]

glandulous *adj.* ANAT = **glandular** *adj.* 1 [14thC. From Latin *glandulosus*, from *glandula* (see GLAND[1]).] —**glandulously** *adv.*

glans /glanz/ (*plural* **glandes** /glándeez/) *n.* **1. glans, glans penis** TIP OF PENIS the rounded tip of a penis **2. glans, glans clitoridis** TIP OF CLITORIS the erectile tissue at the tip of a clitoris [Mid-17thC. From Latin, 'acorn'. From its shape.]

glare /glair/ *vi.* (**glares, glaring, glared**) **1.** STARE STONILY to stare intently and angrily **2.** LOOK ANGRILY to express or signal anger, disapproval, contempt, or another negative emotion by giving a steady stare **3.** BE UNPLEASANTLY BRIGHT to shine brightly and intensely, often dazzlingly **4. STAND OUT OBTRUSIVELY** to be very conspicuous, blatant, or obtrusive ○ *Mistakes glared from every page of the report.* ■ *n.* **1. ANGRY LOOK** a prolonged stare, usually expressing anger, disapproval, contempt, or another negative emotion **2. EXCESSIVE BRIGHTNESS** dazzling or uncomfortable brightness ○ *a screen on the monitor to reduce glare* **3. MEDIA SPOTLIGHT** excessive attention from the media **4. GAUDY ORNAMENTATION** gaudy coloration or decoration [13thC. From Middle Low German *glaren* 'to gleam'.]

glaring /gláiring/ *adj.* **1. OBVIOUS** very obvious, or easily seen or detected ○ *a report full of glaring mistakes* **2. ANGRY** expressing anger, disapproval, contempt, or another negative emotion ○ *a glaring look of sheer contempt* **3. UNPLEASANTLY BRIGHT** intensely or dazzlingly bright **4. GARISH** gaudy or brash, especially in a tasteless way ○ *painted in glaring oranges and greens* —**glaringly** *adv.* —**glaringness** *n.*

glary /gláiri/ (**-ier, -iest**) *adj.* **1. STARING** staring steadily and often angrily ○ *glary eyes* **2. EXCESSIVELY BRIGHT** dazzlingly or uncomfortably bright ○ *a glary computer screen*

Glasgow /gláazgō, glázgō/ **1.** city on the River Clyde, southwestern Scotland. An industrial and commercial centre, it has a cathedral and three universities. Population: 616,430 (1996). **2.** council area in west-central Scotland. Population: 623,850 (1996). Area: 175 sq. km/68 sq. mi. Official name **City of Glasgow**

Glasgow kiss *n.* a very aggressive head butt directed at the face, especially the nose, of another person (*slang humorous*)

glasnost /glássnost/ *n.* a policy that commits a government or organization to greater accountability, openness, discussion, and freer disclosure of information than previously, especially that of Mikhail Gorbachev in the former Soviet Union. ◊ **perestroika** [Late 20thC. From Russian, literally 'publicness'.]

glass /glaass/ *n.* **1. TRANSPARENT SOLID SUBSTANCE** a hard, usually transparent, substance that shatters easily and is used for making such objects as windows, bottles, and lenses. It is made by melting sand in combination with other oxides such as lime or soda without crystallizing them. **2. UNCRYSTALLIZED SUBSTANCE RESEMBLING GLASS** a solid substance similar to glass formed by melting and cooling without crystallizing **3. GLASS CONTAINER** a container without a handle made from glass, for drinking from **4. MEASURE AMOUNT IN GLASS** the amount a drinking glass holds **5.** HOUSEHOLD = **glassware 6. GARDENING PROTECTING COVER** a cloche, greenhouse, or other insulating material used to protect germinating plants ○ *Keep the seedlings under glass for the first four weeks.* **7.** = looking glass **8. BAROMETER** a barometer (*dated*) **9.** = magnifying glass **10.** = volcanic glass **11.** = fibreglass ■ *adj.* **OF GLASS** made from or fitted with glass ■ *vt.* (**glasses, glassing, glassed**) **1. COVER WITH GLASS** to cover or fit sth with glass ○ *glassed the porch* **2. INSERT INTO A GLASS CONTAINER** to put sth into a glass container or one made of a material resembling glass ○ *glassed the specimens in formalin* **3. CUT SB USING GLASS** to injure sb with a drinking glass or a broken part of a drinking glass, usually in the face (*slang*) [Old English *glæs*. Ultimately from a prehistoric Germanic word that is also the ancestor of English *glare* and German *Glas* 'glass'.]

Glass /glaass/, **Philip** (*b.* 1937) US composer. He is

AKG London
Philip Glass

known for his minimalist compositions, including the opera *Einstein on the Beach* (1976).

glass blowing *n.* the forming or shaping of a glass object by blowing air through a tube into a mass of semimolten glass —**glass blower** *n.*

glass case *n.* a display cabinet made mainly of glass and used to exhibit objects of interest or value

glass ceiling *n.* an unofficial but real impediment to sb's advancement into upper-level management positions because of discrimination based on the person's gender, age, race, ethnicity, or sexual preference [From the idea that it is an invisible barrier]

glass chin *n.* = glass jaw

glass cloth *n.* **1. CLOTH FOR DRYING GLASS CONTAINERS** a cloth, usually made of closely woven linen, used for drying glasses and dishes **2. CLOTH FOR POLISHING** a polishing cloth with fine particles of glass in it

glass cutter *n.* **1. IMPLEMENT FOR CUTTING GLASS** a tool used to cut glass or to etch designs into glass **2. SB WHO CUTS GLASS** sb whose job is to cut glass or to make cut glass

glassed-in *adj.* made using glass panes ○ *a glassed-in conservatory*

glass eel *n.* a larval form of the American or European eel with a flattened transparent body, found in the Atlantic Ocean

glasses /gláassiz/ *npl.* **1. OUTER EYEWEAR** a pair of sight-correcting or protective lenses set in frames that fit over the ears and sit on the bridge of the nose **2. BINOCULARS** a pair of binoculars

glass eye *n.* an artificial eye made from glass, or material similar to glass, so as to resemble a natural eye

glass fibre *n.* = fibreglass 4

glassfish /gláass fish/ (*plural* **glassfish** *or* **glassfishes**) *n.* **1. TROPICAL FISH POPULAR FOR AQUARIUMS** a small transparent tropical fish found along the coasts and rivers of Africa and the Indian and western Pacific oceans that is commonly kept as an aquarium fish. Genus: *Chanda*. **2. PACIFIC FOOD FISH** a slender, almost transparent, food fish belonging to one of 14 species found in the northwestern Pacific Ocean. Family: Salangidae.

glassful /gláassfool/ *n.* = glass *n.* 4

glass harmonica *n.* a set of drinking glasses or glass bowls, filled to graduated levels with water, that produce sounds of different pitches when their rims are rubbed with a moist finger. It was popular as a musical instrument in the 18th century when various mechanical versions also existed, including one designed by Benjamin Franklin.

glasshouse /gláass howss/ (*plural* **-houses** /-howziz/) *n.* **1.** = greenhouse **2. MILITARY PRISON** a military prison or detention centre (*slang*) **3. MEDIA PROMINENCE** a public position that brings sb a high level of media attention and scrutiny

glassine /gla seén/ *n.* a transparent paper treated with a glaze to make it greaseproof and resistant to the passage of air, and used for book jackets and food packaging

glass jaw *n.* in boxing, a jaw that is highly vulnerable to an opponent's punches (*informal*) [From the idea that it is easily broken]

glassmaker /gláass maykǝr/ *n.* sb whose job is to make glass or glass objects —**glassmaking** *n.*

glass snake *n.* a limbless lizard, or one with vestigial limbs, of Europe, Asia, and North America that can, as a defence mechanism, snap off its tail to confuse predators. Genus: *Ophisaurus*. [From its brittle tail]

glassware /gláass wair/ *n.* objects made of glass considered as a group

glass wool *n.* fine-spun glass fibres formed into a woolly mass and used for insulation, as air filters, or in the manufacture of fibreglass

glasswork /gláass wurk/ *n.* **1. FITTING OF GLASS** the technique or result of cutting and fitting glass, especially glass panes for windows, doors, and conservatories **2. MAKING OF GLASS** the production or

manufacture of glass or glass objects **3.** = glassware —**glassworker** *n.*

glassworks /gláass wurks/ (*plural* **-works**) *n.* a factory for the manufacture of glass or glass objects

glasswort /gláass wurt/ (*plural* **-wort** *or* **-worts**) *n.* a plant with fleshy stems and small leaves that grows in salt marshes and was formerly a source of the soda used in making glass. Genus: *Salicornia*.

glassy /gláassi/ (**-ier, -iest**) *adj.* **1. SMOOTH AND SLIPPERY** having a highly smooth, slippery, often reflective, surface **2. LIKE GLASS** resembling glass in being smooth, reflective, or transparent **3. BLANKLY EXPRESSIONLESS** lacking expression or animation ○ *a blank glassy look* —**glassily** *adv.* —**glassiness** *n.*

glassy-eyed *adj.* having a blank staring expression

Glastonbury /glástǝnbǝri/ historic market town in Somerset, southern England. The site of a 10th-century abbey and an Iron Age lake village, it also hosts an annual music festival. Population: 8,100 (1993).

Glaswegian /glaaz weéjǝn/ *n.* sb who lives in or was born or brought up in Glasgow, Scotland [Early 19thC. Formed from GLASGOW, on the model of NORWEGIAN.] —**Glaswegian** *adj.*

Glauber's salt /glówbǝrz-/, **Glauber salt** *n.* a colourless crystalline sodium sulphate. It is used in solar energy systems, in making dyes, glass, and paper, and as a laxative. [Mid-18thC. Named after the German chemist Johann Rudolf *Glauber* (1604–68), who first produced it.]

glaucoma /glaw kṓmǝ/ *n.* eye disorder marked by abnormally high pressure within the eyeball that leads to damage of the optic disc and, if not treated, causes impaired vision and sometimes blindness [Mid-17thC. Directly or via Latin from Greek *glaukōma*, from *glaukos* (see GLAUCOUS).] —**glaucomatous** *adj.*

glauconite /gláwkǝ nīt/ *n.* a clayey green mineral consisting of a silicate of iron, potassium, and aluminium, and used as a fertilizer [Mid-19thC. Via German *Glaukonit* from Greek *glaukos* (see GLAUCOUS).] —**glauconitic** /gláwkǝ níttik/ *adj.*

glaucous /gláwkǝss/ *adj.* **1. COVERED IN GREYISH POWDER** covered in a greyish, whitish, or bluish waxy or powdery substance that rubs off easily, e.g. the bloom on grapes **2. COLOURS GREYISH-GREEN OR BLUE** having a dull greyish-green or blue colour [Late 17thC. Formed from Latin *glaucus* 'blue-grey, green', which came from Greek *glaukos*.]

glaucous gull *n.* a large gull with a white head and tail and a light-grey back and wings that is found in northern regions. Genus: *Larus hyperboreus*.

glaur /glawr/ *n.* *Scotland* soft or slimy mud (*nonstandard*) [15thC. Origin unknown.] —**glaury** *adj.*

glaze /glayz/ *v.* (**glazes, glazing, glazed**) **1.** *vt.* **CERAMICS COVER WITH FINISH LIKE GLASS** to put a clear or coloured coating on a ceramic object and fire it in a kiln, in order to fix the colouration, make it watertight, or give it a shiny appearance **2.** *vt.* **COOK COAT WITH MILK OR EGG** to brush food with milk, egg, or sugar before baking in order to produce a shiny brown finish **3.** *vt.* **PAINTING COAT OIL PAINTING** to give sth, especially an oil painting, a transparent or semitransparent coating in order to enhance or slightly alter the colour tones **4.** *vt.* **COVERINGS GIVE PROTECTIVE COVERING TO MATERIAL** to place a protective or decorative coating on sth, especially a natural material such as leather, cotton, or paper **5.** *vti.* **MAKE OR BECOME GLASSY IN APPEARANCE** to become, or cause the eyes to become, unfocused and expressionless as a result of loss of interest, distraction, or tiredness **6.** *vt.* **METEOROL COVER WITH ICE** to put a thin layer of ice on sth **7.** *vt.* **CONSTR FIT STH WITH GLASS** to fit glass into or over sth, especially a window, door, or picture ■ *n.* **1. CERAMICS COVERING RESEMBLING GLASS** a shiny, smooth, transparent, or coloured glassy coating on a ceramic object, produced by firing the treated object in a kiln, or the substance or process employed to achieve this **2. COOK COATING FOR FOOD** a shiny brown finish on food or the substance used for achieving this effect **3. PAINTING COATING FOR OIL PAINTING** a transparent or semitransparent coating on sth, especially an oil painting, used to enhance or slightly alter the colour tones, or the substance used to achieve this effect

4. COVERINGS **PROTECTIVE COVERING ON MATERIAL** a protective or decorative covering on sth, especially a natural material such as leather, cotton, or paper, or the substance used for making this kind of coating **5.** US METEOROL = **glaze ice** [14thC. Formed from GLASS, on the model of GRAZE from GRASS.] —**glazer** *n.*

glaze over *vi.* to become unfocused and expressionless as a result of loss of interest, distraction, or tiredness (*refers to eyes*) ○ *Her eyes glazed over as the sedative began to take effect.*

glaze ice, **glazed frost** *n.* a thin coating of ice formed when rain or moisture in the air comes into contact with a surface that is cold enough to cause it to freeze. US term **glaze** *n.* 5

glazier /gláyzi ər/ *n.* sb whose job is to fit glass, especially in windows and doors

glazing /gláyzing/ *n.* **1.** HARD SHINY COATING the glaze coating on an object **2.** COVERING OF STH WITH GLAZE an act or the process of putting a glaze on sth **3.** GLASS FOR WINDOW glass in general, especially the type of glass used in doors or windows or glass that has been fitted in windows or doors **4.** FITTING OF STH WITH GLASS an act or the process of fitting glass into sth

glazing bar *n.* a wooden or metallic strip used to support or separate panes of glass in windows and doors

GLC *abbr.* **1.** Greater London Council **2.** gas-liquid chromatography

GLCM *abbr.* ground-launched cruise missile

gleam /gleem/ *vi.* (**gleams, gleaming, gleamed**) **1.** SHINE BRIGHTLY to shine brightly and continuously **2.** FLASH FOR SHORT TIME to flash, flicker, or appear briefly or indistinctly ■ *n.* **1.** BRIGHT SHINE a steady bright shine **2.** FLASH OF LIGHT a beam of light, especially one that is reflected, dim, or coming from an indistinct source **3.** BRIEF SHOW OF STH a slight or momentary indication of sth ○ *a gleam of interest* [Old English *glǣm.* Ultimately from a prehistoric Germanic word that is also the ancestor of English *glimmer* and *glimpse.*] —**gleamer** *n.* ◇ **a gleam in sb's eye** sth at the very earliest stage of planning or development

gleaming /gléeming/ *adj.* shining, especially with health, cleanliness, or newness ○ *gleaming black hair* —**gleamingly** *adv.*

glean /gleen/ (**gleans, gleaning, gleaned**) *v.* **1.** *vt.* ACCUMULATE STH to obtain information in small amounts over a period of time **2.** *vti.* AGRIC GATHER AFTER HARVEST to go over a field or area that has just been harvested and gather by hand any usable parts of the crop that remain [14thC. Via Old French *glener* from late Latin *glennare*, of Celtic origin.] —**gleaner** *n.*

gleanings /gléeningz/ *npl.* **1.** THINGS COLLECTED objects or ideas that have been gathered or amassed over a period of time, especially when they form a collection or comprehensive whole **2.** AGRIC HARVEST LEFTOVERS the usable parts of a crop that are left behind in a harvested field or area and can be gathered in by hand

gleba /gléebə/ (*plural* **-bae** /-bee/) *n.* the mass of tissue in which spores are formed in the fruiting bodies of certain fungi such as truffles and puffballs [Mid-19thC. From Latin (see GLEBE).]

glebe /gleeb/ *n.* **1.** ARABLE LAND land or soil, especially when considered as a source of abundant natural produce (*literary*) **2.** CHURCH LAND a piece of land belonging to a church and given over temporarily to a member of the clergy to provide additional income [14thC. From Latin *gleba* 'clod'.]

glee /glee/ *n.* **1.** GREAT DELIGHT joyful or animated delight **2.** GLOATINGLY JUBILANT FEELING jubilant, often smug pleasure, especially as a result of sb else's bad luck or failure **3.** MUSIC SONG FOR UNACCOMPANIED VOICES a part song for three or more unaccompanied voices of a type that first became popular in England in the 18th century [Old English *glēo.* Ultimately from a prehistoric Germanic word meaning 'merriment'.]

glee club *n.* US a choral society that concentrates on singing short part songs

gleeful /gléef'l/ *adj.* **1.** JOYFULLY HAPPY very happy or pleased **2.** GLOATINGLY JUBILANT jubilant and smugly pleased, especially as a result of sb else's bad luck or failure —**gleefully** *adv.* —**gleefulness** *n.*

gleet /gleet/ *n.* **1.** INFLAMMATION OF URETHRA inflammation of the urethra, accompanied by a discharge of pus and mucus, and characteristic of a late stage in the development of gonorrhoea **2.** DISCHARGE OF PUS a discharge of pus and mucus in a late stage of gonorrhoea [14thC. Via Old French *glette* 'slime' from Latin *glittus* 'sticky'.]

glei *n.* = gley

Gleichschaltung /glíkh shaltoong/ *n.* the forced standardization and complete suppression of all opposition in the political, social, and economic life and institutions of a country by an oppressive government or regime [Mid-20thC. From German.]

glen /glen/ *n.* a long narrow valley, especially in Scotland [15thC. From Scottish Gaelic *gleann.*] ◇ **in the glens** in the heartland of Scotland

Glencoe /glén kó/ mountain pass in the Scottish Highlands where, in 1692, Campbell soldiers massacred 38 men of the MacDonald clan. Length: 8 km/5 mi.

Gleneagles /glen éeg'lz/ picturesque valley in Perth and Kinross, Scotland, the site of a well-known golf course

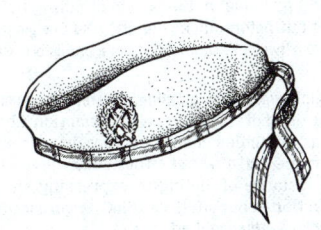

Glengarry

glengarry /glen gárri/ (*plural* **-ries**) *n.* a small brimless hat with a crown creased from front to back and usually a pair of ribbons hanging from the back. It forms part of the uniform of certain Scottish regiments and is sometimes worn as part of Scottish highland dress. [Mid-19thC. Named after *Glengarry* in the Highlands of Scotland, where it originated.]

AKG London

John Glenn

Glenn /glen/, **John** (*b.* 1921) US astronaut and senator. He was the first US astronaut to orbit the earth (1962), and the oldest astronaut ever to go into space (1998). He was first elected a Democratic US senator from Ohio in 1975. Full name **John Herschel Glenn, Jr.**

glenoid /glée oyd/ *adj.* **1.** SHAPED LIKE SMALL CUP shaped like a small shallow cup or socket **2.** ANAT OF SHOULDER SOCKET relating to the cup-shaped socket in the shoulder that holds the head of the humerus [Early 18thC. Via French *glénoïde* from, ultimately, Greek *glēnē* 'eyeball, socket'.]

Glenrothes /glen róthiss/ new town in Fife, Scotland, designated in 1948. It is the administrative centre of Fife council area. Population: 38,650 (1991).

gley /glay/, **glei** *n.* a sticky bluish-grey clay soil or soil layer that forms in heavily water-logged areas [Early 20thC. From Ukrainian *gleĭ.*]

glia /glée ə/ *n.* the network of supporting tissue and fibres that nourishes nerve cells within the brain and spinal cord. It comprises several layers of cells and makes up about 40% of the total volume of nerve tissue. US term **neuroglia** [Late 19thC. From Greek (see GLIADIN).] —**glial** *adj.*

gliadin /glí ədin/, **gliadine** /-deen/ *n.* any of several simple cereal proteins, e.g. those from wheat or rye [Mid-19thC. Via French from Greek *glia* 'glue', from Greek *gloios* 'glutinous substance'.]

glib /glib/ *adj.* **1.** SLICK fluent in a superficial or insincere way ○ *a glib talker* **2.** SUPERFICIAL shallow and lacking thought or preparation ○ *a glib generalization* **3.** CASUAL AND RELAXED easy, unconcerned, and informal in attitude ○ *a glib smile* [Late 16thC. Origin uncertain: perhaps from, ultimately, Middle Low German *glibberich* 'slippery, smooth', of unknown origin.] —**glibly** *adv.* —**glibness** *n.*

glide /glīd/ *v.* (**glides, gliding, glided**) **1.** *vti.* MOVE SMOOTHLY to move, or cause sth to move, in a smooth, effortless, and often graceful way ○ *seals gliding through the water* **2.** *vi.* CHANGE STATE SMOOTHLY to pass smoothly, slowly, or gradually into a specified state ○ *gliding in and out of consciousness* **3.** *vti.* AIR LAND WITHOUT USING ENGINE to bring an aircraft in to land without using the engine, or come in to land in this way **4.** *vi.* MUSIC USE PORTAMENTO to slide from one note to another in music **5.** *vi.* PHON MAKE INTERMEDIATE SPEECH SOUND to produce an intrusive speech sound when moving from one point of articulation to the next **6.** *vt.* CRICKET = **glance** *v.* 6 ■ *n.* **1.** DANCE SMOOTH MOVEMENT a smooth, effortless, and often graceful movement **2.** DANCE SMOOTH FLOWING DANCE a dance characterized by smooth flowing movement **3.** DANCE DANCE STEP a dance step characterized by smooth flowing movement **4.** AIR LANDING WITHOUT USING ENGINE a controlled aircraft descent using no engine power **5.** GEOG SLOW-MOVING CALM WATER a stretch of calm, slowly flowing water in a river or large stream **6.** MUSIC = **portamento 7.** MUSIC EXTENSION FOR TROMBONE a piece of metal tubing used to extend the length of a trombone so that lower notes can be produced **8.** PHON INTERMEDIATE SPEECH SOUND an intrusive speech sound produced when a speaker is moving from one point of articulation to the next, e.g. the /w/ sound in the middle of 'going' **9.** PHON = **semivowel 10.** CRICKET = **glance** *v.* 6 **11.** CRYSTALS = **slip**[1] *n.* 7 **12.** FURNITURE METAL DISC ON FURNITURE LEG BOTTOM a metal or plastic disc fixed to the bottom of the leg of a piece of furniture, to facilitate moving it across the floor **13.** FURNITURE METAL TRACK FOR DRAWER a metal track along which a drawer can be slid in or out easily [Old English *glīdan.* Ultimately from a prehistoric Germanic word that is also the ancestor of English *glissade* and *glitch.*]

glide path *n.* the prescribed descent of an aircraft coming in to land that is shown to the pilot by means of a radio beam and acts as an aid to navigation

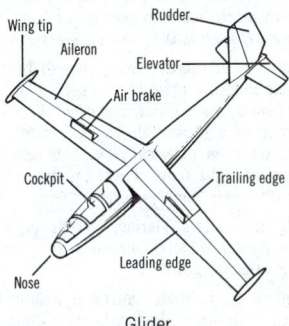

Wing tip | Rudder
Aileron | Elevator
Air brake
Cockpit | Trailing edge
Leading edge
Nose

Glider

glider /glídər/ *n.* **1.** AIR AIRCRAFT WITH NO ENGINE an engineless aircraft that flies by riding air currents. It becomes airborne by being towed up by an aeroplane or by being catapulted into the air from the ground. ◊ **sailplane 2.** ZOOL = **flying phalanger**

glide slope *n.* AIR = **glide path** *n.*

glide time *n.* NZ a system of working with flexitime

glim /glim/ *n.* (*archaic slang*) **1.** LIGHT SOURCE sth such as a candle or lamp that is a source of light **2.** LIGHT FROM CANDLE light given off by a candle, lamp, or other light source [Late 17thC. Origin uncertain: perhaps a shortening of GLIMMER.]

glimmer /glímmər/ *vi.* (**-mers, -mering, -mered**) **1.** EMIT DIM GLOW to emit a faint or intermittent light **2.** BE PRESENT TO SMALL EXTENT to be present faintly or in only a small amount ○ *Hope still glimmered in their hearts.* ■ *n.* **1.** FAINT FLASHING LIGHT a faint or intermittent glowing light ○ *a glimmer of campfires in the distance* **2.** SMALL AMOUNT OF STH a faint sign or small amount of sth ○ *a glimmer of interest* [14thC. Origin uncertain: probably from the ancestor of Swedish *glimra* 'to glimmer'.]

glimmering /glímmərıng/ *n.* = **glimmer** *n.* 2 ■ *adj.* EMITTING DIM GLOW emitting a faint or intermittent light

glimpse /glimps/ *n.* **1.** BRIEF LOOK a quick or incomplete look or sighting of sb or sth **2.** SMALL INDICATION a small, brief, or indistinct indication or appearance of sth ■ *v.* (**glimpses, glimpsing, glimpsed**) **1.** *vt.* CATCH BRIEF SIGHT OF to see sb or sth briefly or incompletely **2.** *vi.* TAKE BRIEF LOOK to have a quick or incomplete look at or through sth **3.** *vi.* EMIT FAINT LIGHT to give off a faint or intermittent light (*archaic*) [14thC. Ultimately from a prehistoric Germanic word that is also the ancestor of English *gleam* and *glimpse*.]

glint /glint/ *vi.* (**glints, glinting, glinted**) FLASH BRIEFLY to gleam or flash, especially brightly or momentarily ○ *Anger glinted in her eyes.* ■ *n.* **1.** BRIEF FLASH a slight or momentary gleam or flash ○ *a glint of daylight through the curtains* **2.** SLIGHT INDICATION a slight sign or indication of sth ○ *a glint of humour in his eyes* **3.** SHININESS OR GLOSSINESS a shiny or glossy appearance [15thC. Origin uncertain: probably an alteration of earlier *glent* 'to gleam', of Scandinavian origin.]

glioma /glī ṓmə/ (*plural* **-mata** /-mətə/ *or* **-mas**) *n.* a tumour composed of connective tissue (**neuroglial tissue**) of the nervous system and affecting the brain or spinal cord [Late 19thC. Formed from Greek *glia* (see GLIADIN).] —**gliomatous** *adj.*

glissade /gli saád/ *n.* **1.** BALLET GLIDING BALLET STEP a gliding ballet step in which one foot slides forwards, backwards, or to one side **2.** ACT OF SLIDING ON SNOW a controlled slide down a snowy slope made without skis by sb in a standing or crouching position ■ *vi.* (**-sades, -sading, -saded**) **1.** BALLET MAKE GLIDING BALLET STEP to perform a glissade in ballet **2.** TO SLIDE ON SNOW to slide down a snowy slope in a controlled manner without skis in a standing or crouching position [Mid-19thC. From French, formed from Old French *glisser* 'to slide', from, ultimately, Old Dutch *glissen*.] —**glissader** *n.*

glissando /gli sándō/ (*plural* **-di** /-dee/ *or* **-dos**) *n.* **1.** SLIDING MOVEMENT ON KEYBOARD OR HARP an act of sliding a finger or thumb up or down a keyboard or harp strings from one note to another **2.** SLIDING MOVEMENT ON VIOLIN OR TROMBONE an act of sliding a finger along a string instrument's fingerboard or slowly moving a trombone's slide in and out to create a smooth change in pitch between two notes [Late 19thC. Via Italian from, ultimately, Old French *glisser* (see GLISSADE).]

glisten /glíss'n/ *vi.* (**-tens, -tening, -tened**) **1.** BE SHINY AND WET-LOOKING to shine brightly, or reflect light from a wet surface ○ *leaves glistening after the rain* **2.** HAVE SHEEN to have a glossy sheen (*refers to hair or an animal's pelt*) ■ *n.* BRIGHT SHINE a bright shine or reflection of light from a wet surface [Old English *glisnian*. Ultimately from a prehistoric Germanic word.]

glister /glístər/ (**-ters, -tering, -tered**) *vi.* to glitter brightly (*archaic*) [14thC. Origin uncertain: probably from Middle Low German *glistern*.]

glitch /glich/ *n.* **1.** SMALL PROBLEM a minor hitch or technical problem ○ *glitches in the software* **2.** ELEC ENG UNWANTED ELECTRONIC SIGNAL a sudden unwanted electronic signal such as results from a power surge or a temporary irregular supply of power [Mid-20thC. Origin uncertain: probably via Yiddish *glitsh* 'slip' from, ultimately, Old High German *glītan* 'to glide'.] —**glitchy** *adj.*

glitter /glíttər/ *vi.* (**-ters, -tering, -tered**) **1.** SPARKLE to sparkle or shimmer brightly ○ *an evening gown glittering with sequins* **2.** SHINE WITH EMOTION to look bright or expressive with an emotion such as anger or love (*refers to eyes*) **3.** BE VIVACIOUS to exhibit liveliness and charm ○ *a radiant personality who glittered at every event she attended* **4.** BE DAZZLING to be characterized by the presence of sb or sth glamorous ○ *The event glittered with Hollywood stars.* ■ *n.* **1.** SPARKLY DECORATION small pieces of reflective material, e.g. sequins **2.** SPARKLING LIGHT bright sparkling light **3.** GLAMOUR dazzling glamour ○ *the glitter of a command performance at the opera* [14thC. From Old Norse *glitra*.] —**glitteringly** *adj.* —**glittery** *adj.*

glitterati /glíttə raáti/ *npl.* famous, rich, or fashionable people thought of as a group, especially those who are frequently photographed by the press [Mid-20thC. Humorous blend of GLITTER and LITERATI.]

glitz /glits/ *n.* **1.** GLAMOUR glamour, especially that associated with show business or celebrities **2.** FLASHY SHOW OF WEALTH extravagant and often tasteless display, especially of wealth [Late 20thC. Back-formation from GLITZY.]

glitzy /glítsi/ (**-ier, -iest**) *adj.* **1.** GLAMOROUS glamorous, especially in relation to show business or celebrities **2.** SHOWY extravagant and often tasteless, especially in the display of wealth [Mid-20thC. Origin uncertain: probably formed from German *glitzern* 'to glitter'.] —**glitziness** *n.*

Gliwice /gli vítsi/ industrial city with many fine old buildings in Katowice Province, southern Poland, west of the city of Katowice. Population: 214,000 (1995).

gloaming /glṓming/ *n.* the period of fading light after sunset but before dark (*literary*) [Old English *glōmung*, from *glōm* 'twilight'. Ultimately from a prehistoric Germanic word.]

gloat /glōt/ *vi.* (**gloats, gloating, gloated**) BE SMUGLY HAPPY to feel or express smug self-satisfaction about sth such as an achievement, a possession, or sb else's misfortune ■ *n.* ACT OF FEELING SMUGLY HAPPY the act or an instance of feeling or expressing smug self-satisfaction about sth [Late 16thC. Origin uncertain.] —**gloater** *n.* —**gloatingly** *adv.*

glob /glob/ *n.* an amount of sth soft or semiliquid (*informal*) [14thC. Origin uncertain: perhaps from Latin *globus* (see GLOBE).] —**globby** *adj.*

global /glṓb'l/ *adj.* **1.** WORLDWIDE relating to or happening throughout the whole world **2.** OVERALL taking all the different aspects of a situation into account **3.** COMPUT RELATING TO WHOLE OF SYSTEM covering or affecting the whole of a computer system, program, or file **4.** SPHERICAL shaped like a globe or sphere —**globally** *adv.*

globalise *vti.* = **globalize**

globalism /glṓb'lizəm/ *n.* the belief that political policies should take worldwide issues into account before focusing on national or state concerns, or the advocacy of this belief —**globalist** *n.*

globalization /glṓbəlī záysh'n/, **globalisation** *n.* **1.** GLOBAL ADOPTION OF SOCIAL INSTITUTIONS the process by which social institutions become adopted on a global scale **2.** OPERATION AT INTERNATIONAL LEVEL the process by which a business or company becomes international or starts operating at an international level

globalize /glṓbəlīz/ (**-izes, -izing, -ized**), **globalise** (**-ises, -ising, -ised**) *vti.* **1.** MAKE STH BECOME ADOPTED GLOBALLY to become, or cause sth, especially social institutions, to become adopted on a global scale **2.** BECOME OR MAKE STH BECOME INTERNATIONAL to become, or cause sth, especially a business or company, to become international or start operating at the international level —**globalizer** *n.*

global village *n.* the whole world considered as a single community served by electronic media and information technology

global warming *n.* an increase in the world's temperatures, believed to be caused in part by the greenhouse effect and depletion of the ozone layer

globe /glōb/ *n.* **1.** MAP OF EARTH ON SPHERE a hollow sphere representing the Earth and illustrated with the continents, seas, and islands, especially one showing and labelling the countries **2.** EARTH the planet Earth **3.** HOLLOW SPHERICAL OBJECT a rounded hollow object, especially one made of glass, e.g. a cover for a lamp, or a goldfish bowl **4.** PART OF MONARCH'S REGALIA a hollow sphere, usually made of gold or another precious metal, that forms part of a monarch's regalia and symbolizes the power or sovereignty of the ruler **5.** *Scotland, Can, ANZ* LIGHT BULB a light bulb ■ *vti.* (**globes, globing, globed**) MAKE INTO OR BECOME GLOBE to form, or cause sth to form, a globe [Mid-16thC. Directly or via Old French from Latin *globus* 'ball, sphere'.]

globe amaranth *n.* an ornamental garden plant with colourful whorls of leaves and flower heads made up of several distinct blossoms. Latin name: *Gomphrena globosa.*

globe artichoke *n.* = **artichoke**

globefish /glṓb fish/ (*plural* **-fish** *or* **-fishes**) *n.* **1.** = **puffer** **2.** = **porcupine fish** [From the puffer's shape when inflated]

globeflower /glṓb flowər/ *n.* a poisonous plant with ball-shaped flowers consisting of large white, pale-yellow, or orange sepals that almost entirely enclose the smaller petals. Genus: *Trollius.*

globe thistle *n.* a plant native to Asia and the Mediterranean with jagged-edged leaves and large white or bluish ball-shaped flowers. Genus: *Echinops.*

globetrot /glṓb trot/ (**-trots, -trotting, -trotted**) *vi.* to travel frequently and to a great variety of distant destinations [Back-formation from GLOBETROTTER]

globetrotter /glṓb trottər/ *n.* sb who travels frequently and to a great variety of distant destinations

globigerina /glṓbijə reénə/ (*plural* **-nas** *or* **-nae** /-nee/) *n.* a marine protozoan with a spiny rounded spiral shell. Genus: *Globigerina.* [Mid-19thC. From modern Latin, genus name, from Latin *globus* 'GLOBE' + *gerere* 'to carry', because it carries around its globe-shaped shell.] —**globigerinal** *adj.*

globigerina ooze *n.* a deposit on the ocean floor that consists of globingerina shells and is found almost worldwide

globin /glṓbin/ *n.* a colourless protein component of the oxygen-carrying pigments myoglobin and haemoglobin [Late 19thC. Shortening of HAEMOGLOBIN.]

globoid /glṓ boyd/ *adj.* BALL-SHAPED shaped like a ball ■ *n.* BALL-SHAPED PART a ball-shaped part, especially one found in plant granules

globose /glṓbōss/, **globous** /glṓ bəss/ *adj.* = **globoid** [15thC. From Latin *globosus*, from *globus* (see GLOBE).] —**globosely** *adv.* —**globosity** /glō bóssəti/ *n.*

globular /glóbyoolər/ *adj.* **1.** SPHERICAL having the shape of a ball or globule **2.** HAVING GLOBULES containing or consisting of globules [Mid-17thC. Formed from Latin *globolus* (see GLOBULE).] —**globularity** /glóbbyoo lárrəti/ *n.* —**globularly** /glóbbyooləlri/ *adv.*

globular cluster *n.* an approximately spherical cluster of densely-packed stars, located within a spherical halo around the Milky Way galaxy

globule /glóbbyool/ *n.* a small ball-shaped object, especially one that is liquid or semiliquid [Mid-17thC. Via French from Latin *globulus*, literally 'little globe', from *globus* 'GLOBE'.]

globuliferous /glóbbyoo líffərəss/ *adj.* composed of, containing, or producing globules

globulin /glóbbyoolin/ *n.* a simple protein belonging to a class that is found in plant and animal tissue. Globulins are soluble in weak salt solutions and form a mass when heated.

glochidium /glō kíddi əm/ (*plural* **-a** /-di ə/) *n.* **1.** **glochidium, glochid** BARBED HAIR OR BRISTLE a barbed hair or bristle that grows on plants such as the prickly pear or among the spores on ferns **2.** MUSSEL LARVA the parasitic larva of certain mussels that has hooks or suckers that it uses to attach itself to the fins or gills of fish. Family: Unionidae. [Late 19thC. Via modern Latin from, ultimately, Greek *glōkhis* 'arrowhead'.] —**glochidial** *adj.* —**glochidiate** /glō kíddi ət/ *adj.*

glockenspiel /glókən shpeel/ *n.* a percussion instrument consisting of a set of tuned metallic bars, played by striking the individual bars with small light hammers [Early 19thC. From German, literally 'bell-play'.]

glogg /glog/ *n.* a hot punch consisting of brandy, red wine, and sherry, and flavoured with sugar, spices, fruit pieces, and blanched almonds. It was originally served in Scandinavia at Christmas. [Early 20thC. From Swedish *glögg*.]

glomerate /glómmərət/ *adj.* **1.** MADE INTO COMPACT BALL formed into a tight ball or cluster **2.** WOUND INTO TIGHT BALL tightly wound together, like a ball of string [Late

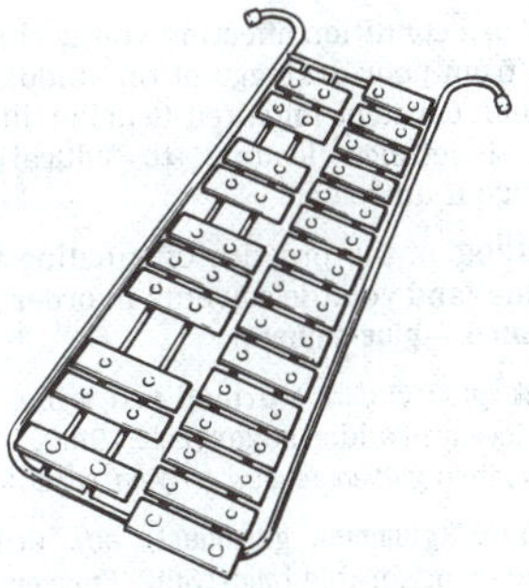

Glockenspiel

18thC. From Latin *glomerare* 'to make into a ball', from *glomus* 'ball of thread'.]

glomerule /glómmə rool/ *n.* **1.** HEAD OF FLOWER a flat-topped flower head formed by a compact cluster of short-stalked flowers **2.** SPORE CLUSTER a cluster of spores formed into a ball shape [Late 18thC. Via French from modern Latin *glomerulus* (see GLOMERULUS).] —**glomerulate** /glo mérrələt/ *adj.*

glomerulonephritis /glō mérrəlō nə frítiss/ *n.* an inflammatory disease affecting the clusters of capillaries (**glomeruli**) in the cortex of a kidney

glomerulus /glō mérrələss/ (*plural* **-li** /-lī/) *n.* **1.** CLUSTER OF NERVES OR BLOOD VESSELS a tightly packed cluster of blood vessels, nerve fibres, or other cells **2.** ROUND STRUCTURE IN KIDNEY a round cluster of interconnected capillaries found in the cortex of a kidney, that remove body waste to be excreted as urine [Mid-19thC. Via modern Latin, literally 'little ball', from Latin *glomus* 'ball of thread'.]

gloom /gloom/ *n.* **1.** MURKY DARKNESS a state of darkness or partial darkness, especially one where shadows or poor visibility create a cheerless or dispiriting atmosphere **2.** DESPONDENCY a feeling or atmosphere of despair, despondency, or misery ■ *v.* (**glooms, glooming, gloomed**) **1.** *vi.* BE DESPONDENT to feel or look despondent or miserable **2.** *vti.* MAKE OR BECOME DARK to become, or cause sth to become, dark [13thC. Origin unknown.] ◇ **gloom and doom** a feeling or expression of despondency and a belief that disaster is about to strike

gloomy /gloómi/ (**-ier, -iest**) *adj.* **1.** MURKILY DARK dark in a way that creates a cheerless or dispiriting atmosphere **2.** SAD sad and hopeless in offering little prospect that things will improve **3.** DESPONDENT feeling sad and without hope, often with a morbid or uninterested outlook on life —**gloomily** *adv.* —**gloominess** *n.*

gloop /gloop/ *n.* semiliquid sticky or messy material (*informal*) US term **goop** [Late 20thC. An imitation of the sound it makes when poured or handled.]

glop /glop/ *n.* *US* (*informal*) **1.** SOFT MASS a soft lump or mixture of sth, especially unappetizing food ○ *a glop of cold, greasy mashed potatoes* **2.** STH WORTHLESS sth such as a piece of music or writing that is considered to be oversentimental or of little value [Early 20thC. (As GLOOP).] —**gloppy** *adj.*

Gloria /gláwri ə/ *n.* **1.** CHRISTIAN RELIGIOUS WORDS a hymn or set of words in Latin that begins with the word 'Gloria' and is used in the Christian liturgy to praise God **2.** MUSICAL SETTING OF GLORIA the words of the Gloria set to music [15thC. From Latin, 'glory'.]

Gloria in Excelsis /-ek sélsiss/ *n.* **1.** CHRISTIAN RELIGIOUS WORDS a hymn or set of words in Latin that begins with the words 'Gloria in Excelsis' and is used in the Christian liturgy to praise God **2.** MUSICAL SETTING OF GLORIA IN EXCELSIS the words of Gloria in Excelsis set to music [From Latin, literally 'Glory in the High Places']

Gloria Patri /-paátree/ *n.* **1.** CHRISTIAN RELIGIOUS WORDS a short hymn or set of words in Latin that begins with the words 'Gloria Patri' and is used in the Christian liturgy to praise God **2.** MUSICAL SETTING OF GLORIA PATRI the words of Gloria Patri set to music [From Latin, literally 'Glory to the Father']

glorified /gláwri fīd/ *adj.* described in much more grandiose or fanciful terms than are warranted ○ *They call it an antique auction, but it's really just a glorified car-boot sale.*

glorify /gláwri fī/ (**-fies, -fying, -fied**) *vt.* **1.** MAKE APPEAR SUPERIOR to cause sth to seem more pleasant, important, or desirable than is actually the case **2.** EXTOL to praise sb or sth highly **3.** RELIG PRAISE DEITY to worship or offer praise to a deity —**glorification** /gláwrifi káysh'n/ *n.* —**glorifier** /gláwri fī ər/ *n.*

gloriole /gláwri ōl/ *n.* a halo around sb's head [Mid-19thC. Via French from Latin *gloriola*, literally 'little glory', from *gloria* (see GLORY).]

gloriosa /glawri ṓssə/ (*plural* **-riosas** *or* **-riosa**) *n.* a tropical climbing plant of the lily family that has large brightly coloured, yellow, orange, or red flowers, and is popular as a greenhouse plant. Genus: *Gloriosa.* [Via its modern Latin genus name, from Latin *gloriosus* (see GLORIOUS)]

glorious /gláwri əss/ *adj.* **1.** EXCEPTIONALLY LOVELY beautiful in a way that inspires wonder or joy ○ *glorious summer weather* **2.** OUTSTANDING so good or distinguished as to merit praise and lasting fame ○ *a glorious career* **3.** ENJOYABLE highly enjoyable **4.** INEBRIATED uproariously drunk (*archaic informal*) [14thC. Via Anglo-Norman and Old French *glorios* from Latin *gloriosus*, from *gloria* 'glory'.] —**gloriously** *adv.* —**gloriousness** *n.*

Glorious Revolution *n.* the overthrow of King James II in 1688 that established the power of Parliament over the monarch

Glorious Twelfth *n.* the first day of the grouse-shooting season on 12 August

glory /gláwri/ *n.* (*plural* **-ries**) **1.** EXALTATION the fame, admiration, and honour that is given to sb who does sth important **2.** ACHIEVEMENT OR DISTINCTION sth that brings or confers admiration, praise, honour, or fame **3.** PRAISE OF DEITY praise and thanksgiving offered as an act of worship to a deity ○ *Glory to God in the highest.* **4.** AWESOME SPLENDOUR majesty or splendour **5.** ASTOUNDING BEAUTY beauty that inspires feelings of wonder or joy ○ *the glory of a bright spring morning* **6.** HEAVEN the idealized beauty and bliss of heaven **7.** ARTS, CHR HALO a halo around sb's head ■ *interj.* EXPRESSING SURPRISE used to express great surprise, shock, dismay, or pleasure (*dated*) [13thC. Via Anglo-Norman and Old French *glorie* from Latin *gloria*.] ◇ **glory be** used to express great surprise, shock, dismay, or pleasure (*dated*) ◇ **go to glory** to die (*dated*) ◇ **in your glory** in a state of great happiness, satisfaction, or triumph

glory in *vt.* to derive great pride, pleasure, amusement, or satisfaction from sth

glory-box *n.* *ANZ* a collection of household goods that a woman collects to use when she is married (*dated*)

glory-of-the-snow (*plural* **glory-of-the-snow** *or* **glory-of-the-snows**) *n.* a small bulbous plant of the lily family, native to the eastern Mediterranean and western Asia but now cultivated in many regions for its early blue flowers. Latin name: *Chionodoxa luciliae.*

Glos. *abbr.* Gloucestershire

gloss[1] /gloss/ *n.* **1.** SHININESS a shiny quality, especially on a smooth surface **2.** DECEPTIVE AND SUPERFICIAL ATTRACTIVENESS an attractive appearance that often conceals sth unattractive or inferior **3.** = **gloss paint 4.** MAKE-UP a make-up or cosmetic designed to impart a shine ○ *lip gloss* ■ *vt.* (**glosses, glossing, glossed**) **1.** MAKE SHINY to apply a coating or gloss to a surface to make it shine **2.** USE GLOSS PAINT ON to apply gloss paint to sth [Mid-16thC. Origin uncertain.]

gloss over *vt.* to leave out negative information on purpose, or address a subject superficially to make it appear more attractive or acceptable

gloss[2] /gloss/ *n.* **1.** EXPLANATORY WORD OR PHRASE a short definition, explanation, or translation of a word or phrase possibly unfamiliar to the reader, often located in a page margin or collected in an appendix or glossary **2.** INTERPRETATION an interpretation or explanation of sth ○ *Her account provides an interesting gloss on the theme of widowhood.* ■ *vt.* (**glosses, glossing, glossed**) **1.** EXPLAIN WORD OR PHRASE to give a short definition, explanation, or translation of a word or phrase that may be unfamiliar to the reader **2.** INSERT EXPLANATIONS IN A TEXT to add or enter the necessary glosses in a manuscript or piece of writing **3.** GIVE DELIBERATELY MISLEADING EXPLANATION OF STH to interpret or explain sth in a deliberately misleading or negative way [Mid-16thC. Via Old French *glose* from, ultimately, medieval Latin *glossa* 'obscure word', from Greek *glōssa*, 'tongue, language' (source of English *epiglottis* and *polyglot*).]

gloss. *abbr.* glossary

glossa /glóssə/ (*plural* **-sae** /-see/ *or* **-sas**) *n.* **1.** ANAT TONGUE a tongue (*technical*) **2.** INSECTS INSECT'S MOUTH STRUCTURE a structure resembling a tongue in the mouth of an insect [Late 19thC. Via modern Latin from Greek *glōssa* (see GLOSS[2]).] —**glossal** *adj.*

glossary /glóssəri/ (*plural* **-ries**) *n.* an alphabetical collection of specialist terms and their meanings, usually in the form of an appendix to a book [14thC. From Latin *glossarium*, from *glossa* (see GLOSS[2]).] —**glossarial** /glo sáiri əl/ *adj.* —**glossarially** *adv.* —**glossarist** /glóssərist/ *n.*

glossectomy /glo séktəmi/ (*plural* **-mies**) *n.* partial or total removal by surgery of the tongue

glosseme /gló seem/ *n.* the smallest meaningful unit of a language [Early 20thC. From Greek *glōssema* 'word requiring explanation', from *glōssa* (see GLOSS[2]).]

glossitis /glo sítiss/ *n.* inflammation of the tongue [Early 19thC. Formed from Greek *glōssa* (see GLOSS[2]).] —**glossitic** /glo síttik/ *adj.*

glossography /glo sóggrəfi/ *n.* the writing of glosses, glossaries, or commentaries as part of a text (*formal*) [Early 17thC. Coined from Greek *glōssa* (see GLOSS[2]) + -GRAPHY.] —**glossographer** /glo sóggrəfər/ *n.*

glossolalia /glóssō láyliə/ *n.* **1.** RELIG = **speaking in tongues 2.** PSYCHOL NONSENSE SPEECH nonsensical or invented speech, especially resulting from a trance or schizophrenia [Late 19thC. Coined from Greek *glōssa* (see GLOSS[2]) + -LALIA.]

glossopharyngeal /glóssō farin jée əl/ *adj.* relating to the tongue and pharynx [Early 19thC. Coined from Greek *glōssa* (see GLOSS[2]) + PHARYNGEAL.]

glossopharyngeal nerve *n.* either of the ninth pair of cranial nerves, which activate the muscles of the tongue, pharynx, and parotid gland

gloss paint *n.* a paint that gives a smooth shiny durable surface, used especially as a final coat on wood

glossy /glóssi/ *adj.* (**-ier, -iest**) **1.** SHINY AND SMOOTH having a smooth shiny surface or texture ○ *a glossy coat is the sign of a healthy animal* **2.** SUPERFICIALLY STYLISH creating a superficial impression of wealth, beauty, or fashionable elegance (*informal*) ○ *a glossy lifestyle that conceals years of financial struggle* ■ *n.* (*plural* **-ies**) **1.** PHOTOGRAPHY PHOTO WITH A SHINY FINISH a photograph printed on shiny smooth paper ○ *Please provide an 8 x 10 glossy.* **2.** PUBL = **glossy magazine** —**glossily** *adv.* —**glossiness** *n.*

glossy magazine *n.* a magazine containing high-quality colour photographs, especially a fashion magazine, printed on smooth-coated paper. Also called **glossy**. US term **slick** *n.* 2

glost firing /glóst-/ *n.* the final high-temperature firing of ceramic ware once it has been coated with glaze, during which the glaze is melted and fused onto the pot [*Glost* probably an alteration of GLOSS[1]]

glottal /glótt'l/ *adj.* **1.** ANAT OF THE GLOTTIS relating to the glottis **2.** PHON USING THE GLOTTIS IN SPEECH used to describe a speech sound that is produced by wholly or partially closing the glottis

glottal stop *n.* a consonantal speech sound created by closing and then opening the glottis before a vowel, which produces a sudden audible release of air. In some languages such as Arabic glottal stops are part of the standard consonant system.

glottis /glóttiss/ (*plural* **-tises** *or* **-tides** /-tti deez/) *n.* **1.** OPENING BETWEEN THE VOCAL CORDS the elongated opening between the vocal cords at the upper part of a vertebrate's windpipe (**larynx**). The glottis is open during breathing but is closed by the epiglottis during swallowing. **2.** VOICE BOX all of the anatomy of the larynx that is involved in producing the voice in a human or vertebrate animal [Late 16thC. Via modern Latin from, ultimately, Greek *glōtta*, a variant of *glōssa* (see GLOSS[2]).]

Gloucester /glóstər/ cathedral city on the River Severn in Gloucestershire, west-central England. Population: 105,800 (1995).

Gloucestershire /glóstərshər/ largely rural county in west-central England, on the border with Wales. Population: 552,700 (1995). Area: 2,642 sq. km/1,024 sq. mi.

glove /gluv/ n. **1.** SHAPED COVERING FOR THE HAND a shaped covering for the hand that includes five separated sections for the thumb and fingers, and extends to the wrist or the elbow **2.** = **gauntlet**[1] n. **3.** PROTECTIVE GLOVE a padded glove worn to protect the hand in boxing, baseball, and cricket ■ vt. (**gloves, gloving, gloved**) PUT A GLOVE ON STH to cover the hand with a glove, or cover sth with sth that is like a glove ○ *Gloved and hatted, the electrician climbed the power pole.* [Old English glōf. Ultimately from a prehistoric Germanic word meaning 'hand.'] —**gloveless** adj. ◇ **the gloves are off** used to indicate that a course of action is about to be pursued in a ruthless and uncompromisingly aggressive way ○ *The gloves are off in the political debate.*

glove box n. **1.** = **glove compartment 2.** BOX FOR HANDLING TOXIC MATERIALS a sealed container that allows radioactive or toxic substances to be handled safely using a pair of gloves attached to openings in its sides

glove compartment n. a small enclosed storage space in the dashboard of a vehicle

glove puppet n. a puppet that fits over the hand like a glove and is operated by the user's thumb and fingers. US term **hand puppet**

Glover /glúvvər/, **Denis James Matthews** (1912–80) New Zealand writer. He is the author of prose and poetry including *Enter Without Knowing* (1964).

glow /glō/ n. **1.** LIGHT FROM STH HOT a light produced by sth that has been heated to a high temperature but is not in flame ○ *the glow of the embers in the grate* **2.** SOFT STEADY LIGHT a soft steady light, especially one without heat or flames ○ *the glow of the neon lights* **3.** SOFT WARM REFLECTED LIGHT a soft warm reflected light ○ *the golden glow of the tapestries on the far wall* **4.** ROSINESS OF COMPLEXION a brightness or redness in sb's complexion, e.g. because of exercise or good health ○ *the healthy glow that exercise gives you* **5.** REDNESS OF EMBARRASSMENT a redness of the face or complexion, especially one caused by embarrassment ○ *face suffused with a glow of shame* **6.** HAPPY FEELING a sense of happiness or wellbeing ○ *a warm glow of satisfaction* ■ vi. (**glows, glowing, glowed**) **1.** EMIT LIGHT AND HEAT to emit light as a result of being extremely hot ○ *The embers of the fire still glowed in the grate.* **2.** EMIT A SOFT STEADY LIGHT to emit a soft steady light without heat or flames ○ *the neon signs glowing red and blue* **3.** REFLECT LIGHT SOFTLY to emit a soft warm reflected light ○ *the walls glowing orange and gold in the afternoon sun* **4.** SHINE WITH HEALTH OR HAPPINESS to show the bright eyes and smooth skin that are a sign of good health, contentment, or high spirits **5.** BE FLUSHED WITH EMBARRASSMENT to have a blood rush to the face, especially because of embarrassment **6.** FEEL WARM AND CONTENTED to feel a pleasant warm sensation owing to happiness, satisfaction, or love ○ *The winning team glowed with pride.* [Old English glōwan. Ultimately from a prehistoric Germanic word that is probably also the ancestor of English glower.]

glower /glówər/ vi. (**-ers, -ering, -ered**) GLARE SILENTLY to stare or look at sb or sth with sullen anger or strong resentment ■ n. ANGRY LOOK a sullen or resentful stare or look [15thC. Origin uncertain: perhaps from a Scandinavian word that had the same prehistoric Germanic ancestor as English glow.] —**gloweringly** adv.

glowing /glṓ ing/ adj. **1.** SHINING SOFTLY AND STEADILY emitting a soft steady light **2.** REDDISH-GOLD rich, strong, or bright in colour, especially when reddish or gold ○ *the glowing colours of autumn* **3.** FULL OF PRAISE praising sb or sth in very warm appreciative terms ○ *glowing reports of the performance* **4.** ROSY red or rosy as a result of excitement, wellbeing, or good health —**glowingly** adv.

glow plug n. a plug fitted to a diesel engine that makes it easier to start in cold weather by warming it up

glowworm /glṓ wurm/ n. a larva of some types of firefly, or a beetle of a closely related family, that emits greenish light from organs in its abdomen. Families: Lampyridae and Phengodidae.

gloxinia /glok sínni ə/ n. a tropical American plant popular as a house plant for its large colourful bell-shaped flowers. Genus: *Sinningia.* [Early 19thC. Named after the 18thC German botanist Benjamin *Gloxin,* who first described it.]

gloze /glōz/ (**glozes, glozing, glozed**) v. **1.** vt. GLOSS OVER STH to attempt to underplay or minimize sth unpleasant or embarrassing ○ *tried to gloze over the scandalous story* **2.** vti. USE FLATTERY to use flattery on sb (*archaic*) [13thC. Via French glose from, ultimately, Latin glossa (see GLOSS[2]).]

gluc- prefix. = **gluco-** (*used before vowels*)

glucagon /glóokə gon/ n. a hormone produced by the pancreas that raises the blood sugar level by promoting the conversion of glycogen to glucose in the liver [Early 20thC. Coined from GLUCO- + Greek *agōn,* the present participle of *agein* 'to lead'.]

gluco- prefix. glucose ○ *glucocorticoid* [From GLUCOSE]

glucocorticoid /glóokō cáwrti koyd/ n. a steroid hormone (**corticoid**) that controls the metabolism of carbohydrates, proteins, and fats. Glucocorticoids have anti-inflammatory properties useful in treating rheumatoid arthritis.

gluconeogenesis /glóokō neé ə jénnəssiss/ n. the production of glucose by the liver from substances other than carbohydrates, e.g. proteins and fats —**gluconeogenetic** /glóokō neé əjə néttik/ adj.

Glucose

glucose /glóokōz/ n. **1.** BIOCHEM SUGAR ENERGY SOURCE a simple sugar produced in plants by photosynthesis and in animals by the conversion of carbohydrates, proteins, and fats. The commonest form, dextrose, is used by all living organisms. Formula: $C_6H_{12}O_6$. **2.** FOOD SYRUPY MIXTURE a syrup containing dextrose, maltose, dextrin, and water that is obtained from starch and used in food manufacture and in alcoholic fermentation [Mid-19thC. Via French from Greek *gleukos* 'sweet wine'.]

glucosidase /gloo kóssi dayz/ n. an enzyme such as maltase that hydrolyses glucosides

glucoside /glóokō sīd/ n. a glycoside with glucose as the sugar component, which it yields upon reacting chemically with water —**glucosidal** adj. —**glucosidic** /glóokō síddik/ adj. —**glucosidically** adv.

glucosuria /glóo kō sóoriə/ n. = **glycosuria** —**glucosuric** /glóo kō sóorik/ adj.

glucuronic acid an acid derived from glucose, important in human metabolism for its ability to combine with certain toxic substances, rendering them harmless. Formula: $OC_6H_9O_6$. [Early 20thC. Coined from GLUCO- on the model of GLYCURONIC.]

glue /gloo/ n. **1.** ANIMAL-BASED ADHESIVE an adhesive substance obtained by boiling animal parts such as bones, hides, horns, and hooves **2.** ADHESIVE a natural or synthetic substance used as an adhesive **3.** STH THAT UNITES PEOPLE a unifying factor or influence ○ *Mutual love and understanding is the glue that holds this family together.* ■ vt. (**glues, gluing, glued**) **1.** STICK THINGS TOGETHER to stick things together or reconstitute sth using an adhesive substance ○ *It took hours to glue the vase back together.* **2.** KEEP SB STILL to cause sb to remain still because of concentrating on sth with full attention (*informal; often passive*) ○ *You've been glued to that computer all day!* [13thC. Via French glu from, ultimately, Latin *gluten* (source of English *agglutinate* and *gluten*).] —**gluey** adj. —**gluily** adv. —**glueiness** n.

glue ear n. a condition affecting young children that results from poor drainage of the middle ear. It is a common cause of impaired hearing during early years, sometimes leading to educational disadvantage if untreated.

glue-sniffing n. the practice of inhaling the fumes from glues and volatile solvents in order to become intoxicated —**glue-sniffer** n.

gluhwein /glóo vīn/ n. warmed red wine, flavoured with spices and added sugar [Late 19thC. From German *Glühwein,* from *glühen* 'to glow' + *Wein* 'wine'.]

glum /glum/ (**glummer, glummest**) adj. quietly melancholic or miserable [Mid-16thC. From an earlier verb meaning 'to look sullen', which evolved from GLOOM.] —**glumly** adv. —**glumness** n.

glume /gloom/ n. BOT either of a pair of dry leaves at the base of the spikelet in an ear of grass [Late 18thC. From Latin *gluma* 'husk'.] —**glumaceous** /gloo máyshəss/ adj.

gluon /glóo on/ n. a theoretical elementary particle without mass, thought to be involved in binding the subatomic particles (**quarks**) together [Late 20thC. Formed from GLUE.]

glut /glut/ n. OVERSUPPLY a larger supply of sth than is needed, especially of a crop or product ○ *There is usually a glut of fresh vegetables in August.* ■ vt. (**gluts, glutting, glutted**) **1.** OVERSUPPLY STH to supply a market with an excess of sth, especially a product, leading to a fall in price ○ *Cheaper products from abroad glutted the market, lowering profits.* **2.** GIVE SB ENOUGH OR TOO MUCH to feed or supply sb with enough or more than enough of sth [14thC. Origin uncertain: probably via Old French *gloutir* 'to swallow' from Latin *gluttire* (see GLUTTON).]

glutaeus n. = **gluteus**

glutamate /glóotə mayt/ n. a salt or ester of glutamic acid, especially its sodium salt (**monosodium glutamate**)

Glutamic acid

glutamic acid /gloo támmik-/, **glutaminic acid** /glootə mínnik-/ n. an amino acid found in plant and animal proteins that can also be synthesized by humans and animals. It is used in the form of monosodium glutamate as a flavouring in food. Formula: $C_5H_9NO_4$. [*Glutamic* from GLUTEN + AMINE + -IC]

Glutamine

glutamine /glóotə meen/ n. an amino acid found in proteins that can also be synthesized by humans and animals. It is used in medicines and in biochemical research. Formula: $C_5H_{10}N_2O_3$. [Late 19thC. Blend of GLUTAMIC ACID and AMINE.]

glutaminic acid *n.* = **glutamic acid**

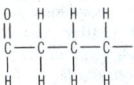

Glutaraldehyde

glutaraldehyde /gloŏotə rál̃di hī̃d/ *n.* an oily water-soluble liquid used as a disinfectant, a tanning agent, and a biological fixative. Formula: $C_5H_8O_2$. [Mid-19thC. Blend of *glutaric* (formed from GLUTEN) + ALDEHYDE.]

glutathione /gloŏotə thī̃on/ *n.* a chemical compound (**peptide**) found in plant and animal tissues that consists of glutamic acid, cysteine, and glycine. It is important in biological oxidation-reduction reactions and the activation of some enzymes. Formula: $C_{10}H_{17}N_3O_6S$. [Early 20thC. Coined from *glutamic* + THIO- + -ONE.]

glutei plural of **gluteus**

gluten /gloŏot'n/ *n.* a protein combination found in some cereals, especially wheat. It makes dough elastic, and enables it to rise by trapping gas. People who have coeliac disease are allergic to gluten and must avoid it in their diets. [Late 16thC. Via French from Latin (see GLUE).]

gluteus /gloŏoti əss/ (*plural* **-i** /-ī̃/), **glutaeus** (*plural* **-i**) *n.* any of the three large buttock muscles that move the thigh in humans, especially the gluteus maximus. The other two muscles are the gluteus medius and the gluteus minimus. [Late 17thC. From modern Latin, formed from Greek *gloutos* 'buttock'.] —**gluteal** /gloŏoti əl/ *adj.*

gluteus maximus /gloŏotiəss máksiməss/ (*plural* **glutei maximi** /gloŏoti ī̃ máksi mī̃/) *n.* the outermost of the three large gluteus muscles that form each buttock in humans [*Maximus* from Latin, 'largest']

glutinous /gloŏotinəss/ *adj.* having a sticky consistency ○ *glutinous rice*

glutton /glútt'n/ *n.* **1.** GREEDY PERSON sb who eats and drinks to excess **2.** ZOOL = **wolverine** [13thC. Via Old French *gluton* from, ultimately, Latin *gluttire* 'to swallow', from *gula* 'throat' (source of English *gullet*).] —**gluttonous** *adj.* —**gluttonously** *adv.* ◇ **a glutton for punishment** sb who deliberately takes on, and appears to need or enjoy, difficulty, discomfort, or stress

gluttony /glútt'ni/ *n.* the act or practice of eating and drinking to excess. Gluttony is one of the seven deadly sins in Christian tradition.

glyc- *prefix.* = **glyco-**

glyceride /glíssə rī̃d/ *n.* an ester formed by the combination of glycerol with an acid. The occur widely in animal and vegetable fats and oils. [Mid-19thC. Formed from GLYCERIN.]

glycerin /glíssərin/, **glycerine** *n.* a thick, sweet, odourless, colourless, or pale yellow liquid obtained from fats and oils as a by-product of soap manufacture. Used as a solvent, antifreeze, plasticizer, drug medium, and sweetener, and in the manufacture of soaps, cosmetics, inks, lubricants, and dynamite. Formula: $C_3H_8O_3$. [Mid-19thC. From French, formed from Greek *glukeros*, an alteration of *glukus* (see GLYCO-).]

glycerol /glíssə rol/ *n.* glycerin (*technical*) [Late 19thC. Formed from GLYCERIN.]

glyceryl /glíssəril/ *n.* a chemical group derived from glycerol by removing or replacing hydroxide, especially a trivalent group CH_2CHCH_2 [Mid-19thC. Formed from GLYCERIN + -YL.]

glyceryl trinitrate *n.* = **nitroglycerin**

glycine /glī̃ss een/ *n.* a sweet crystalline amino acid that is found in most proteins and can also be

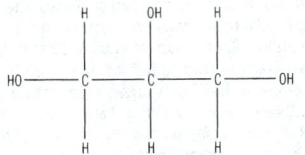

Glycerol

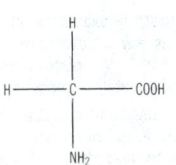

Glycine

synthesized by humans and animals. It acts as a neurotransmitter. Formula: $C_2H_5NO_2$. [Mid-19thC. Formed from Greek *glukus* (see GLYCO-).]

glyco-, **glyc-** *prefix.* **1.** sugar ○ *glycosuria* **2.** glycogen ○ *glycolysis* [From Greek *glukus* 'sweet' (source of English *liquorice*). Ultimately from an Indo-European base that is also the ancestor of *glucose* and *dulcet*.]

glycogen /glī̃kəjən/ *n.* a white compound (**polysaccharide**) stored in the liver and muscles of humans and animals and easily converted to glucose as a source of energy. Formula: $(C_6H_{10}O_5)_n$. —**glycogenic** /glī̃kə jénnik/ *adj.*

glycogenesis /glī̃kō jénnəssiss/ *n.* the formation or conversion of glycogen in the body —**glycogenetic** /glī̃ kōjə néttik/ *adj.*

glycogenolysis /glī̃ kōjə nóllississ/ *n.* the breakdown of glycogen, especially to glucose, in the bodies of humans and animals —**glycogenolytic** /glī̃ kō jénnə líttik/ *adj.*

glycol /glī̃ kol/ *n.* = **ethylene glycol** [Mid-19thC. Formed from GLYCERIN.] —**glycolic** *adj.*

glycolic acid /glī̃t kóllik-/ *n.* a colourless crystalline compound found in unripe grapes, sugar cane, and sugar beet. Used in tanning and the manufacture of pesticides, pharmaceuticals, adhesives, and plasticizers. Formula: $C_2H_4O_3$.

glycolipid /glī̃ kō líppid/ *n.* a lipid that contains a carbohydrate group, especially glucose or galactose

glycolysis /glī̃t kóllassiss/ *n.* the breakdown of a compound such as glycogen or glucose by enzymes, producing pyruvic or lactic acid and releasing energy for use in the body. This metabolic process takes place in nearly all living cells. —**glycolytic** /glī̃ kō líttik/ *adj.*

glycoprotein /glī̃ kō prṓ teen/ *n.* a complex protein in which the nonprotein part is a carbohydrate

glycoside /glī̃ kō sī̃d/ *n.* a sugar derivative that breaks down into a sugar and a nonsugar compound (**aglycone**). Some glycosides such as digitoxin are used medicinally. [Mid-20thC. Formed from *glycose*, a variant of GLUCOSE.] —**glycosidic** /glī̃ kō síddik/ *adj.*

glycosuria /glī̃kōs syoŏori ə/ *n.* the presence of sugar in the urine, usually a sign of diabetes [Mid-19thC. Coined from *glycose* (see GLYCOSIDE) + -URIA.] —**glycosuric** *adj.*

glycosylation /glī̃kō sī̃ láysh'n/ *n.* the addition of a carbohydrate to an organic molecule [Mid-20thC. Coined from *glycose* (see GLYCOSIDE) + -YL + -ATION.]

Glyndebourne /glī̃nd bawrn/ site of an annual international opera festival held in the village of Glynde in East Sussex, southern England

glyph /glif/ *n.* **1.** ARCHIT **CARVED GROOVE IN ANCIENT GREEK ARCHITECTURE** an ornamental carved channel or groove, especially a vertical one like those on a Doric frieze **2.** HIST **CARVED SYMBOL OR CHARACTER** a symbol or character, especially one that has been incised or carved out in a stone surface like the characters of the ancient Mayan writing system **3.** COMPUT **CHARACTER IN FONT** the symbol or symbols that form a single character in a font [Late 18thC. Via French *glyphe* from Greek *gluphē* 'carving', from *gluphein* 'to carve'.] —**glyphic** *adj.*

glyptic /glíptik/ *adj.* relating to the art of engraving or carving, especially on precious stones [Early 19thC. Directly or via French *glyptique* from Greek *gluptikos*, from *gluptēs* 'carver', from *gluphein* (see GLYPH).]

glyptics /glíptiks/ *n.* = **glyptography** (*takes a singular verb*)

glyptograph /glíp tō graaf/ *n.* an engraving or carving on a precious stone [Late 18thC. Coined from Greek *gluptos* 'carved' + -GRAPH.]

glyptography /glip tóggrəfi/ *n.* the art or process of engraving or carving on precious stones —**glyptographer** *n.* —**glyptographic** /glíp tō gráffik/ *adj.* —**glyptographical** /-gráffik'l/ *adj.*

gm *abbr.* gram

GM *abbr.* **1.** general manager **2.** George Medal **3.** grand master **4.** EDUC grant-maintained **5.** MIL guided missile **6.** GENETICS genetic modification **7.** genetically modified

GMO *n.*, *abbr.* genetically modified organism

GMP *abbr.* BIOL guanosine monophosphate

GMS *abbr.* EDUC grant-maintained status

GMT *abbr.* Greenwich Mean Time

GMW *abbr.* gram-molecular weight

gn *abbr.* guinea

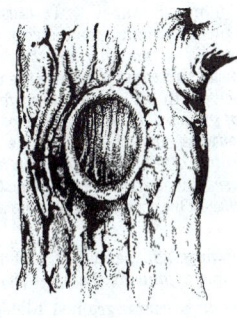

Gnarl

gnarl[1] /naarl/ *n.* a hard lump, knot, or swelling on a tree trunk or branch [Early 19thC. Back-formation from GNARLED.]

gnarl[2] /naarl/ (**gnarls, gnarling, gnarled**) *vi.* to snarl or growl (*archaic*) [Late 16thC. Formed from *gnar* 'to snarl, growl', an imitation of the sound.]

gnarled /naarld/ *adj.* **1.** KNOTTED AND TWISTED twisted and full of knots ○ *an ancient gnarled tree* **2.** TWISTED, MISSHAPEN, OR WEATHER-BEATEN twisted, misshapen, or weather-beaten because of age, hard work, or illness ○ *gnarled hands* [Early 17thC. Alteration of *knurled*.]

gnash /nash/ (**gnashes, gnashing, gnashed**) *vt.* to grind your teeth together, especially in pain, anger, or frustration [15thC. Origin uncertain: perhaps from an earlier verb *gnast*, of Scandinavian origin, or, alternatively, an imitation of the sound.]

gnat /nat/ *n.* a small two-winged biting fly such as a black fly or a midge [Old English *gnætt*. Ultimately from an Indo-European word that is also the ancestor of English *gnaw*.]

gnatcatcher /nát kachər/ *n.* a small American songbird with a long tail and slender bill that feeds on insects. Genus: *Polioptila*.

gnathic /náthik/, **gnathal** /náth'l/ *adj.* relating to the jaw [Late 19thC. Formed from Greek *gnathos* 'jaw'.]

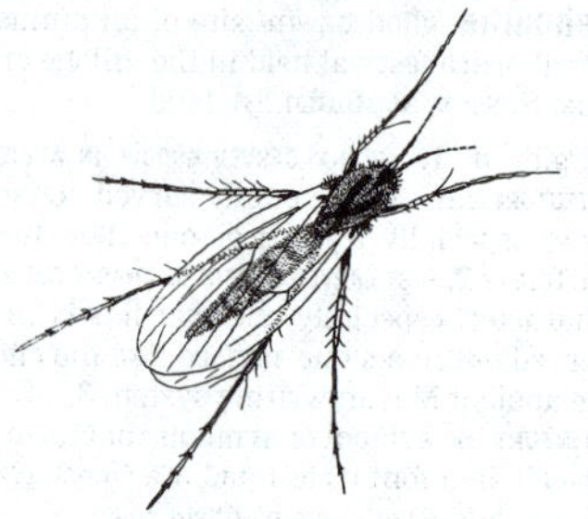

Gnat

gnathion /náythi on/ *n.* the lowest point on the midline of the lower jaw [Late 19thC. From Greek *gnathos* (see GNATHIC).]

gnathite /náy thīt/ *n.* a mouthpart similar to a jaw that is used for grasping or chewing by insects, lobsters, and other arthropods [Late 19thC. From Greek *gnathos* (see GNATHIC).]

gnathostome /náythə stōm/ *n.* a vertebrate that has a mouth with jaws, as do all vertebrates except agnathans such as lampreys and hagfish. Superclass: Gnathostomata. [Early 20thC. Coined from Greek *gnathos* (see GNATHIC) + *stoma* 'mouth'.]

-gnathous *suffix.* having a particular kind of jaw ○ *prognathous* [Formed from Greek *gnathos* 'jaw'. Ultimately from an Indo-European base meaning 'jaw', which is also the ancestor of English *chin.*]

gnaw /naw/ *v.* (**gnaws, gnawing, gnawed, gnawed** *or* **gnawn** *archaic* /nawn/) **1.** *vti.* CHEW AT STH to chew or bite on sth persistently, often reducing it gradually to a particular state ○ *a terrier gnawing away at a huge bone* **2.** *vt.* MAKE STH BY CHEWING to make sth by grinding with the teeth and chewing ○ *The hamster escaped by gnawing a hole in its cage.* **3.** *vt.* ERODE to wear sth away often until it reaches a particular shape or size ○ *The wind and waves had gnawed the rocks into fantastic shapes.* **4.** *vi.* CAUSE SB WORRY to cause sb constant anxiety or distress ○ *That question still gnaws at me after all these years.* **5.** *vi.* GRADUALLY REDUCE STH'S POWER to reduce the effectiveness or influence of sth bit by bit ○ *a profound sense of unease that gnaws away at our sense of wellbeing* ■ *n.* ACT OF GNAWING an act or example of gnawing ○ *Prince trotted off to have a gnaw on his bone.* [Old English *gnagen.* Ultimately from a prehistoric Germanic word thought to suggest the action.] —**gnawable** *adj.* —**gnawer** /náwər/ *n.*

gnawing /náwing/ *adj.* persistent and troubling or uncomfortable ○ *gnawing doubts* —**gnawingly** *adv.*

gneiss /nīss/ *n.* a coarse-grained high-grade metamorphic rock formed at high pressures and temperatures, in which light and dark mineral constituents are segregated into visible bands [Mid-18thC. From German, of uncertain origin: probably an alteration of Old High German *gneisto* 'spark', from its lustre.] —**gneissic** *adj.* —**gneissose** /nīs ōss/ *adj.*

gnocchi /nóki/ *npl.* in Italian or Italian-style cookery, dumplings made of potato, semolina, or flour, usually boiled and served with soup or a sauce [Late 19thC. From Italian, of uncertain origin: perhaps an alteration of *nocchio* 'knot in wood'.]

gnome[1] /nōm/ *n.* **1.** MYTHOL TINY SUPERNATURAL BEING according to old folk tales, one of a race of small beings usually portrayed as hunchbacked men with long white beards who live in the earth guarding treasure **2.** GARDENING = **garden gnome 3.** OFFENSIVE TERM an offensive term deliberately insulting sb thought of as small and, often, ugly (*insult*) [Mid-17thC. Via French from modern Latin *gnomus*, which was coined by PARACELSUS.] —**gnomelike** *adj.* ◇ **the gnomes of Zurich** international bankers and financiers, especially those based in Switzerland (*humorous*)

gnome[2] /nōm/ *n.* a short saying or proverb that expresses a general idea or principle [Late 16thC. Via Greek *gnōmē* 'opinion, judgment' from, ultimately, *gignōskein* 'to know'.]

gnomic /nṓmik/ *adj.* **1.** EPIGRAMMATIC resembling or containing proverbs or other short pithy sayings that express basic truths ○ *his gnomic utterances were widely quoted by journalists* **2.** CRYPTIC opaque or difficult to understand —**gnomically** *adv.*

gnomon /nṓ mon/ *n.* **1.** TIME ARM OF SUNDIAL the arm of a sundial, used to show the time of day by the position of its shadow **2.** GEOM PART OF A PARALLELOGRAM the part of a parallelogram that is left when a smaller similar parallelogram has been taken from its corner [Mid-16thC. Directly or via French or Latin from Greek *gnōmōn* 'indicator', from *gignōskein* (see GNOME[2]).] —**gnomonic** /nō mónnik/ *adj.* —**gnomonically** /-mónnikli/ *adv.*

gnosis /nṓssiss/ *n.* knowledge of spiritual truths reputedly possessed by the ancient Gnostics, who believed them to be essential to salvation [Late 16thC. From Greek *gnōsis* 'investigation, knowledge', from *gignōskein* (see GNOME[2]).]

gnostic /nóstik/ *adj.* relating to knowledge, especially knowledge of spiritual truths [Mid-17thC. See GNOSTIC.]

Gnostic *n.* BELIEVER IN GNOSTICISM sb who believes in Gnosticism ■ *adj.* OF GNOSTICISM relating to Gnosticism [Late 16thC. Via ecclesiastical Latin and Greek *gnōstikos* from, ultimately, *gignōskein* (see GNOME[2]).]

Gnosticism /nóstissizəm/ *n.* a pre-Christian and early Christian religious movement teaching that salvation comes by learning esoteric spiritual truths that free humanity from the material world, believed in this movement to be evil

gnotobiotics /nṓ tō bī óttiks/ *n.* the scientific study of organisms living either in a germ-free or a controlled environment, as when a known contaminant has been introduced [Mid-20thC. Coined from Greek *gnōtos* 'known' + BIOTIC.] —**gnotobiotic** *adj.* —**gnotobiotically** *adv.*

GNP *abbr.* gross national product

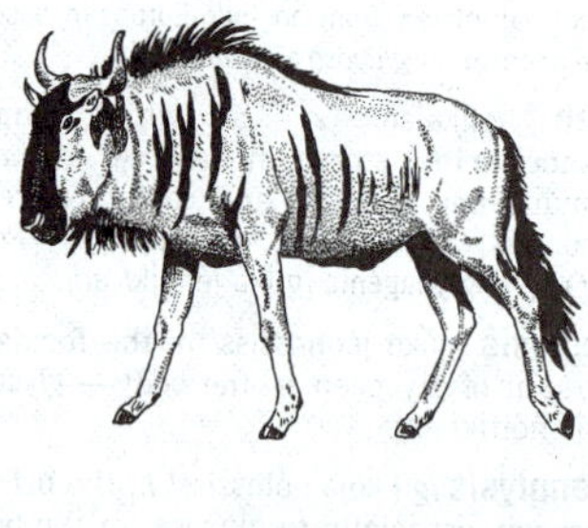

Gnu

gnu /noo/ (*plural* **gnu** *or* **gnus**) *n.* a large African antelope with a head resembling that of an ox, short mane, beard, downward curving horns, and tufted tail. Latin name: *Connochaetes gnou* and *Connochaetes taurinus.* [Late 18thC. Origin uncertain: probably via Dutch *gnoe* from Khoisan.]

GNU *abbr. S Africa* Government of National Unity

GNVQ (*plural* **GNVQs**) *n.* a post-16 qualification designed to provide vocationally orientated skills and knowledge for progression to employment or university. They are available at three levels, foundation, intermediate, and advanced. Full form **General National Vocational Qualification**

go[1] /gō/ (**goes, going, went** /went/, **gone** /gon/, *plural* **gos**) CORE MEANING: a basic intransitive verb of motion expressing movement from an unspecified point of departure or from a place that is already known or assumed ○ *Have you any idea where he went?* ○ *She never went anywhere without her spectacles.* ○ *Johnny went back inside for another coffee.* ○ *I've always wanted to go to Paris.*

1. *vi.* DEPART to leave a place ○ *Please don't go.* ○ *He's going tomorrow.* **2.** *vi.* MOVE TO DO STH to move towards a person or place with the intention of doing sth specific ○ *We had to go and pick up our young son who was playing at a friend's house.* ○ *After the wedding they went to live in Spain.* **3.** *vi.* PROCEED TO AN ACTIVITY to leave a place and proceed towards an activity, often a recreational activity ○ *They go for a jog every morning.* **4.** *vi.* ATTEND to attend a place regularly ○ *She went to evening classes to get more qualifications.* **5.** *vi.* TAKE PART IN to take part in a television or radio programme ○ *The President went on television to defend his government's decision.* **6.** *vi.* LEAD TO to lead to, or begin or end at, a particular place (*refers to a route or travel service*) ○ *Take the road that goes into the city centre.* ○ *The new bus service will go from Edinburgh to London.* **7.** *vi.* ELAPSE to elapse or pass (*refers to time*) ○ *As time went on, he pursued lesser jobs.* **8.** *vi.* BE ALLOTTED TO to be allotted to a particular recipient or used for a particular purpose (*refers to money or other resources*) ○ *The house will go to his surviving children.* ○ *Much of her income went on household bills.* **9.** *vi.* BE GIVEN TO to be given to sb as a quality or attribute ○ *The credit should go to the one who tries hardest.* **10.** *vi.* BE DISCARDED to be eliminated, given up, or got rid of ○ *This old sweater has just got to go!* ○ *Thousands of jobs will have to go, they say, if the company is to prosper.* **11.** *vi.* BE SPENT to be spent or used up ○ *By the end of the evening all the food had gone.* **12.** *vi.* LEAVE A JOB to leave a job or organization ○ *He was costing the company thousands and had to go.* **13.** *vi.* BLEND IN to be suited in a place, or blend or harmonize with other things ○ *They wanted to find a carpet that would go with the existing decor.* ○ *Those trousers just don't go.* **14.** *vi.* FIT IN to fit in a place because of being the right shape or size ○ *I tried to push the package through the letter box but it wouldn't go.* **15.** *vi.* BELONG to have somewhere as a usual or proper place ○ *The towels go in the cupboard in the bathroom.* **16.** *vi.* BE PUT to be put into sth as one of the parts that form it ○ *all the elements that go into making a successful musical* **17.** *vi.* FUNCTION to function or operate ○ *Can you get my car going again?* ○ *Without capital to make it go, our business plan was merely hopes written out on paper.* **18.** *vi.* FAIL to get weaker and begin to fail or give way ○ *My eyesight is starting to go* **19.** *vi.* BREAK DOWN to stop working properly and start to break down ○ *I think the battery may be going – the electrics are starting to play up.* **20.** *vi.* DIE to die (*used euphemistically*) ○ *I'm afraid she has gone.* **21.** *vi.* BECOME to change so as to come to be in a particular state or condition ○ *Their pet's behaviour went out of control.* **22.** *vi.* BE DRESSED OR EQUIPPED AS SPECIFIED to be in a particular state with regard to dress or equipment ○ *They went barefoot on the beach.* **23.** *vi.* PROCEED to proceed or happen in a particular way ○ *How did it go at work today?* ○ *We were trying to figure out what really went wrong.* ○ *The intruder went unchallenged.* **24.** *vi.* MAKE A NOISE AS A SIGNAL to make a noise such as a ring or a knock to attract attention ○ *She had just closed the front door when the phone went.* **25.** *vi.* MAKE A NOISE to make a particular noise ○ *The horn went beep.* ○ *Cows go 'moo'.* **26.** *vi.* REACH A PARTICULAR POINT to proceed to or reach a particular position or level ○ *'The freedom she experienced, the indulgence with which she was treated, went beyond her expectations'.* (Thomas Hardy, *The Mayor of Casterbridge*; 1886) **27.** *vi.* SERVE TO DO STH to be of such a nature or quality as to do sth ○ *It just goes to show how careful you have to be.* **28.** *vi.* COMPARE to compare with other people or things of the same kind ○ *As holidays abroad go, it was probably the best we've ever had.* **29.** *vi.* SOUND to proceed in terms of sound or words (*refers to a piece of music or writing*) ○ *How does that tune go again?* **30.** *vi.* ACCOMPANY to occur with or be present at the same time as sth else ○ *It's not necessarily the case that intelligence and common sense go together.* **31.** *vi.* CIRCULATE to circulate as information around a place or among people ○ *It soon went round the whole village that she had inherited a fortune.* **32.** *vi.* HAVE RECOURSE TO to turn to a procedure as a result of unresolved problems ○ *They couldn't agree, so they went to arbitration.* **33.** *vi.* BE THE AUTHORITY to be necessarily accepted as what will be the case in a given situation ○ *Whatever she says goes in our home.* **34.** *vi.* ENDURE to continue surviving or succeeding in a difficult situation ○ *Human beings can go for much longer without food than without water.* **35.** *vt.* BET IN CARDS to bet or bid in a card game ○ *I go three clubs.* **36.** *vt.* SAY to say sth quoted (*nonstandard*) ○ *So she goes, 'If you want it done then do it yourself'.* **37.** *vi. Carib* WILL will do sth ○ *I go see you tomorrow.* **38.** *vi.* EXPRESSING FUTURE ACTION used to express future action or intent (*used in progressive tenses*) ○ *What are we going to do?* **39.** *n.* ATTEMPT AT STH an attempt or chance to do sth ○ *She passed the exam on the* second go. **40.** *n.* MOVE OR TURN TAKEN a move or turn in a game ○ *It's your go.* **41.** *n.* ENERGY energy and vibrancy (*informal*) ○ *I've had so much more go since changing my diet.* **42.** *adj.* FUNCTIONING ready and operating properly (*informal*) ○ *All systems are go.* [Old English *gān*. Ultimately from an Indo-European word that is also the ancestor of German *gehen* 'to go'.] ◇ **anything goes** used to indicate that anything is to be tolerated or accepted as the norm ○ *In this place almost anything goes!* ◇ **at one go** all at the same time ◇ **on the go** very active and busy ○ *a two-career couple, always on the go* ◇ **have a go (at sth)** to make an attempt at sth (*informal*) ○ *He said that he had never skied before but he was willing to have a go at it.* ◇ **have a go at sb** to attack sb verbally (*informal*) ◇ **make a go of sth** to make a success of sth ○ *They couldn't make a go of the relationship.* ◇ **here we go!** used as a chant by football supporters either when their team is winning or to encourage their team to win ◇ **here we go (again)!** used to express displeasure or resignation that sth, usually sth bad, that has happened before is now happening again ○ *Here we go again! This old car simply won't start.* ◇ **it is all go** used to indicate that there is a lot of activity and hard work happening (*informal*) ○ *It's all go around here!* ◇ **there you go** *US* used to express general encouragement or approval to sb else (*informal*) ◇ **there you go again** used to complain that sb has done sth bad or wrong yet again ○ *There you go again, misinterpreting and twisting what I'm saying* ◇ **to go** to be taken home rather than consumed on the premises ○ *one pizza to go*

go about *v.* **1.** *vt.* TACKLE STH to deal with a problem, assignment, or task **2.** *vt.* CONSTANTLY BEHAVE IN SPECIFIED WAY to spend a lot of time behaving in a specified way ○ *She's been going about causing trouble in the office.* **3.** *vti.* BE WIDELY KNOWN OR CURRENT to be experienced or known by a lot of people, often in a particular place ○ *wild rumours going about London* **4.** *vi.* SAILING CHANGE TACK to change tack in a sailing boat ◇ **there's a lot of it going about** used to indicate that sth is extremely widespread ○ *He's got flu? There's a lot of it going about.*

go after *vt.* to make a deliberate effort to get or find sth seen as desirable or advantageous ○ *I decided to go after a teaching job I saw in the paper.*

go ahead *vi.* to start or continue with sth, especially after a period of uncertainty or delay ○ *We decided to go ahead and start our meal without her.*

go along *vi.* **1.** ACCOMPANY SB to accompany sb on a journey ○ *I decided to go along just to keep her company.* **2.** DEVELOP IN SPECIFIED MANNER to develop or progress in a manner specified, especially favourably (*informal*) ○ *Things were going along reasonably well until she lost her job again.*

go along with *vt.* to accept sth or obey sb, especially reluctantly or to the surprise of others ○ *You can't go along with it – it's breaking the law.*

go around *vti.* **1.** BE WIDELY KNOWN OR SHARED to be experienced or shared by a lot of people ○ *a flu virus that's going around at work* **2.** BE ENOUGH FOR EVERYONE to be able to be distributed to everyone ○ *There aren't enough pens to go around, so you'll have to share.* ◇ **what goes around comes around** used to say that whatever happens now will have an effect in the future (*informal*)

go at *vt.* to attempt sth enthusiastically or energetically ○ *He went at the snow shovelling as if it were a race.*

go away *vi.* **1.** TAKE A HOLIDAY to leave the place where you live, especially in order to take a holiday (*informal*) ○ *Are you going away this summer?* **2.** GET OUT OF HERE used to tell sb to get away from you and leave the place where you are because he or she is annoying you ○ *Go away! I'm busy.* ○ *I just had to tell him to go away, and so he went.*

go back *vi.* **1.** ORIGINATE FROM A TIME to originate from a particular date, period, or time ○ *a tradition that goes back hundreds of years to the time of Henry VIII* **2.** BE RESET AN HOUR EARLIER to be required to be reset an hour earlier, to Greenwich Mean Time from British Summer Time **3.** RETURN TO WORK to return to work after being absent, e.g. because of holidays, illness, or industrial action (*informal*)

go back on *vt.* to change your mind about sth you have agreed or promised to do ○ *You can't go back on what we originally agreed – a deal's a deal.*

go by *v.* **1.** *vi.* PASS IN TIME to move onwards in terms of time ○ *As the years go by he gets more and more mellow* **2.** *vt.* REGARD STH AS TRUE to treat advice or information as reliable or true **3.** *vt.* USE PARTICULAR SOURCE OF INFORMATION to use a particular way of doing sth or finding sth out ○ *All we had to go by was a soggy map.*

go down *vi.* **1.** SINK BENEATH STH to sink beneath the surface of a body of water ○ *An oil tanker went down off the coast of Alaska.* **2.** CRASH to fall from the air and crash ○ *The kite went down in the treetops.* **3.** GO BELOW HORIZON to sink below the horizon ○ *The sun had already gone down by the time we got back.* **4.** SUFFER DISGRACE to be disgraced or ruined (*informal*) ○ *If he goes down, he'll take the whole department with him.* **5.** BE DEFEATED to be defeated in a vote or competition (*informal*) ○ *Manchester United went down 2–3 to Barnsley in the third round.* **6.** SPORTS TO BE RELEGATED in sports, to be relegated or demoted ○ *The local team only just managed to avoid going down this season.* **7.** BE REMEMBERED to be remembered in a specified way ○ *She will surely go down as one of the greatest athletes of all time.* **8.** BE RECEIVED to be received in a particular way ○ *an idea that didn't go down at all well with shareholders* **9.** TAKE PLACE to happen or be happening (*slang*) ○ *Hey, what's going down?* ○ *When the robbery went down, the cops rushed to the scene.* **10.** BE EATABLE OR DRINKABLE to be able to be eaten or drunk, especially easily or enjoyably (*informal*) ○ *With sick children, soup tends to go down more easily than solid foods.* **11.** BECOME ILL WITH STH to become ill with a specified or illness (*informal*) ○ *Most of her class has gone down with the flu.* **12.** COMPUT MALFUNCTION to break down or stop working ○ *Since the airline's computers have gone down, we can't get flight information yet.* **13.** BE SENT TO PRISON to be sent to prison, especially for a specified period (*informal*) **14.** UNIV LEAVE UNIVERSITY AT THE END OF TERM to leave college or university at the end of term or the end of the academic year **15.** BRIDGE FAIL TO ACHIEVE BRIDGE TRICKS in the game of bridge, to fail to attain the number of tricks that has been contracted for

go down on *vt.* to perform oral sex on sb (*slang taboo*)

go for *vt.* **1.** TRY TO OBTAIN STH YOU WANT to make an effort to obtain sth because it is suitable for you or important to you (*informal*) ○ *I really think you should go for that sales job.* **2.** LIKE STH OR SB A LOT to prefer, like, or be interested in a particular thing or person (*informal*) ○ *I don't really go for science fiction.* **3.** CHOOSE STH to choose one particular thing rather than another (*informal*) ○ *I think I'll go for the chocolate cheesecake – how about you?* **4.** ATTACK SB to attack sb physically or verbally **5.** COMMAND A PRICE to be worth or sold for a particular amount ○ *In the end the house went for far less than its market value.* **6.** BE RELEVANT TO SB to apply or be relevant to sb ○ *She needs to be more careful in her work – and that goes for you, too!* ◇ **go for it** not to stop or relax until you aggressively reach your goal (*slang*) ○ *The coach told the team to get out there and go for it.* ◇ **have sth going for you** to be in a situation where sth is useful or helpful to you to a particular extent (*informal*) ○ *She has a lot going for her in the tennis championship, given her season's record.*

go forward *vi.* to be required to be reset an hour later, to British Summer Time from Greenwich Mean Time ○ *The clocks go forward tonight.*

go in *vi.* **1.** BE OBSCURED BY CLOUD COVER to become hidden by clouds ○ *Once the sun went in, it got really cold sitting in the ski lift.* **2.** BE LEARNT to be learnt, remembered, or understood (*informal*) ○ *However many times I read it nothing seems to go in.* **3.** BEGIN AN ATTACK to launch an attack or begin another manoeuvre ○ *After the police went in, things rapidly got out of hand.* **4.** CRICKET BEGIN AN INNINGS in cricket, to begin an innings (*refers to a player or a team*)

go in for *vt.* **1.** ENTER A COMPETITION to enter a competition or sporting event **2.** ENJOY DOING STH to enjoy a particular activity ○ *I don't really go in for team sports myself.* **3.** CHOOSE A CAREER to choose a particular area of study or career ○ *decided to go in for the priesthood*

go into *vt.* **1.** BEGIN A CAREER to begin a job or career in a particular area of activity ○ *She went into advertising and made pots of money.* **2.** LOOK INTO STH to examine or look into sth in detail and with thoroughness **3.** BE A FACTOR OF A NUMBER to be a factor of a particular number or amount ○ *15 won't go into 125.* **4.** BE SPENT ON STH to be used or spent for a particular purpose ○ *Millions have gone into finding a cure.*

go in with *vt.* to begin participating in a scheme or venture with other people ○ *I went in with four friends to start a restaurant.*

go off *v.* **1.** *vi.* BECOME BAD to become bad, stale, or rancid ○ *Milk goes off very quickly in this weather.* **2.** *vi.* DETONATE to explode or be fired **3.** *vi.* BEGIN SOUNDING OR VIBRATING to start to ring, sound, or vibrate ○ *The smoke alarm goes off whenever we make toast.* **4.** *vi.* BE CARRIED OUT to be carried out or conducted in a particular manner ○ *I think the conference went off as well as could be expected.* **5.** *vi.* DEPART to set out, or set out for a particular place ○ *There were endless TV images of soldiers going off to war.* **6.** *vti.* LEAVE PITCH OR STAGE to leave a sports pitch, stage, or other place ○ *The band went off early but came back to play three encores.* **7.** *vi.* START BEHAVING IN PARTICULAR WAY to change behaviour and start behaving in a particular way ○ *When I suggested a few changes he went off into hysterics.* **8.** *vt.* STOP LIKING SB OR STH to stop liking sb or sth previously liked ○ *I soon went off him once he started telling jokes.* ○ *went off the idea once he found out how much it cost* **9.** *vi. Aus* GO WELL to go exceptionally well (*slang*)

go off with *vt.* to begin a relationship with sb, especially abandoning a spouse or partner in order to do this ○ *We were not surprised to learn he'd gone off with his secretary.*

go on *v.* **1.** *vi.* CARRY ON to continue in progress ○ *The dispute went on for another nine months before it was resolved.* **2.** *vi.* OCCUR to happen or take place ○ *I asked him what was going on.* **3.** *vti.* MAKE A PUBLIC ENTRANCE to make an entrance on a sports pitch, stage, or other public place ○ *She went on every night to rapturous applause.* ○ *The team went on the pitch feeling that they'd already won.* **4.** *vi.* TALK TOO MUCH to talk too much and much too long ○ *She's always going on about her yacht.* **5.** *vi.* CONTINUE SPEAKING to continue speaking, especially after a pause ○ *She then went on about the latest international incident.* **6.** *vi.* DO STH AFTERWARDS to do sth after the time or period you are referring to ○ *She finished fourth, but went on to win the championship the following year.* **7.** *vt.* USE AS RELIABLE INFORMATION to use sth as reliable information ○ *The police have very little to go on at this stage.* **8.** *vt.* ENJOY STH to like or enjoy sth (*informal*) ○ *I don't go much on his new haircut.* **9.** *vi.* USED TO EXPRESS ENCOURAGEMENT used to encourage sb to do sth, usually sth the person is reluctant or afraid to try (*informal*) ○ *Go on, you'll have a great time skiing down that hill!* **10.** *vi.* EXPRESSING DISBELIEF used when you are pleading with sb, or when you are expressing pleading disbelief (*informal*) ○ *Oh, go on! I simply don't believe she could have done such a thing!* **11.** *vt.* APPROXIMATE STH to be close to a particular age, time, or number (*used in progressive tenses*) ○ *He must be going on 50.*

go on at *vt.* to criticize or nag sb persistently or at length (*informal*) ○ *He's always going on at me about how scruffy I look.*

go out *vi.* **1.** SOCIALIZE to socialize and enjoy yourself away from home ○ *She loves going out, but he prefers to stay at home.* **2.** FLOW OUTWARDS FROM SHORE to flow away from the shoreline ○ *the tide had gone out* **3.** GO OUT OF STYLE to stop being fashionable ○ *Muttonchop whiskers went out in the late 1800s.* **4.** FINISH GAME to end your part in a game or competition by doing sth you need to do ○ *You need to throw a six to go out.* **5.** BE FORCED OUT OF GAME to be forced to quit a game or competition ○ *The two lowest scoring teams in each round go out.* **6.** DATE SB to date sb, or date each other ○ *They've been going out for six months.* **7.** BE BROADCAST to be broadcast on TV or the radio ○ *The programme went out last night.* **8.** BE EXTINGUISHED to stop burning or functioning ○ *the fire has gone out*

go out to *vt.* **1.** BE BEATEN BY SB IN COMPETITION to be beaten by another team or contestant in a knockout competition ○ *Liverpool went out to Newcastle in the semifinal.* **2.** BE EXTENDED TO SB to be offered or extended to a person or group ○ *Our thoughts go out tonight to the friends and relatives of the victims.*

go over *v.* **1.** *vi.* CHANGE TO NEW SYSTEM to change to a different system or way of doing things ○ *We went over from oil to gas when we got the central heating* replaced. **2.** *vi.* CHANGE ALLEGIANCE to change allegiance and start supporting sb or sth else ○ *In a surprise move, the MP went over to Labour.* **3.** *vt.* EXAMINE STH CAREFULLY to examine or check sth carefully ○ *The police went over the car looking for fingerprints.* **4.** *vt.* REHEARSE AND MEMORIZE to practise or repeat sth in order to learn it ○ *The actors were all busy going over their lines.*

go round *v.* **1.** *vti.* = **go around 2.** *vi.* VISIT SB to go and visit sb ○ *Let's go round and see Dave.*

go through *v.* **1.** *vt.* EXAMINE THOROUGHLY AND PHYSICALLY to examine or inspect sth very carefully ○ *The police went through his luggage but found nothing suspicious.* **2.** *vi.* GAIN OFFICIAL APPROVAL to be accepted or approved officially, after having gone through channels or set procedural stages **3.** *vt.* UNDERGO UNPLEASANTNESS OF SOME KIND to undergo hardship or difficulties, usually in stages and over a period of time ○ *They're going through a series of business setbacks.* **4.** *vt.* CONSUME IN QUANTITY to use, eat, or spend sth, especially a large amount in a short time ○ *They go through hundreds of pounds of groceries a week.* **5.** *vi.* *Aus* LEAVE to leave or depart (*informal*)

go through with *vt.* to carry on with sth until it has been completed or resolved, especially when this requires determination ○ *I'm determined to go through with this court case, come what may.*

go under *vi.* **1.** SINK IN WATER to sink below the surface of the water ○ *I managed to grab him as he went under for the third time.* **2.** FAIL to close down, or be unable to keep going **3.** LOSE CONSCIOUSNESS to lose consciousness, especially after being given an anaesthetic ○ *They began the operation as soon as she'd gone under.*

go up *vi.* **1.** BE BUILT to be constructed ○ *A new supermarket went up where the cinema used to be.* **2.** BE DISPLAYED to be put on display ○ *A notice has gone up saying how we can be contacted.* **3.** DETONATE OR IGNITE to explode or burst into flames ○ *The whole place went up in a matter of seconds.* **4.** UNIV GO TO UNIVERSITY to go to or return to a university at the beginning of a term or academic year

go with *vt.* **1.** BE PART OF STH to be a normal or usual part of sth ○ *The long hours go with the job.* **2.** ADOPT OR FOLLOW AN IDEA to adopt or follow a particular approach or point of view ○ *Just go with the plan as it stands for the time being and we'll see what happens.* **3.** DATE SB to spend time romantically and socially with sb (*informal*) ○ *Anna's been going with Alex for a month now.* **4.** HAVE SEX WITH SB to have sexual intercourse with sb (*informal*)

go without *vt.* to be deprived financially, or be deprived of a particular thing ○ *You'll have to go without breakfast if you want to catch the early train.* ○ *Sometimes the poor family just had to go without.*

go² /gō/ *n.* a Japanese board game played with black and white stones on a surface marked with 19 lines intersecting each other to create 367 crossing points. The object of the game is to capture the larger part of the board and the opponent's stones. [Late 19thC. From Japanese.]

GO *abbr.* MIL general order

goa /gố ə/ *n.* a Tibetan gazelle with a brownish-grey coat, the male of which has backward curving horns. Latin name: *Procapra picticaudata.* [Mid-19thC. From Tibetan *dgoba.*]

Goa /gố ə/ state on the western coast of India. Formerly a Portuguese territory, it was incorporated into India in 1961 and became a separate Indian state in 1987. Capital: Panaji. Population: 1,235,000 (1994). Area: 3,813 sq. km/1,472 sq. mi.

goad /gōd/ *vt.* (**goads, goading, goaded**) **1.** DRIVE SB TO DO STH to provoke or incite sb into action (*often passive*) **2.** PROD WITH A STICK to prod an animal with a long pointed stick ■ *n.* **1.** POINTED ANIMAL PROD a long pointed stick used for prodding cattle and other animals **2.** STIMULUS sth used to motivate sb or stir sb into action [Old English *gād.* Ultimately from a prehistoric Germanic word that also produced Old English *gār* 'spear' (source of English *garlic*).]

─── **WORD KEY: SYNONYMS** ───
See Synonyms at *motive.*

go-ahead *n.* PERMISSION TO PROCEED permission or approval to proceed with sth (*informal*) ○ *Once we get*

the go-ahead from the bank, we can get things moving. ■ *adj.* ENTERPRISING imaginative and ambitious ○ *a young go-ahead company at the forefront of information technology*

goal /gōl/ *n.* **1.** SPORTS TARGET AREA the space or opening into which a ball or puck must go to score points in a game such as football or hockey, usually a pair of posts with a crossbar and often a net ○ *The kick landed just to the left of the goal.* **2.** SPORTS SCORE the score gained by getting the ball or puck into the goal ○ *leading by three goals to two* **3.** SPORTS SUCCESSFUL SHOT a successful attempt at hitting, kicking, throwing, or passing a ball or hitting a puck into or over a goal ○ *one of the greatest goals of all time* **4.** AIM sth that sb wants to achieve ○ *One of my goals for this year is to learn Spanish.* **5.** RACE'S END the end of a race ○ *The runners are still several minutes from the goal.* [14thC. Origin unknown.]

goal area *n.* in soccer, the rectangular area marked out in front of the goal within which goalkeepers may handle the ball

goal difference *n.* in football and other sports, the difference between the number of goals scored for and against a team over a particular period. It is often used as a decider between teams with equal points.

goal-directed *adj.* strongly motivated and highly organized in achieving tasks that are specified in advance

goalie /gốli/ *n.* a goalkeeper (*informal*)

goalkeeper /gốl keepər/ *n.* in games such as football and hockey, a defensive player positioned in or near a goal whose main task is to keep the ball or puck from crossing the goal line into the goal

goal kick *n.* **1.** SOCCER FREE KICK BY THE DEFENDER NEAR THE GOAL a free kick taken from the six-yard-line by a defensive player when the ball has been driven out of play over the end line (**goal line**) by an opposing player **2.** RUGBY ATTACKER'S FREE KICK TO CONVERT A TRY in rugby, a free kick by a member of the attacking team, aimed at clearing the defenders' crossbar and designed to convert a five-point try into a seven-point score

goalless /gốl ləss/ *adj.* **1.** SPORTS WITH NO GOALS without any goals being scored ○ *A goalless semifinal left everyone feeling cheated.* **2.** AIMLESS having no goals to aim for in life or work

goal line *n.* in games such as football and hockey, the line where goalposts are positioned and over which the ball must pass or be carried to make a score. A try or touchdown can be scored anywhere along the line; in other circumstances the ball may also have to pass between the posts.

goalmouth /gốl mowth/ (*plural* **-mouths** /-mowthz/) *n.* in games such as soccer and hockey, the area directly in front of the goal

goal-oriented *adj.* = **goal-directed**

goalpost /gốl pōst/ *n.* either of two posts, usually supporting a crossbar between them, that together mark the boundary of the goal in games such as football and hockey ◇ **move the goalposts** to change the rules or conditions after a project has started or a course of action has been embarked on ○ *We'll never finish the software if Marketing keeps moving the goalposts.*

goalscorer /gốl skawrər/ *n.* a player who scores or has just scored a goal

goanna /gō ánnə/ *n.* a large Australian monitor lizard

Goanna

of which there are several varieties. Genus: *Varanus.* [Mid-19thC. Alteration of IGUANA.]

Goat: Mountain goat

goat /gōt/ (*plural* **goats** *or* **goat**) *n.* **1.** ZOOL HORNED MAMMAL RELATED TO SHEEP an agile ruminant mammal that is related to sheep and has backward curving horns, straight hair, and a short tail. Domestic goats are raised for their wool, meat, and milk. Genus: *Capra.* **2.** LECHER a lecherous man (*insult*) **3.** = **scapegoat** [Old English *gāt.* Ultimately from an Indo-European word that also produced German *Geiß* 'goat'. Originally in the meaning 'she-goat', it came to denote both sexes by the 14thC.] ─ **goatish** *adj.* ◇ **act** *or* **play the goat, act** *or* **play the giddy goat** to behave in a silly way, often intentionally ◇ **get sb's goat** to annoy or irritate sb (*informal*) ○ *Their constant carping over trivia really gets my goat.*

Goat *n.* ZODIAC = **Capricorn**

goat cheese, goat's cheese *n.* cheese made from goat's milk

Goatee: Actor Tom Hanks wearing a goatee

goatee /gō teé/ *n.* a short pointed beard on the chin but not the cheeks [From its resemblance to a goat's beard]

goatfish /gốt fish/ (*plural* **-fish** *or* **-fishes**) *n.* *US* = **red mullet** [From the barbels beneath its mouth]

goatherd /gốt hurd/ *n.* sb who looks after goats

goat moth *n.* a large pale-grey European moth with wood-boring larvae that give off an odour like that of goats. Latin name: *Cossus cossus.*

goatsbeard /gốts beerd/ *n.* **1.** FLOWER LIKE A DANDELION a Eurasian plant, now also growing in the United States, that has woolly stems and large yellow flowers like those of the dandelion. Latin name: *Tragopogon pratensis.* **2.** PLANT WITH WHITE FLOWERS an eastern North American plant that has long spikes of small white flowers. Latin name: *Aruncus dioicus.* [From the down on the seeds]

goat's cheese *n.* = **goat cheese**

goatskin /gốt skin/ *n.* **1.** SKIN OF A GOAT the skin or hide of a goat **2.** INDUST, CLOTHES LEATHER leather made from the skin of a goat **3.** LEATHER WINE FLASK a wine container made from the skin of a goat

goat's milk *n.* milk from a goat, used for drinking and for making cheese

goat's rue *n.* a Eurasian legume plant grown for its white, purple, or pink flowers and used for feeding livestock. Latin name: *Galega officinalis.*

gob¹ /gob/ *n.* CLOT a lump of a soft or wet substance (*slang*) ○ *a huge gob of whipped cream* ■ *vi.* (**gobs, gobbing, gobbed**) SPIT PHLEGM to spit or eject phlegm from the throat (*slang*) [14thC. From Old French *gobe* 'mouthful', from *gober* 'to swallow', of uncertain origin.]

gob² /gob/ *n.* the human mouth (*slang disapproving*) [Mid-16thC. Origin uncertain: perhaps from Scottish, Irish, and Gaelic.]

gob³ /gob/ *n.* waste material from mining, e.g. clay or shale [Mid-19thC. Origin unknown.]

gobbet /góbbit/ *n.* **1.** QUANTITY OF LIQUID a quantity of liquid, often in a sticky blotch ○ *Gobbets of grease covered the top of the stove.* **2.** EXCERPT an extract from a text, especially one chosen for translation or comment in an examination **3.** HUNK OF FOOD a piece or chunk of sth, especially raw meat (*archaic*) [13thC. From Old French *gobet* 'a small gob', from *gobe* (see GOB¹).]

gobble¹ /góbb'l/ (-bles, -bling, -bled) *vt.* **1.** EAT QUICKLY AND GREEDILY to eat sth quickly and greedily ○ *He gobbled up all the pizza.* **2.** USE STH UP to use sth up quickly or in large amounts (*informal humorous*) ○ *watching the payphone gobble her money* [Early 17thC. Origin uncertain: probably formed from GOB¹.]

gobble² /góbb'l/ *vi.* (-bles, -bling, -bled) MAKE THE SOUND OF A TURKEY to make the characteristic gurgling sound of a male turkey, or a sound resembling this ■ *n.*, *interj.* TURKEY SOUND the gurgling sound made by a male turkey [Late 17thC. An imitation of the sound.]

gobbledegook /góbb'ldigook/, **gobbledygook** *n.* language that is difficult or impossible to understand, especially either nonsense or long-winded technical jargon (*informal disapproving*) ○ *This manual is full of gobbledegook.* [Mid-20thC. An imitation of the sound made by a male turkey.]

gobbler /góbblər/ *n.* a male turkey (*informal*)

Gobelin /góbəlin/ *n.* a tapestry produced by the Gobelin factory in Paris, characterized by vivid pictorial scenes

go-between *n.* sb who communicates or mediates between two groups or two individuals during a negotiation, transaction, or secret operation ○ *used as a go-between to ease communication between the enemy generals prior to surrender*

Gobi Desert /góbi-/ desert in northern China and southern Mongolia, the coldest and one of the largest deserts in the world. Area: 1,300,000 sq. km/500,000 sq. mi.

goblet /góbblət/ *n.* **1.** STEMMED DRINKING VESSEL a drinking vessel with a stem and base, especially one of metal or glass **2.** LARGE CUP a large bowl-shaped cup used for drinking in former times (*archaic*) [14thC. From Old French *gobelet* 'small cup', from *gobel* 'cup'.]

goblet cell *n.* a cell shaped like a goblet that secretes mucus. Goblet cells are found in the intestines and respiratory system of mammals and the epidermis of fish.

goblin /góblin/ *n.* in folk tales, a creature resembling a small man of unpleasant appearance, usually evil or mischievous [14thC. Origin uncertain: probably via Anglo-Norman from medieval Latin *gobelinus*, the name of a spirit that supposedly haunted the French town of Évreux in the 12thC.]

gobo /góbō/ (*plural* **gobos** *or* **goboes**) *n.* **1.** MICROPHONE SHIELD a shield that is placed around a microphone to keep out unwanted sounds **2.** LENS SHIELD a black screen placed around the lens of a camera or video camera to keep out unwanted light [Mid-20thC. Origin unknown.]

gobshite /góbshīt/ *n. Ireland, UK* an offensive term for a person despised especially for being unintelligent (*regional taboo insult*) [Mid-20thC. From GOB² + *shite*, a variant of SHIT.]

gobsmacked /góbsmakt/ *adj.* extremely surprised or shocked (*slang*)

gobstopper /góbstopər/ *n.* a large hard sweet that changes colour as it is sucked. US term **jawbreaker** [From GOB², because of its speech-inhibiting size]

gobstruck /góbstruk/ *adj.* = **gobsmacked** (*slang*)

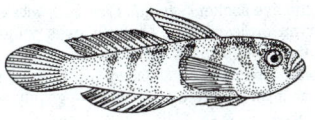

Goby

goby /góbi/ (*plural* **-by** *or* **-bies**) *n.* a small elongated spiny-finned freshwater or marine fish whose pelvic fins form a sucker. Gobies are usually found in burrows or crevices. Family: Gobiidae. [Mid-18thC. Via Latin *gobius* from Greek *kōbios*, the name of a small fish.]

go-by *n.* a slight or snub (*slang*) ○ *She tried to speak but he gave her the go-by.*

go-cart, **go-karts** *n.* **1.** CHILD'S CAR WITH AN ENGINE a light open-framed car large enough for a child or young teenager to sit in, containing a small engine and used for racing **2.** MOTOR SPORTS = **kart**

god /god/ *n.* **1.** SUPERNATURAL BEING one of a group of supernatural male beings in some religions, each of which is worshipped as the personification or controller of some aspect of the universe ○ *Thor, the Norse god of thunder.* ◊ **goddess** *n.* 1 **2.** FIGURE OR IMAGE a representation of a god, used as an object of worship ○ *the little bronze god standing in a niche above the altar.* ◊ **goddess** *n.* 2 **3.** STH THAT DOMINATES SB'S LIFE sth that is so important that it takes over sb's life (*informal*) ○ *worshipping the false god of fame* **4.** SB ADMIRED AND IMITATED a man who is widely admired or imitated (*informal*) ○ *He was one of the rock music gods of the early Seventies.* ◊ **goddess** *n.* 3 ■ **gods** *npl.* **1.** FATE the entire group of supernatural beings viewed as deciding human fate **2.** THEATRE THEATRE GALLERY the highest tier of seats in a theatre (*informal*) [Old English. Ultimately from an Indo-European word, meaning 'that which is invoked', which is also the ancestor of German *Gott* 'god'.]

God *n.* **1.** RELIG SUPREME BEING the being believed in monotheistic religions such as Judaism, Islam, and Christianity to be the all-powerful all-knowing creator of the universe, worshipped as the only god **2.** CHR THE TRINITY one supreme being worshipped by Christians in the form of three persons, Father, Son, and Holy Ghost ■ *interj.* EXPRESSION OF STRONG FEELING used to express or emphasize feelings such as anger, helplessness, and frustration (*sometimes considered offensive*)

Godard /góddaar/, **Jean-Luc** (b. 1930) French film director. A director of the French New Wave, he became influential in the 1960s with films such as *Breathless* (1960) and *Weekend* (1967).

Godavari /gō dáavəri/ river in western India that is sacred to Hindus. It rises in the Western Ghats and empties into the Bay of Bengal. Length: 1,448/900 mi.

god-awful, **God-awful** *adj.* extremely bad or unpleasant (*slang; sometimes considered offensive*) ○ *a god-awful racket*

godchild /gód chīld/ (*plural* **-children**) *n.* sb whose spiritual upbringing is made the responsibility of a godmother or a godfather, or both. This arrangement is usually declared at the person's baptism or christening.

goddaughter /gód dawtər/ *n.* a girl or woman who is sb's godchild

goddess /gódd ess/ *n.* **1.** SUPERNATURAL BEING one of the group of supernatural female beings in some religions, worshipped as the personification or controller of some aspect of the universe. ◊ **god** *n.* 1 **2.** FIGURE OR IMAGE a representation of a goddess, used as an object of worship ○ *the statue of the goddess, standing in the temple's first niche.* ◊ **god** 3. SB ADMIRED AND IMITATED a woman who is widely admired or

imitated, especially for her beauty (*informal*) ○ *a screen goddess.* ◊ **god** *n.* 4

godet /gō dét/ *n.* a triangular piece of material inserted into a skirt or other garment to make it more flared or to widen it [Late 19thC. From French.]

godfather /gód faathər/ *n.* **1.** MAN GODPARENT a man who is sb's godparent **2.** ORGANIZED-CRIME BOSS a man who heads a criminal organization, especially a Mafia leader (*informal*)

── **WORD KEY: CULTURAL NOTE** ──
The Godfather, a film by US director Francis Ford Coppola (1972). Based on the novel by Mario Puzo (1969), it describes the attempts of the Sicilian Corleone family to maintain their control of the New York Mafia when a group of renegade families set up a drug-smuggling ring. It and its two sequels, *The Godfather Part II* (1974) and *The Godfather Part III* (1990), brought new meaning to terms such as 'godfather' and 'consigliere'.

God-fearing *adj.* devout or deeply religious

godforsaken /gódfər sayk'n/ *adj.* depressing, deserted, or empty ○ *The soldiers couldn't wait to get out of that godforsaken desert.*

God-given *adj.* existing or applying as part of the natural order of the universe rather than arranged by humanity

godhead /gód hed/ *n.* the nature or essence of being divine (*formal*)

Godhead /gód hed/ *n.* the Christian God, especially when considered as the Holy Trinity (*formal*)

godhood /gód hood/ *n.* = **godhead** (*formal*)

Godiva /gə dīvə/, **Lady** (1040?–80?) English noblewoman. According to legend, she obtained a remission of heavy local taxes levied by her husband, Leofric, Earl of Chester, by riding naked through the marketplace in Coventry on a horse.

godless /gódləss/ *adj.* **1.** WITHOUT GOD OR A GOD not believing in or worshipping God, or any god (*disapproving*) **2.** WICKED of an evil or immoral character or nature (*formal disapproving*) —**godlessly** *adv.* —**godlessness** *n.*

godlike /gód līk/ *adj.* fit for God or a god, or having the qualities of a god or of God, e.g. superhuman power, beauty, or imagination

godly /gódli/ (-lier, -liest) *adj.* **1.** DEVOUT devoted to or worshipping God (*formal*) **2.** DIVINE fit for God or a god, or having godlike qualities —**godliness** *n.*

godmother /gód muthər/ *n.* a woman who is sb's godparent

godown /gố down/ *n.* a warehouse, especially in India and Malaysia [Late 16thC. Via Portuguese *gudao* from Tamil *kitanku* and Kannada *gadangu* 'store'.]

godparent /gód pairənt/ *n.* sb who is named as a sponsor when a child is baptized. Godparents often maintain close, almost familial relationships with a godchild.

godroon /gə drŏon/ *n.* = **gadroon**

God's Acre /gódz áykər/ *n.* any churchyard or cemetery (*literary*) [From the German *Gottesacker*]

God's country *n.* a nation or piece of land that is dearly loved

godsend /gód send/ *n.* **1.** UNEXPECTED GOOD sth good that happens unexpectedly **2.** STH OR SB VERY USEFUL sth received that proves extremely useful, or sb who arrives and gives much-needed help [Early 19thC. From *God's send* 'sth sent by God': *send* from SEND¹ (noun) in the obsolete sense 'thing sent'.]

God's gift *n.* an extremely admirable, valued, or talented person (*often used ironically*) ○ *He thought he was God's gift to the film industry.*

god slot *n.* a scheduled time for religious programmes on radio or television (*informal; may be considered offensive*)

godson /gód sun/ *n.* a man or boy who is sb's godchild

God's own /gódz ōn/, **Godzone** *n. ANZ* New Zealand or Australia, seen by their inhabitants as specially favoured countries (*informal; often used ironically*) [Shortening of *God's own country*]

God's own country *n.* any country or piece of land seen as chosen and specially favoured

Godspeed /gód speed/ *interj.* used to wish sb a safe journey or successful endeavour (*dated*) [15thC. From *God speed you* 'may God speed you'.]

godsquad /gód skwod/ *n.* a Christian religious group, especially one that enthusiastically recruits new members (*informal humorous or disapproving; may be considered offensive*)

Godwin Austen, Mount /góddwin óstin/ = K2

godwit /gód wit/ *n.* a large wading bird, found worldwide, that has a long slightly upturned bill and long legs and is related to curlews and sandpipers. Genus: *Limosa*. [Mid-16thC. Origin unknown.]

Godzone *n.* = God's own

Goebbels /góbl'z/, **Joseph** (1897–1945) German Nazi politician. He was Adolf Hitler's minister of propaganda (1933–45). Full name **Paul Joseph Goebbels**

goer /gó ər/ *n.* **1.** REGULAR ATTENDER sb who attends performances or other events on a regular basis (*usually used in combination*) ○ *festival-goer* **2.** FAST MOVER a spirited or fast-moving person or animal (*informal*) **3.** PROMISCUOUS PERSON sb who is promiscuous or sexually uninhibited (*slang*)

Goering /góring/, **Göring, Hermann** (1893–1946) German Nazi politician. Adolf Hitler's second in command, he organized Nazi Germany's concentration camps, directed its economy, and planned much of Germany's military strategy in World War II. Full name **Hermann Wilhelm Goering**

Johann Wolfgang von Goethe: Portrait (1826) by Heinrich Christoph Kolbe

Goethe /gótə/, **Johann Wolfgang von** (1749–1832) German writer and scientist. A seminal figure of European literature, he was a prolific writer of poems, novels, plays, criticism, and letters. His masterwork is the dramatic poem *Faust* (1808–32). He was also author of *The Sorrows of Young Werther* (novel, 1774).

goethite /gó thīt/ *n.* an earthy, rust-coloured hydrated iron oxide mineral formed by the alteration of iron minerals [Early 19thC. Named after J. W. von *Goethe* (1749–1832), German writer.]

go-faster *adj.* intended to make a motor vehicle look or sound sporty or fast (*informal*) ○ *a car with go-faster stripes*

gofer /gófər/ *n.* sb who runs errands, especially sb employed to do this and other low-level, basic tasks (*informal*) [Mid-20thC. From a reduced pronunciation of *go for.*]

goffer /góffər/, **gauffer** *vt.* (-fers, -fering, -fered) **1.** HAIR CRIMP HAIR to make hair wavy or crimped using a heated iron or similar device **2.** PRESS FRILLS INTO FABRIC to press pleats into fabric to produce an ornamental frill using a heated iron or similar implement ■ *n.* GOFFERING TOOL a tool used for goffering frills [Late 16thC. From French *gaufrer* 'mark with a decorative tool', from *gaufre* 'honeycomb', from, ultimately, Middle Low German *wafel.*]

Gog and Magog *n.* in the Bible, the name given to the enemies of God's people. In the book of Ezekiel, Gog is named as the ruler of a land named Magog, while Revelations names Gog and Magog as nations that were under Satan's rule.

go-getter /gó géttər/ *n.* sb who is enterprising and forceful (*informal*)

gogga /khókhə/ *n. S Africa* an insect or other small crawling or flying animal (*informal*)

goggle /góggl/ *v.* (-gles, -gling, -gled) **1.** *vi.* STARE WIDE-EYED to stare with eyes wide open, usually in astonishment **2.** *vti.* ROLL THE EYES to roll the eyes about, or roll about in the eye socket ■ *adj.* BULGING bulging from the eye socket ○ *goggle eyes* ■ *n.* WIDE-EYED STARE a staring or leering at sb with eyes wide [14thC. Origin uncertain: probably literally 'to move back and forth repeatedly', formed from assumed *gog* 'to move back and forth', an imitation of the movement.] —**goggly** *adj.*

goggle-box *n.* a television set (*dated informal*)

goggle-eyed *adj.* with staring eyes

goggles /góggl'z/ *npl.* protective glasses, usually made of plastic or glass and fitting tight to the face

go-go *adj. US* **1.** ENERGETIC characterized by energy and forcefulness **2.** FIN SPECULATIVE bringing or expected to bring quick or high returns on any investment ○ *These go-go stocks carry risk and are not for the timid investor.* **3.** DISCO relating to or seen in discotheques or music clubs (*dated*) ■ *n.* MUSIC TYPE OF MUSIC type of US popular music from the 1980s, an amalgamation of disco, funk, and Latin sounds [Doubling of GO, probably referring to French *à gogo* 'galore']

go-go dancer *n.* an energetic and usually scantily dressed dancer providing entertainment in a nightclub or pub (*dated*)

Goiânia /goy áani ə/ capital city of Goiás State in south-central Brazil. Population: 972,766 (1996).

Goidel /góyd'l/ *n.* a Celt who speaks any one of the northern branch of Celtic languages known as Goidelic [Late 19thC. From Old Irish *Goídel* (see GAEL).]

Goidelic /goy déllik/ *n.* the northern branch of the Celtic family of languages, comprising Irish Gaelic, Scottish Gaelic, and Manx —**Goidelic** *adj.*

going /gó ing/ *n.* **1.** ACT OF LEAVING an act of leaving somewhere **2.** CONDITIONS UNDER FOOT the state of the ground as it affects ease and speed of movement, especially for horses in a race ○ *The going is good.* **3.** CONDITIONS FOR PROGRESS conditions for making progress of any kind ○ *The going gets tough when you reach the rocky terrain.* ■ *adj.* **1.** SUCCESSFUL currently operating successfully **2.** ACCEPTED AS STANDARD currently accepted as standard or valid ○ *the going rate for platinum* **3.** EXISTING currently in existence or available ○ *the best going*

going-over (*plural* **goings-over**) *n.* (*informal*) **1.** THOROUGH EXAMINATION a thorough examination or check ○ *They gave the results a thorough going-over before making their report.* **2.** OVERHAUL an action by which sth is thoroughly improved or restored to a previous condition such as an act of cleaning, polishing, or dusting sth ○ *The house got a complete going-over before the arrival of the in-laws.* **3.** SCOLDING OR BEATING a verbal scolding or physical beating

goings-on /gó ingz-/ *npl.* events or activities, especially of a noteworthy or suspicious nature (*informal*)

goiter *n. US* = goitre

goitre /góytər/ *n.* enlargement of the thyroid gland appearing as a swelling of the front of the neck. Iodine deficiency is one of several causes. [Early 17thC. From French, from, ultimately, Latin *guttur* 'throat'.] —**goitrous** /góytrəss/ *adj.*

go-kart, **go-cart** *n.* **1.** MOTOR SPORTS = kart **2.** = go-cart *n.* **1**

Golan Heights /gó lan-/ disputed upland region on the border between Israel and Syria, northeast of the Sea of Galilee. Administered by Syria until 1967, it was first occupied and then, in 1981, annexed by Israel. Highest peak: 2,224/7,294 ft. Area: 1,250 ft/485 sq. mi.

gold /góld/ *n.* **1.** MINERALS SOFT YELLOW METALLIC ELEMENT a soft heavy yellow metal that is highly valued and widely used to make jewellery, often in alloy form. The most ductile and malleable metal, it is corrosion-resistant and is found in underground veins and alluvial deposits. Symbol Au **2.** COLOURS DEEP RICH YELLOW HUE a deep rich yellow colour that resembles that of the metal gold **3.** THINGS MADE OF GOLD things made of gold, e.g. coins or pieces of jewellery **4.** WEALTH much money or wealth **5.** SPORTS GOLD MEDAL a gold medal (*informal*) **6.** ARCHERY BULL'S EYE the bull's

eye of a target, which is usually gilt ■ *adj.* **1.** OF OR LIKE GOLD made of, covered with, or looking like gold, often as a symbol of high quality or achievement **2.** OF RICH DEEP YELLOW HUE of a deep rich yellow colour **3.** INDICATIVE OF TOP RECORDING SALES used to describe a golden replica of a recording that has achieved exceptionally high sales, the replica being presented to the recording artist or artists. Sales of an album must exceed 250,000 copies, or 500,000 in the United States, and those of a single, 500,000, or one million in the United States. [Old English. Ultimately from an Indo-European word that is also the ancestor of English *yellow* and *gild.*]

Whoopi Goldberg

Goldberg /góldbərg/, **Whoopi** (b. 1949) US actor. Her films include *The Color Purple* (1985) and an Academy Award-winning performance in *Ghost* (1990). Real name **Caryn Johnson**

gold brick *n.* a brick or other thing that appears to be made of gold but is not actually valuable [From the gold rush era in the United States, when cheaters sold fake gold bricks, or sold real gold bricks but later replaced them with fake ones]

Gold Coast /góld kōst/ **1.** city on the Pacific coast, southeastern Queensland, Australia. It straddles the border between Queensland and New South Wales. Population: 311,932 (1996). **2.** former name for **Ghana** (1874–1957)

Goldcrest

goldcrest /góld krest/ *n.* a small, very active, olive-green songbird with a yellow-and-black crown, common in Europe. Latin name: *Regulus regulus.*

gold digger *n.* **1.** SB WHO COURTS SB FOR MONEY sb, who pursues personal relationships in order to obtain wealth (*insult*) **2.** GOLD MINER a miner looking for gold deposits —**gold-digging** *n.*

gold disc *n.* **1.** MUSIC TOP SELLING RECORD a golden replica of a recording that has achieved exceptionally high sales. Sales of an album must exceed 250,000 copies, or 500,000 in the United States, and those of a single 500,000, or one million in the United States. US term **gold record 2.** COMPUT MASTER DISC FOR CD the master disc from which a CD-ROM is made

gold dust *n.* **1.** PARTICLES OF GOLD small particles of gold occurring naturally **2.** = alyssum

golden /góld'n/ *adj.* **1.** COLOURED LIKE GOLD with the deep rich yellow colour or sheen of gold ○ *golden hair* **2.** MADE OF GOLD made largely or wholly of gold ○ *a golden crown* **3.** EXCELLENT especially good ○ *a golden opportunity* **4.** IDYLLIC when there is general or individual success, happiness, or prosperity ○ *the* *golden years of their lives* **5. FAVOURED** very popular or successful, or likely to become so ○ *the golden boys and girls of the downhill ski circuit* **6. 50TH** that is fiftieth in a series ○ *golden jubilee* —**goldenly** *adv.*

golden age *n.* **1. PERIOD OF EXCELLENCE** a period of great prosperity or achievement, especially in the arts **2. EARLIEST AND BEST AGE** the first age of the world in classical mythology, characterized by idyllic happiness and innocence

golden ager /-áygər/ *n.* *US* sb over retirement age

golden Alexanders (*plural* **golden Alexanders**) *n.* a perennial North American plant of the carrot family that has small yellow flowers and is found in woods and meadows. Latin name: *Zizia aurea.* (*takes a singular or plural verb*) [*Alexanders* of uncertain origin: probably from medieval Latin (*petroselinum*) *Alexandrinum* 'horse-parsley', named after ALEXANDER III]

golden anniversary *n.* a fiftieth anniversary, e.g. of a wedding, or its celebration

golden aster *n.* a North American plant with yellow flowers resembling those of daisies. Genus: *Chrysopsis.*

Golden Bay /góldən-/ bay on the northern coast of the South Island, New Zealand. It extends 40 km/25 mi. from Farewell Spit in the west to Separation Point in the east.

golden brown *n.* a yellowish-brown colour —**golden-brown** *adj.*

golden-brown alga *n.* a freshwater or marine alga that is yellow to golden-brown in colour. Division: *Chrysophyta.* (*often used in the plural*)

golden calf *n.* an unworthy object that is esteemed or worshipped, especially money [From the golden calf made by Aaron and worshipped by the Israelites (Exodus 32)]

golden chain *n.* = laburnum

Golden Delicious *n.* a variety of eating apple with greenish or yellowish skin and a soft sweet flesh

golden eagle *n.* a large dark-brown eagle that has golden-brown feathers on its head and neck. It is found in mountainous areas of the northern hemisphere. Latin name: *Aquila chrysaetos.*

goldeneye /góld'n ī/ *n.* **1. BLACK-AND-WHITE DUCK** a black-and-white diving duck with yellow eyes. There are two species, both found in northern regions. Latin name: *Bucephala clangula* and *Bucephala islandica.* **2. INSECT WITH YELLOW EYES** an insect with yellow eyes and delicate lacy wings. Family: Chrysopidae.

Golden Fleece *n.* in Greek mythology, the fleece of the winged ram Chrysomallus, kept in a sacred grove by King Aeëtes, from where it was stolen by Jason

Golden Gate Bridge

Golden Gate Bridge long suspension bridge across the entrance to San Francisco Bay, California, United States. It was opened in 1937 and links San Francisco with Marin County.

golden hamster *n.* a small mammal with tan fur, a short tail, and large cheek pouches for storing food that is often kept as a pet or used as a laboratory animal. The widespread domestic population came from a single female and 12 young caught in Syria in 1930. Latin name: *Mesocricetus auratus.*

golden handcuffs *npl.* generous benefits promised to an employee on joining a company to discourage

him or her from leaving to work elsewhere (*informal*)

golden handshake *n.* a large sum of money given to an employee to compensate for the loss of a job or compulsory early retirement (*informal*)

golden hello *n.* a large sum of money given after an employment contract has been signed, offered as an inducement to sb to take up a new job or join an organization (*informal*)

Golden Horde *n.* the Mongol army that invaded and dominated large parts of eastern Europe in the 13th century

Golden Horn /góldən háwrn/ inlet of the Bosporus, in the European part of Turkey, that forms the harbour of Istanbul. Length: 8 km/5 mi.

golden jubilee *n.* a 50th anniversary, especially of a public event

golden lion tamarin *n.* a small monkey with brilliant golden fur and mane, found in the coastal forests of Brazil. Although its survival is endangered, a 1996 zoo breeding programme successfully reintroduced it into its natural habitat. Latin name: *Leontopithecus rosalia.*

golden mean *n.* **1. MODERATION** the middle course that avoids extremes in either direction **2. ARTS** = **golden section**

golden nematode *n.* a small worm that can infest potato fields, causing severe damage to crops and loss of productive farm land. Latin name: *Heterodera rostochiensis.*

golden oldie *n.* a song that was popular in the past and has remained popular or become popular again (*informal*)

golden oriole *n.* a songbird found in warmer European and Asian climates, the male of which has bright yellow plumage with a black tail and wings, while the female is yellowish-green. Latin name: *Oriolus oriolus.*

golden parachute *n.* an employment agreement that gives generous benefits to a senior executive who is forced to leave a company (*informal*)

golden pheasant *n.* a brightly coloured long-tailed pheasant native to the mountainous regions of China and Tibet and often seen in aviaries elsewhere. Latin name: *Chrysolophus pictus.*

golden plover *n.* a northern European shorebird with brown and black plumage and gold spots on its head and back. It migrates seasonally as far as the Mediterranean coast. Latin name: *Pluvialis apricaria.*

golden retriever *n.* a medium-sized dog of a breed with soft cream to golden hair. Its companionable nature makes it a popular family pet.

goldenrod /góld'n rod/ (*plural* **-rods** *or* **-rod**) *n.* a tall-stemmed, late summer-blooming plant with clusters of small yellow flowers. It is widespread in Europe and North America. Genus: *Solidago.*

golden rule *n.* **1. ESSENTIAL RULE** any basic rule that must be followed **2. RULE OF CONDUCT** the rule of conduct that advises people to treat others in the same manner as they wish to be treated themselves **3. MATH** = **rule of three**

goldenseal /góld'n seel/ *n.* a small perennial woodland plant of the buttercup family that has small greenish flowers and is native to eastern North America. Its thick yellow rootstock is used in herbal medicine for its healing and antiseptic properties. Latin name: *Hydrastis canadensis.*

golden section *n.* **ARTS** the proportion arising from the division of a straight line into two, so that the ratio of the whole line to the larger part is exactly the same as the ratio of the larger part to the smaller part. It is considered to be the most aesthetically pleasing proportion.

golden share *n.* a controlling share retained by a government in a company that has been taken out of public ownership and privatized

golden syrup *n.* a clear yellow syrup used in baking and for desserts. It is a traditional accompaniment for steamed sponge pudding and the main ingredient of the filling of treacle tart. It is made of

sucrose, glucose, and fructose or three different types of sugar, with natural flavouring and colouring such as caramel.

golden triangle *n.* the part of Southeast Asia where Laos, Thailand, and Myanmar (formerly Burma) meet and where much opium is grown

golden wattle *n.* a small Australian acacia tree that has a slender trunk and masses of golden-yellow flowers in spring. It is the floral emblem of Australia. The tree is often grown as an ornamental and for the fragrance of its flowers, and its bark is used in tanning leather. Latin name: *Acacia pycantha.*

goldfield /góld feeld/ *n.* an area with gold mines

goldfinch /góld finch/ *n.* a small finch with yellow and black markings, found in North America, Europe, and Asia. Genus: *Carduelis.*

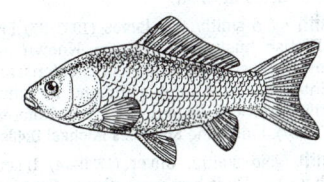
Goldfish

goldfish /góldfish/ (*plural* **-fish** *or* **-fishes**) *n.* a small orange-red freshwater fish native to eastern Asia but commonly kept in aquariums, ponds, and tanks. It is related to the carps and minnows. Latin name: *Carassius auratus.*

goldfish bowl *n.* **1. BOWL FOR GOLDFISH** a clear glass or plastic bowl in which to raise and keep goldfish **2. PLACE WITHOUT PRIVACY** a situation or place that is always open to public view or scrutiny

gold leaf *n.* gold that is beaten out into very thin sheets and used for gilding and lettering

Emma Goldman

Goldman /góldmən/, **Emma** (1869–1940) Russian-born US anarchist. A fiery writer and lecturer, she was imprisoned and deported (1919) for her radical political activities in the United States, and wrote the autobiographical *Living my Life* (1931).

gold medal *n.* a medal that is made of gold or sth representing gold, given as a first prize for excellence or winning a competition —**gold medalist** *n.*

gold mine *n.* **1. PLACE FOR MINING GOLD** a place where gold is mined **2. RICH SOURCE** a rich source of sth valuable, especially easily obtained wealth ○ *Some of the smaller shops are little gold mines.* —**gold-miner** *n.* —**gold-mining** *n.*

gold plate *n.* **1. ITEMS MADE OF GOLD** bowls, goblets, and other utensils made of gold **2. THIN LAYER OF GOLD** a thin coating of gold on another metal, usually produced by electroplating

gold-plated *adj.* having a thin coating of gold, usually produced by electroplating —**gold-plate** *vt.*

gold record *n. US* MUSIC = **gold disc**

gold reserve *n.* a fund of gold in coins or bullion held by a central bank and regarded as providing a foundation for a paper currency and security for borrowing

gold rush *n.* **1.** RUSH TO A NEW GOLDFIELD a sudden wave of migration to new territory because gold has been discovered there. One of the most famous gold rushes was to the Klondike in Yukon, Canada, from 1896. **2.** RUSH FOR NEW WEALTH a sudden rush to make money from a new source or by a new means

────── WORD KEY: CULTURAL NOTE ──────

The Gold Rush, a film by director and actor Charles Chaplin (1925). Set during the California gold rush of 1849, it places Chaplin's gentle and sensitive Tramp character in the materialistic, amoral environment of a mining town to great comic effect. In one famous scene, Chaplin is reduced to eating his shoes, but eventually he strikes it rich and returns home a wealthy man.

goldsmith /góld smith/ *n.* sb who makes articles out of gold or deals in them

Goldsmith /góld smith/, **Sir James** (1933–97) French-born British business executive. Known for his flamboyant lifestyle as much as his extensive business interests, he used his fortune to fund conservative political causes, e.g. the Referendum Party (1994). Full name **Sir James Michael Goldsmith**

Goldsmith /góld smith/, **Oliver** (1730–74) Irish-born British writer. He is best remembered for his novel *The Vicar of Wakefield* (1766) and his comedy *She Stoops to Conquer* (1773).

goldsmith beetle *n.* a beetle of the scarab family that has a metallic gold colour. Latin name: *Cotalpa lanigera*.

gold standard *n.* a system of defining monetary units in terms of their value in gold, usually accompanied by the free circulation of gold and free exchange of currency into it

goldstone /góld stōn/ *n.* MINERALS = **aventurine**

goldthread /góld thred/ *n.* a low-growing evergreen plant that is common in mossy woods or swamps in North America and Europe. The yellow rootstock has provided a popular traditional remedy for inflammation. Genus: *Coptis*.

golem /gṓləm, góy-/ *n.* in Jewish legend, a creature made of clay and brought to life by magical incantations. The most famous was the golem made by the Maharal, Rabbi Loew, in the 16th century to defend the Jews of Prague from a pogrom. [Late 19thC. From Yiddish *goylem*, from Hebrew *golem* 'shape, mass'.]

golf /golf/ *n.* GAME WITH BALL AND CLUBS an outdoor game in which an array of specially designed clubs with long shafts are used to hit a small ball from a prescribed starting point into a hole. The object of the game is to complete the course in as few strokes as possible. ■ *vi.* (**golfs, golfing, golfed**) PLAY GOLF to play the game of golf [15thC. Origin uncertain: perhaps from Dutch *kolf* 'club'.]

Golf *n.* the NATO phonetic alphabet code word for the letter 'G', used in international radio communications

golf ball *n.* a small hard ball used for playing golf

golf cart *n.* a motorized vehicle used to drive around on a golf course during play

golf club *n.* **1.** STICK FOR HITTING GOLF BALLS a specially designed club with a long shaft and a metal or wooden head, used in golf to strike the ball **2.** GOLFERS' ASSOCIATION an association of people who play golf, usually on the same course **3.** PREMISES OF GOLFERS' ASSOCIATION the premises or facilities used by a golf club

golf course *n.* an area of land designed for playing the game of golf

golfer /gólfər/ *n.* sb who plays the game of golf

golfing /gólfing/ *n.* the activity of playing golf (*often used before a noun*) ○ *a golfing umbrella*

golf links *npl.* a golf course situated beside the sea

golf widow *n.* a woman whose husband or partner spends many hours playing golf (*informal*)

Golgi apparatus /gólji-/, **Golgi body**, **Golgi complex** *n.* a membranous structure in the cytoplasm of cells consisting of layers of flattened sacs. It functions in the processing and transporting of proteins. [Early 20thC. Named after Camillo *Golgi* (1844–1926), Italian histologist.]

Golgotha /gólgəthə/ site outside the city of Jerusalem where Jesus Christ was crucified, according to the Bible. Hebrew for **Calvary**

goliard /gṓli ərd/ *n.* in 12th- and 13th-century Western Europe, a wandering scholar who was noted for writing bawdy and satirical Latin verses, and for buffoonery and riotous living [Late 15thC. From Old French, 'glutton', via Latin *gula* from Sanskrit *gir-ami*.]

goliath /gə líf əth/, **Goliath** *n.* a gigantic or over-powering opponent or competitor ○ *a corporation regarded as the goliath of the oil industry* [Late 16thC. The name of the giant killed by David in the Bible (1 Samuel 17).]

Goliath *n.* in the Bible, a giant Philistine who was slain by David using a sling and a stone

Goliath beetle *n.* a very large tropical African scarab beetle that can measure up to 15 cm/6 in in length and has bold black, white, and brown markings. Latin name: *Goliathus giganteus*.

Goliath frog *n.* a very large frog of central Africa that can measure up to 30 cm/12 in. Latin name: *Rana goliath*.

golliwog /góli wog/, **golliwogg** *n.* an offensively grotesque cloth doll with a black face and hair and brightly coloured clothes. Now rarely made, the dolls are offensive to Black people, as is the term itself. (*offensive*) [Late 19thC. Named after a fictional character in books by US writer and illustrator Florence Upton (1873–1922).]

golly[1] /gólli/ *interj.* used to express surprise, amazement, or anxiety, or for emphasis (*dated informal*) ○ *Golly, we're in real trouble now!* [Late 18thC. Alteration of GOD.]

golly[2] /gólli/ (*plural* **-lies**) *n.* a golliwog (*informal offensive*) [Mid-20thC. Shortening.]

gomasio /go mássi ō/, **ghomasio** *n.* a seasoning mixture made of ground sesame seeds and salt, used especially in Japanese cookery

gombeenism /góm beenizəm/, **gombeen** /góm been/ *n.* *Ireland* money-lending at extortionate rates [Mid-19thC. See GOMBEEN MAN.]

gombeen man *n.* *Ireland* **1.** MONEY-LENDER a money-lender who charges exorbitant interest **2.** ENTREPRENEUR a small-time entrepreneur [Gombeen from Anglo-Irish, from Irish *gaimbín* 'usury']

gombroon /gómbroon/ *n.* pottery made in Iran and elsewhere in imitation of white Chinese porcelain [Late 17thC. Named after *Gombroon*, a port in Iran, now called Bandar Abbas.]

Gomorrah /gə mórrə/ *n.* a place or society marked by evil, depravity, and promiscuousness (*disapproving*) [Early 20thC. Named after an ancient biblical city destroyed by God because of its wickedness (Genesis 19).]

gon- *prefix.* = **gono-** (*used before vowels*)

-gon *suffix.* a figure having a particular number of angles ○ *undecagon* ○ *polygon* [Via Greek *-gōnon* from, ultimately, *gōnia* 'angle, corner'. Ultimately from an Indo-European word meaning 'knee, bend', which is also the ancestor of English *knee* and *genuflect*.]

gonad /gṓ nad, gónnad/ *n.* an organ that produces reproductive cells (**gametes**), e.g. a testis or an ovary [Late 19thC. From modern Latin *gonad*, stem of *gonas*, from Greek *gonos* 'seed, generation'.] —**gonadal** /gṓ náyd'l, go-/ *adj.* —**gonadic** /gṓ náddik, go-/ *adj.*

gonadotrophic /gónnədə trṓfik/, **gonadotropic** /-tróppik/ *adj.* stimulating or acting on the gonads [Mid-20thC. Coined from GONAD + TROPHIC or -TROPIC.]

gonadotrophin /gónnədə trṓfin/, **gonadotropin** /-trṓpin/ *n.* a hormone secreted by the pituitary gland, and in some mammals by the placenta during pregnancy, that influences gonadal activity, including the onset of sexual maturity and regulation of reproductive activity [Mid-20thC. Coined from GONAD + TROPHIN or -TROPIN.]

gonadotropic *adj.* = **gonadotrophic**

gonadotropin *n.* = **gonadotrophin**

Gonaïves /gō nív/ town in western Haiti, situated 109 km/68 mi. northwest of Port-au-Prince. Population: 63,291 (1992).

Goncourt /góN koor/, **Edmond de** (1822–96) French novelist and diarist. He collaborated with his brother Jules de Goncourt (1830–70) on works including a 40-year journal of French social and literary life. Full name **Edmond Louis Antoine de Goncourt**

Gondola

gondola /góndələ/ *n.* **1.** VENETIAN CANAL BOAT a narrow flat-bottomed boat, used on the canals of Venice, that has a curved prow and stern and is moved along with a long pole **2.** AIR CAR BELOW A BALLOON a basket or cabin suspended from a balloon or airship, for carrying people or equipment **3.** CABLE CAR a car or cabin suspended from cables, especially one attached to a ski lift **4.** COMM ISLAND OF SHELVES a free-standing shelving unit forming an island for displaying goods in a supermarket or other self-service shop [Mid-16thC. Via Venetian Italian from Rhaeto-Romance *gondolà* 'to roll, rock'.]

gondolier /góndə leér/ *n.* sb who propels a gondola through the water, especially on the canals of Venice

Gondwanaland /gon dwaánə land/ ancient landmass, consisting of the southern part of the super-continent of Pangaea. Comprising South America, Africa, peninsular India, Australia, and Antarctica, it began to break up approximately 200 million years ago. ◊ **Laurasia, Pangaea**

gone past participle of **go** ■ *adj.* **1.** ABSENT absent after leaving somewhere ○ *She has been gone for hours.* **2.** IRRECOVERABLE beyond hope of recovery ○ *All hopes for a truce are gone.* **3.** USED UP having been completely used up ○ *If the milk is all gone, we'll drink our coffee black.* **4.** ADVANCED IN TIME more advanced than a particular time or age ○ *It's gone six and we'll be late.* **5.** PREGNANT having been pregnant for a particular number of months ○ *She's eight months gone.* **6.** DEAD no longer living (*informal*) **7.** UNEASY giving a sensation of giddiness or sinking in the stomach **8.** INFATUATED affected by a strong feeling of attraction towards sb (*informal*) ○ *He's gone on your sister.* **9.** EXHILARATED excited or exhilarated, e.g. while listening to music (*slang*)

goner /gónnər/ *n.* sb or sth beyond hope of recovery, especially sb who is dead or about to die (*slang; used with the indefinite article*) ○ *It looks like he's a goner.* [Mid-19thC. Coined from GONE + -ER.]

gonfalon /gónfələn/ *n.* a banner suspended from a crossbar, often with an edge cut like streamers, used especially as the standard of some medieval Italian republics or carried in church processions [Late 16thC. Via Italian *gonfalone* from Frankish, ultimately from prehistoric Germanic words meaning 'war' and 'banner'.]

gonfalonier /gónfələ neér/ *n.* **1.** GONFALON CARRIER sb who carries a gonfalon **2.** MEDIEVAL ITALIAN MAGISTRATE the chief magistrate of some medieval Italian republics, who carried the republic's gonfalon

gong /gong/ *n.* **1.** RESONANT BRONZE PLATE a circular bronze plate that makes a resonant sound when struck with a mallet, used especially as an orchestral percussion instrument or to summon people to meals **2.** WARNING BELL a round metal bell that is struck by a mechanically operated hammer, used especially as

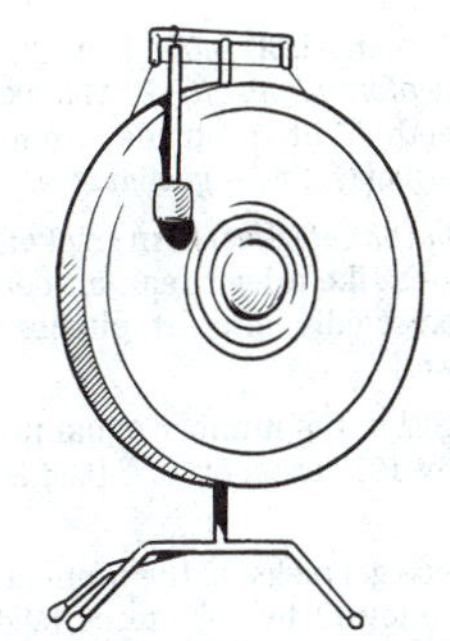

Gong

an alarm **3.** MEDAL a medal or decoration (*slang*) ■ *v.* (**gongs, gonging, gonged**) **1.** *vi.* SOUND LIKE A GONG to sound resonantly like a gong **2.** *vt.* SUMMON to summon sb with a gong [Early 17thC. From Malay, an imitation of the sound of striking a gong.]

Gongorism /góng gərìzəm/ *n.* a style in Spanish literature characterized by ornate devices, classical allusions, and deliberate obscurity [Early 19thC. Named after the Spanish poet *Góngora* y Argote (1561–1627).] —**Gongoristic** /góng gə rístik/ *adj.*

gonidium /gō níddi əm/ (*plural* **-a** /-ə/) *n.* **1.** ALGAL REPRODUCTIVE CELL an asexual reproductive cell in some algae, e.g. a zoospore **2.** ALGAL CELL IN LICHEN a chlorophyll-containing algal cell in the body (**thallus**) of a lichen [Mid-19thC. From modern Latin, from Greek *gonos* 'offspring'.] —**gonidial** /gō níddi əl/ *adj.*

gonif *n.* = **ganef**

goniometer /gṓni ómmitər/ *n.* **1.** INSTRUMENT FOR MEASURING ANGLES an instrument for measuring angles, especially those between crystal faces **2.** RADIO SIGNAL DIRECTION FINDER a device for establishing the bearing of an incoming radio signal [Mid-18thC. From French *goniomètre*, from Greek *gonia* 'angle' + METER.] —**goniometric** /gṓni ə métrik/ *adj.* —**goniometrical** /-méttrik'l/ *adj.* —**goniometry** /gṓni ómmətri/ *n.*

gonion /gṓni on/ *n.* the point on either side of the lower jaw where it turns upwards [Late 19thC. From French, from Greek *gonia* 'angle'.]

goniotomy /gṓni óttəmi/ (*plural* **-mies**) *n.* an operation to treat glaucoma by cutting into the narrow angle between the back of the cornea and the root of the iris to allow drainage of aqueous humour

gonk /gongk/ (**gonks, gonking, gonked**) *vti.* COMPUT to lie about sth or embellish the truth, especially in an online conversation in a chat room (*slang*) ○ *Are you gonking me?* [Mid-20thC. An invented word.] —**gonk** *n.*

gonna /gónnə, gúnnə/ *contr.* going to (*nonstandard*) [Early 20thC. Alteration.]

gono-[1] *prefix.* sexual, generative, semen, or seed [From Greek *gonos* or *gonē* 'generation, offspring, seed']

gono-[2] *prefix.* sex, seed, reproduction ○ *gonophore* [From Greek *gonos* 'offspring, procreation'. Ultimately from an Indo-European base meaning 'to beget', which is also the ancestor of English *kin*, *genus*, and *germ*.]

gonococcus /gónnə kókəss/ (*plural* **-ci** /gónnə kóksī/) *n.* a spherical bacterium that causes gonorrhoea. Latin name: *Neisseria gonorrhoeae.* [Late 19thC. From GONORRHOEA + COCCUS.] —**gonococcal** /gónnə kók'l/ *adj.* —**gonococcic** /gónnə kóksik/ *adj.*

gonof *n.* = **ganef**

gonopore /gónnə pawr/ *n.* an external reproductive pore in some insects and worms through which reproductive cells are secreted

gonorrhoea /gónnə rée ə/, **gonorrhea** *n.* a sexually transmitted disease that causes inflammation of the genital mucous membrane, burning pain when urinating, and a discharge. It is caused by a gonococcus bacterium. [16thC. Via modern Latin from Greek *gonorrhoia*, literally 'flowing of semen', from *gonos* 'semen'.] —**gonorrhoeal** *adj.*

-gony *suffix.* **1.** origin ○ *cosmogony* **2.** method of reproduction ○ *schizogony* [Formed from Greek *gonos* 'offspring, procreation' (see GONO-)]

gonzo /gónzō/ *adj.* (*slang*) **1.** *US* IDIOSYNCRATICALLY SUBJECTIVE characterized by subjective interpretation and exaggeration ○ *Gonzo journalism is unlike the work of the impartial observer.* **2.** UNCONVENTIONAL unusual or strange [Late 20thC. Origin uncertain: perhaps from Italian, 'foolish', or Spanish *ganso* 'goose, fool'.]

goo /goo/ *n.* (*informal*) **1.** STH STICKY any sticky substance, typically sth unpleasant **2.** EXCESS EMOTION cloying emotionalism [Early 20thC. Origin uncertain: perhaps an abbreviation of BURGOO.]

good /go͝od/ (**better** /béttər/, **best** /best/) CORE MEANING: an adjective indicating that sth is approved of or desirable ○ *It's a good idea to change your password now and again.* ○ *It's good to talk.*

1. *adj.* OF HIGH QUALITY of a high quality or standard, either on an absolute scale or in relation to another or others ○ *The meal wasn't good.* ○ *He'll make a very good doctor.* ○ *I smashed one of my good plates.* **2.** *adj.* SUITABLE having the appropriate qualities to be sth or to fit a particular purpose ○ *Futons make good chairs as well as beds.* ○ *The bicycle is good for short trips.* **3.** *adj.* SKILLED possessing the necessary skill or talent to do sth ○ *I'm not a very good driver.* ○ *She's good at science.* **4.** *adj.* VIRTUOUS having or showing an upright and virtuous character ○ *You're a good man, Joe.* **5.** *adj.* KIND having or showing a kind and generous disposition ○ *She was always very good to me.* **6.** *adj.* AFFORDING PLEASURE affording pleasure or comfort ○ *He's a man who insists on the finer things in life: good food, good books, and the theatre.* **7.** *adj.* UNDAMAGED having undergone no deterioration or damage ○ *I smelled the meat and found it was still good.* **8.** *adj.* AMPLE sufficiently large, or providing more than enough of sth ○ *Between them they have a good income.* **9.** *adj.* HONOURABLE worthy of honour or high esteem ○ *They come from a good family.* **10.** *adj.* VALID acceptable as true or genuine and sufficient for the purpose ○ *There had better be a good explanation for this mess.* ○ *Don't travel unless your insurance is good.* **11.** *adj.* HELPFUL helping sb to organize thoughts or make decisions ○ *She gave me some good advice.* **12.** *adj.* PLEASANT pleasant to look at ○ *Don't let her good looks distract you from her intelligence.* **13.** *adj.* BENEFICIAL beneficial to health or wellbeing ○ *Eating lots of fruit is good for you.* **14.** *adj.* FAVOURABLE suitable and likely to produce the right results or conditions ○ *a good time to have a holiday* **15.** *adj.* THOROUGH that goes to the fullest extent of the action ○ *Take a good look round.* **16.** *adj.* FIN FINANCIALLY ADVANTAGEOUS financially or commercially advantageous or reliable ○ *I made a few good investments last year.* **17.** *adj.* GENUINE that is what it appears to be ○ *a good ten pound note* **18.** *adj.* OBEDIENT well behaved and obedient ○ *The children are always good when we take them out.* **19.** *adj.* WELL MANNERED socially correct ○ *very good behaviour* **20.** *adj.* ABLE TO DO MORE remaining in operation or effect, or able to continue doing sth ○ *The car will be good for another 6,000 miles.* **21.** *adj.* FIN ABLE TO PAY able to pay or contribute sth, or to allow a sum to be drawn ○ *He's good for at least £1,000.* **22.** *adj.* FIN THAT WILL BE PAID that the debtor is expected to honour in full ○ *a good debt* **23.** *adj.* PRODUCING A RESULT able to produce a particular result ○ *John is always good for a laugh.* **24.** *adj.* SIZABLE considerable in extent or size ○ *a good selection of books on computers* **25.** *adj.* FULLY at least a particular time or length ○ *It's a good 30 years since we met.* **26.** *adj.* RACKET GAMES WITHIN BOUNDS inside the required area for the shot to be allowed ○ *The umpire said that the ball was good.* **27.** *adj.* USED IN EXCLAMATIONS used in exclamations of surprise, dismay, or other strong feelings (*informal*) ○ *Good heavens! I've won first prize!* **28.** *adj.* HEALTHY well in health (*informal; in UK usually used in negative statements*) ○ *I'm not feeling too good so I'll stay at home.* ○ *'How are you?' 'Good'.* **29.** *interj.* USED TO EXPRESS SATISFACTION used to express satisfaction or pleasure in sth that has just been said, or to confirm it ○ *'They've just arrived'.'Good'.* **30.** *n.* BENEFICIAL EFFECT sth resulting in a beneficial effect or state ○ *the common good* ○ *What good will complaining do?* **31.** *n.* = **goodness** *n.* 1 **32.** *n.* POSITIVE PART the positive part or aspect of sth ○ *You have to take the good with the bad in this agreement.* **33.** *n.* STH WORTH HAVING sth worth having or achieving ○ *Let's work for the future good of the nation.* **34.** *npl.* VIRTUOUS PEOPLE those who are virtuous and upright ○ *the great and the good.* ◆ **goods** [Old English *god*, from a prehistoric Germanic word meaning 'to unite', which is also the ancestor of English *gather*] ◇ **be (all) to the good** to be to sb's benefit ◇ **be up to no good** to be in the process of doing or planning sth wrong or illegal (*informal*) ◇ **for good** permanently from the time in question ○ *They've gone for good.* ◇ **give as good as you get** to contend as effectively as your opponent ○ *Her tennis opponent is tough, but she can give as good as she gets.* ◇ **good and** completely and entirely (*informal*) ○ *I'll get up in the morning when I'm good and ready, and not before.* ◇ **make good** to become successful, often after an unpromising start ○ *Though he didn't do very well at school, he made good as a businessman.* ◇ **make good sth 1.** to perform sth successfully ○ *We must make good our attempt to win the trophy.* **2.** to carry out sth intended or promised ○ *She made good her promise to repay the money on time.* **3.** to compensate for sth, especially for damage or loss ○ *They made good the damage they had accidentally caused.* **4.** to demonstrate the truth or correctness of sth ○ *If you cannot make good these charges, the defendant will not stand trial.* ◇ **throw good money after bad** to put more money, better used elsewhere, into a bad investment ○ *If you have the car repaired again, you'll just throw good money after bad.* ◇ **to the good** richer by a particular amount of money ○ *By the end of the day, we were 50 pounds to the good.*

good afternoon *interj.* used when people meet or part, or begin or end a telephone conversation, during the afternoon

Good Book *n.* the Christian Bible

goodbye /go͝od bī/ *interj.* FAREWELL used when people part or end a telephone conversation ○ *With the hurricane approaching, it's goodbye to our holiday at the seaside.* ■ *n.* ACT OF LEAVING an act of making a farewell ○ *It's time to say our goodbyes and catch the plane.* [Late 16thC. From *God be with you.*]

good cause *n.* **1.** CHARITY sth or sb deserving help, especially a charity **2.** LEGAL REASON a sufficient legal standard or reason

good day *interj.* used when people meet or part, or begin or end a telephone conversation, during daylight hours (*formal*)

good evening *interj.* used to convey good wishes when people meet or part, or begin or end a telephone conversation, during the evening

good faith *n.* honesty of intention ○ *an effort to fulfill the contract in good faith.*

good-for-nothing *n.* LAZY PERSON sb who is perceived as lazy and irresponsible (*insult*) ■ *adj.* LAZY lazy and irresponsible

Good Friday *n.* the Christian holy day observed on the Friday before Easter, commemorating the death of Jesus Christ on the Cross (**Crucifixion**) [*Good* in the sense of 'holy']

Good Friday plant *n.* = **moschatel**

good guy *n.* *US* sb who is good or law-abiding, especially in a Western, crime novel, or film (*informal*)

goodhearted /go͝od haártid/ *adj.* having or showing a kind and generous nature —**goodheartedly** *adv.* —**goodheartedness** *n.*

Good Hope, Cape of /go͝od hṓp/ ◆ **Cape of Good Hope**

good-humoured *adj.* disposed to be cheerful and friendly, or reflecting such an attitude —**good-humouredly** *adv.*

goodie *n.* = **goody**[1]

Good King Henry (*plural* **Good King Henrys** *or* **Good King Henry**) *n.* a weed of the goosefoot family that has arrow-shaped leaves and small green flowers. Latin name: *Chenopodium bonus-henricus.*

good life *n.* a life of carefree comfort and luxury ○ *living the good life in Palm Springs*

good-looking *adj.* having a pleasant personal, especially facial, appearance —**good-looker** *n.*

WORD KEY: SYNONYMS

good-looking, attractive, beautiful, handsome, lovely, pretty

CORE MEANING: having a pleasing facial appearance **good-looking** used of either men or women to indicate pleasing looks; **attractive** used in a similar way to *good-looking*. It is also used to describe people who are not conventionally good-looking but who are still very appealing, especially to members of the opposite sex; **beautiful** most often used to describe women or girls whose appearance is very pleasing, especially in a way that is generally considered ideal or perfect; **handsome** used to talk about men whose appearance is very pleasing, especially men who have strong, rugged-looking features. It can also be used to describe women who have strong, imposing features; **lovely** most often used to talk about women who are very pleasing to look at but possibly not beautiful; **pretty** used to talk about women and especially girls who are very attractive, usually in a way that is not conventionally beautiful.

---

good looks *npl.* a pleasant personal appearance, especially facial appearance

goodly /góodli/ (-lier, -liest) *adj.* **1.** SOMEWHAT LARGE moderately large in quantity or extent **2.** ATTRACTIVE having a fine appearance (*archaic*) **3.** PLEASANT of a pleasing quality (*archaic*) ○ *the goodly fellowship of the prophets* —**goodliness** *n.*

goodman /góodmən/ (*plural* -men /-mən/) *n.* (*archaic*) **1.** MAN IN CHARGE OF A HOUSEHOLD the man in charge of a household or family, especially a married man **2.** **goodman, Goodman** POLITE ALTERNATIVE FOR MR formerly used as a polite form of address before the surname of a man who was not a gentleman or nobleman, especially a yeoman

good morning *interj.* used to convey good wishes when people meet or part, or begin or end a telephone conversation, during the morning

good name *n.* **1.** REPUTATION sb's reputation for honesty and integrity **2.** *South Asia* LAST NAME sb's last name or family name

good nature *n.* a pleasant and obliging disposition

good-natured *adj.* having or showing a pleasant and obliging disposition —**good-naturedly** *adv.* —**good-naturedness** *n.*

goodness /góodnəss/ *n.* **1.** GOOD QUALITY the quality of being good **2.** VIRTUOUSNESS personal virtue or kindness **3.** GOOD PART the nutrition or other benefit to be derived from sth ○ *Vegetables lose a lot of their goodness if you overcook them.* ■ *interj.* USED TO EXPRESS SURPRISE used to express surprise or amazement, or for emphasis ○ *For goodness sake, stop that!* ◇ **goodness knows** used to indicate bafflement or lack of knowledge about sth ○ *Goodness knows what they're doing out there at midnight.*

goodnight *interj.* used to convey good wishes when people part or end a telephone conversation at night, especially at bedtime

good-o *interj.* = good-oh

good offices *npl.* help or support, especially help in resolving a dispute

good-oh, good-o *interj.* used to express approval or agreement (*informal*)

good oil *n. Aus* reliable information (*informal*) ○ *He gave me the good oil for Saturday's race.*

good old boy, good ol' boy, good ole boy *n. US* stereotype of a man who is part of a peer group and conforms to the behaviour characteristic of the group, especially applied to a white man in parts of the rural southern United States. The good old boy is often perceived as a caricature of the relaxed, convivial, conservative American southern white man. (*often offensive*)

goods /góodz/ *npl.* **1.** MERCHANDISE articles for sale or use, often those produced for later consumption, as opposed to services (*takes a singular or plural verb*) **2.** PORTABLE PROPERTY portable personal property **3.** MERCHANDISE MOVED BY RAIL merchandise that is transported, especially by rail, as opposed to passengers (*often used before a noun*) **4.** STH PROMISED sth promised or expected (*informal*) ○ *You can rely on her to come up with the goods.* **5.** GENUINE ARTICLE sth that is genuinely what it should be (*slang; takes*

a singular or plural verb) **6.** INCRIMINATING EVIDENCE information or evidence that will incriminate sb (*slang*)

Good Samaritan *n.* sb who voluntarily helps others who are in trouble [From the parable of the Good Samaritan (Luke 10:30–37), who helps a man beaten by robbers]

goods and services tax *n.* in Canada and New Zealand, a value-added tax charged on all goods and services

good-sized *adj.* rather large in size ○ *The recipe called for a good-sized piece of chocolate.*

good-tempered *adj.* having or showing a placid disposition —**good-temperedly** *adv.* —**good-temperedness** *n.*

good-time girl *n.* a young woman whose chief aim is to pursue pleasure

good turn *n.* a friendly act that helps or benefits sb else ○ *One good turn deserves another.*

goodwife /góod wíf/ (*plural* -wives /góod wívz/) *n.* (*archaic*) **1.** HOUSEWIFE the woman in charge of a household or family, especially a married woman **2.** POLITE ALTERNATIVE FOR MRS formerly used as a polite form of address before the surname of a woman who was not a gentlewoman or noblewoman, especially a yeoman's wife

goodwill /góod wíl/ *n.* **1.** FRIENDLY DISPOSITION friendly disposition towards sb or sth (*often used before a noun*) ○ *a goodwill gesture* **2.** WILLINGNESS cheerful willingness to do sth **3.** ACCT NONTANGIBLE VALUE OF BUSINESS the value of a business over and above its tangible assets **4.** CHARITY SHOP a shop that sells donated goods in order to raise money for charity

Goodwin Sands /góodwin-/ a dangerous area of sandbanks at the entrance to the Strait of Dover, off the southern coast of Kent, England. Length: 16km/ 10 mi.

Goodwood /góodwŏŏd/ country estate and racecourse in West Sussex, England, near Chichester

good word *n.* a comment recommending sb or made in favour or defence of sb ○ *He promised to put in a good word for me.*

goody[1] /góodi/, **goodie** /góoddi/ *n.* (*plural* -ies) **1.** STH SWEET TO EAT sth desirable, especially sth sweet to eat (*often used in the plural*) **2.** SB GOOD a good or law-abiding person, especially in a Western or a crime thriller ■ *interj.* USED TO INDICATE DELIGHT used to express great pleasure (*informal*) ○ *Oh goody, ice cream!* [Coined from GOOD + -Y]

goody[2] /góodi/, **Goody** *n.* = goodwife (*archaic*) [Mid-16thC. Pet form.]

goody-goody *n.* (*plural* goody-goodies) = goody two-shoes ■ *adj.* SMUGLY VIRTUOUS irritatingly well-behaved or smugly virtuous (*informal*) [Mid-19thC. Reduplication of GOODY[1].]

goody two-shoes (*plural* **goody two-shoes**) *n.* sb smugly well-behaved, irritatingly virtuous, or sanctimonious (*informal*) [Mid-20thC. From the name of a character in a children's book perhaps by Oliver Goldsmith.]

gooey /góo i/ (-ier, -iest) *adj.* **1.** STICKY sticky and soft ○ *gooey chocolate cake* **2.** SENTIMENTAL cloyingly sentimental (*informal*) ○ *a gooey romantic novel*

goof /góof/ *n.* (*informal*) **1.** MISTAKE a mistake or blunder ○ *A colossal goof caused the whole computer system to crash.* **2.** UNINTELLIGENT PERSON an unintelligent or incompetent person (*insult*) ■ *v.* (**goofs, goofing, goofed**) (*informal*) **1.** *vi.* MAKE MISTAKE to make a thoughtless or unintelligent mistake **2.** *vt.* BOTCH to spoil sth through incompetence or lack of intelligence [Early 20thC. Origin uncertain: probably from dialect *goff* 'simpleton'.]

goof around *vi. US* to behave in a playful or silly way (*informal*) ○ *Once the pressure of exams was off, the students just goofed around.*

goof off *v. US* to waste time instead of working (*informal*) ○ *The crew goofed off when the boss left early.*

goofball /góof bawl/ *n. US* **1.** UNINTELLIGENT PERSON a silly or unintelligent person (*insult*) **2.** DRUG PILL a barbiturate or other drug in the form of a pill (*slang*)

goofy /góofi/ (-ier, -iest) *adj.* **1.** SILLY silly or unintelligent (*informal insult*) **2.** STICKING OUT used to describe teeth that protrude from the mouth (*informal*) —**goofily** *adv.* —**goofiness** *n.*

googly /góogli/ (*plural* -glies) *n.* in cricket, an off-break ball that looks like a leg break on delivery and so moves unexpectedly after it pitches [Early 20thC. Origin unknown.]

googol /góo gol/ *n.* the number equal to the numeral 1 followed by 100 zeros, or 10^{100} [Mid-20thC. Invented word.]

googolplex /góo gol pleks/ *n.* the number equal to the numeral 1 followed by 10^{100} zeros [Mid-20thC. From GOOGOL + Latin *plexus* 'intricate, braided'.]

gook /gook/ *n. US* a highly offensive term for an Asian person or sb of Asian descent (*slang offensive*) [Mid-20thC. Origin unknown.]

gooly /góoli/ (*plural* -lies), **goolie** *n.* a testicle (*informal humorous; usually used in the plural*) [Mid-20thC. Linked to Hindi *goli* 'ball, bullet'.]

goon /goon/ *n.* **1.** CLUMSY PERSON sb who is clumsy or uncouth (*insult*) **2.** SB WHO ACTS SILLY sb who acts in a silly or bizarre manner for amusement (*informal*) **3.** *US* THUG a professional gangster whose work is beating up or terrorizing people [Mid-19thC. Origin uncertain: perhaps from *goon(e)y*, variant of *gony* 'simpleton'; or from Alice the Goon, a character invented by the US cartoonist, E. C. Segar (1894–1938).]

goonda /góondə/ *n. S Asia* in the Indian subcontinent, a ruffian or hooligan [Early 20thC. From Hindi *gunṇḍā* 'rascal'.]

gooney /góoni/ (*plural* -neys), **gooney bird** *n.* an albatross, especially the black-footed albatross. Latin name: *Diomedea nigripes*. [Late 16thC. Origin unknown.]

goop /goop/ *n.* **1.** *US* = gloop (*informal*) **2.** UNINTELLIGENT PERSON an unintelligent or inane person (*slang insult*) [Early 20thC. Variant of GOOF.] —**goopy** *adj.*

goosander /goo sándər/ *n.* a waterfowl found in Europe and North America that has a narrow serrated bill and a dark head and white body in the male. Latin name: *Mergus merganser.* = **common merganser** [Early 17thC. Probably ultimately from GOOSE + Old Norse *andar-*, stem of *ond* 'duck'.]

Goose

goose /gooss/ *n.* (*plural* **geese** /geess/) **1.** LONG-NECKED WATER BIRD a large waterfowl with a long neck and webbed feet, noted for its seasonal migrations and distinctive honking sound. Geese resemble swans but have shorter necks. Subfamily: Anserinae. **2.** FEMALE GOOSE a female goose. ◊ **gander 3.** FOOD FLESH OF THE GOOSE the flesh of the goose, cooked and eaten as food **4.** SILLY PERSON sb who is silly **5.** TAILOR'S IRON an iron with a long curved handle, used by tailors for pressing and smoothing cloth **6.** PROD IN THE BUTTOCKS a poke between or pinch on the buttocks (*slang*) ■ *vt.* (**gooses, goosing, goosed**) (*slang*) **1.** PROD SB IN THE BUTTOCKS to poke or pinch sb on the buttocks **2.** *US* SPUR SB TO ACTION to spur sb on to action [Old English *gōs*. Ultimately from an Indo-European word.] ◇ **kill the goose that lays the golden eggs** to destroy sth that is or has been a regular, dependable source of profit or benefit

goose barnacle *n.* a barnacle that has a flattened shell, feathery appendages, and a fleshy stalk that it uses to attach itself to surfaces, especially floating wood. Genus: *Lepas.*

---

a at; aa father; aw all; ay day; air hair; ə about, edible, item, common, circus; e egg; ee eel; hw it; i it, happy; ī ice; 'l apple; 'm rhythm; 'n fashion; o odd; ō open; oo good; oo pool; ow owl; oy oil; th thin; th this; u up; ur urge;

Gooseberry

gooseberry /go͝oz bəri/ (*plural* -ries) *n*. **1.** SPINY FRUIT BUSH a spiny fruit bush, native to Europe and Asia, that produces green or sometimes red edible berries. Latin name: *Ribes uva-crispa*. **2.** FRUIT OF GOOSEBERRY the acid-tasting fruit of a gooseberry plant, usually eaten cooked and sweetened (*often used before a noun*) ○ *gooseberry pie* **3.** UNWANTED EXTRA PERSON an unwanted single person with a couple or a group otherwise made up of couples (*informal*) ○ *I don't want to play gooseberry.* [Mid-16thC. *Goose* of uncertain origin: perhaps from GOOSE, or by folk etymology from French *groseille* 'redcurrant'.]

goose bumps *npl*. US = **goose pimples**

gooseflesh /go͝oss flesh/ *n*. = **goose pimples**

goosefoot /go͝oss fo͝ot/ *n*. a weed with small greenish flowers and berries, and leaves that resemble a goose's foot. Genus: *Chenopodium*.

goosegog /go͝oz gog/ *n*. a gooseberry (*informal*) [Early 19thC. *Gog* a variant of GOB.]

goosegrass /go͝oss graass/ *n*. BOT an annual plant of Europe and Asia with slender sprawling stems, narrow leaves, and tiny white flowers. Its spiny round fruits cling to animals and clothing. Latin name: *Galium aparine*. US term **cleavers**

gooseneck /go͝oss nek/ *n*. sth curved like a goose's neck or U-shaped such as a pipe joint or a flexible neck on a lamp (*often used before a noun*) ○ *a gooseneck lamp*

gooseneck barnacle *n*. = **goose barnacle**

goose pimples *npl*. temporary pimples on the skin brought on by cold or fear, or by sudden excitement, and caused by contraction of connective tissues (**papillae**) at the base of hairs. US term **goose bumps** —**goose-pimply** *adj*.

goose step *n*. a military marching step performed with straight legs swung high in a forward movement —**goose-step** *vi*.

goosy /go͝ossi/ (-ier, -iest), **goosey** (-ier, -iest) *adj*. **1.** RESEMBLING A GOOSE similar to a goose **2.** HAVING GOOSE PIMPLES affected by goose pimples, or the nervousness or fear that can cause them (*informal*) **3.** SILLY behaving in a silly or scatterbrained way

gopher /gófər/ *n*. **1.** BURROWING RODENT a small short-tailed rodent of North and Central America that has fur-lined cheek pouches and short legs. It digs sizable burrows. Family: Geomyidae. **2.** COMPUT SYSTEM PROVIDING INTERNET LINKS an Internet system that organizes files into menus containing links to text files, graphic images, databases, and additional menus (*often used before a noun*) ○ *a gopher site* [Late 18thC. Origin uncertain: perhaps from Canadian French *gaufre* 'honeycomb', referring to the burrows made by the animals. For computing sense, alteration of GOFER, from the idea that it tunnels from place to place.]

gopherwood /gófər wo͝od/ *n*. **1.** = **yellowwood 2.** WOOD OF NOAH'S ARK in the Bible, the wood from which Noah's ark was made, or the tree from which it came [Early 17thC. *Gopher* from Hebrew *gōpher*.]

Gorakhpur /gáwrək po͝or/ industrial city in Uttar Pradesh State, northern India. It is a major railway junction and trading centre. Population: 506,000 (1991).

goral /gáwrəl/ *n*. a small short-horned antelope found in the rugged country of the Himalayas and adjacent Southeast Asia. Genus: *Nemorhaedus*. [Mid-19thC. From a Himalayan language.]

gorb /gawrb/ *n*. *Ireland* a glutton [Early 19thC. Origin unknown.]

Mikhail Gorbachev

Gorbachev /gáwrbə chof/, **Mikhail** (b. 1931) Soviet statesman. As general secretary of the Soviet Communist Party (1985–91) and president (1988–91), he initiated democratic reforms that precipitated the disintegration of the Soviet Union and the end of the Cold War. He won the Nobel Peace Prize in 1990. Full name **Mikhail Sergeyevich Gorbachev**

Gorbals /gáwrb'lz/ suburb of Glasgow, Scotland, on the southern bank of the River Clyde

gorblimey /gawr blĭmi/ *interj*. = **cor blimey** [Late 19thC. Alteration of *God blind me* (see COR BLIMEY).]

Gordian knot /gáwrdi ən-/ *n*. a problem for which it is very difficult to find a solution [Late 16thC. From the knot of *Gordius*, king of Gordium, that was to be loosed only by the future ruler of Asia: Alexander the Great sliced through it.]

Nadine Gordimer

Gordimer /gáwrdimər/, **Nadine** (b. 1923) South African novelist. Her works examined the tensions of apartheid in South Africa. She won the Nobel Prize in literature in 1991.

Gordon /gáwrd'n/, **Adam Lindsay** (1833–70) Azores-born Australian poet. He wrote about Australian rural life in such collections as *Bush Ballads and Galloping Rhymes* (1870).

Gordon Bennett /gáwrd'n bénnit/ *interj*. used to express surprise or annoyance (*dated informal*) [Late 20thC. Alteration of GORBLIMEY and from James *Gordon Bennett* (1841–1918), American publisher and sports promoter.]

Gordon setter /gáwrd'n-/ *n*. a gun dog with a long black-and-tan coat, belonging to a breed developed in Scotland [Mid-19thC. Named after Alexander *Gordon*, 4th Duke of Gordon (1743–1827), who promoted the breed.]

gore[1] /gawr/ (**gores, goring, gored**) *vt*. to pierce the flesh of a person or animal with horns or tusks [14thC. Origin uncertain: perhaps a variant of *gore* 'spear', from Old English *gār* (source of English *garlic*).]

gore[2] /gawr/ *n*. thick coagulating blood, especially blood shed as a result of violence [Old English *gor* 'dirt, dung', from prehistoric Germanic. The meaning 'blood' first appeared in the mid-16thC.]

gore[3] /gawr/ *n*. a triangular piece of cloth used, e.g., in making a loose skirt [Old English *gāra*, of uncertain origin] —**gored** *adj*.

Gore /gawr/ town on the River Mataura on the South Island, New Zealand. It is a centre of agriculture and light industry. Population: 10,296 (1996).

gorge /gawrj/ *n*. **1.** NARROW VALLEY a deep narrow, usually rocky valley **2.** CONTENTS OF STOMACH the contents of the stomach, especially when they are perceived as rising in the throat out of disgust or anger **3.** MIL ENTRANCE TO OUTWORK a narrow entrance at the rear of an outwork in a fortification **4.** OBSTRUCTION IN PASSAGE a mass of sth obstructing a passage, especially a mass of ice obstructing a river **5.** HAWK'S CROP the crop of a hawk ■ *v*. (**gorges, gorging, gorged**) **1.** *vti*. EAT GREEDILY to eat sth greedily and to excess ○ *They gorged on chocolates.* ○ *They sat at the counter gorging meat and potatoes.* **2.** *vt*. EAT to devour sth greedily ○ *They sat at the counter gorging meat and potatoes.* **3.** *vt*. = **engorge** *v*. 1 [14thC. From French, 'throat', from Latin *gurge* 'abyss, whirlpool'.]

gorgeous /gáwrjəss/ *adj*. **1.** BEAUTIFUL outstandingly beautiful or richly coloured ○ *dressed in gorgeous silks* **2.** PLEASING very pleasant (*informal*) ○ *a gorgeous spring morning* [15thC. From Old French *gorgias* 'stylish, elegant, of uncertain origin: perhaps formed from *gorge* 'throat' (see GORGE), because the neck can be adorned with stylish things.] —**gorgeously** *adv*. —**gorgeousness** *n*.

gorget /gáwrjit/ *n*. **1.** MIL ARMOUR FOR THROAT a crescent-shaped piece of armour for protecting the throat **2.** CLOTHES PART OF NUN'S HEADDRESS the part of a nun's headdress that covers the neck and shoulders **3.** ACCESSORIES NECKLACE a circular or crescent-shaped ornament worn round the neck **4.** ZOOL COLOURED BAND ON THROAT a band or patch of distinctive colour on the throat of a bird or other animal [15thC. From Old French *gorgete*, from *gorge* 'throat' (see GORGE).]

Gorgon /gáwrgən/ *n*. **1.** MYTHOL GREEK MONSTER in Greek mythology, a monstrous woman with snakes for hair, who turned those who looked at her into stone **2.** gorgon, Gorgon TERRIFYING WOMAN a woman regarded as very frightening or ugly (*insult*) [14thC. From Latin *Gorgon-*, stem of *Gorgo*, from Greek *Gorgō*, from *gorgos* 'terrible'.]

gorgonian /gawr góni ən/ *n*. a coral with a flexible horny branched skeleton. Family: Gorgonacea. [Mid-19thC. Formed from modern Latin *Gorgonia*, genus name, ultimately from Latin *Gorgon-* (see GORGON), referring to its power to turn to stone.] —**gorgonian** *adj*.

Gorgonian /gawr góni ən/ *adj*. relating to or resembling a mythological female monster called a Gorgon

gorgonize /gáwrgə nīz/ (**-izes, -izing, -ized**), **gorgonise** (**-ises, -ising, -ised**) *vt*. to petrify or mesmerize sb (*literary*)

Gorgonzola /gáwrgən zṓlə/, **gorgonzola** *n*. a moist Italian blue cheese with a strong flavour [Late 19thC. Named after *Gorgonzola*, the Milanese village where the cheese was first made.]

Gorilla

gorilla /gə ríllə/ *n*. **1.** ZOOL LARGEST APE the largest ape, native to central Africa, with a relatively short but very powerful body and coarse dark hair. Latin name: *Gorilla gorilla*. **2.** THUG a large or brutal person, especially a hired thug (*informal*) [Mid-19thC. Via modern Latin from Greek *gorillas*, from, ultimately, an assumed African word meaning 'wild or hairy man'.]

Gorki /gáwrki/ former name for **Nizhi Novgorod**

Gorky /gáwrki/, **Gorki, Maksim** (1868–1936) Russian writer. His works inaugurated Socialist Realism, and include the play *The Lower Depths* (1902) and an autobiographical trilogy (1915–23). Pseudonym of **Aleksei Maksimovich Peshkov**

Görlitz /gúrlits/ industrial city in Saxony State, east-central Germany, on the border with Poland. Population: 77,600 (1989).

gormandize /gáwrmən dīz/ (-izes, -izing, -ized), **gormandise** (-ises, -ising, -ised) vti. to eat food gluttonously [Mid-16thC. Ultimately from French *gourmandise* 'gluttony', from *gourmand* (see GOURMAND).] —**gormandizer** n.

gormless /gáwrmləss/ adj. lacking intelligence, common sense, or initiative (informal) [Mid-19thC. Variant of *gaumless*, literally 'lacking understanding', from *gaum* 'understanding, heed', from Old Norse *gaumr* 'heed'.]

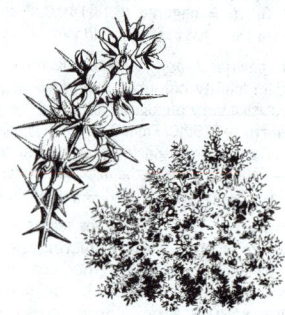
Gorse

gorse /gawrss/ (plural **gorses** or **gorse**) n. a shrub with fragrant yellow flowers, thick green spines, and black pods. Genus: *Ulex*. [Old English *gors*. Ultimately from an Indo-European word meaning 'to be prickly or rough'.]

Gorton /gáwrt'n/, **Sir John Grey** (b. 1911) Australian statesman. He was a Liberal Party politician and prime minister of Australia (1968–71).

gory /gáwri/ (-rier, -riest) adj. **1.** BLOODY covered with blood or gore **2.** ATTENDED BY BLOODSHED involving much bloodshed **3.** HORRIBLE arousing horror or terror ◦ *the gory details* —**gorily** adv. —**goriness** n.

Gosford /gósfərd/ coastal city in eastern New South Wales, Australia, situated 85 km/53 mi. north of Sydney. Population: 144,840 (1996).

gosh /gosh/ interj. used to express surprise, amazement, or pleasure (informal) [Mid-18thC. Substitution for GOD.]

Goshawk

goshawk /góss hawk/ n. a large fierce hawk with broad rounded wings and a long tail, found in Europe and North America. Latin name: *Accipiter gentilis*. [12thC. From Old English *goshafoc*, from *gos* + *hafoc*, earlier forms of GOOSE and HAWK.]

gosling /gózling/ n. a young goose [15thC. From Old Norse *gøslingr*, from *gas* 'goose'.]

go-slow n. a protest by industrial workers in which they deliberately work slowly. US term **slowdown**

gospel /gósp'l/ n. **1.** SET OF BELIEFS a set of beliefs held strongly by a group or person **2.** ABSOLUTE TRUTH sth believed to be absolutely and unquestionably true **3.** = gospel music

Gospel /gósp'l/ n. **1.** TEACHINGS OF JESUS CHRIST the teachings of Jesus Christ and the story of his life **2.** BOOK OF BIBLE any of one the biblical books Matthew, Mark, Luke, or John **3.** BIBLE EXTRACT an extract from one of the Gospels read as part of a Christian religious service [Old English *gōdspel*, literally 'good news', from *gōd* 'good' + *spel* 'tidings' (see SPELL), ultimately a translation of Greek *euaggelion*]

gospeller /góspələr/ n. **1.** GOSPEL READER sb who reads the Gospel in a Christian religious service **2.** PREACHER OF THE GOSPEL sb who preaches the Gospel (disapproving)

gospel music n. highly emotional evangelical vocal music that originated among African American Christians in the southern United States and was a strong influence in the development of soul music

gospel side n. in a Christian church, the left side of the altar as faced by the congregation. ◊ epistle side

gospel truth n. = gospel n. 2

Gosport /góspawrt/ town in Hampshire, southern England, on Portsmouth harbour. It is an English Channel port and the site of naval installations. Population: 74,800 (1995).

goss n. gossip (slang) ◦ *all the latest goss* [Shortening of GOSSIP]

gossamer /góssəmər/ n. **1.** FINE COBWEBS a fine film of cobwebs, often seen floating in the air or covered with dew on the ground **2.** DELICATE FABRIC fabric or gauze that is delicate, sheer, and soft **3.** STH SHEER AND DELICATE sth delicate, sheer, and filmy [14thC. Origin uncertain: probably from GOOSE + SUMMER, a period of mild autumn weather when goose was in season and such webs were often seen in the air.] —**gossamery** adj.

gossan /góss'n, gózz'n/, **gozzan** /gózz'n/ n. a yellow or red layer on the surface of minerals rich in iron oxide, produced by alteration and leaching of sulphide ores [Late 18thC. Origin uncertain: probably from Cornish, formed from *gōs* 'blood'.]

Gosse /goss/, **Sir Edmund William** (1849–1928) English writer. Among his numerous works of literary criticism, biography, and poetry, he is best remembered for his autobiographical *Father and Son* (1907).

gossip /góssip/ n. **1.** CONVERSATION ABOUT PERSONAL MATTERS conversation about personal or intimate rumours or facts, especially when malicious **2.** CASUAL CONVERSATION informal and chatty conversation or writing about recent and often personal events ◦ *They had a good gossip in the pub.* **3.** HABITUAL TALKER sb given to spreading personal or intimate information about other people ■ vi. (-sips, -siping, -siped) SPREAD RUMOURS to tell people rumours or personal or intimate facts about other people, especially maliciously ■ n. WOMAN FRIEND a close woman friend (archaic) [Old English *godsibb* 'godparent', later 'close friend', from *god* 'god' + *sibb* 'relative' (source of *sibling*). The underlying meaning is 'chat with a close friend'.] —**gossiper** n. —**gossipry** n. —**gossipy** adj.

——— **WORD KEY: REGIONAL NOTE** ———

Gossip originally meant 'godmother' or 'sponsor in baptism', and illustrates a phenomenon called 'semantic degradation', where a word of high prestige loses some or all of its value. Many dialect words meaning 'to gossip' also mean 'to scold or nag'.

———

gossip column n. a regular feature in a magazine or newspaper where rumours and personal or intimate facts about celebrities are exposed —**gossip columnist** n.

gossipmonger /góssip mung gər/ n. sb who is a gossip

gossoon /go soón/ n. Ireland a young boy (informal) [Late 17thC. Via Irish from French *garçon* (see GARÇON).]

gossypol /góssi pol/ n. a substance extracted from cotton seeds that has been shown to inhibit the production of sperm and has been studied for possible use as a contraceptive. Formula: $C_{30}H_{30}O_8$. [Late 19thC. Formed from modern Latin *Gossypium*, genus name of the cotton plant, from Latin *gossypion* 'cotton tree'.]

got past participle, past tense of **get**

Göta Canal /yốtə-/ waterway in southwestern Sweden, linking Gothenburg on the western coast with Stockholm on the Baltic coast. Length: 558 km/347 mi.

gotcha /góchə/ interj. used to indicate that sb has been successfully tricked or caught out in some way, or to indicate comprehension of sth (informal) [Mid-20thC. From a pronunciation of *got you*.]

goth /goth/ n. **1.** SB BARBARIC sb who is uncivilized or barbaric **2.** **goth, Goth** MUSIC MUSICAL STYLE a style of popular music that combines elements of heavy metal with punk **3.** **goth, Goth** FASHION FASHION OF DARK CLOTHES AND MAKE-UP a style of fashion popular among men and women in the 1980s, characterized by black clothes, heavy silver jewellery, black eye make-up and lipstick, and often pale face make-up **4.** **goth, Goth** SB FOLLOWING GOTHIC MUSIC AND FASHION sb who follows gothic music and fashion

Goth n. a member of an ancient Germanic people who settled south of the Baltic and from the 3rd to the 5th centuries founded kingdoms in many parts of the Roman Empire [Old English *gotan* 'Goths'. From late Latin *Gothi*, of prehistoric Germanic origin.]

Goth. abbr. Gothic

Gotham /góthəm/ n. a nickname for New York City

Gothenburg /góth'n burg/, **Göteborg** seaport and industrial city on the River Göta estuary in southwestern Sweden. It is the second largest city and principal port of Sweden. Population: 449,189 (1995).

gothic /góthik/ adj. UNCIVILIZED barbarous or uncivilized ■ n. **1.** MUSIC, FASHION = gothic n. 2, goth n. 3 **2.** PRINTING SIMPLE TYPEFACE a simple sans serif typeface with strokes of uniform width **3.** PRINTING HEAVY ANGULAR TYPEFACE a heavy bold angular early typeface —**gothically** adv. —**gothicness** n.

——— **WORD KEY: CULTURAL NOTE** ———

American Gothic, a painting by US artist Grant Wood (1930). It portrays an elderly, rather dour farming couple standing in front of a gothic-style farmhouse. Initially criticized as a cruel caricature of country folk, it is now one of the best-known and most popular of all American paintings. A generic term, *American gothic*, came to mean very hard-working, conservative, and rigidly self-disciplined. It is one of the relatively few such terms whose meaning derives not merely from the title of a painting but from the visual representation in the painting.

AKG London
Gothic: Interior of Cologne Cathedral, Germany (begun 1248)

Gothic adj. **1.** ARCHIT OF MEDIEVAL ARCHITECTURAL STYLE belonging to a style of architecture used in Western Europe from the 12th to the 15th centuries, and characterized by pointed arches, flying buttresses, and high curved ceilings **2.** ARTS OF MEDIEVAL ARTISTIC STYLE belonging to a style of music, painting, or sculpture practised in parts of Europe from the 12th to the 15th centuries **3.** HIST OF MIDDLE AGES relating to the Middle Ages **4.** **Gothic, gothic** LITERAT OF EERIE FICTION STYLE belonging to a genre of fiction characterized by gloom and darkness, often with a grotesque or supernatural plot unfolding in an eerie or lonely location such as a ruined castle **5.** PEOPLES OF THE GOTHS relating to or typical of the Goths, or their language or culture ■ n. LANG EXTINCT LANGUAGE OF ANCIENT GOTHS an extinct language formerly spoken by the ancient Goths in parts of Scandinavia and around the Baltic Sea. It is one of the East Germanic group of the Germanic branch of Indo-European. —**Gothically** adv. —**Gothicness** n.

Gothic arch n. a pointed arch, as found in Gothic churches

Gothicise vt. = Gothicize

gothicism /góthi sizəm/ n. crudeness of style or manner, or an example of crudeness

Gothicism *n.* use of the Gothic style of architecture, art, or literature —**Gothicist** *n.*

Gothicize /góthi sīz/ (**-cizes, -cizing, -cized**), **Gothicise** (**-cises, -cising, -cised**) *vt.* to make sth Gothic in style —**Gothicizer** *n.*

Gothic Revival *n.* a style of architecture based on a reintroduction of the Gothic style, popular in the 18th and 19th centuries

Gotland /góttlənd/, **Gottland** island and county of Sweden, situated in the Baltic Sea about 80 km/50 mi. from the mainland. Capital: Visby. Population: 58,120 (1995). Area: 3,140 sq. km/1,212 sq. mi.

gotta /góttə/ *vi.* used as a written representation of 'got to', reflecting popular pronunciation (*informal*) [Early 20thC. From a pronunciation of *got to*.]

gotten *US* past participle of **get**

götterdämmerung /góttər dámmərŏong/, **Götterdämmerung** *n.* **1.** MYTHOL DESTRUCTION OF GERMAN GODS in Germanic mythology, the destruction of the gods after battle with the forces of doom **2.** VIOLENT END OF REGIME the overthrow or violent ending of a regime or institution [Early 20thC. From German, 'twilight of the gods'.]

Göttingen /gótingən/ university town in Lower Saxony, central Germany. It is situated about 89 km/55 mi. south of Hanover. Population: 127,900 (1994).

gouache /gŏo áash/ *n.* **1.** PAINTING TECHNIQUE a method of painting in which opaque watercolours are mixed with gum **2.** PAINT USED IN GOUACHE the paint used in the gouache technique **3.** A GOUACHE PAINTING a painting done with gouache [Late 19thC. Via French from Italian *guazzo*, 'puddle', of uncertain origin: probably via Latin *aquatio* from, ultimately, *aqua* 'water' (see AQUA).]

Gouda[1] /gówdə/ *n.* a mild Dutch cheese, typically sold in a flattened sphere covered in wax [Mid-19thC. Named after GOUDA, where it is made.]

Gouda[2] /gówdə/ city in South Holland Province, western Netherlands. Famous for its cheese, it is situated about 21 km/13 mi. northeast of Rotterdam. Population: 69,916 (1994).

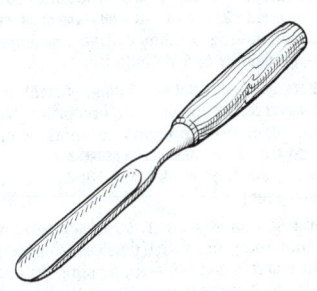

Gouge

gouge /gowj/ *vti.* (**gouges, gouging, gouged**) **1.** CARVE OUT HOLE to cut or scoop a hole or groove in sth, usually using a sharp tool **2.** FORM ROUGHLY BY CUTTING to form sth by roughly cutting it out of surrounding material **3.** *US* OVERCHARGE SB to cheat sb or act dishonestly by demanding an unreasonably high price for services or goods (*informal*) **4.** INJURE SB'S EYE to attack sb's eye with the thumb ■ *n.* **1.** WOODWORK CHISEL WITH CONCAVE BLADE a chisel with a concave blade used for cutting grooves and holes in wood **2.** SMALL HOLE a mark, groove, or hole, usually made with a pointed tool **3.** *US* ACT OF OVERCHARGING an instance of paying too much or being charged exorbitantly for goods or services (*informal*) **4.** GEOL ROCK FRAGMENTS clay material produced by the grinding together of rock surfaces in a fault or within a mineral vein [Late 15thC. Via French from late Latin *gubia*, variant of *gulbia*, of Celtic origin.] —**gouger** *n.*

goujon /gŏojən/ *n.* a long strip of fish or chicken coated in egg and breadcrumbs and deep-fried [Mid-20thC. From French, 'gudgeon' (see GUDGEON), so called from the shape of the strips.]

goulash /gŏol ash/ *n.* **1.** COOK HUNGARIAN STEW a stew of Hungarian origin, made with beef, veal, lamb, or pork and seasoned with paprika **2.** BRIDGE DEALING OF CARDS a way of dealing cards that have already been arranged in a specific order, without shuffling them first [Mid-19thC. From Hungarian *gulyás*, a shortening of *gulyás hús* 'herdsman's meat'.]

Goulburn /gŏol burn/ city in eastern New South Wales, Australia. It is the commercial centre of a rural district. Population: 21,293 (1996).

Gould /gŏold/, **Shane** (*b.* 1956) Australian swimmer. She won five medals at the 1972 Olympics and retired from competitive swimming at age 16. Full name **Shane Elizabeth Gould**

gourami /gŏo ráami/ (*plural* **-mi** *or* **-mis**) *n.* a freshwater fish of Southeast Asia, many species of which are capable of breathing air and are often kept in aquariums. Family: Anabantidae. [Late 19thC. Via Malay *gurami* 'freshwater carp' from Javanese *graméh*.]

Gourd

gourd /gŏord/ *n.* **1.** HARD-SKINNED FRUIT a hard-skinned fleshy fruit produced by several different plants related to cucumbers and marrows, eaten when ripe or dried and used as decoration, bowls, or cups **2.** GOURD-PRODUCING PLANT a plant that produces gourds [14thC. Via Anglo-Norman *gurde* from, ultimately, Latin *cucurbita* (source also of English *courgette*).]

gourde /gŏord/ *n.* **1.** HAITIAN CURRENCY UNIT the basic unit of currency in Haiti. See table at **currency 2.** NOTE WORTH A GOURDE a note worth one gourde [Mid-19thC. Via Haitian Creole from French *gourd* 'dull, heavy', from Latin *gurdus* 'dolt', later 'dull, blunt'.]

gourmand /gŏormənd/ *n.* sb who loves food and often eats excessively or greedily [15thC. From French, 'glutton', of uncertain origin.]

gourmandise /gŏormən deéz/ *n.* an appreciation of good food and drink [Mid-16thC. From French, formed from *gourmand* 'glutton'.]

gourmet /gŏor may/ *n.* FOOD FOOD EXPERT sb who has an expert knowledge and an enjoyment of good food and drink ■ *adj.* COOK OF SPECIAL FOOD relating to or preparing high-quality food that is sophisticated, expensive, rare, or meticulously prepared [Early 19thC. From French, an alteration (influenced by *gourmand* 'GOURMAND') of Middle French *groumet* 'servant, vintner's assistant', from English *groom*.]

gout /gowt/ *n.* **1.** DISEASE CAUSING SWOLLEN JOINTS a metabolic disorder mainly affecting men in which excess uric acid is produced and deposited in the joints, causing painful swelling, especially in the toes and feet **2.** BLOB a large blob or clot of sth, usually of blood [13thC. Via Old French *goute* from Latin *gutta*, literally 'drop of liquid'; so called from the idea that gout was caused by drops of a morbid fluid in the blood.]

gouty /gówti/ (**-ier, -iest**) *adj.* **1.** WITH GOUT resulting from or causing gout **2.** AFFECTED BY GOUT affected by or tending to contract gout —**goutiness** *n.*

gov. /guv/ *abbr.* **1.** government **2.** governor

govern /gúvv'n/ (**-erns, -erning, -erned**) *v.* **1.** *vti.* POL HAVE POLITICAL AUTHORITY to be responsible officially for directing the affairs, policies, and economy of a state, country, or organization **2.** *vt.* CONTROL STH to control, regulate, or direct sth **3.** *vt.* RESTRAIN control sth by restraint **4.** *vt.* HAVE INFLUENCE OVER to have or exercise an influence over sth **5.** *vt.* MECH ENG CONTROL SPEED OF to maintain the speed of an engine or keep it from going above a specific level by controlling the fuel or steam supply **6.** *vt.* LAW BE LAW FOR to be the defining rule for sth **7.** *vt.* GRAM DETERMINE FORM OF WORD to dictate the inflection, mood, or case of another word [13thC. Via Old French *governer* and Latin *gubernare* from Greek *kubernan* 'to steer' (source of English *cybernetics*), of unknown origin.] —**governable** *adj.*

governance /gúvv'nənss/ *n.* **1.** MANNER OF GOVERNMENT the system or manner of government **2.** STATE OF GOVERNING A PLACE the act or state of governing a place **3.** AUTHORITY control or authority (*formal*)

governess /gúvvərnəss/ *n.* especially in former times, a woman employed to teach children in their own homes, and sometimes also to care for the children [15thC. From Old French *governeresse*, feminine of *governeour* 'governor'.]

governessy /gúvvərnəssi/ *adj.* like a strict or prim governess

governing body (*plural* **governing bodies**) *n.* a group of people appointed to supervise and regulate a field of activity or an establishment

government /gúvv'nmənt/ *n.* **1.** POL POLITICAL AUTHORITY a group of people who have the power to make and enforce laws for a country or area **2.** POL STYLE OF GOVERNMENT a type of political system **3.** POL THE STATE VIEWED AS RULER the state and its administration viewed as the ruling political power **4.** POL BRANCH OF GOVERNMENT a branch or agency of a government, taken as the whole (*informal*) **5.** CONTROL OF STH the management or control of sth **6.** GRAM DETERMINATION OF INFLECTION the determination of the inflection, mood, or case of a word by another word **7.** EDUC POLITICAL SCIENCE political science as a subject of study ■ *adj.* OF GOVERNMENT relating to or provided by a government, usually a national government —**governmental** /gúvv'n mént'l/ *adj.* —**governmentally** /-mént'li/ *adv.*

—— **WORD KEY: USAGE** ——
Singular or plural? Like many collective nouns, **government** can be used with a singular or plural construction, depending on whether the emphasis is on the government as a body making joint decisions or on the individuals that constitute it.

governmentalize /gúvv'n mént'l īz/ (**-izes, -izing, -ized**), **governmentalise** (**-ises, -ising, -ised**) *vt.* to put a sphere of activity under the power of the government

governmentese /gúvv'nmən teéz/ *n.* language that is full of difficult jargon, thought to be typical of language used by government, e.g. in regulations and laws

Government House *n.* in Australia, the official residence of the Governor-General

governor /gúvv'nər/ *n.* **1.** GOVERNING BODY MEMBER a member of a governing body of an institution **2.** POL GOVERNING OFFICIAL an appointed or elected official who governs a state, colony, or province for a specified term **3.** CRIMINOL PRINCIPAL PRISON OFFICER the principal officer in charge of a prison. US term **warden 4.** AUTHORITY FIGURE an authority figure such as an employer or boss (*informal*) **5.** MECH ENG REGULATING DEVICE a device for regulating the speed of an engine **6.** REPRESENTATIVE OF BRITISH CROWN IN AUSTRALIA the representative of the British crown in Australia at the level of state government. The Governor must officially approve all legislation passed by the state parliament.

governor general (*plural* **governors general** *or* **governor generals**) *n.* **1.** CROWN REPRESENTATIVE the representative of the British Crown in some countries of the Commonwealth of Nations **2.** TOP GOVERNOR a governor who has authority over deputy governors —**governor-generalship** *n.*

governorship /gúvvərnərship/ *n.* the position, duties, or term of office of a governor

Governors Island island in New York Bay, just south of the tip of Manhattan Island, that was used as a military post until the 19th century. Area: 70 hectares/175 acres.

govt *abbr.* government

gowan /gów ən/ *n. Scotland* any yellow or white field flower, especially a daisy [Late 16thC. Origin uncertain: probably an alteration of *golland* 'buttercup', from a Scandinavian source.]

Gower Peninsula /gów ər-/ rocky peninsula on the coast of Swansea district, southern Wales. Length: 24 km/15 mi.

gowk /gowk/ *n.* an offensive term for sb considered unintelligent or awkward (*regional informal*) [14thC. From Old Norse *gaukr*, originally in sense 'cuckoo'.]

gown /gown/ *n.* **1.** CLOTHES **ELEGANT OR FORMAL DRESS** a woman's full-length elegant or formal dress for special occasions **2.** CLOTHES **LONG ROBE** a long robe, often dark in colour, worn on official occasions by people such as judges, professors, university graduates, and barristers **3.** CLOTHES **LOOSE OUTER GARMENT** a loose cloak or robe such as that worn by surgeons that is worn to protect clothes **4.** UNIV **MEMBERS OF A UNIVERSITY COLLECTIVELY** the members of a university regarded as distinct from the rest of a town's population ■ *vt.* **(gowns, gowning, gowned) DRESS IN GOWN** to dress sb in a loose robe [14thC. Via Old French *goune* from late Latin *gunna* 'fur or leather garment', of unknown origin.]

gownsman /gównzmən/ (*plural* **-men** /-mən/) *n.* a man, e.g. an academic who wears a gown for professional reasons

Francisco Goya: Self-portrait

Goya /góy ə/, **Francisco de** (1746–1828) Spanish painter. One of the greatest Spanish masters, he was known for his naturalistic tapestry designs, portraits, and several series of satirical etchings, including *The Caprices* (1797–99). Full name **Francisco José de Goya y Lucientes**

GP *n.* MED **FAMILY DOCTOR** a doctor who deals with patients' general medical problems, either at a surgery or, sometimes, at patients' homes. Full form **general practitioner** ■ *abbr.* **1.** MED general practice **2.** MUSIC general pause **3.** SPORTS Grand Prix

Gp. *abbr.* STOCK EXCH group

GPI *n.* a condition that occurs in the late stages of syphilis and is characterized by dementia, speech difficulty, and inability to move. Full form **general paralysis of the insane**

GPMU *abbr.* Graphical, Paper, and Media Union

GPO *abbr.* HIST General Post Office

gps, GPS *n.* NAVIG **SATELLITE NAVIGATION SYSTEM** a worldwide navigation system that uses information received from orbiting satellites. Full form **Global Positioning System** ■ *abbr.* **1.** gallons per second **2.** *Aus* EDUC Great Public Schools

GPU *n.* the Soviet secret police, from 1922 to 1923. Full form **Gosudarstvennoe politicheskoe upravlenie** [From Russian, 'State Political Directorate']

GQ *abbr.* General Quarters

gr. *abbr.* **1.** grade **2.** grain **3.** gram **4.** gross

Gr. *abbr.* **1.** Greece **2.** Greek

Graafian follicle /graáfi ən-/ *n.* a small fluid-filled sac **(vesicle)** containing a maturing ovum. Graafian follicles are found in the ovaries of mammals. ◊ **ovisac** [Mid-19thC. Named after the Dutch anatomist Regnier de *Graaf* (1641–73), who discovered the vesicles.]

grab /grab/ *v.* **(grabs, grabbing, grabbed) 1.** *vt.* **GRASP STH** to grasp sth quickly, suddenly, or forcefully ○ *Grab a pen and sit down.* **2.** *vti.* **TRY TO GRASP** to try to grasp sth that is hard to reach or in short supply ○ *Stop grabbing or I won't give you any.* **3.** *vt.* **SEIZE STH** to take sth violently or dishonestly ○ *grab the money and run* **4.** *vt.* **HAVE EMOTIONAL IMPACT ON SB** to appeal to, attract, impress, or affect sb emotionally (*informal*) ○ *The film didn't really grab me.* **5.** *vt.* **HURRIEDLY GET STH** to obtain sth quickly and without difficulty (*informal*) ○ *I'll just grab a bite to eat.* **6.** *vi.* *US* **TAKE HOLD SUDDENLY** to take hold suddenly or intermittently ○ *The brakes grabbed and the car went into a skid.* ■ *n.* **1. GRABBING** the act of grabbing sth ○ *He made a grab at my arm.* **2. STH GRABBED** sth that is grabbed **3. DEVICE FOR GRABBING** an apparatus or device used for grasping hold of sth **4. GRABBING ABILITY** the ability or capacity to hold sth fast [Late 16thC. Origin uncertain: probably from Middle Dutch or Middle Low German *grabben*. Ultimately from a prehistoric base that is also the ancestor of English *grasp*.] —**grabbable** *adj.* —**grabber** *n.* ◇ **up for grabs** available for the first comer to take or use (*informal*)

WORD KEY: SYNONYMS

See Synonyms at ***catch***.

grab bag *n.* **1.** *US* = **lucky dip 2. MISCELLANEOUS COLLECTION** sth composed of miscellaneous or mismatched components (*informal*)

grab bar *n.* a bar attached to a wall to provide a grip, e.g. near a bath or next to a toilet for people who have difficulty in standing up

grabbing /grábbing/ *adj.* with a character or way of behaving that attempts to obtain a lot of sth, especially money or sth abstract like people's attention (*usually used in combination*)

grabble /grább'l/ **(-bles, -bling, -bled)** *vi.* **1. GROPE ABOUT** to scratch or search about with the hands **2. SPRAWL** to tumble or fall to the ground on all fours [Late 16thC. Origin uncertain: probably from Dutch *grabbelen*, from *grabben*.] —**grabbler** *n.*

grabby /grábbi/ **(-bier, -biest)** *adj.* pushy and grasping (*informal insult*) —**grabbiness** *n.*

graben /graàbən/ *n.* a broad valley, especially a rift valley [Late 19thC. From German *Graben*, literally 'ditch'.]

Grable /gráyb'l/, **Betty** (1916–73) US actor, dancer, and singer. She was a star of musical films in the 1940s. Full name **Elizabeth Ruth Grable**

grab rail *n.* = **grab bar**

grace /grayss/ *n.* **1. ELEGANCE** elegance, beauty, and smoothness of form or movement **2. POLITENESS** dignified, polite, and decent behaviour ○ *She fended off queries with her usual grace.* **3. GENEROSITY OF SPIRIT** a capacity to tolerate, accommodate, or forgive people **4.** CHR **PRAYER AT MEALTIMES** a short prayer of thanks to God said before, or sometimes after, a meal **5.** FIN = **grace period 6. PLEASING** a pleasing and admirable quality or characteristic (*usually plural*) **7.** CHR **GIFT OF GOD TO HUMANKIND** in Christianity, the infinite love, mercy, favour, and goodwill shown to humankind by God **8.** CHR **FREEDOM FROM SIN** in Christianity, the condition of being free of sin, e.g. through repentance to God **9.** MUSIC = **grace note** ■ *vt.* **(graces, gracing, graced) 1. CONTRIBUTE PLEASINGLY** to make a pleasing contribution to an event, often by attending it (*often used ironically*) ○ *So good of you to grace us with your presence.* **2. ADD ELEGANCE** to add elegance, beauty, or charm to sth **3.** MUSIC **ORNAMENT** to add ornamental or decorative notes to a piece of music [12thC. Via Old French from Latin *gratia* (source of English *gracious*), from *gratus* 'pleasing' (see GRATEFUL).] ◇ **fall from grace** to lose a favoured or privileged position ◇ **with (a) bad grace** in a rude bad-tempered way ◇ **with (a) good grace** in a polite and willing way

Grace /grayss/ *n.* used as a title when addressing a duke, duchess, or archbishop

Grace /grayss/, **Patricia** (*b.* 1937) New Zealand writer. Her fiction weaves traditional Maori motifs into modern narratives, and includes *Potiki* (1986).

Grace, W. G. (1848–1915) English cricketer. The dominant player of the Victorian era, he played for Gloucester, London County, and England in his 43-year career, and remains one of the legends of the game. Full name **William Gilbert Grace**

grace-and-favour *n.* *UK* a property, e.g. a flat, owned by the British monarch who allows sb to live in it rent-free as a mark of special favour or gratitude

grace cup *n.* a cup of wine or liquor passed round at the end of a meal for a final toast

graceful /gráyssf'l/ *adj.* **1. ELEGANT AND BEAUTIFUL** showing elegance, beauty, and smoothness of form or movement **2. POISED AND DIGNIFIED** marked by poise, dignity, and politeness —**gracefully** *adv.* —**gracefulness** *n.*

graceless /gráyssləss/ *adj.* **1. WITHOUT ELEGANCE** lacking elegance in form or movement **2. LACKING DIGNITY** bad-mannered and undignified —**gracelessly** *adv.* —**gracelessness** *n.*

grace note *n.* a note added to a piece of music as an embellishment, usually played quickly before a principal note and written smaller than a normal note on the page

grace period *n.* the extra time allowed before having to pay a debt or complete a transaction

Graces *n.* in Greek mythology, three sister goddesses, Aglaia, Euphrosyne, and Thalia, who have the power to grant charm, happiness, and beauty

gracile /gráss ɪl/ *adj.* gracefully slender and slight (*literary*) [Early 17thC. From Latin *gracilis*, of unknown origin.] —**gracileness** *n.* —**gracility** /grə sílləti/ *n.*

gracious /gráyshəss/ *adj.* **1. KIND AND POLITE** full of tact, kindness, and politeness ○ *a gracious refusal* **2. CONDESCENDINGLY POLITE** condescendingly indulgent and generous to perceived inferiors **3. ELEGANT AND COMFORTABLE** luxurious and elegant ○ *gracious living* **4.** CHR **HAVING DIVINE GRACE** displaying divine grace, mercy, or compassion ■ *interj.* **EXPRESSING SURPRISE** used to express surprise, dismay, or indignation [13thC. Via Old French from Latin *gratiosus* 'agreeable', from *gratia* 'grace' (see GRACE).] —**graciously** *adv.* —**graciousness** *n.*

grackle /grák'l/ *n.* **1. N AMERICAN BLACKBIRD** a noisy North American blackbird with metallic black plumage and a long keel-shaped tail. Genus: *Quiscalus.* **2. STARLING** a European and Asian starling with mostly black plumage. Genus: *Gracula.* [Late 18thC. Via modern Latin *Gracula*, genus name, from Latin *graculus* 'jackdaw'. Ultimately from an Indo-European word meaning 'to croak', which is also the ancestor of English *crow* and *crane*.]

grad /grad/ *n.* a graduate (*informal*) [Shortening]

grad. *abbr.* **1.** gradient **2.** EDUC graduated

gradable /gráydəb'l/ *adj.* **1. ABLE TO BE GRADED** capable of being graded **2.** GRAM **ALLOWING VARIATION OF DEGREE** capable of having a comparative and superlative form —**gradability** /gráydə bílləti/ *n.*

gradate /grə dáyt/ **(-dates, -dating, -dated)** *v.* **1.** *vti.* **CHANGE IMPERCEPTIBLY** to pass imperceptibly from one shade or degree of intensity to another, or cause sth to do this **2.** *vt.* **ARRANGE IN DEGREES** to arrange sth in steps, grades, or ranks [Mid-18thC. Back-formation from GRADATION.]

gradation /grə dáysh'n/ *n.* **1. SERIES OF DEGREES** a series of gradual and progressive degrees, steps, or stages **2. SINGLE DEGREE** a degree, step, or stage in a gradual progression **3. DISCRETE ARRANGEMENT** the arrangement of sth according to size, rank, or quality **4. COLOUR CHANGE** the gradual and progressive change from one colour or tone to another **5.** PHON **VOWEL CHANGE** a change in the length or quality of a vowel within a word, signifying a change in function such as tense or number **6.** GEOG **LEVELLING OF LAND** the process of levelling land by erosion or deposition of sediment [Late 16thC. Directly or via French from the Latin stem *gradation-*, literally 'making steps', from *gradus* (see GRADE).] —**gradational** *adj.* —**gradationally** *adv.*

grade /grayd/ *n.* **1. LEVEL IN A SCALE OF PROGRESSION** a level, step, or stage in a scale of progression, quality, or size (*often used in combination*) ○ *low-grade ore* **2. MARK SHOWING A LEVEL** a mark to indicate a level, step, or stage in a process **3.** EDUC **YEAR IN SCHOOL** a class or year in the US and Canadian school systems ○ *She'll be in the tenth grade this year.* **4.** EDUC **MARK FOR QUALITY OF WORK** a mark or rating given for work in school or college, usually using the descending scale of A, B, C, D, E, and F ○ *She got a good grade for her essay.* **5. RANK** a rank or class **6. PEOPLE IN RANK** a group of people of the same rank **7.** FOOD **FOOD CLASSIFICATION** a category indicating the relative quality of food as determined by the US Department of Agriculture ○ *grade A eggs* **8.** *US* **GRADIENT** a gradient or slope, especially on a road or railroad **9.** MATH **UNIT OF ANGLE** a unit of angle equal to 0.9° **10.** PHON **VOWEL FORM** a form of vowel morpheme when a vowel varies owing to

gradation ■ vt. (grades, grading, graded) 1. ARRANGE BY DEGREES to arrange or classify things or people according to rank, quality, or level 2. US ASSIGN A GRADE to assign a mark or rating, e.g. to a student's work 3. TRANSP MAKE A ROAD LEVEL to level a road or railway by adjusting its gradients [Early 16thC. Via French from Latin *gradus* 'step, stage' (source also of English *degree*). Ultimately from an Indo-European base meaning 'to walk', which is the ancestor of *progress* and *transgress*).]
◇ **make the grade** to meet the required standard

─── **WORD KEY: ORIGIN** ───
The Latin word *gradus* from which **grade** is derived, and its related verb *gradi* 'to walk, go', are also the sources of English *aggression*, *congress*, *degrade*, *degree*, *digress*, *gradient*, *gradual*, *ingredient*, *progress*, *retrograde*, and *transgress*.

grade crossing *n.* US = **level crossing**

graded sediment *n.* a sediment deposited on land or the seabed in which there is an upward gradation of the grains from coarse to fine

gradely /gráydli/ *adj.* EXCELLENT decent, fine, and respectable (*regional*) ■ *adv.* APPROPRIATELY promptly and properly (*regional*) [13thC. From Old Norse *greiðligr*, from *greiðr* 'ready, prompt'.]

grader /gráydər/ *n.* 1. SB WHO OR STH THAT GRADES a person who or machine that grades sth 2. US EDUC STUDENT a student in a particular grade in school ○ *first graders* 3. CONSTR EARTH LEVELLER a machine with a wide blade that levels earth, used in road construction

grade school *n.* US an elementary or primary school

gradient /gráydi ənt/ *n.* 1. STEEPNESS the rate at which the steepness of a slope increases 2. SLOPE an upward or downward slope, e.g. in a road or railway 3. PHYS MEASURE OF CHANGE a measure of change in a physical quantity such as temperature or pressure over a specified distance 4. BIOL RATE OF GROWTH any of a series of changes in the rate of growth or metabolism of an organism, cell, or organ 5. MATH SLOPE ON A CURVE the slope of a line or a tangent at any point on a curve ■ *adj.* SLOPING sloping evenly and uniformly [Mid-17thC. Partly via Latin *gradient-*, the present participle stem of *gradi* 'to walk', (from *gradus* 'step'; see GRADE), and partly formed from GRADE on the model of 'quotient'.]

gradient post *n.* a small post with arms to represent gradients that is used beside a railway line to indicate where the gradient changes

gradin /gráydin/, **gradine** *n.* 1. STEP NEAR AN ALTAR a raised step above or behind an altar 2. STEP ON A SLOPE one of a set of steps arranged on a slope [Mid-19thC. Via French from Italian *gradino*, literally 'small step', from *grado* 'step', from Latin *gradus* (see GRADE).]

gradual /grájjoo əl/ *adj.* 1. HAPPENING SLOWLY proceeding or developing slowly by stages or degrees ○ *a gradual improvement* 2. CHANGING SLOWLY changing slowly ○ *a gradual incline* ■ *n.* CHR 1. SUNG VERSES in some Christian services, a set of scriptural verses sung after the epistle at Communion 2. RELIGIOUS MUSIC BOOK a book of music for the sung parts of the Communion Service [15thC. From medieval Latin *gradualis*, from Latin *gradus* 'step' (see GRADE).] —**gradualness** *n.*

gradualism /grájjoo əlizəm/ *n.* 1. GRADUAL CHANGE the principle, theory, or policy of allowing change, especially political change, to take place gradually rather than suddenly or drastically 2. GEOL THEORY OF ROCK CHANGE the theory that change in rocks and fossils happens by a gradual historical process — **gradualist** *n., adj.* —**gradualistic** /grájjoo ə lístik/ *adj.*

gradually /grájjoo əli/ *adv.* in a way that proceeds or develops slowly by steps or degrees

graduand /grájjoo and/ *n.* a student who is about to graduate from university [Late 19thC. From medieval Latin *graduandus*, literally 'sb on whom a degree is being conferred', from *graduare* (see GRADUATE).]

graduate *n.* /grájjoo ət/ 1. EDUC HOLDER OF A DEGREE sb who has obtained a first degree from a university or college 2. US EDUC SB WHO HAS COMPLETED A COURSE OF STUDIES sb who has obtained a diploma or degree after completing a course of study, e.g. from high school 3. US CONTAINER WITH MARKINGS a container such as a flask or tube with graduated markings that is used for measuring liquids ■ *v.* /grájjoo ayt/

(-ates, -ating, -ated) 1. *vi.* UNIV RECEIVE DEGREE to receive a degree from a university or college 2. *vi.* MOVE UP to move upwards from one level or activity to another ○ *I've graduated from skiing to snowboarding.* 3. *vt.* MARK WITH DEGREES OR LEVELS to mark sth with units of measurement 4. *vt.* SORT BY DIFFERENCES to sort sth into groups according to quality, size, or type ■ *adj.* /grájjoo ət/ EDUC = **postgraduate** —**graduator** /grájjoo aytər/ *n.*

graduated /grájjoo aytid/ *adj.* 1. IN STAGES divided into regular steps or stages 2. MEASURE MARKED WITH LINES marked with lines to enable measurement 3. FIN BASED ON INCOME used to describe or relating to a system of taxation under which those with the greatest income or assets pay the highest percentage of tax

graduation /grájjoo áysh'n/ *n.* 1. EDUC COMPLETION OF STUDIES the completion of a degree ○ *the number of credits required for graduation* 2. EDUC DEGREE CEREMONY a ceremony in which degrees are awarded to students who have successfully completed their studies ○ *attended her grandson's graduation* 3. MEASURE MARK ON AN INSTRUMENT a unit of measurement or division marked on an instrument 4. MEASURE DIVIDING PROCESS the process of marking or dividing sth according to quantity or quality

gradus /gráddəss/ *n.* 1. MUSIC MUSICAL EXERCISE BOOK a book of musical exercises arranged in order of difficulty 2. POETRY POETRY AID a dictionary designed to aid in writing Greek or Latin verse [Mid-18thC. Shortening of *Gradus ad Parnassum* 'Steps to Parnassus', the title of a manual of Latin composition for students.]

Graec- *prefix.* = **Graeco-** (*used before vowels*)

Graecise *vt.* = **Graecize**

Graecism /gréess izzəm/, **Grecism** *n.* 1. GREEK IDIOM an idiom of the Greek language used in another language, often for stylistic effect 2. GREEK STYLE AND SPIRIT Greek style, spirit, or characteristics as related to Greek culture, arts, architecture, and philosophy [Late 16thC. From medieval Latin *Græcismus*, from *Græcus* 'Greek'.]

Graecize /gréess īz/ (-cizes, -cizing, -cized), **Graecise** (-cises, -cising, -cised), **Grecize** (-cizes, -cizing, -cized) *vt.* to make sth Greek or Hellenic in style or form so that it becomes characteristic of the culture, civilization, or language of the ancient Greeks

Graeco- *prefix.* Greece, Greek ○ *Graeco-Roman* [From Latin *Graecus* (see GREEK)]

Graeco-Roman, **Greco-Roman** *adj.* 1. ANCIENT GREEK AND ROMAN relating to, or typical of, both ancient Greece and ancient Rome or the influence of their civilizations 2. WRESTLING RELATING TO A WRESTLING HOLD used to describe a style of wrestling allowing no hold below the waist and no use of the legs to obtain a fall

Graf /graaf/, **Steffi** (*b.* 1969) German tennis player. She turned professional at age 13, and went on to become only the fifth player to win the tennis Grand Slam (1988). She won five singles titles at Wimbledon.

graffiti /grə féeti/ *n.* drawings or writing that is scratched, painted, or sprayed on walls or other surfaces in public places (*takes a singular or plural verb*) [Mid-19thC. From Italian, plural of *graffito* (see GRAFFITO).]

graffitist /grə féetist/ *n.* sb who makes graffiti

graffito /grə féet ō/ (*plural* -ti /-ti/) *n.* 1. WRITTEN MARK ON WALL an instance of graffiti scratched, painted, or sprayed on a surface (*formal*) 2. ARCHAEOL ANCIENT INSCRIPTION an ancient drawing or inscription on a wall or rock surface [Mid-19thC. From Italian, literally 'scribbling', via *graffio* 'scratching' from, ultimately, Latin *graphium* 'stylus', from Greek *grapheion*, from *graphein* 'to write' (see GRAPHIC).]

graft¹ /graaft/ *n.* 1. SURG TRANSPLANTED TISSUE a piece of living tissue or an organ that is transplanted to a part of a patient's body, either from a donor or another part of the patient's body. Grafts are used to replace damaged or diseased tissue or organs. 2. BOT PLANT TISSUE JOINED TO ANOTHER PLANT a piece of living tissue from the shoot of a plant that is joined to the stem and root system of another plant, resulting in the growth of a single plant 3. SURG, BOT GRAFT LOCATION the place where tissue is implanted by means of a graft 4. BOT GRAFTED PLANT a plant that is the product

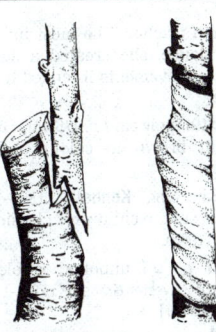
Graft

of a graft 5. JOINING PROCESS the process of joining one thing to another ■ *vt.* (grafts, grafting, grafted) 1. SURG TRANSPLANT TISSUE to transplant a piece of living tissue or an organ to a part of a patient's body. The tissue or organ may be either from a donor or from another part of the patient's body. 2. BOT UNITE PLANT TISSUE to join a piece of tissue from a part of one plant to the stem and root system of another plant to produce desirable characteristics such as vigour or resistance to disease in the new plant 3. JOIN DISSIMILAR THINGS to join two things that do not share a natural relationship or affinity for each other [15thC. Via Old French *grafe* 'pencil' (from a perceived similarity with the shoot of a plant), from late Latin *graphium* 'writing implement, stylus' (see GRAFFITO).] — **grafter** *n.*

graft² /graaft/ *n.* 1. HARD WORK hard work (*informal*) 2. CHEATING BY A CORRUPT INDIVIDUAL the use of dishonest or illegal means to gain money or property by sb in a position of power or in elected office 3. MONEY OBTAINED CORRUPTLY sth obtained illegally by taking advantage of high position or office ■ *v.* (grafts, grafting, grafted) (*informal*) 1. *vi.* WORK HARD to work hard 2. *vti.* GET BY DECEIT to obtain money or property by deceit [Mid-19thC. Origin uncertain: perhaps from GRAFT¹, the underlying idea being 'digging'.] —**grafter** *n.*

Grafton /gráftən/ city in northeastern New South Wales, Australia. It is an agricultural and regional service centre. Population: 16,562 (1996).

Katharine Graham

Graham /gráy əm/, **Katharine** (*b.* 1917) US newspaper executive. She was publisher of the *Washington Post* (1969–79). Born **Katharine Meyer**

Graham, Martha (1893–1991) US dancer, chore-

Martha Graham: Performing in *Judith* (1957)

ographer, and teacher. The most influential figure in modern dance, she created a dance language using flexible movements intended to express emotional power.

graham cracker /gráy əm-/ *n.* *US* a flat dry sweetened biscuit, light brown in colour and made from graham flour

Grahame /gráy əm/, **Kenneth** (1859–1932) British writer. He wrote the children's classic *The Wind in the Willows* (1908).

graham flour *n.* *US* unbolted whole-wheat flour [Named after Dr Sylvester *Graham* (1794–1851), an American dietary reformer]

Graham Land /gráy əm-/ northern section of the Antarctic peninsula, part of the British Antarctic Territory

Grahamstown /gráy əmz town/ city in Eastern Cape Province, southern South Africa, situated about 97 km/60 mi. northeast of Port Elizabeth. Population: 75,000 (1985).

grail /grayl/ *n.* sth that is eagerly sought after

Grail *n.* CHR according to medieval legend, the cup said to be used by Jesus Christ at the Last Supper, and by Joseph of Arimathea to collect his blood and sweat at the Crucifixion. It was sought after by medieval knights. [14thC. Via Old French *grael* from medieval Latin *gradalis* 'dish', of uncertain origin.]

grain /grayn/ *n.* **1.** AGRIC **CEREALS** cereal crops **2.** BOT **SMALL SEED** a small hard seed or fruit **3.** **TINY SINGLE PIECE** a tiny individual piece of sth, e.g. sand or salt **4.** **SMALL AMOUNT** a tiny amount of sth ○ *He doesn't have one grain of common sense!* **5.** **PATTERN IN MATERIAL, ESPECIALLY WOOD** the arrangement, direction, or pattern of the fibres in wood, leather, stone, or paper, typically aligned along a single axis ○ *When painting, follow the grain of the wood.* **6.** MEASURE **UNIT OF WEIGHT** the smallest unit of weight in the avoirdupois (1/7000 pound) and apothecaries' systems (1/5760 pound), equal to approximately 0.065 grams **7.** TEXTILES **DIRECTION OF THREADS** the line of the threads in a fabric **8.** INDUST **SIDE OF LEATHER** the side of leather from which hair has been removed **9.** CHEM **SMALL CRYSTAL** a small crystal, especially one forming part of a crystalline solid **10.** **BASIC QUALITY** the basic quality or characteristic of sth or sb **11.** PHOTOGRAPHY **PHOTOGRAPHIC PARTICLE** any of the small particles in a photographic emulsion that form an image, limiting the extent of possible enlargement **12.** TV, ELEC ENG **ELECTRICAL INTERFERENCE AFFECTING TELEVISION IMAGE** the granular effect on a television image caused by unwanted electrical signals **13.** SPACE TECH **PROPELLANT FOR ROCKET** a mass of solid propellant for a rocket or missile **14.** CHEM **DYE** red or purple dye made from cochineal insects (*archaic*) ■ *v.* (**grains, graining, grained**) **1.** *vti.* **GRANULATE** to break down into small particles or grains, or make sth break down into small particles **2.** *vt.* **MIMIC PATTERN OF WOOD** to paint or stain a material with a pattern similar to wood or leather **3.** *vt.* CRAFT **TREAT LEATHER** to soften or raise the pattern of leather **4.** *vt.* INDUST **REMOVE HAIR** to remove the hair from leather **5.** *vt.* **GIVE A GRAINY APPEARANCE** to give sth a rough or granular appearance **6.** *vt.* AGRIC **FEED GRAIN** to feed grain to an animal [13thC. Via Old French from Latin *granum* 'seed'. Ultimately from an Indo-European word that is also the ancestor of *corn* and *kernel*.] —**grainer** *n.* ◇ **go against the grain** be contrary to sb's natural inclinations, wishes, or feelings

WORD KEY: ORIGIN

The Latin word *granum* from which **grain** is derived is also the source of English *filigree, garner, granary, grange, granite, gravy, grenade, ingrained,* and *pomegranate.*

grain alcohol *n.* alcohol made from a fermented cereal

grained /graynd/ *adj.* having grain of a particular type

grainfield /gráyn feeld/ *n.* a field in which grain is grown

Grainger /gráynjər/, **Percy** (1882–1961) Australian-born US pianist and composer. His 400 compositions, many based on folk music, include *Green Bushes* (1921) and *Shepherds Hey* (1922). Born **George Percy Grainger.** Full name **Percy Aldridge Grainger**

grains of paradise *npl.* the peppery brown seeds of a West African plant, formerly used in veterinary medicine and for adding piquancy to mulled wine and other drinks *Aframomum melegueta*

grain weevil *n.* a small beetle that feeds on and damages cereal grains. Latin name: *Calendra granaria.*

grain whisky *n.* whisky that is made from any fermented cereal other than malted barley

grainy /gráyni/ (**-ier, -iest**) *adj.* **1.** PHOTOGRAPHY **NOT CLEAR** unclear and poorly defined because of a large grain size or overenlargement **2.** **RESEMBLING GRAINS** resembling or composed of grains **3.** **NOT SMOOTH** having a granular rather than a smooth texture **4.** **LIKE WOOD GRAIN** resembling the grain of wood, leather, stone, or paper —**graininess** *n.*

grallatorial /grállə táwri əl/ *adj.* used to describe a bird that has long legs adapted for wading [Mid-19thC. Via modern Latin *grallatorius* from Latin *grallator* 'stilt-walker', from *grallae* 'stilts'.]

gram[1] /gram/ *n.* a metric unit of mass, equal to 0.001 kg or equivalent to approximately 0.035 oz. Symbol g [Late 18thC. Via French *gramme* and late Latin *gramma* from Greek *gramma* 'small weight'.]

gram[2] /gram/ *n.* any of various edible beans, e.g. the chickpea, lentil, or mung bean, used as food [Early 18thC. Via obsolete Portuguese *gram* from Latin *granum* (see GRAIN).]

gram. *abbr.* **1.** grammar **2.** GRAM grammatical

-gram *suffix.* **1.** sth written, drawn, or recorded ○ *trigram* ○ *oscillogram* **2.** a message delivered by a third party ○ *telegram* ○ *kissagram* [From Greek *gramma*; related to *graphein* 'to write' (see GRAPHIC)]

grama /graámə/, **gramma, grama grass, gramma grass** *n.* a pasture grass that grows in western North America and South America. Genus: *Bouteloua.* [Mid-19thC. Via American Spanish from, ultimately, Latin *gramen* 'grass' (see GRAMINEOUS).]

gramarye /grámməri/, **gramary** *n.* (*archaic*) **1.** **MAGIC** magic and enchantment **2.** **KNOWLEDGE** skill in grammar or learning [14thC. From Anglo-Norman *gramarie* 'Latin grammar', a variant of Old French *gramaire* (see GRAMMAR).]

gram atom *n.* a quantity of a chemical element whose mass in grams is the same as its atomic weight

gram calorie *n.* = **calorie** *n.* 1

gram equivalent *n.* the quantity of a substance whose mass in grams is the same as its chemical equivalent weight

gramercy /grə múrssi/ *interj.* (*archaic*) **1.** **EXPRESSION OF THANKS** used as an expression of thanks **2.** **EXPRESSION OF WONDER** used as an expression of surprise or wonder [14thC. From Old French *grant merci*, literally '(God give you) great reward'.]

gramicidin /grámmi sídin/, **gramicidin D** *n.* an antibiotic too toxic for internal use but widely sold as an ingredient of various ointments, creams, and eye and ear drops [Mid-20thC. Coined from GRAM-POSITIVE + -CIDE + -IN.]

gramineous /grə mínni əss/, **graminaceous** /grámmi náyshəss/ *adj.* **1.** **IN GRASS FAMILY** belonging to the grass family **2.** **GRASSY** resembling grass (*technical*) [Mid-17thC. Via Latin *gramineus* from *gramin-*, the stem of *gramen* 'grass, fodder'. Ultimately from an Indo-European word meaning 'to devour', ancestor also of English *cress, gastric,* and *gangrene.*] —**gramineousness** *n.*

graminivorous /grámmi nívvərəss/ *adj.* that feeds on grass (*technical*) [Mid-18thC. Coined from Latin *gramin-*, the stem of *gramen* 'grass' (see GRAMINEOUS) + -VOROUS.]

gramma /graámə/ *n.* BOT = **grama**

grammar /grámmər/ *n.* **1.** **RULES FOR LANGUAGE** the system of rules by which words are formed and put together to make sentences **2.** **PARTICULAR SET OF LANGUAGE RULES** the rules for speaking or writing a particular language, or a particular analysis of the rules of language ○ *Spanish grammar* ○ *case grammar* **3.** **QUALITY OF LANGUAGE** the spoken or written form of language sb uses, as related to accepted standards of correctness **4.** **GRAMMAR BOOK** a book dealing with the grammar of a language **5.** **ANALYTICAL SYSTEM** a systematic treatment of the elementary principles of a subject and their interrelationships [14thC. Via Old French *gramaire* and Latin *grammatica* from, ultimately, Greek *grammatikos*, 'relating to letters', from *grammat-*, the stem of *gramma* 'written character, letter' (see -GRAM).]

grammarian /grə máiri ən/ *n.* **1.** **GRAMMAR EXPERT** sb who is very skilled in grammar **2.** **WRITER ON GRAMMAR** a writer on grammar, especially one who espouses prescriptive rules

grammar school *n.* **1.** **ACADEMIC SECONDARY SCHOOL** in Britain and some Commonwealth countries, a state secondary school teaching children who are traditionally selected for high academic ability **2.** *US* **GRADE SCHOOL** an elementary school

grammatical /grə máttik'l/ *adj.* **1.** **IN GRAMMAR** in or relating to the rules of grammar **2.** **CORRECT IN TERMS OF GRAMMAR** conforming to the accepted rules of grammar [Early 16thC. Via late Latin *grammaticalis* from, ultimately, Greek *grammatikos* (see GRAMMAR).] —**grammaticality** /grə mátti kálləti/ *n.* —**grammatically** /grə máttikli/ *adv.* —**grammaticalness** *n.*

grammatology /grámmə tólləji/ *n.* the study of writing systems [Mid-20thC. Coined from Greek *grammat-*, the stem of *gramma* 'written letter' + -LOGY.] —**grammatologic** /grámmətə lójjik/ *adj.* —**grammatological** /-lójjik'l/ *adj.* —**grammatologist** /grámmə tólləjist/ *n.*

gramme *n.* = **gram**

gram molecule *n.* a quantity of a molecular chemical compound whose mass in grams is the same as its molecular weight —**gram-molecular** *adj.*

Grammy /grámmi/ *tdmk.* a service mark for an award given annually for achievement in the recorded music industry

Gram-negative, **gram-negative** *adj.* used to describe bacteria that lose the colour of a gentian violet stain, used in Gram's method of classifying bacteria

gramophone /grámmə fōn/ *n.* a record player (*dated*) [Late 19thC. Alteration of PHONOGRAM.]

grampa /grám paa/ *n.* a grandfather (*informal; usually used by or to children*) [Contraction of GRANDPAPA]

Grampian Mountains /grámpi ən-/ mountain range in central Scotland that forms a natural division between the Highlands and Lowlands. The highest peak is Ben Nevis, 1,343 m/4,406 ft.

Grampian Region /grámpi ən-/ former region in northeastern Scotland that included the present-day council areas of Aberdeenshire and Moray

Grampians /grámpi ənz/ group of rugged red sandstone mountains in western Victoria, Australia. The highest peak is Mount William, 1,168 m/3,832 ft.

Grampians National Park /grámpi ənz-/ national park in western Victoria, Australia, established in 1984. It contains the Grampians, a group of rugged sandstone mountains. Area: 1,670 sq. km/645 sq. mi.

Gram-positive, **gram-positive** *adj.* used to describe bacteria that retain the colour of a gentian violet stain, according to Gram's method of classifying bacteria

gramps /gramps/ *n.* a grandfather (*informal; usually used by or to children*) [From a contraction of GRANDPAPA]

grampus /grámpəss/ (*plural* **-pus** *or* **-puses**) *n.* a large grey dolphin with a blunt snout, short flippers, and a tall dark grey fin. It is widely distributed throughout warm seas. Latin name: *Grampus griseus.* [Early 16thC. Alteration of Old French *graspeis*, from medieval Latin *crassus piscis*, literally 'fat fish'.]

Gram's method /grámz-/, **Gram's stain** *n.* a technique used to classify bacteria according to their ability to lose or retain the colour of a gentian violet stain, applied within the framework of an established test procedure. The retention or loss of stain indicates a particular cell-wall structure and distinguishes two types of bacteria. [Late 19thC. Named after the Danish physician H. C. J. *Gram* (1853–1938), who developed it.]

gran /gran/ *n.* a grandmother (*informal; usually used by or to children*) [Mid-19thC. Shortening.]

grana plural of **granum**

Granada /grə naádə/ city and capital of Granada Province in the autonomous region of Andalusia, southern Spain. It is the site of the Alhambra, a Moorish palace and citadel. Population: 272,738 (1995).

granadilla /gránnə dílla/ *n.* **1.** PLANTS **PASSION FRUIT PLANT** a tropical passionflower with edible egg-shaped fruit. Latin name: *Passiflora quadrangularis.* **2.** FOOD **FRUIT OF THE GRANADILLA** the fruit that grows on the granadilla [Early 17thC. From Spanish, literally 'little pomegranate', formed from *granada* 'pomegranate'.]

granary /gránnəri/ (*plural* **-ries**) *n.* **1.** GRAIN WAREHOUSE a warehouse or storeroom for grain **2.** GRAIN-GROWING REGION a region where grain is abundant [Late 16thC. From Latin *granarium*, from *granum* (see GRAIN).]

Granary *tdmk.* a trademark for bread that contains whole grains of wheat and has a nutty flavour

Gran Chaco /gran chákō/ thinly populated region in south-central South America, extending from southern Bolivia through Paraguay to northern Argentina. Area: 647,500 sq. km/250,000 sq. mi.

grand /grand/ *adj.* **1.** OUTSTANDING outstanding and impressive in appearance, extent, or style ○ *making a grand entrance* **2.** IMPRESSIVE impressive, ambitious, and far-reaching ○ *a grand plan* **3.** WORTHY OF RESPECT worthy of great respect by virtue of exceptional ability or high rank ○ *among the grandest orchestras of our time* **4.** HAUGHTY self-important or haughty ○ *His friends always act a bit grand around me.* **5.** WONDERFUL wonderful, enjoyable, and memorable ○ *We had a grand time.* **6.** PRINCIPAL main or principal ○ *And now we move into the Grand Banqueting Hall.* **7.** TERRIFIC respected and admirable (*informal*) ○ *She's a grand lass.* ■ *n.* (*informal*) **1.** MONEY **1,000 POUNDS** a thousand pounds ○ *made ten grand on the deal* **2.** MUSIC = **grand piano** [Early 16thC. Via Old French from Latin *grandis* 'full grown', of unknown origin.] —**grandly** *adv.* —**grandness** *n.*

grand- *prefix.* one generation further removed ○ *grandniece* [From GRAND]

granda /gránda/ *n.* UK, Scotland, Ireland a name for a grandfather (*regional informal*) [Variant of GRANDDAD]

grandad *n.* = granddad

grandaddy *n.* = granddaddy

grandam /grándəm/, **grandame** *n.* a grandmother or woman who is no longer young (*archaic*) [13thC. From Anglo-French *graund dame* 'grandmother', literally 'great lady'.]

grand-aunt *n.* = great-aunt

grandbaby /gránd baybi/ *n.* a grandchild who is still a baby

Grand Bahama /gránd bə haámə/ island of the western Bahamas in the Atlantic Ocean off the eastern coast of Florida. Population: 40,898 (1990). Area: 1,114 sq. km/430 sq. mi.

Grand Banks /-bángks/ shallow section of the Atlantic Ocean, off southeastern Newfoundland, Canada, that is an important fishing region. Area: 282,500 sq. km/109,000 sq. mi.

Grand Canal main thoroughfare of Venice, Italy. There are almost 200 palaces on the banks of the canal. Length: 3 km/2 mi.

Grand Canyon

Grand Canyon /-kánnyən/ spectacular natural gorge carved by the Colorado River in northwestern Arizona. Its width varies from 8 to 29 km/5 to 18 mi., and its depth can exceed 1.6 km/1 mi. Length: 443 km/227 mi.

Grand Canyon National Park national park in northern Arizona, established in 1919. Its primary feature is the Grand Canyon of the Colorado River. Area: 4,930 sq. km/1,904 sq. mi.

grandchild /gránd chīld/ (*plural* **-children** /-children/) *n.* a child of your son or daughter

Grand Coulee Dam /-koóli-/ dam in Washington State on the Columbia River, 145 km/90 mi. west of Spokane. Completed in 1942, it is the world's largest concrete structure and a major source of hydroelectric power. Height: 168 m/550 ft.

granddad /grán dad/, **grandad** *n.* (*informal*) **1.** GRANDFATHER a grandfather **2.** TERM FOR MAN PAST MIDDLE AGE used as a rather disrespectful name for a man of advanced years (*sometimes considered offensive*)

granddaddy /grán dadi/ (*plural* **-dies**), **grandaddy** (*plural* **-dies**) *n.* **1.** GRANDFATHER a grandfather (*informal*) **2.** FIRST ONE sth considered the oldest, first, or most important of its time

granddaughter /grán dawtər/ *n.* a daughter of your son or daughter

grand duchess *n.* **1.** GRAND DUKE'S SPOUSE the wife or widow of a grand duke **2.** HIGH NOBLEWOMAN a woman who holds a rank just below that of a queen **3.** RUSSIAN PRINCESS in tsarist Russia, a daughter of a tsar, or a daughter of a tsar's descendants

grand duchy *n.* a country, territory, or estate that has a grand duke or a grand duchess as its ruler

grand duke *n.* **1.** HIGH-RANKING NOBLEMAN a nobleman who holds a rank just below that of a king **2.** RUSSIAN NOBLE in tsarist Russia, a brother, son, uncle, or nephew of a tsar

grande dame /graáNd dám/ *n.* a socially important, dignified, and usually older woman [From French, 'great lady']

Grande Dixence Dam /-díks'nss-/ concrete dam on the River Dixence, southwestern Switzerland. Completed in 1962, it is one of the world's highest dams. Height: 284 m/932 ft.

grandee /gran deé/ *n.* **1.** SB WITH POWER TO PERSUADE sb highly influential and respected, especially a politician **2.** SPANISH OR PORTUGUESE NOBLEMAN a high-ranking Spanish or Portuguese nobleman [Late 16thC. Via Spanish and Portuguese *grande* from Latin *grandis* 'great' (source of English *grand*).]

grandeur /gránjər/ *n.* the quality of being great or grand and very impressive [Early 16thC. From French, formed from *grand* (see GRAND).]

grandfather /gránd faathər/ *n.* **1.** FATHER OF YOUR PARENT the father of your father or mother **2.** ANCESTOR a man who is sb's ancestor **3.** USED TO ADDRESS MAN used as a name for a man considered to be advanced in years (*dated informal*) **4.** W Country WOODLOUSE a woodlouse (*informal*) —**grandfatherly** *adj.*

grandfather clause *n.* **1.** HIST VOTING RIGHTS CLAUSE a clause in some US Southern states' constitutions that waived electoral literacy requirements for descendants of those allowed to vote before 1867, in effect enabling illiterate white people to vote while excluding illiterate Black people. It was declared unconstitutional in 1915. **2.** LAW EXEMPTING CLAUSE a clause in prohibitive legislation that makes exceptions for those already engaged in the activity that it bans or regulates

Grandfather clock

grandfather clock *n.* a large clock in a tall case that stands on the floor. = **longcase clock**

grand final *n.* the last round in a series of contests, competitions, or sports matches

grand finale *n.* the closing spectacular scene or section of a performance or other show

Grand Guignol /gaáN gee nyól/ *n.* THEATRE a sensational drama, often structured in short scenes with violent or horrific subject matter, that aims to horrify its audience [Early 20thC. From *Le Grand Guignol*, the name of a theatre in Paris that specialized in short sensational dramas.] —**grand guignol** *adj.*

grandiloquence /gran dílləkwənss/ *n.* a pompous or lofty manner of speaking or writing [Late 16thC. Formed from Latin *grandiloquus* 'speaking grandly', from *grandis* 'great' + *loqui* 'to speak'.] —**grandiloquent** *adj.* —**grandiloquently** *adv.*

grandiose /grándi ōss/ *adj.* **1.** PRETENTIOUS AND POMPOUS pretentious, pompous, and imposing **2.** MAGNIFICENT impressive and magnificent **3.** OVERLY COMPLEX too complicated and unrealistic ○ *a grandiose plan* [Mid-19thC. Via French from Italian *grandioso* 'imposing', from *grande* 'great', from Latin *grandis*.] —**grandiosely** *adv.* —**grandioseness** *n.* —**grandiosity** /grándi óssəti/ *n.*

grandioso /grándi óss ō/ *adj.*, *adv.* in a grand or imposing style (*used as a musical direction*) [Late 19thC. From Italian, 'grandly'.]

grand jury *n.* in US and Canadian law, a panel of 12 to 23 jurors called to decide whether there are grounds for a criminal prosecution in a case. Grand juries began in England in the 13th century and were abolished in 1948. —**grand juror** *n.*

grandkid /gránkid/ *n.* a grandchild (*informal*)

grand larceny *n.* a robbery or theft of money or property with a value over the amount specified by law to constitute petty larceny

grandma /grán maa/ *n.* a name for a grandmother (*informal*) [Late 18thC. Shortening.]

grand mal /graán mál/ *n.* a serious form of epilepsy in which there is loss of consciousness and severe convulsions. ◊ **petit mal** [From French, literally 'great illness']

Grand Manan Island /-mə nán-/ island at the entrance to the Bay of Fundy in southwestern New Brunswick, southeastern Canada. Area: 137 sq. km/53 sq. mi.

grand master, **grandmaster** *n.* **1.** CHESS TOP CHESS PLAYER a champion chess player who plays at an international level **2.** SB OUTSTANDING sb who is at the highest level of ability or achievement in a particular field **3.** GROUP HEAD a head of a brotherhood of knights, or of a fraternal organization such as the Masons

grandmother /grán muthər/ *n.* **1.** PARENT'S MOTHER the mother of your father or mother **2.** ANCESTOR a woman who is sb's ancestor **3.** USED TO ADDRESS WOMAN used to address a woman of advanced years (*dated informal; sometimes considered offensive*) —**grandmotherly** *adj.*

grandmother clock *n.* a clock in a tall case that stands on the floor, smaller than a grandfather clock

Grand National *n.* a famous steeplechase, held annually at Aintree in Liverpool since 1839. Competitors have to negotiate 31 fences around a 7.2 km/4 mi. 855 yd racecourse.

grandnephew /grán néf yoo/ *n.* a son of sb's nephew or niece

grandniece /grán neéss/ *n.* a daughter of sb's nephew or niece

grand old man *n.* a man usually past middle age who is respected for his contribution to some field of activity such as politics, music, or sport ○ *the grand old man of British jazz*

grand opera *n.* an opera on a serious dramatic theme in which all the words are sung and there is no spoken dialogue

grandpa /grán paa/ *n.* (*informal*) **1.** GRANDFATHER a name for a grandfather **2.** MAN PAST MIDDLE AGE a slightly disrespectful name for man of advanced years (*sometimes considered offensive*)

grandpapa /gránpə paa/ *n.* a grandfather (*dated*)

grandparent /gránd pairənt/ *n.* the mother or father of your mother or father —**grandparental** /gránd pə rént'l/ *adj.* —**grandparenthood** /gránd pairənt hŏŏd/ *n.*

Grand piano

grand piano *n.* a large piano in which the strings are fixed horizontally behind the keyboard in a long harp-shaped frame

Grand Pré /gron práy, graaN-/ village in central Nova Scotia, Canada, on Minas Basin, the site of Grand Pré National Historic Park

Grand Prix /grón prée/ (*plural* **Grand Prix** *or* **Grands Prix** /grón prée/) *n.* **1. IMPORTANT CAR RACE** any one of a number of important international annual races for racing cars, held to decide the world motor-racing championship **2. IMPORTANT SPORTS COMPETITION** any one of various competitions in a variety of sports that have the same importance and prestige as a Grand Prix in motor-racing [From French, literally 'big prize']

Grand Remonstrance *n.* the document issued by the Long Parliament in 1640 that listed problems with the King's government, abuses of power already rectified, and desired reforms

grandsire /gránd sīr/ *n.* **1. GRANDFATHER** a grandfather (*archaic*) **2. ANCESTOR** a man who is sb's ancestor (*archaic or literary; often used in the plural*) **3. MAN PAST MIDDLE AGE** a man of advanced years (*archaic*) **4. METHOD OF CHANGE-RINGING** in bell-ringing, a method of change-ringing using an odd number of bells

grand slam *n.* **1. SPORTS WINNING OF ALL MAJOR COMPETITIONS** in some sports, e.g. tennis and golf, the winning of all of a specified group of major competitions by one player or team in one year **2. SPORTS MAJOR COMPETITION** any one of a specified group of major competitions in a particular sport **3. CARDS WINNING OF ALL TRICKS** in bridge and similar card games, the winning of all 13 tricks in a game by one player or pair of players, or a contract to do so **4. BASEBALL 4 RUNS** in baseball, a home run made when all the bases are loaded

grandson /gránd sun/ *n.* a son of your son or daughter

grandstand /gránd stand/ *n.* **1. STRUCTURE FOR SPECTATORS' SEATS** an open building or platform, usually with a roof, containing rows of seats for spectators at a sports stadium or racecourse **2. SPECTATORS IN A GRANDSTAND** the spectators sitting in a grandstand ■ *adj.* **UNOBSTRUCTED** clear, close, and unobstructed ○ *We had a grandstand view of the proceedings.* ■ *vi.* (**-stands, -standing, -standed**) *US, Can* **SEEK ATTENTION OR ADMIRATION** to show off in order to impress people, especially spectators ○ *Stop your grandstanding and sit down, so we can watch the show.* —**grandstander** *n.*

grandstand finish *n.* a finish to a race or competition that is exciting because the outcome is unclear until the very end [So called because the outcome is decided at the finish line, which is typically in front of the grandstand]

grand total *n.* a final and complete total of all amounts to be added

grand tour *n.* **1. TOUR OF EUROPEAN CITIES** in the past, a tour of the main European cities and cultural centres undertaken by young upper-class Englishmen as a way of completing their education **2. TOUR OF SEVERAL PLACES** a trip or tour that takes in visits to several places, or a visit that allows a complete inspection of all parts of one place

Grand Trunk Canal canal linking the rivers Mersey and Trent in England. It is also linked to the Bridge-water Canal. Length: 150 km/93 mi.

grand-uncle *n.* = **great-uncle**

Grand Union Canal canal in southern and central England connecting the River Thames near London with the Midlands

grange /graynj/ *n.* **1. LARGE FARMHOUSE** a large farmhouse or country house with other buildings such as stables or barns attached to it **2. GRANARY OR BARN** a large farm building used for storing grain or hay (*archaic*) [13thC. Via French from medieval Latin *granica villa*, literally 'grain house' (the original sense in English), from Latin *granum* (see **GRAIN**).]

Grange *n.* the Patrons of Husbandry, an association of US farmers founded in 1867 for their mutual support

grangerise *vt.* = **grangerize**

grangerize /gráynjə rīz/ (**-izes, -izing, -ized**), **grangerise** (**-ises, -ising, -ised**) *vt.* **1. INSERT BOOK'S PICTURES INTO OTHER BOOK** in the past, to illustrate a book with pictures cut out of another book or books **2. TAKE BOOK'S PICTURES FOR OTHER BOOK** in the past, to cut pictures out of a book or books in order to illustrate another one [Late 19thC. Named after the English biographer James *Granger* (1723–76), whose *Biographical History of England* had blank pages for illustrations.] —**grangerizer** *n.*

grani- *prefix.* grain, seed ○ *granivorous* [From Latin *granum* (see **GRAIN**)]

granita /grə néetə/ *n.* a type of sweetened flavoured water ice with a grainy texture, sometimes served as a refresher between courses rather than as a dessert [Mid-19thC. From Italian, the feminine form of *granito* (see **GRANITE**).]

granite /gránnit/ *n.* **1. MINERALS COARSE-GRAINED IGNEOUS ROCK** a coarse-grained igneous rock made up of feldspar, mica, and at least 20 per cent quartz. It is used extensively in building. **2. TOUGHNESS** determination or toughness of character **3. SPORTS STONE USED IN CURLING** the rounded stone used in the sport of curling [Mid-17thC. Via Italian *granito*, literally 'grainy', from, ultimately, Latin *granum* (see **GRAIN**).] —**granitic** /grə níttik/ *adj.* —**granitoid** /gránni toyd/ *adj.*

graniteware /gránnit wair/ *n.* **1. SPECKLED POTTERY** a type of earthenware with a speckled glaze that gives it the appearance of granite **2. SPECKLED IRON DISHES** iron articles, e.g. pots and bowls, coated with a glaze that gives a finish with the appearance of granite

granivorous /grə nívvərəss/ *adj.* ZOOL that eats seeds

granny /gránni/ (*plural* **-nies**), **grannie** *n.* **1. GRANDMOTHER** a grandmother (*informal*) **2. WOMAN OF ADVANCED YEARS** a slightly disrespectful name for a woman of advanced years **3. FUSSY PERSON** an annoyingly fastidious or fussy person (*insult*) **4. BUILDING CHIMNEY COVERING** a revolving cap on a chimney pot **5. = granny knot 6.** *NZ* **GRANNY SMITH** a Granny Smith apple (*informal*) [Mid-17thC. Shortening of *grannam*, a common pronunciation of **GRANDAM**.]

granny annexe *n.* = **granny flat**

granny-bashing *n.* violence against or an assault on a woman of advanced years, especially for the purpose of robbery (*informal*)

granny bond *n.* a type of savings bond that is index-linked to inflation. Originally, such bonds could be bought only by people over the official retirement age.

granny dress *n.* a type of long dress in a style considered to have been worn by earlier generations of women that was popular in the late 1960s and early 1970s

granny-dumping *n.* the abandonment of a senior citizen who is in deteriorating mental or physical health by a family member or members in a public place (*disapproving*)

granny flat *n.* a small self-contained flat that is in or attached to a house and is considered suitable for an elderly parent to live in independently of the rest of the family. US term **mother-in-law apartment**

granny gear *n.* the lowest gear on a bicycle that makes it possible to pedal up steep inclines (*informal*)

granny glasses *npl.* spectacles consisting of small lenses set in gold or steel frames

granny knot *n.* a reef knot incorrectly tied and therefore likely to come apart

Granny Smith *n.* a type of eating apple with green skin and crisp white flesh [Late 19thC. From the nickname of Maria Ann *Smith* (1801–70), who first grew the apple in her garden in Sydney, Australia.]

granny specs *npl.* = **granny glasses** (*informal*)

grano- *prefix.* granite ○ *granolith* [Via German from, ultimately, Italian *granito* (see **GRANITE**)]

granodiorite /gránnō dī ə rīt/ *n.* a coarse-grained igneous rock containing plagioclase and orthoclase, whose composition is intermediate between granite and diorite —**granodioritic** /gránnō dī ə ríttik/ *adj.*

granola /grə nólə/ *n.* a breakfast cereal consisting of rolled oats mixed with other ingredients such as brown sugar, dried fruit, nuts, honey, and sesame seeds [Early 20thC. Originally a trade name.]

granolith /gránnə lith/ *n.* a paving material made from cement and granite chips —**granolithic** /gránnə líthik/ *adj.*

granophyre /gránn ō fīr/ *n.* a medium-grained light-coloured igneous rock consisting mainly of crystals of feldspar and quartz that have crystallized together [Late 19thC. From German *Granophyr*, from *Granit* 'granite' + *Porphyr* 'porphyry'.] —**granophyric** /gránn ō fírrik/ *adj.*

Gran Paradiso /gram párrə deézō/ mountain in the Western Alps, northern Italy, situated within the Gran Paradiso National Park. Height: 4,061 m/13,323 ft.

grant /graant/ *vt.* (**grants, granting, granted**) **1. COMPLY WITH A REQUEST** to carry out or comply with a request for sth **2. ALLOW STH AS A FAVOUR OR PRIVILEGE** to give sb sth or allow sb to have sth, especially as a favour or privilege ○ *She refused to grant any interviews.* **3. AGREE THE TRUTH OF STH** to acknowledge that what sb else has said, or what a person thinks sb else is thinking, is true ○ *He's a hard worker, I grant you, but hardly managerial material.* **4. LAW TRANSFER STH LEGALLY** to transfer property or rights in a legal transaction ■ *n.* **1. MONEY GIVEN FOR A PURPOSE** a sum of money given by the government, a local authority, or some other organization to fund such things as education, research, or home improvements **2. GIFT** anything that is given to sb as a favour or privilege, or the giving of it ○ *a land grant* **3. LAW TRANSACTION** sth transferred from one person to another in a legal transaction, or the transaction itself **4. LAW TRANSFER DOCUMENT** a legal document recording a transaction in which sth is transferred from one person to another **5. AREA OF LAND** in the United States, a unit of territory in New Hampshire, Maine, or Vermont [13thC. From Old French *granter*, a variant of *creanter* 'to guarantee', via assumed Vulgar Latin *credentare* from, ultimately, Latin *credere* (see **CREDIBLE**).] —**grantable** *adj.* —**granter** *n.* ◇ **take sb for granted** to fail to realize or appreciate the value of sb ◇ **take sth for granted 1.** to assume that sth is true without checking **2.** to fail to appreciate or realize the value of sth

———— WORD KEY: SYNONYMS ————
See Synonyms at *give*.

Ulysses S. Grant

Grant /graant/, **Ulysses S.** (1822–85) US statesman and 18th president of the United States. As the Union army's greatest general, he led his troops to victory in the US Civil War. His Republican administration

(1869–77) is regarded as one of the most corrupt in US history. Full name **Hiram Ulysses Simpson Grant**

grant aid *n.* financial help provided to a school or other educational establishment by central government

grant-aid *vt.* to give grant aid to sb or sth

grant-aided school *n.* a school in which independent managers control the appointment of the teachers and the religious instruction given, and are required to pay part of the upkeep costs

granted /graántid/ *adv., conj.* used when acknowledging the truth of sth sb has said or is thinking

grantee /graán teé/ *n.* sb to whom sth is transferred in a legal transaction

Granth /grunt/ *n.* one of the sacred scriptures of Sikhism [Late 18thC. Via Hindi from Sanskrit *granthaḥ* 'book', literally 'binding'.]

Grantham /gránthəm/ historic market town in Lincolnshire, eastern England. Population: 32,200 (1991).

grant-in-aid (*plural* **grants-in-aid**) *n.* a sum of money given as funding by a central government to a local government, or by central or local government to a department or institution

grant-maintained school *n.* a self-governing school funded directly by central government rather than a local education authority

grantor /graán táwr, graán̄tər/ *n.* sb from whom sth is transferred in a legal transaction

granular /gránnyoŏlər/ *adj.* **1.** MADE UP OF GRAINS consisting of small grains or particles **2.** WITH TEXTURE OF GRANULES appearing to consist of or be covered in small grains or particles [Late 18thC. Formed from late Latin *granulum* (see GRANULE).] —**granularity** /gránnyoŏ lárrəti/ *n.* —**granularly** /gránnyoŏlərli/ *adv.*

granulate /gránnyoŏ layt/ (**-lates, -lating, -lated**) *v.* **1.** *vti.* MAKE INTO SMALL PARTICLES to form or cause sth to form into small grains or particles **2.** *vti.* BECOME OR MAKE GRAINY IN TEXTURE to become rough and grainy in texture or appearance, or give sth a rough and grainy texture or appearance **3.** *vi.* MED FORM HEALING WOUND TISSUE to form the type of tissue that grows over healing wounds (**granulation tissue**) [Mid-17thC. Formed from late Latin *granulum* (see GRANULE).] —**granulative** /gránnyoŏlətiv/ *adj.* —**granulator** /gránnyoŏ laytər/ *n.*

granulated sugar /gránnyoŏ laytid-/ *n.* white sugar in the form of a coarse powder with large particles

granulation /gránnyoŏ láysh'n/ *n.* **1.** MAKING OF SMALL PARTICLES the formation of small grains or particles **2.** GRAINY TEXTURE a grainy texture or appearance **3.** SMALL LUMP any one of the individual small lumps that, together, give sth a rough grainy texture or appearance **4.** MED FORMATION OF TISSUE OVER HEALING WOUND the formation of the type of tissue that grows over healing wounds (**granulation tissue**) or the tissue itself **5.** ASTRON CELLULAR APPEARANCE OF SUN'S SURFACE the cellular appearance of the Sun's disc when seen at high magnification [Early 17thC. Formed from late Latin *granulum* (see GRANULE).]

granulation tissue *n.* connective tissue in the form of small grainy particles along with masses of tiny blood vessels that forms over healing wounds

granule /grán yool/ *n.* **1.** SMALL PARTICLE a small grain or particle **2.** GEOL SMALL ROCK FRAGMENT a mineral or rock particle that is the size of a small grain **3.** ASTRON TEMPORARY BRIGHT REGION ON SUN'S SURFACE a temporary bright region on the Sun's surface, typically having an approximate diameter of 1,000 km/320 mi [Mid-17thC. From late Latin *granulum*, literally 'small seed', from Latin *granum* (see GRAIN).]

granulite /gránnyoŏ līt/ *n.* a coarse-grained metamorphic rock in which the minerals are of roughly equal size —**granulitic** /gránnyoŏ líttik/ *adj.*

granulocyte /gránnyoŏlə sīt/ *n.* a white blood cell that contains many granular particles in its cytoplasm —**granulocytic** /gránnyoŏlə síttik/ *adj.*

granuloma /gránnyoŏ lómə/ (*plural* **-mas** *or* **-mata** /-lómətə/) *n.* a small mass of granulation tissue caused by chronic infection —**granulomatous** *adj.*

granulose /gránnyoŏ lōss/ *adj.* **1.** MADE UP OF SMALL PARTICLES consisting of small grains or particles **2.** WITH THE TEXTURE OF GRANULES appearing to consist of or be covered in small grains or particles

granulosis /gránnyoŏ lóssiss/ *n.* a virus disease affecting insect larvae in which the infected cells contain tiny granular particles

granum /gráynəm/ (*plural* **-na** /gráynə/) *n.* a stack of thin layers in a chloroplast in which the green pigment chlorophyll is contained [Late 19thC. Via German from Latin, 'seed' (see GRAIN).]

Granville-Barker /gránvil baárkər/, **Harley** (1877–1946) British actor, producer, and dramatist. He managed London theatres, wrote plays about social problems, and published a famous series of prefaces to Shakespeare's plays (1927–46).

Grape

grape /grayp/ *n.* **1.** EDIBLE FRUIT an edible green or purple berry with sweet juicy flesh that grows in bunches on a vine. It may be eaten fresh or used to make wine or grape juice. Raisins, sultanas, and currants are dried grapes. **2.** = **grapevine** *n.* **1** **3.** PLANT WITH FRUIT RESEMBLING GRAPES a plant that produces fruit resembling grapes in some way ○ *Oregon grape* **4.** BEVERAGES WINE the drink wine (*humorous*) **5.** ARMS = **grapeshot** **6.** COLOURS DARK PURPLE COLOUR a dark purple colour ■ *adj.* COLOURS DARK PURPLE IN COLOUR of a dark purple colour [13thC. From Old French, 'bunch of grapes', ultimately from a prehistoric Germanic word meaning 'hook' (as used to harvest grapes), which was also the ancestor of English *cramp*, *crimp*, and *grapnel*.]

————— **WORD KEY: CULTURAL NOTE** —————
The Grapes of Wrath, a novel by US writer John Steinbeck (1939). A sympathetic portrayal of the plight of the rural poor during the Depression and an attack on capitalism, it tells of the tribulations suffered by the Joad family when they leave drought-stricken Oklahoma in search of work. It was made into a film by John Huston in 1940.

grape fern *n.* any one of various ferns with fronds that bear clusters of spore capsules similar to grapes. Genus: *Botrychium*.

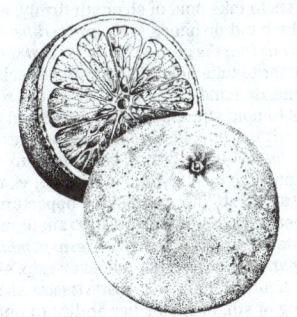
Grapefruit

grapefruit /gráyp froot/ (*plural* **-fruits** *or* **-fruit**) *n.* **1.** LARGE YELLOW OR PINKISH CITRUS FRUIT a large round yellow or pinkish citrus fruit with very tart juicy edible flesh ○ *grapefruit juice* **2.** CITRUS TREE an evergreen tree, related to oranges and lemons, that has dense dark green foliage, large white flowers, and produces grapefruit. Latin name: *Citrus paradisi*. [Early 19thC. Probably so called because the fruit grows in bunches, like grapes.]

grape hyacinth *n.* a perennial plant belonging to the lily family with dense clusters of cup-shaped, usually blue, flowers. Genus: *Muscari*.

grape ivy *n.* a South American evergreen climbing plant commonly kept as a house plant. Latin name: *Rhoicissus rhomboidea*.

grapeshot /gráyp shot/ *n.* a number of small iron balls fired simultaneously from a cannon in order to kill enemy soldiers [From the resemblance of the bunches of shot to a cluster of grapes]

grape sugar *n.* a fruit sugar obtained from grapes

grapevine /gráyp vīn/ *n.* **1.** VINE THAT BEARS GRAPES a vine on which grapes grow. Genus: *Vitis*. **2.** PATH ALONG WHICH INFORMATION SPREADS the path of communication along which news, gossip, or rumour passes unofficially from person to person within a group, organization, or community (*informal*) ○ *I heard on the office grapevine that she was leaving.*

grapey /gráypi/ (**-ier, -iest**), **grapy** (**-ier, -iest**) *adj.* looking or tasting like a grape or grapes —**grapiness** *n.*

graph[1] /graaf, graf/ *n.* DIAGRAM SHOWING VARYING QUANTITIES a diagram used to indicate relationships between two or more variable quantities. The quantities are measured along two axes, usually at right angles. A graph may consist, e.g., of a line joining points plotted between coordinates, a series of parallel bars or boxes, or a circle divided into wedges. ■ *vt.* (**graphs, graphing, graphed**) PUT DATA ON A GRAPH to represent data by means of a graph, or add data to a graph [Late 19thC. Shortening of *graphic formula*.]

graph[2] /graaf, graf/ *n.* a symbol, letter, or combination of letters used in writing to represent the smallest discrete unit of speech [Mid-20thC. From Greek *graphē* (see GRAPHIC).]

graph- *prefix.* = **grapho-** (*used before vowels*)

-graph *suffix.* **1.** sth written or drawn ○ *digraph* ○ *zincograph* **2.** an instrument for writing, drawing, or recording ○ *pantograph* ○ *seismograph* [Via French from, ultimately, Greek *graphein* 'to write' (see GRAPHIC)]

grapheme /grá feem/ *n.* any of a set of written symbols, letters, or combinations of letters that represent the same sound, e.g. f in 'fat', ph in 'photo', and gh in 'tough' —**graphemic** /gra feémik/ *adj.* —**graphemically** /-ikli/ *adv.*

graphemics /gra feémiks/ *n.* = **graphology** *n.* **2** (*takes a singular verb*)

-grapher *suffix.* one who writes, draws, or records ○ *calligrapher* ○ *cinematographer* [Formed from late Latin *-graphus*, via Greek *-graphos* from *graphein* 'to write' (see GRAPHIC)]

graphic /gráffik/ *adj.* **1.** VIVIDLY DETAILED including a number of vivid descriptive details, especially exciting or unpleasant ones ○ *her graphic description of the accident* **2.** SHOWN IN WRITING representing sth such as a sound by means of letters or other written symbols. 'Moo', 'woof', and 'miaow' are graphic representations of the sounds made by cows, dogs, and cats respectively. **3.** SHOWN IN PICTURES representing sth in the form of pictures or images **4.** MATH RELATING TO GRAPHS given in the form of a graph or diagram, or relating to graphs or diagrams **5.** OF GRAPHIC ARTS relating to the graphic arts **6.** OF GRAPHICS relating to graphics **7.** GEOL CONTAINING CRYSTALS LIKE LETTERS containing crystal structures that resemble letters ■ *n.* (*often used in the plural*) **1.** COMPUT PICTURE PRODUCED BY COMPUTER a picture, design, or visual display of data produced by a computer program **2.** PUBL BOOK ILLUSTRATION an illustration or diagram in a book or magazine **3.** CINEMA, TV DISPLAYED TEXT OR DRAWING IN FILM any part of a film that consists of illustration and text, e.g. titles, credits, or drawings [Mid-18thC. Via Latin from, ultimately, Greek *graphein* 'to write'. Ultimately from an Indo-European word meaning 'to scratch', which is also the ancestor of English *carve*.] —**graphically** *adv.* —**graphicness** *n.*

graphicacy /gráffikəssi/ *n.* the ability to use and understand such things as symbols, diagrams, plans, and maps [Mid-20thC. Formed from GRAPHIC, on the model of *literacy*.]

graphical /gráffik'l/ *adj.* MATH = **graphic** *adj.* **4**

graphical user interface *n.* a user interface on a computer that relies on icons, menus, and a mouse rather than on typing in commands

graphic arts *npl.* any of the artistic processes such as drawing, calligraphy, engraving, and printmaking that are based on the use of lines rather than colour —**graphic artist** *n.*

graphic design *n.* the art of integrating text, typography, and illustrations in the production of books and magazines —**graphic designer** *n.*

graphic equalizer *n.* a device, e.g. on a radio or CD player, that allows adjustments to be made to the strength of sounds of different frequencies. The variable levels of the sounds are often displayed electronically in graphical format.

graphic novel *n.* a fictional story for adults published in the form of a comic strip

graphics /gráffiks/ *n.* (*takes a singular verb*) **1.** DIAGRAMS AND ILLUSTRATIONS the presentation of information in the form of diagrams and illustrations as opposed to words and numbers **2.** COMPUT DISPLAY OF COMPUTER DATA AS SYMBOLS the art and science of storing, manipulating, and displaying computer data in the form of pictures, diagrams, graphs, or symbols **3.** ARCHIT, ENG MATHEMATICAL DRAWING the science of drawing sth in accordance with mathematical principles, e.g. in architecture and engineering ■ *npl.* ARTS = **graphic arts**

graphics tablet *n.* a device consisting of an electronic pen and an electronically sensitive surface, used to enter pictures or designs into a computer by drawing them

graphite /gráf īt/ *n.* a soft, dark grey or black form of carbon that occurs naturally as a mineral and is also produced industrially. It conducts electricity. Graphite is used in batteries, lubricants, polishes, electric motors, nuclear reactors, and carbon fibres, and, mixed with clay, is the lead of pencils. [Late 18thC. From German *Graphit*, from Greek *graphein* 'to write' (see GRAPHIC).] —**graphitic** /grə fíttik/ *adj.*

graphitize /gráffi tīz/ (-**tizes**, -**tizing**, -**tized**), **graphitise** (-**tises**, -**tising**, -**tised**) *vt.* **1.** MAKE INTO GRAPHITE to convert sth into graphite **2.** COVER OR COMBINE WITH GRAPHITE to coat sth with graphite, or mix graphite into it — **graphitizable** *adj.* —**graphitization** *n.*

graphology /gra fóllǝji/ *n.* **1.** PSYCHOL PSYCHOLOGICAL STUDY OF HANDWRITING the study of handwriting, especially in order to make an assessment of an individual's personality from characteristic patterns or features of his or her writing **2.** LING LINGUISTIC STUDY OF WRITING the study of writing systems and their relationship to the sound systems of languages —**graphological** /gráffǝ lójjik'l/ *adj.* —**graphologist** /gra fóllǝjist/ *n.*

graph paper *n.* paper on which a series of usually equally spaced vertical and horizontal intersecting lines has been imprinted to facilitate the drawing of graphs and diagrams

-graphy *suffix.* **1.** a method of writing or making an image by means of a particular process or technique ○ *chirography* ○ *radiography* **2.** writing about or study of a particular subject ○ *biography* ○ *ethnography* [Via Latin *-graphia* from, ultimately, Greek *graphein* 'to write' (see GRAPHIC)]

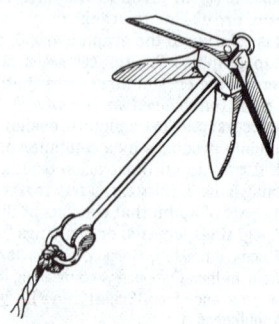

Grapnel

grapnel /grápn'l/ *n.* **1.** DEVICE WITH HOOKS a device consisting of an iron shaft with several hooks at one end and a rope at the other by which it can be thrown to attach itself to sth **2.** NAUT ANCHOR FOR A SMALL BOAT an anchor with three or more arms, especially one for anchoring a small boat [14thC. Via Anglo-Norman from Old French *grapon*, from *grape* 'hook' (see GRAPE).]

grappa /gráppǝ/ (*plural* -**pas** *or* -**pa**) *n.* an Italian brandy that is distilled from what remains of grapes after they have been pressed for wine-making [Late 19thC. From Italian, literally 'grape stalk, brandy'. Ultimately from a prehistoric Germanic word that is also the ancestor of English *grape*.]

Stephane Grappelli

Grappelli /grǝ pélli/, **Stephane** (1908–97) French musician, known for his playing of the violin in the jazz style.

grapple /grápp'l/ *v.* (-**ples**, -**pling**, -**pled**) **1.** *vi.* SEIZE AND STRUGGLE WITH SB to grab hold of sb and struggle with him or her in a hand-to-hand fight **2.** *vi.* STRUGGLE TO DEAL WITH STH to struggle with sth that is difficult to deal with, e.g. a problem that is difficult to solve or a concept or theory that is difficult to grasp **3.** *vt.* GRAB SB to grasp hold of sb **4.** *vt.* HOLD STH WITH A HOOKED DEVICE to hook or hold sth with a grapnel or other hooked device ■ *n.* **1.** = **grapnel** *n.* 1 **2.** STRUGGLE a close struggle **3.** WRESTLING GRIP OR HOLD in wrestling, a grip or hold on an opponent [14thC. From Old French *grapil*, literally 'small hook', from *grape* 'hook' (see GRAPE).] —**grappler** *n.*

grappling /grápling/ *n.* = **grapnel** *n.* 1

grappling iron, **grappling hook** *n.* = **grapnel** *n.* 1

graptolite /gráp tō līt/ *n.* any one of various small floating sea animals that lived in colonies that existed between about 550 million and 325 million years ago and are now found as fossils. Graptolite fossils are often used to date rocks. Orders: Graptoloidea and Dendroidea. [Mid-19thC. Coined from Greek *graptos* (the past participle of *graphein* 'to write'; see GRAPHIC) + -LITH. So called because their fossils leave marks like pencil marks on the surrounding rocks.]

grapy *adj.* = **grapey**

Grasmere /gráass meer/ village and lake in Cumbria, England

grasp /graasp/ *v.* (**grasps**, **grasping**, **grasped**) **1.** *vt.* TAKE HOLD OF STH to take hold of sb or sth firmly, especially with the hand or hands ○ *He grasped her arm and led her out into the garden.* **2.** *vi.* TRY TO TAKE HOLD OF STH to attempt to take hold of sb or sth, especially with the hand or hands ○ *he grasped at the rope* **3.** *vt.* HOLD STH to hold sth, especially in the hand or hands ○ *She rushed into the room with a letter grasped in her hand.* **4.** *vt.* TAKE AN OPPORTUNITY to take the opportunity to do sth when it arises **5.** *vi.* TRY TO TAKE OPPORTUNITY to attempt to take the opportunity to do sth when it arises **6.** *vt.* UNDERSTAND STH to manage to understand sth ○ *I just can't grasp what you're getting at.* ■ *n.* **1.** HAND GRIP a hold or grip, especially in the hand or hands **2.** UNDERSTANDING sb's understanding of sth, or his or her ability to understand sth ○ *a poor grasp of the facts* **3.** ABILITY TO ACHIEVE STH ability to achieve or get sth ○ *Success was within her grasp.* **4.** CONTROL power or control ○ *in the tyrant's grasp* [14thC. Origin uncertain; ultimately from a prehistoric Germanic word that is also the ancestor of English *grab*.] —**graspable** *adj.*

— WORD KEY: SYNONYMS —
See Synonyms at *catch*.

grasper /gráaspǝr/ *n.* **1.** GREEDY PERSON sb who is greedy for money **2.** SB WHO GRASPS sb who grasps sth

grasping /gráasping/ *adj.* greedy for money —**graspingly** *adv.* —**graspingness** *n.*

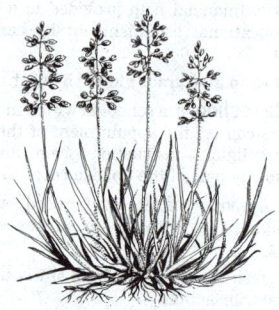

Grass: Annual meadow grass

grass /graass/ *n.* **1.** (*plural* **grasses** *or* **grass**) GREEN PLANT THAT FORMS LAWNS a low green narrow-leaved plant that grows in fields and gardens, is eaten by animals such as cows and sheep, and is used to make lawns and playing fields **2.** GRASS-COVERED AREA an area of grass, e.g. a lawn or pasture **3.** HOLLOW-STEMMED GREEN PLANT a plant with hollow jointed stems and long narrow, usually green leaves and tiny flowers arranged in spikes. Grasses include important food plants such as wheat, oats, barley, rice, rye, maize, millet, and sorghum as well as sugar cane and bamboo. Family: Gramineae. **4.** PLANT RESEMBLING GRASS a green plant such as goosegrass or knotgrass not related to the true grasses **5.** MARIJUANA the drug marijuana (*slang*) **6.** INFORMER sb who informs on sb else, especially to the police (*slang*) ■ *v.* (**grasses**, **grassing**, **grassed**) **1.** *vti.* COVER OR BECOME COVERED WITH GRASS to become covered with grass, or to cause ground to become covered with grass **2.** *vi.* BE INFORMER to inform on sb, especially to the police (*slang*) **3.** *vt.* AGRIC FEED AN ANIMAL ON GRASS to put an animal into a pasture to feed on grass **4.** *vt.* BRING OPPONENT DOWN to make an opponent fall to the ground [Old English *graes*. Ultimately from an Indo-European word that is also the ancestor of English *green* and *grow*.] ◇ **not let the grass grow under your feet** to act without delay or wasting time ◇ **put sb out to grass** to impose retirement on sb

— WORD KEY: CULTURAL NOTE —
Leaves of Grass, a collection of verse by US poet Walt Whitman (1855–92). Whitman constantly revised and expanded this collection to create a work that celebrates all aspects of human life from politics to the natural world and from procreation to mortality. Both its subject matter and its self-consciously modern style, based on long, loosely rhymed lines, were highly influential.

grass up *vt.* to inform on sb, especially to the police (*slang*)

Günter Grass

Grass /grass/, **Günter** (*b.* 1927) German writer and political activist. His novels such as *The Tin Drum* (1963) combine fantasy and symbolism with the theme of the materialism of modern life. He has also campaigned for the Social Democratic Party in Germany.

grass box *n.* the container attached to a lawnmower that catches the grass cuttings. US term **grass catcher**

grass carp *n.* a plant-eating fish, originally from Russia and China, used for keeping waterweeds under control. Latin name: *Ctenopharyngodon idella*.

grass catcher *n. US* = **grass box**

grass cloth *n.* cloth made from loosely woven plant fibres

grass court *n.* a grass-covered tennis court

grass-green *adj.* of the same colour as green grass — **grass green** *n.*

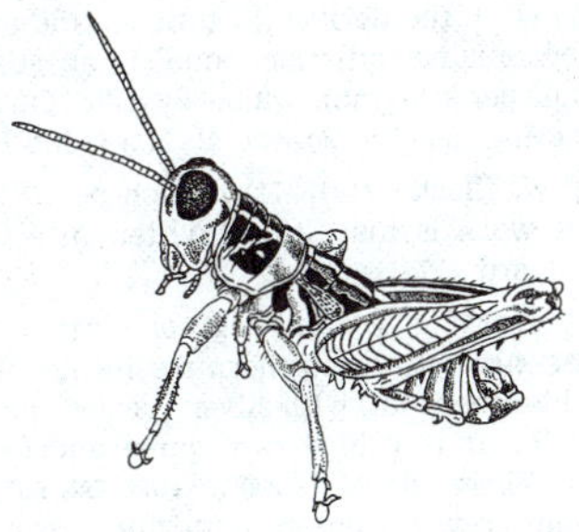

Grasshopper

grasshopper /gráass hopər/ *n.* **1.** INSECTS **JUMPING INSECT** a slender plant-eating flying and jumping insect that produces a buzzing or whirring sound by rubbing its back legs against its forewings. Order: Orthoptera. **2.** BEVERAGES **CREAMY COCKTAIL** a cocktail consisting of crème de menthe, crème de cacao, and cream ■ *adj.* **NOT ABLE TO FOCUS** unable to concentrate on one thing for very long ○ *have a grasshopper mind* [14thC. Formed from earlier *grasshop*, from Old English *gærshoppa*.]

grassland /gráass land/ *n.* **1. GRASS-COVERED LAND** land on which grass or low green plants are the main vegetation **2. PASTURE LAND** land kept for pasture or for the production of forage crops

grass moth *n.* a small straw-coloured night-flying moth that spends the daytime clinging to grass stems. Family: Pyralidae.

grass-of-Parnassus *n.* a white-flowered plant of the saxifrage family found in marshes and on wet moorland. Latin name: *Parnassia palustris.*

grass roots *npl.* **1. ORDINARY PEOPLE** the ordinary people in a community or the ordinary members of an organization, as opposed to the leadership **2. BASIS OF STH** the origin, basis, fundamental aim, or basic meaning of sth ○ *the grass roots of socialism*

grassroots /gráass roots/, **grass-roots** *adj.* coming from, formed by, or involving the ordinary people in a community, or the ordinary members of an organization, as opposed to the leadership

grass snake *n.* a nonpoisonous dark green snake found in Europe, North Africa, and Asia. It is the commonest snake in Europe. Genus: *Natrix.*

grass tree *n.* an eastern Australian tree that has a thick unbranching trunk with a tuft of leaves like grass at the top. Genus: *Xanthorrhoea.*

grass widow *n.* a woman whose husband is frequently away from home or who has completely deserted her [Originally denoting a discarded mistress, thought of as having made love in a field]

grass widower *n.* a man whose wife is frequently away from home or who has completely deserted him

grassy /gráassi/ (**-ier, -iest**) *adj.* **1. GRASS-COVERED** covered with grass **2. LIKE GRASS** looking, tasting, or feeling like grass

grate[1] /grayt/ *n.* **1. BARS IN FRONT OF FIRE** a framework of metal bars used to keep solid fuel such as coal or wood within a fireplace, stove, or furnace **2. FIREPLACE** a fireplace, stove, or furnace **3. BARS OVER OPENING** a framework of bars covering and blocking an opening **4.** MINING **SIEVE FOR GRADING ORE** an iron plate with holes in it for grading crushed ore [14thC. Via Old French from, ultimately, Latin *cratis* 'wickerwork' (see CRATE).]

grate[2] /grayt/ (**grates, grating, grated**) *v.* **1.** *vti.* **MAKE INTO OR BECOME SMALL PIECES** to shred sth by rubbing it against a rough surface or a tool with sharp-edged holes in it, or be shredded in this way ○ *He chose a cheese that grates easily.* **2.** *vti.* **MAKE NOISE OF RUBBING OR VIBRATING** to make a rough, vibrating, or creaking sound by being rubbed together, or cause things to make such a sound by rubbing them against each other ○ *Grasshoppers make their characteristic sound by grating their back legs against their wings.* **3.** *vi.* **IRRITATE** to be a source of irritation ○ *His constant sniggering really grates on me.* **4.** *vt.* **SAY STH IN HARSH VOICE** to say sth in a harsh rasping voice [14thC. From Old French *grater* 'to scrape', ultimately from a prehistoric Germanic word that is also the ancestor of English *scratch*.] —**grated** *adj.*

grateful /gráytf'l/ *adj.* **1. FEELING THANKS** having the desire or reason to thank sb ○ *I'm very grateful to you for your help.* ○ *He received a grateful letter from them, saying how much they appreciated his support.* **2. COMFORTING** giving pleasure or comfort (*archaic or literary*) [Mid-16thC. Formed from earlier *grate* 'pleasing, thankful', from Latin *gratus* (source also of English *grace, disgrace*, and *gratitude*).] —**gratefully** *adv.* —**gratefulness** *n.*

grater /gráytər/ *n.* **1. DEVICE WITH SHARP-EDGED HOLES** a device with many sharp-edged holes against which sth such as cheese can be rubbed to reduce it to shreds or fine particles **2. SB WHO GRATES** a person who grates sth

graticule /grátti kyool/ *n.* **1. TRANSPARENT OVERLAY GRID** a grid of lines on glass or other transparent material used for measuring features on a map, photograph, or diagram placed beneath it. US term **reticle 2. LINES ON MAP** the grid of latitudinal and longitudinal lines on a map [Late 19thC. Via French from, ultimately, Latin *craticula*, literally 'small grid', from *cratis* (see CRATE).]

gratification /gráttifi káysh'n/ *n.* **1. SATISFACTION** pleasure or satisfaction **2. STH SATISFYING** sth that gives pleasure or satisfaction **3. ACT OF PLEASING OR SATISFYING** the act of giving sb pleasure or satisfaction **4. TIP** a gratuity (*archaic*)

gratify /grátti fī/ (**-fies, -fying, -fied**) *vt.* **1. PLEASE** to make sb feel pleased or satisfied (*often passive*) **2. FULFIL A DESIRE** to satisfy a desire [15thC. Directly or via French *gratifier* from Latin *gratificari*, from *gratus* 'agreeable' (see GRATEFUL).] —**gratifier** *n.* —**gratifying** *adj.* —**gratifyingly** *adv.*

gratin /grátt aN/ (*plural* **-tins** *or* **-tin**) *n.* **1. TOPPING OF BREADCRUMB OR MELTED CHEESE** a crust of browned breadcrumbs or melted grated cheese on top of food. ◊ **au gratin 2. DISH WITH BREADCRUMB OR CHEESE CRUST** a cooked dish with a breadcrumb or melted cheese crust [Mid-17thC. From French, formed from Old French *grater* (see GRATE[2]).]

gratin dish *n.* a container used for cooking or serving a gratin

gratinee /grátti náy/ *adj.* cooked or served with browned breadcrumbs or melted grated cheese on top. ◊ **au gratin** [Early 20thC. From French *gratinée*, the feminine past participle of *gratiner* 'to cook au gratin'.]

grating[1] /gráyting/ *n.* **1. METAL GRILLE** a framework of metal bars covering an opening **2.** = **diffraction grating**

grating[2] /gráyting/ *adj.* **1. ROUGH** unpleasantly rough, harsh, or vibrating **2. IRRITATING** causing irritation ■ **gratings** *npl.* **SMALL GRATED PIECES** shreds or fine particles produced by grating sth —**gratingly** *adv.*

gratis /gráttiss, gráy-, gráa-/ *adj., adv.* received or given without cost or payment [15thC. From Latin, literally 'out of kindness', formed from *gratia* (see GRACE).]

gratitude /grátti tyood/ *n.* a feeling of being thankful to sb for doing sth ○ *I'd like to find some way of expressing my gratitude to her for all she did.* [15thC. Directly or via French from Latin *gratitudo*, from *gratus* (see GRATEFUL).]

gratuitous /grə tyóo itəss/ *adj.* **1. UNNECESSARY** unnecessary and unjustifiable ○ *gratuitous remarks* **2. FREE** received or given without payment or obligation **3. WITHOUT RETURN BENEFIT** not requiring any benefit or compensation in return [Mid-17thC. Via French from Latin *gratuitus* 'freely given', from *gratus* (see GRATEFUL).] —**gratuitously** *adv.* —**gratuitousness** *n.*

gratuity /grə tyóo əti/ (*plural* **-ties**) *n.* **1. MONEY GIVEN IN APPRECIATION** a small gift, usually of money, given to sb such as a waiter as thanks for service given **2.** MIL **MONEY GIVEN ON RETIREMENT** a sum of money given to sb, especially a member of the armed forces, when he or she retires [15thC. Via French *gratuité* from medieval Latin *gratuitas* 'gift', from Latin *gratus* (see GRATEFUL). The word originally denoted the gift of God's grace.]

gratulatory /gráttyoolətəri/ *adj.* expressing congratulations (*formal*)

graupel /grówp'l/ *n.* small soft white ice particles that fall as hail or snow [Late 19thC. From German, literally 'small hulled corn', ultimately from a Slavonic word.]

grav /grav/ *n.* a unit of acceleration that corresponds to the standard acceleration of free fall. Symbol **g** [Shortening of GRAVITY]

gravadlax /grávvəd laks/ *n.* = **gravlax**

gravamen /grə váy men/ (*plural* **-vamens** *or* **-vamina** /-vámminə/) *n.* **1. SUBSTANCE OF ACCUSATION** the most serious part of an accusation or charge made against an accused person **2. GRIEVANCE** a grievance against sb (*formal*) [Early 17thC. Via medieval Latin 'grievance', literally 'obligation', from, ultimately, Latin *gravare* 'to weigh upon', from *gravis* 'heavy' (see GRAVE[2]).]

grave[1] /grayv/ *n.* **1. BURIAL PLACE OF DEAD BODY** a hole dug in the ground for a dead person's body, or the place where a dead person's body is buried ○ *She goes every week to put fresh flowers on her husband's grave.* ○ *as silent as the grave* **2. LAST RESTING PLACE** any final resting place ○ *the sunken ship's watery grave* **3. DEATH** the end of life ○ *health care from the cradle to the grave* ○ *went to an early grave* **4. END OF STH** the end or destruction of sth ○ *the grave of his ambition* [Old English *græf*. Ultimately from an Indo-European word meaning 'to scratch, dig' that is also the ancestor of English *groove, grub*, and *engrave*.] —**graveless** *adj.* ◇ **turn in his** *or* **her grave** used to emphasize how displeased or upset sb who is dead would be if he or she knew what was happening

grave[2] /grayv/ (**graver, gravest**) *adj.* **1. SERIOUS IN MANNER** solemn and serious in manner **2. HAVING SERIOUS EFFECT** very important and with serious consequences, and therefore needing to be thought about carefully **3. WITH POSSIBLE HARM OR DANGER** causing, involving, or arising from a threat of danger or harm or other bad consequences ○ *Things are looking pretty grave here as the air raid sirens wail.* [15thC. Via French from Latin *gravis* 'heavy' (source also of English *gravity* and *grief*). Ultimately from an Indo-European base that is also the ancestor of English *baryon, brute*, and *guru*.] —**gravely** *adv.* —**graveness** *n.*

grave[3] /graav/ *n.* **MARK INDICATING PRONUNCIATION** a mark used to indicate pronunciation in some languages, consisting of a little line sloping downwards to the right above a letter, as in ò and è. ◊ **acute, circumflex** ■ *adj.* **WITH A GRAVE ACCENT** having or being a grave ○ *e grave* [Early 17thC. From French, 'heavy' (see GRAVE[2]).]

grave[4] /grayv/ (**graves, graving, graved, graved** *or* **graven** /gráyv'n/) *vt.* **1. FIX STH IN MIND** to fix sth firmly in the mind (*literary*) ○ *graved it in her mind* **2. ENGRAVE STH** to carve or engrave sth (*archaic*) [Old English *grafan* 'to dig, carve'. The underlying meaning is 'to engrave on the mind'.]

grave[5] /grayv/ (**graves, graving, graved**) *vt.* to clean the bottom of a wooden ship and coat it with pitch [15thC. Origin uncertain: probably from French dialect *grave* 'sand, shore', from Old French (see GRAVEL), because the work was done while the ship was hauled up on a beach.]

grave[6] /graáv ay/ *adv.* to be played seriously or solemnly (*used as a musical direction*) [Late 16thC. Via Italian from Latin *gravis* 'heavy' (see GRAVE[2]).] —**grave** *adj.*

grave accent /graáv-/ *n.* = **grave**[3]

graveclothes /gráyv klōthz/ *npl.* the clothes or other wrappings that a dead body is buried in

gravedigger /gráyv diggər/ *n.* sb employed to dig graves

gravel /grávv'l/ *n.* **1. SMALL STONES** small stones used for paths or for making concrete **2.** GEOL **ROCK FRAGMENTS** a deposit or stratum of loose fragmentary sedimentary material **3.** MED **SMALL PARTICLES IN KIDNEY OR BLADDER** hard particles in the kidney or bladder that are much smaller than kidney stones and can pass through the urinary tract without causing a blockage, although they may cause severe pain ■ *vt.* (**-els, -elling, -elled**) **1. COVER STH WITH GRAVEL** to cover a surface with gravel **2. BEWILDER SB** to puzzle or confuse sb [13thC. From Old French *gravel*, from *grave* 'pebbles, shore', of Celtic origin.]

gravel-blind *adj.* almost totally sightless (*literary; considered offensive in most contexts*) [Modelled on SAND-BLIND]

gravelly /grávv'li/ *adj.* **1. GRATING** sounding rough or harsh ○ *a gravelly voice* **2. LIKE GRAVEL** like or covered with gravel **3. WITH GRAVEL** made or manufactured with gravel

graven /gráyv'n/ past participle of **grave**[4]

graven image *n.* a carving representing a god (*literary*)

graveolent /gráyvi ələnt/ *adj.* having a strong unpleasant smell (*formal*) [Early 17thC. From the Latin stem *graveolent-*, literally 'having a strong smell'.]

graver /gráyvər/ *n.* a tool used for carving or engraving

grave robber *n.* sb who steals things from graves or tombs, usually either valuable artefacts or corpses for dissection

Graves /graav/ *n.* a white or red wine from the district of Graves in southwestern France

Graves /grayvz/, **Robert** (1895–1985) British poet and novelist. A classical scholar, he was also a prolific writer of poetry and fiction. His works include *Goodbye to All That* (1929), *I, Claudius* (1934), and *The White Goddess* (1947). Full name **Robert Ranke Graves**

Graves' disease /gráyvz-/ *n.* an inflammatory disorder of the thyroid gland commonly associated with protrusion of the eyes [Mid-19thC. Named after the Irish physician Robert J. *Graves* (1796–1853), who was one of the first to describe the condition.]

Gravesend /gráyvz énd/ port on the River Thames in Kent, southeastern England. Population: 92,900 (1994).

graveside /gráyv sīd/ *n.* the area surrounding a grave (*often used before a noun*) ○ *a graveside service*

gravesite /gráyv sīt/ *n.* the place where sb's grave is

gravestone /gráyv stōn/ *n.* an ornamental piece of stone put at the head of a grave, on which are written the name, birth date, and death date of the person buried there

graveyard /gráyv yaard/ *n.* **1. AREA WHERE PEOPLE ARE BURIED** a piece of ground, sometimes beside a church, set aside for people to be buried in **2. DUMPING PLACE** a place where old, unwanted, useless objects, especially old cars, are left

graveyard poetry *n.* sad reflective poems about death, often set in graveyards and typically by 18th century English writers —**graveyard poet** *n.*

graveyard shift *n.* a shift of work running through the early hours of the morning, especially one running from midnight till eight o'clock the following morning, or the workers on such a shift

gravid /grávvid/ *adj.* carrying young or eggs (*technical*) [Late 16thC. From Latin *gravidus*, from *gravis* 'heavy' (see GRAVE[2]).] —**gravidity** /grə víddəti/ *n.* —**gravidly** *adv.* —**gravidness** *n.*

gravida /grávvidə/ (*plural* **-das** *or* **-dae** /grávvidee/) *n.* a pregnant woman (*technical*) ◊ **multigravida, primigravida** [Mid-20thC. From Latin, the feminine form of *gravidus* (see GRAVID).]

gravimeter /grə vímmitər/ *n.* **1. DEVICE FOR MEASURING GRAVITATION** an instrument for measuring variations in the strength of the Earth's gravitational field from one place to another **2. DEVICE FOR MEASURING RELATIVE DENSITY** an instrument used to measure the relative density of a substance [Late 18thC. From French *gravimètre*, from Latin *gravis* (see GRAVE[2]).]

gravimetric /grávvi métrik/ *adj.* **1. RELATING TO MEASUREMENT OF WEIGHT** relating to or using the measurement of weight **2. OF CHEMICAL ANALYSIS AND WEIGHT** relating to chemical analysis involving the measurement of the weights of substances used in and produced by a chemical reaction. ◊ **volumetric 3. MEASURING GRAVITATIONAL VARIATIONS** relating to the measurement of variations in the strength of the Earth's gravitational field from one place to another — **gravimetrical** *adj.* —**gravimetrically** *adv.*

gravimetry /grə vímmətri/ *n.* **1. MEASUREMENT OF WEIGHT** the measurement of density or weight **2. MEASUREMENT OF GRAVITATIONAL DIFFERENCES** the measurement of variations in the strength of the Earth's gravitational field from one place to another [Mid-19thC. Formed from GRAVIMETER.]

graving dock *n.* = **dry dock** [From GRAVE[5]]

gravitas /grávvi tass, -taas/ *n.* a serious and solemn attitude or way of behaving (*formal*) [Early 20thC. From Latin (see GRAVITY).]

gravitate /grávvi tayt/ (**-tates, -tating, -tated**) *v.* **1.** *vi.* **MOVE STEADILY TOWARDS STH** to move gradually and steadily to or towards sb or sth as if drawn by some force or attraction ○ *guests slowly gravitating to the kitchen* **2.** *vti.* PHYS **MOVE BECAUSE OF GRAVITY** to move or cause sth to move under the influence of the force of gravity [Mid-17thC. From modern Latin *gravitat-*, the stem of *gravitare*, from Latin *gravitas* (see GRAVITY).] —**gravitater** *n.* —**gravitative** *adj.*

gravitation /grávvi táysh'n/ *n.* **1. MOVING IN DIRECTION OF STH** a gradual and steady movement to or towards sb or sth as if drawn by some force or attraction **2.** PHYS **FORCE THAT ATTRACTS THINGS** the mutual force of attraction between all particles or bodies that have mass — **gravitational** *adj.* —**gravitationally** *adv.*

gravitational field *n.* the region of space around an object that has mass, within which another object that has mass experiences the force of attraction

gravitational lens *n.* a large celestial object, such as a galaxy, whose gravitational field focuses or distorts the light from another object beyond it

gravitational wave *n.* a hypothetical wave, predicted by relativity theory, that travels at the speed of light and propagates a gravitational field

graviton /grávvi ton/ *n.* a hypothetical particle with zero charge and rest mass that is considered to be the quantum particle of the gravitational interaction [Mid-20thC. Formed from GRAVITATION.]

gravity /grávvəti/ *n.* **1.** ASTRON **GRAVITATIONAL FORCE OF EARTH** the attraction due to gravitation that the Earth or another celestial body exerts on an object on or near its surface **2.** PHYS = **gravitation** *n.* 2 **3. SERIOUSNESS OR SIGNIFICANCE** the serious nature of sth because e.g. of the worrying or significant consequences it has or could have **4. SERIOUS BEHAVIOUR** solemnity and seriousness in sb's attitude or behaviour **5. HEAVINESS** the quality of being heavy **6. HEAVINESS** the heaviness of sth (*formal*) [15thC. Via French *gravité* from Latin *gravitas* 'heaviness', from *gravis* (see GRAVE[2]).]

WORD KEY: CULTURAL NOTE

Gravity's Rainbow, a novel by US writer Thomas Pynchon (1973). Set in Europe during World War II, it describes the attempts of various interest groups to exploit the extrasensory powers of US soldier Tyrone Slothrop, whose sexual encounters reliably predict the impact sites of German V2 rockets. It is noted for its extraordinary erudition, broad range of styles, and complex characterization.

gravity feed *n.* a mechanism or process for supplying sth such as fuel to a boiler or materials to a manufacturing process by their downward movement under the influence of gravity —**gravity-fed** *adj.*

gravlax /gráv laks/ *n.* a Scandinavian dish consisting of thin slices of dried salmon marinated in sugar, salt, pepper, and herbs, especially dill, and usually served as an appetizer [Mid-20thC. From Swedish or Norwegian *gravlaks*, literally 'buried salmon' (because originally the fish was marinated in a hole in the ground).]

gravure /grə vyóor, -vyáwr/ *n.* **1.** = **intaglio** *n.* 4 **2. PLATE OR PRINT** a plate used in or a print produced by intaglio printing **3.** = **photogravure** [Late 19thC. From French, formed from *graver* 'to engrave'. Ultimately from a prehistoric Germanic word that was also the ancestor of English *grave*[4] and *engrave*.]

gravy /gráyvi/ (*plural* **-vies**) *n.* the juices produced by meat while it is being roasted, fried, or grilled, or a sauce made with these juices or another liquid and poured over cooked meat and vegetables [14thC. From Old French *grave*, of uncertain origin; perhaps a misreading of *grane* 'stew, sauce', probably ultimately from Latin *granum* (see GRAIN).]

gravy boat *n.* a small jug, usually long and narrow, in which gravy and other sauces are served

gravy ring *n. Ireland* a doughnut

gravy train *n.* a way of getting a large amount of money or other benefits for very little effort (*informal*) ○ *scrambling to get on the gravy train*

gray[1] *adj., n.* US = **grey**

gray[2] /gray/ *n.* the derived SI unit for the absorbed dose of ionizing radiation, equal to an absorption of 1 joule per kilogram. Symbol **Gy** [Late 20thC. Named after the English radiobiologist L. H. *Gray* (1905–65).]

Gray /gray/, **Thomas** (1716–71) British poet. His most famous work is his 'Elegy Written in a Country Churchyard' (1751).

grayling /gráyling/ (*plural* **-lings** *or* **-ling**) *n.* **1.** ZOOL **FISH RESEMBLING TROUT** a northern freshwater fish that resembles the trout, with silvery scales and a large dorsal fin. It is valued as a game and food fish. Genus: *Thymallus*. **2.** INSECTS **EUROPEAN BUTTERFLY** a common grey European butterfly. Latin name: *Eumenis semele*.

graymail *n.* US = **greymail**

Graz /graats/ city and capital of Styria Province on the River Mur in southeastern Austria. Population: 237,810 (1991).

graze[1] /grayz/ (**grazes, grazing, grazed**) *v.* **1.** *vti.* **EAT GRASS IN FIELDS** to eat grass and other green plants in fields, or eat the grass and plants of a particular field or fields **2.** *vt.* **ALLOW ANIMALS TO EAT GRASS** to allow animals such as cows and sheep to eat grass in fields ○ *Her ranch now grazes 100,000 head of cattle.* **3.** *vt.* **USE LAND FOR FEEDING ANIMALS** to allow animals such as cows and sheep to eat the grass and green plants of a particular field or fields ○ *We usually graze those two fields over there.* **4.** *vi.* FOOD **EAT SNACKS** to eat snacks throughout the day instead of proper meals, especially while working (*slang*) **5.** *vi.* **EAT FOOD IN SUPERMARKET** to eat food from the shelves of a supermarket while shopping without subsequently paying for it at the checkout (*slang*) **6.** *vi.* TV **CHANGE TV CHANNELS** to switch television channels frequently without watching much of any programme (*slang*) **7.** *vi.* **KEEP STOPPING AND STARTING** to perform an activity in a desultory manner, e.g. by picking up and putting down magazines without reading much of any one (*slang*) [Old English *grasian*, from *græs* (see GRASS)] —**grazeable** *adj.* —**grazer** *n.*

graze[2] /grayz/ *v.* (**grazes, grazing, grazed**) **1.** *vti.* **TOUCH STH LIGHTLY** to touch against the surface of sth lightly in passing **2.** *vt.* **BREAK THE SKIN SLIGHTLY** to damage the surface of the skin of a part of the body slightly when it is rubbed against sth rough and hard ■ *n.* **1. SLIGHT BREAK IN SKIN** slight and shallow damage to the skin caused by rubbing against sth rough and hard **2. TOUCH OF STH** the act of rubbing sth or touching it lightly ○ *the graze of a bullet* [Late 16thC. Origin uncertain; perhaps from GRAZE[1], with the idea of cropping grass very short.]

grazier /gráyzi ər, -zhər/ *n.* **1. CATTLE FARMER** sb who owns a farm on which cattle are raised and fattened for market **2.** *Aus* **SHEEP OR CATTLE FARMER** a large-scale farmer who raises sheep or cattle

grazing /gráyzing/ *n.* **1. FOOD FOR COWS AND SHEEP** grass and green plants for animals such as cows and sheep to eat **2. LAND WITH GRASS** land with grass suitable for animals such as cows and sheep to feed on **3. EATING OF SNACKS** the eating of snacks throughout the day instead of proper meals, especially while working (*slang*) **4. EATING OF FOOD IN SUPERMARKET** the eating of food from the shelves of a supermarket while shopping without subsequently paying for it at the checkout (*slang*) **5. CHANGING OF TV CHANNELS** the switching of television channels frequently without watching much of any programme (*slang*) **6. FREQUENTLY STOPPING AND STARTING** performing an activity in a desultory manner, e.g. by picking up and putting down magazines without reading much of any one (*slang*)

grazioso /grátsi ósso, graa-/ *adv.* in a graceful way (*used as a musical direction*) [Early 19thC. From Italian.] —**grazioso** *adj.*

grease *n.* /greess/ **1.** FOOD **ANIMAL FAT** thick soft animal fat, e.g. from cooked meat **2. THICK LUBRICANT** a thick oily substance, especially one used to make machinery run smoothly **3. HAIR OIL FOR HAIR** an oily substance used as a cosmetic for the hair **4. AGRIC OILY WOOL** untreated wool from sheep that still contains its natural oils, or the natural oils in this wool **5. BRIBERY** bribes or bribery (*slang*) **6. LONG-HAIRED MOTORCYCLISTS** long-haired motorcyclists (*dated slang insult*) ■ *vt.* /greess, greez/ (**greases, greasing, greased**) **1. PUT GREASE ON STH** to put grease on sth, e.g. in order to make it move smoothly or to stop sth else sticking to it **2. MAKE STH EASIER OR QUICKER** to make sth such as progress or promotion easier or quicker (*informal*) ○ *His mother's money certainly greased his path to the boardroom.* [13thC. Via Anglo-Norman *grece*, from, ultimately, Latin *crassus* 'fat, thick' (source of English *crass*).] ◇ **grease sb's palm** *or* **hand** to bribe sb to do sth (*informal*)

greaseball /greéss bawl/ *n.* sb habitually dirty or unkempt who has greasy hair (*slang insult*)

grease gun *n.* **ENG** a hand-held device for forcing grease into machinery to lubricate it

grease monkey *n.* an offensive term for a mechanic, especially one who works on motor vehicles or aircraft (*slang offensive*)

greasepaint /greéss paynt/ *n.* a thick, greasy, or waxy form of coloured make-up used by actors

grease pencil *n.* a pencil containing a core of a waxy coloured substance that can write on glossy surfaces

greaseproof /greéss proof/ *adj.* not allowing oil or grease to soak into it or pass through it

greaseproof paper *n.* paper that does not allow oil or grease to soak into it or pass through it and is used especially in cooking, preparing, or wrapping food. US term **waxed paper**

greaser /greéssər, greézər/ *n.* **1. MECHANIC OR ENGINEER** sb whose job involves greasing machinery, especially a mechanic who works on motor vehicles or a ship's engineer (*slang*) **2. LONG-HAIRED MOTORCYCLIST** a usually young, long-haired, leather-jacketed motorcyclist, especially a member of a motorcycle gang (*slang insult*) **3. SB WHO TRIES TO GAIN FAVOUR** sb who tries to gain the favour or approval of a superior by flattery or grovelling (*slang insult*)

greasewood /greéss wood/ *n.* **1. SPINY N AMERICAN SHRUB** a spiny shrub that grows in desert areas of western North America and yields an oil that is used as a fuel. Latin name: *Sarcobatus vermiculatus*. **2. SHRUB RELATED TO GREASEWOOD** a shrub that is similar to or related to the greasewood, e.g. the creosote bush

greasy /greéssi, greézi/ (**-ier, -iest**) *adj.* **1. MADE OF GREASE** consisting of grease or sth with the consistency of grease **2. THICK WITH GREASE** covered with or containing grease, often a lot of grease or too much of it **3. HAVING EXCESSIVE NATURAL OILS** producing or containing a lot of natural oils **4. PRODUCED BY GREASE** caused by grease or sth with the consistency of grease **5. SLIPPERY** difficult to move, walk, or drive on because of wetness or iciness **6. SMARMY** unpleasantly and insincerely flattering, friendly, or grovelling — **greasily** *adv.* —**greasiness** *n.*

greasy spoon *n.* a small, cheap, and often dirty café, especially one that serves fried food (*informal*)

great /grayt/ *adj.* **1. IMPRESSIVELY LARGE** very large and impressive **2. LARGE IN NUMBER** large in number or with many parts ○ *a great crowd of well-wishers* **3. BIGGER THAN OTHERS** larger or more important than others of the same kind **4. MUCH** extreme or more than usual ○ *It gives me great pleasure to introduce our speaker tonight.* **5. LASTING A LONG TIME** lasting a long time, or covering a long distance **6. IMPORTANT** very significant or important **7. EXCEPTIONALLY TALENTED** with exceptional talents, or having made remarkable achievements **8. POWERFUL** powerful and influential **9. GOOD AT STH** able to do sth very well, or very skilful with sth (*informal*) ○ *Alice is great at spelling.* **10. VERY GOOD** very good or pleasing (*informal*) ○ *It was great to hear your news.* **11. USEFUL** very useful or suitable for a particular task (*informal*) ○ *This cast-iron pan is great for doing pancakes.* **12. BEING A GOOD EXAMPLE OF STH** doing sth often, enjoying sth very much, or being a very good example of sth ○ *Joe's a great one for the soaps – he never misses an episode.* **13. USED FOR EMPHASIS** used to emphasize how much of a quality sb or sth has (*informal*) ○ *Their new house is a great*

big place out in the country. ○ *I can't wear this – there's a dirty great hole in the front!* **14. PREGNANT** pregnant (*archaic*) ■ *n.* **1. SB GREAT** sb whose fame or influence has proved to be long-lasting ○ *one of the all-time greats of blues music* **2. MUSIC PART OF PIPE ORGAN** the principal division of a pipe organ ■ *adv.* **VERY WELL** very well (*informal*) ○ *That's it; you're doing great.* ○ *Steve and I get along just great.* [Old English *grēat* 'thick, coarse'. Ultimately from a prehistoric Germanic word that is also the ancestor of English *grit, groat,* and *grout.*] —**greatly** *adv.* —**greatness** *n.*

──── **WORD KEY: CULTURAL NOTE** ────

The Great Gatsby, a novel by US writer F. Scott Fitzgerald (1925). Set on Long Island, New York, it is the story of enigmatic businessman Jay Gatsby, a symbol of the American obsession with wealth and status, whose attempts to revive a relationship with an old girlfriend lead to his downfall. It was made into films by Elliott Nugent in 1949 and by Jack Clayton in 1974. Terms such as *Gatsbyesque*, obsessed with social status and the acquisition of great riches, derive directly from the book title and the character.

great- *prefix.* **1. BEING A PARENT OF GRANDPARENT** being a parent of sb's grandparent **2. BEING GRANDCHILD'S CHILD** being a child of one of sb's grandchildren

great ape *n.* any of the larger apes such as the gorilla, chimpanzee, or orang-utan

Great Attractor *n.* a large aggregation of galaxies, approximately 150 to 350 million light years away, whose gravitational pull might account for the unexpected motions of many galaxies including our own

great auk *n.* a large flightless sea bird that was native to northern Atlantic coasts until it was hunted to extinction in the middle of the 19th century. Latin name: *Pinguinus impennis.*

great-aunt *n.* an aunt of sb's father or mother

Great Australian Bight wide inlet of the Indian Ocean off the southern coast of Australia. It stretches 1,100 km/685 mi. from Cape Pasley in Western Australia to Cape Carnot in South Australia.

Great Barrier Reef chain of coral reefs in the Coral Sea, located off the coast of Queensland, Australia. The largest deposit of coral in the world, the reef extends for 2,010 km/1,250 mi. Area: 348,600 sq. km/134,600 sq. mi.

Great Bear *n.* = Ursa Major

Great Bear Lake freshwater lake in Canada's Northwest Territories, lying astride the Arctic Circle. It is the world's eighth largest lake. Area: 31,153 sq. km/12,028 sq. mi. Depth: 410 m/1,345 ft.

great black-backed gull *n.* a large sea bird with a white head and body and black wings that is native to the shores of the North Atlantic. Latin name: *Larus marinus.*

great blue heron *n.* a large long-legged long-necked North American heron with greyish-blue plumage. Latin name: *Ardea herodias.*

Great Britain the largest island of the British Isles in northwestern Europe. It includes England, Scotland, and Wales. ♦ **United Kingdom**

great circle *n.* a circle on the surface of a sphere such as the Earth that has a radius equal to the radius of the sphere, and whose centre is also the sphere's centre. ◇ **small circle**

greatcoat /grayt kōt/ *n.* a long thick heavy overcoat worn especially by soldiers

great crested grebe *n.* a large diving waterfowl of Europe, Africa, Asia, and Australia with no tail and a ruff on its head that is expanded during courtship rituals. Latin name: *Podiceps cristatus.*

Great Dane *n.* a very large dog with long legs, a square head and deep muzzle, and short hair, belonging to a breed originating in Germany [Because it was developed in Germany, whose inhabitants were formerly called Danes]

Great Depression *n.* a drastic decline in the world economy resulting in mass unemployment and widespread poverty that lasted from 1929 until 1939

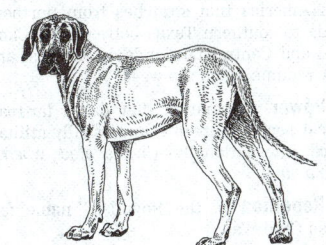

Great Dane

great divide *n.* **1. MAJOR DEMARCATION** a major demarcation between two contrasting things, especially life and death **2. LINE BETWEEN LIFE AND DEATH** the boundary between life and death

Great Divide *n.* = Continental Divide

Great Dividing Range /grayt di víding raynj/ system of mountain ranges and plateaus in Queensland, New South Wales, and Victoria, extending along the eastern border of Australia. The highest point is Mount Kosciusko, 2,228 m/7,310 ft.

greater celandine *n.* a yellow-flowered plant of the poppy family. It yields an orange-coloured latex used to treat eye and skin disorders. Latin name: *Chelidonium majus.* US term **celandine.** ◊ **lesser celandine**

Greater Sunda Islands /-súndə-/ ♦ **Sunda Islands**

greatest common divisor *n.* = highest common factor

Great Glen rift valley in Scotland that extends southwestwards from the Moray Firth to Loch Linnhe. It contains Loch Lochy and Loch Ness. Length: 156 km/97 mi.

great-grandchild *n.* a son or daughter of your grandchild

great hearted /grayt haártid/ *adj.* **1. LARGE-SPIRITED** with a generous and forgiving nature **2. UNDAUNTED** not easily frightened or dispirited —**great heartedly** *adv.*

Great Indian Desert = Thar Desert

Great Karoo ♦ Karoo

Great Lake the largest natural freshwater lake in Australia, on the island of Tasmania, near the Great Western Tiers. Area: 114 sq. km/44 sq. mi.

Great Lakes

Great Lakes group of five freshwater lakes in north-central North America, interconnected by natural and artificial channels. The largest group of lakes in the world, they are Lakes Superior, Michigan, Huron, Erie, and Ontario. Area: 244,108 sq. km/94,251 sq. mi.

Great Leap Forward *n.* the attempt by the People's Republic of China from 1958 to 1960 to modernize agriculture by labour-intensive methods

great mountain buttercup *n.* NZ = Mount Cook lily

great-nephew *n.* a son of sb's nephew or niece

great-niece *n.* a daughter of sb's nephew or niece

great northern diver *n.* **BIRDS** a large black-and-white diving bird especially found in North America. Latin name: *Gavia immer.* US term **common loon**

great organ *n.* the main keyboard of an organ, and the pipes and mechanism relating to it. ◊ **choir organ**

Great Plains vast high plateau region in central North America that stretches from northeastern Canada to southern Texas between the Canadian Shield and Central Lowlands on the east and the Rocky Mountains on the west

Great Power *n.* a nation that has a far-reaching political, social, economic, and usually military influence internationally (*hyphenated when used before a noun*)

Great Rebellion *n.* the Royalists' name for the English Civil War

Great Rift Valley depression extending more than 4,830 km/3,000 mi. from the valley of the River Jordan in Syria to Mozambique, forming the most extensive rift in the earth's surface. The area is marked by a chain of seas and lakes and a series of volcanoes.

Great Russian *n.* **1.** LANG RUSSIAN LANGUAGE the Russian language (*dated*) **2.** PEOPLES RUSSIAN a member of the main Russian-speaking ethnic group in Russia ■ *adj.* OF THE RUSSIAN PEOPLE relating to or belonging to the Great Russian people

Great St Bernard Pass /-s'nt búrnərd-, -sáN bər naárd-/ mountain pass in western Europe, on the border between Valais, central Switzerland, and Aosta Province, Piedmont, northern Italy. Founded in the 11th century, it is named after the hospice founded at its summit by the French monk St Bernard. Height: 2,468 m/8,090 ft.

Great Salt Lake shallow body of salt water in northwestern Utah, near Salt Lake City. It is the largest salt lake in North America. Area: 4,403 km/1,700 sq. mi.

Great Sandy Desert desert in northwestern Australia that contains large areas of sand dunes and salt marshes and some grassland. Area: 310,000 sq. km/150,000 sq. mi.

Great Schism *n.* **1.** TIME OF TWO POPES the period between 1378 and 1415 when there were rival popes, one reigning in Rome and the other in Avignon **2.** HISTORICAL SEPARATION OF CHURCHES the separation of the Roman Catholic and Eastern Orthodox churches in 1054, as a result of theological disagreement

Great Seal *n.* in the United Kingdom, the seal kept in the charge of the Lord Chancellor or, formerly, the Lord Keeper of the Seal, and used in sealing important state papers

great skua *n.* a large brown predatory seabird of the North Atlantic that feeds on fish, eggs, and other adult birds. Latin name: *Catharacta skua*.

Great Slave Lake freshwater lake in the Northwest Territories, northwestern Canada. It is the deepest lake in North America. Depth: 614 m/2,015 ft. Area: 28,570 sq. km/11,031 sq. mi.

Great Smoky Mountains National Park national park in the southeastern United States, in western North Carolina and eastern Tennessee. Established in 1930, it contains some of the highest peaks in eastern North America. Area: 2,106 sq. km/813 sq. mi.

great tit *n.* a large common Eurasian tit with a short bill, and yellow, black, and white markings. Latin name: *Parus major*.

Great Trek *n.* a mass movement between 1836 and 1844 of Boer cattlemen in South Africa from the Cape to the north that eventually resulted in the establishment of the Transvaal and the Orange Free State

great-uncle *n.* an uncle of your father or mother

Great Victoria Desert desert in the states of Western Australia and South Australia, consisting of sand dunes, salt lakes, and low scrubland. Area: 650,000 sq. km/250,000 sq. mi.

Great Wall *n.* **1.** ASTRON IMMENSE GALACTIC SUPERCLUSTER a huge expanse of thousands of galaxies arranged in a supercluster that forms the largest system of astronomical objects observed in the universe **2.** = **Great Wall of China**

Great Wall of China

Great Wall of China *n.* a vast Chinese defensive fortification begun in the 3rd century BC and running along the northern border of the country for 2400 km/1500 mi

Great War *n.* = World War I

great white shark *n.* a large shark of warm and tropical waters that is grey-brown with white underparts. It preys on large fish, marine mammals, and carrion, and has a reputation for eating human beings. Latin name: *Carcharodon carcharias*.

Great Yarmouth /-yaárməth/ port and holiday resort on the eastern coast of Norfolk, eastern England. It is an important terminal for freight from continental Europe. Population: 46,400 (1991).

great year *n.* a period of about 25,800 years, representing a complete cycle of the precession of the equinoxes

greave /greev/ *n.* a piece of armour worn from the ankle to the knee (*usually used in the plural*) [14thC. From Old French *greve* 'calf, shin'.]

Grebe

grebe /greeb/ (*plural* **grebes** *or* **grebe**) *n.* a freshwater diving bird with lobed toes that is a strong swimmer. Family: Podicipedidae. [Mid-18thC. From French *grèbe*.]

Grecian /greesh'n/ *adj.* **1.** IN ANCIENT GREEK STYLE relating to or typical of the ancient Greek style of architecture or sculpture **2.** = **Greek** *adj.* 1 ■ *n.* **1.** HELLENIST a Hellenist (*dated*) **2.** = **Greek** *n.* 1 —**Grecianize** *vt.*

Grecism *n.* = **Graecism**

Greco /grékō/, **El** (1541–1614) Greek-born Spanish painter. His works combine the baroque style with exaggerated mannerism, and are characterized by lambent lighting and elongated figures. Real name **Domenikos Theotokopoulos**

Greco- *prefix.* = **Graeco-**

Greco-Roman *adj.* = **Graeco-Roman**

Greece /greess/ country in southeastern Europe, on the southernmost part of the Balkan Peninsula and numerous islands in the Aegean, Ionian, and Mediterranean seas. Language: Greek. Currency: drachma. Capital: Athens. Population: 10,493,000 (1996). Area: 131,957 sq. km/50,949 sq. mi. Official name **Hellenic Republic**

greed /greed/ *n.* **1.** EATING OF TOO MUCH the habit of eating to excess, or the desire to do so **2.** STRONG DESIRE FOR MORE an overwhelming desire to have more of sth such as money than is actually needed [Late 16thC. Back-formation from GREEDY.]

Greece

greedy /greédi/ (**-ier, -iest**) *adj.* **1.** EATING TOO MUCH eating to excess, or wanting to do so **2.** STRONGLY DESIRING MORE THAN REQUIRED having an overwhelming desire to have more of sth such as money than is actually needed [Old English *grædig*. Ultimately from a prehistoric Germanic base meaning 'hunger, greed'.] —**greedily** *adv.* —**greediness** *n.*

greedy guts /greédi guts/ (*plural* **-yguts**) *n.* sb who eats to excess, or wants to do so (*informal*)

greegree *n.* = **grigri**

Greek /greek/ *n.* **1.** SB FROM GREECE sb who was born in or brought up in Greece, or who has Greek citizenship **2.** LANGUAGE OF GREECE the official language of Greece and part of Cyprus, spoken by about 12 million people. ◊ **Ancient Greek, Demotic, Katharevousa, Late Greek, modern Greek** ■ *adj.* **1.** OF GREECE OR GREEKS relating to or typical of Greece, or its people or culture **2.** LANG OF THE GREEK LANGUAGE relating to the Greek language **3.** CHR OF GREEK ORTHODOX CHURCH relating to or belonging to the Greek Orthodox Church [Old English *grecas*. Ultimately from Latin *Graecus*, from Greek *Graikos*, the prehistoric name for the Hellenic people.] ◊ **beware of Greeks bearing gifts** be careful of possible treachery from sb who appears to be kind ◊ **it's (all) Greek to me** used to say that you cannot understand sth

Greek Catholic *n.* **1.** MEMBER OF EASTERN ORTHODOX CHURCH a member of the Eastern Orthodox Church **2.** MEMBER OF UNIAT GREEK CHURCH a member of the Uniat Greek Church

Greek Church *n.* = **Greek Orthodox Church**

Greek cross *n.* a cross consisting of four arms of the same length

Greek key *n.* an ornate pattern for a cornice or border consisting of lines that change direction at right angles to form a continuous band

Greek Orthodox Church *n.* **1.** NATIONAL CHURCH OF GREECE the national church of Greece, an independent section of the Eastern Orthodox Church **2.** = **Orthodox Church**

Greek salad *n.* a salad of tomatoes, lettuce, cucumber, olives, oregano, and feta cheese

green /green/ *adj.* **1.** COLOURS GRASS-COLOURED of a colour in the spectrum between yellow and blue, like the colour of grass **2.** HAVING EDIBLE GREEN LEAVES consisting of or containing green leaves of vegetables ○ *a green salad* **3.** GRASSY OR LEAFY consisting of or containing grass, plants, or foliage **4.** green, Green POL ADVOCATING PROTECTION OF THE ENVIRONMENT supporting or promoting the protection of the environment **5.** ENVIRON MADE WITH LITTLE ENVIRONMENTAL HARM produced in an environmentally and ecologically friendly way, e.g. by using renewable resources **6.** FOOD NOT RIPE unripe or not mature ○ *green bananas* **7.** FOOD UNSMOKED still raw, not yet smoked **8.** UNSEASONED newly cut and still unseasoned (*refers to leather*) ○ *green wood* **9.** UNTANNED not yet tanned (*refers to leather*) **10.** METALL UNFIRED not yet fired **11.** JEALOUS envious or jealous **12.** SICKLY-LOOKING pale and sickly-looking, especially as a result of nausea **13.** INNOCENT naive and lacking in experience, especially because of being new to sth **14.** NEW young, new, recent, or fresh ■ *n.* **1.** COLOURS THE COLOUR OF GRASS a primary colour between yellow and blue in the spectrum, like the colour of grass **2.** GREEN COLOURING a green pigment or dye **3.** GREEN CLOTH green fabric or clothing **4.** STH GREEN a green object **5.** GRASSY AREA an area of ground that is covered with grass, especially a public or communal area **6.** *Scotland* GRASSY AREA BELONGING TO HOUSE an area of grass belonging to a house or block of flats. ◊ **back green 7.** SPORTS GRASSY AREA FOR BOWLING an area of grass that is maintained for bowling and similar games **8.** GOLF GRASSY AREA SURROUNDING A GOLF HOLE the closely mown area at the end of a fairway on a golf course on which the hole for the ball is located **9.** FOLIAGE foliage used for decoration. US term **greens 10. green, Green** ADVOCATE OF PROTECTION OF ENVIRONMENT sb who supports or promotes the protection of the environment, especially a member of a political party concerned with environmental issues **11.** *US* MONEY cash or paper money (*slang*) ■ *v.* (**greens, greening, greened**) **1.** *vti.* BECOME OR MAKE GREEN to become green, or make sth green **2.** *vt.* PLANT TREES IN to plant trees and develop parks in urban areas **3.** *vti.* BECOME AN ENVIRONMENTAL ADVOCATE to become, or make sb become, aware of environmental issues [Old English *grene*. Ultimately from a prehistoric Germanic base that is also the ancestor of English *grass* and *grow*.] —**greenish** *adj.* —**greenly** *adv.* ◊ **go green** to become actively interested in environmental issues and support environmental causes

green alga *n.* an alga found mostly in fresh water. Division: *Chlorophyta*.

greenback /greén bak/ *n.* *US* a US bank note of any denomination (*slang*)

Green Bay /greén-/ city in Brown County, northeastern Wisconsin, on the southern shores of Lake Michigan. Population: 102,708 (1994).

green bean *n.* a type of bean such as French beans or runner beans that is eaten complete with its pod

green belt *n.* **1.** UNDEVELOPED LAND AROUND A CITY a strip of undeveloped land around a city that cannot be built on because of government legislation preventing urban sprawl **2.** IRRIGATED LAND BORDERING A DESERT an irrigated area of land on the edge of a desert, designed to prevent any further encroachment by the desert

Green Beret *n.* (*informal*) **1.** SPECIAL FORCES MEMBER a US Special Forces soldier **2.** COMMANDO a British commando [From the regulation green beret worn by members]

greenbottle /greén bot'l/, **greenbottle fly** *n.* a fly that is metallic green in colour and lays its eggs in rotting vegetation or flesh. Genus: *Lucilia*.

green card *n.* **1.** US IDENTITY CARD in the United States, an identity card and work permit issued to nationals of other countries **2.** DRIVING INSURANCE DOCUMENT an insurance document for motorists driving abroad **3.** BRITISH DISABLED PERSON'S IDENTITY CARD in the United Kingdom, an identity card issued by the government to a disabled person —**green-carder** *n.*

green dragon *n.* a tuberous North American plant that has divided leaves and small green flowers arranged along a stalk enclosed in a tight green sheath. Latin name: *Arisaema dracontium*.

Graham Greene

Greene /greén/, **Graham** (1904–91) British writer. His major novels, including *Brighton Rock* (1938) and *The Power and the Glory* (1940), incorporate themes of spiritual and moral struggle. Full name **Henry Graham Greene**

green earth *n.* PAINTING = **terre verte**

greenery /greénəri/ *n.* **1.** GREEN PLANTS growing green foliage and plants **2.** LEAVES AND BRANCHES AS DECORATION

green leaves and small branches from trees and shrubs used for decoration. US term **evergreens**

green-eyed monster *n.* jealousy or envy personified

greenfield /greén feeld/ *adj.* relating to or situated in a piece of open land that has not been built on

greenfinch /greén finch/ (*plural* **-finches** *or* **-finch**) *n.* a European green-grey and yellow finch. Latin name: *Carduelis chloris*.

green fingers *npl.* a natural ability to make plants grow well. US term **green thumb** —**green-fingered** *adj.*

greenfly /greén flī/ (*plural* **-flies** *or* **-fly**) *n.* a green winged aphid that is a pest of garden plants, houseplants, and crops

greengage /greén gayj/ *n.* **1.** KIND OF PLUM TREE a variety of plum tree that has roundish sweet green fruits. Latin name: *Prunus domestica italica*. **2.** PLUM FRUIT the fruit of the greengage tree [Early 18thC. *Gage* from the name of Sir William *Gage*, who introduced it to England.]

greengrocer /greén grôssər/ *n.* **1.** FRUIT AND VEGETABLE SELLER sb who sells fresh fruit and vegetables. ◊ **grocer 2. greengrocer, greengrocer's** (*plural* **-cer's**) FRUIT AND VEGETABLE SHOP a shop that sells fresh fruits and vegetables. ◊ **grocer 3.** AUSTRALIAN CICADA a large bright-green Australian cicada. Latin name: *Cyclochila australasiae*.

greengrocery /greén grôssəri/ *n.* (*plural* **-ies**) **1.** = **greengrocer** *n.* **2** **2.** GREENGROCER'S TRADE the trade or profession of a greengrocer ■ **greengroceries** *npl.* FOOD SOLD BY GREENGROCER fresh fruit and vegetables sold by a greengrocer

greenhead /greén hed/ *n.* a male mallard duck

greenheart /greén haart/ (*plural* **-hearts** *or* **-heart**) *n.* **1.** TROPICAL AMERICAN TREE an evergreen tropical American tree of the laurel family with dark greenish wood. Latin name: *Ocotea rodiaei*. **2.** TREE RESEMBLING THE GREENHEART any of a number of trees similar to the true greenheart. ◊ **African greenheart 3.** GREENHEART TREE WOOD the wood of any of the greenheart trees

greenhorn /greén hawrn/ *n.* sb who is naive and unsophisticated

——— **WORD KEY: SYNONYMS** ———
See Synonyms at *beginner*.

greenhouse /greén howss/ (*plural* **-houses** /-howziz/) *n.* a glass or transparent plastic structure, often on a metal or wooden frame, in which plants that need heat, light, and protection from the elements are grown

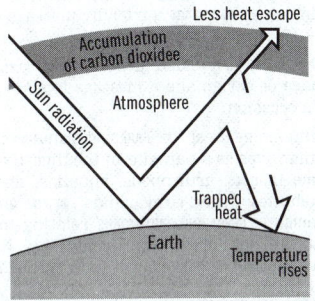
Greenhouse effect

greenhouse effect *n.* warming of the Earth's surface as a result of atmospheric pollution by gases. It is now feared that the warming effects are being undesirably increased, causing climate changes and melting polar icecaps.

greenhouse gas *n.* a gas such as carbon dioxide, ozone, or water vapour that contributes to the warming of the Earth's atmosphere by reflecting radiation from the Earth's surface

greenie /greéni/ *n.* *Aus* a conservationist or environmentalist (*informal*)

greening /greéning/ *n.* a type of apple that is green when ripe [Early 17thC. Origin uncertain: probably from Dutch *groeninc*, a variety of apple.]

green keeper *n.* sb who manages and maintains a golf course or bowling green. US term **greenskeeper**

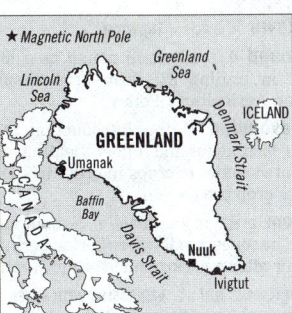
Greenland

Greenland /greénlənd/ island situated between the North Atlantic and Arctic oceans. The largest island in the world, it is a self-governing part of Denmark. Capital: Nuuk. Population: 58,000 (1996). Area: 2,175,600 sq. km/840,000 sq. mi. —**Greenlander** *n.*

Greenlandic /greén lándik/ *n.* INUIT DIALECT a dialect of Inuit spoken in Greenland by about 60,000 people ■ *adj.* **1.** OF GREENLAND DIALECT relating to the dialect Greenlandic **2.** OF GREENLAND relating to or typical of Greenland or its people or culture

Greenland right whale *n.* ZOOL = **bowhead**

Greenland Sea section of the Atlantic Ocean off the coast of northeastern Greenland that is covered by pack ice for most of the year

green light *n.* **1.** SIGNAL TO PROCEED a light that is green in colour and is used as a signal at intersections for vehicles or pedestrians to proceed **2.** PERMISSION TO BEGIN permission to start work on sth, especially a project or plan

greenling /greénling/ (*plural* **-lings** *or* **-ling**) *n.* a fish of coastal waters in the northern Pacific Ocean with large pectoral fins, a large head, and a skin flap over each eye. Family: Hexagrammidae.

greenmail /greén mayl/ *n.* BUSINESS PRESSURE BY THREAT OF TAKEOVER the purchase of enough of a company's shares to threaten it with takeover, thereby forcing the company to buy back the stock at a higher price to avoid the takeover. ◊ **blackmail, greymail** ■ *vt.* (**-mails, -mailing, -mailed**) GREENMAIL SB to subject a company to greenmail [Late 20thC. From GREEN 'money' + BLACKMAIL.] —**greenmailer** *n.*

green man *n.* an illuminated green symbol of a walking man at a pedestrian crossing that indicates that it is safe to cross

green manure *n.* a growing crop that is ploughed directly back into the soil to act as a fertilizer

green monkey *n.* a small olive green African monkey that lives in large troops in woodlands or on the edge of savanna grasslands. Latin name: *Cercophithecus aethiops sabaeus*.

green monkey disease *n.* MED = **Marburg disease**

Green Mountains mountain range in the Appalachian system, extending from Canada into western Massachusetts. The highest point is Mount Mansfield, 1,339 m/4,393 ft.

Greenock /greénək/ seaport on the Firth of Clyde, southwestern Scotland, the birthplace of James Watt. Population: 50,013 (1991).

greenockite /greénə kīt/ *n.* a yellowish crystalline mineral consisting of cadmium sulphide [Mid-18thC. Named after Charles Murray Cathcart, Lord *Greenock*.]

green paper *n.* in the United Kingdom or Canada, a document that contains the government's policy proposals that are to be discussed in Parliament. ◊ **white paper**

Green Party *n.* a British political party formed in 1985 whose primary policy is the protection of the environment

Greenpeace /greén peess/ *n.* an international organization that advocates the protection of the environment and takes nonviolent action to achieve its aims

green pepper *n.* an unripe sweet pepper eaten raw or cooked. Latin name: *Capsicum annuum*. ◊ **red pepper**

green plover *n.* BIRDS = lapwing

green pound *n.* the British pound as a unit of exchange in trading EU farm produce under the Common Agricultural Policy

green revolution *n.* the introduction of modern farming techniques and higher-yielding, more pest-resistant varieties of crops in order to significantly increase crop production

greenroom /gréen room, -rŏŏm/ *n.* a room in a studio, theatre, or concert hall where performers may relax before or after a performance or appearance

greens /greenz/ *npl.* **1.** VEGETABLES WITH GREEN LEAVES AND STEMS vegetables with green leaves and stems, e.g. cabbage and spinach **2.** *US* = **green** *adj.* **⧫ 3.** *US* GREEN-COLOURED CLOTHING green clothing, e.g. US Army uniforms or operating room scrubs (*informal*)

greensand /gréen sand/ *n.* sandstone flecked with the dark-green clay mineral glauconite

greenshank /gréen shangk/ (*plural* -shanks *or* -shank) *n.* a large sandpiper of Europe and Asia with long greenish legs. Latin name: *Tringa nebularia.*

greensickness /gréen siknəss/ *n.* = **chlorosis** *n.* **2** — **greensick** *adj.*

greenskeeper /gréenz keepər/ *n.* *US* = **green keeper**

greenstick fracture *n.* a bone fracture usually occurring in children, in which one side of the bone is broken and the other side is bent [*Greenstick* from GREEN 'immature' + STICK because it resembles a stick]

greenstone /gréen stōn/ *n.* **1.** GEOL GREEN IGNEOUS ROCK a green igneous rock containing the minerals feldspar and hornblende **2.** VARIETY OF JADE a dark New Zealand variety of jade used especially in Maori weapon and jewellery making

greenstrip *n.* *US* a firebreak on open grassland, planted with vegetation that does not burn easily

greensward /gréen swawrd/ *n.* a grass-covered piece of ground, or an area of turf (*archaic or literary*)

greentailing *n.* environmentally responsible retailing that involves the sale of products with the least impact on the environment or that increases the ecological awareness of the consumer (*informal*) [Coined from GREEN + *tailing* from retail]

green tea *n.* tea made from leaves that have been dried but not fermented, and that is pale green in colour. **◊ black tea**

green thumb *n.* *US, Can* = **green fingers**

green turtle *n.* a large marine turtle of warm waters, sometimes killed for food. It comes to land only to bask, sleep, and lay eggs. Latin name: *Chelonia mydas.* [From its green shell]

green vitriol *n.* = **ferrous sulphate**

greenware /gréen wair/ *n.* dry clay pieces before they have been fired

greenway /gréen way/ *n.* *US* a stretch of undeveloped land close to an urban area that is kept for recreational use

Greenway /gréen way/, **Francis Howard** (1777–1837) British-born Australian architect. He was transported to Australia for forgery in 1814, and there designed numerous public buildings in New South Wales.

green-wellie *adj.* used to describe or relating to rich upper-class British people who enjoy country pursuits (*informal*) [From the stereotype of the clothing worn by such people]

Greenwich /grénnich, -ij/ borough of London, on the southern bank of the River Thames. It is the site of the prime meridian, which passes through the Royal Greenwich Observatory. Population: 211,410 (1995).

Greenwich Mean Time, **Greenwich Time** *n.* the time in a zone that includes the 0° meridian of Greenwich, London, used formerly as the main standard from which the time in other zones is calculated

Greenwich Village *n.* a residential area in lower Manhattan, once popular with bohemians, artists, and writers and now a tourist attraction

greenwood /gréen wŏŏd/ *n.* a forest or woods in the summer when the leaves are green. It is the trad-

itional location for stories about outlaws such as Robin Hood. (*archaic*)

green woodpecker *n.* a large European woodpecker with green feathers and a red crown, often found feeding on the ground. Latin name: *Picus viridis.*

Germaine Greer

Greer /greer/, **Germaine** (b. 1939) Australian writer and feminist. She launched her career as a passionate advocate of women's empowerment with her first book, *The Female Eunuch* (1970).

greet¹ /greet/ (greets, greeting, greeted) *vt.* **1.** WELCOME SB to welcome sb in a cordial and usually conventional way **2.** ADDRESS SB COURTEOUSLY to address sb in a polite and usually conventional way on meeting **3.** ADDRESS SB IN A LETTER to address a person or group at the start of a letter using a set formula **4.** REPLY TO STH to receive or respond to sth in a particular way ○ *the news was greeted with dismay* **5.** BECOME NOTICEABLE to become perceptible to sb, especially by way of the senses such as vision, hearing, or smell ○ *The smell of a cake baking greeted them.* [Old English *gretan*. Ultimately from a prehistoric West Germanic word meaning 'to resound'.]

greet² /greet/ *vi.* (greets, greeting, greeted) *Scotland* (*nonstandard*) **1.** WEEP to cry or weep **2.** COMPLAIN to complain whiningly ■ *n. Scotland* (*nonstandard*) **1.** WEEPING an act of crying or weeping **2.** COMPLAINING an act of complaining whiningly [Partly from Old English *grētan* (see GREET¹), partly from *grēotan* 'to cry', from, ultimately, prehistoric Germanic]

greeter *n.* sb employed to greet customers in a restaurant or similar business

greeting /gréeting/ *n.* **1.** FRIENDLY GESTURE a cordial and often conventional gesture or expression used when welcoming, meeting, or addressing sb **2.** WELCOMING SB an act of welcoming or addressing sb with a greeting ■ *npl.* MESSAGE a friendly message or good wishes [Old English *grēting*]

greetings card *n.* a folded piece of heavy paper with an image or design and a message to sb to mark a special occasion

gregarine /gréggə reen/ *n.* PARASITIC PROTOZOAN a protozoan that lives as a parasite in the digestive tracts of some insects, arthropods, annelids, and other invertebrates. Order: Gregarinida. ■ *adj.* **gregarine, gregarinian** OF GREGARINE PROTOZOANS relating to or belonging to the order that comprises the gregarines [Mid-19thC. Formed from modern Latin *Gregarina*, genus name, from Latin *gregarius* (see GREGARIOUS).]

gregarious /gri gáir əss/ *adj.* **1.** FRIENDLY very friendly and sociable **2.** ZOOL LIVING COMMUNALLY used to describe organisms that live in groups **3.** PLANTS GROWING TOGETHER used to describe plants that grow in clusters [Mid-17thC. Formed from Latin *gregarius*, from *grex* 'flock'.] —**gregariously** *adv.* —**gregariousness** *n.*

─── **WORD KEY: ORIGIN** ───

The Latin word *grex* from which *gregarious* is derived is also the source of English *aggregate*, *congregation*, and *egregious*.

Gregg /greg/, **Sir Norman McAlister** (1892–1966) Australian ophthalmologist. He discovered the link between rubella during pregnancy and birth defects.

Gregorian calendar /gri gáwri ən-/ *n.* the calendar introduced in 1582 by Pope Gregory XIII that is still in use and is a modification of the previous Roman calendar. **◊ Julian calendar, Hegira calendar**

Gregorian chant *n.* a liturgical chant of the Roman Catholic Church that is sung without accompaniment [From its supposedly having been introduced by Pope *Gregory* I]

Gregorian telescope *n.* an astronomical telescope that has a concave primary mirror with a central hole through which light is reflected from a smaller secondary concave mirror [Mid-18thC. Named after the Scottish mathematician J. *Gregory* (1638–75) who invented it.]

Gregory I /gréggəri/, **St** (540?–604) Pope. As pope (590–604), he sent St Augustine to England to lead the country's conversion to Christianity. He is said to have introduced Gregorian chant into the Roman Catholic liturgy. Known as **Gregory the Great**

greisen /gríz'n/ *n.* a granite-derived rock consisting of mica and quartz [Late 19thC. From German, probably formed from *greis* 'grey with age'.]

gremlin /grémlin/ *n.* a tiny imaginary mischievous creature that is blamed for faults in tools, machinery, and electronic equipment (*informal*) [Early 20thC. Origin uncertain: probably modelled on GOBLIN, first used by airforce personnel in World War II.]

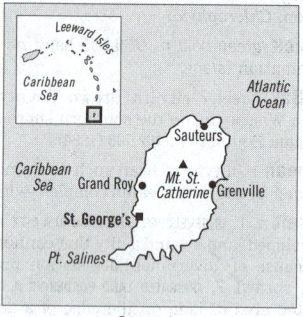

Grenada

Grenada /gri náydə, gre naádə/ independent state in the southeastern Caribbean Sea, comprising the island of Grenada and some of the southern Grenadines. Language: English. Currency: East Caribbean dollar. Capital: St George's. Population: 95,535 (1997). Area: 344 sq. km/133 sq. mi. —**Grenadian** /grə náydi ən/ *n., adj.*

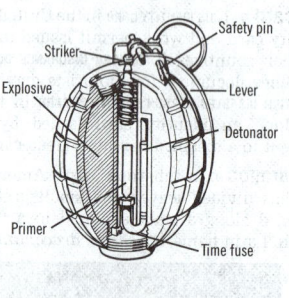

Grenade

grenade /gri náyd/ *n.* **1.** HAND-THROWN BOMB a small bomb that is thrown by hand or shot from a rifle or other weapon **2.** SEALED GLASS PROJECTILE a sealed glass projectile that breaks on impact, releasing tear gas or chemicals to put out fires [Mid-16thC. From French, an alteration of *grenate* 'pomegranate' (influenced by Spanish *granada*), from *pome grenate*. The powder capsules in a grenade were thought to resemble the seeds in the fruit.]

grenadier /grénnə deer/ (*plural* -diers *or* -dier) *n.* **1.** GRENADE-CARRYING SOLDIER formerly, a soldier armed with grenades **2.** TALL STRONG SOLDIER formerly, a soldier assigned to a special company of a regiment on the basis of exceptional height and ability **3.** ZOOL BOTTOM-DWELLING FISH a bottom-dwelling marine fish with a tapering body and no tail fin. Family: Macrouridae. **4.** BIRDS EAST AFRICAN FINCH an East African finch with purple patches, a red beak, and a tapering tail. Latin name: *Uraeginthus ianthinogaster.* **5.** BIRDS AFRICAN WEAVERBIRD an African weaverbird with a black head and bright red plumage on its crown and back.

Latin name: *Euplectes orix*. [Late 17thC. Formed from GRENADE.]

Grenadier, **Grenadier guard** n. SOLDIER IN GUARDS a British soldier belonging to the first regiment of the Guards Division, the troops of the Royal Household ■ **Grenadiers** npl. BRITISH REGIMENT in the British army, the first regiment of the Guards Division, the troops of the Royal Household

grenadine[1] /grénnə deen/ n. **1.** POMEGRANATE SYRUP a syrup made from pomegranates, used especially in cocktails **2.** RED-ORANGE a reddish-orange colour ■ adj. RED-ORANGE of a reddish-orange colour [Late 19thC. From French (*sirop de*) *grenadine*, from *grenade* (see GRE-NADE).]

grenadine[2] /grénnə deen/ n. a dress fabric of silk or wool woven like gauze [Mid-19thC. From French, 'silk having a texture like grain', from, ultimately, *grain* (see GRAIN).]

Grenoble /grə nőb'l/ industrial city and capital of Isère Department, in the Rhône-Alpes Region, southeastern France. Population: 150,758 (1990).

grenz rays npl. low-energy x-rays produced by electrons accelerated through less than 25 kilovolts [*Grenz* from German *Grenze* 'boundary']

Gresham's law /gréshəmz-/, **Gresham's theorem** n. the theory that bad money drives good money out of circulation because a currency of lower intrinsic value will be used whilst one of higher intrinsic value will be hoarded [Mid-19thC. Named after Sir Thomas *Gresham* (1519?-79), the founder of the Royal Exchange, sub-financial advisor to Queen Elizabeth I.]

Gretna Green /grétnə-/ village in Dumfries and Galloway, southwestern Scotland. It used to be a popular place for eloping couples from England to be married without parental consent. Population: 3,149 (1991).

grevillea /grə vílliə/ (plural **-leas** or **-lea**) n. an ornamental evergreen tree or shrub native to Australia and New Caledonia. Genus: *Grevillea*. [Mid-19thC. From modern Latin, genus name, named after the Scottish horticulturist Charles Francis *Greville* (1749–1809).]

grew past tense of **grow**

grey /gray/ adj. OF THE COLOUR OF ASH having the colour of ash or lead ○ *a dull grey sky* ○ *city workers in grey suits* ■ n. **1.** COLOUR OF ASH the colour of ash or lead **2.** PIGMENT MADE FROM BLACK AND WHITE a pigment or dye that is formed from a combination of black and white and is or is near to the colour of ash or lead ○ *Use greys and blues to emphasize the mood.* **3.** GREY CLOTHING fabric or clothing that is grey in colour **4.** **grey**, **Grey** CONFEDERATE SOLDIER a soldier of the Confederacy in the American Civil War. ◊ blue n. ⁊ **5.** STH GREY a grey object [Old English *gr_æg*, ultimately from a prehistoric Germanic base that is also the ancestor of English *grizzle*; in the sense 'soldier', from the colour of their uniforms] —**greyness** n.

Grey /gray/, **Sir Edward, 1st Viscount Grey of Fallodon** (1862–1933) British statesman. A member of the Liberal Party, he was secretary of state for foreign affairs (1905–16).

Grey, **Sir George Edward** (1812–98) Portugese-born British explorer and colonial administrator. He was governor of South Australia (1840–45), and governor (1845–53, 1861–68) and premier (1877–79) of New Zealand.

Grey, Lady Jane, Queen of England (1537–54). The great-granddaughter of Henry VII, she was named as the successor of Edward VI in 1553. She ruled for only nine days before being forced to abdicate, and was executed for treason.

grey area n. **1.** UNCLEAR SITUATION a situation, subject, or category of sth that is unclear or hard to define or classify **2.** STH THAT CANNOT BE CLASSIFIED a part of sth that does not belong to any specific category but contains features of more than one **3.** ECONOMICALLY DEPRESSED UK REGION in the United Kingdom, a part of the country suffering from high unemployment

greyback /gráy bak/ n. an animal, bird, fish, or insect with a grey back

greybar land /gráy baar-/ n. the state of waiting for the grey bar graphic device on a computer screen slowly to fill up as a time-consuming computer process nears completion (informal)

greybeard /gráy beerd/ n. **1.** ELDERLY MAN an elderly man (dated) **2.** CONTAINER FOR ALCOHOL an earthenware container for alcohol —**greybearded** adj.

grey eminence n. = éminence grise

grey fox n. a fox with a grey and red coat that is found in woodlands throughout the United States and Central America. Latin name: *Urocyon cinereoargenteus*.

Grey Friar n. a monk of the Franciscan order [From the colour of the order's habit]

greyhen /gráy hen/ (plural **-hens** or **-hen**) n. a female black grouse

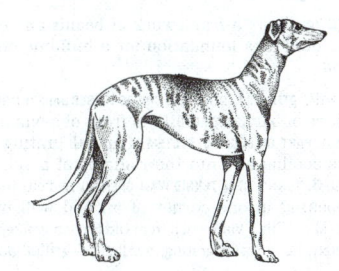

Greyhound

greyhound /gráy hownd/ n. a tall slim fast-running dog with a smooth coat, narrow head, and long legs, widely used for racing [Old English *grīghund*. Grey-ultimately from a prehistoric Germanic base that is also the ancestor of Old Norse *grey* 'bitch'.]

greyish /gráy ish/ adj. slightly or somewhat grey in colour

grey jay n. a North American bird of the crow family that is grey in colour with black markings on the head. It inhabits coniferous forests, especially spruce forests. Latin name: *Perisoreus canadensis*.

greylag /gráy lag/, **greylag goose** n. a common Eurasian wild goose that is a light brownish-grey in colour with a large orange or pink bill. It is the ancestor of the domestic farm goose. Latin name: *Anser anser*. [Early 18thC. From GREY + dialect *lag* 'goose', of unknown origin.]

greymail /gráy mayl/ n. a manoeuvre used by the defence in a spy trial whereby the government is threatened with the revelation of national secrets unless the case against the defendant is dropped. ◊ **blackmail**, **greenmail** [Late 20thC. Modelled on BLACK-MAIL.]

grey market n. **1.** STOCK EXCH TRADING IN SHARES BEFORE ISSUE trading in new shares before they have been officially issued on the stock exchange **2.** COMM SECRET TRADING IN GOODS clandestine but legal trading in goods either at excessively high prices or at prices well below the manufacturer's recommended price. ◊ **black market**

grey matter n. **1.** INTELLIGENCE intelligence or brains (informal) **2.** BROWNISH-GREY TISSUE WITHIN BRAIN brownish-grey nerve tissue consisting mainly of nerve cell bodies within the brain and spinal cord. ◊ **white matter**

Greymouth /gráyməth/ town on the western coast of the South Island, New Zealand. A former gold-mining town, it is now the commercial centre of a mining and industrial region. Population: 10,191 (1996).

grey mullet n. any fish of approximately 70 species that occur throughout the world in tropical and temperate seas. Some are caught for food. Family: Mugilidae. US term **mullet**

grey squirrel n. a large tree squirrel of North America, Great Britain, Ireland, and South Africa that has grey fur with a reddish tinge in the legs and head. Latin name: *Sciurus carolinensis*. ◊ **red squirrel**

greywacke /gráy wakə/ n. a conglomerate rock composed of well-rounded pebbles cemented by a sandy infill [Late 18thC. From German *Grauwacke* 'grey sandstone'.]

grey wagtail n. a small songbird, found in Europe, Asia, and Africa, with a grey back and head, yellow underside, and a long tail that it wags to keep its balance. Latin name: *Motacilla cinerea*.

grey water n. ENVIRON waste water from sinks, baths, and kitchen appliance

greywether /gráy wethər/ n. GEOL = sarsen

grey whale n. a large baleen whale of coastal waters of the North Pacific that has no dorsal fin but a line of bumps along part of its back. Latin name: *Eschrichtius gibbosus*.

grey wolf n. a large intelligent highly social wild dog of North America, Europe, and Asia, varying in colour from white in the north of its range to black in the south. Latin name: *Canis lupus*.

gribble /gríbb'l/ n. a small marine crustacean of the woodlouse family that burrows into submerged wooden structures. Genus: *Limnoria*. [Late 18thC. Origin uncertain.]

gricer /gríssər/ n. a train spotter (dated) [Mid-20thC. Origin unknown.]

grid /grid/ n. **1.** MAPS REFERENCE LINES ON A MAP a network of evenly spaced horizontal and vertical lines on a map, used as a basis for finding specific points **2.** ADJACENT SQUARES a network of squares formed by horizontal and vertical lines **3.** GRATING MADE OF BARS a set of parallel or crisscrossing bars that form a grating **4.** UTIL NETWORK a network of cables, lines, or pipes for distributing electricity, gas, or water **5.** UTIL = national grid **6.** ELECTRON ENG CONTROL ELECTRODE the part of a electronic valve that controls the flow of current between the other electrodes, usually constructed as a metal screen or coil **7.** MOTOR SPORTS = starting grid **8.** AMERICAN FOOTBALL = gridiron n. 3 [Mid-19thC. Shortening of GRIDIRON.] —**gridded** adj.

grid bias n. a fixed voltage applied between the control electrode and the cathode in an electronic valve

gridder /grídder/ n. US an American football player (informal) [Early 20thC. Formed from GRID.]

griddle /grídd'l/ n. **1.** HEATED COOKING SURFACE a heavy flat metal plate heated and used for cooking food, especially batter mixtures **2.** SIEVE USED BY MINERS a sieve with a base formed from a wire mesh, used by miners ■ vt. (**-dles**, **-dling**, **-dled**) COOK STH ON A GRIDDLE to cook sth on a flat hot surface [Pre-12thC. From Old French *gredil* 'gridiron', from, ultimately, Latin *cratis* 'crate'.]

gridiron /gríd⊤ərn/ n. **1.** = grill[1] **2.** GRATING a structure consisting of parallel bars **3.** AMERICAN FOOTBALL AMERICAN FOOTBALL FIELD a field marked with parallel white lines, on which American football is played **4.** AMERICAN FOOTBALL AMERICAN FOOTBALL the game of American football (informal) **5.** THEATRE STRUCTURE ABOVE A THEATRE STAGE a structure of beams or bars above a theatre stage from which lighting and scenery are suspended [13thC. Alteration of GRIDDLE, by association with IRON.]

gridlock /gríd lok/ n. **1.** TRAFFIC JAM a traffic jam in which congestion at one or two road junctions affects a wide area so that traffic is unable to move in any direction **2.** DEADLOCK a situation in which no progress can be made —**gridlocked** adj.

grid reference n. a reference, usually using numbers or letters, that specifies a position on a map or chart by referring to the superimposed grid

grief /greef/ n. **1.** INTENSE SORROW great sadness, especially as a result of a death **2.** CAUSE OF INTENSE SORROW the cause of intense, deep, and profound sorrow, especially a specific event or situation **3.** TROUBLE annoyance or trouble (informal) [Pre-12thC. Via Anglo-Norman *gref* from Old French *grief* 'grieved', from *grever* (see GRIEVE).] ◊ **come to grief** to suffer misfortune or ruin ◊ **good grief!** used to express surprise, exasperation, or dismay (dated informal)

grief-stricken adj. deeply affected by sadness

Edvard Grieg

Grieg /greeg/, **Edvard** (1843–1907) Norwegian composer. His work was permeated by the melodies and harmonies of Norwegian folk music. He was a noted composer of songs, and wrote the music to Henrik Ibsen's *Peer Gynt* (1875). Full name **Edvard Hagerup Grieg**

grievance /gréevənss/ n. **1.** STH THOUGHT REASON ENOUGH TO COMPLAIN a cause for complaint or resentment that may or may not be well-founded **2.** RESENTMENT bitterness or anger at having received unfair treatment **3.** FORMAL OBJECTION a formal complaint made on the basis of sth that sb feels is unfair

grieve[1] /greev/ (**grieves, grieving, grieved**) v. **1.** vti. EXPERIENCE INTENSE SORROW to experience great sadness, e.g. at a death **2.** vt. MAKE SAD to cause great sadness to sb [Pre-12thC. Via Old French *grever* 'to burden' from Latin *gravare*, from *gravis* 'heavy, grave' (source of English *gravity*).] —**griever** n.

grieve[2] /greev/ n. Scotland a farm supervisor or manager [Old English *grǣfa*]

grievous /gréevəss/ adj. **1.** VERY SERIOUS extremely serious or significant **2.** SEVERE very bad or severe — **grievously** adv. —**grievousness** n.

grievous bodily harm n. CRIMINAL LAW serious physical injury intentionally done to sb

Griffin

griffin /gríffin/, **griffon, gryphon** n. a mythical monster with the head and wings of an eagle and the body and tail of a lion [13thC. Via Old French *grifoun* from Latin *gryphus*, from Greek *grups*.]

Griffin /gríffin/, **Walter Burley** (1876–1937) US-born Australian architect. In collaboration with his wife, Marion Griffin (1871–1961), he designed the new Australian capital city, Canberra (1914–35).

griffon /gríffən/ n. **1.** SMALL DOG a small dog like a terrier belonging to a breed with wiry hair and a short muzzle **2.** MYTHOL = **griffin** [Late 18thC. Via French from Old French *grifoun* (see GRIFFIN).]

griffon vulture n. a large light-coloured vulture with dark wing and tail feathers, found in southern Europe, North Africa, and the Middle East. Genus: *Gyps*.

grigri /gree gree/ (plural **-gris**), **greegree** (plural **-grees**), **gris-gris** (plural **gris-gris**) n. an African talisman or fetish [Late 18thC. Via American Spanish from Caribbean *grugru* 'palm'.]

grike /grīk/, **gryke** n. a deep cleft in a bare limestone rock surface. ◊ **clint** [Late 18thC. Origin unknown.]

grill[1] /gril/ vti. (**grills, grilling, grilled**) COOK UNDER OR OVER DIRECT HEAT to cook food or be cooked by direct heat ■ n. PLATE FOR GRILLING flat plate made of parallel metal bars used for grilling ■ vt. (**grills, grilling, grilled**) INTERROGATE to interrogate or cross-examine sb in a persistent manner (*informal*) ■ n. INDUST GRIDIRON PATTERN a pattern made on a surface by a grill or gridiron ■ vti. (**grills, grilling, grilled**) SUBJECT TO GREAT HEAT to subject sb or sth or be subjected to great heat, especially from the sun ■ n. **1.** FOOD FOOD COOKED ON GRILL a dish or portion of food cooked on a grill **2.** COOK RESTAURANT SERVING GRILLED FOOD an establishment that serves food cooked on a grill **3.** PART OF COOKER RADIATING HEAT a device in or on a cooker that radiates heat downwards. US term **broiler** [Mid-17thC. From French *griller*, from *grille* (see GRILLE).] —**griller** n.

──── **WORD KEY: SYNONYMS** ────
See Synonyms at *question*.

grill[2] n. = **grille**

grillage /gríllij/ n. a framework of beams and crossbeams built as a foundation for a building on soft ground

grille /gril/, **grill** n. **1.** BUILDING CRISSCROSSED BARS a pattern or lattice of bars, especially in front of a window **2.** AUTOMOT PART OF COOLING SYSTEM a metal grating that allows cooling air into the radiator of a vehicle's engine **3.** TENNIS REAL TENNIS WALL OPENING in real tennis, the opening in one corner of an end wall of the court [Mid-17thC. Via French from Old French *graille*, from, ultimately, Latin *cratis* 'grating, hurdle'.] —**grilled** adj.

grillroom /gríl room, -rôom/ n. = **grill**[1] n. 2

grillwork /gríl wurk/ n. = **grille** n. 1

grilse /grilss/ (plural **grilses** or **grilse**) n. a salmon the first time it returns from the sea [15thC. Origin unknown.]

grim /grim/ (**grimmer, grimmest**) adj. **1.** DEPRESSING depressingly gloomy ○ *a grim economic forecast* **2.** FORBIDDING forbidding and unattractive in appearance ○ *a grim mining town of Great Depression times* **3.** STERNLY SERIOUS stern in a frightening and unnerving way ○ *a grim, set look on his face* **4.** UNPLEASANT extremely unpleasant, distressing, or sinister ○ *a grim accident scene* **5.** IRONIC disquietingly ironic ○ *a grim reminder of humankind's penchant for folly* **6.** ILL unwell, especially as a result of overindulgence in alcohol (*informal*) **7.** SHODDY very low in quality (*informal*) ○ *put in a pretty grim performance* [Old English. Ultimately from a prehistoric Germanic word that is also the ancestor of English *grumble* and Spanish *grima* 'fright' (source of English *grimace*).] —**grimly** adv. —**grimness** n.

grimace /grímməss, gri máyss/ n. EXPRESSION ON FACE contorted twisting of the face that expresses disgust or pain ■ vi. (**-aces, -acing, -aced**) MAKE A GRIMACE to twist the face in a grimace [Mid-17thC. Via French *grimache* from Spanish *grimazo* 'caricature', from *grima* (see GRIM).] —**grimacer** n. —**grimacingly** adv.

Grimaldi /gri máldi/ n. ASTRON a very large, dark-floored enclosure near the western edge of the moon, approximately 220 km/135 mi. in diameter

grimalkin /gri máwlkin, -málkin/ n. an old female cat [Late 16thC. From GREY + obsolete *malkin* 'cat' (from a pet form of the female names *Maud* or *Matilda*).]

grime /grīm/ n. ACCUMULATED DIRT dirt or soot, usually accumulated in a black layer or ingrained into a surface ■ vt. (**grimes, griming, grimed**) COVER WITH GRIME to coat sth with dirt or soot [13thC. From Middle Low German *greme*.]

Grimm /grim/, **Jakob** (1785–1863) German philologist and folklorist. He was the founder of comparative linguistics, and formulated Grimm's Law. In collaboration with his brother, Wilhelm Karl Grimm (1786–1859), he collected old German folk tales and published them in collections now known as *Grimm's Fairy Tales* (1812–22). Full name **Jakob Ludwig Karl Grimm**

Grim Reaper n. a personification of death, shown as a cloaked man or skeleton holding a scythe

grimy /grími/ (**-ier, -iest**) adj. heavily soiled, usually with dirt or soot —**grimily** adv. —**griminess** n.

──── **WORD KEY: SYNONYMS** ────
See Synonyms at *dirty*.

grin /grin/ vi. (**grins, grinning, grinned**) SMILE BROADLY to smile broadly, usually showing the teeth ■ n. BROAD SMILE a broad smile that usually shows the teeth [Old English *grennian* 'to bare your teeth'. Ultimately from an Indo-European base meaning 'to be open', ancestor also of English *groan*. The underlying idea is 'opening the mouth'.] —**grinner** n. ◇ **grin and bear it** to tolerate sth unpleasant without complaining (*informal*)

grind /grīnd/ v. (**grinds, grinding, ground**) **1.** vti. PULVERIZE STH to crush sth into very small pieces by rubbing it between two hard surfaces, or to be crushed in this way **2.** vti. MAKE A RASPING NOISE to rub two surfaces together with a grating noise or make a grating noise by rubbing things together ○ *He ground the gears every time he shifted.* **3.** vt. PUSH DOWN WITH TWISTING MOTION to push sth down firmly or crush sth on a surface with a twisting or rotating motion ○ *ground the cigarette out on the pavement* **4.** vt. US = **mince 5.** vt. SMOOTH OR SHARPEN STH to make sth smooth or sharp by rubbing it against an abrasive surface **6.** vi. MOVE NOISILY to move with a grating noise **7.** vt. TURN A HANDLE TO RUN STH to operate sth such as a barrel organ by turning its handle **8.** vi. LABOUR AT STH to study or work hard, especially too hard (*informal*) **9.** vi. DANCE EROTICALLY to dance erotically with a circling of the hips (*informal*) ■ n. **1.** STH BORING AND REPETITIVE sth that is routine, dull, and tedious (*informal*) **2.** GRINDING an act of grinding **3.** GRINDING NOISE a grating noise like that of sth grinding **4.** TEXTURE the texture of sth that is ground **5.** US HARD WORKER sb who works or studies too hard (*informal*) **6.** EROTIC DANCE MOVEMENT an erotic circling and thrusting of the hips in dancing (*informal*) [Old English *grindan*]

grind down vt. to weaken sb gradually by persistent oppression

grind on vi. to continue in an unrelenting way

grind out vt. **1.** DO STH BY ROTE to perform or produce sth mechanically as a result of boredom or excessive familiarity with the process **2.** SAY WITH ROUGH VOICE to say sth with a rough or grating voice **3.** PUT STH OUT BY CRUSHING to extinguish sth by crushing it on a surface with a twisting motion

grinder /grīndər/ n. **1.** SB OR STH THAT GRINDS sb or sth that grinds sth ○ *a coffee grinder* **2.** TOOTH a molar tooth [Old English *grindere*. Originally, 'sb who grinds anything in a mill'.]

grinding /grínding/ adj. **1.** OPPRESSIVE oppressive and relentless ○ *grinding poverty* **2.** GRATINGLY NOISY characterized by a grating sound —**grindingly** adv.

grindstone /grīnd stōn/ n. **1.** STONE WHEEL FOR SHARPENING an abrasive wheel that sharpens or polishes sth **2.** STONE FOR SHARPENING any stone used for sharpening or polishing sth **3.** = **millstone** ◇ **have** or **keep your nose to the grindstone** to keep working hard without taking a break

gringo /gríng gō/ (plural **-gos**) n. an offensive term used in Spain and Latin America to refer to an English-speaking foreigner (*slang insult*) [Mid-19thC. From Spanish, 'foreigner'.]

griot /gree ō, gri ót/ n. a member of a caste of professional oral historians in the Mali Empire [Early 19thC. From French.]

grip /grip/ n. **1.** GRASPING OR HOLDING ACTION an act of taking or keeping a firm hold of sth **2.** MANNER OF HOLDING the way that sb holds sth ○ *a firm grip* **3.** GRASP a grasp or hold of sth **4.** = **handgrip** n. 2 **5.** = **handgrip** n. 3 **6.** HOLDING DEVICE any device for holding sth firmly **7.** ABILITY NOT TO SLIP the ability of sth to adhere to a surface without slipping **8.** CONTROL power over sb or sth ○ *The dictator had millions of lives in his grip.* **9.** COMPREHENSION a proper understanding of sth **10.** HAIR = **hairgrip 11.** SMALL SUITCASE a bag or small holdall **12.** CINEMA, TV MEMBER OF FILM TEAM a stagehand on a film or television set who moves equipment **13.** THEATRE STAGEHAND sb who moves sets and props in a theatre ■ v. (**grips, gripping, gripped**) **1.** vt. GRASP STH FIRMLY to take or keep a firm hold of sth **2.** vti. STICK TO STH to adhere to a surface without slipping **3.** vt. TAKE CHARGE OF SB OR STH to take control of sb or sth ○ *I was gripped by a sudden, awful realization* **4.** vt. CAPTURE INTEREST to capture sb's interest, imagination, or attention ○ *a performance that gripped the audience* [Partly from Old English *gripe* 'grasp' and partly from Old English *gripa* 'handful', both ultimately from the same prehistoric Germanic base] —**gripper** n. ◇ **get to grips**

with sth to begin to understand and deal with sth ◇ **lose your grip** to stop being as effective or as much in control as formerly

―――――― **WORD KEY: SYNONYMS** ――――――
See Synonyms at **catch**.

gripe /grīp/ v. (**gripes, griping, griped**) **1.** vi. **GRUMBLE CONSTANTLY** to complain continually and irritatingly (informal) **2.** vti. **EXPERIENCE OR CAUSE STOMACH PAINS** to experience or cause sb to suffer severe stomach pains (informal) **3.** vi. **SAIL INTO THE WIND** to sail into the wind against the action of the helm ■ n. **MINOR COMPLAINT** a minor but irritating grievance (informal) ■ npl. **MOORING ROPES** ropes that hold a boat to a dock [Old English grīpan 'to seize'. Ultimately from a prehistoric Germanic base that was also the ancestor of English grip and grope. The sense 'to complain' probably evolved from 'to cause stomach pain'.] —**griper** n.

―――――― **WORD KEY: SYNONYMS** ――――――
See Synonyms at **complain**.

gripe water n. a medicine given to babies to relieve colic

griping /grīping/ adj. sudden, sharp, and intense (refers to stomach pain)

grippe /grip/, **grip** n. influenza (archaic) [Late 18thC. From French, literally 'seizure'.] —**grippy** adj.

gripping /grípping/ adj. holding the interest and attention completely

Griqua /greékwə/ (plural **-qua** or **-quas**), **Grikwa** (plural **-kwa** or **-kwas**) n. **1.** **PEOPLES SOUTH AFRICAN OF MIXED DESCENT** a member of a group of people of mixed African and European descent in South Africa **2.** **LANG GRIQUA LANGUAGE** the language spoken by the Griqua people [Mid-18thC. From Nama.]

Gris /greess/, **Juan** (1887–1927) Spanish-born French artist. After 1906 he lived in Paris, where he was much influenced by cubism. In addition to paintings and collages, he designed sets for Diaghilev's ballets. Real name **José Vittoriano González**

Grisaille: *David and Goliath* by Andrea Mantegna

AKG London

grisaille /gri záyl, -zī/ n. **1.** **PAINTING TECHNIQUE** a method of painting that uses shades of grey **2.** **WORK IN GRISAILLE STYLE** a work of art produced by the grisaille method [Mid-19thC. From French, from gris 'grey'.]

griseofulvin /grízzi ō foólvin, gríss-, -fúlvin, gríssi ō fúlvin/ n. an antibiotic used to treat external fungal infections, obtained from a fungus Penicillium griseofulvum [Mid-20thC. Coined from modern Latin griseofulvum, species name (from medieval Latin griseus 'grey' + Latin fulvus 'reddish-yellow') + -IN.]

grisette /gri zét/ n. **1.** **YOUNG FRENCH WOMAN** formerly, a young working-class French woman **2.** **EDIBLE TOADSTOOL** a species of edible fungus with a grey, orange, or brown cap. Latin name: Amanita fulva and Amanita vaginata. [Early 18thC. From French, from gris 'grey'.]

gris-gris n. = grigri

griskin /grískin/ n. lean meat from a loin of pork [Late 17thC. Literally 'small pig', from obsolete grice 'pig', from Old Norse gríss.]

grisly /grízzli/ (**-lier, -liest**) adj. gruesomely unpleasant or creating a sense of horror [12thC. Ultimately from a prehistoric West Germanic base denoting 'terror', which was also the ancestor of Old English āgrīsan 'to terrify'.] —**grisliness** n.

grison /gríss'n, gríz-/ (plural **-sons** or **-son**) n. a South American weasel that has striking grey, white, and black markings, and is sometimes used to hunt chinchillas. There are two species. Latin name: Galictis vittata and Galictis cuja. [Late 18thC. From French, from gris 'grey'.]

grist /grist/ n. **1.** **GRAIN GROUND INTO FLOUR** grain that is ground into flour **2.** **GRAIN PRODUCED AT ONE GRINDING** the quantity of grain that is ground in one batch **3.** **BREWING MALT** malt grain that is used for brewing [Old English. Ultimately from a prehistoric Germanic base that was also the ancestor of English grind.] ◇ **grist to the mill, grist to sb's mill** a potential source of advantage or profit to sb

gristle /gríss'l/ n. tough cartilage, especially in meat prepared for eating [Old English, of unknown origin]

gristly /gríssli/ (**-tlier, -tliest**) adj. consisting of, containing, or resembling gristle —**gristliness** n.

gristmill /gríst mil/ n. a mill where grain or corn is ground

grit /grit/ n. **1.** **SAND OR STONE GRAINS** small pieces of sand or stone **2.** **GRINDSTONE** a piece of sandstone used as a grindstone **3.** **TEXTURE OF GRAINS** the texture of stone used for grinding **4.** **PARTICLE SIZE** a measure of the size of particles ○ coarse grit **5.** **FIRMNESS OF CHARACTER** determination or strength of character ■ vt. (**grits, gritting, gritted**) **1.** **CLENCH TEETH** to clench the teeth, especially when under stress **2.** **COVER WITH GRIT** to cover sth with grit, especially an icy road [Old English grēot. Ultimately from a prehistoric Germanic base that is also the ancestor of English groats 'husked grain'.]

grits /grits/ npl. **1.** **US COARSELY GROUND MAIZE** coarsely ground hulled maize that is boiled and eaten hot with butter, especially at breakfast in the southern United States (takes a singular or plural verb) **2.** **GRAIN WITH HUSKS REMOVED** grain that has had its husks removed or been coarsely ground [Late 16thC. Plural of obsolete grit 'chaff', from Old English grytta 'coarse meal'.]

gritstone n. = grit n. 2

gritter /gríttər/ n. a vehicle that spreads grit or salt on icy roads

gritty /grítti/ (**-tier, -tiest**) adj. **1.** **RESOLUTE** courageous, resolute, or persistent **2.** **REALISTIC** having a stark realism **3.** **LIKE OR WITH GRIT** resembling, containing, or covered with grit —**grittily** adv. —**grittiness** n.

grizzle[1] /grízz'l/ vti. (**-zles, -zling, -zled**) **BECOME OR MAKE GREY** to make sth grey, or become grey ■ n. **1.** **COLOURS GREY** a grey colour **2.** **GREY HAIR** hair that is grey or streaked with grey **3.** **GREY WIG** a grey-coloured wig [14thC. From Old French grisel, from gris 'grey'.]

grizzle[2] /grízz'l/ vi. (informal) **1.** **CRY AND WHINE** to cry and whine quietly and persistently (refers to young children) **2.** **GRUMBLE** to complain annoyingly and persistently [Mid-18thC. Origin uncertain: perhaps ironically from earlier Grizel 'patient Griselda', the proverbial meek wife.] —**grizzler** n.

grizzled /grízz'ld/ adj. **1.** **STREAKED WITH GREY** streaked with grey, especially with grey hair **2.** **GREY-HAIRED** having hair that is grey or streaked with grey

grizzly bear, **grizzly** n. a variety of brown bear found in northwestern North America that has brown fur tipped with white. Latin name: Ursus arctos horribilis.

groan /grōn/ n. **1.** **MOURNFUL SOUND** a long low cry expressing pain or misery **2.** **LOUD CREAKING SOUND** a loud creaking sound of sth affected by pressure ○ the ship's timbers groaned and creaked **3.** **GRIEVANCE** an aggrieved complaint (informal) ■ v. (**groans, groaning, groaned**) **1.** vi. **MOAN** to utter a moan **2.** vt. **EXPRESS WITH GROAN** to express sth by means of a groan **3.** vi. **MAKE A LOUD CREAKING SOUND** to make a loud creaking sound as a result of pressure **4.** vi. **COMPLAIN** to complain in an aggrieved way (informal) [Old English grānian. Ultimately from an Indo-European base meaning 'to be open', which is also the ancestor of English grin, the underlying idea being 'open-mouthed'.] —**groaner** n. —**groaningly** adv.

groats /grōts/ npl. grain, especially oats, that has been crushed or has had the husks removed (takes a singular or plural verb) [14thC. From Old English grotan; related to grit.]

grobag n. = growbag

grocer /grōssər/ n. **1.** **FOOD SELLER** sb who owns or runs a shop selling food and other household goods. ◊ **greengrocer** **2.** **grocer, grocer's** (plural **-cer's**) **FOOD SHOP** a shop that sells food and other household goods. US term **grocery store**. ◊ **greengrocer** [13thC. Via Old French grossier from medieval Latin grossarius 'wholesale dealer', from grossus 'large' (source of English gross).]

grocery /grōssəri/ n. (plural **-ies**) **1.** = grocer n. 2 **2.** **GROCER'S TRADE** the trade or profession of a grocer ■ **groceries** npl. **FOOD SOLD IN GROCER'S** goods, especially food, sold in a grocer's shop

grockle /grók'l/ n. W Country a derogatory term for a tourist, especially one from the Midlands or North of England (informal insult) [Mid-20thC. Invented word.]

grody /grōdi/ (**-dier, -diest**) adj. US disgusting or extremely unpleasant (slang) [Mid-20thC. Formed by alteration from GROTESQUE.]

grog /grog/ n. **1.** **HOT ALCOHOLIC DRINK** a mixture of alcohol, especially rum, and water **2.** **ANZ ALCOHOLIC DRINK** a beverage that contains alcohol (informal) [Mid-18thC. Shortening of Old Grogram, the nickname of Admiral Edward Vernon (from the grogram cloak he wore), who introduced the practice of watering down rum served to sailors.]

groggy /gróggi/ (**-gier, -giest**) adj. feeling weak or dizzy, especially because of illness, or overindulgence —**groggily** adv. —**grogginess** n.

grogram /grógrəm/ n. a stiff fabric of silk and wool or mohair. ◊ **grosgrain** [Mid-16thC. From French gros grain 'coarse grain'.]

Groin

groin /groyn/ n. **1.** **AREA BETWEEN THIGHS AND ABDOMEN** the area between the tops of the thighs and the abdomen **2.** **GENITALS** the genitals, especially the testicles **3.** US = groyne **4.** **ARCHIT EDGE BETWEEN VAULTS** a curved line forming the edge between two intersecting vaults [14thC. Origin uncertain: possibly from Old English grynde 'depression, hole', the underlying idea being 'depression between the thighs'.]

grommet /grómmit, grúm-/, **grummet** /grúm-/ n. **1.** **PROTECTIVE EYELET** a protective eyelet in a material that prevents tearing either of the material or of a rope passed through it **2.** **REINFORCEMENT AROUND EYELET** a small ring of metal or plastic that reinforces an eyelet **3.** **SAILING RING TO FASTEN A SAIL** a ring used to fasten the edge of a sail to its stay **4.** **MED TUBE FOR DRAINING EAR** a small tube for draining the middle ear of sb who has glue ear [Early 17thC. From obsolete French gromette 'curb of a bridle', from gourmer 'to curb'.]

gromwell /grómmwəl, -wel/ n. a hairy flowering plant of the borage family that produces hard smooth white seeds. Genus: Lithospermum. [13thC. Anglicization of Old French gromil, of uncertain origin: perhaps from a variant of graine 'grain' + mil 'millet', from Latin milium.]

Gromyko /grə meékō/, **Andrey** (1909–89) Soviet statesman. He was foreign minister (1957–85) and head of state (1985–88) of the Soviet Union during the Cold War. Full name **Andrey Andreyevich Gromyko**

Groningen /grōningən, grónn-/ city in the northeastern Netherlands, capital of Groningen Province, on the Hunze River. Population: 170,535 (1994).

groom /groom, groŏm/ n. **1.** = bridegroom **2.** **EQU SB WHO CARES FOR HORSES** sb whose job is to look after horses by cleaning them and their stables **3.** **OFFICER IN ROYAL HOUSEHOLD** any of various officers in a royal household ■ v. (**grooms, grooming, groomed**) **1.** vt. **CARE FOR**

AN ANIMAL'S APPEARANCE to clean and brush or comb an animal **2.** *vti.* ZOOL CLEAN ITS BODY to clean the fur, skin, or feathers of another animal or of itself, often with the tongue (*refers to an animal, especially a dog or cat*) **3.** *vt.* CARE FOR YOUR PERSONAL APPEARANCE to keep sb else's or your own personal appearance neat **4.** *vt.* TRAIN to train and prepare sb for a particular position **5.** *vt.* SKIING MAKE A PATH IN SNOW to clear a path or track in snow by compacting the snow [12thC. Origin uncertain: possibly from assumed Old English *groma* 'boy, male servant', related to *grow.*] —**groomer** *n.*

WORD KEY: REGIONAL NOTE

It is possible – although not likely – that a bridegroom has wondered why sb going to be married is called **groom**, a name more often associated with sb who looks after horses. In fact, his title has a very interesting history. In the early Middle Ages, *bryde* was both male and female. Then *guma*, meaning 'man', was added to differentiate him from his wife. He should, therefore, be called *bridegoom*. It is likely that *goom* became *groom* by a process of folk etymology, in the same way that *asparagus* became *sparrow grass* in folk speech.

groomsman /gro͝omzmən, gro͞om-/ (*plural* **-men** /-mən/) *n.* a man who is an attendant to a bridegroom

Groote Eylandt /gro͞ot īlənd/ island in the Gulf of Carpentaria, off the northeastern coast of the Northern Territory of Australia. Population: 14,209 (1996). Area: 2,285 sq. km/882 sq. mi.

groove /groov/ *n.* **1.** NARROW PASSAGE a narrow channel or path in a surface **2.** TRACK CUT IN A RECORD a spiral track cut into a vinyl record along which the needle of the record player passes **3.** MOUNTAINEERING, GEOG ROCK CLEFT a cleft in rock **4.** REGULARLY FOLLOWED PROCEDURE a routine into which sb has settled (*informal*) **5.** ACTIVITY FITTED TO SB an activity or situation suited to sb's talents or tastes (*slang*) **6.** MUSIC MUSICAL BEAT a strong beat or rhythm in music (*slang*) ■ *v.* (**grooves, grooving, grooved**) **1.** *vt.* MAKE A GROOVE to cut a groove in a surface **2.** *vti.* MUSIC PLAY MUSIC RHYTHMICALLY to play jazz or dance music with a strong beat (*slang*) [14thC. From Dutch *groeve*. Ultimately from the same prehistoric Germanic base as English *grave*[1].] —**groover** *n.* ◇ **in the groove** MUSIC playing or performing in a highly accomplished manner (*dated slang*)

groovy /gro͞ovi/ (**-ier, -iest**) *adj.* **1.** FASHIONABLE used, often as an exclamation, to describe sb or sth that is fashionable, excellent, or pleasing (*dated slang*) **2.** UNFASHIONABLE used ironically of sth that is unfashionable or out of touch with modern youth culture (*slang*) [Mid-20thC. From the phrase *in the groove*, originally referring to the grooves on a vinyl record.] —**groovily** *adv.* —**grooviness** *n.*

grope /grōp/ *v.* (**gropes, groping, groped**) **1.** *vi.* SEARCH BY FEELING to search for sth blindly or uncertainly by feeling with the hands **2.** *vi.* BE WITHOUT GUIDANCE to strive blindly or uncertainly for sth ○ *groping for inspiration* **3.** *vt.* EXPLORE UNCERTAINLY to feel your way forward slowly and hesitantly, e.g. in the dark ○ *They groped their way back out of the tunnel.* **4.** *vt.* FONDLE SB to caress or touch sb's body for sexual pleasure, often roughly, awkwardly, or without the person's consent (*informal*) ○ *A young couple were groping one another in the back row.* ■ *n.* **1.** ACT OF GROPING an act or instance of groping **2.** A FONDLE a rough or unsolicited caress or touch for sexual pleasure (*informal*) [Old English *grāpian* 'to grasp at'. Ultimately from the same prehistoric Germanic base as English *grip* and *gripe*.] —**groper** *n.* —**gropingly** *adv.*

groper /grṓpər/ *n.* ANZ a heavy-bodied large-jawed food fish that lives in tropical and temperate seas. Family: Serranidae. [Late 19thC. Variant of GROUPER.]

Gropius /grṓpi əss/, **Walter** (1883–1969) German-born US architect and educator. A pioneer of the international style, he directed the Bauhaus design school in Weimar, Germany (1919–28). As head of Harvard University's architecture department (1938–52) he trained a generation of US architects in the modernist idiom. Full name **Walter Adolph Gropius**

grosbeak /grṓss beek/ *n.* a finch found in Europe and North America with a large beak that it uses to crush seeds. Some classifications also include the New World cardinals. Family: Fringillidae and

AKG London

Walter Gropius

Emberizidae. [Late 17thC. From French *grosbec*, literally 'large-beak'.]

groschen /grṓsh'n, grṓ-/ (*plural* **-schen**) *n.* **1.** AUSTRIAN CURRENCY UNIT a minor unit of currency in Austria, one hundred of which are worth a schilling. See table at **currency 2.** COIN WORTH ONE GROSCHEN a coin worth one groschen **3.** COIN WORTH TEN PFENNIGS a coin in Germany worth 10 pfennigs (*informal*) **4.** OLD GERMAN COIN a silver coin issued in various regions of Germany from the 13th century [Early 17thC. Via German from, ultimately, medieval Latin *(denarius) grossus* 'thick (penny)'.]

grosgrain /grṓ grayn/ *n.* a heavy corded silk or rayon fabric used mainly for trimmings and ribbons. ◊ **grogram** [Mid-19thC. From French, literally 'coarse grain', which is also the source of English *grogram*.]

gros point /grṓ-/ *n.* US term **raised point 1.** EMBROIDERY STITCH a large half cross-stitch used in embroidery **2.** EMBROIDERY embroidery done with gros point [From French *gros point (de Venise)*, literally 'large stitch (from Venice)', applied to a type of lace first manufactured in Venice]

gross /grōss/ *adj., adv.* WITHOUT DEDUCTIONS before any usual deductions such as tax or expenses have been made ■ *adj.* **1.** OBVIOUSLY WRONG flagrantly wrong or unmitigated ○ *a gross breach of the rules* **2.** VULGAR vulgar or coarse **3.** WITHOUT GOOD TASTE OR APPRECIATION not sensitive to, or not able to appreciate, the finer things in life **4.** EXTREMELY OVERWEIGHT overweight to an unhealthy or repellent degree (*informal*) **5.** LUXURIANT growing thickly or densely **6.** *US* DISGUSTING disgusting or highly unpleasant (*informal*) ■ *n.* **1.** (*plural* **gross**) MEASURE TWELVE DOZEN a quantity of 144 or twelve dozen **2.** SUM BEFORE DEDUCTIONS a total, especially a total amount of money before usual deductions are made ■ *vt.* (**grosses, grossing, grossed**) EARN MONEY to earn or make an amount of money as profit before usual deductions are made [14thC. Via French from late Latin *grossus* 'bulky, coarse' (source of English *engross* and *grocer*).] —**grossly** *adv.* —**grossness** *n.*

gross out *vt. US* to be disgusting or repellent to sb (*slang*) ○ *language that really grossed me out*

gross anatomy *n.* a branch of anatomy dealing with body parts that are visible to the naked eye

gross domestic product *n.* the total value of all goods and services produced within a country in a year, minus net income from investments in other countries

Grossglockner /gross glóknər/ mountain in southern Austria, in the Hohe Tauern range, part of the Eastern Alps. The highest point in Austria, it rises to a height of 3,797 m/12,457 ft.

gross national product *n.* the total value of all goods and services produced within a country in a year, including net income from investments in other countries

gross-out *n. US* sth considered disgusting or repellent (*slang*)

gross profit *n.* the difference between sales revenue and the cost of goods sold

grossularite /gróssyo͝olə rīt/, **grossular** /gróssyo͝olər/ *n.* a yellow, green, or brown garnet found in chalky rock. The green variety often used as a gemstone. [Early 19thC. Via German from modern Latin *grossularia* 'gooseberry' (because of the gem's colour), from French *groseille* (a possible source of English *gooseberry*).]

grosz /grōsh/ (*plural* **groszy** /grṓshi/ *or* **grosze**) *n.* **1.** POLISH CURRENCY UNIT a minor unit of Polish currency, one hundred of which are worth one zloty. See table at **currency 2.** COIN WORTH ONE GROSZ a coin worth one grosz [Mid-20thC. Via Polish *grosz* and Czech *groš* from medieval Latin *(denarius) grossus* (see GROSCHEN).]

grot[1] /grot/ *n.* dirt, mess, or rubbish (*informal*) [Mid-20thC. Back-formation from GROTTY.]

grot[2] /grot/ *n.* a grotto (*literary*) [Early 16thC. Via French *grotte* from Italian *grotta* (see GROTTO).]

grotesque /grō tésk/ *adj.* **1.** DISTORTED distorted, especially in a strange or disturbing way ○ *The flames cast grotesque shadows on the wall.* **2.** INCONGRUOUS seeming strange or ludicrous through being out of place or unexpected **3.** ARTS BLENDING REALISTIC AND FANTASTIC relating to or typical of a style of art that mixes the realistic and the fantastic ■ *n.* **1.** ARTS ART MIXING REALISTIC AND FANTASTIC a style of art, especially in 16th-century Europe, in which representations of real and fantastic figures are mixed **2.** ARTS GROTESQUE ARTISTIC PIECE a piece of art in the grotesque style **3.** STH GROTESQUE sb or sth considered to be grotesque [Mid-16thC. Via French *crotesque* from Italian *grottesca* 'like a grotto', from *grotta* 'grotto', referring to the fanciful wall paintings found in excavated Roman ruins (see GROTTO).] —**grotesquely** *adv.* —**grotesqueness** *n.*

grotesquerie /grō téskəri/, **grotesquery** (*plural* **-ries**) *n.* **1.** GROTESQUE QUALITY the grotesque quality of sth **2.** STH STRANGE OR FANTASTIC sth grotesque, especially a piece of art in the grotesque style

grotto /gró tō/ (*plural* **-toes** *or* **-tos**) *n.* **1.** CAVE a cave, especially one with interesting natural features **2.** IMITATION CAVE an imitation cave, especially as an ornamental shelter in a formal garden [Early 17thC. Via Italian *grotta* from, ultimately, Latin *crypta* (see CRYPT).]

grotty /grótti/ (**-tier, -tiest**) *adj.* (*informal*) **1.** DIRTY OR SHABBY distastefully dirty, shabby, or in poor condition **2.** GENERALLY UNPLEASANT generally unpleasant or despicable **3.** UNWELL physically unwell [Mid-20thC. Formed from GROTESQUE.] —**grottily** *adv.* —**grottiness** *n.*

grouch /growch/ *vi.* (**grouches, grouching, grouched**) COMPLAIN to complain or grumble (*informal*) ■ *n.* (*informal*) **1.** COMPLAINT an instance of complaining **2.** COMPLAINER sb who is habitually bad-tempered or complaining **3.** BAD MOOD a mood characterized by complaining or sulking ○ *a day-long grouch* [Late 19thC. Variant of earlier *grutch*, of uncertain origin: possibly from Old French *groucher* (see GRUDGE).] —**grouchily** *adv.* —**grouchiness** *n.* —**grouchy** *adj.*

ground[1] /grownd/ *n.* **1.** LAND SURFACE the surface of the land **2.** EARTH the earth or soil **3.** LAND FOR A PURPOSE an area of land used for a particular purpose (*often used in the plural*) ○ *burial ground* **4.** BATTLE AREA the land held or fought over in battle ○ *The partisans retreated, yielding ground to the government troops.* **5.** SUBJECT an area of knowledge or debate ○ *Most of the ground had been covered in an earlier lecture.* **6.** FOUNDATION a reason or basis (*often used in the plural*) ○ *There are grounds for believing his story.* **7.** PAINTING PAINTING SURFACE an underlying surface or prepared area that paint is applied to **8.** BACKGROUND a background, e.g. the background of a painting or the background colour of a flag **9.** PAINTING FIRST COAT OF PAINT a first coat of paint applied to a surface being decorated **10.** SEA BOTTOM the bottom of the sea, a river, or a lake **11.** CRICKET AREA BEFORE STUMPS the area that a batsman must stand in, measuring from the popping crease to the stumps ○ *He was run out before he could regain his ground.* **12.** MUSIC = **ground bass 13.** *US* ELEC ENG = **earth** ■ **grounds** *npl.* **1.** SURROUNDING LAND the land surrounding and belonging to a building (*sometimes singular*) **2.** BEVERAGES DREGS the sediment or dregs of a drink, especially coffee ■ *adj.* ON THE GROUND happening, living, or operating on the ground ○ *ground crews* ■ *v.* (**grounds, grounding, grounded**) **1.** *vt.* GIVE SB FOUNDATION to teach sb the basics about sth ○ *He had been well grounded in the techniques.* **2.** *vt.* SUPPORT STH to base ideas, arguments, or beliefs on sth ○ *Her beliefs are grounded on an unshakable faith.* **3.** *vt.* AIR STOP A PILOT OR PLANE FLYING to prevent or forbid an aircraft or aviator from flying ○ *Bad weather grounded all outgoing flights.* **4.** *vt.* FORBID TO GO OUT to restrict sb to a place, especially a child to his or her home, as a punishment (*informal*) ○ *My dad grounded me for a week.*

5. *vti.* SAILING **RUN VESSEL AGROUND** to become stranded in a vessel or cause a vessel to become stranded by running aground ○ *The ferry grounded on a reef.* **6.** *vi.* **LAND ON THE GROUND** to land on the ground or hit the ground **7.** *vt.* **PUT STH ON THE GROUND** to put sth on the ground ○ *ground your rifles* **8.** *vt.* **FIX** to fix sth on or in sth else as a foundation ○ *The fence posts are grounded in concrete.* **9.** *vti.* BASEBALL **HIT A BALL TO THE GROUND** to strike a ball so that it hits or rolls along the ground **10.** *vt. US* ELEC ENG = **earth 11.** *vt.* PAINTING **PREPARE A PAINTING SURFACE** to apply a preparatory coat to a surface that is to be painted [Old English *grund*] ◇ **break fresh** *or* **new ground** to do or discover sth new ◇ **get (sth) off the ground** to get sth started or operating ◇ **hit the ground running** to begin to deal with a new situation with great energy and without delay, generally because of good prior preparation (*informal*) ◇ **hold** *or* **stand your ground** to stick resolutely to decisions, attitudes, or principles in the face of pressure to abandon them ◇ **run sb** *or* **sth to ground** to find sb or sth finally, after a long and determined search ◇ **suit sb down to the ground** to be perfectly suited to or suitable for sb ◇ **the moral high ground** a position of moral superiority in relation to other people ◇ **thin on the ground** few in number or rare

ground^2 /grownd/ past participle, past tense of **grind**

groundbait /grównd bayt/ *n.* bait thrown into water to attract fish [Mid-17thC. Originally a bait used in bottom-fishing.]

ground bass *n.* a short bass part continually repeated as the basis for a changing melody

ground beetle *n.* = **carabid**

groundbreaker /grównd braykər/ *n.* sb or sth that invents, discovers, or develops sth new

groundbreaking /grównd brayking/ *adj.* new and pioneering or innovative [Early 20thC. From the expression *break ground* 'turn the first spade of earth for a new building'.]

groundburst /grównd burst/ *n.* an explosion of a bomb or warhead on the ground rather than in the air

ground cherry *n.* **1. FRUIT WITH A PAPERY HUSK** a small round cherry-shaped fruit that has a papery husk **2. PLANT WITH EDIBLE BERRIES** a plant found mainly in North America on which ground cherries grow. Genus: *Physalis.*

ground cloth *n.* = **groundsheet**

ground control *n.* the staff and equipment on the ground that monitor or guide the flight of an aircraft or spacecraft (*takes a singular or plural verb*)

ground cover *n.* plants that grow densely and close to the ground, especially growing wild in a forest or deliberately planted in a garden to prevent weeds or soil erosion

ground crew *n.* people working in aviation, especially technicians or mechanics, who do not normally work in the air

grounded /grówndid/ *adj.* having a secure feeling of being in touch with reality and personal feelings

ground elder *n.* BOT a perennial plant, native to Europe and Asia, with white flowers and underground creeping stems, regarded as a weed. Latin name: *Aegopodium podagraria.* US term **goutweed**

ground floor *n.* the floor of a building that is level with or nearest to street level ◇ **in on the ground floor** involved in sth, especially a business venture, at the earliest stage

ground fog *n.* fog lying at or near ground level

ground frost *n.* a temperature of 0°C or lower as registered on a thermometer touching the ground

ground game *n.* hunted animals that cannot fly, e.g. hares and deer

ground glass *n.* **1. ROUGHENED GLASS** glass with a roughened nontransparent surface produced by abrading or etching **2. GLASS PARTICLES** glass that has been ground into fine particles, used as an abrasive, especially on glasspaper

groundhog /grównd hog/ *n.* ZOOL = **woodchuck**

Groundhog Day *n.* 2 February in the United States and Canada, when groundhogs emerge from hibernation to test the weather. In sunshine, they supposedly sense a late spring and return to their burrows. The day is celebrated annually in Punxsutawney, Pennsylvania.

grounding /grównding/ *n.* **1. BASICS** training in or knowledge of the basics of sth ○ *had a good grounding in maths* **2.** TRANSP **BUMP IN ROAD STRANDING VEHICLE** an incident when a vehicle, especially a low-loading lorry with a long wheelbase, is stranded on a hump or hump-backed bridge in the road

ground ivy *n.* an invasive evergreen ivy native to Europe and Asia and naturalized in North America. It has scalloped leaves and small purple-blue flowers. Latin name: *Glechoma hederacea.*

groundless /grówndləss/ *adj.* not based on evidence or reason and not justified or true —**groundlessly** *adv.* —**groundlessness** *n.*

groundling /grówndling/ *n.* **1.** BIOL **ANIMAL OR PLANT NEAR THE GROUND** an animal or plant that lives on or near the ground, or at the bottom of a river, lake, or the sea **2.** THEATRE **STANDING SPECTATOR** a member of an Elizabethan theatre audience standing in front of the stage in the cheapest part of the theatre (*archaic*) **3.** AIR **AVIATION WORKER ON GROUND** a member of the ground crew at an airport or airforce base (*slang*)

ground loop *n.* a sharp involuntary turn made by an aircraft that is taxiing, taking off, or landing, caused by unbalanced drag

groundmass /grównd mass/ (*plural* **-masses**) *n.* in some kinds of rock, the fine-grained base rock in which larger crystals are embedded

groundnut /grównd nut/ *n.* **1.** (*plural* **-nuts** *or* **-nut**) **N AMERICAN CLIMBING PLANT** a North American climbing vine with fragrant brownish flowers and edible tubers. Latin name: *Apios americana.* **2. EDIBLE TUBER OF GROUNDNUT PLANT** the edible tuber of a groundnut plant **3. PLANT WITH EDIBLE TUBERS** a plant that produces underground pods or tubers containing edible nuts **4.** FOOD = **peanut**

groundnut oil *n.* a mild cooking oil extracted from peanuts

ground pine *n.* **1. PLANT WITH PINE SMELL** a variety of bugle plant, native to Europe and North Africa, that has two-lipped yellow flowers with red spots. The flowers smell of pine if crushed. Latin name: *Ajuga chamaepitys.* **2. N AMERICAN MOSS** a North American moss with spore-producing tissues grouped in cones. Genus: *Lycopodium.*

ground plan *n.* **1.** ARCHIT **PLAN OF FLOOR OF BUILDING** a scale drawing of a floor of a building, especially the ground floor **2. FIRST PLAN** a preliminary plan or general outline of sth ○ *a ground plan for corporate expansion*

ground plum *n.* a flowering plant native to central and western regions of the United States, with edible green fruits that resemble plums. Genus: *Astragalus.*

ground rent *n.* rent paid by a person who leases land for a specified term, especially with a view to building on it

ground rule *n.* (*often used in the plural*) **1. FUNDAMENTAL RULE** a basic rule of procedure ○ *Let's establish a few ground rules before we go any further.* **2.** SPORTS **SPECIFIC RULE** a sports rule that is specific to a particular place of play

groundsel /grównds'l/ *n.* a yellow-flowered plant native to Europe and Asia, generally regarded as a weed. Genus: *Senecio.* [Old English *grundeswylige*, an alteration of *gundeswilgie*, literally 'pus-swallower', because of its use in poultices]

groundsheet /grównd sheet/ *n.* a sheet of waterproof material placed on the ground to protect a sleeping bag or the floor of a tent from ground dampness. US term **ground cloth**

groundsill /grównd sil/ *n.* the joist that is nearest the ground in a timber structure

groundskeeper /grówndz keepər/ *n.* = **groundsman** —**groundskeeping** *n.*

ground sloth *n.* an extinct ground-dwelling sloth that lived in North, Central, and South America, and is believed to be the ancestor of modern tree sloths. Family: Megalonychoidea.

groundsman /grówndzmən/ (*plural* **-men** /-mən/) *n.* sb who maintains a playing field or the grounds of a property. US term **groundskeeper**

ground speed *n.* the speed of a flying aircraft measured in relation to the ground it is travelling over and used for calculating flight times

ground squirrel *n.* a ground-dwelling burrowing rodent related to the tree squirrels and found in North America, Europe, Africa, and Asia. Family: Sciuridae.

ground staff *n.* SPORTS workers who maintain a playing field (*takes a singular or plural verb*)

ground state *n.* PHYS the state of lowest energy for a particle, atom, molecule, or system

ground stroke *n.* in tennis, a shot played from any part of the court after the ball has bounced

ground substance *n.* the solid, semi-solid, or liquid material that exists between the cells in connective tissue, cartilage, or bone

groundswell /grównd swel/ *n.* **1. DEEP WAVES** a deep wide up-and-down movement of the sea, often caused by a far-off storm or an earthquake **2. RISING FEELING** a strong growth of feeling or opinion that is evident but not always attributable to a specific source ○ *a groundswell of public opinion against the new measures*

ground water *n.* water held underground in soil or permeable rock, often feeding springs and wells

ground wave *n.* a radio wave transmitted directly from a transmitter to a receiver, without reflection from the ionosphere

groundwork /grównd wurk/ *n.* basic preparatory tasks that form a foundation for sth else

ground zero *n.* the point on the surface of land or water that is precisely the site of detonation of a nuclear weapon, or the point immediately above or below it

group /groop/ *n.* **1. SET OF PEOPLE OR THINGS** a number of people or things considered together or regarded as belonging together **2. PEOPLE WITH STH IN COMMON** a number of people sharing sth in common such as an interest, belief, or political aim ○ *an unemployed workers' group* **3.** MUSIC **BAND OF MUSICIANS** a small number of musicians, especially in pop music, who play together as a unit **4.** COMM **COMPANIES UNDER COMMON CONTROL** a number of companies all controlled by a single company or common owner **5.** ARTS **SET OF FIGURES IN ARTISTIC WORK** a number of figures forming a distinct unit in a painting, sculpture, or other artistic composition **6.** MIL **SET OF SEVERAL MILITARY UNITS** a military formation made up of several complementary units **7.** AIR FORCE **AIR FORMATION BETWEEN SQUADRON AND WING** an air force formation made up of two or more squadrons, but smaller than a wing **8.** CHEM **COLLECTION OF ATOMS** a collection of atoms that is a distinct chemical unit, such as the hydroxy group **9.** CHEM **COLLECTION OF SIMILAR ELEMENTS** a set of chemical elements classified according to the vertical column they occupy in the periodic table. There are 18 such groups, and elements in the same group have similar properties. ○ *the alkaline earth group of elements* **10.** GEOL **SET OF ROCK FORMATIONS** a collection of rock formations that date from the same geological era and are considered as a stratigraphic unit **11.** MATH **MATHEMATICAL SET UNDER AN OPERATION** a set of mathematical entities that are related by a particular operation. For example, consecutive numbers are a group under addition but not under multiplication. (*often used before a noun*) ■ *vti.* (**groups, grouping, grouped**) **FORM GROUP** to come together as a unit, or to bring people or things together to form a unit ○ *onlookers grouped in ones and twos on the sidelines* ■ *adj.* **OF GROUPS** relating to groups or forming a group ○ *group holidays* [Late 17thC. Via French *groupe* from Italian *gruppo*, 'group, knot'. Ultimately from a prehistoric Germanic word.] —**groupable** *adj.*

group captain, Group Captain *n.* AIR FORCE an officer in the Royal Air Force senior to a wing commander and junior to an air commodore

group dynamics *n.* the interpersonal processes, conscious and unconscious, that take place in the course of interactions among a group of people (*takes a singular verb*)

grouper /groópər/ (plural **-pers** or **-per**) n. a heavy-bodied large-jawed food fish that lives in tropical and temperate seas. Family: Serranidae. [Early 17thC. From Portuguese garupa.]

groupie /groópi/ n. (informal) **1. ADORING FAN** an enthusiastic fan of a pop group, especially a teenager seeking sexual intercourse with the object of her adulation **2. ENTHUSIASTIC FAN** any enthusiastic fan or supporter

grouping /groóping/ n. a set of people or things gathered into a group

Group of Eight full form of **G8**

group practice n. a medical, dental, or veterinary practice operated by several doctors, dentists, or vets working together

group theory n. the study of the formation and properties of mathematical groups. It has applications in the study of the symmetry of molecules and crystal shapes.

group therapy n. the treatment of psychological problems by placing patients in groups and, under the guidance of a trained therapist, encouraging them to discuss their problems with each other —**group therapist** n.

groupthink /groóp thingk/ n. conformity in thought and behaviour among the members of a group, especially an unthinking acceptance of majority opinions

groupuscule /groópə skyool/ n. a small political group, especially a splinter group of extremists or activists regarded as marginal (disapproving) [Mid-20thC. From French, 'very small group', formed from groupe on the model of corpuscule.]

groupware /groóp wair/ n. software designed to be shared collaboratively by a number of users on a network. It may offer such features as e-mail, scheduling capabilities, and file distribution.

Grouse

grouse[1] /growss/ (plural **grouse**) n. BIRDS a large game bird that nests on the ground on moors and in forests. Most species are reddish-brown in colour with feathered feet and legs. Family: Tetraonidae. [Early 16thC. Origin uncertain: perhaps from Latin gruta, name of a game bird, or grus 'crane', or from Welsh grugiar 'heath hen'.]

━━━━━ **WORD KEY: SYNONYMS** ━━━━━
See Synonyms at **complain**.

grouse[2] /growss/ vi. (**grouses**, **grousing**, **groused**) COMPLAIN to complain in a grumbling, often self-serving way (informal) ■ n. GRUMBLE a grumbling complaint (informal) [Early 19thC. Origin uncertain: perhaps from Old French grouchier 'to grumble' (see GRUDGE).] —**grouser** n.

grout /growt/ n. **1. MORTAR FOR FILLING GAPS** thin mortar used to fill gaps, especially between tiles **2. PLASTER** fine plaster used to finish ceilings and walls ■ **grouts** npl. **1. DREGS** the sediment that lies at the bottom of a liquid **2. FOOD GROATS** groats (archaic) ■ vt. (**grouts**, **grouting**, **grouted**) APPLY GROUT TO to use grout to fill gaps, especially between tiles, or to finish a ceiling or wall [Old English grūt. Ultimately from a prehistoric Germanic word that was also the ancestor of English grit and groats.] —**grouter** n.

grove /grōv/ n. **1. GROUP OF TREES** a small wood ○ a hazel grove **2. AGRIC PLANTATION** a plantation of trees grown for their produce [Old English grāf, of unknown origin]

grovel /gróvv'l/ (**-els**, **-elling**, **-elled**) vi. **1. BEHAVE SERVILELY** to act in a servile way, showing exaggerated and false respect in order to please sb or out of fear ○ I've already apologized but now he wants me to grovel. **2. CRAWL** to crawl or lie face down on the ground in humility or fear **3. WALLOW** to indulge in sth unworthy (literary) [Late 19thC. From obsolete groof 'face downward', from, ultimately, Old Norse á grúfu, from grúfa 'proneness', of unknown origin.] —**groveller** n. —**grovellingly** adv.

grow /grō/ (**grows**, **growing**, **grew** /groo/, **grown** /grōn/) v. **1.** vi. **GET BIGGER** to become larger in size through natural development **2.** vi. **BECOME LARGER** to expand or become larger in any way ○ The number of members will grow rapidly. **3.** vi. **INCREASE** to increase in degree ○ Excitement is growing. **4.** vi. **BE ABLE TO DEVELOP NATURALLY** to be capable of developing naturally and remaining in a naturally healthy state ○ Flowers won't grow in this soil. **5.** vi. **BE PRODUCT OF STH** to develop from sth else ○ Hatred grew out of mutual ignorance. **6.** vi. **BECOME** to move from one condition to another, especially gradually ○ The night grew cold. **7.** vt. **CAUSE TO GROW** to make sth, especially plants, grow and develop ○ We grow tomatoes in the greenhouse. **8.** vt. **DEVELOP NATURALLY** to produce sth as part of a natural process, or allow it to be produced ○ He thought he might grow a moustache. **9.** vt. **EXPAND** to develop, expand, and stimulate sth, especially a business, a line of business, or an economic market ○ She was brought in to grow the firm's market share. [Old English grōwan. Ultimately from an Indo-European word that is also the ancestor of English green and grass.]

━━━━━ **WORD KEY: USAGE** ━━━━━
Object of the verb: Metaphorical uses of **grow** as a transitive verb are widely disliked: grow the economy and grow a stock portfolio, for example, strike many as uncouth, even wrong. There are no grounds for objecting to literal physical senses of the transitive verb: grow a beard, grow corn. Nor are there grounds for objecting to metaphorical uses of the intransitive verb: The economy grew rapidly.

grow into vt. to develop in size, maturity, or capability to suit sth

grow on vt. **1. GRADUALLY BECOME PLEASING TO** to become gradually more acceptable or pleasing to sb **2. BECOME APPARENT TO** to become gradually more apparent or powerful to sb

grow out of vt. to become too mature or too big in size for sth

grow up vi. **1. BECOME ADULT** to develop into an adult **2. BEHAVE MORE MATURELY** to behave in a more mature and sensible way **3. COME INTO EXISTENCE** to come into existence and develop ○ A town had grown up at the junction of the two rivers.

growbag /grō bag/, **grobag** n. a plastic sack filled with compost and nutrients as a container for growing plants in [Mid-20thC. Variant of Gro-bag, a trademark.]

grower /grōw ər/ n. a person or organization growing plants of a particular kind, especially as a commercial enterprise

growing pains npl. **1. ADOLESCENT PAIN** pains in the limbs that adolescents are sometimes affected by, thought to be caused by rapid bodily growth **2. EARLY PROBLEMS** problems associated with the early stages of sth such as a developing project

growing point n. the area in a plant where the cells are actively dividing to produce new tissue in the stems and roots

growing season n. the time of year during which annual plants, especially farm crops, develop to maturity. It may be defined according to mean air temperature or the absence of frost.

growl /growl/ v. (**growls**, **growling**, **growled**) **1.** vti. **MAKE HOSTILE SOUND** to make, or communicate sth by means of, a low nonverbal sound in the throat that expresses hostility **2.** vti. **SPEAK IN HOSTILE WAY** to speak, or say sth, in a deep voice that expresses impatience or hostility ○ He was growling at the children. **3.** vi. **MAKE RUMBLING NOISE** to make a low rumbling noise ■ n. **1. ANIMAL'S HOSTILE NOISE** the low throaty noise made by a hostile animal, especially a dog **2. HOSTILE UTTERANCE** sth said in a hostile throaty voice [Mid-

17thC. Origin uncertain: probably from Old French grouler, of prehistoric Germanic origin; ultimately an imitation of the sound.] —**growling** adj. —**growlingly** adv. —**growly** adj.

growler /grówlər/ n. **1.** Can **SMALL ICEBERG** a small iceberg with very little showing above water **2. GROWLING PERSON OR ANIMAL** a person or animal that growls

grown past participle of **grow** ■ adj. **HAVING MATURED** having developed and matured

grown-up adj. **1. FULLY MATURE** fully developed and mature **2. FOR ADULTS** relating to or for adults ■ n. (plural **grown-ups**) **ADULT** an adult person (usually used by or to children) ○ Ask a grown-up to put it in the oven for you.

growth /grōth/ n. **1. GROWING PROCESS** the process of becoming larger and more mature through natural development ○ A child needs protein for healthy growth. **2. INCREASE** an increase in numbers, size, power, or intensity **3. STH THAT GROWS** sth that grows or has grown ○ three days' growth of beard on his chin **4.** MED **ABNORMAL TISSUE** an abnormal formation of tissue such as a tumour growing in or on an organ ■ adj. **EXPANDING** in the process of expanding or developing, especially rapidly ○ growth industries

growth factor n. a substance produced by cells that stimulates them to multiply. When produced in excessive amounts, a growth factor may be associated with abnormal growth such as that seen in cancer.

growth hormone n. a hormone, made and stored in the pituitary gland in the brain, that stimulates protein synthesis and the growth of the long bones of the limbs

growth regulator n. a natural or synthetic preparation that promotes or inhibits plant growth

growth ring n. a sheath of cells forming concentric rings in the cross-section of a woody stem or trunk, and representing the result of the yearly growth spurt that begins in the spring. The age of a tree can be determined by counting its growth rings.

growth substance n. a chemical produced by a plant that regulates its growth and development, and is usually made in the shoot tip and transported to other regions

groyne n. a structure resembling a wall built out into a river or the sea to protect the shore from erosion. US term **groin** [Late 16thC. From obsolete groin 'pig's snout', which came via Old French from Latin grunnire 'to grunt' (see GRUNION).]

grozer /grōzar/ n. N England a gooseberry (informal)

GRP abbr. glass-reinforced plastic

grub /grub/ v. (**grubs**, **grubbing**, **grubbed**) **1.** vt. **DIG UP** to dig up or pull sth out of the ground, especially without proper tools ○ grubbing up potatoes **2.** vt. **CLEAR GROUND** to remove roots and stumps from an area of ground **3.** vi. **SEARCH ON GROUND** to search on or in the ground for sth **4.** vi. **SEARCH LABORIOUSLY** to search for sth laboriously, usually by moving things and looking under things ○ grubbing in the archives for evidence **5.** vi. **TOIL** to work hard, especially at sth dull or arduous ■ n. **1. INSECTS LARVA** the worm-like larva of various insects, especially beetles **2. FOOD** food, especially a meal (informal) [14thC. From assumed Old English grybban. Ultimately from an Indo-European word meaning 'to scratch, dig' that was also the ancestor of English grave[1], groove, and engrave. In the sense 'food', perhaps from the eating of larvae by birds.] —**grubber** n.

grubby /grúbbi/ (**-bier**, **-biest**) adj. **1. DIRTY** dirty or slovenly **2. HAVING GRUBS** infested with grubs **3. CONTEMPTIBLE** disliked or despised, especially for being sordid or dishonourable ○ articles in his grubby little newssheet —**grubbily** adv. —**grubbiness** n.

━━━━━ **WORD KEY: SYNONYMS** ━━━━━
See Synonyms at **dirty**.

grub-kick n. a kick in rugby that makes the ball travel along the ground

grub screw n. a small screw with no head, used to fix a movable part in position

grubstake /grúb stayk/ n. **1.** US, Can MINING **MONEY ADVANCED TO PROSPECTOR** supplies or money given to a prospector in return for a share in any profits **2.** COMM **ADVANCE FOR STARTING UP BUSINESS** money or materials given to sb starting a business in return for a share in any profits ■ *vt.* (**-stakes, -staking, -staked**) *US, Can* **ADVANCE MONEY TO** to give money or supplies to sb in business in return for a share of any profits [Mid-19thC. From GRUB 'food' + STAKE².] —**grub-staker** *n.*

Grub Street *n.* the world of literary hackwork and those who work at it [Named after a former street in London, once well known for its population of hack writers]

grudge /gruj/ *n.* **RESENTMENT** a feeling of resentment or ill will, especially one lasting for a long time ■ *vt.* (**grudges, grudging, grudged**) **1.** **GIVE RELUCTANTLY** to allow or give sth reluctantly ○ *He wouldn't grudge working late if he knew it was important.* **2.** **ENVY** to be envious or resentful of sb for sth [14thC. From Old French *grouchier* 'to grumble' (possible source of English *grouch* and *grouse²*). Probably ultimately of prehistoric Germanic origin.] —**grudger** *n.*

grudge match *n.* **SPORTS** a match between players or teams who have a long-standing animosity between them or who have a particular score to settle

grudging /grújjing/ *adj.* done or given reluctantly, or doing or giving sth reluctantly —**grudgingly** *adv.*

gruel /grooʻəl/ *n.* a thin porridge made by boiling meal, especially oatmeal, in water [14thC. From Old French, ultimately of prehistoric Germanic origin.]

gruelling /grooʻəling/ *adj.* extremely arduous or exhausting [Mid-19thC. From GRUEL in the obsolete verb sense 'to punish', from the idea of giving gruel as a punishment.] —**gruellingly** *adv.*

gruesome /grooʻssəm/ *adj.* involving or depicting death or injury in a disturbing or sickening way [Late 16thC. Formed from obsolete *grue* 'to shudder', of Scandinavian origin.] —**gruesomely** *adv.* —**gruesomeness** *n.*

gruff /gruf/ *adj.* **1.** **SURLY** abrupt, angry, or impatient in manner or speech **2.** **HARSH-SOUNDING** harsh-sounding or throaty ○ *a gruff voice* [15thC. From Flemish or Dutch *grof*, 'rough, harsh'.] —**gruffly** *adv.* —**gruffness** *n.*

grumble /grúmb'l/ *v.* (**-bles, -bling, -bled**) **1.** *vi.* **EXPRESS DISSATISFACTION** to complain or mutter in a discontented way **2.** *vt.* **SAY AS COMPLAINT** to say sth as a complaint ○ *Some entrants grumbled that there wasn't enough time.* **3.** *vi.* **MAKE RUMBLING NOISES** to make rumbling or growling noises ○ *thunder grumbling in the distance* ■ *n.* **1.** **COMPLAINT** a complaint or expression of discontent **2.** **RUMBLING NOISE** a rumbling or growling noise [Late 16thC. Origin uncertain: probably from Middle Dutch *grommelen* 'to mumble, grunt'. Ultimately from the same prehistoric Germanic base as English *grim* and *grimace*.] —**grumbler** *n.* —**grumbly** *adj.*

─── **WORD KEY: SYNONYMS** ───
See Synonyms at *complain*.

grumbling /grúmbling/ *n.* **COMPLAINT** a muted complaint or protest ○ *grumblings of discontent* ■ *adj.* **TENDING TO COMPLAIN** with a tendency to complain —**grumblingly** *adv.*

grummet *n.* = grommet

grump /grump/ *n.* **SB IN A BAD MOOD** sb who is bad-tempered or sullen (*informal*) ■ **grumps** *npl.* **BAD-TEMPERED MOOD** a bad-tempered or sullen mood (*informal*) ○ *a fit of the grumps* ■ *vi.* (**grumps, grumping, grumped**) **COMPLAIN** to complain or be sullen (*informal*) [Early 18thC. An imitation of the sound of someone expressing displeasure.]

grumpy /grúmpi/ *adj.* (**-ier, -iest**) *adj.* bad-tempered or sullen —**grumpily** *adv.* —**grumpiness** *n.*

Grundyism /grúndi izəm/ *n.* a prudish narrow-minded attitude towards other people (*disapproving*) [Mid-19thC. From the name of 'Mrs Grundy', a character in Thomas Moreton's play *Speed the Plough* (1798), who was noted for her prudish attitude.]

grunge /grunj/ *n.* **1.** **FILTH** filth or rubbish (*informal*) **2.** MUSIC **KIND OF ROCK MUSIC** a variety of rock music that emerged in the 1980s in the United States and owes much to punk and heavy metal (*often used before a noun*) ○ *grunge rock* **3.** FASHION **UNKEMPT FASHION STYLE** a style of dress, popularized by fans of grunge music, typified by second-hand clothes worn in layers, heavy footwear, unkempt hair, and an overall scruffy appearance ○ *designer grunge* **4.** *US* **SB OB-**

JECTIONABLE sb who is regarded as undesirable, especially sb who is or looks dirty (*slang insult*) [Mid-20thC. Back-formation from GRUNGY.]

grungy /grúnji/ *adj.* (**-gier, -giest**) *adj.* **1.** **DIRTY OR INFERIOR** dirty, shabby, inferior, or otherwise undesirable (*informal*) **2.** MUSIC, FASHION **OF GRUNGE MUSIC OR FASHIONS** relating to or typical of grunge music or grunge fashions [Mid-20thC. Origin uncertain: perhaps a blend of GRUBBY and DINGY.]

grunion /grúnyən/ *n.* a small fish, native to the coastal waters of California and Mexico, that spawns on beaches. Latin name: *Leuresthes tenuis*. [Early 20thC. Origin uncertain: probably from Spanish *gruñón*, literally 'grunter', from, ultimately, Latin *grunnire* 'to grunt'. Ultimately from an Indo-European word that is the ancestor of English *grunt* and *grudge*.]

grunt¹ /grunt/ *v.* (**grunts, grunting, grunted**) **1.** *vi.* **MAKE NOISE OF OR LIKE A PIG** to make the half-nasal, half-throaty noise that a pig makes **2.** *vti.* **SAY STH IN THROATY BURST** to make a deep sound in the throat as an annoyed, half-hearted, or inattentive response to what sb has said, or to indicate or say sth in this way ○ *He grunted in acknowledgment of my greeting.* ■ *n.* **1.** **NOISE OF OR LIKE PIG** a half-throaty, half-nasal noise that a pig makes, or a speech sound that resembles it **2.** ZOOL **MARINE FISH** a bony tropical marine fish that grunts when taken out of the water. Some species have patterns of bright colours. Family: Pomadasyidae. [Old English *grunettan*. Ultimately from an Indo-European word that is also the ancestor of English *grudge* and *grunion*.] —**grunter** *n.*

grunt² /grunt/ *n.* *US* MIL an infantryman in the United States Army or Marine Corps, especially one serving in Vietnam [Mid-20thC. From earlier *grunt* 'unskilled assistant, dogsbody', alteration of *ground*, from *ground man* 'low-ranking railway worker'.]

gruntled /grúnt'ld/ *adj.* pleased or happy (*informal humorous*) [Early 20thC. Back-formation from DISGRUNTLED.]

Grus /grooss/ *n.* a small constellation of the southern hemisphere situated between Tucana and Piscis Austrinus

Gruyère /grooʻ yair/ *n.* a hard cheese with occasional holes in it, originally made in Switzerland, that has a mild nutty slightly sweet flavour. It is often used in cooking, e.g. in fondues. [Early 19thC. Named after *Gruyère*, the town in Switzerland where it was first produced.]

gryke *n.* = grike

gryphon /gríff'n/ *n.* MYTHOL = griffin

GS *abbr.* **1.** General Secretary **2.** MIL general staff

GSO *abbr.* MIL General Staff Officer

gsoh *abbr.* good sense of humour (*used in personal columns*)

G-spot *n.* a highly sensitive small area in the vagina that, when stimulated, gives extreme sexual pleasure (*informal*) [Late 20thC. Shortening of *Gräfenberg spot*, named after Ernst *Gräfenberg* 1881–1957, the German gynaecologist who first identified this spot.]

GSR *abbr.* galvanic skin response

GSS *abbr.* Government Statistical Service

GST *abbr.* goods and services tax

Gstaad /gə shtaʻat/ *n.* alpine ski resort in Bern Canton, western Switzerland. Population: 2,500 (1980).

G-string *n.* a piece of material covering only the pubic area, supported by a narrow cord between the buttocks and around the waist. It is worn, e.g. by striptease dancers. [Late 19thC. Origin uncertain.]

G-suit *n.* a close-fitting garment worn by pilots and astronauts that counters the blackout effects of high acceleration by applying pressure to the legs and lower body, thereby reducing blood supply loss to the head [Mid-20th C. Shortening of *gravity-suit*.]

GT *abbr.* Gran Turismo (*used as part of the name of a fast car*) [Italian, 'grand touring']

GTC, **g.t.c.** *abbr.* COMM good till cancelled

gtd *abbr.* guaranteed

GTT *abbr.* MED glucose tolerance test

gtt. *abbr.* PHARM drops (*on prescriptions*) [Latin, *guttae*]

GU, **g.u.** *abbr.* genitourinary

guacamole /gwaʻakə mōʻli/ *n.* avocado mashed or puréed with tomato and lightly spiced with chilli, and served as a dip or in salads [Early 20thC. Via American Spanish from Nahuatl *ahuacamolli*, literally 'avocado paste'.]

guacharo /gwaʻacha rō/ (*plural* **-ros**) *n.* = oilbird [Early 19thC. Via American Spanish *guácharo* from, ultimately, Quechua *wáhcha* 'orphan'.]

Guadalajara /gwaʻadələ haʻarə/ city in west-central Mexico, capital of Jalisco State, and the country's second largest city. Founded in 1530, it is a holiday resort and commercial centre. Population: 1,628,617 (1990).

Guadalcanal /gwaʻadəlkə nál/ mountainous island in the southwestern Pacific Ocean. It is the largest island of the Solomon Islands. In World War II, heavy fighting took place there between the United States and Japanese forces. Area: 5,336 sq. km/2,060 sq. mi.

Guadalquivir /gwaʻadəlkwi veʻer/ river in Andalusia, southern Spain. It rises in the Sierra de Segura and flows southwestwards through Córdoba and Seville before emptying into the Gulf of Cádiz. Length: 602 km/374 mi.

Guadalupe Hidalgo /gwaʻadə loʻop hi dálgō/ former name for **Gustavo A. Madero**

Guadalupe Mountains mountain range of the Rocky Mountains that runs from New Mexico to Texas. The highest peak is Guadalupe Peak, 2,667 m/8,749.

Guadeloupe /gwaʻadə loʻop/ an overseas department of France consisting of a group of islands in the eastern Caribbean. Capital: Basse-Terre. Population: 418,000 (1993). Area: 1,780 sq. km/687 sq. mi.

Guadiana /gwa dyaʻanə/ river that rises south of Madrid, Spain, and flows westwards to Portugal. It forms part of the southern border between the two countries before emptying into the Gulf of Cádiz. Length: 829 km/515 mi.

guaiac /gwíʻ ak, -ək/ *n.* = guaiacum *n.* 3

guaiacol /gwíʻ ə kol/ *n.* a yellowish oily liquid extracted from guaiacum resin or wood creosote and used medicinally as an expectorant, antiseptic, and local anaesthetic. Formula: $C_7H_8O_2$. [Mid-19thC. Coined from GUAIACUM + -OL.]

guaiacum /gwíʻ əkəm/ *n.* **1.** TREES **TROPICAL AMERICAN TREE** a tropical American evergreen tree with small leaves that grow in clusters. One species yields the resin that contains guaiacol. Genus: *Guaiacum*. ◊ **lignum vitae** **2.** INDUST **GUAIACUM WOOD** the hard dense oily wood of the guaiacum tree **3.** PHARM **GUAIACUM RESIN** the brownish-green resin of the guaiacum tree, used in medicine and in making varnishes [Mid-16thC. Via modern Latin, genus name, from American Spanish *guayacán*, from Taino.]

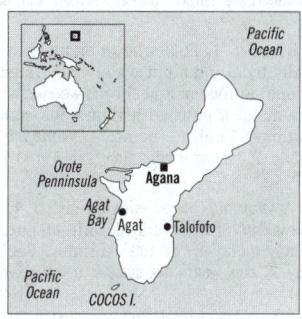

Guam

Guam /gwaam/ island and tourist resort in the northwestern Pacific Ocean. An unincorporated territory of the United States, it is the largest of the Mariana Islands. Capital: Agana. Population: 156,974 (1996). Area: 541 sq. km/209 sq. mi. —**Guamanian** /gwaa máyni ən/ *n., adj.*

guan /gwaan/ *n.* a large tree-dwelling fruit-eating bird found in Central and South America. Family: Cracidae. [Late 17thC. Via American Spanish from Miskito *kwamu*.]

guanaco /gwə naá kō/ (*plural* **-cos**) *n.* a South American animal that looks like, and is related to, the domesticated llama and alpaca. It lives in the arid regions of the Andes mountains. Latin name: *Lama guanaco.* [Early 17thC. Via Spanish from Quechua *huanacu.*]

guanethidine /gwaa néthi deen/ *n.* a drug used in its sulphate form in the treatment of high blood pressure. Formula: $C_{10}H_{22}N_4$. [Mid-20thC. Blend of GUANIDINE and ETHYL.]

Guangdong /gwáng dóong/ province of southern China, on the South China Sea. Capital: Guangzhou. Population: 66,890,000 (1994). Area: 197,100 sq. km/76,100 sq. mi.

Guangzhou /gwáng jō/ capital of Guangdong Province and the chief port in southeastern China. It lies about 129 km/80 mi. northwest of Hong Kong. A major international trade fair is held here twice yearly. Population: 3,560,000 (1993).

guanidine /gwaáni deen/ *n.* a strongly alkaline substance found in urine as a product of protein metabolism and also found in plant tissues. It is used in the manufacture of plastics and resins. Formula: CH_5N_3. [Mid-19thC. Coined from GUANO + -IDE + -INE.]

guanine /gwaá neen/ *n.* a component of nucleic acids that pairs with cytosine to carry hereditary information in DNA and RNA in cells. Chemically, it is a purine derivative. Formula: $C_5H_5N_5O$. Symbol **G** [Mid-19thC. Coined from GUANO + -INE.]

guano /gwaá nō/ *n.* **1.** ANIMAL DROPPINGS accumulated droppings of birds, bats, and seals, occurring where large established colonies of these animals are situated **2.** AGRIC GUANO FERTILIZER fertilizer consisting of dried bird or bat droppings, and rich in nutrients, including urates, oxalates, and phosphates, or a synthetic fertilizer with properties similar to those of natural guano [Early 17thC. Via American Spanish from Quechua *huanu* 'dung'.]

guanosine /gwaánō seen/ *n.* a nitrogen-containing compound formed from guanine and the sugar ribose. Formula: $C_{10}H_{13}N_5O_5$. [Early 20thC. Coined from GUANINE + RIBOSE + -INE.]

guanosine monophosphate *n.* a constituent of the nucleic acids DNA and RNA that plays a part in various metabolic reactions and is composed of guanosine linked to a phosphate group

guanosine triphosphate *n.* a constituent of the nucleic acids DNA and RNA that participates in various metabolic reactions, including the formation of proteins, and consists of guanosine linked to three phosphate groups

Guantánamo Bay /gwan taánəmō-/ sheltered inlet of the Caribbean Sea, southeastern Cuba. It is the site of a major US naval base. Area: 78 sq. km/30 sq. mi.

guanylic acid /gwaa níllik-/ *n.* = **guanosine monophosphate** [Late 19thC. *Guanylic* coined from GUANOSINE + -YL + -IC.]

guar /goó aa/ *n.* **1.** PLANTS INDIAN FODDER PLANT a plant originally from India but widely cultivated in arid conditions as fodder and for its seeds, which are used to make a gum with numerous commercial applications. Latin name: *Cyamopsis tetragonolobus.* **2.** INDUST = **guar gum** [Late 19thC. From Hindi *guār.*]

guarani /gwaárəni/ (*plural* **-nies** *or* **-nis**) *n.* **1.** CURRENCY UNIT OF PARAGUAY the standard unit of currency of Paraguay, made up of 100 centimos. See table at **currency 2.** COIN WORTH ONE GUARANI a coin worth one guarani

Guarani /gwaáərə neé/ (*plural* **-ni** *or* **-nis**) *n.* **1.** PEOPLES MEMBER OF NATIVE S AMERICAN PEOPLE a member of a Native South American people who live in parts of Paraguay, Uruguay, Bolivia, and Brazil, and belong to the Tupi-Guaranian group of peoples **2.** LANG LANGUAGE OF PARAGUAY an official language of Paraguay, also spoken in other parts of central South America. It is one of the Tupi-Guarani branch of the Andean-Equatorial family of Native South American languages. About three million people speak Guarani. [Mid-20thC. Via Spanish *Guaraní* from *Guarini*, the name of a Native South American people of Paraguay.] —**Guarani** *adj.*

guarantee /gárrən teé/ *n.* **1.** ASSURANCE sth that assures a particular outcome ○ *There's no guarantee that the plan will work.* **2.** COMM PROMISE OF QUALITY a formal promise that a product will be repaired free of charge if it breaks or fails within a stated period, or that substandard work will be redone ○ *a five-year guarantee.* **3.** COMM CERTIFICATE STATING PROMISE OF QUALITY a document setting out a promise of quality made by a manufacturer or the provider of a service **4. guarantee** LAW PROMISE TO BE RESPONSIBLE FOR ANOTHER a formal promise by one person to take responsibility for the debts or obligations of another person if that person fails to meet them **5.** LAW SB RECEIVING FORMAL ASSURANCE a person or company given an assurance that sb's debts or obligations will be dealt with **6.** = **guarantor** ■ *vt.* (**-tees, -teeing, -teed**) **1.** ASSURE to promise sth or make sth certain ○ *We can't guarantee availability of seats on tomorrow's flight.* **2.** COMM PROMISE QUALITY OF GOODS OR SERVICES to give a formal, usually printed promise that a product will be repaired free of charge if it fails within a specified period, or that substandard work will be redone **3.** LAW TO ACCEPT RESPONSIBILITY FOR SB to promise to fulfil another person's debts or obligations if that person fails to meet them [Late 17thC. Alteration (on the model of GUARANTY) of earlier *garant*, from Old French (see GUARANTY).]

guarantor /gárrən táwr/ *n.* sb who gives a guarantee, especially a formal promise to be responsible for sb else's debts or obligations [Mid-19thC. Formed from GUARANTEE.]

WORD KEY: SYNONYMS

See Synonyms at ***backer.***

guaranty /gárrən tee/ *n.* (*plural* **-ties**) **1.** LAW = **guarantee** *n.* 4 **2.** SECURITY sth used as security for a formal promise **3.** PLEDGING the giving of sth as security for a promise **4.** = **guarantor** ■ *vt.* (**-ties, -tying, -tied**) LAW = **guarantee** *v.* 3 [Early 16thC. Via Anglo-Norman *guarantie* from Old French *garantir* 'to warrant', from *garant* (see WARRANT).]

guard /gaard/ *vt.* (**guards, guarding, guarded**) **1.** PROTECT to protect sb or sth against danger or loss **2.** PREVENT ESCAPE OF to watch over and prevent the escape of sb held captive ○ *Two police officers were guarding the prisoner.* **3.** CONTROL PASSAGE THROUGH PLACE to watch over and control passage through an entrance or across a boundary ○ *All of the mountain passes are guarded by troops.* **4.** PUT PROTECTIVE COVER ON to equip a machine or device with a protective cover **5.** CONTROL to control or restrain sth such as speech or behaviour ○ *guard your tongue* **6.** *US* BASKETBALL HAMPER OPPONENT in basketball, to prevent an opponent from scoring or playing effectively **7.** ESCORT to escort sb (*archaic*) ■ *n.* **1.** PROTECTOR a person or group that protects, watches over, restrains, or controls sb or sth ○ *The prisoner broke away from his guards.* **2.** CEREMONIAL ESCORT a usually mounted or motorized group forming a ceremonial escort **3.** RAIL RAILWAY EMPLOYEE IN CHARGE OF PASSENGERS a railway employee who is in charge of a train and whose job is to check tickets, announce stops, and attend to passengers' needs and safety. US term **conductor 4.** ACT OF GUARDING an act of guarding sb or sth or the responsibility of guarding sb or sth **5.** PROTECTIVE DEVICE a device or part intended to protect the user against injury ○ *a guard on a lathe* **6.** WAY TO PROTECT SB OR STH any means of protection ○ *The pension is index-linked as a guard against inflation.* **7.** DEFENCE a defensive posture or state of mind ○ *Her guard was up.* **8. guard, Guard** MIL SOLDIER in the British army and other armies, a soldier who belongs to any regiment originally formed to provide protection for the sovereign **9.** *Ireland* GARDAI a member of the Garda (*informal*) **10.** BODY PROTECTION a piece of tough material worn to protect a part of the body from injury **11.** BASKETBALL DEFENSIVE POSITION IN BASKETBALL either of the two players in basketball who regularly defend the backcourt and initiate attacks **12.** CRICKET BATSMAN'S STANCE IN CRICKET in cricket, a position taken by a batsman when ready to receive a bowled ball [15thC. From French *garde* (noun) and *garder* (verb), both ultimately from a prehistoric Germanic base that is also the ancestor of English *ward, warden,* and *wary.*] ◇ **mount** *or* **stand guard** to keep a watch or defensive posture ◇ **off (your) guard** having relaxed the usual precautions against attack ◇ **on (your) guard** prepared against attack

WORD KEY: SYNONYMS

See Synonyms at ***safeguard.***

guard against *vt.* to be wary of sth or take precautions against it

guardant /gaárdənt/, **gardant** *adj.* having the face turned towards the observer (*refers to an animal on a coat of arms*) ○ *a lion guardant* [Late 16thC. From French *gardant*, the present participle of *garder* (see GUARD).]

guard cell *n.* either of two specialized cells bordering pores in the epidermis of leaves that move to control the size of the aperture in response to changes in water levels. The guard cells and pore are called the stoma, and are situated on the underside, and sometimes the top side, of leaves and on young shoots.

guard dog *n.* a dog used for guarding property or people

guarded /gaárdid/ *adj.* wary, cautious, or noncommittal —**guardedly** *adv.* —**guardedness** *n.*

WORD KEY: SYNONYMS

See Synonyms at ***cautious.***

guard hair *n.* the long coarse outer hair on mammals that forms a protective layer over the softer underfur

guardhouse /gaárd howss/ (*plural* **-houses** /-howziz/) *n.* a building used to house soldiers acting as guards and as a place for detaining military prisoners

Guardi /gwaárdi/, **Francesco** (1712–93) Italian painter. He painted romantic landscapes of his native city, Venice, which are characterized by lively line and colour and a mood of fantasy.

guardian /gaárdi ən/ *n.* **1.** PROTECTOR a person who watches over or protects sb or sth, or an organization with a protecting role **2.** LAW LEGALLY RESPONSIBLE INDIVIDUAL sb who is legally appointed to look after the affairs of another, especially those of a minor **3.** CHR SUPERIOR IN FRANCISCAN HIERARCHY a superior in a Franciscan monastery ■ *adj.* PROTECTING acting as sb's protector [15thC. From Anglo-Norman *gardein*, from, ultimately, Old French *garder* (see GUARD).] —**guardianship** *n.*

guardian angel *n.* **1.** PROTECTOR sb seen as the special protector of sb's interests (*informal*) **2.** PERSONAL ANGEL an angel believed to look after a particular individual

Guardian Angel *n.* a member of a vigilante group that patrols the streets of a city as a volunteer crime prevention squad. New York was the birthplace of the first such group.

guard of honour *n.* **1.** FORMAL ESCORT a body of troops acting as a formal escort for sb important during a ceremony **2.** FOOD PAIR OF LAMB JOINTS INTERLEAVED two racks of lamb joints arranged for roasting with bone ends curved inwards and interleaved. For presenting at table, paper frills are often placed on the bone ends.

guardrail /gaárd rayl/ *n.* **1.** SAFETY RAIL a rail acting as a safety barrier at the side of a staircase, road, or deck of a ship **2.** RAIL EXTRA RAIL GIVING TRAIN STABILITY an additional rail laid close inside the main running rail on tight curves and at points to help a train's wheels stay on the track

guard ring *n.* a ring worn to stop another ring from slipping off the finger

guardroom /gaárd room, -rōom/ *n.* a room used by soldiers acting as guards and as a place for detaining military prisoners

guardsman /gaárdzmən/ (*plural* **-men** /-mən/) *n.* a soldier who belongs to any of several regiments of the British army originally formed to provide protection for the sovereign

guard's van *n.* a compartment, usually at the rear of a train, in which the guard travels

guar gum /goó aar-/ *n.* gum extracted from the seeds of the guar plant, added to processed food as a thickener and stabilizer and also used in paper manufacture

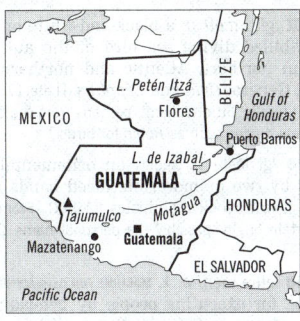

Guatemala

Guatemala /gwaˈtə maalə/ the third largest country in central America, bordered on the north and east by Belize, Mexico, and the Gulf of Honduras and on the south and west by Honduras and El Salvador. About two thirds of the total land area of Guatemala is mountainous. Language: Spanish. Currency: quetzal. Capital: Guatemala City. Population: 11,685,695 (1997). Area: 108,889 sq. km/42,042 sq. mi. Official name **Republic of Guatemala** —**Guatemalan** adj., n.

Guatemala City capital city of Guatemala, located in the south-central part of the country. It is the largest city in Central America and the nation's economic centre. It was the capital of the United Provinces of Central America between 1823 and 1834. Population: 1,167,495 (1994).

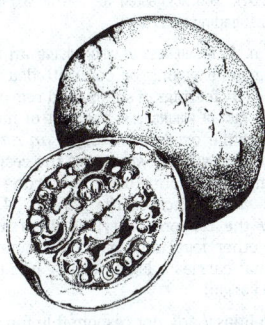

Guava

guava /gwaˈavə/ n. 1. FOOD TROPICAL FRUIT the large pear-shaped edible fruit of a tropical American tree that has red or yellow-green skin and cream or pink flesh, and is eaten raw or often made into jam 2. TREES TROPICAL TREE BEARING GUAVAS a small tropical American tree related to the myrtle, that has guavas as fruit. Genus: *Psidium*. [Mid-16thC. Alteration of Spanish *guayaba*, of Caribbean Native American origin.]

guayule /gwə yooˈli/ n. 1. SHRUB THAT PROVIDES RUBBER a bushy shrub found in the southwestern United States and Mexico whose sap is a source of rubber. Latin name: *Parthenium argentatum*. 2. RUBBER rubber made from the sap of the guayule shrub [Early 20thC. Via American Spanish from Nahuatl *cuauhuli*, literally 'gum tree'.]

gubbins /gúbbinz/ npl. ODDMENTS bits and pieces (*informal*) ■ n. gubbins (*plural* -binses) NAMELESS GADGET a gadget or device whose name sb does not know or has forgotten (*informal*) [Mid-16thC. From obsolete *gobbon* 'fragment', from Old French.]

gubernatorial /gooˈbərnə táwri əl/ adj. relating to, involving, belonging to, or typical of a governor, especially a United States governor [Mid-18thC. Formed from Latin *gubernator* 'governor', from *gubernare* (see GOVERN).]

guck /guk/ n. any slimy, oily, gooey, or otherwise unpleasant substance (*informal*) [Mid-20thC. Origin uncertain: perhaps a blend of GOO and MUCK.]

guddle /gúdd'l/ n. Scotland MESS a state of untidiness or confusion, or an untidy place (*informal*) ■ vi. (-dles, -dling, -dled) Scotland TO FISH WITH HANDS to use the hands to catch fish by groping under the water from the banks of a river ○ *guddling for trout* [Mid-17thC. Origin unknown.]

gudgeon[1] /gújjən/ n. 1. SMALL FISH a small European freshwater fish that belongs to the minnow family and is often used as bait. Latin name: *Gobio gobio*. 2. SB SILLY sb who is easily duped (*slang*) ■ vt. (-eons, -eoning, -eoned) CHEAT SB to dupe or cheat sb (*slang*) [14thC. Via Old French *goujon* from, ultimately, Latin *gobius* (see GOBY).]

gudgeon[2] /gújjən/ n. a socket that a pin fits into, e.g. the pin of a hinge or the pivoting bolt of a ship's rudder [15thC. From Old French *goujon*, literally 'little gouge', from late Latin *gubia* (see GOUGE).]

gudgeon pin n. a pin in a piston of an internal-combustion engine attaching to the little end of a connecting rod. US term **wrist pin**

guelder rose /géldər/ n. a deciduous bushy Eurasian shrub with lacy clusters of white flowers that are followed by bunches of rounded red fruit. Latin name: *Viburnum opulus*. [Late 16thC. Named after the Dutch province of *Gelderland*, where the flower originated.]

Guelph[1], **Guelf** n. a member of a political party in medieval Italy that supported the authority of the pope and opposed the Ghibellines, who supported the Holy Roman Emperor's claim to rule Italy [Late 16thC. Via Italian *Guelfo* from Middle High German *Welf*, name of a leading dynasty of the Holy Roman Empire.] —**Guelphism** n.

Guelph[2] /gwelf/ industrial city on the Speed River in southeastern Ontario, Canada, 96 km/60 mi. west of Toronto. Population: 95,821 (1996).

guenon /gwén nən, gə nón/ n. a small long-tailed African monkey that lives in trees. Genus: *Cercopithecus*. [Mid-19thC. From French, of uncertain origin.]

guerdon /gúrd'n/ n. REWARD a reward or recompense (*literary*) ■ vt. (-dons, -doning, -doned) GIVE REWARD TO to give sb a reward or recompense (*literary*) [14thC. Via Old French from medieval Latin *widerdonum* 're-payment', a partial translation of Old High German *widarlōn*, literally 'giving back'.]

guereza /gə rézzə/ (*plural* -zas) n. a large long-haired monkey that lives in the forests of East and Central Africa. Latin name: *Colobus abyssinicus*. [Mid-19thC. Origin uncertain.]

guerilla n. = guerrilla

Guernica /gúrnikə, gur neékə/ town near Bilbao in the Basque Country, northern Spain. An important centre of Basque culture, it was bombed in 1937 by German aircraft during the Spanish Civil War. Population: 16,400 (1989).

guernsey /gúrnzi/ (*plural* -seys) n. 1. guernsey, Guernsey AGRIC DAIRY COW a light-brown and white dairy cow that produces rich milk, belonging to a breed originating on the island of Guernsey 2. CLOTHES SWEATER a hand-knitted woollen sweater of a type that sailors and fishermen typically wear 3. Aus SPORTS SPORTS JERSEY a sleeveless woollen shirt or jumper worn by a football player ◇ **get a guernsey**, **be given a guernsey** Aus to be congratulated for sth or have your efforts acknowledged in some way

Guernsey /gúrnzi/ island in the English Channel, the second largest of the Channel Islands. Dairy farming, tourism, and banking are the main trades. Capital: St Peter Port. Population: 58,867 (1991). Area: 64 sq. km/25 sq. mi.

guerrilla /gə ríllə, ge-/, **guerilla** n. a member of an irregular paramilitary unit, usually with some political objective such as the overthrow of a government. Guerrillas usually operate in small groups to harass and carry out sabotage. ○ *guerrilla warfare* [Early 19thC. From Spanish, 'raiding party, skirmish', from *guerra* 'war'. Ultimately from a prehistoric Germanic word that is also the ancestor of English *war*.]

guess /gess/ v. (guesses, guessing, guessed) 1. vt. PREDICT to form an opinion about sth without enough evidence to make a definite judgment ○ *She guessed the playing card he'd turn up*. 2. vt. CONCLUDE CORRECTLY to arrive at a correct answer or to conjecture about sth ○ *I guessed it would be you*. 3. vi. FORM OPINION to form an opinion without knowing for sure 4. vi. FIND CORRECT ANSWER to be correct in your thinking about what might be the case 5. vt. US, Can SUPPOSE to think or suppose sth ○ *I guess I'll have the steak*. ■ n. 1. OPINION an opinion or answer arrived at by guessing ○ *My guess is she'll head for home*. 2. ACT OF GUESSING an act or the process of guessing ○ *Have another guess*. [13thC. Of Scandinavian origin; ultimately from a prehistoric Germanic word meaning 'to try to get'.] —**guessable** adj. —**guesser** n. ◇ **anybody's** or **anyone's guess** sth that cannot be reliably predicted (*informal*)

guesstimate /géstimət/ n. ESTIMATE BASED ON CONJECTURE an estimate based largely on incomplete information or evidence (*informal*) ■ vti. (-mates, -mating, -mated) MAKE CONJECTURE ABOUT to make an estimate of sth based largely on incomplete evidence or information (*informal*) [Mid-20thC. A blend of GUESS and ESTIMATE.]

guesswork /géss wurk/ n. the process of making guesses, or the conclusions arrived at by guessing

guest /gest/ n. 1. RECIPIENT OF HOSPITALITY sb who receives hospitality at the home of sb else 2. SB ENTERTAINED AT ANOTHER'S EXPENSE sb who receives entertainment such as a meal or attendance at a social event that is paid for by sb else ○ *Club members are allowed to sign two people in as guests*. 3. CUSTOMER sb who pays to use the facilities of a hotel, restaurant, or other establishment 4. SB ASKED TO JOIN OTHERS sb who is invited by an organization or institution to receive hospitality ○ *We have a distinguished guest at the meeting tonight*. 5. BROADCAST SB MAKING SPECIAL APPEARANCE sb who appears in a radio or television programme who does not appear on it regularly ○ *our special guest for tonight's show* 6. ZOOL ANIMAL USING ANOTHER'S NEST a creature, especially an insect, that shares the shelter of another or lives alongside the other as a parasite ■ vi. (guests, guesting, guested) BROADCAST MAKE SPECIAL APPEARANCE to appear as a guest on a radio or television programme ■ adj. 1. APPEARING AS GUEST appearing or invited as a guest 2. FOR GUESTS for guests to use [13thC. From Old Norse *gestr*. Ultimately from an Indo-European word meaning 'stranger' that is also the ancestor of English *host*, *hostile*, and *xenophobia*.] ◇ **be my guest** used to tell people that they are welcome to do as they please (*informal*)

guest beer n. a beer kept on draught in a bar for a limited period only as an addition to the usual beers

guesthouse /gést howss/ (*plural* -houses /-howziz/) n. 1. SMALL HOTEL a small hotel or private home that offers accommodation to paying guests 2. US HOUSE FOR VISITORS a small house used to accommodate visitors to a main house

guest night n. an evening on which nonmembers are welcome to participate in the activities of a club or society

guest of honour n. sb invited to attend a gathering or event who is seen as highly important or the most important of the invited guests

guestroom /gést room, -rŏŏm/, **guest room** n. a bedroom for visitors who stay for a short time

guest worker n. a foreign national allowed to come and work, but not take up permanent residence, in another country

AKG London

Che Guevara

Guevara /gə vaˈarə/, **Che** (1928–67) Argentine-born South American revolutionary leader. A radical political theorist and guerrilla fighter, he played a significant part in Fidel Castro's revolution (1956–59) and early administration in Cuba. He was executed while planning an uprising in Bolivia. Real name **Ernesto Guevara de la Serna**

guff /guf/ n. (*informal*) 1. FOOLISH TALK nonsense or empty talk 2. Scotland SMELL a smell, especially a bad one [Early 19thC. Thought to suggest a whiff of bad smelling air.]

guffaw /gə fáw/ *vi.* (**-faws, -fawing, -fawed**) LAUGH LOUDLY to laugh loudly and raucously ■ *n.* RAUCOUS LAUGH a loud and raucous laugh [Early 18thC. An imitation of the sound.]

Peggy Guggenheim

Guggenheim /go͝oggən hīm/, **Peggy** (1898–1979) US art collector and philanthropist. She helped to promote the careers of such avant-garde artists as Max Ernst and Jackson Pollock and was one of the earliest collectors of surrealist and abstract art.

GUI /go͞o i/ *abbr.* COMPUT graphical user interface

guidance /gī́d'ns/ *n.* **1.** LEADERSHIP leadership or direction **2.** ADVICE advice or counselling, especially counselling given to students on academic matters **3.** SYSTEMS THAT CONTROL FLIGHT the systems and devices that control the flight of an aircraft, missile, or spacecraft ○ *onboard guidance*

guide /gīd/ *v.* (**guides, guiding, guided**) **1.** *vti.* SHOW SB THE WAY to lead sb in the right direction **2.** *vt.* STEER to steer a vehicle or animal **3.** *vt.* HELP SB LEARN STH to teach sb or oversee training in sth ○ *An instructor will be appointed to guide you through the course.* **4.** *vt.* RUN ORGANIZATION to control the affairs of an organization or body **5.** *vt.* ADVISE OR INFLUENCE to advise or counsel sb, or influence the way sb behaves or acts ○ *Be guided by your conscience.* ■ *n.* **1.** SB WHO SHOWS THE WAY sb who leads others in the right direction **2.** SB WHO LEADS TOURISTS sb who supervises a tour **3.** INFLUENCE ON DECISION sb who or sth that strongly affects the decisions and behaviour of another ○ *Her grandmother's wisdom was her guide throughout life.* **4.** GUIDEBOOK a guidebook to a place. = **guidebook** **5.** SOURCE OF INFORMATION a publication or a section of a magazine or newspaper giving information on a subject ○ *a TV guide* **6.** CONTROLLING DEVICE a device that controls the movement or operation of a machine **7.** **guide, Guide** SCOUTING MEMBER OF GIRLS' SCOUTING ORGANIZATION a member of the Guides, a worldwide scouting organization for girls **8.** MIL SOLDIER CONTROLLING MARCH a soldier stationed at the side of a column of marching soldiers to control alignment and lead the way [14thC. From Old French *guider*, ultimately of prehistoric Germanic origin.] —**guidable** *adj.*

WORD KEY: SYNONYMS

guide, conduct, direct, lead, steer, usher

CORE MEANING: to show sb the way to somewhere

guide used to talk about a situation where sb shows sb else or a group of people the way somewhere, or gives a tour of a particular place. It is used especially when the person showing the way has personal knowledge of the place and is able to supply detailed information; **conduct** used when the person showing the way has some kind of authority or specialized knowledge, for example the guide in a museum; **direct** used to talk about one person showing another the way somewhere, usually without going there with that person; **lead** used to suggest that the person showing the way is out in front of the person or people being shown the way, and often implying that he or she is in charge or control; **steer** used in a similar way to 'guide', especially to talk about showing sb to a particular place or location; **usher** used specifically to talk about showing sb to a seat in a place such as a church, theatre, or restaurant.

guidebook /gī́d bo͝ok/ *n.* a book containing information for tourists about a country, area, city, or institution

guided missile /gī́did-/ *n.* a self-propelled missile that can be steered in flight by remote control or by an onboard homing device

guide dog *n.* a dog trained to lead a sightless person

guideline /gī́d līn/ *n.* **1.** OFFICIAL ADVICE an official recommendation indicating how sth should be done or what sort of action should be taken in a particular circumstance **2.** LINE MARKING CORRECT POSITION a line that shows a correct position, route, or alignment, e.g. a fine line printed as an aid to lining up text or illustrations on a page

guidepost /gī́d pōst/ *n.* a direction sign at a roadside

guide rope *n.* a rope attached to an object or to another rope or cable and used to manoeuvre it into position or to steady a load

guideway /gī́d way/ *n.* a groove or channel that controls the direction in which a moving object travels

guide word *n.* *US* = **catchword**

guiding /gī́ding/ *n.* *UK, Can* the activities of the Guides, members of a worldwide scouting movement for girls

guiding light *n.* sb who or sth that serves as a guide, example, or inspiration

Guido d'Arezzo /gwéedō da rétsō/ (990?–1033?) Italian monk and music theorist. He introduced the four-line staff and the system of using syllables to name the notes of the scale.

guidon /gī́d'n/ *n.* a regimental flag or pennant, or the soldier who carries it [Mid-16thC. Via French from Italian *guidone*, from *guida* 'guide'.]

guild /gild/, **gild** *n.* **1.** ASSOCIATION OF PEOPLE WITH SIMILAR INTERESTS a club, society, or other organization of people with common interests or goals **2.** MEDIEVAL TRADE ASSOCIATION an association of merchants or craftspeople in medieval Europe, formed to give help and advice to its members and to make regulations and set standards for a particular trade **3.** GROUP OF ORGANISMS a group of organisms that use the same environmental resources in a similar way [14thC. Origin uncertain: probably from Middle Low German and Middle Dutch *gilde*, of the same prehistoric Germanic origin as German *Geld* 'money'. Probably named from the members' subscriptions.] —**guildship** *n.*

guilder /gíldər/ *n.* **1.** CURRENCY UNIT OF NETHERLANDS the standard unit of currency of the Netherlands, made up of 100 cents. See table at **currency** **2.** GUILDER COIN a coin worth one guilder **3.** OLD COIN a gold or silver coin formerly used as a unit of currency in Germany, Austria, or the Netherlands [15thC. Alteration of Dutch *gulden*, literally 'golden'.]

Guildford /gílfərd/ cathedral city on the River Wey in Surrey, southern England. It is the site of the University of Surrey. Population: 126,200 (1994).

guildhall /gíld hawl/ *n.* **1.** TOWN HALL a name given to the town hall in some towns **2.** GUILD'S MEETING PLACE the meeting place of a modern or medieval guild

guildsman /gíldzmən/ (*plural* **-men** /-mən/) *n.* a man who is member of a guild

guild socialism *n.* a socialist movement in Great Britain in the early 20th century advocating state ownership of industry but with each branch managed by guilds of workers —**guild socialist** *n.*

guildswoman /gíldz wo͝omən/ (*plural* **-men** /-wimin/) *n.* a woman who is a member of a guild

guile /gīl/ *n.* a cunning, deceitful, and treacherous quality or type of behaviour, or particular skill and cleverness in tricking or deceiving people [13thC. Via Old French from Old Norse.] —**guileful** *adj.* —**guilefully** *adv.* —**guilefulness** *n.*

guileless /gī́l ləss/ *adj.* having or showing no deceit or expectation of being deceived —**guilelessly** *adv.* —**guilelessness** *n.*

WORD KEY: SYNONYMS

See Synonyms at ***naive***.

Guilin /gwáy lín/ city in northeastern Guangxi Zhuangzu, southern China. A small industrial centre, it is located in a scenic limestone region made famous by Chinese classical painters and poets. Population: 364,130 (1990).

guillemot /gíllī mot/ *n.* a black-and-white or greyish narrow-billed diving sea bird of the auk family, found in northern Atlantic and northern Pacific waters. Genera: *Uria* and *Cepphus*. [Late 17thC. From French, literally 'little William', perhaps from the custom of using male names such as *Robin* for birds.]

guilloche /gi lṓsh/ *n.* ARCHIT an ornamental border formed by two or more interlaced bands round a series of interlocking circles [19thC. From French, of uncertain origin: possibly the personal name *Guillaume* 'William'.]

guillotine /gíllə teen/ *n.* **1.** MACHINE FOR BEHEADING PEOPLE a machine for executing people by beheading, consisting of a vertical wooden frame with grooves for a heavy sliding blade to be dropped from a height onto a person's neck. It became famous for its use during the French Revolution. **2.** EXECUTION BY GUILLOTINE execution by means of the guillotine **3.** INSTRUMENT FOR CUTTING METAL OR PAPER a cutting instrument, especially one for cutting sheet metal or paper, consisting of a platform with a blade attached to one side that is pulled down like a lever **4.** TIME LIMIT ON LEGISLATIVE DEBATE a limit on the time available for debate on a piece of legislation, designed to speed up parliamentary proceedings and prevent opponents of the legislation obstructing its progress ■ *vt.* (**-tines, -tining, -tined**) **1.** BEHEAD SB to execute sb using a guillotine **2.** CUT METAL OR PAPER WITH MACHINE to cut sth such as paper or sheet metal using a guillotine **3.** LIMIT LEGISLATIVE DEBATE to set a time limit on the discussion of a piece of legislation [Late 18thC. Named after the French physician Joseph-Ignace *Guillotin* (1738–1814), who suggested its use as a more humane means of beheading in 1789.]

guilt /gilt/ *n.* **1.** AWARENESS OF WRONGDOING an awareness of having done wrong or committed a crime, accompanied by feelings of shame and regret ○ *feelings of guilt* **2.** FACT OF WRONGDOING the fact of having committed a crime or done wrong ○ *an admission of guilt* **3.** RESPONSIBILITY FOR WRONGDOING the responsibility for committing a crime or doing wrong ○ *Some of the guilt must attach to the parents.* **4.** LAW LEGAL CULPABILITY the responsibility, as determined by a court or other legal authority, for committing an offence that carries a legal penalty [Old English *gylt*, of unknown origin]

guiltless /gíltləss/ *adj.* not responsible for a crime or wrongdoing, or not deserving blame or criticism —**guiltlessly** *adv.* —**guiltlessness** *n.*

guilt trip *n.* an exaggerated feeling or display of shame and regret, usually lasting for a considerable time (*informal*)

guilty /gílti/ (**-ier, -iest**) *adj.* **1.** RESPONSIBLE FOR WRONGDOING responsible for a crime, wrong action, or error and deserving punishment, blame, or criticism ○ *He was guilty of a serious error of judgment.* **2.** LAW OFFICIALLY FOUND RESPONSIBLE FOR CRIME found and declared responsible for committing an offence by a court or other legal authority **3.** ASHAMED OF WRONGDOING aware of having done wrong or committed a crime and regretful and ashamed about it ○ *I still feel guilty about having forgotten your birthday.* **4.** SHOWING GUILT indicating or suggesting that sb feels guilt, has done wrong, or has sth to hide ○ *a guilty look on his face* **5.** CAUSING GUILT causing or likely to cause emotions of shame and regret ○ *a guilty secret* —**guiltily** *adv.* —**guiltiness** *n.*

guilty conscience *n.* a feeling of having done wrong, especially sth that is hidden from others or denied

guimpe /gimp, gamp/ *n.* **1.** SHORT BLOUSE a short blouse designed to be worn under a dress or pinafore **2.** PART OF NUN'S HABIT a starched cloth that covers the neck and shoulders and is worn by some nuns as part of their habit **3.** = **gimp**[1] *n.* [Mid-19thC. From French, from Old French *guimple* 'wimple'.]

Guin. *abbr.* Guinea

guinea /gínni/ *n.* **1.** OLD UNIT OF BRITISH CURRENCY a gold coin worth 21 shillings (£1.05p) that was a British unit of currency between 1663 and 1813 **2.** AMOUNT EQUIVALENT TO £1.05 an amount equivalent to £1.05 or 21 shillings, the value of a guinea [Mid-16thC. Because they were first made for trade with the African country of *Guinea* and made from Guinean gold.]

a at; aa father; aw all; ay day; air hair; ə about, edible, item, common, circus; e egg; ee eel; hw when; i it, happy; ī ice; 'l apple; 'm rhythm; 'n fashion; o odd; ō open; o͝o good; o͞o pool; ow owl; oy oil; th thin; th this; u up; ur urge;

Guinea

Guinea /gínni/ republic on the Atlantic coast in western Africa, between Guinea-Bissau and Sierra Leone. It became independent from France in 1958. Language: French. Currency: Guinean franc. Capital: Conakry. Population: 7,405,375 (1997). Area: 245,857 sq. km/94,926 sq. mi. Official name **Republic of Guinea** —**Guinean** adj., n.

Guinea-Bissau

Guinea-Bissau /gínni bi sów/ republic on the Atlantic coast in western Africa, between Senegal and Guinea. It became independent from Portugal in 1974. Language: Portuguese. Currency: Guinea-Bissau peso. Capital: Bissau. Population: 1,096,000 (1996). Area: 36,125 sq. km/13,948 sq. mi. Official name **Republic of Guinea-Bissau**

guinea fowl n. a plump short-tailed bird with a bare head and neck, typically black with white speckles, and related to the pheasant. It is native to Africa, but bred worldwide for food. Subfamily: Numidinae. [18thC. Named after the GUINEA coast of Africa.]

guinea hen n. a female guinea fowl

Guinea pig

guinea pig n. **1.** RODENT KEPT AS PET a plump short-eared furry domesticated rodent, native to South America, that is larger than a hamster, widely kept as a pet, and used as a subject in scientific experiments. Latin name: *Cavia porcellus*. **2.** SB OR STH EXPERIMENTED ON sb or sth used as the subject of an experiment, or used for any kind of test or trial [17thC. Named after GUINEA in Africa, probably from confusion with *Guiana* in South America.]

guinea worm n. a long thin worm, found in Africa and Asia, that lives as a parasite under the skin of people and animals and can grow to several feet in length. Latin name: *Dracunculus medinensis*. [Late 17thC. Named after the *Guinea* coast of Africa.]

Guinevere /gwínni veer/ n. in English legend, she was the wife of King Arthur and the lover of the knight Sir Lancelot

Guinness /gínniss/, **Sir Alec** (b. 1914) British actor. He won an Academy Award for *The Bridge on the River Kwai* (1957). Among his numerous other roles, he was identified particularly closely with John Le Carré's fictional hero George Smiley.

Guinness /gínness/, **Arthur** (1725–1803) Irish brewer. In the late 1700s he developed a dark version of porter that still bears his name.

guipure /gi pyoóə/ n. a heavy large-patterned lace that is not made on a mesh base but joined together by threads [Mid-19thC. From French *guiper* 'to cover with cloth or yarn', from, ultimately, a prehistoric Germanic word meaning 'to wind round'.]

guiro /gweéro/ (plural **-ros**) n. a musical instrument, popular throughout Central and South America, made from a gourd with grooves cut into its surface that creates a rasping sound when a stick is scraped across it [Late 19thC. From Spanish, literally 'gourd'.]

guise /gīz/ n. **1.** DECEPTIVE OUTWARD APPEARANCE a false outward appearance ○ *hiding her treacherous intentions under the guise of friendship* **2.** FORM OR APPEARANCE a shape or form, especially a changed one, in which sth presents itself or is presented ○ *old ideas in a new guise* **3.** COSTUME a style of dress or personal appearance [14thC. Via French from, ultimately, a prehistoric Germanic word that is also the ancestor of English *wise* 'manner', the original sense in English.]

guiser /gízə/ n. Scotland one of a group of children who go around their neighbourhood at Hallowe'en offering to perform sth, usually a song, in return for money or food [15thC. Formed from *guise* 'to dress up', from GUISE.] —**guising** n.

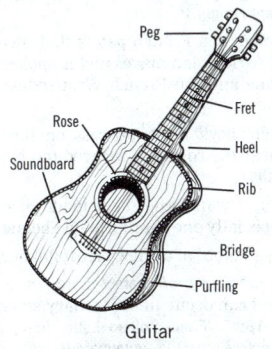

Guitar

guitar /gi taár/ n. a musical instrument with a long neck, a flat body shaped like a figure of eight, and usually six strings that are plucked or strummed [Early 17thC. Via Spanish *guitarra* from Greek *kithara* 'cithara', an ancient musical instrument (source also of English *zither*).] —**guitarist** n.

guitarfish /gi taár fish/ (plural **-fishes** or **-fish**) n. a ray found in tropical and subtropical seas, with large curving pectoral fins that give its body a guitar shape when seen from above. Family: Rhinobatidae.

Guitry /geé tree/, **Sacha** (1885–1957) Russian-born French dramatist and actor. He wrote approximately 130 plays, in many of which he, his wife, and his father played leading roles. Real name **Alexandre Georges Guitry**

Guiyang /gwáy yáng/ industrial city in southern China and capital of Guizhou Province. Population: 1,530,000 (1991).

Guizhou /gwáy jó/ province in southwestern China, dominated by a high plateau. Capital: Guiyang. Population: 34,580,000 (1994). Area: 174,000 sq. km/67,200 sq. mi.

Gujarat /goójjə raát/ state in western India, bordered in the northwest by Pakistan and in the south and southwest by the Arabian Sea. Capital: Gandhinagar. Population: 44,235,000 (1994). Area: 196,024 sq. km/75,685 sq. mi.

Gujarati /goójjə raáti/ (plural **-ti**), **Gujerati** (plural **-ti**) n. **1.** INDIAN LANGUAGE a language spoken in the Indian states of Gujarat and Maharashtra and in southern parts of Pakistan. It belongs to the Indic group of the Indo-Iranian branch of Indo-European. Gujarati is spoken by about 35 million people. **2.** MEMBER OF INDIAN PEOPLE a member of a people living mainly in the Indian state of Gujarat [Early 19thC. From Hindi.] —**Gujarati** adj.

Gujranwala /goój raán wulə/, **Gujrānwāla** city in northeastern Pakistan, in the Punjab Province. A commercial centre, it is situated about 64 km/40 mi. north of Lahore. Population: 658,753 (1981).

gulag /goól ag/ n. **1.** POLITICAL PRISON IN FORMER USSR a prison or labour camp in the former Soviet Union, to which opponents of the government were sent **2.** PRISON CAMP NETWORK IN FORMER USSR the network of political prisons and labour camps in the former Soviet Union **3.** FORMER SOVIET DEPARTMENT ADMINISTERING PRISONS the department of the former Soviet security service that was responsible for running the network of political prisons **4.** PRISON FOR DISSENTERS any place that dissenters are sent to, or the isolating or imprisoning of dissenters [Mid-20thC. From Russian, an acronym of *Glavnoe upravlenie ispravitelno-trudovykh lagerei* 'Chief Administration for Corrective Labour Camps'.]

gulch /gulch/ n. US, Can a small rocky ravine, especially one with a fast-flowing stream running through it (often used in placenames) [Mid-19thC. Origin uncertain: perhaps from obsolete *gulch* 'to gush'.]

gulden /goóldən/ (plural **-dens** or **-den**) n. = guilder [Late 19thC. From German and Dutch (source of English *guilder*), 'golden'.]

gules /gyoolz/ n. the colour red on a coat of arms [14thC. From Old French *go(u)les* 'red fur neckpiece', a plural use of *go(u)le* (see GULLET).]

gulf /gulf/ n. **1.** INLET OF SEA a large inlet of a sea similar to a bay but often longer and more enclosed by land (often used in placenames) ○ *the Gulf of Mexico* **2.** WIDE HOLE a deep wide hole in the ground **3.** VAST DIFFERENCE a great difference, e.g. in points of view, regarded as dividing or separating people or groups [14thC. Via French *golfe* from, ultimately, Greek *kolfos*, originally 'bosom', hence 'bag, trough between waves, abyss'.]

Gulf States n. **1.** OIL-PRODUCING COUNTRIES BORDERING PERSIAN GULF the countries that border the Persian Gulf, considered as an economic or geopolitical unit, especially as oil producers. The Gulf States include Iran, Iraq, Kuwait, Saudi Arabia, Bahrain, Qatar, the United Arab Emirates, and Oman. **2.** US STATES BORDERING GULF OF MEXICO the states of the southern United States that border the Gulf of Mexico, including Florida, Alabama, Mississippi, Louisiana, and Texas

Gulf Stream /gúlf streem/ warm current of the Atlantic Ocean, originating in the Gulf of Mexico and flowing northeastwards along the coast of North America towards Newfoundland

Gulf War n. **1.** CONFLICT IN GULF INVOLVING US FORCES the war that took place in the Persian Gulf between United Nations forces and Iraq, following the invasion of Kuwait by Iraq in August 1990. Fighting took place in January and February 1991 and resulted in the withdrawal of Iraq from Kuwait. **2.** = **Iran-Iraq War**

Gulf War syndrome n. a group of medical symptoms, including fatigue, skin disorders, and muscle pains, experienced by some soldiers who fought in the Gulf War of 1991. These conditions are believed by some people to have been caused by exposure to pesticides, vaccines, and chemical and biological warfare agents.

gulfweed /gúlf weed/ n. a brown seaweed that forms thick floating masses in tropical Atlantic waters. Genus: *Sargassum*.

gull[1] /gul/ n. a fairly large web-footed white-and-grey sea bird with a yellow beak. Gulls are the commonest birds in coastal North America and Europe. Genus: *Larus*. [15thC. From Celtic.] —**gullery** n.

gull[2] /gul/ vt. (**gulls, gulling, gulled**) DECEIVE to trick or deceive sb (archaic) (often passive) ■ n. A DUPE sb who is easily deceived (archaic) [Mid-16thC. Origin unknown.]

Gullah /gúllə/ (plural **-lahs** or **-lah**) n. **1.** AFRICAN AMERICANS OF SE US COAST a member of a people of African descent

Gull

who live along the coasts of South Carolina, Georgia, and northern Florida, and on the neighbouring Sea Islands **2.** CREOLE LANGUAGE OF GULLAH PEOPLE the creole language of the Gullah people. It is a form of English that has been influenced by several West African languages in its vocabulary, pronunciation, and grammatical structure. About 300,000 people speak Gullah. [Mid-18thC. Origin uncertain: perhaps an alteration of *Angola* or from *Gola*, a people of Sierra Leone and Liberia.] —**Gullah** *adj.*

gullet /gúllit/ *n.* **1.** THROAT the oesophagus or throat **2.** INDENTATION IN A PROTOZOAN a groove or indentation in the protoplasm of certain protozoans that has a function in the intake of food [14thC. From Old French *goulet*, literally 'little throat', from *go(u)le* 'throat', from Latin *gula* (source also of English *glutton*).]

gullible /gúlləb'l/ *adj.* tending to trust and believe people, and therefore easily tricked or deceived [Early 19thC. Formed from GULL[2].] —**gullibility** /gùllə bílləti/ *n.* —**gullibly** /gúlləbli/ *adv.*

Gullitt /hóòllit/, **Ruud** (*b.* 1962) Suriname-born Dutch footballer and manager. He won 65 caps for his country and captained the triumphant 1988 European Championship side.

gullwing /gúll wing/ *adj.* UPWARD-OPENING hinged at the top and opening upwards (*refers to a type of car door*) ■ *n.* UPWARD-SLANTING AIRCRAFT WING an aircraft wing in which the section attached to the fuselage slants upwards and the outer section is horizontal, or an aircraft with such a wing

gully /gúlli/ *n.* (*plural* **-lies**) **1.** SMALL VALLEY a channel or small valley, especially one carved out by persistent heavy rainfall **2.** NARROW MOUNTAIN PASSAGE a narrow passage between two rocky slopes on a mountain **3.** CHANNEL MADE FOR WATER a gutter, open drain, or other artificial channel for water, especially one at a roadside **4.** NARROW PATH a narrow path between buildings or fences (*regional*) **5.** CRICKET FIELDING POSITION a fielding position between the last of the slips and point, or a fielder in this position ○ *standing at gully* **6.** CHANNEL BY BOWLING LANE the channel on either side of a ten-pin bowling lane ■ *vti.* (**-lies, -lying, -lied**) CUT OUT CHANNELS to wear away channels in land or soil, or be worn into channels, by heavy rainfall [Mid-17thC. From French *goulet* (see GULLET).]

gulosity /gyoo lóssəti/ *n.* gluttony or greed (*archaic*) [15thC. From late Latin *gulositas* from, ultimately, Latin *gula* 'throat, appetite'.]

gulp /gulp/ *v.* (**gulps, gulping, gulped**) **1.** *vt.* SWALLOW FAST to swallow sth greedily, hurriedly, or frantically, taking in large amounts at a time ○ *She gulped down her coffee and grabbed her coat.* **2.** *vi.* GASP to gasp or choke **3.** *vi.* MAKE SWALLOWING MOTION to make a swallowing movement with the throat, especially because of being frightened or nervous ○ *He gulped and looked around nervously for the exit.* **4.** *vi.* MAKE SWALLOWING SOUND to make a loud swallowing sound with the throat, especially because of drinking too fast ■ *n.* **1.** SWALLOWING MOTION OR SOUND a swallowing movement or noise made with the throat **2.** AMOUNT SWALLOWED a quantity of sth, especially drink, consumed in one large swallow [15thC. Origin uncertain: probably from Middle Dutch *gulpen* 'to swallow, guzzle'.] —**gulper** *n.* —**gulpingly** *adv.*

gulp back *vt.* to attempt to stifle tears or sobs

gum[1] /gum/ *n.* **1.** BOT STICKY PLANT SUBSTANCE THAT HARDENS a sticky substance found inside some plants, especially trees, that hardens when it is exposed to air and dissolves when put in water **2.** BOT ANY STICKY PLANT SUBSTANCE any sticky substance found inside plants, e.g. resins **3.** STH STICKY any sticky substance or deposit **4.** INDUST ADHESIVE glue made from or containing a sticky plant substance, or any soft synthetic glue used for sticking paper or other lightweight materials **5.** PLANTS TREE PRODUCING GUM any of numerous trees that produce gum. Genera: *Eucalyptus* and *Liquidambar* and *Nyssa*. **6.** CHEWING GUM chewing gum (*informal*) **7.** CHEWY SWEET a chewy fruit-flavoured sweet ■ *vt.* (**gums, gumming, gummed**) STICK STH TO STH ELSE to stick sth to sth else, with or without gum or glue [14thC. Via Old French *gomme*, from, ultimately, Greek *kommi*, from Egyptian *kemai*.]

gum up *vt.* to block or immobilize sth with a sticky substance that prevents parts from moving ○ *eyes all gummed up* ◇ **gum up the works** to bring everything to a halt, usually by being obstructive or incompetent (*informal*)

gum[2] /gum/ *n.* the firm flesh that surrounds the roots of the teeth (*often used in the plural*) [Old English *goma*, of uncertain origin]

gum accroides *n.* = **acaroid gum**

gum ammoniac *n.* = **ammoniac**

gum arabic *n.* a sticky substance taken from some acacia trees and used as an ingredient in adhesives, confectionery, and medicines [Because the trees that produce it grow in the Middle East and near Arabia]

gumbo /gúmbō/ (*plural* **-bos**) *n.* **1.** PLANTS = **okra** *n.* 1, **okra** *n.* 2 **2.** FOOD THICK STEW WITH OKRA a stew of fish, poultry, or meat that has been thickened with okra **3.** *US* STICKY SOIL silty soil that turns very sticky and muddy when it becomes wet, and is found throughout the central United States **4.** *US* MIXTURE a mixture or hotchpotch (*informal*) ○ *The band played a gumbo of Cajun, zydeco, and jazz music.* [Early 19thC. From Louisiana French *gombo*, of African, probably Bantu origin.]

Gumbo /gúmbō/ *n.* a French patois that incorporates aspects of African languages and is spoken in parts of Louisiana and the French West Indies —**Gumbo** *adj.*

gumboil /gúm boyl/ *n.* an abscess on the gum, especially near the root of a decayed tooth. Technical name **parulis**

gum boot *n.* a waterproof boot made of rubber or plastic, especially one coming to just below the knee

gumdrop /gúm drop/ *n.* a chewy fruit-flavoured sweet

gumma /gúmmə/ (*plural* **-mata** /-mətə/) *n.* a rubbery tumour that can occur in the tertiary stage of syphilis [Early 18thC. From modern Latin, from, ultimately, Greek *kommi* (see GUM[1]).] —**gummatous** *adj.*

gummite /gúmmīt/ *n.* a brownish-yellow to orange mixture of naturally occurring hydrated oxides of uranium, thorium, and lead [Mid-19thC. Coined from GUM[1] (because of its appearance) + -ITE.]

gummosis /gə móssiss/ *n.* the production of too much gum by a tree, especially a fruit tree, as a result of infection, a wound, or adverse weather [Late 19thC. Coined from GUM[1] + -OSIS.]

gummous /gúmməss/ *adj.* **1.** RESEMBLING GUM sticky like the gum from a tree **2.** HAVING GUM containing gum

gummy[1] /gúmmi/ (**-mier, -miest**) *adj.* **1.** STICKY LIKE GUM like gum, especially in being sticky or thick and slow-flowing **2.** STUCK OR BLOCKED WITH GUM covered, clogged, or stuck together with a sticky substance of some kind —**gumminess** *n.*

gummy[2] /gúmmi/ (**-mier, -miest**) *adj.* with only the gums showing, but no teeth, usually because the person concerned has no teeth —**gummily** *adv.*

gum nut *n. Aus* the hard seed pod of a eucalyptus tree

gump /gump/ *vi.* to muddle through difficult situations thanks to a series of lucky chances [Late 20thC. From the 1994 film *Forrest Gump*.]

WORD KEY: CULTURAL NOTE

Forrest Gump, a film by US director Robert Zemeckis (1994). It is the sentimental tale of a mentally ill boy who grows up to become a sports star, war hero, and successful businessman thanks to his uncomplicated worldview, traditional moral values, and uncanny ability to be in the right place at the right time.

gum plant *n.* a yellow-flowered North American plant with sticky flower heads or leaves. Genus: *Grindelia*.

gumption /gúmpsh'n/ *n.* (*informal*) **1.** COMMON SENSE practical common sense and presence of mind ○ *Luckily, he had the gumption to call the police.* **2.** COURAGE TO ACT the courage to take what action is needed ○ *He wouldn't have the gumption to say so, even if he disagreed.* [Early 18thC. Originally Scots, of uncertain origin: perhaps formed from obsolete *gome* 'attention, heed', of Scandinavian origin.]

gum resin *n.* a naturally occurring mixture of gum and resin taken from some plants and trees, e.g. the yellow pigment gamboge

gumshield /gúm sheeld/ *n.* a hard plastic cover that fits inside sb's mouth over the teeth and gums, worn as protection from injury by people involved in contact sports such as boxing and rugby. US term **mouth guard**

gumshoe /gúm shoo/ *n. US* a detective, especially a private investigator (*informal*) [Early 20thC. Originally in the sense 'galosh'; the modern meaning arose from the idea of moving with stealth, as if wearing gumshoes.]

gum tree *n.* any of numerous trees that produce gum. Genera: *Eucalyptus* and *Liquidambar* and *Nyssa*. ◇ **up a gumtree** in a difficult or impossible situation (*informal*)

gum turpentine *n.* = **turpentine**

gumwood /gúm wòòd/ *n.* wood from any gum tree, especially a eucalyptus tree

gun /gun/ *n.* **1.** WEAPON THAT FIRES BULLETS a weapon, from a small handheld pistol to a large piece of artillery, with a metal tube through which bullets or missiles are fired by an explosive charge **2.** DEVICE THAT FIRES STH any tool or instrument that forces sth out under pressure **3.** SHOT FROM GUN a shot fired from a gun, e.g. as a military salute or a signal for a race to begin, or the sound of the shot ○ *Wait for the gun.* **4.** SB WITH GUN sb who is armed with a gun (*informal*) ○ *the fastest gun in the West* **5.** *US* ACCELERATOR a vehicle's accelerator (*informal*) ○ *Give it the gun.* **6.** HUNTER a member of a party of hunters armed with shotguns ■ *vt.* (**guns, gunning, gunned**) PRESS THROTTLE to rev up an engine (*informal*) [14thC. Origin uncertain: probably from a pet form of the Scandinavian female name *Gunnhildr* (itself from *gunnr* 'battle' + *hildr* 'war'), from the custom of giving women's names to weapons.] ◇ **go great guns** to be working, operating, or doing sth at great speed or very effectively and successfully ◇ **jump the gun 1.** to start a race before the starting gun goes off **2.** to act prematurely ◇ **stick to your guns** to refuse to change your plans or opinions even though under attack

gun down *vt.* to shoot and kill or severely injure sb (*informal*)

gun for *vt.* (*informal*) **1.** INTEND TO HARM to set out to attack or criticize sb, or bring about sb's downfall **2.** INTEND TO GET to plan or intend to get sth for yourself ○ *She's gunning for a position in the Paris office.*

gunboat /gún bōt/ *n.* a small fast ship with large guns mounted on it, used e.g. by coastguards

gunboat diplomacy *n.* negotiations between nations that involve threats to use military force

gun carriage *n.* a platform with wheels on which a large military gun is mounted and transported or on which a coffin is laid during state funerals

gun control *n.* legal measures to control, license, review, put conditions on, or restrict the ownership of firearms by members of the public

guncotton /gún kot'n/ *n.* = **nitrocellulose**

gun dog *n.* **1.** HUNTER'S OR GAMEKEEPER'S DOG a dog trained to find game and to bring back any game shot by a hunter or gamekeeper **2.** DOG OF HUNTING BREED a dog of a breed such as a pointer that is traditionally regarded as suitable for training as a hunter's or gamekeeper's dog

gunfight /gún fīt/ *n.* a fight between two or more people armed with handguns, especially in the days of the Wild West —**gunfighter** *n.*

gunfire /gún fīr/ *n.* shots fired from a gun or guns, or the sound of shots

gunflint /gún flint/ *n.* a small piece of flint that ignites the gunpowder in an old-fashioned flintlock gun

gunge /gunj/ *n.* an unpleasantly sticky, slimy, or messy semi-liquid substance (*informal*) [Mid-20thC. Origin uncertain: perhaps thought to suggest stickiness, or perhaps a blend of GOO and SPONGE.] —**gungy** *adj.*

gung ho /gúng hố/ *adj.* (*informal*) (*hyphenated when used before a noun*) **1. WANTING TO FIGHT** eager to fight, especially in a military conflict **2. VERY KEEN** extremely or excessively enthusiastic or eager [Mid-20thC. From Mandarin Chinese *honghé*, literally 'work together' (a motto of the US marines in Asia in World War II), a shortening of *gōngyèhézuòshè* 'Chinese Industrial Cooperative Society'.]

gunite /gúnn īt/ *n.* a concrete building material that is sprayed from a high-pressure gun onto a mould, or over reinforced concrete or steel in light construction [Early 20thC. Coined from GUN + -ITE, originally as a trademark.]

gunk /gungk/ *n.* a greasy messy near-solid mass (*informal*) [Mid-20thC. Originally the trademark of a degreasing solvent, probably thought to suggest lumpy grease.] —**gunky** *adj.*

gun lobby *n.* lobbyist groups who argue for the right of ordinary members of the public to buy and own guns, and who resist legislative attempts to put conditions on the ownership and availability of firearms and ammunition

gunlock /gún lok/ *n.* the mechanism by which the gunpowder charge was exploded in early types of gun, such as flintlock, matchlock, or wheel lock

gunman /gúnmən/ *n.* (*plural* -**men** /-mən/) *n.* **1. MAN WITH GUN** a man armed with a gun, especially a criminal or an assassin **2. SKILFUL SHOOTER** a man skilled in firing guns

gunmetal /gún mett'l/ *n.* **1. GREY BRONZE FOR CANNONS** a dark grey bronze formerly used to make cannons **2. ANY DARK GREY METAL** any of various dark grey alloys formerly widely used to make household and industrial items and especially children's toys **3. gunmetal, gunmetal grey** COLOURS DARK GREY COLOUR a dark grey colour with a tinge of blue —**gunmetal-grey** *adj.*

Gunn /gun/, **Mrs Aeneas** (1870–1961) Australian writer. She is author of *We of the Never Never* (1908), a best-selling account of life on a remote Australian farm. Born **Jeannie Taylor**

gunnel[1] *n.* = gunwale

gunnel[2] /gúnn'l/ (*plural* -**nels** *or* -**nel**) *n.* a small fish that is similar to an eel and is found in coastal areas of the Atlantic and Pacific oceans. Family: Pholidae. [Late 17thC. Origin unknown.]

Gunnell /gúnn'l/, **Sally** (*b.* 1966) British athlete. She dominated 400-metre hurdle running in the 1990s. Full name **Sally Janet Gunnell**

gunner /gúnnər/ *n.* **1. SOLDIER WHO FIRES LARGE GUN** a soldier who operates a large gun **2. NCO WITH GUN-RELATED RESPONSIBILITIES** a warrant officer in the British navy or the United States Marines who is responsible for training gun operators and running the ammunition stores **3. ARTILLERY SOLDIER** a soldier in an artillery regiment, especially a private

gunnera /gúnnərə/ (*plural* -**as**) *n.* a tropical plant with huge leaves that resemble the leaves of a palm, especially a gigantic South American variety. Genus: *Gunnera*. [Late 18thC. From modern Latin, genus name, named after the Norwegian botanist J.E. *Gunnerus*, (1718–73).]

gunnery /gúnnəri/ *n.* **1. SCIENCE OF GUNS AND THEIR USE** the knowledge and techniques involved in the effective use of guns or in their design and construction **2. USE OF GUNS** the use of guns, especially of large guns in battle

gunny /gúnni/ (*plural* -**nies**) *n.* **1. COARSE CLOTH** coarse jute or hemp cloth, commonly used for making sacks **2. SACK** a sack made from such cloth. US term **gunnysack** [Early 18thC. From Hindi *gonī*.]

gunnysack /gúnni sak/ *n.* = gunny *n.* 2

gunplay /gún play/ *n.* the shooting of guns, especially by armed criminals

gunpoint /gún poynt/ *n.* the muzzle of a firearm ◇ **at gunpoint** under the threat of being shot and killed if orders are not obeyed

gunpowder /gún powdər/ *n.* an explosive mixture of potassium nitrate, charcoal, and sulphur, formerly used as the charge in firearms, and still used in fireworks and other explosives, e.g. in quarry blasting

Gunpowder Plot *n.* a conspiracy by a group of Roman Catholics, including Guy Fawkes, to blow up Parliament in 1605

gunpowder tea *n.* a kind of Chinese green tea with individual leaves rolled into small pellets

gunroom /gún room, -rŏom/ *n.* **1. ROOM FOR GUNS** a room in a house where guns are kept, especially shotguns **2. NAVY OFFICERS' QUARTERS** the quarters of midshipmen and junior officers on a ship in the British navy

gunrunning /gún running/ *n.* the smuggling of illegal arms into a country, usually in order to supply terrorist or insurrectionist organizations —**gunrunner** *n.*

gunship /gún ship/ *n.* a military aircraft, usually a helicopter, that is fitted with guns for intrinsic use against ground targets

gunshot /gún shot/ *n.* **1. GUN'S NOISE** the sound of a gun being fired **2. BULLETS FIRED** bullets or shot fired from a gun **3. GUN'S RANGE** the maximum distance that a bullet fired from a gun can travel

gun-shy *adj.* **1. TIMID** extremely cautious, timid, or wary of taking risks **2. SCARED OF GUNS** afraid of guns or the noise they make when fired

gunslinger /gún slingər/ *n.* an armed fighter or criminal, especially in the frontier days of the Wild West (*informal*) —**gunslinging** *n.*

gunsmith /gún smith/ *n.* sb who makes and repairs firearms, or sells them in a shop

gunstock /gún stok/ *n.* the shaped wooden or metal handle of a rifle that is pressed against the shoulder when the rifle is being fired

Guntur /gŏon tŏor/ *city in the River Krishna delta, in Andhra Pradesh State, southeastern India. Population: 273,000 (1991).

gunwale /gúnn'l/ *n.* the top edge of a ship's sides that forms a ledge round the whole ship above the deck (*often used in the plural*) [15thC. From GUN + *wale* 'strip, stripe' (from Old English *walu*); because it was used in the past to support guns.]

guppy /gúppi/ (*plural* -**pies**) *n.* a small freshwater fish with a brightly coloured tail, native to the West Indies and South America, that is popular in aquariums and produces live young, rather than eggs. Latin name: *Poecilia reticulata*. [Early 20thC. Named after the Reverend R. J. Lechmere *Guppy* (1836–1916), who sent the first specimen from Trinidad to the British Museum.]

Gupta /gŏoptə/ *n.* an Indian dynasty of the 3rd to 6th centuries that established a loose empire in much of the subcontinent [Late 19thC. Named after *Chandragupta*, the dynasty's founder.]

Gur /gŏo ər/ *n.* a group of around 70 languages, including Mossi, Dagomba, and Mamprusi, spoken in western parts of Central Africa. It is a branch of the Niger-Congo family of African languages. About 10 million people speak one of the languages classified as being in the Gur group. —**Gur** *adj.*

gurdwara /gúrd waarə/ *n.* a Sikh temple or other place of worship where Sikh scriptures are kept [Early 20thC. From Punjabi *gurduārā*.]

gurgle /gúrg'l/ *v.* (-**gles**, -**gling**, -**gled**) **1.** *vi.* MAKE BUBBLING NOISE to make the deep bubbling noise that liquid makes when it is poured from a bottle **2.** *vti.* MAKE BUBBLING WATER SOUND to make a bubbling sound in the throat, or to say sth with a bubbling sound ■ *n.* GURGLING SOUND the sound or act of gurgling [Mid-16thC. Via assumed Vulgar Latin *gurguliare* from Latin *gurgulio* 'gullet' (source of English *gorge* and *regurgitate*).] —**gurglingly** *adv.*

Gurindji /ŏorinji/ *npl.* NATIVE AUSTRALIAN PEOPLE a Native Australian people living in northern parts of Central Australia ■ *n.* GURINDJI LANGUAGE the language of the Gurindji

Gurkha /gúrkə/ *n.* **1. MEMBER OF HINDU PEOPLE** a member of a Hindu people living mainly in Nepal, with small communities in Bhutan **2. GURKHA IN ARMY** a Gurkha serving in the British or Indian army [Early 19thC. From Nepalese *Gurkha*, a place name.] —**Gurkha** *adj.*

Gurkhali /gur kaáli/ *n.* the language of the Gurkhas, a member of the Indic branch of the Indo-European family of languages [Late 19thC. Formed from Nepalese *Gurkha* (see GURKHA).] —**Gurkhali** *adj.*

Gurmukhi /gŏo ə mŏoki/ *n.* the script in which Punjabi is written [Late 19thC. From Punjabi.]

gurn (gurns, gurning, gurned) *vi.* = girn

gurnard /gúrnərd/ (*plural* -**nards** *or* -**nard**) *n.* **1. FISH WITH SPINY FINS** a widely distributed spiny-finned marine fish with an armoured head and sets of pectoral fins modified for crawling on the sea bottom. Family: Triglidae. **2.** = **flying gurnard** [14thC. From Old French *gornart*, from, ultimately, Latin *grunnire* 'to grunt', from the sound it makes when caught.]

gurney /gúrni/ (*plural* -**neys**) *n.* US = trolley [Late 19thC. Origin uncertain: perhaps named after J.T. *Gurney* of Boston who patented a new cab design in 1883. Originally used for a type of cab.]

guru /gŏo roo/ (*plural* -**rus**) *n.* **1. HINDU OR SIKH RELIGIOUS TEACHER** in Hinduism and Sikhism, a religious leader or teacher **2. LEADER OF RELIGIOUS GROUP** a spiritual leader or intellectual guide for a religious group or movement especially one being described as nonmainstream **3. SB INFLUENTIAL** sb who is prominent and influential in a specific field and sets a trend or starts a movement ○ *a meeting of the world's software gurus* **4. INDIVIDUAL'S REVERED TEACHER AND COUNSELLOR** a teacher or counsellor in spiritual or intellectual matters who is especially revered and followed by an individual [Early 17thC. From Sanskrit, 'elder, teacher'.]

gush /gush/ *vti.* (gushes, gushing, gushed) **1. FLOW OUT FAST** to flow out, or to send a liquid out, rapidly and in large quantities **2. SPEAK, BEHAVE, OR SAY EFFUSIVELY** to speak or behave in an extremely or exaggeratedly enthusiastic, affectionate, or sentimental way ○ *'Your children are simply delightful!', she gushed.* ■ *n.* **1. FLOW OF LIQUID** a fast or copious flow of liquid from somewhere **2. EMOTIONAL OUTBURST** an outburst of overenthusiastic or overemotional speech or behaviour [14thC. Origin uncertain: probably an imitation of the sound of liquid gushing.] —**gushing** *adj.* —**gushingly** *adv.*

gusher /gúshər/ *n.* **1. FREE-FLOWING OIL WELL** an oil well from which oil flows freely and in large amounts, without having to be pumped **2. EFFUSIVE PERSON** sb who tends to speak or behave in an exaggeratedly emotional way

gushy /gúshi/ (-**ier**, -**iest**) *adj.* characterized by overenthusiastic or over-emotional speech or behaviour —**gushily** *adv.* —**gushiness** *n.*

Gusset

gusset /gússit/ *n.* **1. INSET PIECE OF FABRIC** a piece of fabric, usually triangular in shape, inserted in a garment where added strength or freedom of movement is needed **2. FLAT PLATE REINFORCING A JOINT** a flat, often triangular plate, usually of steel or plywood, used to connect and reinforce a joint where several members meet at different angles, e.g. in a pitched roof **3. CHAIN MAIL AT AN ARMOUR JOINT** a section of chain mail protecting the unarmoured joints of a suit of armour ■ *vt.* (-**sets**, -**seting**, -**seted**) FIT STH WITH A GUSSET to fit a garment, a wooden joint, or a suit of armour with a gusset [14thC. From French *gousset*, literally 'little pod', from *gousse* 'pod, shell', of unknown origin.]

gussy up /gússi úp/ (**gussies up, gussying up, gussied up**) *vt. US* to dress sb in fancy clothes, or decorate sth elaborately (*informal*) (*often passive*) ○ *all gussied up in a frilly dress* ○ *The city was gussied up for the visit of the mayor.* [Mid-20thC. *Gussy* of uncertain origin: perhaps from Australian slang *gussie* 'an effeminate man', a pet form of the male first name *Augustus*.]

gust /gust/ *n.* **1. BURST OF WIND** a sudden violent rush of wind **2. EMOTIONAL OUTBURST** an outburst of emotion such as anger ■ *vi.* (**gusts, gusting, gusted**) **BLOW IN BURSTS** to blow, or be blown by the wind, in sudden violent bursts [Late 16thC. From Old Norse *gustr*, from *gjósa* 'to gush'.]

gustation /gu stáysh'n/ *n.* the action of tasting, or the sense or faculty of taste (*formal*) [Late 16thC. Directly or via French from the Latin stem *gustation-*, from *gustare* 'to taste'.]

gustatory /gústətəri/, **gustatorial** /gústə táwri əl/ *adj.* relating to the sense of taste or to the action or experience of tasting sth (*formal*) [Late 17thC. Formed from Latin *gustare* (see GUSTATION).] —**gustatorily** *adv.*

Gustav II Adolph /gŏŏst aav/, **King of Sweden** (1594–1632). As king (1611–32) he led Protestantism forces during the Thirty Years' War (1618–48). He is regarded as the founding father of modern Sweden. Known as **the Lion of the North**

gusto /gústō/ *n.* lively enthusiasm or enjoyment [Early 17thC. Via Italian from Latin *gustus* 'taste'.]

gut /gut/ *n.* **1. ALIMENTARY CANAL** the whole of the alimentary canal in people and animals, from the mouth to the anus, or the lower part of it, (**the intestine**), from the stomach to the anus **2. ABDOMEN** sb's belly, especially if it is noticeably large (*slang disapproving*) ○ *I've got to work off this gut.* **3. PLACE WHERE INSTINCTS ARE FELT** sb's deepest instinctively felt emotions or responses, as distinct from rational or logical responses (*often used in the plural*) ○ *a gut reaction* **4.** = **catgut 5. FISHING CORD** cord made of fibrous material taken from silkworms, used to make fishing lines ■ **guts** *npl.* **1. INTESTINES** the insides of a person or animal, especially the intestines **2. STRENGTH OF CHARACTER** courage or boldness (*slang*) **3. INNER OR CENTRAL PARTS** the inner or central parts of sth such as the working parts of a machine or the basic principles that a theory is based on ■ *vt.* (**guts, gutting, gutted**) **1. REMOVE AN ANIMAL'S INSIDES** to remove the insides of a dead animal **2. DESTROY A BUILDING'S INTERIOR** to destroy the internal parts of a building, leaving only the outer walls standing ○ *The factory was completely gutted in the fire.* **3. EMPTY** to remove all the internal fixtures and furnishings from a room or building **4. TAKE EXTRACTS FROM A TEXT** to select extracts from a piece of writing for use elsewhere [Old English *guttas*. Ultimately from an Indo-European word meaning 'to pour', which was also the ancestor of English *funnel*. The underlying meaning is 'tube through which sth flows'.] ◇ **bust a gut** to struggle or work exceptionally hard to get sth done (*slang*) ◇ **hate sb's guts** to dislike sb very much (*informal*)

GUT /gut/ *abbr.* PHYS Grand Unified Theory

gutbucket /gút bukit/ *n.* **1. HOME-MADE BASS** a home-made instrument played like a double bass, made by fixing a stick to an upturned basin and stretching a string along its length **2. KIND OF JAZZ** a simple but highly emotional style of jazz or blues [Early 20thC. Originally a bucket used for carrying beer, or for catching the slops from a barrel, later used for the instrument made from the bucket.]

Gutenberg /gŏŏt'n burg/, **Johannes** (1400?–68) German printer. He is credited with the invention of movable type, which he used in his Mainz printing press to print the 42-line Bible, known as the Gutenberg Bible. Full name **Johannes Gensfleisch Gutenberg**

Guthrie /gúthri/, **Sir Tyrone** (1900–71) British stage director. He was closely identified with the Old Vic-Sadler's Wells Company in the 1940s and 1950s, and founded the Tyrone Guthrie Theatre in Minneapolis, Minnesota, in 1963. Full name **Sir William Tyrone Guthrie**

Popperfoto

Johannes Gutenberg: 15th-century engraving showing Gutenberg (left foreground) printing the Gutenberg Bible (1456?)

Guthrun *n.* MYTHOL = **Gudrun**

gut job *n. US* the restoration or repair of a building that includes the removal and rebuilding of the interior (*informal*)

gutless /gútləss/ *adj.* lacking in courage and determination —**gutlessness** *n.*

WORD KEY: SYNONYMS

See Synonyms at ***cowardly***.

gut rehabilitation, **gut renovation** *n. US* = **gut job** (*informal*)

guts *n.* a very greedy person (*informal; takes a singular verb*)

WORD KEY: SYNONYMS

See Synonyms at ***courage***.

gutsy /gútsi/ (**-ier, -iest**) *adj.* (*informal*) **1. COURAGEOUS** showing courage, boldness and determination **2. DONE WITH EMOTION** done or performed with a great deal of vigour, passion, or emotion **3. GREEDY** greedy or gluttonous —**gutsily** *adv.* —**gutsiness** *n.*

gutta /gúttə/ (*plural* **-tae** /-tee/) *n.* **1. ORNAMENT CARVED ON A DORIC ENTABLATURE** one of a series of ornaments shaped like drops that are attached to the underside of a Doric entablature **2. DROP OF MEDICINE** a drop of medicine (*dated*) (*formerly used in the instructions on prescriptions to indicate the dose to be taken*) [14thC. From Latin, 'drop'.]

gutta-percha /gúttə púrchə/ *n.* **1. PLIABLE SUBSTANCE MADE FROM LATEX** a soft pliable substance made from the latex taken from a Malaysian tree, used in golf balls, for waterproofing substances, and as insulation for electrical wires **2. TREE FROM WHICH GUTTA-PERCHA COMES** a tree from which gutta-percha is taken. Genera: *Palaquium* and *Payena*. [Mid-19thC. Alteration (by influence of Latin *gutta* 'drop') of Malay *getah perca*, literally 'gum strips of cloth', because it resembles cloth.]

guttate /gútt ayt/, **guttated** /gútt aytid/ *adj.* BIOL having or resembling drops or spots [Early 19thC. From Latin *guttatus*, from *gutta* (see GUTTA).]

guttation /gu táysh'n/ *n.* the oozing out of water droplets from the uninjured surface of a plant leaf

gutted /gúttid/ *adj.* **1. WITH INSIDES REMOVED** with the insides taken out, ready to be sold ○ *the price for round haddock and gutted haddock* **2. VERY DISAPPOINTED** desperately disappointed or upset (*informal*) ○ *They were absolutely gutted when they lost the match.*

gutter /gúttər/ *n.* **1. RAINWATER CHANNEL ON A ROOF** a metal or plastic channel on a roof for carrying away rainwater **2. RAINWATER CHANNEL ON A ROAD** a channel at the edge of a road that carries water into a drain **3. POOR OR DEGRADED STATE** an impoverished and degraded existence or way of life ○ *She dragged me out of the gutter and made me respect myself.* **4.** BOWLING **CHANNEL ON TEN-PIN BOWLING LANE** the channel on either side of a ten-pin bowling lane **5.** PRINTING **INNER MARGINS OF BOOK** the blank space formed by the inner margins of two facing pages of a book **6.** STAMPS **SPACE BETWEEN STAMPS ON SHEET** the space between the printed design of one stamp and the next one on the sheet, where the perforations lie ■ *v.* (**-ters, -tering, -tered**) **1.** *vi.* **MELT QUICKLY** to burn down more quickly than usual because the melting wax has formed a channel on one side (*refers to a candle*) **2.** *vi.* **FLICKER** to flicker when on the point of being extinguished **3.** *vt.* **FORM CHANNELS IN** to wear away channels in the surface of sth **4.** *vi.* **TRICKLE** to run in a narrow stream or trickle ○ *The overflow was guttering down the wall.* ■ *adj.* **OF THE WORST KIND** of the most vulgar, corrupt, or morally degraded kind (*disapproving*) ○ *the gutter press* [13thC. From Anglo-Norman *gotere*, from, ultimately, Latin *gutta* 'drop' (source of English *gout*). The underlying sense is of sth along which 'drops' of water run.]

gutter out *vi.* **1. STOP BURNING** to go out after flickering for a while ○ *Most of the candles guttered out.* **2. COME TO A GRADUAL FINISH** to come to an end finally, after gradually declining ○ *The peace process had all but guttered out.*

gutter ball *n.* in ten-pin bowling, a ball that, when bowled, rolls into the gutter and does not knock over any pins

guttering /gúttəring/ *n.* **1. ROOF GUTTERS** the gutters on a roof **2. CHANNELS USED AS GUTTERS** metal or plastic channels used as gutters

gutter press *n.* low-quality newspapers and magazines that deal mostly with scandal and gossip, rather than serious news

guttersnipe /gúttər snīp/ *n.* (*insult*) **1. DIRTY CHILD WITHOUT MEANS** a child who wears dirty ragged clothes, has rough manners, and lives in the streets **2. SB FROM LOWER CLASS** sb with a rough or vulgar manner, especially sb with a lower-class background [Mid-19thC. The modern sense evolved from 'the common snipe' (a bird that likes wet muddy conditions) via 'street cleaner'.] —**guttersnipish** *adj.*

guttural /gúttərəl/ *adj.* **1. GRUFF-SOUNDING** characterized by harsh and grating speech sounds made in the throat or towards the back of the mouth **2.** PHON = **velar** *adj.* 1 ■ *n.* **GUTTURAL SPEECH SOUND** a speech sound produced in the throat or at the back of the mouth [Late 16thC. Directly or via French from medieval Latin *gutturalis*, from Latin *guttur* 'throat'.] —**gutturalism** *n.* —**gutturality** *n.* —**gutturally** *adv.* —**gutturalness** *n.*

gutturalize /gúttərə līz/ (**-izes, -izing, -ized**), **gutturalise** (**-ises, -ising, -ised**) *v.* **1.** *vt.* **SAY IN GUTTURAL WAY** to pronounce a speech sound in the throat or towards the back of the mouth **2.** *vti.* **SPEAK OR SAY HARSHLY** to speak or say sth in a harsh rasping way —**gutturalization** *n.*

gutty /gútti/ (*plural* **-ties**) *n. Scotland* a plimsoll (*informal; usually in plural*) [20thC. From GUTTA-PERCHA, because it is made of rubber.]

guv /guv/ *n.* (*informal*) **1. TERM OF ADDRESS FOR A SUPERIOR MAN** used as a familiar term of address by one man to another, especially to one in a superior position **2. BOSS** used by men and women as an informal term of address for their boss [Mid-19thC. Shortening of GUVNOR.]

guvnor /gúvnər/ *n.* (*dated informal*) **1.** = **guv** *n.* 1 **2. FATHER** formerly used by upper-class young men as an informal term, and a term of address, for their fathers ○ *The guvnor won't increase my allowance.* [Mid-19thC. Representing a pronunciation of GOVERNOR.]

guy[1] /gī/ *n.* **1. MAN** a man (*informal*) **2. PERSON** sb of either sex, especially one of a group of people (*informal*) **3. MODEL BURNT ON BONFIRE** a home-made model of a man, like a scarecrow, originally intended as an effigy of Guy Fawkes, usually made by children and burnt on a fire on 5 November in Britain ○ *'Penny for the guy!'* **4. ODDLY DRESSED PERSON** a person dressed in very odd or very shabby clothes (*archaic informal*) ■ *vt.* (**guys, guying, guyed**) **POKE FUN AT** to make fun of sb or sth, especially by a comical imitation ■ *n.* scarecrow (*regional informal*) [Early 19thC. From *Guy Fawkes* (see GUY FAWKES NIGHT).]

guy[2] /gī/ *n.* = **guyrope** ■ *vt.* (**guys, guying, guyed**) **SUPPORT WITH GUYROPES** to support or anchor sth using ropes, cables, or chains [14thC. Origin uncertain: probably from a Low German word that is, perhaps, also the source of Dutch *gei* and German *Geitau* 'brail' (a type of rope).]

Guy. *abbr.* Guyana

Guyana

Guyana republic on the North Atlantic coast of South America bordered on the northwest by Venezuela, on the southwest by Brazil and on the east by Surinam. Formerly a British colony, it gained independence in 1966. Language: English. Currency: Guyana dollar. Capital: Georgetown. Population: 711,759 (1997). Area: 215,000 sq. km/83,000 sq. mi. Official name **Cooperative Republic of Guyana** —**Guyanese** *adj.*, *n.*

Guy Fawkes Night *n.* = **Bonfire Night** [Named after *Guy Fawkes* (1570–1606), one of the conspirators who tried to blow up Parliament (see GUNPOWDER PLOT)]

guyot /gee ṓ/ *n.* a flat-topped underwater mountain, commonly found in the Pacific Ocean and considered to be an extinct volcano [Mid-20thC. Named after Arnold Henri *Guyot*, (1807–84), a Swiss-born US geologist and geographer.]

guyrope /gí rōp/, **guyline** *n.* a rope, wire, or chain tightened to hold sth in position, e.g. any of the ropes pulled tight to keep a tent up

guywire /gí wīr/ *n.* US = **guyrope**

guzzle /gúzz'l/ (**-zles**, **-zling**, **-zled**) *vti.* to eat or drink sth greedily, or consume sth rapidly and in large quantities (*informal*) [Late 16thC. Origin uncertain: perhaps from Old French *gosillier* 'to chatter, vomit', from, ultimately, late Latin *geusiae* 'cheeks'.] —**guzzler** *n.*

GW *symbol.* gigawatt

Gwalior /gwáali awr/ city near Agra in Madhya Pradesh State, central India. Population: 692,982 (1991).

gweduc *n.* ZOOL = **geoduck**

gweilo /gwī lṓ/ *n. Hong Kong* a foreigner from the West (*informal*)

Gwelo /gweēlṓ/ former name for **Gweru** (since 1982)

Gwent /gwent/ former county in southeastern Wales, approximately equivalent to the modern-day county of Monmouthshire

Gweru /gwáy roo/ city on the River Gweru, in central Zimbabwe. It is a commercial, manufacturing, and transportation centre. Population: 124,735 (1992).

Gwyn /gwin/, **Gwynn, Nell** (1650–87) English actor. A leading performer in Restoration comedies, she became the mistress of Charles II and bore him two sons. Full name **Eleanor Gwyn**

Gwynedd /gwínneth/ mountainous county in northwestern Wales, dominated by Snowdonia National Park. Area: 3,867 sq. km/1,494 sq. mi. Population: 118,000 (1995).

gwyniad /gwínni ad/ (*plural* **-ads** *or* **-ad**) *n.* a variety of freshwater white fish found mainly in Lake Bala in Wales [Early 17thC. From Welsh, from *gwyn* 'white'.]

Gy *symbol.* NUCLEAR PHYS gray

gybe /jīb/, **jibe** *vti.* NAUT **1.** SWING ACROSS BOAT to swing, or to make a fore-and-aft sail swing, across from one side of the boat to the other when sailing before the wind **2.** CHANGE DIRECTION IN SAILING SHIP to change direction, or cause a sailing ship to change direction, by turning away from the wind, as a result of a fore-and-aft-sail gybing ■ *n.* ACTION OF GYBING a sudden shift of a sail back and forth or a change in direction [Late 17thC. From obsolete Dutch *gÿben*.]

gym /jim/ *n.* **1.** GYMNASIUM a gymnasium (*informal*) **2.** PHYSICAL EDUCATION physical education, especially as a school subject (*informal*) **3.** CHILD'S CLIMBING FRAME a sturdy metal or hard plastic frame designed for children's outdoor play and exercise (*often used in combination*) [Late 19thC. Shortening.]

gymkhana /jim ka'anə/ *n.* **1.** HORSE-RIDING EVENT a community-based outdoor event with various activities relating to horse-riding **2.** ATHLETICS MEETING OR FACILITY a place where a sporting event or contest is held (*dated*) [Mid-19thC. Alteration (by influence of words such as GYMNAST) of Urdu *gendkānah*, literally 'ball house'. Originally used for a public sports facility.]

Exercise bench

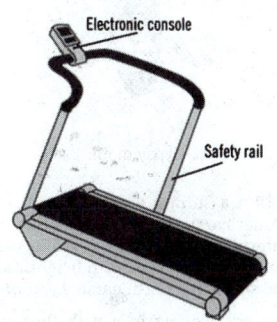

Treadmill

Electronic console

Safety rail

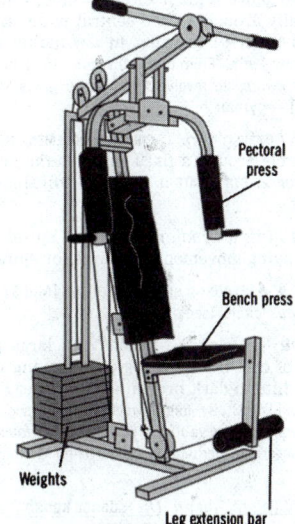

Weight trainer

Pectoral press

Bench press

Weights

Leg extension bar

Gymnasium: Typical equipment used in a gymnasium

gymnasium /jim náyzi əm/ (*plural* **-ums** *or* **-a**) *n.* a hall equipped for physical exercise or physical training of various kinds, e.g. in a school or a private club [Late 16thC. Via Latin, 'school', from, ultimately, Greek *gumnazein* 'to exercise naked' (a custom in ancient times), hence 'to train', from *gumnos* 'naked'.]

gymnast /jím nast/ *n.* sb who is good at gymnastics, especially sb involved in gymnastics as a competitive sport [Late 16thC. Directly or via French from Greek *gumnastēs* 'trainer of athletes', from *gumnazein* (see GYMNASIUM).]

gymnastic /jim nástik/ *adj.* **1.** INVOLVING GYMNASTICS relating to or involving gymnastics ○ *gymnastic equipment* **2.** INVOLVING ATHLETICISM involving or demonstrating athleticism and agility ○ *a gymnastic dancing style* [Late 16thC. Via Latin from Greek *gumnastikos*, from *gumnazein* (see GYMNASIUM).] —**gymnastically** *adv.*

gymnastics /jim nástiks/ *n.* (*takes a singular verb*) **1.** PHYSICAL TRAINING USING GYMNASTIC EQUIPMENT physical training using equipment such as bars, rings, and vaulting horses, designed to develop agility and muscular strength **2.** COMPETITIVE SPORT USING GYMNASTIC EQUIPMENT the competitive sport in which athletes perform a series of exercises on pieces of gymnastic equipment ■ *npl.* **1.** PHYSICAL EXERCISES movements, exercises, or activities that involve feats of physical strength and agility **2.** ACTIONS DEMONSTRATING AGILITY AND SKILL the performance of a series of complex mental or physical operations of a particular kind, usually rapidly and with great agility and skill ○ *verbal gymnastics*

gymnosperm /jímnə spurm/ *n.* a woody vascular plant such as a conifer, cycad, or gingko in which the ovules are carried naked on the scales of a cone. ◊ **angiosperm** [Mid-19thC. Via modern Latin *gymnospermus* from Greek *gumnospermos*, literally 'naked seed'.] —**gymnospermous** /jímnə spúrməss/ *adj.* —**gymnospermy** /gímnə spurmi/ *n.*

Gympie /gímpi/ town in southeastern Queensland, Australia, that is an agricultural centre. Population: 10,813 (1996).

gym rat *n.* sb who spends a great deal of time exercising or playing a sport at a gymnasium (*informal*)

gym shoe *n.* = **plimsoll**

gymslip /jím slip/ *n.* a schoolgirl's sleeveless dress worn over a blouse as part of a school uniform

gyn. *n.*, *adj.*, *abbr.* gynaecology

gyn- *prefix.* = **gyno-** (*used before vowels*)

gynae /gíni/ *adj.* gynaecological (*informal*) ■ *n.* (*informal*) **1.** GYNAECOLOGIST a gynaecologist **2.** GYNAECOLOGY gynaecology or the department of a hospital that deals with this [Mid-20thC. Shortening.]

gynaec-, **gynaeco-** *prefix.* woman ○ *gynaecology* [From Greek *gunaik-*, the stem of *gunē* (see GYNO-)]

gynaecocracy /jínni kókrəssi, gíni-/ (*plural* **-racies**) *n.* an actual or theoretical political dominance by women, or a political system that gives supremacy to women

gynaecoid /jínni koyd, gíni-/ *adj.* physically resembling or typical of a woman ○ *a gynaecoid pelvis*

gynaecol. *abbr.* **1.** gynaecological **2.** gynaecologist **3.** gynaecology

gynaecological /gínikə lójjik'l/, **gynaecologic** /gínikə lójjik/ *adj.* relating to women's health, especially to diseases of the reproductive organs

gynaecology[1] /gíni kólləji/ *n.* the branch of medicine that deals with women's health, especially with the health of women's reproductive organs —**gynaecologist** *n.*

gynaecology[2] /gínə kólləji/ *n.* gynaecology, or the department of a hospital that deals with this speciality (*informal*) = **gynecology**

gynaecomastia /jínni kō mástiə, gíni-/ *n.* enlarged breasts on a man caused by hormonal imbalance or hormone therapy [Mid-19thC. Coined from GYNAECO- + Greek *mastos* 'breast'.]

gynaecopathy /jínni kóppəthi, gíni-/ (*plural* **-pathies**) *n.* any disease that affects only women

gynaephobia /jínnə fōbiə, gínə-/ *n.* an irrational and pathological fear of women

gynandromorph /ji nándrə mawrf/ *n.* creature, especially an insect, that has both male and female characteristics in a way abnormal for its species [Late 19thC. Coined from GYNANDROUS + MORPH.] —**gynandromorphic** /ji nándrə máwrfik/ *adj.* —**gynandromorphous** /-máwrfəss/ *adj.* —**gynandromorphism** /-máwrfizəm/ *n.* —**gynandromorphy** /ji nándrə mawrfi/ *n.*

gynandrous /jī nándrəss/ *adj.* BOT used to describe flowers such as orchids that have pistils and stamens united in a column [Early 19thC. Formed from Greek *gunandros* 'of doubtful sex', from *gunē* 'woman, female' + the stem *andr-* 'man'.]

gynarchy /jī naarki, gī-/ (*plural* **-chies**) *n.* = **gynae-cocracy** —**gynarchic** /jī naarkik, gī-/ *adj.*

-gyne *suffix.* **1.** female ○ *androgyne* **2.** female reproductive organ ○ *trichogyne* [From Greek *gunē* (see GYNO-)] —**gynous** *suffix.* —**gyny** *suffix.*

gyneco- US = **gynaeco-**

gynecocracy *n.* US = **gynaecocracy**

gynecol. US = **gynaecol.**

gynecology *n.* US = **gynaecology**

gyno- *prefix.* **1.** female reproductive organ ○ *gynophore* **2.** woman ○ *gynocracy* [From Greek *gunē* 'woman'. Ultimately from the Indo-European word for 'woman', which is also the ancestor of English *queen* and *banshee*.]

gynocracy /jī nókrəssi, gī-/ (*plural* **-cies**) *n.* = **gynaecocracy**

gynodioecious /jínnō dī éeshəss, gīnō-/ *adj.* used to describe a plant species that has bisexual flowers on some plants and single-sex flowers on others — **gynodioecism** /jínō dī éessizəm, gīnō-/ *n.*

gynoecium /jī néessi əm, gī-/ (*plural* **-a** /-ə/) *n.* the carpels of a plant considered together [Mid-19thC. From an alteration (influenced by Greek *oikos* 'house') of modern Latin *gynaeceum* 'women's apartments', from the neuter of Greek *gunaikeios* 'of women', from *gunē* 'woman'.]

gynogenesis /jīnə jénnəssiss, gīnə-/ *n.* the development of an embryo without fusion of the egg and sperm nuclei, so that the embryo has only maternal chromosomes

gynophore /jínə fawr, gīnə-/ *n.* a pistil stalk that has its gynoecium raised above the rest of the flower — **gynophoric** /jínə fórrik, gīnə-/ *adj.*

Gyor /dyur, dyör/ town and river port in northwestern Hungary, situated on the River Danube, about halfway between Budapest and Vienna. Population: 127,000 (1995).

gyp[1] /jip/, **gip** *vt.* (**gyps, gypping, gypped; gips, gipping, gipped**) CHEAT to cheat sb, especially by overcharging (*informal*) ■ *n.* **1.** CHEATER sb who cheats or swindles people (*insult*) **2.** SCAM a scheme to trick or swindle people (*informal; sometimes considered offensive*) [Late 19thC. Origin uncertain: perhaps a derogatory shortening of GYPSY.] —**gypper** *n.*

gyp[2] /jip/, **gip** *n.* pain, especially if sharp or severe (*informal*) ○ *His arthritis was giving him gyp.* [Late 19thC. Contraction of GEE UP.]

gyppo /jíppō/ (*plural* **-pos**) *n.* **1.** OFFENSIVE TERM an offensive term for a Romany (*slang offensive*) **2.** OFFENSIVE TERM an offensive term for an Egyptian, formerly used especially by British troops stationed in North Africa (*dated slang offensive*) [Early 20thC. Alteration of GYPSY and EGYPTIAN.]

gyppy tummy /jíppi-/ (*plural* **gyppy tummies**) *n.* a stomach upset with a bout of diarrhoea, especially one happening to a Western visitor in a hot Eastern country (*informal; sometimes considered offensive*) [*Gyppy*, a variant of GYPPO an offensive term for 'Egyptian', because the condition was common in the Middle East]

gypsiferous /jip síffərəss/ *adj.* containing gypsum

gypsophila /jip sóffilə/ *n.* a plant of the carnation family native to the Mediterranean, with delicate tiny white or pink flowers on long branching stalks. It is popular in bouquets. Genus: *Gypsophila.* [Late 18thC. From modern Latin, genus name, literally 'chalk-

loving', from Greek *gupsos* 'chalk', because it grows in chalky soil.]

gypsum /jípsəm/ *n.* **1.** WHITE MINERAL a naturally occurring colourless or white mineral, hydrated calcium sulphate, that is used to make cement, plaster of Paris, chalk, and agricultural fertilizers. Formula: $CaSO_4.2H_2O$. **2.** PLASTERBOARD plasterboard (*informal*) [14thC. Via Latin from Greek *gupsos* 'chalk, gypsum'.]

gypsy /jípsi/ (*plural* **-sies**) *n.* sb who has a nomadic or unconventional lifestyle

Gypsy (*plural* **-sies**), **Gipsy** (*plural* **-sies**) *n.* an offensive term for a member of the Romany people (*offensive*) [Mid-16thC. Shortening of EGYPTIAN, because Gypsies were once thought to have come from Egypt.] — **Gypsy** *adj.*

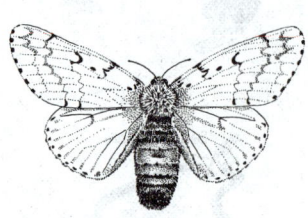

Gypsy moth

gypsy moth *n.* a European tussock moth, common in North America since the 19th century, where its hairy caterpillar has become a serious pest of trees. The caterpillar is greyish with bright red and blue spots and stiff hairs. Latin name: *Lymantria dispar.*

gyral /jírəl/ *adj.* moving in a path that is spiral or circular —**gyrally** *adv.*

gyrate /jī ráyt/ *vi.* (**-rates, -rating, -rated**) MOVE IN CIRCLE OR SPIRAL to move with a circular or spiral motion, especially around a fixed central point ■ *adj.* BIOL GROWING IN A SPIRAL growing in a winding spiral or coil [Early 19thC. From late Latin *girat-*, the past participle stem of *gyrare*, 'to revolve', from Latin *gyrus* 'circle' (see GYRUS).] —**gyrator** *n.*

gyration /jī ráysh'n/ *n.* **1.** CIRCULAR MOVEMENT movement in a circle around a fixed centre ○ *the gyration of the rotor* **2.** STH GYRATE a spiral or coil-shaped thing or part

gyratory /jī ráytəri/ *adj.* moving in a spiral or circle or involving movement in a circle or spiral

gyre /jīr/ *n.* a circle or spiral (*literary*) [Mid-16thC. From Latin *gyrus* 'circle' (see GYRUS).]

gyrfalcon /júr fawlkən, -folkən/ *n.* a large powerful falcon of cold northern regions, varying in colour from white to dark brown. Latin name: *Falco rusticolus.* [14thC. By folk etymology (by association with Latin *gyrare* 'to revolve') from Old French *gerfaucon; ger-* of uncertain origin: perhaps from Old High German *gir* 'vulture'.]

gyro /jírō/ (*plural* **-ros**) *n.* US = **doner kebab** [Late 20thC. From modern Greek *guros*, literally 'turning'.]

gyro- *prefix.* **1.** spinning or rotating in a circle ○ *gyrostatics* **2.** gyroscope, gyroscopic ○ *gyrostabilizer* [From Greek *guros* 'ring, circle']

gyrocompass /jírō kumpəss/ *n.* a navigational compass fitted with a gyroscope instead of a magnet

gyromagnetic /jírō mag néttik/ *adj.* relating to or caused by the magnetism produced by the spinning motion of a charged particle ○ *gyromagnetic effect*

gyromagnetic ratio *n.* PHYS the ratio of the magnetic moment to the angular momentum of a system

gyron /jírən/, **giron** *n.* in heraldry, a triangular form made by two blinds drawn from the edge of an escutcheon to meet at the fesse-point and occupying half of the quarter [Late 16thC. From French, literally 'gusset'; ultimately from a prehistoric Germanic word that is also the source of English *gore*[2].]

gyroplane /jírō playn/ *n.* an aircraft fitted with an unpowered rotor for producing lift. ◊ **autogiro**

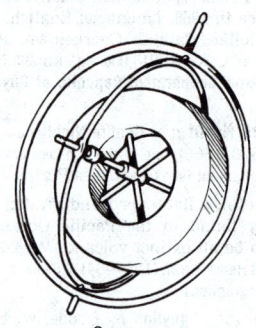

Gyroscope

gyroscope /jírə skōp/ *n.* a device consisting of a rotating heavy metal wheel pivoted inside a circular frame. The wheel's rotation enables it to retain its original orientation in space when the frame turns. Gyroscopes are used in compasses and other navigational aids, and in stabilizing mechanisms on ships and aircraft. —**gyroscopic** /jírə skóppik/ *adj.* —**gyroscopically** /-skóppikli/ *adv.*

gyrostabilizer /jírō stáybə līzər/ *n.* a stabilizing system that uses gyroscopes to compensate and reduce the rolling or pitching motion of a ship or aircraft

gyrostat /jírō stat/ *n.* a type of gyroscope or gyrostabilizer in which the rotating wheel is pivoted within a rigid case [Late 19thC. Coined from GYRO- + Greek *statos* 'standing'.]

gyrostatics /jírō státtiks/ *n.* the science that deals with rotating bodies (*takes a singular verb*) —**gyrostatic** /jírō státtik/ *adj.* —**gyrostatically** /-státtikli/ *adv.*

gyrus /jírəss/ (*plural* **-ri** /-rī/) *n.* any of the rounded ridges on the outer layer of the brain [Mid-19thC. Via Latin, literally 'circle', from Greek *guros* 'ring, circle' (source of English *gyro-*).]

Gyumri /gyoŏmri/ city in northwestern Armenia, the country's second most populated urban area. Population: 123,000 (1990). Former name **Leninakhan**

gyve /jīv/ *n.* LEG SHACKLE a shackle or fetter, usually for the leg (*archaic*) (*usually used in plural*) ■ *vt.* (**gyves, gyving, gyved**) SHACKLE to shackle or fetter sb, especially by the leg (*archaic*) [13thC. Origin unknown.]

h¹ /aych/ (plural **h's**), **H** (plural **H's** or **Hs**) n. **1.** 8TH LETTER OF ENGLISH ALPHABET the eighth letter of the modern English alphabet **2.** SPEECH SOUND CORRESPONDING TO THE LETTER 'H' the speech sound that corresponds to the letter 'H' **3.** LETTER 'H' WRITTEN a written representation of the letter 'H'

h² symbol. **1.** Planck's constant **2.** hecto-

H symbol. **1.** ELECTRON ENG henry **2.** CHEM hydrogen **3.** PHYS enthalpy **4.** Hamiltonian **5.** magnetic field strength

h. abbr. **1.** h., H. harbour **2.** h., H. hard **3.** h., H. hardness **4.** h., H. height **5.** h., H. high **6.** h., h hit **7.** hospital **8.** horizontal **9.** MUSIC horn **10.** hour **11.** hundred **12.** husband

ha¹ /haa/, **hah** interj. **1.** EXPRESSING VARIOUS EMOTIONS used to express surprise, triumph, scorn, or happiness, depending on the way the speaker says it **2.** REPRESENTING LAUGHTER a word repeated to represent in writing the sound of laughter [13thC. An imitation of the sound.]

ha² symbol. hectare

h.a. abbr. hoc anno

Haakon VII /háwk on/, **King of Norway** (1872–1957). On the dissolution of the union between Sweden and Norway, he was elected king in 1905.

haar /haar/ n. in eastern England and Scotland, a cold mist or fog off the North Sea coast, or rolling in from the North Sea (regional) [Late 17thC. Origin uncertain: perhaps from Old Norse hárr 'hoar, hoary'.]

Haarlem /háarləm/, **Harlem** city in North Holland province, western Netherlands, 20 km/12 mi. west of Amsterdam. Population: 149,788 (1992).

Hab. abbr. Habakkuk

Habakkuk /hábbəkək/, **Habacuc** n. **1.** BIBLICAL HEBREW PRIEST in the Bible, a Hebrew priest who lived in the seventh century BC **2.** BOOK OF THE BIBLE one of the prophetic books of the Bible. See table at **Bible**

habanera /hábbə náirə/ n. **1.** SLOW DANCE a slow dance in two-four time, originally from Cuba **2.** MUSIC DANCE MUSIC FOR HABANERA a piece of music for the habanera, which has a characteristic dotted rhythm [Late 19thC. From Spanish habanera, 'Havana'.]

hab. corp. abbr. LAW habeas corpus

habdabs /háb dabz/ npl. a fit of extreme anxiety or irritation (informal) [Mid-20thC. Origin unknown.]

habdalah /hav dáalə/, **havdalah** n. a Jewish ceremony that marks the end of the Sabbath or another holy day, or a prayer said during the ceremony [Mid-18thC. From Hebrew habdālāh 'separation, division'.]

habeas corpus /háybi əss káwrpəss/ n. a writ issued in order to bring sb who has been detained into court, usually for a decision on whether the detention is lawful [From Latin, literally 'you may have the body']

Haber-Bosch process /háabər bósh-/ n. CHEM = **Haber process** [Named after the German chemists Fritz Haber (1869–1934) and Karl Bosch (1874–1940)]

haberdasher /hábbər dashər/ n. **1.** DEALER IN SEWING ARTICLES sb who deals in small articles used in sewing, e.g. thread, ribbons, and buttons **2.** US DEALER IN MEN'S CLOTHING sb who owns or works in a store that sells men's clothing and accessories [14thC. Probably from

Anglo-Norman hapertas 'small items of merchandise', of unknown origin.]

haberdashery /hábbər dashəri/ (plural **-ies**) n. **1.** GOODS SOLD BY A HABERDASHER the items sold by a haberdasher **2.** SHOP SELLING HABERDASHERY a shop, or a department in a larger store, that sells haberdashery

habergeon /hábbərjən/ n. a sleeveless chain mail jacket worn under armour [14thC. From French haubergeon, from Old French hauberc, literally 'a little hauberk' (see HAUBERK).]

Haber process /háabər-/ n. a commercial process for catalytically producing ammonia from atmospheric nitrogen and hydrogen at high temperature and pressure [See HABER-BOSCH PROCESS]

habile /hábbil, hábbeel/ adj. able to do sth with ease (literary) [Late 15thC. Via French from Latin habilis 'able, easy to hold' (source of English able), from habere 'to have, hold'.]

habiliment /hə bíllimənt/ n. GARMENT OR GARMENTS clothing, or an item of clothing (formal) (usually used in the plural) ■ **habiliments** npl. **1.** SPECIALIZED EQUIPMENT the equipment and gear needed for a task or activity **2.** SPECIAL CLOTHES items of clothing associated with sb's work or position, or an occasion [Early 17thC. From Old French habillement, from habiller 'to fit out', from habile (see HABILE). The sense 'clothing' developed in French, probably by association with 'habit'.]

habilitate /hə bílli tayt/ (**-tates, -tating, -tated**) v. **1.** vi. PREPARE FOR POSITION to qualify for employment or an office (formal) **2.** vt. US EQUIP A MINING OPERATION to provide a mine with the equipment and money needed for operation **3.** vt. CLOTHE to clothe sb in a particular way (literary) [Early 17thC. From medieval Latin habilitare, from habilitas 'ability', from habilis (see HABILE).] —**habilitation** /hə bílli táysh'n/ n. —**habilitator** /hə bílli taytər/ n.

habit /hábbit/ n. **1.** STH DONE ALL THE TIME an action or behaviour pattern that is regular, repetitive, and often unconscious ○ I really need to get into the habit of writing down what I spend. ○ He has a really annoying habit of finishing your sentences for you. **2.** ADDICTION an addiction to a drug (slang) **3.** RELIG CLOTHING OF RELIGIOUS ORDER a long loose gown, usually black, brown, grey, or white, traditionally worn by nuns and monks **4.** CLOTHES = **riding habit 5.** BOT, ZOOL GROWTH PATTERN the characteristic appearance, behaviour, or growth pattern of a plant or animal **6.** SHAPE OF A CRYSTAL the characteristic growth pattern or shape of a crystal **7.** ATTITUDE sb's attitude or general disposition ■ vt. (**-its, -iting, -ited**) CLOTHE SB SPECIALLY to dress sb in clothing distinctive to a particular position or office (literary) [12thC. Via Old French abit from Latin habitus from, ultimately, habere 'to have, wear'.] ◇ **kick the habit** to become free of an addiction, or stop doing sth that has been a long-standing practice

——— WORD KEY: SYNONYMS ———
habit, custom, tradition, practice, routine, wont
CORE MEANING: established pattern of behaviour
habit sth that is done on such a regular basis that it becomes normal to act in this way and can be difficult to stop. It can be used to suggest that sth is done compulsively; **custom** sth that sb regularly does at a particular time or on a particular occasion. It is also used to describe sth that is an established action or pattern of behaviour for a particular community or group of people; **tradition** an established action or pattern of

behaviour in a particular community or group of people, especially one that has existed for a long time and is considered an important part of a particular culture or way of life; **practice** an established way of doing sth, especially a way that has developed through experience and knowledge; **routine** a sequence of actions that is regularly followed on a day-to-day basis, sometimes with the suggestion that this is monotonous and tedious; **wont** a formal or literary word used to describe sth that sb does regularly or habitually.

——— WORD KEY: ORIGIN ———
The Latin word habere from which **habit** is derived was used reflexively to mean 'to be', and so its past participle habitus came to be used as a noun for 'how you are', that is, your 'state' or 'condition'. Subsequently this developed along the lines of both 'outward condition or appearance', hence 'clothing', and 'inner condition, quality, nature, character', and later came to mean 'usual way of behaving'. (The notion of adapting a verb meaning 'to have' to express 'how you are, how you comport yourself' is duplicated in English 'behave').

habitable /hábbitəb'l/ adj. considered fit to be lived in ○ A lot of structural work will be needed before the house is habitable. [14thC. Via Old French from Latin habitabilis, from habitare 'to possess, inhabit' (see HABITAT).] —**habitability** /hábbitə bílləti/ n. —**habitableness** /hábbitəb'lnəss/ n. —**habitably** /-təbli/ adv.

habitant /hábbitənt/ n. **1.** INHABITANT sb living in a place **2.** Can, US N AMERICAN FARMER OF FRENCH ORIGIN a farmer of French descent living in Canada or the United States [15thC. From French, from the present participle of Old French habiter 'to dwell', from Latin habitare (see HABITAT).]

habitat /hábbi tat/ n. **1.** HOME ENVIRONMENT the natural conditions and environment, e.g. forest, desert, or wetlands, in which a plant or animal lives **2.** TYPICAL LOCATION the place in which a person or group is usually found **3.** ARTIFICIALLY CREATED ENVIRONMENT a sealed controlled environment in which people can live, e.g. to do research on the sea floor [Late 18thC. 3rd person present singular form of Latin habitare 'to possess, inhabit', literally 'to keep having' (source also of English inhabit), from habere 'to have'.]

habitation /hábbi táysh'n/ n. **1.** OCCUPANCY the occupancy of a place by people or animals **2.** LIVING PLACE a place in which to live ○ The squirrels found a new habitation in a hollow tree. **3.** DWELLINGS a group of dwellings and their inhabitants ○ There is little evidence remaining of the ancient habitation. [14thC. Via Old French from, ultimately Latin habitare (see HABITAT).] —**habitational** adj.

habit-forming adj. capable of causing a physiological or psychological need in sb

habitual /hə bíchoo əl/ adj. **1.** REGULAR done regularly and frequently **2.** PERSISTING IN SOME BEHAVIOUR continuing in some practice as a result of an ingrained tendency **3.** CHARACTERISTIC typical of sb's character or behaviour ○ She tackled the problem with her habitual single-mindedness. —**habitually** adv. —**habitualness** n.

——— WORD KEY: SYNONYMS ———
See Synonyms at **usual**.

habituate /hə bíchoo ayt/ (**-ates, -ating, -ated**) v. **1.** vt. MAKE SB USED TO STH to accustom a person or animal to sth through prolonged and regular exposure (*formal*) ○ *People living in cities become habituated to crowds.* **2.** *vti.* PSYCHOL **LEARN OR TEACH SB TO IGNORE STH** to learn or teach a person or animal not to respond to a stimulus that is frequently repeated **3.** *vi.* **BECOME ACCUSTOMED TO** to become dependent on or less affected by a medical or illegal drug through frequent use [16thC. From late Latin *habituare* 'to bring into a state', from Latin *habitus* (see HABIT).]

habituation /hə bíchoo áysh'n/ *n.* **1. GETTING USED TO STH** the act of becoming accustomed to sth through prolonged and frequent exposure (*formal*) **2.** PSYCHOL **DECREASED RESPONSE TO REPEATED STIMULUS** a basic form of learning in which an organism's response to a repeated stimulus decreases in strength **3. DRUG TOLERANCE OR DEPENDENCY** tolerance to or dependence on a medical or illegal drug, through frequent and prolonged use

habitude /hábbi tyood/ *n.* a tendency to act in a particular way (*literary*) —**habitudinal** /hábbi tyoōdin'l/ *adj.*

habitué /hə bítyoo ay/ (*plural* **-bitués**) *n.* sb who visits a place regularly [Early 19thC. From French, from the past participle of *habituer*, from late Latin *habituare* (see HABITUATE).]

habitus /hábbitəss/ (*plural* **-tus**) *n.* the general appearance, posture, or physical state of a patient, especially with regard to susceptibility to disease [Late 19thC. From Latin (see HABIT).]

haboob /hə boōb/ *n.* a violent sandstorm or dust storm that sweeps across the deserts of northern Africa and Arabia and the plains of India [Late 19thC. From Arabic *habub* 'violent storm'.]

Habsburg *n.* HIST = **Hapsburg**

habu /haá boo/ (*plural* **-bus**) *n.* a large poisonous snake native to Okinawa and neighbouring Pacific islands. Latin name: *Trimeresurus flavoviridis.* [Late 19thC. From Japanese.]

HAC *abbr.* Honourable Artillery Company

háček /haá chek/ *n.* a mark (ˇ) placed over a letter in some Slavic and other languages to indicate a change in pronunciation. In Czech, e.g., if placed over the letter 'c' it changes the sound to 'ch'. [Mid-20thC. From Czech, literally 'small hook', formed from *hak* 'hook'.]

hachure /ha shyoōr/ *n.* **SHORT LINE SHOWING A SLOPE** any of the short parallel lines used for shading on a map to indicate the direction and steepness of a slope ■ *vt.* (**-chures, -churing, -chured**) **SHADE** to shade a map with hachure lines to show the direction and steepness of slopes [Mid-19thC. From French, formed from *hacher* 'to mark with hatches' (see HATCH[3]).]

hacienda /hássi éndə/ *n.* **1. LARGE ESTATE** a large estate, farm, or ranch in Spain or Spanish-speaking parts of America **2. HOUSE ON A LARGE ESTATE** the main residence on a hacienda [Mid-18thC. Via Spanish, 'domestic work, large estate', from Latin *facienda* 'things needing to be done', from *facere* 'to do' (see FACT).]

hack[1] /hak/ *v.* (**hacks, hacking, hacked**) **1.** *vti.* **CUT USING REPEATED BLOWS** to cut or chop sth by striking it with short repeated blows using a sharp tool such as a knife or an axe **2.** *vt.* **CLEAR A WAY** to open a path by cutting through an obstruction ○ *I had to hack my way through the bureaucracy to get the job done.* **3.** *vt.* **CHOP OFF OR INTO PARTS** to cut, shape, or divide sth roughly or carelessly (*informal*) ○ *He's hacked a whole chunk off that article I wrote for the magazine.* **4.** *vi.* COMPUT **GET INTO A COMPUTER SYSTEM** to explore and manipulate the workings of a computer or other technological device or system, either for the purpose of understanding how it works or to gain unauthorized access **5.** *vt.* **COPE WITH STH** to succeed at or endure sth (*informal*) ○ *I wonder if he can hack it.* **6.** *vi.* **MAKE A COUGHING NOISE** to cough persistently in short dry bursts with a rasping noise **7.** *vt.* **KICK FOOTBALL PLAYER'S SHINS** to commit a foul by kicking the shins of an opposing player in rugby or football **8.** *vt.* BASKETBALL **HIT A BASKETBALL PLAYER'S ARM** to commit a foul in basketball by striking another player on the arm ■ *n.* **1. QUICK CHOP** a short violent blow with a sharp tool **2. COUGHING NOISE** a short dry cough **3. CUT MADE BY HACKING STH** a rough cut made by a quick blow with a sharp tool, e.g. a notch in a tree made with an axe **4. TOOL FOR HACKING** a tool, e.g. a pickaxe, used for chopping sth or breaking up hard ground **5. WOUND FROM A KICK** a wound from being kicked **6. DISABLING KICK IN FOOTBALL** a kick on the shins in rugby or football, meant to disable a player temporarily **7.** COMPUT **SUCCESSFUL EFFORT** an extremely good, often very time-consuming, work effort that produces exactly what is needed (*informal*) [Old English *haccian* 'to cut in pieces'. Ultimately from a prehistoric West Germanic word.]

hack[2] /hak/ *n.* **1. HORSE FOR RIDING** a horse for riding or driving **2. OLD HORSE** a horse that is in bad condition through age or overwork **3. HORSE FOR HIRE** a horse that is hired out **4. HORSE RIDE** a ride on a horse, usually through the countryside **5. DRUDGE** sb who does dull and tedious work **6. HIRED WRITER** a writer paid to produce routine often down-market writing, e.g. for newspapers or films (*disapproving*) **7.** POL **LOYAL PARTY WORKER** a political party member who serves the party unquestioningly (*disapproving*) **8.** *US* **TAXI** a taxi (*informal*) ■ *v.* (**hacks, hacking, hacked**) **1.** *vti.* **TAKE HORSE RIDE** to ride a horse, or go on a horse ride, for pleasure, usually through the countryside **2.** *vi. US* **DRIVE A TAXI** to drive a taxi (*informal*) **3.** *vi.* EQU **GO RIDING** to ride a horse for exercise at a normal pace ■ *adj.* **TRITE** lacking quality and originality ○ *The film had a really hack plot.* [Early 18thC. Shortening of HACKNEY.]

hack[3] /hak/ *n.* **1. FEEDING RACK** a rack on which fodder for cattle is placed **2. FEEDING POST FOR HAWKS** in falconry, a board from which a hawk takes meat **3. PILE OF BRICKS** a pile or row of unfired bricks that have been laid out to dry [Late 16thC. Variant of HATCH[1].]

hackamore /hákə mawr/ *n. US* a bridle without a bit but with an adjustable band by which a rider can exert pressure on a horse's nose, used especially to break young horses [Mid-19thC. By folk etymology (by association with HACK[2]) from Spanish *jaquima*, from, ultimately, Arabic *šaqīmah* 'restraint, bit'.]

hackberry /hákbəri/ (*plural* **-ries**) *n.* a North American tree of the elm family that has soft yellowish wood, small flowers, and small round or egg-shaped dark-red edible fruit. Latin name: *Celtis occidentalis.* [Mid-18thC. Variant of *hagberry* 'bird cherry'; *hag* of Scandinavian origin.]

hackbut /hák but/ *n.* = **harquebus** [15thC. From French *haquebut(e)*, alteration of *haquebusche*, from Middle Dutch *hakebus*, literally 'hook-gun', from *hake(n)* 'hook' + *bus(se)* 'gun', from the hook cast on the gun as a fixture.] —**hackbuteer** /hákbə teér/ *n.* —**hackbutter** /hák buttər/ *n.*

hacker /hákər/ *n.* **1.** COMPUT **SB ACCESSING ANOTHER'S COMPUTER** sb who uses computer expertise to gain unauthorized access to a computer system belonging to another, either to learn about the system or to examine its data **2.** COMPUT **COMPUTER ENTHUSIAST** sb who is very interested or skilled in computer technology and programming **3.** *US* SPORTS **AMATEUR PLAYER** sb who enjoys a sport but is not very good at it **4. SB WHO CHOPS** sb who cuts or chops sth

hackie /háki/ *n. US* a taxi driver (*informal*)

hacking cough /hàking-/ *n.* a repeated cough that is short, dry, and rasping [Late 19thC. From HACK[1].]

hacking jacket, **hacking coat** *n.* a tweed or woollen jacket with side or back vents and a full skirt, worn for horse riding

hackle[1] /hák'l/ *n.* **1.** BIRDS **BIRD'S NECK FEATHER** any of the long slender feathers on the neck or lower back of a male bird, especially a fowl **2.** ANGLING **FEATHERS USED IN A FISHING FLY** a tuft of feathers from the neck of a bird used in making an artificial fly for fishing **3.** ANGLING **FISHING FLY MADE FROM FEATHERS** an artificial fly for fishing made from the neck feathers of a bird **4.** MIL **FEATHERED ORNAMENT** an ornament made of feathers worn in the headdress of some Highland regiments **5.** TEXTILES **FLAX COMB** a steel comb with long teeth used to comb out flax, hemp, or jute fibres ■ **hackles** *npl.* **HAIRS ON AN ANIMAL'S NECK** the hairs on the back of the neck and along the spine of an animal, especially a dog or cat, that stand on end when it is threatened or angry ■ *vt.* (**-les, -ling, -led**) **1.** ANGLING **PUT FEATHERS ON A FISHING FLY** to trim an artificial fly with the neck feathers from a bird **2.** TEXTILES **COMB FLAX BEFORE SPINNING** to comb out flax, hemp, or jute fibres using a hackle [15thC. Variant of earlier *heckle*, probably from an Old English word meaning literally 'little hook', from the prehistoric Germanic ancestor of English *hook*.] —**hackler** *n.* ◇ **make sb's hackles rise** to produce anger or hostility in sb

hackle[2] /hák'l/ (**-les, -ling, -led**) *vti.* to mangle sth by cutting it roughly [Late 16thC. From HACK[1].]

hackly /hákli/ (**-lier, -liest**) *adj.* having a rough jagged surface

hackmatack /hákmə tak/ *n. US* TREES **1.** = **tamarack 2.** = **balsam poplar** [Late 18thC. From Algonquian *akemantek* 'snowshoe wood'.]

hackney /hákni/ (**-neys, -neying, -neyed**) *n.* **1. VEHICLE FOR HIRE** a car, carriage, or similar vehicle providing a taxi service **2. HORSE FOR RIDING** a horse for riding or driving [13thC. Origin uncertain: probably named after *Hackney*, area of northeastern London where horses were formerly grazed.] —**hackneyism** *n.*

hackneyed /hák nid/ *adj.* made commonplace and stale by overuse ○ *the same old hackneyed sales talk*

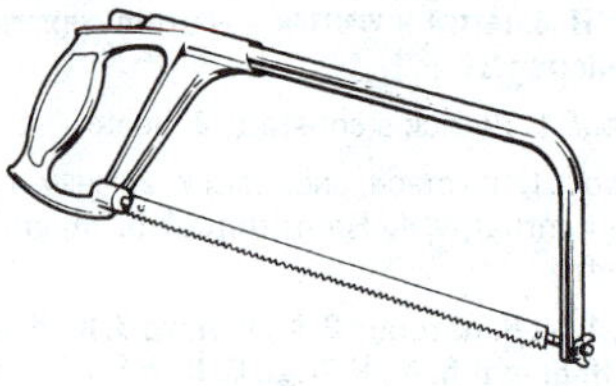

Hacksaw

hacksaw /hák saw/ *n.* **SAW FOR CUTTING METAL** a handsaw with a small-toothed steel blade stretched taut across a frame, used for cutting metal ■ *vt.* (**-saws, -sawing, -sawed, -sawn** /hák sawn/ *or* **-sawed**) **CUT STH WITH A HACKSAW** to cut sth using a hacksaw

hacktivism /háktivizzəm/ *n.* the activity of breaking into and sabotaging the computer system of a government or organization via the Internet as a form of political protest ○ *'The apparent increase in hacktivism may be due in part to the growing importance of the Internet as a means of communication'.* (*Wired website*; April 1999) [Late 20thC. Formed from HACKER + ACTIVISM.] —**hacktivist** *n.*

hackwork /hák wurk/ *n.* ordinary literary, artistic, or professional work that sb is hired to do (*disapproving*)

had past tense, past participle of **have**

hadaway /háddə wáy/ *interj. N England* used to urge sb to hurry [Origin uncertain: perhaps alteration of *hold away*]

haddock /háddək/ (*plural* **-dock** *or* **-docks**) *n.* a North Atlantic fish that is related to but smaller than the cod. It is a popular food fish. Latin name: *Melanogrammus aeglefinus.* [14thC. Via Anglo-Norman *hadoc* from Old French *(h)adot*, whose origin is unknown.]

hade /hayd/ *n.* GEOL **ANGLE OF A FAULT PLANE** the angle between the vertical plane and a plane containing a vein, fault, or lode ■ *vi.* (**hades, hading, haded**) **SLOPE FROM THE VERTICAL** to be at an angle to the vertical [Late 17thC. Origin uncertain; perhaps from a dialect form of HEAD.]

Hades /háy deez/ *n.* **1. GREEK UNDERWORLD** in Greek mythology, the underworld kingdom inhabited by the souls of the dead **2. GREEK GOD OF THE UNDERWORLD** in Greek mythology, the god of the underworld and husband of Persephone. Roman equivalent **Pluto 3. hades, Hades HELL** hell (*informal*) [Late 16thC. From Greek *Haidēs* god of the dead; ultimate origin unknown.] —**Hadean** /háydi ən/ *adj.*

Hadhramaut /haádrə máwt/, **Hadramaut** coastal region in the southern Arabian peninsula, shared between Yemen and Oman. The ancient civilization that flourished there is called 'Hazarmaveth' in the Bible. Area: 155,400 sq. km/60,000 sq. mi.

Hadith /háddith/, **hadith** *n.* the collected traditions, teachings, and stories of the prophet Muhammad, accepted as a source of Islamic doctrine and law second only to the Koran [Early 18thC. From Arabic *hadīt* 'tradition'.]

hadj *n.* = hajj

hadji *n.* = hajji

Hadlee /háddli/, **Sir Richard John** (*b.* 1948) New Zealand cricketer. He was an all-rounder who in 1990 set a world record of 431 Test wickets.

hadn't /hádd'nt/ *contr.* had not

Hadramaut = Hadhramaut

Hadrian /háydri ən/, **Emperor of Rome** (76–138). As emperor (117–38) he ended Rome's policy of territorial expansion.

Hadrian's Wall

Hadrian's Wall /háydri ənz/ *n.* a fortified wall built from the Solway Firth to the mouth of the River Tyne in the early 2nd century AD as a defence against invasion by the Picts. It was built on the orders of Roman emperor Hadrian and marked the northern boundary of the Roman Empire.

hadron /háddron/ *n.* an elementary particle that is subject to the strong nuclear interaction [Mid-20thC. Coined from Greek *hadros* 'bulky' + -ON.] —**hadronic** /ha drónnik, hə-/ *adj.*

hadrosaur /háddrə sawr/, **hadrosaurus** /-sáwrəss/ (*plural* **-uses**) *n.* an amphibious plant-eating dinosaur with a snout resembling a duck's bill and strong hind legs for walking in swamps. Hadrosaur fossils have been found in sediments from the Upper Cretaceous period. Genus: *Anatosaurus.* [Late 19thC. From modern Latin *hadrosaurus*, formed from Greek *hadros* 'bulky' + *sauros* 'lizard'.]

hadst /hadst/ *vt.* 2nd person present singular of **have** (*archaic*)

haecceity /hek se·é əti, heek-, hīk-/ *n.* PHILOS the essential property that makes an individual uniquely that individual [Mid-17thC. From medieval Latin *heicceitas*, formed from Latin *haec*, feminine singular form of *hic* 'this'.]

Haeckel /hék'l/, **Ernst** (1834–1919) German zoologist and evolutionist. He was an early advocate of Charles Darwin, and is chiefly remembered for producing genealogical trees of species development. Full name **Ernst Heinrich Philipp August Haeckel**

Haeckel's law /hék'lz, heé-/ *n.* the theory proposing as a law that an embryo in each stage of development resembles an organism that its species descended from [Late 19thC. Named after Ernst Heinrich HAECKEL.]

haem /heem/ *n.* the deep red, nonprotein portion of haemoglobin that contains iron [Early 20thC. Back-formation from HAEMOGLOBIN.]

haem- *prefix.* = haemo- (*used before vowels*)

haemagglutinate /hee·mə glóoti nayt/ (**-nates, -nating, -nated**) *vti.* to cause red blood cells to clump together, or become clumped together —**haemagglutination** /hee·mə glóoti náysh'n/ *n.*

haemagglutinin /hee·mə glóotinin/ *n.* an agent such as a virus or an antibody that causes red blood cells to clump together

haemal /heem'l/ *adj.* **1.** OF BLOOD found in or associated with the blood or blood vessels **2.** ASSOCIATED WITH HEART'S POSITION located on or associated with the side of the body where the heart and major arteries and veins are found [Mid-19thC. From Greek *haima* 'blood'.]

haemangioma /hi mánji óˉmə/ (*plural* **-mata** /-mətə/ *or* **-mas**) *n.* a benign tumour or birthmark consisting of a dense, often raised cluster of blood vessels in the skin

haemapheresis /hee·mə fe·éressiss/ *n.* MED = apheresis

haemat- *prefix.* = haemato- (*used before vowels*)

haematein /hee·mə teé in/ *n.* a chemical compound consisting of reddish-brown crystals, used to stain samples for microscope study. Formula: $C_{16}H_{12}O_6$.

haematic /hee máttik/ *adj.* relating to or acting on blood

haematin /heé·mətin/ *n.* a bluish- to brownish-black compound derived from the decomposition of haemoglobin. Formula: $C_{34}H_{33}N_4O_5Fe$.

haematinic /hee·mə tínnik/ *adj.* used to describe a drug or other agent that causes an increase in the amount of haemoglobin in the blood

haematite /heé·mə tīt/ *n.* a mineral that is an important iron ore and occurs as black, brown, or red crystals or in a massive uncrystallized form, often in very large deposits. Formula: Fe_2O_3. [15thC. Via Latin *hematites* and Greek, 'blood-like stone'.] —**haematitic** /heé·mə títtik/ *adj.*

haemato- *prefix.* blood ○ *haematoblast* [From Greek *haimat-*, the stem of *haima*]

haematoblast /hee máttō blast/ *n.* an immature blood cell, especially a red blood cell

haematocrit /heé·mə tō krit/ *n.* **1.** PERCENTAGE OF BLOOD THAT IS CELLS the percentage of a blood sample that consists of red blood cells, measured after the blood has been centrifuged and the cells compacted **2.** CENTRIFUGE THAT COMPACTS RED BLOOD CELLS a centrifuge used to compact the red blood cells in a blood sample in order to determine the percentage of the blood that consists of cells [Late 19thC. Coined from HAEMATO- + Greek *kritēs* 'judge' (see CRITIC).]

haematogenesis /heé·mə tō jénnəssiss/ *n.* = haematopoiesis —**haematogenic** /heé·mə tō jénnik/ *adj.*

haematogenous /hee·mə tójjinəss/ *adj.* **1.** MAKING BLOOD producing blood **2.** OF BLOOD originating in or derived from blood **3.** SPREAD BY BLOOD spread by means of blood

haematology /hee·mə tólləji/ *n.* the branch of medicine devoted to the study of blood, blood-producing tissues, and diseases of the blood —**haematologic** /heé·mətə lójjik/ *adj.* —**haematologically** /-lójjikli/ *adv.* —**haematologist** /hee·mə tólləjist/ *n.*

haematoma /hee·mə tōˉmə/ (*plural* **-mas** *or* **-mata** /-mətə/) *n.* a semisolid mass of blood in the tissues, caused by injury, disease, or a clotting disorder

haematophagous /hee·mə tóffəgəss/ *adj.* feeding on blood [Mid-19thC. Coined from HAEMAT- + Greek *phagein* 'to eat'.]

haematopoiesis /heé·mə tō poy e·éssiss/, **haemopoiesis** /heé·mō-/ *n.* the formation of red blood cells in the blood-forming tissues of the body [Mid-19thC. Coined from HAEMAT- + *poiēsis* 'making'.] —**haematopoietic** /-poy éttik/ *adj.*

haematoxylin /hee·mə tóksilin/ *n.* a chemical compound in the form of yellow or red crystals, derived from logwood and used as a pigment in inks, dyes, and stains. Formula: $C_{16}H_{14}O_6 \cdot 3H_2O$. [Mid-19thC. Formed from modern Latin *Haematoxylum*, genus name of logwood, from the Greek stem *haimat-* 'blood' + *xulon* 'wood'.]

haematozoon /hee·mə tō zóˉ on/ (*plural* **-a** /-zóˉ ə/) *n.* a parasitic protozoan or other microorganism that lives in blood —**haematozoal** *adj.*

haematuria /hee·mə tyoóri ə/ *n.* the presence of blood in the urine, as a result of injury to or disease of the kidneys, ureters, bladder, or urethra. ◊ **haemoglobinuria** [Early 19thC. Coined from HAEMAT- + Latin *urina* 'urine'.] —**haematuric** *adj.*

-haemia *suffix.* = -aemia

haemic /heé·mik/ *adj.* relating to blood [Mid-19thC. From Greek *haima* 'blood'.]

haemo- *prefix.* blood ○ *haemolysis* [From Greek *haima*, of unknown origin]

haemochromatosis /heé·mō krōˉmə tóssiss/ *n.* a genetic disorder in which there is excess accumulation of iron in the body leading to damage of many organs, especially the liver and pancreas [Late 19thC. Coined from HAEMO- + Greek *khroma* 'colour'.]

haemocoel /heé·mə seel/ *n.* a body cavity in spiders, crustaceans, and other arthropods through which the blood or haemolymph circulates [Mid-19thC. Coined from HAEMO- + Greek *koilos* 'hollow'.]

haemocyanin /heé·mō sīˉ ənin/ *n.* a bluish pigment found in the blood or haemolymph of certain arthropods and molluscs that functions like haemoglobin, transporting oxygen to tissues [Late 19thC. Coined from HAEMO- + Greek *kuan(e)os* 'dark blue' + -IN.]

haemocyte /heé·mō sīt/ *n.* blood cell (*technical*) [Early 20thC. Coined from HAEMO- + Greek *kutos* 'receptacle'.]

haemodialysis /heé·mō dī álləsiss/ *n.* dialysis of the blood (*technical*)

haemoflagellate /heé·mō flájjə layt/ *n.* a flagellate protozoan that lives as a parasite in blood

haemoglobin /heé·mə glóˉbin/ *n.* an iron-containing protein in red blood cells that combines reversibly with oxygen and transports it from the lungs to body tissues

haemoglobinuria /heé·mə glóˉbi nyoóri ə/ *n.* the presence in the urine of haemoglobin that has been freed from red blood cells. ◊ **haematuria** —**haemoglobinuric** *adj.*

haemolymph /heé·mōlimf/ *n.* a fluid in certain invertebrates that functions like the blood in vertebrates [Late 19thC. Coined from HAEMO- + Latin *lympha* 'clear liquid'.] —**haemolymphatic** /heé·mō lim fáttik/ *adj.*

haemolyse /heé·mə līz/ (**-lyses, -lysing, -lysed**) *vti.* to destroy red blood cells and release haemoglobin, or undergo destruction and release haemoglobin [Early 20thC. HAEMO- + *-lyse*, a variant of -LYZE.]

haemolysin /heé·mō líssin, hi móllissin/ *n.* a bacterial toxin, antibody, or other agent that destroys red blood cells, releasing free haemoglobin

haemolysis /hi móllississ/ *n.* the destruction of red blood cells and the release of the haemoglobin they contain —**haemolytic** /heé·mə líttik/ *adj.*

haemolytic anaemia *n.* anaemia that results from the destruction of red blood cells and may be caused by bacteria, genetic disorders, or toxic chemicals

haemophilia /heé·mə filli ə/ *n.* a disorder linked to a recessive gene on the X-chromosome and occurring almost exclusively in men and boys, in which the blood clots much more slowly than normally, resulting in extensive bleeding from even minor injuries [Late 19thC. Coined from HAEMO- + Greek *philia* 'friendship', formed from Greek *philos* 'dear'.]

haemophiliac /heé·mə fílliak/ *n.* sb who has haemophilia

haemophilic /heé·mə fíllik/ *adj.* **1.** OF HAEMOPHILIA relating to, resembling, or affected with haemophilia **2.** MICROBIOL PREFERRING BLOOD used to describe bacteria that are adapted to thrive in blood or a medium rich in blood

haemopoiesis *n.* = haematopoiesis

haemoptysis /hi móptississ/ *n.* the coughing up of blood or mucus containing blood (*technical*) [Mid-17thC. Coined from HAEMO- + Greek *ptysis* 'act of spitting'.]

haemorrhage /hémmərij/ *n.* MED **1.** EXCESSIVE BLEEDING the loss of blood from a ruptured blood vessel, either internally or externally **2.** UNCONTROLLED LOSS a large uncontrolled loss of sth valuable ○ *a haemorrhage of cash that threatened the firm* ■ *v.* (**-rhages, -rhaging, -rhaged**) **1.** *vi.* MED BLEED HEAVILY to bleed profusely and uncontrollably **2.** *vti.* LOSE STH VALUABLE to experience a sudden, uncontrolled, and massive loss of sth valuable ○ *The failed business had been haemorrhaging money for months.* [15thC. Via Old French or Medieval Latin *emorsagia*, from Greek *haimorrhagia*, from *haima* 'blood' + *rhēgnunai*, 'break, burst'.] —**haemorrhagic** /hémmə rájjik/ *adj.*

haemorrhagic fever *n.* a viral infection such as dengue or Ebola that results in fever, chills, and profuse internal bleeding from the capillaries

haemorrhoidectomy /hémməroy déktəmi/ (*plural* **haemorrhoidectomies** *or* **hemorrhoidectomies**) *n.* a surgical procedure to remove haemorrhoids

haemorrhoids /hémmə roydz/ *npl.* painful varicose veins in the canal of the anus —**haemorrhoidal** /hémmə róyd'l/ *adj.*

haemosiderin /heémō síddərin/ *n.* a protein that stores iron

haemostasis /heémō stáyssiss/, **hemostasis, haemostasia** /heémō stáyzi ə/, **hemostasia** *n.* **1.** STOPPING OF BLEEDING the stopping of bleeding or haemorrhaging in an organ or body part **2.** STOPPING OF BLOOD FLOW the stopping of the blood flow through an organ or body part

haemostat /heémō stat/, **hemostat** *n.* **1.** SURG SURGICAL CLAMP a surgical instrument that stops bleeding by clamping a blood vessel **2.** CHEM CHEMICAL ANTIBLEEDING AGENT a chemical agent that stops bleeding

haemostatic /heémō státtik/, **hemostatic** *adj.* STOPPING BLOOD FLOW stopping or slowing down the flow of blood ■ *n.* HAEMOSTATIC AGENT an agent that stops or slows down the flow of blood

haere mai /hírə mī/ *interj.* *NZ* used to welcome sb [Mid-18thC. From Maori, literally 'come hither'.]

hafiz /haáfiz/ *n.* the title used to address sb who has committed the Koran to memory [Mid-17thC. Via Persian from Arabic *ḥāfiẓ* 'guardian'.]

hafnium /háfni əm/ *n.* a bright silvery metallic chemical element found in zirconium ores. It is used to absorb neutrons in nuclear reactor rods and in the manufacture of tungsten filaments. Symbol **Hf** [Early 20thC. From modern Latin, formed from *Hafnia*, the Latin name for Copenhagen, Denmark, where the element was discovered.]

haft /haaft/ *n.* HANDLE the handle of a knife, axe, or other weapon or tool (*literary*) ■ *vt.* (**hafts, hafting, hafted**) PROVIDE WITH HANDLE to fit a weapon or tool with a handle (*literary*) [Old English *hæft(e)*. From a prehistoric Germanic base that also produced English *heave*.] —**hafter** *n.*

haftarah /haáftə raa/ (*plural* **-rahs** *or* **-roth** /-rōt/ *or* **-rot**), **haftorah** (*plural* **-rahs** *or* **-roth** *or* **-rot**), **haphtarah** (*plural* **-rahs** *or* **-roth** *or* **-rot**) *n.* a reading from the Prophets following each lesson from the Torah in synagogue services on the Sabbath [Early 18thC. From Hebrew *hapẖṭārāh* 'conclusion'.]

hag[1] /hag/ *n.* **1.** OFFENSIVE TERM an offensive term that deliberately insults a woman's appearance, temperament, and age **2.** WITCH a witch, especially one late in life **3.** ZOOL = **hagfish 4.** A WOMAN DEMON a demon in the shape of a woman (*archaic*) [14thC, but rare before the 16thC. Origin uncertain: perhaps shortening of Old English *hægtesse* 'witch', from a prehistoric Germanic word that also produced German *Hexe* 'witch'.] —**haggish** *adj.*

hag[2] /hag/ *n.* *N England, Scotland* **1.** SOLID PLACE IN BOG a relatively firm spot in a bog **2.** BOGGY AREA a boggy area on a moor [Mid-17thC. From Old Norse *hǫgg* 'gap', originally 'cutting, blow'.]

Hag. *abbr.* BIBLE Haggai

Hagar /háy gaar, -gər/ *n.* in the Bible, an Egyptian servant of Sarah who bore Sarah's husband, Abraham, a son named Ishmael (Genesis 16, 21:1–21) [From Hebrew *Haghar*]

hagbut /hágbut/ *n.* = **harquebus** [Variant of HACKBUT] —**hagbuteer** /hágbu teér/ *n.* —**hagbutter** /hágbutər/ *n.*

hagfish /hág fish/ (*plural* **-fish** *or* **-fishes**) *n.* a primitive jawless marine fish with an elongated body and a sucking mouth that it uses for feeding off other fishes. Family: Myxinidae.

Haggadah /hə gaádə/ (*plural* **-dahs** *or* **-doth** /-dōth/), **Haggada** (*plural* **-das** *or* **-doth**) *n.* **1.** RABBINIC LITERATURE ON BIBLICAL STORIES those sections of the Talmud and other rabbinic literature that deal with biblical narrative and stories and legends on biblical themes rather than with religious law and regulations **2.** BOOK CONTAINING THE PASSOVER SERVICE the service for the ritual meal (**Seder**) celebrated by Jews at Passover, or the book containing this service. It includes the story of the Exodus from Egypt. **3.** STORY OF ISRAELITES' EXODUS FROM EGYPT the account of the Exodus of the Israelites from Egypt that is central to the Jewish Passover ritual [Mid-19thC. From Hebrew *haggādāh* 'tale', formed from *higgīd* 'to tell'.] —**haggadic** /hə gáddik/ *adj.*

Haggai /hággī, hággay ī/ *n.* **1.** HEBREW PROPHET in the Bible, a Hebrew prophet who urged the Israelites to rebuild their temple in Jerusalem in prophecies believed to have been made in 520 BC **2.** BOOK OF THE BIBLE a book of the Bible that tells the story of the rebuilding of the Israelites' temple after their return to Jerusalem from exile in Babylon and records Haggai's prophecies. See table at **Bible** [From Hebrew]

haggard /hággərd/ *adj.* **1.** TIRED-LOOKING AND THIN IN THE FACE showing signs of tiredness, anxiety, or hunger on the face, e.g. dark rings around the eyes **2.** WILD wild and unruly in appearance **3.** UNMANAGEABLE used in falconry to describe a hawk that has reached maturity before being captured and is therefore wild and unmanageable ■ *n.* HAWK a captured wild adult hawk [Late 16thC. From French *hagard* 'untamed' (used of hawks), perhaps ultimately from a prehistoric Germanic word meaning 'hedge'; the underlying meaning would be 'like a wild hawk of the woods'.] —**haggardly** *adv.* —**haggardness** *n.*

Haggard /hággərd/, **Sir H. Rider** (1856–1925) British novelist. He wrote *King Solomon's Mines* (1885) and *She* (1887). Full name **Sir Henry Rider Haggard**

haggis /hággiss/ (*plural* **-gises**) *n.* a Scottish dish made from lamb or, less commonly, beef offal mixed with suet, oats, onions, herbs, and spices and packed into a round sausage skin and usually boiled. Haggis is traditionally cooked in a cleaned sheep's stomach, but artificial casings are now frequently used. Vegetarian versions are now also produced. [15thC. Origin uncertain.]

WORD KEY: ORIGIN

One possible source of ***haggis*** is Middle English *haggen*, meaning 'to chop', a northern variant of HACK[1]. From this view, its name would refer to its chopped-up contents. An alternative possibility is Old French *agace*, meaning 'magpie'. This is supported by a parallel semantic development of English 'pie', which originally meant 'magpie' but was apparently applied to a 'pastry case with a filling' from the notion that the collection of edible odds and ends in a pie resembles the collection of trinkets assembled by the acquisitive magpie. The miscellaneous assortment of sheep's entrails and other ingredients in a haggis therefore would represent the magpie's hoard.

haggle /hágg'l/ *v.* (**-gles, -gling** *or* **-gled, -gled**) **1.** *vi.* TRY TO SETTLE ON A PRICE to argue over sth, e.g. a price or contract, in order to reach an agreement **2.** *vti.* CUT ROUGHLY to cut sth roughly (*regional*) ■ *n.* ARGUMENT LEADING TO AGREEMENT an argument over sth in an attempt to reach an agreement [Late 16thC. Literally 'to keep chopping', from Middle English *haggen* 'to chop', a variant of HACK[1]. The modern meaning may have developed via the idea of 'chopping away' at a price.] —**haggler** *n.*

hagio- *prefix.* saints, holy ○ *hagiolatry* ○ *hagioscope* [From Greek *hagios* 'holy']

hagiocracy /hággi ókrəssi/ (*plural* **-cies**) *n.* **1.** GOVERNMENT BY HOLY PEOPLE government by saints, prophets, or other holy people **2.** PLACE GOVERNED BY HOLY PEOPLE a state or community governed by holy people

Hagiographa /hággi óggrəfə/ *n.* the last of the three main parts into which the Hebrew Bible is divided [Late 16thC. Via late Latin from Greek *hagios* 'holy' + *grapha* 'writings'.]

hagiographer /hággi óggrəfər/, **hagiographist** /-fist/ *n.* **1.** BIOGRAPHER OF SAINTS sb who writes biographies of the saints **2.** REVERENTIAL BIOGRAPHER sb who writes biographies that treat their subjects with undue reverence **3.** WRITER OF PART OF THE HEBREW BIBLE any of the writers of the Hagiographa

hagiography /hággi óggrəfi/ (*plural* **-phies**) *n.* **1.** BIOGRAPHY OF SAINT biography of a saint or the saints **2.** BIOGRAPHY REVERING ITS SUBJECT biography that treats its subject with undue reverence —**hagiographic** /hággi ə gráffik/ *adj.*

hagiolatry /hággi óllətri/ *n.* the worship or idolizing of saints

hagiology /hággi ólləji/ (*plural* **-gies**) *n.* **1.** WRITINGS ABOUT SAINTS literature about the lives of the saints **2.** BIOGRAPHY OF A SAINT a biography of a saint, or a collection of such biographies **3.** LIST OF SAINTS an authoritative list of saints **4.** COLLECTION OF SACRED WRITINGS a collection or history of sacred writings —**hagiologic** /hággi ə lójjik/ *adj.* —**hagiologist** /hággi óllə jist/ *n.*

hagioscope /hággi ə skōp/ *n.* a narrow opening in an interior wall of a church that allows members of the congregation seated at the sides to see the altar —**hagioscopic** /hággi ə skóppik/ *adj.*

hag-ridden *adj.* **1.** TORMENTED BY FEAR plagued by fear or mental anguish (*literary*) **2.** OFFENSIVE TERM MEANING HARASSED BY WOMEN an offensive term referring to a man troubled or dominated by women (*offensive*)

Hague, The /thə háyg/ city in the western Netherlands, seat of the Dutch government and capital of South Holland Province. Population: 444,661 (1993).

hah *interj.* = **ha**

ha-ha[1], **haw-haw** *interj.* **1.** REPRESENTATION OF LAUGHTER used in writing to indicate the sound of sb laughing **2.** USED TO MOCK SB used to tease or ridicule sb (*informal*) ○ *'Where is it?''Ha-ha, wouldn't you like to know?'* [Old English. An imitation of the sound.]

ha-ha[2], **haw-haw** *n.* a deep ditch or steep change in level, sometimes supported by a wall, that marks the boundary of a large garden but is not visible from within it [Early 18thC. From French; presumably from a cry of surprise when finding one.]

hahnium /haáni əm/ *n.* dubnium or hassium (*dated*) Symbol **Hn** [Late 20thC. Named after Otto *Hahn* (1879–1968), German chemist.]

Haida /hídə/ (*plural* **-da** *or* **-das**) *n.* **1.** PEOPLES MEMBER OF A NATIVE N AMERICAN PEOPLE a member of a Native North American people living along the coast of British Columbia in Canada, the adjoining Alaskan coast, and the islands lying off these areas. The Haida are particularly noted for their intricately carved dugout canoes and miniature totems. **2.** LANG HAIDA LANGUAGE the language of the Haida, now spoken by very few people [Early 20thC. From Haida, 'people'.] —**Haida** *adj.* —**Haidan** *adj.*

Haidar Ali /hídər aáli/ (1722–82) Indian soldier and ruler. Sultan of Mysore (1759–82), he waged war against the British in India and was defeated by Sir Eyre Coote (1781–82).

Haifa /hífə/ city and chief seaport of Israel, situated in the northern part of the country. Population: 252,300 (1996).

haik /hīk, hayk/, **haick** *n.* a loose-fitting garment made from a rectangle of cloth, usually white, that is wrapped around the head and body. It is worn by men and women in North Africa. [Early 18thC. From Arabic *ḥā'ik*.]

Haikou /hí kṓ/ capital of Hainan Province in China, on the northern side of the island of Hainan. Population: 280,153 (1990).

haiku /hí koo/ (*plural* **-ku**) *n.* a form of Japanese poetry with 17 syllables in three unrhymed lines of five, seven, and five syllables, often describing nature or a season [Late 19thC. From Japanese, shortening of *haikai no ku*, literally 'not serious verse'.]

hail[1] /hayl/ *n.* **1.** PELLETS OF ICE small balls of ice and hardened snow that fall like rain **2.** POURING DOWN OF STH HARMFUL a barrage of sth, e.g. missiles or insults ■ *vi.* (**hails, hailing, hailed**) RAIN ICE PELLETS to rain small balls of ice or hardened snow [Old English *hagol, hægl*. Ultimately from an Indo-European word that also produced Greek *kakhlēx* 'pebble'.]

hail[2] /hayl/ *vt.* (**hails, hailing, hailed**) **1.** GREET to welcome or greet sb upon meeting ○ *We hailed each other like long-lost buddies.* **2.** ACCLAIM to praise or approve a person, action, or accomplishment with enthusiasm ○ *The press hailed her as a child prodigy.* **3.** SHOUT OR SIGNAL FOR ATTENTION to attract the attention of sb or sth, e.g. a taxi or ship, by calling or signalling ■ *n.* **1.** GREETING an expression of greeting or acclamation **2.** SHOUT OR SIGNAL a shout or signal to attract attention ■ *interj.* EXCLAMATION OF GREETING used to greet, welcome, or acclaim sb (*archaic or literary*) [12thC. Variant of HALE[1], originally used as an interjection for wishing sb good health.] —**hailer** *n.* ◇ **within hail** near enough to hear a shout or see a signal (*dated*)

hail from *vt.* to live in or come from a particular place, especially as a birthplace or place of origin ○ *Her husband hails from Manchester.*

Haile Selassie I /híli sə lássi/, **Emperor of Ethiopia** (1892–1975). He led the Ethiopian revolution in 1916 and was a modernizing emperor (1930–36, 1942–74). Born **Ras Tafari Makonnen**

hail-fellow-well-met *adj.* EXCESSIVELY FRIENDLY very friendly, especially in a way that presumes an intimacy that does not exist ■ *n.* VERY FRIENDLY PERSON an exuberantly friendly person [From the greeting *Hail, fellow! Well met!*]

Hail Mary (*plural* **Hail Marys**) *n.* a Roman Catholic prayer to the Virgin Mary based on Gabriel's and Elizabeth's greetings to her as recorded in the Gospel of Luke in the Bible. Churchgoers are often required to repeat the prayer as a penance, given in the sacrament of reconciliation. [Translation of medieval Latin *Ave, Maria*, the opening words of the prayer]

Hailsham /háylshəm/, **Quintin Hogg, 2nd Viscount, Baron Hailsham of St Marylebone** (b. 1907) British statesman. First elected to parliament in 1938, he held many government posts, and was Lord Chancellor (1970–74, 1979–87). Full name **Quintin McGarel Hogg**

hailstone /háyl stōn/ *n.* a pellet of ice and hardened snow that falls like rain

hailstorm /háyl stawrm/ *n.* a storm that includes a downpour of hail

Hainan /hí nán/ province in southeastern China comprising the island of Hainan in the South China Sea. Capital: Haikou. Population: 7,110,000 (1994). Area: 34,300 sq. km/13,240 sq. mi.

Haiphong /hí fóng/ city and seaport in northern Vietnam, on the Red River delta. Population: 1,447,523 (1989).

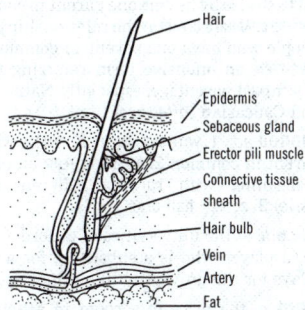

Hair: Cross-section of hair follicle

hair /hair/ *n.* **1.** STRANDS GROWING ON THE HEAD OR BODY the mass of fine flexible protein strands that grow from follicles on the skin of a person or animal, especially those on sb's head **2.** SINGLE STRAND any of the fine strands that grow on the skin of a person or animal ○ *The rug was covered with dog hairs.* **3.** BOT GROWTH ON A PLANT RESEMBLING HAIR a thin flexible growth on a plant resembling a human or animal hair **4.** TEXTILES FABRIC fabric made from animal hair **5.** TINY AMOUNT a tiny amount or degree [Old English *hær*. Ultimately from a prehistoric Germanic word that also produced German *Haar*. There is no general Indo-European word for 'hair'.] —**hairless** *adj.* ◇ **be tearing your hair out** to be very irritated or frustrated ◇ **have sb by the short hairs** to have sb in your control or power ◇ **not turn a hair** to remain completely calm ◇ **split hairs** to argue about or give undue significance to fine distinctions and details

hairball /hair bawl/ *n.* a ball of hair that accumulates in the stomach of some animals, e.g. cats and cows, when they clean themselves. It often causes indigestion and retching.

hairbreadth *n.* = **hair's-breadth** ■ *adj.* VERY NARROW exceedingly narrow

hairbrush /hair brush/ *n.* a brush for smoothing and styling hair

hair cell *n.* a sensory cell with fine projections resembling hairs, especially one in the inner ear that transmits information on sound or movement to the brain

haircloth /hair kloth/ *n.* a thick coarse fabric made from horse's or camel's hair, used in upholstery

haircut /hair kut/ *n.* **1.** CUTTING OF SB'S HAIR a session in which sb's hair is cut **2.** WAY SB'S HAIR IS CUT the shape or style in which sb's hair is cut ○ *How do you like my new haircut?*

hairdo /hair doo/ (*plural* **-dos**) *n.* the way in which sb's hair has been cut or styled (*informal*)

hairdresser /hair dresser/ *n.* **1.** SB WHOSE WORK IS STYLING HAIR sb who cuts, styles, colours, or curls hair as a profession **2.** HAIRDRESSER'S PLACE OF BUSINESS a shop or salon where a hairdresser works

hairdressing /hair dressing/ *n.* **1.** CARE OF THE HAIR the cutting, styling, colouring, or curling of hair **2.** HAIRDRESSER'S PROFESSION the occupation of a hairdresser **3.** HAIR CARE PRODUCT a preparation, e.g. an oil or gel, used to style or care for the hair

hair dryer *n.* a device that uses heated air for drying hair, either hand-held or in the shape of a dome that fits over the head

haired /haird/ *adj.* having hair of a particular length, colour, type, or style (*used in combination*) ○ *long-haired*

hair follicle *n.* a small tubular pit in the outer layer of skin (**epidermis**) enclosing the base of a growing hair

hairgrip /hair grip/ *n.* a small metal or plastic pin bent double, used to grip the hair and keep it in place. US term **bobby pin**

hairline /hair līn/ *n.* **1.** WHERE HAIR BEGINS ON HEAD the line across the top of the forehead behind which the hair grows **2.** THIN LINE a very narrow line that is barely visible **3.** PRINTING THIN STROKE a very thin line on a typeface, or a typeface containing thin lines **4.** TEXTILES FABRIC WITH FINE STRIPES a textile pattern of very thin stripes, usually one thread wide, or a fabric with such stripes

hairnet /hair net/ *n.* a circular piece of fine netting with an elastic edge, worn to hold the hair in place, especially in bed

hairpiece /hair peess/ *n.* a wig, toupee, or other piece of false hair, worn to conceal hair loss or to add bulk or length to sb's natural hair

hairpin /hair pin/ *n.* **1.** BENT WIRE FOR HOLDING HAIR a U-shaped piece of metal wire used to hold the hair in place **2.** STH WITH A SHARP BEND sth with a U-shape resembling a hairpin, especially a sharp bend in a road **3.** MUSIC SYMBOL FOR CRESCENDO OR DIMINUENDO a long V-shaped mark used in written music to indicate an increase or decrease in loudness (*informal*)

hair-raising *adj.* causing intense fear or excitement ○ *Landing on that makeshift runway was the most hair-raising experience of my life.* —**hair-raiser** *n.* —**hair-raisingly** *adv.*

hair's-breadth *n.* a very small margin or distance

hair shirt *n.* **1.** HAIRCLOTH SHIRT a shirt made from a harsh scratchy haircloth that was once worn next to the skin by religious people as a form of self-imposed punishment **2.** PERSONAL PUNISHMENT a self-imposed punishment in the form of private suffering

hair slide *n.* a decorative clip with a hinged back used to hold hair in place

hair space *n.* the thinnest space used to separate words and letters in typesetting

hairsplitting /hair splitting/ *n.* ARGUING OVER DETAILS overattention to unimportant details and fine distinctions, especially in an argument ○ *Whether it was five past or ten past is just hairsplitting: you kept me waiting for over an hour.* ■ *adj.* CONCERNED TOO MUCH WITH DETAILS giving undue significance to fine distinctions and details [From the phrase *split hairs* 'to make too fine distinctions'] —**hairsplitter** *n.*

hair spray *n.* a substance sprayed onto the hair to hold it in place

hairspring /hair spring/ *n.* a very fine coiled spring that controls the movement of the balance wheel in a watch or clock

hairstreak /hair streek/ *n.* a brown or greyish tropical American butterfly with delicate streaks on the underside of its wings and fine tails resembling hairs on its hind wings. Subfamily: Theclinae.

hair stroke *n.* a very fine line in writing or printing

hairstyle /hair stīl/ *n.* the way in which sb's hair is cut and arranged ○ *How do you like my new hairstyle?* —**hairstyling** *n.* —**hairstylist** *n.*

hairtail /hair tayl/ *n.* a predatory fish of warm seas with a long narrow body and many sharp teeth. Family: Trichiuridae. US term **cutlass fish**

hair trigger *n.* **1.** SENSITIVE TRIGGER a gun trigger that needs very little pressure to activate it **2.** QUICK RESPONSE a response or mechanism that reacts to the slightest provocation or impulse (*hyphenated before a noun*) [From the thin spring that it activates]

hair weave *n.* the process of braiding false hair to sb's own hair in order to conceal hair loss

hairweaving /hair weeving/ *n.* the interweaving of a hairpiece with sb's own hair, often done to disguise hair loss —**hairweave** *vt.* —**hairweaver** *n.*

hairworm /hair wurm/ *n.* a long slender aquatic worm whose larva lives as a parasite on arthropods. Phylum: Nematomorpha.

hairy /hairi/ (**-ier, -iest**) *adj.* **1.** COVERED WITH HAIR covered with hair or filaments resembling hair **2.** MADE OF HAIR made of hair, or similar in texture to sth made of hair **3.** FRIGHTENING filled with dangers or difficulties (*informal*) —**hairiness** *n.*

hairy vetch *n.* a type of vetch with hairy stems and purplish flowers that is native to Europe and Asia. It is widely grown for ground cover and forage. Latin name: *Vicia villosa*.

hairy woodpecker *n.* a common North American woodpecker with black and white markings that, except for its long bill and larger size, looks like the downy woodpecker

Haiti

Haiti /háyti/ republic occupying the western third of the island of Hispaniola in the northern Caribbean. Language: French, Haitian Creole. Currency: gourde. Capital: Port-au-Prince. Population: 6,732,000 (1996). Area: 27,750 sq. km/10,714 sq. mi. Official name **Republic of Haiti**

Haitian /háysh'n, haa éesh'n/ *n.* **1.** PEOPLES SB FROM HAITI sb who was born or brought up in Haiti, or who has Haitian citizenship **2.** LANG = **Haitian Creole** —**Haitian** *adj.*

Haitian Creole *n.* the French-based creole spoken on the island of Haiti. It has about four million speakers. —**Haitian Creole** *adj.*

Haitink /hí tingk/, **Bernard** (b. 1929) Dutch conductor. One of the leading conductors of the later 20th century, he led the Amsterdam Concertgebouw Orchestra (1958–63) and the London Philharmonic Orchestra (1967–79).

haj *n.* = **hajj**

haji *n.* = **hajji**

hajj /haj/ (*plural* **hajjes**), **hadj** (*plural* **hadjes**), **haj** (*plural* **hajes**) *n.* the pilgrimage to Mecca, Saudi Arabia, that is a principal religious obligation of adult Muslims [Late 17thC. From Arabic, 'pilgrimage'.]

Hajjaj /ha jáj/ *n.* the governor of the eastern provinces of India during the Arab Umayyad dynasty, the first time the Indian subcontinent was occupied by a Muslim force

hajji /hájji/ (*plural* **-jis**), **hadji** (*plural* **hadjis**), **haji** (*plural* **-is**) *n.* a Muslim who has made the pilgrimage to Mecca (*also used as a title*) [Early 17thC. Directly or via

Turkish from Persian *ḥājī* 'pilgrim', formed from Arabic *ḥajj* 'pilgrimage'.]

haka /haákə/ *n.* **1.** MAORI DANCE a traditional Maori war dance with vocal accompaniment by the dancers **2.** DANCE PERFORMED BY SPORTS TEAM a version of the traditional haka performed by a sports team, especially the New Zealand rugby team [Mid-19thC. From Maori.]

hake /hayk/ (*plural* **hake** *or* **hakes**) *n.* a marine fish similar to the cod, with two dorsal fins and an elongated body. It is a valuable food fish. Genus: *Merluccius.* [15thC. Origin uncertain: perhaps shortening of assumed *hakefish*, from dialectal *hake* 'hook', from Old Norse *haki*, from the shape of its lower jaw.]

hakea /haáki ə, háy-/ *n.* a shrub or tree of Australia that bears hard woody fruit. Genus: *Hakea.* [Mid-19thC. From modern Latin, named after C. L. von *Hake* (1745–1818), German amateur botanist.]

hakim[1] /hə keém/, **hakeem** *n.* a Muslim doctor who uses traditional remedies [From Arabic *ḥakīm* 'wise man']

hakim[2] /haákim/ *n.* a Muslim judge, ruler, or administrator [Early 17thC. From Arabic *ḥākim* 'ruler'.]

Hakluyt /hák loot/, **Richard** (1552?–1616) English geographer. His works on English naval exploration include *Divers Voyages Touching the Discovery of America and the Islands Adjacent* (1582).

Hakodate /haákō daá tay/ seaport on Tsugaru Strait in southern Hokkaido, Japan. Population: 307,249 (1990).

haku /haá k-/ *n. Hawaii* a crown made of fresh flowers

hal- *prefix.* = **halo-** (*used before vowels*)

Halacha /hə laákə/, **Halakha, Halakhah** *n.* the body of Jewish law beginning with the Pentateuch and developed by the rabbis [Mid-19thC. From Hebrew *hă lāḵāh* 'law'.]

halal /hə laál, hállal/ *adj.* SUITABLE FOR MUSLIMS used to describe meat from animals that have been slaughtered in the ritual way prescribed by Islamic law, or relating to such meat ■ *n.* HALAL MEAT halal meat ■ *vt.* (**-lals, -lalling, -lalled**) SLAUGHTER ANIMALS IN THE ISLAMIC WAY to slaughter animals for meat in the ritual way prescribed by Islamic law [Mid-19thC. From Arabic *ḥalāl* 'lawful'.]

halala /hə laálə/ (*plural* **-la** *or* **-las**) *n.* **1.** MINOR UNIT OF SAUDI ARABIAN CURRENCY a minor unit of currency in Saudi Arabia, one hundred of which are worth one rial. See table at **currency 2.** COIN WORTH ONE HALALA a coin worth one halala [Mid-20thC. From Arabic.]

halation /hə láysh'n/ *n.* **1.** FUZZY GLOW IN A PHOTOGRAPH a blurred bright patch around a light source on a photographic image. It is caused by light being reflected off the film base and back onto the light-sensitive layer. **2.** HALO ROUND A BRIGHT TELEVISION IMAGE a patch or ring of glowing light round a bright object on a television screen [Mid-19thC. Coined from HALO + -ATION.]

Halberd

halberd /hálbərd/, **halbert** /-bərt/ *n.* an axe blade and pick with a spearhead on top, mounted on a long handle and used as a weapon in the 15th and 16th centuries [15thC. Via French from, ultimately, Middle High German *helmbarde*, from *helm* 'handle' + *barde* 'hatchet'.] —**halberdier** /hálbər deér/ *n.*

halcyon /hálssi ən/ *adj.* TRANQUIL tranquil and free from disturbance or care (*literary*) ■ *n.* **1.** MYTHOL MYTHOLOGICAL BIRD THAT CALMED THE SEA in Greek mythology, a bird resembling the kingfisher, believed to have had the power to calm the waves at the time of the winter solstice when it nested at sea **2.** KINGFISHER a kingfisher (*literary*) [14thC. Via Latin from Greek *(h)alkuōn* 'mythical bird', of unknown origin.]

halcyon days *npl.* **1.** TRANQUIL HAPPY TIME a time of happiness and tranquillity (*literary*) **2.** CALM DAYS AT WINTER'S START two weeks of calm weather during the winter solstice

Haldane /háwld ayn/, **J. B. S.** (1892–1964) British geneticist. He specialized in the mathematics of natural selection and on haemophilia and colour blindness. He wrote for specialist and popular audiences and was a noted Marxist in the 1930s and 1940s. Full name **John Burdon Sanderson Haldane**

Haldane /háwl dayn/, **Richard Burdon, Viscount Haldane of Cloane** (1856–1928) British philosopher and statesman. He is principally remembered for his term as secretary of state for war (1905–12), when he laid plans for troop mobilization prior to World War I.

hale[1] /hayl/ (**haler, halest**) *adj.* in robust good health ○ *hale and hearty* [Old English *hāl* 'whole, healthy' (also the source of modern English *whole*), later reinforced by Old Norse *heill*] —**haleness** *n.*

hale[2] /hayl/ (**hales, haling, haled**) *vt.* **1.** HAUL SB OR STH to pull or drag sb or sth with great effort (*archaic*) **2.** MAKE SB GO SOMEWHERE to compel sb to go somewhere, especially to court [13thC. Via Old French *haler* from Old Norse *hala*.] —**haler** *n.*

haler /haálər/ (*plural* **halers** *or* **haleru** /-lə roo/) *n.* **1.** MINOR UNIT OF CZECH CURRENCY a minor unit of currency of the Czech Republic, one hundred of which are worth one koruna. See table at **currency 2.** COIN WORTH A HALER a coin worth a haler [Mid-20thC. Via Czech from Middle High German *haller* 'silver coin', named after *Hall*, a Swabian town where they were minted.]

Haley /háyli/, **Bill** (1927–81) US musician. He drew on his background in country and western and rhythm and blues in recording some of the first rock-and-roll hits, including 'Rock Around the Clock' (1955), with the Comets, the band he formed in 1952. Full name **William John Haley**

half /haaf/ *n.* (*plural* **halves** /haavz/), *adj., det., pron.* ONE OF TWO EQUAL PARTS either of two equal or nearly equal parts into which a whole can be divided ○ *Arrange the apricot halves, skin uppermost, in a gratin dish.* ○ *The recession began in the second half of 1990.* ○ (adj) *You don't have to pay for the first half hour.* ○ (det) *I'll pay half the bill.* ○ (pron) *I invited 20, but only half showed up.* ■ *adj.* TIME 30 MINUTES AFTER used to describe the time 30 minutes after a stated hour (*informal*) ○ *They're arriving for dinner at half six.* ■ *n.* (*plural* **halves** /haavz/) **1.** SPORTS PLAYING PERIOD either of two periods of play into which some games are divided ○ *We started off well but failed to score in the second half.* **2.** HALF FARE a fare costing more or less half the ordinary amount, e.g. for a child or senior citizen, on public transport ○ *Two and two halves please.* **3.** HALF A PINT half a pint of beer or other alcoholic drink ■ *adj., adv.* PARTIAL to some extent but not complete or completely ○ (adj) *She gave me a half-smile* ○ (adv) *She was half laughing, half crying* ■ *n.* (*plural* **halves** /haavz/) EDUC SCHOOL TERM either of two parts of an academic year ○ *We've got exams at the end of the half.* US term **semester** ■ *adj., adv.* EQUALLY in equal parts ○ (adj) *We each have half ownership in the building.* ○ (adv) *He's half French, half Spanish.* [Old English *healf.* Ultimately from a prehistoric Germanic word that also produced German *halb*. The original meaning was 'side'.] ◇ **by half** to a too great extent ○ *I don't trust him – he's too friendly by half.* ◇ **go halves (with sb)** to share sth equally with sb ○ *If we go halves on the petrol the journey shouldn't be too expensive.* ◇ **not do things by halves** to do things thoroughly and often on a large scale ◇ **not half 1.** not at all ○ *Mmm! This cake's not half bad!* **2.** much less than half ○ *She's not half as busy as you are.* ○ *This isn't half the fun I thought it would be.* **3.** used as an understatement to indicate enthusiasm (*informal*) ○ *Just look at them – his new girlfriend can't half dance!*

WORD KEY: USAGE

Singular or plural? The noun ***half*** is singular, but the word is treated as plural when it is followed by a plural noun (with or without *of*) or when it refers back to a plural: *Half the people are late. The other half of them aren't coming at all. At least half are behaving inexcusably.* With many singular nouns, ***half*** can be used in the form *half a share, half of a share*, or *a half share.*

half-and-half *adj.* WITH HALF OF EACH containing half each of two things ■ *adv.* IN HALF in two equal portions ■ *n.* (*plural* **half-and-halfs**) **1.** TWO THINGS MIXED EQUALLY a mixture of two things in equal parts **2.** MIXTURE OF ALCOHOLIC BEVERAGES an alcoholic drink made up of equal parts of stout and beer or bitter and mild

half-arsed /-aárst/ *adj.* (*slang offensive*) **1.** OFFENSIVE TERM badly organized or carried out **2.** WEAK lacking forcefulness or effectiveness

halfback /haáf bak/ *n.* **1.** PLAYER FORWARD OF THE LAST DEFENSIVE LINE a player in a team sport who is positioned just in front of the last defensive line **2.** SOCCER MIDFIELDER a midfielder in soccer (*dated*) **3.** POSITION OF A HALFBACK the position of sb playing as a halfback **4.** RUGBY PLAYER BEHIND THE SCRUM either of the two players positioned immediately behind the scrum in rugby

half-baked *adj.* (*informal*) **1.** POORLY PLANNED not well thought out and likely to fail **2.** UNINTELLIGENT lacking the ability to act with reason and common sense ○ *That's about what you'd expect from a department run by a load of half-baked idealists.*

halfbeak /haáf beek/ *n.* a small fish with a short upper jaw and long lower jaw, found in warm seas, lakes, and rivers. Family: Hemiramphidae.

half binding *n.* a type of bookbinding in which the back and sometimes the corners of a book are bound in one material and the sides in another

half-blood *n.* **1.** HALF-BROTHER OR HALF-SISTER sb who is related to sb else by having one parent in common **2.** RELATIONSHIP SHARING ONE PARENT the relationship between two people who have one parent in common **3.** *US* OFFENSIVE TERM an offensive term referring to sb of racially mixed parentage, especially Native American and Caucasian (*offensive*)

half-blooded *adj.* **1.** WITH ONE PARENT IN COMMON with only one parent in common **2.** OFFENSIVE TERM an offensive term meaning with racially different parents (*offensive*) **3.** ZOOL = **half-bred**

half-blue *adj.* at the universities of Oxford and Cambridge, a player who is a substitute for a blue or who plays for the university in a minor sport

half board *n.* the price of a room in a hotel for a night with breakfast and one main meal included (*hyphenated when used before a noun*)

half boot *n.* a boot that reaches anywhere from the top of the ankle to mid-calf

half-bound *adj.* used to describe a book that is bound on the back and sometimes the corners in one material and on the sides in another

half-bred *adj.* ZOOL used to describe a domestic animal that has only one parent of a known pedigree

half-breed *n.* **1.** OFFENSIVE TERM an offensive term referring to a person of mixed racial parentage, especially Native American and Caucasian (*offensive*) **2.** ZOOL OFFSPRING OF ONLY ONE PUREBRED PARENT a domestic animal with only one parent of known pedigree **3.** ZOOL, BOT HYBRID ANIMAL OR PLANT an animal or plant that is a hybrid product of two distinct types

half-brother *n.* a son of one of your parents by a different partner

half-caste *n.* an offensive term referring to sb of mixed racial parentage (*offensive*) —**half-caste** *adj.*

half cock *n.* a position on a single-action firearm in which the hammer is half-raised and locked so that the trigger cannot be pulled ◇ **go off at half cock 1.** to fail because of poor planning, timing, or preparation **2.** to do or say sth before thinking about it

half-cocked *adj.* **1.** WITH THE TRIGGER IN LOCKED POSITION used to describe a single-action firearm with the hammer half-raised and locked so that the trigger cannot be pulled **2.** UNPREPARED lacking adequate planning, thought, or preparation

half-crown *n.* a silver coin in Britain that was worth two shillings and sixpence. It was withdrawn in 1971 when the currency was decimalized.

half-cut *adj.* rather drunk (*informal*)

half-day *n.* either the morning or the afternoon of a normal working day, especially when taken as a holiday

half-dead *adj.* tired and worn-out (*informal*)

half-dollar *n.* a US coin worth 50 cents

half gainer *n.* a type of dive in which the diver jumps from the board facing forwards and then does a half backward somersault to enter the water headfirst, facing the board

half-hardy *adj.* used to describe a plant that can survive outdoors in mild frosts

half-hearted *adj.* with little enthusiasm and no real interest in the result —**half-heartedly** *adv.* —**half-heartedness** *n.*

half hitch *n.* a knot made by looping a piece of rope round an object then passing the end of the rope round itself and through the loop

half-holiday *n.* either the morning or afternoon of a working day taken as a holiday

half-hour *n.* **1.** 30 MINUTES a period of 30 minutes **2.** POINT IN TIME HALFWAY BETWEEN HOURS the point in time 30 minutes after the start of an hour ○ *Isn't that clock supposed to chime on the half-hour?* —**half-hourly** *adv., adj.*

half-inch *n.* HALF AN INCH a measurement of length equal to half an inch or roughly 13 mm ■ *vt.* Cockney STEAL to steal (*slang*)

half-jack *n.* S Africa a flat pocket-sized bottle of alcohol, usually brandy (*informal*)

half-length *adj.* **1.** PAINTING SHOWN ABOVE THE WAIST used to describe a portrait depicting the subject from the waist up but including the hands **2.** CLOTHES REACHING TO THE KNEE coming down to the knee rather than the ankles ■ *n.* PORTRAIT FROM WAIST UP a portrait depicting the subject from the waist up but including the hands

half-life (*plural* **half-lives**) *n.* **1.** PHYS TIME TAKEN TO LOSE HALF OF RADIOACTIVITY the time a radioactive substance takes to lose half its radioactivity through decay. Symbol $T\frac{1}{2}$ **2.** PHYSIOL TIME TAKEN TO LOSE HALF OF DRUG the time it takes for half a given amount of a substance such as a drug to be removed from living tissue through natural biological activity

half-light *n.* the soft dim light seen at dawn and dusk

half-line, **half line** *n.* MATH = **ray**[1] *n.* 4

half-marathon *n.* a race on foot covering 21.243 km/13 mi. 352 yd

half-mast *n.* FLAG POSITION AS A TRIBUTE TO SB the position, roughly halfway down a flagpole, to which a flag is lowered as a sign of respect when an important person dies ■ *vt.* (**half-masts**, **half-masting**, **half-masted**) LOWER A FLAG AS A TRIBUTE to position a flag roughly halfway down a flagpole as a mark of respect when an important person dies

half measure *n.* an inadequate or ineffectual action

half-moon *n.* **1.** MOON SEEN AS A SEMICIRCLE the moon when only half its face is illuminated during the first or last quarter **2.** STH SEMICIRCULAR anything with the shape of a semicircle or crescent **3.** AREA OF THE FINGERNAIL a pale semicircle at the base of the fingernail

half nelson *n.* a hold in which a wrestler passes an arm under the opponent's arm from behind to the back of the neck and then levers the opponent's arm backwards [From the fact that only one arm is held, not both, as in a full nelson]

half note *n.* US = **minim**

halfpenny /háypni, -pəni/ *n.* (*plural* **-ny** *or* **-nies**) a former British coin worth half an old or new penny, finally withdrawn in 1985

halfpennyworth /háypni wurth, háypərth/ *n.* **1.** HIST STH AVAILABLE FOR HALF A PENNY an amount that could be bought for half a penny **2.** TINY AMOUNT a very small amount

half-pie *adj.* NZ partly or poorly done (*informal*) [*Pie* perhaps from Maori *pai* 'good']

halfpipe *n.* SPORTS a large frozen snow structure in the shape of the bottom half of a pipe, built for freestyle snowboarding

half-price *n.* HALF USUAL PRICE half the usual price ■ *adj., adv.* FOR HALF THE PRICE at half the regular price

half rhyme *n.* an imperfect rhyme where there is a similarity in the sounds but not the identity of stressed vowels that is found in full rhymes

half seas over *adj.* somewhat drunk (*dated informal*) [From the idea of being halfway over the sea, i.e. neither completely sober nor completely drunk]

half-sister *n.* a daughter of one of your parents by a different partner

half-size *n.* a size that is halfway between two whole-numbered sizes ○ *Do you have half-sizes in this style?*

half-slip *n.* a woman's undergarment that hangs from the waist and is worn as a lining for a skirt or dress

half sole *n.* a sole on a shoe that covers the wide part at the front of the base

half-sole (**half-soles**, **half-soling**, **half-soled**) *vt.* to put a new half sole on a shoe or boot

half step *n.* US MUSIC = **semitone**

half term *n.* a short holiday for schools halfway through an academic term (*hyphenated when used before a noun*)

half tide *n.* the time during which the tide is halfway between its high and low levels

Half-timbered

half-timbered *adj.* built with a visible frame of wooden beams as well as plaster, stone, or brick. Many Tudor buildings were half-timbered. —**half-timbering** *n.*

half-time *n.* a short break between the halves of a game during which players rest

half title *n.* **1.** TITLE ON THE PAGE BEFORE THE TITLE PAGE the title of a book printed on the right-hand page before the main title page **2.** TITLE PRECEDING SECTION OF BOOK a title printed on a separate page at the beginning of a section of a book

halftone /háaf tōn/ *n.* **1.** INTERMEDIATE SHADE a shade or tone halfway between light and dark **2.** PRINTING PROCESS FOR REPRODUCING SHADING IN PRINT a photoengraving process by which shading is produced by photographing an image through a screen, then etching a plate so that the shading is reproduced as dots

half-track *n.* a military vehicle with wheels on the front axles and Caterpillar™ treads on the axles that supply motive power

half-truth *n.* a statement that includes only some of the relevant facts or information and so is intended or likely to be misleading

half volley *n.* STROKE IN BALL OR RACKET GAMES a stroke or shot that makes contact with the ball immediately after it has bounced ■ *vti.* **half-volley** (**half-volleys**, **half-volleying**, **half-volleyed**) STRIKE A BALL IMMEDIATELY AFTER BOUNCE to strike a ball immediately after it has bounced

halfway /háaf wáy/ *adv., adj.* **1.** BETWEEN at or to the middle point between two things in space or time ○ *reach the halfway point* **2.** ONLY PART WAY to only some extent, degree, or distance

halfway house *n.* **1.** COMPROMISE a combination of the qualities of two things that may not be as good as either of them ○ *The style is a sort of halfway house between late romanticism and early modernism.* **2.** REHABILITATION CENTRE a hostel or centre designed to ease people back into society after their release

from an institution, e.g. prison or a psychiatric hospital **3.** HALFWAY TO THE END OF STH the halfway point in progress towards a goal **4.** STOPPING PLACE a resting place for travellers halfway through a long journey

halfwit /háaf wit/ *n.* an offensive term for sb who behaves in a thoughtless or unintelligent way (*informal insult*) —**half-witted** /haaf wíttid/ *adj.* —**half-wittedly** *adv.* —**half-wittedness** *n.*

half-yearly *adv., adj.* done or happening every six months or in the middle of the calendar or financial year

halibut /hállibət/ (*plural* **-buts** *or* **-but**) *n.* a large edible flatfish of the northern Atlantic and Pacific oceans. Genus: *Hippoglossus.* [15thC. From an earlier form of HOLY + dialect *butt* 'flatfish' (from Middle Low German or Middle Dutch), perhaps because it was eaten on holy days.]

Halicarnassus /hálli kaar nássəss/ ancient city in the southwestern part of present-day Turkey. It was the site of the Mausoleum, the tomb of King Mausolus, which was one of the Seven Wonders of the World.

halide /háylīd, hállid/, **halid** /hállīd, -lid/ *n.* a chemical compound of a halogen with another element or group of atoms [Late 19thC. Coined from HALOGEN + -IDE.]

Halifax /hálli faks/ **1.** manufacturing town in Yorkshire, northern England, that grew up as a centre of textile making. Population: 91,069 (1991). **2.** Atlantic seaport and capital of Nova Scotia Province, Canada. Population: 332,518 (1996).

haliplankton /hálli plangktən/ *n.* plankton found in the sea

halite /háylīt, hállit/ *n.* a colourless or white mineral found on dried-up lake beds in the form of cubic crystals. It is mined for use as table salt and to make chlorine. Formula: NaCl. [Mid-19thC. Coined from Greek *hals* 'salt' + -ITE.]

halitosis /hálli tóssiss/ *n.* = **bad breath** [Late 19thC. Coined from Latin *halitus* 'breath' + -OSIS.]

hall /hawl/ *n.* **1.** ENTRANCE ROOM an entrance room in a house, flat, or building, with doors leading to other rooms **2.** CORRIDOR a connecting passage or corridor with doors leading to other rooms **3.** BUILDING WITH A LARGE PUBLIC ROOM a building with a large room used for public events or activities such as meetings, entertainment, and exhibitions **4.** LARGE ROOM a large room in a building such as a school, university, or castle, used for such purposes as dining or receptions **5.** LARGE HOUSE the main house on a large estate **6.** = **hall of residence 7.** DINING ROOM a large dining room in a university, college, or school [Old English. Ultimately from a prehistoric Germanic base meaning 'to cover, conceal', the underlying meaning being 'roofed space'.]

Hall /hawl/, **Ben** (1837–65) Australian bushranger, He led several daring raids on mail coaches and banks in New South Wales. Full name **Benjamin Hall**

Hall, John (1824–1907) English-born New Zealand statesman. He was the prime minister of New Zealand (1879–82). His government extended the right to vote to all males.

Hall, Ken (1901–44) Australian film director. He directed early Australian comedies, including *On Our Selection* (1932). Full name **Kenneth George Hall**

Hall, Sir Peter (b. 1930) British theatre director. He led the Royal Shakespeare Company (1960–68), Covent Garden Opera (1969–71) and the National Theatre (1973–88). Full name **Sir Peter Reginald Frederick Hall**

Hall, Rodney (b. 1935) Australian novelist and poet. His works include *Captivity Captive* (1988).

Hall, Roger Leighton (b. 1939) British-born New Zealand playwright. His plays include *Middle Age Spread* (1978).

hallah *n.* JUDAISM = **challah**

Halle /hállə/ city in central Germany, situated on the River Saale 50 km/31 mi. northwest of Leipzig. Population: 311,400 (1990).

Hallé /hállay/, **Sir Charles** (1819–95) German-born British conductor and pianist. He founded the Hallé Orchestra in Manchester in 1858.

Hallel /haa layl, hállel/, **hallel** *n.* Psalms 113 to 118, recited during the Jewish morning service at festivals as an expression of joy [Early 18thC. From Hebrew, 'praise'.]

hallelujah /hálli loóyə/, **halleluiah, alleluia** /álli-/ *interj.* **1. USED TO EXPRESS PRAISE TO GOD** used to express praise or thanks to God **2. USED TO EXPRESS RELIEF** used to express relief, welcome, or gratitude ○ *Hallelujah! The old car finally started on the fifth try.* ■ *n.* **1. CRY OF 'HALLELUJAH!'** a thankful cry of 'hallelujah!' **2. HYMN OF PRAISE** a song or piece of religious music expressing praise to God [Old English, via Latin from, ultimately, Hebrew *hallĕlūyāh*, literally 'praise ye the Lord']

Haller /hállər/, **Albrecht von** (1707–77) Swiss biologist. He published his neurological and physiological learning in *Elements of the Physiology of the Human Body* (1757–66).

Halley /hálli, háwli/, **Edmond** (1656–1742) British astronomer. He is chiefly remembered for calculating the period of orbit (76 years) of the comet now named after him.

halliard *n.* = **halyard**

Hall-Jones /háwl jónz/, **William** (1851–1936) English-born New Zealand statesman. A Liberal Party politician, he was briefly prime minister of New Zealand in 1906. He was the first premier to be officially called prime minister.

Hallmark

hallmark /háwl maark/ *n.* **1. MARK OF QUALITY** a mark showing that sth is of high quality **2. DISTINGUISHING MARK** a feature of sth that distinguishes it from others ○ *Discreet service is the hallmark of a fine restaurant.* **3. OFFICIAL MARK ON PRECIOUS METAL** a mark stamped on articles made of gold, silver, or platinum to show that the metal used meets the proper standards of purity ■ *vt.* **(-marks, -marking, -marked) STAMP WITH A MARK OF QUALITY** to stamp an article made of gold, silver, or platinum to show that the metal used meets the proper standards of purity [Early 18thC. Named after *Goldsmiths' Hall* in London, where the Goldsmiths' Company assayed and stamped gold and silver articles.]

hallo /hə ló/ *n.* (*plural* **-los**) = **hello** ■ *interj., n.* (*plural* **-los**), *vti.* (**-los, -loing, -loed**) = **halloo**

halloa *interj., n., vti.* = **halloo**

hall of residence *n.* a campus building where students live while attending a college or university. US term **dormitory**

halloo /hə loó/, **halloa** /hə ló/ *interj.* **1. CALL TO ATTRACT ATTENTION** used to try to attract sb's attention **2. CALL TO URGE ON HUNTING DOGS** used to spur on dogs in a hunt ■ *n.* (*plural* **-loos**; *plural* **-loas**) **CRY OF 'HALLOO!'** a cry of 'halloo!' used to attract attention or spur on dogs ■ *v.* (**-loos, -looing, -looed; -loas, -loaing, -loaed**) **1.** *vi.* **CALL OUT 'HALLOO!'** to utter a call of 'halloo!' **2.** *vt.* **SPUR ON WITH HALLOOS** to spur hunting dogs on by shouting halloos **3.** *vt.* **SHOUT STH** to shout out sth to sb [Late 17thC. Alteration of earlier *holla*, from French *holà*.]

hallow /hálló/ (**-lows, -lowing, -lowed**) *vt.* **1. MAKE HOLY** to make sb or sth holy **2. RESPECT GREATLY** to have great respect or reverence for sb or sth [Old English *hālgian*. Ultimately from an Indo-European base that is also the ancestor of English *holy, whole,* and *health*.] —**hallower** *n.*

hallowed /hállód/ *adj.* **1. SANCTIFIED** holy or kept for religious use ○ *buried in hallowed ground* **2. RESPECTED** regarded with great respect or reverence ○ *the hallowed pages of our country's history* —**hallowedness** *n.*

Hallowe'en /hállō eén/, **Halloween** *n.* the night of 31 October, the eve of All Saints' Day, originally celebrated by Celtic peoples but now popular in the United States, Canada, and the United Kingdom. Traditionally, children dress up as witches or ghosts and go from door to door asking for sweets and threatening to play tricks if refused. [Late 18thC. Shortening of *All Hallow Even*, from ALLHALLOWMAS + EVEN.]

Hallowmas /hállō mass/ *n.* = **All Saints' Day** (*archaic*) [14thC. Shortening of ALLHALLOWMAS.]

hall stand *n.* a piece of furniture, usually kept in the hall of a house, where people can hang their coats, hats, and umbrellas. US term **hall tree**

Hallstatt /hál stat/, **Hallstattian** /hal státti ən/ *adj.* relating to or typical of a European culture of the late Bronze Age and early Iron Age [Mid-19thC. Named after the town of *Hallstatt* in Austria, where a large burial site of the period was found.]

hall tree *n.* US = **hall stand**

halluces plural of **hallux**

hallucinate /hə loóssi nayt/ (**-nates, -nating, -nated**) *vti.* to imagine seeing, hearing, or otherwise sensing people, things, or events that are not present or actually occurring at the time [Early 19thC. From Latin *hallucinari* 'to dream, be distracted'.] —**hallucinator** *n.* —**hallucinative** /hə loóssinətiv/ *adj.*

hallucination /hə loóssi náysh'n/ *n.* **1. FALSE SENSE PERCEPTION** the perception of sb or sth that is not really there, often as a symptom of a psychiatric disorder or as a response to certain drugs **2. STH IMAGINED** sth that sb imagines seeing, hearing, or otherwise sensing when it is not present or actually occurring at the time (*often used in the plural*) —**hallucinational** *adj.*

hallucinatory /hə loóssinətəri/ *adj.* **1. RELATING TO FALSE SENSE PERCEPTION** relating to or involving the belief that sth is being seen, heard, or otherwise sensed when it is not present or actually occurring **2. CAUSING FALSE SENSE PERCEPTION** causing sb to believe that he or she is seeing, hearing, or otherwise sensing things that are not present or actually occurring at the time

hallucinogen /hə loóssinə jen/ *n.* a substance, especially a drug, that causes hallucinations, e.g. LSD —**hallucinogenic** /hə loóssinə jénnik/ *adj.*

hallucinosis /hə loóssi nóssiss/ *n.* a psychiatric disorder that involves hallucinations

hallux /hálləks/ (*plural* **-luces** /hállyoō seez/) *n.* the big toe on the human foot, or the first digit on the hind foot of some mammals, birds, reptiles, and amphibians (*technical*) [Mid-19thC. Via modern Latin from Latin *hallus*.]

hallux valgus *n.* an abnormal bending of the big toe in which its tip points towards the little toe and its base sticks out on the inner edge of the foot [*Valgus* from Latin 'bowlegged']

hallway /háwl way/ *n.* = **hall** *n.* 1, **hall** *n.* 2

halm *n.* = **haulm**

halma /hálmə/ *n.* a board game similar to Chinese chequers [Late 19thC. From Greek, 'leap'. Ultimately from an Indo-European word that is also the ancestor of English *salient* and *assail*.]

Halmahera /hálmə heérə/ the largest island of the Moluccas, in Indonesia, situated on the equator. Area: 17,780 sq. km/6,865 sq. mi.

halo /háylō/ *n.* (*plural* **-loes** *or* **-los**) **1. CIRCLE OF LIGHT AROUND A SAINT'S HEAD** a ring or circle of light around the head of a saint in a religious painting **2. IMAGINED AURA OF GLORY** an aura of glory imagined to surround sb or sth famous or revered **3. STH RESEMBLING A RING OF LIGHT** sth that resembles or suggests a ring of light **4. ASTRON LIGHT CIRCLE AROUND MOON OR SUN** a circle of light around the Moon or Sun, caused by light refracting from ice crystals in the atmosphere **5. ASTRON BODY OF STARS** a thinly populated spherical region of stars and other luminous objects surrounding a galaxy ■ *vt.* (**-los, -loing, -loed**) **SURROUND WITH HALO** to surround sb or sth with a halo [Mid-16thC. Via medieval Latin from, ultimately, Greek *halos* 'disc around the Sun or Moon'.]

halo- *prefix.* **1.** salt ○ *halobiont* **2.** halogen ○ *halocarbon* [Via French from, ultimately, Greek *hals*. Ultimately

from the Indo-European word for 'salt', which is also the ancestor of English *salt* and *saline*.]

halobiont /hállō bí ont/ *n.* an organism that lives in a salty environment, especially the sea —**halobiontic** /hállō bí óntik/ *adj.*

halocarbon /hállō kaárbən/ *n.* a compound, e.g. fluorocarbon, containing carbon and a halogen

halocline /hállō klín/ *n.* a vertical gradient in the saltiness of the ocean

halo effect *n.* the tendency to judge sb as being totally good because one aspect of his or her character is good [From the halos of angels]

halogen /hálləjən/ *n.* **ELECTRONEGATIVE CHEMICAL ELEMENT** any of the five electronegative elements, fluorine, chlorine, iodine, bromine, or astatine ■ *adj.* **USING HALOGEN** used to describe lamps or heat sources having a filament surrounded by halogen vapour ○ *a halogen uplighter/bulb* [Mid-19thC. So called because the elements readily form salts when combined with metals.]

halogenate /hálləjə nayt/ (**-nates, -nating, -nated**) *vt.* to treat sth or combine it with a halogen —**halogenation** /hálləjə náysh'n/ *n.*

halon /háy lon/ *n.* a stable halocarbon used to put out fires

haloperidol /hállō pérri dol/ *n.* a drug used as a tranquillizer, especially in the treatment of schizophrenia, mania, organic psychoses, delirium tremens, and behavioural disorders in children. Formula: $C_{21}H_{23}ClFNO_2$. [Mid-20thC. Coined from HALO- + PIPERIDINE + -OL.]

halophile /hállō fíl/ *n.* a plant that thrives in salty soil —**halophilic** /hállō fíllik/ *adj.*

halophyte /hállō fít/ *n.* a plant capable of growing in salty soil —**halophytic** /hállō fíttik/ *adj.* —**halophytism** /hállō fítizəm/ *n.*

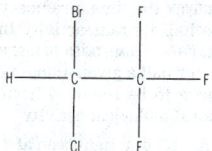
Halothane

halothane /hállō thayn/ *n.* a colourless liquid used as an inhaled anaesthetic. Formula: $C_2HBrClF_3$. [Mid-20thC. Coined from HALO- + ETHANE.]

haloumi /hə loómi/ (*plural* **-mis**) *n.* a salty white Greek cheese with a tough rubbery texture that is usually grilled until a crust has formed on both sides and eaten hot

Hals /halss/, **Frans** (1580?–1666) Flemish-born Dutch painter. He was known principally as a painter of lighthearted portraits. His work includes *The Laughing Cavalier* (1624).

halt¹ /hawlt, holt/ *n.* **1. TEMPORARY STOP** an end or temporary stop ○ *The sudden rain brought the game to a halt.* **2. SMALL RAILWAY STATION** a small, often rural, station, especially one that has no ticket office or public toilets ■ *interj.* **COMMAND USED TO MAKE SB STOP** used to command sb to stop ○ *Halt! Identify yourself!* ■ *vti.* (**halts, halting, halted**) **STOP** to stop, or make sb or sth stop [Late 16thC. From German *halten* 'to stop, hold'.]

halt² /hawlt, holt/ *vi.* (**halts, halting, halted**) **1. ACT HESITANTLY** to act or behave without certainty or confidence **2. BE DEFECTIVE** to have defects or inconsistencies in logical development or in poetic rhythm **3. OFFENSIVE TERM** an offensive term meaning to have mild, moderate, or severe difficulty in walking (*archaic offensive*) ■ *npl.* **OFFENSIVE TERM** an offensive term referring to people who have difficulty in walking (*offensive*) ■ *adj.* **OFFENSIVE TERM** an offensive term meaning walking with difficulty (*archaic offensive*) [Old English *healtian* 'to walk with a limp']

halter[1] /háwltər, hólt-/ *n.* **1.** ROPE OR LEATHER DEVICE FOR A HORSE an arrangement of ropes or leather straps put over the head of an animal, especially a horse, and used to lead it **2.** BACKLESS GARMENT a woman's garment, worn between the shoulders and waist, that fastens or passes behind the neck and leaves the arms, shoulders, and back bare ○ *wore shorts and a halter on hot summer days* **3.** ROPE FOR HANGING SB a rope with a noose, used to hang sb **4.** HANGING death by hanging ○ *destined for the halter* ■ *vt.* (*-ters, -tering, -tered*) **1.** PUT A HALTER ON to put a halter on an animal **2.** HANG SB to execute sb by hanging [From Old English *hælftre*. Ultimately from a prehistoric Germanic word meaning 'to hold on to', which is also the ancestor of English *helm* and *halberd*.]

halter[2] *n.* = **haltere**

haltere /hál teer/ (*plural* **-teres** /-teér eez/), **halter** /háltər/ (*plural* **-teres**) *n.* either of a pair of projecting parts in insects of the fly family that are rudimentary hind wings and are used to maintain balance in flight [Mid-16thC. From Greek. Formed from *hallesthai* 'to jump'. The word originally denoted weights athletes held in their hands to gain extra impetus in jumping.]

haltertop /háwltər top, hólt-/ *n.* CLOTHES = **halter**[1] *n.* 3

halting /háwlting, hólting/ *adj.* **1.** CONTAINING FREQUENT STOPS hesitant or done with frequent irregular pauses ○ *halting speech* **2.** OFFENSIVE TERM an offensive term meaning having difficulty in walking (*archaic offensive*) —**haltingly** *adv.* —**haltingness** *n.*

halutz *n.* = **chalutz**

halva /hálvə, hál vaa/, **halvah** *n.* a confection, originally from the Middle East, made from crushed sesame seeds and honey with various flavourings such as chocolate or nuts [Mid-17thC. Via Turkish from, ultimately, Arabic *halwā*.]

halve /haav/ (**halves, halving, halved**) *v.* **1.** *vt.* DIVIDE IN TWO to divide sth into two equal parts **2.** *vt.* SPLIT EQUALLY to divide sth equally between two people **3.** *vti.* REDUCE BY HALF to reduce sth by half, or be reduced by half **4.** *vt.* GOLF SCORE EVENLY AT to draw at a hole or match by playing the same number of strokes as an opponent [14thC. Formed from HALF.]

halves plural of **half**

halyard /hállyərd/, **halliard** *n.* a rope used to raise or lower sth, e.g. a sail or flag [14thC. Alteration of earlier *halier*, from *halen* 'to pull', from Old French *haler* (see HAUL).]

ham[1] /ham/ *n.* **1.** MEAT FROM A PIG'S THIGH meat cut from the thigh of the hind leg of a pig after curing by salting or smoking ○ *a slice of ham* ○ *a ham sandwich* **2.** PIG'S THIGH the thigh of the hind leg of a pig **3.** BACK OF THE LEG the back of sb's leg from the knee up to and including the buttock **4.** HOLLOW AREA BEHIND THE KNEE a hollow area behind sb's knee [Old English *hamm* 'back of the knee'. The meaning developed from 'back of the knee' to 'back of the thigh' to 'thigh'.]

ham[2] /ham/ *n.* SB WHO OVERACTS sb, especially an actor, who performs in an exaggerated showy style ■ *vti.* (**hams, hamming, hammed**) OVERACT to behave, overact, or perform a role in an exaggerated showy style [Late 19thC. Origin uncertain: possibly a shortening of *ham-fatter* 'amateurish actor', which might derive from blackface minstrels' practice of cleaning their faces with ham fat after the show.]

ham[3] /ham/ *n.* a licensed amateur radio operator [Early 20thC. Origin uncertain: perhaps a shortening of AMATEUR.]

Ham in the Bible, he was the second son of Noah and was formerly considered to be the ancestor of the Hamite people (Genesis 10:1)

Hama /haám aa/, **Hamāh** ancient city in west-central Syria, 121 km/75 mi. southwest of Aleppo. Population: 254,000 (1992).

hamadryad /hámmə drî əd, -ad/ *n.* **1.** MYTHOL WOOD NYMPH in Greek and Roman mythology, a minor deity who lives in a tree and dies when the tree dies **2.** ZOOL = king cobra [14thC. Via Latin from the Greek stem *Hamadruad-*, from *hama* 'together' + *Druas* (see DRYAD).]

hamadryas baboon /hámmə drî əss-/ *n.* a baboon native to northeastern Africa and Arabia that was

sacred to the ancient Egyptians. The adult male has a long silvery mane. Latin name: *Papio hamadryas*. [Late 19thC. Via modern Latin from Latin *Hamadryas* (see HAMADRYAD).]

hamal /hə maál/, **hammal, hamaul** *n.* sb who works as a porter or servant in a Muslim country [Mid-18thC. From Arabic *hammāl*, formed from *hamala* 'to carry'.]

Hamamatsu /hámmə mát soo/ coastal manufacturing city in southern Honshu, Japan. Population: 534,624 (1990).

hamantasch /haámən tash/ (*plural* **-taschen** /-tash'n/) *n.* a triangular pastry filled with spiced dried fruit or poppy seeds and eaten during the Jewish feast of Purim [From Yiddish, from *Haman*, the persecutor of the Jews in the Book of Esther (in the Bible) + *tasch*, from German *Tasche* 'bag, pocket']

hamartia /hə maárti ə/ *n.* LITERAT a defect in the character of the protagonist of a tragedy that brings about his or her downfall [Late 18thC. From Greek *hamartia* 'error, sin', from *hamartanein* 'to miss the mark, make a mistake'.]

hamate /háy mayt/ *adj.* HAVING A HOOK SHAPE shaped like a hook ■ *n.* HOOKED BONE IN THE WRIST a hook-shaped bone in the wrist [Early 18thC. From Latin *hamatus*, from *hamus* 'hook'.]

hamaul *n.* = **hamal**

Hamburg /hám burg/ city and major seaport in north-central Germany, situated on the rivers Elbe and Alster. Population: 1,703,800 (1994).

hamburger /hám burgər/ *n.* **1.** *US* MINCED BEEF minced beef **2.** CAKE OF MINCED MEAT a flat cake of minced meat, usually beef, that is grilled or fried and usually served in a bun **3.** MINCED-BEEF SANDWICH a sandwich containing a flat cake of grilled or fried minced beef or other meat in a bun, usually with other ingredients such as lettuce and condiments [Late 19thC. Formed from *Hamburg steak*, named after HAMBURG, Germany.]

hame /haym/ *n.* either of a pair of metal or wooden bars curved to fit over the neck of a draught animal and to which the traces are attached [14thC. From Middle Dutch.]

Hamersley Range /hámmərzli ráynj/ range of mountains in northwestern Western Australia, containing large iron ore deposits

hametz /ha méts, kha-/ *n.* JUDAISM = **chametz**

ham-fisted *adj.* = **ham-handed** (*informal*) —**ham-fistedly** *adv.* —**ham-fistedness** *n.*

ham-handed *adj.* **1.** CLUMSY clumsy with the hands (*informal*) **2.** HAVING BIG HANDS having hands that are very large —**ham-handedly** *adv.* —**ham-handedness** *n.*

Hamhung /haám hoóng/, **Hamhŭng** industrial city in South Hamgyŏng Province, North Korea. Population: 701,000 (1987).

Hamilton /hámm'ltən/ **1.** industrial town in central Scotland, near Glasgow. Population: 49,991 (1991). **2.** seaport and capital of the British dependency of Bermuda, situated on Bermuda Island. Population: 1,100 (1991). **3.** Canadian city situated at the western end of Lake Ontario. Population: 650,400 (1996). **4.** city in the western North Island, New Zealand, situated on the Waikato River

Hamilton, Lady Emma (1765–1815) British woman. She is remembered as the mistress of Horatio Nelson, with whom she had a child, Horatia (1801–81). Born Emma Lyon

Hamilton, James, 3rd Marquis and 1st Duke of Hamilton (1606–49) Scottish nobleman. He led an army into England in support of Charles I but was defeated at Preston by Oliver Cromwell (1648).

Hamilton, Sir William (1788–1856) Scottish philosopher. His *Lectures on Metaphysics and Logic* (1860) introduced Kant to English readers.

Hamilton, Sir William Rowan (1805–65) Irish mathematician. He introduced the method of quaternions into algebra and helped to discover the wave theory of light.

Hamiltonian function /hámmil tóni ən/ *n.* a mathematical function used to describe the dynamics of a system, e.g. particles in motion, that uses momentum and spatial coordinates. Symbol *H* [Mid-

19thC. Named after the Irish mathematician Sir William Rowan HAMILTON.] —**Hamiltonianism** *n.*

Hamilton Island island and tourist destination, situated 1,160 km/719 mi. north of Brisbane off the eastern coast of Queensland, Australia

Hamite /hámm īt/ *n.* a member of a group of peoples who live in various parts of North Africa [Mid-19thC. Named after HAM.]

Hamitic /ha míttik, hə-/ *n.* GROUP OF AFRICAN LANGUAGES a group of languages spoken in parts of northeastern Africa that is sometimes regarded as a branch of the Afro-Asiatic family of African languages. About six million people speak a Hamitic language. ■ *adj.* **1.** OF THE HAMITES relating to or typical of the Hamites, their culture, or their language **2.** OF OR IN HAMITIC relating to the Hamitic group of languages

Hamito-Semitic /hámmitō-/ *n., adj.* = **Afro-Asiatic** (*no longer used technically*)

hamlet /hámmlət/ *n.* **1.** SMALL VILLAGE a small village or group of houses **2.** ANTHROP GROUP OF HOMESTEADS a group of homesteads or households [14thC. Via Old French *hamelet* 'small village' from, ultimately, *ham* 'village'. Ultimately from a prehistoric West Germanic word that is also the ancestor of English *home*.]

hammal *n.* = **hamal**

Hammarskjöld /hámmər shoóld/, **Dag** (1905–61) Swedish diplomat. He was known as a skilful mediator as secretary general of the United Nations (1953–61), and won a Nobel Peace Prize posthumously in 1961.

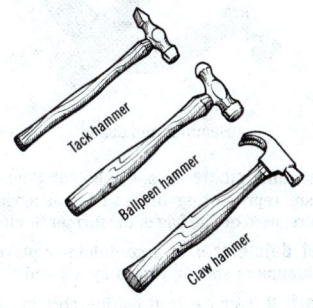

Tack hammer / Ballpeen hammer / Claw hammer

Hammer

hammer /hámmər/ *n.* **1.** POUNDING TOOL a hand tool consisting of a shaft with a metal head at right angles to it, used mainly for driving in nails and beating metal **2.** MECHANICAL STRIKING TOOL a powered mechanical striking tool used, e.g., in forging metal ○ *a steam hammer* **3.** STRIKING PART a part that strikes another in various devices, e.g. in a piano or striking clock **4.** ARMS PART OF GUN the part of the firing mechanism of a gun that delivers the impact that detonates the cartridge **5.** SPORTS OBJECT FOR THROWING IN A SPORTS EVENT a heavy metal ball attached to a handle of flexible wire, thrown in an athletics field event **6.** SPORTS = hammer throw **7.** AUCTIONEER'S GAVEL a gavel used by an auctioneer **8.** ANAT = malleus ■ *v.* (**-mers, -mering, -mered**) **1.** *vti.* POUND STH IN to force sth such as a nail into sth else by pounding it with a hammer **2.** *vt.* BEAT INTO SHAPE to beat sth with a hammer, especially to shape it ○ *hammering tin into bowls* **3.** *vt.* CAUSE STH TO BE REMEMBERED to cause sth to be remembered, realized, or understood by repeating it forcefully and frequently ○ *They had caution hammered into them by the driving instructor.* **4.** *vti.* HIT STH HARD AND REPEATEDLY to hit or strike sth hard and repeatedly ○ *hammering at the door* **5.** *vi.* PRODUCE A RHYTHMICAL MOVEMENT OR BEAT to produce fast, powerful, rhythmical movements or beats **6.** *vt.* DAMAGE STH SEVERELY to inflict serious damage on sth **7.** *vt.* GIVE SB A BEATING to beat or batter sb severely (*informal*) **8.** *vt.* DEFEAT SB BY LARGE MARGIN to inflict a convincing defeat on sb, especially an opponent in a competitive sport (*informal*) ○ *Our team got hammered in last week's game.* **9.** *vt.* CRITICIZE SB OR STH HEAVILY to subject sb or sth to severe criticism (*informal*) ○ *The critics really hammered his last play.* **10.** *vt.* FORMALLY DECLARE INSOLVENT to announce the insolvency of a member of the Stock Exchange, who is then not allowed to trade **11.** *vt.* CAUSE STOCK EXCHANGE MARKET TO DROP to cause a Stock Exchange market to drop by suddenly selling a security or securities in large quantities [Old English *hamor*. From a prehistoric Germanic word meaning 'stone, stone tool' that is also the ancestor of English *heaven*.] —**hammerer** *n*. ◇ **go** *or* **come under the hammer** to be up for auction or sale ◇ **go at it hammer and tongs 1.** to do sth with maximum energy and force **2.** to fight or argue violently

hammer away at *vt*. to work hard, determinedly, and steadily at sth ○ *hammering away at the new novel*
hammer out *vt*. **1.** SHAPE WITH A HAMMER to shape or reshape metal with a hammer **2.** AGREE ON OR ESTABLISH to agree on or establish sth after prolonged discussion or argument ○ *hammer out a revised contract* **3.** PLAY MUSIC ENERGETICALLY to play a piece of music on a piano energetically and forcefully ○ *She can really hammer out a tune.*

Hammer /hámmər/, **Armand** (1898–1990) US industrialist, art collector, and philanthropist. He established trade links with the Soviet Union in the 1920s and increased his personal fortune as the chair and CEO of Occidental Petroleum (1956–89). He made major philanthropic gifts to US art and educational institutions.

Hammer and sickle

hammer and sickle *n*. a symbol of Soviet Communism representing industrial and agricultural workers, used on the flag of the former Soviet Union

hammer dulcimer *n*. a large dulcimer played with light hammers and supported by a stand

Hammerfest /hámmər fest/ fishing port in northern Norway, the northernmost town in Europe. Population: 6,934 (1990).

hammerhead /hámmər hed/ (*plural* **-heads** *or* **-head**) *n*. **1.** TROPICAL AFRICAN WADING BIRD a large brown wading bird of tropical African wetlands, ponds, and lakes that has a prominent crest on the back of its head. Latin name: *Scopus umbretta*. **2.** = hammerhead shark **3.** AFRICAN FRUIT BAT a fruit bat native to Africa, the male of which has an enlarged square head and a muzzle shaped like the head of hammer. Latin name: *Hypsignathus monstrosus*.

hammerheaded /hámmər héddid/ *adj*. having a head shaped like a hammer

Hammerhead shark

hammerhead shark *n*. a shark with a head that has a lateral extension on each side with an eye at the end. Genus: *Sphyrna*.

hammerkop /hámmər kop/ (*plural* **-kops** *or* **-kop**) *n*. = **hammerhead** *n*. **1** [Mid-19thC. From Afrikaans *hamerkop*, literally 'hammerhead'.]

hammerlock /hámmər lok/ *n*. a wrestling hold in which an opponent's arm is twisted upwards behind

the back [Possibly because the position of the wrestler's arms resembles the head of a claw hammer]

hammer throw *n*. a field event in which competing athletes try to throw a heavy metal ball attached to a handle of flexible wire as far as they can

hammertoe /hámmər tō/ *n*. **1.** TOE CONDITION an abnormal condition of a toe in which the joint between the two small bones of the toe is permanently bent downwards in a claw shape **2.** TOE IN AN ABNORMAL CONDITION a toe affected by hammertoe

hammock /hámmək/ *n*. a hanging bed made of canvas or netting and suspended at both ends by ropes tied between two supports [Mid-16thC. Via Spanish *hamaca* from Taino.]

Hammond /hámmənd/, **Dame Joan Hood** (1912–96) New Zealand-born Australian opera singer. She was a soprano who performed regularly at Covent Garden and with major opera companies around the world. She was also a championship golfer and swimmer.

Hammurabic code /hámmoŏ ráabik-/ *n*. the first known code of law, written down in the 18th century BC by Hammurabi, king of Babylonia

hammy /hámmi/ (**-mier, -miest**) *adj*. performing sth such as a role in an exaggerated showy style (*informal*) —**hammily** *adv*. —**hamminess** *n*.

Hampden /hámdən/, **John** (1594–1643) English statesman. He was the most notable of five MPs whose attempted imprisonment by Charles I in 1642 sparked the Civil War.

hamper¹ /hámpər/ *vt*. (**-pers, -pering, -pered**) IMPEDE to prevent the free movement or action of sb or sth ■ *n*. SHIP'S EQUIPMENT equipment on board a ship that is essential but likely to get in the way [14thC. Origin unknown.] —**hamperer** *n*.

———— **WORD KEY: SYNONYMS** ————
See Synonyms at **hinder**.

hamper² /hámpər/ *n*. **1.** LARGE FOOD BASKET a large basket with a cover that is used for carrying food, especially for picnics **2.** *US* = laundry basket [14thC. Via Anglo-Norman *hanaper* 'basket for holding goblets' from Old French *hanap* 'goblet', of Germanic origin.]

Hampshire¹ /hámpshər/ (*plural* **-shires** *or* **-shire**) *n*. **1.** BLACK-AND-WHITE PIG a black-and-white pig of a breed developed in the United States from stock imported from Hampshire, England **2.** HORNLESS BLACK-FACED SHEEP a large English sheep of a breed with a black face and no horns [Mid-17thC. Named after the English county where the breed originated.]

Hampshire² /hámpshər/ county in southern England, bordering the English Channel. Population: 1,622,000 (1996). Area: 3,769 sq. km/1,455 sq. mi.

Hampshire Down *n*. = **Hampshire¹** n. **2**

Hampton /hámptən/ city and port in southeastern Virginia, situated on the Hampton Roads opposite Norfolk. It is the home of Langley Air Force Base and Hampton University. Population: 139,628 (1994).

Hampton Court /hámptən káwrt/ royal palace by the River Thames in southwestern London, mainly dating from the Tudor period

Hamster

hamster /hámstər/ *n*. **1.** ZOOL SMALL RODENT WITH CHEEK POUCHES a small Eurasian rodent with a short tail and large cheek pouches for storing food. Golden hamsters are often kept as pets. Family: Muridae. **2.** COMPUT MOUSE DEVICE WITH NO CORD a cordless mouse device for a computer that operates through an

infrared connection [Early 17thC. Via German from Old High German *hamustro*, possibly of Slavonic origin.]

hamstring /hám string/ *n*. **1.** ANAT LEG TENDON either of the two prominent common tendons of the three ham muscles behind the knee **2.** ANAT = hamstring muscle **3.** ZOOL TENDON IN AN ANIMAL'S LEG a large tendon at the back of the hock of an animal's hind leg ■ *vt*. (**-strings, -stringing, -strung** /-strung/, **-strung** /hám strung/) **1.** CUT THE HAMSTRING to cut the hamstring of a person or animal causing inability to use the leg normally (*often considered offensive*) **2.** THWART to make sb or sth powerless or ineffective ○ *hamstrung by lack of funds*

hamstring muscle *n*. any of three muscles at the back of the thigh that control certain leg movements, e.g. flexing the knee

hamstrung past tense, past participle of **hamstring**

Hamsun /hámsoōn/, **Knut** (1859–1952) Norwegian author. His best known work is *Growth of the Soil* (1917). He won a Nobel Prize in literature in 1920. Pseudonym of **Knut Pedersen**

hamulus /hámyoŏləss/ (*plural* **-li** /-lī/) *n*. a hook-shaped part at the end of a bone [Early 18thC. From Latin, 'small hook', from *hamus* 'hook'.] —**hamular** *adj*. —**hamulate** *adj*. —**hamulose** *adj*. —**hamulous** *adj*.

hamza /hámzə/, **hamzah** *n*. the sign (ʔ) used in Arabic script to represent a glottal stop [Early 19thC. From Arabic.]

Han /han/ (*plural* **Han** *or* **Hans**) *n*. **1.** ANCIENT CHINESE DYNASTY a member of a Chinese dynasty that ruled from 206 BC to AD 220 and was responsible for systematizing Chinese bureaucracy, promoting Confucianism, and consolidating Chinese government and territory **2.** = Han Chinese [Mid-18thC. From Chinese *Hàn*.] —**Han** *adj*.

Han Chinese (*plural* **Han Chinese**) *n*. a member of the largest ethnic group in China, making up approximately 93% of the Chinese population —**Han Chinese** *adj*.

Hancock /hán kok/, **Lang** (1909–92) Australian mineral prospector and industrialist. He is regarded as the founder of the Australian iron ore industry. Full name **Langley George Hancock**

Hancock, Tony (1924–68) British comedian. Known for his lugubrious demeanour, he first came to stardom with the radio show *Hancock's Half Hour* (1954–61). Full name **Anthony John Hancock**

hand /hand/ *n*. **1.** END OF THE HUMAN ARM the part of the human arm below the wrist, consisting of a thumb, four fingers, and a palm and capable of holding and manipulating things **2.** ANIMAL PART CORRESPONDING TO THE HUMAN HAND the part of an animal's limb that corresponds to a human hand in shape or function **3.** POINTER ON A CLOCK a pointer on a clock, watch, dial, or gauge **4.** PLAYER'S CARDS the cards dealt to a player in a card game ○ *a losing hand* **5.** ROUND IN A CARD GAME a round in a card game **6.** CARD PLAYER in cards, sb who plays a particular card game **7.** INFLUENCE the influence or directing action of sb or sth **8.** PART IN DOING STH a share in the performance of an action ○ *Who else had a hand in this?* **9.** HELP help to do sth ○ *Give me a hand moving this table.* **10.** OFFER OF AGREEMENT a sign of agreement or acceptance, especially of an offer of marriage ○ *Here's my hand on it.* **11.** SIDE side or direction ○ *surrounded by enemies at every hand* **12.** CLAP a round of applause ○ *a big hand for our next contestant* **13.** *US* TEXTILES = handle *n*. **4** **14.** POSSESSION OR POWER the possession, power, responsibility, or care of sb ○ *Your future is in your own hands.* **15.** DEGREE OF CLOSENESS TO A SOURCE a degree of closeness to actual involvement in sth being talked about ○ *I heard about it at third hand.* **16.** SAILOR a member of the crew of a vessel ○ *Attention, all hands!* **17.** SB DOING OR MAKING STH sb who does or makes sth, especially with a particular level of competence or experience ○ *I'm not much of a hand at hanging wallpaper.* ○ *an old hand at whitewater rafting* **18.** WORKER a worker, especially one doing manual work ○ *a farm hand* **19.** HANDWRITING sb's handwriting ○ *an admirably clear hand* **20.** SKILL ability or skill ○ *She has a good hand for gardening.* **21.** APPROACH OR METHOD a distinctive way of doing sth ○ *the bungling hand of an amateur* **22.** MEASURE OF A HORSE'S HEIGHT a measure of the height of a horse, equal to 10.2 cm/4 in **23.** PRINTING = **index 24.** BUNCH OF STH a bunch of sth, especially bananas **25.** CUT OF PORK a cut of pork from the front leg of the animal ■ *v.* (hands, handing, handed). **1.** *vt.* PASS BY HAND to pass sth to sb by hand ○ *She handed me a glass.* **2.** *vt.* LEAD BY THE HAND to help or lead sb by the hand ○ *She handed her aunt into the taxi.* **3.** *vti.* FURL to furl a sail [Old English, of prehistoric German origin] —**handless** *adj.* ○ **at hand 1.** nearby **2.** about to happen ◇ **be hand in glove (with sb)** to cooperate with sb, usually for some secret or illegal purpose ◇ **change hands** to pass to a different owner ◇ **force sb's hand** to pressure sb to do sth against his or her will or earlier than planned ◇ **hand in hand 1.** in close cooperation **2.** inseparably closely **3.** holding hands ◇ **(from) hand to mouth** with barely enough to live on for your daily needs ◇ **hold sb's hand** to provide reassurance, guidance, and support to sb ◇ **in hand 1.** under control **2.** remaining or unused ◇ **not turn a hand (to do sth)** *US* make no attempt to help sb ◇ **off sb's hands** no longer sb's responsibility or problem ◇ **on hand** near and available ◇ **on the one hand...on the other hand** used to present two conflicting aspects of a situation ○ *On the one hand we have plenty of time, but on the other hand our resources are limited.* ◇ **out of hand** immediately and without consideration or explanation ◇ **out of sb's hands** have no influence over future developments ○ *It's out of my hands.* ◇ **take sb** or **sth in hand** to begin to bring sb or sth under control ◇ **the upper hand** the advantage in a given situation ◇ **try your hand at sth** to make an attempt at sth, usually for the first time ◇ **turn your hand to sth** to do sth for the first time and be competent at it

hand down *vt.* **1.** BEQUEATH to pass sth on to a later generation or time **2.** PASS CLOTHES ON to pass clothes on from an older to a younger child **3.** *US, Can* PRONOUNCE A VERDICT OR SENTENCE to decide on a verdict or sentence and announce it in court

hand in *vt.* **1.** SUBMIT STH to give or submit sth to sb ○ *She handed in her notice.* **2.** SURRENDER STH to return or surrender sth, especially sth lost or illegal

hand off *vt.* in rugby, to push or hold an opponent away or deflect a tackle with an open hand

hand on *vt.* to pass sth to the next person or generation

hand out *vt.* **1.** DISTRIBUTE to distribute or give sth by hand **2.** AWARD to administer or award sth

hand over *v.* **1.** *vt.* SURRENDER SB OR STH to surrender sb, or give sth away to sb else ○ *Hand over the money and nobody gets hurt.* **2.** *vti.* BROADCAST TRANSFER A COMMENTARY to transfer control of a commentary during a broadcast to sb else ○ *I'll now hand you over to our match commentator.*

hand axe *n.* a chipped stone tool rounded at one end and pointed at the other, used for a variety of purposes during the Lower and Middle Palaeolithic periods

handbag /hánd bag/ *n.* **1.** WOMAN'S SMALL BAG a small bag, with or without a strap or handle, used by women to carry personal items such as keys, money, and cosmetics **2.** TRAVELLING BAG a small light travelling bag that is easily carried by hand ■ *vt.* (-bags, -bagging, -bagged) ATTACK VERBALLY to make a strong verbal attack on sb or sth (*informal; refers to a woman*)

handball /hánd bawl/ *n.* **1.** PROHIBITED HANDLING OF FOOTBALL in football, a rule infringement committed when a player other than a goalkeeper inside his or her penalty area uses a hand to control the ball **2.** BALL GAME PLAYED AGAINST A WALL a game for two or four people in which players hit a small hard ball against a wall with their hands **3.** BALL USED IN HANDBALL the small hard rubber or synthetic ball used in the game of handball **4.** GOAL-SCORING BALL GAME a team game similar to basketball in which players dribble the ball and pass it, and goals are scored by hitting the ball into the goal with the hand —**handballer** *n.*

handbarrow /hánd barrō/ *n.* a flat rectangular board for transporting loads that has a pair of handles at either end and is carried by two people

handbell /hánd bel/ *n.* a small bell held in the hand to be rung, often one of a tuned set used to play a musical piece or to practise ring-changing

handbill /hánd bil/ *n.* a small sheet of paper with a notice or advertisement printed on it, distributed by hand

handblown /hánd blōn/ *adj.* used to describe glassware blown using a hand-held tube ○ *a handblown vase*

handbook /hánd book/ *n.* **1.** REFERENCE BOOK a reference book, especially one small enough to be carried in the hand, giving concise information on a particular subject ○ *Where's my handbook of English–French expressions?* **2.** MANUAL a concise manual explaining how sth works or how to use it. US term **manual 3.** SHORT TRAVEL GUIDE a concise guide designed to help travellers and tourists find their way around a region, city, or other geographical location [Early 19thC. A translation of German *Handbuch*, which in turn was translated from medieval Latin *manualis liber* 'manual'.]

handbrake /hánd brayk/ *n.* **1.** HAND-OPERATED BRAKE a brake operated manually by a lever, used to prevent a vehicle from rolling when stationary or parked. US term **emergency brake 2.** HANDLEBAR BRAKES either of two manual brakes on the handlebars of a bicycle or motorcycle, used to slow or stop the vehicle

handbreadth /hánd bredth, -bretth/, **hand's-breadth** /hándz-/ *n.* the width of a hand, used as an approximate measure of length

h & c *abbr.* hot and cold (water)

handcart /hánd kaart/ *n.* a small cart with two or four wheels, pulled or pushed by hand

handclap /hánd klap/ *n.* a clapping of the hands, done to gain attention, applaud, or keep a rhythm. ◊ **slow handclap**

handclasp /hánd klaasp/ *n. US* = **handshake**

handcraft /hánd kraaft/ *n.* = **handicraft n. 3** ■ *vt.* (-crafts, -crafting, -crafted) MAKE BY HANDICRAFT to make sth using manual skill

handcuff /hánd kuf/ *npl.* **handcuffs** DEVICE FOR RESTRAINING THE HANDS a pair of strong usually metal rings joined by a chain or bar, placed as a restraint around sb's wrists and locked ■ *vt.* (-cuffs, -cuffing, -cuffed) **1.** PUT IN HANDCUFFS to restrain sb by using handcuffs **2.** MAKE INEFFECTIVE to make sb or sth ineffective ○ *handcuffed by bureaucratic regulations*

handedness /hándidnəss/ *n.* **1.** USE OF A FAVOURITE HAND the tendency to prefer the use of one hand over the other **2.** CHEM PROPERTY OF BEING ASYMMETRIC the property of some objects whereby they cannot be superimposed on their mirror images

George Frederick Handel

Handel /hánd'l/, **George Frederick** (1685–1759) German-born British composer. He is best known for his oratorio *Messiah* (1742) and the orchestral suites *Music for the Royal Fireworks* (1749) and *Water Music* (1717).

handfeed /hánd feed/ (-feeds, -feeding) *vt.* **1.** GIVE FOOD TO SB BY HAND to feed a person or an animal by hand **2.** FEED A MACHINE BY HAND to feed material into a machine by hand rather than by means of an automatic or machine feed

handful /hánd fool/ *n.* **1.** AMOUNT CONTAINED BY THE HAND an amount that can be held in the hand **2.** SMALL AMOUNT OR NUMBER a small amount or number of people or things ○ *Only a handful of students turned up for the lecture.* **3.** SB OR STH DIFFICULT a sb or sth that is difficult to cope with or control (*informal*) ○ *Together those two are a real handful!*

WORD KEY: CULTURAL NOTE

A Handful of Dust, a novel by writer Evelyn Waugh (1934). One of Waugh's early satires, it tells the story of Tony Last, a haughty country gent whose wife leaves him for a young socialite. His response is to set off on an ill-advised expedition to South America, where he ends up the captive of an eccentric local with a penchant for Dickens.

---

hand glass *n.* **1.** MAGNIFYING GLASS a magnifying glass with a handle for holding in the hand **2.** HAND MIRROR a small mirror for holding in the hand (*dated*) **3.** = **cold frame**

hand grenade *n.* a small bomb designed to be thrown by hand and detonated by a time fuse

handgrip /hánd grip/ *n.* **1.** = **grip n. 2 2.** HANDLE a handle or the part of sth that can be held with the hand ○ *My motorbike needs a new handgrip.* **3.** COVERING FOR A HANDLE a piece of material that covers a handle and makes it easier to keep hold of **4.** TRAVELLING BAG a small light travelling bag that is easily carried by hand

handgun /hánd gun/ *n.* a gun that can be held and fired in one hand

hand-held *adj.* **1.** HELD IN THE HAND made to be operated while held in the hand **2.** CINEMA, TV SHOT WITH A PORTABLE CAMERA filmed with a camera that is carried by the operator rather than mounted on a support ○ *black-and-white hand-held footage*

handhold /hánd hōld/ *n.* **1.** STH TO HOLD ON TO sth for sb climbing to grasp for support, e.g. a projecting piece of rock or a fissure in a cliff face **2.** GRIP a firm grip with the hand or hands

handholding /hánd hōlding/ *n.* the giving of reassurance and guidance to sb

handicap /hándi kap/ *n.* **1.** HINDRANCE sth that hinders or is a disadvantage to sb or sth **2.** SPORTS BALANCED CONTEST a contest in which individual competitors are given an advantage or disadvantage in an attempt to give every contestant an equal chance ○ *a handicap race* **3.** SPORTS ADDED ADVANTAGE OR DISADVANTAGE an advantage or disadvantage given to a competitor in a handicap **4.** GOLF GOLFER'S COMPENSATION IN STROKES a compensation in strokes given to a golfer on the basis of skill in past performances **5.** PHYSICAL OR MENTAL CHALLENGE a particular way in which sb is physically or mentally challenged (*often considered offensive*) ■ *vt.* (-caps, -capping, -capped) **1.** HINDER to hinder or be a disadvantage to sb or sth **2.** GIVE SPORTS HANDICAPS to give an advantage or disadvantage to a competitor in a contest [Mid-17thC. From *hand in cap* 'betting game in which contestants place their hands in a hat with their wagers'.]

WORD KEY: ORIGIN

In the original game of *handicap*, one contestant put up an item of personal property against sth belonging to the other contestant, offering to exchange the one for the other. An umpire adjudicated on the difference in value between the two articles. The contestants then placed their hands in a hat, along with some forfeit money, and the way in which they withdrew their hands – full or empty – signified whether they accepted the adjudication. If they both either accepted or rejected it, the umpire got the forfeit money; if they disagreed, the one who accepted it got the money. The application to horseracing arose in the 18th century from the notion of an umpire adjudicating on the weight disadvantage to be given to a particular horse.

---

handicapped /hándi kapt/ *adj.* PHYSICALLY OR MENTALLY CHALLENGED physically or mentally challenged (*often considered offensive*) ■ *npl.* OFFENSIVE TERM an offensive term for people who are physically challenged (*offensive*)

handicapper /hándi kappər/ *n.* **1.** SB WHO ASSIGNS SPORTS HANDICAPS sb who assigns handicaps to competitors in a contest **2.** SB WHO PREDICTS THE WINNER OF A HORSE RACE sb who tries to forecast the outcome of a horse race, especially one who provides published advice to people betting

handicraft /hándi kraaft/ *n.* **1.** CRAFT a craft or occupation in which manual skill is needed, e.g. weaving **2.** OBJECT MADE BY HAND sth made using manual skill **3.** MANUAL SKILL skill in making things with the

hands [13thC. An alteration of HANDCRAFT, modelled on HANDIWORK.] —**handicrafter** *n.*

handily /hándili/ *adv.* **1.** CONVENIENTLY in a convenient way ○ *handily close to the station* **2.** SKILFULLY in a skilful way **3.** US EASILY in an easy way ○ *She took the second set handily.*

handiwork /hándi wurk/ *n.* **1.** SB'S ACTION action taken by sb, or the result of sb's action ○ *The broken window was the handiwork of local vandals.* **2.** WORK DONE BY HAND work done or produced by hand **3.** SKILL WITH WHICH STH IS DONE the skill with which sth is done, especially manual skill [From Old English *handgeweorc*, from *hand* 'hand' + *geweorc*, literally 'body of work', from *weorc* (see WORK)]

hand-jam *n.* CLIMBING an act of wedging the hand into a rock crack to aid in climbing

handkerchief /hángkər chif, -cheef/ (*plural* **-chiefs** *or* **-chieves** /-cheevz/) *n.* **1.** CLOTH FOR WIPING THE NOSE a square of cloth or absorbent paper used mainly to wipe areas of the face, especially the nose **2.** *US* = kerchief

hand-knit *vti.* to knit sth by hand, not on a machine

handle /hánd'l/ *n.* **1.** PART FOR HOLDING OR OPERATING STH a part of a thing by which it is held, moved, or operated **2.** NAME sb's name (*slang*) ○ *What's your handle?* **3.** MEANS an opportunity, pretext, or means of doing sth **4.** TEXTILES FEEL OF TEXTILE the feel of a textile, used to determine its quality. US term **hand** *n.* 13 **5.** *US* GAMBLING TOTAL AMOUNT BET the total sum of money bet on a race, series of races, or other event ■ *v.* (**-dles**, **-dling**, **-dled**) **1.** *vt.* TOUCH to touch, pick up, or move sth with the hands ○ *Don't handle the merchandise.* **2.** *vt.* OPERATE to operate or make use of sth with the hands **3.** *vt.* TAKE CHARGE OF to take care of or be responsible for sth ○ *Who handles the import side of the business?* **4.** *vt.* DEAL WITH to deal with or cope with sb or sth ○ *She's good at handling difficult customers.* **5.** *vt.* BE MANAGER OF to manage or supervise sb ○ *He handles a string of professional boxers.* **6.** *vt.* BE ABOUT STH to discuss or deal with a subject ○ *The novel handles the theme of unrequited love in an original way.* **7.** *vt.* TRADE IN to deal in particular goods **8.** *vi.* RESPOND TO CONTROL to respond to control or use, often in a particular way ○ *The little yacht handled like a dream.* [Old English. The noun is *handle* and the verb *handlian*, both of which were formed from *hand* 'hand'.] —**handleability** /hánd'lə bílləti/ *n.* —**handleable** /hánd'ləb'l/ *adj.* —**handleless** /hánd'l ləss/ *adj.* ◇ **fly off the handle** to lose your temper, especially without justification (*informal*) ◇ **get a handle on sth** to understand a situation fully or be able to control it fully ○ *It's a difficult problem to get a handle on.*

Handlebar moustache: William II, Emperor of Germany and King of Prussia (photographed in 1898)

handlebar moustache /hánd'l baar-/ *n.* a thick broad moustache that curls up at the ends like handlebars

handlebars /hánd'l baarz/ *npl.* a bar with handles at each end, used to steer a vehicle such as a bicycle or motorcycle

handler /hándlər/ *n.* **1.** ANIMAL TRAINER sb who trains or manages animals that perform in films, television programmes, or judged shows **2.** SB USING A TRAINED DOG sb who uses a specially trained dog, e.g. in the police or armed forces **3.** BOXER'S TRAINER a boxer's trainer or second **4.** MANAGER sb who manages the career of sb or the running of sth **5.** SB WORKING WITH STH sb who works or deals with a particular thing ○ *a baggage handler for an airline*

handling /hándling/ *n.* **1.** WAY SB HANDLES STH the way in which sb handles or deals with sth ○ *The report criticized his handling of the affair.* **2.** TREATMENT the way in which a subject is treated or dealt with in a written work or other work of art **3.** COMM TRANSPORT AND PACKAGING the transport and packaging of goods ○ *The cost includes a charge for handling.* **4.** RECEIVING STOLEN GOODS the receiving of goods known to be stolen. US term **fencing**

handmade /hánd máyd/ *adj.* made by hand, not by machine ○ *handmade furniture*

handmaid /hánd mayd/, **handmaiden** /-mayd'n/ *n.* **1.** WOMAN SERVANT a woman or girl servant (*archaic*) **2.** STH HELPFUL sth that provides help or support in a subsidiary role (*literary*) ○ *Hard work and focus are the handmaids of genius.* [The underlying meaning is 'sb who is at hand when needed']

hand-me-down *n.* **1.** USED GARMENT an item of clothing, usually outgrown, passed down from a family member or friend to another **2.** STH PREVIOUSLY DISCARDED sth taken up or used by a person or group that has been used before and discarded

hand-off *n.* in rugby, a pushing or holding away of an opponent or a deflection of a tackle with an open hand

hand organ *n.* = barrel organ

handout /hánd owt/ *n.* **1.** CHARITABLE GIFT sth such as money or food given as charity to sb in need **2.** DOCUMENT DISTRIBUTED TO A GROUP a document, such as a press release, an advertisement, or material accompanying a meeting or lecture that is distributed to a group

handover /hándōvər/ *n.* **1.** SURRENDERING a surrendering of sb, or a giving away of sth to sb else ○ *the handover of power to the civilian authorities* **2.** BROADCAST TRANSFER OF COMMENTARY a transfer of the control of the commentary during a broadcast to sb else

handpick /hánd pík/ (**-picks**, **-picking**, **-picked**) *vt.* **1.** CHOOSE SB OR STH CAREFULLY to choose sb or sth carefully and personally, e.g. members of a team **2.** PICK OR HARVEST BY HAND to pick or harvest sth by hand, not by machine

hand plant *n.* in skateboarding, a move in which the board is held to the feet with one hand while performing a handstand on a ramp or obstacle with the other [Late 20thC]

hand press *n.* a printing press operated by hand

handprint /hánd print/ *n.* a mark or impression made by the palm of the hand and fingers

hand puppet *n.* *US* = glove puppet

handrail /hánd rayl/ *n.* a rail to hold with the hand for support, e.g. at the side of stairs or a ramp

handsaw /hánd saw/ *n.* a saw for use with one hand

hand's-breadth *n.* = handbreadth

hands down *adv.* **1.** EASILY without encountering any problems, obstacles, or opposition **2.** UNQUESTIONABLY without any doubt whatsoever ○ *they won hands down*

hands-down *adj.* accepted without any question [From horse-racing, when a jockey wins by such a wide margin that he can relax his grip on the reins]

handsel /hánss'l/, **hansel** *n.* (*archaic*) **1.** GOOD-LUCK GIFT a gift given for good luck at the beginning of sth, especially a new year **2.** FIRST PAYMENT a first payment for sth, or the first money taken in by a new business ■ *vt.* (**-sels**, **-selling**, **-selled**) (*archaic*) **1.** GIVE GOOD-LUCK GIFT TO to give sb a good-luck gift at the beginning of sth, especially a new year **2.** INAUGURATE to begin or launch sth with ceremony **3.** USE FOR FIRST TIME to use sth or do sth for the first time [14thC. A blend of Old English *handselen* 'a handing over' and Old Norse *handsal*, literally 'giving the hand'.]

handset /hánd set/ *n.* the part of a telephone that is held in the hand and contains the parts used for speaking into and listening to

handshake /hánd shayk/ *n.* **1.** GRIP WITH THE HAND a gesture of gripping and shaking another person's hand, used as a greeting or farewell and to seal an agreement **2.** COMPUT EXCHANGE OF SIGNALS an exchange of signals between a computer and another computer or external device indicating that a link is and communication is possible

handshaking /hánd shayking/ *n.* the exchanging of signals between a computer and another computer or external device indicating that a link is established and communication is possible

hands-off *adj.* not wanting or needing to interfere in or control sth ○ *The boss operates a hands-off policy with respect to the day-to-day running of the business.*

handsome /hánssəm/ *adj.* **1.** GOOD-LOOKING with good-looking facial features or a pleasing general appearance **2.** GENEROUS amounting to a higher sum than expected [Mid-16thC. The underlying meaning is 'handy, skilled'.] —**handsomeness** *n.*

——— **WORD KEY: SYNONYMS** ———
See Synonyms at ***goodlooking***.

handsomely /hánssəmli/ *adv.* in an amount that is more than expected

hands-on *adj.* **1.** USING STH involving the actual use of sth ○ *Learning computer skills is a hands-on process.* **2.** INVOLVING PHYSICAL TOUCHING involving physical touching of sth ○ *The children's science museum has many hands-on exhibits.* **3.** PERSONALLY INVOLVED giving personal attention to or taking personal control of sb or sth ○ *She's very much a hands-on manager.*

handspike /hánd spīk/ *n.* a metal bar used as a lever [Early 16thC. Alteration of Dutch *handspaak*, from *hand* 'hand' + *spaak* 'spoke'.]

handspring /hánd spring/ *n.* a gymnastic movement in which sb flips the body forwards or backwards and lands briefly on the hands before continuing the flip so as to land on the feet again

handstand /hánd stand/ *n.* an act of balancing the body on the hands with the legs straight up in the air

hand-to-hand *adj.* taking place at close quarters and involving bodily contact —**hand-to-hand** *adv.*

hand-to-mouth *adj.* POOR having barely enough money or food for daily needs ■ *adv.* IN POVERTY with only just enough money or food for daily needs [From the idea that everything sb earns goes to meet the immediate need for food]

handwork /hánd wurk/ *n.* work done by hand, not by a machine —**handworker** *n.*

handwoven /hánd wóv'n/ *adj.* **1.** WOVEN BY HAND LOOM woven on a hand-operated loom, not a mechanical one **2.** WOVEN BY HAND woven using the hands

handwringing /hánd ringing/ *n.* **1.** DEMONSTRATION OF CONCERN the demonstration or expression of concern about sth, often without any constructive action being taken **2.** NERVOUS CLASPING OF THE HANDS the repeated clasping and squeezing of the hands together as a result of anxiety or grief

handwrite /hánd rīt/ (**-writes**, **-writing**, **-wrote** /-rōt/, **-written** /-ritt'n/) *vt.* to use a writing implement such as a pen or pencil to put words on paper

handwriting /hánd rīting/ *n.* **1.** WRITING DONE BY HAND writing done by hand using a pen or pencil **2.** MANNER OF WRITING sb's individual way of writing by hand ○ *I recognized my father's handwriting on the envelope.* [Early 16thC. Translation of Latin *manuscriptum*.]

handwrought /hánd ráwt/ *adj.* shaped by hand, especially by hammering

handy /hándi/ (**-ier**, **-iest**) *adj.* **1.** CONVENIENT located in a convenient place, especially nearby and easy to reach **2.** USEFUL useful or easy to use **3.** SKILFUL skilful at doing a number of different things —**handiness** *n.*

handyman /hándi man/ (*plural* **-men** /-men/) *n.* **1.** SB WHO DOES SMALL JOBS sb who earns money by doing a variety of small jobs **2.** SB SKILFUL sb who has the experience and skill to perform a variety of small jobs

hang /hang/ *v.* (**hangs**, **hanging**, **hung** /hung/) **1.** *vti.* SUSPEND to suspend or fasten sth so that it is held up from above and not supported from below **2.** *vt.* FIX ON HINGES to fix sth such as a door on hinges so that it can move freely **3.** (*past and past participle* **hanged**) *vti.* KILL SB WITH ROPE to kill sb or yourself by fastening a rope round the neck and removing any other support for the body, or die in this way, especially as a form of legal execution **4.** *vt.* **DECORATE WITH STH** to decorate or furnish a place or object with sth ○ *hang the Christmas tree with lights and decorations* **5.** *vt.* **PUT UP WALLPAPER** to fix wallpaper onto walls **6.** *vti.* **DISPLAY A PAINTING** to put pictures or paintings on display, or be put on display **7.** *vt.* **LET DROOP** to let sth, especially the head, droop ○ *They should hang their heads in shame.* **8.** *vt.* **SUSPEND A GUTTED ANIMAL** to suspend meat or a recently killed game animal until the flesh begins to decompose slightly and becomes more tender and highly flavoured **9.** *vi.* **LAW PREVENT A JURY FROM DECIDING** to prevent a jury from reaching a verdict (*usually used in the passive*) **10.** *vti.* **BASEBALL PITCH A BALL THAT FAILS TO BREAK** in baseball, to pitch the ball in such a way that it fails to break, or be pitched in this way **11.** (*past and past participle* **hanged**) *vt.* **EXCLAMATION INDICATING ANNOYANCE** used as a euphemism for damn (*dated informal*) ○ *Hang it all!* ○ *I'll be hanged if I'll let them get away with this!* **12.** *vt.* **US MAKE A TURN** to make a particular turn, especially when driving a car (*informal*) ○ *Hang a right at the next street.* **13.** *vi.* **BE UNRESOLVED** to be unresolved or in doubt ○ *His academic future hangs in the balance.* **14.** *vti.* **FOLD OR DROOP** to fold or bend sth over or across sth, or be folded or bent over or across sth **15.** *vi.* **DRAPE** to drape from a point of suspension in a particular way ○ *The jacket hung badly on her.* **16.** *vi.* **ELAPSE SLOWLY** to pass by or elapse slowly ○ *Time hung heavily when she was away.* **17.** *vi.* **COMPUT ALLOW NO INPUT OR OUTPUT** to refuse additional input and be unable to generate output until re-booted (*refers to a computer*) ■ *n.* **1.** **WAY OF HANGING STH** the way that sth hangs **2.** **SLOPE** a downward slope **3.** **EXHIBITION OF ARTWORK** an exhibition of artwork, especially paintings [Old English *hangian* (intransitive), from a prehistoric West Germanic base] ◇ **get the hang of sth** to learn a skill or activity thoroughly ◇ **not give or care a hang (for** *or* **about sb** *or* **sth)** to be completely unconcerned or indifferent about sb or sth (*dated informal*)

hang about *vi.* = hang around (*informal*) ■ *interj.* **WAIT** used to ask or command sb to wait (*informal*)

hang around *vi.* **1.** **WASTE TIME** to loiter or waste time **2.** **ASSOCIATE REGULARLY** to spend time regularly with sb ○ *He hangs around with the drama crowd.*

hang back *vi.* to show reluctance to do sth

hang in *vt.* US to endure or persevere in doing sth (*informal*) ○ *She hung in as long as she could.*

hang on *v.* **1.** *vi.* **HOLD ON TIGHTLY** to hold on tightly to sth **2.** *vi.* **KEEP GOING** to persist in an endeavour in spite of obstacles or difficulties **3.** *vt.* **DEPEND ON STH** to depend on sth **4.** *vi.* **WAIT** to wait or show patience for a short time **5.** *vt.* **LISTEN CLOSELY TO** to listen attentively to what sb says

hang onto *vt.* = hang on v. 1, **hang on** v. 4

hang out *v.* **1.** *vt.* **SUSPEND OUTSIDE** to put sth outside, e.g. on a line, pole, or balcony, so that it will dry or so that it can be seen **2.** *vi.* **BE AROUND SOMEWHERE** to be regularly present somewhere (*informal*) **3.** *vi.* US **SPEND TIME SOMEWHERE** to spend time somewhere in a casual or relaxed way (*informal*) **4.** *vi.* **ASSOCIATE** to spend time regularly with sb (*informal*)

hang over *v.* **1.** *vt.* **BE IMMINENT FOR** to be imminent or threatening for, or be unwelcomely associated with, sb or sth **2.** *vi.* **BE POSTPONED** to be put off to a later date ○ *Our holiday plans will hang over until next year.*

hang together *vi.* to be consistent or cohesive

hang up *v.* **1.** *vt.* **SUSPEND** to put sth on a peg, hook, nail, or hanger **2.** *vti.* **REPLACE A PHONE IN ITS CRADLE** to end a telephone call by returning the receiver to its original position, often abruptly

hang upon *vt.* = hang on, hang on v. 5

hangar /hángər/ *n.* a large building in which aircraft are kept or repaired [Late 17thC. Via French, 'shed', from Old French *hangard*, possibly from medieval Latin *angarium* 'shed for shoeing horses', or of prehistoric Germanic origin.]

hangdog /háng dog/ *adj.* having an expression that indicates guilt or sadness [Late 17thC. Originally referring to sb who deserved to be hanged like a dog.]

hanger /hángər/ *n.* **1.** **PEG OR HOOK FOR HANGING STH** a support from which sth can be hung, e.g. a peg or hook **2.** **FRAME FOR HANGING A GARMENT** a triangular frame of metal, wood, or plastic over which clothes can be draped

for storage or display **3.** **SB WHO HANGS STH** sb who hangs or suspends sth **4.** **SMALL WOOD** a small wood on the side of a hill **5.** **SHORT SWORD** a short sword worn on a belt

hanger-on (*plural* **hangers-on**) *n.* sb who latches on to a richer or more prominent person or group in the hope of personal gain

Hang-glider

hang-glider *n.* an aircraft without an engine that consists of a rigid frame in the shape of a wing, with the pilot usually suspended in a harness below the wing. Hang-gliders can be launched by foot, with the pilot running down a slope, or by being towed by a truck, winch, or ultralight aircraft. — **hang-gliding** *n.*

hangi /húngi, hángi/ (*plural* **-i**) *n.* NZ **1.** **PIT FOR OUTDOOR COOKING** a pit for cooking food outdoors using hot stones and damp cloths **2.** **FEAST** a feast consisting of food cooked in a hangi [Mid-19thC. From Maori.]

hanging /hánging/ *n.* **1.** **METHOD OF KILLING** the act of killing sb by putting the neck in a noose and re-moving the support, especially as a form of legal execution **2.** **FABRIC HUNG ON A WALL** a drapery, tapestry, or decorative fabric hung on a wall (*often used in the plural*) ■ *adj.* **1.** **PUNISHABLE BY DEATH** punishable by death, or seen as deserving the death penalty ○ *a hanging offence* **2.** **SEVERE OR UNMERCIFUL** tending to impose severe punishments, especially the death penalty ○ *a hanging judge* **3.** **AT THE TOP OF A SLOPE** positioned at the top of a steep slope or height

hanging indent, **hanging indentation** *n.* an indenting of all the lines of a paragraph of text except the first

hanging wall *n.* the rocks that hang over a seam of coal or other mineral vein

hangman /hángmən/ (*plural* **-men** /-mən/) *n.* **1.** **EXECUTIONER** an official who carries out the death penalty of hanging **2.** **GAMES LETTER GAME** a game in which one player has to guess a word, letter by letter, while the other player draws a sketch of a hanged person. To win, the player has to guess the word before the drawing is complete.

hangnail /háng nayl/ *n.* a small piece of skin partly detached from the side or base of a fingernail [Late 17thC. By folk etymology from *agnail* 'corn on the foot', from Old English *angnægl*, from *ang-*, from a prehistoric Germanic word meaning 'tight', + NAIL.]

hangover /háng ōvər/ *n.* **1.** **ILLNESS AFTER DRINKING** the symptoms of headache, nausea, thirst, and sickness that result from drinking too much alcohol **2.** **ASPECT ROOTED IN THE PAST** sth that remains from an earlier time

Hang Seng index /háng séng-/ *n.* an index based on the relative prices of selected shares on the Hong Kong Stock Exchange

Hangul /háng gŏŏl/, **hangul** *n.* the alphabet used for Korean writing [Mid-20thC. From Korean *han kul*, literally 'Korea alphabet'.]

hang-up *n.* **1.** **CONTINUING ANXIETY ABOUT STH** a psychological or emotional problem or fixation about sth (*informal*) **2.** **CAUSE OF PROBLEMS** a persistent impediment or source of delay ○ *Bureaucratic inefficiency was the main hang-up.*

Hangzhou /háng jṓ/ *seaport and capital city of Zhejiang Province in southeastern China. Population: 1,340,000 (1991).

Han Jiang /hán jyáng/, **Han** river of central China, a

tributary of the River Yangtze and major trade artery. Length: 1,532 km/952 mi.

hank /hangk/ *n.* **1.** **LOOSE BALL OF STH** a piece of sth such as hair, rope, or wool that has been wrapped round itself to form a loose ball **2.** **SAILING ATTACHMENT FOR A SAIL** a ring-shaped fitting that can be opened to secure the leading edge of a sail **3.** **MEASURE LENGTH OF STH** a length of yarn when reeled. A hank of cotton is 767 m/840 yd. [14thC. From Old Norse *hönk*, from a prehistoric Germanic word that is also the ancestor of English *hook*.]

hanker /hángkər/ (**-kers, -kering, -kered**) *vi.* to want sth very badly and persistently ○ *hankering after something I can't have* [Early 17thC. Origin uncertain: possibly from Dutch dialect *hankeren*.] —**hankerer** *n.*

hankie /hángki/, **hanky** (*plural* **-kies**) *n.* a handkerchief (*informal*) [Late 19thC. Shortening.]

hanky-panky /-pángki/ *n.* **1.** **FRIVOLOUS SEXUAL BEHAVIOUR** frivolous and slightly indecent sexual activity **2.** **SUSPICIOUS ACTIVITY** illicit or suspicious behaviour [Mid-19thC. An alteration, via the form *hokey-pokey*, of HOCUS POCUS, the earliest uses of the word being for 'juggling, conjuring'.]

Hannibal /hánnib'l/ city and port in eastern Missouri, on the Mississippi River. It was the boyhood home of Mark Twain. Population: 18,004 (1990).

Hannibal (247–183 BC) Carthaginian general. At the beginning of the Second Punic War (218–202 BC), he marched across the Alps to northern Italy with elephants and a 40,000-strong army. It was one of the most famous military exploits in history. He was less successful in a subsequent African campaign against Scipio, and died in exile.

Hanoi /ha nóy/ capital city of Vietnam, located in the north of the country. Population: 2,154,900 (1993).

Hanover /hánnōvər, ha nṓfər/ *n.* the royal house of Great Britain from 1714, when the elector of Hanover ascended the British throne as George I, until 1901, when Queen Victoria died

Hanoverian /hánnō veéri ən/ *adj.* **1.** **OF HOUSE OF HANOVER** relating to or characteristic of the British rulers from 1714 to 1901 **2.** **OF HANOVER** relating to or typical of Hanover, Germany, or of its inhabitants or culture ■ *n.* **HANOVERIAN MONARCH** a supporter or monarch of the British Hanoverian line

Hansa /hánssə, hánzə/, **Hanse** /hanss/ *n.* **1.** = Hanseatic League **2.** **FEE FOR HANSA MEMBERSHIP** the fee paid by a new member of the Hansa [12thC. From Old High German, 'troop, company'.]

Hansard /hán saard/ *n.* the official published reports of proceedings in the British or Canadian parliaments or of similar legislative bodies in the Commonwealth [Late 19thC. Named after the British printer Luke *Hansard* (1752–1828), who first published it.]

Hanse *n.* = Hansa

Hanseatic /hánssi áttik/ *adj.* relating to the Hanseatic League or one of the towns in it [Early 17thC. From medieval Latin *Hanseaticus*, from *Hansa* (see HANSA).]

Hanseatic League *n.* an organized network of towns in northern Europe from the 15th to the 16th centuries that protected each other and promoted trade with each other

hansel *n.* = handsel

Hansen's disease /hánss'nz-/ *n.* = leprosy [Early 20thC. Named after the Norwegian physician Gerhard *Hansen* (1841–1921), who described it.]

hansom /hánssəm/, **hansom cab** *n.* a covered two-

Hansom

wheeled vehicle drawn by one horse and carrying two passengers inside while the driver sits outside on a raised seat at the rear [Mid-19thC. Named after the British architect Joseph Aloysius Hansom (1803–82), who patented an improved design of cab in 1834.]

hantavirus n. a virus belonging to a group that affects small rodents and can be passed to humans by inhalation or ingestion of their secretions or excreta. Symptoms include fever, headache, nausea, and vomiting.

Hants. /hants/ abbr. Hampshire

Hanukkah /hánnəkə, haÿan-, xaÿan-/, **Hanukah, Chanukah, Chanukkah** n. an eight-day Jewish festival beginning on the 25th day of Kislev in December and commemorating the rededication to Judaism of the Temple in Jerusalem. The temple was rededicated in 165 BC after a period during which it had been used for the worship of Greek gods under Antiochus Epiphanes.

Hanuman /húnnoÿo maÿan/ n. **1. Hanuman, hanuman** SACRED MONKEY a slender long-tailed langur monkey of southern Asia, considered sacred in India. Latin name: *Presbytis entellus.* **2.** INDIAN RELIG MONKEY CHIEF in Hinduism, a leader of monkeys who assists Rama **3.** HINDU MONKEY GOD a popular Hindu monkey god depicted in the epic Sanskrit poem Ramayana [Early 19thC. From Sanskrit, literally 'large-jawed'.]

hao /how/ (plural **hao**) n. **1.** SUBUNIT OF VIETNAMESE CURRENCY a minor currency unit of Vietnam, ten of which are worth one dong. See table at **currency 2.** COIN WORTH A HAO a coin worth one hao [Mid-20thC. From Vietnamese.]

haole /hówli/ n. sb, especially a white person, who lives in Hawaii but is not a Polynesian [Mid-19thC. From Hawaiian.] —**haole** adj.

hap[1] /hap/ n. HAPPENING a happening or occurrence (archaic) ■ vi. (**haps, happing, happed**) HAPPEN to happen or occur (archaic) [13thC. From Old Norse happ.]

hap[2] /hap/ n. Scotland COVERING sth used to cover a person or bed, e.g. a cloak or quilt ■ vt. (**haps, happing, happed**) Scotland, US WEAR WARM CLOTHES to wrap up in warm clothes (regional) [13thC. Origin uncertain: perhaps from Scandinavian.]

hapax legomenon /háppaks lə gómmi non, -nən/ (plural **hapax legomena** /-nə/) n. a word of which there is only one recorded use [Mid-17thC. From Greek, 'said only once'.]

ha'penny /háypni/ (plural **-nies**) n. = halfpenny [Mid-16thC. Contraction.]

haphazard /hap házzərd/ adj. happening or done in a way that has not been planned [Late 16thC. From HAP[1] + HAZARD, literally 'hazard of chance'.] —**haphazardly** adv. —**haphazardness** n.

haphtarah n. JUDAISM = haftarah

hapl- prefix. = haplo- (used before vowels)

hapless /háppləss/ adj. unlucky or unfortunate — **haplessly** adv. —**haplessness** n.

haplite /hápplīt/ n. = aplite —**haplitic** /hap líttik/ adj.

haplo- prefix. **1.** single ○ haplology **2.** haploid ○ haplont [From Greek haplous. Ultimately from an Indo-European word that is also the ancestor of English simple.]

haplography /hap lóggrəfi/ n. the accidental omission of a letter or syllable that should be repeated, e.g. 'mispell' for 'misspell' [Late 19thC]

haploid /hápployd/ adj. **haploid, haploidic** WITH SINGLE SET OF CHROMOSOMES having a single set of unpaired chromosomes ■ n. ORGANISM WITH UNPAIRED CHROMOSOMES a cell or organism with a single set of unpaired chromosomes [Early 20thC]

haplology /hap lólləji/ n. the accidental omission of one or more repeated syllables or sounds when speaking [Late 19thC] —**haplologic** /hápplə lójjik/ adj.

haplont /há plont/ n. an organism, especially an algal plant, that is haploid at one stage of its life cycle [Early 20thC. Coined from HAPLOID + -ONT.] —**haplontic** /ha plóntik/ adj.

haplosis /ha plóssiss/ n. the production of haploids during cell division (**meiosis**) [Coined from HAPLOID + -OSIS]

haply /háppli/ adv. used to express the possibility or hope that sth is or will be the case (archaic) ○ 'I will kiss thy lips; haply some poison yet doth hang on them' (William Shakespeare, Romeo and Juliet; 1594)

ha'p'orth /háypərth/ (plural **ha'p'orth**) n. = halfpennyworth [Late 17thC. Contraction.]

happen /háppən/ v. (**-pens, -pening, -pened**) **1.** vi. OCCUR to take place ○ How did it happen? **2.** vt. DO STH BY CHANCE to do sth by chance and without a previous plan ○ If you happen to see him, give him these keys. **3.** vi. AFFECT SB to affect sb or sth, especially in an unpleasant way ○ If anything happens to me, you'll regret it. **4.** vi. OCCUR BY CHANCE to occur or exist by chance ■ adv. N England PERHAPS used to suggest that sth may occur or be the case ○ Happen we'll go for a walk. [14thC. Formed from HAP[1].]
happen along, happen by vi. US to appear or pass by chance or unexpectedly (informal)
happen on vt. to discover or encounter sth or sb by chance
happen upon vt. = happen on

happenchance /háppən chaanss/ n. = happenstance [Mid-20thC. Alteration of HAPPENSTANCE.]

happening /háppəning/ n. **1.** OCCURRENCE sth that occurs **2.** ARTISTIC PERFORMANCE an improvised or informal performance or demonstration, often dramatic in form and using audience participation (informal) ■ adj. FASHIONABLE at the forefront of what is fashionable and exciting (informal)

happenstance /hápp'n stanss/ n. a chance occurrence or event [Late 19thC. Blend of HAPPENING and CIRCUMSTANCE.]

happi coat /háppi-/ n. an open Japanese jacket that has wide loose sleeves and is usually tied with a sash, or a fashion garment resembling this [Late 19thC. Happi from Japanese.]

happily /háppili/ adv. **1.** FORTUNATELY used to indicate that sth that could have been difficult or disastrous is luckily the reverse ○ Happily, no one was hurt. **2.** WILLINGLY with willingness ○ I'd happily contribute. **3.** IN A HAPPY WAY in a pleased, contented, or joyful way

happy /háppi/ (**-pier, -piest**) adj. **1.** FEELING PLEASURE feeling or showing pleasure, contentment, or joy ○ happy smiling faces **2.** CAUSING PLEASURE causing or characterized by pleasure, contentment, or joy ○ a happy childhood **3.** SATISFIED feeling satisfied that sth is right or has been done right ○ Are you happy with your performance? **4.** WILLING willing to do sth ○ I'd be only too happy to help. **5.** FORTUNATE resulting in sth pleasant or welcome ○ a happy coincidence **6.** TIPSY slightly drunk (informal) **7.** USED IN GREETINGS used in formulae to express a hope that sb will enjoy a special day or holiday ○ Happy birthday! **8.** TOO READY TO USE STH inclined to use a particular thing too readily or be too enthusiastic about a particular thing (used in combination) ○ trigger-happy [14thC. Formed from HAP[1].] —**happiness** n.

happy event n. the birth of a baby (informal)

happy-go-lucky adj. tending not to worry about the future

happy hardcore n. uplifting hardcore music, often achieving its emotional effect by the use of piano riffs over straightforward rhythms

happy hour n. a period of time, usually in the late afternoon or early evening, during which a pub or bar serves alcoholic drinks at reduced prices

happy hunting ground n. **1.** HUNTING AND FEASTING PARADISE among some Native American peoples, a place of peace and abundance to which people go after death **2.** PLACE WITH ABUNDANT SUPPLY a place that provides plenty of sth desired

happy medium n. a satisfying compromise

Hapsburg /háps burg/, **Habsburg** /hábz-/ n. a member of a German royal family, prominent between the 13th and 20th centuries in Europe, that included rulers of the Holy Roman Empire, Spain, and Austria-Hungary

hapten /háptən/, **haptene** /háp teen/ n. an antigen that can stimulate production of antibodies only in combination with a specific protein [Early 20thC. Formed from Greek haptein 'to fasten'.]

haptic /háptik/ adj. relating to the sense of touch [Late 19thC. From Greek haptikos, from haptesthai 'to grasp, touch', from haptein 'to fasten'.]

haptoglobin /háptə glóbin/ n. any of several plasma proteins that combine with free haemoglobin in the bloodstream [Mid-20thC. Coined from Greek haptein 'to fasten' + GLOBIN.]

haptotropism /háptō trópizəm/ n. BIOL = thigmotropism [Late 19thC. Coined from Greek haptein 'to fasten' + -TROPISM.]

hapu /haÿa pool/ n. NZ a principal social unit of Maori society, consisting of a group of extended families holding land in common that forms a division of a tribe [Mid-19thC. From Maori.]

hapuka /haÿa poÿokə/ (plural **-kas** or **-ka**) n. NZ ZOOL = groper [Mid-19thC. From Maori.]

hara-kiri /hárrə kírri, -keÿer ri/ n. a traditional form of suicide, sometimes ritually performed as a point of honour in Japan, involving disembowelment with a sword [Mid-19thC. From Japanese, literally 'belly-cutting'.]

Harald I /hárrəld/, **King of Norway** (850?–933?). He unified Norway in a long military campaign culminating in the Battle of Hafrsfiord (about 885). Known as **Harald the Fairhaired**

harangue /hə ráng/ vti. (**-rangues, -ranguing, -rangued**) ADDRESS SB LOUDLY AND FORCEFULLY to criticize or question sb or try to persuade sb to do sth in a forceful angry way ■ n. FORCEFUL CRITICISM OR PERSUASION a loud, forceful, and angry speech criticizing sb or trying to persuade sb to do sth [15thC. Via French from medieval Latin harenga of uncertain origin: possibly ultimately from prehistoric Germanic.] —**haranguer** n.

Harare /hə raÿari/ capital city of Zimbabwe, located in the northeastern part of the country. Population: 1,184,169 (1992).

harass /hárrəss, hə ráss/ (**-rasses, -rassing, -rassed**) vt. **1.** KEEP BOTHERING OR ATTACKING SB to persistently annoy, attack, or bother sb **2.** EXHAUST AN ENEMY WITH REPEATED ATTACKS to exhaust an enemy by repeatedly attacking [Early 17thC. From French harasser, from harer 'to set a dog on (by crying 'hare')', ultimately of uncertain origin: perhaps from Old High German haren.] —**harasser** n.

harassed /hárrəst, hə rást/ adj. stressed and anxious because of having a lot of things to do or worry about

harassment /hárrəssmənt, hə rássmənt/ n. behaviour that threatens or torments sb, especially persistently

Harbin /haÿar bín/ capital city of Heilongjiang Province in northeastern China. Population: 2,830,000 (1991).

harbinger /haÿarbinjər/ n. SB OR STH THAT ANNOUNCES STH sb or sth that foreshadows or anticipates a future event ■ vt. (**-gers, -gering, -gered**) HERALD STH to herald or foreshadow sb or sth [12thC. From Old French herberger, from herbergier 'to provide shelter for an army', ultimately from prehistoric Germanic words meaning 'army' and 'protect'.]

harbor n., vti. US = harbour

harbour /haÿarbər/ n. **1.** PORT part of a body of water near a coast in which ships can anchor safely (often used in placenames) **2.** PLACE OF REFUGE any place that is safe and sheltered ■ v. (**-bours, -bouring, -boured**) **1.** vt. KEEP STH IN MIND to continue to think privately about an emotion or thought for a long time ○ had harboured a secret fear of the dark since childhood **2.** vt. SHELTER SB to provide sb with shelter or sanctuary **3.** vti. NAUT KEEP A SHIP IN HARBOUR to take shelter in a harbour, or shelter a ship in a harbour [Old English herebeorg 'lodging', literally 'army shelter', ultimately from a prehistoric Germanic word that is also the ancestor of English harbinger] —**harbourer** n.

harbourage /haÿarbərij/ n. = harbour n. 1, harbour n. 2

harbour master n. an official who supervises and administers the general activities of a port or harbour

harbour seal *n.* a small seal that is greyish-black with paler spots and lives on the northern coasts of North America, Europe, and Asia. Latin name: *Phoca vitulina.*

hard /haard/ *adj.* **1.** NOT EASILY BENT firm, stiff, or rigid and not easily cut, pierced, or bent ○ *a hard mattress* **2.** DIFFICULT OR AWKWARD difficult or awkward to do or achieve ○ *a hard decision* **3.** DIFFICULT TO UNDERSTAND difficult to understand or explain **4.** INVOLVING EFFORT involving a great deal of labour or effort ○ *a hard climb* **5.** PERFORMING ENERGETICALLY acting or producing sth with energy or industriousness ○ *a hard worker* **6.** MIGHTY using a lot of force or violence **7.** DEMANDING AND STRICT making inflexible and heavy demands ○ *a hard taskmaster* **8.** PROBLEMATIC difficult and full of problems ○ *a hard life* **9.** UNSYMPATHETIC showing little or no sympathy, compassion, or gentleness ○ *She's as hard as nails.* **10.** RESENTFUL marked by resentment or bitterness ○ *no hard feelings* **11.** REAL OR TRUE demonstrably real, true, or certain ○ *cold, hard facts* **12.** PENETRATING seeming to penetrate and discover intentions or thoughts ○ *a hard stare* **13.** TOUGH tough, violent, and ruthless ○ *a hard man* **14.** POL RADICAL politically radical or extreme ○ *the hard left* **15.** SEVERE marked by weather conditions such as extreme cold or severe storms ○ *a hard winter* **16.** VISUALLY HARSH harsh and glaring to the sight **17.** TOUGHENED rough or leathery, and unyielding ○ *hard skin* **18.** CHEM CONTAINING MINERAL SALTS containing mineral salts and preventing soap from lathering well **19.** FIRM OR CRISP IN TEXTURE having a crisp, firm, or stale crust or texture **20.** ERECT stiff and erect (*informal*) **21.** = hard-core *adj.* 2 **22.** PHYS READILY ABLE TO PENETRATE SUBSTANCES used to describe radiation, especially high frequency X-rays, that has a high energy and is thus readily able to penetrate substances including metals, or relating to this ○ *hard vacuum* **23.** FIN STRONG AND STABLE stable in value and in demand by currency traders **24.** FIN IN CASH in the form of coins and paper money rather than, e.g., cheques **25.** BEVERAGES HIGH IN ALCOHOL having a high alcoholic content, especially alcohol produced by distillation **26.** DRUGS ADDICTIVE AND DANGEROUS TO HEALTH highly addictive and particularly dangerous to the health **27.** PHON PRONOUNCED LIKE 'K' OR 'G' used to describe the consonants 'c' and 'g' when they are pronounced with a 'k' sound, as in 'come', and a 'g' sound, as in 'go'. ◊ **soft** ■ *adv.* **1.** FORCEFULLY with a lot of force ○ *hit the ball hard* **2.** INTENSELY to an extreme degree ○ *pulled the truck over hard* **3.** ENERGETICALLY with vigour and energy or industriousness ○ *worked hard* **4.** WITH CONCENTRATION with great mental concentration **5.** WITH DIFFICULTY with effort and great difficulty **6.** COMPACTLY into a solid or compact state ○ *set hard* **7.** PAINFULLY in a way that causes anguish or hardship ○ *hit hard by the recession* **8.** SLOWLY slowly and with difficulty ○ *hatred that dies hard* ■ *n.* **1.** BEACH WHERE BOAT CAN LAND a beach or slope that is convenient for hauling vessels out of water **2.** ROAD a road across a foreshore [Old English *heard.* Ultimately meaning 'resistant to pressure', from an Indo-European word meaning 'strength', which is also the ancestor of English *democracy.*] ◊ **be hard on sb 1.** to treat sb severely **2.** to be unfortunate for sb ◊ **be hard put to do sth** to find it difficult to do sth ◊ **hard by** close by

─── **WORD KEY: SYNONYMS** ───

hard, difficult, strenuous, tough, arduous, laborious

CORE MEANING: requiring effort or exertion

hard a general word used to describe sth that requires effort or exertion to do or achieve; **difficult** similar in meaning to *hard,* but suggesting more complexity and a need for skill or patience; **strenuous** used to describe sth that requires a great deal of physical effort and stamina; **tough** used to describe sth that is extremely difficult or strenuous; **arduous** a fairly formal word used to describe sth that requires great energy, effort, and often physical exertion to do or achieve; **laborious** a fairly formal word, emphasizing the need for physical effort and great exertion in order to do sth, and also suggesting tedium.

─── **WORD KEY: CULTURAL NOTE** ───

Hard Times, a novel by writer Charles Dickens (1854) was the story of the loveless upbringing of Tom and Louisa Gradgrind to contrast the soullessness of utilitarianism, as personified by their father Thomas Gradgrind, with the natural warmth and generosity of the

human spirit, symbolized by their adopted sister Sissy Jupe, a member of a travelling circus.

hard-and-fast *adj.* unable to be changed or adapted [Originally a nautical phrase referring to a ship run aground]

Hardanger Fjord /haard angǝr fyáwrd/ large fjord on the southwestern coast of Norway. Length: 183 km/114 mi.

hard-ass *n.* US sb who is perceived as inflexible and uncompromising (*slang offensive*) —**hard-assed** *adj.*

hardback /haard bak/ *n.* a book with a rigid cover

hardbake /haard bayk/ *n.* almond toffee

hardball /haard bawl/ *n.* **1.** *US* = baseball **2.** *US, Can* RUTHLESS BEHAVIOUR tough or ruthless behaviour, especially in politics or business (*informal*) ○ *These guys play hardball.*

hard-bitten *adj.* tough and experienced

hardboard /haard bawrd/ *n.* thin stiff sheets of compressed sawdust and wood chips

hard-boiled *adj.* **1.** COOKED UNTIL FIRM used to describe an egg boiled until the yolk and white are firm **2.** UNSENTIMENTAL tough, realistic, and unsentimental (*informal*) —**hard-boil** *vt.*

hardboot /haard boot/ (**-boots, -booting, -booted**) *vt.* = coldboot

hardbound /haard bownd/ *adj.* bound as a book in a stiff cover

hard case *n.* **1.** TOUGH PERSON sb who is tough and ruthless (*hyphenated when used before a noun*) **2.** *Aus* UNCONVENTIONAL PERSON sb who is unconventional and colourful (*dated informal*)

hard cheese *interj.* used to comment on, and express a lack of sympathy for, sb's misfortune (*informal*)

hard coal *n.* = anthracite

hard copy *n.* data from a computer that is printed out, usually on paper, rather than read from the screen

hard core *n.* **1.** COMMITTED NUCLEUS OF A GROUP the most committed, faithful, and active members of a group or organization **2.** MUSIC TYPE OF FAST ROCK MUSIC a type of dance music notable for its repetitive rhythmic synthesized sounds and fast tempo **3.** TRANSP FOUNDATION FOR ROADS OR PAVING stones and other rubble used to form a foundation under roads or paving

hard-core *adj.* **1.** UNCOMPROMISING uncompromising and committed **2.** SHOWING EXPLICIT SEX depicting sexual acts in an explicit way

hardcover /haard kuvvǝr/ *n.* = hardback

hard disk, hard drive *n.* a rigid disk inside a computer that is magnetized to hold a large quantity of computer data and programs

hard-edge *adj.* used to describe a US style of abstract painting that arose in the 1960s and is marked by sharply outlined coloured forms

hard-edged *adj.* realistic, direct, and uncompromising

harden /haard'n/ *v.* (**-ens, -ening, -ened**) **1.** *vti.* BECOME OR MAKE HARD to become hard, firm, or solid, or make sth become hard, firm, or solid ○ *The glue hardened overnight.* **2.** *vti.* MAKE OR BECOME LESS SYMPATHETIC to become or make sb become more tough, callous, or unfeeling **3.** *vti.* MAKE OR BECOME MORE DETERMINED to become or make sb become more determined and resolute **4.** *vti.* MAKE OR BECOME STRONGER to become or make sb or sth become stronger or more resistant **5.** *vi.* COMM STABILIZE to become stable after fluctuation ○ *Prices are hardening.* ■ *adj.* *Carib* STUBBORN stubborn and disobedient or intransigent

harden off *vti.* to accustom a plant grown indoors to outdoor conditions by gradually exposing it to cold, wind, or sunlight before planting it out, or become accustomed to outdoor conditions in this way

hardened /haard'nd/ *adj.* sufficiently experienced to have become blasé about sth that most people would find unpleasant or difficult

hardener /haard'nǝr/, **hardening** /haard'ning/ *n.* an ingredient or element that makes sth hard, e.g. a substance added to paint to make it more durable

hardening of the arteries *n.* loss of elasticity in the walls of the arteries, formerly believed to be a major cause of heart disease (*dated; no longer used technically*)

hard-fisted *adj.* not generous with money

hardhack /haard hak/ (*plural* **-hacks** *or* **-hack**) *n.* a North American shrub that belongs to the rose family and has short downy leaves and tapering clusters of small pink or white flowers. Latin name: *Spiraea tomentosa.* [Mid-19thC. Origin uncertain: perhaps literally 'hard to hack', from HARD + HACK.]

hardhanded /haard hándid/ *adj.* showing little or no sympathy or pity —**hardhandedness** *n.*

hard hat *n.* **1.** PROTECTIVE HELMET a helmet made of metal or plastic worn for protection by workers in a factory or on a construction site **2.** *US* WORKER a construction worker (*informal*) **3.** *US* CONSERVATIVE a politically very conservative patriot (*informal*)

hardheaded /haard héddid/ *adj.* behaving in a shrewd, tough, and logical way that is not influenced by emotions —**hardhead** *n.* —**hardheadedly** *adv.* —**hardheadedness** *n.*

hardheads /haard hedz/ *n.* a variety of knapweed found in grasslands that has dense reddish-purple flower heads. Latin name: *Centaurea nigra.* US term **knapweed**

hardhearted /haard haártid/ *adj.* showing no sympathy for other people's feelings —**hardheartedly** *adv.* —**hardheartedness** *n.*

hard-hitting *adj.* direct and uncompromising ○ *a hard-hitting documentary*

Hardie /haardi/, **Keir** (1856–1915) British politician. He founded the Scottish Labour Party (1888), the first labour party in Britain. Full name **James Keir Hardie**

Hardie Boys /haardi bóyz/, **Sir Michael** (*b.* 1931) New Zealand lawyer and statesman. He became governor-general of New Zealand in 1996.

hardihood /haardihŏŏd/ *n.* **1.** RESOLUTENESS the quality of being tough and able to withstand difficulty or hard work **2.** AUDACITY bold audacity

Warren G. Harding

Harding /haarding/, **Warren G.** (1865–1923) US statesman and 29th President of the United States. A conservative Republican from Ohio elected on the promise of a 'return to normalcy' after World War I, he presided (1921–23) over a federal administration distinguished primarily by its flagrant corruption. Full name **Warren Gamaliel Harding**

hard labour *n.* a sentence of compulsory work imposed in addition to a term of imprisonment, not used as a sentence in the United Kingdom since 1948

hard landing *n.* **1.** AIR UNCONTROLLED LANDING an uncontrolled landing by an aircraft or spacecraft that results in its being damaged or destroyed **2.** ECON ECONOMIC DOWNTURN AFTER SUCCESS a downward trend in economic activity after a period of expansion

hardline /haard lín/ *adj.* inflexible and uncompromising —**hardliner** *n.*

hard lines *interj.* used to comment that sb is or has been unfortunate (*dated*) (*often used ironically*)

hardly /haardli/ CORE MEANING: an adverb with negative meaning, used to indicate that sth is true or exists to a very minimal extent ○ *She lived so privately, hardly anyone even spoke to her* ○ *Though we hardly* *knew him, we could sense his good humour.* ○ *I looked out of the window; it was hardly raining.* **adv. 1. NOT** indicates that sth is almost entirely untrue or impossible ○ *We are hardly going to give up with success in view.* ○ *It's hardly likely that I would tell you.* **2. ONLY WITH DIFFICULTY** only with great awkwardness, difficulty, or embarrassment ○ *I was so shocked I could hardly speak.* **3. SELDOM** indicates that sth seldom occurs (*used with a negative such as 'without'*) ○ *Hardly a day passes without acclaim for this exciting new invention.* **4. AS SOON AS** indicates that one event follows quickly after another ○ *Hardly had I rung the bell when the bolt was shot back.* **5. USED TO DISAGREE** used to indicate surprise, disagreement or annoyance ○ *'I thought you were going at about sixty miles an hour'.'Well, hardly. Maybe forty'.* [13thC. Coined from HARD + -LY. Originally 'vigorously, with energy', hence 'not easily', hence 'almost not'.]

──── **WORD KEY: USAGE** ────

Grammar: *Hardly*, like *barely* and *scarcely*, has a negative force, rendering unnecessary the use of another negative in the clause or sentence: *I can [not: can't] hardly see you.* Note that *when* and not *than* is used in any continuation of the sentence: *Hardly [or barely or scarcely] had I begun to speak when [not than] she interrupted me.* (After *no sooner*, however, *than* is correct.) *Hardly* is limited to these special uses; the routine adverb from the adjective *hard* is *hard*: *They are all working hard to get ready for their exams.*

hard man *n.* a man who is perceived as vicious and ruthless, probably with criminal tendencies

hard mouth *n.* a horse's mouth that is insensitive to pressure from the bit, or a horse's ability to resist this pressure —**hard-mouthed** *adj.*

hardness /háardnəss/ *n.* **1. FIRMNESS, SOLIDITY, AND COMPACTNESS** the state or quality of being firm, solid, and compact **2. UNYIELDING TOUGHNESS** the state or quality of being tough and unyielding **3. CHEM WATER QUALITY** the degree to which water contains mineral salts **4. METALL, MEASURE DEGREE TO WHICH A METAL IS HARD** the degree to which a metal may be scratched, abraded, indented, or machined, measured according to any of several scales

hard news *n.* news that concerns specific events and is strictly factual —**hard-news** *adj.*

hard-nosed *adj.* tough, realistic, and unsentimental (*informal*)

hard of hearing *adj.* unable to hear as much as others do (*often considered offensive*)

hard-on *n.* an erect penis (*slang taboo*)

hard palate *n.* the bony front portion of the roof of the mouth

hardpan /háard pan/ *n.* a layer of hard matter, especially clay, that lies under soft soil and that plant roots cannot penetrate

hard-pressed *adj.* **1. WITHOUT SUFFICIENT RESOURCES** under a lot of pressure and without sufficient resources **2. HAVING DIFFICULTY** finding sth very difficult

hard put *adj.* **hard put, hard put to it** not easily able to do sth or, more generally, to cope

hard rock *n.* a form of rock music that has simple lyrics and a strong insistent beat, and that is usually very loud

hardrock /háard rok/ *adj. Can* relating to the extraction of minerals from igneous and metamorphic rocks by blasting or drilling

hard sauce *n. US* = **brandy butter**

hard science *n.* any science in which data can be precisely quantified and theories tested. Physics, chemistry, geology, and astronomy are hard sciences.

hard sell *n.* a direct, aggressive, and insistent way of selling or advertising. ◊ **soft sell**

hard-shell, **hard-shelled** *adj. US* rigid and uncompromising in attitude

hard-shell clam *n.* = **quahog**

hardship /háard ship/ *n.* **1. DIFFICULTIES** difficulty or suffering caused by a lack of sth, especially money **2. CAUSE OF HARDSHIP** sth that causes hardship

hard shoulder *n.* an area at the side of a motorway where a vehicle can stop in an emergency

hardstand /háard stand/ *n. US* = **hard standing**

hard standing *n.* a hard surface on which aircraft or heavy motor vehicles may be parked. US term **hardstand**

hard stuff *n.* sth that is intoxicating, addictive, and potentially very dangerous to the health (*informal*)

hardtack /háard tak/ *n.* a hard thin unsalted bread or biscuit formerly eaten aboard ships and as military rations

hard up *adj.* short of money (*informal*)

hardware /háard wair/ *n.* **1. TOOLS AND IMPLEMENTS** tools and implements that are typically made of metal, e.g. hinges, hammers, and cutlery **2. COMPUT COMPUTER EQUIPMENT AND PERIPHERALS** the equipment and devices that make up a computer system as opposed to the programs that are used on it **3. MIL MILITARY WEAPONS** heavy military weapons and equipment **4. ARMS GUN** a gun or guns (*informal*)

hard-wearing *adj.* not easily damaged or worn out through constant use

hard wheat *n.* a kind of wheat with hard kernels and a high gluten content that is used to make the flour for bread

hardwire /háard wīr/ (**-wires, -wiring, -wired**) *vt.* to build a function into a computer with hardware rather than programming

hardwood /háard wŏŏd/ *n.* **WOOD LIKE OAK** wood from a broad-leaved tree, e.g. oak, ash, or birch, as opposed to from a conifer ■ *adj.* **TREE PRODUCING HARDWOOD** a tree that produces hardwood

hard word *n.* (*informal*) **1. DISMISSAL** dismissal from employment **2. Ireland REPRIMAND** a reprimand or unfair criticism ◇ **put the hard word on sb** *ANZ* to put pressure on sb to do sth (*informal*)

hardy /háardi/ (**-dier, -diest**) *adj.* **1. ROBUST** sufficiently robust to withstand fatigue, hardship, or adverse physical conditions **2. PLANTS NOT SENSITIVE TO COLD** used to describe plants that are able to live outdoors during the winter ○ *a hardy shrub* **3. COURAGEOUS** courageous and daring [13thC. From French *hardi*, from *hardir* 'to become bold', from a prehistoric Germanic word that is also the ancestor of English *hard*.] —**hardily** *adv.* —**hardiness** *n.*

Hardy /háardi/, **Oliver** (1892–1957) US actor. He appeared with Stan Laurel in a series of classic films in the 1920s and 1930s.

Hardy, Thomas (1840–1928) British novelist and poet. He wrote brooding novels of the West Country including *The Mayor of Casterbridge* (1886), and from the 1890s devoted himself to poetry.

Hardy, Thomas Masterman (1769–1839) British sailor. He was flag captain of the *Victory* at the Battle of Trafalgar (1805), and attended Nelson as he was dying.

hard yards *npl. Aus* hard work (*informal*) ○ *He had to do the hard yards drumming up support.*

Hardy-Weinberg law /háardi wīn burg-/, **Hardy-Weinberg distribution** *n.* a principle of genetics stating that gene frequencies remain constant from one generation to the next if mating is random and there are no outside influences such as mutation and immigration [Mid-20thC. Named after the British mathematician G. H. *Hardy* (1877–1947) and the German physician Wilhelm *Weinberg* (1862–1937), who each formulated the law independently in 1908.]

hare /hair/ *n.* (*plural* **hare** *or* **hares**) **LARGE MEMBER OF RABBIT**

Hare

FAMILY a fast-running animal that resembles a rabbit but is larger, has longer ears and legs, and does not burrow. Genus: *Lepus*. ■ *vi.* (**hares, haring, hared**) **RUN FAST** to run or move very fast [Old English *hara*, from a prehistoric Germanic word of uncertain origin: probably ultimately from an Indo-European word meaning 'grey', from its colour]

Hare /hair/, **Sir David** (b. 1947) British playwright. His plays explore political and moral themes in contemporary Britain, and include the trilogy *Racing Demon* (1989), *Murmuring Judges* (1991), and *The Absence of War* (1993).

hare and hounds, **hare and hounds race** *n.* an outdoor game in which one group of players, the hounds, follow a trail of scattered scraps of paper left by another group of players, the hares. The hares attempt to reach a designated point before the hounds catch them.

Harebell

harebell /hair bel/ *n.* a low-growing plant found in northern temperate regions that has narrow leaves and blue bell-shaped flowers. Latin name: *Campanula rotundiflora*. [Perhaps because the plant grows in places frequented by hares]

harebrained /hair braynd/ *adj.* impractical and likely to fail (*insult*)

Hare Krishna /hárri-/ *n.* **1. HINDU RELIGIOUS GROUP** a religious group that bases its practice on worship of the god Krishna **2. MEMBER OF HARE KRISHNA** sb who is a member of Hare Krishna [Late 20thC. From Sanskrit, 'O Lord Krishna', a chant used by devotees.]

harelip /hair lip/ *n.* an offensive term for a facial deformity, now rare, in which sb born with the upper lip in two parts has had the separation incompletely rectified by surgery. It is often associated with a cleft palate. (*offensive*) —**harelipped** *adj.*

harem /haáirəm, haá reem, haa reém/ *n.* **1. WOMEN'S PART OF A HOUSE** the separate private quarters reserved for wives and concubines in a Muslim home **2. GROUP OF WOMEN** the wives and concubines who live in a harem **3. ZOOL GROUP OF ANIMALS** a group of female animals of the same species associated for breeding purposes with one male **4. WOMEN FOLLOWERS** any group of women admirers or followers (*humorous*) (*sometimes considered offensive*) [Mid-17thC. Via Turkish from, ultimately, Arabic *haram* 'prohibited (place), women's quarters'.]

harem pants *npl.* women's trousers made of soft thin cloth and having wide legs that are gathered at the ankle

Harer /haárər/, **Härer, Harar** city in eastern Ethiopia, the centre of a coffee-growing area. Population: 77,202 (1989).

hare's-foot (*plural* **hare's-foot** *or* **hare's-foots**), **hare's-foot clover** *n.* a clover that grows on sandy soil and has white or pink flowers almost hidden by its calyx. Latin name: *Trefolium arvense*. [From the soft hair about the flowers, giving the plant the appearance of a hare's foot]

harestail /hairz tayl/ *n.* a variety of cotton grass that grows on moors and has a single flower head [From the similarity of the plant to a hare's tail]

harewood /hair wŏŏd/ *n.* the greenish-coloured wood of the sycamore maple, used in making furniture [Late 17thC. *Hare* by folk etymology from German dialect *Ehre*, from, ultimately, Latin *acer* 'maple, sycamore'.]

Hargrave /haár grayv/, **Lawrence** (1850–1915) English-born Australian aviator and explorer. He designed several primitive aircraft.

Hargreaves /haár greevz/, **James** (1720–78) British inventor. His invention of the spinning jenny in 1764 heralded a new era in industrial history.

haricot /hárrikō/ n. **1. WHITE BEAN** a small white oval dried bean, cooked and eaten as a vegetable **2. PLANT PRODUCING EDIBLE SEEDS** a bean plant whose seeds are dried and stored as haricots. Latin name: *Phaseolus vulgaris.* **3. = French bean** [Mid-17thC. From French, of uncertain origin: probably from Nahuatl *ayacotli.*]

Harijan /húrrijən/ n. a member of a class of people in India whose touch was formerly considered to defile a Hindu of a higher caste [Mid-20thC. From Sanskrit, literally 'God's people', an appellation introduced by M. K. Gandhi.]

harissa /hə ríssə/ n. a hot spicy oily paste used as an ingredient in North African and Middle Eastern cooking or served as an accompaniment for dishes, especially for couscous

hark /haark/ (**harks, harking, harked**) vi. to listen to sth or sb (*literary or humorous*) [12thC. Origin uncertain: probably from assumed Old English *heorcnian*, from a prehistoric Germanic word that is also the ancestor of English *hearken* and *hear.*]
hark back vi. **1. REVERT TO STH** to think or speak again about sth from the past **2. BE SIMILAR TO A PAST THING** to be similar in some respects to sth in the past

harken vi. = **hearken**

harl /haarl/ vt. (**harls, harling, harled**) Scotland **COVER BUILDING** to cover the exterior walls of a building with lime and gravel or sand ■ n. Scotland **MIXTURE FOR COVERING BUILDINGS** a mixture of lime and gravel or sand used for covering a building's exterior walls [13thC. Origin unknown.]

Harlech /haárlək/ village in Gwynedd, northwestern Wales, dominated by the ruins of its castle. Population: 1,500 (1994).

Harlem Globetrotters /haárləm glób trottərz/ npl. a US basketball team that tours widely to play exhibition matches during which the team displays skilled comic manoeuvres

harlequin /haárləkwin/ n. **CLOWN** a clown or buffoon ■ adj. **HAVING MULTICOLOURED SHAPES** varied in colour and having a pattern of irregular shapes [Late 16thC. Via obsolete French from *Hellequin,* legendary leader of night-raiding demon horsemen.]

Harlequin n. Harlequin, harlequin a comic dramatic character featured in the Italian commedia dell'arte and the English harlequinade, usually shown wearing multicoloured diamond-patterned tights and a black mask

harlequinade /haárləkwi náyd/ n. **1. ENTERTAINMENT FEATURING A HARLEQUIN** a pantomime, play, or other performance featuring a harlequin as a character **2. CLOWNISH BEHAVIOUR** the action of clowning around or acting in a silly way

harlequin bug n. a black bug of North and Central America that has black and red markings and feeds on cabbages and similar plants. Latin name: *Murgantia histrionica.*

harlequin duck n. a small duck native to North America, Iceland, and eastern Siberia that dives for its food and has blue and red plumage with black and white markings. Latin name: *Histrionicus histrionicus.*

Harley Street /haárli-/ n. a street in central London famous for the number of eminent doctors who have practices there

harling n. Scotland **BUILDING** = **harl**

harlot /haárlət/ n. a prostitute (*archaic or literary*) [13thC. From Old French, 'vagabond, rogue, beggar', of unknown origin.]

Harlow /haárlō/ town in Essex, southeastern England, designated a 'New Town' in 1947. Population: 73,000 (1995).

harm /haarm/ n. **DAMAGE OR INJURY** physical or mental damage or injury ■ vt. (**harms, harming, harmed**) **INJURE SB OR STH** to injure or damage sb or sth physically, mentally, or morally [Old English *hearm,* from a prehistoric Germanic word meaning 'harm, grief']

WORD KEY: SYNONYMS
harm, damage, hurt, injure, wound
CORE MEANING: to weaken or impair sth or sb
harm a general term meaning to cause physical, emotional, or mental impairment or deterioration of health in living things. It can also refer to weakening or impairing sth such as a system; **damage** a slightly narrower term meaning to weaken or spoil objects or plants, not usually used with reference to people or animals. It can also refer to weakening or impairing sth abstract such as a chance or sb's reputation; **hurt** a general word meaning to cause pain and physical damage to people and animals. It can also mean upsetting or offending sb; **injure** to cause physical damage to a person or animal, usually serious enough to cause at least a temporary loss of function or use. Like *damage,* it can also apply to abstract things such as sb's reputation or pride; **wound** a narrower term than *hurt* meaning to cause physical damage to sb, especially as a result of the use of a weapon, a violent incident, or a serious accident. It can also refer to upsetting or offending sb.

---

harmattan /haar mátt'n/ n. an extremely dry dusty wind from the Sahara that blows towards the western coast of Africa, especially between November and March [Late 17thC. From Twi *haramata,* of uncertain origin: possibly from Arabic *ḥaram* 'evil or prohibited (thing)' (source of *harem*).]

harmful /haármf'l/ adj. causing damage or injury ○ *The plant is harmful to humans.* —**harmfully** adv. —**harmfulness** n.

harmless /haármləss/ adj. **1. UNOBJECTIONABLE** not likely to cause offence or upset ○ *Don't worry; he's harmless enough.* **2. NOT DANGEROUS** not likely to cause damage or injury —**harmlessly** adv. —**harmlessness** n.

harmonic /haar mónnik/ adj. **1. PRODUCED BY HARMONY** relating to, produced, or marked by harmony **2. RELATING TO INTEGRAL MULTIPLE OF FREQUENCY** used to describe a frequency that is an integral multiple of a fundamental frequency ■ n. **1. MULTIPLE OF A FUNDAMENTAL FREQUENCY** a single oscillation having a frequency that is an integral multiple of a fundamental frequency, e.g. 220 Hz and 330 Hz are both harmonics of 110 Hz **2. OVERTONE ON A STRINGED INSTRUMENT** an overtone produced on an instrument, e.g. by lightly touching a vibrating string at a point where the string to either side will continue to vibrate [Late 16thC. Via Latin *harmonicus* from Greek *harmonika* 'theory of music', from *harmonia* (see HARMONY).]

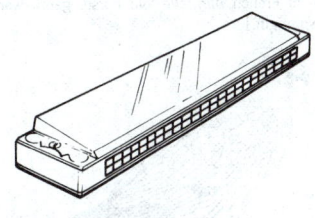

Harmonica

harmonica /haar mónnikə/ n. a musical instrument consisting of a small narrow metal case containing a set of metal reeds that are made to sound by exhaling or inhaling air past them. ◊ **glass harmonica** [Mid-18thC. Via Italian *armonica* from Latin *harmonicus* HARMONIC.]

harmonic analysis n. MATH the representation of a periodic function by a series of sines and cosines, especially by a Fourier series

harmonic distortion n. the unwanted presence of distorted frequencies at the output of an electronic device, e.g. the output of an audio amplifier

harmonic mean n. the reciprocal of the arithmetic mean of the reciprocals of a finite set of numbers

harmonic minor scale n. a version of the minor scale in which the seventh note is raised by a semitone, both ascending and descending

harmonic motion n. = **simple harmonic motion**

harmonic progression n. any sequence of numbers whose reciprocals form an arithmetic progression, e.g. 1/2, 1/5, 1/8, 1/11

harmonics /haar mónniks/ n. the branch of science that deals with the physical properties of musical sound (*takes a singular verb*)

harmonic series n. any infinite series of numbers constructed by adding the numbers in a harmonic progression to one another, e.g. 1/2+1/5+1/8+ 1/11

harmonious /haar móni əss/ adj. **1. RELATING TO HARMONY** relating to or sounding in harmony **2. BLENDING PLEASANTLY** having a pleasing combination of parts or colours **3. SHOWING ACCORD** characterized by friendly agreement or accord —**harmoniously** adv. —**harmoniousness** n.

harmonise vti. = **harmonize**

harmonist /haármənist/ n. **1. MAKER OF HARMONY** sb who creates musical harmony well **2. SB STUDYING PARALLEL TEXTS** sb who researches and tries to find similarities in parallel texts, especially the four Gospels —**harmonistic** /haármə nístik/ adj. —**harmonistically** /-nístikli/ adv.

harmonium /haar móni əm/ n. a type of organ in which a pair of bellows operated by the player's feet blow air into the reeds to produce sound [Mid-19thC. Via French from either Latin *harmonia* 'harmony' or Greek *harmonios* 'harmonious'.]

harmonize /haármə nīz/ (**-nizes, -nizing, -nized**), **harmonise** (**-nises, -nising, -nised**) v. **1.** vti. **BLEND PLEASINGLY** to blend pleasingly, be in a pleasant combination, or make things combine pleasantly **2.** vt. **MAKE SYSTEMS SIMILAR** to make rules, regulations, or systems similar or in accord with each other **3.** vt. **ADD HARMONY TO A MELODY** to provide a harmony for a melody **4.** vi. **PLAY IN HARMONY** to sing or play musical instruments together in harmony —**harmonizable** adj. —**harmonization** /haármo nī záysh'n/ n. —**harmonizer** /haármə nīzər/ n.

harmonized sales tax n. in the Canadian provinces of Nova Scotia, New Brunswick, and Newfoundland, a tax combining the goods and services tax and the provincial sales tax

harmony /haárməni/ (*plural* **-nies**) n. **1. PLEASING COMBINATION OF SOUNDS** a pleasing combination of musical sounds **2. HAPPY AGREEMENT** a situation in which there is agreement **3. PLEASANTNESS IN THE ARRANGEMENT OF PARTS** a pleasing effect produced by an arrangement of things, parts, or colours **4. STUDY OF CHORDS IN MUSIC** the study of the way in which musical chords are constructed and function in relation to one another **5. NOTES SUNG OR PLAYED TOGETHER** any combination of notes that are sung or played at the same time. Changing harmony is one of the most characteristic features of Western music, providing momentum and richness to the melody. **6. STUDY OF TEXTS** a study or collation of the similarities in parallel texts, particularly the four Gospels **7. PARALLEL TEXT** a book or manuscript in which several versions of the same text, often a biblical text, are laid out in parallel columns ○ *a Gospel harmony* [14thC. Via French *harmonie* from Greek *harmonia* 'agreement, concord', from *harmozein* 'to fit together'.]

Harnack /haárn ak/, **Adolf von** (1851–1930) German theologian. One of the leading Protestant scholars of his day, he advocated a return to biblical Christianity. His major work was *History of Dogma* (1886–90).

harness /haárnəss/ n. **1. LEATHER STRAPS FOR AN ANIMAL** a set of straps fixed together and fitted to an animal such as a horse so that it can be attached to a cart or carriage for pulling **2. STRAPS FITTED TO A PERSON** an arrangement of straps fitted to sb to fasten the person to sth or to keep the person in position **3. ARMOUR** the armour worn by a soldier, or by a mounted soldier and the soldier's horse (*archaic*) ■ vt. (**-nesses, -nessing, -nessed**) **1. FIT AN ANIMAL WITH A HARNESS** to fit a horse with a harness on an animal **2. GET CONTROL OF AND USE STH** to gain control of sth and use it for some purpose **3. FIT SB WITH ARMOUR** to equip sb with

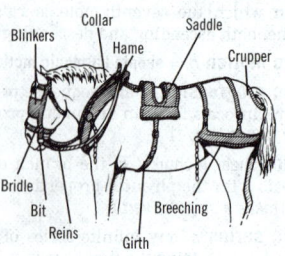

Harness

armour (*archaic*) [13thC. Via Old French *harneis* from assumed Old Norse *hernest* 'provisions for an army', from *herr* 'army'.] —**harnesser** *n*. ◇ **in harness 1.** doing your usual work **2.** working together cooperatively with a person or group

harness horse *n*. a horse that is used to pull a vehicle or for racing

harness race *n*. a horse race in which specially bred horses pull small carriages around a course wearing special harnesses to ensure that they move as required by rule

Harney Peak /haárni-/ mountain in the Black Hills, southwestern South Dakota, and the highest point in the state. Height: 2,207 m/7,242 ft.

Harold I /hárrəld/, **King of the English** (*d.* 1040) Danish-born English monarch. He was the illegitimate son of Canute II, and ruled England (1037–40) in constant strife against his half-brother, Hardecanute. Known as **Harold Harefoot**

Harold II, King of the English (1020?–66). The last Saxon king of England (1064–66), he was killed fighting William the Conqueror at the Battle of Hastings.

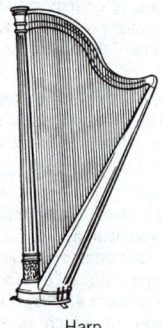

Harp

harp /haarp/ *n*. **1.** TRIANGULAR STRINGED INSTRUMENT a triangular-shaped instrument that has a curved neck and strings stretched between the neck and the body, at an angle to the sound box. The modern orchestral harp is large and played by a seated player. **2.** HARMONICA a reed harmonica (*informal*) ■ *vi.* (**harps, harping, harped**) PLAY THE HARP to play the harp [Old English *hearpe*, from prehistoric Germanic] —**harper** *n*. —**harpist** *n*.

harp on *vti.* to repeat or stress sth in a way that becomes tiresome

harpoon /haar poon/ *n*. WEAPON SIMILAR TO SPEAR a long

Harpoon

pointed piece of metal that is attached to a cord and thrown or fired from a gun in order to capture whales or other large sea animals ■ *vt.* (**-poons, -pooning, -pooned**) CATCH STH USING HARPOON to catch a whale or other large sea animal using a harpoon [Early 17thC. From Old French *harpon* 'clamp', from *harpe* 'dog's claw, clamp' from, ultimately, Greek *harpē* 'sickle'.] —**harpooneer** /haár poo neér/ *n*. —**harpooner** /haar poónər/ *n*.

harp seal *n*. a brownish-grey earless seal that is whitish when very young and lives in coastal regions and on ice floes of the North Atlantic Ocean. It was formerly hunted for its fur but is now protected from large-scale commercial hunting. Latin name: *Pagophilus groenlandicus*. [*Harp* from the shape of the seal's markings]

harpsichord /haárpsi kawrd/ *n*. a keyboard instrument resembling a piano and having horizontal strings plucked by leather or quill points connected to the keys. It was superseded by the piano in the 19th century. [Early 17thC. From French *harpechorde*, from Latin *harpa* 'harp' + *chorda* 'string'.] —**harpsichordist** *n*.

Harpur /haárpər/, **Charles** (1813–68) Australian poet and playwright. Considered by many to be Australia's first major poet, he wrote *The Bushranger* (1853).

harpy /haárpi/ (*plural* -**pies**) *n*. an offensive term for a woman that deliberately insults her attitude towards others in the pursuit of personal goals (*insult*) [From HARPY]

Harpy /haárpi/ (*plural* -**pies**) *n*. in Greek mythology, a monster that was half woman half bird of prey. The Harpies were thought to live on the Strophades Islands and carry out acts of vengeance on behalf of the gods. [14thC. Directly or via French from Latin *harpyia*, from Greek *harpuiai* (plural) 'snatchers', from *harpazein* 'to seize'.]

harpy eagle *n*. a huge eagle with a black back, white underparts, and a grey head with a double crest, native to lowland forests from southern Mexico to northern Argentina. It feeds on monkeys, sloths, opossums, and snakes. Latin name: *Harpia harpyja*.

harquebus /haárkwibəss, -kwə-/, **arquebus** /aár-/ *n*. an early type of portable gun supported on a tripod by a hook, or on a forked post [Mid-16thC. Via French (*h*)*arquebuse* from, ultimately, Middle Dutch *hakebus*, Middle High German *hake(n)būhse*, or Middle Low German *hakebusse*, literally 'hook-gun' (because supported by a hook); see HACKBUT.] —**harquebusier** /-seer/ *n*.

harridan /hárridən/ *n*. an offensive term for a woman that deliberately insults her age and temperament (*offensive*) [Late 17thC. Origin uncertain: perhaps an alteration of French *haridelle* 'old horse, gaunt woman', of unknown origin.]

Harrier

harrier[1] /hárri ər/ (*plural* -**ers** *or* -**er**) *n*. a slender hawk with long wings and tail that hunts by flying low over marshland and grassland to catch mice, snakes, frogs, and fish. Genus: *Circus*. [Mid-16thC. Formed from *harrow* 'to rob', variant of HARRY; later influenced by HARRIER[3].]

harrier[2] /hárri ər/ *n*. **1.** ZOOL DOG FOR RABBIT HUNTING a small hound, resembling a foxhound, used for hunting hares or rabbits **2.** ATHLETICS RUNNER a cross-country runner (*often used in the name of athletics clubs*) [15thC. Origin uncertain: perhaps formed from HARE

(later influenced by HARRIER[3]) on the model of French *lévrier* 'greyhound', literally 'dog for hunting hares'.]

harrier[3] *n*. sb who harries sb with repeated verbal or physical attacks, or sb who raids or pillages a place

Harris /hárriss/ the southern part of the island of Lewis in the Outer Hebrides, Scotland. It is famous for its tweed. Area: 500 sq. km/193 sq. mi.

Harris, Sir Arthur Travers (1892–1984) British airman. Commander-in-chief of the RAF Bomber Command (1942–45), he supervised the bombing of Germany's industrial heartland during World War II. Known as **Bomber Harris**

Harris, Max (*b.* 1921) Australian writer and publisher. A founder of the avant-garde journal *Angry Penguins*, he wrote the verse collection *The Angry Eye* (1973). Full name **Maxwell Henley Harris**

Harris, Rolf (*b.* 1930) Australian artist and entertainer. He had several hit records and presented television shows in Australia and the United Kingdom.

Harrisburg /hárriss burg/ city and capital of Pennsylvania, located in the southern part of the state. Population: 52,376 (1990).

Benjamin Harrison

Harrison /hárriss'n/, **Benjamin** (1726?–91) American patriot. A longtime member of the Virginia House of Burgesses (1749–75), he presided over the Continental Congress (1774–77) and signed the Declaration of Independence (1776). He was governor of Virginia (1781–84).

Harrison, Benjamin (1833–1901) US statesman and 23rd President of the United States. The grandson of William Henry Harrison, he was a Republican senator (1881–87) before his election as president. His administration (1889–93) enacted protectionist tariffs and other pro-business legislation.

Harrison, George (*b.* 1943) British musician. The lead guitarist with The Beatles, he later turned to solo music projects and film production.

Harrison, Sir Rex (1908–90) British actor. He starred in comedies including *Blithe Spirit* (1945) and *My Fair Lady* (1964), for which he won an Academy Award. Full name **Sir Reginald Carey Harrison**

Harrison, Tony (*b.* 1937) British poet. Known for his adaptations of Greek drama, his poetical works include 'Earthworks' (1964) and 'V' (1985).

William Henry Harrison

Harrison, William Henry (1773–1841) US statesman and 9th President of the United States. He was elected president in 1840 on the strength of his military successes against the Native North Americans and in the War of 1812, but died after one month in office.

Harris tweed /hárris-/ n. a thick woven woollen cloth that is traditionally made in Harris in the Western Isles of Scotland

Harrogate /hárrəgət/ spa town in North Yorkshire, northern England. It has 87 mineral springs. Population: 149,700 (1994).

Harrovian /hə róvi ən/ n. sb educated or being educated at Harrow School [Early 19thC. Formed from modern Latin *Harrovia* 'Harrow'.] —**Harrovian** adj.

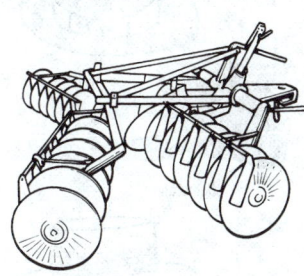

Harrow

harrow[1] /hárrō/ n. FARM MACHINE FOR BREAKING UP SOIL a piece of farm equipment with sharp teeth or discs that is used to break up soil and clods of dirt and to even up a ploughed field ■ vti. (-rows, -rowing, -rowed) BREAK UP LAND to break up land by pulling a harrow over it, or be broken up with a harrow [12thC. From Old Norse *herfi*.] —**harrower** n.

harrow[2] vt. = **harry** (archaic)

harrowing /hárrō ing/ adj. evoking feelings of fear, horror, or disgust ○ *harrowing scenes of hurricane devastation*

Harrow School /hárrō-/ n. a public school for boys in northwestern London. It was founded in 1571.

harrumph /hə rúmf/ (-rumphs, -rumphing, -rumphed) vti. 1. MUTTER CRITICAL REMARKS to make comments of criticism and displeasure, often muttering so that listeners are aware of the tone but cannot hear the exact words 2. CLEAR THE THROAT to clear the throat, or make a noise that resembles the sound of clearing the throat [Mid-20thC. An imitation of the sound.]

harry /hárri/ (-ries, -rying, -ried), **harrow** archaic /hárrō/ (-rows, -rowing, -rowed) vt. 1. CAUSE DISTRESS BY REPEATED ATTACKS to cause sb mental, emotional, or physical distress by repeated verbal or physical attacks ○ *The crows have harried the cat so badly that it no longer goes outside.* 2. RAID OR PILLAGE to raid or pillage an area, or a town or village, especially during a war [Old English *hergian* 'to ravage (literally as an army does)', from a prehistoric Germanic word meaning 'army', which is also the ancestor of English *harangue* and *herald*]

harsh /haársh/ adj. 1. DIFFICULT TO ENDURE difficult to live in or endure because very uncomfortable or inhospitable ○ *a rugged and harsh environment* ○ *a harsh winter* ○ *harsh prison conditions* 2. SEVERELY CRITICAL severely scrutinizing, critical, and rigid in manner 3. PUNITIVE extremely exacting to the point of being punitive ○ *Harsh penalties will be imposed.* 4. JARRING jarring or unpleasant to the senses [14thC. Origin uncertain: perhaps from Scandinavian.] —**harshen** vti. —**harshly** adv. —**harshness** n.

Harsha /haársha/ n. a descendant of the Guptas in India, who created a loose empire in northern India between AD 616 and 654

harslet n. = **haslet**

hart /haart/ (plural **harts** or **hart**) n. a male deer, especially a male red deer over five years of age [Old English *heor(o)t*. Ultimately from an Indo-European word meaning 'horn, head', which is also the ancestor of English *carrot*, *rhinoceros*, and *reindeer*.]

Hart /haart/, **Pro** (b. 1928) Australian painter, noted for his naive style and his depictions of life in and around the central Australian town of Broken Hill. Real name **Kevin Charles Hart**

hartal /haar taál, hur taál, haár taal/ n. S Asia in the Indian subcontinent, a closing of shops and suspending of work, especially as an indication or means of political protest [Early 20thC. From Hindi *hartāl*, literally 'shop locking'.]

Hartebeest

hartebeest /haárti beest/ (plural **-beests** or **-beest**) n. a large social antelope of African sub-Saharan grasslands that is fawn to dark brown in colour, with high shoulders, a sloping back, and a long head with large ringed horns. Genus: *Alcelaphus*. [Late 18thC. From obsolete Afrikaans, 'deer, hart', literally 'hart-beast'.]

Hartlepool /haártli pool/ industrial town and seaport in northeastern England. Population: 92,200 (1995).

Hartley /haártli/, **David** (1732–1813) British politician and inventor. He assisted Benjamin Franklin in drafting the Treaty of Paris (1783) and invented a house fire-proofing system.

Hartnell /haártnəl/, **Norman** (1901–79) British couturier. He was known for his tailored women's suits, elaborate gowns, and, most notably, Elizabeth II's wedding dress. Full name **Norman Bishop Hartnell**

Hartog /haár tog/, **Dirk** (fl. 16th–17th centuries) Dutch navigator. His Dutch East India Company expedition to Java in 1616 instead reached Australia, where he made the earliest recorded exploration of the west coast.

hart's-tongue (plural **hart's-tongues** or **hart's-tongue**) n. a Eurasian evergreen fern that has narrow undivided fronds bearing rows of spore-producing organs. Latin name: *Phyllitis scolopendrium*. [Translation of medieval Latin *lingua cervi* (from the shape of its fronds)]

harum-scarum /háirəm skáirəm/ adj. exhibiting reckless disorganized abandon ○ *Her outfit looks harum-scarum, but it's a planned effect.* [Late 17thC. Origin uncertain: probably a rhyming alteration of HARE (verb) + SCARE.] —**harum-scarum** adv.

haruspex /hə rú speks/ (plural **-pices** /-spi seez/), **aruspex** /ə rú-/ (plural **-pices**) n. in ancient Rome, a priest who attempted to foretell the future, especially by examining the entrails of animals [15thC. From Latin, of uncertain origin: perhaps literally 'sb who looks at entrails'.]

Harvard system /haárvərd-/ n. a bibliographic reference system in academic publishing, in which the author and date are given in the text, and the full reference is supplied in a general list of references

Harvard University /haárvərd-/ the oldest university in the United States, founded in 1636 in Massachusetts

harvest /haárvist/ n. 1. QUANTITY OF CROP the quantity of a crop that is gathered or ripens during a particular season ○ *a record harvest of wheat for Canada's grain farmers* ○ *Variations in the world harvest can be tracked to 0.1 per cent.* 2. CROP THAT IS GATHERED OR RIPENS the crop that is gathered or ripens during a particular season ○ *A few days of rain can destroy an entire harvest of strawberries.* 3. SEASON IN WHICH CROPS ARE GATHERED the season during which crop plants mature and crops are gathered 4. CONSEQUENCES OF PREVIOUS ACTION the results of past or prior actions or behaviour ■ v. (-vests, -vesting, -vested) 1. vti. GATHER CROP to gather a crop for use or sale ○ *The wood is harvested sustainably.* 2. vt. GATHER NONPLANT ITEMS to collect sth other than a plant crop,

e.g. fish raised commercially in a hatchery 3. vt. REAP RESULTS to reap the results of past or prior actions or behaviour, whether good or bad ○ *In the aftermath of a violent civil war the beleaguered people harvested nothing but sorrow.* [Old English *hærfest* 'autumn' ('time for gathering crops'). Ultimately from an Indo-European word meaning 'to gather', which is also the ancestor of English *carpet* and *scarce*.] —**harvestable** adj.

harvester /haárvist ər/ n. 1. MACHINE THAT GATHERS CROPS a machine that gathers crops from the fields, especially a combine harvester 2. SB WHO GATHERS CROPS sb who gathers crops, especially by hand ○ *Coffee harvesters are at risk from the bites of poisonous spiders.*

harvest festival n. a Christian service of thanksgiving after a completed harvest

harvest fly n. a cicada, native to the United States, that sings loudly near the end of the summer. Genus: *Tibicen*.

harvest home n. 1. GATHERING OF HARVEST the gathering of the harvest, especially its safe completion 2. CELEBRATION OF HARVEST a celebration of the completion of the harvest (hyphenated when used before a noun) ○ *a harvest-home dance*

harvestman /haárvist mən/ (plural **-men** /-mən/) n. 1. INSECTS = **daddy longlegs** n. 2 2. AGRIC AGRICULTURAL LABOURER an agricultural labourer, especially, before agriculture became mechanized, one who left home to find work at harvest time

harvest moon n. the full moon nearest to the autumnal equinox. It rises for several nights at nearly the same time at points successively further north on the eastern horizon.

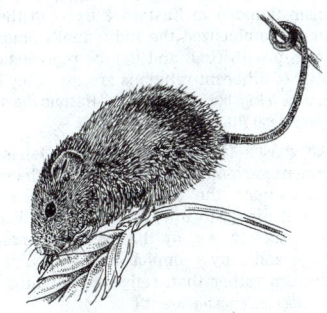

Harvest mouse

harvest mouse n. a small reddish-brown Eurasian mouse that often lives in fields of corn and other grain. Latin name: *Micromys minutus*.

Harvey /haárvi/, **William** (1578–1657) English physician. He discovered the circulation of the blood, and formally published his work on the circulatory system in 1628.

Harwich /hárrij, -ich/ town and seaport in Essex, eastern England, an important ferry terminal

Harwood /haár wŏŏd/, **Gwen** (1920–95) Australian poet. Influenced by the philosophy of Wittgenstein, her published works include *The Lion's Bride* (1981) and *Bone Scan* (1990). Born **Gwendoline Nessie Foster**

Harz Mountains /haárts-/ mountain range in central Germany, between the Elbe and Weser rivers south of Brunswick. The highest peak is Brocken. Height: 1,141 m/3,743 ft.

has 3rd person present singular of **have**

has-been n. sb who was popular or important in the past but is now largely forgotten (informal) ○ *It's hard to be a hero one day and a has-been the next.*

Hašek /hásh ek/, **Jaroslav** (1883–1923) Czechoslovakian writer. He is best known for his four-volume unfinished satirical novel *The Good Soldier Schweik* (1920–23).

hash[1] /hash/ n. 1. hash, hash mark SYMBOL # the symbol #, especially on a telephone keypad or a computer keyboard. US term **pound sign** 2. COOK FRIED DISH OF POTATOES AND MEAT a dish made of cooked potatoes or other vegetables, usually combined with chopped-up pieces of cooked meat, and reheated, usually by frying until golden brown ○ *corned-beef hash* ■ vt.

(hashes, hashing, hashed) COMPUT APPLY ALGORITHM TO A STRING to apply an algorithm to a character string, especially in order to find an address of a record [Late 16thC. From French *hacher* 'to hack, cut into small pieces', from *hache* 'axe' (see HATCHET).] ◇ **make a hash of sth** to do sth very badly (*informal*) ○ *I made a real hash of the exam – I couldn't answer any questions.* ◇ **settle sb's hash** to assert yourself over sb, especially sb hostile or troublesome (*informal*) **hash out, hash over** *vt. US* = **thrash out** ○ *They hashed out their differences with an arbitrator*

hash² /hash/ *n.* hashish (*slang*) [Mid-20thC. Shortening.]

hash browns *npl. US* cooked potatoes that are chopped up, sometimes with onions, and fried until golden brown. Occasionally, hash browns are formed into small cakes or patties.

HaShem /hásh em/ *n.* in Judaism, a substitute word used when referring to God in contexts other than prayers or scriptural readings, because the name for God is too holy for such use [From Hebrew, literally 'the name']

hashish /háshish, há sheesh, ha sheesh/, **hasheesh** /há sheesh, ha sheesh/ *n.* a purified resin, prepared from the flowering tops of the female cannabis plant, that is smoked or chewed for its narcotic and intoxicating properties and is widely illegal [Late 16thC. From Arabic *ḥašīš*, literally 'dry herb, powdered hemp' (source of English *assassin*).]

hash mark *n.* = **hash¹** *n.* 1 ■ AMERICAN FOOTBALL LINE FOR FOOTBALL POSITION a line indicating how close to a sideline a football may be at the start of a play

Hasid /hássid/ (*plural* **-sidim** /-dim/), **Hassid** (*plural* **-sidim**), **Chassid** (*plural* **-sidim**), **Chasid** (*plural* **-sidim**) *n.* a member of a Jewish movement of popular mysticism founded in Eastern Europe in the 18th century. It emphasized the individual's emotional relationship with God, and is now represented by a number of different religious groups. [Early 19thC. From Hebrew *ḥāsīd*, literally 'pious'.] —**Hasidic** /ha síddik/ *adj.* —**Hasidism** /ha síddizəm/ *n.*

Haskalah /háskə láa/, **Haskala** *n.* the Jewish enlightenment movement, originating in 18th-century Germany under the influence of Moses Mendelssohn. It aimed to integrate Jews into Western European society, e.g. by the use of German, not Yiddish, and by emphasizing secular intellectualism rather than religious learning. [From Hebrew *haśkālāh* 'enlightenment']

hasky /háski/ *adj.* (*regional informal*) **1.** DRY without rain **2.** QUICK-TEMPERED sarcastic or quick-tempered [Mid-17thC. Formed from variant of HARSH.]

haslet /háyzlət, házlət/, **harslet** /háarzlət/ *n.* meat loaf, well seasoned with herbs, made from the offal of pigs [14thC. From Old French *hastelet*, literally 'small piece of meat roasted on a spit', from *haste* 'spit', of uncertain origin.]

hasn't /házz'nt/ *contr.* has not

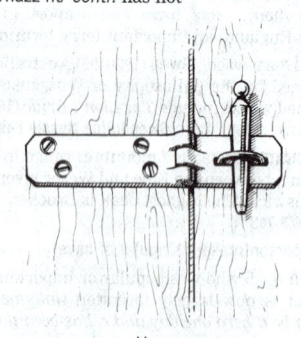

Hasp

hasp /haasp/ *n.* HINGED METAL FASTENING a hinged metal fastening that fits over a staple and is secured by a pin, bolt, or padlock ■ *vt.* (**hasps, hasping, hasped**) CLOSE STH WITH A HASP to close sth, especially a door or window, with a hasp [Old English *hæpse* 'fastening' (*hæpsian*, verb), from prehistoric Germanic]

Hassan II /hə saán/, **King of Morocco** (*b.* 1929. Educated in France, he ruled Morocco from 1961. Full name **Muhammad Hassan**

Hassid *n.* = **Hasid**

hassium /hássi əm/ *n.* an extremely rare, unstable chemical element produced in high-energy atomic collisions. Symbol **Hs** [Late 20thC. From modern Latin, from Latin *Hassias* 'Hesse', German state where it was discovered.]

hassle /háss'l/ *n.* DIFFICULTY, TROUBLE, OR AGGRAVATION a source or the experience of aggravation or annoying difficulty (*informal*) ○ *It's just not worth the hassle.* ■ *vt.* (**-sles, -sling, -sled**) KEEP BOTHERING OR ANNOYING SB to bother or annoy sb, especially by continually asking that person to do sth (*informal*) ○ *Stop hassling me about washing the car.* [Late 19thC. Origin uncertain: perhaps a blend of HAGGLE and TUSSLE. Originally a dialect verb meaning 'to hack at'.]

hassock /hássək/ *n.* **1.** CUSHION ON WHICH TO KNEEL a thick firm cushion used for kneeling on, especially in church **2.** GRASS CLUMP a thick clump of grass **3.** *US* FURNITURE = **pouf** [Old English *hassuc* 'clump of grass', of unknown origin]

hast /hast/ *vt.* 2nd person present singular of **have** (*archaic*)

haste /hayst/ *n.* GREAT SPEED great speed, especially in situations where time is limited (*formal*) ○ *Make haste, or you will be very late! ○ The general proceeded with haste to his headquarters.* ■ *vti.* (**hastes, hasting, hasted**) HURRY to hasten (*archaic literary*) [13thC. Via Old French from a prehistoric Germanic word.]

hasten /háyss'n/ (**-tens, -tening, -tened**) *v.* **1.** *vt.* SPEED STH UP to make sth happen more quickly ○ *A holiday would hasten his recovery.* **2.** *vi.* GO SOMEWHERE QUICKLY to go somewhere quickly or without delay **3.** *vi.* DO STH IMMEDIATELY to do or say sth without delay, often in order to correct what might otherwise be a misleading impression ○ *'But she's perfectly right', he hastened to add.* ◇ **more haste less speed** a way of saying that it is not worth rushing sth because too many mistakes will be made

Hastings /háystingz/ *historic* seaside town in East Sussex, southern England. The Battle of Hastings (1066) was fought nearby. Population: 82,600 (1995).

Hastings, Warren (1732–1818) British statesman and colonial administrator. As the first governor-general of India (1774–85), he secured British rule and enacted legal and administrative reforms. His impeachment in parliament for high crimes and misdemeanours (1788–95) exonerated him, but destroyed his career and his fortune.

hasty /háysti/ (**-ier, -iest**) *adj.* done, taking place, or acting in a hurry because of impetuosity or lack of time ○ *a hasty marriage* —**hastily** *adv.* —**hastiness** *n.*

hasty pudding *n.* a type of sweet milk pudding made with flour, semolina, or tapioca [*Hasty* of uncertain origin: perhaps because the pudding can be made speedily]

hat /hat/ *n.* **1.** HEAD COVERING a covering for the head, worn for protection from the weather or as a fashion accessory ○ *The children hung their hats and coats up when they came in.* **2.** AREA OF RESPONSIBILITY used for a single area of interest, knowledge, or responsibility in an individual with many interests and responsibilities ○ *She put on her accountant's hat and gave the committee some suggestions for maximizing profits.* [Old English *hæt(t)* 'hat, head-covering', via a prehistoric Germanic word meaning 'hood, cowl' from an Indo-European base meaning 'to cover', which is also the ancestor of English *hood*] —**hatted** *adj.* ◇ **hang up your hat 1.** to retire from work ○ *When this project's finished he's going to hang up his hat and retire to the country.* **2.** to settle down to a calmer, more stable lifestyle following an extended period of stress or activity ○ *Children of military personnel move so frequently that they'd like to find just one place in which to hang up their hats.* ◇ **hats off to sb** a way of saying that sb has gained your respect or admiration ◇ **keep sth under your hat** to keep sth secret ◇ **my hat!** a way of saying that sth is ridiculous or not true (*dated*) ◇ **pass the hat round** to collect contributions for sb or sth ◇ **pull sth out of the hat** to do, accomplish, make, or get sth as if by a magic trick when the resources appear to be unavailable (*informal*) ◇ **take your hat off to sb** to acknowledge admiration or respect for sb ○ *You have to take your hat off to her – she's stuck by him for 25 years.* ◇ **talk through your hat** to talk nonsense

Skullcap

Top hat

Pillbox

Fedora

Deerstalker

Boater

Bowler

Trilby

Astrakhan

Stovepipe

Cloche

Beret

Hat

○ *You're talking through your hat, and I don't take a word of it seriously.* ◇ **throw your hat into the ring** to volunteer to take part in a particular contest ○ *I didn't think I'd get the job, but I decided to throw my hat into the ring anyway.*

hatband /hát band/ *n.* a thin strip of leather, cloth, ribbon, or other material that is fixed round a hat just above the brim

hatbox /hát boks/ *n.* a large hard box with a removable or liftable lid, used for storing, carrying, and protecting a hat or hats

hatch¹ /hach/ *n.* **1.** TYPE OF DOOR a door cut into the floor or ceiling of sth, especially on a boat or an aircraft. It is lifted to provide access to the area below or above it. A hatch may also provide access to an attic or cellar in a building. **2.** SMALL HOLE BETWEEN TWO ROOMS a small connecting hole in a wall between two rooms, or the small doors that cover this hole ○ *an escape hatch* ○ *There's a serving hatch between the kitchen and the living room.* [Old English *hæcc* 'lower half of a door, wicket'. From a prehistoric Germanic base of unknown origin that is also the ancestor of Dutch *hek* 'gate'.]

hatch² /hach/ *v.* (**hatches, hatching, hatched**) **1.** *vi.* **BREAK OPEN FOR RELEASE OF YOUNG** to break open so that the young inside may be released **2.** *vi.* **COME OUT OF EGG** to emerge from an egg **3.** *vt.* **CAUSE YOUNG TO EMERGE FROM EGG** to cause a young organism, e.g. a chick, fish, or insect, to emerge from its egg ○ *Birds hatch their chicks by sitting on the nests.* **4.** *vt.* **SECRETLY DEVISE A PLOT** to secretly devise a plot, plan, or scheme, usually an illicit or illegal one, or one that is ill-advised in some way ■ *n.* **YOUNG ORGANISMS NEWLY HATCHED** a group of young organisms, e.g. chicks, fish, or insects, that have just recently emerged from eggs ○ *This hatch contains more males than females.* [15thC. Origin uncertain.]

hatch out *vi.* to hatch from an egg

hatch³ /hach/ (**hatches, hatching, hatched**) *vti.* in graphic art, to mark or cover sth with parallel crossed lines to show shading, or be marked in this way [15thC. From French *hacher* 'to chop', from *hache* 'axe' (see HATCHET).] —**hatching** *n.*

Hatchback

hatchback /hach bak/ *n.* a type of car with a door at the back that is hinged from the roof to allow easy access to storage space behind the rear seats. The storage space usually has a removable shelf between the top of the seats and the rear window, which hides what is being kept below. ○ *a five-door hatchback*

hatchery /hácheri/ (*plural* **-ies**) *n.* a place where fish or poultry eggs are hatched commercially under artificial conditions ○ *a fish hatchery*

Hatchet

hatchet /háchit/ *n.* a small axe that can be used with one hand ○ *wield a hatchet* [14thC. From French *hachette*, literally 'small axe', from *hache* 'axe' (source of English *hash¹*), from medieval Latin *hapia*, from prehistoric Germanic.] ◇ **bury the hatchet** to make peace with sb after a disagreement ○ *They fell out years ago, but it looks as if they've finally decided to bury the hatchet.* ◇ **do a hatchet job on sb** *or* **sth** criticize sb or sth unfairly, especially in print (*informal*) ○ *The reviewer did a hatchet job on the author of the novel.*

hatchet face *n.* an unpleasantly long thin face with sharp or gaunt features —**hatchet-faced** *adj.*

hatchet man *n.* **1.** **SB EMPLOYED TO MAKE CUTS** sb who is employed to do sth unpopular or unscrupulous, especially to make cuts in staff or funding (*informal*) **2.** *US, Can* **HIRED KILLER** sb who is hired to murder another person (*slang*)

hatchling /háchling/ *n.* a bird, fish, insect, or other organism that has just hatched from an egg

hatchment /háchmənt/ *n.* a diamond-shaped panel bearing the coat of arms of sb who has died [Early 16thC. Origin uncertain: probably from obsolete French *hachement*, alteration of Old French *acesmement* 'adornment', from *acesmer* 'to adorn', of unknown origin.]

hatchway /hach way/ *n.* = **hatch¹** *n.* **2**

hate /hayt/ *v.* (**hates, hating, hated**) **1.** *vt.* **DISLIKE SB OR STH INTENSELY** to dislike sb or sth intensely, often in a way that evokes feelings of anger, hostility, or animosity ○ *Love her or hate her, you have to admit she's got a great singing voice.* ○ *Having come to hate her husband, the defendant admits that she attempted to poison him.* **2.** *vti.* **HAVE STRONG DISTASTE FOR** to have strong distaste or aversion for sth, sb, or sth that has to be done ○ *I hate this show; it's so boring.* ○ *They hate cleaning out the stable every day.* ○ *I hate to say it, but I know we're going to lose.* ■ *n.* **1.** **FEELING OF INTENSE DISLIKE OR ANGER** a feeling of intense dislike, anger, hostility, or animosity ○ *You could see the hate in his eyes.* **2.** **STH HATED** sth that is hated [Old English *hete* (noun) and *hatian* (verb). Ultimately from an Indo-European word perhaps meaning 'strong feeling', which is also the ancestor of English *heinous*.] —**hateable** *adj.* —**hated** *adj.* —**hater** *n.*

——— **WORD KEY: SYNONYMS** ———
See Synonyms at *dislike*.

hateful /hayt f'l/ *adj.* **1.** **SPITEFULLY MALEVOLENT** characterized by malevolence or spite **2.** **EVOKING FEELINGS OF HATRED** eliciting feelings or reactions of hatred, detestation, or abhorrence —**hatefully** *adv.* —**hatefulness** *n.*

hate mail *n.* mail that expresses the sender's anger about sth, usually towards the recipient, in a threatening or offensive way

Hatfield /hat feeld/ *n.* town in Hertfordshire, southeastern England, designated a 'New Town' in 1948. Population: 31,104 (1991).

hatful /hat fool/ *n.* a large quantity or number of sth ○ *received a hatful of compliments on the performance*

hath /hath/ 3rd person present singular of **have** (*archaic*)

Hathaway /háthə way/, **Anne** (1556–1623) English wife of Shakespeare. She was born into a farming family, and married William Shakespeare, eight years her junior, in 1582.

hatha yoga /háthə-, húttə-/ *n.* a low-impact yoga that helps to regulate breathing by exercises consisting of postures and stretches intended to sustain healthy bodily functioning and induce emotional calmness [From Sanskrit, literally 'force yoga']

hatpin /hat pin/ *n.* a long thin pin, often with a decoration at the end, that is pushed through a hat and into the hair to keep the hat securely on the head

hatred /háytrid/ *n.* a feeling of intense dislike, anger, hostility, or animosity [12thC. From HATE + a suffix formed from Old English *ræden* 'state, condition' (found also in English *kindred*).]

——— **WORD KEY: SYNONYMS** ———
See Synonyms at *dislike*.

Hatshepsut /hat shép soot/, **Queen of Egypt** (1520?–1483? BC). She crowned herself pharaoh in 1503 BC after years of ruling jointly with her husband, Thutmose II, and his son, Thutmose III.

hat stand *n.* a tall free-standing piece of furniture

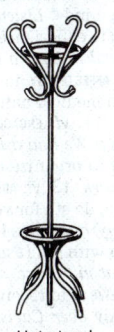
Hat stand

consisting of a base with a pole fixed into it with hooks round the top on which hats, coats, and umbrellas can be hung

hatter /háttər/ *n.* sb who makes and sells hats

Hatteras, Cape /-háttərəss/ promontory projecting into the Atlantic Ocean in eastern North Carolina renowned for treacherous weather conditions

Hattersley /háttərzli/, **Roy, Lord** (*b.* 1932) British politician. Elected to parliament in 1964, he was deputy leader of the Labour Party (1983–92), and was made a life peer in 1997. Full name **Roy Sydney George, Lord Hattersley**

hat trick *n.* a series of three wins or successes, especially three goals scored by the same player in a game of football [Origin uncertain: probably from the former cricketing practice of awarding a hat to a bowler who took three wickets with three consecutive balls]

hauberk /háw burk/ *n.* a long, sleeveless, tunic made of chain mail. It was originally intended as protection just for the neck and shoulders but it developed into a longer tunic in the 12th and 13th centuries. [13thC. Via Old French *hau(s)berc* from a prehistoric Germanic word meaning literally 'neck-protector', the first element of which is also the ancestor of English *hawse*.]

haugh /haw, haakh/ *n.* *Scotland* a low-lying stretch of land in a river valley, often unproductive because of frequent flooding [Origin uncertain: probably from Old English *healh* 'corner, nook, small hollow in a slope']

Haughey /háwhi/, **Charles** (*b.* 1925) Irish politician. He was leader of the Fianna Fáil party (1979–92) and prime minister of Ireland (1979–81, 1982, and 1987–92).

haughty /háwti/ (**-tier, -tiest**) *adj.* behaving in a superior, condescending, or arrogant way ○ *She always took a haughty tone with the landlady.* [Mid-16thC. Formed from archaic *haught*, from French *haut(e)* 'high'.] —**haughtily** *adv.* —**haughtiness** *n.*

haul /hawl/ *v.* (**hauls, hauling, hauled**) **1.** *vt.* **MOVE STH WITH EFFORT** to transport sth that is heavy and bulky from one place to another **2.** *vt.* **PULL OR DRAG STH** to pull or drag sth with continuous and laborious movements **3.** *vt.* **SAILING CHANGE COURSE** to change a vessel's course so as to sail closer to the wind **4.** *vi.* **NAUT BLOW CLOSER TO BOW** to blow from a direction that is closer to a vessel's bow **5.** *vt.* **SHIPPING HOIST INTO DRY DOCK** to hoist a vessel from the water into a dry dock, e.g. to make repairs ■ *n.* **1.** **STOLEN ITEMS** goods that have been stolen, or the value of these stolen goods ○ *The haul was mainly silver and paintings.* **2.** **CONFISCATED CONTRABAND** illegal goods that are confiscated by the authorities **3.** **FISHING SINGLE CATCH OF FISH** the amount of fish caught in a single catch **4.** **TRANSP DISTANCE STH IS TRANSPORTED** a distance over which sth is transported or pulled, or which sb travels with difficulty [13thC. Variant of HALE.] ◇ **haul sb over the coals** to reprimand sb severely

——— **WORD KEY: SYNONYMS** ———
See Synonyms at *pull*.

haul off *vi.* to manoeuvre a vessel in order to avoid sth

haul up *vt.* to force sb to appear before a court or some other disciplinary body for judgment

haulage /háwlij/ *n.* **1.** **TRANSPORTING GOODS** the business or process of transporting goods, usually by road or rail **2.** **COST OF TRANSPORTING GOODS** the cost of transporting goods, or the rate charged for transporting goods

hauler /háwlər/ *n.* *US* = **haulier**

haulier /háwli ər/ *n.* a person or company whose business is transporting goods, especially by road. US term **hauler**

haulm /hawm/, **halm** *n.* **1.** **STEMS OR STALKS** the stems or stalks of grain, beans, peas, potatoes, or grasses, especially after harvesting and used for thatching or litter **2.** **SINGLE STEM** a single stem of grain, beans, peas, potatoes, or grasses [Old English *h(e)alm*. Ultimately from an Indo-European word that is also the ancestor of English *culm* and *calamus*.]

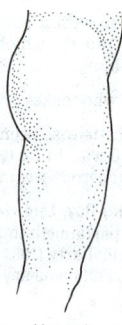

Haunch

haunch /hawnch/ n. **1.** HIP, BUTTOCK, AND UPPER THIGH the part of the body comprising the hip, buttock, and upper thigh ○ *She sat back on her haunches.* **2.** FOOD, ZOOL ANIMAL LEG one of the back legs of a four-legged animal, either when it is alive, or as a cut of meat **3.** ARCHIT UPPER PART OF ARCH the upper curving part of either side of an arch [12thC. Via French *hanche* from prehistoric Germanic.]

haunt /hawnt/ vt. (**haunts, haunting, haunted**) **1.** PARANORMAL APPEAR TO SB AS A GHOST to frequent a place or appear to sb in the form of a ghost or other supposed supernatural being **2.** DISCOMFIT SB BY UNPLEASANT REMINDERS to cause sb unease, worry, or regret by continual presence or recurrence in his or her life ○ *haunted by doubt* **3.** VISIT SOMEWHERE CONTINUALLY to go often to a place ○ *She no longer haunts the late-night bars and prefers to stay at home.* ■ n. PLACE SB OFTEN VISITS a place that sb likes and often visits ○ *a holiday away from the usual tourist haunts* [12thC. Via French *hanter* 'to frequent a place' (literally 'as a home') from, ultimately, a prehistoric Germanic word that is also the ancestor of English *home*.] —**haunter** n.

haunted /háwntid/ adj. **1.** PARANORMAL FREQUENTED BY A GHOST inhabited by or visited regularly by a ghost or other supposed supernatural being **2.** STRANGELY TERRIFIED IN APPEARANCE looking strangely frightened or worried

haunting /háwnting/ adj. evoking strong emotion, especially a sense of sadness, that persists for a long time ○ *a haunting testament to war's destruction* — **hauntingly** adv.

Hauraki Gulf /how ráki-/ bay on the northeastern coast of North Island, New Zealand. The city of Auckland is located on its southwestern shore. Area: 2290 sq. km/884 sq. mi.

Hausa /hówssə/ (plural **-sa** or **-sas**) n. **1.** PEOPLES MEMBER OF W AFRICAN PEOPLE a member of a people living mainly in northern Nigeria and southern Niger **2.** LANG LANGUAGE OF EASTERN W AFRICA a language widely spoken in Nigeria, Niger, and other parts of eastern West Africa. It is one of the Chadic branch of the Afro-Asiatic family of languages. Hausa is spoken by about 25 million native speakers, with approximately a further 40 million people using it as a second language. **3.** SPIRITUAL TRADITION OF NIGERIA the tradition combining elements of Islam and of local religious beliefs associated with the Hausa, after the collapse of the Songhay Empire [Early 19thC. From Hausa.] —**Hausa** adj.

hausfrau /hówss frow/ (plural **-fraus**) n. a traditional housewife, conventionally believed to be interested mostly in her home and family (disapproving; offensive in some contexts) ○ *She wanted a career, not a life as a hausfrau.* [Late 18thC. From German, from *Haus* 'house' and *Frau* 'wife, woman'.]

Haussmann /óss man/, **George-Eugène, Baron** (1809–91) French town planner. His redesign of Paris in the 1850s and 1860s, with its broad avenues and parks, influenced urban design around the world.

haustellum /haw stélləm/ (plural **-la** /-lə/) n. the tip of the proboscis, or elongated mouthpart, that is adapted for sucking food in many insects, e.g. flies [Early 19thC. From modern Latin, literally 'small scoop', from Latin *haustrum* 'scoop' from, ultimately, *haurire* 'to draw up' (source of English *exhaust*).]

haustorium /haw stáwri əm/ (plural **-a** /-i ə/) n. a food-absorbing structure of a parasitic plant or fungus. It penetrates host tissues and obtains food and water from a host plant. [Late 19thC. Formed from Latin *haustor* 'water-drawer, drinker', from, ultimately, *haurire* 'to draw up' (see HAUSTELLUM).]

hautboy /ó boy, hó-/ (plural **-boys**), **hautbois** (plural **-bois**) n. **1.** PLANTS TYPE OF STRAWBERRY a strawberry, native to central Europe and Asia, with large fruit. Latin name: *Fragaria moschata.* **2.** MUSIC OBOE an oboe (archaic) [Mid-16thC. From French *hautbois* 'oboe' (source of English *oboe*), from *haut* 'high' (from its high pitch) + *bois* 'wood', from Germanic.]

haute couture /ót-/ n. exclusive and expensive clothing made for an individual customer by a fashion designer, or the industry that produces such clothing [Early 20thC. From French, literally 'high dressmaking'.]

haute cuisine /ót-/ n. classic high-quality French cooking (hyphenated when used before a noun) [Early 20thC. From French, literally 'high cooking'.]

haute école /ót ay kol/ n. the skill and art of expert horsemanship [Mid-19thC. From French, literally 'high school'.]

hauteur /ō túr/ n. a haughty manner, feeling, or quality (formal) [Early 17thC. From French, from *haute* 'high', feminine of *haut*, from, ultimately, Latin *altus* (source of English *altitude* and *haughty*).]

haut monde /ó mónd/ n. the highest stratum of society, international or domestic, and those in it ○ *a denizen of the haut monde, invited to every international ball and gala* [Mid-19thC. From French, literally 'high world'.]

Havana[1] /hə vánnə/ capital, port, and largest city of Cuba, on the northwestern coast of the country. Population: 2,241,000 (1995). —**Havanan** adj., n.

Havana[2], **Havana cigar** n. a high-quality cigar made in Cuba

Havant /hávv'nt/ seaside town in Hampshire, southern England. Population: 46,510 (1991).

Havarti /hə váarti/ n. a moist pale semi-hard cheese with lots of tiny holes and a slightly rubbery texture, made in Denmark. It has a mild buttery flavour. [Mid-20thC. Named after *Havarti*, the farm of Hanne Nielsen, the 19th-century Danish cheese maker who popularized it.]

havdalah n. = habdalah

have (stressed) /hav/; (unstressed) /həv, əv/ (**has** (stressed) /haz/; (unstressed) /həz, əz/, **having, had** /had/, **had** (stressed) /had/; (unstressed) /həd, əd/) CORE MEANING: a verb indicating that sb possesses sth, either materially or as a characteristic or attribute ○ *She has a small cottage in the country.* ○ *He has beautiful eyes.*
1. vt. OWN STH to be the owner or possessor of sth ○ *I don't have a lot of money.* **2.** vt. POSSESS A CHARACTERISTIC to be the possessor of a quality or characteristic ○ *She had long blonde hair.* **3.** v. FORMS PERFECT TENSES used to form the following tenses or aspects: the present perfect, the past perfect, the future perfect, and the continuous forms of these (used before the past participle of a verb or at the beginning of a question, or with 'got' to indicate possession) ○ *I have finished my dinner, thank you.* ○ *Have you finished yet?* ○ *I have got a new car.* **4.** v. EXPRESSES COMPULSION expresses compulsion, obligation, or necessity ○ *We have to do the economic analysis.* **5.** v. EXPRESSES CERTAINTY expresses conviction or certainty ○ *There just has to be a solution to the problem.* **6.** vt. RECEIVE to receive or obtain sth ○ *I had a Christmas card from him.* **7.** vt. EAT STH to eat or drink sth ○ *We have breakfast at eight.* **8.** vt. THINK OF STH to think of sth, or hold sth in the mind ○ *Listen! I have a good idea.* **9.** vt. EXPERIENCE STH to experience or undergo sth ○ *He went to the carnival to have a good time.* ○ *I had a shock.* **10.** vt. BE AFFECTED BY to be affected by sth, especially sth of a medical nature ○ *I've had the flu for the last week.* **11.** vt. ENGAGE IN STH to engage or participate in sth ○ *We had a long talk about cars.* **12.** vt. ARRANGE STH to organize or arrange sth ○ *We had a party last week.* **13.** vt. ARRANGE FOR STH TO BE DONE to arrange for sth to be done by you or on your behalf ○ *I've just had my hair cut.* **14.** vt. TOLERATE STH to tolerate or put up with sth (usually used in negative statements) ○ *I won't have such behaviour any longer!* **15.** vt. RECEIVE SB to receive sb as a guest ○ *We had Mother to stay over Christmas.* **16.** vt. BRING A CHILD INTO EXISTENCE to be the parent of a child, or conceive, carry, or give birth to a child ○ *She's had three children and now she's having another one.* **17.** vt. PUT SB OR STH SOMEWHERE to put or place sb or sth in a particular place ○ *I'll have you two in the front row, please.* **18.** vt. UNDERGO STH to be the victim of an unpleasant action or experience ○ *I had my car stolen.* **19.** vt. MAKE STH HAPPEN to direct or cause sb to do sth, or cause sth to happen ○ *If you see him tomorrow, have him call me.* **20.** vt. CHEAT SB to cheat or outwit sb (usually passive) ○ *I think you'll find that you've been had in this deal.* **21.** npl. **haves** PRIVILEGED PEOPLE people who are rich and privileged, especially compared with those who are not [Old English *habban.* Ultimately from an Indo-European word meaning 'to grasp', which is also the ancestor of English *capable* and *heave*.] ◇ **has** or **had it** declares or asserts, or declared or asserted ○ *Rumour has it that they are planning to get engaged.* ◇ **have done with sth** to finish with sth ○ *Let's put everything else in this box and have done with it.* ◇ **have had it 1.** to have no prospect of success ○ *We've had it now.* **2.** to be too worn out, damaged, or exhausted to function properly (informal) ○ *I'm afraid this printer has just about had it.* ○ *I've had it – you go on, I'm turning back.* ◇ **have had it with** to have lost patience with sb or sth ○ *I've had it with delays.* ◇ **have it coming** to be about to receive punishment or retribution, or deserve it ○ *He has it coming to him.* ◇ **have it in for sb** to hold hard feelings against sb and intend to do that person harm ○ *She has it in for him, and you can expect her to seek revenge soon.* ◇ **have it out (with sb)** to engage in a spirited, aggressive argument over an issue with sb ○ *OK, let's have it out now and get this settled once and for all.* ◇ **have to do with 1.** to be relevant to ○ *Does your question have anything to do with the topic under discussion?* **2.** to have a friendship or relationship with ○ *She will have nothing to do with him any more.* ◇ **have what it takes** to have the necessary skills, personality, or attitude to be successful at sth ○ *He doesn't really have what it takes to be a professional actor.* ◇ **let sb have it** to deliver an attack on sb ○ *He refused to change his behaviour, and in the end I let him have it.* ◇ **never had it so good** to have not possessed so many benefits before ○ *Look at these sales figures – we've never had it so good!* ◇ **not having any** refusing to take part or become involved in sth ○ *They tried to involve him in the conspiracy, but it soon became clear that he wasn't having any.*

— WORD KEY: USAGE —
See Usage note at **do**.

have on vti. to have an article of clothing on your body

have up vt. to cause sb to appear for trial (informal) ○ *He was had up for breaking and entering.*

Havel /hávvel/, **Václav** (b. 1936) Czech statesman and dramatist. He was a dissident playwright who became a leader of the Charter 77 democracy movement under Communist rule. After the democratic revolution in 1989 he became president of Czechoslovakia (1989) and then of the Czech Republic (1993).

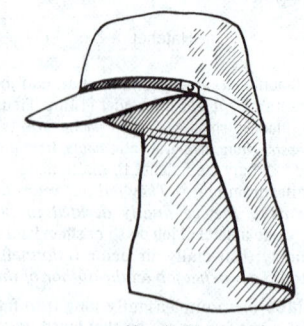

Havelock

havelock /háv lok/ n. a light-coloured cover for a soldier's cap, with a flap extending over the back of the neck to protect the head and neck from the sun [Mid-19thC. Named after Sir Henry *Havelock* (1795–1857), a British major-general who served in India; he introduced it as part of his troops' uniform.]

haven /háyv'n/ *n.* **1.** SHELTERED PLACE a place sought for rest, shelter, or protection ○ *a haven for wildlife* **2.** NAUT ANCHORAGE a harbour or port facility where ships and boats come in and tie up (*literary*) [Pre-12thC. From Old Norse *höfn*, literally 'place that holds (ships)'.]

have-nots *npl.* people who are not rich or privileged, especially compared with those who are ○ *a country with the highest income inequality between the haves and have-nots*

haven't /háv'nt/ *contr.* have not

haver /háyvər/ *n., interj.* **haver, havers** *Scotland, N England* NONSENSE nonsense ■ *vi.* (**-ers, -ering, -ered**) **1.** *Scotland, N England* TALK NONSENSE to talk nonsense **2.** VACILLATE to be unable to make a choice or come to a decision [Early 18thC. Origin unknown.]

Haverfordwest /hávvərfərd wést, haárfərd-/ market town in Pembrokeshire, southwestern Wales. It is the administrative centre of the county. Population: 13,700 (1994). Welsh **Hwlffordd**

haversack /hávvər sak/ *n.* a strong bag carried on the back or the shoulder, used especially by travellers or hikers [Mid-18thC. Via French *havresac* from obsolete German *Habersack*, from *Haber* 'oats' + *Sack* 'bag'; originally used by cavalrymen to hold oats for their horses.]

Haversian canal /hə vúrsh'n-, hə vúrssi ən-/ *n.* a tiny longitudinal channel in bone tissue. The canals form a network that contains blood vessels and nerve fibres. [Mid-19thC. Named after Clopton *Havers* (1650?-1702), the English physician and anatomist who discovered them.]

Haversian system *n.* a Haversian canal along with the concentric layers of compact bone surrounding it

haversine /hávvər sīn/ *n.* in mathematics, half the value of the versed sine [Late 19thC. Contraction of *half versed sine*.]

havildar /hávv'l daar/ *n.* in the Indian subcontinent, an army or police officer with a rank equivalent to sergeant [Late 17thC. Via Urdu *hawildār* from Persian *hawāl(a)dār*, literally 'charge holder'.]

havoc /hávvək/ *n.* **1.** DEVASTATION widespread damage, destruction, or devastation ○ *the havoc wreaked by the storm* **2.** CHAOS a condition or situation of disruptive chaos [15thC. From Anglo-Norman (*crier*) *havok* '(to cry) havoc', signal to an army to seize plunder, alteration of Old French *havo(t)* 'pillage', of uncertain origin: probably from prehistoric Germanic.]

Havre, Le /lə aávrə/ city and seaport, Seine-Maritime Department, northwestern France, situated on the English Channel 177 km/110 mi. northwest of Paris. Population: 197,219 (1990).

Havre de Grace /hávvər də gráss/ city in northeastern Maryland, on Chesapeake Bay at the mouth of the Susquehanna River. Population: 10,092 (1996).

haw[1] /haw/ *n.* **1.** = **hawthorn 2.** FRUIT OF HAWTHORN the round or oval fruit of the hawthorn, usually red or yellow and containing seeds [Old English *haga*, of uncertain origin: perhaps the same word as Old English *haga* 'hedge'.]

haw[2] /haw/ *n.* UTTERANCE SHOWING HESITATION a sound that people make when they are hesitating to speak ■ *vi.* (**haws, hawing, hawed**) MAKE HESITATING SOUND to make a sound indicative of hesitation while speaking [Mid-17thC. An imitation of the sound.]

haw[3] /haw/ *n.* = **nictitating membrane** [Early 16thC. Origin unknown.]

haw[4] /haw/ *interj.* used to command an animal or a team of animals to turn left [Late 17thC. Origin unknown.]

Hawaii /hə wî í/ state of the United States in the northern Pacific Ocean, consisting of eight main islands and over 100 others. Capital: Honolulu. Population: 1,183,723 (1997). Area: 16,729 sq. km/6,459 sq. mi. ■ the largest island in the state of Hawaii. Population: 120,317 (1990). Area: 10,443 sq. km/4,028 sq. mi.

Hawaii-Aleutian Standard Time *n.* the standard time in the time zone centred on longitude 150° W, which includes an area of the Pacific Ocean that includes Hawaii and the western Aleutian Islands. It is ten hours earlier than Universal Coordinated Time.

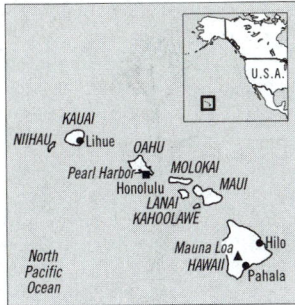

Hawaii

Hawaiian /hə wî ən, -i ən/ *n.* **1.** PEOPLES SB FROM HAWAII sb who was born in or brought up in the US state of Hawaii, especially sb of Melanesian or Tahitian descent **2.** LANG LANGUAGE SPOKEN IN HAWAII a language spoken in Hawaii and other neighbouring islands, belonging to the Polynesian branch of the Austronesian family of languages. Hawaiian is spoken by about 70,000 people. —**Hawaiian** *adj.*

Hawaiian appliqué *n.* an appliqué developed in Hawaii, consisting of a large central motif, from a design cut from folded paper, which is applied to a foundation fabric and made into a quilt. Traditional Hawaiian appliqué is made in two solid colours, typically red, green, orange, or blue on white.

Hawaiian English *n.* a variety of English spoken in Hawaii

WORD KEY: WORLD ENGLISH

Hawaiian English is the English language as used, mainly in speech, in Hawaii, a state of the United States. It ranges from Hawaii Pidgin English to standard US English, and is influenced by Hawaiian, a Polynesian language, and by the languages of immigrants from China, Japan, and the Philippines among others, as well as by usage from the US mainland. Expressions from Hawaiian include *aloha* 'love, sympathy, welcome, farewell', *haole* 'foreigner, especially a Caucasian', *heiau* 'a temple', *hula* (a graceful swaying dance), *kahuna* (a traditional priest or shaman), *lei* (a garland of flowers), *wahine* 'a girl, a woman'. Hybrid expressions are commonplace, usually with the Hawaiian element first, as in *aloha party*, *kukui nut*, *Waikiki Beach*, and *Waimea Arboretum*.

Hawaiian goose *n.* = **nene**

Hawaiian guitar *n.* a small steel-strung guitar with a sliding glass or metal bar that fits across the strings in order to change the pitch of the whole instrument. It is usually played horizontally on a stand, and the strings are plucked with a thimble.

Hawaiian shirt *n.* a short-sleeved shirt with brightly coloured designs, often featuring Hawaiian motifs, printed on it

Hawaii Standard Time, **Hawaii Time** *n.* = **Hawaii-Aleutian Standard Time**

haway /ha wáy/ *interj. N England* used as a greeting (*informal*)

Haweswater /háwz wawtər/ lake in Cumbria, northern England, now enlarged and used as a reservoir

Hawfinch

hawfinch /háw finch/ (*plural* **-finches** *or* **-finch**) *n.* a Eurasian bird that has a thick conical silvery beak, brown plumage, black-and-white wings, and a white-tipped tail. Latin name: *Coccothraustes coccothraustes*. [*Haw* from HAW[1]]

haw-haw *n.* = **ha-ha**[1], **ha-ha**[2]

Hawick /háw ik/ historic town in the Scottish Borders district on the River Teviot. Population: 15,812 (1991).

hawk[1] /hawk/ *n.* **1.** BIRDS BIRD OF PREY a diurnal bird of prey, typically having broad wings, a short hooked bill, strong talons, and a long tail. Subfamilies: Accipitridae and Buteoninae. **2.** POL, MIL SB FAVOURING FORCE sb who favours the use of military force in implementing foreign policy rather than diplomatic solutions. ◊ **dove 3.** AGGRESSIVE COMPETITOR a fiercely competitive, aggressive, predatory, or combative person ○ *a marketing hawk who wanted to put the competition out of business* ■ *v.* (**hawks, hawking, hawked**) **1.** *vi.* HUNT HUNT WITH HAWKS to hunt for prey on the wing, or hunt for prey using hawks and similar birds of prey **2.** *vti.* BIRDS ATTACK ON THE WING to pursue or attack while flying in a way similar to that of a hawk ○ *big brown bats hawking at small prey* ○ *tiny birds hawking insects in the morning sky* [Old English *h(e)afoc*. Ultimately from an Indo-European word meaning 'to grasp' (see HAVE).] —**hawker** *n.* —**hawking** *n.*

hawk[2] /hawk/ *v.* (**hawks, hawking, hawked**) **1.** *vi.* CLEAR THE THROAT to clear the throat noisily **2.** *vt.* COUGH UP PHLEGM to clear the throat and noisily cough up phlegm ■ *n.* **1.** ATTEMPT AT CLEARING THROAT a noisy attempt to clear the throat of phlegm **2.** SALIVA OR PHLEGM saliva or phlegm, especially when sb spits it out [Late 16thC. Origin uncertain: probably an imitation of the sound.]

hawk[3] /hawk/ (**hawks, hawking, hawked**) *vti.* to engage in selling merchandise on the street or from door to door [14thC. Origin uncertain: probably a back-formation from *hawker*, probably from Middle Low German *höker*, from *höken* 'to peddle'.] —**hawker** *n.*

hawk[4] /hawk/ *n.* a metal square with a wooden handle underneath, used by a plasterer to hold wet plaster or mortar before applying it to a surface [15thC. Origin uncertain: perhaps the same word as HAWK[1].]

hawkbill *n.* = **hawksbill**

hawkbit /háwk bit/ (*plural* **-bits** *or* **-bit**) *n.* a perennial plant found in grasslands that has yellow flowers and lobed leaves. There are three varieties. Genus: *Leontodon.* [Early 18thC. Blend of HAWKWEED and DEVIL'S BIT.]

Hawke /hawk/, **Bob** (*b.* 1929) Australian politician. He was leader of the Australian Labor Party and prime minister of Australia (1983–91). Full name **Robert James Lee Hawke**

Hawke Bay bay on the eastern coast of North Island, New Zealand. It extends from Mahia Peninsula in the north to Cape Kidnappers in the south.

Hawker /háwkər/, **Harry George** (1889–1921) Australian aviator. He was chief test pilot with the Sopwith Aviation Company (1913–20) and a designer of early aircraft.

Hawke's Bay /háwks-/ administrative region of New Zealand, located in eastern North Island and bordering Hawke Bay. Population: 144,292 (1996). Area: 21,178 sq. km/8,177 sq. mi.

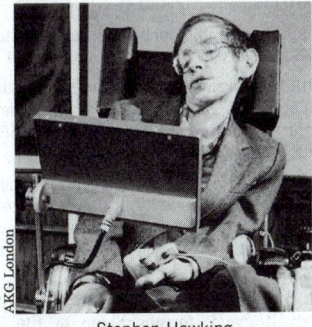

Stephen Hawking

Hawkesbury /háwksbəri/ river in eastern New South Wales, Australia, which rises in the Great Dividing Range. Length: 480 km/300 mi.

hawk-eyed *adj.* quick to see things that are not obvious, often as a result of having very keen eyesight ○ *The hawk-eyed appraiser spotted a tiny chip in the antique teapot.*

Hawking /háwking/, **Stephen** (*b.* 1942) British physicist and mathematician. His research focused on space-time and unified field theory. His lectures, films, and books, including his best-selling *A Brief History of Time* (1988), made difficult concepts in physics accessible to the public. Full name **Stephen William Hawking**

hawkish /háwkish/ *adj.* favouring the use of military force in implementing foreign policy rather than diplomatic solutions. ◊ **dovish**

Hawk moth

hawk moth *n.* a moth with a thick body and long narrow wings that enable it to hover over flowers and feed on their nectar. Family: Sphingidae.

Hawk owl

hawk owl *n.* an owl with a long slender tail and brownish speckled plumage that resembles a hawk when in flight. It is found in North America and northern Eurasia. Latin name: *Surnia ulula.*

hawk's beard (*plural* **hawk's beards** *or* **hawk's beard**) *n.* a plant with small yellow flowers resembling those of the dandelion. Genus: *Crepis.*

hawksbill /háwks bil/ (*plural* **-bills** *or* **-bill**), **hawksbill turtle, hawkbill** (*plural* **-bills** *or* **-bill**) *n.* a tropical sea turtle, reaching 61 cm/2 ft in length and now classified as endangered, that has a yellowish-brown shell of overlapping plates once valued as a source of tortoiseshell. Latin name: *Eretmochelys imbricata.* [From the shape of its mouth, likened to a hawk's beak]

hawk's-eye *n.* a semiprecious gemstone that is a dark blue variety of the mineral crocidolite

Hawksmoor /háwksmoŏr, -mawr/, **Nicholas** (1661–1736) British architect. He was a pupil of Sir Christopher Wren and assistant to Sir John Vanbrugh. His finest work includes All Souls, Oxford (1729).

hawkweed /háwk weed/ (*plural* **-weed** *or* **-weeds**) *n.* a composite plant that is typically hairy and has yellow or orange rayed flowers. Genus: *Hieracium.* [Translation of Latin *hieracium*, from Greek *ierakion*, from *ierax* 'hawk']

Haworth /hów ərth/ historic village in West Yorkshire, northern England, former home of the Brontë family. Population: 4,956 (1991).

Haworth, Sir Norman (1883–1950) British biochemist. He was awarded the Nobel Prize in chemistry with Paul Karrer in 1937 for his research into the struc-

Hawkweed

ture of vitamin C. Full name **Sir Walter Norman Haworth**

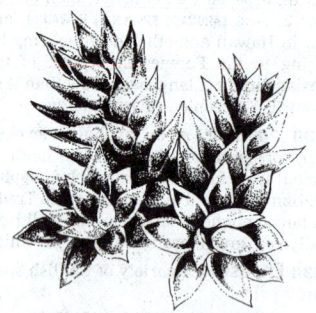

Haworthia

haworthia /haw wáwthi ə/ (*plural* **-as** *or* **-a**) *n.* a succulent herb, native to South Africa, with densely overlapping, often warty leaves, clustered in rosettes. Genus: *Haworthia.* [Named after Adrian Hardy Haworth (1768–1833), who wrote extensively on succulent plants]

hawse /hawz/ *n.* **1.** LOCATION OF SHIP'S HAWSEHOLES the area of a ship in which the hawseholes are to be found **2.** = **hawsehole 3.** SPACE BETWEEN BOW AND ANCHOR the space between the bow and the anchors of a ship lying at anchor **4.** ANCHOR DEPLOYMENT the way in which a ship's anchor lines are deployed, starboard and port, when both are deployed together at the same time ■ *vi.* (**hawses, hawsing, hawsed**) PITCH VIOLENTLY WHEN AT ANCHOR to pitch violently when lying at anchor [Origin uncertain: either 13thC, from Old Norse *hals,* or from Old English *h(e)als,* both 'neck, ship's prow'. Ultimately from an Indo-European word meaning 'to revolve'.]

hawsehole /háwz hōl/ *n.* an opening in the bow of a ship through which a large heavy line is passed for towing or mooring the ship

hawsepipe /háwz pīp/ *n.* a pipe on each side of a ship's bow for use in deploying and weighing anchor, with the anchor lines running through each pipe

hawser /háwzər/ *n.* a large heavy cable that is used when mooring or towing a ship [13thC. From Anglo-Norman *haucer,* from Old French *haucier* 'to hoist', literally 'to make high', ultimately from Latin *altus* 'high' (see ALTITUDE).]

hawser-laid *adj.* used to describe rope composed of three strands, each of which has been made by being twisted in a left-handed direction. The three strands are then twisted together in a right-handed direction.

hawthorn /háw thawrn/ *n.* a thorny tree or shrub of the rose family that has clusters of white or pink flowers and small reddish fruits. Genus: *Crataegus.*

Hawthorne /háw thawrn/, **Nathaniel** (1804–64) US writer. His novels and short stories frequently deal with Puritan sin and atonement, and include *The Scarlet Letter* (1850). Born **Nathaniel Hathorne**

Hawthorne effect /háw thawrn-/ *n.* social research findings attributable to the attention of researchers to the subjects of their research rather than to factors significant to the research topic. An example would be when variables of both a positive and a negative nature produce the same effect. [Mid-20thC. Named after the *Hawthorne* plant of the Western Electric

Nathaniel Hawthorne

Company in Cicero (Chicago, Illinois), where it was first observed.]

hay /hay/ *n.* CUT AND DRIED GRASS grass or other plants that are cut, dried, and then often used as fodder ○ *a bale of hay* ■ *v.* (**hays, haying, hayed**) **1.** *vi.* CUT, BALE, AND STORE HAY to mow hay and bale or roll it, and then store it ○ *He's been haying all day.* **2.** *vt.* FEED WITH HAY to feed animals with hay [Old English *hēg,* literally 'sth that can be cut down'. Ultimately from an Indo-European word meaning 'to hew, strike', which is also the ancestor of English *haggle, hew,* and *hoe.*] ◇ **a roll in the hay** an instance of having sex with sb (*slang*) ◇ **hit the hay** to go to bed (*informal*) ○ *We hit the hay at nine, completely exhausted.* ◇ **make hay while the sun shines** to take advantage of all opportunities when they present themselves (*informal*)

— WORD KEY: CULTURAL NOTE —
The Hay Wain, a painting by artist John Constable (1821). The most popular of Constable's many depictions of his native Suffolk, it shows a hay cart crossing a river. By combining a bold style with close observation of nature, Constable creates a realistic image of an idealistic world, in which humans and nature are in close harmony.

haybox /háy boks/ *n.* an insulated box, originally filled with hay, used to allow food that has been boiled to finish cooking without more fuel

haycock /háy kok/ *n.* a cone-shaped pile of hay that is left in a field until it is dry enough to be stored

Hayden /háyd'n/, **Bill** (*b.* 1933) Australian statesman. The leader of the Australian Labor Party (1978–83), he served as governor-general of Australia (1989–96). Full name **William George Hayden**

Hay diet /háy-/ *n.* a way of eating in which protein and carbohydrate foods are not eaten at the same time, claimed to be helpful for digestive complaints and weight loss [Mid-20thC. Named after William Howard Hay (1866–1940), who devised it.]

Haydn /hīd'n/, **Joseph** (1732–1809) Austrian composer. His hundreds of symphonies, concertos, string quartets, and operas helped define the classical style, and include the popular oratorio *The Creation* (1798). Full name **Franz Joseph Haydn**

Hayek /hī ek/, **Friedrich A. von** (1899–1992) German-born British economist. An influential advocate of an unfettered free market, he led the Chicago school's monetarist attack on Keynesian economics. He shared a Nobel Prize in economics in 1974. Full name **Friedrich August von Hayek**

Rutherford B. Hayes

Hayes /hayz/, **Rutherford B.** (1822–93) US statesman and 19th president of the United States. A Republican, he reformed the civil service and withdrew the last federal troops from the Reconstruction South during his presidential term (1877–81). Full name **Rutherford Birchard Hayes**

hay fever *n.* an allergic reaction to pollen that irritates the upper respiratory tract and the eyes, resulting in symptoms including a runny and itchy nose, itchy and watering eyes, and sneezing. Technical name **pollinosis**

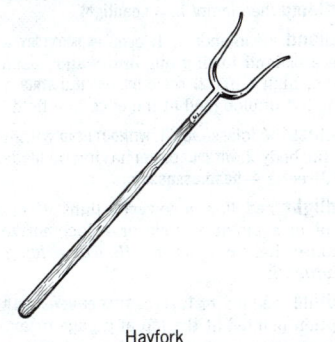

Hayfork

hayfork /háy fawrk/ *n.* **1.** = **pitchfork 2.** HAY-MOVING MACHINE a machine-operated fork for moving hay

hayloft /háy loft/ *n.* a loft for storing hay over a stable or a barn

haymaker /háy maykər/ *n.* **1.** AGRIC WORKER PROCESSING HAY an agricultural worker whose job it is to cut, turn, toss, spread, or carry hay after it has been mown **2.** AGRIC MACHINE PROCESSING HAY a machine for breaking down stems of hay to improve the drying process **3.** BOXING POWERFUL SWINGING PUNCH a powerful swinging punch, especially in a boxing match (*slang*) **4.** CRICKET SWEEPING STROKE WITH BAT in cricket, a sweeping stroke with the bat

haymow /háy mō/ *n.* **1.** = **hayloft 2.** QUANTITY OF HAY STORED IN BARN a quantity of hay stored in a barn or loft

hayrack /háy rak/ *n.* **1.** RACK HOLDING FEED a rack that holds hay and from which livestock feed **2.** RACK ON CART a rack attached to a cart to increase its capacity for carrying hay **3.** CART WITH HAYRACK a cart fitted with a hayrack

hayrick /háy rik/ *n.* = **haystack**

hayseed /háy seed/ *n.* **1.** GRASS SEED FROM HAY grass seed that is shaken out of hay **2.** PIECES OF GRASS pieces of grass or straw that fall from hay **3.** *US, Can* OFFENSIVE TERM an offensive term that deliberately insults sb's rural base or background and his or her intelligence and level of sophistication (*informal insult*)

haystack /háy stak/ *n.* a large pile of hay, especially one that is built in the open and covered with thatch for winter storage

Haywards Heath /háywərdz heeth/ market and dormitory town in West Sussex, southern England. Population: 28,923 (1991).

haywire /háy wīr/ *adj.* functioning erratically, or not functioning at all (*informal*) ○ *A powerful magnet can make the television set go haywire.* [From the springy nature of wire used to tie up bundles of hay, and sometimes for makeshift repairs]

Hayworth /háywərth/, **Rita** (1918–87) US actor. A dancer from her childhood, she appeared in films including *Gilda* (1946). Real name **Margarita Carmen Cansino**

hazard /házzərd/ *n.* **1.** POTENTIAL DANGER sth that is potentially very dangerous **2.** ENG DANGEROUS OUTCOME a dangerous or otherwise unwanted outcome, especially one resulting from the failure of an engineered system **3.** GAMBLING DICE GAME a dice game resembling craps **4.** GOLF OBSTACLE ON GOLF COURSE a natural or constructed obstacle on a golf course, e.g. a bunker or a lake **5.** TENNIS RECEIVER'S SIDE IN REAL TENNIS in real tennis, the receiver's side of the court **6.** CUE GAMES SCORING STROKE IN BILLIARDS a scoring stroke in billiards, made when a ball is pocketed, either a ball other than the striker's (**winning hazard**) or the striker's cue ball itself (**losing hazard**) ■ *vt.* (**-ards, -arding, -arded**) **1.** SUGGEST TENTATIVELY to offer a tentative explanation of sth ○ *Would anyone like to*

hazard a guess as to what this could possibly mean? **2.** RISK LOSS OF STH to chance or risk sth, especially in order to gain sth else [13thC. Via Old French *hasard* 'game of chance played with dice' from, ultimately, Arabic *az-zahr*, literally 'the die' or 'the chance'.]

hazard light *n.* either of a pair of car lights, usually the indicators, that flash on and off to warn other drivers of potential danger

hazardous /házzərdəss/ *adj.* potentially very dangerous to living beings or the environment —**hazardously** *adv.* —**hazardousness** *n.*

hazardous waste *n.* a by-product of manufacturing processes or nuclear processing that is toxic and presents a potential threat to people and the environment

hazard pay *n. US* = **danger money**

hazard warning light *n.* = **hazard light**

haze /hayz/ *n.* **1.** PARTICLES IN THE ATMOSPHERE mist, cloud, or smoke suspended in the atmosphere and obscuring or obstructing the view **2.** VAGUE OBSCURING FACTOR sth that is vague and serves to obscure sth **3.** DISORIENTED MENTAL OR PHYSICAL STATE a mental or physical state or condition when feelings and perceptions are vague, disorienting, or obscured ■ *vi.* (**hazes, hazing, hazed**) BECOME SATURATED WITH PARTICLES to become filled with suspended atmospheric particulate matter such as pollution ○ *It's going to be hot and muggy and in the afternoon it will begin to haze over.* [Early 18thC. Origin uncertain: probably a back-formation from HAZY.]

hazel /háyz'l/ *n.* (*plural* **-zels** *or* **-zel**) **1.** TREES SMALL TREE WITH EDIBLE NUTS a shrub or small tree of the birch family that has edible brown nuts. Genus: *Corylus*. **2.** INDUST WOOD OF HAZEL the wood of the hazel tree **3.** FOOD = **hazelnut 4.** COLOURS LIGHT BROWN COLOUR a light-brown colour with a tinge of green or gold, like a ripe hazelnut ■ *adj.* COLOURS HAZEL-COLOURED of the colour hazel [Old English *hæsel*. Ultimately from an Indo-European word.]

hazelnut /háyz'l nut/ *n.* an edible nut from a hazel tree

Hazlitt /házlit/, **William** (1778–1830) British essayist. He is regarded as one of the most brilliant English prose stylists. His collections of essays include *Table Talk* (1821–22) and *The Spirit of the Age* (1825).

hazy /háyzi/ (**-ier, -iest**) *adj.* **1.** VISUALLY OBSCURED unclear, especially because partially obscured or obstructed by mist, cloud, or smoke **2.** IMPRECISE not specific or clearly remembered **3.** NOT KNOWLEDGEABLE showing a lack of understanding or knowledge [Early 17thC. Origin unknown. Originally in the sense 'foggy'.] —**hazily** *adv.* —**haziness** *n.*

Hazzard /házzərd/, **Shirley** (*b.* 1931) Australian-born US writer. Her novels include *The Transit of Venus* (1980).

Hb *abbr.* haemoglobin

HB *abbr.* hard black (*used of pencil lead*)

HBC *abbr.* Hudson's Bay Company

H-beam *n.* a structural steel member shaped like an H in section. It is similar to an I-beam.

HBM *abbr.* **1.** Her Britannic Majesty **2.** His Britannic Majesty

H-bomb *n.* = **hydrogen bomb**

HC *abbr.* House of Commons

HCF, **hcf** *abbr.* highest common factor

HCG *abbr.* human chorionic gonadotrophin

HCI *abbr.* human-computer interaction

hcp *abbr.* handicap

hd *abbr.* **1.** hand **2.** head

HD *abbr.* **1.** hard disk **2.** heavy-duty **3.** high density **4.** hard drive

hdbk *abbr.* handbook

HDL *abbr.* high-density lipoprotein

hdqrs *abbr.* headquarters

HDTV *abbr.* high-definition television

hdw. *abbr.* hardware

he[1] (*stressed*) /hee/; (*unstressed*) /hi, i/ *pron.* MALE NOT REFERRED TO BY NAME used to refer to a male person

or animal who has been previously mentioned or whose identity is known (*used as the subject of a verb*) ■ *n.* MALE ANIMAL OR BOY a male animal or boy, especially used of a new baby ○ *Is your puppy a he or a she?* [Old English *he*. Ultimately from an Indo-European word meaning 'this (here)', which is also the ancestor of English *hence*, *here*, and *her*.]

he[2] /hay/ *n.* the fifth letter of the Hebrew alphabet, represented in the English alphabet as 'h'. See table at **alphabet** [Mid-17thC. From Hebrew *hē*'.]

He *symbol.* helium

HE *abbr.* **1.** His Eminence **2.** His Excellency

head /hed/ *n.* **1.** ANAT TOP PART OF BODY the topmost part of a vertebrate body, where the brain, eyes, nose, ears, mouth, and jaws are situated **2.** ZOOL MOST FORWARD SECTION OF BODY the section of the body of an invertebrate that is forward of all other segments **3.** CENTRE OF INTELLECT the centre of a human being's faculties of intellect, emotion, and reasoning ○ *She worked out a solution in her head.* ○ *Use your head, and don't panic!* ○ *a good head for figures* **4.** ARTS REPRESENTATION OF HUMAN HEAD an artistic, photographic, or televised representation or image of a human being's face, hair, eyes, mouth, nose, and ears **5.** LEADER OF OTHERS sb who is in charge of, has responsibility for, and supervises others **6.** EDUC = **headteacher 7.** CRISIS POINT a critical juncture in a situation or series of events, at which time some action must be taken, however painful ○ *The dispute came to a head at the monthly meeting.* **8.** MORE IMPORTANT END the more important end of sth ○ *Our guest sat at the head of the table.* **9.** TOP OF LONG THIN OBJECT the wider, often flattened, top of a long thin object ○ *He hit the nail on the head.* **10.** HIGHEST PART the highest or uppermost part of sth ○ *the head of the valley* **11.** BEVERAGES FROTH ON BEER the froth that forms on the top of beer when it is poured into a glass **12.** (*plural* **head**) COUNTABLE UNIT a single unit in a number of people or animals, especially when they are being counted ○ *500 head of cattle* **13.** MEASURE OF DISTANCE the height or length of a head, used as a measure of distance between two individuals, especially racehorses at the winning post ○ *The favourite won by a head.* **14.** BOT FLOWER OR VEGETABLE the top of a plant where a flower or a cluster of leaves grows **15.** MED TOP OF PIMPLE OR BOIL the visible pus-filled centre of a pimple or boil **16.** DRUGS DRUG USER sb who habitually uses drugs (*slang*) **17.** MED HEADACHE a headache (*informal*) ○ *I've got a terrible head.* **18.** GEOG SOURCE OF RIVER the source of a river or stream **19.** GEOG PROMONTORY a headland that juts out into the sea or other stretch of water (*often used in placenames*) **20.** COINS OBVERSE OF COIN the side of a coin that shows a leader's head or other main design **21.** ELEC ENG ELECTROMAGNETIC RECORDING DEVICE the part of a machine such as a tape recorder that uses, e.g., magnetic tape to record, read, or erase sounds, images, or data (*often used in the plural*) **22.** COMMUNICATION SECTION IN SPEECH OR TEXT one of the main sections or topics of a written or spoken discourse **23.** PRINTING TITLE a heading such as like a newspaper headline or before a section in a text **24.** NAUT SHIP'S TOILET a lavatory on a ship (*slang*) **25.** MUSIC PART OF DRUM the stretched membrane of a drum or tambourine **26.** PHYS REQUIRED HEIGHT OF LIQUID SURFACE the height that the surface of a liquid has to be above a specified level to produce a stated pressure at the specified level **27.** PHYS PRESSURE OF LIQUID the pressure at the lower of two points in a column of liquid resulting from the difference in height **28.** PHYS PRESSURE the pressure exerted by a liquid or gas ○ *a head of steam* **29.** MINING PART OF COAL MINE a passage where coal is mined underground **30.** TRANSP TERMINAL the destination point of a transport route **31.** MECH ENG DEVICE FOR HOLDING CUTTING TOOLS a part of a boring or turning machine, e.g. a lathe, that holds cutting tools to the work in progress **32.** ENG = **cylinder head 33.** *Carib* STATE OF MIND sb's specified state of mind at a given time, especially as perceived by others ○ *Wha' head you pushing?* **34.** ORAL SEX an act of performing oral sex on sb (*slang taboo*) ■ *v.* (**heads, heading, headed**) **1.** *vt.* CONTROL OTHERS OR ORGANIZATION to be in the first position of authority and exercise control over people or an organization **2.** BE AT FRONT OF GROUP to be at the front or the top of sth ○ *The mayor headed the procession as it entered the town.*

○ *The list was headed by some very well-known names.* **3.** *vi.* **GO IN CERTAIN DIRECTION** to move or go in a specified direction or to a specified position ○ *He headed towards the station.* ○ *I think we're heading for trouble here.* **4.** *vt.* **CAUSE TO GO SOMEWHERE** to make sth move in a specified direction or to a certain place ○ *The pilot headed the plane in a northeasterly course.* **5.** *vt.* PRINTING **BE OR GIVE A HEADING** to act as or supply a heading on a written page ○ *A short quotation heads each chapter of this book.* ○ *Let's head the letter with our logo.* **6.** *vt.* FOOTBALL **HIT WITH HEAD** to use the head to hit a ball ○ *He headed the ball into the goal.* [Old English *hēafod.* Ultimately from an Indo-European word that is also the ancestor of English *captain, cattle, chapter,* and *chief.*] ◇ **above sb's head** too difficult for sb to understand ◇ **be head and shoulders above sb** to be notably superior to sb ◇ **be off your head** to be mentally disturbed ◇ **give sb his** *or* **her head** to relax control or supervision of sb ◇ **go off your head** to become completely irrational (*informal*) ◇ **go to sb's head 1.** to make sb conceited or overconfident **2.** to make sb dizzy or light-headed ○ *The champagne went right to my head.* ◇ **head over heels 1.** in a headfirst rolling movement **2.** completely ○ *They fell head over heels for each other.* ◇ **keep your head** to remain calm or unexcited ◇ **let sb have his** *or* **her head = give sb his** *or* **her head** ◇ **lose your head** to panic or lose self-control ◇ **over sb's head = above sb's head**

head off *v.* **1.** *vt.* **INTERCEPT** to stop a person or animal from proceeding in a particular direction by placing yourself between the person or animal and the goal sought ○ *Let's try and head the robbers off at the pass.* ○ *We took a short cut to head her off before she reached the station.* **2.** *vt.* **FORESTALL** to try in advance to prevent sth from taking place, or to prevent sb from doing sth, that might prove difficult or unpleasant ○ *We need to head off any attempt to have the matter raised again in committee.* **3.** *vi.* **GO** to go, or leave a place and go, in a particular direction ○ *The others headed off down the hill while we stayed to enjoy the view a little longer.*

headache /héd ayk/ *n.* **1.** MED **PAIN IN THE HEAD** a pain in the head caused, e.g., by dilation of cerebral arteries or muscle tightness **2. SOURCE OF WORRY** sth that causes worry or difficulty (*informal*) —**headachy** *adj.*

headband /héd band/ *n.* a band of material that is worn round the head across the forehead, especially to keep hair off the face

headbang /héd bang/ (**-bangs, -banging, -banged**) *vi.* to dance to heavy metal music by moving the head violently backwards and forwards to the beat of the music (*slang*)

headbanger /héd bangər/ *n.* **1. FAN OF HEAVY METAL MUSIC** sb whose favourite music is heavy metal (*slang*) **2. headbanger, heidbanger** *Scotland* **VERY UNINTELLIGENT PERSON** sb who is very unintelligent or completely unreasonable (*informal insult*)

headboard /héd bawrd/ *n.* an upright board, often padded or covered in fabric, used to form the head of a bed

head boy *n.* a boy in the senior years at a secondary school who has been elected to represent the school and to act as a role model for younger pupils

head-butt /héd but/ *vt.* (**head-butts, head-butting, head-butted**) **HIT SB WITH HEAD** to hit sb a deliberate hard blow with the forehead or the top of the head ■ *n.* **BLOW WITH THE HEAD** a deliberate blow with the forehead or the top of the head

headcase /héd kayss/ *n.* an offensive term that deliberately shows contempt for or ridicules sb's mental condition (*informal insult*)

headcheese /héd cheez/ (*plural* **-cheeses** *or* **-cheese**) *n. US, Can* = **brawn** [*Cheese* from the ingredients being pressed together as in cheese-making]

head cold *n.* a viral infection of the nose, throat, and bronchial tubes, characterized by coughing, sneezing, headaches, and nasal congestion

head collar *n.* = **headpiece** *n.* 3

head count *n.* the process of counting the people in a group one by one, or the number arrived at by this process ○ *After a head count, we found there were 265 people in the hall.*

headdress /héd dress/ *n.* a decorative covering worn on the head, usually as a sign of rank, for ceremonial purposes, or as personal display

headed /héddid/ *adj.* **1. WITH A HEADING** with a heading, e.g. a letterhead, title, or similar inscription **2. WITH A PARTICULAR HEAD** with a specified kind of head or heads (*usually used in combination*) **3. WITH HAIR OF PARTICULAR KIND** with a specified colour or type of hair (*usually used in combination*) **4. WITH A PARTICULAR TEMPERAMENT** with a specified temperament, characteristic, or ability (*usually used in combination*)

header /héddər/ *n.* **1.** SOCCER **SHOT OR PASS WITH HEAD** a deliberate use of the head to play, pass, or shoot the ball in football ○ *He scored with a flying header.* **2. HEADLONG FALL** a headlong plunge or fall **3.** PRINTING **HEADING FOR PAGE** a heading for each page of a word-processed or faxed document, usually automatically inserted and consisting of text or a page number **4.** COMPUT **PLACE FOR INFORMATION ABOUT MESSAGE** a place at the top of a piece of electronic mail where the sender can state what a message is about and where it is being sent from and to **5.** CONSTR **CROSSWISE BRICK IN WALL** a brick or stone positioned crosswise in a wall and level with its outer surface **6.** INDUST **MAKER, FITTER, OR REMOVER OF TOPS** a person who, or a machine that, makes, fits, or removes the tops of sth **7.** ENG = **header tank**

header tank *n.* a raised tank that ensures a constant pressure or supply of fluid to a system, especially water to a central heating system

headfast /héd faast/ *n.* a mooring rope at the bow of a ship

headfirst /héd fúrst/ *adv., adj.* **WITH THE HEAD LEADING** in a movement or position where the head is in front of the rest of the body and is the first thing that reaches, enters, or strikes sth ○ *He insisted on going down the slide headfirst.* ○ *taking a headfirst dive into the pool* ■ *adv.* **RASHLY AND THOUGHTLESSLY** abruptly and without taking time to think about or prepare for sth ○ *They rush into things headfirst and think about the consequences afterwards.*

headful /hédfòòl/ *n.* **1. LARGE AMOUNT** a large amount of sth that has been learned, thought, or imagined (*informal*) ○ *a headful of facts* **2. MASS OF HAIR** a thick mass of hair ○ *a headful of curls*

head gate *n.* **1. UPSTREAM GATE OF LOCK** the gate that controls the flow of water into the upstream end of a canal lock **2.** = **floodgate**

headgear /héd geer/ *n.* **1.** CLOTHES **STH COVERING THE HEAD** sth worn on the head, especially a hat ○ *sporting some very natty headgear* **2.** MINING **HOISTING MECHANISM AT MINESHAFT** an apparatus at the top of a mineshaft for lifting things out of and lowering them into a mine **3.** RIDING **PART OF HARNESS** the part of a harness that fits over a horse's head

head girl *n.* a girl in the senior years at a secondary school who has been elected to represent the school and to act as a role model for younger pupils

headhunt /héd hunt/ (**-hunts, -hunting, -hunted**) *v.* **1.** *vt.* BUSINESS, HR **RECRUIT SB FROM ANOTHER COMPANY** to recruit, or attempt to recruit, an executive or highly valued employee from one company to fill a similar position in another enterprise ○ *The agency headhunted her to work for an American bank.* **2.** *vi.* ANTHROP **COLLECT HEADS** to seek, collect, and preserve the heads of enemies as trophies or ceremonial objects

headhunter /héd huntər/ *n.* **1.** BUSINESS, HR **RECRUITMENT AGENT** sb whose job is to seek personnel for a company from other firms **2.** ANTHROP **SB WHO COLLECTS HEADS** a member of a people practising headhunting

headhunting /héd hunting/ *n.* **1.** BUSINESS, HR **RECRUITMENT FROM OTHER COMPANIES** the business of recruiting people who already hold positions in companies to fill similar positions in other enterprises **2.** ANTHROP **HEAD-COLLECTING** the practice among some peoples of cutting off the heads of enemies killed in battle and preserving them as trophies or ceremonial objects

heading /hédding/ *n.* **1. TITLE** sth that forms the head, top, edge, or front of sth, especially as a title for a paragraph, section, chapter, or page ○ *The chapter headings are to be set in 24-point bold.* **2. CATEGORY OF SUBJECT MATTER** any of the divisions into which the subject matter of a document, discourse, or discussion is divided ○ *That information definitely comes under the heading of matters not to be aired in public.* **3.** NAVIG **COURSE** the direction in which a ship or aircraft is travelling, often given as a compass bearing ○ *If we continue on our present heading we should sight land in one hour.* **4.** MINING **MINE TUNNEL** a horizontal tunnel in a mine, or the end of such a tunnel

headlamp /héd lamp/ *n.* = **headlight**

headland /hédd̦lənd/ *n.* **1.** GEOG **PROMONTORY** a narrow piece of land jutting out into water, usually with steep, high cliffs **2.** AGRIC **UNPLOUGHED STRIP** a strip of land left unploughed at the edge of a field

headless /héddləss/ *adj.* **1. WITHOUT HEAD** without a head on the body **2. WITHOUT LEADER** having no leader, guide, or director —**headlessness** *n.*

headlight /héd līt/ *n.* a powerful light attached to the front of a motor vehicle or a locomotive, or the beam of light cast by it ○ *He was driving without headlights.*

headline /héd līn/ *n.* **1.** PRESS **TITLE OF NEWSPAPER ARTICLE** a caption printed at the top of a page or article in a newspaper, usually in large heavy letters and often summarizing the content that follows it ○ *an article with the headline 'Sharp Fall in Share Prices'* **2.** PRINTING **LINE AT TOP OF PAGE** a line printed at the top of a page of a book or document giving the page number and sometimes other information such as the title or the author's name ■ **headlines** *npl.* PRESS, BROADCAST **MAIN NEWS ITEMS** the most important items of news covered by a newspaper or a news broadcast ○ *Her name has seldom been out of the headlines since she announced her intention to sue.* ○ *We bring you the headlines every hour on the hour.* ■ *vt.* (**-lines, -lining, -lined**) **1.** PRESS **PROVIDE PROMINENT HEADING** to give a prominent title or caption to sth ○ *They headlined the story POP STAR ENTERS HOSPITAL.* **2.** *US* **PUBLICIZE AS STAR** to present sb as the leading attraction of a show **3.** *US* ARTS **APPEAR AS STAR** to appear as the leading attraction of a show

headliner /héd līnər/ *n. US* a performer who is advertised as a leading attraction in a show

head-load *n. S Africa* **STH CARRIED ON PORTER'S HEAD** a burden carried on the head of a porter ■ *vt. S Africa* **CARRY STH ON HEAD** to transport sth by carrying it on the head

headlock /héd lok/ *n.* a hold in which a wrestler tightly grips an arm around an opponent's head

headlong /héd long/ *adv., adj.* **1. WITH HEAD FOREMOST** with the head in front of the rest of the body, especially in a rapid uncontrolled movement **2. MOVING FAST AND OUT OF CONTROL** moving or travelling in a fast uncontrolled way **3. WITH TOO MUCH HASTE** acting, happening, or done in an impetuous way with little or no thought for the consequences ○ *She had thrown herself headlong into an even worse situation.* ■ *adj.* **VERY STEEP** very steep (*archaic*) [14thC. By folk etymology from earlier *headling*, by association with *-long* 'foremost', in, for example SIDELONG.]

head louse *n.* a louse that lives on a human head among the hair, feeding by sucking blood and gluing its eggs to the hair shafts near the skin surface. Latin name: *Pediculus humanus capitis.*

headman /hédmən, héd man/ (*plural* **-men** /-mən, -men/) *n.* **1. CHIEF** the leader of a community or village in some small-scale societies **2. LEADER** a leader or overseer

headmaster /hed maástər/ *n.* a man who is in charge of a school —**headmasterly** *adj.* —**headmastership** *n.*

headmistress /hed místrəss/ *n.* a woman who is in charge of a school —**headmistressy** *adj.*

head money *n.* **1. BOUNTY** a reward paid for the capture or killing of a fugitive or outlaw **2. POLL TAX** a tax on each person (*archaic*)

headmost /héd mōst/ *adj.* forward to the greatest extent

headnote /héd nōt/ *n.* a brief note at the top of a chapter or a page that summarizes what follows, especially points of law or a legal decision

head of programming *n.* an executive who is responsible for the selection of television or radio programmes. US term **program director**

head of state *n.* the chief representative of a country or state, who may or may not also be the head of government

head of the river *n.* **1.** ROWING REGATTA a regatta held on a river involving a series of races for rowing crews **2.** VICTOR IN REGATTA the winner of a regatta held on a river

head-on *adv., adj.* WITH FRONT FACING FORWARDS with the front facing towards sth ○ *We were sailing head-on into the teeth of the gale.* ○ *a head-on collision* ■ *adv.* WITHOUT EVASION OR COMPROMISE making no attempt to avoid the dangers or difficulties involved in sth ■ *adj.* UNCOMPROMISING involving direct, fundamental, and uncompromising opposition ○ *He tried to avoid a head-on clash with his business partner.*

head over heels *adv.* rolling or turning so that the feet are in the air and the head below them so as to land on the back or the feet [From earlier *heels over head*] ◇ **head over heels in love** completely and rapturously in love

headphones /héd fōnz/ *npl.* a pair of listening devices joined by a band across the top of the head and worn in or over the ears

headpiece /héd peess/ *n.* **1.** PRINTING DESIGN AT TOP OF PAGE an ornamental design printed at the beginning of a text **2.** CLOTHES HEAD PROTECTOR a covering for the head, especially a protective one **3.** EQU BRIDLE PART the part of a horse's bridle that fits around the head

head pin *n.* = **kingpin** *n.* 4

headquarter /hed kwáwrtər/ (**-ters, -tering, -tered**) *v. US* (*informal*) **1.** *vt.* PROVIDE WITH BASE to provide sb with a centre of operations ○ *They headquartered their office in a former barracks.* **2.** *vi.* BE BASED to set up a headquarters ○ *She headquartered in Paris.*

headquarters /hed kwáwrtərz, héd kwawrtərz/ *npl.* (*takes a singular or plural verb*) **1.** BUSINESS HEAD OFFICE the administrative centre from which the affairs of an organization are directed **2.** MIL COMMANDER'S OPERATIONAL BASE a military commander's central office, from which operations are controlled and orders issued ○ *Napoleon's headquarters were in a disused windmill.* ○ *Headquarters is on the radio; they want to know our precise position.*

headrace /héd rayss/ *n.* a channel conveying water to a water wheel or turbine

headrail /héd rayl/ *n.* **1.** CUE GAMES STARTING END OF BILLIARD TABLE the end of the table from which a game of billiards is started, nearest the baulk line **2.** SAILING RAILING ON SAILING SHIP a railing on a sailing vessel extending from the rear of the bow to the back of the figurehead

headreach /héd reech/ *n.* DISTANCE MADE TO WINDWARD the distance that a sailing boat makes to windward when tacking ■ *vt.* (**-reaches, -reaching, -reached**) OUTDISTANCE OTHER BOAT to make a better distance than another boat when tacking

head register *n.* the higher register or falsetto of men's and boys' singing voices in which tone production is concentrated in the head and assisted by sympathetic vibration of the nasal and skull cavities

headrest /héd rest/ *n.* an often padded support for the head, usually on the back of a seat, especially in a motor vehicle

head restraint *n.* an adjustable headrest fitted to the back of a seat of a motor vehicle, designed to prevent neck injuries in an accident

head rhyme *n.* = **alliteration**

headroom /héd room, -rŏŏm/ *n.* the space or clearance overhead, e.g. in a room, doorway, the interior of a motor vehicle, or the underside of a bridge ○ *There's plenty of headroom in this car, even in the back seat.*

headsail /héd sayl/ *n.* a sail attached to or set forward of the foremast

headscarf /héd skaarf/ (*plural* **-scarves** /-skaarvz/) *n.* a woman's scarf in the form of a square of fabric, for wearing on the head or tied round the neck

head sea *n.* waves or a current running in a direction opposite to the course of a ship

headset /héd set/ *n.* a pair of earphones, often with a small mouthpiece attached to enable two-way communication

headshaking /héd shayking/ *n.* a series of side-to-side movements of the head, communicating or suggesting sth such as disagreement, doubt, or refusal ○ *I noticed a lot of headshaking in the audience as you made that claim.*

headship /hédship/ *n.* **1.** EDUC POST OF HEAD TEACHER a position as the principal of a school **2.** POSITION OF LEADER sb's position or authority as a leader

headshot /héd shot/ *n.* **1.** PHOTOGRAPHY, CINEMA PHOTO OF HEAD a photograph or cinematic shot of a head, especially a person's head **2.** ARMS GUNSHOT TO HEAD a gunshot aimed to hit the head of a person or animal

headshrinker /héd shringkər/ *n. US* a psychiatrist (*dated informal insult*)

headsman /hédzmən/ (*plural* **-men** /-mən/) *n.* a public executioner who beheaded prisoners condemned to death

headsquare /héd skwair/ *n.* = **headscarf**

head staggers *n.* a disease in cattle or horses characterized by loss of balance or staggering (*regional; takes a singular or plural verb*) ◇ **get** *or* **take** *or* **have the head staggers** to lose your temper or your composure (*regional humorous*)

headstand /héd stand/ *n.* a position in gymnastics or yoga in which the body is balanced upside down on the head, usually using the hands for support

head start *n.* an advantage in a competition or endeavour ○ *A good education gives you a head start when it comes to getting a job.*

headstock /héd stok/ *n.* an assembly or part of a machine, especially in a lathe, that holds and supports a revolving part

headstone /héd stōn/ *n.* **1.** GRAVESTONE a slab of stone placed at the head of a grave as a memorial to the person or people buried there **2.** ARCHIT = **keystone**

headstream /héd streem/ *n.* a stream that is the source, or one of the sources, of a river

headstrong /héd strong/ *adj.* self-willed and determined not to follow orders or advice —**headstrongly** *adv.* —**headstrongness** *n.*

heads up *interj. US* a command to watch out, especially for danger from overhead, e.g. a falling object or a ball coming through the air

heads-up *n. US* **1.** WARNING an early warning to sb that sth, typically sth undesirable, is soon to happen ○ *gave the law firm a heads-up on the impending subpoena* **2.** STH REQUIRING ATTENTION sth that requires alert attention ■ *adj. US* ALERT AND RESOURCEFUL showing quick resourcefulness and alertness in doing or observing sth

head teacher *n.* sb who is in charge of the teaching staff of a school and who oversees its day-to-day running

head-to-head *adv., adj.* WITH A DIRECT ENCOUNTER in or involving direct contact or confrontation ■ *adv.* WITH HEADS ADJACENT placed or arranged with heads adjacent ○ *We put the beds head-to-head.* ■ *n.* DIRECT ENCOUNTER a direct and immediate encounter

head trip *n. US* (*dated slang*) **1.** MENTALLY STIMULATING EXPERIENCE an experience that stimulates or excites sb mentally **2.** STH DONE FOR PERSONAL GRATIFICATION sth done or a way of behaving that is intended mainly for personal gratification

head-up display *n.* a display of instrument data projected onto a screen at eye level so that a pilot or driver does not have to look down to see it. US term **heads-up display**

head voice *n.* MUSIC = **head register**

head waiter *n.* the person in charge of a group of servers at a restaurant. The head waiter is often also responsible for taking reservations and seating customers.

head wall *n.* a cliff forming one end of a valley

headwaters /héd wawtərz/ *npl.* the streams that make up the beginnings of a river

headway /héd way/ *n.* **1.** PROGRESS progress towards achieving sth ○ *We're unable to make much headway with the project.* **2.** FORWARD MOVEMENT movement or rate of progress forwards **3.** = **headroom** **4.** TRANSP DIFFERENCE IN TIME OR DISTANCE the interval or distance between two vehicles, trains, or ships travelling in the same direction along the same route ◇ **make headway** to make progress in doing sth or going somewhere

headwind /héd wind/ *n.* a wind blowing against the direction of travel

headword /héd wurd/ *n.* a word or phrase that forms a heading at the start of a text and is usually printed in distinctive type, especially a main entry word in a dictionary

headwork /héd wurk/ *n.* **1.** MENTAL EFFORT mental activity or effort **2.** ARCHIT ARCHITECTURAL DECORATION decoration on the keystone of an arch

heady /héddi/ (**-ier, -iest**) *adj.* **1.** EXHILARATING causing or involving a feeling of energy, confidence, and elation **2.** INTOXICATING causing a feeling of light-headedness or intoxication **3.** IMPETUOUS impulsive and rash in behaviour —**headily** *adv.* —**headiness** *n.*

heal /heel/ (**heals, healing, healed**) *v.* **1.** *vt.* CURE FROM AILMENT to make a person or injury healthy and whole **2.** *vi.* REPAIR NATURALLY to be repaired and restored naturally, e.g. by the formation of scar tissue ○ *The broken bone seems to be healing up quite nicely.* **3.** *vt.* SETTLE OR RECTIFY to repair or rectify sth that causes discord and animosity ○ *Unless she can heal the rift within her party, she stands little chance in the election.* **4.** *vti.* MORALLY PURIFY to get rid of a wrong, evil, or spiritual affliction [Old English *hǣlan*. Ultimately from a prehistoric Germanic base that is also the ancestor of English *health* and *whole*.] —**healable** *adj.*

heal-all *n.* = **selfheal**

healer /héelər/ *n.* sb who cures or treats illnesses or injuries, often using spiritual rather than scientific methods

Healey /héeli/, **Denis, Baron Healey of Riddlesden** (*b.* 1917) British politician. A Labour MP from 1952, he was Chancellor of the Exchequer (1974–79) and deputy leader of the Labour Party (1980–83). Full name **Denis Winston Healey**

healing /héeling/ *n.* PROCESS OF CURING OR BECOMING WELL the process of curing sb or sth, or of becoming well ○ *spiritual healing* ■ *adj.* CURATIVE with the effect of curing or improving sth ○ *the healing process*

health /helth/ *n.* **1.** MED PRESENCE OR ABSENCE OF WELLBEING the general condition of the body or mind, especially in terms of the presence or absence of illnesses, injuries, or impairments **2.** OVERALL CONDITION OF STH the general condition of sth in terms of soundness, vitality, and proper functioning ○ *There is concern about the financial health of the company.* **3.** DRINKING TOAST a toast drunk to wish for sb's wellbeing and prosperity ○ *Here's a health to Her Majesty!* ■ *adj.* **1.** MED DEVOTED TO GENERAL WELLBEING with the function of maintaining physical and mental wellbeing among the general public and the administration of medical and related services **2.** GOOD FOR PEOPLE promoting physical and mental wellbeing [Old English *hǣlþ*. Ultimately from a prehistoric Germanic base that is also the ancestor of English *heal* and *whole*, the underlying idea being of 'wholeness'.]

health camp *n. NZ* a camp for children who need health care, usually located on the coast

health care *n.* the provision of medical and related services aimed at maintaining good health in individuals or the public, especially through the prevention and treatment of disease

healthcare /hélth kair/ *adj.* concerned with or involved in providing physical and mental services, preventive medicine, and treatment to individuals or the public

healthcare assistant /hélth kair-/ *n.* sb with no specialized training employed in a hospital or other healthcare facility to perform basic nursing-support tasks such as bedmaking or giving patients baths. US term **nurses' aide**

health centre *n.* **1.** LOCAL HEADQUARTERS FOR HEALTHCARE SERVICES a place, operated by a local authority, that houses a medical practice and other healthcare services **2.** PLACE OFFERING STUDENT HEALTH SERVICES a place, operated by a school or university, that houses a medical practice and other healthcare services for students

health farm *n.* a commercial establishment similar to a hotel, usually rural, that offers ways of improving health and fitness, e.g. a controlled diet, exercise, and massage. US term **health spa**

health food *n.* food that is considered to be more beneficial to health than ordinary food, especially products that are organically grown or without chemical additives

healthful /hélthf'l/ *adj.* beneficial to physical or mental health —**healthfully** *adv.* —**healthfulness** *n.*

WORD KEY: USAGE

See Usage note at ***healthy.***

health insurance *n.* insurance to cover the costs or losses incurred if an insured person falls ill

health salts *npl.* mineral salts, e.g. magnesium sulphate, used as a mild laxative

Health Service Commissioner /hélth surviss kə míshənər/ *n.* a senior British official who investigates complaints about services provided by healthcare authorities that have not been satisfactorily resolved at a lower level

health spa *n.* = **health farm**

health visitor *n. UK* a trained nurse who gives medical care and advice to people in their homes, especially to mothers of babies and young children, senior citizens, and to physically challenged people

healthy /hélthi/ (**-ier, -iest**) *adj.* **1.** IN GOOD CONDITION in good physical or mental condition **2.** BENEFICIAL TO HEALTH helping to maintain or bring about good health ○ *a healthy diet* ○ *This is not a very healthy place to live.* **3.** SUGGESTIVE OF GOOD HEALTH showing that sb is in good health **4.** MORALLY OR PSYCHOLOGICALLY SOUND showing or encouraging moral or psychological soundness **5.** FUNCTIONING WELL in a prosperous and efficient condition ○ *My bank balance isn't looking very healthy at the moment.* **6.** CONSIDERABLE large, usually satisfyingly large, in size or quantity (*informal*) —**healthily** /hélthili/ *adv.* —**healthiness** /hélthinəss/ *n.*

WORD KEY: USAGE

healthy or **healthful**? It is sometimes argued that ***healthy*** should be used only to describe a living being that is in good health, and that ***healthful*** is the word for such things as habits or foods that promote good health. There is nothing wrong with observing this distinction, but there is also nothing wrong with using ***healthy*** as a synonym for ***healthful***, as reputable writers have been doing for centuries.

Heaney /héeni/, **Seamus** (*b.* 1939) British poet. His poems explored the relationship of his native Northern Irish culture and language, and were collected in volumes including *North* (1975) and *The Spirit Level* (1995). One of the leading English-language poets of his generation, he won a Nobel Prize in literature in 1995. Full name **Seamus Justin Heaney**

heap /heep/ *n.* **1.** ROUNDED PILE a large number of things lying on top of one another, or a large quantity of material, forming a roughly rounded shape ○ *They'd left all their dirty clothes in a heap on the floor.* ○ *All that was left of the building was a heap of rubble.* **2.** STH OLD OR BATTERED sth that is old, dilapidated, or untidy-looking, especially an old building or car (*informal*) ○ *You'll never get to Scotland in this old heap.* **3.** LARGE AMOUNT a large quantity or amount (*informal*) (*often used in the plural*) ○ *Don't worry, we've got heaps of time.* ○ *I've got a heap of things to see to before I can go home.* ■ *vt.* (**heaps, heaping, heaped**) **1.** PUT IN A PILE to collect or arrange sth into a loose pile ○ *heaping the stuff all together in the middle of the yard* **2.** PILE UP to load or put a lot of sth into a shallow container, forming a roughly rounded mound **3.** GIVE IN ABUNDANCE to give or supply sth in large quantities or amounts ○ *They heaped scorn on my suggestion.* [Old English *hēap*. Ultimately from a prehistoric Germanic base that is also the ancestor of Dutch *hoop* 'hope', the underlying idea being of sth forlorn.] ◇ **all of a heap** into a state of shock, surprise, or confusion (*informal*) ○ *The news was totally unexpected and it knocked me all of a heap.*

heap up *v.* **1.** *vti.* FORM INTO HEAP to accumulate sth, or be gathered, into a roughly rounded mound **2.** *vt.* COLLECT to collect or acquire sth in large amounts

heaped /heept/ *adj.* containing sth in an amount large enough to rise up in a small heap. US term **heaping**

heaping /heéping/ *adj. US* = **heaped**

heaps /heeps/ *npl. Aus* TROUBLE trouble, opposition, or adverse criticism (*informal*) ○ *I copped heaps for resigning from the team when I did.* ■ *adv.* VERY MUCH very much or greatly (*informal*) ○ *I feel heaps better since I went to the doctor.*

hear /heer/ (**hears, hearing, heard, heard** /hurd/) *v.* **1.** *vti.* PERCEIVE SOUNDS to perceive or be able to perceive sound **2.** *vti.* GET TO KNOW STH to be informed of sth, especially by being told about it **3.** *vt.* LISTEN TO STH to listen to sb or sth ○ *I'm sure I've heard him on the radio.* **4.** *vti.* UNDERSTAND to understand fully by listening attentively ○ *Did you hear what I just said?* ○ *I won't stand for it, do you hear?* **5.** *vt.* LAW PRESIDE OVER STH to consider sth officially as a judge, commissioner, or member of a jury ○ *the judge who heard the case* **6.** *vt.* CHR ATTEND MASS to attend Mass in a Roman Catholic church ○ *The congregation heard Mass at ten o'clock.* [Old English *hīeran*. Ultimately from a prehistoric Germanic word (source also of German *hören*) of uncertain origin.] —**hearable** *adj.* —**hearer** *n.* ◇ **hear, hear!** used as an exclamation to show great approval

hear from *vt.* to receive a communication, e.g. a letter or telephone call, from a person, place, or organization

hear of *vt.* to consider sth as a possibility ○ *She wouldn't hear of their paying their own way.*

hear out *vt.* to continue listening until sb or sth has finished

hearing /heéring/ *n.* **1.** AWARENESS OF SOUND the perception of sound, made possible by vibratory changes in air pressure on the ear drums ○ *My hearing's going, so you'll have to speak louder.* **2.** EARSHOT the range within which sth can be heard ○ *She moved out of hearing and I lost the end of the sentence.* **3.** CHANCE TO BE HEARD an opportunity to be heard, especially a chance to state an opinion or fact ○ *All I want is for my views to get a fair hearing.* **4.** LAW TRIAL the trial of a case in a court of law **5.** LAW PRELIMINARY EXAMINATION OF ACCUSED a preliminary judicial examination of an accused person to decide whether the case should proceed to trial **6.** LAW SESSION TO HEAR EVIDENCE a session of an investigative or legislative body at which witnesses are heard ◇ **hard of hearing** unable to hear well

hearing aid *n.* a small amplifying device to enable sb to hear better, usually worn in or behind the ear

hearing dog *n.* a dog trained to help a deaf or hearing-impaired person by indicating that it has heard a certain sound, e.g. the ringing of a telephone or doorbell

hearing-impaired *adj.* with a reduced or deficient ability to hear

hearing loss *n.* a measurable reduction of the ability to hear or distinguish sounds, especially of a specific frequency

hearken /haárkən/ (**-kens, -kening, -kened**), **harken** (**-kens, -kening, -kened**) *vi.* to listen and pay attention (*archaic*) [Old English *he(o)rcnian* (from an earlier form of HARK), by folk etymology from association with HEAR] —**hearkener** *n.*

Hearne /hurn/, **Samuel** (1745–92) British explorer. Working for the Hudson's Bay Company, he was the first European to travel overland to the North American coast on the Arctic Ocean (1770–72).

hearsay /heér say/ *n.* SECOND-HAND INFORMATION information that is heard from other people ■ *adj.* HEARD SECOND-HAND being or containing information heard from other people [Mid-16thC. Translation of Old French *par oïr dire*, literally 'by hear say'.]

hearsay evidence *n.* evidence consisting of testimony about other people that is not based on direct or personal knowledge. Hearsay evidence is not usually admissible in a court of law.

hearse /hurss/ *n.* a vehicle in which a coffin is carried to a funeral or a dead body is taken away [13thC. Originally 'toothed frame for holding candles over coffins', via French *herse* from, ultimately, Latin *hirpex* 'rake, harrow', of uncertain origin: probably from Oscan *hirpus* 'wolf', from the teeth.]

WORD KEY: ORIGIN

Agricultural harrows in the Middle Ages were typically toothed triangular frames, so the word for a harrow came to be applied in French to a triangular toothed frame for holding candles, as used in a church, and particularly as placed over a coffin at funeral services. This was the meaning of ***hearse*** when English acquired it, and it only gradually developed via 'canopy placed over a coffin' and 'coffin, bier' to the modern sense 'funeral vehicle' (first recorded in the mid-17thC).

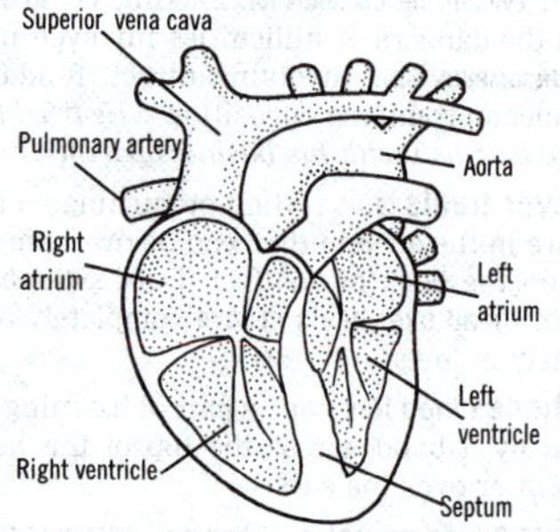

Heart: Human heart

heart /haart/ *n.* **1.** PHYSIOL BLOOD-PUMPING ORGAN a hollow muscular organ that pumps blood around the body, in humans situated in the centre of the chest with its apex directed to the left **2.** ANAT POSITION OF CHEST ABOVE HEART the area on the front of the human body that corresponds roughly to the position of the heart **3.** BASIS OF EMOTIONAL LIFE the human heart, considered as the source and centre of emotional life, where the deepest and sincerest feelings are located and an individual is most vulnerable to pain **4.** CHARACTER sb's essential character ○ *He's an awkward cuss, but he's got a very good heart.* **5.** COMPASSION the ability to feel humane and altruistic feelings ○ *If she had any heart she would forgive him.* **6.** AFFECTION affection, love, or warm admiration ○ *The chorus's singing won the hearts of the audience.* **7.** SPIRIT the capacity for courage and determination ○ *The team played with a lot of heart.* ○ *They put their whole hearts into making a go of the business.* **8.** DISPOSITION a mood, mental state, or frame of mind **9.** ESSENTIAL PART OF STH the distinctive, significant, and characteristic centre of sth ○ *the heart of rural England* **10.** PLANTS PART OF VEGETABLE AROUND CORE the often tasty or succulent compact central part of a vegetable, e.g. a lettuce or cabbage, where the leaves curl in tightly ○ *palm hearts* ○ *artichoke hearts* **11.** FOOD ANIMAL HEART USED AS FOOD the heart of an animal that is cleaned and trimmed, then roasted, stewed, or braised as food **12.** SYMBOLIC DEPICTION OF HEART a simplified and conventionalized picture of a heart as a rounded, roughly triangular shape, often used to signify love **13.** CARDS PLAYING CARD any one of a suit of cards marked with a symbolic depiction of one or more hearts. ◊ **hearts 14.** BELOVED PERSON sb who is dearly loved ○ *Come to me, dear heart.* [Old English *heorte*. Related to German *Herz*.] ◇ **at heart** in essence or reality, and despite contrary appearances ◇ **break sb's heart** to cause sb intense unhappiness and suffering ◇ **do sb's heart good** to make sb feel happy or satisfied ◇ **eat your heart out 1.** to brood about sth that makes you feel unhappy (*informal*) **2.** to be consumed with envy ◇ **from the bottom of your heart** with the utmost sincerity ◇ **have sb's welfare** *or* **interests at heart** to have sb's wellbeing or interests in mind ◇ **heart and soul** completely, or with the greatest devotion ◇ **in your heart of hearts** in your deepest inner feelings ◇ **learn** *or* **know sth by heart** to memorize or have memorized sth ◇ **lose heart** to become discouraged ◇ **not have the heart to do sth** to be unable to bring yourself to do sth that is liable to hurt sb else ◇ **set your heart on sth, have your heart set on sth** to have sth as your ambition or greatest wish ◇ **take heart** to become encouraged and more confident ◇ **take sth to heart 1.** to take sth seriously **2.** to be upset by sth ◇ **wear your heart on your sleeve** to reveal your feelings openly ◇ **with all your heart** completely or very willingly

WORD KEY: ORIGIN

The Indo-European ancestor of ***heart*** is also the ultimate source of English *cardiac, concord, cordial, courage, quarry,* and *record.*

WORD KEY: CULTURAL NOTE

Heart of Midlothian, a novel by Scottish writer Sir Walter Scott (1818). Widely regarded as Scott's best novel, it is set in the 1730s and tells the story of Effie Deans, who is wrongfully accused of the murder of a child. The title refers to the site of Effie's incarceration: the Tolbooth prison in Edinburgh, in the county of Midlothian.

heartache /haárt ayk/ *n.* a powerful feeling of sorrow, anguish, or regret

heart attack *n.* **1.** MED **DAMAGE TO HEART** a sudden, serious, painful, and sometimes fatal interruption of the heart's normal functioning, especially due to a blockage in the coronary artery **2. SUDDEN SHOCK** a sudden severe shock (*informal*) ○ *I had a heart attack when I looked in the drawer and saw that the money was gone.*

heartbeat /haárt beet/ *n.* **1. CONTRACTION OF HEART MUSCLE** a vigorous contraction of the lower chambers of the heart that drives blood through the body **2. CONTINUOUS PULSATION OF HEART** the continuous pulsating movement and sound made by a beating heart ○ *Her rapid heartbeat gradually slowed.* **3. DRIVING FORCE** the driving force behind sth

heart block *n.* a condition in which the nerve impulses that control the heartbeat are abnormal so that the ventricles and the atria no longer beat in time with one another

heartbreak /haárt brayk/ *n.* intense unhappiness or grief

heartbreaker /haárt braykər/ *n.* sb who or sth that makes people very unhappy, especially sb with whom many people fall in love and by whom they are subsequently hurt

heartbreaking /haárt brayking/ *adj.* causing intense sadness or distress —**heartbreakingly** *adv.*

heartbroken /haárt brōkən/ *adj.* feeling intensely unhappy or disappointed because of sth that has happened ○ *The children were heartbroken when we had to cancel the trip.* —**heartbrokenly** *adv.* —**heartbrokenness** *n.*

heartburn /haárt burn/ *n.* an uncomfortable burning sensation in the lower chest, usually caused by stomach acid flowing back into the lower end of the oesophagus [Formed from HEART in the obsolete sense 'stomach']

heart disease *n.* an abnormal condition of the heart or the blood vessels supplying it that impairs cardiac functioning

hearten /haárt'n/ (**-ens, -ening, -ened**) *vt.* to make sb feel more cheerful and hopeful [Formed from HEART in the obsolete sense 'to encourage']

heartening /haárt'ning/ *adj.* giving sb optimism or encouragement

heart failure *n.* **1. END OF HEARTBEAT** cessation of the normal functioning of the heart, leading to death ○ *He died from heart failure at 92, while gardening.* **2. HEART INSUFFICIENCY** a condition in which the heart cannot pump blood in sufficient volume to meet the needs of the body, causing breathlessness, enlargement of the liver, swollen ankles, and other symptoms

heartfelt /haárt felt/ *adj.* arising from strong and sincere emotion

hearth /haarth/ *n.* **1. FLOOR OF FIREPLACE** the floor of a fireplace, especially when it extends into the room **2. HOME AND FAMILY LIFE** the fireplace of a home, thought of as a symbol of the home and the life of the family who live in it **3.** METALL **PART OF FOUNDRY FURNACE** the lowest part of a foundry furnace where molten metal collects or ore is smelted [Old English *heorþ*. Ultimately from a prehistoric Germanic word, (which also produced German *herd*), of uncertain origin.]

hearth rug *n.* a rug for the floor in front of a fireplace

hearthside /haárth sīd/ *n.* = **fireside**

hearthstone /haárth stōn/ *n.* **1. STONE FORMING HEARTH** a large stone used to form the hearth in a fireplace **2. CLEANSING STONE FOR HEARTHS** a soft variety of stone or a compound of pipeclay and stone used to clean and whiten fireplaces and doorsteps

heartily /haártili/ *adv.* **1. ENTHUSIASTICALLY** in a sincere and enthusiastic way **2. GOOD-NATUREDLY** in a loud, vigorous, good-natured way **3. COMPLETELY** in a full and complete way **4. HUNGRILY** with a good appetite

heartland /haárt land/ *n.* a central area of a country or region, or an area of it that has special economic, political, military, or sentimental significance

heartless /haártləss/ *adj.* having or showing no pity or kindness —**heartlessly** *adv.* —**heartlessness** *n.*

heart-lung machine /haárt lúng mə sheen/ *n.* a machine that is used to take over the functions of the heart and lungs in pumping and oxygenating the blood, chiefly during heart surgery

heart massage *n.* = **cardiac massage**

heart murmur *n.* an unusual sound coming from the heart that can be detected by a stethoscope and may indicate the presence of a heart defect

heart of palm *n.* the terminal bud of the cabbage palm, cooked and served as a vegetable or in salads

heart rate *n.* the number of heartbeats occurring within a specified length of time

heartrending /haárt rending/ *adj.* causing intense sadness or distress, especially in sympathy with sb else's unhappiness or hardship —**heartrendingly** *adv.*

hearts /haarts/ *n.* **1. SUIT OF CARDS** a suit of cards marked with red heart symbols (*takes a singular or plural verb*) **2. CARD GAME** a card game in which players try to avoid winning cards of the suit hearts or the queen of spades, or else to win all of these (*takes a singular verb*)

heart-searching *n.* a thorough and often painful examination of your own conscience, feelings, or motives

heartsease /haárts eez/ (*plural* **-eases** *or* **-ease**) *n.* a pansy, especially the wild pansy. Latin name: *Viola tricolor.*

heartsick /haárt sik/ *adj.* deeply disappointed or sad ○ *I'm heartsick when I think of how things ought to have been.* —**heartsickness** *n.*

heart-smart *adj.* used to describe food that is low in fat and cholesterol and therefore reduces the risk of heart disease (*informal*)

heartsore /haárt sawr/ *adj.* extremely sad or regretful (*archaic or literary*)

heartstrings /haártstringz/ *npl.* sb's feelings, especially tender emotions [*String* in the obsolete sense 'tendon', from the earlier belief that tendons brace the heart]

heartthrob /haárt throb/ *n.* sb who is thought to be extraordinarily attractive, especially a young film star or singer (*dated informal*)

heart-to-heart *adj.* **VERY FRANK AND INTIMATE** frank and intimate, often about personal matters ■ *n.* **FRANK TALK** a frank, intimate conversation

heart urchin *n.* a variety of sea urchin with a heart-shaped body. Genus: *Echinocardium.*

heartwarming /haárt wawrming/ *adj.* inspiring warm or kindly feelings, usually by showing life and human nature in a positive and reassuring light

heartwood /haárt wŏŏd/ *n.* the wood at the centre of a tree trunk or branch that is older, darker, and harder than the wood surrounding it

heartworm /haárt wurm/ (*plural* **-worms** *or* **-worm**) *n.* **1.** ZOOL **PARASITIC WORM** a parasitic filarial worm that lives in the heart and associated blood vessels of members of the dog family, and occasionally in cats and seals **2.** VET **HEART INFECTION IN DOGS** an infection of the heart in members of the dog family, and occasionally in cats and seals, that is caused by parasitic worms

hearty /haárti/ *adj.* (**-ier, -iest**) **1. SINCERE AND ENTHUSIASTIC** sincere and expressed in a cheerful, enthusiastic way **2. LOUD AND ENTHUSIASTIC** done in an unrestrainedly loud, vigorous, but usually good-humoured way **3. HEALTHY** showing physical health, strength, and vigour **4. STRONGLY FELT** sincerely and strongly felt **5. SUBSTANTIAL AND NOURISHING** substantial, or giving great satisfaction and nourishment ○ *I need a hearty breakfast to get my day started.* **6. OVERLOUD AND OVERENTHUSIASTIC** annoyingly or boorishly loud or boisterous, and usually overenthusiastic about sport or outdoor activities (*informal*) ■ *n.* (*plural* **-ies**) **BOISTEROUS SPORTING TYPE** sb who behaves in a loud boisterous way and is usually very enthusiastic about sport or outdoor activities (*informal insult*) —**heartiness** *n.* ◇ **my hearties** comrades, addressed especially to fellow sailors (*archaic*)

heat /heet/ *n.* **1. ENERGY PERCEIVED AS TEMPERATURE** a form of transferred energy that arises from the random motion of molecules and is felt as temperature, especially as warmth or hotness. Heat is transmitted by conduction, convection, or radiation. ○ *There was virtually no heat coming from the fire.* Symbol **Q** **2. DEGREE OF HOTNESS** the perceptible degree of hotness ○ *The heat in that kitchen is absolutely unbearable.* ○ *At what heat do I cook this?* **3. SOURCE OF HIGHER TEMPERATURE** a source of warmth, e.g. to cook sth or to keep a building warm ○ *The heat turns off automatically when the room reaches a certain temperature.* **4. INTENSE EMOTION** emotional intensity, especially in the form of anger or excitement ○ *I replied with some heat that my conscience was perfectly clear.* ○ *in the heat of the moment* **5. TIME OF MOST ACTIVITY AND EXCITEMENT** the period or phase of sth at which activity and excitement is at its most intense ○ *During the heat of the campaign, many rash promises were made.* **6.** FOOD **SPICY HOTNESS FELT IN MOUTH** the hot or burning sensation produced in the mouth by certain spicy foods **7.** ZOOL **SEXUALLY RECEPTIVE STAGE** a time during a female mammal's reproductive cycle when she is fertile and ready to mate **8.** SPORTS, GAME **PRELIMINARY ROUND** one of several preliminary rounds before a race or contest, especially one in which competitors are eliminated, or one that determines the main event's starting order **9. MENTAL PRESSURE** psychological pressure on a person or group, especially to produce or achieve sth (*informal*) ○ *We're beginning to feel the heat as the deadline gets closer and closer.* **10.** *US* **CRITICISM** harsh criticism or reproach (*slang*) ○ *What's your problem? Can't you take the heat?* **11.** CRIMINOL **INTENSE POLICE ACTIVITY** intensive police activity carried out in order to catch criminal suspects (*slang*) **12.** *US* CRIMINOL **POLICE** the police (*slang*) ■ *vti.* (**heats, heating, heated**) **RAISE TEMPERATURE** to become or make sth warm or hot [Old English *hǣtu*. Ultimately from a prehistoric Germanic word that was formed from a word meaning 'hot' (the ancestor of English *hot*).] —**heatless** *adj.* ◇ **turn on** *or* **up the heat (on sb)** to apply increased pressure on sb (*slang*)

heat up *vti.* **1. MAKE OR BECOME HOTTER** to make sth hotter, or become hotter **2. MAKE OR BECOME MORE INTENSE** to become or make sth more intense, exciting, or excited

heat barrier *n.* = **thermal barrier**

heat capacity *n.* the quantity of heat required to raise the temperature of one mole or gram of a substance by one degree Celsius. Symbol *C*

heat death *n.* a condition of a closed system in which energy is uniformly distributed throughout it, with none available for use. The universe might ultimately suffer heat death if the universe is a closed system.

heated /heétid/ *adj.* **1. MADE WARM** made warm by artificially generated heat **2. INTENSE OR ANGRY** showing emotional intensity or anger —**heatedness** *n.*

heatedly /heétidli/ *adv.* with anger or emotional intensity

heat engine *n.* a machine that transforms heat into mechanical power, e.g. a steam or petrol engine

heater /heétər/ *n.* **1. HEATING DEVICE** a device that uses fuel to produce heat in order to make sth else warm or hot, especially a device to heat the air in a room or vehicle **2. HEATING ELEMENT IN VALVE** an element in a valve that carries the current for heating a cathode **3.** *US* **HANDGUN** a revolver or other handgun (*dated slang*)

heat exchanger *n.* a device, e.g. a car radiator, that transfers heat from one medium to another, usually by conduction through a solid barrier

heat exhaustion *n.* a condition of physical weakness or collapse often accompanied by nausea, muscle cramps, and dizziness, that is caused by exposure to intense heat

heath /heeth/ n. **1.** GEOG GRASSY AND SHRUBBY UNCULTIVATED LAND a tract of uncultivated, open land with infertile, often sandy soil covered with rough grasses and small shrubs or heather **2.** PLANTS LOW EVERGREEN SHRUB a plant of a family that includes heather and some other low-growing evergreen shrubs with small bell-shaped flowers, commonly found on heaths. Genera: *Erica* and *Calluna*. **3.** INSECTS BROWN BUTTERFLY a butterfly with coppery-brown wings. Genus: *Coenonympha*. [Old English *hǣp*. Ultimately from a prehistoric Germanic base meaning 'unploughed land', which is also the ancestor of German and Dutch *heide*, and English *heathen*.]

Heath /heeth/, **Edward** (*b.* 1916) British statesman. A Conservative MP from 1950, he was prime minister of Great Britain (1970–74) during a period of industrial unrest and Britain's accession to the European Economic Community. Full name **Sir Edward Richard George Heath**. Known as **Ted Heath**

heathcock /heeth kok/ n. the male of the black grouse (*archaic*)

heathen /heeth'n/ n. **1.** OFFENSIVE TERM an offensive term that deliberately insults sb who does not acknowledge the God of the Bible, Torah, or Koran **2.** OFFENSIVE TERM an offensive term that deliberately insults sb's nonbelief in religion, way of life, or degree of knowledge [Old English *hǣpen*. Ultimately from a prehistoric Germanic word meaning 'inhabiting heaths', hence 'uncivilized', from a word meaning 'heath' (source also of English *heath*).] —**heathen** adj. —**heathenish** adj. —**heathenishly** adv. —**heathenishness** n. —**heathenize** vti.

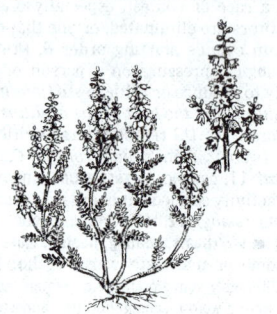

Heather

heather /heth'r/ n. **1.** PLANTS SMALL-FLOWERED SHRUB a low shrubby evergreen plant with spiky leaves and small bell-shaped purple, pink, or white flowers, that grows in clusters on heaths and mountainsides in Europe and Asia. Latin name: *Calluna vulgaris*. **2.** COLOURS PURPLE COLOUR a purple colour tinged with pink and blue ■ adj. COLOURS OF PURPLE COLOUR of a purple colour tinged with pink and blue [14thC. By folk etymology from earlier Scottish and northern English *hadder* or *hathir*, by association with HEATH (on which it grows), of unknown origin.] —**heathery** adj.

heather grass n. a European perennial grass with flat hairless leaves. Latin name: *Sieglingia decumbens*. [Because it grows in the same places as heather]

heather mixture n. a textile made of interwoven yarns of various colours, especially the colours of heather

heath-fowl n. a black grouse (*archaic*) [Because it lives on heaths]

heath grass n. = heather grass

heath hen n. **1.** FEMALE BLACK GROUSE the female of the black grouse **2.** US EXTINCT GROUSE an extinct grouse native to New England and related to the prairie chicken. Latin name: *Typanuchus cupido cupido*.

Heath Robinson /heeth róbbinss'n/ adj. constructed or improvised in a way that looks ramshackle and wildly implausible, especially through being overelaborate or overingenious (*humorous*) ○ *It's a bit Heath Robinson, but it ought to stop the sausages rolling off the barbecue.* US term **Rube Goldberg** [Early 20thC. Named after W. *Heath Robinson* (1872–1944), a British humorous artist whose illustrations featured such devices.]

Heathrow Airport /heeth rṓ-/ the largest and busiest airport serving London, situated on the western outskirts of the capital

heating /heeting/ n. **1.** PROCESS OF WARMING STH the operation of warming sth, e.g. food, a room, or the interior of a building **2.** EQUIPMENT THAT CREATES HEAT the equipment that produces heat to warm sth, e.g. a central heating system ○ *The heating doesn't come on again until six o'clock in the evening.*

heating element n. an insulated or covered wire whose high resistance to an electrical current causes its temperature to rise, providing heat to surrounding materials, e.g. an electric blanket

heating pad n. a fabric-covered pad that encloses an electric heating element and is used to apply heat to various parts of the body

heat island n. an urban area where the air temperature is consistently higher than in the surrounding region because of the generation and retention of heat created by human activity and human-made structures

heat lightning n. lightning seen near the horizon, especially on hot evenings, without the sound of thunder. It is thought to be a reflection of lightning on clouds. The thunder accompanying the lightning is too distant to be heard.

heat of combustion n. the amount of heat produced when one mole of a substance is burned in oxygen

heat-proof adj. not damaged or affected when exposed to heat, e.g. in an oven or over a flame

heat prostration n. = heat exhaustion

heat pump n. a mechanical or chemical device used to heat and air-condition buildings

heat rash n. = prickly heat

heat-seal vt. to make packaging material, usually a thin clear plastic film, airtight around sth by applying heat and pressure

heat-seeking adj. able to detect and follow infrared radiation from heat ○ *The aircraft was brought down by a heat-seeking missile.*

heat shield n. a coating or structure designed to protect against the effects of very high temperatures, especially the coating that protects spacecraft during re-entry into the Earth's atmosphere

heat sink n. a device, often a metal plate, that conducts and dissipates unwanted heat generated by an electronic component or power supply

heatstroke /heet strōk/ n. a condition caused by prolonged exposure to high temperatures, in which people experience high fever, headaches, hot dry skin, physical exhaustion, and sometimes physical collapse and coma

heat-treat vt. METALL to bring metal to the desired hardness by alternately heating and cooling it — **heat treatment** n.

heat wave n. a period of unusually hot weather

heave /heev/ v. (**heaves, heaving, heaved**) **1.** vt. MOVE USING MUCH EFFORT to pull, push, lift, or throw sth heavy by exerting great physical effort, especially in a concentrated or concerted burst ○ *We picked up the sack between us and heaved it into the truck.* **2.** vi. EXERT PHYSICAL EFFORT IN RHYTHMIC BURST to exert great physical effort, especially in concentrated or concerted rhythmic bursts, when pulling on a rope or attempting to move sth heavy ○ *All together now, heave!* ○ *We heaved and heaved, but the car remained firmly stuck in the mud.* **3.** vt. DIRECT BY TOSSING STH to throw sth fairly heavy in a particular direction, often in a casual way (*informal*) ○ *Heave the empty boxes into that corner.* **4.** vi. RISE AND FALL RHYTHMICALLY to rise and fall in a rhythmic or spasmodic way ○ *After the long run his chest was heaving, and he was covered in sweat.* **5.** vi. MAKE A SUDDEN INVOLUNTARY MOVEMENT to move in a violent involuntary motion, often associated with feelings of nausea ○ *The sight made my stomach heave.* ○ *The boat heaved to the port side.* **6.** vti. VOMIT to vomit sth up, or try to vomit (*informal*) **7.** vt. LABORIOUSLY UTTER STH to utter a sound, especially with a long outflow of breath or with effort and pain ○ *We can heave a sigh of relief now that the waiting is over.* **8.**

(*past* hove) vti. NAUT MOVE A SHIP to move or make a ship move in a particular direction **9.** (*past* hove) vi. APPEAR to become visible, like a ship appearing over the horizon ○ *An enemy ship hove into sight.* ○ *Gradually, the end of summer hove into sight.* **10.** vt. GEOL DISPLACE HORIZONTALLY to displace rock strata or a mineral lode in a horizontal direction, usually by the intersection of other strata or another lode ■ n. **1.** EFFORTFUL BURST a burst of physical effort to pull on sth or move sth heavy ○ *We gave one final heave and the tree began to topple over.* **2.** THROW an act of throwing sth fairly heavy, or the distance sth is thrown **3.** UP-AND-DOWN MOVEMENT a rhythmical or spasmodic movement that rises and falls **4.** GEOL HORIZONTAL DISPLACEMENT rock strata or a lode that is displaced horizontally **5.** ACT OF VOMITING an act of or attempt at vomiting (*informal*) ■ interj. Carib USED TO REPORT FIGHT in Trinidad, used to report that a fight has started (*informal*) ■ npl. VOMITING ATTACK an attack of vomiting or retching (*slang*) [Old English *hebban* 'to lift'. Ultimately from a prehistoric Germanic word (source also of German *heben*).] —**heaver** n.

――――――― **WORD KEY: SYNONYMS** ―――――――
See Synonyms at *throw*.

heave down vt. to turn a boat over for cleaning
heave to vti. to bring a ship to a stop ○ *We hove to about a cable's length from her stern.*

heave-ho /heev hṓ/ interj. NAUT COMMAND TO PULL used to command or encourage sailors to pull together on a rope ■ n. DISMISSAL OR REJECTION dismissal from sth, or rejection by sb (*informal*) ○ *He's just been given the heave-ho from his job.*

heaven /hevv'n/ n. **1.** Heaven, heaven RELIG PERFECT DWELLING PLACE AFTER DEATH a place or condition of supreme happiness and peace where good people are believed to go after death, and, especially in Christianity, the dwelling place of God and the angels **2.** BLISSFUL EXPERIENCE an experience of blissful happiness ○ *It's heaven not to have get up early in the morning.* ○ *This place would be heaven, if it weren't for the people who live here.* **3.** SKY OVERARCHING EARTH the sky by day or at night as seen from Earth (*often used in the plural*) ○ *After weeks of drought the heavens opened.* **4.** Heaven, heaven CHR POWER OF GOD in Christian belief, the power of God to direct events on earth ○ *Heaven protect us!* ○ *a gift from heaven* ■ interj. heaven, heavens EXPRESSING ASTONISHMENT used to express great surprise, annoyance, or gratitude (*informal*) ○ *Good heavens, is that the time?* [Old English *heofon*, of uncertain origin] ◇ **for heaven's sake** used to express annoyance or exasperation ◇ **heaven knows** used to emphasize the truth of what sb is saying ○ *Heaven knows, I've warned you about that already.* ◇ **heaven (only) knows** used to emphasize the fact that sb is unable even to make a reasonable guess at sth unknown or mysterious ○ *Heaven only knows what he's done with my keys.* ◇ **move heaven and earth** to do everything possible to make sth happen

heavenly /hevv'nli/ (**-lier, -liest**) adj. **1.** CHR OF GOD AND HEAVEN belonging to the heaven and God of Christian belief ○ *A heavenly voice spoke to him out of the clouds.* **2.** LOVELY supremely delightful, delicious, or beautiful (*informal*) ○ *The chocolate mousse was heavenly.* ○ *a sweet little cottage with the most heavenly view* **3.** IN THE SKY in the sky or space as seen from Earth —**heavenliness** n.

heavenly body n. ASTRON = celestial body

heaven-sent adj. happening or arriving at just the right time to help or benefit sb greatly

heavenward /hevv'nwərd/, **heavenwards** /-wərdz/ adv., adj. moving or directed upwards towards the sky or heaven ○ *He rolled his eyes heavenward, shrugged his shoulders, and said 'That's the way the cookie crumbles!'*

heaves /heevz/ n. a chronic lung disorder in horses marked by difficulty in breathing and believed to be caused by dust, moulds, or other air pollutants. The heaves resembles asthma in human beings. (*informal; takes a singular or plural verb*)

heavier-than-air adj. unable to float in air because it weighs more than the air it displaces, and thus only able to fly under power using aerodynamic lift

heavily /hévvili/ *adv.* **1.** WITH GREAT WEIGHT with a great weight **2.** LABORIOUSLY in a slow, clumsy, or laborious way **3.** SEVERELY in a severe, onerous, or comprehensive way **4.** IN LARGE NUMBERS in large numbers or quantities **5.** SADLY in a sad and resigned way ○ *'It was my fault', he replied heavily.* **6.** SERIOUSLY in a serious or enthusiastic way (*informal*) ○ *I didn't know you were heavily into astrology.*

heaviness /hévvinəss/ *n.* the condition of being heavy

Heaviside /hévvi sīd/, **Oliver** (1850–1925) British physicist. He predicted the existence of the ionosphere and contributed to the development of radio communications.

Heaviside layer /hévvi sīd-/ *n.* = **E layer** [Early 20thC. Named after Oliver HEAVISIDE, its discoverer.]

heavy /hévvi/ *adj.* (**-ier, -iest**) **1.** WEIGHING A LOT weighing a relatively large amount and thus difficult to lift, carry, or move ○ *Daddy can't carry you any more, you're too heavy.* ○ *We put heavy stones on the corners of the rug to stop it blowing away.* **2.** PRESENT IN LARGE AMOUNTS occurring or produced in large amounts or in greater amounts than normal **3.** FULL, THICK, OR DENSE involving or using a larger amount of material or having a thicker, denser texture than usual **4.** ABUNDANTLY USING STH using or consuming sth a great deal **5.** NEEDING STRENGTH needing much strength and effort ○ *heavy road work* **6.** DEMANDING difficult to fulfil or cope with, and often burdensome or oppressive **7.** BUSY filled with a large or larger than normal amount of activity, business, or commitments **8.** POWERFUL struck or striking with a great deal of weight or force **9.** BROAD AND DARK thick and dark-coloured, or made with thick dark lines **10.** EXPLICIT intended to give emphasis to sth and to make the meaning or intention obvious **11.** UNSUBTLE lacking subtlety or delicacy ○ *heavy sarcasm* **12.** FLESHY large and solidly fleshy ○ *a huge, heavy body* **13.** CLUMSY typical of sb who is large and who moves slowly and deliberately or clumsily **14.** SOUNDING LOUD AND DULL loud and dull in sound, as if produced by sth large hitting or falling onto sth **15.** INDUST EXTENSIVELY PRODUCING OR REFINING STH involved in large-scale industrial processes requiring large premises and a lot of equipment **16.** RUGGED AND STRONG specially adapted for rough work or for carrying large loads ○ *heavy excavating equipment* **17.** MIL LARGE-CALIBRE firing large-calibre ammunition **18.** MIL, NAVY WITH LARGE WEAPONS carrying more or larger guns and armaments than is standard **19.** SAD sad, or likely to make sb feel sad **20.** SERIOUS AND REQUIRING CONCENTRATION requiring concentrated attention to be understood or appreciated ○ *a heavy novel* **21.** TURGID difficult and requiring effort rather than being pleasurable ○ *I'm trying to finish reading the novel, but it's heavy going.* **22.** STRICT strict or severe in behaviour **23.** VIOLENT using or prepared to use violence (*informal*) **24.** POWERFUL AND LINGERING strong and lingering in smell ○ *a heavy odour of leeks* **25.** NAUT ROUGH with large waves causing difficulties for boats **26.** METEOROL DARK AND OVERCAST dark in colour and threatening rain or snow **27.** METEOROL SULTRY AND THREATENING sultry and overcast, as if threatening a storm or thunder **28.** FOOD HARD TO DIGEST large in quantity and difficult to digest **29.** MUSIC WITH POWERFUL BEAT used to describe rock music with a powerful, insistent beat **30.** SERIOUS AND OPPRESSIVE significant, oppressively serious, or emotionally demanding (*slang*) ○ *I had a heavy scene with my friend tonight.* **31.** CHEM WITH HIGH ATOMIC WEIGHT with a higher than normal atomic weight **32.** PHYS WITH HIGH SPECIFIC GRAVITY with a higher than normal specific gravity **33.** MUDDY wet, muddy, and not able to be travelled over at high speed ○ *Reports from the racecourse indicate that the going is heavy.* ■ *n.* (*plural* **-ies**) **1.** ARTS VILLAIN a villain in a play, film, or other dramatic performance ○ *He played the heavy in a couple of westerns.* **2.** SB WHO IS VIOLENT sb hired to persuade people, by threats or violence, to do sth (*slang; often used in the plural*) ○ *He sent in a bunch of heavies to do his dirty work.* **3.** PRESS BROADSHEET a broadsheet newspaper (*informal; often used in the plural*) ○ *None of the heavies ran the story.* **4.** US IMPORTANT PERSON sb who is important or influential (*informal*) **5.** US SPORTS HEAVYWEIGHT a heavyweight, e.g., a heavyweight boxer (*informal*) **6.** *Scotland* STRONG BITTER BEER a type of bitter brown beer ■ *adv.* HEAVILY in a heavy way [Old English *hefig*. Ultimately from a prehistoric Germanic word meaning 'weighty' (ancestor also of Dutch *hevig*), from, ultimately, a word meaning 'to lift' (source also of English *heave*).]

heavy breather *n.* **1.** NUISANCE CALLER sb who makes anonymous nuisance calls, breathing loudly into the telephone in a way that is intended to suggest sexual excitement or a physical threat **2.** NOISY BREATHER sb who breathes noisily or with difficulty, usually because of a medical condition —**heavy breathing** *n.*

heavy chain *n.* either of the larger polypeptide chains in an antibody. ◊ **light chain**

heavy cream *n.* US cream with a high fat content that can be whipped to make it thicker

heavy-duty *adj.* **1.** TOUGH AND DURABLE designed for hard wear or use in rough conditions **2.** SERIOUS more serious, substantial, or intensive than usual (*informal*) ○ *a heavy-duty meeting*

heavy-footed *adj.* slow, lumbering, or clumsy in walking

heavy-handed *adj.* **1.** PHYSICALLY OR SOCIALLY CLUMSY lacking skill or delicacy in handling objects or dealing with people **2.** HARSH AND OPPRESSIVE relying on force or intimidation to exercise authority —**heavy-handedly** *adv.* —**heavy-handedness** *n.*

heavy-hearted *adj.* feeling or showing sadness (*literary*) —**heavy-heartedly** *adv.* —**heavy-heartedness** *n.*

heavy hydrogen *n.* an isotope of hydrogen with a mass number greater than 1, especially deuterium

heavy-laden *adj.* carrying a heavy burden, e.g. of sorrow or guilt (*literary*)

heavy lifting *n.* the lifting of heavy objects

heavy metal *n.* **1.** MUSIC TYPE OF ROCK MUSIC a style of loud rock music with a very strong beat (*hyphenated when used before a noun*) **2.** METALL METAL WITH HIGH RELATIVE DENSITY a metal, often toxic to organisms, that has a relative density of 5.0 or higher, e.g. lead, mercury, copper, and cadmium

heavy oil *n.* a mixture of hydrocarbons distilled from coal tar that is heavier than water

heavy particle *n.* = **baryon**

heavyset /hévvi sét/ *adj.* with a compact and powerful-looking build

heavy spar *n.* a mineral form of barium sulphate. Formula: $BaSO_4$.

heavy water *n.* water that has had its hydrogen atoms replaced with the hydrogen isotope deuterium. It is used in some nuclear reactors. Formula: D_2O.

heavy-water reactor *n.* a nuclear reactor in which heavy water is used as a moderator

heavyweight /hévvi wayt/ *n.* **1.** BOXING BOXER IN HIGHEST WEIGHT CATEGORY a boxer of the heaviest weight class. Professional heavyweight boxers must weigh more than 79.5 kg/175 lbs. **2.** SPORTS CONTESTANT IN HEAVIEST WEIGHT CLASS a contestant in the heaviest weight class of a sport **3.** HEAVY PERSON OR THING sb or sth whose weight is considerably above the average **4.** SB OR STH POWERFUL OR INFLUENTIAL a person or organization with considerable power or influence, usually in a specified area (*informal*)

Heb. *abbr.* **1.** Hebrew **2.** BIBLE Hebrews

hebdomad /hébdə mad/ *n.* (*formal*) **1.** GROUP OF SEVEN a group of seven people or things **2.** WEEK a period of seven days [Mid-16thC. Via late Latin from the Greek stem *hebdomad-* 'the number seven, a period of seven days', from *hepta* 'seven' (source of English *heptagon*).]

hebdomadal /heb dómməd'l/ *adj.* occurring on a weekly basis (*formal*)

Hebdomadal Council *n.* the governing body of Oxford University

hebe /héebi/ *n.* a flowering evergreen shrub with drooping spikes of blue, mauve, or white flowers and overlapping leaves resembling scales. Genus: *Hebe.* [Mid-20thC. Named after HEBE.]

Hebe /héebi/ *n.* in Greek mythology, the goddess of youth and the daughter of Zeus and Hera. She married Hercules. [Early 17thC. From Greek *Hēbē*, literally 'youthful prime'.]

Hebei /hŏ báy/ province in northern China. Its territories include the economic heartland of ancient Chinese civilization. Capital: Shijiazhuang. Population: 63,880,000 (1994). Area: 188,000 sq. km/72,600 sq. mi.

hebetate /hébbi tayt/ (**-tates, -tating, -tated**) *adj.* used to describe a plant part that has a blunt or soft point [Late 16thC. From Latin *hebetat-*, the past participle stem of *hebetare*, from the stem *hebet-* 'blunt, dull', of unknown origin.]

hebetic /hi béttik/ *adj.* occurring at or concerning puberty (*formal*) [From Greek *hēbētikos*, from, ultimately, *hēbē* 'youth', from *Hēbē* 'HEBE']

hebetude /hébbi tyood/ *n.* mental lethargy (*literary*) [Early 17thC. From late Latin *hebetudo*, from the Latin stem *hebet-* 'dull', of unknown origin.]

Hebr. *abbr.* **1.** Hebrew **2.** BIBLE Hebrews

Hebraic /hi bráy ik/, **Hebraical** /-ik'l/ *adj.* relating to the Hebrews or their language or culture [14thC. Via late Latin from Greek *Hebraikos*, from *Hebraios* (see HEBREW).] —**Hebraically** *adv.*

Hebraicism /hi bráyisizəm/ *n.* = **Hebraism**

Hebraise *vti.* = **Hebraize**

Hebraism /hée brayizəm/ *n.* a characteristic feature of the Hebrew language, especially one borrowed by another language, or sth frequently found among the Hebrew people or their culture [Late 16thC. Via French or modern Latin from late Greek *Hebraismos*, from *Hebraios* (see HEBREW).]

Hebraist /hée bray ist/ *n.* a scholar who specializes in the study of Hebrew —**Hebraistically** /hée bray ístikli/ *adv.*

Hebraize /hée bray īz/ (**-izes, -izing, -ized**), **Hebraise** (**-ises, -ising, -ised**) *v.* **1.** *vt.* MAKE RESEMBLE HEBREW to give a language or culture Hebrew characteristics **2.** *vi.* BECOME LIKE HEBREW to adopt Hebrew idioms or customs [Mid-17thC. From late Greek *Hebraizein*, from *Hebraios* (see HEBREW).] —**Hebraization** /hée bray ī záysh'n/ *n.* —**Hebraizer** /hée bray īzər/ *n.*

Hebrew /hée broo/ *n.* **1.** LANG ONE OF OFFICIAL LANGUAGES OF ISRAEL one of the official languages of Israel, also spoken in the United States and parts of Europe. It is one of the Canaanitic subgroup of the Semitic group of the Afro-Asian family of African languages. Hebrew is spoken by about five million people. **2.** PEOPLES, HIST = **Israelite** ■ *adj.* LANG, HIST = **Hebraic** [13thC. Via Old French *ebreu* from, ultimately, late Greek *Hebraios*, from Aramaic *ibrāy*, a rendering of Hebrew *ibrī* 'Israelite', literally 'sb from the other side (of the Euphrates river)'.]

Hebrew calendar *n.* = **Jewish calendar**

Hebrews /hée brooz/ *n.* in the Bible, an epistle that is thought to have been written towards the end of the first century AD (*takes a singular verb*) See table at **Bible**

Hebrew Scriptures *npl.* the Bible of Judaism, consisting of the Pentateuch, the Prophets, and the Hagiographa. ◊ **Torah**

Hebrides /hébbrə deez/ collective name for the islands off the western coast of Scotland, comprising an outer chain of islands, the Outer Hebrides, separated by a sea channel from the Inner Hebrides nearer the mainland —**Hebridean** /hébbri dée ən/ *adj., n.*

Hecate /hékəti/, **Hekate** *n.* in Greek mythology, the goddess of darkness and the underworld. She was the daughter of the Titans Perses and Asteria. [Late 16thC. From Greek *Hekatē*, a form of *hekatos* 'far-darting'.]

hecatomb /hékə tōm, hékə toom/ *n.* **1.** ANCIENT GREEK OR ROMAN SACRIFICE a public sacrifice and feast in ancient Greece or Rome, originally involving the slaughter of 100 oxen **2.** GREAT SACRIFICE any large-scale sacrifice (*literary*) [Late 16thC. Via Latin from Greek *hekatombē*, from *hekaton* 'hundred' + *bous* 'ox'.]

heck /hek/ *interj.* EXPRESSING IRRITATION OR EMPHASIS used as a mild way of expressing annoyance or frustration, or emphasizing a statement (*informal*) ○ *Oh heck, I suppose that means we can't go.* ■ *n.* EXCLAMATION sometimes used as a less offensive alternative for the word 'hell' (*informal*) ○ *What the heck is going on?* [Late 19thC. Euphemistic alteration of HELL.] ◇ **a heck of a, one heck of a** used to indicate that sth is particularly large, intense, or impressive (*informal*) ○ *There's a heck of a lot still to do before closing time.*

heckelphone /hék'l fōn/ *n.* a bass musical instrument of the oboe family, in pitch between the cor anglais and the bassoon [Early 20thC. From German *Heckelphon*, named after the German instrument-maker Wilhelm *Heckel* (1856–1909), its inventor. Modelled on SAXOPHONE.]

heckle /hék'l/ *v.* (**-les, -ling, -led**) **1.** *vti.* **INTERRUPT SB WITH SHOUTING** to shout remarks, insults, or questions in order to disconcert sb who is making a speech or giving a performance ○ *I don't mind being heckled, but when they start throwing things it does rather put me off.* **2.** *vt.* **DRESS FLAX OR HEMP** to comb flax or hemp ■ *n.* **COMB FOR FLAX OR HEMP** a comb used for dressing flax or hemp [14thC. Variant of HACKLE. The underlying idea of the interrupting sense is 'scratching, irritating'.]

heckler /héklər/ *n.* sb who deliberately interrupts a speaker or performer by shouting

hect- *prefix.* = **hecto-** (*used before vowels*)

hectare /hék taar, hék tair/ *n.* a metric unit of area equal to 100 ares or 10,000 sq. m (2.471 acres) [Early 19thC. From French, from Greek *hekaton* 'hundred' + French *are* 'unit of area', from Latin *area* 'open space' (source of English *area*).]

hectic /héktik/ *adj.* **1.** **CONSTANTLY BUSY AND HURRIED** characterized by continual activity and haste, the lack of any time to rest or relax, and a sense of things barely under control ○ *Things have been a bit hectic at work this week.* **2.** MED **FEVERISH** symptomatic of or involving a recurrent afternoon fever, especially one accompanying tuberculosis ○ *hectic fever* ○ *a hectic flush* [14thC. Via Old French *etique* from, ultimately, Greek *hektikos* 'habitual, consumptive', from, ultimately, Greek *ekhein* 'to have'.]

hecto- *prefix.* one hundred ○ *hectogram.* Symbol **h** [Via French from Greek *hekaton.* Ultimately from the Indo-European word for 'hundred', which is also the ancestor of English *hundred* and *centum.*]

hectocotylus /héktō kóttiləss/ (*plural* **-li** /-lī/) *n.* a tentacle with which male octopuses and related molluscs transfer sperm to the female during mating [Mid-19thC. From modern Latin, genus name (given in the mistaken belief that the tentacles were separate organisms), from French *hecto-* 'HECTO-' + Greek *kotulē* 'cup, sth hollow'.]

hectogram /héktō gram/, **hectogramme** *n.* a metric unit of mass equal to 100 grams [Late 18thC. From French *hectogramme*, from *hecto-* 'HECTO-' + -GRAM.]

hectolitre /hékto leetər/ *n.* a metric unit of capacity equal to 100 litres [Early 19thC. From French, from *hecto-* 'HECTO-' + LITRE.]

hectometre /héktō meetər/ *n.* a metric unit of length equal to 100 metres [Early 19thC. From French *hectomètre*, from *hecto-* 'HECTO-' + METRE.]

hector /héktər/ *vti.* (**-tors, -toring, -tored**) **SPEAK IN INTIMIDATING WAY** to speak to sb in a loud, threatening, or domineering tone intended to intimidate ■ *n.* **BULLY** a bully (*archaic or literary*) [Mid-17thC. From HECTOR. The name became associated with a London gang.]

Hector *n.* in Greek mythology, the main Trojan hero in the Trojan War and the son of King Priam and Queen Hecuba. He was killed by Achilles. [14thC. Via Latin from Greek *Hektōr*, literally 'holding fast', ultimately from *ekhein* 'to hold'.]

Hecuba /hékyŏŏbə/ *n.* in Greek mythology, the queen of Troy and wife of King Priam. She had 16 children, including Cassandra, Hector, and Paris. [Via Latin from Greek *Hekabē*]

he'd (*stressed*) /heed/; (*unstressed*) /hid, id/ *contr.* **1.** **HE HAD** he had **2.** **HE WOULD** he would

heddle /hédd'l/ *n.* one of the sets of vertical cords or wires in the frame on a loom that guides the warp threads [Early 16thC. Origin uncertain: perhaps from Old English *hefeld*, related to English *heave.*]

hedge /hej/ *n.* **1.** **ROW OF SHRUBS** a close-set row of bushes, usually with their branches intermingled, forming a barrier or boundary in a garden, park, or field **2.** FIN **PROTECTIVE METHOD** a means of protection against sth, especially a means of guarding against financial loss ○ *a hedge against inflation* **3.** **EVASIVE STATEMENT** an evasive or noncommittal statement ■ *v.* (**hedges, hedging, hedged**) **1.** *vt.* **PUT BUSHES AROUND STH** to put a row of intermingled shrubs around an area of ground **2.** *vi.* **WORK ON HEDGES** to work at repairing, trimming, or planting a hedge, especially on a farm **3.** *vt.* **RESTRICT STH** to restrict the scope or applicability of sth by means of sth else, e.g. a set of regulations, conditions, or qualifications ○ *It was a promise, but hedged in with so many ifs and buts that I wouldn't rely on it.* **4.** *vi.* **BE EVASIVE** to avoid answering a question directly or definitely ○ *She could have given a straight answer, but instead she hedged.* **5.** *vi.* FIN **TRY TO OFFSET POSSIBLE LOSSES** to take measures to offset any possible loss on a financial transaction, especially by investing in counterbalancing securities as a guard against price fluctuations [Old English *hegg.* Ultimately from a prehistoric Germanic word meaning 'to grasp'.] —**hedgy** *adj.*

Hedgehog

hedgehog /héj hog/ *n.* **1.** ZOOL **SMALL SPINY ANIMAL** any of various small mammals of Europe, Africa, and Asia that have a small pointed head and a round body with stiff spines on the back. Hedgehogs eat insects, eggs, and mice, frogs, and other small animals, and can roll into a ball when attacked to protect themselves by means of their spines. Family: Erinaceidae. **2.** MIL **DEFENCE AGAINST LANDING CRAFT** an underwater obstacle designed to keep landing craft from reaching a beach by ripping holes in the hulls

WORD KEY: REGIONAL NOTE

Modern traffic has drastically reduced the hedgehog population in Britain. Once, these little quadrupeds were found in all areas and names for them proliferated. They included *furze-pig, hedge-boar, hedge-hock, prickly-backed urchin, urchin* and, thanks to Beatrix Potter, *Mrs Tiggywinkle.* Some people confuse hedgehogs and porcupines. The porcupine was not originally a native of Europe and is related to the squirrel family.

hedgehop /héj hop/ (**-hops, -hopping, -hopped**) *vi.* to fly very low above the ground, often so low that the aircraft must ascend to avoid obstacles on the ground —**hedgehopper** *n.*

hedgerow /héj rō/ *n.* a row of bushes or small trees forming a hedge, especially round a field or along a country road or path

hedge-school *n.* in 17th- and 18th-century Ireland, an unofficial school for Catholic children designed to evade legal restrictions on their education, often held out of doors

hedge sparrow *n.* = **dunnock**

hedonic /hee dónnik/ *adj.* **1.** **OF PLEASURE** concerned with pleasure **2.** **HEDONISTIC** characteristic of or relating to hedonism or hedonists [Mid-17thC. From Greek *hēdonikos*, from *hēdonē*, 'pleasure'.]

hedonism /héed'nizəm, hédd'nizəm/ *n.* **1.** **SEEKING OF PLEASURE** a devotion, especially a self-indulgent one, to pleasure and happiness as a way of life **2.** PHILOS **PHILOSOPHY OF PLEASURE** a philosophical doctrine that holds that pleasure is the highest good or the source of moral values [Mid-19thC. From Greek *hēdonē* 'pleasure'.] —**hedonist** *n.* —**hedonistic** /héedə nístik, héddə-/ *adj.* —**hedonistically** /-nístikli/ *adv.*

-hedron *suffix.* a figure or crystal having a particular number or kind of surfaces ○ *pentahedron* [Via modern Latin from, ultimately, Greek *hedra* 'face' (see CATHEDRAL)] —**-hedral** *suffix.*

heebie-jeebies /heébi jeébiz/ *npl.* uncomfortable nervous or anxious feelings (*slang*) ○ *There's something about thick fog that gives me the heebie-jeebies.* [Early 20thC. Coined by the US cartoonist Billy DeBeck (1890–1942) in his comic strip *Barney Google.*]

heed /heed/ *vti.* (**heeds, heeding, heeded**) **PAY ATTENTION TO ADVICE** to give serious attention to a warning or advice and take it into account when acting ■ *n.* **SERIOUS ATTENTION** serious attention paid to sb or to sth such as a warning, piece of advice, or request [Old English *hēdan*, ultimately from a prehistoric Germanic word] —**heeder** *n.*

heedful /heédf'l/ *adj.* paying attention to sb or to sth such as a warning, piece of advice, or danger —**heedfully** *adv.* —**heedfulness** *n.*

heedless /heédləss/ *adj.* not paying attention to sb or to sth such as a warning, piece of advice, or danger —**heedlessly** *adv.* —**heedlessness** *n.*

heehaw /heé haw/ *n.* **1.** **DONKEY'S BRAY** the natural sound made by a donkey **2.** **NOISY LAUGH** an unrefined noisy laugh (*informal*) ■ *vi.* (**-haws, -hawing, -hawed**) **1.** **BRAY LIKE DONKEY** to make a natural heehaw **2.** **LAUGH NOISILY** to laugh in an unrefined noisy way [Early 19thC. An imitation of the sound.]

heel[1] /heel/ *n.* **1.** PHYSIOL **BACK PART OF FOOT** the back part of a person's foot immediately below the ankle, or the same part of an animal's foot or paw **2.** CLOTHES **BACK OF SHOE OR SOCK** the part of a sock, stocking, shoe, or boot that covers the back part of sb's foot **3.** CLOTHES **BACK OF UNDERSIDE OF SHOE** the back, usually thicker, portion of the underside of a shoe or other footwear that raises the foot off the ground ○ *I'll need to get new heels on these boots.* **4.** PHYSIOL **THICKER PART OF PALM** the thicker part of the palm of the hand, located next to the wrist **5.** CLOTHES **PART OF GLOVE** the part of a glove that covers the part of the palm located next to the wrist **6.** FOOD **BREAD CRUST** a crusty end of a loaf of bread **7.** FOOD **CHEESE RIND** the hard rind from a wedge of cheese **8.** GOLF **PART OF GOLF CLUB** the part of the head of a golf club where the shaft is attached **9.** MUSIC **END OF VIOLIN BOW** the end of a violin bow that is held while playing the violin **10.** GARDENING **PIECE ATTACHED TO CUTTING** a small piece of a plant stem or tuber left attached to a cutting to promote the growth of new roots **11.** SAILING **BOTTOM OF MAST** the bottom end of a ship's or boat's mast **12.** NAUT **STERN** the stern end of a ship's keel **13.** **OFFENSIVE TERM** an offensive term, especially for a man, that deliberately insults sb's behaviour (*informal insult*) ■ **heels** *npl.* CLOTHES **HIGH HEELS** high-heeled shoes ■ *v.* (**heels, heeling, heeled**) **1.** *vt.* **FIT OR REPAIR SHOE'S HEEL** to fit, replace, or repair the heel of a shoe or boot **2.** *vi.* **FOLLOW BY SB'S HEELS** to follow closely at sb's heels when commanded (*refers to dogs*) **3.** *vt.* EQU **DIG HEELS INTO MOUNT** to hit or prod an animal being ridden with the heel **4.** *vi.* DANCING **MOVE HEELS IN DANCE** to move the heels in time with music, or touch the ground with the heels when dancing **5.** *vt.* GOLF **MISHIT GOLF BALL** to mishit a golf ball with the heel of a club **6.** *vt.* FOOTBALL **KICK BALL** to kick a ball with the heel, especially in rugby to pass the ball out of the scrummage using the heel [Old English *hēla.* Ultimately from a prehistoric Germanic word that is also the ancestor of English *hough.*] —**heelless** *adj.* ◇ **cool** *or* **kick your heels** to wait or be kept waiting for a long time (*informal*) ◇ **dig in your heels** to hold stubbornly to a position or attitude ◇ **(hard) on the heels of sb** *or* **sth 1.** close behind sb or sth **2.** soon after sb or sth ◇ **show (sb) a clean pair of heels** to run away from sb ◇ **take to your heels** to run off ◇ **to heel 1.** directly behind the person with whom a dog is walking **2.** under control or discipline ◇ **turn on your heel** to turn round suddenly

heel[2] /heel/ *vti.* (**heels, heeling, heeled**) **LEAN TO ONE SIDE** to lean over to one side so far as to be in danger of capsizing, or cause a ship or boat to lean in this way ○ *The ship heeled in the wind.* ■ *n.* **SIDEWAYS LEAN** a leaning to one side, or the degree to which a ship or boat is leaning [Late 16thC. Alteration of Middle English *helden* (taken to be a past participle), from Old English *hieldan* 'to lean or bend'.]

heel-and-toe *adj.* ATHLETICS **CONSTITUTING WALKING NOT RUNNING** used to describe walking or racing that requires the heel of one foot to touch the ground before the toe of the other is lifted from the ground

■ *vi.* (**heel-and-toes, heel-and-toeing, heel-and-toed**) MOTOR SPORTS **PRESS BRAKE AND ACCELERATOR** to operate the brake and accelerator pedals at the same time with one foot, usually to keep the engine revolutions high when shifting to a lower gear while racing

heelball /heél bawl/ *n.* a black waxy substance used by shoemakers to blacken the edges of the heels and soles of shoes and boots, or a similar substance used for making brass-rubbings

heelbar /heél baar/ *n.* a small shop or a counter in a large shop where repairs are made to shoe soles and heels, often while the customer waits

heel bone *n.* the quadrangular bone that forms the heel of the foot. Technical name **calcaneus**

heeled /heeld/ *adj.* with a heel or heels, often of a specified type (*often used in combination*) ○ *a high-heeled shoe*

heeler /heélər/ *n.* **1.** **SB OR STH THAT HEELS SHOES** a person or machine that fits, replaces, or repairs the heels of shoes or boots ○ *the quickest heeler in the shoe factory* **2.** *Aus* **HERDING DOG** an Australian sheep or cattle dog that herds by biting at the heels of the animals

heel in (**heels in, heeling in, heeled in**) *vt.* to place a bare-root plant at a sharp angle in a holding bed and cover the roots with soil until it can be planted properly [Old English *helian* 'to conceal'; ultimately from a prehistoric Germanic word that is also the ancestor of English *hell*. Originally spelt *hele*; the current spelling arose by association with HEEL[1].]

heelpiece /heél peess/ *n.* the part of a sock, stocking, shoe, or boot that fits round the heel of the foot

heelpost /heél pōst/ *n.* a post to which the hinges of a gate or door are attached

heeltap /heél tap/ *n.* **1.** **DRINK LEFT IN GLASS** a small quantity of an alcoholic drink remaining at the bottom of a glass after the rest has been swallowed **2.** **LAYER OF MATERIAL IN SHOE HEEL** a layer of leather or other material in the heel of a shoe or boot

Hefei /hő fáy/ capital city of Anhui Province, west of Nanjing, eastern China. Population: 1,000,000 (1991).

Hefner /héfnər/, **Hugh** (*b.* 1926) US publisher. He founded *Playboy* in 1953, and through the magazine a string of related nightclubs. His own much publicized hedonistic lifestyle epitomized the sexual revolution of the 1960s and 1970s. Full name **Hugh Marston Hefner**

heft /heft/ *vt.* (**hefts, hefting, hefted**) *US, UKdial* **1.** **LIFT STH** to lift up sth heavy, especially with a burst of effort ○ *He hefted the load onto his back and slowly started up the mountain.* **2.** **ESTIMATE WEIGHT OF STH** to lift sth in order to estimate its weight ■ *n. US, UKdial* **GREAT WEIGHT** substantial heaviness or bulk [15thC. Originally as the noun. Of uncertain origin; probably from HEAVE, modelled on pairs of words such as *cleave, cleft*.] —**hefter** *n.*

hefty /héfti/ (**-ier, -iest**) *adj.* **1.** **POWERFULLY BUILT** big and strong in physique **2.** **HEAVY** large and heavy to lift **3.** **EXPENSIVE** involving a large sum of money **4.** **FORCEFUL** delivered with or characterized by great force and power **5.** **STRENUOUS** requiring a lot of effort to do **6.** **LARGER THAN USUAL** much larger than is usual or required —**heftily** *adv.* —**heftiness** *n.*

Hegel /háyg'l/, **G. W. F.** (1770–1831) German philosopher. His idealist metaphysics exerted an enormous influence on 19th-century European thought. His works include *The Phenomenology of Mind* (1807) and the *Encyclopedia of the Philosophical Sciences in Outline* (1817). Full name **Georg Wilhelm Friedrich Hegel** —**Hegelian** /hi gáyli ən/ *adj., adj., n.*

Hegelianism /hi gáyli ənizzəm/ *n.* the philosophy of G.W.F. Hegel, which proposes a unified solution to all philosophical problems through development of a reasoning process that ultimately interprets reality by way of the dialectic method

hegemony /hi gémməni, -jémməni/ *n.* control or dominating influence by one person or group over others, especially by one political group over society or one nation over others (*formal*) [Mid-16thC. From Greek *hēgemonia* 'leadership', ultimately from *hēgisthai* 'to lead'.] —**hegemonic** /héggə mónnik, héjjə-/ *adj.* —**hegemonism** *n.* —**hegemonist** /hi gémmənist, -jémmə-/ *n.*

hegira /héjjirə, hi jīrə/, **hejira** *n.* a flight or withdrawal from somewhere, especially to escape from danger [Late 16thC. Via medieval Latin from Arabic *hijra*, literally 'the leaving of home and friends'.]

Hegira /héjjirə, hi jīrə/, **Hejira** *n.* **1.** **MUHAMMAD'S WITHDRAWAL FROM MECCA** the withdrawal of the Prophet Muhammad from Mecca to Medina to escape persecution **2.** **MUSLIM ERA** the Muslim era, dated from the first day of the lunar year in which Muhammad's withdrawal to Medina took place. This was 16 July, AD 622 in the Gregorian calendar.

heh /hay/ *interj.* used to express surprise or in order to attract attention [14thC. Natural exclamation.]

Heian /háyən/ *adj.* characteristic of or relating to Japan from AD 794–1185, when Confucianism and other Chinese influences were at their height [Late 19thC. From Japanese *Heian-kyo*, now Kyoto, former capital of Japan.]

Heidegger /hī degər/, **Martin** (1889–1976) German philosopher. He greatly influenced the development of phenomenology and existentialism in the 20th century. His most important work is *Being and Time* (1927).

Heidelberg man *n.* an extinct early human of the Pleistocene epoch that is known mainly from a fossilized jawbone [Early 20thC. Named after the city of HEIDELBERG in southwestern Germany, near where a jawbone from Heidelberg man was found.]

heifer /héffər/ *n.* a young cow, especially one that has never had a calf [Old English *heahfore*, of unknown origin]

Heifetz /hīfits/, **Jascha** (1901–87) Lithuanian-born US violinist. Noted for his technical mastery, he was considered one of the greatest classical violinists of his time.

heigh /hay/ *interj.* used to express encouragement or approval [14thC. Natural exclamation.]

heigh-ho /-hṓ/ *interj.* used to express boredom, disappointment, or weary resignation ○ *Heigh-ho. Here we go again.*

height /hīt/ *n.* **1.** **LENGTH UPWARDS** the distance between sb or sth's lowest point and highest point ○ *a steep cliff about 70 m in height* **2.** **DISTANCE ABOVE STH** the distance that sb or sth is above the ground, sea, or another reference point **3.** **NOTICEABLE TALLNESS** the condition of being noticeably high or tall compared to others ○ *His height makes him stand out in a crowd.* **4.** **HIGH POSITION** a high place or position, especially one where sb can see a view or how high up he or she is (*often used in the plural*) **5.** **HIGHEST POINT** the top or highest point of sth ○ *When you reach the height, you'll get a marvellous view.* **6.** **HIGH LEVEL** a high level of intensity or severity (*often used in the plural*) ○ *Their arrogance is reaching new heights.* **7.** **HIGHEST LEVEL** the time of greatest intensity, activity, importance, or success ○ *She was at the height of her powers.* **8.** **EXTREME** the most extreme example of sth ○ *It was the height of folly to have gone there on your own.* ■ **heights** *npl.* **HILLS OR MOUNTAINS** an area of hilly or mountainous terrain, especially one that is noticeably elevated above the surrounding region (*often used in placenames*) [Old English *hēhþu* 'the highest part'. Ultimately from a prehistoric Germanic word that is also the ancestor of English *high*.]

WORD KEY: CULTURAL NOTE

Wuthering Heights, a novel (1847) by writer Emily Brontë. Brontë's only novel, it is the story of a foundling, Heathcliff, whose mistreatment at the hands of his adoptive family leads him to seek revenge later in life. The novel is noted for its evocative descriptions of the Yorkshire moors, its complex morality, and its intensity of feeling.

heighten /hīt'n/ (**-ens, -ening, -ened**) *vti.* **1.** **MAKE OR BECOME GREATER** to make sth such as a feeling or emotion greater or more intense, or become greater or more intense ○ *His attempts to reassure them served only to heighten their fears.* **2.** **MAKE OR BECOME HIGHER** to make sth higher, or become higher ○ *As protection, they heightened the city walls by a further three feet.* **3.** **APPEAR BRIGHTER OR MAKE STH BRIGHTER** to make sth such as a colour appear brighter or stronger, or appear to become brighter or stronger ○ *The sunlight heightened the flush on her cheeks.* —**heightened** *adj.* —**heightener** *n.*

height of land *n. Can* a ridge of high land that is a watershed

Heimdall /háym daal/, **Heimdal, Heimdallr** /háym daalər/ *n.* in Norse mythology, a giant warrior who was the god of light and dawn [From Old Norse *Heimdallr*, from *heimr* 'home, world' + *dallr*, of uncertain origin: perhaps related to Old English *deall* 'bold']

Heimlich manoeuvre /hīmlik-/ *n.* a emergency method for treating choking that uses an upward thrust immediately below the breastbone to expel food or another blockage from the windpipe [Late 20thC. Named after the American surgeon Henry J. *Heimlich* (born 1920), who devised it.]

Heine /hīnə/, **Heinrich** (1797–1856) German poet. One of Germany's greatest lyric poets, he spent his last 25 years in France. The poems in his *Book of Songs* (1827) inspired numerous musical settings by leading European composers.

Heinkel /hīngk'l/, **Ernst** (1888–1958) German engineer. He designed aircraft used by the German air force in both world wars, and built the first jet-propelled plane (1939). Full name **Ernst Heinrich Heinkel**

Heinlein /hīn līn/, **Robert** (1907–88) US writer. His many works of science fiction, known for their technological sophistication, include *Stranger in a Strange Land* (1961). Full name **Robert Anson Heinlein**

heinous /háynəss/ *adj.* shockingly evil or wicked [14thC. From Old French *haineus*, from *hair* 'to hate', ultimately from a prehistoric Germanic word that is also the ancestor of English *hate*.] —**heinously** *adv.* —**heinousness** *n.*

heir /air/ *n.* **1.** **LEGAL INHERITOR OF STH** sb who receives or who has by law the right to receive the property, position, or title of another when that person dies **2.** **RECIPIENT OF TRADITION** sb who or sth that inherits sth such as a tradition, problem, or characteristic from a predecessor ○ *Our generation is the unfortunate heir to decades of pollution.* [14thC. Via Old French *(h)eir* from, ultimately, Latin *heres*.] —**heirless** *adj.* —**heirship** *n.*

heir apparent (*plural* **heirs apparent**) *n.* **1.** **UNDOUBTED LEGAL HEIR** an heir whose entitlement to receive an inheritance cannot be altered by the birth of another heir **2.** **EXPECTED SUCCESSOR** sb who is expected to inherit another's position, status, or influence

heir at law (*plural* **heirs at law**) *n.* the heir of sb's property under the law if that person dies without a valid will

heiress /áirəss/ *n.* a woman or girl who receives or has by law the right to receive the property, position, or title of another when that person dies

heirloom /áir loom/ *n.* **1.** **STH HANDED DOWN** sth valuable that has been in the possession of a family for a long time and has been passed on from one generation to the next **2.** **LAW STH INHERITED BY LAW** an item of personal property that is attached to the estate that the legal heir will inherit [LOOM[2], in an obsolete sense 'tool, utensil']

heir presumptive (*plural* **heirs presumptive**) *n.* an heir whose entitlement to an inheritance will cease if another heir is born whose entitlement is greater

Heisenberg /hīz'n burg/, **Werner** (1901–76) German physicist. He directed Germany's development of an atomic bomb during World War II. His most important research in theoretical physics included work on quantum theory and his discovery of the uncertainty principle. He won the Nobel Prize in 1932.

Heisenberg uncertainty principle *n.* = **uncertainty principle** [Named after the German physicist Werner HEISENBERG (1901–76), who deduced it]

heist /hīst/ *n. US, Can* **THEFT** a theft or robbery, especially of money or valuables, usually involving the use of weapons (*slang*) ■ *vt.* (**heists, heisting, heisted**) *US, Can* **STEAL STH** to steal or rob sth, especially money or valuables, usually while carrying weapons (*slang*) [Mid-19thC. Representing a local American pronunciation of HOIST.] —**heister** *n.*

heita /háy taal/ *interj. S Africa* used as a friendly

greeting among young Black men and boys in South Africa (*informal*) ♦ **sharp**

heitiki /hay teeki/ *n. NZ* a Maori fertility symbol (**tiki**) carved from greenstone in the shape of a foetus, worn as a neck ornament [Mid-19thC. From Maori, literally 'hanging image'.]

hejira, **Hejira** *n.* = **hegira**, **Hegira**

Hekate *n.* = **Hecate**

Heke Pokai /héke páwku/, **Hone** (1810?–50) Maori chief. He was head of the Ngapuhi people and a strong opponent of British colonial government in New Zealand.

Hekla /hékla/ active volcano in southwestern Iceland. Height: 1,491 m/4,892 ft.

Hel /hel/, **Hela** /hé laa/ *n.* **1. NORSE GODDESS OF THE DEAD** in Norse mythology, the daughter of Loki, and the goddess of the dead and the underworld **2. NORSE UNDERWORLD** in Norse mythology, the underworld of the dead [From Old Norse, related to English *hell*]

HeLa cell /héela-/, **Hela cell** *n.* a cell from a strain of human cervical cancer cells that is used in medical and biological research [Mid-20thC. Acronym formed from the name of *Henrietta Lacks*, the patient from whom the original cells were taken.]

held past tense, past participle of **hold**

Heldentenor /hélden tə nawr/ *n.* a tenor or tenor voice with a robust dramatic quality that is suited especially for heroic roles in the operas of Richard Wagner [Early 20thC. From German, literally 'hero tenor'.]

Helen /héllən/, **Helen of Troy** *n.* in Greek mythology, the daughter of Zeus and Leda and the most beautiful woman in Greece. Her husband was Menelaus, the king of Sparta. Her abduction by Paris sparked the Trojan War.

Helena /héllənə/ city and capital of Montana, located in the western part of the state. Population: 24,569 (1990).

Helena, St (248?–328?) Roman empress. She was the mother of Constantine I. Among her religious pilgrimages, she visited Jerusalem about 325, where she founded the Church of the Holy Sepulchre and is said to have discovered the True Cross.

Helene /hə leeni/ *n.* a very small natural satellite of Saturn, discovered in 1980. It is irregular in shape, with a maximum dimension of 36 km/22 mi. and occupies an intermediate orbit.

helenium /hi leeni əm/ (*plural* **-ums** *or* **-um**) *n.* a plant of the daisy family that is native to North and South America and has yellow or dark reddish flowers, or in cultivated varieties sometimes bicoloured flowers. Genus: *Helenium.* [Early 17thC. Via modern Latin from Greek *helenion*, perhaps named after HELEN OF TROY.]

Helensvale /héllənz vayl/ town in southeastern Queensland, Australia, a residential, tourist, and cattle grazing centre. Population: 13,823 (1996).

heli /hélli/ (*plural* **-is**) *n.* a rotary-wing aircraft (*informal*) [Shortening of HELICOPTER]

heli- *prefix.* helicopter ○ *helipad* [From HELICOPTER]

heliacal /hi lf ək'l/ *adj.* used to describe the rising or setting of a star that occurs at the same time as the rising or setting of the sun, because of their near conjunction [Mid-16thC. Via late Latin *heliacus* from, ultimately, Greek *hēlios* 'sun'.] —**heliacally** *adv.*

helianthemum /heeli ánthəməm/ *n.* any of various evergreen perennials native to the United States, Europe, and Asia Minor with white, yellow, pink, or orange flowers. Genus: *Helianthemum.* [Early 19thC. From modern Latin, formed from Greek *hēlios* 'sun' + *anthemon* 'flower' (because the flower turns to follow the path of the sun).]

helianthus /heeli ánthəss/ (*plural* **-thuses** *or* **-thus**) *n.* a tall perennial plant related to the sunflower with yellow flowers resembling those of the daisy. Some cultivated varieties have double flowers. Genus: *Helianthus.* [Late 18thC. From modern Latin, formed from Greek *hēlios* 'sun' + *anthos* 'flower' (because the flower turns to follow the path of the sun).]

heliborne /hélli bawrn/ *adj.* transported by helicopter

helic- *prefix.* = **helico-** (used before vowels)

helical /héllik'l/ *adj.* in the shape of a helix or spiral [Late 16thC. From Latin *helix* (see HELIX).] —**helically** *adv.*

helical gear *n.* a gear whose teeth are formed to curve along a spiral path on the surface of the gear on an axis oblique to the axis of the gear itself

helices plural of **helix**

helichrysum /hélli krízəm/ (*plural* **-sums** *or* **-sum**) *n.* an annual or perennial plant of the daisy family grown especially for its variously coloured flowers that retain their colour when dried. Genus: *Helichrysum.* [Mid-16thC. From Latin, literally 'golden spiral'.]

helico- *prefix.* helix, spiral ○ *helicograph* [From Greek *helik-*, the stem of *helix* (see HELIX)]

helicograph /héllikō graaf, -graf/ *n.* an instrument for drawing spiral curves on a flat surface

helicoid /hélli koyd/ *adj.* BIOL SPIRAL shaped or coiled like a spiral (*technical*) ○ *a helicoid shell* ■ *n.* GEOM SPIRAL SURFACE a spiral geometric surface that resembles a thread on a screw [Late 17thC. From Greek *helicoidēs*, from *helix* 'HELIX'.] —**helicoidal** /hélli kóyd'l/ *adj.* —**helicoidally** /-kóyd'li/ *adv.*

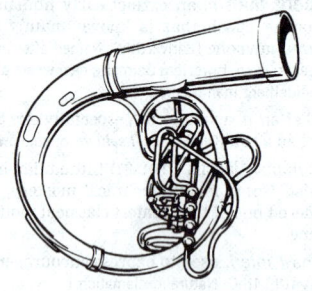

Helicon

helicon /héllikən, -kon/ *n.* a large bass tuba that encircles the player's body, used in marching bands [Late 19thC. From *Helicon;* influenced by HELIX (because of the shape).]

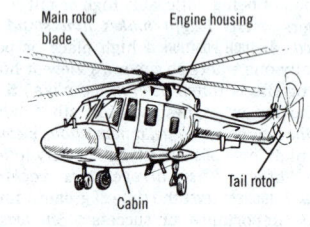

Main rotor blade · Engine housing · Tail rotor · Cabin

Helicopter

helicopter /hélli koptər/ *n.* AIRCRAFT WITH ROTORS an aircraft without wings that moves by means of large blades (**rotors**) that spin round above it. It can fly vertically and horizontally and can hover. ■ *vti.* (**-ters, -tering, -tered**) FLY IN HELICOPTER to travel or transport sb or sth in a helicopter ○ *The survivors were helicoptered to a hospital.* [Late 19thC. From French *hélicoptère,* from Greek *helix* 'spiral' + *pteron* 'wing'.]

helicopter gunship *n.* a large heavily armed helicopter used to protect troops on the ground

heliculture /hélli kulchər/ *n.* the science or the profession of raising snails for food [From modern Latin *Helix,* a genus of spiral-shelled molluscs (from Greek *helix* 'HELIX') + CULTURE] —**helicultural** /hélli kulchərəl/ *adj.* —**heliculturalist** /-kulchərəlist/ *n.*

helideck /hélli dek/ *n.* a deck on sth such as a ship or offshore oil platform that is used as a landing site for helicopters

helio- *prefix.* sun ○ *heliostat* [From Greek *hēlios* (source of English *helium*). Ultimately from the Indo-European word for 'sun', which is also the ancestor of *sun* and *solar*.]

heliocentric /heeli ō séntrik/, **heliocentrical** /-séntrik'l/ *adj.* **1. WITH THE SUN CENTRAL** with the sun at the centre ○ *a heliocentric orbit* **2. FROM CENTRE OF SUN** measured from or considered as if viewed from the centre of the sun —**heliocentrically** /-séntrikli/ *adv.* —**heliocentricity** /-sen tríssəti/ *n.*

heliodor /heeli ō dawr/ *n.* a clear yellow variety of beryl found in southwestern Africa, used as a gemstone [Early 20thC. Coined from HELIO- + Greek *dōron* 'gift'.]

heliograph /heeli ə graaf, -graf/ *n.* **1.** COMMUNICATION SIGNALLING APPARATUS an apparatus that is used to send messages in Morse code by flashes of reflected sunlight **2.** ASTRON PHOTOGRAPHING APPARATUS an apparatus used to photograph the sun —**heliographer** /heeli óggrəfər/ *n.* —**heliographic** /heeli ə gráffik/ *adj.*

heliolatry /heeli óllətri/ *n.* worship of the sun —**heliolater** *n.* —**heliolatrous** *adj.*

heliolithic /heeli ō líthik/ *adj.* used to describe a culture or society characterized by worship of the sun and the construction of monuments or temples using huge stones (**megaliths**)

heliometer /heeli ómmitər/ *n.* a refracting telescope with a divided objective that is used to measure small angular distances between celestial objects or points on the moon —**heliometric** /heeli ə méttrik/ *adj.* —**heliometrical** /-méttrik'l/ *adj.* —**heliometrically** /-méttrikli/ *adv.* —**heliometry** /heeli ómmətri/ *n.*

heliophyte /heeli ō fīt/ *n.* a plant that can survive and grow in direct sunlight or that grows best in direct sunlight

Heliopolis /heeli óppəliss/ city of ancient Egypt, northeast of present-day Cairo in the Nile delta. The great temple there was the centre of sun worship, and reached the height of its influence in the 13th century BC.

Helios /heeli oss/ *n.* in Greek mythology, the god of the sun. The son of Hyperion and Thea, he drove his golden chariot across the sky from east to west each day. Roman equivalent **Sol**

helioseismology /heeli ō sīz móllǝji/ *n.* the scientific study of the sound waves in the sun's atmosphere

heliosphere /heeli ō sfeer/ *n.* a spherical region round the sun, approximately 100 astronomical units in radius, outside which interstellar space begins

heliostat /heeli ō stat/ *n.* an instrument with an automatically rotated mirror that reflects the sun's light in a constant direction, used to measure the sun's radiation [Mid-18thC. From modern Latin *heliostata* or French *héliostat,* both from Greek *hēlios* 'sun' + *statos* 'standing'.] —**heliostatic** /heeli ō státtik/ *adj.*

heliotaxis /heeli ō táksiss/ *n.* movement towards or away from sunlight in an organism that is able to move about freely —**heliotactic** /-táktik/ *adj.*

heliotherapy /heeli ō thérrəpi/ *n.* treatment of illness by exposure to direct sunlight

heliotrope /heeli ə trōp/ *n.* (*plural* **-tropes** *or* **-trope**) **1.** PLANTS PLANT WITH PURPLE FLOWERS any of various hairy herbaceous plants or shrubs of the borage family, especially a South American species cultivated for its small, very fragrant purple flowers. Genus: *Heliotropium.* **2.** PLANTS FLOWER THAT TURNS TOWARDS SUN any of a number of plants with flowers that turn towards the sun **3.** COLOURS BLUISH COLOUR a bluish-purple colour **4.** MINERALS = **bloodstone 5.** CIV ENG SURVEYING INSTRUMENT an instrument used in geodesic surveying to reflect the sun's rays over long distances ■ *adj.* COLOURS OF BLUISH COLOUR of a bluish-purple colour [Pre-12thC. Via Latin *heliotropium* from Greek *heliotropion,* literally 'sun turning'.]

heliotropism /heeli óttrəpizəm/ *n.* growth towards sunlight by a plant. ◊ **phototropism** —**heliotropic** /heeli ə tróppik/ *adj.* —**heliotropical** *adj.* —**heliotropically** *adv.*

heliozoan /heeli ō zō ən/ *n.* a free-living, usually freshwater, protozoan that has a spherical shell and radiating projections (**pseudopodia**). Class: Heliozoa. [Late 19thC. From modern Latin *Heliozoa,* class name, from Greek *hēlios* 'sun' + *zōion* 'animal'.] —**heliozoic** *adj.*

helipad /hélli pad/ *n.* an area where helicopters take off and land

heliport /hélli pawrt/ *n.* an airport designed for helicopters

heli-skiing *n.* skiing in which skiers are taken to a usually remote ski slope by helicopter

helistop /hélli stop/ *n.* a place where helicopters can take off and land, usually without the support facilities found at a heliport

helium /heéli əm/ *n.* a nonflammable inert gas that is colourless and odourless. Symbol **He** [Late 19thC. From Greek *hēlios* 'sun' (because its existence was deduced from its emission line in the solar spectrum).]

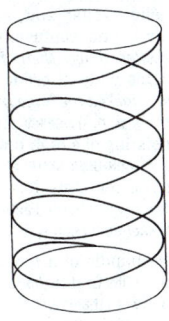
Helix

helix /heéliks/ (*plural* **helices** /hélli seez/ *or* **helixes**) *n.* **1.** SPIRAL OR COIL sth in the form of a spiral or coil, e.g. a corkscrew or a coiled spring **2.** GEOM SPIRAL CURVE a mathematical curve that lies on a cylinder or cone and makes a constant angle with the straight lines lying in the cylinder or cone **3.** ANAT RIM OF EAR the rim of the external ear [Mid-16thC. Via Latin from Greek.]

hell /hel/ *n.* **1.** **hell, Hell** PLACE OF PUNISHMENT AFTER DEATH according to many religions, the place where the souls of people who are damned suffer eternal punishment after death **2.** **hell, Hell** DEVILISH POWER according to some religions, Satan or the powers of evil that live in hell **3.** UNDERWORLD according to some religions, the place where the spirits of all people go after death **4.** SUFFERING OR ITS CAUSE a state or place of extreme pain or misery, or sth or sb that causes extreme pain or misery ○ *Finals are absolute hell.* ○ *She went through hell until she heard they were safe.* ■ *interj.* EXPRESSING ANNOYANCE used to express annoyance or surprise (*sometimes considered offensive*) ○ *Hell! I've lost the key.* [Old English *hel(l).* Ultimately from an Indo-European word meaning 'to conceal', which is also the ancestor of English *conceal, occult, eucalyptus,* and *apocalypse.*] ◇ **a hell of a, one hell of a** used as an intensifier (*informal*) ◇ **come hell or high water** whatever difficulties there may be ◇ **from hell** of the worst sort imaginable (*informal*) ○ *The bus ride in the snowstorm was a trip from hell.* ◇ **give sb hell 1.** to scold sb severely (*informal*) **2.** to cause sb trouble or pain (*informal*) ◇ **hell for leather** extremely rapidly and often recklessly (*informal*) ◇ **hell to pay** serious trouble or punishment that is sure to result from sth (*informal*) ◇ **(just) for the hell of it** just for amusement or excitement (*informal*) ◇ **like hell 1.** very fast or very intensely (*informal*) **2.** used to emphasize disagreement or denial (*informal*) ◇ **play (merry) hell with sth** to cause harm, disruption, or damage to sth (*informal*) ◇ **raise hell 1.** to object to sth strongly and loudly (*informal*) **2.** to cause a noisy disturbance (*informal*) ◇ **the hell 1.** used to emphasize annoyance (*informal*) **2.** used to emphasize disagreement or denial (*informal*)

he'll (*stressed*) /heel/; (*unstressed*) /eel, il/ *contr.* **1.** HE WILL he will **2.** HE SHALL he shall

Helladic /he láddik/ *adj.* associated with or characteristic of the Bronze Age civilization that flourished in Greece from 3000 to 1100 BC [Early 19thC. From Greek *Helladikos,* from *Hellas* 'Greece'.]

Hellas /héllass/ *n.* **1.** GREECE the ancient name for Greece **2.** ASTRON PLAIN ON MARS an extensive plain on the surface of Mars in the southern hemisphere, approximately 1800 km/1100 mi. across

hellbender /hél bendər/ *n.* a large, dark grey salamander found in rivers in eastern and central parts of the United States. Latin name: *Cryptobranchus alleganiensis.*

hell-bent *adj.* absolutely determined to do sth, regardless of the consequences

hellcat /hél kat/ *n.* an offensive term that deliberately insults a woman's temper and suggests that she is violent (*offensive*)

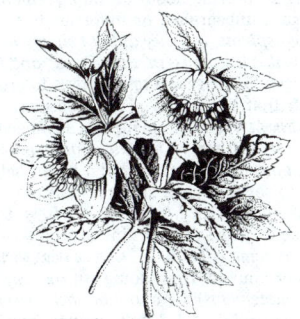
Hellebore

hellebore /hélli bawr/ (*plural* **-bores** *or* **-bore**) *n.* **1.** EARLY-FLOWERING PLANT an early-flowering, often poisonous perennial plant, native to Europe and Asia, that has large divided leaves and drooping white, pink, dark purple, or sometimes green flowers. The Christmas rose is a hellebore. Genus: *Helleborus.* **2.** GREENISH-FLOWERED PLANT any of various poisonous plants of North America with greenish flowers. Genus: *Veratrum.* [Pre-12thC. Via Old French *ellebre* from, ultimately, Greek *helleboros.*]

helleborine /hélliba rīn, -reen/ *n.* an orchid native to temperate northern areas and often occurring in woodland. Genera: *Epipactis* and *Cephalanthera.* [Late 16thC. Directly or via French from Latin *(h)elleborine,* from Greek 'a plant like hellebore'.]

Hellen /héllən/ *n.* in Greek mythology, a king of Thessaly and ancestor of the ancient Hellenic peoples

Hellene /hélleen/, **Hellenian** /he leéni ən/ *n.* (*formal*) **1.** ANCIENT GREEK an ancient Greek **2.** SB FROM MODERN GREECE sb who was born or brought up in modern Greece [Mid-17thC. From Greek *Hellēn* 'a Greek'.]

Hellenic /-leénik, he lénnik/ *adj.* PEOPLES OF ANCIENT GREECE relating to or typical of ancient Greece, or its people, languages, or culture ■ *n.* LANG GROUP OF GREEK LANGUAGES the branch of Indo-European consisting of the ancient and modern forms of Greek [Mid-17thC. From Greek *Hellēnikos,* from *Hellēn* (see HELLENE).] —**Hellenically** *adv.*

Hellenise *vti.* = **Hellenize**

Hellenism /héllənizəm/ *n.* **1.** ANCIENT GREEK CULTURE the culture and civilization of ancient Greece, especially in the period after Alexander the Great when it spread to other parts of the Mediterranean and Middle East and North Africa **2.** ADMIRATION FOR ANCIENT GREEK CULTURE the enthusiasm for or adoption of ancient Greek culture or customs **3.** GREEK CHARACTERISTIC a Greek custom or idiom **4.** GREEK NATIONAL CHARACTER the national character of the Greeks [Early 17thC. From Greek *Hellēnismos* (see HELLENIZE).]

Hellenist /héllənist/ *n.* **1.** GREEK EXPERT sb who is a specialist in the study of Greek language, literature, culture, or history, or sb who has a great enthusiasm for things Greek **2.** HIST ADOPTER OF GREEK WAYS sb, especially a Jew, who adopted Greek customs, language, and culture during the 4th to 1st centuries BC [Early 17thC. From Greek *Hellēnistēs* (see HELLENIZE).]

Hellenistic /héllə nístik/ *adj.* **1.** OF ANCIENT GREEK CIVILIZATION characteristic of or concerned with ancient Greek civilization from the late 4th to 1st centuries BC **2.** OF GREEKS characteristic of or associated with the Greeks **3.** PREFERRING GREEK CULTURE enthusiastic for or adopting ancient Greek culture or customs ○ *the Hellenistic Jews of Alexandria* —**Hellenistically** *adv.*

Hellenize /héllə nīz/ (**-nizes, -nizing, -nized**), **Hellenise** (**-nises, -nising, -nised**) *vti.* to adopt the language and culture of the ancient Greeks, or make sth such as a culture more like that of the ancient Greeks [Early 17thC. From Greek *Hellēnizein,* to make Greek', from *Hellēn* (see HELLENE).] —**Hellenization** /héllə nī záysh'n/ *n.* —**Hellenizer** /héllə nīzər/ *n.*

heller /héllər/ (*plural* **-ler**) *n.* **1.** OLD GERMAN OR AUSTRIAN COIN any of several obsolete German or Austrian coins **2.** = **haler** [Late 16thC. From German, ultimately named after the town of *Schwäbisch Hall* in Germany, where it was first minted.]

hellfire /hél fīr/ *n.* FIERY PUNISHMENT IN HELL punishment in hell, often described as eternal torment in the flames of hell's fires ■ *adj.* EMPHASIZING PUNISHMENT IN HELL detailing the punishment sinners can expect in hell in a vigorous and emotional way

hellgrammite /hélgrə mīt/ *n.* US the large aquatic carnivorous larva of the North American dobsonfly, often used as fish bait [Mid-19thC. Origin unknown.]

hellhole /hél hōl/ *n.* a terrifying, unbearable, or evil place

hellhound /hél hownd/ *n.* **1.** FIEND a fiend or fiendish, wicked person **2.** MYTHOL HOUND GUARDING HELL a hound said to guard the gates of hell, especially in Greek mythology

hellish /héllish/ *adj.* **1.** VILE so wicked or cruel that it seems characteristic of the devil **2.** OF HELL like, from, or typical of hell **3.** DREADFUL extremely unpleasant or difficult (*informal*) ○ *The exam was absolutely hellish.* ■ *adv.* EXTREMELY used as an intensifier (*informal*) ○ *hellish difficult* —**hellishly** *adv.* —**hellishness** *n.*

Popperfoto
Lillian Hellman

Hellman /hélmən/, **Lillian** (1905–84) US playwright. She was known for her powerful moral dramas such as *Watch on the Rhine* (1941) and *Toys in the Attic* (1960). Full name **Lillian Florence Hellman**

hello /hə ló, he ló/, **hallo** /hə ló, ha ló/, **hullo** /hə ló, hu ló/ *interj., n.* (*plural* **-los**) **1.** WORD USED AS GREETING a word used to greet sb you meet, to answer a telephone call, or to begin a radio or television programme ○ *Hello. Nice to meet you.* ○ *After we had all said our hellos, we settled down to eat.* **2.** WORD TO ATTRACT ATTENTION a word used to attract attention ○ *Hello! Is there anyone in?* **3.** WORD EXPRESSING SURPRISE a word used to express surprise ○ *Hello! What's that doing here?* [Late 19thC. Origin uncertain; probably ultimately from French *holá,* literally 'stop there!', used to attract attention.]

hell-raiser *n.* sb whose idea of having a good time involves behaving in ways that other people consider drunken, rowdy, and disruptive

Hell's Angel *n.* a member of a Californian gang of motorcyclists, mostly men, typically dressing in denim and leather and originally noted for violent antisocial behaviour, or a member of any similar gang elsewhere

helluva /hélləvə/ *adj.* used as an intensifier (*informal*) ○ *a helluva party* [Early 20thC. Representing 'hell of a'.]

helm[1] /helm/ *n.* **1.** NAUT SHIP'S STEERING APPARATUS the apparatus used to steer a ship, especially the wheel or handle (**tiller**) by which the rudder is turned **2.** POSITION OF CONTROL a position of leadership or control within an organization, country, or enterprise ○ *The failing company needed a new chief at its helm.* ■ *vt.* (**helms, helming, helmed**) **1.** NAUT STEER SHIP to be at the helm of a ship steering it **2.** DIRECT STH to be at the head of an organization, country, or enterprise directing it [Old English *helma,* from a prehistoric Germanic word meaning 'handle' that is also the ancestor of English *halter* and *helve*] —**helmless** *adj.*

helm[2] /helm/ *n.* **HELMET** an ancient or medieval helmet (*archaic or literary*) ■ *vt.* **(helms, helming, helmed) PROVIDE SB WITH HELMET** to provide a soldier or knight with a helmet (*archaic or literary*) [Old English. Ultimately from a prehistoric Germanic word meaning 'to conceal or cover', which is also the ancestor of English *hell* and *helmet*.]

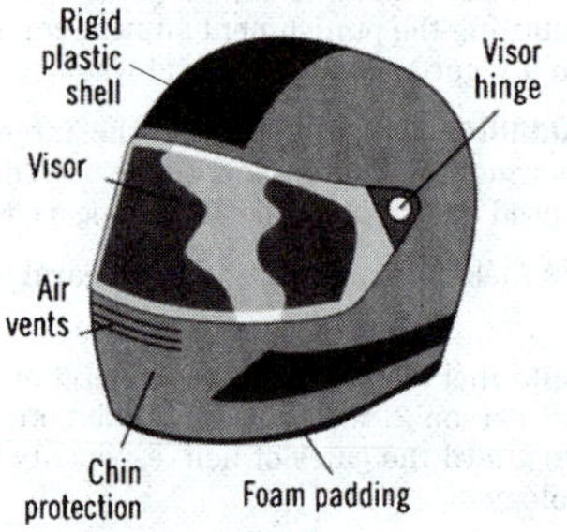
Rigid plastic shell
Visor hinge
Visor
Air vents
Chin protection
Foam padding
Helmet: Crash helmet

helmet /hélmit/ *n.* **1. HARD PROTECTIVE HEAD COVERING** a hat or other head covering made of a hard material and worn to protect the head from injury, often part of a uniform, suit of armour, or protective clothing **2. PROTECTIVE HAT** any of various types of hat worn to give protection, e.g. against cold weather or the heat of the sun **3.** BIOL **PART SHAPED LIKE HELMET** a part of an organism, e.g. a flower's sepal or corolla, resembling a helmet [15thC. From Old French, diminutive of *helme* 'helmet'. Ultimately from the same prehistoric Germanic word as English *helm*.] —**helmeted** *adj.*

helminth /hélminth/ *n.* any of various parasitic worms, e.g. a fluke, nematode, or tapeworm [Mid-19thC. From Greek *helminth-* 'intestinal worm'.] —**helminthoid** *adj.*

helminthiasis /hélmin thī́ əssiss/ *n.* infestation by parasitic worms, or a disease caused by this

helminthic /hel mínthik/ *adj.* **1. OF PARASITIC WORMS** caused by or relating to flukes, nematodes, or other parasitic worms **(helminths) 2. USED AGAINST PARASITIC WORMS** eradicating or expelling parasitic worms ■ *n.* = **vermifuge**

helminthology /hélmin thólləji/ *n.* the scientific study of parasitic worms —**helminthologist** *n.*

Helmont /hél mont/, **Jan Baptista van** (1580–1644) Flemish chemist and physiologist. An early experimental chemist, he invented the term 'gas'.

helmsman /hélmzmən/ (*plural* **-men** /-mən/) *n.* **1.** NAUT **STEERSMAN** sb who steers a ship **2. LEADER** sb who directs an organization, country, or enterprise ○ *the country's helmsman in the crisis* —**helmsmanship** *n.*

helo /héllō/ (*plural* **-os**) *n.* (*informal*) **1. HELICOPTER** a rotary-winged aircraft **2. HELIPORT** an airport designed for helicopters [Mid-20thC. Shortening and alteration.]

Héloïse /éllō eez/ (1098?–1164) French abbess. Her love affair with Peter Abelard, and their subsequent separation and correspondence, provided one of the world's great love stories.

helot /héllət/ *n.* a serf or enslaved person [Late 16thC. Via Latin *Helotes* from Greek *Heilōtes*, said to be named after *Helos*, a town in Laconia whose inhabitants were enslaved.] —**helotage** *n.*

Helot *n.* in ancient Sparta, a member of a class of serfs claimed as property by the state but assigned to individual Spartans to work on their land [Late 16thC. (See HELOT).]

helotism /héllətizəm/ *n.* **1.** POL **SOCIOPOLITICAL SYSTEM** a political or social system in which one group, class, or nation is systematically oppressed by another **2.** BIOL **ANIMAL SYMBIOSIS** a type of symbiosis found especially among ants, in which one species acts as workers for another, dominant species

help /help/ *v.* **(helps, helping, helped) 1.** *vti.* **ASSIST SB WITH ACTIVITY** to make it easier for sb to do sth, or possible for sb to do sth that one person cannot do alone, by providing assistance of some sort ○ *Let me help you with those packages.* ○ *Can you help me solve this problem?* **2.** *vti.* **ADVISE** to provide sb with advice, directions, or other information ○ *I wonder if you could help me? I'm trying to find Belmont Road.* **3.** *vti.* **BE USEFUL** to make sth easier or more likely ○ *It would help if you didn't keep shaking the ladder.* ○ *Would a degree help me get a better job?* **4.** *vti.* **MAKE THINGS BETTER** to bring about an improvement in sth unpleasant, unbearable, or unfortunate ○ *I took a couple of aspirins, but they didn't help my headache.* ○ *You look ridiculous in that dress, and the hat doesn't help.* **5.** *vti.* **PROVIDE FOR SB'S NEEDS** to provide sb with sth that he or she needs, especially money **6.** *vti.* **ADVANCE STH** to promote the advancement or improvement of sth ○ *Opening a new sports centre won't cut out teenage crime, but it might help.* **7.** *vt.* **SERVE SB** to serve sb in a shop, restaurant, or other establishment ○ *Can I help you, sir?* **8.** *vt.* **SERVE FOOD** to give sb or yourself a serving of food ○ *He helped himself to some cake.* **9.** *vt.* **KEEP SB FROM DOING STH** to keep sb or yourself from doing sth (*usually used in negative statements*) ○ *We couldn't help overhearing your conversation.* ○ *I didn't want to laugh, but I couldn't help myself.* **10.** *vt.* **PREVENT STH** to prevent sth from happening (*usually used in negative statements*) ○ *The child couldn't have helped the accident.* ■ *n.* **1. ASSISTANCE** sth that is done for or given to sb in order to make sth easier, possible, or better ○ *I could do with some help in the kitchen.* **2. SB OR STH THAT ASSISTS** sb who or sth that provides aid or assistance to sb else ○ *The headaches are pretty bad, but the aspirins are a help.* **3. WAY OUT OF STH** a way of avoiding doing sth or of undoing sth (*often used in negative statements*) ○ *Well, there's no help for it now but to start digging.* **4. SB PAID TO CLEAN** sb who is paid to help with the housework in another person's home **5. SERVANTS COLLECTIVELY** domestic servants as a group (*takes a singular or plural verb*) ○ *told us that the help have to eat in the kitchen* ■ *interj.* **CALL FOR ASSISTANCE** used to call for assistance when sb is in danger or difficulty [Old English *helpan*, ultimately from a prehistoric Germanic word] —**helper** *n.* ◇ **help yourself** take sth for your own use, usually without permission

WORD KEY: USAGE

can't help but Traditionally, speakers and writers had a choice between, for example, *can't help doing* and *can't [or cannot] but do.* The latter is now very uncommon. *Can't help but do* is often seen, but it is a redundant, improper mixture of the two forms, and should be avoided in favour of *can't help doing.*

help out *vti.* to give sb some help, e.g. by doing some work or giving money

help desk *n.* a service providing technical help and support for people using a computer package or network

helper T cell, helper cell *n.* a white blood cell that is part of the body's immune response, recognizing foreign antigens and stimulating the production of cells to control them

helpful /hélpf'l/ *adj.* providing or willing to provide assistance, information, or other aid ○ *You might find this book helpful.* —**helpfully** *adv.* —**helpfulness** *n.*

helping /hélping/ *n.* an amount of food served to sb at one time

helping hand *n.* sth done to assist sb else

helpless /hélpləss/ *adj.* **1. NEEDING HELP** unable to manage without help **2. DEFENCELESS** unprotected and unable to provide an adequate defence against an attack **3. UNABLE TO ACT EFFECTIVELY** unable to do anything to protect sb or prevent sth happening ○ *He was helpless to stop the assault.* **4. UNRESTRAINED** unable to exert control or restraint ○ *His jokes had us absolutely helpless.* —**helplessly** *adv.* —**helplessness** *n.*

helpline /hélp līn/ *n.* a telephone service that provides advice or information to people who phone up with problems or inquiries

Helpmann /hélpmən/, **Sir Robert Murray** (1909–86) Australian ballet dancer and choreographer. He was principal dancer and choreographer at Sadler's Wells Ballet in the 1930s and 1940s, and later joined the Australian Ballet (1964–76).

helpmate /hélp mayt/ *n.* a helpful companion or partner, especially a spouse

helpmeet /hélp meet/ *n.* a helpmate, especially a wife (*archaic; sometimes considered offensive*) [Late 17thC. From MEET[2] 'suitable', from the biblical phrase 'an help meet for him' (Genesis 2:18, 20).]

Helsingør /hélseng úr/ town and seaport in eastern Denmark on the island of Zealand, the setting of William Shakespeare's play *Hamlet.* Population: 43,302 (1992).

Helsinki /hel síngki/ capital city and chief seaport of Finland, situated on the Gulf of Finland in the south of the country. Population: 497,542 (1991).

helter-skelter /héltər skéltər/ *adv., adj.* **1. HURRIEDLY OR HURRIED** with hurry and confusion ○ *The rabbits rushed helter-skelter down their burrows.* **2. HAPHAZARDLY OR HAPHAZARD** without order or organization ○ *The winds had knocked the huge trees helter-skelter all over the park.* ■ *n.* **1. SPIRAL SLIDE** a fairground amusement consisting of a high tower with a spiral slide round it **2. CONFUSED STATE** a hurried or disorganized situation or state [Late 16thC. A playful formation thought to suggest hurried action, perhaps formed on Middle English *skelten* 'to come, go'.]

helve /helv/ *n.* the handle of a tool such as an axe, pick, or hammer [Old English *helfe.* Ultimately from a prehistoric Germanic word that is also the ancestor of English *halter* and, probably, *helm*[1].]

Helvellyn /hel véllin/ mountain in the Lake District of Cumbria, northwest England. Height: 950 m/3,118 ft.

Helvetian /hel veésh'n/ *n.* **1. SB FROM SWITZERLAND** sb who was born in or is a citizen of Switzerland **2.** HIST **MEMBER OF HELVETII** a member of the ancient Celtic people the Helvetii ■ *adj.* **1. SWISS** relating to or typical of Switzerland **2.** HIST **OF HELVETII** relating to or typical of the Helvetii [Mid-16thC. From Latin *Helvetia* 'Switzerland', from *Helvetius* 'of or with the Helvetii'.]

Helvetic /hel véttik/ *adj.* **1. SWISS** relating to or typical of Switzerland **2.** CHR **OF SWISS PROTESTANTISM** following or relating to the religious teachings of Ulrich Zwingli and other Swiss Protestant reformers ■ *n.* PEOPLES **SB FROM SWITZERLAND** sb who was born or brought up in Switzerland, or who has Swiss citizenship [Early 18thC. (See HELVETIAN).]

Helvetii /hel veéshi ī/ *npl.* a Celtic people who originally came from southern Germany and migrated to Helvetia where they settled during the second century BC [Late 19thC. From Latin.]

Helvétius /hel veéshi əss/, **Claude Adrien** (1715–71) French philosopher. *De l'esprit* (1758), his major work, was denounced and publicly burned for its insistence that self-interest alone drives human actions.

hem[1] /hem/ *n.* **1. FOLDED FABRIC EDGE** a neat nonfraying edge on sth made of cloth, e.g. at the bottom of a skirt or dress, made by folding the fabric over and stitching it down **2.** = **hemline** *n.* 1 ■ *v.* **(hems, hemming, hemmed) 1.** *vti.* **MAKE HEM ON STH** to fold over and stitch down fabric to make a hem on sth ○ *hem curtains* **2.** *vt.* **ENCLOSE SB OR STH** to surround and enclose sb or sth ○ *The small yard was hemmed about by a tall hedge.* [Old English, related to Old Frisian *hemme* 'enclosed land']

hem in *vt.* to confine and restrict sb or sth

hem[2] /hem/ *interj., n.* **NOISE MADE IN THROAT** a word used to represent the sound made by sb clearing his or her throat or coughing quietly in order to attract attention, warn sb else, or hide embarrassment or uncertainty ■ *vi.* **(hems, hemming, hemmed) HESITATE IN SPEECH** to make the sound 'hem' or otherwise hesitate in speech [15thC. An imitation of the sound.] ◇ **hem and haw** to hesitate while speaking or deciding about sth

hem-[1] *prefix.* US = **haemo-**

hem-[2] *prefix.* US = **haem-**

hema- *prefix.* US = **haema-**

he-man (*plural* **he-men**) *n.* a strong, muscular man (*informal*)

hemat- *prefix.* US = **haemat-**

hemato- *prefix.* US = **haemato-**

heme /heem/ *n.* US = **haem**

Hemel Hempstead /hémm'l hémpstid/ town in Hertfordshire, south-central England, designated a 'New Town' in 1947. Population: 79,235 (1991).

hemeralopia /hémmərə lŏpi ə/ n. impaired vision in daylight (*technical*) [Early 18thC. Via modern Latin from Greek *hēmeralōps*, literally 'day-blind eye'.] —**hemeralopic** /-lóppik/ *adj.*

hemerocallis /hémmə rō kálliss/ n. = **day lily** [Mid-17thC. From Greek *hēmerokallis* 'lily that flowers for a day', from *hēmera* 'day' + *kallos* 'beauty'.]

hemi- *prefix.* half, partial ○ *hemihydrate* ○ *hemimetabolous* [From Greek *hēmi-*. Ultimately from an Indo-European word that is also the ancestor of English *semi-* and *sand-blind*.]

-hemia *suffix. US* = **-haemia**

hemicellulose /hémmi séllyŏŏ lŏss, -lŏz/ n. any of a group of polysaccharides found in plants, especially in the cell wall [So called because it is less complex than cellulose]

hemichordate /hémmi káwr dayt/ n. a marine animal resembling a worm that has a rudimentary cartilaginous skeleton (**notochord**) and numerous gill slits. Phylum: Hemichordata. [Late 19thC. From modern Latin *Hemichordata*, phylum name, from Greek *hemi-* 'HEMI-' + Latin *chorda* 'CORD'.] —**hemichordate** *adj.*

hemicycle /hémmi sīk'l/ n. a structure or arrangement that has a semicircular shape (*formal*) [15thC. Via French and Latin from Greek *hēmikuklion* 'semicircle'.] —**hemicyclic** /hémmi sĭklik, -sĭklik/ *adj.*

hemidemisemiquaver /hémmi démmi sémmi kwáyvər/ n. MUSIC a note with a time value equal to half a demisemiquaver or one sixty-fourth of a semibreve. US term **sixty-fourth note**

hemihedral /hémmi heédrəl/ *adj.* used to describe crystals that have only half the number of faces needed for complete symmetry [Mid-19thC. Coined from HEMI- + *-hedral* from -HEDRON.]

hemihydrate /hémmi hī drayt/ n. a hydrate, e.g. plaster of Paris, that consists of two parts compound to one part water

hemimetabolous /hémmi mə tábbələss/, **hemimetabolic** /hémmi metə bóllik/ *adj.* used to describe winged insects that lack complete metamorphosis, as do grasshoppers, whose increasingly larger nymphs approach adult form without going through a pupal stage

hemimorphic /hémmi máwrfik/ *adj.* used to describe crystals that do not have a horizontal axis of symmetry, so that the top and bottom of the crystal display different forms [Mid-19thC. Coined from HEMI- + Greek *morphē* 'form'.]

Ernest Hemingway

Hemingway /hémming way/, **Ernest** (1899–1961) US writer. He wrote fiction including *A Farewell to Arms* (1929) and *For Whom the Bell Tolls* (1940) in a distinctive terse style that complemented his own macho image and made him one of the century's leading novelists. He won the Nobel Prize in literature in 1954. Full name **Ernest Miller Hemingway**

hemiola /hémmi ŏlə/ n. a rhythmic alternation of two notes in the place of three, or three notes in place of two [14thC. Via medieval Latin *hemiolia* from Greek *hēmiolia* 'in the ratio of one and a half to one', from *holos* 'whole'.]

hemiplegia /hémmi pleéji ə/ n. total or partial inability to move, experienced on one side of the body, and caused by brain disease or injury. ◊ **paraplegia, quadriplegia** [Early 17thC. Via modern Latin from Greek *hēmiplēgia*, from *plēgē* (see -PLEGIA).] —**hemiplegic** *adj., n.*

hemipode /hémmi pōd/, **hemipod** /-pod/ n. a small round-bodied ground-dwelling bird of the grasslands of Africa, Australasia, and southern Europe and Asia. Family: Turnicidae. [Mid-19thC. From modern Latin HEMI- + Greek *podos* 'foot'.]

hemipteran /hi míptərən/ n. INSECT BELONGING TO BUG ORDER any insect that has mouthparts adapted for piercing and sucking and two pairs of wings, belonging to an order that includes stinkbugs, bedbugs, and other true bugs. Order: Hemiptera. ■ *adj.* = **hemipterous** [Late 19thC. Formed from modern Latin *Hemiptera*, order name, literally 'with half a wing', from Greek *pteron* 'wing'; from the partly hardened forewings of bugs.]

hemipterous /hi míptərəss/ *adj.* relating to or belonging to an order of insects that have mouthparts adapted for piercing and sucking [Early 19thC. From modern Latin *Hemiptera* (see HEMIPTEROUS).]

hemisphere /hémmi sfeer/ n. **1.** HALF OF THE EARTH one half of the Earth, especially a half north or south of the equator or west or east of the prime meridian **2.** HALF OF SPHERE one half of a sphere or of anything spherical in shape **3.** ANAT = **cerebral hemisphere 4.** ASTRON HALF OF CELESTIAL SPHERE either half of the celestial sphere north or south of the celestial equator [14thC. Via French or Latin from Greek *hēmisphairion*, from *sphaira* 'SPHERE'.] —**hemispheric** /hémmi sférrik/ *adj.* —**hemispherically** /-sférrikli/ *adv.*

hemistich /hémmi stik/ n. half of a line of poetry, usually separated from the rest by a caesura [Late 16thC. Via late Latin *hemistichium* from Greek *hēmistikhion*, from *stikhos* 'STICH'.]

hemizygous /hémmi zígəss/ *adj.* having only one of a specified pair of genes, as, e.g., do the unpaired X chromosomes of male mammals

hemline /hém līn/ n. **1.** CLOTHES' BOTTOM EDGE the bottom edge of a skirt, dress, or coat **2.** HEIGHT OF HEM the height of the hem of an item of women's clothing, especially the typical height of hems on fashionable women's clothing during a certain period ○ *Hemlines are up again.*

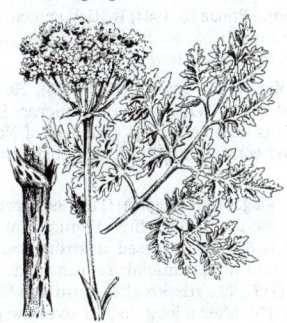
Hemlock

hemlock /hém lok/ n. (*plural* **-locks** *or* **-lock**) n. **1.** POISONOUS PLANT a very poisonous herbaceous plant of the carrot family that has small white flowers and finely cut leaves. Latin name: *Conium maculatum*. US term **poison hemlock 2.** POISON a poison obtained from the fruit of the hemlock plant. Hemlock was used in ancient Greece to execute people. Socrates was forced to drink hemlock when he was condemned to death. **3.** EVERGREEN TREE an evergreen tree of the pine family that has small cones and short blunt needles. Genus: *Tsuga*. ◊ **western hemlock 4.** HEMLOCK WOOD the wood of the hemlock tree [Old English *hymlic(e)*, *hemlic*, of unknown origin]

hemlock fir, hemlock spruce n. = **hemlock** n. **2**

hemmer /hémmər/ n. **1.** SEWER OF HEMS sb who hems clothes or other items **2.** DEVICE FOR SEWING HEMS a sewing machine attachment for sewing hems

hemo- *prefix. US* = **haemo-**

hemorrhoids *npl.* = **haemorrhoids**

hemp /hemp/ n. **1.** PLANTS PLANT WITH TOUGH FIBRES a plant native to Asia, widely grown for the tough fibres obtained from its stems and as the source of marijuana or cannabis **2.** TEXTILES TOUGH FIBRE FROM HEMP PLANT the tough fibre from the stems of the hemp plant, used in making canvas, rope, paper, and cloth **3.** TEXTILES TOUGH FIBRE FROM PLANTS any of several types of strong fibre obtained from plant stems and used like hemp **4.** DRUGS NARCOTIC DRUG FROM HEMP PLANT any of several narcotic drugs made from various parts of the hemp plant, smoked, chewed, eaten, or drunk to produce a mildly euphoric reaction and illegal in many countries. ◊ **bhang, cannabis, ganja, hashish, marijuana, dagga** [Old English *henep*. Ultimately from an Indo-European word that is also the ancestor of Greek *kannabis* (source of English *cannabis* and *canvas*).] —**hempen** *adj.*

hemp agrimony n. a tall Eurasian or North African plant with clusters of red, pink, or purple composite flowers and leaves like those of the hemp plant. Latin name: *Eupatorium cannabinum*.

hemp nettle n. **1.** FLOWERING PLANT a bristly Eurasian plant resembling the nettle, with red, pink, purple, or white two-lipped flowers and serrated leaves, now naturalized in the United States. Latin name: *Galeopsis tetrahit*. **2.** BRISTLY PLANT any of several Eurasian bristly plants that resemble the nettle. Genus: *Galeopsis*.

hemstitch /hém stich/ n. **1.** STITCH USED FOR HEMMING a small overcast stitch used to secure a hem **2.** DECORATIVE STITCH a decorative stitch used to ornament the edge of a cloth, in which, after horizontal threads are removed, vertical threads are gathered in small regular bunches ■ *vti.* (**-stitches, -stitching, -stitched**) EDGE STH WITH HEMSTITCH to hem or decorate an edge of cloth using hemstitch —**hemstitcher** n.

hen /hen/ n. **1.** AGRIC DOMESTIC FOWL an adult female domestic fowl **2.** BIRDS FEMALE BIRD any adult female bird **3.** MARINE BIOL FEMALE AQUATIC ANIMAL the female of some aquatic animals, e.g. the octopus, crab, and lobster **4.** OFFENSIVE TERM an offensive term that deliberately insults a woman's personality, activity, and age (*offensive dated*) **5.** *Scotland* WAY OF ADDRESSING WOMAN OR GIRL an affectionate or familiar term of address used to a woman or girl (*informal*) [Old English *henn*. Ultimately from an Indo-European word with the basic meaning 'to sing' that is also the ancestor of Latin *cantare* (source of English *canticle* and *chant*).] —**hennish** *adj.* —**hennishly** *adv.* —**hennishness** *n.* ◊ **rare as hen's teeth, scarce as hen's teeth** extremely valuable and hard to find

Henan /hŏ nán/ densely populated province in eastern China, including important sites of early Chinese civilization. Capital: Zhengzhou. Population: 90,270,000 (1994). Area: 167,000 sq. km/64,500 sq. mi.

hen-and-chickens (*plural* **hen-and-chickens** *or* **hens-and-chickens**) n. any of several plants, especially the houseleek, producing new plants as offsets that grow at the end of horizontal shoots or runners from the main plant [From the resemblance to young chicks surrounding the mother hen]

Henare /hénnəri/, **Sir James** (1911–89) New Zealand soldier. He commanded the Maori Battalion during World War II.

henbane /hén bayn/ n. a poisonous Eurasian plant of the nightshade family with hairy, sticky leaves, a strong unpleasant smell, and greenish-yellow flowers. It is a source of the drugs hyoscyamine and scopolamine. Latin name: *Hyoscyamus niger*.

henbit /hén bit/ n. a plant of the mint family with small white or reddish-purple lipped flowers. It was originally native to Europe and Asia, but is now naturalized in the United States. Latin name: *Lamium amplexicaule*. [*Bit* in the obsolete sense 'morsel of food']

hence /henss/ *adv.* **1.** BECAUSE OF THIS from this cause, or for this reason (*formal*) ○ *I lent him money before, and he never paid it back; hence my reluctance to lend him more.* ○ *Her grandfather was Polish, hence her interest in Polish culture* **2.** LATER THAN NOW later than the present time (*formal*) ○ *I'm sure the company will be in a much better financial position a year hence.* **3.** AWAY FROM HERE away from this place (*archaic*) ○ *Get you hence.* ○ *Hence! I never want to* *clap eyes on you again!* [13thC. Formed from Old English *heonan* 'hence' + the adverb suffix -s (as in 'backwards', 'besides'). Ultimately from an Indo-European demonstrative pronoun meaning 'this' that is also the ancestor of English *he*.]

henceforth /hénss fáwrth/, **henceforward** /-fáwrwərd/, **henceforwards** *adv.* from this time forwards (*formal*)

henchman /hénchmən/ (*plural* -men) *n.* 1. SUPPORTER OF SOMEONE DUBIOUS a supporter or associate of sb in a dubious cause, e.g. a member of a criminal's entourage, or sb whose status comes from supporting a politician (*disapproving*) 2. LOYAL FOLLOWER a loyal supporter or follower, especially of sb who holds a high office or position 3. PAGE OR SQUIRE a page or squire to sb of high rank (*archaic*) [14thC. *Hench* from Old English *hengest* 'stallion'.]

hencoop /hén koop/ *n.* a cage, hutch, or small building where hens or other domestic birds are kept

hendeca- *prefix.* forming words that signify eleven of sth such as sides, facets, or units [From Greek *hendeka* 'eleven']

hendecasyllable /hén dekə silləb'l/ *n.* a line of verse that consists of 11 syllables —**hendecasyllabic** /hén dekəsi lábbik, hen dékəsi lábbik/ *adj.*

hendiadys /hen dī ədiss/ *n.* a literary device expressing an idea by means of two words linked by 'and', instead of by a grammatically more complex form such as an adverb qualifying an adjective. Everyday examples of hendiadys are the expressions 'nice and soft', rather than 'nicely soft', and 'good and tight'. [Late 16thC. From medieval Latin, coined from Greek *hen dia duoin* 'one through two'.]

Jimi Hendrix

Hendrix /héndriks/, **Jimi** (1942–70) US musician. A virtuoso blues-rock guitarist, he was known for songs like 'Wild Thing' and albums including *Are You Experienced?* (1967). His charismatic stage performance was captured in the film *Woodstock* (1970). Full name **James Marshall Hendrix**

henequen /hénnikin/, **henequin** *n.* 1. PLANTS MEXICAN PLANT a tropical American plant that has large thick fibrous leaves shaped like swords and is found chiefly in the Yucatan peninsula of Mexico. Latin name: *Agave fourcroydes*. 2. TEXTILES FIBRE OBTAINED FROM HENEQUEN PLANT the reddish fibre obtained from the leaves of the henequen plant, used in making rope, twine, and coarse fabric. ◊ sisal [Early 17thC. Via Spanish from perhaps, ultimately, Arawakan.]

henge /henj/ *n.* a prehistoric oval or circular area, often bounded by a mound or ditch, that contains standing stones or wooden pillars that were erected during the Neolithic or Bronze Age [Mid-18thC. Back-formation from STONEHENGE.]

Hengist /héng gist/ (*d.* 488) Saxon leader. With his brother Horsa (*d.* 455), he is said to have led a Saxon force to England in about 449, and to have ruled the Anglo-Saxons in Kent, England, until his death.

hen harrier *n.* a slender, long-winged bird of prey that lives in open moorland and marshlands in northern Europe and North America and preys on small animals. Latin name: *Circus cyaneus*. US term **northern harrier**

henhouse /hén howss/ (*plural* -houses /-howziz/) *n.* a shelter or small shed where hens or other domestic birds are housed

Henle's loop /hénliz-/ *n.* ANAT = loop of Henle

henna /hénnə/ *n.* 1. PLANTS SHRUB a shrub of the loose-strife family that grows in Asia and North Africa and has fragrant white or reddish flowers and leaves that are used to make a dye. Latin name: *Lawsonia inermis*. 2. MANUF RED DYE a strong red dyestuff made from the leaves of the henna plant, used primarily as a hair dye. Henna is also used to stain the skin or nails, in cosmetics, and in colouring fabric. 3. COLOURS REDDISH-BROWN COLOUR a rich reddish-brown colour ■ *adj.* COLOURS OF REDDISH-BROWN COLOUR of a rich reddish-brown colour ■ *vt.* (-nas, -naing, -naed) COLOURS COLOUR STH WITH HENNA to dye or colour sth with henna [Early 17thC. From Arabic *ḥinnā'*.]

hennery /hénnəri/ (*plural* -ies) *n.* a place or farm where hens or other domestic birds are bred, reared, or kept

hen night *n.* a party or evening out for a woman who is about to be married, attended only by her women friends (*sometimes considered offensive*) ◊ **stag night**

henotheism /hénnə thi izəm/ *n.* the worship of one god, e.g. as the special god of a social group or occupation, while acknowledging or believing in the existence of other gods [Mid-19thC. Coined from the Greek stem *heno-* 'one' + *theos* 'god' + -ISM.] —**henotheist** *n.* —**henotheistic** /hénnə thi ístik/ *adj.*

hen party *n.* a celebration or night out that is exclusively for women (*sometimes considered offensive*)

henpeck /hén pek/ (-pecks, -pecking, -pecked) *vt.* an offensive term meaning to annoy or torment a husband or partner through continual nagging and fault-finding (*offensive*) [Back-formation from *henpecked*, from the hens' practice of plucking the cock] —**henpecked** *adj.*

Henrietta Maria /hénri éttə mə reé ə/ (1609–69) French-born queen consort of Charles I of England. After her marriage to Charles I (1625), her involvement in British politics made her highly unpopular.

hen run *n.* an enclosed area within which hens or other domestic birds can move about freely

henry /hénri/ (*plural* -ries) *n.* the SI unit of electrical inductance, equal to an electrical potential of one volt induced in a closed circuit by a current varying uniformly by one ampere per second. Symbol **H** [Late 19thC. Named after Joseph HENRY.]

Henry /hénri/, **Prince** (*b.* 1984) British prince. He is the younger son of Charles, Prince of Wales, and Diana, Princess of Wales. Known as **Harry**

Henry I, King of the English (1068–1135). He was the youngest son of William the Conqueror. His reign (1100–35) is notable for his conquest of Normandy (1106) and consolidation of his English and French realms.

Henry II, King of the English (1133–89) French-born English monarch. The first Plantagenet English king (1154–89), he imposed a strong central administration and judicial reform and annexed Ireland (1171–72). His knights murdered Thomas à Becket (1170) after a long dispute over the power of the church.

Henry III, King of England (1207–72). The son of King John, he began his long reign (1216–72) at the age of nine. His rule was marked by tensions with the nobility, which came to a head in 1264 with Simon de Montfort's rebellion; this was defeated in 1265 and royal power restored.

Henry IV, King of England (1367–1413). The son of John of Gaunt, he was the first Lancastrian English king. His reign (1399–1413) was marked by baronial revolts, Owen Glendower's Welsh rebellion (1400–09), and conflicts with Parliament over royal finance. Born **Henry Bolingbroke**

Henry V, King of England (1387–1422). He was the son of Henry IV. During his reign (1413–22) he invaded France, winning the Battle of Agincourt (1415) against superior forces, conquering Normandy (1417–20), and being declared heir to the French throne (1420).

Henry VI, King of Germany and Holy Roman Emperor (1165–97). As German king (1169–97) he conquered and annexed Sicily (1194).

Henry VI, King of England (1421–71). The son of Henry V, he lost all of England's French possessions except Calais during his reign (1422–61, 1470–71). His ineffectual leadership at home sparked the Wars of the Roses (1455–85).

Henry VII, King of England (1457–1509). He ended the Wars of the Roses by defeating Richard III at Bosworth (1485), and founded the Tudor dynasty. His reign (1485–1509) was noted for national unity and efficient government administration. Born **Henry Tudor**

Henry VIII, King of England and Ireland (1491–1547). He succeeded his father, Henry VII. During his reign (1509–47), he broke with the Catholic Church (1534) and assumed control over the Church of England. He is notorious for his six marriages and execution of two of his wives.

Henry (the Lion), Duke of Saxony and Duke of Bavaria (1129?–95). He expanded his territories to the east of Saxony and challenged the power of the Holy Roman Empire, but lost his duchies in 1180 to Frederick I.

Henry, Lenny (*b.* 1958) British comedian. A popular television performer, his appearances included *Tiswas* (1979–82) and *The Lenny Henry Show* (1984–95).

Henson /hénss'n/, **Jim** (1936–90) US puppeteer. He invented the Muppets, which appeared on the television programmes *Sesame Street* and *The Muppet Show* (1976–81). Full name **James Maury Henson**

hent /hent/ (**hents, henting, hented**) *vt.* to take hold of sb or sth (*archaic*) [Old English *hentan*. Ultimately from a prehistoric Germanic word.]

hep[1] /hep/ (**hepper, heppest**) *adj.* hip (*dated slang*)

hep[2] /hep/ *n.* hepatitis (*informal*)

heparin /héppərin/ *n.* a polysaccharide present in living tissue, especially the lungs and liver, that functions naturally as an anticoagulant and is used medicinally to treat thrombosis [Early 20thC. Coined from obsolete *hepar* 'sulphur compound' (which came via late Latin from Greek *hēpar* 'liver') + -IN.] —**heparinoid** *adj.*

hepat- *prefix.* = **hepato-** (*used before vowels*)

hepatectomy /héppə téktəmi/ (*plural* -mies) *n.* surgical removal of all or part of the liver

hepatic /hi páttik/ *adj.* 1. ANAT, MED OF THE LIVER relating to or affecting the liver 2. COLOURS LIVER-COLOURED of a deep brownish-red colour like that of liver 3. BOT OF OR LIKE LIVERWORT FAMILY relating to, belonging to, or resembling the members of the liverwort family of flowerless green plants ■ *n.* 1. PHARM DRUG FOR TREATING LIVER DISEASE any of several drugs that combat diseases of the liver 2. PLANTS = liverwort [14thC. Via Latin from Greek *hēpatikos*, from the stem *hēpat-* 'liver'.]

hepatica /hi páttikə/ *n.* any of a group of woodland plants of northern temperate regions, related to the buttercup, that have three-lobed leaves and white, lilac, or purple flowers. Genus: *Hepatica*. [15thC. Via medieval Latin from Greek *hēpatikos* (see HEPATIC); from the shape of the leaves.]

hepatitis /héppə títiss/ *n.* inflammation of the liver, causing fever, jaundice, abdominal pain, and weakness

hepatitis A *n.* a relatively mild form of hepatitis that is caused by a virus and transmitted through contaminated food and water. ◊ **hepatitis B**

hepatitis B *n.* a sometimes chronic or fatal form of hepatitis that is caused by a virus and transmitted through contact with infected blood, blood products, and bodily fluids. ◊ **hepatitis A**

hepato- *prefix.* liver ○ *hepatotoxic* [From Greek *hēpat-*, the stem of *hēpar*. Ultimately from the Indo-European word for 'liver' that is also the ancestor of English *gizzard*.]

hepatocellular /héppətō séllyōōlər, hi páttə séllyōōlər/ *adj.* relating to liver cells

hepatocyte /hi páttə sīt, héppətə-/ *n.* a cell of the liver

hepatogenous /héppə tójjənəss/ *adj.* originating in the liver

hepatoma /héppə tṓmə/ (*plural* -mas *or* -mata /-mətə/) *n.* a tumour of the liver

hepatomegaly /héppətō méggəli, hi páttə-/ n. enlargement of the liver

hepatotoxic /héppətō tóksik, hi páttə-/ adj. a condition in which the liver is damaged

hepatotoxicity /héppətō tok síssəti, hi páttə-/ (plural -ties) n. 1. DAMAGE TO THE LIVER a condition in which the liver is damaged 2. ABILITY TO DAMAGE THE LIVER the capacity or tendency of sth to damage the liver

hepatotoxin /héppətō tóksin, hi páttə-/ n. a substance that causes damage to the liver

Audrey Hepburn

Hepburn /hép burn/, **Audrey** (1929–93) Belgian-born US actor. She starred in numerous films, including *Funny Face* (1957) and *Breakfast at Tiffany's* (1961). During her last years she was a roving ambassador for UNICEF. Real name **Edda van Heemstra Hepburn-Ruston**

Katharine Hepburn

Hepburn, Katharine (b. 1907?) US actor. She was known for her roles as strong-willed heroines, and won Academy Awards for *Morning Glory* (1933), *Guess Who's Coming to Dinner* (1967), *The Lion in Winter* (1968), and *On Golden Pond* (1981). Full name **Katharine Houghton Hepburn**

hepcat /hép kat/ n. sb who is considered to be cool, especially a jazz fan in the 1940s (dated slang)

Hephaestus /hi féestəss/, **Hephaistos** n. in Greek mythology, the son of Hera and Zeus and the god of fire and fire-based arts such as metalwork. Roman equivalent **Vulcan**

Hepplewhite: 18th-century elbow chair decorated with the Prince of Wales's feathers

Hepplewhite /hépp'l wīt/ adj. IN 18C FURNITURE STYLE in or relating to the style of the 18th-century English cabinet-maker George Hepplewhite. Pieces typically have graceful curving lines and delicate

inlays, often featuring floral or ribbon designs. Open chairbacks, heart- or shield-shaped, are a feature of the style. ■ n. FURNITURE IN 18C STYLE furniture or a piece of furniture made by or in the style of Hepplewhite

Hepplewhite /hépp'l wīt/, **George** (d. 1786) British furniture designer. He produced over 300 designs in *The Cabinet-Maker and Upholsterer's Guide* (1788) that are characterized by a combination of simplicity and delicacy.

hept- prefix. = **hepta-** (used before vowels)

hepta- prefix. seven ○ heptahedron [From Greek hepta. Ultimately from the Indo-European word for 'seven' that is also the ancestor of English seven and septet.]

heptachlor /héptə klawr/ n. a pesticide containing chlorine

heptad /hép tad/ n. set or series of seven [Mid-17thC. From the Greek stem heptad- 'the number seven', from hepta 'seven'.]

heptagon /héptəgən/ n. a two-dimensional shape with seven angles and seven sides [Late 16thC. Via French heptagone or medieval Latin heptagonum from, ultimately, Greek heptagōnos 'having seven angles'.] —**heptagonal** /hep tággənəl/ adj.

heptahedron /héptə heedrən/ (plural -drons or -dra /-heedrə/) n. a solid figure with seven plane faces —**heptahedral** adj.

heptamerous /hep támmərəss/ adj. used to describe plant parts, e.g. petals or sepals, that grow or are arranged in groups of seven

heptameter /hep támmitər/ n. a line of poetry or verse composed of seven metric feet [Late 19thC. Via late Latin from Greek heptametron, from hepta 'seven' + metron 'metre'.] —**heptametrical** /héptə méttrik'l/ adj.

heptane /hép tayn/ n. an isomeric form of an organic chemical obtained from petroleum, especially a colourless flammable liquid alkane hydrocarbon used as a solvent and anaesthetic and to determine octane ratings. Formula: C_7H_{16}.

heptarch /hép taark/ n. one of the seven rulers in a heptarchy

heptarchy /hép taarki/ (plural -chies) n. 1. GOVERNMENT BY SEVEN RULERS government by seven rulers or leaders 2. STATE WITH SEVEN RULERS a state governed by seven rulers or one divided into seven parts, each ruled by a different head —**heptarchic** /hep taárkik/ adj. —**heptarchical** adj.

Heptarchy /hép taarki/ n. the association consisting of the seven English kingdoms of Kent, Sussex, Wessex, Essex, Northumbria, East Anglia, and Mercia during the period from the 5th to the 9th centuries AD

heptastich /héptəstik/ n. a seven-line stanza or poem

Heptateuch /héptə tyook/ n. the first seven books of the Bible, comprising Genesis, Exodus, Leviticus, Numbers, Deuteronomy, Joshua, and Judges. ◊ **Hexateuch, Pentateuch** [Late 17thC. Via late Latin from Greek heptateukhos, from hepta 'seven' + teukhos 'book'.]

heptathlon /hep táthlən, -lon/ n. an athletic competition, often for women, in which each contestant must compete in seven events, which are typically the javelin, hurdles, high jump, long jump, shot put, sprint, and 800-metre race. ◊ **pentathlon, decathlon** [Late 20thC. Coined from HEPTA- + Greek athlon 'contest'.] —**heptathlete** /hep táth leet/ n.

heptose /héptōss, -ōz/ n. any of a group of carbohydrates that are simple sugars (**monosaccharides**) with seven carbon atoms per molecule

Hepworth /hép wurth/, **Dame Barbara** (1903–75) British sculptor. Many of her works, e.g. the Dag Hammarskjöld Memorial (1964) at the U.N. headquarters in New York, are massive abstract shapes in stone or wood, pierced by holes. Full name **Dame Jocelyn Barbara Hepworth**

her (stressed) /hur/; (unstressed) /hər, ər/ pron., det. 1. WOMAN OR GIRL NOT REFERRED TO BY NAME used to refer to a woman, girl, or female animal who has been previously mentioned or whose identity is known (used as the object of a verb or preposition) ○ (det) Tell her I'll be there in ten minutes. ○ (det) We left

Dame Barbara Hepworth: Working on the plaster model for the bronze sculpture *Rock (Porthcurno)*

the report with her. ○ (det) What is her name? ○ (pron) He handed her the car keys. ○ (pron) I know it's her. 2. COUNTRY used to refer to a country or nation when it has been mentioned or its identity is known (formal) ○ (det) Britain's dealings with her EU partners have often been complex. 3. MACHINE used to refer to a car, machine, or ship ○ (pron) Fill her up, will you? ○ (det) Sea water washed across her decks. [Old English hire. Ultimately from an Indo-European demonstrative pronoun meaning 'this' that is also the ancestor of English he and hence.]

her. abbr. 1. heraldic 2. heraldry

Hera /heérə/ n. in Greek mythology, the wife of Zeus and goddess of marriage. She was often portrayed as jealous and resentful of infidelity. Roman equivalent **Juno**

Heracles /hérrə kleez/, **Herakles** n. in Greek mythology, the son of Zeus and a mortal woman, Alcmene. He was noted for his courage and great strength and was required to perform 12 near-impossible labours. Roman equivalent **Hercules** —**Heraclean** /hérrə kleé ən/ adj.

Heraclid /hérrəklid/ (plural -clidae /-klīdi/) n. in Greek mythology and ancient Greek history, sb who was descended, or claimed descent from, the hero Heracles —**Heraclidan** /hérrə klīd'n/ adj.

Heraclitus /hérrə klítəss/ (fl. 500? BC) Greek philosopher. He was an early metaphysician. Only fragments remain of his major work, *On Nature*. —**Heraclitean** /hérrə klíshi ən/ adj.

Heraclius /he rákli əss/, **Emperor of the Byzantine Empire** (575?–641). He came to power in a coup (610) after deposing Phocas. He successfully repelled a Persian invasion (622–28), and reclaimed the True Cross (630), an important Christian relic.

Herakles n. = **Heracles**

herald /hérrəld/ n. 1. BRINGER OF NEWS sb who brings or announces important news 2. SIGN OF WHAT WILL HAPPEN sb or sth that is a forerunner of sth or gives an indication of sth that is going to happen (literary) 3. OFFICIAL MESSENGER an official messenger and representative of a king or leader in former times 4. HERALDIC OFFICIAL an official who is concerned with heraldry, ranked between the king-of-arms and the pursuivant 5. OFFICIAL AT MEDIEVAL TOURNAMENTS sb who performed official duties at medieval tournaments and jousting contests ■ vt. (-alds, -alding, -alded) 1. SIGNAL STH to give or be a sign that sth is going to happen 2. WELCOME SB OR STH to welcome or announce sb or sth with enthusiasm [14thC. Via Old French herault from a prehistoric Germanic compound meaning 'commander of the army', whose elements are also the ancestors of English harangue, harbour, and wield.]

—— **WORD KEY: CULTURAL NOTE** ——
The Sydney Morning Herald, a newspaper published in Sydney since 1831. One of Australia's most widely read and influential broadsheets. It is commonly referred to as 'The Herald'.

heraldic /hə ráldik, he-/ adj. belonging or relating to heraldry or heralds —**heraldically** adv.

herald moth n. a nocturnal hibernating moth of northern Europe marked by mottled brown forewings and dull grey hind wings. Latin name: *Scoliopteryx libatrix*.

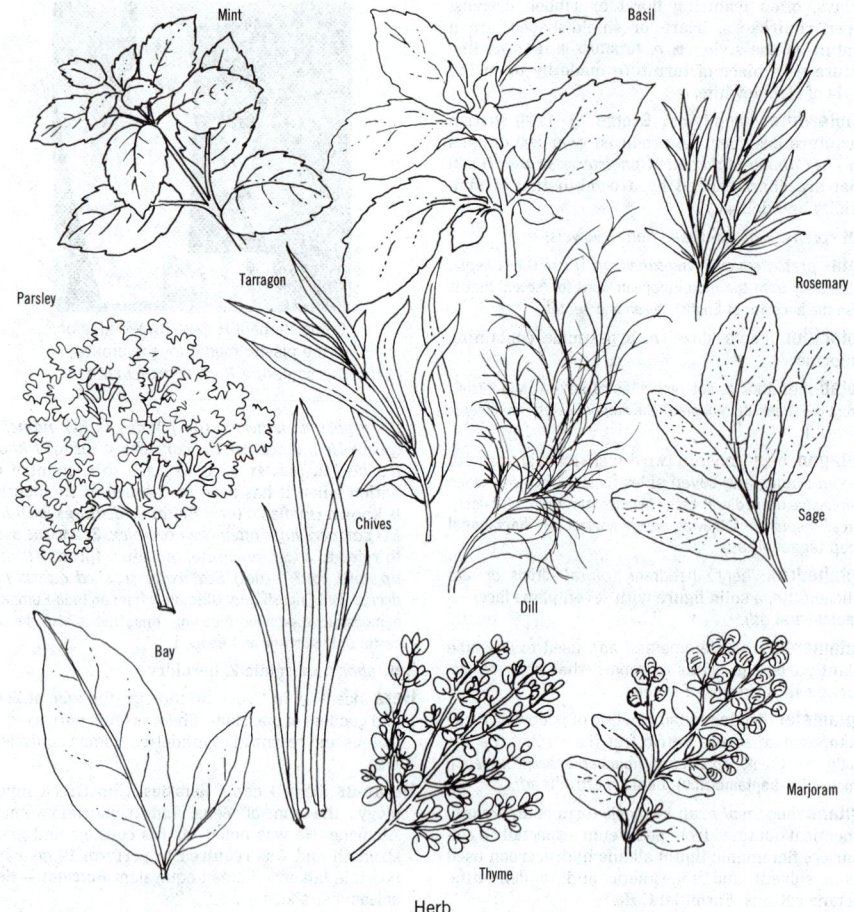

Mint

Basil

Parsley

Tarragon

Rosemary

Chives

Sage

Dill

Bay

Marjoram

Thyme

Herb

heraldry /hérrəldri/ (*plural* **-ries**) *n.* **1.** STUDY OF COATS OF ARMS the profession or study of the devising and granting of coats of arms and of determining who is entitled to bear them **2.** COATS OF ARMS coats of arms and the symbols and conventions connected with them **3.** POMP pomp and ceremony

heralds' college *n.* = **college of arms**

herb /hurb/ *n.* **1.** CULINARY AND MEDICINAL PLANT a low-growing aromatic plant used fresh or dried for seasoning in cooking, for its medicinal properties, or in perfumes. Sage and rosemary are herbs. (*often used before a noun*) **2.** BOT PLANT WITHOUT WOODY STEMS a seed-producing flowering plant that does not produce woody stems and that forms new stems and leaves each season **3.** DRUGS MARIJUANA marijuana (*slang*) [13thC. Via Old French *erbe* from Latin *herba* 'grass, herb'.]

herbaceous /hər báyshəss/ *adj.* **1.** WITHOUT WOODY STEMS used to describe plants or plant parts that are fleshy and wither after each growing season, as opposed to plants such as trees that grow woody stems and are persistent **2.** RESEMBLING LEAVES similar to leaves in colour and general appearance **3.** OF AROMATIC PLANTS relating to aromatic herbs such as sage, dill, or thyme [Mid-17thC. From Latin *herbaceus*, from *herba* 'grass, herb'.] —**herbaceously** *adv.*

herbaceous border *n.* a flower bed that is mainly planted with perennial plants rather than with annuals

herbage /húrbij/ *n.* **1.** HERBACEOUS PLANTS herbaceous plants, especially their leafy or succulent and edible parts **2.** VEGETATION GROWING IN FIELDS grass and other vegetation growing in fields, pasture land, and meadows [14thC. From Old French *herbage* from medieval Latin *herbagium*, from Latin *herba* 'grass, herb'.]

herbal /húrb'l/ *adj.* OF AROMATIC HERBS characteristic of, consisting of, or made with aromatic herbs ■ *n.* BOOK LISTING HERBS a book that lists individual herbs and describes their particular properties and possible uses [Early 16thC. From medieval Latin *herbalis*, from Latin *herba* 'grass, herb'.]

herbalist /húrbəlist/ *n.* **1.** SB KNOWLEDGEABLE ABOUT HERBS sb who grows, collects, sells, or dispenses aromatic herbs, especially those considered to have medicinal properties **2.** *S Africa* TRADITIONAL DOCTOR a traditional doctor who uses herbs and other medicines to remedy illness and discomfort **3.** BOTANIST a botanist, especially one concerned with the classification of plants (*archaic*)

herbal medicine *n.* **1.** TREATMENT WITH HERBS a system of medical treatment based on the properties of medicinal herbs **2.** MEDICINE FROM HERBS a medication made from a herb or herbs

herbarium /hur báiri əm/ (*plural* **-ums** *or* **-a** /-áiri ə/) *n.* **1.** COLLECTION OF DRIED PLANTS a collection of dried plants, especially one in which the plants have been mounted, systematically classified, and labelled for use in scientific studies **2.** HOME OF DRIED PLANT COLLECTION a building, room, or other place where a herbarium is kept [Late 18thC. From late Latin, formed from Latin *herbarius* 'herbalist', from *herba* 'grass, herb'.] —**herbarial** *adj.*

herb bennet /-bénnit/ *n.* a common wild plant of Europe, Asia, and North Africa that has small yellow flowers, long hairy stems, and hooked seeds. Its sweet-smelling roots were formerly used medicinally and thought to give protection against the devil. Latin name: *Geum urbanum*. Also called **wood avens**

herb Christopher (*plural* **herbs Christopher**) *n.* = **baneberry** [Translation of medieval Latin *herba Christophori*. Named after St CHRISTOPHER.]

herbed /hurbd/ *adj.* flavoured with herbs

Herbert /húrbərt/, **George** (1593–1633) English poet and clergyman. A friend of Francis Bacon and John Donne, he wrote poetry that was published posthumously in *The Temple* (1633).

Herbert, Xavier (1901–84) Australian novelist. His works include *Poor Fellow My Country* (1975), the longest novel ever published in Australia. Full name **Alfred Francis Xavier Herbert**

herb Gerard /-jérr aard/ (*plural* **herbs Gerard**) *n.* = **ground elder** [Named after St *Gerard* of Toul (935?–994), whom people with gout prayed to]

herbicide /húrbi sīd/ *n.* a chemical preparation designed to kill plants, especially weeds, or to inhibit their growth —**herbicidal** /húrbi sīd'l/ *adj.* —**herbicidally** /-sīd'li/ *adv.*

herbivore /húrbi vawr/ *n.* an animal that feeds only or mainly on grass and other plants [Mid-19thC. From French, or back-formation from HERBIVOROUS.]

herbivorous /hur bívvərəss/ *adj.* eating only or mainly grass or other plants, or relating to the eating of such plants [Mid-17thC. From modern Latin *herbivorus*, literally 'eating grass', from Latin *herba* 'grass, herb'.]

herb of grace *n.* rue (*archaic*) [From the formal identity between the plant name RUE and RUE 'regret, repentance', a different word]

herb Paris (*plural* **herbs Paris**) *n.* a tall woodland plant that grows throughout Europe, characterized by a whorl of four leaves and a single greenish-yellow flower similar to an eight-pointed star. The flower is made up of four sepals and four petals, and the fruit is a single black berry. Latin name: *Paris quadrifolia*. [Partial translation of medieval Latin *herba paris*, literally 'herb of a pair', probably because the configuration of its leaves resembles a true lover's knot]

herb Robert /-róbbərt/ (*plural* **herbs Robert**) *n.* a common plant of the cranesbill family native to temperate northern Europe and Asia, with red-tinged leaves and stems and small pink or purple flowers. The stems and the leaves, which are divided and delicate, have a strong and rather unpleasant odour. Latin name: *Geranium robertianum*. [Translation of medieval Latin *herba Roberti*. The identity of the *Robert* after whom the plant is named is uncertain, perhaps *Robert*, Duke of Normandy, or St *Robert*.]

herby /húrbi/ (**-ier**, **-iest**) *adj.* **1.** WITH HERBAL TASTE OR SMELL tasting or smelling of herbs **2.** OF AROMATIC HERBS associated with aromatic or medicinal herbs **3.** FULL OF GROWING HERBS with a lot of growing herbs or grass

Herculaneum /húrkyoŏ láyni əm/ ancient Roman town near modern Naples, destroyed with its neighbour Pompeii in the eruption of Vesuvius in AD 79

herculean /húrkyoŏ lée ən, hur kyoóli ən/ *adj.* **1.** NEEDING GREAT STRENGTH OR EFFORT requiring a great deal of strength, effort, stamina, or resources **2.** herculean, Herculean CONNECTED WITH HERCULES associated with or resembling Hercules

Hercules /húrkyoŏ leez/ *n.* **1.** MYTHOL ROMAN MYTHOLOGICAL HERO in Roman mythology, the son of Jupiter and a mortal woman, Alcmene. He was noted for his courage and great strength and was required to perform 12 near-impossible tasks, called the labours of Hercules. Greek equivalent **Heracles 2.** (*plural* **-les** *or* **-leses**) VERY STRONG MAN a man with great or unusual strength **3.** ASTRON NORTHERN CONSTELLATION a large northern constellation between Lyra and Corona Borealis

hercules beetle *n.* an exceptionally large South American beetle of the scarab family that can grow to over 15 cm/6 in in length. The male has two large projecting horns. Latin name: *Dynastes hercules*.

Hercules' club *n.* **1.** TREE RELATED TO GINSENG a small tree or shrub of the ginseng family, native to the southeastern United States, that has prickly leaves and bark that has medicinal properties. Latin name: *Aralia spinosa*. **2.** TREE RELATED TO CITRUS a small spiny tree or shrub related to the citrus family and native to the southern United States, with bark and berries that have medicinal properties. Latin name: *Zanthoxylum clava-herculis*.

Hercynian /hur sínni ən/ *adj.* relating to the period during the late Palaeozoic era when some of the major European mountain ranges were being formed [Late 16thC. Formed from Latin *Hercynia (silva)*, from Greek *Herkunios drumos*, the name given to a forested mountain region situated between the Carpathian Mountains and the River Rhine.]

herd[1] /hurd/ *n.* **1.** AGRIC LARGE GROUP OF DOMESTIC ANIMALS a large number of domestic animals, especially cattle, often of the same breed, that are kept, driven, or reared together **2.** ZOOL LARGE GROUP OF WILD ANIMALS a large number of wild animals of the same kind that live, feed, and travel as a group **3.** LARGE GROUP OF

PEOPLE a large group of people, often with a common interest, purpose, or bond ○ *herds of eager shoppers* **4.** ORDINARY PEOPLE ACTING AS GROUP ordinary people, considered as acting or thinking as a group and lacking the ability to think as individuals (*disapproving*) ○ *She was never one to follow the herd.* ■ *v.* (**herds, herding, herded**) **1.** *vt.* AGRIC CONTROL GROUP OF ANIMALS to drive, keep, or look after domestic animals as a group **2.** *vt.* MOVE OR COLLECT A GROUP to move people or animals somewhere as a group, or collect them into a group ○ *We were herded onto buses.* **3.** *vi.* FORM OR MOVE IN A GROUP to gather together or go somewhere as a group [Old English *heord.* Ultimately from an Indo-European word meaning 'row, group' that is also the ancestor of German *Herde.*]

herd[2] /hurd/ *n.* sb who looks after domestic animals (*archaic; usually used in combination*) ◊ **cowherd, goatherd, shepherd** [Old English *hirdi.* Ultimately from the same prehistoric Germanic word that produced HERD[1] 'group of animals'.]

herd-book /húrd bòok/ *n.* a book that gives details of the pedigrees of domestic animals, especially cattle or pigs

herder /húrdər/ *n. US* = **herdsman** *n.* 2

Herder /húrdər/, **Johann Gottfried von** (1744–1803) German philosopher and critic. An important figure in the development of German romanticism, his most important work is *Outline of a Philosophy of the History of Man* (1784–91).

herd instinct *n.* the innate desire to belong to or be associated with a group, or to imitate the general behaviour of a group

herdsman /húrdzmən/ (*plural* **-men**) *n.* **1.** REARER OF LIVESTOCK sb who owns or breeds cattle or other livestock **2.** SB WHO TENDS ANIMALS sb who tends or drives domestic animals in groups, especially on open pasture or land. US term **herder** *n.* [Alteration of Old English *heordman* 'herdsman' on the model of such words as *craftsman*]

herd tester *n. NZ* sb who examines the health of dairy cows and who sees that the production of milk and butterfat is carried out under the prescribed hygienic conditions

Herdwick /húrdwik/ *n.* a hardy sheep with thick coarse wool belonging to a breed originating in the Lake District [Early 19thC. From obsolete *herdwick* 'pasturage', literally 'herdsman's place'.]

here /heer/ CORE MEANING: an adverb used to refer to this place or this time ○ *How long have you been waiting here?* ○ *Winter is here.*

adv. **1.** THIS PLACE in, at, or to the place where you are, or at a place near you ○ *Have you been here before?* ○ *Come and sit here, beside me.* **2.** POINT OR STAGE used to draw attention to a particular point or stage in a situation ○ *I want to say here, before I go further, that only part of the credit should be mine.* **3.** NOW indicates a situation or event that is happening at the present time ○ *The time for celebrations is here.* **4.** INDICATES AN OFFER indicates that sb is offering sth to sb ○ *Here are some general guidelines.* ○ *Here's my card.* **5.** INTRODUCES STH used to introduce or draw attention to a topic ○ *Now, here is a question for everybody.* **6.** LIFE ON EARTH used to refer to people in general and their life on Earth ○ *Where did we come from? Why are we here? That's the big question.* [Old English *hēr.* Ultimately from an Indo-European demonstrative pronoun meaning 'this' that is also the ancestor of English *he* and *hence.*] ◇ **(the) here and now** used to emphasize that you are talking about the present time ○ *I'm entitled to an explanation, and I want one here and now.* ◊ *He outlined all sorts of schemes, but hadn't much practical advice about the here and now.* ◇ **here and there** in different places or at different points ○ *She'd picked up some general knowledge here and there.* ◇ **here goes** used to indicate that sb is about to perform an action ○ *This is my first move on the chessboard – here goes!* ◇ **here we go again** used to indicate that an event or situation is, tiresomely or irritatingly, about to repeat itself ○ *Here we go again – making a mountain out of a molehill.* ◇ **neither here nor there** not important or relevant ○ *Why she wants this is neither here nor there, but we have to decide how we're going to reply.*

hereabouts /heérə bówts/, **hereabout** /heérə bowt/ *adv.* near here, or in this neighbourhood or area

hereafter /heer àaftər/ *adv.* (*formal*) **1.** AFTER THE PRESENT TIME from now on or at a time in the future ○ *He believes this to be a universal law of nature; and we may hope hereafter to see the law proved true.* ○ *No one of us knows what may happen hereafter.* **2.** IN ANY FOLLOWING PART in any following part of an article or document ○ *Here is established a Commerce Technology Advisory Board (hereafter in this section referred to as the 'Advisory Board').* ■ *adv., n.* LIFE AFTER DEATH the life that is thought by some to exist after death (*formal*) ○ *(adv.) Mercy and forgiveness will be ours hereafter.* ○ *(n.) Your deeds will be judged in the hereafter.*

hereby /heer bī́, heer bī/ *adv.* by means of this declaration, document, or ruling (*formal*) ○ *I hereby renounce all claim to the estate.*

hereditable /hi rédditəb'l/ *adj.* capable of being inherited [15thC. From obsolete French *héréditable* or medieval Latin *hereditabilis,* both from ecclesiastical Latin *hereditare* 'to inherit' (see HEREDITAMENT).] —**hereditability** /hi rédditə bíllәti/ *n.*

hereditament /hérri díttəmənt/ *n.* **1.** INHERITABLE PROPERTY a piece of property that can be inherited **2.** AUTOMATICALLY INHERITED PROPERTY a piece of property that passes automatically to a legal heir unless a will specifies otherwise [15thC. From medieval Latin *hereditamentum,* from ecclesiastical Latin *hereditare* 'to inherit', from the Latin stem *hered-* 'heir'.]

hereditarian /hi réddi táiri ən/ *n.* sb who believes that inherited characteristics play a more important part in forming people's characters and determining human behaviour than do environmental and social factors. ◊ **environmentalist** —**hereditarian** *adj.* —**hereditarianism** *n.*

hereditary /hi rédditəri/ *adj.* **1.** GENETICS PASSED ON GENETICALLY passed genetically, or capable of being passed genetically, from one generation to the next **2.** HANDED DOWN THROUGH GENERATIONS handed down, or legally capable of being handed down, through generations by inheritance **3.** HAVING INHERITED STATUS holding a right, function, or property by right of inheritance **4.** TRADITIONALLY HELD possessed by or characteristic of both ancestors and descendants although not physically transmitted ○ *the family's hereditary fondness for city life* **5.** RELATING TO INHERITANCE relating to inheritance or heredity **6.** MATH, LOGIC SHARING A RELATIONSHIP OR PROPERTY sharing or transmitting a particular relationship or property [15thC. From Latin *hereditarius,* from *hereditas* 'inheritance' (see HEREDITY).] —**hereditarily** *adv.* —**hereditariness** *n.*

heredity /hi rédditi/ (*plural* **-ties**) *n.* GENETICS **1.** PASSING ON OF GENETIC FACTORS the passing on of genetic factors such as the colour of hair or eyes from one generation to the next, resulting in similarities between members of one family or strain **2.** SET OF INHERITED CHARACTERISTICS the complete set of inherited characteristics of an organism [Mid-16thC. Directly or via French from Latin *hereditas* 'inheritance', from the stem *hered-* 'heir'.]

Hereford[1] /hérrifərd/ *n.* a hardy cow that has a distinctive red coat with white markings, belonging to a breed originating in England and bred for beef [Early 19thC. Named after *Hereford* the English county where the animal was first bred.]

Hereford[2] /hérrifərd/ historic cathedral city in Herefordshire, western England. Population: 49,500 (1995).

Hereford and Worcester former county in western England. It was formed in 1974 by amalgamating the historic counties of Herefordshire and Worcestershire and disbanded in 1998. Population: 1,213,400 (1995). Area: 3,926 sq. km/1,515 sq. mi.

Herefordshire /hérrifərdshər/ county in western England. It was disbanded in 1974 and reinstated as a unitary authority in 1998.

herein /heer ín/ *adv.* (*formal*) **1.** IN THIS DOCUMENT in this document, article, or proceeding ○ *Disclaimer: The views represented herein do not necessarily represent the views of the moderators.* **2.** IN THIS RESPECT introduces a clause in which sb states an opinion about the nature or cause of sth or goes on to give further detail ○ *People are not always conscious of the effect their behaviour is having on others, and herein lies the main problem.*

hereinafter /heérin àaftər/ *adv.* later in this document, article, or proceeding (*formal*) ○ *the European Monetary Institute (hereinafter referred to as EMI)*

hereinbefore /heérinbi fáwr/ *adv.* earlier in this document, article, or proceeding (*formal*)

hereinto /heer ín too, heérin tóo/ *adv.* into this matter, situation, or place (*formal*)

hereof /heer óv/ *adv.* of or concerning this (*formal*)

hereon /heer ón/ *adv.* following immediately after this (*archaic*)

Herero /hə ráirō, háirərō/ (*plural* **-ro** *or* **-ros**) *n.* **1.** PEOPLES MEMBER OF AFRICAN PEOPLE a member of a largely cattle-rearing people living mainly in Namibia and Botswana **2.** LANG LANGUAGE OF HERERO PEOPLE a Bantu language spoken by the Herero people. It belongs to the Benue-Congo group of the Niger-Congo family of African languages, and is spoken by about 25,000 people. [Mid-19thC. From Bantu.] —**Herero** *adj.*

heresiarch /hə reézi aark/ *n.* sb who leads or instigates a heretical religious group or movement [Mid-16thC. Via ecclesiastical Latin from ecclesiastical Greek *hairesiarkhēs,* from Greek *hairesis* 'choice, group' (see HERESY) + *-arkhēs* 'ruler' (see -ARCH).]

heresy /hérrəssi/ (*plural* **-sies**) *n.* **1.** RELIG UNORTHODOX RELIGIOUS OPINION an opinion or belief that contradicts established religious teaching, especially one that is officially condemned by a religious authority **2.** RELIG HOLDING OF UNORTHODOX RELIGIOUS BELIEF the holding of, or adherence to, an opinion or belief that contradicts established religious teaching, especially one that is officially condemned by religious authorities ○ *guilty of heresy* **3.** UNORTHODOX OPINION an opinion or belief that does not coincide with established or traditional theory, especially in philosophy, science, or politics **4.** HOLDING OF UNORTHODOX OPINION the holding of an unorthodox opinion that is in conflict with established or traditional theory [12thC. Via Old French from, ultimately, Greek *hairesis* 'choice, sect', from *haireisthai* 'to choose'. The underlying idea is of sb's choice of a way of thinking.]

heretic /hérrətik/ *n.* **1.** RELIG SB WHO HOLDS UNORTHODOX RELIGIOUS BELIEF sb who holds or adheres to an opinion or belief that contradicts established religious teaching, especially one that is officially condemned by religious authorities **2.** SB WITH UNCONVENTIONAL BELIEFS sb whose opinions, beliefs, or theories in any field are considered by others in that field to be extremely unconventional or unorthodox [14thC. Via Old French from, ultimately, Greek *hairetikos* 'able to choose', from *haireisthai* (see HERESY).]

hereto /heer tóo/ *adv.* to this document, proceeding, or matter (*formal*)

heretofore /heértoo fáwr/ *adv.* up until this time (*formal*) ○ *He had more liberty now than he had known heretofore.*

hereunder /heer úndər/ *adv.* (*formal*) **1.** AFTER THIS after this introduction, heading, or sentence **2.** BY THE TERMS OF THIS by the terms of this instruction, agreement, or ruling

hereunto /heer ún too/ *adv.* to this document, proceeding, or matter (*formal*)

hereupon /heérə pón/ *adv.* **1.** AT THIS immediately after or in response to this ○ *Hereupon the entire delegation left.* **2.** ON THIS MATTER on this point, subject, or matter (*formal*) ○ *retired to deliberate before pronouncing hereupon*

Hereward the Wake /hérriwərd thə wáyk/ (*fl.* 1070) Anglo-Saxon rebel. He attacked the Norman conquerors of England at Peterborough (1070), and defended his stronghold at the Isle of Ely (1071).

herewith /heer wíth, heer wíth/ *adv.* **1.** WITH THIS COMMUNICATION with this letter or other written, typed, or printed message ○ *Herewith the documents you requested.* **2.** BY THIS STATEMENT by this statement, ruling, or document (*formal*) ○ *I herewith pronounce sentence of banishment.*

Herez /hə réz/, **Heriz** /hə ríz/ *n.* a Persian rug of high quality that is woven with a pattern of flowers or trees [Named after *Heris,* an Iranian town]

heriot /hérri ət/ *n.* in feudal England, a tribute or gift, often a prized animal or a treasured possession, given by a tenant's or villein's family to his lord at the tenant's death [Old English *heregeatwa*, literally 'army trappings'. In origin, the word referred to the return of weapons.]

heritable /hérritəb'l/ *adj.* **1.** ABLE TO BE INHERITED able to be passed on to an heir by the laws of inheritance **2.** ABLE TO INHERIT having the legal right or qualification to inherit sth [14thC. From French, formed from *hériter* 'to inherit', from ecclesiastical Latin *hereditare* (see HEREDITAMENT).] —**heritability** /hérritə bílləti/ *n.* —**heritably** /hérritəbli/ *adv.*

heritage /hérritij/ *n.* **1.** STH SB IS BORN TO the status, conditions, or character acquired by being born into a particular family or social class ○ *the responsibilities that were his heritage* **2.** RICHES OF PAST a country's or area's history and historical buildings and sites that are considered to be of interest and value to present generations (*often used before a noun*) ○ *the town's heritage trail* **3.** STH PASSING FROM GENERATION TO GENERATION sth such as a way of life or traditional culture that passes from one generation to the next in a social group ○ *The celebration of Passover is part of the Jewish heritage.* **4.** LEGAL INHERITANCE property or land that is or can be passed on to an heir [13thC. From Old French, formed from *hériter* (see HERITABLE).]

heritor /hérritər/ *n.* an inheritor of property by law (*archaic or technical*) [15thC. Via Anglo-Norman from French *héritier*, from *hériter* (see HERITABLE).]

heritress /hérritrəss/, **heritrix** /-triks/ (*plural* **-trices** /-trī seez/ *or* **-trixes**) *n.* a woman or girl who is inheritor of property by law (*archaic or technical*)

Heriz *n.* TEXTILES = **Herez**

herl /hurl/ *n.* **1.** FEATHER BARB the barb or barbs of a feather used for trimming an artificial fishing fly **2.** FISHING FLY a fishing fly trimmed with a barb or barbs of a feather [Origin uncertain: probably from Middle Low German *herle* 'fibre of hemp or flax']

herm /hurm/, **herma** /húrmə/ (*plural* **-mae** /-mee/ *or* **-mai** /-mī/) *n.* a square pillar topped with a bust, usually of the god Hermes, used as a marker in ancient Greece and Rome, and as an ornament in classical architecture [Late 16thC. Via Latin from Greek *Hermēs* HERMES.]

Herman /húrmən/, **Sali** (1898–1993) Swiss-born Australian painter. He is known for his depictions of Sydney slums. Full name **Sali Yakubowitsch Herman**

hermaphrodite /hur máffrə dīt/ *n.* **1.** BIOL ORGANISM HAVING BOTH SEXES a plant or animal having both male and female reproductive organs and secondary sexual characteristics **2.** PHYSIOL PERSON HAVING BOTH SEXES sb who has both male and female elements of genital structure and both male and female secondary sexual characteristics **3.** SB OR STH COMBINING CONTRADICTORY ELEMENTS sb or sth that combines two very different elements or qualities, or seems to belong to two different classifications at once ■ *adj.* WITH HERMAPHRODITE'S CHARACTERISTICS having the characteristics of a hermaphrodite [15thC. Via Latin from Greek *Hermaphroditos* HERMAPHRODITUS.] —**hermaphrodism** *n.* —**hermaphroditic** /hur máffrə díttik/ *adj.* —**hermaphroditical** /-díttik'l/ *adj.* —**hermaphroditically** /-díttikli/ *adv.* —**hermaphroditism** *n.*

hermaphrodite brig *n.* a two-masted sailing vessel with a square-rigged foremast and a square-rigged topsail above a fore-and-aft rig on the mainmast

Hermaphroditus /hur máffrə dítəss/ *n.* in Greek mythology, the son of Hermes and Aphrodite, whose body was merged with the body of the nymph Salmacis to become half male and half female

hermeneutic /húrmə nyóotik/, **hermeneutical** /-nyóo tik'l/ *adj.* **1.** OF INTERPRETATION OF TEXTS relating to or consisting in the interpretation of texts, especially the books of the Bible **2.** SERVING TO EXPLAIN serving to interpret or explain sth (*formal*) [Late 17thC. From Greek *hermēneutikos* 'of interpreting', from *hermēneuein* 'to interpret', from *hermēneus* 'interpreter'.] —**hermeneutically** *adv.* —**hermeneutist** *n.*

hermeneutics /húrmə nyóotiks/ *n.* (*takes a singular verb*) **1.** SCIENCE OF INTERPRETING TEXTS the science and methodology of interpreting texts, especially the books of the Bible **2.** THEOLOGY OF RELIGIOUS CONCEPTS the branch of theology that is concerned with explaining or interpreting religious concepts, theories, and principles **3.** PHILOSOPHY OF HUMAN BEHAVIOUR AND SOCIETY the branch of philosophy that is concerned with the study and interpretation of human behaviour, structures of society, and how people function within these structures **4.** DISCUSSION OF MEANING OF LIFE in existentialism, deliberation on the meaning and purpose of life

Hermes /húr meez/ *n.* in Greek mythology, the messenger of the gods and a son of Zeus. He was the patron of athletes, thieves, and trade, and was usually depicted with wings on his cap and sandals. Roman equivalent **Mercury**

Hermes Trismegistus /-tríssmə jístəss, -gístəss/ *n.* a name given to the Egyptian god Thoth by Greek neo-Platonists, who regarded him as a teacher of religion, magic, and alchemy

hermetic /hur méttik/, **hermetical** /-méttik'l/ *adj.* **1.** AIRTIGHT so tightly or perfectly fitting as to exclude the passage of air **2.** PROTECTED FROM OUTSIDE INFLUENCE protected from or preventing any outside interference or influence ○ *lead a solitary, hermetic existence* **3.** HARD TO UNDERSTAND obscure and difficult for outsiders to understand **4. hermetic, Hermetic** INVOLVING ALCHEMY OR MAGIC associated with alchemy or magic [Mid-17thC. From modern Latin *hermeticus*, from HERMES TRISMEGISTUS. The meaning 'airtight' comes from a magic seal supposedly invented by Hermes Trismegistus.] —**hermetically** *adv.*

hermit /húrmit/ *n.* **1.** SB WHO CHOOSES TO LIVE ALONE sb who chooses to live alone and to have little or no contact with other people **2.** CHR, HIST EARLY CHRISTIAN LIVING APART FROM SOCIETY sb who, in early Christian times, chose to reject material things and to live apart from the rest of society, especially in order to be completely devoted to God [12thC. Via Old French *hermite* or medieval Latin *heremita* from Greek *erēmitēs*, from *erēmia* 'desert', from *erēmos* 'solitary'.] —**hermitic** /hur míttik/ *adj.* —**hermitical** *adj.* —**hermitically** *adv.*

hermitage /húrmitij/ *n.* **1.** PLACE WHERE HERMIT LIVES a building or shelter where a hermit lives, or where a group of people live an isolated religious life **2.** ISOLATED PLACE a place of isolation or solitude where sb can live apart from society [13thC. From Old French, from *hermite* 'hermit' (see HERMIT).]

Hermitage /húrmitij/ *n.* a museum in St Petersburg, Russia, that contains one of the world's major collections of paintings. The nucleus of its collection was the art collection of Catherine the Great.

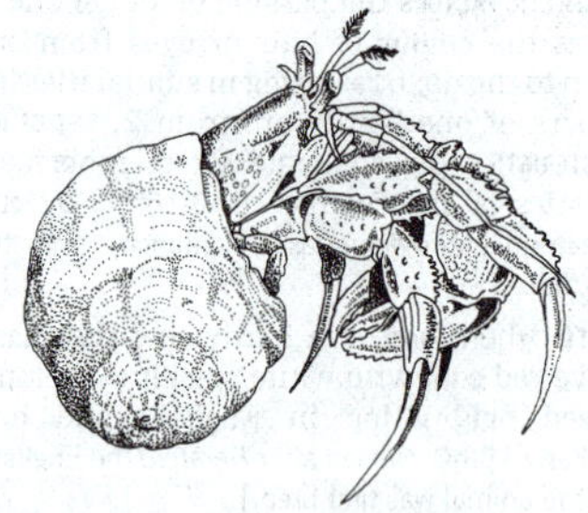

Hermit crab

hermit crab *n.* a soft-bodied crab that takes over an empty mollusc shell, usually a whelk shell, and carries it around on its back for protection and to retire into. It starts off with a small shell that, as it grows, is discarded for increasingly larger ones, so that it may change shells several times during its lifespan. Order: Decapoda.

hermit thrush *n.* a brownish North American songbird with a speckled breast, reddish tail, and a distinctive spiralling song reminiscent of the sound of a flute. Latin name: *Catharus guttatus.*

Hermon, Mount /-húrmən/ the highest peak in the Anti-Lebanon Mountains, on the Syria-Lebanon border. It has many associations with ancient Palestine. Height: 2,814 m/9,232 ft.

hern /hurn/ *n.* a heron (*archaic or literary*) [14thC. Variant of HERON.]

hernia /húrni ə/ (*plural* **-as** *or* **-ae** /-ee/) *n.* a condition in which part of an internal organ projects abnormally through the wall of the cavity that contains it, especially the projection of the intestine from the abdominal cavity. It may be present at birth, especially in the region of the navel, or caused by muscular strain or injury, or result from a congenital weakness in the cavity wall. ◊ **hiatus hernia** [14thC. From Latin. Ultimately from an Indo-European word meaning 'gut' that is also the ancestor of English *yarn* and Greek *khorion* 'afterbirth' (source of English *chorion*).] —**hernial** *adj.*

herniate /húrni ayt/ (**-ates, -ating, -ated**) *vi.* to project through an abnormal opening in the wall of a body cavity, or through a normal or potential opening that has become abnormally enlarged (*refers to an organ or body part*) —**herniated** *adj.* —**herniation** /húrni áysh'n/ *n.*

herniorrhaphy /húrni órrəfi/ (*plural* **-phies**) *n.* the surgical repair of an abnormal opening in the wall of a body cavity

hero /héerō/ (*plural* **-roes**) *n.* **1.** REMARKABLY BRAVE PERSON sb who commits an act of remarkable bravery or who has shown great courage, strength of character, or another admirable quality ○ *a war hero* **2.** SB ADMIRED sb who is admired and looked up to for outstanding qualities or achievements ○ *heroes of the war against poverty.* ◊ **superhero 3.** LITERAT, CINEMA MAIN CHARACTER IN FICTIONAL PLOT the principal man or boy character in a film, novel, or play, especially one who plays a vital role in plot development or around whom the plot is structured ○ *'Whether I shall turn out to be the hero of my own life, or whether that station will be held by anybody else, these pages must show'.* (Charles Dickens, *David Copperfield*; 1849–50) ◊ **antihero 4.** MYTHOL LEGENDARY MAN WITH SUPERHUMAN POWERS in classical mythology, a man, especially the son of a god and a mortal, who is famous for possessing some extraordinary gift, e.g. superhuman strength ○ *the Greek heroes* **5.** *US* FOOD LONG SANDWICH a sandwich made from a long roll or loaf of bread, typically with a filling of meat and cheese with lettuce and tomato [Mid-16thC. Via Latin from Greek *hērōs* 'hero, warrior'. Possibly related to Latin *servare* 'to protect' (see SERVE).]

Hero /héerō/ *n.* in Greek mythology, a priestess of Aphrodite whose lover Leander swam the Hellespont to visit her every night, and who drowned herself after he drowned in the strait

Hero (of Alexandria) /héer ō əv állig záandri ə/ (AD 20?–62?) Greek mathematician and inventor. He designed numerous mechanical devices and devised a formula for calculating the area of a triangle.

Herod (the Great) /hérrəd thə gráyt/, **King of Judea** (73–4 BC). Born in Palestine and supported by the Romans, he ruled Judea (37 BC–4 BC) over a period of relative prosperity. He is remembered in Jewish and Christian tradition as a tyrant and, according to the Bible, ordered the massacre of every male baby in Jerusalem (Matthew 2:16).

Herod Agrippa I /hérrəd ə gríppə/, **King of Judea** (10? BC–AD 44). He was the grandson of Herod the Great. As the Roman-appointed king of Judea (41–44), he adopted policies favourable to the Jews. He is said in the New Testament to have imprisoned St Peter and executed St James.

Herod Agrippa II (27–93?) Roman ruler in Palestine. The son of Herod Agrippa I, he was the Roman-appointed ruler in northern Palestine, where he supported Rome during the Jewish revolt (66–73).

Herod Antipas /hérrəd ánti pass/ (21 BC–AD 39) Galilean leader. The son of Herod the Great, he was tetrarch of Galilee and Perea (4 BC–AD 39) and ordered the execution of John the Baptist (Mark 6:14–29).

Herodotus /hə róddətəss/ (484?–425? BC) Greek historian. Known as 'the father of history', his anecdotal *History* includes a description of the war between the Greeks and Persians in the 5th century BC.

heroic /hi rṓ ik/, **heroical** /-rṓ ik'l/ *adj.* **1.** COURAGEOUS showing great bravery, courage, or determination ○ *a heroic fight against a disease* **2.** SUITABLE FOR A HERO characteristic of or suitable for a hero **3.** LARGE OR EXTREME large, extensive, or extreme, often daunting in aspect or done in response to a desperate situation ○ *heroic measures to save a person's life* **4.** MYTHOL RELATING TO MYTHICAL HERO characteristic of or involving the heroes of legend or mythology **5.** POETRY IN OR OF HEROIC VERSE written in or characteristic of heroic verse. ◊ **mock-heroic 6.** SCULPTURE LARGER THAN LIFE-SIZE used to describe a piece of sculpture that is larger than life-size. ◊ **colossal 7.** FLAMBOYANT exaggerated and flamboyant (*archaic*) —**heroically** *adv.* —**heroicalness** *n.* —**heroicness** *n.*

heroic age *n.* a time in a culture's mythology when heroes were believed to exist, especially the time in ancient Greek legend up to and including the return from Troy

heroical *adj.* = heroic

heroic couplet *n.* two lines of verse in iambic pentameters that rhyme, usually part of a series of rhyming pairs

heroic drama *n.* a type of play popular during the Restoration period, especially one written by John Dryden, generally involving a warrior hero who must find a way to resolve a dilemma. This often involves finding a way of preserving both his honour and his love for a woman.

heroic metre *n.* = heroic verse

heroic quatrain *n.* a four-line unit of verse in which each line consists of five iambic feet and either alternate or adjacent lines rhyme

heroics /hi rṓ iks/ *npl.* **1.** OVERDRAMATIC BEHAVIOUR OR TALK rash, inappropriate, or extravagantly courageous behaviour or talk ○ *There is no room for heroics on this expedition.* **2.** = heroic verse

heroic stanza *n.* four lines of verse in which the first and third lines and the second and fourth lines rhyme

heroic tenor *n.* = Heldentenor

heroic verse *n.* a verse form used in epic poetry or other narrative poetry on heroic subjects, especially the ancient Greek and Latin hexameter, the iambic pentameter, or the alexandrine

heroin /hérrō in/ *n.* a white powder derived from morphine that is a highly addictive narcotic drug. It is prohibited for medical use in most countries, but in the UK can be used in terminal cases where patients are in severe pain. (*often used before a noun*) [Late 19thC. From German. Coined from Greek *hērōs* 'hero, warrior' (see HERO), reputedly because of the delusions of heroism that affect those who use it.]

heroine /hérrō in/ *n.* **1.** REMARKABLY BRAVE WOMAN a woman who commits an act of remarkable bravery or who has shown great courage, strength of character, or another admirable quality **2.** ADMIRED WOMAN a woman who is admired or looked up to for her qualities or achievements ○ *heroines of the women's suffrage movement* **3.** LITERAT, CINEMA MAIN WOMAN CHARACTER IN FICTIONAL PLOT the principal woman or girl character in a film, novel, or play, especially one who plays a vital role in plot development or around whom the plot is structured

heroism /hérrō izəm/ *n.* remarkable physical or moral courage

heron /hérrən/ *n.* any of several long-legged wading

Heron

birds with long necks and tapered beaks that live in a range of freshwater habitats and feed mainly on fish, frogs, and small mammals. They have rather untidy-looking drooping feathers, and many species have crested heads. Family: Ardeidae. [14thC. Via Old French from a prehistoric Germanic word that is also the ancestor of Swedish *häger* 'heron'.]

heronry /hérrənri/ (*plural* **-ries**) *n.* an area where herons nest and raise their young

Herophilus /heer óffiləss/ (335?–280? BC) Greek anatomist. Considered the founder of scientific anatomy, he is known for his detailed description of the brain and nervous system.

hero worship *n.* **1.** GREAT ADMIRATION FOR SB great admiration for sb, especially if it borders on the excessive **2.** MYTHOL WORSHIPPING OF HEROES the ancient Greek or Roman practice of worshipping a mythological hero or heroes

hero-worship *vt.* to admire sb, often to the extent of obsession —**hero-worshipper** *n.*

herp. *abbr.* herpetology

herpes /húr peez/ *n.* a viral infection causing small painful blisters and inflammation, most commonly at the junction of skin and mucous membrane in the mouth or nose or in the genitals [14thC. Via Latin from, ultimately, Greek *herpein* 'to creep'. Ultimately from an Indo-European word meaning 'to creep' that is also the ancestor of English *serpent*.]

herpes simplex /-sím pleks/ *n.* either of two viral diseases marked by clusters of small watery blisters, one affecting the area of the mouth and lips and the other the genitals [From modern Latin, literally 'simple herpes']

herpesvirus /húr peez vírəss/ *n.* any of various related DNA-containing animal viruses that replicate in cell nuclei and cause such diseases as chickenpox, herpes, and shingles

herpes zoster /-zóstər/ *n.* shingles (*technical*) [From modern Latin; *zoster* via Latin from Greek, 'girdle']

herpet. *abbr.* herpetology

herpetic /hər péttik/ *adj.* OF HERPES relating to, affected by, or indicative of herpes ■ *n.* SB WITH HERPES sb who has any form of herpes (*technical*)

herpetol *abbr.* herpetology

herpetology /húrpi tólləji/ *n.* the scientific study of reptiles and amphibians [Early 19thC. Coined from Greek *herpeton* 'creeping thing, reptile', from *herpein* 'to creep' (see HERPES) + -O- + -LOGY.] —**herpetologic** /húrpitə lójjik/ *adj.* —**herpetological** *adj.* —**herpetologically** *adv.* —**herpetologist** /húrpi tólləjist/ *n.*

Herr /hair, hur/ (*plural* **Herren** /hérrən/) *n.* the German equivalent of 'Mister', used as a title before a surname or profession [Mid-17thC. From German.]

Herrenvolk /hérrən folk/ *n.* in Nazi ideology the Germans as a master race (*often considered offensive*) [Mid-20thC. From German, literally 'master people'.]

Herrick /hérrik/, **Robert** (1591–1674) English poet. Ordained in 1623, he wrote over 1,200 religious and secular poems published in *Hesperides* (1648).

herring /hérring/ (*plural* **-rings** *or* **-ring**) *n.* **1.** FISH OF N ATLANTIC a small edible fish with silvery scales that lives in large shoals in the North Atlantic and is commercially very important to the area's fishing industry. Latin name: *Clupea harengus.* ◊ **red herring 2.** FISH RELATED TO HERRING any fish related to and resembling the herring. Family: Clupeidae. [Old English *hāring*, of prehistoric West Germanic origin]

herringbone /hérringbōn/ *n.* **1.** PATTERN OF INTERLOCKING V SHAPES a regular geometric pattern made by placing two contrasting rows of slanting lines or blocks together so that they form rows of Vs, zigzags, or chevrons. The technique is used in bricklaying, textiles, parquet flooring, weaving, and embroidery. **2.** TEXTILES FABRIC WITH HERRINGBONE PATTERN fabric woven in a herringbone pattern (*often used before a noun*) ○ *a herringbone jacket* **3.** SKIING METHOD FOR ASCENDING ON SKIS a method for climbing a slope by facing the peak, with skis pointing out at an angle, and moving them upwards one step after the other ■ *v.* (**-bones, -boning, -boned**) **1.** *vti.* DECORATE STH WITH HERRINGBONE to decorate or make sth such as cloth with a her-

ringbone pattern **2.** *vi.* SKIING GO UP SLOPE ON SKIS to ascend a slope on skis using the herringbone method

herringbone bond *n.* a type of decorative bricklaying in which the bricks are placed at an angle to one another to form a herringbone pattern

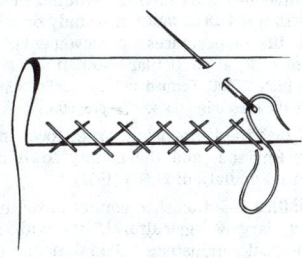

Herringbone stitch

herringbone stitch *n.* an embroidery stitch made with overlapping cross stitches that form a zigzag line, often used as a border stitch or hemming stitch

herring choker *n.* Can sb from New Brunswick, or, less often, the Maritime Provinces in Canada (*informal*)

herring gull *n.* a common gull that is widespread throughout the northern hemisphere, with a body that is mainly white, a grey back, and grey wings with black tips. Latin name: *Larus argentatus.*

Herriot /hérri ət/, **Édouard** (1872–1957) French statesman. He served as premier of France (1924–25, 1926, 1932) and was imprisoned (1942–45) for resisting the Vichy government during World War II.

Herriot, James (1916–95) British author. A television series, *All Creatures Great and Small* (1977–80), was made of his popular series of books about his experiences as a veterinarian in Yorkshire.

hers /hurz/ *pron.* **1.** STH BELONGING TO HER indicates that sth belongs or relates to a woman, girl, or female animal who has been previously mentioned or whose identity is known ○ *She drew my face to hers and kissed me.* ○ *I knew an uncle of hers.* **2.** BELONGING TO A COUNTRY belonging to or associated with a country or nation when its identity is known (*formal*) **3.** BELONGING TO A MACHINE belonging to or associated with a car, machine, or ship [14thC. Formed from HER + -'S.]

Herschel /húrsh'l/, **Caroline** (1750–1848) German-born British astronomer. She worked with her brother William Herschel on numerous astronomical investigations. She discovered eight comets and three nebulae. Full name **Caroline Lucretia Herschel**

Herschel, Sir John Frederick William (1792–1871) British astronomer. The son of William Herschel, he furthered his father's systematic studies of the heavens, studied the stars of the southern hemisphere, and invented a photographic fixing agent.

Herschel, Sir William (1738–1822) German-born British astronomer. Assisted in his researches by his sister Caroline Herschel, he pioneered the study of stars. He catalogued double stars and nebulae and discovered the planet Uranus (1781). Born **Friedrich Wilhelm Herschel**

herself (*stressed*) /hər sélf/; (*unstressed*) /ər sélf/ CORE MEANING: the form of 'her' used in reflexive and emphatic contexts ○ *She did it herself.*
pron. **1.** REFERRING TO FEMALE SUBJECT OF VERB used to refer to the same woman, girl, or female animal as the subject of the verb ○ *She put her hand on the rail to support herself.* ○ *She decided to treat herself.* **2.** USED FOR EMPHASIS used to emphasize or clarify which woman, girl, or female animal is being referred to, often introducing a note of surprise or awe ○ *I received a letter from the author herself.* **3.** ALONE OR WITHOUT HELP used to show that a woman, girl or female animal is alone or unaided ○ *sitting by herself in the garden* ○ *wrote the song herself* **4.** COUNTRY used to refer to a nation or country whose identity is known (*formal*) ○ *Britain is causing problems for herself with this policy.* **5.** MACHINE used to refer to a car, machine, or ship **6.** NORMAL SELF her normal self

in terms of personality, health, or behaviour ○ *She's not herself today – I don't know what's the matter with her.*

herstory /húrstəri/ (*plural* **-ries**) *n.* **1. HISTORY FROM WOMEN'S PERSPECTIVE** history as it affects women or looked at from the point of view of women, especially in contrast to conventional treatment of history, seen in feminist terms as having favoured men **2. LIFE EXPERIENCES OF WOMAN OR WOMEN** the study or recording of the life experiences, achievements, or expectations of a particular woman or group of women [Late 20thC. Formed on the model of HISTORY as if *his-* were the masculine possessive pronoun.]

Hertford /haàrtfərd/ historic market town in south-eastern England, and the county town of Hertfordshire. Population: 21,665 (1991).

Hertfordshire /haàrtfərdshər/ county in southeastern England, largely agricultural, but with modern technological industries. Population: 1,001,200 (1995). Area: 1,634 sq. km/632 sq. mi.

Herts. /haarts/ *abbr.* Hertfordshire

hertz /hurts/ (*plural* **hertz**) *n.* the SI unit of frequency equal to one cycle per second. Symbol **Hz** [Late 19thC. Named after Heinrich HERTZ.]

Hertz /hurts/, **Heinrich** (1857–94) German physicist. He was the first to produce electromagnetic waves under laboratory conditions, leading to the development of the telegraph and radio. The unit of frequency, hertz, is named after him. Full name **Heinrich Rudolf Hertz**

Hertzian wave /húrtsi ən-, háirtsi ən-/ *n.* a radio wave (*archaic*) [See HERTZ]

Hertzog /húrts og/, **J. B. M.** (1866–1942) South African politician. He founded the Nationalist Party (1914). As South African prime minister (1924–39), he secured the rights of Dutch-descended Afrikaners in South Africa while pursuing a policy of racial segregation. Full name **James Barry Munnik Hertzog**

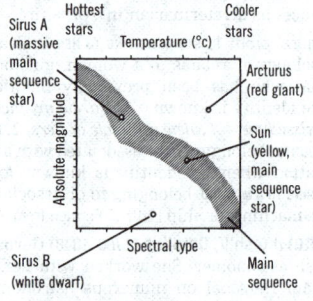

Hertzsprung-Russell diagram

Hertzsprung-Russell diagram *n.* a graph that plots the brightness of stars against their spectral type or colour

Hervey Bay /haárvi-/ town located on a bay of the same name in southern Queensland, Australia. Population: 32,054 (1996).

Herzog /húrts og/, **Werner** (*b.* 1942) German film director. He created powerful dramas about characters in the grip of anguish or obsession, including *Aguirre, The Wrath of God* (1972) and *Fitzcarraldo* (1982). Real name **Werner Stipetic**

he's (*stressed*) /heez/; (*unstressed*) /eez/ *contr.* **1. HE IS** he is ○ *He's not the man I saw.* **2. HE HAS** he has ○ *He's finished his lunch.*

Hesione /hi sí əni/ *n.* in Greek mythology, a princess whom Hercules rescued from a sea monster

hesitant /hézzitənt/ *adj.* hesitating or reluctant to do or say sth because of indecision or lack of confidence —**hesitance** *n.* —**hesitancy** *n.* —**hesitantly** *adv.*

─── **WORD KEY: SYNONYMS** ───

See Synonyms at *unwilling.*

hesitate /hézzi tayt/ (**-tates, -tating, -tated**) *vi.* **1. BE SLOW TO ACT** to be slow in doing sth, or pause while doing or saying sth, often because of uncertainty or doubt **2. NOT BE EAGER TO DO STH** to be reluctant to do or say sth ○ *If you're puzzled by anything, don't hesitate to ask.* [Early 17thC. From Latin *haesitat-*, the past participle

stem of *haesitare* 'to stick fast', from *haerere* 'to stick' (source of English *adhere* and *cohere*).] —**hesitater** *n.* —**hesitatingly** *adv.* —**hesitative** /hézzi taytiv/ *adj.*

─── **WORD KEY: SYNONYMS** ───

hesitate, pause, falter, stumble, waver, vacillate

CORE MEANING: to show uncertainty or indecision

hesitate to take or cause a short break in an activity, as a result of uncertainty or reluctance to continue; **pause** to cause an interruption in an activity that is already under way. It can be used to describe an interruption that is intentional, for example to allow sb time to do sth. It can also be used to describe an interruption that is due to hesitation or uncertainty; **falter** used to describe a series of short stoppages and a failure to run smoothly, for example because of nervousness, fear, awkwardness, or incompetence; **stumble** meaning the same as *falter*, used especially to talk about hesitation and noticeable awkwardness in saying sth; **waver** to hesitate or be undecided about a course of action, sometimes after the course of action has begun; **vacillate** used to describe a process of indecision and hesitation that involves veering between extremes.

hesitation /hézzi táysh'n/ *n.* **1. ACT OF HESITATING** the act of hesitating or pausing **2. RELUCTANCE** the state of being reluctant or undecided

Hesperian /he speéri ən/ *adj.* **1. WESTERN** belonging to or connected with the west (*literary*) **2. OF HESPERIDES** relating to the Hesperides [Late 15thC. Via Latin from Greek *hesperios* 'western', from *hesperos* 'western, evening' (see HESPERIDES).]

Hesperides /he spérri deez/ *npl.* **1. MYTHOLOGICAL GREEK NYMPHS** in Greek mythology, the daughters of Atlas and Hesperus and the guards of a tree bearing golden apples from which Hercules was required to gather fruit as one of his twelve labours **2. ISLANDS OF GREEK MYTHOLOGY** in Greek mythology, islands far to the west in which a tree with golden apples grew [Late 16thC. From Greek, the plural of *hesperis* 'western', from *hesperos* 'western, evening'. Ultimately from an Indo-European base that also produced English *west* and *vespers.*] —**Hesperidean** /héspə ríddi ən/ *adj.*

hesperidin /he spérridin/ *n.* a white or colourless crystalline glycoside obtained from citrus fruits and used medicinally to treat capillary disease [Mid-19thC. Coined from the Greek stem *hesperid-* 'western' (see HESPERIDES) + -IN.]

hesperidium /héspə ríddi əm/ *n.* a fruit, e.g. a citrus fruit, made up of a thick leathery rind and soft segmented pulp [Mid-19thC. Coined from HESPERIDES, with reference to the golden apples, + -IUM.]

Hesperus /héspərəss/ *n.* the planet Venus, especially just after sunset when it shines brightly (*literary*) [From Latin, from Greek *hesperos* 'western, evening']

Hess /hess/, **Rudolf** (1894–1987) German Nazi deputy leader. Adolf Hitler's private secretary and deputy in the 1920s and 1930s, he was captured as a prisoner of war in Scotland (1941), convicted of war crimes at Nuremberg (1945–46), and imprisoned for life in Spandau Prison, West Berlin. Full name **Walter Richard Rudolf Hess**

Hesse /hess, héssə/ state and historic duchy in west-central Germany. Largely an agricultural region, it is drained by the Rhine and Main rivers in the west and, in the northeast, by the River Weser.

Hesse, Hermann (1877–1962) German novelist and poet. His spiritually probing novels include *Siddhartha* (1922) and *Steppenwolf* (1927). He was awarded the Nobel Prize for literature in 1946.

hessian /héssi ən/ *n.* a coarse strong fabric made from jute or hemp and used for making bags and in upholstery. It was also formerly used as a backing for linoleum. [Late 19thC. Named after the German state of *Hesse*, where the fabric originated. Compare the origins of DENIM, JERSEY, and WORSTED.]

Hessian /héssi ən/ *n.* **1. PEOPLES SB FROM HESSE** sb who lives in or was born or brought up in the central German state of Hesse **2. MIL GERMAN MERCENARY SOLDIER** a German mercenary soldier, especially one from the kingdom of Hesse, who fought for the British army during the American War of Independence or the Napoleonic Wars ■ *adj.* **OF HESSE** relating to or typical of Hesse, or its people or culture

Hessian boot *n.* a men's knee-high boot with a tasselled top, first worn by Hessian soldiers and fashionable at the beginning of the 19th century

Hessian fly *n.* a small fly of the gallfly family that lays its eggs on the stems of grain plants, where the larvae bore into the stems and weaken them. It causes severe damage to crops, especially wheat, barley, and rye. Latin name: *Mayetiola destructor.* [From having been inadvertently brought to North America by Hessian troops]

hessite /héss īt/ *n.* a grey metallic mineral composed of silver telluride [Mid-19thC. Named after the Russian chemist G. H. *Hess* (1802–50).]

hessonite /héssə nīt/ *n.* = essonite

hest /hest/ *n.* sb's order, command, or pressing request (*archaic*) [Old English *hǽs.* Possibly from an Indo-European word meaning 'to set in motion' that is also the ancestor of Latin *citare* 'to urge' (see CITE).]

Hester /héstər/, **Joy St Clair** (*b.* 1920) Australian artist. She is noted for her expressionistic pen and gouache works.

Hestia /hésti ə/ *n.* in Greek mythology, the goddess of the hearth. Roman equivalent **Vesta**

Heston /hést'n/, **Charlton** (*b.* 1923) US actor. He specialized in heroic roles that capitalized on his rugged good looks and powerful physique, and won an Academy Award for *Ben-Hur* (1959). In his later years he made frequent public appearances on behalf of conservative political causes. Real name **John Charlton Carter**

Hesychast /héssi kast/ *n.* a member of a school of meditative devotion developed by monks of the Greek Orthodox Church on Mount Athos —**Hesychastic** /héssi kástik/ *adj.*

het /het/ *n.* a heterosexual person (*slang disapproving*) [Shortening]

hetaera /hi teérə/ (*plural* **-rae** /-ree/ *or* **-ras**), **hetaira** /-tírə/ (*plural* **-rai** /-rī/ *or* **-ras**) *n.* one of a special class of women who were used by the men of ancient Greece as prostitutes, and who were valued as intelligent, witty, educated, and highly cultured companions [Early 19thC. From Greek, the feminine form of *hetairos* 'companion'. Ultimately from an Indo-European word that is also the ancestor of English *idiot* and *sodality.*] —**hetaeric** *adj.*

hetaerism /hi teérizəm/, **hetairism** /-tír-/ *n.* **1. LIFE AS OR WITH CONCUBINE** the social condition or institution of concubinage **2. CUSTOM OF SHARING SEXUAL PARTNERS** the practice in some societies of sharing spouses or sexual partners —**hetaerist** *n.* —**hetaeristic** /héttə rístik/ *adj.*

heter- *prefix.* = hetero- (*used before vowels*)

hetero /héttərō/ *n.* (*plural* **-os**) **HETEROSEXUAL PERSON** sb who is heterosexual (*informal*) ■ *adj.* **HETEROSEXUAL** heterosexual (*informal*) [Mid-20thC. Shortening.]

hetero- *prefix.* **1.** different, other ○ *heterochromatic* **2.** containing atoms of different kinds ○ *heterocyclic* [From Greek *heteros* 'other'. Ultimately from an Indo-European word meaning 'one of two'.]

heteroatom /héttərō atəm/ *n.* a noncarbon atom in a heterocyclic compound

heterocercal /héttərō súrk'l/ *adj.* used to describe a fish's tail in which the vertebral column bends upwards and extends into the upper and larger lobe of the tail-fin, as in some sharks [Mid-19thC. Coined from HETERO- + Greek *kerkos* 'tail'.]

heterochromatic /héttərō krə máttik/ *adj.* containing many different colours —**heterochromatism** /héttərō krómatizəm/ *n.*

heterochromatin /héttərō krómatin/ *n.* chromatic material that contains few genes but stains readily with basic dyes and appears as nodules between chromosomes. ◊ **euchromatin**

heterochromosome /héttərō krómassōm/ *n.* a chromosome consisting mainly of heterochromatin, especially a sex chromosome

heterochromous /héttərō krómass/ *adj.* used to describe plant parts that exhibit different colours

heteroclite /héttərə klīt/, **heteroclitic** /-klíttik/ *adj.* **OF UNUSUAL FORMATION** used to describe a word that is formed in an unusual or irregular way ■ *n.* IR-

REGULARLY FORMED WORD a word that is formed in an unusual or irregular way [Late 15thC. Via late Latin from Greek *heteroklitos*, from *heteros* 'the other one of two' + *klīnein* 'to lean' (source of English *climax*).]

heterocyclic /héttərō sīklik, -síklik/ *adj.* used to describe or relating to a ring system composed of atoms in which at least one is not a carbon atom

heterodactylous /héttərō dáktiləss/, **heterodactyl** /-dákt'l/ *adj.* used to describe the feet of certain birds, e.g. the trogons, in which the first and second toes point backwards and the third and fourth toes point forwards. ◊ **zygodactyl**

heterodont /héttərə dont/ *adj.* used to describe a mammal that has teeth of different types, e.g. incisors, canines, premolars, and molars

heterodox /héttərə doks/ *adj.* at variance with established or accepted beliefs or theories, especially in the field of religion (*formal*) [Early 17thC. Via late Latin from Greek *heterodoxos*, from *heteros* 'the other one of two' + *doxa* 'opinion' (source of English *doxology*).]

heterodoxy /héttərə doksi/ (*plural* **-ies**) *n.* (*formal*) **1.** DISAGREEMENT WITH ESTABLISHED OPINIONS the condition of being at variance with established or accepted beliefs or theories, especially in the field of religion **2.** UNORTHODOX OPINION an opinion, belief, or theory that is at variance with established or accepted ones

heterodyne /héttərə dīn/ *vt.* (**-dynes, -dyning, -dyned**) COMBINE RADIO-FREQUENCY WAVES to combine a received radio-frequency wave with a wave of a different frequency to produce frequencies equal to the sum of and the difference between the original two signals ■ *adj.* INVOLVING COMBINED RADIO WAVES consisting of, produced by, or operated by heterodyning signals

heteroecious /héttə rō éeshəss/ *adj.* used to describe a parasite such as a tapeworm that lives in two or more hosts in the course of its life cycle [Late 19thC. Coined from HETERO- + Greek *oikia* 'house'.] —**heteroecism** /héttərō éessizəm/ *n.*

heterogamete /héttə rō gámmeet/ *n.* **1.** EITHER OF UNITING REPRODUCTIVE CELLS either of two reproductive cells (**gametes**) that differ in size, structure, and function, and that unite in the process of reproduction, e.g. the small sperm and large ova in humans **2.** SEX-DETERMINING REPRODUCTIVE CELL a reproductive cell produced by the sex that carries the chromosomes that determine the sex of the offspring

heterogametic /héttə rōgə méttik/ *adj.* **1.** PRODUCING TWO DIFFERENT REPRODUCTIVE CELLS used to describe the sex that produces reproductive cells (**gametes**) of two different types, one type producing males and the other females **2.** OF HETEROGAMETES relating to heterogametes

heterogamy /héttə róggəmi/ *n.* **1.** BIOL UNION OF DISSIMILAR REPRODUCTIVE CELLS in sexual reproduction, the union of two types of sex cell (**heterogamete**) that are dissimilar in size, structure, and function **2.** BIOL ALTERNATING OF FORMS OF REPRODUCTION the alternation of sexual and asexual reproduction in certain species, e.g. aphids, in which every other generation is produced from the female with no need for a male **3.** BOT HAVING DIFFERENT FLOWERS ON ONE PLANT the production on the same plant of two kinds of flower, one bearing both male and female organs and the other bearing only female organs or being asexual —**heterogamic** /héttərō gámmik/ *adj.* —**heterogamous** /héttə róggəməss/ *adj.*

heterogeneity /héttərō jə née əti, -náyəti/ *n.* **1.** DIVERSITY the diverse nature of sth **2.** CHEM HETEROGENEOUS STATE the state of being chemically heterogeneous

heterogeneous /héttərō jéeni əss/, **heterogenous** /héttə rójjənəss/ *adj.* **1.** CONSISTING OF DISSIMILAR PARTS consisting of parts or individual elements that are unrelated or unlike each other **2.** UNRELATED not related or similar **3.** CHEM WITH TWO OR MORE PHASES used to describe a chemical substance that has two or more phases [Early 17thC. Formed from medieval Latin *heterogeneus*, from Greek *heterogenēs*, literally 'other kind', from *heteros* 'other' + *genos* 'kind'.] —**heterogeneously** *adv.* —**heterogeneousness** *n.*

heterogenesis /héttərō jénnəssiss/ *n.* the appearance of a mutation in a population

heterogenetic /héttərō jə néttik/ *adj.* **1.** OF HETEROGENESIS relating to heterogenesis **2.** BIOL FROM DISPARATE ANCESTORS derived from ancestors not closely related **3.** MUTATING reproducing by heterogenesis —**heterogenetically** *adv.*

heterogenic /héttərō jéenik/ *adj.* used to describe a reproductive cell (**gamete**), individual, or population that has more than one variant (**allele**) of a particular gene

heterogenous /héttə rójjənəss/ *adj.* **1.** = **heterogeneous** **2.** MED NOT FROM THE SAME BODY originating outside the body, from another individual or species [Late 17thC. Variant of HETEROGENEOUS.] —**heterogeny** *n.*

heterogony /héttə róggəni/ *n.* a life cycle involving alternating parasitic and free-living generations —**heterogonous** *adj.* —**heterogonously** *adv.*

heterograft /héttə rō graaft/ *n.* a graft of living tissue from one animal to another of a different species

heterography /héttə róggrəfi/ (*plural* **-phies**) *n.* **1.** DIFFERENT LETTERS FOR SAME SOUND the use of different letters or groups of letters to represent the same sound or sounds **2.** WRITING SYSTEM WITH HETEROGRAPHY a writing system that uses different combinations of letters to represent the same sound or sounds [Late 18thC. Coined from HETERO- + -GRAPHY on the model of ORTHOGRAPHY.] —**heterographic** /héttərō gráffik/ *adj.*

heterokaryon /héttərō kárri ən/ (*plural* **-a** /-ri ə/) *n.* a cell that has two or more genetically different nuclei

heterokaryosis /héttə rō kárri ṓssiss/ *n.* the presence in a cell of two or more nuclei of different genetic origin. Heterokaryosis occurs naturally in certain fungi when cells fuse but their nuclei do not, and can be induced artificially to study the interaction of cellular components of different species. —**heterokaryotic** /héttərō kárri óttik/ *adj.*

heterologous /héttə rólləgəss/ *adj.* **1.** MED FROM DIFFERENT SPECIES derived or taken from a different species **2.** IMMUNOL NOT CORRESPONDING used to describe an antigen and an antibody that do not correspond to each other **3.** BIOL IN ABNORMAL LOCATION not normally found in the particular part of the body in which it has been found **4.** BIOL DIFFERING IN STRUCTURE AND ORIGIN used to describe organisms or parts that differ from each other in structure or origin [Mid-19thC. Coined from HETERO- + Greek *logos* 'relation, ratio'.] —**heterologously** *adv.*

heterolysis /héttə rólləssiss/ *n.* **1.** CHEM FORMATION OF OPPOSITELY CHARGED PARTICLES the breaking of a chemical bond in a compound, producing particles or ions of opposite charge, e.g. the formation of sodium and chloride ions in a salt solution **2.** BIOL CELL DESTRUCTION the destruction of cells or proteins of one species by the action of enzymes or lysins from another, e.g. when the blood of one species causes the red blood cells of another species to rupture —**heterolytic** /héttərə líttik/ *adj.*

heteromerous /héttə rómmərəss/ *adj.* **1.** BIOL WITH DIFFERENT PARTS with parts of different types **2.** BOT WITH DIFFERENT NUMBERS OF PARTS with flowers that do not have the same number of petals in each case, or with other parts that are made up of different numbers of elements

heteromorphic /héttərō máwrfik/, **heteromorphous** /-máwrfəss/ *adj.* **1.** BIOL TAKING DIFFERENT FORMS DURING LIFE CYCLE taking different forms at different stages of its life cycle **2.** GENETICS OF DIFFERENT SIZE OR SHAPE differing in size or shape, as the X and Y sex chromosomes do **3.** BIOL, PATHOL ABNORMAL differing in shape, size, or structure from the normal form of an organism **4.** PATHOL INVOLVING ABNORMAL FORM characterized by an abnormal form or forms —**heteromorphism** /héttərō máwrfizəm/ *n.* —**heteromorphy** /héttə rō mawrfi/ *n.*

heteronomous /héttə rónnəməss/ *adj.* **1.** POL UNDER OTHER LAWS subject to other laws or rules or to laws and rules imposed by other people or institutions **2.** BIOL GROWING OR DEVELOPING DIFFERENTLY used to describe parts of an organism that have different modes of development, growth, and different functions [Early 19thC. Coined from HETERO- + Greek *nomos* 'law'.] —**heteronomously** *adv.* —**heteronomy** /héttə rónnəmi/ *n.*

heteronym /héttərōnim/ *n.* either of two or more words that are spelt the same, but differ in meaning and often in pronunciation, e.g. 'bow' (a ribbon) and 'bow' (of a ship) [Late 19thC. Coined from HETERO- + *-nym*.] —**heteronymous** /héttə rónnəməss/ *adj.* —**heteronymy** /-əmi/ *n.*

heteroousian /héttərō óozi ən/, **heterousian** /héttə róozi ən/ *n.* in Christian theology, sb who believes that God the Father and God the Son are not formed of the same substance [Late 17thC. Formed from Greek *heter(o)ousios*, literally 'other substance', from *heteros* 'other' + *ousia* 'substance'.] —**heteroousian** *adj.*

heterophyllous /héttərō fílləss/ *adj.* used to describe plants such as the sassafras tree that have different shapes of leaves on the same plant —**heterophylly** /héttə róffili/ *n.*

heteroplasty /héttərō plasti/ (*plural* **-ties**) *n.* **1.** GRAFTING FROM SB OR STH ELSE a surgical procedure to graft or transplant tissues or organs from one person or animal to another **2.** = **heterograft** —**heteroplastic** /héttərō plástik/ *adj.*

heteroploid /héttərō ployd/ *adj.* WITH ABNORMAL CHROMOSOME NUMBER with a number of chromosomes that is, unusually, not an exact multiple of the basic chromosome number for that species ■ *n.* HETEROPLOID CELL a heteroploid cell or organism

heteropolar /héttərō pṓlər/ *adj.* CHEM = **polar** —**heteropolarity** /héttərō pō lárrəti/ *n.*

heteropteran /héttə róptərən/ *n.* an insect, e.g. a bedbug or another true bug, with mouthparts adapted for piercing and sucking, and partially hardened forewings with membranous tips. Order: Heteroptera. [Mid-19thC. Coined from HETERO- + Greek *pteron* 'wing'.] —**heteropteran** *adj.*

heterosexism /héttərō séksizəm/ *n.* discrimination against gays and lesbians by heterosexuals —**heterosexist** /héttərō séksist/ *n., adj.*

heterosexual /héttərō sékshoo əl/ *n.* SB SEXUALLY DESIRING OPPOSITE SEX sb who sexually desires members of the opposite sex ■ *adj.* **1.** DESIRING OPPOSITE SEX sexually desiring members of the opposite sex **2.** INVOLVING BOTH SEXES relating to sexual desire or sexual relations between people of opposite sexes —**heterosexually** *adv.*

heterosexuality /héttərō sékshoo álləti/ *n.* sexual desire or sexual relations between people of opposite sexes

heterosis /héttə rṓssiss/ *n.* BIOL = **hybrid vigour** [Mid-19thC. From Greek *heterōsis*, literally 'making different', from *heteros* 'different'.]

heterosporous /héttərō spáwrəss, -róspərəss/ *adj.* producing two types of spore, microspores and megaspores, on the same plant —**heterospory** /héttərō spáwri, -róspəri/ *n.*

heterostyly /héttərō stīli/ *n.* BOT the possession of styles of different lengths on different plants of the same species, which is an aid to cross-pollination by insects —**heterostyled** /héttərō stīld/ *adj.* —**heterostylous** /héttərō stīləss/ *adj.*

heterotrophic /héttərō tróffik/ *adj.* obtaining nourishment by digesting plant or animal matter, as animals do, as opposed to photosynthesizing food, as plants do —**heterotroph** /héttərō trōf/ *n.* —**heterotrophy** /-trōfi/ *n.*

heterotypic /héttə rō típpik/, **heterotypical** /-típpik'l/ *adj.* differing from the standard or normal type in an organism

heterousian *n., adj.* = **heteroousian**

heterozygous /héttə rō zīgəss/ *adj.* used to describe a cell or organism that has two or more different versions (**alleles**) of at least one of its genes. The offspring of such an organism may thus differ with regard to the characteristics determined by the gene or genes involved, depending on which version of the gene they inherit. —**heterozygote** /héttə rō zī gōt/ *n.*

heth /het, heth, khet, kheth/, **cheth** *n.* the eighth letter of the Hebrew alphabet, represented in the English alphabet as 'h'. See table at **alphabet** [Early 19thC. From Hebrew *ḥēth*.]

hetman /hétmən/ (*plural* **-mans**) *n.* = **ataman** [Mid-18thC. Via Polish, of uncertain origin: probably from German *Hauptmann* 'headman, captain'.]

het up *adj.* extremely excited as a result of anticipation, anger, or anxiety (*informal*) [*Het* originally the past participle of HEAT]

heuchera /hyoókərə, hóy-/ *n.* a plant native to North America but grown elsewhere that has sprays of small, usually red, flowers and low-growing heart-shaped leaves. Genus: *Heuchera*. [Late 19thC. From modern Latin, named after the German botanist J. H. *Heucher* (1677–1747).]

heulandite /hyoólən dīt/ *n.* a mineral of the zeolite family, consisting of a hydrated silicate of calcium, sodium, and aluminium, occurring in rock cavities as long white, yellow, red, or brown crystals [Early 19thC. Formed from the name of the English mineralogist H. *Heuland* (1777–1856).]

heuristic /hyoo rístik/ *adj.* **1.** EDUC ENCOURAGING DISCOVERY OF SOLUTIONS relating to or using a method of teaching that encourages learners to discover solutions for themselves **2.** PHILOS, SCI INVOLVING TRIAL AND ERROR using or arrived at by a process of trial and error rather than set rules **3.** COMPUT ABLE TO CHANGE used to describe a computer program that can modify itself in response to the user, e.g. a program for checking spelling ■ *n.* LOGIC PROCEDURE FOR GETTING SOLUTION a helpful procedure for arriving at a solution but not necessarily a proof [Early 19thC. Alteration of Greek *heuriskein* 'to find' (source of English *eureka*).] —**heuristically** *adv.*

heuristics /hyoo rístiks/ *n.* a method of solving a problem for which no formula exists, based on informal methods or experience, and employing a form of trial and error (**iteration**) (*takes a singular verb*)

hevea /heévi ə/ *n.* a tree native to the Amazon jungle, whose bark contains a milky sap that provides rubber. The best known species is the rubber tree, widely planted throughout the tropics as a source of natural rubber. Genus: *Hevea*. [Late 19thC. Via modern Latin from Quechua *hyeve*.]

Hevesy /hévveshi/, **Georg von** (1885–1966) Hungarian chemist. A Nobel Prize winner (1943), he pioneered the use of radioactive trace elements to study the chemical processes of living organisms. Full name **Georg Charles von Hevesy**

hew /hyoo/ (**hews, hewing, hewed, hewn** *or* **hewed**) *v.* **1.** *vti.* CUT DOWN OR UP to cut, break, or destroy sth, especially wood or stone, with a cutting implement, especially an axe **2.** *vt.* MAKE BY CUTTING OR CARVING to form or create sth by cutting wood or stone ○ *hewed a path through the forest* **3.** *vt.* SEVER FROM STH ELSE to cut sth off from a larger block or mass **4.** *vti.* HIT WITH SWORD to strike sb with a sword or axe ○ *He hewed at his enemies with his claymore.* [Old English *hēawan*, of prehistoric Germanic origin] —**hewer** *n.*

hew to *vt. US, Can* to conform closely to sth, e.g. a code or procedure (*formal*)

Hewett /hyoó it/, **Dorothy** (b. 1923) Australian writer. She wrote plays, poems, and a novel. Her controversial play *The Chapel Perilous* (1971) was banned for many years. Full name **Dorothy Coade Hewett**

Hewish /hyoó ish/, **Antony** (b. 1924) British astronomer. He shared the Nobel Prize in physics (1974) for his discovery of the class of stars known as pulsars.

hex /heks/ *n.* **1.** CURSE a curse or evil spell **2.** BRINGER OF BAD LUCK sb believed to bring bad luck or misfortune ■ *vt.* (**hexes, hexing, hexed**) **1.** CURSE OR BEWITCH to put a curse or spell on sb or sth **2.** HAVE BAD EFFECT ON to appear to have a bad effect on sth, as if it were cursed or bewitched ○ *A string of accidents hexed their first attempt to climb the mountain.* [Mid-19thC. Via Pennsylvanian German from German *Hexe* 'witch'.] —**hexer** *n.*

hex. *abbr.* **1.** hexagon **2.** hexagonal

hex- *prefix.* = **hexa-** (*used before vowels*)

hexa- *prefix.* six ○ *hexapod* [From Greek *hex*. Ultimately from the Indo-European word for 'six' that is also the ancestor of English *six* and *sextet*.]

hexachlorophene /héksə kláwrə feen/ *n.* a white odourless organic compound that has antiseptic properties and is used as an antibacterial agent in soaps and toothpaste and as an antiseptic in deodorants. Formula: $(C_6HCl_3OH)_2CH_2$. [Late 20thC. Coined from HEXA- + CHLORO- + Greek *phaino-* 'shining'.]

hexachord /héksə kawrd/ *n.* a series of six adjacent diatonic notes forming the basis of medieval and classical Greek music theory. There were three variants, the so-called natural, hard, and soft hexachords, which approximate to the modern C major, G major, and F major scales respectively.

hexadecimal /heksə déssim'l/ *adj.* COMPUT BASED ON NUMBER 16 used to describe a number system based on the number 16, in which the letters A to F are used as digits in addition to the digits 0 to 9. It is used especially to represent binary code in computers. ■ *n.* **1.** NUMBER WITH BASE 16 a number expressed using the base 16 rather than, e.g., the usual base 10 **2.** NOTATION FOR NUMBERS WITH BASE 16 the notation used to represent numbers with a base 16

hexagon /héksəgən/ *n.* a two-dimensional figure that has six sides [Late 16thC. Via late Latin *hexagonum* from, ultimately, Greek *hexagōnos* 'six-cornered', from *hexa-* 'six'.]

hexagonal /hék sággən'l/ *adj.* **1.** GEOM SIX-SIDED with six straight sides and six angles **2.** GEOM CONTAINING OR BASED ON HEXAGON containing a hexagon, or having a hexagon as a base **3.** CRYSTALS HAVING A SIX-SIDED CROSS SECTION belonging to one of the seven crystal systems, the members of which are six-sided in cross section, are elongated perpendicular to that cross section, and have sixfold symmetry about the long axis —**hexagonally** *adv.*

hexagram /héksə gram/ *n.* **1.** GEOM SIX-POINTED GEOMETRIC FIGURE a six-pointed star-shaped figure formed by extending the sides of a regular hexagon until they meet at six points **2.** EASTERN RELIG PATTERN OF SIX LINES any of the 64 possible combinations of six broken or unbroken lines, used in divination, especially in the *I Ching*

hexahedron /héksə heédrən/ *n.* a three-dimensional geometrical figure that has six plane faces, e.g. a cube [Late 16thC. From Greek *hexaedron*, neuter singular of *hexaedros*, literally 'six-sided', from *hexa-* 'six'.] —**hexahedral** *adj.*

hexahydrate /héksə hī drayt/ *n.* a crystalline compound, each molecule of which contains six loosely bound water molecules (**water of crystallization**) from which the water escapes when the compound is heated, leaving the compound unchanged

hexamerous /hek sámmərəss/, **hexameral** /-sámmərəl/ *adj.* with parts, especially petals or stamens, arranged in sets of six —**hexamerism** *n.*

hexameter /hek sámmitər/ *n.* a line of verse that has six metrical feet, usually all in the same or a related metre. The classical Greek and Latin epic poems the *Iliad*, *Odyssey*, and *Aeneid* are composed in dactylic hexameters. [14thC. Via Latin from Greek *hexametros* 'of six measures', from *hexa-* 'six' + *metron* 'measure'.] —**hexametric** /héksə méttrik/ *adj.*

hexamine /héksə meen/ *n.* a type of solid camping fuel sold in blocks [Mid-20thC. Contraction of *hexamethylenetetramine*, an antibacterial agent.]

hexane /hék sayn/ *n.* a volatile hydrocarbon found in petroleum that is a major ingredient of petrol and is commonly used as a solvent. Formula: C_6H_{14}.

Hexapla /héksəplə/ *n.* an ancient version of the Hebrew Scriptures, compiled by the early Christian theologian, Origen, that contains six parallel versions of the text [Early 17thC. From *(ta) hexapla*, its Greek title, the neuter plural of *hexaplous* 'sixfold', from *hexa-* 'six'.]

hexapody /hek sáppədi/ (*plural* **-dies**) *n.* a line of poetry consisting of six feet [Coined from HEXA- + -POD on the model of words such as TETRAPODY.] —**hexapodic** /héksə pódik/ *adj.*

hexastich /héksə stik/, **hexastichon** /hek sásti kon/ (*plural* **-cha** /-kə/) *n.* a unit of verse, e.g. a stanza or a short poem, that contains six lines [Late 16thC. Via modern Latin *hexastichon* from Greek, 'of six rows', from *hexa-* 'six' + *stichos* 'row'.]

hexastyle /héksə stíl/ *adj.* ARCHIT WITH SIX COLUMNS with six architectural columns, or in the form of six columns ■ *n.* ARCHIT CONSTRUCTION WITH SIX COLUMNS a building, or a portico or other part, that has six columns

Hexateuch /héksə tyook/ *n.* the first six books of the Bible, comprising Genesis, Exodus, Leviticus, Numbers, Deuteronomy, and Joshua. ◊ **Heptateuch, Pentateuch** [Late 19thC. Coined from HEXA- + Greek *teuchos* 'book', on the model of *Pentateuch*.]

hexavalent /héksə váylənt/ *adj.* with a chemical valency of six

hexcentric /héksə séntrik/ *n.* a six-sided metal chock used in rock climbing

hexosan /hék sō san/ *n.* a complex carbohydrate (**polysaccharide**) found in the cell walls of plants that breaks down to form a hexose. Formula: $C_6H_{10}O_5$.

hexose /héksōz, -sōss/ *n.* a simple sugar, e.g. glucose, that contains six carbon atoms per molecule

hex sign *n.* any one of various stylized signs incorporating a circle and other elements used to ward off evil or bad luck [See HEX]

hexyl /héks'l/ *n.* an organic group or radical derived from hexane and containing six carbon atoms. Formula: C_6H_{13}.

hey /hay/ *interj.* **1.** DEMANDING ATTENTION used to get sb's attention (*informal*) **2.** EXPRESSING VARIOUS EMOTIONS used to express surprise, irritation, or dismay **3.** US GREETING used as a greeting (*informal*) [12thC. Natural exclamation.]

heyday /háy day/ *n.* the time of sb's or sth's greatest success, popularity, or power [Late 16thC. By folk etymology from earlier *heyda* 'hurrah' (by association with DAY), of uncertain origin: probably an extension of HEY, modelled partly on Low German *heida*.]

Heysen /hīz'n/, **Sir Hans** (1877–1968) German-born Australian painter. A landscape artist, he is best known for his watercolour paintings of eucalyptus forests. Full name **Sir Wilhelm Ernst Hans Franz Heysen**

Heywood /háywood/, **Thomas** (1574?–1641) English dramatist. He wrote more than 220 comedies and tragedies, notably *A Woman Killed with Kindness* (1603).

hf *abbr.* half

Hf *symbol.* hafnium

HF *abbr.* **1.** hard firm (*used to indicate hardness of lead on pencils*) **2.** RADIO high frequency

h.f. *abbr.* high frequency

HFC *abbr.* hydrofluorocarbon

hg[1] *abbr.* BIOCHEM haemoglobin

hg[2] *symbol.* MEASURE hectogram

HG *abbr.* **1.** Her Grace **2.** LANG High German **3.** His Grace **4.** Home Guard

hgb. *abbr.* haemoglobin

HGH *abbr.* human growth hormone

hgt *abbr.* height

HGV *abbr.* heavy goods vehicle

hgwy *abbr.* highway

hh *abbr.* hands (*used as a measure of a horse's height*)

HH *abbr.* **1.** double hard (*used to indicate hardness of lead on pencils*) **2.** Her Highness **3.** His Highness **4.** LAW Her Honour **5.** LAW His Honour **6.** RELIG His Holiness

H-Hour *n.* the appointed time for a military event, e.g. a planned attack, to take place [*H* abbreviation for 'hour']

hi /hī/ *interj.* **1.** HELLO! used as an informal greeting (*informal*) **2.** ATTRACTING ATTENTION used to attract sb's attention (*archaic informal*) [12thC. Natural exclamation.]

HI *abbr.* **1.** MAIL Hawaii **2.** Hawaiian Islands **3.** MED hearing-impaired

hiatal /hī áyt'l/ *adj.* relating to an opening, gap, or aperture in an organ of the body

hiatal hernia *n. US* = hiatus hernia

hiatus /hī áytəss, hi-/ (*plural* **-tuses** *or* **-tus**) *n.* **1.** UNEXPECTED GAP a break in sth where there should be continuity **2.** ANAT OPENING an opening or aperture in an organ, e.g. the opening in the diaphragm for the oesophagus **3.** LING SEPARATION BETWEEN CONSECUTIVE VOWELS a break in pronunciation between two vowels that are next to each other in consecutive syllables without an intervening consonant, as in 're-examine' **4.** PRINTING OMISSION a gap where sth is missing, especially in manuscripts [Mid-16thC. From Latin, 'gaping, opening', from *hiare* 'to gape', from, ultimately, an Indo-European word that is also the ancestor of English *yawn*.]

hiatus hernia *n.* a hernia in which the part of the stomach around the oesophagus entrance is forced up into the chest cavity through the normal opening in the diaphragm for the oesophagus. Hiatus hernia is associated with heartburn and can usually be corrected by surgery. US term **hiatal hernia**

hibachi /hi baáchi/ (*plural* **-chis**) *n.* a portable barbecue of Japanese design, with a base for the fire with vents under it, and one or more adjustable cooking racks [Mid-19thC. From Japanese, literally 'fire bowl'.]

hibakusha /hi baákoōshə/ (*plural* **-sha** *or* **-shas**) *n.* sb who survived the atomic bombing of Hiroshima or Nagasaki in 1945 [Mid-20thC. From Japanese, literally 'sb who suffers an explosion'.]

hibernaculum /híbər nákyōōləm/ (*plural* **-la** /-lə/) *n.* **1.** ZOOL HIBERNATION PLACE the winter den of a hibernating animal or insect **2.** BOT BUD COVER the covering of a plant bud that protects it during its dormant phase [Late 17thC. From Latin, from *hibernare* (see HIBERNATE).]

hibernal /hī búrn'l/ *adj.* relating to winter as one of the six divisions of the year used to describe ecological communities [Early 17thC. From late Latin *hibernalis*, from *hibernus* 'wintry'.]

hibernate /híbər nayt/ (**-nates, -nating, -nated**) *vi.* **1.** BIOL PASS WINTER ASLEEP to be in a sleep-like dormant state over the winter while living off reserves of body fat, with a decrease in body temperature and pulse rate and slower metabolism. Animals that hibernate include bears, bats, and many amphibians. **2.** BECOME LESS ACTIVE to become less active, especially by staying at home rather than going out to socialize (*informal humorous*) [Early 19thC. From Latin *hibernare*, from *hiberna* 'winter quarters', a noun use of a form of *hibernus* 'wintry'.] —**hibernation** /híbər náysh'n/ *n.* —**hibernator** /híbər naytər/ *n.*

Hibernia /hī búrni ə/ *n.* Ireland (*archaic or literary*) [From Latin, 'Ireland', alteration of *Iverna*, which came via Greek *I(w)ernē* from Celtic]

Hibernian /hī búrni ən/ *adj.* relating to or typical of Ireland (*archaic or literary*) —**Hibernian** *n.*

Hibernicism /hī búrnissizəm/, **Hibernianism** /-búrni ənizzəm/ *n.* an Irish word, expression, or idiom in the English language

Hiberno- *prefix.* Irish [Formed from medieval Latin *Hibernus* 'Irish', from Latin *Hibernia* 'HIBERNIA']

Hiberno-English *n.* the variety of English spoken in Ireland with features from Irish Gaelic, including intonation and some Gaelic words and phrases —**Hiberno-English** *adj.*

Hibiscus

hibiscus /hī brískəss, hi-/ *n.* a shrub or small tree of the mallow family that has large brightly-coloured flowers with prominent stamen tubes. It is pollinated by birds. Genus: *Hibiscus.* [Early 18thC. Via Latin from Greek *hibiskos*, 'marshmallow', perhaps of Celtic origin.]

HIB vaccine /híb-/ *n.* a vaccine that protects against the bacterium that causes meningitis, usually given in the first year of life

---

hic /hik/ *interj.* used to represent the sound of a hiccup [Late 19thC. An imitation of the sound.]

hiccup /híkup/, **hiccough** *n.* **1.** MED CONVULSIVE GASP an abrupt involuntary contraction of the diaphragm that causes an intake of breath and closes the sound-producing folds at the top of the windpipe (**vocal cords**), resulting in a convulsive gasp **2.** GULPING SOUND the gulping sound that accompanies a hiccup, or a sound like this **3.** HITCH IN ARRANGEMENTS a temporary setback to sb's plans or arrangements (*informal*) ■ **hiccups, hiccoughs** *npl.* GULPING INTAKES OF BREATH an attack of repeated involuntary spasms of the diaphragm, resulting in periodic noisy gulps of breath ■ *v.* (**-cups, -cuping** *or* **-cupping, -cuped** *or* **-cupped; -coughs, -coughing, -coughed**) **1.** *vi.* PRODUCE HICCUP to have a spasm of the diaphragm resulting in a hiccup **2.** *vi.* MAKE HICCUP NOISES to make the sound of, or a sound like, a hiccup **3.** *vt.* TALK WHILE HICCUPPING to say sth while hiccupping [Late 16thC. An imitation of the sound.]

hic jacet /hik jáysət, -jákət/ an inscription often found on gravestones, meaning 'here lies' [From Latin]

hick /hik/ *n.* BUMPKIN an unsophisticated and uncultured rural or small-town person (*informal insult*) ■ *adj.* RURAL, RUSTIC, AND UNSOPHISTICATED remote from big cities and lacking in sophistication (*informal insult*) [Mid-16thC. From *Hick*, an old pet-form of the male name 'Richard'.]

Hick /hik/, **Graeme** (*b.* 1966) Rhodesian-born British cricketer, who is a batsman for Worcestershire and England. He scored his hundredth first-class century in 1998, the second youngest cricketer to do so.

hickey /híki/ (*plural* **-eys** *or* **-ies**) *n.* **1.** *US, Can* = **doohickey** (*informal*) **2.** *US, Can* = **lovebite** (*informal*) **3.** *US, Can* PIMPLE a pimple (*informal*) **4.** PRINTING PRINTING ERROR a printing error or imperfection [Early 20thC. Origin unknown.]

US Signal Corps
Wild Bill Hickok

Hickok /híkok/, **Wild Bill** (1837–76) US law enforcer, gunfighter, and scout. He was a Union spy and scout during the US Civil War and later a Kansas marshal known for his marksmanship. His touring Buffalo Bill's Wild West Show (1872–73) was a popular attraction. Real name **James Butler Hickok**

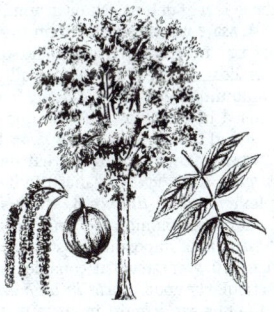
Hickory

hickory /híkəri/ (*plural* **-ries**) *n.* **1.** TREES N AMERICAN NUT TREE a deciduous North American tree of the walnut family with compound leaves and nuts that are edible in some species. Genus: *Carya.* **2.** INDUST HICKORY WOOD the hard light-coloured wood of a hickory tree, used in tool handles and agricultural implements **3.** HICKORY STICK a walking stick or switch

---

made of hickory wood [Late 17thC. From Algonquian, a shortening of *pockerchicory*, *pohickery*, a type of walnut.]

hid past tense, past participle of **hide**[1]

hidalgo /hi dálgō/ (*plural* **-gos**) *n.* a man belonging to the lowest rank of Spanish nobility [Late 16thC. From Spanish, a contraction of *hijo de algo*, literally 'son of sth'.]

Hidalgo /hi dálgō/ state in east-central Mexico. Capital: Pachuca. Population: 2,100,000 (1995). Area: 20,987 sq. km/8,103 sq. mi.

hidden past participle of **hide**[1] —**hiddenness** *n.*

hidden agenda *n.* a plan, motive, or aim underlying sb's actions that is kept secret from others

hiddenite /híd'n īt/ *n.* a rare green variety of the mineral spodumene, used as a gemstone. It is an aluminium lithium silicate found in hydrothermal deposits. [Late 19thC. Formed from the name of US mineralogist W. E. *Hidden*, who discovered it.]

hidden tax *n.* = indirect tax

hide[1] /hīd/ *v.* (**hides, hiding, hid** /hid/, **hidden** /híd'n/ *or* **hid**) **1.** *vti.* MOVE OUT OF SIGHT to conceal yourself, or sth or sb else, from view **2.** *vt.* KEEP SECRET to prevent sth from becoming known **3.** *vt.* BLOCK VIEW OF STH to obscure sth by passing, or passing sth, in front of it, or by being temporarily or permanently in front of it ○ *The clouds hid the sun for a while.* **4.** *vt.* TURN AWAY to turn away or cover the face or eyes with the hands, e.g., so that the expression cannot be seen or in order to avoid seeing sth ■ *n.* HUNT, LEISURE WILDLIFE OBSERVATION POST a place, often constructed to look like part of the natural environment, where sb can hide in order to observe, or sometimes shoot, wild animals. US term **blind** *n.* 3 [Old English *hȳdan.* Ultimately from a prehistoric West Germanic word that is also the ancestor of English *hoard, huddle,* and *hut.*]
hide out *vi.* to be in, or go into, hiding

hide[2] /hīd/ *n.* **1.** ANIMAL SKIN the skin of some larger animals, e.g. deer, cow, or buffalo (*often used in combination*) **2.** HUMAN SKIN a person's skin (*informal*) ○ *'A vengeance on your crafty wither'd hide!'* (William Shakespeare, *The Taming of the Shrew*; 1593) [Old English *hȳd.* Ultimately from an Indo-European word that is also the ancestor of *hide*[1] and of Latin *cutis* (source of English *cuticle*) , the underlying idea being 'covering'.] ◇ **neither hide nor hair of sb** *or* **sth** no trace of sb or sth ◇ **tan sb's hide** to beat or whip sb (*informal*)

hide[3] /hīd/ *n.* in Old English law, a measure of land equal to 120 acres [Old English *hīd*, 'measure of land for supporting a family', of prehistoric Germanic origin]

hide-and-seek *n.* a children's game in which one player lets the others hide, and then tries to find them

hideaway /hídə way/ *n.* a secluded place of retreat or concealment

hidebound /híd bownd/ *adj.* **1.** NARROW-MINDED AND CONSERVATIVE unwilling to countenance new ideas or new ways of doing things (*disapproving*) **2.** AGRIC WITH DRY, STIFF SKIN with skin that is dry, stiff, and closely attached to the flesh, as a result of poor feeding ○ *hidebound cattle* **3.** TREES WITH TOO STIFF BARK with bark that is so inflexible that normal growth is restricted

hideous /híddi əss/ *adj.* **1.** HORRIBLE TO SEE extremely unpleasant or horrible to see **2.** HORRIBLE TO HEAR frighteningly horrible to hear ○ *a hideous shriek* **3.** MORALLY REPULSIVE morally repulsive or disgusting **4.** CAUSING SUFFERING causing a great deal of suffering [14thC. From Anglo-Norman *hidous* and Old French *hidos*, from *hi(s)de* 'fear'.] —**hideousness** *n.*

hideously /híddi əssli/ *adv.* **1.** FRIGHTENINGLY OR REVOLTINGLY in an extremely unpleasant, frightening, or revolting way **2.** EXTREMELY to a frightening or revolting extent

hideout /híd owt/ *n.* a place where sb is hiding, especially sb wanted by the police

hidey-hole /hídi hōl/, **hidy-hole** *n.* a place of concealment for sb or sth (*informal*) [*Hidey* a variant of HIDING]

hiding[1] /híding/ *n.* a place where sb is hiding or can hide, or the state of being hidden [From HIDE[1]]

hiding[2] /híding/ *n.* the punishment of being beaten

(*informal*) [From HIDE[2]] ◇ **on a hiding to nothing** in a situation in which there is no chance of success

hidrosis /hi drṓssiss, hī-/ *n.* **1.** SWEAT PRODUCTION the production or excretion of sweat (*technical*) **2.** DISEASE OF SWEAT GLANDS a skin disease that affects the sweat glands [Mid-19thC. From Greek, from *hidrōs* 'sweat'.] —**hidrotic** /-dróttik/ *adj.*

hidy-hole *n.* = **hidey-hole**

hie /hī/ (**hies, hieing** *or* **hying, hied**) *vi.* to go somewhere in a hurry (*archaic*) [Old English, of unknown origin]

hiemal /hī əm'l/ *adj.* relating to or occurring in winter (*formal*) [Mid-16thC. From Latin *hiemalis*, from *hiems* 'winter'.]

hier- *prefix.* = **hiero-** (*used before vowels*)

hierarch /hīr aark/ *n.* sb of high rank in a hierarchy, especially a priestly hierarchy [15thC. Via medieval Latin *hierarcha* from Greek *hierarkhēs*, literally 'ruling sacred person', from *hieros* 'sacred' + *arkhēs* 'ruling'.]

hierarchical /hīr áarkik'l/, **hierarchic** /hīr áarkik/ *adj.* **1.** RIGIDLY GRADED IN ORDER relating to or arranged in a formally ranked order **2.** RELIG ADMINISTERED BY RANKED CLERGY administered by a hierarchy composed of members of the clergy —**hierarchically** *adv.*

hierarchize /hīr aar kīz/ (**-chizes, -chizing, -chized**), **hierarchise** (**-chises, -chising, -chised**) *vt.* to arrange sth, e.g. an organization, in graduated ranks — **hierarchization** /hīr aar kī záysh'n/ *n.*

hierarchy /hīr aarki/ (*plural* **-chies**) *n.* **1.** FORMALLY RANKED GROUP an organization or group whose members are arranged in ranks, e.g. in ranks of power and seniority **2.** FORMAL GRADING OF A GROUP categorization of members of a group according to the importance of each **3.** BIOL ANIMAL GROUP ORGANIZATION a form of social organization in animals in which different members of a group possess different levels of status, affecting their feeding and mating behaviour **4.** RELIG RANKED GROUP OF CLERGY a body of clergy organized into ranks **5.** BIOL SUBSET WITHIN A RANKED SYSTEM a subset within a classification system, e.g. that for plants or animals **6.** CONTROLLING GROUP IN FORMAL ORGANIZATION those who are in charge of a formally organized group, especially the priests in control of the Roman Catholic Church or a local part of it

hieratic /hīr áttik/, **hieratical** /-áttik'l/ *adj.* **1.** RELIG OF PRIESTS relating to priests **2.** LING OF ANCIENT WRITING SYSTEM relating to a cursive version of ancient Egyptian hieroglyphics **3.** ARTS IN STYLIZED FORM fixed, formal, and stylized in a traditional way, e.g. as ancient Egyptian art is ■ *n.* LING ANCIENT WRITING SYSTEM a cursive version of ancient Egyptian hieroglyphics [Mid-17thC. Via Latin *hieraticus* from Greek *hieratikos* 'priestly', from *hiereus*, literally 'sacred person', from *hieros* 'sacred'.] —**hieratically** *adv.*

hiero- *prefix.* holy, sacred ○ *hierocracy* [From Greek *hieros*. Ultimately from an Indo-European word denoting strong feeling that is also the ancestor of English *irate*, *iron*, and *oestrus*.]

hierocracy /hīr ókrəssi/ (*plural* **-cies**) *n.* **1.** CLERICAL GOVERNMENT government by clergy **2.** RULING CLERGY a body of clergy that rules a place or country — **hierocratic** /hīrō kráttik/ *adj.*

hierodule /hīrə dyool/ *n.* in ancient Greece, an enslaved person kept in or associated with a temple, especially a prostitute [Mid-19thC. Via Latin *hierodulus* from Greek *hierodoulos* 'temple slave', from *hieron*, literally 'sacred place', from *hieros* 'sacred' + *doulos* 'slave'.] —**hierodulic** /hīrə dyóolik/ *adj.*

hieroglyph /hīrəglif/ *n.* a symbol or picture used in a writing system to denote an object, concept, sound, or sequence of sounds, originally and especially in the writing system of ancient Egypt [Late 16thC. Back-formation from HIEROGLYPHIC.]

hieroglyphic /hīrə glíffik/ *adj.* **1. hieroglyphic, hieroglyphical** IN HIEROGLYPHS relating to or written in hieroglyphs **2.** HARD TO READ difficult to read (*informal*) ■ *n.* = **hieroglyph** [Late 16thC. Directly or via French *hiéroglyphique*, from Late Latin *hieroglyphicus* from Greek *hierogluphikos*, literally 'sacred carving', from *hieros* 'sacred' + *gluphē* 'carving', because hieroglyphs were associated with priests.] —**hieroglyphically** *adv.*

hieroglyphics /hīrə glíffiks/ *n.* PICTURE WRITING SYSTEM a writing system that uses symbols or pictures to denote objects, concepts, or sounds, originally and especially in the writing system of ancient Egypt (*takes a singular verb*) ■ *npl.* STH HARD TO DECIPHER writing that is difficult to decipher, or other indecipherable symbols (*informal*) (*takes a plural verb*)

Hieroglyph: Detail of wall painting in the tomb of Inherkha, Thebes, Egypt (1279BC–1212BC)

hierogram /hīrō gram/ *n.* a symbol with religious significance

Hieronymian /hīrə nímmi ən/, **Hieronymic** /-nímmik/ *adj.* relating to St Jerome [Mid-17thC. Formed from Latin *Hieronymus* 'JEROME'.]

hierophant /hīrō fant/ *n.* **1.** EXPLAINER OF MYSTERIES sb who interprets and expounds the meaning of obscure and mysterious matters, especially sacred doctrines or mysteries **2.** INTERPRETER OF EVENTS sb who explains or comments on everyday matters (*formal*) **3.** ANCIENT GREEK PRIEST a priest who revealed the mysteries at the annual festival of Eleusis in ancient Greece [Late 17thC. Via late Latin *hierophanta* from Greek *hierophantēs*, literally 'sacred person who reveals sth' from *hieros* 'sacred' + *phen-*, the stem of *phainein* 'to reveal'.] —**hierophantic** /hīrə fántik/ *adj.* —**hierophantically** /-fántikli/ *adv.*

hifalutin *adj.* = **highfalutin**

hi-fi /hī fī/ (*plural* **hi-fis**) *n.* **1.** HIGH-QUALITY AUDIO EQUIPMENT a set of high-quality equipment for reproducing and usually recording sound, which may include a CD player, tape deck, turntable, tuner, amplifier, and speakers **2.** = **high fidelity** [Mid-20thC. Shortening of HIGH FIDELITY.]

higgledy-piggledy /hígg'ldi pígg'ldi/ *adj.* DISORGANIZED disorganized and untidy ■ *adv.* MESSILY in a disorganized, untidy state ○ *'Jasper had already unpacked her young lady's things and laid them higgledy-piggledy in the spacious wardrobe'.* (L. T. Meade, *A Very Naughty Girl*; 1907) [Late 16thC. Origin uncertain: probably from the idea of pigs being messy, or being huddled together when herded.]

high /hī/ *adj.* **1.** OF GREAT HEIGHT extending a long way from bottom to top, especially when viewed from the bottom **2.** ABOVE SB OR STH situated in a position above the onlooker or above sb or sth else referred to ○ *The window was too high for him to see in.* **3.** IN HEIGHT ABOVE STH above or stretching upwards from a known base level such as sea or ground level ○ *ten feet high* **4.** ABOVE AVERAGE greater than the normal or average, e.g. in quantity, number, quality, intensity, or cost, or well above a smaller or lower level or amount ○ *a high cost of living* **5.** MUSIC RAISED IN PITCH raised in pitch towards the upper end of a range of sound ○ *can hit the high notes* **6.** METEOROL BLOWING STRONGLY blowing with a great deal of force ○ *a high wind* **7.** ADVANCED advanced in development or complexity ○ *high finance* **8.** BETTER superior in quality, character, or morals ○ *sets a high example* **9.** WITH ELEVATED RANK important in status or rank ○ *a high official* **10.** VERY FAVOURABLE considering sb or sth to be particularly good ○ *held in high esteem* **11.** AT A PEAK at the busiest or most important stage ○ *high summer* **12.** HAPPY animated and cheerful ○ *in high spirits* **13.** OVEREXCITED overexcited or overstimulated **14.** DRUGS INTOXICATED under the influence of alcohol or drugs (*slang*) **15.** FOOD STRONG-SMELLING OR STRONG-TASTING with a very strong smell or taste, either because it is pleasantly mature or because it has overmatured and has begun to go bad **16.** GEOG FAR FROM EQUATOR at a considerable distance either north or south of the equator ○ *high latitude* **17.** PHON WITH TONGUE RAISED IN MOUTH formed with the back of the tongue close, or relatively close, to the roof of the mouth ○ *high vowel sounds* **18. high, High** CHR RITUALISTIC favouring or involving formal and elaborate ritual and ceremonial **19.** MECH ENG PRODUCING TOP SPEEDS resulting in a relatively large number of revolutions of the driven part as compared with the driving part in a transmission gear, and giving the top speed of travel or rotation ■ *adv.* WAY UP at, in, or into a high position ○ *The balloon rose high in the sky.* ■ *n.* **1.** TOP PLACE a high level or position ○ *an all-time high* **2.** METEOROL = **anticyclone 3.** METEOROL TOP TEMPERATURE the highest temperature reached or expected to be reached in a particular period ○ *Today's high will be in the nineties.* **4.** ELATED STATE a state of euphoria (*informal*) **5.** INTOXICATED STATE a state of intoxication by drugs or alcohol **6.** EDUC HIGH SCHOOL a high school (*informal*) ○ *She goes to Kinross High.* **7.** *US* MECH ENG = **top** (*informal*) [Old English *hēah*. Ultimately from a prehistoric Germanic word that is also the ancestor of German *hoch* and Dutch *hoog*.] ◇ **high and dry 1.** stranded and abandoned, and perhaps helpless **2.** beyond the reach of water ◇ **high and mighty** arrogant and self-important ◇ **run high** to be at a level of great intensity

WORD KEY: CULTURAL NOTE

High Noon, a film by US director Fred Zinnemann (1952). In this classic Western, lawman Will Kane (Gary Cooper) valiantly awaits and then confronts a killer seeking revenge for his recent incarceration. Shot in real time, the film's suspense is heightened by close-ups of Kane's anxious expressions and of clocks ticking steadily towards the moment of truth.

highball /hī bawl/ *n.* *US* BEVERAGES SPIRITS WITH WATER OR CARBONATED DRINK a long drink consisting of spirits mixed with ice and water or a carbonated drink ■ *vti.* (**-balls, -balling, -balled**) TRANSP GO AT HIGH SPEED to travel, or drive a vehicle, at high speed (*slang*) [From the earlier sense 'a type of poker played with balls and a tall glass receptacle']

high beam *n.* *US* = **full beam**

high blood pressure *n.* abnormally high arterial blood pressure. It encompasses abnormal elevation of either systolic pressure, the peak blood pressure with each beat, or diastolic pressure, the running pressure between heart beats, or both.

highborn /hī bawrn/ *adj.* born into an aristocratic family (*literary*)

highboy /hī boy/ *n.* *US* = **tallboy**

high brass *n.* brass consisting of 65 per cent copper and 35 per cent zinc

highbred /hī bred/ *adj.* **1.** AGRIC FROM GOOD STOCK born of or descended from superior breeding stock **2.** REFINED showing or having refined manners (*archaic*)

highbrow /hī brow/ *adj.* INTELLECTUAL dealing with serious subjects, especially cultural subjects, in an intellectual way ○ *'conceits which would be only highbrow wisecracks in inferior writing have fused into a form that can only be called inevitable, the way it should be'* (Northrop Frye, *The Bush Garden*; 1972) ■ *n.* INTELLECTUAL PERSON sb with highbrow interests or tastes [From the idea that a high forehead signifies greater brain power] —**highbrowism** *n.*

highchair /hī cháir/ *n.* a small chair with long legs and often a detachable tray, for older babies and toddlers to use at mealtimes

High Church *n.* a section of the Anglican Church that stresses the essential unity of Anglican Christianity with Roman Catholicism and Orthodoxy, holds traditional views about the sacraments, and favours ritual and ceremony

high-class *adj.* **1.** FOR THE RICH appealing to the rich or sophisticated, and therefore usually expensive **2.** SOPHISTICATED showing or having the kind of sophistication associated with wealth

high comedy *n.* comedy with humour depending on witty dialogue and a clever plot rather than slapstick

high command *n.* **1.** SENIOR OFFICERS the senior officers in a country's armed forces, who jointly take decisions on strategy and tactics **2.** MILITARY HEADQUARTERS the main headquarters of a military force

High Commission *n.* the embassy of one country of the Commonwealth of Nations in another Commonwealth country

High Commissioner *n.* **1.** AMBASSADOR the chief representative of a country of the Commonwealth of Nations in another Commonwealth country **2.** HEAD OF INTERNATIONAL COMMISSION the person leading an international commission

high-concept *adj.* used to describe a film that contains features likely to attract a large audience, e.g. big stars, fast action, and glamour

high country *n.* lands that are in a mountainous region, but not so high as to have no pastoral or agricultural use (*hyphenated when used before a noun*)

high court *n.* in the United States, a principal or supreme court, especially the Supreme Court of the United States

High Court *n.* **1.** MOST SENIOR COURT a country's principal court, especially the High Court of Justice in England and Wales, or the High Court of Justiciary in Scotland **2.** FEDERAL SUPREME COURT in Australia, the federal supreme court and final court of appeal **3.** MAIN CIVIL AND CRIMINAL COURT in New Zealand, a civil and criminal court inferior to the Court of Appeal but superior to the District Courts **4.** HIGHEST STATE COURT in India, the highest court of a state

High Court of Justice *n.* the principal court for civil cases in England and Wales

High Court of Justiciary *n.* the principal criminal court in Scotland

high day *n.* a day of religious celebration (*archaic*) ◇ **on high days and holidays** on special occasions

high-definition television *n.* a television system with twice the scanning capacity of normal television systems, allowing for far greater definition and less flickering

high-end *adj.* sophisticated and discerning, or likely to appeal to sophisticated and discerning people

high-energy *adj.* **1.** CHEM RELEASING A LOT OF ENERGY used to describe chemical reactions that take place with the release of substantial amounts of energy **2.** FOOD PROVIDING ENERGY EASILY used, especially in marketing, to describe foods that can be broken down by the body to provide a ready supply of energy, e.g. glucose drinks or high-sugar items such as honey

high-energy physics *n.* = particle physics

Higher /híˈər/ *n.* **1.** SCOTTISH SCHOOL EXAMINATION in Scotland, an examination in a single subject, usually taken after five or six years of secondary education (*often used before a noun*) **2.** EXAM PASS in Scotland, a pass in a Higher examination

higher criticism *n.* the establishment of the sources of biblical texts, using the techniques of textual criticism —**higher critic** *n.*

higher education *n.* education generally begun after Highers or A-levels, usually carried out at a university or college, and involving study for a degree, diploma, or similar advanced qualification

higher law *n.* a moral law or ethical principle that is believed to be of greater validity than earthly law

higher learning *n.* education or study at university level (*formal or literary*)

higher mathematics *n.* mathematics at an abstract and sophisticated level, including number theory and topology (*takes a singular verb*)

higher-up *n.* sb in a position of authority or at a higher level in a hierarchy (*informal*)

highest common factor *n.* the highest number that can be exactly divided into each member of a set of numbers. The highest common factor of 12, 60, and 84 is 12. US term **greatest common divisor**

high explosive *n.* a liquid or solid substance that undergoes explosive decomposition (**detonation**) without burning to produce a large release of energy. High explosives are used for rock blasting and have military applications.

highfalutin /hífə loˈotin, -tʼn/, **hifalutin, highfaluting** /-loˈoting/ *adj.* affecting a grand style in an un-

convincing way (*informal*) [Mid-19thC. Origin of *falutin* uncertain: perhaps from *fluting*, the present participle of FLUTE.]

high fashion *n.* = haute couture

high fidelity *n.* extremely high-quality sound reproduction with minimal distortion, achieved with electronic equipment (*hyphenated when used before a noun*)

high-five *n.* US an informal greeting or gesture of elation or victory in which sb slaps a raised palm against the raised palm of sb else (*slang*) —**high-five** *vti.*

high-flier, high-flyer *n.* sb who enjoys great success, especially professional success, or who seems destined for great achievement

high-flown *adj.* giving an unconvincing appearance of being elegant, refined, or exalted ○ '*a warning against high-flown pretensions*' (Henry James, *Roderick Hudson*; 1876)

high-flyer *n.* = high-flier

high frequency *n.* a radio frequency in the range 3–30 MHz or of wavelength 10–100 metres (*hyphenated when used before a noun*)

high gear *n.* US = top gear

High German *n.* the form of German spoken originally in the southern part of the country that gave rise to a literary and cultured form of the language that has become standard German —**High-German** *adj.*

high-grade *adj.* of a high quality, especially because of purity or concentration of contents

high ground *n.* **1.** RAISED AREA an area of land higher than its surroundings **2.** SUPERIORITY a position of superiority or advantage over others

high-handed *adj.* overbearing and inconsiderate of other people's views or sensibilities —**high-handedly** *adv.* —**high-handedness** *n.*

high-hat *adj.* SNOBBISH snobbish and arrogant (*archaic informal*) ■ *n.* SNOB a snob (*archaic informal*) ■ *vti.* (**high-hats, high-hatting, high-hatted**) US, Can BEHAVE SNOBBISHLY to treat sb in a haughty, disdainful way (*dated*)

high-hat cymbals *npl.* a pair of cymbals on a stand, with the upper one made to rise and fall against the lower one by the drummer's foot

high heels *npl.* women's shoes with tall slender heels that raise the back of the foot off the ground

High Holidays, High Holy Days *npl.* the Jewish festivals of Rosh Hashana and Yom Kippur, along with the days in between

high horse *n.* an attitude of arrogance and haughty disregard for others (*informal*) ○ *is on her high horse this morning* ○ *told him to get off his high horse*

high hurdles *n.* a track event for men, in which the athletes cover a distance of 110 m outdoors, jumping over hurdles 107 cm/42 in high (*takes a singular or plural verb*)

highjack *v.* = hijack

high jinks /híˈjingks/, **hijinks** *n.* good-humoured boisterousness, frequently including mischievousness and pranks (*informal*) (*takes a singular or plural verb*)

high jump *n.* a sporting event in which the athletes run forward to gain momentum, and then jump over a horizontal pole. The pole is raised higher in each successive round until all competitors have failed to get over it. —**high jumper** *n.* —**high jumping** *n.* ◇ **be for the high jump** to be about to be scolded, punished severely, or dismissed from a job (*informal*)

highland /híˈlənd/ *n.* HILLY LAND hilly ground, higher than its surroundings ■ **highlands** *npl.* HILLY AREA an area or region that is largely hilly or mountainous. ◇ **Highlands** ■ *adj.* RELATING TO HIGHLANDS relating to or coming from highlands

Highland[1] *adj.* relating to, found in, or originating from the Scottish Highlands

Highland[2] /híˈlənd/ council area of northern Scotland. Population: 208,300 (1995). Area: 25,784 sq. km/9,955 sq. mi.

Highland cattle *npl.* a smallish breed of hardy cattle with long shaggy reddish brown hair and long curved horns, originally bred in the Highlands of Scotland

Highland Clearances *npl.* the forcible removal of tenants from their land by many 18th- and 19th-century landlords in the Scottish Highlands, usually to introduce sheep farming

Highland dress *n.* a modern version of the traditional clothing of Highland men, comprising a tartan kilt, a sporran, knee-length socks, a tweed or plain wool jacket, and brogues. Highland dress is worn, e.g., by some Scottish regiments, by pipe bands, and by some Scotsmen or men of Scottish descent, especially on special occasions.

highlander /híˈləndər/ *n.* sb who was born in or lives in a highland area

Highlander *n.* sb who was born or who lives in the Scottish Highlands

Highland fling *n.* an energetic Scottish solo dance originally danced by men in Highland dress, but now also by women and children, most frequently in competitions at Highland Games

Highland Games *n.* an outdoor meeting at which there are competitions in various sports, e.g. tossing the caber, in Scottish dancing, and in piping (*takes a singular or plural verb*)

Highlands /híˈləndz/ mountainous area of mainland Scotland, north and west of a line from Dumbarton in the west to Stonehaven in the east

high-level *adj.* involving participation by people at a high level in their organization or country, e.g. politicians, civil servants, or company directors

high-level language *n.* a computer programming language that has syntax and grammar crudely approximating a natural language, e.g. English, and requires translation to a low-level language that a computer can recognize. The pioneering high-level languages, FORTRAN, COBOL, and ALGOL, have largely been supplanted by BASIC, FORTH, PASCAL, and C, especially for educational and personal-computer applications.

high-level waste *n.* radioactive waste material retaining sufficient activity that it needs to be continuously cooled

high life *n.* the luxurious lifestyle of fashionable society (*often used ironically*)

highlife /híˈlîf/ *n.* a style of music that blends West African elements with American jazz forms and is popular in West Africa

highlight /híˈlît/ *n.* **1.** BEST PART the most memorable, important, or exciting part of an experience or event **2.** REPRESENTATIVE PART an exemplary extract from a larger work that, along with others, is meant to represent it ○ *gave us highlights of the President's speech* **3.** PAINTING, PHOTOGRAPHY CONTRASTING PALE AREA an area in a very light tone in a painting or photograph that provides contrast, illumination, or the appearance of illumination **4.** PHOTOGRAPHY REFLECTION the reflection of a light source in a picture, e.g. the reflection of a studio light in shiny hair or the reflection of light in sb's eye ■ **highlights** *npl.* HAIR LIGHT STREAKS IN HAIR strands of hair that are deliberately made lighter than the rest of the hair ■ *vt.* (**-lights, -lighting, -lighted**) **1.** EMPHASIZE to draw attention to sth, or make sth particularly prominent or noticeable ○ *The report highlights the problems of inner-city areas.* **2.** MARK WITH HIGHLIGHTER to mark sth, e.g. parts of a text, with a highlighter pen **3.** HAIR PUT STREAKS IN to put highlights in sb's hair **4.** PAINTING ADD LIGHT AREAS IN to add highlights to parts of a picture to provide contrast, illumination, or the appearance of illumination

highlighter /híˈlîtər/ *n.* **1.** MARKER PEN a broad-tipped felt pen, often with transparent, brightly coloured ink, for marking important passages of text **2.** COSMETICS FACE COSMETIC a cosmetic for the face that is used to emphasize features such as the eyes or cheekbones

high-low *n.* **1.** CARDS VARIANT OF POKER a variety of poker in which both high and low hands win **2.** BRIDGE SIGNAL IN BRIDGE a signal to a bridge partner to lead a particular suit

highly /híli/ adv. **1.** EXTREMELY very much ○ *highly likely to succeed* **2.** FAVOURABLY very favourably ○ *highly regarded* **3.** IN HIGH PLACE in a high position or rank ○ *highly placed officials who denied the story* **4.** GREATLY to a great extent or in many ways ○ *highly improbable*

highly-strung adj. by nature tense, nervous, or easily upset. US term **high-strung**

high-maintenance adj. requiring an excessive amount of attention or effort to maintain (*informal*)

High Mass n. an elaborate Roman Catholic Mass in which a choir sings much of the service. It is usually celebrated by more than one priest.

high-minded adj. having or showing high moral principles —**high-mindedly** adv. —**high-mindedness** n.

highmost /hí mōst/ adj. highest (*literary*)

high-muck-a-muck /hí múkə múk/, **high-muckety-muck** /-múkəti-/ n. US sb in a position of importance and authority who behaves in an overbearing way (*informal*) [Mid-19thC. Origin uncertain: probably by folk etymology from Chinook Jargon *hiyu muckamuck*, literally 'ten portions of choice whalemeat', by association with HIGH.]

Highness /hínəss/ n. a title and style of address for members of a royal family other than a sovereign

high noon n. **1.** NOON EXACTLY the exact moment of noon **2.** PEAK OF ACHIEVEMENT the high point or most creative part of sb's career or achievements **3. high noon, High Noon** CRUCIAL TIME a time of confronting a serious problem or making a hard decision

high-octane adj. **1.** ENERGY WITH HIGH OCTANE CONTENT used to describe fuel that has a high octane content **2.** DYNAMIC showing or demanding a high degree of commitment and effort in a drive for success (*informal*)

high-pitched adj. **1.** AT TOP OF SOUND RANGE towards the upper end of the range of audible sound **2.** BUILDING WITH STEEP SLOPE having a very steep slope **3.** EMOTIONAL extremely emotional and intense **4.** FORMAL AND ELABORATE in a formal and flowery style

high places npl. positions of power, authority, or influence

high-powered, **high-power** adj. **1.** BUSINESS DYNAMIC possessing great energy and impressive ability, especially as displayed in a professional environment ○ *a high-powered sales pitch* **2.** INFLUENTIAL having a lot of power or influence **3.** OPTICS GREATLY ENLARGING giving a high magnification **4.** TECH VERY POWERFUL operating much more powerfully, or able to handle material of greater complexity and more quickly, than others of the same type

high-pressure adj. **1.** TECH OPERATING AT GREATER THAN NORMAL PRESSURE using, or designed to withstand, forces exerted by liquid or gas at pressures higher than normal atmospheric pressure **2.** STRESSFUL causing stress, e.g. from deadlines or excessive demands ○ *She's at her best in high-pressure situations.* **3.** PERSISTENT aggressively persistent in seeking to bring about a result

high priest n. **1.** MAIN PROPONENT the leading figure propounding a doctrine or ideology **2.** JUDAISM JEWISH CHIEF PRIEST a chief priest, especially the head of the priestly caste at the time of the Temple in Jerusalem **3.** CHR MORMON PRIEST a man who is a priest in the Church of the Latter Day Saints, belonging to the order of Melchizedek —**high priesthood** n.

high priestess n. **1.** RELIG WOMAN RELIGIOUS LEADER a woman who leads a religion, or a religious group **2.** MAIN PROPONENT the leading woman propounding a doctrine or ideology

high profile n. a prominent position or presence in the public eye

high-profile adj. in or intended to be in the public eye, e.g. to attract attention, support, or business

high relief n. a version of relief sculpture in which the carving projects from the background to more than half its natural depth (*hyphenated when used before a noun*)

High Renaissance n. the period in European art between about 1490 and 1520, when the work of Leonardo da Vinci, Michelangelo, Raphael, and other great artists reached the highest point of Renaissance perfection

high resolution n. the use in a video display or printed image of a large number of dots or lines to portray an image in great detail (*hyphenated when used before a noun*)

high-rise adj. **1.** ARCHIT MULTISTOREY consisting of several storeys, but usually fewer than for a skyscraper **2.** TRANSP WITH HIGH HANDLEBARS used to describe a child's bicycle that has small wheels, very high handlebars, and a long narrow seat ■ n. **1.** ARCHIT TALL BUILDING a multistorey building **2.** TRANSP HIGH-RISE BICYCLE a child's high-rise bicycle

high-risk recreation n. a recreational activity that involves an element of danger, e.g. hang-gliding, skydiving, bungee jumping, and whitewater rafting. Experiencing the sensation of risk is an important motive for participation.

high road n. **1.** TRANSP MAIN ROAD a main road, usually in a town or village **2.** DIRECT ROUTE the easiest or most direct way to somewhere

high roller n. US, Can (*slang*) **1.** FIN BIG SPENDER a person or organization that spends money freely and extravagantly **2.** LEISURE GAMBLER a gambler who plays for high stakes —**high-rolling** adj.

high school n. **1.** SECONDARY SCHOOL a secondary school, for pupils aged 11 to 16, 17, or 18 **2.** UPPER SECONDARY SCHOOL in the United States a school that includes grades 9 or 10 to 12

high seas npl. the open ocean, not under any nation's jurisdiction

high season n. the most popular time of year for holidays, when resorts are at their busiest. US term **peak season**

high sign n. US a secret signal, often prearranged, given as a warning or to convey information

high society n. the fashionable wealthy classes in society

high-sounding adj. grandiose and pretentious but unlikely to come to anything

high-spirited adj. lively and full of fun or mischief —**high-spiritedly** adv. —**high-spiritedness** n.

high spot n. the most memorable, important, or exciting part of an experience or event (*informal*)

high-stakes adj. in which sb is likely to win or lose a great deal ○ *'Everyone is getting in the starting blocks for a high-stakes fight'. (The Washington Post; November 1998)*

high-sticking n. in ice hockey, the offence of holding the hockey stick higher than is allowed by the rules

high street, **High Street** n. **1.** MAIN STREET IN TOWN a principal street where the main shops are located **2.** ECON RETAIL TRADE the ordinary retail sector of the national economy (*informal*) **3.** ECON CONSUMERS GENERALLY the public, when viewed as consumers (*informal*)

high-strung adj. US, Can = **highly-strung**

high style n. the most up-to-date and stylish fashion, especially in clothing (*hyphenated when used before a noun*)

high table n. a table in a large dining hall in some schools and university colleges at which the staff, principal teachers, or fellows sit

hightail /hí tayl/ (**-tails**, **-tailing**, **-tailed**) vti. to rush away from a place (*slang*) [With reference to the erect tail of a fleeing animal]

high tea n. a meal served in the late afternoon or early evening, consisting of a cooked dish, usually hot, with bread and butter, cakes, and tea

high tech, **hi-tech** n. **1.** TECH ADVANCED TECHNOLOGY advanced technology and state-of-the-art techniques, especially in electronic engineering **2.** DESIGN PLAIN AND SIMPLE DESIGN a style of architecture and interior design that makes use of metal, glass, and plastic in a simple utilitarian way —**high-tech** adj.

high technology n. = high tech n. 1

high-tension adj. ELEC designed for or operating at high voltage

high-test adj. ENERGY = high octane

high tide n. **1.** GEOG HIGHEST POINT OF TIDE the tide at its highest level **2.** NAUT MOMENT OF HIGHEST TIDE the time when the tide reaches its highest level **3.** PEAK OF STH the culmination or high point of sth

high-toned adj. culturally, morally, or socially superior (*dated*)

high treason n. treason against sb's own sovereign or country

high-up n. sb who holds a senior position in an organization (*informal; usually used in the plural*)

highveld /hí velt/ n. the high-altitude grassy plateau of Gauteng and neighbouring provinces in the northern part of South Africa [Late 19thC. Partial translation of Afrikaans *hoëveld*.]

high-voltage adj. ELEC involving a voltage higher than 650 volts

high water n. GEOG, NAUT **1.** = high tide n. 1, high tide n. 2 **2.** HIGHEST WATER LEVEL the highest level reached by any stretch of water, e.g. during a flood (*hyphenated when used before a noun*) **3.** TIME OF HIGHEST WATER the time when the water level of a river or other stretch of water is at its highest

high-water mark n. **1.** GEOG, NAUT HIGHEST WATER LEVEL the highest level reached by any natural stretch of water, principally by the sea at high tide, but also, e.g., a river during a flood **2.** GEOG, NAUT MARK SHOWING HIGHEST LEVEL a mark drawn to indicate the highest level reached by any natural stretch of water **3.** PEAK OF STH a high point in an enterprise ○ *Winning the book award was the high-water mark in her career.*

high-water pants npl. US trousers that are too short, especially because the person wearing them has grown out of them (*informal*)

highway /hí way/ n. **1.** TRANSP PUBLIC ROAD any public road (*formal*) (*often used before a noun*) **2.** US, Can TRANSP MAIN ROAD a principal road, especially one that connects towns or cities and is part of a numbered system (*often used before a noun*) **3.** DIRECT WAY a direct route or course ○ *the highway to fame*

Highway Code n. a government-published booklet containing rules and information relating to the use of public roads, or the body of conventions that govern road use

highwayman /hí waymən/ (*plural* **-men** /-mən/) n. formerly, sb who forced people travelling by road to stop, usually at gunpoint, and robbed them

highway patrol n. the law enforcement agency that patrols the public highways in some states of the United States

highway robbery n. US = daylight robbery (*informal*)

High Weald /hí weeld/ region between the North and South Downs, covering the counties of East and West Sussex, Kent, and Surrey, southeastern England. Area: 1,460 sq. km/569 sq. mi.

high wire n. a tightrope stretched high above the ground on which circus performers balance and perform acrobatics

high-wire adj. holding the possibility of great risk, e.g. to life or reputation

High Wycombe /hí wíkəm/ furniture-making town in Buckinghamshire, south-central England. Population: 71,718 (1991).

HIH abbr. **1.** Her Imperial Highness **2.** His Imperial Highness

hijack /hí jak/, **highjack** vt. (**-jacks**, **-jacking**, **-jacked**) **1.** SEIZE AIRCRAFT, SHIP, OR TRAIN to take control of a public transport vehicle, e.g. a passenger aircraft, while in transit, taking the people on board hostage, and diverting it to another destination **2.** STOP A VEHICLE TO ROB IT to seize a motor vehicle, e.g. an armoured car carrying money, in order to rob it of its contents **3.** STEAL STH FROM A SEIZED VEHICLE to steal merchandise, money, or any other items from a hijacked motor vehicle **4.** STEAL IDEA to take sb else's idea and use it, especially to the exclusion or detriment of the person from whom it was taken (*informal*) ■ n. = hijacking [Early 20thC. Origin uncertain.] —**hijacker** n.

hijacking /hí jaking/ n. the forcible seizure of a public transport vehicle, e.g. a passenger aircraft, while in transit, taking those on board hostage, and compelling diversion of the vehicle to another destination

hijinks *npl.* = **highjinks**

hike /hīk/ *v.* (**hikes, hiking, hiked**) **1.** *vti.* **TAKE A LONG WALK** to go for a long walk in the countryside, usually for pleasure **2.** *vti.* **MIL GO ON A TRAINING MARCH** to march in a training exercise **3.** *vt.* **RAISE AMOUNT OF STH** to increase taxes, prices, or the level or quantity of sth suddenly and by a large amount ○ *rumours that the banks plan to hike up interest rates* **4.** *vt.* **PULL STH UPWARDS** to pull or raise sth with a sudden strong movement ■ *n.* **1.** **PLEASURABLE LONG WALK** a long walk, usually across country for pleasure **2.** **SUDDEN LARGE INCREASE IN STH** a sudden large increase in prices, taxes, or the level or quantity of sth ○ *an unexpected hike in interest rates* [Early 19thC. Origin uncertain: perhaps an alteration of HITCH.] ◇ **take a hike** *US* to leave abruptly, or, more often, used to tell sb who is unwelcome to leave (*slang*)

hike out *vi.* Can, US SAILING to lean backwards over the side of a sailboat to counterbalance the wind in the sails and keep the boat flat in the water

hike up *vti.* to move up or become moved up from the proper position ○ *Her coat had hiked up at the back*

hiker /hīkər/ *n.* sb who takes long walks in the country, usually for pleasure

hilarious /hi laíri əss/ *adj.* causing great amusement [Early 19thC. Formed from Latin *hilaris* 'cheerful', from Greek *hilaros*.] —**hilariously** *adv.* —**hilariousness** *n.*

───── **WORD KEY: SYNONYMS** ─────
See Synonyms at *funny*.

hilarity /hi lárrəti/ *n.* amusement or merry laughter [15thC. Via French *hilarité* from Latin *hilaritas*, from *hilaris* (see HILARIOUS).]

Hilary term /hílləri-/ *n.* the spring term at Oxford University and the Inns of Court [Late 16thC. Named after *Hilarius*, bishop of Poitiers, France (died 367), whose Anglican feast day is 13 January.]

Hilbert /hílbərt/, **David** (1862–1943) German mathematician. He is best known for reducing geometry to a series of abstract equations, thereby giving it a more mathematical foundation.

Hildegard (of Bingen) /híldə gaard əv bíngən/, St (1098–1179) German writer and composer. She is remembered for her book of visions, *Scivias* (1141–52), and for the devotional music and poetry she wrote.

hili plural of **hilus**

hill /hil/ *n.* **1.** **HIGH LAND** an area of land, usually rounded in shape, that is higher than the surrounding land but not as high as a mountain ○ *the hills north of Tavistock* **2.** **GRADIENT IN ROAD** a slope or gradient in a road ○ *You'll need to drop into second gear for this hill.* **3.** **PILE OF EARTH** a pile of sth such as earth ■ *vt.* (**hills, hilling, hilled**) **MAKE EARTH INTO PILE** to pile up earth, especially around the base of plants [Old English *hyll*. Ultimately from an Indo-European word meaning 'to be prominent' that is also the ancestor of English *column*, *culminate*, and *excellent*.] —**hiller** *n.* ◇ **over the hill** at an age considered too advanced in years for sth or supposedly past the prime of life

Hill *n.* Capitol Hill (*informal*) ○ *has worked on the Hill for two years*

Hill /hil/, **Archibald** (1886–1977) British physiologist. He was joint winner of the Nobel Prize in physiology or medicine in 1922 for his research into the production of heat in muscle contractions. Full name **Archibald Vivian Hill**

Hill, David (1802–70) British photographer and painter. He is remembered for his collaboration with Robert Adamson on the production of about 1,500 photographs. Full name **David Octavius Hill**

Hill, Ernestine (1899–1972) Australian author. She wrote the novels *The Great Australian Loneliness* (1937) and *My Love Must Wait* (1941).

Hill, Graham (1929–75) British racing driver. The father of Damon Hill, he was winner of the Grand Prix World Championship (1962, 1968) and the Indianapolis 500 (1966). Full name **Norman Graham Hill**

Hillary /hílləri/, **Sir Edmund** (b. 1919) New Zealand mountaineer and explorer. On 29 May 1953, he and Tenzing Norgay became the first climbers to reach the summit of Mount Everest. Full name **Sir Edmund Perceval Hillary**

hillbilly /híl bili/ (*plural* **-lies**) *n.* US a term used by people from the country to describe themselves with pride, but used by others as an insult to mean sb ignorant and unsophisticated (*informal*) (*offensive in some contexts*) [Early 20thC. *Billy* pet-form of the name *William*.]

hillbilly music *n.* a variety of country music, especially the music of the Appalachian Mountains, that features fiddles, banjos, guitars, and hammer dulcimers

hill climb *n.* a competition in which car or motorcycle drivers compete to set the fastest time in reaching the top of a steep slope

hill country *n.* NZ hilly country, or such land used as pasture for sheep or cattle

hillcrest /híl krest/ *n.* the summit or the highest ridge of a hill

Hilliard /hílli ərd/, **Nicholas** (1547–1619) British painter and goldsmith. The founder of the English school of painting miniatures, his portraits include Mary, Queen of Scots, and Elizabeth I.

hill myna, **hill mynah** *n.* a black bird belonging to the starling family and native to southern Asia, often kept as a cage bird because of its ability to mimic human words. Latin name: *Gracula religiosa*.

hillock /híllək/ *n.* a small hill or mound —**hillocked** *adj.* —**hillocky** *adj.*

Hills hoist /hílz-/ *n.* Aus a metal structure consisting of a pole surmounted by a rotating metal frame that supports clothes lines [Named after its inventor, Lance Hill]

hillside /híl sīd/ *n.* the slope or side of a hill

hill station *n.* a village or government office in the northern hills or low mountain ranges of the Indian subcontinent, established by the British as respite from the summer heat for officials and their families

hilltop /híl top/ *n.* the summit of a hill

hilly /hílli/ (**-ier, -iest**) *adj.* **1.** **WITH MANY HILLS** having many hills ○ *hilly countryside* **2.** **WITH STEEP SLOPE** having a steep incline

hilt /hilt/ *n.* the handle of a sword, knife, or dagger [Old English *hilt(e)*. Ultimately from a prehistoric Germanic word that is perhaps also the ancestor of English *helve*.] ◇ **(up) to the hilt** to the maximum

Hilton Head /hílton héd/ ◇ **Sea Islands**

hilum /hīləm/ (*plural* **-la** /hílə/) *n.* a scar on the seed of a plant indicating where it was attached to the ovule [Mid-17thC. From Latin, 'trifle'. The current meanings evolved from the belief that the Latin word originally meant 'sth that adheres to a bean'.]

hilus /hīləss/ (*plural* **-li** /-lī/) *n.* an opening through which blood vessels and nerves enter and leave an organ. US term **hilum** [Mid-19thC. From modern Latin, an alteration of HILUM.]

him (*stressed*) /him/; (*unstressed*) /im/ *pron.* used to refer to a man, boy, or male animal who has been previously mentioned or whose identity is known (*used as the object of a verb or preposition*) ○ *She handed him the phone without a word.* ○ *John closed the door behind him.* ○ *It's him, I know it's him.*

HIM *abbr.* **1.** Her Imperial Majesty **2.** His Imperial Majesty

Himalaya /hímmə láy ə/, **Himalayas** /-əz/ mountain system in Asia, forming the northern boundary of the Indian subcontinent. Its highest peak, and the highest mountain in the world, is Mount Everest,

8,848 m/29,028 ft. Length: 2,414 km/1,500 mi. —**Himalayan** *adj.*

Himalaya

Himalia /hi maáli ə/ *n.* a small natural satellite of Jupiter, discovered in 1904. It is approximately 180km/112 mi. in diameter. [Late 20thC. Origin uncertain: probably via Greek *himalis*, a name for DEMETER, the goddess of agriculture, fertility, and marriage, from, ultimately, *himalios* 'abundant'.]

himation /hi mátti on/ *n.* a loose outer garment worn by men and women in ancient Greece, consisting of a large rectangular piece of cloth draped over one shoulder and under the opposite arm [Mid-19thC. From Greek, literally 'small garment', formed from *hima* 'garment', from *hennunai* 'to clothe'.]

Himmler /hímmlər/, **Heinrich** (1900–45) German Nazi politician. The head of the Nazi police forces (1936–45), he committed suicide rather than face trial for his part in the Holocaust.

himself (*stressed*) /him sélf/; (*unstressed*) /im sélf/ CORE MEANING: the form of 'him' used in reflexive and emphatic contexts ○ *After a final struggle with himself, he handed the papers over.* ○ *If he himself doesn't know what he's doing, I don't see how I can help her.* ○ *He did it himself.*
pron. **1.** **REFERRING TO MALE SUBJECT OF VERB** used to refer to the same man, boy, or male animal as the subject of the verb ○ *He decided to treat himself.* ○ *his sense of pride in himself* **2.** **USED FOR EMPHASIS** used to emphasize or clarify which man, boy, or male animal is being referred to, often introducing a note of surprise or awe ○ *a visit from the Prince himself* **3.** **ALONE OR WITHOUT HELP** used to show that a man, boy, or male animal is alone or unaided ○ *sitting by himself in a corner* ○ *tied his shoelaces himself* **4.** **NORMAL SELF** his normal self in terms of personality, health, or behaviour ○ *not feeling himself* **5.** *Scotland, Ireland* **IMPORTANT MALE PERSON** an important, or often self-important, man or boy (*informal; often used ironically*) ○ *Himself is wanting a word.*

Himyarite /hímmyə rīt/ *n.* (*plural* **-ites** or **-ite**) MEMBER OF ANCIENT ARABIAN PEOPLE a member of an ancient people who lived in southern parts of the Arabian Peninsula ■ *adj.* **RELATING TO HIMYARITES** relating to or typical of the Himyarites or their culture [Mid-19thC. Formed from *Himyar*, the name of a legendary king of Yemen.] —**Himyarite** *adj.*

Himyaritic /hímmyə ríttik/ *n.* an extinct language spoken by the ancient Himyarites in southwestern Arabia. It belongs to the Semitic branch of the Afro-Asiatic family of African languages. —**Himyaritic** *adj.*

Hinayana /heenə yaánə/ *n.* the form of Buddhism, mainly found in Sri Lanka and Southeast Asia, characterized by adherence to the early Pali scriptures and the nontheistic pursuit of purification through Nirvana [Mid-19thC. From Sanskrit, literally 'lesser vehicle'. From its fewer followers when compared with MAHAYANA Buddhism.] —**Hinayanist** *n.* —**Hinayanistic** *adj.*

Hinchinbrook Island /hínchinbròōk-/ island off the northeastern coast of Australia, near the town of Caldwell in northern Queensland. Area: 394 sq. km/152 sq. mi.

Hinckley /híngkli/ town in Leicestershire, central England, situated in the southeast of the county. Population: 40,608 (1991).

Hincks /hingks/, **Sir Francis** (1807–85) Irish-born Canadian colonial administrator. He advocated a bicultural nation and cofounded the Reform Party in 1841.

hind[1] /hīnd/ adj. at or forming the back part of an animal ○ *the hind legs of a donkey* [13thC. Origin uncertain: probably a shortening of Old English *behindan* 'BEHIND'.]

hind[2] /hīnd/ n. **1.** FEMALE DEER a female red deer **2.** SPOTTED MARINE FISH a spotted marine fish that is a type of groper, found in the Atlantic Ocean. Genus: *Epinephelus*. [Old English. Ultimately from an Indo-European word meaning 'hornless' that is also the ancestor of English *scant*.]

Hind. abbr. **1.** Hindi **2.** Hindu **3.** Hindustan **4.** Hindustani

hindbrain /hīnd brayn/ n. the rearmost part of the brain in a vertebrate embryo that develops into the cerebellum, pons, and medulla oblongata

Hindemith /hīndə mit/, **Paul** (1895–1963) German composer and violinist. A pioneer of *Gebrauchsmusic*, a utilitarian approach to composition, he also wrote ballets, concertos, and operas, including *Mathis der Maler* (1938).

Hindenburg /hīndən burg/, **Paul von** (1847–1934) Prussian-born German statesman. A general in World War I, he became second president of the German Republic in 1925, and appointed Hitler chancellor in 1933.

Hindenburg line n. a strong defensive line of fortifications built by the German Army near the border between France and Belgium in 1916–17 and breached by an Allied offensive in 1918 [Early 20thC. Named after Paul von HINDENBURG, who devised the plan.]

hinder[1] /hīndər/ vti. (**hinders, hindering, hindered**) GET IN THE WAY OF to delay or obstruct the development or progress of sb or sth ○ *A heavy snowfall has hindered rescuers' attempts to reach the stranded climbers.* ■ n. SPORTS INTERFERENCE WITH BALL in squash and handball, an opponent's accidental interference, preventing fair and unobstructed return of the ball [Old English *hindrian*. Ultimately from a prehistoric Germanic word that is also the ancestor of English *behind*. The underlying idea is of keeping sth or sb behind.] —**hinderer** n.

—— **WORD KEY: SYNONYMS** ——
hinder, block, hamper, hold back, impede, obstruct
CORE MEANING: to put difficulties in the way of progress **hinder** to delay or slow down the progress of sth, either accidentally or by deliberate interference; **block** to cause a complete stoppage of progress; **hamper** to create or cause restraints or obstacles that may make action or progress extremely difficult; **hold back** an expression used to describe the prevention or restriction of the advance of sb or sth; **impede** a fairly formal word used to describe the prevention of progress, usually to a greater extent than is suggested by 'hinder' or 'hamper'; **obstruct** used to suggest a serious delay in action or progress to a much greater extent than 'hinder', and often, like 'block', a complete stoppage.

hinder[2] /hīndər/ adj. at or towards the rear of sth ○ *at the hinder end of the conference* [Old English. Origin uncertain: perhaps a shortening of Old English *hinderweard* 'backward'.]

Hindi /hīndi/ n. an official language of India that developed from a literary form of Hindustani and is widely used as a lingua franca in many parts of the world. Of the Midland subgroup of the Indic group of the Indo-Iranian branch of Indo-European, Hindi is spoken by about 200 million native speakers, and by about 700 million people as a second language. [Early 19thC. From Urdu *hindī*, from *Hind* 'India'.] —**Hindi** adj.

hindmost /hīnd mōst/ adj. farthest back or last (*dated*)

Hindoo n., adj. = Hindu (*archaic*) ■ adj. HINDU Hindu (*archaic*) —**Hindooism** n.

hindquarter /hīnd kwawrtər/ n. BACK PART OF CARCASS either of the two back quarters of a carcass of beef, lamb, veal, or mutton consisting of one leg and one or two ribs ■ **hindquarters** npl. REAR OF FOUR-LEGGED

ANIMAL the hind legs and adjoining parts of a four-legged animal

hindrance /hīndrənss/ n. **1.** STH IN THE WAY sb or sth that prevents or makes it difficult for sb to do sth **2.** OBSTRUCTION OF PROGRESS the act of obstructing progress

hindsight /hīnd sīt/ n. the ability or opportunity to understand and judge an event or experience after it has occurred ○ *With hindsight we should have chosen a warmer colour for the dining room.* ○ *easy to say with the benefit of hindsight*

Hindu /hín doo, hín doo/ n. **1.** FOLLOWER OF HINDUISM sb who practices the religion of Hinduism **2.** SB FROM HINDUSTAN sb who was born in or brought up in the Indian region of Hindustan ■ adj. **1.** OF HINDUISM relating to or following Hinduism **2.** OF HINDUS OR THEIR CULTURE relating to or typical of Hindus or their culture **3.** RELATING TO INDIA OR ITS PEOPLE relating to or found in India, especially Hindustan, or its people or culture [Mid-17thC. Via Urdu from Persian *Hindū*, from *Hind* 'India'.]

Hinduism /hín doo izəm/ n. the religion of India and the oldest of the worldwide religions, characterized by a belief in reincarnation and the essential unity of forms and theories. Hinduism has a large pantheon of gods and goddesses, and traditionally had a caste system.

Hindu Kush /hín doo koōsh, hin doo-/ mountain system in central Asia mainly in Afghanistan but extending into Jammu and Kashmir. The highest peak is Tirich Mir, 7,690 m/25,230 ft. Length: 800 km/500 mi.

Hindustan /hín doo staan/ n. a loosely defined term that usually refers to the northern Hindi-speaking region of India, stretching from the Himalayas southwards to the Deccan and from Assam in the east to Punjab in the west. The term is sometimes used to indicate the Ganges Plain, or sometimes the whole of India or the Indian subcontinent.

Hindustani n. GROUP OF INDIAN LANGUAGES a group of Indian languages and dialects that includes all forms of both Urdu and Hindi ■ adj. **1.** RELATING TO HINDUSTAN relating to Hindustan or its language, people, or culture **2.** LANGUAGE OF HINDUSTANI relating to the group of languages and dialects that includes all forms of both Urdu and Hindi [Early 17thC. Via Urdu from Persian *Hindūstānī*, literally 'of the Indian country'.]

Hindustani music n. *South Asia* the classical music of northern India

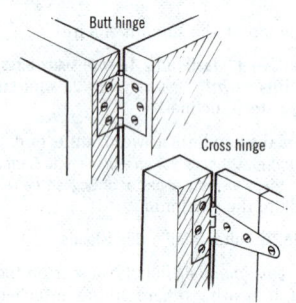

Hinge

hinge /hinj/ (**hinges, hinging, hinged**) n. **1.** JOINT THAT FASTENS DOOR TO FRAME a movable joint of metal or plastic used to fasten two things, e.g. a box and its lid, together and allow one of them to pivot ○ *The hinges on the door need oiling.* **2.** ZOOL LIGAMENT FOR PIVOTING a part in animals that operates like a hinge, as does the ligament that opens and closes the two halves of a clam or other bivalve mollusc **3.** ANAT = **hinge joint 4.** STH VITAL TO OUTCOME sth on which a subsequent action or outcome depends **5.** STICKY PAPER STRIP a thin gummed paper strip that is folded in half to affix postage stamps to the pages of an album [13thC. Origin uncertain: probably from a prehistoric Germanic word that is also the ancestor of English *hang*.] —**hingeless** adj.

hinge on vt. to depend completely on sth ○ *The success of the plan hinges on your full cooperation.*

hinge joint n. a joint, e.g. a knee or elbow joint, that

allows movement in only one plane. Technical name **ginglymus**

Hinkler /híngklər/, **Bert** (1892–1933) Australian aviator. In 1928 he completed the first solo flight from London to Darwin, Australia, in the record time of 16 days. Full name **Herbert John Louis Hinkler**

hinny /hínni/ (plural **-nies**) n. the offspring of a stallion and a female ass [Early 17thC. Via Latin *hinnus* from Greek (g)*innos*.]

Hinshelwood /hínsh'l woŏd/, **Sir Cyril Norman** (1897–1967) British chemist. He was joint winner of the Nobel Prize in chemistry (1956) for his research into the kinetics of chemical chain reactions.

hint /hint/ vi. (**hints, hinting, hinted**) SUGGEST STH INDIRECTLY to convey an idea or information in a roundabout way ○ *The President hinted that he might not seek a second term.* ■ n. **1.** INDIRECT SUGGESTION an idea or information conveyed in a roundabout way ○ *Our daughter has been dropping hints that she'd like a guitar for her birthday.* **2.** PIECE OF ADVICE a useful piece of advice, or a practical suggestion ○ *The book had lots of useful hints on how to grow vegetables.* **3.** VERY SMALL AMOUNT an amount or trace of sth that is so small that it can only just be noticed ○ *The walls need a hint of yellow.* [Early 17thC. Origin uncertain: probably an alteration of obsolete *hent* 'grasp'. Originally meaning 'opportunity', the underlying idea is of sth that may be seized.] —**hintingly** adv. ◇ **take the hint** to understand what is being implied or suggested and to act accordingly

hinterland /híntər land/ n. **1.** LAND ADJACENT TO WATER the land that lies next to coastline or a river **2.** AREA SURROUNDING CITY a region, including communities and rural areas, that surrounds a city and depends on it economically and culturally ○ *an analysis of Milan and its hinterland* **3.** REMOTE COUNTRY REGION a region that is remote from cities or their cultural influence [Late 19thC. From German, from *hinter* 'behind' + *Land* 'land'.]

hip[1] /hip/ n. **1.** SIDE OF BODY BELOW WAIST the region on either side of the body between the waist and the thigh **2.** = **hip joint 3.** ARCHIT ROOF ANGLE the angle formed where two adjacent sides of a sloping roof meet **4.** POINTED END OF OBSTACLE in skateboarding, the place where a ramp or obstacle comes to a point [Old English *hype*. Ultimately from a prehistoric Germanic word that is also the ancestor of German *Hüfte* 'hip'.]

hip[2] /hip/ n. = rosehip [Old English *hēope*. Ultimately from an Indo-European word meaning 'thorn'.]

hip[3] /hip/ (**hipper, hippest**) adj. aware of and influenced by the latest fashions in clothes, music, or ideas (*slang*) ○ *He's one hip dude.* [Early 20thC. Alteration of earlier HEP, of uncertain origin: perhaps from Wolof *hepi* 'to be aware'.] —**hiply** adv. —**hipness** n. ◇ **be hip to sth** US to be aware of sth that is going on (*informal*)

hipbone /híp bōn/ n. either of the two large bones forming the sides of the pelvis and made up of the ilium, ischium, and pubis, fused together in adults. Technical name **innominate bone**

hip boot n. a boot reaching to the hip, usually worn by people who fish

hip flask n. a small flat metal flask, usually containing an alcoholic beverage, that can be carried in a pocket

hip hip hooray interj. used as a cheer to express joy or approval of sb or sth [*Hip* of unknown origin]

hip-hop n. a form of popular culture that started in the United States in the 1980s in African American inner-city areas. Its elements include rap music, graffiti art, and breakdancing. [From HIP[3]]

hip-huggers /-huggərz/ npl. US = hipsters

hip joint n. the joint formed between the head of the thigh bone and the hipbone

Hipparchus /hi paarkəss/ (190?–120? BC) Greek astronomer and mathematician. The inventor of trigonometry, he also produced the earliest known star catalogue and discovered the precession of the equinoxes.

hippeastrum /híppi ástrəm/ n. a plant belonging to the daffodil family and native to Central and South America, often grown for its huge red or pink funnel-shaped flowers. Genus: *Hippeastrum*. ◇ amar-

yllis [Early 19thC. From modern Latin, formed from Greek *hippeus* 'horseman' + *astron* 'star'.]

hipped /hipt/ *adj.* having hips, especially of a particular kind (*usually used in combination*) ○ *narrow-hipped*

hipped roof *n.* = **hip roof**

hippie /híppi/, **hippy** (*plural* **-pies**) *n.* a young person, especially in the 1960s, who rejected accepted social and political values and proclaimed a belief in universal peace and love. Hippies often dressed unconventionally, lived communally, and used psychedelic drugs. (*informal*) [Mid-20thC. Formed from HIP[3].] —**hippiedom** *n.* —**hippiehood** *n.* —**hippieness** *n.*

hippo /híppō/ (*plural* **-pos**) *n.* a hippopotamus (*informal*) [Late 19thC. Shortening.]

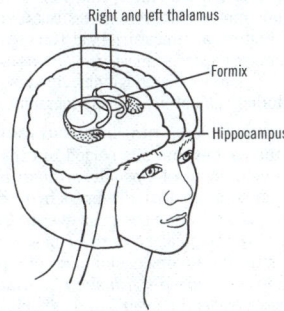

Right and left thalamus

Formix

Hippocampus

Hippocampus

hippocampus /híppō kámpəss/ (*plural* **-pi** /-pī/) *n.* **1.** MYTHOL SEA CREATURE IN MYTHS a mythological sea creature with the head and forelegs of a horse and the tail of a fish **2.** ANAT AREA OF BRAIN ASSOCIATED WITH MEMORY either of two curved ridges of tissue in the brain, located in the floor of the cavity (**ventricle**) within each of the cerebral hemispheres and concerned with basic drives, emotions, and short-term memory. Together with the hypothalamus, the hippocampi and their connections form part of the limbic system. [Late 16thC. Via Latin from Greek *hippokampos*, from *hippos* (see HIPPO-) + *kampos* 'sea monster'.] —**hippocampal** *adj.*

hippocras /híppō krass/ *n.* a medieval drink of spiced wine sweetened with honey [14thC. Via Old French *hypocras* from medieval Latin (*vinum*) *Hippocraticum*, literally '(wine of) Hippocrates'. Named after HIPPOCRATES, because he supposedly invented the filter used for straining the wine.]

Hippocrates /hi pókrə teez/ (460?–377? BC) Greek physician. Known as the father of medicine, he gave his name to the Hippocratic Oath. —**Hippocratic** /híppə kráttik/ *adj.*

Hippocratic oath *n.* an oath taken by newly qualified doctors to observe the ethical standards of their profession, specifically to seek to preserve life [Because Hippocrates was the supposed author of such an oath]

hippodrome /híppə drōm/ *n.* **1.** STADIUM USED FOR HORSE-RACING an open-air stadium in ancient Greece or Rome with an oval track that was used for horse or chariot racing **2.** VARIETY THEATRE a variety theatre or circus (*dated*) [Late 16thC. Via French and Latin from Greek *hippodromos*, from *hippos* (see HIPPO-) + *dromos* 'racecourse'.]

hippogriff /híppə grif/ *n.* a monster from Greek mythology with the body of a horse and the head, wings, and claws of a griffin [Mid-17thC. Via French *hippogriffe* from Italian *ippogrifo*, from Greek *hippos* (see HIPPO-) + Italian *grifo* 'GRIFFIN'.]

Hippolyta /hi póllitə/ *n.* in Greek mythology, a queen of the Amazons. The daughter of Ares, the god of war, she was killed by Hercules when, as one of his labours, he took her girdle.

hippopotamus /híppə póttəməss/ (*plural* **-muses** *or* **-mi** /-mī/) *n.* a large amphibious mammal of the rivers of eastern equatorial Africa that has a large head with a wide mouth, short legs, and a thick grey skin. Latin name: *Hippopotamus amphibius*. [Mid-16thC. Via Latin from Greek *hippopotamos*, from *hippos* 'horse' + *potamos* 'river'.]

Hippopotamus

hippy[1] *n.* = **hippie**

hippy[2] /híppi/ (**-pier**, **-piest**) *adj.* having wide hips

hip roof *n.* a roof with sloping ends as well as sides

hipster /hípstər/ *n.* sb who is up-to-date with the latest fashions in music, clothes, and social attitudes, especially sb who is interested in modern jazz (*dated slang*) [Formed from HIP[3] + -STER]

hipsters /hípstərz/ *npl.* trousers that end at the hips instead of the waist. US term **hip-huggers** [Formed frm HIP[1] + -STER]

hiragana /heerə gáanə/ *n.* a cursive set of symbols or ideograms (**kana**) used by the Japanese for polite, informal, or casual writing, e.g. in newspapers and general literature. ◊ **kana, katakana** [Early 19thC. From Japanese, literally 'plain syllabary'.]

hire /hīr/ *v.* (**hires, hiring, hired**) **1.** *vti.* GIVE SB WORK to employ sb to work for you, or pay sb to do a job for you **2.** *vt.* PAY FOR THE USE OF STH to rent sth from sb for a period of time ○ *hired the village hall for the wedding reception* ■ *n.* ACT OF HIRING STH OR SB the activity of renting sth to sb or of making the services of sb available to another for pay [Old English *hȳr*. Ultimately from a prehistoric Germanic word that is also the ancestor of German *Heuer* 'sailor's wages'.] —**hirable** *adj.*

— **WORD KEY: SYNONYMS** —

hire, rent, let, lease, charter

CORE MEANING: to get or grant the temporary use of sth in return for payment

hire to get or grant the temporary use of sth in return for payment, usually for a fairly short period of time; **rent** to get or grant the temporary use of property for residential or commercial purposes in return for payment. It can also be used to talk about other items such as cars or television sets. It usually suggests that the arrangement will last for a longer period of time than *hire* does; **let** to grant the temporary use of property, whether for residential or commercial purposes, in exchange for payment; **lease** to get or grant the temporary use of sth for a specified period in return for periodic payments under the terms of a contract, known as a 'lease'; **charter** used to mean *hire* when referring to a large vehicle or boat or ship, usually meant for exclusive use.

hire out *vt.* to rent sth to sb, or make the services of sb available to another for pay

hireling /hírling/ *n.* sb who works only for money, especially sb who will do menial and unpleasant tasks (*disapproving*)

hire purchase *n.* a financing arrangement enabling sb to take possession of an expensive item while making regular payments on it, with legal ownership transferred only after it is paid for. US term **installment plan**

hi-res /hí réz/ *adj.* high-resolution and therefore showing a lot of detail (*informal*) ○ *a hi-res graphic* [Shortening]

Hiri Motu /heeri mō too/ *n.* a pidginized form of Motu that has now acquired the status of one of the official languages of Papua New Guinea. Hiri Motu is spoken by about 150,000 people. —**Hiri Motu** *adj.*

hiring fair /híring-/ *n.* a gathering formerly held in rural areas for hiring farm labourers

Hirohito /heeri heetō/, **Emperor of Japan** (1901–89) His reign (1926–89) was the longest in Japanese history.

He renounced the belief that Japanese rulers are divine at the end of World War II (1945) and oversaw the transition to a constitutional monarchy.

Hiroshige /heerō shee gay/ (1797–1858) Japanese artist. One of the most prolific and popular Japanese artists of the 19th century, he is known for his serene woodblock prints, particularly of landscapes. Full name **Ando Hiroshige**

hirple /húrp'l/ (**-les, -ling, -led**) *vi.* Scotland to walk with a limp [15thC. Origin uncertain: probably from or related to Old Norse *herpast* 'to suffer from cramps'.]

— **WORD KEY: REGIONAL NOTE** —

Rural dialects abound in words such as *hirple* that describe different kinds of lameness, although they are no longer as precise as they once were. Other words associated with lameness include *backy, bockedy, cammy, gammy,* and *nought-and-carry-one.*

hirsute /húr syoot/ *adj.* **1.** PHYSIOL WITH A LOT OF HAIR having a large amount of hair ○ *a hirsute young man* **2.** BOT COVERED WITH STIFF HAIRS used to describe a plant or plant part covered with long stiff hairs ○ *a hirsute leaf* [Early 17thC. From Latin *hirsutus* 'shaggy'.] —**hirsuteness** *n.*

hirsutism /húr syootizəm/ *n.* an abnormal growth of hair, e.g. on a woman's face or body

hirudin /hi roódin/ *n.* a substance produced by the salivary glands of leeches that prevents blood from clotting [Early 20thC. Formed from Latin *hirudo* 'leech'.]

his (*stressed*) /hiz/; (*unstressed*) /iz/ *det., pron.* indicates sth belonging or relating to a man, boy, or male animal who has been previously mentioned or whose identity is known ○ *He stood at the sink washing his hands.* ○ *The fault was all his.* ○ *I went to school with a cousin of his.*

His-an /hí sán/ city and capital of Shaanxi province, central China, situated on the southern bank of the Wei approximately 130 km/80 mi. above its junction with the Huang

Hispanic /hi spánnik/ *n.* = **Hispanic American** ■ *adj.* **1.** OF SPAIN AND SPANISH PEOPLE relating to or typical of Spain, or its people or culture **2.** OF SPANISH-SPEAKING PEOPLE relating to or typical of Spanish-speaking people or their culture **3.** OF PEOPLE OF SPANISH DESCENT relating to or typical of people descended from Spanish or Latin-American people or their culture [Late 16thC. From Latin *Hispanicus*, from *Hispania* 'Spain'.]

Hispanic American *n.* sb who was born in or is a citizen of the United States and who is of Spanish or Latin American descent —**Hispanic-American** *adj.*

Hispanicise *vt.* = **Hispanicize**

Hispanicism /hi spánnisizəm/ *n.* a Spanish word, expression, or other linguistic feature that has been adopted into another language

Hispanicist /hi spánnisist/ *n.* a scholar of the languages and cultures of Spain and Spanish-speaking countries

Hispanicize /hi spánni sīz/ (**-cizes, -cizing, -cized**), **Hispanicise** (**-cises, -cising, -cised**) *vt.* to make sb or sth Spanish in character, style, or culture —**Hispanicization** /hi spánni sī záysh'n/ *n.*

Hispanism /híspənizəm/ *n.* = **Hispanicism** [Mid-20thC. Formed from Latin *Hispania* 'Spain'.]

Hispanist /híspənist/ *n.* = **Hispanicist**

Hispano /hi spánnō, hi spaán ō, híspə nō/ (*plural* **-nos**) *n.* sb of Spanish descent who lives in the southwestern United States. Many Hispanos are descended from people who lived in the region before its annexation by the United States. [Mid-20thC. Shortening of HISPANO AMERICAN.]

Hispano-American *n.* = **Hispanic American** —**Hispano-American** *adj.*

hispid /híspid/ *adj.* rough, especially covered with stiff hairs or bristles ○ *a hispid leaf* [Mid-17thC. From Latin *hispidus*.] —**hispidity** /his pídditi/ *n.*

hiss /hiss/ *v.* (**hisses, hissing, hissed**) **1.** *vi.* MAKE 'S' SOUND to make a sound like a loud continuous 's' ○ *the sound of car tyres hissing over a wet road* **2.** *vti.* SHOW NEGATIVE OPINION OF STH to show disapproval or dislike of sb or sth, e.g. a performance, by making a hissing sound **3.** *vti.* WHISPER LOUDLY to whisper loudly and angrily ○ *'Stop biting your nails', she hissed.* ■ *n.* **1.** SOUND LIKE 'S' a sound like a loud continuous 's' ○ *the hiss of escaping air* **2.** SOUND EXPRESSING DISAPPROVAL a hissing sound used to express disapproval or dislike of sth or sb ○ *The news was greeted with a hiss.* [14thC. An imitation of the sound.] —**hisser** *n.*

Hiss /hiss/, **Alger** (*b.* 1904) US lawyer and government official. A former senior State Department official, he was accused by Whittaker Chambers (1948) of spying for the Soviet Union, and imprisoned for perjury despite his protestations of innocence.

hisself *(stressed)* /hiz sélf/; *(unstressed)* /iz sélf/ *pron.* = **himself** *(nonstandard)*

hist. *abbr.* **1.** histology **2.** historic **3.** historical **4.** history

hist- *prefix.* = **histo-** (*used before vowels*)

histaminase /hi stámmi nayz, -nayss/ *n.* an enzyme found in the digestive system that inactivates histamine and certain diamines

histamine /hístə meen/ *n.* an amine compound released by cells of the body's immune system in allergic reactions that causes irritation, contraction of smooth muscle, stimulation of gastric secretions, and dilation of blood vessels. Formula: $C_5H_9N_3$. [Early 20thC. A blend of HISTIDINE and AMINE.] —**histaminic** /hístə mínnik/ *adj.*

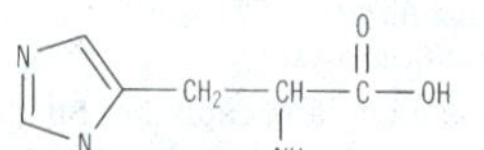

Histidine

histidine /hístə deen/ *n.* an essential amino acid involved in the growth and repair of tissues and important as the iron-binding site for haemoglobin. Formula: $C_6H_9N_3O_2$.

histiocyte /hísti ə sīt/ *n.* a large immobile scavenging cell (**macrophage**) found in connective tissue —**histiocytic** /hísti ə síttik/ *adj.*

histo- *prefix.* living tissue ○ *histochemistry* [From Greek *histos* 'web'; related to *histanai* 'to set up' (see APOSTASY)]

histochemistry /híst ō kémmistri/ *n.* the biochemistry of cells and tissues —**histochemical** *adj.* —**histochemically** *adv.*

histocompatibility /hístōkəm páttə bílləti/ *n.* the degree of similarity between certain antigens (**histocompatibility antigens**) that determines the degree of success of a tissue graft or blood transfusion —**histocompatible** /hístōkəm páttəb'l/ *adj.*

histocompatibility antigen *n.* an antigen occurring on the surface of tissue cells that is used in self-identification and determines the acceptance of a tissue graft or blood transfusion

histodialysis /hístō dī álləssiss/ *n.* = **histolysis**

histogenesis /hístō jénnəssiss/ *n.* the formation and development of tissues and organs from undifferentiated cells —**histogenetic** /hístōjə néttik/ *adj.* —**histogenetically** *adv.* —**histogenic** /híst ō jénnik/ *adj.* —**histogenically** *adv.*

histogram /hístə gram/ *n.* a statistical graph of a frequency distribution in which vertical rectangles of different heights are proportionate to corresponding frequencies

histology /hi stólləji/ *n.* a branch of anatomy concerned with the study of the microscopic structures of animal and plant tissue —**histologic** /hístə lójjik/ *adj.* —**histological** *adj.* —**histologically** *adv.* —**histologist** /hi stóllәjist/ *n.*

histolysis /hi stólləssiss/ *n.* the breakdown and disintegration of bodily tissue —**histolytic** /hístə líttik/ *adj.* —**histolytically** *adv.*

histone /híst ōn/ *n.* a protein whose molecules organize and pack the DNA in chromosomes into the greatly condensed form (**chromatin**) it normally adopts. There are five types, together constituting about half the mass of chromosomes. [Late 19thC. From German *Histon*, of uncertain origin: perhaps from Greek *histanai* or from *histos* (see HISTO-).]

histopathology /hístōpə thólləji/ *n.* a branch of pathology concerned with the study of the microscopic changes in diseased tissues —**histopathologic** /hístō páthə lójjik/ *adj.* —**histopathological** *adj.* —**histopathologically** *adv.* —**histopathologist** /hístōpə thólləjist/ *n.*

histophysiology /hístō fízzi ólləji/ *n.* a branch of physiology concerned with the structure and function of tissues —**histophysiologic** /hístō fízzi ə lójjik/ *adj.* —**histophysiological** *adj.*

histoplasmosis /hístō plaz mṓssiss/ *n.* a severe disease of the lungs with symptoms resembling flu, caused by the fungus *Histoplasma capsulatum* [Early 20thC. Formed from modern Latin *Histoplasma*, genus name.]

historian /hi stáwri ən/ *n.* **1.** STUDENT AND SCHOLAR OF HISTORY sb who is knowledgeable in history and who may write about or teach it **2.** RECORDER OF EVENTS sb who writes an account of historical events [15thC. From French *historien*, from Latin *historia*, on the model of *logicien* 'logician' (see HISTORY).]

historiated /hi stáwri aytid/ *adj.* used to describe decorative initials in books or maps and plans that are illustrated with symbolic flowers and animals or symbols in the form of flowers or animals [Late 19thC. Directly or via French from medieval Latin *historiare* 'to adorn (with historical scenes), relate', from Latin *historia* (see HISTORY).]

historic /hi stórrik/ *adj.* **1.** SIGNIFICANT IN HISTORY important in or affecting the course of history ○ *Yalta, scene of the historic meeting between Roosevelt, Stalin, and Churchill* ○ *a historic decision affecting world peace* **2.** = **historical** *adj.* 1

historical /hi stórrik'l/ *adj.* **1.** EXISTING OR HAPPENING IN THE PAST existing, happening, or relating to the past ○ *an important historical personage* **2.** USED IN THE PAST worn or used by people in the past ○ *historical uniforms of the 18th century* **3.** SUPPORTED BY FACTS FROM HISTORY based on or describing people who lived in the past or events that happened in the past ○ *historical fiction* ○ *a historical film* **4.** RELATING TO STUDY OF HISTORY relating to or involving the study of history **5.** RELATING TO THE EVOLUTION OF PHENOMENA relating to the gradual change and development of phenomena, e.g. languages or societies ○ *historical sociology* —**historicalness** *n.*

historical geology *n.* a branch of geology that deals with the geological history of the earth

historical linguistics *n.* the study of language as it changes and develops through time

historically /hi stórrikli/ *adv.* **1.** REGARDING HISTORY according to or with reference to history or its course ○ *The law will prove to be historically significant.* **2.** MANY TIMES BEFORE used to indicate that sth has happened often in the past ○ *Historically, a rise in interest rates slows the rate of inflation.*

historical materialism *n.* the part of Marx's theory of dialectical materialism that maintains that the development of social thought and institutions is based on material economic forces

historical novel *n.* a novel set in the past that includes real events and people from that period

historical present *n.* the present tense used to narrate actions that happened in the past to make them seem more vivid

historicise *vt.* = **historicize**

historicism /hi stórrissizəm/ *n.* **1.** THEORY THAT NATURAL LAWS GOVERN HISTORY the belief that natural laws beyond human control determine historical events **2.** BELIEF IN UNIQUENESS OF HISTORICAL PERIODS the theory that each period of history has its own unique beliefs and values and can only be understood in its historical context —**historicist** *n.*

historicity /hístəríssəti/ *n.* the state or fact of being historically authentic

historicize /hi stórri sīz/ (**-cizes, -cizing, -cized**), **historicise** (**-cises, -cising, -cised**) *vt.* to give sth the appearance of historical truth —**historicization** /hi stórri sī záysh'n/ *n.*

Historic Places Trust *n.* the statutory body in New Zealand whose duty it is to preserve historic sites, especially those of the Maori

historiography /hi stáwri óggrəfi/ *n.* **1.** METHODS OF HISTORICAL RESEARCH the principles, theories, or methods of historical research or writing **2.** THE WRITING OF HISTORY the writing of history based on scholarly disciplines such as the analysis and evaluation of source materials **3.** AVAILABLE DATA ON HISTORICAL TOPIC the existing findings and interpretations relating to a particular historical topic **4.** HISTORICAL LITERATURE a body of historical literature [Mid-16thC. Via medieval Latin from Greek *historiographia*, from *historia* (see HISTORY) + *graphia* 'writing'.] —**historiographic** /hi stáwri ə gráffik/ *n.* —**historiographical** *adj.* —**historiographically** *adv.*

history /hístəri/ (*plural* **-ries**) *n.* **1.** WHAT HAS HAPPENED IN THE PAST the past events of a period in time or in the life or development of a people, an institution, or a place **2.** STUDY OF THE PAST the branch of knowledge that records and analyses past events **3.** RECORD OF EVENTS a chronological account of past events of a period or in the life or development of a people, an institution, or a place ○ *a history of Byzantium* **4.** PERSONAL BACKGROUND the events and experiences of an individual's past ○ *We don't know very much about her personal history.* **5.** SCI SYSTEMATIC RECORD OF NATURAL PHENOMENA an account of related natural phenomena based on observation and investigation (*archaic*) ○ *a history of volcanoes* **6.** INTERESTING PAST an interesting or colourful past ○ *The car has a bit of a history attached to it.* **7.** STH NO LONGER IMPORTANT sth that belongs to the past and is no longer important ○ *The scandal is history, as far as I'm concerned.* **8.** SB NO LONGER IMPORTANT sb who has suffered total loss of power, high position, or importance (*slang*) ○ *If he's found guilty of bribery, he's history.* **9.** LITERAT HISTORICAL PLAY a play that deals with historical events **10.** LITERAT LIFE STORY a narrative that deals with the events of a fictional character's life (*archaic*) [15thC. Via Latin from Greek *historia* 'history, knowledge, narrative' (source of English *story*), from *histōr* 'learned man'.] ◇ **be ancient history** to be sth that happened a long time ago, or perhaps only recently in the past, and is no longer important or relevant

histrionic /hístri ónnik/, **histrionical** /-ónnik'l/ *adj.* **1.** OVERDRAMATIC overdramatic in reaction or behaviour ○ *Paul gave a histrionic sigh and slumped in his chair.* **2.** THEATRE RELATING TO ACTING relating to acting or actors (*formal*) [Mid-17thC. From late Latin *histrionicus*, from the Latin stem *histrion-* 'actor'.] —**histrionically** *adv.*

histrionics /hístri ónniks/ *n.* OVERDONE EMOTION exaggerated emotional behaviour done for show or to get a reaction from sb (*takes a singular or plural verb*) ○ *Let's hope there won't be any histrionics when you tell them.* ■ *npl.* THEATRE DRAMATIC PERFORMANCES performances of dramatic works (*formal; takes a plural verb*)

hit /hit/ *v.* (**hits, hitting, hit**) **1.** *vti.* STRIKE SB OR STH DELIBERATELY to strike sb or sth deliberately with the hand or sth held in it ○ *He hit me on the jaw with a good solid punch.* **2.** *vti.* COME INTO CONTACT to come into violent contact with sth ○ *His van skidded and hit a parked car.* **3.** *vt.* SPORTS MAKE BALL MOVE to make sth such as a ball move by striking it with a bat or racket ○ *She kept hitting the ball over the fence into the next garden.* **4.** *vt.* STRIKE BUTTON OR KEY to press or push a button or part of a machine (*informal*) ○ *Try to hit the keys smoothly.* **5.** *vt.* SPORTS MAKE A SCORE WITH BALL to score points in a sport by striking a ball well or delivering it successfully to a target ○ *You'll need to hit a home run to win.* ○ *She hit the first goal in the second minute of the game.* **6.** *vt.* STRIKE TARGET to reach an intended target with a ball or missile **7.** *vti.* COME TO MIND to realize or become conscious of sth ○ *It suddenly hit him that he was unlikely to see her again.* **8.** *vt.* GIVE SB INFORMATION to tell sb sth that may be of interest (*slang*) ○ *'Do you want to know what I think?' 'Okay, hit me'.* **9.** *vt.* AFFECT SB OR STH BADLY to have an adverse effect on sb or sth ○ *The rise in interest rates is going to hit exporters hard.* **10.** *vt.* **ARRIVE AT SPECIFIED LEVEL** to reach a particular level on a scale ○ *Unemployment has hit the 2 million mark.* **11.** *vt.* **PRODUCE STH ACCURATELY** to render or represent sth accurately ○ *hit a high C* **12.** *vt.* **CONFORM TO STH** to conform to or agree with sth ○ *Your comments hit a sympathetic note.* **13.** *vt.* **REACH A PLACE** to reach a particular place (*informal*) ○ *You'll hit a toll-free road about five miles farther on.* **14.** *vi.* **HAPPEN** to take place, usually with undesirable or adverse effects (*informal*) ○ *The storm hit before we could get home.* **15.** *vt.* **VIEW WEB PAGE** to visit or view a particular web page (*informal*) **16.** *vt.* CRIMINOL **TO KILL SB USING HIRED HAND** to murder sb, especially by employing a professional killer (*slang*) ○ *One of the croupiers got hit last night.* ■ *n.* **1. HARD BLOW** a hard blow delivered with the hand or sth held in it ○ *She gave it a good hit.* **2. COLLISION** a violent impact between things **3. STH THAT HITS TARGET** a ball or missile that successfully strikes the target ○ *We've taken a couple of hits, but nothing serious.* **4.** BASEBALL = **base hit** **5. SUCCESS** sb who or sth that is popular and successful ○ *The band had a big hit with their last CD.* ○ *The clown was a hit with the kids.* **6.** DRUGS **EFFECT OF DRUG** a sense of a drug's effect (*slang*) **7. STH GIVEN** a single item given or taken, e.g. a drink or a card at the game of twenty-one (*slang*) **8.** CRIMINOL **PROFESSIONAL KILLING** a murder, especially one committed by a professional killer (*slang*) **9.** COMPUT **ACCESSING OF DATABASE OR INTERNET FILE** an instance of a user retrieving an item from a database or contacting a file, e.g. a home page, through the Internet ○ *Her home page has received 3,000 hits since she opened it last month.* [Pre-12thC. From Old Norse *hitta* 'to find'. Originally used in the Old Norse sense (which survives in HIT ON), the underlying idea of its current meaning is 'to reach'.] —**hittable** *adj.* ◇ **hit it off** to get on very well with sb (*informal*)

hit back *vi.* to retaliate against sb or sth for an attack

hit on, hit upon *vt.* to think of a solution to a problem ○ *She then hit on the idea of painting the inside of the box black.*

hit out *vi.* **1. CRITICIZE SB** to criticize sb or sth severely ○ *The bishop hit out at their human rights record.* **2. TRY TO STRIKE SB** to try to strike sb repeatedly ○ *When the baby is in a tantrum, she hits out at people trying to comfort her.*

hit up *v.* **1.** *vt.* **ASK** to ask sb for sth (*slang*) ○ *How come you're suddenly hitting me up for the cab fare?* **2.** *vi.* *ANZ* **WARM UP BEFORE A GAME** in racket games, to hit the ball back and forth without scoring points, in order to warm up before a game

hit-and-miss *adj.* done in a careless haphazard way ○ *The survey was hit-and-miss, so we cannot trust the results.* US term **hit-or-miss**

hit-and-run *adj.* **1.** LAW **NOT STOPPING AFTER CAUSING AN ACCIDENT** used to describe or relating to a road accident in which the driver who has hit another person or motor vehicle leaves the scene without stopping ○ *a hit-and-run driver* **2. FAST AND WITHOUT WARNING** relying on surprise and speed to overcome an enemy ○ *Three fighter planes launched a hit-and-run attack at dawn.* ■ *n.* **HIT-AND-RUN ACCIDENT** a hit-and-run road accident

hitch /hich/ *v.* (**hitches, hitching, hitched**) **1.** *vti.* TRANSP **HITCHHIKE** to hitchhike a ride (*informal*) ○ *We hitched down through Italy in three days.* **2.** *vt.* **JOIN STH POWERED TO STH ELSE** to connect two things so that one can move the other, e.g. a horse to a wagon or a trailer to a car **3.** *vt.* **FASTEN STH TO STOP IT** to fasten or tie sth temporarily to keep it from moving away ○ *Hitch the boat to the dock before the current catches it.* ■ *n.* **1. OBSTACLE** an obstacle in the way of progress ○ *There's been a slight technical hitch.* **2. MEANS OF CONNECTING TWO THINGS** a device used to connect two things, e.g. a ball on a vehicle for connecting a trailer **3. KNOT THAT UNTIES EASILY** a knot that can be easily untied, used for temporarily securing a line to sth **4. TUG** a sudden pull on sth [14thC. Origin unknown.] —**hitcher** *n.*

hitch up *vt.* to pull up an article of clothing

Hitchcock /hích kok/, **Sir Alfred** (1899–1980) British film director. A prolific director and master of suspense, his films include *The Thirty-Nine Steps* (1935), *Rebecca* (1940), and *Psycho* (1960). Full name **Sir Alfred Joseph Hitchcock**

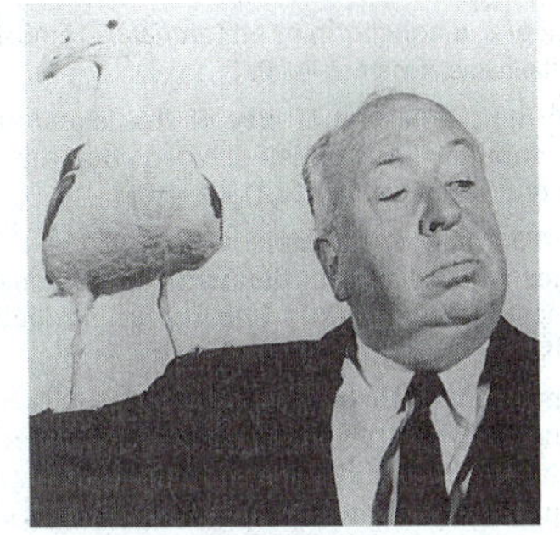

Sir Alfred Hitchcock

hitchhike /hích hīk/ (**-hikes, -hiking, -hiked**) *vti.* to get a ride from a passing vehicle, usually by standing at the side of the road and holding out the hand with the thumb raised —**hitchhiker** *n.*

hitching post *n.* a post or rail used to tie the reins of a horse to

hi-tech /hī ték/ *n., adj.* = **high tech, high-tech**

hither /híthər/ *adv.* **HERE** to this place (*archaic*) ○ *Come hither, child.* ■ *adj.* **ON NEAR SIDE** on the near side of sth (*archaic*) [Old English *hider*. Ultimately from an Indo-European word meaning 'here, this'.]

hithermost /híthərmōst/ *adj.* nearest this direction (*archaic*)

hitherto /híthər tóo, híthər too/ *adv.* up to the present time or the time in question ○ *Hitherto most people had paid cash.*

hitherward /híthərwərd/, **hitherwards** /-wərdz/ *adv.* in this direction (*archaic*)

hit in (*plural* **hits in**) *n.* in hockey, a hit from the sideline awarded to the opposition when the team in possession of the ball fails to keep it on the pitch

Hitler /hítlər/, **Adolf** (1889–1945) Austrian-born German Nazi leader. He cofounded the Nazi party in Germany (1919) and became chancellor in 1933. His invasion of Poland in 1939 led to the outbreak of World War II. He implemented anti-Semitic policies that led to the Holocaust.

Hitlerism /hítlərizəm/ *n.* the extreme nationalistic ideology and fascistic policies developed by the Nazi Party under Adolf Hitler —**Hitlerist** *n.* —**Hitlerite** *adj.*

hit list *n.* (*informal*) **1. LIST OF PROBLEMS NEEDING ELIMINATING** a list of things or people who are considered problems to be dealt with in the near future **2.** CRIMINOL **LIST OF POSSIBLE MURDER VICTIMS** a list of potential murder victims

hit man *n.* a hired assassin (*slang*)

hit-or-miss *adj.* = **hit-and-miss**

hit out (*plural* **hit outs** *or* **hits out**) *n.* in hockey, a hit taken from the 16-yard line that is awarded to the defence when the attacking team hit the ball over the goal line without scoring a goal

hit parade *n.* a list of the best-selling pop records in the previous week (*dated*)

hit squad *n.* (*slang*) **1. HIRED KILLERS** a team of hired assassins or other killers **2. HIRED PROBLEM SOLVERS** a team of experts sent in to solve serious problems

Hittite /híttīt/ *n.* **1.** PEOPLES **MEMBER OF ANCIENT ANATOLIAN PEOPLE** a member of an ancient people of Anatolia whose empire flourished in parts of western Asia during the second millennium BC **2.** LANG **EXTINCT ANATOLIAN LANGUAGE** an extinct language spoken in Anatolia, parts of Syria, and the surrounding areas during the second millennium BC. Linguists agree that it is an Indo-European language, but, despite evidence from ample cuneiform inscriptions, there is no consensus over which branch of Indo-European it belongs to. [Mid-16thC. Formed from Hebrew *Ḥittīm*, from Hittite *Hatti*.] —**Hittite** *adj.*

hit-up *n.* *ANZ* RACKET GAMES = **knock-up**

HIV *n.* either of two strains of a retrovirus, HIV-1 or HIV-2, that destroys the immune system's helper T cells, the loss of which causes Aids. Full form **human immunodeficiency virus**

hive /hīv/ *n.* **1. HOME FOR BEES** a shelter in which a colony of social bees, especially honeybees, builds its nest **2. COLONY OF BEES** a colony of honeybees ■ *v.* (**hives, hiving, hived**) **1.** *vti.* **PUT BEES INTO HIVE** to gather in a hive, or cause bees to gather in a hive ○ *hive a swarm* **2.** *vt.* **KEEP HONEY IN HIVE** to store honey in a hive **3.** *vt.* **KEEP STH TO USE LATER** to store sth for later use **4.** *vi.* **LIVE CLOSELY TOGETHER** to live closely in a group [Old English *hȳf*. Ultimately from an Indo-European word meaning 'round container', which also produced Latin *cupa* 'barrel' (source of English *coop*).] —**hiveless** *adj.* ◇ **a hive of industry** *or* **activity** a very busy, active place

hive off *vt.* **1. SPLIT STH OFF FROM WHOLE** to separate sth from the whole or from a larger group, e.g. to divert work to a subsidiary company or to split a branch of knowledge into different areas **2. MAKE NATIONALIZED INDUSTRY PRIVATE** to transfer an industry from governmental to private ownership

hives /hīvz/ *n.* MED = **urticaria** [Early 16thC. Originally a Scottish dialect word, of unknown origin.]

HIV-negative *adj.* having taken a test that revealed no antibodies to HIV in the bloodstream

HIV-positive *adj.* shown by a test for antibodies to HIV in the bloodstream to be infected with the HIV virus

hiziki *n.* = **hijiki**

HJ *abbr.* hic jacet (*on gravestones*) [Latin, 'here lies']

HK *abbr.* **1.** Hong Kong (*international vehicle registration*) **2.** House of Keys

HKJ *abbr.* (Hashemite Kingdom of) Jordan (*international vehicle registration*)

hl *symbol.* hectolitre

HL *abbr.* House of Lords

HLA *n.* the major antigen compatibility complex in humans that is genetically determined and is involved in cell self-identification and histocompatibility. Full form **human lymphocyte antigen**

HLL *abbr.* high-level language

hm *abbr.* hectometre

h'm /m, hm/ *interj.* used to represent a sound made while pausing during a conversation to consider sth ○ *H'm, it'll take about two weeks.* [Mid-19thC. An imitation of the sound.]

HM *abbr.* **1.** headmaster **2.** headmistress **3.** MUSIC heavy metal **4.** Her Majesty **5.** His Majesty

HMAS *abbr.* **1.** Her Majesty's Australian ship **2.** His Majesty's Australian ship

HMCS *abbr.* **1.** Her Majesty's Canadian Ship **2.** His Majesty's Canadian Ship

HMF *abbr.* **1.** Her Majesty's Forces **2.** His Majesty's Forces

HMG *abbr.* **1.** Her Majesty's Government **2.** His Majesty's Government

HMI *abbr.* **1.** EDUC Her Majesty's Inspector (of Schools) **2.** human-machine interface

Hmong /máwng, hə máwng/ (*plural* **Hmongs** *or* **Hmong**) *n.* **1.** PEOPLES **MEMBER OF PEOPLE OF S CHINA** a member of a people living in southern parts of China and northern parts of Laos, Thailand, and Vietnam, where they tend to inhabit the more remote, mountainous areas of these regions **2.** LANG **LANGUAGE SPOKEN IN S CHINA** a language spoken in parts of southern China and by scattered communities in Laos, Thailand, Vietnam, and the United States. Hmong forms one main branch of the Miao-Yao language family. Over five million people speak Hmong. —**Hmong** *adj.*

HMS, **H.M.S.** *abbr.* **1.** Her Majesty's Service **2.** Her Majesty's Ship **3.** His Majesty's Service **4.** His Majesty's Ship

HMSO *abbr.* **1.** Her Majesty's Stationery Office **2.** His Majesty's Stationery Office

Hn symbol **Hn**

HNC *n.* a qualification in a technical subject that is recognized by many professional and technical establishments. Full form **Higher National Certificate**

HND *n.* a post-school vocational award higher than the National Diploma. It requires the equivalent of two years' full-time study and is generally regarded as roughly equivalent to a university pass degree. Full form **Higher National Diploma**

zh vision In foreign words: kh German Bach; aN French vin; aaN French blanc; ö German schön, French feu; oN French bon; öN French un; ü French rue Stress marks: ´ as in secret \séek rət\; academic \àkə démmik\

ho[1] /hō/ (*plural* **hos** *or* **hoes**) *n.* **1. PROSTITUTE** a prostitute (*slang*) **2. OFFENSIVE TERM** an offensive term for a woman (*slang offensive*) [Late 20thC. Pronunciation of WHORE.]

ho[2] /hō/ *interj.* **1. EXPRESSING VARIOUS EMOTIONS** used to express surprise, triumph, admiration or derision, depending on the way the speaker says it **2. CALL FOR ATTENTION** used to attract sb's attention **3. USED TO POINT OUT STH** used to draw sb's attention to sth (*used in combinations*) ○ *Land ho!*

Ho *symbol.* holmium

HO, **H.O.** *abbr.* **1.** head office **2.** Home Office

ho. *abbr.* house

Ho. *abbr.* BIBLE Hosea

h.o. *abbr.* COMM hold over

Hoad /hōd/, **Lew** (1934–94) Australian tennis player. He won the Wimbledon singles championship in 1956 and 1957. Full name **Lewis Alan Hoad**

hoar /hawr/ *adj.* white or greyish white in colour, usually as a result of age or frost (*literary*) [Old English *hār*. Ultimately from an Indo-European word meaning 'shine', which also produced English *hue* and German *heiter* 'merry'.]

hoard /hawrd/ *vti.* (**hoards, hoarding, hoarded**) **STORE A SUPPLY OF STH** to collect and store, often secretly, a large quantity of sth such as food or money for use in the future ■ *n.* **SECRET STORE** a store of sth such as food or money that has been hidden for use in the future [Old English *hord*. Ultimately from an Indo-European word that is also the ancestor of English *hide* and *obscure*.]

WORD KEY: SYNONYMS

See Synonyms at ***collect***.

hoarding /háwrding/ *n.* **1.** = **billboard**[1] *n.* ○ *an advertising hoarding* **2. TALL WOODEN SCREEN ROUND BUILDING SITE** a tall wooden fence used to screen off a building site [Early 19thC. Formed from obsolete *hoard*, of uncertain origin: probably from, ultimately, Old French *hurder* 'to enclose', from *hurt* 'palisade', of prehistoric Germanic origin.]

hoar frost *n.* the white frost that forms on grass or leaves in the morning when the dew freezes

hoarhound *n.* = **horehound**

hoarse /hawrss/ (**hoarser, hoarsest**) *adj.* **1. SOUNDING ROUGH** sounding rough and grating **2. WITH HARSHLY GRATING VOICE** having a rough, harsh, grating voice [Old English *hās*, of prehistoric Germanic origin] —**hoarsely** *adv.* —**hoarseness** *n.*

hoarsen /háwrss'n/ (**-ens, -ening, -ened**) *vti.* to become hoarse, or make the voice hoarse

hoary /háwri/ (**-ier, -iest**) *adj.* **1. OVERUSED** old and stale from overuse ○ *Not that hoary old chestnut about the chicken crossing the road?* **2. WHITE WITH AGE** used to describe hair that has become white or grey with age **3.** BIOL **COVERED WITH PALE HAIRS** covered with grey or white hairs ○ *a plant with hoary leaves* —**hoarily** *adv.* —**hoariness** *n.*

hoary marmot *n.* a marmot found in the mountains of northwestern North America, with a greyish coat and a shrill cry. Latin name: *Marmota caligata.*

hoatching /hṓching/ *adj. Scotland* full of people or things (*informal*) [Origin unknown]

hoatzin *n.* a South American bird with brownish plumage, a very small crested head, and a specialized digestive system for leaves. Young birds have a clawlike digit on each wing, used for climbing and swimming. Latin name: *Opisthocomus hoazin.* [Mid-17thC. Via American Spanish from Nahuatl *uatzin*, of uncertain origin: probably an imitation of the sound made by the bird.]

hoax /hōks/ *n.* **DECEPTION** an act intended to trick people into believing sth is real that is not ■ *vt.* (**hoaxes, hoaxing, hoaxed**) **DECEIVE PEOPLE** to trick people into believing sth is real that is not [Late 18thC. Origin uncertain: probably an alteration of HOCUS.] —**hoaxer** *n.*

hob[1] /hob/ *n.* **1. COOKING SURFACE** a flat surface containing cooking rings, hotplates, or burners, either on top of a cooker or as a separate appliance **2. PLACE TO KEEP PANS WARM** a small shelf or rack level with the top of the grate of a fireplace on which to set pans to keep them warm [Late 17thC. Alteration of earlier *hub*, of unknown origin.]

hob[2] /hob/ *n.* a hobgoblin or elf (*archaic*) [15thC. Formed from the name *Robert* or *Robin*.]

Hobart /hṓ baart/ capital city of the island state of Tasmania in Australia, located on the River Derwent. Population: 126,118 (1996).

Hobbema /hóbbimə/, **Meindert** (1638–1709) Dutch painter. A specialist in detailed Dutch landscapes, his most famous work is *The Avenue, Middelharnis* (1689).

Hobbes /hobz/, **Thomas** (1588–1679) English philosopher and political theorist. In *Leviathan* (1651) he advocated absolute monarchy as the only means of controlling clashing human interests and desires and guaranteeing their rights of self-preservation and happiness. —**Hobbesian** /hóbzi ən/ *adj., n.* —**Hobbism** *n.* —**Hobbist** *adj., n.*

hobbit /hóbbit/ *n.* a member of an imaginary kind of good-natured little people who have brown furry legs and live underground. Hobbits are the creation of writer J.R.R. Tolkien, whose most famous hobbit is Bilbo Baggins, the hero of *The Hobbit*. [Mid-20thC. Coined by J.R.R. Tolkien.]

hobble /hóbb'l/ *v.* (**-bles, -bling, -bled**) **1.** *vi.* **LIMP ALONG** to walk haltingly and unsteadily, taking short steps **2.** *vt.* **LIMIT HORSE'S MOVEMENT** to tie the legs of a horse loosely together with a rope or strap to prevent it from moving away **3.** *vt.* **RESTRICT SB'S ACTIONS** to put restrictions on sb or sth to slow or prevent progress ■ *n.* **1. UNSTEADY WALK** a halting unsteady walk **2. ROPE OR STRAP** sth such as a loop of rope or a strap used to tie the legs of a horse [13thC. Origin uncertain: probably from Low German.]

hobbledehoy /hóbb'ldi hóy/ *n.* a clumsy or rude young man (*archaic*) [Mid-16thC. Origin unknown.]

hobble skirt *n.* a long skirt designed to be full at the hips but narrow at the ankles, first popular between 1910 and 1914

Hobbs /hobz/, **Jack** (1882–1963) British cricketer. With a career total of 61,237 runs, including 197 centuries, he was the first cricketer to be knighted (1953).

hobby /hóbbi/ (*plural* **-bies**) *n.* **1. ENJOYABLE ACTIVITY** an activity engaged in for pleasure and relaxation during spare time ○ *Our oldest boy's hobby is flying kites.* **2.** BIRDS **SMALL GREY FALCON** a small grey falcon with chestnut legs that breeds in Europe and Asia and winters in Africa. Its speed and deftness make it popular as a hunting bird. Latin name: *Falco subbuteo.* [13thC. Origin uncertain: probably from *Hobin*, a variant of the name *Robin*. Originally a nickname for a horse, the word in its main current meaning is a shortening of HOBBYHORSE.]

hobbyhorse /hóbbi hawrss/ *n.* **1. TOY HORSE FROM A STICK** a toy consisting of a long stick with the shape of a horse's head at one end **2. HORSE FIGURE USED IN FOLK DANCES** a representation of a horse that a Morris dancer or mummer wears around the waist so that it appears that the horse is being ridden **3. FAVOURITE TOPIC** a favourite subject about which sb will talk given the slightest opportunity

hobgoblin /hób góblin, hób goblin/ *n.* **1.** = **goblin 2. STH TROUBLING** a source of fear or worry [*Hob* from HOB[2]]

hobnail /hób nayl/ *n.* a short nail with a broad head that is used to protect the soles of boots ○ *the sound of hobnails on stone barracks stairs*

hobnob /hób nob/ (**-nobs, -nobbing, -nobbed**) *vi.* to socialize in a familiar manner with sb, especially sb considered to be of a higher social class (*disapproving*) ○ *hobnobbing with the rich and famous* [Mid-18thC. Origin uncertain: probably from obsolete *hob or nob*, literally 'have or not have'. Originally in the meaning 'to drink together' (perhaps from the notion of buying alternate rounds).]

hobo /hṓbō/ (*plural* **-boes**) *n.* sb who is poor and homeless, especially sb who travelled around the United States looking for work in the 1920s and 1930s by hiding on freight trains [Late 19thC. Origin unknown.]

hobson-jobson /hóbss'n jóbss'n/ *n.* the assimilation of the sound of a word or words into the sound system of another language, as occurred when the French 'vin blanc' became the English 'plonk' [Late 19thC. From the title of an Anglo-Indian glossary by Yule and Burnell, from Arabic *Yā Ḥasan! Yā Ḥusayn!* 'O Hasan! O Husain!', a cry used at Muslim ceremonies.]

Hobson's choice /hóbss'nz-/ *n.* a choice between what is offered and nothing at all [Mid-17thC. Named after the English liveryman Thomas *Hobson* (1554–1631), who would only let his customers take the horse nearest the door.]

Ho Chi Minh City the largest city of Vietnam, located in the south of the country. Population: 4,22,300 (1993). Former name **Saigon**

hock[1] /hok/ *n.* **1.** ZOOL **ANIMAL'S LOWER LEG JOINT** the joint in the hind leg of a four-legged animal such as a horse or cow, corresponding to the human ankle **2.** BIRDS **FOWL'S ANKLE** the ankle joint in the leg of a fowl **3.** FOOD **LEG OF MEAT** a cut of cured meat, especially ham, taken from the lower joint of the leg immediately above the foot. It contains a comparatively small amount of meat but has a good flavour and jelly properties and is often used in stocks and soups. [16thC. Shortening of obsolete *hockshin*, from Old English *hōhsinu*, literally 'heel-sinew', from *hōh* 'heel' (related to English *heel*).]

hock[2] /hok/ *n.* German white wine, especially from the Rhineland and strictly from Hochheim in the Rheingau [Early 17thC. Shortening of obsolete English *hockamore*, an Anglicization of German *Hochheimer*, from *Hochheim*, a German town that is a centre of wine production.]

hock[3] /hok/ (**hocks, hocking, hocked**) *vt.* to deposit sth as security against money borrowed, with the risk of losing it if the money is not paid back by a certain time (*slang*) [Mid-19thC. From Dutch *hok* 'prison', hence 'debt'.] ◇ **in hock 1.** left as security against money borrowed (*slang*) ○ *With so many things in hock, the shelves were quite bare.* **2.** in debt (*informal*) ○ *in hock to finance an expensive car* **3.** in prison (*informal*)

hockey /hóki/ *n.* **1. FIELD SPORT PLAYED WITH STICKS** a field sport played between two teams of 11 players, using wooden sticks with curved ends. The aim is to hit a small hard ball into the opposing goal. ○ *a hockey player.* US term **field hockey 2.** *US* = **ice hockey 3.** *US, Can* = **street hockey** [Early 16thC. Origin uncertain.]

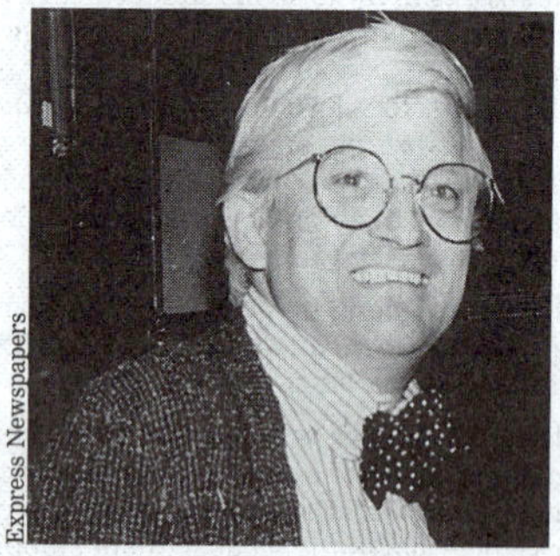
Express Newspapers

David Hockney

Hockney /hókni/, **David** (*b.* 1937) British painter. He was closely associated with the Pop Art movement. His fascination with water inspired 'swimming pool' paintings such as *A Bigger Splash* (1967).

Hocktide /hók tīd/ *n.* a festival that used to be celebrated on the second Monday and Tuesday after Easter, originally for the purpose of raising money [15thC. *Hock-*, 'the beginning of the second week after Easter', of unknown origin.]

hocus /hṓkəss/ (**-cuses, -cusing** *or* **-cussing, -cused** *or* **-cussed**) *vt.* (*archaic*) **1. DECEIVE** to deceive or trick sb **2. DOPE SB** to incapacitate a person or animal with drugs **3. ADD DRUG TO ALCOHOLIC DRINK** secretly to add a drug to an alcoholic drink [Late 17thC. Shortening of HOCUS-POCUS.]

hocus-pocus /-pṓkəss/ *n.* (*plural* **hocus-pocuses** *or* **hocus-pocusses**) **1. CONJURER'S INCANTATION** a phrase or chant used by a magician or conjurer during a performance **2. MAGIC TRICK** a trick performed by a magician or conjurer **3. TRICKERY** a hoax or trickery ○ *The negotiations were ruined by the parties' hocus-pocus.* **4. CONJURER** a juggler or magician (*dated*) ■ *vti.* (**hocus-pocuses** *or* **hocus-pocusses, hocus-pocusing** *or* **hocus-pocussing, hocus-pocused** *or* **hocus-pocussed**) **DECEIVE** to deceive or trick sb ○ *It was something to* *see a rookie player hocus-pocus an old pro.* [Formed from pseudo-Latin *hax pax max Deus adimax*, used by conjurers to impress audiences. Originally in the meaning of 'conjurer, trickster'.]

hod /hod/ *n.* **1.** TROUGH ON A POLE a V-shaped tray on the end of a long pole, usually carried on the shoulder. It is used to carry bricks, mortar, and other building materials. **2.** = **coal scuttle** [Late 16thC. Originally a dialect word meaning 'pannier, basket', from Old French *hotte*, of prehistoric Germanic origin.]

hod carrier *n.* sb hired to carry bricks and mortar in a hod

hodden /hódd'n/ *n. Scotland* a type of coarse, undyed, homespun woollen fabric produced in Scotland [Late 16thC. Origin unknown.]

Hoddle /hódd'l/, **Glenn** (*b.* 1957) British footballer and manager. He spent most of his playing career with Tottenham (1976–86). He won 53 international caps, and was England manager (1996–99).

Hodge /hoj/ *n.* a name used to represent a typical agricultural labourer (*archaic*) [14thC. Shortening and alteration of the first name *Roger*.]

hodgepodge /hój poj/ *n.* = **hotchpotch** [14thC. Variant of HOTCHPOTCH, perhaps by association with HODGE.]

Hodgkin /hójkin/, **Alan** (*b.* 1914) British physiologist. He shared the Nobel Prize in physiology or medicine (1963) for his research into the chemical processes of nerve impulses. Full name **Alan Lloyd Hodgkin**

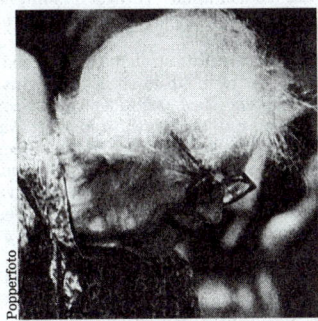
Popperfoto

Dorothy Mary Hodgkin

Hodgkin, Dorothy Mary (1910–94) Egyptian-born British chemist. She was awarded the Nobel Prize in chemistry (1964) for work on X-rays, molecular science, and penicillin. Born **Dorothy Mary Crowfoot**

Hodgkin, Thomas (1798–1866) British pathologist. He was the first person to detect the glandular disease of the lymph tissue later named Hodgkin's disease.

Hodgkins /hójkinz/, **Frances Mary** (1869–1947) New Zealand painter. Noted for her watercolour still lifes and landscapes, she spent most of her working life in Europe.

Hodgkin's disease /hójkinz-/ *n.* a malignant form of lymphoma marked by progressive enlargement of the lymph nodes and spleen and sometimes of the liver [Mid-19thC. Named after Thomas HODGKIN.]

hodman /hódmən/ (*plural* -**men** /-mən/) *n.* = **hod carrier**

hodometer /hō dómmitər/ *n.* = **odometer**

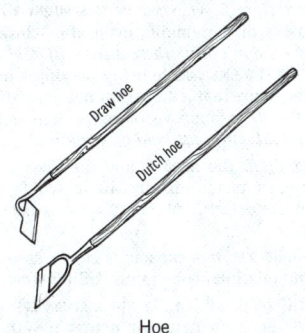
Draw hoe
Dutch hoe

Hoe

hoe /hō/ *n.* WEEDING TOOL a garden implement used for weeding or turning over soil. It consists of a long pole with a small flat metal blade set into one end

at an angle. ■ *vti.* (**hoes, hoeing, hoed**) DIG USING HOE to dig or weed using a hoe [14thC. Via Old French *houe* from assumed Frankish, 'to cut', from a prehistoric Germanic word meaning 'to cut down', which is also the ancestor of English *haggle*.] —**hoer** *n.*

hoedown /hố down/ *n. Southern US, Can* **1.** COUNTRY DANCE a noisy lively dance, especially a square dance, or a party that includes square dancing **2.** MUSIC DANCE MUSIC music used at or intended for use at a hoedown [From the idea of stopping work]

Hofei /hố fáy/ = **Hefei**

hog /hog/ *n.* **1.** ZOOL PIG a full-grown domestic pig, especially a castrated male pig **2.** US MEMBER OF THE PIG FAMILY any of various mammals of the pig family, including both domesticated and wild species, e.g. the wild boar. Family: Suidae. **3.** hog, hogg YOUNG SHEEP a young sheep that is older than a lamb and that has not yet been sheared (*regional*) **4.** NAUT SHIP'S BROOM a broom used to clean the bottom of a ship while it is in the water ■ *v.* (**hogs, hogging, hogged**) **1.** *vt.* TAKE AN EXCESS OF STH to take more of sth or keep sth for longer than is fair or polite (*informal*) ○ *He's been hogging the middle lane for the past two miles.* **2.** *vt.* ARCH THE BACK to arch the back upwards **3.** *vt.* EQU TRIM A HORSE'S MANE to trim the mane of a horse very short, causing it to stand up like the bristles of a hog's back **4.** *vti.* NAUT WARP to cause the keel or plank of a ship to curve upwards in the middle, or curve in this way **5.** *vt.* NAUT SCRUB WITH A BROOM to clean a ship's bottom with a broom while the ship is in the water [Pre-12thC. Origin uncertain: perhaps ultimately from Celtic. The word probably originally applied in English to the age of a pig or sheep.] —**hoglike** *adj.*
◇ **go the whole hog** to do sth wholeheartedly or completely and without restraint (*slang*)

hogan /hốgən/ *n.* a traditional Navajo dwelling made of wood and mud, with a roof of earth [Late 19thC. From Navajo.]

Hogan /hốgən/, **Ben** (1912–97) US golfer. He won over 60 major golfing tournaments including four US Open championships (1948, 1950, 1951, 1953). Full name **William Benjamin Hogan**

Hogan, Paul (*b.* 1940) Australian actor. Originally a television performer, he starred in the film *Crocodile Dundee* (1986) and cowrote and produced *Crocodile Dundee II* (1988).

Hogarth /hố gaarth/, **William** (1697–1764) British painter and engraver. He is best known for his series of satirical engravings, including *A Rake's Progress* (1732–35). —**Hogarthian** /hō gáarthi ən/ *adj.*

hogback /hóg bak/ *n.* GEOG a steep and narrow low ridge produced by the erosion of the softer surrounding rock strata

hog badger *n.* a nocturnal badger native to Southeast Asia that has an elongated snout with which it roots for insects and grubs. Latin name: *Arctonyx collaris.* [Hog from its cloven hooves]

hog cholera *n. US* = **swine fever**

hogfish /hógfish/ (*plural* -**fish** *or* -**fishes**) *n.* **1.** FISH OF CORAL REEFS a fish in the wrasse family found on tropical coral reefs and often brightly coloured, especially one with the first three spines of its dorsal fin thickened and elongated. Latin name: *Lachnolaimus maximus.* **2.** = **pigfish** [Hog from the grunting sound it makes]

hogg *n.* = **hog** *n.* **3** (*regional*)

Hogg /hog/, **James** (1770–1835) Scottish poet. A shepherd turned writer, he wrote ballads and the novel *The Private Memoirs and Confessions of a Justified Sinner* (1824).

hogget /hóggit/ *n.* **1.** ANZ, UK, US = **hog** *n.* **3** (*regional*) **2.** YOUNG SHEEP'S WOOL the wool from a sheep 12 to 14 months old

hoggish /hóggish/ *adj.* greedy, selfish, or slovenly — **hoggishly** *adv.* —**hoggishness** *n.*

Hogmanay /hógmə nay, hógmə náy/ *n. Scotland* New Year's Eve as celebrated in Scotland and in parts of northern England [Early 17thC. Origin uncertain: probably from Norman dialect *hoguinané*, said when exchanging New Year's gifts, from Old French *aguillanneuf*, a contraction of *accueillis l'an neuf* 'welcome the new year'.]

hognosed skunk /hógnōzd-/ *n.* a large skunk of Central and South America that has a broad white stripe down its back and a snout resembling a hog's with which it roots for insects and grubs. Latin name: *Conepatus mesoleucas.*

hognose snake /hógnōz-/, **hognosed snake** *n.* a nonvenomous North American snake with a stout body and an upturned snout resembling a hog's that is used for burrowing. Genus: *Heterodon.* [Hognose from its upturned snout]

hognut /hóg nut/ *n.* = **pignut**

hog peanut *n.* a North American vine of the legume family that has clusters of white or pinkish flowers and edible, fleshy, single-seeded pods that ripen on or beneath the ground. Latin name: *Amphicarpaea bracteata.*

hog's back *n.* = **hogback**

Hog's Back /hógz bak/ ridge in Surrey, southeastern England, running between the towns of Guildford and Farnham. Height: 154 m/505 ft.

hogshead /hógz hed/ *n.* **1.** LIQUID MEASURE a unit of capacity for liquids or dry goods, used especially for alcohol, having various units but typically 54 imperial gallons or 63 US gallons **2.** LARGE CASK a large cask or barrel, especially one having a capacity of one hogshead [14thC. Literally 'head of a hog' (the reason for the name is unknown).]

hog-tie *vt. US* **1.** TRUSS to tie the legs of an animal or the feet and hands of a person together **2.** IMPEDE to hamper sb in his or her actions, or impede the progress of sth (*informal*)

hogwash /hóg wosh/ *n.* **1.** NONSENSE rubbish or nonsense (*informal*) ○ *What a pile of hogwash!* **2.** PIGSWILL leftovers of food that are given to pigs to eat

Hogweed

hogweed /hóg weed/ *n.* any of several coarse weeds such as sow thistle and knotweed

Hohhot /hố hót/ capital city of Inner Mongolia, an autonomous region in northeastern China. Population: 652,534 (1990).

ho hum /hố húm/ *interj.* used to express boredom, disappointment, or resignation (*informal*) ○ *Ho hum, off we go, I suppose.* [Thought to suggest a yawn]

hoick /hoyk/ (**hoicks, hoicking, hoicked**) *vti.* to pull or lift sth or sb violently or suddenly (*informal*) [Late 19thC. Origin uncertain: perhaps a variant of HIKE 'to pull up'.]

hoicks /hoyks/ *n.* a shout in hunting, used to urge hounds to move along faster [Early 17thC. Origin unknown.]

hoi polloi /hóypə lóy, hóy pólloy/ *n.* ordinary people as opposed to the wealthy, well-educated, and cultivated elite [From Greek, literally 'the many']

hoisin sauce /hóysin-/ *n.* a dark sweet and spicy sauce of thick consistency made from fermented soy beans and used to flavour Chinese dishes and as a condiment [Hoisin from Chinese (Cantonese), literally 'delicacy of the sea']

hoist /hoyst/ *vt.* (**hoists, hoisting, hoisted**) LIFT UP to raise or lift sb or sth up, especially using a mechanical device such as a winch ■ *n.* **1.** DEVICE FOR LIFTING a mechanical device or apparatus such as a winch or elevator designed for lifting people or heavy objects **2.** LIFTING UP an act of hoisting sb or sth **3.** SHIPPING SIGNAL a message or signal conveyed from ship to ship by flags hoisted up the mast **4.** MEASURE OF A SAIL the height of a sail or flag [16thC. Alteration of *hoise*, itself an alteration of obsolete *heise*, of uncertain origin: probably from Dutch *hijsen* or Low German *hissen* 'to raise'.] —**hoister** *n.*

WORD KEY: SYNONYMS

See Synonyms at ***raise***.

hoity-toity /hóyti tóyti/ *adj.* arrogant and self-important (*informal*) [Alteration and repetition of obsolete *hoit* 'to romp', of uncertain origin. Originally in the meaning of 'flighty behaviour'.]

Hokan /hṓkən/ *n.* a group of Native American languages of the southwestern United States, including Chumash, Yuman, and other languages and linguistic groups [Early 20thC. Formed from Hokan *hok* 'two'.] —**Hokan** *adj.*

hoke /hōk/ (**hokes, hoking, hoked**) *vt.* to introduce highly melodramatic or broadly comic elements into a story, play, or speech, in order to captivate an audience [Early 20thC. Back-formation from HOKUM.]

hokey /hṓki/ (**-ier, -iest**) *adj.* (*informal*) **1.** *US, Can* **CONTRIVED** obviously contrived or clearly not genuine **2.** *US* **CORNY** corny, sentimental, or melodramatic [Mid-20thC. Formed from HOKE or HOKUM.] —**hokeyness** *n.* —**hokily** *adv.*

hokey cokey /hṓki kṓki/ *n.* a dance, done especially by children, in which a circle of people sing out the instructions for movements that they perform at the same time. US term **hokey-pokey** [Origin uncertain: perhaps by repetition and alteration from HOKEY]

hokey-pokey /hṓki pṓki/ (*plural* **hokey-pokeys**) *n.* **1.** *NZ* **TOFFEE** a kind of toffee, most often encountered as an ingredient in a flavour of ice cream **2.** *US* = **hokey cokey** [Origin unknown]

Hokkaido /ho kīdō/ the second largest island of Japan, situated north of the main island of Honshu. Population: 5,643,647 (1990). Area: 83,520 sq. km/32,247 sq. mi.

hokku /hó koo/ (*plural* **-ku**) *n.* = **haiku** [Late 19thC. From Japanese, 'opening verse (of a sequence of comic verses)'.]

hokum /hṓkəm/ *n. US* **1. RUBBISH** sth that on the surface appears to be true or credible but is in fact meaningless or untrue (*informal disapproving*) ○ *a load of hokum* **2. UNNECESSARY THEATRICS** highly melodramatic or broadly comedic elements introduced into a story, play, or speech, in order to captivate an audience [Early 20thC. Origin uncertain: perhaps a blend of HOCUS-POCUS and BUNKUM.]

hol- *prefix.* = **holo-** (*used before vowels*)

holandric /hō lándrik, ho-/ *adj.* used to describe genetic traits carried on the Y chromosome and therefore carried and inherited only by males [Mid-20thC. Coined from HOLO- + ANDRO- + -IC.]

Holarctic /hō laárktik, ho-/ *adj.* found in or typical of the regions of North America and Eurasia combined, which share many faunal characteristics

Holbein (the Elder) /hól bīn thi éldər/, **Hans** (1460?–1524) German painter. The father and teacher of Hans Holbein the Younger, his most famous work is the St Sebastian Altar, Munich (1493).

Holbein (the Younger) /hól bīn thə yúng gər/, **Hans** (1497–1543) German painter. The son of Hans Holbein the Elder, he is best remembered for his portraits of the court of Henry VIII.

hold[1] /hōld/ *v.* (**holds, holding, held** /held/) **1.** *vt.* **GRASP STH** to take sth firmly and retain it in the hand or arms **2.** *vt.* **LIFT AND KEEP IN POSITION** to carry, lift, or support temporarily an object or part of the body in a particular position ○ *Hold the rope a bit higher.* **3.** *vt.* **FIX** to keep sth fixed in a particular position ○ *The picture is held in place by two large hooks.* **4.** *vt.* **EMBRACE** to bring or have sb within an embrace or supported by the arms **5.** *vt.* **CONTAIN** to be the place where sth is or can be kept ○ *a basket to hold all your sewing equipment* **6.** *vt.* **KEEP IN CUSTODY** to keep sb in a particular place or condition, especially in custody **7.** *vt.* **DELAY** to cause delay to sb ○ *What held you so long?* **8.** *vt.* **RETAIN** to retain or reserve sth for later use or collection by sb else ○ *Ask if they can hold the tickets for us at the box office.* **9.** *vt.* **REFRAIN** to refrain from doing or saying sth ○ *The captain told his soldiers to hold their fire.* **10.** *vt.* **STOP LEAVING** to stop sth leaving or happening at the appointed time, usually for a particular purpose ○ *The conductor held the train so that we could board.* **11.** *vt.* MIL **KEEP BY FORCE** to keep possession of sth by force, especially while under attack ○ *The insurgents held the town for some time before retreating.* **12.** *vt.* **HAVE CERTAIN CAPACITY** to contain or be able to contain a particular number or amount ○ *This cup holds eight ounces.* **13.** *vt.* **BE ABLE TO CONSUME** to consume sth, especially alcohol, without ill effect **14.** *vt.* **ARRANGE** to arrange, take part in, or observe an activity or event ○ *They hold a party every Friday night.* **15.** *vt.* **POSSESS** to have the right to sth as a possession or achievement ○ *The author holds the copyright to this book.* **16.** *vt.* **HAVE PARTICULAR POSITION** to fulfil the duties of a particular title, office, or position ○ *She has held the position of Director since 1994.* **17.** *vti.* **KEEP PROMISE** to keep a promise, or make sure that sb keeps a promise or is true to a stated intention ○ *The lawyer held to his promise to bring them to justice.* **18.** *vt.* **BELIEVE OR FEEL** to have a particular belief, opinion, or feeling ○ *As Jefferson expressed it in the Declaration of Independence, 'We hold these truths to be self-evident'.* **19.** *vt.* **REGARD** to regard sb or sth in a particular way ○ *She holds her professor in very high esteem.* **20.** *vt.* **HAVE A PARTICULAR BEARING** to keep or carry the body or a part of it in a particular attitude or position ○ *The old general holds himself stiffly.* **21.** *vt.* **ENGROSS** to engage or captivate sb or sb's attention ○ *She held their attention with the dramatic tale of her rescue.* **22.** *vt.* LAW **DECIDE LEGALLY** to decide or lay down sth legally or authoritatively ○ *The appeals court held that the lower court acted properly.* **23.** *vt.* MUSIC **SUSTAIN** to keep singing or playing a note or a chord without stopping ○ *The trumpeter held the note for at least a full minute.* **24.** *vi.* **PERSIST** to continue in a particular state or course ○ *I can't believe this run of bad luck will hold.* ○ *The snow still holds on the mountains.* **25.** *vi.* **REMAIN FIRM** to remain fast or firm and not break or give way ○ *The dam held throughout the flooding.* ○ *I don't think the rope is going to hold for much longer.* **26.** *vi.* **STAND FIRM** to maintain a position against attack or opposition ○ *Their defensive line held, despite heavy losses.* **27.** *vi.* **REMAIN VALID** to remain in force or continue to be valid ○ *Many old sayings still hold true.* **28.** *vi.* **STAY FINE** continue to be fine and, e.g., not rain, snow, or become cold (*refers to the weather*) ○ *We're meant to be going to a picnic on Saturday so I hope the weather holds.* **29.** *vt.* **LEASE PROPERTY** to maintain the right to use property by some kind of tenure, e.g. a lease or easement ○ *They held the farm under a very long lease.* **30.** *vti.* COMMUNICATION **WAIT ON TELEPHONE** to wait during a telephone call and not break the connection, usually so that the person being called can speak to sb else or transfer the call ○ *Could you hold, please, while I try to connect you?* ○ *Hold the line please.* ■ *n.* **1. GRASP ON STH** the act or position of grasping or keeping possession of sth ○ *a firm hold on the child's arm* ○ *no hold on reality* **2.** WRESTLING **WRESTLING TECHNIQUE** a position or manner of grasping an opponent in wrestling **3. STH GIVING SUPPORT** sth that may be grasped or used as a support ○ *There were few holds on the sheer rock face.* **4. STH THAT RESTRAINS** a structure or receptacle used for keeping sth in check, e.g. a lock on a canal **5. CONTROL OVER SB** a controlling power or influence ○ *a firm hold on the public's imagination* **6. DELAYING STH** an act of delaying or restraining sth, or an order to effect this ○ *Because of excessive traffic, there was a hold put on the plane's takeoff.* ○ *Put a hold on their dinner order.* **7.** MUSIC **MUSIC NOTATION** a symbol appearing above or below a note or rest, signalling that it can be prolonged beyond its prescribed time **8. PRISON** a prison cell or place of confinement **9. STRONGHOLD** a fortified place in a castle or other structure (*dated*) [Old English *haldan, healdan*, from a prehistoric Germanic word meaning 'to guard, watch', which is also the ancestor of English *behold* and *halt*] ◇ **get hold of sb** *or* **sth** to succeed in finding sb or obtaining sth ◇ **hold good** to apply, or be true or valid ◇ **hold it** used to tell sb to stop or wait ◇ **hold sth against sb** to resent sth that sb has done and to bear a grudge because of it ◇ **on hold 1.** COMMUNICATION waiting to be connected or reconnected to sb during a telephone call **2.** into or in a state of suspension or postponement ◇ **no holds barred** with no restrictions on what is allowed or included

hold back *v.* **1.** *vti.* **RESTRAIN** to keep back or restrain sb from doing sth ○ *His shyness holds him back from making friends.* **2.** *vt.* **KEEP BACK** to withhold sth or retain sth within your own control ○ *accused of holding back vital information* ○ *holding back tears*

WORD KEY: SYNONYMS

See Synonyms at ***hinder***.

hold down *vt.* to do enough in a job or position to keep it (*informal*) ○ *He can't even manage to hold down one job, let alone two!*

hold forth *vi.* to speak at length and sometimes tediously on a particular subject ○ *holding forth for hours about their flash new car*

hold in *vt.* **1. KEEP IN CHECK** to keep back or in check ○ *It was nearly impossible to hold in the hounds until the hunt began.* **2. RESTRAIN EMOTIONS** to suppress sth such as an emotion or feeling ○ *They held in their emotions throughout the crisis.*

hold off *v.* **1.** *vti.* **REFRAIN** to refrain from doing sth ○ *We decided to hold off until after the election.* ○ *It might be wise to hold off making any decisions until after the results come out.* **2.** *vt.* **RESIST** to keep sb or sth away, or prevent sb from approaching too close ○ *A handful of soldiers held off several enemy attacks.* **3.** *vi.* **NOT HAPPEN** to not produce bad weather conditions after threatening to do so ○ *The rain held off, and the barbecue went ahead as planned.*

hold on *vi.* **1. WAIT** to wait for a short while ○ *Hold on, and let's see if we can sort out this problem.* **2. PERSIST** to continue on a course of action or direction, or maintain sth such as a set of principles or a particular state of mind ○ *He held on until he knew all was lost.* ○ *The scientist held on to her theory and finally proved it correct.*

hold out *v.* **1.** *vt.* **EXTEND** to stretch out or extend a part of the body, or offer sth to sb in doing this ○ *She held out her hand.* **2.** *vi.* **LAST** to keep up or continue to be in supply ○ *The water supply will hold out only until tomorrow night.* **3.** *vi.* **ENDURE** to continue to resist and not give in to sth ○ *We managed to hold out for three days against the enemy.* **4.** *vi.* **RESIST** to refuse to settle sth or accept sth until all demands or conditions are met ○ *holding out for a 6% pay rise*

hold over /hṓldōvər/ *vt.* **1. DEFER** to postpone action on or consideration of sth until a later date **2. NOT LET SB FORGET STH** to blackmail sb with information, or not let sb forget sth embarrassing or shameful in order to have power over him or her (*informal*) ○ *You're not going to keep holding that over me, are you?*

hold together *vti.* to remain united, or cause a group of people to remain united, often despite problems or disagreements ○ *He held the family together single-handed.* ○ *It was nothing more than a desire to earn money that held them together.*

hold up *v.* **1.** *vt.* **CAUSE DELAY** to cause sb or sth to be late or take longer than intended ○ *Minor disagreements hold up any negotiation.* ○ *I was held up in traffic.* **2.** *vt.* CRIMINOL **ROB** to rob a person or place using violence or threats, usually at gunpoint **3.** *vt.* **PRESENT** to show or display sb or sth for a specific reason ○ *The firefighter was held up as a good example of bravery.* **4.** *vi.* **ENDURE** to continue to function or survive ○ *How's the bike holding up?* ○ *You've been holding up well under the strain.* **5.** *vi.* **REMAIN SAME** to remain or be maintained at a particular level or in a particular state ○ *Prices have not held up well in this recession.* **6.** *vi.* **STAND UP TO SCRUTINY** to remain persuasive or convincing even after closer examination ○ *I don't think these ideas will hold up.* **7.** *vi.* BRIDGE **NOT PLAY HIGH CARD** to delay playing a high card in order to prevent a suit from being established

hold with *vt.* to approve or agree with sth ○ *She doesn't hold with that kind of thinking.*

hold[2] /hōld/ *n.* the area below the deck of a ship or the area inside an aircraft in which cargo is carried [Late 16thC. Alteration of HOLE, influenced by HOLD[1].]

holdall /hṓld awl/ *n.* a capacious bag or case used for carrying miscellaneous items. US term **carryall**

holdback /hṓld bak/ *n.* **1. STH THAT HINDERS** sth that prevents sb from doing or achieving sth or that prevents an event or plan from going ahead **2. DEVICE ON A WAGON OR CARRIAGE** a device on the shaft of a wagon or carriage that attaches to the horse's harness, allowing the horse to hold back or back up the vehicle 3. STH HELD BACK sth withheld, usually wages or money

hold button *n.* a button on a telephone that allows sb to put a caller on hold

Holden /hṓldən/, **William** (1918–81) US actor. He was a popular clean-cut hero in many 1940s and 1950s Hollywood films such as *Sunset Boulevard* (1950) and *Bridge on the River Kwai* (1957).

holder /hṓldər/ *n.* **1.** CONTAINER sth designed to hold another thing (*often used in combination*) ○ *a candle holder* **2.** OWNER sb who owns, occupies, or is in possession of sth, e.g. property or a title ○ *the current holder of the world title* **3.** FIN SB WITH A PROMISE OF PAYMENT sb in possession of and legally entitled to receive payment on or negotiate a note, bill, or cheque

Hölderlin /hṓldər lin/, **Friedrich** (1770–1843) German poet. His works include a translation of Sophocles' *Antigone* and the novel *Hyperion* (1797–99). Full name **Johann Christian Friedrich Hölderlin**

holdfast /hṓld faast/ *n.* **1.** CLAMP a device such as a clamp or grip designed to hold sth securely **2.** BOT PLANT'S MEANS OF ATTACHING ITSELF an organ at the base of a seaweed, aquatic plant, or fungus that attaches the organism to a surface **3.** FIRM GRASP the action or fact of holding sth fast or firmly

holding /hṓlding/ *n.* **1.** LEASED LAND a piece of land that is leased from sb else, especially when used for agricultural purposes **2.** PROPERTY legally owned property of any kind, but especially stocks or bonds (*often used in the plural*) **3.** SPORTS ILLEGAL USE OF THE ARMS use of the arms to hold or obstruct an opponent when such use is not allowed in the rules of a sport or game, e.g. in boxing **4.** PSYCHOL SENSE OF SECURITY the ability of a therapist or parent to make a client or child feel contained and secure during times of growth or change

holding company *n.* a company that has a controlling interest in one or more other companies through ownership of stocks or bonds

holding operation *n.* a procedure or operation designed to maintain the present situation as it is

holding pattern *n.* **1.** AIR WAITING PATH OF PLANE a usually circular pattern held by an aircraft while awaiting permission to land **2.** LIMBO a state of suspended action or progress ○ *He's in a holding pattern until he knows whether he's been given the scholarship.*

holdover *n.* ARTS a performer or a presentation such as a play or series of concerts that continues beyond the term originally agreed

holdup /hṓld up/ *n.* **1.** CRIMINOL ROBBERY an act of robbing a person or place using violence or threats, usually at gunpoint **2.** DELAY an act of causing sb or sth to be late or take longer than planned ○ *Travel was slowed by holdups on the M40.* **3.** BRIDGE WITHHOLDING OF CARD the holding back of a card rather than playing it to take a trick early in the play of a hand

WORD KEY: SYNONYMS

See Synonyms at ***theft***.

hole /hōl/ *n.* **1.** CAVITY a hollow space in a solid object or area ○ *The hole had filled with water.* **2.** APERTURE a gap or opening in or through sth ○ *a hole in my socks* **3.** BURROW a hollowed-out area in the earth where an animal such as a rabbit or mouse lives ○ *a rabbit hole* **4.** UNPLEASANT PLACE TO BE a dark or dirty place, especially a place where sb lives (*informal*) **5.** FLAW a fault or flaw in sth such as logic, an argument, or a position ○ *But there are so many holes in her theory.* **6.** AWKWARD SITUATION an awkward or embarrassing situation (*informal*) **7.** PRISONER'S CELL a prison cell or dungeon (*informal*) **8.** ELECTRON ENG MOBILE SPACE IN SEMICONDUCTOR a space normally occupied by an electron in the lattice structure of a semiconductor material that is mobile and can act as a carrier of a positive charge **9.** GOLF TARGET IN GOLF a small round cavity or cup on a golf course into which the ball is hit **10.** GOLF AREA OF GOLF COURSE a part of a golf course that consists of a tee, a fairway, and a green with a hole and is a basic element in scoring. A golf course usually has 18 holes. ■ *v.* **(holes, holing, holed) 1.** *vti.* PERFORATE to make a hole or holes in sth ○ *This new device holes a ream of paper perfectly.* **2.** *vt.* GOLF PUT IN A HOLE to hit or drive a ball into one of the holes of a golf course **3.** *vi.* GO INTO A HOLE to go or climb into a hole [Old English *hol* 'hollow', ultimately of uncertain origin: probably from an Indo-European word meaning 'to hide' (ancestor of English *conceal*)] ◇ **make a hole in sth** to use up a large part of sth (*informal*) ○ *The monthly rent makes a considerable hole in my salary.* ◇ **pick holes in sth** to find fault with sth, often over minor imperfections

hole out *vi.* to hit a golf ball into a hole

hole up *vi.* **1.** HIDE AWAY to hide away somewhere (*slang*) **2.** SHELTER to go into a hole, cave, or other similar place to shelter or hibernate

hole-and-corner *adj.* secret or secretive ○ *hole-and-corner activities*

hole in one (*plural* **holes in one**) *n.* a shot in golf that enters the hole directly from the tee

hole-in-the-wall (*plural* **holes-in-the-wall**) *n.* (*informal*) **1.** MODEST ESTABLISHMENT a small unpretentious out-of-the-way place such as a little restaurant or other business **2.** CASH DISPENSER an automatic cash dispenser located in the outside wall of a bank or other building

holey /hṓli/ *adj.* having or full of holes

Holi /hṓli/ *n.* the Hindu festival of spring that honours the time when Krishna paid amorous attention to young women tending cows. As part of the celebrations people spray coloured water over each other. [Late 17thC. From Hindi *holī*.]

holiday /hólli day, -di/ *n.* **1.** DAY OF LEISURE a day taken off or set aside for leisure and enjoyment, when sb is exempt from work or normal activity **2.** PERIOD OF LEISURE a period of time free from work or normal activity and given over to leisure and recreation ○ *the summer holidays* ○ *whilst we were on holiday in Spain* ○ *a holiday resort.* US term **vacation 3.** LEGAL DAY OFF a day set aside by law, statute, or custom as exempt from regular work or business activities, e.g. Christmas Day or a bank holiday **4.** HOLY DAY the day or days of a religious festival ■ *vi.* **(-days, -daying, -dayed)** SPEND HOLIDAY to go on or spend a holiday. US term **vacation** *v.* [Old English *hāligdæg*, literally 'holy day', a day set aside as a religious festival, and hence when no work was done]

Holiday /hólli day/, **Billie** (1915–59) US jazz singer. Known for her emotionally charged renditions of popular songs, she collaborated with Count Basie and Artie Shaw. Her autobiography *Lady Sings the Blues* (1956) was later made into a film. Real name **Eleanora Fagan McKay Holiday**. Known as **Lady Day**

holiday camp *n.* a purpose-built site, often by the sea, that provides accommodation, organized leisure activities, and facilities for people who come for a holiday

holidaymaker /hólli day maykər, -di-/ *n. UK, ANZ* sb who is on holiday. US term **vacationer**

holier-than-thou /hṓli ər-/ *adj.* SELF-RIGHTEOUS aggressively or offensively pompous or self-righteous (*informal*) ○ *Her holier-than-thou attitude puts people off.* ■ *n.* SELF-RIGHTEOUS PERSON OR ORGANIZATION an aggressively or offensively pompous or self-righteous person or organization (*informal*) ○ *The chairman is regarded as one of the bigger holier-than-thous.*

holiness /hṓlinəss/ *n.* the state or quality of being holy

Holiness *n.* a title used in addressing or referring to the Pope

holism /hṓlizəm/ *n.* **1.** PHILOS PHILOSOPHICAL THEORY the view that a whole system of beliefs must be analysed rather than simply its individual components **2.** MED THEORY OF HEALTH the theory of the importance of taking all of sb's physical, mental, and social conditions, not just physical symptoms, into account in the treatment of illness [Early 20thC. Coined from Greek *holos* 'whole' + -ISM.] —**holist** *n.*

holistic /hō lístik/ *adj.* including or involving all of sth, especially all of sb's physical, mental, and social conditions, not just physical symptoms, in the treatment of illness —**holistically** *adv.*

holland /hólland/ *n.* a type of strong smooth linen fabric used especially for upholstery [14thC. Named after HOLLAND, where it was originally produced.]

Holland /hólland/ **1.** = **Netherlands 2.** former administrative division of Lincolnshire, England, known as the Parts of Holland. It was abolished in 1974.

Holland, Sir Sidney George (1893–1961) New Zealand statesman. Elected to parliament in 1940, he became leader of the National Party (1947) and prime minister of New Zealand (1949–57).

hollandaise sauce /hóllən dáyz-/, **hollandaise** *n.* a rich creamy piquant sauce made from butter, egg yolks, and vinegar or lemon juice. It is served with many different foods, especially fish. [*Hollandaise* from French, the feminine of *Hollandais* 'Dutch']

Hollander /hólləndər/ *n.* sb born, brought up, or living in the Netherlands (*dated*)

Hollands /hólləndz/ *n.* genever, or Dutch gin (*archaic*) [Late 18thC. Formed from obsolete Dutch *Hollandsch genever* 'Dutch gin'.]

holler /hóllər/ *vti.* **(-lers, -lering, -lered)** SHOUT to call out or shout sth (*informal*) ○ *If you need me, just holler!* ■ *n.* (*informal*) **1.** LOUD CRY a loud cry or shout **2.** *US* WORK SONG a type of work song originally sung by enslaved and labouring Black American people [Late 17thC. Origin uncertain: probably ultimately from both Old French *halloer* 'to pursue with shouting', an imitation of the sound, and French *holà* 'stop!', from *ho* 'ho' + *là* 'there'.]

hollow /hóllō/ *adj.* **1.** NOT SOLID having empty space inside ○ *The tree trunk was hollow inside.* **2.** CONCAVE sunk deep into the surface of sth **3.** NOT FULL-TONED resonating or echoing as if in an empty space ○ *It gave a huge, hollow, booming sound.* **4.** INSINCERE not sincere, genuine, or significant ○ *He gave a hollow laugh.* **5.** HUNGRY having the feeling of an empty stomach ■ *n.* **1.** CAVITY a hollow or concave place or area, as in a tree trunk or sb's back ○ *The child held the chick in the hollow of his hand.* **2.** VALLEY a sunken or low-lying area of the earth's surface ■ *v.* **(-lows, -lowing, -lowed) 1.** *vt.* MAKE A CAVITY IN STH to form sth by removing contents to leave a concave area or cavity **2.** *vti.* MAKE OR BECOME HOLLOWED to make sth hollow or become hollow ○ *eyes hollowed from lack of sleep* ■ *adv.* HOLLOWLY in a hollow way ○ *Their voices rang hollow in the emptied streets.* [Old English *holh* 'hollow place, hole, cave', of uncertain origin: probably from a prehistoric Germanic word that is also the ancestor of English *hole*] —**hollowly** *adv.* —**hollowness** *n.*

WORD KEY: SYNONYMS

See Synonyms at ***vain***.

WORD KEY: CULTURAL NOTE

The Hollow Men, a poem by US-born British writer T. S. Eliot (1925). One of Eliot's most pessimistic works, it depicts a barren, ghostly land peopled by soulless beings. Its imagery and concern with the sterility of modern civilization link it to 'The Waste Land', but in 'The Hollow Men' the message, conveyed in short lines and repetitive phrases, is more direct and bereft of any hope of redemption. The oft-quoted words 'This is the way the world ends/ Not with a bang but a whimper' come from this poem.

Hollows /hólloz/, **Fred** (1930–93) New Zealand-born Australian ophthalmologist. He was a pioneer of the treatment of trachoma among Aboriginal Australians and founder of eye health programmes in a number of developing countries. Full name **Frederick Cossom Hollows**

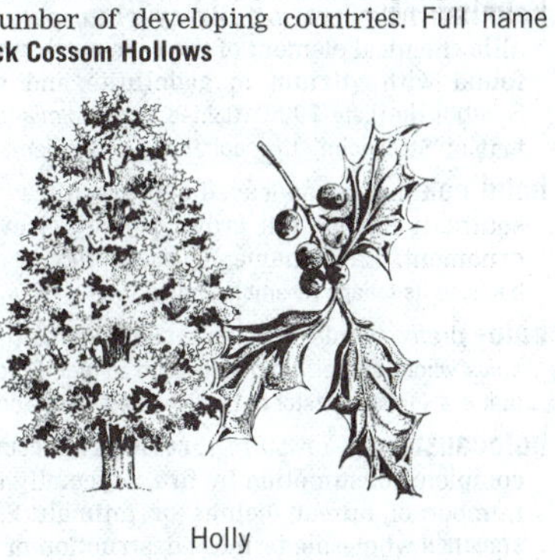

Holly

hollowware /hóllō wair/ *n. US* articles of tableware and kitchenware such as pots, bowls, cups, vases, and jugs that are hollow, as opposed to items such as plates and saucers

holly /hólli/ (*plural* **-lies**) *n.* **1. EVERGREEN SHRUB WITH RED BERRIES** an evergreen tree or shrub with glossy, prickly leaves and bright red berries. Genus: *Ilex.* **2. DECORATIVE FOLIAGE** the leaves and berries of holly used especially as a Christmas decoration [12thC. Shortening of Old English *hole(g)n*, from prehistoric Germanic.]

Holly /hólli/, **Buddy** (1938–59) US musician. His band, the Crickets, was one of the earliest rock-and-roll groups, and helped establish the standard lineup of two guitars, bass, and drums. His hit songs included 'That'll Be the Day' and 'Peggy Sue' (both 1957). Real name **Charles Hardin Holley**

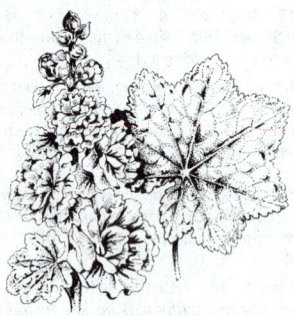

Hollyhock

hollyhock /hólli hok/ *n.* a plant of the mallow family that has very tall hairy stems and is often grown for its spikes of variously coloured flowers. Latin name: *Alcea rosea.* [13thC. From an alteration of HOLY (perhaps from its being connected with a saint) + obsolete *hock* 'mallow', of unknown origin.]

holly oak *n.* = **holm oak** [Because its foliage resembles holly]

Hollywood[1] /hólliwŏŏd/ *n.* the US film industry as a whole

Hollywood[2] /hólliwŏŏd/ district of Los Angeles, California, a centre of the US film and television industry

holm[1] /hōm/, **holme** *n.* **1. FLAT LAND BY RIVER** low-lying flat land next to a river or stream **2. SMALL ISLAND** a small island in a river, lake, estuary, or near the coastal mainland [Old English, from Old Norse *holmr* 'islet in a bay, meadow'. Ultimately from an Indo-European base meaning 'to be prominent' (ancestor of English *hill*).]

holm[2] /hōm/ *n.* **1.** = **holm oak 2. HOLLY** a holly plant (*regional*) [14thC. Alteration of obsolete *hollin*, from Old English *hole(g)n*, an earlier form of HOLLY.]

holme *n.* = **holm**[1]

Holmes à Court /hōmz ə kawrt/, **Robert** (1937–90) South African-born Australian business executive. He was the head of the Bell Group Ltd, one of Australia's largest companies during the 1980s. He was also an art collector and horse breeder. Full name **Michael Robert Hamilton Holmes à Court**

holmic /hólmik/ *adj.* resembling or containing the metallic element holmium

holmium /hólmi əm/ *n.* a silvery-white malleable metallic chemical element of the rare-earth group often found with yttrium in gadolinite and monazite. Symbol **Ho** [Late 19thC. Coined from *Holmia* (a Latinized form of 'Stockholm', the capital city of Sweden), + -IUM.]

holm oak *n.* a broad-leaved evergreen tree native to southern Europe but grown widely elsewhere for ornament. Latin name: *Quercus ilex.* [From HOLM[2] because its foliage resembles holly]

holo- *prefix.* whole, complete ○ *hologynic* [From Greek *holos* 'whole, entire'. Ultimately from an Indo-European word that is also the ancestor of English *solid, safe,* and *catholic*.]

holocaust /hóllə kawst/ *n.* **1. COMPLETE DESTRUCTION BY FIRE** complete consumption by fire, especially of a large number of human beings or animals **2. TOTAL DESTRUCTION** wholesale or mass destruction of any kind **3. BURNT OFFERING** a sacrifice that is totally consumed by fire [13thC. Via Old French *holocauste* from, ultimately, Greek *holokaustos*, literally 'burned whole', from, ultimately,

kaiein 'to burn'.] —**holocaustal** /hóllə kawst'l/ *adj.* —**holocaustic** /-káwstik/ *adj.*

──── **WORD KEY: ORIGIN** ────

Holocaust was originally used in English for a 'burnt offering', a 'sacrifice completely consumed by fire' (Mark 12:33, 'more than all whole burnt offerings and sacrifices', in the Authorized Version of the Bible, was translated by William Tyndale in 1526 as 'a greater thing than all holocausts and sacrifices'). John Milton is the first English writer recorded as using it in the wider sense 'complete destruction by fire', in the late 17th century, and in the succeeding centuries several precedents were set for its modern application to 'nuclear destruction' and 'mass murder' — Bishop Ken, for instance, wrote in 1711 'Should general Flame this World consume ... An Holocaust for Fontal Sin', and Leitch Ritchie in 1833 refers to Louis VII making 'a holocaust of thirteen hundred persons in a church'. The specific application to the mass murder of the Jews by the Nazis during World War II was introduced by historians during the 1950s, probably as an equivalent to Hebrew *ḥurban* and *shoah* 'catastrophe' (used in the same sense).

Holocaust /hóllə kawst/ *n.* the systematic extermination of millions of European Jews, Romany people, Slavs, intellectuals, gay people, and political dissidents by the Nazis and their allies during World War II. In popular usage, especially in the United States, Holocaust refers particularly to the extermination of European Jews. ○ *Holocaust survivors*

Holocene /hóllō seen/ *n.* the most recent epoch of the Quaternary period, extending to the present day [Late 19thC. From French from an earlier form of HOLO- + Greek *kainos* 'new, recent'.] —**Holocene** *adj.*

holocrine /hóllō krin, -krīn/ *adj.* relating to a gland such as a sebaceous gland whose secretions are derived from the substance of the gland itself

holoenzyme /hóllō én zīm/ *n.* an active enzyme comprising a protein and coenzyme

hologram /hóllə gram/ *n.* **1. THREE-DIMENSIONAL PHOTOGRAPHIC IMAGE** a three-dimensional image of an object that is a photographic record of light interference patterns produced using a photographic plate and light from a laser **2. HOLOGRAM IMAGE** the image produced by a hologram

holograph /hóllə graf, -gräf/ *n.* **1. ORIGINAL MANUSCRIPT** a manuscript or other document entirely handwritten by its author. This term is used especially in reference to manuscripts and letters, and to unwitnessed wills. **2.** = **hologram** *n.* 1, **hologram** *n.* 2 ■ *adj.* **IN THE HANDWRITING OF THE AUTHOR** used to describe a manuscript or other document wholly written in the handwriting of its author [Early 17thC. Via late Latin *holographus* from Greek *holographos*, literally 'written whole'.]

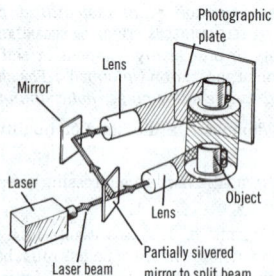

Holography

holography /ho lóggrəfi/ *n.* a method of recording and showing a three-dimensional image of an object using a photographic plate and light from a laser — **holographic** /hóllə gráffik/ *adj.* —**holographically** /-gráffikli/ *adv.*

hologynic /hóllō jínnik, -gínnik/ *adj.* used to describe genetic traits that are inherited and passed on only by females [Coined from HOLO- + Greek *gunē* 'woman' (see GYNO-) + -IC]

holohedral /hóllō heédrəl/ *adj.* used to describe crystals having all the faces required for complete symmetry

holometabolism /hóllōmə tábbəlizəm/ *n.* the condition of developing by metamorphosing from a distinct larval into a distinct adult stage —**holometabolous** *adj.*

holomorphic /hóllō máwrfik/ *adj.* = **holohedral** —**holomorphism** *n.*

holophrastic /hóllō frástik/ *adj.* containing the idea of a sentence or phrase in one word, e.g. 'good-bye' [Mid-19thC. Coined from HOLO- + Greek *phrastikos*, from *phrazein* 'to tell'.]

holophyte /hólə fīt/ *n.* an organism that synthesizes complex organic molecules by photosynthesis

holophytic /hóllə fíttik/ *adj.* able to synthesize complex organic molecules by photosynthesis. ◆ **holozoic**

holoplankton /hóllō plángktən/ *n.* organisms that remain free-swimming plankton throughout their life cycle

holothurian /hóllō thyoóri ən/ *n.* a marine invertebrate animal (**echinoderm**) of the class that includes the sea cucumber. Holothurians have a mouth surrounded by tentacles at one end, an anus at the other, and a body that contains calcitic material but is not rigid. Class: Holothuroidea. [Mid-19thC. Formed from modern Latin *Holothuria*, genus name, from Latin *holothurion*, a marine creature.] —**holothurian** *adj.*

holozoic /hóllō zṓ ik/ *adj.* obtaining nutrition from other organisms or organic matter, as most animals do. ◆ **holophytic**

holp /hōlp/ past tense of **help** (*archaic*)

holpen /hṓlpən/ past participle of **help** (*archaic*)

hols /holz/ *n.* holidays, especially school holidays or sb's main annual holiday (*informal*) ○ *during the hols* [Early 20thC. Contraction of *holidays*.]

Holst /hōlst/, **Gustav** (1874–1934) British composer. He is best remembered for his popular orchestral suite *The Planets* (1914–16). Full name **Gustav Theodore Holst**

Holstein /hól stīn/, **Holstein-Friesian** *n.* = **Friesian** [Mid-19thC. Named after the region, formerly of the Netherlands, now of northern Germany, from which it originates.]

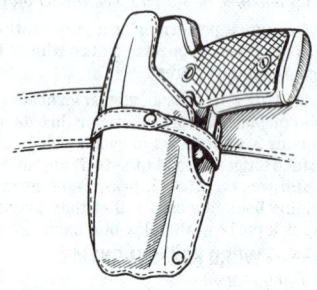

Holster

holster /hṓlstər/ *n.* **GUN HOLDER** a holder for a pistol, usually worn on the hip or shoulder ■ *vt.* (**-sters, -stering, -stered**) **PUT GUN IN HOLDER** to put a pistol in a holster [Mid-17thC. Origin uncertain: probably from Dutch, from, ultimately, an Indo-European word meaning 'to cover' (ancestor of English *conceal*).] —**holstered** *adj.*

holt[1] /hōlt/ *n.* **1. WOODED AREA** a wood or copse (*archaic*) **2. WOODED HILL** a wooded hill (*regional*) [Old English, of prehistoric Germanic origin]

holt[2] /hōlt/ *n.* the lair of an otter, or, sometimes, of some other burrowing animal [14thC. Variant of HOLD 'the action of holding', hence 'protecting sth'.]

Holt /hōlt/, **Harold** (1908–67) Australian statesman. He entered the House of Representatives as a Liberal Party politician (1935), and served as prime minister of Australia (1966–67). Full name **Harold Edward Holt**

holus-bolus /hṓləss bṓləss/ *adv.* all at once or all together (*dated informal*) [Mid-19thC. Origin uncertain: possibly pseudo-Latin for 'whole bolus', or humorously representing Greek *holos bōlos* 'the whole lump' (see BOLUS).]

holy /hṓli/ *adj.* (**-lier, -liest**) **1.** SACRED relating to, belonging to, or coming from a divine being or power ○ *holy relics* **2.** SAINTLY devoted to the service of God, a god, or a goddess **3.** PURE morally and spiritually perfect and of a devoutly religious character ○ *a holy man* **4.** CONSECRATED dedicated or set apart for religious purposes ○ *these holy grounds* **5.** AWE-INSPIRING of a unique character, evoking reverence ○ *Gettysburg is a holy place for many Americans.* ■ *n.* (*plural* **-lies**) **1.** HOLY THING sth sanctified or venerated **2.** HOLY PERSON a devoutly religious, saintly person ■ *interj.* USED IN EXPRESSIONS OF SURPRISE used in various expressions to show surprise (*informal*) ○ *Holy smoke!* [Old English *hālig*, from a prehistoric Germanic word that is the ancestor of English *whole*, the underlying idea being 'unimpaired'] —**holily** *adv.*

Holy Alliance *n.* an alliance among Russia, Prussia, and Austria in 1815 advocating government according to Christian principles

Holy Ark *n.* = **ark** *n.* 4

Holy City *n.* **1.** RELIG JERUSALEM Jerusalem as a city of great religious significance **2.** CHR HEAVEN heaven in Christian tradition

Holy Communion *n.* CHR = **Communion**

Holy Cross *n.* in Christianity, the cross that Jesus Christ died on

holy day *n.* a day set aside for the celebration of a religious festival

holy day of obligation *n.* a Roman Catholic festival on which Catholics are required to attend mass and abstain from certain types of work

Holy Family *n.* in Christianity, the young Jesus Christ, his mother Mary, and Mary's husband, St Joseph, especially as represented in art

Holy Father *n.* in the Roman Catholic Church, the Pope

Holy Ghost *n.* = **Holy Spirit**

Holy Grail *n.* = **Grail**

Holyhead /hólli héd, hólli hed/ **1.** island in northwestern Wales also called Holy Island, situated off the island and county of Anglesey. Area: about 36 sq. km/14 sq. mi. **2.** seaport and resort on the northern coast of Holyhead Island, northwestern Wales. Population: 11,800 (1991). Welsh **Caergybi**

Holy Innocents' Day *n.* in the Christian church, 28 December, the day that commemorates the order given by Herod to massacre all baby boys in Bethlehem

Holy Island 1. = **Lindisfarne 2.** a small island in the Irish Sea off the northwestern coast of Wales, near Anglesey. Area: 62 sq. km/24 sq. mi.

Holy Joe /-jṓ/ *n.* (*dated slang*) **1.** CLERGYMAN a clergyman **2.** SB SANCTIMONIOUS a sanctimonious or self-righteous person

Holy Loch /hṓli lókh/ sea loch near Dunoon, on the Firth of Clyde, Scotland

Holyoake /hṓli ōk/, **Sir Keith** (1904–83) New Zealand statesman. A National Party politician, he served as prime minister of New Zealand (1957, 1960–72) and was the first politician to become governor-general (1977–80). Full name **Sir Keith Jacka Holyoake**

Holy Office *n.* **1.** COMMITTEE OF CARDINALS a permanent committee of the Roman Catholic College of Cardinals that deals with doctrine and morals. It was established in 1542, and was also called the Inquisition. In 1965 its title was changed to Congregation for the Doctrine of the Faith. **2.** HIST = **Inquisition**

holy of holies *n.* **1.** INNER SANCTUM FOR ARK the inner chamber inside the Sanctuary in the Jewish Temple in Jerusalem, where the Ark of the Covenant was kept **2.** SACRED PLACE any place considered to be especially sacred

holy orders *npl.* **1.** RITE OF ORDINATION the rite or sacrament of ordination as a Christian minister or priest **2.** MINISTER'S OR PRIEST'S RANK the rank or position of a Christian minister or priest **3.** ROMAN CATHOLIC OR ANGLICAN RANKS in the Roman Catholic Church, the ranks of priest, deacon, and subdeacon, or in the Anglican Church, the ranks of bishop, priest, and deacon

Holy Roller *n.* an offensive term for a member of a Christian group that worships in what is perceived to be an ecstatic or frenzied way, with shouting, bodily movements, and trances (*slang offensive*) [From the movement of the body during worship]

Holy Roman Empire *n.* an empire in Germany and northern Italy (800–1806). Initially a revival of the Western Roman Empire, it became confined to Germany, and the emperor's authority was negligible after 1254. From 1438 the imperial crown, although elective, was held almost continuously by the Hapsburg family. ◊ **Roman Empire**

Holy Saturday *n.* in Christianity, the Saturday preceding Easter Sunday

Holy Scripture *n.* the Christian Bible, or a particular part of it that is being cited or referred to

Holy See *n.* **1.** PAPACY in the Roman Catholic Church, the see of the Pope as Bishop of Rome **2.** PAPAL COURT in the Roman Catholic Church, the government departments, jurisdiction, and authority of the Vatican

Holy Sepulchre *n.* in Christianity, the tomb in which the body of Jesus Christ was laid after the Crucifixion

Holy Spirit *n.* in Christianity, the third person of the Trinity, understood as the spiritual force of God

holystone /hṓli stōn/ *n.* DECK SCOURER a piece of soft sandstone used for scouring the decks of ships ■ *vt.* (**-stones, -stoning, -stoned**) CLEAN WITH HOLYSTONE to scour the deck of a ship with a holystone [*Holy* perhaps because it is used while kneeling]

Holy Synod *n.* the governing body of any of the Eastern Orthodox Christian churches

holy terror *n.* sb who is especially difficult or frightening to deal with (*informal*) ○ *That child is a holy terror.*

Holy Thursday *n.* **1.** ASCENSION DAY in the Anglican Church, Ascension Day, the 40th day after Easter **2.** MAUNDY THURSDAY in the Roman Catholic Church, Maundy Thursday, the Thursday before Easter commemorating the Last Supper and the day before Jesus Christ was crucified

holytide /hṓli tīd/ *n.* a period having particular religious significance (*archaic*) [12thC. *Tide* from TIDE in the obsolete sense of 'period of time'.]

Holy Trinity *n.* CHR = **Trinity**

holy war *n.* a war undertaken in the name of a particular religion

holy water *n.* water that has been blessed by a priest and is used in a church for blessings, baptisms, and other holy rituals

Holy Week *n.* in the Christian calendar, the final week of Lent, beginning on Palm Sunday and including Ash Wednesday, Maundy Thursday, Good Friday, and Holy Saturday

Holy Writ *n.* sacred Christian writings, especially the Bible

Holy Year *n.* in the Roman Catholic Church, a period of remission from sin declared by the Pope with certain conditions attached, usually at 25 year intervals

hom- *prefix.* = **homo-** (*used before vowels*)

homage /hómmij/ *n.* **1.** DEFERENCE a show of reverence and respect towards sb **2.** HIST VASSAL'S RESPECT DUE TO LORD a formal public acknowledgment of allegiance on the part of a vassal towards a feudal lord [13thC. From Old French, of uncertain origin: probably from *homme* 'man', from the allegiance of one person to another.]

hombre /ómbray/ *n. US* a man (*informal*) [Mid-19thC. Via Spanish from Latin *homo* 'human being' (source of English *homicide*).]

homburg /hóm burg/ *n.* a man's felt hat with an upturned brim and a lengthwise crease in the crown [Late 19thC. Named after the town in western Germany where it was first worn.]

home /hōm/ *n.* **1.** RESIDENCE the place where a person, family, or household lives **2.** FAMILY GROUP a family or any other group that lives together ○ *Theirs was a happy home, full of love.* **3.** BIRTHPLACE where sb was born or brought up or feels he or she belongs ○ *Home is York.* **4.** NATIVE HABITAT the place where sth is most common or indigenous, or where sth had its origins **5.** SAFE PLACE a place where a person or animal can find refuge and safety or live in security **6.** PLACE OF ASSISTANCE an establishment where sb who is in need of care, rest, or medical attention can stay or find help ○ *My grandmother moved into a home.* **7.** GRAVE the place where sb is imagined to dwell after death (*literary*) **8.** SPORTS GOAL the place or point that must be hit in order to score in many games, or that must be reached in order to be safe from attack **9.** BASEBALL = **home plate** ■ *adj.* **1.** DOMESTIC related in some way to sb's own home or country **2.** OF A HOUSEHOLD for or belonging to or produced in a dwelling or household ○ *She loved her son's home cooking.* **3.** NATIVE happening in or coming from sb's native territory or permanent base, especially a sports team's own ground ○ *The home team usually has the advantage in a game.* **4.** EFFECTIVE to the point, or central to achieving a goal ○ *She won the argument with that home thrust.* **5.** PRINCIPAL belonging or relating to the headquarters of a business or enterprise ○ *She was promoted to the company's home office.* ■ *adv.* **1.** AT OR TO SB'S HOME at or to the house, household, or country where sb lives ○ *He desperately wanted to get home.* **2.** EFFECTIVELY to the point or desired goal ○ *Her criticisms of his behaviour hit home.* **3.** TO THE CENTRE to the centre or heart of sth, or as far as possible into a desired position ○ *In one stroke, she drove the nail home.* ■ *v.* (**homes, homing, homed**) **1.** *vi.* GO HOME to go back to the house, household, or country where sb lives **2.** *vi.* RETURN HOME to return home, especially to fly home accurately (*refers to animals and birds*) **3.** *vi.* DWELL to have a home and live in it (*dated*) **4.** *vt.* TAKE OR SEND HOME to take or send sb or sth home (*dated*) **5.** *vt.* PROVIDE WITH A HOME to give a home to sb or sth (*dated*) [Old Englsh *hām*, from, ultimately, a prehistoric Germanic word meaning 'home', which is also the ancestor of English *hamlet* and *hangar*] —**homelike** *adj.* ◇ **at home 1.** ready to receive visitors **2.** at ease or in a familiar and friendly place **3.** having knowledge of or familiarity with a subject or activity ◇ **home and dry** with sth successfully completed

WORD KEY: USAGE

home or **house**? Many consider ***home*** an affectation when used anywhere that ***house*** would be appropriate (*Home for Sale*). ***Home*** is nonetheless useful to express the idea of dwelling places of various sorts, including flats and other dwellings that are not accurately described as houses. ***House***, in many contexts, suggests a single-family dwelling. For example, if *The tornado destroyed 17 homes* is meant to convey that 17 residential structures were demolished, the word should have been ***houses***. *Most homes in town lost electricity*, however, no doubt refers to households of all descriptions, so here ***homes*** is the better choice.

WORD KEY: CULTURAL NOTE

Home Alone, a film by US director Chris Columbus (1990). A comedy set in Chicago at Christmas time, it portrays the adventures of a young boy, Kevin (Macauley Culkin), who is inadvertently left at home by his family when they go on vacation in Europe. Delighting in his new-found independence, the boy manages not only to take care of himself but also to outwit a pair of hapless burglars. In US popular culture, *Home Alone* soon came to mean not only children left alone by negligent travelling parents but also the parents themselves, as this headline indicates: '"Home Alone" Parents Indicted by States on 64 Criminal Counts' (*The Washington Post* 10 February, 1993).

home in *vi.* **1.** PROCEED TOWARDS TARGET to locate and proceed straight towards a target **2.** DIRECT ATTENTION TO STH to direct all attention or energy towards sth ○ *She instinctively homed in on the weakest aspects of the production.*

Home (of the Hirsel) /hyoom/, **Sir Alec Douglas-Home, Baron** (1903–95) British statesman and prime minister. First elected to Parliament as a Conservative in 1931, he became the 14th Earl of Home in 1951, but renounced his peerage to become prime minister (1963–64). He was twice foreign secretary. Full name **Sir Alexander Federick Douglas-Home**

home banking *n.* an electronic banking system that allows a customer to carry out transactions at home

homebody /hốm bodi/ (*plural* -**ies**). *n.* sb who likes to stay at home rather than go out a lot (*informal*)

homebound /hốm bownd/ *adj. US* = **housebound**

homeboy /hốm boy/ *n. US* a man or boy from sb's home town, state, or neighbourhood, especially sb who shares that person's own culture and customs (*slang*)

homebred /hốm bréd/ *adj.* **1.** BRED AT HOME bred or raised at home **2.** UNSOPHISTICATED without worldly experience

home-brew *n.* an alcoholic beverage, especially beer, that has been brewed at home for personal consumption —**home-brewed** *adj.*

homebuyer /hốm bī ər/ *n.* sb who is buying or interested in buying a house or flat

homecoming /hốm kuming/ *n.* the arrival home of sb who has been away ○ *a party to celebrate his homecoming*

Home Counties the counties nearest to London, England, usually taken to include Kent, Surrey, Essex, Buckinghamshire, Berkshire, Hertfordshire, and East and West Sussex. Middlesex, formerly included, is now part of London.

home economics *n.* the science or study of food, diet, cookery, childcare, and other subjects related to the running of a home, as taught in schools

home farm *n.* the farm on an estate with a number of farms that produces food for the owner

home fries *npl. US* boiled sliced potatoes fried in butter or oil, sometimes with onions and seasonings

home from home *n.* a place in which sb feels as comfortable and relaxed as at home

home front *n.* the civilian effort and activity at home in support of a war waged abroad ○ *and on the home front valiant efforts are being made to get the harvest in on time*

homegirl /hốm gurl/ *n. US* a girl or woman from sb's home town, state, or neighbourhood, especially one who shares that person's own culture and customs (*slang*)

homegrown /hốm grốn/ *adj.* **1.** GROWN IN SB'S OWN GARDEN grown in sb's own garden or on sb's own land **2.** LOCALLY PRODUCED produced by or coming from the area or region in question ○ *homegrown talent*

home guard *n.* **1.** VOLUNTEER FORCE a local volunteer force designed to defend an area while the regular army is fighting elsewhere **2.** MEMBER OF A VOLUNTEER FORCE a member of a home guard

Home Guard *n.* **1.** VOLUNTEER ARMY IN UK an army of volunteer civilians formed in the UK during World War II to help protect and police the UK. It was disbanded in 1957. **2.** MEMBER OF VOLUNTEER ARMY a member of the Home Guard

home help *n.* **1.** PAID DOMESTIC HELPER sb who is paid to help sb with domestic tasks **2.** DOMESTIC AID SERVICE a service provided by a local authority to help people in need with domestic tasks they cannot perform

homeland /hốm land/ *n.* **1.** NATIVE COUNTRY the country where sb was born or where sb lives and feels that he or she belongs **2.** HIST SELF-GOVERNING TERRITORY FOR BLACK PEOPLE any of the partially self-governing regions of South Africa created and set aside for the Black population under the former policy of racial apartheid

homeless /hốmləss/ *adj.* WITH NO HOME without a home of any kind ■ *npl.* PEOPLE WITH NO HOME people without a home of any kind —**homelessness** *n.*

homely /hốmli/ (-**lier**, -**liest**) *adj.* **1.** COSY simple, comfortable, and unpretentious, as if it were sb's home or part of one **2.** UNPRETENTIOUS IN MANNER having a simple, unpretentious, and warm-hearted manner **3.** *US* NOT GOOD-LOOKING plain or less than pleasing in appearance ○ *a rather homely face* —**homeliness** *n.*

homemade /hốm máyd/ *adj.* **1.** MADE AT HOME made at home using traditional methods rather than by a manufacturer ○ *Have you tried some of my homemade marmalade?* **2.** MAKESHIFT roughly or crudely constructed to perform a specific function or purpose, especially by an individual in his or her home

Home Office *n.* in the United Kingdom, the department of the government that is responsible for domestic and internal affairs

homeopathy /hốmi óppəthi/, **homoeopathy** *n.* a complementary disease treatment system in which a patient is given minute doses of natural drugs that in larger doses would produce symptoms of the disease itself. The system was created by Dr Samuel Hahnemann (1755–1843) on the assumption that like can be cured by like. —**homeopath** /hốmi ə path/ *n.* —**homeopathic** /hốmi ə páthik/ *adj.* —**homeopathically** *adv.* —**homeopathist** /hốmi óppəthist/ *n.*

homeostasis /hốmi ō stáyssiss/, **homoeostasis** *n.* a state of equilibrium, or a tendency to reach equilibrium. Such equilibrium may be reached or maintained metabolically through biochemical reactions within a cell or organism, or socially and psychologically within an individual, group, or population. [Early 20thC. Coined from HOMEO- + Greek *stasis* 'standing still' (see STASIS).] —**homeostatic** /-státtik/ *adj.*

homeotherm /hốmi ə thurm/, **homoeotherm**, **homoiotherm** /hō móyə-/ *n.* an organism whose stable body temperature is generally independent of the temperature of its surrounding environment [Late 19thC. Coined from HOMEO- + Greek *thermē* 'heat' (see THERM).] —**homeothermic** /hốmi ō thúrmik/ *adj.* —**homeothermy** /hốmi ō thurmi/ *n.*

home page *n.* **1.** WEBSITE OPENING PAGE the opening page of an Internet website **2.** PERSONAL SITE ON INTERNET sb's personal website on the Internet, often containing personal data, photographs, or contact information

home plate *n.* a flat slab marking the area over which a pitcher must throw the ball for a strike and on which a base runner must land in order to score

home port *n.* the place of registry or regular base of a ship

homer /hốmər/ *n.* **1.** ZOOL HOMING PIGEON a homing pigeon (*informal*) **2.** *US* BASEBALL HOME RUN a home run in baseball (*informal*) **3.** ELECTRON ENG HOMING DEVICE a device that provides signals for guiding missiles, ships, or aircraft to their destinations

Homer /hốmər/ city in southern Alaska on the southeastern shore of Cook Inlet. Population: 4,608 (1996).

Homer (fl. 8th century BC) Greek poet. He is credited as the author of the great epics, the *Iliad* and the *Odyssey*.

home range *n.* the specific geographical area to which an animal generally restricts its activities

Homeric /hō mérrik/ *adj.* **1.** OF HOMER relating to or belonging to Homer, his work, or his times ○ *'Thus vain and false are the mere human surmises and doubts which clash with Homeric writ!'* (Alexander William Kinglake, *Eothen*; 1844) **2.** OF HOMER'S GREEK relating to the early form of ancient Greek used in Homer's poetry **3.** HEROIC characteristic or worthy of a hero (*literary*) [Early 17thC. Via Latin from Greek *Homērikos*, from *Homēros* HOMER.] —**Homerically** *adv.*

Homeric laughter *n.* loud continuous laughter, like that of the gods in Homer's epic poems (*literary*)

Homeric simile *n.* = **epic simile**

home rule *n.* **1.** SELF-GOVERNMENT the principle or practice of self-government by a part of a larger country or commonwealth such as a municipality, colony, territory, or principality **2.** PARTIAL AUTONOMY OF US CITIES in the United States, the partial autonomy granted to cities and some counties, under which they manage their own affairs, in accordance with the Constitution

Home Rule *n.* the political aim of the Irish nationalists between 1870 and 1920 in their struggle to secure self-government for Ireland

home run *n.* in baseball, a hit that allows a player to make a circuit of all four bases and score a run, usually by hitting the ball out of the playing area

Home Secretary *n.* the head of the Home Office, in charge of internal and domestic affairs

homesick /hốm sik/ *adj.* feeling sadness and longing to be at home with family and friends when away from them —**homesickness** *n.*

homespun /hốm spun/ *adj.* **1.** PLAIN AND SIMPLE simple and unpretentious **2.** CRAFT MADE BY HAND AT HOME spun or woven by hand at home **3.** CLOTHES, HOUSEHOLD MADE OF HOMESPUN FABRIC made of fabric woven or spun by hand at home ■ *n.* TEXTILES **1.** ROUGH CLOTH a coarse plain cloth woven from homespun thread **2.** ROUGH CLOTH WOVEN ON POWER LOOM a cloth similar to homespun, but woven on an automatic or electric loom

homestay /hốm stay/ *n.* **1.** *US* TIME SPENT WITH A FOREIGN FAMILY a visit to sb's home in a foreign country, often a stay by an exchange student in a family's home (*informal*) **2.** ANZ BED AND BREAKFAST bed-and-breakfast accommodation in a private home as opposed to a guesthouse

homestead /hốm sted/ *n.* **1.** HOUSE, OUTBUILDINGS, AND LAND a house, especially a farmhouse, with its dependent buildings and land, considered as a whole **2.** *US* LAW RESIDENCE EXEMPT FROM FORCED SALE in the United States, a house, adjoining land, and buildings declared as the owner's fixed residence and therefore exempt from seizure and forced sale for the recovery of debts **3.** ANZ MANAGER'S HOUSE in Australia and New Zealand, the home of the manager or owner of a large farm **4.** *US* HIST LAND CLAIMED BY SETTLER in the United States or Canada, a piece of land occupied by a settler or squatter under the terms of the US Homestead Act or the Canadian Dominion Lands Act

homesteader /hốm stedər/ *n.* **1.** OWNER OF HOMESTEAD sb who owns and manages a homestead **2.** *US, Can* SETTLER GRANTED GOVERNMENT LAND in the United States and Canada, sb who settles and farms land under the terms of either the US Homestead Act or the Canadian Dominion Lands Act

home straight *n. US* term **home stretch 1.** LAST SECTION OF RACECOURSE the part of a racecourse between the last turn and the finishing line **2.** LAST STAGE OF UNDERTAKING the last part of a journey, task, or operation ○ *We're on the home straight now.*

home stretch *n. US* = **home straight**

home teacher *n.* a teacher employed by the state system to teach in their own homes children with medical conditions that prevent them from going to school. US term **visiting teacher**

home town *n.* the town or city where sb was born, spent his or her childhood, or lives on a long-term basis

home truth *n.* an unpleasant but true fact about sb's character or behaviour that he or she is told by sb else

home unit *n. ANZ* = **unit** *n.* 6

home video *n.* **1.** WATCHING OF VIDEOS AT HOME the watching of commercial videotapes at home **2.** VIDEO RECORDING MADE AT HOME a video recording produced at home, often a recording of family celebrations and events

homeward /hốmwərd/ *adv.* **homeward, homewards** TOWARDS HOME in the direction of home ○ *homeward bound* ■ *adj.* GOING HOME going home, or in the direction of home

homework /hốm wurk/ *n.* **1.** EDUC SCHOOL WORK DONE AT HOME school work that pupils do at home or outside lesson times **2.** PRELIMINARY OR PREPARATORY WORK facts that are found out about a particular subject, especially in preparation for writing or talking about it (*informal*) **3.** PAID WORK DONE AT HOME work done at home for money, especially piecework ◇ **do your homework** to do all the necessary research and preparation for sth in a thorough manner

homey[1] /hốmi/ (-**ier**, -**iest**), **homy** (-**ier**, -**iest**) *adj.* feeling as comfortable and familiar as sb's own home ○ *a homey little hotel* —**homeyness** *n.*

homey[2] /hốmi/ *n. US* = **homeboy, homegirl** (*slang*) [Late 20thC. Shortening and alteration.]

homicidal /hómmi síd'l/ *adj.* capable of or intending to kill another human being unlawfully —**homicidally** *adv.*

homicide /hómmi sīd/ *n.* **1.** KILLING OF SB the act or an instance of unlawfully killing another human being **2.** SB WHO HAS COMMITTED HOMICIDE sb who has killed another human being unlawfully [13thC. Via French from Latin *homicidium* and Latin *homicida*, both from *homo* 'human being' (see HOMINOID) + *caedere* 'to kill' (see -CIDE).]

homiletic /hómmi léttik/, **homiletical** /-léttik'l/ *adj.* **1.** RELATING TO HOMILETICS relating to the art of writing and preaching sermons **2.** RELATING TO HOMILIES relating to, or in the style of, a sermon or homily [Mid-17thC. Via late Latin from, ultimately, Greek *homilein* 'to associate with, converse', from *homilos* 'crowd' (see HOMILY).] —**homiletically** *adv.*

homiletics /hómmi léttiks/ *n.* the art of writing and preaching sermons (*takes a singular verb*)

homily /hómmili/ (*plural* **-lies**) *n.* **1.** MORAL OR RELIGIOUS LECTURE a sermon on a moral or religious topic **2.** MORALIZING SPEECH a speech or other piece of writing with a moralizing theme [14thC. Via Old French *omilie* from, ultimately, Greek *homilia* 'sermon', from *homilos* 'crowd'. Ultimately from an Indo-European word meaning 'together' that is also the ancestor of English *same*.] —**homilist** *n.*

homing /hṓming/ *adj.* **1.** ZOOL RELATING TO ABILITY TO RETURN HOME relating to or possessing the ability to find the way home after travelling a long distance **2.** AEROSP ABLE TO GUIDE ITSELF TO TARGET used to describe a missile or aircraft that has equipment that enables it to guide itself to its target

homing guidance *n.* a system that enables a missile or aircraft to guide itself to its target

homing pigeon *n.* a pigeon, used in racing and carrying messages, that is trained to return to its roost

hominid /hómminid/ *n.* MEMBER OF A PRIMATE FAMILY INCLUDING HUMANS a primate belonging to a family of which the modern human being is the only species still in existence. Family: Hominidae. ■ *adj.* OF HOMINIDS relating to the hominids [Late 19thC. Via modern Latin *Hominidae*, family name, from, ultimately, Latin *homo* 'human being' (see HOMINOID).]

hominization /hómmi nī záysh'n/, **hominisation** *n.* the theorized evolutionary development of human characteristics that set hominids apart from other primates [Mid-20thC. Via French from Latin *homin-*, the stem of *homo* 'human being' (see HOMINOID).]

hominoid /hómmi noyd/ *adj.* **1.** SIMILAR TO HUMAN resembling a human being **2.** OF HUMAN BEINGS AND APES belonging or relating to the superfamily that includes human beings and apes. Superfamily: Hominoidea. [Early 20thC. Formed from Latin *homin-*, the stem of *homo* 'human being', literally 'earthling'. Ultimately from an Indo-European word meaning 'earth', also the ancestor of English *human* and *humble*.]

hominy /hómmini/ (*plural* **-nies**) *n.* US dried hulled kernels of maize that are eaten boiled [Early 17thC. Contraction of Virginia Algonquian *uskatahomen*.]

hominy grits *npl.* US FOOD grits (*dated*)

homo /hṓmō/ (*plural* **-mos**) *n.* an offensive term referring to a man who is homosexual (*dated slang offensive*) [Early 20thC. Shortening.]

homo- *prefix.* alike, same ○ *homograph* [From Greek *homos*. Ultimately from an Indo-European word meaning 'one', which is also the ancestor of English *same*, *some*, *similar*, and *hetero-*.]

homocentric /hṓmō séntrik, hómmō-/ *adj.* used to describe circles and spheres that have the same centre

homocercal /hṓmō súrk'l, hómmō-/ *adj.* used to describe a fish that has a tail with two symmetrical lobes that extend beyond the end of the vertebral column, or a tail of this kind

homochromatic /hṓmō krō máttik, hómmō-/ *adj.* = **monochromatic** *adj.* 1

homochromous /hṓm ō krṓməss, hómm ō-/ *adj.* being of just one colour [Mid-19thC. Coined from HOMO- + Greek *khrōma* 'colour'.]

homocyclic /hṓmō síklik, hómmō-, -síklik/ *adj.* used to describe a chemical compound in which molecules take the form of a ring in which all the atoms are the same

homodont /hṓmə dont, hómmə-/ *adj.* used to describe vertebrates that have teeth that are all similar in shape and not of different shapes as in most nonmammalian vertebrates [Late 19thC. Coined from HOMO- + the Greek stem *odont-* 'tooth'.]

homoeo- *prefix.* similar, alike ○ *homoeotherm* [From Greek *homoios* 'similar', from *homos* 'same' (see HOMO-)]

homoeopathy *n.* = **homeopathy**

homoeostasis *n.* = **homeostasis**

homoeotherm *n.* = **homeotherm**

Homo erectus /hṓmō i réktəss/ *n.* an extinct ancestor of the modern human being (**Homo sapiens**) living approximately 1.5 million years ago and known by fossils to have had an upright stature, a smallish brain, and a low forehead [From modern Latin, literally 'upright man']

homoerotic /hṓmō i róttik, hómmō-/ *adj.* relating to or characterized by homosexual eroticism

homoeroticism /hṓmō i róttisizəm/, **homoerotism** /hṓmō érrətizəm/ *n.* eroticism that is focused on or inspired by people of the same sex

homogametic /hṓmogə méttik/ *adj.* producing gametes that have the same type of sex chromosome

homogamy /ho móggəmi/ *n.* the condition of a flower in which male and female organs mature at the same time —**homogamous** /ho móggəməss/ *adj.*

homogenate /ho mójjənət, -nayt/ *n.* a substance produced by homogenizing

homogeneity /hṓmōjə née əti, hómmō-, -náyəti/ *n.* **1.** QUALITY OF BEING THE SAME the quality of being of the same or a similar nature **2.** QUALITY OF BEING UNIFORM the quality of having a uniform appearance or composition [Early 17thC. From medieval Latin *homogeneitas*, from *homogeneus* (see HOMOGENEOUS).]

homogeneous /hṓmə jéeni əss, hómmə-/ *adj.* **1.** OF SAME KIND having the same kind of constituent elements, or being similar in nature **2.** HAVING UNIFORM COMPOSITION having a uniform composition or structure [Mid-17thC. Formed from medieval Latin *homogeneus*, from Greek *homogenēs*, literally 'of the same kind'.] —**homogeneously** *adv.* —**homogeneousness** *n.*

homogenize /ho mójjə nīz/ (**-nizes, -nizing, -nized**), **homogenise** (**-nises, -nising, -nised**) *v.* **1.** *vt.* GIVE MILK OR CREAM EVEN CONSISTENCY to emulsify the fat particles in milk or cream so as to give it an even consistency **2.** *vti.* BECOME OR MAKE HOMOGENEOUS to become or cause sth to become homogeneous [Late 19thC. Formed from HOMOGENEOUS.] —**homogenization** /ho mójjə nī záysh'n/ *n.* —**homogenizer** /ho mójjə nīzər/ *n.*

homogenous /ho mójjənəss/ *adj.* = **homogeneous** —**homogenously** *adv.*

homogeny /ho mójjəni/ *n.* a similarity in individuals, organs, or parts caused by a common ancestry [Late 19thC. Coined from HOMO- + -GENY.]

homograft /hómmə graaft/ *n.* a graft of tissue from one organism to another of the same species. ◊ **allograft**

homograph /hómmə graaf/ *n.* a word that is spelt in the same way as one or more other words but is different in meaning, e.g. the verb 'project' and the noun 'project'. ◊ **homophone, homonym** —**homographic** /hómmə gráffik/ *adj.*

Homo habilis /hṓmō hábbiliss/ *n.* an extinct ancestor of the modern human being (**Homo sapiens**) living approximately 1.5 million years ago and characterized by its ability to make and use tools [From modern Latin, literally 'skilful man']

homoio- *prefix.* = **homoeo-**

homoiotherm *n.* = **homeotherm**

Homoiousian /hṓ moy óossi ən/ *n.* CHRISTIAN BELIEVING JESUS CHRIST IS NOT GOD a Christian who believes that Jesus Christ is of a similar, but not identical, substance to God. ◊ **Homoousian** ■ *adj.* OF DOCTRINE OF HOMOIOUSIANS relating to the doctrine of the Homoiousians. ◊ **Homoousian** [Late 17thC. Formed from Greek *homoiousios* 'of similar substance', from *homoios* 'similar' + *ousia* 'substance'.] —**Homoiousianism** *n.*

homologate /hO móllə gayt/ (**-gates, -gating, -gated**) *v.* **1.** *vti.* LAW CONFIRM STH to confirm or sanction the validity of sth **2.** *vt.* CARS OFFICIALLY RECOGNIZE CAR MODEL OR COMPONENT to give official recognition to a prototype car or car component, thus allowing it to be used in a motor race [Early 16thC. Via medieval Latin *homologare* 'to agree', from, ultimately, Greek *homologos* 'agreeing' (see HOMOLOGOUS).] —**homologation** /ho móllə gáysh'n/ *n.*

homological /hṓmə lójjik'l, hómmə-/ *adj.* = **homologous** —**homologically** *adv.*

homologize /ho móllə jīz/ (**-gizes, -gizing, -gized**), **homologise** (**-gises, -gising, -gised**) *vt.* to make sth have a similar or related structure, position, function, or value to sth else —**homologizer** *n.*

homologous /ho mólləgəss/ *adj.* **1.** SIMILAR sharing a similar or related structure, position, function, or value **2.** BIOL HAVING SAME ORIGIN BUT DIFFERENT FUNCTION sharing the same origin but having a different function, as do, e.g., the wing of a bird and the fin of a fish **3.** CHEM OF RELATED CHEMICAL COMPOUNDS relating to a series of organic chemical compounds such as a methylene group, each of which differs from the preceding by the addition of a constant component **4.** MED HAVING IDENTICAL TISSUE produced from identical tissue [Mid-17thC. Via medieval Latin from Greek *homologos* 'agreeing', literally 'speaking the same', from *homos* 'same' and *legein* 'to speak'.]

homolographic /ho móllə gráffik, hómmələ-/ *adj.* MAPS = **equal-area** [Mid-19thC. Alteration (under the influence of *homo-*) of *homalographic*, from Greek *homalos* 'even, level' + -GRAPHIC.]

homologue /hómmə log/ *n.* **1.** BIOL HOMOLOGOUS PART OR ORGAN a part or organ that has the same evolutionary origin as another but differs in function, e.g. a bird's wing in relation to the fin of a fish **2.** CHEM HOMOLOGOUS COMPOUND a homologous chemical compound [Mid-19thC. Via French from, ultimately, Greek *homologos* 'agreeing' (see HOMOLOGOUS).]

homology /ho mólləji/ *n.* **1.** BIOL LIKENESSES BETWEEN ANIMALS similar characteristics in two animals that are a product of descent from a common ancestor rather than a product of a similar environment **2.** CHEM SIMILARITY BETWEEN COMPOUNDS the correspondence between chemical compounds in a homologous series [Early 17thC. Via late Latin from Greek *homologia* 'agreement', from *homologos* (see HOMOLOGOUS.)]

homolosine projection /ho móllə sīn-, hō-/ *n.* a map of the Earth's surface that distorts the oceans in order to represent the continents with a minimum of distortion [Coined from HOMOLOGRAPHIC + SINE, because it is a homolographic projection based on sinusoidal curves]

homolysis /ho mólləssiss, hō-/ *n.* the breakdown of a molecule into neutral atoms or radicals —**homolytic** /hṓmmə líttik, hṓmə-/ *adj.*

homonym /hómmənim/ *n.* **1.** WORD WITH SAME SPELLING OR SOUND a word that is spelt or pronounced in the same way as one or more other words but has a different meaning. 'Fleet' (group of vehicles) and 'fleet' (swift), 'plane' and 'plain', and the verb 'sow' (plant seeds) and the noun 'sow' (female pig) are homonyms of three types. ◊ **homograph, homophone** **2.** SB WITH SAME NAME sb with the same name as sb else **3.** BIOL DUPLICATE TAXONOMIC NAME a taxonomic name that is the same as one already designating a different species or genus and cannot therefore be used [Late 17thC. Via Latin *homonymum* from, ultimately, Greek *homonumos* (see HOMONYMOUS).] —**homonymic** /hómmə nímmik/ *adj.* —**homonymity** /-nímməti/ *n.* —**homonymy** *n.*

homonymous /hə mónniməss/ *adj.* **1.** OF HOMONYMS relating to homonyms or in the form of a homonym ○ *The words 'peace' and 'piece' are homonymous.* **2.** HAVING SAME NAME having the same name as sb or sth else [Early 17thC. Via Latin from, ultimately, Greek *homōnumos*, literally 'having the same name', from *onuma* 'name' (see ONOMASTIC).] —**homonymously** *adv.*

Homoousian /hṓmō óossi ən/ *n.* CHRISTIAN BELIEVING JESUS CHRIST IS GOD a Christian who believes that Jesus Christ is of the same substance as God, in accordance with the Council of Nicaea's definition of the Trinity. ◊ **Homoiousian** ■ *adj.* OF DOCTRINE OF HOMOOUSIANS relating to the doctrine of the Homoousians. ◊ **Homoiousian** [Mid-16thC. Formed from Greek *homoousios* 'of the same substance', from *homos* 'same' + *ousia* 'substance'.] —**Homoousianism** *n.*

homophile /hṓmō fīl, hómmō-/ *adj.* **1.** ADVOCATING GAY AND LESBIAN RIGHTS supporting the rights of gay and lesbian people and appreciating their culture **2.** GAY OR LESBIAN relating to or being gay or lesbian ■ *n.* SB GAY OR LESBIAN a gay man or lesbian woman, or a supporter of gay and lesbian rights

homophobia /hŏmō fŏbi ə, hómmō-/ *n.* an irrational hatred, disapproval, or fear of homosexuality, gay and lesbian people, and their culture [Mid-20thC. Coined from HOMOSEXUAL + -PHOBIA.]

homophobic /hŏmō fŏbik, hómmō-/ *adj.* showing an irrational hatred, disapproval, or fear of homosexuality, gay and lesbian people, and their culture —**homophobe** *n.*

homophone /hómmə fōn/ *n.* **1.** WORD WITH SAME PRONUNCIATION a word that is pronounced in the same way as one or more other words but is different in meaning and sometimes spelling, as are 'hair' and 'hare'. ◊ **homograph, homonym 2.** LETTER WITH SAME SOUND a letter or diphthong that has the same sound as one or more other letters or diphthongs [Early 17thC. From Greek *homophōnos* 'having the same sound'.]

homophonic /hómmə fónnik/ *adj.* **1.** LING SOUNDING THE SAME sharing the same sound **2.** MUSIC RELATING TO HOMOPHONY relating to part music in which the parts move together in simple harmonization —**homophonically** *adv.*

homophony /hə móffəni/ *n.* **1.** LING IDENTICAL PRONUNCIATION OF WORDS the quality of having the same pronunciation as one or more other words with a different origin and meaning **2.** MUSIC HOMOPHONIC MUSIC music of a largely chordal style in which there is no independence of voice parts, but rather a simple harmonization of a melody [Mid-18thC. From Greek *homophōnia* 'unison', from *homophōnos* (see HOMOPHONE).]

homoplastic /hŏmō plástik, hómmō-/ *adj.* used to describe a tissue graft that is obtained from a member of the same species as the recipient —**homoplastically** *adv.*

homopolar /hŏmō pōlər, hómmō-/ *adj.* having uniform polarity —**homopolarity** /hŏmō pō lárrəti, hómmō-/ *n.*

homopteran /ho móptərən, hō-/ *n.* INSECT SUCKING PLANT JUICES THROUGH MOUTHPARTS any insect that has the ability to suck plant juices through its mouthparts, e.g. the cicada, scale insect, or aphid. Order: Homoptera. ■ *adj.* OF HOMOPTERANS being or relating to a homopteran [Mid-19thC. From modern Latin *Homoptera*, order name, from Greek *homos* 'same' and *pteron* 'wing'. So called because their wings have a uniform texture.]

Homo sapiens /-sáppi enz, -sáypi-/ *n.* the species of modern human beings, the only extant species of the family that also included other species named Homo. Family: Hominidae. [From modern Latin, literally 'wise man']

homoscedastic /hŏmōski dástik, hómmō-/ *adj.* characterized by equal statistical variances [Early 20thC. Coined from HOMO- + Greek *skedastos* 'able to be scattered', from *skedannunai* 'to scatter'. Ultimately from an Indo-European base that also produced English *scatter* and *shingle*.] —**homoscedasticity** /hŏmōski dass tíssəti, hómmō-/ *n.*

homosexual /hŏmō sékshoo əl, hómmə-/ *n.* SB ATTRACTED TO SAME SEX sb who is sexually attracted to members of his or her own sex ■ *adj.* **1.** ATTRACTED TO SAME SEX sexually attracted to members of the same sex **2.** OF HOMOSEXUALITY relating to sexual attraction or activity among members of the same sex

homosexuality /hŏmō sék shoo álləti, hómmə-/ *n.* sexual attraction to, and sexual relations with, members of the same sex

homosporous /ho móspərəss, hō-, hŏmə spáwrəss/ *adj.* producing asexual spores of only one type

homotaxis /hŏmō táksiss, hómmō-/ *n.* a similarity of composition, arrangement, or fossil content among rock strata of different ages or locations —**homotaxial** *adj.* —**homotaxially** *adv.* —**homotaxic** *adj.*

homothallic /hŏmō thállik, hómmō-/ *adj.* used to describe a plant that has both male and female reproductive organs on one thallus and is therefore able to fertilize itself —**homothallism** *n.*

homozygote /hŏmō zígōt, hómmō-/ *n.* an organism that has two identical genes at the same place on two corresponding chromosomes —**homozygotic** /hŏmō zī góttik, hómmō-/ *adj.*

homozygous /hŏmō zígəss, hómmō-/ *adj.* having two identical genes at the corresponding loci of homologous chromosomes —**homozygously** *adv.*

Homs /homz/ historic city in western Syria, situated on the River Orontes. Population: 518,000 (1992).

homunculus /ho múng kyŏoləss/ (*plural* **-li** /-lī/), **homuncule** /ho múng kyool/ *n.* **1.** VERY SMALL HUMAN BEING a diminutive human being without any deformity of physiology **2.** MINIATURE PERSON INSIDE EGG OR SPERM in early biological theory, the fully formed human being that was thought to exist inside an egg or spermatozoon [Mid-17thC. From Latin *homunculus*, literally 'little person', from *homo* (see HOMINOID).] —**homuncular** /ho múng kyŏolər/ *adj.*

homy *adj.* = **homey**[2]

hon /hun/ *n.* US = **honey** *n.* **3** (*informal*) [Early 20thC. Shortening.]

hon. *abbr.* **1.** honorary **2.** honourable

Hon. *abbr.* Honourable

honan /hŏ nán/ *n.* a rough-woven raw silk fabric, originally from China [Early 20thC. Named after Honan, a province of northern China where the fabric was originally manufactured.]

honcho /hónchō/ *n.* (*plural* **-chos**) US SB IN CHARGE sb who is in charge of a project or situation, or of other people (*slang*) ◦ *Who's the head honcho around here?* ■ *vt.* (**-chos, -choing, -choed**) US BE IN CHARGE OF STH to manage or organize people or events (*slang*) ◦ *He's the one who honchoed their election campaign.* [Mid-20thC. From Japanese *hanchō* 'group leader'. The term was adopted by US soldiers during the Korean War.]

Hond. *abbr.* Honduras

Honduras

Honduras /hon dyŏorəss/ republic in Central America, with coastlines on the Caribbean Sea and the Pacific Ocean. Language: Spanish. Currency: lempira. Capital: Tegucigalpa. Population: 5,666,000 (1996). Area: 112,088 sq. km/43,277 sq. mi. Official name **Republic of Honduras** —**Honduran** /hon dyŏorən/ *adj.*, *n.*

Honduras, Gulf of inlet of the Caribbean Sea, situated between southern Belize, eastern Guatemala, and northern Honduras

hone[1] /hōn/ *vt.* (**hones, honing, honed**) **1.** IMPROVE STH WITH REFINEMENTS to bring sth to a state of increased intensity, excellence, or completion, especially over a period of time **2.** SHARPEN BLADE ON WHETSTONE to sharpen a blade on a fine whetstone ■ *n.* **1.** WHETSTONE a fine-grained sedimentary rock used as a whetstone for sharpening razors and other cutting tools. Emery and silicon carbide products are now largely used instead. **2.** MACHINE TOOL a tool with a rotating abrasive head, used to bore holes [Old English *hān* 'whetstone'. Ultimately from an Indo-European word meaning 'to sharpen', which may also be the ancestor of English *cone*.] —**honer** *n.*

hone[2] /hōn/ *vi.* (**hones, honing, honed**) (*regional*) **1.** WANT VERY MUCH to long for sb or sth **2.** COMPLAIN CONTINUOUSLY to complain about sb or sth, especially in a whining manner [Early 17thC. From Old French *hognier* 'to grumble', of uncertain origin.]

Honecker /hón ekər/, **Erich** (1912–94) German statesman. He served as secretary general of East Germany from 1971 until he was ousted in 1989, a year before the fall of the Berlin Wall.

Honegger /hónnigər/, **Arthur** (1892–1955) French composer. He was a member of the Paris based group of composers known as 'Les Six'. His works include *Pacific 231* (1923) and *King David* (1921).

honest /ónnist/ *adj.* **1.** MORALLY UPRIGHT never cheating, lying, or breaking the law **2.** TRUTHFUL OR TRUE expressing or embodying the truth **3.** IMPARTIAL presenting information in an impartial way **4.** REASONABLE IN A PARTICULAR SITUATION reasonable and acceptable, given the circumstances ◦ *an honest mistake* **5.** UNPRETENTIOUS having simple manners and no pretensions ◦ *honest country folk* **6.** RESPECTABLE respectable and virtuous (*dated*) [13thC. Via Old French from Latin *honestus* 'honourable', from *honos* 'honour' (source of English *honour*).] —**honestness** *n.* ◊ **honest to God** *or* **goodness 1.** used to express surprise or shock **2.** used to emphasize the truth of a statement

honest broker *n.* a person, country, or organization that mediates in disputes [Translation of German *ehrlicher Makler*, a phrase describing the German statesman Otto von Bismarck (1815–98)]

honestly /ónnistli/ *adv.* **1.** FAIRLY OR JUSTLY in a way that is fair, just, truthful, and morally upright **2.** GENUINELY really and truly ◦ *Can you honestly say that you care?* ■ *interj.* USED TO EXPRESS SURPRISE used to express surprise, annoyance, or disapproval

honest-to-God, **honest-to-goodness** *adj.* completely real or authentic (*informal*) ◦ *You made a real, honest-to-God mess of that.*

honesty /ónnisti/ (*plural* **-ties**) *n.* **1.** MORAL UPRIGHTNESS the quality, condition, or characteristic of being fair, just, truthful, and morally upright **2.** TRUTHFULNESS truthfulness, candour, or sincerity ◦ *In all honesty, I really didn't know.* **3.** PLANTS PLANT WITH FLAT PAPERY SEED PODS a hardy European plant with purplish or white flowers and flat silvery seed pods that are often used for indoor decoration. Latin name: *Lunaria annua*.

honewort /hŏn wurt/ *n.* a European plant that has clusters of small white flowers. Latin name: *Trinia glauca*. [Mid-17thC. *Hone*, of unknown origin.]

honey /húnni/ *n.* **1.** FOOD SWEET STICKY SUBSTANCE MADE BY BEES a sweet sticky golden-brown fluid produced by bees from the nectar of flowers, used especially in cooking or spread on bread **2.** SWEET SUBSTANCE MADE BY OTHER INSECTS a sweet sticky substance produced from nectar by insects other than bees **3.** US, Can AFFECTIONATE TERM OF ADDRESS a term of affection or endearment used to address sb (*informal*) **4.** US SB VERY NICE sb who is considered to be very nice or sweet (*informal*) **5.** US STH EXTREMELY GOOD an object, situation, or idea that is exceptionally good (*informal*) ◦ *That's a honey of a motorboat!* **6.** COLOURS YELLOWISH-BROWN COLOUR a yellowish-brown colour, like that of honey ■ *adj.* COLOURS OF YELLOWISH-BROWN COLOUR yellowish-brown in colour, like honey ■ *vt.* (**-eys, -eying, -eyed** *or* **-ied**) US TALK FLATTERINGLY TO SB to talk to sb in an affectionate and flattering way, especially insincerely and for selfish reasons (*informal*) [Old English *hunig*, of prehistoric Germanic origin]

honey badger *n.* = **ratel** [From its fondness for honey]

honey bear *n.* = **kinkajou** [From its practice of sucking honey from the nests of bees]

honeybee /húnni bee/ *n.* a honey-producing bee that lives in organized groups and has been domesticated for its honey and beeswax since ancient times. Latin name: *Apis mellifera*.

honeybun /húnni bun/, **honeybunch** /-bunch/ *n.* US, Can = **honey** *n.* **3** (*informal*)

honey-buzzard *n.* a bird of prey that is native to Europe and feeds on honey from bees' nests. Latin name: *Perno apivorus*.

honeycomb /húnni kōm/ *n.* **1.** STRUCTURE OF SIX-SIDED CELLS a collection of hexagonal cells constructed of wax by bees inside a hive or nest in which honey is stored, eggs are laid, and larvae develop **2.** FOOD CELLS CONTAINING HONEY EATEN AS FOOD a structure made up of waxy hexagonal cells containing honey that is extracted from a bees' hive or nest and eaten by animals and humans **3.** STH RESEMBLING HONEYCOMB an object resembling a honeycomb in pattern or structure, especially by consisting of a network of hexagons **4.** TEXTILES HONEYCOMB-PATTERNED FABRIC a soft fabric woven in a pattern of ridges and hollows similar to those in a honeycomb, usually used for towels and bedcovers ■ *vt.* (**-combs, -combing, -combed**) **1.** PROVIDE STH WITH HOLES to fill a wall, cliff, or structure with many cavities **2.** INFILTRATE STH THOROUGHLY to infiltrate

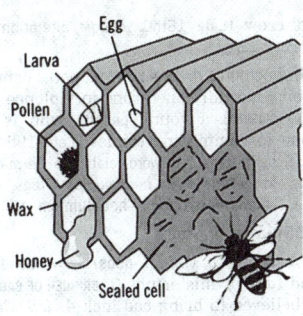

Honeycomb

a place or organization thoroughly ○ *an intelligence agency honeycombed by double agents* [Possibly so called because the arrangement of the plates hanging from the roof of a hive resembles a comb with its teeth] — **honeycombed** *adj.*

honeycomb moth *n.* = wax moth

honey creeper *n.* **1.** SMALL TROPICAL AMERICAN BIRD a small tropical American bird that has brightly-coloured plumage and a long slender beak for sucking nectar from flowers. Family: Coerebidae. **2.** SMALL HAWAIIAN BIRD a Hawaiian bird that resembles the honey creeper of tropical America. Family: Drepanididae.

honeydew /húnni dyoo/ *n.* **1.** INSECTS SWEET SUBSTANCE PRODUCED BY APHIDS a sweet sticky substance deposited on leaves by aphids and certain other insects as a by-product of the juices they suck from plants **2.** BOT SWEET SUBSTANCE EXUDED BY PLANTS a sweet sticky substance produced by the leaves of some plants **3.** FOOD = honeydew melon [From the belief that the substance was distilled from the air like dew] —**honeydewed** *adj.*

honeydew melon *n.* a melon with sweet green flesh and a smooth greenish-white rind. Latin name: *Cucumis melo*.

honeyeater /húnni eetər/ *n.* a slender bird, found from Australia to Hawaii, that has a long beak and a long brush-tipped tongue for extracting nectar from flowers. Family: Meliphagidae.

honeyed /húnnid/, **honied** *adj.* **1.** INGRATIATING intended to flatter or soothe **2.** PLEASANT-SOUNDING sweet and pleasant to hear **3.** SWEETENED WITH HONEY containing or sweetened with honey —**honeyedly** *adv.*

honey fungus *n.* a mushroom that has a golden or brown cap and is edible when cooked. It grows in small tight clusters at the base of trees, and is possibly the most serious fungal parasite affecting coniferous trees. Latin name: *Armillaria mellea*. [From its colour]

honey guide *n.* **1.** BIRDS SMALL TROPICAL BIRD FEEDING ON BEESWAX a small bird of tropical African and Asian forests that feeds on the wax and larvae remaining after people or animals have removed the honey from bees' nests. Family: Indicatoridae. **2.** BOT MARKINGS ON FLOWER dots or lines on the perianth of a flower that guide insects towards the nectar. They are sometimes only visible to the human eye in ultraviolet photographs.

honey locust *n.* a thorny tree native to eastern North America with compound leaves and long pods containing a sweet pulp. Genus: *Gleditsia*.

honeymoon /húnni moon/ *n.* **1.** HOLIDAY FOR NEWLY-MARRIED COUPLE a holiday taken by a newly-married couple, usually immediately following the wedding or reception **2.** PERIOD OF GOOD FEELING a short period of harmony or goodwill at the beginning of a relationship, especially in politics or business ■ *vi.* (-moons, -mooning, -mooned) GO ON HONEYMOON to go on holiday just after getting married [Originally in the sense 'waning affection', from the idea that although married love is at first as sweet as honey, it soon wanes like the moon] —**honeymooner** *n.*

honey mouse *n.* a small Australian marsupial with a very long snout adapted for feeding on pollen and honey, a long tail, and light brown fur with dark stripes. Latin name: *Tarsipes spenserae*.

honey myrtle *n.* an Australian plant with flowers that consist of clusters of pink or purple hairy spikes. Genus: *Melaleuca*.

honey plant *n.* a plant that provides bees with nectar

honey-sucker *n.* = honey mouse

Honeysuckle

honeysuckle /húnni suk'l/ *n.* **1.** CLIMBING SHRUB WITH FRAGRANT FLOWERS a climbing shrub that has twining stems and fragrant tubular flowers with spreading twin-petal lobes. Genus: *Lonicera*. **2.** AUSTRALIAN PLANT an Australian plant with flowers that grow in spike-shaped clusters. Genus: *Banksia*. **3.** *Ireland* FUCHSIA a fuchsia plant [Old English *hunigsūce*, from HONEY + SUCK. So called from the belief that bees extract honey from it.]

honeysuckle ornament *n.* = anthemion

honey-sweet *adj.* sounding or appearing sweet and attractive

hong /hong/ *n.* in 19th-century Canton, a business owned by foreigners [Early 18thC. From Chinese *háng*, dialectal (Guangdong) *hòhng* 'row, trade'.]

hongi /hóng ee/ *n.* a Maori greeting in which two people rub noses [Mid-19thC. From Maori.]

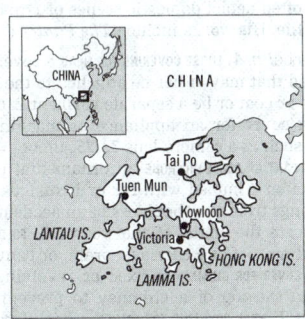

Hong Kong

Hong Kong /hóng kóng/ seaport and major commercial centre on the southeastern coast of China. A former British colony, it is now a Chinese Special Administrative Region. Population: 6,189,800 (1995). Area: 1,076 sq. km/415 sq. mi.

Hong Kong English *n.* a variety of English spoken in Hong Kong

──── **WORD KEY: WORLD ENGLISH** ────

Hong Kong English is the English language as used in Hong Kong, ranging from forms close to British, US, and Australian usage to those influenced by and mixed with Cantonese, the language of some 98% of the population. Hong Kong English pronunciation is 'non-rhotic', that is, 'r' is not pronounced in such words as *art*, *door*, and *worker*. It generally shares features with English as used in mainland China, Taiwan, and Singapore: e.g. glottal stops replacing the /p, t, k/ consonants at the ends of such words as *map*, *pat*, and *tack*. In grammar, there is a tendency to use the present tense when describing events in the past and future ('When I see him in school yesterday' and 'Tomorrow I ask him about it'). Hong Kong English has three sources of distinctive vocabulary. The first is represented by items taken directly from Chinese (especially Cantonese), e.g. *gweilo* 'ghost man/person' for 'a European', and *feng shui* 'wind-water', denoting a system of laws that govern spatial relationships with respect to the flow of energy, used in situating buildings advantageously. The second vocabulary source is represented by items that translate Chinese words and phrases, such as *dragon boat*, a long decorated boat configured as a dragon, used in racing

at festivals, and *snakehead*, a smuggler of illegal immigrants from mainland China. A third vocabulary source is represented by items common to former British colonies, especially in Asia, e.g. *expat* (English), short for 'expatriate', *godown* (probably from Tamil), 'warehouse', and *shroff* (from Arabic through Indian languages), 'cashier'.

honied *adj.* = honeyed

honi soit qui mal y pense /ónni swaá kee mál ee pónss/ the French motto of the Order of the Garter, meaning 'shame upon him who thinks evil of it' [From French]

Honiton lace /hónnitən-, húnni-/, **Honiton** *n.* lace with a pattern of sprigs of flowers [Named after *Honiton* in Devon, where it was first made]

honk /hongk/ *n.* **1.** CRY OF GOOSE the raucous sound made by a goose **2.** SOUND OF CAR HORN the sound made by a car horn **3.** SOUND RESEMBLING GOOSE OR CAR HORN any sound, e.g. a laugh or a blowing of the nose, that resembles the sound made by a goose or a car horn ■ *v.* (honks, honking, honked) **1.** *vi.* PRODUCE HONK to let out or give out a honk **2.** *vti.* SOUND CAR HORN to cause a car horn to make a honk [Mid-19thC. An imitation of the sound.]

honker /hóngkər/ *n.* **1.** SB OR STH THAT HONKS a person, animal, or object, e.g. a goose or a car horn, that makes a honking sound **2.** LARGE NOSE a nose, especially a large one (*informal*) **3.** *Can* CANADA GOOSE a Canada goose (*informal*)

honky /hóngki/ (*plural* **-kies**), **honkie** (*plural* **-kies**), **honkey** (*plural* **-keys**) *n. US* an offensive term that deliberately insults a Caucasian (*slang offensive*) [Origin uncertain: possibly from Wolof (an African language) *honq* 'pink'; perhaps also influenced by HUNKY.]

honky-tonk /hóngki tongk/ *n.* **1.** *US* CHEAP NIGHTCLUB a cheap, noisy, and often disreputable bar or nightclub (*slang*) **2.** RAGTIME PIANO-PLAYING a style of ragtime with a heavy beat, usually played on an upright piano with a tinny sound **3.** COUNTRY MUSIC a style of country music associated with honky-tonks ○ *honky-tonk blues* ■ *vi.* (honky-tonks, honky-tonking, honky-tonked) *US* VISIT HONKY-TONKS to frequent cheap noisy bars and nightclubs [Late 19thC. Origin unknown.]

Honolulu /hónnə loŏ loo/ urban area and capital of Hawaii, located on Oahu Island, Hawaii. Population: 365,272 (1990).

honor *n., vt. US* = honour

honorarium /ónnə ráiri əm/ (*plural* **-ums** *or* **-a** /-ə/) *n.* an amount of money paid to sb, especially a professional person, for providing a service [Mid-17thC. Via Latin, 'gift made on being admitted to a post of honour', from, ultimately, *honor* 'HONOUR'.]

──── **WORD KEY: SYNONYMS** ────
See Synonyms at **wage**.

honorary /ónnərəri/ *adj.* **1.** AWARDED AS HONOUR given, elected, or awarded for outstanding service or distinguished achievements, rather than for the completion of formal educational or legal requirements **2.** SYMBOLIZING HONOUR CONFERRED representing the bestowal of an honour or distinction on sb **3.** UNPAID holding an office awarded as an honour and receiving no payment for services provided in that office **4.** NOT LEGALLY ENFORCEABLE dependent on sb's sense of honour and honesty for fulfilment, rather than on a legal agreement

honorary white *n.* formerly, in South Africa, a foreign visitor not considered white but granted the rights of whites under the apartheid regime

honorific /ónnə ríffik/ *adj.* CONFERRING OR SHOWING HONOUR given as a mark of distinction, or reflecting esteem and respect ■ *n.* **1.** TITLE OF RESPECT a title of respect, e.g. 'The Honourable', used in speech or writing **2.** GRAM GRAMMATICAL FORM ACKNOWLEDGING INFERIORITY OF SPEAKER a phrase or word, e.g. a pronoun or a verb inflection, that is used to show respect to sb of a higher status

──── **WORD KEY: REGIONAL NOTE** ────

In parts of Britain with large populations originating in the Indian subcontinent, the honorific *-gi*, or occasionally *-ji* (both pronounced like the letter 'G'), is added to an English name or title as a mark of respect, giving, for example, *Marygi* or *Professorgi*.

honoris causa /ho náwriss kówzə/ *adv.* as a mark of honour (*formal*) ○ *a doctorate in humane letters conferred honoris causa* [From Latin, 'for the sake of honour']

honour /ónnər/ *n.* **1. PERSONAL INTEGRITY** strong moral character or strength, and adherence to ethical principles ○ *It's a matter of honour.* **2. RESPECT** great respect and admiration **3. DIGNITY OR DISTINCTION** personal dignity that sometimes leads to recognition and glory ○ *Although defeated, he accepted the loss with honour* **4. REPUTATION** sb's good name or good reputation ○ *My honour is at stake.* **5. WOMAN'S REPUTATION** a woman's virginity or reputation for chastity (*dated*) **6. SOURCE OF PRIDE** sb or sth that brings respect or glory and is a source of pride to sb or sth else ○ *Your achievements are an honour to your parents and school.* **7. MARK OF DISTINCTION** sth such as a gift, award, or gesture that signifies high achievement or respect **8. GREAT PRIVILEGE** a special privilege that is cherished, e.g. an opportunity to be introduced to sb admired or respected or an opportunity to serve a worthy cause ○ *It is indeed an honour to have you here today.* **9. MEN'S CODE OF INTEGRITY** a code of integrity in some societies, e.g. in feudal Europe and medieval Japan, that men upheld by force of arms **10.** GOLF **RIGHT TO TEE OFF FIRST** the right to drive off first from the tee in golf ■ *npl.* **1. honours, Honours** EDUC **ACADEMIC DISTINCTION** official recognition of academic excellence given to students by colleges and universities at graduation **2. honours** BRIDGE **FOUR OR FIVE HIGHEST CARDS** four or five of the highest cards, especially the ace, king, queen, jack, and ten of the trump suit ■ *vt.* **(-ours, -ouring, -oured) 1. ESTEEM SB OR STH** to have or show great respect and admiration for sb or sth **2. DISTINGUISH, EXALT, OR ENNOBLE SB** to recognize sb publicly or elevate sb's status officially, usually by giving that person a title or an award **3. PAY TRIBUTE TO SB** to praise publicly and pay respect to sb who has died **4. DIGNIFY PERSON OR EVENT** to give prestige to sb or sth such as an occasion by choosing to appear, accompany, or take part **5.** FIN **TREAT STH AS MONEY** to accept a cheque or other financial instrument as money or as a substitute for money and pay it when it is due ○ *The bank won't honour a cheque without a signature.* **6. KEEP PROMISE** to keep a promise or fulfil the terms of an agreement or contract **7.** DANCE **BOW TO DANCING PARTNER** to bow to another dancer in square dancing [12thC. Via Old French from Latin *honor-*, the stem of *honos* (source also of English *honest*), of unknown origin.] —**honourer** *n.* —**honourless** *adj.* ◇ **do sb the honour of doing sth** to make sb feel proud and pleased by agreeing to do sth for that person (*formal*) ○ *Will you do me the honour of dancing the last waltz with me?* ◇ **do the honours** to act as host or hostess by doing sth for a group of guests, e.g. pouring wine, carving meat, or cutting a cake (*informal*) ◇ **honour bound** obliged by a promise or ethical principles to do sth ◇ **in honour of sb** *or* **sth** in recognition of or for the glorification of sb or sth ○ *I'd like to propose a toast in honour of the bride and groom.* ◇ **on your honour 1.** staking your reputation on sth ○ *On my honour, I will tell the truth, the whole truth, and nothing but the truth.* **2.** being trusted to act in a particular way ○ *You are on your honour to behave well while I am gone.*

Honour *n.* used as a form of address to a judge ○ *Your Honour, may we approach the bench?*

honourable /ónnərəb'l/ *adj.* **1. HAVING PERSONAL INTEGRITY** guided by, or with a reputation for having, strong moral and ethical principles **2. DESERVING OR GAINING HONOUR** worthy of or winning honour, respect, recognition, or glory **3. MORALLY UPRIGHT** upright and moral in intent (*formal*) ○ *I hope his intentions are honourable.* —**honourability** /ónnərə bílləti/ *n.* —**honourableness** /ónnərəb'lnəss/ *n.* —**honourably** *adv.*

Honourable *adj.* **1. USED AS TITLE OF RESPECT** used as a title of respect before sb's name to indicate entitlement to respect because of an official position held or to address a parliamentary colleague ○ *My honourable friend has spoken on this matter before.* **2. USED AS COURTESY TITLE FOR NOBILITY** used as a courtesy title in the United Kingdom for the children of some members of the aristocracy

honourable discharge *n.* an official dismissal from the armed forces, signifying that all duties have been honourably fulfilled

honourable mention *n.* an official or public commendation, usually granted to sb who has done well in a competition but not actually won an award

Honour Moderations *npl.* at Oxford University, the first set of public examinations in certain subjects according to which students are awarded first, second, or third class honours

Honours List *n.* a list of individuals who have been or are to be awarded honours such as a peerage or membership of a chivalric order by the British monarch

honours of war *npl.* **1. PRIVILEGES ACCORDED TO DEFEATED ENEMY** certain privileges that are accorded members of a defeated army **2. RESPECT TO DEAD SOLDIER** marks of respect paid by troops at the burial of another soldier

honour system *n.* a system under which people are relied on to be honest without direct supervision

Hons *abbr.* Honours

Hon. Sec. *abbr.* Honorary Secretary

Honshu /hón shoo/ the largest and most populous island of Japan. Area: 230,940 sq. km/89,166 sq. mi. Population: 99,254,194 (1990).

hooch[1] /hooch/, **hootch** *n. US* cheap alcohol, especially illegally distilled spirits (*slang*) [Late 19thC. Shortening of *hoochinoo*, from *Hoochinoo*, a Tlingit village in Alaska where illegal liquor was made, from Tlingit *xutsnu:wú*, literally 'brown bear's fort'.]

hooch[2] /hooch/ *interj. Scotland* used to express exhilaration in traditional Scottish dancing

Hooch /hooch/, **Pieter de** (1629–84) Dutch painter. His works often depict domestic scenes of 17th-century Dutch life. His works include *The Pantry* (?1658).

hood[1] /hŏŏd/ *n.* **1. LOOSE COVERING FOR HEAD** a covering for the head that may either be attached to the neck of a cloak or coat or be a separate garment **2. COVER FOR DEVICE** a cover for an appliance or machine, or a device such as a camera lens **3.** *US* AUTOMOT = **bonnet** *n.* 2 **4. PART OF ACADEMIC ROBE** an ornamental piece of cloth, often trimmed with fur or luxurious fabric, that hangs from the shoulders of an academic robe to indicate the status of the wearer **5. FOLDING ROOF** the folding roof of a carriage, pram, or convertible car **6. COVER FOR CHIMNEY** a fixed or revolving cover fitted to the top of a chimney to prevent downdraught **7. HEAD COVERING FOR FALCON** a bag placed over the head of a falcon to keep it calm when it is not hunting **8.** ZOOL **GROWTH OR MARKING ON ANIMAL'S HEAD** a crest, marking, or other conspicuous part on the head of an animal ■ *vt.* **(hoods, hooding, hooded) COVER STH WITH HOOD** to cover the head of a person, animal, or bird with a hood [Old English *hōd*. Ultimately from an Indo-European base meaning 'to cover', which is also the ancestor of English *hat* and *heed*.] —**hoodless** *adj.* —**hoodlike** /hŏŏd līk/ *adj.*

hood[2] /hŏŏd/ *n. US* a hoodlum (*slang*) [Late 19thC. Shortening.]

Hood /hŏŏd/, **Samuel, 1st Viscount** (1724–1816) British admiral. He was famed for his role in the defeat of the French off St Kitts (1782) and Dominica (1784).

-hood *suffix.* **1.** quality, state, condition ○ *knighthood* **2.** a group of people ○ *brotherhood* [Old English *-hād* (related to German *-heit*)]

hooded /hŏŏddid/ *adj.* **1. COVERED BY A HOOD** covered by or having a hood **2. PARTLY HIDDEN** partly concealed or covered ○ *dark, hooded eyes* **3.** ZOOL **HAVING CREST** having a crest, markings, or a specialized structure on the head —**hoodedness** *n.*

hooded crow *n.* a crow of Europe and Asia with a black head, tail, and wings, and a grey body. It is a subspecies of the carrion crow. Latin name: *Corvus corone cornix*.

hooded seal *n.* a large grey-spotted seal of the North Atlantic and Arctic oceans. The mature male has an inflatable sac near its nose that it uses in fighting. Latin name: *Cystophora cristata*.

hoodie crow /hŏŏdi-/, **hoodie** /hŏŏdi/ *n. Scotland* a hooded crow [Late 18thC. *Hoodie* alteration and diminutive of *hooded*.]

hoodlum /hŏŏdləm/ *n.* **1. GANGSTER** a petty criminal or gangster, especially one prone to violence **2. YOUNG VANDAL OR CRIMINAL** a young person who is violent or prone to committing crimes [Late 19thC. Origin uncertain: perhaps from a word related to German dialect *hudelum* 'disorderly' or *huddelumpe* 'rags, careless person'.] —**hoodlumish** *adj.* —**hoodlumism** *n.*

hood mould *n.* = **dripstone**

hoodoo /hŏŏ doo/ *n.* (*plural* **-doos**) **1.** = **voodoo 2. BAD LUCK** bad luck or misfortune **3. BRINGER OF BAD LUCK** sb or sth believed to bring bad luck **4.** *US, Can* **ODDLY-SHAPED ROCK COLUMN** in the western United States and Canada, a column of rock that has been weathered into a strange shape ■ *vt.* **(-doos, -dooing, -dooed) JINX SB OR STH** to appear to bring bad luck or misfortune to sb or sth [Late 19thC. Origin uncertain: possibly an alteration of VOODOO.] —**hoodooism** *n.*

hoodwink /hŏŏd wingk/ **(-winks, -winking, -winked)** *vt.* **1. TRICK SB** to deceive or dupe sb, especially by being clever or cunning **2. BLINDFOLD SB** to put a blindfold on sb (*archaic*) **3. CONCEAL STH** to conceal or hide sth (*archaic*) —**hoodwinker** *n.*

hooey /hŏŏ i/ *n.* empty or nonsensical talk or ideas (*informal*) [Early 20thC. Origin unknown.]

hoof /hoof, hŏŏf/ *n.* (*plural* **hooves** /hoovz, hŏŏvz/ *or* **hoofs**) **1. ANIMAL'S FOOT OF HORNY MATERIAL** the foot of a horse, deer, cow, or similar animal, covered with horny material **2. HORNY COVERING OF FOOT** the horny material covering the feet of animals such as horses, deer, and cattle **3. ANIMAL WITH HOOVES** an animal such as a horse, deer, or cow that has hooves **4. HUMAN FOOT** the foot of a human being (*slang humorous*) ■ *vt.* **(hoofs, hoofing, hoofed) 1. TRAVEL DISTANCE ON FOOT** to walk a specified distance (*slang*) **2. KICK SB OR STH** to kick or trample a person or animal [Old English *hōf*. Ultimately from an Indo-European word.] —**hoofless** *adj.* ◇ **hoof it 1.** to walk (*slang*) **2.** to dance (*slang*) ◇ **on the hoof 1.** alive and not yet butchered **2.** without sufficient thought or attention (*informal*) **3.** while moving around or doing sth else (*informal*) ○ *eating lunch on the hoof*

hoofed /hooft, hŏŏft/, **hooved** /hoovd, hŏŏvd/ *adj.* having hooves, or having hooves of a particular size and type

hoofer /hŏŏfər, hŏŏfər/ *n. US* a professional dancer, especially a tap dancer (*slang*)

hoofprint /hŏŏf print, hŏŏf-/ *n.* an imprint of an animal's hoof

hoo-hah /hŏŏ haa/, **hoo-ha** *n.* a loud noisy fuss, controversy, or disturbance (*slang*) [Mid-20thC. Origin uncertain: probably from Yiddish *hu-ha*, ultimately an imitation of the sound.]

hook /hŏŏk/ *n.* **1. BENT PIECE OF METAL** a bent or curved piece of metal or other material, used to attach, suspend, fasten, or lift another object **2. STH RESEMBLING HOOK** sth resembling a curved piece of metal, especially a plant or animal part **3.** ANGLING = **fish-hook 4.** AGRIC = **sickle** *n.* 1 **5. TRAP OR SNARE** a stratagem for trapping or snaring sb **6. STH THAT ATTRACTS** a means of attracting or interesting sb, especially a potential customer (*informal*) **7.** BOXING **SHORT SWINGING BLOW** in boxing, a short blow to an opponent delivered with a swing and a bent arm **8.** GOLF **GOLF SHOT CURVING SHARPLY** a golf shot that swerves sharply from right to left in the case of a right-handed player **9.** BASKETBALL = **hook shot 10.** CRICKET **LEG-SIDE SHOT IN CRICKET** in cricket, a shot with the bat held parallel to the ground that sends the ball towards the leg side **11. CREST OF BREAKING WAVE** the crest of a wave that is about to break **12.** ICE HOCKEY **ACT OF RESTRAINING ICE HOCKEY PLAYER** the act of using an ice hockey stick to prevent another player from moving freely **13. PART OF LETTER** in writing or printing, a short curve of a letter that extends above or below the line ○ *the hook of the 'g'* **14.** MUSIC **CATCHY REFRAIN** a pleasing and easily remembered refrain in a pop song ■ *v.* **(hooks, hooking, hooked) 1.** *vti.* **FASTEN WITH HOOK** to fasten by means of hooks or hooks and eyes **2.** *vt.* **ATTACH ONE THING TO ANOTHER** to attach one thing to another by means of a specially designed mechanical device ○ *hook the trailer to the car* **3.** *vti.* **BEND LIKE HOOK** to curve or cause sth to curve in the shape of a hook

○ *The road hooks sharply to the left.* **4.** *vt.* **ENSNARE STH** to catch or ensnare sth using a hook **5.** *vt.* **CATCH SB'S ATTENTION** to attract and hold sb's interest or attention **6.** *vt.* DRUGS **MAKE SB ADDICTED** to cause sb to become addicted or dependent on sth, especially a drug (*slang*) **7.** *vt.* BOXING **HIT SB WITH CURVING BLOW** in boxing, to deliver a sharp curving blow to an opponent, using a curved or bent arm **8.** *vt.* GOLF **STRIKE SWERVING BALL IN GOLF** in golf, to strike the ball so that it swerves sharply from right to left in the case of a right-handed player **9.** *vt.* BASKETBALL **SHOOT BALL IN BASKETBALL** in basketball, to shoot the ball by sweeping the hand upwards and farther away from the basket while moving sideways towards the basket **10.** *vt.* RUGBY **KICK BALL BACKWARDS IN RUGBY SCRUM** in rugby, to kick the ball backwards out of a scrum to the fly half **11.** *vt.* CRICKET **STRIKE CRICKET BALL TOWARDS LEG SIDE** in cricket, to strike the ball towards the leg side with the bat held parallel to the ground **12.** *vt.* ICE HOCKEY **RESTRAIN PLAYER WITH ICE HOCKEY STICK** to use an ice hockey stick to prevent another player from moving freely **13.** *vi.* **BE PROSTITUTE** to work as a prostitute (*slang*) **14.** *vt.* **GORE SB OR STH** to gore a person or animal with the horns or tusks **15.** *vt.* AGRIC **CUT STH WITH SICKLE** to cut grass or similar plants with a sickle **16.** *vt.* CRAFT **MAKE RUG** to make a rug by pulling pieces of wool through holes in stiff canvas using a special hook **17.** *vt.* **STEAL STH** to seize and steal sth (*slang*) [Old English *hōc*. Ultimately from an Indo-European word meaning 'hook, tooth', which is also the ancestor of English *hack* and *heckle*.] —**hookless** *adj.* ◇ **by hook or by crook** by some means or other ◇ **hook it** to run away (*dated slang*) ◇ **hook, line, and sinker** to a complete and total degree (*informal*) ○ *They fell for the story hook, line, and sinker.* ◇ **off the hook 1.** free of a difficult situation (*informal*) **2.** with the receiver off its cradle so that no telephone calls can be received ◇ **sling your hook** to go away (*slang; usually used as a command*)

hook up *v.* **1.** *vt.* **CONNECT ELECTRONIC DEVICES** to connect two or more electronic devices ○ *Is the microphone hooked up?* **2.** *vti.* **GET TOGETHER** to meet and become associated, or cause sb to meet and become associated with sb else (*informal*)

hookah /hŏŏkə/ *n.* an Asian pipe for smoking tobacco or marijuana, consisting of a flexible tube with a mouthpiece attached to a container of water through which smoke is drawn and cooled [Mid-18thC. Via Urdu from Arabic *ḥukka* 'jar'.]

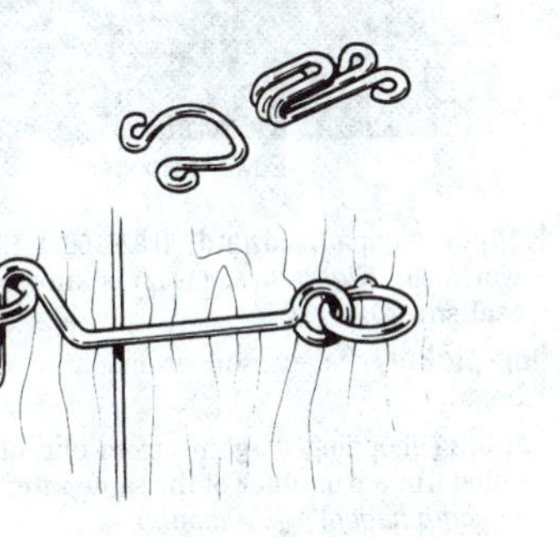

Hook and eye: Clothes fastener (top) and latch (bottom)

hook and eye (*plural* **hooks and eyes**) *n.* **1.** **CLOTHES FASTENER** a fastening for clothes consisting of a small hook inserted into a metal or thread loop **2.** *US* **LATCH** a latch for a gate or door consisting of a metal hook inserted into a screw eye

hookcheck *n.* ICE HOCKEY = **hook** *n.* 12

Hooke /hŏŏk/, **Robert** (1635–1703) British scientist and architect. He is best known for the formulation of Hooke's Law, the theory of elasticity.

hooked /hŏŏkt/ *adj.* **1.** **SHAPED LIKE HOOK** bent or shaped like a hook **2.** **HAVING HOOK AT END** ending in a hook **3.** CRAFT **MADE USING YARN HOOK** made by hooking yarn through canvas **4.** DRUGS **ADDICTED** addicted to a drug (*slang*) **5.** **OBSESSED WITH SB OR STH** in love with or compulsively attracted to sb, or obsessed with sth (*slang*)

hooker[1] /hŏŏkər/ *n.* a prostitute (*informal*) [Mid-19thC. Origin uncertain: possibly from an earlier meaning 'sneak thief'.]

hooker[2] /hŏŏkər/ *n.* **1.** **SB OR STH THAT HOOKS** a person, animal, or object that catches sth by hooking it **2.** RUGBY **RUGBY PLAYER** a front row forward who hooks the ball out of the scrum

hooker[3] /hŏŏkər/ *n.* **1.** **FISHING BOAT** a commercial fishing vessel that uses hooks and lines instead of nets **2.** **EX-CARGO BOAT** a large cargo boat with several sails, formerly used off the western coast of Ireland and now used as a pleasure craft [Mid-17thC. From Dutch *hoeker*, a shortening of Middle Dutch *hoeckboot* 'fishing boat', from *hoec* 'fish-hook'.]

Hooker /hŏŏkər/, **Joseph** (1814–79) US general. Known as an aggressive leader, he was put in command of the Army of the Potomac (1863). Known as **Fighting Joe**

Hooker, Sir William Jackson (1785–1865) British botanist. He wrote extensively on botany and became the first director of Kew Gardens, London (1841–65).

hookey *n.* = **hooky**

hooknose /hŏŏk nōz/ *n.* a nose with a noticeable curve, like an eagle's beak —**hooknosed** *adj.*

hook shot *n.* a shot that is made by sweeping the hand upwards and farther away from the basket while moving sideways towards the basket

hook-tip *n.* a moth that has forewings ending in a hooked point. Genus: *Daepana.*

hookup /hŏŏk up/ *n.* **1.** UTIL **LINK BETWEEN SOURCE AND USER** a connection allowing a user access to a utility such as electricity, gas, or water ○ *a gas hookup* **2.** ELECTRON ENG **ELECTRONIC SYSTEM** a number of items of electronic equipment designed to operate together (*informal*) **3.** **RELATIONSHIP** an alliance between people, groups, or things, especially an unlikely one (*informal*) ○ *a bizarre hookup between political enemies over an issue* **4.** ANGLING **CATCH IN OFFSHORE FISHING** in offshore big game fishing, an act of catching a fish on the end of the line

hookworm /hŏŏk wurm/ *n.* **1.** **PARASITIC WORM** a blood-sucking, disease-causing nematode worm that bores through the skin, attaching itself to the intestinal walls with its hooked mouthparts. Family: Ancylostomatidae. **2.** = **ancylostomiasis**

hookworm disease *n.* = **ancylostomiasis**

hooky /hŏŏki/, **hookey** *n.* absence, especially from school, without permission (*informal*) [Mid-19thC. Origin uncertain: perhaps from HOOK in the meaning 'to run away'.] ◇ **play hooky** to be absent without permission, especially from school (*informal*)

hooley /hŏŏli/ (*plural* **-leys**) *n. NZ, Ireland* a noisy merry party (*informal*) [Late 19thC. Origin unknown.]

hooligan /hŏŏligən/ *n.* an aggressive young man, especially one acting as part of a group, who commits acts of vandalism and violence in public places (*informal*) [Late 19thC. Origin uncertain: possibly from *Hooligan*, surname of a fictional rowdy Irish family in a music-hall song, and name of a comic Irish character in a cartoon.]

hooliganism /hŏŏligənizəm/ *n.* acts of vandalism and violence in public places, committed especially by youths

hoon /hoon/ *n. ANZ* (*informal*) **1.** **LOUT** a lout or hooligan **2.** **SPEEDING DRIVER** sb, especially a young man, who drives fast and recklessly **3.** **HIGHSPEED DRIVE** an act of driving fast and recklessly ■ *vi.* (**hoons, hooning, hooned**) *ANZ* **DRIVE TOO FAST** to drive fast and recklessly (*informal*) [Mid-20thC. Origin unknown.]

hoop /hoop/ *n.* **1.** **RING HOLDING BARREL TOGETHER** the metal or wooden ring used to hold the staves of a barrel in place **2.** **LARGE RING-SHAPED TOY** a large light ring of wood, metal, or plastic used as a toy or exercise aid **3.** **PAPER-COVERED RING JUMPED THROUGH IN CIRCUS** a large light ring, often with paper stretched over it, through which circus animals or performers jump **4.** ACCESSORIES **SUPPORT FOR PETTICOAT OR SKIRT** a lightweight cane, wire, or whalebone ring, or a structure made of several such rings, used, especially formerly, to stiffen a woman's skirt or petticoat **5.** CLOTHES **WIDE STIFF PETTICOAT OR SKIRT** a petticoat or skirt stiffened by cane, wire, or whalebone rings **6.** SEW **BAND FOR KEEPING EMBROIDERY FABRIC TAUT** either of a pair of wooden or metal bands used to keep fabric taut when it is being embroidered **7.** **EARRING** an earring formed from a continuous ring of metal **8.** **CIRCULAR PART OF FINGER RING** the part of a ring that the finger fits through **9.** BASKETBALL **METAL RING HOLDING NET IN BASKETBALL** in basketball, the metal ring from which an open-bottomed net is suspended, through which the ball is thrown in order to score points **10.** SPORTS **CROQUET WICKET** in croquet, a metal arch through which the ball is driven ■ *vt.* (**hoops, hooping, hooped**) **PUT HOOP ROUND STH** to surround sth with a hoop or band [Old English *hōp*, of prehistoric West Germanic origin] ◇ **jump, go through hoops (for sb)** to go to extreme lengths to gain favour with sb or to carry out sb's wishes (*informal*)

hooper /hoopər/ *n.* sb who makes or repairs barrels

hoopla[1] /hŏŏp laa/ *n.* a fairground game in which a player tries to throw a small hoop over a prize in order to win it [Early 20thC. Formed from HOOP, under the influence of HOOPLA[2].]

hoopla[2] /hŏŏp laa/ *n. US* **1.** **LOUD CELEBRATION** noisy excited commotion or joyous celebrating (*informal*) **2.** **GREAT PUBLIC UPROAR** a great amount of public fuss, commotion, or uproar with attendant publicity or media interest (*slang*) **3.** **MISLEADING TALK** intentionally misleading talk or propaganda (*informal*) [Late 19thC. Origin uncertain: perhaps from French *houp-là* 'upsy-daisy'!]

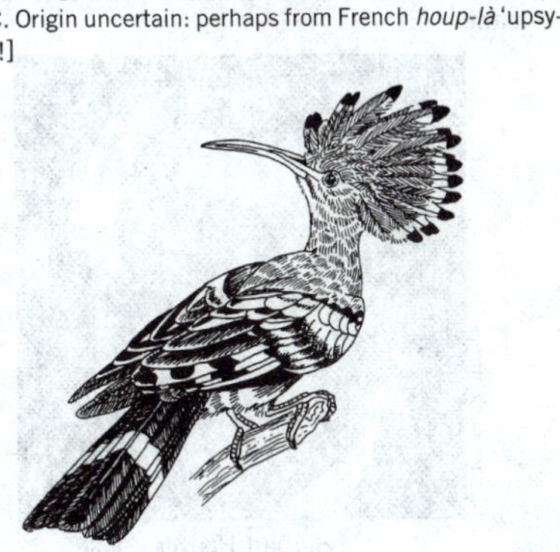

Hoopoe

hoopoe /hŏŏ poo/ (*plural* **-poes** *or* **-poe**) *n.* a Eurasian bird with a pinkish-brown head and back, a very prominent crest, a downward-curving bill, and a loud cry. Latin name: *Upupa epops.* [Mid-17thC. Alteration of earlier *hoop*, via Old French *huppe* from, ultimately, Latin *upupa*, an imitation of the bird's cry.]

hoop pine *n.* an Australian timber tree with rough bark. Latin name: *Araucaria cunninghamii.*

hoop skirt *n.* a long full skirt held out in the shape of a bell by a series of connected hoops, fashionable in the 18th and early 19th centuries

hoop snake *n.* any harmless North American snake such as the mud snake that was once believed to be able to take its tail in its mouth and roll along like a hoop

hooray /hŏŏ ráy/, **hoorah** /-ráa/, **hurray** /hə ráy, hŏŏ ráy/ *interj.* **USED AS SHOUT OF JOY** used as a shout of happy excitement, victory, or jubilation ■ *n.* **SHOUT OF JOY** a shout of happy excitement, victory, or jubilation [Late 17thC. Alteration of HURRAH.]

Hooray Henry /hŏŏ ray hénnri/ *n.* a young upper-class man, generally educated at public school, who wears conservative clothes and behaves and speaks in a loud, extrovert manner (*informal*)

hooroo /hŏŏ roo/ *interj. ANZ* = **goodbye** (*dated informal humorous*) [Early 20thC. Alteration of HURRAH.]

hoosegow /hŏŏss gow/ *n. US* a jail (*slang*) [Early 20thC. From Mexican Spanish *jusgado*, from Spanish *juzgado*, 'courtroom', from the past participle of *juzgar* 'to judge', from Latin *judicare* (see JUDGE).]

hoot /hoot/ *n.* **1.** **OWL'S CRY** the long sad-sounding cry of some owls **2.** **SOUND LIKE OWL'S CRY** a sound similar to an owl's cry, e.g. the sound made by a train whistle or car horn **3.** **LAUGHING SOUND** a cry, especially of laughter, derision, or scorn **4.** **SB OR STH HILARIOUS** a highly amusing person, object, or situation (*slang*) ■ *v.* (**hoots, hooting, hooted**) **1.** *vi.* **EMIT HOOT** to emit or produce a hoot **2.** *vi.* **MAKE LAUGHING SOUND** to utter a sound of laughter, derision, or scorn **3.** **SOUND CAR HORN** to cause a car horn to make a hoot **4.** *vt.* **DRIVE PERFORMER OFF STAGE** to drive a public performer or speaker off a stage by jeering **5.** *vt.* EXPRESS FEELING WITH JEERS to express a feeling such as contempt, derision, or scorn by jeering [12thC. Origin uncertain: perhaps an imitation of the sound.] ◇ **not care** *or* **give a hoot** not care at all

hootch *n.* = **hooch**[1]

hootenanny /hoot'n anni/ (*plural* **-nies**) *n.* US (*informal*) **1.** PERFORMANCE BY FOLK SINGERS an informal or impromptu performance by folk singers, in which the audience participates **2.** UNNAMED OBJECT an object or gadget for which the name is not known [Early 20thC. Origin unknown.]

hooter /hootər/ *n.* **1.** SB OR STH THAT HOOTS a person, animal, or object that hoots, especially a horn **2.** LARGE NOSE a nose, especially a large one (*slang humorous*) ■ **hooters** *npl.* US OFFENSIVE TERM an offensive term for a woman's large breasts, especially when large (*slang offensive*)

hoot owl *n.* an owl that has a hooting call

hoots /hoots/ *interj.* Scotland used to express impatience, disbelief, or annoyance (*informal*)

hooved *adj.* = **hoofed**

Hoover /hoovər/ *tdmk.* a trademark for a vacuum cleaner

Library of Congress

Herbert Hoover

Hoover /hoovər/, **Herbert** (1874–1964) US statesman and 31st president of the United States. A Republican president (1929–33), he opposed government assistance during the Great Depression. This made him unpopular, and he was defeated after one term by Franklin D. Roosevelt. Full name **Herbert Clarke Hoover**

Hoover Dam /hoovər dám/ dam on the Colorado River, on the Arizona-Nevada border, completed in 1936. Height: 221 m/726 ft.

hooves plural of **hoof**

hop[1] /hop/ *v.* (**hops, hopping, hopped**) **1.** *vi.* JUMP LIGHTLY ON ONE FOOT to jump lightly or quickly, especially on one foot **2.** *vi.* JUMP LIGHTLY WITH ALL FEET to move in a series of small jumps using both or all feet **3.** *vti.* LEAP OVER STH to jump quickly or lightly over sth **4.** *vi.* LIMP to walk with a limp **5.** *vi.* GET ON OR OFF to move quickly or lightly into, onto, out of, or off sth, especially a vehicle (*informal*) **6.** *vt.* US, Can JUMP ABOARD to get on a plane, train, bus, or other vehicle, usually quickly or after a sudden decision to do so (*informal*) ○ *hop a plane to California* **7.** *vt.* US RAIL RIDE TRAIN WITHOUT TICKET to ride on a train secretly without paying (*informal*) **8.** *vt.* AIR JOURNEY BY PLANE to make a journey by aeroplane, especially over a sea or ocean (*informal*) ■ *n.* **1.** SMALL QUICK JUMP a small jump on one, both, or all feet **2.** AIR FLIGHT a flight or leg of a flight in an aeroplane (*informal*) ○ *a short hop from New York to Chicago* **3.** LEISURE DANCE a social occasion at which people dance together, usually to popular music (*dated informal*) **4.** US SPORTS BOUNCE a bounce or rebound of a ball [Old English *hoppian* 'to leap, limp', from a prehistoric Germanic base that is also the ancestor of English *hip*[1]. The sense 'to jump on one foot' dates from the early 18thC.] ◇ **catch sb on the hop** to find sb unprepared (*informal*) ◇ **keep sb on the hop** to keep sb busy and alert (*informal*)

hop[2] /hop/ *n.* **1.** PLANTS CLIMBING VINE a climbing vine of the mulberry family that has lobed leaves and green female flowers arranged in spikes that look like pine cones. Latin name: *Humulus lupulus*. **2.** US DRUGS DRUG a narcotic drug such as opium (*dated slang*) ■ **hops** *npl.* BEVERAGES DRIED HOP FLOWERS the

dried flowers of the hop plant, used in brewing to add a distinctive bitter taste to beer [15thC. From Middle Low German or Middle Dutch *hoppe*.]

hop up *vt.* (*slang*) **1.** US INTOXICATE WITH DRUGS to make sb excited, or intoxicated, especially with drugs (*often passive*) **2.** US, Can AUTOMOT = **soup up**

hop, skip, and jump *n.* a short distance ○ *It's just a hop, skip, and jump to the station.*

hop, step, and jump *n.* **1.** ATHLETICS = **triple jump 2.** = **hop, skip, and jump**

HOP *abbr.* high oxygen pressure

hop clover *n.* US = **hop trefoil**

hope /hōp/ *vti.* (**hopes, hoping, hoped**) WANT OR EXPECT STH to have a wish to have or do sth or for sth to happen or be true, especially sth that seems possible or likely ■ *n.* **1.** CONFIDENT DESIRE a feeling that sth desirable is likely to happen ○ *The research offers hope to sufferers.* **2.** LIKELIHOOD OF SUCCESS a chance that sth desirable will happen or be possible ○ *There's not much hope that things will improve.* **3.** WISH OR DESIRE sth that sb wants to have or do or wants to happen or be true ○ *My hope is that she will change her mind.* **4.** SOURCE OF SUCCESS OR RELIEF sb or sth that seems likely to bring success or relief ○ *We have to do this, it's our only hope.* **5.** TRUST a feeling of trust (*archaic*) [Old English *hopian* 'to hope' and *hopa* 'hope', of uncertain origin: probably from Low German] —**hoper** *n.*

Hope /hōp/, **A. D.** (b. 1907) Australian poet and critic. An influential writer, his works include *The Wandering Islands* (1955) and *Collected Poems* (1972). Full name **Alec Derwent Hope**

hope chest *n.* US = **bottom drawer**

hopeful /hōpf'l/ *adj.* **1.** HAVING HOPE feeling fairly sure that sth that is wanted will happen **2.** GIVING HOPE making sb feel confident that sth desirable will happen **3.** SHOWING HOPE showing a desire for sth ■ *n.* SB DESIRING SUCCESS sb who wants to achieve sth, especially sb who hopes to be successful in acting, music, sport, politics, or some other endeavour —**hopefulness** *n.*

hopefully /hōpfəli/ *adv.* **1.** IN HOPEFUL WAY in a way that shows sb's hope of having or receiving sth **2.** IT IS HOPED used to indicate that sb hopes sth will happen or will be the case

——— **WORD KEY: USAGE** ———

Sentence adverb : Many adverbs that express a wish or comment, for example *clearly*, *obviously*, and *thankfully*, are routinely used to qualify a whole sentence: *They clearly haven't understood the issue*; *Obviously, there is a problem*; *Thankfully, they didn't arrive too late.* Many people object when *hopefully* is used in this way — in, for example, *Hopefully, someone can resolve this* — typically on the grounds that there is no one present in the sentence who is meant to be doing the hoping. This argument would tell against a number of the well-established sentence adverbs as well. For example, in *They clearly haven't understood the issue*, 'they' are not finding anything clear. The grounds on which to object to the sentence-adverbial *hopefully* may be illogical, therefore, but many well-educated, well-spoken people revile it regardless. A recommendation often made is to replace the word with *it is to be hoped*. That, however, strikes many people as stilted and even worse than *hopefully*. Frequently the best choice is *let's hope*.

Hopeh /hṓ páy/ = **Hebei**

hopeless /hōpləss/ *adj.* **1.** WITH NO HOPE OF SUCCESS unable to succeed or improve, or be resolved, helped, or cured **2.** DESPAIRING feeling no hope, or showing that sb has no hope **3.** VERY BAD showing a complete lack of ability, competence, or efficiency —**hopelessness** *n.*

hopelessly /hōpləssli/ *adv.* **1.** IN WAY SHOWING LACK OF HOPE in a way that shows sb has no hope of success, relief, or of getting what he or she wants **2.** VERY BADLY actually or supposedly to too great a degree to be improved or of use

hophead /hóp hed/ *n.* **1.** US DRUG ADDICT sb addicted to a narcotic drug such as heroin (*slang*) **2.** ANZ DRUNKARD sb who is frequently or usually drunk (*informal*)

Hopi (*plural* **-pi** *or* **-pis**) *n.* **1.** PEOPLES MEMBER OF NATIVE N AMERICAN PEOPLE a member of a Native North American people of northeastern Arizona **2.** LANG NATIVE N

AMERICAN LANGUAGE a language spoken in northeastern Arizona that is one of the Shoshonean group of the Uto-Aztecan branch of the Aztec-Tanoan family of Native North American languages. Hopi is spoken by about 5,000 people. [Late 19thC. From Hopi, literally 'peaceable'.] —**Hopi** *adj.*

Hopkins /hópkinz/, **Sir Anthony** (b. 1937) Welsh actor. His films include *Silence of the Lambs* (1991), *Remains of the Day* (1993), and *Shadowlands* (1993).

Hopkins, Sir Frederick (1861–1947) British biochemist. He was joint winner of the Nobel Prize in physiology or medicine (1929) for research into the role of vitamins in diet. Full name **Sir Frederick Gowland Hopkins**

Hopkins, Gerard Manley (1844–89) British poet. He was a technical innovator and is best remembered for his poem 'The Wreck of the Deutschland' (1875).

hoplite /hóp līt/ *n.* a heavily armed foot soldier in ancient Greece [Early 19thC. From Greek *hoplitēs*, from *hoplon* 'weapon', from *hepein* 'to care for, work at'.] —**hoplitic** /hop líttik/ *adj.*

hoplology /hop lólləji/ *n.* the study of weapons and armour [Late 19thC. Coined from Greek *hoplon* 'weapon' (see HOPLITE) and -LOGY.] —**hoplologist** *n.*

hopper[1] /hóppər/ *n.* **1.** TECH FUNNEL-SHAPED DISPENSER a large funnel-shaped container for storing and dispensing grain, fuel, or other materials **2.** RAIL, FREIGHT VEHICLE THAT DISCHARGES LOAD THROUGH FLOOR a wagon or railroad car with sloping floors designed to carry dry bulk goods such as grain or cement that are discharged through an opening in the bottom **3.** SB OR STH THAT HOPS sb who or sth that hops **4.** INSECTS JUMPING INSECT a jumping insect such as a leafhopper, treehopper, froghopper, or planthopper. Order: Homoptera.

hopper[2] /hóppər/ *n.* a machine used to harvest hops

UPI/Corbis-Bettmann

Edward Hopper

Hopper /hóppər/, **Edward** (1882–1967) US artist. His work, e.g. *Nighthawks* (1942) is known for its stark realism.

hop-picker *n.* a person or machine that harvests hops

hopping /hópping/ *n.* going from one place of a specified kind to another of the same kind (*usually used in combination*) ○ *job-hopping*

hopping mad *adj.* extremely angry (*informal*) [Hopping from the bodily movements often accompanying extreme anger]

hopple *vt.*, *n.* = **hobble** *v.* **2**, **hobble** *n.* **2** [Late 16thC. Origin uncertain: probably from Low German.] —**hoppler** *n.*

hoppy /hóppi/ (**-pier, -piest**) *adj.* with a strong taste of hops

hopsack /hóp sak/ *n.* **1.** FABRIC FOR CLOTHING a coarsely woven cotton or woollen fabric used to make clothes **2.** FABRIC FOR SACKS a coarse fabric of hemp or jute, used to make sacks or bags

hopscotch /hóp skoch/ *n.* a children's game in which players hop along squares marked in a pattern on the ground to pick up a small object thrown into one of the squares [Early 19thC. From SCOTCH in the sense 'scratched line'. The game was formerly called *scotch-hoppers* and *hop-scot*.]

hop trefoil *n.* a plant of northern temperate grasslands that is related to peas, beans, and clover and has yellow flowers that resemble hops. Latin name: *Trifolium campestre*. US term **hop clover**

Hopscotch

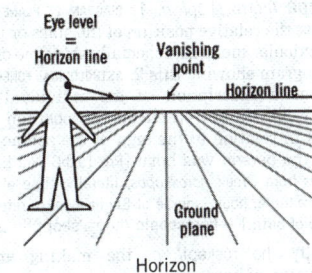

Eye level = Horizon line
Vanishing point
Horizon line
Ground plane

Horizon

hor. *abbr.* **1.** horizon **2.** horizontal **3.** horology

hora /háwrə/, **horah** *n.* **1.** DANCE CIRCLE DANCE a traditional dance of Israel and Romania, performed in a circle **2.** MUSIC MUSIC FOR HORA the traditional music to which the hora is danced [Late 19thC. From Romanian *horă* and Hebrew *hōrāh*.]

Horace /hórrəss/ (65–8 BC) Roman poet. The son of a slave, he was educated in Rome and Athens, and became the preeminent lyric poet of his time. His most famous works are *Odes* (23 BC) and *Epistles* (20? BC). Full name **Quintus Horatius Flaccus**

Horae /háwr ee/ *n.* in ancient Greece, the goddesses of the seasons and the order of nature

horah *n.* = hora

horal /háwrəl/ *adj.* hourly (*formal*) [Early 18thC. From late Latin *horalis*, from Latin *hora* (see HOUR).]

horary /háwrəri/ *adj.* (*formal*) **1.** RELATING TO HOUR relating to an hour or hours **2.** HOURLY hourly [Early 17thC. From medieval Latin *horarius*, from Latin *hora* (see HOUR).]

Horatian /hə ráysh'n/ *adj.* written by or in the style of the ancient Roman poet Horace ◇ *Alexander Pope's Horatian odes* [Early 17thC. From Latin *Horatianus*, from Quintus *Horatius* Flaccus, Latin name of HORACE.]

Horatian ode *n.* an ode that has several stanzas, each of which has the same rhythmic pattern

horde /hawrd/ *n.* **1.** THRONG a large group of people (*often used in the plural*) **2.** ANTHROP NOMADIC GROUP a group of nomads, especially of a people who live by hunting and foraging for food (**hunter-gatherers**) **3.** ZOOL SWARM OR PACK a large group of insects or other animals moving in a mass ■ *vi.* (**hordes, hording, horded**) **1.** FORM OR LIVE IN CROWD to gather together, move, or live in a large crowd or mass **2.** ANTHROP LIVE IN GROUP to live together in a nomadic group [Mid-16thC. Directly and via French and German from Polish *horda*, from, ultimately, Turkish *ordu* 'camp, army' (source of English *Urdu*).]

Hordern /háwrdərn/, **Sir Michael** (1911–95) British actor. An accomplished Shakespearean and film actor, his films include *The Spy Who Came in From the Cold* (1965).

horehound /háwr hownd/, **hoarhound** *n.* **1.** PLANTS MINT PLANT EASING COUGHS a bitter perennial mint of Europe and Asia that has downy leaves, square stems, and small white flowers whose juice was used as a flavouring and is used in cough remedies. Latin name: *Marrubium vulgare.* **2.** STH PREPARED FROM HOREHOUND an extract of the horehound plant, or sth flavoured with it, e.g. cough drops [Old English *hāre hūne*, from *hār* 'HOAR' + *hūne* 'horehound', of unknown origin]

horizon /hə ríz'n/ *n.* **1.** PLACE WHERE EARTH MEETS SKY the line in the furthest distance where the land or sea seems to meet the sky **2.** ASTRON CIRCLE ON APPARENT SPHERE OF SKY a circle formed on the celestial sphere by a plane tangent to a point on the earth's surface **3.** ASTRON CIRCLE ON CELESTIAL SPHERE a circle formed on the celestial sphere by a plane through the centre of the earth and parallel to the tangent of a point on the earth's surface **4.** GEOG DISTINCT LAYER OF SOIL a layer of soil having characteristics that distinguish it from other layers **5.** ARCHAEOL GEOLOGICAL LAYER a distinct layer of rock or geological deposit within a stratum that can be dated, e.g. by its fossil content ■ **horizons** *npl.* RANGE OF EXPERIENCE the range or limits of sb's interests, knowledge, or experience [14thC.

Via Old French *orizon(te)* from, ultimately, Greek *horizōn (kuklos)*, literally 'limiting (circle)', present participle of *horizein* 'to limit', from *horos* 'limit'.] —**horizonal** *adj.*

horizontal /hórri zónt'l/ *adj.* **1.** LEVEL parallel to the horizon **2.** MEASURED IN HORIZONTAL PLANE measured or operating in a plane parallel to the horizon **3.** LYING DOWN lying down or in a reclining position (*informal*) **4.** BUSINESS BEING OR HAVING SAME STATUS being at or having the same level within a group of people ◇ *a horizontal promotion* **5.** BUSINESS APPLIED TO ALL applied equally to all members, parts, or aspects of sth ◇ *a horizontal bonus* **6.** OF HORIZON relating to the horizon ■ *n.* STH HORIZONTAL a horizontal line, surface, or position [Mid-16thC. From French, or modern Latin *horizontalis*, from the late Latin stem *horizont-* of *horizon* 'horizon', from Greek *horizōn* (see HORIZON).] —**horizontality** /hórri zon tálləti/ *n.* —**horizontalness** /hórri zónt'lnəss/ *n.* —**horizontally** /-zónt'li/ *adv.*

horizontal bar *n.* **1.** RAISED METAL BAR a metal bar fixed in a horizontal position and used for gymnastic exercises **2.** GYMNASTICS EVENT a competitive gymnastics event involving feats of skill and strength on the horizontal bar

horizontal mobility *n.* a change in social situation that does not involve a change in social status

hormogonium /háwrmə gṓni əm/ (*plural* **-a** /-ə/) *n.* a section of a filament of blue-green algae that detaches and reproduces by cell division [Late 19thC. From modern Latin, from Greek *hormos* 'chain' + *gonos* 'generation, seed' (see GONAD).]

hormone /háwr mōn/ *n.* **1.** BIOCHEM REGULATING CHEMICAL IN BODY a chemical substance produced in the body's endocrine glands or certain other cells that exerts a regulatory or stimulatory effect, e.g. in metabolism **2.** PLANTS REGULATING CHEMICAL IN PLANTS a non-nutrient substance synthesized by plants that regulates growth and development **3.** INSECTS REGULATING CHEMICAL IN INSECTS a substance produced in the body of an insect that regulates various aspects of growth and development such as the change from larva to adult **4.** CHEM SYNTHETIC REGULATING CHEMICAL a synthetic chemical that acts like a hormone [Early 20thC. Formed from Greek *hormōn*, present participle of *horman* 'to set in motion', from *hormē* 'assault'.] —**hormonal** /hawr mṓn'l/ *adj.* —**hormonally** /-mṓn'li/ *adv.*

hormone replacement therapy *n.* treatment to maintain previous levels of the hormone oestrogen in women during and after the menopause, e.g. to avoid bone weakness (**osteoporosis**) and protect against heart attacks. Full form of **HRT**. US term **estrogen-replacement therapy**

Hormuz, Strait of /hawr mooz, háwrmŏŏz/ narrow waterway between Iran and the Arabian Peninsula, linking the Persian Gulf with the Arabian Sea. Formerly **Ormuz**

horn /hawrn/ *n.* **1.** CARS, EMERGENCIES NOISE-MAKING WARNING DEVICE a device, e.g. in a car, that produces a loud noise as a warning or signal (*often used in combination*) **2.** ZOOL PROJECTION ON ANIMAL'S HEAD one of a permanent pair of pointed projections on the head of certain mammals, e.g. the cow, sheep, or antelope, made of a sheath of hardened protein over bone **3.** ZOOL PROJECTION FROM NOSE OF RHINOCEROS a solid outgrowth of keratin and fused hair from the nasal bone of a rhinoceros **4.** ZOOL PROJECTION RESEMBLING HORN any of various hard, pointed, or horn-shaped projections on animals, birds, reptiles, fish, or insects **5.** MUSIC BRASS MUSICAL INSTRUMENT a wind instrument

usually made of brass and consisting of a long tube with a flared end that produces a sound when the player's lips vibrate together into the mouthpiece **6.** MUSIC JAZZ INSTRUMENT any wind instrument played in a jazz band (*informal*) **7.** MUSIC SIMPLE WIND INSTRUMENT a simple or early type of musical instrument made from an animal's horn **8.** INDUST HARD SUBSTANCE OF HORNS the hard substance that covers an animal's horns, consisting mainly of a tough protein (**keratin**) **9.** STH MADE OF HORN sth made with a piece of horn or from a synthetic substance resembling it **10.** PROJECTION ON DEVIL'S HEAD either of a pair of parts resembling an animal's horns supposed to grow on the head of a cuckold or the devil **11.** HORN-SHAPED THING sth shaped like a horn, e.g. either of the tips of a crescent moon, the pommel of a saddle, or the pointed end of an anvil **12.** GEOG SHARP PEAK a sharp pyramid-shaped mountain peak **13.** GEOG HORN-SHAPED AREA a horn-shaped body of water or land **14.** ERECTION an erection of the penis (*slang taboo*) **15.** US UTIL TELEPHONE a telephone (*slang*) ■ *vt.* (**horns, horning, horned**) **1.** PROVIDE WITH HORNS to give sth a horn or horns **2.** ATTACK WITH HORNS to butt or gore sb with the horns **3.** *Carib, US* HAVE SEX WITH SB ELSE'S PARTNER to make a cuckold of sb by having a sexual relationship with the spouse or partner (*informal*) [Old English. Ultimately from an Indo-European base meaning 'horn, head'.] ◇ **draw in your horns 1.** to spend or invest less money than usual or before **2.** to adopt a less active or less assertive position ◇ **on the horns of a dilemma** faced with making a decision between two things or two courses of action, each of which is problematic or unattractive

— **WORD KEY: ORIGIN** —
The Indo-European ancestor of *horn* is also the ultimate source of English *carrot, corn, cornea, corner, cornet, cranium, ginger, hart, hornet, keratin, rhinoceros,* and *triceratops.*

horn in *vi.* to intrude, interfere, or get involved in sth without invitation (*informal*)

Horn, Cape /hawrn/ cape at the southern tip of South America, on an island now belonging to Chile. It was notorious for shipwrecks in the age of sailing ships.

hornbeam /háwrn beem/ *n.* **1.** TREES TREE WITH SMOOTH BARK a tree that has smooth greyish bark and hard white wood. Genus: *Carpinus.* **2.** INDUST WOOD OF HORNBEAM the hard white wood of the hornbeam tree

hornbill /háwrn bil/ *n.* a noisy tropical bird that has a very large curved bill with a horny protuberance. Hornbills are often found in large groups. Family: Bucerotidae.

hornblende /háwrn blend/ *n.* a variety of a silicate mineral (**amphibole**) ranging in colour from dark green to black and containing aluminium, calcium, iron, magnesium, and sodium [Late 18thC. From German, literally 'horn blende'.] —**hornblendic** /hawrn bléndik/ *adj.*

hornbook /háwrn bŏŏk/ *n.* a page of text formerly made for the teaching of reading, usually printed with the alphabet, letter combinations, and a religious passage, and covered with a thin layer of horn

Horne /hawrn/, **Donald** (b. 1921) Australian writer and academic. His most famous work is *The Lucky Country* (1964). Full name **Donald Richmond Horne**

horned /hawrnd/ *adj.* having a horn or horns, or one or more projections that resemble horns

horned lizard *n.* a small insect-eating lizard of the desert regions of the southwestern United States and Mexico that has a flattened body, a short tail, and spikes like horns on its head. Genus: *Phrynosoma.*

horned owl *n.* a large owl that has prominent ear tufts resembling horns. Latin name: *Bubo virginianus.*

horned pout *n.* = hornpout

horned toad *n.* = horned lizard

horned viper *n.* a poisonous snake of the desert regions of the Near East and Africa that has spines on its head that look like horns. Latin name: *Cerastes cornutus.*

hornet /háwrnit/ *n.* a large social stinging wasp that builds large group nests underground or hanging from a tree. Family: Vespidae. [Old English *hyrnet(u)*. Ultimately from an Indo-European word that is also the ancestor of English *horn*.]

hornet's nest *n.* a highly controversial issue or situation that is likely to lead to confrontation, opposition, or argument

hornfels /háwrn felz, -fels/ (*plural* **-fels**) *n.* a fine-grained metamorphic rock composed of silicate minerals and formed through the action of heat and pressure on shale [Mid-19thC. From German, literally 'horn rock'.]

horn fly *n.* a small bloodsucking black fly that is a pest of cattle. Latin name: *Haematobia irritans*. [*Horn* from its sucking blood from the base of the horns of cattle]

hornist /háwrnist/ *n.* a musician who plays a horn

horn-mad *adj.* extremely angry or enraged (*archaic*) [The word originally described the rage of horned beasts]

horn of plenty *n.* **1.** = **cornucopia 2.** FUNGI **HORN-SHAPED EDIBLE FUNGUS** a funnel-shaped, black and brown edible fungus found in deciduous woodland in autumn. Latin name: *Craterellus cornucopioides*.

hornpipe /háwrn pīp/ *n.* **1.** DANCE **SAILORS' DANCE** a lively British dance traditionally performed by sailors **2.** MUSIC **MUSIC ACCOMPANYING HORNPIPE** the music for a hornpipe, or an orchestral piece based on this **3.** MUSIC **REED INSTRUMENT** a musical instrument with a single reed and a mouthpiece made of horn, traditionally used to play the music for a hornpipe

hornpout /háwrn powt/ *n.* a small North American fish with a large head and eight barbels. Latin name: *Ictalurus nebulosus*.

horn-rims, **horn-rimmed glasses** *npl.* spectacles with frames made from dark-coloured horn or a synthetic substance made to resemble this —**horn-rimmed** *adj.*

hornstone /háwrn stōn/ *n.* = **hornfels** [Early 18thC. Translation of German *Hornstein*, literally 'horn stone'.]

hornswoggle /háwrn swogg'l/ (**-gles, -gling, -gled**) *vt.* *US* to cheat, trick, or deceive sb (*informal*) [Early 19thC. Origin unknown.]

horntail /háwrn tayl/ *n.* an insect that resembles a wasp and whose larvae burrow in wood. The female has a specialized egg-laying organ (**ovipositor**) used to lay eggs in wood. Family: Siricidae.

hornworm /háwrn wurm/ *n.* the caterpillar of certain hawkmoths, with a projection on its tail that resembles a horn. Hornworms are often destructive agricultural pests.

hornwort /háwrn wurt/ *n.* a rootless aquatic plant that grows in branching submerged masses and has finely dissected leaves and tiny flowers. Genus: *Ceratophylum*. [Modelled on Greek *keratophullon*, literally 'horn leaf'; from the appearance of its branching stem]

horny /háwrni/ (**-ier, -iest**) *adj.* **1. AS TOUGH AS HORN** hard or rough like horn **2. OF OR LIKE HORN** made of or resembling horn **3. FEELING SEXY** sexually excited, or easily aroused sexually (*informal*) **4. LOOKING SEXY** sexually attractive (*informal*) **5. WITH HORNS** having a horn or horns —**hornily** *adv.* —**horniness** *n.*

horol. *abbr.* **1.** horological **2.** horology

horologe /hórrə loj/ *n.* any device used to tell the time, e.g. a clock or sundial (*formal*) [13thC. Via Old French *or(i)loge* from, ultimately, Greek *hōrologion*, literally 'little time-telling (instrument)', ultimately from *hōra* 'time, hour' (source of English *hour*).]

horologist /ho rólləjist/, **horologer** *n.* **1.** TIME **STUDIER OF TIME** sb who studies the science of measuring time **2.** CRAFT **CLOCKMAKER** sb skilled in making clocks and watches

Horologium /háwrə lōji əm/ *n.* a faint constellation of the southern hemisphere situated between Hydrus and Eridanus

horology /ho rólləji/ *n.* **1.** TIME **TIME MEASUREMENT** the study or science of measuring time **2.** CRAFT **CLOCKMAKING** the art or skill of making clocks, watches, and other devices for telling the time [15thC. Coined from Greek *hōra* 'time, hour' (source of English *hour*) + -LOGY.] — **horologic** /hórrə lójjik/ *adj.* —**horological** *adj.* —**horologically** *adv.*

horoscope /hórrə skōp/ *n.* **1. DIAGRAM OF PLANETARY RELATIONSHIP** the relative position of the stars or planets at a particular moment, especially sb's time of birth, or a diagram showing this **2. ASTROLOGICAL FORECAST** an astrologer's description of an individual's personality and future based on the position of the planets in relation to the sign of the zodiac under which the person was born [Pre-12thC. Via Latin *horoscopus* from Greek *hōroskopos*, literally 'time observer', from *hōra* 'time, hour' (source of English *hour*), referring to the time of birth.] —**horoscopic** /hórrə skóppik/ *adj.*

horoscopy /ho róskəpi/ *n.* the making and interpretation of horoscopes

horrendous /ho réndəss, hə-/ *adj.* **1. DREADFUL** sufficiently unpleasant, frightening, or shocking as to provoke horror **2. VERY LARGE** very large, great, or high, often unreasonably or excessively so (*informal*) ○ *horrendous prices* [Mid-17thC. Formed from Latin *horrendus* 'to be shuddered at', a form of *horrere* (see HORRIBLE).]

horrendously /ho réndəssli, hə-/ *adv.* to a very great, and often unreasonable or excessive, degree

horrent /hórrənt/ *adj.* standing on end like bristles (*archaic*) ○ *'With bright imblazonrie, and horrent arms'* (John Milton, *Paradise Lost*; 1667) [Mid-17thC. From Latin *horrent-*, the present participle stem of *horrere* (see HORRIBLE).]

horrible /hórrəb'l/ *adj.* **1. VERY UNPLEASANT** very bad, very unpleasant, or caused by anxiety or fear about sth bad ○ *a horrible smell* **2. CAUSING HORROR** sufficiently frightening, distressing, or shocking as to provoke horror ○ *a horrible crime* **3. NASTY** unkind, rude, or badly-behaved (*informal*) [13thC. Via Old French *(h)orrible* from Latin *horribilis*, from *horrere* 'to bristle, shudder with fear at' (source of English *horror* and *ordure*).] —**horribleness** *n.*

horribly /hórrəbli/ *adv.* **1. IN UNPLEASANT WAY** in an unpleasant, disagreeable, distressing, or shocking way **2. VERY** to a great or excessive extent ○ *horribly late*

horrid /hórrid/ *adj.* **1. NASTY** callously unkind or nasty (*informal*) ○ *a horrid thing to say* **2. CAUSING DISGUST** provoking disgust or extreme displeasure ○ *a horrid taste* **3. CAUSING HORROR** dreadful, shocking, or frightening enough to cause horror ○ *a horrid accident* **4. BRISTLY** rough, shaggy, or bristly (*archaic*) [Late 16thC. From Latin *horridus* 'bristly, rough, horrid', from *horrere* (see HORRIBLE).] —**horridly** *adv.* —**horridness** *n.*

horrific /ho ríffik, hə-/ *adj.* frightening or disturbing enough to cause horror [Mid-17thC. Directly or via French *horrifique* from Latin *horrificus*, from *horrere* (see HORRIBLE).] —**horrifically** *adv.*

horrify /hórri fī/ (**-fies, -fying, -fied**) *vt.* **1. CAUSE SB TO FEEL HORROR** to make sb feel horror, disgust, or fright **2. DISMAY SB** to make sb shocked or dismayed [Late 18thC. From Latin *horrificare*, literally 'to cause horror', from, ultimately, *horrere* (see HORRIBLE).] —**horrification** /hórifi káysh'n/ *n.* —**horrified** /hórri fīd/ *adj.* —**horrifying** /-fī ingli/ *adj.* —**horrifyingly** /-fī ingli/ *adv.*

horripilation /ho rippi láysh'n/ *n.* the standing on end of sb's hair, e.g. because of fear or cold [Mid-17thC. From the late Latin stem *horripilation-*, from, ultimately, Latin *horripilare* 'to become hairy', from *horrere* 'to stand on end' (see HORRIBLE) + *pilus* 'hair'.]

horror /hórrər/ *n.* **1. INTENSE FEAR OR SHOCK** a very strong, painful feeling of fear, shock, or disgust **2. INTENSE DISLIKE OR DISMAY** a feeling of distress or distaste **3. STH CAUSING HORROR** sth, or an aspect of sth, that causes a feeling of great fear or disgust ○ *the horrors of war* **4. STH UNPLEASANT** a very unpleasant or unattractive thing (*informal*) ○ *The new building is an absolute horror.* **5. SB CAUSING DISLIKE** a disagreeable or ill-mannered person, especially a badly-behaved child (*informal*) ■ **horrors** *npl.* (*informal*) **1. FEELING OF TERROR** a feeling of great fear, anxiety, or hopelessness **2.** = **delirium tremens** ■ *adj.* CINEMA, LITERAT **GROTESQUE AND TERRIFYING** used to describe a genre of motion picture or literature intended to thrill viewers or readers by provoking fear or revulsion through the portrayal of grotesque, violent, or supernatural events. ◊ **horror story** [14thC. Directly or via Old French *(h)orrour* from Latin *horror*, from *horrere* (see HORRIBLE).]

horror story *n.* **1.** LITERAT **FRIGHTENING FICTIONAL TALE** a story that is intended to frighten people, usually by describing gruesome or supernatural events **2. REPORT OF HORRIFYING EXPERIENCE** a true account of sth very unpleasant or shocking

horror-struck, **horror-stricken** *adj.* suddenly shocked, frightened, or dismayed

hors concours /áwr koN kóor/ *adj.* in the capacity or manner of sb who is not competing [From French, literally 'out of the competition']

hors de combat /áwr də kóm baa/ *adj.* out of action and often in a seriously wounded condition [From French, literally 'out of the fight']

hors d'oeuvre /awr dúrv/ (*plural* **hors d'oeuvre** *or* **hors d'oeuvres**) *n.* a small portion of food served cold or hot before a meal to stimulate the appetite [From French, literally 'outside the work']

horse /hawrss/ *n.* **1.** ZOOL **FOUR-LEGGED SOLID-HOOFED ANIMAL** a large four-legged animal with a mane, tail, hooves, and a long head. Horses are kept as domestic animals for riding, pulling vehicles, and carrying loads. Latin name: *Equus caballus*. **2.** ZOOL **STALLION OR GELDING** an adult male horse **3.** ZOOL **ANIMAL OF THE HORSE FAMILY** an animal, e.g. a donkey or zebra, that belongs to the family including the horse. Family: Equidae. **4.** GYMNASTICS = **vaulting horse 5. FRAME OR SUPPORT** a type of frame or support, especially one mounted on four legs **6.** ARMY **MOUNTED SOLDIERS** soldiers riding horses (*takes a singular or plural verb*) **7.** GEOL **ROCK MASS IN AN ORE VEIN** a mass of rock located in an ore vein **8.** DRUGS **HEROIN** heroin (*dated slang*) **9.** AUTOMOT **HORSEPOWER** horsepower (*informal; usually used in the plural*) ■ **horses** *npl.* **HORSERACING** horseracing, especially as a gambling activity (*informal*) ■ *v.* (**horses, horsing, horsed**) **1.** *vt.* **GIVE SB A HORSE** to provide sb with a horse **2.** *vti.* RIDING **PUT OR GET ON A HORSE** to put a rider on a horse's back, or mount a horse **3.** *vi.* ZOOL **BE IN HEAT** to be ready to mate with a male horse (*refers to a mare*) [Old English *hors*, from a prehistoric Germanic word of uncertain origin] ◇ **get on your high horse** to adopt an arrogant attitude ◇ **flog a dead horse** to pursue a topic or course of action that is likely to be totally unproductive ◇ **from the horse's mouth** from a well-informed and reliable source ◇ **look a gift horse in the mouth** to criticize sth that has been given to you

horse around, **horse about** *vi.* to play or fool around in a boisterous manner

horse-and-buggy *adj.* adhering to things, fashions, or ideas that are old-fashioned and out of date [From the obsolescence of this means of transport]

horseback /háwrss bak/ *adj., adv.* on a horse's back ◇ **on horseback** sitting on or riding a horse

horse bean *n.* = **broad bean** [From its use as fodder for horses]

horsebox /háwrss boks/ *n.* a vehicle, e.g. a lorry or railway car, used to transport horses. US term **horsecar** *n.*

horse brass *n.* a flat, usually circular, polished brass ornament originally attached to a horse's harness and now sometimes hung on walls or beams in houses or bars for decoration

horsecar /háwrss kaar/ *n.* *US* = **horsebox**

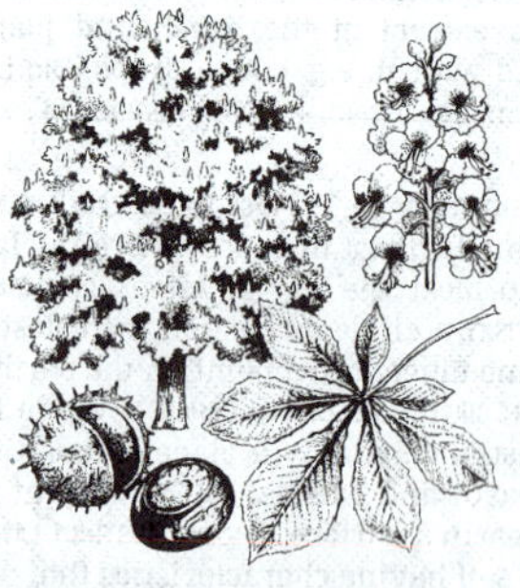

Horse chestnut

horse chestnut *n.* **1.** TREES **TREE WITH LARGE SHINY BROWN SEEDS** a large tree of Europe and Asia that has five-lobed leaves, conical clusters of flowers, and shiny brown seeds that resemble nuts. Latin name: *Aesculus hippocastanum*. **2.** **A FRUIT OF HORSE CHESTNUT TREE** the shiny brown inedible fruit of the horse chestnut tree. ◊ **conker 3.** INDUST **HORSE CHESTNUT WOOD** the soft wood of the horse chestnut tree [Translation of obsolete modern Latin *Castanea equina*; *equina* 'horse' perhaps because the leaf stalk bears the image of a horse's hock and foot with shoe and nails]

horsefeathers /háwrss fethərz/ *n., interj. US* nonsense (*humorous slang; takes a singular verb*) [Early 20thC. Alteration of HORSESHIT.]

horseflesh /háwrss flesh/ *n.* **1.** EQU **HORSES OR HORSE** horses collectively **2.** FOOD **MEAT FROM A HORSE** the flesh of a horse, especially when sold or eaten as meat

horsefly /háwrss flī/ (*plural* **-flies**) *n.* a large two-winged fly, the female of which sucks the blood of horses and other mammals. Genus: *Tabanus*.

Horse Guards *npl.* CAVALRY REGIMENT FORMING SOVEREIGN'S BODYGUARD a cavalry regiment that, with the Life Guards, forms the Household Cavalry responsible for guarding the sovereign, especially during public ceremonies ■ *n.* HEADQUARTERS OF HORSE GUARDS the headquarters of the Horse Guards in Whitehall, London

horsehair /háwrss hair/ *n.* **1.** INDUST LONG HAIR FROM A HORSE hair from a horse's mane and tail, used to upholster furniture, to fill mattresses, and to make cloth **2.** TEXTILES **HORSEHAIR CLOTH** fabric woven from the hair of a horse's mane and tail

horsehair worm *n.* = **hairworm** [*Horsehair* from its form, likened to a hair of a horse]

Horsehead nebula /háwrss hed-/ *n.* a dark nebula in the constellation Orion, shaped like a horse's head

horsehide /háwrss hīd/ *n.* the tough thick skin of a horse, or leather made from a horse's skin

horse latitudes *npl.* either of two regions at sea near the latitudes 30° S and 30° N marked by high atmospheric pressure and light variable winds or calms [Late 18thC. Origin uncertain.]

horselaugh /háwrss laaf/ *n.* a loud, coarse, and often scornful laugh

horseleech /háwrss leech/ *n.* a large freshwater leech. Genus: *Haemopis*. [*Horse* in animal and plant names usually denotes 'large size' or 'coarseness', the horse typifying a large creature]

horseless carriage *n.* a motor car, at a time when horse-drawn vehicles were still the usual form of transport (*archaic*)

horse mackerel *n.* a swift torpedo-shaped fish found in the Atlantic Ocean, the Mediterranean Sea, and the Black Sea. Latin name: *Trachurus trachurus*. [See HORSELEECH]

horseman /háwrssmən/ (*plural* **-men** /-mən/) *n.* a man who rides or is riding a horse, especially a man who does so with skill

horsemanship /háwrssmən ship/ *n.* skill in riding horses

horsemint /háwrss mint/ *n.* **1.** N AMERICAN MINT a coarse North American mint that has showy yellow flowers with purple spots. Latin name: *Monarda punctata*. **2.** EURASIAN WILD MINT a hairy wild mint of Europe and Asia that has elongated clusters of small pinkish-purple flowers. Latin name: *Mentha longifolia*. [See HORSELEECH]

horse mushroom *n.* an edible and highly esteemed mushroom that resembles cultivated mushrooms but is larger and has a smell of almonds. Latin name: *Agaricus arvensis*. [See HORSELEECH]

horse nettle *n.* a coarse prickly North American weed of the nightshade family with white or blue flowers and yellow berries. Latin name: *Solanum carolinese*. [See HORSELEECH]

horse opera *n.* a Western film (*informal*) [*Horse* from the ubiquity in such works of horses; *opera* from the use of dramatic music and themes]

horse pistol *n.* a large pistol formerly used by horsemen and carried in a holster

horseplay /háwrss play/ *n.* rough, boisterous, playful behaviour

horsepower /háwrss powər/ *n.* a unit of power equal in the United Kingdom to 550 foot-pounds per second and in the United States to 745.7 watts [*Horse* from one such unit being supposedly equivalent to the work rate of a horse]

horserace /háwrss rayss/ *n.* a race between horses ridden by jockeys on a flat circuit or over obstacles

horseracing /háwss rayssing/ *n.* a sport in which horses ridden by jockeys race against each other, usually with spectators and others betting on the result

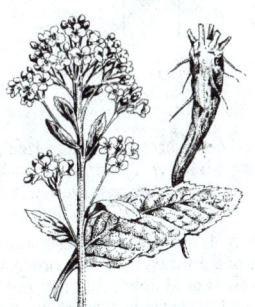

Horseradish

horseradish /háwrss radish/ *n.* **1.** PLANTS **PLANT WITH PUNGENT ROOTS** a tall coarse plant that has white flowers and thick white pungent roots. Latin name: *Amoracia lapathifolia*. **2.** FOOD **HORSERADISH ROOT AS FOOD** the long slim pungent root of the horseradish plant used in cookery, especially peeled and grated to make a hot, sharp-tasting sauce often served with beef [See HORSELEECH]

horse sense *n.* common sense (*informal*)

horseshit /háwrss shit/ *n.* **1.** *US* OFFENSIVE TERM an offensive term for nonsense (*slang offensive*) **2.** OFFENSIVE TERM an offensive term for the excrement of a horse (*offensive*)

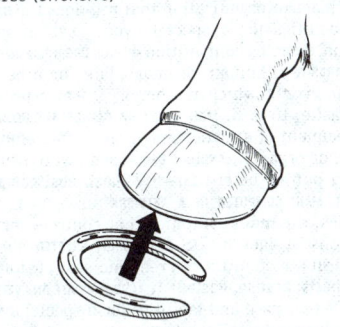

Horseshoe

horseshoe /háwrss shoo/ *n.* **1.** EQU **PROTECTION FOR A HORSE'S HOOF** a flat U-shaped piece of iron nailed to the bottom of a horse's hoof to protect it against hard surfaces. Horseshoes are regarded as symbols of good luck. **2.** GOOD-LUCK TOKEN a representation of a horseshoe regarded as a symbol of good luck **3.** HORSESHOE-SHAPED THING sth that has the curved shape of a horseshoe ◊ '... *every known superstition in the world is gathered into the horseshoe of the Carpathians* ...' (Bram Stoker, *Dracula*; 1897) ■ *vt.* (**-shoes, -shoeing, -shoed**) EQU = **shoe** *v.* 1 —**horseshoer** *n.*

horseshoe arch *n.* an arch that narrows slightly below the upper rounded part. Horseshoe arches are characteristic of the Islamic architecture of southern Spain and North Africa.

horseshoe bat *n.* a bat that has a horseshoe-shaped appendage that surrounds the nostrils. Horseshoe bats are found in Europe, but most abundantly in the tropics and subtropics. Family: Rhinolophidae.

horseshoe crab *n.* a large marine arthropod of eastern North America and Asia that has a stiff pointed tail and rounded brown body resembling a horseshoe. Class: Merostomata.

Horseshoe Falls /háwrss shoo-/ crescent-shaped Canadian section of the Niagara Falls on the US-Canadian border. Height: 49 m/161 ft.

horseshoes /háwrss shooz/ *n. US* LEISURE a game in which players throw horseshoes at a post and score points based on how close they land to the post (*takes a singular verb*)

horse show *n.* a sporting event in which horses and usually riders are judged on their skills in a variety of competitions such as riding or jumping

horsetail /háwrss tayl/ *n.* **1.** PLANTS **NONFLOWERING PLANT** a nonflowering plant that has a hollow jointed stem, tiny thin leaves, and spore-producing cones produced at the top of the stems. Genus: *Equisetum*. **2.** HIST **TURKISH EMBLEM OF RANK** a former emblem of rank of Turkish pashas in the Ottoman Empire

horse-trading *n.* negotiation that involves bargaining and mutual compromise, often some shrewdness, and sometimes unscrupulous tactics such as secret or unofficial deals —**horse-trade** *vi.* —**horse-trader** *n.*

horsewhip /háwrss wip/ *n.* **1.** WHIP FOR A HORSE a whip formerly used to keep a horse under control, e.g. when being driven, and usually made of a long strip of leather attached to a short handle **2.** *Carib* ZOOL **W INDIAN SNAKE** a long thin snake common in the forests of Trinidad and frequently found in bushes near homes ■ *vt.* (**-whips, -whipping, -whipped**) BEAT SEVERELY to flog a person or animal with a horsewhip or with sth similar, usually as a punishment —**horsewhipper** *n.*

horsewoman /háwrss woomən/ (*plural* **-en** /-wimin/) *n.* a woman who rides or is riding a horse, especially one who does so with skill

horsey /háwrssi/ (**-ier, -iest**), **horsy** (**-ier, -iest**) *adj.* **1.** RELATING TO HORSES belonging to, relating to, or characteristic of a horse **2.** LOOKING LIKE A HORSE heavy, awkward, and unattractive in appearance **3.** INTERESTED IN HORSES very fond of horses and interested in activities involving horses such as riding, racing, showjumping, or hunting —**horsiness** *n.*

Horsham /háwrshəm/ town in West Sussex, England, combining light industry, service industries, and agriculture. Population: 39,894 (1991).

horst /hawrst/ *n.* an elevated block of the Earth's crust forced upwards between faults [Late 19thC. From German, 'heap, mass'.]

horsy *adj.* = **horsey**

hort. *abbr.* **1.** horticulture **2.** horticultural

hortative /háwrtətiv/ *adj.* = **hortatory** (*formal*) [Early 17thC. Via Latin *hortativus* from, ultimately, *hortari* 'to exhort' (see HORTATORY).] —**hortatively** *adv.*

hortatory /háwrtətəri/ *adj.* urging, encouraging, or strongly advising a course of action to sb (*formal*) [Late 16thC. Via late Latin *hortatorius* from, ultimately, Latin *hortari* 'to urge strongly, exhort' (source of English *exhort*).] —**hortatorily** *adv.*

horticulture /háwrti kulchər/ *n.* **1.** BOT, GARDENING **CULTIVATION OF GARDENS** the science, skill, or occupation of cultivating plants, especially flowers, fruit, and vegetables, in gardens or greenhouses **2.** ANTHROP **SIMPLE AGRICULTURE WITHOUT MANY TOOLS** a simple form of agriculture based on working small plots of land without using draught animals, ploughs, or irrigation [Late 17thC. Formed from Latin *hortus* 'garden' (source of English *orchard*). Ultimately from an Indo-European word meaning 'to enclose', which is also the ancestor of English *yard* and *garden*.] —**horticultural** /háwrti kúlchərəl/ *adj.* —**horticulturally** *adv.* —**horticulturist** *n.*

Horus /háwrəss/ *n.* in Egyptian mythology, the god of the sun, the sky, and goodness, usually depicted as having a falcon's head. Horus was the son of Isis and Osiris.

Hos. *abbr.* Hosea

hosanna /hō zánnə/, **hosannah** *n., interj.* a cry of praise to God [Pre-12thC. Via late Latin from Greek *hōsanna*, from Rabbinic Hebrew *hŏsă'nā*, shortening of Hebrew *hōšĭ'ā-nnā* 'save, (we) pray' (Psalm 118:25).]

Hosay /hō sáy/, **Hosein** /hō sáyn/ *n.* an Islamic religious festival held on the tenth day of the month of Moharram celebrating the martyrdom of Imam Hosein. In Port of Spain, Trinidad, floats depicting religious sites and figures are paraded through the streets and thrown into the sea as a symbol of the vanity of worldly things.

hose /hōz/ *n.* FLEXIBLE TUBE a flexible tube or pipe, often made of rubber or plastic, through which fluids such as water or petrol can flow ■ *npl.* **1.** *US* CLOTHES LEG COVERING a skintight leg covering such as stockings or socks (*takes a plural verb*) **2.** CLOTHES, HIST TIGHT-FITTING TROUSERS a garment formerly worn by men, fitting closely to the legs and attaching to a doublet ■ *vt.* (**hoses, hosing, hosed**) **1.** DIRECT WATER ON SB OR STH to spray, soak, wash, or rinse sth or sb with water from a hose **2.** *US* TRICK SB to deceive or trick sb (*slang*) [Old English *hosa* 'leg covering, husk' (hence 'flexible tube'). Ultimately from an Indo-European word meaning 'to cover', which is also the ancestor of English *hut, scum,* and *sky*.]

Hosea /hō zée ə/ *n.* in the Bible, a short prophetic book. See table at **Bible**

Hosein *n.* = **Hosay**

hosel /hṓz'l/ *n.* the socket in the head of a golf club where the shaft is attached [Late 19thC. Formed from HOSE + the suffix *-el* 'small' (from Latin *-ellus*).]

hosepipe /hṓz pīp/ *n.* a long hose for domestic use, e.g. in watering gardens or washing cars

hoser /hṓzər/ *n. Can* an offensive term for a person who is considered to be unintelligent and vulgar, especially a man whose main interests are ice hockey and drinking beer (*insult offensive slang*)

hosier /hṓzi ər/ *n.* sb who makes or sells hosiery (*archaic*)

hosiery /hṓzi əri/ *n.* socks, stockings, and tights, considered collectively

hosp. *abbr.* hospital

hospice /hóspiss/ *n.* **1.** MED, SOC WELFARE NURSING HOME FOR THE DYING a usually small residential institution for terminally ill patients where treatment focuses on the patient's wellbeing rather than a cure and includes drugs for pain management, sometimes periods at home, and often spiritual counselling **2.** HIST REFUGE FOR TRAVELLERS AND DESTITUTE in former times, a place where pilgrims, travellers, and the homeless or destitute were offered lodging, usually by a religious order [Early 19thC. Via French from Latin *hospitium* 'guesthouse, hospitality', from the stem *hospit-* of *hospes* 'host, guest' (source of English *host*[1]).]

hospitable /ho spíttəb'l, hóspitəb'l/ *adj.* **1.** TREATING VISITORS WELL friendly, welcoming, and generous to guests or strangers ○ *That's very hospitable of you.* **2.** AGREEABLE pleasant, agreeable, and providing what sb needs to live comfortably ○ *a hospitable climate* [Late 16thC. From French, from obsolete *hospiter* 'to receive a guest', from, ultimately, the Latin stem *hospit-* of *hospes* (see HOST[1]).] —**hospitableness** *n.* —**hospitably** *adv.*

hospital /hóspit'l/ *n.* **1.** MED BUILDING FOR MEDICAL CARE an institution where people receive medical, surgical, or psychiatric treatment and nursing care **2.** PLACE OF REPAIR a place where sth is mended **3.** SOC WELFARE CHARITABLE HOME OR SCHOOL a charitable institution providing shelter, care, or education for orphaned children, senior citizens, or the homeless or destitute (*archaic*) [13thC. Via Old French, 'hostel', from medieval Latin *hospitale* 'guesthouse, inn', from the Latin stem *hospit-* of *hospes* (see HOST[1]).]

Hospital /hóspit'l/, **Janette Turner** (*b.* 1942) Australian novelist, who was the author of *The Last Magician* (1992).

hospital-acquired infection *n.* a disease caught while being treated in hospital for sth else ○ *'Each year, nearly 90,000 patients in the United States die of a hospital-acquired infection...'* (*New York Times Magazine*; February 1998)

hospital corner *n.* either of the corners at the foot of a bed in which the bedclothes are tucked under the mattress in neat triangular folds [*Hospital* from its use in hospitals]

Hospitaler *n.* US = **Hospitaller**

hospitality /hóspi tálləti/ *n.* a friendly welcome and kind or generous treatment offered to guests or strangers

hospitality suite *n.* a room or suite of rooms where invited guests or clients of a company, delegates to a conference, or other official visitors are welcomed and provided with free refreshments

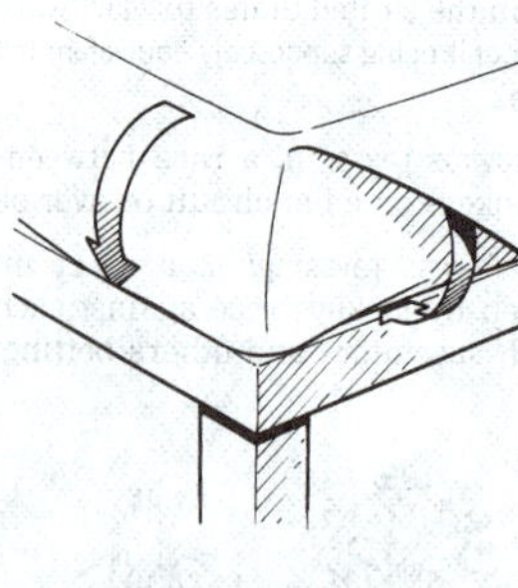

Hospital corner

hospitalize /hóspita līz/ (**-izes, -izing, -ized**), **hospitalise** (**-ises, -ising, -ised**) *vt.* to admit sb to hospital for treatment, diagnosis, or observation, usually as an inpatient —**hospitalization** /hóspita lī záysh'n/ *n.*

Hospitaller *n.* **1.** RELIG, HIST MEMBER OF A CRUSADING ORDER a member of a military religious order, the Knights of the Hospital of St John, founded in the late 11th century by European crusaders to care for sick pilgrims in Jerusalem **2. hospitaller, Hospitaller** RELIGIOUS OR CHARITABLE CARER a member of a religious order or charitable institution involved in the care of the sick, especially in hospital [14thC. Via Old French *hospitalier* from medieval Latin *hospitalarius*, from *hospitale* 'guesthouse, inn' (see HOSPITAL).]

hospodar /hóspə daar/ *n.* a prince or governor of Moldavia or Wallachia during the time of Ottoman rule [Late 16thC. Via Romanian from Ukrainian.]

host[1] /hōst/ *n.* **1.** SB ENTERTAINING GUESTS sb who invites, welcomes, and entertains guests, often providing them with food and drink **2.** BROADCAST SB INTRODUCING GUESTS ON A SHOW sb who presents a television or radio programme in which invited guests take part, e.g. a chat show or game show **3.** PLACE WHERE AN EVENT IS HELD a place or organization that provides the space and facilities for a special event, e.g. an international sporting competition **4.** BIOL ORGANISM INFECTED BY A PARASITE a human, animal, plant, or other organism in or on which another organism, especially a parasite, lives **5.** MED GRAFT OR TRANSPLANT RECIPIENT the recipient of a transplanted or grafted embryo, tissue, or organ **6.** LANDLORD OF AN INN sb who owns or runs a pub or hotel (*dated*) **7. host, host computer** COMPUT MAIN COMPUTER IN A NETWORK in a computer network, the main computer that controls certain functions or files **8.** *US* RESTAURANT GREETER sb employed in a restaurant to greet and seat customers ■ *vt.* (**hosts, hosting, hosted**) **1.** ACCOMMODATE AN EVENT to provide the space and facilities for a special event, e.g. an international sporting competition **2.** BROADCAST INTRODUCE GUESTS ON A SHOW to act as the host of a television or radio programme **3.** ENTERTAIN GUESTS to be the host of a social or official gathering **4.** COMPUT CREATE A WEBSITE FOR SB to provide the service of creating a website on the Internet for sb [13thC. Via Old French *(h)oste* 'host, guest' from the Latin stem *hospit-* of *hospes* (source of English *hospital* and *hotel*), of uncertain origin: probably from *hostis* 'stranger, enemy'.]

host[2] /hōst/ *n.* **1.** LARGE GROUP a very large number of people or things **2.** MIL ARMY an army (*archaic*) [14thC. Via Old French from Latin *hostis* 'stranger, enemy' (in medieval Latin, 'army') (source of English *hostile*).]

Host, host *n.* the bread or wafer consecrated and eaten during the Christian ceremony of Communion [14thC. Via Old French *(h)oiste* from Latin *hostia* 'sacrificial animal, victim'.]

hosta /hóstə/ *n.* a perennial shade-loving plant with broad ribbed leaves and clusters of tubular white, blue, or lilac flowers. Genus: *Hosta.* US term **plantain lily** [Early 19thC. From modern Latin (genus name), named after Nicolaus T. *Host* (1761–1834), an Austrian botanist.]

hostage /hóstij/ *n.* **1.** CAPTIVE HELD FOR RANSOM sb held prisoner by a person or group, e.g. a criminal or a terrorist organization, until certain demands are met or money is handed over **2.** SB MANIPULATED BY ANOTHER a person or group of people whose freedom of action is restricted or controlled by a more powerful organization by implied threats or other means **3.** SECURITY OR PLEDGE a person or thing given or held as security (*archaic*) [13thC. From Old French *(h)ostage*, from late Latin *obsidiatus* 'hostageship', literally 'sitting in the way of', from, ultimately, *sedere* 'to sit'.] ◇ **a hostage to fortune** a remark or action that could potentially lead to trouble or difficulty and so is better avoided

host computer *n.* = **host**[1] *n.* 7

hostel /hóst'l/ *n.* **1.** = **youth hostel 2.** SUPERVISED LODGING FOR WORKERS OR EX-OFFENDERS a place where supervised lodging is provided to workers, juvenile offenders, or ex-offenders **3.** ACCOMMODATION FOR HOMELESS accommodation for people who are homeless **4.** CHEAP INN an inexpensive inn or place of lodging [13thC. From Old French *(h)ostel*, from medieval Latin *hospitale* 'guesthouse, inn' (see HOSPITAL).]

hosteler *n.* US = **hosteller**

hosteling *n.* US = **hostelling**

hosteller /hóst'lər/ *n.* **1.** HOSTEL LODGER sb who stays at hostels while travelling, especially a young person who stays at youth hostels **2.** LANDLORD OF INN sb who owns or runs an inn or a cheap hotel (*archaic*)

hostelling /hóst'ling/ *n.* staying at hostels, especially youth hostels, while travelling around for pleasure

hostelry /hóst'lri/ (*plural* **-ries**) *n.* a hotel, pub, or inn (*archaic or humorous*)

hostess /hṓstiss, hō stéss/ *n.* **1.** WOMAN ENTERTAINING GUESTS a woman who invites, welcomes, and entertains guests, often providing them with food and drink **2.** BROADCAST WOMAN INTRODUCING GUESTS ON SHOW a woman who presents a television or radio programme in which invited guests take part, e.g. a chat show or game show **3.** PAID DANCE PARTNER a woman who is paid to be a man's dancing partner at a nightclub or dance hall **4.** *US* WOMAN GREETER IN A RESTAURANT a woman who is employed in a restaurant to greet and seat customers **5.** *US* TRANSP WOMAN ATTENDANT FOR PASSENGERS a woman who is employed to provide for the safety and comfort of passengers on an aircraft, ship, train, or bus ■ *vti.* (**-esses, -essing, -essed**) ACT AS HOSTESS to act as the hostess to an event, or perform the duties of a hostess [12thC. From Old French *(h)ostesse*, from *(h)oste* 'host' (see HOST[1]).]

hostile /hós tīl/ *adj.* **1.** VERY UNFRIENDLY showing or feeling hatred, enmity, antagonism, or anger towards sb **2.** AGAINST strongly opposed to sb or sth ○ *hostile to the idea* **3.** MIL RELATING TO AN ENEMY relating to, characteristic of, or belonging to an enemy, especially in warfare ○ *hostile fire* **4.** ADVERSE not favourable to life, health, development, or success ○ *a hostile environment* **5.** COMM AGAINST A MANAGEMENT'S WILL opposed by the owner or management of a corporation ○ *a hostile takeover* ■ *n.* **1.** MIL ENEMY an enemy in warfare **2.** HOSTILE PERSON sb who is antagonistic or opposed to sb or sth [Late 16thC. Directly or via French from Latin *hostilis*, from *hostis* 'enemy, stranger' (source of English *host*[2]).] —**hostilely** *adv.*

hostile witness *n.* LAW a witness called by an opposing party who gives evidence against that party

hostility /ho stílləti/ *n.* (*plural* **-ties**) **1.** INTENSE AGGRESSION OR ANGER a feeling or attitude of hatred, enmity, antagonism, or anger towards sb **2.** STRONG OPPOSITION strong opposition to sb or sth **3.** HOSTILE ACT an aggressive act against sb ■ **hostilities** *npl.* MIL ATTACKS open acts of warfare

hostler /ósslər/, **ostler** *n.* = **ostler**

hot /hot/ *adj.* (**hotter, hottest**) **1.** VERY WARM at a high, relatively high, or very high temperature ○ *the hottest day of the year* **2.** TOO WARM FOR COMFORT feeling warmer than normal or desirable **3.** FOOD VERY SPICY OR PEPPERY spicy or peppery enough to cause a burning sensation in the mouth or throat **4.** CAUSING CONTROVERSY causing much discussion, disagreement, or controversy ○ *a hot topic* **5.** UNPLEASANT OR DANGEROUS unpleasant or uncomfortable because of antagonism, trouble, or danger (*informal*) ○ *It got too hot for him to handle.* **6.** QUICKLY ANGERED easily provoked or aroused ○ *a hot temper* **7.** INTENSE OR VIOLENT felt, done, or expressed with forceful, intense energy ○ *hot competition* **8.** COLOURS INTENSE very bright and vivid ○ *hot pink* **9.** CLOSE following sb or sth very closely ○ *hot on the trail* **10.** REQUIRING ATTENTION requiring immediate attention and offering potential success or good fortune ○ *a hot tip* **11.** CURRENT OR TOPICAL very recent or new and therefore of interest or importance ○ *hot off the press* **12. EXCITING** new, fresh, and exciting (*informal*) ○ *a hot new talent* **13. SUCCESSFUL** very popular or successful (*informal*) ○ *one of the hottest items in the range* **14. KNOWLEDGEABLE** having or showing great skill or knowledge (*informal*) ○ *not very hot at maths* **15. US LUCKY** very lucky, e.g. in gambling (*informal*) **16. WISE** very good, wise, or sensible (*informal*) ○ *That idea's not so hot.* **17. WELL** well or good (*informal*) ○ *I don't feel too hot.* **18. NEAR THE ANSWER OR A MISSING OBJECT** very close to sth to be found or discovered in a hunting or guessing game (*informal*) ○ *You're getting hotter.* **19. KEEN** enthusiastically eager (*informal*) ○ *She's really hot on jazz.* **20. STRICT** very strict about sth (*informal*) ○ *He's hot on getting the paperwork right.* **21. PHYSICALLY ATTRACTED** physically attracted or aroused (*slang*) ○ *She's hot on him.* **22. PHYSICALLY ATTRACTIVE** physically attractive or exciting (*slang*) **23. STOLEN** obtained illegally, especially by stealing (*slang*) ○ *hot jewels* **24. ON THE RUN** wanted by the police (*slang*) ○ *a hot suspect* **25. US EAGER** full of activity, energy, enthusiasm, or excitement **26. MUSIC INVENTIVE AND EXCITING** with strong rhythms or exciting improvisation (*informal*) **27. CARS POWERFUL** very fast and powerful (*slang*) **28. ELEC LIVE** electrically charged ○ *a hot wire* **29. NUCLEAR PHYS RADIOACTIVE** dangerously radioactive **30. BIOL INFECTIOUS OR LETHAL** extremely infectious or lethal, or containing infectious viruses **31. US ANGRY** angry or agitated about sth (*informal*) **32. PHYS IN AN ELEVATED ENERGY STATE** in an elevated energy state, usually caused by nuclear processes ○ *a hot atom* **33. US ABSURD** funny, absurd, or unbelievable (*slang*) ■ **hots** *npl.* **DESIRE** strong physical desire (*informal*) ■ *adv.* **INTENSELY** in an eager, intense, or angry way ○ *They argued hot and long.* [Old English *hāt*, from a prehistoric Germanic word that is also the ancestor of English *heat*] —**hotness** *n.* ◇ **blow** *or* **run hot and cold** to keep changing your mind, e.g. by being enthusiastic about sth then unenthusiastic (*slang*) ◇ **hot to trot** eager and willing (*slang*)

hot up *vti.* **1. INTENSIFY** to make sth more intense, active, or exciting, or increase in intensity, activity, or excitement (*informal*) **2. INCREASE POWER** to make sth faster or more powerful, or increase in speed or energy

hot air *n.* impressive or boastful talk about achievements or intentions that has no substance (*informal*)

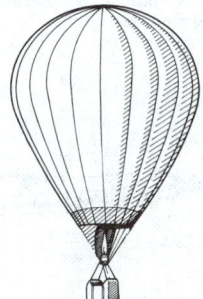

Hot-air balloon

hot-air balloon *n.* a lighter-than-air craft in which a compartment for pilot and passengers is suspended from a large nylon balloon that holds heated air or helium

hotbed /hót bed/ *n.* **1. CENTRE OF ACTIVITY** an environment where sth flourishes or happens frequently, especially sth undesirable **2. GARDENING HEATED GLASS-COVERED SOIL BED** a planting bed covered with glass and heated with electricity or by the action of fermenting manure to aid in quick germination of seeds and growth of plants

hot-blooded *adj.* easily angered, excited, or physically aroused —**hot-bloodedness** *n.*

hot button ◇ **press sb's hot button** to provoke a strong immediate reaction, usually a predictable one

hotch /hoch/ (**hotches, hotching, hotched**) *vi.* Scotland to be surrounded by or full of a swarm of sth [14thC. Origin uncertain: perhaps from Old French *hoch(i)er* 'to shake' (source of English *hotchpot*), from prehistoric Germanic.]

hotchpot /hóch pot/ *n.* in law, the gathering together of property belonging to different people in order to divide it equally [14thC. Ultimately from Old French *hochepot* 'hotchpotch', from *hocher* 'to shake' (see HOTCH) + *pot* 'pot' (from assumed Vulgar Latin *pottus*, source of English *pot*).]

hotchpotch /hóch poch/ *n.* **1. JUMBLE** a mixture of several unrelated things **2. STEW** a stew consisting of a varied mixture of ingredients, usually mutton and vegetables [Late 16thC. Rhyming alteration of HOTCH-POT.]

hot comb *n.* a comb that can be heated, usually electrically, and used to style or straighten the hair

hot-comb *vt.* to style or straighten the hair using a hot comb

hot cross bun *n.* a sweet bun containing yeast, spices, and dried fruit and marked with a cross on the top, traditionally eaten hot on Good Friday

hot dog *n.* **SAUSAGE IN BREAD ROLL** a type of long sausage typically served hot on a bread roll with toppings such as fried onions, mustard, or ketchup ■ *interj. US* **EXPRESSION OF ENTHUSIASTIC PLEASURE** used to express strong approval, delight, or surprise (*informal*)

hot-dog (**hot-dogs, hot-dogging, hot-dogged**) *vi. US* to perform difficult, dangerous, or acrobatic stunts in a showy or impressive manner in skiing, surfing, and similar sports (*slang*) —**hot-dogger** *n.* —**hot-dogging** *n.*

hotel /hō tél/ *n.* **1. PLACE FOR AN OVERNIGHT STAY** a building or commercial establishment where people pay for lodgings, meals, and sometimes other facilities or services **2. Aus PUB** an establishment that sells alcoholic beverages **3. S Asia RESTAURANT** a restaurant **4. COMMUNICATION CODE WORD FOR LETTER 'H'** the NATO phonetic alphabet code word for the letter 'H', used in international radio communications [Mid-17thC. Via French *hôtel* from Old French *hostel* 'lodging, hostel', from medieval Latin *hospitale* (see HOSPITAL).]

hotelier /hō télli ay, -télli ər/ *n.* sb who owns or runs a hotel [Early 20thC. Via French *hôtelier* from Old French *hostelier* 'hosteler', from, ultimately, medieval Latin *hospitale* (see HOSPITAL).]

hotelling *n.* **BUSINESS** the practice of providing temporary desk space for an employee [From the idea that a hotel is a temporary place to stay]

hot fence *n. NZ* an electric fence round a farm

hot flash *n. US* = **hot flush**

hot flush *n.* a sudden hot feeling, sometimes accompanied by sweating and redness of the face, experienced by some women during the menopause and caused by an endocrine imbalance. US term **hot flash**

hotfoot /hót foot, hót foot/ *adv.* with great haste ◇ **hotfoot it** to go with great haste and eagerness, usually on foot (*informal*)

hot-gospeller *n.* sb who preaches religion or spreads propaganda in a very forceful or enthusiastic manner (*informal; offensive in some contexts*)

hothead /hót hed/ *n.* sb who acts hastily without thinking or who is too easily angered or excited

hotheaded /hót héddid/ *adj.* too easily angered or excited and usually acting impetuously —**hot-headedly** *adv.* —**hotheadedness** *n.*

hothouse /hót howss/ *n.* (*plural* **-houses** /-howziz/) **1. GARDENING HEATED GREENHOUSE** a heated building, usually with glass walls and roof, in which tropical or delicate plants can grow at a stable warm temperature **2. CENTRE OF ACTIVITY** a place where a particular thing flourishes and develops, usually in an intensive way ○ *a hothouse of technological innovation* ■ *adj.* **SENSITIVE** sensitive and delicate (*informal*) ○ *hothouse views on political strategy*

hothousing /hót howzing/ *n.* a programme of providing children with intensive education

hot key *n.* a key or combination of keys on a computer keyboard that provide a short cut for performing a particular function

hotline /hót līn/ *n.* **1. DIRECT TELEPHONE LINK TO A SERVICE** a telephone number that enables members of the public to make direct contact with a special service offering information, advice, or help, usually on a

serious or urgent matter **2. COMMUNICATIONS LINK BETWEEN LEADERS** a telephone connection or similar link that allows direct communication between heads of government or other important people, especially in an emergency

hotly /hótli/ *adv.* **1. ANGRILY** in an angry way **2. FIERCELY** in an intense and committed way ○ *hotly contested*

hot-melt *n.* a fast-drying adhesive applied in a molten state

hot metal *n.* **1. METAL PRINTING TYPE** printing type cast from molten metal in a crucible beside the printing machine **2. METHOD OF PRINTING** printing using hot metal type

hot money *n.* funds transferred from one form of currency to another in order to take advantage of better exchange rates

hot pants *npl.* **1. CLOTHES TIGHT SHORTS** very brief close-fitting shorts for women, first fashionable in the early 1970s **2. PHYSICAL DESIRE** very strong physical desire (*slang*)

hot plate *n.* **1. HEATED COOKING SURFACE** a flat heated surface, usually part of a cooker, on which food can be cooked **2. DEVICE FOR KEEPING FOOD WARM** a portable device with a flat heated surface on which food can be heated or kept warm

hotpot /hót pot/ *n.* a stew of meat and vegetables, e.g. lamb, onion, and potatoes, cooked slowly in the oven in a covered container

hot pot *n.* a small heated pot of boiling water or broth used to cook pieces of food at the table, especially in Asian cookery

hot potato *n.* a sensitive or controversial issue that is awkward or difficult to deal with

hot press *n.* a machine used to apply heat and pressure to a material such as paper or cloth —**hot-press** *vt.*

hot rod *n.* a car that has been modified to make it go very fast (*slang*)

hot-rod (**hot-rods, hot-rodding, hot-rodded**) *v.* (*slang*) **1.** *vt.* **INCREASE A CAR'S POWER** to modify a car or its engine to make it very fast or powerful **2.** *vi.* **DRIVE** to drive a hot rod

hot-rodder *n.* sb who drives a hot rod (*slang*)

hot seat ◇ **in the hot seat** facing or liable to face criticism or difficult questioning ○ *in the hot seat after the latest round of allegations*

hot shoe *n.* a camera accessory used to connect the camera and an electric flash

hotshot /hót shot/ *n.* a successful, important, or highly skilled person, especially one who is showily confident (*informal*)

hot spot *n.* **1. MIL PLACE OF POTENTIAL UNREST** an area where fighting or trouble is likely to break out **2. LEISURE CENTRE OF ENTERTAINMENT** a place that is a centre of entertainment and social activity, e.g. a lively nightclub (*informal*) **3. ENG SMALL AREA OF INTENSE HEAT** a small area of sth, e.g. an engine, that is at a much higher temperature than the rest **4. GEOG AREA OF GEOTHERMAL ACTIVITY** a part of the Earth's surface subject to greater than usual geothermal activity

hot spring *n.* a spring of water heated by geothermal energy. ◊ **geyser**

hotspur /hót spur/ *n.* a rash or impetuous person [From *Hotspur*, the nickname of Henry Percy (1364–1403), English rebel]

hot stuff *n.* **1. VERY GOOD PERSON OR THING** sb who or sth that is particularly impressive, attractive, exciting, or important (*informal*) **2. ATTRACTIVE PERSON** a physically attractive person (*informal*) **3. SEXUALLY EXPLICIT THING** sth, e.g. a book or photograph, that is particularly erotic or pornographic

Hottentot /hótt'n tot/ (*plural* **-tot** *or* **-tots**) *n.* (*dated offensive*) **1. PEOPLES KHOIKHOI** a former name of the Khoikhoi people **2. LANG KHOIKHOI LANGUAGE** the language of the Khoikhoi people [Late 17thC. Ultimately from Dutch, of uncertain origin: probably originally a formula in a Nama song used by Dutch sailors to refer to the people themselves.]

Hottentot fig *n.* a low-growing succulent plant that has purplish or yellowish flowers resembling daisies, and edible fruit. It is native to South Africa, but is now grown in many frost-free places. Latin name: *Carpobrotus edulis*.

hot ticket *n.* sb who or sth that is very popular at a particular time

hotting /hótting/ *n.* performing difficult or dangerous high-speed stunts and manoeuvres in a stolen car (*slang*)

hottish /hóttish/ *adj.* fairly but not excessively hot

hot toddy *n.* = **toddy**

hot tub *n.* a large round bathtub filled with hot water for one or more people to relax, bathe, or socialize in

hot war *n.* armed conflict between groups or nations, as opposed to political hostility. ◊ **cold war**

hot water *n.* a situation of trouble or difficulty, usually resulting from doing sth wrong (*informal*)

hot-water bottle *n.* a container, usually made of rubber, filled with hot water and used to warm a bed or part of the body

hot-wire (**hot-wires**, **hot-wiring**, **hot-wired**) *vt.* to start a car by bringing the ignition wires into contact (*informal*)

Houdan /hoo dan/ *n.* a breed of domestic fowl that has black and white plumage and a characteristic full crest [Late 19thC. Named after *Houdan*, village in the French department of Seine-et-Oise, where the breed originated.]

hough /hok/ *n.* **1.** ZOOL = **hock**¹ **1 2.** *Scotland* FOOD **CUT OF BEEF** a cut of beef from the leg, used in stewing ■ *vt.* **HAMSTRING** to hamstring an animal [Old English *hōh* 'heel', from prehistoric Germanic]

hou high /hō-/ *n. Hong Kong* a state of intoxication or excitement, e.g. from a drug (*slang*)

hou inch *n. Hong Kong* sb who is aloof or arrogant (*slang insult*)

hoummos /hóommooss/ *n.* = **hummus**

hound /hownd/ *n.* **1.** ZOOL **DOG BRED FOR HUNTING** a dog originally bred for hunting, with floppy ears, short hair, and a deep bark (*often used in combination*) **2.** ZOOL **DOG** any domestic dog, especially one viewed with disapproval (*informal*) **3.** **UNPLEASANT PERSON** a contemptible or despicable person (*dated*) **4.** **EN-THUSIAST** sb who pursues, seeks, or collects sth with great enthusiasm or determination (*informal*) ■ *vt.* (**hounds**, **hounding**, **hounded**) **1.** **PURSUE DOGGEDLY** to follow, chase, or pester sb in a persistent or re-lentless manner **2.** **URGE OR NAG SB** to urge or force sb to do sth by nagging or harassment ○ *he was hounded out of office by a hostile press* [Old English *hund* 'dog'. Ultimately from an Indo-European base.] — **hounder** *n.*

WORD KEY: ORIGIN

The Indo-European word that is the ancestor of **hound** is also the ultimate source of English *canary, canine, chenille, corgi, cynic, dachshund,* and *kennel.*

houndfish /hównd fish/ (*plural* -**fish** *or* -**fishes**) *n.* a small shark or dogfish

hounds /howndz/ *npl.* the part of a ship's masthead that supports the topmast and the rigging [15thC. By folk etymology from *hune* 'wooden projection below a masthead', of uncertain origin: probably from Old Norse *húnn* 'knob at the top of a masthead'.]

hound's-tongue *n.* a coarse plant of the borage family, native to Europe and Asia, that has small reddish-purple flowers and spiny clinging fruit. Latin name: *Cynoglossum.* [Translation of Latin *cyno-glossus* 'dog-tongued', from the shape and texture of its leaves, likened to the tongue of a dog]

houndstooth check /hówndz tooth-/, **hound's-tooth check** *n.* a fabric design of small jagged checks

hour /owr/ *n.* **1.** 60 MINUTES 3,600 seconds, or one of 24 equal parts of a day **2.** 60-MINUTE INTERVAL SHOWN ON A TIMEPIECE one of the intervals of 60 minutes shown on a clock or watch ○ *There's a bus at 20 past the hour.* **3.** TIME OF DAY time of day, with emphasis on the general portion of day or night being referred to ○ *at this unearthly hour* **4.** REGULAR TIME FOR STH a time at which sth usually takes place or is done ○ *my lunch hour* **5.** SIGNIFICANT PERIOD a period during which

sth particularly significant happens ○ *Enjoy your hour of glory while it lasts.* **6.** TIME OF SUCCESS a time when sb is powerful, successful, or famous ○ *This is your hour, so seize the opportunity!* **7.** TIME OF DEATH the time when sb is going to die ○ *As he started falling, he thought his hour had surely come.* **8.** MEASURE, NAVIG MEASURE OF LONGITUDE a measure of longitude equal to 15 degrees or one twenty-fourth of a great circle [12thC. Via Old French *houre* from Latin *hora*, from Greek *hōra* 'time period, season'. Ultimately from an Indo-European word meaning 'season', which is also the ancestor of English *year*.] ◇ **at any hour** at any time, day or night ◇ **of the hour** enjoying the highest degree of relevance, importance, or popularity at the current moment or particular time ○ *She is clearly the woman of the hour.*

hour angle *n.* ASTRON the angle, measured positively westwards, between the plane containing the observer and the Earth's poles and the plane containing a particular celestial body and the Earth's poles

hour circle *n.* ASTRON a great circle passing through the poles of the celestial sphere and intersecting the celestial equator at right angles, containing a point on the celestial sphere such as a star

Hourglass

hourglass /ówr glaass/ *n.* a time-measurement device consisting of two transparent bulbs connected by a narrow tube and containing an amount of sand that takes a specified time to flow between the bulbs after inversion

hourglass figure *n.* a woman's body shape, curving out above and below a narrow waist like the shape of an hourglass

hour hand *n.* the shorter, wider hand of a nondigital clock or watch, which indicates the hour

houri /hóori/ *n.* **1.** ISLAM YOUNG WOMAN IN PARADISE in Islamic belief, one of the beautiful young women who attend Muslim men in paradise **2.** LOVELY WOMAN an attractive woman (*dated; sometimes considered offensive*) [Mid-18thC. Via French from, ultimately, Arabic *ḥawrā'* 'woman with dark eyes'.]

hourly /ówrli/ *adj.* **1.** EACH HOUR happening at sixty-minute intervals ○ *hourly news* **2.** OCCURRING A LOT happening frequently or continually ○ *hourly changes* **3.** CALCULATED BY THE HOUR calculated as a par-ticular amount for each hour worked ○ *hourly wages* **4.** PAID BY THE HOUR working for pay that is calculated as a particular amount for each hour worked ■ *adv.* **1.** SOON at any time shortly from now ○ *Her arrival is expected hourly.* **2.** OFTEN frequently or continually ○ *The situation is changing hourly.* **3.** BY THE HOUR with a particular amount being paid for each hour worked

hours /owrz/ *npl.* **1.** LONG TIME a long but unspecified amount of time (*informal*) **2.** TIMES FOR DOING PARTICULAR THINGS the times of day during which particular things are done ○ *during school hours* **3.** TIME IN A 24-HOUR CLOCK the time of day, when using a 24-hour clock ○ *The flight leaves at 1300 hours.* **4.** CANONICAL HOURS the canonical hours taken as a whole

Housatonic /hoossə tónnik/ river in northwestern Massachusetts and Connecticut, rising in the Berk-shire Hills. Length: 240 km/150 mi.

house /howss/ *n.* **1.** DWELLING a building made for people to live in, especially one built for a single group of occupants **2.** OCCUPANTS OF A HOUSE all of the people who are in a house at one time, particularly the people

who usually live there **3.** COMMUNITY DWELLING a build-ing in which a community of people lives **4.** BUILDING FOR ANIMALS a building where animals are kept, es-pecially in a zoo ○ *the monkey house* **5.** PLACE WHERE PEOPLE PAY TO EAT a place where members of the public pay for food, drink, or entertainment, e.g. a res-taurant or club ○ *the speciality of the house* **6.** THEATRE THEATRE a theatre, or the audience at a theatre ○ *The dancers performed to an appreciative house.* **7.** BUSI-NESS BUSINESS OPERATION a company or a corporation creating or selling a particular product ○ *a pub-lishing house* **8.** EDUC DIVISION OF SCHOOL any of the groups into which the pupils of some schools are divided. In residential schools this is based on the actual boarding houses where the pupils live. **9.** **house, House** POL LEGISLATIVE GROUP a legislative group in a government or the place where it meets **10.** FAMILY LINE a family line, including ancestors and descendants, especially a royal family ○ *the House of Windsor* **11.** ZODIAC DIVISION OF THE ZODIAC one of the 12 divisions of the zodiac in astrology **12.** ZODIAC ZODIAC SIGN WHERE A PLANET LIES the sign of the zodiac in which a planet is found at a specific time **13.** SPORTS CURLING TARGET an area of concentric circles at either end of an ice rink marked out for curling, with the target in its centre ■ *interj.* USED TO CLAIM WIN AT BINGO shouted by people playing bingo to claim that they have the full set of numbers needed to win a game (*informal*) ■ *vt.* (**houses**, **housing**, **housed**) **1.** GIVE SOME-WHERE TO LIVE to provide sb with a place to live **2.** CONTAIN to contain, keep, or store sth **3.** NAUT PUT AWAY SAFELY to put sth away safely, e.g. oars or an anchor [Old English *hūs*, of prehistoric Germanic origin] ◇ **on the house** given free by sb who would normally be paid ◇ **bring the house down** to provoke a great deal of laughter or applause ◇ **like a house on fire** very well, successfully, quickly, or strongly ○ *They got on like a house on fire.* ◇ **play house** *US* to take part in a children's game of pretending to be a family, with children playing the roles of both adults and children (*informal*) ◇ **put your house in order** to organize your life properly

WORD KEY: USAGE

See Usage note at **home.**

house agent *n.* = **estate agent**

house arrest *n.* a form of legal confinement in which people who have been arrested are not allowed to leave their own homes

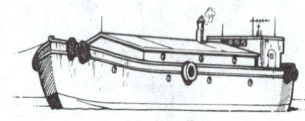

Houseboat

houseboat /hówss bōt/ *n.* a boat, especially a flat-bottomed river boat or barge, that is permanently moored and used as a house

housebound /hówss bownd/ *adj.* unable to go out of doors because of illness or difficulty in travelling, or because of severe weather

houseboy /hówss boy/ *n.* a term, often considered offensive, referring to a man, especially in Africa or the Indian subcontinent, employed to perform various household tasks

housebreak /hówss brayk/ *vt.* (-**breaks**, -**breaking**, -**broke** /-brōk/, -**broken** /-brōkən/) *US* = **housetrain** ■ *n. US* = **break-in**

house call *n. US* a visit made by a doctor or other professional to a patient or client at home

housecarl /hówss kaarl/ *n.* any one of the household warriors of an early English or Danish nobleman or king [Old English *hūscarl*, from Old Norse *húskarl*, from *hús* 'house' + *karl* 'man']

housecoat /hówss kōt/ *n.* a woman's outer garment, often loose and comfortable, worn at home

housefather /hówss faathər/ *n.* a man who is responsible for a group of young people living in an institution such as a hostel

housefly /hówss flī/ (*plural* **-flies**) *n.* a common fly that lives in and around human dwellings in most parts of the world and is responsible for spreading numerous diseases. Latin name: *Musca domestica*.

house guest *n.* sb who stays in sb else's home as a guest

household /hówss hōld/ *n.* **PEOPLE WHO LIVE TOGETHER** the people who live together in a single home ■ *adj.* **1. BELONGING TO A HOUSEHOLD** relating to, belonging to, or used in a household **2. FAMILIAR TO ALL** very widely known ○ *Thanks to the media, their personal problems are household knowledge.*

Household Cavalry *n.* the cavalry regiments, the Horse Guards and the Life Brigade, responsible for guarding the UK sovereign, especially during public ceremonies

householder /hówss hōldər/ *n.* sb who owns or rents a house, either alone or as the head of a family

household gods *npl.* the deities believed to protect the home and its inhabitants, especially in the religion of ancient Rome. ♦ **lares and penates**

household name *n.* sb or sth that most people know about

household troops *npl.* soldiers who accompany and guard a sovereign

household word *n.* a popular saying, the name of a famous person, or an event that is very well known

househusband /hówss huzbənd/ *n.* a man who does not go out to work but stays at home to manage a household [Mid-20thC. Modelled on HOUSEWIFE.]

housekeeper /hówss keepər/ *n.* **1. SB LOOKING AFTER HOUSE** sb who carries out the work of looking after a house and the people who live there **2. SB LOOKING AFTER SB ELSE'S HOUSE** sb employed to carry out or manage the work of looking after sb else's house and the people who live there

housekeeping /hówss keeping/ *n.* **1. HOUSEHOLD MAINTENANCE** the maintenance of a household, or the range of tasks involved in this **2. MONEY FOR RUNNING HOUSEHOLD** money used to pay for the things needed in maintaining a household ○ *Perhaps we could save a little extra from the housekeeping.* **3.** *US* **MANAGEMENT OF PROPERTY AND EQUIPMENT** the management and upkeep of equipment and property for a business or other organization **4.** COMPUT **MAINTENANCE OF COMPUTER SYSTEM** the performance of routine tasks needed to keep a computer system working efficiently, e.g. deletion of unwanted files

House Leader *n. Can* a member of the Canadian government who initiates and supervises business in the legislature

houseleek /hówss leek/ *n.* any one of various European flowering succulent plants that have rosettes of leaves at the base of the stems. Genus: *Sempervivum*. [So called because it was formerly planted on walls and roofs, in the belief that it protected the house from lightning]

house lights *npl.* the lights inside a theatre or auditorium that illuminate the area where the audience sits

housemaid /hówss mayd/ *n.* a woman employed to do housework (*dated*)

housemaid's knee *n.* a swelling of the fluid-filled sac in front of the kneecap, caused by kneeling too much

houseman /hówssmən/ (*plural* **-men** /-mən/) *n.* a hospital intern (*dated*)

house martin *n.* a small swallow, native to Europe, China, and Africa that has blue-black feathers, a white rump, and a forked tail. Latin name: *Delichon urbica*. [From its habit of nesting under the eaves of houses]

housemaster /hówss maastər/ *n.* a man who is in charge of the students living together in a house at a private boys' school

housemate /hówss mayt/ *n.* sb who shares a house with one or more other people who are not relatives

housemistress /hówss mistrəss/ *n.* a woman who is in charge of the students living together at certain prep schools and colleges

housemother /hówss muthər/ *n.* a woman who is responsible for a group of young people living in an institution such as a boarding house or a private school

house mouse *n.* a grey or brownish-grey mouse that is common worldwide and is a household pest. Latin name: *Mus musculus*.

house music *n.* a style of dance music first developed by adding electronic beats to disco records, and later characterized by the addition of repetitive vocals, extracts from other recordings, or synthesized sounds [Origin uncertain: probably named after the *Warehouse*, a nightclub in Chicago in the United States, where this style of music originated]

House of Assembly *n.* **1. LAW-MAKING BODY IN A COMMONWEALTH COUNTRY** the law-making body or lower house of the legislature in some countries of the Commonwealth of Nations **2. LOWER HOUSE OF STATE PARLIAMENT** the lower house of the state parliament in South Australia and Tasmania

house of cards *n.* sth that is unstable and likely to fall down, like a structure built of playing cards

House of Commons *n.* the lower house of Parliament in the United Kingdom and Canada

house of correction *n.* an institution where people convicted of minor offences were imprisoned in the past

house officer *n. UK* a junior doctor at a hospital. ◊ **intern** *n.* 1

house of God *n.* = **house of worship**

house of ill repute, **house of ill fame** *n.* a brothel (*dated*)

House of Keys *n.* the lower house of the legislature of the Isle of Man

House of Lords *n.* the nonelected upper house of Parliament in the United Kingdom, made up of hereditary peers, life peers, and certain bishops

House of Representatives *n.* **1. LOWER HOUSE OF CONGRESS** the lower house of Congress and of most state legislatures in the United States **2. AUSTRALIAN FEDERAL PARLIAMENT** the lower house of the federal parliament of Australia **3. PARLIAMENT OF NEW ZEALAND** in the past, the lower chamber of the New Zealand Parliament, now its sole chamber

House of the People *n.* = **Lok Sabha**

house of worship, **house of God** *n.* a church, temple, synagogue, or other building used for religious services

house organ *n.* a magazine published by a business or other organization for its employees or customers, containing information about the company, its products, and its employees

housepainter /hówss payntər/ *n. US* sb who paints houses for a living

house party *n.* **1. PARTY AT SB'S HOME** a party at sb's home at which the guests stay overnight or for several days, especially at a wealthy person's country house **2. GUESTS AT A HOUSE PARTY** the group of guests attending a house party

houseplant /hówss plaant/ *n.* a decorative plant grown indoors, especially one that would die if planted outdoors in a cold climate

house-proud *adj.* taking pride in the appearance of your home and its state of cleanliness or repair, sometimes in an excessive or fussy way

house rule *n.* a rule, usually not one of the regular rules in a game, that is observed in a casino or among a group of friends

house-sit *vti.* to live in temporarily and take care of sb else's house and property while that person is away

house sitter *n.* sb who lives in and takes care of a house while its usual occupants are away [Modelled on BABYSITTER]

Houses of Parliament, London, designed by Sir Charles Barry (1840–60)

Houses of Parliament *npl.* **1. PARLIAMENTARY BUILDINGS** the building in which the House of Commons and the House of Lords meet and work **2. COMMONS AND LORDS AS ONE** the House of Commons and the House of Lords considered together ○ *The bill will go before the Houses of Parliament this year.*

house sparrow *n.* a small hardy brown and grey bird with a black throat, originally European and Asian but now common in many areas of the world. Latin name: *Passer domesticus*. [From its habit of living in or near human settlements]

house-to-house *adj.* going or done from one house to the next ○ *a house-to-house search*

housetop /hówss top/ *n.* the very top or roof of a house

housetrain /hówss trayn/ (**-trains**, **-training**, **-trained**) *vt.* to teach a domestic animal to excrete outdoors or in a particular place. US term **housebreak** *v.* — **housetrained** *adj.*

housewarming /hówss wawrming/, **housewarming party** *n.* a party that sb gives to celebrate moving into a new house

housewife /hówss wīf/ (*plural* **-wives** /-wīvz/) *n.* a woman who does not go out to work but stays at home to manage a household

housewifely /hówss wīfli/ *adj.* **1. OF OR FOR A HOUSEWIFE** relating to, belonging to, done by, or thought appropriate for a housewife **2. NEAT AND TIDY** showing the qualities traditionally thought appropriate for a housewife, e.g. tidiness and careful management of money

housework /hówss wurk/ *n.* tasks such as dusting, vacuuming, washing clothes, and cooking that are regularly done in a house

housey-housey /hówssi hówssi/ *n.* the game of bingo (*dated*) [Alteration of HOUSE]

housing[1] /hówzing/ *n.* **1. ACCOMMODATION** houses and other buildings where people live, considered collectively ○ *Decent housing is often hard to find.* **2. PROVISION OF ACCOMMODATION** the provision of places to live ○ *Housing of the homeless is our first priority.* **3. ENG MACHINE'S PROTECTIVE STRUCTURE** a frame or structure that protects part of a machine ○ *a wheel housing* **4. WOODWORK PLACE WHERE A PIECE FITS** a slot, groove, or hole in one piece of wood into which another piece is fitted **5. NICHE FOR A STATUE** a small recess or hollow in which a statue can be placed

housing[2] /hówzing/ *n.* **1. COVERING FOR A HORSE'S BACK** a piece of cloth that covers the back of a horse, used for protection or decoration **2. HORSE TRAPPINGS** the ornamental trappings for a horse (*often used in the plural*) [Mid-17thC. Formed from Old French *houce*, from medieval Latin *hultia* 'protective covering', ultimately of prehistoric Germanic origin.]

housing association *n.* a nonprofit-making organization that provides houses and flats at fair rents

housing estate *n.* a planned area of houses or flats, usually built at the same time to a similar design, sometimes with a number of small shops

housing project *n. US* a group of houses or flats built with public money for low-income families

housing scheme *n. Scotland* a housing estate built by a local authority, originally made up of homes to be rented by council tenants

Housman /hówssmən/, **A. E.** (1859–1936) English poet and scholar. His verse collections include *A Shropshire Lad* (1896) and *Last Poems* (1922). Full name **Alfred Edward Housman**

Houston /hyóóstən/ city in Texas, the fourth largest city in the United States. Population: 1,630,553 (1990).

houting /hówting/ (*plural* **-ings** *or* **-ing**) *n.* an edible European fish of the whitefish family that lives in salt water but produces its young in fresh water. Latin name: *Coregonus oxyrhynchus*. [Late 19thC. Via Dutch from Middle Dutch *houtic*, of uncertain origin.]

Houyhnhnm /hoo inəm/ *n.* a wise being looking like a horse in *Gulliver's Travels* by Jonathan Swift [Early 18thC. Coined as an imitation of the sound of a horse's neigh.]

HOV *abbr.* high-occupancy vehicle

hove past participle of **heave** *v.* **8.** past tense of **heave** *v.* **9** (*literary*)

hovel /hóvv'l/ *n.* a small, dirty, or poorly built house [14thC. Origin uncertain: perhaps from Low German.]

hover /hóvvər/ *vi.* (**-ers, -ering, -ered**) **1.** FLOAT IN THE AIR to float in the air without moving very far from the same spot **2.** BE FLYING IN ONE SPOT to stay in the air in the same position by rapidly beating the wings (*refers to birds*) **3.** WAIT NEAR SB OR STH to wait near a person or place, usually in a nervous, inquisitive, or expectant way **4.** BE UNDECIDED to be unable to decide between alternatives **5.** BE IN AN UNSTABLE CONDITION to be in a condition that is neither one of two alternatives nor the other ○ *He hovered between life and death.* **6.** STAY AROUND THE SAME LEVEL to stay near a particular point, changing only slightly ○ *Inflation has been hovering around the same level for several months.* ■ *n.* ACT OF HOVERING an act or the condition of floating in the air without moving very far from the same spot [14thC. Formed from obsolete *hove* 'to linger', of unknown origin.] —**hoverer** *n.* —**hoveringly** *adv.*

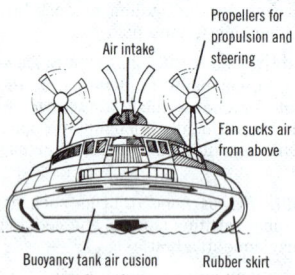

Propellers for propulsion and steering
Air intake
Fan sucks air from above
Buoyancy tank air cusion
Rubber skirt

Hovercraft

hovercraft /hóvvər kraaft/ (*plural* **-crafts** *or* **-craft**) *n.* a vehicle that can travel over land and water supported by a cushion of air that it creates by blowing air downwards

hoverfly /hóvvər flī/ (*plural* **-flies**) *n.* a fly that feeds on nectar and has a hovering style of flight. Many resemble wasps in colouring. Family: Syrphidae.

hover mower *n.* a type of lawn mower with horizontally rotating blades that uses a cushion of downwards-directed air to lift itself slightly above the ground

hoverport /hóvvər pawrt/ *n.* a place where hovercrafts load and unload [Mid-20thC. Coined from HOVERCRAFT + AIRPORT.]

how[1] /how/ *adv.* **1.** IN WHAT WAY used to ask or report questions or to introduce statements about the manner in which sth happens or is done ○ *How do I open the window here?* ○ *I don't know how you manage to sew so neatly.* **2.** TO WHAT EXTENT used to ask or report questions or to introduce statements about the quantity or degree of sth ○ *How high is the roof?* ○ *Tell me honestly how serious the situation is.* **3.** WHAT IS STH LIKE used to ask or report questions or to introduce statements about the quality or success of sth ○ *How was the film?* **4.** USED IN EXCLAMATIONS used in exclamations to emphasize a word or statement ○ *How beautiful she was!* ■ *rel adv.* IN WHATEVER WAY used to indicate that it does not matter in what way sb does sth ○ *Fix it how you want – just as long as it gets fixed.* ■ *conj.* THAT used to mention a fact or event ○ *Do you remember how we were ridiculed and derided?* [Old English *hū.* Ultimately from an Indo-European base that is also the ancestor of English *what, when, where, why,* and *who.*] ◇ **and how** used to show strong agreement with or to emphasize sth that has just been said (*informal*) ◇ **how about 1.** used to make a suggestion (*informal*) ○ *How about some lunch?* **2.** used to change the subject of conversation (*informal*) ○ *That's enough of my ideas. How about your own policies?* ◇ **how are you?, how are you doing?** used to ask about sb's health, or simply as a greeting when you meet sb, especially sb already known ◇ **how come?** used to ask the reason for sth (*informal*) ○ *How come the meeting's been cancelled?* ◇ **how do you do?** used when meeting sb for the first time

how[2] *n.* = **howe**[2]

Howard /hów ərd/, **Catherine, Queen of England** (1520?–42). The fifth wife of Henry VIII (1540–42), she was beheaded when her premarital affairs were revealed.

Howard, Sir Ebenezer (1850–1928) British town planner. He introduced the garden city model of urban development, first applying his principles in Letchworth (1903) and Welwyn Garden City (1919).

Howard, John (1726–90) British penal reformer. He persuaded Parliament to pass two acts of law (1774) designed to improve prison conditions.

Howard, John (*b.* 1939) Australian statesman. Elected to parliament as a Liberal Party politician in 1974, he became prime minister of Australia in 1996. Full name **John Winston Howard**

Howard, Leslie (1893–1943) British actor. He is best known for his roles as Henry Higgins in *Pygmalion* (1938) and Ashley Wilkes in *Gone With the Wind* (1939). Real name **Leslie Howard Steiner**

Howard, Trevor (1916–88) British actor. An accomplished stage and screen performer, his films include *Brief Encounter* (1945) and *Mutiny on the Bounty* (1962). Full name **Trevor Wallace Howard**

howbeit /how beé it/ *adv.* HOWEVER however or nevertheless (*formal*) ■ *conj.* THOUGH although (*archaic*) [14thC. Formed from HOW + BE + IT, meaning literally 'however it may be'.]

Howdah

howdah /hówdə/ *n.* a large seat for several people, often with a canopy, that rests on the back of an elephant [Late 18thC. Via Urdu *haudah* from Arabic *hawdaj* 'litter carried by a camel'.]

how-do-you-do *n.* **1.** GREETING a greeting or welcome ○ *got to business as soon as the how-do-you-dos were finished* **2.** BOTHERSOME SITUATION a difficult or unsatisfactory situation (*informal*) ○ *a fine how-do-you-do* [From the greeting *how do you do?*]

howdy /hówdi/ *interj. US* used as a greeting (*informal*) [Early 19thC. Shortening of *how d'ye,* a variant of *how do you do?*]

howe[1] /how/ *n. Scotland* a hollow or valley (*often used in placenames*) ○ *'We sat down, therefore, in a howe of the hillside'* (Robert Louis Stevenson, *Kidnapped;* 1886). [Pre-12thC. Variant of HOLE.]

howe[2] /how/, **how** *n.* a small prominent hill (*regional*) [14thC. From Old Norse *haugr* 'mound', from a prehistoric Germanic word that is also the ancestor of English *high.*]

Howe /how/, **Sir Geoffrey, Baron of Aberavon** (*b.* 1926) British politician. He served as Chancellor of the Exchequer (1979–83) and Foreign Secretary (1983–89) in Margaret Thatcher's government. Full name **Richard Edward Geoffrey Howe**

Howe, William, 5th Viscount (1729–1814) British military commander. Second in command at the Battle of Bunker Hill (1775), he became commander in chief of the British Army in North America (1776–78).

howe'er /how áir/ *contr.* however (*literary*) [Contraction of HOWEVER]

however /how évvər/ CORE MEANING: an adverb introducing some form of contrast ○ *I'm not sure how effective the campaign has been. I do however think that it has been distinctively different.*
    1. *adv.* TO WHATEVER DEGREE used to indicate that no matter what happens, a situation remains the same ○ *However objective it may believe itself to be, it is still only an opinion.* **2.** *rel adv.* IN WHATEVER WAY used to indicate that it does not matter in what way sb does sth ○ *Peel and prepare the potatoes however you like.* **3.** *adv.* HOW used as an emphatic form of 'how' ○ *What a surprise to see you! However did you find us?*

howff /howf, hōf/, **howf** *n. Scotland* a place where people often go to meet, especially a public house [Early 18thC. Origin uncertain: possibly from Dutch *hof* 'enclosure, garden'.]

howitzer /hówitsər/ *n.* a cannon with a bore diameter greater than 30 mm and a maximum elevation of 60 degrees that fires projectiles in a curved trajectory. Self-propelled or towed, it also has a muzzle velocity lower than that of a gun. [Late 17thC. Via Dutch *houwitser* from, ultimately, Czech *haufnice* 'catapult', from *hauf* 'heap' (of stones), of prehistoric Germanic origin.]

howk /hōk/ (**howks, howking, howked**) *vti. Scotland* to dig, or dig sth up or out (*informal*) [14thC. Variant of earlier *holk,* related to Low German *holken* 'to hollow out', and to English *hole* and *hollow.*]

howl /howl/ *v.* (**howls, howling, howled**) **1.** *vi.* MAKE A WAVERING SOUND to make a long wavering or whining sound ○ *a coyote howling* **2.** *vi.* CRY OUT to cry out in pain, anger, or distress **3.** *vi.* ROAR WITH LAUGHTER to laugh loudly and unrestrainedly (*slang*) **4.** *vt.* CALL OUT to call sth out in a long wavering way ■ *n.* **1.** LONG MOANING CRY a long sad wavering cry **2.** LOUD CRY a cry of pain, anger, or distress **3.** DRAWN-OUT WAVERING SOUND a long high loud wavering noise ○ *the howl of the wind* **4.** STH OR SB HILARIOUS an extremely funny person or thing (*slang*) [13thC. Origin uncertain: probably ultimately an imitation of the sound, and possibly related to English *owl.*]

howl down *vt.* to prevent sb or sth from being heard by making loud cries of protest or mockery

howler /hówlər/ *n.* **1.** LAUGHABLE MISTAKE a mistake that is so bad that it is funny (*informal*) **2.** SB OR STH THAT HOWLS sb who or sth that makes a howling noise **3.** ZOOL = **howler monkey**

howler monkey *n.* any one of various tropical mainly leaf-eating monkeys of Central and South America that live in trees and have a very loud booming call. Genus: *Alouatta.*

howling /hówling/ *adj.* **1.** LOUD AND WAVERING making a loud high wavering noise ○ *a howling gale* **2.** DISMALLY DESOLATE dismal, or empty of human beings (*literary*) ○ *alone in the howling desert* **3.** VERY GREAT extreme or great in degree (*informal*) ○ *Our presentation was a howling success!* ■ *n.* NOISE a succession of long high wavering noises, e.g. animal cries or the sound of a strong wind ○ *the howling of the wind* —**howlingly** *adv.*

Howlin' Wolf /hówlin wóòlf/ (1910–76) US musician. He was an electric blues singer who profoundly influenced rock'n'roll during its early years. His most famous song was 'Smokestack Lightnin' (1956). Real name **Chester Arthur Burnett**

howsit /hówzit/ *interj. S Africa* a greeting used when meeting sb (*informal*) [Shortening of *how is it?*]

howsoever /hówsō évvər/ *adv.* however (*formal or archaic*)

how-to *adj.* giving practical information and instructions on the way to do sth (*informal*) ○ *another how-to guide on home decorating*

howzat /hów zat/ *interj.* shouted at a cricket umpire by players claiming that a batsman is out (*informal*) [Late 20thC. Alteration of *how's that?*]

Hoxha /hójjə/, **Enver** (1908–85) Albanian statesman. Founder of the Albanian Communist Party (1941), he served as prime minister (1944–54), foreign minister (1946–53), and first secretary of the Communist Party (1943–85).

hoya /hóyə/ *n.* = **waxplant** [Mid-19thC. From modern Latin, genus name, from the name of the English gardener Thomas *Hoy* (died 1821).]

Hoy and West Mainland /hóy ənd wést-/ designated National Service Area in Orkney, Scotland. The Old Man of Hoy is a pillar-shaped rock just off the coast of the island of Hoy.

hoyden /hóyd'n/ *n.* an offensive term that deliberately insults a young woman's self-control and thoughtfulness (*dated offensive*) [Late 17thC. Origin uncertain: probably from Dutch *heiden* 'lout, heathen'.]

Hoyle /hoyl/, **Sir Fred** (*b.* 1915) British astronomer and writer. An expert in astrophysics, he has written books on astronomy and works of science fiction. Full name **Sir Frederick Hoyle**

hp *abbr.* horsepower

HP *abbr.* **1.** Houses of Parliament **2.** hire purchase **3.** BOT hardy perennial **4.** high pressure

h.p. *abbr.* **1.** high pressure **2.** hire purchase

HPV *n.*, *abbr.* human papilloma virus

HQ, **h.q.** *abbr.* headquarters

hr *abbr.* hour

HR *abbr.* **1.** Home Rule **2.** human resources **3.** *US* homeroom

H.R. *abbr.* House of Representatives

HRE *abbr.* **1.** Holy Roman Emperor **2.** Holy Roman Empire

HREOC *abbr.* Human Rights and Equal Opportunities Commission

HRH *abbr.* **1.** Her Royal Highness **2.** His Royal Highness

HRM *abbr.* human resource management

hrs *abbr.* hours

HRT *abbr.* hormone replacement therapy

Hs *symbol.* hassium

HS *abbr.* **1.** High School **2.** Home Secretary

HSC *abbr.* Higher School Certificate

HSE *abbr.* Health and Safety Executive

HSH *abbr.* **1.** Her Serene Highness **2.** His Serene Highness

Hsien Nien /syén nyén/ *n.* = **Chinese New Year**

HSRC *abbr.* Human Sciences Research Council

HST *abbr.* **1.** harmonized sales tax **2.** high-speed train **3.** hypersonic transport

ht *abbr.* **1.** heat **2.** height

HT *abbr.* **1.** half-time **2.** ELEC ENG high tension **3.** high tide

HTH *abbr.* hope this helps

HTLV *abbr.* human T-cell lymphotropic virus

HTLV-I *n.* a virus associated with cancers of the lymphatic system. Full form **human T-cell lymphotropic virus I**

HTLV-II *n.* a virus associated with leukaemia. Full form **human T-cell lymphotropic virus II**

HTML *n.*, *abbr.* COMPUT hypertext markup language

Hts *abbr.* GEOG Heights

HTTP *abbr.* COMPUT hypertext transfer protocol

huaca /wáakə/ *n.* any one of the sacred spirits and powers whom Native South American peoples of the Andes believe to live in caves, rocks, and other natural formations [Early 17thC. From Spanish *huaca guaca* from Quechua *waca*, 'god of the house'.]

Huang He /hwáng hố/ China's second longest river,

flowing through the north-central part of the country. Length: 4,667 km/2,900 mi.

huarache /wə ráa chee/ *n.* a sandal originally worn in Mexico, with the upper part made of woven leather straps [Late 19thC. Via Mexican Spanish from, probably, Japanese *warachi* 'straw sandal'.]

hub /hub/ *n.* **1.** CENTRAL PART the central part of a wheel or a similar device that rotates, e.g. a propeller **2.** CENTRE OF ACTIVITY a place that is a centre of activity or interest **3.** **hub**, **hub airport** AIR CENTRAL AIRPORT IN A NETWORK a central airport that passengers can fly to from smaller local airports in order to catch an international or long-distance flight [Early 16thC. Origin uncertain; probably an alteration of HOB; the underlying meaning is perhaps 'lump, mass'.]

hubba-hubba /húbbə húbbə/ *interj.* *US* used to express approval, enthusiasm, or pleasure (*dated slang*) [Mid-20thC. Origin uncertain.]

Hubble /húbb'l/, **Edwin** (1889–1953) US astronomer. Through his study of galaxies he proved the universe to be larger than had previously been thought, and still expanding. The Hubble Space Telescope is named after him. Full name **Edwin Powell Hubble**

hubble-bubble /húbb'l-/ *n.* = **hookah** [Early 17thC. Alteration of BUBBLE.]

Hubble constant /húbb'l/, **Hubble's constant** *n.* the ratio that expresses the rate of the universe's expansion, equal to the speed at which galaxies appear to be moving away from the Earth divided by their distance [Mid-20thC. Named after the US astronomer Edwin P. HUBBLE, who discovered the relationship.]

Hubble's law *n.* the law holding that the speed at which distant galaxies are moving away from the Earth is proportional to their distance from the observer [Mid-20thC. See HUBBLE CONSTANT.]

Hubble Telescope: A space shuttle astronaut repairs the Hubble Telescope

Hubble Telescope, **Hubble Space Telescope** *n.* a telescope mounted on a satellite that orbits the Earth, used to observe distant parts of the universe and photograph them. It was launched in 1990. [Late 20thC. Named in honour of Edwin P. HUBBLE.]

hubbub /húbbub/ *n.* **1.** CONFUSION OF VOICES a confused din, especially a number of voices speaking at once **2.** EXCITED FUSS a fuss or period of excitement [Mid-16thC. Origin uncertain: probably from Celtic.]

hubby /húbbi/ (*plural* **-bies**) *n.* a husband (*informal*) [Late 17thC. Alteration of HUSBAND.]

hubcap /húb kap/ *n.* a round cover that protects the outside of the central part of a vehicle's wheel

Hubei /hoō báy/ province in central China comprising both mountainous territory and the lake-studded plain of the Yangtze River. Capital: Wuhan. Population: 57,190,000 (1994). Area: 187,500 sq. km/72,394 sq. mi.

hubris /hyoóbriss, hoō-/ *n.* **1.** PRIDE excessive pride or arrogance **2.** EXCESSIVE AMBITION the excessive pride and ambition that usually leads to the downfall of a hero in classical tragedy [Late 19thC. From Greek.] —**hubristic** /hyoo bristik, hoo-/ *adj.* —**hubristically** /-bristikli/ *adv.*

huckaback /húkə bak/, **huck** /huk/ *n.* a coarse absorbent type of cotton or linen fabric used mainly for towels [Late 17thC. Origin unknown.]

huckleberry /húk'lbəri/ (*plural* **-ries**) *n.* **1.** PLANT LIKE A BLUEBERRY a North American shrub that is related to the blueberry and bears edible fruit. Genus:

Gaylussacia. **2.** FRUIT the edible, dark blue fruit of the huckleberry [Late 16thC. Origin uncertain: probably an alteration of *hurtleberry* 'whortleberry'.]

huckster /húkstər/ *n.* **1.** AGGRESSIVE SALESPERSON sb who uses aggressive methods to sell or promote sth **2.** RETAILER sb who sells small articles, especially a street pedlar ■ *v.* (**-sters**, **-stering**, **-stered**) **1.** *vt.* PEDDLE MERCHANDISE to sell or peddle sth **2.** *vti.* SELL AGGRESSIVELY to use aggressive methods to sell or promote sth [12thC. Origin uncertain: perhaps from Middle Dutch *hokester*, from *hoeken* 'to peddle'.]

HUD *abbr.* head-up display

Huddersfield /húddərz feeld/ industrial town in West Yorkshire, northern England, which grew up as a centre of the woollen textile industry. Population: 119,000 (1994).

huddle /húdd'l/ *n.* **1.** TIGHT GROUP a group of people or things gathered closely together **2.** BRIEF TALK a quick private talk or gathering (*informal*) ■ *v.* (**-dles**, **-dling**, **-dled**) **1.** *vti.* GATHER TIGHTLY TOGETHER to gather together in a tightly packed group, or make people or things do this ○ *The small crowd of spectators huddled together for warmth.* **2.** *vi.* CROUCH to draw your arms and legs tightly into your body, or move in close to sth, often for shelter or comfort ○ *He huddled in a doorway to get out of the rain.* **3.** *vi.* TALK PRIVATELY to gather privately to confer, make plans, or gossip (*informal*) **4.** *vt.* DO STH HASTILY to make or put together sth carelessly or hastily [Late 16thC. Origin uncertain: perhaps from Low German *hudeln* 'to crowd together', ultimately from an Indo-European base meaning 'to cover, conceal'.]

Hudibrastic /hyoódi brástik/, **hudibrastic** *adj.* mock-heroic, especially written in the style or metre used by Samuel Butler in his poem *Hudibras*

Hudson /húdss'n/ river in eastern New York State, and the longest in the state, flowing into the sea at New York City. Length: 492 km/306 mi.

Hudson, Rock (1925–85) US actor. He was a handsome romantic lead in films such as *Pillow Talk* (1959). Real name **Roy Harold, Jr Scherer**

Hudson Bay almost landlocked inland sea of east-central Canada, rich in wildlife. Native Americans and Inuit are the chief inhabitants of the region. Area: 730,000 sq. km/280,000 sq. mi. Depth: 258 m/846 ft.

Hudson's Bay blanket *n.* *Can* a wool blanket, usually cream-colored with distinctive red, black, yellow, and indigo stripes. First introduced as a trade item in the 18th century, it is still made today. [Late 19thC. So called because it was originally traded by the *Hudson's Bay* Company.]

Hudson's Bay Company /húdss'nz-/ *n.* a fur-trading company chartered in England in 1670 to trade in North America and later much involved in fur trading, exploring, and claiming territory for the British crown [Late 17thC. So called because its original charter was to trade in the areas of North America adjacent to Hudson Bay.]

Hudson Strait body of water in northeastern Canada connecting Hudson Bay with the Atlantic Ocean and separating Baffin Island from northern Quebec. Depth: 880 m/2,890 ft. Length: 720 km/450 mi.

hue /hyoo/ *n.* **1.** COLOUR a colour ○ *flowers of every hue* **2.** SHADE OF COLOUR a specific shade of a particular colour ○ *a pleasing hue of green* **3.** COLOURS PROPERTY OF A COLOUR a property of a colour that enables it to be perceived, e.g. as red or green and that is determined by its dominant wavelength **4.** TYPE a type or kind in a particular range ○ *All hues of political opinion should be represented in the discussions.* **5.** ASPECT an aspect, or the way that sth looks ○ *This puts a completely different hue on the matter.* [Old English *hē(o)w*, of prehistoric Germanic origin]

Hue /hway/ historic city in central Vietnam on the River Huong, near the South China Sea. The Nguyen royal capital from 1802 to 1945, it was heavily damaged during the Vietnam War. Population: 260,489 (1989).

hue and cry /hyoo-/ *n.* **1.** UPROAR a great uproar or commotion about sth **2.** PURSUIT in the past, a pursuit of sb accused of a crime, with the pursuers calling on bystanders to join in the chase [From Anglo-Norman *hu e cri*, literally 'outcry and cry'. *Hu* 'outcry' is from Old French *huer* 'to shout', an imitation of the sound of hunting or battle cries.]

-hued *suffix.* of a particular colour or number of colours ○ *the many-hued rainbow* ○ *a rose-hued sunset*

huff /huf/ *n.* FIT OF THE SULKS a brief mood of anger or resentment at sth sb has done ■ *v.* (**huffs, huffing, huffed**) **1.** *vti.* ANGER SB OR GET ANGRY to anger or offend sb, or become angry or offended **2.** *vi.* BLOW OR PANT to blow, pant, or breathe laboriously **3.** *vti.* BOARD GAMES REMOVE OPPONENT'S PIECE to remove an opponent's draughtsman from the board as a penalty for failing to make an obligatory capture [Late 16thC. An imitation of the sound of blowing.] ◇ **huff and puff 1.** to blow or pant, or do this while moving with great difficulty **2.** to make noisy but empty threats, or raise objections without any intention of taking action

huffy /húffi/ (**-ier, -iest**) *adj.* easily offended or put into a huff —**huffily** *adv.* —**huffiness** *n.*

hug /hug/ *v.* (**hugs, hugging, hugged**) **1.** *vt.* EMBRACE AFFECTIONATELY to put your arms round sb's body and hold the person tight to show affection or pleasure **2.** *vt.* PUT YOUR ARMS ROUND to clasp your arms round a part of your own body ○ *hugging her knees to her chest* **3.** *vr.* PUT YOUR ARMS ROUND YOURSELF to put your arms round your own body, especially to keep warm **4.** *vr.* CONGRATULATE YOURSELF to congratulate yourself or show great delight **5.** *vt.* KEEP CLOSE to remain in close linear proximity to sth while moving in a forward direction ○ *The boat hugged the coastline.* ■ *n.* AFFECTIONATE EMBRACE an affectionate embrace [Mid-16thC. Origin uncertain: probably from a Scandinavian source.] —**huggable** *adj.* —**hugger** *n.*

huge /hyooj/ (**huger, hugest**) *adj.* **1.** ENORMOUS very big in size or amount **2.** LARGE IN SCOPE very large in scope or scale ○ *huge talent* **3.** SIGNIFICANTLY SUCCESSFUL very important or successful (*informal*) ○ *This band are going to be huge.* [12thC. Shortening of Old French *ahuge*, of unknown origin.] —**hugeness** *n.*

hugely /hyóoji/ *adv.* to a great degree ○ *hugely successful*

huggermugger /húggər mugər/ *n.* MUDDLED MESS a disorderly mess or muddle ■ *adj.* **1.** DISORDERED confused or jumbled **2.** SECRETIVE clandestine or secret [Early 16thC. Origin uncertain.] —**huggermugger** *adv.*

Huggins /húgginz/, **Sir William** (1824–1910) British astronomer. He revolutionized astronomy by using spectroscopy to study the chemical constituents, motions, and velocities of stars.

Langston Hughes

Hughes /hyooz/, **Langston** (1902–67) US writer. A leader of the Harlem Renaissance, he incorporated the rhythms of jazz into his poems and stories about Black urban life. Full name **James Mercer Langston Hughes**

Hughes, Richard (1900–76) British writer. He wrote *Danger* (1924), the BBC's first radio drama, and *A High Wind in Jamaica* (1929). Full name **Richard Arthur Warren Hughes**

Hughes, Robert (b. 1938) Australian art critic and writer. His best known works include *The Shock of the New* (1980) and *The Fatal Shore* (1987). Full name **Robert Studley Forrest Hughes**

Hughes, Ted (1930–98) British poet. He was poet laureate (1984–98) and married the poet Sylvia Plath in

1956. His works include *Lupercal* (1960) and *Wodwo* (1967). Full name **Edward James Hughes**

Hughes, Thomas (1822–96) British writer. His novel *Tom Brown's Schooldays* (1857) was based on his experiences at Rugby School.

Hughes, William Morris (1862–1952) English-born Australian statesman. He was expelled from the Labor Party (1916) and served as prime minister of Australia (1917–22) for the Nationalist Party.

Hugo /hyóogō/, **Victor** (1802–85) French poet, novelist, and dramatist. A leading writer of the 19th century, he wrote *The Hunchback of Notre Dame* (1831) and *Les misérables* (1862). Full name **Victor Marie Hugo**

Huguenot /hyóogənō/ *n.* FRENCH PROTESTANT a French Protestant, especially in the 16th and 17th centuries ■ *adj.* OF THE FRENCH PROTESTANT CHURCH relating to, belonging to, or typical of the French Protestant Church [Mid-16thC. From French, an alteration (based on the name of Besançon *Hugues*, leader of a Swiss political movement) of obsolete *eiguenot*, from ultimately, Swiss German *Eidgenosse* 'confederate', literally 'oath-companion'.] —**Huguenotism** /hyóogə notizəm/ *n.*

huh /hu/ *interj.* **1.** EXPRESSION OF SURPRISE OR DISDAIN used to show surprise, inquiry, disdain, or lack of interest **2.** INVITATION TO AGREE used after giving an opinion to invite comment, especially agreement ○ *Great shot, huh?* [Early 17thC. A natural exclamation.]

hui /hóo ee/ (*plural* **hui**) *n.* NZ a social gathering in a Maori community [Mid-19thC. From Maori and Hawaiian.]

huia /hóoyə/ (*plural* **-a**) *n.* a New Zealand bird, now thought to be extinct, with tail feathers that were much prized by Maoris. Latin name: *Heteralocha acutirostris.* [Mid-19thC. From Hawaiian; an imitation of the sound of its whistle.]

hula /hóolə/ *n.* POLYNESIAN DANCE a Polynesian or Hawaiian dance, often accompanied by drumming and chanting, in which the performers move their hips back and forth and make miming gestures with their hands ■ *vi.* (**-las, -laing, -laed**) PERFORM A HULA to dance a hula [Early 19thC. From Hawaiian.]

Hula-Hoop *tdmk.* a trademark for a plastic ring that is placed around the waist and kept twirling by rhythmically moving the hips

hulk /hulk/ *n.* **1.** SB BIG sb who is big, powerful, and often clumsy **2.** EMPTY HULL the empty hull of a ship that has been wrecked or is too old to be sailed **3.** UNWIELDY SHIP a heavy ship that is difficult to steer **4.** SHELL OF A STRUCTURE the shell of any old, abandoned, or burnt-out structure or vehicle **5.** OLD SHIP USED AS PRISON an old, permanently moored ship, used in the 19th century as a prison (*often used in the plural*) ■ *vi.* (**hulks, hulking, hulked**) MOVE CLUMSILY to move in a clumsy or awkward way [Pre-12thC. Origin uncertain: probably via Anglo-Latin *hulcus* from Greek *holkas* 'merchant barge, ship that is towed', from *helkein* 'to pull'.]

hulking /húlking/, **hulky** /-ki/ (**-ier, -iest**) *adj.* large, bulky, and often clumsy

hull /hul/ *n.* **1.** BODY OF SHIP the body of a ship, excluding other parts, e.g. the masts and engines **2.** BODY OF A VEHICLE the main body of a large vehicle such as a tank or aeroplane **3.** AEROSP ROCKET CASING the external casing of a rocket, missile, or spaceship **4.** CALYX ON A STRAWBERRY the calyx on a strawberry that stays attached to the fruit when it is picked but is not eaten **5.** OUTER COVERING the outer covering of a seed or fruit ■ *vt.* (**hulls, hulling, hulled**) **1.** TAKE OFF A STRAWBERRY CALYX to remove the calyx from a strawberry **2.** REMOVE THE OUTER RIND FROM FRUIT to remove the outer rind or shell from a fruit or vegetable [Old English *hulu.* Ultimately from an Indo-European base meaning 'to cover, conceal', which is also the ancestor of English *helmet, hole,* and *hell.*]

Hull /hul/ industrial and port city in northeastern England, situated on the Humber Estuary. Its full name is Kingston upon Hull. Population: 268,600 (1995).

Hull, Bobby (b. 1939) Canadian ice hockey player. He played left wing for the Chicago Blackhawks (1957–72) and was the first to score over 50 goals in a season. Full name **Robert Marvin Hull**

Hull, Cordell (1871–1955) US statesman. He was secretary of state from 1933 to 1944 and was awarded the Nobel Peace Prize in 1945.

hullabaloo /húlləbə lóo/, **hullaballoo** *n.* noisy excitement or fuss [Mid-18thC. Alteration of earlier *holloballo*, from *holla*, an early variant of HELLO.]

hullo *interj., n.* = **hello**

Hulme /hyoom/, **Denny** (1936–94) New Zealand motor-racing driver. He won the 1967 Formula One world championship. Full name **Dennis Clive Hulme**

Hulme, Keri (b. 1947) New Zealand writer. She won the Booker Prize in 1985 for her first novel, *The Bone People* (1983).

hum /hum/ *v.* (**hums, humming, hummed**) **1.** *vi.* MAKE A DRONING SOUND to make a steady prolonged droning sound ○ *bees humming* **2.** *vti.* SING WITH THE LIPS CLOSED to sing with lips closed and without words, or sing sth in this way **3.** *vi.* GIVE OFF A LOW STEADY SOUND to be filled with a low, continuous, indistinct noise ○ *a room that hummed with strange electronic equipment* **4.** *vi.* BE EXTREMELY BUSY to be very busy or active (*informal*) ○ *This place is really humming.* **5.** *vi.* STINK to smell unpleasantly (*informal*) ■ *n.* **1.** DRONING NOISE a steady droning sound **2.** BAD SMELL an unpleasant smell (*informal*) ■ *interj.* EXPRESSION OF DISPLEASURE OR INDECISION a low sound made to express displeasure, doubt, surprise, or indecision [14thC. An imitation of the sound.] ◇ **hum and haw** to hesitate while speaking or deciding about sth

human /hyóomən/ *adj.* **1.** OF PEOPLE relating to, involving, or typical of human beings ○ *human nature* ○ *human frailty* **2.** MADE UP OF PEOPLE composed of people ○ *the human race* ○ *a human chain of protesters* **3.** COMPASSIONATELY KIND showing kindness, compassion, or approachability **4.** IMPERFECT having the imperfections and weaknesses of a human being rather than a machine or divine being ○ *Remember he's only human, so don't expect too much.* ■ *n.* PERSON a human being [14thC. Via French *humain* from Latin *humanus.*] —**humanness** *n.*

------- **WORD KEY: CULTURAL NOTE** -------
The Human Comedy, a collection of novels and stories by French writer Honoré de Balzac (published 1833–50). By linking his novels and stories through the use of common themes and characters, Balzac planned an oeuvre that would portray the human species in all stages of its development and aspects of its behaviour. At the time of his death, the collection included a hundred novels and stories and about fifty incomplete works.

human being *n.* **1.** MEMBER OF THE HUMAN SPECIES a member of the species to which men and women belong. Latin name: *Homo sapiens.* **2.** PERSON a person, viewed especially as having imperfections and weaknesses ○ *I'm a human being, not a machine.*

humane /hyoo máyn/ *adj.* **1.** COMPASSIONATE showing the better aspects of the human character, especially kindness and compassion **2.** INVOLVING MINIMAL PAIN without inflicting any more pain than is necessary **3.** WITH AN EMPHASIS ON LIBERAL VALUES with an emphasis on respect for other people's views [15thC. Variant of HUMAN.] —**humanely** *adv.* —**humaneness** *n.*

human ecology *n.* a branch of sociology that studies the relationships between human beings and their natural and social environments

human engineering *n.* = **ergonomics**

humane society *n.* any one of various organizations that promote compassionate treatment of animals

human ethology *n.* the study of human behaviour, especially aggressive and submissive behaviour in social contexts

human factors engineering *n.* = **ergonomics**

human immunodeficiency virus *n.* full form of **HIV**

human interest *n.* an element in sth, especially a news report, that is about sb's personal life or feelings and is expected to appeal to the public's sympathy or curiosity —**human-interest** *adj.*

humanise *vt.* = **humanize**

humanism /hyóomənizəm/ *n.* **1.** BELIEF IN A HUMAN-BASED MORALITY a system of thought that is based on the values, characteristics, and behaviour that are believed to be best in human beings, rather than on any supernatural authority **2. CONCERN FOR PEOPLE** a concern with the needs, wellbeing, and interests of people **3. humanism, Humanism RENAISSANCE CULTURAL MOVEMENT** the secular cultural and intellectual movement of the Renaissance that spread throughout Europe as a result of the rediscovery of the arts and philosophy of the ancient Greeks and Romans — **humanist** /hyoo̅o̅mənist/ *n., adj.* —**humanistic** /hyoo̅o̅mə-nístik/ *adj.* —**humanistically** /-nístikli/ *adv.*

humanitarian /hyoo̅o̅ mánni táiri ən/ *adj.* **1. CARING** committed to improving the lives of other people ○ *a humanitarian organization* **2. HUMAN** involving and affecting human beings, especially in a harmful way (*informal*) ○ *a humanitarian disaster* ■ *n.* **1. CARING PERSON** sb who is committed to improving the lives of other people **2. SB BELIEVING IN HUMANITARIANISM** sb who believes in a philosophical theory of humanitarianism [Mid-19thC. Formed from HUMAN, on the model of UNITARIAN and EGALITARIAN.]

humanitarianism /hyoo̅o̅ mánni táiri ənizəm/ *n.* a commitment to improving the lives of other people — **humanitarianist** *n.*

humanities /hyoo̅o̅ mánnətiz/, **Humanities** *npl.* **1. LIBERAL ARTS** the liberal arts as subjects of study, as opposed to the sciences **2. CLASSICAL STUDIES** the study of the language and literature of the ancient Greeks and Romans

humanity /hyoo̅o̅ mánnəti/ *n.* **1. HUMAN RACE** the human race considered as a whole **2. QUALITIES OF A HUMAN BEING** the qualities or characteristics considered as a whole to be typical of human beings **3. KINDNESS** kindness or compassion for others

humanize /hyoo̅o̅mə nīz/ (**-izes, -izing, -ized**), **humanise** (**-ises, -ising, -ised**) *vti.* **1. MAKE OR BECOME HUMAN** to make sth human or like humans, or become human or like humans **2. MAKE OR BECOME HUMANE** to make or become humane in character, characteristics, or nature —**humanization** /hyoo̅o̅mə nī záysh'n/ *n.* —**humanizer** /-nīzər/ *n.*

humankind /hyoo̅o̅mən kínd/ *n.* all human beings considered as a whole ○ *'Human kind cannot bear very much reality'.* (T. S. Eliot, *Four Quartets, Burnt Norton*; 1935)

humanly /hyoo̅o̅mənli/ *adv.* **1. WITHIN THE LIMITS OF HUMAN ABILITY** within the limits of human ability and knowledge ○ *They did all that was humanly possible to save him.* **2. IN A WAY TYPICAL OF HUMANS** in a way generally considered to be typical of humans **3. ACCORDING TO HUMAN EXPERIENCE** as far as human knowledge or experience can judge

humanmade /hyoo̅o̅mən mayd/ *adj.* made by human beings and not occurring naturally ○ *'Human-made materials gradually deteriorate even when exposed to unpolluted rain, but acid rain accelerates this process'.* (United States Environmental Protection Agency website; April 1999) = **manmade**

human nature *n.* the typical character that all human beings share, often seen as being imperfect

humanoid /hyoo̅o̅mə noyd/ *adj.* **RESEMBLING A HUMAN** used to describe a being from another planet that has the appearance or characteristics of a human ■ *n.* **HUMAN-LIKE CREATURE FROM ANOTHER PLANET** a being from another planet that has the appearance or characteristics of a human [Early 20thC. Formed from HUMAN + -OID.]

human papilloma virus *n.* a virus that causes warts in the genital area of humans

human resources *n.* **EMPLOYEE RECRUITMENT AND MANAGEMENT** the field of business concerned with recruiting and managing employees (*takes a singular verb*) ○ *a career in human resources* ■ *npl.* **PERSONNEL** all the people who work in a business or organization, considered as a whole (*takes a plural verb*)

human rights *npl.* the rights that are considered by most societies to belong automatically to everyone, e.g. the rights to freedom, justice, and equality (*sometimes singular*)

Humber Estuary /húmbər éstyoŏri/ navigable estuary separating Yorkshire and Lincolnshire, eastern England. The rivers Trent, Yorkshire, Ouse, and Hull flow into it. Length: 64 km/39 mi.

Humberside /húmbər sīd/ former county of northeastern England (1974–96), formed from parts of Yorkshire and Lincolnshire

humble /húmb'l/ *adj.* (**-bler, -blest**) **1. MODEST** modest and unassuming in attitude and behaviour **2. RESPECTFUL** feeling or showing respect and deference towards other people **3. LOWLY** relatively low in rank and without pretensions ○ *of humble origins* ■ *vt.* (**-bles, -bling, -bled**) **1. MAKE SB FEEL LESS IMPORTANT** to make sb feel less proud or convinced of his or her own importance **2. DEGRADE** to lower sb in rank or importance [13thC. Via Old French *(h)umble* from Latin *humilis* 'lowly' (source of English *humiliate*), from *humus* 'earth'; the underlying idea is 'close to the ground'.] — **humbleness** *n.* —**humbly** *adv.*

humblebee /húmb'l bee/ *n.* = **bumblebee** [15thC. Origin uncertain: probably an alteration of Middle Low German *hummelbē*, literally 'humming bee', from *hummel* 'hum, buzz' + *bē* 'bee'.]

humbled /húmb'ld/ *adj.* made to feel less important, proud, or confident

humble pie *n.* a pie made in the past using the entrails of a newly killed animal, especially a deer (*archaic*) [Mid-17thC. Alteration (modelled on HUMBLE) of earlier *umble pie*, from *umbles* 'edible animal entrails', via French dialect *nombles* from, ultimately, Latin *lumbulus* 'small loin'.] ◇ **eat humble pie** to apologize or admit you have been wrong, especially in a way that makes you feel humiliated

humbling /húmbling/ *adj.* making sb lose confidence, self-importance, or pride —**humblingly** *adv.*

Humboldt /húm bōlt/, **Alexander, Freiherr von** (1769–1859) German explorer and naturalist. He is best known for his encyclopedic account of the physical universe, *The Cosmos* (1845–62). Full name **Friedrich Wilhelm Heinrich Alexander Humboldt**

Humboldt Current /húm bōlt-/ *n.* a cold current of the South Pacific Ocean that flows north along the coastline of South America [Named after the German scientist Baron Friedrich von *Humboldt* (1769–1859), who explored the coasts of Central and South America in the early 19thC]

humbug /húm bug/ *n.* **1. NONSENSE** sth that is silly or makes no sense **2. DECEPTION** sth that is meant to deceive or cheat people **3. FRAUD** sb who deceives others by taking on a false identity or pretending to have a certain background or skills **4. BOILED SWEET** a boiled mint-flavoured sweet, usually decorated with stripes ■ *vti.* (**-bugs, -bugging, -bugged**) **DECEIVE** to take part in a deception, or deceive sb ■ *interj.* **NONSENSE!** used to express the opinion that sth is nonsense or deception (*archaic*) [Mid-18thC. Origin unknown.]

humdinger /húmdingər/ *n.* an exceptional or outstanding person or thing (*slang*) [Early 20thC. Origin uncertain: probably from HUM in the sense of an approving murmur + *dinger* 'superlative thing' (formed from DING in the sense 'to beat, excel').]

humdrum /húm drum/ *adj.* dull because of being too familiar and lacking variety [Mid-16thC. Origin uncertain: probably an expressive alteration of HUM.]

Hume /hyoom/, **Basil, Cardinal** (b. 1923) British Roman Catholic cardinal. He became Archbishop of Westminster in 1976, the first Benedictine monk to hold this office. Full name **George Basil Hume**

Hume, David (1711–76) Scottish philosopher and historian. His major works were *A Treatise of Human Nature* (1739–40) and *An Enquiry Concerning Human Understanding* (1748).

Hume, John (b. 1937) Northern Irish politician. The leader of the Social Democratic and Liberal Party from 1979, he was joint winner of the 1998 Nobel Peace Prize for his contribution to the Northern Irish peace process.

humectant /hyoo méktənt/ *n.* **ABSORBENT SUBSTANCE** a substance such as a skin lotion that absorbs or helps retain moisture ■ *adj.* **MOISTURE-ABSORBING** capable of absorbing or retaining moisture [Early 19thC. Formed from Latin *(h)umectare* 'to moisten', from *(h)umectus* 'moist', from *(h)umere* 'to be moist' (see HUMID).]

humeral /hyoo̅o̅mərəl/ *adj.* relating to, involving, or located in the humerus of the upper arm or forelimb ○ *a humeral injury*

humeral veil *n.* a silk shawl covering the shoulders and hands, worn by a Roman Catholic priest while holding sacred vessels

humerus /hyoo̅o̅mərəss/ (*plural* **-i** /-rī/) *n.* the long bone of the human upper arm or in a forelimb in other animals [14thC. From Latin, 'upper arm'. Ultimately from an Indo-European word meaning 'shoulder'.]

humic /hyoo̅o̅mik/ *adj.* relating to, involving, containing, or typical of humus [Mid-19thC. Formed from HUMUS.]

humid /hyoo̅o̅mid/ *adj.* with a relatively high level of moisture in the air [14thC. From Latin *(h)umidus*, from *(h)umere* 'to be moist'. Ultimately from an Indo-European word meaning 'wet', which is also the ancestor of English *wake, humour,* and *hygro-*.] —**humidly** *adv.* —**humidness** *n.*

— WORD KEY: SYNONYMS —
See Synonyms at **wet**.

humidex /hyoo̅o̅mi deks/ *n.* **Can** an index of the level of discomfort likely to be experienced as a result of the combined effects of humidity and heat [Late 20thC. Contraction of *humidity index.*]

humidifier /hyoo míddi fī ər/ *n.* a device or machine that keeps the air moist inside an enclosed space

humidify /hyoo míddi fī/ (**-fies, -fying, -fied**) *vt.* to make sth, especially the air, more moist or damp — **humidification** /hyoo míddifi káysh'n/ *n.*

humidistat /hyoo míddi stat/ *n.* an instrument that measures or controls the relative humidity of air [Early 20thC. Formed from HUMIDITY, on the model of THERMOSTAT.]

humidity /hyoo míddəti/ *n.* **1. ATMOSPHERIC MOISTURE** the amount of moisture in the air **2. HIGH MOISTURE LEVEL** the condition of having a high amount of moisture in the air **3.** = **relative humidity**

humidor /hyoo̅o̅mi dawr/ *n.* a container, often a box or jar, in which tobacco products, especially cigars, can be stored to prevent them from drying out [Early 20thC. Formed from HUMID, on the model of CUSPIDOR.]

humify /hyoo̅o̅mi fī/ (**-fies, -fying, -fied**) *vti.* to turn a substance into humus, or turn into humus

humiliate /hyoo mílli ayt/ (**-ates, -ating, -ated**) *vt.* to damage sb's dignity or pride, especially publicly [Mid-16thC. From late Latin *humiliare*, from Latin *humilis* (see HUMBLE).] —**humiliating** *adj.* —**humiliatingly** *adv.* — **humiliator** *n.*

humiliation /hyoo mílli áysh'n/ *n.* **1. LOSS OF DIGNITY** the feeling or condition of being lessened in dignity or pride **2. LESSENING OF SB'S DIGNITY** the act of damaging sb's dignity or pride **3. STH THAT HUMILIATES** sth that damages sb's pride or dignity

humility /hyoo mílləti/ *n.* the quality of being modest or respectful [13thC. Via French *humilité* from Latin *humilitas*, from *humilis* (see HUMBLE).]

hummable /húmməb'l/ *adj.* memorable and melodious enough to make people want to hum it (*informal*)

Hummel /hoŏm'l/, **Johann** (1778–1837) German composer and pianist. He was a pupil of Mozart and is best known for his work on piano finger technique, *Klavierschule* (1828). Full name **Johann Nepomuk Hummel**

Hummingbird

hummingbird /húmming burd/ *n.* a small brightly-coloured bird of North, Central, and South America that can beat its wings rapidly, making a humming sound and allowing it to hover. Family: Trochilidae.

humming top *n.* a child's spinning top that makes a humming sound as it spins

hummock /húmmək/ *n.* **1. SMALL HILL** a small hill or mound **2. ICE RIDGE** a ridge of ice in an ice field [Mid-16thC. Origin unknown. Originally a nautical term for a coastal hillock.] —**hummocky** *adj.*

hummus /hŏŏmmŏŏss/, **humus, hoummos** *n.* a Middle Eastern dip made with mashed chickpeas, tahini, oil, lemon juice, and garlic, combined into a thick paste [Mid-20thC. From Arabic *ḥummuṣ* 'chickpea'.]

humongous /hyoo múng gəss/, **humungous** *adj.* extremely large in size or amount (*informal*) [Mid-20thC. Origin uncertain: perhaps a blend of HUGE and MONSTROUS.] —**humongously** *adv.*

humor *n., vt.* US = humour

humoral /hyóoməral/ *adj.* relating to, involving, or typical of body fluids, especially blood serum

humoresque /hyóomə résk/ *n.* a light or whimsical piece of music, especially in 19th-century music [Late 19thC. Alteration of German *Humoreske*, from *Humor* 'humour', from English.]

humorist /hyóomərist/ *n.* **1. COMIC WRITER** sb who writes or performs comic material **2. FUNNY PERSON** sb known to be amusing and to have a quick wit

humorous /hyóomərəss/ *adj.* **1. FUNNY** amusing, or intended to make people laugh **2. WITTY** witty, or able to make people laugh —**humorously** *adv.* —**humorousness** *n.*

—— WORD KEY: SYNONYMS ——
See Synonyms at *funny*.

humour /hyóomər/ *n.* **1. FUNNY QUALITY** the quality or content of sth, e.g. a story, performance, or joke, that elicits amusement and laughter **2. ABILITY TO SEE STH IS FUNNY** the ability to see that sth is funny, or the enjoyment of things that are funny ○ *He has no sense of humour.* **3. FUNNY THINGS AS A GENRE** writings and other material created to make people laugh **4. SB'S USUAL TEMPERAMENT** sb's character or usual attitude ○ *a writer of melancholy humour* **5. MOOD** a temporary mood or state of mind **6. HIST BODY FLUID** according to medieval science and medicine, any of the four main fluids of the human body, blood, yellow bile, black bile, or lymph, that determined a person's mood and temperament (*archaic*) ■ *vt.* (**-mours, -mouring, -moured**) **1. DO WHAT SB WANTS** to do what sb wants in order to keep him or her happy **2. COMPLY** to act in accordance with sth (*archaic*) [14thC. Via Anglo-Norman from Latin *humor* 'body fluid', from *humere* 'to be wet' (see HUMID).]

humoured /hyóomərd/ *adj.* with a particular character or frame of mind (*usually used in combination*) ○ *good-humoured*

humourless /hyóomərləss/ *adj.* **1. WITHOUT A SENSE OF HUMOUR** lacking a sense of humour **2. NOT FUNNY** having no amusing aspect —**humourlessly** *adv.* —**humourlessness** *n.*

hump /hump/ *n.* **1. ZOOL BUMP ON AN ANIMAL'S BACK** a rounded protuberance on the back of some animals, e.g. camels and some cattle **2. MED CURVE OF THE BACK** a pronounced convex curvature of sb's upper spine resulting from injury or disease, a congenital abnormality, or an accumulation of fat **3. BUMP IN THE SURFACE OF STH** a rounded protruding mass such as a mound of earth ■ *v.* (**humps, humping, humped**) **1.** *vt.* **MOVE STH WITH EFFORT** to carry sth heavy with difficulty (*informal*) **2.** *vti.* **HAVE SEX** to have sexual intercourse with sb (*slang offensive*) **3.** *vt.* **MAKE STH INTO A HUMP** to form sth into a hump [Mid-17thC. Origin uncertain: probably from or related to Dutch *homp* or Low German *humpe*.] ◇ **over the hump** past the worst or most difficult part of sth ◇ **the hump** a mood of annoyance, resentment, or unhappiness (*informal*)

humpback /húmp bak/ *n.* **1.** = **hunchback 2.** ZOOL = **humpback whale 3.** CIV ENG = **humpback bridge 4.** ZOOL = **pink salmon**

humpback bridge, **hump-backed bridge** *n.* a small narrow bridge with a steep approach and descent

humpback salmon *n.* = **pink salmon** [*Humpback* because

the male develops a humped back during the breeding season]

Humpback whale

humpback whale, **humpback** *n.* a large dark grey or black whale, up to 15.2 m/50 ft long, with a humped back and long white flippers, that feeds by sieving plankton and fish through baleen plates. Humpback whales communicate with one another using distinctive complex sounds that can travel over considerable distances. Latin name: *Megaptera novaeangliae*.

Humperdinck /hŏŏmpər dingk/, **Engelbert** (1854–1921) German composer. He wrote numerous operas, the most famous of which, *Hänsel und Gretel* (1893), was first conducted by Richard Strauss.

humph /humf/ *interj.* used to express annoyance, doubt, or dissatisfaction [Mid-16thC. A natural exclamation.]

Humphries /húmfriz/, **Barry** (b. 1934) Australian writer and performer. He is best known as the creator of the comic characters Dame Edna Everage and Sir Les Patterson. Full name *John Barry Humphries*

humpty-dumpty /húmpti dúmpti/ (*plural* **humpty-dumpties**) *n.* a short dumpy person [Late 18thC. From the nursery-rhyme character *Humpty-Dumpty*, whose name is of uncertain origin: perhaps playfully based on HUMP and DUMPY.]

humpy[1] /húmpi/ (**-ier, -iest**) *adj.* **1. WITH HUMPS** having or full of humps **2. IRRITABLE** feeling irritable and easily annoyed (*informal*) —**humpiness** *n.*

humpy[2] /húmpi/ (*plural* **-ies**) *n. Aus* a small, crudely constructed hut or shelter in the bush [Mid-19thC. From Aboriginal *yumbi*, influenced by HUMP.]

humungous *adj.* = **humongous**

humus[1] /hyóoməss/ *n.* a dark brown organic component of soil that is derived from decomposed plant and animal remains and animal excrement. Humus improves the water-retaining properties of soil, making it more fertile and workable. [Late 18thC. From Latin, 'soil'.]

humus[2] *n.* FOOD = **hummus**

Hun /hun/ *n.* **1. PEOPLES MEMBER OF AN EARLY ASIAN NOMADIC PEOPLE** a member of a nomadic people, probably originating in northern central Asia, who invaded China in the 3rd century BC and then spread westwards to Asia and Europe. During the 4th century AD, under their leader, Attila, they overran much of the Roman Empire. **2. BARBARICALLY CRUEL PERSON** a barbaric destructive person **3.** HIST **OFFENSIVE TERM** an offensive term to refer to a German person or the German people, especially by the Allies during World Wars I and II (*dated slang offensive*) [Old English *Hūne*, via a prehistoric Germanic word from late Latin *Hunni*, from, ultimately, Sogdian *xwn*.]

hunch /hunch/ *n.* **1. FEELING** an intuitive feeling about sth **2. STOOP** a curved posture of the body with the head down and shoulders forwards **3.** MED = **hump** *n.* **2 4. PIECE** a large lump or slice of sth (*archaic*) ■ *vti.* (**hunches, hunching, hunched**) **BEND UPPER BODY FORWARDS** to bend the head down and the shoulders forwards, e.g. because of bad posture, illness, or the cold ○ *a typist hunching over the keyboard* ○ *hunched her shoulders against the wind* [15thC. Origin unknown.]

hunchback /húnch bak/ *n.* **1. SB WITH HUMP ON BACK** sb who has a hump on his or her back **2. HUMPED BACK** a

back that shows a pronounced curvature of the spine —**hunchbacked** *adj.*

—— WORD KEY: CULTURAL NOTE ——
The Hunchback of Notre Dame, a novel by French writer Victor Hugo (1831). In this richly evocative medieval tragedy, Quasimodo, the hunchbacked bell-ringer at the Cathedral of Notre Dame in Paris, falls in love with a beautiful girl, Esmerelda. When corrupt priest Claude Frollo's harassment of Esmerelda results in her being executed for sorcery, Quasimodo murders Frollo by pushing him off the bell tower.

hundred /húndrəd/ *n.* **1. NUMBER 100** the number 100 **2. GROUP OF 100** a group of a hundred objects or people **3. LARGE NUMBER** an unspecified large number (*usually used in the plural*) ○ *attended by hundreds* **4. NUMBER THIRD FROM DECIMAL POINT** the number that is three places to the left of the decimal point in Arabic notation **5. POSITION THIRD FROM DECIMAL POINT** the position that is three places to the left of the decimal point in Arabic notation **6.** CRICKET **100 RUNS** a score of 100 runs by a batsman **7.** HIST **COUNTY SUBDIVISION** a historical subdivision of English, Irish, and some North American counties ■ **hundreds** *npl.* **1. NUMBERS 100 TO 999** the numbers 100 to 999 **2. YEARS OF A CENTURY** the years of a particular century, regarded as those beginning with a particular number ○ *the seventeen hundreds* [Old English. Ultimately from an Indo-European word that is related to Latin *centum* (source of English *cent* and *century*.]

hundred per cent *adv.* (*informal*) **1. TOTALLY** in a complete or full way **2. COMPLETELY WELL** completely fit and healthy

hundreds-and-thousands *npl.* tiny multicoloured sugar strands used for decorating cakes

hundredth /húndrədth/ *n.* one of 100 equal parts of sth

hundredweight /húndrəd wayt/ *n.* **1. WEIGHT OF 112 LB, USED IN UK** a unit of mass in the British imperial system equal to 112 lb (50.80 kg) **2. WEIGHT OF 100 LB, USED IN US** a unit of mass in the US customary system equal to 100 lb (45.36 kgs) **3.** = **metric hundredweight** [Early 16thC. The exact weight has varied from time to time; it was probably originally 100 pounds.]

Hundred Years' War *n.* a series of wars fought between England and France from 1337 to 1453 that resulted in the final expulsion of England from all French territories except Calais

hung[1] past participle, past tense of **hang**

hung[2] *adj.* unable to form a majority and therefore make decisions or reach a verdict ○ *a hung jury* ○ *a hung parliament*

Hung. *abbr.* **1.** Hungarian **2.** Hungary

Hungarian /hung gáiri ən/ *n.* **1. PEOPLES SB FROM HUNGARY** sb who was born or brought up in Hungary, or who is a Hungarian citizen **2.** LANG **OFFICIAL LANGUAGE OF HUNGARY** the official language of Hungary, also spoken in parts of neighbouring countries, belonging to one of the Ugric subgroups of the Finno-Ugric branch of the Uralic family of languages. It is spoken by about 14 million people. —**Hungarian** *adj.*

Hungarian goulash *n.* = **goulash**

Hungary

Hungary /húng gəri/ republic in central Europe, first united as a country around AD1000. Language: Hungarian. Currency: forint. Capital: Budapest. Population: 10,225,000 (1995). Area: 93,030 sq. km/35,919 sq. mi. Official name **Republic of Hungary**

hunger /húng gər/ n. **1.** NEED TO EAT the need or desire for food **2.** STARVATION lack of food leading to illness or death ○ *children dying of hunger* **3.** CRAVING a great need or desire for sth ○ *a hunger for knowledge* ■ vi. (**-gers, -gering, -gered**) CRAVE to feel a very strong need or desire for sth [Old English *hungur*, from prehistoric Germanic]

hunger march n. a march organized by unemployed people to draw attention to their plight

hunger strike n. a refusal to eat over a period of time as a form of protest, especially by a prisoner — **hunger striker** n.

hungover /hung óvər/, **hung over** adj. suffering from the aftereffects of drinking too much alcohol

hungry /húng gri/ (**-grier, -griest**) adj. **1.** WANTING TO EAT wanting or needing food **2.** AVID wanting or desiring sth very much ○ *hungry for new experiences* **3.** AMBITIOUS having great ambition or a powerful desire to win (*informal*) ○ *They won because they were hungrier than we were.* **4.** CAUSING HUNGER using up a lot of energy and making sb feel hungry ○ *hungry work* [Old English *hungrig*, related to *hungur* (see HUNGER)] —**hungrily** adv. —**hungriness** n. ◇ **go hungry** to go without food

hung up adj. (*informal*) **1.** OBSESSED obsessed with sb or sth ○ *He's completely hung up on her.* **2.** WORRIED in a state of worry or anxiety over sth ○ *hung up over minor details*

hunk /hungk/ n. **1.** CHUNK a large piece of sth such as bread or cheese that is cut or torn off a larger portion **2.** MALE WITH A GOOD PHYSIQUE used to describe a man who is well-built and very physically impressive (*informal*) [Early 19thC. Origin uncertain: perhaps from Flemish *hunke* 'piece of food'.]

hunker /húngkər/ (**-kers, -kering, -kered**) vi. to squat down close to the ground [Early 18thC. Origin uncertain.]

hunkers /húngkərz/ npl. the hips, buttocks, and upper thighs of humans or animals (*dated informal*) [Mid-18thC. Origin uncertain: probably from HUNKER in the sense of 'thing with which you hunker'.]

hunky /húngki/ (**-ier, -iest**) adj. masculine, well-built, and very physically attractive (*informal*)

hunky-dory /-dáwri/ adj. absolutely fine or satisfactory (*informal*) [Origin uncertain: probably an alteration of *hunky* 'all right', from obsolete *hunk* 'place where a game player is safe from capture', from Dutch *honk* 'home']

Hunnish /húnnish/ adj. **1.** RELATING TO HUNS typical of or relating to the Huns **2. Hunnish, hunnish** DESTRUCTIVELY CRUEL destructive and barbarous

hunt /hunt/ v. (**hunts, hunting, hunted**) **1.** vt. SEEK PREY to pursue an animal with the aim of capturing or killing it for sport or food ○ *Cats hunt mice and small birds.* **2.** vt. SEEK OUT to search for and try to capture sb **3.** vi. SEARCH to search persistently for sth difficult to find ○ *hunting for his missing keys* **4.** vt. HOUND SB to seek out and harass or persecute sb **5.** vi. HUNT CHASE ANIMALS WITH HOUNDS to engage in a sport involving the pursuit of an animal, usually a fox, on horseback and with the aid of hounds **6.** vt. HUNT USE ANIMAL IN BLOOD SPORT to use a horse or hounds for the purpose of chasing and killing game, typically a fox **7.** vt. HUNT HUNT IN A PARTICULAR PLACE to search a particular area for animals to capture or kill for sport or food **8.** vi. ENG OSCILLATE ABOUT POSITION to oscillate about a fixed point ■ n. **1.** ACT OF SEARCHING the act of looking for sb or sth carefully, thoroughly, and persistently **2.** HUNT SEEKING OF PREY a pursuit of animals to capture or kill them for sport or food ○ *a deer hunt* **3.** HUNTING EXPEDITION an organized event in which riders and hounds, pursue a fox or deer with the aim of killing it for sport **4.** ORGANIZED GROUP OF HUNTERS a group of people engaged in hunting as a sport ○ *She joined the local hunt.* [Old English *huntian*, from prehistoric Germanic] ◇ **hunt high and low for sb** *or* **sth** to search extremely thoroughly for sb or sth

Hunt /hunt/, **Geoff** (b. 1947) Australian squash player. He won the World Open title in 1976, 1977, 1979, and 1980. Full name **Geoffrey Brian Hunt**

Hunt, Holman (1827–1910) British painter. He was a cofounder of the Pre-Raphaelite Brotherhood (1848) and his works include *The Scapegoat* (1854) and *May Morning on Magdalen Tower* (1889). Full name **William Holman Hunt**

Hunt, James (1947–93) British racing driver. Formula One World Champion in 1976, he retired from racing in 1979 and took up motor racing commentary. Full name **James Simon Wallis Hunt**

Hunt, Leigh (1784–1859) British poet. He was a friend of Keats, Byron, and Shelley. His works include two volumes of collected poems (1832, 1844) and his *Autobiography* (1850). Full name **James Henry Leigh Hunt**

Hunt, Sam (b. 1946) New Zealand poet. A writer and performer of popular verse, his works include *South into Winter* (1973).

huntaway /húntə way/ n. NZ a sheepdog that is trained to drive sheep forward from a position behind them

hunted /húntid/ adj. startled and panic-stricken, as if being pursued or hunted ○ *a hunted look*

hunter /húntər/ n. **1.** PREDATOR a person or animal that hunts birds or animals for food or sport **2.** HORSE a powerful fast horse that is bred for and used in hunting **3.** DOG a dog that is specially bred for and used in hunting **4.** SEEKER sb who seeks out sb or sth specific, especially as an occupation or hobby **5.** WATCH a watch with a hinged metal cover to protect the watch face

--- WORD KEY: CULTURAL NOTE ---

The Heart is a Lonely Hunter, a novel by US writer Carson McCullers (1940). A work about isolation, alienation, and the search for love, it is the story of four lonely individuals, all of whom find themselves drawn to a local boy who is unable to hear or speak. The novel's central irony is that the boy is even more isolated than they are, his loneliness eventually leading him to suicide.

Hunter /húntər/, **Bill** (b. 1941) Australian actor. His films include *Newsfront* (1978). Full name **William Hunter**

Hunter, John (1728–93) Scottish anatomist and surgeon. Through his study of anatomy, biology, physiology, and pathology, he established surgery as a modern scientific discipline.

Hunter, William (1718–83) Scottish obstetrician. He introduced the dissection of cadavers as part of medical training. His advances in obstetrics led to its recognition as a branch of medicine.

hunter-gatherer n. a member of a society in which people live by hunting and gathering only, with no crops or livestock being raised for food

hunter-killer adj. used to describe a naval force consisting of an antisubmarine warfare carrier and its associated elements

hunter's moon n. the first full moon directly following the harvest moon

hunting /húnting/ n. **1.** KILLING OF ANIMALS FOR SPORT the sport or practice of pursuing and killing or capturing wild animals **2.** SEEKING OUT the process of searching carefully for sth, usually over a period of time ○ *job hunting*

hunting and gathering n. seeking game and edible plants for subsistence, as practised by pre-agricultural and nomadic people, rather than raising livestock and crops for food

Huntingdon town in eastern England, the former county town of Huntingdonshire

Huntingdonshire /húntingdənshər/ historic former county in eastern England, now part of Cambridgeshire. Population: 149,600 (1995).

hunting ground n. **1.** HUNT AREA FOR HUNTING a place where hunting takes place or that is suitable for hunting **2.** SOURCE OF STH a source of useful or desired objects or information ○ *The town is a great hunting ground for antiques.*

hunting horn n. a horn used to give signals during hunting, especially foxhunting

hunting knife n. a broad knife used for killing or gutting game

hunting spider n. = wolf spider

Huntington's chorea /húntingtənz ko rée ə/ n. a hereditary disorder of the nervous system that manifests as jerky involuntary movements in early middle age, with behavioural changes and progressive dementia [Late 19thC. Named after the American neurologist George *Huntington* (1851–1916), who first described it.]

hunting watch n. = hunter n. 5

huntress /húntrəss/ n. a woman or goddess who hunts

hunt saboteur n. sb who believes that fox-hunting is cruel and travels to hunts in order to try and prevent them from proceeding

huntsman /húntsmən/ (*plural* **-men** /-mən/) n. **1.** HUNT HUNT OFFICIAL an official who is in charge of the hounds belonging to a hunt **2.** HUNT HUNTING MAN a man who hunts, either for a living or for a pastime **3.** ZOOL = **huntsman spider**

huntsman spider n. a large spider with a light brown or grey hairy body that lives in hot and tropical regions. Family: Sparassidae.

Huon pine /hyoó on-/ n. a large coniferous tree that grows in South America, Australia, and Southeast Asia and is used for timber. Latin name: *Dacrydium franklinii*. [Early 19thC. Named after the River *Huon* in southern Tasmania, where it was first found.]

hup /hup/ interj. used when lifting or raising sth (*informal*) [Mid-20thC. Origin uncertain: perhaps an alteration of *hep*, used when marching to mark time, of unknown origin.]

huppah n. = chuppah

Hurd /hurd/, **Douglas** (b. 1930) British Conservative politician. He served as Northern Ireland secretary (1984), home secretary (1985), and foreign secretary (1989–95). Full name **Douglas Richard Hurd**

hurdies /húrdiz/ npl. Scotland the buttocks or haunches [Mid-16thC. Origin unknown.]

hurdle /húrd'l/ n. **1.** SPORTS FRAME FOR RUNNER TO JUMP one of a number of light barriers over which runners have to jump in some athletics events **2.** SPORTS RACE OVER BARRIERS an athletics event in which runners have to race to clear a series of light barriers **3.** DIFFICULTY OR OBSTACLE a difficulty or obstacle that has to be overcome **4.** FENCE a light framework made of intertwined branches or wattle that is used as a temporary fence **5.** HORSERACING FENCE USED IN HORSE RACE a fence of intertwined branches or wattle that horses race over, or a race over fences of this type **6.** HIST FRAME FOR CONVICTS a frame on which traitors were dragged and paraded before the public before being executed (*archaic*) ■ v. (**-dles, -dling, -dled**) **1.** vi. SPORTS RACE OVER HURDLES to run in an athletics event in which hurdles must be jumped **2.** vt. SPORTS CLEAR RACING BARRIER to clear a barrier in a race **3.** vt. OVERCOME A DIFFICULTY to overcome an obstacle or difficulty **4.** vt. FENCE AREA to fence off an area with hurdles [Old English *hyrdel*. Ultimately from an Indo-European word meaning 'to turn' that is also the ancestor of English *grate*[1] and *grille*.] —**hurdler** n.

Hurdy-gurdy

hurdy-gurdy /húrdi gúrdi, húrdi gurdi/ (*plural* **hurdy-gurdies**) n. **1.** BARREL ORGAN a mechanical musical instrument such as a barrel organ that is played by turning a handle **2.** MEDIEVAL MUSICAL INSTRUMENT a medieval stringed musical instrument played by turning a wheel with one hand and depressing keys on a keyboard with the other. Sound was produced by adding violin-bow rosin to the outer edge of the wheel, which made the strings vibrate when it was turned against them. [Mid-18thC. An imitation of the sound.]

hurl /hurl/ *v.* **(hurls, hurling, hurled) 1.** *vt.* **FLING STH** to throw sth with great force **2.** *vt.* **YELL STH** to utter sth with great violence or vehemence ○ *hurling abuse* **3.** *vti.* BASEBALL **PITCH** to pitch a baseball **4.** *vi.* **VOMIT** to vomit, especially with considerable force (*slang*) ■ *n.* **1. STRONG THROW** a forceful throw, or the act of throwing sth with great force **2.** *Scotland* TRANSP **RIDE IN VEHICLE** a ride in any vehicle with wheels [12thC. Origin uncertain: probably suggests the action.] —**hurler** *n.*

WORD KEY: SYNONYMS

See Synonyms at ***throw***.

hurley /húrli/ *n. Ireland* the game of hurling [Early 19thC. Fomed from HURL.]

hurley *n.* a long wooden stick with a curved end used in the game of hurling

hurling /húrling/ *n.* an Irish field sport resembling hockey and lacrosse that is played with broad sticks and a leather ball that is passed from player to player through the air

hurly-burly /húrli burli/ *n.* noisy and bustling activity [Alteration of *hurling and burling*, a playful formation ultimately based on HURL]

Huron /hyŏŏrən, -on/ (*plural* **-ron** *or* **-rons**) *n.* PEOPLES a member of a confederacy of four Native North American peoples who originally lived around the Great Lakes but today live in Quebec, Ontario, and Oklahoma. During the 17th century, the Huron population was greatly reduced by continual warring with the Iroquois and the arrival of smallpox and other European diseases. [Mid-17thC. From French, literally 'boar', from Old French *hure* 'bristling hair'.] —**Huron** *adj.*

Huron, Lake /hyŏŏrən/ second largest of the Great Lakes, lying between the state of Michigan, United States, and the province of Ontario, Canada. Area: 59,600 sq. km/23,000 sq. mi. Depth: 229 m/751 ft.

hurrah **(-rahs, -rahing, -rahed)** *interj.* = **hooray** [Late 17thC. Alteration of archaic *huzza* (see HUZZAH).]

hurray *interj., vi.* = **hooray**

Hurrian /hŏŏri ən/ *n.* **1.** PEOPLES **MEMBER OF ANCIENT SYRIAN PEOPLE** a member of an ancient people who lived in Syria and Mesopotamia around 1500 BC **2.** LANG **LANGUAGE OF HURRIAN** the language of the Hurrians. Its affinities are unknown. [Early 20thC. Formed from Hittite and Assyrian *Harri* and *Hurri*.] —**Hurrian** *adj.*

hurricane /húrrikən, -kayn/ *n.* **1.** METEOROL **SEVERE STORM** a severe tropical storm with torrential rain and winds above 119 km/74 mi. per hour. Hurricanes originate in areas of low pressure in equatorial regions of the Atlantic or Caribbean, then strengthen, travelling northwest, north, or northeast. **2.** METEOROL **HIGH WIND** a wind with speeds above 119 km/74 mi. per hour and a force of 12 or above on the Beaufort scale **3. FAST FORCEFUL THING** sb or sth resembling a violent storm in force, speed, or effect [Mid-16thC. Via Spanish *huracán* from Taino *hurakán* 'god of the storm'.]

hurricane deck *n.* a deck on a ship with a cover from the sun

hurricane lamp *n.* an oil or paraffin lamp with a glass cover to prevent the wick from being extinguished in wind or rain

hurried /húrrid/ *adj.* done, made, or performed too quickly because of a real or perceived lack of time —**hurriedly** *adv.* —**hurriedness** *n.*

hurry /húrri/ *v.* **(-ries, -rying, -ried) 1.** *vi.* **RUSH** to move or do sth with great or excessive speed because of a real or perceived lack of time **2.** *vt.* **SPEED UP** to make or encourage sb or sth to act with greater speed ■ *n.* **1. HASTE** a state in which sb is doing sth or moving at a great or excessive speed ○ *We were in such a hurry we left the tickets behind.* **2. URGENCY** the need to do sth quickly ○ *What's the hurry?* [Early 17thC. Origin uncertain; perhaps suggests the action.] —**hurrying** *adj.* —**hurryingly** *adv.* ◇ **in a hurry** readily or willingly (*informal*)

hurry-scurry *n.* an undue rush to do sth [Mid-18thC. Repetition of HURRY.]

hurst /hurst/ *n.* a wood (*archaic*) [Old English *hyrst*, from a prehistoric Germanic word]

hurt /hurt/ *v.* **(hurts, hurting, hurt) 1.** *vt.* **INJURE SB OR STH** to cause physical pain in sb or in yourself or part of the body ○ *hurt his back when he fell down* **2.** *vti.* **CAUSE PAIN** to experience physical pain, or cause sb to experience physical pain ○ *Ouch! That hurts!* **3.** *vti.* **UPSET** to feel emotional pain, or make sb feel emotional pain ○ *hurt by his unkind remarks* **4.** *vti.* **IMPAIR** to have a negative effect on sth ○ *This could hurt her chances of re-election.* **5.** *vi.* **EXPERIENCE DIFFICULTIES** to undergo or experience difficulties or setbacks, e.g. in business or financial affairs (*informal*) ○ *too much competition, so the business is really hurting* ■ *n.* **1. PAIN** emotional or mental pain or suffering ○ *after all the hurt he's caused* **2. INJURY** an injury or wound, whether emotional or physical ○ *old hurts* ■ *adj.* **1. INJURED** injured or in physical pain **2. UPSET** feeling or showing emotional pain or suffering [12thC. From Old French *hurter* 'to ram, collide', probably ultimately from prehistoric Germanic.] —**hurter** *n.*

WORD KEY: SYNONYMS

See Synonyms at ***harm***.

hurtful /húrtf'l/ *adj.* causing emotional pain or suffering —**hurtfully** *adv.* —**hurtfulness** *n.*

hurtle /húrt'l/ **(-tles, -tling, -tled)** *vi.* to move or travel at very high speed [13thC. Formed from HURT.]

husband /húzbənd/ *n.* **SPOUSE** the man to whom a woman is married ■ *vt.* **(-bands, -banding, -banded) BE THRIFTY WITH STH** to use and manage sth economically, e.g. resources or money [Pre-12thC. From Old Norse *húsbóndi* 'man in charge of the house, farmer', from *hús* 'house' + *bóndi* 'dweller', present participle of *búa* 'to dwell'.] —**husbandage** *n.* —**husbander** *n.*

husbandman /húzbəndmən/ (*plural* **-men** /-mən/) *n.* a farmer (*archaic*)

husbandry /húzbəndri/ *n.* **1.** AGRIC **FARMING** the science, skill, or art of farming **2. FRUGAL MANAGEMENT** the frugal and sensible management of resources

hush /hush/ *vti.* **(hushes, hushing, hushed) MAKE SB BE QUIET** to become silent, or make sb become quiet or silent ■ *interj.* **BE QUIET** used as a request or demand for silence ■ *n.* **SILENCE** a stillness or silence, especially after a period of noise or in expectation of sth [Mid-16thC. Origin uncertain; probably a back-formation from archaic *husht* 'silent', earlier 'hush!', a natural exclamation.] **hush up** *vt.* to prevent sth, especially sth dishonourable or discreditable, from becoming publicly known (*informal*)

hushaby /húshə bī/ *interj.* used to lull a child to sleep [Mid-18thC. Coined from HUSH + *-aby* as in *lullaby*.]

hush-hush *adj.* secret or confidential (*informal*)

hush money *n.* money paid as a bribe not to disclose information (*informal*)

Hush Puppies *tdmk.* a trademark for a type of soft shoe

husk /husk/ *n.* **1.** BOT **OUTER PLANT COVERING** the outer membranous covering of some fruits, nuts, and grains **2. USELESS OUTER SHELL** an empty outer shell or covering that no longer serves any useful purpose [14thC. Origin uncertain: perhaps from Low German *hūske* 'little house, cover'.] —**husker** *n.*

husk tomato *n.* = **ground cherry**

husky[1] /húski/ *adj.* **(-ier, -iest) 1. THROATY** hoarse and dry, either naturally or as a result of illness or emotion ○ *a husky voice* **2.** *US* **BURLY AND COMPACT IN PHYSIQUE** with a solid, burly, strong, and compact physique ○ *a husky boy* **3. RELATING TO HUSKS** containing or resembling husks ■ *n.* CLOTHES **PADDED WAISTCOAT** a short padded or quilted waistcoat [Mid-16thC. Formed from HUSK.] —**huskily** *adv.* —**huskiness** *n.*

husky[2] /húski/ (*plural* **-kies**) *n.* a large long-haired dog with a curled tail and pricked-up ears, originally bred in Arctic regions and trained to pull sleds [Mid-19thC. Origin uncertain: probably a shortening and alteration of ESKIMO, the original name being *Eskimo dog*.]

huss /huss/ *n.* the edible flesh of the European dogfish [15thC. Origin unknown.]

Huss /huss/, **John** (1372?–1415) Bohemian religious reformer. He was burnt at the stake for supporting the teachings of the English reformer, Wycliffe. His execution led to the outbreak of the Hussite Wars (1419–34).

hussar /hŏŏ zaar/ *n.* **1. EUROPEAN CAVALRY SOLDIER** a soldier in any European light cavalry unit in the 18th and 19th centuries that adopted an ornate uniform similar to that of the Hungarian cavalry in the 15th century **2. HUNGARIAN CAVALRY MEMBER** a member of the Hungarian cavalry in the 15th century [Mid-16thC. Via Hungarian *huszár* 'light horseman' from, ultimately, Italian *corsaro* 'corsair'.]

Hussein I /hŏŏ sáyn/, **King of Jordan** (1935–99). Throughout his reign (1952–99), he was a moderating influence in Middle East politics.

Hussein, Saddam (*b.* 1937) Iraqi president. As leader of the Baath party, he became president in 1979. Two years after the end of the Iran-Iraq War (1980–88), his invasion of Kuwait led to the Gulf War.

Hussite /hússīt/ *n.* a follower of the teachings of the Bohemian nationalist and religious reformer John Huss (1372?-1415) —**Hussitism** /hússitizəm/ *n.*

hussy /hússi/ (*plural* **-sies**) *n.* an offensive term that deliberately insults a woman's manner or behaviour (*insult*) [Mid-16thC. Contraction of HOUSEWIFE (the original sense).]

hustings /hústingz/ *npl.* **1. ELECTIONEERING ACTIVITIES** the political activities, e.g. speech-making and the organization of public rallies, that take place before an election **2. ELECTION PLATFORM FORMERLY USED** in Great Britain before 1872, a platform from which parliamentary candidates were nominated and addressed electors (*archaic*) [Pre-12thC. From Old Norse *húsþing* 'council held by a king and his immediate followers', from *hús* 'house' + *þing* 'meeting'.]

hustle /húss'l/ *v.* **(-tles, -tling, -tled) 1.** *vt.* **PROPEL** to convey sb roughly or hurriedly from a place ○ *hustled her into a waiting car* **2.** *vi.* **HURRY** to go somewhere or do sth fast or hurriedly (*informal*) ○ *We'd better hustle, or we'll be late.* **3.** *vt.* **DEAL WITH STH FAST** to deal with sth hurriedly ○ *Let's hustle this project along.* **4.** *vti.* *US* CRIMINOL **SOLICIT CUSTOMERS IN SHADY DEALS** to solicit customers in shady or illegal deals, e.g. as a prostitute (*slang*) **5.** *vt.* *US* **SELL STH AGGRESSIVELY** to sell sth aggressively, e.g. drinks in a bar **6.** *vti.* *US* CRIMINOL **ENGAGE IN SMALL-TIME ILLEGAL DEALS** to engage in small-time crooked dealing, e.g. petty theft (*slang*) ■ *n.* **NOISY ACTIVITY** lively, noisy, continual activity ○ *enjoyed the hustle of the big city* [Late 17thC. From Dutch *hutselen* 'to shake or toss', literally 'to shake repeatedly', ultimately from *hotsen* 'to shake'.]

hustler /hússlər/ *n.* CRIMINOL **1. PETTY CRIMINAL** sb who engages in illegal activities, e.g. petty theft or illegal gambling, on a small scale (*informal*) **2.** *US* **PROSTITUTE** a prostitute, especially a streetwalker or one who solicits in bars (*slang*)

hut /hut/ *n.* **ONE-ROOM BUILDING** a small single-storey building, often made of wood, that is used as a simple house or shelter, or for storage, temporary accommodation, or leisure or community activities ○ *a scout hut* ■ *vt.* **(huts, hutting, hutted) PROVIDE WITH HUTS** to provide huts for a place, especially for accommodation [Mid-16thC. Via French *hutte* from High German *hütte*, of uncertain origin.]

hutch /huch/ *n.* **1. CAGE** a small shelter, usually constructed from wire and wood, for keeping small animals such as rabbits **2.** *US* HOUSEHOLD **CHINA CABINET** a cupboard with drawers and usually open shelves on top, often used for storing and displaying dishes and kitchen utensils [12thC. Via French *huche* from medieval Latin *hutica*, of unknown origin.]

Hutchinson-Gilford syndrome /húchins'n gílfərd-/ *n.* MED = **progeria** [Named after the British physicians Sir Jonathan *Hutchinson* (1828–1913) and Hastings *Gilford* (1861–1941)]

hutment /hútmənt/ *n.* a group of huts forming a military encampment

Hutton /hútt'n/, **James** (1726–97) Scottish geologist. He outlined the principles of uniformitarianism in *Theory of the Earth* (1795).

Hutt Valley /hút válli/ urbanized region in the south

of the North Island, New Zealand, near the city of Wellington

Hutu /hoͦo tooͦ/ (*plural* **-tu** *or* **-tus**) *n.* **1.** PEOPLES MEMBER OF A RWANDAN AND BURUNDIAN PEOPLE a member of a people who make up the majority of the population of Rwanda and Burundi. ◊ Tutsi **2.** LANG LANGUAGE OF RWANDA AND BURUNDI a language spoken in Rwanda and Burundi that is one of the Bantu group of the Niger-Congo family of African languages. Hutu is spoken by about 14 million people. [Mid-20thC. From a Bantu language.] —**Hutu** *adj.*

hutzpah *n.* = **chutzpah**

Huxley /húksli/, **Aldous** (1894–1963) British novelist and essayist. His novels include *Point Counter Point* (1928), *Brave New World* (1932), and *Eyeless in Gaza* (1936). Full name **Aldous Leonard Huxley**

Huxley, Andrew (*b.* 1917) British physiologist. He was joint winner of the Nobel Prize in physiology or medicine (1963) for his work on nerve impulses. Full name **Andrew Fielding Huxley**

Huxley, Sir Julian (1887–1975) British biologist. He was the first director-general of UNESCO (1947–48) and the author of *Essays of a Biologist* (1923). Full name **Sir Julian Sorrell Huxley**

Huxley, T. H. (1825–95) British biologist. A supporter of Darwin, he wrote *Zoological Evidences as to Man's Place in Nature* (1863) and *Collected Essays* (1893–94). Full name **Thomas Henry Huxley**

Huygens' eyepiece /híganz-/ *n.* an eyepiece consisting of two planoconvex lenses with their flat sides towards the eye, fitted mainly on optical instruments that are used for observation rather than measurement [Mid-19thC. Named after the Dutch physicist and astronomer Christiaan *Huygens* (1629–95), who invented it.]

Huygens' principle *n.* PHYS the proposition that every point on a wavefront acts as a source of secondary waves of light and that the wavefront at a later time is the envelope of these secondary waves [See HUYGENS' EYEPIECE]

huzzah /hoͦo záa, hə-/ (**-zahs**, **-zahing**, **-zahed**) *n.* = **hooray** (*archaic*) [Late 16thC. Variant of *huzza*, of uncertain origin: perhaps a sailor's work-chant when hauling on ropes; or related to German *Hussa*, a hunting cry.]

HV *abbr.* **1.** MED health visitor **2.** ELEC high voltage

h.v. *abbr.* high voltage

HVAC *abbr.* heating, ventilating, and air conditioning

hvy *abbr.* heavy

HW *abbr.* **1.** hazardous waste **2.** high water **3.** hot water **4.** hit wicket

h.w. *abbr.* hit wicket

Hwange National Park /hwáng gi-/ the largest national park in Zimbabwe, established in 1929. Area: 14,651 sq. km/5,657 sq. mi.

HWM *abbr.* high-water mark

hwy *abbr.* highway

hwyl /hoͦoi l/ *n.* NZ ENTHUSIASM good spirit or enthusiasm (*informal*) ■ *interj.* NZ USED AS GREETING used as a toast or to say goodbye (*informal*) [From Welsh]

Hyacinth

hyacinth /hí ə sinth/ *n.* a plant of the lily family, native to the northeastern Mediterranean, cultivated widely for its spikes of highly fragrant pink, white, or blue flowers. Latin name: *Hyacinthus orientalis*. [Mid-16thC. Via French and Latin from Greek

huakinthos 'plant sprung from the blood of HYACINTHUS', also 'blue stone' (source of English *jacinth*).] —**hyacinthine** /hī ə sín thīn/ *adj.*

hyacinth bean *n.* a deciduous woody-stemmed leguminous climbing plant with attractive pink or white flowers. Latin name: *Dolichos lablab*.

hyacinth orchid *n.* a leafless Australian orchid that has dark pink flowers with white spots and usually grows near eucalyptus trees. Latin name: *Dipodium punctatum*.

Hyacinthus /hí ə sínthəss/ *n.* a young boy in Greek mythology who was loved and accidentally killed by the god Apollo, who made a flower grow on the spot where the boy died

Hyades /hí ə deez/ *n.* a cluster of over 200 stars in the constellation Taurus. Its five brightest members form a V-shaped group that is visible to the naked eye.

hyaena *n.* = **hyena**

hyal- *prefix.* = **hyalo-** (*used before vowels*)

hyalin /hí ə lin/ *n.* a clear glassy material found in hyaline cartilage or formed as a product of some skin diseases

hyaline /hí ə lin, -leen, -līn/ *adj.* clear, translucent, and containing no fibres or granular material

hyaline cartilage *n.* the most common type of cartilage, consisting of a bluish-white elastic material containing fine collagen fibres that provides flexibility and support at the joints. Hyaline cartilage is found at the ends of the long bones and in the nose and the larynx, and forms most of the foetal skeleton.

hyaline membrane disease *n.* = **respiratory distress syndrome**

hyalite /hí ə līt/ *n.* a clear colourless variety of the semiprecious gemstone opal

hyalitis /hí ə lítiss/ *n.* inflammation of the transparent jelly (**vitreous humour**) that fills the chamber of the eye behind the lens

hyalo- *prefix.* glass, glassy ○ *hyaloplasm* [From Greek *hualos* 'glass', of unknown origin]

hyaloid /hí ə loyd/ *adj.* clear and glassy in appearance

hyaloid membrane *n.* a transparent insubstantial membrane surrounding the transparent jelly (**vitreous humour**) of the eye and separating it from the retina

hyaluronic acid /hí əlooͦ rónnik-/ *n.* a viscous slippery complex sugar that lubricates joints and helps maintain the shape of the eyeballs. It is present in connective tissue, and also plays a role in the healing of wounds. [*Hyaluronic* from HYALOID (because the substance was first isolated in the vitreous humour) + *uronic* 'connected with urine']

hyaluronidase /hí əlooͦ rónnidayss, -dayz/ *n.* an enzyme that breaks down hyaluronic acid, increasing the permeability of connective tissues

hybrid /híbrid/ *n.* **1.** BOT PLANT RESULTING FROM CROSSING a plant produced from a cross between two plants with different genetic constituents. Hybrids from crosses between crop varieties are often stronger and produce better yields than the original stock. **2.** ZOOL ANIMAL RESULTING FROM CROSS-SPECIES MATING an animal that results from the mating of parents from two distinct species or subspecies **3.** COMPOUND sth made up of a mixture of different elements **4.** LING WORD DERIVED FROM TWO LANGUAGES a word that has derived from two different languages, e.g. 'appendicitis', in which 'appendic' is from Latin and 'itis' is from Greek **5.** AUTOMOT USING TWO FUELS a vehicle with an engine that runs on electricity and petrol, which it can alternate between ■ *adj.* **1.** BIOL CROSSBRED bred from two distinct species or subspecies **2.** CONTAINING MIXED ELEMENTS made up of different elements or components ○ *a hybrid literary form* **3.** BEING A HYBRID being or relating to a hybrid **4.** ELECTRON ENG UNUSUAL AS AN ELECTRONIC CIRCUIT used to describe an electronic circuit that consists of two or more components not ordinarily combined with one another, e.g. a circuit that has integrated circuitry, transistors, and valves **5.** ELECTRON ENG WITH MULTIPLE INTEGRATED CIRCUITRY used to describe an electronic circuit containing more than one integrated circuit, all of which are

attached to the same ceramic substrate [Early 17thC. From Latin *hybrida*, of uncertain origin: probably from Greek *hubrida* 'mongrel'.] —**hybridism** *n.* —**hybridist** *n.* —**hybridity** /hī bríddəti/ *n.*

hybrid antibody *n.* an artificial antibody synthesized to attach to two different antigens

hybrid bill *n.* **1.** PUBLIC AND PRIVATE BILL in Parliament, a bill with some provisions affecting the public domain and others affecting private interests. ◊ private bill, public bill **2.** LAW a bill encompassing a number of largely unrelated subject areas

hybrid computer *n.* a computer employing both analog and digital techniques

hybridize /híbri dīz/ (**-izes**, **-izing**, **-ized**), **hybridise** (**-ises**, **-ising**, **-ised**) *vti.* to generate a new form of plant or animal, either by human intervention or naturally, by combining the genes of two different species or subspecies —**hybridizable** *adj.* —**hybridization** /híbri dī záysh'n/ *n.* —**hybridizer** /híbri dīzər/ *n.*

hybridoma /híbri dómə/ *n.* a hybrid cell produced by the fusion of a tumour cell with a normal antibody-producing cell, which then proliferates and yields large amounts of a monoclonal antibody

hybrid rock *n.* rock formed when molten magma incorporates solid material from the rock through which it flows, yielding a mixture of rock types

hybrid vigour *n.* the increased growth, disease resistance, and fertility seen in hybrid species. Mules, the offspring of mares and donkeys, are stronger and longer-lived than the parent animals.

hyd. *abbr.* hydraulics

hydathode /hída thōd/ *n.* a pore in the outer layer of a leaf that secretes water when the rate of transpiration is low, e.g. in humid conditions [Late 19thC. From Greek *hudat-*, stem of *hudōr* 'water', + *hodos* 'way'.]

hydatid /hídətid/, **hydatid cyst** *n.* a cyst formed in human tissue that contains the larvae of a tapeworm [Late 17thC. Via modern Latin from Greek *hudatis* 'drop of water, watery vesicle', from *hudat-*, stem of *hudōr* 'water'.]

hydatid disease *n.* a condition resulting from the presence of hydatid cysts in the liver, lungs, or brain, which can cause malignancies, blindness, epilepsy, and fever

hydnocarpate /hídnō kaͦar payt/ *n.* a salt of hydnocarpic acid

hydnocarpic acid /hídnō kaͦarpik-/ *n.* a fatty acid containing a carbon ring in its structure, occurring as glycerides in chaulmoogra oil. Formula: $C_{16}H_{28}O_2$. [*Hydnocarpic* from *hydnocarpus*, plant yielding an oil containing this acid, ultimately from Greek *hudnon* 'truffle' + *karpos* 'fruit', from the fruit's appearance]

hydr- *prefix.* = **hydro-** (*used before vowels*)

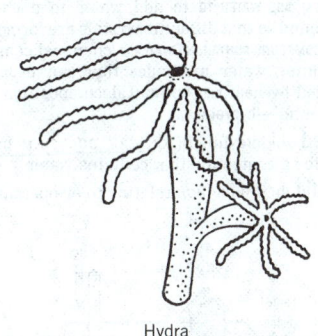

Hydra

hydra /hídrə/ (*plural* **-dras** *or* **-drae** /-drī/) *n.* a freshwater polyp with a cylindrical body at one end and a mouth surrounded by tentacles at the other. Genus: *Hydra*. [Late 18thC. Via modern Latin, genus name, from, ultimately, Greek *hudra* 'water snake'.]

Hydra *n.* **1.** ASTRON LARGEST CONSTELLATION the largest constellation, between Leo in the northern hemisphere and Centaurus in the southern hemisphere **2.** MYTHOL MANY-HEADED MONSTER a monster in Greek mythology that had nine heads and was killed by Hercules.

When one head was cut off, another grew instantly in its place.

hydracid /hī drássid/ n. an acid in which the hydrogen atoms are bound to an atom other than oxygen, e.g. hydrochloric acid

hydragogue /hídrə gog/ n. a laxative that acts osmotically by drawing water into the intestinal canal from the blood, thereby softening the contents. Epsom salts was once the principal hydragogue but has now been superseded by complex sugars such as lactulose that work in the same way. [Mid-17thC. Via late Latin *hydragogus* from Greek *hudragōgos* 'conveying water', from the stem *hudr-* 'water'.]

hydra-headed adj. with many heads or parts like heads

hydralazine /hī drállə zeen/ n. a drug that lowers blood pressure, usually given with drugs that cause increased urine output [Mid-20thC. Coined from HYDRO + PHTHALIC ACID + AZINE.]

hydrangea /hī dráynjə/ n. an erect or climbing evergreen or deciduous shrub, native to Asia, that has large clusters of white, pink, or blue flowers in a variety of shapes. Genus: *Hydrangea*. [Mid-18thC. From modern Latin, genus name, literally 'water pot'; from its cup-shaped seed pod.]

hydrant /hídrənt/ n. an upright pipe, usually in a street, connected to a water main with a valve to which a hose can be attached, e.g. by the fire services [Early 19thC. Formed from HYDRO-.]

hydranth /hí dranth/ n. the sedentary form in the life cycle of a cnidarian such as a sea anemone or a hydra [Late 19thC. From HYDRA + Greek *anthos* 'flower'.]

hydrarch /hí draark/ adj. used to describe the development of a sequence of ecological stages that begins in a freshwater habitat such as a pond [Early 20thC. Coined from HYDRO- + Greek *arkhē* 'beginning'.]

hydrargyrum /hī draárjirəm/ n. CHEM ELEM mercury (*archaic*) [Mid-16thC. Via modern Latin from, ultimately, Greek *hydrarguros*, from the stem *hudr-* 'water' + *arguros* 'silver'.]

hydrase /hí drayss, -drayz/ n. an enzyme that catalyses the addition or removal of water

hydrastine /hī dráss teen, -tin/ n. a poisonous white substance extracted from the thick yellow roots of the goldenseal plant, once used medicinally to stop haemorrhaging, shrink the uterus, and reduce inflammation of mucous membranes. Formula: $C_{21}H_{21}NO_6$. [Mid-19thC. Formed from *hydrastis*, plant genus name, formed from HYDRO- + *astis*, of unknown origin.]

hydrastinine /hī drásti neen, -nin/ n. an organic compound forming colourless crystals, soluble in water and resembling hydrastine in its medicinal properties. Formula: $C_{11}H_{13}NO_3$.

hydrate /hí drayt, hī dr-yt/ vt. (-drates, -drating, -drated) 1. GIVE WATER TO to provide water for sb or sth in order to re-establish or maintain a correct fluid balance 2. CHEM ADD WATER TO to add water to a chemical compound so that different crystals are formed ■ n. CHEM COMPOUND CONTAINING WATER a chemical compound containing water molecules that can usually be expelled by heating, without decomposition of the compound —**hydrator** n.

hydrated /hí draytid, hī dráytid/ adj. CHEM used to describe a compound that contains water

hydraulic /hī dróllik/ adj. relating to or operated by a

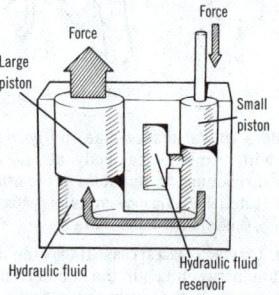

Hydraulic: Cross-section of hydraulic mechanism

device in which pressure applied to a piston is transmitted by a fluid to a larger piston, giving rise to a larger force [Early 17thC. Via Latin *hydraulicus* from Greek *hudraulikos*, from *hudōr* 'water' + *aulos* 'pipe'.] —**hydraulically** adv.

hydraulic brake n. a brake in which force applied to a pedal is transmitted to the brake pads by an enclosed liquid, usually a glycol mixture

hydraulic coupling n. an arrangement in which two pistons of different sizes are connected by an enclosed fluid that can transmit pressure from one piston to the other

hydraulic press n. a device in which a relatively small force applied to a piston results in movement of a larger piston to which it is hydraulically coupled by an enclosed liquid. A hydraulic press is often the key part of machinery that forces materials to flow plastically into a preformed shape.

hydraulic ram n. 1. HYDRAULIC-PRESS PISTON the larger working piston of a hydraulic press 2. RESERVOIR WATER-LEVEL CONTROLLING DEVICE a device that uses the kinetic energy of a flow of water to raise water to a reservoir that is higher than the water source itself

hydraulics /hī drólliks/ n. the study of water or other fluids at rest or in motion, especially with respect to engineering applications (*takes a singular verb*)

hydrazide /hídrə zīd/ n. a compound formed when one of the hydrogen atoms in hydrazine is replaced by a radical containing the CO moiety [Late 19thC. Coined from HYDR- + AZO- + -IDE.]

Hydrazine

hydrazine /hídrə zeen/ n. a highly reactive colourless liquid or white crystalline solid made from sodium hypochlorite and ammonia, used in rocket fuel. Formula: $H_2N.NH_2$. [Late 19thC. Coined from HYDR- + AZO- + -INE.]

hydrazoic acid /hídrə zṓ ik-/ n. a colourless liquid that is highly toxic and explosive in the presence of oxygen. Formula: HN_3. [*Hydrazoic* coined from HYDR- + AZO- + -IC]

hydric /hídrik/ adj. 1. WITH MUCH WATER containing or using considerable amounts of water 2. ECOL VERY WET used to describe or relating to an environment that is extremely wet

hydride /hí drīd/ n. a chemical compound formed between hydrogen and a more electropositive atom, e.g. sodium hydride, or via a covalent bond, e.g. boron hydride. Hydrides can also be formed with transition metals such as platinum and palladium.

hydrilla /hī dríllə/ n. (*plural* -las or -la) a plant that grows underwater in large masses and oxygenates the water. Introduced into the southern United States, it has proliferated to such an extent that in some places it chokes fish and blocks water traffic. Genus: *Hydrilla*. [Early 19thC. From modern Latin, genus name, literally 'little hydra', from Latin *hydra* (see HYDRA).]

hydriodic acid /hídri óddik-/ n. a colourless or pale yellow strong acid formed when hydrogen iodide gas dissolves in water [*Hydriodic* coined from HYDR- + IODINE + -IC]

hydro[1] /hídrō/ (*plural* -dros) n. 1. HYDROELECTRIC POWER PLANT a power plant that generates electricity using water pressure 2. HYDROELECTRIC POWER power generated using water pressure 3. *Can* ELECTRIC POWER electricity from an electric utility ○ *the hydro bill* [Early 20thC. Shortening of HYDROELECTRIC.]

hydro[2] /hídrō/ (*plural* -dros) n. a hotel, resort, or clinic offering hydropathic treatment [Late 19thC. Shortening of *hydropathic treatment*.]

hydro- prefix. 1. water, liquid, moisture ○ *hydrobiology* 2. hydrogen ○ *hydrocarbon* [From Greek *hudr-*, the stem of *hudōr* 'water'. Ultimately from the Indo-European word for 'water', which is also the ancestor of English *water*, *undulate*, *otter*, and *vodka*.]

hydroacoustics /hídrō ə koóstiks/ n. the branch of acoustics that studies how sound travels in water (*takes a singular verb*)

hydrobiology /hídrō bī ólləji/ n. the branch of biology that studies aquatic animals and plants —**hydrobiological** /hídrō bī ə lójjik'l/ adj. —**hydrobiologist** /hídrō bī ólləjist/ n.

hydrobromic acid /hídrō brṓmik-/ n. a colourless or pale yellow strong acid formed when hydrogen bromide gas is dissolved in water

hydrocarbon /hídrō kaárbən/ n. an organic chemical compound containing only hydrogen and carbon atoms, arranged in rows, rings, or both, and connected by single, double, or triple bonds. Hydrocarbons constitute a very large group including alkanes, alkenes, and alykynes. —**hydrocarbonaceous** /-kaarbə náyshəss/ adj. —**hydrocarbonic** /-kaar bónnik/ adj. —**hydrocarbonous** /-kaárbənəss/ adj.

hydrocele /hídrō seel/ n. an abnormal accumulation of watery liquid in a body cavity, especially in the sac round the testes. It is a painless condition that can be treated surgically by drainage of the fluid.

hydrocellulose /hídrō séllyoólōss/ n. a gelatinous substance formed when cellulose is mixed with water, acids, or alkalis, e.g. in the manufacture of paper or rayon

hydrocephalus /hídrō séffələss, -kéffələss/, **hydrocephaly** /hídrō séffəli, -kéffəli/ n. an abnormal increase of cerebrospinal fluid round the brain, resulting in infants in an enlargement of the head because the bones of the skull are still unfused. The fluid is blocked by a congenital condition or a disease, and can be drained into the abdominal cavity. [Late 17thC. Via modern Latin from, ultimately, Greek *hudōr* 'water' + *kephalē* 'head'.] —**hydrocephalic** /hídrō sə fállik, -kə-/ adj. —**hydrocephaloid** /hídrō séffə loyd, -kéffə/ adj. —**hydrocephalous** /-séffələss, -kéffə-/ adj.

hydrochloric acid /hídrə klórrik-/ n. a strong colourless acid formed when hydrogen chloride gas dissociates in water, used in industrial and laboratory processes. Hydrochloric acid is also produced in the stomach, where it initiates the digestion of proteins.

hydrochloride /hídrō kláwr īd/ n. a salt formed when hydrochloric acid reacts with an organic base, e.g. aniline

hydrochlorothiazide /hídrō kláwrō thī ə zīd/ n. a drug used in the treatment of fluid retention and high blood pressure

hydrocolloid /hídrō kólloyd/ n. a substance that forms a gel when mixed with water —**hydrocolloidal** /hídrōkə lóyd'l/ adj.

hydrocoral /hídrə kórrəl/ n. a marine multicellular organism that lives in colonies and builds calcareous skeletons within which the animals live. Order: Milleporina and Stylasterina.

hydrocortisone /hídrə káwrtizōn/ n. 1. PHYSIOL HORMONE ASSOCIATED WITH INFLAMMATION a steroid hormone secreted by the adrenal glands in response to tissue damage causing inflammation. It is important in the stress reaction and in regulating blood sugar and fat deposition. 2. PHARM HYDROCORTISONE DRUG a synthetic form of hydrocortisone used as a drug to treat inflammatory and allergic conditions and adrenal failure

hydrocracking /hídrō kraking/ n. an industrial process in which the action of hydrogen under high pressure fragments long-chain hydrocarbons to produce more volatile compounds, e.g. petrol and paraffin

hydrocyanic acid /hídrō sī ánnik-/ n. a colourless weak acid that smells of almonds, formed when hydrogen cyanide is dissolved in water

hydrodynamic /hídrō dī námmik/, **hydrodynamical** /-námmik'l/ adj. 1. OF LIQUIDS' MECHANICAL PROPERTIES relating to the mechanical properties of liquids 2. MOVED BY LIQUID operated by a moving liquid —**hydrodynamically** adv.

hydrodynamics /hídrō dī námmiks/ n. the area of fluid dynamics that is concerned with the study of liquids (takes a singular verb) —**hydrodynamicist** /-námmissist/ n.

hydroelectric /hídrō i léktrik/ adj. 1. GENERATED BY WATER POWER generated by converting the pressure of falling or running water to electricity by means of a turbine coupled to a generator 2. OF HYDROELECTRIC POWER GENERATION relating to the generation of electricity by means of water pressure —**hydroelectrically** adv.

hydrofluoric acid /hídrō floo óorrik-/ n. an extremely poisonous corrosive colourless liquid formed by solution of hydrogen fluoride in water. It is used to etch glass, treat metal surfaces, and clean masonry.

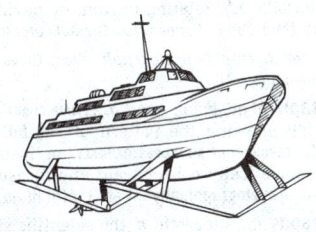

Hydrofoil

hydrofoil /hídrə foyl/ n. 1. HIGH-SPEED BOAT a boat with wing-shaped blades fixed to struts under the hull that lift the boat out of the water as speed increases 2. WING-SHAPED BLADE ON HYDROFOIL a wing-shaped blade that lifts a hydrofoil out of the water

hydroforming /hídrō fawrming/ n. 1. CHEM ENG CONVERSION OF HYDROCARBONS a high-temperature process in which hydrogen, with other catalysts, causes certain hydrocarbons to break down, lose hydrogen, and rearrange themselves into aromatic or cyclic forms. It is used in the petroleum industry to impart better antiknock properties to petrol. 2. METALL METAL SHAPING PROCESS a process in which sheet metal is shaped by a punch forced against a flexible shaped block resting on a fluid-filled bag

hydrogel /hídrə jel/ n. a thick fluid like a jelly, formed by the addition of a substance to water

hydrogen /hídrəjən/ n. a highly reactive colourless gas, the lightest chemical element and the most abundant in the universe, occurring mainly in water and in most organic compounds. Hydrogen is widely used in many industrial processes, especially in the production of ammonia and in the reduction of metal ores to metals. Symbol **H** [Late 18thC. From French hydrogène, from Greek hudōr 'water' + French -gène (see -GEN).] —**hydrogenous** /hī drójjənəss/ adj.

hydrogenase /hī drójjə nayss, -nayz/ n. an enzyme that catalyses reduction reactions by hydrogen

hydrogenate /hī drójjə nayt/ (-ates, -ating, -ated) vt. to add hydrogen to a compound in a chemical reaction —**hydrogenation** /hī dróffə náysh'n/ n. —**hydrogenator** /hī drójjə naytər/ n.

hydrogen bomb n. an explosive weapon of mass destruction in which huge amounts of energy are released by the fusion of hydrogen nuclei

hydrogen bond n. an electrostatic interaction between molecules of compounds in which hydrogen atoms are bound to electronegative atoms, e.g. oxygen and nitrogen. The attraction between water molecules due to hydrogen bonds accounts for the relatively high boiling point of water.

hydrogen bromide n. a colourless gas usually made by combination of hydrogen and bromine in the presence of a catalyst such as platinum. It forms hydrobromic acid in water solution. Formula: HBr.

hydrogen carbonate n. a salt of carbonic acid in which one hydrogen atom has been replaced, usually by a metal

hydrogen chloride n. a colourless fuming corrosive gas made by heating sodium chloride with sulphuric acid or by a combination of hydrogen and chlorine at high temperatures. Hydrogen chloride, which forms hydrochloric acid in water, is used in the manufacture of PVC. Formula: HCl.

hydrogen cyanide n. an extremely poisonous colourless liquid or gas with a characteristic smell of almonds that is formed by the reaction between an acid and a metal cyanide. Formula: HCN.

hydrogen embrittlement n. a process in which a metal is weakened by incorporation of hydrogen in or below its surface, e.g. during plating or etching

hydrogen fluoride n. a colourless corrosive liquid formed by the action of sulphuric acid on a metal fluoride. Hydrofluoric acid is formed when it dissolves in water. Formula: HF.

hydrogen iodide n. a colourless gas formed by direct reaction of hydrogen and iodine in the presence of a catalyst, usually platinum. Formula: HI.

hydrogen ion n. a positively charged ion of hydrogen that is formed by the removal of an electron from a hydrogen atom and is present in solutions of acids in water. The degree to which a compound produces hydrogen ions in solution is measured on the pH scale, 1 being highly acidic, 7 being neutral, and 14 being highly alkaline.

hydrogenize /hī drójjə nīz/ (-nizes, -nizing, -nized), **hydrogenise** (-nises, -nising, -nised) vt. = hydrogenate —**hydrogenization** /hī drójjə nī záysh'n/ n.

hydrogenolysis /hídrəjə nólləssiss/ n. the breaking of a bond in a molecule of an organic compound by the action of hydrogen, accompanied by the addition of a hydrogen atom to each of the fragments

hydrogenous /hī drójjənəss/ adj. containing hydrogen

hydrogen peroxide n. a colourless viscous unstable liquid that readily decomposes in water and oxygen. A strong oxidizing agent, it is used as a bleach, as a mild antiseptic, and as a component in rocket fuel. Formula: H_2O_2.

hydrogen sulphate n. a salt containing the ion HSO_4O^-, formed when one hydrogen atom is removed from sulphuric acid by reaction with a metal, metal salt, or organic group

hydrogen sulphide n. a colourless flammable poisonous gas with a characteristic smell of rotten eggs that is formed by the action of a mineral acid such as hydrochloric acid on a metal sulphide. North Sea gas contains hydrogen sulphide, and so do volcanic emissions. Formula: H_2S.

hydrogen sulphite n. a salt containing the ion HSO_3^-

hydrogen tartrate n. a salt or ester of tartaric acid, e.g. potassium hydrogen tartrate, that forms deposits in wine vats

hydrogeology /hídrō ji ólləji/ n. a branch of geology that studies the movement of subsurface water through rocks, either as underground streams or percolating through porous rocks. Hydrogeology also considers the effect of moving water on rocks, including their erosion. —**hydrogeologic** /hídrō ji ə lójjik/ adj. —**hydrogeological** /-lójjik'l/ adj. —**hydrogeologist** /hídrō ji ólləjist/ n.

hydrograph /hídrə graaf, -graf/ n. a graph showing the change through time in the amount of water flowing down a river

hydrography /hī dróggrəfi/ n. the scientific study of seas, lakes, and rivers, especially the charting of tides and changes in coastal bathymetry or the measurement and recording of river flow —**hydrographer** n. —**hydrographic** /hídrə gráffik/ adj. —**hydrographically** /hídrə gráffikli/ adv.

hydroid /hí droyd/ n. 1. MARINE INVERTEBRATE ANIMAL a marine invertebrate animal with an internal body cavity that lives in colonies, forming growths like tufts. Order: Hydroida. 2. POLYP an asexual polyp that is part of the life cycle of hydrozoans [Mid-19thC. Formed from HYDRA.]

hydrokinetic /hídrō ki néttik, -kī-/, **hydrokinetical** /-néttik'l/ adj. 1. OF HYDROKINETICS relating to or involving hydrokinetics 2. OF FLUID IN MOTION relating to, involving, or typical of fluids in motion

hydrokinetics /hídrō ki néttiks, -kī-/ n. the branch of physics concerned with the scientific study of the properties and behaviour of fluids in motion (takes a singular verb)

hydrolase /hídrə layz, -layss/ n. an enzyme that controls hydrolysis, e.g. an esterase [Early 20thC. Formed from HYDROLYSIS.]

hydrologic cycle /hídrə lójjik-/, **hydrological cycle** /-lójjik'l-/ n. the water cycle (technical)

hydrology /hī drólləji/ n. the scientific study of the properties, distribution, use, and circulation of the water of the earth and the atmosphere in all of its forms —**hydrologist** n.

hydrolysate /hī dróllə sayt/ n. a substance produced by hydrolysis

hydrolyse /hídrə līz/ (-lyses, -lysing, -lysed) vti. to undergo hydrolysis, or make a substance undergo hydrolysis [Late 19thC. Formed from HYDROLYSIS on the model of ANALYSIS, ANALYSE.] —**hydrolysable** adj. —**hydrolysation** /hídrə līz záysh'n/ n.

hydrolysis /hī drólləssiss/ n. a chemical reaction in which a compound reacts with water, causing decomposition and the production of two or more other compounds, e.g. the conversion of starch to glucose —**hydrolytic** /hídrə líttik/ adj. —**hydrolytically** adv.

hydrolyze vti. US = hydrolyse

hydromagnetics /hídrō mag néttiks/ n. = magnetohydrodynamics (takes a singular verb) —**hydromagnetic** adj.

hydromancy /hídrō manssi/ n. the attempt to find out about future events or unknown knowledge by studying the appearance or movement of water —**hydromancer** n. —**hydromantic** /hídrō mántik/ adj.

hydromechanics /hídrō mi kánniks/ n. = hydrodynamics (takes a singular verb) —**hydromechanical** adj.

hydromedusa /hídrōmi dyoóssə/ (plural -sae /hídrōmi dyoóssee/) n. a free-swimming marine invertebrate animal, resembling a tiny jellyfish, that is the reproductive stage of a hydroid

hydromel /hídrō mel/ n. a drink made of honey mixed in water. If allowed to ferment, it turns into mead. (archaic) [15thC. Via Latin hydromeli from Greek hudromeli, literally 'water honey', from meli 'honey'.]

hydrometallurgy /hídrō me tállərji/ n. the extraction of metals from ores by treating them with aqueous chemical solutions, including extraction by electrolysis and ion exchange —**hydrometallurgical** /hídrō metə lúrjik'l/ adj.

hydrometeor /hídrō méeti ər/ n. a weather condition caused by condensation of water in the atmosphere, e.g. rain, snow, or fog —**hydrometeorological** /hídrō méeti ərə lójjik'l/ adj. —**hydrometeorologist** /hídrō méeti ə rólləjist/ n. —**hydrometeorology** /-rólləji/ n.

hydrometer /hī drómmitər/ n. a device used to determine the specific gravity, or density, of a liquid, e.g. battery acid. It consists typically of a sealed graduated tube containing a weighted bulb. —**hydrometric** /hídrō méttrik/ adj. —**hydrometrically** /-méttrikli/ adv. —**hydrometry** /hī drómmətri/ n.

hydromorphic /hídrō máwrfik/ adj. relating to or typical of a soil that has built up in the presence of excess water

hydronium ion n. = hydroxonium ion

hydropathy /hī dróppəthi/ n. the treatment of injuries or disease by applying water both internally and externally —**hydropath** /hídrō páth/ n. —**hydropathic** /hídrō páthik/ adj. —**hydropathical** /hídrō páthik'l/ adj. —**hydropathically** /-páthikli/ adv.

hydroperoxide /hídrōpə rók sīd/ n. an intermediate compound formed during the oxidation of unsaturated organic substances and containing the group -OOH

hydrophane /hídrə fayn/ n. a translucent form of opal that has a pearly lustre and becomes transparent in water —**hydrophanous** /hī dróffənəss/ adj.

hydrophilic /hídrō fíllik/ adj. dissolving in, absorbing, or mixing easily with water —**hydrophile** /hídrə fíl/ n. —**hydrophilicity** /hídrōfi líssəti/ n.

hydrophobia /hídrō fóbi ə/ n. **1.** = rabies **2.** FEAR OF FLUIDS an extremely intense aversion to water, especially the fear of drinking water or other liquids

hydrophobic /hídrō fóbik/ adj. **1.** AFRAID OF WATER relating to or affected by an extreme fear of water **2.** CHEM NOT COMPATIBLE WITH WATER not dissolving in, absorbing, or mixing easily with water —**hydrophobe** /hídrəfōb/ n. —**hydrophobicity** /hídrōfō bíssəti/ n.

hydrophone /hídrəfōn/ n. an electronic receiver that can pick up sound travelling through water by converting acoustic energy into electromagnetic waves. It is used, e.g. to track submarines.

hydrophyte /hídrə fít/ n. a plant that will only grow in water or in a very damp environment —**hydrophytic** /hídrə fíttik/ adj.

hydroplane /hídrō playn/ n. **1.** FAST BOAT a motorboat designed so that it rises up out of the water at high speed and skims along the surface **2.** VANE ON SUBMARINE a horizontal vane on a submarine, used to control its vertical movement ■ vi. (**-planes, -planing, -planed**) **1.** SKIM THE SURFACE to skim along on the surface of the water, especially in a hydroplane **2.** to skid on a wet road because a film of surface water prevents a vehicle's tyres from making firm contact with the road surface. = **aquaplane**

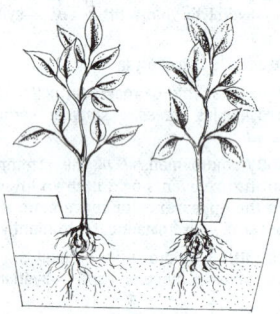

Hydroponics

hydroponics /hídrō pónniks/ n. the growing of plants in a nutrient liquid with or without gravel or another supporting medium (takes a singular verb) [Mid-20thC. Coined from HYDRO- + Greek ponos 'work' + -ICS.] —**hydroponic** adj. —**hydroponically** adv. —**hydroponicist** /-pónnissist/ n. —**hydroponist** /hí dróppənist/ n.

hydropower /hídrō powər/ n. electric power generated using water power

hydroquinone /hídrōkwi nốn/, **hydroquinol** n. a white crystalline compound used as a photographic developer, in paints, in motor oils, and in some medicines. Formula: $C_6H_4(OH)_2$.

hydroscope /hídrə skōp/ n. an optical instrument for observing objects that are deep beneath the surface of a body of water. It is constructed from a series of mirrors encased in a tube. —**hydroscopic** /hídrə skóppik/ adj. —**hydroscopical** /-skóppik'l/ adj. —**hydroscopically** /-skóppikli/ adv.

hydroski /hídrō skee/ n. a hydrofoil on a seaplane, usually ski-shaped and retractable, used to give extra lift on takeoff

hydrosol /hídrə sol/ n. a colloidal solution in which the particles are suspended in water [Mid-19thC. Coined from HYDRO- + SOLUTION.] —**hydrosolic** /hídrə sóllik/ adj.

hydrospace /hídrə spayss/ n. the area beneath the surface of the seas

hydrosphere /hídrə sfeer/ n. the portion of the earth's surface that is water, including the seas and water in the atmosphere —**hydrospheric** /hídrə sférrik/ adj.

hydrostat /hídrō stat/ n. a device designed to regulate the height of fluid in a column or container

hydrostatic /hídrō státtik/, **hydrostatical** /-státtik'l/ adj. **1.** OF FLUIDS AT REST relating to, involving, or typical of fluids that are at rest and the forces and pressures they exert **2.** OF HYDROSTATICS relating to, involving, or

typical of hydrostatics [Mid-17thC. Origin uncertain: probably from modern Latin hydrostaticus or formed from its source Greek hudrostatēs 'hydrostatic balance', from statikos 'causing to stand'.] —**hydrostatically** adv.

hydrostatics /hídrō státtiks/ n. the scientific study of the equilibrium of liquids at rest and the forces and pressures exerted by them (takes a singular verb)

hydrotaxis /hídrō táksiss/ n. the response of an organism or cell to the presence of water or moisture, usually detected as movement —**hydrotactic** /-táktik/ adj.

hydrotherapeutics /hídrō thérrə pyoótiks/ n. the scientific study and theory of the external use of water for healing (takes a singular verb) —**hydrotherapeutic** adj.

hydrotherapy /hídrō thérrəpi/ n. the treatment of disease by the external use of water, e.g. by exercising weakened limbs in a pool —**hydrotherapist** n.

hydrothermal /hídrō thúrm'l/ adj. relating to or produced by extremely hot water, as are, e.g., rock formations —**hydrothermally** adv.

hydrothorax /hídrō tháw raks/ n. an abnormal build-up of fluid in a pleural cavity, e.g. as a result of failing circulation caused by heart disease [Late 18thC. From modern Latin, from Latin thorax 'chest'.] —**hydrothoracic** /hídrō thaw rássik/ adj.

hydrotropism /hí dróttrəpizəm/ n. movement in a plant, e.g. by roots, towards or away from a source of water —**hydrotropic** /hídrō tróppik/ adj. —**hydrotropically** /-tróppikli/ adv.

hydrous /hídrəss/ adj. **1.** CONTAINING WATER containing water or moisture **2.** MIXED WITH WATER containing or combined chemically with water molecules

hydroxide /hí drók síd/ n. a compound containing the hydroxyl group -OH, specifically an acid or base containing the hydroxyl ion. Formula: OH⁻.

hydroxide ion n. = **hydroxyl**

hydroxonium ion /hídrók sốni əm ī ən/, **hydronium ion** n. the positive ion that is formed by the addition of a proton to a water molecule, usually in solutions of acids. Formula: H_3O^+. [Early 20thC. Hydronium coined from HYDRO- + oxonium, from OXY- on the model of AMMONIUM.]

hydroxy /hí dróksi/ adj. containing one or more hydroxyl groups

hydroxyapatite /hí dróksi áppə tít/ n. naturally occurring hydrated calcium phosphate, the mineral constituent of bone and enamel. Formula: $Ca_5(PO_4)_3OH$.

hydroxyl /hí dróksil/ n. the negative ion formed by the attachment of an oxygen atom and a hydrogen atom. Formula: OH⁻. [Mid-19thC. Coined from HYDRO- + OXY- + -YL.] —**hydroxylic** /hí drok síllik/ adj.

hydroxylamine /hí dróksilə meén, hī dróksil ámmin/ n. a colourless crystalline compound that decomposes at room temperature and explodes on heating, used as a reducing agent and in the synthesis of organic molecules. Formula: NH_2OH.

hydroxylate /hī dróksi layt/ (**-ates, -ating, -ated**) vt. to introduce hydroxyl into a compound —**hydroxylation** /hī dróksi láysh'n/ n.

hydroxyl ion n. = **hydroxyl**

hydroxyproline /hī dróksi prố leen/ n. an amino acid derived from proline residues within protein molecules, occurring in gelatin and collagen

hydrozoan /hídrō zố ən/ n. a marine or freshwater invertebrate animal such as a polyp or jellyfish. Class: Hydrozoa. [Late 19thC. Formed from modern Latin Hydrozoa, class name, literally 'water animals', from Greek zōia, the plural of zōion 'animal' (source of English zoology).]

Hydrus /hídrəss/ n. a constellation in the southern hemisphere near the south celestial pole

Hyena

hyena /hī eénə/, **hyaena** n. a carnivorous scavenging mammal resembling a dog, with a sloping back and loping gait, found in Africa and southern Asia. Family: Hyaenidae. [14thC. Directly or via Old French hyene from Latin hyaena, from Greek huaina, the feminine of hus 'pig'.] —**hyenic** adj.

hyetal /hí ət'l/ adj. relating to rain, or having high rainfall [Mid-19thC. Formed from Greek huetos 'rain'.]

hyeto- prefix. rain ○ hyetograph [From Greek huetos, from huein 'to rain']

hyetograph /hí ətō graaf, -graf/ n. **1.** RAIN CHART a chart or graph showing the pattern of rainfall in an area **2.** DEVICE THAT MEASURES RAINFALL an instrument that automatically collects rain and measures its amount —**hyetographically** /hí ətō gráffikli/ adv.

hyetography /hí ə tóggrəfi/ n. the scientific study of rainfall, including its distribution and variation over a specific area

Hygeia /hī jeéə/ n. in Greek mythology, the goddess of health. The daughter of Asclepius, she is often represented as a maiden feeding a snake.

Hygiea /hī jeé ə/ n. the fourth-largest asteroid, discovered in 1849. It has a diameter of approximately 420 km.

hygiene /hí jeen/ n. **1.** PRESERVATION OF HEALTH the science dealing with the preservation of health **2.** CLEANLINESS the practice or principles of cleanliness [Late 17thC. Directly or via French hygiène from modern Latin (ars) hygieina, literally 'healthful art', a partial translation of Greek hugieinē tekhnē; the first word came ultimately from hugiēs 'healthy'.]

hygienic /hī jeének/ adj. **1.** OF CLEANLINESS relating to the scientific study or principles of cleanliness **2.** PROMOTING HEALTH promoting health or cleanliness **3.** GERM-FREE clean or free from disease-causing microorganisms —**hygienically** adv.

hygienics /hī jeéniks/ n. = **hygiene** 1 (takes a singular verb)

hygienist /hí jeenist/ n. sb who has studied and become a specialist in the maintenance of hygiene

hygro- prefix. moisture, humidity ○ hygrometer [From Greek hugros 'moist'. Ultimately from an Indo-European base that is also the ancestor of English humid.]

hygrograph /-graf/ n. an automatic hygrometer that records the humidity of the air

hygrometer /hī grómmitər/ n. an instrument used to measure humidity —**hygrometric** /hígrə méttrik/ adj. —**hygrometrically** /-métrikli/ adv.

hygrophilous /hī gróffiləss/ adj. adapted to growing in damp places

hygrophyte /hígrə fít/ n. PLANTS = **hydrophyte** —**hygrophytic** /hígrə fíttik/ adj.

hygroscope /hígrə skōp/ n. an instrument that shows changes in the humidity of the air but does not measure the changes

hygroscopic /hígrə skóppik/, **hygroscopical** /-skóppik'l/ adj. capable of easily absorbing moisture, e.g. from the air —**hygroscopically** adv. —**hygroscopicity** /hígrəskō píssəti/ n.

hygrostat /hígrə stat/ n. = **humidistat**

Hyksos /híksoss/ (plural **-sos**) n. a member of an ancient nomadic Asian group of people, probably of Semitic ancestry, who conquered and ruled Egypt between 1720 BC and 1560 BC [Early 17thC. Via Greek

Huksōs from Egyptian *heqa khoswe* 'foreign rulers'.] —**Hyksos** *adj.*

hyla /hī́lə/ *n.* a tree frog of a genus found all over the world. Genus: *Hyla*. [Mid-19thC. Via modern Latin, genus name, from Greek *hulē* 'wood'.]

hylo- *prefix.* matter ○ *hylotheism* [From Greek *hulē* 'wood, matter']

hylomorphism /hī́lə máwrfizəm/ *n.* the belief that all material objects are made up of matter, which is only potential, and form, which makes the object an actuality

hylotheism /hī́lə thée izəm/ *n.* the belief that God and the material world are the same

hylozoism /hī́lə zṓ izəm/ *n.* the belief that all matter is living [Late 17thC. Coined from HYLO- + Greek *zōē* 'life' + -ISM.] —**hylozoic** /hī́lə zṓ ik/ *adj.*

hymen /hī́ men/ *n.* a thin mucous membrane that completely or partially covers the opening of the vagina [Mid-16thC. Directly or via French from late Latin, from Greek *humēn* 'membrane'.]

Hymen /hī́men/ *n.* in Greek mythology, the god of marriage, often represented as a youth holding a torch

hymeneal /hī́ me née əl/ *adj.* OF MARRIAGE relating to, involving, or typical of marriage (*literary*) ■ *n.* WEDDING SONG a song or poem celebrating a wedding (*literary*) [Early 17thC. Formed from Latin *hymenaeus* 'wedding song, wedding', from Greek *humenaios*, from *Humēn* HYMEN.] —**hymeneally** *adv.*

hymenium /hī́ méeni əm/ (*plural* **-a** /-ni ə/ *or* **-ums**) *n.* a layer of spore-bearing structures within or on the surface of the fruiting body of a fungus [Early 19thC. Via modern Latin from Greek *humenion*, literally 'small membrane', from *humēn* 'membrane' (source of English *hymen*).] —**hymenial** *adj.*

hymenopteran /hī́mə nóptərən/, **hymenopteron** *n.* an insect such as the wasp, ant, and sawfly that has two pairs of membranous wings and a very thin waist and that lives in socially complex colonies. Order: Hymenoptera. [Mid-19thC. Formed from modern Latin *Hymenoptera*, order name, from the neuter plural of Greek *humenopteros* 'membrane-winged', from *humēn* 'membrane' + *-pteros* from *pteron* 'wing'.] —**hymenopteran** *adj.* —**hymenopterous** *adj.*

hymn /him/ *n.* **1.** RELIGIOUS SONG a song of praise to God, a god, or a saint **2.** SONG OF PRAISE a song of praise to sb or sth other than a deity ■ *v.* (**hymns, hymning, hymned**) **1.** *vt.* SING IN PRAISE to sing in praise of sb or sth **2.** *vi.* SING HYMNS to sing songs of praise [Pre-12thC. Via Latin *hymnus* from Greek *humnos* 'song in praise of gods or heroes', of uncertain origin: perhaps formed from *Humēn* HYMEN.] —**hymnic** /hímnik/ *adj.*

hymnal /hímnəl/ *n.* a book of church hymns

hymnist /hímnist/ *n.* sb who composes hymns

hymnody /hímnədi/ (*plural* **-dies**) *n.* **1.** COMPOSING OF HYMNS the composing or singing of hymns **2.** HYMNS COLLECTIVELY hymns collectively, usually a group that share a specific characteristic such as time of composition or use in a particular church [Early 18thC. Via medieval Latin *hymnodia* from Greek *humnōidia* 'singing of hymns', from *humnos* 'song in praise of gods or heroes' (see HYMN).]

hymnology /him nólləji/ (*plural* **-gies**) *n.* **1.** STUDY OF HYMNS the study of religious hymns **2.** = **hymnody** —**hymnologic** /hímnə lójjik/ *adj.* —**hymnological** /-lójjik'l/ *adj.* —**hymnologist** /him nólləjist/ *n.*

hyoid /hī́ oyd/ *adj.* OF THE HYOID BONE relating to or involving the U-shaped hyoid bone ■ *n.* = **hyoid bone** [Early 19thC. Via French *hyoïde* from, ultimately, Greek *huoeidēs* 'shaped like the Greek letter upsilon', from *hu* 'the letter upsilon'.]

hyoid bone *n.* a U-shaped bone positioned at the base of the tongue and above the thyroid cartilage that supports the tongue and its muscles

hyoscine /hī́ ō seen/ *n.* CHEM = **scopolamine** [Late 19thC. Formed from modern Latin *Hyoscyamus* (see HYOSCYAMINE).]

hyoscyamine /hī́ ō sī́ ə meen/ *n.* a poisonous alkaloid, resembling atropine and used medicinally in similar ways, that occurs naturally in henbane and belladonna. Formula: $C_{17}H_{23}NO_3$. [Mid-19thC. Formed from modern Latin *Hyoscyamus*, genus name of the henbane, from Greek *huoskuamos*, literally 'pig's bean', from the genitive of *hus* 'pig' + *kuamos* 'bean'.]

hyp. *abbr.* **1.** hypotenuse **2.** hypothesis **3.** hypothetical

hyp- *prefix.* = **hypo-** (*used before vowels*)

hypabyssal /híppə bíss'l/ *adj.* used to describe igneous rocks, especially in the form of dikes or sills, created when molten magma rose to the surface of the earth but solidified before reaching it —**hypabyssally** *adv.*

hypaesthesia *n.* an abnormally reduced sensitivity to touch [Late 19thC. From modern Latin, literally 'condition of sensation being below normal', from Greek *aisthēsis* 'sensation'.] —**hypaesthetic** /-théttik, -/ *adj.*

hypaethral /hi péethrəl, hī-/ *adj.* with no roof or a roof that is partly open to the sky, in the style, e.g. of a classical temple [Late 18thC. Formed from Latin *hypaethrus* 'in the open air', from Greek *hupaithros*, literally 'under the air', from *aithēr* 'air' (source of English *ether*).]

hypallage /hī pálləji/ *n.* a figure of speech in which the usual relations of words or phrases are interchanged [Late 16thC. Via late Latin from Greek *hupallagē*, literally 'interchange', from *allag-*, the stem of *allassein* 'to exchange', from *allos* 'other'.]

hypanthium /hī pánthi əm/ (*plural* **-a** /hī pánthi ə/) *n.* the flat or cup-shaped area that bears the stamens, petals, and sepals of some plants, e.g. a rose or cherry [Mid-19thC. From modern Latin, literally 'structure under the flower', from Greek *anthos* 'flower' (source of English *anther*).] —**hypanthial** *adj.*

Hypatia /hī páyshə/ (375–415) Greek philosopher. A follower of Plato, she taught in Alexandria where she was renowned for her learning. Considered a pagan by many Christians, she was murdered by an Alexandrian mob.

hype[1] /hīp/ *n.* **1.** PUBLICITY greatly exaggerated publicity intended to excite public interest in sth such as a film or theatrical production **2.** SB OR STH OVERPUBLICIZED sb who or sth that is extensively publicized **3.** DECEPTION a deception or dishonest scheme ■ *vt.* (**hypes, hyping, hyped**) **1.** PUBLICIZE to promote sb or sth with intense publicity **2.** ARTIFICIALLY BOOST SALES to boost sales of a pop recording artificially by employing people to buy quantities of it at numerous outlets [Early 20thC. Origin uncertain: partly a back-formation from HYPERBOLE and from slang *hyper* 'sb giving short change' (from HYPER-). First recorded in the senses 'instance of short-changing' and 'to short-change'.]

hype[2] /hīp/ *n.* (*slang*) **1.** HYPODERMIC a hypodermic needle or injection **2.** DRUG ADDICT a drug addict

hyped up *adj.* highly stimulated or excited, especially by drugs (*slang*) [Early 20thC. *Hyped* formed from a shortening of HYPODERMIC.]

hyper /hī́pər/ *adj.* (*informal*) **1.** EXCESSIVELY ACTIVE behaving in an overexcited or hyperactive way **2.** EXCITABLE easily excited, or having a highly strung temperament [Mid-20thC. Shortening of HYPERACTIVE.]

hyper- *prefix.* **1.** over, above, beyond ○ *hyperextension* **2.** excessive, abnormally high ○ *hypertension* [From Greek *huper* 'above, beyond'. Ultimately from an Indo-European base that is also the ancestor of English *over* and *super*.]

hyperacidity /hī́pərə síddəti/ *n.* a condition in which there is abnormal production of stomach acid, usually associated with the formation of a peptic or duodenal ulcer

hyperactive /hī́pər áktiv/ *adj.* abnormally active, restless, and lacking the ability to concentrate for any length of time, especially as a result of deficit disorder —**hyperaction** /-áksh'n/ *n.* —**hyperactively** /-áktivli/ *adv.* —**hyperactivity** /hī́pər ak tívvəti/ *n.*

hyperaemia /hī́pər éemi ə/ *n.* an abnormally high level of blood in some part of the body —**hyperaemic** /hī́pər éemik/ *adj.*

hyperaesthesia /hī́ pər eess théezi ə/ *n.* an abnormally heightened sensitivity of some part of the body, e.g. the skin, or any of the senses [Mid-19thC. From modern Latin, literally 'condition of extreme sensation', from Greek *aisthēsis* 'sensation'.] —**hyperaesthetic** /-théttik/ *adj.*

hyperbaric /hī́pər bárrik/ *adj.* relating to, involving, occurring at, or operating at pressures higher than normal [Mid-20thC. Coined from HYPER- + Greek *baros* 'heavy' (source of English *barometer*) + -IC.] —**hyperbarically** *adv.*

hyperbaton /hī púrbə ton/ *n.* a figure of speech in which the expected word order is inverted for emphasis, e.g. in 'you I hate' [Mid-16thC. Via Latin from Greek *huperbaton* 'overstepping', from *huperbainein* 'to step over', from *bainein* 'to step, walk'.]

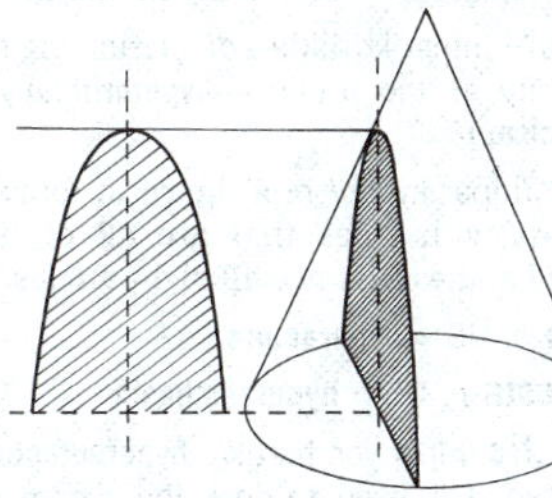

Hyperbola

hyperbola /hī púrbələ/ (*plural* **-las** *or* **-le** /hī púrbəlee/) *n.* a conic section formed by a point that moves in a plane so that the difference in its distance from two fixed points in the plane remains constant [Mid-17thC. Via modern Latin from Greek *huperbolē* 'excess' (see HYPERBOLE).]

hyperbole /hī púrbəli/ *n.* deliberate and obvious exaggeration used for effect, e.g. 'I could eat a million of these' [15thC. Via Latin from Greek *huperbolē* 'excess', literally 'overthrow', from *ballein* 'to throw'.]

hyperbolic /hī́pər bóllik/, **hyperbolical** /-bóllik'l/ *adj.* **1.** OF HYPERBOLA relating to, involving, or typical of a hyperbola **2.** OF GEOMETRIC SYSTEM produced by or relating to a geometric system in which two lines can pass through any point in a plane without intersecting a specific line in the same plane **3.** OF HYPERBOLIC FUNCTION connected with or relating to a hyperbolic function **4.** OF HYPERBOLE relating to, involving, or typical of hyperbole —**hyperbolically** *adv.*

hyperbolic function *n.* any of six functions analogous to trigonometric functions but related to a hyperbola rather than a circle. Hyperbolic functions include the hyperbolic sine, hyperbolic cosine, hyperbolic tangent, hyperbolic cotangent, hyperbolic secant, and hyperbolic cosecant.

hyperbolize /hī púrbə līz/ (**-lizes, -lizing, -lized**), **hyperbolise** (**-lises, -lising, -lised**) *vti.* to use deliberate and obvious exaggeration for effect, or describe sth in obviously exaggerated terms

hyperboloid /hī púrbə loyd/ *n.* a mathematical surface whose sections parallel to one coordinate plane form ellipses and those parallel to the other two coordinate planes form hyperbolas

hyperborean /hī́pər báwri ən/ *adj.* **1.** OF FAR NORTHERN REGIONS relating to, typical of, or in the far northern regions **2.** OF ARCTIC PEOPLES relating to or typical of peoples who live in the Arctic [Late 16thC. From late Latin *hyperboreanus*, from Latin *hyperboreus*, from Greek *huperbore(i)os*, from *boreios* 'northern' or *Boreas* 'north wind'.]

Hyperborean /hī́pər báwri ən/ *n.* in Greek legend, a member of a people who lived beyond the north wind in a land that was always sunny and warm

hypercalcaemia /hī́pər kal séemiə/ *n.* an abnormally high amount of calcium in the blood. US term **hypercalcemia** —**hypercalcaemic** *adj.*

hypercapnia /hī́pər káppni ə/ *n.* an abnormally high level of carbon dioxide in the blood [Early 20thC. From modern Latin, literally 'condition of excessive smoke', from Greek *kapnos* 'smoke'.] —**hypercapnic** *adj.*

hypercharge /hī́pər chaarj/ *n.* a property of elementary particles that is calculated by adding together a particle's baryon number and its quantum property of strangeness [Mid-20thC. Contraction of *hyperonic charge* (*hyperonic* being formed from HYPERON).]

hypercholesterolaemia /hī́pərkə léstərə léemi ə/ *n.* an abnormally high level of cholesterol in the blood. US term **hypercholesterolemia** —**hypercholesterolaemic** *adj.*

hypercorrect /hípərkə rékt/ *adj.* **1.** EXCESSIVELY CORRECT too greatly concerned about correctness **2.** SHOWING HYPERCORRECTION showing or being the result of hypercorrection —**hypercorrectly** *adv.* —**hypercorrectness** *n.*

hypercorrection /hípərkə réksh'n/ *n.* a grammatical mistake or mispronunciation made by correcting sth that is not actually wrong, e.g. saying 'between you and I' instead of 'between you and me'

hypercritical /hípər kríttik'l/ *adj.* criticizing sb or sth too severely or too much —**hypercritically** *adv.* —**hypercriticism** *n.*

hypercube /hípər kyoob/ *n.* a figure in four or more dimensions with sides that are all of the same length and angles that are all right angles

hyperemia *n.* US = hyperaemia

hyperesthesia *n.* US = hyperaesthesia

hypereutectic /hípər yoo téktik/, **hypereutectoid** /hípər yoo ték toyd/ *adj.* used to describe a compound or alloy that contains a minor component in a higher proportion than in the mixture of the same elements that has the lowest melting point

hyperextension /hípərik sténsh'n/ *n.* the movement of a limb beyond its normal range —**hyperextend** *vt.* —**hyperextended** *adj.*

hyperfine structure /híər fīn-/ *n.* the splitting of lines in a spectrum into two or more closely spaced fine lines, caused by magnetic interactions within atoms

hyperfocal distance /hípərfōk'l-/ *n.* the distance between a camera lens and the closest object that is in focus when the lens is focused at infinity

hypergamy /hī púrgəmi/ *n.* a custom in some societies that requires a woman to marry a man of a higher social class than the one to which she belongs

hyperglycaemia /hípər glī seémi ə/ *n.* an abnormally high level of sugar in the blood. US term **hyperglycemia** —**hyperglycaemic** *adj.*

hypergolic /hípər góllik/ *adj.* used to describe a rocket propellant that ignites on contact with an oxidizer [Mid-20thC. Coined from German *Hypergol* 'hypergolic fuel', from *hyper-* 'hyper-' + *erg-* 'work' (from Greek *ergon*) + *-ol* (see -OL).] —**hypergol** /hípər gol/ *n.* —**hypergolically** /hípər góllikli/ *adv.*

hyperhidrosis /-hī-/ *n.* excessive sweating, either generalized or localized to a particular part of the body

hypericum /hī pérrikəm/ *n.* a herbaceous plant that grows in temperate regions, e.g. St John's wort. Genus: *Hypericum*. [15thC. Via Latin, genus name, from Greek *hupereikon*, from *huper* 'over' + *ereikē* 'heath, heather'.]

hyperinflation /hípərin fláysh'n/ *n.* very high and rapid monetary inflation, or the period during which this occurs —**hyperinflationary** *adj.*

hyperinsulinism /hípər ínsyŏolinizəm/ *n.* an abnormally high level of insulin in the blood, causing hypoglycaemia

Hyperion /hī peéri ən/ *n.* **1.** ASTRON MOON OF SATURN the seventh moon of Saturn, discovered in 1848 **2.** MYTHOL TITAN in Greek mythology, one of the Titans. He was the son of Gaea and Uranus and the father of Helios, god of the sun, Selene, goddess of the moon, and Eos, goddess of the dawn.

hyperirritability /hípər írritə bílləti/ *n.* an abnormally extreme response to stimuli —**hyperirritable** /hípər írritəb'l/ *adj.*

hyperkeratosis /hípər kérrə tốssiss/ *n.* an excessive thickening of the outer layer of the skin —**hyperkeratotic** /-tóttik/ *adj.*

hyperkinesia /hípər ki neézi ə, -kī-/, **hyperkinesis** /-neéssiss, -kī-/ *n.* **1.** ABNORMAL MOVEMENT abnormally increased movement in a muscle, e.g. in a spasm **2.** HYPERACTIVITY excessive activity in children, e.g. those affected by attention deficit disorder [Mid-19thC. *Hyperkinesis*, literally 'extreme movement', coined from HYPER- + Greek *kinēsis* 'movement' (see KINESIS); *hyperkinesia*, coined from HYPERKINESIS + -IA.] —**hyperkinetic** /-néttik, -kī-/ *adj.*

hyperlink *n.* a word, symbol, image, or other element in a hypertext document that links to another such element in the same document or in another hypertext document. The hyperlink is activated with a mouse click.

hyperlipaemia /hípərli peémi ə/ *n.* an excessive level of fats or lipids in the blood. US term **hyperlipemia** —**hyperlipaemic** *adj.*

hyperlipidaemia /hípər líppi deémi ə/ *n.* = **hyperlipaemia**. US term **hyperlipidemia**

hypermarket /hípər maarkit/ *n.* a very large self-service store that sells products usually sold in department stores as well as those sold in supermarkets, e.g. clothes, hardware, electrical goods, and food [Late 20thC. Translation of French *hypermarché*, from *marché* 'market', from Latin *mercatus* (see MARKET).]

hypermedia /hípər meedi ə/ *n.* COMPUT a hypertext system that supports the linking of graphics, audio and video elements, and text. The World Wide Web has many aspects of a complete hypermedia system.

hypermeter /hī púrmitər/ *n.* a line or metric foot of poetry that has one or more syllables in addition to those usually occurring in a metric foot or completed line of verse [Mid-17thC. Via late Latin *hypermetrus* from Greek *hupermetros* 'beyond measure', from *metron* 'measure'.] —**hypermetric** /hípər méttrik/ *adj.* —**hypermetrical** /-méttrik'l/ *adj.*

hypermetropia /hípər mi trópi ə/, **hypermetropy** /-méttrəpi/ *n.* = **hyperopia** (*technical*) [Mid-19thC. From modern Latin, formed from Greek *hupermetros* 'beyond measure', from *metron* 'measure' (see METRE).] —**hypermetropic** /-mi tróppik/ *adj.* —**hypermetropical** /-tróppik'l/ *adj.*

hypermnesia /hípərm neézi ə/ *n.* an unusually powerful ability to remember exactly, sometimes a symptom of a psychiatric disorder [Mid-19thC. From modern Latin, literally 'condition of extreme memory', from Greek *mnēsis* 'memory'.] —**hypermnesic** *adj.*

hypernym /hípərnim/ *n.* LING = **superordinate** *n.* 1

hyperon /hípə ron/ *n.* a kind of baryon, a comparatively massive elementary particle that may be unstable or partially stable and is short-lived [Mid-20thC. Coined from HYPER- + -ON.]

hyperopia /hípər ópi ə/ *n.* long-sightedness (*technical*) —**hyperopic** /-óppik/ *adj.*

hyperostosis /hípər oss tốssiss/ *n.* an abnormal growth or thickening of bone [Mid-19thC. From modern Latin, literally 'condition of excessive bone', from Greek *osteon* 'bone' (source of English *osteo-*).] —**hyperostotic** /-tóttik/ *adj.*

hyperparasite /hípər párrə sīt/ *n.* a parasite living on another parasite —**hyperparasitic** /hípər párrə síttik/ *adj.* —**hyperparasitism** /hípər párrəsitizəm/ *n.*

hyperparathyroidism /hípər parə thī roydizəm/ *n.* an abnormally high level of parathyroid hormone in the body, causing various disorders including kidney damage

hyperphagia /hípər fáyji ə/ *n.* a condition in which sb compulsively overeats over a long period —**hyperphagic** *adj.*

hyperphysical /hípər fízzik'l/ *adj.* not governed by the natural laws of physics —**hyperphysically** *adv.*

hyperpituitarism /hípərpi tyŏo itərizəm/ *n.* excessively high activity of the pituitary gland, sometimes causing abnormal bodily growth —**hyperpituitary** *adj.*

hyperplane /hípər playn/ *n.* a figure in hyperspace that is the three-dimensional equivalent of a plane in ordinary space

hyperplasia /hípər pláyzi ə/ *n.* abnormal growth in a part of the body, caused by an excessive multiplication of cells —**hyperplastic** /-plástik/ *adj.*

hyperploid /hípər ployd/ *adj.* having an extra chromosome or section of a chromosome, e.g. in Down's syndrome, in which there is an extra copy or segment of chromosome 21 —**hyperploidy** *n.*

hyperpnoea /hípərp neé ə, hípər-/ *n.* unusually deep or fast breathing, e.g. after physical exertion. = **hyperpnoea**. US term **hyperpnea** [Mid-19thC. From modern Latin, literally 'extreme breathing', from Greek *pnoē* 'breathing'.] —**hyperpnoeic** *adj.*

hyperpyrexia /hípər pī réksi ə/ *n.* a very high fever [Late 19thC. From modern Latin, literally 'extreme fever', from *pyrexia* 'fever' (see PYREXIA).] —**hyperpyretic** /-réttik/ *adj.* —**hyperpyrexial** /-réksi əl/ *adj.*

hyperrealism /hípər reéəlizəm/ *n.* a style in the visual arts that uses realism to achieve a striking effect rather than photographic representation of real life —**hyperrealist** /hípər reéəlist/ *adj.*, *n.* —**hyperrealistic** /hípər reeə lístik/ *adj.*

hypersensitive /hípər sénssətiv/ *adj.* **1.** EASILY UPSET very easily upset or offended **2.** MED SUSCEPTIBLE easily affected by a drug, allergen, or other agent —**hypersensitiveness** *n.* —**hypersensitivity** /hípər sénssə tívvəti/ *n.*

hypersexual /hípər sékshoo əl/ *adj.* interested in or engaging in sexual activity to an abnormal extent —**hypersexuality** /hípər sekshoo álləti/ *n.*

hypersonic /hípər sónnik/ *adj.* relating to or moving at a speed of at least five times the speed of sound —**hypersonically** *adv.*

hyperspace /hípər spayss/ *n.* **1.** MATH SPACE OF MORE THAN THREE DIMENSIONS space with more than three dimensions **2.** THEORETICAL DIMENSION in science fiction, a theoretical dimension in which things not physically possible in ordinary space such as intergalactic travel can happen —**hyperspatial** /hípər spáysh'l/ *adj.*

hypersthene /hípərs theen/ *n.* a green, brown, or black pyroxene mineral, consisting of silicate of magnesium and iron [Early 19thC. From French *hypersthène*, literally 'extremely strong (mineral)', from Greek *sthenos* 'strength'.] —**hypersthenic** /hípərs thénnik/ *adj.*

hypersurface /hípər surfiss/ *n.* a mathematical surface in hyperspace, analogous to a surface in three-dimensional space

hypertension /hípər ténsh'n/ *n.* **1.** HIGH BLOOD PRESSURE abnormally high blood pressure **2.** ARTERIAL DISEASE arterial disease accompanied by high blood pressure

hypertext /hípər tekst/ *n.* a system of storing images, text, and other computer files that allows direct links to related text, images, sound, and other data

hypertext markup language *n.* the markup language used for creating documents on the World Wide Web

hypertext transfer protocol *n.* the client/server protocol that defines how messages are formatted and transmitted on the World Wide Web

hyperthermia /hípər thúrmi ə/ *n.* abnormally high body temperature, especially when induced for therapeutic reasons [Late 19thC. From modern Latin, literally 'condition of extreme heat', from Greek *thermē* 'heat'.] —**hyperthermal** *adj.* —**hyperthermic** *adj.*

hyperthyroidism /hípər thī roy dizzəm/ *n.* **1.** EXCESSIVE THYROID HORMONES the overproduction of thyroid hormones at dangerously high levels **2.** THYROID CONDITION the condition in which basal metabolism increases as a result of overactivity of the thyroid gland —**hyperthyroid** *adj.*

hypertonic /hípər tónnik/ *adj.* **1.** CHEM HAVING HIGHER OSMOTIC PRESSURE having a higher osmotic pressure than another fluid **2.** MED EXCESSIVELY TENSE used to describe a body part, e.g. a muscle or artery, that is under abnormally high tension —**hypertonia** /hípər tốni ə/ *n.* —**hypertonicity** /hípərtō níssəti/ *n.*

hypertrophy /hī púrtrəfi/ *n.* **1.** BIOL ENLARGEMENT BY CELL GROWTH a growth in size of an organ through an increase in the size, rather than the number, of its cells **2.** UNNECESSARY COMPLEXITY exaggerated or unnecessary growth or complexity ◆ *vti.* (-**phies**, -**phying**, -**phied**) BIOL GET BIGGER BY CELL GROWTH to grow larger through an increase in the size, rather than the number, of cells —**hypertrophic** /hípər trốffik/ *adj.*

hyperventilate /hípər vénti layt/ (-**lates**, -**lating**, -**lated**) *vi.* to breathe unusually deeply or rapidly because of anxiety or organic disease and in excess of the body's requirements, causing too much loss of carbon dioxide

hyperventilation /hípər venti láysh'n/ *n.* unusually deep or rapid breathing, caused by extreme anxiety or an organic disease, that leads to loss of carbon dioxide from the blood and often faintness

hypervitaminosis /hípər víttəmi nốssiss/ *n.* a condition in which abnormal effects are caused by taking in too much of one or more vitamins

hypha /hífə/ (*plural* **-phae** /hífee/) *n.* a thread-like part of the vegetative portion of a fungus [Mid-19thC. Via modern Latin from Greek *huphē* 'web'.] —**hyphal** *adj.*

hyphen /híf'n/ *n.* DASH SHOWING WORD BREAK a punctuation mark (-) used at the end of a line when a word must be divided, or to link elements in a compound word or phrase ■ *vt.* (**-phens, -phening, -phened**) = **hyphenate** [Early 17thC. Via late Latin from late Greek *huphen* 'sign joining two syllables or words' (literally 'under one'), from, ultimately, *hupo* HYPO- + *hen*, the neuter of *heis* 'one'.]

hyphenate /hífə nayt/ (**-ates, -ating, -ated**) *vt.* to separate or join words or parts of words using a hyphen —**hyphenation** /hífə náysh'n/ *n.*

hyphenated /hífə naytid/ *adj.* **1.** WITH HYPHEN split or joined by a hyphen **2.** WITH HYPHEN IN SURNAME having a surname containing two or more family names connected by a hyphen **3.** *US* BELONGING TO TWO CATEGORIES belonging to a group of people identified in two ways that may be joined as one term

hypn- *prefix.* = **hypno-** (*used before vowels*)

hypnagogic /hípnə gójjik/, **hypnogogic** *adj.* in or relating to the state of drowsiness immediately before sleep [Late 19thC. From French *hypnagogique*, literally 'of leading to sleep', from Greek *hupno-* HYPNO- + *agōgos* 'leading' (from *agein* 'to lead'; see AGONY).]

hypnagogic image *n.* sth of the nature of hallucination seen or imagined by sb just before falling asleep

hypno- *prefix.* **1.** sleep ○ *hypnopompic* **2.** hypnosis ○ *hypnoanalysis* [From Greek *hupnos*. Ultimately from an Indo-European word meaning 'to sleep', which is also the ancestor of English *soporific* and *insomnia*.]

hypnoanalysis /hípnō ə nálləsiss/ (*plural* **-ses** /-seez/) *n.* psychoanalysis carried out on people who are in a state of hypnosis —**hypnoanalytic** /hípnō ánnə líttik/ *adj.*

hypnogenesis /hípnō jénnəsiss/ *n.* the process of inducing sleep or a state of hypnosis —**hypnogenetic** /híppnō jə néttik/ *adj.* —**hypnogenetically** /-néttikli/ *adv.*

hypnogogic *adj.* = **hypnagogic**

hypnoid /híp noyd/, **hypnoidal** /hip nóyd'l/ *adj.* relating to, involving, or resembling sleep or hypnosis

hypnology /hip nólləji/ *n.* the scientific study of sleep or hypnosis —**hypnologic** /híppnə lójjik/ *adj.* —**hypnologist** /hip nólləjist/ *n.*

hypnopaedia /hípnə peédi ə/ *n.* sleep-learning (*technical*) = **hypnopaedia** [Mid-20thC. Coined from HYPNO- + Greek *paideia* 'education' (source of English *encyclopedia*).]

hypnopedia *n.* US = **hypnopaedia**

hypnopompic /hípnə pómpik/ *adj.* involving, typical of, or in the state between sleeping and waking [Early 20thC. Coined from HYPNO- + Greek *pompē* 'a sending away' (source of English *pomp*) + -IC.]

Hypnos /híp noss/ *n.* in Greek mythology, the god of sleep, and the father of Morpheus, god of dreams [From Greek *Hupnos*, literally 'sleep']

hypnosis /hip nóssiss/ (*plural* **-ses** /-seez/) *n.* **1.** SLEEP-LIKE CONDITION a sleep-like condition that can be artificially induced in people, in which they can respond to questions and are very susceptible to suggestions from the hypnotist **2.** PUTTING PEOPLE IN SLEEP-LIKE CONDITION the technique or practice of inducing a state of hypnosis in people

hypnotherapy /híppnō thérrəpi/ *n.* the use of hypnosis in treating illness, e.g. in dealing with physical pain or psychological problems —**hypnotherapist** *n.*

hypnotic /hip nóttik/ *adj.* **1.** OF SLEEP OR HYPNOSIS relating to, involving, or producing sleep or hypnosis **2.** SUSCEPTIBLE TO HYPNOSIS susceptible to being hypnotized **3.** FASCINATING so fascinating that the attention of people watching or listening is absorbed completely (*informal*) ■ *n.* **1.** STH CAUSING SLEEP a drug or other agent that causes sleep or drowsiness **2.** SB EASILY HYPNOTIZED sb who is susceptible to being hypnotized [Early 17thC. Via French *hypnotique* from, ultimately, Greek *hupnōtikos* 'putting to sleep', from *hupnoun* 'to put to sleep', from *hupnos* 'sleep'.] —**hypnotically** *adv.*

hypnotise *vt.* = **hypnotize**

hypnotism /hípnətizəm/ *n.* **1.** = **hypnosis** *n.* 2 **2.** THEORY OF HYPNOSIS the theory and practice of hypnotizing people [Mid-19thC. Shortening of *neuro-hypnotism*.] —**hypnotist** *n.*

hypnotize /hípnə tīz/ (**-tizes, -tizing, -tized**), **hypnotise** (**-tises, -tising, -tised**) *vt.* **1.** PUT SB INTO HYPNOSIS to put sb into the sleep-like state of hypnosis **2.** FASCINATE to fascinate or charm sb utterly —**hypnotizability** /hípnə tīzə bílləti/ *n.* —**hypnotizable** /hípnə tīzəb'l/ *adj.* —**hypnotization** /híppnə tī záysh'n/ *n.* —**hypnotizer** /hípnə tīzər/ *n.*

hypo[1] /hípō/ (*plural* **-pos**) *n.* a hypodermic syringe or injection (*informal*) [Early 20thC. Shortening of HYPODERMIC.]

hypo[2] /hípō/ *n.* sodium thiosulphate, used in photographic processing as a fixing agent (*informal*) [Mid-20thC. Shortening of *hyposulphite*, another name for thiosulphate.]

hypo- *prefix.* **1.** under, below ○ *hypodermis* **2.** abnormally low ○ *hypotonia* **3.** in a lower state of oxidation [From Greek *hupo*. Ultimately from an Indo-European word meaning 'under', which is also the ancestor of English *up*, *above*, and *opal*.]

hypoacidity /hípō ə síddəti/ *n.* an abnormally low level of acidity, especially in the stomach

hypoallergenic /hípō állər jénnik/ *adj.* not likely to cause an allergic reaction

hypoblast /hípə blast/ *n.* the inner germ layer of an embryo, which develops into the endoderm —**hypoblastic** /hípə blástik/ *adj.*

hypocalcaemia /hípō kal seémi ə/ *n.* an abnormally low level of calcium in the blood. US term **hypocalcemia** —**hypocalcaemic** *adj.*

hypocaust /hípō kawst/ *n.* a system of central heating used by the ancient Romans, in which hot air from an underground furnace circulated beneath floors and between double walls [Late 17thC. Via Latin *hypocaustum* from Greek *hupokauston* 'place heated from below', from *kaiein* 'to burn' (source of English *caustic*).]

hypocentre /hípō sentər/ *n.* ARMS = **ground zero**

hypochlorite /hípə kláwrīt/ *n.* a salt or ester of hypochlorous acid

hypochlorous acid /hípə kláwrəss-/ *n.* a weak unstable greenish-yellow acid that occurs only in solution or in its salts, formed when chlorine dissolves in water. It is commonly used in bleach and disinfectants. Formula: HOCl.

hypochondria /hípə kóndri ə/ *n.* IMAGINED ILLNESS an abnormal, usually long-term preoccupation with health and bodily sensations, accompanied by a deluded conviction of having a serious disease without objective evidence ■ plural of **hypochondrium** [Mid-16thC. Via late Latin (plural) 'upper abdomen', formerly believed to be the seat of melancholy, from, ultimately, Greek *hupokhondrios*, literally 'under the cartilage of the breastbone', from *khondros* 'cartilage'.]

hypochondriac /hípə kónndri ak/ *n.* PSYCHOL SB WITH IMAGINARY ILLNESS sb who is excessively preoccupied with health and persistently believes that he or she is ill or in danger of becoming ill ■ *adj.* **1.** PSYCHOL BELIEVING IN NONEXISTENT ILLNESS excessively preoccupied with health and persistently believing in a nonexistent illness, or relating to the attitudes or state of mind of sb with this condition **2.** ANAT OF THE HYPOCHONDRIUM relating to, involving, or typical of the hypochondrium —**hypochondriacal** /hípə kon drīək'l/ *adj.* —**hypochondriacally** /hípə kon drī əkli/ *adv.*

hypochondriasis /hípə kon drī əssiss/ (*plural* **-ases** /-seez/) *n.* = **hypochondria** *n.*

hypochondrium /hípə kóndri əm/ (*plural* **-a** /hípə kóndriə/) *n.* the area of the upper abdomen on either side of the epigastrium below the lower ribs [Mid-17thC. Back-formation from HYPOCHONDRIA (which was originally a plural form).]

hypocorism /hī pókərizəm/ *n.* **1.** PET NAME a pet name, especially a diminutive or abbreviated form of sb's full name (*formal*) **2.** USE OF PET NAME the use of a pet name to address sb, instead of his or her full name [Early 16thC. Via late Latin *hypocorisma* from Greek *hupokorisma*, from *hupokorizesthai* 'to play the child', from, ultimately, *korē* 'child'.] —**hypocoristic** /hípə kawr rístik/ *adj.* —**hypocoristical** /-rístik'l/ *adj.* —**hypocoristically** /-rístikli/ *adv.*

hypocotyl /hípə kóttil/ *n.* the part of an embryo plant lying between its cotyledons and its radicle [Late 19thC. Coined from HYPO- + COTYLEDON.] —**hypocotylous** /hípə kóttiləss/ *adj.*

hypocrisy /hi pókrəssi/ (*plural* **-sies**) *n.* **1.** FEIGNED HIGH PRINCIPLES the false claim to or pretence of having admirable principles, beliefs, or feelings ○ *It would be sheer hypocrisy for them to turn round and do what they criticise in others.* **2.** HYPOCRITICAL ACT an act or instance of hypocrisy ○ *the legion hypocrisies of the party opposite* [12thC. Via Old French *ypocrisie* from, ultimately, Greek *hupokrisis* 'acting a part', from *hupokrinesthai* 'to dispute subordinately, act a part', literally 'to separate under', from *krinein* 'to separate'.]

hypocrite /híppəkrit/ *n.* sb who gives a false appearance of having admirable principles, beliefs, or feelings ○ *nothing but a bunch of hypocrites* [12thC. Via Old French *ypocrite* from, ultimately, Greek *hupokritēs* 'actor, pretender', from *hupokrinesthai* (see HYPOCRISY).]

hypocritical /híppə kríttik'l/ *adj.* showing, originating from or of the nature of hypocrisy ○ *It would be hypocritical of me to congratulate you on defeating me.* —**hypocritically** *adv.*

hypocycloid /hípə sī kloyd/ *n.* a curve traced by a point on the circumference of a circle as it rolls along the inside circumference of another circle —**hypocycloidal** /hípə sī klóyd'l/ *adj.*

hypoderm *n.* = **hypodermis**

hypodermal /hípə dúrm'l/ *adj.* **1.** OF HYPODERMIS relating to the layer of fatty tissue (**hypodermis**) beneath the skin **2.** UNDER THE SKIN located beneath the skin

hypodermic /hípə dúrmik/ *adj.* ANAT INVOLVING AREA BENEATH SKIN relating to or involving the area of tissue lying beneath the skin ■ *n.* INJECTION OR NEEDLE USED a hypodermic injection, needle, or syringe (*informal*) [Mid-19thC. Coined from HYPO- + Greek *derma* 'skin' (source of English *-derm*) + -IC.] —**hypodermically** *adv.*

hypodermic injection *n.* an injection into tissue under the skin

hypodermic needle *n.* **1.** NEEDLE FOR INJECTIONS a thin hollow needle used with a syringe, suitable for administering hypodermic injections **2.** SYRINGE COMPLETE WITH NEEDLE a hypodermic syringe to which a needle has been fitted (*informal*)

hypodermic syringe *n.* a plastic or glass syringe to which a thin hollow needle is attached, used to inject medicine under the skin or to withdraw fluids, especially blood, from under the skin

hypodermis /hípə dúrmiss/, **hypoderm** /hípə durm/ *n.* **1.** ANAT TISSUE UNDER SKIN the layer of fatty tissue beneath the skin **2.** ZOOL SKIN BENEATH ANIMAL'S SHELL the epidermis of some animals, e.g. arthropods, that secretes a shell or other outer covering **3.** BOT CELLS UNDER PLANT SURFACE the usually supportive and protective layer of cells immediately under the outer covering of a plant [19thC. Coined from HYPO- + *-dermis*, on the model of EPIDERMIS.]

hypoeutectic /hípō yoo téktik/, **hypoeutectoid** /-tékt oyd/ *adj.* containing less of the minor component in a mixture or alloy than in the mixture of the same elements that has the lowest melting point

hypogastrium /hípə gástri əm/ (*plural* **-a** /-tri ə/) *n.* the part of the front of the human abdomen that lies below the navel [Late 17thC. Via modern Latin from Greek *hupogastrion* 'lower part of the belly', literally 'under-belly', from the stem *gastr-* 'belly' (source of English *gastric*).] —**hypogastric** *adj.*

hypogea plural of **hypogeum**

hypogeal /hípə jeé əl/, **hypogean** /-jeé ən/, **hypogeous** /-jeé əss/ *adj.* **1.** UNDERGROUND happening or living below ground **2.** BOT REMAINING UNDERGROUND remaining below ground while the stem of the plant grows. ◊ **epigeal** [Late 17thC. Formed from late Latin *hypogeus*, from Greek *hupogeios* 'underground', from *gē* 'ground, earth' (source of English *geo-*).] —**hypogeally** *adv.*

hypogene /hípə jeen/ *adj.* used to describe rocks that are formed or lying beneath the earth's surface [Mid-19thC. Coined from HYPO- + -GENE.] —**hypogenic** /hípə jénnik/ *adj.*

hypogenous /hī pójjənəss/ *adj.* on or growing on the undersurface of sth, e.g. a leaf

hypogeous /hīpə jée əss/ *adj.* = **hypogeal**

hypogeum /hīpə jée əm/ (*plural* **-a** /-jée ə/) *n.* an underground room or space in an ancient building, or an ancient underground burial chamber [Mid-17thC. Via Latin from Greek *hupogeion*, originally a form of *hupogeios* 'underground' (see HYPOGEAL).]

hypoglossal /hīpə glóss'l/ *adj.* **1. UNDER THE TONGUE** beneath or on the underside of the tongue **2. RELATING TO HYPOGLOSSAL NERVE** relating to or involving the hypoglossal nerve [Mid-19thC. Formed from *hypoglossus* 'either of the hypoglossal nerves', from HYPO- + Greek *glōssa* 'tongue' (source of English *gloss* 'translation').]

hypoglossal nerve *n.* either of the 12th pair of cranial nerves that serve the muscles of the tongue

hypoglycaemia /hīpō glī seémi ə/ *n.* the medical condition of having an abnormally low level of sugar in the blood. US term **hypoglycemia**

hypogynous /hī pójjinəss/ *adj.* used to describe a flower such as a buttercup that has its petals, sepals, or other parts situated below and apart from its ovary [Early 19thC. Formed from modern Latin *hypogynus*, from *hypo-* 'below' + Greek *gunē* 'woman', used to mean 'pistil'.] —**hypogyny** /hī pójjini/ *n.*

hypolimnion /hīpō límni ən/ (*plural* **-nia** /-ni ə/) *n.* the lower and colder layer of water in a lake, largely stagnant and remaining at a constant temperature [Early 20thC. Coined from HYPO- + Greek *limnion* 'small lake', from *limnē* 'lake'.]

hypomania /hīp ō máyni ə/ *n.* a condition of mild mania or abnormal excitement, especially when part of a bipolar manic-depressive cycle —**hypomanic** /-mánnik/ *adj.*

hyponasty /hīpə nasti/ *n.* greater than normal growth on the underside of a plant part, causing the part to bend upwards [Late 19thC. Coined from HYPO- + Greek *nastos* 'pressed close, compact'.] —**hyponastic** /hīpə nástik/ *adj.* —**hyponastically** /-nástikli/ *adv.*

hyponym /hīpənim/ *n.* a word whose meaning is both narrower than and included in the meaning of a more general term. The words 'tulip' and 'rose' are hyponyms of 'flower'. ◊ **superordinate** —**hyponymy** /hī pónnimi/ *n.*

hypophyge /hī póffiji/ *n.* = **apophyge** [From Greek *hupophugē* 'evasion, flight from under', from *phugē* 'flight']

hypophysectomy /hīpōfi séktəmi/ (*plural* **-mies**) *n.* surgical removal of the pituitary gland

hypophysis /hī póffissis/ (*plural* **-ses** /-seez/) *n.* the pituitary gland (*technical*) [Late 17thC. Via modern Latin from Greek *hupophusis* 'offshoot', literally 'growth from under', from *phusis* 'growth' (source of English *physic*).] —**hypophyseal** /hīpə fízzi əl/ *adj.*

hypopituitarism /hīpəpi tyoóitərizəm/ *n.* failure of the pituitary gland to produce hormones, especially a deficiency in growth hormone, which can result in dwarfism —**hypopituitary** *adj.*

hypoplasia /hīpō pláyzi ə/, **hypoplasty** /hīpō plasti/ *n.* the failure of an organ or body part to grow or develop fully —**hypoplastic** /hīpō plástik/ *adj.*

hypoploid /hīpə ployd/ *adj.* having a chromosome number slightly less than the diploid number —**hypoploidy** *n.*

hypopnea *n.* = **hypopnoea**

hypopnoea /hī pópni ə/ *n.* breathing that is abnormally shallow and slow. US term **hypopnea** [Via modern Latin from Greek, formed from *pnoia* 'breathing'] —**hypopnoeic** /hī pop neé ik/ *adj.*

hyposensitivity /hīpō sénssi tívvəti/ *n.* an abnormally low sensitivity to stimuli such as allergens —**hyposensitive** *adj.*

hypostasis /hī póstəssiss/ (*plural* **-ses** /-seez/) *n.* **1.** MED **SETTLING OF BODY FLUID** the abnormal settling of fluid in an organ or other part of the body, as a result of poor circulation, in patients kept in bed, and after death **2.** PHILOS **ESSENCE** the essence or reality of sth **3.** CHR **ONE OF TRINITY** any of the three persons of the Christian Trinity **4.** CHR **ESSENTIAL NATURE OF JESUS CHRIST** the essential nature of Jesus Christ, in which the divine and the human are believed to be combined [Early 16thC. Via late Latin from Greek *hupostasis* 'sediment, foundation', later 'essence', from *huphistasthai* 'to stand under, support', from *histasthai* 'to stand'.] —**hypostatic** /hīpə státtik/ *adj.* —**hypostatical** /-státtik'l/ *adj.* —**hypostatically** /-státtikli/ *adv.*

hypostatize /hī póstə tīz/ (**-tizes, -tizing, -tized**), **hypostatise** (**-tises, -tising, -tised**), **hypostasize** (**-sizes, -sizing, -sized**), **hypostasise** (**-sises, -sising, -sised**) *vt.* **1. GIVE IDEA CONCRETE EXISTENCE** to treat sth conceptual as if it is real **2. PERSONIFY** to personify or embody sth —**hypostatization** /hī póstə tī záysh'n/ *n.* —**hypostasization** *n.*

hypostyle /hīpə stīl/ *adj.* **WITH ROOF ON COLUMNS** with a roof or ceiling that rests on many columns ■ *n.* **COLUMNED SPACE** a building or space with a roof or ceiling that rests on columns [Mid-19thC. From Greek *hupostulos* 'resting upon pillars', literally 'pillar under', from *stulos* 'pillar'.]

hypotaxis /hīpō táksiss/ *n.* the subordinate status of one clause in relation to another separated from it by a subordinating conjunction [Late 19thC. From Greek *hupotaxis* 'subjection', from *hupotassein* 'to arrange under', from *tassein* 'to arrange'.] —**hypotactic** /-táktik/ *adj.*

hypotension /-ténsh'n/ *n.* abnormally low blood pressure —**hypotensive** /-ténssiv/ *adj., n.*

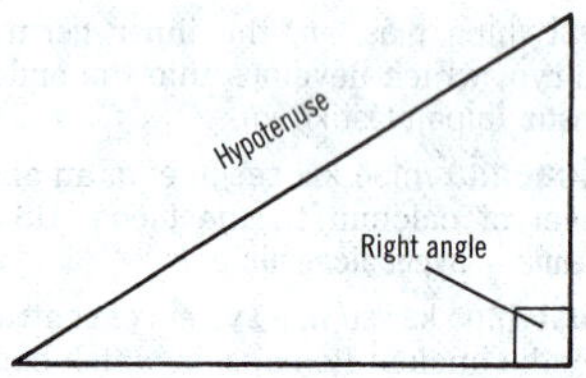

Hypotenuse

hypotenuse /hī póttə nyooz/ *n.* the longest side of a right-angled triangle, opposite the right angle [Late 16thC. Via Latin *hypotenusa* from Greek *hupoteinousa* '(line) stretching under (the right angle)', from the present participle of *hupoteinein* 'to stretch under', from *teinein* 'to stretch'.]

hypoth. *abbr.* **1.** hypothesis **2.** hypothetical

hypothalamus /hīpō thálləməss/ (*plural* **-mi** /-mī/) *n.* a central area on the underside of the brain, controlling involuntary functions such as body temperature and the release of hormones —**hypothalamic** /hīpōthə lámmik/ *adj.*

hypothecate /hī póthə kayt/ (**-cates, -cating, -cated**) *vt.* to pledge property or goods as security for a debt without surrendering ownership [Early 17thC. From medieval Latin *hypothecare*, from late Latin *hypotheca* 'deposit', from Greek *hupothēkē*, from *hupotithenai* 'to deposit as a pledge'.] —**hypothecation** /hī póthə káysh'n/ *n.* —**hypothecator** /hī póthə kaytər/ *n.*

hypothermal /hīpō thúrm'l/ *adj.* **1.** MED **OF HYPOTHERMIA** relating to, involving, or typical of hypothermia **2. FORMED UNDERGROUND** used to describe rocks and minerals formed deep underground at high temperatures

hypothermia /hīpō thúrmi ə/ *n.* **1. ABNORMALLY LOW BODY TEMPERATURE** dangerously low body temperature caused by prolonged exposure to cold **2. DELIBERATELY REDUCED BODY TEMPERATURE** lower-than-normal body temperature induced medically, e.g. to slow a patient's metabolism during heart surgery [Late 19thC. Coined from HYPO- + Greek *thermē* 'heat' (source of English *thermal*) + -IA.] —**hypothermic** *adj.*

hypothesis /hī póthəssiss/ (*plural* **-ses** /-seez/) *n.* **1. THEORY NEEDING INVESTIGATION** a tentative explanation for a phenomenon, used as a basis for further investigation ○ *The hypothesis of the big bang is one way to explain the beginning of the universe.* **2. ASSUMPTION** a statement that is assumed to be true for the sake of argument ○ *That is what would logically follow if you accepted the hypothesis.* **3.** LOGIC **ANTECEDENT CLAUSE** the antecedent of a conditional statement [Late 16thC. Via late Latin from Greek *hupothesis* 'foundation, base', literally 'placing under', from *thesis* 'placing'.] —**hypothesist** *n.*

hypothesize /hī póthəsīz/ (**-sizes, -sizing, -sized**), **hypothesise** (**-sises, -sising, -sised**) *vti.* to offer sth as or form a hypothesis ○ *Let us, for the moment, hypothesize that the earth is flat.* —**hypothesizer** *n.*

hypothetical /hīpə théttik'l/, **hypothetic** /-théttik/ *adj.* assumed or proposed for further investigation ○ *The question is purely hypothetical.* —**hypothetically** *adv.*

hypothetical imperative *n.* an imperative that depends on a condition, e.g. 'be kind to people if they are kind to you'. ◊ **categorical imperative**

hypothyroid /hīpō thī royd/ *adj.* relating to, characteristic of, or affected by hypothyroidism

hypothyroidism /hīpō thī roydizzəm/ *n.* a deficiency or the bodily condition resulting from a deficiency in the production of thyroid hormones by the thyroid gland, resulting in a slowing of the metabolic rate. A severe deficiency can result in myxoedema.

hypotonic /hīpə tónnik/ *adj.* **1. LACKING MUSCLE TONE** with low or diminished muscle tone or tension **2. LOWER IN OSMOTIC PRESSURE** with a lower osmotic pressure than another fluid —**hypotonia** /-tṓni ə/ *n.* —**hypotonicity** /hīpətə níssəti/ *n.*

hypoventilate /hīpō vénti layt/ (**-lates, -lating, -lated**) *vi.* to breathe in an abnormally slow and shallow way

hypoventilation /hīpō vénti láysh'n/ *n.* abnormally slow and shallow breathing leading to a dangerous build-up of carbon dioxide in the blood

hypoxaemia /hī pok seémi ə/ *n.* inadequate oxygen in the blood. US term **hypoxemia** [Late 19thC. Coined from HYP- + OXYGEN + -AEMIA.] —**hypoxaemic** *adj.*

hypoxanthine /hīpə zán theen, -thin/ *n.* a white powdery substance that is a by-product of metabolism in plants and animals. Formula: $C_5H_4N_4O$.

hypoxemia *n.* US = **hypoxaemia**

hypoxia /hī póksi ə/ *n.* an inadequacy in the oxygen reaching the body's tissues [Mid-20thC. Coined from HYP- + OXYGEN + -IA.] —**hypoxic** *adj.*

hypso- *prefix.* height ○ *hypsometer* [From Greek *hupsos*; ultimately related to *hupo* 'under, below' (see HYPO-)]

hypsography /hip sóggrəfi/ (*plural* **-phies**) *n.* = **hypsometry** —**hypsographic** /hipsə gráffik/ *adj.* —**hypsographical** /-gráffik'l/ *adj.*

hypsometer /hip sómmitər/ *n.* **1. INSTRUMENT FOR MEASURING ALTITUDE** an instrument that uses the boiling point of water at different altitudes to measure the elevation of a given point on the earth's surface **2. INSTRUMENT MEASURING TREE HEIGHT** an instrument for calculating the heights of trees by using the principles of geometric triangulation

hypsometry /hip sómmətri/ *n.* the measurement of the elevation of land above sea level —**hypsometric** /hipsə méttrik/ *adj.* —**hypsometrical** /-méttrik'l/ *adj.* —**hypsometrically** /-méttrikli/ *adv.* —**hypsometrist** /hip sómmətrist/ *n.*

hyrax /hī raks/ (*plural* **-raxes** *or* **-races** /hīrə seez/) *n.* a small gregarious plant-eating mammal that resembles a rabbit with short ears and has toenails resembling hooves. Hyraxes live around the Mediterranean Sea and in southwestern Asia. Family: Procaviidae. [Mid-19thC. Via modern Latin from Greek *hurax* 'shrew-mouse', of unknown origin.]

hyson /hīss'n/ *n.* a Chinese green tea [Mid-18thC. From Chinese *xīchūn*, literally 'bright spring'.]

hyssop /híssəp/ *n.* **1. AROMATIC HERB** a fragrant blue-flowered plant of Europe and Asia, similar to mint, cultivated since medieval times as a medicinal herb and still used today in aromatherapy and alternative medicine. Latin name: *Hyssopus officinalis.* **2. PLANT SIMILAR TO HYSSOP** a plant related to or similar to true hyssop **3. BIBLICAL PLANT** an unidentified plant whose twigs are described in the Bible as being used to sprinkle water during Hebrew religious ceremonies [Pre-12thC. Via Latin *hyssopus* from Greek *hussōpos*, of uncertain origin: probably from Semitic.]

hyster- *prefix.* = **hystero-** (*used before vowels*)

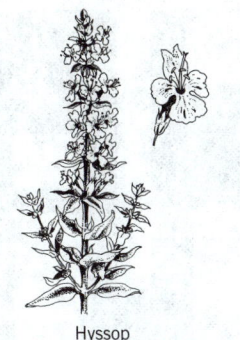

Hyssop

hysterectomy /hístə réktəmi/ (*plural* **-mies**) *n.* a surgical operation to remove a woman's uterus — **hysterectomize** /hístə réktə mīz/ *vt.*

hysteresis /hístə reéssiss/ *n.* a delayed response by an object to changes in the forces acting on it, especially magnetic forces [Late 19thC. From Greek *husterēsis* 'deficiency', from *husterein* 'to be behind, come late', from *husteros* 'late'.] —**hysteretic** /hístə réttik/ *adj.*

hysteria /hi steéri ə/ *n.* **1.** EMOTIONAL INSTABILITY CAUSED BY TRAUMA an emotionally unstable state brought about by a traumatic experience **2.** STATE OF EXTREME EMOTION a state of extreme or exaggerated emotion such as excitement or panic, especially among large numbers of people ○ *press hysteria about ministerial sleaze* **3.** LAUGHING OR CRYING uncontrollable laughter or crying **4.** PSYCHIAT CONVERSION DISORDER conversion disorder (*dated*) [Early 19thC. Formed from Latin *hystericus* (see HYSTERIC).]

──── **WORD KEY: CULTURAL NOTE** ────
Studies in Hysteria, a book by Austrian psychologists Joseph Bauer and Sigmund Freud (1895). A pioneering work in the field of psychoanalysis, it suggests that hysterical symptoms are the result of the memory's suppression of earlier traumatic events. The authors recommend that patients recall and confront these experiences in the hope of achieving catharsis.

hysteric /hi stérrik/ *adj.* = **hysterical** *adj.* **1**, **hysterical** *adj.* **2**, **hysterical** *adj.* **3** ■ *n.* SB WITH HYSTERIA sb affected by hysteria (*dated*) (*sometimes considered offensive*) [Mid-17thC. Via Latin *hystericus* from Greek *husterikos* 'suffering in the uterus', from *hustera* 'uterus' (see HYSTERO-). From the belief that hysteria was caused by malfunction of the uterus.]

hysterical /hi stérrik'l/ *adj.* **1.** AFFECTED BY HYSTERIA in a state of hysteria ○ *hysterical with grief* **2.** RELATING TO HYSTERIA relating to, caused by, or subject to hysteria **3.** UNCONTROLLABLE impossible to hold back or control ○ *hysterical sobbing coming from the next room* **4.** EXTREMELY FUNNY causing uncontrollable laughter (*informal*) ○ *one hysterical sketch after another* — **hysterically** *adv.*

hysterics /hi stérriks/ *n.* (*takes a singular or plural verb*) **1.** LAUGHTER a state of uncontrollable laughter (*informal*) ○ *had them in hysterics with her stories* **2.** STATE OF HYSTERIA a state of hysteria or an episode of hysterical behaviour

hystero- *prefix.* **1.** uterus ○ *hysterotomy* **2.** hysteria ○ *hysterogenic* [From Greek *hustera* 'womb'. Ultimately from an Indo-European word that is also the ancestor of English *uterus*.]

hysterogenic /hístərə jénnik/ *adj.* bringing about a state of emotional instability or hysteria

hysteron proteron /hístə ron próttə ron/ *n.* a figure of speech in which the order of words or phrases is the reverse of what is usual, e.g. 'photographed in white and black' [Mid-16thC. Via late Latin from Greek *husteron proteron* 'latter first'.]

hysterotomy /hístə róttəmi/ (*plural* **-mies**) *n.* a surgical incision into a woman's uterus, especially in order to carry out a caesarean section

Hz *symbol.* hertz

i¹ /ī/ (plural **i's**), **I** (plural **I's** or **Is**) n. **1.** 9TH LETTER OF ENGLISH ALPHABET the ninth letter of the modern English alphabet **2.** SPEECH SOUND CORRESPONDING TO 'I' the speech sound that corresponds to the letter 'I' **3.** LETTER 'I' WRITTEN a written representation of the letter 'I'

i² symbol. **1.** MATH the imaginary number $\sqrt{-1}$ **2.** one **3.** CHEM van't Hoff's factor

I¹ pron. a pronoun used by a speaker or writer to refer to himself or herself (used as the subject of a verb) [Old English ic. Via prehistoric Germanic from an Indo-European word meaning 'I', which is also the ancestor of English ego and egotism.]

I², **i** n. the Roman numeral for one

I³ symbol. **1.** electric current **2.** CHEM ELEM iodine **3.** CHEM ionization potential **4.** QUANTUM PHYS isospin **5.** PHYS moment of inertia **6.** one **7.** LOGIC a particular affirmative categorical statement **8.** MATH unit matrix

I⁴ abbr. Italy (international vehicle registration)

i. abbr. **1.** incisor **2.** indicate **3.** BANKING interest **4.** GRAM intransitive **5.** island **6.** isle

I. abbr. **1.** Imperial **2.** (single column) inch (of an advertisement) **3.** incumbent **4.** independence **5.** Independent **6.** India **7.** Indian **8.** Inspector **9.** Institute **10.** Instructor **11.** intelligence **12.** International **13.** interpreter **14.** Ireland **15.** Irish **16.** Island **17.** Isle **18.** issue **19.** Italian

-i- used as a connector to join word elements ○ fossiliferous [Via Old French from Latin]

IA abbr. Institute of Actuaries

Ia. abbr. Iowa

i.a. abbr. in absentia

-ia suffix. **1.** place names ○ Australia ○ India **2.** a plural ○ Saturnalia **3.** diseases or medical conditions ○ dyslexia **4.** classes or genera ○ mammalia ○ gardenia **5.** things belonging to or associated with sth ○ memorabilia [Directly or via modern Latin from Latin and Greek]

IAA abbr. **1.** indoleacetic acid **2.** International Advertising Association

IAAF abbr. International Amateur Athletic Federation

IAB abbr. **1.** Industrial Advisory Board **2.** Industrial Arbitration Board

IABA abbr. International Amateur Boxing Association

IACP abbr. International Association of Chiefs of Police

IAEA abbr. International Atomic Energy Agency

IAF abbr. Indian Air Force

IAL abbr. International Algebraic Language

-ial suffix. connected with or belonging to sth ○ secretarial ○ imperial [Directly or via French from Latin -ialis and -iale, adjective suffixes]

IAM abbr. **1.** Institute of Administrative Management **2.** internal auditory meatus

iamb /ī am/, **iambic** /ī ámbik/ n. a unit of rhythm in poetry, consisting of one short or unstressed syllable or group followed by one long or stressed syllable. 'The ploughman homeward plods his weary way' consists of five iambs. [Mid-19thC. Anglicized form of IAMBUS.] —**iambic** adj.

iambic pentameter /ī ámbik/ n. the most common rhythm in English poetry, consisting of five iambs in each line. 'The quality of mercy is not strained' is an iambic pentameter.

iambus (plural **-buses** or **-bi**) n. = **iamb** [Late 16thC. Via Latin from Greek iambos 'iamb, lampoon', from iaptein 'to attack in words'. From the tradition that iambic verse was first used by satirists.]

-ian suffix. belonging to, coming from, being involved in, or being like sth ○ Italian ○ Smithsonian ○ mathematician [Directly or via French -ien from Latin -ianus, which was formed by adding the adjective suffix -anus to nouns with stems ending in i]

Iapetus /ī áppitəss/ n. a natural satellite of Saturn, discovered in 1671. It is 1,436 km in diameter and occupies an outer orbit.

IARC abbr. International Agency for Research on Cancer

IARU abbr. International Amateur Radio Union

IAS abbr. **1.** image analysis system **2.** COMPUT immediate access store **3.** Indian Administrative Service **4.** AIR indicated air speed

Iaşi /yaáshi/ city and capital of the county of the same name in eastern Romania, situated on a tributary of the River Prut. Population: 342,994 (1992).

-iasis (plural **-iases**) suffix. forms words for diseases characterized by or caused by sth specified ○ filariasis [Coined from -i- + Latin or Greek -asis, used to form nouns of state or process]

IATA /ee aátə, ī-/ abbr. International Air Transport Association

-iatric suffix. of a particular field of medicine ○ psychiatric

-iatrics suffix. a particular field of medicine ○ paediatrics

iatrogenic /ī áttrō jénnik/ adj. used to describe a symptom or illness brought on unintentionally by sth that a doctor does or says ○ iatrogenic disorders [Early 20thC. Coined from Greek iatros 'doctor' + -GENIC.] —**iatrogenically** adv.

-iatry suffix. a particular field of medicine or medical treatment ○ psychiatry [From Greek -iatreia 'art of healing', from iatros 'doctor']

IAU abbr. **1.** International Association of Universities **2.** International Astronomical Union

IB abbr. **1.** COMM in bond **2.** incendiary bomb **3.** industrial business **4.** International Baccalaureate **5.** invoice book

ib. abbr. ibidem

IBA abbr. **1.** Independent Broadcasting Authority **2.** indolebutyric acid **3.** International Bar Association **4.** Investment Bankers' Association

IBD abbr. **1.** inflammatory bowel disease **2.** ion-beam deposition

I-beam n. a metal beam or girder that is shaped like a capital 'I' in cross section

Iberia /ī beéri ə/ n. **1.** = **Iberian Peninsula** (the) **2.** ANCIENT CAUCASIAN REGION an ancient region in the Caucasus, roughly equivalent to present-day eastern Georgia

Iberian /ī beéri ən/ n. **1.** MEMBER OF ANCIENT PEOPLE a member of one of the ancient peoples who lived either on the Iberian Peninsula or in the Transcaucasian state of Iberia **2.** SB FROM IBERIAN PENINSULA sb who lives in or was born or brought up in Spain or Portugal ■ adj. **1.** OF ANCIENT IBERIANS relating to or typical of the ancient peoples who lived either on the Iberian Peninsula or in the Transcaucasian state of Iberia **2.** OF IBERIAN PENINSULA relating to or typical of Spain or Portugal, or their people or culture [Early 16thC. Formed from Latin Iberia 'land of the Iberes', from Greek Ibēres 'Spaniards'.]

Iberian Peninsula /ī beéri ən-/ peninsula in southwestern Europe, divided into Spain and Portugal, together with Gibraltar

iberis /ī beériss/ n. any of several low-growing Mediterranean plants, widely grown for their white, pink, or purple flowers. Genus: Iberis. [Mid-18thC. From modern Latin, genus name, of uncertain origin: perhaps via Greek ibēris 'kind of pepperwort' from Ibēres 'Spaniards', because several species come from Spain.]

Ibero- prefix. Iberia or Iberian

Ibex

ibex /ī beks/ (plural **ibexes** or **ibex**) n. a wild mountain goat with long knobbly backward-curving horns that lives in Europe, Asia, and northern Africa. Genus: Capra. [Early 17thC. From Latin, of uncertain origin.]

IBF abbr. International Boxing Federation

IBG abbr. interblock gap

Ibibio /i bíbbi ō/ (plural **-o** or **-os**) n. **1.** PEOPLES MEMBER OF AFRICAN PEOPLE a member of a people living in southeastern parts of Nigeria, especially in the region around the port of Calabar **2.** LANG LANGUAGE OF IBIBIO the language of the Ibibio belonging to the Benue-Congo group of languages. About two million people speak Ibibio. [Early 19thC. From Ibibio.] —**Ibibio** adj.

ibid. /íbbid/ abbr. ibidem

ibidem /íbbi dem/ adv. used to cite the same book, publication, chapter, or page previously cited [Mid-18thC. From Latin, 'in the same place', from ibi 'there' + -dem 'that'.]

-ibility (plural **-ibilities**) suffix. = **-ability** [Via French -ibilité from the Latin stem -ibilitat-, from -ibilis]

ibis /ī biss/ (plural **ibises** or **ibis**) n. a gregarious wading bird with a downward-curving bill. Ibises live in warm and tropical climates. Family: Threskiornithidae. [14thC. Via Latin from, ultimately, Egyptian hbj.]

-ible suffix. = **-able** [From Latin -ibilis, adjective suffix]

Iblis /íbliss/ n. = **Eblis**

IBM abbr. intercontinental ballistic missile

Ibis

Ibo /ēˈēbō/ (*plural* **Ibo** *or* **Ibos**), **Igbo** /ˈigbō/ (*plural* **-bo** *or* **-bos**) *n.* **1.** PEOPLES **MEMBER OF NIGERIAN PEOPLE** a member of a people living in parts of western Africa, especially in southeastern Nigeria. During the 1960s, the Ibo formed the breakaway state of Biafra. Fighting with Nigerian troops and severe famine led to enormous loss of life and the Ibo capitulated in 1970. **2.** LANG **LANGUAGE OF IBO** a language spoken in southern parts of Nigeria and in some areas of Niger. It is one of the Kwa group of the Niger-Congo family of African languages. Ibo is spoken by about 17 million people. [Mid-18thC. From Ibo.] —**Ibo** *adj.*

IBRD *abbr.* International Bank for Reconstruction and Development

IBS *abbr.* irritable bowel syndrome

AKG London

Henrik Ibsen

Ibsen /ˈibssˈn/, **Henrik** (1828–1906) Norwegian playwright. The pioneering psychological realism of such works as *A Doll's House* (1879) and *Hedda Gabler* (1890) had a profound impact on 20th-century drama. Full name **Henrik Johan Ibsen**

Ibuprofen

ibuprofen /ī byoo prōˈfen/ *n.* a drug used to relieve pain and reduce inflammation, widely used in the treatment of arthritis and rheumatism. It is a member of a class of drugs known as NSAIDs, nonsteroidal anti-inflammatory drugs, which also includes aspirin. Formula: $C_{13}H_{18}O_2$. [Mid-20thC. Coined from ISO- + BUTYL + PROPIONIC + an alteration of PHENYL.]

i/c *abbr.* **1.** in charge (of) **2.** in command

ICA *abbr.* **1.** **ICA, ICAEW** Institute of Chartered Accountants in England and Wales **2.** Institute of Contemporary Arts **3.** International Coffee Agreement **4.** International Commodity Agreement **5.** International Cooperation Administration

ICAO *abbr.* **1.** International Civil Aeronautics Organization **2.** International Civil Aviation Organization

Icarus /ˈikərəss/ *n.* **1.** MYTHOL **CHARACTER IN GREEK MYTHOLOGY** in Greek mythology, the son of Daedalus, who drowned in the sea while attempting to escape from Crete after the sun melted his wings of wax and feathers **2.** ASTRON **ASTEROID** an asteroid whose orbit is within 30 million km/19 million mi. of the sun, closer than any other orbiting object —**Icarian** /i káiri ən/ *adj.*

ICBM *abbr.* intercontinental ballistic missile

ICC *abbr.* International Chamber of Commerce

ice /īss/ *n.* **1.** **FROZEN WATER** water that has frozen into solid form ○ *puddles turning to ice* **2.** **EXPANSE OF FROZEN WATER** an area, layer, or body of frozen water ○ *a polar bear far out on the ice* **3.** **SUBSTANCE LIKE ICE** any substance resembling ice, e.g. the frozen form of carbon dioxide, known as dry ice **4.** **PIECES OF FROZEN WATER** ice, either crushed or in cubes, used to cool drinks or food **5.** **FOOD** = **water ice 6.** **ICE CREAM** an ice cream (*often used on signs*) ○ *hot dogs, burgers, and ices* **7.** SPORTS **SKATING SURFACE** a prepared frozen surface for ice skaters or ice-hockey players **8.** **COLDNESS** animosity or excessive formality between people ○ *The room's atmosphere turned to ice when the two adversaries met.* **9.** **DIAMONDS** diamonds, or jewellery in general, especially stolen merchandise (*slang*) **10.** DRUGS **ILLEGAL DRUG** a concentrated form of the drug methamphetamine (*slang*) ■ *adj.* **MADE OF ICE** made of, containing, using, or for use on ice ○ *an ice cube* ○ *an ice sculpture* ○ *an ice axe* ■ *v.* (**ices, icing, iced**) **1.** *vi.* **FREEZE UP** to sustain freezing and the development of a thin coating of ice on the surface ○ *The bridge iced, making it dangerous.* ○ *Bridges ice before roads.* **2.** *vt.* **PUT ICING ON CAKE** to cover sth such as a cake with icing **3.** *vt.* **COOL A DRINK** to chill a drink with ice, or stir ice cubes into it [Old English *īs.* From prehistoric Germanic, of uncertain origin.] ◇ **break the ice** to overcome the initial restraint felt by people who have just met or who are meeting under awkward circumstances ◇ **cut no ice** to fail to impress or make a difference ◇ **on ice 1.** in abeyance or in a state of being postponed **2.** being chilled in a freezer, refrigerator, or among ice cubes ◇ **on thin ice** in an unsafe, difficult, or vulnerable situation (*informal*)

ice over *vi.* to become covered with a layer of ice ○ *As soon as the loch iced over, people were out there with their skates.*

ice up *vi.* to become coated with a layer of ice ○ *The car's windscreen will ice up if you don't put it in the garage.*

ICE *abbr.* **1.** ice, compress, elevation (*used as a treatment for injuries and bruises*) **2.** Institution of Civil Engineers **3.** internal-combustion engine **4.** International Cultural Exchange

Ice. *abbr.* **1.** Iceland **2.** Icelandic

ice age *n.* any of the periods in the Earth's history when temperatures fell worldwide and large areas of the Earth's surface were covered with glaciers

Ice Age *n.* the most recent ice age during which most of the northern hemisphere was covered with glaciers, occurring during the Pleistocene epoch

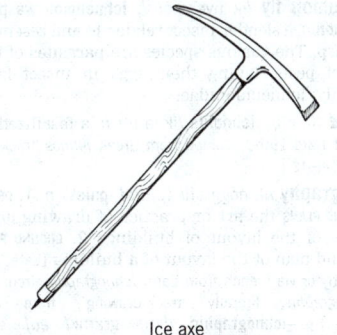

Ice axe

ice axe *n.* a lightweight tool resembling an axe, used by mountaineers to cut handholds and footholds in ice and provide additional balance during a slide down a snow-covered slope

ice bag *n.* a waterproof bag filled with ice and held against an injured part of the body to ease pain or reduce swelling

ice beer *n.* beer brewed by a process that freezes the beer and removes some of the ice, thus increasing the beer's alcohol content

iceberg /ˈīss burg/ *n.* **1.** **MASS OF FLOATING ICE** a large mounded mass of ice that has broken away from a glacier and floats in the sea, with the greater part of its bulk under the water **2.** *US* **SB WITH COOL MANNER** sb who is unemotional or unfriendly (*informal*) [Late 18thC. From Dutch *ijsberg*, literally 'ice mountain'.]

iceberg lettuce *n.* a large round kind of lettuce with pale crisp juicy leaves, somewhat like cabbage leaves, that form a tight head when the lettuce is mature

iceblink /ˈīss blingk/ *n.* a yellowish glow in the sky, occurring when sunlight is reflected by a distant ice field

ice blue *adj.* of a very pale blue colour —**ice blue** *n.*

iceboat /ˈīssbōt/ *n.* = **icebreaker** *n.* **2**

icebound /ˈīss bownd/ *adj.* unable to move because of being covered with or surrounded by ice

icebox /ˈīss boks/ *n.* **1.** *US, Can* = **refrigerator 2.** **FREEZER COMPARTMENT** a small freezer compartment inside a refrigerator **3.** **COOL CONTAINER FOR FOOD** an insulated container or cabinet filled with ice and used to keep food and drinks cool and fresh

icebreaker /ˈīss braykər/ *n.* **1.** **STH THAT RELAXES GROUP** sth such as a joke or game used to ease the initial tension, restraint, or awkwardness of a meeting or social gathering **2.** SHIPPING **SHIP FOR BREAKING ICE** a ship with a reinforced bow used to break up ice and cut a passage through frozen navigable waters **3.** **TOOL FOR BREAKING ICE** any tool designed to break up ice, e.g. a small hammer with a sharpened head

ice bucket *n.* **1.** **ICE-CUBE CONTAINER** a container in which ice cubes are kept cold, ready to be served in drinks **2.** **WINE COOLER** a container, sometimes on a stand, filled with ice cubes or a mixture of ice and water and used to keep a bottle of wine cool

icecap /ˈīss kap/ *n.* a thick permanent covering of ice and snow extending outwards in every direction, e.g. from the North and South Poles or from a mountain top

ice-cold *adj.* extremely cold

ice cream *n.* **1.** **FROZEN DESSERT** a sweet frozen dessert or snack traditionally made with cream and egg yolks and flavoured with a variety of fruits or other extracts **2.** **SERVING OF ICE CREAM** a serving of ice cream, especially an ice-cream cone [Alteration of *iced cream*]

ice-cream cone, **ice-cream cornet** *n.* **1.** **CONE-SHAPED WAFER** a hollow cone-shaped wafer designed to hold a serving of ice cream **2.** **CONE-SHAPED WAFER CONTAINING ICE CREAM** an ice-cream cone containing a serving of ice cream

ice-cream soda *n.* a refreshment consisting of ice cream in any kind of fizzy drink, sometimes with the addition of a flavoured syrup, and served in a tall glass

iced /īst/ *adj.* **1.** **CHILLED OR WITH ICE** chilled or poured over ice cubes **2.** **WITH ICING** decorated with icing ○ *iced buns*

ice dancing *n.* figure skating in which a pair of

Express Newspapers

Ice dancing: Jayne Torvill and Christopher Dean

skaters perform routines based on ballroom dancing, and in which the height of lifts is restricted in competition. Competitive ice dancing also requires that the two skaters remain in close physical contact throughout their routine. —**ice-dance** *vi.* —**ice dancer** *n.*

icefall /íss fawl/ *n.* **1.** FROZEN WATERFALL a waterfall that has frozen solid **2.** SLOPING FACE OF A GLACIER a face of a glacier on which the gradient is so steep that the ice breaks up into a jumble of blocks. ◊ **serac** [Modelled on WATERFALL]

ice fall *n.* an avalanche or fall of isolated chunks of ice from a mountain side

ice field *n.* a large, flat expanse of ice formed where the land surface is level, therefore making it easy for ice to accumulate

ice fish *n.* any of various related medium-sized spiny-finned Antarctic fish that have semitransparent scaleless bodies and a low oxygen requirement that makes them well suited to cold waters. Family: Chaenichthyidae.

ice floe *n.* a sheet of floating ice smaller than an ice field

ice foot *n.* a permanent band of ice along the coast of a polar region

ice hockey *n.* a game played on ice by two teams of six skaters. Points are scored by hitting a rubber disc (**puck**) into the opposing team's goal with a long flat-bladed stick. US term **hockey**

icehouse /íss howss/ (*plural* **-houses** /-howziz/), **ice house** *n.* a building where ice is made, stored, and sometimes sold

Icel. *abbr.* **1.** Iceland **2.** Icelandic

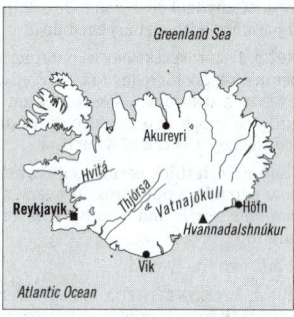

Iceland

Iceland /íslənd/ island republic in the North Atlantic Ocean, 300 km/185 mi. east of Greenland and 1,000 km/620 mi. west of Norway. Language: Icelandic. Currency: króna. Capital: Reykjavik. Population: 269,697 (1997). Area: 103,000 sq. km/39,800 sq. mi. Official name **Republic of Iceland** —**Icelander** *n.*

Icelandic /íss lándik/ *adj.* OF ICELAND relating to or typical of Iceland, or its people or culture ■ *n.* LANG LANGUAGE OF ICELAND the North Germanic language of modern Iceland

Iceland moss *n.* a greyish-brown lichen found in the Arctic and northern Europe, grown as a food and also used medicinally. Latin name: *Cetraria islandica.* [From the fact that it is found in ICELAND]

Iceland poppy *n.* a poppy of Arctic regions, often grown for its white or yellow flowers on leafless stems. Latin name: *Papaver nudicaule.* [From the fact that it is found in ICELAND]

Iceland spar *n.* a transparent form of calcite used in optical instruments for its refractive properties [From the fact that it is found in ICELAND]

ice lolly *n.* flavoured water ice or ice cream frozen onto a stick

ice machine *n.* a machine that produces ice cubes

iceman /íss man/ (*plural* **-men** /-men/) *n.* an explorer or mountaineer experienced in travelling on ice

ice needle *n.* a tiny needle-shaped ice crystal that forms in cold moist air and gathers with others into masses resembling clouds, often at high altitudes and in otherwise clear weather

Iceni /ī seé nī/ *npl.* an ancient people of Britain who, under Queen Boudicca, attempted to overthrow the Romans in AD 61. The Romans fought off the Iceni and Boudicca committed suicide.

ice pack *n.* **1.** MED ICE USED FOR AN INJURY an ice-filled cloth or bag held against an injured part of the body to ease pain or reduce swelling **2.** GEOG PACK ICE an area of pack ice

ice pick *n.* a lightweight hand-held pick for chipping away or breaking up ice

ice plant *n.* **1.** PLANTS PLANT WITH THICK LEAVES AND PINK FLOWERS a clump-forming plant with thick, pale-green leaves and flat heads of pink flowers on long stalks. Latin name: *Sedum spectabile.* **2.** PLANT WITH GLISTENING LEAVES a low-growing succulent plant native to southern Africa with pink or white flowers and leaves that are covered with fine protruding sacs that glisten like ice crystals. Latin name: *Mesembryanthemum crystallinum.*

ice point *n.* the temperature, 0°C or 32°F, at which water freezes under a pressure of one atmosphere

ice rink *n.* an area of frozen water used by ice-skaters, ice-hockey players, and curlers, especially an enclosed prepared surface

ice road *n. Can* a stretch of road that runs on a frozen body of water

ice sheet *n.* a thick covering of ice over a large area that remains for a long period of time

ice shelf *n.* a thick mass of ice covering coastal land and extending out over the sea so that the extended portion floats

ice show *n.* an entertainment performed by skaters on ice

ice skate *n.* a boot with a metal blade fitted along the length of its sole, allowing the wearer to glide over an ice-covered surface

ice-skate (**ice-skates, ice-skating, ice-skated**) *vi.* to glide over an ice-covered surface on ice skates — **ice-skater** *n.*

ice skating *n.* the sport or pastime of using ice skates to glide over an ice-covered surface

ice volcano *n.* a volcano-like formation composed of plastic ice magma, found on the two moons of Uranus

ice water *n.* **1.** US DRINK OF CHILLED WATER very cold water or water chilled in a refrigerator or with ice cubes, served as a drink **2.** MELTED ICE water produced when ice melts

ICFTU *abbr.* International Confederation of Free Trade Unions

I.Chem.E. *abbr.* Institution of Chemical Engineers

I Ching /eé chíng/ *n.* **1.** CHINESE SYSTEM OF FORTUNE-TELLING an ancient Chinese system of divination, based on a book of Taoist philosophy and expressed in hexagrams chosen at random and interpreted to answer questions and give advice **2.** BOOK OF I CHING the book containing the symbols used in I Ching divination and an accompanying text that the reader may consult for help in interpreting the symbols [Late 19thC. From Chinese, literally 'Book of Changes'.]

ichneumon fly /ik nyoómən-/, **ichneumon wasp, ichneumon** *n.* a slender insect related to and resembling a wasp. The various species are parasites of many insect pests, laying their eggs in insect larvae. Family: Ichneumonidae.

ichnite /ík nīt/, **ichnolite** /íknə līt/ *n.* a fossilized footprint [Mid-19thC. Coined from Greek *ikhnos* 'track, footprint' + -ITE.]

ichnography /ik nógrəfi/ (*plural* **-phies**) *n.* **1.** DRAWING GROUND PLANS the art or practice of drawing ground plans of the layout of buildings **2.** GROUND PLAN a ground plan of the layout of a building [Late 16thC. Directly or via French from Latin *ichnographia*, from Greek *ikhnographia*, literally 'track-drawing', from *ikhnos* 'track'.] —**ichnographic** /íknə gráffik/ *adj.* —**ichnographical** *adj.* —**ichnographically** *adv.*

ichnology /ik nólləji/ *n.* the scientific study of fossilized footprints [Mid-19thC. Coined from Greek *ikhnos* 'track, footprint' + -LOGY.] —**ichnological** /íknə lójjik'l/ *adj.*

ichor /í kawr/ *n.* **1.** MED DISCHARGE FROM SORE a watery or slightly bloody discharge from a wound or an ulcer **2.** MYTHOL GREEK GODS' BLOOD the fluid said to run, instead of body fluid, through the veins of the gods in Greek mythology [Mid-17thC. From Greek *ikhōr*, of unknown origin.] —**ichorous** /íkərəss/ *adj.*

ichth. *abbr.* ichthyology

ichthus /íkthəss/, **ichthys** /-thiss/ *n.* a simple symbol that resembles a fish, consisting of two curves that bisect each other. It is a symbol of Christianity. [From Greek *ikhthus* 'fish']

ichthy- *prefix.* = ichthyo- (used before vowels)

ichthyo- *prefix.* fish ○ *ichthyology* [Via Latin from, ultimately, Greek *ikhthus* 'fish']

ichthyofauna /íkthi ə fáwnə/ *n.* all fish that live in a particular area —**ichthyofaunal** *adj.*

ichthyoid /íkthi oyd/ *n.* a fish, or a vertebrate such as a lamprey or hagfish that is similar to a fish — **ichthyoid** *adj.* —**ichthyoidal** /íkthi óllǝjist/ *adj.*

ichthyol. *abbr.* ichthyology

ichthyology /íkthi ólləji/ *n.* the branch of zoology that deals with the scientific study of fish —**ichthyologic** /íkthi ə lójjik/ *adj.* —**ichthyological** *adj.* —**ichthyologically** *adv.* —**ichthyologist** *n.*

ichthyophagous /íkthi óffəgəss/ *adj.* eating or feeding on fish

ichthyornis /íkthi áwrniss/ *n.* a prehistoric toothed bird, similar to a gull, that lived during the Cretaceous period. Genus: *Ichthyornis.* [Late 19thC. From modern Latin, genus name, literally 'fish-bird', from Greek *ikhthus* 'fish' + *ornis* 'bird' (source of English *ornitho-*).]

ichthyosaur /íkthi ə sawr/, **ichthyosaurus** /íkthi ə sáwrəss/ (*plural* **-ruses** *or* **-ri** /-sáwr ī/) *n.* a prehistoric reptile with a long snout and paddle-shaped limbs that lived in the sea during the Mesozoic era. Order: Ichthyosauria. [Mid-19thC. From modern Latin *Ichthyosauria*, order name, literally 'fish-lizards', from Greek *ikhthus* 'fish' + *sauros* 'lizard'.] —**ichthyosaurian** /íkthi ə sáwri ən/ *adj.*

ichthyosis /íkthi óssiss/ *n.* a disease that causes the skin to become dry, thick, and scaly

ichthys *n.* = ichthus

-ician *suffix.* one who practises or specializes in ○ *musician* ○ *statistician* [From Old French *-icien*, from *-ique* (see -IC)]

icicle /íssik'l/ *n.* **1.** HANGING ICE a hanging tapered rod of ice, formed when dripping water freezes **2.** SB VERY RESERVED sb who is aloof or unemotional (*informal*) [14thC. From ICE + obsolete *ickle* 'icicle', from Old English *gicel*, of prehistoric Germanic origin.]

icily /íssili/ *adv.* in a very aloof or unfriendly manner

iciness /íssinəss/ *n.* **1.** BEING COVERED WITH ICE the state of being covered with ice **2.** EXTREME COLDNESS extreme coldness, usually to the point of freezing ○ *the wind's iciness* **3.** UNFRIENDLINESS extreme aloofness or unfriendliness of manner ○ *the iciness of her tone*

icing /íssing/ *n.* **1.** FOOD GLAZING FOR CAKES a sugar-based decorative coating for cakes, either soft or hardened, made by mixing powdered sugar with water or another binding substance and often other ingredients or flavourings **2.** METEOROL FORMATION OF ICE the formation of ice on surfaces, e.g. on aircraft or ships ○ *Some roads will be liable to icing.* **3.** ICE HOCKEY SHOOTING PUCK INTO OPPOSING TERRITORY in ice hockey, the action of shooting the puck out of defensive territory and far into the opposing team's territory ◊ **the icing on the cake** sth additional that makes sth that was already good even better

icing sugar *n.* powdered white sugar used to make icing, for sweetening, or for sprinkling. US term **confectioners' sugar**

ICJ *abbr.* International Court of Justice

icky /íki/ (**-ier, -iest**) *adj.* (*informal*) **1.** NASTY generally nasty or unpleasant ○ *I had an icky feeling in their presence.* **2.** STICKY disgustingly and messily sticky **3.** SENTIMENTAL sentimental in a silly or childish way ○ *a script with some pretty icky lines* [Early 20thC. Origin uncertain.] —**ickiness** *n.*

ICM abbr. **1.** Institute of Credit Management **2.** Intergovernmental Committee for Migrations (*part of the UN*)

Icon: Eastern Orthodox icon of *Christus Acheiropoietus* in the Cathedral of the Assumption, Moscow

icon /ˈīˌkon/ *n.* **1.** **icon, ikon** RELIG **IMAGE OF HOLY PERSON** a holy picture, carving, or statue of Jesus Christ, the Virgin Mary, or a saint, especially an oil painting on a wooden panel, used in worship in the Eastern Orthodox churches **2.** **SB FAMOUS FOR STH** sb or sth widely and uncritically admired, especially sb or sth symbolizing a movement or field of activity ○ *the all-time rock 'n' roll icon.* **3.** COMPUT **PICTURE ON COMPUTER SCREEN** a small image on a computer screen that represents sth, e.g. a program or device that is activated by a mouse click or a trash bin for unwanted files ○ *Open the program by clicking on its icon.* **4.** COMMUNICATION **RECOGNIZABLE SYMBOL** a picture or symbol that is universally recognized to be representative of sth ○ *The icon of a walking person is the international symbol to indicate that it's safe to cross the street.* [Mid-16thC. Via Latin from Greek *eikōn* 'likeness, image'. Ultimately from an Indo-European word meaning 'to be like'.]

icon- *prefix.* = **icono-**

iconic /ˈī kónnik/ *adj.* **1.** **CHARACTERIZED BY FAME** relating to or characteristic of sb or sth admired as an icon ○ *Their fame has grown to iconic proportions.* **2.** RELIG **TYPICAL OF A RELIGIOUS ICON** relating to or characteristic of a religious icon ○ *iconic images* **3.** SCULPTURE **CONVENTIONAL** made in a conventional style or pose, especially that of ancient Greek statues of athletes — **iconically** *adv.*

iconic memory *n.* a form of memory in which objects are retained briefly but clearly as a visual image after the stimulus has been removed. It develops between the ages of two and six when a child begins to use images to stand for objects.

icono- *prefix.* icon, image ○ *iconolatry* ○ *iconoscope* [From Greek *eikōn*]

iconoclasm /ˈī kónnə klazəm/ *n.* **1.** **CHALLENGE TO TRADITION** a challenge to and overturning of traditional beliefs, customs, and values **2.** RELIG **BREAKING OF RELIGIOUS IMAGES** the destruction of religious images used in worship, or opposition to their use in worship

iconoclast /ˈī kónnə klast/ *n.* **1.** **SB CHALLENGING TRADITION** sb who challenges or overturns traditional beliefs, customs, and values **2.** RELIG **DESTROYER OF RELIGIOUS IMAGES** sb who destroys religious images used in worship or is opposed to their use in worship **3.** HIST **HERETIC IN GREEK ORTHODOX CHURCH** a member of an 8th-century movement in the Greek Orthodox Church that tried to end the use of icons [Mid-17thC. Via medieval Latin *iconoclastes* from medieval Greek *eikonoklastēs* 'image-breaker', from *eikōn* (see ICON) + *klan* 'to break'.] — **iconoclastic** /ˈī kónnə klástik/ *adj.* — **iconoclastically** /-klástikli/ *adv.*

iconography /ˈīkə nóggrəfi/ *n.* **1.** COMMUNICATION **SET OF RECOGNIZED IMAGES** the set of symbols or images used in a particular field of activity, e.g. music or cinema, and recognized by people as having a particular meaning ○ *In the 1960s, peace signs and long hair were part of the iconography of rebellion.* **2.** PAINTING **SYMBOLS IN PAINTING** the symbols and images used conventionally in a genre of painting, or the study and interpretation of these symbols and images ○ *the iconography used in Renaissance paintings of the Virgin and Child* **3.** **IMAGES OF SB OR STH SPECIFIC** the

collection, description, or study of images of sb or sth specific — **iconographer** *n.* — **iconographic** /ˈī kónnə gráffik/ *adj.* — **iconographical** /-gráffik'l/ *adj.*

iconolatry /ˈīkə nóllətri/ *n.* the worshipping of religious images rather than of what they represent (*disapproving*) — **iconolater** *n.*

iconology /ˈīkə nólləji/ *n.* **1.** **STUDY OF SYMBOLS** the study of artistic images and their symbolism and interpretation **2.** **IMAGES COLLECTIVELY** images or symbols, or the images or symbols used in a particular field of activity — **iconological** /ˈī kónnə lójjik'l/ *adj.* — **iconologist** /ˈīkə nóllǝjist/ *n.*

iconoscope /ˈī kónnə skōp/ *n.* an early form of television camera tube in which an image is converted into electrical impulses [Mid-19thC. The earliest meaning of the word was 'instrument for giving an impression of depth to flat pictures'.]

iconostasis /ˈīkə nóstəssiss/ (*plural* **-ses** /-seez/), **iconostas** /ˈī kónnə stass/ (*plural* **-tases**) *n.* a screen on which icons are mounted, used in Eastern Orthodox churches to separate the area around the altar from the main part of the church [Mid-19thC. From modern Greek *eikonostasis*, literally 'place where images stand'.]

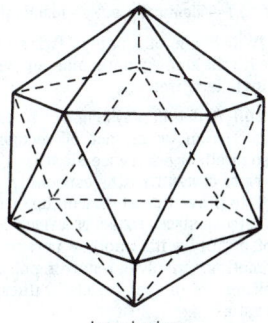

Icosahedron

icosahedron /ˈīkəssə héedrən/ (*plural* **-drons** *or* **-dra** /-héedrə/) *n.* a solid geometric figure having 20 sides or faces [Late 16thC. Via late Latin *icosahedrum* from Greek *eikosaedron*, from *eikosi* 'twenty' + *hedra* 'base'.] — **icosahedral** *adj.*

icositetrahedron /ˈīkəssi téttrə héedrən/ (*plural* **-drons** *or* **-dra** /-edrə/) *n.* a solid geometric figure having 24 sides or faces [Mid-19thC. Coined from Greek *eikosi* 'twenty' + *tetra-* 'four' + -HEDRON.]

ICPO *abbr.* International Criminal Police Organization

ICR *abbr.* **1.** COMPUT intelligent character recognition **2.** Institute for Cancer Research

ICRC *abbr.* International Committee of the Red Cross

ICS *abbr.* **1.** instalment credit selling **2.** Institute of Chartered Shipbrokers **3.** International Chamber of Shipping **4.** investors' compensation scheme

-ics *suffix.* **1.** a science, art, or knowledge ○ *physics* ○ *mathematics* **2.** an activity or action ○ *callisthenics* [From -IC + -S; translation of Greek *-ika* 'matters pertaining to a certain subject', hence used as name of treatises]

icteric /ik térrik/ *adj.* affected with, relating to, or resembling jaundice

icterus /íktərəss/ *n.* jaundice (*technical*) [Early 18thC. Via Latin from Greek *ikteros*, of unknown origin.] — **icteric** /ik térrik/ *adj.*

ictus /íktəss/ (*plural* **-tuses** *or* **-tus**) *n.* **1.** MED **SEIZURE** a seizure (*technical*) **2.** POETRY **STRESS ON SYLLABLES** the stress that falls on syllables in poetic rhythm [Early 18thC. From Latin, originally the past participle of *icere* 'to strike', of unknown origin.] — **ictal** *adj.*

ICU *abbr.* intensive care unit

ICWA *abbr.* Institute of Cost and Works Accountants

icy /íssi/ (**-ier**, **-iest**) *adj.* **1.** **ICE-COVERED** covered in ice, or involving the presence of ice **2.** **VERY COLD** extremely cold, like ice ○ *Your hands are icy.* **3.** **UNFRIENDLY** very aloof or unfriendly ○ *his reserved manner and icy voice*

id /id/ *n.* in Freudian psychoanalytic theory, the part of the psyche that is unconscious and the source of primitive instinctive impulses and drives. The

other parts of the psyche are the ego and the superego. [Early 20thC. From Latin, 'it'; translation of German *es*.]

I'd /īd/ *contr.* **1.** **I HAD** I had ○ *I'd forgotten you were coming.* **2.** **I WOULD** I would or should

ID[1] *abbr.* **1.** identification **2.** infectious disease(s) **3.** **ID, i.d.** inner diameter **4.** **ID, i.d.** inside diameter or internal diameter **5.** internal diameter **6.** Intelligence Department **7.** **ID, i.d.** ANAT intradermal **8.** MAIL Idaho

ID[2] (**IDs, IDing, IDed**) *vt.* to identify sb, or check sb's identity (*informal*) ○ *police to ID the suspect*

id. *abbr.* idem

Id. *abbr.* Idaho

-id *suffix.* **1.** objects, especially meteors, that appear to come from a specified constellation ○ *Perseids* **2.** PHYS particular kinds of particle or body ○ *energid* **3.** ZOOL a member of a zoological family ○ *camelid* **4.** a member of a dynasty ○ *Abbasid* [Directly or via French *-ide* from Latin *-ides*, from Greek *-idēs* 'offspring of']

IDA *abbr.* International Development Association

Ida. *abbr.* Idaho

Idaho

Idaho /ídəhō/ state in the western United States bordered by Montana, Nevada, Oregon, Utah, Washington, and Wyoming, and British Columbia, Canada. Capital: Boise. Population: 1,210,232 (1997). Area: 216,456 sq. km/83,574 sq. mi. — **Idahoan** /ídə hō ən, ídə hō ən/ *adj., n.*

Id al-Adha /íd al a daá/ *n.* an important Islamic annual festival, the Feast of the Sacrifice, commemorating Abraham's sacrifice of the lamb in place of his son Isaac

Id al-Fitr /íd al fíttrə/ *n.* an important Islamic annual festival and public holiday, the Feast of Breaking the Fast, marking the end of the Ramadan fast

Ida Mountains /ídə-/ mountain range in northwestern Turkey, southeast of the ancient site of Troy. The highest peak is Mount Gargarus, 1,767 m/5,797 ft.

IDB *abbr.* **1.** S Africa illicit diamond buyer **2.** S Africa illicit diamond buying **3.** Industrial Development Bank

IDC *abbr.* industrial development certificate

ID card *n.* a card identifying its carrier, having on it such information as name, age, and often an address and a physical description or photograph (*informal*)

IDD *abbr.* **1.** TELECOM international direct dialling **2.** insulin-dependent diabetes

IDDD *abbr.* international direct distance dialling

-ide *suffix.* **1.** class of elements or compounds ○ *actinides* **2.** organic compound derived from another compound ○ *anhydride* [From OXIDE]

idea /ī déeə/ *n.* **1.** **OPINION** a personal opinion or belief ○ *Do you have any ideas on how the problem should be tackled?* **2.** **SUGGESTION** a thought to be presented as a suggestion ○ *It was her idea to plant daisies.* **3.** **IMPRESSION** an impression or knowledge of sth ○ *We have no idea how much it would cost.* **4.** **PLAN** a realization of a possible way of doing sth or of sth to be done ○ *Watching the beaver building its dam gave me an idea.* **5.** **AIM** the aim or purpose of a project or plan ○ *The idea of the new scheme is to keep young people in school.* **6.** **GIST** the gist or précis of sth such as a book, report, project, or plan ○ *give you only a broad idea now, with a detailed outline* *to follow* 7. THOUGHT a thought about or mental picture of sth such as a future or possible event ○ *Sometimes the idea of having to speak in public is worse than actually doing it.* 8. CONCEPT a concept that exists in the mind only ○ *discussing the idea of morality* 9. MENTAL IMAGE a mental image that reflects reality 10. MOTIF a theme or motif that forms the basis of a piece of music throughout its development [14thC. Via Latin from Greek, 'look', formed from *idein* 'to see' (source of English *identity*). The meaning developed in Greek from 'appearance' via 'image' to 'mental image, notion'.] —**idealess** *adj.* ◇ **get ideas** to become ambitious or begin thinking undesirable thoughts (*informal*) ◇ **have no idea** to know nothing at all, especially about a particular subject ◇ **what's the big idea?** used, often angrily, to ask about sb's intention or about what is happening

ideal /ī dēe əl/ *n.* 1. PERFECT EXAMPLE an excellent or perfect example of sth or sb, or sth that is considered a perfect example ○ *By her third film, she had become the world's ideal of beauty and grace.* 2. PRINCIPLE a standard or principle to which people aspire ○ *political ideals* 3. IMAGINARY OBJECT OR CONCEPT a concept that exists in the imagination only ■ *adj.* 1. BEST serving as the best or most perfect example 2. PERFECT perfect but existing only in the imagination ○ *In an ideal world, such horrors wouldn't happen.* 3. EXCELLENT excellent or perfectly suitable ○ *A later meeting would be ideal for me.* [15thC. Directly or via French *idéal* from late Latin *idealis*, from Latin *idea* (see IDEA). The English word originally meant 'existing as an archetype'.] —**idealless** *adj.* —**idealness** *n.*

ideal gas *n.* a hypothetical gas that obeys the gas laws perfectly at all temperatures and pressures

idealise *vt.* = **idealize**

idealism /ī dēe əlizəm/ *n.* 1. BELIEF IN PERFECTION belief in and pursuit of perfection as an attainable goal ○ *youthful idealism* 2. LIVING BY HIGH IDEALS aspiring to or living in accordance with high standards or principles 3. PHILOS BELIEF THAT MATERIAL THINGS ARE IMAGINARY the philosophical belief that material things do not exist independently but only as constructions in the mind

idealist /ī dēe əlist/ *n.* 1. SB WITH HIGH IDEALS sb who aspires to or lives in accordance with high standards or principles 2. IMPRACTICAL PERSON sb who rejects practical considerations in favour of the pursuit of perfection ○ *too much of an idealist to compromise with her opponents* 3. PHILOS BELIEVER IN PHILOSOPHICAL IDEALISM a believer in a philosophy holding that material objects do not exist independently of the mind —**idealistic** /ī dēe ə lístik/ *adj.* —**idealistically** *adv.*

ideality /ídi állәti/ *n.* 1. CONDITION OF BEING IDEAL the condition or quality of being ideal 2. STATUS AS IDEA existence as an idea only, rather than as a concrete object

idealize /ī dēe ə līz/ (-izes, -izing, -ized), **idealise** (-ises, -ising, -ised) *vt.* to think of or represent sb or sth as being perfect, ignoring any imperfections that exist or may exist in reality ○ *paintings that idealize feminine beauty* —**idealization** /-lī záysh'n/ *n.* —**idealizer** /ī dēe ə līzər/ *n.*

idealized /ī dēe ə līzd/, **idealised** *adj.* thought of or presented as perfect, and ignoring, hiding, or smoothing out any flaws or defects that exist or may exist in reality ○ *an idealized view of human relationships* ○ *an idealized, disclike shape*

ideally /ī dēe əli/ *adv.* 1. IN AN IDEAL SITUATION if everything were perfect or as desired ○ *Ideally, I'd like to finish the job by next week.* 2. PERFECTLY in a perfect manner ○ *She is ideally suited to the post.* 3. THEORETICALLY in theory or in the imagination

ideate /ídi ayt/ (-ates, -ating, -ated) *vti.* to form an idea of sth, or form ideas [Early 17thC. From medieval Latin *ideat-*, the past participle stem of *ideare* 'to form an idea or conception', from Latin *idea* (see IDEA).] —**ideation** /ídi áysh'n/ *n.* —**ideational** /-áysh'nəl/ *adj.* —**ideationally** *adv.* —**ideative** /ídi ətiv, -i aytiv/ *adj.*

idée fixe /ée day féeks/ (*plural* **idées fixes** /ée day fíks/) *n.* an idea that remains fixed and unchanging in the mind and often becomes an obsession [From French, literally 'fixed idea']

idée reçue /ée day rə syóo/ (*plural* **idées reçues** /-syóo/) *n.* a conventional or commonplace idea [From French, literally 'received idea']

idem /íddem, í-/ *pron.* the same, especially a book, article, or chapter previously referred to [14thC. From Latin, 'same' (see IDENTITY).]

idempotent /ī dem pōt'nt, ī démpətənt/ *adj.* remaining unchanged when multiplied by itself [Late 19thC. From Latin *idem* 'same' (see IDENTITY) + the stem *potent-* 'powerful' (source of English *potent*).]

identic /ī déntik/ *adj.* 1. POL WITH THE SAME DIPLOMATIC FORM used to describe diplomatic notes sent, or diplomatic action taken, by two or more governments in exactly the same form 2. IDENTICAL identical (*archaic*) [Mid-17thC. From medieval Latin *identicus* 'identical', from *ident-*, combining form of Latin *idem* 'same' (see IDENTITY).]

identical /ī déntik'l/ *adj.* 1. ALIKE IN EVERY WAY exactly the same as or equal to sth else, or alike in every respect 2. ONE AND THE SAME being one single person or thing though appearing in different guises or disguises [Late 16thC. Formed from medieval Latin *identicus*, from *ident-*, combining form of Latin *idem* 'same' (see IDENTITY).] —**identically** *adv.* —**identicalness** *n.*

identical twin *n.* one of a pair of twins of the same sex and with the same genetic makeup who develop from a single fertilized egg

identification /ī déntifi káysh'n/ *n.* 1. CONNECTION OF IDENTITY the action or an act of recognizing and naming sb or sth or otherwise identifying him, her, or it 2. PROOF OF IDENTITY sth, especially a card or document, to prove that sb is who he or she claims to be 3. PSYCHOL STRONG FEELING OF AFFINITY a powerful feeling of affinity with another person or group, which sometimes involves regarding sb as a model and adopting his or her beliefs, values, or other characteristics

identification card *n.* = **identity card**

identification parade *n.* a group of people, including a suspect, shown by police to a witness to a crime in order to discover whether the witness can identify the person who committed it. US term **lineup** *n.* 3

identifier /ī dénti fī ər/ *n.* a symbol that identifies, indicates, or names a body of data

identify /ī dénti fī/ (-fies, -fying, -fied) *vt.* 1. RECOGNIZE AND NAME to recognize sb or sth and to be able to say who or what he, she, or it is 2. CONSIDER AS THE SAME to consider two or more things as being entirely or essentially the same [Mid-17thC. Directly or via French *identifier* from medieval Latin *identificare*, literally 'to make the same', from *ident-* (see IDENTITY).] —**identifiability** /ī dénti fī ə bílləti/ *n.* —**identifiable** /-fī əb'l/ *adj.* —**identifiably** *adv.*

identify with *v.* 1. *vt.* FEEL AFFINITY WITH to feel a strong sympathetic or imaginative bond with sb or sth and a sense of understanding and sharing his, her, or its nature or concerns 2. ASSOCIATE ONE THING WITH ANOTHER to consider sb or sth as closely linked with sb or sth, e.g. a school of thought or political movement (*often passive*)

Identikit /ī déntikit/ *tdmk.* a trademark for a set of pictures showing varied facial features that can be combined to produce a human likeness, e.g. of a missing person or of a criminal suspect

identity /ī déntəti/ (*plural* -ties) *n.* 1. WHAT IDENTIFIES SB OR STH who sb is or what sth is, especially the name sb or sth is known by. ◊ **individuality** 2. SB'S ESSENTIAL SELF the set of characteristics that sb recognizes as belonging uniquely to himself or herself and constituting his or her individual personality for life 3. SAMENESS the fact or condition of being the same or exactly alike 4. *ANZ* CELEBRITY sb who is well known in a particular field of activity (*informal*) 5. MATH EQUATION TRUE FOR ALL ITS VARIABLES a mathematical equation that remains valid whatever values are taken by its variables 6. MATH = **identity element** [Late 16thC. From Late Latin *identitas*, from *ident-*, combining form of Latin *idem* 'same', from *id* 'that'.]

identity card *n.* a card carrying the holder's name, address, date of birth, and other particulars, together with a photograph, that serves as proof of his or her identity for official purposes. US term **identification card**

identity crisis *n.* 1. ANXIETY ABOUT SOCIAL ROLE a period during which sb feels great anxiety and uncertainty about his or her identity and role in life and society, typically experienced in adolescence or middle age 2. ANXIETY OF GROUP a period of anxiety or confusion about the nature, aims, and role of a group, organization, or business

identity element *n.* an element of a set that leaves other elements unchanged when combined with them

identity matrix *n.* a square matrix that has the numeral 1 in each position on the principal diagonal and 0 in all other positions

identity parade *n.* CRIMINOL = **identification parade**

ideo- *prefix.* forms words whose meaning involves ideas ○ *ideomotor* [Via French from, ultimately, Greek *idea* (see IDEA)]

ideogram /íddi ə gram/, **ideograph** /íddi ə graaf, -graf/ *n.* 1. SYMBOL IN WRITING SYSTEM a symbol used in some writing systems, e.g. those of Japan and China, that directly but abstractly represents the thing or concept itself rather than the word for it 2. GRAPHICAL SYMBOL a symbol or graphical character, e.g. '@' or '&', used to represent a word —**ideogrammatic** /íddi əgrə máttik/ *adj.* —**ideogrammatically** /-máttikli/ *adv.* —**ideographic** /íddi ə gráffik/ *adj.* —**ideographically** /-gráffikli/ *adv.*

ideography /íddi óggrəfi/ *n.* the use of graphical symbols to convey ideas

ideological /ídi ə lójjik'l/, **ideologic** /-lójjik/ *adj.* based on a particular ideology, or relating to an ideology or to ideologies, especially to ideologies that conflict —**ideologically** *adv.*

ideologist /ídi óllәjist/ *n.* 1. BELIEVER IN SYSTEM OF IDEAS sb who advocates or supports a particular ideology 2. SB WHO WORKS ON BELIEF SYSTEM sb who devises or revises an ideology

ideologue /ídi ə log/ *n.* an ideologist, especially a particularly zealous or doctrinaire supporter of an ideology [Early 19thC. From French *idéologue*, back-formation from *idéologie* (see IDEOLOGY).]

ideology /ídi óllәji/ (*plural* -gies) *n.* 1. SYSTEM OF SOCIAL BELIEFS a closely organized system of beliefs, values, and ideas forming the basis of a social, economic, or political philosophy or programme 2. MEANINGFUL BELIEF SYSTEM a set of beliefs, values, and opinions that shapes the way an individual or a group such as a social class thinks, acts, and understands the world [Late 18thC. From French *idéologie*, literally 'science of ideas', from *idéo-* 'ideo-' + *-logie* '-logy'.]

ideomotor /ídi ə mōtər/ *adj.* used to describe body movements triggered by thoughts rather than by external stimuli

ides /īdz/, **Ides** *n.* in the ancient Roman calendar, the name given to the 15th day of March, May, July, and October, or the 13th day of any other month (*takes a singular or plural verb*) [12thC. Directly or via French from Latin *idus* (plural), of uncertain origin: perhaps from Etruscan.]

-idine *suffix.* a chemical compound related to another compound ○ *histidine* [From -IDE + -INE]

idio- *prefix.* private, individual, proper, or distinctive ○ *idiolect* ○ *idiomorphic* [From Greek *idios* 'one's own, private'. Ultimately from an Indo-European base meaning 'self', which is also the ancestor of English *self*, *ethnic*, and *custom*.]

idioblast /íddi ō blast/ *n.* a specialized plant cell that differs considerably from others in the same area of tissue. An idioblast is usually thick-walled and lacks chlorophyll. —**idioblastic** /-blástik/ *adj.*

idiocy /íddi əssi/ *n.* 1. LACK OF INTELLIGENCE extreme lack of intelligence or foresight 2. UNINTELLIGENT ACT an extremely unintelligent or thoughtless act 3. AN OFFENSIVE TERM an offensive term in a now disused classification system for mental disability (*dated offensive*) [Early 16thC. Formed from IDIOT; perhaps modelled on words such as ACCURACY.]

idioglossia /íddi ō glóssi ə/ *n.* 1. CHILDHOOD SPEECH DEFECT a developmental speech defect in which a child substitutes different sounds for the correct ones, so that speech is intelligible only to parents or others closely involved with the child **2. PRIVATE LANGUAGE** the invention and use of language by a child or closely involved siblings such as twins that is unintelligible to anyone else [Late 19thC. Formed from Greek *idioglōssos*, literally 'of distinct tongue', from *idios* 'distinct' + *glossa* 'tongue'.]

idiographic /íddi ō gráffik/ *adj.* concentrating on particular cases and the unique traits or functioning of individuals, rather than on broad generalizations about human behaviour. Idiographic research methods in psychology include the case study, which is characterized by the distinctiveness of each case. ◊ **nomothetic**

idiolect /íddi ə lekt/ *n.* an individual person's vocabulary and particular and unique way of using language [Mid-20thC. Coined from IDIO- + DIALECT.] —**idiolectal** /íddi ə lékt'l/ *adj.*

idiom /íddi əm/ *n.* **1. FIXED EXPRESSION WITH NONLITERAL MEANING** a fixed, distinctive, and often colourful expression whose meaning cannot be understood from the combined meanings of its individual words, e.g., 'to have sb in stitches' **2. NATURAL WAY OF USING A LANGUAGE** the way of using a particular language that comes naturally to its native speakers and involves both knowledge of its grammar and familiarity with its usage **3. STYLISTIC EXPRESSION OF PERSON OR GROUP** the style of expression of a specific individual or group **4.** ARTS **DISTINGUISHING ARTISTIC STYLE** the characteristic style of an artist or artistic group [Late 16thC. Directly or via French *idiome* from late Latin *idioma*, from Greek, 'property, peculiarity', from, ultimately, *idios* (see IDIO-).]

idiomatic /íddi ə máttik/, **idiomatical** /-máttik'l/ *adj.* **1. CHARACTERISTIC OF NATIVE-SPEAKER USE** characteristic of, or in keeping with, the way a language is ordinarily and naturally used by its native speakers **2. OF THE NATURE OF AN IDIOM** having a meaning not deducible from the combined meanings of the words that make it up ○ *an idiomatic phrase* **3.** ARTS **CHARACTERISTIC OF PARTICULAR STYLE** characteristic of a particular style, or using a particular and distinctive style, especially in the arts —**idiomatically** *adv.* —**idiomaticness** *n.*

idiomorphic /íddi ō máwrfik/ *adj.* used to describe minerals that occur naturally in the form of fully developed crystals —**idiomorphically** *adv.* —**idiomorphism** *n.*

idiopathic /íddi ō páthik/ *adj.* used to describe a disease or disorder that has no known cause —**idiopathically** *adv.* —**idiopathy** /íddi óppəthi/ *n.*

idiophone /íddi ō fōn/ *n.* a percussion instrument, e.g. a gong or xylophone, that is made from resonating material that does not have to be tuned —**idiophonic** /íddi ō fónnik/ *adj.*

idiosyncrasy /íddi ō síngkrəssi/ (*plural* **-sies**) *n.* **1. QUIRK** a way of behaving, thinking, or feeling that is peculiar to an individual or group, especially an odd or unusual one **2.** MED **UNUSUAL RESPONSE TO STH** an unusual or exaggerated reaction to a drug or food that is not caused by an allergy [Early 17thC. Directly or via French *idiosyncrasie* from Greek *idiosugkrasia*, literally 'personal mixing together', from, ultimately, *krasis* 'mixing'.] —**idiosyncratic** /íddi ō sing kráttik/ *adj.* —**idiosyncratically** /-sing kráttikli/ *adv.*

idiot /íddi ət/ *n.* **1. OFFENSIVE TERM** an offensive term that deliberately insults sb else's intelligence (*insult*) **2. OFFENSIVE TERM** an offensive term in a now disused classification system for sb with an IQ of about 25 or under and a mental age of less than three years (*dated offensive*) [14thC. Via French from, ultimately, Greek *idiōtēs* 'private person, layperson lacking specialized knowledge', from *idios* (see IDIO-).]

idiot board *n.* a placard, projector, or continuous roll of paper that prompts a television performer with lines to be spoken (*slang*)

idiot box *n.* television or a television set (*slang*) [*Idiot* from the belief that watching too much television causes stupidity]

idiot card *n.* TV = **idiot board** (*slang*)

idiotic /íddi óttik/ *adj.* an offensive term that deliberately insults sb else's behaviour (*insult*) —**idiotically** *adv.* —**idioticalness** *n.*

idiot-proof *adj.* constructed or designed so as not to fail or go wrong even if misused

idiot savant /éedi ō sa voN, íddi ət sávvənt/ (*plural* **idiot savants** *or* **idiots savants**) *n.* an offensive term used to describe sb who has a psychiatric disorder or a learning problem but who is exceptionally gifted in one particular area, e.g. rapid mental calculation, architectural drawing, or remembering facts (*offensive*) [From French, literally 'learned idiot']

idiot tape *n.* a tape for a typesetting machine that contains text but no formatting except markers for new paragraphs

idle /īd'l/ *adj.* (**idler, idlest**) **1. LAZY** lazy and unwilling to work **2. NOT WORKING OR IN USE** not working, operating, producing, or in use **3. FRIVOLOUS** serving no serious purpose, or frivolous and a waste of time **4. NOT EARNING MONEY** not being used to yield a financial return ○ *idle funds* **5. UNFOUNDED** having no basis in fact ○ *idle gossip* **6. INEFFECTIVE** unlikely to be carried out or impossible to put into effect ○ *idle threats* ■ *n.* CARS **SPEED OF ENGINE WITH GEAR DISENGAGED** the speed of a motor vehicle engine that is running but is not in gear, or the way it runs ■ *v.* (**idles, idling, idled**) **1.** *vti.* **PASS TIME AIMLESSLY** to be lazy and avoid work, or to pass the time lazily doing nothing in particular **2.** *vi.* **MOVE SLOWLY AND AIMLESSLY** to move in slow and lazy or aimless way **3.** *vti.* **RUN WITHOUT APPLYING POWER** to run gently with the gear disengaged, or to allow an engine to do this **4.** *vt. US, Can* **MAKE UNEMPLOYED** to make workers unemployed or inactive [Old English *īdel* 'worthless, empty', from a prehistoric Germanic word of unknown origin] —**idleness** *n.* —**idly** *adv.*

WORD KEY: SYNONYMS

See Synonyms at ***vain***.

idle pulley, idler pulley *n.* a freely rotating pulley wheel that guides or takes up slack from a drive belt by pressing against it

idler /īdlər/ *n.* **1. LAZY PERSON** sb who avoids work or who spends time in a lazy or relaxed fashion **2.** MECH ENG = **idle wheel**

idler pulley *n.* = **idle pulley**

idler wheel *n.* = **idle wheel**

idle time *n.* a period during which a device, machine, or employee is temporarily inactive

idle wheel, idler wheel *n.* **1. MECHANISM THAT TRANSMITS MOTION** a gear wheel or roller placed between two others to transmit motion between them without changing their speed or direction or to provide support **2.** = **idle pulley**

idli /íddli/ *npl. S Asia* steamed rice cakes eaten for breakfast, especially in southern India [Mid-20thC. From Malayalam and Kannada *iḍḍali*.]

idocrase /īdə krayz, -krayss/ *n.* MINERALS = **vesuvianite** [Early 19thC. From Greek *eidos* 'form' (see IDOL) + *krasis* 'mixture'.]

idol /īd'l/ *n.* **1. OBJECT OF ADORATION** sb or sth greatly and often fanatically admired and loved (*disapproving*) **2.** RELIG **OBJECT WORSHIPPED AS GOD** sth such as a statue or carved image that is worshipped as a god **3.** RELIG **FORBIDDEN OBJECT OF WORSHIP** in monotheistic religions, any object of worship other than the one God [13thC. Via French *idole* from, ultimately, Greek *eidōlon* 'image', from *eidos* 'form, shape' (source of English *idyll* and *kaleidoscope*).]

idolater /ī dóllətər/ *n.* **1. WORSHIPPER OF IDOLS** sb who worships idols (*disapproving*) **2. EXTREME ADMIRER** a fanatical admirer of sb or sth [14thC. Formed from French *idolâtre*, from, ultimately, Greek *eidōlolatrēs*, literally 'image worshipper', from *eidōlon* (see IDOL).]

idolatress /ī dóllətrəss/ *n.* a woman who worships idols (*dated disapproving*)

idolatry /ī dóllətri/ *n.* **1. IDOL WORSHIP** the worship of idols or false gods (*disapproving*) **2. EXTREME ADMIRATION** extreme admiration or fanatical devotion to sb or sth [13thC. Via French *idolâtrie* from, ultimately, Greek *eidōlolatreia*, literally 'image-worship', from *eidōlon* (see IDOL).] —**idolatrous** *adj.* —**idolatrously** *adv.*

idolize /īdə līz/ (**-izes, -izing, -ized**), **idolise** (**-ises, -ising, -ised**) *vt.* **1. ADMIRE FANATICALLY** to feel great admiration and respect for, or be fanatically devoted to, sb or sth **2. WORSHIP AS IDOL** to worship sth or sb as an idol (*disapproving*) —**idolization** /īdə lī záysh'n/ *n.* —**idolizer** /īdə līzər/ *n.*

IDP *abbr.* integrated data processing

Idriess /éedrəss/, **Ion** (1890–1979) Australian novelist. His novels include *Flynn of the Inland* (1932). Full name **Ion Llewellyn Idriess**

idyll /ídd'l, īd'l/ *n.* **1. EXPERIENCE OF SERENE HAPPINESS** an experience or period of serene and carefree happiness, usually in beautiful surroundings and often in the context of a romantic relationship **2. TRANQUIL CHARMING SCENE** a scene or event characterized by tranquillity, simple beauty, and innocent charm, usually in a rural setting **3.** ARTS **LITERARY PIECE ABOUT CHARMING RURAL LIFE** a short work in verse or prose, a painting, or a piece of music depicting simple pastoral or rural scenes and the life of country folk, often in idealized terms [Late 16thC. Via Latin *idyllium* 'pastoral poem' from Greek *eidullion*, literally 'small picture', from *eidos* (see IDOL).]

idyllic /i díllik, ī d-/ *adj.* **1. SERENELY BEAUTIFUL AND HAPPY** serenely beautiful, untroubled, and happy **2. LIKE AN IDYLL** like an idyll, especially in having a simple, unspoilt, and especially rural charm

idyllically /i díllikli, ī-/ *adv.* in a simple and idealized way

idyllist /ídd'list, īd'list/ *n.* a writer, composer, or painter of idylls

IE *abbr.* LING Indo-European

i.e. *abbr.* that is to say [Latin, *id est* 'that is']

-ie *suffix.* **1.** one that is small or dear ○ *doggie* ○ *auntie* **2.** one having a particular character ○ *sweetie* **3.** one having to do with ○ *townie*

IEE *abbr.* Institution of Electrical Engineers

-ier *suffix.* = **er**

if /if/ CORE MEANING: a conjunction used to indicate the circumstances that would have to exist in order for an event to happen ○ *You can come with us if you want to.* ○ *Are you thinking of buying a new car? If so, talk to us first.*

1. *conj.* **USED IN INDIRECT QUESTIONS** used to introduce in indirect speech a question that in direct speech requires the answer 'yes' or 'no' ○ *He asked the hotel receptionist if it was possible to hire a car.* **2.** *conj.* **MODIFYING A STATEMENT** used to indicate a modification to a statement, usually to add sth negative or to indicate that there is less of sth than originally expected ○ *The report will be with you at the end of the week, if not before.* ○ *a gallant, if misguided attempt* **3.** *conj.* **INTRODUCING AN EXCLAMATION** used to introduce an exclamation expressing surprise or dismay ○ *If she isn't the most selfish person I've met!* **4.** *n.* **DOUBT** a doubt or uncertainty ○ *There is rather a large if about whether or not she'll finish her degree.* **5.** *n.* **CONDITION** a condition or qualification ○ *I'm not very happy about the ifs that have been put into the contract.* [Old English *gif*, from a prehistoric Germanic word of unknown origin] ◇ **ifs and buts** excuses or protests ◇ **ifs, ands, or buts** *US* excuses or protests ◇ **if only** used to introduce the expression of a hopeless wish or regret ○ *If only you had told me sooner.*

WORD KEY: USAGE

When to use **if and when** This expression is often used in cases where ***if*** or ***when*** alone would be enough, but there are occasions on which both are needed to convey condition about both likelihood and timing of an eventuality; in the sentence *Arrange repairs if and when necessary*, omission of ***if*** could imply that repairs are always necessary at some point, and omission of ***when*** could fail to make the point that repairs should be done promptly.

WORD KEY: USAGE

Ambiguous construction: In *We have hundreds, if not thousands, of items in stock*, the ***if not*** fairly plainly means 'or even'. In *It's a clever idea, if not a practical one*, it fairly plainly means 'although not'. But in *He's good-looking, if not really handsome*, it is unclear which of those meanings is intended — at least out of context. Often it is clear what ***if not*** means only because the context shows what the phrase must mean. Where it will not be clear, another wording is preferable and can be easily found.

IF *abbr.* ELECTRON ENG intermediate frequency

IFC *abbr.* International Finance Corporation (*of the UN*)

Ife /eé fay/ city in southwestern Nigeria, situated 87 km/54 mi. east of Ibadan. Population: 225,500 (1990).

IFF *abbr.* MIL Identification, Friend, or Foe

iffy /íffi/ (**-fier, -fiest**) *adj.* (*informal*) **1.** DUBIOUS OR SUSPICIOUS of doubtful and probably low quality, not to be relied on, or arousing suspicion **2.** DOUBTFUL doubtful and undecided about sth —**iffiness** *n.*

Ifni /eéfni/ former overseas province of Spain, now part of Morocco, situated on the southwestern coast of the country. Sidi Ifni is the only city. Area: 1502 sq. km/580 sq. mi.

IFOR, Ifor *abbr.* MIL implementation force

IFR *abbr.* instrument flying regulations

Ig *abbr.* immunoglobulin

IG *abbr.* Inspector General

IgA *n.* a class of antibodies, found in respiratory and alimentary secretions as well as in saliva and tears, that help the body to neutralize harmful bacteria and viral antigens [Shortening of *immunoglobulin A*]

IGB *abbr.* S Africa illicit gold buying

Igbo *n., adj.* = **Ibo**

IgD *n.* a class of antibodies, present on most cell surfaces and predominant in B cells, that help the body to resist antigens. ◊ **B cell** [Shortening of *immunoglobulin D*]

IgE *n.* a class of antibodies, abundant in tissues, that help the body to expel intestinal parasites and cause allergic reactions in response to antigens [Shortening of *immunoglobulin E*]

IgG *n.* a class of antibodies, predominant in serum, that pass through the placental wall into foetal circulation and help to prepare the immune system for the period of infancy [Shortening of *immunoglobulin G*]

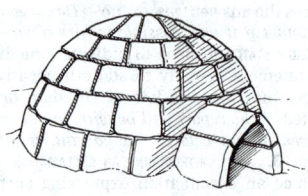

Igloo

igloo /íggloo/ *n.* **1.** DOME-SHAPED INUIT HOUSE an Inuit dwelling, usually dome-shaped and built from blocks of packed snow **2.** DOME-SHAPED SHELTER any small dome-shaped shelter or structure [Mid-19thC. From Inuit *iglu* 'house'.]

IgM *n.* a class of antibodies, circulating in the blood and secretions, that help the body to resist viruses [Shortening of *immunoglobulin M*]

IGM *abbr.* CHESS International Grandmaster

ign. *abbr.* **1.** ignites **2.** ignition **3.** unknown [Latin *ignotus*]

Ignatius Loyola /ig náyshəss loy ólə, -lóyələ/, **St** (1491–1556) Spanish priest who was cofounder of the Society of Jesus (Jesuits) in 1534. He also produced a Jesuit training manual, *Spiritual Exercises* (1548).

igneous /ígni əss/ *adj.* **1.** FORMERLY MOLTEN used to describe rock formed under conditions of intense heat or produced by the solidification of volcanic magma on or below the Earth's surface **2.** RELATING TO FIRE connected with or characteristic of fire (*formal*) [Mid-17thC. Formed from Latin *igneus*, from *ignis* 'fire' (see IGNITE).]

ignescent /ig néss'nt/ *adj.* giving off sparks when struck, as a flint does [Early 19thC. From Latin *ignescent-*, the present participle stem of *ignescere* 'to catch fire', from *ignis* 'fire' (see IGNITE).]

ignes fatui plural of **ignis fatuus**

ignimbrite /ígnim brīt/ *n.* a volcanic rock consisting of droplets of lava and glass that were welded together by intense heat [Mid-20thC. Coined from Latin *ignis* 'fire' (see IGNITE) + the stem *imbr-* 'rain' + -ITE; from its formation from the deposits of a cloud of volcanic ash.]

ignis fatuus /ígniss fáttyoo əss/ (*plural* **ignes fatui** /íg neez fáttyoo ī/) *n.* **1.** = **will-o'-the-wisp 2.** ILLUSORY THING sth, e.g. a hope or an aim, that proves illusory or leads sb astray (*literary*) [From Latin, literally 'foolish fire'; from its erratic movements]

ignite /ig nít/ (**-nites, -niting, -nited**) *v.* **1.** *vti.* LIGHT FIRE OR BEGIN TO BURN to set fire to sth, or catch fire **2.** *vti.* CHEM HEAT GAS UNTIL IT BURNS to heat a gas to the temperature at which it begins to burn **3.** *vt.* AROUSE EMOTION IN to cause a strong emotion to arise or show itself in sb [Mid-17thC. From Latin *ignit-*, the past participle stem of *ignire* 'to set on fire', from *ignis* 'fire' (source of English *igneous*).] —**ignitability** /ig nítə bílləti/ *n.* —**ignitable** /ig nítəb'l/ *adj.* —**igniter** /-tər/ *n.*

ignition /ig nísh'n/ *n.* **1.** CHEM PROCESS OF IGNITING the process of setting sth on fire **2.** MECH ENG MEANS OF STARTING ENGINE a mechanism that determines when, where, and how a spark is delivered to an engine cylinder to ignite the fuel and start or run the engine **3.** MECH ENG SPARK THAT IGNITES FUEL-AIR MIXTURE a spark in an internal-combustion engine that ignites and explodes a mixture of fuel and air

ignition point *n.* the temperature at which a substance begins to burn and will remain alight

ignoble /ig nób'l/ *adj.* **1.** DISHONOURABLE dishonourable, ungenerous, and contrary to the high standards of conduct expected of sb **2.** NOT OF THE NOBILITY not belonging to the nobility (*formal*) [15thC. Directly or via French from Latin *ignobilis*, literally 'not noble', from (*g*)*nobilis* 'noble' (see NOBLE).] —**ignobility** /ígnō bílləti/ *n.* —**ignobly** /ig nób'li/ *adv.*

—————— **WORD KEY: SYNONYMS** ——————
See Synonyms at *mean*.

ignominious /ígnə mínni əss/ *adj.* **1.** SHAMEFUL involving a total loss of dignity and pride and making sb or sth appear shamefully weak and ineffective **2.** DESPICABLE deserving condemnation and contempt (*formal*) —**ignominiously** *adv.* —**ignominiousness** *n.*

ignominy /ígnəmini/ (*plural* **-ies**) *n.* **1.** DISGRACE AND DISHONOUR a total loss of dignity and self-respect or an incurring of public disgrace **2.** STH DISGRACEFUL a disgraceful act (*formal*) [Mid-16thC. Directly or via French *ignominie* from Latin *ignominia*, literally 'lacking name', from *nomin-*, the stem of *nomen* 'name, reputation'.]

ignoramus /ígnə ráyməss/ *n.* an offensive term that deliberately insults sb else's intelligence level (*insult*) [Late 16thC. Via modern Latin, 'we ignore', from Latin, a form of *ignorare* (see IGNORE).]

ignorance /ígnərənss/ *n.* **1.** LACK OF KNOWLEDGE lack of knowledge or education **2.** UNAWARENESS unawareness of sth, often of sth important

ignorant /ígnərənt/ *adj.* **1.** LACKING KNOWLEDGE lacking knowledge and education in general or in a specific subject **2.** UNAWARE unaware of sth ○ *ignorant of the danger* **3.** RESULTING FROM LACK OF KNOWING caused by a lack of understanding or experience ○ *an ignorant mistake* **4.** *Carib* QUARRELSOME quarrelsome and aggressive —**ignorantly** *adv.* —**ignorantness** *n.*

ignore /ig náwr/ (**-nores, -noring, -nored**) *vt.* **1.** REFUSE TO NOTICE to refuse to notice or pay attention to sb or sth **2.** *Aus* REJECT INDICTMENT to reject a bill of indictment on the grounds of insufficient evidence [Early 17thC. Directly or via French *ignorer*, from Latin *ignorare* 'not to know, to ignore', ultimately from (*g*)*noscere* 'to know' (source of English *notice*).] —**ignorable** *adj.* —**ignorer** *n.*

IGO *abbr.* inter-governmental organization

Igorot /íggə rót, eégə-/ *n.* (*plural* **-rot** *or* **-rots**) PHILIPPINE PEOPLE a member of a people living in the mountainous northern part of the island of Luzon in the Philippines ■ *adj.* OF THE IGOROT relating to or typical of the Igorot or their culture [Early 19thC. From Spanish *Ygolote*, from the local name.]

Iguaçu /íg waa soó/ river in southern Brazil and northeastern Argentina. Length: 1,200 km/745 mi.

Iguaçu Falls

Iguaçu Falls waterfalls on the Iguaçu River. In the wet season they form a single waterfall over 4 km/2.5 mi. wide and up to 80 m/260 ft high.

Iguana

iguana /i gwaánə/ (*plural* **-nas** *or* **-na**) *n.* a large plant-eating tropical lizard, chiefly found in South and Central America, with a serrated fringe or crest running along its back from head to tail. Family: Iguanidae. [Mid-16thC. Via Spanish from Arawak *iwana*.] —**iguanian** *adj., n.*

iguanodon /i gwaánə don/ *n.* a large long-tailed plant-eating dinosaur of the Jurassic and early Cretaceous periods. Genus: *Iguanodon*. [Early 19thC. Formed from IGUANA + -*odon*, from Greek, variant of the stem *odont-* 'tooth'; from the similarity of its teeth to those of an iguana.]

IGY *abbr.* International Geophysical Year

IHC *abbr.* NZ intellectually handicapped child

Ihimaera, Witi (*b.* 1944) New Zealand novelist. His collection of short stories *Pounamou, Pounamou* (1972) was the first work by a Maori writer to be published in English in New Zealand. Full name **Witi Tame Ihimaera**

ihp *abbr.* indicated horsepower

ihram /ee raám/ *n.* **1.** WHITE ROBE WORN BY MECCA PILGRIMS a white cotton robe worn by men when they are pilgrims to Mecca, formed from pieces of cloth wound around the waist and over the shoulder **2.** HOLY STATE OF PILGRIM WEARING IHRAM the state of holiness conferred or symbolized by the wearing of the ihram [Early 18thC. From Arabic *'iḥrām*.]

iid *abbr.* STATS independent identically distributed (*used of two or more random variables*)

IJsselmeer /íss'l meer/ shallow freshwater lake in the northern Netherlands that occupies part of what was formerly the Zuider Zee. The River IJssel flows into it.

ikat /ee kaat, i kát/ *n.* a technique for making patterned fabric by using tie-dyed yarn [Mid-20thC. From Malay, literally 'to tie, fasten'.]

IKBS *abbr.* intelligent knowledge-based system

ikebana /ík ay baánə, íki-/ *n.* the Japanese art of arranging flowers in a formal balanced composition [Early 20thC. From Japanese, literally 'living flowers'.]

Ike Taiga /í kay tīgə/ (1723–76) Japanese painter. His works, using ancient forms of calligraphy, are in the Bunjinga style.

ikon *n.* = **icon** *n.* 1

IL *abbr.* 1. MAIL Illinois 2. Israel (*international vehicle registration*)

il- *prefix.* = **in-**[1], **in-**[2] (*used before l*)

ilang-ilang *n.* = **ylang-ylang**

-ile[1] *suffix.* of, relating to, capable of ○ *pulsatile* ○ *protrusile* [Via Old French from Latin *-ilis*]

-ile[2] *suffix.* a portion of a particular size in a frequency distribution ○ *quartile* ○ *percentile* [Origin uncertain]

ilea plural of **ileum**

ILEA /ílli ə/ *abbr.* Inner London Education Authority

ileac /ílli ak/, **ileal** /ílli əl/ *adj.* 1. OF THE ILEUM relating to the ileum 2. MED OF ILEUS relating to ileus [Early 19thC. Alteration of ILIAC on the model of ILEUM and ILEUS.]

ileitis /ílli ítiss/ *n.* inflammation of the ileum

ileostomy /ílli óstəmi/ (*plural* **-mies**) *n.* 1. OPERATION MAKING OPENING TO ILEUM the surgical operation of making an opening through the abdominal wall into the ileum, so that waste can be discharged out of the body without passing through the colon 2. SURGICAL OPENING TO ILEUM a surgical opening through the abdominal wall into the ileum

Ilesa /i láyshə/, **Ilesha** town in Kwara State, southwestern Nigeria, situated approximately 24 km/15 mi. southeast of Oshogbo. Population: 342,000 (1992).

ileum /ílli əm/ (*plural* **-a** /-ə/) *n.* the third and lowest portion of the small intestine, extending from the jejunum to the pouch-shaped caecum at the beginning of the large intestine [Late 17thC. From medieval Latin, variant of Latin *ilium* 'entrails', perhaps from association with *ileus* (see ILEUS).]

ileus /ílli əss/ *n.* the inability of the contents of the intestines to pass through them owing to physical obstruction, or muscular inadequacy, often accompanied by extreme pain and vomiting [Late 17thC. Via Latin from Greek *ileos* 'colic', of uncertain origin: probably formed from *eilein* 'to hold in check'.]

ilex /í leks/ *n.* 1. PLANT OF HOLLY GENUS any tree or shrub belonging to a genus whose best-known member is the holly tree. Genus: *Ilex*. 2. = **holm oak** [From Latin, 'holm oak']

Ilfracombe /ílfrə koom/ seaside resort in northern Devon, England. Population: 10,429 (1991).

ilia plural of **ilium**

iliac /ílli ak/ *adj.* relating to the ilium and its surroundings [Early 16thC. From late Latin *iliacus* 'relating to colic', from Latin *ilia* (see ILIUM).]

Iliad /ílli əd/ *n.* an ancient Greek epic poem, describing the siege and capture of Troy, ascribed to Homer, and probably composed by oral tradition over the centuries prior to 700 BC [Early 17thC. Via the Latin stem *Iliad-* from Greek *Ilias* 'of Troy', from *Ilion* 'Troy'.] —**Iliadic** /ílli áddik/ *adj.*

Iliamna /ílli ámnə/ volcanic peak in southwestern Alaska, situated on the western side of Cook Inlet. Height: 3,053 m/10,016 ft.

Iliamna, Lake the largest lake in Alaska, situated in the southwest of the state, west of Cook Inlet. Area: 2,647 sq. km/1,022 sq. mi.

ilium /ílli əm/ (*plural* **-a** /-ə/) *n.* the wide flat upper portion of the pelvis that is connected to the base of the vertebral column. The ilium is a separate bone at birth but later becomes fused with two other bones to form the hip bone (**innominate bone**). [14thC. From Latin, the classical Latin plural meaning 'groin, flanks, entrails'. Originally, the English word denoted the ILEUM.]

ilk *n.* SORT kind or sort (*informal*) ○ *'save forlorn hopes and their ilk'* (Stephen Crane, *The Red Badge of Courage*; 1895) ■ *det. Scotland* = **ilka** [Old English *ilca* 'same', a compound whose parts are descended from an Indo-European word meaning 'same' and a prehistoric Germanic word meaning 'form' (also the ancestor of English *each*)] ◇ **of that ilk** *Scotland* from, living in, or, usually, laird or owner of a place whose name is identical to your surname

ilka /ílkə/, **ilk** /ilk/ *det. Scotland* each or every [12thC. Originally two words. From dialect *ilk* 'each' (from Old English *ylc*) + A.]

Ilkeston /ílkstən/ town in Derbyshire, central England, situated 13 km/8 mi. northwest of Nottingham. Population: 35,134 (1991).

ill /il/ *adj.* 1. UNWELL not in good health, having a disease, or feeling unwell or nauseous 2. HARMFUL resulting in harm, pain, or trouble for sb or sth 3. UNKIND unkind and unfriendly ○ *ill feeling* 4. UNFAVOURABLE predicting a bad future or outcome 5. MORALLY BAD resulting from the actual or supposed moral badness of sb or sth ○ *of ill repute* 6. BAD not up to the expected or required standard, e.g. of behaviour or competence ■ *adv.* 1. BADLY badly, inadequately, or inappropriately ○ *prisoners who were ill treated* 2. UNFAVOURABLY in an adverse or unfavourable way or so as to reflect badly on sb or sth ○ *It boded ill for the future.* 3. WITH DIFFICULTY only with great difficulty and trouble ○ *She can ill afford the time at present.* ■ *n.* 1. HARM evil or harm, especially as a fate wished on sb ○ *don't wish others ill* 2. UNFAVOURABLE OPINION an unfavourable opinion of sb or sth ○ *spoke ill of them* ○ *thought ill of them* 3. MISFORTUNE trouble or misfortune, or a troublesome or distressing experience (*archaic*) 4. ILLNESS a disease or sickness (*archaic*) [12thC. From Old Norse *illr* 'evil, difficult', *illa* 'badly', and *ilt* 'evil', of unknown origin. 'Unwell' dates from the 15thC.]

WORD KEY: USAGE

ill or **sick**? In general, someone who is or who feels ***ill*** is unwell in some way, whereas someone who is or who feels ***sick*** is vomiting or about to vomit. On the other hand, ***ill*** has limitations of use that are filled by ***sick***; in particular, ***ill*** is less common in attributive position before a noun, and it is more natural to say *a sick child* than *an ill child*. So too there are set expressions in which ***sick*** is used but not ***ill***, for example *sick leave, sick note, to go sick*.

I'll /īl/ *contr.* I will or shall

ill. *abbr.* 1. illustrated 2. illustration 3. illustrator

Ill. *abbr.* Illinois

ill-advised *adj.* not wise, prudent, or sensible —**ill-advisedly** /íl əd vízidli/ *adv.*

ill-affected *adj.* hostile or unfriendly towards sb or sth (*formal*)

ill-assorted, **ill-sorted** *adj.* mismatched or incompatible

ill at ease *adj.* uncomfortable and nervous

illation /i láysh'n/ *n.* (*formal*) 1. INFERENCE an inference drawn from sth 2. ACT OR PROCESS OF INFERRING STH the act or process of making an inference [Mid-16thC. From the Latin stem *illation-*, from *illat-* (see ILLATIVE).]

illative /i láytiv, íllə-/ *adj.* 1. INFERENTIAL involving or relating to the making of inferences (*formal*) 2. STATING INFERENCE expressing or preceding an inference 3. OF CASE OF FINNISH NOUN expressing motion towards sth. It is usually translated into English using the prepositions 'into' or 'towards'. (*used to describe a noun case in Finnish and some other languages*) ■ *n.* 1. CASE OF FINNISH NOUN the illative case in Finnish and similar languages 2. STH THAT STATES INFERENCE a word, phrase, or morpheme that expresses an inference [Late 16thC. From Latin *illativus*, from *illat-*, the past participle stem of *inferre* 'to infer' (see INFER).] —**illatively** *adv.*

Illawarra /íllə wórrə/ division in southeastern New South Wales, southeastern Australia, situated approximately 48 km/30 mi. south of Sydney. Population: 33,478 (1991).

ill-bred *adj.* rude, impolite, or otherwise showing a lack of good manners or the results of a bad upbringing —**ill-breeding** *n.*

ill-conceived *adj.* not based on good planning, especially not having an aim or goal that is likely to be successfully achieved

ill-considered *adj.* done or made unwisely or without sufficient thought about the consequences

ill-defined *adj.* not clearly or sharply defined, or not clearly thought out

ill-disguised *adj.* apparent or visible, especially in sb's expression, voice, or manner, because any attempt to conceal it is unsuccessful or perfunctory ○ *her ill-disguised contempt for them*

ill-disposed *adj.* having an unfriendly or hostile attitude towards sb or sth

ill-dressed *adj.* dressed in shabby, badly fitting, or unsuitable clothes

illegal /i léeg'l/ *adj.* 1. LAW AGAINST THE LAW forbidden by law 2. SPORTS, GAME AGAINST THE RULES not allowed by the rules of sth such as a game 3. COMPUT NOT PERMITTED BY COMPUTER not permitted in a computer program ■ *n.* ILLEGAL IMMIGRANT sb who has entered a country illegally [Early 17thC. Directly or via French from medieval Latin *illegalis* 'not legal', from *legalis* 'legal' (see LEGAL).] —**illegally** *adv.*

illegality /ìllee gálləti/ (*plural* **-ties**) *n.* 1. FACT OF BEING ILLEGAL the fact of being forbidden by law or by the rules of sth 2. UNLAWFUL ACT an act that is against the law

illegible /i léjjəb'l/ *adj.* impossible or very difficult to read —**illegibility** /i léjjə bílləti/ *n.* —**illegibly** /i léjjəbli/ *adv.*

illegitimate /íllə jíttəmət/ *adj.* 1. AGAINST LAW OR RULES not carried out, made, or constituted in accordance with the law, the rules governing a particular activity, or social norms and customs 2. BORN OUT OF WEDLOCK born to parents who are not married to each other 3. LOGIC NOT CORRECTLY REASONED not correctly inferred or reasoned [Mid-16thC. Formed from late Latin *illegitimus*, from *legitimus* (see LEGITIMATE).] —**illegitimacy** *n.* —**illegitimately** *adv.*

ill-fated *adj.* ending in, or doomed to, disaster

ill-favoured *adj.* 1. UNATTRACTIVE unattractive in appearance, especially having an unattractive face 2. OBJECTIONABLE offensively objectionable (*literary*) —**ill-favouredly** *adv.* —**ill-favouredness** *n.*

ill feeling *n.* animosity or resentment towards sb, sth, or each other

ill-founded *adj.* with no sound basis in fact or logic

ill-gotten *adj.* acquired dishonestly or illegally ○ *ill-gotten gains*

ill health *n.* the state of being in poor physical or mental condition

ill humour *n.* a bad mood or bad temper —**ill-humoured** *adj.*

illiberal /i líbbərəl/ *adj.* 1. NARROW-MINDED narrow-minded and intolerant of ideas and behaviour that vary from an inflexibly conservative standard 2. UNGENEROUS lacking in generosity (*formal*) [Mid-16thC. Via French from Latin *illiberalis* 'sordid, mean' (literally 'not liberal'), from *liberalis* 'liberal' (see LIBERAL).] —**illiberality** /i líbbə rálləti/ *n.* —**illiberally** /i líbbərəli/ *adv.*

illicit /i líssit/ *adj.* 1. ILLEGAL not allowed by the law 2. UNACCEPTABLE BY PREVAILING SOCIAL STANDARDS considered wrong or unacceptable by prevailing social customs or standards [Early 16thC. Directly or via French *illicite* from Latin *illicitus* 'not licit', from *licitus* 'licit' (see LICIT).] —**illicitly** *adv.* —**illicitness** *n.*

Illimani /éelyi mánni/ mountain in western Bolivia, situated south of La Paz. The highest peak is Nevada Illimani, 6,462 m/21,201 ft.

illimitable /i límmitəb'l/ *adj.* with no limits or bounds (*formal*) —**illimitability** /i límmitə bílləti/ *n.* —**illimitably** /i límmitəbli/ *adv.*

Illinois[1] /ílli nóy/ *n.* (*plural* **-nois**) MEMBER OF NATIVE N AMERICAN CONFEDERACY a member of a confederacy of Native North American peoples who originally lived in an area covering northern Illinois, eastern Iowa, and southern Wisconsin, now inhabiting a reservation in northeastern Oklahoma ■ *adj.* OF ILLINOIS CONFEDERACY relating to or typical of the Illinois confederacy, its people, or their culture

Illinois[2] /íllə nóy/ 1. state in north-central United States, bordered by Indiana, Iowa, Kentucky, Missouri, Wisconsin, and Lake Michigan. Capital: Springfield. Population: 11,895,849 (1997). Area: 150,007 sq. km/57,918 sq. mi. 2. river in northern Illinois formed by the joining of the Des Plaines and Kankakee rivers. Length: 680 km/420 mi.

Illinoisan /ílli nóyən, -nóyz'n/, **Illinoisian** /-nóyzi ən/ *adj.* relating to or typical of the state of Illinois, or its people or culture

Illinois Waterway system of rivers and canals in Illinois that connects Lake Michigan at Chicago

Illinois

with the Mississippi River at Grafton. Length: 523 km/325 mi.

illiquid /i líkwid/ *adj.* **1.** FIN HARD TO CONVERT INTO CASH not easily convertible into cash **2.** NOT HAVING ENOUGH CASH without sufficient ready cash —**illiquidity** /ílli kwíddəti/ *n.*

illite /íllīt/ *n.* a clay mineral of the mica group found in shale and mudstone, consisting of hydrated silicate of potassium and aluminium [Mid-20thC. Named after ILLINOIS[2] (US state where it was first found).] —**illitic** /i líttik/ *adj.*

illiteracy /i líttərəssi/ (*plural* **-cies**) *n.* **1.** READING INCAPACITY an inability to read and write **2.** LACK OF KNOWLEDGE OF A SUBJECT lack of education and knowledge in a particular subject **3.** ERROR IN SPEECH OR WRITING a basic or gross error in reading, writing, or speaking that suggests limited knowledge of language or grammar

illiterate /i líttərət/ *adj.* **1.** OFFENSIVE TERM an offensive term used to describe people who are not able to read and write (*offensive*) **2.** UNEDUCATED with an inadequate education in or knowledge of a particular subject, or none at all ○ *artistically illiterate* **3.** MAKING MANY LANGUAGE MISTAKES full of, or making many basic errors in the use of language ○ *illiterate prose* ■ *n.* OFFENSIVE TERM an offensive term for sb who lacks education and knowledge, especially sb who cannot read or write (*offensive*) [15thC. From Latin *illiterat(t)us*, literally 'not lettered', from *lit(t)eratus* 'lettered, learned' (see LITERATE).] —**illiterately** *adv.* —**illiterateness** *n.*

ill-judged *adj.* showing a lack of good judgment or an incorrect assessment of a situation

ill-mannered *adj.* rude or impolite —**ill-manneredly** *adv.*

ill nature *n.* a bad-tempered, unpleasant, or unkind disposition

ill-natured /-náychərd/ *adj.* bad-tempered, unpleasant, or unkind —**ill-naturedly** *adv.* —**ill-naturedness** *n.*

illness /ílnəss/ *n.* **1.** DISEASE OR SICKNESS a disease, sickness, or other such indisposition **2.** BAD HEALTH a state of bad health

illocution /íllə kyoósh'n/ *n.* an action such as naming, threatening, warning, or promising that is carried out simply by saying the appropriate words [Mid-20thC. Coined by the philosopher J. L. Austin from IL + LOCUTION.] —**illocutionary** *adj.*

illogical /i lójjik'l/ *adj.* **1.** NOT FOLLOWING RULES OF LOGIC not following the rules of logic, or not following logically from a previous premise, statement, or action **2.** UNREASONABLE apparently unreasonable or perverse, especially in not being or not giving the expected response —**illogicality** /i lójji kálləti/ *n.* —**illogically** /i lójjikli/ *adv.*

ill-omened /-ṓmənd/ *adj.* accompanied by signs suggesting disaster or failure

ill-sorted *adj.* = ill-assorted

ill-starred *adj.* doomed to end in failure or disaster (*formal*) [From the astrological belief that an unpropitious arrangement of the celestial bodies at the time of a birth or the start of an undertaking predetermined an unhappy outcome]

ill-tempered *adj.* having or showing an irritable mood or disposition —**ill-temperedly** *adv.*

ill-timed *adj.* done or occurring at the wrong time and thus not having the desired effect

ill-treat *vt.* **1.** ABUSE to behave cruelly or unkindly towards a person or animal **2.** MISUSE to misuse sth or give sth rough treatment —**ill-treatment** *n.*

——————— **WORD KEY: SYNONYMS** ———————
See Synonyms at ***misuse***.

illume /i loóm, i lyoóm/ (**-lumes, -luming, -lumed**) *vt.* to cast illumination on sth (*archaic literary*) [Early 17thC. Contraction of ILLUMINE.]

illuminance /i loóminənss/ *n.* the amount of light, evaluated according to its capacity to produce visual stimulation, that reaches a unit of surface area during a unit of time. It is measured in lux. Symbol E_v

illuminant /i loóminənt/ *n.* sth that gives off or provides light [Mid-17thC. From Latin *illuminant-*, the present participle stem of *illuminare* (see ILLUMINATE).]

illuminate /i loómi nayt/ *v.* (**-nates, -nating, -nated**) **1.** *vti.* SHINE LIGHT ON STH to make sth visible or bright with light, or be lit up **2.** *vt.* DECORATE WITH LIGHTS to decorate sth with lights for a celebration **3.** *vt.* CLARIFY to make sth clear, or easier to understand and appreciate **4.** *vti.* ENLIGHTEN SB to provide sb with knowledge or with intellectual or spiritual enlightenment (*literary; often passive*) **5.** *vt.* PRINTING ADD COLOURED ELEMENTS TO PAGE to add coloured letters, illustrations, and designs to a manuscript or the borders of a page **6.** *vt.* CAUSE TO LOOK HAPPY AND ANIMATED to make sth, especially sb's face, look happy and animated ■ *n.* SB ENLIGHTENED sb who has or claims to have special enlightenment (*archaic*) [15thC. From Latin *illuminat-*, the past participle stem of *illuminare* 'to light up', ultimately from the stem *lumin-* 'light' (source of English *luminous*).] —**illuminated** *adj.* —**illuminative** *adj.* —**illuminator** *n.*

illuminati /i loómi naáti/, **Illuminati** *npl.* any of various groups of people in history claiming to have received special religious or spiritual enlightenment, especially an 18th-century German secret society with deist and republican ideas. The name was also applied to several groups in 18th-century France, a group of religious enthusiasts in 16th-century Spain, and the Rosicrucians. [Late 16thC. Via Italian from Latin, plural of *illuminatus*, past participle of *illuminare* (see ILLUMINATE).]

illuminating /i loómi nayting/ *adj.* informative and enlightening, often by revealing or emphasizing facts that were previously obscure —**illuminatingly** *adv.*

Illumination: Title page of the manuscript *Augustinus Questiones in Heptateuchon* (8th century)

illumination /i loómi náysh'n/ *n.* **1.** ACT OF ILLUMINATING the provision of light to make sth visible or bright, or the fact of being lit up **2.** USABLE LIGHT the amount or strength of light available in a place or for a purpose **3.** CLARIFICATION AND EXPLANATION the process of clarifying or explaining sth **4.** ENLIGHTENMENT intellectual or spiritual enlightenment **5.** PRINTING ORNAMENTATION OF PAGE a coloured letter, design, or illustration decorating a manuscript or page, or the art or act of decorating written texts **6.** PHYS = illuminance **7.** DECORATIVE STREET LIGHT a group of coloured lights used to decorate streets and public buildings, especially at Christmas or other festive occasions —**illuminational** *adj.*

illumine /i loómin/ (**-mines, -mining, -mined**) *vti.* to illuminate sb or sth, or become illuminated (*literary*) [14thC. Via French *illuminer* from Latin *illuminare* (see ILLUMINATE).] —**illuminable** *adj.*

illuminism /i loóminizəm/ *n.* the beliefs held by illuminati, especially their belief in or claim to special enlightenment

illus. *abbr.* **1.** illustrated **2.** illustration **3.** illustrator

ill-use *vt.* = ill-treat *v.* 1 —**ill-usage** *n.*

ill-used /-yoózd/ *adj.* cruelly or harshly treated

illusion /i loózh'n/ *n.* **1.** STH WITH DECEPTIVE APPEARANCE sth that deceives the senses or mind, e.g. by appearing to exist when it does not or appearing to be one thing when it is in fact another **2.** DECEPTIVE POWER OF APPEARANCES the ability of appearances to deceive the mind and senses or the capacity of the mind and senses to be deceived by appearances **3.** FALSE IDEA a false idea, conception, or belief concerning sth **4.** PSYCHOL MISTAKEN SENSORY PERCEPTION a misinterpretation of an experience of sensory perception, especially a visual one, where the stimuli are objectively present and the mistaken perception is due to physical rather than psychological causes. ◊ **hallucination** **5.** TEXTILES FINE GAUZE a fine gauze used for trimming. ◊ **tulle** [14thC. Via French from, ultimately, Latin *illus-*, past participle stem of *illudere* 'to play at', ultimately from *ludus* 'play, sport' (source of English *ludicrous*).] —**illusionary** *adj.* —**illusionless** *adj.*

——————— **WORD KEY: USAGE** ———————
See Usage note at ***allusion***.

illusionism /i loózh'nizəm/ *n.* the use of pictorial techniques to create illusions. ◊ **trompe l'oeil**

illusionist /i loózh'nist, i lyoó-/ *n.* **1.** MAGICIAN a performer of magical tricks **2.** PAINTING PAINTER WHO MAKES PICTORIAL ILLUSIONS an artist who creates pictorial illusions —**illusionistic** /i loózh'n ístik/ *adj.* —**illusionistically** /-ístikli/ *adv.*

illusive /i loóssiv, i lyoó-/ *adj.* = illusory [Early 17thC. From medieval Latin *illusivus* 'deceptive', from the Latin stem *illus-* (see ILLUSION).] —**illusively** *adv.* —**illusiveness** *n.*

illusory /i loózəri, i loóss-/ *adj.* produced by, based on, or consisting of an illusion [Late 16thC. Directly or via French *illusoire* from ecclesiastical Latin *illusorius* 'ironical, of mocking character', from the Latin stem *illus-* (see ILLUSION).] —**illusorily** *adv.* —**illusoriness** *n.*

illustrate /íllə strayt/ (**-trates, -trating, -trated**) *v.* **1.** *vt.* ARTS ACCOMPANY WITH PICTURES to provide explanatory or decorative pictures to accompany a printed, spoken, or electronic text ○ *The book was illustrated with diagrams.* **2.** *vti.* FULLY EXPLAIN to clarify sth by giving examples or making comparisons **3.** *vt.* BE CHARACTERISTIC OF to be a good example of sth, or serve to demonstrate sth and make it clear ○ *a case that illustrates the need for legislation* [Early 16thC. From Latin *illustrat-*, the past participle stem of *illustrare* 'to light up', from *lustrare* (source of English *lustre*).] —**illustratable** *adj.* —**illustrator** *n.*

illustration /íllə stráysh'n/ *n.* **1.** PICTURE THAT COMPLEMENTS TEXT a drawing, photograph, or diagram that accompanies and complements a printed, spoken, or electronic text **2.** ARTS PROVISION OF PICTURES ACCOMPANYING TEXT the art or process of producing or providing pictures to accompany a text **3.** STH THAT HELPS EXPLAIN an example or comparison that helps to clarify or explain sth —**illustrational** *adj.*

illustrative /ílləstrətiv, i lús-, íllə straytiv/ *adj.* serving to illustrate or explain sth —**illustratively** *adv.*

illustrious /i lústri əss/ *adj.* extremely distinguished and deservedly famous [Mid-16thC. Formed from Latin *illustris* 'bright, famous', from *illustrare* (see ILLUSTRATE).] —**illustriously** *adv.* —**illustriousness** *n.*

illuviation /i loóvi áysh'n/ *n.* the process by which materials such as colloids and salts are washed from an upper layer of soil to a lower one [Early 20thC. Coined from IL- + -*luviation* (as in ELUVIATION).] —**illuviated** /i loóvi aytid/ *adj.*

illuvium /i loóvi əm/ (*plural* **-ums** *or* **-a** /-vi ə/) *n.* colloids, salts, and other material washed from an upper to a lower layer of soil [Early 20thC. From modern Latin, from -*luvium* (as in ALLUVIUM).]

ill will *n.* a feeling or attitude of hostility, unfriendliness, or dislike towards sb ○ *They bore us no ill will.*

ill-wisher *n.* sb who wishes misfortune or evil to come to another person

Illyrian /i lírri ən, i léeri ən/ *n.* **1.** PEOPLES **HISTORICAL INHABITANT OF EASTERN ADRIATIC COAST** a member of any of the related peoples who, for over a thousand years from the late third century BC, occupied the Adriatic coastal regions from Albania northwards. The Illyrians were conquered by the Romans around 33 BC. **2.** LANG **EXTINCT LANGUAGE OF ILLYRIANS** an extinct language that was spoken in Illyria in ancient times. It is agreed that it was an Indo-European language, and generally thought to be related to Albanian. ■ *adj.* **CHARACTERISTIC OF ILLYRIA** relating to or characteristic of Illyria, its people, or extinct language [Mid-16thC. Formed from Latin *Illyrius*, from *Illyria*.]

ilmenite /ílmə nīt/ *n.* a mineral, usually found in basic metamorphic and igneous rocks, consisting of a mixed oxide of iron and titanium [Early 19thC. Named after the *Ilmen* Mountains in the southern Urals, Russia, where it was found.]

ILO *abbr.* International Labour Organization

Iloilo /éelō éelō/ city and capital of Iloilo Province, Philippines, situated in the southeastern part of the Iloilo Strait. Population: 309,505 (1990).

Ilorin /i lórrən/ city and capital of Kwara State, southwestern Nigeria, situated approximately 274 km/170 mi. northeast of Lagos. Population: 420,000 (1991).

ILS *abbr.* AEROSP instrument landing system

I'm /īm/ *contr.* I am

IM *abbr.* **1.** CHESS International Master **2.** MED intramuscular

i.m. *abbr.* MED intramuscular

im- *prefix.* = **in-**[1], **in-**[2] (*used before b, m, and p*)

image /ímmij/ *n.* **1. ACTUAL OR MENTAL PICTURE** a picture or likeness of sb or sth, produced either physically by a sculptor, painter, or photographer, or conjured in the mind **2.** OPTICS **LIKENESS SEEN OR PRODUCED** the likeness of sb or sth that appears in a mirror, through a lens, or on the retina of the eye, or that is produced electronically on a screen **3. SB CLOSELY RESEMBLING SB ELSE** sb who or sth that is very like sb or sth else in appearance ○ *She's the image of her grandmother.* **4. CONSPICUOUS EXAMPLE** an extremely typical or extreme example of sth **5.** LITERAT **EXAMPLE OF FIGURATIVE LANGUAGE** a figure of speech, especially a metaphor or simile **6.** MATH **SET OF FUNCTION'S VALUES** the value of a mathematical function corresponding to a specific value of the function's variable ■ *vt.* (**-ages, -aging, -aged**) **1. CREATE IMAGE OF** to produce a physical or mental image of sth **2.** MED **MAKE VISUAL IMAGE OF BODY STRUCTURES** to produce a visual representation of bodily structures, using X-rays, ultrasound, radioactivity, heat, or magnetism and, usually, computerized scanning devices, as an aid to diagnosis and treatment **3. PICTURE IN MIND** to form a mental image of sth **4. DESCRIBE STH IN VISUAL TERMS** to describe vividly or in visual terms **5. TYPIFY** to embody or typify sth [12thC. Via French from Latin *imago* 'likeness' (source of English *imagine*). Originally 'statue, figurine'.] —**imageable** *adj.* —**imageless** *adj.* —**imager** *n.*

image compression *n.* COMPUT a technique based on fractal mathematics for reducing the amount of digitized information needed to store a visual image such as a film electronically

image converter *n.* an optical-electronic device that reproduces an image formed by invisible radiation such as ultraviolet and infrared on a photoemissive surface as a visible-light image on a luminescent surface

image intensifier *n.* an optical-electronic device that amplifies an image formed by visible radiation on a photoemissive surface to present an enhanced image on a luminescent surface

image-maker *n.* sb employed to create a favourable public image of a business, organization, product, or public figure

image orthicon /-áwrthi kon/ *n.* a television camera tube in which an electron image on a photoemissive surface is focused onto a target for scanning

imagery /ímmijəri/ (*plural* **-ries**) *n.* **1.** LITERAT **METAPHORS AND SIMILES** the figurative language, especially metaphors and similes, used in poetry, plays, and other literary works **2. IMAGES IN THE MIND** a set of mental pictures produced by the memory or imagination or conjured up by a stimulus ○ *Her dreams were filled with surreal imagery.* **3.** ARTS **IMAGES IN ARTISTIC WORK** the pictorial images found in works of art such as paintings and sculptures **4. IMAGES COLLECTIVELY** a group or set of images considered together ○ *studying the CAT-scan imagery*

image tube *n.* an optical-electronic device that converts invisible radiation into a visible image, as in an image converter, or amplifies visible radiation into an enhanced image, as in an image intensifier

imaginable /i májjinəb'l/ *adj.* capable of being conceived or imagined ○ *the worst meal imaginable* —**imaginability** /i májjinə bílləti/ *n.* —**imaginably** /i májjinəbli/ *adv.*

imaginary /i májjinəri/ *adj.* **1. IN THE MIND** existing only in the mind, not in reality **2.** MATH **RELATING TO IMAGINARY NUMBERS** relating to or containing imaginary numbers, or being the coefficient of the imaginary part in a complex number. ◊ **imaginary number, complex number** ■ *n.* MATH = **imaginary number** [14thC. From Latin *imaginarius*, from *imagin-*, the stem of *imago* (see IMAGE).] —**imaginarily** *adv.* —**imaginariness** *n.*

imaginary number *n.* MATH a complex number in the form $a + ib$ where i is the square root of minus one, and b is not equal to zero. ◊ **real number**

imaginary part *n.* MATH the real number, b, in the complex number $a + ib$, where $i = \sqrt{-1}$

imagination /i májji náysh'n/ *n.* **1. ABILITY TO VISUALIZE** the ability to form images and ideas in the mind, especially of things never seen or never experienced directly **2. CREATIVE PART OF THE MIND** the part of the mind where ideas, thoughts, and images are formed **3. RESOURCEFULNESS** the ability to think of ways of dealing with difficulties or problems —**imaginational** *adj.*

imaginative /i májjinətiv/ *adj.* **1. SKILLED AT VISUALIZING OR THINKING ORIGINALLY** good at thinking of new ideas or at visualizing things that have not been seen or experienced **2. ORIGINAL** new and original or not likely to have been easily thought up by sb else ○ *an imaginative solution to a long-standing problem* **3. UNLIKELY** seeming untrue, implausible, or unlikely (*often used ironically*) **4. OF THE IMAGINATION** relating to the ability to form images and ideas in the mind, or to think of new things —**imaginativeness** *n.*

imaginatively /i májjinətivli/ *adv.* in a new and original way that would not have occurred readily to most people

imagine /i májjin/ *v.* (**-ines, -ining, -ined**) **1.** *vti.* **FORM AN IMAGE IN THE MIND** to form an image or idea of sth in the mind ○ *I can just imagine his reaction!* **2.** *vt.* **SEE OR HEAR STH UNREAL** to see or hear sth that is not there, or to think sth that is not true ○ *There's nothing there — you're imagining things!* **3.** *vt.* **ASSUME STH** to suppose or assume sth ■ *interj.* **imagine, imagine that EXPRESSION OF SURPRISE** used to express surprise [14thC. Via French from Latin *imaginare* 'to make an image of' and *imaginari* 'to picture to yourself', both formed from *imagin-*, the stem of *imago* (see IMAGE).] —**imaginer** *n.* —**imagining** *n.*

imagined /i májjind/ *adj.* existing only as an idea, thought, or assumption, not in reality

imaging /ímmijing/ *n.* **1. TECHNIQUE FOR MAKING IMAGES** any of several often computerized techniques, e.g. X-rays, ultrasound, radioactivity, heat, or magnetism, used to obtain images of bodies or body parts for diagnosis, emergency rescue, or surveillance **2.** PSYCHOL, ALTERN MED **USE OF MENTAL IMAGES** the use of mental images to ease pain, alter the course of disease processes, or help in achieving a goal

imagism /ímmijizzəm/ *n.* POETRY a literary movement of early 20th-century US and English poets that sought to modernize poetic language by the use of ordinary language, free verse, and precise everyday imagery —**imagist** *n.* —**imagistic** /ímmi jístik/ *adj.* —**imagistically** /-jístikli/ *adv.*

imago /i máy gō, i maá gō/ (*plural* **-goes** *or* **-gines** /i májjə neez/) *n.* **1.** INSECTS **SEXUALLY MATURE ADULT INSECT** an insect in its sexually mature adult state **2.** PSYCHOL **IDEALIZED MENTAL PICTURE** in psychoanalysis, an unconscious idealized mental picture, especially of a parent, that is formed early in life and retained in adulthood [Late 18thC. From Latin (see IMAGE).]

imam /i maám, i mám/, **imaum** /i maám, i máwm/ *n.* **1. LEADER OF MOSQUE PRAYERS** a man who leads the prayers in a mosque **2. imam, Imam RELIGIOUS LEADER DESCENDED FROM MUHAMMAD** any of various Islamic religious leaders regarded as direct descendants of Muhammad or Ali and appointed by Allah **3. ISLAMIC COMMUNITY LEADER** a leader of an Islamic community **4. ISLAMIC SCHOLAR** a respected Islamic scholar, especially a founder of a school of theology or law [Early 17thC. From Arabic *'imām*, literally 'leader'.]

imamate /i maá mayt/ *n.* **1. IMAM'S POSITION OR PERIOD OF OFFICE** the title or position of an imam, or the period sb spends as an imam **2. IMAM'S TERRITORY** the area for which an imam is leader

IMarE *abbr.* Institute of Marine Engineers

imaret /i maá ret/ *n.* a place providing food and shelter for travellers and pilgrims in Turkey [Early 17thC. Via Turkish from Arabic *'imāra* 'building'.]

Imari /i maári/ *n.* a Japanese porcelain that is brightly decorated, especially with a floral design [Late 19thC. Named after the port of *Imari* in Kyushu, Japan, from which it was exported.]

imbalance /im bállənss/ *n.* **1. UNEVENNESS OF EMPHASIS** an unevenness, inequality, or bias existing between two or more people or things, especially in their degree of emphasis, proportions, or function **2. STATE OF DISHARMONY** a lack of harmony or an inability to function well or harmoniously, or sth causing this state ○ *a hormonal imbalance*

imbecile /ímbə seel, ímbə sīl/ *n.* **1. OFFENSIVE TERM** an offensive term that deliberately insults sb's level of intellect (*insult*) **2. OFFENSIVE TERM** offensive term in an absolute classification system for an IQ between 25 and 50 and a mental age of between two and seven years (*dated offensive*) [15thC. Via French from Latin *imbecillus*, literally 'without support', from *baculum* 'stick, staff'. The underlying meaning is 'weak, powerless'.] —**imbecilic** /ímbə síllik/ *adj.* —**imbecility** /-sílləti/ *n.*

imbed /im béd/ *vt.* = **embed**

imbibe /im bīb/ (**-bibes, -bibing, -bibed**) *v.* **1.** *vti.* **DRINK STH** to drink sth, especially alcohol (*formal or humorous*) **2.** *vt.* **ABSORB IDEAS** to take sth into the mind as if drinking a liquid (*literary*) **3.** *vt.* **TAKE STH IN AS IF DRINKING** to take in sth as if drinking it (*literary*) **4.** *vti.* **ABSORB STH** to absorb moisture, gas, light, or heat (*formal*) [14thC. From Latin *imbibere*, literally 'to drink in', from *bibere* 'to drink'.] —**imbiber** *n.*

imbibition /ím bi bísh'n/ *n.* CHEM the absorption or adsorption of sth, such as liquid or heat, by a mixture (**colloid**) such as a gel [15thC. From the medieval Latin stem *imbibition-* 'absorption, infusion', from Latin *imbibere* (see IMBIBE).] —**imbibitional** *adj.*

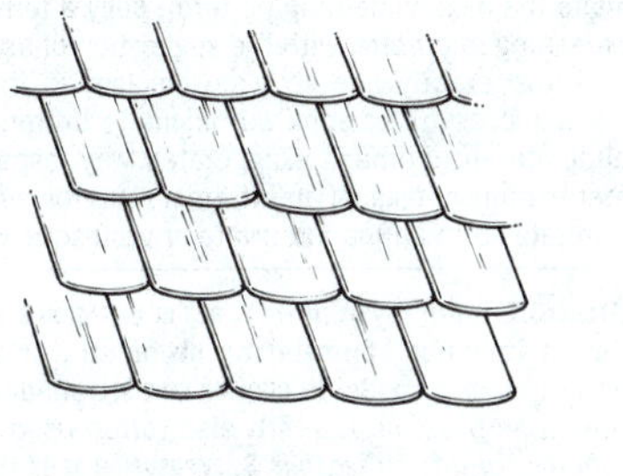

Imbricate

imbricate *adj.* /ímbri kət, ímbri kayt/ **1.** ARCHIT **CONSISTING OF OVERLAPPING TILES** consisting of overlapping tiles or slates **2.** BOT, ZOOL **OVERLAPPING LIKE ROOF TILES** used to describe plant or animal parts that overlap in a regular pattern ■ *vti.* /ímbri kayt/ (**-cates, -cating, -cated**) **OVERLAP OR BE OVERLAPPING** to lay things so that they overlap in layers, or to be overlapping in layers, in a similar way to roof tiles [Mid-17thC. From Latin *imbricare* 'to cover with pantiles', from *imbric-*, the stem of *imbrex* 'roof-tile', from *imber* 'rain'.] —**imbricated** /ímbri kaytid/ *adj.* —**imbrication** /ímbri káysh'n/ *n.*

imbroglio /im bróli ō/ (*plural* **-glios**) *n.* a confusing, messy, or complicated situation, especially one that involves disagreement or intrigue (*formal or literary*) [Mid-18thC. From Italian, from *brogliare* 'to mix up', probably from Old French *brouillier* (see BROIL[2]).]

imbrue /im bróo/ (**-brues, -bruing, -brued**) *vt.* to stain sth, especially with blood (*archaic or literary*) [Early 16thC. From Old French *embruer* 'to soil or spatter', of uncertain origin: perhaps from assumed Vulgar Latin *imbiberare*, from Latin *bibere* 'to drink'.] —**imbruement** *n.*

imbue /im byóo/ (**-bues, -buing, -bued**) *vt.* **1. FILL WITH A PARTICULAR QUALITY** to make sth or sb rich with a particular quality (*usually passive*) ○ *imbued with a strong sense of patriotism* **2. SOAK STH WITH STH** to saturate sth with a substance, especially dye (*formal*) [Late 16thC. From Latin *imbuere* 'to moisten, stain', of unknown origin.]

IMCO *abbr.* Intergovernmental Maritime Consultative Organization

IMechE *abbr.* Institution of Mechanical Engineers

IMF *abbr.* International Monetary Fund

IMHO *abbr.* in my humble opinion (*used in e-mail communications*)

imidazole /ímmi dázzōl, i míddəzōl/ *n.* an organic white crystalline base that inhibits the action of histamine. Formula: $C_3H_4N_2$. [Late 19thC. Coined from IMIDE + AZO- + -OLE.]

imide /ímmīd/ *n.* any of a class of organic compounds containing the NH group combined with an acid group and derived from ammonia [Mid-19thC. From French, alteration of *amide* (see AMIDE).] —**imidic** /i míddik/ *adj.*

imine /ímmeen, i méen/ *n.* any of a class of organic compounds containing the NH group combined with a nonacid group and derived from ammonia [Late 19thC. Alteration of AMINE, on the model of IMIDE.]

IMinE *abbr.* Institution of Mining Engineers

imipramine /i míprə meen/ *n.* a chemical with a three-ring (**tricyclic**) molecular structure, used as a drug in the treatment of depression. Formula: $C_{19}H_{24}N_2$. [Mid-20thC. Blend of IMINE, PROPYL, and AMINE.]

imit. *abbr.* 1. imitation 2. imitative

imitate /ímmi tayt/ (**-tates, -tating, -tated**) *vt.* **1. FOLLOW SB'S EXAMPLE** to use sb or sth as a model, attempting to copy an existing method, style, or approach **2. MIMIC SB** to copy sb's behaviour, voice, or manner, especially in order to make fun of him or her **3. BE OR LOOK LIKE STH** to be or look like sth else ○ *a case of life imitating art* [Mid-16thC. From Latin *imitari*, of unknown origin.] —**imitable** *adj.* —**imitability** /ímmitə bílləti/ *n.* —**imitator** /ímmi taytər/ *n.*

WORD KEY: SYNONYMS

imitate, copy, emulate, mimic, take off, ape

CORE MEANING: to adopt the behaviour of another person

imitate the most wide-ranging term; **copy** a term similar in meaning to *imitate*, with the suggestion of attempting to behave exactly like sb else; **emulate** to imitate sb who is successful or admired; **mimic** to imitate sb in a deliberate and perhaps exaggerated way, especially in order to amuse; **take off** an informal term for *mimic*; **ape** to imitate sb in an inappropriate or grotesque way.

imitation /ímmi táysh'n/ *n.* **1. ACT OF IMITATING STH** the act or an instance of imitating sb or sth, or of using sth or sb as a model **2. COPY OR FAKE** sth made to be as much as possible like sth else (*often used before a noun*) ○ *imitation leather* **3. IMPRESSION OF SB** the act of mimicking sb, or an impression of sb **4.** MUSIC **REPETITION OF A MUSICAL MOTIF** the repetition of a musical idea such as a melody or rhythmic figure in another part, often at another pitch and sometimes with variation ■ *adj.* **NOT GENUINE** synthetic, intended as a copy of sth, or not genuine —**imitational** *adj.*

imitative /ímmitətiv/ *adj.* **1. ATTEMPTING TO COPY STH** designed to be like sth else, but usually inferior to the original **2. INVOLVING IMITATION** involving or practising imitation **3.** = **onomatopoeic** —**imitatively** *adv.* —**imitativeness** *n.*

IMM *n., abbr.* **1.** International Mercantile Marine **2.** International Monetary Market

immaculate /i mákyoolət/ *adj.* **1. CLEAN** absolutely clean, tidy, and free from blemishes **2. FAULTLESS** showing faultless perfection [15thC. From Latin *immaculatus*, literally 'without stain', from, ultimately, *macula* 'blemish' (source of English *mackle*), of unknown origin.] —**immaculacy** *n.* —**immaculateness** *n.* —**immaculately** *adv.*

Immaculate Conception *n.* **1. VIRGIN MARY'S SINLESSNESS** the Roman Catholic doctrine that the Virgin Mary's soul was free from the stain of original sin from the moment of her soul's conception. The term does not, contrary to popular belief, refer to the conception of Jesus Christ. **2. FEAST OF THE IMMACULATE CONCEPTION** the feast of the Immaculate Conception, celebrated in the Roman Catholic Church on 8 December

immanent /ímmənənt/ *adj.* **1. WITHIN STH** existing within or inherent in sth (*formal*) **2.** RELIG **EXISTING IN ALL PARTS OF THE UNIVERSE** existing in, and extending into, all parts of the created world [Mid-16thC. From late Latin *immanere*, literally 'to dwell within', from Latin *manere* 'to remain or dwell'.] —**immanence** *n.* —**immanency** *n.* —**immanently** *adv.*

immanentism /ímmənəntizzəm/ *n.* the belief that God exists in, and extends into all of, the created universe, including the individual —**immanentist** *adj., n.* —**immanentistic** /ímmənən tístik/ *adj.*

Immanuel /i mánnyoo əl/, **Emmanuel** *n.* the Messiah, referred to in Jewish and Christian scriptures, whom Christians believe to be Jesus Christ [15thC. Via late Latin and Greek from Hebrew *'immānū'ēl*, literally 'with us is God'.]

immaterial /ímmə téeri əl/ *adj.* **1. NOT RELEVANT** lacking relevance or importance **2. HAVING NO PHYSICAL SUBSTANCE** not made of matter or not physically real [14thC. From late Latin *immaterialis*, from *materialis* (see MATERIAL).] —**immateriality** /ímmə téeri álləti/ *n.* —**immaterialness** /ímmə téeri əlnəss/ *n.* —**immaterially** /-téeri əli/ *adv.*

immaterialise *vt.* = **immaterialize**

immaterialism /ímmə téeri əlizzəm/ *n.* a metaphysical doctrine holding that the material world does not exist except as ideas or perceptions in the mind, or that only spirits and nonphysical things exist

immaterialize /ímmə téeri ə līz/ (**-izes, -izing, -ized**), **immaterialise** (**-ising, -ising, -ised**) *vt.* to take away the physical substance of sth and make it spiritual or intangible —**immaterialization** /ímmə téeri ə lī záysh'n/ *n.*

immature /ímmə tyóor, ímmə chóor/ *adj.* **1. NOT FULLY DEVELOPED** young, and not fully grown or developed **2. CHILDISH** lacking the wisdom or emotional development normally associated with adults (*disapproving*) **3. STYLISTICALLY CRUDE AND IMPERFECT** not yet having attained the perfection of a later, or fully developed, style ○ *an example of the artist's immature period* [Mid-16thC. From Latin *immaturus*, literally 'not ripe', from *maturus* (see MATURE).] —**immaturely** *adv.* —**immaturity** *n.* —**immatureness** *n.*

immeasurable /i mézhərəb'l/ *adj.* too large or too much to be measured —**immeasurability** /i mézhərə bílləti/ *n.* —**immeasurably** /i mézhərəbli/ *adv.* —**immeasurableness** /-b'lnəss/ *n.*

immed. *abbr.* immediate

immediate /i méedi ət/ *adj.* **1. WITHOUT PAUSE OR DELAY** happening or done at first, at once, or without delay ○ *the problem requires immediate attention* **2. NEAREST** nearest in time, space, or relationship ○ *only my immediate family were invited* **3. CURRENT** urgent or pressing, and so needing to be dealt with before anything else **4. HAVING A DIRECT EFFECT** affecting sth directly, without anything intervening **5.** PHILOS **KNOWN FROM EXPERIENCE** relating to sth that is known about from personal experience or by intuition **6.** LOGIC **DERIVED FROM A SINGLE PREMISE** used to describe an inference derived from a single premise, without any middle term, and often by conversion of a categorial statement. An example is 'some cows are brown, therefore some brown things are cows'. [14thC. Directly or via French from late Latin *immediatus*, literally 'not separated', from Latin *mediatus*, the past participle of *mediare* (see MEDIATE).] —**immediacy** /i mídi əsi/ *n.* —**immediateness** *n.*

immediate annuity *n.* FIN an annuity whose payments begin less than one year after it is bought. ◊ **deferred annuity**

immediate constituent *n.* the first level into which a linguistic unit is analysed, e.g. the subject and predicate as parts of a sentence

immediately /i méedi ətli/ *adv.* **1. AT ONCE** without delay or without pausing beforehand **2. VERY CLOSELY** very closely in space or time **3. DIRECTLY** directly, and without anyone or anything in between ■ *conj.* **AS SOON AS** as soon as, or at the moment that

immemorial /ímmi máwri əl/ *adj.* so old that it seems always to have existed ○ *have known them since time immemorial* ○ *immemorial customs of the nation* [Early 17thC. From medieval Latin *immemorialis*, literally 'not belonging to memory', from Latin *memoria* (see MEMORY).] —**immemorially** *adv.*

immense /i ménss/ *adj.* **1. HUGE** very large in extent or degree ○ *an immense desert* ○ *immense relief* **2. UNABLE TO BE MEASURED** too large to be measurable **3. EXCELLENT** very good or showing excellence (*informal*) [15thC. Via French from Latin *immensus*, literally 'not measured', from *mensus*, the past participle of *metiri* (see MEASURE).] —**immensely** *adv.* —**immenseness** *n.* —**immensity** *n.*

immensely *adv.* to a very great extent or degree ○ *she was immensely rich*

immerse /i múrss/ (**-merses, -mersing, -mersed**) *v.* **1. COMPLETELY COVER STH IN LIQUID** to put sth into a liquid so that the liquid's surface covers it completely **2.** *vr.* **OCCUPY YOURSELF TOTALLY WITH STH** to become completely occupied with sth, giving all your time, energy, or concentration to it **3.** *vt.* CHR **BAPTIZE SB** to baptize sb, especially in the Baptist Church, by lowering the person's head and upper body, or sometimes the whole body, into water [Early 17thC. From Latin *immers-*, the past participle stem of *immergere*, literally 'to plunge into', from *mergere* (see MERGE).]

immerser /i múrssər/ *n.* an immersion heater (*informal*)

immersion /i múrsh'n/ *n.* **1. COMPLETE INVOLVEMENT** involvement in sth that completely occupies all the time, energy, or concentration available **2.** EDUC **INTENSIVE LANGUAGE TEACHING** an intensive method of teaching sb a language, in which all teaching is carried out in the language that is being learned ○ *an immersion course in Gaelic* **3. PLACING OF STH UNDER LIQUID** the dipping of sth into a liquid so that it is completely covered **4.** CHR **BAPTISM BY DIPPING BODY IN WATER** the practice, especially in the Baptist Church, of baptism by lowering a person's head and upper body, or sometimes the whole body, into water **5.** ASTRON **DISAPPEARANCE OF A CELESTIAL BODY BEFORE AN ECLIPSE** the movement of a celestial body, such as the Moon, into the shadow of another body, causing an eclipse

immersion heater *n.* an electric water heater with the heating element completely submerged in the water, especially one that is part of a domestic hot-water tank

immersionism /i múrsh'nizəm/ *n.* the belief that immersion is the only true method of baptism

immesh /i mésh/ (**-meshes, -meshing, -meshed**) *vt.* = **enmesh**

immigrant /ímmigrənt/ *n.* **1. SB COMING TO SETTLE IN A COUNTRY** sb who has come to a country and settled there **2.** BOT, ZOOL **PLANT OR ANIMAL IN A NEW PLACE** a plant or animal that establishes itself in a place where it was not found before ■ *adj.* **SETTLING IN ANOTHER COUNTRY** relating to those who have come to settle in another country

immigrate /ímmi grayt/ (**-grates, -grating, -grated**) *vi.* **1. COME AND SETTLE IN A COUNTRY** to enter a new country for the purpose of settling there **2.** BOT, ZOOL **ARRIVE FROM ELSEWHERE** to become established in a new environment [Early 17thC. From Latin *immigrare*, literally 'to move into', from *migrare* (see MIGRATE).] —**immigrator** *n.* —**immigratory** *adj.*

immigration /ímmi gráysh'n/ *n.* **1. ARRIVAL OF SETTLERS IN A NEW COUNTRY** the act of people entering into a new country to settle permanently **2. PASSPORT CONTROL**

a at; aa father; aw all; ay day; air hair; ə about, edible, item, common, circus; e egg; ee eel; hw when; i it, happy; ī ice; 'l apple; 'm rhythm; 'n fashion; o odd; ō open; ōō good; oo pool; ow owl; oy oil; th thin; th this; u up; ur urge;

the control point at an airport, seaport, or border crossing where people entering a country must stop to have their passports officially checked **3. Immigration** *US* INS the United States Immigration and Naturalization Service **(INS)** (*informal*) **—immigrational** *adj.*

imminent /ímminənt/ *adj.* about to happen or threatening to happen [Early 16thC. From Latin *imminere*, literally 'to hang over', from *minere* (see EMINENT).] **—imminence** *n.* **—imminently** *adv.* **—imminentness** *n.*

immiscible /i míssəb'l/ *adj.* used to describe two or more liquids that will not mix together to form a single homogenous substance [Late 17thC. From late Latin *immiscibilis*, literally 'not subject to mixing', from Latin *miscere* 'to mix'.] **—immiscibility** /i míssə bíllәti/ *n.* **—immiscibly** /i míssəbli/ *adv.*

immitigable /i míttigəb'l/ *adj.* incapable of being alleviated, weakened, or softened (*literary*) [Late 16thC. From late Latin *immitigabilis*, from Latin *mitigare* (see MITIGATE).] **—immitigability** /i míttigə bíllәti/ *n.* **—immitigableness** /i míttigəb'lnəss/ *n.* **—immitigably** /-bli/ *adv.*

immittance /i mítt'ns/ *n.* the joint concept of electrical admittance and impedance [Mid-20thC. Blend of IMPEDANCE and ADMITTANCE.]

immix /i míks/ (**-mixes, -mixing, -mixed**) *vt.* to mix or blend sth in (*archaic*) [15thC. Back-formation from earlier *immixt* 'commingled', from Latin *immixtus*, the past participle of *immiscere*, literally 'to mix in', from *miscere* 'to mix'.] **—immixture** *n.*

immobile /i mṓ bīl/ *adj.* **1.** MOTIONLESS without moving ○ *he stood perfectly immobile for a few seconds* **2.** INCAPABLE OF MOTION unable to move or be moved [14thC. Via French from Latin *immobilis*, literally 'not moving', from *mobilis* (see MOBILE).] **—immobility** /ímmō bíllәti/ *n.*

immobilise *vt.* = **immobilize**

immobilize /i mṓbi līz/ (**-lizes, -lizing, -lized**), **immobilise** (**-lises, -lising, -lised**) *vt.* **1.** MAKE MOTIONLESS to make sb or sth completely still (*often passive*) **2.** PUT A MACHINE OUT OF ACTION to make a machine or device stop working, or adjust or damage it so that it cannot be made to work **3.** MED KEEP THE BROKEN PART OF A LIMB STILL to rest a joint, or keep the parts of a fractured limb fixed in place so that they are unable to move **4.** FIN TAKE OUT OF CIRCULATION to withdraw money or other capital from circulation to establish a reserve **—immobilization** /i mṓbi lī záysh'n/ *n.*

immobilizer, immobiliser *n.* an electronic security device that can be fitted to a motor vehicle, to stop the engine working and prevent the vehicle from being stolen

immoderate /i móddərət/ *adj.* going beyond what is healthy, moral, appropriate, or socially acceptable (*formal*) [14thC. From Latin *immoderatus*, literally 'not restrained', from *moderatus* (see MODERATE).] **—immoderacy** *n.* **—immoderately** *adv.* **—immoderateness** *n.* **—immoderation** /i móddə ráysh'n/ *n.*

immodest /i móddist/ *adj.* **1.** BOASTFUL boasting, or tending to boast a great deal **2.** INDECENT likely to embarrass, offend, or shock people, especially because of open references to sexual matters or exposure of parts of the body that are normally covered [Late 16thC. Directly or via French from Latin *immodestus*, from *modestus* 'kept within due measure'.] **—immodestly** *adv.* **—immodesty** *n.*

immolate /ímmə layt/ (**-lates, -lating, -lated**) *vt.* **1.** KILL AS A SACRIFICE to kill a person or an animal, e.g. as a ritual sacrifice, or to commit suicide as a protest, especially by burning (*formal*) **2.** SACRIFICE STH HIGHLY VALUED to give up sth that is highly valued (*literary*) [Mid-16thC. From Latin *immolare* 'to sprinkle with meal', from *mola* 'meal, millstone'; from the custom of sprinkling sacrificial victims with meal.] **—immolation** /ímmə láysh'n/ *n.* **—immolator** /ímmə laytər/ *n.*

immoral /i mórrəl/ *adj.* contrary to accepted moral principles **—immorality** /ímə rállәti/ *n.* **—immorally** /i mórrəli/ *adv.*

immoralist /i mórrəlist/ *n.* sb who engages in immoral acts, who rejects moral values, or who urges others to behave immorally

immortal /i máwrt'l/ *adj.* **1.** ABLE TO LIVE OR LAST FOREVER able to have eternal life or existence **2.** FAMOUS very famous and likely to be remembered for a long time ■ *n.* **1.** SB OR STH FAMOUS sb or sth famous that people will remember for a long time (*often used in the plural*) **2. immortal, Immortal** A GOD a god who lives for ever, especially a god of ancient Greece or Rome [14thC. From Latin *immortalis*, literally 'not subject to death', from *mortalis* (see MORTAL).] **—immortality** /ímmawr tállәti/ *n.* **—immortally** /i máwrtəli/ *adv.*

immortalise *vt.* = **immortalize**

immortalize /i máwrt'l īz/ (**-izes, -izing, -ized**), **immortalise** (**-ises, -ising, -ised**) *vt.* **1.** MAKE SB'S MEMORY LIVE ON to make sb or sth famous for a very long time, especially as the subject of a work of art such as a painting, novel, or film **2.** GIVE ETERNAL LIFE TO to elevate a mortal person to the state of divinity or bestow eternal life on sb **3.** BIOL CAUSE TO REPRODUCE INDEFINITELY to cause sth such as human cells to reproduce indefinitely **—immortalization** /i máwrt'l ī záysh'n/ *n.*

immortelle /ímmawr tél/ *n.* PLANTS = **everlasting** *n.* 2 [Mid-19thC. From French, shortened from *fleur immortelle*, literally 'undying flower'.]

immotile /i mṓ tīl/ *adj.* BOT, ZOOL used to describe a plant or animal part that cannot move **—immotility** /ímmō tíllәti/ *n.*

immovable /i móovəb'l/, **immoveable** *adj.* **1.** UNABLE TO BE MOVED fixed in a permanent position, or incapable of being moved **2.** OF FIXED OPINION sticking firmly to an opinion or decision **3.** ALWAYS OCCURRING ON THE SAME DATE used to describe a religious festival that always falls on the same date each year, like, e.g., Christmas, but unlike Easter ■ *n.* **immovable, immoveable** LAW BUILDING OR LAND property that consists of land or buildings (*often used in the plural*) **—immovability** /i móovə bíllәti/ *n.* **—immovableness** /i móovəb'lnəss/ *n.* **—immovably** /-bli/ *adv.*

immun. *abbr.* **1.** immunity **2.** immunization **3.** immunology

immune /i myóon/ *adj.* **1.** IMMUNOL SAFE FROM A PARTICULAR DISEASE protected from getting a particular disease because of natural resistance, resistance acquired after catching the disease before, or resistance conferred by inoculation ○ *immune to smallpox* **2.** IMMUNOL RELATING TO DISEASE RESISTANCE relating to a body's resistance to disease, or the creation of resistance **3.** NOT SUBJECT TO OR RESPONSIBLE FOR exempt from sth that others are subject to or made to endure or perform ○ *immune from prosecution* **4.** NOT AFFECTED BY STH not sensitive or susceptible to sth ○ *immune to flattery* [Late 19thC. From Latin *immunis* 'exempt from public service', from *munis* 'ready for service' (related to English *municipal*).]

immune complex /ímmyóonō kómpleks/, **immunocomplex** *n.* a combination of a disease-causing agent **(antigen)** and its corresponding antibody that plays a role in some types of immune responses and may be associated with autoimmune disease

immune response *n.* **1.** RESPONSE OF THE IMMUNE SYSTEM the overall activity of the body's immune system following the arrival of a disease-causing agent **(antigen) 2.** BIOLOGICAL DEFENCE SYSTEM OF AN ORGANISM the integrated defence mounted by an organism against a disease-causing agent **(antigen)**, including the production of antibodies and white blood cells designed to destroy the antigen or render it harmless

immune system *n.* the interacting combination of all the body's ways of recognizing cells, tissues, objects, and organisms that are not part of itself, and initiating the immune response to fight them

immunise *vt.* = **immunize**

immunity /i myóonəti/ (*plural* **-ties**) *n.* **1.** IMMUNOL RESISTANCE TO DISEASE a body's ability to resist a particular disease, whether existing naturally or as a result of inoculation or previous infection **(acquired immunity)**. In active immunity, the body itself produces appropriate antibodies and lymphocytes, while in passive immunity, antibodies are introduced from another source, as from mother to foetus. ○ *immunity to smallpox* **2.** FREEDOM FROM RESPONSIBILITY OR PUNISHMENT exemption or protection from sth unpleasant, such as a duty or penalty, to which others are subject ○ *immunity from prosecution*

immunize /ímmyoo nīz/ (**-nizes, -nizing, -nized**), **immunise** (**-nises, -nising, -nised**) *vt.* **1.** IMMUNOL MAKE SB RESISTANT TO A DISEASE to make sb resistant to a particular disease, especially by inoculation ○ *immunized against tuberculosis* **2.** GRANT SB EXEMPTION give sb exemption or protection from sth to which others are subject, especially in a criminal matter under investigation **—immunization** /ímmyoo nī záysh'n/ *n.* **—immunizer** /ímmyoo nīzər/ *n.*

immuno- *prefix.* immune, immunity ○ *immunodeficiency* [From IMMUNE]

immunoassay /ímmyóonō ássay/ *n.* the use of disease-causing agents **(antigens)** and their corresponding antibodies to detect and analyse various chemical substances **—immunoassayist** *n.*

immunochemistry /ímmyóonō kémmistri/ *n.* the branch of chemistry dealing with the chemical reactions of immunity **—immunochemical** /-kémmik'l/ *adj.*

immunocompetence /ímmyóonō kómpitənss/ *n.* the ability of the body to develop an immune response in the presence of a disease-causing agent **(antigen) —immunocompetent** *adj.*

immunocomplex *n.* IMMUNOL = **immune complex**

immunocompromised /ímmyóonō kómprə mīzd/ *adj.* lacking an adequate immune response as a result of disease, exposure to radiation, or treatment with immunosuppressive drugs

immunodeficiency /ímmyóonō di físh'nssi/ (*plural* **-cies**) *n.* the inability, either inborn or acquired, of the body to produce an adequate immune response to fight disease **—immunodeficient** *adj.*

immunodepression /ímmyóonō di présh'n/ *n.* = **immunosuppression**

immunodiagnosis /ímmyóonō dī əg nṓssiss/ (*plural* **-noses** /-seez/) *n.* the diagnosis of disease by studying the antibodies in a sample of blood serum **—immunodiagnostic** /-nóstik/ *adj.*

immunoelectrophoresis /ímmyóonō i léktrō fə réessiss/ *n.* the separation and identification of proteins using precipitates formed by specific immunological reactions **—immunoelectrophoretic** /-fə réttik/ *adj.* **—immunoelectrophoretically** *adv.*

immunofluorescence /ímmyóonō floor réss'nss/ *n.* the labelling of antibodies or disease-causing agents **(antigens)** with a fluorescent dye in order to identify or locate them in a tissue sample **—immunofluorescent** *adj.*

immunogenetics /ímmyóonō jə néttiks/ *n.* the discipline that studies the genetic basis of the immune system. This study is especially important in organ transplantation, where a close genetic match of tissue lowers the likelihood of organ rejection. (*takes a singular verb*) **—immunogenetic** *adj.* **—immunogeneticist** /-jə néttissist/ *n.*

immunogenic /ímmyóonō jénnik/ *adj.* creating immunity or an immune response **—immunogenically** *adv.* **—immunogenicity** /-jə nísseti/ *n.*

immunoglobulin /ímmyóonō glóbbyóolin/ *n.* BIOCHEM a glycoprotein with a high molecular weight that acts like an antibody and is produced by white blood cells during an immune response. Immunoglobulins are found in blood serum, the respiratory and digestive tracts, and body secretions, and they are grouped into five classes on the basis of their structure and physiological activity.

immunohaematology /ímmyóonō héemə tólləji/ *n.* the discipline concerned with all aspects of immunology relating to the blood, including blood groups and blood disorders **—immunohaematologic** /-heemətə lójjik/ *adj.* **—immunohaematological** *adj.*

immunohematology /ímmyóonō heemə tólləji/ *n.* MED US = **immunohaematology**

immunol. *abbr.* immunology

immunology /ímmyoo nólləji/ *n.* the scientific study of the way the immune system works in the body, including allergies, resistance to disease, and acceptance or rejection of foreign tissue **—immunologic** /ímmyoonə lójjik/ *adj.* **—immunological** /-lójjik'l/ *adj.* **—immunologically** /-lójjikli/ *adv.* **—immunologist** /ímmyoo nólləjist/ *n.*

immunopathology /ímmyóonōpə thólləji/ *n.* the study of disorders of the immune system and the resulting diseases or allergies —**immunopathologic** /ímmyōōnō páthə lójjik/ *adj.* —**immunopathological** /-lójjik'l/ *adj.* — **immunopathologist** /ímmyōōnō pə thóllǝjist/ *n.*

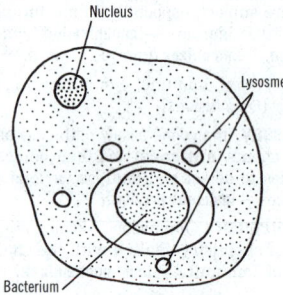

Immunoreaction: Section of immune cell ingesting and degrading disease-causing bacterium

immunoreaction /i myóōnō ri áksh'n/ *n.* the reaction between a disease-causing agent (**antigen**) and its specific antibody, either as the body's immune response or as part of a laboratory procedure — **immunoreactive** /-áktiv/ *adj.* —**immunoreactivity** /i myōōnō ri ak tívvǝti/ *n.*

immunosuppression /ímmyōōnō sǝ présh'n/ *n.* the inhibition of the immune response, usually deliberately by administering drugs to prevent rejection of transplanted organs, but sometimes resulting from disease, as in the case of AIDS — **immunosuppressant** /-sǝ préss'nt/ *adj., n.* —**immunosuppressive** /-préssiv/ *adj., n.*

immunotherapy /ímmyōōnō thérrǝpi/ *n.* treatment of disease or other disorders by strengthening the body's immune system, e.g. by administering antibodies —**immunotherapeutic** /ímmyōōnō thérrǝ pyóōtik/ *n.*

immure /i myōōr/ (**-mures, -muring, -mured**) *vt.* **1.** IMPRISON SB to confine sb in prison (*literary*) (*usually passive*) **2.** SHUT SB AWAY to shut away or seclude sb (*formal*) (*often passive*) **3.** ENCLOSE STH to enclose sth in a wall or surround sth with walls (*archaic*) [Late 16thC. Directly or via French *emmurer* from Latin *immurare*, literally 'to wall in', from *murus* 'wall'.] —**immurement** *n.*

immutable /i myōōtǝb'l/ *adj.* not changing or not able to be changed [15thC. From Latin *immutabilis*, literally 'unchanging', from *mutare* 'to change'.] —**immutability** /i myōōtǝ bílląti/ *n.* —**immutableness** /i myōōtǝb'lnǝss/ *n.* —**immutably** /-bli/ *adv.*

IMO *abbr.* **1.** International Meteorological Organization **2.** International Miners' Organization **3.** in my opinion (*used in e-mail communications*)

imp /imp/ *n.* **1.** NAUGHTY FAIRY in children's stories, a small mischievous creature resembling a fairy **2.** MISCHIEVOUS CHILD a high-spirited or mischievous child **3.** DEMON a small demon or devil ■ *vt.* (**imps, imping, imped**) REPAIR A HAWK'S FEATHERS to repair the broken wing of a hawk or falcon by grafting on new feathers [Old English *impa* 'young shoot, scion' and *impian* 'to graft', both ultimately from Greek *emphuein*, literally 'to emplant', from *phuein* 'to grow, plant']

IMP *abbr.* **1.** COMPUT interface message processor **2.** BRIDGE International Match Point

imp. *abbr.* **1.** GRAM imperative **2.** GRAM imperfect **3.** **imp., IMP.** imperial **4.** GRAM impersonal **5.** import **6.** important **7.** imported **8.** importer **9.** imprimatur

Imp. *abbr.* **1.** Imperator **2.** Imperatrix

impact *n.* /ím pakt/ **1.** ACTION OF HITTING the action of one object hitting another **2.** FORCE OF COLLISION the force with which one object hits another **3.** EFFECT the strong effect that sth or sb has ■ *vti.* /im pákt/ (**-pacts, -pacting, -pacted**) **1.** STRIKE STH to strike sth with force **2.** HAVE AN EFFECT ON STH to have an immediate and strong effect on sth or sb [Early 17thC. From Latin *impactus*, the past participle of *impingere* (see IMPINGE).] —**impaction** /im páksh'n/ *n.*

— **WORD KEY: USAGE** —

Impact, noun and verb: The noun *impact*, in its figurative meaning, should normally convey some sense of powerful or dramatic consequence, and should not just be an

---

alternative word for *effect* or *impression*. To use it in a context like *he had an impact on everyone in the room* — except in highly unusual circumstances — is to devalue the word. Many careful users of the language strongly dislike the verb *impact* in any figurative sense whatsoever, regardless of whether the verb is followed by *on*: both, for example, *this impacts the company favourably* and *this impacts on the company* are courting contempt. The verb is undeniably common in business communication, but anyone who hopes to achieve an effect that is even faintly literary should avoid it in favour of *affect*, *change*, or the like. Use of the verb is uncontroversial only in physical senses: *The car impacted the railing.*

impact adhesive *n.* a powerful glue that begins to form a bond as soon as the two coated surfaces are brought together

impacted /im páktid/ *adj.* **1.** DENT WEDGED SIDEWAYS UNDER THE GUM wedged sideways against a barrier, usually the root of another tooth, and thus unable to break through the gum (*refers to an unerupted tooth*) **2.** MED WITH BROKEN ENDS JAMMED TOGETHER with the broken ends jammed tightly together by the initial trauma (*refers to a bone fracture*) **3.** DIFFICULT TO MOVE unable to be moved, usually because of being jammed in a narrow space

impact printer *n.* a printing device in which ink is pressed onto the paper by the printing element, as it is in a traditional typewriter

impact statement *n.* a written statement outlining the effects of sth on a particular person or place ○ *a consumer impact statement*

impact zone *n.* in surfing, the best and at the same time most dangerous position on a wave, where the water is about to separate into droplets

impair /im paír/ (**-pairs, -pairing, -paired**) *vt.* to lessen the quality, strength, or effectiveness of sth [14thC. Via Old French *empeirier* from assumed Vulgar Latin *empejorare*, literally 'to make worse', from Latin *pejor* 'worse'.] —**impairable** *adj.* —**impairer** *n.*

impaired /im paírd/ *adj.* with sth specified that is absent or lessened, either temporarily or permanently (*usually used in combination*) ○ *hearing-impaired*

impairment /im paírmǝnt/ *n.* **1.** LESSENING OR ABSENCE OF ABILITY a lessening or the absence of a particular physical or mental function **2.** ACT OF DAMAGING STH the causing of injury or harm to sth, such as the health of a particular area of the body or mind, or the function of a machine

Impala

impala /im paálǝ/ (*plural* **-las** *or* **-la**) *n.* a large reddish-brown African antelope with long curved horns that makes spectacular leaps when alarmed. Latin name: *Aepyceros melampus*. [Late 19thC. From Zulu *impala*.]

impale /im páyl/ (**-pales, -paling, -paled**), **empale** (**-pales, -paling, -paled**) *vt.* **1.** SPEAR to pierce sb or sth with a pointed object (*often passive*) **2.** FENCE IN to surround sth with a fence (*archaic*) **3.** HERALDRY COMBINE COATS OF ARMS to combine two coats of arms on a single shield, divided by a vertical stripe (**pale**) [Mid-16thC. Directly or via French *empaler* from medieval Latin *impalare*, literally 'to put on a stake', from *palus* 'stake'.] —**impalement** *n.* —**impaler** *n.*

impalpable /im pálpǝb'l/ *adj.* (*formal*) **1.** UNABLE TO BE TOUCHED OR SENSED not capable of being touched, or not

---

capable of being perceived by the senses **2.** HARD TO UNDERSTAND difficult to understand or grasp [Early 16thC. Directly or via French from late Latin *impalpabilis*, literally 'not touchable', from *palpare* 'to touch gently'.] —**impalpability** /im pálpǝ bílląti/ *n.* —**impalpably** /im pálpǝbli/ *adv.*

impanation /ímpǝ náysh'n/ *n.* according to some denominations of Christianity, the presence of the body and blood of Jesus Christ in bread and wine that has been consecrated for the service of Communion [Mid-16thC. From medieval Latin *impanare* 'to embody in bread', from Latin *panis* 'bread'.]

impanel /im pánn'l/ (**-els, -elling, -elled**), **empanel** (**-els, -elling, -elled**) *vt.* LAW **1.** LIST PEOPLE AS POSSIBLE JURORS to draw up a list of people to be selected for jury service **2.** SELECT A JURY FROM A LIST to select a jury from a list of eligible persons [15thC. From Anglo-Norman *empaneller* 'to put on a list', from *panel* 'list', 'jury list' (see PANEL).]

imparity /im párrǝti/ (*plural* **-ties**) *n.* = disparity *n.* 1 [Mid-16thC. From late Latin *imparitas*, from Latin *impar* 'unequal', from *par* 'equal'.]

impart /im paárt/ (**-parts, -parting, -parted**) *vt.* **1.** COMMUNICATE to communicate information or knowledge **2.** GIVE A QUALITY TO STH to give sth a particular quality [Mid-16thC. Via Old French *impartir* from Latin *impartire*, literally 'to give a share in', from *pars* 'part'.] —**impartation** /ím paar táysh'n/ *n.*

impartial /im paársh'l/ *adj.* having no direct involvement or interest and not favouring one person or side more than another —**impartiality** /im paárshi álląti/ *n.* —**impartially** /im paársh'li/ *adv.* —**impartialness** /-sh'lnǝss/ *n.*

impartible /im paártǝb'l/ *adj.* LAW not to be divided up [Late 16thC. From late Latin *impartibilis*, literally 'not divisible', from *partire* (see PART).] —**impartibility** /im paártǝ bílląti/ *n.* —**impartibly** /im paártǝbli/ *adv.*

impassable /im paássǝb'l/ *adj.* **1.** IMPOSSIBLE TO USE impossible to travel on or through, e.g. because of being in bad condition or being blocked by snow **2.** IMPOSSIBLE TO OVERCOME impossible to solve or overcome ○ *impassable obstacles to peace* —**impassability** /im paássǝ bílląti/ *n.* —**impassableness** /im paássǝb'lnǝss/ *n.* —**impassably** /-bli/ *adv.*

impasse /am paáss, ám paass, im paáss, ím paass/ *n.* a point at which no further progress can be made or agreement reached ○ *talks have reached an impasse* [Mid-19thC. From French, formed from *im-* 'not' + *passer* (see PASS).]

impassion /im pásh'n/ (**-sions, -sioning, -sioned**) *vt.* to arouse strong feelings in sb (*usually passive*) [Late 16thC. From Italian *impassionare*, from *passione* 'passion', from the late Latin stem *passion-* (see PASSION).]

impassioned /im pásh'nd/ *adj.* expressing or revealing strong feelings —**impassionedly** *adv.* —**impassionedness** *n.*

impassive /im pássiv/ *adj.* **1.** EXPRESSIONLESS showing no emotion, especially on the face **2.** DEVOID OF ALL EMOTION feeling no emotions at all, either positive or negative [Early 17thC. The literal meaning is 'without suffering or passion'.] —**impassively** *adv.* —**impassiveness** *n.* —**impassivity** /ímpǝ sívvǝti/ *n.*

— **WORD KEY: SYNONYMS** —

impassive, apathetic, phlegmatic, stolid, stoical, unmoved
CORE MEANING: showing no emotional reponse or interest
impassive suggesting the absence of any outward sign of emotion, whether of facial expression, gesture, or action; **apathetic** often used in a derogatory way and suggesting a failure to respond because of a total lack of interest and a state of inertia; **phlegmatic** a formal word indicating that sb has the kind of temperament that makes him or her generally unemotional and difficult to arouse; **stolid** describes sb who is unemotional and not easily excited or upset; **stoical** used approvingly to describe sb who accepts problems and difficulties without complaining or getting upset; **unmoved** describes sb's reaction if no emotion, surprise, or excitement is shown in a situation where this would normally have been expected.

impaste /im páyst/ (**-pastes, -pasting, -pasted**) *vt.* to cover sth thickly with paste, paste, or crust (*literary*) [Mid-16thC. From Italian *impastare*, literally 'to

---

paste on', from *pasta* (see PASTE).] —**impastation** /ìmpass táysh'n/ *n.*

impasto /im pástō/ *n.* **1.** TECHNIQUE OF PAINTING THICKLY the technique of applying paint so thickly that brush or knife strokes can be seen **2.** PAINT THICKLY APPLIED paint applied so thickly that brush or knife strokes can be seen [Late 18thC. From Italian, the past participle of *impastare* (see IMPASTE).]

impatience /im páysh'nss/ *n.* **1.** ANNOYANCE AT WAITING irritation at having to wait or at sb or sth that causes a wait **2.** EAGERNESS eagerness to do sth immediately, and unwillingness to wait

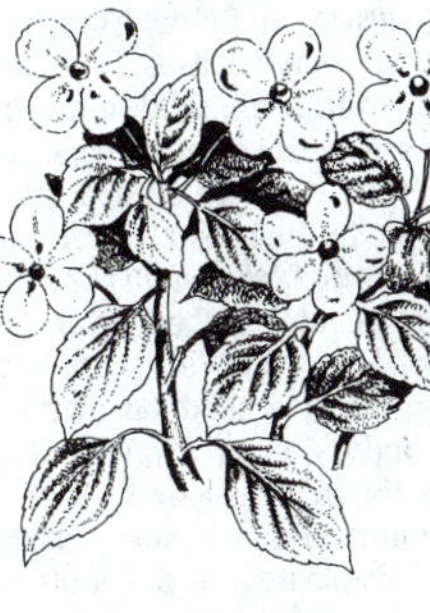

Impatiens

impatiens /im páyshi enz, -pátti-/ (*plural* **-tiens**) *n.* = **busy Lizzie** [Late 18thC. Via modern Latin, genus name, from Latin, literally 'impatient' (see IMPATIENT); so called because the capsules tend to burst open when touched.]

impatient /im páysh'nt/ *adj.* **1.** ANNOYED AT WAITING annoyed by being kept waiting or by being delayed **2.** EAGER eager to do sth immediately, and unwilling to wait **3.** SHOWING IMPATIENCE showing annoyance at being kept waiting, or keenness to get on with sth **4.** EASILY ANNOYED unable to tolerate a particular thing and easily annoyed by it ○ *he was impatient of formalities* [14thC. Via French from the Latin stem *impatient-*, literally 'not enduring', from *pati* 'to suffer'.] —**impatiently** *adv.*

impeach /im peéch/ (**-peaches, -peaching, -peached**) *vt.* **1.** *US* ACCUSE AN OFFICIAL OF AN OFFENCE in the United States, to charge a serving government official with serious misconduct while in office **2.** *US* CAST OUT OF PUBLIC OFFICE to remove sb, especially a president, from public office because of having committed high crimes and misdemeanours (*formal*) **3.** LAW ACCUSE OF A SERIOUS CRIME to accuse sb of a crime, especially treason or another crime against the state **4.** LAW BRING CHARGES AGAINST SB to charge sb with a crime or misdemeanour **5.** DISPARAGE to question sb's good character (*formal*) [14thC. Via Old French *empecher* from late Latin *impedicare* 'to catch, entangle', from *pedica* 'fetter, snare'.] —**impeacher** *n.* —**impeachment** *n.*

impeachable /im peéchəb'l/ *adj.* **1.** WORTHY OF A CRIMINAL TRIAL serious enough for the offender to be brought to trial (*refers to a crime or charge*) ○ *an impeachable offence* **2.** *US* ABLE TO BE CHARGED in the United States, subject to a charge of crime and therefore liable to being brought to trial —**impeachability** /im peéchə bílləti/ *n.*

impeccable /im pékəb'l/ *adj.* **1.** PERFECT so perfect or flawless as to be beyond criticism ○ *she had impeccable taste* **2.** RELIG FREE FROM SIN so perfect in character as to be incapable of sinning [Mid-16thC. From Latin *impeccabilis*, literally 'not liable to sin', from *peccare* 'to sin'.] —**impeccability** /im pékə bílləti/ *n.* —**impeccably** /im pékəbli/ *adv.*

impecunious /ìmpi kyóoni əss/ *adj.* having little or no money, and so unable to lead a comfortable life (*formal*) [Late 16thC. Formed from obsolete *pecunious* 'wealthy', from Latin *pecunia* (see PECUNIARY).] —**impecuniosity** /ìmpi kyòoni óssəti/ *n.* —**impecuniously** /ìmpi kyóoni əssli/ *adv.* —**impecuniousness** *n.*

impedance /im peéd'nss/ *n.* **1.** PREVENTION OF PROGRESS sth that delays or prevents progress, or the preventing of progress (*formal*) **2.** ELEC OPPOSITION TO THE FLOW OF ALTERNATING CURRENT the opposition in a circuit to the flow of alternating current, consisting of resistance and reactance. Symbol *Z* **3.** ACOUSTICS RATIO OF SOUND PRESSURE TO VELOCITY the ratio of the sound pressure in a medium to the velocity of the particles in the medium. ◊ **immittance**

impede /im peéd/ (**-pedes, -peding, -peded**) *vt.* to interfere with the movement, progress, or development of sth or sb [Late 16thC. From Latin *impedire* 'to shackle the feet' (ultimately related to *pes* 'foot').] —**impeder** *n.*

WORD KEY: SYNONYMS

See Synonyms at ***hinder.***

impediment /im péddimənt/ *n.* **1.** IMPAIRMENT an impairment, especially one affecting speech **2.** OBSTACLE sth that hinders progress in some way **3.** (*plural* **-ments** *or* **-menta**) LAW LEGAL OBSTRUCTION the reason a legal contract, e.g. a marriage, cannot be entered into [14thC. From Latin *impedimentum* 'hindrance', from *impedire* (see IMPEDE).] —**impedimental** /im péddi mént'l/ *adj.* —**impedimentary** /-méntəri/ *adj.*

impedimenta /im péddi méntə/ *npl.* **1.** OBSTRUCTIONS obstacles, hindrances, or obstructions to progress (*literary*) **2.** ARMY MILITARY EQUIPMENT equipment and baggage carried by soldiers (*formal*) **3.** plural of **impediment** *n.* 3 [Early 17thC. From Latin, literally 'hindrances', plural of *impedimentum* (see IMPEDIMENT).]

impedor /im peédər/ *n.* any circuit component that has impedance [Formed from IMPEDANCE, on the model of RESISTOR]

impel /im pél/ (**-pels, -pelling, -pelled**) *vt.* **1.** FORCE TO DO to force sb to do sth, or make sb feel the need to do sth (*usually passive*) ○ *I felt impelled to protest* **2.** CAUSE TO MOVE to start or keep sth or sb moving in a particular direction (*formal*) [15thC. From Latin *impellere*, literally 'to drive towards', from *pellere* 'to beat'.]

impeller /im péllər/ *n.* the rotating part that transmits motion in a centrifugal pump, turbine, or blower

impend /im pénd/ (**-pends, -pending, -pended**) *vi.* **1.** BE CLOSE TO HAPPENING to be threateningly close to happening (*formal*) **2.** HANG MENACINGLY to hover or hang above sth, usually in a threatening way (*literary*) [Late 16thC. From Latin *impendere*, literally 'to hang over', from *pendere* 'to hang'.] —**impendence** *n.* —**impendency** *n.* —**impendent** *adj.* —**impending** *adj.*

impending /im pénding/ *adj.* about to happen

impenetrable /im pénnitrəb'l/ *adj.* **1.** IMPOSSIBLE TO GET IN OR THROUGH not able to be passed through or entered ○ *The woods formed an impenetrable barrier.* **2.** INCOMPREHENSIBLE impossible to understand or discern ○ *impenetrable legal jargon* **3.** CLOSED TO INFLUENCE not open to intellectual or moral influences, impressions, or ideas [15thC. Via French from Latin *impenetrabilis*, from *penetrabilis* (see PENETRABLE).] —**impenetrability** /im pénnitrə bílləti/ *n.* —**impenetrably** /-bli/ *adv.*

impenitent /im pénnit'nt/ *adj.* NOT SORRY having or showing no regret or sorrow for sin or misbehaviour ■ *n.* UNREPENTING PERSON sb who is unrepentant [15thC. From the ecclesiastical Latin stem *impaenitent-*, from *paenitent-* (see PENITENT).] —**impenitence** *n.* —**impenitency** *n.* —**impenitently** *adv.*

impennate /im pénnayt/ *adj.* used to describe a bird that has small wings that are incapable of supporting flight but are adapted for swimming

imper. *abbr.* GRAM imperative

imperative /im pérrətiv/ *adj.* **1.** NECESSARY absolutely necessary or unavoidable ○ *It is imperative that justice is seen to be done.* **2.** COMMANDING forceful and demanding the obedience and respect of others (*formal*) **3.** GRAM USED FOR GIVING ORDERS used to express a command or request, e.g. the verb form 'come' in 'Come here!' ■ *n.* **1.** PRIORITY sth that must be done ○ *The general's imperative was to conquer or die.* **2.** **imperative, imperative mood** GRAM WAY OF COMMANDING the form of a verb used to give an order **3.** GRAM VERB EXPRESSING A COMMAND OR REQUEST a verb in the imperative mood, such as 'close' in 'Please close the door' [15thC. From late Latin *imperativus*, literally 'specially ordered', from Latin *imperare* 'to command', from *parare* 'to prepare'.] —**imperatively** *adv.* —**imperativeness** *n.*

imperator /ìmpə ráa tawr/ *n.* **1.** ROMAN GENERAL a victorious military commander during the time of the Roman Republic **2.** HIST ROMAN EMPEROR the head of state of the Roman Empire **3.** ABSOLUTE RULER an absolute ruler or commander [Mid-16thC. From Latin, literally 'commander', formed from *imperare* (see IMPERATIVE).] —**imperatorial** /im pérrə táwri əl/ *adj.*

imperceptible /ìmpər séptəb'l/ *adj.* very slight or gradual ○ *an imperceptible touch of the hand* —**imperceptibility** /ìmpər séptə bílləti/ *n.* —**imperceptibly** /-bli/ *adv.*

imperceptive /ìmpər séptiv/ *adj.* lacking the ability to notice things or to understand sb or sth —**imperceptively** *adv.* —**imperceptiveness** *n.* —**imperceptivity** /ìmpər sep tívvəti/ *n.*

impercipience /ìmpər síppi ənss/ *n.* a lack of perception (*formal*) ○ *the impercipience of the egotist* —**impercipient** *adj.*

imperf. *abbr.* **1.** GRAM, BOT imperfect **2.** STAMPS imperforate

imperfect /im púrfikt/ *adj.* **1.** FAULTY having a fault or defect **2.** NOT COMPLETE lacking a part **3.** BOT NOT ABLE TO REPRODUCE used to describe a flower that lacks either a stamen or a pistil and is therefore unable to reproduce **4.** MUSIC NOT PERFECT used to describe a musical interval other than the fourth, fifth, or octave **5.** MUSIC ENDING ON 5TH NOTE OF SCALE used to describe a cadence ending on the 5th note of the scale (**dominant**) rather than on the first note (**tonic**) **6.** GRAM EXPRESSING INCOMPLETE ACTION used to describe a verb or tense that denotes past action going on but not completed **7.** LAW UNENFORCEABLE unable to be enforced ■ *n.* GRAM **1.** VERB TENSE a grammatical tense used for expressing incomplete or habitual action in the past **2.** VERB FORM a form of a verb used to express the imperfect tense [14thC. Alteration of *imperfit*, from French *imparfait*, from Latin *imperfectus*, from *perfectus* 'perfect' (see PERFECT).] —**imperfectly** *adv.* —**imperfectness** *n.*

imperfect fungus *n.* a fungus that forms only asexual spores (**conidia**). Order: Fungi Imperfecti.

imperfection /ìmpər féksh'n/ *n.* **1.** FAULT sth that makes a person or thing less than perfect **2.** FAULTINESS the possession of faults or defects

WORD KEY: SYNONYMS

See Synonyms at ***flaw.***

imperfective /ìmpər féktiv/ *adj.* INDICATING INCOMPLETE ACTION used to describe a verb aspect expressing action that is not completed. ◊ **perfective** ■ *n.* **1.** VERB ASPECT the imperfective aspect of the verb **2.** VERB FORM a verb form belonging to the imperfective aspect —**imperfectively** *adv.*

imperforate /im púrfərit/ *adj.* **1.** WITHOUT AN OPENING with no perforation or opening **2.** ANAT PARTIALLY OR COMPLETELY CLOSED lacking an opening of the normal size, especially because of abnormal development **3.** STAMPS WITH NO HOLES produced without the perforations that allow easy tearing or division ■ *n.* STAMPS STAMP WITHOUT PERFORATIONS a stamp without perforations around it —**imperforation** /im pùrfə ráysh'n/ *n.*

imperia plural of **imperium**

imperial /im peéri əl/ *adj.* **1.** BELONGING TO EMPIRE OR EMPEROR concerning or involving an empire or its ruler **2.** INDICATING A COUNTRY'S AUTHORITY involving or relating to the authority of a country over colonies or other countries **3.** SUPREMELY POWERFUL holding supreme power ○ *All are subject to the imperial power of the state.* **4.** GRAND very grand or majestic **5.** SUPERIOR better in quality or larger in size **6.** MEASURE OF BRITISH NON-METRIC SET OF MEASURES belonging or conforming to the non-metric system of weights and measures legally established in Britain that includes the foot, pound, and gallon ■ *n.* **1.** PRINTING PAPER SIZE the largest of the traditional US and British paper sizes. The US imperial measures 584 x 838 mm/23 x 33 in and the British imperial 559 x 762 mm/22 x 30 in, untrimmed. **2.** RELATIVE OF AN EMPEROR OR EMPRESS a person belonging to an imperial family (*formal*) **3.** HAIR SMALL BEARD a tuft or point of hair grown on the chin or below the lower lip. This style was made fashionable by the French Emperor Napoleon III. **4.** ANTIQUES TRUNK FOR LUGGAGE a chest fitted into the top of a coach to store travellers' bags, or the part of a coach's roof where this chest fits **5.** MONEY OLD RUSSIAN COIN a former gold coin of Russia worth about eight rubles **6.** BEVERAGES LARGE WINE BOTTLE a wine bottle containing the equivalent of eight standard bottles, used for red Bordeaux [14thC. Via French from Latin *imperialis*, from *imperium* 'rule, empire' (see EMPIRE).] —**imperially** *adv.*

imperial gallon *n.* = **gallon** *n.* 1

imperialism /im péeri əlizəm/ *n.* **1. BELIEF IN EMPIRE-BUILDING** the policy of extending the rule or influence of a country over other countries or colonies **2. DOMINATION BY AN EMPIRE** the political, military, or economic domination of one country over another **3. TAKEOVER AND DOMINATION** the extension of power or authority over others in the interests of domination ○ *cultural imperialism* —**imperialist** *n., adj.* —**imperialistic** /im péeri ə lístik/ *adj.* —**imperialistically** /-lístikəli/ *adv.*

Imperial Valley /im péeri əl-/ valley in southeastern California, part of a larger valley that extends into Mexico. It is a rich agricultural area. Length: 97 km/60 mi.

imperil /im pérrəl/ (**-ils, -illing, -illed**) *vt.* to put sth or sb in danger (*dated formal*) —**imperilment** *n.*

imperious /im péeri əss/ *adj.* haughty and domineering [Mid-16thC. From Latin *imperiosus*, from *imperium* 'rule, empire' (see EMPIRE).] —**imperiously** *adv.* —**imperiousness** *n.*

imperishable /im pérrishəb'l/ *adj.* **1. THAT WILL NOT DECAY** not liable to become spoilt, weak, or damaged through time and wear **2. LONG-LASTING** not forgotten or ignored over time (*literary*) ○ *The imperishable quality of great literature distinguishes it from humbler writing.* —**imperishability** /im pérrishə bílləti/ *n.* —**imperishableness** /im pérrishəb'lnəss/ *n.* —**imperishably** /-bli/ *adv.*

imperium /im péeri əm/ (*plural* **-ria** /-ri ə/) *n.* **1. SUPREME POWER** supreme or imperial power (*formal*) **2. LAW LEGAL RIGHT TO COMMAND** the use of the power of the state to enforce the law **3. EMPIRE** an area controlled by a supreme power (*formal or literary*) [Mid-17thC. From Latin, literally 'rule, empire' (see EMPIRE).]

impermanent /im púrmənənt/ *adj.* that will change, go away, disappear, or fade —**impermanence** *n.* —**impermanency** *n.* —**impermanently** *adv.*

impermeable /im púrmi əb'l/ *adj.* not permitting the passage of liquid, gas, or other fluid. ◊ **impervious** —**impermeability** /im púrmi ə bílləti/ *n.* —**impermeableness** /im púrmi əb'lnəss/ *n.* —**impermeably** /-bli/ *adv.*

impermissible /ímpər míssəb'l/ *adj.* that cannot or will not be allowed —**impermissibility** /ímpər míssə bílləti/ *n.* —**impermissibly** /ímpər míssəbli/ *adv.*

impers. *abbr.* GRAM impersonal

impersonal /im púrs'nəl/ *adj.* **1. NOT PERSONALIZED** not referring to individuals or reflecting personalities but focusing on events and facts ○ *an impersonal style of reporting* **2. ANONYMOUS** not considering people as individuals ○ *an impersonal bureaucracy* **3. COLD AND ALIENATING** making a person feel insignificant and ignored as an individual ○ *the service in the restaurant was brisk and impersonal* **4. WITHOUT HUMAN TRAITS** without any human characteristics or personality **5.** GRAM **NOT SPECIFIC** used to describe a clause or construction that includes a personal pronoun that does not refer to a specific person or thing, such as 'it is raining' or 'you shouldn't drink and drive' —**impersonality** /im púrsənálləti/ *n.* —**impersonally** /im púrss'nəli/ *adv.*

impersonalize /im púrs'nə līz/ (**-izes, -izing, -ized**), **impersonalise** (**-ises, -ising, -ised**) *vt.* to make sth neutral, lacking in human warmth, or without reference to individuals —**impersonalization** /im púrss'nə lī záysh'n/ *n.*

impersonate /im púrssə nayt/ (**-ates, -ating, -ated**) *vt.* **1. MIMIC** to mimic the voice, appearance, and manners of another person, especially in order to entertain **2.** LAW **ACT A PART** to pretend to be another person, especially in order to deceive [Early 17thC. Formed from Latin *persona* 'person' (see PERSON), on the model of INCORPORATE.] —**impersonation** /im púrssə náysh'n/ *n.* —**impersonator** /im púrssə naytər/ *n.*

impertinence /im púrtinənss/, **impertinency** /im púrtinənssi/ (*plural* **-cies**) *n.* **1. IMPUDENCE** boldness and rudeness, especially to a superior **2. STH CHEEKY** a disrespectful action or comment **3. IRRELEVANCE** lack of relevance to the matter in hand (*formal*)

impertinent /im púrtinənt/ *adj.* (*formal*) **1. CHEEKY** showing a bold or rude lack of respect, especially to a superior **2. IRRELEVANT** not appropriate or relevant [14thC. Directly or via French from the late Latin stem *impertinent-* 'not pertinent', from the Latin stem *pertinent-* 'pertinent' (see PERTINENT); 'disrespectful' evolved in the 17thC, via the idea of presumptuously going beyond what is relevant to yourself.] —**impertinently** *adv.*

imperturbable /ímpər túrbəb'l/ *adj.* not easily worried, distressed, or agitated ○ *The doctor's imperturbable manner soothed the distressed patient.* [15thC. From late Latin *imperturbabilis*, from *perturbare* 'to disturb' (see PERTURB).] —**imperturbability** /ímpər túrbə bílləti/ *n.* —**imperturbableness** /ímpər túrbəb'lnəss/ *n.* —**imperturbably** /-bli/ *adv.*

impervious /im púrvi əss/ *adj.* **1. NOT RESPONSIVE** remaining unmoved and unaffected by other people's opinions, arguments, or suggestions ○ *The directors were impervious to the growing resentment among the staff.* **2. NOT LETTING STH THROUGH** not allowing passage into or through sth [Mid-17thC. Formed from Latin *impervius*, from *pervius* (see PERVIOUS).] —**imperviously** *adv.* —**imperviousness** *n.*

impetigo /ímpi tígō/ *n.* a contagious infection of the skin characterized by blisters that form yellow-brown scabs. It is caused by staphylococcal and streptococcal bacteria. [14thC. From Latin, where it was formed from *impetere* (see IMPETUS).] —**impetiginous** /ímpi tíjjinəss/ *adj.*

impetrate /ímpi trayt/ (**-trates, -trating, -trated**) *vt.* to request sth in an earnest manner, especially in prayer, or to obtain sth in this way (*archaic or formal*) [15thC. From Latin *impetrare* 'to achieve or procure', from *patrare* 'to bring about' (source of English *perpetrate*).] —**impetration** /ímpi tráysh'n/ *n.* —**impetrative** /ímpitrətiv/ *adj.* —**impetrator** /-traytər/ *n.*

impetuosity /im péttyoo óssəti/ (*plural* **-ties**) *n.* (*formal*) **1. TENDENCY TO RASHNESS** a tendency to act rashly **2. IMPULSIVE ACTION** an act performed on the spur of the moment after little or no consideration

impetuous /im péttyoo əss/ *adj.* **1. ACTING IMPULSIVELY** acting on the spur of the moment, without considering the consequences **2. DONE ON IMPULSE** done without thought as a reaction to an emotion or impulse **3. VIOLENT** moving with great force and energy (*literary*) [14thC. Via French *impétueux*, from late Latin *impetuosus*, from *impetus* (see IMPETUS).] —**impetuously** *adv.* —**impetuousness** *n.*

impetus /ímpitəss/ *n.* **1. PUSH** sth that provides energy or motivation to accomplish sth or to undertake sth **2.** PHYS **FORCE** a force that causes the motion of an object to overcome resistance and maintain its velocity [Mid-17thC. From Latin, literally 'assault, force', from *impetere* 'to assail', from *petere* 'to go towards, seek'.]

impf. *abbr.* GRAM, BOT imperfect

imp. gal., **imp. gall.** *abbr.* imperial gallon

impi /ímpi/ (*plural* **impi** *or* **impies**) *n.* *S Africa* a band of armed Zulu warriors or soldiers in precolonial times [Mid-19thC. From Zulu.]

impiety /im pī əti/ (*plural* **-ties**) *n.* **1.** RELIG **LACK OF RELIGIOUS RESPECT** a lack of due reverence for God or religion **2.** RELIG **UNGODLY ACT** an act that shows a lack of religious respect or devotion **3. LACK OF RESPECT** a lack of respect or dutifulness (*formal or archaic*) [Late 16thC. Directly or via French *impiété*, from Latin *impietas*, from *impius* (see IMPIOUS).]

impinge /im pínj/ (**-pinges, -pingeing, -pinged**) *vi.* **1. STRIKE** to strike or hit sth ○ *Loud noise can impinge on the eardrum, causing temporary hearing impairment.* **2. INTERFERE** to affect the limits of sth, especially a right or law, often causing some kind of restriction (*formal*) ○ *Members claimed that cancelling the ballot impinged on their voting rights.* [Mid-16thC. From Latin *impingere* 'to strike or drive in forcibly', from *pangere* 'to drive or fix in' (source of English *page*).] —**impingement** *n.* —**impinger** *n.*

impious /ímpi əss, im pí əss/ *adj.* **1.** RELIG **SHOWING LACK OF RELIGIOUS RESPECT** not showing due reverence for God or sth holy **2. DISRESPECTFUL** showing a lack of respect for sb or sth (*formal or archaic*) [Mid-16thC. Formed from Latin *impius*, from *pius* 'pious' (see PIOUS).] —**impiously** *adv.* —**impiousness** *n.*

impish /ímpish/ *adj.* wicked in a playful way, without causing serious harm —**impishly** *adv.* —**impishness** *n.*

implacable /im plákəb'l/ *adj.* impossible to pacify or to reduce in strength or force (*formal*) ○ *an implacable foe* ○ *an implacable ice storm* [15thC. From Latin *implacabilis*, from *placabilis* 'easily appeased', from *placare* 'to calm' (see PLACATE).] —**implacability** /im plákə bílləti/ *n.* —**implacableness** /im plákəb'lnəss/ *n.* —**implacably** /-bli/ *adv.*

implant *v.* /im plaánt/ (**-plants, -planting, -planted**) **1.** *vt.* **ESTABLISH HABITS OR NOTIONS** to fix sth deeply in sb's mind or consciousness as a behaviour pattern, thought, or belief **2.** *vt.* **INSERT** to fit or fix sth small into sth larger, which then encases it ○ *Gold fillings, implanted in his front teeth, flashed when he smiled.* **3.** *vt.* **BURY** to fix sth in the ground, especially so that it grows **4.** *vt.* SURG **EMBED** to embed sth such as a mechanical device in the body ○ *The hormone pellets are invisibly implanted just below the skin.* **5.** *vi.* GYN **BECOME EMBEDDED** to become embedded in the lining of the womb ■ *n.* /ím plaant/ SURG **STH INSERTED DURING SURGERY** sth inserted or embedded in the tissues or organs of the body during a surgical procedure, such as encapsulated drugs or fluid-filled sacs to replace or augment breast tissue —**implantable** /im plaántəb'l/ *adj.* —**implanter** /im plaántər/ *n.*

implantation /ím plaan táysh'n/ *n.* **1. BEING OR BECOMING IMPLANTED** the state of being or process of becoming fixed or embedded in sth **2.** SURG **SURGICALLY IMPLANTING IN THE BODY** the insertion or embedding of sth into body tissues or organs during a surgical procedure **3.** GYN **ATTACHMENT OF AN EMBRYO** the process by which or stage at which an embryo becomes embedded in the lining of the womb

implausible /im pláwzəb'l/ *adj.* hardly likely to be true, acceptable, or possible —**implausibility** /im pláwzə bílləti/ *n.* —**implausibleness** /im pláwzəb'lnəss/ *n.* —**implausibly** /-bli/ *adv.*

implead /im pleéd/ (**-pleads, -pleading, -pleaded**) *vti.* to bring a lawsuit against an individual or organization in court [14thC. From Anglo-Norman *empleder*, ultimately from Old French *plaidier* (see PLEAD).] —**impleadable** *adj.* —**impleader** *n.*

implement *n.* /ímplimənt/ **1. TOOL** a useful article of equipment, usually a specially shaped object to do a particular task ○ *writing implements* **2. REQUIREMENT** sth needed in order to achieve sth (*formal*) ■ *vt.* /ímpli ment/ (**-ments, -menting, -mented**) **1. CARRY OUT OR FULFIL** to put sth into effect or action ○ *The plan has yet to be fully implemented.* **2. GIVE TOOLS TO** to provide or equip sb with the tools or other means to do sth (*formal*) [15thC. From late Latin *implementum* 'filling', from Latin *implere*, literally 'to fill in', from *plere* 'to fill'.] —**implemental** /ímpli mént'l/ *adj.* —**implementation** /ímpli men táysh'n/ *n.* —**implementer** /ímpli mentər/ *n.*

implicate /ímpli kayt/ (**-cates, -cating, -cated**) *vt.* **1. CONNECT WITH STH** to show that sb or sth played a part in or is connected to an activity, such as a crime **2. IMPLY** to imply or involve sth as a consequence (*formal*) ○ *Do you not see that his words implicate an error on my part?* **3. ENTANGLE OR INTERWEAVE** to wreathe, twist, or knit things together (*literary*) [15thC. From Latin *implicat-*, the past participle stem of *implicare* 'to entangle, involve' (the original sense in English), from *plicare* 'to fold' (source of English *ply*).]

implication /ímpli káysh'n/ *n.* **1. INDIRECT SUGGESTION** sth that is implied as a natural consequence of sth else ○ *It is important to consider the wider implications of making such a decision.* **2. IMPLICIT UNDERSTANDING** the state of implying or being implied, without being plainly expressed **3. INVOLVEMENT** the involvement or entanglement of sb in sth ○ *his implication in the crime* **4.** LOGIC **LOGICAL RELATION** in logic, a relationship between two propositions that holds when both propositions are true and fails when the first is true but the second is false —**implicational** *adj.*

implicative /im plíkətiv, ímpli kaytiv/ *adj.* tending to imply or implicate (*formal*) —**implicatively** *adv.*

implicit /im plíssit/ *adj.* **1. IMPLIED** not stated, but understood in what is expressed ○ *Asking us when we would like to start was an implicit acceptance of our terms.* **2. ABSOLUTE** not affected by any doubt or uncertainty ○ *implicit faith* **3. CONTAINED** present as a necessary part of sth ○ *Confidentiality is implicit in the relationship between doctor and patient.* [Late 16thC. Directly or via French *implicite* from Latin *implicitus* 'entangled', from *implicare* (see IMPLICATE).] —**implicitly** *adv.*

implied /im plíd/ *adj.* involved, understood, or suggested without expressly being stated ○ *implied criticisms*

implode /im plṓd/ (**-plodes, -ploding, -ploded**) *vti.* PHYS to collapse inwardly with force, as a result of the external pressure being greater than the internal pressure, or to cause sth to collapse inwardly [Late 19thC. Formed from Latin *plodere* 'to clap', on the model of EXPLODE.]

implore /im pláwr/ (**-plores, -ploring, -plored**) *vt.* (*formal*) **1. BEG EARNESTLY** to plead with sb to do sth ○ *The tenants implored their landlord not to sell the building.* **2. REQUEST EARNESTLY** to beg or pray for sth [Early 16thC. Directly or via French *implorer* from Latin *implorare* 'to call upon with tears', from *plorare* 'to weep'.] —**imploration** /ímplə ráysh'n, ím plaw-/ *n.* —**imploratory** /im pláwrətəri/ *adj.* —**implorer** /-pláwrər/ *n.*

imploring /im pláwring/ *adj.* earnestly asking for sth ○ *an imploring look* —**imploringly** *adv.*

implosion /im plṓzh'n/ *n.* PHYS the violent inward collapse of a vessel or structure resulting from the external pressure being greater than the internal pressure [Late 19thC. Formed from IMPLODE, on the model of EXPLOSION.]

implosive /im plṓssiv, -plṓziv/ *adj.* PHYS indicating or relating to violent inward collapse —**implosively** *adv.*

imply /im plí/ (**-plies, -plying, -plied**) *vt.* **1. SUGGEST** to make sth understood without expressing it directly **2. INVOLVE** to involve sth as a necessary part or condition ○ *Such impressive exam results imply good teaching and study methods.* [14thC. Via Old French *emplier* from Latin *implicare* 'to entangle or involve' (the original sense in English) (see IMPLICATE).]

impolite /ímpə lít/ *adj.* not showing proper manners or respect [Early 17thC. From Latin *impolitus*, from *politus* 'polished' (see POLITE).] —**impolitely** *adv.* —**impoliteness** *n.*

impolitic /im póllətik/ *adj.* likely to be disadvantageous and therefore not advisable (*formal*) ○ *It would be impolitic to refuse.* —**impoliticly** *adv.* —**impoliticness** *n.*

imponderabilia /im póndərə bílli ə/ *npl.* matters or factors whose importance or effect cannot be assessed (*literary*) [Early 20thC. From modern Latin, literally 'things that cannot be weighed', ultimately from Latin *ponderare* 'to weigh' (see PONDER).]

imponderable /im póndərəb'l/ *adj.* **NOT MEASURABLE** not quantifiable in terms of importance or effect ○ *Sheer inspiration remains an imponderable force in cultural and technological developments.* ■ *n.* **STH IMPOSSIBLE TO CALCULATE** an event, factor, or other matter whose importance or effects cannot be calculated (*often used in the plural*) ○ *just another of life's imponderables* —**imponderability** /im póndərə bílləti/ *n.* —**imponderableness** /im póndərəb'lnəss/ *n.* —**imponderably** /-bli/ *adv.*

import *vt.* /im páwrt/ (**-ports, -porting, -ported**) **1.** COMM **BRING IN FROM ABROAD** to bring sth or cause sth to be brought in from another country, usually for commercial or industrial purposes **2. BRING IN FROM OUTSIDE** to bring in sth, such as knowledge or expertise, from an outside source **3.** COMPUT **TRANSFER DATA** to transfer data from one location to another in a computer or from one computer to another in a computer network, especially when a change of format is required **4. IMPLY** to mean sth, often in addition to what is actually expressed (*formal*) ○ *What does the legal motion really import here?* ■ *n.* /ím pawrt/ **1.** COMM **STH BROUGHT FROM ABROAD** sth that is brought into one country from another, usually for commercial or industrial purposes **2. IDEA OR PERSON BROUGHT IN** an idea, practice, or person brought in from the outside ○ *The new accounting system is an import from the private sector.* **3.** COMM **IMPORTATION** the bringing in of sth from abroad or an outside source ○ *Most governments forbid the import of such goods.* **4. TRUE SIGNIFICANCE** the meaning or significance of sth ○ *a foreign policy decision of great import* [15thC. From Latin *importare* 'to carry or bring in', used in medieval Latin to mean 'to convey a meaning, be significant', from *portare* 'to carry'.] —**importability** /im páwrtə bílləti/ *n.* —**importable** /im páwrtəb'l/ *adj.*

importance /im páwrt'nss/ *n.* **1. SIGNIFICANCE** considerable value, relevance, or interest ○ *It is difficult to overestimate the importance of this breakthrough to medical science.* **2. HIGH RANK** high position, rank, or reputation in society

important /im páwrt'nt/ *adj.* **1. HAVING VALUE OR SIGNIFICANCE** worthy of note or consideration, especially for its interest, value, or relevance ○ *an important scientific discovery* ○ *an important author* **2. HIGH-RANKING** with high social position or influence among people **3. POMPOUS** seeming to assume more status, significance, or value than is actually due ○ *strode into the room with an important air* [15thC. From medieval Latin *important-*, present participle stem of *importare* (see IMPORT).] —**importantly** *adv.*

importation /ím pawr táysh'n/ *n.* **1.** COMM **ACT OF IMPORTING** the bringing in of goods or commodities from another country **2. STH BROUGHT IN FROM ELSEWHERE** any thing, person, or service from another country, separate source, or external organization

importer /im páwrtər/ *n.* a person or company that buys goods or services from abroad and then sells them in the domestic market

importunate /im páwrtyŏonət/ *adj.* (*formal*) **1. DEMANDING AND PERSISTENT** continually asking for sth, especially in a forceful, insistent, or troublesome manner ○ *importunate requests for a loan* **2. URGENT OR PRESSING** requiring immediate attention and action ○ *importunate requests for medical aid* [Early 16thC. Formed from Latin *importunus* (see IMPORTUNE).] —**importunately** *adv.* —**importunateness** *n.*

importune /im páwr tyoon, ím pawr tyŏon/ *vt.* (**-tunes, -tuning, -tuned**) (*formal*) **1. BOTHER INSISTENTLY** to ask sb continually, repeatedly, or forcefully for sth, especially in a troublesome way **2. MAKE AN IMMORAL REQUEST** to ask sb to have sexual relations in exchange for money ■ *adj.* **IMPORTUNATE** persistent or pressing [Mid-16thC. From French *importuner* or medieval Latin *importunari*, from Latin *importunus* 'inconvenient, unseasonable', from *Portunus*, god of harbours (source of English *opportune*).] —**importunacy** /im páwrtyŏonəssi/ *n.* —**importunely** /ím páwr tyoonli, -pawr tyŏonli/ *adv.* —**importuner** /im páwr tyoonər, ím pawr tyŏonər/ *n.*

importunity /ím pawr tyŏonəti/ (*plural* **-ties**) *n.* (*formal*) **1. WEARISOME PERSISTENCE** the fact of being troublesomely demanding or insistent **2. PERSISTENT DEMAND** a demand made repeatedly or insistently

impose /im pṓz/ (**-poses, -posing, -posed**) *v.* **1.** *vt.* **LEVY OR ENFORCE** to lay down sth compulsory, such as a tax or a punishment **2.** *vt.* **INSIST ON** to make people agree to sth or comply with sth by having superior strength or authority ○ *It broke his heart to see Western culture imposed on this dignified people.* **3.** *vti.* **INCONVENIENCE SB** to give people extra work or difficulties by forcing your company or your personal concerns on them **4.** *vt.* PRINTING **ARRANGE PAGES** to order the pages of sth such as a book or magazine for printing **5.** *vt.* **PASS OFF ON SB** to use deceit or fraud to give sth to sb or to persuade sb to accept sth **6.** *vt.* RELIG **LAY ON HANDS** to bless sb, e.g. in confirmation or ordination, by laying hands on the person's head [15thC. Via French *imposer* (influenced by *poser* 'to put') from Latin *imponere* 'to place on or into', from *ponere* 'to place' (source of English *component*).] —**imposable** *adj.* —**imposer** *n.*

imposing /im pṓzing/ *adj.* large and stately, creating an impression of grandeur [Mid-17thC. The original meaning was 'insistent, dictatorial'.] —**imposingly** *adv.* —**imposingness** *n.*

imposition /ímpə zísh'n/ *n.* **1. EXTRA TROUBLE** a request or task, especially a time-consuming one, that is unreasonably expected of sb **2. ENFORCED DUTY** a tax, fee, or penalty that is imposed on people **3. ESTABLISHING OR ENFORCING OF STH** the official or legal process of laying down sth compulsory such as a tax, fee, or penalty **4.** PRINTING **ARRANGEMENT OF PAGES** the setting up and ordering of pages for printing **5. DECEPTION** a deception or fraud (*literary*) **6.** RELIG **BLESSING** the laying of hands on sb's head in a religious sacrament such as ordination or confirmation

impossibility /im póssə bílləti/ (*plural* **-ties**) *n.* **1. STH IMPOSSIBLE** a situation that cannot happen, or anything that cannot exist or cannot be done ○ *Living without water is a physical impossibility.* **2. FACT OF BEING IMPOSSIBLE** the likelihood that sth will not happen or cannot be achieved ○ *the impossibility of finding another job close to home*

impossible /im póssəb'l/ *adj.* **1. NOT POSSIBLE** that cannot exist or cannot be done ○ *an impossible task* **2. TOO DIFFICULT** very difficult to deal with and apparently without a solution ○ *The situation was impossible: I couldn't be honest without offending one of them.* **3. UNENDURABLE** unbearably difficult or not possible to endure ○ *the humidity was impossible* **4. NOT BELIEVABLE** ridiculous or unreasonable, because it could not be true [14thC. Directly or via French from Latin *impossibilis*, from *possibilis* 'possible' (see POSSIBLE).] —**impossibleness** *n.*

impossibly /im póssəbli/ *adv.* **1. INFURIATINGLY** to an infuriating or intolerable degree (*informal*) **2. EXTREMELY** to an extent that is almost unbelievable ○ *impossibly thin slices* **3. NOT BY ANY MEANS** in a way that could not be done or could not happen

impost[1] /ím pōst/ *n.* **1.** FIN **CUSTOMS DUTY** a tax or other payment levied on goods brought into a country **2.** HORSERACING **HANDICAP WEIGHT** the weight a horse must carry, including that of the jockey, in a handicap race [15thC. From Italian *imposta*, feminine past participle of *imporre* 'to impose' used as a noun, from Latin *imponere* (see IMPOSE).]

impost[2] /ím pōst/ *n.* ARCHIT the top part of a pillar, column, or wall, which may be decorated or moulded and on which a vault or arch rests [Mid-16thC. Via French from, ultimately, Latin *impostus*, *impositus*, the past participle of *imponere* (see IMPOSE).]

imposter *n.* = **impostor**

imposthume *n.* = **impostume**

impostor /im póstər/, **imposter** *n.* sb who pretends to be sb else in order to deceive or cheat. An impostor uses sb else's name or documents. [Late 16thC. Via French *imposteur* from, ultimately, Latin *impositor*, from *imponere* (see IMPOSE). The underlying sense is of 'putting on' a false identity.]

impostume /im pós tyoom/, **imposthume** *n.* a cyst or pus-containing abscess found in or on any part of the body (*archaic*) [14thC. From Old French *empostume*, ultimately from Greek *apostēmai* 'to withdraw' (referring to the gathering or 'withdrawal' of pus into an abscess).]

imposture /im póschər/ *n.* the act of pretending to be sb else in order to trick people, or an occasion on which this is done (*formal*) [Mid-16thC. Via French from late Latin *impostura*, literally 'a putting on', ultimately from *imponere* (see IMPOSE).]

impotence /ímpətənss/, **impotency** /-tənssi/ *n.* **1.** MED **SEXUAL INABILITY** the inability of a male to perform sexual intercourse, usually because erection of the penis cannot be achieved or sustained **2. WEAKNESS** the lack of strength or power to do anything ○ *We lamented our impotence as we watched the business gradually deteriorate.*

impotent /ímpətənt/ *adj.* **1.** MED **SEXUALLY UNABLE** unable to perform sexual intercourse, usually because erection of the penis cannot be achieved or sustained **2. POWERLESS** without the strength or power to do anything effective or helpful [14thC. Via French from the Latin stem *impotent-*, from *potent-* 'powerful' (see POTENT).] —**impotently** *adv.*

impound /im pównd/ (**-pounds, -pounding, -pounded**) *vt.* **1. KEEP IN A CONFINED PLACE** to lock sth such as an illegally parked car in an enclosure or compound **2.** LAW **TAKE INTO LEGAL CUSTODY** to take goods or possessions into official custody **3.** LAW **WITHHOLD LEGALLY** to withhold sth by legal means **4.** CIV ENG **HOLD A WATER SUPPLY** to save and collect water in a dam or reservoir [15thC. Literally 'to put into a pound', formed from POUND[3] 'enclosed place'.] —**impoundable** *adj.* —**impoundage** *n.* —**impounder** *n.* —**impoundment** *n.*

impoverish /im póvvərish/ (**-ishes, -ishing, -ished**) *vt.* (*formal*) **1. MAKE POOR** to cause sb or sth to be poor or poorer (*often passive*) **2. SPOIL OR REDUCE IN QUALITY** to take away some part or quality belonging to sth, leaving it in a worse or weaker condition ○ *a vocabulary impoverished by technical jargon* **3.** AGRIC

zh vision In foreign words: kh German Bach; aN French vin; aaN French blanc; ö German schön, French feu; oN French bon; öN French un; ü French rue Stress marks: ´ as in secret \séek rət\; academic \ákə démmik\

MAKE LESS RICH OR FERTILE to take away the nutrients and richness from sth such as soil [15thC. From Old French *empoveriss-*, a stem of *empov(e)rier*, from *povre* 'poor' (see POOR).] —**impoverisher** *n.* —**impoverishment** *n.*

impracticable /im práktikəb'l/ *adj.* **1. NOT POSSIBLE** that cannot be carried out effectively **2. UNUSABLE** not in a fit condition for use **3. INTRACTABLE** impossible or almost impossible to deal with (*archaic*) —**impracticability** /im práktikə bílləti/ *n.* —**impracticableness** /im práktikəb'lnəss/ *n.* —**impracticably** /-bli/ *adv.*

impractical /im práktik'l/ *adj.* **1. NOT WORKABLE** that will not work effectively or be without problems when put into practice **2. NO GOOD AT DOING EVERYDAY THINGS** not able to perform practical tasks or deal easily with practical matters ○ *She is a brilliant academic, but completely impractical around the house.* —**impracticality** /im prákti kálləti/ *n.* —**impractically** /im práktikli/ *adv.* —**impracticalness** /-práktik'lnəss/ *n.*

imprecate /ímpri kayt/ (**-cates, -cating, -cated**) *vti.* to call down sth bad or harmful, especially a curse, on sb (*formal*) [Early 17thC. From Latin *imprecari*, from *precari* 'to pray' (see PRAY).] —**imprecator** *n.* —**imprecatory** /ímpri kaytəri/ *adj.*

imprecation /ímpri káysh'n/ *n.* (*formal*) **1. CURSE** an oath or curse **2. CURSING SB** the calling down of harm on sb **3. SWEARING** swearing or blasphemy

imprecise /ímpri síss/ *adj.* not exact or accurate —**imprecisely** *adv.* —**impreciseness** *n.* —**imprecision** /-sízh'n/ *n.*

impregnable /im prégnəb'l/ *adj.* **1. IMPOSSIBLE TO BREAK INTO** too strong to be captured or opened by force ○ *an impregnable fortress* **2. UNBEATABLE** unable to be shaken or destroyed by any outside influence ○ *impregnable faith* [15thC. From Old French *imprenable*, which was formed from *prenable* 'takeable', from *prendre* 'to take', from Latin *prehendere* The *-g-* spelling may have been modelled on words like DEIGN and REIGN.] —**impregnability** /im prégnə bílləti/ *n.* —**impregnableness** /im prégnəb'lnəss/ *n.* —**impregnably** /-bli/ *adv.*

impregnate *vt.* /ím preg nayt/ (**-nates, -nating, -nated**) **1. SATURATE** to incorporate a chemical into a porous material such as wood or cloth, especially by soaking it thoroughly with a liquid (*usually passive*) **2. FILL** make sth express or contain a particular quality or idea throughout (*literary*) **3.** BIOL **MAKE PREGNANT** to make a female pregnant ■ *adj.* /im prégnət/ **1. SATURATED** infused or saturated with sth **2.** BIOL **PREGNANT** pregnant or fertilized [Early 17thC. From late Latin *impregnat-*, the past participle stem of *impregnare*, ultimately from Latin *praegnas* 'pregnant' (see PREGNANT).] —**impregnation** /ím preg náysh'n/ *n.* —**impregnator** /ím prég naytər/ *n.*

impresa /im práyzə/, **imprese** /im práz/ *n.* a design, usually with a motto, representing a particular person or thing, e.g. on a coat of arms (*archaic*) [Late 16thC. From Italian, literally 'undertaking, device', from *imprendere* 'to undertake', ultimately from Latin *prendere* 'to take, grasp'.]

impresario /ímprə saári ō/ (*plural* **-os**) *n.* **1. ENTERTAINMENT MANAGER** a producer or promoter of commercial entertainment ventures, especially in musical theatre **2. BUSINESS HEAD OF AN OPERA OR BALLET COMPANY** sb in charge of an opera or ballet company who is responsible for business affairs, contracting artists, and commissioning new works **3. ENTERTAINER** a showman [Mid-18thC. From Italian, 'sb who undertakes', formed from *impresa* (see IMPRESA).]

imprescriptible /ímpri skríptəb'l/ *adj.* impossible to remove or violate [Late 16thC. From medieval Latin *imprescriptibilis*, from Latin *praescript-*, past participle stem of *praescribere* 'to direct in writing' (see PRESCRIBE).] —**imprescriptibility** /ímpri skríptə bílləti/ *n.* —**imprescriptibly** /ímpri skríptəbli/ *adv.*

imprese *n.* = **impresa** (*archaic*) [Late 16thC. Via French from Italian *impresa* (see IMPRESA).]

impress[1] *v.* /im préss/ (**-presses, -pressing, -pressed**) **1.** *vti.* **INFLUENCE DEEPLY OR PLEASE GREATLY** to bring about a strong or lasting effect, usually favourable, on the mind or feelings of sb (*often passive*) ○ *We were not impressed by the way we were treated.* **2.** *vt.* **MAKE CLEARLY UNDERSTOOD** to make sure that sb has a clear and lasting understanding, memory, or mental image of sth ○ *She impressed on every child her expectation of complete honesty.* **3.** *vt.* **PRESS A SHAPE INTO STH** to make a pattern, design, or mark on sth by pressing or stamping **4.** *vt.* ELECTRON ENG **APPLY A VOLTAGE** to apply a voltage to an electronic circuit or device ■ *n.* /ím press/ **STAMP** a characteristic mark (*literary*) [14thC. From French *empresser*, from Latin *impressus*, past participle of *imprimere* 'to press in', from *premere* 'to press' (see PRESS).] —**impresser** *n.* —**impressible** /im préssəb'l/ *adj.* —**impressibility** /im préssə bílləti/ *n.*

impress[2] /im préss/ (**-presses, -pressing, -pressed**) *vt.* **1. SEIZE** to seize by force for public use **2.** HIST **FORCE TO SERVE** to compel people to serve in a navy or army, especially by arbitrary means ○ *It was a common practice to impress seamen from coastal towns* [Late 16thC. Formed from PRESS[2] 'to force into service'.]

impression /im présh'n/ *n.* **1. WHAT STAYS IN SB'S MIND** a lasting effect, opinion, or mental image of sb or sth ○ *I made a bad impression by arriving late for the interview.* **2. GENERAL IDEA** a belief about or understanding of sth ○ *I was under the impression that they were married.* **3. PRESSED-IN SHAPE** a pattern, design, or mark made by sth hard being pressed onto sth softer ○ *The intruder's boots had left an impression in the mud.* **4.** ARTS **IMITATING OF SB** entertainment in which a performer mimics the way a well-known person speaks and behaves, usually in a humorous or exaggerated way **5.** DENT **MOULD TAKEN OF TEETH** a mould taken of the teeth and surrounding gums on which dentures, restorations, or dental appliances are constructed **6.** PRINTING **COPIES OF A BOOK** all the copies of a book printed at one time, or the printing of these **7.** PRINTING **COPY OF A BOOK** a printed copy of a book —**impressional** *adj.* —**impressionally** *adv.*

impressionable /im présh'nəb'l/ *adj.* ready to accept or be impressed by the experiences, opinions, and personalities of other people —**impressionability** /im présh'nə bílləti/ *n.* —**impressionableness** /im présh'nəb'lnəss/ *n.*

impressionism /im présh'nizəm/, **Impressionism** *n.* **1.** PAINTING **SCHOOL OF PAINTING** a style of painting that concentrates on the general tone and effect produced by a subject without elaboration of details. Monet and Renoir were practitioners of impressionism. **2.** MUSIC **MUSIC EXPRESSING IMPRESSIONS AND FEELINGS** a style of music, especially of late 19th- and early 20th-century France, characterized by the use of rich harmonies and tones rather than form to express scenes or emotions. Debussy and Ravel were practitioners of impressionism.

impressionist /im présh'nist/ *n.* **1. impressionist, Impressionist** PAINTING, MUSIC **PRACTITIONER OF IMPRESSIONISM** an artist or composer who paints pictures or writes music in the style of impressionism, especially one active in France at the end of the 19th century **2.** THEATRE, TV **ENTERTAINER** a performer who mimics the way well-known people speak and behave, usually in a humorous and exaggerated way [Late 19thC. In the sense 'practitioner of impressionism', from French *impressioniste*, originally a derisive name stemming from the title of Monet's *Impression: soleil levant* 'Impression: rising sun'.]

impressionistic /im préshə nístik/ *adj.* **1. UNDETAILED** giving a broad picture or general idea rather than an exact description **2.** PAINTING, MUSIC **LIKE IMPRESSIONIST ART OR MUSIC** concerning, involving, or in the style of impressionism or the impressionists in painting or music —**impressionistically** *adv.*

impressive /im préssiv/ *adj.* that makes a deep and usually favourable impression on the mind or senses —**impressively** *adv.* —**impressiveness** *n.*

impressment /im préssmənt/ *n.* the seizing of property or people and forcing them into public use or service (*formal*) [Late 18thC. Formed from IMPRESS[2].]

imprest /ím prest/ *n.* **1.** FIN **ADVANCE OF MONEY** an advance payment of money, especially to sb who is to carry out some business for the state **2.** FIN **LOAN TO DRAW ON** a loan, usually in the form of a petty cash account, that can be drawn upon as needed **3.** NAVY, MIL **ADVANCE PAYMENT** a payment formerly made in advance to a British soldier or sailor upon enlistment [Mid-16thC. Formed from obsolete *prest* 'loan', from Old French, formed in turn from *prester* 'to lend', ultimately from Latin *praesto* 'at hand' (source of English *presto*).]

imprimatur /ímpri maátər, -máytər/ *n.* **1. APPROVAL** authority to do, say, or especially print sth (*formal*) **2. OFFICIAL LICENCE** an authorization allowing a book or other work to be published, now usually confined to works sanctioned by the Roman Catholic Church [Mid-17thC. From Latin, literally 'let it be printed'.]

imprimis /im prímiss/ *adv.* in the first place (*formal*) [15thC. From Latin, from *in primis*, literally 'among the first things'.]

imprint *n.* /ímprint/ **1. PRESSED-IN SHAPE** a pattern, design, or mark that is made by pressing sth down on or into sth else **2.** PUBL **PRINTED PUBLICATION DETAILS** the name and address of the publisher and printer as shown at the front of a book **3. SPECIAL MARK** a printed or stamped sign on an object, e.g. to indicate its origin **4. LASTING EFFECT** an effect that remains and is recognizable for a long time ○ *The years of occupation left their imprint on all the inhabitants.* ■ *v.* /im prínt/ (**-prints, -printing, -printed**) **1.** *vt.* **MARK BY PRESSING** to put a shape or design on sth, e.g. the surface of an object, using a stamp or printing device **2.** *vt.* **CAUSE TO REMAIN** to fix an image, memory, opinion, or idea in a vivid or lasting way ○ *The scene was imprinted on her memory.* **3.** *vi.* ZOOL **ESTABLISH SOCIAL ATTACHMENTS** to learn an attraction to members of the same species or substitutes very early in life. ◊ **imprinting** —**imprinter** *n.*

imprinting /im prínting/ *n.* ZOOL a form of rapid learning very early in an animal's social development that results in strong behavioural patterns of attraction to members of its own species, especially parents. Imprinting was first described by Konrad Lorenz in 1937 when he trained young ducks and geese to follow him and regard him as their mother. [15thC. Originally in the sense 'the printing of books'; used by Lorenz to translate his term, German *Prägung*.]

imprison /im prízz'n/ (**-ons, -oning, -oned**) *vt.* to lock sb up in prison [13thC. From Old French *emprisoner*, from *prison* (see PRISON).] —**imprisoner** *n.* —**imprisonment** *n.*

improbable /im próbbəb'l/ *adj.* not likely to happen or to be true —**improbability** /im próbbə bílləti/ *n.* —**improbableness** /im próbbəb'lnəss/ *n.* —**improbably** /-bli/ *adv.*

improbity /im próbəti/ *n.* lack of moral scruples or honesty (*formal*)

impromptu /im prómp tyoo/ *adj.* **DONE OR SAID SPONTANEOUSLY** not prepared or planned in advance ○ *an impromptu speech* ■ *adv.* **WITHOUT PRIOR THOUGHT OR PREPARATION** in an unrehearsed way ■ *n.* **1.** MUSIC **SHORT SOLO PIECE** a short instrumental piece whose style gives an impression of improvisation. Such pieces were a highly developed and popular form in the 19th century. **2. STH SPONTANEOUS OR UNREHEARSED** sth done or said without planning [Mid-17thC. Via French from Latin *in promptu* 'at hand, in readiness', from *promptus* (see PROMPT).]

improper /im próppər/ *adj.* **1. UNSUITABLE** not appropriate to the context, the nature of the case, or the purpose in view (*formal*) **2. RUDE** not in accordance with accepted good manners or decorum **3.** LAW **IRREGULAR** not in accordance with the accepted standards of sth such as a profession ○ *the improper handling of funds* —**improperly** *adv.* —**improperness** *n.*

improper fraction *n.* a fraction in which the numerator is equal to or greater than the denominator, such as 6/4

impropriate *vt.* /im própri ayt/ (**-ates, -ating, -ated**) **PUT UNDER LAY CONTROL** to put ecclesiastical property or tithes in lay hands ■ *adj.* /im própri ət/ **UNDER LAY CONTROL** in the hands of lay people (*refers to ecclesiastical property*) [Early 16thC. From the past participle of Anglo-Latin *impropriare* 'to appropriate', ultimately from Latin *proprius* 'own' (see PROPER).] —**impropriation** /im própri áysh'n/ *n.* —**impropriator** /im própri aytər/ *n.*

impropriety /ímprə prí əti/ (*plural* **-ties**) *n.* conduct not considered correct, moral, or appropriate in a given context

improve /im proóv/ (**-proves, -proving, -proved**) *v.* **1.** *vti.* **MAKE OR BECOME BETTER** to make sth better in quality or condition, or to become better ○ *His health is improving daily.* **2.** *vt.* **INCREASE THE VALUE OF** to make property, such as land or buildings, more valuable

a at; aa father; aw all; ay day; air hair; ə about, edible, item, common, circus; e egg; ee eel; hw when; i it, happy; ī ice; 'l apple; 'm rhythm; 'n fashion; o odd; ō open; ōō good; oo pool; ow owl; oy oil; th thin; th this; u up; ur urge;

3. *vt.* USE WELL to make good use of or employ sth to advantage [Early 16thC. From Anglo-Norman *emprower* 'to make a profit' (the original sense in English), from Old French *prou* 'profit', from late Latin *prode* 'profitable' (see PROUD).] —**improvability** *n.* —**improvable** /im pro͞ovəb'l/ *adj.* —**improvableness** /-pro͞ovəb'lnəss/ *n.* —**improvably** /-əbli/ *adv.* —**improver** /-vər/ *n.*

improve on, improve upon *vt.* to do better or be better than a particular thing, especially a previous standard or record ○ *improved on her previous time by four seconds*

improvement /im pro͞ovmənt/ *n.* 1. GETTING OR MAKING BETTER the process of making sth better or of becoming better ○ *an improvement on her past performance* 2. CHANGE OR ADDITION a change or addition that makes sth better 3. ADVANCE IN VALUE an increase in value, especially in the value of land or property 4. CHANGE THAT APPRECIATES VALUE a change or addition, especially to property or land, that increases value ○ *home improvements*

improvident /im próvvidənt/ *adj.* (*formal*) 1. UNCONCERNED ABOUT FUTURE NEEDS failing to put money aside or give any thought to forward planning 2. WITHOUT FORESIGHT not sensible, cautious, or wise [15thC. Literally 'not foreseeing', ultimately from the late Latin stem *provident-* 'foreseeing' (see PROVIDENT).] —**improvidence** *n.* —**improvidently** *adv.*

improvisation /ímprə vī záysh'n/ *n.* 1. IMPROVISED PIECE OR PERFORMANCE sth performed or done without any preparation or set text to follow 2. CREATING AND PERFORMING SIMULTANEOUSLY the skill or creative process of creating and performing sth without any preparation or set text to follow —**improvisational** *adj.* —**improvisationally** *adv.*

improvise /ímprə vīz/ (-vises, -vising, -vised) *vti.* 1. ARTS MAKE STH UP ON THE SPOT to act or compose sth, especially a sketch, play, song, or piece of music, without any preparation or set text to follow 2. SUBSTITUTE to make a substitute for sth out of the materials that happen to be available at the time ○ *If you haven't got a hammer, we'll have to improvise.* [Early 19thC. Directly or via French from Italian *improvvisare*, ultimately from Latin *improvisus* 'unforeseen', from *providere* 'to foresee' (see PROVIDE).] —**improvisatorial** /ímprə vīzə táwri əl/ *adj.* —**improvisatory** /ímprə vī záytəri/ *adj.* —**improviser** /ímprə vīzər/ *n.*

imprudence /im pro͞od'nss/ *n.* a lack of wisdom, judgment, or discretion

imprudent /im pro͞od'nt/ *adj.* showing no care, forethought, or judgment (*formal*) —**imprudently** *adv.*

impudence /ímpyo͝odənss/, **impudency** /-dənssi/ *n.* 1. DELIBERATE RUDENESS behaviour that shows a lack of respect and shameless boldness 2. PIECE OF IMPUDENCE a rude or disrespectful remark or act

impudent /ímpyoodənt/ *adj.* showing a lack of respect and excessive boldness [14thC. From the Latin stem *impudent-*, from *pudens* 'ashamed, modest', present participle of *pudere* 'to feel or make ashamed' (source of English *pudendum*).] —**impudently** *adv.* —**impudentness** *n.*

impugn /im pyóon/ (-pugns, -pugning, -pugned) *vt.* to suggest that sb or sth cannot be trusted or respected (*formal*) ○ *Far be it from me to impugn his motives, but...* [14thC. From Latin *impugnare* 'to fight against' (the original sense in English), from *pugnare* 'to fight' (see PUGNACIOUS).] —**impugnable** *adj.* —**impugnation** /ím pug náysh'n/ *n.* —**impugner** /im pyóonər/ *n.* —**impugnment** /-mənt/ *n.*

impulse /ím pulss/ *n.* 1. FORCE DRIVING STH FORWARD a driving force producing a forward motion 2. FORWARD MOTION the motion produced by a driving force 3. SUDDEN URGE a sudden desire, urge, or inclination (*often used before a noun*) 4. INSTINCTIVE DRIVE an instinctive drive or natural tendency 5. MOTIVE a motivation or reason for a specific activity 6. PHYS FORCE ACTING OVER TIME a measure of momentum arrived at by multiplying the average force acting on a body by the length of time it acts 7. PHYSIOL NERVE OR MUSCLE SIGNAL a progressive wave of biochemically generated energy that travels along a nerve fibre or muscle and stimulates or inhibits activity [Mid-17thC. From Latin *impulsus*, past participle of *impellere* (see IMPEL).]

impulsion /im púlsh'n/ *n.* 1. ACT OR INSTANCE OF URGING the act of urging or forcing sb into action, or an instance of this 2. MOVEMENT OR THRUSTING FORCE a movement that comes from being pushed or thrust, or the force that creates this movement 3. SUDDEN DESIRE a sudden desire, inclination, or urge

impulsive /im púlssiv/ *adj.* 1. INCLINED TO ACT ON SUDDEN URGES having a tendency to act on sudden urges or desires 2. SPONTANEOUS based on or motivated by impulse 3. PHYS COMING IN BURSTS acting or coming in short bursts 4. ACOUSTICS SHORT AND PERCUSSIVE used to describe a sound that is of short duration and composed of a wide range of frequencies —**impulsively** *adv.* —**impulsiveness** *n.* —**impulsivity** /im pul ssívvəti/ *n.*

impunity /im pyóonəti/ *n.* exemption from punishment, harm, or recrimination [Mid-16thC. From Latin *impunitas*, from *impunis* 'without punishment', from *poena* 'punishment'.]

impure /im pyóor/ *adj.* 1. CONTAMINATED unclean because containing sth harmful 2. ADULTERATED combined with sth of inferior quality 3. SINFUL tainted with sin 4. HAVING MIXED STYLES combining a mixture of styles, or derived from more than one source 5. COLOURS MIXED WITH OTHER COLOURS being mixed with other colours or with black or white [15thC. From Latin *impurus*, from *purus* 'pure' (see PURE).] —**impurely** *adv.* —**impureness** *n.*

impurity /im pyóorəti/ (*plural* -ties) *n.* 1. LACK OF PURITY the state or quality of being impure 2. CONTAMINANT a substance that adulterates or contaminates sth ○ *drinking water that was found to contain impurities* 3. ELECTRON ENG STH ADDED TO A SEMICONDUCTOR a small amount of a substance added to a pure semiconductor to control its electrical conductivity

imputation /ímpyo͝o táysh'n/ *n.* 1. ACT OF IMPUTING the act of accusing sb of sth, or of attributing a result to a particular cause 2. ACCUSATION an accusation of wrongdoing or an attribution of blame

impute /im pyóot/ (-putes, -puting, -puted) *vt.* 1. ATTRIBUTE A BAD ACTION to attribute a usually undesirable action or event to sb ○ *'He had married her with that bad past life hidden behind him, and she had no faith left to protest his innocence of the worst that was imputed to him'.* (George Eliot, *Middlemarch*; 1872) 2. ATTRIBUTE A QUALITY to attribute a quality to a person, cause, or source ○ *'it was charity to impute some of her unbecoming indifference to the languor of ill-health'* (Jane Austen, *Emma*; 1816) 3. LAW CHARGE SB RESPONSIBLE FOR ANOTHER'S CRIME to bring legal charges against sb because a person that he or she is responsible for has committed an offence 4. RELIG EXTEND A QUALITY TO SB ELSE to regard a quality such as righteousness that applies to sb as also applying to another person associated with him or her [14thC. Via French *imputer* from Latin *imputare* 'to bring into the reckoning', from *putare* 'to reckon' (source of English *putative*).] —**imputable** *adj.* —**imputative** *adj.* —**imputer** *n.*

impv *abbr.* GRAM imperative

IMS *abbr.* 1. Indian Medical Service 2. Institute of Management Services

in /in/ CORE MEANING: a grammatical word indicating that sth or sb is within or inside sth ○ (prep) *The dinner's in the oven.* ○ (adv) *I called by, but you weren't in.*

1. *prep.* INDICATES A PLACE indicates that sth happens or is situated somewhere ○ *He spent a whole year in Russia.* 2. *prep.* INDICATES A STATE indicates a state or condition that sth or sb is experiencing ○ *The banking industry is in a state of flux.* 3. *prep.* INDICATES AFTER after a period of time that will pass before sth happens ○ *She should be well enough to leave in a week or two.* 4. *prep.* DURING indicates that sth happens during a period of time ○ *He crossed the desert in 39 days.* 5. *prep.* INDICATES HOW STH IS EXPRESSED indicates the means of communication used to express sth ○ *I managed to write the whole speech in French.* 6. *prep.* INDICATES SUBJECT AREA indicates a subject or field of activity ○ *She graduated with a degree in biology.* 7. *prep.* AS A CONSEQUENCE OF while doing sth or as a consequence of sth ○ *In reaching for a glass he knocked over the ashtray.* 8. *prep.* COVERED BY indicates that sth is wrapped or covered by sth ○ *The floor was covered in balloons and toys.* 9. *prep.* INDICATES HOW SB IS DRESSED indicates that sb is dressed in a particular way ○ *She was dressed in a smart suit.* 10. *prep.* ZOOL PREGNANT WITH pregnant with ○ *The cows were in calf.* 11. *adv.* ALIGHT indicates that a fire is alight ○ *It was so cold that we had to keep the fire in all night.* 12. *adv.* HAVE INNINGS indicates that a team or player in sports has an innings, e.g. in cricket ○ *Any volunteers to go in first?* 13. *adj.* FASHIONABLE fashionable or popular ○ *Inline skates are the in thing.* 14. *adj.* INTO OFFICE indicates that a party or group has achieved or will achieve power or authority ○ *Everyone was very optimistic when the new party got in.* [Old English] ◇ **have it in for, have got it in for** to dislike sb and want to do that person harm ○ *Ever since I got the job the boss has had it in for me.* ◇ **in between** between ○ *Normal light consists of a wave that vibrates up and down, side to side, and every direction in between.* ◇ **in for** indicates that sb will experience sth, e.g. a surprise or a shock ○ *Little did she know what she was in for.* ◇ **in on** having knowledge about or involvement in sth ○ *The whole class was in on the plans for the surprise party.* ◇ **in that** introduces an explanation of a statement ○ *Action Park is unusual in that it fights lawsuits tenaciously and settles none.* ◇ **in with** associated with or friendly with ○ *a reporter perhaps too much in with the politicians to be objective* ○ *He's been getting in with a bad crowd.* ◇ **the ins and outs** all the detailed facts and points about sth ○ *I don't know all the ins and outs of the matter, but she's leaving.*

In *symbol.* CHEM ELEM indium

in. *abbr.* in., in MEASURE inches

in-[1] *prefix.* not ○ *insensitive* ○ *incomplete* [From Latin]

in-[2] *prefix.* in, into, towards, within ○ *infighting* ○ *inbound* [From Latin]

-in *suffix.* 1. a neutral chemical compound ○ *fibroin* ○ *digitalin* ○ *thrombin* 2. antibiotic ○ *streptothricin* 3. pharmaceutical ○ *warfarin* 4. toxic substance ○ *botulin* 5. antigen ○ *bacterin* 6. = **-ine** ○ *hyalin* [From IN, Latin *in* 'in, into, on, during, against', or *in-* 'not']

inability /innə bílləti/ *n.* a lack of the ability, means, or power to do sth ○ *his inability to face the truth*

in absentia /in əb sénti ə/ *adv.* in the absence of the person or persons concerned (*formal*) [From Latin, literally 'in absence']

inaccessible /innək séssəb'l/ *adj.* 1. DIFFICULT TO GET TO difficult or impossible to gain access to or reach 2. DIFFICULT TO ACHIEVE difficult or impossible to afford or attain 3. HARD TO UNDERSTAND difficult or impossible to understand [15thC. Directly or via French from late Latin *inaccessibilis*, from *accessibilis* 'accessible'.] —**inaccessibility** /innək séssə bílləti/ *n.* —**inaccessibly** /-séssəbli/ *adv.*

inaccuracy /in ákyo͝orəssi/ (*plural* -cies) *n.* 1. LACK OF ACCURACY lack of accuracy or correctness 2. MISTAKE an error or mistake

WORD KEY: SYNONYMS

See Synonyms at ***mistake***.

inaccurate /in ákyo͝orət/ *adj.* not accurate or correct —**inaccurately** *adv.* —**inaccurateness** *n.*

inaction /in áksh'n/ *n.* 1. FAILURE TO ACT failure to take action when action is necessary ○ *'But in a nation that demands action, Congress has become the master of inaction.'* (National Public Telecommunity Network, *Bush speeches in campaign '92*) 2. ABSENCE OF ACTIVITY lack of activity, especially laziness or idleness

inactivate /in ákti vayt/ (-vates, -vating, -vated) *vt.* to make sth inactive or unable to function —**inactivation** /in ákti váysh'n/ *n.*

inactive /in áktiv/ *adj.* 1. NOT TAKING ACTION taking no action or not taking part in action that others are involved in 2. NOT BEING USED OR OPERATED not in use, or not functioning or operating 3. LAZY OR SEDENTARY not involving or taking part in physical activity 4. GEOG DORMANT used to describe a volcano that is not erupting but not extinct 5. MIL NOT IN ACTIVE SERVICE not taking part in, or not being used for, active military service 6. CHEM INERT having little or no chemical reactivity 7. CHEM HAVING LOW RADIOACTIVITY having low or zero radioactivity 8. BIOL BIOLOGICALLY INERT having little if any discernible effect on living things as a result of the loss of some property such as the ability to infect or create antigens **9.** MED **NOT DEVELOPING OR GIVING SYMPTOMS** used to describe a disease that is present in the body but not developing or not producing any symptoms —**inactively** *adv.* —**inactivity** /in ak tívvəti/ *n.*

inadequacy /in áddikwəssi/ (*plural* **-cies**) *n.* **1. STATE OF NOT BEING ADEQUATE** the failure to be adequate, e.g. to reach a required or expected standard **2. FAULT** a flaw or weakness that reveals inadequacy

inadequate /in áddikwət/ *adj.* failing to reach an expected or required level or standard ○ *inadequate supplies of food* —**inadequately** *adv.* —**inadequateness** *n.*

inadmissible /ínnəd míssəb'l/ *adj.* not admissible or allowable, especially in a court of law —**inadmissibility** /ínnəd missə bílləti/ *n.* —**inadmissibly** /ínnəd míssəbli/ *adv.*

inadvertence /ínnəd vúrt'nss/, **inadvertency** /ínnəd vúrt'nssi/ (*plural* **-cies**) *n.* **1. CARELESSNESS** carelessness or lack of attention **2. OVERSIGHT** an oversight or result of carelessness

inadvertent /ínnəd vúrt'nt/ *adj.* **1. RESULTING FROM CARELESSNESS** done unintentionally or without thinking **2. CARELESS** failing to pay enough attention or take enough care [Mid-17thC. Formed from Latin *advertent-*, present participle stem of *advertere* 'to turn the mind to' (see ADVERT).]

inadvertently /ínəd vúrt'ntli/ *adv.* without intending to or without realizing

inadvisable /ínnəd vízəb'l/ *adj.* not to be advised or recommended —**inadvisability** /ínnəd vízə bílləti/ *n.* —**inadvisably** /ínnəd vízəbli/ *adv.*

in aeternum /ín ee t/ *adv.* eternally or forever (*formal*) [From Latin, literally 'in eternal']

inalienable /in áyli ənəb'l/ *adj.* not able to be transferred or taken away, e.g. because of being protected by law (*formal*) —**inalienability** /in áyli ənə bílləti/ *n.* —**inalienably** /in áyli ənəbli/ *adv.*

inalterable /-óltə-/ *adj.* not able to be changed —**inalterability** /in áwltərə bílləti, -óltə-/ *n.* —**inalterably** /in áwltərəbli, -óltə-/ *adv.*

inamorata /in ámmə raátə/ (*plural* **-tas**) *n.* a woman whom sb loves or with whom sb has a romantic relationship (*literary*) [Late 16thC. From Italian, feminine of *inamorato* (see INAMORATO).]

inamorato /in ámmə raátō/ (*plural* **-tos**) *n.* a man whom sb loves or with whom sb has a romantic relationship (*literary*) [Late 16thC. From Italian, past participle of *inamorare* 'to fall in love', from *amore* 'love', from Latin *amor* (source of English *amorous*).]

inane /i náyn/ *adj.* **1. SILLY OR UNINTELLIGENT** having little sense or importance **2. INSUBSTANTIAL** empty, insubstantial, or void ■ *n.* **EMPTINESS** great emptiness, especially the perceived emptiness of outer space (*archaic*) [Mid-16thC. From Latin *inanis* 'empty, lacking sense'.] —**inanely** *adv.* —**inaneness** *n.*

inanimate /in ánnimət/ *adj.* **1. NOT LIVING** not alive **2. NOT LIVELY** not active, energetic, or lively ○ *'She had relapsed once more into the vacant inanimate creature who had opened the gate to us'.* (Wilkie Collins, *The Law and the Lady*; 1875) **3. RELATING TO NOUNS FOR NONLIVING THINGS** belonging to the category of nouns that refer to things and concepts considered to be without life [15thC. From late Latin *inanimatus* 'lifeless', from Latin *animatus*, past participle of *animare* 'to animate' (see ANIMATE).] —**inanimately** *adv.* —**inanimateness** *n.*

inanition /ínnə nísh'n/ *n.* **1. EXHAUSTION DUE TO STARVATION** exhaustion caused by lack of food or water or as a result of disease **2. LETHARGY** lethargy or lack of vitality (*literary*) **3. EMPTINESS** emptiness such as the absence of moral standards or intellectual substance (*formal*) [14thC. From the late Latin stem *inanition-*, from, ultimately, Latin *inanis* (see INANE).]

inanity /i nánnəti/ (*plural* **-ties**) *n.* **1. MEANINGLESS QUALITY** meaninglessness or senselessness that suggests a lack of understanding or intelligence **2. SILLINESS** silliness or foolishness **3. STH INANE** sth such as a silly remark that demonstrates or suggests inanity **4. EMPTY QUALITY** emptiness such as the imagined void of outer space (*archaic*)

inappellable /ínnə péllәb'l/ *adj.* unable to be challenged or appealed against (*formal*) [Early 19thC. From obsolete French *inappelable*, from *appeler* (see APPEAL).]

inappetence /in áppitənss/, **inappetency** /-tənssi/ *n.* lack of appetite (*formal*) —**inappetent** *adj.*

inapplicable /ínnə plíkəb'l/ *adj.* not applicable, suitable, or relevant —**inapplicability** /ínnə plikə bílləti/ *n.* —**inapplicably** /ínnə plíkəbli/ *adv.*

inapposite /in áppəzit/ *adj.* unsuitable or out of place (*formal*) —**inappositely** *adv.* —**inappositeness** *n.*

inappreciable /ínnə préeshəb'l/ *adj.* too small to be noticed or significant —**inappreciably** *adv.*

inappreciative /ínnə préeshətiv/ *adj.* feeling or showing no appreciation —**inappreciatively** *adv.* —**inappreciativeness** *n.*

inapproachable /ínnə próchəb'l/ *adj.* impossible to approach —**inapproachability** /ínnə prṓchə bílləti/ *n.* —**inapproachably** /ínnə próchəbli/ *adv.*

inappropriate /ínnə própri ət/ *adj.* not fitting, timely, or suitable —**inappropriately** *adv.* —**inappropriateness** *n.*

inapt /in ápt/ *adj.* **1. NOT SUITABLE** not suitable or appropriate **2. UNSKILLED** lacking aptitude, capability, or skill —**inaptitude** /in ápti tyood/ *n.* —**inaptly** *adv.* —**inaptness** *n.*

inarch /i naárch/ (**-arches, -arching, -arched**), **enarch** (**-arches, -arching, -arched**) *vt.* to graft part of one plant onto another without separating it from its parent [Early 17thC. Coined from IN- + ARCH, because the graft forms an arch between its parent and the new stock.]

inarguable /in aár gyoo əb'l/ *adj.* impossible to deny or take an opposing view about —**inarguably** *adv.*

inarticulate /in aar tíkyoolət/ *adj.* **1. EXPRESSING ONESELF POORLY** not good at choosing the right words or speaking fluently **2. NOT UNDERSTANDABLE** not understandable as speech or language **3. NOT EFFECTIVELY EXPRESSED** not clearly or effectively expressed **4. NOT SPOKEN ABOUT** not expressed, or not able to be expressed in words **5. UNABLE TO SPEAK** lacking the power to speak, especially because of feeling strong emotion **6.** ZOOL **NOT JOINTED** used to describe certain body parts that have no joints or segments, e.g. the bones of the skull **7.** MARINE BIOL **HAVING A SHELL WITHOUT A HINGE** used to describe a class of brachiopods that have shells without a hinge and are held together only by muscles and the body wall [Early 17thC. Originally in the sense 'without joints'.] —**inarticulately** *adv.* —**inarticulateness** *n.* —**inarticulacy** *n.*

inartistic /in aar tístik/ *adj.* **1. NOT CONFORMING TO THE RULES OF ART** not in accordance with the principles of art **2. NOT INTERESTED IN THE ARTS** having no appreciation of or sensitivity to the arts **3. LACKING ARTISTIC SKILL** possessing or demonstrating little or no artistic talent —**inartistically** *adv.*

inasmuch as /ínnəz múch əz/ *conj.* **1. BECAUSE** used to introduce an explanation or reason ○ *'This was an idle and unpractical question, inasmuch as the answer was not forthcoming.'* (Henry James, *Confidence*) **2. IN SO FAR AS** used to introduce a comment that limits the extent of sth [*Inasmuch* from IN + AS + MUCH, modelled on French *en tant* 'in so much']

inattention /ínnə ténsh'n/ *n.* failure to take proper care or give enough attention to sth

inattentive /ínnə téntiv/ *adj.* not paying attention or taking proper care —**inattentively** *adv.* —**inattentiveness** *n.*

inaudible /in áwdəb'l/ *adj.* not loud enough to be heard —**inaudibility** /in áwdə bílləti/ *n.* —**inaudibly** /in áwdəbli/ *adv.*

inaugural /i náwgyoorəl/ *adj.* **1. RELATING TO AN INAUGURATION** relating to or marking the official beginning of sth **2. FIRST OF SEVERAL** being the first of a series, such as the first issue of a magazine [Late 17thC. From French, formed from *inaugurer* 'to inaugurate', from Latin *inaugurare* (see INAUGURATE).]

inaugurate /i náwgyoo rayt/ (**-rates, -rating, -rated**) *vt.* **1.** POL **SWEAR FORMALLY INTO OFFICE** to place sb in office with a formal ceremony **2. OPEN CEREMONIALLY** to open or mark the beginning of sth such as a new building with a formal ceremony or dedication **3. PUT INTO OPERATION** to initiate sth or put it into operation, especially in a formal or official manner [Late 16thC. From Latin *inaugurare* 'to foretell the future from birds' flight', later 'to install in office after observing the omens', from *augurari* (see AUGUR).] —**inaugurator** *n.* —**inauguratory** /in áwgyoorətəri/ *adj.*

inauguration /i náwg yoo ráysh'n/ *n.* **1.** POL **INDUCTION INTO OFFICE** the formal placing of sb in an official position, especially the President of the United States, or a ceremony held for this purpose **2. CEREMONIAL OPENING OF STH** a formal ceremony to open or mark the beginning of sth such as a new building **3. PUTTING STH INTO OPERATION** the act of bringing sth into service or putting it into operation, or an occasion on which this is done

inauspicious /in aw spíshəss/ *adj.* suggesting that the future is not very promising or that success is unlikely —**inauspiciously** *adv.* —**inauspiciousness** *n.*

inauthentic /ín aw théntik/ *adj.* not authentic or genuine —**inauthenticity** /ín aw then tíssəti/ *n.*

inbd *abbr.* TRANSP inboard

in-between *adj., adv.* **INTERMEDIATE** falling between others ○ *one of his in-between moods when you don't know what he'll say* ■ *n.* **SB OR STH INTERMEDIATE** sb or sth that falls between others ○ *the oldest, the youngest, and the in-between*

inboard /ín bawrd/ *adj.* **1. LOCATED INSIDE A BOAT'S HULL** located inside the hull of a boat, not fitted to the outside **2. HAVING AN INBOARD ENGINE** having an inboard engine ■ *n.* **BOAT WITH AN INBOARD MOTOR** a boat that has an inboard motor ■ *adv.* **AWAY FROM THE SIDES** more towards the centre of an aircraft or boat than towards the sides or edges

inborn /ín bawrn/ *adj.* inherited from parents or possessed from birth [Old English. Originally in the sense 'native, indigenous'; the current sense dates from the early 16thC.]

inbound[1] /ín bownd/ *adj.* arriving, incoming, or heading towards an airport, port, or station [Late 19thC. From IN + BOUND.]

inbound[2] (**-bounds, -bounding, -bounded**) *vti.* in basketball, to put the ball back into play by passing it from out of bounds to a player on the court [Late 20thC. Back-formation from INBOUNDS.]

inbounds /ín bowndz/ *adj.* BASKETBALL involving returning the basketball into play ○ *on the ensuing inbounds play*

inbounds line *n.* in American football, either of the two broken lines that run the length of the pitch

inbreathe /in breeth/ (**-breathes, -breathing, -breathed**) *vt.* **1. INHALE** to take sth into the airways by breathing in **2. INSPIRE** to inspire sb or infuse sb with sth (*literary*) [14thC. Modelled on Latin *inspirare* 'to breathe into' (source of English *inspire*).]

inbred /ín bred/ *adj.* **1. INNATE** existing naturally, through being possessed from birth or inherited from parents **2.** GENETICS **PRODUCED BY INBREEDING** produced by the mating of closely related individuals of a species ■ *n.* GENETICS **FORM RESULTING FROM INBREEDING** a person or an animal whose health and intelligence are affected because his, her, or its ancestors were too closely related to each other

inbreed /in bréed/ (**-breeds, -breeding, -bred** /-bréd/, **-bred**) *v.* **1.** *vti.* GENETICS **MATE CLOSELY RELATED INDIVIDUALS** to mate closely related individuals of a species with each other, especially over many generations **2.** *vt.* **CREATE OR PRODUCE** to cause sth to develop in sb —**inbreeder** *n.*

inbreeding /ín breeding/ *n.* the mating of closely related individuals of a species, especially over many generations. It may be done deliberately to enhance desired traits in livestock or pets but increases the risk of inherited defects.

in-built *adj.* **1. INNATE** existing as part of sb's character **2. FITTED INSIDE STH** fitted inside sth or existing as a part of it

inby /in bí/ *adv., adj. Scotland* **1. FURTHER INSIDE HOUSE** further in, especially further inside a house (*nonstandard*) **2. TO FARMHOUSE** to or towards a house, especially the main or only house on a piece of land such as a farm [Early 18thC. From IN + BY.]

inc. *abbr.* **1.** included **2.** including **3.** inclusive **4.** income **5.** incomplete **6. inc., Inc.** *US* BUSINESS incorporated **7.** increase

Inca /íngkə/ (*plural* **-ca** *or* **-cas**) *n.* **1.** MEMBER OF A NATIVE S AMERICAN PEOPLE a member of a Native South American people whose huge empire, based in Peru and covering the entire Andean region, flourished from the 12th century AD until the mid-16th century. The Incas were sophisticated engineers, architects, and artists who had a highly complex social structure. The descendants of the Incas form roughly 50% of today's population of Peru. **2.** INCA KING a king, noble, or ruler of the Inca empire [Late 16thC. From Quechua, literally 'royal person'.] —**Inca** *adj.* —**Incaic** /ing káyik/ *adj.* —**Incan** /íngkən/ *adj.*

incalculable /in kálk yōōləb'l/ *adj.* **1.** TOO GREAT TO MEASURE too great or numerous to be measured **2.** IMPOSSIBLE TO FORESEE too uncertain to assess or plan for in advance —**incalculability** /in kálkyōōlə bílləti/ *n.* —**incalculably** /in kálkyōōləbli/ *adv.*

incalescent /ínkə léss'nt/ *adj.* becoming warmer or hotter (*technical*) [Mid-17thC. From Latin *incalescent-*, the present participle stem of *incalescere* 'to get hotter', ultimately from *calere* 'to be hot' (source of English *chafe*).] —**incalescence** *n.*

in camera *adv., adj.* **1.** IN A COURT CLOSED TO THE PUBLIC in a court from which the public is barred **2.** IN A JUDGE'S CHAMBERS in a judge's private chambers rather than in open court **3.** IN PRIVATE in private or in secret [From late Latin, literally 'in the chamber']

incandesce /ín kan déss/ (**-desces, -descing, -desced**) *vti.* to give off light as a result of being heated to a high temperature, or to cause sth to give off light in this way [Late 19thC. Back-formation from INCANDESCENT.]

incandescence /ín kan déss'nss/, **incandescency** /-s'nssi/ *n.* **1.** EMISSION OF LIGHT BY A HOT OBJECT the emission of light by an object as a result of its being heated to a high temperature **2.** LIGHT FROM A HOT OBJECT the light produced by an object heated to a high temperature **3.** EMOTIONAL INTENSITY intensity of emotion such as anger or romantic passion

incandescent /ín kan déss'nt/ *adj.* **1.** GLOWING WITH HEAT emitting light as a consequence of being heated to a high temperature **2.** GLOWING BRIGHTLY shining or glowing brightly **3.** SHOWING INTENSE EMOTION feeling or displaying intense emotion such as anger or romantic passion [Late 18thC. Directly or via French from Latin *incandescere* 'to glow', from *candescere* 'to become white', from *candidus* (see CANDID).] —**incandescently** *adv.*

incandescent lamp *n.* an electric lamp that produces light from an electrically heated filament

incantation /ín kan táysh'n/ *n.* **1.** USE OF SUPPOSEDLY MAGIC WORDS the ritual chanting or use of supposedly magic words **2.** SET OF SUPPOSEDLY MAGIC WORDS a set of words spoken or chanted as a supposedly magic spell [14thC. Via French from, ultimately, Latin *incantare* 'to chant', from *cantare* 'to sing'.] —**incantational** *adj.*

incapable /in káypəb'l/ *adj.* **1.** LACKING NECESSARY ABILITY lacking the ability, character, or strength required to do sth **2.** NOT GOOD ENOUGH unable to function or perform adequately **3.** UNABLE TO LOOK AFTER SELF not able to look after yourself ○ *exhausted and incapable* **4.** IMPOSSIBLE too extreme for sth to be possible ○ *damage incapable of being repaired* **5.** LEGALLY INELIGIBLE legally disqualified or ineligible [Late 16thC. Directly or via French from late Latin *incapabilis*, from *capabilis* 'capable' (see CAPABLE).] —**incapability** /in káypə bílləti/ *n.* —**incapableness** *n.* —**incapably** /-bli/ *adv.*

incapacitant /ínkə pássitənt/ *n.* a substance such as tear gas that can temporarily incapacitate sb, used especially in riot control and biological warfare

incapacitate /ínkə pássi tayt/ (**-tates, -tating, -tated**) *vt.* **1.** DEPRIVE OF EFFECTIVENESS to deprive sb or sth of power, force, or effectiveness **2.** LAW OFFICIALLY RULE SB OUT to disqualify sb or make sb legally ineligible —**incapacitation** /ínkə passi táysh'n/ *n.*

incapacity /ínkə pássəti/ (*plural* **-ties**) *n.* **1.** INABILITY OR INEFFECTIVENESS lack of ability, force, or effectiveness **2.** PHYSICAL OR MENTAL CHALLENGE a physical or mental challenge **3.** LEGAL DISQUALIFICATION a legal or official disqualification [Early 17thC. Directly or via French *incapacité* from late Latin *incapacitas*, from Latin *capacitas* 'capacity' (see CAPACITY).]

incapsulate *vti.* = **encapsulate**

in-car *adj.* fitted or provided inside a car

incarcerate /in káarssə rayt/ (**-ates, -ating, -ated**) *vt.* (*formal*) **1.** IMPRISON to put sb in prison **2.** CONFINE to place sb in a place or situation of confinement [Early 16thC. From medieval Latin *incarcerat-*, past participle stem of *incarcerare*, from *carcer* 'prison'.] —**incarceration** /in kaárssə ráysh'n/ *n.* —**incarcerator** /in káarssə raytər/ *n.*

incardinate /in káardi nayt/ (**-nates, -nating, -nated**) *vt.* **1.** MOVE A PRIEST TO A NEW DISTRICT to transfer a Roman Catholic priest to a new district under the authority of a different bishop **2.** MAKE A PRIEST A CARDINAL to promote a member of the Roman Catholic clergy to the position of cardinal **3.** MAKE A PRIEST MOST SENIOR to promote a Roman Catholic priest to the position of most senior member of the clergy within a particular church or area [Early 17thC. From late Latin *incardinat-*, past participle stem of *incardinare* 'to ordain as chief priest', from Latin *cardinalis* (see CARDINAL).] —**incardination** /in kaárdi náysh'n/ *n.*

incarnadine /in káarnə dīn/ *adj.* CRIMSON of a crimson or blood red colour (*literary*) ■ *n.* CRIMSON COLOUR the colour crimson or the colour of blood (*literary*) ■ *vt.* (**-dines, -dining, -dined**) MAKE CRIMSON to tinge or stain sth crimson or blood red (*literary*) [Late 16thC. Via French from Italian *incarnatino* 'carnation', literally 'flesh-colour', ultimately from the Latin stem *carn-* 'flesh' (see CARNAL).]

incarnate *adj.* /in káarnət/ **1.** MADE HUMAN having a bodily form, especially a human form **2.** PERSONIFIED being the epitome of sth ○ *an adviser who is discretion incarnate* **3.** BOT PINK OR RED used to describe plant parts that are pink or crimson ■ *vt.* /in káar nayt/ (**-nates, -nating, -nated**) **1.** SHOW IN HUMAN FORM to give sth a bodily form, especially a human form **2.** PERSONIFY to be the epitome or personification of sth **3.** CAUSE TO HAPPEN to bring about or realize sth that exists as an idea or theory only [14thC. From ecclesiastical Latin *incarnatus*, past participle of *incarnari* 'to be made flesh', from the Latin stem *carn-* 'flesh' (see CARNAL).] —**incarnator** /in káar naytər/ *n.*

incarnation /ín kaar náysh'n/ *n.* **1.** PERSONIFICATION OF STH sb or sth personifying, representing, or typifying a quality or idea **2.** ONE LIFE IN A SERIES OF LIVES one of a succession of lives or periods spent in the body of a particular animal or person **3.** MANIFESTATION OF A GOD a god's or spirit's appearance in human or animal form

Incarnation *n.* in Christianity, God's taking human form as Jesus Christ

in case ♦ **case**

incase *vt.* = **encase** —**incasement** *n.*

incautious /in káwshəss/ *adj.* careless, rash, or lacking in caution —**incautiously** *adv.* —**incautiousness** *n.* —**incaution** *n.*

incendiarism /in séndi ərizəm/ *n.* inflammatory talk or provocative behaviour designed or likely to cause civil unrest (*formal*)

incendiary /in séndi əri/ *adj.* **1.** ARMS CONTAINING CHEMICALS THAT CAUSE FIRE containing highly flammable substances that will cause a fire on impact **2.** LIKELY TO CATCH FIRE able to catch fire spontaneously or cause a fire easily **3.** INCITING CIVIL UNREST designed or likely to cause civil unrest **4.** RELATING TO ARSON relating to or involving the illegal burning of property ■ *n.* (*plural* **-ies**) **1.** **incendiary, incendiary bomb** ARMS BOMB DESIGNED TO CAUSE A FIRE a bomb or missile containing a highly flammable substance such as napalm, designed to cause a fire on impact **2.** SB INCITING TROUBLE sb who stirs up trouble or violence, especially for political motives (*formal*) **3.** ARSONIST sb who illegally sets fire to property (*formal*) [15thC. From Latin *incendiarius*, from *incendium* 'conflagration', from *incendere* (see INCENSE[1]).]

incense[1] /in senss/ *n.* **1.** SUBSTANCE BURNT FOR ITS FRAGRANT SMELL a substance, usually fragrant gum or wood, that gives off a pleasant smell when burnt **2.** SMOKE OR FRAGRANCE FROM INCENSE the smoke or fragrant smell produced when incense is burnt **3.** FRAGRANCE a pleasant smell **4.** PRAISE praise or adulation ■ *v.* (**-censes, -censing, -censed**) **1.** *vti.* HONOUR A GOD WITH INCENSE to honour a god by burning incense **2.** *vt.* PERFUME WITH INCENSE to perfume sth with incense [13thC. Via French *encens* from ecclesiastical Latin *incensum*, a form of *incensus*, past participle of Latin *incendere* 'to set fire to', from the base of *candere* 'to glow'.] —**incensation** /in sen sáysh'n/ *n.*

incense[2] /in sénss/ (**-censes, -censing, -censed**) *vt.* to make sb extremely angry [15thC. From French *encenser*, from *encens*, or ecclesiastical Latin *incensare*, from *incensum* (see INCENSE[1]).] —**incensement** *n.*

incense cedar *n.* **1.** EVERGREEN TREE a coniferous evergreen tree of the cypress family with resinous scaly leaves, flattened branches, and aromatic wood. Different species occur in the Americas, Asia, and New Zealand. Genera: *Austrocedrus* and *Calocedrus* and *Libocedrus*. **2.** FRAGRANT WOOD OF THE INCENSE CEDAR TREE the aromatic wood of the incense cedar tree, often used to scent rooms or drawers, or to keep away moths. Its resistance to decay makes it useful for decking and fence posts, and it is also used to make pencils.

incensory /ín senssəri/ (*plural* **-ries**) *n.* RELIG = **censer** [Early 17thC. From medieval Latin *incensorium*, from ecclesiastical Latin *incensum* (see INCENSE[1]).]

incentive /in séntiv/ *n.* STH THAT ENCOURAGES SB TO ACTION sth that encourages or motivates sb to do sth ■ *adj.* ENCOURAGING OR MOTIVATING serving to encourage or motivate sb [Early 17thC. From Latin *incentivum*, literally 'sth that sets the tune', ultimately from *incinere* 'to sound', from *canere* 'to sing'.] —**incentively** *adv.*

WORD KEY: SYNONYMS

See Synonyms at ***motive***.

incentivise = **incentivize**

incentivize /in sénti vīz/ (**-izes, -izing, -ized**), **incentivise** (**-ises, -ising, -ised**) *vt.* to motivate sb by offering an incentive such as a higher rate of pay (*informal*)

incept /in sépt/ (**-cepts, -cepting, -cepted**) *vi.* UNIV to enrol at a university, especially to begin studying for a master's degree or doctorate (*dated formal*) [15thC. From Latin *incept-*, past participle stem of *incipere* 'to begin' (see INCIPIENT).] —**inceptor** *n.*

inception /in sépsh'n/ *n.* **1.** BEGINNING the beginning of sth (*formal*) **2.** UNIV ENROLMENT AT UNIVERSITY enrolment as a university student, especially one studying for a master's degree or doctorate (*dated formal*) [15thC. Directly or via French from the Latin stem *inception-*, ultimately from *incipere* (see INCIPIENT).]

inceptive /in séptiv/ *adj.* **1.** INITIAL representing or coming at the beginning of sth (*formal*) **2.** LING EXPRESSING THE IDEA OF STARTING used to describe a verb or verb form that, in some languages, indicates the beginning of an action ■ *n.* LING **1.** INCEPTIVE ASPECT the inceptive aspect of verbs **2.** INCEPTIVE VERB a verb in the inceptive aspect [Early 17thC. From late Latin *inceptivus*, ultimately from Latin *incipere* (see INCIPIENT).] —**inceptively** *adv.*

incertitude /in súrti tyood/ *n.* **1.** DOUBT doubt or uncertainty **2.** LACK OF SELF-CONFIDENCE lack of confidence in yourself [15thC. Directly or via French from late Latin *incertitudo*, from *certitudo* 'certitude' (see CERTITUDE).]

incessant /in séss'nt/ *adj.* continuing for a long time without stopping [15thC. Directly or via French from the late Latin stem *incessant-*, from *cessare* 'to stop' (see CEASE).] —**incessancy** *n.* —**incessantly** *adv.*

incest /ín sest/ *n.* sexual activity between two people who are considered, for moral and genetic reasons, too closely related to have such a relationship. Incest is regarded as a serious taboo in almost every society, although cultures differ as to the extent to which marriages are allowed between relatives. [13thC. From Latin *incestus*, from *castus* (see CHASTE).]

incestuous /in sést yoo əss/ *adj.* **1.** RELATING TO OR INVOLVING INCEST relating to or involving a sexual relationship between two people who are considered, for moral and genetic reasons, too closely related to have such a relationship **2.** GUILTY OF INCEST having had a sexual relationship with sb considered to be too close a relative **3.** UNHEALTHILY EXCLUSIVE OF OTHERS unhealthily intimate or interconnected, especially so as to exclude the involvement or influence of others ○ *an incestuous friendship* **4.** BORN OF PARENTS WHO COMMITTED INCEST born as the result of an incestuous relationship (*archaic*) —**incestuously** *adv.* —**incestuousness** *n.*

inch[1] /inch/ *n.* **1.** MEASURE UNIT OF LENGTH a unit of length equal to 2.54 cm/$\frac{1}{12}$ of a foot. Symbol " **2.** SMALL AMOUNT a very small amount, degree, or distance **3.** METEOROL **AMOUNT OF RAIN OR SNOW** a fall of enough rain or snow to cover a surface to a depth of one inch **4.** METEOROL **UNIT OF ATMOSPHERIC PRESSURE** a unit of atmospheric pressure equal to that needed to maintain a mercury column one inch high in a barometer ■ *vti.* **(inches, inching, inched) MOVE SLOWLY** to move or cause sb or sth to move very slowly or by small degrees [Pre-12thC. From Latin *uncia* 'one twelfth', from *unus* 'one' (source of English *unit* and *ounce*).]

inch[2] /inch/ *n.* in Scotland and Ireland, a small island (*often used in place names*) [15thC. From Scottish Gaelic *innis* 'island'.]

inchmeal /ínch meel/ *adv.* in very small stages or progressions [Mid-16thC. From INCH[1] + -MEAL.]

inchoate /in kṓ ət/ *adj.* (*formal*) **1. JUST BEGINNING** just beginning to develop **2. IMPERFECTLY FORMED** only partly formed **3. CHAOTIC** lacking structure, order, or organization [Mid-16thC. From Latin *inchoatus*, past participle of *inchoare*, variant of *incohare* 'to begin'.] —**inchoately** *adv.* —**inchoateness** *n.* —**inchoation** /in kō áysh'n/ *n.*

inchoative /in kṓ ətiv/ *adj., n.* GRAM = **inceptive** *adj.* 2, **inceptive** *n.* 1, **inceptive** *n.* 2

inchworm /ínch wurm/ *n.* = **measuring worm**

incidence /ínssidənss/ *n.* **1. RATE OF OCCURRENCE OF STH** the frequency with which sth occurs **2. INSTANCE OR MANNER OF STH HAPPENING** an instance of sth happening, or the manner in which it happens **3.** PHYS, MATH **IMPACT ON A SURFACE** the impact that sth moving, e.g. a ray of light or a projectile, makes with a surface

incident /ínssidənt/ *n.* **1. EVENT** sth that happens, especially a single event **2. VIOLENT OCCURRENCE** a public occurrence, especially a violent one ○ *an incident outside a nightclub* **3. EVENT WITH POTENTIALLY SERIOUS CONSEQUENCES** an event that may result in a crisis, especially in international matters ■ *adj.* **1. RELATED TO STH** accompanying sth or occurring as a consequence of it (*formal*) **2.** PHYS **COMING INTO CONTACT WITH SURFACE** coming into contact with a surface [15thC. Directly or via French from, ultimately, Latin *incidere* 'to fall upon or happen to', from *cadere* 'to fall'.]

incidental /ínssi dént'l/ *adj.* **1. RELATED OR ACCOMPANYING** related to or accompanying sth more important **2. OCCURRING BY CHANCE** occurring by chance or without intention **3. OCCASIONAL** unimportant or occasional **4. RESULTING FROM STH** occurring as a result of sth (*formal*) ■ *n.* **MINOR ITEM** sth that is occasional or unimportant such as a minor expense

incidentally /ínssi dént'li/ *adv.* **1. BY THE WAY** used to introduce additional information such as sth that the speaker has just thought of **2. BY CHANCE** by chance or by accident

incidental music *n.* music that accompanies the action of a film, play, or television programme, as distinct from theme music or songs that feature in a musical

incinerate /in sínnə rayt/ **(-ates, -ating, -ated)** *vti.* to burn to ashes, or cause sth to burn to ashes, especially in an incinerator [15thC. From medieval Latin *incinerare*, from *ciner-*, stem of *cinis* 'ashes'.] —**incineration** /in sínnə ráysh'n/ *n.*

incinerator /in sínnə raytər/ *n.* a furnace for destroying things by burning them, especially one used to burn rubbish

incipient /in síppi ənt/ *adj.* beginning to appear or develop [Mid-17thC. From Latin *incipient-*, present participle stem of *incipere* 'to undertake or begin', from *capere* 'to take'.] —**incipience** *n.* —**incipiently** *adv.*

incipit /ínssipit, ínki-/ *n.* the opening word or words of a medieval manuscript or an early printed book, by which it is often known in the absence of a title [Late 19thC. From Latin, literally 'it begins', a form of *incipere* (see INCIPIENT).]

incisal /in sīz'l/ *adj.* relating to the cutting edge of a tooth [Early 20thC. Formed from INCISOR.]

incise /in sīz/ **(-cises, -cising, -cised)** *vt.* **1.** ARTS **ENGRAVE OR CARVE** to carve or engrave a pattern or design into sth **2.** SURG **CUT** to cut into sth [Mid-16thC. From French *inciser*, from Latin *incis-*, past participle stem of *incidere* 'to cut into', from *caedere* 'to cut'.]

incised /in sīzd/ *adj.* used to describe a leaf with edges that are deeply and sharply indented

incision /in sízh'n/ *n.* **1.** SURG **CUT OR ACT OF CUTTING** a cut or the act of cutting, especially when performed by a surgeon **2.** BOT **LEAF'S DEEPLY INDENTED EDGE** a sharp indentation in the edge of a leaf **3. FACT OF BEING INCISIVE** the fact or quality of being quick to understand or able to express sth clearly

incisive /in sīssiv/ *adj.* **1. QUICK TO UNDERSTAND** quick to understand, analyse, or act **2. EXPRESSING OR EXPRESSED CLEARLY** characterized by clear and direct expression **3. HURTFUL** designed to be cutting, unkind, or hurtful —**incisively** *adv.* —**incisiveness** *n.*

incisor /in sīzər/ *n.* one of the flat sharp-edged teeth in the front of the mouth, used for cutting and tearing food [Late 17thC. From medieval Latin *dens incisor*, literally 'cutter tooth', formed from Latin *incis-* (see INCISE).]

incitation *n.* = **incitement**

incite /in sīt/ **(-cites, -citing, -cited)** *vt.* to stir up feelings in or provoke action by sb [15thC. Via French *inciter* from Latin *incitare* 'to hasten or urge on', from *citare* 'to set in motion' (see CITE).] —**inciter** *n.*

incitement /in sītmənt/, **incitation** /ín sī táysh'n/ *n.* **1. PROVOCATION** the stirring up of feelings or the provoking of action, especially militancy or violence **2. STH THAT INCITES** sth that stirs up feelings or provokes action

incivility /ínssi víllәti/ (*plural* **-ties**) *n.* **1. RUDE BEHAVIOUR OR LANGUAGE** rude or impolite behaviour or language **2. RUDE ACT OR REMARK** a rude or impolite act or remark [Mid-16thC. From Latin *incivilis*, from *civilis* (see CIVIL).]

incl. *abbr.* **1.** including **2.** inclusive

inclement /in klémmənt/ *adj.* **1.** METEOROL **NOT PLEASANT OR MILD** unpleasant in being stormy, rainy, or snowy **2. SHOWING LITTLE MERCY** showing little or no mercy (*formal*) [Mid-16thC. Directly or via French *inclément* from the Latin stem *inclement-*, literally 'not clement', from *clement-* (see CLEMENT).] —**inclemency** *n.* —**inclemently** *adv.*

inclinable /in klīnəb'l/ *adj.* **1. HAVING A PARTICULAR TENDENCY** inclined to behave in a particular way **2. IN FAVOUR** likely to agree or approve (*formal*)

inclination /ínkli náysh'n/ *n.* **1. WAY SB FEELS ABOUT STH** a feeling that pushes sb to make a particular choice or take a particular decision **2. TENDENCY** a tendency to do or prefer sth, or a desire for sth **3. DEVIATION FROM LINE OR PLANE** the tilting of sth away from a line or surface, or the degree to which it is tilted **4. SLOPE** a sloping surface **5. TILTING OF STH** a bending of sth, e.g. a bowing of the head **6.** GEOM **ANGLE ON GRAPH** the angle between a line on a graph and the positive direction of the x-axis **7.** GEOM **SMALLER ANGLE** the smaller angle between two lines or planes **8.** ASTRON **ANGLE OF ORBIT** the angle between a planet's orbit and the apparent orbit of the Sun in relation to the Earth **9.** PHYS = **dip** —**inclinational** *adj.*

incline *vti.* /in klīn/ **(-clines, -clining, -clined) 1. BE OR MAKE LIKELY TO ACT** to tend, or make sb tend, towards a particular belief or course of action **2. ANGLE OR BE ANGLED** to lie at an angle or put sth at an angle **3. BEND** to bend sth, especially the head or body when bowing or nodding ■ *n.* /ín klīn/ **1. SLOPE** a slope or sloping surface **2.** RAIL = **inclined railway** [14thC. Via Old French *encliner* from Latin *inclinare* 'to lean towards', from *clinare* 'to lean' (source of English *decline*).] —**incliner** /in klīnər/ *n.*

inclined /in klīnd/ *adj.* **1. MOTIVATED TO DO STH** moved or persuaded to do sth ○ *I'm not inclined to listen to any more of this.* **2. TALENTED IN A PARTICULAR AREA** naturally talented or interested in a particular field or area **3. SLANTED OR FORMING AN ANGLE** sloping or forming an angle with sth else

inclined railway *n.* a railway system, used on particularly steep gradients, in which the trains are hauled by cable

inclinometer /ínkli nómmitər/ *n.* **1. DEVICE FOR MEASURING INCLINATION** an instrument that measures angles or slopes such as the angle of an aircraft relative to the ground **2. DEVICE FOR FINDING AN INCLINATION** an instrument used to determine the angle made by the Earth's magnetic field relative to the horizontal plane [Mid-19thC. Coined from Latin *inclinare* (see INCLINE) + -METER.]

inclose *vt.* = **enclose** —**inclosable** *adj.* —**incloser** *n.* —**inclosure** *n.*

include /in klo͞od/ **(-cludes, -cluding, -cluded)** *vt.* **1. CONTAIN** to have sth as a constituent element **2. BRING INTO GROUP** to make sb or sth part of a group [15thC. From Latin *includere* 'to shut in or enclose', from *claudere* 'to shut'.] —**includable** *adj.*

WORD KEY: USAGE

See Usage note at ***comprise***.

included /in klo͞odid/ *adj.* **1. CONTAINED WITHIN A GROUP** forming part of a group or whole **2.** BOT **NOT PROTRUDING** used to describe the stamens or carpels of a flower that do not protrude beyond the edges of the petals **3.** GEOM **LOCATED BETWEEN INTERSECTING LINES** formed by and contained in two intersecting lines —**includedness** *n.*

including /in klo͞oding/ *prep.* used to introduce examples of people or things forming part of a particular group or whole ○ *It will cost you £39.95 including VAT.*

inclusion /in klo͞ozh'n/ *n.* **1. PRESENCE IN GROUP** the addition of sb or sth to, or the presence of sb or sth in, a group or mixture **2. SB OR STH INCLUDED** sb or sth included in a group or mixture **3.** GEOL **SUBSTANCE TRAPPED INSIDE MINERAL** a solid, liquid, or gas contained within a mineral or rock **4.** METALL a particle of foreign material within a piece of metal **5.** BIOL **FOREIGN BODY IN CELL** a nonliving mass such as a starch grain or droplet of fat in the cytoplasm or nucleus of a cell **6.** MATH **RELATION BETWEEN SETS** the relation between two classes or sets when the second is a subset of the first [Early 17thC. Formed from the Latin stem *inclus-*, past participle stem of *includere* (see INCLUDE).] —**inclusionary** *adj.*

inclusion body *n.* MED a mass of virus particles inside a cell, formerly used in the diagnosis of some viral infections

inclusive /in klo͞ossiv/ *adj.* **1. INCLUDING THE SPECIFIED LIMITS** used to indicate that a span of time or a range within a series includes the dates, times, or other items stated at the beginning and end of the span ○ *the period from October 1 to July 31, inclusive* **2. INCLUDING MANY THINGS** including many things or everything **3.** GRAM **INCLUDING SPEAKER AND PERSON ADDRESSED** used to describe a pronoun that includes the speaker and the person or persons spoken to. In English, "we" is the only inclusive pronoun. **4.** LOGIC **BEING TYPE OF SENTENCE IN LOGIC** used to describe a sentence in logic (**disjunction**) containing two propositions of which at least one and possibly both can be true. ◊ **exclusive** [Late 16thC. From medieval Latin *inclusivus*, from Latin *inclus-* (see INCLUDE).] —**inclusively** *adv.* —**inclusiveness** *n.*

incoercible /ínkō úrssəb'l/ *adj.* not giving in to force or pressure from others

incog. *abbr.* incognito

incogitant /in kójjitənt/ *adj.* inconsiderate or thoughtless (*formal*) [Early 17thC. From the Latin stem *incogitant-*, literally 'unthinking', from *cogitare* 'to think' (see COGITATE).]

incognita /in kog ne͞etə/ *adj., adv.* with the identity disguised or hidden, e.g., under an assumed name (*used to describe a woman or girl*) [Late 17thC. From Italian, feminine of *incognito* 'incognito'.] —**incognita** *n.*

incognito /in kog ne͞etō/ *adj., adv.* **IN DISGUISE** with the identity disguised or hidden, e.g. under an assumed name ■ *n.* (*plural* **-tos**) **1. SB INCOGNITO** sb who is acting or travelling incognito **2. DISGUISE** the character, disguise, or name assumed by sb who is incognito [Mid-17thC. Via Italian from Latin *incognitus* 'unknown', from *cognitus*, past participle of *cognoscere* 'to learn', from *noscere* 'to know'.]

incognizant /in kógnizənt/ *adj.* not knowing, realizing, or being aware (*formal*) —**incognizance** *n.*

incoherence /ínkō he͞erənss/ *n.* a lack of logical organization in the way sth is thought out or expressed that makes it difficult to understand

incoherent /ín kō he͞erənt/ *adj.* **1. LACKING CLARITY OR ORGANIZATION** not clearly expressed or well thought out, and consequently difficult to understand **2. UNABLE TO SPEAK OR EXPRESS CLEARLY** unable to express thoughts or feelings clearly or logically **3.** NOT COHESIVE not sticking together as a mass **4.** PHYS OUT OF PHASE having the same frequency but not the same phase —**incoherently** *adv.*

incombustible /ínkəm bústəb'l/ *adj.* NOT COMBUSTIBLE not capable of being burnt ■ *n.* STH INCOMBUSTIBLE an incombustible object, material, or substance [15thC. From medieval Latin *incombustibilis*, from *combustibilis* 'combustible' (see COMBUSTIBLE).] —**incombustibility** /ínkəm bústə bílləti/ *n.* —**incombustibly** /-bústəbli/ *adv.*

income /ín kum/ *n.* **1.** MONEY RECEIVED OVER PERIOD the amount of money received over a period of time either as payment for work, goods, or services, or as profit on capital **2.** INFLOW a coming in or flowing in [14thC. From Old Norse *innkoma* 'arrival'; in later use from IN + COME.]

income bond *n.* a bond paying a rate of return in proportion to the issuer's income

income group *n.* a section of the population grouped by income, e.g. for the purpose of market research

incomer /ín kummər/ *n.* sb who settles in a place where he or she was not born

incomes policy *n.* an economic policy that seeks to control inflation by controlling wage levels

income support *n.* a social security payment made to unemployed people and people on low incomes. It was introduced in 1986 to replace supplementary benefit.

income tax *n.* a tax paid on money made from employment, business, or capital (*hyphenated when used before a noun*)

incoming /ín kumming/ *adj.* **1.** ARRIVING arriving, coming in, or entering **2.** TAKING UP NEW JOB about to take up a particular job or office **3.** BEING RECEIVED being received or taken in ■ *n.* ARRIVAL an arrival or entrance (*formal*) ■ **incomings** *npl.* INCOME sums of money earned or received

incommensurable /ínkə ménshərəb'l/ *adj.* **1.** IMPOSSIBLE TO MEASURE not capable of being compared or measured, especially because lacking a common quality necessary for a comparison to be made **2.** MATH HAVING NO COMMON FACTOR having no common factor or measure other than 1 ■ *n.* STH INCOMMENSURABLE sth that cannot be compared or measured, especially a quality or a mathematical value [Mid-16thC. From late Latin *incommensurabilis*, from *commensurabilis* 'commensurable'.] —**incommensurability** /ínkə ménshərə bílləti/ *n.* —**incommensurably** /ínkə ménshərəbli/ *adv.*

incommensurate /ínkə ménshərət/ *adj.* **1.** NOT PROPORTIONATE not proportionate to or up to the level of sth **2.** = **incommensurable** *adj.* 1 —**incommensurately** *adv.* —**incommensurateness** *n.*

incommode /ínkə mṓd/ (**-modes, -moding, -moded**) *vt.* to bother or inconvenience sb (*formal*) [Late 16thC. Directly or via French *incommoder* from Latin *incommodare*, from *commodus* 'convenient' (see COMMODIOUS).]

incommodious /ínkə mṓdi əss/ *adj.* (*formal*) **1.** UNCOMFORTABLY CRAMPED uncomfortably lacking in space **2.** CAUSING INCONVENIENCE causing trouble or inconvenience —**incommodiously** *adv.* —**incommodiousness** *n.*

incommodity /ínkə móddəti/ (*plural* **-ties**) *n.* bother or inconvenience, or sth that causes it (*formal*) [15thC. Via French *incommodité* from, ultimately, Latin *commodus* 'convenient' (see COMMODIOUS).]

incommunicable /ínkə myoṓnikəb'l/ *adj.* **1.** IMPOSSIBLE TO CONVEY not capable of being expressed or conveyed to others **2.** NOT TALKATIVE tending not to say much or give much information away (*archaic*) [Mid-16thC. From late Latin *incommunicabilis* 'not to be passed on', from *communicabilis* 'communicable'.] —**incommunicability** /ínkə myoṓnikə bílləti/ *n.* —**incommunicably** /ínkə myoṓnikəbli/ *adv.*

incommunicado /ínkə myoṓni kaádō/ *adj.* prevented by circumstances or by force from communicating with other people [Mid-19thC. From Spanish *incomunicado*, from *incomunicar* 'to deprive of communication', from Latin *communicare* (see COMMUNICATE).] —**incommunicado** *adv.*

incommunicative /ínkə myoṓnikətiv/ *adj.* unwilling to communicate or provide information —**incommunicatively** *adv.* —**incommunicativeness** *n.*

incommutable /ínkə myoṓtəb'l/ *adj.* not able to be changed, exchanged for sth else, or reduced in severity (*formal*) [15thC. From Latin *incommutabilis* 'unchangeable', from *commutare* (see COMMUTE).] —**incommutability** /ínkə myoṓtə bílləti/ *n.* —**incommutableness** /ínkə myoṓtəb'lnəss/ *n.* —**incommutably** *adv.*

incomparable /in kómpərəb'l/ *adj.* **1.** UNEQUALLED IN QUALITY so excellent, outstanding, or unique as to have no equal **2.** IMPOSSIBLE TO COMPARE WITH STH ELSE impossible to compare with sth else, or with each other, because there is no basis on which a comparison could be made [15thC. Via French from Latin *incomparabilis* 'that cannot be equalled', from *comparare* (see COMPARE).] —**incomparability** /in kómpərə bílləti/ *n.* —**incomparableness** /in kómpərəb'lnəss/ *n.* —**incomparably** *adv.*

incompatibility /ínkəm páttə bílləti/ (*plural* **-ties**) *n.* **1.** INABILITY TO COOPERATE OR COEXIST a basic inability to cooperate, coexist, or function in combination with sb or sth else **2.** CONFLICTING QUALITY a quality or feature that renders sb or sth incompatible with sb or sth else

incompatible /ínkəm páttəb'l/ *adj.* **1.** UNABLE TO COOPERATE OR COEXIST unable to exist, cooperate, blend, or get along with sb or sth else because of basic differences **2.** UNABLE TO BE HELD SIMULTANEOUSLY unable to be held simultaneously with another position or office by one individual **3.** IMMUNOL LIKELY TO BE REJECTED BY DONOR used to describe a tissue transplant or blood that is likely to be rejected by a recipient's immune system **4.** PHARM NOT SUITABLE FOR USE IN COMBINATION used to describe two or more drugs that should not be used in combination because, e.g., they would counteract each other **5.** BOT NOT ABLE TO BE POLLINATED OR GRAFTED used to describe plants or varieties that cannot be successfully cross-pollinated or grafted onto each other **6.** LOGIC CONTRADICTORY used to describe two propositions that cannot both be true at the same time **7.** MATH MATHEMATICALLY INCONSISTENT not mathematically consistent ■ *n.* SB OR STH INHARMONIOUS sb or sth that is not compatible with sb or sth else [15thC. From medieval Latin *incompatibilis*, from *compati* 'to suffer together'.] —**incompatibleness** *n.* —**incompatibly** *adv.*

incompetent /in kómpitənt/ *adj.* **1.** BAD AT DOING STH lacking the skills, qualities, or ability to do sth properly **2.** LAW LACKING NECESSARY STATUS not having the necessary legal status, validity, or powers for the purpose in question ■ *n.* SB BAD AT DOING STH sb who lacks the skills, qualities, or ability to do sth properly [Late 16thC. Via French *incompétent* from the late Latin stem *incompetent-*, literally 'not competent', from *competere* (see COMPETE).] —**incompetence** *n.* —**incompetently** *adv.*

incomplete /ínkəm pleét/ *adj.* **1.** LACKING A PART lacking sth such as a particular part that properly or desirably belongs with it **2.** UNFINISHED not yet finished or fully developed [14thC. From Latin *incompletus*, literally 'not finished', from *completus* (see COMPLETE).] —**incompletely** *adv.* —**incompleteness** *n.* —**incompletion** /-pleésh'n/ *n.*

incomplete fracture *n.* a fracture that does not go all the way through a bone

incompliant /ínkəm plí ənt/ *adj.* unwilling to to be flexible and accommodating or to comply with sth (*formal*) —**incompliance** *n.* —**incompliantly** *adv.*

incomprehensible /in kómpri hénssəb'l/ *adj.* **1.** BEYOND UNDERSTANDING impossible or very difficult to understand **2.** LIMITLESS lacking or incapable of having limits (*archaic*) [14thC. From Latin *incomprehensibilis*, literally 'not comprehensible', from *comprehendere* (see COMPREHEND).] —**incomprehensibility** /in kómpri hénssə bílləti/ *n.* —**incomprehensibleness** /in kómpri hénssəb'lnəss/ *n.* —**incomprehensibly** *adv.*

incomprehension /in kómpri hénsh'n/ *n.* an inability or failure to understand, or a state of bewilderment resulting from this

incomprehensive /in kómpri hénssiv/ *adj.* limited in scope (*formal*) —**incomprehensively** *adv.* —**incomprehensiveness** *n.*

incompressible /ínkəm préssəb'l/ *adj.* difficult or impossible to compress —**incompressibility** /ínkəm préssə bílləti/ *n.* —**incompressibleness** /ínkəm préssəb'lnəss/ *n.* —**incompressibly** /-bli/ *adv.*

inconceivable /ínkən seévəb'l/ *adj.* **1.** UNIMAGINABLE impossible to imagine or to grasp mentally and understand **2.** EXTREMELY UNLIKELY so unlikely as to be beyond belief or thought impossible ○ *It's inconceivable that they should have made the same mistake twice.* —**inconceivability** /ínkən seévə bílləti/ *n.* —**inconceivableness** /ínkən seévəb'lnəss/ *n.* —**inconceivably** *adv.*

inconcinnity /ínkən sínnəti/ *n.* inelegance or unsuitability caused by not being in proportion or not harmonizing with other things (*formal*) [Early 17thC. From Latin *inconcinnitas*, literally 'not well joined', from *concinnus* (see CONCINNITY).]

inconclusive /ínkən kloóssiv/ *adj.* not producing a clear-cut result, firm conclusion, or decisive proof of sth —**inconclusively** *adv.* —**inconclusiveness** *n.*

incondite /in kóndit, -dīt/ *adj.* crude, poorly constructed, or unpolished (*formal*) [Mid-16thC. From Latin *inconditus*, literally 'not put together', from *condere* (see ABSCOND).] —**inconditely** *adv.*

incongruent /in kóng groo ənt/ *adj.* not corresponding in structure or content [15thC. From the Latin stem *incongruent-*, literally 'not in agreement', from *congruens*, the present participle of *congruere* (see CONGRUENT).] —**incongruence** *n.* —**incongruently** *adv.*

incongruity /ínkən groó əti/ (*plural* **-ties**) *n.* **1.** INCONGRUOUSNESS the fact of being incongruous **2.** STH OUT OF PLACE sth that does not seem to fit in with or be appropriate to its context

incongruous /in kóng groo əss/ *adj.* **1.** UNSUITABLE OR ODD unsuitable, strange, or out of place in a particular setting or context **2.** INCONSISTENT WITH STH not in accord or consistent with sth [Early 17thC. From Latin *incongruus*, literally 'not in agreement', from *congruus* (see CONGRUOUS).] —**incongruously** *adv.* —**incongruousness** *n.*

inconsecutive /ínkən sékyootiv/ *adj.* not following in order one after another —**inconsecutively** *adv.* —**inconsecutiveness** *n.*

inconsequence /in kónsikwənss/ *n.* lack of relevance and significance

inconsequent /in kónsikwənt/ *adj.* not following as a natural or logical result [Late 16thC. From the Latin stem *inconsequent-*, literally 'not following', from *consequens*, the present participle of *consequi* (see CONSEQUENT).] —**inconsequently** *adv.* —**inconsequentness** *n.*

inconsequential /in kónssi kwénsh'l/ *adj.* **1.** UNIMPORTANT of little or no importance **2.** = **inconsequent** [Early 17thC. Formed from IN- + CONSEQUENTIAL.] —**inconsequentiality** /in kónssi kwénshi állәti/ *n.* —**inconsequentialness** /in kónsi kwénsh'lnəss/ *n.* —**inconsequentially** /-sh'li/ *adv.*

inconsiderable /ínkən síddərəb'l/ *adj.* **1.** SMALL small in size, amount, or value (*often used with 'not'*) **2.** UNWORTHY OF CONSIDERATION so unimportant as to be not worth considering (*formal*) [Late 16thC. Directly or via French from late Latin *inconsiderabilis*, literally 'unimaginable', from Latin *considerare* (see CONSIDER).] —**inconsiderableness** *n.* —**inconsiderably** *adv.*

inconsiderate /ínkən síddərət/ *adj.* lacking thought or consideration for other people and their feelings [15thC. From Latin *inconsideratus*, literally 'not thinking', from *consideratus*, the past participle of *considerare* (see CONSIDER).] —**inconsiderately** *adv.* —**inconsiderateness** *n.* —**inconsideration** /ínkən síddə ráysh'n/ *n.*

inconsistency /ínkən sístənssi/ (*plural* **-cies**), **inconsistence** /ínkən sístənss/ *n.* **1.** LACK OF CONSISTENCY the fact of being inconsistent **2.** INCONSISTENT THING sth that contradicts sth else or that is not in keeping with it

inconsistent /ínkən sístənt/ *adj.* **1.** CONTAINING CONFLICTING OR CONTRADICTORY ELEMENTS containing elements that conflict with or contradict each other **2.** VARYING AND UNPREDICTABLE unpredictable or unreliable in being likely to behave differently or achieve a different result if a particular situation is repeated **3.** CONFLICTING OR INCOMPATIBLE WITH STH conflicting with or not corresponding to sth such as a rule, principle, or expectation **4.** MATH **LACKING COMMON VALUES IN AN EQUATION** not having a common set of values for the unknowns in an equation —**inconsistently** *adv.*

inconsolable /ínkən sṓləb'l/ *adj.* so deeply distressed that nobody can offer any effective comfort [Late 16thC. Directly or via French from Latin *inconsolabilis*, from *consolare* (see CONSOLE).] —**inconsolability** /ínkən sṓlə bíllәti/ *n.* —**inconsolableness** /ínkən sṓləb'lnəss/ *n.* —**inconsolably** /-sṓləbli/ *adv.*

inconsonant /in kónssənənt/ *adj.* not in harmony or not compatible with sth else (*formal*) —**inconsonance** *n.* —**inconsonantly** *adv.*

inconspicuous /ínkən spíkyoo əss/ *adj.* not easily seen or noticed [Early 17thC] —**inconspicuously** *adv.* —**inconspicuousness** *n.*

inconstant /in kónstənt/ *adj.* **1. UNFAITHFUL** not faithful in relationships (*literary*) **2. CHANGEABLE** likely to change frequently and unpredictably [15thC. Directly or via Old French from the Latin stem *inconstant-*, literally 'not standing firm', from *constare* (see CONSTANT).] —**inconstancy** *n.* —**inconstantly** *adv.*

incontestable /ínkən téstəb'l/ *adj.* impossible to question or dispute [Late 17thC. Directly or via French from medieval Latin *incontestabilis*, literally 'unanswerable', from *contestari* (see CONTEST).] —**incontestability** /ínkən téstə bíllәti/ *n.* —**incontestableness** /-téstəb'lnəss/ *n.* —**incontestably** /-téstəbli/ *adv.*

incontinence /in kóntinənss/, **incontinency** /in kóntinənssi/ *n.* **1.** MED **INABILITY TO CONTROL URINATION OR DEFECATION** an inability to control urination or defecation, so that either may take place involuntarily **2. LACK OF SEXUAL CONTROL** lack of sexual restraint or self-control **3. LACK OF MODERATION** lack of moderation in an action or emotion (*literary*)

incontinent[1] /in kóntinənt/ *adj.* **1.** MED **UNABLE TO CONTROL BLADDER OR BOWELS** unable to control the bladder or bowels and liable to urinate or defecate involuntarily **2. LACKING SEXUAL CONTROL** lacking restraint in sexual matters, or engaging in premarital or extramarital sex **3. UNRESTRAINED** unrestrained and uncontrolled (*literary*) [14thC. Directly or via French from the Latin stem *incontinent-*, literally 'not holding together', from *continere* (see CONTAIN).] —**incontinently** *adv.*

incontinent[2] /in kóntinənt/ *adv.* immediately, or abruptly and hastily (*archaic*) [15thC. From Old French *incontinent*, from late Latin *in continenti (tempore)* 'in continuous (time)' (i.e., without a break), from *continens*, the present participle of *continere* (see CONTAIN).]

incontrollable /ínkən trṓləb'l/ *adj.* = **uncontrollable** —**incontrollably** *adv.*

incontrovertible /ín kontrə vúrtəb'l/ *adj.* certain, undeniable, and not open to question —**incontrovertibility** /ín kontrə vúrtə bíllәti/ *n.* —**incontrovertibleness** /ín kóntrə vúrtəb'lnəss/ *n.* —**incontrovertibly** *adv.*

inconvenience /ínkən veéni ənss/ *n.* **1. LACK OF CONVENIENCE** the quality or fact of being inconvenient or causing discomfort, difficulty, or annoyance **2. AN ANNOYANCE** sth that causes difficulties or annoyance ■ *vt.* (**-iences, -iencing, -ienced**) **CAUSE DIFFICULTY TO** to cause sb difficulties, especially relatively minor or unnecessary ones, or involving unwanted extra effort, work, or trouble

inconvenient /ínkən veéni ənt/ *adj.* causing or involving difficulties or unwanted extra effort, work, or trouble [Mid-17thC. Via Old French from the Latin stem *inconvenient-* 'incongruous', literally 'not fitting together', from *convenire* (see CONVENE).] —**inconveniently** *adv.*

inconvertible /ínkən vúrtəb'l/ *adj.* FIN **1. NOT EXCHANGEABLE FOR GOLD** not exchangeable for gold or silver **2. NOT EXCHANGEABLE FOR FOREIGN CURRENCY** not exchangeable for the currency of another country [Mid-17thC. Directly or via French from late Latin *inconvertibilis*, literally 'unchangeable', from *convertire* (see CONVERT).] —**inconvertibility** /ínkən vúrtə bíllәti/ *n.* —**inconvertibleness** /ínkən vúrtəb'lnəss/ *n.* —**inconvertibly** *adv.*

inconvincible /ínkən vínssəb'l/ *adj.* impossible or very difficult to convince —**inconvincibility** /ínkən vínssə bíllәti/ *n.* —**inconvincibleness** /ínkən vínsəb'lnəss/ *n.* —**inconvincibly** *adv.*

incoordinate /ínkō áwrdinət/ *adj.* lacking co-ordination —**incoordinately** *adv.*

incoordination /ínkō áwrdi náysh'n/ *n.* **1.** MED **INABILITY TO CONTROL MUSCLES** an inability to control voluntary muscular movements **2. INCONSISTENT APPROACH** lack of organization or a consistent approach (*formal*)

incorp. *abbr.* incorporated

incorporate *v.* /in káwrpə rayt/ (**-rates, -rating, -rated**) **1.** *vti.* **JOIN WITH STH THAT EXISTS** to unite or combine sth with, or include it within, sth already formed **2.** *vti.* **MERGE THINGS** to merge, or to combine one thing with another, so as to form a united whole **3.** *vti.* COMM **FORM OR BECOME CORPORATION** to form a corporation, or to give sth the legal form of a corporation **4.** *vt.* **GIVE REAL FORM TO** to give material form to sth (*formal*) ■ *adj.* /in káwrpərət/ **1. UNITED** merged into a united whole (*formal*) **2.** COMM **LEGALLY A CORPORATION** legally established as a corporation [14thC. From late Latin *incorporare*, literally 'to make into a body', from *corpus* 'body' (see CORPUS).] —**incorporable** /in káwrpərəb'l/ *adj.* —**incorporation** /in káwrpə ráysh'n/ *n.* —**incorporative** /in káwrpərətiv/ *adj.* —**incorporator** /-raytər/ *n.*

incorporated /in káwrpə raytid/ *adj.* **1. LEGALLY CONSTITUTED AS A CORPORATION** constituted in the legal form of a corporation **2. COMBINED AS ONE WHOLE** combined or merged into one thing —**incorporatedness** *n.*

incorporeal /in kawr páwri əl/ *adj.* **1. WITHOUT PHYSICAL BEING** without a physical body, or existing solely as a spirit (*formal*) **2.** LAW **ATTACHED TO STH MATERIAL** used to describe a legal entity that has no material existence of its own but is connected to an actual object such as a patent or copyright [15thC. Formed from Latin *incorporeus*, literally 'having no body', from *corpus* 'body' (see CORPUS).] —**incorporeality** /in kawr páwri állәti/ *n.* —**incorporeally** /in kawr páwri əli/ *adv.* —**incorporeity** /in káwrpə reé əti/ *n.*

incorrect /ínkə rékt/ *adj.* **1. ERRONEOUS** wrong, false, or inaccurate **2. UNFITTING** not appropriate, suitable, or proper [15thC. Directly or via French from Latin *incorrectus*, literally 'uncorrected', from *correct-*, the past participle stem of *corrigere* (see CORRECT).] —**incorrectly** *adv.* —**incorrectness** *n.*

incorrigible /in kórrijəb'l/ *adj.* **1. IMPOSSIBLE TO CHANGE** impossible to correct or reform ○ *incorrigible cynics* **2. UNRULY AND UNMANAGEABLE** very difficult to control or keep in order ■ *n.* **SB OR STH INCORRIGIBLE** sb or sth that is impossible or very difficult to change [14thC. Directly or via French from Latin *incorrigibilis*, literally 'not able to be corrected', from *corrigere* (see CORRECT).] —**incorrigibility** /in kórrijə bíllәti/ *n.* —**incorrigibly** /in kórrijəbli/ *adv.*

incorrupt /ínkə rúpt/ *adj.* **1. UNSULLIED** morally pure and uncorrupted (*formal*) **2. NOT DECOMPOSED** unaffected by decay or spoiling (*archaic*) **3. FREE OF MISTAKES** without errors or alterations (*formal*) [14thC. From Latin *incorruptus*, literally 'not destroyed', from *corruptus* (see CORRUPT).] —**incorruption** /-rúpsh'n/ *n.* —**incorruptly** /-rúptli/ *adv.*

incorruptible /ínkə rúptəb'l/ *adj.* **1. INCAPABLE OF BEING CORRUPTED** incapable of being morally corrupted, especially incapable of being bribed or motivated by selfish or base interests **2. NOT SUBJECT TO DECOMPOSITION** incapable of being affected by decay or decomposition —**incorruptibility** /ínkə rúptə bíllәti/ *n.* —**incorruptibly** *adv.*

incr. *abbr.* **1.** increase **2.** increased **3.** increasing **4.** increment

increase *vti.* /in kreéss, íng kreess/ (**-creases, -creasing, -creased**) **MAKE OR BECOME LARGER OR GREATER** to make sth or become larger in number, quantity, or degree ■ *n.* /íng kreess, in kreéss/ **1. RISE IN STH** a rise to a greater number, quantity, or degree, or the amount by which sth is increased **2. BECOMING OR MAKING LARGER OR GREATER** the process of becoming or of making sth larger in number, quantity, or degree [14thC. Via Old French *encreistre* from Latin *increscere*, from *crescere* 'to grow' (see CRESCENT).] —**increasable** *adj.* —**increaser** /-ər/ *n.*

WORD KEY: SYNONYMS

increase, expand, enlarge, extend, augment, intensify, amplify

CORE MEANING: make larger or greater

increase a general word meaning to become larger or greater; **expand** to make larger, usually in scope as well as size. It can also be used to talk about making sth such as an account or report seem larger or more substantial by adding more details; **enlarge** make bigger; **extend** to make larger in terms of length or to cause to cover a wider area; **augment** to add to sth in order to make it larger or more substantial; **intensify** to cause sth such as an emotion or reaction to be stronger or more extreme; **amplify** to make a sound louder. It can also be used to talk about making an effect greater.

increasingly /in kreéssingli/ *adv.* ever increasing over time ○ *'As Election Day approaches, there is no front-runner, and the insults and accusations from both sides have been increasingly frequent and bellicose.'* (Susan K. Livio, *Election '96: Senate Race*; 1996)

increate /ínkri áyt, -ət/ *adj.* existing without having been created (*archaic or literary*) [Mid-16thC. From Latin *increatus*, literally 'not created', from *creatus*, the past participle of *creare* (see CREATE).] —**increately** *adv.*

incredible /in kréddəb'l/ *adj.* **1. BEYOND BELIEF** impossible or very difficult to believe **2. MORE THAN THOUGHT POSSIBLE** unexpectedly or astonishingly large or great (*informal*) ○ *There's an incredible amount of food still left.* **3. AMAZING** very surprising ○ *It's incredible how many people have turned up.* **4. EXCELLENT** extraordinarily good, talented, or enjoyable (*informal*) [15thC. From Latin *incredibilis*, literally 'not believable', from *credere* 'to believe'.] —**incredibility** /in kréddə bíllәti/ *n.* —**incredibly** /-kréddəbli/ *adv.*

incredulity /ínkrə dyoólәti/ *n.* a state or feeling of disbelief

incredulous /in kréddyoōləss/ *adj.* **1. UNWILLING TO BELIEVE** unable or unwilling to believe sth or completely unconvinced by it **2. SHOWING DISBELIEF** showing or characterized by disbelief [Late 16thC. Formed from Latin *incredulus*, literally 'not believing', from *credulus* (see CREDULOUS).] —**incredulously** *adv.* —**incredulousness** *n.*

increment /íngkrimənt/ *n.* **1. INCREASE IN STH** an addition to or increase in the amount or size of sth, especially one of a series of small, often regular or planned increases, e.g. to a salary **2. ACT OF INCREASING** the act or process of increasing **3.** MATH **SMALL CHANGE IN MATHEMATICAL VALUE** a small positive or negative change in the value of a mathematical variable or function [15thC. From Latin *incrementum* 'growth, increase', from *increscere* (see INCREASE).] —**incremental** /íngkri mént'l/ *adj.* —**incrementally** *adv.*

incrementalism /íngkri mént'lizəm/ *n.* = **gradualism**

increscent /in kréss'nt/ *adj.* showing a lighted surface area, especially that of the Moon, that is increasing in size [Late 16thC. From Latin *increscere* (see INCREASE).]

incriminate /in krímmi nayt/ (**-nates, -nating, -nated**) *vt.* **1. MAKE APPEAR GUILTY** to provide evidence of sb's guilt or make sb appear guilty of a crime or mistake **2.** LAW **ACCUSE OF WRONGDOING** to accuse sb of a crime or error [Mid-18thC. From late Latin *incriminat*, the past participle stem of *incriminare*, literally 'to make criminal', from *crimen* (see CRIME).] —**incriminating** *adj.* —**incrimination** /in krímmi náysh'n/ *n.* —**incriminator** /in krímmi naytər/ *n.* —**incriminatory** /in kríminətəri/ *adj.*

incross /ín kross/ *n.* **INBRED ORGANISM** an organism produced through inbreeding within the same strain or breed ■ *vti.* (**-crosses, -crossing, -crossed**) **PRODUCE BY INBREEDING** to produce an organism by inbreeding or to be produced in this way. ◊ **outcross**

in-crowd *n.* a small, fashionable, and exclusive or influential group, especially one that others want to be part of because of its prestige (*informal*)

incrust *vti.* = **encrust**

incrustation *n.* = **encrustation**

incubate /íngkyoō bayt/ (**-bates, -bating, -bated**) *v.* **1.** *vti.* ZOOL **SIT ON EGGS** to keep eggs warm by sitting on them so that the embryos inside can develop and hatch, or to be kept warm in this way **2.** *vti.* MED **KEEP BABY IN INCUBATOR** to keep a premature or unwell baby inside a controlled environment in order to keep it alive and assist its growth and development, or to be kept in such an environment **3.** *vti.* MICROBIOL **GROW MICROORGANISMS IN CONTROLLED ENVIRONMENT** to keep cells or microorganisms at a controlled temperature in or on a medium so that they multiply, or to be kept in or on such a medium **4.** *vi.* **DEVELOP IN FAVOURABLE**

ENVIRONMENT to be kept, or to develop while being kept, in a favourable environment, e.g. under a parent bird's body, in a incubator, or in a growth medium **5.** *vti.* MED BUILD UP DISEASE-PRODUCING GERMS to develop an infection, through the reproduction of germs, to the point at which the first signs of a disease appear, or to be developed in this way **6.** *vti.* GRADUALLY BRING STH INTO BEING to form or develop sth, such as a plan or an idea, slowly and quietly over a period of time, or to be formed or developed in this way [Mid-17thC. From Latin *incubare*, literally 'to lie down on', from *cubare* 'to lie down'.] —**incubative** *adj.* —**incubatory** *adj.*

incubation /íngkyoo báysh'n/ *n.* **1.** PROCESS OF INCUBATING OR BEING INCUBATED the process of incubating sth such as an egg or an idea, the process of being incubated, or the period of time taken by either process **2.** MED MAINTENANCE OF BABY IN CONTROLLED ENVIRONMENT the keeping of a premature or unwell baby in an environment in which the temperature, humidity, and oxygen levels can be easily controlled **3.** MICROBIOL CONTROLLED GROWTH OF MICROORGANISMS the maintenance of cells or microorganisms under a controlled temperature in or on a medium so that they can multiply **4.** MED GROWTH OF DISEASE-CAUSING MICROORGANISMS the development of an infection inside the body to the point at which the first signs of disease become apparent **5.** GRADUAL DEVELOPMENT the slow development of sth, especially through thought and planning **6.** = **incubation period** —**incubational** *adj.*

incubation period *n.* the period between the time sb is infected with a disease and the appearance of its first symptoms

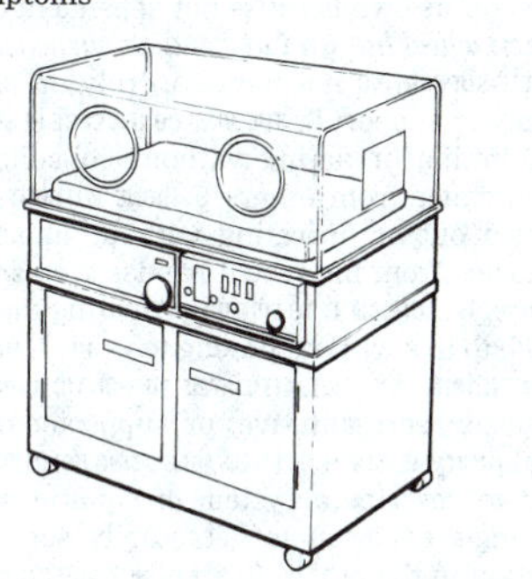

Incubator

incubator /íngkyoo baytər/ *n.* **1.** MED HOSPITAL APPARATUS FOR PREMATURE BABIES a hospital apparatus, usually a transparent box, in which a premature or unwell baby is kept in a controlled environment to protect it from infection and assist its growth and development. Incubators regulate temperature, humidity, and oxygen levels. **2.** ZOOL DEVICE TO NURTURE STH an apparatus in which the temperature is kept at a constant level so that eggs can be artificially hatched or cells and microorganisms can multiply in or on a growth medium

incubus /íngkyoobəss/ (*plural* **-bi** /-bī/ *or* **-buses**) *n.* **1.** MYTHOL MALE DEMON HAVING SEX WITH WOMEN a male demon that was believed in medieval times to have sexual intercourse with women while they were asleep **2.** CAUSE OF MENTAL DISTRESS sth that causes sb much worry or anxiety, especially a nightmare or obsession (*literary*) [14thC. Via late Latin, 'nightmare', from, ultimately, Latin *incubare* 'to lie down on'. The underlying meaning is 'one that lies down on another'.]

incudes plural of **incus**

inculcate /ín kul kayt/ (**-cates, -cating, -cated**) *vt.* to fix sth firmly in sb's mind through frequent and forceful repetition [Mid-16thC. From Latin *inculcat-*, the past participle stem of *inculcare*, literally 'to stamp in', from *calcare* 'to tread on, press in' (see CAULK).] —**inculcation** /ín kul káysh'n/ *n.* —**inculcator** /ín kul kaytər/ *n.*

inculpable /in kúlpəb'l/ *adj.* free of guilt and blame (*formal*) [Late 15thC. From late Latin *inculpabilis*, literally 'not guilty', from *culpare* (see CULPABLE).] —**inculpability** /in kúlpə bílləti/ *n.* —**inculpableness** /in kúlpəb'lnəss/ *n.* —**inculpably** *adv.*

inculpate /ín kul payt/ (**-pates, -pating, -pated**) *vt.* to incriminate sb or put the blame for sth on sb (*formal*) [Late 18thC. From late Latin *inculpat-*, the past participle stem of *inculpare*, literally 'to put blame on', from Latin *culpa* 'blame, fault' (source of English *culpable* and *culprit*).] —**inculpation** /ín kul páysh'n/ *n.* —**inculpative** /in kúlpətiv/ *adj.* —**inculpatory** /-təri/ *adj.*

incult /in kúlt/ *adj.* coarse, uncouth, and without culture or refinement (*archaic*) [Late 16thC. From Latin *incultus*, literally 'uncultivated', from *cultus*, the past participle of *colere* 'to inhabit, cultivate, worship'.]

incumbency /in kúmbənssi/ (*plural* **-cies**) *n.* (*formal*) **1.** TENURE OF OFFICE the period of time during which sb occupies an official post **2.** OFFICIAL POST an official position, especially in a church or political organization **3.** EXISTENCE AS A DUTY the obligatory nature of sth or the fact of its being a duty or obligation that must be performed **4.** OBLIGATION sth such as a duty that is necessary or obligatory

incumbent /in kúmbənt/ *adj.* **1.** OBLIGATORY necessary as a result of a duty, responsibility, or obligation (*formal*) ○ *It is incumbent on me to ensure that our generous hosts should not go unthanked.* **2.** IN OFFICE currently holding a position or office **3.** ON TOP OF STH resting, lying, or leaning on sth (*archaic or technical*) ○ *incumbent strata* ■ *n.* SB IN OFFICE sb currently holding an official post, especially in a church or political organization ○ *He took comfort in the fact that incumbents are often offered the chance of serving a second term of office.* [15thC. From Latin *incumbent-*, the present participle stem of *incumbere*, literally 'to lie in or on', from *-cumbere* 'to lie down'.] —**incumbently** *adv.*

incumber *vt.* = **encumber**

incunabula /ínkyoo nábbyoolə/ *npl.* the early stages or beginnings of sth (*literary*) [Early 19thC. From Latin, 'swaddling clothes, infancy', from *cunae* 'cradle'. Ultimately from an Indo-European word meaning 'place to lie' that is also the ancestor of English *cemetery*.]

incunabulum /ínkyoo nábbyooləm/ (*plural* **-la** /-lə/), **incunable** /in kyóonəb'l/ *n.* PRINTING a book printed from movable type before 1501 [Early 19thC. From Latin, singular of *incunabula* (see INCUNABULA).]

incur /in kúr/ (**-curs, -curring, -curred**) *vt.* **1.** ACQUIRE A BURDEN to become burdened with sth such as a debt **2.** EXPERIENCE STH UNPLEASANT to suffer sth such as sb's anger or a financial loss as a result of an action ○ *incur their wrath* [15thC. Via Old French *encourir* from Latin *incurrere*, literally 'to run into', from *currere* 'to run' (see CURRENT).] —**incurrable** *adj.* —**incurrence** *n.*

incurable /in kyóorəb'l/ *adj.* **1.** IMPOSSIBLE TO CURE not possible to cure **2.** IMPOSSIBLE TO CHANGE not possible to change ■ *n.* SB OR STH IMPOSSIBLE TO CURE sb or sth with an illness or condition that cannot be cured [14thC. Directly or via French from late Latin *incurabilis*, literally 'not curable', from *cura* (see CURE).] —**incurability** /in kyoorə bílləti/ *n.* —**incurableness** /in kyóorəb'lnəss/ *n.* —**incurably** *adv.*

incurious /in kyóori əss/ *adj.* showing no curiosity about or interest in sth —**incuriosity** /in kyoori óssəti/ *n.* —**incuriously** /in kyóori əssli/ *adv.* —**incuriousness** *n.*

incurrent /in kúrrənt/ *adj.* flowing or running inwards into sth [Late 16thC. From Latin *incurrere* (see INCUR).]

incursion /in kúrsh'n/ *n.* **1.** RAID a brief, hostile, and usually sudden invasion of sb's territory **2.** UNWELCOME INTRUSION the act of flowing, running, or intruding into sth, usually with unpleasant or damaging effects (*formal*) [15thC. Directly or via Old French from the Latin stem *incursion-*, literally 'a running in', from *incurs-*, the past participle stem of *incurrere* (see INCUR).] —**incursive** /in kúrssiv/ *adj.*

incurvate *vti.* /ínkur vayt/ (**-vates, -vating, -vated**) = **incurve** ■ *adj.* /in kúr vayt/ INWARDLY CURVED curved or bending inwards [Late 16thC. From Latin *incurvat-*, the past participle stem of *incurvare*, literally 'to bend inwards' from *curvus* (see CURVE).] —**incurvation** /ínkur váysh'n/ *n.* —**incurvature** /in kúrvəchər/ *n.*

incurve /in kúrv/ *vti.* (**-curves, -curving, -curved**) CURVE INWARDS to curve inwards, or to give sth an inward curve ■ *n.* INWARD CURVE a curve that bends inwards —**incurved** *adj.*

incus /íngkəss/ (*plural* **-cudes** /in kyóod eez/) *n.* ANAT a small bone, shaped like an anvil, found in the middle ear of mammals between the malleus and stapes bones. ◊ **malleus, stapes** [Mid-17thC. From Latin *incus* 'anvil', from, ultimately, *incudere* (see INCUSE).] —**incudal** /íngkyood'l/ *adj.* —**incudate** /íng kyoo dayt/ *adj.*

incuse /in kyóoz/ *adj.* STAMPED INTO COIN AS A DESIGN hammered, stamped, or impressed on a coin as a design ■ *n.* STAMPED-IN COIN DESIGN a design stamped, hammered, or impressed on a coin ■ *vt.* (**-cuses, -cusing, -cused**) IMPRESS COIN DESIGN to hammer or stamp a design on a coin [Early 19thC. From Latin *incus-*, past participle stem of *incudere*, literally 'to hammer on', from *cudere* 'to beat'.]

IND *abbr.* **1.** India (*international vehicle registration*) **2.** in God's Name [Latin *in nomine Dei*]

ind., ind *abbr.* **1.** independence **2.** independent **3.** index **4.** indicative **5.** indirect **6.** industrial **7.** industry

Ind., Ind *abbr.* **1.** Independent **2.** India **3.** Indian **4.** Indiana **5.** Indies

indaba /in daabə/ *n. S Africa* **1.** MEETING OR CONFERENCE a long political meeting, conference, or consultation, originally held with or among indigenous peoples of southern Africa **2.** PROBLEM a problem or serious matter for sb to think about or deal with (*informal*) [Early 19thC. From 'discussion'.]

indamine /índə meen/ *n.* an organic base that forms blue or green salts and is used in making dyes [Late 19thC. Coined from IND- + AMINE.]

indebted /in déttid/ *adj.* **1.** IN DEBT owing money to sb **2.** OBLIGATED TO SB obliged or grateful to sb for sth such as assistance or a favour received [13thC. Alteration of Old French *endetté*, the past participle of *endetter*, literally 'to put in debt', from *dette* (see DEBT).]

indebtedness /in déttidnəss/ *n.* **1.** STATE OF BEING IN SB'S DEBT the condition of owing money to sb or owing sb thanks **2.** AMOUNT OWED the total amount sb owes

indecency /in deéss'nsi/ (*plural* **-cies**) *n.* **1.** OFFENSIVENESS offensiveness according to accepted standards, especially in sexual matters **2.** INDECENT ACT an act that offends against accepted standards of decency

indecent /in deéss'nt/ *adj.* **1.** OFFENDING PUBLIC MORAL STANDARDS unacceptable and offensive to accepted standards, especially in sexual matters **2.** IMPROPER inappropriate under the circumstances and disapproved of by others ○ *The funeral was arranged with indecent haste.* [Late 16thC. Directly or via French from the Latin stem *indecent-*, literally 'not fitting', from *decens* (see DECENT).] —**indecently** *adv.*

indecent assault *n.* a sexual assault on sb that does not involve rape

indecent exposure *n.* the criminal offence of deliberately displaying part of the body, usually the genitals, to sb else in public

indeciduous /índi sídd yoo əss/ *adj.* evergreen (*technical*)

indecipherable /índi sífərəb'l/ *adj.* impossible or very difficult to read or understand —**indecipherability** /índi sífərə bílləti/ *n.* —**indecipherableness** *n.* —**indecipherably** *adv.*

indecision /índi sí<u>zh</u>'n/ *n.* inability to reach a decision or uncertainty resulting from sb's inability or refusal to reach a decision [Mid-18thC. From French *indécision*, literally 'indecisiveness', from *décision* 'decision'.]

indecisive /índi síssiv/ *adj.* **1.** UNABLE TO DECIDE unable or reluctant to make decisions generally or to come to a decision about sth in particular **2.** WITHOUT A CLEAR OUTCOME not producing a clear result, especially a clear victory for sb —**indecisively** *adv.* —**indecisiveness** *n.*

indeclinable /índi klínəb'l/ *adj.* GRAM existing in one form only and having no grammatical inflections, e.g. no plural form [15thC. Via French from Latin *indeclinabilis*, literally 'not declinable', from *declinare* (see DECLINE).] —**indeclinably** *adv.*

indecorous /in dékərəss/ *adj.* rather rude or shocking because of being considered socially unacceptable [Late 17thC. Formed from Latin *indecorus*, literally 'not seemly', from *decorus* (see DECOROUS).] —**indecorously** *adv.* —**indecorousness** *n.*

indecorum /índi káwrəm/ *n.* **1.** IMPROPER BEHAVIOUR behaviour that offends against what is socially acceptable and polite **2.** INDECOROUS ACT an indecorous action [Late 16thC. From Latin, formed from *indecorus* (see INDECOROUS).]

indeed /in de͞ed/ CORE MEANING: an adverb indicating agreement with or confirmation of sth ○ *He is indeed an actor.* ○ *'Do you know that man?' 'Indeed I do'.* *adv.* 1. WHAT IS MORE used to introduce a statement that strengthens or adds to a point just made ○ *I am willing, indeed eager, to speak on your behalf.* 2. FOR EMPHASIS used to give additional emphasis to a descriptive word or phrase (*used at the end of a clause*) ○ *The news, I learned, was grim indeed.* 3. EMPHASIZE A QUESTION used to emphasize a question and usually to express surprise or doubt at the same time (*often used as a question itself*) [14thC. From IN + DEED; the underlying meaning is 'in fact'.]

indef. *abbr.* indefinite

indefatigable /índi fáttigəb'l/ *adj.* never showing any sign of getting tired or of relaxing an effort [Early 17thC. Directly or via obsolete French *indéfatigable* from, ultimately, Latin *defatigare* 'to tire out', from *fatigare* (source of English *fatigue*).] —**indefatigability** /índi fáttigə bílləti/ *n.* —**indefatigableness** *n.* —**indefatigably** *adv.*

indefeasible /índi fe͞ezəb'l/ *adj.* LAW impossible to annul, make void, or forfeit —**indefeasibility** /índi fe͞ezə bílləti/ *n.* —**indefeasibleness** /índi fe͞ezəb'lnəss/ *n.* —**indefeasibly** /-fe͞ezəbli/ *adv.*

indefectible /índi féktəb'l/ *adj.* (*formal*) 1. ENDURING not affected by decay or failure 2. FLAWLESS without fault or imperfection [Mid-17thC. Formed from obsolete *defectible* 'liable to fail', from late Latin *defectibilis* from *defectus* (see DEFECT).] —**indefectibility** /índi féktə bílləti/ *n.* —**indefectibly** /índi féktəbli/ *adv.*

indefensible /índi fénssəb'l/ *adj.* 1. PERMITTING NO EXCUSE too bad or blameworthy to be in any way justified or excused ○ *indefensible conduct* 2. UNABLE TO BE PROTECTED incapable of being defended from attack 3. INVALID not based on fact, proof, or sound reasoning ○ *an indefensible argument* —**indefensibility** /índi fénssə bílləti/ *n.* —**indefensibleness** *n.* —**indefensibly** *adv.*

indefinable /índi fínəb'l/ *adj.* impossible or very difficult to describe, define, or analyze —**indefinability** /índi fínə bílləti/ *n.* —**indefinableness** *n.* —**indefinably** *adv.*

indefinite /in déffənət/ *adj.* 1. UNLIMITED not fixed or limited in length, size, duration, or quantity 2. NOT CLEAR not clear or not precisely defined or fixed 3. VAGUE AND UNCERTAIN unable or unwilling to give a clear indication of thoughts or plans 4. BOT TOO MANY TO COUNT consisting of units that are too numerous to be counted precisely ○ *indefinite stamens* 5. BOT GROWING AT TIP continuing to grow at the tip of the main stem instead of terminating in a flower bud. US term **indeterminate** [Mid-16thC. From Latin *indefinitus*, literally 'having no limits', from *definire* 'to define'.] —**indefiniteness** *n.*

indefinite article *n.* a word such as 'a' or 'an' in English that designates a noun referring to sth that has not been mentioned before and is simply any one of its kind ○ *Choose a book and write a review of it.*

indefinite integral *n.* an integral that when differentiated equals a given function

indefinitely /in déffənətli/ *adv.* 1. FOR UNSPECIFIED LENGTH OF TIME for a length of time that has no fixed or obvious end 2. UNSPECIFICALLY OR VAGUELY in a general and unspecific or vague and imprecise way

indefinite pronoun *n.* a pronoun, such as 'someone', 'nothing', or 'anything' in English, that does not refer to a particular person or thing

indehiscent /índi híss'nt/ *adj.* not opening up to release seeds when ripe —**indehiscence** *n.*

indelible /in délləb'l/ *adj.* 1. IMPOSSIBLE TO REMOVE OR ALTER physically impossible to rub, wash out, or alter 2. CONTAINING AN INDELIBLE SUBSTANCE containing indelible ink or lead ○ *an indelible pencil* 3. PERMANENT impossible to remove and therefore remaining forever [15thC. Directly or via French *indélébile* from Latin *indelebilis*, literally 'not defaceable', from *delere* 'to blot out, deface'.] —**indelibility** /in déllə bílləti/ *n.* —**indelibleness** /in délləb'lnəss/ *n.* —**indelibly** *adv.*

indelicate /in déllikət/ *adj.* 1. TACTLESS OR OFFENSIVE tactless, crude, or too frank, and therefore causing or likely to cause offence 2. PHYSICALLY UNREFINED crude, rough, or coarse in texture or appearance —**indelicacy** *n.* —**indelicately** *adv.* —**indelicateness** *n.*

indemnify /in démni fī/ (**-fies, -fying, -fied**) *vt.* 1. INSURE AGAINST LOSS to provide sb with protection, especially financial protection, against possible loss, damage, or liability 2. REIMBURSE AFTER LOSS to pay compensation to sb for damage, loss, or liability incurred [Early 17thC. Formed from Latin *indemnis*, literally 'not injured', from *damnum* 'injury'.] —**indemnification** /in démnifi káysh'n/ *n.* —**indemnifier** /in démni fī ər/ *n.*

indemnity /in démnəti/ (*plural* **-ties**) *n.* 1. INSURANCE protection or insurance against possible loss or damage 2. LAW EXEMPTION FROM PENALTIES legal exemption from penalties or liabilities 3. COMPENSATION a compensation paid for loss or damage [15thC. Via French from late Latin *indemnitas* 'security for damage', from Latin *indemnis* (see INDEMNIFY).]

indemonstrable /índi mónstrəb'l/ *adj.* impossible to prove or demonstrate (*formal*) —**indemonstrability** /índi mónstrə bílləti/ *n.* —**indemonstrableness** /índi mónstrəb'lnəss/ *n.* —**indemonstrably** /-mónstrəbli/ *adv.*

indene /ín deen/ *n.* a colourless liquid obtained from coal tar and petroleum that is used in making synthetic resins. Formula: C_9H_8. [Late 19thC. Coined from INDOLE + -ENE.]

indent[1] *v.* /in dént/ (**-dents, -denting, -dented**) 1. *vti.* PRINTING BEGIN LINE IN FROM MARGIN to start a line or row some distance in from the margin 2. *vt.* FORM RECESS IN to form a deep recess in sth (*often passive*) 3. *vt.* NOTCH to make jagged, notched, or serrated edges in sth 4. *vt.* US FIT NOTCHED EDGES to join together two notched pieces of sth 5. *vt.* TEAR COPIED DOCUMENT IN HALF to tear a document, especially one containing two copies of the same text, in half along an irregular line 6. *vt.* DRAW UP IN DUPLICATE to draw up a document in two or more exact copies 7. *vti.* ORDER USING OFFICIAL FORM to place an order for supplies using an official form 8. *vt.* COMM ORDER FOREIGN GOODS to place an order for foreign goods, usually through an agent ■ *n.* /ín dent, in dént/ 1. PRINTING SPACE SET IN FROM MARGIN a blank space left between the margin and the beginning of a line or row 2. INDENTURE an indenture (*archaic*) 3. ORDER OF FOREIGN GOODS an order for foreign goods, usually placed through an agent 4. OFFICIAL ORDER FOR SUPPLIES a requisition or official order for supplies [14thC] —**indented** /in déntid/ *adj.* —**indenter** /in déntər/ *n.*

indent[2] *vt.* /in dént/ (**-dents, -denting, -dented**) MAKE DENT IN to press sth inwards to form a dent ■ *n.* /ín dent, in dént/ = **dent** *n.* 1 [14thC. Formed from IN- + DENT.]

WORD KEY: ORIGIN

Etymologically, English has two separate words *indent*, although they have converged to a considerable extent over the centuries (particularly in the virtually shared derivative *indentation*). The one meaning 'to make a hole or depression in' is simply a derivative of *dent*. *Indent* 'to make notches in', however, owes its origin to Latin *dens* 'tooth'. This formed the basis of an Anglo-Latin verb *indentare* that denoted the drawing up of a contract between two parties on two identical documents that were cut along a matching line of notches or 'teeth' that could subsequently be rejoined to prove their authenticity. A particular use of such contracts was between master craftsmen and their trainees, who hence became known as *indentured* apprentices.

indentation /ín den táysh'n/ *n.* 1. NOTCH OR RECESS a notch, recess, or hollowed-out place in sth such as an edge, a boundary line, or a coast 2. JAGGED EDGE a series of notches or recesses, or the edge formed by this 3. PRINTING LEAVING SPACE AT BEGINNING OF LINE the leaving of space between the margin and the beginning of a line or row, or the blank space left 4. ACT OF INDENTING the act of indenting sth or the fact of being indented

indenture /in dénchər/ *n.* 1. CONTRACT WITH APPRENTICE a contract committing an apprentice or servant to serve a master for a specific period of time (*often plural*) 2. WRITTEN AGREEMENT a written contract or agreement between two or more parties 3. DUPLICATE DOCUMENT WITH TORN EDGE a document written in duplicate on a single sheet and torn in half so that the edges of the two resulting copies could be matched up to prove their authenticity 4. AUTHORIZED LIST an official list or inventory that has been authenticated for use as a voucher 5. INDENTATION an indentation (*archaic*) ■ *vti.* CONTRACT SB FOR SERVICES to commit sb to work as an apprentice or servant for a specified period of time by means of indentures —**indentureship** *n.*

indentured servant *n.* US an immigrant to North America during the 17th to 19th centuries who contracted to work for an employer for a number of years in exchange for passage and accommodation

independence /índi péndənss/ *n.* freedom from dependence on or control by another person, organization, or state

Independence Day *n.* US a national holiday in the United States, celebrated on 4 July, to commemorate the signing of the Declaration of Independence in 1776

independency /índi péndənssi/ (*plural* **-cies**) *n.* 1. INDEPENDENCE independence (*archaic*) 2. FREE TERRITORY an independent state or territory

Independency *n.* CHR the principle or policy that each local Christian church or congregation should be free of external ecclesiastical control

independent /índi péndənt/ *adj.* 1. NOT CONTROLLED BY ANOTHER free from the authority, control, or domination of sb or sth else, especially not controlled by another state or organization and able to self-govern 2. ABLE TO FUNCTION BY ITSELF able to operate or stand on its own because not dependent on another ○ *Each wheel has an independent suspension system.* 3. SELF-SUPPORTING not forced to rely on another for money or support 4. SHOWING CONFIDENCE IN SELF capable of thinking or acting without consultation with or guidance from others 5. DONE WITHOUT OBSTRUCTION carried out or operating without interference or influence from interested parties ○ *an independent counsel* 6. SUFFICIENT TO LIVE ON providing the means on which to live without having to work 7. **independent, Independent** POL NOT AFFILIATED TO POLITICAL PARTY not a member, representative, or supporter of any political party 8. MATH NOT SOLVABLE USING SOLUTION TO ANOTHER used to describe a system of equations in which no single equation is necessarily solved using a solution to the others 9. STATS NOT AFFECTING OTHER VARIABLES in statistics, distributed in such a way that the value taken on by one variable leaves all others unaffected 10. LOGIC NOT DEPENDENT ON AXIOM OR PROPOSITION not proved from another logical axiom or proposition ■ *n.* 1. SB OR STH UNAFFECTED BY OTHERS sb or sth that is free from control, dependence, or interference 2. **independent, Independent** POL NONPARTY POLITICIAN sb, especially a politician, who is not a member of, does not represent, or does not support any political party —**independently** *adv.*

Independent *n.* 1. CHR SUPPORTER OF SELF-GOVERNING CHRISTIAN CHURCH sb who believes that each Christian church or congregation should be free of external ecclesiastical control. Originally, Independents were members of a religious and political movement in 17th-century England that resulted in the organization of the Baptist and Congregationalist churches. 2. = **independent** *n.* 2

independent clause *n.* GRAM a clause that can stand on its own as a sentence, such as 'She'll go on holiday' in the sentence 'She'll go on holiday if she can raise the money'

independent invention *n.* ANTHROP an invention arrived at independently, even though another group of people may have created the same invention in a different place at a different time

independent school *n.* EDUC a school that is not financed or run by a local authority or the government

independent variable *n.* 1. MATH VARIABLE DETERMINING VALUE OF OTHERS the variable in a mathematical statement whose value, when specified, determines the value of another variable or other variables 2. STATS VARIABLE MANIPULATED IN AN EXPERIMENT a variable that is manipulated in an experiment in order to observe the effect on another variable

in-depth *adj.* giving careful consideration to all details and aspects of a subject —**in depth** *adv.*

indescribable /índi skríbəb'l/ *adj.* **1.** IMPOSSIBLE TO DESCRIBE impossible or very difficult to describe ○ *an indescribable sensation* **2.** SO GREAT AS TO DEFY DESCRIPTION so intense or extreme as to defy description ○ *indescribable joy* —**indescribability** /índi skríbə bílləti/ *n.* —**indescribableness** /índi skríbəb'lnəss/ *n.* —**indescribably** *adv.*

indestructible /índi strúktəb'l/ *adj.* impossible or very difficult to destroy —**indestructibility** /índi strúktə bílləti/ *n.* —**indestructibleness** /índi strúktəb'lnəss/ *n.* —**indestructibly** *adv.*

indeterminable /índi túrminəb'l/ *adj.* **1.** IMPOSSIBLE TO FIND OUT DEFINITELY impossible to determine or ascertain exactly **2.** IMPOSSIBLE TO ANSWER OR SETTLE impossible to resolve, answer, or settle [15thC. From late Latin *indeterminabilis*, literally 'not definable', from *determinare* (see DETERMINE).] —**indeterminableness** *n.* —**indeterminably** *adv.*

indeterminacy principle *n.* = uncertainty principle

indeterminate /índi túrminət/ *adj.* **1.** NOT KNOWN EXACTLY not known exactly, or impossible to work out **2.** VAGUE not definite, precise, or clear **3.** UNPREDICTABLE without a predictable result or outcome **4.** MATH HAVING NO NUMERICAL MEANING having no numerical value or meaning, e.g. the expressions '0/0' or '0°' **5.** MATH WITH AN INFINITE NUMBER OF SOLUTIONS having an infinite number of solutions **6.** BOT = indefinite [14thC. From Latin *indeterminatus*, literally 'not defined', from *determinare* (see DETERMINE).] —**indeterminacy** /índi túrminəsi/ *n.* —**indeterminately** *adv.* —**indeterminateness** *n.* —**indetermination** /índi túrmi náysh'n/ *n.*

indeterminate sentence *n.* a prison sentence that has a wide term, e.g. from one to five years, the date of release being determined by the prisoner's conduct and other factors

indeterminate vowel *n.* = schwa

indeterminism /índi túrminizəm/ *n.* the philosophical theory that human beings have free will and their actions are not always and completely determined by previous events. ♢ **determinism** —**indeterminist** *n.* —**indeterministic** /índi túrmi nístik/ *adj.*

index /ín deks/ *n.* (*plural* **-dexes** *or* **-dices** /-di seez/) **1.** PUBL ALPHABETICAL REFERENCE LIST IN BOOK an alphabetical list, usually at the end of a book, of people, places, or topics, giving the numbers of the pages on which they are mentioned **2.** CATALOGUE an ordered list of the items that make up a collection, e.g. the books in a library, usually including details of where to find them **3.** PUBLICATION LISTING ARTICLES a periodical or book that lists articles or other published works alphabetically by subject or author **4.** = thumb index **5.** INDICATOR an indicator or sign of sth ○ *One index of the situation's gravity is the severance of diplomatic relations.* **6.** TECH POINTER a pointer or needle, especially on a piece of scientific equipment **7.** PRINTING PRINTING CHARACTER a character ☞ used by printers to draw attention to a paragraph, section, or note **8.** MATH = exponent *n.* 4 **9.** MATH NUMBER GIVEN AS SUPERSCRIPT a number or variable given as a superscript before a square-root sign showing which root is to be taken **10.** MATH SUBSCRIPT OR SUPERSCRIPT IDENTIFYING AN ELEMENT a subscript or superscript numeral that identifies a particular element or range in a set or sequence **11.** NUMBER EXPRESSING RELATIONSHIP a scale, or a number on a scale, that expresses the price, value, or level of sth in comparison to sth else or to a previously established base number ■ *v.* **1.** *vti.* MAKE INDEX FOR to compile an index for sth such as a book **2.** *vt.* PUT IN AN INDEX to enter sth such as a name, title, subject, or quotation in an index **3.** *vt.* INDICATE to be a sign or indicator of sth (*formal*) **4.** *vt.* ECON MAKE INDEX-LINKED to make sth index-linked [Late 16thC. From Latin *index* 'forefinger', literally 'pointer'. Ultimately from an Indo-European base meaning 'to show'.] —**indexer** *n.*

Index *n.* = Index Librorum Prohibitorum

indexation /ín dek sáysh'n/ *n.* the linking of wages, pensions, or other remuneration to an index representing the cost of living, so that they are automatically adjusted up or down as that rises or falls

index case *n.* the first documented case of an illness in an epidemiological study

index finger *n.* the finger next to the thumb [From Latin *index* 'forefinger' (see INDEX)]

index fossil *n.* the fossil of an organism that is specific to a particular geological age and is used for dating or identifying rocks or rock layers in which it is found

index fund *n.* a mutual fund composed of companies listed in an important stock market index in order to match the market's overall performance

Index Librorum Prohibitorum /-IT bráwrəm prŏ híbbi táwrəm/ *n.* a list formerly compiled by the Roman Catholic Church of books and publications that Church members were forbidden to read [From Latin, 'list of forbidden books']

index-linked *adj.* adjusted up or down as the cost-of-living index rises or falls

index-linking *n.* = indexation

index number *n.* a number used to indicate the change in a value or quantity, e.g. a price or unemployment, when compared to the level of that value or quantity at an earlier time. The base level is usually arbitrarily set at 100, and the increase or decrease in index numbers over time is often expressed as a percentage change.

Index of Industrial Production *n.* a report produced by the Central Statistical Office showing the performance of the main British industries

index of refraction *n.* = refractive index

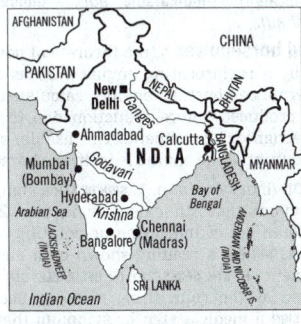

India

India[1] /índi ə/ country in southern Asia, the second largest in the world by population and the seventh largest by area. Language: Hindi, English. Currency: rupee. Capital: New Delhi. Population: 966,783,171 (1997). Area: 3,095,472 sq. km/1,195,063 sq. mi. Official name **Republic of India**

India[2] /índi ə/ *n.* the NATO phonetic alphabet code word for the letter 'I', used in international radio communication

India ink *n.* US = Indian ink

Indiaman /índi əmən/ (*plural* **-men** /-mən/) *n.* a large merchant sailing ship that was formerly used to transport goods to and from India [Early 18thC. From INDIA + MAN 'ship', as in *man of war*.]

Indian /índi ən/ *n.* **1.** SB FROM INDIA sb who was born or brought up in the Republic of India, or who has Indian citizenship **2.** NATIVE AMERICAN a Native American (*offensive*) **3.** OFFENSIVE TERM an offensive term for any of the languages of Native Americans (*offensive*) ■ *adj.* **1.** RELATING TO INDIA relating to India or its peoples, languages, or culture **2.** RELATING TO NATIVE AMERICANS relating to Native Americans or their languages or cultures (*offensive*) [13thC. From *India*, from, ultimately, Greek, 'the region of the Indus river', which came via Old Persian *Hindu* 'Indus' from Sanskrit *síndhu*.]

——— WORD KEY: USAGE ———

Sensitivity trap: Initially the term *Indian* was applied to the earliest inhabitants of the American continents because Columbus and other early European explorers, having arrived at North America's east coast, believed they had reached India by a new route. As a name thus applied in error by conquerors, *Indian* may well be regarded as insensitive or even offensive. Some of the people in question prefer to be called *American Indians* and some prefer the term *Native American*, this last choice being the one that is least likely to cause offence.

Indiana

Indiana /índi ánnə/ state in the north-central United States, bordered by Illinois, Kentucky, Michigan, Ohio, and Lake Michigan. Capital: Indianapolis. Population: 5,864,108 (1997). Area: 94,327 sq. km/36,420 sq. mi. —**Indianan** *n., adj.*

Indian agent *n.* an official in the United States or, formerly, in Canada, acting as a government representative to communities of Native North Americans

Indianapolis /índi ə náppəlis/ capital of Indiana, in the central part of the state, southwest of Fort Wayne on the White River. It is the largest city in the state. Population: 746,737 (1996).

Indian cholera *n.* the disease cholera

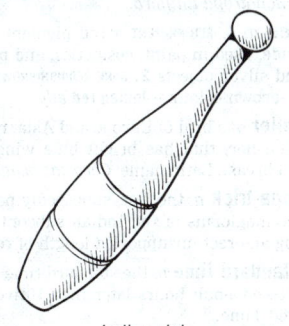

Indian club

Indian club *n.* a club shaped like an elongated bottle, used in gymnastics and juggling

Indian corn *n.* = maize [From its cultivation by Native Americans]

Indian English *n.* a variety of English spoken in India

——— WORD KEY: WORLD ENGLISH ———

Indian English is the English language as used in India since the 17th century. Traditionally the term has referred to the English usage of the entire subcontinent (former 'undivided India'), but today the term is technically limited to the Republic of India, in which English has multiple legislated roles: as an associate official language (Hindi being the official one); as a national language alongside Hindi, Bengali, and Tamil (it being the state language of the states of Manipur, Meghalaya, Nagaland, and Tripura); as the official language of eight Union territories, including the Andaman and Nicobar Islands, Delhi, and Pondicherry. Indian English has many distinct spoken varieties owing to the influence of regional languages such as Bengali, Hindi, and Tamil. Finally, it is notable for its strong ongoing contribution to English literature. Indian English has been the source of many loan words in World English: *bangle, chutney, bungalow, chintz, dinghy, dungaree, juggernaut, pundit,* and *shampoo.* Indian English expressions often combine English words into compounds that are not self-explanatory outside the national culture: for example, *Eve-teasing* (harassment of women), *head-bath* (a hair wash), *Himalayan blunder* (a huge mistake), and *tiffin room* (a snack shop). See SOUTH ASIAN ENGLISH.

Indian file *n.* single file (*dated offensive*) [From a Native American custom of walking in single file]

Indian giver *n.* US sb who gives sth and then asks for its return (*informal offensive*) [Possibly from a Native American custom of exchanging gifts of equal value]

Indian hemp *n.* **1.** = **hemp** **2.** PERENNIAL PLANT a perennial North American plant of the dogbane family whose roots can be used as a laxative and emetic. Latin name: *Apocynum cannabinum.*

Indian ink *n.* US term **India ink** **1.** BLACK PIGMENT USED IN INK the black pigment, usually shaped into cakes or sticks, from which Indian ink is made **2.** LIQUID BLACK INK a liquid black ink made from a pigment that is a mixture of lampblack and a binding agent [From its originally being brought to Europe from China and Japan via India]

Indian meal *n. US* = **cornmeal**

Indian Mutiny *n.* a rebellion of Indian soldiers against British rule in 1857–58

Indian Ocean ocean situated east of Africa, south of Asia, west of Australia, and north of Antarctica. Its greatest known depth is 7,725 m/25,344 ft. Area: 73,427,800 sq. km/28,350,500 sq. mi.

Indian Pacific *n.* the train service in Australia that runs between Perth, on the shore of the Indian Ocean, and Sydney, on the shore of the Pacific Ocean

Indian paintbrush *n.* a wild plant of the figwort family, found in North America, with brightly coloured bracts that look like flowers. Latin name: *Castileja linariaefolia.*

Indian pipe *n.* a perennial North American and Asian woodland plant whose single white stem and nodding flower resemble a tobacco pipe. Latin name: *Monotropa uniflora.*

Indian red *n.* **1.** RED PIGMENT a red pigment made of iron oxide, used in paint, cosmetics, and polish for gold and silver objects **2.** DARK REDDISH-BROWN a dark reddish-brown colour —**Indian red** *adj.*

Indian roller *n.* a bird of Europe and Asia, related to the kingfisher, that has bright blue wings and a chestnut breast. Latin name: *Coracias benghalensis.*

Indian rope-trick *n.* the feat, supposedly performed by some magicians of the Indian subcontinent, of climbing an erect unsupported length of rope

Indian Standard Time *n.* the standard time in India. It is five-and-a-half hours later than Universal Coordinated Time.

Indian Subcontinent large region in southern Asia, including the countries of Bangladesh, the Republic of India, and Pakistan

Indian summer *n.* **1.** MILD AUTUMN WEATHER a period of mild sunny weather occurring in autumn in the northern hemisphere **2.** TIME OF CALM a calm or productive and enjoyable period towards the end of sb's life or the end of a process, period, or activity [Origin uncertain: perhaps because it was first noticed in areas inhabited by Native Americans]

Indian tobacco *n.* a very poisonous North American annual plant of the bluebell family that has oval toothed leaves and small purplish flowers followed by swollen seed capsules. Native North American peoples once smoked the leaves as a remedy for respiratory symptoms. Latin name: *Lobelia inflata.*

Indian-wrestle (**Indian-wrestles, Indian-wrestling, Indian-wrestled**) *vti.* to attempt to force down an opponent's upraised arm or to throw a standing opponent off balance

Indian wrestling *n.* a form of wrestling in which one opponent attempts to force down another's upraised arm or to throw a standing opponent off balance

India paper *n.* **1.** THIN PAPER a thin fine paper originally made in Asia, used for prints and illustrations **2.** = **Bible paper**

India print *n.* a fabric made in India that has colourful block patterns on it

India rubber *n.* INDUST rubber (*dated*)

Indic /índik/ *n.* a group of over 500 languages of the Indian subcontinent, forming a major division of Indo-Iranian that includes Hindi, Urdu, Assamese, Bengali, Gujarati, Sinhalese, Punjabi, Sanskrit, and the Dardic languages. Over 700 million people speak one of the languages classified as Indic. ◊ **Iranian** [Mid-19thC. Via Latin *Indicus* from Greek *Indikos*, from *Indos* 'the Indus river'.] —**Indic** *adj.*

indic. *abbr.* **1.** indicating **2.** GRAM indicative **3.** indicator

indican /índikən/ *n.* **1.** CHEMICAL IN URINE a substance formed in the intestine by bacterial action and excreted in urine and sweat. High levels in urine may indicate obstruction of the intestine. Formula: $C_8H_6NO_4SK$. **2.** CHEMICAL IN PLANTS an off-white, crystalline, sugar derivative found in plants that was the original source of indigo dye. Formula: $C_{14}H_{17}NO_6$. [Mid-19thC. Coined from Latin *indicum* 'indigo' + -AN[1].]

indicant /índikənt/ *n.* sth that indicates sth [Early 17thC. From Latin *indicare* (see INDICATE).]

indicate /índi kayt/ (**-cates, -cating, -cated**) *v.* **1.** *vt.* POINT TO to point sth out or point to sth **2.** *vt.* SHOW EXISTENCE OR TRUTH OF to be or provide a sign or symptom of sth **3.** *vt.* REGISTER MEASUREMENT to register a measurement, e.g. of speed or temperature **4.** *vt.* SHOW WHAT SB THINKS OR INTENDS to state or show an opinion, feeling, instruction, or intention, especially briefly or indirectly **5.** *vt.* SHOW WHAT SHOULD BE DONE to make sb think that sth should be done or used (*usually used in the passive*) ○ *In a case like this, a firm approach is indicated.* **6.** *vti.* GIVE SIGNALS AS DRIVER to signal your intentions to other vehicles when driving, especially before turning or moving to the left or right **7.** *vt.* MED SHOW PRESENCE OF DISEASE to point out the presence of, or remedy for, a disease or syndrome [Early 17thC. From Latin *indicare* 'to point towards, show', from *dicare* 'to proclaim' (source of English *preach* and *abdicate*).] —**indicatable** *adj.* —**indicatory** /in díkətəri/ *adj.*

indicated horsepower *n.* the theoretical power produced by a reciprocating engine such as a steam or internal-combustion engine, calculated as the power produced before reduction due to friction and mechanical movement. The usable, reduced-power output of the engine is its brake horsepower.

indication /índi káysh'n/ *n.* **1.** SIGN OF STH a sign, signal, or symptom that sth exists or is true **2.** ACT OF INDICATING an act of indicating or pointing to sth **3.** READING INSTRUMENT a reading shown on a measuring instrument **4.** STH NECESSARY OR DESIRABLE sth that is indicated as the right thing to do or use **5.** MED MEDICAL SIGN a medical sign or symptom that shows the presence of a disease or a remedy for it —**indicational** *adj.*

WORD KEY: SYNONYMS

See Synonyms at ***sign***.

indicative /in díkətiv/ *adj.* **1.** INDICATING EXISTENCE OR TRUTH showing, suggesting, or pointing out that sth exists or is true **2.** GRAM RELATING TO BASIC MOOD OF VERBS relating to verbs in simple objective statements ■ *n.* GRAM **1.** BASIC MOOD OF A VERB the basic mood of a verb in languages such as English, used for ordinary objective statements **2.** VERB IN BASIC MOOD a verb used in a simple statement of fact —**indicatively** *adv.*

indicator /índi kaytər/ *n.* **1.** DRIVER'S SIGNAL a device on a motor vehicle, usually a flashing light, that indicates that the driver is turning or moving to the left or right **2.** STH THAT SHOWS WHAT CONDITIONS ARE sth observed or calculated that is used to show the presence or state of a condition or trend **3.** MEASURING INSTRUMENT an instrument or gauge that measures sth and registers the measurement **4.** STH GIVING INFORMATION sth such as a light, sign, or pointer that gives information, e.g. about which direction to follow **5.** CHEM CHEMICAL SHOWING PRESENCE OF STH a substance such as litmus that shows the presence or concentration of a particular material or chemical **6.** ECOL = **indicator organism**

indicator diagram *n.* a graph showing the variation of pressure and volume in a cylinder of a reciprocating engine

indicator organism *n.* an organism whose presence or absence in an environment indicates particular conditions there, e.g. its oxygen level or the presence of a contaminating substance

indices plural of **index**

indicia plural of **indicium**

indicial /in dísh'l/ *adj.* acting as or relating to a sign or indication of sth (*formal*)

indicium /in díssi əm/ (*plural* **-a** /-si ə/) *n.* a sign indicating the presence or nature of sth, e.g. a medical condition [Early 17thC. From Latin, where it was formed from *indic-*, the stem of *index* (see INDEX).]

indicolite /índikə līt/ *n.* a blue-coloured tourmaline used as a gemstone [Early 19thC. Coined from Latin *indicum* 'indigo' + -LITE.]

indict /in dít/ (**-dicts, -dicting, -dicted**) *vt.* **1.** FORMALLY CHARGE ACCUSED PERSON to charge sb formally with commission of a crime **2.** ACCUSE OF A WRONG to accuse sb of wrongdoing [14thC. Via Anglo-Norman *enditer* from, ultimately, Latin *indicere* 'to proclaim', literally 'to say in', from *dicere* 'to say'. The spelling *indict*, dating from the 17thC., was modelled on medieval Latin *indictare* 'to indict'.] —**indictee** /indī tée/ *n.* —**indicter** /in dítər/ *n.* —**indictor** *n.*

indictable /in dítəb'l/ *adj.* **1.** LIABLE TO INDICTMENT liable to be charged with a criminal offence **2.** MAKING SB LIABLE TO INDICTMENT making sb liable to be charged with commission of a crime ○ *an indictable offence*

indiction /in díksh'n/ *n.* a cyclical period of 15 years begun during the reign of Constantine the Great in the later Roman Empire at the end of which property was evaluated for taxation [14thC. From the Latin stem *indiction-* 'declaration', from *indictus*, past participle of *indicere* 'to declare' (see INDICT); from the declaration fixing the valuation on which tax was assessed.] —**indictional** /in díksh'nəl/ *adj.*

indictment /in dítmənt/ *n.* **1.** STATEMENT OR FACT THAT ACCUSES a statement or indication that sth is wrong or sb is to blame ○ *a stinging indictment of our prison system* **2.** CRIMINAL LAW ACT OF INDICTING SB the act of indicting sb or the condition of being indicted **3.** CRIMINAL LAW FORMAL CHARGE OF CRIMINAL WRONGDOING a formal accusation of a serious crime **4.** ACCUSATION OF CRIMINAL CONDUCT a formal accusation of criminal conduct **5.** CRIMINAL LAW ACCUSATION BY LORD ADVOCATE IN SCOTLAND in Scotland, an accusation of crime brought by the Lord Advocate

indie /índi/ *n.* INDEPENDENT COMPANY a small independent business enterprise, especially one related to music (*slang*) ■ *adj.* ISSUED BY SMALL COMPANIES issued by small independent record companies, or playing the sort of music recorded by such companies (*slang*) [Early 20thC. Shortening of INDEPENDENT.]

Indiennes /índi én/ *n.* fabric with small brightly coloured French provincial patterns that are hand-printed using carved blocks. It was originally imported from India. [Late 19thC. Ultimately from French (*à l'*)*indienne*, literally '(in the) Indian (style)'.]

indifference /in díffrənss/ *n.* **1.** LACK OF INTEREST IN STH lack of interest, care, or concern **2.** UNIMPORTANCE lack of importance or significance ○ *It's a matter of complete indifference to me whether you go or stay.* **3.** LOW QUALITY ordinariness or lack of quality

indifferent /in díffrənt/ *adj.* **1.** WITHOUT CARE OR INTEREST showing no care or concern for, or interest in, sb or sth ○ *She was indifferent to their criticism.* **2.** FAVOURING NEITHER SIDE without bias or preference for one person, group, or thing rather than another **3.** ONLY AVERAGE average or low in quality **4.** BIOL UNDIFFERENTIATED not specialized or differentiated in cells or tissues **5.** SCI NEUTRAL neutral and having no properties that are affected by a process or reaction **6.** OF NO IMPORT lacking importance or significance (*archaic*) [14thC. Directly or via Old French from the Latin stem *indifferent-* 'making no difference', from *different-*, present participle stem of *differre* 'to differ'.]

indifferentism /in díffrəntizəm/ *n.* the belief that variations in doctrine and practice within a religion are unimportant

indifferently /in díff rəntli/ *adv.* **1.** WITHOUT INTEREST without showing interest or concern **2.** NOT WELL not very well **3.** EQUALLY without differences or exceptions (*formal*)

indigen *n.* = **indigene**

indigence /índijənss/ *n.* extreme poverty in which the basic necessities of life are lacking (*formal*)

WORD KEY: SYNONYMS

See Synonyms at ***poverty***.

indigene /índi jeen/, **indigen** /índijən/ *n.* sb who was born in a place or location or sth that was produced in or grows in or belongs naturally to a place or location (*formal*) [Late 16thC. Via French *indigène* from Latin *indigena* 'native' (see INDIGENOUS).]

indigenize /in díjji nīz/ (**-izes, -izing, -ized**), **indigenise** (**-ises, -ising, -ised**) *vti.* to increase the use of local inhabitants for a task previously done by people from another country, usually the home country of an employing company —**indigenization** /in díjji nī záysh'n/ *n.*

indigenous /in díjjinəss/ *adj.* **1.** BELONGING TO A PLACE originating in and typical of a region or country **2.** NATURAL natural or inborn (*formal*) [Mid-17thC. From Latin *indigena*, literally 'born in', from *gignere* 'to beget'. Ultimately from an Indo-European word that is also the ancestor of English *gender*.] —**indigenity** /índi jénniti/ *n.* —**indigenously** /in díjjinəssli/ *adv.*

——— **WORD KEY: SYNONYMS** ———
See Synonyms at *native*.

indigenous people *n.* the people who occupy a region at the time of its contact with colonial powers or the outside world

indigent /índijənt/ *adj.* EXTREMELY POOR lacking the necessities of life, such as food, clothing, and shelter (*formal*) ■ *n.* DESTITUTE PERSON sb who is very poor (*formal*) [14thC. Via Old French from Latin *indigent-*, present participle stem of *indigere*, literally 'to lack in', from *egere* 'to need'.] —**indigently** *adv.*

indigested *adj.* = undigested

indigestible /índi jéstəb'l/ *adj.* **1.** DIFFICULT TO DIGEST difficult or impossible to digest **2.** HARD TO UNDERSTAND hard to take in or understand (*informal*) [15thC. Directly or via French from late Latin *indigestibilis*, from *digestibilis* 'digestible'.] —**indigestibility** /índi jéstə bílləti/ *n.* —**indigestibly** *adv.*

indigestion /índi jéschən/ *n.* difficulty in digesting food, resulting in such symptoms as belching, heartburn, or stomach pains. Technical name **dyspepsia** [14thC. Directly or via Old French from the late Latin stem *indigestion-*, from *digestion-* (see DIGESTION).]

indigestive /índi jéstiv/ *adj.* experiencing or resulting from indigestion

indignant /in dígnənt/ *adj.* angry or annoyed at the unfairness or unreasonableness of sb or sth [Late 16thC. From Latin *indignant-*, present participle stem of *indignari* 'to regard as unworthy', ultimately from *dignus* 'worthy' (see DIGNITY).] —**indignantly** *adv.*

indignation /índig náysh'n/ *n.* anger or annoyance because sb or sth seems unfair or unreasonable [14thC. Directly or via Old French from the Latin stem *indignation-*, from *indignari* (see INDIGNANT).]

——— **WORD KEY: SYNONYMS** ———
See Synonyms at *anger*.

indignity /índígnəti/ (*plural* **-ties**) *n.* a humiliating loss of dignity or self-esteem [Late 16thC. Directly or via French *indignité* from Latin *indignitas*, from *indignus* 'unworthy'.]

Indigo: Synthetic indigo

indigo /índigō/ *n.* (*plural* **-gos** *or* **-goes**) **1.** BLUE DYE a blue dye, once obtained from plants, but now usually made synthetically **2.** PLANT YIELDING INDIGO DYE a tropical plant of the pea family with fronds of pointed leaves and spikes of red or purple flowers, a source of indigo dye. Genus: *Indigofera*. **3.** DEEP PURPLISH-BLUE COLOUR a deep purplish-blue colour that lies towards one end of the visible spectrum, between blue and violet ■ *adj.* DEEP PURPLISH-BLUE of a deep purplish-

blue colour [Mid-16thC. Via Portuguese from, ultimately, Greek *indikon*, literally 'the Indian substance', a form of *Indikos* 'Indian', from *Indos* 'the River Indus'.]

indigo bird *n.* an East African weaverbird, the male of which has deep purplish-black feathers, found in gardens and in the wild. Genus: *Hypochera*.

indigo blue *n.* = indigo

indigo bunting *n.* a North American finch found in hedgerows and at the margins of woods, the male of which has brilliant indigo feathers. Latin name: *Passerina cyanea*.

indigo snake *n.* a large deep-blue snake, found from the southern United States to South America, that preys on small mammals but is harmless to humans. Latin name: *Drymarchon corais*.

indigotin /in díggətin, índi gótin/ *n.* = indigo *n.* 1 [Mid-19thC. Coined from INDIGO + -IN.]

indirect /índi rékt, índī-/ *adj.* **1.** NOT IN STRAIGHT LINE not in a direct line, course, or path **2.** NOT IMMEDIATE OR INTENDED not occurring as an immediate or intended effect or consequence **3.** DEVIOUS not obvious or straightforward in approach **4.** INVOLVING INTERMEDIATE STAGES not obtained or proceeding from an immediate or straightforward relationship [14thC. Directly or via Old French from medieval Latin *indirectus* 'not direct', from Latin *directus* (see DIRECT).] —**indirectness** *n.* —**indirectly** *adv.*

indirect cost *n.* a business expense that is not directly connected with a particular product or operation

indirect discourse *n.* = indirect speech

indirection /índə réksh'n, índī réksh'n/ *n.* **1.** LACK OF DIRECTNESS lack of directness in a path, course, or procedure **2.** AIMLESSNESS lack of a goal or goals **3.** STH NOT HONEST AND STRAIGHTFORWARD an approach or action that is devious or deceitful

indirect labour *n.* work that is not considered in determining costs per unit in producing or manufacturing sth, e.g. work done by clerical or maintenance staff

indirect lighting *n.* reflected or diffused light used to avoid glare or shadows

indirect object *n.* the recipient of the action shown by a verb and its direct object, e.g. 'the cat' in 'She gave the cat a meal'

indirect proof *n.* LOGIC proof of a conclusion by showing that assuming its negation will lead to a contradiction

indirect question *n.* a question reported in indirect speech, e.g. 'He asked why you were not there'

indirect speech *n.* a report of sth said or written that conveys what was said, but not the exact words in their original form, as in 'She said she would join us later'

indirect tax *n.* a tax levied on goods or services, instead of directly on companies and individuals

indiscernible /índi súrnəb'l/ *adj.* impossible to see or to understand —**indiscernibility** /índi súrnə bílləti/ *n.* —**indiscernibly** /índi súrnəbli/ *adv.*

indiscipline /in díssəplin/ *n.* lack of control or discipline

indiscreet /índi skreét/ *adj.* lacking tact or discretion [15thC. From Latin *indiscretus* 'unseparated, undistinguished' (see DISCREET).] —**indiscreetly** *adv.* —**indiscreetness** *n.*

indiscrete /índi skreét/ *adj.* not divided into parts or appearing not to consist of separate parts [Early 17thC. From Latin *indiscretus* 'unseparated, undistinguished', from *discretus* (see DISCRETE).] —**indiscretely** *adv.* —**indiscreteness** *n.*

indiscretion /índi skrésh'n/ *n.* **1.** TACTLESS LACK OF JUDGMENT lack of tact or good judgment **2.** STH UNWISE sth said or done that is tactless or unwise ○ *apologizing for past indiscretions* —**indiscretionary** *adj.*

indiscriminate /índi skrímminət/ *adj.* **1.** UNSELECTIVE making no careful distinctions or choices **2.** HAPHAZARDLY RANDOM random, haphazard, or confused —**indiscriminately** *adv.* —**indiscriminateness** *n.* —**indiscrimination** /índi skrímmi náysh'n/ *n.* —**indiscriminative** *adj.*

indispensable /índi spénssəb'l/ *adj.* **1.** NECESSARY necessary, essential, or not to be dispensed with **2.** HAVING TO BE FACED unavoidable, especially as a duty ■ *n.* ESSENTIAL sth that is essential and cannot be dispensed with —**indispensability** /índi spénssə bílləti/ *n.* —**indispensableness** /índi spénssəb'lnəss/ *n.* —**indispensably** *adv.*

——— **WORD KEY: SYNONYMS** ———
See Synonyms at *necessary*.

indispose /índi spóz/ (**-poses, -posing, -posed**) *vt.* **1.** SICKEN to make sb ill (*archaic*) **2.** MAKE UNFIT to make sb unfit for sth (*formal*) **3.** MAKE AVERSE TO STH to make sb dislike the prospect of sth or be unwilling to do sth (*formal*) [Mid-17thC]

indisposed /índi spózd/ *adj.* (*formal*) **1.** SICK too ill to do sth **2.** UNWILLING TO SAY OR DO STH unwilling to say or do sth, especially because of a feeling of annoyance

indisposition /índispə zísh'n/ *n.* (*formal*) **1.** MINOR ILLNESS an illness that is not serious **2.** RELUCTANCE reluctance or unwillingness to do sth

indisputable /índi spyoot əb'l/ *adj.* impossible to doubt, question, or deny [Mid-16thC. From late Latin *indisputabilis* 'not disputable', from Latin *disputabilis* (see DISPUTABLE).] —**indisputability** /índi spyootə bílləti/ *n.* —**indisputableness** /índi spyootəb'lnəss/ *n.* —**indisputably** *adv.*

indissoluble /índi sóllyoob'l/ *adj.* incapable of being dissolved, broken, or undone —**indissolubility** /índi sóllyoo bílləti/ *n.* —**indissolubly** /índi sóllyoobli/ *adv.*

indistinct /índi stíngkt/ *adj.* **1.** UNCLEAR giving an unclear impression to the sight or hearing **2.** VAGUE not clearly remembered, understood, or thought out [Mid-16thC. From Latin *indistinctus* 'not distinct', from *distinctus* (see DISTINCT).] —**indistinctly** *adv.* —**indistinctness** *n.*

indistinctive /índi stíngktiv/ *adj.* without any distinguishing qualities or features —**indistinctively** *adv.*

indistinguishable /índi stíng gwishəb'l, índə-/ *adj.* **1.** VERY LIKE SB OR STH ELSE impossible to tell apart from sb or sth else ○ *His handwriting is indistinguishable from his father's.* **2.** INDISTINCT very hard to see, hear, or understand —**indistinguishability** /índi stíng gwishə bílləti/ *n.* —**indistinguishably** /índi stíng gwishəbli/ *adv.*

indite /in dīt/ (**-dites, -diting, -dited**) *vt.* to write or compose sth such as a poem, letter, or speech (*archaic or literary*) [14thC. From Old French *enditer*, literally 'to compose in words in', from, ultimately, Latin *dictare* 'to compose in words' (see DICTATE).]

indium /índi əm/ *n.* a soft silvery-coloured rare metallic chemical element, often found in zinc and tin ores, used in alloys, transistors, and electroplating. Symbol **In** [Mid-19thC. Coined from INDIGO + -IUM. From two indigo lines in its spectrum.]

indiv., individ. *abbr.* individual

individual /índi víddyoo əl/ *n.* **1.** PARTICULAR PERSON a particular person, distinct from others in a group **2.** SEPARATE THING a separate entity or thing **3.** BIOL SEPARATE ORGANISM an independent organism separate from a group ■ *adj.* **1.** SEPARABLE FROM OTHERS singular and separable from others in a group or class **2.** OF OR FOR ONE PERSON belong to, relating to, or intended for one person only **3.** VERY DISTINCTIVE strikingly personal, unusual, or distinctive [15thC. From medieval Latin *individualis*, from Latin *individuus* 'not divisible', from, ultimately, *dividere* 'to divide'.]

individualise *vt.* = individualize

individualism /índi víddyoo əlizəm/ *n.* **1.** PURSUIT OF PERSONAL GOALS the pursuit of personal happiness and independence rather than collective goals or interests **2.** PERSONAL TRAIT a personal peculiarity or trait **3.** POL POLITICAL BELIEF IN IMPORTANCE OF INDIVIDUAL the belief that society exists for the benefit of the individual, who must not be constrained by government interventions or made subordinate to collective interests

individualist /índi víddyoo əlisst/ *n.* **1.** INDEPENDENT THINKER sb who thinks or behaves independently **2.** BELIEVER IN INDIVIDUALISM sb who believes in the social or political philosophy of individualism —**individualistically** /índi vidyoo ə lístikli/ *adv.*

individuality /índi vidyoo álləti/ (*plural* **-ties**) *n.* **1.** INDIVIDUAL TRAIT OR CHARACTER a specific personality, character, or characteristic that distinguishes one person or thing from another **2.** STATE OF BEING AN INDIVIDUAL the state or condition of being separate from others

individualize /índi víddyoo ə līz/ (**-izes, -izing, -ized**), **individualise** (**-ises, -ising, -ised**) *vt.* **1.** GIVE INDIVIDUAL CHARACTER TO to give sb or sth a character that is separate and distinct from other people or things **2.** TREAT INDIVIDUALLY to consider or treat sb or sth specifically, as distinct from other people or things **3.** ADAPT TO INDIVIDUAL REQUIREMENTS to make, adapt, or modify sth to suit a particular person —**individualization** /índi víddyoo ə lī záysh'n/ *n.* —**individualizer** /índi víddyoo ə līzər/ *n.*

individually /índi víddyoo əli/ *adv.* as a separate person or entity, not as part of a group or class

individual medley *n.* a swimming race divided into three or four equal parts, in each of which the swimmers must use a particular stroke such as backstroke, freestyle, breaststroke, or butterfly

individuate /índi víddyoo ayt/ (**-ates, -ating, -ated**) *vt.* to make sb or sth separate and distinct from others (*formal*) [Early 17thC. From medieval Latin *individuat-*, past participle stem of *individuare*, from Latin *individuus* (see INDIVIDUAL).] —**individuator** *n.*

individuation /índi vidyoo áysh'n/ *n.* **1.** ACT OF MAKING SEPARATE the act or process of making sb or sth separate and distinct from others **2.** PSYCHOL PROCESS OF PSYCHOLOGICAL DEVELOPMENT in Jungian psychology, the process of the development of the self, achieved by resolving the conflicts arising at life's transitional stages, in particular the transition from adolescence to adulthood. Jung believed this process could not be completed until middle age.

indivisible /índi vízzəb'l/ *adj.* **1.** NOT SEPARABLE not capable of being separated into parts **2.** MATH NOT MULTIPLE OF NUMBER not capable of being divided by a given number without leaving a remainder [14thC. From late Latin *indivisibilis* 'not divisible', from *divisibilis* 'divisible'.] —**indivisibility** /índi vizə bílləti/ *n.* —**indivisibly** /índi vízzəbli/ *adv.*

indn *abbr.* indication

indo- *prefix.* Forms the name of chemical compounds derived from or related to indigo ○ *indoxyl* [From INDIGO]

Indo- *prefix.* **1.** India ○ *Indo-Pacific* **2.** Indic ○ *Indo-Iranian* [From INDIA and INDIC]

Indo-Canadian *n.* a Canadian person of Indian descent, or one who was born in India —**Indo-Canadian** *adj.*

Indochina

Indochina /índō chínə/ peninsula of southeastern Asia that includes Myanmar, Thailand, Cambodia, Vietnam, Laos, and the Malay Peninsula. In a narrower sense it refers only to Cambodia, Laos, and Vietnam. —**Indochinese** /índō chī neezí/ *adj., n.*

indocile /in dó sīl/ *adj.* resisting discipline or instruction [Early 17thC. Directly or via French from Latin *indocilis* 'difficult to teach', from *docilis* (see DOCILE).] —**indocility** /índō sílləti/ *n.*

indoctrinate /in dóktri nayt/ (**-nates, -nating, -nated**) *vt.* to teach sb a belief, doctrine, or ideology thoroughly and systematically, especially with the aim of discouraging independent thought or the acceptance of other opinions [Early 17thC. From Old French *en-*

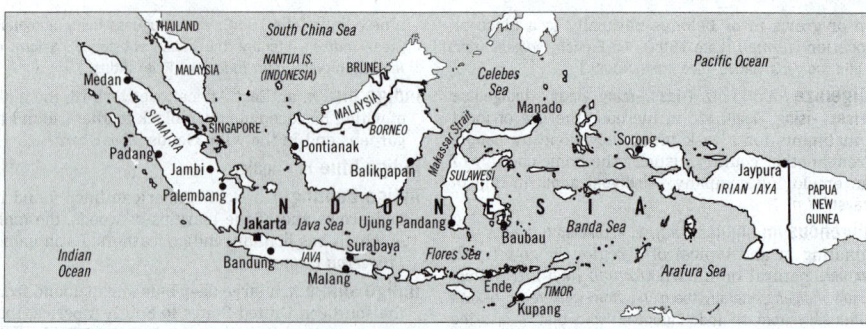

Indonesia

doctriner, literally 'to teach in', from medieval Latin *doctrinare* 'to teach'.] —**indoctrination** /in dóktri náysh'n/ *n.* —**indoctrinator** /in dóktri naytər/ *n.*

Indo-European /índō-/ *n.* **1.** FAMILY OF EUROPEAN AND ASIAN LANGUAGES a family of languages conventionally divided into the following branches: Balto-Slavonic, Germanic, Italic, Indo-Iranian, Celtic, Greek, Albanian, Armenian, Anatolian, and Tocharian. This language family, now spoken from India to western Europe, includes many modern languages, e.g. English, French, German, Spanish, Russian, Hindi, and Urdu. ◊ **satem, centum, Proto-Indo-European 2.** SPEAKER OF INDO-EUROPEAN LANGUAGE sb who speaks any of the Indo-European languages —**Indo-European** *adj.*

Indo-Iranian *n.* a group of languages spoken in the north of the Indian subcontinent and in parts of the Middle East, forming a branch of Indo-European and dividing into two subgroups, Indic and Iranian. About 800 million people speak one of the languages classified as Indo-Iranian. —**Indo-Iranian** *adj.*

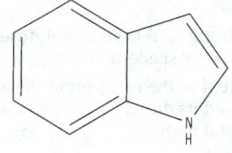

Indole

indole /índōl/, **indol** /-dol/ *n.* a crystalline compound that occurs in plants and in the intestines. It can also be derived from coal tar and is used in perfumes and as a reagent. Formula: C_8H_7N. [Mid-19thC. Coined from IND- + -OLE.]

indoleacetic acid /índōlə seétik-, -ə séttik-/ *n.* a plant hormone that stimulates growth and root formation in stems. Formula: $C_{10}H_9NO_2$. [*Indoleacetic* coined from INDOLE + ACETIC]

indolebutyric acid /índōl byoo tírrik-/ *n.* a synthetic plant hormone that stimulates growth in stems. Formula: $C_{12}H_{13}O_2N$. [*Indolebutyric* coined from INDOLE + BUTYRIC]

indolent /índələnt/ *adj.* **1.** LAZY lethargic and not showing any interest or making any effort **2.** MED PAINLESS AND SLOW TO CHANGE used to describe a disease or condition that is slow to develop or be healed, and causes no pain [Mid-17thC. From the late Latin stem *indolent-* 'insensitive to pain', from *dolent-*, present participle stem of *dolere* 'to suffer pain'.] —**indolence** *n.* —**indolently** *adv.*

Indology /in dólla ji/ *n.* the study of the history, culture, or philosophy of the Indian subcontinent [Late 19thC. Coined from INDO- + -LOGY.] —**Indologist** *n.*

indomethacin /índō méthəssin/ *n.* a drug used to relieve pain, fever, and inflammation, especially from arthritis. Formula: $C_{19}H_{16}ClNO_4$. [Mid-20thC. Coined from INDOLE + METHYL + ACETIC + -IN.]

indomitable /in dómmitəb'l/ *adj.* brave, determined, and impossible to defeat or frighten [Mid-17thC. From late Latin *indomitabilis* 'untamable', from *domitare* 'to tame' (source of English *daunt*).] —**indomitability** /in dómmitə bílləti/ *n.* —**indomitableness** /in dómmitəb'lnəss/ *n.* —**indomitably** /-bli/ *adv.*

Indon. *abbr.* Indonesian

Indonesia /índə neézi ə/ island republic of southeastern Asia, the fourth most populous country in the world. It consists of more than 13,670 islands, 6,000 of which are inhabited. Language: Bahasa Indonesia. Currency: rupiah. Capital: Jakarta. Population: 209,774,138 (1997). Area: 1,919,317 sq. km/741,903 sq. mi. Official name **Republic of Indonesia**

Indonesian /índō neézi ən/ *n.* **1.** PEOPLES SB FROM INDONESIA sb who was born or brought up in Indonesia, or who is a citizen of Indonesia **2.** LANG = Bahasa Indonesia —**Indonesian** *adj.*

indoor /ín dáwr/ *adj.* situated or done within a building [Early 18thC. From IN + DOOR, replacing earlier *within door(s)*; from the use of *door* as a metaphor for building (as in *next door*).]

indoor air quality *n.* the condition of the air inside buildings, including the extent of pollution caused by smoking, dust, mites, mould spores, radon, and gases and chemicals from materials and appliances

indoor-outdoor *adj.* designed to be used inside or outside a building

indoors /ín dáwrz/ *adv.* into or inside a building [Late 18thC. Formed from INDOOR.]

Indo-Pacific /índō-/ *n.* a group of about 700 languages spoken in New Guinea and the surrounding islands. Three million people speak an Indo-Pacific language.

Indore /in dáwr/ **1.** former state, now part of Madhya Pradesh, central India **2.** city in western Madhya Pradesh, central India, situated 547 km/340 mi. northeast of Mumbai (Bombay). Population: 1,086,673 (1991).

indorse (**-dorses, -dorsing, -dorsed**) *vt.* = endorse

indoxyl /in dóksil/ *n.* a crystalline compound found in plants and animals that, when oxidized, is a source of indigo dye. Formula: C_8H_7NO. [Late 19thC. Coined from IND- + OXY- + -YL.]

Indra /índrə/ *n.* in Vedic mythology, a powerful warrior god and the ruler of the sky and weather. He became a subordinate god in later Hindu mythology.

indraught /ín draaft/ *n.* an inward flow or current of air

indrawn /ín dráwn/ *adj.* **1.** DRAWN IN drawn in or pulled in **2.** UNRESPONSIVE unresponsive or extremely reserved

indri /índri/, **indris** /índriss/ (*plural* **-dris**) *n.* a large rare black-and-white lemur of Madagascar, with large eyes, silky fur, and a rudimentary tail. Latin name: *Indri indri*. [Mid-19thC. From Malagasy *indry!* 'look!' or *indry izy!* 'there he is!', wrongly taken to be the name of the animal, which in Malagasy is *babakoto*.]

indubitable /in dyoobitəb'l/ *adj.* obvious or definitely true, and not to be doubted (*formal*) [Early 17thC. Directly or via French from Latin *indubitabilis* 'not doubtful', ultimately from *dubitare* 'to doubt' (source of English *doubt*).] —**indubitability** /in dyoobitə bílləti/ *n.* —**indubitably** /in dyoobitəbli/ *adv.*

induc. *abbr.* induction

induce /in dyo͞oss/ (**-duces, -ducing, -duced**) *v.* **1.** *vt.* **PERSUADE TO DO STH** to persuade or influence sb to do or think sth **2.** *vt.* PSYCHOL **PRODUCE MENTAL OR PHYSICAL STATE** to cause or bring about a thought, feeling, or physical condition **3.** *vti.* OBSTET **HASTEN BIRTH OF BABY** to make the process of labour or the birth of a baby start by a medical intervention, usually by administering a drug, before it happens naturally **4.** *vt.* LOGIC **REASON FROM OBSERVATION** to make a statement based on the observation of facts **5.** *vt.* PHYS **PRODUCE BY INDUCTION** to produce an electric current or a magnetic field by induction [14thC. From Latin *inducere* 'to lead into, persuade', from *ducere* 'to lead'.]

induced drag *n.* the drag force created by the lift of an aircraft

inducement /in dyo͞oss mənt/ *n.* **1. STIMULUS OR INCENTIVE** sth that gives sb a reason to do sth, especially sth that is offered as an incentive **2. INDUCING ACTION** the act of inducing sth

WORD KEY: SYNONYMS

See Synonyms at ***motive***.

induct /in dúkt/ (**-ducts, -ducting, -ducted**) *vt.* **1. FORMALLY ADMIT TO OFFICE** to install sb formally in a position or office **2. INTRODUCE NEW IDEAS TO** to introduce sb to new beliefs, knowledge, or ideas **3.** *US* **ENLIST FOR MILITARY SERVICE** to formally enlist sb for service in the military **4.** = **induce** *v.* 5 [14thC. From Latin *inductus*, past participle of *inducere* 'to lead into' (see INDUCE).]

inductance /in dúktənss/ *n.* **1. PROPERTY OF ELECTRIC CIRCUIT** the property of an electric circuit or device whereby an electromotive force is created by a change of current in it or in a circuit near it. Symbol **L** **2.** = **inductor** *n.* 2

inductile /in dúktīl/ *adj.* not pliable or yielding [Mid-18thC. Formed from IN- + DUCTILE.] —**inductility** /índuk tíllәti/ *n.*

induction /in dúksh'n/ *n.* **1. PROCESS OF INDUCING STH** the process of inducing a state, feeling, or idea **2.** OBSTET **PROCESS OF HASTENING BABY'S BIRTH** the act or the process of medically hastening, or inducing, the birth of a baby **3. ACT OF INDUCTING SB** the act or process of inducting sb into a position or an organization **4.** LOGIC **CONCLUSION BASED ON EVIDENCE** a generalization based on observed instances, or the making of such generalizations, in the usual working method of scientists **5.** PHYS **CREATION OF ELECTRIC OR MAGNETIC FORCES** the process by which electric or magnetic forces are created in a circuit by being in proximity to an electric or magnetic field or a varying current without physical contact **6.** *US* MIL **ACT OF ENLISTING SB** the act of formally enlisting sb into military service **7.** EMBRYOL **PROCESS IN DEVELOPMENT OF EMBRYO** the process by which one part of an embryo affects the development of another, e.g. through the diffusion of hormones **8.** CHEM **SYNTHESIS OF ENZYME** the process by which the production of an enzyme is stimulated by the increased concentration of the substance it acts on **9.** MATH **PROCESS OF MATHEMATICAL PROOF** a process for proving propositions with variables limited to positive integers by showing that the smallest instance is true and each following instance is derived from the one before —**inductional** *adj.*

induction coil *n.* a transformer that produces an intermittent high-voltage current from a low-voltage direct current by means of several wire windings and, often, a soft iron core

induction hardening *n.* a process by which the outer surface of a metal is hardened by rapid heating and cooling

induction heating *n.* a process for raising the temperature of a metal by inducing an electric current within it

induction motor *n.* an alternating-current electric motor powered by the interaction of a varying magnetic field in its windings with the current induced in the rotor

inductive /in dúktiv/ *adj.* **1.** PHYS **OF ELECTRIC OR MAGNETIC INDUCTION** involving, operating by, or caused by electric or magnetic induction **2.** PSYCHOL **PRODUCING MENTAL OR PHYSICAL STATE** relating to the process of inducing a feeling, idea, or state **3.** LOGIC **REACHING A CONCLUSION BASED ON OBSERVATION** generalizing to produce a universal claim or principle from observed instances **4.** BIOL **AFFECTING ANOTHER EMBRYONIC PART** producing an effect on another embryonic part by induction —**inductively** *adv.* —**inductiveness** *n.*

inductor /in dúktər/ *n.* **1. AGENT OF INDUCTION** sb or sth that inducts **2. PART OF CIRCUIT GENERATING FORCE** a part of an electric circuit, usually a coil, in which an electromotive force is generated by inductance **3. COMPONENT CAUSING INDUCTANCE** an electrical or electronic component designed to cause or work on inductance

indue (**-dues, -duing, -dued**) *vt.* = **endue**

indulge /in dúlj/ (**-dulges, -dulging, -dulged**) *v.* **1.** *vti.* **HAVE OR PERMIT A TREAT** to allow sb or yourself to have or do sth enjoyable **2.** *vi.* **DRINK ALCOHOL** to permit yourself to drink alcohol, especially to excess (*dated informal*) **3.** *vt.* BUSINESS **GIVE DEBTOR TIME TO PAY** to allow a debtor time to pay a bill [Early 17thC. From Latin *indulgere* 'to allow space or time for, give rein to', of unknown origin.] —**indulger** *n.*

indulged /in dúljd/ *adj.* pampered, spoiled, or catered to

indulgence /in dúljənss/ *n.* **1. YIELDING TO SB'S WISH** the gratification of or yielding to a wish **2. STH ALLOWED AS LUXURY** sth that sb lets himself or herself or sb else have, especially a luxury **3. TOLERANT ATTITUDE** a kind or tolerant attitude towards sb **4.** CHR **REMISSION OF PUNISHMENT FOR SIN** in Roman Catholicism, a grant by the pope of partial remission of time to be spent in purgatory or of some other consequence of a sin. In the Middle Ages, a practice of selling indulgences grew up. **5.** BUSINESS **TIME FOR REPAYMENT** time given to a debtor to repay a bill

indulgent /in dúljənt/ *adj.* permissive, tolerant, or humouring sb's wishes —**indulgently** *adv.*

induline /índyo͝o līn/, **indulin** /índyoo līn/ *n.* any one of a large group of blue dyes resembling indigo [Late 19thC. Coined from INDO- + -ULE + -INE.]

indult /in dúlt/ *n.* CHR a dispensation from the pope that allows a special exception to Roman Catholic church law [15thC. Via French from late Latin *indultum* 'grant, concession', from *indultus*, past participle of *indulgere* 'to indulge' (see INDULGE).]

indumentum /índyo͝o méntəm/ (*plural* **-ta** /-tə/ *or* **-tums**), **indument** /índyo͝omənt/ *n.* a covering of hairs on a plant, or of hair, fur, or feathers on an animal [Mid-19thC. From Latin *indumentum* 'garment', from *induere* 'to put on'.]

induna /in do͞onə/ *n.* *S Africa* a Black advisor or overseer, such as a counsellor of a tribal chief or a supervisor in a mine, factory, or farm [Mid-19thC. From Zulu.]

induplicate /in dyo͞oplikət, -kayt/ *adj.* used to describe a bud or leaf that has its edges bent or folded inwards, so as to touch but not overlap [Early 19thC. Coined from IN- + DUPLICATE.] —**induplication** /in dyo͞opli káysh'n/ *n.*

indurate *vti.* /índyo͝o rayt/ (**-rates, -rating, -rated**) **MAKE OR BECOME HARD** to make sth hard or to become hard (*literary or technical*) ■ *adj.* /índyoo rət/ **FEELING NO COMPASSION** unsympathetic or unfeeling (*literary*) [Mid-16thC. From Latin *indurat-*, past participle stem of *indurare* 'to make hard', from *durus* 'hard'.] —**indurative** /in dyo͞orə tiv/ *adj.*

induration /índyo͝o ráysh'n/ *n.* **1. HARDENING** the process of hardening sth or of becoming hard (*literary or technical*) **2.** GEOL **HARDENING OF GEOLOGICAL SEDIMENT** the process by which a soft geological sediment becomes hard **3.** MED **HARDNESS IN BODY TISSUE** a hardness in body tissue, especially a tumour

Indus[1] /índəss/ river in Asia. It rises in western Tibet and flows northwest across Jammu and Kashmir and then southwest through Pakistan to the Arabian Sea. Length: 2,900 km/1,800 mi.

Indus[2] *n.* a faint constellation visible in the Southern Hemisphere

indus. *abbr.* **1.** industrial **2.** industry

indusium /in dyo͞ozi əm/ (*plural* **-a** /-zi ə/) *n.* **1.** BOT **PROTECTIVE COVERING** a membrane on the underside of a fern leaf that protects developing spores **2.** BIOL **PROTECTING AND COVERING MEMBRANE** an enveloping protective membrane [Early 18thC. From Latin, 'tunic', from *induere* 'to put on (a garment)'.] —**indusial** *adj.*

industrial /in dústri əl/ *adj.* **1. OF INDUSTRY** relating to, used in, or created by industry **2. WITH MANY DEVELOPED INDUSTRIES** having a large quantity of highly developed industries **3. OF INDUSTRY'S WORKFORCE** relating to or involving workers in industry ■ **industrials** *npl.* **SHARES IN INDUSTRIAL COMPANIES** the shares and interest-bearing securities of industrial companies —**industrially** *adv.*

industrial accident *n.* an accident, often causing serious injury, that is job-related in that it usually happens on a work site, e.g. a factory floor or a construction site

industrial action *n.* any protest action, e.g. as a strike, undertaken by employees against working conditions, layoffs, or other grievances. US term **job action**

industrial archaeology *n.* the study of sites, buildings, and equipment used by industries in the past

industrial award *n.* a judgment made by an Australian Industrial Commission or a similar body in settlement of a dispute between employees and employers

industrial democracy *n.* the partial or complete management of an industrial workplace by those employed in it

industrial design *n.* the art of designing the shape, size, or appearance of manufactured objects

industrial development certificate *n.* a document issued by the Department of the Environment that must accompany an application made to a local authority for permission to build or extend a factory

industrial disease *n.* a disease affecting people as a result of the work they do

industrial engineering *n.* the study and practice of designing industrial operations

industrial espionage *n.* the secret removal, copying, or recording of confidential or valuable information in a company for use by a rival concern or a competitor

industrial estate *n.* a large area of land, usually on the edge of a town, where factories and businesses are concentrated in accordance with local planning regulations. US term **industrial park**

industrialisation *n.* = **industrialization**

industrialise *vti.* = **industrialize**

industrialism /in dústri əlizəm/ *n.* the organization of an economy or a society around extensive manufacturing, rather than around agriculture, the production of handicrafts, or commerce

industrialist /in dústri əlist/ *n.* sb who owns or controls an industrial concern, or has a major share in one

industrialization /in dústri əlī záysh'n/, **industrialisation** *n.* the adoption of industrial methods of production and manufacturing by a country or group, with all the associated changes in lifestyle, transport, and other aspects of society

industrialize /in dústri ə līz/ (**-izes, -izing, -ized**), **industrialise** (**-ises, -ising, -ised**) *vti.* to adapt a country or group to industrial methods of production and manufacturing, across a wide area, with all the accompanying social changes, or to be adapted in this way

industrial medicine *n.* a branch of medicine that specializes in the prevention or treatment of diseases, stresses, or hazards in the workplace

industrial melanism *n.* the increase in the numbers of animals, especially moths, with dark coloration in places where industries create a lot of black smoke and predators more easily feed on lighter individuals

industrial misconduct *n.* irregular or negligent conduct by an employee in a workplace, which may result in a penalty

industrial park *n.* *Aus, US* = **industrial estate**

industrial psychology *n.* the study of human behaviour and attitudes in the workplace —**industrial psychologist** *n.*

industrial relations *npl.* **1. LINKS BETWEEN WORKERS AND MANAGERS** the relationship between management and employees in an industrial company **2. RELATIONS BETWEEN ORGANIZED MANAGEMENT AND LABOUR** the relations and procedures between employers' organizations and trade unions that are institutionalized in an industrial society

Industrial Revolution n. the social and economic changes in Great Britain, Europe, and the United States that began in the second half of the 18th century and involved widespread adoption of industrial methods of production. The specialization of tasks, the concentration of capital, and the centralization of workforces were important aspects of these changes, which first affected Great Britain.

industrial sociology n. the study of relationships and structures in industrial organizations

industrial-strength adj. used to describe materials or chemicals that are strong or of a quality suitable for use in industry

industrial tribunal n. a court that rules on disputes between employees and management

industrial union n. a trade union made up of workers with different occupations who are all employed in one industry

Industrial Workers of the World n. an international trade union with socialist aims that was founded in the United States in 1905 and lost influence after the 1920s

industrious /in dústri əss/ adj. hard-working, conscientious, and energetic —**industriously** adv. —**industriousness** n.

industry /índəstri/ (plural -**tries**) n. **1. LARGE-SCALE PRODUCTION** organized economic activity connected with the production, manufacture, or construction of a particular product or range of products **2. WIDESPREAD ACTIVITY** an activity that many people are involved in, especially one that has become excessively commercialized or standardized ○ *the heritage industry* **3. HARD WORK** diligent hard work (*formal or literary*) ○ *a hive of industry* [15thC. Directly or via Old French *industrie* from Latin *industria* 'diligence', from *industrius* 'diligent', literally 'building in', from assumed *-struus* 'building'.]

industry-wide adj. cutting across an entire field of commercial activity

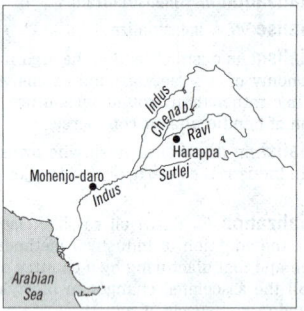

Indus Valley Civilization: Map of the Indus River Valley

Indus Valley Civilization n. a Bronze-Age civilization that flourished in the lower Indus River Valley, mainly in present-day Pakistan and northern India, from about 2500 to 1700 BC. It was the earliest known civilization in South Asia and, with Mesopotamia and Egypt, one of the earliest anywhere in the world.

indwell /in dwél/ (-**dwells**, -**dwelling**, -**dwelled** or -**dwelt**, -**dwelled** or -**dwelt** /in dwélt/) vti. to inhabit, infuse, or abide within a person, community, or place (*literary*) [14thC. Formed from IN- + DWELL.] —**indweller** n.

-ine suffix. of, relating to, made of ○ *crystalline* ○ *murrhine* (Directly or via Old French from Latin *-inus* and, ultimately, Greek *-inos*]

inebriant /i neébri ənt/ n. CAUSE OF DRUNKENNESS sth that causes drunkenness or intoxication ■ adj. **INTOXICATING** capable of making sb drunk or intoxicated in some other way (*archaic or literary*) [Early 19thC. Formed from INEBRIATE, on the model of INTOXICANT.]

inebriate /i neé bri ayt/ vt. (-**ates**, -**ating**, -**ated**) **1. MAKE INTOXICATED** to cause sb to become drunk or in-

toxicated **2. EXCITE** to make sb excited or exhilarated (*formal*) ■ n. **INTOXICATED PERSON** sb who is drunk or intoxicated (*archaic or literary*) ■ adj. **INTOXICATED** drunk or intoxicated (*archaic or literary*) [15thC. From Latin *inebriatus*, past participle of *inebriare*, literally 'to make drunk in', from *ebriare* 'to make drunk', from *ebrius* 'drunk'.] —**inebriation** /i neé bri áysh'n/ n. —**inebriety** /ínni brí əti/ n.

inebriated /i neébri aytid/ adj. drunk or intoxicated (*formal*)

inedible /in éddəb'l/ adj. unfit for consumption as food —**inedibility** /in éddə bílləti/ n. —**inedibly** /in éddəbli/ adv.

—— **WORD KEY: USAGE** ——
See Usage note at *eatable*.

inedited /in éddit id/ adj. not having been edited or published [Mid-18thC. Formed from IN- + EDIT + -ED.]

ineducable /in éddyōōkəb'l/ adj. impossible to educate (*archaic*) —**ineducability** /in éddyōōkə bílləti/ n.

ineffable /in éffəb'l/ adj. incapable of being expressed in words (*formal*) [15thC. Directly or via French from Latin *ineffabilis* 'unutterable', from, ultimately, *effari* 'to speak out', from *fari* 'to speak' (source of English *fable*).] —**ineffability** /in éffə bílləti/ n. —**ineffableness** /in éffəb'lnəss/ n. —**ineffably** /in éffəbli/ adv.

ineffaceable /ínni fáyssəb'l/ adj. incapable of being erased or removed (*formal*) —**ineffaceability** /ínni fáyssə bílləti/ n. —**ineffaceably** /ínni fáyssəbli/ adv.

ineffective /ínni féktiv/ adj. **1. NOT PRODUCING DESIRED RESULT** not producing the desired result or effect **2. LACKING COMPETENCE** incompetent or inept —**ineffectively** adv. —**ineffectiveness** n.

ineffectual /ínni fékchoo əl/ adj. **1. INCOMPETENT OR INDECISIVE** not competent, decisive, or authoritative enough to achieve desired aims **2. INCAPABLE OF GENERATING DESIRED OUTCOME** not able to produce a satisfactory outcome —**ineffectuality** /ínni fékchooálla ti/ n. —**ineffectually** /ínni fékchoo əli/ adv. —**ineffectualness** /ínni fékchoo əlnəss/ n.

inefficacious /in efi káyshəss/ adj. not having a positive or useful effect (*formal*) —**inefficaciously** adv. —**inefficaciousness** n. —**inefficacity** /-kássəti/ n. —**inefficacy** /in éffikəssi/ n.

inefficient /ínni físh'nt/ adj. performing tasks in a way that is not organized or fails to make the best use of sth, especially time —**inefficiency** (plural -**cies**) n.

inelastic /ínni lástik/ adj. **1. NOT STRETCHY** unable to return quickly to its original shape and size after being bent, stretched, or squashed **2. NOT EASILY CHANGED** unable to incorporate changes or adapt to new circumstances easily **3. PHYS NOT AFFECTING TRANSLATIONAL KINETIC ENERGY** used to describe a collision that does not lead to an overall loss of translational kinetic energy **4. ECON INSENSITIVE TO PRICE CHANGES** used to describe supply or demand that is not affected by fluctuations in price

inelegant /in élligənt/ adj. **1. UNSTYLISH** lacking grace, sophistication and good taste in appearance or behaviour **2. LACKING PRECISION** unnecessarily complicated or long —**inelegance** n.

ineligible /in éllijəb'l/ adj. not legally entitled or qualified to do, be, or get sth —**ineligibility** n.

ineluctable /ínni lúktəb'l/ adj. unable to be escaped from or avoided (*literary*) [Early 17thC. From Latin *ineluctabilis*, from in'not' + *eluctari*'struggle out of'.] —**ineluctability** /-lúktə bílləti/ n. —**ineluctably** /-lúktəbli/ adv.

inept /i népt/ adj. **1. UNABLE TO HANDLE JOB** lacking competence or skill for a particular task **2. TOTALLY INAPPROPRIATE** not in keeping with what is right or proper for the circumstances [Mid-16thC. From Latin *ineptus*, literally 'not suitable', from *aptus* (see APT).] —**ineptitude** /i népti tyood/ n. —**ineptly** adv. —**ineptness** n.

inequable /in ékwəb'l/ adj. not fair or uniform [Early 18thC. From Latin *inaequabilis*, from *aequabilis* 'equable' (see EQUABLE).]

inequality /ínni kwólləti/ (plural -**ties**) n. **1. DIFFERENCE IN STATUS** social or economic disparity between people

or groups **2. LACK OF EQUAL TREATMENT** unequal opportunity or treatment based on social or economic disparity **3. STATE OF BEING UNEQUAL** the condition or an instance of not being equal **4. UNEVENNESS ON SURFACE** variability or unevenness in the surface of sth **5. MATH STATEMENT INDICATING UNEQUAL QUANTITIES** a mathematical statement indicating that two quantities are not equal, represented by the symbols <, >, and ≠, meaning less than, greater than, and not equal to. An unconditional inequality is one that is true for all values of a variable, while a conditional inequality is false for some values of a variable. [15thC. From Old French *inequalité*, from, ultimately, Latin *aequalis* (see EQUAL).]

inequitable /in ékwitəb'l/ adj. showing bias or favouritism (*formal*) —**inequitableness** n. —**inequitably** adv.

inequity /in ékwəti/ (plural -**ties**) n. **1. UNFAIR TREATMENT** lack of fairness or justice (*formal*) **2. UNFAIR SITUATION OR ACTION** a situation or action that is not fair

ineradicable /ínni ráddikəb'l/ adj. impossible to get rid of —**ineradicability** /ínni ráddikə bílləti/ n. —**ineradicableness** /ínni ráddikəb'lnəss/ n. —**ineradicably** /-bli/ adv.

inerrant /in érrənt/ adj. **1. INCAPABLE OF MISTAKES** incapable of making a mistake (*literary*) **2. CORRECT** containing no mistakes [Mid-17thC. From the Latin stem *inerrant-*, literally 'not wandering', from *errare* (see ERR).] —**inerrancy** n.

inert /i núrt/ adj. **1. MOTIONLESS** not moving or able to move **2. CHEM NONREACTIVE** not readily changed by chemical or biological reaction **3. SLUGGISH OR UNMOTIVATED** lacking in energy or motivation [Mid-17thC. From Latin *inert-*, the stem of *iners*, literally 'having no skill', from *ars* 'skill, art'. The underlying meaning is 'useless, ineffective'.] —**inertly** adv. —**inertness** n.

inert gas n. = **noble gas**

inertia /i núrshə/ n. **1. APATHY** inability or unwillingness to move or act **2. PHYS RESISTANCE TO CHANGE** the property of a body by which it remains at rest or continues moving in a straight line unless acted upon by a directional force [Early 18thC. From Latin, 'lack of skill, inactivity', formed from *iners* (see INERT).] —**inertial** adj. —**inertially** adv.

inertial confinement fusion n. NUCLEAR PHYS nuclear fusion achieved by firing high-energy lasers or particle beams at small pellets, typically containing deuterium and sometimes also tritium

inertial force n. a hypothetical force postulated by an observer who is being accelerated in order to analyse motion using Newton's laws

inertial guidance, **inertial navigation** n. navigation by conversion of the accelerations experienced into distances and directions. It is used on aircraft, spacecraft, or missiles that use devices such as gyroscopes, accelerometers, and computers to calculate and adjust course.

inertia selling n. the practice of sending unsolicited goods to people's homes and demanding payment if the goods are not returned [From the idea that people will usually pay for the items rather than go to the trouble of returning them]

inescapable /ínni skáypəb'l/ adj. impossible to avoid —**inescapably** adv.

in esse /-éssi/ adj. having actual existence as opposed to potential existence [From Latin, literally 'in existence']

inessential /ínni sénsh'l/ adj. **1. NOT ESSENTIAL** not absolutely necessary **2. WITHOUT ESSENCE** without substance or being ■ n. STH INESSENTIAL sth that is unnecessary —**inessentiality** /ínni sénshi álləti/ n.

inessive /in éssiv/ n. in the grammar of languages such as Finnish, a case of nouns and pronouns used to indicate the location of sth [Late 19thC. Formed from Latin *inesse* 'to be in or at', from *esse* 'to be'.]

inestimable /in éstiməb'l/ adj. **1. INCALCULABLE** too great to calculate its extent, magnitude, or amount **2. INVALUABLE** of such great worth that a value cannot be placed upon it [14thC. Via French from Latin *inaestimabilis*, literally 'not calculable', from *aestimare* (see ESTIMATE).] —**inestimability** /in éstimə bílləti/ n. —**inestimableness** /in éstimab'lnəss/ n. —**inestimably** /in éstimabli/ adv.

inevitable /in évvitəb'l/ *adj.* UNAVOIDABLE impossible to avoid or to prevent from happening ■ *n.* STH CERTAIN sth that is certain to happen [15thC. From Latin *inevitabilis*, literally 'not avoidable', from *evitare* 'to shun'.] —**inevitability** /in évvitə bílləti/ *n.* —**inevitableness** *n.* —**inevitably** /-bli/ *adv.*

inexact /ínnig zákt/ *adj.* **1.** NOT FULLY ACCURATE not entirely accurate **2.** SLAPDASH not thorough or careful —**inexactitude** /ínnig zákti tyood/ *n.* —**inexactly** *adv.* —**inexactness** *n.*

inexcusable /ínnik skyóozəb'l/ *adj.* impossible to pardon or justify [15thC. From Latin *inexcusabilis*, literally 'not excusable', from *excusare* (see EXCUSE).] —**inexcusability** /ínnik skyóozə bílləti/ *n.* —**inexcusableness** /ínnik skyóozəb'lnəss/ *n.* —**inexcusably** /-bli/ *adv.*

inexhaustible /ínnig záwstəb'l/ *adj.* **1.** EVERLASTING impossible to use up **2.** NOT GETTING TIRED showing no sign of tiring —**inexhaustibility** /ínnig záwstə bílləti/ *n.* —**inexhaustibleness** /ínnig záwstəb'lnəss/ *n.* —**inexhaustibly** /-bli/ *adv.*

inexistent /ínnig zístənt/ *adj.* not in existence [Mid-16thC. Via the late Latin stem *inexistent-* from, ultimately, Latin *existere* (see EXIST).]

inexorable /in éksərəb'l/ *adj.* **1.** UNSTOPPABLE impossible to stop (*formal*) **2.** ADAMANT AND PITILESS not moved by anyone's attempts to plead or persuade [Mid-16thC. Via French from, ultimately, Latin *exorare* 'to prevail upon', from *orare* 'to pray' (see ORATION).] —**inexorability** /in éksərə bílləti/ *n.* —**inexorableness** /in éksərəb'lnəss/ *n.* —**inexorably** /-bli/ *adv.*

inexpedient /ínnik spéedi ənt/ *adj.* not recommended or prudent (*formal*) —**inexpedience** *n.* —**inexpediently** *adv.*

inexpensive /ínnik spénssiv/ *adj.* not costing much money —**inexpensively** *adv.* —**inexpensiveness** *n.*

inexperience /ínnik spéeri ənss/ *n.* **1.** LACK OF EXPERIENCE the lack of skills or knowledge that people learn over a period of time **2.** LACK OF SOPHISTICATION lack of sophistication about worldly ways [Late 16thC. Via French from late Latin *inexperientia*, literally 'lack of experience', from Latin *experientia* (see EXPERIENCE).] —**inexperienced** *adj.*

inexpert /in ékspurt/ *adj.* lacking in skill or experience [15thC. Via Old French from Latin *inexpertus*, literally 'not experienced', from *expertus*, the past participle of *experiri* (see EXPERIENCE).] —**inexpertly** *adv.* —**inexpertness** *n.*

inexpiable /in ékspi əb'l/ *adj.* so bad that it cannot be atoned for [15thC. From Latin *inexpiabilis* 'that cannot be atoned for', from *expiare* (see EXPIATE).] —**inexpiableness** *n.* —**inexpiably** *adv.*

inexplicable /ínnik splíkəb'l, in éksplikəb'l/ *adj.* incapable of being explained or justified [15thC. Directly or via French from Latin *inexplicabilis*, from *explicare* (see EXPLICATE).] —**inexplicability** /ínnik splíkə bílləti, in éksplikə-/ *n.* —**inexplicableness** /ínnik splíkəb'lnəss, in éksplikə-/ *n.* —**inexplicably** /ínnik splíkəbli, in éksplik-/ *adv.*

inexplicit /ínnik splíssit/ *adj.* not expressed or shown fully, openly, and unambiguously

inexpressible /ínnik spréssəb'l/ *adj.* impossible to put into words —**inexpressibility** /ínnik spréssə bílləti/ *n.* —**inexpressibleness** /ínnik spréssəb'lnəss/ *n.* —**inexpressibly** /ínnik spréssəbli/ *adv.*

inexpressive /ínnik spréssiv/ *adj.* conveying no feeling —**inexpressively** *adv.* —**inexpressiveness** *n.*

inexpugnable /ínnik spúgnəb'l/ *adj.* **1.** IMPREGNABLE impossible to take by force **2.** UNBEATABLE impossible to overcome [15thC. Via French from Latin *inexpugnabilis*, from *expugnare*, literally 'to fight off', from pugnare 'to fight'.] —**inexpugnability** /ínnik spúgnə bílləti/ *n.* —**inexpugnableness** /ínnik spúgnəb'lnəss/ *n.* —**inexpugnably** /-bli/ *adv.*

inexpungible /ínnik spúnjəb'l/ *adj.* impossible to remove or cancel out

inextensible /ínnik sténssəb'l/ *adj.* impossible to stretch to a greater length —**inextensibility** /ínnik sténssə bílləti/ *n.*

in extenso /in ik sténssō/ *adv.* at its full length ○ *quote a passage in extenso* [From Latin, literally 'at a stretch']

inextinguishable /ínnik stíng gwishəb'l/ *adj.* impossible to extinguish or suppress —**inextinguishableness** *n.* —**inextinguishably** *adv.*

inextirpable /ínnik stúrpəb'l/ *adj.* impossible to remove or destroy (*literary*) [Early 17thC. From Latin *inex(s)tirpabilis*, from *ex(s)tirpare* (see EXTIRPATE).] —**inextirpableness** *n.*

in extremis /in ik streémiss/ *adv.* IN DESPERATE CIRCUMSTANCES in desperate circumstances, especially at the point of death ■ *adj.* NEAR DEATH on the point of death [From Latin, literally 'in the extremes']

inextricable /ínnik stríkəb'l, in ékstrikəb'l/ *adj.* **1.** IMPOSSIBLE TO ESCAPE FROM impossible to get free from **2.** IMPOSSIBLE TO DISENTANGLE impossible to unentangle or undo **3.** HOPELESSLY COMPLEX hopelessly involved or complex [Mid-16thC. From Latin *inextricabilis* 'that cannot be disentangled', from *extricare* (see EXTRICATE).] —**inextricability** /ínnik stríkə bílləti, in ékstrikə-/ *n.* —**inextricableness** /ínnik stríkəb'lnəss, in ékstrikəb'l-nəss/ *n.* —**inextricably** /ínnik stríkəbli, in ékstrikəbli/ *adv.*

INF *n., abbr.* intermediate-range nuclear forces

inf. *abbr.* **1.** infantry **2.** inferior **3.** GRAM infinitive **4.** infinity **5.** informal **6.** information **7.** infra

Inf. *abbr.* infantry

infallible /in fálləb'l/ *adj.* **1.** NOT ERRING incapable of making a mistake **2.** INCAPABLE OF FAILING certain not to fail **3.** RELIG UNERRING IN DOCTRINE incapable of being mistaken in matters of doctrine and dogma [15thC. From medieval Latin *infallibilis*, from Latin *fallere* 'to deceive, disappoint' (source of English *fail*).] —**infallibility** /in fállə bílləti/ *n.* —**infallibleness** /in fálləb'lnəss/ *n.* —**infallibly** /-bli/ *adv.*

infamous /ínfəməss/ *adj.* **1.** NOTORIOUS having an extremely bad reputation **2.** ABOMINABLE so bad as to earn sb an extremely bad reputation [14thC. From medieval Latin *infamosus*, a variant of Latin *infamis* 'of ill repute', literally 'having no fame', from *fama* (see FAME).] —**infamously** *adv.*

infamy /ínfəmi/ (*plural* **-mies**) *n.* **1.** NOTORIETY the disgrace to sb's reputation caused by an infamous act or behaviour **2.** SHAMEFUL OR CRIMINAL CONDUCT shameful or criminal conduct or character **3.** EVIL DEED a publicly known infamous act or event [15thC. From French *infamie*, from, ultimately, Latin *infamis* (see INFAMOUS).]

infancy /ínfənssi/ *n.* **1.** BABYHOOD the condition or time of childhood before a baby walks or talks **2.** BEGINNING an early stage of development for an idea, project, or enterprise **3.** LAW TIME OF BEING MINOR the condition or time in which a young person is not legally considered an adult

infant /ínfənt/ *n.* **1.** BABY a very young child that can neither walk nor talk **2.** EDUC YOUNG SCHOOLCHILD a schoolchild between the ages of five and seven **3.** LAW LEGAL MINOR a young person legally considered a minor ■ **infants** *npl.* EDUC INFANT DEPARTMENT OF SCHOOL the infant department of a primary school (*informal*) ■ *adj.* JUST BEGINNING in an early stage of development [14thC. Via French *enfant* from, ultimately, Latin *infans*, literally 'not speaking', from *fari* 'to speak'.] —**infanthood** *n.*

infanta /in fántə/ (*plural* **-tas**) *n.* **1.** SPANISH OR PORTUGUESE PRINCESS in the past, the daughter of a Spanish or Portuguese king **2.** INFANTE'S WIFE the wife of an infante [Late 16thC. From Spanish and Portuguese, feminine of *infante* (see INFANTE).]

infante /in fánti/ (*plural* **-tes**) *n.* in the past, a son, other than the heir to the throne, of a Spanish or Portuguese king, especially the second son [Mid-16thC. Via Spanish and Portuguese from Latin *infans* 'child' (see INFANT).]

infanticide /in fánti sīd/ *n.* **1.** MURDER OF INFANT the killing of an infant **2.** KILLING OF BABIES the practice of killing newborn babies **3.** KILLER OF INFANT sb who kills an infant —**infanticidal** /in fánti sīd'l/ *adj.*

infantile /ínfən tīl/ *adj.* **1.** CHILDISH showing a lack of maturity **2.** RELATING TO INFANTS relating to infants or infancy **3.** GEOG IN FIRST STAGE OF EROSION in the earliest stage of erosion —**infantility** /ínfən tílləti/ *n.*

infantile paralysis *n.* poliomyelitis (*dated*)

infantilise *vt.* = **infantilize**

infantilism /in fántilizəm/ *n.* childish or immature behaviour

infantilize /in fánti līz/ (**-izes, -izing, -ized**), **infantilise** (**-ises, -ising, -ised**) *vt.* **1.** KEEP FROM MATURING to make sb infantile or to keep sb in an infantile state **2.** TREAT AS A BABY to treat sb as or consider sb to be infantile —**infantilization** /in fánti lī záysh'n/ *n.*

infant mortality rate *n.* the number of infant deaths during the first year of life per thousand live births

infantry /ínfəntri/ (*plural* **-tries**) *n.* the soldiers or a unit of soldiers who are trained to fight on foot [Late 16thC. From French *infanterie*, from, ultimately, Italian *infante* 'youth, foot soldier', from Latin *infans* (see INFANT).]

infantryman /ínfəntrimən/ (*plural* **-men** /-mən/) *n.* a soldier in the infantry

infant school *n.* a school, or part of a school, for children between the ages of four or five and seven

infarct /in fáarkt/ *n.* an area of tissue that has recently died as a result of the sudden loss of its blood supply, e.g. following blockage of an artery by a blood clot [Late 19thC. From modern Latin *infarctus*, from the past participle stem of Latin *infarcire*, literally 'to cram in', from *farcire* 'to stuff'.]

infarction /in fáarksh'n/ *n.* **1.** INFARCT FORMATION the formation of an infarct **2.** = **infarct**

infatuate /in fáttyoo ayt/ (**-ates, -ating, -ated**) *vt.* **1.** MAKE ENAMOURED to inspire a thoughtless or excessive passion in sb for another person or thing **2.** MAKE SB IRRATIONAL to make sb behave irrationally as a result of a great, often temporary passion for sb or sth [Mid-16thC. From Latin *infatuat-*, the past participle stem of *infatuare*, literally 'to make foolish', from *fatuus* 'foolish' (source of English *fatuous*).]

infatuated /in fáttyoo aytid/ *adj.* **1.** HOPELESSLY IN LOVE preoccupied with and foolishly in love with sb **2.** PASSIONATE ABOUT STH utterly captivated and obsessed by sth —**infatuatedly** *adv.*

infatuation /in fáttyoo áysh'n/ *n.* **1.** THOUGHTLESS PASSION a great, often temporary, and irrational passion for sb or sth **2.** OBJECT OF SB'S INFATUATION the person or object that sb is infatuated with

WORD KEY: SYNONYMS

See Synonyms at ***love***.

infauna /in fáwnə/ *npl.* organisms that live in tubes or burrows beneath the surface of the sea floor [Early 20thC. Coined from IN- + FAUNA.] —**infaunal** *adj.*

infeasible /in feézəb'l/ *adj.* not practical or easily achieved —**infeasibility** /in feézə bílləti/ *n.* —**infeasibleness** /in feézəb'lnəss/ *n.* —**infeasibly** /-bli/ *adv.*

infect /in fékt/ (**-fects, -fecting, -fected**) *vt.* **1.** MED CAUSE INFECTION IN to contaminate or cause infection in sb or sth with a disease-producing agent **2.** MED CAUSE COMMUNICABLE DISEASE IN to give sb a communicable disease **3.** ENTER PERSON OR ANIMAL to invade and live in the body of a person or animal (*refers to microorganisms or endoparasites*) **4.** AFFECT to corrupt or adversely affect sb or sth **5.** INFLUENCE SB'S FEELINGS to communicate an emotion such as enthusiasm or fear to sb **6.** COMPUT CONTAMINATE COMPUTER WITH VIRUS to copy to a computer system a computer virus that is capable of damaging the system's programs or data [14thC. From Latin *infect-*, the past participle stem of *inficere* 'to stain, dye', literally 'to dip in', from *facere* 'to do, put'.] —**infected** *adj.* —**infector** *n.*

infection /in féksh'n/ *n.* **1.** MED STATE OF BEING INFECTED the reproduction and proliferation of microorganisms within the body **2.** MED INFECTING OF OTHERS the transmission of infectious microorganisms from one person to another **3.** BIOL INFECTING MICROORGANISM an infecting microorganism or agent **4.** MED DISEASE a communicable disease **5.** MORAL CORRUPTION sth that corrupts sb morally **6.** TRANSMISSION OF FEELINGS the communication of emotions or attitudes between people

infectious /in fékshəss/ *adj.* **1.** MED COMMUNICABLE used to describe a disease that is capable of being passed from one person to another **2.** MED CAUSED BY BACTERIA caused by bacteria, viruses, or other microorganisms **3.** BIOL CAUSING INFECTION bringing about infection **4.** AFFECTING FEELINGS OF OTHERS capable of affecting the emotions and attitudes of others —**infectiously** adv. —**infectiousness** n.

infectious hepatitis n. = hepatitis A

infectious mononucleosis n. glandular fever (technical)

infective /in féktiv/ adj. **1.** CAPABLE OF INFECTING capable of producing an infection **2.** AFFECTING FEELINGS capable of affecting the emotions and attitudes of others —**infectiveness** n. —**infectivity** /ín fek tívvəti/ n.

infelicitous /ínfə líssitəss/ adj. inappropriate to the situation or purpose —**infelicitously** adv.

infelicity /ínfə líssəti/ (plural **-ties**) n. **1.** INAPPROPRIATENESS the inappropriateness of sth, especially an expression, to a particular situation **2.** STH INAPPROPRIATE sth inappropriate to a situation or purpose, especially an expression [Early 17thC. From Latin infelicitas 'unhappiness', from felix 'happy'. The underlying meaning is 'an unfortunate expression'.]

infer /in fúr/ (**-fers, -ferring, -ferred**) v. **1.** vti. CONCLUDE STH ON THE BASIS OF REASONING to conclude sth on the basis of evidence or reasoning **2.** vt. SUGGEST to suggest or lead to sth as a conclusion **3.** vt. IMPLY to imply or suggest sth [Early 16thC. From Latin inferre, literally 'to bring in', from ferre 'to carry'.] —**inferable** adj. —**inferably** adv. —**inferrer** n.

—————— **WORD KEY: SYNONYMS** ——————
See Synonyms at **deduce**.

inference /ínfərənss/ n. **1.** CONCLUSION a conclusion drawn from evidence or reasoning **2.** LOGIC REASONING PROCESS the process of reasoning from a premise to a conclusion **3.** IMPLICATION sth that is implied [Late 16thC. From medieval Latin inferentia, from Latin inferre (see INFER).] —**inferential** /ínfə rénsh'l/ adj. —**inferentially** /-rénsh'li/ adv.

inferior /in féeri ər/ adj. **1.** LOWER IN STANDING lower or low in rank, standing, or degree **2.** NOT AS GOOD lower in quality or value **3.** MEDIOCRE failing to meet a standard of quality, ability, or achievement **4.** ANAT LOWER IN BODY used to describe a body part or organ situated beneath another similar part **5.** BOT BELOW A CALYX used to describe a plant ovary located below a calyx **6.** ASTRON BETWEEN EARTH AND SUN orbiting or taking place between the Earth and the Sun. Mercury and Venus are designated as inferior planets. **7.** PRINTING PRINTED BELOW THE LINE written or printed at a slightly lower level than the rest of the characters in a line, e.g. the '2' in 'CO₂' ■ n. **1.** LOWER RANKING PERSON sb of lower status, rank, or quality **2.** PRINTING SUBSCRIPT CHARACTER a character printed or written below the line [15thC. From Latin, 'lower', from inferus 'below'. Ultimately from an Indo-European word meaning 'beneath' that is also the ancestor of English under and infernal.] —**inferiority** /in féeri órrəti/ n. —**inferiorly** /in féeri ərli/ adv.

inferiority complex n. an overdeveloped sense of being inferior to others. In extreme cases it can manifest itself in either withdrawn or aggressive social behaviour.

infernal /in fúrn'l/ adj. **1.** RELATING TO UNDERWORLD relating to hell or the underworld **2.** DIABOLICAL IN NATURE so wicked or cruel as to be worthy of hell **3.** VERY ANNOYING extremely annoying or unpleasant (informal) [14thC. From Old French, from, ultimately, Latin infernus 'lower, the underworld'. Ultimately from an Indo-European word meaning 'beneath' that is also the ancestor of English under and inferior.] —**infernally** adv.

inferno /in fúrnō/ (plural **-nos**) n. **1.** CONFLAGRATION a fire or a place that is burning fiercely **2.** HELLISH PLACE a place or situation that is reminiscent of hell [Mid-19thC. Via Italian, 'hell', from late Latin infernus (see INFERNAL).]

—————— **WORD KEY: SYNONYMS** ——————
See Synonyms at **fire**.

infertile /in fúr tīl/ adj. **1.** STERILE physically incapable of conceiving offspring **2.** NOT PRODUCING CROPS incapable of producing crops **3.** NOT FERTILIZED used to describe an egg that has not been fertilized [Late 16thC. Directly or via French from late Latin infertilis, literally 'not bearing', from fertilis (see FERTILE).] —**infertilely** adv. —**infertility** /ínfər tílləti/ n.

infest /in fést/ (**-fests, -festing, -fested**) vt. **1.** TAKE OVER PLACE to overrun a place in large numbers and become threatening, harmful, or unpleasant **2.** LIVE AS A PARASITE ON to live as a parasite on or in sth [Mid-16thC. Directly or via French infester from Latin infestare 'to attack', from infestus 'hostile'.] —**infestation** /ín fe stáysh'n/ n. —**infested** /in féstid/ adj. —**infester** n.

infibulate /in fíbbyoō layt/ (**-lates, -lating, -lated**) vt. to close the vagina partially by stitching it, or closing it with a clasp. The clitoris is often removed at the same time. ◊ **female circumcision** [Early 17thC. From Latin infibulat-, past participle stem of infibulare 'to fasten with a pin', from fibula (see FIBULA).] —**infibulation** /in fíbbyoō láysh'n/ n.

infidel /ínfid'l/ n. (disapproving) **1.** RELIG, HIST HEATHEN sb who has no belief in the religion of the speaker or writer, especially Christianity or Islam **2.** RELIG NONBELIEVER sb who has no religious beliefs [15thC. Directly or via French infidèle from Latin infidelis, literally 'unbelieving', from fidelis 'faithful', from fides (see FAITH).]

infidelity /ínfi délləti/ (plural **-ties**) n. **1.** UNFAITHFULNESS unfaithfulness or disloyalty, especially to a sexual partner **2.** UNFAITHFUL ACT an act of unfaithfulness or disloyalty, especially to a sexual partner **3.** DISBELIEF lack of religious faith (disapproving) [14thC. From French infidélité, from, ultimately, Latin infidelis (see INFIDEL).]

infield /ín feeld/ n. **1.** CRICKET NEAR WICKET IN CRICKET area of a cricket field that is close to the wickets **2.** BASEBALL DIAMOND the area of a baseball field bounded by home plate and the three bases **3.** BASEBALL PLAYERS IN INFIELD the defensive baseball players in the infield considered together. They are the first, second, and third basemen and the shortstop. **4.** HORSERACING AREA WITHIN A RACETRACK the area bounded by a racetrack **5.** AGRIC, HIST FARMLAND CLOSE TO A FARMHOUSE the farmland close to a farmhouse that is regularly manured and cropped

infielder /ín feeldər/ n. a defensive baseball player in the infield

infighting /ín fīting/ n. **1.** INTERNAL SQUABBLING conflict or rivalry between associates or members of the same organization **2.** SPORTS FIGHTING AT CLOSE RANGE boxing or fighting at close range —**infighter** n.

infill /ín fil/ n. **1.** BUILDING IN SPACES BETWEEN BUILDINGS the filling of gaps, especially of vacant areas between existing buildings ■ vt. (**-fills, -filling, -filled**) BUILD IN GAPS to build new buildings in gaps between existing buildings —**infilling** n.

infiltrate /ínfil trayt/ vti. (**-trates, -trating, -trated**) **1.** MIL BREAK THROUGH SECRETLY to cross or send sb into enemy territory without the enemy's knowledge ○ infiltrate troops behind enemy lines **2.** GET IN POSITION TO DO HARM to establish sb or become established within a place or organization with the intention of doing harm or gathering information ○ activists were infiltrated into local parties **3.** CHEM PERMEATE FLUID THROUGH A SUBSTANCE to pass through a substance by filtration, or make a liquid or gas pass through a substance by filtration ■ n. MED ABNORMAL ACCUMULATION a substance such as fat that passes into tissues and cells and forms an abnormal accumulation [Mid-18thC. Formed from IN- + FILTRATE.] —**infiltration** /ínfil tráysh'n/ n. —**infiltrative** /ínfil traytiv/ adj. —**infiltrator** /-traytər/ n.

infimum /ínfimom/ (plural **-fima** /-mə/) n. a number less than or equal to all elements of a set, thus a lower bound, but greater than or equal to all other lower bounds of the set [Mid-20thC. From Latin, literally 'lowest part'.]

infin. abbr. GRAM infinitive

infinite /ínfinət/ adj. **1.** NOT MEASURABLE without any limits that can be measured or realized **2.** EXCEEDINGLY GREAT very great in size, number, degree, or extent ○ he took infinite pains over it **3.** MATH GREATER THAN ANY ASSIGNED VALUE greater in number, size, or scope than any arbitrarily assigned value **4.** MATH WITH UNLIMITED SPATIAL EXTENT extending indefinitely or having unlimited spatial extent **5.** MATH WITH INFINITE ELEMENTS having an infinite number of terms or elements **6.** MATH IN ONE-TO-ONE RELATIONSHIP able to be put into a one-to-one correspondence with a subset of itself ■ n. STH INFINITE sth that is infinite, e.g. space [14thC. Via Old French from Latin infinitus, literally 'not bounded', from finitus 'finished, finite'.] —**infinitely** adv. —**infiniteness** n.

Infinite n. used to refer to God

infinite loop n. a series of instructions in a computer program containing errors that make it repeat endlessly

infinitesimal /ínfini téssim'l/ adj. **1.** TINY very small in number, amount, or degree **2.** MATH CLOSE TO ZERO able to assume values arbitrarily close to but greater than zero ■ n. INFINITESIMAL NUMBER an infinitesimal number or function [Mid-17thC. Formed from modern Latin infinitesimus 'the number in a series corresponding to infinity' (as when calculating fractions), from Latin infinitus (see INFINITE).] —**infinitesimally** adv.

infinitesimal calculus n. MATH = calculus n. 1

infinitive /in fínnitiv/ n. a form of a verb with no reference to a particular tense, person, or subject. In English, an infinitive is usually preceded by the word 'to', as in 'to see'. [15thC. From late Latin infinitivus, from Latin infinitus, literally 'not bounded' (see INFINITE). The underlying meaning is 'not limited by person or number'.] —**infinitival** /in fínni tīv'l/ adj. —**infinitivally** /in fínni tīvəl-/ adv.

infinitude /in fínni tyood/ n. **1.** BOUNDLESSNESS the infinite nature of sth **2.** VERY LARGE NUMBER OF STH a very great number, degree, or extent of sth [Mid-17thC. Formed from Latin infinitus 'infinite' (see INFINITE), on the model of MAGNITUDE.]

infinity /in fínnəti/ (plural **-ties**) n. **1.** STH WITHOUT LIMITS limitless time, space, or distance ○ beyond the Earth lay infinity **2.** STH TOO GREAT TO COUNT an amount or number so great that it cannot be counted ○ an infinity of stars **3.** STATE OF BEING INFINITE the state or quality of being infinite **4.** MATH CONCEPT OF BEING ALWAYS UNLIMITED the concept of being unlimited by always being larger than any imposed value or boundary. For some purposes this may be considered as being the same as one divided by zero. **5.** GEOM GEOMETRIC POINT AT INFINITE DISTANCE a part of a geometric figure situated an infinite distance from the observer, e.g. the hypothetical point at which parallel lines meet in Euclidean geometry **6.** OPTICS INFINITELY DISTANT POINT a point sufficiently far from a lens or mirror that the light emitted from it falls in parallel rays on the surface [14thC. From French infinité, from, ultimately, Latin infinitus (see INFINITE).]

infirm /in fúrm/ adj. **1.** NOT STRONG lacking strength and vitality, e.g. because of sickness or age **2.** IRRESOLUTE lacking firmness of character or a strong will **3.** BUILDING STRUCTURALLY UNSOUND having a structure that is not sound **4.** LAW LEGALLY UNSOUND invalid or not supported, e.g. a title to property or a claim ■ npl. PEOPLE WHO ARE NOT STRONG people who lack strength and vitality, e.g. because of sickness or age (sometimes considered offensive) [14thC. From Latin infirmus, literally 'not strong', from firmus 'firm'.] —**infirmly** adv. —**infirmness** n.

—————— **WORD KEY: SYNONYMS** ——————
See Synonyms at **weak**.

infirmary /in fúrməri/ (plural **-ries**) n. a hospital or area within an institution where sick and injured people are cared for [15thC. From medieval Latin infirmaria, from Latin infirmus (see INFIRM).]

infirmity /in fúrməti/ (plural **-ties**) n. **1.** LACK OF STRENGTH lack of strength and vitality **2.** CHARACTER FLAW a weakness or failing in sb's character **3.** MINOR ILLNESS any medical condition that causes a lack of strength or vitality

infix /ín fiks/ vt. (**-fixes, -fixing, -fixed**) **1.** FIX STH FIRMLY IN STH ELSE to insert sth into another thing in order to secure it **2.** INSTIL to secure sth firmly in the mind **3.** GRAM PUT AN ELEMENT IN WORD to insert a linking element into a word. In the word acidophilus, '-o-' is an infix. ■ n. GRAM AFFIX IN MIDDLE an affix inserted into the middle of a word [Early 16thC. Partly from IN + FIX; partly from Latin infix-, the past participle stem of infigere, literally 'to fasten in', from figere (see FIX).] —**infixation** /ínfik sáysh'n/ n. —**infixion** /in fíksh'n/ n.

infl. abbr. **1.** inflammable **2.** inflorescence **3.** influence **4.** influenced

in flagrante delicto /in flə gránti di líktō/, **in flagrante** informal adv. **1.** IN A CRIMINAL ACT in the act of committing an offence **2.** HAVING SEX in the act of having sexual relations, especially illicit sexual relations [From Latin, literally, 'in the heat of the crime']

inflame /in fláym/ (**-flames, -flaming, -flamed**) *v.* **1.** *vt.* **PROVOKE A POWERFUL RESPONSE IN** to excite sb to an intense emotion such as anger or jealousy **2.** *vt.* **MAKE STH STRONGER** to make sth, e.g. anger or jealousy, become more intense **3.** *vti.* MED **SWELL AND TURN RED** to become red and swollen, or to make bodily tissue become red and swollen, in response to injury or infection [14thC. Via Old French *enflammer* from Latin *inflammare*, from *flamma* 'flame'.] —**inflamed** *adj.* —**inflamer** *n.*

inflammable /in flámməb'l/ *adj.* **1. EASILY SET ON FIRE** quickly and easily set on fire and burned. ◊ **flammable 2. EASILY ROUSED** easily made angry or passionate ■ *n.* **FLAMMABLE ITEM** sth that is quickly and easily set on fire and burned [Early 17thC. From medieval Latin *inflammabilis* 'liable to inflammation', from Latin *inflammare* (see INFLAME).] —**inflammability** /in flámmə bíllәti/ *n.* —**inflammableness** /in flámməb'lnəss/ *n.* —**inflammably** /-bli/ *adv.*

inflammation /ínflə máysh'n/ *n.* **1.** MED **SWOLLEN REDDENED STATE** swelling, redness, heat, and pain produced in an area of the body as a reaction to injury or infection **2. HEIGHTENING OF EMOTION** a heightening or stirring up of emotion

inflammatory /in flámmətəri/ *adj.* **1. PROVOCATIVE** liable to arouse strong emotions, especially anger **2.** MED **RELATING TO INFLAMMATION** caused or characterized by inflammation —**inflammatorily** *adv.*

inflammatory bowel disease *n.* a disease causing inflammation of the bowel, typically Crohn's disease or ulcerative colitis

inflatable /in fláytəb'l/ *adj.* **BLOW-UP** made of expandable material that can be filled with gas or air ■ *n.* **BLOWN-UP OBJECT** sth, e.g. a ball, mattress, or boat, that can be filled with air or gas

inflate /in fláyt/ (**-flates, -flating, -flated**) *vti.* **1. EXPAND WITH AIR** to fill sth, e.g. a ball, mattress or boat, with air or gas, or to be filled with air or gas **2. MAKE STH APPEAR GREATER** to exaggerate the size or importance of sth, or to become exaggerated in size or importance **3.** ECON **INCREASE PRICES OR MONEY SUPPLY** to cause inflation in prices or the money supply, or to undergo inflation [15thC. From Latin *inflat-*, the past participle stem of *inflare*, literally 'to blow into', from *flare* (see FLATULENT).] —**inflator** *n.*

inflated /in fláytid/ *adj.* **1. UNDESERVEDLY GREAT** greater than is justified or normal ○ *an inflated sense of her own importance* **2.** ECON **EXCESSIVELY HIGH** excessively or abnormally high **3. PRETENTIOUS** exaggerated or pompous in expression **4. BLOWN UP** expanded with air or gas —**inflatedly** *adv.* —**inflatedness** *n.*

inflation /in fláysh'n/ *n.* **1.** ECON **HIGHER PRICES** an increase in the supply of currency or credit relative to the availability of goods and services, resulting in higher prices **2. BEING INFLATED** the act of inflating sth or the condition of being inflated **3. BEING PUFFED UP WITH PRIDE** being puffed up with pride

inflationary /in fláysh'nəri/ *adj.* relating to or causing economic inflation ○ *inflationary policies*

inflationary spiral *n.* a continuous economic cycle of higher prices causing higher wages, which in turn cause even higher prices

inflationism /in fláysh'nizzəm/ *n.* the advocacy or policy of deliberately causing economic inflation through an increase in the supply of available currency and credit —**inflationist** *adj., n.*

inflect /in flékt/ (**-flects, -flecting, -flected**) *v.* **1.** *vt.* **VARY THE PITCH OF THE VOICE** to change the pitch or tone of the voice **2.** *vti.* GRAM **CHANGE A WORD FORM** to change the form of a word, e.g. to show a change in tense, mood, gender, or number, or to be changed in this way **3.** *vt.* **BEND** to make sth turn from a direct line or course [15thC. From Latin *inflectere*, literally 'to bend in', from *flectere* (see FLEXIBLE).] —**inflectable** *adj.* —**inflected** *adj.* —**inflective** *adj.* —**inflector** *n.*

inflection /in fléksh'n/, **inflexion** *n.* **1. CHANGE IN PITCH** a change in the tone or pitch of the voice **2.** GRAM **WORD CHANGE** a change in the form of a word to show a grammatical change such as tense, mood, gender, or number **3.** GRAM **ALTERED FORM OF WORD** an altered form of a word, e.g. one showing a change in tense, mood, gender, or number, or the part of the word that changes in this way **4. BENDING** a turning from a straight line or course, or a more general change in direction **5.** GEOM = **point of inflection** —**inflectional** *adj.* —**inflectionally** *adv.* —**inflectionless** *adj.*

inflection point *n. US* GEOM = **point of inflection**

inflexed /in flékst/ *adj.* BOT used to describe a plant part that is bent inwards or downwards towards the stem [Mid-17thC. Formed from Latin *inflex-*, the past participle stem of *inflectere* (see INFLECT).]

inflexible /in fléksəb'l/ *adj.* **1. UNBENDING** adhering firmly to a viewpoint or principle **2. IMPOSSIBLE TO CHANGE** firmly established and impossible to change ○ *an inflexible rule* **3. RIGID** stiff and bent only with difficulty [15thC. From Latin *inflexibilis*, literally 'not able to bend', from *flex-*, the past participle stem of *flectere* (see FLEXIBLE).] —**inflexibility** /in fléksə bílləti/ *n.* —**inflexibleness** /in fléksəb'lnəss/ *n.* —**inflexibly** *adv.*

inflexion *n.* = **inflection**

inflict /in flíkt/ (**-flicts, -flicting, -flicted**) *vt.* **1. CAUSE SUFFERING** to cause damage, harm, or unpleasantness to sb or sth ○ *inflicted heavy casualties on the enemy forces* **2. FORCE ON SB** to impose a burden on another [Mid-16thC. From Latin *inflict-*, the past participle stem of *infligere*, literally 'to strike upon', from *fligere* 'to hit' (source also of English *conflict, afflict,* and *profligate*).] —**inflictable** *adj.* —**inflicter** *n.* —**infliction** /in flíksh'n/ *n.* —**inflictive** /-tiv/ *adj.*

in-flight *adj.* taking place or provided for passengers during an aircraft journey ○ *in-flight entertainment*

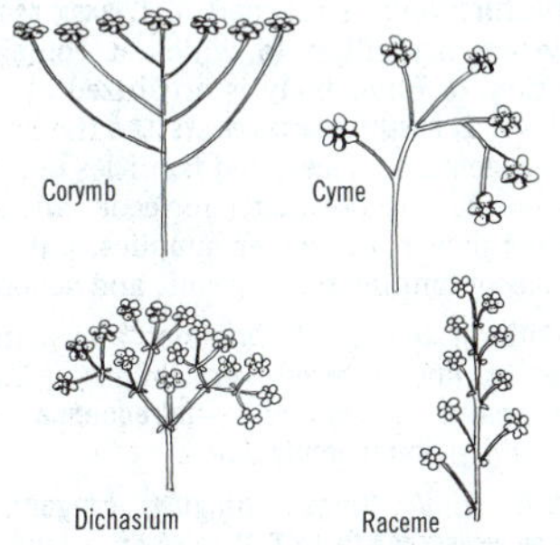
Corymb
Cyme
Dichasium
Raceme

Inflorescence

inflorescence /ínflə réss'nss/ *n.* BOT **1. FLOWERING PART OF A PLANT** a flowering structure that consists of more than one flower and usually comprises distinct individual flowers **2. WAY FLOWERS GROW** the arrangement or manner in which flowers develop on a stalk **3. FLOWERING** the budding and flowering of a plant [Mid-18thC. From modern Latin *inflorescentia*, from, ultimately, Latin *inflorescere*, literally 'to come into flower', from *florescere* 'to begin to flower'.]

inflow /in flō/ *n.* **1. STH THAT FLOWS IN** sth that flows in somewhere ○ *an inflow of fresh water into a lake* **2. INFLUX** an instance or process of sth flowing in ○ *the inflow of visitors to the site* **3. PLACE WHERE AN INFLOW OCCURS** the point at which sth flows in —**inflowing** *n.*

influence /in floo ənss/ *n.* **1. EFFECT ON STH** the effect of sth on a person, thing, or event ○ *Picasso's influence on the course of 20th-century art* **2. POWER TO SWAY** the power that sb has to affect other people's thinking or actions by means of argument, example, or force of personality ○ *She came under the influence of one of her teachers.* **3. SPECIAL ADVANTAGE** the power or authority that comes from wealth, social status, or position **4. SB WHO CAN SWAY ANOTHER** sb or sth able to affect the course of events or sb's thinking or action ○ *He's a bad influence on you.* **5. STARS' EFFECT ON PEOPLE** in astrology, an emanation that is believed to come from the stars and planets and to affect human characteristics, personality, and actions ■ *vt.* (**-ences, -encing, -enced**) **1. SWAY** to persuade or sway sb ○ *What influenced you in your choice of career?* **2. AFFECT** to have the power to affect sth ○ *the factors that influence a nation's development* [14thC. From medieval Latin *influentia*, from, ultimately, Latin *influere*, literally 'to flow in', from *fluere* (see FLUENT).] —**influenceable** *adj.* —**influencer** *n.* ◇ **under the influence** intoxicated by having drunk alcohol (*informal*)

influent /in floo ənt/ *n.* GEOG a stream flowing into a lake or larger river [15thC. From Latin *influent-*, the present participle stem of *influere* (see INFLUENCE).]

influential /in floo énsh'l/ *adj.* having a great deal of power to sway people —**influentially** *adv.*

influenza /in floo énzə/ *n.* **1.** MED **WIDESPREAD VIRAL ILLNESS** a viral illness producing a high temperature, sore throat, runny nose, headache, dry cough, and muscle pain. The illness is widespread, especially during winter months, and can sometimes be fatal. **2.** VET **VIRAL ILLNESS OF ANIMALS** a viral disease of domestic animals, usually characterized by fever and respiratory problems [Mid-18thC. Via Italian from medieval Latin *influentia* (see INFLUENCE), apparently from the belief that epidemics were due to the influence of the stars.] —**influenzal** *adj.*

influx /in fluks/ *n.* **1. ARRIVAL IN LARGE NUMBERS** a sudden arrival of a large number of people or things ○ *dealing with the influx of tourists into the city* **2. INFLOW** a flowing in, especially of a stream or river [Late 16thC. Via late Latin *influxus* from Latin, the past participle of *influere* (see INFLUENCE).]

influx control *n.* the control over the movement of Blacks into urban areas exerted by government under the system of rigid pass laws in South Africa during apartheid

info /ínfō/ *n.* information (*informal*) [Early 20thC. Shortening.]

infold *vt.* = **enfold**

infomediary /ínfō meédiəri/ *n.* a website providing specialist information on behalf of both the producers of goods and their customers

infomercial /ínfō múrsh'l/ *n.* a commercial advertisement on television that is made to appear like a full-length interview or documentary programme [Late 20thC. Blend of INFORMATION and COMMERCIAL.]

infonesia /ínfō neésiə/ *n.* an inability to remember an item of information or its location, especially on the Internet (*informal*)

inform /in fáwrm/ (**-forms, -forming, -formed**) *v.* **1.** *vt.* **COMMUNICATE INFORMATION TO** to communicate information or knowledge to sb (*often passive*) ○ *The police informed us of the accident.* **2.** *vr.* **LEARN ABOUT STH** to familiarize yourself with a subject **3.** *vi.* **TELL THE POLICE** to give confidential or incriminating information to the authorities about sb else's activities, especially to the police **4.** *vt.* ARTS **UNDERLIE AND ANIMATE STH** to be an essential characteristic of sth ○ *His religious beliefs inform his entire work.* **5.** *vt.* **GIVE STRUCTURE TO** to give structure or substance to sth (*formal*) [14thC. Via Old French *enformer* from Latin *informare*, literally 'to give form to', from *forma* (see FORM). The underlying meaning is 'to shape sb's mind, instruct'.]

informal /in fáwrm'l/ *adj.* **1. FREE OF CEREMONY** relaxed and casual rather than ceremonious and stiff **2. UNOFFICIAL** not officially prepared, organized, or sanctioned ○ *The two sides in the conflict held informal talks.* **3.** CLOTHES **CASUAL AND EVERYDAY** suitable for casual or everyday situations ○ *informal dress* **4.** LANG **COLLOQUIAL** more appropriate in spoken than written form —**informality** /ínfər málləti/ *n.* —**informally** /in fáwrməli/ *adv.*

informal economy *n.* economic activities organized without government approval, outside mainstream industry and commerce

informal vote *n. ANZ* a spoiled ballot paper

informant /in fáwrmənt/ *n.* **1. SB WHO SUPPLIES INFORMATION** sb who gives information to sb, often a newspaper **2. INFORMER** sb who gives confidential or incriminating information to the police about sb

informatics /ínfər máttiks/ *n.* INFO SCI = **information science** (*takes a singular verb*) [Mid-20thC. Formed from INFORMATION, on the model of Russian *informatika*.]

information /ínfər máysh'n/ *n.* **1. KNOWLEDGE** definite knowledge acquired or supplied about sth or sb ○ *a bulletin giving the latest information on the trial* **2. GATHERED FACTS** the collected facts and data about a particular subject **3.** *US* = **directory enquiries 4. MAKING FACTS KNOWN** the communication of facts and knowledge **5.** COMPUT **COMPUTER DATA** computer data that has been organized and presented in a systematic fashion to clarify the underlying meaning **6.** LAW **FORMAL CRIMINAL ACCUSATION** a formal accusation of a crime brought before a court or magistrate —**informational** *adj.* —**informationally** *adv.*

information age *n.* a period characterized by widespread electronic access to information through the use of computer technology

information appliance *n.* a small, portable, digital information processing machine designed to function on an electronic network

information processing *n.* the organization, manipulation, and distribution of data, nowadays typically carried out by computers

information retrieval *n.* the process used to systematically store and retrieve computerized data

information science *n.* the study of the processes involved in the collection, categorization, and distribution of data, particularly with reference to computer data

information superhighway *n.* the developing worldwide computer network that includes the Internet, private networks, and proprietary online services. It permits the rapid sending of many different forms of data, including voice, video, and text.

information technology *n.* the use of technologies from computing, electronics, and telecommunications to process and distribute information in digital and other forms

information theory *n.* the mathematical study of the transmission, reception, storage, and retrieval of information based on the statistical analysis of communication between humans and machines

informative /in fáwrmətiv/ *adj.* providing useful information —**informatively** *adv.* —**informativeness** *n.*

informatory /in fáwrmətəri/ *adj.* providing useful information (*dated*) —**informatorily** *adv.*

informed /in fáwrmd/ *adj.* **1.** HAVING KNOWLEDGE showing, having, or based on knowledge or understanding of a situation or subject ○ *informed criticism* **2.** FULLY AWARE based on a proper knowledge and understanding of a situation or subject ○ *an informed decision* —**informedly** /in fáwrmidli/ *adv.*

informed consent *n.* agreement by a patient to undergo an operation or medical treatment or take part in a clinical trial after being informed of and having understood the risks involved

informer /in fáwrmər/ *n.* **1.** SECRET PROVIDER OF INFORMATION ABOUT A CRIME sb who provides the police or authorities with information about criminal activities **2.** PROVIDER OF INFORMATION sb or sth that provides information about a subject or situation

infotainment /ínfō táynmənt/ *n.* television programmes that deal with serious issues or current affairs in an entertaining way [Late 20thC. Blend of INFORMATION and ENTERTAINMENT.] —**infotainer** *n.*

infra /ínfrə/ *adv.* a term used in an explanatory note to refer a reader to a point later in a text, especially in the phrase 'vide infra' (*formal*) ◊ **supra** [Late 19thC. From Latin.]

infra- *prefix.* below, beneath, inferior ○ *infrasonic* ○ *infraclass* [From Latin *infra* 'below'. Ultimately from an Indo-European word that is also the ancestor of English *under, inferior,* and *infernal.*]

infraclass /ínfrə klaass/ *n.* a taxonomic category of organisms that is above an order and below a subclass

infracostal /ínfrə kóst'l/ *adj.* lying below the ribs

infract /in frákt/ (**-fracts, -fracting, -fracted**) *vt.* to fail to obey or fulfil a law, contract, or agreement [Late 18thC. From Latin *infractus*, the past participle stem of *infringere* 'to destroy'.] —**infractor** *n.*

infraction /in fráksh'n/ *n.* a failure to obey or fulfil a law, contract, or agreement [15thC. Directly and via Middle French, from Latin *infractio*, from *infractus* (see INFRACT).]

infra dig /ínfrə díg/ *adj.* below the standard of social behaviour that sb usually maintains (*informal*) [Early 19thC. Shortening of Latin *infra dignitatem*.]

infrahuman /ínfrə hyóomən/ *adj.* in the system of classifying living organisms, belonging to a lower order than human beings

infrangible /in fránjəb'l/ *adj.* (*formal*) **1.** IMPOSSIBLE TO BREAK OR SEPARATE unable to be broken or separated into pieces **2.** NOT TO BE IGNORED unable to be disregarded or violated [Late 16thC. Directly or via French from medieval Latin *infrangibilis*, from *in-* 'not' + *frangibilis* 'breakable'.] —**infrangibility** /in fránjə bílləti/ *n.* —**infrangibleness** /in fránjəb'lnəss/ *n.* —**infrangibly** *adv.*

infrared /ínfrə réd/ *n.* PORTION OF INVISIBLE SPECTRUM the portion of the invisible electromagnetic spectrum consisting of radiation with wavelengths in the range 750 nm to 1 mm, between light and radio waves ○ *infrared radiation* ■ *adj.* RELATING TO INFRARED RADIATION using, producing, or affected by infrared radiation [Late 19thC. Because it lies below the red end of the visible spectrum.]

infrared astronomy *n.* the study of celestial objects with wavelengths in the infrared range. Infrared sources within our galaxy include cool gas giants and the galactic centre.

infrared photography *n.* photography with film that is sensitive to infrared radiation, used, e.g., for taking pictures at night or in haze and in detecting camouflaged objects

infrasonic /ínfrə sónnik/ *adj.* **1.** RELATING TO SOUND INAUDIBLE TO HUMANS relating to sound at frequencies below 20 Hz, which cannot be heard by human beings but can be felt as vibration **2.** RELATING TO INFRASONIC WAVES OR VIBRATIONS using or produced by infrasonic waves or vibrations —**infrasonically** *adv.*

infrasound /ínfrə sownd/ *n.* sound at frequencies below 20 Hz, which cannot be heard by humans but can be felt as vibration

infrastructure /ínfrə strukchər/ *n.* **1.** BASIC ORGANIZATION the system according to which a company, organization, or other body is organized at the most basic level **2.** PUBLIC SERVICES OR SYSTEMS the large-scale public systems, services, and facilities of a country or region that are necessary for economic activity, including power and water supplies, public transport, telecommunications, roads, and schools

infrequent /in fréekwənt/ *adj.* not appearing, happening, or encountered very often ○ *Her visits became more infrequent.* —**infrequence** *n.* —**infrequency** *n.* —**infrequently** *adv.*

infringe /in frínj/ (**-fringes, -fringing, -fringed**) *v.* **1.** *vt.* DISOBEY OR DISREGARD STH to fail to obey a law or regulation or observe the terms of an agreement **2.** *vti.* ENCROACH ON SB'S RIGHTS OR PROPERTY to take over land, rights, privileges, or activities that belong to sb else, especially in a minor or gradual way ○ *infringing on our personal freedom* [Mid-16thC. From Latin *infringere* 'to damage', from *frangere* 'to break' (source of English *fracture*).] —**infringer** *n.*

infringement /in frínjmənt/ *n.* **1.** BREACH OF A LAW OR RIGHT a failure to obey a law or regulation **2.** ENCROACHMENT an encroachment on land, rights, privileges, or activities that belong to sb else, especially in a minor or gradual way

infundibula plural of **infundibulum**

infundibuliform /ín fun díbbyóoli fawrm/ *adj.* used to describe a flower or other plant part that resembles a funnel in shape

infundibulum /ín fun díbbyóoləm/ (*plural* **-la** /-lə/) *n.* a funnel-shaped opening, passage, or structure in vertebrates such as the stalk connecting the pituitary gland to the brain or the opening of a Fallopian tube into the ovary [Mid-16thC. From Latin, 'funnel', from *infundere* 'to pour in' (source of English *infuse*).] —**infundibular** *adj.* —**infundibulate** /ín fun díbbyóo layt, -lət/ *adj.*

infuriate /in fyóori ayt/ (**-ates, -ating, -ated**) *vt.* to make sb extremely angry [Mid-17thC. From medieval Latin *infuriare*, from *furiare* 'to anger', from *furia* 'fury'.] —**infuriated** *adj.* —**infuriatedly** *adv.* —**infuriating** *adj.* —**infuriatingly** *adv.*

infuse /in fyóoz/ (**-fuses, -fusing, -fused**) *v.* **1.** *vt.* PERVADE to fill sth with a strong emotion such as hatred, enthusiasm, or desire (*often passive*) **2.** *vt.* INTRODUCE STH INTO SB'S MIND to fix an emotion, belief, or quality gradually but firmly in sb's mind **3.** *vti.* STEEP IN LIQUID to soak tea or herbs in liquid in order to extract the flavour or some other property **4.** *vt.* MED GIVE A LIQUID USING A DRIP to introduce a solution such as saline, sucrose, or glucose into a vein, body cavity, or the intestinal tract in order to treat or feed sb using a drip. ◊ **transfuse** [15thC. Via Old French *infuser* from, ultimately, Latin *infundere* 'to pour in', from *fundere* 'to pour'.] —**infuser** *n.*

infusible /in fyóozəb'l/ *adj.* **1.** MED USABLE IN A DRIP able to be introduced into the body through a drip **2.** SUITABLE FOR INFUSING suitable for soaking in liquid to make an infusion ○ *infusible herbs* —**infusibility** /in fyóozə bílləti/ *n.*

infusion /in fyóozh'n/ *n.* **1.** ACT OF INFUSING STH the act of of soaking sth in a liquid in order to extract sth soluble **2.** MED ADMINISTERING OF A LIQUID THROUGH A DRIP the introduction of a solution such as saline, sucrose, or glucose through a drip in order to treat or feed a patient **3.** LIQUID MADE BY INFUSING STH a liquid such as tea that is made by infusing sth **4.** MED LIQUID ADMINISTERED THROUGH A DRIP a solution introduced into the body by infusion **5.** INTRODUCTION OF STH NEEDED the addition of a new or necessary quality or element to sth ○ *an infusion of private capital into the project* [14thC. Via Old French from Latin *infusio*, from the past participle stem of *infundere* (see INFUSE).]

infusorial earth /ínfyoo záwri əl-/ *n.* = **diatomaceous earth**

-ing[1] *suffix.* **1.** forming the present participle of verbs ○ *raining* **2.** forming adjectives from words other than verbs ○ *swashbuckling* [Alteration of earlier *-ende*, from Old English]

-ing[2] *suffix.* **1.** action or process ○ *rowing* ○ *cooking* **2.** result of (*archaic*) [Old English *-ung, -ing*]

-ing[3] *suffix.* sb or sth that has a particular character ○ *gelding* [Old English, 'belonging to, of the line of']

ingather /in gáthər/ (**-ers, -ering, -ered**) *v.* **1.** *vt.* COLLECT A HARVEST to gather in a harvest of sth **2.** *vi.* CONVERGE to come together or assemble (*formal or literary*) —**ingatherer** *n.*

ingenious /in jéeni əss/ *adj.* **1.** INVENTIVE possessing cleverness and imagination **2.** CLEVER AND EFFECTIVE clever, original, and effective ○ *an ingenious solution* [15thC. Via Middle French *ingénieux* from Latin *ingeniosus*, from *ingenium* 'mind' (source of English *engine*).] —**ingeniously** *adv.* —**ingeniousness** *n.*

ingénue /ánzhə nyoo/ *n.* a girl or young woman who is naive and lacks experience or understanding of life [Mid-19thC. Via French from, ultimately, Latin *ingenuus* (see INGENUOUS).]

ingenuity /ínjə nyóo əti/ (*plural* **-ties**) *n.* cleverness and originality [Late 16thC. From Latin *ingenuitas*, from *ingenuus* (see INGENUOUS).]

ingenuous /in jénnyoo əss/ *adj.* **1.** INNOCENT AND UNWORLDLY showing innocence and a lack of worldly experience **2.** SEEMING HONEST appearing honest and direct [Late 16thC. From Latin *ingenuus* 'native, freeborn, honest', from *gignere* 'to beget'. Ultimately from an Indo-European word that also produced English *kin*.] —**ingenuously** *adv.* —**ingenuousness** *n.*

WORD KEY: SYNONYMS

See Synonyms at ***naive***.

ingest /in jést/ (**-gests, -gesting, -gested**) *vt.* to take sth such as food or liquid into the body by swallowing or absorbing it [Early 17thC. From the past participle stem of Latin *ingerere* 'to carry in', from *gerere* 'to carry'.] —**ingestion** /in jéschən/ *n.* —**ingestive** /-jéstiv/ *adj.*

ingesta /in jéstə/ *npl.* food or liquid taken into the body by swallowing or absorbing [Early 18thC. From Latin *ingestus*, the past participle of *ingerere* (see INGEST).]

Ingham /íngəm/ town in northeastern Queensland, Australia, a major centre of sugar production. Population: 5,012 (1996).

ingle /íng g'l/ *n.* a fireplace, or an open fire burning in a fireplace (*archaic*) [Early 16thC. Origin uncertain: perhaps from Gaelic *aingeal* 'fire, light'.]

inglenook /íng g'l nòok/ *n.* **1.** RECESS BESIDE A FIREPLACE a recess for a seat or bench beside a large fireplace, sometimes covered by the chimney-breast **2.** FIRESIDE SEAT a seat built in an inglenook, especially one of two benches facing each other

inglorious /in gláwri əss/ *adj.* **1.** SHAMEFUL bringing shame or dishonour **2.** NOT FAMOUS not having received recognition, and so unknown or obscure (*archaic or literary*) [Mid-16thC. From Latin *inglorius*, from *gloria* 'glory'.] —**ingloriously** *adv.* —**ingloriousness** *n.*

ingoing /ín gō ing/ *adj.* **RELATING TO ARRIVAL** relating to entering a place or taking up a new position ■ *n.* **PAYMENT FOR PREVIOUS TENANT'S FIXTURES** an amount paid by a new tenant for fixtures left by the previous tenant (*often used in the plural*)

ingot /íng gət/ *n.* **1. METAL CASTING** a metal casting that is shaped for easy working or for recasting, typically in an oblong **2. MOULD FOR CASTING INGOTS** a mould used for the casting of ingots [14thC. Origin uncertain: probably formed from Old English *in* 'in' + *gotan*, past participle of *gēotan* 'to pour'.]

ingot iron *n.* very pure iron that is produced in the same way as steel but using methods that reduce the carbon, manganese, and silicon content

ingraft /in gráaft/ (**-grafts, -grafting, -grafted**) *vt.* = **engraft** —**ingraftation** /in gráaf táysh'n/ *n.* —**ingraftment** /in gráaftmənt/ *n.*

ingrain /in gráyn/ *vt.* (**-grains, -graining, -grained**) **IMPRESS STH ON SB'S MIND** to impress a feeling, belief, or experience firmly and indelibly on sb's mind (*usually passive*) ○ *The sight is still ingrained on my memory.* ■ *adj.* **1.** = **ingrained 2.** TEXTILES **PREDYED** dyed before being spun or woven ■ *n.* TEXTILES **1. PREDYED YARN OR FIBRE** yarn or fibre that is dyed before being spun or woven **2. PREDYED RUG OR CARPET** a rug or carpet made of yarn or fibre that is dyed before being spun or woven [15thC. Formed from GRAIN, from its application to certain insects and the dye produced by them.]

ingrained /in gráynd/ *adj.* **1. WORKED DEEP INTO STH** worked into the surface, pores, or fibres of sth and very difficult to remove ○ *ingrained dirt* **2. IMPRESSED ON SB'S MIND** firmly fixed in sb's mind and only removed or challenged with difficulty **3. HABITUAL** long-established or confirmed in a habit or practice —**ingrainedly** /in gráynidli/ *adv.* —**ingrainedness** /-id-nəss/ *n.*

ingrate /ín grayt, in gráyt/ *n.* **UNGRATEFUL PERSON** sb who does not show or express gratitude (*formal or literary*) ■ *adj.* **UNGRATEFUL** showing no gratitude (*formal or literary*) [15thC. Via Old French from Latin *ingratus*, 'ungrateful', from *in-* 'not' + *gratus* 'grateful'.]

ingratiate /in gráyshi ayt/ (**-ates, -ating, -ated**) *vr.* to try to enter sb's favour, especially in order to gain an advantage ○ *It's no use trying to ingratiate yourself with me.* [Early 17thC. From Italian *ingraziare*, from *in grazia* 'into favour', from Latin *in gratiam*, from, ultimately, *gratia* 'favour' (source of English *grace*).] —**ingratiation** /in gráyshi áysh'n/ *n.* —**ingratiatory** /in gráyshi ətəri/ *adj.*

ingratiating /in gráyshi ayting/ *adj.* **1. SEEKING TO PLEASE SB** designed to win sb's approval, especially in order to gain an advantage **2. PLEASING** agreeable or giving pleasure (*archaic or literary*) —**ingratiatingly** *adv.*

ingratitude /in grátti tyood/ *n.* failure to show or express gratitude [14thC. Directly or via Old French from Latin *ingratitudo*, from *ingratus* 'ungrateful', from *gratus* 'grateful'.]

ingredient /in gréedi ənt/ *n.* **1. ITEM IN RECIPE** any of the component parts of a mixture, especially in cooking **2. ELEMENT REQUIRED FOR STH** any of the different elements required for a situation, relationship, or plan ○ *What are the ingredients for a happy marriage?* [15thC. From, ultimately, Latin *ingredi* 'to enter' (source of English *ingress*), from *gradi* 'to step'.]

Ingres /áng grə/, **Jean-Auguste-Dominique** (1780–1867) French artist. He was a leading exemplar of neoclassicism in such paintings as *Grande Odalisque* (1814).

ingress /ín gress/ *n.* **1. ENTRY** entry into a place **2. RIGHT OF ENTRY** the right to enter a place **3. ENTRANCE** a way of entering a place [15thC. From Latin, 'entrance', from *ingredi* 'to enter', from *gradi* 'to walk'.]

ingressive /in gréssiv/ *adj.* **1. OF ENTRY** relating to entry into or the entrance to a place **2.** PHON **PRONOUNCED BY INHALING** used to describe a speech sound that is pronounced by inhaling rather than exhaling **3.** GRAM = **inceptive** *n.* 1, **inceptive** *n.* 2 ■ *n.* PHON **INGRESSIVE SPEECH SOUND** a speech sound pronounced by inhaling ■ *adj.* GRAM = **inceptive** *adj.* 2 —**ingressiveness** *n.*

in-group *n.* a group of people who show loyalty and preferential treatment to one another because they share common interests, beliefs, and attitudes

ingrowing /ín grō ing/ *adj.* growing or appearing to grow inwards. An ingrowing toenail does not actually grow inwards: inflamed tissue around the edge of the nail grows over it.

ingrown /ín grōn/ *adj.* **1.** MED **GROWN INTO THE FLESH** that has or appears to have grown into the flesh. ◊ **ingrowing 2. NATURAL TO SB** having become a natural part of sb's character over a long period of time **3. INWARD-LOOKING** inward-looking and preoccupied with personal or local interests —**ingrownness** *n.*

ingrowth /ín grōth/ *n.* **1. GROWTH INTO THE FLESH** growth or apparent growth into the flesh. ◊ **ingrowing 2. STH INGROWN** sth that grows inwards, e.g. a hair

ings /ingz/ *npl.* *N England* low-lying land

inguinal /íng gwin'l/ *adj.* located in or affecting the groin [15thC. From Latin *inguinalis*, from *inguen* 'groin'.]

ingulf /in gúlf/ (**-gulfs, -gulfing, -gulfed**) *vt.* = **engulf** —**ingulfment** *n.*

ingurgitate /in gúrji tayt/ (**-tates, -tating, -tated**) *vt.* to swallow large amounts of food greedily (*formal or literary*) [Late 16thC. From, ultimately, Latin *ingurgitare* 'to pour in, gorge yourself', from *gurges* 'gulf', from the sense 'engulf'.] —**ingurgitation** /in gúrji táysh'n/ *n.*

Ingush /ing goósh/ (*plural* **-gushes** *or* **-gush**) *n.* a member of an ethnic group that lives mainly in the Russian provinces of Ingushetia and Chechnya [Early 20thC. From Russian, the name of the former autonomous area.]

INH *tdmk.* a trademark for a drug used to treat tuberculosis

inhabit /in hábbit/ (**-its, -iting, -ited**) *v.* **1.** *vt.* **LIVE IN A PLACE** to live in or occupy a particular place (*often passive*) **2.** *vt.* **BE FOUND** to be found in or pervade sth ○ *the fears that inhabited each waking moment* **3.** *vi.* **RESIDE PERMANENTLY** to reside permanently in a place (*archaic*) [14thC. Via Old French *enhabiter* from Latin *inhabitare*, from *habitare* 'to possess, dwell', from *habere* 'to hold, have' (source of English *habit*).] —**inhabitability** /in hábbitə bílləti/ *n.* —**inhabitable** /in hábbitəb'l/ *adj.* —**inhabitation** /in hábbi táysh'n/ *n.* —**inhabiter** /in hábbitər/ *n.*

inhabitancy /in hábbitənssi/ (*plural* **-cies**), **inhabitance** /in hábbitənss/ *n.* living in a place as an inhabitant (*archaic*)

inhabitant /in hábbitənt/ *n.* a person or animal that lives in a particular place or area

inhabited /in hábbitid/ *adj.* lived in, especially by human beings

inhalant /in háylənt/ *adj.* **BREATHED IN** breathed in through the nose or mouth as a medicine or for its soothing effect ■ *n.* **MEDICINE THAT IS INHALED** a substance in the form of a vapour or gas that is inhaled, especially as a medicine or for its soothing effect

inhalation /ínhə láysh'n/ *n.* **1. BREATH TAKEN IN** an intake of breath through the nose or mouth into the lungs **2. STH INHALED** a substance in the form of a vapour or gas that is inhaled, especially as a medicine or for its soothing effect [Early 17thC. From medieval Latin, from, ultimately, Latin *inhalare*, 'to breathe upon' (see INHALE).] —**inhalational** *adj.*

inhalator /ínhə laytər/ *n.* MED **1.** = **respirator 2.** = **inhaler**

inhale /in háyl/ (**-hales, -haling, -haled**) *vti.* to breathe in, or to draw a gas, liquid, or solid into the lungs through the nose or mouth [Early 18thC. Either by back-formation from INHALATION, or from Latin *inhalare* 'to breathe upon', from *halare* 'to breathe' (by contrast with EXHALE in English).]

inhaler /in háylər/ *n.* **1. DEVICE FOR INHALING MEDICINE** a small device used for inhaling medicine in the form of a vapour or gas in order to ease a respiratory condition such as asthma or to relieve nasal congestion **2. SB WHO INHALES** sb who inhales or who inhales sth

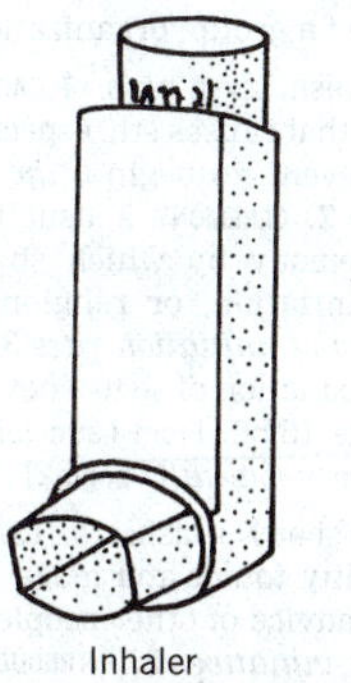

Inhaler

inharmonious /ín haar mṓni əss/ *adj.* **1. DISCORDANT** lacking in harmony or sounding unpleasant **2. UNHAPPY** characterized by disagreement and conflict **3. CLASHING** clashing or not matching —**inharmoniously** *adv.* —**inharmoniousness** *n.*

inharmony /in háarməni/ *n.* lack of harmony, accord, or agreement

inhaul /ín hawl/, **inhauler** /ín hawlər/ *n.* a rope used to haul or hold in a sail

inhere /in héer/ (**-heres, -hering, -hered**) *vi.* to be a natural and integral part of sth (*formal*) [Mid-16thC. From Latin *inhaerere*, from *haerere* 'to stick'.] —**inherence** /in héerənss, -hérrənss/ *n.* —**inherency** *n.*

inherent /in hérrənt, -héerənt/ *adj.* unable to be considered separately from the nature of sth because of being innate or characteristic ○ *the risks inherent in investing in the stock market* [Late 16thC. From, ultimately, Latin *inhaerere* 'to stick to' (see INHERE).] —**inherently** *adv.*

inherit /in hérrit/ (**-its, -iting, -ited**) *v.* **1.** *vti.* **RECEIVE STH WHEN SB DIES** to become the owner of sth when sb dies in accordance with legal succession or the terms of a will or as the result of a bequest or legacy **2.** *vt.* **RECEIVE A CHARACTERISTIC OR QUALITY FROM A PARENT** to receive a characteristic or quality as a result of its being passed on genetically **3.** *vt.* **GET STH FROM A PREDECESSOR** to take sth over from the person or group who previously lived in a place or did a job [14thC. Via Old French *enheriter* 'to make an heir' from late Latin *inhereditare* 'to inherit', from *hereditare*, from Latin *heres* 'heir'.] —**inheritor** *n.*

inheritable /in hérritəb'l/ *adj.* **1.** LAW = **heritable 2.** BIOL **ABLE TO BE PASSED ON GENETICALLY** used to describe a characteristic or quality that can be transmitted genetically from parent to offspring **3. ABLE TO INHERIT** having the right to inherit sth (*archaic*) [15thC. Via Anglo-French *enheritable* 'able to be made heir' from Old French *enheriter* 'to make an heir' (see INHERIT).] —**inheritability** /in hérritə bílləti/ *n.* —**inheritableness** /in hérritəb'lnəss/ *n.*

inheritance /in hérritənss/ *n.* **1.** LAW **INHERITED WEALTH OR TITLE** money, property, or a title that has been inherited or is to be inherited **2.** LAW **OWNERSHIP OR SUCCESSION BY HEREDITY** hereditary ownership of wealth or a title, or the succession to wealth or a title **3.** LAW **RIGHT TO INHERIT** the right of an heir to inherit wealth or a title when an ancestor dies **4. HERITAGE** sth that is inherited from the past **5.** BIOL **TRANSMISSION OF GENETICALLY CONTROLLED CHARACTERISTICS** the transmission of genetically controlled characteristics or qualities from parent to offspring **6.** COMPUT **CREATION OF AN OBJECT WITH THE SAME VARIABLES** a feature of programming whereby a new object can be created from existing objects and, as a consequence of creation, possess the variables and methods of the parent object [15thC. From Old French *enheritaunce*, from *enheriter* 'to make an heir' (see INHERIT).]

inheritance tax *n.* a tax levied on property received by inheritance or legal succession, calculated according to the value of the property received

inhesion /in héezh'n/ *n.* the state of being a natural and integral part of sth (*formal*) [Mid-17thC. From late Latin *inhaesio*, from the past participle stem of Latin *inhaerere* 'to stick'.]

inhibin /in híbbin/ *n.* a hormone secreted by the testis and ovary that inhibits the pituitary's production of follicle-stimulating hormone and helps control gamete and blood cell production, growth, and development [Mid-20thC. Coined from Latin *inhibere* 'to hinder' + -IN.]

inhibit /in híbbit/ (**-its, -iting, -ited**) *vt.* **1. HOLD STH IN CHECK** to stop sth from continuing or developing ○ *changes in spending patterns that are likely to inhibit the growth of the economy* **2. CONSTRAIN** to prevent sb from behaving or speaking freely or unself-consciously **3.** CHEM **STOP OR RESTRICT A CHEMICAL REACTION** to prevent or slow down a chemical reaction **4.** BIOL **INTERFERE WITH A BODILY PROCESS OR ORGAN** to slow down or adversely affect a bodily process or the action of an organ **5.** ELECTRON ENG **PREVENT A SIGNAL OR EVENT** to prevent a specific signal or event from occurring **6.** FORBID STH to forbid sth (*archaic*) [15thC. From the past participle stem of Latin *inhibere* 'to hinder', from *habere* 'to hold'.] —**inhibitable** *adj.* —**inhibitive** *adj.*

inhibited /in híbbitid/ *adj.* unable to behave spontaneously or express feelings openly, especially with regard to sexuality and the body —**inhibitedly** *adv.* —**inhibitedness** *n.*

inhibiter *n.* = **inhibitor**

inhibition /ìn hi bísh'n/ *n.* **1.** FEELING THAT INHIBITS SB a feeling or belief that prevents sb from behaving spontaneously or speaking freely **2.** STH THAT INHIBITS sth that inhibits, or the act of inhibiting **3.** PSYCHOL INHIBITED MENTAL STATE a mental state in which sb's activity or behaviour is inhibited. ◊ **repression 4.** PSYCHOL DIMINISHED RESPONSE TO A STIMULUS in Pavlovian conditioning, the progressive weakening of a response to a stimulus after repeated presentations of the stimulus **5.** CHEM IMPEDING CHEMICAL REACTION the slowing down or prevention of a chemical reaction **6.** BIOL OBSTRUCTION OF A BODILY PROCESS OR ORGAN the suppression or blocking of a bodily process or the action of an organ **7.** SUSPENSION ORDER FROM BISHOP in the Church of England, an order from a bishop suspending a member of the clergy from his or her duties [14thC. Via Old French from Latin *inhibitio*, from *inhibere* 'to hinder' (see INHIBIT).]

inhibitor /in híbbitər/, **inhibiter** *n.* **1.** CHEM SUBSTANCE SLOWING A CHEMICAL REACTION a substance that stops or slows a chemical reaction ○ *a rust inhibitor* **2.** BIOCHEM SUBSTANCE HALTING A BIOLOGICAL PROCESS a substance that slows or halts a metabolic or physiological process, e.g. by preventing the activity of an enzyme **3.** STH THAT INHIBITS STH sb or sth that inhibits sb or sth else

in-home *adj.* available in sb's home

inhospitable /ìn ho spíttəb'l, in hóspit-/ *adj.* **1.** NOT WELCOMING not welcoming or friendly **2.** HARSH harsh and difficult to live or work in ○ *an inhospitable climate* [Late 16thC. From French, from *in-* 'not' + *hospitable* (see HOSPITABLE).] —**inhospitableness** *n.* —**inhospitably** *adv.* —**inhospitality** *n.*

in-house *adj.* LOCATED WITHIN A COMPANY working, carried out, or existing within a company or organization ■ *adv., n.* WITHIN A COMPANY within a company or organization

inhuman /in hyóomən/ *adj.* **1.** VERY CRUEL showing great cruelty and a lack of humanity **2.** UNFEELING giving an impression of being cold and unfeeling **3.** NOT HUMAN not seeming to be human, or not typical of human beings [15thC. Directly or via Middle French from Latin *inhumanus*, from *in-* 'not' + *humanus* 'human'.] —**inhumanly** *adv.* —**inhumanness** *n.*

inhumane /ìn hyoo máyn/ *adj.* lacking compassion, and causing excessive suffering [15thC. Originally from INHUMAN; later from IN- + HUMANE.] —**inhumanely** *adv.*

inhumanity /ìn hyoo mánnəti/ (*plural* **-ties**) *n.* **1.** GREAT CRUELTY great cruelty and lack of humanity **2.** CRUEL ACT an act of great cruelty [15thC. Via Old French from Latin *inhumanitas*, from *inhumanus* (see INHUMAN).]

inhume /in hyóom/ (**-humes, -huming, -humed**) *vt.* to bury a dead body (*formal or literary*) [Early 17thC. From Latin *inhumare*, from *humus* 'earth' (source of English *humble*).] —**inhumation** /ìn hyoo máysh'n/ *n.* —**inhumer** /in hyóomər/ *n.*

inimical /i nímmik'l/ *adj.* **1.** NOT FAVOURABLE unfavourable for sth ○ *activities inimical to the public good* **2.** HOSTILE showing hostility [Early 16thC. Via late Latin *inimicalis* from Latin *inimicus* 'unfriendly' (source of English *enemy*), from *in-* 'not' + *amicus* 'friend'.] —**inimicality** /i nìmmi kálləti/ *n.* —**inimically** /i nímmikli/ *adv.* —**inimicalness** /i nímmik'lnəss/ *n.*

inimitable /i nímmitəb'l/ *adj.* impossible to imitate, especially because of being unique to a particular person or group ○ *She carried it off in her usual inimitable style.* [15thC. Directly or via French from Latin *inimitabilis*, from *in-* 'not' + *imitabilis* 'capable of being imitated'.] —**inimitability** /i nìmmitə bílləti/ *n.* —**inimitableness** /i nímmitəb'lnəss/ *n.* —**inimitably** *adv.*

inion /ínni ən/ *n.* ANAT a projection of the occipital bone that forms a slight lump at the back of the skull just above the neck [Early 19thC. From Greek, 'nape of the neck'.]

iniquitous /i níkwitəss/ *adj.* immoral, especially in a way that results in great injustice or unfairness —**iniquitously** *adv.* —**iniquitousness** *n.*

iniquity /i níkwəti/ (*plural* **-ties**) *n.* **1.** INJUSTICE OR IMMORALITY great injustice or extreme immorality **2.** IMMORAL ACT a grossly immoral act [13thC. Via Old French from Latin *iniquitas*, from *iniquus* 'unjust', from *in-* 'not' + *aequus* 'equal' (source of English *equity*).]

init. *abbr.* initial

initial /i nísh'l/ *adj.* **1.** COMING AT THE START coming first, or present at the beginning of an event or process ○ *My initial feeling was one of shock.* **2.** COMING FIRST IN A WORD relating to or used as the first letter or letters of a word ■ *n.* **1.** FIRST LETTER OF A NAME the first letter of the name of a person, place, or organization **2.** PRINTING LARGE ORNATE FIRST LETTER the large and often highly decorative first letter of a verse, paragraph, or page, especially as seen in illuminated manuscripts **3.** BOT PLANT-TISSUE CELL a cell in the growing point (**meristem**) of a plant that gives rise to cells that will develop into different plant tissues ■ **initials** *npl.* FIRST LETTERS OF SB'S NAMES the first letter of each of the names of a person, place, or organization, used as an abbreviation or means of identification ■ *vt.* (**-tials, -tialling, -tialled**) MARK STH WITH INITIALS to sign or mark a document with initials, especially in order to show approval or give authorization [Early 16thC. From Latin *initialis*, from *initium* 'beginning' (source of English *commence*).] —**initialer** *n.*

initialise *vti.* = **initialize**

initialism /i nísh'lizəm/ *n.* an abbreviation made up of initial letters that are all pronounced separately, e.g. UN for United Nations

initialize /i níshə līz/ (**-izes, -izing, -ized**), **initialise** (**-ises, -ising, -ised**) *vti.* to prepare a piece of computer hardware or software such as a printer, modem, or timer for use, often by resetting a memory location to its initial value —**initialization** /i nìshə lī záysh'n/ *n.* —**initializer** /i níshə līzər/ *n.*

initially /i nísh'li/ *adv.* at first or to begin with

initial public offering *n.* FIN a first-time sale of company securities on a stock exchange to public investors

Initial Teaching Alphabet *n.* an alphabet of 44 symbols, each representing a single sound in English, used to teach children to read

initiate *vt.* /i níshi ayt/ (**-ates, -ating, -ated**) **1.** MAKE STH START to cause sth, especially an important event or process, to begin ○ *to initiate talks* **2.** TEACH SB ABOUT STH NEW to introduce sb to a new activity, interest, or area ○ *initiated me into the joys of snowboarding* **3.** INTRODUCE SB INTO GROUP to allow sb take part in a ritual or ceremony in order to become a member of a group, organization, or religion ■ *n.* /i níshi ət/ **1.** SB INITIATED INTO A GROUP sb who has been recently admitted to a group, organization, or religion after participating in a ritual or ceremony **2.** SB NEWLY INTRODUCED TO STH sb recently introduced to a new activity, interest, or area ■ *adj.* /i níshi ət/ **1.** RECENTLY INITIATED belonging or relating to those who have been recently introduced to a new activity, interest, or area **2.** HAVING SECRET OR SPECIAL KNOWLEDGE knowing the secrets of a group, organization, or religion [Mid-16thC. From the past participle stem of Latin *initiare* 'to begin', from *initium* 'beginning' (see INITIAL).] —**initiator** *n.*

initiated /i níshi aytid/ *npl.* those who know about sth that seems difficult or complicated, or who know the secrets of a group, organization, or religion

initiation /i nìshi áysh'n/ *n.* **1.** ACTION THAT MAKES STH START action that causes sth, especially an important process or event, to begin ○ *the initiation of legal proceedings* **2.** CEREMONY a usually secret or mysterious ceremony by which sb is admitted to a group, organization, or religion (*sometimes used before a noun*) ○ *initiation rites* **3.** INTRODUCTION TO STH NEW the introduction of sb to a new activity, interest, or area [Late 16thC. From Latin *initiatio*, from the past participle stem of *initiare* 'to begin'.]

initiative /i níshətiv, i níshi-/ *n.* **1.** ABILITY TO ACT ON YOUR OWN the ability to act and make decisions without the help or advice of other people ○ *You'll just have to use your initiative.* **2.** INTRODUCTORY STEP the first step in a process that, once taken, determines subsequent events ○ *decided to take the initiative* **3.** PLAN a plan or strategy aimed at tackling a particular problem ○ *a peace initiative* **4.** ADVANTAGEOUS POSITION a favourable position that allows sb to take pre-emptive action or control events ○ *lose the initiative* **5.** POL RIGHT TO INTRODUCE NEW LEGISLATION the right to bring a new law or measure before a legislative body **6.** POL PROPOSAL OF LEGISLATION BY CITIZENS a process valid in many US states and in Switzerland that allows citizens to propose legislation by petition ■ *adj.* OF INITIATION used in or relating to initiation (*formal*) [Late 18thC. Via French from the past participle stem of Latin *initiare* 'to begin'.]

initiatory /i níshi ətəri, i níshətəri/ *adj.* **1.** BEGINNING occurring at or related to the beginning of sth **2.** FOR INITIATION used in or characteristic of an initiation [Early 17thC]

inj. *abbr.* **1.** injection **2.** injury

inject /in jékt/ (**-jects, -jecting, -jected**) *v.* **1.** *vti.* MED PUT FLUID INTO THE BODY WITH A SYRINGE to introduce a drug, vaccine, or other fluid into part of the body using a syringe **2.** *vt.* FORCE LIQUID OR GAS INTO STH to force a liquid or gas through a small opening into a confined space ○ *They inject an insulating foam into the cavity between the walls.* **3.** *vt.* ADD STH TO SITUATION to introduce a particular quality or element into a situation ○ *an attempt to inject a little levity into the proceedings* **4.** *vt.* SPACE TECH PUT A ROCKET OR SATELLITE IN ORBIT to put a rocket or satellite in orbit or a spacecraft on a trajectory to its destination [Late 16thC. From, ultimately, Latin *inicere* 'to throw in', from *iacere* 'to throw' (source of English *ejaculate*).] —**injectable** *adj.*

injectant /in jéktənt/ *n.* an injected substance

injection /in jéksh'n/ *n.* **1.** MED INJECTED DOSE OF A DRUG a dose of a particular drug in liquid form that is injected into the body with a syringe **2.** MED INTRODUCTION OF FLUID WITH A SYRINGE the introduction of fluid into the body by means of a syringe **3.** AUTOMOT SPRAYING FUEL INTO AN ENGINE the process of spraying fuel through a pump into the inlet manifold or cylinder of an internal-combustion engine, eliminating the need for a carburettor **4.** ADDITION OF STH TO SITUATION the introduction of a particular quality or element into a situation ○ *a cash injection* **5.** PROVISION OF MONEY a provision of money for a country, organization, project, or person in financial need **6.** ALGEBRA ONE-TO-ONE MAPPING OF SETS a one-to-one mapping of two sets such that each element of each set corresponds to only one element of the other set **7.** TECH INTRODUCTION OF FLUID INTO A CAVITY a process for introducing a fluid such as a plastic under pressure into a cavity **8.** SPACE TECH PUTTING A SATELLITE INTO ORBIT the insertion of an artificial satellite into orbit or a space probe on a trajectory **9.** SPACE TECH MOMENT OF SATELLITE INSERTION the moment or place at which insertion of a satellite or probe occurs [15thC. Directly or via Middle French from Latin *injectio*, from *inicere* 'to throw in' (see INJECT).] —**injective** /in jéktiv/ *adj.*

injection moulding *n.* a manufacturing process in which heated material (**thermoplastic**) is forced under pressure into a water-cooled mould —**injection-moulded** *adj.*

in-joke *n.* a joke that is shared and understood only by a particular group of people

injudicious /ìnjoo díshəss/ *adj.* lacking in judgment or discretion —**injudiciously** *adv.* —**injudiciousness** *n.*

Injun /ínjən/ *n.* an offensive term for a Native North American (*dated offensive*) [Late 17thC. Represents colloquial and dialectal pronunciation of INDIAN.]

injunction /in júngksh'n/ *n.* **1.** LAW COURT ORDER a court order that requires sb involved in a legal action to do sth or refrain from doing sth **2.** COMMAND a command or order, especially from sb in a position of authority **3.** ACT OF ORDERING SB the act of ordering sb to do or not to do sth [15thC. From late Latin *injunctio*, from *injungere* 'to enjoin', from *jungere* 'to join'.]

injure /ínjər/ (**-jures, -juring, -jured**) *vt.* **1.** HURT SB OR STH to cause physical hurt or damage to a person, animal, or body part **2.** OFFEND SB to cause sb distress by an unkind action or words **3.** LAW DO LEGAL WRONG TO SB to wrong sb by word or deed in such a way that redress by legal means is available **4.** DAMAGE SB'S REPUTATION to damage sb's reputation, career, or chances of success [15thC. Via Old French *injurier* from Latin *injuriare*, from *injuria* (see INJURY).] —**injurable** *adj.* —**injurer** *n.*

━━━━━ **WORD KEY: SYNONYMS** ━━━━━
See Synonyms at **harm**.

injurious /in jóori əss/ *adj.* **1.** CAUSING INJURY causing harm, hurt, damage, or distress **2.** DAMAGING SB'S REPUTATION damaging sb's reputation, career, or chances of success [15thC. Via Middle French *injurios* from Latin *injuriosus*, from *injuria* (see INJURY).] —**injuriously** *adv.* —**injuriousness** *n.*

injury /ínjəri/ (*plural* -**ries**) *n.* **1.** PHYSICAL DAMAGE physical damage to the body or a part of the body ○ *They escaped without injury.* **2.** WOUND a specific instance of physical damage to part of the body ○ *a serious back injury* **3.** LAW HARM TO SB'S REPUTATION harm caused to sb's career or reputation by scandal, rumour, or defamation **4.** LAW INFRINGEMENT OF SB'S RIGHTS the violation of sb's rights, against which legal action can be taken [14thC. Via Anglo-Norman from Latin *injuria* 'a wrong', from *injurius* 'unjust', from *in-* 'not' + *jus* 'justice'.]

injury benefit *n.* a weekly payment made under the National Insurance system to sb injured while at work, the amount of which is calculated according to the seriousness of the injury

injury time *n.* extra time allowed at the end of some matches, especially football and rugby, to compensate for time spent attending to injured players during the game

injustice /in jústiss/ *n.* unfair or unjust treatment of sb, or an instance of this [14thC. Via Old French from Latin *injustitia*, from *injustus* 'unjust', from *in-* 'not' + *justus* 'just'.]

ink /ingk/ *n.* **1.** LIQUID FOR WRITING, DRAWING, OR PRINTING a coloured liquid or paste used for writing, printing, or drawing **2.** ZOOL LIQUID EJECTED BY OCTOPUS OR SQUID a dark brown liquid (**sepia**) ejected from a gland (**ink sac**) near the anus by most cephalopods, including the octopus and the squid, to distract predators **3.** US PRINT PUBLICITY publicity, especially in the print media (*slang*) ○ *The stunt got him all kinds of ink.* ■ *vt.* (**inks, inking, inked**) **1.** MARK STH WITH INK to write or draw with ink on a piece of paper or other surface **2.** ADD INK to coat sth with ink or apply ink to sth, usually in preparation for printing **3.** US SIGN A CONTRACT to put or obtain a signature on a contract or other document (*informal*) [13thC. Via Old French *enque* from, ultimately, Greek *enkauston* 'purple ink', from *enkaiein* 'to burn in', from the process of encaustic painting.] —**inker** *n.*

ink in *vt.* **1.** ADD INK TO A DRAWING to go over the pencil lines of a drawing or design in ink **2.** SPREAD INK to spread ink on a surface in preparation for printing

Inkatha /in ka'ata/ *n.* a Zulu political party that was founded in South Africa in 1975

inkberry /ingk berri/ (*plural* -**ries**) *n.* **1.** EVERGREEN SHRUB an upright evergreen shrub native to eastern North America with small black fruits and oblong to oval dark green leaves that may be smooth-edged or have serrated tips. Latin name: *Ilex glabra*. **2.** BLACK FRUIT the small black rounded fruit of an inkberry **3.** BOT = **pokeweed** [Mid-18thC. From the use of the berries for making ink.]

inkblot /ingk blot/ *n.* **1.** INK STAIN a stain or spot of spilled ink **2.** PSYCHOL PATTERN IN THE RORSCHACH TEST any of the ten abstract patterns resembling an inkblot used in the Rorschach test

inkblot test *n.* PSYCHOL = **Rorschach test**

ink-cap *n.* a mushroom with a conical cap, on the underside of which are gills that dissolve into an inky black pulp after the spores mature. Species include the common ink-cap and the edible shaggy ink-cap or lawyer's wig. Genus: *Coprinus*. US term **inky cap**

inkhorn /ingk hawrn/ *n.* OLD INK CONTAINER a small portable ink container made from horn or a similar material and used in former times ■ *adj.* TOO LEARNED excessively scholarly in style or language, especially in the use of terms derived from Latin and Greek

in-kind *adj.* US **1.** IN GOODS OR SERVICES in the form of goods or services rather than in cash **2.** GIVING BACK

AN EQUIVALENT AMOUNT giving sth that is equivalent to what has been received

ink-jet printer *n.* a printer that prints using particles or droplets of electrically charged ink from a matrix of tiny ink jets

inkle /íngk'l/ *n.* a narrow linen tape used for trimmings, or the yarn used in this tape [Mid-16thC. Origin unknown: possibly from Dutch *enkel* 'single', from its narrowness.]

inkling /íngkling/ *n.* **1.** FAINT IDEA a vague idea or suspicion about a fact, event, or person ○ *I had no inkling that he was unhappy.* **2.** HINT an indication of how to go about sth ○ *Could you give me some inkling of where to look?* [Early 16thC. From an obsolete English verb of unknown origin meaning 'to utter in an undertone', hence, 'to hint'.]

ink mouse *n.* S England ZOOL a bat (*informal*)

ink sac *n.* a large gland with an opening close to the anus of most cephalopods, including the octopus and squid, from which ink (**sepia**) is ejected to distract predators

inkstand /ingk stand/ *n.* **1.** STAND FOR WRITING MATERIALS a rack or stand that is kept on a desk and contains pots of ink, pens, and other writing materials **2.** = **inkwell**

inkwell /ingk wel/ *n.* a small container for ink, especially one that fits into a hole in a desk

inky /íngki/ (-**ier**, -**iest**) *adj.* **1.** COVERED IN INK consisting of or covered in ink **2.** DARK black or dark blue in colour

inky cap *n.* US = **ink-cap**

INLA *abbr.* Irish National Liberation Army

inlace /in láyss/ *vt.* = **enlace**

inlaid /ín láyd, in layd/ *adj.* **1.** SET INTO A SURFACE set into the surface of wood or another material, usually to provide decoration **2.** DECORATED decorated with an inlaid pattern

inland /ínlənd/ *adj.* **1.** NOT NEAR A COAST OR BORDER in or relating to the part of a country that is not near the coast or a border **2.** WITHIN A COUNTRY occurring within a country, rather than between countries ■ *adv.* IN OR INTO THE INTERIOR OF COUNTRY in or towards the interior of a country ■ *n.* INTERIOR OF A COUNTRY the interior of a country [Old English]

inland bill *n.* a bill that is both drawn and payable in the United Kingdom

Inland Revenue *n.* a government body responsible for the collection and administration of direct taxes such as income tax and corporation tax

Inland Sea /ínlənd-/ arm of the Pacific Ocean, in Japan, between the islands of Honshu, Shikoku, and Kyushu. Length: 386 km/240 mi.

in-law /ín law/ *n.* a relative by marriage (*informal*)

inlay *vt.* /ín láy, in lay/ (-**lays**, -**laying**, -**laid**) **1.** SET STH INTO A SURFACE to set pieces of material such as wood, ivory, or stone into previously cut slots in a surface to form a decorative pattern **2.** DECORATE STH WITH AN INLAID DESIGN to decorate sth such as a piece of furniture by setting pieces of wood, stone, ivory, or other material into its surface ■ *n.* /ín lay/ **1.** PIECES OF MATERIAL SET INTO A SURFACE pieces of material such as wood, ivory, or stone set into the surface of a piece of furniture to form a decorative pattern **2.** DECORATIVE PATTERN a decorative pattern formed by inlaying **3.** DENT GOLD OR PORCELAIN FILLING FOR TOOTH a filling made of gold or porcelain that is inserted into a cavity in a tooth and cemented in position —**inlayer** *n.*

inlet /ín let/ *n.* **1.** NARROW OPENING IN A COASTLINE a narrow stretch of water reaching inland from a sea or lake **2.** STRETCH OF WATER BETWEEN TWO ISLANDS a narrow stretch of water between two islands **3.** SEW PIECE OF EXTRA FABRIC a piece of fabric put into the seam of a garment to make it bigger or for decoration **4.** TECH PASSAGE OR VALVE an opening through which liquid or gas enters a machine or other device ■ *vt.* (-**lets**, -**letting**, -**let**) = **inlay** v. 1, **inlay** v. 2 [13thC. Originally in the sense 'permission to enter'.]

inlier /ín īˌər/ *n.* a rock formation in which older rocks are completely surrounded by younger rocks. ◊ **outlier** [Mid-19thC. Formed from IN- + *lier*, modelled on OUTLIER.]

in-line *adj.* used to describe a device or machine in which similar parts are located together and in a straight line, e.g. the cylinders in an internal-combustion engine

In-line skate

in-line skates *npl.* roller skates with each boot mounted on a single line of three or four narrow wheels

in loc. cit. *adv.* = **loc. cit.**

in loco parentis /in lókō pə réntiss/ *adv.* having or taking on the responsibilities of a parent when dealing with sb else's child [From Latin]

inly /ínnli/ *adv.* (*literary*) **1.** INWARDLY in an inwards way **2.** INTIMATELY with deep or intimate understanding

inlying /ín īˌ ing/ *adj.* situated within a country or region

inmate /ín mayt/ *n.* sb who has been confined within a prison or a psychiatric hospital [Late 16thC. Formed from IN + MATE 'companion'.]

in medias res /in meèdi ass ráyz/ *adv.* straight in or into the middle of a sequence of events, especially in a literary narrative that has no introduction (*formal*) [From Latin, 'into the midst of things']

in memoriam /ín mi máwri əm/ *prep.* in memory of or in memory (*used in epitaphs and obituaries*) [From Latin]

inmesh *vt.* = **enmesh**

inmigrant /ín mīgrənt/ *adj.* FROM ANOTHER PART OF THE SAME COUNTRY coming from a different part of the same country ■ *n.* SB FROM WITHIN THE SAME COUNTRY sb who travels from a different part of the same country

inmigrate /ín mī grayt/ (-**grates**, -**grating**, -**grated**) *vi.* to travel to a place from a different part of the same country —**inmigration** /ín mī gráysh'n/ *n.*

inmost /ín mōst/ *adj.* = **innermost** [Old English *innemest*, from *inne* 'in' + *mest* 'most']

inn /in/ *n.* **1.** PUB a small hotel or pub offering food and sometimes accommodation (*often used in pub names*) ○ *a country inn* **2.** HIST HOTEL a place providing food and lodging for travellers (*dated*) **3.** RESIDENCE FOR STUDENTS formerly, a hall of residence for students, especially those studying law [Old English from, ultimately, an Indo-European word meaning 'in' which is also the source of English *in*]

innards /ínnərdz/ *npl.* (*informal*) **1.** INTERNAL ORGANS the internal organs of the body, especially the intestines **2.** INTERNAL PARTS OF A MACHINE the internal working parts of a machine or mechanical device [Early 19thC. Alteration of INWARDS (plural noun)]

innate /i náyt/ *adj.* **1.** PRESENT FROM BIRTH relating to qualities that a person or animal is born with **2.** INTEGRAL forming an integral part of sth **3.** PHILOS COMING FROM THE MIND coming directly from the mind rather than being acquired by experience or from external sources ○ *an innate sense of justice* **4.** BOT JOINED TO THE FILAMENT BY THE BASE used to describe an anther that is joined to the filament by its base only **5.** BOT ORIGINATING WITHIN THE THALLUS forming an integral part of the thallus [15thC. From Latin *innatus*, the past participle of *innasci* 'to be born in', from *nasci* 'to be born' (source of English *nature*).] —**innately** *adv.* —**innateness** *n.*

innate releasing mechanism *n.* a process within the central nervous system of animals that, in response to certain stimuli, causes the animal to produce instinctive behaviour. An example is the way that chicks of some birds peck at the red dot on the adult's beak.

inner /ínnər/ *adj.* **1. NEAR OR CLOSER TO THE CENTRE** located near or closer to the centre of sth ○ *the inner city* **2. BEING OR OCCURRING INSIDE** located or happening on the inside of sth ○ *an inner door* **3. OF THE MIND** relating to sb's private feelings or happening in sb's mind ○ *his quiet exterior that hid an inner confidence* **4. NOT OBVIOUS** needing to be examined closely or thought about in order to be seen or understood ○ *searching for the inner meaning of the text* **5. PRIVILEGED** most privileged or influential ○ *the inner circle* ■ *n.* **1. PART OF TARGET** the part of a target, especially of a dartboard, surrounding the bull's-eye **2. HIT** a hit on the inner [Old English *innera*. Ultimately from an Indo-European word meaning 'in' that is also the source of English *enter*.] —**innerly** *adv.* —**innerness** *n.*

inner bar *n.* all the barristers that comprise the King's or Queen's Counsel. ◊ **outer bar** [From their precedence over ordinary barristers]

inner child *n.* PSYCHOL an adult's conception of himself or herself as a child, often used as a tool in therapeutic processes to explore feelings about the person's childhood

inner city *n.* the central or innermost parts of a city, particularly when associated with social problems such as inadequate housing and high levels of crime and unemployment (*hyphenated when used before a noun*)

inner-directed *adj.* guided by personal beliefs rather than by norms imposed by society

inner ear *n.* the fluid-filled part of the ear, including the cochlea, which is responsible for hearing, and the semicircular canals, which control balance

Inner Light *n.* in Quaker belief, the presence of God as a guiding force within the human soul

inner man *n.* ◊ **inner woman 1. A MAN'S SOUL** the soul or the spiritual or intellectual part of a man **2. A MAN'S APPETITE** the appetite of a man (*humorous*)

Inner Mongolia Autonomous Region administrative region of northern China, bordered on the north by Russia and Mongolia. Population: 22,840,000 (1995). Area: 1,177,500 sq. km/454,600 sq. mi.

innermost /ínnər mōst/ *adj.* **1. MOST CENTRAL** most important, private, or personal ○ *innermost thoughts* **2. FARTHEST FROM THE OUTSIDE** taking place or being situated farthest from the outside

inner planet *n.* any of the four planets Mercury, Venus, Earth, or Mars whose orbits lie closest to the Sun and are within the asteroid belt. ◊ **outer planet**

inner product *n.* MATH = **scalar product**

inner sole *n.* a foot-shaped piece of leather, sheepskin, or synthetic material worn inside a shoe or boot to provide a better fit or added warmth. ◊ **insole**

inner space *n.* **1. AREA BENEATH THE SURFACE OF THE SEA** environment that exists beneath the surface of the sea **2. MENTAL REALM** sb's inner spiritual or psychological depths

innerspring /ínnər spring/ *adj.* US = **interior-sprung**

Inner Temple *n.* a law society that, together with Gray's Inn, Lincoln's Inn, and the Middle Temple, forms the Inns of Court

inner tube *n.* a hollow rubber ring filled with compressed air that fits inside a pneumatic tyre

innervate /ínnur vayt/ (**-vates, -vating, -vated**) *vt.* **1. SUPPLY NERVES TO A BODY ORGAN** to distribute nerves to an organ or body part **2. STIMULATE A MUSCLE, ORGAN, OR BODY PART** to cause a muscle, organ, or other part of the body to act —**innervation** /innur váysh'n/ *n.* —**innervational** /-sh'nəl/ *adj.*

innerve /i núrv/ (**-nerves, -nerving, -nerved**) *vt.* to provide sth with nervous energy

innerwear /ínnər wair/ *n.* clothing that is worn next to the skin, such as a vest or a slip

inner woman *n.* ◊ **inner man 1. A WOMAN'S SOUL** the soul or the spiritual or intellectual part of a woman **2. A WOMAN'S APPETITE** the appetite of a woman (*humorous*)

inning /ínning/ *n.* **1. BASEBALL BASEBALL DIVISION** one of the divisions of a game of baseball or softball during which each team bats until it makes three outs. Nine innings is standard for baseball, seven for softball, but extra innings are played if the score remains tied. **2. CIV ENG RECLAMATION OF LAND FROM THE SEA** the reclamation of marshy or flooded land from the sea (*archaic*) [Old English *innung*, from *innian* 'to put in', from *in* (see IN). In sport, from the sense of 'in possession of the game'.]

innings /ínningz/ (*plural* **-nings**) *n.* **1. CRICKET TURN AT BATTING** the turn of a cricket player or team at batting **2. CRICKET RUNS SCORED DURING AN INNINGS** the runs scored during the turn of a cricket player or team at batting **3. PERIOD OF SUCCESS** a period of opportunity or success, or a long active life or career ○ *He's had a good innings, and he's looking forward to retirement.*

Innisfail /ínnəs fayl/ coastal town in northeastern Queensland, Australia, a fishing port and sugar-growing centre. Population: 8,987 (1996).

innit /ínnit/ *interj.* used as a tag question at the end of a statement (*nonstandard*) ○ *Nice weather, innit?* [Mid-19thC. Alteration.]

innkeeper /ín keepər/ *n.* sb who owns or manages an inn

innocence /ínnəsənss/ *n.* **1. LAW ABSENCE OF GUILT** the state of not being guilty of a crime or offence **2. LAW LAWFULNESS** the state of being permitted by law **3. HARMLESSNESS** harmlessness in intention **4. FREEDOM FROM SIN** freedom from sin or evil **5. LACK OF WORLDLY EXPERIENCE** a lack of experience of the world, especially when this results in a failure to recognize the harmful intentions of other people **6. IGNORANCE** ignorance of the serious consequences of sth such as an act or remark [14thC. Via Old French from Latin *innocentia*, from *innocens* (see INNOCENT).]

innocency /ínnəsənssi/ (*plural* **-cies**) *n.* an innocent action or quality (*archaic*)

innocent /ínnəsənt/ *adj.* **1. LAW NOT GUILTY** not guilty of a crime or offence **2. LAW WITHIN THE LAW** permitted by or acting within the law ○ *an innocent bystander* **3. HARMLESS IN INTENTION** not intended to cause harm ○ *an innocent remark* **4. UNCORRUPTED** pure and uncorrupted by evil, sin, or experience of the world **5. NAIVE** more trusting or naive than most people through lack of experience of life or failure to recognize the motives of others **6. IGNORANT OF STH** having very little or no knowledge of sth ○ *innocent of the finer points of etiquette* **7. LACKING IN STH** completely lacking in a particular quality ○ *innocent of any artistic skill* ■ *n.* **1. BLAMELESS PERSON** a blameless vulnerable person, especially a very young child **2. NAIVE PERSON** a simple, naive, or inexperienced person [14thC. Via Old French from Latin *innocens*, from *in-* 'not' + the present participle of *nocere* 'to harm'.] —**innocently** *adv.*

Innocent III /ínnəss'nt/, Pope (1160?–1216). As pope (1198–1216) he exercised considerable power over the European political rulers of the day, launched the Fourth Crusade (1204), and summoned the Fourth Lateran Council (1215).

innocuous /i nókyoo əss/ *adj.* **1. UNLIKELY TO OFFEND** not intended to cause offence or provoke a strong reaction and unlikely to do so ○ *an innocuous comment* **2. HARMLESS** harmless in effect ○ *an innocuous-seeming white powder* [Late 16thC. From Latin *innocuus*, from *in-* 'not' + *nocuus* 'hurtful', from *nocere* 'to harm'.] —**innocuously** *adv.* —**innocuousness** *n.*

innominate /i nómminət/ *adj.* **1. NAMELESS** without a name (*formal*) **2. UNNAMED** anonymous (*literary*) [Mid-17thC. From late Latin *innominatus*, from *in-* 'not' + *nominatus* (see NOMINATE).]

innominate artery *n.* a short artery rising from the arch of the aorta towards the right upper part of the body. It divides to form the right common carotid artery, which supplies blood to the head, and the right subclavian artery, which supplies blood to the right arm.

innominate bone *n.* a hipbone (*technical*) [Because early anatomists could not think of anything it resembled]

innominate vein *n.* either of two large veins on opposite sides of the neck that join to form the

superior vena cava, one of the two veins taking blood to the heart

innovate /ínnə vayt/ (**-vates, -vating, -vated**) *vti.* to introduce a new way of doing sth or a new device [Mid-16thC. From Latin *innovat-*, from *innovare* 'to renew', from *novus* 'new'.]

innovation /ínnə váysh'n/ *n.* **1. ORIGINATION** the act or process of inventing or introducing sth new **2. NEW IDEA OR METHOD** sth newly invented or a new way of doing things ○ *suspicious of fax machines and other technological innovations* —**innovational** *adj.*

innovative /ínnə vaytiv, ínnəvətiv/ *adj.* new and original or taking a new and original approach [Early 17thC.] —**innovatively** *adv.* —**innovativeness** *n.*

Innu /ínnoo/ (*plural* **-nu**) *n.* **1. PEOPLES ONE OF AN ALGONQUIAN PEOPLE** a member of an Algonquian people living in northern Quebec and Labrador **2. LANG LANGUAGE OF THE INNU** the Algonquian language of the Innu people —**Innu** *adj.*

innuendo /ínnyoo éndō/ (*plural* **-does** *or* **-dos**) *n.* **1. HINT OF STH IMPROPER** an indirect remark or gesture that usually carries a suggestion of impropriety ○ *'"I suppose Mary Garth admires Mr. Lydgate," said Rosamund, not without a touch of innuendo.'* (George Eliot, *Middlemarch*; 1872) **2. LAW INTERPRETATION OF POSSIBLY LIBELLOUS LANGUAGE** an interpretation of words that are claimed to be libellous where the meaning is not obvious, in a legal action for libel or slander **3. LAW GLOSS FOR A TECHNICAL LEGAL WORD** an explanation of a technical legal word, usually given in brackets [Mid-16thC. From Latin *innuendo* 'by intimation', from *innuere* 'to nod to, signify'.]

innumerable /i nyoomərəb'l/ *adj.* too many to be counted [14thC. Via Latin *innumerabilis* from, ultimately, *numerus* 'number'.] —**innumerability** /i nyoomərə bílləti/ *n.* —**innumerableness** /i nyoomərəb'lnəss/ *n.* —**innumerably** /i nyoomərəbli/ *adv.*

innumerate /i nyoomərət/ *adj.* lacking a basic knowledge of mathematics and unable to use numbers in calculation [Mid-20thC. Formed from NUMERATE.]

inobservance /ínnəb zúrvənss/ *n.* **1. LACK OF ATTENTION** lack of heed or attention **2. DISREGARD FOR RULE OR LAW** failure to comply with sth, especially a rule, law, or custom —**inobservant** *adj.* —**inobservantly** *adv.*

inobtrusive /ínnəb troóssiv/ *adj.* = **unobtrusive**

inoculable /i nókyoōləb'l/ *adj.* able to be prevented by inoculation —**inoculability** /i nókyoōlə bílləti/ *n.*

inoculant /i nókyoōlənt/ *n.* = **inoculum**

inoculate /i nókyoō layt/ (**-lates, -lating, -lated**) *vt.* **1. MED PROTECT SB AGAINST DISEASE** to inject or introduce a serum, antigen, or a weakened form of a disease-producing pathogen into sb's body in order to create immunity to the disease ○ *inoculated every child against polio* **2. BIOL ADD MICROORGANISMS TO A CULTURE** to introduce microorganisms into a culture medium [15thC. From Latin *inoculare* 'to graft on a plant part' (the original sense in English), from *oculus* 'bud, eye', the underlying idea being 'implanting sth into an individual'.] —**inoculation** *n.* —**inoculative** /i nókyoōlətiv/ *adj.* —**inoculator** /-laytər/ *n.*

inoculum /i nókyoōləm/ (*plural* **-ula** /-lə/) *n.* material injected into sb or sth to create resistance to a disease [Early 20thC. Formed from Latin *inoculare* 'to inoculate' (see INOCULATE), modelled on COAGULUM.]

inodorous /in ódərəss/ *adj.* having no smell

in-off *n.* a shot in snooker in which the ball hits another ball before falling into a pocket

inoffensive /ínnə fénssiv/ *adj.* not causing harm, annoyance, or offence ○ *the remark was inoffensive enough* —**inoffensively** *adv.* —**inoffensiveness** *n.*

inofficious /ínnə físhəss/ *adj.* LAW violating standards of morality or natural affection, especially failing to give an heir a just share of the inheritance ○ *an inofficious will* [Early 17thC. From Latin *inofficiosus* 'undutiful, not obliging', from *officium* 'duty'.] —**inofficiously** *adv.* —**inofficiousness** *n.*

inoperable /in óppərəb'l/ *adj.* **1. SURG TOO FAR ADVANCED FOR EFFECTIVE SURGERY** having advanced to a stage at which surgical intervention would serve no useful purpose **2. NOT PRACTICAL** not practical or workable —

inoperability /in óppərə bílləti/ *n.* —**inoperableness** /in óppərəb'lnəss/ *n.* —**inoperably** *adv.*

inoperative /in óppərətiv/ *adj.* **1. NOT WORKING** not functioning properly or as usual **2. INEFFECTIVE OR UNENFORCEABLE** not effective or no longer valid or able to be enforced —**inoperatively** *adv.* —**inoperativeness** *n.*

inopportune /in óppər tyoon/ *adj.* happening at a bad moment or an inconvenient time —**inopportunely** *adv.* —**inopportuneness** *n.* —**inopportunity** /in óppə tyoōnəti/ *n.*

inordinate /in áwrdinət/ *adj.* **1. EXCESSIVE** beyond reasonable limits in amount or degree ○ *'capable of expressing an inordinate degree of unreason'* (Henry James, *Roderick Hudson*; 1876) **2. UNRESTRAINED** showing a lack of restraint or control (*archaic or literary*) [14thC. Via Latin *inordinatus* 'not orderly, out of order' from, ultimately, *ordo* 'order'.] —**inordinacy** *n.* —**inordinately** *adv.* —**inordinateness** *n.*

inorg. *abbr.* inorganic

inorganic /ín awr gánnik/ *adj.* **1. NOT ANIMAL OR VEGETABLE** composed of minerals rather than living material **2. CHEM WITHOUT CARBON** used to describe chemical compounds that contain no carbon, excluding the oxides of carbon, carbon disulphide, cyanides, and their associated acids and salts —**inorganically** *adv.*

inorganic chemistry *n.* the branch of chemistry relating to inorganic compounds

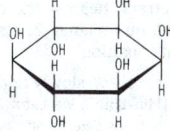

Inositol

inositol /i nóssi tol/ *n.* a cyclic alcohol that has nine related forms, one of which occurs in plants and animals and functions as a growth factor. Formula: $C_6H_{12}O_6$. [Late 19thC. Coined from Greek *inos* 'sinew' + -ITE + -OL.]

inotropic /ínnə tróppik, ínə-/ *adj.* having an effect on the force of muscular contraction ○ *an inotropic drug* [Early 20thC. Coined from Greek *inos* 'sinew, tendon' + -TROPIC.]

inpatient /ín paysh'nt/, **in-patient** *n.* **PERSON STAYING IN HOSPITAL** sb receiving medical treatment that requires a stay in hospital ■ *adj.* **FOR INPATIENTS** relating to, designed for, or used by inpatients [Mid-18thC]

in perpetuum /ín pur péttyoo əm/ *adv.* **LAW** forever [From Latin]

in personam /ín pur sónəm/ *adj., adv.* **LAW** made about or directed at a person rather than at property. ◊ **in rem** [From Latin, literally 'against a person']

in petto /ín péttō/ *adj.* **CHR** not disclosing publicly the name of a cardinal appointed by the pope [Late 17thC. From Italian, literally 'in the breast'.]

inphase /ín fayz/ *adj.* of the same electrical phase

in posse /ín póssi/ *adj.* potentially rather than in reality [From Latin]

inpouring /ín pawring/ *n.* a sudden flowing in of a large amount of sth

in-process *adj.* in the process of being manufactured

in propria persona /ín própri ə pur sónə/ *adv.* **LAW** in person, especially when unrepresented by a lawyer [From Latin, literally 'in your own person']

input /ín poŏt/ *n.* **1. CONTRIBUTION** a contribution to sth, especially comments or suggestions made to a group **2. STH GOING IN** sth that enters a process or situation from the outside and is then acted upon or integrated ○ *sensory input* **3. ELECTRON ENG ELECTRICITY DRIVING A MACHINE** power, electrical energy, or an elec-

trical signal that enters a device and is usually recovered in the form of work or some other output effect **4. COMPUT COMPUTER TERMINAL** a terminal or connection where data enters a computer ■ *v.* (**-puts, -putting, -putted** *or* **-put**) **1.** *vti.* **CONTRIBUTE INFORMATION** to provide information to help sb make a decision (*informal*) **2.** *vt.* **COMPUT ENTER DATA** to enter data into a computer

input/output *n.* the hardware or software that controls the passage of information into and out of a computer or computer component

inq. *abbr.* inquiry

inquest *n.* **1. FORMAL INVESTIGATION** an official inquiry held by a coroner into the facts of a case such as a sudden unexpected death or the discovery of sth valuable that might be treasure trove **2. INQUIRY INTO WHAT WENT WRONG** an investigation of the facts of a situation, particularly one that had an undesired outcome (*literary*) [14thC. Via Old French *enqueste* from Latin *inquesta*, which was formed from *inquirere* 'to enquire' (source of English *enquire*).]

inquietude /in kwí ə tyood/ *n.* a worried or restless state of mind (*literary*) [15thC. Via Late Latin *inquietudo* from, ultimately, Latin *quietus* 'quiet' (source of English *quiet*).]

inquiline /íngkwi līn/ *n.* an animal that lives in the nest or home of another species [Mid-17thC. Via Latin *inquilinus* 'tenant, lodger' from *incolere* 'to inhabit', from *colere* 'to dwell' (source of English *colony* and *culture*).]

inquire /in kwír/ (**-quires, -quiring, -quired**), **enquire** (**-quires, -quiring, -quired**) *v.* **1.** *vti.* **ASK** to ask a question ○ *inquire about a job* ○ *The secretary inquired whether I intended to stay on another year.* **2.** *vi.* **TRY TO FIND OUT THE FACTS** to try to discover the facts of a case [13thC. Via Old French *enquerre* from, ultimately, Latin *inquirere* 'to inquire into', from *quaerere* 'to seek' (source of English *query* and *question*).]

inquire after, **enquire after** *vt.* to ask for news about sb's health or welfare

——————— **WORD KEY: USAGE** ———————

See Usage note at *enquire.*

inquiring /in kwíring/, **enquiring** *adj.* **1. EAGER TO LEARN** eager to learn new things **2. LOOKING QUESTIONING** appearing to want to know or learn sth ○ *an inquiring glance from the attendant* —**inquiringly** *adv.*

inquiry /in kwíri/ (*plural* **-ies**), **enquiry** (*plural* **-ies**) *n.* **1. OFFICIAL REVIEW** a formal investigation to determine the facts of a case **2. REQUEST FOR INFORMATION** a request for information

inquisition /íngkwi zísh'n/ *n.* **1. PERIOD OF INTENSE QUESTIONING** a succession of detailed and relentless questions **2. HARSH INVESTIGATION** an inquiry or investigation that is harsh or unfair [14thC. Via Old French *inquisicion* from Latin *inquirere* 'to inquire' (see INQUIRE).] —**inquisitial** *adj.* —**inquisitionist** *n.*

Inquisition *n.* an organization in the Roman Catholic Church founded in the 13th century to find, question, and sentence those who did not hold orthodox religious beliefs. The Spanish Inquisition lasted until the 19th century and was known for its harsh punishments and use of torture.

inquisitive /in kwízzətiv/ *adj.* **1. INQUIRING** eager for knowledge **2. TOO CURIOUS** too curious about other people's business [14thC. Via Old French from, ultimately, Latin (see INQUIRE).] —**inquisitively** *adv.* —**inquisitiveness** *n.*

inquisitor /in kwízzitər/ *n.* **1. INTERROGATOR** sb who asks a succession of relentless and searching or hostile questions **2. inquisitor, Inquisitor** **HIST ROMAN CATHOLIC QUESTIONER** an official working for the Inquisition [Early 16thC. (See INQUIRE).]

inquisitorial /in kwízzə táwri əl/ *adj.* **1. OF OR LIKE AN INQUISITION** resembling a formal inquiry, especially in using rigorous or relentless questioning **2. HAVING JUDGE AND PROSECUTOR AS THE SAME PERSON** used to describe a trial in which one person is both judge and prosecutor —**inquisitorially** *adv.* —**inquisitorialness** *n.*

inquorate /in kwáw rayt/ *adj.* having too few people present to provide a quorum and therefore unable to make an official decision [Late 20thC. Coined from QUORUM.]

in re /in reé, in ráy/ *prep.* with regard to [From Latin, literally 'in the matter of']

in rem /in rém/ *adj.* **LAW** made about or directed at property rather than a person. ◊ **in personam** [From Latin, literally 'against a thing']

in rerum natura /in ráiroŏm na toŏrə/ *adv.* in the nature of things [From Latin]

in-residence *adj.* **US** officially connected with a university or other institution, often as a teacher or lecturer, but allowed time for original creative work ○ *She completed her book while serving as poet-in-residence at a small college.*

INRI *abbr.* Jesus of Nazareth, King of the Jews (*used as an inscription over the head of the crucified Jesus Christ*) [Latin, Iesus Nazarenus Rex Iudaeorum]

inro /ínrō/ (*plural* **-ro**) *n.* a small ornamented box worn hanging from the sash of a kimono with compartments for holding cosmetics, perfumes, and medicines [Early 17thC. From Japanese *in*, 'seal' + *ro*, 'basket'.]

inroad /ínrōd/ *n.* **RAID** a sudden attack on an enemy camp (*archaic*) ■ **inroads** *npl.* **ENCROACHMENT** a gradual encroachment on or of sth ○ *young companies using electronic sales methods have made inroads into traditional markets* [Mid-16thC. Coined from IN + *road* 'a riding, raid'.]

inrush /ín rush/ *n.* a sudden flooding or flowing in

INS *abbr.* International News Service

ins. *abbr.* **1.** inscription **2. ins., Ins.** inspector **3.** insulation **4.** insurance

insalivate /in sálli vayt/ (**-vates, -vating, -vated**) *vt.* to mix food with saliva in the process of chewing —**insalivation** /in sálli váysh'n/ *n.*

insalubrious /ínssə loŏ bri əss/ *adj.* not pleasant, healthy, or wholesome (*formal*) —**insalubriously** *adv.* —**insalubrity** *n.*

insane /in sáyn/ *adj.* **1. PSYCHIAT LEGALLY CONSIDERED AS PSYCHIATRICALLY DISORDERED** legally incompetent or irresponsible because of a psychiatric disorder **2. LACKING REASONABLE THOUGHT** showing a complete lack of reason or foresight (*informal*) ■ *npl.* **PSYCHIAT PEOPLE LEGALLY CONSIDERED AS PSYCHIATRICALLY DISORDERED** persons who are legally incompetent or irresponsible because of a psychiatric disorder (*dated*) [Mid-16thC. From Latin *insanus*, from *sanus* 'healthy, sane'.] —**insanely** *adv.* —**insaneness** *n.*

insanitary /in sánnitəri/ *adj.* dirty or unhygienic and thus likely to cause disease —**insanitariness** *n.* —**insanitation** /in sánni táysh'n/ *n.*

insanity /in sánnəti/ (*plural* **-ties**) *n.* **1. LACK OF REASON OR GOOD SENSE** extreme foolishness or an act that demonstrates it **2. LAW** legal incompetence or irresponsibility because of a psychiatric disorder

insatiable /in sáyshəb'l/ *adj.* always needing more and impossible to satisfy [15thC. Via Old French from, ultimately, Latin *satiare* 'to fill' (see SATIATE).] —**insatiability** /in sáyshə bílləti/ *n.* —**insatiableness** /in sáyshəb'lnəss/ *n.* —**insatiably** *adv.*

insatiate /in sáyshi ət/ *adj.* insatiable (*literary*) [15thC. From Latin *insatiatus* 'not satisfied' (see SATIATE).] —**insatiately** *adv.* —**insatiateness** *n.*

inscape /ín skayp/ *n.* the distinctive and essential inner quality of sth, especially a natural object or a scene in nature [Mid-19thC. Origin uncertain, probably modelled on LANDSCAPE.]

inscribe /in skríb/ (**-scribes, -scribing, -scribed**) *vt.* **1. PUT WRITING ON STH** to write, print, or engrave words or letters on a surface **2. WRITE STH ON A LIST** to add a name to a list or book **3. WRITE A DEDICATION ON STH** to write a signed message to sb in a book or on a photograph, often when presenting it as a gift **4. GEOM DRAW A GEOMETRIC FIGURE WITHIN ANOTHER** to draw a geometric figure within another so that all of the second figure lies within the first and touches it at as many points as possible ○ *inscribe a circle within a square* [15thC. From Latin *inscribere* 'to write on', from *scribere* 'to write'.] —**inscribable** *adj.* —**inscriber** *n.*

inscription /in skrípsh'n/ *n.* **1. WRITING** words or letters written, printed, or engraved on a surface **2. DEDICATION** a signed message written in a book or on a photograph, often when it is being presented as a gift [14thC. Via Latin from *inscribere* 'to write on'.] —**inscriptional** *adj.*

inscriptive /in skríptiv/ *adj.* relating to or constituting an inscription —**inscriptively** *adv.*

inscrutable /in skrо́otəb'l/ *adj.* hard to interpret because not expressing anything obviously ○ *his inscrutable expression* [16thC. Via Old French from ecclesiastical Latin *inscrutabilis*, from Latin *scrutari* 'to search, investigate' (source of English *scrutiny*).] —**inscrutability** /in skrо́otə bílləti/ *n.* —**inscrutableness** /in skrо́otəb'lnəss/ *n.* —**inscrutably** *adv.*

INSEAD, **Insead** *abbr.* Institut européen d'administration des affaires

inseam /ín seem/ *n.* *US* = **inside leg** [Late 19thC]

insect /ín sekt/ *n.* **1.** ZOOL **SMALL SIX-LEGGED ANIMAL** an air-breathing invertebrate animal (**arthropod**) that has well-defined segments, e.g. a head, thorax, abdomen, two antennae, three pairs of legs, and usually two sets of wings. Class: Insecta. **2. STH LIKE AN INSECT** a small animal that resembles an insect, e.g. a spider or centipede (*not used technically*) **3. CONTEMPTIBLE PERSON** an unimportant person viewed with contempt (*insult*) [Early 17thC. Via Latin *insectum* from *insecare* 'to cut up', from *secare* 'to cut' (source of *dissect* and *segment*).] —**insectan** /in séktən/ *adj.*

insectarium /ínsek táiri əm/ (*plural* **-ums** *or* **-a** /-ə/), **insectary** (*plural* **-ries**) *n.* a place for breeding or observing insects

insecticide /in sékti sīd/ *n.* a chemical substance used to kill insects —**insecticidal** /in sékti sī́d'l/ *adj.* —**insecticidally** *adv.*

insectivore /in sékti vawr/ *n.* **1. SMALL INSECT-EATING MAMMAL** a small nocturnal mammal that feeds primarily on insects. Moles, shrews, and hedgehogs are all insectivores. **2. PLANT OR ANIMAL EATING INSECTS** any plant or animal that feeds primarily on insects [Mid-19thC. From modern Latin *Insectivora*, name of the order, from *insecta* 'insect' (see INSECT) + *-vorus* '-eating'.]

insectivorous /ínsek tívvərəss/ *adj.* **1.** ZOOL **FEEDING ON INSECTS** feeding on insects, as some birds and small mammals do **2.** BOT **ABLE TO TRAP INSECTS** adapted for or capable of trapping insects as food, as the pitcher plant does

insecure /ínssi kyо́or/ *adj.* **1. NOT CONFIDENT** anxious and lacking in self-confidence **2. NOT SAFE** unsafe and unprotected ○ *insecure premises that are vulnerable to thieves* **3. LIKELY TO FALL** liable to fall down or fall off ○ *an insecure walkway* [Mid-17thC. From medieval Latin *insecurus*, 'unsafe'.] —**insecurely** *adv.* —**insecureness** *n.* —**insecurity** *n.*

insecurity (*plural* **-ties**) *n.* **1. BEING INSECURE** the state of being unsafe or insecure **2. UNSAFE FEELING** a state of mind characterized by self-doubt and vulnerability **3. INSECURE PHENOMENON** an instance or cause of being insecure —**insecurity** *n.*

inselberg /ínz'l burg/ *n.* an isolated hill or mountain, often heavily eroded on its lower slopes, rising abruptly from a plain [Early 20thC. From German, literally 'island mountain'.]

inseminate /in sémmi nayt/ (**-nates, -nating, -nated**) *vt.* to put sperm into the reproductive tract of a female [Early 17thC. From *inseminare* 'to implant', which was formed from, ultimately, *semen* 'seed'.] —**insemination** /in sémmi náysh'n/ *n.*

insensate /in sén sayt, -sət/ *adj.* **1. WITHOUT FEELING** inanimate and thus unable to feel anything **2. COLD AND HEARTLESS** entirely lacking in sympathetic feeling or human kindness (*literary*) **3. THOUGHTLESS** lacking in common sense or reasonable thought (*literary*) [15thC. From ecclesiastical Latin *insensatus* (see SENSATE).] —**insensately** *adv.* —**insensateness** *n.*

insensible /in sénssəb'l/ *adj.* **1.** = **insensate** *adj.* 1 **2. NOT CONSCIOUS** without feeling or consciousness **3. NOT AWARE OR RESPONSIVE** unaware of or unresponsive to sth **4. UNNOTICEABLE** so small or gradual as to be almost imperceptible ○ *an insensible shift in emphasis* [14thC. Via Old French from Latin *insensibilis* 'imperceptible', from *sensus* 'perception' (see SENSE).] —**insensibility** /in sénssə bílləti/ *n.* —**insensibleness** /in sénssəb'lnəss/ *n.* —**insensibly** *adv.*

insensitive /in sénssətiv/ *adj.* **1. THOUGHTLESS** insufficiently aware of other people's feelings and unable to respond to them appropriately **2. NOT REACTING PHYSICALLY** not responsive to a physical stimulus such as touch or sound **3. INDIFFERENT AND UNRESPONSIVE** indifferent to the importance of sth and therefore not responding to it —**insensitively** *adv.* —**insensitiveness** *n.* —**insensitivity** /in sénssə tívvəti/ *n.*

insentient /in sénshənt/ *adj.* without life, consciousness, or perception —**insentience** *n.*

inseparable /in séppərəb'l/ *adj.* **1. ALWAYS TOGETHER** sharing a close friendship and always seen or found together ○ *the two girls became inseparable* **2. UNABLE TO BE SEPARATED** so closely linked as to be impossible to consider separately ○ *reading and the ability to spell will seem inseparable* —**inseparability** /in séppərə bílləti/ *n.* —**inseparableness** /in séppərəb'lnəss/ *n.* —**inseparably** *adv.*

insert *vt.* /in súrt/ (**-serts, -serting, -serted**) **1. PLACE STH INSIDE STH** to put sth inside or into sth else ○ *insert the screws in the holes already drilled* **2. ADD STH TO STH** to add new material to the body of sth, especially a text ■ *n.* /ín surt/ **1.** PRESS **ADVERTISING SUPPLEMENT IN A MAGAZINE** a supplement in the form of a single sheet or booklet placed inside a magazine or newspaper, usually as advertising **2.** SEW **ADDED PART** a piece of fabric, usually contrasting, that is sewn into a main piece [15thC. From Latin *serere* 'to join' (source of English *series*).] —**insertable** *adj.* —**inserter** *n.*

insertion /in súrsh'n/ *n.* **1. ADDITION** the act of putting sth into sth else **2. STH ADDED** material that is inserted into a text **3.** ANAT, BOT **ATTACHMENT POINT** the point of attachment of sth, e.g. a leaf to its stem or a muscle to a bone it moves **4.** GENETICS **INSERTED GENETIC MATERIAL** a segment of DNA that is inserted into a gene sequence **5.** SPACE TECH = **injection** *n.* 8, **injection** *n.* 9 —**insertional** *adj.*

insertion stitch *n.* an embroidery stitch that joins two pieces of fabric together and decorates the gap between them

in-service *adj.* **1. HAPPENING WHEN EMPLOYED FULL TIME** taking place while sb is employed full time ○ *an in-service training programme* **2. WORKING AS FULL-TIME EMPLOYEE** employed full time, especially in a particular job

insessorial /in se sáwri əl/ *adj.* used to describe birds that are adapted, or have feet that are adapted, for perching [Mid-19thC. Formed from modern Latin *Insessores*, former name for the order of perching birds, from *insidere* 'to sit on' (see INSIDIOUS).]

inset *vt.* /in sét/ (**-sets, -setting, -set**) **PLACE A SMALLER THING IN A LARGER THING** to insert sth into a larger thing, e.g. a gem in a crown, or a small map in the corner of a larger map ■ *n.* /ín set/ **1. SMALL THING PLACED IN STH LARGER** sth inserted into a larger thing ○ *a map of the state with city maps as insets* **2.** GEOG **CHANNEL** a place where sth flows in, especially the tide

INSET /ín set/, **Inset** *abbr.* in-service education of teachers

inshallah /in shállə/, **insh'allah** *interj.* an expression meaning 'if God wills', used to suggest that sth in the future is uncertain [Mid-19thC. From Arabic *in šā 'Allāh*, literally 'if God wills (it)'.]

inshore /in shawr/ *adj.* **NEAR THE COAST** near or towards the coast ○ *inshore waters* ■ *adv.* **TOWARDS THE COAST** towards the coast from the direction of the sea

inshrine /in shrín/ (**-shrines, -shrining, -shrined**) *vt.* = **enshrine**

inside /in síd, ín sīd/ CORE MEANING: a grammatical word indicating the interior part of sth, the part that is enclosed by or surrounded with sth, or the place or part within ○ (adv) *I opened the door and looked inside.* ○ (adj) *his inside jacket pocket* ○ (n) *I looked round the room, gnawing the inside of my cheek nervously.* ○ (prep) *The jewels are kept inside a locked box.*

1. *adj., prep.* **WITHIN AN ORGANIZATION** happening or coming from within an organization ○ *They had access to inside information about the takeover bid.* ○ *things that were going on inside the committee* **2.** *adv., prep.* **RELATING TO INNER FEELINGS** indicating emotions that are not expressed ○ *She doesn't like to look inside and face up to what she's really like.* ○ *Seeing her like that had snapped something inside him.* **3.** *prep.* **WITHIN A TIME** done in a period of time less than the one stated ○ *We managed to completely redecorate the room inside seven hours.* **4.** *adj.* **AT THE EDGE OF THE ROAD** nearest the edge of the road **5.** *adv.* **IN PRISON** serving time in prison (*informal*) ○ *He was inside for three years.* **6.** *n.* **INNER EDGE** the part of a road or path farthest from the centre ○ *was forced to overtake him on the inside* **7.** *n.* **PRIVILEGED ACCESS** a position that gives access to privileged information ○ *information from someone on the inside* **8.** *npl.* **insides** ANAT **INTERNAL ORGANS** the internal organs of the body, especially the stomach and bowels (*informal*) [15thC] ◇ **inside of** within a particular period of time ◇ **inside out** with the part that is normally inside facing outwards ◇ **know sth inside out** to know sth extremely well

inside job *n.* a crime carried out by or with the help of sb who works for the individual or organization concerned (*informal*)

inside lane *n.* the section of a multiple-lane road nearest to the left, used by vehicles being overtaken and those turning off the road

inside leg *n.* US term **inseam 1.** CLOTHES **INSIDE TROUSER LEG SEAM** the inner seam of a pair of trousers, from the crotch to the bottom of the trouser leg **2. MEASUREMENT OF INSIDE LEG** the measurement of a trouser leg's inner seam

insider /in sídər/ *n.* sb who is accepted as a member of a group and who knows all about its inner workings

insider trading *n.* profitable trading in securities that is done using access to privileged information. Such trading is usually illegal.

inside track *n.* **1.** SPORTS **INNER LANE OF RACETRACK** the lane of an oval racetrack nearest the centre and thus shorter than the outer lanes **2. POSITION OF ADVANTAGE** an advantageous position

insidious /in síddi əss/ *adj.* slowly and subtly harmful or destructive [Mid-16thC. Via Latin *insidiosus* from *insidiae* 'ambush', from *insidere* 'to sit on, lie in wait', from *sedere* 'to sit' (source of English *sedentary, session, reside,* and *seance*).] —**insidiously** *adv.* —**insidiousness** *n.*

insight /ín sīt/ *n.* **1. PERCEPTIVENESS** the ability to see clearly and intuitively into the nature of a complex person, situation or subject **2. CLEAR PERCEPTION** a clear perception of sth ○ *thanked him for his remark and told him it was an interesting insight* **3.** PSYCHOL **SELF-AWARENESS** the ability of a person to understand and find solutions to his or her personal problems **4.** PSYCHIAT **PERCEPTION THAT HALLUCINATIONS ARE NOT REAL** the perception, lacking in some psychiatric disorders such as schizophrenia, that symptoms such as delusions and hallucinations are not objective [Old English]

insightful /ín sītf'l/ *adj.* containing or capable of clear and subtle perceptions about a subject [Early 20thC] —**insightfully** *adv.* —**insightfulness** *n.*

insight meditation *n.* = **vipassana**

insigne /in sígni/ singular of **insignia** (*literary*)

insignia /in sígni ə/ (*plural* **-a** *or* **-as**) *n.* **1. OFFICIAL SYMBOL** a badge of authority or membership of a group **2. IDENTIFYING MARK** an identifying mark or sign [Mid-17thC. From Latin *insignis* 'marked', from *signum* 'sign'.]

insignificant /ínssig níffikənt/ *adj.* **1. WITHOUT IMPORTANCE** too small and unimportant to be relevant ○ *statistically insignificant* **2. WITHOUT MEANING** having little or no meaning **3. POWERLESS** lacking in power or status —**insignificance** *n.* —**insignificantly** *adv.*

insincere /ínssin séer/ *adj.* not genuine and not reflecting true feelings —**insincerely** *adv.* —**insincerity** /ínssin sérrəti/ *n.*

insinuate /in sínnyoo ayt/ (**-ates, -ating, -ated**) *v.* **1.** *vti.* **IMPLY STH** to hint at sth unpleasant or suggest it indirectly and gradually **2.** *vr.* **WORM YOUR WAY IN** to introduce yourself gradually and cunningly into a position, especially a place of confidence or favour [Early 16thC. From Latin *insinuare*, from *sinus* 'curve' (source of English *sine*). The underlying sense is 'to work in a roundabout way'.] —**insinuatingly** *adv.* —**insinuative** /in sínnyoo ətiv/ *adj.* —**insinuator** /-aytər/ *n.*

insinuation /in sínnyoo áysh'n/ *n.* **1. SLY HINT** sth unpleasant artfully and indirectly suggested to another person **2. ACT OF INSINUATING** the act of hinting

a at; aa father; aw all; ay day; air hair; ə about, edible, item, common, circus; e egg; ee eel; hw when; i it, happy; ī ice; 'l apple; 'm rhythm; 'n fashion; o odd; ō open; о́o good; oo pool; ow owl; oy oil; th thin; th this; u up; ur urge;

sth unpleasant or suggesting it indirectly and gradually

insipid /in síppid/ *adj.* **1. DULL** dull because lacking in character and lively qualities ○ *'that insipid languor that results from the removal of all passions from the mind'* (David Hume) **2. FLAVOURLESS** bland and without flavour [Early 17thC. Directly or via French from late Latin *insipidus* 'tasteless', from *sapidus* 'having a flavour'.] —**insipidity** /inssi píddəti/ *n.* —**insipidly** /in síppidli/ *adv.* —**insipidness** *n.*

insist /in síst/ (**-sists, -sisting, -sisted**) *vti.* **1. MAINTAIN STH AGAINST OPPOSITION** to state or demand sth firmly in spite of disagreement or resistance from others ○ *She insisted that he was wrong.* ○ *Please, you must take it, I insist!* **2. DECLARE STH PERSISTENTLY** to state sth firmly and steadfastly ○ *They insist on punctuality.* ○ *he insisted there was nothing to worry about* [Late 16thC. From Latin *insistere* 'to persist', from *sistere* 'to stand, cause to stand'.]

insistence /in sístənss/, **insistency** /-tənssi/ *n.* continued assertion of sth despite disagreement from others ○ *the UN's insistence that the resolution must be accepted*

insistent /in sístənt/ *adj.* **1. PERSISTENT** persistent in maintaining or demanding sth ○ *she was most insistent* **2. DEMANDING ATTENTION** persistently calling for or compelling attention ○ *insistent pleas* —**insistently** *adv.*

in situ /in síttyoo/ *adv., adj.* in its natural or original place ○ *a useful tool for studying cell proliferation in situ under normal and pathological conditions* [From Latin]

insnare *vt.* = **ensnare**

insobriety /ínssō brí əti/ *n.* lack of moderation, especially in drinking

insofar as /in sō fáar əz/ *conj.* used to introduce a statement that explains or qualifies a previous statement (*formal*)

insol. *abbr.* insoluble

insolate /ínsō layt/ (**-lates, -lating, -lated**) *vt.* to expose sth to sunlight [Early 17thC. From Latin *insolare*, from *sol* 'sun' (source of English *solar*).]

insolation /ínssō láysh'n/ *n.* **1. EXPOSURE TO SUNLIGHT** exposure of sth to sunlight **2.** MED **SUNSTROKE** sunstroke (*technical*) **3.** ASTROPHYS **RATE OF SOLAR RADIATION** the rate of solar radiation received per unit area

insole /ínssōl/ *n.* **1. SHOE LINING** the inner lining of a shoe **2. PAD INSIDE SHOE** a thin removable liner placed inside a shoe to make it warmer or more comfortable or to prevent the buildup of odour

insolent /ínssələnt/ *adj.* showing an aggressive lack of respect in speech or behaviour [14thC. From Latin *insolens* 'unusual, arrogant', from *solere* 'to be accustomed'.] —**insolence** *n.* —**insolently** *adv.*

insolubilize /in sóllyŏŏbə līz/ (**-lizes, -lizing, -lized**), **insolubilise** (**-lises, -lising, -lised**) *vt.* to make sth incapable of being dissolved in a liquid —**insolubilization** /in sóllyŏŏbə lī záysh'n/ *n.*

insoluble /in sóllyŏŏb'l/ *adj.* **1. NOT DISSOLVABLE** incapable of being dissolved in a liquid **2. IMPOSSIBLE TO SOLVE** not able to be solved —**insolubility** /in sóllyŏŏ bílləti/ *n.* —**insolubleness** /in sóllyŏŏb'lnəss/ *n.* —**insolubly** *adv.*

insolvable /in sólvəb'l/ *adj.* = **insoluble** *adj.* 2

insolvency /in sólvənssi/ (*plural* **-cies**) *n.* the condition of being unable to pay debts, or an instance of this

insolvent /in sólvənt/ *adj.* **1.** FIN **BANKRUPT** unable to pay debts **2.** LAW **OF BANKRUPTCY** relating to people or businesses that are bankrupt ■ *n.* FIN **BANKRUPT PERSON** sb who is unable to pay his or her debts

insomnia /in sómni ə/ *n.* inability to fall asleep or to remain asleep long enough to feel rested, especially as a problem continuing over time [Early 17thC. Coined from Latin *insomnis* 'sleepless', from *somnus* 'sleep'.] —**insomniac** /-ni ak/ *adj., n.*

insomuch as /ínssō múch az/ *conj.* used to introduce an explanation or reason

insomuch that *conj.* used to indicate the extent to which sth is true or is the case

insouciance /in sóossi ənss/ *n.* cheerful lack of anxiety or concern [Early 19thC. Via French from *soucier*, 'to care', formed from Latin *solicitare* 'to trouble' (source of English *solicit*).]

insouciant /in sóossi ənt/ *adj.* cheerfully unconcerned or unworried about sth [Early 19thC. From French, from *souciant*, present participle of *soucier* 'to care', from Latin *sollicitare* 'to disturb'.]

insoul *vt.* = **ensoul**

insp. *abbr.* **1.** inspected **2. insp., Insp.** inspector

inspan /in spán/ (**-spans, -spanning, -spanned**) *vt.* *S Africa* to harness an animal to a vehicle [Early 19thC. Via Afrikaans from Dutch *inspannen*. Ultimately from a prehistoric Germanic word meaning 'to bind, stretch', which is also the ancestor of English *span*[1] and *span*[2].]

inspect /in spékt/ (**-spects, -specting, -spected**) *vt.* **1. LOOK AT STH CRITICALLY** to examine sth carefully in order to judge its quality or correctness ○ *She took the cheese out of the refrigerator and inspected it for mould.* **2. SURVEY STH** to examine or review sth officially ○ *The barracks is inspected every day.* [Early 17thC. From Latin *inspicere*, from *specere* 'to look at'.] —**inspectable** *adj.* —**inspective** *adj.*

inspection /in spéksh'n/ *n.* **1. CRITICAL EXAMINATION** a critical examination of sb or sth aimed at forming a judgment or evaluation **2. OFFICIAL EXAMINATION** an official and authoritative examination of sth ○ *a motor vehicle inspection* [14thC. Via French from, ultimately, Latin *inspect-* (see INSPECT).]

inspection arms *n.* a position in which a rifle is held diagonally in front of the body with the muzzle pointing upwards to the left and the rifle chamber open for inspection

inspector /in spéktər/ *n.* **1. OFFICIAL EXAMINER** an official who examines sth in order to judge its quality or compliance with rules or the law **2. POLICE OFFICER OF MIDDLE RANK** a police officer of the rank above a sergeant and below a superintendent —**inspectoral** *adj.* —**inspectorial** /ín spek táwri əl/ *adj.* —**inspectorship** /in spéktər ship/ *n.*

inspectorate /in spéktərət/ *n.* **1. GROUP OF INSPECTORS** a group or department of inspectors **2. INSPECTOR'S DISTRICT** an area supervised by an inspector **3. INSPECTOR'S DUTIES** the office or duties of an inspector

inspector general (*plural* **inspectors general**) *n.* **1. HEAD OF INSPECTORS** an official who is the head of an inspectorate **2.** MIL **MILITARY INSPECTOR** a military officer who investigates and reports on organizational matters

insphere *vt.* = **ensphere**

inspiration /ínspi ráysh'n/ *n.* **1. STIMULUS TO DO CREATIVE WORK** sth that stimulates the human mind to creative thought or to the making of art ○ *found inspiration in the landscape around her* **2. THING THAT INSPIRES** sb or sth that inspires sb ○ *His book is an inspiration to all would-be travellers.* **3. CREATIVENESS** the quality of being stimulated to creative thought or activity, or the manifestation of this ○ *a moment of inspiration* **4. GOOD IDEA** a sudden brilliant idea **5.** RELIG **DIVINE INFLUENCE** divine guidance and influence on human beings **6.** PHYSIOL **BREATHING IN** the drawing of air into the lungs [14thC. Via Old French from Latin *inspiratio*.]

inspirational /ínspi ráysh'nəl/ *adj.* **1. BRINGING INSPIRATION** bringing or showing creative stimulus **2. STIMULATING PEOPLE TO ACHIEVE** stimulating people into greater efforts or more enthusiasm or more creative behaviour ○ *an inspirational leader* —**inspirationally** *adv.*

inspirator /ínspi raytər/ *n.* a device for drawing in a gas or vapour [Late 19thC. Formed from INSPIRE.]

inspiratory /in spírətəri/ *adj.* relating to the process of breathing in, or used in breathing in [Late 18thC. Formed from INSPIRE.]

inspire /in spír/ (**-spires, -spiring, -spired**) *v.* **1.** *vti.* **STIMULATE SB TO DO STH** to encourage people into greater efforts or greater enthusiasm or creativity **2.** *vt.* **PROVOKE A FEELING** to arouse a particular feeling in sb **3.** *vt.* **CAUSE CREATIVE ACTIVITY** to stimulate sb to do sth, especially creative work or the making of art **4.** *vti.* PHYSIOL **BREATHE IN** to inhale air or a gas into the lungs [14thC. Via Old French *enspirer* from Latin *inspirare*, from *spirare* 'to breathe' (source of English *spirit*).] —**inspirable** *adj.* —**inspirative** *adj.* —**inspirer** *n.*

inspired /in spírd/ *adj.* **1. EXTRAORDINARILY GOOD** brilliant and creative ○ *an inspired rendition of a classic song* ○ *She was an inspired teacher.* **2. MOTIVATED BY STH** based on a particular motive or example (*usually used in combination*) ○ *a Jesuit-inspired curriculum*

inspiring /in spíring/ *adj.* making sb feel more enthusiastic, confident, or stimulated —**inspiringly** *adv.*

inspirit /in spírrit/ (**-its, -iting, -ited**) *vt.* to give energy or courage to sb (*archaic or literary*) —**inspiriter** *n.* —**inspiritingly** *adv.*

inspissate /in spíss ayt/ (**-sates, -sating, -sated**) *vti.* to become thicker in consistency or to cause sth to thicken, especially by boiling or evaporation [Early 17thC. From Latin *inspissare* 'to thicken', from *spissus* 'thick'.] —**inspissator** /inspiss aytər/ *n.*

INST *abbr.* in the name of the Holy Trinity [Latin, *in nomine Sanctae Trinitaris*]

inst. *abbr.* **1.** COMM instant **2.** instantaneous **3. inst., Inst.** institute **4. inst., Inst.** institution **5.** institutional

instability /ínstə bílləti/ *n.* **1. BEING UNSTABLE** the quality of being unstable, erratic, or unpredictable **2. NOT STEADY** lack of steadiness or firmness

install /in stáwl/, **instal** *v.* (**-stalls, -stalling, -stalled; -stals, -stalling, -stalled**) **1.** *vt.* **FIT OR CONNECT STH** to put machinery or equipment into place and make it ready for use **2.** *vt.* COMPUT **LOAD SOFTWARE** to load software onto a computer **3.** *vt.* **PLACE SB IN OFFICE** to appoint sb to a particular position or to induct sb formally into office **4.** *vr.* **SETTLE IN** to settle yourself comfortably somewhere ■ *n.* COMPUT **ACT OF LOADING SOFTWARE** the act of loading software onto a computer ○ *'I opted for the full install, which can involve anything up to 72Mb of space'.* (*Internet Magazine*; November 1998) [15thC. Directly or via Old French *installer* from medieval Latin *installare* 'to place in office', from *stallum* 'stall'.] —**installer** *n.*

installant /in stáwlənt/ *n.* sb who appoints another person to a particular position, or who formally inducts another person into office

installation /ínstə láysh'n/ *n.* **1. ACT OF INSTALLING EQUIPMENT** the process of putting a piece of equipment or machinery in place and setting it up ready for use **2. PLACE WITH EQUIPMENT** a place housing equipment or machinery for a particular use ○ *a communications installation* **3. STH THAT HAS BEEN INSTALLED** a piece or system of equipment that has been put in place and made ready for use **4.** MIL **MILITARY BASE** a military base or camp ○ *The artillery installation on the island is marked in red on the map.* **5. APPOINTING OF SB TO POSITION** the act of appointing sb to a particular position or of inducting sb formally into office **6.** ARTS **ART EXHIBIT** an artwork assembled by the artist involving the arrangement of three-dimensional objects or the use of paint and other media directly on walls or floors ○ *an installation using video monitors and empty bottles*

installment *n.* *US* = **instalment**

installment plan *n.* *US* = **hire purchase**

instalment /in stáwlmənt/ *n.* one of the parts of sth that appears or is presented at intervals ○ *published in instalments* ○ *'The working documents now circulating are but the latest instalment of a debate that first surfaced in the 1970s'.* (Art Weissman, *Pulse of the People*; 1997) [Mid-18thC. Via Anglo-Norman *estallment* from Old French *estaler* 'to fix, place'.]

instance /ínstənss/ *n.* **1. ILLUSTRATION** an example of a particular situation or event ○ *cited several instances of his being untruthful* **2. EVENT** an occurrence of sth ○ *we can overlook it in this instance* **3. REQUEST** a request or demand (*archaic*) **4.** LAW **LEGAL ACTION** a legal proceeding or lawsuit ■ *vt.* (**-stances, -stancing, -stanced**) **GIVE AS AN EXAMPLE** to offer sth as an example [14thC. Via French *instance* and medieval Latin *instantia* from, ultimately, Latin *instans* 'present' (see INSTANT).] ◇ **for instance** as an example ◇ **in the first instance** used to indicate sth that is or happens first, before other events or stages (*formal*)

instancy /ínstənssi/ *n.* **1. URGENCY** the need for sth to be done without delay, or insistence that it be done **2. LACK OF DELAY** immediateness or lack of delay

instant /ínstənt/ *adj.* **1. IMMEDIATE** happening immediately, without delay ○ *She demanded instant service.* **2.** FOOD **QUICK TO PREPARE** quickly and easily prepared, often premixed, precooked, or powdered ○ *instant coffee* **3. SUDDEN** achieving a particular status very suddenly and effortlessly ○ *the play was an instant success* **4. URGENT AND PRESSING** requiring immediate attention or an immediate response ○ *an instant need for help* **5.** COMM **FROM THIS MONTH** happening in the current month ○ *your letter of the 13th instant* **6. CURRENT** present or current (*archaic*) ■ *n.* **1. SHORT TIME** an extremely brief period of time ○ *for an instant* **2. MOMENT IN TIME** a particular moment in time ○ *The instant I saw his face I knew that something was wrong.* **3.** FOOD **INSTANT PRODUCT** a quickly prepared item of food or drink ■ *adv.* **INSTANTLY** instantly (*literary*) [15thC. Via Old French from Latin *instare* 'to be present', from *stare* 'to stand'.] —**instantness** *n.*

instantaneous /ínstən táyni əss/ *adj.* **1. HAPPENING IMMEDIATELY** occurring immediately or almost immediately **2.** MATH **OF VALUE AT GIVEN INSTANT** indicating the value of sth at a given moment in time, expressed as the average value of a varying quantity over an infinitesimally small time interval ○ *instantaneous velocity* [Mid-17thC. Via medieval Latin *instantaneus* from Latin *instans* 'present' (see INSTANT).] —**instantaneity** /in stántə náy əti, -née əti/ *n.* —**instantaneously** /ínstən táyni əssli/ *adv.* —**instantaneousness** *n.*

instantiate /in stánshi ayt/ (**-ates, -ating, -ated**) *vt.* to provide an example to support or explain sth [Mid-20thC. Formed from INSTANCE.]

instantly /ínstəntli/ *adv.* **1. IMMEDIATELY** immediately and without delay **2. URGENTLY** urgently or insistently (*archaic*) ■ *conj.* **AS SOON AS** happening or done immediately after sth else ○ *I phoned instantly I heard you were back.*

instant-on *adj.* including a device that allows for a rapid start-up, eliminating the need for a warm-up period

instant replay *n. US* = **action replay**

instar /ín staar/ *n.* in the life cycle of an arthropod such as an insect, a stage between two successive moults [Late 19thC. From Latin 'form, image'.]

instate /in stáyt/ (**-states, -stating, -stated**) *vt.* to establish sb in office —**instatement** *n.*

in statu quo /in státtoo kwṓ/ *adv.* in the same state [From Latin *in statu quo ante*, literally 'in the (same) state as before']

instauration /ín staw ráysh'n/ *n.* (*formal*) **1. RENOVATION** the restoration of sth that has lapsed or fallen into decay **2. FOUNDING** the founding or establishment of sth [Early 17thC. From Latin *instaurare* 'to renew' (source of English *store*).] —**instaurator** /ín staw raytər/ *n.*

instead /in stéd/ *adv.* as a replacement or substitute for sth [13thC. Formed from IN + *stede* 'place'.] ◇ **instead of** as an alternative to, or substitute for, sth

instep /ín step/ *n.* **1.** ANAT **UPPER MIDDLE AREA OF THE FOOT** the arched middle portion of the human foot between the ankle and toes, especially its upper surface **2.** CLOTHES **MIDDLE PART OF A SHOE** the part of a shoe that covers the middle portion of the foot [15thC. Origin unknown.]

instigate /ínsti gayt/ (**-gates, -gating, -gated**) *vt.* **1. GET STH STARTED** to cause a process to start **2. START TROUBLE** to cause trouble, especially by urging sb to do sth destructive or wrong [Mid-16thC. From Latin *instigare*.] —**instigation** *n.* —**instigative** *adj.* —**instigator** *n.*

instil /in stíl/ (**-stils, -stilling, -stilled**) *vt.* **1. IMPART STH GRADUALLY** to impress ideas, principles, or teachings gradually on sb's mind ○ *I tried to instil self-respect in my students.* **2. DRIP LIQUID INTO STH** to pour medicine or another liquid into sth drop by drop [15thC. From Latin *instillare*, from *stilla* 'drop'.] —**instillation** /ínsti láysh'n/ *n.* —**instiller** /in stíllər/ *n.* —**instilment** /-mənt/ *n.*

instill *vt. US* = **instil**

instinct /in stingkt/ *n.* **1. BIOLOGICAL DRIVE** an inborn pattern of behaviour characteristic of a species and shaped by biological necessities such as survival and reproduction **2. STRONG NATURAL IMPULSE** a powerful impulse that feels natural rather than reasoned ○ *followed his instincts and took to his heels* **3. KNACK** a natural gift or skill ○ *an instinct for putting people at ease* ■ *adj.* **FILLED** completely filled or imbued with sth (*formal*) ○ *a look instinct with compassion* [15thC. Via Latin *instinctus* 'impulse' from *instinguere* 'to incite', from *stinguere* 'to sting, goad' (source of English *distinct* and *extinct*).]

instinctive /in stíngktiv/ *adj.* **1. INVOLUNTARY** relating to, prompted by, or based on a strong natural impulse ○ *an instinctive fear of water* **2. NATURAL** having a particular quality or skill spontaneously and without effort or instruction ○ *an artist with an instinctive feel for colour* ○ *an instinctive cook* —**instinctively** *adv.*

instinctual /in stíngktyoo əl/ *adj.* relating to or prompted by a basic biological need [Early 20thC. Formed from INSTINCT + *-ual*, adjective suffix.] —**instinctually** *adv.*

institute /ínsti tyoot/ *vt.* (**-tutes, -tuting, -tuted**) **1. START STH** to start or initiate sth in an official or formal way ○ *institute legal proceedings* **2. APPOINT SB** to appoint sb to an office, especially a religious one **3. SET STH UP** to set up or establish sth ■ *n.* **1. ORGANIZATION WITH A SPECIALIZED GOAL** an organization for promoting sth, such as art, science, or the well-being of a group **2. PLACE FOR ADVANCED STUDY** an educational institution, especially one concerned with technical subjects **3. RULE** an established principle or rule ■ **institutes** *npl.* LAW **LAW SUMMARY** a summary of laws [14thC. From Latin *instituere* 'to establish', from *statuere* 'to set up', from *stare* 'to stand' (source of English *constant* and *stage*).] —**instituter** *n.*

institution /ínsti tyóosh'n/ *n.* **1. IMPORTANT ORGANIZATION** a large organization such as a college, hospital, or bank that is influential in the community **2. ESTABLISHED PRACTICE** an established law, custom, or practice ○ *the institution of marriage* **3. STARTING OF STH** the act of initiating or establishing sth **4. LONG-ESTABLISHED PERSON OR THING** sb or sth that has been well-known and established in a place for many years (*informal*) **5. PLACE OF CARE OR CONFINEMENT** a place where people with mental or physical disabilities are cared for **6.** FIN **LARGE AND POWERFUL INVESTOR** a large financial organization, e.g. a pension fund, that has considerable resources to make investments ○ *a mutual fund available only to institutions* —**institutional** *adj.* —**institutionally** *adv.* —**institutionary** *adj.*

institutionalism /ínsti tyóosh'nəlizəm/ *n.* a belief in the merits of established customs and systems —**institutionalist** *n.*

institutionalize /ínsti tyóosh'nə līz/ (**-izes, -izing, -ized**), **institutionalise** (**-ises, -ising, -ised**) *vt.* **1. PUT SB INTO AN INSTITUTION** to put sb into an institution such as a children's home, nursing home, or prison **2. ESTABLISH STH AS NORMAL** to make sth an established custom or an accepted part of the structure of a large organization or society **3. MAKE INTO OR LIKE INSTITUTION** to convert sth into an institution or make sth resemble an institution —**institutionalization** /ínsti tyóosh'nə lī záysh'n/ *n.*

institutionalized /ínsti tyóosh'nə līzd/ *adj.* **1. ESTABLISHED AS NORMAL** having become an established custom or an accepted part of the structure of a large organization or society because it has existed for so long **2. DEPENDENT ON THE ROUTINE OF INSTITUTION** lacking the will or ability to think and act independently because of having spent a long time in an institution such as a psychiatric hospital or prison

institutive /ínsti tyootiv/ *adj.* serving to establish or being established —**institutively** *adv.*

in-store *adj.* happening, available, or situated within a large store, e.g. a supermarket or department store ○ *an in-store bakery*

instr. *abbr.* **1.** instruction **2.** instructor **3.** instrument **4.** GRAM, MUSIC instrumental

instruct /in strúkt/ (**-structs, -structing, -structed**) *v.* **1.** *vti.* **TRAIN SB** to teach sb a subject or how to do sth **2.** *vt.* **DIRECT SB** to tell sb to do sth, especially with authority or as an order **3.** *vt.* **OBTAIN LEGAL REPRESENTATION** to ask or authorize a lawyer to act on your behalf and supply him or her with relevant information **4.** *vt.* **GIVE SB INFORMATION** to inform sb about sth, especially in a formal or official manner ○ *We were instructed that the meeting had been postponed.* [15thC. From Latin *instruct-*, the past participle stem of *instruere* 'to prepare, equip', from *struere* 'to build'.] —**instructible** *adj.*

WORD KEY: SYNONYMS

See Synonyms at ***teach***.

instruction /in strúksh'n/ *n.* **1. TEACHING OR THINGS TAUGHT** teaching in a particular subject or skill, or the facts or skills taught ○ *driving instruction* **2. TEACHING PROFESSION OR PROCESS** the profession of teaching or the teaching process **3. ORDER** a spoken or written statement of what must be done, especially delivered formally, with official authority, or as an order ○ *acting on instructions we received* **4.** COMPUT **COMMAND** a code that tells a computer to perform a specific operation ■ **instructions** *npl.* **1. LIST OF THINGS TO DO** printed information about how to do, make, assemble, use, or operate sth ○ *The instructions are printed on the back of the packet.* **2.** LAW **BRIEFING TO LAWYER** the relevant information about a legal case given by a client to a solicitor or a solicitor to a barrister —**instructional** *adj.*

instructive /in strúktiv/ *adj.* providing useful information or insight into sth —**instructively** *adv.* —**instructiveness** *n.*

instructor /in strúktər/ *n.* sb who teaches sth, often a sport or a practical skill ○ *a ski instructor* —**instructorship** *n.*

instrument /ínstrōōmənt/ *n.* **1.** SCI **TOOL** a tool or mechanical device, especially one used for precision work in science, medicine, or technology **2.** MUSIC **OBJECT THAT PRODUCES MUSIC** an object used to produce musical notes, e.g. by blowing through an opening, plucking or rubbing its strings, or striking it **3.** MEASURE **MEASURING DEVICE** a device that measures or controls sth, such as a speedometer or voltometer **4. MEANS OF DOING STH** sth or sb used as a means of achieving a desired result or accomplishing a particular purpose (*usually used in the singular*) ○ *The secret police were the state's instrument for controlling the populace.* **5. OBJECT USED FOR SOME PURPOSE** an object that has been or could be used for some purpose (*formal*) ○ *hit on the head by a blunt instrument* **6.** LAW **DOCUMENT** a legal document (*formal*) ■ *vt.* (**-ments, -menting, -mented**) **1.** MUSIC **ARRANGE MUSIC** to write or arrange a piece of music for performance on musical instruments **2.** SCI **SUPPLY WITH MEASURING DEVICES** to equip sth with instruments for measurement or control [13thC. Via Old French from Latin *instrumentum*, from *instruere* 'to prepare'.]

instrumental /ínstrōō mént'l/ *adj.* **1.** MUSIC **FOR INSTRUMENTS, NOT VOICES** played on one or more musical instruments and not sung or accompanied by singing **2. CONNECTED WITH INSTRUMENTS** done with or produced by an instrument or instruments **3. MAKING STH HAPPEN** playing an important part in achieving a result or accomplishing a purpose ○ *she was instrumental in getting the legislation passed* **4.** GRAM **INDICATING THE MEANS OF DOING STH** describing a noun case that indicates sth is used for a purpose or is the means by which sth is done **5.** PHILOS **OF INSTRUMENTALISM** relating to instrumentalism ■ *n.* **1.** MUSIC **MUSIC PLAYED BY INSTRUMENTS** a piece of music, or part of a piece of music, that is played by one or more musical instruments and is not sung or accompanied by singing **2.** GRAM **NOUN FORM INDICATING THE MEANS OF DOING STH** the form (**case**) of a noun indicating that sth is used for a purpose or is the means of doing sth, or a noun in this form —**instrumentally** *adv.*

instrumentalism /ínstrōō mént'lizəm/ *n.* PHILOS the view that theories are useful tools for making predictions but cannot be literally true or false

instrumentalist /ínstrōō mént'list/ *n.* **1.** MUSIC **PLAYER OF INSTRUMENT** sb who plays a musical instrument **2.** PHILOS **PROPONENT OF INSTRUMENTALISM** a supporter or advocate of instrumentalism ■ *adj.* PHILOS **FOR INSTRUMENTALISM** supporting or advocating instrumentalism

instrumentality /ínstrōō men tálləti/ (*plural* **-ties**) *n.* (*formal*) **1. ACTION OR USE** sb's action or the use of sb or sth in getting sth done ○ *'But for her instrumentality, the fatal knowledge would not have been imparted'.* (Elizabeth Gaskell, *Some Passages from the History of the Chomley Family*; 1865) **2.** *US* POL **SECTION** in the United States, a subbranch of a department or agency ○ *a department, agency, or instrumentality of the executive, legislative, and judicial branches of the federal government* [Mid-17thC]

instrumental learning *n.* PSYCHOL a form of learning that takes place as a direct consequence of a reward or pleasant outcome for the learner

instrumentation /ínstroo̖ men táysh'n, ínstrəmən-/ *n.* **1.** MUSIC **ARRANGEMENT FOR MUSICAL INSTRUMENTS** the composition or arrangement of music for performance, in which a combination of musical instruments is specified **2.** MUSIC **MUSICAL INSTRUMENTS USED** the particular instruments that are to perform a piece of music **3. EQUIPMENT FOR CONTROL OR OPERATION** a set of instruments used for a particular purpose, e.g. operating a machine or controlling an aircraft **4. USE OF INSTRUMENTS** the use of instruments as tools or for measurement or control **5. MAKING INSTRUMENTS** the design, development, or manufacture of instruments for use in science, medicine, technology, or industry **6. MEANS** the means or agency through which sth is done (*formal*)

instrument board *n.* = **instrument panel**

instrument flying *n.* the flying of an aircraft using only information obtained from instruments rather than from what the pilot can see

instrument landing *n.* landing an aircraft while relying on information from instruments rather than from looking out of the aircraft's window

instrument panel *n.* a set of instruments mounted at the front of a machine or in front of sb driving or steering a motor vehicle, aircraft, or ship

insubordinate /ínssə báwrdinət/ *adj.* **DISOBEDIENT OR REBELLIOUS** refusing to obey orders or submit to authority ■ *n.* **DISOBEDIENT OR REBELLIOUS PERSON** sb who refuses to obey orders or submit to authority —**insubordinately** *adv.* —**insubordination** /ínssə báwrdə náysh'n/ *n.*

insubstantial /ínssəb stánsh'l/ *adj.* **1. SMALL AND WEAK** not very large, solid, or strong **2. NOT TANGIBLE** not existing in reality ○ *an insubstantial apparition* —**insubstantiality** /ínssəb stanshi álləti/ *n.* —**insubstantially** /ínssəb stánsh'li/ *adv.*

insufferable /in súffərəb'l/ *adj.* so annoying, unpleasant, or uncomfortable that it is unbearable —**insufferably** *adv.* —**insufferableness** *n.*

insufficiency /ínssə físh'nssi/ (*plural* **-cies**) *n.* **1. NOT ENOUGH** a smaller number or lesser amount than is needed ○ *an insufficiency of provisions for a long cruise* **2.** MED **UNFITNESS OR FAILURE** inability or failure to perform competently, adequately, or normally ○ *cardiac insufficiency* **3. FAILURE TO MEASURE UP** a failure to meet some standard or requirement ○ *the insufficiency of the causes presented to explain this phenomenon*

insufficient /ínssə físh'nt/ *adj.* not enough in amount or quality to satisfy some purpose or standard ○ *we were given insufficient notice* —**insufficiently** *adv.*

insufflate /ínssə flayt, in súf layt/ (**-flates, -flating, -flated**) *vt.* **1. BLOW INTO STH** to blow or breathe into sth (*formal*) **2.** MED **BLOW STH INTO A BODY CAVITY** to blow sth, e.g. air, powder, or gas, into the lungs or some other body cavity in the course of medical treatment **3.** CHR **BLOW ON SB** to blow or breathe on sth or sb as part of a Christian religious sacrament or ritual such as baptism or exorcism, to symbolize the Holy Spirit [Late 17thC. Latin *insufflat-*, from *insufflare*, from *sufflare* 'to blow up' (source of English *soufflé*).] —**insufflation** /ínssə fláysh'n/ *n.* —**insufflator** /ínssə flaytər/ *n.*

insulant /ínssyoo̖lənt/ *n.* material that insulates sth

insular /ínssyoo̖lər/ *adj.* **1. LIMITED IN OUTLOOK** concerned only with your own country, society, or way of life and not interested in new ideas or different cultures **2. NOT CLOSE TO OTHERS** physically or emotionally removed from others **3. OF ISLANDS** relating to or originating in an island **4.** ANAT **OF ISLANDS OF CELLS** relating to a collection of cells or tissue reminiscent of an island [Mid-16thC. Via French *insulaire* from late Latin *insularis*, from Latin *insula* 'island'.] —**insularism** *n.* —**insularity** /ínssyoo lárrəti/ *n.* —**insularly** /ínssyoo̖lərli/ *adv.*

insulate /ínssyoo layt/ (**-lates, -lating, -lated**) *vt.* **1. PREVENT THE PASSAGE OF STH** to prevent or reduce the passage of heat, electricity, or sound into, from, or through sth, especially by surrounding it with some material **2. PROTECT OR ISOLATE SB** to protect or isolate sb from sth, especially from sth unpleasant or undesirable [Mid-16thC. Formed from Latin *insula* 'island'.]

insulating tape *n.* a thin strip of adhesive material that can be wrapped round bare wires or electrical connections to stop electricity from passing from them to sb or sth that touches them. US term **friction tape**

insulation /ínssyoo̖ láysh'n/ *n.* **1. MATERIAL THAT INSULATES** sth that prevents or reduces the passage of heat, electricity, or sound, e.g. a special material or a layer of air. Cork, glass fibre, rubber, and plastic are all used as insulation. **2. PREVENTION OF CONDUCTION** the act of covering or surrounding sth to prevent or reduce the passage of heat, electricity, or sound **3. PROTECTION** protection or isolation from sth

insulative /ínssyoo̖lətiv, -laytiv/ *adj.* preventing or reducing the passage of heat, electricity, or sound

insulator /ínssyoo̖ laytər/ *n.* a material or device that prevents or reduces the passage of heat, electricity, or sound

insulin /ínssyoo̖lin/ *n.* a hormone secreted by the islets of Langerhans in the pancreas that regulates the level of glucose in the blood. Deficiency in production results in diabetes mellitus. [Early 20thC. Coined from Latin *insula* 'island' (source of English *isle* and *isolate*), after the 'islets of Langerhans'.]

insulin shock, **insulin reaction** *n.* a severe drop in blood sugar resulting from an excess of insulin and marked by sweating, dizziness, trembling, and eventual coma

insult /in súlt/ *v.* (**-sults, -sulting, -sulted**) **1.** *vti.* **BE OFFENSIVE** to say or do sth rude or insensitive that offends sb else **2.** *vt.* **SHOW CONTEMPT** to say or do sth suggesting a low opinion of sb or sth ○ *Don't insult me by offering me pity.* ■ *n.* **1. OFFENSIVE WORDS OR ACTION** a remark or action that offends sb, usually because it is rude or insensitive **2. STH SHOWING CONTEMPT** behaviour or words implying a low opinion of sb, e.g. a payment that is much less than expected or deserved ○ *The article is an insult to the intelligence of the reader.* **3.** MED **INJURY OR AN INJURING AGENT** an injury or trauma to the body or sth that causes such harm [Mid-16thC. Via French *insulter* from Latin *insultare*, literally 'to keep jumping on', which was formed from, ultimately, *salire* 'to jump'.] —**insulter** *n.*

insulting /in súlting/ *adj.* causing offence because it is rude or insensitive or suggests a low opinion of sb or sth —**insultingly** *adv.*

insuperable /in soo̖pərəb'l/ *adj.* impossible to overcome, get rid of, or deal with successfully ○ *battling against insuperable odds* [14thC. Via Old French from, ultimately, Latin *superare* 'to overcome', from *super* 'above' (source of English *superior*, *sovereign*, *soprano*, and *sirloin*).] —**insuperability** /in soo̖pərə bílləti/ *n.* —**insuperableness** /in soo̖pərəb'lnəss/ *n.* —**insuperably** /-bli/ *adv.*

insupportable /ínssə páwrtəb'l/ *adj.* **1. IMPOSSIBLE TO ENDURE** too great, unpleasant, or difficult to bear ○ *an insupportable claim* **2. UNJUSTIFIABLE** impossible to justify or defend —**insupportableness** *n.* —**insupportably** *adv.*

insurable /in shoo̖rəb'l, -sháwr-/ *adj.* INSUR able to be covered or protected by insurance —**insurability** /in shoo̖rə bílləti, -sháwrə-/ *n.*

insurable interest *n.* a demonstrable interest in sth covered by an insurance policy, the loss of which would cause deprivation or financial loss. Insurable interest must be shown whenever sb takes out an insurance policy or makes a claim.

insurance /in shoo̖rənss, -sháwr-/ *n.* **1.** INSUR **FINANCIAL PROTECTION AGAINST LOSS OR HARM** an arrangement by which a company gives customers financial protection against loss or harm, e.g. theft or illness, in return for payment (**premium**) **2. A MONEY PAID BY AN INSURANCE COMPANY** the sum of money that an insurance company pays or agrees to pay if a specified undesirable event occurs **3.** INSUR **PREMIUM** the payment made to obtain insurance ○ *My car insurance has gone up again.* **4.** INSUR **INSURANCE BUSINESS** the commercial business of providing insurance **5. MEANS OF PROTECTION** an act, measure, or provision that gives protection against some undesirable event or risk ○ *provided a map as insurance against getting lost* [15thC. Via Old French *enseurance*.]

insurance policy (*plural* **insurance policies**) *n.* a written contract between an insurance company and a person or organization requiring insurance against loss or harm. The insurance policy sets out the terms and conditions of the agreement, specifying the risks for which compensation or costs will be paid.

insure /in shoo̖r, -sháwr/ (**-sures, -suring, -sured**) *v.* **1.** *vti.* **COVER STH WITH INSURANCE** to agree formally that, for a sum of money paid to a company, the company will pay compensation or costs if some specified harm or loss occurs to sb or sth ○ *the ring was insured for £5,000* **2.** *vi.* **PROTECT AGAINST RISK** to get protection from sth undesirable that might happen, usually by making contingency plans or taking precautionary or preventive measures **3.** *vt. US* = **ensure** [15thC. Variant of ENSURE.]

WORD KEY: USAGE

See Usage note at ***assure***.

insured /in shoo̖rd, -sháwrd/ *adj.* **COVERED BY INSURANCE** covered by insurance ■ *n.* **OBJECT OF INSURANCE** sb or sth covered by insurance ○ *the signature of the insured*

insurer /in shoo̖rər, -sháwr-/ *n.* a company or individual providing insurance

insurgency /in súrjənssi/ (*plural* **-cies**), **insurgence** /-jənss/ *n.* **1. REBELLION** a rebellion or uprising against a government **2. STATE OF REBELLION** the state of being in rebellion

insurgent /in súrjənt/ *n.* **REBEL** sb who rebels against authority or leadership, especially sb belonging to a group involved in an uprising against the government or ruler of a country ■ *adj.* **REBELLIOUS** rebelling against authority or leadership, especially against the government or ruler of a country [Mid-18thC. From Latin *insurgent-*, formed from *insurgere* 'to rise up', from *surgere* 'to rise'.] —**insurgently** *adv.*

insurmountable /ínssər mówntəb'l/ *adj.* impossible to overcome or deal with successfully —**insurmountability** /ínssər mowntə bílləti/ *n.* —**insurmountably** /ínssər mówntəbli/ *adv.*

insurrection /ínssə réksh'n/ *n.* rebellion against the government or rulers of a country, often involving armed conflict [15thC. From the Latin stem *insurrection-*, from *insurgere* 'to rise up'.] —**insurrectional** *adj.* —**insurrectionary** *n., adj.* —**insurrectionism** *n.* —**insurrectionist** *n., adj.*

insusceptible /ínssə séptəb'l/ *adj.* **1. NOT AFFECTED** not likely to be affected or influenced by sth **2. NOT SUBJECT TO STH** not able to undergo some process —**insusceptibility** /ínssə séptə bílləti/ *n.* —**insusceptibly** /ínssə séptəbli/ *adv.*

inswing /ín swing/ *n.* in cricket, the curve of a bowl from the batter's off to leg side [Early 20thC. Back-formation from INSWINGER.]

inswinger /ín swingər/ *n.* **1.** CRICKET **BALL CURVING INWARDS** a ball that curves through the air from the batter's off to leg side **2.** SOCCER **CURVING BALL** a ball kicked, particularly from a corner, that curves through the air towards the goal

int. *abbr.* **1.** (military) intelligence **2.** intercept **3.** interest **4.** interim **5.** interior **6.** GRAM interjection **7.** intermediate **8.** internal **9. int., Int.** international **10.** interpreter **11.** intersection **12.** interval **13.** interview **14.** GRAM intransitive

intact /in tákt/ *adj.* **1. NOT DAMAGED** whole and undamaged ○ *Only two of the original plates remained intact.* **2. COMPLETE** without any missing parts or elements **3.** ANAT **WITHOUT ANY REMOVED PARTS** having all bodily parts in place and undamaged [15thC. From Latin *intactus* 'untouched', which was formed ultimately from *tangere* 'to touch' (see TANGIBLE).] —**intactly** *adv.* —**intactness** *n.*

Intaglio: Ancient Egyptian granite carving

intaglio /in taáli ŏ, -tálli ŏ/ (*plural* **-glios** *or* **-gli** /in taál ee/) *n.* **1.** HOLLOWED-OUT DESIGN a carving made by cutting a hollowed-out design into some material such as stone **2.** CARVING OF INTAGLIOS the process or art of carving hollowed-out designs in material such as stone **3.** CARVED GEM a gem in which a hollowed-out design has been carved **4.** PRINTING PRINTING WITH INCISED PLATES a printing technique in which the design is cut into the plate rather than protruding from it. Intaglio printing includes engraving, etching, and drypoint. **5.** PRINTING INCISED PRINTING PLATE a printing plate into which the design is cut or incised [Mid-17thC. Via Italian from, ultimately, *intagliare* 'to engrave', from *tagliare* 'to cut'.]

intake /ín tayk/ *n.* **1.** AMOUNT TAKEN IN an amount taken in or consumed ○ *increase your intake of fluids* **2.** PEOPLE TAKEN IN the number of people admitted to a place or organization at a particular time or the people themselves. The term often refers to those entering an educational establishment at the beginning of an academic year. ○ *The college has increased its intake of mature students.* **3.** TAKING IN STH the process of taking in some substance, especially by eating or drinking **4.** OPENING THROUGH WHICH FLUID PASSES an opening through which fluid enters a duct or contained area, e.g. that of a jet engine ○ *the fuel intake*

intangible /in tánjəb'l/ *adj.* **1.** NON-MATERIAL without material qualities, and so not able to be touched or seen **2.** HARD TO DESCRIBE difficult to define or describe clearly, but nonetheless perceived ■ *n.* STH UNQUANTIFIABLE an unquantifiable quality or asset ○ *such intangibles as duty* [Early 17thC. Via medieval Latin *intangibilis*, or formed from TANGIBLE.] —**intangibility** /in tánjə bílləti/ *n.* —**intangibleness** /in tánjəb'lnəss/ *n.* —**intangibly** /-bli/ *adv.*

intangible asset *n.* a business asset, e.g. a firm's customer goodwill, that is of value although it is not directly quantifiable in terms of goods produced or sold

Intarsia: Panel (1506) in the Palazzo Ducale, Mantua, Italy

intarsia /in taárssi ə/ (*plural* **-as**) *n.* **1.** CRAFT WOOD INLAY wood inlay using different colours of wood, common in the Italian Renaissance **2.** CRAFT MAKING OF INTARSIAS the art or process of making intarsias, e.g. for wall panels **3.** KNITTING WAY OF KNITTING knitting with two or more coloured yarns in which the new colour is introduced by twisting around the old, left hanging until it is needed again [Mid-19thC. Via German and Italian from, ultimately, Arabic *tarsī*.]

integer /íntijər/ *n.* **1.** WHOLE NUMBER any positive or negative whole number or zero **2.** WHOLE THING a whole unit or entity (*technical*) [Early 16thC. From Latin 'complete, whole' (source of English *entire*). Ultimately from an Indo-European base meaning 'to touch'.]

integral /íntigrəl, in téggrəl/ *adj.* **1.** NECESSARY OR CONSTITUENT being an essential part of sth or any of the parts that make up a whole ○ *Adequate funding is integral to the success of the venture.* ○ *mealtimes are an integral part of family life* **2.** MADE UP OF PARTS composed of parts that together make a whole **3.** COMPLETE without missing parts or elements **4.** ARITH OF AN INTEGER relating to an integer **5.** MATH RELATING TO INTEGRALS relating to mathematical integrals or integration ■ *n.* MATH **1.** = definite integral **2.** = indefinite integral [Mid-16thC. Via French from, ultimately, Latin *integer* 'whole'.] —**integrality** /ínti grálləti/ *n.* —**integrally** /íntigrəli, in téggrəli/ *adv.*

integral calculus *n.* a branch of mathematics dealing with integrals and differential equations, used to determine areas, volumes, and lengths, and in many areas of applied mathematics

integrand /ínti grand/ *n.* a mathematical function or equation to be integrated [Late 19thC. From Latin *integrandus* 'to be integrated', from *integrare* 'to integrate', from *integer* 'whole'.]

integrant /íntigrənt/ *adj.* PART OF WHOLE part of a whole (*formal*) ■ *n.* INTEGRAL PART an integral part of sth (*formal*)

integrate /ínti grayt/ (**-grates**, **-grating**, **-grated**) *v.* **1.** *vti.* FIT IN WITH A GROUP to become an accepted member of a group and its activities, or to help sb do this **2.** *vti.* MAKE INTO A WHOLE to join two or more objects or make sth part of a larger whole, or to become joined or combined in this way **3.** *vt.* MAKE OPEN TO ALL to make a group, community, place, or organization and its opportunities available to all, regardless of race, ethnic group, religion, gender, or social class **4.** *vt.* MATH FIND A MATHEMATICAL INTEGRAL to find the definite or indefinite integral of a function or equation [Mid-17thC. From Latin *integrat-*, from *integrare* 'to make whole', from *integer* 'whole'.] —**integrable** /íntigrəb'l/ *adj.* —**integrability** /íntigrə bílləti/ *n.* —**integrative** /ínti graytiv/ *adj.*

integrated /íntigraytid/ *adj.* **1.** COMBINED OR COMPOSITE made up of elements or parts that work well together ○ *an integrated transport system* **2.** COMBINING DISSIMILAR THINGS bringing together processes or functions that are normally separate **3.** OPEN TO ALL PEOPLE open to everyone, without restrictions based on race, ethnicity, religion, gender, or social class

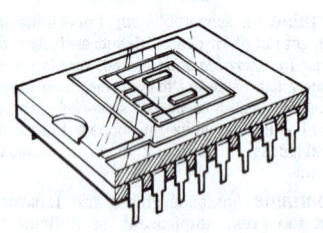

Integrated circuit

integrated circuit *n.* an extremely small complex of electronic components contained on a thin chip or wafer of semiconducting material such as silicon —**integrated circuitry** *n.*

integration /ínti gráysh'n/ *n.* **1.** EQUAL ACCESS FOR ALL the process of opening a group, community, place, or organization to all, regardless of race, ethnicity, religion, gender, or social class **2.** ACCEPTANCE INTO A COMMUNITY becoming an accepted member of a group or community **3.** COMBINATION a combination of parts or objects that work together well **4.** MATH MATHEMATICAL OPERATION the mathematical process of finding the solution of a differential equation or a function whose differential equation is known **5.** PSYCHOL ORGANIZATION OF PERSONALITY TRAITS the process of coordinating separate personality elements into a bal-

anced whole or producing behaviour compatible with sb's environment

integrationist /ínti gráysh'nist/ *n.* WORKER FOR INTEGRATION a supporter or activist who works to promote and maintain integration ■ *adj.* FAVOURING INTEGRATION supporting or promoting racial integration

integrator /ínti graytər/ *n.* **1.** COMPUT COMPUTER DEVICE a computer component that performs numerical integration to solve differential equations **2.** SB OR STH THAT INTEGRATES sb or sth that brings about integration

integrity /in téggrəti/ *n.* **1.** POSSESSION OF FIRM PRINCIPLES the quality of possessing and steadfastly adhering to high moral principles or professional standards **2.** COMPLETENESS the state of being complete or undivided (*formal*) ○ *the territorial integrity of a nation.* **3.** WHOLENESS the state of being sound or undamaged (*formal*) ○ *Their refusal to participate in the experiment will undermine its integrity.* [15thC. Via Old French from Latin *integritas*, from *integer* 'whole'.]

integument /in téggyŏomənt/ *n.* an outer protective layer or part of an animal or plant, e.g. a shell, rind, husk, or skin [Early 17thC. Via Latin *integumentum* from *integere* 'to cover up', from *tegere* 'to cover' (source of English *tile* and *detect*).] —**integumental** /in téggyŏo mént'l/ *adj.* —**integumentary** /in téggyŏo méntəri/ *adj.*

intellect /íntə lekt/ *n.* **1.** MENTAL ABILITY sb's ability to think, reason, and understand ○ *appeals to the intellect rather than the emotions* ○ *a highly developed intellect* **2.** INTELLIGENT PERSON a very intelligent and knowledgeable person ○ *The commission called on some of our ablest intellects in its search for solutions.* [14thC. Via Old French from Latin *intellect-*, from *intellegere* 'to perceive' (see INTELLIGENT).]

intellection /íntə léksh'n/ *n.* (*formal*) **1.** THINKING thinking, reasoning, or other mental activity **2.** RESULT OF THINKING a thought or an idea —**intellective** /íntə léktiv/ *adj.* —**intellectively** *adv.*

intellectual /íntə lékchoo əl/ *adj.* **1.** RELATING TO THINKING relating to or involving the mental processes of abstract thinking and reasoning rather than the emotions **2.** INTELLIGENT AND KNOWLEDGEABLE having a highly developed ability to think, reason, and understand, especially in combination with wide knowledge **3.** FOR INTELLIGENT PEOPLE intended for, appealing to, or done by intelligent people ○ *intellectual pursuits* ■ *n.* INTELLIGENT PERSON sb with a highly developed ability to reason and understand, especially if also well educated and interested in the arts or sciences or enjoying activities involving serious mental effort [15thC. Via Old French from late Latin *intellectualis*, from *intellectus* 'intellect', from *intellegere* 'to perceive' (see INTELLIGENT).] —**intellectuality** /íntə lekchoo álləti/ *n.* —**intellectually** /íntə lékchoo əli/ *adv.* —**intellectualness** /-əlnəss, -léktyoo-/ *n.*

intellectualise *vti.* = intellectualize

intellectualism /íntə lékchoo əlizəm/ *n.* **1.** PSYCHOL EXERCISE OF POWER TO THINK the development and use of the ability to think, reason, and understand **2.** TOO MUCH ATTENTION TO THINKING overemphasis on intellectual processes or pursuits **3.** PHILOS BELIEF THAT KNOWLEDGE COMES FROM REASONING the doctrine that all that can truly be called knowledge is derived from reasoning —**intellectualist** *n.* —**intellectualistic** /íntə lékchoo ə lístik/ *adj.* —**intellectualistically** /-lístikli/ *adv.*

intellectualize /íntə lékchoo ə līz/ (**-izes**, **-izing**, **-ized**), **intellectualise** (**-ises**, **-ising**, **-ised**) *v.* **1.** *vti.* CONSIDER STH RATIONALLY to analyse, deal with, or explain sth by thinking or reasoning exclusively **2.** *vi.* THINK to think or reason **3.** *vti.* MAKE OR BECOME INTELLECTUAL to make sb or sth intellectual or to become intellectual ○ *intellectualized poetry* **4.** *vt.* PSYCHOL REASON AWAY PROBLEMS to protect yourself unconsciously from the emotional stress that would come from dealing with fears or problems by reasoning them away —**intellectualization** *n.* —**intellectualizer** *n.*

intellectual property *n.* original creative work manifested in a tangible form that can be legally protected, e.g. by a patent, trademark, or copyright

intelligence /in téllijənss/ *n.* **1.** ABILITY TO THINK AND LEARN the ability to learn facts and skills and apply them, especially when this ability is highly developed **2.** SECRET INFORMATION information about secret plans or activities, especially those of foreign governments, the armed forces, business enemies, or criminals **3. GATHERING OF SECRET INFORMATION** the collection of secret military or political information **4. PEOPLE GATHERING SECRET INFORMATION** an organization that gathers information about the secret plans or activities of an adversary or potential adversary and the people involved in gathering such information **5. INTELLIGENT SPIRIT** an entity capable of rational thought, especially one that does not have a physical form —**intelligential** /in télli jénsh'l/ *adj.*

intelligence quotient *n.* full form of **IQ**

intelligencer /in téllijənssər/ *n.* sb who provides or gathers information, especially about secret plans or activities (*archaic*)

intelligent /in téllijənt/ *adj.* **1. MENTALLY ABLE** having intelligence, especially to a highly developed degree **2. SENSIBLE OR RATIONAL** showing or resulting from an ability to think and understand things clearly and logically ○ *an intelligent solution* **3.** COMPUT **ABLE TO STORE AND PROCESS DATA** with built-in electronic processing and data storage ability ○ *an intelligent terminal* **4.** COMPUT **SELF-REGULATING** programmed to be able to adjust itself to changes in its environment and make deductions from information it processes [Early 16thC. From Latin *intelligent-*, formed from *intellegere* 'to perceive, discern', from *inter-* 'between' + *legere* 'to choose, read' (source of English *select* and *legible*).] —**intelligently** *adv.*

WORD KEY: SYNONYMS

intelligent, bright, quick, smart, clever, able, gifted

CORE MEANING: having the ability to learn and understand

intelligent a general word used to describe a person or animal who is quick to learn and understand; **bright** an informal word used to describe sb who is mentally alert and responsive; **quick** an informal word emphasizing the ability to recognize or understand things quickly; **smart** an informal word similar to *bright*, but also implying mental resourcefulness; **clever** having the capacity to learn quickly, often implying mental resourcefulness, but also cunning or ingenuity; **able** a word used, especially in educational circles, of children who are intelligent; **gifted** describes sb who has an exceptional talent, especially sb artistic or creative. Also used, especially in educational circles, of children who are exceptionally intelligent and learn easily.

intelligentsia /in télli jéntsi ə/ *n.* the most intelligent, intellectual, or highly educated members of a society or community, especially those who are interested in the arts, literature, philosophy, and politics [Early 20thC. Via Russian *intelligentsiya* from Latin *intelligentia* 'intelligence'.]

intelligible /in téllijəb'l/ *adj.* **1. UNDERSTANDABLE** capable of being understood ○ *his ideas were barely intelligible* **2.** PHILOS **UNDERSTANDABLE BY THE MIND ALONE** perceptible only by the mind, not the senses [14thC. Via Old French from Latin *intelligibilis*, from *intellegere* 'to perceive' (see INTELLIGENT).] —**intelligibility** /in téllijə bílləti/ *n.* —**intelligibleness** /in téllijəb'lnəss/ *n.* —**intelligibly** *adv.*

Intelsat /ín tel sat/, **INTELSAT** *n.* **1.** an international organization whose membership includes the telecommunications agencies of most countries and that owns the communications satellites that orbit the Earth. Full form **International Telecommunication Satellite Organization** **2. TELECOMMUNICATIONS SATELLITE** a telecommunications satellite launched by Intelsat

intemperance /in témpərənss/ *n.* **1. EXCESSIVE INDULGENCE** the satisfying of an unacceptable or excessive desire, especially excessive drinking of alcohol **2. LACK OF SELF-CONTROL** lack of self-control **3.** METEOROL **BAD WEATHER** severity of weather conditions or climate (*formal*)

intemperate /in témpərət/ *adj.* **1. DRINKING TO EXCESS** drinking too much alcohol, especially frequently **2. LACKING SELF-CONTROL** having or showing a lack of self-control, especially in expressing feelings or satisfying physical desires **3.** METEOROL **TOO HOT OR COLD** extremely or unpleasantly hot or cold (*formal*) —**intemperately** *adv.* —**intemperateness** *n.*

intend /in ténd/ (**-tends, -tending, -tended**) *v.* **1.** *vti.* **MEAN TO DO STH** to have sth in mind as a plan ○ *I really intended to write, but I didn't have time.* **2.** *vt.* **DO OR SAY FOR SOME PURPOSE** to do, say, or produce sth with a particular purpose, use, target, or group of people in mind ○ *a dictionary intended for schoolchildren* **3.** *vt.* **MEAN STH** to signify or indicate sth through speech or behaviour ○ *What impression did he intend to give us with such a remark?* [14thC. Via Old French from Latin *intendere*, from *in-* 'towards' + *tendere* 'to stretch'.]

intendance /in téndənss/ *n.* **1. ADMINISTRATIVE DEPARTMENT** a public department or administrative office in some countries **2.** = **intendancy** *n.* 1

intendancy /in téndənssi/ (*plural* **-cies**) *n.* **1. WORK OF AN INTENDANT** the role or functions of an intendant **2. INTENDANTS AS A GROUP** intendants considered collectively **3. ADMINISTRATIVE AREA** the department or district administered by an intendant

intendant /in téndənt/ *n.* an official or administrator in some countries, especially in the past in France, Spain, and Portugal, and currently in parts of Latin America [Mid-17thC. Via Old French from Latin *intendent-*, formed from *intendere* (see INTEND).]

intended /in téndid/ *adj.* **1. ENVISIONED** aimed at or designed for ○ *We were unable to reach our intended destination* **2. PLANNED** planned for the future **3. DELIBERATE** said or done deliberately ■ *n.* **FUTURE HUSBAND OR WIFE** the person to whom sb is engaged to be married (*dated or humorous*) ○ *He cherished the letter from his intended.* —**intendedly** *adv.*

intending /in ténding/ *adj.* planning to be or become sth

intendment /in téndmənt/ *n.* the meaning of sth, especially a word or term, according to law

intens. *abbr.* 1. intensifier 2. intensify 3. intensive

intense /in ténss/ *adj.* **1. EXTREME** great, strong, or extreme in a way that can be felt ○ *intense heat* **2. EFFORTFUL OR ACTIVE** involving great effort or much activity ○ *showed intense dedication to the task* **3. CONCENTRATED** narrowly focused or concentrated ○ *an intense stare* **4. PASSIONATE** feeling or showing strong and deeply felt emotions in a serious way ○ *a very intense young student* [15thC. Via Old French from Latin *intensus*, the past participle of *intendere* 'to stretch out' (see INTEND).] —**intenseness** *n.*

intensely /in ténssli/ *adv.* **1. EXTREMELY** very much **2. STRONGLY** strongly or brightly ○ *intensely pink curtains* **3. PENETRATINGLY** in a fixed and penetrating way **4. PASSIONATELY** with great passion and enthusiasm

intensifier /in ténssi fī ər/ *n.* **1.** GRAM **WORD INDICATING HOW MUCH STH APPLIES** a word or phrase, e.g. 'definitely', 'quite', or 'hardly', that indicates the relative degree to which sth applies, as in 'quite good' or 'hardly enough' **2. SB OR STH THAT INTENSIFIES** sb or sth that makes sth larger, sharper, or stronger

intensify /in ténssi fī/ (**-fies, -fying, -fied**) *vti.* **1. MAKE OR BECOME GREATER** to make sth greater or stronger, or to increase in strength or degree ○ *media interest intensified as the week progressed* **2. INCREASE EFFORT OR CONCENTRATION** to do sth with greater effort or more activity or to become more concentrated —**intensification** /in ténssifi káysh'n/ *n.*

WORD KEY: SYNONYMS

See Synonyms at ***increase***.

intension /in ténsh'n/ *n.* **1.** LOGIC **MEANING OF EXPRESSION** the meaning of an expression as opposed to what it refers to. The intension of the word 'human' is the property of being human, whereas it has as its reference, or extension, human beings as a group. **2. INTENSITY** intensity (*formal*) **3. INTENSIFICATION** intensification (*formal*) [Early 17thC. From the Latin stem *intension-*, from *intendere* 'to stretch out, become tense'.] —**intensional** *adj.* —**intensionally** *adv.*

intensional object *n.* LOGIC a concept, property, or proposition as opposed to an individual, set, or truth value, which are the extensional counterparts of intensional objects

intensity /in ténssəti/ (*plural* **-ties**) *n.* **1. QUALITY OF BEING INTENSE** the strength, power, force, or concentration of sth ○ *The pain increased in intensity.* **2. INTENSE MANNER** a passionate and serious attitude or quality ○ *a rare emotional intensity in her work* **3.** PHYS **MAGNITUDE OF ENERGY** the strength of a source of energy, e.g. light, electricity, or sound, per unit area, mass, or time

intensive /in ténssiv/ *adj.* **1. CONCENTRATED** involving concentrated effort, usually in order to achieve sth in a comparatively short time ○ *an intensive course in German* **2.** AGRIC **INCREASING PRODUCTION** relating to a form of agriculture in which scientific and technological methods, e.g. the use of chemicals that boost growth or crop yields, are used to increase productivity **3. MAKING HEAVY USE OF** requiring or using a great deal of a particular thing ○ *capital-intensive* **4.** GRAM **INDICATING HOW MUCH** used to describe a word or phrase, e.g. 'extremely', that emphasizes or intensifies the word that it modifies ■ *n.* GRAM **WORD INDICATING HOW MUCH** a word or phrase, e.g. 'extremely', that emphasizes or intensifies the word that it modifies —**intensively** *adv.* —**intensiveness** *n.*

intensive care *n.* the monitoring, care, and treatment of patients who are critically ill or critically injured, or the part of a hospital where this care takes place. The monitoring is usually done by electronic means, so that essential corrective action can be taken with a minimum of delay. ○ *One of the survivors is still in intensive care.*

intensive care unit *n.* a department of a hospital that is designed and equipped for the monitoring, care, and treatment of critically ill or critically injured patients

intent /in tént/ *n.* **1. PLAN OR PURPOSE** sth planned or the purpose that accompanies a plan ○ *'My intent is to use our attractive domestic market as the basis of a muscular free trade policy that will strengthen America's global economic reach...'* (National Public Telecomputing Network, *Bush speeches in campaign '92*; 1992) **2.** LAW **STATE OF MIND** sb's state of mind when deliberately committing or planning to commit an illegal act **3. CONNOTATION** the meaning or significance of sth, especially when it is not explicitly expressed ■ *adj.* **1. WITH FIXED ATTENTION** with full attention or effort concentrated or focused on one thing ○ *Intent on her work, she lost track of the time.* **2. DETERMINED** showing great determination to do sth ○ *They are intent on catching the early train.* [13thC. Via Old French *entent* from, ultimately, Latin *intendere* (see INTEND).] —**intently** *adv.* —**intentness** *n.* ◇ **to all intents and purposes** in effect the same, although not actually the same

intention /in ténsh'n/ *n.* **1. AIM OR OBJECTIVE** sth that sb plans to do or achieve ○ *State your intentions.* **2. QUALITY OF PURPOSEFULNESS** the quality or state of having a purpose in mind ○ *She acted without intention.* ■ **intentions** *npl.* **SB'S MARRIAGE PLANS** sb's plans with respect to marriage (*dated*) ○ *What are your intentions towards my daughter?* [14thC. Via Old French from the Latin stem *intention-*, from *intendere* (see INTEND).]

intentional /in ténsh'nəl/ *adj.* **1. DELIBERATE** done on purpose, not by accident **2.** PHILOS **INVOLVING THOUGHTS ABOUT OBJECTS** involving thoughts, e.g. beliefs or desires, about different kinds of objects, including those that have no actual existence —**intentionality** /in ténshə nálləti/ *n.* —**intentionally** /in ténsh'nəli/ *adv.*

inter /in túr/ (**-ters, -terring, -terred**) *vt.* to bury the body or ashes of a cremated body in a grave or tomb (*formal*) [15thC. Via Old French *enterer*, ultimately from IN + Latin *terra* 'earth'.]

inter. *abbr.* intermediate

inter- *prefix.* 1. between, among ○ *interlinear* ○ *interstate* ○ *intercut* 2. mutual, reciprocal ○ *interchange* 3. involving two or more groups ○ *international* [Directly and via Old French *entre* from Latin *inter* 'between, among' (source of English *internal* and *entrails*). Ultimately from an Indo-European word meaning literally 'more in'.]

interabang *n.* PRINTING = **interrobang**

interact /íntər ákt/ (**-acts, -acting, -acted**) *vi.* **1. ACT ON EACH OTHER** to have an effect on sth else or one another **2. COMMUNICATE OR WORK TOGETHER** to be or become involved in communication, social activity, or work with sb else or one another

interactant /íntər áktənt/ *n.* sb or sth that interacts in some way (*formal*)

interaction /íntər áksh'n/ *n.* **1. COMMUNICATION OR COLLABORATION** communication between or joint activity involving two or more people **2.** RECIPROCAL ACTION the combined or reciprocal action of two or more things that have an effect on each other and work together **3.** PHYS FORCE BETWEEN ELEMENTARY PARTICLES any of the four fundamental forces acting between elementary particles, namely gravitational, electromagnetic, strong, and weak —**interactional** *adj.*

interactionism /íntər ákshʼnizəm/ *n.* PHILOS in Western metaphysics, the theory that the mind and the body act on each other

interactive /íntər áktiv/ *adj.* **1.** COMMUNICATING OR COLLABORATING involving the communication or collaboration of people or things **2.** COMPUT WITH USER-MACHINE COMMUNICATION allowing or involving the exchange of information or instructions between a person and a machine such as a computer or a television **3.** COMPUT OPERATOR-CONTROLLED operating on instructions entered by sb at a keyboard or other input device —**interactively** *adv.* —**interactivity** /íntər aktívvitee/ *n.*

inter alia /íntər áyli ə, -ááli-, -álli-/ *adv.* among other things (*formal*) ○ *budget funds for two new schools inter alia* [From Latin]

inter alios /íntər áyli ōss, -ááli-, -álli-/ *adv.* among other people (*formal*) [From Latin]

interallied /íntər állīd/ *adj.* involving the combined or mutual action of allies, especially in a war

interbreed /íntər breéd/ (**-breeds, -breeding, -bred** /-bréd/, **-bred**) *vti.* **1.** BREED WITH OTHER GROUPS to produce offspring by mating with a member of a different breed or species, or to mate an animal of one species or variety with one of another **2.** BREED WITHIN A NARROW GROUP to breed or make sth breed within a closed population or narrow range of types

interbroker dealer /íntər brṓkər-/ *n.* sb who facilitates stock-exchange dealings between other brokers and dealers

intercalary /in túrkələri/ *adj.* **1.** INSERTED INTO THE CALENDAR added to the calendar year to keep calendar years concurrent with solar years. In the Gregorian calendar 29 February is an intercalary day in leap years. **2.** INDICATING A YEAR WITH ADDITION used to describe a year to which an intercalary day or month has been added. A leap year is an intercalary year. **3.** INSERTED OR INTRODUCED put into sth else, or inserted between other parts (*formal*) [Early 17thC. Via Latin *intercalarius* from *intercalare* (see INTERCALATE).]

intercalate /in túrkə layt/ (**-lates, -lating, -lated**) *v.* **1.** *vt.* INSERT EXTRA TIME INTO THE CALENDAR to insert an extra day or month into a calendar year to keep it consistent with the solar year **2.** *vti.* INSERT OR INTRODUCE to place sth into sth else, inserting it between other elements, or to be placed between other elements (*formal*) [Early 17thC. From Latin *intercalat-*, from *intercalare*, from *calare* 'to proclaim'.] —**intercalation** /in túrkə láyshʼn/ *n.* —**intercalative** /in túrkələtiv, in túrkə laytiv/ *adj.*

intercaste /ínter kaást/ *adj.* *S Asia* across caste boundaries

intercede /íntər seéd/ (**-cedes, -ceding, -ceded**) *vi.* **1.** PLEAD FOR SB to plead with sb in authority on behalf of sb else, especially sb who is to be punished for sth **2.** SPEAK FOR SB to speak in support of sb involved in a dispute **3.** MEDIATE IN A DISPUTE to attempt to settle a dispute between others [Late 16thC. Via Latin *intercedere* from *cedere* 'to give way' (see CEDE).] —**interceder** *n.*

intercellular /íntər séllyŏŏlər/ *adj.* BIOL existing between cells ○ *an intercellular substance*

intercept /íntər sépt/ *v.* (**-cepts, -cepting, -cepted**) **1.** *vti.* INTERRUPT PROGRESS to prevent people or objects from reaching their destination or target by stopping, diverting, or seizing them ○ *the contraband was intercepted by police at the dock* **2.** *vt.* SPORTS GET THE BALL in sports, to gain possession of a ball intended for an opponent **3.** *vt.* GEOM MARK EXTENT to include part of a curve, surface, or solid between two points or lines ■ *n.* **1.** MATH DISTANCE BETWEEN THE ORIGIN AND AXIS CROSSING the distance from the origin of a coordinate system to the point where a curve or surface crosses an axis **2.** ACT OF INTERCEPTING the intercepting of sth, especially a radio transmission, a missile, or an aircraft **3.** ASTRON DIFFERENCE BETWEEN CALCULATED AND OBSERVED ALTITUDE the difference between the calculated and observed altitude of a celestial object [15thC. From Latin *intercept-*, formed from *intercipere*, from *capere* 'to seize'.] —**interceptive** /íntər séptiv/ *adj.*

intercepter *n.* = **interceptor**

interception /íntər sépshʼn/ *n.* **1.** INTERCEPTING SB OR STH the act or an instance of intercepting sb or sth **2.** STH INTERCEPTED sth intercepted, especially a passed ball that is intercepted by an opponent while it is in the air

interceptor /íntər séptər/, **intercepter** *n.* **1.** AIR FORCE FAST FIGHTER PLANE a fast, very manoeuvrable fighter plane designed to intercept enemy aircraft **2.** ARMS GUIDED MISSILE a guided missile designed to intercept enemy missiles or spacecraft **3.** ONE THAT INTERCEPTS sb or sth that intercepts

intercession /íntər séshʼn/ *n.* **1.** INTERCEDING the action of pleading on sb's behalf **2.** TRYING TO RESOLVE CONFLICT the action of attempting to settle a dispute **3.** PRAYER OR PETITION prayer to God, a god, or a saint on behalf of sb or sth [15thC. Via Old French from the Latin stem *intercession-*, from *intercedere* (see INTERCEDE).] —**intercessional** *adj.* —**intercessor** /íntər séssər, -sessər/ *n.* —**intercessorial** /íntərssə sáwri əl/ *adj.* —**intercessory** /íntər séssəri/ *adj.*

interchange /íntər cháynj/ *v.* (**-changes, -changing, -changed**) **1.** *vti.* SWITCH OR SWAP PLACES to put each of two things in the place of the other or to change places with sth else **2.** *vti.* ALTERNATE OR FOLLOW EACH OTHER to arrange things alternately in a series or to be arranged in this way **3.** *vt.* EXCHANGE THINGS to give sth to sb and receive a similar thing from the same person in return ■ *n.* **1.** EXCHANGE OF THINGS an exchange of things, especially ideas, opinions, or information, among people **2.** ALTERNATION the action of alternating or changing places **3.** TRANSP ROAD INTERSECTION a major road junction where vehicles can, by means of slip roads, bridges, and underpasses, change from one road to another without stopping or crossing other traffic [14thC. Via Old French *entrechangier*.] —**interchanger** /íntər cháynjər/ *n.*

interchangeable /íntər cháynjəbʼl/ *adj.* capable of being switched, exchanged, or used in place of another or each other —**interchangeability** /íntər chaynjə bílləti/ *n.* —**interchangeably** *adv.*

intercity /íntər sítti/ *adj.* involving, connecting, or occurring between two or more cities

Intercity *tdmk.* a trademark for a fast rail service between major towns and cities, or a train providing this service

intercoastal /íntər kṓstʼl/ *adj.* connecting or occurring between ports on different coasts or two or more coastlines

intercollegiate /íntərkə leéjət/ *adj.* involving or occurring between the members of two or more colleges or universities ○ *intercollegiate sports*

intercolumniation /íntərkə lúmni áyshʼn/ *n.* a system used to space columns in a colonnade, based on the use of their diameters as a measurement

intercom /íntər kom/ *n.* a system or device for transmitting sound from one part of a building, aircraft, or ship to another [Mid-20thC. Shortening of *intercommunication system*.]

intercommunal /íntərkə myŏŏnʼl/ *adj.* existing or occurring between the members of two or more communities

intercommunicate /íntərkə myŏŏni kayt/ (**-cates, -cating, -cated**) *vi.* **1.** TALK TO EACH OTHER to communicate with each other **2.** ALLOW PASSAGE FROM ONE TO ANOTHER to be connected to sth else or each other, especially to another room by means of a door in the dividing wall ○ *intercommunicating hotel rooms* —**intercommunication** /-myŏŏni káyshʼn/ *n.* —**intercommunicative** /íntərkə myŏŏnikətiv/ *adj.* —**intercommunicator** /-kaytər/ *n.*

intercommunion /íntərkə myŏŏnyən/ *n.* **1.** CHR AGREEMENT ALLOWING JOINT COMMUNION an arrangement between different Christian denominations enabling members to receive the Communion at each other's services **2.** CLOSE ASSOCIATION a close association or relationship between people or groups, especially one that involves mutual participation or action

interconnect /íntərkə nékt/ (**-nects, -necting, -nected**) *vti.* **1.** JOIN ONTO ONE ANOTHER to be joined to sth else or to a number of joined things, or to make sth part of such a network (*often passive*) ○ *the rooms are interconnected to form a suite* **2.** RELATE THINGS to show a relationship between two or more things, or to be related —**interconnection** /-nékshʼn/ *n.*

interconnective /íntərkə néktiv/ *adj.* connecting or capable of connecting with sth else or with each other —**interconnectivity** /íntərkə nék tívvəti/ *n.*

intercontinental /íntər konti néntʼl/ *adj.* **1.** BETWEEN CONTINENTS involving or occurring between two or more continents **2.** GOING TO ANOTHER CONTINENT going from one continent to another

intercontinental ballistic missile *n.* a ballistic missile with a range of about 3,000 to 8,000 nautical miles

interconversion /íntərkən vúrshʼn/ *n.* the conversion of two or more things, e.g. chemicals, into one another —**interconvert** /-kən vúrt/ *vt.* —**interconvertibility** /íntərkən vurtə bílləti/ *n.* —**interconvertible** /íntərkən vúrtəbʼl/ *adj.*

intercooler /íntər koolər/ *n.* a heat exchanger that cools a fluid between successive stages of compression or chemical reaction

intercostal /íntər kóstʼl/ *adj.* situated or occurring between the ribs ○ *an intercostal nerve* [Late 16thC. Coined from Latin *costa* 'side, rib'.]

intercourse /íntər kawrss/ *n.* **1.** MUTUAL DEALINGS communication or exchanges between people or groups, especially conversation or social activity **2.** = **sexual intercourse** [15thC. Via Old French *entrecours* 'commerce', from Latin *intercursus*, literally 'running between', from *currere* 'to run' (source of English *courier*, *current*, and *cursive*).]

intercrop /íntər króp, -krop/ (**-crops, -cropping, -cropped**) *vti.* to grow different crops in the same field, usually in alternate rows, or to plant a crop between the rows of another crop —**intercrop** /íntər krop/ *n.*

intercultural /íntər kúlchərəl/ *adj.* involving or occurring between different cultures or between people with different cultural backgrounds —**interculturally** *adv.*

intercurrent /íntər kúrrənt/ *adj.* **1.** MED OCCURRING DURING OTHER DISEASE occurring during and changing the course of an already existing disease ○ *treating an intercurrent infection* **2.** SIMULTANEOUS OR INTERVENING occurring at the same time as sth else or during the period between two other events (*formal*) [Early 17thC. From Latin *intercurrent-*, from *intercurrere*, literally 'to run between', from *currere* 'to run'.] —**intercurrence** *n.* —**intercurrently** *adv.*

intercut /íntər kút/ (**-cuts, -cutting, -cut**) *vt.* to alternate scenes or shots of a film or insert one scene into another during the editing process, usually to show different events taking place at the same time

interdenominational /íntər di nommi náyshʼnəl/ *adj.* involving, occurring between, or open to people from different religious groups

interdental /íntər déntʼl/ *adj.* **1.** DENT BETWEEN THE TEETH existing between or designed for use between the teeth **2.** PHON WITH THE TONGUE BETWEEN THE TEETH made by placing the tip of the tongue between the teeth ■ *n.* PHON SOUND MADE WITH TONGUE BETWEEN TEETH a sound made by putting the tip of the tongue between the teeth —**interdentally** *adv.*

interdepartmental /íntər dee paart méntʼl/ *adj.* involving or occurring between different departments of the same organization or the people who work in them —**interdepartmentally** *adv.*

interdependent /íntərdi péndənt/ *adj.* **1.** DEPENDING ON EACH OTHER unable to exist or survive without each other ○ *interdependent organisms* **2.** WITH MUTUALLY DEPENDENT ELEMENTS relying on mutual assistance, support, cooperation, or interaction among constituent elements or members —**interdepend** *vi.* —**interdependence** *n.* —**interdependently** *adv.*

interdict /íntər díkt/ *n.* **1.** LAW PROHIBITIVE ORDER a court order that prohibits sth **2.** *Scotland* COURT ORDER BANNING STH TEMPORARILY a court order that bans some action that has been complained of as being against the law until the matter is tried in the proper court **3.** CHR **EXCLUSION FROM CHURCH SACRAMENTS** a ban imposed by a pope, church council, or bishop that excludes a person, group, or nation from the sacraments of the Roman Catholic Church. In the past the interdict was used to enforce obedience. ■ *vt.* (**-dicts, -dicting, -dicted**) **1.** LAW **BAN BY LAW** to prohibit sth or forbid sb from doing sth, especially in accordance with civil or ecclesiastical law **2.** *US* LAW **PREVENT ILLEGAL ENTRY** to prevent sb or sth entering a country illegally ○ *Patrols will be increased along the border to interdict smugglers.* **3.** MIL **PREVENT ENEMY USE** to keep an enemy from using an area by troop movements or other means [13thC. Via Old French *entredit* from Latin *interdictum*, formed from *interdicere* 'to prohibit', from *dicere* 'to speak'.] —**interdiction** /íntər díksh'n/ *n.* —**interdictor** /-díktər/ *n.* —**interdictory** /-díktəri/ *adj.*

interdigital /íntər díjjit'l/ *adj.* ELECTRON ENG in the form of two series of parallel strips that fit together like the fingers of clasped hands —**interdigitally** *adv.*

interdigitate /íntər díjji tayt/ (**-tates, -tating, -tated**) *vti.* to fit together like the fingers of clasped hands or to place or hold objects together in such a pattern —**interdigitation** /íntər dijji táysh'n/ *n.*

interdisciplinary /íntər díssiplinəri, -dissi plínnəri/ *adj.* involving two or more academic subjects or fields of study

interest /íntrəst/ *n.* **1. CURIOSITY OR CONCERN** a feeling of curiosity or concern about sth that makes the attention turn towards it ○ *an interest in art* **2. QUALITY THAT ATTRACTS ATTENTION** a power, quality, or aspect of sth that attracts attention, concern, or curiosity ○ *it's of no interest to me* **3. ENJOYABLE THING** sth that sb enjoys doing (*often used in the plural*) ○ *My leisure interests include sailing, music, reading, and walking.* **4. BENEFIT OR ADVANTAGE** the good, benefit, or advantage of sb or sth ○ *in the interests of peace* **5. INVOLVEMENT** sb's involvement with sth that makes its progress or success important to him or her ○ *took a personal interest in the progress of the project* **6.** FIN **BORROWING CHARGE OR PAYMENT FOR MONEY USE** a charge made for a loan or credit facility, or a payment made by a bank or other financial institution for the use of money deposited in an account **7.** COMM **SHARE IN STH** a legal right to claim a share in sth, especially in a business or property, or the business or property itself **8. CONNECTION** a personal or commercial connection with sth or sb, especially when this prevents sb from being objective or impartial ○ *had to declare a conflict of interest* ■ **interests** *npl.* **INFLUENTIAL GROUP** a group of people in business or society who have the same aims or support the same cause, especially a powerful or influential group ■ *vt.* (**-ests, -esting, -ested**) **1. GET SB'S ATTENTION** to attract or hold sb's attention or arouse sb's curiosity or concern ○ *It may interest you to know that the building used to be a mortuary.* **2. MAKE SB WANT STH** to make sb want to have or buy sth, do sth, or become involved with sth ○ *I tried to interest him in helping with the preparations.* [15thC. Via Old French from Latin 'it matters', from *interesse*, literally 'to be in the middle', from *esse* 'to be'.]

interested /íntrəstid/ *adj.* **1. CURIOUS OR CONCERNED** paying attention to sth or devoting time to sth because of curiosity, concern, or enjoyment **2. WANTING STH** involved or wanting to be involved in sth ○ *interested parties can call the free number* **3. AFFECTED OR INVOLVED** having a legal right or share in sth or a personal or commercial connection with sth —**interestedly** *adv.* —**interestedness** *n.*

interest group *n.* **1. OCCUPATIONAL GROUP** an occupational group such as a business organization, trade union, or professional association that is concerned mainly with the economic interests of its members **2. PEOPLE WITH SHARED INTEREST** a group of people who share an interest in sth such as a subject of study

interesting /íntrəsting/ *adj.* **1. AROUSING CURIOSITY OR ATTENTION** arousing curiosity, attracting or holding attention, or provoking thought **2. NOT BORING** enjoyable because of being varied, challenging, stimulating, or exciting

interface /íntər fayss/ *n.* **1. COMMON BOUNDARY** the surface, place, or point where two things touch each other or meet **2.** CHEM **BOUNDARY BETWEEN THINGS** a common boundary between objects or different phases of a substance ○ *an oil-water interface* **3. POINT OF INTERACTION** the place, situation, or way in which two things or people act together or affect each other or the point of connection between things **4.** COMPUT **BOUNDARY ACROSS WHICH DATA PASSES** a common boundary shared by two devices, or by a person and a device, across which data or information flows, e.g. the screen of a computer **5.** COMPUT **LINKING SOFTWARE** software that links a computer with another device, or the set of commands, messages, images, and other elements allowing communication between computer and operator **6.** ELECTRON ENG **LINKING DEVICE** an electronic device or circuit or other point of contact between two pieces of equipment ■ *vti.* (**-faces, -facing, -faced**) **1. HAVE OR GIVE COMMON BOUNDARY** to touch or meet at a surface, place, or point, or to make things join in this way **2. INTERACT** to act together or affect each other or to make things or people interact **3.** COMPUT **SERVE AS INTERFACE** to connect or serve as an interface for two or more pieces of equipment —**interfacial** /íntər fáysh'l/ *adj.* —**interfacially** /-fáysh'li/ *adv.*

interfacing /íntər fayssing/ *n.* a fabric that is used to stiffen or support collars, cuffs, or other parts of a garment

interfaith /íntər fáyth/ *adj.* involving or occurring between people of different religious faiths

interfere /íntər féer/ (**-feres, -fering, -fered**) *vi.* **1. MEDDLE IN OTHERS' AFFAIRS** to participate in the affairs of others, especially by offering unwanted or unhelpful advice or by trying to resolve others' disputes ○ *It's not advisable to interfere in a private quarrel.* **2. HAVE AN UNDESIRABLE EFFECT** to delay, hinder, or obstruct the natural or desired course of sth ○ *The weather interfered with our plans.* **3.** COMMUNICATION **CAUSE INTERFERENCE** to cause electronic interference **4.** PHYS **AFFECT DISPLACEMENT OR AMPLITUDE** to act together to increase, decrease, or cancel out displacement or amplitude **5.** EQU **HIT A HOOF AGAINST A LEG** to hit one hoof against the opposite hoof or leg while walking (*refers to horses*) **6. TOUCH ILLICITLY** to touch sb sexually in a way contrary to law or moral standards (*dated*) [15thC. Via Old French *s'entreferir* 'to strike each other', ultimately from Latin *ferire* 'to strike'.] —**interferer** *n.*

interference /íntər féeranss/ *n.* **1. MEDDLING IN OTHERS' AFFAIRS** involvement in sth without any invitation or justification ○ *he deeply resented any interference in his private life* **2. HINDRANCE** hindrance or obstruction that prevents a natural or desired outcome **3.** COMMUNICATION **SIGNAL THAT INTERFERES** an unwanted signal that disrupts radio, telephone, or television reception **4.** PHYS **PROCESS OF WAVE INTERACTION** a process in lightwave transmission in which two or more waves are superimposed in such a way that they produce higher peaks, lower troughs, or a new wave pattern **5.** AMERICAN FOOTBALL **LEGAL BLOCKING** in American football, the legal blocking of defensive players to protect and make way for the player carrying the ball —**interferential** /íntərfə rénsh'l/ *adj.* ◇ **run interference 1.** AMERICAN FOOTBALL to carry out legal blocking of defensive players to protect and make way for the player carrying the ball **2.** *US* to contribute help or support to sb or sth, especially by preventing others from acting as a hindrance (*informal*)

interfering /íntər féering/ *adj.* deliberately becoming involved in other people's affairs in a way that is not needed and is unwelcome —**interferingly** *adv.*

interferometer /íntərfə rómmitər/ *n.* a device that uses an interference pattern to determine wave frequency, length, or velocity —**interferometric** /íntər feerə méttrik/ *adj.* —**interferometrically** /-méttrikli/ *adv.* —**interferometry** /-rómmətri/ *n.*

interferon /íntər féer on/ *n.* a complex protein (**glycoprotein**) that is produced by cells in response to a virus or bacterium and that inhibits virus development [Mid-20thC. Coined from INTERFERE + -ON.]

interfertile /íntər fúr tīl/ *adj.* able to interbreed with other species or subspecies and produce viable offspring —**interfertility** /íntərfər tílləti/ *n.*

interfile /íntər fīl/ (**-files, -filing, -filed**) *vt.* to put an item or items among similar items in a file

interflow /íntər flṓ/ (**-flows, -flowing, -flowed**) *vi.* to merge into a single stream

interfluent /íntər flóo ənt/ *adj.* **1. FLOWING TOGETHER** merging into a single stream **2. FLOWING BETWEEN** flowing between things or places [Mid-17thC. From Latin *interfluent-*, the present participle stem of *interfluere* 'to flow together', from *fluere* 'to flow'.]

interfluve /íntər floov/ *n.* **1. LINE SEPARATING DRAINAGE AREAS** the ridge line separating two river catchments **2. LINE MARKING A DIVIDE IN WATER FLOW** a line joining points on one side of which water will flow to one river whilst on the other side water will flow to another river [Early 20thC. Back-formation from *interfluvial*.] —**interfluvial** /íntər flóovi əl/ *adj.*

interfuse /íntər fyóoz/ (**-fuses, -fusing, -fused**) *vti.* to mingle, blend, or fuse thoroughly, or to mix two or more things in this way [Late 16thC. From Latin *interfus-*, formed from *interfundere*, literally 'to pour together', from *fundere* 'to pour'.] —**interfusion** /íntər fyóozh'n/ *n.*

intergalactic /íntərgə láktik/ *adj.* situated, happening, or moving between galaxies, or involving two or more galaxies —**intergalactically** *adv.*

intergenerational /íntər jennə ráysh'nəl/ *adj.* occurring between, involving, or affecting people of two or more generations

interglacial /íntər gláysi əl, -gláysh'l/ *n.* a period of warmer climate separating two periods of glaciation and displaying a characteristic sequence of changes in vegetation. The term is used especially for several such periods that occurred during the Pleistocene epoch, lasting from 1.8 million to 10,000 years ago. ◊ **interstadial** —**interglacial** *adj.*

intergovernmental /íntər guvvərn mént'l, -guvvər-/ *adj.* involving representatives of or concerning relations between two or more governments —**intergovernmentally** *adv.*

intergrade *vi.* /íntər gráyd/ (**-grades, -grading, -graded**) ZOOL **CHANGE BY STAGES** to be transformed from one form to another through a series of stages or forms that involve partial transitions ■ *n.* /íntər grayd/ **1. TRANSITIONAL FORM** a transitional form or stage **2.** GEOG **TRANSITIONAL SOIL HORIZON** a transitional soil horizon between two distinctive soils —**intergradient** *adj.* —**intergradation** /íntər gray dáysh'n/ *n.*

intergroup /íntər gróop/ *adj.* involving members of two or more racial or social groups, or concerned with relations between groups

intergrowth /íntər grōth/ *n.* growth of one thing into or within another thing, or among other things, or the result of such growth

interim /íntərim/ *adj.* **1. HAVING TEMPORARY EFFECT** serving as a temporary measure until sth more complete and permanent can be established **2.** POL **HOLDING TEMPORARY OFFICE** serving temporarily until a permanent replacement can be elected or appointed ■ *n.* **INTERVENING TIME** a period of time between two occurrences or periods ○ *in the interim* [Mid-16thC. From Latin, 'meanwhile'.]

interim dividend *n.* a dividend paid by a company before the end of its financial year

interionic /íntər ī ónnik/ *adj.* situated between or involving two or more ions

interior /in téeri ər/ *n.* **1. INSIDE PART** the inside of sth ○ *the interior of the church was dark* **2. INSIDE OF A BUILDING OR ROOM** the inside of a building or room considered especially with regard to its decoration and furnishing **3. PART FARTHEST IN FROM THE EDGE** the part of sth that is far or farthest from its edge, boundary, or surface, especially the part of a country or continent that is remote or farthest from the coast **4. PICTURE OF THE INSIDE OF A ROOM** a painting or photograph of the inside of a room **5. INSIDE SET OR SCENE** a setting or actual location that represents the inside of a building, or a scene filmed inside a building ■ *adj.* **1. LOCATED INSIDE** located or occurring inside sth, or suitable for the inside of sth **2. CENTRAL** remote or farthest from the edge, boundary, or surface of sth, especially from the coast of a country or continent **3. OCCURRING IN THE MIND** taking place within sb's mind and usually not expressed out loud [15thC. Directly or via French *intérieur* from Latin *interior*, literally 'more in the midst of', from *inter* 'between' (see INTER-).] —**interiority** /in teeri órrəti/ *n.* —**interiorly** /in téeri ərli/ *adv.*

Interior *n.* **COUNTRY'S INTERNAL AFFAIRS** in the United States and some other countries, the internal affairs of the nation, especially as opposed to its foreign affairs ■ *adj.* OF INTERNAL AFFAIRS relating to the internal affairs of a country, especially as opposed to its foreign affairs

interior angle *n.* **1.** ANGLE INSIDE A POLYGON the angle formed between two adjacent sides of a polygon and lying in its interior. The sum of the interior angles of any polygon is equal to the number of its sides minus two and multiplied by 180°. **2.** ANGLE WITHIN INTERSECTING LINES any of the four angles formed in the area between two lines by a third line that intersects them (**transversal**)

interior decoration *n.* **1.** = interior design **2.** DECORATIONS AND FURNISHINGS the way that a room or building is decorated and furnished **3.** WALLPAPERING AND PAINTING the skill or trade of sb who specializes in wallpapering and painting interiors —**interior decorator** *n.*

interior design *n.* the art or process of planning the decoration and furnishings of a room or building. US term **interior decoration** —**interior designer** *n.*

interiorize /in teéri ə rīz/ (**-izes, -izing, -ized**), **interiorise** (**-ises, -ising, -ised**) *vt.* = internalize —**interiorization** /in teéri ə rī záysh'n/ *n.*

interior monologue *n.* an extended passage in a story or novel that expresses what a character is thinking and feeling. ◊ **stream of consciousness, soliloquy**

Interior Salish /-sáylish/ (*plural* **Interior Salish**) *n.* a member of a Native North American people who originally lived in parts of British Columbia, northern Washington, northern Idaho, and western Montana. Today a small community of approximately 5,000 Interior Salish live on a reservation in Montana. —**Interior Salish** *adj.*

interior-sprung *adj.* having many helical springs inside a thick padded cover. US term **innerspring**

inter-island /íntər-/ *adj.* occurring between islands, or involving two or more islands

interj. *abbr.* interjection

interjacent /íntər jáyss'nt/ *adj.* being in a position between sth and sth else (*formal*) [Mid-16thC. From Latin *interjacent*-, the present participle stem of *interjacere* 'to lie between', from *jacere* 'to lie' (source of English *adjacent*).]

interject /íntər jékt/ (**-jects, -jecting, -jected**) *vti.* to say or insert sth in a way that interrupts what is being said or discussed [Late 16thC. From Latin *interject*-, the past participle stem of *interjicere* 'to interpose', literally 'to throw between', from *jacere* 'to throw'.] —**interjector** *n.* —**interjectory** *adj.*

interjection /íntər jéksh'n/ *n.* **1.** EXCLAMATION EXPRESSING EMOTION a sound, word, or phrase that expresses a strong emotion such as pain or surprise but otherwise has no meaning **2.** COMMENT MADE ABRUPTLY sth said loudly and abruptly or inserted in a text, especially sth that interrupts what is being said or discussed —**interjectional** *adj.* —**interjectionally** *adv.*

interkinesis /íntərki neéssiss, -kī-/ *n.* the period of rest between meiotic cell divisions, similar to the interphase stage in mitosis

interlace /íntər láyss/ (**-laces, -lacing, -laced**) *v.* **1.** *vti.* WEAVE TOGETHER to join together or interweave, often in an intricate pattern, by crossing over each other, or to cause two or more things to do this **2.** *vt.* BREAK UP STH WITH STH ELSE to break up the flow or relieve the monotony of sth by occasionally inserting sth different such as jokes in a serious talk [14thC. From Old French *entrelacier*, literally 'to lace together', from *lacier* 'to lace'.] —**interlacement** *n.*

interlaced /íntər láyst/ *adj.* ELECTRON ENG refreshing the image on a monitor screen by scanning first all odd and then all even numbered lines

interlaced scanning *n.* a technique used in television and computer monitors in which high vertical resolution is achieved by scanning all odd and then all even numbered lines

interlanguage /íntər lángwidj/ *n.* LANG a form of language typically produced by learners of a second language or foreign language, which combines elements of two or more languages

interlard /íntər laárd/ (**-lards, -larding, -larded**) *vt.* to vary or interrupt speech or writing by interspersing other contrasting words [Mid-16thC. From French *entrelarder* 'to mix alternating layers of fat into lean meat', from *larde* 'lard'.]

interlay /íntər láy/ *vt.* (**-lays, -laying, -laid** /-láyd/, **-laid**) PUT STH BETWEEN STH to lay or layer sth between sth else ■ *n.* INSERTED LAYER sth laid between two surfaces

interleaf /íntər leef/ (*plural* **-leaves** /-leevz/) *n.* an extra sheet or page, usually a blank one, inserted into a book

interleave /íntər leév/ (**-leaves, -leaving, -leaved**) *vt.* to add extra sheets or pages, usually blank ones, between the pages of a book, e.g. to allow for notes or to protect illustrations [Mid-17thC. Formed from INTER- + LEAF.]

interleukin /íntər loókin/ *n.* a chemical found in white blood cells that stimulates them to fight infection [Late 20thC. Coined from INTER- + LEUCOCYTE + -IN.]

interleukin-1 /íntər lookin-/ *n.* an interleukin secreted by antigen-activated macrophages that stimulates the production of other factors that activate the immune system

interleukin-2 /íntər lookin-/ *n.* an interleukin that stimulates T-cells and is used in the treatment of cancer

interlibrary loan /íntər líbrəri-/ *n.* **1.** BOOK-BORROWING SYSTEM a system by which libraries and library users can borrow books from other libraries **2.** BORROWING OF A BOOK a borrowing of a book through an interlibrary loan system **3.** BOOK BORROWED a book borrowed through an interlibrary loan system

interline[1] /íntər lín/ (**-lines, -lining, -lined**) *vt.* to write or print words between the lines of writing or printing in a text or document [15thC. From medieval Latin *interlineare*, from Latin *linea* (see LINE[1]).] —**interlineation** /íntər línni áysh'n/ *n.*

interline[2] /íntər lín/ (**-lines, -lining, -lined**) *vt.* to put an extra lining, usually of a stiffer material, between the fabric and the lining of a piece of clothing [15thC. Formed from INTER- + LINE[2].]

interlinear /íntər línni ər/, **interlineal** /-línni əl/ *adj.* **1.** INSERTED BETWEEN LINES inserted between the lines of a text or document **2.** HAVING ALTERNATING VERSIONS OF TEXT written or printed with different versions of the same text on alternate or succeeding lines [14thC. Via medieval Latin *interlinearis* from, ultimately, Latin *linea* (see LINE[1]).] —**interlinearly** *adv.*

Interlingua /íntər líng gwə/ *n.* a made-up language designed to facilitate international communication, based on the common elements of living Latinate languages [Early 20thC. Coined from INTER- + Latin *lingua* 'tongue, language'.]

interlining /íntər líning/ *n.* an extra lining inserted between the fabric and lining of a piece of clothing to provide extra thickness or warmth, or the fabric used for this

interlink /íntər língk/ (**-links, -linking, -linked**) *vti.* to connect sth with sth else in several ways, or to be connected together in several ways

interlock /íntər lók/ *vti.* (**-locks, -locking, -locked**) **1.** FIT TOGETHER CLOSELY to fit or fasten two or more things together closely and firmly, especially by means of parts that mesh, hook, or dovetail together, or to be fitted together in this way **2.** OPERATE AS A UNIT to connect together as parts in such a way that all must move or operate if one does, or to be connected in this way ■ *n.* /íntər lok/ **1.** CONNECTING AND COORDINATING DEVICE a device or mechanism that connects different parts or components of sth such as a piece of machinery in order to coordinate and synchronize their action **2.** CLOSE CONNECTION a close connection by means of parts that fit or fasten together closely and firmly **3.** TEXTILES TIGHTLY-KNITTED FABRIC a fabric made with tightly-knitted stitches **4.** SEW CANVAS FOR NEEDLEPOINT a type of canvas used for needlepoint that has the warp and weft threads knotted together to prevent movement **5.** COMPUT COMPUTER SECURITY DEVICE a security device such as a password system designed to prevent unauthorized use of a computer ■ *adj.* TEXTILES TIGHTLY-KNITTED knitted with close, tight stitches

interlocking directorates *npl.* boards of directors that have enough members in common to place the companies that they oversee under the same control

interlocution /íntərlō kyoósh'n/ *n.* a discussion or conversation involving two or more people (*formal*) [Mid-16thC. From the Latin stem *interlocution*-, from *interlocut*-, the past participle stem of *interloqui* 'to interrupt', literally 'to speak between', from *loqui* (see LOQUACIOUS).]

interlocutor /íntər lókyoótər/ *n.* **1.** SB DISCUSSING sb who takes part in a discussion or conversation (*formal*) **2.** MINSTREL SHOW PERFORMER a performer in a minstrel show who acted as the presenter and stood in the middle and bantered with the end men [Early 16thC. From modern Latin, formed from Latin *interlocut*-, the past participle stem of *interloqui* 'to interrupt', literally 'to speak between', from *loqui* (see LOQUACIOUS).]

interlocutory /íntər lókyoótəri/ *adj.* **1.** INVOLVING DISCUSSION involving or characteristic of conversation or discussion (*formal*) **2.** LAW ISSUED PROVISIONALLY issued provisionally during a lawsuit

interloper /íntər lōpər/ *n.* **1.** INTRUDER sb who enters a place or joins a group or gathering without any right to do so **2.** SB WHO INTERFERES sb who interferes in other people's affairs, especially selfishly [Late 16thC. Modelled on earlier *landloper* 'vagabond', from Middle Dutch *landlooper*, literally 'land-runner', from *land* 'land' + *loopen* 'to run'. The word originally meant 'an unauthorized trader'.]

interlude /íntər lood/ *n.* **1.** INTERVENING PERIOD OF TIME a relatively short period of time between two longer periods, during which sth happens that is different from what has happened before and what follows **2.** ARTS ENTERTAINMENT DURING A PERFORMANCE BREAK a short play, piece of music, or other entertainment performed during a break in the performance of a long work [14thC. From medieval Latin *interludium*, literally 'in-between-play' (because it was originally performed between the acts of a long medieval mystery play), from Latin *ludus* 'play'.]

intermarriage /íntər márrij/ *n.* **1.** MARRIAGE BETWEEN DIFFERENT GROUPS marriage between members of different religious, social, or racial groups, or an instance of this **2.** MARRIAGE WITHIN A GROUP marriage between people who belong to the same religious, social, or racial group, or an instance of this [Early 17thC. The word was used earlier in the general sense 'marriage'.]

intermarry /íntər márri/ (**-ries, -rying, -ried**) *vi.* **1.** MARRY MEMBER OF ANOTHER GROUP to marry a member of a different religious, social, or racial group **2.** MARRY WITHIN A GROUP to marry within a religious, social, or racial group [Early 17thC. The word was used earlier in the general sense 'to marry'.]

intermediary /íntər meédi əri/ *n.* (*plural* **-ies**) **1.** GO-BETWEEN sb who goes from one person or group to another, carrying messages or trying to bring about agreement **2.** MEANS OR MEDIUM sth that functions as a means or medium for bringing sth about ■ *adj.* **1.** MEDIATING acting as a messenger or mediator between two or more people or groups **2.** LYING IN BETWEEN lying or occurring between two different forms, states, points, or extremes [Late 18thC. Via French *intermédiaire* from, ultimately, Latin *intermedius* (see INTERMEDIATE[1]).]

intermediate[1] /íntər meédi ət/ *adj.* **1.** BEING IN BETWEEN lying or occurring between two different forms, states, points, or extremes ○ *an intermediate course* **2.** GEOL CONTAINING BETWEEN 55% AND 66% SILICA used to describe an igneous rock with a silica content of between 55 per cent and 66 per cent ■ *n.* **1.** STH BETWEEN TWO OTHER THINGS sth that lies or occurs between two different forms, states, points, or extremes **2.** = intermediary *n.* **1** **3.** CHEM CHEMICAL FOR FURTHER REACTIONS a chemical compound that is formed during a chemical reaction and is used in another reaction to obtain another compound **4.** CHEM SHORT-LIVED CHEMICAL COMPONENT a molecule, ion, or free radical that exists for a short time during a chemical reaction [15thC. Directly or via French from medieval Latin *intermediatus*, from Latin *intermedius*, from *medius* 'middle'.] —**intermediately** *adv.* —**intermediateness** *n.*

intermediate[2] /íntər meédi ayt/ (**-ates, -ating, -ated**) *vi.* to act as a go-between or mediator between two or more people or groups [Early 16thC. Formed from INTER-

+ MEDIATE.] —**intermediation** /íntər meédi áysh'n/ n. —**intermediator** /íntər meédi aytər/ n.

intermediate-acting adj. having a period of therapeutic activity that is between that of long-acting and short-acting drugs

intermediate bulk container n. a portable container for transporting liquids or solids that holds 500 to 1,000 litres/110 to 220 gallons or 500 to 1,500 kg/1,100 to 3,300 lb. It is intermediate in size between a drum and a tanker load.

intermediate court n. Aus a court at the middle level of the state court hierarchy in Australia, below the supreme courts but above the magistrates' courts. Intermediate courts include the county courts in Victoria, district courts in New South Wales, Western Australia, and Queensland, and local courts elsewhere.

intermediate frequency n. the frequency that an incoming signal is changed to in a heterodyne receiver prior to amplification

intermediate host n. an animal that is the host for an immature parasite, which then moves on to a different host before reproducing

intermediate-level waste n. radioactive waste from reactors and processing plants that is solidified, mixed with concrete, and stored in drums. These drums are then placed for long-term storage in waste repositories.

intermediate-range ballistic missile n. a ballistic missile that has a range of 1,200 to 1,600 km/750 to 1,000 mi. ◊ **intercontinental ballistic missile**

intermediate school n. **1.** US = junior high, middle school **2.** NZ SCHOOL FOR 11–13 YEAR-OLDS in New Zealand, a school that takes children between the ages of 11 and 13

intermediate technology n. simple technology that is environmentally sensitive and based on local resources

intermediate treatment n. care for children affected by emotional or personality disorders, or psychiatric conditions that do not require hospitalization but do require close monitoring

intermediate vector boson n. an elementary particle that transmits weak interactions between other elementary particles. The three postulated intermediate vector bosons, the W^+, W^-, and Z^0 particles, have all been observed.

intermedin /íntər meédin/ n. PHYSIOL = **melanocyte-stimulating hormone** [Mid-20thC. Coined from modern Latin (pars) intermedia 'intermediate (part) (of the pituitary)' (from Latin intermedius) + -IN.]

interment /in túrmənt/ n. the burial of a dead body or the ashes of a cremated body (formal) [14thC. Formed from INTER.]

intermesh /íntər mésh/ (-meshes, -meshing, -meshed) vti. to engage or mesh with one another, or to cause sth such as the teeth of cogwheels to do so

intermetallic /íntərmi tállik/ adj. consisting of two or more metals in specific proportions

intermezzo /íntər métsō, -médzō/ (plural -zos or -zi /-métsi, -médzi/) n. **1.** SHORT MOVEMENT IN A LONGER MUSICAL WORK a short piece of music that is performed between longer movements of an extended musical composition **2.** SHORT PIECE OF MUSIC a short musical composition, usually for solo piano **3.** = **interlude** n. 2 [Late 18thC. Via Italian from Latin intermedius 'intermediate', from medius 'middle'.]

interminable /in túrminəb'l/ adj. so long and boring or frustrating as to seem endless ◊ interminable delays [14thC. Directly or via French from late Latin interminabilis, literally 'unending', from Latin terminare (see TERMINATE).] —**interminability** /in túrminə bílləti/ n. —**interminably** /-minəbli/ adv.

intermingle /íntər míng g'l/ (-gles, -gling, -gled) vti. to mix sth together with sth else, or to become mixed together ◊ the scents of jasmine and honeysuckle intermingled

intermission /íntər mísh'n/ n. **1.** = **interval** n. 3 **2.** PAUSE a pause in, or temporary discontinuation of, an activity [15thC. Directly or via French from the Latin stem intermission-, from intermiss-, the past participle stem of intermittere (see INTERMIT).]

intermit /íntər mít/ (-mits, -mitting, -mitted) vti. (formal) **1.** DISCONTINUE to discontinue doing sth temporarily, or to be discontinued temporarily **2.** PAUSE to stop or cause sth to stop for a short time or for short intervals [Mid-16thC. From Latin intermittere 'to interrupt', literally 'to send between', from mittere (see MISSION).] —**intermittor** n. —**intermittingly** adv.

intermittent /íntər mítt'nt/ adj. happening or coming from time to time [Mid-16thC. From Latin intermittere 'to interrupt' (see INTERMIT).] —**intermittence** n. —**intermittently** adv.

——————— WORD KEY: SYNONYMS ———————
See Synonyms at **periodic**.

intermittent claudication n. a cramping pain, induced by exercise and relieved by rest, that is caused by inadequate blood supply to the affected muscles, usually the calves

intermittent current n. a unidirectional current that is interrupted periodically

intermittent fever n. a fever that rises and falls and then returns, occurring in diseases such as malaria

intermix /íntər míks/ (-mixes, -mixing, -mixed) vti. = **intermingle** [Mid-16thC. From Latin intermixtus, the past participle of intermiscere, literally 'to mix together', from miscere (see MIXED).] —**intermixable** adj.

intermodal /íntər mṓd'l/ adj. TRANSPORTABLE BY VARIOUS MEANS used to describe containers designed to be transferred from one mode of transport to another while in transit, e.g. from a train to a ship to a lorry ■ n. GOODS CONTAINER a container for goods that can be transferred from one mode of transport to another during shipment without being unpacked

intermodulation /íntər moddyoō láysh'n/ n. the undesired interaction of electronic signals or complex wave components to produce waves with frequencies equal to the sums and differences of integral multiples of the frequencies of the signals

intermolecular /íntərmə lékyoōlər/ adj. occurring between molecules, or involving two or more molecules —**intermolecularly** adv.

intermontane /íntər mon táyn/ adj. used to describe basins lying between two mountain ranges, and often filling up with sediment washed down from them [Early 19thC. Formed from INTER- + MONTANE.]

intermural /íntər myoōrəl/ adj. involving participants from two or more educational institutions, athletic clubs, or other groups. ◊ **intramural** [Modelled on INTRA-MURAL]

intern /in túrn/, **interne** v. (-terns, -terning, -terned) **1.** vt. DETAIN SB to detain sb in confinement as being a security threat **2.** vi. US WORK AS AN INTERN to work as an intern, especially in a hospital ■ n. **1.** US, Can, Aus JUNIOR HOSPITAL DOCTOR a junior doctor at a hospital **2.** US TRAINEE sb who works as a low-level assistant or trainee in an occupation in order to gain practical experience [Mid-19thC. The noun is via French interne; the verb via interner, both ultimately from Latin internus (see INTERNAL).]

internal /in túrn'l/ adj. **1.** LOCATED INSIDE located within or affecting the inside of sth, especially the inside of the body ◊ internal organs **2.** INTENDED FOR USE INSIDE effective when used or suitable for use inside sth, especially the inside of the body **3.** SELF-CONTAINED OR SELF-GENERATING existing, evident in, or arising from the nature, structure, or qualities that sb or sth has ◊ internal cohesion **4.** OCCURRING WITHIN A COUNTRY originating, operating, or located within a country's borders ◊ internal affairs **5.** MENTAL involving or existing within the mind or spirit ◊ internal conflict **6.** OCCURRING WITHIN AN ORGANIZATION working at or carried out within an organization or institution such as a school, college, or university ◊ internal e-mail [15thC. Directly or via Old French internel from medieval Latin internalis, from Latin internus 'inwards, within', from inter (see INTER-).] —**internality** /in túrnáləti/ n. —**internally** /in túrn'li/ adv. —**internalness** /-n'lnəss/ n.

internal-combustion engine n. an engine in which fuel is burnt in combustion chambers within the engine instead of in an external furnace and in which the energy released moves one or more pistons

internal ear n. = inner ear

internal energy n. the total kinetic energy of the atoms and molecules of a system plus the potential energy of their mutual interaction. An increase in internal energy manifests as a rise in temperature or a change in phase. Symbol U

internalize /in túrnə līz/ (-izes, -izing, -ized), **internalise** (-ises, -ising, -ised) vt. **1.** ADOPT OTHERS' BELIEFS to adopt the beliefs, values, and attitudes of others, either consciously or unconsciously **2.** KEEP A PROBLEM INSIDE to deal with an emotion or conflict by thinking about it rather than expressing it openly —**internalization** /in túrnə lī záysh'n/ n.

internal medicine n. the branch of medicine concerned with the diagnosis and nonsurgical treatment of diseases affecting the internal organs, and with preventive medicine

internal resistance n. the resistance within a source of electrical current such as a cell or generator

internal respiration n. the metabolic use of oxygen by a cell to produce energy, resulting in the release of carbon dioxide

internal rhyme n. a rhyme in which one of the rhyming words is within the line of poetry and the other is at the end of the same line or within the next line

internal secretion n. a secretion, especially a hormone, that is absorbed into the blood directly after production

internal wave n. a waveform that develops below the surface of a body of water where two water masses with different densities meet. An internal wave can develop in an estuary where salt water lies underneath less dense river water.

internat. abbr. international

international /íntər násh'nəl/ adj. **1.** INVOLVING SEVERAL COUNTRIES involving two or more countries or their citizens **2.** CROSSING NATIONAL BOUNDARIES extending beyond or across national boundaries **3.** OF RELATIONS AMONG NATIONS concerned with relations between nations ■ n. **1.** CONTEST BETWEEN TEAMS FROM DIFFERENT COUNTRIES a sports contest between teams or players from two or more countries, especially a football or rugby match between teams representing two countries **2.** MEMBER OF AN INTERNATIONAL TEAM a member of a team representing his or her country in an international event —**internationality** /íntər násh'n álləti/ n. —**internationally** /-násh'nəli/ adv.

International /íntər násh'nəl/ n. any of four international Socialist, Communist, or Anarchist organizations formed in 1864, 1889, 1919, and 1938 respectively

International Atomic Time n. a precisely determined system of measuring time in which a second is defined in terms of atomic events that are known to a high degree of accuracy

International Bank for Reconstruction and Development n. = World Bank

International Brigade n. any of seven mainly Communist and Socialist forces of volunteers from many different countries that fought on the Republican side during the Spanish Civil War

International Court of Justice n. the chief judicial body of the United Nations, empowered to resolve international disputes between member nations who submit a case to the court

International Criminal Police Organization n. full form of **Interpol**

International Date Line n. an internationally agreed imaginary line running roughly along the 180° meridian of longitude. To the east of the line the date is one day earlier than to the west.

International Development Association n. a specialized agency of the United Nations that provides credit to nations on easier terms than the World Bank

Internationale /íntər náshə naál/ n. a revolutionary Socialist song written in France in 1871 and adopted as the anthem of the First, Second, and Third Internationals. A Russian version was the national anthem of the Soviet Union until 1944. [Early 20thC. From French *(chanson) internationale* 'international (song)'.]

International Finance Corporation *n.* a specialized agency of the United Nations that is affiliated with the World Bank and promotes private enterprise in developing nations by providing risk capital

International Gothic *n.* a style of painting and other visual art that emerged in Europe with the increasing exchange of ideas and techniques among European artists towards the end of the 14th century

International Grandmaster *n.* a chess player who has achieved the highest ranking awarded to a participant in international competitions

internationalise *vt.* = internationalize

internationalism /íntər násh'nəlizəm/ *n.* **1.** COOPERATION BETWEEN COUNTRIES a policy or spirit of cooperation and mutual understanding between countries **2.** INTEREST IN OTHER COUNTRIES a willingness and ability to understand and respect the concerns, attitudes, and ways of life of other countries **3.** INTERNATIONAL CHARACTER OR QUALITY the international character or quality of sb or sth

internationalist /íntər násh'nəlist/ *n.* **1.** ADVOCATE OF INTERNATIONAL COOPERATION sb who favours greater cooperation and understanding between countries **2.** SB INTERESTED IN OTHER COUNTRIES sb who is interested in other countries and understands and respects their peoples' concerns, attitudes, and ways of life ■ *adj.* FAVOURING INTERNATIONAL COOPERATION favouring greater cooperation and understanding between countries

internationalize /íntər násh'nə līz/ (-izes, -izing, -ized), **internationalise** (-ises, -ising, -ised) *vt.* **1.** MAKE STH INTERNATIONAL to make sth international in character, structure, or outlook **2.** PUT STH UNDER INTERNATIONAL CONTROL to place sth under the protection or control of several countries instead of one country —**internationalization** /íntər násh'nə līˈzáysh'n/ *n.*

international law *n.* the accepted rules that govern countries in their relations with other countries

International Master *n.* a chess player who has achieved a high ranking in international competitions that is below that of an International Grandmaster

International Modernism *n.* = International Style

International Monetary Fund *n.* a specialized agency of the United Nations that seeks to promote international monetary cooperation and the stabilization of national currencies and help nations resolve balance of payment problems

International Phonetic Alphabet *n.* a system of letters and marks, based for the most part on the letters of the Roman alphabet, that is used internationally to represent the speech sounds of languages

International Practical Temperature Scale *n.* a scientific temperature scale, expressed in degrees Celsius, that has eleven fixed temperature reference points, including the boiling point of oxygen and the freezing point of gold

international relations *npl.* RELATIONS BETWEEN COUNTRIES political and other dealings between two or more countries ■ *n.* STUDY OF RELATIONS BETWEEN COUNTRIES the branch of political science that studies the relations between countries (*takes a singular verb*)

international sea and swell scale *n.* = Douglas scale

International Standards Organization *n.* an international organization established in 1947 to standardize such things as units of measurement and the meanings of technical terms

International Style *n.* an early 20th-century architectural style in the United States and Europe that favoured the use of simple geometric lines, spacious interiors, and materials such as steel and reinforced concrete

International System (of Units) *n.* an internationally accepted system of units of measurement used for scientific work. The basic units are the metre, kilogram, second, kelvin, mole, ampere, and candela, these being the basic quantities of length,

International Style: Studio building (1925) at the Bauhaus, Dessau, Germany

mass, time, temperature, amount of substance, electric current, and luminous intensity.

International Telecommunication Union *n.* a specialized agency of the United Nations that promotes international cooperation in telecommunications and allots radio frequencies for various purposes. It was founded in 1865 and affiliated with the United Nations in 1947.

international telegram *n.* a message sent by telephone or telex from the United Kingdom to another country, where it is delivered in written or printed form

international unit *n.* an internationally agreed unit of the amount of a biologically active substance such as a hormone or vitamin required to produce a specific response

interne *n.* US = intern

internecine /íntər neé sīn/ *adj.* **1.** INTERNAL occurring within a group or organization **2.** MUTUALLY DESTRUCTIVE damaging or injuring participants on both sides of a conflict or struggle [Mid-17thC. From Latin *internecinus* 'deadly', from *internecare* 'to exterminate', literally 'to kill completely', from *necare* 'to kill', from *nex* 'death' (source of English *pernicious*).]

──── **WORD KEY: ORIGIN** ────
The original meaning of *internecine* is 'attended by great slaughter'. Its modern connotations of 'conflict within a group', which can be traced back to the 18th century (Samuel Johnson in his *Dictionary* (1755) defined it as 'endeavouring mutual destruction'), arose from the standard interpretation of *inter-* as 'among, between', but in fact in the case of Latin *internecinus* it was being used simply to add emphasis.

internee /íntər neé/ *n.* sb who is confined in prison, a concentration camp, or other place, especially during a war

internesia /íntər neézhə/ *n.* US an inability to remember either the location or information contained in a Web site (*informal*) [Combination of INTERNET + AMNESIA]

Internet /íntər net/ *n.* a network that links computer networks all over the world by satellite and telephone, connecting users with service networks such as e-mail and the World Wide Web

Internet protocol *n.* the standard that controls the routing and structure of data transmitted over the Internet

Internet service provider *n.* a business that provides access to the Internet, usually for a monthly fee. Some large providers offer users a wide range of news, information, and entertainment services.

interneuron /íntər nyoˈor on/ *n.* a short nerve cell in the central nervous system that connects the nerve cells in a reflex arc, e.g. a sensory nerve to a motor nerve —**interneuronal** /-nyoˈorən'l/ *adj.*

internist /ín turnist/ *n.* a doctor who specializes in the diagnosis, prevention, and nonsurgical treatment of diseases affecting the internal organs [Early 20thC. Formed from INTERNAL + -IST.]

internment /ín túrnmənt/ *n.* the confinement of sb regarded as a security threat in a prison, concentration camp, or other place, especially during a war

internode /íntər nōd/ *n.* **1.** BOT STEM SECTION BETWEEN TWO NODES the part of a plant stem between two nodes **2.** ANAT NERVE CELL PART the part of the axon of a nerve cell that lies between the nodes of Ranvier. The internode is covered by the myelin sheath, which is absent at the nodes. [Mid-17thC. From Latin *internodium*, from *nodus* 'knot'.] —**internodal** /íntər nṓd'l/ *adj.*

inter nos /íntər nóss/ *adv.* between or among ourselves [From Latin]

internship /ín turn ship/ *n.* US the position of an intern or a period of time working as one

internuncial /íntər núnsh'l/ *adj.* **1.** ANAT CONNECTING used to describe nerve cells that connect one nerve cell to another **2.** CHR OF A PAPAL INTERNUNCIO acting as or connected with an internuncio of the Roman Catholic Church —**internuncially** *adv.*

internuncio /íntər núnshi ō/ (*plural* -os) *n.* **1.** PAPAL AMBASSADOR a diplomatic representative of the pope ranking below a nuncio **2.** GO-BETWEEN a messenger or go-between (*formal*) [Mid-17thC. Via Italian *internunzio* from Latin *internuntius*, literally 'intermediate messenger', from *nuntius* (see NUNCIO).]

interoceanic /íntər ōshi ánnik/ *adj.* occurring between or connecting two or more oceans

interoffice /íntər óffiss/ *adj.* occurring between offices or involving two or more offices in the same organization ○ *an interoffice memo*

interp. *abbr.* interpreter

interpellant /íntər péll'nt/ *adj.* ASKING QUESTION asking a question in a parliament on some aspect of government policy (*formal*) ■ *n.* SB ASKING QUESTION a member of a parliament who asks a question on some aspect of government policy (*formal*) [Mid-19thC. Via French from, ultimately, Latin *interpellare* (see INTERPELLATE).]

interpellate /in túrpə layt/ (-lates, -lating, -lated) *vt.* to interrupt a parliamentary debate by asking a question on some aspect of government policy [Late 19thC. From Latin *interpellare*, literally 'to thrust yourself between', from *-pellare* 'to thrust yourself', a variant of *pellere* 'to push, drive' (see PULSE[1]).] —**interpellation** /in túrpə láysh'n/ *n.* —**interpellator** /in túrpə laytər/ *n.*

interpersonal /íntər púrss'nəl/ *adj.* concerning or involving relationships between people —**interpersonally** *adv.*

interphalangeal /íntərfə lánji əl/ *adj.* situated between the bones of the fingers or toes

interphase /íntər fayz/ *n.* the period during which a cell is not actively dividing, when other activities such as DNA synthesis take place

interplanetary /íntər plánnitəri/ *adj.* situated, happening, or moving between planets or involving two or more planets

interplay /íntər play/ *n.* the way in which two or more people or things repeatedly act on and react to each other

interplead /íntər pleéd/ (-pleads, -pleading, -pleaded *or* -pled, -pleaded *or* -pled /íntər pléd/) *vi.* to go to trial to resolve which of several claimants has the right to claim money or property held by a third party [Mid-16thC. From Anglo-Norman *enterpleder*, literally 'to plead together', from *pleder* (see PLEAD).]

interpleader /íntər pleédər/ *n.* a trial to resolve which of several claimants can sue for money or property held by a third party. The third party institutes an interpleader to avoid several individual proceedings. [Mid-16thC. From Anglo-Norman *enterpleder* (see INTERPLEAD).]

Interpol /íntər pol/ *n.* an association of national police forces, established in 1923, that promotes cooperation and mutual assistance in apprehending international criminals and criminals who flee abroad to avoid justice. The headquarters of Interpol is in Paris. Full form **International Criminal Police Organization**

interpolate /in túrpə layt/ (-lates, -lating, -lated) *v.* **1.** *vt.* INSERT STH INTO STH ELSE to add sth, often sth unnecessary, between the existing elements or items of sth else **2.** *vt.* ADD WORDS TO A TEXT to add a comment or extra words to a written text, often altering or falsifying the meaning **3.** *vt.* ALTER TEXT to alter or deliberately falsify a text by adding a comment or extra words to it **4.** *vti.* INTERRUPT BY SAYING STH to say sth that interrupts what sb else is saying **5.** *vt.* MATH ESTIMATE THE VALUE OF A MATHEMATICAL FUNCTION to estimate the value of a mathematical function that lies between known values, often by means of a graph [Early 17thC. From Latin *interpolare*, literally 'to polish up'. The underlying meaning is 'to add new material so as make a book appear more recent'.] —**interpolation** /in túrpə láysh'n/ *n.* —**interpolative** /in túrpələtiv/ *adj.* —**interpolator** /in túrpə laytər/ *n.*

interpose /íntər pṓz/ (**-poses, -posing, -posed**) *v.* **1.** *vti.* INTERRUPT BY SAYING STH to say sth that interrupts what sb else is saying **2.** *vt.* PLACE BETWEEN PEOPLE OR THINGS to place yourself or sth else between two people or things **3.** *vti.* INTERVENE WITH STH to intervene or interfere in a situation such as a dispute [Late 16thC. From French *interposer*, an alteration (influenced by *poser* 'to place') of Latin *interponere*, literally 'to place between', from *ponere* (see POSITION).] —**interposable** *adj.* —**interposal** *n.* —**interposer** *n.* —**interposition** /íntərpə zísh'n/ *n.*

interpret /in túrprit/ (**-prets, -preting, -preted**) *v.* **1.** *vt.* FIND THE MEANING OF STH to establish or explain the meaning or significance of sth **2.** *vt.* ASCRIBE A MEANING TO to ascribe a particular meaning or significance to sth ○ *I interpreted his gesture as an invitation.* **3.** *vt.* PERFORM STH IN PARTICULAR WAY to perform sth such as a play or piece of music in a way that conveys particular ideas or feelings about it **4.** *vti.* LANG TRANSLATE STH to translate what is said in one language into another so that speakers of different languages can communicate **5.** *vt.* COMPUT EXECUTE A COMPUTER PROGRAM to convert instructions in a computer program written in a high-level language into machine language and execute them, one instruction at a time [14thC. Directly or via French *interpréter* from Latin *interpretari* 'to explain', from *interpret-*, the stem of *interpres* 'broker, explainer, translator'.] —**interpretable** *adj.* —**interpretability** /in túrpritə bílləti/ *n.* —**interpretably** /in túrpritəbli/ *adv.*

interpretation /in túrpri táysh'n/ *n.* **1.** ESTABLISHMENT OF MEANING an explanation or establishment of the meaning or significance of sth **2.** ASCRIPTION OF PARTICULAR MEANING an ascription of a particular meaning or significance to sth **3.** PERFORMANCE OF STH the way in which an artistic work, e.g. a play or piece of music, is performed so as to convey a particular understanding of the work **4.** TRANSLATION the oral translation of what is said in one language into another, so that speakers of different languages can communicate **5.** *Scotland* EDUC COMPREHENSION a comprehension exercise **6.** EXPLANATORY INFORMATION AT PLACE OF INTEREST explanatory information to help people understand what they are seeing or encountering at a place of interest —**interpretational** *adj.*

interpretative *adj.* = **interpretive**

interpreter /in túrpritər/ *n.* **1.** TRANSLATOR sb who translates orally what is said in one language into another language, so that speakers of different languages can communicate **2.** PERFORMER EXPRESSING PARTICULAR IDEAS sb who performs sth such as a play or piece of music in a way that expresses particular ideas or feelings about it **3.** COMPUT PROGRAM EXECUTING INSTRUCTIONS a computer program that translates the instructions in a program written in a high-level computer language into machine language and executes them, processing one instruction at a time —**interpretership** *n.*

interpretive /in túrpritiv/, **interpretative** /in túrpritətiv/ *adj.* relating to, involving, or providing an interpretation or explanation of sth —**interpretively** *adv.*

interpretive centre, interpretation centre *n.* = **visitor centre**

interprovincial /íntərprə vínsh'l/ *adj.* occurring between provinces, or connecting or involving two or more provinces

interpupillary /íntər pyóopələri/ *adj.* between the pupils of the eyes

interquartile range /íntər kwáwr tīl-/ *n.* a measure of the spread of a group of values equal to the difference between the upper limit for the lower quarter and the lower limit for the upper quarter

interracial /íntər ráysh'l/ *adj.* occurring between or involving different races —**interracially** *adv.*

interregional /íntər reéj'nəl/ *adj.* occurring between regions or involving two or more regions

interregnum /íntər régnəm/ (*plural* **-nums** *or* **-na** /-régnə/) *n.* **1.** TIME BETWEEN ONE REIGN AND THE NEXT the period of time between the end of one reign or regime and the beginning of the next **2.** TIME WITHOUT GOVERNMENT OR CONTROL a period of time during which there is no government, control, or authority **3.** INTERRUPTION a pause or gap in any continuous activity or series [Late 16thC. From Latin, 'period between kingships', from *regnum* (see REIGN). Originally the English word denoted the 'temporary authority in place between reigns'.] —**interregnal** /íntər régn'l/ *adj.*

interrelate /íntərri láyt/ (**-lates, -lating, -lated**) *vti.* to have a relationship in which each person or thing depends on or is affected by the others, or to cause people or things to have such a relationship —**interrelation** /-láysh'n/ *n.* —**interrelationship** *n.*

interrenal /íntər reén'l/ *adj.* situated between or connecting the kidneys

interrobang /in térrə bang/, **interabang** *n.* a punctuation mark used at the end of, or sometimes in place of, an utterance that is both question and exclamation, especially to indicate disbelief [Mid-20thC. Blend of INTERROGATION MARK and BANG[1] (printers' slang for an exclamation mark).]

interrog. *abbr.* **1.** interrogate **2.** interrogation **3.** interrogative

interrogate /in térrə gayt/ (**-gates, -gating, -gated**) *vt.* **1.** QUESTION SB THOROUGHLY to question sb thoroughly, often in an aggressive or threatening manner and especially as part of a formal inquiry, e.g. in a police station or courtroom **2.** COMPUT REQUEST A RESPONSE FROM A COMPUTER PART to transmit a request for information to a device or program with the expectation that an immediate response will trigger further interaction [15thC. From Latin *interrogare*, literally 'to ask in the presence of', from *rogare* (see ROGATION).] —**interrogatee** /in térrə gay teé/ *n.* —**interrogator** /in térrə gaytər/ *n.*

interrogation /in térrə gáysh'n/ *n.* **1.** THOROUGH QUESTIONING the act or process of questioning sb closely, often in an aggressive manner, especially as part of an official inquiry or trial **2.** QUERY a question (*formal*) **3.** COMPUT TRANSMISSION OF A SIGNAL TO A COMPUTER the transmission of a signal to a device or program that triggers a response —**interrogational** *adj.*

interrogation mark *n.* = **question mark**

interrogative /íntə róggətiv/ *adj.* **1.** QUESTIONING questioning or seeming to question sb or sth **2.** GRAM USED TO ASK A QUESTION consisting of or used in asking a question ■ *n.* GRAM **1.** WORD USED TO ASK A QUESTION a word or particle that is used to form a question, e.g. 'who', 'what', or 'where' **2.** FORM OF QUESTION the form of a sentence that is used to ask a question —**interrogatively** *adv.*

interrogatory /íntə róggətəri/ *adj.* ASKING A QUESTION asking a question, used to ask a question, or in the form of a question (*formal*) ■ *n.* (*plural* **-ries**) **1.** QUESTION a question or series of questions **2.** LAW FORMAL WRITTEN QUESTION a formal written question asked during a legal proceeding and usually answered under oath —**interrogatorily** *adv.*

interrogee /in térrə geé/ *n.* sb who is being subjected to interrogation

interrupt /íntə rúpt/ *v.* (**-rupts, -rupting, -rupted**) **1.** *vti.* HALT A SPEAKER OR SPEAKER'S UTTERANCE to halt the flow of a speaker or of a speaker's utterance with a question or remark **2.** *vti.* DISTURB SB OR SB'S WORK to disturb sb who is busy doing sth, causing him or her to stop **3.** *vt.* CAUSE STH TO STOP to cause a break in the flow of sth or put a temporary stop to sth **4.** *vt.* TAKE A BREAK FROM to discontinue doing sth temporarily **5.** *vt.* OBSTRUCT A VIEW to obstruct or block a view ■ *n.* COMPUT **1.** SIGNAL TO SUSPEND OPERATION a signal to a computer processor to suspend the operation it is currently doing in favour of the operation that produced the interrupt signal **2.** INTERRUPT A SIGNAL CIRCUIT the circuit that conveys an interrupt signal [14thC. From Latin *interrupt-*, the past participle stem of *interrumpere* 'to break apart', from *rumpere* (see RUPTURE).] —**interruptible** *adj.* —**interruptive** *adj.* —**interruptively** *adv.* —**interrupter** *n.*

interrupted cadence *n.* MUSIC a cadence that does not end with the expected chord of the tonic but moves from the dominant to the more unstable submediant or subdominant

interrupted screw *n.* a screw whose thread is broken in one or more places by a lengthways slot that enables a partial turn to lock or unlock the screw

interruption /íntə rúpsh'n/ *n.* **1.** STH THAT INTERRUPTS the act of interrupting sb, or sth that interrupts sb who is saying or doing sth **2.** BREAK IN ACTIVITY a pause, break, or temporary halt in an ongoing activity or process

interscholastic /íntərskə lástik/ *adj.* occurring between, involving, or representing two or more schools —**interscholastically** *adv.*

inter se /íntər sáy, íntər seé/ *adv., adj.* between or among themselves [From Latin]

intersect /íntər sékt/ (**-sects, -secting, -sected**) *v.* **1.** *vti.* CROSS to cross sth, or to cross each other **2.** *vt.* GO THROUGH STH to follow a path across or through sth **3.** *vti.* OVERLAP to overlap or have things in common with sth or each other **4.** *vti.* GEOM, MATH HAVE POINTS IN COMMON to overlap geometrically so that a point or set of points is common to two or more figures [Early 17thC. From Latin *intersect-*, the past participle stem of *intersecare*, literally 'to cut between', from *secare* (see SECTION).]

intersection /íntər séksh'n/ *n.* **1.** ACT OF INTERSECTING the act or fact of intersecting **2.** CROSSROADS a place where two roads or paths cross each other **3.** CROSSING POINT the place or point where two things cross each other **4.** OVERLAPPING an overlapping between two things such as different personal interests or political positions **5.** GEOM COMMON POINT a point or set of points common to two or more intersecting geometric figures **6.** MATH SET OF COMMON ELEMENTS a set that consists of all of the elements common to two or more other sets, thus being the largest set contained in all of the others —**intersectional** *adj.*

interservice /íntər súrviss/ *adj.* occurring among the various branches of the armed forces

intersex /íntər seks/ *n.* an organism with characteristics of both sexes

intersexual /íntər sékshoo əl/ *adj.* **1.** OCCURRING BETWEEN MALES AND FEMALES occurring between males and females or affecting their relations **2.** ZOOL HAVING MALE AND FEMALE CHARACTERISTICS having characteristics of both sexes —**intersexualism** *n.* —**intersexuality** /-sekshoo álləti/ *n.* —**intersexually** /íntər sékshoo əli/ *adv.*

interspace *n.* /íntər spayss/ SPACE OR INTERVAL a space or interval of time between two things ■ *vt.* /íntər spáyss/ (**-spaces, -spacing, -spaced**) **1.** PUT STH BETWEEN TWO THINGS to put sth in the spaces or gaps between things **2.** INSERT SPACES BETWEEN to put spaces or breaks between things —**interspatial** /íntər spáysh'l/ *adj.* —**interspatially** /-spáyshəli/ *adv.*

interspecific /íntərspə siffik/ *adj.* **1.** CREATED FROM DIFFERENT SPECIES created by crossing different species **2.** MINERALS OCCURRING BETWEEN DIFFERENT SPECIES occurring between or involving different species

intersperse /íntər spúrss/ (**-sperses, -spersing, -spersed**) *vt.* **1.** BREAK STH'S CONTINUITY to break up the continuity or flow of sth with sth else **2.** PUT HERE AND THERE to put or insert sth here and there among or in sth else [Mid-16thC. From Latin *interspers-*, the past participle stem of *interspergere*, literally 'to scatter between', from *spargere* 'to scatter' (source also of English *disperse* and *sparse*).] —**interspersedly** /íntər spúrssidli/ *adv.* —**interspersion** /-spúrsh'n/ *n.*

interstadial /íntər stáydi əl/ *adj.* relating to a short period of relatively warmer climate within an ice age [Early 20thC. Coined from INTER- + Latin *stadium* 'stage'.]

interstate *adj.* /íntər stáyt/ OCCURRING BETWEEN STATES occurring between, connecting, or involving two or more states ■ *n.* /íntər stayt/ **interstate, Interstate** MAJOR MOTORWAY BETWEEN CITIES a limited-access road that forms part of the federally funded system of motorways connecting the major cities of the United States ■ *adv. Aus* **TO OR IN ANOTHER STATE** to or in another state or states

interstation /íntər stáysh'n/ *adj.* occurring between or connecting stations

interstellar /íntər stéllər/ *adj.* situated, happening, or moving between stars, or involving two or more stars

intersterile /íntər stérrīl/ *adj.* not capable of interbreeding —**intersterility** /íntərstə rílləti/ *n.*

interstice /in túrstiss/ *n.* **1. SMALL SPACE** a small opening, crack, or gap between two things **2.** CRYSTALS **A SPACE IN A CRYSTAL LATTICE** a gap between neighbouring atoms in the lattice of a crystal **3.** ANAT **SPACE IN BODY TISSUE** a small space in a tissue or between parts of the body [15thC. Via French from Latin *interstitium*, from *intersistere*, literally 'to stand still in the middle', from *sistere* 'to cause to stand', from *stare* (see STAND).]

interstitial /íntər stísh'l/ *adj.* **1.** MINERALS **RELATING TO GAPS** forming, situated in, or relating to one or more small openings, gaps, or cracks **2. OCCURRING BETWEEN OTHER MINERALS** located in or creating a space between other minerals **3.** CHEM **OF A COMPOUND CONTAINING METALS AND NONMETALS** relating to a compound, e.g. a carbide, in which ions or atoms of a nonmetal occupy positions in a metal lattice. Interstitial compounds generally have metallic characteristics. **4.** ANAT **OCCURRING BETWEEN TISSUES** lying between parts of an organ or between groups of cells or tissues. The interstitial cells between mammalian testicles are responsible for secreting male sex hormones. ■ *n.* **UNSOLICITED ADVERTISEMENT ON THE INTERNET** an unsolicited page of advertisement on the World Wide Web that briefly precedes a selected page —**interstitially** *adv.*

interstitial-cell-stimulating hormone *n.* = **luteinizing hormone**

intertestamental /íntər testə mént'l/ *adj.* during, from, or relating to the period between the composition of the last books of the Hebrew Scriptures, called Old Testament by Christians, and the first books of the New Testament of the Bible

intertextuality /íntər tekstyoo álləti/ *n.* the relationship that exists between different texts, especially literary texts, or the reference in one text to others —**intertextual** /íntər tékstyoo əl/ *adj.* —**intertextually** *adv.*

intertexture /íntər tékschər/ *n.* **1. INTERWOVEN OBJECT OR MATERIAL** an object or material that has been made by interweaving two or more things **2. INTERWEAVING OR BEING INTERWOVEN** an act of interweaving two or more things, or the fact of being interwoven [Mid-17thC. Formed from Latin *intertext-*, the past participle stem of *intertexere*, literally 'to weave together', from *texere* (see TEXT).]

intertidal /íntər tíd'l/ *adj.* occurring within or forming the area between high and low tide levels in a coastal zone —**intertidally** *adv.*

intertribal /íntər tríb'l/ *adj.* occurring between tribes or involving two or more tribes —**intertribally** *adv.*

intertrigo /íntər trígō/ *n.* the inflammation of two skin surfaces that are in constant contact. It is caused by friction or sweat. [Early 18thC. Via Latin, 'chafing of the skin', from assumed *interterere*, literally 'to rub together', from *terere* 'to rub'.]

intertropical /íntər tróppik'l/ *adj.* located or occurring between the Tropic of Capricorn and Tropic of Cancer

intertwine /íntər twín/ (**-twines, -twining, -twined**) *vti.* **1. TWIST OR BE TWISTED TOGETHER** to twist two or more things together, or to be or become twisted together or with sth else **2. LINK OR BECOME LINKED TOGETHER** to link or involve sth with sth else, or to become linked or involved with each other ○ *Their lives had intertwined.* —**intertwinement** *n.*

intertwist /íntər twíst/ (**-twists, -twisting, -twisted**) *vti.* = **intertwine** *v.* 1

interunion /íntər yóonyən/ *adj.* occurring between or involving two or more unions, especially trade unions

interurban /íntər úrbən/ *adj.* occurring between, connecting, or involving two or more towns or cities

interval /íntərv'l/ *n.* **1. INTERVENING PERIOD OF TIME** a period of time between one event and the next **2. INTERVENING DISTANCE** the distance between one thing and another **3. BREAK IN PERFORMANCE** a break between parts of a musical or theatrical performance or cinema showing. = **intermission** *n.* 1 **4.** MUSIC **DIFFERENCE IN MUSICAL PITCH** the musical distance between the pitches of two notes **5.** MATH **ALL NUMBERS BETWEEN TWO NUMBERS** a set containing all the real numbers or points between two specified real numbers or points, which are called the endpoints. If the set includes the endpoints it is a closed interval, and if it excludes the endpoints it is an open interval. [14thC. Via Old French *entreval(e)* from, ultimately, Latin *intervallum*, literally 'space between ramparts or palisades', from *vallum* 'rampart' (source of English *wall*).] —**intervallic** /íntər vállik/ *adj.* ◇ **at intervals 1.** at different points in time **2.** at various locations

intervalometer /íntərvə lómmitər/ *n.* a device that is designed to activate a mechanism automatically and at regular intervals, especially one that operates a camera shutter [Mid-20thC. Coined from INTERVAL + -METER.]

interval signal *n.* a particular piece of music or other sound that a radio station uses as its own peculiar identifying signal, broadcasting it between and sometimes during programmes

interval training *n.* a method of training, especially in athletics, that involves alternating between aerobic and nonaerobic exercise in the same session

intervene /íntər véen/ (**-venes, -vening, -vened**) *vi.* **1. ACT TO PRODUCE CHANGE** to take some action or get involved in sth in order to change what is happening, especially to prevent sth undesirable ○ *the referee had to intervene to stop the fight* **2. HAPPEN SO AS TO IMPEDE** to occur and as a result stop or delay sth from happening **3. ELAPSE** to elapse between one point in time and another ○ *the intervening years* **4. BE SITUATED IN BETWEEN** to be located between two things **5. BREAK INTO A CONVERSATION** to break into a conversation or discussion **6.** LAW **ENTER A LAWSUIT** to enter a lawsuit as a third party in order to protect your own interests **7.** ECON **ACT TO MANIPULATE ECONOMIC MARKETS** to take economic action that is designed to counter a trend in a market, especially in order to stabilize a country's currency [Late 16thC. From Latin *intervenire*, literally 'to come between', from *venire* (see VENUE).]

intervenor /íntər véenər/, **intervener** *n.* a party that enters a lawsuit as a third party in order to protect its interests

intervention /íntər vénsh'n/ *n.* **1. ACTION AFFECTING ANOTHER'S AFFAIRS** an action undertaken in order to change what is happening or might happen in another's affairs, especially in order to prevent sth undesirable **2.** ECON **MARKET MANIPULATION** economic action that is designed to counter a trend in a market, especially in order to stabilize a country's currency **3. BUYING OF SURPLUS BY EU** the purchase of agricultural produce by the European Union when the market price falls below a certain level (**intervention price**) because there is a surplus

interventionism /íntər vénsh'nizəm/ *n.* **1.** POL **INVOLVEMENT IN ANOTHER COUNTRY'S AFFAIRS** political interference or military involvement by one country in the affairs of another **2.** ECON **GOVERNMENT INTERFERENCE IN ECONOMIC MATTERS** action by a government to influence and improve the country's economic situation or some aspect of it —**interventionist** *n., adj.*

interventricular /íntər ven tríkyòolər/ *adj.* situated or occurring between the ventricles of the heart

intervertebral /íntər vúrtibrəl/ *adj.* situated or occurring between the vertebrae of the backbone —**intervertebrally** *adv.*

intervertebral disc *n.* one of the flexible plates of cartilage connecting adjacent vertebrae of the backbone that impart flexibility and act as shock absorbers to protect the spinal cord from impact, e.g. when running

interview /íntər vyoo/ *n.* **1. MEETING FOR ASKING QUESTIONS** a meeting during which sb is asked questions, e.g. by a prospective employer, a journalist, or a researcher **2. RECORD OF AN INTERVIEW** a transcript, report on, or recording of an interview ■ *v.* (**-views, -viewing, -viewed**) **1.** *vt.* **ASK SB QUESTIONS** to ask sb a series of questions in an interview **2.** *vi.* **PERFORM IN AN INTERVIEW** to speak and answer in a particular way in an interview ○ *she always interviews well* [Early 16thC. From obsolete French *entrevue*, from *entrevoir*, literally 'to see each other', from *voir* 'to see', from Latin *videre* (see VISIBLE).] —**interviewable** *adj.*

interviewee /íntər vyoo ée/ *n.* sb who is the subject of an interview

interviewer /íntər vyoo ər/ *n.* sb who conducts an interview or interviews

inter vivos /íntər vée voss/ *adv., adj.* LAW from one living person to another [From Latin, literally 'between the living']

intervocalic /íntərvō kállik/ *adj.* used to describe a speech sound occurring or inserted between vowels, e.g. between one word that ends with a vowel and another word that starts with a vowel —**intervocalically** *adv.*

interwar /íntər wáwr/ *adj.* occurring between two wars, especially between World War I and World War II

interweave /íntər wéev/ (**-weaves, -weaving, -wove** /-wṓv'n/, **-woven** /-wṓv/) *vti.* **1. WEAVE TOGETHER** to weave sth into or with sth else, or to be woven together, into, or with sth else **2. COMBINE** to combine sth with sth else, or to be combined with sth —**interweavement** *n.* —**interweaver** *n.*

intestacy /in téstəssi/ *n.* the condition of having died without having made a legally valid will

intestate /in tést ayt/ *adj.* **1. LEAVING NO LEGALLY VALID WILL** not having made a legally valid will **2. NOT WILLED TO SB** not having been assigned to sb in a legally valid will ■ *n.* **SB LEAVING NO LEGALLY VALID WILL** sb who has died without having made a legally valid will [14thC. Directly or via French *intestat* from Latin *intestatus* 'not having made a will', from *testari* 'to make a will'.]

intestinal /in téstin'l/ *adj.* **1. LOCATED IN THE INTESTINES** found in or affecting the intestines **2. THE INTESTINES** characteristic of, forming part of, or relating to the intestines —**intestinally** *adv.*

intestinal flora *npl.* bacteria present in a healthy intestine that complete digestion, synthesize vitamin K, and create an acid environment that prevents infection by harmful bacteria

intestine /in téstin/ *n.* that part of the digestive system between the stomach and the anus or cloaca that digests and absorbs food. In mammals, the small intestine digests and absorbs food from the stomach, and the large intestine then absorbs most of the remaining water in the food. (*often used in the plural*) [15thC. Via French from, ultimately, Latin *intestinus* 'internal', from *intus* 'within'. Ultimately from an Indo-European word that is also the ancestor of English *endo-*.]

intifada /ínti faádə/ *n.* the Palestinian uprising in the West Bank and Gaza Strip that started in 1987 in protest against the continued Israeli occupation [Late 20thC. From Arabic *intifāḍa*, literally 'a shaking off'.]

intimacy /íntiməssi/ (*plural* **-cies**) *n.* **1. CLOSE RELATIONSHIP** a close personal relationship **2. QUIET ATMOSPHERE** a quiet and private atmosphere **3. DETAILED KNOWLEDGE** a detailed knowledge resulting from a close or long association or study **4. PRIVATE UTTERANCE OR ACTION** a private and personal utterance or action **5. SEXUAL ACT** a sexual act or sexual intercourse (*used euphemistically*)

intimate[1] /íntimət/ *adj.* **1. CLOSE** having, involving, or resulting from a close personal relationship **2. QUIET** quiet and private or secluded, enabling people to feel relaxed with each other **3. PRIVATE AND PERSONAL** so private and personal as to be kept secret or discussed only with a close friend or relative **4. SEXUAL** involving or having a sexual relationship (*used euphemistically*) **5. WORN NEXT TO THE SKIN** intended to be worn next to the skin or in a private setting **6. THOROUGH** very great and detailed as a result of extensive study or close experience ○ *an intimate knowledge of the workings of government* **7. CLOSELY CONNECTED** very close because of the influence of one thing on another ○ *the intimate connection between power and corruption* **8. INNERMOST** relating to or involving the innermost nature of sth ■ *n.* **CLOSE**

FRIEND a close personal friend [Early 17thC. From late Latin *intimatus*, the past participle of *intimare* (see INTIMATE²).] —**intimately** *adv.* —**intimateness** *n.*

intimate² /ínti mayt/ (**-mates, -mating, -mated**) *vt.* **1. HINT QUIETLY** to hint at sth or let sth be known in a quiet, indirect, or subtle way **2. ANNOUNCE** to announce sth formally [Early 16thC. From late Latin *intimare* 'to make known', from *intimus* 'innermost'. Ultimately from the Indo-European word for 'in', which is also the ancestor of English *in* and *inter-*.] —**intimater** *n.*

intimation /ínti máysh'n/ *n.* **1. HINT** a subtle hint or sign of sth **2. ANNOUNCEMENT** a formal announcement of sth

intime /oN teém/ *adj.* small, quiet, and private or secluded [Early 17thC. Via French, 'intimate', from Latin *intimus* 'innermost' (see INTIMATE²).]

intimidate /in tímmi dayt/ (**-dates, -dating, -dated**) *vt.* **1. PERSUADE OR DISSUADE BY FRIGHTENING** to persuade sb to do sth or dissuade sb from doing sth by frightening him or her, e.g. by means of violence or blackmail **2. DAUNT** to create a feeling of fear, awe, or inadequacy in sb [Mid-17thC. From medieval Latin *intimidare*, literally 'to put in fear', from Latin *timidus* 'fearful'.] —**intimidation** /in tímmi dáysh'n/ *n.* —**intimidatory** /in tímmi dáytəri/ *adj.*

intinction /in tíngksh'n/ *n.* CHR the act of dipping the Communion bread into the wine so that the person taking Communion receives both [Late 19thC. From the late Latin stem *intinction-* from Latin *intingere* 'to dip in', from *tingere* (see TINGE).]

intine /ín tin, ín teen/ *n.* the inner wall of a pollen grain or spore [Mid-19thC. Formed from Latin *intimus* 'innermost' (see INTIMATE²), on the model of 'extine'.]

intitule /in títtyool/ (**-ules, -uling, -uled**) *vt.* to give a title to an act of Parliament [15thC. Via French *intituler* from, ultimately, late Latin *intitulare* 'to entitle', from Latin *titulus* (see TITLE).]

intl *abbr.* international

into *(stressed)* /ín too/; *(unstressed)* /íntə, íntŏŏ/ CORE MEANING: a preposition indicating that sb or sth is or moves inside sth, either physically or figuratively ○ *I released the balloon into the air.* ○ *in case you get into difficulties* ○ *I decided to go into the army.* ○ *When did you go into partnership with them?* *prep.* **1. INDICATES MOVEMENT** moving or putting sth from outside to the interior or inner part of sth ○ *He stuck his hand into his pocket and pulled out a pencil.* **2. INDICATES MOVEMENT TO THE MIDST OF** indicates that sth or sb moves to the middle of sth and becomes part of it or is surrounded by it ○ *He leapt into the water.* **3. INDICATES ENTRY** indicates entering a state, career, or period of time ○ *She decided to go into marketing.* ○ *He went on working until he was well into his seventies.* ○ *The fire department burst into action.* **4. INDICATES CONTACT WITH** indicates coming up against sth accidentally ○ *I happened to bump into him last night quite by chance.* **5. INDICATES CHANGE** indicates becoming a new entity, shape, or form as a result of a change or transformation ○ *change water into wine* ○ *The caterpillar changes into a butterfly.* **6. INDICATES RESULT** indicates a situation resulting from sb's persuasion ○ *My friends talked me into getting this haircut.* **7.** ARITH **INDICATES DIVIDEND** indicates the division of numbers ○ *9 into 63 equals 7.* **8. DIVIDED** indicates that sth is divided so that it becomes several smaller parts ○ *She divided the cake into six, and gave each of us a slice.* **9. ENTHUSIASTIC ABOUT** indicates interest in or enthusiasm about sth (*informal*) ○ *I was really into tennis that summer.* [Old English *in(n)tō*, from IN + TO]

intolerable /in tóllərəb'l/ *adj.* **1. IMPOSSIBLE TO BEAR** so bad, difficult, or painful that it cannot be endured ○ *the pain was intolerable* **2. VERY UNPLEASANT** very unpleasant or annoying —**intolerability** /in tóllərə bíllәti/ *n.* —**intolerably** /-bli/ *adv.*

intolerant /in tóllərənt/ *adj.* **1. EASILY ANNOYED** easily angered or annoyed when things do not go as expected or desired **2. UNACCEPTING OF DIFFERENCES** refusing to accept people who are different or live differently, e.g. people of different races or religions **3. UNABLE TO TOLERATE STH** not able to endure or tolerate sth —**intolerance** *n.* —**intolerantly** *adv.*

intonate /íntō nayt/ (**-nates, -nating, -nated**) *vt.* **1. SAY IN PARTICULAR WAY** to say sth in a particular tone of voice **2.** PHON **SPEAK WITH VARYING PITCH** to speak with the rising and falling pitch that is typical of ordinary speech **3.** PHON **PRONOUNCE A CONSONANT WITH VOICING** to pronounce a consonant with a vibration of the vocal cords, as English speakers do when they pronounce the consonant 'v' as opposed to the consonant 'f' [Late 18thC. From medieval Latin *intonat-*, the past participle stem of *intonare* 'to intone' (see INTONE).]

intonation /íntō náysh'n/ *n.* **1.** PHON **PITCH OF THE VOICE** the rising or falling pitch of the voice when sb says a word or syllable, or the rising and falling pattern of speech generally **2. INTONING** a saying or chanting of sth in a solemn or serious way, or sth said or chanted in this way **3.** MUSIC **ACCURACY OF PITCH** accuracy of pitch in performing music **4.** MUSIC **BEGINNING OF A PLAINSONG** the opening phrase of a piece of plainsong, sung by a soloist or just a few members of the choir —**intonational** *adj.*

intonation contour, intonation pattern *n.* LING the pattern of rising and falling pitch in speech that helps to distinguish between questions, statements, and other types of speech

intone /in tṓn/ (**-tones, -toning, -toned**) *v.* **1.** *vt.* **SAY** to say sth, especially in a slow and serious or solemn way (*formal*) **2.** *vti.* **CHANT A PRAYER** to recite a prayer or other religious words in a chanting monotone **3.** *vt.* MUSIC **START A PLAINSONG** to sing the opening phrase of a piece of plainsong [14thC. Directly or via Old French *entoner* from medieval Latin *intonare*, literally '(to sing) in tone', from Latin *tonus* 'tone' (see TONE).] —**intonement** *n.* —**intoner** *n.*

in toto /in tṓt ō/ *adv.* in its entirety or as a whole ○ *The salary's nothing special, but when you consider compensation in toto it's quite attractive.* [From Latin]

intoxicant /in tóksikənt/ *n.* **INTOXICATING THING** sth that causes physical or psychological intoxication, e.g. an alcoholic drink or great power ■ *adj.* **CAPABLE OF INTOXICATING** capable of making sb intoxicated

intoxicate /in tóksi kayt/ (**-cates, -cating, -cated**) *v.* **1.** *vt.* **MAKE DRUNK OR STUPEFIED** to make sb drunk with alcohol or stupefied with drugs or other substances **2.** *vt.* **EXCITE** to make sb intensely excited or overjoyed, often so much so that the person becomes irrational **3.** *vti.* PATHOL **POISON** to poison sb (*technical*) [15thC. From medieval Latin *intoxicat-*, the past participle stem of *intoxicare* 'to poison', from Latin *toxicum* 'poison' (see TOXIC).] —**intoxicable** *adj.* —**intoxicative** /-kaytiv/ *adj.* —**intoxication** /-káysh'n/ *n.* —**intoxicator** /-kaytər/ *n.*

intoxicated /in tóksi kaytid/ *adj.* **1. DRUNK** drunk or stupefied (*formal or humorous*) **2. EXCITED** intensely excited or overjoyed, often so much so that a person becomes foolish or irrational —**intoxicatedly** *adv.*

intoxicating /in tóksi kayting/ *adj.* **1. CAPABLE OF MAKING SB DRUNK** capable of making sb drunk or stupefied (*formal*) **2. EXCITING** capable of making sb intensely excited or overjoyed, often so much so that the person becomes irrational —**intoxicatingly** *adv.*

intr. *abbr.* GRAM intransitive

intra- *prefix.* within or inside ○ *intranasal* [Directly or via modern Latin 'on the inside, within', from late Latin, from Latin *intra*. Ultimately from an Indo-European word that is also the ancestor of English *enter* and *entero-*.]

intra-arterial *adj.* within or introduced into an artery or arteries —**intra-arterially** *adv.*

intra-articular *adj.* within or introduced into a joint of the body

intra-atomic *adj.* existing or occurring within an atom or atoms, rather than between atoms

intracardiac /íntrə kaárdi ak/ *adj.* within or introduced into the heart —**intracardially** /íntrə kaárdi əli/ *adv.*

intracellular /íntrə séllyŏŏlər/ *adj.* within a cell or cells —**intracellularly** *adv.*

intracerebral /íntrə sérrəbrəl/ *adj.* existing or taking place inside the main part of the brain or cerebrum —**intracerebrally** *adv.*

Intracoastal Waterway /íntrə kṓst'l-/ a system of protected waterways, including rivers, bays, coastal sounds, and canals, in the eastern and southeastern United States, made up of the Atlantic Intracoastal Waterway and the Gulf Intracoastal Waterway. Length: 4,000 km/2,500 mi.

intracompany /íntrə kúmpəni/ *adj.* within the same company or between employees or divisions of the same company

intracranial /íntrə kráyni əl/ *adj.* within or introduced into the skull —**intracranially** *adv.*

intractable /in tráktəb'l/ *adj.* **1. STRONG-WILLED AND REBELLIOUS** resisting attempts to control, correct, or influence (*formal*) **2. DIFFICULT TO DEAL WITH** difficult to deal with or solve **3. DIFFICULT TO MANIPULATE** difficult to shape or manipulate [15thC. From Latin *intractabilis*, from *tractabilis* (see TRACTABLE).] —**intractability** /in tráktə bíllәti/ *n.* —**intractably** /in tráktəbli/ *adv.*

WORD KEY: SYNONYMS

See Synonyms at ***unruly***.

intracutaneous /íntrə kyoo táyni əss/ *adj.* = **intradermal** —**intracutaneously** *adv.*

intradermal /íntrə dúrm'l/, **intradermic** /-mik/ *adj.* within or introduced between the layers of the skin —**intradermally** *adv.*

intradermal test *n.* a test for immunity or allergic sensitivity involving the injection of small amounts of a test material into the skin through a fine needle. The development of swelling or inflammation at the injection site indicates allergy to the material injected.

intradermic *adj.* = **intradermal**

intrados /in tráy doss/ (*plural* **-dos** *or* **-doses**) *n.* the inner curve of an arch [Late 18thC. From French, from Latin *intra* 'within' + French *dos* 'back' (from Latin *dorsum*; see DORSAL).]

intragenic /íntrə jénnik/ *adj.* located or occurring within the same gene

intralingual /íntrə líng gwəl/ *adj.* occurring within a single language

intramolecular /íntrə mə lékyŏŏlər/ *adj.* existing or occurring within a single molecule —**intramolecularly** *adv.*

intramural /íntrə myŏŏrəl/ *adj.* **1. WITHIN COLLEGE** occurring within or involving members of a single college or university, instead of members of or teams from various colleges or universities **2.** ANAT **WITHIN WALL TISSUE** within the tissue of the wall of a blood vessel or another hollow body part

intramuscular /íntrə múskyŏŏlər/ *adj.* within or into the substance of a muscle —**intramuscularly** *adv.*

intranasal /íntrə náyz'l/ *adj.* within or introduced into the nose —**intranasally** *adv.*

intranational /íntrə násh'nəl/ *adj.* existing or occurring within the boundaries of a single nation, rather than involving different nations

intranet /íntrə net/ *n.* a network of computers, especially one using World Wide Web conventions, that can be accessed only by an authorized set of users, e.g. those within a single company

intrans. *abbr.* GRAM intransitive

intransigence /in tránssijənss, -zi-, -traánssi-, -zi-/, **intransigeance** *n.* firm or unreasonable refusal even to consider changing a decision or attitude

intransigent /in tránssijənt, -zijənt/, **intransigeant** *adj.* **REFUSING TO COMPROMISE** firmly or unreasonably refusing even to consider changing a decision or attitude ■ *n.* **UNYIELDING PERSON** sb who firmly or unreasonably refuses to compromise or change an attitude or decision, especially in politics (*formal*) [Late 19thC. Via French from Spanish *los intransigentes*, extreme political party (literally 'the uncompromising ones'), ultimately from *transigir* 'to compromise', from Latin *transigere* 'to come to an agreement' (see TRANSACTION).] —**intransigently** *adv.*

intransitive /in tránssitiv/ *adj.* GRAM **WITH NO DIRECT OBJECT** without a direct object, e.g. the verb 'die' in the sentence 'He was slowly dying' ■ *n.* GRAM **VERB WITHOUT A DIRECT OBJECT** a verb that does not take a direct object [Early 17thC. From late Latin *intransitivus*, literally 'not passing over', from *transitivus* 'transitive, passing over'.] —**intransitively** *adv.* —**intransitiveness** *n.*

intranuclear /ìntrə nyóokli ər/ *adj.* **1.** NUCLEAR PHYS **WITHIN ATOMIC NUCLEUS** existing or occurring within the nucleus of an atom **2.** CELL BIOL **WITHIN CELL NUCLEUS** existing or occurring within the nucleus of a cell

intraocular /ìntrə ókyoolər/ *adj.* within or introduced into the inside of the eyeball —**intraocularly** *adv.*

intraperitoneal /ìntrə pérritō née əl/ *adj.* within or introduced into the peritoneal cavity —**intraperitoneally** *adv.*

intrapersonal /ìntrə púrss'nəl/ *adj.* relating to the internal aspects of a person, especially emotions. ◊ **interpersonal** —**intrapersonally** *adv.*

intrapreneur /ìntrəprə núr/ *n.* an employee with a flair for innovation and risk-taking who is given unusual freedom to develop products or subsidiary businesses within a company. ◊ **entrepreneur** [Late 20thC. Coined from INTRA- + ENTREPRENEUR.] —**intrapreneurial** *adj.* —**intrapreneurialism** *n.* —**intrapreneurially** *adv.*

intraspecific /ìntrəspə síffik/, **intraspecies** /-spéesh eez, -spéess-/ *adj.* existing within a single species or confined to members of one species

intrauterine /ìntrə yóotə rīn/ *adj.* existing, occurring, or designed to be used inside the womb

intrauterine device *n.* a plastic or metal device that is inserted into the cavity of the womb in order to prevent pregnancy

intravascular /ìntrə váskyoolər/ *adj.* within the blood vessels or a similar system in animals or plants —**intravascularly** *adv.*

intravenous /ìntrə véenəss/ *adj.* **1. WITHIN VEIN** existing or occurring inside a vein, or administered into a vein **2. USED TO ADMINISTER TREATMENT** used in administering fluids or medicines into the veins —**intravenously** *adv.*

intraventricular /ìntrə ven tríkyoolər/ *adj.* within or introduced into a ventricle, such as one in the heart or brain —**intraventricularly** *adv.*

intravital /ìntrə vít'l/, **intravitam** /-vée tam/ *adj.* occurring in or used on a living cell or organism [Late 19thC. Formed from modern Latin *intra vitam* 'within life'.] —**intravitally** *adv.*

in-tray *n.* a tray on sb's desk for papers that have not yet been dealt with

intrazonal /ìntrə zōn'l/ *adj.* used to describe a soil that has a well-developed and differentiated set of soil characteristics (**profile**), determined by the nature of the parent material and age of the soil

intreat *vti.* = **entreat**

intrench *vti.* = **entrench**

intrepid /in tréppid/ *adj.* fearless and persistent in the pursuit of sth (*dated or humorous*) [Late 17thC. Directly or via French *intrépide* from Latin *intrepidus*, literally 'not agitated', from *trepidus* 'agitated' (source of English *trepidation*).] —**intrepidity** /ìntrə píddəti/ *n.* —**intrepidly** /in tréppidli/ *adv.*

WORD KEY: SYNONYMS

See Synonyms at ***bold***.

intricacy /íntrikəssi/ (*plural* **-cies**) *n.* **1. COMPLEXITY** the complex character of sth that has many details, parts, or other elements **2. COMPLEX THING** sth that is complex and has many details, parts, or other elements (*often used in the plural*)

intricate /íntrikət/ *adj.* **1. WITH MANY PARTS** containing many details or small parts that are skilfully made or assembled **2. COMPLEX AND DIFFICULT** with many interrelated elements, parts, or factors so as to be complex and difficult to understand or resolve [15thC. From Latin *intricatus*, past participle of *intricare* 'to entangle, perplex', from *tricae* 'impediments, tricks' (see TRICK).] —**intricately** *adv.* —**intricateness** *n.*

intrigant /íntrigənt/, **intriguant** *n.* (*archaic*) **1. SECRET PLOTTER** sb who devises secret plots or schemes **2. CLANDESTINE LOVER** sb who carries on a secret love affair

intrigue *n.* /ín treeg, in tréeg/ **1. SECRET PLOTTING** secret scheming or plotting **2. SECRET PLOT** a secret scheme or plot **3. SECRET LOVE AFFAIR** a secret love affair (*archaic*) ■ *v.* /in tréeg/ (**-trigues, -triguing, -trigued**) **1.** *vt.* **INTEREST SB** to make sb greatly interested or curious **2.** *vi.* **SCHEME** to scheme or use underhand methods to achieve sth **3.** *vi.* **HAVE SECRET LOVER** to carry on a secret love affair (*archaic*) [Early 17thC. Via French from Italian *intrigo*, from *intrigare* 'to entangle' (source of the verb), from Latin *intricare* (see INTRICATE).] —**intriguer** /in tréegər/ *n.* —**intriguingly** *adv.*

intrinsic /in trínssik/, **intrinsical** /-trínssik'l/ *adj.* **1. BASIC AND ESSENTIAL** belonging to sth as one of the basic and essential elements that make it what it is **2. OF ITSELF** by or in itself, rather than because of its associations or consequences **3.** ANAT **FOUND IN BODY PART** occurring wholly within or belonging wholly to a part of the body, e.g. an organ [15thC. Via French *intrinsèque* from late Latin *intrinsecus* 'inward', from assumed Latin *intrim* 'within'.] —**intrinsically** *adv.*

intrinsic factor *n.* a protein produced in the stomach that promotes the absorption of vitamin B_{12} in the small intestine. Insufficient intrinsic factor results in pernicious anaemia.

intro /íntrō/ *n.* an introduction, especially the opening few bars of a piece of pop music (*informal*) [Early 19thC. Shortening.]

intro. *abbr.* **1.** introduction **2.** introductory

intro- *prefix.* **1.** in, into ○ *intromission* **2.** inward ○ *introvert* [From Latin *intro*; ultimately related to *intra* (see INTRA-)]

introd. *abbr.* **1.** introduction **2.** introductory

introduce /ìntrə dyóoss/ (**-duces, -ducing, -duced**) *v.* **1.** *vt.* **ACQUAINT WITH SB ELSE** to present yourself or another person to sb else and become acquainted with that person **2.** *vt.* **GIVE AUDIENCE FORETASTE** to tell an audience a little about what or whom they are going to see or hear **3.** *vt.* **BRING IN STH NEW** to bring sth to a place, into existence, or into operation for the first time **4.** *vt.* **CAUSE TO EXPERIENCE STH NEW** to make sb aware of sth for the first time, or give sb a first experience of sth **5.** *vt.* **PREFACE WITH STH ELSE** to begin sth with a preface of some sort, especially one designed to get people's attention **6.** *vt.* **TALK ABOUT STH NEW** to mention sth for the first time **7.** *vt.* POL **PRESENT LEGISLATION FORMALLY** to present proposed legislation formally to an assembly, so that it can be debated and voted on **8.** *vt.* **INSERT** to insert sth into sth else **9.** BOT, ZOOL **BRING IN NEW SPECIES** to place or establish an individual or species of plant or animal in a new habitat or environment [15thC. Origin uncertain: either from Latin *introducere* 'to lead in', from *ducere* 'to lead', or a back-formation from INTRODUCTION.] —**introducer** *n.* —**introducible** *adj.*

introduction /ìntrə dúksh'n/ *n.* **1. EXPLANATORY SECTION AT BEGINNING** a section at the beginning of a book or of another piece of writing, e.g. one that summarizes what it is about or sets the scene **2. STH GIVING BASIC FACTS** a book or course of study that gives sb basic facts or skills in a field **3. MAKING ACQUAINTANCE** the act of formally presenting sb or yourself to sb else and becoming acquainted **4. PRESENTATION** the act of presenting sb or sth to an audience, assembly, or other group **5. FIRST EXPERIENCE** sb's first experience of sth **6.** MUSIC **BEGINNING OF PIECE OF MUSIC** the opening passage of a piece of music, or the opening movement in a suite **7. BRINGING IN STH NEW** the act of bringing sth to a place, into existence, into operation, or into an activity for the first time **8. STH BROUGHT IN** sth brought in from elsewhere or created **9. INSERTION** the insertion of sth somewhere [14thC. Directly or via French from the Latin stem *introduction-*, from *introduct-*, the past participle stem of *introducere* (see INTRODUCE).]

introductory /ìntrə dúktəri/ *adj.* **1. GIVING FORETASTE** telling a little about what is to come **2. PROVIDING THE BASICS** providing the basic facts or skills **3. INITIAL** made or used when sth begins or is first introduced [14thC. Directly or via Old French *introductoire* from late Latin *introductorius*, from *introduct-* (see INTRODUCTION).] —**introductorily** *adv.* —**introductoriness** *n.*

introgression /ìntrə grésh'n/ *n.* the incorporation of genes from one species into the gene pool of another as a result of hybridization [Mid-17thC. Coined from INTRO- + *-gression* as in PROGRESSION, originally in the general sense 'going in'.] —**introgressant** /ìntrə gréss'nt/ *adj.* —**introgressive** /-gréssiv/ *adj.*

introit /ín troyt/, **Introit** *n.* **1. PART OF ROMAN CATHOLIC MASS** the part of the Roman Catholic Mass consisting of psalm verses and the Gloria Patri, said or sung when the priest first approaches the altar **2. PART OF ANGLICAN SERVICE** a psalm or hymn sung as the minister enters the church at the beginning of the Anglican service of Holy Communion [15thC. Via French from medieval Latin *introitus*, from Latin, 'entrance', the past participle of *introire* 'to go in', from *ire* 'to go'.] —**introital** /in tróyt'l/ *adj.*

introjection /ìntrə jéksh'n/ *n.* PSYCHOL the unconscious adoption by sb of the values or attitudes of sb else, whom that person wants to impress or be accepted by [Mid-19thC. Coined from INTRO- + *-jection* as in PROJECTION.] —**introject** /ìntrə jékt/ *vt.*

intromission /ìntrə mísh'n/ *n.* the inserting or admitting of sth into sth else (*formal*) [Mid-16thC. Directly or via French from the medieval Latin stem *intromission-*, from, ultimately, Latin *intromittere* (see INTROMIT).] —**intromissive** /ìntrə míssiv/ *adj.*

intromit /ìntrə mít/ (**-mits, -mitting, -mitted**) *vt.* to cause or allow sth to enter sth else (*formal*) [15thC. From Latin *intromittere* 'to send in', from *mittere* 'to send' (see MISSION).] —**intromissibility** /ìntrə míssə bílləti/ *n.* —**intromissible** /-b'l/ *adj.* —**intromitter** /-míttər/ *n.*

intron /ín tron/ *n.* a section of DNA in a cell that is not expressed as an amino acid or messenger RNA. ◊ **exon** [Late 20thC. Coined from INTRAGENIC + -ON.]

introrse /in tráwrss/ *adj.* pointing and opening inwards, as the anthers of some flowers do, releasing pollen towards the centre of the flower [Mid-19thC. From Latin *introrsus*, a contraction of *introversus*, from *versus*, the past participle of *vertere* 'to turn'.] —**introrsely** *adv.*

introspect /ìntrə spékt/ (**-spects, -specting, -spected**) *vi.* to undertake a detailed mental self-examination of feelings, thoughts, and motives [Late 17thC. Directly or via Latin *introspectare*, literally 'to look into repeatedly', from *introspect-*, past participle stem of *introspicere* 'to look into', from *specere*.]

introspection /ìntrə spéksh'n/ *n.* the detailed mental self-examination of feelings, thoughts, and motives, especially when this is regarded as unhealthy or obsessive —**introspectional** *adj.*

introspectionism /ìntrə spéksh'nizəm/ *n.* a school of psychology concentrating on the study of immediate subjective experience. ◊ **behaviourism** —**introspectionistic** /ìntrə spékshə nístik/ *adj.*

introspective /ìntrə spéktiv/ *adj.* tending to make or containing a detailed examination of sb's feelings, thoughts, and motives

introspective psychology *n.* = **introspectionism**

introversion /ìntrə vúrsh'n/ *n.* **1.** PSYCHOL **INTEREST IN SELF** the tendency to be more interested in your own feelings and thoughts than in the people and world around you. ◊ **extroversion 2.** MED **ORGAN'S TURNING IN ON ITSELF** a turning inwards of a hollow organ such as the womb into itself [Mid-17thC. Formed from INTROVERT on the model of such pairs as *evert, eversion*.]

introvert *n.* /ìntrə vurt/ **1. RESERVED PERSON** a shy person who tends not to socialize much **2.** PSYCHOL **SB INTERESTED IN OWN SELF** sb who tends to be more interested in his or her own feelings and thoughts than in other people and the outside world ■ *adj.* = **introverted** [Mid-17thC. From modern Latin *introvertere*, literally 'to turn in', from Latin *vertere* 'to turn' (see VERSUS).]

introverted /ìntrə vúrtid/ *adj.* **1. SHY** tending to be shy and quiet or ill at ease in a group **2.** PSYCHOL **INTERESTED IN OWN FEELINGS** interested more in your own feelings, thoughts, and motives than in other people and the world around you **3.** MED **TURNED INTO ITSELF** turned into itself or pulled back inside a larger part

intrude /in tróod/ (**-trudes, -truding, -truded**) *v.* **1.** *vi.* **INVADE SB'S PRIVACY** to disturb sb's peace or privacy by going where you have not been invited or are not welcome **2.** *vi.* **HAVE UNPLEASANT EFFECT** to have an unpleasant or undesired effect on sth **3.** *vt.* **ADD STH UNPLEASANT** to add or mention sth inappropriate or unwanted (*formal*) **4.** *vti.* GEOL **MOVE INTO ROCK FORMATION** to move in a molten state into a pre-existing rock formation, or force molten rock into a pre-existing rock formation [15thC. Partly from Latin *intrudere* 'to thrust in', from *trudere* 'to thrust'; partly a back-formation from INTRUSION.]

intruder /in tróodər/ *n.* **1. SB WHO ENTERS ILLEGALLY** sb who enters a building or property illegally, usually in order to commit a crime **2. UNWELCOME PERSON** sb who is somewhere where he or she is not welcome or has not been invited

intrusion /in tro͞ozh'n/ *n.* **1.** DISTURBANCE a disturbing of sb's peace or privacy by an unwelcome arrival or presence **2.** STH UNWELCOME an unwelcome presence or effect that disturbs or upsets sth **3.** LAW UNLAWFUL ENTRY an illegal entry into a place, often by force, in order to commit a crime (*formal*) **4.** GEOL INTRUDED ROCK a body of igneous rock, often massive with associated linear dykes and sills, that has moved while molten into older solid rocks with subsequent alteration of those rocks. Dartmoor is a granite intrusion. **5.** GEOL MOVEMENT OF MOLTEN ROCK the movement of molten rock (**magma**) into pre-existing rock [14thC. Directly or via French from the medieval Latin stem *intrusion-*, from Latin *intrus-*, past participle stem of *intrudere* (see INTRUDE).] —**intrusional** *adj.*

intrusive /in tro͞ossiv/ *adj.* **1.** INTRUDING causing a disturbance or having an unpleasant effect **2.** GEOL FORMED BY INTRUSION used to describe a rock formed by having moved while in a molten state into pre-existing rocks **3.** PHON OF CONNECTING SPEECH SOUND used to describe a speech sound that is introduced between two words only to facilitate more fluent pronunciation —**intrusively** *adv.* —**intrusiveness** *n.*

intrust *vt.* = **entrust**

intubate /íntyo͞o bayt/ (**-bates, -bating, -bated**) *v.* MED **1.** *vti.* INSERT TUBE IN WINDPIPE to insert a tube through the vocal cords and into the windpipe in order to provide sb's lungs with oxygen, usually during surgery under anaesthesia **2.** *vt.* INSERT TUBE IN SB to treat sb by inserting a tube into the windpipe so that oxygen can be supplied to the lungs [Late 19thC. Coined from IN- + Latin *tuba* 'tube' + -ATE.] —**intubation** /ìntyo͞o báysh'n/ *n.*

INTUC /ín tuk/ *abbr.* Indian National Trade Union Congress

intuit /in tyo͞o it/ (**-its, -iting, -ited**) *vt.* to be aware of or know sth without having to think about it or learn it [Mid-19thC. Back-formation from INTUITION.] —**intuitable** *adj.*

intuition /íntyoo ísh'n/ *n.* **1.** KNOWING STH INSTINCTIVELY the state of being aware of or knowing sth without having to discover or perceive it, or the ability to do this **2.** INSTINCTIVE BELIEF sth known or believed instinctively, without actual evidence for it **3.** PHILOS IMMEDIATE KNOWLEDGE immediate knowledge of sth [15thC. Directly or via French from the late Latin stem *intuition-* 'consideration', ultimately from Latin *intueri* 'to look upon', from *tueri* 'to look'.] —**intuitional** *adj.* —**intuitionally** *adv.*

intuitionism /íntyoo ísh'nizəm/ *n.* **1.** PHILOS DOCTRINE OF INTUITIVE PERCEPTION the doctrine that asserts that a perceived object is intuitively known to be real **2.** ETHICS ETHICAL PRINCIPLES UNDERSTOOD THROUGH INTUITION the doctrine that knowledge of goodness or obligation and the principles governing them can be discerned through intuition **3.** LOGIC, MATH MATHEMATICAL THEORY a theory in the foundation of mathematics that holds that only proofs constrained by certain restrictions are permitted. ◊ **formalism, logicism**

intuitive /in tyo͞o itiv/ *adj.* **1.** KNOWN AUTOMATICALLY known directly and instinctively, without being discovered or consciously perceived **2.** KNOWING BY INSTINCT knowing things instinctively —**intuitively** *adv.* —**intuitiveness** *n.*

intumesce /íntyo͞o méss/ (**-mesces, -mescing, -mesced**) *vi.* to become enlarged or swollen as a result of increased flow of blood or other fluids [Late 18thC. From Latin *intumescere* 'to swell up', from *tumescere* (see TUMESCENT).]

intumescence /íntyo͞o méss'nss/ *n.* **1.** MED SWELLING WITH FLUID a swelling or increase in the volume of part of the body as a result of increased flow of blood and other fluids **2.** MED SWOLLEN PART a part of the body that is swollen with blood or another fluid **3.** CHEM SWELLING OF COMPOUND the swelling of a crystalline compound on heating, often with the release of water vapour —**intumescent** *adj.*

intussuscept /íntəssə sépt/ (**-cepts, -cepting, -cepted**) *vti.* to undergo, or cause part of a tubular structure to undergo, a partial sliding into itself, e.g. as part of the intestine sometimes does [Early 19thC. Back-formation from INTUSSUSCEPTION.] —**intussusceptive** *adj.*

intussusception /íntəssə sépsh'n/ *n.* **1.** MED TELESCOPING OF TUBULAR ORGAN a sliding of a portion of a tubular organ into another portion, especially a condition of the bowel in which this happens, creating swelling that leads to obstruction **2.** BOT CELL WALL GROWTH the growth of the surface area of a cell wall by the incorporation of particles into the wall [Early 18thC. Directly or via French from the modern Latin stem *intussusception-*, from Latin *intus* 'within' + the stem *susception-* 'undertaking', from *suscept-* (see SUSCEPTIBLE).]

intwine *vti.* = **entwine**

intwist *vt.* = **entwist**

Inuit /ínno͞o it, -yo͞o-/ (*plural* **-it** *or* **-its**), **Innuit** (*plural* **-it** *or* **-its**) *n.* **1.** PEOPLES ARCTIC OR GREENLAND PEOPLE a member of any of several aboriginal peoples who live in coastal regions of the Canadian Arctic and in Greenland. The Inuit are related to the Yupik of Alaska and northeastern Siberia. **2.** LANG LANGUAGE OF INUIT any of the languages of the Inuit, constituting one of the three branches of the Eskimo-Aleut family of languages. Inuit is spoken by about 60,000 people. ◊ **Inuktitut** [Mid-18thC. From Inuit, the plural of *inuk* 'person'.] —**Inuit** *adj.*

WORD KEY: USAGE

See Usage note at ***Eskimo.***

inukshuk /i no͞ok sho͞ok/ *n. Can* rocks piled up to look like a person from a distance, used as a marker or guidepost by the Inuit [From *Inuit*]

Inuktitut /i no͞oktətoot/ *n.* a language of the Inuit, especially those in the eastern Arctic. ◊ **Inuit** [Late 20thC. From Inuit, literally 'the Inuit way'.]

inulase /ínnyo͞o layz, -layss/ *n.* an enzyme that brings about the breakdown of inulin [Late 19thC. Coined from INULIN + -ASE.]

inulin /ínnyo͞o lin/ *n.* a fructose sugar found in the roots and tubers of various plants and is used medically in a test that assesses whether the kidneys are functioning properly [Early 19thC. Coined from Latin *inula* 'elecampane' + -IN.]

inunction /in úngksh'n/ *n.* **1.** MED RUBBING IN OF OIL the rubbing in of oil or ointment **2.** RELIG ANOINTING the anointing of sb with oil as part of a religious ceremony (*formal*) [15thC. Via the Latin stem *inunction-* from, *inunguere* 'to anoint' (literally 'to smear on'), from *unguere* 'to smear' (see UNGUENT).]

inundate /ín un dayt, ínnən-/ (**-dates, -dating, -dated**) *vt.* **1.** OVERWHELM to overwhelm sb with a huge quantity of things that must be dealt with **2.** FLOOD to flood a place with water (*formal*) [Late 16thC. Back-formation from INUNDATION.] —**inundator** *n.* —**inundatory** /ín úndətəri/ *adj.*

inundation /ín un dáysh'n, ínnən-/ *n.* **1.** FLOOD a flood of water (*formal*) **2.** OVERWHELMING ACCUMULATION an accumulation of an overwhelming amount of things that sb has to deal with [15thC. Directly or via Old French *inondacion* from the Latin stem *inundation-*, from *inundare*, literally 'to flow onto', ultimately from *unda* 'wave' (see UNDULATE).]

Inupiat /i no͞opi at, -nyo͞o-/ *npl.* an Inuit people who live along the Beaufort Sea and Chukchi coast of the Arctic Ocean [Late 20thC. From Inuit *inuk* 'person' + *piaq* 'genuine'.]

inurbane /ín ur báyn/ *adj.* lacking good manners or sophistication —**inurbanely** *adv.* —**inurbanity** /ín ur bánnəti/ *n.*

inure /i nyo͝or/ (**-ures, -uring, -ured**) *v.* **1.** *vt.* HARDEN SB TO STH to make sb used to sth unpleasant over a period of time, so that he or she no longer is bothered or upset by it **2.** *vi.* LAW COME INTO EFFECT to come into operation or effect [15thC. From assumed Anglo-Norman *eneurer*, literally 'to accustom by use', ultimately from assumed *eure* 'use', from Latin *opera* 'work'.] —**inurement** *n.*

inurn /in úrn/ (**-urns, -urning, -urned**) *vt.* **1.** PUT ASHES IN URN to place a cremated body's ashes in an urn **2.** BURY to put a dead body in a grave (*formal*) —**inurnment** *n.*

in utero /in yo͞otər ō/ *adv., adj.* in or while still inside a woman's womb [From Latin]

inutile /in yo͞o tīl/ *adj.* pointless or useless (*literary*) [15thC. Via French from Latin *inutilis*, from *utilis* 'useful' (see UTILITY).] —**inutilely** *adv.* —**inutility** /ínnyoo tílləti/ *n.*

inv. *abbr.* **1.** invariable **2.** invented **3.** invention **4.** inventor **5.** invoice

in vacuo /in vákyoo ō/ *adv.* **1.** CHEM IN VACUUM in a vacuum **2.** LAW IN ISOLATION in isolation, without considering any evidence [From Latin]

invade /in váyd/ (**-vades, -vading, -vaded**) *v.* **1.** *vti.* ENTER COUNTRY BY MILITARY FORCE to enter a country by force with or as an army, especially in order to conquer it **2.** *vt.* ENTER AND SPREAD THROUGH to enter and spread throughout sth completely **3.** *vt.* GO SOMEWHERE IN NUMBERS to enter or be present in a place in great numbers **4.** *vt.* SPOIL to spoil sth by interfering, interrupting, or reducing it **5.** *vti.* MED CAUSE DISEASE to enter and spread gradually throughout a part of the body, causing harm or damage **6.** *vti.* BOT GROW RAPIDLY AND HARMFULLY to become established and spread rapidly in an area, crowding out the pre-existing plants [15thC. Directly or via Old French *invader* from Latin *invadere* 'to go in', from *vadere* 'to go' (source of English *evade*).] —**invadable** *adj.* —**invader** *n.*

invaginate /in vájji nayt/ (**-nates, -nating, -nated**) *vti.* to push the wall of a cavity or hollow organ inwards or one section of a hollow organ into another, like a glove finger pushed into itself [Mid-17thC. Back-formation from INVAGINATION.]

invagination /in vájji náysh'n/ *n.* **1.** MED PUSHING STH INSIDE ITSELF the pushing of sth into itself or partially inside out, like a glove finger pushed into itself, or the condition of sth that results from this **2.** MED INVAGINATED ORGAN a hollow organ or body part that has been pushed back inside itself **3.** CELL BIOL INFOLDING OF CELL STRUCTURE the process of folding a portion of a cell structure inwards, as when the cell membrane turns inwards during phagocytosis **4.** EMBRYOL FORMING OF HOLLOW GROWTH INSIDE the pushing inwards of a layer of cells to produce a hollow ingrowth in sth, as when the wall of the blastula forms the gastrula [Mid-17thC. From medieval Latin *invaginare* 'to sheathe', from Latin *vagina* 'sheath' (source of English *vagina*).]

invalid[1] /in vállid/ *adj.* **1.** LAW NOT LEGAL not legally binding or enforceable **2.** LOGIC FLAWED not acceptable or correct because of being based on a mistake or employing flawed reasoning [Mid-16thC. From Latin *invalidus* 'not strong', from *validus* 'strong' (see VALID).]

invalid[2] /ínvəlid, -leed/ *n.* **1.** MED SB WITH CHRONIC DISEASE sb who has a chronic disease or a medical disorder and needs care **2.** OFFENSIVE TERM an offensive term for sb with physical disabilities (*dated offensive*) ■ *adj.* **1.** AFFECTED BY CHRONIC DISEASE having a chronic disease or medical disorder **2.** FOR SB WITH CHRONIC DISEASE for sb who has a chronic disease or medical disorder ■ *vt.* (**-valids, -validing, -valided**) **1.** CAUSE TO HAVE CHRONIC DISEASE to cause sb to have a chronic disease or medical disorder **2.** SEND HOME BECAUSE OF ILLNESS to send sb away or home for good, especially from the armed forces, because of chronic illness or severe injury [Mid-17thC. From INVALID[1].]

invalidate /in válli dayt/ (**-dates, -dating, -dated**) *vt.* **1.** MAKE NOT LEGAL to deprive sth of its legal force or value **2.** SHOW TO BE WRONG to prove that sth is wrong or make sth worthless —**invalidation** /in válli dáysh'n/ *n.* —**invalidator** /in válli daytər/ *n.*

WORD KEY: SYNONYMS

See Synonyms at ***nullify.***

invalidism /ínvəlidizəm, -leed-/ *n.* **1.** CHRONIC ILLNESS chronic illness or medical disorder **2.** LIVING LIKE INVALID an abnormal preoccupation with the state of personal health that causes sb to live like an invalid. ◊ **hypochondriosis**

invalidity /ínvə líddəti/ *n.* **1.** LOGIC UNSOUNDNESS a lack of soundness or accuracy that results from an error in reasoning **2.** LAW LACK OF LEGALITY the condition of not being legally binding or enforceable

invalidity benefit *n.* an allowance paid by the government to sb whose long-term illness has prevented him or her from working for at least six months. ◊ **disability benefit**

invaluable /in vállyoo əb'l/ *adj.* extremely useful or valuable —**invaluableness** *n.* —**invaluably** *adv.*

Invar /in vaar/ *tdmk.* a trademark for an iron, nickel, and carbon alloy that is used for making watch springs

invariable /in váiri əb'l/ *adj.* NEVER CHANGING never changing or varying ■ *n.* MATH CONSTANT QUANTITY a mathematical quantity that is a constant —**invariability** /in váiri ə bílləti/ *n.* —**invariableness** /in váiri əb'lnəss/ *n.*

invariably /in váiri əbli/ *adv.* always or almost always

invariant /in váiri ənt/ *adj.* **1.** = **invariable** *adj.* **2.** MATH UNCHANGING used to describe a quantity or set of quantities that is not changed by a designated mathematical operation such as the transformation of coordinates ■ *n.* MATH UNCHANGING RELATIONSHIP a relationship that is not changed by a designated mathematical operation such as the transformation of coordinates —**invariance** *n.* —**invariancy** *n.*

invasion /in váyzh'n/ *n.* **1.** MIL ATTEMPT TO CONQUER a hostile entry of an armed force into a country's territory, especially with the intention of conquering it **2.** ARRIVAL IN LARGE NUMBERS the arrival of large numbers of people or things at one time ○ *an invasion of tourists* **3.** SPOILING a spoiling of sth by interfering with it or taking some of it away **4.** SPREAD OF STH HARMFUL the arrival or spread of sth that causes damage or harm **5.** MED SPREAD OF DISEASE the spread of disease-causing organisms or malignant cells in the body **6.** BOT AGGRESSIVE SPREAD OF PLANT the aggressive spread of a plant species in an area, stifling the growth of pre-existing species [15thC. Directly or via French from the late Latin stem *invasion-*, from Latin *invas-*, past participle stem of *invadere* (see INVADE).]

invasive /in váyssiv/ *adj.* **1.** MIL ATTACKING involving or mounting a military attack on a territory, especially with a view to conquering it **2.** INTRUDING involving an intrusion or infringement, e.g. of sb's privacy or rights **3.** MED ATTACKING ADJACENT TISSUE having or showing a tendency to spread from the point of origin to adjacent tissue, as some cancers do **4.** SURG INTO PATIENT'S BODY done by inserting sth into or operating on the body through an incision or a natural orifice **5.** BOT GROWING AGGRESSIVELY growing aggressively in an area and stifling the growth of pre-existing plants —**invasively** *adv.* —**invasiveness** *n.*

invective /in véktiv/ *n.* ABUSIVE LANGUAGE an abusive expression, or language used to attack or blame sb (*formal*) ■ *adj.* USING ABUSE using abusive language (*formal*) [15thC. Directly or via French *invectif* from late Latin *invectivus* 'abusive', from, ultimately, Latin *invehere* 'to carry in', from *vehere* 'to carry'.] —**invectively** *adv.* —**invectiveness** *n.*

inveigh /in váy/ (**-veighs, -veighing, -veighed**) *vi.* to speak angrily in criticism of or protest at sth (*formal*) [15thC. From Latin *invehere* (see INVECTIVE).] —**inveigher** *n.*

inveigle /in váyg'l, -vée-/ (**-gles, -gling, -gled**) *vt.* **1.** PERSUADE to charm or entice sb into doing sth that he or she would not otherwise have done ○ *inveigled me into making the trip* **2.** OBTAIN BY PERSUASION to obtain sth by persuading sb to give it [15thC. From Anglo-Norman *envegler*, an alteration of French *aveugler* 'to deprive of sight', ultimately from assumed Vulgar Latin *aboculus*, literally 'without eye', from Latin *oculus* 'eye'.] —**inveiglement** *n.* —**inveigler** *n.*

invent /in vént/ (**-vents, -venting, -vented**) *vt.* **1.** CREATE STH NEW to be the first to think of, make, or use sth **2.** MAKE UP to make up sth false, e.g. a false excuse [15thC. From Latin *invent-*, past participle stem of *invenire* 'to come upon', from *venire* 'to come' (see VENUE).] —**inventable** *adj.*

invention /in vénsh'n/ *n.* **1.** CREATED THING a thing that sb has created, especially a device or process **2.** ACT OF CREATING the creation of sth new **3.** LIE a lie, or the telling of lies (*used euphemistically*) **4.** CREATIVE ABILITY the talent to create new things **5.** MUSIC SHORT INSTRUMENTAL WORK a short instrumental work, usually for keyboard, that has two or three parts and employs the technique of counterpoint —**inventional** *adj.* —**inventionless** *adj.*

inventive /in véntiv/ *adj.* **1.** SKILLED AT INVENTING good at creating new things **2.** DISPLAYING CREATIVITY displaying creativity or imagination in its design **3.** INVOLVED IN INVENTION involved in or concerned with invention —**inventively** *adv.* —**inventiveness** *n.*

inventor /in véntər/ *n.* sb who invents sth, especially a new device or process

inventory /ínvəntəri/ *n.* (*plural* **-ries**) **1.** LIST OF ITEMS a list of things, especially items of property **2.** ACCT RECORD OF ASSETS a record of a business's current assets, including property owned as well as merchandise on hand and the value of work in progress and work completed but not sold **3.** ASSETS a company's assets as a whole, or the value of them **4.** STOCK OF GOODS the merchandise or stock that a store or company has on hand **5.** = **stocktaking** ■ *vt.* (**-ries, -rying, -ried**) MAKE INVENTORY OF to make an inventory of items, or enter a particular item on an inventory [15thC. From medieval Latin *inventorium*, an alteration of late Latin *inventarium*, literally 'list of what is found', from, ultimately, Latin *invenire* (see INVENT).] —**inventoriable** *adj.* —**inventorial** /ínvən táwri əl/ *adj.* —**inventorially** *adv.*

inveracity /ínvə rássəti/ (*plural* **-ties**) *n.* a lie, or the telling of lies (*humorous*)

Invercargill /ínvər kaárg'l/ city on the southern coast of the South Island, New Zealand. Situated on the River Waihopai, it is the commercial centre of a farming district. Population: 49,306 (1996).

Inverclyde /ínvər klíd/ council area near Glasgow, Scotland. Population: 89,990 (1993).

inverness *n.* a long overcoat with a rounded collar and a detachable cape [Mid-19thC. Named after INVERNESS.]

Inverness /ínvər néss/ industrial and market town in northern Scotland, at the northeastern end of the Caledonian Canal. Population: 62,647 (1991).

inverse /in vúrss, ín vurss/ *adj.* **1.** OPPOSITE OR REVERSING opposite to or reversing sth **2.** MATH INVOLVING OPPOSITELY AFFECTED VARIABLES involving two variables that are in a mathematical relationship where, when one increases, the other decreases and vice versa ■ *n.* **1.** OPPOSITE sth that is a total opposite **2.** MATH ELEMENT OF SET either of two elements of a set that when added together give 0, one being the negative of the other, e.g. 3 and –3 **3.** MATH = **inverse function 4.** LOGIC OPPOSITE LOGICAL PROPOSITION a logical proposition in which both the subject and the predicate are the opposite of another proposition [15thC. From Latin *inversus*, past participle of *invertere* 'to turn upside down' (literally 'to turn inside-out'), from *vertere* 'to turn' (see VERSE).] —**inversely** *adv.*

inverse function *n.* a mathematical operation or function that exactly reverses another operation or function. Addition and subtraction are inverse functions, as are exponentiation and taking the root of a number.

inversely proportional *adj.* **1.** OPPOSITE opposite in size, degree, or rate of development **2.** MATH CHANGING OPPOSITELY BY SAME FACTOR involving a mathematical relationship in which an increase in one variable by a given factor brings about a decrease by the same factor in another

inverse square law *n.* a natural law in which the magnitude of a physical quantity varies inversely with the square of its distance from its source. The gravitational attraction exerted by the Sun on the planets and the attraction or repulsion exhibited between two magnets are governed by the inverse square law.

inversion /in vúrsh'n/ *n.* **1.** REVERSAL a reversing of the order, arrangement, or position of sth **2.** REVERSED STATE OR THING a state in which the order, arrangement, or position of sth is reversed, or sth in such a state **3.** GRAM = **anastrophe 4.** METEOROL TEMPERATURE INCREASE WITH ALTITUDE a stable atmospheric condition in which air temperature increases vertically upwards through a layer. It is the reverse of normal conditions. **5.** MED INVERTING OF ORGAN abnormal positioning of an organ, especially the abnormal turning inwards or inside out of an organ. This sometimes happens to the womb after childbirth, when part of it is pulled through the cervical canal. **6.** MATH INVERTED RATIO the transformation of a mathematical proportion by inverting the ratio and order of its terms **7.** MUSIC CHANGING OF INTERVAL BY OCTAVE a raising of the lower note of an interval, or a lowering of the upper note, by an octave **8.** MUSIC MOVING OF CHORD TONE a moving of the root tone of a chord to a position other than the lowest **9.** MUSIC REVERSING OF MELODY INTERVALS a converting of all the intervals in a melody from ascending to descending and vice versa **10.** CHEM PRODUCTION OF OPPOSITE OPTICAL ACTIVITY a chemical reaction in which an optically active compound gives a product with opposite optical configuration **11.** GENETICS CHROMOSOMAL MUTATION a chromosomal mutation in which a block of genes in a segment is in reverse order —**inversive** *adj.*

invert *vt.* /in vúrt/ (**-verts, -verting, -verted**) **1.** REVERSE ARRANGEMENT to reverse the order, position, or arrangement of sth **2.** MAKE OPPOSITE to change sth to its opposite or contrary **3.** MUSIC ALTER POSITION OF NOTES to change the position or arrangement of the musical notes in an interval, chord, or melody to produce inversion **4.** CHEM CHANGE OPTICAL CONFIGURATION to convert an optically active isomer into an isomer with the opposite configuration **5.** LOGIC CONVERT LOGICAL PROPOSITION to negate both the subject and predicate of a logical proposition ■ *n.* /ín vurt/ CHEM PRODUCT OF INVERSION a substance obtained by optical inversion. ◊ **invert sugar** ■ *adj.* /ín vurt/ CHEM OPTICALLY INVERTED subjected to optical inversion [Mid-16thC. From Latin *invertere* (see INVERSE).] —**invertible** /in vúrtəb'l/ *adj.* —**invertibility** /-bílləti/ *n.*

invertase /in vúr tayz, -tayss/ *n.* an enzyme that converts sucrose to a mixture of fructose and glucose by catalytic hydrolysis

invertebrate /in vúrtibrət/ *n.* ANIMAL WITHOUT BACKBONE an animal such as an insect or worm that does not have a backbone ■ *adj.* **1.** WITH NO BACKBONE lacking a backbone or spinal column **2.** OF INVERTEBRATES relating to or consisting of animals that lack backbones **3.** LACKING CHARACTER lacking strength of character [Early 19thC. From modern Latin *invertebratus*, literally 'not jointed', from Latin *vertebra* 'joint, vertebra' (see VERTEBRA).]

inverted /in vúrtid/ *adj.* **1.** REVERSED turned upside down, inside out, or back to front **2.** MUSIC WITH FUNDAMENTAL NOTE REPOSITIONED modified so that the fundamental note of the chord is not the lowest note of the chord **3.** MUSIC WITH NOTES IN MIRROR IMAGE with the musical notes so arranged that every ascending interval is made descending and vice versa

inverted comma *n.* any of the punctuation marks ' and ' or " and ", used around quotations, direct speech, and titles and to give special emphasis to particular words. US term **quotation mark**

inverted mordent *n.* a musical ornament consisting of two notes of the same pitch separated by a third note one step above the others

inverted pleat *n.* a flat symmetrical pleat formed by folding the fabric to the front on either side of the section being pleated. It is the reverse of a box pleat.

inverted snob *n.* sb who disdains or is prejudiced against people of a higher social class or the interests, concerns, and tastes of such people —**inverted snobbery** *n.*

inverter /in vúrtər/ *n.* **1.** STH THAT INVERTS sb or sth that inverts or causes an inversion **2.** ELEC ENG DEVICE CONVERTING CURRENT a device that changes direct current into alternating current and is commonly used on boats to operate devices such as radios from batteries

invert sugar *n.* a mixture of glucose and fructose, obtained by the optical inversion of sucrose, that also occurs naturally in fruits and honey. It is used in the food industry.

invest /in vést/ (**-vests, -vesting, -vested**) *v.* **1.** *vti.* BUY SHARES OR BONDS to use money to buy or participate in a business enterprise that offers the possibility of profit, especially by buying shares or bonds **2.** *vti.* DEPOSIT MONEY WITH BANK to deposit money with a bank or other financial institution in an account that pays interest **3.** *vti.* SPEND MONEY ON PROJECT to spend money on sth in the hope of a future return or benefit **4.** *vt.* CONTRIBUTE EFFORT TO STH to contribute time, energy, or effort to an activity or project, or undertaking in the expectation of a benefit **5.** *vt.* GIVE STH A QUALITY to give sb or sth a particular quality or characteristic **6.** *vt.* CONFER STH ON to confer sth such as a power or right on a person or group ○ *The charter invests the directors with the right to spend money as they see fit.* **7.** *vi.* MAKE A PURCHASE to use money to buy sth, especially sth that sb should be able to use for a relatively long time (*informal*) ○ *It's time this family invested in a new car.* **8.** *vt.* INSTALL IN OFFICIAL ROLE to install sb formally or ceremoniously in an official position (*formal*) ○ *The prince was invested in a ceremony held at the castle.* **9.** *vt.* ADORN to dress, clothe, or cover sb or sth with a garment or other covering (*literary*) **10.** *vt.* BESIEGE to lay siege to a place (*archaic*) [Mid-16thC. Directly or via French *investir* from Latin *investire* 'to clothe (in)', ultimately from *vestis* 'clothing' (see VEST). The underlying idea is of 'dressing up' your capital.] —**investable** *adj.*

investigate /in vésti gayt/ (**-gates, -gating, -gated**) *v.* **1.** *vti.* CARRY OUT OFFICIAL ENQUIRY to carry out a detailed examination or enquiry, especially officially, in order to find out about sth or sb ○ *The local police are investigating a murder.* **2.** *vi.* HAVE A LOOK to have a look or go and see what happened ○ *We heard noises downstairs, so Fred went down to investigate.* [Early 16thC. From Latin *investigare*, literally 'to look into for traces', ultimately from *vestigium* 'footprint' (see VESTIGE).] —**investigable** /in véstigəb'l/ *adj.*

investigation /in vésti gáysh'n/ *n.* **1.** EXAMINATION an examination or enquiry into sth, especially a detailed one that is undertaken officially **2.** LOOK ROUND a look round a place or to see what has happened

investigative /in véstigətiv/, **investigatory** /-təri/ *adj.* **1.** SPECIALIZING IN INVESTIGATING responsible for or specializing in investigating **2.** USED IN INVESTIGATION used in or relating to investigation ○ *investigative techniques*

investigator /in vésti gaytər/ *n.* sb who investigates things as a profession, especially sb who investigates crimes or prepares official or confidential reports on people or events. ◊ **private detective**

investiture /in véstichər/ *n.* **1.** INSTALLATION IN POSITION the formal installing of sb in a position or role, especially an official one, or a ceremony held to mark this **2.** LAY APPOINTMENT OF ROMAN CATHOLIC BISHOPS the appointment of bishops in the Roman Catholic Church by a civil ruler instead of by the Church [14thC. Via medieval Latin *investitura* from, ultimately, Latin *investire* 'to clothe (in)' (see INVEST); from clothing the person being installed in the insignia of rank or position.]

investment /in véstmənt/ *n.* **1.** FIN USE OF MONEY FOR FUTURE PROFIT the outlay of money, e.g. by depositing it in a bank or by buying shares in a company, with the object of making a profit **2.** FIN MONEY INVESTED an amount of money invested in sth for the purpose of making a profit **3.** FIN STH INVESTED IN sth such as a company, endeavour, or object that money is invested in with the goal of making a profit **4.** CONTRIBUTION TO ACTIVITY a contribution of sth such as time, energy, or effort to an activity, project, or undertaking, in the expectation of a benefit **5.** PURCHASE a purchase, especially sth that sb should be able to use for a relatively long time (*informal*) **6.** INVESTITURE the formal or ceremonial installing of sb in a role or position, especially an official one (*formal*) **7.** MIL SIEGE a siege or besieging (*archaic*) **8.** ECON MONEY IN COMPANY'S PROPERTY the outlay of money that a company's existing buildings, equipment, and materials is equivalent to **9.** BIOL OUTER LAYERS OF ORGANISM the outer layers of an animal or organ

investment analyst *n.* sb who is employed by a stock exchange business to research other companies and areas of investment for clients

investment company *n. US* a company that holds securities in other companies purely for investment

investment trust *n.* a legal arrangement of investors that invests its capital in securities

investor /in véstər/ *n.* a person, company, or other organization that has money invested in sth, especially one that holds shares in publicly owned corporations

inveterate /in véttərət/ *adj.* **1.** HABITUAL fixed in a habit or practice, especially a bad one **2.** FIRMLY ESTABLISHED firmly established and of long standing [14thC. From Latin *inveteratus*, past participle of *inveterare* 'to become old', from *veter-*, the stem of *vetus* (source of English *veteran* 'old'.] —**inveteracy** *n.* —**inveterately** *adv.* —**inveterateness** *n.*

inviable /in ví əb'l/ *adj.* unable to survive, especially financially or biologically —**inviability** /in ví ə bílləti/ *n.* —**inviableness** *n.* —**inviably** /in ví əbli/ *adv.*

invidious /in víddi əss/ *adj.* **1.** PRODUCING RESENTMENT producing resentment or ill feeling, e.g. by unfairly slighting sb **2.** UNPLEASANT unpleasant because producing or likely to produce jealousy, resentment, or hatred in others [Early 17thC. From Latin *invidiosus*, from *invidia* 'ill will', literally 'looking at (with malice)', ultimately from *videre* 'to look'.] —**invidiously** *adv.* —**invidiousness** *n.*

invigilate /in víjji layt/ (**-lates, -lating, -lated**) *vti.* to supervise an examination, especially in order to prevent cheating. US term **proctor** [Mid-16thC. From Latin *invigilare* 'to watch, be awake in or on account of', ultimately from *vigil* 'watchful' (see VIGIL).]

invigilator /in víjji laytər/ *n.* sb who supervises students at an examination. US term **proctor**

invigorate /in víggə rayt/ (**-ates, -ating, -ated**) *vt.* to fill sb or sth with energy or life (*often passive*) [Mid-17thC. Origin uncertain: probably formed from earlier *invigor*, from, ultimately, Old French *envigourer* 'to make vigorous', from 'vigour'.] —**invigoration** /in víggə ráysh'n/ *n.* —**invigorative** /in víggərətiv/ *adj.* —**invigoratively** *adv.* —**invigorator** *n.*

invigorating /in víggə rayting/ *adj.* filling sb or sth with energy or life —**invigoratingly** *adv.*

invincible /in vínssəb'l/ *adj.* **1.** UNBEATABLE incapable of being defeated or beaten as a result of great strength or skill **2.** TOO DIFFICULT TO OVERCOME so great or difficult as to be impossible to overcome **3.** DEEP-ROOTED too deep-rooted or ingrained to be altered [15thC. Directly or via French from Latin *invincibilis*, from *vincibilis* 'conquerable' (see VINCIBLE).] —**invincibility** /in vínssə bílləti/ *n.* —**invincibleness** /in vínssəb'lnəss/ *n.* —**invincibly** /in vínssəbli/ *adv.*

inviolable /in ví ələb'l/ *adj.* **1.** UNBREAKABLE secure from infringement or breaking **2.** SECURE FROM ATTACK secure from violence or attack [15thC. Directly or via French from Latin *inviolabilis*, from *violabilis* 'that may be injured', from *violare* 'to treat violently' (see VIOLATE).] —**inviolability** /in ví ələ bílləti/ *n.* —**inviolableness** /in ví ələb'lnəss/ *n.* —**inviolably** *adv.*

inviolate /in ví ələt/ *adj.* **1.** UNALTERED not subject to change, damage, or destruction **2.** KEPT PURE kept pure, untouched, or unblemished [15thC. From Latin *inviolatus*, from *violat-*, past participle stem of *violare* 'to treat violently' (see VIOLATE).] —**inviolacy** /in ví ələssi/ *n.* —**inviolately** *adv.* —**inviolateness** *n.*

invisible /in vízzəb'l/ *adj.* **1.** IMPOSSIBLE TO SEE not able to be seen with the eyes **2.** HIDDEN hidden from view **3.** MADE TRANSPARENT MAGICALLY impossible to see as a result of magic or pseudo-scientific processes **4.** NOT EASILY NOTICED not noticed or detected readily **5.** ECON UNRECORDED STATISTICALLY not reflected or reported in economic statistics, or not recorded statistically ■ *n.* **1.** ACCT ITEM NOT IN FINANCIAL STATEMENT an item not reported in a company's financial statement **2.** SB OR STH INVISIBLE sb or sth that is invisible [14thC. Directly or via French from Latin *invisibilis*, from *visibilis* (see VISIBLE).] —**invisibility** /in vízzə bílləti/ *n.* —**invisibleness** /in vízzəb'lnəss/ *n.* —**invisibly** *adv.*

invisible ink *n.* a liquid used to write sth that cannot be seen until the paper is treated in some way, e.g. with heat

invitation /ìnvi táysh'n/ *n.* **1.** OFFER OF STH an offer to come or go somewhere, especially one promising pleasure or hospitality, or the making of such an offer **2.** WRITTEN NOTE a note or other message, especially a printed card, that contains an invitation **3.** ENCOURAGEMENT encouragement to do sth ■ *adj.* OPEN ONLY TO THOSE ASKED open only to people who have been asked personally. US term **invitational**

invitatory /in vítətəri/ *adj.* inviting or encouraging sth

invite *vt.* /in vít/ (**-vites, -viting, -vited**) **1.** ASK TO PARTICIPATE to ask sb to come or go somewhere or to do sth **2.** REQUEST to ask for sth or say that sth should be welcomed ○ *She invited questions from the audience.* **3.** PROVOKE to encourage or provoke sth that might not have happened otherwise ○ *an attitude that invites disaster* ■ *n.* /ín vìt/ INVITATION an invitation (*informal*) [Mid-16thC. Directly or via French *inviter* from Latin *invitare*, of uncertain origin: perhaps literally 'to be pleasant towards', formed from assumed *vitus* 'pleasant'.] —**invitee** /ín vī tée/ *n.* —**inviter** /in vítər/ *n.*

inviting /in víting/ *adj.* suggesting or offering pleasure or enjoyment ○ *Inviting smells were coming from the kitchen.* —**invitingly** /in vítingli/ *adv.* —**invitingness** *n.*

in vitro /in vée trō/ *adj., adv.* in an artificial environment such as a test tube rather than inside a living organism [From Latin, literally 'in glass']

in vitro fertilization *n.* fertilization of an ovum by sperm outside the body when normal conception is not achievable because of a woman's low fertility. After 5 days, this is followed by implantation in the womb.

in vivo /in vée vō/ *adj., adv.* existing or carried out inside a living organism, as in a test or experiment [From Latin, literally 'in the living']

invocate /ínvə kayt/ (**-cates, -cating, -cated**) *vt.* to appeal to sb or to God or a spirit for help (*archaic*) [Mid-16thC. From Latin *invocare* 'to call upon' (see INVOKE).] —**invocative** /in vókətiv/ *adj.*

invocation /ínvə káysh'n/ *n.* **1.** CALLING UPON HIGHER POWER a calling upon a greater power such as God or a spirit for help **2.** RELIG PRAYER a short prayer forming part of a religious service **3.** QUOTING OF STH AS A REASON the act of calling upon or quoting sth such as a law as a reason or justification **4.** INCANTATION SUPPOSEDLY SUMMONING DEMON a casting of a spell in an attempt to make an evil spirit appear, or the spell itself —**invocational** *adj.* —**invocatory** /in vókətəri/ *adj.*

invoice /ín voyss/ *n.* **1.** REQUEST FOR PAYMENT a written record of goods or services provided and the amount charged for them, sent to a customer as a request for payment **2.** SHIPMENT OF GOODS a shipment of goods that is recorded on an invoice ■ *vt.* (**-voices, -voicing, -voiced**) SEND SB AN INVOICE to send sb an invoice for payment [Mid-16thC. Originally the plural of obsolete *invoy*, from obsolete French *envoy* 'sending' (see ENVOY); because the invoice is sent.]

invoke /in vók/ (**-vokes, -voking, -voked**) *vt.* **1.** CALL UPON GREATER POWER to call upon a greater power such as God or a spirit for help **2.** USE IN SUPPORT to quote, rely on, or use sth such as a law in support of an argument or case **3.** ASK FOR to ask or appeal for sth **4.** ATTEMPT TO SUMMON DEMON to call upon an evil spirit to appear, e.g. by casting a spell **5.** AROUSE to create or arouse an idea, emotion, or image [15thC. Via French *invoquer* from Latin *invocare* 'to call upon', from *vocare* 'to call' (see VOCATION).] —**invoker** *n.*

involucre /ínvə lookər, -loo-/ *n.* a ring of modified leaves beneath a flower or flower cluster, as in dandelion or daisy flowers [Late 16thC. Directly or via French from Latin *involucrum* 'wrapper', from *involvere* 'to roll into', from *volvere* 'to roll'.] —**involucral** /ínvə lóokrəl/ *adj.* —**involucrate** /-lóokrət/ *adj.*

involucrum /ínvə lóokrəm/ (*plural* **-cra** /-krə/) *n.* **1.** MED NEW BONE a growth of new bone that forms around a mass of dead or infected bone **2.** BOT = **involucre** [Late 17thC. From Latin (see INVOLUCRE).]

involuntarily /in vóllləntərəli/ *adv.* without wanting or intending to

involuntary /in vólləntəri/ *adj.* **1.** COMPELLED required or exacted against sb's will or wishes **2.** UNCONTROLLABLE spontaneous or automatic, and not controlled or controllable by the mind —**involuntariness** *n.*

involuntary manslaughter *n.* LAW the accidental and unlawful killing of one human being by another without planning of the killing in advance

involuntary muscle *n.* a muscle that acts independently of the will, especially in reflex functions

involute /ínvə loot/ *adj.* **1.** COMPLEX complicated or intricate **2.** BOT ROLLING INWARDS having petals or leaves that roll inwards at the edges **3.** ZOOL TIGHTLY WHORLED used to describe a shell whose axis is hidden by tight whorls ■ *n.* /ínvəloot/ GEOM TYPE OF CURVE a curve traced by the end of a taut thread that cannot be extended as it is wound upon or unwound from another curve ■ *vi.* /ínvə lóot/ (**-lutes, -luting, -luted**) BECOME INVOLUTE to become complex or inwardly rolled, whorled, or curved [Mid-17thC. From Latin *in-*

volutus 'intricate' or, in medieval Latin, 'rolled inwards, forming a spiral', past participle of *involvere* 'to enwrap' (see INVOLVE).] —**involutely** *adv.*

involuted /ínvə lóotid/ *adj.* = involute

involution /ínvə lóosh'n/ *n.* **1.** COMPLICATION an act of making sth complicated or intricate, or the condition of being complicated or intricate **2.** STH COMPLEX sth complicated or intricate **3.** ZOOL DECLINE IN FUNCTION a decline or degeneration in the physiological function of an organ **4.** BIOL INVOLUTE PART an involute part or structure **5.** PHYSIOL DECREASE IN SIZE a return to normal size of a body or body part after expansion **6.** ALGEBRA RAISING OF QUANTITY TO POWER the operation of raising a number, variable, or expression to a specified positive integral power, x^n **7.** GRAM COMPLEX GRAMMATICAL STRUCTURE a complicated grammatical construction **8.** BIOL DEVELOPMENTAL PROCESS FORMING TUBE the process by which certain cells grow inwards over the edge of an organ or part until they rejoin the structure to form a tube. The bladder is formed by involution. —**involutional** *adj.*

involve /in vólv/ (**-volves, -volving, -volved**) *v.* **1.** *vt.* CONTAIN STH to contain or include as a necessary element of sth **2.** *vt.* CONCERN SB to be a matter that concerns or affects sb **3.** *vt.* CAUSE SB TO PARTICIPATE to make sb part of, or make sb take part in, an event or ongoing process **4.** *vt.* IMPLICATE SB to connect a person with sth, especially sth disreputable **5.** *vt.* ENGROSS SB to take up sb's whole attention **6.** *vt.* COMPLICATE STH to make sth complicated or difficult to follow (*often passive*) **7.** *vt.* ENCLOSE STH to envelop sth (*literary*) (*often passive*) **8.** *vr.* COIL UP to coil, wrap, or wind up (*archaic*) [Late 14thC. From Latin *involvere* 'to enfold', from *volvere* 'to roll' (source of English *evolution* and *vault*).] —**involvement** *n.* —**involver** *n.*

involved /in vólvd/ *adj.* **1.** COMPLICATED complicated or difficult to follow **2.** CONNECTED connected with or participating in sth **3.** IN RELATIONSHIP participating in a romantic or sexual relationship —**involvedly** /in vólvdli, -vidli/ *adv.*

involving /in vólving/ *adj.* holding the attention ○ *a highly involving storyline*

invt. *abbr.* inventory

invulnerable /in vúlnərəb'l/ *adj.* **1.** UNABLE TO BE HURT not capable of being wounded, damaged, hurt, or affected ○ *invulnerable to criticism* **2.** SAFE FROM ATTACK not capable of being successfully attacked [Late 16thC. From Latin *invulnerabilis*, from *vulnerare* 'to wound' (see VULNERABLE).] —**invulnerability** /in vúlnərə bílləti/ *n.* —**invulnerableness** /in vúlnərəb'lnəss/ *n.* —**invulnerably** /-vúlnərə bli/ *adv.*

inward /ínwərd/ *adj.* **1.** INSIDE situated within sth **2.** OF THE MIND OR SPIRIT relating to or existing in the mind or spirit **3.** TOWARDS THE INSIDE towards the inside or centre of sth ■ *adv.* US = inwards ■ *n.* THE INSIDE the inner part (*literary archaic*) ○ *'To kiss the tender inward of thy hand'* (William Shakespeare, *Sonnets*; 1609) —**inwardness** *n.*

Inward Light *n.* = Inner Light

inwardly /ínnwərdli/ *adv.* **1.** TO YOURSELF to yourself, or without showing a feeling on the outside **2.** TOWARDS INSIDE on or to the inside

inwards /ínnwərdz/ *adv.* US term inward **1.** TOWARDS THE INSIDE towards the inside or centre of sth ○ *Several windows fell right inwards, through the weight of the snow against them.* **2.** TOWARDS THE MIND OR SPIRIT in, into, or towards the mind or spirit ○ *with thoughts turning inwards* ■ *npl.* INTERNAL ORGANS the internal organs of the body (*archaic or literary*)

inweave /in wéev/ (**-weaves, -weaving, -wove** /-wṓv/, **-woven** /-wṓv'n/) *vt.* to weave sth into a fabric or design

inwrap *vt.* = enwrap

inwreathe *vt.* = enwreathe

in-your-face /-yər-/, **in-yer-face** *adj.* (*slang*) **1.** FORCEFUL expressing opinions in a forceful, sometimes aggressive way ○ *Her approach is a little too in-your-face for my liking.* **2.** SO DIRECT AS TO BE UNIGNORABLE direct or provocative in a way that is designed to attract attention ○ *an in-your-face advertising campaign* [Late 20thC]

Io[1] *symbol.* ionium (*archaic*)

Io[2] /í ō/ *n.* **1.** MYTHOL WOMAN TURNED INTO HEIFER in Greek mythology, the daughter of the river god Inachus, turned into a heifer by the god Zeus to protect her from the jealousy of his wife Hera **2.** ASTRON LARGE MOON OF JUPITER a large natural satellite of Jupiter, discovered in 1601 by Galileo. It is 3,640 km/2,260 m in diameter and remarkable for being volcanically active. [Via Latin from Greek *Iō*]

I/O *abbr.* COMPUT input/output

IOC *n., abbr.* International Olympic Committee

iod- *prefix.* = iodo- (*used before vowels*)

iodate /í ə dayt/ *n.* a salt of iodic acid. The most important salts are sodium and potassium iodates, which are used in medicine. [Early 19thC. Formed from IODIC ACID.]

iodic /í óddik/ *adj.* relating to, containing, or caused by iodine, especially with a valency of five

iodic acid *n.* a colourless or white crystalline solid that is soluble in water and is used in analytical chemistry and as a disinfectant, deodorant, and antiseptic. Formula: HIO_3.

iodide /í ə díd/ *n.* a salt of hydriodic acid that contains the univalent anion ion I⁻. Metallic iodides such as silver, sodium, or potassium iodide are employed in photography and in iodized table salt.

iodinate /í ədi nayt/ (**-nates, -nating, -nated**) *vt.* to treat sth with iodine or an iodine compound, or add or substitute iodine atoms to or in an organic compound —**iodination** /í ədi náysh'n/ *n.*

iodine /í ə deen/ *n.* **1.** CHEM NONMETALLIC CRYSTALLINE HALOGEN ELEMENT a poisonous, dark grey to purple-black, lustrous, and nonmetallic crystalline element in the halogen family used as a germicide and antiseptic and in the preparation of dyes, pharmaceuticals, and tinctures. Radioactive isotopes of iodine are employed as tracers in medicine and industry and in the diagnosis and treatment of certain diseases. Symbol **I 2.** PHARM ANTISEPTIC a mixture of iodine and potassium iodide in alcohol employed as a topical antiseptic [Early 19thC. Formed from French *iode*, from Greek *iōdēs* 'violet-coloured', from *ion* 'violet'; from the purple vapour produced by heated iodine crystals.]

iodise *vt.* = iodize

iodism /í ədizəm/ *n.* a form of poisoning caused by the ingestion of iodine or an iodine compound (*dated*)

iodize /í ə díz/ (**-dizes, -dizing, -dized**), **iodise** (**-dises, -dising, -dised**) *vt.* to treat or combine sth with iodine or an iodine compound —**iodization** /í ə dī záysh'n/ *n.* —**iodizer** /í ə dízər/ *n.*

iodo- *prefix.* iodine ○ *iodophor* [From French *iode* (see IODINE)]

iodoform /í óddə fawrm/ *n.* a yellow volatile crystalline compound with a penetrating odour, used as an antiseptic and in ointments for minor skin diseases. Formula: CHI_3. [Mid-19thC. Coined from IODO- + FORMYL.]

iodophor /í óddə fawr/ *n.* a substance consisting of iodine and a surface-active agent in solution that slowly releases elemental iodine and can be used as a disinfectant [Mid-20thC. Coined from IODO- + -phor, variant of -PHORE.]

iodopsin /í ō dópsin/ *n.* a photosensitive violet pigment in the retinal cones of the eye [Mid-20thC. Coined from Greek *iōdēs* 'violet-coloured' (see IODINE) + OPSIN, on the model of *rhodopsin*.]

iodous /í óddəss/ *adj.* involving, containing, or caused by iodine

iolite /í ō līt/ *n.* = cordierite [Early 19thC. Coined from Greek *ion* 'violet' + -LITE.]

IOM *abbr.* Isle of Man

Io moth /í ō-/ *n.* a large yellow North American moth with a large spot resembling an eye on each of its hind wings. Stinging spines appear on its larvae. Latin name: *Automeris io*. [Named after Io, who was tormented by a gadfly; so called because of the stinging spines of the larvae]

ion /í ən, í ön/ *n.* an atom or group of atoms that has acquired an electric charge by losing or gaining one or more electrons [Mid-19thC. From Greek *ion*,

literally 'moving thing', from the present participle of *ienai* 'to go', from the movement of any ion towards the electrode of opposite charge.]

-ion *suffix.* **1.** action or process ○ *eruption* ○ *erosion* **2.** result of an action or process ○ *abrasion* **3.** condition, state ○ *elation* [Via Old French from the Latin stem -*ion*-]

Iona /í ṓnə/ low-lying island off the southwestern tip of Mull, in the Inner Hebrides, western Scotland. Area: 8.5 sq. km/3 sq. mi.

ion engine *n.* a theoretical rocket engine that derives its thrust from the electrostatic acceleration of a stream of positive ions. Because the engine does not provide enough thrust to escape the Earth's gravity, it could be used only in space.

Popperfoto

Eugene Ionesco

Ionesco /ée ə nésk ō/, **Eugène** (1909–94) Romanian-born French dramatist. He was one of the chief exponents of the Theatre of the Absurd. His plays include *The Chairs* (1952) and *Rhinoceros* (1959).

ion exchange *n.* the interchange of ions of the same charge between a solution and a solid in contact with it —**ion exchanger** *n.*

Ionia /í ṓni ə/ region of ancient western Asia Minor in the Aegean coast that was colonized by the Greeks around 1000 BC

Ionian /í ṓni ən/ *n.* MEMBER OF ANCIENT GREEK PEOPLE a member of an ancient Greek people who lived in Attica around the 10th century BC, before spreading out to many of the coastal regions and islands of the Aegean. They established important cultural and trading centres in their new settlements. ■ *adj.* OF IONIA relating to or typical of Ionia, or its people, dialect, or culture

Ionian Islands /í ṓni ən-/ group of seven Greek islands in the Ionian and Mediterranean seas. Corfu is the capital and largest city in the islands. Population: 191,003 (1991). Area: 2,307 sq. km/891 sq. mi.

Ionian mode *n.* the medieval musical mode corresponding to the modern C major scale

Ionian Sea part of the Mediterranean Sea, situated between the southeastern coast of Italy and western Greece

ionic /í ónnik/ *adj.* relating to or containing matter in the form of charged atoms or groups of atoms

Ionic *n.* **1.** LANG IONIAN DIALECT an extinct dialect of Ancient Greek, that was spoken mainly in Ionia **2.** POETRY METRICAL FOOT a metrical foot used in classical prosody, consisting of two long syllables followed by two short ones (**greater Ionic**) or two short syllables followed by two long ones (**lesser Ionic**) ■ *adj.* **1.** ARCHIT OF ARCHITECTURAL ORDER relating to or typical of the order of architecture characterized by fluted columns and capitals with spiral scroll-shaped ornaments **2.** = Ionian *adj.* **3.** POETRY IN IONIC METRE relating to, typical of, or expressed in Ionic metre [Early 17thC. From Greek *Iōnikos* 'of Ionia'.]

Ionic order *n.* one of the five classical orders of architecture, characterized by fluted columns and capitals with spiral scroll-shaped ornaments

ionic propulsion *n.* motion produced in reaction to the expulsion of a stream of accelerated ions

ion implantation *n.* the use of a stream of electrically accelerated ions to implant impurities on or near the surface of the substrate during the manufacture of a semiconductor

ionisation *n.* = ionization

ionise *vti.* = ionize

ionium /ī óni əm/ *n.* a radioactive isotope of thorium, originally thought to be a new element (*archaic*) Symbol **Io** [Early 20thC. Coined from ION + -IUM, in reference to the supposed new element's ionizing action.]

ionization /ī ə nī záysh'n/, **ionisation** *n.* a process in which an atom or molecule loses or gains electrons, acquiring an electric charge or changing an existing charge

ionization chamber *n.* a device used to detect and measure ionizing radiation, consisting of a gas-filled tube with electrodes at each end between which a voltage is maintained. Radiation that ionizes gas molecules in the tube causes a current between the electrodes, the strength of which is a function of the radiation's intensity.

ionize /ī ə nīz/ (-**izes**, -**izing**, -**ized**), **ionise** (-**ises**, -**ising**, -**ised**) *vti.* to undergo or cause sth to undergo ionization —**ionizable** *adj.*

ionone /ī ənön/ *n.* a yellow liquid smelling of violets that is extracted from plants and used in the production of perfumes. Formula: $C_{13}H_{20}O$. [Late 19thC. Coined from Greek *ion* 'violet' + -ONE.]

ionophore /ī ónnə fawr/ *n.* a chemical compound that increases the permeability of biological membranes to particular ions [Mid-20thC. Coined from ION + -PHORE.]

ionosphere /ī ónnə sfeer/ *n.* four layers of the Earth's upper atmosphere in which incoming ionizing radiation from space creates ions and free electrons that can reflect radio signals, enabling their transmission around the world [Early 20thC. Coined from ION + -SPHERE.] —**ionospheric** /ī ónnə sférrik/ *adj.* —**ionospherically** /-sférrikli/ *adv.*

ionospheric wave *n.* = sky wave

ion propulsion *n.* = ionic propulsion

ion rocket *n.* a rocket powered by an ion engine

iontophoresis /ī óntəfə reéssiss/ *n.* the movement of ions through biological material under the influence of an electric current [Early 20thC. Coined from Greek *iont-*, stem of *iōn*, present participle of *ienai* 'to go' (see ION) + -PHORESIS.] —**iontophoretic** /-fə réttik/ *adj.* —**iontophoretically** /-fə réttikli/ *adv.*

IOOF *abbr.* Independent Order of Oddfellows

iota /ī ótə/ *n.* **1.** 9TH LETTER OF GREEK ALPHABET the 9th letter of the Greek alphabet, represented in the English alphabet as 'i' or 'j'. See table at **alphabet 2.** SMALL AMOUNT a very small amount of sth ○ *anyone with an iota of sense* [Early 17thC. Via Latin from Greek *iōta*, from a Semitic source.]

iotacism /ī ótəsizəm/ *n.* the tendency in speakers of modern Greek to use the sound of iota in place of the sound of other vowel characters such as eta or upsilon [Mid-17thC. Via Latin from Greek *iōtakismos*, from *iōta* (see IOTA).]

IOU /ī ō yoo/ *n.* a written acknowledgment of a debt between the writer and sb else [Representation of 'I owe you']

IOW *abbr.* **1.** Isle of Wight **2.** in other words (*used in e-mail messages*)

Iowa

Iowa /ī əwə/ **1.** state in the north-central United States bordered by Illinois, Minnesota, Missouri, Nebraska, South Dakota, and Wisconsin. Capital: Des Moines. Population: 2,852,423 (1997). Area: 145,754

sq. km/56,276 sq. mi. **2.** river in Iowa that flows southeastwards and empties into the Mississippi River. Length: 530 km/330 mi.

Iowan /ī ō ən, ī ə wən/ *n.* sb who lives in or was born or brought up in the state of Iowa —**Iowan** *adj.*

IP *abbr.* **1.** image processing **2.** Internet protocol

IPA *abbr.* **1.** International Phonetic Alphabet **2.** Institute of Practitioners in Advertising

ipecacuanha /íppi kakyoo ánnə/, **ipecac** /íppi kak/ (*plural* -**cacuanhas** *or* -**cacs**) *n.* **1.** PLANTS S AMERICAN SHRUB a South American shrub, the roots of which are a source of a vomit-inducing medicine (**emetic**). Latin name: *Cephaelis ipecacuanha*. **2.** MED EMETIC an emetic made from the dried roots of the ipecacuanha plant [Early 17thC. Via Portuguese from Tupi *ipe-kaâ-guéne*, literally 'low plant causing vomit'.]

Iphigenia /ífiji nī ə, i fíjji-/ *n.* in Greek mythology, a daughter of Agamemnon. He was prepared to sacrifice her to Artemis in order to gain favourable winds for the Greek fleet to sail for Troy. Differing versions of the myth give different accounts of her fate.

IPL *abbr.* initial program load

IPO *abbr.* initial public offering

Ipoh /eépō/ city and capital of Perak State, western Malaysia. Population: 382,633 (1991).

ippon /i pón, íppon/ *n.* a winning point awarded in judo or karate for perfect technique [Mid-20thC. From Japanese.]

ipse dixit /ípsi díksit/ *n.* sth asserted dogmatically and without proof [Late 16thC. From Latin, 'he himself said it', translating Greek *autos epha*, originally used by Pythagoreans in reference to Pythagoras himself.]

ipsilateral /ípsi láttərəl/ *adj.* being on or affecting the same side of the body [Early 20thC. Alteration of *ipselateral*, from Latin *ipse* 'self, same' + LATERAL.] —**ipsilaterally** *adv.*

ipsissima verba /ip síssimə vúrbə/ *npl.* the precise words used in sth that is quoted [From Latin, 'the very words']

ipso facto /ípsō fáktō/ *adv.* as the result of a particular fact [From Latin, 'by the fact itself']

ipso jure /ípsō joóri/ *adv.* by reason of a particular law [From Latin, 'by the law itself']

Ipswich /ípswich/ **1.** town and administrative centre in Suffolk, England. Population: 114,100 (1995). **2.** city in Queensland, eastern Australia, just outside Brisbane. Population: 117,435 (1996).

IQ *n.* a measure of sb's intelligence, obtained through a series of aptitude tests concentrating on different aspects of intellectual functioning. An IQ score of 100 represents 'average' intelligence. Full form **intelligence quotient**

i.q. *abbr.* idem quod [Latin, 'the same as']

Iqbal /ík bal/, **Sir Muhammad** (1875–1938) Indian philosopher, poet, and political leader. He became president of the Muslim League in 1930, and his separatist political philosophy underpinned the eventual formation of Pakistan.

Iquique /ee keé kay/ seaport, city, and capital of Tarapacá Region, northern Chile, situated 209 km/130 mi. south of the Peruvian border. Population: 145,139 (1992).

Iquitos /ee keé toss/ city and river port in northeastern Peru, situated on the upper River Amazon, 2,040 km/1,268 mi. overland northeast of Lima. Population: 266,175 (1993).

Ir *symbol.* iridium

IR *abbr.* **1.** Inland Revenue **2.** COMPUT information retrieval **3.** infrared (radiation) **4.** Iran (*international vehicle registration*)

Ir. *abbr.* **1.** Ireland **2.** Irish

ir- *prefix.* = **in-**[1], **in-**[2] (*used before r*)

IRA[1] *n.* an organization of Irish nationalists originally set up to strive for an independent Ireland by force of arms and still dedicated to achieving the unity of the island of Ireland. Full form **Irish Republican Army**

IRA[2] *n. US* a plan in the United States that permits individuals to accumulate savings tax free until retirement. Full form **Individual Retirement Account**

iracund /írə kund/ *adj.* easily made angry (*literary*) [Early 19thC. From Latin *iracundus*, from *ira* 'anger' + -*cundus* 'inclined towards' (source of English *jocund*).] —**iracundity** /írə kúndəti/ *n.*

irade /i raádi/ *n.* a written decree of a Muslim ruler, especially, formerly, the Sultan of Turkey [Late 19thC. From Arabic *irādah* 'will, desire, wish'.]

Iran

Iran /i raán, i rán/ republic in southwestern Asia, formerly known abroad as Persia. Language: Farsi. Currency: Iranian rial. Capital: Tehran. Population: 67,540,002 (1997). Area: 1,648,000 sq. km/636,300 sq. mi. Official name **Islamic Republic of Iran**

Iran. *abbr.* Iranian

Iranian /i ráyni ən/ *n.* **1.** LANG LARGE SUBGROUP OF INDO-EUROPEAN LANGUAGES a group of languages spoken in the region northeast of the Persian Gulf. It is a subgroup of the Indo-Iranian branch of Indo-European, and includes Baluchi, Kurdish, and Farsi. About 70 million people speak an Iranian language. **2.** PEOPLES SB FROM IRAN sb who was born or brought up in Iran, or who is a citizen of Iran —**Iranian** *adj.*

Iran-Iraq War *n.* the war fought between Iran and Iraq that lasted from 1980 to 1988, following the invasion of border territory in Iran by Iraq

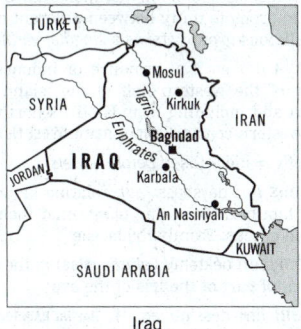
Iraq

Iraq /i raák, i rák/ republic in southwestern Asia, bordered by Turkey, Iran, Saudi Arabia, Kuwait, the Persian Gulf, Jordan, and Syria. Language: Arabic. Currency: Iraqi dinar. Capital: Baghdad. Population: 22,219,289 (1997). Area: 438,317 sq. km/169,235 sq. mi. Official name **Republic of Iraq**

Iraqi /i raáki, i ráki/ *n.* **1.** PEOPLES SB FROM IRAQ sb who was born or brought up in Iraq, or who is a citizen of Iraq **2.** LANG ARABIC DIALECT OF IRAQ the modern dialect of Arabic spoken in Iraq —**Iraqi** *adj.*

irascible /i rássəb'l/ *adj.* **1.** QUICK-TEMPERED easily provoked to anger or outbursts of temper **2.** SHOWING ANGER showing or typical of anger [Mid-16thC. Via French from Latin *irascibilis* 'quick to anger, irritable', from *irasci* 'to grow angry', from *ira* 'anger'.] —**irascibility** /i rássə bílləti/ *n.* —**irascibleness** /i rássəb'lnəss/ *n.* —**irascibly** *adv.*

irate /ī ráyt/ *adj.* **1.** VERY ANGRY feeling great anger **2.** INDICATING ANGER showing or typical of great anger [Mid-19thC. From Latin *iratus* 'enraged', past participle of *irasci* 'to grow angry'.] —**irately** *adv.* —**irateness** *n.*

Irawadi = **Irrawaddy**

IRBM *abbr.* intermediate-range ballistic missile

ire /īr/ *n.* a feeling or display of deep anger or fury (*literary*) [13thC. Via French from Latin *ira* 'anger', of uncertain origin.] —**ireful** *adj.*

WORD KEY: SYNONYMS

See Synonyms at **anger**.

Ire. *abbr.* Ireland

Ireland

Ireland /īrlənd/ **1.** island in northwestern Europe, in the North Atlantic Ocean, west of Great Britain. It comprises the Republic of Ireland and the British province of Northern Ireland. Area: 84,431 sq. km/32,599 sq. mi. **2.** republic occupying the southern, central, and northwestern parts of the island of Ireland. Language: English, Irish Gaelic. Currency: punt. Capital: Dublin. Population: 3,606,952 (1997). Area: 70,273 sq. km/27,133 sq. mi. Official name **Republic of Ireland**

Ireland, Northern ♦ Northern Ireland

Ireland, David (*b.* 1927) Australian novelist. His works include *The Unknown Industrial Prisoner* (1971).

irenic /ī reˈenik, ī rénnik/, **irenical** /ī reˈenik'l, ī rénnik'l/ *adj.* promoting or intended to promote peace (*literary*) [Mid-19thC. From Greek *eirēnikos* 'peaceable, peaceful', from *eirēnē* 'peace'.] —**irenically** *adv.*

irenicon *n.* = eirenicon

irenics /ī reˈeniks, ī rénn-/ *n.* a branch of theology that seeks to promote unity between different churches and religious groups (*takes a singular verb*)

Irian Jaya /írri ən jī ə/ province of Indonesia, consisting of the western half of the island of New Guinea and including islands off its northern and northwestern coasts. Former name **West New Guinea**

irid- *prefix.* = irido- (*used before vowels*)

iridaceous /írri dáyshəss/ *adj.* relating or belonging to the family of flowering plants that includes the iris and crocus. Family: Iridaceae.

iridectomy /írri déktəmi/ (*plural* -**mies**) *n.* the surgical removal of part of the iris of the eye

iridescent /írri déss'nt/ *adj.* **1.** HAVING RAINBOW COLOURS marked by or showing rainbow colours that appear to move and change as the angle at which they are seen changes **2.** LUSTROUS having a lustrous or brilliant appearance or quality —**iridescence** *n.* —**iridescently** *adv.*

iridic[1] /i ríddik, ī-/ *adj.* relating to, involving, or containing the element iridium [Mid-19thC. Formed from IRIDIUM.]

iridic[2] /i ríddik, ī-/ *adj.* relating to or typical of the iris of the eye [Late 19thC. Formed from IRID-, the stem of Iris (see IRIS).]

iridium /i ríddi əm, ī-/ *n.* a brittle silver-white metallic chemical element that forms hard corrosion-resistant alloys used in pen nibs, jewellery, watch and compass pivot bearings, surgical instruments, electrical contacts, and chemical crucibles. The international kilogram standard maintained in Paris is made of an alloy of 10 parts iridium and 90 parts platinum. Symbol **Ir** [Early 19thC. From modern Latin, formed from IRID-, from the rainbow colours of the metal when dissolved in hydrochloric acid.]

irido- *prefix.* **1.** iris ○ *iridotomy* ○ *iridaceous* **2.** rainbow ○ *iridescent* **3.** iridium ○ *iridosmine* [Via Latin from, ultimately, Greek *irid-*, the stem of *iris* (see IRIS)]

iridocyte *n.* a cell in the skin of fish and certain cephalopods that contains guanine and causes iridescence

iridology /írri dólləji/ *n.* a technique in alternative medicine by which diagnosis of various bodily disorders is claimed to be possible by examination of the fine structure of the iris of the eye —**iridologist** *n.*

iridosmine /írri dóss mīn/, **iridosmium** /-dózmi əm/ *n.* an ore and natural alloy of iridium and osmium in which the osmium content exceeds 35 per cent, with traces of platinum, rhodium, ruthenium, iron, and copper [Early 19thC. Blend of IRIDIUM and OSMIUM.]

iridotomy (*plural* -**mies**) *n.* a surgical operation in which the iris of the eye is cut into, nowadays using a laser

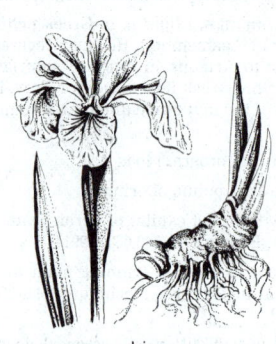

Iris

iris /írriss/ *n.* **1.** ANAT **PART OF EYE** the coloured part of the eye that consists of a muscular diaphragm surrounding the pupil and regulating the light entering the eye by expanding and contracting the pupil **2.** PLANTS **FLOWERING PLANT** a plant with long sword-shaped leaves and large brightly coloured flowers. Genus: *Iris*. **3.** METEOROL **RAINBOW** a rainbow (*literary*) **4.** COLOURS **RAINBOW SHOW OF COLOURS** a show of colours of various hues, like a rainbow **5.** PHOTOGRAPHY = **iris diaphragm** [15thC. Directly, or via modern Latin, from Greek *iris*, *Iris*, 'rainbow' (or the messenger-goddess personifying it), 'iris' (of the eye), 'iris' (the flower).]

iris diaphragm *n.* a diaphragm consisting of adjustable thin plates that control the size of an aperture, especially one used in a camera to control the amount of light allowed to enter

Irish /írish/ *adj.* **1.** OF IRELAND relating to or typical of Ireland, or its people or culture **2.** LANG OF IRISH GAELIC relating to the Irish Gaelic language **3.** LANGUAGE OF ENGLISH DIALECT OF IRELAND relating to the dialect of English spoken in Ireland ■ *npl.* PEOPLES **PEOPLE FROM IRELAND** people who were born or brought up in Ireland, or who have Irish citizenship ■ *n.* LANG = **Irish Gaelic** [13thC. Formed from *Ir-*, stem of Old English *Īras* 'inhabitants of Ireland', of uncertain origin: probably ultimately from Old Irish *Ériu* 'Ireland'.] —**Irishness** *n.*

Irish bull *n.* a statement that is incongruous and ludicrous (*offensive*) [*Irish* from the offensive stereotype of the Irish as foolish, and BULL[1]]

Irish coffee *n.* a hot drink of sweetened coffee containing Irish whiskey and topped with whipped cream

Irish elk *n.* any of various extinct giant large-antlered Eurasian deer of the Pleistocene epoch. Genus: *Megaloceros*.

Irish English *n.* the variety of English spoken in Ireland —**Irish English** *adj.*

WORD KEY: WORLD ENGLISH

Irish English is the English language as used in Ireland since at least the 16th century. For some observers, the terms *Irish English*, *Anglo-Irish*, and *Hiberno-English* mean much the same; for others, the term *Irish English* refers to English throughout Ireland, Anglo-Irish refers to a variety which originated among settlers from England (and has been especially associated with a Dublin élite), and Hiberno-English refers to usage markedly influenced by Irish Gaelic, although all commentators agree that it is difficult to draw a clear line between the various kinds of *Irish English*. Northern Irish

English is generally regarded as a distinct variety of *Irish English* (but is not usually contrasted with a 'Southern Irish English'). Within Northern Ireland, Ulster Scots derives from the settlement (or as it was called at the time, 'plantation') of Scottish Protestants in the North from the early 17th century onwards. *Irish English* is generally 'rhotic' (that is, *r* is pronounced in words such as *art*, *door*, and *worker*) and 'retroflex' (that is, with the tip of the tongue curled back and raised); the 'wh' in words like *why* and *what* is pronounced as 'hw', so that *whales* and *Wales* are clearly distinguished; words like *three* and *those* are commonly pronounced like 'tree' and 'dose' and words like *leave* and *tea* as 'lave' and 'tay'. There are distinctive grammatical forms influenced by Irish Gaelic. First, forms like these are used for emphasis and increased focus: 'It's a fine man he is','It was to help her I went', and 'It's himself was the best player'. Second is the use of *after* and -*ing* to mark an action just completed: 'She's after helping them this very morning'. The third is the omission of *yes* and *no* in answers: 'Did you come yesterday? – I did'; 'Can you see him now? – We can'. Vocabulary adapted from Gaelic includes the now internationally current *banshee* (from *bean sidhe* 'fairy woman'), *colleen* ('young woman', from *cailín*), *kitter* ('left-handed', from *citeóg*), *shillelagh* (a thick stick, from the town of the same name); and *whiskey* or *whisky* (both originally from Gaelic *uisge beatha* 'water of life').

Irish Gaelic *n.* an official language of the Republic of Ireland, spoken mainly in the western parts of the country. It is one of the Goidelic group of the Celtic branch of Indo-European. Irish Gaelic is spoken by about 5,000 people as a first language, with approximately a million others using it as a second language. —**Irish Gaelic** *adj.*

Irish harp *n.* a small diatonic harp constructed with a hollowed willow soundbox

Irishman /írishmən/ (*plural* -**men** /-mən/) *n.* a man who was born in or who lives in Ireland, or who is of Irish descent

Irish moss *n.* an edible red seaweed found on the coasts of Europe and North America, from which a complex carbohydrate food additive (**carrageenan**) is obtained. Latin name: *Chondrus crispus*.

Irish Republican Army *n.* full form of **IRA**

Irishry /írishri/ (*plural* -**ries**) *n.* the people of Ireland collectively (*takes a singular or plural verb*)

Irish Sea body of water situated between Great Britain and Ireland, connecting to the North Atlantic Ocean to the south through St George's Channel and to the north through the North Channel. Area: 103,600 sq. km/40,000 sq. mi.

Irish setter

Irish setter *n.* a setter with a silky reddish coat, originally bred in Ireland

Irish stew *n.* a stew of lamb or mutton, potatoes, and onions

Irish terrier *n.* a terrier with a wiry reddish coat, originally bred in Ireland

Irish water spaniel *n.* a spaniel with a dense curly liver-coloured coat, originally bred in Ireland. It is used in hunting waterfowl.

Irish whiskey *n.* whiskey made in Ireland, principally of barley

Irish wolfhound

Irish wolfhound n. a large powerful hound with a rough shaggy coat, belonging to an ancient breed originally developed in Ireland. The Irish wolfhound is the tallest breed of dog in the world.

Irishwoman /írish wŏŏmən/ (*plural* **-en** /-wimin/) n. a woman who was born in or who lives in Ireland, or who is of Irish descent

iritis /ī rītiss/ n. inflammation of the iris of the eye [Early 19thC. Coined from IRIS + -ITIS.] —**iritic** /ī ríttik/ adj.

irk /urk/ (**irks, irking, irked**) vt. to annoy sb slightly, especially by being tedious [14thC. Earliest sense 'to grow weary or vexed'; originally northern English; origin uncertain: perhaps from Old Norse yrkja 'to work'.]

─── **WORD KEY: SYNONYMS** ───
See Synonyms at **annoy** and **bother**.

irksome /úrksəm/ adj. slightly annoying, especially by being tedious —**irksomely** adv. —**irksomeness** n.

Irkutsk /ur kŏŏtsk, eer-/ city in southern Siberian Russia and capital of Irkutsk Oblast. It is situated on the River Angara, 72 km/45 mi. from the southwestern shore of Lake Baikal. Population: 639,000 (1992).

IRL abbr. **1.** Republic of Ireland (*international vehicle registration*) **2.** in real life (*used in e-mail messages*)

IRO abbr. **1.** Inland Revenue Office **2.** International Refugee Organization **3.** International Relief Organization

iroko /ə rŏkŏ/ (*plural* **-kos**) n. **1.** TREES AFRICAN TREE a hardwood tree of tropical Africa. Genus: *Chlorophora*. **2.** INDUST HARD AFRICAN WOOD the hard brown wood of the iroko tree, often used as a substitute for teak [Late 19thC. From Yoruba.]

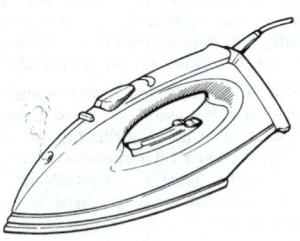

Iron

iron /ī ərn/ n. **1.** CHEM ELEM METALLIC ELEMENT a heavy magnetic malleable ductile lustrous silvery-white metallic element used for a variety of engineering and structural products. It is also present in very small quantities in the blood. It is the fourth most abundant element in the earth's crust and is believed to make up 80 per cent of the planet's core. Symbol **Fe 2.** HEATED TOOL any of various tools made of iron or steel, usually heated before and during use ○ *a soldering iron* **3.** HOUSEHOLD CLOTHES PRESSER a small, usually electrical, appliance with a handle and a flat metal base that is heated for use in pressing clothes and sometimes contains water to make steam **4.** GOLF METAL-HEADED GOLF CLUB any of various golf clubs with metal heads, differentiated by numbers that indicate different angles of the face and lengths of the shaft **5.** EQU = stirrup **6.** US TECH COMPUTER

HARDWARE computer hardware, especially older and larger mainframes (*slang*) ○ *a company with some big iron* **7.** HARSH CHARACTER a strong, unyielding, or hard aspect of sb's nature ■ **irons** npl. RESTRAINTS FOR THE ARMS OR LEGS manacles or fetters for restraining the arms or legs ■ adj. **1.** MADE OF IRON relating to or made of iron **2.** VERY STRONG very strong or hard **3.** TOUGH very robust or tough **4.** UNYIELDING very determined, unyielding, or cruel ■ v. (**irons, ironing, ironed**) **1.** HOUSEHOLD PRESS CLOTHES to press clothes or other fabrics with an iron to remove wrinkles **2.** vt. COVER WITH IRON to cover or clad sth with iron **3.** vt. CRIMINOL FETTER PRISONER to place fetters on a prisoner (*archaic*) [Old English īren, from a prehistoric Germanic word of uncertain origin: probably via Celtic from, ultimately, an Indo-European word that is also the ancestor of English ore] ◇ **have several irons in the fire** to be involved in several different activities at the same time ◇ **pump iron** to do weight-lifting exercises for bodybuilding or fitness (*slang*) ◇ **strike while the iron is hot** to act while circumstances are favourable to a successful outcome

iron out vt. **1.** SMOOTH STH to smooth away wrinkles in a garment or fabric using an iron **2.** SETTLE OR RESOLVE STH to settle a dispute or resolve a problem by removing difficulties

iron age n. in Greek and Roman mythology, an era regarded as the third and last step in humankind's degeneration from the golden age

Iron Age n. the period following the Bronze Age from about 1500 BC onwards in the Middle East, during which iron was increasingly used in making tools and weapons

ironbark /ī ərn baark/ n. any of several species of Australian eucalyptus trees noted for their hard rough bark, e.g. red ironbark. Latin name: *Eucalyptus sideroxylon*.

iron blue n. an insoluble compound used as a blue pigment in paint, ink, and paper dyeing, and in fertilizers. Formula: $Fe_7C_{18}N_{18} \cdot 10H_2O$.

ironbound /ī ərn bownd/ adj. **1.** DECORATED WITH IRON wrapped or decorated with iron bands **2.** HARSH stern or unyielding **3.** RUGGED edged or enclosed with rocks (*literary*) ○ *an ironbound coast*

ironclad /ī ərn klad/ adj. **1.** COVERED OR PROTECTED WITH IRON covered with iron, especially as a protection or armour **2.** STRONG strong, firm, or unyielding **3.** IRREFUTABLE not capable of being attacked or refuted ○ *an ironclad alibi* ■ n. ARMOURED SHIP a 19th-century wooden warship armoured with metal plates

Iron Cross n. the highest German military decoration, instituted in Prussia in 1813 and awarded during World Wars I and II

iron curtain n. an impenetrable barrier to understanding, awareness, or agreement

Iron Curtain n. the militarized border between the Communist bloc and western Europe during the Cold War, or the policy of isolation that prevented western and eastern Europeans from travelling or communicating freely. The Iron Curtain existed from the end of World War II until the fall of eastern European Communist governments between 1989 and 1991. ○ *'From Stettin in the Baltic to Trieste in the Adriatic, an iron curtain has descended across the continent.'* (Sir Winston Churchill, *Fulton, Missouri, Speech*; 1946)

iron grey adj. of a dark grey colour with a greenish hue —**iron grey** n.

iron hand n. strict, harsh, or despotic control —**ironhanded** /īrn hándid/ adj. —**ironhandedness** n.

iron horse n. a steam-powered railway locomotive (*dated*)

ironic /ī rónnik/, **ironical** /-ik'l/ adj. relating to, characterized by, using, or containing irony —**ironically** adv.

ironing /ī ərning/ n. **1.** PRESSING CLOTHES the act of pressing clothes or other fabrics to remove wrinkles **2.** CLOTHES clothes that have been ironed or have to be ironed

ironing board n. a covered, often padded board on legs on which clothes are ironed

ironize /ī ər nīz/ (**-izes, -izing, -ized**), **ironise** (**-ises, -ising, -ised**) v. **1.** vi. USE IRONY to use irony or be ironic **2.** vt. MAKE STH IRONIC to give sth an ironic tone, or make sth ironic in nature

iron lung n. an airtight metal cylinder encasing a patient up to the neck, formerly used to provide help in breathing by alternating air pressure within the cylinder

iron maiden n. a medieval instrument of torture consisting of a hinged box shaped like a human body and lined with spikes that impale sb placed inside as it is closed

iron man n. **1.** STRONG MAN a man of great physical strength and endurance **2.** ANZ, US MEN'S SPORTS COMPETITION an athletic competition for men held at a beach and including a variety of disciplines such as surfing, canoeing, swimming, and running

ironmonger /ī ərn mung gər/ n. UK sb who deals in tools and other articles made chiefly of metal —**ironmongery** n.

iron oxide n. any of the natural or synthetic compounds of iron and oxygen

iron pan n. a hard layer below the surface of sand or gravel in which iron salts from percolating water have precipitated, cementing the grains of the material together

iron pyrites n. = pyrite

iron rations npl. food designed to be used in an emergency, especially by military personnel. US term **iron ration**

ironside /ī ərn sīd/ (*plural* **-sides** /ī ərn sīdz/) n. a man of great physical strength or endurance

Ironside n. a nickname given to King Edmund II of England

ironsides n. = ironside

Ironsides /ī ərn sīdz/ npl. the cavalry regiment led by Oliver Cromwell in the English Civil War

ironstone /ī ərn stŏn/ n. **1.** GEOL IRON-BEARING SEDIMENTARY ROCK any sedimentary rock that contains a large amount of iron ore **2.** CERAMICS WHITE POTTERY a hard and durable variety of white pottery

ironware /ī ərn wair/ n. goods, especially kitchen utensils, made of iron

iron woman n. ANZ, US an athletic competition for women held at a beach and including a variety of disciplines such as surfing, canoeing, swimming, and running

ironwood /ī ərnwŏŏd/ (*plural* **-woods** *or* **-wood**) n. **1.** TREES TREE WITH HARD WOOD any of a range of trees that have very hard wood, e.g. the hornbeam **2.** INDUST HARD WOOD the very hard wood of an ironwood tree

ironwork /ī ərn wurk/ n. sth made of iron, e.g. a gate, especially when it is decorative

ironworker /ī ərn wurkər/ n. **1.** WORKER IN IRONWORKS sb employed in an ironworks **2.** MAKER OF IRONWORK sb who produces ironwork

ironworks /ī ərn wurks/ n. a factory where iron is smelted or large metal goods are made (*takes a singular verb*)

irony /ī rəni/ (*plural* **-nies**) n. **1.** HUMOUR BASED ON OPPOSITES a type of humour based on using words to suggest the opposite of their literal meaning **2.** STH HUMOROUS BASED ON CONTRADICTION sth said or written that uses sardonic humour **3.** INCONGRUITY incongruity between what actually happens and what might be expected to happen, especially when this disparity seems absurd or laughable **4.** INCONGRUOUS THING sth that happens that is incongruous with what might be expected to happen, especially when this seems absurd or laughable **5.** = dramatic irony **6.** = Socratic irony [Early 16thC. Via Latin *ironia* from Greek *eirōneia* 'pretended ignorance', formed from *eirōn* 'dissembler', of uncertain origin: perhaps formed from *eirein* 'to say'.]

Iroquoian /írrə kwóy ən/ n. **1.** LANG NATIVE N AMERICAN FAMILY OF LANGUAGES a family of Native North American languages spoken by Iroquois peoples of eastern North America. Its many languages include Mohawk, Seneca, Cherokee, and Huron. **2.** PEOPLES MEMBER OF NATIVE N AMERICAN PEOPLE a member of any of the Native North American peoples who speak an Iroquoian language —**Iroquoian** adj.

Iroquois /írrə kwoy/ (*plural* **-quois**) *n.* a member of a former confederacy of six Native North American peoples, the Mohawk, Oneida, Seneca, Onondaga, Cayuga, and Tuscarora. Originally settled along the Hudson River Valley, many Iroquois now live in urban areas. [Mid-17thC. Via French from Algonquian.] —**Iroquois** *adj.*

IRQ *abbr.* Iraq (*international vehicle registration*)

irradiant /i ráydi ənt/ *adj.* radiating light or shining brightly [Early 16thC. From Latin *irradiant-*, present participle stem of *irradiare* (see IRRADIATE).]

irradiate /i ráydi ayt/ (**-ates, -ating, -ated**) *vt.* **1.** EXPOSE STH TO RADIATION to expose sb or sth to or treat sb or sth with radiation or streams of particles **2.** PRESERVE FOOD to treat food with electromagnetic radiation to kill microorganisms and slow down the process of ripening and gradual deterioration or rotting **3.** LIGHT STH UP to make sth brighter by shining light onto it **4.** MAKE STH INTELLIGIBLE to make sth intellectually clear **5.** = **radiate** *v.* 4 [Early 17thC. From Latin *irradiat-*, past participle stem of *irradiare* 'to illumine, send out beams', ultimately from *radius* 'ray, beam'.] —**irradiative** /i ráydi ətiv/ *adj.* —**irradiator** /i ráydi aytər/ *n.*

irradiation /i ráydi áysh'n/ *n.* **1.** IRRADIATING the act of irradiating sb or sth, or the state of being irradiated **2.** LIGHTING EFFECT the visual effect by which a brightly lit thing appears larger against a dark background **3.** MED MEDICAL RADIATION the medical use of radiation, e.g. X-rays, gamma rays, or neutrons

irradicable /i ráddikəb'l/ *adj.* incapable of being eradicated [Early 18thC. From medieval Latin *irradicabilis*, from Latin *radicare*, 'to take root', wrongly understood as 'to root out'.] —**irradicably** *adv.*

irrational /i rásh'nəl/ *adj.* **1.** LACKING IN REASON contrary to or lacking in reason or logic **2.** LACKING IN LOGIC unable to think logically **3.** UNABLE TO THINK CLEARLY lacking the normal ability to think clearly, especially because of shock or injury to the brain **4.** MATH CONTAINING IRRATIONAL NUMBER used to describe an expression that contains an irrational number **5.** POETRY CONTAINING METRIC IRREGULARITY used to describe an irregularity in the metre of a classical poem, usually where there is a long foot instead of a short one ■ *n.* **1.** IRRATIONAL PERSON sb who is unable to think and reason clearly or logically **2.** MATH = **irrational number** [15thC. From Latin *irrationalis*, from *rationalis* 'endowed with reason' (see RATIONAL).] —**irrationality** /i rásh'n álləti/ *n.* —**irrationally** /i rásh'nəli/ *adv.* —**irrationalness** /-nəss/ *n.*

irrationalism /i rásh'nəlizəm/ *n.* **1.** ABSENCE OF REASON the state of lacking reason or logic **2.** BELIEF IN FEELINGS the belief that feelings and intuition are more important than reason —**irrationalistic** /i rásh'nə lístik/ *adj.*

irrational number *n.* any real number that cannot be expressed as the exact ratio of two integers, e.g. $\sqrt{2}$ and π

Irrawaddy /írrə wóddi/, **Irawadi** principal river of Myanmar (Burma). Length: 2,100 km/1,300 mi.

irreal /i réel/ *adj.* illusory or not actually existing —**irreality** /írri álləti/ *n.*

irreclaimable /írri kláyməb'l/ *adj.* not able to be reclaimed ○ *an irreclaimable desert* ○ *irreclaimable damages* —**irreclaimability** /írri kláymə bílləti/ *n.* —**irreclaimableness** /írri kláyməb'lnəss/ *n.* —**irreclaimably** *adv.*

irreconcilable /i rékən sīləb'l/ *adj.* **1.** INCOMPATIBLE not capable of being made to agree or coexist with sth else **2.** UNRESOLVABLE incapable of being resolved **3.** IMPLACABLE determinedly hostile and unwilling to accept compromise ■ *n.* **1.** IMPLACABLE PERSON sb who is determinedly hostile or will not accept compromise **2.** INCOMPATIBLE IDEA any of two or more ideas, beliefs, or principles that cannot be made to agree or coexist —**irreconcilability** /i rékən sīlə bílləti/ *n.* —**irreconcilableness** /i rékən sīləb'lnəss/ *n.* —**irreconcilably** /-bli/ *adv.*

irrecoverable /írri kúvvərəb'l/ *adj.* **1.** INCAPABLE OF BEING REGAINED impossible to get back or regain **2.** INCAPABLE OF BEING REPAIRED impossible to repair or remedy —**irrecoverableness** *n.* —**irrecoverably** *adv.*

irredeemable /írri déeməb'l/ *adj.* **1.** FIN UNABLE TO BE PAID OFF that cannot be ended by paying off the principal **2.** FIN NOT RECOVERABLE that cannot be made good once lost **3.** NOT REPAIRABLE impossible to repair **4.** FIN NOT CONVERTIBLE INTO COINS that cannot be converted into coins **5.** CHR INCAPABLE OF REDEMPTION refusing to reform and unable to be saved —**irredeemability** /írri déemə bílləti/ *n.* —**irredeemableness** /írri déeməb'lnəss/ *n.* —**irredeemably** *adv.*

irredentist /írri déntist/ *n.* a member of a group of people who support the return to their country of territories that used to belong to it but are now under foreign rule —**irredentism** *n.*

Irredentist *n.* a member of an Italian organization founded in 1878 that advocated the adding to Italy of Italian-speaking territories that were under foreign control at that time [Late 19thC. From Italian *irredentista*, from *(Italia) irredenta* 'unrecovered (Italy)', from *redento* 'redeemed', from Latin *redemptus* (see REDEMPTION).]

irreducible /írri dyóossəb'l/ *adj.* **1.** INCAPABLE OF BEING DECREASED not able to be made smaller **2.** INCAPABLE OF SIMPLIFICATION not able to be simplified or simplified further **3.** MATH IMPOSSIBLE TO FACTOR INTO LESSER POLYNOMIALS used to describe a polynomial that cannot be factored into two polynomials of a lesser degree **4.** MATH IMPOSSIBLE TO REDUCE TO RATIONAL EXPRESSION used to describe a radical that cannot be reduced to a rational expression —**irreducibility** /írri dyóossə bílləti/ *n.* —**irreducibleness** /írri dyóossəb'lnəss/ *n.* —**irreducibly** *adv.*

irreflexive /írri fléksiv/ *adj.* used to describe a relation in which, if a has the relation to b, then b does not have the relation to a

irreformable /írri fáwrməb'l/ *adj.* **1.** INCAPABLE OF REFORM incapable of being reformed **2.** INCAPABLE OF ALTERATION impossible to revise or alter —**irreformability** /írri fáwrmə bílləti/ *n.*

irrefragable /i réffrəgəb'l/ *adj.* not able to be refuted or disputed (*formal*) [Mid-16thC. From late Latin *irrefragabilis*, from Latin *refragari* 'to oppose, contest'.] —**irrefragability** /i réffrəgə bílləti/ *n.* —**irrefragableness** /i réffrəgəb'lnəss/ *n.* —**irrefragably** *adv.*

irrefrangible /írri fránjəb'l/ *adj.* **1.** INCAPABLE OF BEING DISOBEYED impossible to disobey or violate (*formal*) **2.** INCAPABLE OF BEING BROKEN impossible to break or smash (*formal*) **3.** PHYS INCAPABLE OF BEING REFRACTED used to describe visible light or other radiation that cannot be refracted —**irrefrangibility** /írri fránjə bílləti/ *n.* —**irrefrangibleness** /írri fránjəb'lnəss/ *n.* —**irrefrangibly** *adv.*

irrefutable /írri fyóotəb'l, i réffyòotəb'l/ *adj.* impossible to refute or disprove [Early 17thC. From late Latin *irrefutabilis*, from Latin *refutare* 'to refute'.] —**irrefutability** /írri fyóotə bílləti, i réffyòotə-/ *n.* —**irrefutableness** /írri fyóotəb'lnəss, i réffyòotə-/ *n.* —**irrefutably** *adv.*

irreg. *abbr.* irregular

irregardless /írri gáardləss/ *adv.* = **regardless** (*nonstandard*) [Early 20thC. Origin uncertain: probably a blend of IRRESPECTIVE and REGARDLESS.]

WORD KEY: USAGE

Nonstandard usage: A moment's thought will reveal that since the prefix *ir-* means 'not' (as it does in *irrespective*), and the suffix *-less* means 'without', ***irregardless*** is an illogical double negative. As such it is to be avoided, in favour of *irrespective* or *regardless.*

irregular /i réggyòolər/ *adj.* **1.** NOT OF UNIFORM APPEARANCE not even, uniform, or symmetrical in appearance **2.** OCCURRING AT ODD INTERVALS OF TIME not occurring at equally spaced intervals of time **3.** NONCONFORMING not conforming to common practices **4.** BEHAVING UNACCEPTABLY not conforming to accepted rules or standards of behaviour **5.** MIL UNOFFICIAL not forming part of an official military body **6.** GRAM NOT FORMED BY USUAL GRAMMATICAL RULES not following the usual rules of word formation **7.** MED CONSTIPATED not having a regular daily bowel movement (*used euphemistically*) **8.** BOT HAVING ASYMMETRICAL PARTS not having symmetrical parts ■ *n.* MIL SOLDIER NOT PART OF REGULAR FORCES a soldier who is not part of of an official military body [15thC. Via Old French *irreguler* from medieval Latin *irregularis* 'breaking a rule', from *regularis* 'of a rule' (see REGULAR).] —**irregularly** *adv.*

irregularity /i réggyòo lárrəti/ (*plural* **-ties**) *n.* **1.** BEING IRREGULAR the state of being irregular **2.** IRREGULAR THING sth irregular, e.g. a bump in a road **3.** UNAUTHORIZED THING sth unauthorized or unacceptable by usual standards

irrelative /i réllətiv/ *adj.* **1.** NOT CONNECTED not related or connected **2.** NOT APPLICABLE not relevant

irrelevant /i rélləvənt/ *adj.* not relevant or important —**irrelevance** *n.* —**irrelevancy** *n.* —**irrelevantly** *adv.*

irreligious /írri líjjəss/ *adj.* **1.** LACKING FAITH lacking in any religious faith **2.** AGAINST RELIGION opposed to religion —**irreligiously** *adv.* —**irreligiousness** *n.*

irremeable /i réem' əb'l/ *adj.* not allowing any possibility of return (*archaic or literary*) [Late 16thC. From Latin *irremeabilis*, from *remeare* 'to return'.] —**irremeably** *adv.*

irremediable /írri méedi əb'l/ *adj.* impossible to remedy or put right [Mid-16thC. From late Latin *irremediabilis* 'incurable', from *remediare* 'to cure'.] —**irremediableness** *n.* —**irremediably** *adv.*

irremissible /írri míssəb'l/ *adj.* **1.** UNPARDONABLE not able to be pardoned or excused **2.** OBLIGATORY not able to be avoided or postponed [15thC. Directly or via French from ecclesiastical Latin *irremissibilis* 'unpardonable', from Latin *remiss-*, past participle stem of *remittere* 'to forgive' (see REMISSION).] —**irremissibility** /írri míssə bílləti/ *n.* —**irremissibleness** /írri míssəb'lnəss/ *n.* —**irremissibly** *adv.*

irremovable /írri móovəb'l/ *adj.* incapable of being removed —**irremovability** /írri móovə bílləti/ *n.* —**irremovableness** /írri móovəb'lnəss/ *n.* —**irremovably** *adv.*

irreparable /i réppərəb'l/ *adj.* not able to be repaired or put right ○ *did irreparable damage to the computer* [15thC. Directly or via Old French from Latin *irreparabilis* 'not to be recovered', from *reparare* 'to recover' (source of *repair*).] —**irreparability** /i réppərə bílləti/ *n.* —**irreparableness** /i réppərəb'lnəss/ *n.* —**irreparably** *adv.*

irrepealable /írri péeləb'l/ *adj.* not able to be repealed (*formal*) —**irrepealability** /írri péelə bílləti/ *n.* —**irrepealableness** /írri péeləb'lnəss/ *n.* —**irrepealably** *adv.*

irreplaceable /írri pláyssəb'l/ *adj.* not able to be replaced —**irreplaceability** /írri pláyssə bílləti/ *n.* —**irreplaceableness** /írri pláyssəb'lnəss/ *n.* —**irreplaceably** *adv.*

irrepressible /írri préssəb'l/ *adj.* not able to be controlled ○ *irrepressible high spirits* —**irrepressibility** /írri préssə bílləti/ *n.* —**irrepressibleness** /írri préssəb'lnəss/ *n.* —**irrepressibly** /-bli/ *adv.*

irreproachable /írri próchəb'l/ *adj.* not incurring any reproach or criticism [Mid-17thC. From French *irréprochable*, from *réprochable* 'reproachable'.] —**irreproachability** /írri próchə bílləti/ *n.* —**irreproachableness** /írri próchəb'lnəss/ *n.* —**irreproachably** /-bli/ *adv.*

irresistible /írri zístəb'l/ *adj.* **1.** OVERPOWERING not able to be resisted or successfully opposed **2.** VERY DESIRABLE so desirable as to be very difficult to resist [Late 16thC. From medieval Latin *irresistibilis*, from Latin *resistere* 'to oppose, resist'.] —**irresistibility** /írri zístə bílləti/ *n.* —**irresistibleness** /írri zístəb'lnəss/ *n.* —**irresistibly** /-bli/ *adv.*

irresoluble /írri zóllyòob'l/ *adj.* incapable of being solved, reconciled, or explained [Mid-17thC. From Latin *irresolubilis* 'indissoluble', from *resolvere* 'to melt, thaw, dissolve'.] —**irresolubility** /írri zóllyòo bílləti/ *n.* —**irresolubly** /írri zóllyòobli/ *adv.*

irresolute /i rézzə loot/ *adj.* unsure and unable to take decisions —**irresolutely** *adv.* —**irresoluteness** *n.* —**irresolution** /i rézzə lóosh'n/ *n.*

irresolvable /írri zólvəb'l/ *adj.* **1.** IMPOSSIBLE TO RESOLVE INTO COMPONENT PARTS not able to be broken down into different parts **2.** INCAPABLE OF SOLUTION not able to be solved —**irresolvability** /írri zólvə bílləti/ *n.* —**irresolvableness** /írri zólvəb'lnəss/ *n.* —**irresolvably** /-bli/ *adv.*

irrespective /írri spéktiv/ *adv.* in spite of everything (*informal*) —**irrespectively** *adv.* ◇ **irrespective of** without consideration or regardless of

WORD KEY: USAGE

See Usage note at ***irregardless.***

irresponsible /írri spónssəb'l/ adj. 1. NOT CARING not having or showing any care for the consequences of personal actions 2. LAW INCAPABLE OF RESPONSIBILITY not capable of assuming responsibility 3. NOT ACCOUNTABLE not answerable to a higher authority (archaic) —**irresponsibility** /írri spónssə bílləti/ n. —**irresponsibleness** /írri spónssəb'lnəss/ n. —**irresponsibly** /-bli/ adv.

irresponsive /írri spónssiv/ adj. not responding quickly or favourably —**irresponsively** adv. —**irresponsiveness** n.

irretrievable /írri treévəb'l/ adj. 1. INCAPABLE OF RECOVERY impossible to find or recover 2. INCAPABLE OF REPAIR impossible to repair or put right —**irretrievability** /írri treévə bílləti/ n. —**irretrievableness** /írri treévəb'lnəss/ n. —**irretrievably** /-bli/ adv.

irreverence /i révvərənss/ n. 1. DISRESPECT lack of respect or veneration 2. DISRESPECTFUL THING sth said or done that is disrespectful

irreverent /i révvərənt/ adj. lacking in respect [Mid-16thC. From Latin irreverent-, from the present participle stem of revereri 'to revere, respect' (see REVERE).] —**irreverently** adv.

irreversible /írri vúrssəb'l/ adj. impossible to reverse or undo —**irreversibility** /írri vúrssə bílləti/ n. —**irreversibleness** /írri vúrssəb'lnəss/ n. —**irreversibly** /-bli/ adv.

irrevocable /i révvəkəb'l/ adj. not able to be revoked, undone, or changed [14thC. Directly or via French irrévocable from Latin irrevocabilis 'that cannot be recalled or altered', from revocare 'to recall', later 'retract' (see REVOKE).] —**irrevocability** /i révvəkə bílləti/ n. —**irrevocableness** /i révvək-/ n. —**irrevocably** /-bli/ adv.

irrigate /írri gayt/ (-gates, -gating, -gated) vt. 1. AGRIC SUPPLY AREA WITH WATER to bring a supply of water to a dry area, especially in order to help crops to grow 2. MED WASH STH OUT to make water or liquid medication flow through or over a body part or wound 3. REFRESH STH to make sth fresh [Early 17thC. From Latin irrigat-, past participle stem of irrigare, literally 'to water in', from rigare 'to water'.] —**irrigable** /írrigəb'l/ adj. —**irrigation** /írri gáysh'n/ n. —**irrigational** /-gáysh'nəl/ adj. —**irrigative** /írrigətiv/ adj. —**irrigator** /-gaytər/ n.

irritable /írritəb'l/ adj. 1. EASILY ANNOYED easily annoyed or exasperated 2. MED SENSITIVE extremely sensitive, especially to inflammation 3. BIOL RESPONSIVE TO STIMULI used to describe an organism that is able to respond to stimuli [Mid-17thC. From Latin irritabilis 'easily enraged', from irritare 'to provoke, aggravate'.] —**irritability** /írritə bílləti/ n. —**irritableness** /írritəb'lnəss/ n. —**irritably** /-bli/ adv.

irritable bowel syndrome n. a condition of the bowel in which there is recurrent pain with constipation or diarrhoea or alternating attacks of these

irritant /írritənt/ adj. CAUSING IRRITATION causing irritation, especially physical irritation ■ n. ANNOYANCE sth that causes irritation [Early 17thC. From Latin irritant-, present participle stem of irritare 'to provoke, aggravate'.] —**irritancy** n.

irritate /írri tayt/ (-tates, -tating, -tated) v. 1. vti. ANNOY SB to cause sb to feel annoyance or exasperation, or cause annoyance or exasperation 2. vt. MED INFLAME BODY PART to stimulate a body part excessively, causing a painful reaction, e.g. inflammation 3. vt. BIOL STIMULATE ORGANISM to stimulate an organism so as to provoke a response [Mid-16thC. From Latin irritat-, past participle stem of irritare 'to provoke, aggravate'.] —**irritating** adj. —**irritatingly** adv. —**irritative** adj. —**irritator** n.

———— WORD KEY: SYNONYMS ————
See Synonyms at **annoy**.

irritation /írri táysh'n/ n. 1. ANNOYANCE a feeling of annoyance or exasperation 2. ACT OF ANNOYING the act of causing annoyance or exasperation 3. SB OR STH ANNOYING sth who or sb that causes annoyance or exasperation 4. MED REACTION TO IRRITANT a painful reaction, especially an inflammation, caused by an irritant 5. MED INFLAMING the act of causing a painful reaction, especially an inflammation

irrupt /i rúpt/ (-rupts, -rupting, -rupted) vi. 1. ENTER ABRUPTLY to enter suddenly or violently 2. INCREASE QUICKLY

to increase suddenly and rapidly, e.g. in number [Mid-19thC. From Latin irrupt-, past participle stem of irrumpere 'to break into a place', from rumpere 'to break' (source of English rupture).] —**irruption** /i rúpsh'n/ n.

irruptive /i rúptiv/ adj. 1. BREAKING IN entering suddenly, or likely to enter suddenly 2. GEOL INJECTED INTO ROCK used to describe igneous rock that is injected forcibly into pre-existing rock formations —**irruptively** adv.

IRS abbr. Internal Revenue Service

Irtysh /ir tísh/ ♦ **Ob'**

Irving /úrving/, **Sir Henry** (1838–1905) British actor and theatrical manager. He was known for his Shakespearian roles, and for his 24-year acting partnership with Ellen Terry. Born **John Henry Brodribb**

Cook Neilson
John Irving

Irving, John (b. 1942) US novelist. His works include *The World According to Garp* (1978) and *The Hotel New Hampshire* (1981).

is 3rd person present singular of **be**

IS abbr. 1. COMPUT information services 2. Iceland (international vehicle registration)

is. abbr. 1. island 2. isle

Is. abbr. 1. BIBLE Isaiah 2. GEOG Island (used in place-names) 3. GEOG Isle (used in placenames)

is- prefix. = iso- (used before vowels)

ISA /íssə/ abbr. 1. individual savings account 2. International Standard Atmosphere

Isa. abbr. BIBLE Isaiah

Isaac n. in the Bible, the son of Abraham and Sarah. Offered by his father as a sacrifice to God, he was saved at the last moment by divine intervention. He was the father of Jacob and Esau. (Genesis 21–28)

Isabella I /ízzə béllə/, **Queen of Castile and León** (1451–1504). The heir to the crown of Castile and León, she married Ferdinand of Aragón (1469), bringing about the unification of Spain. As queen of Castile and León (1474–1504), she supported the Inquisition, expelled the Jews from Spain, and defeated Granada, the last Moorish kingdom in Spain. She sponsored Christopher Columbus's voyages. Known as **Isabella the Catholic**

Isabella II, **Queen of Spain** (1830–1904). She ruled from 1833 until she was deposed in 1868. Her reign was marked by political turmoil and insurrection.

Isaiah /ī zí ə/ n. 1. HEBREW PROPHET a Hebrew prophet who lived in the latter half of the 8th century BC. He was the earliest of the major prophets. 2. BOOK IN BIBLE a book of the Bible that contains prophecies and apocalyptic material. It is traditionally thought to have been written by Isaiah. See table at **Bible**

isalobar /ī sállə baar/ n. a contour line on a weather chart joining places where equal changes in atmospheric pressure occurred during a given time interval [Early 20thC. Coined from IS(O)- + ALLO- + Greek baros 'weight', on the model of ISOBAR.]

isatin /íssətin/ n. a water-soluble compound related to indigo and indole that crystallizes as orange needles and is used in the manufacture of vat dyes. Formula: $C_6H_5NO_2$. [Mid-19thC. Coined from Greek isatis 'woad' + -IN.] —**isatinic** /íssə tínnik/ adj.

ISBN abbr. International Standard Book Number

ischaemia /i skeémi ə/, **ischemia** n. an inadequate supply of blood to a part of the body, caused by

partial or total blockage of an artery —**ischaemic** adj.

Ischia /íski ə/ island in west-central Italy, situated in the Tyrrhenian Sea between the Gulf of Gaeta and the Bay of Naples. Its highest point is Mount Epomeo, 789 m/2,589 ft. Population: 17,600 (1990). Area: 47 sq. km/18 sq. mi.

ischium /íski əm/ (plural **-a** /-ə/) n. the lowest and rearmost of the three bones that make up each half of the pelvis [Early 17thC. Via Latin from Greek iskhion 'hip joint'.] —**ischial** adj.

ISD abbr. international subscriber dialling

ISDN n. a digital telephone network that can transmit both voice and data messages. Full form **Integrated Services Digital Network**

ISE abbr. International Stock Exchange

-ise suffix. = -ize

isentrope /íssentrōp/ n. a line on a graph or chart linking points of equal entropy [Back-formation from ISENTROPIC]

isentropic /íssen tróppik/ adj. 1. HAVING CONSTANT ENTROPY used to describe a reaction or process that takes place without a change in entropy 2. OF ISENTROPE relating to an isentrope —**isentropically** adv.

Iseult n. ♦ **Tristan**

-ish suffix. 1. characteristic of, like, tending to ○ churlish ○ babyish ○ bookish 2. of or relating to, from ○ Gaulish 3. somewhat, approximately ○ bluish ○ latish [Old English -isc, of prehistoric Germanic origin]

Isherwood /íshərwŏŏd/, **Christopher** (1904–86) British writer. He described prewar Berlin in two volumes of short stories, *Mr Norris Changes Trains* (1935) and *Goodbye to Berlin* (1939). Full name **Christopher William Bradshaw Isherwood**

Ishiguro /íshi gŏŏr ō/, **Kazuo** (b. 1954) Japanese-born British novelist. He won the Booker Prize for *Remains of the Day* (1989).

Ishmael /ísh mayl/ n. 1. OUTCAST IN BIBLE in the Bible, the son of Abraham, expelled into the desert after the birth of his brother Isaac, the forebear of twelve desert tribes. Muslims regard themselves as his descendants. (Genesis 16–21) 2. OUTCAST an outcast (literary)

Ishmaelite /íshmi ə līt/ n. 1. DESCENDANT OF ISHMAEL a descendant of Abraham's son Ishmael 2. = **Ishmael** n. 2 (literary) —**Ishmaelitish** adj. —**Ishmaelitism** n.

Ishtar /ísh taar/ n. in Babylonian and Assyrian mythology, the queen of heaven and goddess of fertility. Tammuz was her consort. She was worshipped throughout the Middle East under various names, including the Phoenician Astarte.

Isidore (of Seville) /ízzə dawr əv sə víl/, **St** (560?–636) Spanish churchman, theologian, and encyclopedist. He became archbishop of Seville in around 600, and is known for his encyclopedic reference work *Etymologiae*.

isinglass /ízing glaass/ n. 1. INDUST GELATIN USED IN ADHESIVES a transparent or translucent gelatin made from the air bladders of various fish, especially the sturgeon, and used as a clarifying agent and in adhesives and jellies 2. GEOL mica [Mid-16thC. By folk etymology from obsolete early Dutch huysenblas 'sturgeon's bladder' (from huysen 'sturgeon' + blas 'bladder'), applied to the bladder's gelatinous product.]

Isis[1] /íssiss/ n. in Egyptian mythology, the goddess of fertility, generally depicted wearing a cow's horns bearing a golden disc representing the sun. She was the wife of her brother Osiris and the mother of Horus.

Isis[2] /íssiss/ alternative name for the River Thames around Oxford, England

Iskenderun /iss kéndə roon/, **Iskenderon** city in southern Turkey, on the southeastern shore of the Gulf of Iskenderun, situated approximately 96 km/60 mi. southeast of Adana. Population: 154,807 (1990).

isl. abbr. 1. island 2. isle

Islam /íz laam, íss-/ n. 1. MUSLIM RELIGION the religion of Muslims, based upon the teachings of Muhammad during the 7th century and now the second largest of the great religions in number of believers 2.

MUSLIM WORLD Muslim people, their culture, or their countries considered collectively [Early 17thC. From Arabic *islām*, literally 'submission (to God)', from the base of *aslāma* 'he surrendered' (source of English *Muslim* and *salaam* 'peace').] —**Islamic** /iz lámmik, iss-/ *adj.*

Islamabad /iz lámməbad/, **Islāmābād** city and capital of Pakistan, situated northeast of Rawalpindi. Population: 204,364 (1981).

Islamise *vt.* = **Islamize**

Islamism /ízz-, ísslə-/ *n.* = **Islam** *n.* 1

Islamize /ízzlə mīz, ísslə-/ (**-izes, -izing, -ized**), **Islamise** (**-ises, -ising, -ised**) *vt.* **1.** CONVERT TO ISLAM to convert people or countries to Islam **2.** MAKE SUBJECT TO ISLAMIC LAW to cause people, institutions, or countries to follow Islamic law —**Islamization** /ízzlə mī záysh'n, ísslə-/ *n.*

island /īlənd/ *n.* **1.** GEOG LAND SURROUNDED BY WATER an area of land, smaller than a continent, that is completely surrounded by water (*often used in placenames*) **2.** STH LIKE AN ISLAND sth that is like an island because it is isolated or surrounded by sth different ○ *'No man is an island, entire of itself.'* (John Donne, *Devotions upon Emergent Occasions*; 1624) **3.** ANAT ISOLATED BODY PART a body part or group of cells that is different in construction from its surroundings ■ *vt.* (**-lands, -landing, -landed**) **1.** MAKE STH INTO AN ISLAND to form sth into an island **2.** ISOLATE SB to cause sb to feel isolated, e.g. from contact with peers or colleagues **3.** SET WITH ISLANDS to provide a stretch of water with islands (*literary*) [Old English *īegland*, from *īeg* 'island' (ultimately from an Indo-European word meaning 'water') + LAND]

WORD KEY: ORIGIN

Despite their similarity, ***island*** and *isle* have completely different origins. ***Island*** goes back to Old English, whereas *isle* comes from Latin *insula*, meaning 'island'. The resemblance is due to a 16th-century change in the spelling of ***island*** under the influence of the semantically close *isle*.

island arc *n.* an arc-shaped chain of islands, usually found in an area of volcanic or seismic activity

islander /īləndər/ *n.* sb who lives on an island

island-hop *vi.* to travel from island to island within the same chain, especially as part of a holiday (*informal*)

Islands of the Blessed *npl.* MYTHOL = **Hesperides**

Islay /īlə, ī lay/ the southernmost island of the Inner Hebrides, western Scotland. Area: 609 sq. km/235 sq. mi.

isle /īl/ *n.* an island, often a small one (*literary*) [13thC. From Old French *ile* (the variant *isle* later influenced the English word), from Latin *insula* (source of English *insulate* and *peninsula*).]

Isle of Man ◆ **Man, Isle of**

Isle of Wight ◆ **Wight, Isle of**

islet /īlət/ *n.* a small isle or island

islets of Langerhans /-lángər hanss/ *npl.* clusters of endocrine cells found in the pancreas that secrete insulin and glucagon

Islip /ízlip/ **1.** village in Oxfordshire, central England, approximately 10 km/6 mi. north of Oxford **2.** town in Suffolk County, southeastern New York, situated on Long Island. Population: 299,587 (1994).

ism /ízzəm/ (*plural* **isms**) *n.* a movement, doctrine, or system of belief (*informal*) [Late 17thC. From -ISM.]

-ism *suffix.* **1.** action, process ○ *mesmerism* ○ *volcanism* **2.** characteristic behaviour or manner ○ *despotism* **3.** state, condition ○ *conservatism* ○ *gangsterism* **4.** abnormal state ○ *caffeinism* **5.** doctrine, system of beliefs ○ *defeatism* ○ *Calvinism* **6.** prejudice ○ *sexism* **7.** distinctive feature or trait ○ *Southernism* ○ *vulgarism* [Via Old French *-isme* and Latin *-ismus* from Greek *-ismos*]

Ismaili /iz maa éeli/ *n.* a member of a branch of Shiite Muslims whose members believe that Ismail, son of the sixth imam, was the true seventh imam [Mid-19thC. From Arabic, formed from the proper name *'Ismā'īl.*]

Ismailiyya /ízmə éeli ə/ city in northeastern Egypt, situated on Lake Timsah. It is the halfway station on the Suez Canal. Population: 255,000 (1992).

isn't /ízz'nt/ *contr.* is not ○ *It isn't ready yet.*

ISO *abbr.* **1.** Imperial Service Order **2.** International Standards Organization

iso- *prefix.* **1.** equal, uniform ○ *isoelectric* ○ *isogloss* **2.** isomeric ○ *isooctane* **3.** of or for different members of the same species ○ *isoagglutination* [From Greek *isos* 'equal', of unknown origin]

isoagglutination /īssō ə glooti náysh'n/ *n.* the clumping together (**agglutination**) of red blood cells in one individual induced by antibodies in the serum of another individual of the same species —**isoagglutinative** /-ə glóotinətiv/ *adj.*

isoagglutinin /īssō ə glóotinin/ *n.* an antibody from one individual that causes the clumping together (**agglutination**) of red blood cells in another individual of the same species but of a different blood group

isobar /īssō baar/ *n.* **1.** METEOROL LINE SHOWING WEATHER PATTERNS a line drawn on a weather map that connects places with equal atmospheric pressure. Isobars are often used collectively to indicate the movement or formation of weather systems. **2.** PHYS ATOMS WITH THE SAME MASS NUMBER one of two or more atoms or elements having the same mass number but different atomic numbers [Mid-19thC. From Greek *isobaros*, literally 'of equal weight'.] —**isobarism** *n.*

isobaric /īssō bárrik/ *adj.* **1.** WITH CONSTANT ATMOSPHERIC PRESSURE having constant or equal atmospheric pressure **2.** OF ISOBARS relating to isobars

isobaric spin *n.* PHYS = **isospin**

isobath /īssō bath/ *n.* a line on a map of the sea that connects points that are at the same depth [Late 19thC. Coined from ISO- + Greek *bathos* 'depth'.] —**isobathic** /īssō báthik/ *adj.*

isobutane /īssō byóo tayn/ *n.* a colourless gaseous hydrocarbon that is an isomer of butane and is used especially as a fuel and refrigerant. Formula: C_4H_{10}.

isocheim /īssō kīm/, **isochime** *n.* a line on a weather map connecting places that have the same average temperature in winter [Mid-19thC. Coined from ISO- + Greek *kheima* 'winter weather'.] —**isocheimal** /īssō kīm'l/ *adj.* —**isocheimenal** /-kīmən'l/ *adj.*

isochromatic /īssōkrō máttik/ *adj.* **1.** = **orthochromatic** **2.** WITH EQUAL COLOUR OR WAVELENGTH having the same colour or wavelength of light

isochronous /ī sókrənəss/, **isochronal** /-krən'l/ *adj.* **1.** WITH EQUAL FREQUENCY having the same frequency or periodicity **2.** MEASURED AT OR LASTING THE SAME TIME measured or occurring at the same time, or lasting for the same length of time —**isochronously** *adv.*

isochroous /ī sókrō əss/ *adj.* having the same colour throughout [Mid-19thC. Coined from ISO- + Greek *khros* 'colour'.]

isoclinal /īssō klīn'l/ *adj.* **1.** WITH THE SAME SLOPE having the same inclination or slope **2.** GEOL HAVING PARALLEL SIDES having the sides of a geological fold parallel to one another ■ *n.* **1.** = **isocline** **2.** = **isoclinic line**

isocline /īssō klīn/ *n.* **1.** FOLD OF ROCK STRATA a geological fold with rock beds that slope in the same direction **2.** = **isoclinic line** [Late 19thC. From Greek *isoklinēs* 'equally balanced', literally 'leaning equally', from *klinein* 'to lean'.]

isoclinic *adj.* = **isoclinal**

isoclinic line *n.* a line on a map connecting points on the Earth's surface that have the same magnetic dip

isocyanate /īssō sī ə nayt/ *n.* a chemical compound used in resins and adhesives, containing the chemical group -NCO

isocyanide /īssō sī ə nīd/ *n.* a colourless liquid with a very unpleasant odour that contains the chemical group -NC

isodiametric /īssō dī ə méttrik/ *adj.* with diameters or axes of equal length

isodose /īssōdōss/ *n.* a dose of radiation of equal intensity applied to more than one part of the body as a medical treatment

isodynamic /īssō dī námmik/ *adj.* **1.** WITH EQUAL STRENGTH having the same strength or intensity **2.** SHOWING EQUAL MAGNETIC INTENSITY connecting points on a map of the Earth's surface that have the same magnetic intensity [Mid-19thC. Formed from Greek *isodunamos*, literally 'of equal power' + -IC.]

isoelectric /īssō i léktrik/ *adj.* having exactly the same electric potential

isoelectronic /īssō i lek trónnik, -éilek-/ *adj.* with the same number of electrons or the same outer atomic structure —**isoelectronically** *adv.*

isoenzyme /īssō én zīm/ *n.* = **isozyme** —**isoenzymatic** /īssō en zī máttik/ *adj.* —**isoenzymic** /īssō en zímmik/ *adj.*

isogamete /īssō gámmeet/ *n.* a gamete physically identical to another with which it unites to form a zygote —**isogametic** /īssōgə méttik/ *adj.*

isogamy /ī sóggəmi/ *n.* the fusion of isogametes in some algae and fungi during reproduction

isogeneic /īssōjə née ik/ *adj.* = **syngeneic** [Mid-20thC. Alteration of ISOGENIC.]

isogenic /īssō jénnik/ *adj.* having identical genes ○ *an isogenic line* [Mid-20thC. Coined from ISO- + Greek *genea* 'race, stock'.]

isogenous /ī sójjənəss/ *adj.* **1.** WITH THE SAME ORIGIN used to describe bodily organs or parts that have the same or a similar origin **2.** = **isogenic** —**isogeny** *n.*

isogloss /īssō gloss/ *n.* a line on a language map that surrounds an area within which a linguistic usage, e.g. a dialectal word, is found [Early 20thC. Formed from ISO- + Greek *glossa* 'language'.] —**isoglossal** /īssō glóss'l/ *adj.* —**isoglossic** /-glóssik/ *adj.* —**isoglottal** /-glótt'l/ *adj.* —**isoglottic** /-glóttik/ *adj.*

isogonal *adj.* = **isogonic**

isogonal line *n.* = **isogonic line**

isogone /īssəgōn/ *n.* = **isogonic line**

isogonic /īssō gónnik/, **isogonal** /ī sóggən'l/ *adj.* MATH WITH EQUAL ANGLES having equal angles ■ *n.* = **isogonic line** [Mid-19thC. Formed from Greek *isogōnios* 'equiangular'.]

isogonic line *n.* a line on a map of the Earth's surface connecting points at which a compass would give the same deviation from true north

isograft /īssō graaft/ *n.* a tissue graft taken from an individual genetically identical to the recipient of the graft, e.g. from an identical twin

isogram /īssō gram/ *n.* = **isopleth**

isohel /īssō hel/ *n.* a line on a map connecting places that receive the same number of hours of sunshine in the course of a year [Early 20thC. Coined from ISO- + Greek *hēlios* 'sun'.]

isohyet /īssō hī ət/ *n.* a line on a map connecting places that receive the same amount of rainfall in the course of a year [Late 19thC. Coined from ISO- + Greek *huetos* 'rain'.] —**isohyetal** *adj.*

isolate *vt.* /īssə layt/ (**-lates, -lating, -lated**) **1.** SEPARATE SB FROM OTHERS to separate a person or place from others of the same type **2.** MED QUARANTINE SB to keep sb who is infected away from others to prevent the spread of a contagious disease **3.** CUT A PLACE OFF to make a place unreachable from the surrounding area ○ *Heavy snowfalls have temporarily isolated the town.* **4.** FIND A CAUSE OF STH to discover which of a number of possible causes or factors is responsible for a particular phenomenon or problem ○ *He isolated a bug in the software as the cause of the failure.* **5.** BIOL SEPARATE OUT to separate out a chemical or biological material such as a virus or bacterium in order to identify and study it **6.** ELECTRON ENG INSULATE AN ELECTRONIC DEVICE to prevent a circuit or device from interacting with another or with an outside stimulus ■ *n.* /īssələt/ **1.** LONE PERSON OR GROUP a person or group separated or cut off from others **2.** BIOL, CHEM MICROORGANISM GROWN IN A LABORATORY a sample of biological material, especially a microorganism, that has been cultured for study **3.** LING ONLY LANGUAGE OF A FAMILY a language that is the only known surviving member of its language family [Early 19thC. Back-formation from ISOLATED, from French *isolé*, ultimately from late Latin *insulatus* 'made into an island', from Latin *insula* 'island' (see INSULAR).] —**isolable** /īssələb'l/ *adj.* —**isolatable** /īssə laytəb'l/ *adj.* —**isolator** *n.*

isolated /íssə laytid/ *adj.* **1.** OFF BY ITSELF far away from other inhabited areas or buildings **2.** ALONE OR LONELY without enough social contact, friends, or support **3.** RARE happening singly, rarely, or only once and unlikely to recur or prove a continuing problem ○ *an isolated incident*

isolated pawn *n.* in chess, a pawn that is not supported by other pawns of the same colour round it

isolating /íssə layting/ *adj.* LING = analytic

isolation /íssə láysh'n/ *n.* **1.** SEPARATION FROM OTHERS the process of separating sb or sth from others, or the fact of being alone and separated from others **2.** GEOGRAPHICAL REMOTENESS remoteness from other inhabited areas or buildings ◇ **in isolation 1.** separate from other related factors or things ○ *we have to look at the problem in isolation* **2.** alone and physically separated from other people

isolationism /íssə láysh'nizəm/ *n.* **1.** POL AVOIDANCE OF INTERNATIONAL RELATIONS a government policy based on the belief that national interests are best served by avoiding economic and political alliances with other countries **2.** MUSIC TYPE OF ELECTRONIC AMBIENT MUSIC a type of electronic ambient music that is generally produced without beats, creating a soothing ambience with unusual sounds —**isolationist** *n.*, *adj.*

isolative /íssələtiv/ *adj.* **1.** PHON RELATING TO PHONETIC CHANGES relating to a sound change that occurs in all phonetic environments such as in the Great Vowel Shift **2.** CAUSING ISOLATION causing sb or sth to be separated or cut off

Isolde ♦ Tristan

isolecithal /íssō léssith'l/ *adj.* used to describe the eggs of mammals and some other vertebrates in which the yolk is evenly distributed throughout the egg

Isoleucine

isoleucine /íssō loó seen/ *n.* an amino acid, obtained by animals from their diet, that is an isomer of leucine and is found in most proteins. Formula: $C_6H_{13}NO_2$.

isolex /íssō leks/ *n.* a line on a language map that surrounds an area within which a particular word is used [Early 20thC. Coined from ISO- + Greek *lexis* 'word'.]

isoline /íssō līn/ *n.* = isopleth

isologous /ī sólləgəss/ *adj.* used to describe two organic compounds that have the same molecular structure but different atoms of the same valency [Mid-19thC. Formed from ISO- + Greek *logos* 'ratio'.]

isomagnetic /íssō mag néttik/, **isomagnetic line** *n.* a line on a map connecting points of the same magnetic force —**isomagnetic** *adj.*

isomer /íssəmər/ *n.* **1.** CHEMICALLY IDENTICAL MOLECULE WITH A DIFFERENT STRUCTURE one of two or more molecules that have the same number of atoms but have different chemical structures and therefore different properties **2.** NUCLIDE WITH A DIFFERENT ENERGY STATE one of two or more nuclides that have the same mass number and atomic number but different energy states and half-lives [Mid-19thC. Formed from Greek *isomerēs*, literally 'sharing equally'.] —**isomeric** /íssō mérrik/ *adj.*

isomerase /ī sómmə rayss, -rayz/ *n.* an enzyme that converts one isomer into another

isomerism /ī sómmərizəm/ *n.* **1.** EXISTENCE OF ISOMERS the existence of two or more molecules that are isomers **2.** EXISTENCE OF NUCLIDES THAT ARE ISOMERS the existence of two or more nuclides that are isomers

isomerize /ī sómmə rīz/ (**-izes, -izing, -ized**), **isomerise** (**-ises, -ising, -ised**) *vti.* to change sth into an isomer or become an isomer —**isomerization** /ī sómmə rī záysh'n/ *n.*

isomerous /ī sómmərəss/ *adj.* ZOOL, BIOL with parts that are similar in number, markings, or other characteristics

isometric /íssō méttrik/, **isometrical** /-k'l/ *adj.* **1.** EQUAL equal in dimension or measurement **2.** PHYSIOL INVOLVING PUSHING THE MUSCLES AGAINST STH used to describe exercises in which muscles are put under tension but not allowed to contract **3.** CRYSTALS WITH THREE EQUAL AXES used to describe a crystalline system that has three equal axes at right angles to one another **4.** POETRY WITH LINES IN SAME METRE having the same number of metrical feet in each line of poetry **5.** ENG PROJECTED AT THE SAME ANGLE TO AXES projected so that the plane of projection of a three-dimensional drawing is at an equal angle to each of the three axes of the object drawn [Mid-19thC. Formed from Greek *isometria*, literally 'equality of measure'.] —**isometrically** *adv.*

isometrics /íssō méttriks/ *n.* a form of exercise in which the muscles are pushed against sth fixed or against other muscles to strengthen them (*takes a singular or plural verb*)

isometropia /íssōmə trṓpi ə/ *n.* the condition of equal refraction of light by both eyes [Coined from Greek *isometros* 'of equal measure' (from *metron* 'measure') + -OPIA]

isometry /ī sómmətri/ (*plural* **-tries**) *n.* **1.** EQUAL MEASUREMENTS equality of measure **2.** MATH GEOMETRIC TRANSFORMATION a geometric transformation such as the rotation of a plane in which the distance between any two points is preserved

isomorph /íssō mawrf/ *n.* a substance or organism that exhibits similarity in form or appearance to others (**isomorphism**)

isomorphic /íssō máwrfik/ *adj.* **1.** BIOL LOOKING LIKE ANOTHER ORGANISM having the same form or appearance as another organism or the same organism at a different stage in its life cycle **2.** MATH CORRESPONDING used to describe mathematical sets with a one-to-one correspondence so that an operation such as addition or multiplication in one produces the same result as the analogous operation in the other **3.** CHEM = isomorphous —**isomorphically** *adv.*

isomorphism /íssō máwrfizəm/ *n.* **1.** BIOL SIMILARITY IN ORGANISMS similarity in form or appearance between organisms of different ancestry or between different stages in the life cycle of the same organism **2.** CHEM SIMILARITY BETWEEN CHEMICALS similarity in crystalline form between chemicals **3.** MATH CORRESPONDENCE BETWEEN SETS a one-to-one correspondence between sets such that an operation, e.g. addition or multiplication, in one produces the same result as the analogous operation in the other

isomorphous /íssō máwrfəss/ *adj.* used to describe a chemical compound that is able to crystallize in a form similar to another chemical compound

isoniazid /íssō nī əzid/ *n.* a colourless crystalline compound used to treat tuberculosis. Formula: $C_6H_7N_3O$. [Mid-20thC. Formed from ISO- + a contraction of NICOTINIC + HYDRAZIDE, elements of its chemical name.]

isooctane /íssō ók tayn/ *n.* a flammable isomer of octane used to determine the octane number of fuel. Formula: $(CH_3)_3CCH_2$.

isopach /íssō pak/, **isopachyte** /íssō pák īt/ *n.* a line on a map of the Earth's surface connecting points where a rock stratum has equal thickness [Early 20thC. Coined from ISO- + Greek *pachus* 'thick'.]

isophone /íssō fōn/ *n.* a line on a language map surrounding an area within which a particular pronunciation is used

isopiestic /íssō pī éstik/ *adj.* METEOROL = isobaric [Coined from ISO- + Greek *piezein* 'to press, squeeze'] —**isopiestically** *adv.*

isopleth /íssō pleth/ *n.* METEOROL a line on a map connecting points with the same value for variables such as temperature or air pressure [Early 20thC. From Greek *isoplēthēs*, literally 'equal in quantity'.] —**isoplethic** /íssō pléthik/ *adj.*

isopod /íssō pod/ *n.* a small invertebrate animal with a flattened body and seven pairs of legs. Woodlice are isopods but most are marine. Order: Isopoda. [Mid-19thC. From modern Latin *Isopoda*, order name, literally 'equal foot', from the Greek stem *pod-* 'foot'.] —**isopodan** /ī sóppədən/ *adj.* —**isopodous** /ī sóppədəss/ *adj.*

isoprenaline /íssō prénnə leen/ *n.* PHARM = isoproterenol [Mid-20thC. Contraction of *N-isopropylnoradrenaline*, its chemical name.]

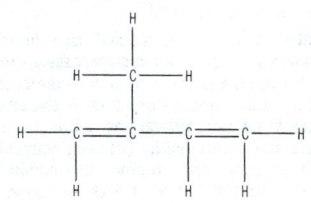

Isoprene

isoprene /íssō preen/ *n.* a colourless flammable liquid hydrocarbon used in making synthetic rubber. Formula: C_5H_8. [Mid-19thC. Formed from ISO- + a contraction of *prophylene*, its chemical name.]

isopropanol /íssō prṓpə nol/ *n.* = isopropyl alcohol

isopropyl /íssō prṓpil/ *n.* a chemical radical isomer of propyl. Formula: C_3H_7.

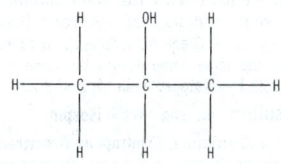

Isopropyl alcohol

isopropyl alcohol *n.* a colourless flammable alcohol used in antifreeze and rubbing alcohol and as a solvent

isoproterenol /íssōprō térrə nol/ *n.* a compound used as a bronchodilator in the treatment of asthma. Formula: $C_{13}H_{17}NO_3$. [Mid-20thC. Contraction of *N-isopropylarterenol*, its chemical name.]

ISO rating *n.* a measure of the sensitivity to light of a material such as photographic film or paper

isorhythm /íssō rithəm/ *n.* a technique of musical composition of the 14th and 15th centuries that uses a repeated rhythmic pattern —**isorhythmic** /íssō ríthmik/ *adj.*

isosceles /ī sóssə leez/ *adj.* **1.** WITH TWO OUT OF THREE SIDES EQUAL used to describe a triangle in which two of the three sides are of equal length **2.** WITH TWO OUT OF FOUR SIDES EQUAL used to describe a trapezium in which the two nonparallel sides are of equal length [Mid-16thC. From late Latin, from Greek *isokelēs*, literally 'equally legged'.]

isoseismal /íssō sízm'l/, **isoseismic** /íssō sízmik/ *adj.* WITH EQUAL EARTHQUAKE INTENSITY relating to or showing equal strength of earthquake shock ■ *n.* LINE SHOWING EQUAL STRENGTH OF EARTHQUAKE a line on a map connecting points of equal strength of earthquake shock

isosmotic /íss oz móttik/ *adj.* CHEM = isotonic *adj.* 2 —**isosmotically** *adv.*

isospin /íssō spin/ *n.* a quantum characteristic of baryons and mesons that relates to the number of different values of electric charge they can have. Symbol I [Mid-20thC. Shortening of ISOBARIC SPIN and ISOTOPIC SPIN.]

isostasy /ɪ sóstəssi/ n. a state of equilibrium between forces such as accumulated ice pushing down on a section of the Earth's surface and those pushing up from below [Late 19thC. Formed from ISO- + Greek *stasis* 'station, stoppage'.] —**isostatic** /ísso státtik/ adj. —**isostatically** /-státtikli/ adv.

isotach /ísso tak/ n. a line on a weather map connecting points where the wind speed is equal [Mid-20thC. Coined from ISO- + Greek *takhos* 'speed'.]

isotactic /ísso táktik/ adj. used to describe a polymer having constituent molecules that give the polymer a repetitive spatial structure [Mid-20thC. Formed from ISO- + Greek *taktos* 'ordered'.]

isotherm /ísso thurm/, **isothermal** /ísso thúrm'l/, **isothermal line** n. 1. METEOROL LINE SHOWING EQUAL TEMPERATURE a line drawn on a weather map that connects places with the same temperature 2. PHYS LINE SHOWING RELATIONSHIP AT THE SAME TEMPERATURE a line on a graph showing the relationship between variables, especially pressure and volume, at a constant temperature [Mid-19thC. From French *isotherme*, literally 'equal heat', from Greek *thermē* 'heat' or *thermos* 'hot'.] —**isothermal** adj. —**isothermally** adv.

isotone /íssətōn/ n. either of two or more atoms with the same number of neutrons but different atomic numbers

isotonic /ísso tónnik/ adj. 1. PHYSIOL OF MUSCLE TENSION AND CONTRACTION relating to the contraction and shortening of a muscle under relatively constant tension, e.g. in weightlifting 2. CHEM WITH EQUAL OSMOTIC PRESSURE relating to or exerting equal osmotic pressure 3. PHYSIOL DESIGNED TO RESUPPLY THE BODY specially formulated to supply the body's chemical needs in situations in which minerals and fluids are used up by the body, e.g. during vigorous exercise —**isotonically** adv. —**isotonicity** /íssə to níssəti/ n.

isotope /íssətōp/ n. either of two or more forms of a chemical element with the same atomic number but different numbers of neutrons [Early 20thC. Coined from ISO- + Greek *topos* 'place', so called because isotopes of the same name occupy the same place in the periodic table.] —**isotopic** /ísso tóppik/ adj.

isotopic spin n. NUCLEAR PHYS = isospin

isotropic /ísso tróppik/, **isotropous** /ɪ sóttrəpəss/ adj. having physical properties that do not vary with direction [Mid-19thC. Formed from ISO- + Greek *tropos* 'turn'.] —**isotropically** adv. —**isotropism** /ísso trópizəm/ n. —**isotropy** /ɪ sóttrəpi/ n.

isozyme /ísso zīm/ n. BIOCHEM one of two or more enzymes that are different chemically but function the same

ISP abbr. Internet service provider

I-spy n. a children's guessing game in which players try to guess which thing in visual range another player has in mind, having been given the first letter of the word

Isr. abbr. Israel

Israel

Israel /íz rayl/ republic in southwestern Asia formed in 1948 as a Jewish state in the historic region of Palestine, on the eastern shore of the Mediterranean Sea. Language: Hebrew, Arabic. Currency: shekel. Capital: Jerusalem. Population: 5,534,670 (1997). Area: 20,700 sq. km/8,000 sq. mi. Official name **State of Israel** —**Israeli** /iz ráyli/ n., adj.

Israelite /ízzri ə līt, ízzrə-/ n. 1. MEMBER OF AN ANCIENT HEBREW PEOPLE a member of the ancient Hebrew people

descended from the biblical patriarch Jacob 2. SB FROM ANCIENT ISRAEL sb who was born in or lived in the ancient kingdom of Israel [14thC. Via late Latin *Israelita*, from Greek *Israēlitēs*, from Hebrew *yiśrə'ēlī*, from *Yiśrā'ēl*.] —**Israelitic** /ízzri ə líttik, ízzrə-/ adj.

Israfil /ízzrə feel/, **Israfel** /-fel/, **Israfeel** /-feel/ n. according to the Koran, the archangel who will herald the end of the world by sounding a trumpet on the Day of Judgment [From Hebrew, 'God heals']

Issachar /íssə kaar/ n. 1. JACOB'S SON in the Bible, a son of Jacob and Leah 2. TRIBE DESCENDED FROM ISSACHAR one of the twelve tribes of Israel, descended from Issachar [Via late Latin from Greek, from Hebrew *Yiśśākhār*]

Issigonis /íssi gónniss/, **Sir Alec** (1906–88) Turkish-born British car designer. He is best known for the Morris Minor (1948) and the Mini (1959). Full name **Sir Alec Arnold Constantine Issigonis**

ISSN abbr. International Standard Serial Number

issuable /íshyoo-/ adj. 1. ALLOWED TO BE ISSUED authorized to be made available for sale or use 2. CAPABLE OF BEING LITIGATED able to be litigated or debated —**issuably** adv.

issuance /íssyoo-, íshyoo-/ n. the act of distributing sth or giving sth out officially

issuant /íssyoo-, íshyoo-/ adj. in heraldry, displaying an animal rising up from sth with only its upper body showing

issue /íssyoo, íshyoo/ n. 1. SUBJECT OF CONCERN a topic for discussion or of general concern ○ *I want to raise several issues at the meeting.* 2. MAIN SUBJECT the central or most important topic in a discussion or debate ○ *The real issue is education.* 3. LAW LEGAL MATTER IN A DISPUTE a legal matter in a dispute between two parties 4. PUBL COPY OF A PUBLICATION a copy of a magazine or newspaper published on a particular date 5. COMM OFFICIAL RELEASE OF STH a set of things such as new stamps or bonds that are made available for sale by an official body at a particular time 6. FIN STOCK MADE AVAILABLE a series of items such as shares in a company that becomes available at the same time 7. ALLOTTING OF STH distribution of sth by an official body ○ *the issue of parking permits* 8. OFFICIAL ALLOTMENT sth officially distributed or supplied, or a specific amount of sth officially supplied ○ *government issue rations* 9. LAW PROGENY the offspring of a person ○ *died without issue* 10. FINAL OUTCOME a final outcome or conclusion of a matter that is usually a solution to a problem or difficulty (dated) ○ *Let's bring our differences to an issue.* 11. MED WOUND PRODUCING DISCHARGE an open wound or ulcer producing pus or blood 12. MED DISCHARGE FROM WOUND pus or blood coming from an open wound or ulcer 13. FIN PROFIT FROM PROPERTY profits made from owning land or buildings 14. SOURCE OF A FLOW a place from which sth flows 15. LIBRARIES SYSTEM FOR TRACKING BOOK LOANS the system in a library used for keeping track of current loans 16. LIBRARIES ITEMS LOANED FROM LIBRARY the number of items, e.g. books or CDs, borrowed from a library at one time ■ v. (-sues, -suing, -sued) 1. vt. SUPPLY STH to supply or distribute sth officially 2. vt. ANNOUNCE STH PUBLICLY to make public sth such as a bulletin, statement, or warning, or deliver it officially to sb ○ *The mayor's office issued a press release.* 3. vt. COMM RELEASE STH FOR SALE to make a set of things such as new stamps or bonds available for sale at a particular time 4. vt. PUBL PUBLISH STH to publish sth such as a newspaper, magazine, or book 5. vi. ORIGINATE to emerge or come out from somewhere ○ *Smoke issued from the burning building.* 6. vi. ARISE FROM A CONDITION to result from or be produced by a particular thing or situation ○ *Our conclusions issue from analysis of the data.* 7. vi. FIN ADD UP AS GAIN to accrue in the form of interest or profit 8. vi. RESULT IN to have as a result (archaic) [13thC. From Old French, ultimately from Latin *exitus*, past participle of *exire* 'to go out' (see EXIT).] —**issueless** adj. —**issuer** n. ◇ **at issue** under discussion or to be decided ◇ **take issue with sb** to disagree with sb about sth

issue price n. the price of new securities when they are first offered to the public

issuing house n. a financial institution that issues shares on behalf of a company that wants to become public

Issyk-Kul /i sík kóol/ lake in northeastern Kyrgyzstan. It has a maximum depth of 700 m/2,300 ft. Area: 6,100 sq. km/2,360 sq. mi.

IST abbr. information sciences technology

-ist suffix. 1. sb who practises a particular skill or profession ○ *psychologist* ○ *etymologist* 2. sb who follows a particular belief or school of thought ○ *idealist* 3. sb associated with a particular action or thing ○ *archivist* ○ *oboist* [Via Old French and Latin from, ultimately, Greek *-istēs*] —**-istic** suffix.

Istanbul /ís tan bóol/, **İstanbul** the largest city in Turkey, situated in the northwest of the country. Population: 7,615,000 (1994). Former name **Byzantium**, **Constantinople**

Isth., **isth.** abbr. isthmus

isthmi plural of **isthmus**

isthmian /íssmi ən, ísth-/ adj. GEOG OF AN ISTHMUS relating to, shaped like, or living in an isthmus joining two larger areas of land ■ n. INHABITANT OF ISTHMUS sb who lives on an isthmus [Early 17thC. Formed from Latin *isthmius*, from Greek *isthmios*.]

Isthmian adj. relating to the Isthmus of Panama or the Isthmus of Corinth

Isthmian Games npl. a sports festival held in ancient Greece on the Isthmus of Corinth that included horse racing and chariot racing

isthmic /íssmik, ísth-/ adj. relating to an isthmus in the body ○ *an isthmic constriction*

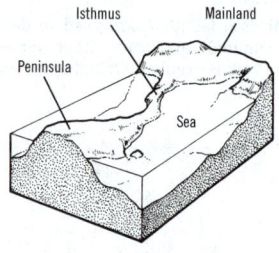

Isthmus

isthmus /íssməss, ísth-/ (plural **-muses** or **-mi** /íssmi/) n. 1. GEOG NARROW CONNECTING STRIP OF LAND a narrow strip of land that joins two larger areas of land ○ *The isthmus connects the continents of North and South America.* 2. ANAT PASSAGE BETWEEN BODY PARTS a narrow connection or passage between parts of the body [Mid-16thC. Via Latin, from Greek *isthmos* 'island'.] —**isthmoid** adj.

istle /ístli/, **ixtle** n. a strong fibre from some tropical American plants such as agave or yucca, used to make rope, baskets, and carpets [Mid-19thC. Via American Spanish *ixtle*, from Nahuatl *ixtli*.]

Istria /ístri ə/ peninsula in northwestern Croatia and southwestern Slovenia, projecting into the Adriatic Sea. Area: 3,885 sq. km/1,500 sq. mi.

ISV abbr. International Scientific Vocabulary

it /it/ CORE MEANING: a pronoun used to refer to an object or an animal, and sometimes a baby ○ *It's a lovely baby.* ○ *They've had the dog a week, and they still haven't thought of a name for it.*

1. pron. INDICATING A PARTICULAR SITUATION used to refer to a situation just described, or to an unspecified or implied situation ○ *He's very upset, but he won't talk about it.* 2. pron. INDICATING A POINT OF VIEW used to indicate feelings or a viewpoint on a particular situation ○ *It's strange how things turn out.* 3. pron. INDICATING STH REPORTED used in the formation of passive sentences reporting a situation ○ *It was reported that several people had been arrested.* 4. pron. INDICATING WEATHER used as the subject of verbs such as 'be', 'get', 'seem', and 'feel' in order to describe sth about the environment, e.g. the temperature or the weather ○ *It's cold and rainy.* 5. pron. INDICATING TIME used to state the time, the time of day, the month, the year, or the season ○ *It's six o'clock.* 6. pron. INDICATING A DESCRIPTION OF AN EXPERIENCE used to refer to life or a particular experience ○ *What's it like being famous?* 7. pron. EMPHASIZING A FOLLOWING CLAUSE

used to draw attention to the person, thing, or clause that immediately follows ○ *It's you who's always complaining!* ○ *It isn't that I don't care.* **8.** *pron.* **INDICATING A CRISIS** the crucial or ultimate point, the perfect situation, person, or thing, or the death or end of sb or sth ○ *When the car turned over I really thought that was it.* **9.** *pron.* **ATTRACTIVE OR SELLING QUALITY** a quality considered by sb to be the most important, e.g. talent, charm, sex appeal, or profitability (*informal*) ○ *You either have it or you don't.* **10.** *pron.* **SEX** sexual intercourse (*slang*) **11.** *n.* GAME **PLAYER IN CHILDREN'S GAMES** in children's informal games, the player who must do sth to the others, e.g. run after and touch them in the game of tag ○ *You're it!* [Old English *hit*, from a prehistoric Germanic base that is also the ancestor of English *he*]

IT *abbr.* information technology

It. *abbr.* Italian

ITA *abbr.* **1.** Independent Television Authority **2. ITA, i.t.a.** initial teaching alphabet

ital. *abbr.* **1.** italic **2.** italics

Ital. *abbr.* **1.** Italian **2.** Italy

Italian /i tállyən/ *n.* **1.** PEOPLES **SB FROM ITALY** sb who was born or brought up in Italy, or who has Italian citizenship **2.** LANGUAGE **LANGUAGE OF ITALY** the official language of Italy and one of the official languages of Switzerland, belonging to the Romance subgroup of the Italic branch of the Indo-European languages. There are about 60 million native speakers of Italian and approximately 60 million using it as a second language. ■ *adj.* **OF ITALY** relating to Italy, or its people or culture [14thC. From Italian *italiano* 'of Italy', from *Italia* 'Italy'.]

Italianate /i tállyə nayt/ *adj.* expressed, done, or made in an Italian style or character

Italian dressing *n.* a salad dressing typically made with oil and vinegar, garlic, and oregano

Italianesque /i tállyə nésk/ *adj.* = **Italianate**

Italian greyhound *n.* a dog resembling a miniature greyhound, belonging to a breed originating in Italy

Italianise *vti.* = **Italianize**

Italianism /i tállyənizəm/ *n.* sth that comes from or is typical of Italy, e.g. a word or phrase that is derived from Italian

Italianize /i tállyə nīz/ (**-izes, -izing, -ized**), **Italianise** (**-ises, -ising, -ised**) *vti.* to make sth Italian in character, or become Italian in character —**Italianization** /i tállyə nī záysh'n/ *n.*

Italian sixth *n.* a three-note chord consisting of an augmented sixth chord and a major third above the root of the chord, used for modulation and for providing colour

Italian sonnet *n.* = **Petrarchan sonnet**

Italian vermouth *n.* a dark-coloured sweet vermouth made in Italy

italic /i tállik/ *adj.* **1. HAVING PRINTED LETTERS SLOPING TO THE RIGHT** printed in or using letters that slope to the right. Italic letters are used, e.g., in book titles or to show emphasis. **2. SLOPING TO RIGHT** handwritten in letters that slope to the right ■ *n.* **ITALIC LETTER** a printed letter that slopes to the right, or a font that uses such letters (*often used in the plural*) [Late 16thC. From the introduction of the style by an Italian printer from Venice in 1501. Originally denoting handwriting.]

Italic *n.* **BRANCH OF THE INDO-EUROPEAN LANGUAGE FAMILY** a branch of the Indo-European language family that includes many former languages of Italy, including Latin and Umbrian ■ *adj.* **1. OF ITALIC** relating to the language family Italic **2. ANCIENT ITALIAN** dating from or used in ancient Italy

italicise *vt.* = **italicize**

Italicism /i tállissizəm/ *n.* a word or phrase that is borrowed from Italian

italicize /i tálli sīz/ (**-cizes, -cizing, -cized**), **italicise** (**-cises, -cising, -cised**) *vt.* to print a word, letter, or document in italics, or change words to an italic font —**italicization** /i tálli sī záysh'n/ *n.* —**italicized** /i tálli sīzd/ *adj.*

Italophile /i tállō fīl/ *n.* sb who loves Italy, Italians, or the Italian way of life —**Italophilia** /i tállō fílli ə/ *n.*

Italy

Italy /íttəli/ republic in southern Europe. Its mainland area projects as a peninsula into the Mediterranean Sea, and it includes, among others, the islands of Elba, Sicily, and Sardinia. Language: Italian. Currency: lira. Capital: Rome. Population: 56,830,508 (1997). Area: 301,323 sq. km/116,341 sq. mi. Official name **Italian Republic**

Itar Tass /eé taar táss/, **ITAR-Tass** *n.* a Russian news agency founded in 1992 to replace Tass, the news agency of the former Soviet Union [Late 20thC. An acronym of Russian *Informatsionnoe telegrafnoe agentsvo Rossii* 'Information Telegraph Agency of Russia' + TASS.]

ITC *abbr.* Independent Television Commission

itch /ich/ *v.* (**itches, itching, itched**) **1.** *vti.* **WANT TO SCRATCH** to have, produce, or cause sb to feel an irritating sensation on the body that provokes a desire to scratch the skin **2.** *vi.* **BE ANXIOUS TO DO STH** to be very eager or impatient to do sth **3.** *vt.* **SCRATCH ITCHY SKIN** to scratch the skin where it itches (*nonstandard*) ■ *n.* **1. FEELING OF WANTING TO SCRATCH** an irritating sensation in the body that provokes a desire to scratch the skin **2. LONGING FOR STH** a restless or uneasy desire for sth **3.** MED **ITCHY SKIN DISORDER** a skin disorder such as scabies that causes the skin to itch [Old English *giccan*, from prehistoric Germanic] —**itchiness** *n.* —**itching** *n.* —**itchy** *adj.*

itch mite *n.* a tiny parasite that burrows into the skin and causes the disease scabies in humans. Latin name: *Sarcoptes scabiei.*

it'd /íttəd/ *contr.* **1.** it would **2.** it had

-ite[1] *suffix.* **1.** mineral, rock, ore, soil, fossil ○ *carnotite* ○ *nummulite* **2.** descendant or follower of ○ *Hamite* ○ *Hussite* **3.** native or resident of ○ *Israelite* ○ *urbanite* **4.** organ, body part, cell, protozoan ○ *sporozoite* **5.** commercial product, explosive ○ *cordite* **6.** product of a chemical process ○ *evaporite* [Via Old French and Latin from Greek *-itēs*]

-ite[2] *suffix.* salt or ester of an acid with a name ending in *-ous* ○ *phosphite* [Alteration of -ATE]

item /ítəm/ *n.* **1. ONE IN A COLLECTION** a single thing in a group or collection of things **2. ONE IN A LIST** one in a list of things **3. BROADCAST OR PUBLISHED REPORT** a piece of information in a news report, e.g. in a newspaper or on television **4.** ACCT **BOOK-KEEPING ENTRY** one entry in a set of financial accounts **5. COUPLE IN A RELATIONSHIP** a couple who are linked in a romantic or sexual relationship (*informal*) ■ *adv.* **INTRODUCING AN ITEM IN LIST** used to introduce an item in a list [Late 16thC. From Latin *item* 'likewise', from *ita* 'thus, so'. Originally used before each article in a list, hence 'separate thing'.]

itemize /ítə mīz/ (**-izes, -izing, -ized**), **itemise** (**-ises, -ising, -ised**) *vt.* to list all of a set of related things ○ *an itemized bill* —**itemization** /ítə mī záysh'n/ *n.* —**itemizer** /ítə mīzər/ *n.*

iterance /íttərənss/ *n.* = **iteration** *n.* 1 [Early 17thC. Formed from Latin *iterare* (see ITERATE).]

iterant /íttərənt/ *adj.* marked by repetition or recurrence [Early 17thC. Formed from *iterant-*, present participle stem of Latin *iterare* (see ITERATE).]

iterate /íttə rayt/ (**-ates, -ating, -ated**) *vt.* to say or do the same thing again [Mid-16thC. From Latin *iterare* 'to repeat', from *iterum* 'again'.]

iteration /íttə ráysh'n/ *n.* **1. REPETITION** an instance or the act of doing sth again **2.** MATH **STEP-BY-STEP PROCESS** a process of achieving a desired result by repeating a sequence of steps and successively getting closer to that result **3.** COMPUT **REPETITION OF STEPS** the repetition of a sequence of instructions in a computer program until a result is achieved **4. NEW VERSION OF STH** a different version of sth, especially a new version of existing computer hardware or software

iterative /íttərətiv/ *adj.* **1.** MATH, LOGIC = **recursive 2.** COMPUT **REPEATING STEPS** using repeated routines in a loop as part of a computer program **3.** GRAM = **frequentative 4. REPETITIVE** repeating again and again —**iteratively** *adv.*

Ithaca /íthəkə/ **1.** island in western Greece, the traditional site of the legendary kingdom of Odysseus. Population: 3,646 (1981). Area: 96 sq. km/37 sq. mi. **2.** city in south-central New York State, south of Cayuga Lake and northwest of Binghamton. Population: 28,507 (1996).

ithyphallic /íthi fállik/ *adj.* **1. OF HYMNS TO BACCHUS** relating to or composed in the metre used in hymns to the ancient Greek god Bacchus **2. SHOWING AN ERECT PENIS IN ART** in sculpture, painting, or other art, having or showing an erect penis ■ *n.* **HYMN** a hymn composed in ithyphallic metre [Early 17thC. Via late Latin *ithyphallicus*, from, ultimately, Greek *ithuphallos* 'phallus carried in procession at festivals of Bacchus', literally 'straight phallus'.]

itinerancy /ī tínnərənssi/, **itineracy** /-rəssi/ *n.* **1. REQUIREMENT TO TRAVEL IN JOB** the fact of travelling, or necessity to travel, from place to place, especially as part of an occupation or profession **2. PEOPLE WITH A CIRCUIT TO COVER** people such as judges or preachers who move from place to place on a circuit **3.** CHR **SYSTEM OF MOVING CLERGY BETWEEN CHURCHES** a system for rotating clergy, especially within the Methodist Church

itinerant /ī tínnərənt/ *adj.* **TRAVELLING ON THE JOB** travelling from place to place, especially to find work or as a part of work ■ *n.* **SB WHO MOVES ROUND** sb who moves from place to place [Late 16thC. From late Latin *itinerant-*, present participle stem of *itinerari* 'to journey', from Latin *itiner-* (see ITINERARY).] —**itinerantly** *adv.*

itinerary /ī tínnərəri/ *n.* (*plural* **-ies**) **1. LIST OF PLACES TO BE VISITED** a plan for a journey listing different places in the order in which they are to be visited **2. RECORD OF A JOURNEY** a written record of a journey to visit different places **3. GUIDEBOOK** a guidebook for travellers ■ *adj.* **INTENDED FOR TRAVELLING** intended or used for the purpose of travelling [15thC. From late Latin *itinerarius*, from Latin *itiner-*, stem of *iter* 'journey, way'.]

itinerate /ī tínnə rayt/ (**-ates, -ating, -ated**) *vi.* to move from place to place on a circuit (*refers to a judge or preacher*) [Early 17thC. From late Latin *itinerari*, from Latin *itiner-* (see ITINERARY).] —**itineration** /ī tínnə ráysh'n/ *n.*

-itis *suffix.* **1.** inflammation, disease ○ *retinitis* **2.** excessive interest in ○ *spectatoritis* [From Greek]

it'll /ítt'l/ *contr.* it will ○ *It'll be so good to see you.*

ITO *abbr.* International Trade Organization

Ito Jakuchu /eétō ja kóo choo/ (1716–1800) Japanese artist. He is known for his meticulously detailed paintings of birds, flowers, and fish.

-itol *suffix.* polyhydric alcohol ○ *inositol* [Coined from -ITE[1] + -OL[1]]

its /its/ *det.* used to indicate that sth belongs or relates to sth ○ *The park changed its policy.* [Late 16thC. Coined from IT + -'S (possessive).]

it's /its/ *contr.* **1.** it is ○ *It's perfect.* **2.** it has ○ *It's been rebuilt.*

itself /it sélf/ CORE MEANING: a reflexive pronoun used to refer back to the subject of a verb or for emphasis *pron.* **1. USED TO REFER BACK TO STH** used to refer back to the subject of a verb ○ *His ignorance finally revealed itself.* **2. USED TO EMPHASIZE STH** used to emphasize the thing that is referred to ○ *The house itself was cheap compared to the land.* **3. ITS NORMAL SELF** the way it usually feels or behaves ○ *The dog's not itself since we moved to the city.*

itsy-bitsy /ítsi bítsi/, **itty-bitty** /ítti bítti/ *adj.* extremely small (*informal*) [Alteration of LITTLE + BIT]

WORD KEY: REGIONAL NOTE

Dialects, like all varieties of English, use a number of reduplicated forms. Many of these are associated with babytalk, and the compound ***itsy-bitsy*** could have been popularized by the nursery rhyme 'Itsy bitsy spider'.

Other rhyming phrases associated with smallness are *teeny weeny* and *teensy weensy*. Dialect terms for 'little' include *dinky*, *titchy*, and *totty*.

ITU *abbr.* **1.** MED intensive therapy unit **2.** International Telecommunication Union

ITV *abbr.* Independent Television

IU *abbr.* **1.** immunizing unit **2.** PHARM international unit

IUCD *abbr.* intrauterine contraceptive device

IUD *abbr.* intrauterine device

-ium *suffix.* chemical element, radical, or ion ○ *californium* [From modern Latin, an alteration of *-um*]

IV[1] *abbr.* **IV, i.v. 1.** intravenous **2.** intravenously

IV[2] (*plural* **IVs** *or* **IV's**) *n.* US **1.** MEDICAL INJECTION OF LIQUID the injection of quantities of a therapeutic fluid such as blood, plasma, saline, or glucose directly into sb's vein at an adjustable rate **2.** EQUIPMENT FOR INJECTING A LIQUID the equipment used to administer an IV [Mid-20thC. Abbreviation of INTRAVENOUS.]

Ivan III /ívən/, **Grand Prince of Muscovy** (1440–1505). As the grand duke of Muscovy (1462–1505), he declared himself 'sovereign of all Russia' (1472) and greatly expanded his empire. He ended Muscovy's subjection to the Tatars (1480). Known as **Ivan the Great**

Ivan IV, Tsar of Russia (1530–84). The grand duke of Moscow, he became the first tsar of Russia (1547–84). He expanded his empire into the Urals and Siberia and instigated major internal reforms, but he is remembered in history for the extreme despotism of his last twenty years. Known as **Ivan the Terrible**

Ivanovo /i vaánəvə/ city in central Russia, situated approximately 233 km/145 mi. northeast of Moscow. Population: 482,000 (1992).

I've /īv/ *contr.* I have

-ive *suffix.* tending to or performing ○ *illustrative* [Via Old French from Latin *-ivus*]

IVF *abbr.* in vitro fertilization

ivied /ívid/ *adj.* covered or overgrown with ivy

ivory /ívəri/ *n.* (*plural* **-ries**) **1.** MATERIAL OF ELEPHANT'S TUSKS a hard cream-coloured substance (**dentine**) that forms the tusks of animals such as the elephant, walrus, and sperm whale and was formerly used to carve small decorative objects **2.** STH MADE OF IVORY an object made of ivory, e.g. a figurine of a person or animal **3.** COLOURS CREAMY WHITE a creamy-white colour, like that of an elephant's tusk ■ **ivories** *npl.* **1.** PIANO KEYS the keys of a piano (*informal*) **2.** TEETH sb's teeth (*slang*) **3.** DICE dice (*slang*) ■ *adj.* CREAM-COLOURED of a creamy white colour, like that of an elephant's tusk [13thC. Via Old French *ivurie* from Latin *ebur*, of uncertain origin: probably ultimately from Egyptian *ab* 'ivory, elephant'.]

ivory-billed woodpecker *n.* a large, nearly extinct woodpecker of the southern United States and Cuba that has black-and-white plumage, a red crest in the male, and an ivory-coloured bill. Latin name: *Campephilus principalis*.

ivory black *n.* a black pigment made from burnt ivory

Ivory Coast /ívəri-/ former name for **Côte d'Ivoire**

ivory gull *n.* a small white Arctic gull that nests on rocky cliffs and winters on the edge of the pack ice. Latin name: *Pagophila eburnea*.

ivory nut *n.* the hard white nut of the ivory palm, the inner part (**endosperm**) of which is used in making buttons or other small items

ivory palm, **ivory-nut palm** *n.* a low-growing palm tree of Brazil and Peru that yields ivory nuts. Latin name: *Phytelephas macrocarpa*.

ivory tower *n.* a state or situation in which sb is sheltered from the practicalities or difficulties of ordinary life [Translation of French *tour d'ivoire*] —**ivory-towered** /ívəri tówərd/ *adj.*

IVR *abbr.* international vehicle registration

ivy /ívi/ (*plural* **ivies** *or* **ivy**) *n.* **1.** EVERGREEN CLIMBING PLANT

Ivy

an evergreen climbing plant with woody stems and green, green-and-yellow, or green-and-white leaves that grows easily on walls or trees or along the ground. Genus: *Hedera*. **2.** PLANT SIMILAR TO THE IVY any climbing plant that resembles the true ivy, e.g. the Boston ivy, Japanese ivy, poison ivy, or ground ivy [Old English *ifig*, from a prehistoric Germanic word of uncertain origin]

Ivy League *n.* GROUP OF PRESTIGIOUS US UNIVERSITIES a group of prestigious and respected universities in the northeastern United States consisting of Brown, Columbia, Cornell, Dartmouth, Harvard, Princeton, the University of Pennsylvania, and Yale ■ *adj.* OF THE IVY LEAGUE relating to the Ivy League or students of the universities of the Ivy League ○ *an Ivy League education* [*Ivy* from the presumption that the universities' walls were ivy-clad on account of their great age] —**Ivy Leaguer** *n.*

iw *abbr.* inside width

Iwo /ée̅wō/ city in southwestern Nigeria, just north of Ibadan. Population: 319,500 (1991).

IWW *abbr.* Industrial Workers of the World

Ixion /ik sī́ ən/ *n.* in Greek mythology, a king of Thessaly who was bound to a perpetually turning wheel by Zeus as punishment for making sexual advances to Hera

ixtle *n.* = istle

Iyar /ée yaar/ *n.* the second month of the Jewish religious calendar and the eighth month of the Jewish civil calendar, falling approximately in April and May [Mid-18thC. From Hebrew *iyyār*.]

-ize *suffix.* **1.** to cause to be, make ○ *formalize* **2.** to treat with or as ○ *chromize* ○ *lionize* **3.** to become, become like ○ *crystallize* **4.** to engage in ○ *extemporize* [Via Old French *-iser* and Latin *-izare* from Greek *-izein*] —**ization** *suffix.*

Izhevsk /i zhéfsk/ city and capital of Udmurtia, eastern Russia, located on the River Izh. Population: 650,700 (1992).

Izmir /ízmeer/, **İzmir** city and seaport in western Turkey. Population: 1,757,414 (1990). Former name **Smyrna**

Izmit /ízmit/, **İzmit** city in northwestern Turkey, situated on the Gulf of Izmit. Population: 256,882 (1990).

izzard /ízzərd/ *n.* the letter 'z' (*archaic*) [Mid-18thC. Alteration of ZED.]

J j

j¹ /jay/ (*plural* **j's**), **J** (*plural* **J's** *or* **Js**) *n.* **1.** 10TH LETTER OF ENGLISH ALPHABET the tenth letter of the modern English alphabet **2.** SPEECH SOUND CORRESPONDING TO LETTER 'J' the speech sound that corresponds to the letter 'J' **3.** LETTER 'J' WRITTEN a written representation of the letter 'J'

j² *symbol.* **1.** the imaginary number √⁻1 **2. j, J** PHYS electric current density

J¹ *symbol.* PHYS joule

J² *abbr.* CARDS jack

J. *abbr.* **1.** PRESS Journal **2.** LAW Judge **3.** LAW Justice

JA *abbr.* **1.** Jamaica (*international vehicle registration*) **2.** LAW Judge Advocate

Ja. *abbr.* January

J/A, JA *abbr.* joint account

jaap /yaap/ *n.* S Africa a person from a rural area who is seen as unsophisticated or unintelligent by urban people (*insult*)

jab /jab/ *vti.* (**jabs, jabbing, jabbed**) **1.** PUSH SHARPLY to make a short punching movement, or push sth with a short punching movement **2.** MAKE SHORT FAST PUNCH to make a short fast punch at an opponent, e.g. in boxing ■ *n.* **1.** PUNCHING MOVEMENT a short sharp punching movement **2.** SHORT SHARP PUNCH a short sharp punch, as used in boxing **3.** INJECTION an injection (*informal*) US term **shot¹** *n.* **14** [Early 19thC. Originally a Scottish variant of *job* 'to pierce, thrust', an imitation of the sound of a brief forcible action.]

Jabalpur /júbb'l poór/ city in central India. It is a major commercial centre. Population: 739,961 (1991). Former name **Jubbulpore**

jabber /jábbər/ *vti.* (**-bers, -bering, -bered**) TALK VERY FAST to talk or say sth rapidly, so that it is incomprehensible ■ *n.* RAPID SPEECH rapid speech that is incomprehensible [15thC. Supposedly imitative of the sound made by sb talking in this way.] —**jabberer** *n.*

jabberwocky /jábbər woki/ (*plural* **-ies**) *n.* speech or writing that is meaningless and often deliberately whimsical or humorous [Early 20thC. From 'Jabberwocky', nonsense poem by English writer Lewis Carroll, from his book *Through the Looking Glass* (1872).]

Jabiru

jabiru /jábbə roó/ (*plural* **-rus** *or* **-ru**) *n.* **1.** LARGE WHITE TROPICAL STORK a large tropical stork of Central and South America that has white plumage and a naked head. Latin name: *Jabiru mycteria*. **2.** LARGE BLACK-AND-WHITE AUSTRALIAN STORK a large black-and-white stork inhabiting the north and east of Australia. Latin

name: *Xenorhynchus asiaticus*. [Late 18thC. From Tupi-Guarani *jabirú* 'swollen-necked', with reference to the large neck typical of the tropical storks.]

Jabiru /jábbə roó/ town in northern Australia, situated inside Kakadu National Park in the Northern Territory. It is a mining town and tourist resort. Population: 1,694 (1996).

jaborandi /jábbə rándi/ (*plural* **-dis** *or* **-di**) *n.* **1.** TROPICAL AMERICAN SHRUB a tropical American shrub of the rue family. Genus: *Pilocarpus*. **2.** DRIED LEAVES USED AS MEDICINE the dried leaves of the jaborandi tree that yield the drug pilocarpine [Early 17thC. From Portuguese, from Tupi-Guarani *jaburandi*, literally 'sb who spits', from the increased saliva of those who chew the leaves.]

jabot /zhábbō/ (*plural* **-bots**) *n.* **1.** RUFFLE ON WOMEN'S CLOTHING an edging of ruffles at the upper front of a blouse or dress **2.** RUFFLE ON MEN'S CLOTHING formerly, a set of ruffles attached to the neckband and falling in tiers down the front of a man's shirt [Early 19thC. From French, 'bird's crop', 'shirt-frill', of uncertain origin: probably from a Proto-Romance base meaning 'crop, gullet'.]

jaboticaba /ja bótti ka'aba/ (*plural* **-bas** *or* **-ba**) *n.* a Brazilian evergreen tree of the myrtle family cultivated for its clusters of fruit. Latin name: *Myrciaria cauliflora*. [Early 17thC. Via Portuguese from Tupi *iauoti'kaua*.]

Jacamar

jacamar /jákə maar/ (*plural* **-mars** *or* **-mar**) *n.* a South and Central American bird with a very long bill and bright blue or green feathers. Jacamars feed on insects and butterflies and lay their eggs in holes in the ground. Family: Galbulidae. [Early 19thC. From French, of uncertain origin: probably from Tupi.]

Jaçana

jaçana /jássə na'a, jə ka'anə/ *n.* BIRDS a water bird found in tropical and subtropical parts of the world

that has short rounded wings and tail and long toes that enable it to walk on floating plants. Male jaçanas incubate the eggs and raise the young birds. Family: Jacanidae. [Mid-18thC. Via Portuguese *jaçanã* from Tupi-Guarani *jasanã*.]

jacaranda /jákə rándə/ (*plural* **-das** *or* **-da**) *n.* **1.** TREES PLANT WITH FERNY LEAVES a tree or shrub of tropical America with ferny leaves, purple flowers, and pleasant-smelling wood. It is widely cultivated in Australia and South Africa. Genus: *Jacaranda*. **2.** INDUST WOOD FROM JACARANDA the pleasant-smelling wood of the jacaranda tree [Mid-18thC. From Portuguese, from Tupi-Guarani *jakara'na*.]

jacinth /jássinth, jáyss-/ (*plural* **-cinths** *or* **-cinth**) *n.* = hyacinth [13thC. From Old French *iacinte* or medieval Latin *iacintus*, an alteration of Latin *hyacinthus* (see HYACINTH).]

jack¹ /jak/ *n.* **1.** MECH ENG DEVICE FOR LIFTING STH HEAVY a portable device that uses a mechanical or hydraulic lifting system to raise heavy objects, especially cars, a short distance **2.** CARDS PLAYING CARD a playing card ranking between a ten and a queen, with a picture of a young man on it **3.** ELEC ENG ELECTRICAL SOCKET a female socket designed to receive a male plug for completing a circuit **4.** GAME OBJECT USED IN JACKS a small, usually metal object with six points that is used in the game of jacks **5.** BOWLS TARGET BALL USED IN LAWN BOWLING a small, usually white ball that players aim at in bowling **6.** ZOOL MALE ANIMAL the male of various animals, especially the donkey **7.** US = jackrabbit **8.** NAUT FLAG ON A SHIP a small flag displayed to indicate the nationality of a ship **9.** ZOOL TROPICAL FISH a warm-water marine fish that has a forked tail. Genus: *Caranx*. **10.** BRACE ON MAST either one of a pair of wooden braces (**crosstrees**) at the head of a topgallant mast used to hold the mast stays away from the mast **11.** LABOURER a labourer, or sb who does odd jobs (*usually used in combination*) **12.** COOK DEVICE THAT TURNS SPIT a device that mechanically turns a spit over an open fire **13.** *US* MONEY money (*slang*) **14.** *US* APPLEJACK applejack ■ *vt.* (**jacks, jacking, jacked**) **1.** MECH ENG RAISE STH WITH JACK to raise a heavy object a short distance using a jack **2.** *US* CRIMINOL ROB SB to steal sth, especially a car, from sb (*slang*) **3.** PRISE STH OPEN to open sth by prising it apart (*slang*) ○ *Who jacked the door?* [14thC. Originally a nickname for *John*, hence a name for an ordinary man, hence applied to things taking the place of a man or saving human labour. The sense of 'small' developed in the 16thC.] ◇ **every man jack** every single person

jack around *vi.* to waste time, loaf, or act irresponsibly (*slang*) ○ *Stop jacking around and get to work!*

jack in *vt.* **1.** STOP DOING STH to stop doing an activity or job (*informal*) **2. jack in, jack into** TO CONNECT TO STH to connect sb or sth electronically to sth (*slang*) ○ *We're jacked into the Internet.*

jack off *vti.* *US* to masturbate yourself or sb else (*slang taboo*)

jack up *v.* **1.** *vt.* MECH ENG LIFT STH WITH JACK to use a jack to lift a heavy object, especially a motor vehicle, off the ground **2.** *vt.* INCREASE AMOUNT OF STH to increase sth, especially a price or salary, often to an unreasonably high level **3.** *vti.* DRUGS INJECT ILLEGAL DRUGS to inject a drug, especially heroin, intravenously (*slang*) **4.** *vi.* Aus REFUSE TO OBEY to refuse to comply with instructions (*informal*)

jack² /jak/ *n.* = jak

jack[3] /jak/ *n.* a short sleeveless coat of armour used in the Middle Ages made of canvas covered with metal plates [14thC. Via Old French *jaque* from Spanish or Portuguese *jaco*, of uncertain origin: perhaps from Arabic *shakk*.]

Jackal

jackal /ják awl, ják'l/ (*plural* **-als** *or* **-al**) *n.* **1.** ZOOL **WILD ANIMAL RESEMBLING DOG** a wild mammal resembling a dog, with long legs, large ears, and a bushy tail. It lives in Africa and southern Asia, and eats small animals, insects, and plants. Genus: *Canis*. **2.** SB PERFORMING MENIAL TASKS sb who does unskilled or menial work on sb else's behalf **3.** CRIMINOL SWINDLER sb who works with others to deceive people, especially to swindle them out of money [Early 17thC. From Turkish *çakal*, from Persian *šagāl*.]

jackanapes /jáka nayps/ (*plural* **jackanapes**) *n.* **1.** IMPUDENT PERSON sb who behaves in an impudent, self-centred way (*dated*) **2.** MISCHIEVOUS CHILD a child who behaves mischievously or impertinently (*dated*) **3.** MONKEY a monkey (*archaic*) [Early 16thC. Originally *Jack Napes*, of uncertain origin: perhaps a playful name for a tame ape, with 'n' added by misdivision of *an ape*.]

jackass /ják ass/ *n.* **1.** ZOOL MALE ASS a male donkey or ass (*slang*) **2.** OFFENSIVE TERM an offensive term that deliberately insults sb's intelligence (*slang insult*) [Early 18thC. *Jack* from JACK[1].] —**jackassery** *n.* ◇ **laughing jackass** = **kookaburra**

jack bean *n.* a tropical American climbing plant of the pea family that is grown in the southern United States mainly for forage. It has clusters of purple flowers that produce long pods with edible seeds. Latin name: *Canavalia ensiformis*.

jackboot /ják boot/ *n.* **1.** MIL MILITARY BOOT a type of sturdy long black leather boot that comes up to, or over, the knee, worn especially by the military in Nazi Germany **2.** HARSH TREATMENT military or other rule that is characterized by cruelty, oppression, or arbitrary aggression **3.** RIDING BOOT a heavy boot of hard leather worn for riding [Late 17thC. *Jack* of uncertain origin: probably from *jack*, a medieval iron-plated battle jacket.]

jack-by-the hedge (*plural* **jack-by-the-hedges**) *n.* = **garlic mustard**

jack crevalle *n.* a spiny-finned edible fish that is common off the western coast of Florida, where it is economically important. Latin name: *Caranx hippos*.

jackdaw /ják daw/ *n.* a large noisy bird of the crow family native to Europe and Asia. It is renowned for stealing things, especially shiny objects, which it hides or takes back to its nest. Latin name: *Corvus monedula*. [Mid-16thC. Literally 'untidy Jack' (see DAW).]

Jackeen /ja keen/ *n.* Ireland sb from Dublin who is thought of as well-read, confident, and particularly proud of being from working or lower class origins, or sometimes by non-Dubliners as smugly clever (*offensive in some contexts*) [Mid-19thC. From Anglo-Irish, diminutive of JACK[1].]

jackeroo /jáka roó/ *n.* Aus a young male trainee worker on a sheep or cattle station (*informal*)

jacket /jákit/ *n.* **1.** CLOTHES SHORT COAT a short, usually hip-length or waist-length coat, sometimes forming part of a suit. It usually has long sleeves, pockets, lapels, and fastens at the front with buttons or a zip. **2.** CLOTHES PROTECTIVE CLOTHING sth that is worn on the upper part of the body for protection or support **3.** FOOD POTATO SKIN the outer skin of an unpeeled cooked potato, especially a baked one **4.** PUBL = **dust jacket 5.** US RECORDING = **sleeve**. **3. 6.** COMPUT FLOPPY DISK CASING the casing of a floppy disk **7.** US COMM FOLDER a strong envelope or folder for holding papers or documents **8.** ENG BOILER COVER a cover or outer casing designed to insulate a boiler **9.** INDUST OUTER CASING OF PIPE an outer casing around a pipe that can be filled with steam or hot water to keep the contents of the pipe warm **10.** ARMS OUTER CASING OF BULLET an outer casing on certain bullets and other types of ammunition **11.** SPORTS COAT IDENTIFYING RACING DOG a distinctive coloured coat for an animal, especially a racing greyhound ∎ *vt.* (**-ets, -eting, -eted**) PUT JACKET ON STH to put a jacket on sb or sth, e.g. a book or record [15thC. From French *jaquet*, diminutive of Old French *jacque* 'tunic', from *jacques* 'peasant', from the common name *Jacques*; because peasants wore the garments.]

jacket potato *n.* a potato that has been baked with the skin still on it and is served plain or with a filling

jackfish /ják fish/ (*plural* **-fish** *or* **-fishes**) *n.* a pike, especially a young or small one [Late 16thC. *Jack* from JACK[1] in the meaning of 'small'.]

Jack Frost *n.* a personification of frost, very cold wintry weather, or the effects that frost or cold weather can produce

jackfruit /ják froot/ (*plural* **-fruit** *or* **-fruits**) *n.* **1.** TREES TROPICAL ASIAN TREE a large tree native to tropical Asia, where it is cultivated for its fine-grained yellowish wood and large edible fruits. Latin name: *Artocarpus heterophyllus*. **2.** FOOD = **jak** [Mid-19thC. *Jack* from Portuguese *jaca* (see JAK).]

Jack-go-to-bed-at-noon *n.* PLANTS = **goatsbeard** *n.* 1 [Because the flowers close up at about noon]

jackhammer /ják hammer/ *n.* a hand-held power tool, usually powered by compressed air and used for splitting or drilling rock, or for breaking up paved areas [*Jack* from JACK[1] in the meaning of 'small']

Jackie-O /jáki ó/ *adj.* used to describe a fashion style associated with Jacqueline Kennedy Onassis ○ *wearing a pair of Jackie-O sunglasses* [Mid-20thC]

jack-in-office (*plural* **jacks-in-office**) *n.* sb who behaves in a self-important way, especially a minor official who sticks to the rules without showing any flexibility

jack-in-the-box (*plural* **jacks-in-the-box** *or* **jack-in-the-boxes**) *n.* a child's toy consisting of a puppet on a spring inside a box. The puppet jumps out when a mechanism is triggered to open the lid.

jack-in-the-pulpit *n.* **1.** N AMERICAN PLANT a woodland plant of eastern North America that produces a thick spike of tiny flowers (**spadix**) surrounded by a sheath. Latin name: *Arisaema triphyllum*. **2.** = **cuckoopint**

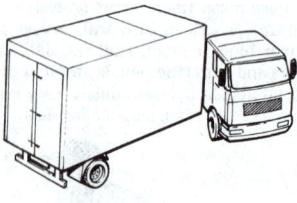

Jackknife: A jackknifed lorry

jackknife /ják nīf/ *n.* (*plural* **-knives**) **1.** FOLDING KNIFE a knife that has a pivoted blade that fits inside the handle when it is not in use **2.** SWIMMING DIVE a dive in which the diver jumps, bends the body at the waist while keeping the legs together and straight, then straightens out to enter the water headfirst ∎ *vi.* (**-knifes, -knifing, -knifed**) **1.** TRANSP FOLD TRAILER IN ON CAB to come to a halt with the trailer at an angle to the cab, as a result of sudden braking or swerving at speed (*refers to articulated lorries*) ○ *The lorry struck a patch of ice and jackknifed.* **2.** SWIMMING DO

JACKKNIFE DIVE to perform a jackknife dive [Early 18thC. *Jack* of uncertain origin: perhaps from JACK[1].]

jack ladder *n.* = **Jacob's ladder** *n.* 1

Jacklin /jáklin/, **Tony** (b. 1944) British golfer. British Open Champion (1969) and US Open Champion (1970), he later captained Europe's Ryder Cup team (1983–89).

jack-of-all-trades (*plural* **jacks-of-all-trades**) *n.* sb who can do various kinds of work

jack-o'-lantern *n.* **1.** LANTERN MADE FROM PUMPKIN a lantern made from a hollowed-out pumpkin that has facial features cut out of it, used as a part of Halloween decoration **2.** = **will-o'-the-wisp**

jack pine *n.* a pine tree of northern North America that has a narrow trunk, short needles arranged in pairs, and curving cones. It has soft wood that is used especially for paper pulp. Latin name: *Pinus banksiana*.

jack plane *n.* a large joinery plane used for rough planing of wood and other surfaces [*Jack* from JACK[1] in the sense of 'instrument']

jackpot /ják pot/ *n.* **1.** GAMBLING CASH PRIZE an amount of money won in a competition or lottery, or as a payout from a fruit machine or other kind of gambling machine **2.** CARDS TOTAL AMOUNT BET ON POKER HANDS an accumulated stake in poker games that can be competed for only by players holding a pair of jacks or a better hand [Late 19thC. *Jack* from the necessity of holding a pair of jacks or better to compete for the pot in poker.] ◇ **hit the jackpot** to achieve great success, especially financially

jack rabbit *n.* a large hare native to the prairies of western North America, with long hind legs and extremely long ears. Genus: *Lepus*. [*Jack* from JACKASS, because of its long ears.]

jack rafter *n.* any one of a set of sloping timber beams spanning between the eaves and the hip rafter of a roof. Each rafter is of a different length to fit the changing dimension of the roof plane. ['Jack' from JACK[1] in the sense of 'small']

Jack Robinson [Origin unknown] ◇ **before you can** *or* **could say Jack Robinson** without the slightest delay or hesitation (*informal*)

Jack Russell, **Jack Russell terrier** *n.* a small terrier with short legs and a white coat with patchy markings in black, brown, or tan, or a combination of these colours [Early 20thC. Named after John (Jack) Russell (1795–1883), the English clergyman who introduced the breed.]

jacks /jaks/ *n.* a game involving picking up small metal or plastic pieces in a particular sequence between bouncing or throwing and catching a ball (*takes a singular verb*) [Early 19thC. Shortening of JACKSTONES.]

jackscrew /ják skroo/ *n.* = **screwjack**

jackshaft /ják shaaft/ *n.* a short shaft that transmits power from a motor or engine to a machine

jacksie /jáksi/, **jacksy** (*plural* **-sies**) *n.* the buttocks or anus (*informal*) [Late 19thC. Colloquial use of JACK[1].]

jacksmelt /ják smelt/ (*plural* **-smelts** *or* **-smelt**) *n.* an edible and commercially important fish of the silverside family, found in North Pacific coastal waters of North America. Latin name: *Atherinopsis californiensis*.

jacksnipe /ják snīp/ (*plural* **-snipe** *or* **-snipes**) *n.* a small wading bird with a fairly short bill and legs and dark plumage. It breeds in swamps and bogs in the far north of Europe and Asia. Latin name: *Limnocryptes minimus*. [So called because of its small size (see JACK[1])]

Jackson /jáks'n/, **Andrew** (1767–1845) US statesman and 7th President of the United States. His army defeated the British at New Orleans during the War of 1812. As Democratic president (1829–37), he opposed the Bank of America and greatly strengthened the presidency. Known as **Old Hickory**

Jackson, Glenda (b. 1936) British actor and politician. She played in numerous Royal Shakespeare Company productions and in films, winning two Academy Awards, before becoming a Labour MP (1992).

Andrew Jackson

Jackson, Marjorie (*b.* 1932) Australian sprinter. She won two gold medals at the 1952 Olympic Games.

Jackson, Michael (*b.* 1958) US entertainer. He was the youngest brother in The Jackson Five before embarking on a successful solo singing career. His album *Thriller* (1982) broke sales records.

Stonewall Jackson

Jackson, Stonewall (1824–63) US general. He was one of the most successful Confederate commanders during the US Civil War (1861–65). Real name **Thomas Jonathan Jackson**

jackstay /ják stay/ *n.* **1.** ROD TO SECURE SAIL a rod attached to a horizontal beam (**yard**) on a mast, used for securing a sail **2.** SUPPORT a support for the ring (**parrel**) that holds a boom to a mast

jackstone /ják stōn/ *n.* a small piece of metal or plastic used in the game of jacks

jackstones /ják stōnz/ *n.* = **jacks** (*takes a singular verb*) [Early 19thC. Named with reference to the small size of the 'stones' (see JACK¹), originally little pebbles or bones.]

jackstraw /ják straw/ *n.* **1.** THIN PLAYING STICK a small thin stick used in the game of jackstraws **2. jackstraws** GAME OF SKILL a game that involves trying to remove a small thin stick (**jackstraw**) from a pile of others without disturbing any of the rest of them (*takes a singular verb*) [Late 16thC. Named because of its small size and also after *Jack Straw*, a 14thC English political rebel, with the sense of 'worthless person'; also 'man of straw'.]

jacksy /jáksi/ *n.* = **jacksie**

Jack Tar *n.* a sailor (*dated informal*) [JACK¹ with the sense 'everyman', *tar* from shortening of *tarpaulin*, used to make the sailors' hats]

Jack-the-lad *n.* a cocky and flashy young man (*informal*) [From the nickname of *Jack Sheppard*, an 18thC thief]

Jack-the-rags (*plural* **Jack-the-rags**) *n.* Wales Jack-the-lad (*informal*)

Jack the Ripper /ják thə rippər/ (*fl.* 1880s) British murderer. He was the notorious unknown killer of six prostitutes in London's East End between August and November 1888.

Jacob¹ /jáykəb/ *n.* in the Bible, the second son of Isaac and Rebekah, and the grandson of Abraham. He tricked his older brother, Esau, out of his father's blessing, and had a vision of ascent into heaven that came to be called 'Jacob's ladder' (Genesis 25–35).

Jacob² /jáykəb/, **Jacob sheep** *n.* a sheep with two or four horns and a cream-coloured fleece with dark-brown patches on it. The fleece is popular with spinners and handloom weavers. [Mid-17thC. Named after JACOB², who kept piebald sheep, described in the Bible, *Genesis* 30:39.]

Jacobean /jákə beé ən/ *adj.* **1.** HISTORY OF JAMES I relating to King James I or to the period of his English reign (1603–25). **2.** FURNITURE OF FURNITURE STYLE in the style of furniture fashionable during the reign of King James I. Pieces were typically quite bulky and were usually made from dark carved oak, often with Gothic motifs. **3.** ARCHIT OF ARCHITECTURAL STYLE in the style of architecture produced during the reign of King James I. It is transitional between the Gothic and Renaissance periods, retaining some Gothic motifs, but also anticipating the reverence for the classical that typifies later design. ■ *n.* HISTORY CONTEMPORARY OF JAMES I sb, especially a prominent person, who lived during the reign of King James I of England [Late 18thC. From ecclesiastical Latin *Jacobus* 'James'.]

Jacobean lily *n.* a flowering plant of the amaryllis family that is native to Mexico, widely cultivated for its bright-red single flower. Latin name: *Sprekelia formosissima*. [Named in honour of St James]

jacobin /jákəbin/ *n.* a variety of pigeon with feathers over the neck and head that grow in the opposite direction to the others, giving it the appearance of having a hood [Late 17thC. From French *jacobine*, femininine of *Jacobin* (see JACOBIN).]

Jacobin /jákəbin/ *n.* **1.** HISTORY FRENCH REVOLUTIONARY EXTREMIST a member of a group of left-wing extremists founded during the French Revolution. In 1793, they overthrew the more moderate republicans, the Girondists, and this allowed Robespierre, the leader of the group, to begin the Reign of Terror and to install revolutionary measures. **2.** POL LEFT-WING EXTREMIST a political radical, especially one who holds extreme left-wing views **3.** CHR FRIAR a French Dominican friar ■ *adj.* HISTORY OF FRENCH JACOBINS relating to the Jacobins of the French Revolution, or to their policies [From Old French, from ecclesiastical Latin *Jacobus*, originally a Dominican friar associated with the church of St Jacques in Paris, where the Jacobins were established] —**Jacobinic** /jákə bínnik/ *adj.* —**Jacobinical** /-bínnik'l/ *adj.* —**Jacobinically** /-bínnikli/ *adv.* —**Jacobinism** /jákəbinizəm/ *n.*

Jacobite /jákə bīt/ *n.* **1.** HISTORY SUPPORTER OF JAMES II AND VII sb who supported the Roman Catholic King James II of England and VII of Scotland and his descendants in the Stuart claim to the British throne **2.** CHR EASTERN CHURCH MEMBER a member of any of the Monophysite churches, especially of Syria ■ *adj.* HISTORY OF JACOBITES relating to the Stuart claim to the British throne or to those who supported the Stuart claim [Late 17thC. From ecclesiastical Latin *Jacobus* (see JACOBEAN).] —**Jacobitic** /jákə bíttik/ *adj.* —**Jacobitical** /-bíttik'l/ *adj.* —**Jacobitism** /jákə bītizəm/ *n.*

Jacob's ladder *n.* **1.** NAUT ROPE LADDER a ladder, used especially on ships, whose rungs are held together by ropes or chains, thus allowing it to be rolled up and stored in a small space **2.** PLANTS N AMERICAN PLANT a North American wild or garden plant that has blue or white flowers and leaves divided into several leaflets in an arrangement similar to a ladder. Genus: *Polemonium*. [Named with reference to the story of Jacob's vision of a ladder reaching to heaven (Genesis 28 :12)]

Jacob's staff *n.* a medieval instrument for measuring distance [Alludes to St James (ecclesiastical Latin *Jacobus* 'James'), one of whose symbols is a pilgrim's staff, or to the staff of Jacob (Genesis 30:10)]

jaconet /jákənit/ *n.* a cotton fabric that is like muslin but slightly heavier and is used for clothing and bandages [Mid-18thC. Anglicization of *Jagannāth(purī)* in India, where it originated.]

jacquard /ják aard/ *n.* **1.** WEAVING TECHNIQUE a technique for producing intricate patterns in material by means of punched cards that give instructions to use or withhold various colours of thread **2.** LOOM ATTACHMENT a loom attachment with punched cards that makes jacquard patterns **3.** = **jacquard loom 4.** PATTERNED MATERIAL a fabric that has been woven with a jacquard pattern [Mid-19thC. Named after its inventor J. M. JACQUARD.]

Jacquard /ják aard/, **Joseph Marie** (1752–1832) French inventor. His invention of the jacquard loom (1801–08), the first mechanical loom for weaving complex patterns, was an inspiration for modern computer programming.

jacquard loom *n.* a loom with an attachment for making jacquard patterns

Jacques-Cartier /zhák kaárti ay/ river that flows south into the St Lawrence River just south of Quebec City in southern Quebec, Canada. Length: 113 km/70 mi.

jactitation /jákti táysh'n/ *n.* **1.** MED UNCONTROLLED THRASHING a state of thrashing around uncontrollably, usually brought on by extremely high temperature, or occasionally by psychiatric disorders **2.** LAW HARMFUL LIE a false boast or claim, especially one that is intended to harm another **3.** BOASTING the act of boasting or exaggerating (*literary*) [Mid-17thC. From Latin *jactitare* 'to bring forward in public, boast', literally 'to throw repeatedly over and over', from, ultimately, Latin *jacere* 'to throw'.]

Jacuzzi /jə koózi/ *tdmk.* a trademark for a whirlpool bath with a system of underwater jets that deliver water under pressure in order to massage and invigorate the body

jade¹ /jayd/ *n.* **1.** SEMIPRECIOUS STONE either of two different minerals, nephrite or jadeite, varying in colour from a deep green to yellow and brown to white, mainly used for making ornaments and jewellery (*often used before a noun*) ○ *a jade necklace* **2.** JADE OBJECTS objects made of jade, collectively ○ *a collector of jade* ■ *n.*, *adj.* COLOURS = **jade green** [Late 16thC. Via French *l'ejade* from Spanish *piedra de ijada* 'stone of the flanks', thought to cure pain in the renal areas, ultimately from Latin *ilia* 'flanks'.]

--- **WORD KEY: ORIGIN** ---

Despite *jade*'s close association with China and Japan, its name has no Asian connections. It is of Latin origin, and started life as a description of the stone's medical applications. Latin *ilia* denoted the 'sides of the lower torso', the 'flanks', the part of the body where the kidneys are situated. A derivative of it passed eventually into Spanish as *ijada*. It was thought in former times that jade could cure pain in the renal area, so the Spanish called it *piedra de ijada*, literally 'stone of the flanks'. In due course this was reduced to simply *ijada*. French took it over as *ejade*, but subsequently *l'ejade* 'the jade' became *le jade*, from which English *jade* is derived. (*Jade*'s alternative name, *nephrite*, is based on the same idea: it comes from Greek *nephros* 'kidney').

jade² /jayd/ *n.* **1.** TIRED OLD HORSE an old horse, especially one that is worn out through overwork (*dated*) **2.** OFFENSIVE TERM an offensive term for a woman that deliberately insults her temperament or her morality (*offensive dated*) ■ *vti.* (**jades, jading, jaded**) MAKE OR BECOME EXHAUSTED to wear sb out or become exhausted, especially through overwork (*dated*) [14thC. Origin unknown.]

jaded /jáydid/ *adj.* **1.** BORED no longer interested in sth, often because of having been overexposed to it **2.** TIRED exhausted, especially through overwork —**jadedly** *adv.* —**jadedness** *n.*

jade green *n.* a pale milky green colour, like that of some types of jade —**jade-green** *adj.*

jadeite /jáyd īt/ *n.* a usually greenish pyroxene mineral consisting of sodium aluminium silicate, occurring only in metamorphic rocks. It is the source of the most precious jade and is found mainly in Myanmar. —**jaditic** /jay díttik/ *adj.*

j'adoube /zha doób, zhə doób/ *interj.* an expression used by a chess player who is about to adjust a piece on the board, to ensure that this will not be counted as an official move [Early 19thC. From French, literally 'I dub' (touch on the shoulder).]

jaeger /jáygər/ *n.* **1.** BIRDS PREDATORY SEA BIRD any of several mostly brownish or grayish predatory sea birds with narrow wings, found in the northern Pacific and Atlantic. Genus: *Stercorarius*. **2.** HUNT HUNTER a hunter, especially in Germany and Switzerland [Mid-19thC. Anglicization of German *Jäger* 'huntsman', from *jagen* 'to hunt, pursue'.]

Jaén /haa én/ capital city of Jaén Province in southern Spain. It is an industrial centre. Population: 101,938 (1991).

Jaffa /jáffə/, **Jaffa orange** *n.* a variety of large thick-skinned juicy orange [Late 19thC. Named after *Jaffa* (TEL-AVIV YAFO), where this fruit was first cultivated.]

Jaffna /jáfnə/ port and capital city of Northern Province, in northern Sri Lanka. Population: 129,000 (1990).

jag[1] /jag/ *n.* **1.** JAGGED PROJECTION a sharp projection, especially of rock **2.** NOTCH a notch or indentation in sth, e.g. a leaf **3.** TEAR IN CLOTHING a deliberate tear in a garment or piece of material that reveals a different material underneath (*archaic*) **4.** *Scotland* INJECTION an injection (*informal*) ■ *vt.* (**jags, jagging, jagged**) CUT STH UNEVENLY to cut notches in sth, or cut sth unevenly [14thC. Origin uncertain, possibly from, ultimately, Arabic *az-zagaye* 'lance, javelin'.]

jag[2] /jag/ *n.* (*informal*) **1.** PERIOD OF INTOXICATION a period of intoxication by drugs or alcohol **2.** DRUNKEN STATE the state of being intoxicated from drugs or alcohol **3.** BINGE a period of time spent doing sth in an uncontrolled or excessive way [Late 16thC. Origin unknown.]

JAG *abbr.* Judge Advocate General

jagged /jággid/ *adj.* **1.** WITH SHARP POINTS having sharp protruding parts or points ○ *jagged peaks of the distant mountains* **2.** UNEVEN having rough and uneven edges or surfaces ○ *a hastily drawn, jagged portrait* —**jaggedly** *adv.* —**jaggedness** *n.*

Mick Jagger

Jagger /jággər/, **Mick** (*b.* 1943) British rock musician and songwriter. He founded, with Keith Richards, the Rolling Stones, and wrote many of their hits, including 'Satisfaction' (1965). Full name **Michael Phillip Jagger**

jaggery /jággəri/ *n.* unrefined brown sugar made in Southeast Asia from the sap of the date palm [Late 16thC. From Portugese *xagara*, from, ultimately, Sanskrit *śarkarā* 'sugar'.]

jaggy /jággi/ (**-gier, -giest**) *adj.* (*informal*) **1.** JAGGED jagged **2.** *Scotland* PRICKLY prickly and irritating to the skin

Jaguar

jaguar /jággyoo ər/ *n.* a large cat related to the leopard but with a shorter tail and black spots inside black rings on its tawny coat. It lives mainly in the forests of southern North America, Central America, and northern South America. Latin name: *Panthera onca.* [Early 17thC. From Portuguese, from Tupi *jaguara* and Guarani *yaguará* 'carnivorous animal'.]

jaguarundi /jágwə rúndi/, **jaguarondi** /-róndi/ *n.* a small slender cat of Central and South America that has a brownish, greyish, or reddish coat and small ears. Latin name: *Felis yagouaroundi.* ◊ **eyra** [Mid-19thC.

Coined from Portuguese *jaguar* (see JAGUAR) + *undi* 'dark'.]

Jah /jaa/ *n.* God, especially in Rastafarianism [Mid-16thC. From Hebrew *Yāh*, a shortening of *Yahweh* 'Jehovah'.]

Jahveh, **Jahweh** *n.* = **Yahweh**

jai alai /hī ə lī/ *n.* a version of the game pelota, for two or four players. ◊ **pelota** [Early 20thC. From Spanish, from Basque *jai* 'festival' + *alai* 'merry'.]

Jai Hind /ja hínd/ *interj. S Asia* an Indian slogan meaning 'victory to India', shouted especially at political rallies or given as a greeting [Mid-20thC. From Hindi, from *jai* 'long live'! + *Hind* 'India'.]

jail /jayl/, **gaol** *n.* **1.** PLACE WHERE CRIMINALS ARE KEPT a secure place for keeping people found guilty of crimes or awaiting legal judgment **2.** LIFE AS A PRISONER the state of being kept in a jail ○ *sentenced to three years jail.* ◊ **prison** ■ *vt.* (**jails, jailing, jailed; gaols, gaoling, gaoled**) **1.** SEND SB TO JAIL to sentence sb to spend time in a jail ○ *The judge jailed her for three months.* **2.** LOCK SB IN JAIL to keep sb in a jail or other secure place ○ *prisoners who were jailed in a dungeon* [13thC. 'Gaol' via Old North French *gaiole* 'jail', via Old French *jaiole*, from Latin *caveola*, diminutive of *cavea* 'cage'.]

jailbait /jáyl bayt/ *n.* an offensive term for a minor under the age of consent who is sexually desirable to sb older (*slang offensive*)

jailbird /jáyl burd/ *n.* a current or former prisoner, especially sb with more than one experience of prison (*slang*)

jailbreak /jáyl brayk/ *n.* a forceful escape from jail or prison

jailer /jáylər/, **jailor, gaoler** *n.* sb who is in charge of prisoners in a jail, or who is in overall charge of a jail

jail fever *n.* typhus (*dated*)

jailhouse /jáyl howss/ *n. US* a jail (*informal*)

jailor *n.* = **jailer**

Jain /jīn, jayn/, **Jaina** /jínə, jáynə/ *n.* BELIEVER IN JAINISM sb who believes in or practises Jainism ■ *adj.* OF JAINISM relating to Jains or Jainism [Late 18thC. From Hindi, from Sanskrit *jaina* 'of a conqueror'.]

Jainism /jīnizəm, jáyn-/ *n.* an ancient branch of Hinduism that rejects the notion of a supreme being and advocates a deep respect for all living things. Some adherents refuse to wash for fear of killing creatures on the body. —**Jainist** *adj.*

Jaipur /jī poór/ capital city of Rajasthan State, northern India. It is a major commercial and manufacturing centre. Population: 1,454,678 (1991).

jak /jak/, **jack** *n.* the large greenish bulbous fruit produced by the jackfruit tree. It can weigh up to 27 kg/60 lb and has highly nutritious seeds. [Late 16thC. Via Portuguese *jaca* from Malayalam *cakka*.]

Jakarta /jə kaártə/ capital and largest city of Indonesia, located in the centre of the country, on the northwestern coast of the island of Java. Population: 9,160,5000 (1995). Former name **Batavia**

jakes /jayks/ (*plural* **jakeses** *or* **jakes**) *n.* **1.** *UK, US* LAVATORY a lavatory, especially an outside one or one without running water (*regional archaic informal*) **2.** *SW England* HUMAN EXCREMENT human faeces, urine, or excrement generally (*informal*) [Mid-16thC. Origin uncertain: perhaps from the male forename *Jacques*, or *Jack's* (see JACK[1]).]

Jalalabad /jə laálə bad/, **Jalālābād** city in eastern Afghanistan, on the River Kabul

Jalandhar /jállən daar/ ◆ **Jullunder**

jalap /jálləp/ *n.* a Mexican twining plant of the convolvulus family, the dried tubers of which have a purgative effect. Latin name: *Ipomoea purga.* [Mid-17thC. Via French from an abbreviation of Spanish *purga de Jalapa*, named after the Mexican city of *Jalapa*, where the plant flourished.] —**jalapic** /jə láppik/ *adj.*

jalapeño /hállə páy nyō/ (*plural* **-ños**), **jalapeño pepper** *n.* a small hot pepper that is green or red when ripe and is used extensively in Mexican cooking. Latin name: *Capsicum annuum.* [Mid-20thC. From Mexican Spanish.]

jalopy /jə lóppi/ (*plural* **-ies**) *n.* a rickety or battered old car (*dated informal*) [Early 20thC. Origin unknown.]

jalouse /jə looz/ (**-louses, -lousing, -loused**) *vt. Scotland* to suspect that sth is the case (*nonstandard*) [Late 17thC. From French *jalouser* 'to envy, be jealous of'.]

Jalousie

jalousie /zhálloo zee/ *n.* a shutter or window covering consisting of a set of angled parallel slats that can be opened to various degrees to control the amount of light or air passing through [Mid-18thC. From French, literally 'jealousy', by extension a type of window-covering or shutter.]

jam[1] /jam/ *v.* (**jams, jamming, jammed**) **1.** *vt.* PUSH STH IN FORCIBLY to push sth into a tight space with force ○ *jammed the clothes into the wardrobe* **2.** *vt.* FILL STH UP to fill a place with people or things pressed closely together ○ *The fans jammed the streets to see their heroes.* ○ *jammed the fridge with delicacies* **3.** *vti.* STOP WORKING to cause a piece of machinery or equipment to stick or stop working, or undergo such a stoppage ○ *The photocopier jammed when I was in the middle of using it.* **4.** *vt.* BLOCK STH UP to block up sth that functions as an exit, passage, or means of escape ○ *Leaves had jammed the drains and gutters.* **5.** *vt.* PUT ON BRAKES HARD to apply the brakes of a car suddenly and hard **6.** *vt.* CRUSH PART OF BODY to injure a part of the body, especially by squeezing or squashing it ○ *I jammed my finger in the door.* **7.** *vt.* BROADCAST INTERFERE WITH BROADCASTING SIGNALS to block a radio or TV signal, usually by broadcasting other signals on the same frequency **8.** *vt.* TELECOM OVERWHELM SWITCHBOARD to overwhelm a switchboard with telephone calls **9.** *vt.* RECORDING MAKE TAPE IMPOSSIBLE TO COPY to put a blocking device on sth, especially a prerecorded video tape, in order to prevent it from being copied **10.** *vi.* MUSIC IMPROVISE MUSIC TOGETHER to play music, especially jazz, rock, or pop, in an improvised way, often in a group ■ *n.* **1.** = **traffic jam 2.** DIFFICULT SITUATION a difficult, awkward, or embarrassing situation (*informal*) ○ *a cash shortage that's got the company in a jam* **3.** STOPPAGE an instance of sth being blocked or prevented from functioning ○ *a paper jam in the photocopier* **4.** BROADCAST SIGNAL BLOCKAGE a blockage of radio or television signals **5.** RECORDING DEVICE TO PREVENT COPYING a device that prevents sth, especially a prerecorded video tape, from being copied **6.** MUSIC = **jam session** (*informal*) [Early 18thC. Origin uncertain, perhaps imitative of the action of pushing. Music senses perhaps from Mandingo and Black West African English *jama* 'crowd gathering', and Wolof *jaam* 'enslaved person'.] —**jammable** *adj.* —**jammer** *n.*

jam[2] /jam/ *n.* FRUIT SPREAD a spread made from fruit boiled with sugar. Pectin is often added to help it set. ■ *vt.* (**jams, jamming, jammed**) MAKE FRUIT INTO JAM to make fruit into jam by boiling it with sugar [Mid-18thC. Origin uncertain: possibly from the idea of crushing or 'jamming' fruit into jars.]

Jam. *abbr.* **1.** Jamaica **2.** BIBLE James

Jamaica /jə máykə/ island country situated south of Cuba in the northern Caribbean Sea. It is the third largest island of the Greater Antilles. Language: English. Currency: Jamaican dollar. Capital: Kingston. Population: 2,615,581 (1997). Area: 10,991 sq. km/4,244 sq. mi. —**Jamaican** *n., adj.*

Jamaica pepper *n.* = **allspice** *n.* 2

Jamaica rum *n.* a slowly fermented rum that has a dark colour and a strong flavour

jamb /jam/, **jambe** *n.* **1.** UPRIGHT SUPPORT either of the upright parts of a door or window frame or the sides of a fireplace **2.** INSIDE SURFACE the inside vertical

Jamaica

face of an opening [14thC. Via Italian *gamba* or Old French *jambe* 'leg', from, ultimately, Greek *kampē* 'bend, joint'.]

jambalaya /jámbə líˈə, júmbə-/ *n.* a Creole dish of rice with a mixture of fish and meat such as shrimps, chicken, ham, and spicy sausage [Late 19thC. Via Louisiana French from Provençal *jambalaia* 'stewed mixture of rice and fowl'.]

Jambi /jámbi/ city and port in western Indonesia, on the island of Sumatra. It is the capital of Jambi Province. Population: 301,359 (1990).

jamboree /jámbə reeˈ/ *n.* **1.** BIG CELEBRATION a large-scale planned celebration with various events and entertainments **2.** INTERNATIONAL MEETING OF SCOUTS OR GUIDES a large gathering of members of the Scout or Guide movement, often on an international scale [Mid-19thC. Origin uncertain.]

James[1] /jaymz/ *n.* in the Bible, an epistle believed to have been written by James, a brother or relative of Jesus Christ. See table at **Bible**

James[2] /jaymz/ river in western Virginia, formed at Iron Gate by the joining of the Cowpasture and Jackson rivers. Length: 547 km/340 mi.

James, St (*fl.* AD 1st century) One of the 12 apostles, he was a member of the inner circle of Jesus Christ's disciples. He was the son of Zebedee and Salome and the brother of St John. (Matthew 4:21). Known as **St James the Great**

James, St (*fl.* AD 1st century) He was a relative of Jesus Christ, and is identified in the New Testament as a leader of the early Christian church in Jerusalem. (Mark 6:3). Known as **St James the Just**

James, St (*d.* AD 62?). One of the 12 apostles, he was the son of Alphaeus. (Matthew 10:3). Known as **St James the Less**

James I, King of Aragón (1208–76). He captured the Balearic Islands (1229–35) and Valencia (1238) from the Moors. Known as **James the Conqueror**

James I, King of England, Scotland, and Ireland (1566–1625). He was king of Scotland as James VI (1567–1625), and succeeded to the English throne in 1603. He authorized the King James Bible.

James II, King of England, Scotland, and Ireland (1633–1701). His Roman Catholicism occasioned political conflict before and during his reign (1685–88), and he was deposed in the Revolution of 1688–89 by his nephew and son-in-law William III.

James VI /jaymz/ ♦ **James I**

P. D. James

James, P. D., Baroness James of Holland Park (*b.* 1920) British novelist. Her best-selling crime novels include *The Black Tower* (1975) and *Original Sin* (1994). Full name **Phyllis Dorothy James**

James Bay southern extension of Hudson Bay, between western Quebec and northeastern Ontario, Canada. Area: 32,000 sq. km/12,350 sq. mi.

Jameson /jaymsˈn/, **Sir Leander** (1853–1917) British-born South African politician. He led the Jameson Raid, an attempt to overthrow the Boer government in the Transvaal (1895). Full name **Sir Leander Starr Jameson**

Jamestown Island /jáymz town-/ island in eastern Virginia, on the James River. It was the site of Jamestown village, the first permanent settlement of English colonists in North America.

jaminder *n.* = **zamindar**

jam jar *n.* **1.** JAR FOR JAM a glass jar with a lid containing jam **2.** CAR a car (*slang*)

jammies /jámmiz/ *npl.* pyjamas (*informal; often used by or to children*) [Late 20thC. Shortening and alteration.]

Jammu and Kashmir /júmmoo-/ section of the disputed territory of Kashmir in the northern part of the Indian subcontinent that has been under Indian control since 1972

jammy[1] /jámmi/ (**-mier**, **-miest**) *adj.* **1.** STICKY WITH JAM covered in or filled with jam **2.** LUCKY lucky (*informal*) **3.** EXCELLENT excellent or profitable (*slang*)

jammy[2] /jámmi/ (*plural* **-mies**) *n.* S Africa an old car (*slang humorous*) [Origin uncertain: perhaps from rhyming slang *jam jar*]

jam-pack *vt.* to fill a container or place extremely tightly or to capacity (*informal*)

jam session *n.* a period of time spent making improvised music, especially jazz, rock, or pop music, as practice, for fun, or to experiment with new songs or techniques

Jamshedpur /júm shed poórˈ/ city in eastern India, on the Subarnarekha River, in Bihar State. Population: 478,950 (1991).

Jan, Jan. *abbr.* January

Janáček /yánnə chekˈ/, **Leo** (1854–1928) Czech composer. His music was influenced by traditional Czech folk songs, and includes the operas *Jenufa* (1904) and *The Cunning Little Vixen* (1924).

Jandal /jándˈl/ *tdmk. NZ* a trademark for a very open sandal that has a thong between the big toe and the other toes

Janeite /jáyn īt/ *n.* sb who is an expert on or admirer of the life and works of the English novelist Jane Austen

JANET /jánnit/ *n.* an Internet-linked computer network used by academics and researchers, especially those affiliated to universities and institutes of higher education [Acronym formed from *Joint Academic Network*]

jangle /jáng gˈl/ *vti.* (**-gles**, **-gling**, **-gled**) **1.** MAKE A METALLIC SOUND to make a harsh metallic noise, or cause sth made of metal to make such a noise ○ *heard his keys jangling* **2.** IRRITATE SB'S NERVES to put sb's nerves on edge, or be tense and on edge ○ *The shock jangled her nerves.* ■ *n.* **1.** METALLIC SOUND a harsh metallic noise **2.** ARGUMENT a disagreement or quarrel (*dated*) [13thC. From Old French *jangler* 'to chatter', of uncertain origin: possibly from prehistoric Germanic.] —**jangler** *n.* —**jangly** *adj.*

janissary /jánnissəri/ (*plural* **-ies**), **janizary** /-zəri/ (*plural* **-ies**) *n.* **1.** HIST TURKISH SOLDIER a member of the Turkish sultan's elite personal guard from the 14th century until 1826. Janissaries were recruited from Christians in the Balkans and disbanded as part of 19th-century reforms. **2.** DEVOTED FOLLOWER a loyal follower or supporter [Early 16thC. Via French *janissaire* from, ultimately, Turkish *yeniçeri*, literally 'new troops'.]

janitor /jánnitər/ *n.* **1.** US, Can, Scotland = **caretaker 2.** DOORKEEPER a doorkeeper (*archaic*) [Mid-16thC. From Latin, 'door person', from *janua* 'door'. The caretaking sense developed in the early 18thC.] —**janitorial** /jánni táwri əl/ *adj.*

janizary *n.* = **janissary**

jankers /jángkərz/ *n.* punishment for a serviceman

or servicewoman who has committed a military offence (*slang*) [Early 20thC. Origin unknown.]

Jan Mayen /yan míˈ ən/ island of Norway, lying between Norway and Greenland in the Arctic Ocean. Area: 373 km/144 mi. Length: 63 km/39 mi.

Jansen /jánssˈn/, **Cornelis** (1585–1638) Dutch theologian. He was the founder of the Roman Catholic reform movement known as Jansenism. His work *Augustinus* (1640) was condemned as heretical.

Jansenism /jánss'nizəm/ *n.* a religious movement of the 17th and 18th centuries based on the theological views of Cornelius Jansen, who maintained that there can be no good act without divine will or the grace of God [Mid-17thC. Named after Cornelius *Jansen* (1585–1638), Bishop of Ypres in France.] —**Jansenist** *n.* —**Jansenistic** /jánssə nístik/ *adj.* —**Jansenistical** /jánssə nístik-/ *adj.*

jansky /jánski/ (*plural* **-skys**) *n.* a unit used to indicate the strength of radio sources in astronomy, equal to 10^{-26} watts per square metre per hertz. Symbol **Jy** [Mid-20thC. Named after the US radio engineer Karl C. *Jansky* (1905–50), who discovered radio waves in outer space.]

January /jánnyoŏ əri, jánnyoŏri/ (*plural* **-ys**) *n.* the first month of the year in the Gregorian calendar. It is 31 days long. [Pre-12thC. From Latin *Januarius* (*mensis*), first month of the Roman year, literally 'month of Janus', from *Janus* (see JANUS).]

Janus /jáynəss/ *n.* **1.** MYTHOL ROMAN GOD SHOWN WITH TWO FACES the Roman god of beginnings, of the past and the future, and of gates, doorways, and bridges, and of peace. He is traditionally depicted as having two faces looking in opposite directions, suggesting not only vigilance, but also fair-mindedness. Unusually, he has no Greek counterpart. **2.** ASTRON SATELLITE OF SATURN the tenth satellite of Saturn

Janus-faced *adj.* insincere or hypocritical (*literary*)

Jap /jap/ *n.* a highly offensive term for a Japanese person (*slang insult*)

Jap. *abbr.* Japanese

japan /jə pán/ *n.* **1.** BLACK VARNISH a lacquer that, when used to coat wood or metal, gives a glossy black finish **2.** VARNISHED OBJECTS decorative work that has been coated with japan or a similar kind of varnish ■ *vt.* (**-pans**, **-panning**, **-panned**) APPLY JAPAN TO STH to varnish an object with japan [Late 17thC. Named after JAPAN, where it was originally made.]

Japan

Japan /jə pán/ constitutional monarchy in eastern Asia, comprising four large islands and more than 1,000 lesser adjacent islands. Language: Japanese. Currency: yen. Capital: Tokyo. Population: 125,688,711 (1997). Area: 377,750 sq. km/145,850 sq. mi.

Japan, Sea of sea lying between Japan and mainland Asia, connected to the Sea of Okhotsk, the Pacific Ocean, and the East China Sea. Area: 1,000,000 sq. km/390,000 sq. mi.

Japan clover *n.* an annual plant originally native to China and Japan, but now widely grown in the southeastern United States as a forage crop. It has compound leaves divided into many leaflets and small pink flowers. Latin name: *Lespedeza striata*.

Japan Current ♦ **Kuroshio**

Japanese /jáppə neézˈ/ *n.* (*plural* **-nese**) **1.** PEOPLES SB FROM JAPAN sb who was born or brought up in Japan, or who has Japanese citizenship **2. LANG OFFICIAL LANGUAGE OF JAPAN** the official language of Japan, also spoken in parts of Brazil and North America. Its linguistic affiliations are disputed. Some linguists consider it to be an isolate, others relate it to the Altaic family or to Korean. About 126 million people speak Japanese. ■ *adj.* **OF JAPAN OR JAPANESE** relating to or typical of Japan, or its people, culture, or language

Japanese andromeda *n.* an ornamental shrub originally native to Japan but now widely grown for its early-blooming clusters of white bell-shaped flowers. Latin name: *Pieris japonica*.

Japanese beetle *n.* a shiny green and brown scarab beetle that was accidentally introduced into the eastern United States where it has become a serious pest. The larvae eat the roots of grasses and cereal crops and the adults feed on leaves and fruits.

Japanese cedar *n.* = **cryptomeria**

Japanese clover *n.* = **Japan clover**

Japanese garden *n.* a garden designed according to formal Japanese rules, distinguished by its use of foliage plants, rocks, sand, and wooden garden paths, bridges, and pavilions

Japanese iris *n.* an ornamental plant originally native to Japan but now widely grown for its large-petalled, brightly coloured red flowers. Latin name: *Iris kaempferi*.

Japanese maple *n.* a small Asian maple that is widely cultivated for its reddish deeply lobed leaves and purple flowers. Latin name: *Acer palmatum*.

Japanese millet *n.* a coarse Asian annual grass that has edible seeds and is grown for fodder. Latin name: *Echinochloa frumentacea*.

Japanese persimmon *n.* **1. TREES ASIAN FRUIT TREE** an Asian tree that produces large edible red or orange fruit. Latin name: *Diospyros kaki*. **2. FOOD FRUIT OF JAPANESE PERSIMMON** the large edible red or orange fruit of the Japanese persimmon tree. It is bitter when unripe and retains its green calyx even when ripe.

Japanese plum *n.* **1. TREES ASIAN PLUM TREE** a widely cultivated Asian tree with yellow or red fruit. Latin name: *Prunus salicina*. **2. FOOD FRUIT OF JAPANESE PLUM** the fruit of the Japanese plum tree, often pickled and used in cooking, or dried as a health food

Japanese quince *n.* an Asian ornamental shrub of the rose family cultivated for its bright red or pink flowers and edible round white, yellow, or green fruit. Latin name: *Chaenomeles japonica*.

Japanese umbrella pine *n.* a coniferous tree native to central Japan, widely grown elsewhere for ornament. Its leaves grow in pairs fused along their entire lengths and arranged in whorls like the ribs of an umbrella. Latin name: *Sciadopitys verticillata*.

Japan wax, Japan tallow *n.* a hard yellow wax obtained from certain berries. It is used in making candles, matches, soap, polish, food packaging, and as a substitute for beeswax.

jape /jayp/ *n.* **JEST** a joke or an act of mischief (*archaic*) ■ *vti.* (**japes, japing, japed**) **MAKE MISCHIEF** to joke, trick, or make fun of sth (*archaic*) [14thC. From Old French *japer* 'to yelp', influenced by *gaber* 'to mock'.] —**japer** *n.* — **japery** *n.*

Japheth /jáy feth/ *n.* in the Bible, the third son of Noah and brother of Shem and Ham. He was traditionally regarded as the ancestor of a number of non-Semitic peoples of the Mediterranean (Gen 10:1–5).

Japlish /jáplish/ *n.* Japanese with many adoptions of English words, phrases, or idioms [Mid-20thC. Blend of JAPANESE and ENGLISH.]

japonica /jə pónnikə/ *n.* **1.** = **Japanese quince 2.** = **camellia** *n.* 1 [Early 19thC. From modern Latin, feminine form of *Japonicus* 'of Japan'.]

Jaques-Dalcroze /zhák dal króz/, **Emile** (1865–1950) Swiss music teacher and composer. He was the originator of eurhythmics.

jar[1] /jaar/ *n.* **1. STORAGE CONTAINER** a cylindrical container, usually one that has a wide mouth and a lid but no spout, typically made of glass, plastic, or earthenware ○ *pickle jars* **2.** = **jarful 3. ALCOHOLIC DRINK** a glass of beer or other alcoholic drink (*informal*) ■

vt. (**jars, jarring, jarred**) **PUT STH IN JAR** to put sth into a jar, often sealing it in [Late 16thC. Via French *jarre* from Arabic *jarra*.]

jar[2] /jaar/ *v.* (**jars, jarring, jarred**) **1.** *vti.* **IRRITATE** to have an irritating or upsetting effect on sb's nerves or mind ○ *Her constant moaning jars my nerves.* **2.** *vt.* **DISTURB SB** to have a sudden unsettling effect on sb ○ *He needs something to jar him out of his reverie.* **3.** *vi.* **CLASH** to look or seem bad or inappropriate in the context of sth else ○ *The ultramodern dormitories jar with the older, Gothic classroom buildings.* **4.** *vti.* **GRATE** to make, or cause sth to make, a harsh grating noise **5.** *vti.* **SHAKE** to start vibrating, or cause sth to start vibrating ○ *When the furnace comes on it jars the table.* **6.** *vt.* **INJURE STH** to cause injury to a body part by jolting it ○ *Sam jarred his neck in a car accident.* ■ *n.* **1. PHYSICAL JOLT** an act of knocking against sth with a sudden blow **2. GRATING SOUND** a harsh grating noise [Late 15thC. Origin uncertain: probably in some part imitative of discordant sound.] —**jarring** *adj.* —**jarringly** *adv.*

jar[3] /jaar/ *n.* the state of being open or ajar (*archaic*) [Late 17thC. Later form of CHAR, from Old English *cerr* 'turn (of work)'.] ◇ **on the jar** ajar (*dated*)

jarbox /ja'ar boks/ *n.* *Ireland* a sink (*informal*)

jardinière /zha'ardini áir, zha'ardin yáir/ *n.* a large, usually decorative flower pot or other holder for plants [Mid-19thC. From French, literally 'female gardener'.]

jarful /ja'arfool/ *n.* the amount a jar holds, or the contents of a jar

jargon[1] /ja'argən/ *n.* **1. SPECIALIST LANGUAGE** language that is used by a particular group, profession, or culture, especially when the words and phrases are not understood or used by other people ○ *typesetters' jargon* **2. UNINTELLIGIBLE LANGUAGE** pretentious or meaningless language (*disapproving*) ○ *Cut the jargon and get to your point.* **3.** = **pidgin** ■ *vi.* = **jargonize** *v.* 2 [14thC. From Old French *jargoun*, of uncertain origin.] —**jargoneer** /ja'argə ne'er/ *n.* —**jargonist** /ja'argənist/ *n.* —**jargonistic** /-nístik/ *adj.*

jargon[2] /ja'ar gon/, **jargoon** /jaar go'on/ *n.* a colourless, pale, or smoky zircon [Mid-18thC. Via French from Italian *giargone* and, ultimately, from Persian *zargūn* 'gold-coloured'.]

jargonize /ja'argə nīz/ (**-izes, -izing, -ized**), **jargonise** (**-ises, -ising, -ised**) *v.* **1.** *vt.* **TURN LANGUAGE INTO JARGON** to convert ordinary language into jargon **2.** *vi.* **USE JARGON** to talk in jargon —**jargonization** /ja'argə nī záysh'n/ *n.*

jargoon *n.* = **jargon**[2]

jari *n.* = **zari**

jarl /yaarl/ *n.* a chieftain or nobleman in medieval Scandinavia [Early 19thC. From Old Norse *jarl* 'earl', of unknown origin.] —**jarldom** *n.*

Jarlsberg /ya'arlz burg/ *n.* a type of mild pale-yellow Norwegian cheese that has large holes in it

Jarman /ja'armən/, **Derek** (1942–94) British film director and painter. His experimental films, some with homoerotic themes, include *Sebastiane* (1976), *Jubilee* (1978), and *Caravaggio* (1986).

jarosite /járrə sīt/ *n.* a secondary mineral in iron-containing ores, yellow to brown in colour and consisting of a hydrous sulphate of iron and potassium [Mid-19thC. Named after the *Jarosa* ravine in southern Spain, where it was first found.]

jarrah /járrə/ *n.* **1. TREES AUSTRALIAN TREE** a eucalyptus tree of southwestern Australia with dark reddish hard wood. Latin name: *Eucalyptus marginata*. **2. INDUST JARRAH WOOD** the timber of the jarrah tree, used in flooring and building [Mid-19thC. From Aboriginal *djarryl, jerrhyl*.]

Jarrow /járrō/ industrial town and port on the River Tyne, in northeastern England. It is in the unitary council of South Tyneside, in Tyne and Wear. The *Jarrow March* in 1934 was by 200 jobless people protesting about lack of work. Population: 29,325 (1991).

Jarry /zhárri/, **Alfred** (1873–1907) French dramatist and poet. The best known of his surrealist and absurdist works is the play *Ubu roi* (1896), a satire on bourgeois conventions.

Jaruzelski /yárroo zélski/, **Wojciech** (*b.* 1923) Polish statesman and general. As Communist prime minister (1981–85) and president (1985–90) of Poland, he resisted liberal reforms, but in 1990 was defeated by Lech Walesa in free elections. Full name **Wojciech Witold Jaruzelski**

Jas. *abbr.* James

Jasmine

jasmine /jázmin, jássmin/ (*plural* **-mines** *or* **-mine**), **jessamine** /jéssəmin/ (*plural* **-mines** *or* **-mine**) *n.* **1. SCENTED PLANT** a tropical or subtropical climbing plant with fragrant white, yellow, or red flowers. Jasmines are often grown as house or garden plants, and for use in making perfumes. Genus: *Jasminum*. **2. SCENT** perfume made from the oil of a variety of jasmine [Mid-16thC. Via French *jasmin, jessemin* from, ultimately, Persian *yāsaman*.]

jasmine tea *n.* black tea flavoured with jasmine blossoms

Jason /jáyss'n/ *n.* in Greek mythology, a prince who led a group of heroes on his ship, the *Argo*, on a quest to obtain the Golden Fleece and bring it back to Greece

jaspé /jás pay/ *adj.* used to describe fabric that resembles jasper, especially in being streaked or veined with different colours [Mid-19thC. From French past participle of *jasper* 'to marble'.]

jasper /jáspər/ *n.* an impure form of chalcedony, usually coloured red by iron impurities, used for jewellery and ornaments [13thC. Via Anglo-French *jaspre* from Latin *iaspidem*, from Greek *iaspis* 'jasper', from, ultimately, a Semitic source.]

Jat /jaat/ *n.* a member of an Indo-European people living in the Punjab, other areas of northwestern India, and parts of Pakistan [Early 17thC. From Hindi *Jāt*.]

jato /jáytō/, **JATO** *n.* an auxiliary jet or rocket designed to aid the combined thrust of aircraft jet engines during take-off. Full form **jet-assisted take-off**

jaundice /jáwndiss/ *n.* **1. ILLNESS CAUSING YELLOW SKIN** a condition in which there is yellowing of the whites of the eyes, skin, and mucous membranes, caused by bile pigments in the blood. It is a symptom of liver diseases such as hepatitis and cirrhosis, or of a blocked bile duct, and sometimes occurs temporarily in new-born babies whose livers are slightly immature. Technical name **icterus 2. CYNICAL STATE OF MIND** an attitude that is characterized by cynical hostility, jealousy, or prejudice ■ *vt.* (**-dices, -dicing, -diced**) **1. MAKE SB CYNICAL** to alter sb's attitude for the worse, especially when it results in cynical hostility, jealousy, or prejudice **2. AFFECT SB WITH JAUNDICE** to affect sb with jaundice, as a symptom of liver disease [14thC. From Old French *jaunice*, from *jaune* 'yellow'.] —**jaundiced** *adj.*

jaunt /jawnt/ *n.* **EXCURSION** a trip, especially a short one taken for fun or pleasure ■ *vi.* (**jaunts, jaunting, jaunted**) **TAKE SHORT TRIP** to go on a short journey, usually for pleasure [Late 16thC. Origin unknown.]

jaunting car *n.* a lightweight two-wheeled open vehicle pulled by a single horse and having lengthwise seats positioned so that passengers either face each other or sit back-to-back. It was formerly widely used in Ireland.

jaunty /jáwnti/ (**-tier, -tiest**) *adj.* **1. CAREFREE** happy, carefree, and confident **2. CASUAL** fashionable and eye-catching in a casual way **3. POLITE** genteel and mannerly (*archaic*) [Mid-17thC. From French *gentil* 'polite, kind'. The sense of 'carefree' did not develop until late 17thC.] —**jauntily** *adv.* —**jauntiness** *n.*

Jaurès /zhō réss/, **Jean** (1859–1914) French politician and newspaper editor. Cofounder and editor of the newspaper *L'Humanité* (1904), he also helped found the French Socialist Party (1905).

Jav. *abbr.* **1.** Javanese **2. Jav., jav.** ATHLETICS javelin

java /jáávə/ *n. US* coffee, especially brewed coffee as opposed to instant coffee (*informal*) [Mid-19thC. From JAVA².]

Java¹ /jáávə, jáávə/ island in southeastern Asia, the most populous island in Indonesia. Population: 114,733,500 (1995). Area: 310,000 sq. km/120,000 sq. mi.

Java² /jáávə/ *n.* a variety of rich coffee grown on Java and the surrounding islands

Java³ /jáávə/ *tdmk.* a high-level computer programming language that allows small application programs to be downloaded from a server to a client along with the data that each program processes

Java man *n.* a fossil human found in Java and elsewhere in Indonesia, taken to be from the Palaeolithic Age. The body and limbs of Java man are very similar to those of Homo sapiens, but the brain and skull are smaller.

Javanese /jáávə néez/ (*plural* **-nese**) *n.* **1.** PEOPLES SB FROM JAVA sb who was born or who lives on the Indonesian island of Java **2.** LANG LANGUAGE SPOKEN ON JAVA a language spoken on the Indonesian island of Java. It belongs to the Western branch of the Austronesian family of languages. Over 70 million people speak Javanese. —**Javanese** *adj.*

Java sparrow *n.* a small Indonesian weaverbird that has grey and pink feathers and a stout red beak, popular as a cage and aviary bird. Latin name: *Padda oryzivora*.

javelin /jávvəlin/ *n.* **1.** SPEAR a long thin piece of wood, plastic, or metal with a pointed end, used as a weapon or thrown in field competitions **2.** THROWING CONTEST a field event in which competitors try to throw a javelin as far as possible [15thC. Via Middle French *javeline*, diminutive of Old French *javelot*, possibly from, ultimately, a Celtic source, ancestor of Welsh *gaflach* 'feathered lance'.]

javelina /hávvə léenə/ *n. US* ZOOL = peccary [Early 19thC. Alteration of Spanish *jabalina*, the feminine of *jabalí* 'wild boar', from Arabic *jabalī*.]

Javelle water /jáw'l-, jə vél-/, **Javel water** *n.* a solution of sodium hypochlorite, used as a bleach and disinfectant. Formula: NaOCl. [Early 19thC. Named after *Javelle*, a village on the outskirts of Paris, where the solution was first used.]

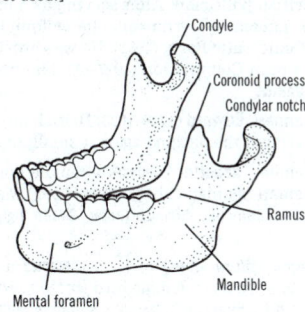

Jaw

jaw /jaw/ *n.* **1.** ZOOL TOOTH-BEARING BONE either of the upper or lower bones that anchor the teeth and form the structural basis of the mouth in vertebrates. In humans and other higher vertebrates, the upper jaw is known as the maxilla and the lower the mandible. **2.** ZOOL INVERTEBRATE BITING PART an invertebrate body part with a function or structure similar to a vertebrate jaw **3.** MECH ENG GRIPPING PART either of two hinged parts of a tool or machine used to grip objects securely **4.** FACE PART the lower, mobile part of the human face ◦ *a strong square jaw* **5.** IMPUDENCE cheeky or impudent talk (*slang*) **6.** LONG TALK a long conversation or discussion (*slang*) **7.**

MORALIZING TALK a moralizing talk or lecture (*slang*) ■ **jaws** *npl.* **1.** GEOG NATURAL ENTRANCE a narrow opening in sth such as a cave, gorge, canyon, or other natural feature **2.** DANGEROUS PLACE a situation that is dangerously close to sth horrible or frightening ■ *vi.* (**jaws, jawing, jawed**) (*slang*) **1.** TALK AT LENGTH to talk or gossip, usually at length **2.** MORALIZE to give a moralizing talk or lecture [14thC. Origin uncertain: possibly from Old French *joe* 'cheek', or from a prehistoric Germanic word, ancestor of *chew*.]

Jawara /jáávwərə/, **Sir Dawda** (*b.* 1924) Gambian statesman. He was the first prime minister (1965–70) and president (1970–94) of the Gambia. Full name **Sir Dawda Kairaba Jawara**

jawbone /jáw bōn/ *n.* BONE IN JAW a bone in the jaw, especially the lower jaw. ◊ **mandible, maxilla** ■ *vt.* (**-bones, -boning, -boned**) *US* PERSUADE SB FORCEFULLY to coerce sb to comply with sth by using the authority of high office (*informal*) —**jawboner** *n.*

jawbreaker /jáw braykər/ *n.* **1.** LANGUAGE UNPRONOUNCEABLE WORD a long word that is difficult to pronounce (*informal*) **2.** CONSTR CRUSHING MACHINE a machine that crushes rocks using powerful jaws **3.** *US* FOOD = **gobstopper** (*informal*)

jawed /jáwd/ *adj.* having jaws of a particular kind (*used in combination*) ◦ *slack-jawed*

jawing /jáwing/ *n.* an act of nagging at or scolding sb (*regional slang*)

— **WORD KEY: REGIONAL NOTE** —
Dialects, like the standard language, have many synonyms for *scolding*, *nagging*. Among the most widespread alongside **jawing** are *blathering, cackling, cagmagging, calleting, canting, chackling, chamming, chittering, jaffocking, jandering*, and *mithering*. Many of these are also used for *gossip*.

jaw-jaw *n.* TALKING talking or a conversation, especially when long-winded and pointless (*informal*) ■ *vi.* (**jaw-jaws, jaw-jawing, jaw-jawed**) RAMBLE ON to talk, especially in a long-winded way or without any obvious purpose (*informal*)

jawline /jáw līn/ *n.* the shape of sb's lower jaw

Jaws of Life *tdmk.* a trademark for a pneumatically operated metal device resembling pincers that is inserted into the body of a severely damaged motor vehicle and then opened to access people trapped inside

Jay

jay /jay/ *n.* **1.** BIRDS NOISY BIRD any of several related birds of the crow family that are typically noisy, often brightly coloured, and known for their intelligence. Family: Corvidae. **2.** SB THOUGHTLESSLY TALKATIVE a heedless or chattering person (*informal*) [13thC. Via Old French *jay* from Latin *gaius*, of uncertain origin: perhaps from the male forename *Gaius*.]

Jayawardene /jĭ́ ə wáárdənə/, **J. R.** (1906–96) Sri Lankan statesman. The leader of the United National Party from 1970, he was prime minister (1977–78) and president (1978–89) of Sri Lanka. Full name **Junius Richard Jayawardene**

Jaycee /jáy seé/ *n.* in North America, Australia, and New Zealand, a member of a junior chamber of commerce, an organization for young people that promotes leadership and business skills [Mid-20thC. From the initial letters of *Junior Chamber*.]

jaywalk /jáy wawk/ (**-walks, -walking, -walked**) *vi.* to cross a road or street anywhere other than at designated crossing places. It is a violation of law in

some places, though rarely enforced. [Early 20thC. Based on JAY in the sense 'heedless person'.] —**jaywalker** *n.* —**jaywalking** *n.*

jazz /jaz/ *n.* **1.** SYNCOPATED POPULAR MUSIC popular music that originated among Black people in New Orleans in the late 19th century and is characterized by syncopated rhythms and improvisation. It has since developed various styles. Jazz originally drew on ragtime, gospel, Black spiritual songs, West African rhythms, and European harmonies. **2.** STUFF unnamed related things or belongings (*slang*) ◦ *Collect up the books and the rest of your jazz and let's get going.* **3.** LIVELINESS animated enthusiasm or vivacity (*slang*) **4.** *US* NONSENSE information or ideas regarded as untrue, misconceived, or misleading (*slang disapproving*) ◦ *Don't be fooled if she starts giving you that jazz about being broke.* ■ *vi.* (**jazzes, jazzing, jazzed**) PLAY OR DANCE TO JAZZ to play or dance to jazz music [Early 20thC. Origin uncertain: perhaps from Bantu *jaja*, earlier *jas* 'to make dance, excite, exaggerate'.] —**jazzer** *n.*

— **WORD KEY: ORIGIN** —
The term *jazz* originated in the southern United States (it is first recorded in 1909, applied to a type of ragtime dance), and it is tempting to speculate that its ancestor crossed the Atlantic in the slave-ships from Africa. This may have cropped up earlier in US English in the form *jasm*, meaning 'energy', which is first recorded in 1860. The link has not been established, but it adds weight to the idea that 'liveliness, lively activity' (which probably also lies behind the word's sexual connotations) is the ancestral meaning of *jazz*, rather than any musical application. In the absence of any certain origin, various colourful alternative theories have been put forward – for example, that *jazz* came from the nickname of a certain Jasbo Brown, an itinerant musician along the banks of the Mississippi (*Jasbo* perhaps being an alteration of *Jasper*).

jazz up *vt.* **1.** ENHANCE to make sb or sth more interesting or decorative (*informal*) ◦ *jazzed up his wardrobe with some Hawaiian shirts* **2.** MUSIC ENLIVEN MUSIC to make a piece of music more lively, especially by quickening the tempo or adding improvisations

jazz age *n.* the era that immediately followed World War I and lasted until the beginning of the Depression in the United States, during which jazz increased in popularity. It was a reaction to the austerity and hardship of the war and was characterized by extravagance and hedonism.

jazz band *n.* a band that plays jazz, usually consisting of five or more instruments including one or more solo wind instruments and a rhythm section consisting of piano, double bass, and drums

jazzfest /jáz fest/ *n.* a festival of jazz music

jazz-fusion *n.* = **jazz-rock**

jazzman /jáz man/ (*plural* **-men** /-men/) *n.* a man who plays or writes jazz music

jazz-rock *n.* jazz music that incorporates elements of rock music, especially its heavy, repetitive beats and electronic amplification

jazzy /jázzi/ (**-ier, -iest**) *adj.* **1.** SHOWY showy, bright, and colourful (*informal*) **2.** JAZZED UP TO APPEAL exaggerated and unrestrained, especially in an attempt to make sth more appealing (*informal*) **3.** LIKE JAZZ in the style of jazz music, especially with the syncopated rhythms of jazz —**jazzily** *adv.* —**jazziness** *n.*

Jb *abbr.* BIBLE Job

JC *abbr.* **1.** LAW jurisconsult **2.** Justice Clerk

J.C. *abbr.* **1.** Jesus Christ **2.** Julius Caesar

JCB *tdmk.* a trademark for a machine with a large shovel at the front and a digging arm at the back, used in excavating and in moving earth and rubble

JCL *n.* a powerful computer language for writing a script used to control the execution of programs in batch processing systems. Full form **job control language**

J cloth *tdmk.* a trademark for a disposable cloth used for cleaning, dusting, washing dishes, and other domestic jobs

JCR *abbr.* junior common room

JCS *abbr.* MIL Joint Chiefs of Staff

jct. *abbr.* junction

JD[1] *abbr.* **1.** Juris Doctor **2.** juvenile delinquent **3.** EDUC Diploma in Journalism

JD[2] *symbol* Jordan dinar

Jdt *abbr.* BIBLE Judith

jealous /jélləss/ *adj.* **1.** ENVIOUS feeling bitter and unhappy because of another's advantages, possessions, or luck **2.** SUSPICIOUS OF RIVALS feeling suspicious about a rival's or competitor's influence, especially in regard to a loved one **3.** WATCHFUL possessively watchful of sth ○ *keeps a jealous guard on his research* **4.** DEMANDING LOYALTY demanding exclusive loyalty or adherence (*archaic*) ○ *a jealous god.* [13thC. Via Old French *gelos* from Latin *zelosus*, from, ultimately, Greek *zelos* 'jealousy', also 'enthusiasm' (source of English *zeal*).] —**jealously** *adv.* —**jealousness** *n.*

jealousy /jélləssi/ *n.* **1.** BEING JEALOUS jealous feelings or behaviour **2.** (*plural* **-ies**) JEALOUS IMPULSE an instance of feeling jealous ○ *a man of many jealousies*

jean /jeen/ *n.* a strong twill cotton that is used in making work clothes, uniforms, overalls, and jeans ○ *a jean jacket* [15thC. Via Old French *Janne* from medieval Latin *Janua*, the Italian city (Genoa) where the cloth was first made. Known in 16thC England as 'jean fustian'.]

jeans /jeenz/ *npl.* casual trousers with raised seams and often with back pockets sewn on, made from denim, jean, or some other strong fabric

jebel /jébb'l/, **djebel, gebel** *n.* a hill or mountain in the Middle East or North Africa (*often used in place-names*) [Mid-19thC. From Arabic *jabal* 'mountain'.]

jeelie /jeéli/, **jeely** *n. Scotland* jam or jelly (*nonstandard*) ○ *You may call it a jam sandwich, but it will always be a jeelie piece to me.* [Variant of JELLY]

Jeep /jeep/ *tdmk.* a trademark for a four-wheel-drive vehicle suitable for rough terrain

jeepers /jeépərz/, **jeepers creepers** *interj.* used to express surprise (*dated informal*) [Early 20thC. Alteration of JESUS.]

jeepney /jeépni/ (*plural* **-neys**) *n.* a Jeep or similar vehicle that has been converted into a small bus, used in the Philippines as a form of public transport [Mid-20thC.]

jeer /jeer/ *vti.* (**jeers, jeering, jeered**) EXPRESS DERISION VOCALLY to shout or laugh at sb or sth as an expression of disgust, scorn, or other displeasure ■ *n.* DERISIVE SHOUT a mocking or scornful laugh or shout [Mid-16thC. Origin uncertain: perhaps from Dutch *gieren* 'to cry, roar (with laughter)'.] —**jeerer** *n.* —**jeeringly** *adv.*

Jeeves /jeevz/ *n.* a handy and reliable person known for providing ready solutions to problems (*informal*) [Mid-20thC. From *Jeeves*, a character in the novels of P. G. WODEHOUSE.]

jeez /jeez/ *interj.* used to express surprise, enthusiasm, or annoyance (*slang*) [Early 20thC. From a shortening of JESUS.]

Library of Congress

Thomas Jefferson

Jefferson /jéffərss'n/, **Thomas** (1743–1826) US statesman and 3rd President of the United States. He was the author of the Declaration of Independence. As Democratic Republican president (1801–09), he strengthened the executive branch of government.

Jeffrey /jéffri/, **Francis, Lord Jeffrey** (1773–1850) British critic and jurist. He edited (1802–29) the influential

Edinburgh Review, which he used as a platform to attack the romantic poets.

Jeffrey pine /jéffri-/ *n.* a pine tree of the western United States that has long needles grouped in threes. Latin name: *Pinus jeffreyi.* [Mid-19thC. Named after John *Jeffrey*, Scottish plant collector.]

jehad *n.* = jihad

Jehoshaphat /ji hóshə fat/ *n.* in the Bible, a king of Judea who succeeded Asa and formed an alliance with Ahab of Israel against Syria. (1, 2 Kings; 2 Chronicles).

Jehovah /ji hóvə/ *n.* JUD-CHR = God [Mid-16thC. From medieval Latin *Iehoua*, mistaken transliteration of *YHWH*, using vowel points of Hebrew *ădōnāy* 'my lord', incorrectly supposed substitution for the name too sacred to pronounce.]

Jehovah's Witness *n.* a member of a religious group that believes in the imminence of Jesus Christ's personal reign on Earth and rejects secular law where it appears to conflict with the divine. Jehovah's Witnesses reject the doctrine of the Trinity.

Jehovist /ji hóvist/ *n.* **1.** = Yahwist **2.** INTERPRETER OF BIBLICAL WORD sb who believes that the Hebrew word 'YHVH' in the Bible was pronounced like 'Jehovah' —**Jehovism** *n.* —**Jehovistic** /jeé hō vístik/ *adj.*

Jehu /jeé hyoo/ *n.* a fast or reckless driver (*informal*) [Early 17thC. Named after the King of Israel who drove 'furiously' (2 Kings 9:20).]

jejunal /ji joón'l/ *adj.* relating to the middle part of the small intestine (**jejunum**)

jejune /ji joón/ *adj.* **1.** BORING uninteresting and intellectually undemanding **2.** CHILDISH lacking maturity or sophistication ○ *jejune chatter about concepts beyond their understanding* **3.** WITHOUT PROPER NOURISHMENT lacking or not providing proper nourishment **4.** BARREN not very fertile [Early 17thC. From Latin *jejunus* 'fasting, meagre'. The late 19thC sense 'childish' arose perhaps from a mistaken belief that 'jejune' came from Latin *juvenis* or French *jeune* 'young'.] —**jejunely** *adv.* —**jejuneness** *n.* —**jejunity** *n.*

jejunostomy /ji joo nóstəmi/ (*plural* **-mies**) *n.* **1.** OPENING UP OF PART OF INTESTINE a surgical operation that creates access from the outside of the body into the middle part of the small intestine (**jejunum**) so that nourishment can be directly introduced **2.** OPENING INTO INTESTINE the opening formed in a jejunostomy

jejunum /ji joónəm/ *n.* the section of the small intestine that is situated between the duodenum and the ileum and whose main function is the absorption of nutrients from digested food [Mid-16thC. From medical Latin, from Latin *jejunus* 'fasting', so called because it is usually found to be empty after death.]

Jekyll /jeék'l/, **Gertrude** (1843–1932) British landscape gardener and writer. Her garden designs, many in collaboration with the architect Edward Lutyens, and her writings were highly influential.

Jekyll and Hyde /jék'l ənd híd/ (*plural* **Jekyll and Hydes**) *n.* sb who has two distinct personalities, one good and the other evil [Late 19thC. From *The Strange Case of Dr. Jekyll and Mr. Hyde,* 1886, by R. L. Stevenson.]

jell /jel/ (**jells, jelling, jelled**), **gel** (**gels, gelling, gelled**) *v.* **1.** *vti.* SOLIDIFY to become, or cause a substance to become, set or firm **2.** *vti.* TAKE SHAPE to become, or cause sth to become, fixed or more definite in shape or form **3.** *vi.* GET ON WELL TOGETHER to bond in a way that gives rise to mutual cooperation ○ *'It's fun being with a bunch of guys who are fighting through adversity and jelling together'.* (*The Philadelphia Inquirer*; 1997) [Mid-18thC. Back-formation from JELLY.]

jellaba /jélləbə, jə laábə/, **djellaba** *n.* a long, loose, sleeved garment with a hood, of a type worn in Morocco and other parts of North Africa [Early 19thC. From Moroccan Arabic *jellāb(a).*]

jellied /jéllid/ *adj.* set in jelly, or covered with a thin layer of jelly ○ *jellied tomato salad*

jellify /jélli fī/ (**-fies, -fying, -fied**) *vti.* to turn, or cause a substance to turn, into jelly —**jellification** /jéllifi káysh'n/ *n.*

Jell-O /jéllō/ *tdmk. US* a trademark for a gelatin-based dessert

jelly[1] /jélli/ *n.* (*plural* **-lies**) **1.** WOBBLY DESSERT a transparent semi-solid fruit-flavoured dessert made from gelatin **2.** FRUIT JUICE BOILED TO SPREADABLE CONSISTENCY a fruit preserve that is made by boiling fruit juice, sugar, and sometimes pectin until it has a semisolid consistency **3.** THICKENED MEAT STOCK a savoury semi-solid food made from gelatin boiled with meat stock ○ *calf's foot jelly* **4.** SUBSTANCE WITH JELLY CONSISTENCY any substance that has the consistency of jelly, especially a pharmaceutical preparation ○ *petroleum jelly* **5.** TYPE OF SANDAL a type of sandal, especially a child's sandal, made from transparent flexible plastic (*often used before a noun*) ■ *vti.* (**-lies, -lying, -lied**) THICKEN to set, or cause sth to set, into a jelly [14thC. Via Old French *gelee* 'frost, jelly', from Latin *gelare* 'to freeze' (source of English *congeal*).] ◇ **turn to jelly** to feel shaky because of extreme fear, nervousness, or exhaustion (*informal*)

jelly[2] /jélli/ *n.* gelignite (*informal*) [Mid-20thC. Shortening and alteration.]

jelly baby *n.* a small fruit-flavoured jelly sweet in the shape of a baby

jelly bag *n.* a bag used for straining the juice when making jelly

jellybean /jélli been/ *n.* a small bean-shaped fruit sweet with a hard coating and a soft jelly centre

jellyfish /jélli fish/ (*plural* **-fishes** or **-fish**) *n.* **1.** MARINE BIOL STINGING MARINE ANIMAL an invertebrate marine animal that, in its reproductive stage, has a nearly transparent gelatinous body shaped like an umbrella with trailing tentacles bearing stinging cells. Phylum: Coelenterata. **2.** MARINE BIOL MARINE ANIMAL LIKE JELLYFISH any of various invertebrate marine animals that have bodies similar to that of a true jellyfish, including cnidarians, ctenophores, and siphonophores **3.** WEAK PERSON sb who lacks strength of character (*informal*) ○ *I'm afraid I'm just a jellyfish when it comes to making decisions.*

jelly fungus (*plural* **jelly funguses** or **jelly fungi**) *n.* any of various fungi that grow on trees and have a gelatinous fruiting body. Order: Tremellales.

jelly mould *n.* a shaped container for making jelly

jemmy /jémmi/ *n.* (*plural* **-mies**) LEVER FOR PRISING STH OPEN a short crowbar used as a lever, usually for prising things open. US term **jimmy** *n.* ■ *vt.* (**-mies, -mying, -mied**) OPEN STH WITH JEMMY to force sth open with a jemmy. US term **jimmy** *v.* [Early 19thC. From *Jemmy,* familiar form of the name *James.*]

je ne sais quoi /zhə nə say kwaá/ *n.* an indefinable quality that makes sb or sth more attractive or interesting (*literary or humorous*) [Mid-17thC. From French, literally 'I do not know what'.]

Jenkins /jéngkinz/, **Roy, Baron Jenkins of Hillhead** (b. 1920) British politician. After serving as a minister in two Labour governments, he cofounded the Social Democratic Party (1981). He was president of the European Commission (1977–81). Full name **Roy Harris Jenkins**

Jenner /jénnər/, **Edward** (1749–1823) British physician. He discovered the vaccine against smallpox.

jennet /jénnit/, **genet** *n.* **1.** DONKEY a female donkey **2.** HORSE a small Spanish riding horse [15thC. Via French *genet,* from, ultimately, Spanish Arabic *Genēṭī* 'light horseman'.]

jenny /jénni/ (*plural* **-nies**) *n.* **1.** ZOOL DONKEY a female donkey **2.** BIRDS BIRD a female bird (*often used before a noun*) ○ *a jenny wren* **3.** MANUF = spinning jenny [Early 17thC. From diminutive of names *Jane, Jennifer,* and a feminine version of *Jack,* often used to designate a tool or piece of machinery.]

jenny-longlegs (*plural* **jenny-longlegs**) *n. Scotland* a cranefly (*informal*)

Jenolan Caves /jə nólən-/ cave system in southeastern New South Wales, Australia. Located in the Blue Mountains National Park, the limestone cave system is a major tourist attraction.

jeopard /jéppərd/ (**-ards, -arding, -arded**) *vt.* to put sb or sth in jeopardy (*archaic*) [15thC. Back-formation from JEOPARDY.]

jeopardize /jéppər dīz/ (**-izes, -izing, -ized**), **jeopardise** (**-ises, -ising, -ised**) *vt.* to put sb or sth at risk of being harmed or lost ○ *jeopardizing the entire mission through his indiscretion*

jeopardy /jéppərdi/ *n.* **1.** DANGER the risk of loss, harm, or death ○ *The entire project is in jeopardy.* **2.** LAW CHANCE OF BEING CONVICTED the risk of being convicted when put on trial for a crime [14thC. From Old French *jeu* (from Latin *jocus* 'pastime') + *parti* (past participle of *partir* 'to divide'), literally 'even or divided game'.]

Jer. *abbr.* **1.** BIBLE Jeremiah **2.** Jersey **3.** Jerusalem

Jerboa

jerboa /jur bó ə/ (*plural* **-as**) *n.* **1.** SMALL RODENT OF ASIA AND AFRICA a small nocturnal rodent that lives in arid regions of Asia and Africa and has large ears, a long tufted tail, and long hind legs adapted for leaping. Family: Dipodidae. **2.** SMALL MARSUPIAL OF CENTRAL AUSTRALIA a small marsupial with long hind legs and a long bushy tail that lives in central desert areas of Australia. Genus: *Antechinomys*. [Mid-17thC. Via modern Latin *jerboa* from Arabic *yarbū'(a)* (variant *jarbū*).]

jeremiad /jérri mí əd/ *n.* a long recitation of mournful complaints (*literary*) [Late 18thC. From French *jérémiade*, from *Jérémie* 'Jeremiah' (see JEREMIAH).]

Jeremiah /jérri mí ə/ *n.* **1.** HEBREW PROPHET a Hebrew prophet who lived in Judah in the 7th and 6th centuries BC and was persecuted for prophesying the fall of Judah and Jerusalem and the Israelites' captivity in Babylon **2.** BOOK OF THE BIBLE the book of the Bible that contains the prophecies of Jeremiah. See table at **Bible 3.** NEGATIVE PERSON sb with a gloomy outlook on the present and future

Jerez de la Frontera /he réss də la fron táirə/ city in southwestern Spain, in Cádiz Province, Andalusia. It is the world's sherry wine capital. Population: 182,939 (1991).

Jericho /jérrikō/ town in the West Bank, in the Jordan Valley. It is regarded as the world's oldest town, with remains dating back to 8000 BC and, according to the Bible, was destroyed by Joshua after he led the Israelites back from captivity in Egypt (Joshua 3–8). Population: 25,000 (1994).

jerid /jə réed/ *n.* a javelin used by Persian, Turkish, and Arabian horsemen, especially during the time of the Ottoman Empire [Mid-17thC. From Arabic *jarīd* 'palm branch stripped of its leaves, javelin'.]

jerk[1] /jurk/ *v.* (**jerks, jerking, jerked**) **1.** *vt.* PULL SUDDENLY to pull sb or sth with a sudden strong movement ○ *He jerked her back from in front of the speeding car.* **2.** *vti.* MOVE JOLTINGLY to proceed, or cause sth or sb to proceed, with bumps and jolts ○ *The car jerked forwards.* **3.** *vi.* PHYSIOL MOVE IN SPASM to move in response to muscular spasms (*refers to parts of the body*) **4.** *vt.* SAY STH ABRUPTLY to utter words or sounds suddenly and forcefully, e.g. from excitement ■ *n.* **1.** SUDDEN PULL a sudden and forceful pulling movement ○ *giving the door a jerk* **2.** JOLTING MOVEMENT an abrupt jolting or jarring motion ○ *moving in jerks* **3.** PHYSIOL TWITCH a spasmodic movement in a muscle **4.** *US, Can* OFFENSIVE TERM an offensive term referring contemptuously to sb who behaves foolishly (*slang insult*) **5.** GYM OVERHEAD LIFT IN WEIGHTLIFTING a lift in weightlifting in which a barbell is thrust from shoulder height to above the head ■ **jerks** *npl.* **1.** EXERCISES physical exercises, especially those such as press-ups that can be done without the use of special equipment (*dated informal*) **2.** *US* PHYSIOL SPASMODIC MOVEMENTS involuntary muscular movements often caused by nervousness or excitement [Mid-16thC. Origin uncertain: possibly an

imitation of the sound of a lash, which was its original meaning.] —**jerker** *n.*

jerk off *vti.* an offensive term meaning to masturbate, or masturbate sb else (*taboo offensive*)

jerk[2] /jurk/ *vt.* (**jerks, jerking, jerked**) COOK PRESERVE MEAT IN STRIPS to preserve meat by cutting it into long strips and drying it ■ *adj.* **1.** STRONGLY FLAVOURED AND SPICY made with strongly flavoured spices, including hot peppers and allspice, as a marinade or rub for grilled meats **2.** SPICY AND GRILLED marinated in a jerk sauce and grilled [Early 18thC. Via American Spanish *charquear* from, ultimately, Quechua (Peruvian) *echarquini* 'to prepare dried meat'.]

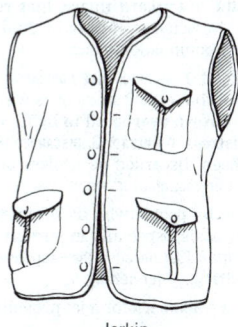
Jerkin

jerkin /júrkin/ *n.* **1.** JACKET a sleeveless coat or jacket worn by men or women **2.** LEATHER TUNIC a man's close-fitting sleeveless tunic, often made of leather, worn in the 16th and 17th centuries [Early 16thC. Origin unknown.]

jerky[1] /júrki/ (**-ier, -iest**) *adj.* moving irregularly with sudden stops and starts —**jerkily** *adv.* —**jerkiness** *n.*

jerky[2] /júrki/ *n.* meat cut into thin strips and dried [Mid-19thC. From American Spanish *charqui*, from Quechua *echarqui* 'dried flesh in long strips'.]

jeroboam /jérrə bó əm/ *n.* a large wine or champagne bottle holding the equivalent of four standard wine bottles, 3 1/108 fl. oz, or a Bordeaux wine bottle equivalent to six bottles, 4.5 1/162 fl. oz [Early 19thC. Named after *Jeroboam*, 'a mighty man of valour' (I Kings 11:28).]

Jerome /jə róm/, **St** (342?–420?) Croatian-born monk and scholar. He made the first translation of the Bible from Hebrew into Latin, the Vulgate. Born **Eusebius Hieronymus**

Jerome, Jerome K. (1859–1927) British novelist. He is best known for his humorous novel *Three Men in a Boat* (1889). Full name **Jerome Klapka Jerome**

Jerry /jérri/ (*plural* **-ries**) *n.* an offensive term referring to a German person, especially a German soldier in World War II (*dated slang insult*) [Early 20thC. Alteration of GERMAN.]

jerry-build (**jerry-builds, jerry-building, jerry-built**) *vt.* to build sth as quickly and cheaply as possible, with little regard for quality [*Jerry* of unknown origin] —**jerry-builder** *n.* —**jerry-building** *n.*

jerry can *n.* a flat-sided can with a capacity of approximately 20 1/4.4 gal. of liquid, originally of German design and used in World War II [*Jerry* a shortening of GERMAN]

jersey /júrzi/ (*plural* **-seys**) *n.* **1.** TEXTILES SOFT KNITTED CLOTHING MATERIAL a knitted fabric, usually made with a plain or stocking stitch, used for making clothing **2.** CLOTHES SWEATER a knitted woollen pullover **3.** SPORTS SHIRT FOR PLAYING SPORTS a shirt worn for playing sport, especially a long-sleeved shirt worn by players of team games such as football and rugby [Late 16thC. Named after JERSEY, where the fabric was originally made.]

Jersey[1] /júrzi/ the largest and southernmost of the Channel Islands in the English Channel, a dependency of the British crown. Language: English, French. Capital: St Helier. Population: 84,082 (1991). Area: 117 sq. km/45 sq. mi.

Jersey[2] /júrzi/ (*plural* **-seys**) *n.* a pale brown dairy cow that produces particularly creamy milk, belonging to a breed originating on the island of Jersey

Jerusalem /jə róossələm/ historic city lying at the intersection of Israel and the West Bank. The whole of the city is claimed by Israel as its capital, but this is disputed internationally. Population: 602,100 (1997).

Jerusalem artichoke *n.* **1.** FOOD ROOT VEGETABLE the edible tuber of a North American species of sunflower plant that has reddish-brown knobbly skin and white flesh and is eaten cooked as a vegetable **2.** PLANTS PLANT WITH EDIBLE TUBERS a perennial North American sunflower whose edible tubers are called Jerusalem artichokes. Latin name: *Helianthus tuberosus*. [*Jerusalem* from Italian *girasole*, from *girare* 'to turn' + *sole* 'sun']

Jerusalem cherry *n.* a plant of the nightshade family, native to South America and widely grown as a houseplant for its white flowers and inedible orange or red berries. Latin name: *Solanum pseudocapsicum*.

Jerusalem cricket *n.* a large flightless nocturnal cricket with short spiny legs, found in arid regions of the southwestern United States. Latin name: *Stenopelmatus fuscus*.

Jerusalem oak *n.* a strong-smelling plant of the goosefoot family that grows as a weed in the northern United States and Canada. Latin name: *Chenopodium botrys*.

Jerusalem thorn *n.* a thorny tropical American shrub of the pea family with pinnate leaves and long clusters of yellow flowers. Latin name: *Parkinsonia aculeata*.

Jervis Bay /júrvəss-/ harbour in southeastern Australia, on the eastern coast of New South Wales. The headland on its southern side is part of the Australian Capital Territory. Area: 160 sq. km/60 sq. mi.

jess /jess/ *n.* FALCON'S LEASH STRAP a short strap with a ring for attaching a leash, fastened round one of the legs of a falcon or other trained bird of prey ■ *vt.* (**jesses, jessing, jessed**) FIT BIRD WITH JESS to put a jess on a bird [14thC. Via Old French *ges*, a form of *get* 'act of throwing', from, ultimately, Latin *jacere* 'to throw'.]

Jesse window /jéssi-/ *n.* a window in a church depicting Jesus Christ's lineage from Jesse [Mid-19thC. Named after *Jesse*, father of David and ancestor of Jesus Christ.]

jest /jest/ *n.* **1.** JOKE sth done or said in a playful joking manner (*formal or humorous*) ○ *Forgive my little jest.* **2.** STH JOKED ABOUT an object of scorn or derision (*archaic*) ■ *vti.* (**jests, jesting, jested**) **1.** BE WITTY to act, write, or speak cleverly or humorously about sth (*formal or humorous*) **2.** MAKE FUN OF SB to treat sb with derision or scorn (*archaic*) [13thC. Via Old French *geste* 'romantic exploit' from Latin *gerere* 'to behave, perform', of unknown origin. Originally 'entertainment, heroic poem'.] ◇ **in jest** as a joke

jester /jéstər/ *n.* **1.** ENTERTAINER an entertainer employed at a medieval court to amuse the monarch and guests ○ *the court jester* **2.** SB WHO JOKES sb who is inclined to joke with others

Jesuit /jézzyoo it/ *n.* **1.** MEMBER OF ROMAN CATHOLIC RELIGIOUS ORDER a member of the Society of Jesus, a Roman Catholic religious order engaged in missionary and educational work worldwide. The order was founded by Saint Ignatius of Loyola in 1534 with the aim of defending Catholicism against the Reformation. **2.** Jesuit, jesuit OFFENSIVE TERM an offensive term referring to sb regarded as crafty or scheming, especially sb who uses deliberately ambiguous or confusing words to deceive others (*slang insult*) ■ *adj.* OF JESUITS belonging or relating to the members of the Society of Jesus ○ *a Jesuit priest* [Mid-16thC. From French *jésuite* or modern Latin *Jesuita*, literally 'follower of Jesus', from *Jesus*.] —**Jesuitic** /jézzyoo íttik/ *adj.* —**Jesuitical** /-íttik'l/ *adj.* —**Jesuitically** /-íttik'li/ *adv.* —**Jesuitism** /jézzyoo itizəm/ *n.* —**Jesuitry** /-itri/ *n.*

Jesus Christ /jeézəss-/, **Jesus** *n.* **1.** BIBLE FOUNDER OF CHRISTIANITY a Jewish religious teacher who lived from about 4 BC to AD 33. His life and teachings form the basis of Christianity. Christians believe he is the Son of God. **2.** HUMAN EMBODIMENT OF DIVINE in Christian Science, the highest human embodiment of the divine idea ■ *interj.* SWEARWORD used as a swearword (*slang offensive*)

Jesus freak *n.* an offensive term referring contemptuously to sb who belongs to a youthful evangelical Christian group that is contemporary in tone (*dated slang offensive*)

jet[1] /jet/ *n.* **1.** PRESSURIZED STREAM OF FLUID a thin concentrated stream of liquid, air, or gas that is forced under pressure from a small nozzle or opening **2.** HOLE THROUGH WHICH FLUID IS FORCED a small opening or nozzle for letting out a stream of fluid **3.** AIR = **jet engine** (*often used before a noun*) ○ *using jet technology* **4.** AIR AIRCRAFT an aircraft powered by jet engines (*often used before a noun*) ○ *a jet landing strip* ■ *v.* (**jets, jetting, jetted**) **1.** *vi.* TRAVEL BY AIR to travel by air, especially by modern passenger aircraft ○ *always jetting off to business meetings* **2.** *vti.* FLOW FORCEFULLY IN THIN STREAM to be emitted, or emit sth, in a thin powerful stream ○ *Water jetted from the broken pipe.* [Late 16thC. Via Old French *jeter* 'to throw', from, ultimately, Latin *jacere* 'to throw'.]

───────── **WORD KEY: ORIGIN** ─────────

Jet was originally used in English to mean 'to protrude, stick out'. This sense is best preserved in the related *jetty* 'projecting pier', while the underlying meaning 'to throw' is still present in the related *jettison* 'things thrown overboard'. *Jet* began to be used for 'to spurt out in a forceful stream' in the 17th century. The notion of using such a stream to create forward motion was first encapsulated in the term 'jet propulsion' in the mid-19th century, but it did not take concrete form for nearly a hundred years (the term *jet engine* is not recorded until 1943). Other English words descended from Latin *jacere* include *abject, dejected, eject, inject, interject, jetsam, jettison, jetty, object, project, reject, subject,* and *trajectory.*

jet[2] /jet/ *n.* **1.** MINERALS BLACK MINERAL a dense black variety of the mineral lignite, cut and polished and used for jewellery and other ornaments (*often used before a noun*) ○ *a jet necklace* **2.** COLOURS JET BLACK jet black [14thC. Via Old French *jaiet*, from Latin *gagates*, from Greek *Gagatēs*, named after *Gagai*, the town in Asia Minor where it was found.]

JET /jet/ *abbr.* **1.** Joint European Torus **2.** Joint European Transport

jetbead /jét beed/ *n.* an ornamental shrub of the rose family with white flowers and shiny black berries. Latin name: *Rhodotypos scandens.*

jet black *n.* a very dark black colour —**jet-black** *adj.*

jet boat *n.* a boat powered by an engine that produces a pressurized stream of water directed backwards

jeté /zhə táy/ *n.* a ballet leap from one leg to the other in which one leg is stretched forwards and the other backwards [Mid-19thC. From French, past participle of *jeter* 'to throw'.]

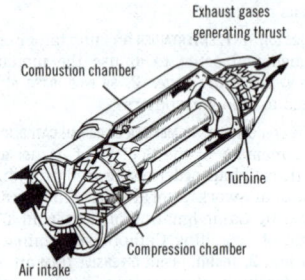

Exhaust gases generating thrust
Combustion chamber
Turbine
Compression chamber
Air intake

Jet engine: Cutaway view

jet engine *n.* an engine, especially one used to propel aircraft, that produces forward thrust by means of a rearward discharge of fluid, usually combustion gases

jet fighter *n.* a fighter plane that is powered by a jet engine or engines

jetfoil /jét foyl/ *n.* a passenger-carrying jet-powered hydrofoil [Late 20thC. Named with reference to its propulsion by water jets.]

jet lag *n.* an internal physical disturbance experienced by air travellers on flights across different time zones. It affects the body's internal clock, disrupting sleeping patterns, eating schedules, and body temperature. —**jet-lagged** *adj.*

jetliner /jét līnər/ *n.* a large passenger aeroplane powered by jet engines [Mid-20thC. Blend of JET[1] and AIRLINER.]

jetpack /jét pak/ *n.* a device fitted with pressurized metal containers that let out jets of gas, worn by astronauts on their back to enable them to move around in space outside a spacecraft

jet plane *n.* an aeroplane powered by jet engines

jet-propelled *adj.* powered by means of engines that use jet propulsion

jet propulsion *n.* forward thrust that results from the rearward discharge of a jet of fluid, especially a jet engine's combustion gases

jetsam /jétsəm/ *n.* **1.** SHIPPING SHIP'S DISCARDED CARGO cargo or equipment that either sinks or is washed ashore after being thrown overboard to lighten the load of a ship in distress. ◊ flotsam **2.** DISCARDED THINGS things that have been discarded as useless or unwanted [Late 16thC. Contraction of JETTISON.]

jet set *n.* wealthy people who travel internationally on a regular basis, especially in pursuit of pleasure (*dated informal*) [*Jet* because they supposedly travel on jets] —**jet-setter** *n.* —**jet-setting** *n.*

Jet Ski *tdmk.* a trademark for a jet-propelled personal watercraft

jet stream *n.* **1.** METEOROL HIGH-LEVEL WINDS a strong permanent high-altitude wind current that moves east in a meandering pattern, affecting the development and movement of weather systems **2.** AEROSP JET ENGINE EXHAUST a flow of exhaust gases produced by a jet engine

jettison /jéttiss'n/ *vt.* (**-sons, -soning, -soned**) **1.** SHIPPING THROW STH OVERBOARD to throw sth from a ship, aircraft, or vehicle **2.** REJECT STH to discard or abandon sth, e.g. an idea or project ○ *plans that had to be jettisoned* ■ *n.* **1.** REJECTION the discarding or rejecting of sth **2.** SHIPPING SHIP'S DISCARDED CARGO the cargo and equipment thrown from a distressed ship to lighten it [15thC. From Anglo-Norman *getteson* 'throwing cargo overboard' (to lighten a ship), from, ultimately, Latin *jectare* 'to throw about'.] —**jettisonable** *adj.*

jetty[1] /jétti/ *n.* (*plural* **-ties**) **1.** DOCK a landing pier **2.** BREAKWATER a wall or other barrier built out into a body of water to shelter a harbour, protect a shoreline from erosion, or redirect water currents [15thC. From Old French *jetee*, literally 'sth thrown (up as a breakwater)', from *jeter* (see JET[1]).]

jetty[2] /jétti/ *adj.* as black as or as shiny as the mineral jet —**jettiness** *n.*

Jetway /jét way/ *tdmk. US* a trademark for an enclosed telescoping walkway between an aeroplane and a terminal building, through which passengers can embark and disembark

jeu d'esprit /zhö de sprée/ (*plural* **jeux d'esprit** /zhö-/) *n.* a witticism, especially one that appears in a work of literature (*literary*) [Early 18thC. From French, literally 'game of spirit or wit'.]

jeunesse dorée /zhö ness dáwray/ *n.* young people who enjoy wealth and privilege (*literary*) [Mid-19thC. From French, literally 'gilded youth'.]

Jevons /jévv'nz/**, William** (1835–82) British economist and mathematician. He introduced the theory of marginal utility, and pioneered the use of mathematics in economics. Full name **William Stanley Jevons**

Jew /joo/ *n.* **1.** RELIG BELIEVER IN JUDAISM sb whose religion is Judaism **2.** PEOPLES MEMBER OF SEMITIC PEOPLE a member of a Semitic people descended from the ancient Hebrews. They are now widely dispersed and share cultural and religious ties based on Judaism. **3.** HIST SB FROM ANCIENT JUDAH sb who lived or was born in ancient Judah **4.** *Jew, jew* AN OFFENSIVE TERM a highly offensive term referring to sb who is regarded as miserly (*dated slang offensive*) ■ *adj.* OFFENSIVE TERM an offensive term indicating that sb or sth belongs or relates to Jews or to Judaism (*offensive*) [Pre-12thC. Via Old French *giu* from Latin *Judaeus*, from, ultimately, Hebrew *yĕhūḏī*, from *yĕhūḏāh* 'Judah', son of the patriarch Jacob, and the tribe descended from him.]

jewel /joo əl/ *n.* **1.** PERSONAL ORNAMENT an ornament, e.g. a ring, necklace, or bracelet, made of a gemstone placed in a setting of gold, silver, or other metal ○ *She wore her best jewels to the ball.* **2.** GEMSTONE a precious stone such as a diamond or sapphire **3.** WATCH BEARING a small crystal or precious stone used as a bearing in a watch **4.** SB OR STH PRIZED a fine example of a particular type of person or thing ○ *Her new teacher's such a jewel!* ■ *vt.* (**-els, -elling, -elled**) ADORN STH WITH JEWELS to equip or decorate sth with jewels [13thC. Via Anglo-Norman *juel* from *jeu* 'game', from Latin *jocus* (source of English *joke*).] ◇ **the jewel in the crown** the best or most outstanding example of sth

jewel beetle *n.* an Australian beetle with an iridescent body that gives it a superficial resemblance to a gemstone. Family: Buprestidae.

jewel box (*plural* **jewel boxes**), **jewel case** (*plural* **jewel cases**) *n.* a hinged plastic case in which a CD is sold and stored

jeweler *n.* US = **jeweller**

jewelfish /joo əl fish/ (*plural* **-fishes** *or* **-fish**) *n.* a brightly coloured African fish that is popular as an aquarium fish. Latin name: *Hemichromis bimaculatus.* ['Jewel' from its irregular speckling of emerald green or sapphire]

jeweller /joo ə lər/ *n.* sb who makes, sells, or repairs jewellery

jeweller's rouge *n.* metal polish in the form of finely ground ferric oxide

jewellery /joo əlri/ *n.* articles worn on the body for decoration, e.g. necklaces, bracelets, earrings, and rings (*often used before a noun*) ○ *a jewellery box*

Jewess /joo iss/ *n.* an offensive term referring to a Jewish woman or girl (*dated offensive*)

jewfish /joo fish/ (*plural* **-fishes** *or* **-fish**) *n.* a large dark spotted fish of the grouper family that has rough scales and is found in warm and tropical seas. Latin name: *Epinephelus itajara.* [Said to have been so called because it was a 'clean' fish in accordance with Jewish dietary law]

Jewish /joo ish/ *adj.* **1.** OF JUDAISM relating to or practising Judaism **2.** OF JEWS belonging or relating to a people descended from the ancient Hebrews —**Jewishly** *adv.* —**Jewishness** *n.*

Jewish calendar *n.* the lunar calendar of the Jewish religious year. It has 12 months, with 13 in leap years, and dates from 3761 BC, considered the year of Creation.

Jewry /joori/ (*plural* **-ries**) *n.* Jewish people in general, or the Jewish religion

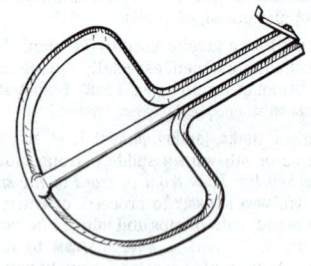

Jew's harp

jew's harp *n.* a small musical instrument held between the teeth and played by plucking a protruding metal tongue. It has a soft twanging sound. [The reason for the name is unknown]

Jezebel /jézzə bel/ *n.* **1.** BIBLE BIBLICAL PRINCESS a Phoenician princess who lived in the 9th century BC. The Bible describes how, as the wife of King Ahab, she introduced tyranny and idolatry into Israel. **2.** *Jezebel, jezebel* OFFENSIVE TERM an offensive term that deliberately insults a woman's sexual activity or interactions (*offensive*)

JFK *abbr.* **1.** John Fitzgerald Kennedy **2.** John Fitzgerald Kennedy International Airport

jg, **j.g.** *abbr.* MIL junior grade

Jhansi /jaánssi/, **Jhānsi** capital city of Jhansi District, central India, in Uttar Pradesh State. Population: 301,304 (1991).

Jhelum /jeéləm/ river in northwestern India and northeastern Pakistan. It runs through the Indian city of Srinagar.

JHVH, **JHWH** *n.* BIBLE = **YHWH**

Jiangsu /jyáng soó/ province in eastern China, bordering on the Yellow Sea. Capital: Nanjing. Population: 70,210,000 (1994). Area: 102,600 sq. km/39,600 sq. mi.

Jiangxi /jyáng sheé/ inland province of southeastern China. Capital: Nanchang. Population: 40,150,000 (1994). Area: 164,800 sq. km/63,600 sq. mi.

jiao /jow/ (*plural* **jiao**) *n.* **1.** **CURRENCY UNIT IN CHINA** a subunit of currency in China, worth one tenth of a yuan. See table at **currency** **2.** **NOTE WORTH ONE JIAO** a note worth one jiao [Mid-20thC. From Chinese *jiăo*.]

jib[1] /jib/ *n.* SAILING a small triangular sail in front of the main or only mast on a sailing ship [Mid-17thC. Origin unknown.] ◇ **the cut of sb's jib** sb's manner and general appearance

jib[2] /jib/ *n.* INDUST the projecting arm of a crane [Mid-18thC. Origin uncertain: perhaps a shortening and alteration of GIBBET.]

jib[3] /jib/ (**jibs, jibbing, jibbed**) *vi.* **1.** **REFUSE TO MOVE** to stop and refuse to move on (*refers to animals*) **2.** **BALK** to be reluctant to do sth [Early 19thC. Origin uncertain.] —**jibber** *n.*

jib boom *n.* an extension of the spar that sticks out from the front of a sailing ship (**bowsprit**) and supports the jib

jibe[1] *n., vti.* = **gibe**

jibe[2] *vti., n.* SAILING = **gybe**

jicama /heékəmə/ *n.* the starchy tuberous root of a tropical plant of the pea family, eaten raw in salads or cooked as a vegetable. Latin name: *Pachyrhizus erosus*. [Early 17thC. Via Mexican Spanish *jícama*, from Nahuatl *xicama*.]

JICRAR /jík raar/ *abbr.* Joint Industry Committee for Radio Audience Research

JICTAR /jík taar/ *abbr.* Joint Industry Committee for Television Advertising Research

Jiddah /jéddə/, **Jedda** city and port in western Saudi Arabia, on the Red Sea, in Al Hijaz state. Population: 1,600,000 (1994 estimate).

jiffy /jíffi/, **jiff** /jif/ *n.* the shortest of moments (*informal*) ○ *I'll be with you in a jiffy.* [Late 18thC. Origin uncertain: perhaps from Bantu *tshipi* 'short'.]

Jiffy /jíffi-/ *tdmk.* a trademark for a padded mailing envelope

jig /jig/ *n.* **1.** DANCE **LIVELY DANCE** a lively folk dance in triple time, especially one with kicking or jumping steps ○ *an Irish jig* **2.** MUSIC **DANCING MUSIC** a piece of music to which a jig is danced **3.** WOODWORK, INDUST **DEVICE FOR HOLDING PIECE OF WORK** the part of a woodworking or metalworking machine that holds the object to be worked on and guides the cutting or drilling tool **4.** ANGLING **WIGGLY FISHING LURE** a fishing lure made to attract a fish's attention through its motion as it is jerked around in the water **5.** MINING **MINERAL-WASHING DEVICE** a device that cleans and separates coal or other excavated minerals from waste material by shaking and washing ■ *v.* (**jigs, jigging, jigged**) **1.** *vti.* **JERK AROUND QUICKLY** to move around, or cause sth to move around, in a quick jerky way **2.** *vi.* DANCE **DANCE A JIG** to dance a lively folk dance in triple time, especially one with kicking or jumping steps **3.** *vt.* WOODWORK, INDUST **CUT OR DRILL STH WITH JIG** to cut or drill a piece of work using a jig as a guide **4.** *vti.* ANGLING **FISH WITH JIG** to fish, or catch a fish, using a jig **5.** *vt.* MINING **CLEAN AND SEPARATE MINERALS WITH JIG** to wash and separate coal or other excavated minerals with a jig [Mid-16thC. Noun of unknown origin. Verb of uncertain origin: perhaps from French *giguer* 'to dance', from *gigue* 'fiddle', from a prehistoric Germanic word.]

jigger[1] /jíggər/ *n.* **1.** MEASURE, BEVERAGES **MEASURE FOR ALCOHOLIC SPIRITS** a measure used for alcoholic spirits, equal to approximately 1.5 fl. oz **2.** WOODWORK, INDUST **JIG OPERATOR** sb who operates a mechanical jig **3.** *US* **STH OR OTHER** an object whose name is not known or cannot be recalled (*informal*) **4.** ANGLING = **jig** *n.* 4 **5.** SAILING **SAIL AT BOAT'S STERN** a small sail near the stern of a small sailing boat **6.** SAILING = **jiggermast** **7.** ENG **DEVICE WORKING WITH JERKING MOTION** a mechanical device, e.g. a drill, that operates with a jerking movement **8.** CUE GAMES **CUE REST** a cue rest in billiards (*informal*) **9.** *Can* ANGLING **FISHING LINE** a short line attached to an unbaited hook, used to catch squid or cod by a jerking motion

jigger[2] *n.* INSECTS = **chigoe** [Late 18thC. Alteration of CHIGGER.]

jiggermast /jíggər maast/ *n.* **1.** **SMALL REAR MAST** the shorter mast near the stern of a small sailing boat **2.** **FOURTH MAST BACK** on a four-masted sailing ship, the mast nearest the stern

jiggery-pokery /jíggəri pókəri/ *n.* devious, deceitful, or dishonest behaviour (*informal*) ○ *All this ridiculous jiggery-pokery going on behind my back!* [Late 19thC. Origin uncertain: said to be an alteration of earlier Scots dialect *joukery-pawkery*; *joukery* formed from *jouk* 'to dodge' and *pawkery* formed from *pawk* 'trick'.]

jiggle /jígg'l/ *vti.* (**-gles, -gling, -gled**) **TO WIGGLE** to move, or cause sth to move, in small rapid movements in any direction ○ *He jiggled the catch.* ■ *n.* **WIGGLY MOVEMENT** a rapid back-and-forth or up-and-down motion ○ *giving the key a quick jiggle in the lock* [Mid-19thC. Blend of JIG and JOGGLE.] —**jiggly** *adj.*

jigsaw /jíg saw/ *n.* **1.** LEISURE **JIGSAW PUZZLE** a jigsaw puzzle **2.** JOINERY **POWER SAW FOR CURVES** a machine saw with a narrow blade, used for cutting curves and shapes ■ *vt.* (**-saws, -sawing, -sawed, -sawed** *or* **-sawn** /-sawn/) JOINERY **CUT STH USING JIGSAW** to cut or shape sth using a jigsaw ■ *adj.* **WITH COMPLEX STRUCTURE** with many interrelating parts or elements forming a complex whole ○ *the jigsaw nature of politics*

jigsaw puzzle *n.* **1.** LEISURE **PICTURE CUT INTO PIECES** a puzzle in the form of interlocking irregularly shaped pieces that make a picture when fitted together **2.** **COMPLEX WHOLE** sth that is made up of many interconnecting parts ○ *help the police to piece together this jigsaw puzzle of motives*

jihad /ji hád/, **jehad** *n.* a campaign waged by Muslims in defence of the Islamic faith against individuals, organizations, or countries regarded as hostile to Islam [Mid-19thC. From Arabic *jihād* 'effort'.]

Jilin /jeé lín/ province in Manchuria, northeastern China. The southeast of the province borders Russia and North Korea. Capital: Changchun. Population: 25,740,000 (1994). Area: 187,000 sq. km/72,200 sq. mi.

jillaroo /jíllə roó/ (*plural* **-roos**) *n. Aus* a woman who is a trainee worker on a sheep or cattle station (*informal*) [Mid-20thC. On the model of JACKAROO.]

jillion /jíllyən/ *n.* a number or amount too great to specify (*informal*) [Mid-20thC. Imaginative formation modelled on BILLION.]

jilt /jilt/ *vt.* (**jilts, jilting, jilted**) **REJECT A LOVER** to break off a romantic relationship with sb abruptly ■ *n.* **SB WHO REJECTS A LOVER** sb who abruptly breaks off a relationship with a lover [Mid-17thC. Origin unknown. Originally 'to deceive, cheat'.]

Jim Crow /jím kró/, **jim crow** *n. US* **1.** **Jim Crow, jim Crow, Jim Crowism, jim Crowism** **RACIAL DISCRIMINATION** the practice of discriminating against Black people, especially by operating systems of public segregation (*informal*) **2.** **TABOO OFFENSIVE TERM** a highly offensive taboo word referring to a Black person (*taboo offensive*) [Mid-19thC. From *Jim Crow*, a Black character in the early 19thC plantation song of that name.]

jimjams /jím jamz/ *npl.* (*informal*) **1.** **DELIRIUM TREMENS** an attack of delirium tremens **2.** **NERVOUSNESS** an attack of nervous anxiety **3.** **PYJAMAS** a pair of pyjamas [Late 19thC. Plural of obsolete *jimjam* 'trivial article, knick-knack', a playful formation.]

jimmy /jímmi/ *n.* (*plural* **-mies**) *US* = **jemmy** *n.* ■ *vt.* (**-mies, -mying, -mied**) *US* = **jemmy** *v.* [Mid-19thC. Alteration of JEMMY.]

Jimmy /jímmi/ *n. Scotland* an informal way of addressing a man whose name is not known (*informal*) ○ *Hey, you, Jimmy!* [Mid-19thC. Familiar form of the forename *James*.]

Jimmy Woodser /-woódzər/ *n. ANZ* (*informal*) **1.** **LONE DRINKER** sb, usually a man, who drinks alone **2.** **DRINK** a drink taken by sb alone [Late 19thC. Origin uncertain: perhaps from *James Wood*, a shearer in New South Wales, or *Jimmy Wood*, a wealthy man; both drank alone.]

jimsonweed /jímss'n weed/ *n. US* = **thorn apple** [Late 17thC. Alteration of *Jamestown*, Virginia, where it was first observed.]

Jinan /jeé nán/ city and capital of Shandong Province on the Huang He, eastern China. Population: 2,320,000 (1991).

jingbang /jíng báng/ *n. Scotland* a thing in its entirety (*informal*) ○ *the whole jingbang* [Mid-19thC. Origin unknown.]

jingle /jíng g'l/ *n.* **1.** **METALLIC TINKLE** a light musical noise like that of small bells or pieces of metal being shaken together **2.** **TUNE ASSOCIATED WITH STH ADVERTISED** a catchy tune or verse, usually one that is played repeatedly to advertise sth ○ *the new jingle for the radio station* ■ *v.* (**-gles, -gling, -gled**) **1.** *vti.* **MAKE A TINKLING SOUND** to make, or cause sth to make, a light musical noise like that of small bells or pieces of metal being shaken together ○ *He jingled the coins in his pocket.* **2.** *vi.* **HAVE AN EASILY REMEMBERED SOUND** to have a sound or rhyme that is catchy or repetitious [14thC. An imitation of the sound of small metallic objects shaken together.] —**jingly** *adj.*

jingo /jíng gō/ (*plural* **-goes**) *n.* a zealous patriot, especially sb who advocates hostility towards other countries [Late 17thC. Origin uncertain: originally a conjurers' term. The modern sense derives from the use of 'by jingo!' in the refrain of a hawkish popular song of the late 19thC.] —**jingoish** *adj.* ◇ **by jingo!** used to express surprise or annoyance (*dated informal*)

jingoism /jíng gō izəm/ *n.* zealous patriotism expressing itself especially in hostility towards other countries —**jingoist** *adj., n.* —**jingoistic** /jíng gō ístik/ *adj.* —**jingoistically** *adv.*

WORD KEY: ORIGIN

The context of the coining of ***jingoism*** was British foreign policy of the late 1870s: the Prime Minister, Benjamin Disraeli, favoured sending in gunboats to halt the advance of the Russian fleet out of their own waters into the Mediterranean; this gave rise to a music-hall song, written in 1878 by G.W. Hunt, the refrain of which went: 'We don't want to fight, yet by Jingo! if we do, We've got the ships, we've got the men, and got the money too'; opponents of the policy picked up on the word *jingo* and used it as an icon of blind patriotism.

Jinja /jínjə/ city in southeastern Uganda, in the Eastern Region, on Lake Victoria. Population: 60,979 (1991).

jink /jingk/ *vi.* (**jinks, jinking, jinked**) **DODGE** to make quick sideways movements in order to evade sb or sth ■ *n.* **DODGING MOVEMENT** a quick evasive movement or manoeuvre [Late 17thC. Origin uncertain: perhaps an imitation of a sudden movement.]

Jinnah /jínnə/, **Muhammad Ali** (1876–1948) Indian and Pakistani statesman. He became president of the Muslim League in India in 1935. His campaign for a separate Muslim state resulted in the creation of Pakistan in 1947, when he became the state's first president and governor-general.

jinni /jínni/ (*plural* **jinn** /jin/), **djinni** (*plural* **djinn**) *n.* in Islamic mythology, a spirit that can take on various human and animal forms and makes mischievous use of its supernatural powers. ◊ **genie** [Early 19thC. From Arabic *jinn*, plural of *jinnī*. The plural form is popularly thought of as the singular.]

jinriksha /jin ríkshə/, **jinricksha** *n.* = **rickshaw** [Late 19thC. From Japanese *jin* 'man' + *riki* 'strength' + *sha* 'vehicle'.]

jinx /jingks/ *n.* **CAUSE OF MISFORTUNE** an unseen force that is thought to bring bad luck, or sb or sth, e.g. a curse, that is thought to bring bad luck ○ *There must be a jinx on this expedition.* ■ *vt.* (**jinxes, jinxing, jinxed**) **BRING MISFORTUNE ON STH** to bring a supposed unseen force of misfortune to bear on sth or sb ○ *the feeling that they had been jinxed in some way* [Early 20thC. Origin uncertain: probably from earlier *jynx* 'the wryneck bird', from its use in witchcraft.] —**jinxed** *adj.*

jipijapa /he'epi ha'apə/ *n.* a stemless plant native to Central and South America that resembles a palm and has large leaves that are used to make panama hats. Latin name: *Carludovica palmata.* [Mid-19thC. Named after *Jipijapa*, a town in Ecuador where it is found.]

JIT *abbr.* MANAGEMT just-in-time

jitter /jíttər/ *vi.* (**-ters, -tering, -tered**) **BEHAVE NERVOUSLY** to behave in a nervous or restless way (*informal*) ■ *n.* ELEC ENG **1. RAPID SIGNAL FLUCTUATION** an undesired rapid movement of electrical signals or images, e.g. on a television or oscilloscope screen, because of circuit instability or faulty components **2. DISTORTION IN DIGITIZED INFORMATION** a distortion in digitally transmitted or recorded sound or images, caused when two devices are not perfectly synchronized, e.g. the recording and playback devices of audio recordings ■ **jitters** *npl.* **NERVOUS ATTACK** feelings of extreme nervousness and agitation (*informal*) ○ *He's got the jitters about his interview tomorrow.* [Early 20thC. Origin uncertain: perhaps from Mandingo *ji-to* 'frightened', from *ji* 'to be afraid'.]

jitterbug /jíttər bug/ *n.* **1. FAST DANCE** a fast energetic jazz dance for couples that was popular in the 1940s **2. JITTERBUG DANCER** sb who dances the jitterbug ■ *vi.* (**-bugs, -bugging, -bugged**) **DANCE JITTERBUG** to dance the jitterbug [Mid-20thC. Origin uncertain: perhaps from Mandingo *jitobaga* 'frightened person' (see JITTER), or *bug* from BUG 'insect'. Originally 'jittery person'.]

jittery /jíttəri/ *adj.* **1. NERVOUS** feeling nervous or agitated **2. JERKY** making rapid jumpy movements —**jitteriness** *n.*

Jivaro /he'evə rō/ (*plural* **-ro** *or* **-ros**) *n.* **1.** PEOPLES **MEMBER OF NATIVE S AMERICAN PEOPLE** a member of a Native South American people living in the tropical forests of Ecuador and northeastern Peru. Their ancestors were noted for their ritual of shrinking and preserving the heads of enemies they had killed. **2.** LANG **LANGUAGE OF JIVARO** the language spoken by the Jivaro. It belongs to the Equatorial branch of the Andean-Equatorial family of American languages. Jivaro is spoken by about 20,000 people. [Mid-19thC. From Spanish *jíbaro*, of uncertain origin: probably from Jivaro *Shuara*.] —**Jivaro** *adj.*

jive /jīv/ *n.* **1.** MUSIC **JAZZ MUSIC** jazz or swing music, especially that of the 1930s and 1940s **2.** DANCE **LIVELY DANCING STYLE** a very lively, uninhibited style of popular dancing, often with a man swinging and throwing a woman. It was originally done to jazz music, and later to rock and roll. **3.** LANGUAGE **JAZZ MUSICIANS' JARGON** the special terminology and slang used by jazz musicians (*slang*) **4.** *US* **INSINCERE TALK** smooth talk that is often deceptive or insincere (*slang*) ■ *v.* (**jives, jiving, jived**) **1.** *vi.* DANCE **DANCE JIVE** to dance in the lively, often acrobatic style associated with jazz music, and later with rock and roll **2.** *vi.* LANGUAGE **TALK JIVE** to use the special terminology and slang of jazz musicians (*slang*) **3.** *vti.* *US* **FLATTER WITH SMOOTH TALK** to flatter or deceive sb with insincere talk (*slang*) ○ *I know when you're jiving me.* ■ *adj.* *US* **INSINCERE** lacking sincerity or honesty (*slang*) ○ *His comments are so jive!* [Early 20thC. Origin uncertain: perhaps from Wolof *jev* 'to talk about sb not present, especially disparagingly'.] —**jiver** *n.*

JJ, JJ. *abbr.* **1.** BIBLE Judges **2.** LAW Justices

Jl *abbr.* **1.** BIBLE Joel **2.** journal

Jl. *abbr.* July

Jm. *abbr.* BIBLE James

Jn *abbr.* BIBLE John

jnd *abbr.* PSYCHOL just noticeable difference

jnr, Jnr *abbr.* junior

jnt *abbr.* joint

jo /jō/ (*plural* **joes**) *n.* *Scotland* sb whom sb else loves (*dated*) [Early 16thC. Scottish form of JOY.]

Jo. *abbr.* BIBLE Joel

Joan of Arc /jōn əv a'ark/, **St** (1412–31) French patriot. She led the French to victory against the English, but was captured and burned at the stake as a heretic. She is the patron saint of France.

João Pessoa /zhwów pe sō ə/ capital city of Paraíba State, in northeastern Brazil. It is a leading trade centre. Population: 497,214 (1991). Former name **Parahyba**

job /job/ *n.* **1. PAID OCCUPATION** an activity such as a trade or profession that sb does regularly for pay, or a paid position doing this ○ *She's got a new job.* **2. TASK** sth that remains to be done or dealt with ○ *I have several jobs to do this afternoon.* **3. ASSIGNMENT** an individual piece of work of a particular nature ○ *We managed to complete the job in under a week.* **4. FUNCTION** the role that sb or sth fulfils ○ *It's her job to look after the finances.* **5. DIFFICULTY** sth that is difficult to accomplish ○ *I had quite a job getting it to start.* **6. QUALITY OF WORK DONE** a completed piece of work of a particular quality ○ *They did a very good job on the exterior.* **7. OBJECT** an object of some kind, especially a manufactured item (*informal*) ○ *one of those big four-wheel-drive jobs* **8. AFFAIR** sth that happens or sth that is done (*informal*) ○ *The party was one of those posh jobs.* **9. CRIME** a criminal act, especially a robbery (*informal*) ○ *not since we did that job in Bermondsey* **10.** COMPUT **PROGRAMMING TASK** a computer programming task run as a single application or unit ■ *v.* (**jobs, jobbing, jobbed**) **1.** *vi.* **WORK OCCASIONALLY** to take occasional or casual work ○ *He jobs as a gardener from time to time.* **2.** *vti.* **DEAL IN WHOLESALE MERCHANDISE** to buy and sell merchandise as a wholesaler or agent **3.** *vt.* **DISTRIBUTE WORK TO OTHERS** to subcontract portions of contract work to others ○ *job out the plumbing work on the house* **4.** *vi.* **PROFIT FROM PUBLIC OFFICE** to make a private gain from working in a public position **5.** *vi.* FIN, HIST **WORK AS STOCKJOBBER** to deal in stocks as a stockjobber (*dated*) [Mid-16thC. Origin uncertain: perhaps from obsolete *job* 'piece', of unknown origin.] ◇ **be a good job** to be a fortunate circumstance (*informal*) ○ *It's a good job you decided to stay in tonight.* ◇ **give sth up as a bad job** to abandon sth that seems unlikely to be going to change for the better ◇ **just the job** exactly what is needed ◇ **on the job 1.** engaged in working **2.** having sex (*slang*)

WORD KEY: SYNONYMS

job, assignment, task, chore, duty

CORE MEANING: a piece of work to be done

job a general word used to describe both a piece of work that sb has chosen to do or one that he or she is obliged to do, for example because it is part of his or her employment. It can also be used to talk about sb's employment; **assignment** a set piece of work given to sb as part of the workload of an occupation or course of study, often with the requirement to finish it within a fixed period of time. It can also be used to mean a post or position that has been allocated to sb; **task** a piece of work that requires effort, often imposed by an employer or someone in authority or by circumstances, but sometimes self-imposed. It is usually either quite short in duration or else has to be finished within a certain time; **chore** a relatively short undertaking, either imposed by sb in authority or self-imposed, requiring effort and indicating some kind of routine. It is often used to indicate that sth is considered tedious and even unpleasant; **duty** used to describe sth that has to be done because of obligations to other individuals or to society.

Job[1] /jōb/ *n.* in the Bible, a righteous man whose faith withstood severe testing by God ○ *have the patience of Job*

Job[2] /jōb/ *n.* the book of the Bible that describes Job's afflictions and eventual reward. See table at **Bible**

job action *n.* *US* = **industrial action**

jobber /jóbbər/ *n.* **1. SB TAKING OCCASIONAL OR CASUAL WORK** sb who does odd jobs or casual work **2.** FIN, HIST = **stockjobber** *n.* 1

jobbery /jóbbəri/ *n.* the corrupt practice of making private gains from public office, or an instance of this

jobbing /jóbbing/ *adj.* working on a casual basis

Jobcentre /jób sentər/ *n.* a local office, run by the government, where jobs are advertised and where people looking for work can receive help and advice

job club *n.* a local association formed, under the auspices of a Jobcentre, to facilitate self-help in the search for work and to monitor progress in finding work

job description *n.* an official written description of the responsibilities and requirements of a specific job, often one agreed between employer and employee

job-hunt (**job-hunts, job-hunting, job-hunted**) *vi.* to look for a job (*informal*) —**job hunter** *n.*

jobless /jóbləss/ *adj.* **UNEMPLOYED** without a job ■ *npl.* **PEOPLE WITHOUT JOBS** unemployed people considered collectively —**joblessness** *n.*

job lot *n.* a miscellaneous collection of articles, especially ones that are bought or sold together ○ *I bought it as a job lot.*

job-related illness *n.* = **industrial disease**

Job's comforter *n.* sb who, though appearing or intending to comfort a distressed person, only succeeds in worsening the situation [From the friends who came to 'comfort' Job in his affliction, counselling him: 'despise not thou the chastening of the Almighty' (Job 5:17)]

job seeker *n.* a person who is actively looking for employment

Jobseeker's Allowance /jób seekərz-/ *n.* money that the government pays to unemployed people who are looking for a job

job-sharing *n.* the dividing up of the responsibilities of a single full-time job between two or more part-time workers —**job-share** *n.*, *vi.*

Job's tears *n.* (*plural* **Job's tears**) **TROPICAL GRASS PLANT** a tropical Asian grass plant with hard white spherical leaves that are used as beads. Latin name: *Coix lacryma-jobi.* ■ *npl.* **WHITE LEAVES USED AS BEADS** the hard white leaves of Job's tears, used as beads [From its round shiny leaves that resemble tears]

jobsworth /jóbz wurth/ *n.* a minor official who insists on following regulations to the letter, especially with the intention of being deliberately obstructive (*informal*) [Late 20thC. From *It's more than my job's worth* (to do whatever is being requested), a phrase supposedly repeated often by such people.]

jock[1] /jok/ *n.* a disc jockey (*informal*) [Late 18thC. Shortening; originally 'jockey'.]

jock[2] /jok/ *n.* (*informal*) **1.** *US* **ATHLETE** an athlete, especially a male athlete in college **2. JOCKSTRAP** a jockstrap [Mid-20thC. Shortening of JOCKSTRAP.]

jock[3] /jok/ (**jocks, jocking, jocked**) *vi.* *Carib* an offensive term meaning to masturbate (*taboo offensive*) [Origin unknown: perhaps originally in the sense 'genitals']

Jock /jok/ *n.* a word used, sometimes disparagingly, to refer to or address a Scottish person, especially a man (*informal; offensive in some contexts*) [From *Jock*, a common Scottish form of John]

jockey /jóki/ *n.* (*plural* **-eys**) **1. RIDER OF RACEHORSE** sb who rides racehorses, especially professionally **2.** *US* **WORKER WITH OR OPERATOR OF STH** sb whose work involves the use or operation of a particular device, vehicle, or object (*informal*) ○ *We desk jockeys need to get out and exercise more.* ■ *v.* (**-eys, -eying, -eyed**) **1.** *vti.* **RIDE RACEHORSE** to ride a racehorse, especially as a professional jockey **2.** *vi.* **TRY TO GAIN ADVANTAGE** to manoeuvre in order to gain an advantage ○ *Watch them all jockeying for promotion.* **3.** *vt.* **MANIPULATE** to trick sb, usually for personal gain ○ *felt she has been jockeyed into doing work for which he gets credit* [Late 16thC. Originally a familiar form of JOCK, indicating 'boy, underling', later 'horse dealer' and hence 'horse rider'.]

Jockey *tdmk.* a trademark for underwear

jock itch *n.* *US* = **dhobi itch**

jockstrap /jók strap/ *n.* an elasticated belt with a pouch at the front, worn by sportsmen to support their genitals or to keep a protective cup in place [Late 19thC. *Jock* from slang *jock* 'genitals', of unknown origin.]

jocose /jə kóss, jō-/ *adj.* (*literary*) **1. FOND OF JOKING** with a playful joking disposition **2. HUMOROUS** playfully humorous in style [Late 17thC. From Latin *jocosus* 'full of joking', from *jocus* 'joke' (source of English *joke*).] —**jocosely** *adv.* —**jocoseness** *n.* —**jocosity** /jə kóssə ti, jō-/ *n.*

jocular /jókyŏŏlər/ *adj.* **1. FOND OF JOKING** with a playful joking disposition **2. HUMOROUS** intended to be funny [Early 17thC. From Latin *jocularis*, literally 'of a little joke', from, ultimately, *jocus* 'joke' (source of English *joke*).] —**jocularity** /jókyŏŏ lárrəti/ *n.* —**jocularly** /jókyŏŏlərli/ *adv.*

jocund /jókənd/ adj. cheerful and full of good humour (literary) [14thC. Via Old French jocond (influenced by Latin jocus 'joke') from Latin jucundus, from juvare 'to please, help'.] —**jocundity** /jə kúndəti/ n. —**jocundly** /jókəndli/ adv.

Jodhpur /jód poór/ city in northwestern India, in the state of Rajasthan. Population: 648,621 (1991).

jodhpurs /jód pərz/ npl. riding breeches that are wide at the hip and narrow round the calves, often with reinforced patches at the knee and thigh where the rider's legs grip the horse [Late 19thC. Named after JODHPUR.]

Jodrell Bank Experimental Station /jóddrəl-/ observatory in southern Cheshire, England, with a giant radio telescope

Joe /jō/, **joe** n. an ordinary man (informal) [Late 18thC. Familiar shortening of forename Joseph.]

Joe Bloggs /-blógz/ n. the average man in the street (informal) US term **Joe Blow**

Joe Blow /jō blō/ n. US, Can, Aus = **Joe Bloggs**

Joel /jō əl/ n. 1. HEBREW PROPHET a Hebrew prophet who lived in the 6th century BC 2. BOOK OF THE BIBLE the book of the Bible that contains the prophecies of Joel, dating from the years following the Israelites' Babylonian exile. See table at **Bible**

joe-pye weed /jō pí-/ n. a tall North American perennial plant with whorled leaves and clusters of small pink or purple flower heads. Latin name: Eupatorium maculatum and Eupatorium purpureum. [Early 19thC. According to tradition, named after Joe Pye, a Native American who mistakenly gathered it in place of the healing herb boneset; the gods turned him into this plant.]

Joe Soap n. a humorous way for sb to refer to himself or herself, especially when feeling put upon (informal)

joey /jō i/ n. Aus a young animal, especially a kangaroo still young enough to be carried in its mother's pouch [Mid-19thC. From Aboriginal joè.]

Joffre /zhóffrə/, **Joseph** (1852–1931) French soldier. He was commander in chief of the French army during World War I until December 1916. Full name **Joseph Jacques Césaire Joffre**

jog /jog/ v. (**jogs, jogging, jogged**) 1. vi. TROT to run at a slow steady pace ○ He jogged across the road to the shop. 2. vi. FITNESS RUN FOR EXERCISE to run at a slow steady pace as a fitness exercise ○ She jogs round the park every morning. 3. vi. GO SLOWLY BUT STEADILY to move along at a slow steady pace ○ The little steam train jogged along the track. 4. vi. PLOD to progress at a slow dull pace ○ How are things? – Oh, you know: jogging along. 5. vt. NUDGE STH to give a light push or shake to sth ○ thought the photo might have jogged your memory ■ n. 1. NUDGE a light push or shake 2. SLOW SPEED a slow steady pace or motion ○ moving along at a jog 3. FITNESS SPELL OF RUNNING a spell of slow steady running for exercise ○ I'm going for a quick jog. [Mid-16thC. Origin uncertain: perhaps an alteration of shaggen 'to jolt'. Originally 'shake up' or 'throw up with a push or jerk'.]

jogging /jógging/ n. a fitness or recreational activity that involves running at a moderate pace, often over long distances

joggle /jógg'l/ n. 1. SHAKING ACTION a gentle shaking motion or action 2. BUILDING MASONRY JOINT a joint between two pieces of masonry or concrete, in which a projection on one fits into a recess of the other ■ v. (-**gles, -gling, -gled**) 1. vti. SHAKE to shake sth gently ○ The table joggled and my drink spilt all over the place. 2. vt. BUILDING JOIN WITH JOGGLE to join pieces of masonry or concrete with a joggle [Early 18thC. Of uncertain origin: perhaps, in building senses, literally 'little jog', ultimately from JAG 'projecting point'; in shaking senses, perhaps literally 'to jog repeatedly', from JOG.]

Jogjakarta /jóg jə kaártə/ city in southwestern Indonesia, on the island of Java. Population: 412,400 (1990).

jog trot n. 1. SLOW RUNNING PACE a slow steady running pace 2. BORING PACE a dull steady pace of life ○ things going on at a jog trot

Johannine /jō hánnīn/ adj. relating to the apostle John or to the books of the Bible attributed to him [Mid-19thC. Formed from late Latin Joannes 'John'.]

john /jon/ n. US a toilet (informal) ○ Where's the john? [Mid-20thC. From John, forename.]

John n. See table at **Bible** 1. GOSPEL IN THE BIBLE the fourth of the gospels of the Bible in which the life and teachings of Jesus Christ are described. It is thought to have been written by St John. 2. EPISTLE OF BIBLE any of the three books of the Bible written in epistle form and traditionally attributed to St John

John /jon/, **St** (d. 101?) Judean apostle. He was one of the 12 disciples of Jesus Christ, and helped organize the early church throughout Palestine and Asia Minor. By tradition he is the author of the fourth Gospel, three Epistles, and Revelations in the Bible.

John, King of England (1167–1216). The youngest son of Henry II, he succeeded his brother Richard I as king (1199–1216). He was forced to issue the Magna Carta in 1215 after demands by the barons of England for constitutional reform. Known as **John Lackland**

John II, King of France (1319–64). He came to the throne in 1350. He was captured by the English (1356) but allowed to return to France to raise a ransom. Failing to do so, he returned to captivity. Known as **John the Good**

John VI, King of Portugal (1769–1826). He fled to Brazil following Napoleon's invasion of Portugal (1807), became King in 1816, and returned to Portugal in 1821. He granted Brazil independence (1822).

John (of Gaunt) /jón əv gáwnt/, **Duke of Lancaster** (1340–99) English soldier and statesman. The fourth son of Edward III, he fought the French and Spanish during the Hundred Years' War. In England he acted as a peacemaker during the reign of his nephew Richard II.

John (of Salisbury) /jón əv sáwlzbəri/ (1115?–80) English churchman, philosopher, and humanist. He was a leader of the 12th-century literary renaissance, and wrote on government, philosophy, and education. Afterwards he became bishop of Chartres. He wrote about the lives of Becket and Anselm.

John (of the Cross) /jón əv thə króss/, **St** (1542–91) Spanish poet and mystic With Teresa of Ávila he founded the contemplative order of Discalced Carmelites (1568) His mystical poems include 'Dark Night of the Soul'. Born **Juan de Yepes y Álvarez,**

John (the Baptist) /jón thə báptist/, **St** (8? BC–AD 27?) Judean prophet. He is described in the gospels as the cousin and precursor of Jesus Christ. He was beheaded at the behest of Salome.

John /jon/, **Augustus** (1878–1961) British painter. The brother of Gwen John, he is known for his portraits of contemporary figures. Full name **Augustus Edwin John**

John, Sir Elton (b. 1947) British rock singer and pianist. His partnership with lyricist Bernie Taupin produced a string of international hit songs. Real name **Reginald Dwight**

John, Gwen (1876–1939) British painter. The sister of Augustus John, many of her works are portraits of women.

John Barleycorn n. (literary or humorous) 1. ALCOHOL PERSONIFIED the personification of alcoholic drink 2. Scotland PERSONIFICATION OF BARLEY barley personified as the source of malt liquor

John Bull /-bool/ n. 1. ENGLAND PERSONIFIED the personification of England and the English people 2. ENGLISHMAN an individual Englishman, especially one regarded as embodying Englishness [Late 18thC. Named after a character representing the English nation in Law is a Bottomless Pit (1712), by J. Arbuthnot.] —**John Bullish** adj. —**John Bullishness** n. —**John Bullism** n.

John Chrysostom /jón kríssəstəm/, **St** (349–407) Syrian-born preacher. He was called 'chrysostomos' (golden-mouthed) because of his oratory. He became patriarch of Constantinople (398–403) but was exiled because of his campaigning against vice.

John Doe /-dó/ n. US 1. ORDINARY MAN an average man affected by everyday events (informal) 2. LAW UNNAMED MAN a man or boy in a legal proceeding whose identity is either not known or not revealed

John Dory /-dáwri/ n. an edible deep-sea fish with a large flat olive-yellow body, long dorsal spines, and large jaws, found in the eastern Atlantic and the Mediterranean. Latin name: Zeus faber.

Johne's disease /yónəz-/ n. a chronic disease of sheep, cattle, and other domestic animals, with symptoms of diarrhoea and loss of weight, caused by a bacterium that is related to the tuberculosis bacterium [Early 20thC. Named after H. A. Johne (1839–1910), German veterinary surgeon, who first described it.]

John Hancock /-hán kok/ n. US sb's signature (informal) [Name of the US statesman who was the first to sign the Declaration of Independence; he signed it in large bold writing]

John Henry n. 1. BLACK FOLKLORE HERO an African American hero in US folklore, renowned for his great strength. He died after beating a steam drill in a contest of endurance. 2. US SIGNATURE sb's signature (informal) [In the sense 'signature' modelled on JOHN HANCOCK]

johnny /jónni/ (plural -**nies**) n. 1. CONDOM a condom (slang) 2. MAN a man or boy (dated informal) 3. US HOSPITAL GOWN a short gown that ties at the back, worn in hospitals by patients [Late 17thC. Diminutive of John.]

Johnny Canuck /jónni kə núk/ n. Can a personification of Canada, in the form of a strong clean-cut young man, often a lumberjack

Johnny-come-lately (plural **Johnny-come-latelies** or **Johnnies-come-lately**) n. a recent arrival at a place, group, position, or point of view (informal) ○ these Johnny-come-latelies and their 'new' ideas

Johnny Reb /-réb/ n. US a Confederate soldier in the American Civil War (archaic informal) [Mid-19thC. Shortening of Johnny Rebel, the name for a Confederate supporter.]

John o'Groats /jón ə gróts/ tourist village on the northeastern tip of Scotland. The journey from John o'Groats to Land's End in Cornwall is reputedly the longest in Great Britain, 1,405 km/873 mi.

John Paul I /jón páwl/, **Pope** (1912–78). He died 34 days after becoming pope in 1978. Born **Albino Luciani**

John Paul II, Pope (b. 1920). In 1978 he became both the first-ever Polish-born pope and the first non-Italian pope since 1522 and is regarded as a traditionalist within the Roman Catholic Church. Born **Karol Wojtyta**

Amy Johnson

Johnson /jónss'n/, **Amy** (1903–41) British flyer. She made record solo flights to Australia (1930), Tokyo (1932), and the Cape of Good Hope and back (1936). She flew the Atlantic in 1936 with her husband and was killed in an air crash.

Johnson, Andrew (1808–75) US statesman and 17th President of the United States. A Democrat, he was Lincoln's vice president (1865), and succeeded to the presidency after Lincoln's assassination in April 1865. As president (1865–69), he survived an impeachment by Republicans opposed to his conciliatory Reconstruction policies.

Lyndon Baines Johnson and Lady Bird Johnson

Johnson, Lyndon Baines (1908–73) US statesman and 36th President of the United States. A Democrat, he was John F. Kennedy's vice president and became president when Kennedy was assassinated, winning a full term the following year. During his presidency (1963–69), increased US involvement in the Vietnam War made him unpopular, and diverted attention from his programme of social reform.

Johnson, Samuel (1709–84) English critic, poet, and lexicographer. His works include his *Dictionary of the English Language* (1755), an edition of Shakespeare (1765), and *Lives of the Poets* (1779–81). He founded two periodicals, *The Rambler* (1750–52) and *The Idler* (1758–60), and his witty conversation is recorded in Boswell's biography of him.

Johnson grass *n.* a coarse perennial variety of sorghum grass, native to Mediterranean regions and often grown as forage. Latin name: *Sorghum halepense.* [Named after William *Johnson,* an Alabama planter]

Johnsonian /jon sóni ən/ *adj.* relating to Samuel Johnson or his works, or written in his style.

Johnston /jónstən/, **George** (1912–70) Australian writer. His novels include *My Brother Jack* (1964) and *Clean Straw For Nothing* (1969). Full name **George Henry Johnstone**

John Thomas *n.* a penis (*slang*) [Origin unknown: originally in the sense 'man-servant']

Johor Strait /jə háwr-/ narrow strait running between Singapore and Malaysia. Previously known as **Johore Strait**

joie de vivre /zhwaá də veévrə/ *n.* energy and love of life [Late 19thC. From French, literally 'joy of living'.]

join /joyn/ *v.* (**joins, joining, joined**) **1.** *vti.* **BRING OR COME TOGETHER** to meet, or make two or more things meet, and become linked or united ○ *where the A4 joins the M4* **2.** *vt.* **FIX TOGETHER** to put or fix two or more things together ○ *Join the wing to the body with glue.* **3.** *vt.* **MAKE CONNECTION BETWEEN THINGS** to establish a connection between two or more things, e.g. by drawing a line between them ○ *Join the dots.* **4.** *vti.* **BECOME PART OF GROUP** to become a member of sth such as a club, social group, company, team, or other organization ○ *I've joined the Mountaineering Club.* **5.** *vt.* **DO THE SAME AS SB** to agree to do the same as sb ○ *I'm sure my colleagues will want to join me in thanking you for your visit today.* **6.** *vt.* **UNITE PEOPLE IN PARTNERSHIP** to bring two or more people into a partnership, e.g. a marriage **7.** *vt.* **MEET SB** to go to meet sb ○ *I'll join you later.* **8.** *vt.* **SHARE SB'S COMPANY** to enter into the company of another person ○ *Do you mind if I join you?* **9.** *vti.* **BE ADJACENT** to be next to sth or to each other ○ *This room joins the bathroom.* ■ *n.* **JOINT** a place where two or more things have been joined ○ *You can hardly see the join.* [13thC. Via Old French *joign-,* present stem of *joindre,* from Latin *jungere* 'to join' (source of English *juncture* and *junta*).] —**joinable** *adj.*

— **WORD KEY: ORIGIN** —
The Indo-European ancestor of *join* is also the ultimate source of English *adjust, conjugal, jostle, joust, jugular, juxtapose, subjugate, yoga,* and *yoke.*

join up *vi.* **1.** **ENLIST IN ARMED FORCES** to enlist as a member of one of the armed forces, especially at the outbreak of hostilities **2.** **MEET FOR JOINT ACTIVITY** to meet sb for a joint activity ○ *They join up with the same friends every year to go on holiday.*

joinder /jóyndər/ *n.* **1.** **ACT OF JOINING** a joining or bringing together of two things (*formal*) **2.** **LAW JOINING OF LEGAL PARTIES** a joining of two parties in a single lawsuit **3.** **LAW COMBINING OF LEGAL PROCEEDINGS** a joining of two causes of action or two defences in a lawsuit **4.** **LAW ACCEPTANCE OF ISSUE** a formal acceptance of an issue offered in a lawsuit [Early 17thC. Via Anglo Norman from Old French *joindre* 'to join'.]

joiner /jóynər/ *n.* **1.** **WOODWORKER IN BUILDING TRADE** sb who is trained or skilled in making the wooden components of buildings, especially the finished woodwork, e.g. door frames and window frames **2.** **ENTHUSIASTIC PARTICIPANT** sb who readily joins clubs, societies, and organizations (*informal*)

joinery /jóynəri/ *n.* **1.** **FINISHED WOODWORK IN BUILDINGS** the visible finished woodwork in a building, e.g. door frames and window frames **2.** **JOINER'S WORK** the work of a joiner, or the techniques that a joiner uses

joint /joynt/ *adj.* **1.** **OWNED IN COMMON** owned in common by two or more people or concerns ○ *joint assets* **2.** **COMBINED** existing and operating in combination ○ *the joint ravages of the weather and the pollution* **3.** **SHARING SAME ROLE** sharing the same role or position with another person or body ○ *My brother and I were appointed joint executors of her will.* **4.** **DONE TOGETHER** done or produced together with others ○ *A joint statement was issued by the three party leaders.* ■ *n.* **1.** **ANAT JUNCTION BETWEEN BONES** any of the parts of the body, e.g. the knee, elbow, or skull, where bones are connected. Many joints have supporting ligaments, protective cartilage, and a particular range of movement, while others, e.g. those between the bones of the vault of the skull, are immobile. **2.** **PLACE WHERE PARTS ARE JOINED** the place where parts or pieces of sth are joined together **3.** **COOK PIECE OF MEAT** a large piece of meat prepared and cooked for several people, especially one that is roasted **4.** **VENUE** a place of entertainment, e.g. a nightclub, especially one considered cheap or disreputable (*slang*) **5.** **DRUGS CANNABIS CIGARETTE** a cigarette containing cannabis (*slang*) **6.** **ZOOL JUNCTION BETWEEN SEGMENTS OF INVERTEBRATE BODY** any of the points of connection between movable segments of the body in an insect, spider, crab, or other invertebrate **7.** **BOT DIVIDING POINT ON PLANT STEM** the place on a plant stem from which a leaf or branch grows **8.** **GEOL CRACK IN ROCK** a crack or fissure in rock, without any looseness or displacement of the surrounding mass **9.** **PUBL HINGE OF BOOK COVER** either of the creases between the spine and the front and back covers of a book, especially a hardback **10.** **A PLACE** a building or dwelling (*slang*) ■ *v.* (**joints, jointing, jointed**) **1.** *vt.* **FIT TOGETHER** to fit or fix parts together by means of a joint **2.** *vt.* **COOK DIVIDE INTO PIECES** to cut a carcass into pieces of meat for cooking **3.** *vt.* **WOODWORK PLANE EDGE OF BOARD** to plane and shape the edge of a board so that it fits with another edge to form a joint **4.** *vi.* **BOT FORM JOINTS DURING GROWTH** to form joints in the stem during the growth process (*refers to cereal plants*) [13thC. From French, past participle of *joindre* 'to JOIN'.] —**jointed** *adj.* — **jointing** *n.* ◇ **out of joint 1.** dislocated or painfully displaced **2.** disturbed or disrupted, usually as a result of some major change or upheaval

joint account *n.* a bank account held in the names of more than one person, typically spouses or partners

Joint Chiefs of Staff *npl.* the most important military advisory group to the President of the United States consisting of the Chiefs of Staff of the Army and Air Force, the commandant of the Marine Corps, and the Chief of Naval Operations

joint defence *n.* a defence strategy in which two or more defendants join and co-operate with one another so that their cases are heard together

jointer /jóyntər/ *n.* **1.** **BUILDING TOOL FOR SHAPING MORTAR** a tool for pointing the mortar in brickwork or stonework after it has been laid **2.** **WOODWORK PLANE FOR SHAPING JOINTS** a long plane used to shape the edges of planks into joints

jointly /jóyntli/ *adv.* in conjunction with, or in co-operation with, a person or organization ○ *The copyright is jointly owned by the composer and the publisher.*

jointress /jóyntrəss/ *n.* **LAW** a woman on whom property has been settled by her husband at the time of their marriage

joint stock *n.* **FIN** stock held jointly, especially in a joint-stock company, a commercial enterprise whose capital is in shares that individual holders may transfer without the consent of the whole body

jointure /jóynchər/ *n.* **LAW** an estate or property settled by a husband on his wife at the time of their marriage, to take effect in the event of his death

joint venture *n.* a business enterprise jointly undertaken by two or more companies, who share the outlay, risks, and profits (*hyphenated when used before a noun*)

jointworm /jóynt wurm/ *n.* the larva of some wasps that forms a weakening swelling at the stem joint of a cereal plant. Family: Eurytomidae.

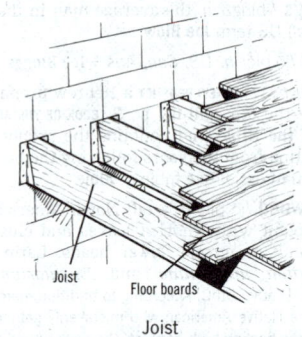

Joist   Floor boards

Joist

joist /joyst/ *n.* any of the parallel beams of wood, metal, or concrete that support a floor, roof, or ceiling [14thC. Via Old French *giste* 'beam supporting a bridge' from, ultimately, Latin *jacere* 'to lie down' (source of English *adjacent*).]

jojoba /hō hóbə/ (*plural* **-bas**) *n.* **1.** **PLANTS DESERT SHRUB YIELDING COSMETIC OIL** a desert shrub or small tree native to Mexico, Arizona, and California, with edible seeds that yield a waxy oil used in shampoos and other cosmetics. Latin name: *Simmondsia chinensis.* **2.** **COSMETICS COSMETIC OIL** the oil derived from the jojoba tree, used in shampoos and other cosmetics (*often used before a noun*) [Early 20thC. Via Mexican Spanish from a Native American word.]

joke /jōk/ *n.* **1.** **FUNNY STORY** a funny story, anecdote, or piece of wordplay that gets passed round and repeated **2.** **STH FUNNY SAID OR DONE** anything said or done to make people laugh ○ *dressed up the dog in a hat and sunglasses as a joke* **3.** **FUNNY EVENT** a funny event or circumstance, or sth to laugh at **4.** **STH INADEQUATE** sb or sth that is laughably inadequate or absurd (*informal*) ○ *The surroundings were pleasant enough but the food was a joke.* ■ *v.* (**jokes, joking, joked**) **1.** *vti.* **MAKE JOKES** to tell funny stories, or say or do things to make sb laugh **2.** *vi.* **NOT BE SERIOUS** to be trying to be amusing, rather than serious or in earnest ○ *We knew he was only joking.* **3.** *vt.* **TEASE** to make fun of sb (*archaic*) [Late 17thC. From Latin *jocus* 'jest, wordplay' (source of English *jocular, juggle,* and *jeopardy*). Originally slang.] ◇ **beyond a joke** having become a serious matter

joker /jókər/ *n.* **1.** **TELLER OR PLAYER OF JOKES** sb who frequently makes jokes or plays jokes on other people **2.** **CARDS CARD BEARING PICTURE OF JESTER** an extra playing card in a pack, bearing a picture of a jester, that in some games can be substituted for other cards **3.** **AMUSING ECCENTRIC PERSON** an amusing, entertaining, or entertainingly eccentric person (*informal*) **4.** **THOUGHTLESS OR INCONSIDERATE PERSON** sb whose thoughtless or inconsiderate action is highly annoying (*informal*) ○ *I'm looking for the joker who double-parked outside my front door.* ◇ **the joker in the pack** an unpredictable element that makes planning or projections difficult (*informal*)

jokey /jóki/ (**-ier, -iest**), **joky** *adj.* good-humoured and amusing, or full of jokes —**jokily** *adv.* —**jokiness** *n.*

jokingly /jókingli/ *adv.* with the intention of making a joke rather than a serious comment or suggestion

joky *adj.* = **jokey**

jolie laide /zhólli léd/ (*plural* **jolies laides** /zhólli léd/) *n.* a woman whose facial features are not pretty in conventional terms, but nevertheless have a distinctive harmony or charm [From French, from *jolie* 'pretty' + *laide* 'ugly']

Joliot-Curie /zhólli ō kyŏóri/, **Frédéric** (1900–58) French physicist. He was the winner of the Nobel Prize in chemistry (1925) with his wife Irène Joliot-Curie (daughter of Marie and Pierre Curie) for producing the first radioisotope artificially. Born **Jean-Frédéric Joliot**

Joliot-Curie, Irène (1897–1956) French physicist. She was joint winner of the Nobel Prize in chemistry (1925) with her husband, Frédéric Joliot-Curie, for producing the first radioisotope artificially. Born **Irène Curie**

Jolley /jólli/, **Elizabeth** (*b.* 1923) British-born Australian writer. Her works include radio plays, short stories, and novels, including *The Well* (1986). Full name **Monica Elizabeth Jolley**

jollification /jóllifi káysh'n/ *n.* the activities of people who are enthusiastically celebrating sth in a happy, friendly way [Early 19thC. Formed from JOLLY.]

jollifications /jóllifi káysh'nz/ *npl.* celebrations or festivities in association with a festival or an auspicious event (*dated*) ○ *I well remember all the jollifications at the end of World War II.*

jollify /jólli fī/ (**-fies, -fying, -fied**) *v.* **1.** *vi.* ENJOY YOURSELF to indulge enthusiastically in happy celebrations (*dated*) **2.** *vt.* MAKE SB OR STH CHEERFUL to make sb cheerful or create a festive atmosphere in sth [Early 19thC. Formed from JOLLY.]

jollities /jóllətiz/ *npl.* celebrations or festivities (*dated*)

jollity /jólləti/ *n.* cheerful, joking, or celebratory behaviour [13thC. From Old French *jolite*, from *joli* (see JOLLY).]

jolly /jólli/ *adj.* (**-lier, -liest**) **1.** FRIENDLY AND CHEERFUL friendly and cheerful, especially in a hearty or exuberant way ○ *a jolly pink-cheeked woman* **2.** HAPPY happily festive in tone or mood (*dated*) **3.** ENJOYABLE bringing pleasure or enjoyment (*dated informal*) ○ *A picnic would be jolly.* ■ *adv.* VERY used to emphasize the extent to which sth is good or bad (*dated informal*) ○ *jolly nice of you to come* [13thC. From Old French *joli* 'merry, pleasant, pretty', of uncertain origin: perhaps from Old Norse *jól* 'yule'.] ◇ **get your jollies** *US* to get pleasure out of sth (*slang*) ◇ **jolly well** a phrase used in annoyance to add emphasis (*dated*) ○ *I'm not jolly well going to stand for it.*

jolly along *vt.* to keep sb happy or cooperative by using flattery or encouragement (*informal*) ○ *Try to jolly her along a little bit longer*

jolly up *vt.* to make a person, place, or situation more lively or cheerful (*dated informal*) ○ *I thought some music might jolly things up a bit.*

jollyboat /jólli bōt/ *n.* a small boat carried on a larger ship, often one kept hoisted at the stern of the ship [Late 17thC. Origin of 'jolly' uncertain: possibly related to YAWL.]

Jolly Roger

Jolly Roger /jólli rójjər/ *n.* the flag traditionally flown by a pirate ship, depicting a white skull and crossbones against a black background [Late 18thC. Origin unknown: *Roger* perhaps from slang use to denote a man or a rogue.]

jolt /jōlt/ *v.* (**jolts, jolting, jolted**) **1.** *vti.* SHAKE OR JERK VIOLENTLY to shake or jerk suddenly and violently, or to make sb or sth shake or jerk suddenly and

violently, especially as a result of a sudden movement **2.** *vi.* BUMP UP AND DOWN to bump up and down or shake from side to side while moving **3.** *vt.* SHAKE OR DISLODGE to knock or shake sb or sth violently enough to cause unsteadiness or loss of balance ○ *A major earthquake jolted the city.* **4.** *vt.* STARTLE INTO REALITY to startle sb out of a daydream, fantasy, or other state of semiawareness ■ *n.* **1.** VIOLENT MOVEMENT a sudden, violent movement or blow ○ *The train moved off again with a series of jolts.* **2.** SHOCK OR REMINDER an emotional shock or a sharp reminder [Late 16thC. Origin unknown: perhaps an alteration of Middle English *jollen* 'to knock' or *jot* 'to bump'.] —**joltingly** *adv.* —**jolty** *adj.*

Jon. *abbr.* BIBLE Jonah

Jonah[1] /jónə/ *n.* **1.** HEBREW PROPHET in the Bible, a Hebrew prophet of the 8th century BC who was swallowed by a great fish and vomited out three days later, unharmed **2.** BOOK IN THE BIBLE a book in the Bible that tells the story of Jonah, whose preaching caused the Assyrians to repent their wickedness. See table at **Bible**

Jonah[2] /jónə/ *n.* sb who is regarded as a bringer of bad luck —**Jonahesque** /jónə ésk/ *adj.*

Jonathan /jónnəthən/ *n.* in the Bible, the eldest son of King Saul and close friend of David, who was killed in battle against the Philistines (1 Samuel 13–2 Samuel 21)

jones /jōnz/ *n.* **1.** *US* DRUG ADDICTION an addiction, especially a heroin addiction (*slang*) **2.** *US* WITHDRAWAL drug withdrawal symptoms, especially from heroin (*slang*) **3.** *US* HABITUAL CRAVING an all-consuming craving or desire for sth (*slang*) **4. jones, Jones** PENIS a penis (*taboo*) [Late 20thC. Origin unknown.]

Jones /jōnz/, **Alan** (*b.* 1947) Australian motor-racing driver. He won the 1980 Formula One world championship.

Jones, Inigo (1573–1652) English architect and stage designer. He introduced the Palladian style into English architecture. His designs include the Queen's House at Greenwich (1616–35).

Jones, John Paul (1747–92) Scottish-born US naval commander. He captured or destroyed many British ships during the American War of Independence.

Joneses /jónziz/ *npl.* neighbours, especially sb's next-door neighbours ○ *keeping up with the Joneses* [Late 19thC. From 'Jones', a common British surname.]

jongleur /zhoN glúr/ *n.* a wandering minstrel of medieval times who travelled about singing the compositions of troubadours or reciting epic poems in noble households or royal courts [Late 18thC. Via French from, ultimately, Latin *joculator* 'jester', from *joculari* (see JUGGLE).]

Jönköping /jón chōping/ city and capital of Jönköping County, in southern Sweden. Population: 113,557 (1993).

Jonquil

jonquil /jóngkwil/ *n.* VARIETY OF NARCISSUS a flowering plant native to southern Europe that is a variety of narcissus. It has intensely fragrant, golden-yellow, short-tubed flowers, is widely cultivated as an ornamental, and is also used in perfumery. Latin name: *Narcissus jonquilla.* ■ *adj.* YELLOW LIKE A JONQUIL with the golden-yellow colour of a jonquil [Early 17thC. Via modern Latin *jonquilla* or French *jonquille* from Spanish *junquillo* 'little rush', from *junco* (see JUNCO). So called because of its resemblance to a rush.]

Jonson /jónss'n/, **Ben** (1573–1637) English playwright and poet. His plays include brilliant comedies such as *Volpone* (1606) as well as classical tragedies. He was poet laureate (1616–25). Full name **Benjamin Jonson**

jootha /jóothə/ *n.* S Asia food that is considered polluted, usually because it has come in contact with sb's saliva

Scott Joplin

Joplin /jópplin/, **Scott** (1868–1917) US composer. He is best known for his ragtime piano music.

Jordaens /yawr dáanss/, **Jacob** (1593–1678) Flemish painter. His large baroque works feature subjects such as banquets, revelry, and genre scenes.

Jordan

Jordan /jáwrd'n/ **1.** kingdom in the Middle East, bordered by Syria, Iraq, Saudi Arabia, the Gulf of Aqaba, Israel, and the West Bank. Language: Arabic. Currency: Jordanian dinar. Capital: Amman. Population: 4,322,255 (1997). Area: 89,556 sq. km/34,578 sq. mi. Official name **Hashemite Kingdom of Jordan 2.** river in southwestern Asia that rises in the Anti-Lebanon Mountains of Lebanon and flows south through the Sea of Galilee before emptying into the Dead Sea. Length: 320 km/200 mi.

Jordan curve *n.* in mathematics, any simple closed curve, e.g. a circle or an ellipse [Early 20thC. Named after the French mathematician M. E. C. *Jordan* 1838–1922.]

Jordan curve theorem *n.* in geometry, a theorem holding that every simple closed curve divides a plane into two regions and serves as their boundary

Jordanian *n.* SB FROM JORDAN sb who was born or brought up in Jordan, or who is a citizen of Jordan ■ *adj.* OF JORDAN relating to or typical of Jordan, or its people or culture

jorts /jawrts/ *npl. Carib* light foods eaten between meals or in place of meals (*informal*)

jorum /jáwrəm/, **joram** *n.* a large drinking bowl or its contents (*archaic*) [Mid-18thC. Origin uncertain: perhaps named after *Joram*, who took silver, gold, and brass vessels to King David (II Samuel 8:10).]

joseph /jōzif/ *n.* a woman's 18th-century riding cloak with a short cape [Mid-17thC. From the coat that *Joseph* left behind in fleeing, Potiphar's wife (Genesis 39:13).]

Joseph /jōzif/ *n.* in the Bible, the son of Jacob and Rachel. He was given a coat of many colours and sold into slavery in Egypt by his jealous brothers (Genesis 30–50).

Joseph /jōzif/, **St** (*fl.* 1st century BC) Biblical figure. In the New Testament he is described as a carpenter of Nazareth and the husband of Mary, the mother of Jesus Christ.

Joseph II, Holy Roman Emperor (1741–90). He was the son of Francis I and Maria Theresa. As emperor (1765–90), he saw his reforms frustrated by insurrection and the distractions of war.

Joseph Bonaparte Gulf /józəf bónə paart-/ inlet of the Timor Sea on the north coast of Australia, extending from Western Australia into the Northern Territory. It is 320 km/200 mi. wide.

Joséphine /józə feen/, Empress of the French (1763–1814). She married the future Napoleon I in 1796 and was empress from 1804 until the childless marriage was dissolved in 1809. Born **Marie Joséphine Rose Tascher de la Pagerie**

Joseph of Arimathea /józif əv árrimə thee ə/, St (*fl.* 1st century AD) According to the Bible, he asked Pontius Pilate for the body of Jesus Christ, and buried it in his own tomb (Matthew 27).

Josephson effect /józifs'n-/ n. the passage of an electric current through a thin insulating layer between two superconducting metals [Late 20thC. Named after the British physicist Brian David *Josephson* b.1940, who predicted it.]

Josephson junction n. in electrical or electronic circuits, a junction that utilizes the Josephson effect, consisting of two superconducting materials separated by a thin insulating layer. In a computer memory, a Josephson junction acts as a high-speed switch.

Josephus /jō seefəss/, **Flavius** (AD37?–100?) Jewish historian and general. His works include a history of the Jewish revolt against Rome (AD66) and a history of the Jews. Born **Joseph Ben Matthias**

josh /josh/ (**joshes, joshing, joshed**) v. US (*informal*) **1.** vti. TEASE SB to make fun of sb in a friendly, good-humoured way **2.** vi. JOKE OR BANTER to joke or indulge in banter with sb [Mid-19thC. Origin unknown: perhaps from *Josh* Billings, pseudonym of US humorist.] —**josher** n. —**joshingly** adv.

Josh. abbr. Joshua

Joshua /jóshoo ə/ n. the book of the Bible that contains a narrative of the Hebrew invasion and partition of Canaan under Joshua's command. See table at **Bible**

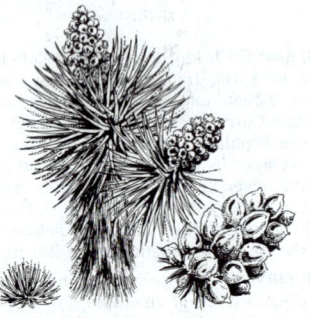

Joshua tree

Joshua tree n. a small tree-shaped yucca with sword-shaped leaves and clusters of white flowers that is native to deserts of the southwestern United States. Latin name: *Yucca brevifolia*. [Mid-19thC. Origin uncertain: probably named after JOSHUA, because the tree's branching shape resembles someone brandishing a spear (Joshua 8:18).]

joss /joss/ n. **1.** CHINESE IDOL an image or statue representing a Chinese deity **2.** LUCK luck or fate (*dated informal*) ○ *Bad joss you breaking your leg.* [Early 18thC. Via Javanese *dejos* from Portuguese *deus* 'god', from Latin.]

josser /jóssər/ n. a man, especially one considered unintelligent or obnoxious (*slang insult*) [Late 19thC. From JOSS.]

joss house n. a Chinese shrine or temple containing images or statues of deities

joss stick n. incense in the form of a stick of dried paste

jostle /jóss'l/ (**-tles, -tling, -tled**) vti. to knock or bump against sb, or to push or elbow sb deliberately, sometimes as an expression of aggression or hostility ○ *We managed to jostle our way to the*

front. [Mid-16thC. Formed from JOUST; the underlying sense is of repeatedly coming together.] —**jostler** n.

jot /jot/ vt. (**jots, jotting, jotted**) WRITE QUICKLY to write sth down hastily for later reference ○ *jotted down the title in her notebook* ■ n. TINY BIT a very small amount [15thC. Via Latin from Greek *iōta* (see IOTA).]

jota /khó taa, hó-/ n. a fast Spanish dance, performed with castanets in triple time, usually to a voice and guitar accompaniment. It is the traditional dance of Aragon. [Mid-19thC. From Spanish.]

jotter /jóttər/, **jotter pad** n. **1.** NOTEPAD a book or pad for making rough notes **2.** *Scotland* EXERCISE BOOK a school exercise book

jotting /jótting/ n. a hastily written note, comment, or observation

Jotun /yót'n, yó toon/, **Jotunn** n. a member of a race of giants with supernatural powers in Norse mythology

Jotunheim /yót'n haym, yó toon-/ n. the home of the giants in Norse mythology [From Old Norse *Jotunheimar*]

joual /zhoo áal, zhwaal/ n. Can a nonstandard, mainly urban dialect of Canadian French containing many English words [Mid-20thC. Via dialectal Canadian French from French *cheval* 'horse'.]

joule /jool/ n. the SI unit of energy or work, equal to the work done when the application point of a one newton force moves one metre in the direction of application. Symbol **J** [Late 19thC. Named after JOULE.]

Joule /jool/, **James** (1818–89) British physicist. He determined the mechanical equivalent of heat. The joule, a unit of energy, is named after him. Full name **James Prescott Joule**

Joule effect n. an increase in heat resulting from the passage of a current through a conductor [Late 19thC (see JOULE).]

jounce /jownss/ vti. (**jounces, jouncing, jounced**) MOVE WHILE BOUNCING to bounce up and down and rock from side to side while moving, or to make sb or sth move in this way ■ n. BOUNCING MOVEMENT a jolting, swaying, bouncing, or rocking movement [15thC. Origin unknown.] —**jouncy** adj.

jour. abbr. **1.** journal **2.** journalist **3.** journeyman

journal /júrn'l/ n. **1.** PUBL MAGAZINE OR PERIODICAL a magazine or periodical, especially one published by a specialist or professional body for its members, containing information and contributions relevant to their area of activity ○ *a medical journal* **2.** DETAILED PERSONAL DIARY sb's written daily record of personal experiences, rather more elaborate and detailed than a diary. **3.** ACCT PRELIMINARY RECORD OF FINANCIAL TRANSACTIONS a book for recording daily transactions, especially in double entry book-keeping, using a formulaic style to ensure their correct entry in a ledger **4.** POL OFFICIAL RECORD the official daily record of proceedings kept by an association or body, especially a legislative body or parliament. The record in the British Parliament is called the Journals. **5.** MECH ENG SECTION OF SHAFT a cylindrical section of a shaft designed to rotate inside a bearing [14thC. Via French, literally 'daily', from, ultimately, late Latin *diurnalis* (see DIURNAL). Originally denoted a book listing the daytime canonical hours.]

journal box n. MECH ENG the metal housing of a journal and its bearing. It often serves as a lubricant store.

journalese /júrn'l eez/ n. the style of writing supposedly associated with journalists, marked by the use of formulaic expressions (*disapproving*)

journalise vti. = journalize

journalism /júrn'lizəm/ n. **1.** REPORTING NEWS FOR THE MEDIA the profession of gathering, editing, and publishing news reports and related articles for newspapers, magazines, television, or radio **2.** NEWS-REPORTING AS A GENRE writing or reporting for the media as a literary genre or style

journalist /júrn'list/ n. sb who works as a writer or editor for a newspaper or magazine or for television or radio

journalistic /júrn'l ístik/ adj. relating to journalism or similar in style to journalism —**journalistically** adv.

journalize /júrn'līz/ (**-izes, -izing, -ized**), **journalise** (**-ises, -ising, -ised**) vti. to keep a journal or record sth in a journal (*formal*) —**journalization** /júrn'l záysh'n/ n. —**journalizer** /júrn'l īzər/ n.

journey /júrni/ n. (*plural* **-neys**) **1.** EXPEDITION SOMEWHERE a trip or expedition from one place to another **2.** PROCESS OF DEVELOPMENT a gradual passing from one state to another regarded as more advanced, e.g. from innocence to mature awareness ○ *a spiritual journey* ■ vi. (**-neys, -neying, -neyed**) TRAVEL to travel to a place or over a particular distance ○ *We are journeying into the unknown.* [12thC. Via Old French *journee* 'day, day's work or travel' (the original senses in English), from, ultimately, Latin *diurnus* (see DIURNAL).] —**journeyer** n.

journeyman /júrnimən/ (*plural* **-men** /-mən/) n. **1.** QUALIFIED ARTISAN an artisan who has completed an apprenticeship and is fully trained and qualified but still works for an employer (*often used before a noun*) ○ *a journeyman electrician* **2.** SB WITH ORDINARY COMPETENCE sb who is a competent and reliable performer or exponent, without being brilliant or outstanding (*often used before a noun*) ○ *a good journeyman violinist* **3.** HIRED WORKMAN a workman hired by the day (*archaic*) [15thC. Literally, someone qualified to work for a daily wage rather than as an apprentice.]

journo /júrnō/ (*plural* **-nos**) n. a journalist (*informal*) [Mid-20thC. Contraction.]

joust /jowst/ n. MEDIEVAL TOURNAMENT a form of combat in medieval times held between two mounted knights in full armour who charged at and tried to unseat each other with a lance ■ vi. (**jousts, jousting, jousted**) **1.** ENGAGE IN A JOUST to take part in a joust **2.** ENGAGE IN A CONTEST to take part in a contest against others ○ *candidates jousting for ninety minutes in a televised debate* [13thC. Via Old French *jouster* 'bring together' from, ultimately, Latin *juxta* 'close, beside' (source of English *adjust* and *juxtaposition*).] —**jouster** n.

J'Ouvert /zhoo váirt/ n. Carib the Monday that is the eve of Mardi Gras, when the festivities begin [From French *jour ouvert*, literally 'the day having been opened']

Jove /jōv/ n. = Jupiter (*literary*) [14thC. Via the stem of Latin *Jovem* from Old Latin *Jovis* (source of English *Jupiter*).] ◇ **by Jove** used to convey surprise, or to emphasize a conviction (*dated*)

jovial /jóvi əl/ adj. cheerful in mood or disposition [Late 16thC. Via French from Latin *jovialis*, from *Jovis* (see JOVE).] —**joviality** /jóvi álləti/ n. —**jovially** /-əli/ adv. —**jovialness** /jóvi əlnəss/ n.

Jovian /jóvi ən/ adj. **1.** MYTHOL RELATING TO GOD JUPITER associated with or characteristic of the god Jupiter **2.** ASTRON RELATING TO THE PLANET JUPITER relating to the planet Jupiter

Jovian planet n. any one of the four major planets, Jupiter, Uranus, Saturn, or Neptune

jowl[1] /jowl/ n. **1.** JAW the jaw, especially the lower jaw **2.** CHEEK a cheek, especially a prominent one [Old English *ceafl*, ultimately from a prehistoric Germanic word]

jowl[2] /jowl/ n. **1.** HANGING PART OF A DOUBLE CHIN a flaccid, plump fold of flesh under sb's chin **2.** HANGING FLESH UNDER AN ANIMAL'S CHIN a dewlap under the neck of cattle or a wattle on the neck of a bird [Old English *ceole*, ultimately from a prehistoric Germanic word]

jowly /jówli/ (**-ier, -iest**) adj. with a fold of flesh hanging under the neck —**jowliness** n.

joy /joy/ n. **1.** GREAT HAPPINESS feelings of great happiness or pleasure, especially of an elevated or spiritual kind **2.** STH THAT BRINGS HAPPINESS a pleasurable aspect of sth, or sth that is seen as a source of happiness ○ *His little granddaughter was a great joy to him.* ■ v. (**joys, joying, joyed**) **1.** vti. REJOICE OR GLADDEN to derive joy from sth, or to give sb joy (*archaic or literary*) **2.** vt. ENJOY to delight in or enjoy sth (*archaic literary*) [12thC. Via French *joie* from, ultimately, Latin *gaudere* 'to rejoice'.] ◇ **no joy** no success (*informal*)

joyance /jóy ənss/ n. feelings or expressions of joy (*archaic or literary*)

James Joyce

Joyce /joyss/, **James** (1882–1941) Irish novelist. His innovative techniques, as in *Ulysses* (1922) and *Finnegans Wake* (1939), make him one of the most influential modern writers. Full name **James Augustine Aloysius Joyce**

Joyce, William (1900–46) British traitor. He was found guilty of treason for the broadcasting of Nazi propaganda to Britain during World War II and hanged. Known as **Lord Haw-Haw**

joyful /jóyf'l/ *adj.* **1.** FEELING OR SHOWING JOY full of joy, or feeling, expressing, or showing joy **2.** WELCOME bringing or causing joy —**joyfully** *adv.* —**joyfulness** *n.*

joyless /jóyləss/ *adj.* lacking in warmth or happiness —**joylessly** *adv.* —**joylessness** *n.*

joyous /jóyəss/ *adj.* (*literary*) **1.** EXPRESSING JOY full of joy, especially of a fervent and unrestrained nature **2.** GIVING JOY making people happy or joyful —**joyously** *adv.* —**joyousness** *n.*

joypop /jóy pop/ (**-pops, -popping, -popped**) *vi.* to take illicit drugs occasionally rather than habitually (*slang*) [Mid-20thC] —**joypopper** *n.*

joyriding /jóy rīding/ *n.* a crime involving stealing a car and driving it dangerously at high speed [Early 20thC] —**joyride** *n.*, *vi.* —**joyrider** *n.*

joystick /jóystik/ *n.* **1.** VEHICLE'S CONTROL LEVER the control lever of an aircraft or of a small motor-powered vehicle **2.** COMPUT LEVER CONTROLLING A CURSOR a hand-held control stick that allows a player to control the movements of a cursor on a VDU screen or a symbol in a video game

JP *abbr.* Justice of the Peace

J particle *n.* = **J/psi particle**

JPG *n.* COMPUT a format for encoding high-resolution graphic images as computer files for storage and transmission. Abbr of **Joint Photographic Group**

Jpn *abbr.* **1.** Japan **2.** Japanese

J/psi particle *n.* an unstable elementary particle of the meson group. It has a large mass, about 6,000 times that of an electron, and is thought to be formed from charmed quarks. [*J* and *psi* represent the 23rd letter of the Greek alphabet]

jr *abbr.* junior

Jr *abbr.* **1.** BIBLE Jeremiah **2.** Junior

JRC *abbr.* Junior Red Cross

JSB *abbr.* joint-stock bank

JSD *abbr.* Doctor of Juristic Science [Latin, *Juris Scientiae Doctor*]

jt *abbr.* joint

Juan Carlos /waán kaár loss/, **King of Spain** (*b.* 1938). He became king following the death of General Franco (1975), presiding over Spain's rapid transition to democracy.

Juan de Fuca, Strait of /joo ən də fyóokə/ body of water lying between Washington State, United States, and Vancouver Island, Canada, connecting the Strait of Georgia and Puget Sound to the Pacific Ocean. Length: 160 km/100 mi.

Juba /joobə/ city in southern Sudan on the River White Nile

jube /joob/ *n.* ANZ a fruit-flavoured chewy sweet (*informal*) [Mid-20thC. Shortening of JUJUBE.]

jubilant /joobilənt/ *adj.* feeling or expressing great delight over a success, achievement, or victory [Mid-17thC. From Latin *jubilantem*, present participle of *jubilare* (see JUBILATE).] —**jubilantly** *adv.*

jubilate /joobi layt/ (**-lates, -lating, -lated**) *vi.* to feel or express immense joy (*archaic*) [Early 17thC. From Latin *jubilatus*, the past participle of *jubilare* 'to call out, to shout for joy'.]

Jubilate /joobi laáti, yoobi laá tay/ *n.* Psalm number 100, which is sung as a canticle in the Roman Catholic and Anglican churches. In the Latin version it begins, 'Jubilate Deo' (Rejoice in the Lord).

jubilation /joobi láysh'n/ *n.* uninhibited rejoicing in the celebration of a victory or success [14thC. From the Latin *jubilationem*, from *jubilare* (see JUBILATE).]

jubilee /joobili, joobi leé/ *n.* **1.** SPECIAL ANNIVERSARY a significant anniversary of an important event such as a wedding or a monarch's succession **2.** JOYFUL TIME a time or season of celebration **3.** CHR YEAR OF INDULGENCE SET BY THE POPE in the Roman Catholic Church, a period set by the Pope, traditionally every 25 years, in which forgiveness of sins is granted in return for acts of piety or repentance **4.** JUDAISM YEAR OF RESTITUTION in Jewish history, a year of restoration or restitution that was proclaimed every fifty years by a countrywide blast of trumpets. During the period, land was left uncultivated, enslaved people were emancipated, and land that had been sold reverted to its former owner. **5.** JUBILATION an act or period of jubilation (*archaic*) [14thC. Via French *jubilé* from Latin *jubilaeus (annus)* '(year) of jubilee', from, ultimately, Hebrew *yōbēl*, literally 'ram', from the ram's horn with which the year of jubilee was proclaimed.]

Jubrān /joo braán/ = **Gibran, Kahlil**

Jud. *abbr.* BIBLE **1.** Judges **2.** Judith

Judaeo- *prefix.* = **Judeo-**

Judah = **Judea**

Judaic /joo dáy ik/, **Judaical** /-ik'l/ *adj.* belonging to or relating to Judaism or Jews [15thC. Via Latin *Judaicus* from Greek *Ioudaikos*, from *Ioudaios* (see JEW).] —**Judaically** *adv.*

Judaica /joo dáy ikə/ *npl.* the Jewish religion, customs, and culture, or artefacts and historical and literary materials that relate to them (*formal*) [Early 20thC. From Latin, neuter plural of *Judaicus* (see JUDAIC).]

Judaise *vti.* = **Judaize**

Judaism /joo day izəm/ *n.* **1.** RELIGION OF THE JEWS the religion of the Jews that has its basis in the Bible and the Talmud. In Judaism, God is the creator of everything and the source of all goodness. **2.** JEWISH WAY OF LIFE Jewish religious practices, customs, and culture as a way of life [14thC. Via ecclesiastical Latin *Judaismus* from Greek *Ioudaismos*, from *Ioudaios* (see JEW).] —**Judaistic** /joo day ístik/ *adj.*

Judaize /joo day īz/ (**-izes, -izing, -ized**), **Judaise** (**-ises, -ising, -ised**) *v.* **1.** *vi.* ADOPT JUDAISM to adopt the Jewish religion and Jewish cultural practices **2.** *vt.* MAKE STH JEWISH to give sth a Jewish character [Late 16thC. Via ecclesiastical Latin *judizare* from Greek *ioudizein*, from *Ioudaios* (see JEW).] —**Judaization** /joo day ī záysh'n/ *n.*

judas /joodəss/, **judas hole** *n.* a peephole or very small window, e.g. in a door [Mid-19thC. Named after JUDAS.]

Judas /joodəss/ *n.* **1.** DISCIPLE WHO BETRAYED JESUS CHRIST IN THE BIBLE one of Jesus Christ's disciples in the new Testament who betrayed him by identifying him with a kiss to the Jewish leaders in exchange for thirty pieces of silver (Luke 22) **2.** TRAITOR a traitor, especially sb who betrays a close friend or a cause or belief (*literary*)

Judas tree *n.* a tree with purplish-red flowers that come out before the leaves. It belongs to the pea family and is native to Europe and Asia. Latin name: *Cercis siliquastrum.* [Mid-17thC. Named after JUDAS from the popular notion that he hanged himself from this tree, and also an alteration of JUDEA, from which the tree originates.]

judder /júddər/ *vi.* (**-ders, -dering, -dered**) SHAKE VIOLENTLY to shake or vibrate violently and rapidly, or to move while shaking ○ *The car juddered along for a few more yards.* ■ *n.* VIOLENT SHAKING a violent, rapid vibration or shaking motion [Mid-20thC. An imitation of the sound.]

judder bar *n.* NZ a ridge built across a road to slow down traffic

Jude /jood/ *n.* **1.** APOSTLE OF JESUS CHRIST one of the twelve Apostles of Jesus Christ, he was the brother of James and author of the Book of Jude in the Bible **2.** BOOK OF THE BIBLE the last epistle of the Bible, probably written in the late 1st century. It reminds Christians of the importance of keeping their faith. See table at Bible

Judeo- *prefix.* Jewish, Judaism ○ *Judeo-Christian* [Via Latin *Judaeus* from Greek *Ioudaios* (see JEW)]

Judeo-Christian *adj.* in the shared tradition of Judaism and Christianity or combining their common beliefs

Judeo-Spanish /joo dézmō/, **Judezmo** *n.*, *adj.* = **Ladino**

Judg. *abbr.* BIBLE Judges

judge /juj/ *n.* **1.** LAW A SENIOR LAWYER a lawyer of high rank who supervises court trials, instructs juries, and pronounces sentence **2.** ADJUDICATOR a person, sometimes one of several, appointed to assess entries or performances in a competition and decide on the winner or winners **3.** SB GIVING AN INFORMED OPINION sb who has an ability to assess quality or give an informed opinion in a particular area of knowledge or experience ○ *a good judge of character* **4.** JUDAISM JEWISH WARRIOR LEADER in Jewish history, any of a succession of warrior leaders who each temporarily held supreme power in Israel between Joshua's death and Saul's succession ■ *v.* (**judges, judging, judged**) **1.** *vt.* LAW ACT AS A LEGAL JUDGE to act as the judge of a legal case **2.** *vt.* BE JUDGE IN A CONTEST to act as a judge in a competition or, as an adjudicator, to pronounce officially on the entries **3.** *vti.* ASSESS to assess the quality of sth or estimate probabilities ○ *Each proposal has to be judged on its individual merits.* **4.** *vt.* CONSIDER OR RECKON to form an opinion of sb or sth, especially after thought or consideration ○ *She was judged to have the best qualifications.* **5.** *vti.* ESTIMATE to measure by guesswork, using the eye or some other sense as a rough guide ○ *You can't always judge people's ages by their voices.* **6.** *vt.* CONDEMN to criticize or condemn sb on moral grounds [12thC. Via Old French *juge* from, ultimately, Latin *judex*, literally 'one who speaks the law', from *jus* 'law, right' (source of English *just*).] —**judger** *n.*

judge advocate *n.* an officer appointed to oversee the proceedings and advise on points of law at a court martial

judgement *n.* = **judgment**

Judges /jújiz/ *n.* a book of the Bible that tells the story of the Israelites from Joshua's death in the 13th century BC to Samuel's birth in the 11th century BC (*takes a singular verb*) See table at Bible

judgment /júj mənt/, **judgement** *n.* **1.** LAW VERDICT the decision arrived at and pronounced by a court of law **2.** LAW OBLIGATION RESULTING FROM A VERDICT an obligation such as a debt that arises as a result of a court's verdict, or a document setting out an obligation of this kind (*often used before a noun*) **3.** DECISION OF A JUDGE the decision reached by one or more judges in a contest ○ *The judgment of the panel must be regarded as final.* **4.** DECISION ON A DISPUTED MATTER an opinion formed or decision reached in the case of a disputed, controversial, or doubtful matter **5.** DISCERNMENT OR GOOD SENSE the ability to form sound opinions and make sensible decisions or reliable guesses ○ *someone with shrewd commercial judgment* **6.** OPINION an opinion formed or given after consideration ○ *a snap judgment* **7.** ESTIMATE BASED ON OBSERVATION an estimate of sth such as speed or distance, made with the help of the eye or some other sense **8.** JUDGING OF STH the judging of a case or a contest **9.** DIVINE PUNISHMENT a misfortune regarded as a divine punishment for folly or sin (*archaic or humorous*) ○ *defeat regarded as a judgment from God for the leader's pride* **10.** LOGIC ACT OF MAKING A STATEMENT the mental act of making or understanding a positive or negative proposition about sth, e.g. in 'a chihuahua is a dog' or 'a lobster is not an insect' [13thC. From Old French *jugement*, from *jugier* 'to judge' (see JUDGE).]

Judgment *n.* **1.** GOD'S JUDGMENT ON AN INDIVIDUAL in Roman Catholic belief, God's decision at the instant of sb's death on whether the soul is to be saved or damned **2.** GOD'S JUDGMENT ON HUMANITY in Jewish, Islamic, and other Christian traditions, God's final judgment of humankind, **(the Last Judgment)** which is to take place at the end of the world

judgmental /juj mént'l/ *adj.* tending to judge or criticize the conduct of other people —**judgmentally** *adv.*

Judgment Day *n.* in Jewish, Christian, and Islamic belief, the day at the end of the world when God delivers his final judgment on humankind

judicable /joódikəb'l/ *adj.* capable of being or liable to be tried in a court of law [Mid-17thC. From late Latin *judicabilis*, from *judicare* (see JUDICATURE).]

judicator /joódi kaytər/ *n.* sb who judges or who acts as a judge (*formal*) [Mid-18thC. Via late Latin from Latin *judicare* (see JUDICATURE).]

judicatory /joódikətəri/ *adj.* **judicatory, judicatorial** LAW RELATING TO A LEGAL SYSTEM relating to a legal system, or to judges or judgment ■ *n.* (*plural* **-ries**) LAW (*formal*) **1.** LEGAL SYSTEM a system of administering justice **2.** LAW COURT a court of law [Late 16thC. From, ultimately, Latin *judicare* (see JUDICATURE).]

judicature /joódikəchər, joo díkəchər/ *n.* **1.** ADMINISTERING OF JUSTICE the administration or dispensation of justice **2.** JUDGE'S OFFICE the power or office of a judge, or a judge's tenure of office **3.** JUDGE'S AREA OF AUTHORITY the area of authority of a judge or a court of law **4.** BODY OF JUDGES a body of judges or of people holding judicial power **5.** SYSTEM OF LAW COURTS a law court, or a system of law courts [Mid-16thC. Via medieval Latin *judicatura* from, ultimately, Latin *judicare* 'to judge', from *judex* (see JUDGE).]

judicial /joo dísh'l/ *adj.* **1.** RELATING TO JUDGES relating or belonging to a body of judges or to the system that administers justice **2.** RELATING TO COURT JUDGMENTS relating to judges in performance of their duties, or to judgment in a court of law **3.** ENFORCED BY A LAW COURT enforced or sanctioned by a court of law **4.** APPROPRIATE TO JUDGES appropriate to a judge or expected of a judge [14thC. From Latin *judicialis*, from *judicium* 'legal proceedings', from *judex* (see JUDGE).] —**judicially** *adv.*

judicial review *n.* **1.** RE-EXAMINATION BY JUDGES a reassessment or re-examination by judges of a decision or proceeding by a lower court or a government department **2.** CONSTITUTIONAL FACILITY FOR REVIEWING LEGISLATION a constitutional right of the court system in some countries to review and cancel government legislation that is held to have been passed illegally

judicial separation *n.* = legal separation

judiciary /joo díshəri, -díshi əri/ *n.* (*plural* **-ies**) **1.** GOVERNMENT BRANCH DISPENSING JUSTICE the branch of a country's central administration that is concerned with dispensing justice **2.** COURT SYSTEM a country's system of law courts **3.** JUDGES IN GENERAL a country's body of judges ■ *adj.* RELATING TO JUDGES relating to courts, judges, and judgment [15thC. From Latin *judiciarius*, from *judicium* (see JUDICIAL).]

judicious /joo díshəss/ *adj.* showing wisdom, good sense, or discretion, often with the underlying aim of avoiding trouble or waste ○ *a little judicious pruning* [Late 16thC. Via French *judicieux* from Latin *judicium* (see JUDICIAL).] —**judiciously** *adv.* —**judiciousness** *n.*

Judith /joódith/ *n.* **1.** HEROINE IN THE BIBLE in the Bible, a Jewish woman who saved the city of Bethulia by beheading the general Holofernes **2.** BOOK OF THE BIBLE a book in the Roman Catholic version of the Bible and the Protestant Apocrypha that tells the story of Judith's heroism in saving her people. See table at **Bible**

judo /joódō/ *n.* a Japanese martial art in which opponents use balance and body weight, with minimal physical effort, to throw or pin each other or hold each other in a lock. Judo was developed from jujitsu, a samurai art, by Jigoro Kano (1860–1938). [Late 19thC. From Japanese, literally 'gentle way'.] —**judoist** *n.*

judogi /joo dōgi/ *n.* the costume worn by participants in judo, made of thick white cotton and consisting

Judo

of a loose jacket secured by a belt and loose trousers. The colour of belt indicates the participant's grade, from the white belt worn by a beginner through various colours to black belt. [Mid-20thC. From Japanese.]

judoka /joó dō kaa/ (*plural* **-kas** *or* **-ka**) *n.* sb who practises the art of judo or who is an expert in it [Mid-20thC. From Japanese.]

judy /joódi/ (*plural* **judies**), **Judy** (*plural* **Judies**) *n.* a girl or woman (*dated slang; sometimes considered offensive*) [Early 19thC. Pet form of the name 'Judith'.]

Judy /joódi/ *n.* the wife of Punch in a traditional Punch-and-Judy puppet show

jug /jug/ *n.* **1.** POURING CONTAINER a deep container for liquids that has a handle and has its rim shaped into a lip or spout for pouring **2.** *US* LARGE LIQUID-CONTAINER a large container for liquids, typically of earthenware or glass, with a handle and a narrow mouth usually closed with a cork **3.** LIQUID CONTAINED IN A JUG the quantity of liquid held in a jug **4.** DRINK OF BEER a drink of beer (*regional*) ○ *going out for a few jugs* **5.** MOUNTAINEERING GOOD HANDHOLD a large, strong, and dependable handhold on a rock climb **6.** PRISON prison or jail (*humorous*) **7.** OFFENSIVE TERM an offensive term for a woman's breast (*dated; considered offensive by many people*) ■ *vt.* (**jugs, jugging, jugged**) **1.** JAIL SB to put sb in jail (*humorous*) **2.** STEW IN AN EARTHENWARE POT to stew meat in a deep earthenware pot [15thC. Origin uncertain: perhaps from *Jug*, an old pet form of the name *Joan*, sometimes given as a nickname to a girl thought not good-looking.]

jugate /joó gayt, joógət/ *adj.* **1.** BOT WITH PAIRED LEAFLETS used to describe leaves that consist of paired leaflets attached to a single leaf stalk **2.** COINS WITH OVERLAPPING PROFILES used to describe heads or busts on coins that are superimposed in profile one on another [Late 19thC. From Latin *jugatus*, past participle of *jugare* 'to join together'.]

jug band *n.* a blues or jazz band featuring jugs as instruments, played by blowing across their rims

Jugendstil /yoógənd shteel/ *n.* the equivalent in Germany and Austria of art nouveau, a style of design that influenced all the visual arts in Europe during the late 19th and early 20th centuries. It is characterized by curvilinearity and the stylization of forms. [Early 20thC. From German, formed from *Jugend* 'youth' (the name of a magazine) + *Stil* 'style'.]

jugged hare *n.* a stew of hare meat, traditionally cooked in an earthenware pot or casserole dish. The sauce is usually thickened with the blood of the hare.

juggernaut /júggər nawt/ *n.* **1.** HUGE LORRY a very large long lorry for transporting goods in bulk **2.** CRUSHING FORCE a force that is relentlessly destructive, crushing, and insensitive [Mid-19thC. From JUGGERNAUT.]

───── **WORD KEY: ORIGIN** ─────

It used to be said, apocryphally, that worshippers of Krishna threw themselves under the wheels of the *Juggernaut* wagon in an access of religious ecstasy, so *juggernaut* came to be used metaphorically in English for an 'irresistible crushing force'. The pejorative British application to large lorries did not become firmly established until the late 1960s.

───────────────────────

Juggernaut *n.* a form of the Hindu god Krishna. A statue of Juggernaut is pulled through the Indian town of Puri every year on a huge chariot during

the festival of Rathayatra. [Mid-17thC. From Sanskrit *Jagannātha*, literally 'protector of the world'.]

juggins /júgginz/ *n.* sb regarded as easy to trick or ingenuous (*dated informal*) [Late 19thC. Origin uncertain: perhaps from the surname 'Juggins'.]

juggle /júg'l/ (**-gles, -gling, -gled**) *v.* **1.** *vti.* KEEP SEVERAL OBJECTS IN THE AIR to keep several objects in motion in the air at the same time by throwing them and catching them in quick succession **2.** *vt.* HAVE DIFFICULTY HOLDING STH to keep adjusting your grip or stance in order to balance objects being held ○ *I was juggling coffee and a plate of sandwiches in one hand.* **3.** *vt.* FIT INTO A SCHEDULE to try to make sth fit into a satisfactory pattern or schedule by careful arranging ○ *parents juggling careers and family life* **4.** *vt.* REARRANGE DATA to manipulate data in order to deceive ○ *juggling the company's books* [14thC. Back-formation from JUGGLER.] —**jugglery** *n.*

Juggler

juggler /júgglər/ *n.* sb who can juggle, especially an entertainer who juggles for a living [Pre-12thC. Via Old French *jogler* from Latin *joculator* 'jester', from *jocus* (see JOKE).]

jugular /júggyʊoolər/ *adj.* **1.** ANAT RELATING TO THE NECK relating to or situated close to the neck or throat **2.** ZOOL WITH PELVIC FINS FURTHER FORWARD used to describe a fish that has pelvic fins in front of the pectoral fins ■ *n.* ANAT = **jugular vein** [Late 16thC. From late Latin *jugularis*, from Latin *jugulum* 'collarbone, throat', from *jugum* (see YOKE).] ◇ **go for the jugular** to make an attack that is intended to be highly destructive and conclusive (*informal*)

jugular vein *n.* any one of four pairs of veins in the neck that drain blood from the head. A larger internal vein is flanked by an external vein on either side of the neck.

jugum /joógəm/ *n.* **1.** INSECTS PART OF AN INSECT'S FOREWING a lobe that sticks out from the base of the forewing of some insects in order to couple it with the hindwing during flight **2.** BOT PAIR OF LEAFLETS a pair of opposed leaflets in a compound leaf [Mid-19thC. From Latin (see YOKE).]

juice /jooss/ *n.* **1.** LIQUID FROM FRUIT OR VEGETABLES the extractable liquid that is contained in fruit or vegetables, or a drink made from this liquid ○ *lemon juice* **2.** BODILY FLUID a natural fluid or secretion of the body **3.** LIQUID FROM COOKING MEAT the liquid that comes from a piece of meat when it is roasted or otherwise cooked **4.** LIQUID EXTRACT any liquid extract or essence, especially from biological material ○ *Pure penicillin was isolated from mould juice.* **5.** FUEL OR POWER fuel, especially petrol for a vehicle, or electricity (*informal*) **6.** ALCOHOL alcoholic drink (*slang*) **7.** *US* MONEY OR INFLUENCE money or influence gained through or utilized in the service of corrupt or criminal activities (*slang*) **8.** *US* LOAN OR INTEREST money lent at an extortionate rate of interest, or the interest extorted (*slang*) ■ *vt.* (**juices, juicing, juiced**) EXTRACT JUICE FROM to extract the juice from a fruit or vegetable [13thC. Via French *jus* from Latin, 'broth, sauce, vegetable juice'.] ◇ **stew in your own juice** to have to suffer the consequences of your actions without any help from others

juice up *vt.* to make sth or sb more lively, exciting, or interesting (*slang*) ○ *juice the party up by bringing in a live band*

juice bar *n.* a café serving freshly prepared fruit juices and other healthy food and drinks

juice box *n.* *US* a small box of fruit juice for one person sold with a straw attached to it

juicehead /jo͞oss hed/ *n.* *US* a heavy drinker or an alcoholic (*slang*)

juicer /jo͞ossər/ *n.* *US* a kitchen appliance, usually electrically powered, for extracting the juice from fruit or vegetables

juicy /jo͞ossi/ (**-ier, -iest**) *adj.* **1.** SUCCULENT containing a lot of juice **2.** PROVIDING INTEREST repaying effort by providing plenty of stimulation and food for thought ○ *I like getting my teeth into a nice juicy problem.* **3.** TITILLATING containing scenes or details that evoke interest because of their sensational nature (*informal*) **4.** LUCRATIVE extremely profitable or productive (*informal*) **5.** SEXUALLY DESIRABLE desirable in a sexual way (*slang*) —**juicily** *adv.* —**juiciness** *n.*

jujitsu /joo jítsoo/, **jiujitsu** *n.* a Japanese system of unarmed fighting devised by the samurai, or the martial art based on it. Judo, aikido, and karate are all developments of jujitsu. (*often used before a noun*) [Late 19thC. From Japanese *jūjutsu*, literally 'gentle skill'.]

juju /jo͞o joo/ *n.* **1.** OBJECT WITH SUPPOSED MAGICAL POWERS an object revered among some West African peoples for the magical powers that it is thought to possess **2.** SUPPOSED MAGIC POWER OF A JUJU the magical or supernatural power associated with a juju **3.** SPELL EFFECTED BY A JUJU a spell put on sth or sb by means of a juju [Early 17thC. From Hausa, of uncertain origin: probably from French *joujou* 'plaything', from *jouer* 'to play', from Latin *jocari*.] —**jujuism** *n.*

jujube /jo͞o joob/ *n.* **1.** TREE WITH RED FRUITS a tree belonging to the buckthorn family that has small yellow flowers and plum-shaped dark-red edible fruits. It has been cultivated throughout Asia since ancient times. Latin name: *Ziziphus jujuba.* **2.** FRUIT OF THE JUJUBE TREE the plum-shaped fruit of the jujube tree, which is sometimes dried like a date **3.** CHEWY SWEET a chewy, usually fruit-flavoured, sweet made of gum or gelatine [14thC. Directly or via French from medieval Latin *jujuba* from, ultimately, Greek *ziziphos*.]

jukebox /jo͝ok boks/ (*plural* **-boxes**) *n.* a coin-operated machine that automatically plays selected records or compact discs

juke joint *n.* *US* a roadside cafe where music is played on a jukebox for dancing (*informal*)

jukskei /yo͝ok skay/ *n.* *S Africa* an outdoor game in which skittle-shaped pegs are thrown at stakes fixed into the ground [Early 19thC. From Afrikaans, literally 'yoke pin' (with which the game was originally played).]

Jul. *abbr.* July

julep /jo͞olip, jo͞o lep/ *n.* = **mint julep** [14thC. Via Old French or medieval Latin from, ultimately, Persian *gulāb* 'rosewater'.]

Julian /jo͞oli ən/ *adj.* **1.** OF JULIUS CAESAR relating to or typical of Julius Caesar **2.** OF THE JULIAN CALENDAR relating to or reckoned according to the Julian calendar

Julian (of Norwich) /jo͞oli ən/ (1342–1416) English mystic. She wrote *Revelations of Divine Love*, an extraordinary record of medieval religious experience.

Juliana /jo͞oli áanə/, **Queen of the Netherlands** (*b.* 1909). She ruled from 1948 to 1980, and abdicated in favour of her eldest daughter Beatrix.

Julian calendar /jo͞oli ən-/ *n.* the twelve-month solar calendar introduced by Julius Caesar in 46 BC, consisting of 365 days, with an extra day every four years. It was replaced by the Gregorian calendar in 1582. ◊ **Gregorian calendar**

Julian date *n.* COMPUT in computer programming, a date expressed as the number of days since January 1 of the current year

julienne /jo͞oli én, zhōoli-/ *adj.* CUT THINLY cut into long thin matchstick strips ■ *n.* CLEAR SOUP WITH VEGETABLE STRIPS a clear soup containing vegetables cut into thin matchstick strips ■ *vt.* (**-ennes, -enning, -enned**) CUT INTO THIN STRIPS to cut vegetables into thin matchstick strips [Early 18thC. From French, from the first name *Jules* or *Julien*.]

Juliet /jo͞oli ət/ *n.* **1.** ASTRON SMALL INNER MOON OF URANUS a small inner natural satellite of Uranus, discovered in 1986 by the spacecraft Voyager 2. It is 84 km/52 mi. in diameter. **2.** COMMUNICATION CODE FOR J the NATO phonetic alphabet code word for the letter 'J', used in international radio communications

Juliet cap *n.* a round close-fitting crocheted net cap for women, sometimes set with pearls. It was fashionable in the 1920s, 1930s, and 1950s for brides and bridesmaids. [Early 20thC. From the heroine of Shakespeare's *Romeo and Juliet*.]

Julius II /jo͞oli əss/, **Pope** (1443–1513). Becoming pope in 1503, he was a powerful ruler and lavish patron of the arts, commissioning Bramante's design for St Peter's and Michelangelo's frescoes for the Sistine Chapel.

Jullundur /jo͝ollǝndər/ city in northwestern India, a major industrial centre. Population: 519,530 (1991).

July /jo͝o lī/ (*plural* **-lies**) *n.* the seventh month of the year in the Gregorian calendar, made up of 31 days [12thC. Via *julie* from Latin *Julius* (referring to Julius CAESAR, who was born in July).]

Jumada /jo͝o máadə/ *n.* in the Muslim calendar, either the fifth or the sixth lunar month in the year [Late 18thC. From Arabic *jumādā*, from *jamada* 'to freeze'.]

jumar /jo͞omər/ *n.* ROPE CLIP a clip or clamp used in rock-climbing or ice-climbing that runs freely up a slack rope but tightens round the rope in response to weight applied from below ■ *vi.* (**-mars, -maring, -mared**) CLIMB USING JUMARS to climb using jumar clamps [Mid-20thC. Origin unknown.]

jumbal /júmb'l/, **jumble** *n.* a light sweet crisp biscuit or cake, traditionally made in the shape of a ring or an S [Early 17thC. Origin uncertain: perhaps an alteration of GIMBAL.]

jumbie /júmbi/ *n.* *Carib* a spirit or ghost [Late 19thC. From Kongo *zumbi* 'fetish'.]

jumble[1] /júmb'l/ *vti.* (**-bles, -bling, -bled**) **1.** PUT THINGS OUT OF ORDER to mix things together indiscriminately so that they are no longer neat or ordered **2.** MUDDLE THINGS UP MENTALLY to muddle things up in the mind ■ *n.* **1.** MUDDLED MASS an untidy or disorganized mass of objects, images, or ideas ○ *His thoughts were all in a jumble.* **2.** ARTICLES FOR JUMBLE SALE unwanted possessions that people hand over for selling at a jumble sale [Early 16thC. Origin uncertain: perhaps thought to suggest the action.]

jumble[2] *n.* = **jumbal**

jumble sale *n.* a sale of clothes and other goods, chiefly second-hand, usually to raise money for charity or for some specific purpose. US term **rummage sale**

jumbo /júmbō/ *n.* **1.** LARGE THING sth or sb that is extra large (*often used before a noun*) ○ *a jumbo helping* **2.** AIR = **jumbo jet** [Early 19thC. From the name of a very large elephant at London Zoo, sold in 1882 to Barnum and Bailey's circus. Perhaps from MUMBO-JUMBO.]

jumboize /júmbō īz/ (**-boizes, -boizing, -boized**), **jumboise** (**-boises, -boising, -boised**) *vt.* to increase the size of a ship, especially a tanker, by inserting a prefabricated central section

jumbo jet *n.* a large wide-bodied commercial aircraft capable of carrying several hundred passengers

jumbuck /júm buk/ *n.* *Aus* a sheep (*informal*) [Early 19thC. Origin unknown.]

Jumna /júmnə/ river in northern India flowing south into the River Ganges at Allahabad. Length: 153 km/95 mi.

jump /jump/ *v.* (**jumps, jumping, jumped**) **1.** *vi.* LEAVE A SURFACE WITH BOTH FEET to bend the knees and push the whole body quickly up off a surface or the ground **2.** *vt.* GET OVER to pass from one side of sth to the other by jumping ○ *jump the fence* **3.** *vti.* SPORTS JUMP AS A SPORTING SKILL in various sports such as horse-riding and skiing, to perform a movement in which the whole body leaves the ground ○ *Make sure you have your skis parallel before you attempt to jump.* **4.** *vi.* MOVE QUICKLY to move quickly in a particular direction ○ *Jump in and I'll give you a lift home.* **5.** *vi.* MAKE A MENTAL LEAP to make an illogical mental leap ○ *His mind keeps jumping from one thing to another.* **6.** *vi.* MOVE JERKILY to move jerkily, in contrast to progressing smoothly or keeping still ○ *Interference was making the picture jump.* **7.** *vi.* START IN SURPRISE to give a start of surprise or fright ○ *The noise made me jump.* **8.** *vi.* RISE SUDDENLY to rise or increase suddenly by a large amount ○ *The Nikkei Index jumped 35 points.* **9.** *vti.* RAIL LEAVE THE RAILS to come off the rails accidentally (*refers to trains*) **10.** *vi.* AIR MAKE A PARACHUTE DESCENT to make a descent by parachute from an aircraft **11.** *vt.* AMBUSH to ambush sb by attacking unexpectedly (*informal*) ○ *The guy jumped me.* **12.** *vt.* VIOLATE AN ENGAGEMENT BY LEAVING to abscond or desert in violation of an engagement, contract, or undertaking **13.** *vti.* OMIT to omit the intervening parts of sth, especially passages of a text, sometimes inadvertently **14.** *vi.* OBEY IMMEDIATELY to carry out orders immediately (*informal*) ○ *When she speaks, you jump.* **15.** *vt.* OFFENSIVE TERM an offensive term meaning to have sexual intercourse with a woman (*offensive slang*) **16.** *vt.* DRIVE THROUGH TRAFFIC LIGHTS to fail to stop at a set of traffic lights (*informal*) **17.** *vt.* *US* BOARD ILLEGALLY to board a train surreptitiously with the intention of travelling on it without paying (*informal*) **18.** *vt.* USURP OWNERSHIP to usurp ownership of a piece of land, especially a mining claim, on the grounds that the owner has abandoned it or not fulfilled the conditions of ownership **19.** *vt.* HELP TO JUMP to support or lift sb who is jumping over sth or down from sth (*archaic*) ○ *'In all their walks he had had to jump her from the stiles'.* (Jane Austen, *Persuasion*; 1818) **20.** *vti.* BRIDGE RAISE A BID to raise a partner's bid to indicate a strong hand **21.** *vt.* BOARD GAMES PASS A PIECE OVER AN OPPONENT'S PIECE in draughts, to capture an opponent's playing piece by passing a piece over it into an empty square ■ *n.* **1.** JUMPING MOVEMENT a jumping movement or the distance jumped ○ *a winning jump of 26 feet* **2.** SPORTS OBSTACLE OR APPARATUS USED IN JUMPING a specially constructed obstacle or other piece of apparatus for use in competitive jumping, e.g. a fence in steeplechasing or a platform from which skiers take off **3.** LEAP OF A PARTICULAR DISTANCE IN SPORTS in field events, a leap of a particular distance or height, or the action of attempting or completing such a leap **4.** SUDDEN RISE a sudden steep rise or increase in an amount ○ *a jump in property prices* **5.** START OF SURPRISE an involuntary movement made when startled **6.** SUDDEN TRANSITION a sudden transition or change of direction, representing a break in continuity or logical progression **7.** PARACHUTE DESCENT a descent by parachute from an aircraft **8.** BOARD GAMES CAPTURE OF AN OPPONENT'S PIECE in draughts, the move of jumping an opponent's piece and capturing it **9.** MATH DISCONTINUOUS NUMERIC INCREASE a point at which a function or a curve undergoes a sudden or major transition [Early 16thC. Origin uncertain: perhaps an imitation of the sound of jumping feet hitting the ground, suggested by *bump* and *thump*.] —**jumpable** *adj.* ◇ **jump to it** to hurry up and carry out orders or instructions (*informal*) ◇ **take a running jump** used dismissively as an instruction to go away (*informal*)

jump at *vt.* to accept a chance or opportunity eagerly ○ *would jump at the chance*

jump on *vt.* to make a sudden physical or verbal attack on sb (*informal*) ○ *Pupils were jumped on for getting a question like that wrong.*

jump up *vi.* to get to your feet immediately

jump ball *n.* a restarting of play in a basketball game, in which the referee throws the ball up high between two opponents who each try to tip it towards a team member

jump bid *n.* in bridge, a bid of one more than is necessary to raise the existing bid

jump cut *n.* in film and television, a sudden abrupt change from one sequence to another

jumped-up *adj.* having been promoted from a lowly position and therefore not entitled to show arrogance or self-importance (*informal insult*)

jumper[1] /júmpər/ *n.* **1.** PERSON OR ANIMAL THAT JUMPS a person or animal that jumps or is trained to jump competitively **2.** *Can* TYPE OF SLEDGE a type of sledge for use over rough terrain **3.** INDUST BORING TOOL a heavy drill used in quarrying that, because of its repeated-impact action, has a jumping motion **4.** ELEC ENG, ELEC WIRE FOR MAKING A CONNECTION a short length of wire for making an electrical connection or for cutting out part of a circuit

jumper[2] /júmpər/ n. **1.** KNITTED GARMENT a knitted garment for the top half of the body, usually with sleeves, made of wool, cotton, or some synthetic fibre, and pulled on over the head **2.** US = pinafore [Mid-17thC. Origin uncertain: probably from 'jump', an alteration of *jupe*, a man's short coat, worn in the 17th and 18th centuries.]

jumper cables npl. US = jump leads

jumping bean n. a seed of some Mexican shrubs when it contains the larva of a small moth. The larva feeds on the seed pulp, making the seed move jerkily. The movements intensify if the seed is warmed, e.g. in the palm of the hand.

jumping gene n. a genetic element that can move from place to place within the chromosomes of an organism. These elements occur in bacteria, plants, and animals and their insertion may inactivate functional genes, causing a type of mutation.

jumping jack n. **1.** ACCORDION-PLEATED FIREWORK a firework that has its gunpowder packed into a pleated tube, so that it jumps along the ground as each segment explodes **2.** US WARMUP EXERCISE a warmup exercise in which the legs are flung apart while the hands are clapped or swung above the head

jumping mouse n. a rodent that looks like a mouse but has long hind legs and a long tail. It is found in Northern temperate regions. Family: Zapodidae.

jumping-off place, **jumping-off point** n. a very remote place, especially a point at the edge of civilization beyond which lies the wilderness

jumping-off point n. **1.** BASE FOR A TRIP a place from which to begin a journey **2.** BASIS FOR BEGINNING a basis on which to begin an enterprise or a discussion **3.** = jumping-off place

jumping plant louse n. a small insect that is a weak flier but has enlarged hind legs for jumping. Found worldwide, it feeds on the sap of plants. Family: Psyllidae.

jumping spider n. a spider found mostly in the tropics that fixes on its prey using an enlarged central pair of eyes, then pounces by rapidly extending its legs. The jumping mechanism depends on sudden elevation in the spider's internal body pressure, and they can achieve distances of several centimetres. Family: Salticidae.

jump jet n. a jet aircraft that takes off and lands vertically

jump jockey n. a jockey specially trained to jump horses over fences and ride in steeplechases, as distinct from a flat-racing jockey

jump leads npl. a pair of electric cables used to start the engine of a vehicle that has a dead battery by connecting it to an external live battery. US term **jumper cables**

jump-off n. **1.** START the start of sth such as a race or a military attack **2.** SHOWJUMPING DECIDING ROUND OF A SHOWJUMPING CONTEST a final extra round of a showjumping competition, in which all the riders who have had clear rounds compete against the clock — **jump off** vi.

jump pass n. a pass that one basketball player makes to another while in mid-jump

jump rope n. US = skipping rope

jump seat n. a folding seat between the front and back seats of a taxicab or similarly large vehicle, or a seat like this for temporary use in an aircraft or train

jump shot n. a basketball shot made with one or both hands by a player who is at the highest point of a jump —**jump shooter** n.

jump-start vt. (jump-starts, jump-starting, jump-started) START A VEHICLE USING JUMP LEADS to start a motor vehicle by attaching it to an external battery using jump leads ■ n. ACTION OF JUMP-STARTING A VEHICLE a jump-starting of a motor vehicle

jump suit n. **1.** WOMAN'S ONE-PIECE SUIT a woman's casual one-piece suit combining top and trousers **2.** PARACHUTIST'S GARMENT a protective zip-up one-piece suit combining long trousers and jacket, worn by a parachutist when jumping

jumpy /júmpi/ (-ier, -iest) adj. **1.** JITTERY very nervous

or anxious **2.** MOVING ERRATICALLY moving jerkily or erratically —**jumpily** adv. —**jumpiness** n.

jun. abbr. junior

Jun. abbr. June

Junagadh /joo náagaad/, **Jūnāgadh** city in western India, in the state of Gujarat. Population: 130,132 (1991).

junco /júngkō/ (plural **-cos**) n. a small North American finch with greyish plumage, a pink bill, and white outer tail feathers. Genus: *Junco*. [Early 18thC. Via Spanish from Latin *juncus* 'rush'.]

junction /júngksh'n/ n. **1.** PLACE WHERE THINGS JOIN a place where two or more objects, e.g. roads or railroad lines, join, meet, or cross **2.** UK TRANSP MOTORWAY EXIT any of a series of numbered points on a motorway at which traffic may join or leave. US term **intersection 3.** ELEC ENG ELECTRICAL CONNECTION a connection between electrical wires or cables **4.** PHYS LAYER BETWEEN METALS a layer of metal separating two metals with different properties and serving as a contact between them, especially in a thermocouple **5.** ELECTRON ENG SEMICONDUCTOR CONTACT a point in a semiconductor device at which regions with different electrical properties come into contact with each other **6.** STATE OR ACT OF JOINING the joining of things or their joined state [Early 18thC. From the Latin stem *junction-*, from *jungere* 'to join' (source of English *join* and *junta*).] —**junctional** adj.

junction box n. an enclosed and protected box inside which electrical circuits are interconnected or branched for distribution

juncture /júngkchər/ n. **1.** POINT IN TIME a point in time, especially an important or critical one **2.** JOINING PLACE a place where two or more things join (formal) **3.** JOINING OF THINGS the joining of one thing with another or their joined state (formal) **4.** LING BREAK BETWEEN WORDS the break between one spoken word and another or the pronunciation features that help a listener to recognize the break, distinguishing, e.g. between 'grey day' and 'grade A' [14thC. From Latin *junctura* 'joint', from *jungere* 'to join'.]

June /joon/ n. the sixth month of the year in the Gregorian calendar, made up of thirty days [Pre-12thC. Via French *juin* from Latin (mensis) *junius* '(month) of Juno'.]

June beetle n. = June bug

Juneberry /joón berri/ (plural **-ries**) n. = serviceberry n. 1, serviceberry n. 2 [Mid-19thC. From the month when it blooms.]

June bug n. a large brown North American flying beetle that is seen in late spring and feeds on leaves. The larvae feed on roots. Subfamily: Melolonthinae.

Carl Gustav Jung

Jung /yŏong/, **Carl Gustav** (1875–1961) Swiss psychiatrist. He broadened Freud's interpretation of the unconscious, and introduced the concepts of introvert and extrovert types and the collective unconscious. —**Jungian** /yŏongi ən/ adj., n.

Jung Chang /jŏong cháng/ (b. 1952) Chinese-born US author of *Wild Swans* (1993), an account of her family's experience in communist China.

Jungfrau /yŏong frow/ mountain in southern Switzerland. Height: 4,158 m/13,642 ft.

jungle /júng g'l/ n. **1.** TROPICAL FOREST an area of tropical rainforest covered with vegetation so dense that it is largely impenetrable **2.** THICKLY COVERED AREA any area covered with dense vegetation **3.** TANGLE a

tangled or confused mass **4.** COMPLEX MATTER a frustratingly or impenetrably complex system **5.** HARSH PLACE a harsh environment characterized by fierce competitiveness or struggle for survival **6.** MUSIC FAST PERCUSSIVE MUSIC a style of 1990s dance music derived from ragga, characterized by a strong beat and rapping. ◊ **drum and bass** [Late 18thC. Via Hindi *jangal*, literally 'wasteland', from Sanskrit *jāngala* 'dry'.]

jungle fever n. a severe form of malaria common in tropical regions, especially Southeast Asia

jungle fowl n. any of various species of wild Asian bird related to the pheasant. Jungle fowl are thought to be the ancestors of the modern domestic fowl. Genus: *Gallus*.

jungle gym n. = climbing frame [Originally a trademark]

jungle juice n. alcohol, especially home-made, poor quality, or very strong alcohol (informal)

junior /joóni ər/ adj. **1.** RELATING TO YOUTH OR CHILDHOOD relating to youth, childhood, or children **2.** junior, Junior YOUNGER younger in age, especially when referring to the younger of two family members, e.g. father and son, who share the same name **3.** LOW IN RANK of relatively low rank or with relatively little experience ○ *a junior minister* **4.** SMALLER smaller than the standard or expected size **5.** EDUC FOR CHILDREN BETWEEN 7 AND 11 relating to or involving schoolchildren between the ages of 7 and 11 ○ *junior school* **6.** US EDUC OF THIRD-YEAR STUDENTS relating to or involving students in the third year of high school or college in the United States ■ n. **1.** YOUNGER PERSON a person younger than another being referred to ○ *My sister is three years my junior.* **2.** LOW-RANKING PERSON sb of relatively low rank or little experience **3.** EDUC STUDENT IN JUNIOR SCHOOL a pupil in a junior school **4.** CHILD a young person, especially sb younger than a teenager **5.** junior, Junior US WAY OF ADDRESSING BOY a form of address used for a boy or young man, affectionately to the son in a family or condescendingly to a stranger (informal; offensive in some contexts) **6.** US EDUC THIRD-YEAR STUDENT a student in the third year of high school or college in the United States **7.** LAW BARRISTER in England and Australia, a barrister who has not yet qualified as a Queen's Counsel [13thC. From Latin, 'younger', formed from *juvenis* 'young'.]

junior college n. US a college offering students a two-year course of study that either terminates in an associate degree or corresponds to the first two years at a four-year college

junior common room n. in some colleges and universities, a room provided for general use by students, as distinct from the senior common room, reserved for staff

junior high, **junior high school** n. US a school that is intermediate between primary school and high school, embracing years six or seven to eight or nine

junior middleweight n. **1.** BOXING WEIGHT in professional boxing, a weight class that is lighter than middleweight and heavier than welterweight, for boxers weighing between 67 and 71 kg/147 and 154 lb **2.** BOXER a boxer who fights at junior middleweight

junior school n. a state-run school for children between the ages of 7 and 11

Juniper

juniper /joónipər/ n. **1.** EVERGREEN PLANT BEARING CONES RESEMBLING BERRIES an evergreen tree or shrub with small purple cones resembling berries that yield juniper

 (caption: AKG London)

oil, used to flavour gin. Genus: *Juniperus.* **2. OIL FROM JUNIPER** the oil from juniper berries [14thC. From Latin *juniperus.*]

junk[1] /jungk/ *n.* **1. RUBBISH** discarded things, or things regarded as worthless or causing clutter (*informal*) **2. USED GOODS FOR SALE** secondhand goods offered for sale (*informal*) **3. CHEAP STUFF** cheap and poorly made goods (*informal*) **4. NONSENSE** meaningless or worthless talk (*informal*) **5. HEROIN** narcotics, especially heroin (*slang*) ■ *vt.* **(junks, junking, junked) DISCARD** to get rid of sth as useless (*informal*) [14thC. Origin uncertain: perhaps via Old French *jonc* 'rush' from Latin *juncus.* Originally in the meaning 'old rope'(perhaps from the use of rushes to make ropes).]

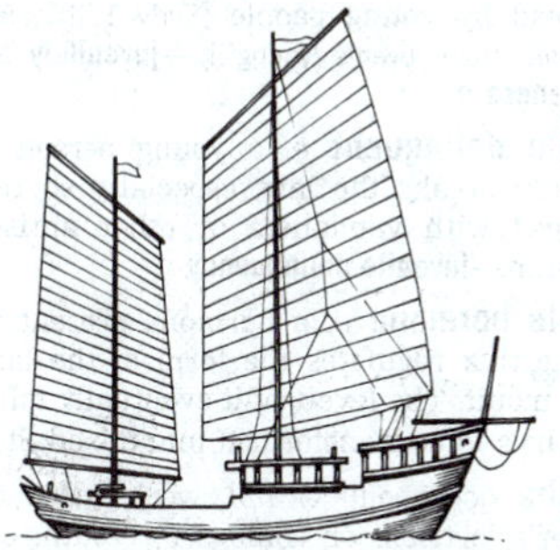

Junk

junk[2] /jungk/ *n.* a flat-bottomed sailing boat, popular in Chinese waters, that is high at the stern and has squarish sails, each supported on several battens [Mid-16thC. Via Portuguese *junco* or Dutch *jonk* from Malay *jong.*]

junk bond *n.* an investment bond that offers the possibility of a high return but at a high risk

Junker /yoŏngkər/ *n.* **1. PRUSSIAN ARISTOCRAT** any of the aristocratic landowners in Prussia, who continued to exercise great political power well into the 20th century **2. OFFENSIVE TERM** an offensive term for a German army officer or official who is considered to be arrogant and dictatorial (*offensive*) [Mid-16thC. From German *Junker*, literally 'young lord'.] —**Junkerdom** *n.* —**Junkerism** *n.*

Junkers /yoŏngkərz/, **Hugo** (1859–1935) German aircraft engineer. His designs include the World War II dive-bomber, the Ju 87 (Stuka).

junket /júngkit/ *n.* **1. EXPENSES-PAID TRIP** a trip taken at sb else's expense, especially one taken by a politician at public expense **2.** *US* **AMUSING OCCASION** an outing, excursion, or party of any kind **3.** FOOD **SET MILK DESSERT** a dessert made from milk that has been set with rennet ■ *v.* **(-kets, -keting, -keted) 1.** *vi.* **HAVE EXPENSES-PAID TRIP** to go on an expenses-paid trip, especially one paid for with public money **2.** *vti. US* **HOLD PARTY** to hold a party or entertain sb with a party [14thC. From French *jonquette*, from *jonc* 'rush', from Latin *juncus.* From being made or served on rushes.] —**junketer** *n.*

junk food *n.* food that does not form part of a well-balanced diet, especially highly processed, high-fat savoury snack items eaten in place of or in addition to regular meals

junkie /júngki/, **junky** (*plural* **-ies**) *n.* **1. DRUG ADDICT** a drug addict, especially sb addicted to heroin (*slang*) **2. ENTHUSIAST** sb whose interest in or liking for sth resembles an addiction (*informal*) ○ *a football junkie*

junk mail *n.* unsolicited mail, especially advertising material

junkman /júngk man/ *n. US* = **rag-and-bone man** (*dated*)

junk shop *n.* **1. SHOP SELLING USED GOODS** a shop selling a variety of secondhand goods **2. LOW-QUALITY ANTIQUE SHOP** a second-rate antique shop

junky /júngki/ *adj.* **(-ier, -iest) WORTHLESS** of very low quality or very little value ■ *n.* = **junkie**

junkyard /júngk yaard/ *n.* a place where junk is collected before being sold or processed

Juno /joŏnō/ (*plural* **-nos**) *n.* **1.** MYTHOL **ROMAN GODDESS** in Roman mythology, the queen of the gods and wife of Jupiter. Greek equivalent **Hera 2. QUEENLY WOMAN** a woman of queenly bearing and imposing beauty — **Junoesque** /joŏnō ésk/ *adj.*

junr, **Junr** *abbr.* junior

junta /júntə, hoŏntə, joŏntə/ (*plural* **-tas**) *n.* (*takes a singular or plural verb*) **1.** POL **NEW RULERS AFTER COUP** a group of military officers who have taken control of a country following a coup d'état **2. SECRET GROUP** a small group of people, especially one secretly assembled for a common goal **3.** POL **LATIN AMERICAN GOVERNMENT BODY** in some parts of Central and South America, a council or other legislative body within the government [Early 17thC. Via Spanish or Portuguese from, ultimately, Latin *jungere* 'to join'.]

junto /júntō, hoŏntō, joŏntō/ *n.* = **junta** *n.* 2 [Early 17thC. Alteration of JUNTA.]

Jupiter /joŏpitər/ *n.* **1.** MYTHOL **ROMAN GOD** in Roman mythology, the king of the gods. Greek equivalent **Zeus 2.** ASTRON **LARGEST PLANET** the largest planet in the solar system, fifth in order from the sun [12thC. From Latin, from the stem *Jov-* 'Jove' + *pater* 'father'.]

Juppé /zhoŏppay/, **Alain** (*b.* 1945) French statesman. A conservative, he was prime minister of France from 1995 to 1997. Full name **Alain Marie Juppé**

Jura /joŏrə/ **1.** island in western Scotland, the fourth largest of the Inner Hebrides. Population: under 200 (1998). Area: 272 sq. km/105 sq. mi. **2.** department in east-central France, in the province of Franche-Comté. Area: 5,053 sq. km/1,951 sq. mi.

jural /joŏrəl/ *adj.* **1.** LAW **RELATING TO LAW** relating to law or the administration of justice **2. RELATING TO RIGHTS** relating to rights or obligations (*formal*) [Mid-17thC. Formed from the Latin stem *jur-* 'law'.] —**jurally** *adv.*

Jura Mountains mountain range situated on the border between France and Switzerland. The highest point is Crêt de la Neige, 1,718 m/5,636 ft. Length: 320 km/200 mi.

Jurassic /joŏ rássik/ *n.* GEOL the period of geological time during which dinosaurs flourished and birds and mammals first appeared, extending from 210 million years to 140 million years ago. It is the middle period of the Mesozoic era. [Mid-19thC. From French *Jurassique*, from *Jura* 'Jura'.] —**Jurassic** *adj.*

jurat /joŏr at/ *n.* **1. AFFIDAVIT STATEMENT** a closing statement on an affidavit, giving details of the parties to it, the witnesses, and the place and time of signing **2. MAGISTRATE** a magistrate in France or the Channel Islands [15thC. From medieval Latin *juratus*, literally 'sworn man', from *jurare* (see JURY).]

juridical /joŏ ríddik'l/, **juridic** /-ríddik/ *adj.* relating to judges, to the administration of the law, or to law in general —**juridically** *adv.*

juridical days *npl.* days on which law courts are in session

jurisconsult /joŏriss kón sult/ *n.* an expert in law who gives advice on legal matters, especially in relation to civil or international law [Early 17thC. From Latin *jurisconsultus*, literally 'skilled in law'.]

jurisdiction /joŏriss díksh'n/ *n.* **1.** LAW **LEGAL AUTHORITY** the authority to enforce laws or pronounce legal judgments **2. RANGE OF LEGAL AUTHORITY** the area over which legal authority extends **3. AUTHORITY** power or authority generally [13thC. Via Old French *jurediction* from the Latin stem *jurisdiction-*, from *jus* 'law' + *dictio* 'saying' (source of English *diction*).] —**jurisdictional** *adj.* —**jurisdictionally** *adv.* —**jurisdictive** *adj.*

jurisp. *abbr.* jurisprudence

jurisprudence /joŏriss proŏd'nss/ *n.* **1. THEORY OF LAW** the philosophy or science of law **2. LEGAL SYSTEM** a system of law or the body of laws applied in a particular country or state **3. BRANCH OF LAW** a branch of law or the law as it applies to a particular area of life — **jurisprudential** /joŏrisproŏ dénsh'l/ *adj.* —**jurisprudentially** /-dénsh'li/ *adv.*

jurisprudent /joŏriss proŏd'nt/ *adj.* **LEGALLY EXPERT** knowledgeable in the science or philosophy of law ■ *n.* = **jurist** [Early 17thC. Via obsolete French from the late Latin stem *jurisprudent-*, from *jus* 'law' + *prudens* 'wise' (source of English *prudent*).]

jurist /joŏrist/ *n.* **1. LEGAL EXPERT** an expert in the science or philosophy of law, especially Roman or civil law **2. LAW STUDENT OR GRADUATE** a student or graduate of law [15thC. Directly or via French from medieval Latin *jurista*, from *jus* 'law, right'.] —**juristic** /-rístik/ *adj.* —**juristical** *adj.* —**juristically** *adv.*

juror /joŏrər/ *n.* **1.** LAW **JURY MEMBER** a member of a jury, especially in a court of law **2. SB TAKING OATH** sb who has sworn an oath, e.g. an oath of allegiance (*formal or literary*) [14thC. Via Anglo-Norman *jurour* and Old French *jureor* from Latin *jurator*, from *jurare* (see JURY).]

jury /joŏri/ (*plural* **-ries**) *n.* **1.** LAW **PEOPLE DECIDING LEGAL CASE** a group of people, usually twelve people, chosen to give a verdict on a legal case that is presented before them in a court of law **2. PEOPLE JUDGING COMPETITION** a group of people who judge a competition [14thC. Via Anglo-Norman and Old French *juree* 'oath, inquest' from, ultimately, Latin *jurare* 'to swear', from *jus* 'law, right'.]

jury box *n.* the part of a court where the jury sits

jury duty *n.* = **jury service**

juryman /joŏrimən/ (*plural* **-men** /-mən/) *n.* a man who is a member of a jury in a court of law

jury nullification *n.* the decision that a jury is, for whatever reason, incapable of sitting

jury-rig **(jury-rigs, jury-rigging, jury-rigged)** *vt.* to build sth in a makeshift way or fit sth out, especially a boat, with makeshift equipment [*jury* of uncertain origin: probably via Old French *ajurie* 'aid' from Latin *adjutare* 'to aid']

jury service *n.* service as a member of a jury in a court of law

jurywoman /joŏri wŏŏmən/ (*plural* **-en** /-wimin/) *n.* a woman who is a member of a jury in a court of law

jus gentium /júss jénti əm/ *n.* international law [From Latin, literally 'law of nations']

jus sanguinis /júss sáng gwiniss/ *n.* the principle in law according to which children's citizenship is determined by the citizenship of their parents [From Latin, literally 'right of blood']

jussive /júsiv/ *adj.* GRAM = **imperative** [Mid-19thC. Formed from Latin *juss-*, the past participle stem of *jubere* 'to command'.]

jus soli /júss sṓl ī/ *n.* the principle in law according to which children's citizenship is determined by the place of their birth [From Latin, literally 'right of soil']

just /just/ *adv.* **1. IN THE IMMEDIATE PAST** a very short time ago ○ *The train has just left.* **2. AT THIS MOMENT** indicating that sb will begin doing sth, or sth will start happening now (*used also with 'about to' and 'going to'*) ○ *I was just about to tell you.* **3. ONLY** only or merely the thing, amount, or situation mentioned ○ *This is just a warning.* **4. BARELY** by only a small degree or margin ○ *I arrived just in time.* **5. USED FOR EMPHASIS** used to emphasize a statement, usually in order to express an emotion ○ *It's just plain wrong.* **6. EXACTLY** precisely the thing, amount, or situation mentioned ○ *It's just what you need.* **7. EXPRESSING AGREEMENT** used as a comment on a statement that has just been made, in order to express agreement ○ *It was exactly what we needed. Wasn't it just!* ■ *adj.* **1. FAIR AND IMPARTIAL** acting with fairness and impartiality **2. MORALLY CORRECT** done, pursued, or given in accordance with what is morally right **3. REASONABLE** valid or reasonable [14thC. Via French *juste* from Latin *justus*, from *jus* 'law, right'.] —**justly** *adv.* —**justness** *n.* ◇ **just about** used to indicate that sth is the case, but only by a very small degree or amount ◇ **just a moment** *or* **second** *or* **minute** used to ask someone to wait for a short time ◇ **just now 1.** a very short time ago **2.** at this very moment ◇ **just so 1.** used to express agreement with or confirmation of a statement that has just been made **2.** done or arranged precisely ○ *They wanted the room decorated just so.*

justice /jústiss/ *n.* **1. FAIRNESS** fairness or reasonableness, especially in the way people are treated or decisions are made **2.** LAW **APPLICATION OF LAW** the legal system or the act of applying or upholding the law **3.** LAW **VALIDITY** validity in law **4. GOOD REASON** sound or good reason **5.** LAW = **justice of the peace** [12thC. Via French from Latin *justitia*, from *justus* 'JUST'.] ◇ **bring sb to justice** to arrest sb to be tried in a court of law ◇ **do justice to sb** *or* **sth 1.** to deal with sb or sth fairly **2.** to convey the true qualities, especially the merits, of sb or sth ◇ **do yourself**

justice to display your own abilities fully or perform to your full potential (*often used in the negative*)

justice of the peace *n.* sb without legal training or qualifications who is appointed to judge minor criminal cases, perform marriages, administer oaths, and refer cases to higher courts

justiciable /ju stíshi əb'l/ *adj.* **1.** LIABLE FOR TRIAL able or required to be tried in a court of law **2.** CAPABLE OF BEING SETTLED IN COURT able to be settled by applying the principles of law —**justiciability** /ju stíshi ə bílləti/ *n.*

justiciary /ju stíshi əri/ *adj.* RELATING TO LEGAL ADMINISTRATION relating to the administration of law ■ *n.* (*plural* **-ies**) SB ADMINISTERING LAW a judge or other officer who administers the law

justifiable /jústi fī əb'l/ *adj.* capable of being shown as reasonable or merited according to accepted standards —**justifiability** /jústi fī ə bílləti/ *n.* —**justifiableness** /-fī əb'lnəss/ *n.* —**justifiably** /-bli/ *adv.*

justifiable homicide *n.* killing that is deemed to be lawful, especially because it is carried out in self-defence or as the only way to prevent a crime

justification /jústifi káysh'n/ *n.* **1.** STH THAT JUSTIFIES sth, e.g. a reason or circumstance, that justifies an action or attitude **2.** GIVING OF REASONS FOR STH the act of justifying sth **3.** PRINTING ALIGNMENT OF MARGINS adjustment of the lengths of spaces between and within words in text in order to make both left and right margins align **4.** CHR CHRISTIAN DOCTRINE the Christian belief that people are absolved from all sin if they believe in Jesus Christ [14thC. Directly or via French from the late Latin stem *justification-*, from *justificare* (see JUSTIFY).]

justificatory /jústifi kaytəri/, **justificative** /-kaytiv/ *adj.* serving or acting to justify sth [Late 16thC. From medieval Latin *justificatorius*, from late Latin *justificare* (see JUSTIFY).]

justify /jústi fī/ (**-fies, -fying, -fied**) *vt.* **1.** MAKE REASONABLE to serve as an acceptable reason or excuse for sth (*often passive*) **2.** GIVE SB REASON to give sb an acceptable reason for taking a particular action (*often passive*) **3.** EXPLAIN to give a reason or explanation why sth was done **4.** PRINTING ALIGN MARGINS OF to adjust the lengths of spaces between and within words in text in order to make both the left and right margins align **5.** CHR FREE FROM SIN to free sb from sinfulness through faith in Jesus Christ or by the grace of

Jesus Christ **6.** LAW GIVE LEGAL REASON FOR to provide a good reason in law for sth, especially for committing the offence that is the subject of a criminal charge [14thC. Via French *justifier* from Latin *justificare* 'to act justly, justify', from Latin *justus* 'JUST'.]

Justinian I /ju stínni ən/, **Emperor of Rome** (482–565). During his reign (527–65) he restored Byzantine power in Rome, northern Italy, and Spain. He revised and systematized Roman law. Known as **Justinian the Great**

just-in-time *n.* a manufacturing and stock-control system in which goods are produced and delivered as they are required. It is designed to eliminate waste and avoid the need for large stocks.

jut /jut/ *vti.* (**juts, jutting, jutted**) STICK OUT to stick out, or make sth stick out, especially beyond the surface or edge of sth ■ *n.* PROJECTING PART sth that sticks out [Mid-16thC. Alteration of JET¹.] —**jutting** *adj.*

jute /joot/ *n.* **1.** INDUST FIBRE coarse fibre from the bark of an Asian tree that is used for making sacking and rope **2.** PLANTS PLANT either of two Asian plants of the linden family that provide jute. Genus: *Corchorus*. [Mid-18thC. Via Bengali *jhuto* from Sanskrit *jūtah* 'matted hair'.]

Jute /joot/ *n.* MEMBER OF GERMANIC PEOPLE a member of a Germanic people from around the Rhine estuary who invaded parts of southeastern England during the fifth century AD. They settled in Kent and the Isle of Wight, where they soon became the dominant people. ◊ **Angle, Saxon** ■ *adj.* RELATING TO JUTES relating to or typical of the Jute people or their culture [Pre-12thC. From Latin *Jutae*, of Germanic origin.] —**Jutish** /jóotish/ *adj.*

Jutland /jútlənd/ peninsula in northern Europe, containing all of mainland Denmark. The base of the peninsula is part of Germany. Length: 338 km/210 mi.

Juvenal /jóov'nəl/ (AD65?–128?) Roman satirist. His sixteen extant *Satires*, which were famously translated by John Dryden, attack the follies and vices of Roman imperial society. Full name **Decimus Junius Juvenalis**

juvenescent /jóovə néssn't/ *adj.* (*literary*) **1.** YOUTHFUL youthful or young-looking **2.** BECOMING A CHILD growing out of infancy and into childhood [Early 19thC. From Latin *juvenescere* 'to grow up'.] —**juvenescence** *n.*

juvenile /jóovə nīl/ *adj.* **1.** YOUTHFUL young or youthful **2.** RELATING TO YOUNG PEOPLE relating to, intended for, or suitable for young people ○ *a juvenile court* **3.** IMMATURE immature or childish ○ *juvenile behaviour* **4.** BIOL NOT YET MATURE used to describe a plant or animal that has not yet reached maturity **5.** BIRDS SEXUALLY IMMATURE used to describe a bird that has developed contour feathers but is not yet sexually mature **6.** GEOL FROM WITHIN THE EARTH used to describe water or gas that has risen to the surface from within the Earth for the first time ■ *n.* **1.** YOUNGSTER a young person **2.** BIOL IMMATURE ANIMAL OR PLANT an animal or plant that has not yet reached maturity **3.** THEATRE ACTOR SUITED TO YOUTHFUL PARTS an actor who plays youthful roles **4.** PUBL BOOK FOR CHILDREN a book intended to be read by young people [Early 17thC. From Latin *juvenilis*, from *juvenis* 'young'.] —**juvenilely** *adv.* —**juvenileness** *n.*

juvenile delinquent *n.* a young person who habitually breaks the law, especially sb repeatedly charged with vandalism or other antisocial behaviour —**juvenile delinquency** *n.*

juvenile hormone *n.* a hormone present in insect larvae that regulates the form of the larva after each moult. The levels of it eventually fall to allow the larva to be transformed into the adult insect.

juvenilia /jóovə nílli ə/ *npl.* works produced in a writer's, artist's, or composer's youth, especially before a mature style has developed

juvenility /jóovə nílləti/ *n.* **1.** JUVENILE QUALITY juvenile quality or state **2.** IMMATURITY foolishly immature behaviour **3.** ACT OF IMMATURITY an act of foolishly immature behaviour (*often used in the plural*)

juxtapose /júkstə pōz/ (**-poses, -posing, -posed**) *vt.* to place two or more things together, especially in order to suggest a link between them or emphasize the contrast between them [Mid-19thC. From French *juxtaposer*, from Latin *juxta* 'close' + French *poser* 'POSE'.] —**juxtaposition** /júkstəpə zísh'n/ *n.* —**juxtapositional** /-zísh'nəl/ *adj.*

JWV *n., abbr.* Jewish War Veterans

Jy *symbol.* Jansky

Jysaitha *n.* INDIAN RELIG in the Hindu calendar, the third month of the year, made up of 29 or 30 days and occurring at about the same time as May and June

Kk

k¹ /kay/ (*plural* **k's**), **K** (*plural* **K's** *or* **Ks**) *n*. **1.** 11TH LETTER OF THE ENGLISH ALPHABET the eleventh letter of the modern English alphabet **2.** SPEECH SOUND CORRESPONDING TO LETTER 'K' the speech sound that corresponds to the letter 'K' **3.** LETTER 'K' WRITTEN a written representation of the letter 'K'

k² *abbr.* **1.** kilo- **2.** knight **3.** knit **4.** SAILING knot

K¹ *symbol.* **1.** PHYS kaon **2.** PHYS kelvin **3.** PHYS kinetic energy **4.** CHEM ELEM potassium

K² *abbr.* **1.** COMPUT kilobyte **2.** kilometre (*informal*) **3.** K, K. CARDS, CHESS king **4.** K, K. MUSIC Köchel (*preceding a number in Köchel's catalogue of Mozart's works*) **5.** MONEY krona **6.** MONEY krone **7.** MONEY kwacha **8.** MONEY kyat **9.** MONEY kopeck **10.** knight **11.** one thousand **12.** FIN one thousand pounds

K2 /kay too͞/ the second highest mountain in the world. It is situated in the Karakorum Range of the western Himalayas on the border between China and the disputed territory of Jammu and Kashmir. Height: 8,611 m/28,251 ft.

ka /kaa/ *n*. in ancient Egypt, the soul of a dead person, said to be able to reside in a statue of that person after death [Late 19thC. From Ancient Egyptian.]

Kaaba /ka͞a'bə/ *n*. a square building inside the great mosque in Mecca, containing a sacred stone (**Black Stone**) said to have been given by God. It is the most holy site in the Islamic religion. [Early 17thC. From Arabic, literally 'the square house'.]

kabala *n*. = kabbalah

Kabardian /kə ba͞a'rdi ən/ *n*. **1.** PEOPLES MEMBER OF A RUSSIAN PEOPLE a member of a people who live in an area to the north of the Caucasus Mountains in southern European Russia **2.** LANG LANGUAGE OF SOUTHERN RUSSIA a language spoken in an area to the north of the Caucasus Mountains in southern European Russia. It belongs to the Abkhazo-Adyghean group of the Caucasian family of languages and is spoken by about 300,000 people. [Late 19thC. From Russian *Kabarda*, a place name.] —**Kabardian** *adj*.

kabbalah /kə ba͞a'lə, kábbələ/ **kabbalah, kabala, cabala, cabbala** *n*. **1.** MYSTICAL JEWISH TEACHINGS a body of mystical Jewish teachings based on an interpretation of the Hebrew scriptures as containing hidden meanings **2.** SET OF MYSTICAL BELIEFS a set of secret or mystical beliefs [Early 16thC. Via medieval Latin from, ultimately, rabbinical Hebrew *qabbalah* 'tradition', from *qibbel* 'to receive, accept'. The underlying idea is 'sth received or handed down'.] —**kabbalism** *n*. —**kabbalist** *n*. —**kabbalistic** /kábbə lístik/ *adj*. —**kabbalistically** /-lístikli/ *adv*.

kabinett /kábbi nét/, **Kabinett** *n*. the lowest grade of high-quality German table wine, typically dry to medium dry [Early 20thC. From German *Kabinettwein*, literally 'cabinet wine'; because the wine was originally kept in a special cellar.]

kabob *n*. = kebab

kabuki /kə bo͞oki/ *n*. traditional Japanese drama in which male actors play both male and female parts [Late 19thC. From Japanese *ka* 'song' + *bu* 'dance' + *ki* 'art, skill'.]

Kabul /ka͞a'bool/ capital city of Afghanistan, located in the centre of the country. Population: 1,424,400 (1988).

Kabyle /kə bíl/ (*plural* **-byles** *or* **-byle**) *n*. **1.** PEOPLES MEMBER OF A N AFRICAN PEOPLE a member of a Berber

Kabuki

people who live in northeastern Algeria **2.** LANG N AFRICAN LANGUAGE a Berber language spoken in northeastern Algeria. It belongs to the Afro-Asiatic family of African languages and is spoken by about three million people. [Mid-18thC. Probably from Arabic *kabā'il* 'tribes'.] —**Kabyle** *adj*.

kaccha /kúchə/ *n*. a pair of short trousers that baptized Sikhs wear as one of the five symbols of religious loyalty (**five Ks**) [From Punjabi]

kachina /kə chéenə/ (*plural* **-nas**) *n*. **1.** NATIVE N AMERICAN SPIRIT any one of the spirits believed by the Native North American Hopi people to be the ancestors of human beings **2.** FIGURE OF A KACHINA a representation of a kachina, usually either a carved wooden doll or a costumed performer in a ceremonial dance [Late 19thC. From Hopi *kacina* 'supernatural'.]

kadaitcha *n*. = kurdaitcha

Kádár /ka͞a'd aar/, **János** (1912–89) Hungarian statesman. He formed a pro-Soviet government following the crushing of the 1956 Hungarian uprising, and exercised supreme power until 1988. Born **János Csermanck**

Kaddish /káddish/ (*plural* **-dishim** /ka díshim/) *n*. a prayer recited at the close of the sections of Jewish religious services, and by close relatives of a deceased person at times of mourning and anniversaries of the death [Early 17thC. From Aramaic *qaddīs* 'holy'.]

Kaduna /kə do͞onə/ capital of Kaduna State, north-central Nigeria, situated about 145 km/90 mi. north of the national capital, Abuja. Population: 309,600 (1992).

Kaffir /káffər/, **Kafir** *n*. **1.** S Africa OFFENSIVE TERM a highly offensive term referring to a black African person (*taboo insult*) **2.** Kaffir, kaffir OFFENSIVE TERM an offensive term referring to a person who is not a Muslim (*slang insult*) **3.** LANG XHOSA the Xhosa language (*dated*) [Mid-16thC. From Arabic *kāfir* 'unbeliever, infidel'.]

kaffir corn *n*. a variety of sorghum cultivated in southern Africa for its grain, used to make beer and as a fodder crop (*sometimes considered offensive*)

kaffiyeh *n*. = keffiyeh

Kafir *n*. = Kaffir

Kafiri /káffəri/ *n*. the language of the Nuri people of Pakistan and Afghanistan. It belongs to the Dardic branch of the Indo-Aryan family of languages. [Early 20thC. See KAFFIR.]

Franz Kafka

Kafka /káfkə/, **Franz** (1883–1924) Czech novelist. His dreamlike works, such as *The Trial* (1925) and *The Castle* (1926), are full of oppression and despair. His major novels were published posthumously by his friend, Max Brod, against Kafka's wishes.

Kafkaesque /káfkə ésk/ *adj*. **1.** OF KAFKA'S WORK relating to or typical of the work of Franz Kafka **2.** IMPERSONAL AND OVERCOMPLEX characterized by seemingly pointless, impersonal, and often disturbing overcomplexity

kaftan *n*. = caftan

Kafue /kaa fo͞o ay/ river in central Zambia, a tributary of the Zambezi. It rises near Zambia's northern border with the Democratic Republic of the Congo. Length: 1,570 km/980 mi.

kagu /ka͞a goo/ *n*. a large greyish flightless bird found only on the Pacific island of New Caledonia. It is now nearly extinct. Latin name: *Rhynochetos jubatus*. [Mid-19thC. From Melanesian.]

kahawai /ka͞ahə wī/ (*plural* **-wais** *or* **-wai**) *n*. a large marine fish of the perch family, similar in appearance to the salmon. It is found in Australia and New Zealand. Latin name: *Arripis trutta*. [Mid-19thC. From Maori.]

kahikatea /kíkə te͞e ə/ *n*. a tall evergreen tree that is native to New Zealand and is an important source of timber. Latin name: *Podocarpus dacrydioides*. [Early 19thC. From Maori.]

Frida Kahlo: Photographed in 1930 by Edward Weston

Kahlo /ka͞a'l ō/, **Frida** (1907–54) Mexican painter. She is known for her idiosyncratic self-portraits that incorporate elements and subject matter inspired by Mexican folk art and her personal life. She was married to the Mexican painter Diego Rivera.

kai /kī/ *n. NZ* food [Mid-19thC. From Maori.]

kaiak *n.* = kayak

Kaieteur Falls /kī´ə toor-/ waterfall in central Guyana, on the Potaro branch of the River Essequibo. Height: 225 m/740 ft.

kaif *n.* = kif

Kaikoura /kī kŏŏra/ town on the northeastern coast of the South Island, New Zealand. It is a fishing, agricultural, and whale-watching centre. Population: 2,207 (1996).

Kaikoura Ranges twin mountain ranges near the northeastern coast of the South Island, New Zealand. The highest point is Tapuaenuku, 2,885 m/9,465 ft.

kail *n.* = kale

kailyard *n.* = kaleyard

kainite /kīn īt, káyn īt/ *n.* a variously coloured mineral that is a sulphate and chloride of magnesium and potassium. It is a source of potassium and is often used as a fertilizer. [Mid-19thC. From German *Kainit*, from German *kainos* 'new, recent'.]

Kaipara Harbour /kī paˊa raa-/ wide harbour on the northwestern coast of the North Island, New Zealand. Area: 520 sq. km/200 sq. mi.

Kairouan /kī ər waˊan/ city in northern Tunisia, capital of Al Qayrawan Governate. Called the City of a Hundred Mosques, it is one of the holiest Muslim cities. Population: 102,600 (1992).

kaiser /kī´zər/ *n.* any one of the former German, Austrian, or Austro-Hungarian emperors, especially the German emperor Wilhelm II, who ruled Germany during World War I [Old English *cāsare*, related to Greek *kaisar* from Latin *Caesar*] —**kaiserdom** *n.* —**kaiserism** *n.*

Kaiser /kī´zər/, **Georg** (1878–1945) German dramatist. He is known for his plays in the expressionist style, including *From Morn to Midnight* (1916), *Gas I* (1918) and *Gas II* (1920).

kaiserin /kī´zərin/ *n.* a German empress or the wife of a German emperor [Late 19thC. From German, feminine form of KAISER.]

kaizen /kī´ zén/ *n.* a Japanese philosophy advocating the need for continuous improvement in a person's personal and professional life [Late 20thC. Japanese, 'improvement'.]

kak /kak/ *interj. S Africa* TABOO SWEARWORD used as a swearword (*taboo offensive*) ■ *n. S Africa* RUBBISH despicable rubbish or downright nonsense (*slang*) [From Afrikaans, 'excrement', from Latin *cacare* 'to defecate']

kaka /kaˊa kaa/ *n.* a species of parrot found in New Zealand and having a long grey bill and greenish-brown plumage. Latin name: *Nestor meridionalis*. [Late 18thC. From Maori.]

Kakadu National Park /kaakə doˊo-/ national park in the Northern Territory, Australia. Area: 20,000 sq. km/7,770 sq. mi.

Kakapo

kakapo /kaˊakə pŏ/ (*plural* -**pos**) *n.* a large flightless nocturnal parrot with green plumage, native to New Zealand. It looks similar to an owl and is now rare. Latin name: *Strigops habroptilus*. [Mid-19thC. From Maori.]

kakemono /kaˊki mŏnˊŏ/ (*plural* -**nos**) *n.* a Japanese wall hanging in the form of a tall narrow scroll, weighted

at the base with a roller and decorated with a painting or with a text in ornamental handwriting [Late 19thC. From Japanese, from *kake*- 'to hang' + *mono* 'thing'.]

kaki /káki/ *n.* = **Japanese persimmon** [Early 18thC. From Japanese.]

kakistocracy /káki stókrəssi/ (*plural* -**cies**) *n.* government by the most unscrupulous or unsuitable people, or a state governed by such people [Early 19thC. From Greek *kakistos* 'worst' + -CRACY.]

kala-azar /kállə ə zaˊar/ *n.* a severe, often fatal, tropical fever caused by a parasite that enters the body via a sandfly bite. Symptoms include acute anaemia, weight loss, and an enlarged liver and spleen. [Late 19thC. From Assamese, from *kala* 'black' + *āzār* 'disease'.]

Kalachakra /kaˊalə chukrə/ *n.* a mandala, traditionally constructed out of grains of sand, depicting Buddhist deities in a portrayal of time. The mandala is destroyed shortly after construction to illustrate the Buddhist teaching of impermanence.

Kalahari Desert /kállə haˊari-/ arid and semiarid region in southern Africa. It occupies much of Botswana and parts of Namibia and South Africa. Area: 712,000 sq. km/275,000 sq. mi.

Kalahari Gemsbok National Park /-gémz bok-/ national park in northwestern South Africa. Area: 9,591 sq. km/3,703 sq. mi.

kalanchoe /kállən kŏˊ i/ *n.* any one of various species of tropical African succulent plant often grown as pot plants for their shiny leaves and clusters of small bright red, pink, or white flowers. Genus: *Kalanchoe*. [Mid-19thC. Via modern Latin from French, ultimately from Chinese *gāláncài*.]

Kalashnikov /kə láshni kof/ *n.* a Russian-manufactured semi-automatic assault rifle that is widely used as a weapon among terrorists and paramilitary organizations [Late 20thC. From Russian, named after M. T. *Kalashnikov*, its developer.]

Kalat /kə laˊat/, **Kalāt** town in western Pakistan, principal town of the Kalat region, in Baluchistan Province. Population: 11,000 (1981).

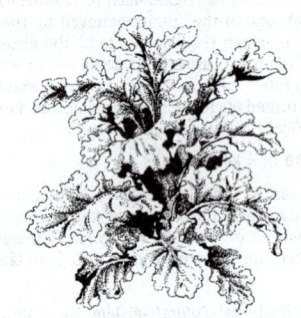

Kale

kale /kayl/, **kail** *n.* **1.** VARIETY OF CABBAGE a hardy heartless variety of cabbage with dark green curly leaves. Latin name: *Brassica oleracea acephala*. **2.** *Scotland* CABBAGE cabbage of any kind **3.** *US* MONEY money (*slang*) [14thC. Scottish variant of COLE.]

kaleidoscope /kə līdəskŏp/ *n.* **1.** OPTICAL TOY an optical toy consisting of a cylinder with mirrors and coloured shapes inside that create shifting symmetrical patterns when the end is rotated **2.** COMPLEX SCENE OR PATTERN a complex, colourful, and shifting pattern or scene **3.** COMPLEX SET OF EVENTS a complex set of events or circumstances [Early 19thC. Coined from Greek *kalos* 'beautiful' + *eidos* 'form' + -SCOPE, literally 'observer of beautiful forms', coined by Sir David Brewster (1781–1868), its inventor.] —**kaleidoscopic** /kə līdə skóppik/ *adj.* —**kaleidoscopically** *adv.*

kalends *npl.* = calends

Kalevala /kaˊalə vaˊalə/ *n.* in Finnish legend, the land of the folk hero Kaleva, whose exploits are recorded in Finnish folk tales

kaleyard /káyl yaard/, **kailyard** *n. Scotland* a kitchen garden (*archaic*) [Mid-16thC. From Scottish, coined from *kale* + *yard*.]

Kaleyard School /káyl yaard-/ *n.* a group of Scottish writers, active from the late 19th to the early 20th century, who wrote romantic portrayals of life in the Scottish Lowlands [*Kaleyard* 'kitchen garden (of a small cottage)', from KALE + YARD; from the writers' portrayal of local town life]

Kalgoorlie-Boulder /kalgŏˊorli-/ city in southern Western Australia, a goldmining centre. Population: 28,087 (1996).

Kali /kaˊali/ *n.* a terrifying Hindu goddess who is the devourer of time. She represents the unpleasant realities of life. [From Sanskrit]

kalif *n.* = caliph

Kalimantan /kálli mántən/ region of the Republic of Indonesia, occupying the southern portion of the island of Borneo. Population: 10,470,800 (1995). Area: 542,700 sq. km/209,500 sq. mi.

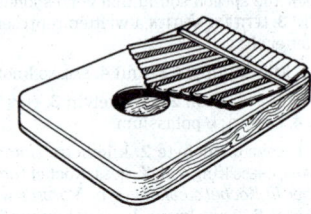

Kalimba

kalimba /kə límbə/ *n.* an African instrument consisting of tuned metal or bamboo bars of varying lengths attached to a soundboard. The bars are plucked to give sound. [Mid-20thC. From Bantu.]

Kalinin /kə leˊenin/ former name for **Tver** (1933–90)

Kaliningrad /kə leˊenin grad/ city in western Russia, on the River Pregolya. It is the capital of Kaliningrad Oblast. Population: 406,000 (1990). Former name **Königsberg** (until 1946)

Kaliyuga /kaˊali yŏˊogə/ *n.* in Hindu philosophy, the age of decadence. It is the fourth and last age in the Hindu cycle of the world. [From Sanskrit]

kallikrein /kálli kreˊe in, kə líkri in/ *n.* an enzyme present in blood, urine, and body tissue that, when activated, dilates blood vessels

Kalmar /kál maar/ port city in southern Sweden, the capital of Kalmar County. It is situated on Kalmarsund opposite the island of Öland. Population: 58,420 (1995).

kalmia /kálmi ə/ *n.* a flowering evergreen shrub, native to North America, that has poisonous leaves and belongs to the heath family. The mountain ash is a kalmia. Genus: *Kalmia*. [Mid-18thC. From modern Latin, genus name, named after the Swedish botanist Pehr Kalm (1716–79).]

Kalmyck /kál muk/, **Kalmuk** /kálmik/ *n.* (*plural* -**mycks** or -**myck**; *plural* -**muks** or -**muk**) **1.** PEOPLES MEMBER OF A SW RUSSIAN PEOPLE a member of a people who live in an autonomous region of southwest Russia. They migrated from northeastern China during the 17th century. **2.** LANG MONGOLIAN LANGUAGE the language spoken by the Kalmyck. It belongs to the Mongolian branch of the Altaic family of languages and is spoken by about 150,000 people. ■ *adj.* **1.** LANGUAGE OF THE LANGUAGE OF THE KALMYCK relating to the Kalmyck language **2.** PEOPLES OF THE KALMYCK relating to the Kalmyck or their culture [Early 17thC. From Russian *Kalmyk*.]

kalpa /kálpə/ *n.* in Hindu philosophy, an immeasurably long period of time. Its length is variable, sometimes described as one complete cycle of the world (**yuga**), sometimes as 1,000 cycles. [Late 18thC. From Sanskrit.]

kalpak *n.* CLOTHES = calpac

kama /kaˊamə/ *n.* sexual pleasure as the third of the four Hindu goals of life [From Sanskrit *kāma* 'love, desire']

kamacite /kámmə sīt/ n. an alloy of nickel and iron found in meteorites [Late 19thC. From Greek *kamak-*, *kamax* 'vine pole' + -ITE.]

Kamakura /káamə koorə/ city southwest of Tokyo, on Sagami Bay, in Kanagawa Prefecture, southeastern Honshu, Japan. Population: 174,307 (1993).

kamala /kə máalə/ n. **1.** EAST INDIAN TREE an East Indian tree that belongs to the spurge family. Latin name: *Mallotus philippinensis*. **2.** POWDER a powder obtained from seeds of the kamala, used as a dye and formerly used to treat worm infestations [Early 19thC. From Sanskrit, probably of Dravidian origin.]

Kamasutra /káamə sóotrə/ n. an ancient Sanskrit text giving instruction on the art of lovemaking [Late 19thC. From Sanskrit, from *kāma* 'love, desire' + *sūtra* 'precept'.]

Kamchatka Peninsula /kam chátkə-/ large peninsula of eastern Russia that separates the Sea of Okhotsk from the Bering Sea and the Pacific Ocean. Area: 518,000 sq. km/200,000 sq. mi.

kame /kaym/ n. a ridge of sand and gravel left by a melting glacier [Late 18thC. From Scottish *kame* 'comb'.]

Kamet, Mount /káamet, kə máyt/ mountain in the Himalayas, in northern India, near the source of the River Jumna. Height: 7,756 m/25,447 ft.

kami /káami/ (plural **-mi**) n. any of the sacred powers that are worshipped in the Shinto religion of Japan. Sometimes personified, they are generally regarded as being the forces that generate life. [Early 17thC. From Japanese.]

kamikaze /kámmi káazi/ n. **1.** AIR FORCE JAPANESE SUICIDE PILOT a World War II Japanese pilot trained for the suicide mission of flying an aircraft packed with explosives into an enemy target, often a ship (often used before a noun) ○ *a kamikaze pilot* **2.** AIR JAPANESE AIRCRAFT an aircraft used by a kamikaze, especially one designed specifically for suicide crashes (often used before a noun) **3.** RECKLESS PERSON sb who behaves in a reckless way, often sb whose actions seem self-defeating or self-destructive (*informal*) ■ adj. RECKLESS reckless, especially seeming to invite failure or self-destruction (*informal*) [Late 19thC. From Japanese, literally 'divine wind'.]

Kampala /kam páalə/ capital city of Uganda, situated in the southern part of the country, near Lake Victoria. Population: 773,463 (1991).

Kampuchea /kámpoo chée ə/ former name for **Cambodia** (1975–89) —**Kampuchean** n., adj.

kana /káanə/ n. **1.** JAPANESE WRITING SYSTEM one of the writing systems used in Japanese. Symbols represent syllables and are often used in conjunction with Japanese pictorial symbols (**kanji**) to change the form of words. ◊ **hiragana, katakana 2.** SYMBOL any one of the syllabic symbols used in kana [Early 18thC. From Japanese.]

Kanak /kə náak/ n. sb who was born in or is a citizen of the French overseas territory of New Caledonia in the South Pacific, and who supports independence from France [Early 20thC. From French *canaque*, of uncertain origin: probably from English *Kanaka* (see KANAKA).] —**Kanak** adj.

Kanaka /kə nákə/ n. HAWAIIAN CITIZEN sb who was born in or is a citizen of Hawaii, especially sb of Polynesian descent ■ adj. OF THE KANAKAS relating to or typical of the Kanakas or their culture [Mid-19thC. From Hawaiian, 'person, human being'.]

kanamycin /kánnə míssin/ n. an antibiotic obtained from a bacterium found in soil, effective against a wide range of serious infections that are resistant to other safer antibiotics [Mid-20thC. From modern Latin *kanamyceticus*.]

Kananga /kə náng gə/ city in the southern Democratic Republic of Congo, capital of Kasai-Occidental Region. Population: 393,030 (1994). Former name **Luluabourg**

Kanarese /kánnə réez/ n. (plural **-rese**) **1.** PEOPLES MEMBER OF AN INDIAN PEOPLE a member of a people living in southwestern India, mainly in the Kanara region **2.** LANG = **Kannada** ■ adj. PEOPLES, GEOG OF KANARA REGION relating to the region of Kanara in southwestern India, or its people or culture

Kanawha /kə náa wə/ river in west-central West Virginia. It rises in northwestern North Carolina and joins the Ohio River at Point Pleasant. Length: 156 km/97 mi.

kanban /kán ban/ n. **1.** ORDER CARD in the just-in-time manufacturing and stock-control system, a card bearing an order for goods, sent to a manufacturer or supplier **2.** = **just-in-time** [Late 20thC. From Japanese 'billboard, sign'.]

Kanchenjunga /kúchən júng gə/ the third highest mountain in the world. It is situated in the Himalayas, on the border between Nepal and Sikkim, India. Height: 8,598 m/28,208 ft.

Wassily Kandinsky: Photographed at the Bauhaus, Dessau, Germany (1930?)

Kandinsky /kan dínski/, **Wassily** (1866–1944) Russian painter. One of the earliest exponents of pure abstraction in art, he wrote *Concerning the Spiritual in Art* (1912), the first treatise on this subject. He taught at the Bauhaus school of design in Weimar and Dessau, Germany (1922–33).

kanga /káng gə/, **khanga** n. a brightly coloured and decorated piece of cotton cloth that women wrap around the body as a garment, originally and especially in East Africa [Mid-20thC. From Kiswahili.]

Kangaroo

kangaroo /káng gə róo/ n. (plural **-roos**) **1.** MARSUPIAL WITH POWERFUL HINDQUARTERS a large leaping animal with powerful hind legs, short forelegs, and a long tail. It is marsupial and is native to Australia and New Guinea. Family: Macropodidae. **2.** Kangaroo RUGBY AUSTRALIAN RUGBY PLAYER a member of the Australian national Rugby League team ■ npl. **1.** Kangaroos SPORTS AUSTRALIAN RUGBY LEAGUE TEAM the Australian national Rugby league team (*informal*) **2.** kangaroos STOCK EXCH AUSTRALIAN SHARES shares in Australian companies (*slang*) ■ vi. (**-roos, -rooing, -rooed**) MOVE JERKILY to make jerky progress in a car as a result of improper use of the clutch or accelerator (*informal*) [Late 18thC. From Aboriginal.]

--- **WORD KEY: CULTURAL NOTE** ---
Kangaroo, a novel by the English writer D. H. Lawrence (1923). Inspired by the author's 1922 visit to Australia, it tells the story of a settler and his wife who become reluctantly involved with local political organizations, including a right-wing political group and its charismatic leader, Kangaroo.

kangaroo court n. an unofficial or mock court set up spontaneously for the purpose of delivering a judgement arrived at in advance, usually one in which a disloyal cohort's fate is decided

kangaroo grass n. a tall Australian species of grass plant used for fodder. Latin name: *Themeda australis*.

Kangaroo Island island off the coast of South Australia. Population: 4,288 (1996). Area: 4,350 sq. km/1,678 sq. mi.

kangaroo paw n. an Australian plant with downy green-and-red flowers. Genus: *Anigozanthos*.

Kangaroo rat

kangaroo rat n. a small nocturnal jumping rodent found in the deserts of the United States and Mexico. It has a long tail and long hind limbs. Genus: *Dipodomys*.

kangaroo vine n. a climbing vine of Australia with shiny green or mottled leaves. Latin name: *Cissus antarctica*.

kangha n. a comb that baptized Sikhs wear in their hair as a symbol of religious loyalty. ◊ **five Ks** [From Punjabi]

KaNgwane /káaəng gwáan ay/ former homeland in northeastern South Africa, created in 1971 and abolished in 1994

kanji /kánji, káanji/ (plural **-ji** or **-jis**) n. **1.** JAPANESE WRITING SYSTEM a Japanese writing system that uses pictorial characters based largely on Chinese ideograms **2.** WRITTEN CHARACTER any one of the characters used in the kanji writing system [Early 20thC. From Japanese, from *kan* 'Chinese' + *ji* 'letter, character'.]

Kannada /káanədə, kán-/ n. INDIAN LANGUAGE a language spoken in some of the southern states of India. It belongs to the Dravidian family of languages and is spoken by about 44 million people. ■ adj. RELATING TO KANNADA relating to the Kannada language

Kano /káanō, káynō/ capital of Kano State, northern Nigeria. Population: 699,900 (1992).

Kanpur /káan poor/, **Kānpur** city in Uttar Pradesh State, northern India, on the River Ganges. Population: 1,958,282 (1991).

Kans. abbr. Kansas

Kansas

Kansas /kánzəss/ state in the western part of the central United States, bordered by Colorado, Missouri, Nebraska, and Oklahoma. Capital: Topeka. Population: 2,594,840 (1997). Area: 213,110 sq. km/82,282 sq. mi. —**Kansan** n., adj.

Kansas City jazz n. a style of big-band jazz music characterized by blues motifs and a relaxed beat

Kant /kant/, **Immanuel** (1724–1804) German philosopher. He is a seminal figure in Western philosophy whose major work is *Critique of Pure Reason* (1781). —**Kantian** /kánti ən/ adj. —**Kantianism** n.

kanzu /kán zoo/ (*plural* **-zus**) *n.* a long garment resembling a robe, usually white and with long sleeves, worn by men in East Africa [Early 20thC. From Kiswahili.]

kaolin /káy əlin/, **kaoline** *n.* fine white clay used in making porcelain and ceramics and in medicine as an absorbent, e.g. in treatments for diarrhoea [Early 18thC. From Chinese *gāoling*, literally 'high hill', named after the hill where it is found.]

kaolinite /káy əli nīt/ *n.* a white or grey mineral that consists of a silicate of aluminium and is the main constituent of kaolin. Formula: $Al_2Si_2O_5(OH)_4$. — **kaolinitic** /káy əli níttik/ *adj.*

kaon /káy on/ *n.* an unstable elementary particle produced as a result of high-energy particle collision. It occurs in both charged and neutral forms and helps to hold protons and neutrons together inside a nucleus. Symbol **K** [Mid-20thC. From *K-meson*, its earlier name.]

kapellmeister /kə pél mīstər/ *n.* the director of a modern choir or, in former times, the director of the orchestra, choir, or opera in the household of a German prince [Late 19thC. From German, from *Kappelle* 'court orchestra' + *Meister* 'master'.]

kaph /kawf/ *n.* the eleventh letter of the Hebrew alphabet, represented in the English alphabet as 'k' or, at the end of a word, as 'kh'. See table at **alphabet** [Early 19thC. From Hebrew, literally 'the palm of the hand'.]

Kapil Dev /káapil dév/ (*b.* 1959) Indian cricketer. A talented all-rounder, he captained India's World Cup winning side (1983) and holds the bowling world record of 432 Test wickets. Full name **Ramlal Nikhanj Kapil Dev**

Kapiti /káppi ti/ urban area in the southwestern part of the North Island, New Zealand. Population: 30,004 (1996).

kapok /káy pok/ *n.* silky fibre obtained from the seed covering of a tropical tree, with numerous uses in the textile industry, e.g. as a stuffing and padding material [Mid-18thC. From Malay.]

kapok bush *n.* a small Australian deciduous tree with bright yellow flowers. Genus: *Cochlospermum*.

Kaposi's sarcoma /kə pōziz-/ *n.* a cancer of connective tissue that causes purplish-red patches on the skin, most commonly found in equatorial Africa and in AIDS patients [Late 19thC. Named after the Hungarian dermatologist M. K. *Kaposi* (1837–1902), who described it.]

kappa /káppə/ *n.* the tenth letter in the Greek alphabet, represented in the English alphabet as 'k' or 'c'. See table at **alphabet** [From Greek]

kaput /kə pŏot, ka pŏot/ *adj.* broken, incapacitated, or not functioning (*informal*) [Late 19thC. Via German *kaputt* from French *capot*, part of a phrase that refers to losing all tricks in the game of piquet.]

kara /kúrrə/ *n.* a steel bangle that baptized Sikhs wear as a symbol of the unity of God. ◊ **five Ks** [From Punjabi]

karabiner /kárrə bénər/, **carabiner** *n.* a large oval or D-shaped metal ring with a spring clip that allows it to be attached to ropes, pitons, and other items of mountaineering equipment [Mid-20thC. Shortening of German *Karabiner-haken* 'spring-hook'.]

Karachay-Cherkessia /kəru chí chair késsi ə/ autonomous republic in southwestern European Russia, bordering Georgia. Cherkessk is the capital. Population: 434,100 (1994). Area: 14,100 sq. km/5,444 sq. mi.

Karachi /kə ráachi/ seaport and largest city of Pakistan, located in the south of the country. Population: 5,180,562 (1981).

karahi /kurí/ *n.* COOK a round frying pan with two handles used to prepare balti, a dish typical of Pakistan cuisine

Karaism /káirə izəm/ *n.* the beliefs of a Jewish denomination (**Karaites**) founded in the 8th century. Its members accept the Bible as the sole source of religious law and reject the Oral and Rabbinical Law. [Late 19thC. From Hebrew *qērāīm* 'Karaites' to 'to read'.] —**Karaite** *n.*

Herbert von Karajan

Karajan /kárrə yaan/, **Herbert von** (1908–89) Austrian conductor. He was the music director of the Berlin Philharmonic Orchestra (1955–89) and director of the Vienna State Opera (1955–64).

Kara-Kalpak /kə ráa kəl paák/ (*plural* **Kara-Kalpaks** or **Kara-Kalpak**) *n.* **1.** PEOPLES MEMBER OF A PEOPLE OF UZBEKISTAN a member of a people who live mainly in the Kara-Kalpak Autonomous Republic in northwestern Uzbekistan **2.** LANG TURKIC LANGUAGE a Turkic language spoken by the Kara-Kalpak. It belongs to the Altaic family of languages and is spoken by about 300,000 people. [Early 18thC. From Kirghiz, from *kara* 'black' + *kalpak* 'cap'.] —**Kara-Kalpak** *adj.*

Karakoram Range: View of the Sind Valley

Karakoram Range /kárrə káwrəm-/ mountain range in the western Himalayas, south-central Asia. Its highest peak is K2, 8,611 m/28,250 ft.

karakul /kárrək'l/, **caracul** *n.* **1.** SHEEP a hardy sheep of a breed from Central Asia, the lambs of which have a soft curly black coat **2.** FLEECE the furry wool from karakul lambs, used especially for making fur coats [Mid-19thC. From Russian, from, in turn, the name of an oasis in Uzbekistan and two lakes in Tajikistan, perhaps ultimately from Turkish.]

Kara Kul /kárrəkŏol/ two lakes in eastern Tajikistan, high on the Pamir plateau near the border with China. They are Great Kara Kul and Little Kara Kul.

Karamanlis /kárrə mánliss/, **Constantine** (1907–98) Greek statesman. Prime minister (1955–63, 1974–80) and president (1980–85, 1990–95), he supervised Greece's transition from military to civilian rule in the 1970s.

Karamea Bight /kárrəmi ə/ large bay on the northwestern coast of the South Island, New Zealand

karaoke /kaárə ŏki, kárro-/ *n.* a form of entertainment in which amateur singers sing popular songs accompanied by prerecorded music from a machine that may also display the words on a video screen [Late 20thC. From Japanese, from *kara* 'empty' + *oke* an abbreviation of *ōkesutora* 'orchestra'.]

Kara Sea /kaárə-/ sea bordering the northwestern coast of Siberian Russia. It is an arm of the Arctic Ocean. Area: 777,000 sq. km/300,000 sq. mi.

karat *n.* US = carat

karate /kə ráati/ *n.* a traditional Japanese form of unarmed combat, now widely popular as a sport, in which fast blows or kicks are used [Mid-20thC. From Japanese, from *kara* 'empty' + *te* 'hand'.]

Karate

karateka /kə ráati ka/ *n.* sb who practises karate or is an expert in karate [From Japanese, literally 'karate person']

Karbala /kaárbələ/, **Karbalā'** city in central Iraq, on the edge of the Syrian Desert. Population: 184,600 (1985).

Karelian /kə réeli ən/ *n.* **1.** LANG FINNISH DIALECT a dialect of Finnish spoken in the northeastern European region of Karelia that formerly belonged to Finland but is now an autonomous republic. It is spoken by around 120,000 people. **2.** PEOPLES CITIZEN OF THE KARELIAN REPUBLIC a native or citizen of the Karelian Republic —**Karelian** *adj.*

Karen /kə rén/ (*plural* **-rens** or **-ren**) *n.* **1.** PEOPLES MEMBER OF AN ASIAN PEOPLE a member of a people who live mainly in southern and eastern Myanmar, formerly Burma **2.** LANG ASIAN LANGUAGE any of the Tibeto-Burman languages spoken in southern and eastern Myanmar. It belongs to the Sino-Tibetan language family and around two million people speak it. [Mid-18thC. From Burmese *ka-reng* 'wild, unclean man'.] —**Karen** *adj.*

Kariba, Lake /kə réebə/ artificial lake on the border between Zambia and Zimbabwe, southern Africa. It was created by building the Kariba Dam across the River Zambezi. Area: 5,180 sq. km/2,000 sq. mi.

Karl-Marx-Stadt /kaarl maárks shtaat/ former name for **Chemnitz** (1953–90)

Karloff /kaár lof/, **Boris** (1887–1969) British actor. He appeared in numerous US horror films, notably as the monster in the film *Frankenstein* (1931). Real name **William Henry Pratt**

Karlovy Vary /kaár lawvi vaári/ city in the northwestern Czech Republic, situated on the River Ohře, west of Prague. Population: 56,292 (1991).

Karlsruhe /kaárlz roŏ ə/ industrial and university city in Baden-Württemberg State, southwestern Germany. Population: 277,700 (1994).

karma /kaármə/ *n.* **1.** EASTERN RELIG EASTERN PHILOSOPHY the Hindu and Buddhist philosophy according to which the quality of people's current and future lives is determined by their behaviour in this and in previous lives **2.** ATMOSPHERE the atmosphere radiated by a place, situation, person, or object (*informal*) **3.** DESTINY destiny or fate in general [Early 19thC. From Sanskrit *karman* 'fate, action'.] —**karmic** *adj.*

Karnak /kaár nak/ village in eastern Egypt, on the River Nile, occupying part of the ancient city of Thebes

Karnataka /kər náatəkə/, **Karnātaka** state in southern India. Capital: Bangalore. Population: 48,150,000 (1994). Area: 191,791 sq. km/74,051 sq. mi. Former name **Mysore**

Karnatak music /kər náatək-/, **Karnatic music** /kər náatik-/ *n.* the classical music of southern India, which often accompanies dance

karoo /kə rŏo/ (*plural* **-roos**) *n.* an arid plateau in southern Africa

Karoo /kə rŏo/, **Karroo** semidesert plateau regions in Western Cape Province, South Africa. Area: 259,000 sq. km/100,000 sq. mi.

kaross /kə róss/ *n.* a blanket made of animal skins, used in southern Africa as either a cloak or a mattress [Mid-18thC. From Afrikaans *karos*, perhaps from Nama.]

Karratha /kə raáthə/ town on the western coast of Western Australia, an industrial centre. Population: 10,057 (1996).

karsey n. = **karzy**

karst /kaarst/ n. a limestone landscape, characterized by caves, fissures, and underground streams [Late 19thC. From German *der Karst*.] —**karstic** adj.

Karttika /kaártikə/ n. in the Hindu calendar, the eighth month of the year, made up of 29 or 30 days and occurring about the same time as October to November

Karumba /kərúmbə/ fishing port on the Gulf of Carpentaria in northwestern Queensland, Australia. Population: 1,043 (1996).

karyo- prefix. cell nucleus ○ *karyoplasm* [Via modern Latin from Greek *karuon* 'nut, kernel']

karyogamy /kárri óggəmi/ n. the fusion of cell nuclei that occurs during fertilization [Late 19thC. Coined from KARY(O)- + -GAMY.] —**karyogamic** /kárri ə gámmik/ adj.

karyogram /kárri ə gram/ n. a photograph or diagram of the chromosomes of a cell in sequence [Mid-20thC. Coined from KARY(O)- + -GRAM.]

karyokinesis /kárri ōki neéssiss, -kī-/ n. BIOL = **mitosis** [Late 19thC] —**karyokinetic** adj.

karyology /kárri ólləji/ n. the study of cell nuclei, especially with reference to chromosomes [Late 19thC] —**karyologic** /kárri ə lójjik/ adj. —**karyological** /-lójjik'l/ adj. —**karyologist** /kárri ólləjist/ n.

karyolymph /kárri ō limf/ n. BIOL = **nuclear sap** [Late 19thC]

karyoplasm /kárri ō plazəm/ n. = **nucleoplasm** [Late 19thC] —**karyoplasmic** /kárri ō plázmik/ adj.

karyosome /kárri ō sōm/ n. a thickened mass of chromatin in a cell nucleus [Late 19thC]

karyotype /kárri ō tīp/ n. 1. CHARACTERISTICS OF CELL CHROMOSOMES the appearance and characteristics of the chromosomes of a cell, especially size, number, and form 2. CELL BIOL PHOTOMICROGRAPH OF CELL CHROMOSOMES a photomicrograph in which a cell's chromosomes are arranged according to size and classification ■ vt. (-types, -typing, -typed) DETERMINE CELL'S KARYOTYPE to determine the karyotype of a cell [Early 20thC] —**karyotypic** /kárri ō típpik/ adj. —**karyotypical** /-típpik'l/ adj. —**karyotypically** adv.

karzy /kaárzi/, **karsey**, **kazi** (plural **-zis**) n. a toilet (slang)

Kasavubu /kássə voó boo/, **Joseph** (1913?–69) Congolese statesman. President of Congo following independence from Belgium (1960), he was overthrown in a coup by Mobutu (1965).

kasbah /káz baa/, **casbah** n. 1. OLDER DISTRICT the older part of a city or town in North Africa or the Middle East, which is often where the markets are situated 2. N AFRICAN FORTRESS a fortress or palace in any of various North African cities or towns

kasha /káshə/ n. a dish of cooked buckwheat resembling porridge, originally from Eastern Europe [Early 19thC. From Russian.]

Kashmir /kash meér/ disputed territory in the northern part of the Indian subcontinent. ◆ Jammu and Kashmir, Kashmir [Azad]

Kashmir, Azad /-aá zad/ section of the disputed territory of Kashmir in the northern part of the Indian subcontinent that has been under Pakistani control since 1972 [*Azad* meaning 'free']

Kashmiri /kash meéri/ n. 1. PEOPLES SB FROM KASHMIR sb who was born in or who is a citizen of Kashmir in Central Asia 2. LANG DARDIC LANGUAGE the official state language of Kashmir, also spoken in neighbouring areas. It is a Dardic language that belongs to the Indic group of languages and is spoken by about five million people. ■ adj. OF KASHMIR relating to Kashmir, its people, language, or culture

kashruth /káshrəth, kash roót/, **kashrut** n. 1. JEWISH LAWS the body of Jewish laws that relate to the preparation and fitness of foods and to items such as textiles and ritual scrolls to be used by Jewish people 2. FITNESS FOR USE BY JEWISH PEOPLE the fitness of an item for use by Jewish people, as determined by reference to kashruth [Early 20thC. From Hebrew 'fitness' especially 'ritual fitness'.]

Kaskaskia /kəss káski ə/ (plural **-kaskias** or **-kaskia**), **Kaskaskias** n. a member of a Native N American people, one of the six that form the Illinois Confederacy —**Kaskaskias** adj.

Kasparov /káspə rof/, **Garry** (b. 1963) Armenian chess player. He became world champion following his defeat of Anatoly Karpov in 1985. Full name **Garry Kimovich Kasparov**. Born **Garri Weinstein**

Kassala /kə saálə/, **Kassalā** city in northeastern Sudan. Population: 98,751 (1983).

Kassel /káss'l/, **Cassel** city in west-central Germany. Population: 201,900 (1994).

kata /káttə/ n. a sequence of movements in some martial arts such as karate, used either for training or to demonstrate technique [Mid-20thC. From Japanese, literally 'model, pattern'.]

katabasis /kə tábbəssiss/ (plural **-bases** /-seez/) n. a retreat, particularly of a military kind (literary) [Mid-19thC. From Greek, from *kata* 'down' + *basis* 'going'.]

katabatic /káttə báttik/ adj. used to describe a wind that moves down a slope, produced by the cooling of air at higher altitudes [Late 19thC. From Greek *katabatikos*, from *katabainein* 'to go down'.]

katabolism n. = **catabolism**

Katahdin, Mount /kə taá dən/ mountain in northern Maine, in Baxter State Park. The highest of its several summits is Baxter Peak, 1,605 m/5,267 ft.

katakana /káttə kaánə/ n. a syllabic form of writing in Japanese that is used principally to transliterate non-Japanese words. ◊ **kana, hiragana** [Early 18thC. From Japanese, from *kata* 'side' + KANA.]

Kathak /kúttək/ n. a form of classical dancing from northern India, used to tell a story [Mid-20thC. From Sanskrit *kathaka* 'storyteller', from *kathā* 'story']

Kathakali /kaáthə kaáli/ n. a form of drama from southern India that interprets stories from Hindu classical literature by combining dance and mime [Early 20thC. From Malayalam *kathakali*, from Sanskrit *kathā* 'story' + Malayalam *kali* 'play'.]

Katharevusa /káthə révvoóssə/ n. a form of modern Greek, used in literature as opposed to everyday speech and writing, that employs some of the features of classical Greek. ◊ **Demotic** [Early 20thC. From Greek *kathareuousa*, ultimately from Greek *katharos* 'pure'.]

Katherine /káthrən/ town in north-central Northern Territory, Australia, a centre of beef production, fruit-growing, and tourism. Population: 7,979 (1996).

Katherine Gorge series of sandstone gorges cut by the River Katherine in the Northern Territory of Australia, northeast of Katherine

Kathmandu = **Katmandu**

Katmai, Mount /kát mī-/ volcano in Katmai National Park and Preserve, Alaska. Height: 2,047 m/6,715 ft.

Katmai National Park and Preserve national park on the Alaska Peninsula, southwestern Alaska. Area: 1,656,475 hectares/4,093,240 acres.

Katmandu /kát man doó/, **Kathmandu** capital city of Nepal, located in the central part of the country. It is situated about 89 km/55 mi. from the border with India. Population: 419,073 (1991).

Katoomba /kə toómbə/ town in southeastern New South Wales, Australia. Population: 17,700 (with Wentworth Falls) (1996).

Katsina /kátsinə/ city in northern Nigeria, the capital of Katsina State. Population: 186,900 (1992).

Kattegat /káttə gat/ strait between the southwestern coast of Sweden and the eastern coast of the Jutland peninsula, Denmark. Length: 225 km/140 mi.

katydid /káyti did/ n. a large green grasshopper that is native to North America and has very long antennae. The males make a shrill sound. Genus: *Microcentrum*. [Late 18thC. An imitation of the sound produced by the male when it rubs its front wings together.]

Katyn Forest /kə teén/ forest in western European Russia, near Smolensk, where the mass grave of thousands of Polish army officers murdered by Soviet security services was discovered in 1943

Katz /kats/, **Sir Bernard** (b. 1911) German-born British biophysicist. He was the joint winner of the Nobel

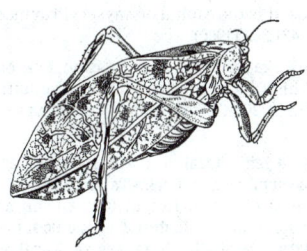

Katydid

Prize for physiology or medicine (1970) for his work on neurotransmitters.

Kauai /kaa wí/ fourth largest island in Hawaii, the northernmost of the main islands. Area: 1,431 sq. km/552 sq. mi.

kaumatua /kow maá too ə/ n. a Maori elder or leader [From Maori *kaumātua* 'adult, elder man or woman']

Kaunas /kównəss/ industrial city in central Lithuania, situated about 97 km/60 mi. west of Vilnius. Population: 415,300 (1995).

Kaunda /kaa oóndə/, **Kenneth** (b. 1924) Zambian statesman. He was president of Zambia from independence in 1964 until 1991. Full name **Kenneth David Kaunda**

kauri /kówri/ n. 1. TREES NEW ZEALAND TREE a large evergreen tree, native to New Zealand, that has oval leaves and is valued for its strong timber. Latin name: *Agathis australis*. 2. INDUST TIMBER the light-coloured wood from the kauri tree 3. = **kauri gum** [Early 19thC. From Maori.]

kauri gum, **kauri resin** n. the brittle resin of the kauri tree that is usually found in fossilized form and is used mainly in varnishes

kava /kaávə/ n. 1. PLANTS POLYNESIAN SHRUB a Polynesian shrub that has clusters of small flowers and belongs to the pepper family. Latin name: *Piper methysticum*. 2. BEVERAGES DRINK a narcotic drink made from the roots of the kava plant [Late 18thC. From Tongan, literally 'bitter'.]

Kaw /kaw/ n. (plural **Kaw** or **Kaws** /kaws/), adj. PEOPLES, LANG = **Kansa**

Kay /kay/, **John** (1704–64) British inventor. He invented the flying shuttle (patented in 1733), which contributed greatly to the mechanization of textile manufacture.

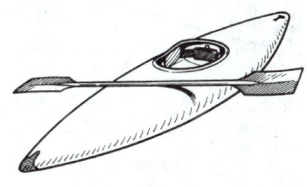

Kayak

kayak /kí ak/, **kaiak** n. 1. SPORTS CANOE a lightweight fibreglass canoe used for leisure and in competitive sport 2. ANIMAL-SKIN BOAT a traditional Inuit boat for one or two people using double-bladed paddles. It is narrow and pointed and consists of a light frame covered with skins. ■ vti. (-aks, -aking, -aked) TRAVEL BY KAYAK to travel or race in a kayak [Mid-18thC. From Inuit *qayaq*.] —**kayaker** n.

kayo /káy ó/ n. (plural **-os**) KNOCKOUT a knockout, especially in boxing ■ vt. (-os, -oing, -oed) KNOCK SB OUT to knock sb out, especially in boxing (slang) [Early 20thC. The pronunciation of KO, a shortening of KNOCKOUT.]

Kayseri /kíssəri/ city in central Turkey, near Mount Argaeus. It is the capital of Kayseri Province. Population: 421,362 (1990).

kazachok /ka'zə chók/ *n.* a Russian folk dance in which high kicks are made from a squatting position [Early 20thC. From Russian, a diminutive of *kazak* 'Cossack'.]

Kazakh /kə zák/, **Kazak** *n.* **1.** PEOPLES MEMBER OF AN ASIAN PEOPLE a member of a Turko-Tatar people of Central Asia, most of whom live in Kazakhstan and who are predominantly Muslim **2.** LANG OFFICIAL LANGUAGE OF KAZAKHSTAN the official language of Kazakhstan in Central Asia, also spoken in parts of Mongolia, China, and Afghanistan. It belongs to the Turkic branch of languages and is spoken by about eight million people. [Mid-19thC. From Russian, from Kazakh *kazak*.] —**Kazakh** *adj.*

Kazakhstan

Kazakhstan /kázzak staʼa/ republic in Central Asia, bounded by Russia, China, Kyrgyzstan, Uzbekistan, Turkmenistan, and the Caspian Sea. Language: Kazakh. Currency: tenge. Capital: Astana. Population: 16,881,793 (1997). Area: 2,717,300 sq. km/ 1,049,155 sq. mi. Official name **Republic of Kazakhstan**

Kazantzakis /kaazaantzákeez/, **Nikos** (1883–1957) Greek writer. His novels include *Zorba the Greek* (1943) and *The Last Temptation of Christ* (1951).

kazatsky /kə zátski/ (*plural* **-skies**), **kazatske** *n.* DANCE = **kazachok**

Kazbek /kaaz bék/ peak on the border of Russia and Georgia in the Caucasus Mountains. Height: 5,037 m/16,526 ft.

kazi *n.* = **karzy**

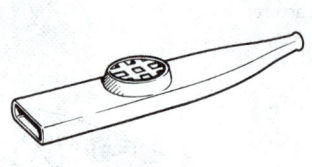

Kazoo

kazoo /kə zoó/ (*plural* **-zoos**) *n.* a toy instrument that makes a buzzing sound, consisting of a tube with a mouthpiece and a hole covered by a thin diaphragm [Late 19thC. An imitation of the sound produced by the instrument.]

KB *abbr.* **1.** COMPUT kilobyte **2.** King's Bench **3.** CHESS king's bishop **4.** Knight Bachelor

KBE *abbr.* Knight (Commander of the Order) of the British Empire

KBP *abbr.* CHESS king's bishop's pawn

kbyte *n., abbr.* COMPUT kilobyte

kc *abbr.* PHYS kilocycle

KC *abbr.* **1.** Kennel Club **2.** King's Counsel **3.** Knight of Columbus

kcal /káy kal/ *abbr.* kilocalorie

KCB *abbr.* Knight Commander of the (Order of the) Bath

KCMG *abbr.* Knight Commander of the Order of St Michael and St George

KCVO *abbr.* Knight Commander of the Royal Victorian Order

kea /keè ə/ *n.* a large New Zealand parrot with brownish-green feathers that lives in mountainous regions and feeds mainly on insects. Latin name: *Nestor notabilis*. [Mid-19thC. From Maori.]

Kean /keen/, **Edmund** (1787–1833) British actor. He was noted for his tragic Shakespearian roles, principally Richard III, Hamlet, Othello, Iago, and Macbeth.

Keating /keéting/, **Paul** (*b.* 1944) Australian statesman. He was Labor prime minister of Australia (1991–96). Full name **Paul John Keating**

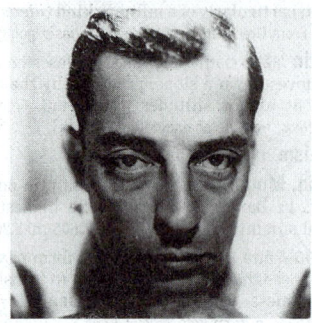

Buster Keaton

Keaton /keét'n/, **Buster** (1895–1966) US silent film comedian. He was a deadpan acrobatic clown in many classic silent films such as *The General* (1927). Real name **Joseph Francis Keaton**

Keats /keets/, **John** (1795–1821) English poet. His lyrical intensity made him one of the most influential of the romantic poets. His great odes were collected in *Lamia, Isabella, The Eve of St Agnes, and Other Poems* (1820). —**Keatsian** /keétsee ən/ *adj.*

kebab /ki báb/, **kabob** /kə baab/ *n.* a selection of small pieces of tender food, e.g. poultry, meat, fish, or seafood, threaded onto a stick and grilled [Late 17thC. From Arabic *kabāb*.]

Keble /keéb'l/, **John** (1792–1866) British churchman and poet. He helped to launch the Oxford Movement, and was also known for his book of poems, *The Christian Year* (1827). Keble College, Oxford, was named in his memory.

Kedah /kédda/ state in northwestern Malaysia, on the Malay Peninsula. Capital: Alur Setar. Area: 9,479 sq. km/3,660 sq. mi.

kedge /kej/ *vti.* (**kedges, kedging, kedged**) MOVE A VESSEL to move a vessel by pulling on a rope or cable attached to a light anchor, or to move in this way ■ *n.* **kedge, kedge anchor** LIGHT ANCHOR a light anchor, especially one that is lodged some distance from a vessel so that the vessel can be pulled towards it [15thC. Origin uncertain: perhaps from CADGE in an earlier sense 'to tie or bind'.]

kedgeree /kéjjə ree/ *n.* **1.** DISH OF RICE, FISH, AND EGGS a dish of British origin based on an Indian dish, consisting of spiced rice with flaked smoked fish and hard-boiled eggs **2.** INDIAN DISH a spicy dish of Indian origin, made from lentils, rice, and sometimes fish [Mid-17thC. From Hindi *khicṛī*.]

keech /keech/ *n.* Scotland excrement (*informal*) [Late 16thC. Origin unknown.]

keek /keek/ *vi.* (**keeks, keeking, keeked**) Scotland PEEP to look at sth, usually in a furtive way or through a narrow opening ■ *n.* Scotland FURTIVE LOOK a brief, often furtive look at sth [14thC. Origin uncertain: perhaps from Middle Dutch or Low German *kīken* 'to peep'.]

keel /keel/ *n.* **1.** NAUT SHIP'S STRUCTURAL ELEMENT the main structural element of a ship, stretching along the centre line of its bottom from the bow to the stern. It may be made of wood or steel and sometimes extends further downwards into the water to provide extra stability. **2.** AIR AIRCRAFT'S STRUCTURAL ELEMENT any structure that looks or acts like a ship's

---

keel, such as the main structural element of an aircraft's fuselage **3.** BIOL RIDGELIKE PART a ridge-shaped part of an organism **4.** NAUT SHIP a ship (*literary*) ■ *vti.* (**keels, keeling, keeled**) NAUT CAPSIZE to capsize a vessel, or to capsize [14thC. From Old Norse *kjölr*.] ◇ **on an even keel** in a stable, steady condition

keel over *v.* **1.** *vi.* COLLAPSE to collapse or fall over, often through exhaustion or illness (*informal*) **2.** *vti.* NAUT = **keel**

keelage /keélij/ *n.* a docking fee for merchant ships, charged by a port

keelboat /keél bōt/ *n.* a covered river boat with a keel and shallow draught but no sail, propelled by rowing, poling, or towing, and used for transporting freight [Late 17thC. Formed from KEEL.]

keelhaul /keél hawl/ (**-hauls, -hauling, -hauled**) *vt.* **1.** DRAG SB UNDER A BOAT to drag sb on a rope from one side of a vessel to the other under the keel as a form of punishment **2.** REBUKE SB to reprimand sb severely (*informal*) [Mid-17thC. From Dutch *kielhalen*.]

keelie /keéli/ *n.* Scotland a rough lower-class man or boy from a town or city, especially a Glaswegian [From Gaelic *gille* (source of English *gillie*). Rare before the 19thC.]

keelson /kéllss'n, keélss'n/, **kelson** /kélss'n/ *n.* a metal or wooden beam attached to the upper side of a boat's keel to reinforce it [13thC. Origin uncertain: probably from Old Norse *kjölsvīn* or from Low German *kielsvīn*.]

keen[1] /keen/ *adj.* **1.** ENTHUSIASTIC very eager and willing ○ *not very keen on the idea* **2.** ATTRACTED attracted to or fond of sb or sth ○ *He's not very keen on tomatoes.* **3.** ACUTE quick to understand things ○ *a keen sense of humour* **4.** SENSITIVE finely tuned and able to sense minor differences, distinctions, or details ○ *a keen sense of smell* **5.** INTENSE intense and lively ○ *keen competition* **6.** SHARP having a sharp cutting edge (*literary*) ○ *a keen razor* **7.** BITING extremely cold and penetrating ○ *a keen wind* **8.** COMM COMPETITIVELY LOW low and therefore competitive ○ *keen prices* **9.** US VERY GOOD fine or very good (*dated slang*) ○ *a keen new bike* [Old English *cēne* 'brave, clever'. Ultimately from a prehistoric Germanic word.] —**keenly** *adv.* —**keenness** *n.*

keen[2] /keen/ *vi.* (**keens, keening, keened**) HOWL IN GRIEF to cry out or wail in grief, especially while lamenting the dead ■ *n.* LAMENT a lamentation for a dead person (*literary*) [Early 19thC. From Irish *caoinim* 'I wail'.] —**keener** *n.*

keep /keep/ *v.* (**keeps, keeping, kept** /kept/) **1.** *vti.* POSSESS to hold or maintain sth in your possession ○ *The sample is yours to keep.* **2.** *vt.* MAINTAIN THE CONDITION OF STH to maintain sth or sb in a particular place or condition ○ *Keep your arm up.* **3.** *vt.* STORE STH to store sth in a place when it is not in use ○ *He keeps the keys in a drawer.* **4.** *vti.* CONTINUE to cause sb or sth to continue in a particular way or activity, or to continue in a particular way ○ *It keeps working even in a power failure.* **5.** *vt.* SAFEGUARD INFORMATION to refrain from telling a secret or other information ○ *keep a secret* **6.** *vt.* SAVE STH to save sth for later use or withhold sth from use ○ *Keep some in reserve.* **7.** *vt.* BE TRUE TO STH to fulfil a promise or other verbal commitment ○ *keep your word* **8.** *vt.* FULFIL A RELIGIOUS DUTY to observe a religious obligation ○ *keep kosher* ○ *keep the Sabbath* **9.** *vt.* MAINTAIN A RECORD to create or maintain sth as a written record ○ *keep a diary* **10.** *vi.* STAY to remain in a particular condition ○ *The stove will keep warm for a while after the fire goes out.* **11.** *vi.* MAINTAIN A COURSE to follow a particular course or direction ○ *Keep straight ahead until the roundabout.* **12.** *vi.* NOT SPOIL to remain fresh or in a usable condition ○ *That fish won't keep in this hot weather.* **13.** *vi.* CONTINUE to do sth repeatedly or continue to do sth ○ *Keep smiling!* **14.** *vi.* NOT REQUIRE ATTENTION to be able to be postponed ○ *I think the dusting will keep till tomorrow.* **15.** *vi.* BE IN PARTICULAR CONDITION to be or remain in a particular condition, especially in terms of health ○ *How are you keeping?* **16.** *vt.* HAVE STH FOR SALE to have sth in stock in order to sell it ○ *Do you keep chainsaw blades?* **17.** *vt.* DETAIN SB to make sb wait or prevent sb from going ○ *Could I keep you for a moment?* **18.** *vt.* LOOK AFTER SB OR STH to take care of a person or animal, providing what is required to live ○ *We've never kept pets.* **19.** *vt.* HAVE AS LIVESTOCK to breed an animal for profit ○ *keep* *cattle* **20.** *vt.* **EMPLOY SB** to employ sb, especially in a household ○ *keep servants* **21.** *vt.* **RUN A BUSINESS OR HOUSEHOLD** to maintain a business, house, or other establishment ○ *He keeps house for the General.* **22.** *vt.* **SUPPORT FINANCIALLY** to provide financially for a spouse or lover (*old*) ■ *n.* **1. MAINTENANCE** food and lodging, or whatever sb needs to live ○ *work for your keep* **2. CASTLE PART** a stronghold, or the innermost fortified part of a castle [Old English *cēpan* 'to take, observe', of unknown origin] ◇ **for keeps** permanently or forever (*informal*) ◇ **keep it up** to continue to do sth ◇ **keep sth to yourself** to refrain from revealing ◇ **keep yourself to yourself** to avoid mixing or communicating with other people

keep at *vt.* **1. CONTINUE DOING STH** to persevere with sth, especially sth difficult or strenuous **2. PESTER SB** to persist in asking sb to do sth (*informal*) ○ *They kept at me to do more and more work in less and less time.*

keep away *v.* **1.** *vt.* **KEEP SB OR STH DISTANT** to prevent sb or sth from going near sb or sth **2.** *vi.* **NOT APPROACH** to avoid going near sth or sb

keep back *vt.* **1. NOT TELL STH** to refrain from telling or revealing sth **2. WITHHOLD STH FOR LATER USE** to hold sth in reserve for later use or for another purpose **3. RESTRAIN STH** to restrain or confine sth to a limit

keep down *v.* **1.** *vt.* **OPPRESS SB OR STH** to maintain sb or sth in an inferior position or in a state of oppression **2.** *vt.* **MAINTAIN STH AT A LOW LEVEL** to maintain sth at a low level, position, or number ○ *Keep the costs down.* **3.** *vi.* **STAY LOW** to stay in a place or position where you cannot be seen **4.** *vt.* **NOT VOMIT STH** to hold food or drink in your stomach without vomiting ○ *He hasn't been able to keep anything down since the operation.*

keep from *vt.* **1. HIDE STH FROM SB** to refrain from disclosing sth to sb **2. RESTRAIN SB** to prevent sb from doing sth **3. SAFEGUARD SB** to protect sb from sth ○ *kept us from harm*

keep in *vt.* **1. REPRESS A FEELING** to repress sth that you feel ○ *keeps in her anger* **2. NOT LET SB LEAVE** to make sb stay in a place, e.g. a schoolchild after class, or a patient in hospital **3. PROVIDE SB WITH STH** to provide sb with a regular supply of sth ○ *money to keep us in petrol*

keep in with *vt.* to maintain a good relationship with sb, often because this might be advantageous

keep off *v.* **1.** *vt.* **PREVENT CONTACT** to prevent sth or sb from having direct contact with sth or sb else **2.** *vti.* **NOT TOUCH** to refrain from direct contact with sth or sb ○ *Keep off the grass!* **3.** *vti.* **NOT CONSUME** to prevent sb from consuming sth or to refrain from consuming sth ○ *I was told to keep off caffeine.* **4.** *vti.* **NOT TALK ABOUT** to prevent sb from discussing sth or to refrain from discussing sth ○ *We kept off the topic of money.* **5.** *vi.* **NOT BEGIN** to fail to start or appear ○ *Let's hope the rain keeps off until the games are over.*

keep on *v.* **1.** *vi.* **CONTINUE** to continue ○ *They just kept on, even after we told them to stop.* **2.** *vt.* **NOT TAKE STH OFF** to continue wearing sth **3.** *vt.* **NOT DISMISS SB** to continue to employ sb **4.** *vi.* **PERSIST IN TALKING ABOUT STH** to talk repetitively or continuously about one thing in a way that makes others bored or annoyed (*informal*)

keep on at *vt.* to pester or nag sb about sth (*informal*)

keep out *vti.* to prevent sb from entering or to refrain from entering a place

keep out of *vti.* **1. PREVENT EXPOSURE** to prevent sb or sth from exposure to sth, or to avoid exposure to sth ○ *keep it out of the rain* **2. AVOID INVOLVEMENT** to prevent sb's involvement in sth, or to avoid involvement in sth ○ *Keep out of her way.*

keep to *vt.* to adhere without deviation to a plan, course, or subject

keep up *v.* **1.** *vt.* **MAINTAIN THE PRESENT LEVEL OF** to maintain sth at its present level, not letting it fall or subside ○ *Keep up the good work.* **2.** *vi.* **STAY EVEN WITH** to go as fast or make the same progress as sb else **3.** *vt.* **MAINTAIN STH IN GOOD CONDITION** to make sure that sth stays in good condition ○ *has a beautiful home but doesn't really keep it up* **4.** *vt.* **DELAY SB'S SLEEP OR BEDTIME** to prevent sb from sleeping or going to bed at night ○ *The music from the party kept us up till dawn.*

keep up with *vt.* **1. REMAIN INFORMED ABOUT STH** to remain abreast of sth that undergoes continuous change or progress **2. STAY IN CONTACT WITH** to stay in contact with sb, especially by letter ○ *I still keep up with a few friends from school.* ◇ **keep up with the Joneses** to maintain a position of equal social status with your neighbours, especially in terms of possessions

keeper /keépər/ *n.* **1. MUSEUM GUARDIAN** sb who is in charge of a museum, gallery, or exhibition **2. WARDEN** sb whose job is to look after or protect animals **3. CARETAKER** sb in charge of a building (*usually used in combination*) ○ *a lighthouse keeper* **4.** CRIMINOL **PRISON GUARD** sb who is responsible for guarding other people, especially in a prison **5. SB KEEPING STH** sb who keeps or maintains sth ○ *a good record keeper* **6. HOLDING DEVICE** a device , such as a clip used to keep sth in place **7.** SPORTS **GOALKEEPER** a goalkeeper or wicketkeeper (*informal*) **8.** PHYS **IRON BAR PLACED ACROSS A MAGNET'S POLES** an iron or steel bar placed across the poles of a permanent horseshoe magnet when it is not in use, to close the magnetic circuit and prevent demagnetization **9.** AMERICAN FOOTBALL **PLAY IN AMERICAN FOOTBALL** in American football, a play in which the quarterback runs towards the goal with the ball —**keepership** *n.*

keeper ring *n.* = **guard ring**

keep fit *n.* a programme of physical exercises designed to keep the body in good condition

keeping /keéping/ *n.* **1. LOOKING AFTER** the act of looking after or caring for sb or sth **2. CHARGE** sb's charge, custody, or possession ○ *It's in the bank's keeping.* ◇ **in keeping with** consistent with or suitable for sth ◇ **out of keeping with** not consistent with or suitable for sth

keepnet /keép net/ *n.* a long cylindrical net with wire hoops attached at regular intervals, placed in water and used to hold fish that have been caught while keeping them alive

keepsake /keép sayk/ *n.* a small item or gift kept because it evokes memories of sb or sth [Late 18thC. The underlying meaning is of sth to be kept 'for the sake of' the giver.]

keeshond /káyss hond/ (*plural* **-honds** *or* **-honden** /-hondən/) *n.* a dog with a dense shaggy blackish-grey coat and a tightly curled tail, belonging to a breed developed in the Netherlands [Early 20thC. From Dutch, literally 'Kees dog', from *Kees* (a pet form of the name *Cornelis* 'Cornelius') + *hond* 'dog'.]

keester *n.* = **keister**

kef *n.* DRUGS = **kif**

keffiyeh /ka feéyə/ *n.* a cotton headdress fastened by a band and worn by Arab men. US term **kaffiyeh**

Keflavik /kéffləvik/ town in southwestern Iceland, situated about 35 km/22 mi. southwest of Reykjavik. Population: 7,605 (1995).

keg /keg/ *n.* **1. SMALL BARREL** a small barrel used for storing liquids **2. CONTENTS OF A KEG** the amount that a keg can hold **3. BEER BARREL** an aluminium barrel that is used for storing and transporting beer [Early 17thC. Alteration of *cag* from, ultimately, Old Norse *kaggi*.]

keg beer *n.* beer that is stored in and served from a pressurized aluminium barrel

keister /keéstər, kīstər/, **keester** /keéstər/ *n.* *US* the buttocks (*humorous slang*) [Late 19thC. Origin unknown.]

Keitel /kīt'l/, **Wilhelm** (1882–1946) German field marshal. Hitler's chief military adviser during World War II, he was executed for war crimes in 1946.

Kejimkujik National Park /kejim ko͞ojik-/ national park and wildlife preserve in southern Nova Scotia, Canada, established in 1974. Area: 403 sq. km/156 sq. mi.

Kekulé formula /kékə lay-/ *n.* the representation of a benzene molecule as a hexagonal ring with alternating single and double bonds linking six carbon atoms, each linked to one hydrogen atom at the vertices [Mid-20thC. Named after the German physicist Friedrich August *Kekulé* (1829–96), who devised it.]

Kelly /kélli/, **Ned** (1855–80) Australian bushranger. Pursued by the police for two years, he was captured and hanged in 1880. He subsequently became a folk hero.

keloid /keé loyd/ *n.* an area of raised pink or red fibrous scar tissue at the edges of a wound or incision [Mid-19thC. From French *chéloïde*, *kéloïde*, from Greek *khēlē* 'crab claw'.] —**keloidal** /kee lóyd'l/ *adj.*

kelp /kelp/ *n.* **1. BROWN SEAWEED** brown seaweed with thick broad fronds. Order: Laminariales. **2. SEAWEED ASH** the ash from kelp or other seaweeds, used as a source of potash and iodine [14thC. Origin unknown.]

kelpie[1] /kélpi/, **kelpy** (*plural* **-pies**) *n.* in Scottish folklore, a malicious water spirit that takes the form of a horse and lures people to death by drowning [Late 17thC. Origin uncertain: perhaps from Gaelic *cailpeach* 'colt, bullock'.]

kelpie[2] /kélpi/ *n.* a smooth-haired dog of an Australian breed of sheepdog [Early 20thC. Named after *King's Kelpie*, the female dog that founded the breed.]

kelson *n.* NAUT = **keelson**

kelt /kelt/ *n.* a salmon that has returned to the river of its birth and recently spawned. In most species, the kelts do not survive, but Atlantic salmon can return to the ocean to spawn another season. [14thC. Origin unknown.]

Kelt *n., adj.* = **Celt** —**Keltic** *adj.*

kelvin /kélvin/ *n.* **UNIT OF ABSOLUTE TEMPERATURE** the SI unit of absolute temperature, equal to 1/273.16 of the absolute temperature of the triple point of water, equivalent to one degree Celsius. A temperature in kelvin may be converted to Celsius by subtracting 273.16. Symbol **K** ■ *adj.* **ON THE KELVIN SCALE** relating to or measured on the Kelvin scale [Early 20thC. Named after the British physicist William Thomson, first Baron KELVIN.]

Kelvin /kélvin/, **William Thomson, 1st Baron** (1824–1907) British physicist. He did pioneering work in thermodynamics and electricity and devised the absolute temperature scale. His work helped develop the law of the conservation of energy. Full name **William Thomson, 1st Baron Kelvin of Largs**

Kelvin scale *n.* a temperature scale on which zero is the lowest possible temperature and the triple point of water is defined as 273.16K. It is based on heat transfer between two sections of a reversible heat engine. [Late 19thC. Named after William Thomson, first Baron KELVIN.]

Kelvinside /kélvin sīd/ *n.* *Scotland* an old-fashioned anglicized accent of Scottish English, widely perceived as affected [Named after *Kelvinside*, an area in Glasgow where the accent is common]

kemp /kemp/ *n.* a short coarse hair or fibre [14thC. From Old Norse *kampr* 'beard, whisker'.] —**kempy** *adj.*

Kempe /kemp/, **Margery** (1373?–1440?) English mystic. She dictated *The Book of Margery Kempe*, an account of her visions and pilgrimages.

Kempe, Rudolf (1910–76) German conductor. He is known for his interpretations of Richard Strauss and Wagner. He conducted the Royal Philharmonic Orchestra (1961–75).

Kempsey /kémpsi/ town in northeastern New South Wales, Australia, a centre of agriculture, timber production, and light industry. Population: 8,630 (1996).

kempt /kempt/ *adj.* tidy and well looked after (*archaic*) [Old English *cemd*, from the past participle of *cemban* 'to comb'. Ultimately from a prehistoric Germanic word that is also the ancestor of English *comb*.]

ken /ken/ *n.* **KNOWLEDGE** sb's knowledge or understanding ○ *It's beyond my ken.* ■ *vti.* (**kens, kenning, kenned** *or* **kent** /kent/, **kenned** *or* **kent**) *Scotland* **KNOW** to know sb or sth [Old English *cennan* 'to make known'. Ultimately from an Indo-European word that is also the ancestor of English *can* and *know*.]

Ken. *abbr.* Kentucky

Kendal /kéndəl/ market town in the Lake District, Cumbria, northwestern England. Population: 23,710 (1991).

Kendal green /kénd'l-/ *n.* **GREEN WOOLLEN CLOTH** a coarse thick green woollen cloth similar to tweed and formerly worn by foresters ■ *adj.* **LIGHT GREYISH GREEN** of a light greyish-green colour [14thC. Named after the town of KENDAL, where the cloth was made.]

Kendo

Popperfoto

kendo /kéndō/ *n.* a Japanese martial art in which people fence using bamboo sticks instead of swords [Early 20thC. From Japanese, literally 'way of the sword'.]

Kendrew /kén droo/, **Sir John** (1917–97) British molecular biologist. He won a joint Nobel Prize in chemistry (1962) for his work in determining the structure of proteins. Full name **Sir John Cowdery Kendrew**

Keneally /kə nálli/, **Thomas** (*b.* 1935) Australian novelist. His book *Schindler's Ark* (1982) won the Booker Prize and was made into a film, *Schindler's List* (1994), by Stephen Spielberg. Full name **Thomas Michael Keneally**

Kenilworth /kénnəl wurth/ market town in Warwickshire, central England. Its ruined castle dates from the early 12th century. Population: 25,461 (1991).

Kennebec /kénnəbék/ river in western Maine that flows south from Moosehead Lake to the Atlantic Ocean. Length: 264 km/164 mi.

Kennedy, Cape /kénnədi/ ♦ **Cape Canaveral**

Kennedy, Mount mountain in the St Elias Range in southwestern Yukon Territory, Canada. Height: 4,238 m/13,905 ft.

Kennedy, Edmund (1818–48) Australian explorer. He was killed by Aboriginals while exploring northern Queensland. Full name **Edmund Besley Court Kennedy**

Jackie Kennedy

John F. Kennedy Library

Kennedy, Jackie (1929–94) US first lady. She married John F. Kennedy in 1953 and as first lady (1961–63) became an international celebrity and style-setter. Her great dignity after her husband's assassination increased public admiration for her. She married Greek shipping magnate Aristotle Onassis in 1968, and after his death in 1975 worked in publishing in New York and continued her lifelong patronage and promotion of the arts. Born **Jacqueline Lee Bouvier**. Full name **Jacqueline Lee Kennedy-Onassis**. Known as **Jackie O**

Kennedy, John F. (1917–63) US statesman and 35th president of the United States. His Democratic administration (1961–63) pursued liberal reforms at home and a hard-line Cold War policy abroad. He was assassinated in Dallas. Full name **John Fitzgerald Kennedy**. Known as **Jack Kennedy**

Kennedy, Joseph P. (1888–1969) US businessman and government official. He was the father of John F., Robert F., and Edward M. Kennedy. He was ambassador to Britain (1938–40). Full name **Joseph Patrick Kennedy**

Kennedy, Nigel (*b.* 1956) British violinist. He is known for his flamboyant style. His repertoire includes classical, jazz, and rock.

Kennedy, Robert F. (1925–68) US politician. Attorney general (1961–64) during the Democratic administration of his brother John F. Kennedy, he was assassinated during his 1968 presidential campaign. Full name **Robert Francis Kennedy**. Known as **Bobby Kennedy**

kennel /kénn'l/ *n.* **1. HUT FOR DOG** a small outdoor structure like a hut, built for a dog to sleep in. US term **doghouse 2. ANIMAL'S LAIR** the lair of a wild animal such as a fox **3. PACK OF DOGS** a pack of hounds or dogs **4. HOVEL** a small house in bad condition (*archaic*) ■ *vti.* (-nels, -nelling, -nelled) **PUT OR STAY IN A KENNELS** to put a dog into a kennels or to stay in a kennels [14thC. Via assumed Anglo-Norman *kenil* from, ultimately, Latin *canis* 'dog' (source of English *canine*).]

Kennelly-Heaviside layer /kénn'li hévvi sīd-/ *n.* PHYS = **E layer** [Early 20thC. Named after the US electrical engineer, Arthur Edwin *Kennelly* (1861–1939) and the British physicist, Oliver *Heaviside* (1850–1925).]

kennels *n.* a place where dogs are bred and trained and where people can leave their dogs while they are away (*takes a singular verb*)

Kenneth I /kénnith/, **King of Scotland** (*fl.* mid-9th century) Around 846 he united the kingdoms of the Scots and the Picts, becoming the first king of Scotland. Known as **Kenneth MacAlpin**

kenning /kénning/ *n.* a metaphorical expression, often a phrase, to denote another word in Old Norse and Old English poetry [Late 19thC. From Old Norse, from *kenna* 'to know'.]

Kenny /kénni/, **Elizabeth** (1886–1952) Australian nurse and therapist. She pioneered alternative treatments for poliomyelitis. Her life story is told in the award-winning film *Sister Kenny* (1947). Known as **Sister Kenny**

keno /keénō/ *n.* US, Aus a game of chance in which players wager on a set of numbers to be drawn at random. It is operated for profit by many states and gaming authorities. [Early 19thC. Via French *quine* 'set of five winning numbers' from Latin *quini* 'five each', from *quinque* 'five'.]

kenosis /ki nőssiss/ *n.* according to Christian belief, Jesus Christ's act of partially giving up his divine status in order to become a man, as recorded in Philippians 2: 6–7 [Late 19thC. From Greek *kenōsis* 'an emptying', from the phrase in *Philippians 2:7 heauton ekenōse* 'emptied himself'.] —**kenotic** /ki nóttik/ *adj.*

kenspeckle /kén spek'l/ *adj.* Scotland easily seen or recognized, or well-known [Mid-16thC. Origin uncertain: probably from Old Norse *kennispeki*, literally 'know wisdom', from *kenna* 'KEN' + *spak* 'wise'.]

kent Scotland past participle, past tense of **ken**

Kent /kent/ county in the southeastern corner of England, and a former Anglo-Saxon kingdom. Maidstone is the administrative centre. Population: 1,551,300 (1995). Area: 3,730 sq. km/1,440 sq. mi.

Kent, William (1686?–1748) English architect and landscape designer. He promoted the Palladian style in architecture and the informal parklike style in garden design.

kente /kénti/, **kente cloth** *n.* a handwoven cloth from Ghana, usually very brightly coloured [Mid-20thC. From Twi, literally 'cloth'.]

kentia /kénti ə/, **kentia palm** *n.* a tall-growing palm tree that is native to Lord Howe Island, Australia, and is widely cultivated for its decorative foliage. Latin name: *Howea forsterana*. [Late 19thC. Coined from modern Latin, named after the British plant collector, William KENT.]

Kentish /kéntish/ *adj.* **1. OF KENT** from or relating to the English county of Kent **2.** LANG **OF THE KENTISH DIALECT** relating to the Kentish dialect ■ *n.* LANG **OLD ENGLISH DIALECT** a dialect of Old English spoken in the extreme southeast of England, probably from around the 5th century AD, recorded in written form from around the 7th century AD. It continued to be spoken in the area into the Middle English period, but was increasingly overtaken by the form of English that

developed from the dialect known as East Midlands. ◊ **Anglian, West Saxon**

kentledge /kéntlij/ *n.* scrap iron or other heavy material used as permanent ballast on ships [Early 17thC. From Old French *quintelage* 'ballast', from *Old French quintal* (see QUINTAL).]

Kentucky

Kentucky[1] /ken túki/ state in the east-central United States, bordered by Illinois, Indiana, Missouri, Ohio, Tennessee, Virginia, and West Virginia. Capital: Frankfort. Population: 3,908,124 (1997). Area: 104,664 sq. km/40,411 sq. mi. —**Kentuckian** *n.*, *adj.*

Kentucky[2] river in central Kentucky that flows northwestwards to join the Ohio River at Carrolton. Length: 417 km/259 mi.

Kentucky bluegrass *n.* a grass native to Africa, Europe, and Asia, naturalized in North America and widely used for pastureland and lawns. Latin name: *Poa pratensis*.

Kentucky coffee tree *n.* a deciduous tree of the legume family with brown pods and compound leaves that is native to eastern North America. Its pulpy seeds were formerly used as a coffee substitute. Latin name: *Gymnocladus dioica*.

Kentucky Derby *n.* a race for three-year-old horses that has been run annually since 1875 at Churchill Downs in Louisville, Kentucky. It is held on the first Saturday in May.

Kenya

Kenya /kényə, keényə/ republic in eastern Africa. It became independent from the United Kingdom in 1963. Language: English, Swahili. Currency: Kenyan shilling. Capital: Nairobi. Population: 27,838,597 (1997). Area: 582,646 sq. km/224,961 sq. mi. Official name **Republic of Kenya** —**Kenyan** *n.*, *adj.*

Kenya, Mount extinct volcano in central Kenya, the second highest mountain in Africa. Height: 5,199 m/17,057 ft.

Kenyatta /ken yáttə/, **Jomo** (1897?–1978) Kenyan statesman. Following the outbreak of the Mau Mau uprising he was imprisoned (1952–61). After independence he became Kenya's first prime minister (1963–64) and president (1964–78). Born **Kamau wa Ngengi**

Kenyon /kényən/, **Dame Kathleen** (1906–78) British archaeologist. She is famous for her excavations at Jericho and Jerusalem.

kephalin *n.* BIOL = **cephalin**

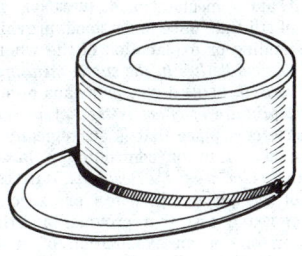

Kepi

kepi /káypi/ *n.* a French military hat with a round flat top and a horizontal peak [Mid-19thC. Via French *képi* from Swiss German *Käppi*, literally 'little cap'.]

Kepler /képlər/, **Johannes** (1571–1630) German astronomer. His three laws of planetary motion include his finding that the planets move around the sun in elliptical orbits.

Kepler's laws /képplərz-/ *npl.* three mathematical statements that describe the movement of the planets in their orbits around the Sun. The first two laws were published in 1609 and the third a decade later. [Late 18thC. Named after the German astronomer, Johannes KEPLER, who discovered them.]

kept past tense, past participle of **keep**

kept woman *n.* a woman who is financially supported by a lover, especially by a married man

Kerala /kérrələ/ state in southwestern India. Capital: Trivandrum. Population: 30,555,000 (1994). Area: 38,864 sq. km/15,005 sq. mi.

kerat- *prefix.* = **kerato-** (used before vowels)

keratectomy /kérrə téktəmi/ (*plural* **-mies**) *n.* surgical removal of part of the cornea

keratin /kérrətin/, **ceratin** *n.* a fibrous insoluble protein that is the main structural element in hair, nails, feathers, and hooves [Mid-19thC. Coined from the stem of Greek *keras* 'horn' + -IN.] —**keratinous** /ke rátt'nəss/ *adj.*

keratinization /kérrəti nī záysh'n, ke rátti nī-/, **keratinisation** *n.* the deposition of keratin in skin cells, e.g. in hair and nails, giving them the texture of horn

keratinize /kérrəti nīz, ke rátti nīz/ (**-izes, -izing, -ized**), **keratinise** (**-ises, -ising, -ised**) *vti.* to convert sth into keratin, or become keratin

keratitis /kérrə títiss/ *n.* inflammation and swelling of the cornea

kerato- *prefix.* **1.** horn-like tissue ○ *keratose* **2.** cornea ○ *keratoplasty* [From Greek *kerat-*, the stem of *keras* 'horn'. Ultimately from an Indo-European base that is also the ancestor of English *horn*, *corn*, and *cranium*.]

keratoid /kérrə toyd/ *adj.* like horn in texture or appearance

keratopathy /kérrə tóppəthi/ *n.* any noninflammatory disorder of the cornea

keratoplasty /kérrətō plasti/ (*plural* **-ties**) *n.* plastic surgery on the cornea, especially corneal grafting —**keratoplastic** /kérrə tō plástik/ *adj.*

keratose /kérrə tōss, -tōz/ *adj.* having a horn-like skeleton, as some sponges have

keratosis /kérrə tóssiss/ (*plural* **-ses** /-seez/) *n.* **1.** HORN-LIKE GROWTH a horn-like growth of hard horn-like tissue on the skin **2.** HORN-LIKE PART a horn-like growth on the skin —**keratotic** /kérrə tóttik/ *adj.*

keratotomy /kérrə tóttəmi/ (*plural* **-mies**) *n.* a surgical cutting of the cornea

kerb /kurb/ *n.* EDGE OF PAVEMENT a raised edge of stone or concrete separating the pavement from the road or street. US term **curb** ■ *vt.* (**kerbs, kerbing, kerbed**) PUT KERB ON STH to provide sth with a kerb. US term **curb** [Mid-17thC. Variant of CURB, in the sense 'an enclosing framework'.]

kerb crawling *n.* the act of driving slowly beside a pavement looking for a prostitute to pick up —**kerb crawler** *n.*

kerb drill *n.* a procedure for crossing a road safely on foot, especially one that is taught to children

kerb market *n.* a stock market that is separate from the stock exchange, originally one operating in the street

kerbstone /kúrb stōn/ *n.* any of the large stones used to make a kerb. US term **curbstone**

Kerch /kyurch/ city and seaport in southern Ukraine, on the eastern shore of the Crimean Peninsula. Population: 176,000 (1990).

kerchief /kúrchif, kúr cheef/ *n.* a square scarf for women, worn round the neck or as a headscarf [13thC. From Anglo-Norman *courchef* or Old French *cueve-chef*, literally 'cover-head'.] —**kerchiefed** *adj.*

Kerensky /kərénski/, **Aleksandr Fyodorovich** (1881–1970) Russian revolutionary leader. He was the head of the 1917 provisional government of Russia from July until the Bolshevik takeover in November 1917.

kerf /kurf/ *n.* a cut or the width of a cut made by an axe, saw, or cutting tool [Old English *cerf*. Ultimately from a prehistoric West Germanic word that is also the ancestor of English *carve*.]

kerfuffle /kər fúff'l/, **carfuffle, kurfuffle** *n.* a noisy disturbance or commotion (*informal*) [Early 19thC. Origin uncertain: perhaps from Gaelic *car* 'twist' + Scots *fuffle* 'fuss'.]

Kerguelen Islands /kúrgilin-/ island group in the southern Indian Ocean, consisting of one main island and about 300 smaller islands and islets. Area: 6,993 sq. km/2,700 sq. mi.

Kermadec Islands /kúrmə dek-/ island group in the southern Pacific Ocean, a dependency of New Zealand. Area: 34 sq. km/13 sq. mi.

Kerman /kur maán/, **Kermān** city in southeastern Iran, the capital of Kerman Province. Population: 311,643 (1991).

kermes /kúr miz/ (*plural* **-mes**) *n.* **1.** INSECTS RED DYESTUFF the dried bodies of female scale insects of the genus *Kermes*, used to produce a purplish-red dye **2.** TREES = **kermes oak** [Late 16thC. Via French *kermès* from Arabic *kirmiz* 'kermes beetle' (source of English *crimson*).]

kermes oak *n.* a small evergreen oak tree native to Europe and Asia that provides a habitat for the scale insects used to make kermes. Latin name: *Quercus coccifera*.

kermis /kúr miss/, **kirmess, kermess** *n.* an annual country fair that used to be held in the Netherlands and northern Germany [Late 16thC. From Dutch, literally 'mass on the anniversary of the church's dedication', from *kerk* 'church' + *misse* 'mass'. From the fair held on this day.]

kern[1] /kurn/, **kerne** *n.* PART OF A CHARACTER the part of a typographical character that projects beyond the body ■ *v.* (**kerns, kerning, kerned; kernes, kerning, kerned**) **1.** *vti.* BRING TYPE TOGETHER to eliminate white space between adjacent letters that may appear too widely separated on a line **2.** *vt.* OVERLAP ADJACENT CHARACTERS to join adjacent printed characters or make them overlap [Late 17thC. Via French *carne* 'corner' from, ultimately, Latin *cardo* 'hinge' (source of English *cardinal*).]

kern[2] /kurn/, **kerne** *n.* a medieval Irish or Scottish light infantryman [14thC. From Irish *ceithearn*.]

kernel /kúrn'l/ *n.* **1.** PLANTS EDIBLE CORE the edible content of a nut or fruit stone **2.** PLANTS CEREAL GRAIN the grain of a cereal that contains a seed and husk **3.** CENTRAL PART the central or most important part of sth ○ *a kernel of self-belief that never wavered* **4.** PHYS ATOM STRIPPED OF ITS ELECTRONS a positively charged atomic nucleus that has lost its valency electrons **5.** COMPUT KEY PORTION OF AN OPERATING SYSTEM the core portion of a computer's operating system that resides in the memory and performs essential functions such as controlling the memory and files and allocating system resources [Old English *cyrnel* 'little seed', from CORN]

Without kerning

AVOKO

Bad kerning

With kerning

AVOKO

Kerning

kerning /kúrning/ *n.* the addition or removal of space between individual characters in a piece of typeset text to improve its appearance or alter its fit

kernite /kúr nīt/ *n.* a colourless or white crystalline mineral that is composed of hydrated sodium borate and is a source of borax and other boron compounds [Early 20thC. Named after *Kern* County, California, where it was discovered.]

kernmantel rope /kúrn mant'l rōp/ *n.* rope made of sheathed nylon fibre that is particularly strong, elastic, and resistant to twisting [20thC. 'kernmantel' from German, literally 'core-casing'. So called because of its fibres within a sheath.]

kero /kérrō/ *n.* ANZ kerosene (*informal*) [Mid-20thC. Shortening.]

kerogen /kérrəjən/ *n.* a fossilized insoluble organic material found in some sedimentary rocks, e.g. oil shales, yielding petroleum products when heated [Early 20thC. Coined from Greek *kēros* 'wax' + -GEN.]

kerosene /kérrə seen/, **kerosine** *n.* US, Can, ANZ a colourless flammable oil distilled from petroleum and used as a fuel for jet engines, heating, cooking, and lighting [Mid-19thC. Coined from Greek *kēros* 'wax' + -ENE or -INE.]

kerplunk /kər plúngk/ *adv., interj.* used to imitate the sound made by sth heavy falling suddenly (*informal*) [An imitation of the sound]

Kerr /kur/, **Sir John** (1914–90) Australian statesman. He was governor-general of Australia (1974–77). In 1975, he dismissed the Labor government led by Gough Whitlam. Full name **Sir John Robert Kerr**

Kerr effect /kúr-/ *n.* **1.** DOUBLE REFRACTION the property of some transparent substances that makes them refract doubly when placed in an electric field **2.** ELLIPTICAL POLARIZATION OF REFLECTED LIGHT the elliptical polarization of plane polarized or unpolarized light when reflected from the polished pole of a magnetized material [Early 20thC. Named after the Scottish physicist, John *Kerr* (1824–1907), who discovered it.]

Kerry[1] /kérri/ (*plural* **-ries**) *n.* a small black bull or dairy cow belonging to a breed that originated in Ireland [Mid-19thC. Named after County KERRY, where the breed originated.]

Kerry[2] /kérri/ county in Munster Province, southwestern Republic of Ireland. Population: 125,863 (1996). Area: 4,701 sq. km/1,815 sq. km.

Kerry blue terrier, Kerry blue *n.* a terrier with a dense but soft wavy bluish-grey coat, belonging to a breed that originated in Ireland [Early 20thC. Named after County KERRY, where the breed originated.]

kersey /kúrzi/ *n.* a smooth woollen fabric used for making coats [14thC. Named after the village of *Kersey* in Suffolk.]

kerseymere /kérrzi meer/ *n.* a fine soft woollen cloth with a fancy twill weave [Late 18thC. Alteration of CASSIMERE by association with KERSEY.]

kerygma /kə rígmə/ *n.* the proclamation of Jesus Christ's teachings, especially as taught in the Gospels [Late 19thC. From Greek *kērugma*, from *kērussein* 'to proclaim'.] —**kerygmatic** /kérrig máttik/ *adj.*

kesh /kaysh/ *n.* the beard and uncut hair traditionally worn by some baptized male Sikhs as one of the symbols of their religion and culture. ◊ **five Ks** [From Punjabi *kes*]

Kesselring /késs'lring/, **Albert** (1885–1960) German field marshal. During World War II he was commander in chief in Italy (1943–45) and the Western Front (1945).

Kestrel

kestrel /késtrəl/ n. a small European and Asian falcon that feeds on small mammals. It can hover in the wind before diving on its prey. Genus: *Falco*. [14thC. Origin uncertain: probably via a dialectal form of French *crécerelle* 'rattle', from Latin *crepitacillum*, literally 'small rattle', from *crepitare* 'to rattle'.]

ket- *prefix.* = keto- (used before vowels)

ketamine /kéttə meen/ n. a white crystalline powder used as a general anaesthetic in human and veterinary medicine. Formula: $C_{13}H_{16}ClNO$.

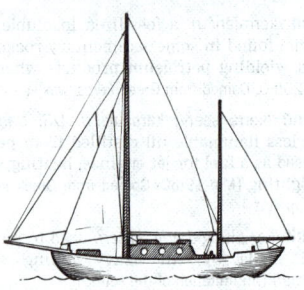

Ketch

ketch /kech/ n. a small sailing ship with two masts [Mid-17thC. Origin uncertain: probably from CATCH.]

ketchup /kéchəp, kéch up/, **catchup** /káchəp, kách up/, **catsup** /kátsəp, káts up/ n. a thick savoury sauce, usually made with tomatoes, that is served cold as a condiment [Late 17thC. Origin uncertain: probably via Malay *kēchap* 'fish sauce' from Chinese (Cantonese) *k'ē chap* 'sauce'.]

ketene /kée teen/ n. a strong-smelling colourless highly reactive toxic gas used as an agent to attach an acetyl group to an organic compound. Formula: C_2H_2O. [Early 20thC. From KETONE + -ENE.]

keto-, **ket-** *prefix.* indicating a chemical compound containing a keto group, C=O, such as ketone ○ *ketosteroid* [From KETONE]

keto form /kéetō-/ n. one of two interconvertible forms of an organic compound, characterized by a carbonyl group attached to two alkyl groups

ketogenesis /kéetō jénnəssiss/ n. the formation or stimulation of the production of ketone bodies, as happens in diabetes —**ketogenic** *adj.*

ketone /kéetōn/ n. an organic compound characterized by a carbon atom doubly bonded to an oxygen atom and to two carbon atoms. The simplest ketone is acetone, an important industrial solvent. [Mid-19thC. From German *Keton*, an alteration of *Aketon* 'acetone'.] —**ketonic** /kee tónnik/ *adj.*

ketone body n. a substance containing ketones produced by fatty acid metabolism. The concentration of ketone bodies in blood and urine increases in starvation, diabetes, and pregnancy.

ketone group n. the carbonyl group, containing carbon atoms doubly bonded to an oxygen atom and linked to the carbon atoms of two other organic groups, a characteristic of all ketones

ketonuria /kéetō nyoóri ə/ n. the presence of ketones in the urine, a dangerous feature of severe and uncontrolled diabetes

ketose /kée tōss, -tōz/ n. a carbohydrate that contains a ketone group

ketosis /kee tóssiss, ki-/ n. the condition resulting from overproduction of ketone bodies —**ketotic** /kee tóttik/ *adj.*

ketoxime /kee tók seem/ n. an organic compound containing a nitrogen atom bonded to a hydroxyl group and a carbon atom, which is bonded to two ketones. It is produced by the reaction between hydroxylamine and a ketone.

Kettering /kéttə ring/ town in Northamptonshire, central England. Population: 79,900 (1995).

kettle /kétt'l/ n. **1.** CONTAINER FOR BOILING WATER a plastic or metal container with a handle, spout, and lid, used for boiling water **2.** METAL POT a metal pot used for cooking, usually one with a lid ○ *a fish kettle* **3.** INDUSTRIAL CONTAINER a large container with no lid that is used for refining metals with a low melting point **4.** GEOL BASIN IN A GLACIAL DRIFT DEPOSIT a steep-sided basin, often a lake or swamp, in a glacial drift deposit, caused by the melting of an ice mass left behind as the glacier retreated [Old English *cetel*. Ultimately via a prehistoric Germanic word from Latin *catillus* 'small cooking pot'.]

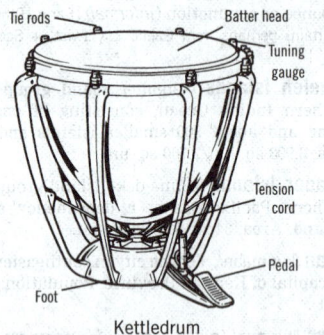

Tie rods — Batter head
— Tuning gauge
Tension cord
Pedal
Foot

Kettledrum

kettledrum /kétt'l drum/ n. a percussion instrument consisting of a large copper or brass drum covered with a parchment skin. Pitch is altered by screws and pedals that increase or decrease the skin's tension. —**kettledrummer** n.

kettle hole n. GEOL = kettle n. 4

kettle of fish n. **1.** DIFFICULT SITUATION an undesirable situation, usually one caused by sb's negligence or incompetence **2.** TYPE OF PERSON OR SITUATION a situation or person to be dealt with (*informal*) ○ *That's a different kettle of fish altogether.*

keV *abbr.* kiloelectronvolt

kevel[1] /kévv'l/ n. a sturdy bitt or bollard for securing the heavier cables on a ship [13thC. Via Old Norman French *keville* 'pin, peg' from Latin *clavicula* 'small key' (source of English *clavicle*).]

kevel[2] /kévv'l/ n. a two-headed hammer, one head with a sharp edge, the other with a point, used for breaking up or shaping stone [Origin unknown]

Kevlar /kév laar/ *tdmk.* a trademark for a reinforcing material used in tyres and bulletproof vests

Kew Gardens /kyoo-/ n. informal name for the Royal Botanic Gardens, Kew, located in western London. They hold the largest collection of plants in the world.

kewpie /kyóopi/ n. a plump doll with rosy cheeks and a curl of hair on its head [Originally a trademark]

kex /keks/ n. the dried stems of a large hollow-stemmed plant such as cow parsnip or chervil [14thC. Origin unknown: perhaps from Celtic]

key[1] /kée/ n. **1.** INSTRUMENT FOR LOCKING AND UNLOCKING a metal bar with notches or grooves that, when inserted into a lock and turned, operates the lock's mechanism **2.** DOOR OR LOCK OPENER a device such as a plastic card with an encoded magnetic strip that operates a door or lock **3.** INSTRUMENT FOR WINDING UP a fitted tool that is turned repeatedly to wind up, set, or calibrate a mechanism **4.** IMPORTANT ASPECT the aspect of sth that, once understood, provides a full understanding or explanation of the whole ○ *The key to this riddle lies in the subtle meanings of the words used.* **5.** MEANS a way or means of achieving sth ○ *Continuity of effort is the key to success.* **6.** STRATEGIC PLACE a place that is strategically vital in gaining access to or controlling a larger area ○ *Istanbul is the key to the Bosporus.* **7.** LIST OF ANSWERS a list of the answers to a test or exercise **8.** EXPLANATORY TEXT a text that provides additional information on, or an explanation of, a work of literature, art, or music **9.** MUSIC TONAL CENTRE the main tonal centre of a musical work, as defined by the relationships between the notes of a scale and the scale's main note **10.** MUSIC MAIN NOTE OF A SCALE the note on which a musical scale begins **11.** MUSIC INSTRUMENT FEATURE the levers on a keyboard instrument that sound a note when pressed, or the metal buttons on a woodwind instrument that alter a note's pitch **12.** MUSIC MUSICAL SCALE a system of related notes in a scale beginning on a particular note ○ *in the key of E* **13.** KEYBOARD BUTTON any of the buttons on a typewriter's or computer's keyboard or keypad that perform an operation when pressed **14.** COMPUT DATABASE FEATURE a field in a database record that uniquely identifies that record **15.** ELEC ENG DEVICE FOR OPERATING CIRCUITS a small manual device for opening, closing, or switching circuits ○ *a telegraph key* **16.** ENG METAL WEDGE OR PIN a metal wedge or pin used to lock together two structural or mechanical components, e.g. a shaft and a hub, to prevent movement relative to each other **17.** CRYPTOGRAPHIC FEATURE in cryptography, the sequence of symbols or characters that defines the makeup of an encoding mechanism **18.** BIOL OUTLINE OF CHARACTERISTICS an outline of the characteristics of an organism, used for taxonomic identification **19.** PHOTOGRAPHY, PAINTING IMAGE FEATURE the tonal value of an image with regard to lightness, darkness, or colour intensity **20.** CONSTR SURFACE PREPARATION the preparing of a surface, usually by making it rough or grooved so that paint or some other finish will stick to it **21.** PITCH OR QUALITY the pitch or quality of an expressive sound, especially the voice ○ *answered in thoughtful key* **22.** MAPS EXPLANATORY LIST an explanatory list of the symbols or abbreviations used on a map or diagram **23.** ARTS MOOD OF AN ART WORK the general mood or style of a work of art, literature, or music **24.** ARCHIT = keystone n. **1 25.** BOT WINGED FRUIT a dry winged fruit like that of an ash or elm tree **26.** BASKETBALL BASKETBALL COURT AREA the area at the ends of a basketball court between the base line and the foul line ■ *adj.* CRUCIAL vital in achieving understanding or success ○ *the key points in the report* ■ *v.* (**keys, keying, keyed**) **1.** *vti.* COMPUT TYPE to use the keyboard of a computer, or input data using it ○ *a solid hour of keying* **2.** *vt.* LOCK STH to lock or adjust sth with a key **3.** *vt.* INDUST PREPARE A SURFACE to prepare a surface, usually by making it rough or grooved, so that paint or another finish will stick to it **4.** *vt.* PROVIDE STH WITH AN EXPLANATION to provide sth with an explanatory list or text **5.** *vt.* MUSIC REGULATE AN INSTRUMENT'S PITCH to regulate the pitch of a musical instrument **6.** *vt.* ADAPT STH to bring sth in line with or make sth consistent with sth else (*often passive*) **7.** *vt.* BUILDING PUT A KEYSTONE IN AN ARCH to provide an arch with a keystone **8.** *vt.* PRINTING MARK ARTWORK to mark artwork, or anything to be reproduced, with symbols that will allow different parts to be correctly aligned for reproduction **9.** *vt.* BIOL IDENTIFY STH to identify an organism or specimen [Old English *cǣg*, of unknown origin]

key in *vt.* to enter data, e.g. a password or PIN, by typing on a keyboard or keypad

key[2] /kee/ n. a small low island of sand or coral, especially in the Gulf of Mexico or the Caribbean [Late 17thC. Via Spanish *cayo* from French *quai* (see QUAY).]

keyboard /kée bawrd/ n. **1.** SET OF KEYS a set of keys laid out in a row or rows, e.g. on a computer, typewriter, piano, or organ **2.** MUSIC MUSICAL INSTRUMENT a musical instrument that has a keyboard, especially an electronic instrument ■ *vti.* (**-boards, -boarding, -boarded**) COMPUT INPUT DATA to enter information into a computer using a keyboard

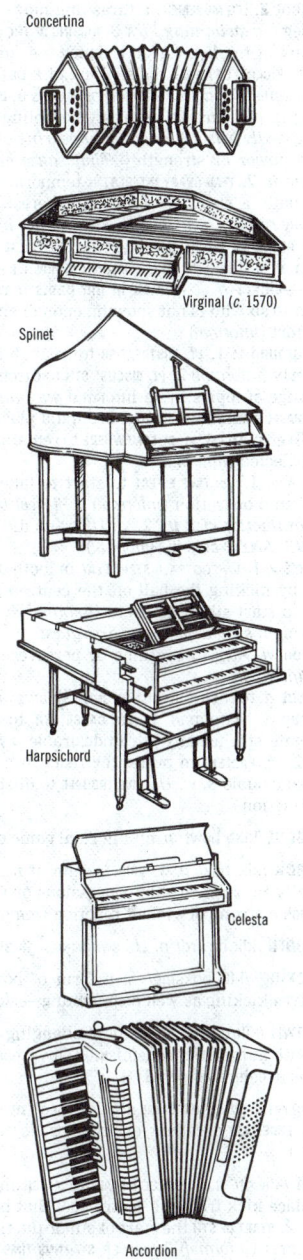

Concertina

Virginal (c. 1570)

Spinet

Harpsichord

Celesta

Accordion

Keyboard: Historical keyboard instruments

keyboarder /keé bawrdər/ n. sb who operates the keyboard of a computer or typesetting machine

keyboardist /keé bawrdist/ n. a musician who plays a keyboard instrument

key card n. a card, usually made of plastic with an encoded magnetic strip, giving access to a door or mechanism

keyed up adj. in a state of great excitement, tension, or nervousness (informal)

key escrow n. a system for encrypting computer data in which the decoding key is held by a third party

key fruit n. BOT = key[1] n. 25

key grip n. the chief grip in a film or stage crew

keyhole /keé hōl/ n. the small hole in a lock into which a key fits

keyhole saw n. = padsaw

keyhole surgery n. surgery performed using instruments that can be introduced into the body through a very small hole and manipulated externally, thus avoiding the need for major incisions

Key Largo /-laárgō/ one of the largest of the Florida Keys, in southeastern Florida, at Biscayne Bay. Length: 48 km/30 mi.

key light n. the main studio or stage light that sets the overall level of light intensity for sth that is being filmed, videotaped, or photographed

key lime, Key lime n. a small tart lime grown in the Florida Keys and Caribbean islands

key money n. a fee paid by a prospective tenant to a landlord or landlady in order to secure a tenancy

Keynes /kaynz/, **John Maynard, 1st Baron Keynes of Tilton** (1883–1946) British economist. He proposed the influential theory that government spending must compensate for insufficient business investment in times of recession. —**Keynesian** n., adj. —**Keynesianism** n.

keynote /keé nōt/ n. 1. MAIN THEME the central or most important point or theme of sth 2. MUSIC = **tonic** n. 4 ■ adj. MOST IMPORTANT containing or outlining the most important themes or policies ■ v. (-notes, -noting, -noted) 1. vti. DELIVER A SPEECH to deliver an important speech to a conference or meeting 2. vt. NOTE IMPORTANT POINTS to outline an important policy in a speech or report [Mid-18thC, in the sense 'first note of a scale', hence, the one that decides what follows]

keynote address n. = keynote speech

keynoter n. sb who delivers the most important speech at a conference or political convention

keynote speech, keynote address n. the most important speech at a conference or political convention

keypad /keé pad/ n. 1. SMALL KEYBOARD a small keyboard, e.g. on a calculator or television remote control, usually with numbers rather than letters on the keys 2. PART OF A KEYBOARD the part of a computer keyboard in which the number and command keys are grouped

keypal /keé pal/ n. US sb with whom regular e-mail is exchanged [Modelled on PENPAL]

key-punch /keé punch/ n. MACHINE FOR PUNCHING HOLES a machine, operated by keyboard, that punches holes in card or paper for use in a data-processing system. Once the primary means of computer input, the keypunch has been made largely obsolete by the computer keyboard. ■ vti. (key-punches, key-punching, key-punched) TO PUNCH HOLES FOR DATA ENTRY to use a key-punch to punch holes in a card or paper tape for data entry into a computer —**key-puncher** n.

key ring n. a metal ring used for keeping keys together, often with a decorative or identifying attachment

key signature n. a group of sharps or flats printed on the staves at the beginning of a piece of music to show the key in which it is to be played

key stage n. any of the four National Curriculum programmes of study that pupils are required to follow. They are key stage 1 (age 5–7), key stage 2 (age 8–11), key stage 3 (age 11–14), and key stage 4 (age 14–16).

keystone /keé stōn/ n. 1. ARCHIT CENTRAL STONE IN AN ARCH the wedge-shaped stone at the highest point of an arch that locks the others in place 2. SUPPORTING ELEMENT sth on which other interrelated things depend ○ friendly alliances that are the keystone of the country's security

────── **WORD KEY: CULTURAL NOTE** ──────

The Keystone Kops, a group of comic characters who appeared in a number of silent films by US director Mack Sennett (1884–1960). A bumbling police squad dressed in oversized uniforms, the Kops usually featured in slapstick chase sequences characterised by superb sight gags and acrobatic stunts.

keystroke /keé strōk/ n. the pressing down of one of the keys on a keyboard, thus activating it

keyway /keé way/ n. a longitudinal slot in two structural or mechanical components, e.g. in the hub or shaft of a wheel, into which a metal wedge or pin can be inserted. When the slots are filled, the two components are locked together so that they will not turn relative to one another.

Key West city in southern Florida, situated on the island of the same name. It is a port and a tourist resort. Population: 24,832 (1990).

key word n. 1. REFERENCE POINT a word used as a reference point for further information or as an indication of the contents of a document 2. CODE WORD a word that is used as a key to a code 3. COMPUT WORD WITH A SPECIAL MEANING TO A COMPUTER a sequence of letters and numbers, often in the form of a common word, with special significance in the context of a computer database or programming or command language

kg symbol. kilogram

KG abbr. Knight of the Order of the Garter

KGB n. the secret police of the former Soviet Union [From Russian, from *Komitet Gosudarstvennoĭ Bezopasnosti* 'Committee of State Security']

kgf symbol. kilogram-force

Khabarovsk /kəba rófsk/ city in eastern Russia, the administrative centre of Khabarovsk Territory. Population: 634,500 (1992).

khaddar /kaádər/, **khadi** /kaádi/ n. a cotton cloth from India that has a plain weave [Early 20thC. From Panjabi *khaddar* or Hindi *khādar, khādī*.]

khaki /kaáki/ adj. COLOURS BROWNISH-YELLOW of a dull brownish-yellow colour ■ n. 1. COLOURS BROWNISH-YELLOW a dull brownish-yellow colour 2. TEXTILES BEIGE CLOTH a tough yellowish-brown fabric often used for making military uniforms [Mid-19thC. Via Urdu *kakī* 'dust-coloured' from, ultimately, Persian *kāk* 'dust'.] —**khaki** adj.

khalif n. = caliph

Khalsa /kaálssə/ n. a strict Sikh religious order founded in 1699 by Guru Gobind Singh [Late 18thC. Via Urdu from, ultimately, Arabic *kāliş* 'pure'.]

khamsin /kam seén, kámsin/, **kamseen, kamsin** n. a dry dusty hot southerly wind that blows from the Sahara across Egypt and over the Red Sea from March to May [Late 17thC. From Arabic *kamāsīn*, from *kamsīn* 'fifty' (because it blows for about fifty days).]

khan[1] /kaan/ n. 1. MEDIEVAL TITLE a medieval title formerly used by Mongol and Turkish rulers in various parts of Asia (usually added to a name) ○ Genghis Khan 2. TITLE OF RESPECT IN CENTRAL ASIA a title of respect taken by various dignitaries in Central Asian countries ○ the Aga Khan [14thC. Via Old French *chan* or medieval Latin *ca(a)nus* from Turkic *kān* 'lord, ruler'.]

khan[2] /kaan/ n. an inn in Turkey and some other Central Asian countries [14thC. From Persian *kān*.]

Imran Khan

Khan /kaan/, **Imran** (b. 1952) Pakistan cricketer. He was four times captain of Pakistan's national team between 1982 and his retirement from cricket in 1992, and also played for Sussex and Worcestershire. Full name **Imran Ahmad Khan Niazi**

Khan, Jahangir (b. 1963) Pakistani squash player. Holder of six world open titles (1981–85, 1988), he was undefeated from April 1981 until November 1986.

khanate /káa nayt/ *n.* **1.** KHAN'S TERRITORY the territory governed by a medieval Chinese emperor or Mongolian or Turkish khan **2.** KHAN'S RANK the position or rank of a khan

khanga /káangə/ CLOTHES = **kanga**

khapra beetle /káaprə-/ *n.* a beetle of Southeast Asia now common in other parts of the world, where it is a pest to grain farmers. Latin name: *Trogoderma granarium.* [*Khapra* via Hindi from Sanskrit *khapara* 'thief']

Kharkov /kaár kof/ the second largest city in Ukraine, capital of Kharkov Oblast. It is situated about 418 km/260 mi. east of Kiev. Population: 1,576,000 (1995).

Khartoum /kaar tóom/ capital city of Sudan and of Khartoum Province. It is situated just south of the confluence of the Blue Nile and White Nile rivers. Population: 476,218 (1983).

khat /kaat/ *n.* **1.** TREES WHITE-FLOWERED SHRUB an evergreen shrub native to Arabia and Africa with white flowers and leaves that have a narcotic effect when chewed or brewed as tea. Latin name: *Catha edulis.* **2.** DRUGS LEAVES OF THE KHAT the leaves of the khat plant, used as a stimulant [Mid-19thC. From Arabic *ḳāt.*]

kheda /kéddə/, **khedah, keddah** *n.* in India and Myanmar, an enclosure used to capture wild elephants [Late 18thC. From Assamese and Bengali *khedā.*]

khedive /ki deév/ *n.* the title of the Turkish viceroys who governed Egypt from 1867 to 1914 while it was under Turkish rule [Mid-19thC. Via French and Ottoman Turkish from Persian *ḵadiiw* 'prince', ultimately from *ḵudā* 'god'.] —**khedival** *adj.* —**khedivate** /kə deévət, -vayt/ *n.*

Khmer /kmair, kə máir/ (*plural* **Khmer** *or* **Khmers**) *n.* **1.** PEOPLES MEMBER OF A CAMBODIAN PEOPLE a member of the main ethnic group in Cambodia **2.** HIST an inhabitant of the ancient Khmer kingdom that flourished in the Mekong valley between the 9th and 13th centuries AD **3.** LANG OFFICIAL LANGUAGE OF CAMBODIA the official language of Cambodia, belonging to the Mon-Khmer group of languages. Khmer is spoken by more than five million people. —**Khmer** *adj.*

Khmer Republic /kmair-/ former name for **Cambodia** (1970–75)

Khmer Rouge /-róozh, -/ *n.* the Cambodian Communist party that seized power in the civil war of 1975 and controlled the country until 1979 [From Khmer *Khmer* 'Kampuchea' + French *rouge* 'red']

Khoikhoi /kóy koy/ (*plural* **-khoi** *or* **-khois**) *n.* **1.** PEOPLES MEMBER OF A NOMADIC AFRICAN PEOPLE a member of a formerly nomadic people now living mainly in Namibia **2. Khoikhoi, Khoi Khoi** LANG NAMIBIAN LANGUAGE a language spoken in Namibia and some parts of western South Africa, belonging to the Khoisan family of African languages and characterized by the use of click consonants. Khoikhoi is spoken by around 55,000 people. [Late 18thC. From Nama, literally 'men of men'.] —**Khoikhoi** *adj.*

Khoisan /kóy saán/, **Khoi-San** *n.* a family of around fifty languages, including Khoikhoi, San, Kwadi, and Sandawe, spoken in parts of Namibia and Botswana and notable for the use of click consonants [Mid-20thC. Blend of KHOIKHOI and SAN.]

Khomeini /kh̲óm ay neé/, **Ruhollah, Ayatollah** (1900–89) Iranian religious leader. He led an Islamic revolution that overthrew the shah (1979), and as virtual head of state introduced a constitution and administration based on Islamic law.

Khrushchev /króoss chof/, **Nikita** (1894–1971) Soviet statesman. In 1953, after Stalin's death, he became first secretary of the Communist Party, and embarked on a programme of de-Stalinization. He was ousted in 1964. The Cuban missile crisis occurred during his administration. Full name **Nikita Sergeyevich Khrushchev**

Khulna /kóolnə/ city and river port in southwestern Bangladesh. It is situated about 145 km/90 mi. southwest of Dhaka. Population: 545,849 (1991).

khuskhus /kúskəss/, **khus-khus** BOT = **vetiver** [Early 19thC. From Urdu and Persian *ḵaskas.*]

Ric Ergenbright/Corbis

Khyber Pass

Khyber Pass /kībər-/ mountain pass in western Asia, the most important pass connecting Afghanistan and Pakistan

kHz *abbr.* kilohertz

Kiama /kī ámmə/ coastal town in southeastern New South Wales, Australia, an administrative centre and tourist resort. Population: 11,711 (1996).

kiang /ki áng/ *n.* a large wild ass native to the Tibetan plateau and the Himalayas. Latin name: *Equus hemionus kiang.* [Mid-19thC. From Tibetan *kyang.*]

kia ora /keé ə áwrə/ *interj.* *NZ* used to greet sb or wish sb good luck [Late 19thC. From Maori, literally 'be well'.]

kibbe /kíbbə/ *n.* a Middle Eastern dish made with minced lamb, pine nuts, and spices [Mid-20thC. From Arabic *kubbah.*]

kibble^1 /kíbb'l/ *n.* a large iron barrel used in wells or mines for lifting water, ore, or refuse to the surface [Via German *Kübel* from, ultimately, Latin *cuppa* (see CUP)]

kibble^2 /kíbb'l/ (**-bles, -bling, -bled**) *vt.* to grind sth, e.g. grain, into small pieces [Late 18thC. Origin unknown.]

kibbutz /ki bóots/ (*plural* **-butzim** /ki boót seem/) *n.* communal farm or factory in Israel run collectively and dedicated to the principle that production work and domestic work are of equal value [Mid-20thC. From modern Hebrew *qibbūṣ* 'gathering'.]

kibbutznik /ki bóotsnik/ *n.* sb who lives and works on a kibbutz

kibe /kīb/ *n.* a chapped or swollen area of skin, usually on the heel and often ulcerated, caused by exposure to cold [14thC. Origin unknown.]

kibitka /ki bítkə/ *n.* **1.** TRANSP RUSSIAN SLEDGE a covered sledge or wagon in Russia **2.** TATAR TENT a tent made of felt used by the Tatars of Central Asia **3.** TATAR FAMILY a family of Tatars [Late 18thC. From Russian.]

kibitz /kíbbits/ (**-itzes, -itzing, -itzed**) *vi.* *US* (*informal*) **1.** INTERFERE to interfere or give unwanted advice, especially when watching a card game **2.** CHAT to chat [Early 20thC. Via Yiddish from German *kiebitsen.*] —**kibitzer** *n.*

kiblah /kíbblə/, **kibla, qibla** *n.* the direction of Mecca that Muslims must face when praying [Mid-17thC. From Arabic *ḳibla*, literally 'that which is opposite'.]

kibosh /kī bosh/ (**-boshes, -boshing, -boshed**) *vt.* to put a stop to sth [Mid-19thC. Origin unknown.] ◇ **put the kibosh on sth** to prevent sth from happening or from being successful (*informal*)

kick /kik/ *v.* (**kicks, kicking, kicked**) **1.** *vti.* STRIKE WITH THE FOOT to strike sth or sb with the foot **2.** *vti.* MOVE WITH THE FOOT to make sth move by striking it with the foot ○ *kick a ball around* **3.** *vti.* MAKE A THRASHING MOVEMENT to make a thrashing movement with the legs, e.g. when fighting or swimming ○ *Hold onto the side of the pool and kick your legs as hard as you can.* **4.** *vti.* RAISE THE LEG HIGH to raise the leg up high in a swift movement, e.g. in a dance ○ *an entire chorus line kicking in unison* **5.** *vi.* ARMS RECOIL to recoil when fired (*refers to firearms*) **6.** *vti.* SPORTS SCORE GOAL in various football games, to score a goal by kicking ○ *He kicked a conversion to win the game.* **7.** *vi.* CRICKET BOUNCE HIGH to bounce up high and quickly (*refers to a cricket ball*) ○ *On this wicket, a pace bowler should be able to make the ball really kick.* **8.** *vi.* OBJECT to show disapproval or object to sth by not cooperating (*informal*) ○ *He kicked against the restrictions.* **9.** *vr.* BLAME to be irritated with yourself (*informal*) ○ *I'm kicking myself for missing the deadline.* ■ *n.* **1.** BLOW WITH THE FOOT a blow with the foot **2.** LEG MOVEMENT a thrashing movement with the leg ○ *a swimming kick* **3.** RAISING OF THE LEG a swift raising of the leg, e.g. in a dance ○ *a high kick* **4.** SPORTS KICKING OF A BALL the striking of a ball with the foot ○ *opted for a kick instead of a pass* **5.** PLEASURE an exciting, pleasurable, or satisfying feeling (*informal*) ○ *She really gets a kick out of appearing on stage.* **6.** POWER power or strength ○ *That sauce has quite a kick to it.* **7.** TEMPORARY INTEREST a temporary interest, especially a strongly absorbing interest (*informal*) ○ *They're on a real health kick at the moment.* **8.** ARMS RECOIL OF A GUN the backward thrust of a gun when it is fired [14thC. Origin unknown.] —**kickable** *adj.* —**kicker** *n.* ◇ **a kick in the pants** a reprimand given to sb who is not showing enough enthusiasm or effort (*informal*)

kick around *v.* **1.** *vt.* MISTREAT SB to treat sb badly and unfairly (*informal*) **2.** *vt.* DISCUSS STH to discuss a topic or range of topics in an informal way (*informal*) **3.** *vti.* TRAVEL AIMLESSLY to travel around a place without any fixed plans **4.** *vi.* BE SOMEWHERE to remain forgotten or neglected (*informal*)

kick in *v.* **1.** *vi.* TAKE EFFECT to start to take effect or come into operation (*informal*) ○ *I'll feel better once the antibiotics kick in.* **2.** *vi.* *US* DIE to die (*slang*) **3.** *vti.* *US, ANZ* = **chip in** (*informal*)

kick off *v.* **1.** *vi.* FOOTBALL START PLAY in football, to start play by kicking the ball off the centre spot **2.** *vti.* BEGIN to start sth or to begin (*informal*) ○ *Let's kick off tonight's show with our first guest.*

kick on *vi.* *ANZ* to continue or persevere in doing sth (*informal*)

kick out *vt.* to throw sb out or send sb away (*informal*)

kick up *v.* (*informal*) **1.** *vt.* CAUSE STH to cause or instigate sth, usually sth undesirable ○ *kick up a fuss* **2.** *vi.* PROTEST to protest or react in a way that causes trouble **3.** *vi.* *US* GIVE TROUBLE to misbehave or malfunction

kickabout /kíkə bowt/ *n.* an informal game of football

kickback /kík bak/ *n.* **1.** BRIBE a sum of money paid illegally in order to gain concessions or favours **2.** REACTION a strong or violent reaction (*informal*)

kickboard /kík bawrd/ *n.* *US* SWIMMING = **float**

kickboxing /kík boksing/ *n.* a form of boxing that involves kicking as well as punching —**kickboxer** *n.*

kickdown /kík down/ *n.* a way of changing gear in a car with automatic transmission, by pressing hard on the accelerator pedal

kicking /kíking/ *n.* THRASHING a severe beating (*informal*) ■ *adj.* EXCELLENT excellent, exciting, or very enjoyable (*slang*)

kickoff /kík of/ *n.* **1.** SOCCER START OF MATCH in football, the place kick from the centre spot that begins the game **2.** START OF STH the start of sth or the time when sth starts (*informal*) **3.** SOCCER STARTING TIME the time at which a game of football is due to start **4.** AMERICAN FOOTBALL START OF A GAME in American football, the kicking of the ball at the beginning of a game, half, or after a touchdown or field goal ◇ **for a kickoff** to begin with, or as the first of several things (*informal*)

kick pleat *n.* an inverted pleat at the lower back of a straight skirt to prevent the wearer from being hampered when walking

kickshaw /kík shaw/ *n.* (*archaic*) **1.** TRINKET a trinket of little value **2.** FOOD DELICACY an exotic food delicacy [Late 16thC. From French *quelque chose* 'sth'.]

kickstand /kík stand/ *n.* a pivoting metal bar on a bicycle or motorcycle that can be pushed down into contact with the ground to keep the vehicle upright when it is stationary [Mid-20thC. So called because it is raised and lowered with the foot.]

kick-start *vt.* (**kick-starts, kick-starting, kick-started**) **1.** MOTORCYCLES START A MOTORCYCLE to start the engine on a motorcycle by stepping down hard on the kick-starter **2.** START STH QUICKLY to start or restart a process or activity quickly and forcefully ○ *policies designed to kick-start an ailing economy* ■ *n.* **1.** MOTORCYCLES = **kick-starter** **2.** FORCEFUL START a course of action that quickly and forcefully starts or restarts a process or activity (*informal*)

kick-starter *n.* the pedal on a motorcycle that starts the engine when it is kicked downwards

kick turn *n.* in skiing, a standing 180° turn made by swivelling each ski separately

kick wheel *n.* a mechanical potter's wheel that is turned by a foot-operated treadle

kid[1] /kid/ *n.* **1.** CHILD a young child (*informal*) **2.** YOUNG GOAT a young goat, antelope, or similar animal **3.** YOUTH a young person (*informal*) **4.** INDUST SOFT LEATHER soft leather made from the skin of a young goat **5.** US TERM OF ADDRESS used as an informal term of address (*informal*) ○ *Here's looking at you, kid.* ■ *adj.* YOUNGER younger, especially of two siblings (*informal*) ○ *his kid sister* ■ *vti.* (**kids, kidding, kidded**) BEAR YOUNG to give birth to a young goat [12thC. From Old Norse *kið.*]

—— WORD KEY: SYNONYMS ——
See Synonyms at *youth*.

—— WORD KEY: REGIONAL NOTE ——
The use of **kid** to mean 'child' was regarded as 'low slang' until the 19th century. In parts of the north of England, **kid** is used as a term of address: *our kid* means 'my youngest brother'.

kid[2] /kid/ (**kids, kidding, kidded**) *v.* **1.** *vti.* SAY STH FOR FUN to say sth that is not true, especially as a joke or to tease sb **2.** *vt.* DECEIVE SB to deceive or mislead sb (*informal*) ○ *don't kid yourself* [Late 16thC. From KID[1].] —**kidder** *n.*

kid[3] /kid/ *n.* a small wooden tub, especially one used for serving food on ships (*archaic*) [Mid-18thC. Origin uncertain: perhaps a variant of KIT.]

Kidderminster /kídderminster/, **Kidderminster carpet** *n.* a type of ingrain carpet originally made in Kidderminster

kiddie *n.* US = **kiddy**

kiddo /kíddō/ (*plural* **-dos** *or* **-does**) *n.* **1.** YOUNG PERSON a child, young person, or friend (*slang*) **2.** TERM OF ADDRESS used as an informal term of address, especially to a young person (*informal*)

Kiddush /kíddəsh, kíddush/ (*plural* **-dushim**), **kiddush** (*plural* **-dushim**) *n.* **1.** BLESSING in Judaism, a special blessing, usually for wine, said before a meal on the eve of the Sabbath or a holiday in order to consecrate the festival **2.** RECEPTION a reception following the recitation of the Kiddush for the congregants, at which drinks and snacks are served [Mid-18thC. From Hebrew *qiddūš* 'sanctification'.]

kiddy /kíddi/ (*plural* **-dies**), **kiddie** *n.* a small child (*informal*)

kid glove *n.* a glove of soft leather made from the skin of a young goat ◇ **handle sb** *or* **sth with kid gloves** to use great care or delicacy when dealing with sb or sth

kidglove /kid glúv/, **kid-glove** *adj.* displaying tact and sensitivity

kidlit /kídlit/ *n.* US literature for children (*informal*) [Late 20thC. Shortening.]

Kidman /kídmən/, **Nicole** (*b.* 1967) Hawaiian-born Australian actor. She has starred in films such as *To Die For* (1994) and *The Portrait of a Lady* (1996).

Kidman, Sir Sidney (1857–1935) Australian landowner. He owned vast plots of grazing land, and was known as the 'Cattle King'.

kidnap /kíd nap/ *vti.* (**-naps, -napping, -napped**) ABDUCT SB to take sb away by force and hold him or her prisoner, usually for ransom ■ *n.* = **kidnapping** [Mid-17thC. From KID[1] + *nap* 'to steal', of uncertain origin: perhaps a variant of NAB. From the practice of abducting children to provide servants for US plantations.] —**kidnapper** *n.*

kidnapping /kíd naping/ *n.* the action or crime of forcefully taking away and holding sb prisoner, usually for ransom. Also called **kidnap**

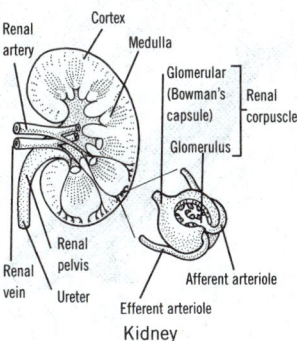

Renal artery — Cortex — Medulla
Glomerular (Bowman's capsule) — Renal corpuscle
Glomerulus
Renal pelvis
Renal vein — Ureter
Afferent arteriole
Efferent arteriole
Kidney

kidney /kídni/ (*plural* **-neys**) *n.* **1.** ANAT WASTE-REMOVING VERTEBRATE ORGAN either of a pair of organs in the abdomen of vertebrates that filter waste liquid resulting from metabolism of the blood, which is subsequently excreted as urine **2.** ZOOL INVERTEBRATE ORGAN the organ in invertebrates that filters waste material for excretion **3.** FOOD ANIMAL KIDNEY AS FOOD the kidney of a pig, calf, ox, or lamb, eaten as meat **4.** KIND a kind, type, or disposition (*dated*) ○ *a person of a very different kidney* [14thC. Origin unknown: perhaps formed from Old English *cod* 'bag'.]

kidney bean *n.* **1.** FOOD PULSE OF THE HARICOT FAMILY a small, usually dark red, edible bean shaped like a kidney **2.** PLANTS PLANT PRODUCING KIDNEY BEANS a widely cultivated annual plant that produces kidney beans. Latin name: *Phaseolus vulgaris.*

kidney-shaped *adj.* in the shape of an oval with a concavity in one side

kidney stone *n.* a small hard mass that forms in the kidney, consisting mainly of phosphates, oxalates, and urates

kidney vetch *n.* = okra

kidology /ki dólləji/ *n.* the use of bluffing or deception (*informal*) [Mid-20thC. From KID[2].]

kidskin /kíd skin/ *n.* = **kid**[1] *n.* 4

kids' stuff *n.* (*informal*) **1.** STH FOR CHILDREN sth considered suitable only for children or immature people **2.** STH EASY OR BORING sth that is very easy or very boring

kidvid /kíd vid/ *n.* US a video for children (*informal*) [Late 20thC. Shortening.]

Kiel /keel/ city and seaport in north-central Germany, the capital of the state of Schleswig-Holstein situated north of Hamburg. Population: 247,700 (1994).

Kiel Canal canal in northwestern Germany connecting the North and Baltic seas. Length: 97 km/60 mi.

kier /keer/ *n.* a vat in which yarn or cloth is bleached or dyed [Late 16thC. From Old Norse *ker* 'tub'.]

Kierkegaard /keérkə gaard/, **Søren** (1813–55) Danish philosopher. His religious philosophy is concerned with individual existence, choice, and commitment, and has profoundly influenced theology and the existential philosophers. His books include *The Concept of Irony* (1841) and *Either/Or* (1843). Full name **Søren Aabye Kierkegaard**

kieserite /keézə rīt/ *n.* a white to yellow crystalline mineral that consists of hydrated magnesium sulphate and is found in large amounts in some salt residues [Mid-19thC. Named after the German physician, Dietrich *Kieser* (1779–1862).]

Kiev /keéyif/ capital and largest city of Ukraine, located in the north-centre of the country. Population: 2,646,000 (1993).

kif /kif/, **kef** /kef/, **kaif** /kayf/ *n.* marijuana, especially in North Africa [Early 19thC. From Arabic *kayf*, *kef* 'pleasure'.]

Kigali /ki gaáli/ capital city of Rwanda, situated on a plateau in the centre of the country, just south of the equator. Population: 234,500 (1993).

kike /kīk/ *n.* US a highly offensive taboo term referring to a Jewish person (*taboo offensive*) [Early 20thC. Origin unknown.]

Kikongo /kee kóng gō/ *n.* LANG = **Kongo**[1] *n.* 2 [Late 19thC. From Kikongo.]

kikumon /kíkə mon, keékə mon/ *n.* the emblem of the Japanese imperial family, in the form of a chrysanthemum [From Japanese]

Kikuyu /ki koõ yoo/ (*plural* **-yu** *or* **-yus**) *n.* **1.** PEOPLES MEMBER OF A RURAL KENYAN PEOPLE a member of an agricultural people living mainly in the highland areas of Kenya, especially around Mount Kenya **2.** LANG AFRICAN LANGUAGE a Benue-Congo language spoken in parts of Kenya, belonging to the Niger-Congo family of African languages. Kikuyu is spoken by about five million people. [Mid-19thC. From Bantu.] —**Kikuyu** *adj.*

Kildare /kil dáir/ county in the province of Leinster in the eastern Republic of Ireland. It borders Dublin to the east. Population: 134,881 (1996). Area: 1,694 sq. km/654 sq. mi.

kilderkin /kílldər kin/ *n.* **1.** OLD LIQUID MEASUREMENT an obsolete British measurement for liquids, equivalent to about 18 gallons or 68 litres **2.** CASK a cask with a capacity of one kilderkin [14thC. From Middle Dutch *kinderkin*, literally 'small quintal'.]

kilim /ki leém, ki lím, keélim/ *n.* a Middle Eastern rug with richly coloured geometric patterns, woven like tapestry, with no pile [Late 19thC. Via Turkish *Kilim* from Persian *gelīm*, coarse-woven blanket.]

Mount Kilimanjaro: View from Amboseli National Park

Kilimanjaro, Mount /kílləmən jaárō/ the highest mountain in Africa, located in northeastern Tanzania. Height: 5,895 m/19,340 ft.

Kilkenny /kil kénni/ county in the province of Leinster, southeastern Republic of Ireland. The county town is Kilkenny. Population: 75,155 (1996). Area: 2,062 sq. km/796 sq. mi.

kill /kil/ *v.* (**kills, killing, killed**) **1.** *vti.* CAUSE SB TO DIE to cause the death of a person or an animal ○ *They were killed in a car crash.* **2.** *vt.* RUIN STH to cause sth to end or be ruined ○ *The remark killed the conversation.* **3.** *vt.* HURT PART OF SB'S BODY to cause severe physical pain or discomfort to sb (*informal*) ○ *My feet are killing me!* **4.** *vt.* OVERPOWER STH SUBTLE OR LESS STRONG to destroy or severely damage an essential, often delicate quality in sth by superimposing sth stronger ○ *Her perfume killed the scent of the roses.* **5.** *vt.* TIRE SB OUT to exhaust sb completely (*informal*) ○ *These stairs kill me every time.* **6.** *vr.* OVEREXERT YOURSELF to push yourself too hard (*informal*; often used ironically) ○ *She was killing herself to get the job done on time.* **7.** *vt.* SWITCH STH OFF to disconnect the power to sth electrical or mechanical so that it stops working (*informal*) ○ *Kill the engine.* **8.** *vt.* MAKE TIME PASS to use up spare time in some activity (*informal*) ○ *They killed a couple of hours at the cinema.* **9.** *vt.* PUBL CUT TEXT to delete a piece of text from a publication or remove a particular amount from a text (*slang*) ○ *We had to kill half a column to make space for the ad.* **10.** *vt.* BLOCK A PLAN to prevent a proposal going through, e.g. the passing of a parliamentary bill **11.** *vti.* BOWL SB OVER to have an overpowering effect on sb, e.g. causing extreme admiration, helpless laughter, or utter amazement (*informal*) ○ *dressed to kill* **12.** *vt.* DRINK ALL OF STH to finish off a bottle of sth, usually an alcoholic beverage (*slang*) **13.** *vt.* SOCCER CONTROL THE BALL to bring a fast-moving ball under instant control **14.** *vt.* US SPORTS HIT A BALL HARD to hit a ball very hard **15.** *vt.* RACKET GAMES MAKE A BALL UNRETURNABLE in racquet games, to hit the ball so hard, with such skill, or in such a direction that your opponent has no chance of returning it ■ *n.* **1. KILLING** the moment or an act of killing sth, especially prey or game, or the bull at the end of a bullfight **2.** HUNT **PREY** the prey killed by an animal or human being **3.** MIL **DESTRUCTION OF ENEMY VEHICLE** the destroying of an enemy vehicle such as a plane, ship, or tank (*slang*) [13thC. From assumed Old English *cyllan*, from a prehistoric Germanic word that is also the ancestor of English *quell*.] ◇ **be in at the kill** to be present at the end of sth or the achievement of an aim, especially when you have worked to cause it

---
WORD KEY: SYNONYMS
---
kill, murder, assassinate, execute, put to death, slaughter, slay, put down, put to sleep
CORE MEANING: to deprive of life
kill a general word used to talk about causing the death of a person or animal; **murder** to take the life of another person in an intentional and often premeditated way that constitutes a serious criminal act; **assassinate** to murder a public figure by means of a sudden surprise attack, often for political or religious reasons; **execute** to take sb's life in accordance with a legal death sentence. It is also used to refer to the instant or summary killing of an enemy, often for political or military reasons; **put to death** to deliberately take sb's life, especially in accordance with a legal death sentence; **slaughter** to kill animals for food, especially animals that have been bred on a farm. It can also be used to refer to brutal and violent killing, usually on a large scale; **slay** a formal or literary word used to refer to killing a person or animal in an intentional and violent way; **put to sleep** a euphemism used to talk about the humane killing of sick or injured animals, especially when done by a vet, used in the same way as 'put down'.

kill off *vt.* **1. COMPLETELY DESTROY STH** to destroy sth utterly, or destroy the remaining members of a group of people or creatures ○ *The spray killed off all the aphids.* **2.** TV, LITERAT **GET RID OF A CHARACTER** to write in the death of a character, especially in a serial or soap opera

Killarney /ki laàrni/ city and tourist centre in the southwestern Republic of Ireland, situated by the Lakes of Killarney. Population: 9,950 (1991).

killdeer /kíl deer/ *n.* a large North American plover that has brown and white plumage, two black breast bands, and a distinctive noisy cry. Latin name: *Charadrius vociferus.* [Mid-18thC. An imitation of the bird's call.]

killer /kíllər/ *n.* **1. SB OR STH THAT KILLS** sb or sth that kills other people or animals intentionally, especially one that does this more than once ○ *a killer crocodile* **2. STH VERY DIFFICULT** sth that is very demanding or difficult (*informal*) ○ *This aerobics class is a killer.* **3. DESTRUCTIVE FORCE, PERSON, OR ORGANISM** sb or sth that destroys or is fatal **4. EXCEPTIONAL THING** sth that is excellent or exceptional (*slang*) ○ *a killer performance*

killer app /-ap/ *n.* COMPUT a computer application of outstanding power, originality, or market reach (*slang*)

killer bee *n.* an aggressive honeybee that was hybridized in Brazil from African and European strains and has spread north into Mexico and southern Texas (*informal*)

killer cell *n.* a T cell that is part of the body's immune system and attacks cells having specific antigens on their surface, e.g. cancer cells and those infected with a virus

killer instinct *n.* **1. URGE TO KILL** a tendency, capacity, or urge to kill **2. STRONG WILL TO WIN** an overpowering drive to succeed, e.g. in business deals or sports, whatever the cost may be to other people

killer T cell *n.* = **killer cell**

killer whale *n.* a black-and-white toothed whale inhabiting colder seas. It grows up to 7.62 m/25 ft long, has a tall dorsal fin, and feeds mainly on fish and squid. Latin name: *Orcinus orca.*

kill fee *n.* US payment made to a writer, photographer, artist, or illustrator by a publisher who has decided not to publish the contracted work

killick /kíllik/, **killock** /kíllək/ *n.* a small anchor, especially one made of a heavy stone [Early 17thC. Origin unknown.]

Killer whale

Killiecrankie, Pass of wooded pass in Perth and Kinross, central Scotland

killifish /kíllifish/ *n.* a fish about the size of a minnow that inhabits fresh and brackish water and is used as an aquarium fish, as bait, and in mosquito control. Family: Cyprinodontidae. [Early 19thC. *Killi* of uncertain origin: perhaps from New York dialect *kill* 'creek, channel', from Dutch *kil* 'channel'.]

killing /kílling/ *n.* **1. SLAYING** the act of causing the death of a human being or an animal **2. QUICK PROFIT** a large and quick profit (*informal*) ■ *adj.* **1. EXHAUSTING** totally exhausting **2. FUNNY** hilariously funny **3. FATAL** causing or resulting in death —**killingly** *adv.*

killing fields *npl.* the site of mass slaughter, e.g. of civilians

---
WORD KEY: CULTURAL NOTE

The Killing Fields, a film by Roland Joffe (1984). Through the true story of US journalist Sydney Schanberg's attempts to trace the Cambodian aide he was forced to leave behind after the fall of Phnom Penh in 1975, Joffe portrays the atrocities perpetrated on the Cambodian people by the Khmer Rouge regime between 1975 and 1978. References such as 'the killing fields of Bosnia' clearly take their linguistic cues from this film title.

killjoy /kíl joy/ *n.* sb whose behaviour prevents other people from having a good time

killock *n.* SAILING = **killick**

Kilmarnock /kil maárnək/ industrial town in East Ayrshire, central Scotland. Population: 44,307 (1991).

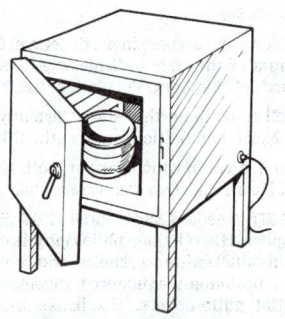
Kiln: Pottery kiln

kiln /kiln, kil/ *n.* INDUSTRIAL OVEN a specialized oven or furnace used for industrial processes such as firing clay for pottery or bricks and for drying materials such as hops or timber ■ *vt.* (**kilns, kilning, kilned**) PROCESS STH IN A KILN to dry, fire, or bake sth in a kiln [Pre-12thC. From Latin *culina*, a variant of *coquina* (source of English *kitchen*).]

Kilner jar /kílnər-/ *tdmk.* a trademark for a glass jar that has an airtight lid and is used for preserving fruit and vegetables

kilo /keélō/ *n.* **1. KILOGRAM** a kilogram. Symbol **k 2.** COMMUNICATION **CODE WORD FOR LETTER 'K'** the NATO phonetic alphabet code word for the letter 'K', used in international radio communications [Mid-19thC. Shortening.]

kilo- *prefix.* **1.** a thousand (10³) ○ *kilogram* **2.** a binary thousand ○ *kilobyte* [Via French from Greek *khilioi* 'thousand']

kilobit /kíllə bit/ *n.* COMPUT 1,024 bits

kilobyte /kíllə bīt/ *n.* COMPUT 1,024 bytes

kilocalorie /kíllō kalləri/ *n.* = **calorie**

kilocycle /kíllō sīk'l/ *n.* a kilohertz (*dated*)

kilogram /kíllə gram/, **kilogramme** *n.* the basic unit of mass in the SI system, equal to 1,000 grams or 2.2046 lbs. Symbol **kg**

kilohertz /kíllō hurts/ *n.* 1,000 hertz

kilometre *n.* 1,000 metres or 0.621 miles

kiloton /kíllō tun/ *n.* **1. 1,000 TONS** 1,000 tons **2. MEASURE OF EXPLOSIVE CAPABILITY** an explosive force equal to 1,000 tons of TNT

kilovolt /kíllə vōlt/ *n.* 1,000 volts

kilowatt /kíllə wot/ *n.* 1,000 watts

kilowatt-hour *n.* a unit of energy equal to the work done by one kilowatt in one hour

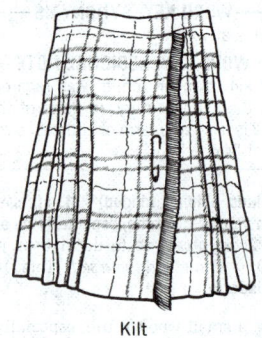
Kilt

kilt /kilt/ *n.* SCOTTISH TARTAN GARMENT an approximately knee-length wrap-around tartan skirt that is part of the traditional Scottish highland dress for men. A variant of it is worn by women and girls. ■ *vt.* (**kilts, kilting, kilted**) **1. TUCK UP A SKIRT** to pull up a skirt and gather it into folds, so as to keep it out of water or mud or to allow more freedom of movement (*dated*) **2. PLEAT GARMENT** to form vertical pleats in the fabric of a garment, usually a skirt [Mid-18thC. From dialect *kilt* 'to tuck up, gird', of Scandinavian origin.]

kilted /kíltid/ *adj.* wearing a kilt

kilter /kíltər/ *n.* good working order or condition ○ *The well pump is out of kilter.* [Mid-17thC. Variant of earlier *kelter*, of unknown origin.]

kiltie /kílti/ *n.* sb wearing a kilt, especially a kilted soldier from a highland regiment (*informal*)

Kimberleys, The /kímbərliz/ plateau region of northwestern Western Australia, near the border with the Northern Territory. The highest point is Mount Hann, 776 m/2,545 ft. Area: 360,000 sq. km/140,000 sq. mi.

kimberlite /kímbər līt/ *n.* a form of igneous rock, found especially in South Africa, composed mainly of peridotite and often containing diamonds [Late 19thC. Named after *Kimberley*, South Africa, a diamond-mining centre.]

kimchi /kímchi/ *n.* a pickle made with vegetables such as cabbage and white radish seasoned with chilli, garlic, and ginger, regarded as the national dish of Korea [Late 19thC. Via Korean *kimch'i* from, ultimately, Chinese.]

Kim Il Sung /kím il súng/ (1912–94) North Korean statesman. As supreme leader of North Korea (1948–94) he tried to reunite Korea in the Korean War (1950–53), and encouraged a personality cult of himself. Born **Kim Song Ju**

kimono /ki mṓnō/ (*plural* **-nos**) *n.* **1. TRADITIONAL JAPANESE GARMENT** a loose, floor-length, traditional Japanese garment that has wide sleeves, wraps in front, and is fastened with a sash **2. WESTERN GARMENT** a Western garment, especially a dressing gown, similar to the Japanese kimono [Late 19thC. From Japanese, formed from *ki* 'wear' + *mono* 'thing'.] —**kimonoed** *adj.*

kin /kin/ *n.* **1. FAMILY GROUP** sb's relatives as a group (*takes a plural verb*) **2. GROUP OR CLASS** a member of a group that shares characteristics with another group ○ *Starfishes and sea urchins are kin.* **3. BLOOD RELATION** sb related by blood ○ *He's not kin but we*

Kimono

consider him one of the family. ■ *adj.* RELATED related to sb [Old English *cyn(n)*. Ultimately from an Indo-European word that is also the ancestor of English *gender, genre, genetic*, and *genesis*.]

-kin *suffix.* little, dear ○ *limpkin* [Origin uncertain: probably from Middle Dutch *-ki(j)n*]

kina /kéenə/ *n.* **1.** CURRENCY OF PAPUA NEW GUINEA the main unit of currency of Papua New Guinea, equal to 100 toeas. See table at **currency 2.** COIN WORTH A KINA a coin worth a kina [Late 20thC. From Tok Pisin.]

Kinabalu, Mount /kínnəbə lóo/ mountain in Malaysia in the state of Sabah, in northern Borneo. It lies in Kinabalu National Park. Height: 4,101 m/13,455 ft.

kinaesthesia /kín eess theézi ə, kīn eess-/, **kinaesthesis** /kín eess théessiss, kīn eess-/ *n.* ANAT the perception or sensing of the motion, weight, or position of the body as muscles, tendons, and joints move [Late 19thC. From Greek *kinein* 'to move' (see KINESIS) + *aisthēsis* 'sensation'.] —**kinaesthetic** *adj.* —**kinaesthetically** *adv.*

kinase /kī nayss, -nayz/ *n.* any of a group of enzymes that catalyze the transfer of a phosphate group from ATP [Early 20thC. Formed from KINETIC + -ASE.]

Kincardineshire /kin kaár dinshər/ former country in eastern Scotland, now part of Aberdeenshire

kincob /kíng kob, -kəb/ *n.* an Indian silk embroidered with gold or silver thread [Early 18thC. From Urdu and Persian *kamkāb* 'gold or silver brocade', an alteration of *kamkā* 'damask silk', ultimately from Chinese words meaning 'gold' and 'flower'.]

kind[1] /kīnd/ *adj.* **1.** COMPASSIONATE having a generous, warm, compassionate nature **2.** GENEROUS showing generosity or compassion **3.** AGREEABLE OR SAFE not harsh, unpleasant, or likely to have destructive effects ○ *a detergent that is kind to the environment* **4.** CARING showing courtesy or caring about sb (*formal*) ○ *my kindest regards to your family* **5.** LOVING full of love (*archaic*) [Old English *gecynde* 'innate', 'natural', from a prehistoric Germanic word that is also the ancestor of English *kin*]

WORD KEY: USAGE

See Usage note at ***kindly***.

kind[2] /kīnd/ *n.* **1.** GROUP OF INDIVIDUALS THAT SHARE FEATURES a group or class of individuals connected by shared characteristics ○ *What kind of fruit is this?* **2.** STH INFERIOR an example of sth, especially if it is seen as inferior or doubtful ○ *Well, you could say it's a kind of tool, but how would you use it?* **3.** ESSENCE OF STH the primary character of sth that determines the class to which it belongs ◇ **kind of** rather, to some extent, or in a way (*informal*) ○ *She seemed kind of upset when I talked to her.* ◇ **in kind 1.** with goods or services and not money **2.** with sth of the same sort that was given ○ *If they attack us, they'll be paid back in kind.* ◇ **of a kind 1.** like sth else in some respects but not enough to be satisfactory **2.** alike, or belonging to the same sort

WORD KEY: USAGE

These kind of When ***kind of*** is followed by a plural word, there is a temptation to precede the whole phrase with a corresponding plural such as *these* or *those*, so that *this kind of thing* becomes *these kind of things*. However, such expressions (and ones on the same pattern employing *sort* or *type*) are widely regarded as ungrammatical. *These kinds of things* or *things of this kind* is to be preferred.

WORD KEY: SYNONYMS

See Synonyms at ***type***.

kinda /kīndə/ *contr.* kind of (*nonstandard*) ○ *It's kinda strange.* [Early 20thC. Alteration.]

kindergarten /kíndər gaart'n/ *n.* *US* a school or class for young children, usually between the ages of four and six, immediately before they begin formal education [Mid-19thC. From German, literally 'children's garden'.]

kind-hearted /-haártid/ *adj.* **1.** FRIENDLY AND GENEROUS BY NATURE sympathetic and kind ○ *She's too kind-hearted to be angry with you for long.* **2.** ARISING FROM KINDNESS showing or arising from a sympathetic and generous nature ○ *a kind-hearted gesture* —**kind-heartedly** *adv.* —**kind-heartedness** *n.*

kindle[1] /kínd'l/ (**-dles, -dling, -dled**) *vti.* **1.** START BURNING to set sth alight, or to begin to burn **2.** BRIGHTEN OR GLOW to make sth glow, or to become bright **3.** IGNITE EMOTION OR INTEREST to become aroused, or to arouse feelings or interest ○ *The programme kindled his interest in antiquarian books.* [12thC. From Old Norse *kynda* 'to catch fire', influenced by Old Norse *kyndill* 'torch, candle'.] —**kindler** *n.*

kindle[2] *n.* ZOOL BROOD OF NEWBORN ANIMALS a brood or a litter, e.g. of kittens ■ *vi.* (**kindles, kindling, kindled**) ZOOL GIVE BIRTH to give birth, especially to baby rabbits

kindliness /kīndliness/ *n.* **1.** AMIABILITY the quality or state of being friendly and generous **2.** MILDNESS OF CLIMATE agreeableness of climate or temperature

kindling /kíndling/ *n.* **1.** FIRE-LIGHTING MATERIAL sth such as a bunch of small dry twigs used to start a fire because it burns easily **2.** MAKING STH BURN the act of making sth start to burn **3.** STIRRING UP OF EMOTION the arousal of sb's interest or feelings

kindly /kīndli/ *adj.* (**-lier, -liest**) **1.** FRIENDLY AND GENEROUS BY NATURE sympathetic and kind **2.** SHOWING SYMPATHY arising from or showing a sympathetic and generous nature **3.** PLEASANT pleasant, mild, or comfortable ■ *adv.* **1.** PLEASE used in polite requests ○ *Kindly take your seats* **2.** IN A KIND WAY showing kindness and considerateness ○ *He kindly accompanied me home.* **3.** TOLERANTLY with tolerance and patience ○ *She kindly disregarded their lack of skill during the first few days.* [Old English]

WORD KEY: USAGE

Often misplaced modifier: ***Kindly*** is not restricted just to *kindness* as such but may also mean, approximately, 'please'. In either case it should modify the action or thing wished for, not some other part of the sentence. Surely the intention of, for example, *May we kindly request that patrons take their seats . . .* is not to point out how kind *we* are in making the request but to encourage patrons to be so kind as to sit down. Thus the sentence should be reworded as *May we request that patrons kindly take their seats.*

kindness /kīndnəss/ *n.* **1.** ABILITY TO BEHAVE KINDLY the practice of being or the capability to be sympathetic and compassionate **2.** COMPASSIONATE ACT an act that shows consideration and caring ○ *How can we thank you for your many kindnesses?*

kindred /kíndrəd/ *adj.* **1.** SIMILAR TO SB OR STH close to sb or sth else because of similar qualities or interests ○ *the kindred relationship between neuroscience and neurology* **2.** RELATED BY BLOOD related to sb by blood (*formal*) ○ *the search for someone kindred to him* ■ *n.* **1.** AFFINITY closeness to sb not related to you by blood based, e.g. on similarity of character or interests ○ *a sense of kindred between the two candidates* **2.** BLOOD RELATIONSHIP relationship by blood or, less strictly, by marriage ○ *occasions that reinforce the ties of kindred* **3.** SB'S FAMILY sb's relatives as a group (*takes a plural verb*) **4.** CLAN a family or group of closely related families, e.g. in the Celtic kin-based social system ○ *The Ui Neill were then the most powerful of the kindreds.* [12thC. Originally spelt *kinrede* (with later appearance of 'd' between 'n' and 'r'), from KIN + Old English *rǣden* 'condition'.] —**kindredness** *n.* —**kindredship** *n.*

kindred spirit *n.* sb who is close to you in character, interests, and temperament

kindy /kíndi/ (*plural* **-dies**), **kindie** *n.* *ANZ* a kindergarten (*informal*) [Mid-20thC. Shortening and alteration.]

kine /kīn/ *npl.* cows or cattle (*archaic*) [Old English *cȳna* 'of the cows', a plural form of *cū*, an earlier form of COW]

kinematics /kínni máttiks/ *n.* a branch of physics that deals with the motion of a body or system without reference to force and mass (*takes a singular verb*) [Mid-19thC. Formed from Greek *kinēmat-*, the stem of *kinēma*, 'motion, movement'.] —**kinematic** *adj.* —**kinematically** *adv.*

kinescope /kínnəskōp, kīnə-/ *n.* *US* = **television tube** [Mid-20thC. Formerly a trademark, formed from KINETIC + -SCOPE.]

kinesics /ki neéssiks, kī-, -neéziks, -/ *n.* the study of the ways in which people use body movements, e.g. shrugging, to communicate without speaking (*takes a singular verb*) [Mid-20thC. Formed from Greek *kinēsis* (see KINESIS).]

kinesiology /ki neéssi ólləji, kī-, -neé zi-, -/ *n.* **1.** STUDY OF THE MOTION OF THE BODY the study of the mechanics of motion with respect to human anatomy **2.** ALTERN MED ALTERNATIVE THERAPY a system of muscle testing that reveals and corrects musculoskeletal imbalances and identifies food sensitivities [Late 19thC. Formed from Greek *kinēsis* (see KINESIS).] —**kinesiologist** *n.*

kinesis /ki neéssiss, kī-/ *n.* the movement of a cell or organism in response to a stimulus such as light. Such movement can be in any direction and its rate depends on the intensity of stimulation. [Early 20thC. From Greek *kinēsis*, 'movement, motion', from *kinein* 'to move' (source of English *cinema* and *telekinesis*).]

-kinesis *suffix.* **1.** motion, activity ○ *psychokinesis* **2.** cell division ○ *diakinesis* [From Greek *kinēsis*, from *kinein* 'to move' (see KINETIC)]

kinesthesia *n.* US = **kinaesthesia**

kinetheodolite /kínnəth' óddə līt/ *n.* an optical instrument that contains a cine camera and provides continuous footage of a moving target, e.g. a missile or satellite, along with its altitude and trajectory [Mid-20thC. Formed from KINESIS + THEODOLITE.]

kinetic /ki néttik, kī-/ *adj.* relating to, caused by, or producing motion [Mid-19thC. From Greek *kinētikos*, 'for putting in motion', from *kinein*, 'to move' (see KINESIS).]

kinetic art *n.* art, especially sculpture, with parts that move, e.g. when blown by the wind or activated by electricity —**kinetic artist** *n.*

kinetic energy *n.* the energy that a body or system has because of its motion. Symbol T, E_k

kinetics /ki néttiks, kī-/ *n.* (*takes a singular verb*) **1.** PHYS = **dynamics** *n.* 3 **2.** CHEM BRANCH OF CHEMISTRY a branch of chemistry that studies rates of reactions

kineto- *prefix.* motion, movement ○ *kinetosome* [From Greek *kinetos* 'moving', from *kinein* 'to move' (see KINETIC)]

kinetoplast /ki néttə plast, kī-/ *n.* a small cell body outside the nucleus and near the base of the flagellum in some protozoans

kinetosome /ki néttə sōm, kī-/ *n.* BIOL = **basal body**

kinfolk /kínfōk/ *npl.* *US* sb's relatives

king /king/ *n.* **1.** MAN OR BOY SOVEREIGN a man or boy who rules as a monarch over an independent state **2.** CHIEF a ruler of a specific group ○ *Jupiter was king of the Roman gods.* **3.** BEST EXAMPLE OF ITS KIND any animal considered as the best, strongest, or biggest of its kind ○ *The lion is variously called the king of beasts or the king of the jungle.* **4.** PRE-EMINENT MAN IN SPECIFIC SPHERE the principal man or pre-eminent male figure in a specific field ○ *King of the chat shows.* **5.** CARDS HIGH FACE CARD any of the four cards in a pack, one in each suit, that carries the picture of a king **6.** CHESS PRINCIPAL CHESS PIECE the most important piece in chess, whose capture wins the game **7.** BOARD GAMES CROWNED PIECE IN DRAUGHTS a piece in the game of draughts that has reached the far side of the board and has been crowned, and may therefore move in any direction ■ *vt.* (**kings, kinging, kinged**) **1.** BOARD GAMES CROWN A PLAYING PIECE to make a piece into a king **2.** CROWN SB KING to make sb a king [Old English *cyning*, from a prehistoric Germanic word that is also the ancestor of English *kin*]

King /king/ *n.* a title used to denote God or Jesus Christ [Old English]

B. B. King

King /king/, **B. B.** (*b.* 1925) US blues musician. He led a blues revival in the 1960s and his rhythm-and-blues hits include 'The Thrill is Gone' (1970) and the album *Live at Cook Country* (1971). Real name **Riley B. King**

Billie Jean King

King, Billie Jean (*b.* 1943) US tennis player. Between 1961 and 1979 she won a record 20 Wimbledon titles. She also won numerous other titles in the United States, France, and Australia. She became the first president of the Women's Tennis Association in 1974.

Martin Luther King, Jr.

King, Martin Luther, Jr. (1929–68) US civil rights leader and clergyman. His non-violent demonstrations against racial inequality led to civil rights legislation. He was awarded the Nobel Peace Prize in 1964 and was assassinated four years later in Memphis, Tennessee.

kingbird /king burd/ *n.* a large American songbird that belongs to the tyrant flycatcher family of birds. Genus: *Tyrannus*.

kingbolt /king bōlt/ *n.* a vertical bolt that joins the body of a carriage, wagon, or railway carriage to the front axle

King Charles spaniel *n.* a small spaniel of a breed with a markedly domed head, snub nose, bulging eyes, floppy ears, and a tan or black coat with white patches [Late 19thC. Named after CHARLES II of England, who was partial to the breed.]

king cobra *n.* a very large poisonous cobra of Southeast Asia and the Philippines that eats other reptiles and can reach a length of 5.5 m/18 ft. Latin name: *Ophiophagus hannah*.

King Country region in the western North Island, New Zealand, lying south of the Waikato region between the western coast and Lake Taupo

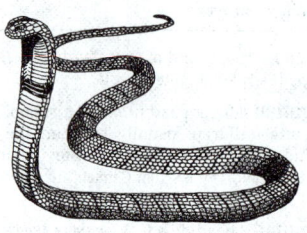

King cobra

king crab *n.* = horseshoe crab

kingcup /king kup/ *n.* a plant of the buttercup family with yellow flowers, especially a marsh marigold

kingdom /kingdəm/ *n.* **1.** MONARCH'S TERRITORY a state or people ruled over by a king or queen **2.** SPHERE OF ACTIVITY a realm or area of activity in which a particular thing is thought to dominate ○ *the kingdom of professional tennis* **3.** SCI HIGHEST CLASSIFICATION FOR NATURAL THINGS any of the three groups, animal, vegetable, and mineral, into which natural organisms and objects are traditionally, as opposed to scientifically, divided [Old English]

kingdom come *n.* **1.** THE NEXT WORLD the next world, or the state after death **2.** END OF THE WORLD the point at which the world comes to an end (*informal*) [Late 18thC. From the phrase *Thy kingdom come* in the Our Father (Matt. 6:10), where *come* is subjunctive, literally 'May Thy kingdom come'.]

kingfish /king fish/ *n.* ZOOL **1.** LARGE EDIBLE FISH a large edible game fish that lives in the warm coastal waters of the Atlantic Ocean. Genus: *Menticirrhus*. **2.** = king mackerel **3.** = opah

Kingfisher

kingfisher /king fishər/ *n.* a brightly coloured bird that usually has a short tail, a long stout bill, and sometimes a crest. It feeds on fish, insects, and other prey. Family: Alcidinidae. [15thC. Originally *king's fisher*.]

King Island island off the northwestern coast of Tasmania, Australia. It is known for its dairy produce. Population: 1,882 (1996). Area: 1,091 sq. km/421 sq. mi.

kinglet /kinglət/ *n.* **1.** BIRDS SMALL N AMERICAN BIRD a small North American bird that is related to the gnatcatchers and to European warblers and has a black-edged yellow or reddish crown. Genus: *Regulus*. **2.** PETTY RULER a minor king, e.g. of a contemptibly small or unimportant kingdom (*insult*)

kingly /kingli/ (**-lier, -liest**) *adj.* **1.** MAGNIFICENT stately and grand, as befits a king ○ *a kingly posture* **2.** ROYAL having or relating to the rank of king ○ *kingly duties* —**kingliness** *n.*

king mackerel *n.* US a mackerel that lives in the warm waters of the Atlantic Ocean and is often caught for sport. Latin name: *Scomber cavalla*.

kingmaker /king maykər/ *n.* sb with the power and connections to influence who is appointed to important positions, usually within a government

king-of-arms (*plural* **kings-of-arms**) *n.* a title given to principal heralds in the British colleges of arms

king of kings, **King of Kings** *n.* **1.** CHR GOD OR JESUS CHRIST a title used for God or Jesus Christ **2.** SUPREME MONARCH a male monarch who rules over other, subordinate kings

king of the castle *n.* **1.** DOMINANT PERSON the most important person in a group or place (*informal*) **2.** CHILDREN'S GAME a game in which a child stands on a piece of higher ground and pushes all other children down

King Peak /king peek/ mountain in the St Elias Range of southwestern Yukon Territory, Canada. Height: 5,221 m/17,130 ft.

king penguin *n.* a large penguin that lives mainly on islands near the Antarctic Circle. Latin name: *Aptenodytes patagonica*.

kingpin /king pin/ *n.* **1.** LEADER the most important person in a group or place (*informal*) **2.** AUTOMOT PART OF AXLE a pivot pin that secures an axle to an axle beam and allows a vehicle to be steered **3.** CRUX OF AN ARGUMENT the most important point in an argument, upon which everything else depends **4.** LEISURE FRONT PIN IN A BOWLING ARRANGEMENT the pin at the apex of a layout of the pins in tenpin bowling, which must be struck at a certain angle if all the pins are to be knocked down

king post *n.* a vertical post that joins the apex of a triangular roof truss to the cross-beam. ◊ **queen post**

Kings /kingz/ *n.* either of two books of the Bible, Kings I and II, that relate the histories of Israel and the kings of Judah (*takes a singular verb*) [Old English]

king salmon *n.* = Chinook salmon

King's Bench *n.* LAW the term used for the Queen's Bench Division when the reigning monarch is a man or boy. ◊ **Queen's bench**

Kings Canyon canyon in central Australia, near Alice Springs in the Northern Territory

King's Counsel *n.* LAW the term used for a Queen's Counsel when the reigning monarch is a man or boy

King's English *n.* standard written or spoken British English, described as the most correct form of the language. It is called the Queen's English when the reigning monarch is a woman.

king's evidence *n.* LAW the term used for queen's evidence when the reigning monarch is a man or boy

king's evil *n.* scrofula (*archaic*) [From the belief that it could be cured by a king's touch]

Kingsford Smith /kingzfərd smith/, **Sir Charles Edward** (1897–1935) Australian aviator. In 1928, with Charles Ulm, he made the first flight across the Pacific Ocean.

king's highway *n.* when the sovereign is a man or boy, any public road (*dated*)

kingship /kingship/ *n.* the office, power, or authority of a king

king-size, **king-sized** *adj.* **1.** EXTRA BIG larger, wider, or longer than the standard version of the same thing **2.** FURNITURE FULL-SIZE used to describe an extra-large size of bed, 1930 x 2032 mm/76 in x 80 in, or bedding made to fit this size of bed **3.** VERY GREAT very great in intensity, scope, or difficulty (*informal*) ○ *a king-size job to finish this weekend*

Kingsley /kingzli/, **Charles** (1819–75) English writer and clergyman. His novels include *Westward Ho!* (1855) and the children's book *The Water Babies* (1863). He was a chaplain to Queen Victoria.

King's Lynn /-lin/ historic town in Norfolk, eastern England, a major seaport in medieval times. Population: 34,900 (1991).

king snake *n.* a nonpoisonous North American constricting snake ranging from 0.6 metres/2 ft to 1.8 metres/6 ft in length and preying on small animals and other snakes. Genus: *Lampropeltis*.

king's peace *n.* in medieval England, the general peace of the kingdom secured by laws enforced in the king's name

King's Proctor *n.* a term used for a Queen's Proctor when the reigning monarch is a man or boy

king's ransom *n.* an enormous sum of money

King's Regulations *npl.* the term used for the Queen's Regulations when the reigning monarch is a man or boy

King's Speech *n.* the term used for the Queen's Speech when the reigning monarch is a man or boy

Kingston upon Hull = **hull** *n.* 1

Kingston-upon-Thames historic town on the River Thames in southeastern England. It is now part of Greater London. Population: 140,100 (1995).

Kingwana /king wáanə/ *n.* a Bantu language spoken in parts of Zaire and widely used as a lingua franca. It is related to Swahili and is a member of the Niger-Congo family of languages. —**Kingwana** *adj.*

kingwood /kíng wŏŏd/ *n.* **1. HARD PURPLISH WOOD** the hard fine-grained purplish wood of a Brazilian tree, used in cabinetwork **2. LEGUMINOUS TREE** the leguminous tree that yields kingwood. Latin name: *Dalbergia cearensis.*

kinin /kínin/ *n.* BIOCHEM **1. BLOOD HORMONE** a polypeptide hormone in the blood that causes dilation of blood vessels and contraction of smooth muscle **2.** = **cytokinin** [Mid-20thC. Origin uncertain: possibly a shortening of BRADYKININ.]

kink /kingk/ *n.* **1. TIGHT COIL** a tight twist or coil in an otherwise straight section of sth such as rope, string, or wire **2. MUSCULAR SPASM** a sudden spasm in a muscle, especially a crick in the neck (*informal*) **3. MINOR DIFFICULTY IN STH** a slight difficulty or holdup in the progress of sth (*informal*) **4. ECCENTRICITY** sth that is eccentric or peculiar in sb's personality or behaviour **5.** *US* **ODD IDEA** a quirky, odd idea or impulse (*informal*) ○ *She got a kink in her head to swim across the Chesapeake Bay alone.* **6. SEXUAL ODDITY** an unusual sexual practice, especially one that might be considered deviant (*slang*) ■ **kinks** *npl. Scotland* **LAUGHTER** convulsions of laughter (*nonstandard*) ○ *had us in kinks with his impressions* ■ *vti.* (**kinks, kinking, kinked**) **MAKE OR BECOME FULL OF TWISTS** to put a kink in sth, or develop a kink [Late 17thC. From Low German *kinke* 'twist in a rope'.]

kinkajou /kíngkə joo/ *n.* a tree-dwelling fruit-eating mammal that lives in Central and South America. It is related to the raccoon and has a long prehensile tail, brownish fur, and large eyes. Latin name: *Potos flavus.* [Late 18thC. Via French *quincajou* from, ultimately, an Algonquian word meaning 'wolverine'.]

kinky /kíngki/ (**-ier, -iest**) *adj.* **1. TIGHTLY COILED** full of tight coils ○ *kinky copper wire* **2. SEXUALLY UNUSUAL** being or engaging in unusual sexual practices that may be considered deviant (*informal*) **3. ECCENTRIC** behaving in an unusual, idiosyncratic way (*informal*) **4. SEXUALLY PROVOCATIVE** intended to be provocative or sexually alluring, usually by being deliberately unusual or bizarre (*dated informal*) —**kinkily** *adv.* —**kinkiness** *n.*

kinnikinnick /kínnikə ník/ *n.* **1. DRIED LEAVES FOR SMOKING** a mixture of the dried leaves of some plants, bark, and sometimes tobacco, smoked in the past by some Native Americans **2. PLANT USED FOR SMOKING** a plant such as sumac or dogwood used for making kinnikinnick [Late 18thC. Ultimately from an Algonquian word meaning 'mixture'.]

Kinnock /kínnək/, **Neil** (*b.* 1942) British politician. He was the leader of the Labour Party from 1983 to 1992. He resigned as Leader of the Opposition after the 1992 general election. Full name **Neil Gordon Kinnock**

kino /keénō/ (*plural* **-nos**) *n.* a red astringent substance resembling resin, obtained by tapping any of several unrelated trees and used medicinally and for tanning in parts of Africa, India, Australia, and the West Indies [Early 19thC. From a West African language.]

Kinross /kin róss/ historic market town in central Scotland, in the former county of Kinross-shire, now part of Perth and Kinross

kin selection *n.* ZOOL natural selection that favours self-sacrificing behaviour towards relatives because, even if the individual dies, those relatives that survive will carry some of its genes

kinsfolk /kínzfōk/ *npl.* sb's relatives

Kinshasa /kin sháassə/ capital city of the Democratic Republic of the Congo, situated on the southern bank of the River Congo. Population: 4,655,313 (1994). Former name **Léopoldville** (until 1966)

kinship /kínship/ *n.* **1. HUMAN RELATIONSHIP** relationship by blood or marriage to another or others **2. RELATEDNESS OF THINGS** relatedness through having characteristics in common, or through coming from the same origin ○ *kinship between Italic and Celtic languages*

Kinski /kínski/, **Klaus** (1926–91) Polish-born German actor. He is best known for his collaborations with the director Werner Herzog in films such as *Nosferatu* (1978) and *Fitzcarraldo* (1982).

kinsman /kínzmən/ (*plural* **-men** /-mən/) *n.* a man or boy who is sb's relative (*formal*) [12thC. From Old English *cynnes mann(um).*]

kinswoman /-wŏŏmən/ (*plural* **-en** /-wimin/) *n.* a woman or girl who is sb's relative (*formal*) [14thC. Modelled on KINSMAN.]

Kintyre /kin tír/ peninsula of western Scotland, between the Firth of Clyde and the Atlantic Ocean The Mull of Kintyre is its southernmost tip. Length: 64 km/40 mi.

kiosk /keé osk/ *n.* **1. SMALL ROOFED STREET STALL** a small permanent or temporary structure in the street from which items such as newspapers and sweets can be bought **2. SMALL STRUCTURE FOR ADVERTISING** a cylindrical structure that stands at a junction or on the street, used to post advertisements and announcements of events **3. TELEPHONE BOOTH** a small booth or shelter in which a public telephone is sited (*dated*) **4. MIDDLE EASTERN GAZEBO** a small open pavilion in the Middle East, especially in a garden [Early 17thC. Via French *kiosque* from Turkish *köşk* 'villa', from Persian *kūšk* 'villa, palace'.]

Kiowa /kí ə waa/ (*plural* **-wa** *or* **-was**) *n.* **1.** PEOPLES **MEMBER OF A NATIVE N AMERICAN PEOPLE** a member of a once-nomadic Native North American people who originally lived in Montana and migrated to an area near the Black Hills. Today, most Kiowa live on a reservation in Oklahoma, which they share with a small community of Kiowa Apache. **2.** LANG **LANGUAGE OF THE KIOWA** the language of the Kiowa people [Early 19thC. Via American Spanish *Caygua* from Kiowa *kygú* (plural).] —**Kiowa** *adj.*

Kiowa Apache *n.* PEOPLES **MEMBER OF A NATIVE NORTH AMERICAN PEOPLE** a member of a Native North American people who originally lived with the Kiowa on the southern Great Plains, sharing a common history and culture, but speaking a different language ■ *adj.* LANG **RELATING TO KIOWA APACHE** relating to the Kiowa Apache people, or their language or culture

kip[1] /kip/ *n. UK* **1. SLEEP** a sleep or a nap (*informal*) **2. BED** a bed or other place to sleep (*slang*) ○ *Is she still in her kip?* ■ *vi.* (**kips, kipping, kipped**) *UK* **SLEEP OR NAP** to sleep or take a nap, often in a makeshift bed (*informal*) [Mid-18thC. From Danish *kippe* 'cheap inn'.]

kip[2] /kip/ *n.* a unit of weight equivalent to 455 kg/1,000 lb [Early 20thC. Formed from an abbreviation of KILO + POUND.]

kip[3] /kip/ (*plural* **kip**) *n.* **1. UNIT OF CURRENCY IN LAOS** the main unit of currency of Laos, equal to 100 at. See table at **currency 2. COIN WORTH A KIP** a coin worth one kip [Mid-20thC. From Thai.]

kip[4] /kip/, **kipskin** /kípskin/ *n.* a hide taken from an immature animal, especially a calf or a lamb [14thC. From Middle Dutch or Middle Low German, 'bundle (of hides)'.]

Kipling /kípling/, **Rudyard** (1865–1936) British writer and poet. His books, many with Indian settings, include *The Jungle Books* (1894, 1895) and *Kim* (1901). He won the 1907 Nobel Prize in literature.

kippa /ki paá/ (*plural* **kippot** /-pót/ *or* **kippoth**) *n.* the skullcap worn by Jewish men and boys for prayer and by Orthodox Jewish men at all times. US term **yarmulke** [Mid-20thC. From modern Hebrew *kippāh.*]

kipper /kíppər/ *n.* **1. SALMON** a male salmon during the spawning season **2. SMOKED HERRING** a fish, usually a herring, that has been cleaned, split open, and then salted and smoked ■ *vt.* (**-pers, -pering, -pered**) **SMOKE FISH** to cure fresh fish, especially herring, by salting and smoking it (*usually passive*) [Old English *cypera* 'spawning salmon', of uncertain origin: perhaps from *coper* 'copper' (from the colour of the fish)] —**kipperer** *n.*

kir /keer/ *n.* an alcoholic drink made by adding cassis to dry white wine [Mid-20thC. Named after Canon Félix *Kir* (1876–1968), mayor of Dijon, France, who supposedly invented the drink.]

kirby grip /kúrbi-/ *tdmk.* a trademark for a grip used to hold sb's hair in place. It consists of a piece of metal bent tightly over into two prongs, with the upper prong ridged.

Kirchhoff /kúrk of/, **Gustav** (1824–87) German physicist. With Robert Bunsen he invented spectroscopy and discovered caesium and rubidium (1860). He formulated Kirchhoff's laws of electrical networks. Full name **Gustav Robert Kirchhoff,**

Kirchner /kúrkhnər/, **Ernst Ludwig** (1880–1938) German artist. Known for his paintings and woodcuts, he was a leading figure in the German expressionist movement Die Brücke (1905–13).

Kirgiz *n.* LANG, PEOPLES = **Kyrgyz**

Kiribati /kírri baáti/ independent state in the west-central Pacific Ocean, part of Micronesia. Language: English. Currency: Australian dollar. Capital: Tarawa. Population: 82,449 (1997). Area: 811 sq. km/313 sq. mi. Official name **Republic of Kiribati**

Kiritimati /kírri ti máati/ island forming part of Kiribati Republic. It is the largest atoll in the Pacific Ocean. Population: 2,537 (1990). Area: 388 sq. km/150 sq. mi.

kirk /kurk/ *n. Scotland* a church [12thC. From Old Norse *kirkja*, from Old English *cir(i)ce*, an earlier form of CHURCH.]

Kirk *n. Scotland* the Church of Scotland, the largest presbyterian church in Scotland

Kirk /kurk/, **Norman** (1923–74) New Zealand statesman. He was Labour prime minister of New Zealand (1972–74). Full name **Norman Eric Kirk**

Kirkcudbright /kur kóobri/ town in Dumfries and Galloway Region, Scotland. Population: 3,588 (1991).

Kirkcudbrightshire /kur kóobrishər/ former county in southwestern Scotland until 1975, now part of Dumfries and Galloway

Kirkwall /kÚrk wawl/ capital and largest town of the Orkney Islands, northern Scotland, on the northern coast of Mainland Island. Population: 6,469 (1991).

Kirlian photography /kúr li ən-/ *n.* PHOTOGRAPHY a photographic process that records the radiation emitted by or the aura surrounding an object in a high-frequency electric field [Late 20thC. Named after Semyon D. and Valentina K. *Kirlian*, Russian technicians who invented the process.]

Kirman /kər maán, keer-/ *n.* a Persian carpet or rug [Late 19thC. Named after *Kirman*, a province in Iran where the rugs were originally made.]

kirmess *n.* = **kermis**

Kirov /keé rof/ city in northeastern European Russia, capital of Kirov Oblast. Population: 487,000 (1990). Former name **Vyatka**

Kirovohrad /ki róvvə grad/ city in central Ukraine, situated southeast of Kiev. Population: 278,000 (1995).

kirpan /keer paán/ *n.* the short sword worn by baptized Sikh men as a symbol of their cultural and religious loyalty. ◊ **five Ks** [Early 20thC. Via Punjabi and Hindi from Sanskrit *kṛpāṇa* 'sword'.]

kirsch /keersh/, **kirschwasser** /keérsh vassər/ *n.* a clear brandy distilled from black cherries, especially in Germany and France [Early 19thC. From German, a shortening of *Kirschwasser*, literally 'cherry-water', from *Kirsche* 'cherry', from assumed Vulgar Latin *cerasia* (source of English *cherry*).]

kirtle /kúrt'l/ *n.* **1. WOMAN'S DRESS** a long gown or skirt worn by women from the Middle Ages to the 17th century **2. 16C MAN'S COAT** a long tunic or coat worn by men until the 16th century [Old English *cyrtel* 'short coat', via prehistoric Germanic from, ultimately, Latin *curtus* 'short, cut short']

Kiruna /keéroonə/ city in Norrbotten County, north-

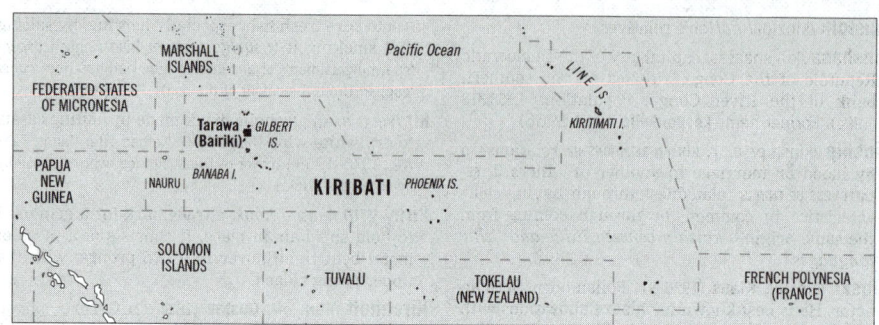
Kiribati

ern Sweden, a region rich in high-quality iron ore. Population: 26,173 (1995).

Kisangani /kíssang gaáni/ capital of Orientale Region, in northern Democratic Republic of the Congo. Population: 417,517 (1994).

kishke /kíshkə/ n. a Jewish dish consisting of a chicken's or cow's intestine stuffed with flour meal, onion, and fat, and then boiled and roasted [Mid-20thC. From Yiddish, from Slavic.]

Kiska Island /kískə-/ island in the Aleutian Islands, southwestern Alaska, the largest and westernmost of the Rat Islands. Area: 285 sq. km/110 sq. mi.

Kislev /kíssləf, kiss lév/ n. the third month of the year in the Jewish civil calendar, and the ninth month in the religious year. It has either 29 or 30 days. [From Hebrew *Kislēw*]

kismet /kíz met, kízmət/ n. **1.** ISLAM ALLAH'S WILL the will of Allah **2.** FATE fate or destiny [Mid-19thC. Via Turkish from Persian *kismat*, from Arabic *kisma(t)* 'lot, portion', from *kasama* 'he divided, allotted'.]

kiss /kiss/ v. (**kisses, kissing, kissed**) **1.** *vti.* BRUSH OR CARESS WITH THE LIPS to touch sb or sth with the lips, either gently or passionately **2.** *vti.* CUE GAMES GLANCE AGAINST ONE ANOTHER in cue games, to touch each other gently when one ball is passing the other, or to touch another ball while passing it **3.** *vt.* TOUCH STH GENTLY to touch or brush against sth lightly (*usually passive*) ○ *oranges kissed by the California sun* ■ n. **1.** CARESS DONE WITH THE LIPS a gentle or passionate touch with the lips **2.** GENTLE PASSING TOUCH a very light, almost imperceptible touch in passing ○ *She felt the kiss of the evening breeze on her skin.* [Old English *cyssan* 'to kiss', from *coss* 'kiss', the old form of the noun] —**kissable** *adj.*

kiss off v. US, Can (*slang*) **1.** *vt.* REJECT SB OR STH to reject sb or sth abruptly ○ *The boss kissed off that idea fast.* **2.** *vt.* BE FORCED TO YIELD STH to be compelled to give sth up ○ *We had to kiss the trip off for lack of money.* **3.** *vi.* GO AWAY to leave immediately or leave sb alone

kissagram /kíssə gram/ n. a delivery service in which the messenger delivers a kiss instead of or as well as the message

kiss and tell n. a book, article, or broadcast interview in which the author or interviewee publicly relates past sexual intimacy with sb

kiss-and-tell *adj.* revealing an earlier sexual experience with sb else, especially when the information, considered to be confidential, is made public (*informal*)

kiss curl n. a small flat curl of hair pressed on the forehead or in front of the ear. US term **spit curl**

kisser /kíssər/ n. **1.** SB WHO KISSES sb who kisses, especially in a particular way ○ *not much of a kisser* **2.** MOUTH sb's mouth (*slang*)

kissing cousin n. sb who is distantly related but known well enough to be kissed on meeting

kissing disease n. glandular fever (*informal*)

kissing gate n. a gate in a V- or U-shaped frame that allows only one person at a time to pass through

kiss of death n. sth or sb whose presence will bring failure or disaster to sth [From the passage in the Bible (Mark 14:44–46) in which Judas kissed Jesus Christ, thereby betraying him]

kiss of life n. (*informal*) **1.** ARTIFICIAL RESPIRATION mouth-to-mouth resuscitation **2.** STH THAT REVIVES STH ELSE sth that revives or restores an enterprise or, less commonly, sb's spirits

kiss of peace n. a gesture, usually either a kiss or handshake, used as a sign of Christian fellowship during Communion

kist[1] n. ARCHAEOL = **cist**

kist[2] /kist/ n. Scotland, S Africa a wooden storage chest variously used for blankets and linen, clothes, or a bride's trousseau [14thC. From Old Norse *kista* (related to Dutch *kist* 'coffin' and German *Kiste* 'box') (see CHEST).]

Kisumu /ki soómoo/ city in southwestern Kenya, on Lake Victoria, a port and capital of Nyanza Province. Population: 201,100 (1991).

Kiswahili /kee swaa heéli/ n. = **Swahili** n. **2** [Mid-19thC. From Bantu, coined from *ki-*, a prefix, + *Swahili*.]

kit /kit/ n. **1.** SET OF THINGS FOR USE TOGETHER a set of articles, tools, or equipment used for a particular purpose **2.** CONTAINER FOR SET the container for a set of things ○ *a sewing kit* **3.** SPECIAL CLOTHING AND EQUIPMENT a special set of clothing and equipment assembled for a member of the armed forces or a sportsperson **4.** SET OF PARTS FOR ASSEMBLING a set of parts ready to be put together [14thC. From Dutch *kitte* 'tankard, jug'. Originally in the meaning 'wooden tub'.] ◇ **get your kit off** to take your clothes off (*slang*)

kit out vt. to provide sb with the clothes, and sometimes also equipment, needed to do sth

kitbag /kít bag/ n. a canvas bag, usually cylindrical, for holding military kit or a similar bag used by civilians, carried on the shoulder

kitchen /kíchin/ n. a room or part of a room or building in which food is prepared and cooked [Pre-12thC. From Latin *coquina* (source of English *cuisine*), and derived from *coquere*, source of English *cook*.]

—— **WORD KEY: REGIONAL NOTE** ——

All languages in the world have borrowed words from English, with **kitchen**, *match*, and *school* being three of the commonest. In many UK dialects, **kitchen** retains an older meaning of 'sauce, savour', illustrating its link with cooking and such words as Latin *coquere* 'to cook': 'Hunger makes the best kitchen'.

kitchen cabinet n. an informal unelected group of advisers to a head of government who are often believed to have more influence than the official cabinet

kitchen Dutch n. S African a colloquial form of Afrikaans that sometimes contains English elements

Kitchener /kíchənər/, **Horatio Herbert, 1st Baron Kitchener of Khartoum and 1st Earl of Broome** (1850–1916) British field marshal and politician. After successful campaigns in Sudan and South Africa, he became war secretary during World War I (1914–16). He was lost with HMS Hampshire, mined near the Orkney Islands. Known as **Lord Kitchener**

kitchenette /kíchi nét/ n. a very small room, or part of another room, fitted out as a kitchen

kitchen garden n. a garden in which vegetables, herbs, and sometimes fruit are grown for the use of a household —**kitchen gardener** n.

kitchen midden n. an area of an archaeological site that contains domestic refuse such as food waste,

broken pottery, and pieces of other household artifacts, indicating long-term human occupation

kitchen tea n. ANZ a women-only party held before a wedding, to which guests bring kitchen equipment as presents for the bride

kitchenware /kíchin wair/ n. utensils used in the kitchen, including pots and pans, mixing bowls, chopping boards, knives, spoons, and gadgets

kite /kīt/ n. **1.** TOY FOR FLYING IN WIND a light framework covered in a thin light material, flown for fun in the wind at the end of a long string **2.** BIRDS SMALL SLIM HAWK a small slim hawk that has long pointed wings and a forked tail. Family: Accipitridae. **3.** SAILING LIGHT SAIL a light sail used in addition to a ship's standard sails **4.** AIR FORCE AEROPLANE an aeroplane (*archaic slang*) ○ *a rickety kite that could barely get off the runway* **5.** FIN FAKE FINANCIAL TRANSACTION a negotiable bill, e.g. a cheque, that is fraudulently used to sustain credit by representing a fictitious monetary transaction (*slang*) **6.** FIN BAD CHEQUE a cheque that is fraudulently written against an account containing insufficient funds and dated so as to allow the perpetrator to take advantage of the time lag required for clearing ■ v. (**kites, kiting, kited**) **1.** *vti.* FIN PASS BAD CHEQUES to write and pass bad cheques in order to sustain credit on a temporary basis, all the time using to advantage the period between writing them and their clearing (*slang*) **2.** *vi.* GLIDE AS IF FLYING to glide and soar like a kite [Old English. From Old English *cȳta* 'kite, bittern'.] —**kiter** n. ◇ **fly a kite 1.** to do sth or speak about sth in order to test public opinion on it (*slang*) **2.** to issue a fraudulent financial document such as a cheque without having enough funds to cover it (*slang*) ◇ **high as a kite 1.** extremely excited or elated (*informal*) **2.** extremely intoxicated or drug-affected (*informal*)

Kite mark /kít maark/ n. the official mark of approval of the British Standards Institution, shaped like a stylized kite, indicating that a manufactured item meets certain standards of quality and reliability

kit fox n. a small slender fox of the western United States that has large ears. It is often regarded as a subspecies of the swift fox. Latin name: *Vulpes macrotis*. [Early 19thC. *Kit* of uncertain origin: probably from *kit*, a shortening of KITTEN.]

kith /kith/ n. sb's friends and acquaintances (*dated*) [14thC. From Old English *cȳþ(þe)*, earlier *cȳþþu* 'knowledge, acquaintance'.] ◇ **kith and kin** sb's friends and relatives

kithara /kíthərə/ n. = **cithara**

kitsch /kich/ n. **1.** ARTISTIC VULGARITY sentimentality, tastelessness, or ostentation in any of the arts ○ *The book jackets were pure kitsch.* **2.** VULGAR OBJECTS collectively, decorative items that are regarded as tasteless, sentimental, or ostentatious in style ○ *tourist shops full of kitsch* [Early 20thC. From German, derived from *kitschen* 'to throw together (a work of art)'.] —**kitschy** *adj.*

kitten /kítt'n/ n. YOUNG CAT the young of a cat ■ *vi.* (**-tens, -tening, -tened**) GIVE BIRTH TO young cats [14thC. Via Old French *chitoun*, diminutive of *chat* 'cat'.] ◇ **have kittens** to become angry, excited, or nervous about sth (*informal*)

kitten heel n. (*usually plural*) **1.** LOW HEEL a low heel on a woman's shoe **2.** LOW-HEELED SHOE a woman's shoe with a low heel

kittenish /kítt'nish/ *adj.* **1.** FRISKY behaving in a lively and playful way, as a kitten does **2.** FLIRTATIOUS coyly flirtatious —**kittenishly** *adv.* —**kittenishness** n.

kittiwake /kítti wayk/ n. (*plural* -**wake** or -**wakes**) n. a gull of northern regions that nests on cliffs and winters on open oceans. Latin names: *Rissa tridactyla* and *Rissa brevirostris*. [Mid-17thC. An imitation of the bird's call.]

kitty[1] /kítti/ (*plural* -**ties**) n. a kitten or cat (*informal*) [Early 18thC. Shortening and alteration of KITTEN.]

kitty[2] /kítti/ (*plural* **kitties**) n. **1.** JOINT POOL OF MONEY a fund of money contributed to by a group of people and used to buy sth in common **2.** CARDS, GAMBLING PROPORTION OF THE OVERALL POT IN POKER a portion of the total amount of money bet by all the players on each hand of poker **3.** GAMBLING POOL OF BETS the amount of money that has been bet by the players in a game

4. BOWLS **JACK** the jack in the game of bowls [Early 19thC. Originally 'small bowl'. See KIT.]

Kitwe /kít way/ copper-mining town in north-central Zambia, north of Lusaka. Population: 338,207 (1990).

Kivu, Lake /keévoo-/ freshwater lake in the Great Rift Valley of Africa, between western Rwanda and the eastern Democratic Republic of the Congo. Area: 2,700 sq. km/1,040 sq. mi.

Kiwi

kiwi /keéwi/ n. (plural **-wi** or **-wis**) **1.** BIRDS **FLIGHTLESS BIRD OF NEW ZEALAND** a nocturnal flightless bird with a long slender beak and no tail that is found only in New Zealand, where it is also the national emblem. Genus: Apteryx. **2. kiwi, Kiwi** PEOPLES **SB FROM NEW ZEALAND** sb who comes from or lives in New Zealand (informal) **3.** BOT **CHINESE VINE WITH EDIBLE FRUIT** a Chinese vine that bears edible fruit with a greenish-brown fuzzy skin and sweet green pulp. Latin name: Actinidia chinensis. **4.** FOOD = **kiwi fruit** ■ adj. **RELATING TO NEW ZEALAND** relating to or typical of New Zealand, its people, or culture (informal) [Mid-19thC. From Maori, an imitation of the bird's cry.]

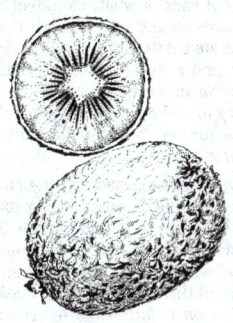

Kiwi fruit

kiwi fruit n. the fruit of the kiwi plant, which has a greenish-brown fuzzy skin and sweet green pulp

KJV abbr. BIBLE King James' Version

KKK abbr. Ku Klux Klan

KKt abbr. CHESS king's knight

KKtP abbr. CHESS king's knight's pawn

kl symbol. kilolitre

KL abbr. Kuala Lumpur

Klagenfurt /kláagən foort/ city and capital of Kärnten Province, southern Austria. It is situated about 100 km/62 mi. southwest of Graz. Population: 89,415 (1991).

Klaipeda /klípidə/ port and city in western Lithuania, on the coast of the Baltic Sea. Population: 202,800 (1995).

Klamath River /kláməth-/ river in the states of Oregon and California, flowing from Upper Klamath Lake into the Pacific Ocean. Length: 400 km/250 mi.

Klan /klan/ n. the Ku Klux Klan (informal) —**Klanism** n.

Klansman /klánzmən/ (plural **-men** /-mən/) n. a member of the Ku Klux Klan

klaxon /kláks'n/ n. a loud electric horn [Early 20thC]

Klee /klay/, **Paul** (1879–1940) Swiss painter. His imaginative and often witty works, some inspired by children's paintings and drawings, had a great influence on modern art.

Kleenex /klée neks/ tdmk. a trademark for a soft facial tissue

Calvin Klein

Klein /klīn/, **Calvin** (b. 1942) US fashion designer. After establishing his own company in 1968, he became known for his understated, sophisticated designs. Full name **Calvin Richard Klein**

Klein, Melanie (1882–1960) Austrian psychoanalyst. She pioneered studies in child psychoanalysis using free-play therapy. She moved to England in 1926.

Klein bottle /klín-/ n. a one-sided surface formed by inserting the small open end of a tapered tube through the side of the tube and upward until it is contiguous with the larger end [Mid-20thC. Named after Felix Klein (1849–1925), German mathematician.]

Klemperer /klémpərər/, **Otto** (1885–1973) German conductor. Noted for his interpretations of Beethoven, Mozart, and Mahler, he moved to the United States in 1933, where he conducted the Los Angeles Symphony Orchestra. From 1959 he conducted the Philharmonia Orchestra of London.

klepht /kleft/ n. one of the Greeks who resisted Turkish rule in Greece from 1456 to 1832 and who lived in the mountains as outlaws and brigands [Early 19thC. From modern demotic Greek klephtēs 'thief', from Greek kleptēs.] —**klephtic** adj.

kleptomania /kléptə máyni ə/ n. an obsessive urge to steal, especially when there is no economic necessity

kleptomaniac /kléptə máyni ak/ n. sb who has an obsessive urge to steal, especially when there is no economic necessity —**kleptomaniacal** /kléptə mə nî ək'l/ adj.

kletterschuh /kléttər shoo/ (plural **-schuhe** or **-schuhs** /-shoo ə/) n. a lightweight climbing boot [Early 20thC. From German, literally 'climbing shoe'.]

klick /klik/ n. Can, US a kilometre (informal) [Mid-20thC. Origin unknown.]

klieg light /kleeg-/ n. a very powerful carbon-arc light used in the past in making films [Early 20thC. Named after John H. Kliegl (1869–1959) and Anton T. Kliegl (1872–1927), German-born US lighting experts and inventors.]

Klimt /klimt/, **Gustav** (1862–1918) Austrian painter. Founder of the Vienna Secession school of painting (1897), he created richly decorated portraits of women.

Klippel /klíppəl/, **Robert** (b. 1920) Australian sculptor. His works include assemblages made with scraps of metal. Full name **Robert Edward Klippel**

klipspringer /klíp springər/ n. a small agile antelope with large ears that lives in mountainous regions of Africa. Latin name: Oreotragus oreotragus. [Late 18thC. From Afrikaans, literally 'cliff-springer, rock-jumper'.]

Klondiker /klón dīkər/, **klondiker** n. Scotland a large factory ship in which fish are processed at sea after being transferred from the smaller fishing boats by which they are caught

kloof /kloof/ n. S Africa a gorge or mountain pass, usually wooded, in southern Africa [Mid-18thC. Via Afrikaans from Dutch clove.]

kludge /klooj/, **kluge** n. PATCHED SOLUTION a makeshift combination of hardware and software put together to solve a computing problem, that, while effective, is usually inelegant and not suitable for manufacture (slang) ■ vt. (**kludges, kludging, kludged; kluges, kluging, kluged**) FIX STH WITH A KLUDGE to solve a computing problem using a kludge (slang) [Mid-20thC. Formed on the model of BOTCH and FUDGE.] —**kludgy** adj.

klutz /kluts/ n. US, Can (slang insult) **1.** OFFENSIVE TERM an offensive term referring to sb who is regarded as physically or socially clumsy **2.** OFFENSIVE TERM an offensive term referring to sb who is regarded as unintelligent [Mid-20thC. Via Yiddish klots 'wooden beam' from German Klotz 'clod'.] —**klutzy** adj.

klystron /klí stron/ n. an electron tube that uses an electric field to generate and amplify microwaves [Mid-20thC. Coined from Greek klus-, stem of kluzein 'to wash or break over', + -TRON.]

km abbr. kilometre

K-meson n. = kaon

km/h abbr. kilometres per hour

kmph abbr. kilometres per hour

kmps abbr. kilometres per second

kn, kn. abbr. **1. kn, kn.** SAILING knot **2.** MONEY krona **3.** MONEY krone

KN abbr. CHESS king's knight

knack /nak/ n. **1.** SKIL an easy, clever way of doing sth or handling a problem ○ I can't get the knack of this software. **2.** PARTICULAR ABILITY a particular skill, especially one that might be innate or intuitive and therefore difficult to teach ○ You certainly have a knack with children. [14thC. Origin uncertain: perhaps from or related to Dutch and Low German knak 'sharp blow, crack', an imitation of the sound. Originally 'trick, deception'.]

WORD KEY: SYNONYMS

See Synonyms at **talent**.

---

knacker /nákər/ n. **1.** SB WHO KILLS HORSES FOR PROFIT sb who makes a living by buying old, worn-out, or injured horses, slaughtering them, and selling their parts, e.g. their flesh and hide **2.** DEMOLITION MERCHANT sb who makes a living by buying unwanted buildings, demolishing them, and selling their materials for scrap ■ **knackers** npl. TESTICLES testicles (slang) ■ vt. (**-ers, -ering, -ered**) TIRE SB OUT to exhaust sb completely (slang) [Early19thC. Originally 'saddler, harness maker', of uncertain origin: probably from Scandinavian.]

knackered /nákərd/ adj. totally exhausted, broken-down, or about to collapse (slang) [Late 19thC. Formed from KNACKER.]

knackwurst /nák wurst/, **knockwurst** /nók wurst/ n. a spicy smoked Continental sausage similar to a frankfurter but shorter and thicker [Mid-20thC. From German, literally 'crack-sausage' (because its skin cracks open when bitten), formed from knacken 'to crack'.]

knag /nag/ n. **1.** KNOT IN WOOD a knot in a piece of wood **2.** WOODEN PEG a peg made of wood [15thC. From Low German knagge 'knot, peg'.]

knap /nap/ (**knaps, knapping, knapped**) vt. to chisel or hammer sth such as a stone so that it breaks into flakes [15thC. Origin uncertain: probably from Low German or Dutch knappen 'to crack', an imitation of the sound.] —**knapper** n.

knapping hammer /nápping hammər/ n. a mason's hammer used for splitting and roughly shaping stone

knapsack /náp sak/ n. a cloth or leather bag with shoulder straps, designed for carrying personal items and supplies on a hiker's back [Early 17thC. From Low German, literally 'eating sack', from knappen 'to bite, eat' + Sack 'sack'.]

knapweed /náp weed/ (plural **-weeds** or **-weed**) n. a thistle plant with purple flowers grouped in a head, and spiny parts just below them. Latin name: Centaurea nigra. [Early 16thC. Alteration of Middle English knopwed, literally 'knob-weed', from knop 'knob', from the shape of its cluster of flowers.]

knar /naar/ n. a knot on a tree or in wood [13thC. Origin uncertain: perhaps from Middle Dutch or Middle Low German knorre.] —**knarred** adj. —**knarry** adj.

knave /nayv/ n. **1.** CUNNING UNTRUSTWORTHY MAN a man who is dishonest and deceitful (archaic insult) **2.** MAN

Knapweed

SERVANT a man of low social position or one who works as a servant (*archaic*) **3.** CARDS = **jack**[1] *n.* **2** [Old English *cnafa* 'boy, male servant', from prehistoric Germanic] —**knavish** *adj.* —**knavishly** *adv.* —**knavishness** *n.*

knavery /náyvəri/ *n.* an action, or behaviour, that is dishonest or deceitful (*archaic*)

knawel /nawl, náw əl/ (*plural* **knawels** *or* **knawel**), **knawe** /naw/ (*plural* **knawes** *or* **knawe**) *n.* a low-growing annual plant of Europe and Asia that has narrow leaves and very small green flowers, usually considered to be a weed. Latin name: *Scleranthus annuus*. [Late 16thC. From German *Knauel* 'knotgrass'.]

knead /need/ (**kneads, kneading, kneaded**) *v.* **1.** *vti.* **WORK DOUGH UNTIL SMOOTH** to fold, press, and stretch a soft substance such as dough or clay, working it into a smooth uniform mass **2.** *vt.* **MASSAGE MUSCLES** to rub, squeeze, or press a part of the body with the hands, e.g. in order to relax the muscles **3.** *vt.* **SHAPE STH WITH THE HANDS** to make or shape sth out of a soft substance by kneading it [Old English *cnedan*. Ultimately from an Indo-European word for knobby objects that is also the ancestor of English *knob* and *knar*.] —**kneadable** *adj.* —**kneader** *n.*

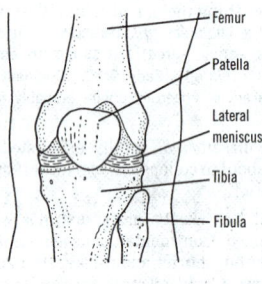

Knee

Femur
Patella
Lateral meniscus
Tibia
Fibula

knee /nee/ *n.* **1.** ANAT **MIDDLE JOINT OF THE HUMAN LEG** the joint of the human leg between the thigh and the lower leg, where the femur and the tibia meet, covered in front by the kneecap (**patella**) **2.** ANAT **WIDER AREA AROUND THE KNEE JOINT** the general area surrounding the knee joint **3.** UPPER LEG the upper surface of the thigh of sb sitting down ○ *Come and sit on my knee.* **4.** CLOTHES **PART OF TROUSERS SURROUNDING THE KNEE** the part of a piece of clothing, especially trousers, that fits around the knee **5.** ZOOL **LEG JOINT IN ANIMALS** the joint between the upper and lower parts of the hind legs in four-legged vertebrates and of the legs in birds **6.** TREES **GROWTH ABOVE WATER FROM A ROOT** a woody outgrowth from the roots of some trees that grow in saturated soils or standing water, which protrudes above the surface and enables them to breathe **7.** **OBJECT THAT LOOKS LIKE A KNEE** sth that resembles the human knee, e.g. a bent pipe ■ *vt.* (**knees, kneeing, kneed**) HIT SB WITH THE KNEE to strike sb with the knee [Old English *cnēow*. Ultimately from an Indo-European word meaning 'to bend' that is also the ancestor of English *genuflect*.] ◇ **bring sb to his** *or* **her knees** to reduce sb to a state of abject weakness and vulnerability or force sb to admit defeat

knee breeches *npl.* = **breeches**

kneecap /née kap/ *n.* **1.** FLAT BONE OVER THE KNEE JOINT a flat triangular bone located at the front of the knee. It protects the knee joint. Technical name **patella 2.** =

kneepad ■ *vt.* (**-caps, -capping, -capped**) CRIMINOL **SHOOT SB IN THE KNEES** to shoot sb deliberately in the knees as a punishment in order to cause lasting difficulty in standing or walking (*informal*)

knee-deep *adj.* **1.** IN AS HIGH AS THE KNEES standing or sunk in sth that reaches up to the knees ○ *be knee-deep in mud* **2.** AS HIGH AS THE KNEES reaching up to the knees ○ *The river was only knee-deep.* **3.** EXTREMELY INVOLVED IN STH completely occupied by or entangled in sth ○ *knee-deep in work*

knee drop *n.* in wrestling, a move in which an opponent is lifted into the air and then dropped over the bent knee of the lifter

knee-high *adj.* UP TO THE KNEES reaching up to the knees ■ *n.* SOCK REACHING KNEE a sock or stocking that comes up as high as the knee

kneehole /née hōl/ *n.* a hole made for the knees in a desk or other piece of furniture

knee jerk *n.* an involuntary contraction of the thigh muscle that produces a sudden extension of the leg, usually in response to a light tap on the tendon below the kneecap

knee-jerk *adj.* (*informal disapproving*) **1.** NOT THOUGHT THROUGH given or occurring immediately and automatically, without thinking, and usually expressing habitual attitude or prejudice ○ *a knee-jerk opinion* **2.** REACTING PREDICTABLY tending to respond in the same way to any situation ○ *a knee-jerk political hack*

kneel /neel/ (**kneels, kneeling, knelt** /nelt/ *or* **kneeled, knelt** *or* **kneeled**) *vi.* to rest on, or get down on, one or both knees [Old English *cnēowlian*, from *cnēow*, an earlier form of KNEE]

kneepad /née pad/ *n.* a covering that protects the knee from injury, especially during sports

kneepan /née pan/ *n.* = **kneecap** *n.* 1

knee sock *n.* a sock that reaches to the knee

knees-up (*plural* **knees-ups**) *n.* UK a lively noisy party, especially one with a lot of dancing (*informal*)

knee-trembler *n.* an act of sexual intercourse performed standing up (*slang*)

kneidel /knáyd'l, knīd'l/ *n.* a small Eastern European dumpling made from potatoes or flour, served in soup or with stew, or filled with a savoury stuffing or fruit [Mid-20thC. From Yiddish *kneydel*, an alteration of Middle High German *knödel* 'dumpling'.]

knell /nel/ *n.* **1.** SLOW BELL RING the sound of a bell rung slowly, associated with solemnity or mourning, used to announce a death or funeral **2.** OMINOUS SIGNAL sth that signals death, disaster, or the end of sth (*literary*) ■ *v.* (**knells, knelling, knelled**) **1.** *vti.* RING A BELL to ring a bell slowly, or produce a slow ringing sound, especially as a sign of mourning or to announce a death or funeral **2.** *vt.* SIGNAL STH OMINOUS to announce or signal sth such as a death, disaster, or the end of sth (*literary*) [Old English *cnyll*, from *cnyllan* 'to strike'. Ultimately from an Indo-European word that is also the ancestor of English *knock* and *knuckle*.]

Kneller /nélbr/, **Sir Godfrey** (1646–1723) German-born English painter. His portrait subjects included several monarchs and many other prominent figures.

knelt past participle, past tense of **kneel**

Knesset /knéss et, knéssit/, **Knesseth** *n.* the parliamentary legislature of Israel. It has one legislative chamber with supreme authority. [Mid-20thC. From Hebrew, literally 'gathering'.]

knew past tense of **know**

Kngwarreye /kəng wúrray/, **Emily Kame** (1910?–96) Australian Aboriginal painter. Her works were part of Australia's contribution to the Venice Biennale in 1997.

Knickerbocker /níkər bokər/ *n.* US **1.** DESCENDANT OF DUTCH IN NEW YORK sb descended from the early Dutch settlers of New York **2.** SB FROM NEW YORK sb who is a native of or lives in the state of New York (*informal*) [Early 19thC. Named after Diedrich Knickerbocker, fictitious author of Washington Irving's *History of New York*.]

knickerbocker glory *n.* a dessert consisting of layers of different flavours of ice cream, fruit, fruit syrups,

jelly, and cream, topped with a wafer biscuit and served in a tall conical glass dish

knickerbockers /níkər bokərz/ *npl.* loose-fitting short breeches gathered at or just below the knee [Mid-19thC. Origin uncertain: perhaps from their resemblance to the Dutchmen's knee breeches in Cruikshank's illustrations in Washington Irving's *History of New York*.]

knickers /níkərz/ *npl.* **1.** PANTIES an undergarment worn by women and girls that covers the body from the waist to the tops of the legs or below and has separate legs or leg-holes **2.** US = **knickerbockers** ■ *interj.* SWEARWORD used as a mild or self-consciously humorous swearword (*informal*) [Late 19thC. Shortening.] ◇ **get your knickers in a twist** to become agitated, excited, or anxious (*informal*)

knick-knack, **nicknack** *n.* a small decorative ornament or object [Late 16thC. Formed from a reduplication of KNACK. From the earlier meaning 'petty trick, artifice'.] —**knick-knackery** *n.*

knickpoint /ník poynt/ *n.* a point along a river's length at which it suddenly begins to flow in a steeper course [Early 20thC. Partial translation of German *Knickpunkt*, from *Knick* 'bend, kink' + *Punkt* 'point'.]

knife /nīf/ *n.* (*plural* **knives** /nīvz/) **1.** TOOL FOR CUTTING OR SPREADING a tool, usually with a sharp blade and a handle, used for cutting, slicing, or spreading **2.** ARMS STABBING WEAPON a knife with a handle and a sharpened blade specifically made to be a weapon ■ *v.* (**knifes, knifing, knifed**) **1.** *vt.* CRIMINOL STAB SB to stab or cut sb with a knife **2.** *vt.* US BETRAY SB to try to bring about sb's downfall in a devious or dishonest way (*informal*) **3.** *vi.* MOVE WITH A SWIFT SMOOTH MOTION to move quickly, forcefully, and cleanly through sth ○ *The hawk knifed through the air.* [Pre-12thC. Origin uncertain: perhaps via Old French *canif* from Basque *kanibet* or *ganibet*, from Latin *canna* 'reed' + Basque *bedoi* 'billhook', *egitai* 'sickle', or *eballe* 'cutter'.] —**knifer** *n.* ◇ **have your knife in** *or* **into sb** to feel hostility and malice towards sb and wish to do him or her harm ◇ **the knives are out (for sb)** there is general hostility towards sb and a desire to cause that person difficulties or harm ◇ **twist** *or* **turn the knife (in the wound)** to try to make a difficult or painful situation even worse for sb ◇ **under the knife** undergoing surgery (*informal*)

knife-edge *n.* **1.** KNIFE'S CUTTING EDGE the cutting edge of the blade of a knife **2.** OBJECT LIKE THE EDGE OF KNIFE an object that is sharp, thin, and narrow **3.** CRITICAL TIME IN A SITUATION a decisive and precarious point in a situation at which it is finely balanced between different possibilities or outcomes ○ *with the future of the project on a knife-edge* **4.** TECH FULCRUM FOR A PRECISE INSTRUMENT a metal wedge whose narrow edge is used as a fulcrum for a scale beam or a lever in a precision instrument

knife pleat *n.* a narrow sharply-creased pleat, usually one of several folded in the same direction, especially in a skirt

knifepoint /nīf poynt/ *n.* the sharp tip of a knife ◇ **at knifepoint** while threatening to stab or cut sb with a knife or being threatened with a knife. ◊ **gunpoint**

knife switch *n.* an electric switch in which a hinged blade is placed between two contact clips

knight /nīt/ *n.* **1.** HIST MEDIEVAL SOLDIER OF HIGH RANK in later medieval Europe, a soldier of noble rank raised to a privileged military status by his king after serving as a page and squire **2.** HIST MEDIEVAL MOUNTED SOLDIER OF LOW RANK in earlier medieval Europe, a tenant of a feudal lord who was required to serve as a soldier on horseback **3.** POL MAN WITH THE TITLE 'SIR' a man who holds a nonhereditary title conferred by a ruler for personal achievement or public service. A British knight has the title 'Sir' before his name. **4.** CHESS HORSE'S HEAD CHESSPIECE a chesspiece shaped like a horse's head that moves two squares horizontally and one vertically or two vertically and one horizontally. Symbol **N 5.** MEMBER OF A BROTHERHOOD a man who belongs to a special group or organization, especially a religious or secret brotherhood **6.** CHAMPION OF A CAUSE a fervent supporter or defender of a cause or belief **7.** PROTECTOR OF A WOMAN a man who is protective and devoted to a woman ■ *vt.* (**knights, knighting, knighted**) MAKE A MAN A KNIGHT to bestow a knighthood on a man [Old English *cniht* 'boy, male attendant', from prehistoric Germanic] ◇ **knight in shining armour** a man who gallantly comes to the rescue of sb in danger or difficulty

knight bachelor (*plural* **knights bachelors** *or* **knights bachelor**) *n.* **1. LOWEST RANK OF KNIGHT** a knight of the lowest rank who is not a member of any of the orders of knighthood **2.** = **bachelor-at-arms**

knight banneret (*plural* **knights bannerets**) *n.* = **banneret**

knight-errant (*plural* **knights-errant**), **knight errant** (*plural* **knights errant**) *n.* **1. WANDERING MEDIEVAL KNIGHT** a medieval knight who travelled around looking for adventure **2. ADVENTUROUS ROMANTIC** a man preoccupied with ideas of adventure and romance —**knight-errantry** *n.*

knighthead /nít hed/ *n.* either of two upright timbers supporting the inner end of the bowsprit of a sailing ship, to which mooring cables or ropes are sometimes attached [Early 18thC. From the fact that it often had a carving of a male head.]

knighthood /nít hŏŏd/ *n.* **1. POSITION OF KNIGHT** the rank, title, or occupation of a knight **2. CHIVALRY AND HONOUR** the qualities of chivalry, bravery, and honour, thought to be characteristic of a knight **3. KNIGHTS** knights considered as a group [Old English]

knightly /nítli/ (**-lier, -liest**) *adj.* relating to knights, or characteristic of a knight, especially in being noble and chivalrous [Old English] —**knightliness** *n.*

knight marshal (*plural* **knights marshal**) *n.* = **marshal** *n.* 5

Knight of Columbus *n.* a member of a benevolent and fraternal organization of Roman Catholic men, founded in the United States in 1882 [Late 19thC. Named after Christopher *Columbus*.]

Knights Hospitallers, Knights of St John of Jerusalem, Knights of the Hospital of St John of Jerusalem *npl.* a military and religious order founded by crusaders in the 12th century to protect a hospital in Jerusalem

Knights of the Round Table *npl.* an order of knights said to have been created by King Arthur that figures prominently in Arthurian legends and chivalric poems [The *Round Table* was where the knights sat. It was circular so that no knight would be seated in a position of superiority.]

Knight Templar (*plural* **Knights Templar**) *n.* HIST a member of a Christian military order that was founded in Jerusalem in 1119 to protect pilgrims after the First Crusade. The order grew wealthy and influential from banking activities before being suppressed by the Pope in 1312.

kniphofia /ni fṓfi ə/ (*plural* **-as** *or* **-a**) *n.* PLANTS = **red-hot poker** [Mid-19thC. Named after the German botanist Johann Hieronymus *Kniphof* (1704–63).]

knish /kə nísh, knish/ *n.* a piece of dough filled with meat, cheese, or potato, baked or fried, and eaten as a snack or appetizer, especially in Jewish-American cooking [Mid-20thC. Via Yiddish from Russian.]

knit /nit/ *v.* (**knits, knitting, knitted** *or* **knit**) **1.** *vti.* **INTERLOCK WOOL LOOPS TO MAKE GARMENT** to interlock loops of wool, using either long needles or a machine, or to make a garment, fabric, or other item by this method **2.** *vti.* **USE A KNIT STITCH** to use a basic plain stitch that forms a flat vertical loop on the front of the piece of knitting ○ *Knit one, purl one.* ◊ **purl 3.** *vti.* **UNITE** to bring people or things together, or come together, in a close association **4.** *vi.* MED **BECOME HEALED** to grow together again after a fracture (*refers to a broken bone*) **5.** *vti.* **BRING THE BROWS CLOSER TOGETHER** to draw the brows together, or be drawn together, in a frown ■ *n.* **1. STH MADE BY KNITTING** a knitted garment or fabric **2. WAY OF KNITTING** a method or style of knitting a garment or fabric **3. PLAIN STITCH** a basic knitting stitch that forms a flat vertical loop on the face of sth being knitted. ◊ **purl** [Old English *cnyttan* 'to tie in knots', from a prehistoric Germanic word that is also the ancestor of English *knot*] —**knittable** *adj.* —**knitter** *n.*

knitting /nítting/ *n.* **1. PRODUCTION OF KNITTED ITEMS** the act or process of making knitted items or fabric by hand-held needles or by machine **2. STH BEING KNITTED** an item that is in the process of being knitted

knitwear /nít wair/ *n.* garments made from knitted fabric

knives plural of **knife**

knob /nob/ *n.* **1. ROUNDED HANDLE OR DIAL** a rounded projecting part attached to a door, drawer, appliance, or other object, used as a handle or a dial or switch **2. ROUNDED PROJECTION** any rounded lump or part projecting from the surface of sth **3. RAISED ORNAMENTAL CARVING** a raised ornament in carved woodwork **4.** GEOG **HILL** a rounded hill **5. SMALL PIECE** a small piece of sth ○ *a knob of butter* **6. OFFENSIVE TERM** an offensive term for a penis (*slang taboo*) ■ *vti.* (**knobs, knobbing, knobbed**) **TABOO TERM MEANING TO HAVE SEX** taboo term meaning to have sexual intercourse, for a man (*slang offensive; refers to a man*) [14thC. From Middle Low German *knobbe* 'knot, knob, bud'.] ◇ **with knobs on 1.** used as a way of returning an insult and supposedly adding greater force to it (*informal; usually used by or to children*) **2.** to a great degree (*informal*)

knobbly /nóbbli/ (**-blier, -bliest**), **knobby** /nóbbi/ (**-bier, -biest**) *adj.* having small hard rounded parts sticking out from the surface [Mid-17thC. Formed from *knobble* 'small knob', from KNOB.]

knobkerrie /nób kerri/, **knobstick** /nób stik/ *n.* a short wooden stick with a knob at one end, used by some South African peoples as a weapon [Mid-19thC. Formed from KNOB + a variant of *kierie*, on the model of Afrikaans *knopkierie*.]

knock /nok/ *v.* (**knocks, knocking, knocked**) **1.** *vi.* **HIT REPEATEDLY** to strike loudly against sth such as a door with the knuckles or an object in order to attract attention ○ *Someone's knocking at the door.* **2.** *vi.* **MAKE A LOUD NOISE BY COLLIDING** to produce a loud and usually repetitive noise by hitting sth ○ *disturbed by a branch knocking against the window all night* **3.** *vti.* **DEAL BLOW** to strike sb or sth with a hard blow ○ *knock in a nail* **4.** *vt.* **PUT IN A PARTICULAR STATE WITH BLOW** to cause sth or sb to be in a particular state, e.g. unconscious or flat on the floor, with a blow ○ *He knocked me off balance.* **5.** *vti.* **COLLIDE OR CAUSE STH TO COLLIDE** to hit against sth, especially accidentally, or cause sth to hit against sth else ○ *The glass broke when I knocked it against the table.* **6.** *vt.* **MAKE STH BY STRIKING** to produce sth, especially a hole, by means of repeated blows **7.** *vt.* **CRITICIZE SB OR STH** to criticize or find fault with sb or sth (*informal*) ○ *Don't knock it until you've tried it.* **8.** *vi.* AUTOMOT **PRODUCE REPEATED RAPPING SOUND** to make a regular rapping noise that is usually caused by faulty fuel combustion (*refers to a vehicle or its engine*) ■ = **knock off** *v.* 8 ■ *n.* **1. BLOW OR COLLISION** a blow struck against sb or sth or a collision with sb or sth **2. SOUND OF KNOCKING** the sound made by sb or sth hitting sth, especially repeatedly **3.** AUTOMOT **REPEATED RAPPING SOUND IN ENGINE** a regular rapping noise made by an engine and usually caused by faulty fuel combustion **4. CRITICISM** a disparaging or critical comment about sb or sth (*informal*) **5. BAD EXPERIENCE** a painful, damaging, or distressing experience (*informal*) **6.** CRICKET **INNINGS** a batsman's innings (*informal*) [Old English *cnocian*, of uncertain origin: thought to be imitative of the sound] ◇ **knock sb cold** to make sb unconscious with a blow (*informal*) ◇ **knock sb dead** to amaze and delight sb with the quality of a performance (*informal*) ◇ **knock sth on the head** to put an end to sth or prevent it from developing any further (*informal*) ◇ **knock sb into the middle of next week** to hit sb very hard (*informal*)

knock about, knock around *v.* (*informal*) **1.** *vt.* **BEAT SB** to abuse sb physically **2.** *vti.* **TRAVEL AROUND** to travel to different places, or to different places within a specific area, especially without a specific itinerary **3.** *vt.* **HAVE A RELAXING TIME** to relax by doing nothing in particular **4.** *vi.* **SPEND TIME** to spend time habitually in the company of sb **5.** *vi.* **BE IN SOME PLACE** to be somewhere in a place or area, though the exact whereabouts are uncertain ○ *I'm sure it's knocking around somewhere in this office.* **6.** *vt.* **DISCUSS STH SPECULATIVELY** to discuss sth casually in order to hear different views **7.** *vt.* **KICK A BALL AROUND** to kick, hit, or throw a ball in an informal game

knock back *vt.* (*informal*) **1.** BEVERAGES **GULP A DRINK DOWN** to drink sth, especially alcohol, very quickly **2. COST SB MUCH MONEY** to cost sb a large amount of money ○ *The repairs knocked me back £500.* **3. TAKE SB ABACK** to come as an unwelcome surprise to sb ○ *The news really knocked me back.* **4.** *ANZ, Scotland* **REJECT SB OR STH** to dismiss or reject sb or sth

knock down *vt.* **1. MAKE SB OR STH FALL** to cause sb or sth to fall to the ground by striking or pushing **2. HIT SB WITH VEHICLE** to hit and injure or kill sb with a moving vehicle **3. DESTROY STRUCTURE** to demolish a building or part of a building **4. DISMANTLE STH** to take sth apart for shipping or storage **5. PRONOUNCE STH SOLD** to show that sth has been sold at an auction by striking a surface with a gavel **6. CUT PRICE OF** to reduce the price of sth (*informal*) ○ *furniture knocked down by 50%* **7. MAKE SB CUT PRICE** to persuade sb to reduce the price of sth

knock off *v.* **1.** *vti.* **STOP WORKING** to finish work at the end of the day, or to stop working or doing sth in order to take a break (*informal*) **2.** *vt.* **CUT PRICE OF** to decrease the price of sth by a particular amount **3.** *vt.* **DEDUCT STH** to deduct sth from sth, especially an amount from a price or a number of points from a score or total **4.** *vt.* **PRODUCE STH WITH EASE OR SPEED** to make or deal with sth easily and quickly (*informal*) ○ *knocks off six or seven articles a month* **5.** *vt.* CRIMINOL **KILL SB** to kill sb, especially intentionally (*slang*) **6.** *vt.* CRIMINOL **ROB OR STEAL** to rob a bank, shop, or other business, or to steal sth (*slang*) **7.** *vt.* *US* COMM **MAKE CHEAP COPY OF PRODUCT** to produce a cheap, sometimes illegal copy of a well-known product (*slang*) **8.** *vt.* **OFFENSIVE TERM** to have sexual intercourse with sb (*slang offensive*) ◇ **knock it off** used to demand that sb stop doing or saying sth (*slang*)

knock on *vti.* in rugby, to make illegal use of the hand or arm to move the ball forwards

knock out *vt.* **1. MAKE SB UNCONSCIOUS BY HITTING** to cause sb to lose consciousness by striking him or her **2. DEFEAT OPPOSING BOXER WITH PUNCH** in boxing, to knock an opponent down for a count of ten, thus winning the match **3. STUPEFY SB WITH DRUGS OR ALCOHOL** to cause sb to lose consciousness or fall asleep by means of drugs or alcohol **4.** SPORTS **ELIMINATE OPPONENT FROM TOURNAMENT** to eliminate an opponent or team from a competition by winning a match or game **5. MAKE STH USELESS** to destroy sth or make it inoperable ○ *The storm knocked out our electricity.* **6. TIRE SB OUT** to exhaust sb completely (*informal*) **7. PRODUCE STH WITH EASE OR SPEED** to make or do sth easily or quickly **8. PLEASE OR IMPRESS SB GREATLY** to overwhelm sb with excitement or pleasure (*informal*) ○ *That music really knocks me out.* **9. SHOCK SB** to cause sb to be greatly shocked (*informal*)

knock together *vt.* to make sth quickly, without much preparation, and often with little care (*informal*)

knock up *v.* **1.** *vt.* **KNOCK ON DOOR TO WAKE SB** to wake sb up by knocking on the door (*slang*) **2.** *vt.* = **knock together** (*informal*) **3.** *vt.* **TIRE SB OUT** to make sb very tired or ill (*slang*) **4.** *vi.* **HIT BALL IN PRACTICE** in racquet games, to hit the ball back and forth in practice with an opponent, especially before beginning a match **5.** *vt.* **SCORE RUNS** in cricket, to score a specific number of runs **6.** *vt.* *US* **OFFENSIVE TERM** an offensive term meaning to make a woman pregnant (*slang offensive*)

knockabout /nókə bowt/ *n.* **1. COMIC PERFORMANCE** a type of comedy characterized by boisterous physical activity, or an actor who specializes in this type of comedy **2. INFORMAL GAME** an informal ball game, especially an informal game of football (*informal*) ■ *adj.* **1. USING SLAPSTICK** characterized by boisterous physical activity **2. STURDY AND INFORMAL** suitable for rough or casual activities

knock-back *n.* *NZ, Scotland* a rejection (*informal*)

knockdown /nók down/ *n.* **1. OVERWHELMING BLOW** a powerful emotional or physical blow **2. PRICE DROP** a reduction in the price of sth **3.** *ANZ* **INTRODUCTION** an introduction to sb (*slang*) ■ *adj.* **1. VERY POWERFUL** having an overwhelmingly powerful or very damaging effect **2. EASILY DISASSEMBLED** made to be taken apart easily **3. DISCOUNTED** reduced or very cheap ○ *a knockdown price*

knocker /nókər/ *n.* **1. FIXTURE FOR KNOCKING ON DOOR** a metal fixture attached with hinges to the door of a house, used for knocking on the door **2. CRITIC** sb who finds fault with sb or sth, especially unfairly (*informal*) ■ **knockers** *npl.* **OFFENSIVE TERM** an offensive term for a woman's breasts (*slang offensive*)

knock-for-knock *adj.* used to describe an agreement between two insurance companies whereby each pays out for damage sustained by its policyholder in an accident involving a policyholder of the other company

knocking copy *n.* advertising material aimed at persuading prospective customers of the inferiority of a rival product or service

knocking-shop *n.* a brothel (*slang*) ['Knocking' formed from KNOCK in the sense 'to have sexual intercourse with']

knock-knee *n.* PERMANENT CONDITION OF LEGS a condition in which the legs are permanently bent so that the knees are close together and the ankles are spread far apart ■ **knock-knees** *npl.* KNEES TURNED INWARDS the knees of sb with knock-knee —**knock-kneed** *adj.*

knockoff /nók of/ *n.* an inexpensive, sometimes illegal copy of a piece of well-known or popular merchandise (*informal*)

knock-on *adj.* SPREADING OUT TO AFFECT OTHERS progressively affecting other people or things related directly or indirectly to whatever was first affected ○ *The knock-on effect will almost certainly cause further factory closures in the area.* ■ *n.* ACT OF HITTING BALL FORWARDS ILLEGALLY in rugby, illegal use of the hand or arm to move the ball forwards

knockout /nók owt/ *n.* **1.** BOXING PUNCH WINNING A BOXING MATCH in boxing, a punch that knocks an opponent down for a count of ten and so wins a contest **2.** BOXING BOXING MATCH WON BY A KNOCKOUT a victory in a boxing match by a knockout **3.** BLOW CAUSING SB TO BECOME UNCONSCIOUS a blow that knocks sb unconscious **4.** SPORTS ELIMINATION COMPETITION a sports competition in which a person or team beaten in one game or match is eliminated from the entire competition **5.** SB OR STH STUNNING sb or sth extremely attractive, good-looking, or enjoyable (*informal*)

knockout drops *npl.* a solution, usually containing chloral hydrate, secretly put in a drink to render the drinker unconscious (*informal*)

knock-up *n.* in racquet games, a practice period with an opponent, especially before the beginning of a match

knockwurst *n.* = knackwurst

knoll[1] /nōl/ *n.* a small rounded hill or mound [Old English *cnoll*, from a prehistoric Germanic base that is also the ancestor of English *knot*] —**knolly** *adj.*

knoll[2] /nōl/ *n.*, *vti.* (**knolls, knolling, knolled**) knell (*archaic*) [14thC. Ultimately from a prehistoric Germanic base that is also the ancestor of English *knell*.]

knop /nop/ *n.* a small decorative knob [14thC. From Middle Low German or Middle Dutch *knoppe* 'knob, knot, button'.] —**knopped** *adj.*

Knossos /nósəss, knóssəss/ ruined city in northern Crete, the centre of the Minoan civilization from about 3000 BC to 1100 BC

knot[1] /not/ *n.* **1.** OBJECT MADE BY TYING A STRAND a usually hard, lump-shaped object formed when a strand of sth, e.g. string or rope, is interlaced with itself or another strand and pulled tight. Knots are mainly used for tying pieces of string, rope, or thread together or securing them to other objects. **2.** WAY OF TYING A LENGTH OF MATERIAL any of a number of set ways of joining or securing lengths of rope, thread, or other strands by tying the material together or around itself **3.** A TANGLE a tightly tangled mass of strands that are hard to separate **4.** DECORATION SHAPED LIKE A KNOT a piece of material such as ribbon or braid tied in a knot or bow and used as a decoration **5.** HARD PATCH ON A TREE a hard patch on a tree out of which a branch or stem grows **6.** DARK WHORL IN CUT TIMBER a hard dark-coloured patch in cut wood at a point where a branch or stem formerly grew out of the tree **7.** LUMP ON A TREE a lump on a tree trunk or branch **8.** MED LUMP IN THE BODY a node, ganglion, lump, or swelling in the body **9.** UNIT OF NAUTICAL OR AIR SPEED a unit of measurement for the speed at which a ship or aircraft travels, equivalent to one nautical mile per hour, approximately 1.85 km per hour/1.15 statute mph **10.** NAUT INDICATOR FOR MEASURING A SHIP'S SPEED a division on a log line used for calculating the speed of a ship **11.** NAUT = nautical mile **12.** TIGHT GROUP a number of people or things grouped closely together **13.** TENSE FEELING a feeling of tightness or

anxiety **14.** PROBLEM a difficult or complex problem ■ *v.* (**knots, knotting, knotted**) **1.** *vti.* MAKE A KNOT to tie sth in a knot, or be tied with a knot **2.** *vti.* TO TANGLE to tangle sth, or become tangled **3.** *vt.* MAKE STH WITH A PATTERN OF KNOTS to produce sth, e.g. a piece of macramé, that consists of a pattern of decorative knots **4.** *vti.* BECOME TENSE to become, or to cause sth to become, tight or tense with anxiety or fear ○ *My stomach knotted up.* [Old English *cnotta*, from a prehistoric Germanic word meaning 'round lump', which is also the ancestor of English *knit* and *knoll*] —**knotter** *n.* ◇ **at a rate of knots** very quickly ◇ **tie the knot** to get married (*informal*) ◇ **tie yourself** *or* **sb (up) in knots** to become completely confused, especially in trying to explain sth, or to make sb completely confused

knot[2] /not/ *n.* a small sandpiper that migrates to the Arctic to breed. Latin name: *Calidris canutus* and *Calidris tenuirostris*. [15thC. Origin unknown.]

knot garden *n.* a herb or flower garden that has its plants arranged in an intricate pattern and some-

Reef knot

Bowline

Surgeon's knot

Clove hitch

Fisherman's bend

Granny knot

Figure of eight

Cow hitch

Heaving line knot

Overhand knot

Sheet bend

Running bowline

Double sheet bend

Whipping

Rolling hitch

Sheepshank

Sheet bend

Bowline on a bight

Knot

times also has trees and bushes trimmed in decorative designs

knotgrass /nót graass/ (*plural* **-grasses** *or* **-grass**) *n.* a creeping plant with prominent nodes on its stems and small pink flowers, considered a troublesome weed. Knotgrass was at one time widely used herbally in an infusion to treat asthma. Latin name: *Polygonum aviculare*. [Early 16thC. 'Knot' from KNOT[1], from its knotted stem.]

knothole /nót hōl/ *n.* a hole in wood where a knot has fallen out or been removed

knotted /nóttid/ *adj.* **1.** TIED OR TANGLED IN KNOTS tied in a knot, tangled up in knots, or made using decorative knots **2.** WOODWORK = knotty *adj.* **2 3.** BOT HAVING STEMS WITH SWELLINGS used to describe a plant that has stems with swellings resembling knots ◇ **get knotted** used to express disagreement or impatience with sb (*slang offensive*)

knotting /nótting/ *n.* a type of decorative weaving such as macramé or tatting, produced by interlacing and tying knots in the wool or thread

knotty /nótti/ (**-tier, -tiest**) *adj.* **1.** FULL OF KNOTS full of tied or tangled knots **2.** WOODWORK MARKED WITH KNOTS containing or marked with many knots ○ *knotty pine* **3.** PUZZLING OR COMPLEX very difficult to understand or solve —**knottily** *adv.* —**knottiness** *n.*

knotweed /nót weed/ (*plural* **-weeds** *or* **-weed**) *n.* = knotgrass

knotwork /nót wurk/ *n.* a type of decorative weaving produced by interlacing and tying knots in the cords

knout /nowt/ *n.* LEATHER WHIP a leather whip formerly used in imperial Russia for flogging ■ *vt.* (**knouts, knouting, knouted**) BEAT SB WITH KNOUT to flog sb using a knout [Mid-17thC. Via French and Russian *knut* from Old Norse *knútr* 'knot'.]

know /nō/ (**knows, knowing, knew** /nyoo/, **known** /nōn/) *v.* **1.** *vti.* HOLD INFORMATION IN THE MIND to have information firmly in the mind or committed to memory ○ *They know the names of all the US presidents.* **2.** *vti.* BE CERTAIN ABOUT STH to believe firmly in the truth or certainty of sth ○ *I know she wouldn't be late without a good reason.* **3.** *vti.* REALIZE STH to be or become aware of sth ○ *I didn't know you cared.* **4.** *vt.* COMPREHEND STH to have a thorough understanding of sth through experience or study ○ *know computers* **5.** *vt.* HAVE ENCOUNTERED SB OR STH BEFORE to be acquainted, associated, or familiar with sb or sth ○ *I have known John for years.* **6.** *vt.* RECOGNIZE DIFFERENCES to be able to perceive the differences or distinctions between things or people ○ *old enough to know right from wrong* **7.** *vt.* IDENTIFY SB OR STH BY A CHARACTERISTIC to recognize sb or sth by a distinguishing characteristic or attribute ○ *I'd know him anywhere by his peculiar laugh.* **8.** *vt.* HAVE SEX WITH SB to engage in sexual intercourse with sb (*archaic*) [Old English *cnāwan*. Ultimately from an Indo-European word that is also the ancestor of English *can* and *cognition*.] —**knowable** *adj.* —**knower** *n.* ◇ **in the know** possessing information that is secret or known only to a small group of people ◇ **you know** used to fill a pause, add emphasis to a statement, or elicit a response from the listener (*informal*) ◇ **you never know** used to indicate that the outcome of events is uncertain and it is possible that sth that seems unlikely could happen

know-all *n.* sb who professes to know more or better than anyone else about everything (*informal*) US term **know-it-all**

know-how *n.* the practical ability and knowledge necessary to do sth (*informal*)

knowing /nó ing/ *adj.* **1.** INDICATING PRIVATE KNOWLEDGE suggesting that sb knows a secret or sth that others are unaware of ○ *a knowing smile* **2.** ASTUTE aware of things and able to act cleverly and judge shrewdly **3.** INTENTIONAL done on purpose —**knowingly** *adv.* —**knowingness** *n.*

know-it-all *n.* US = know-all (*informal*)

knowledgable *adj.* = knowledgeable

knowledge /nóllij/ *n.* **1.** INFORMATION IN MIND general awareness or possession of information, facts, ideas, truths, or principles ○ *Her knowledge and interests are extensive.* **2.** SPECIFIC INFORMATION clear awareness or explicit information, e.g. of a situation or fact ○ *I believe they have knowledge of the circumstances.* **3.** ALL THAT CAN BE KNOWN all the information, facts, truths, and principles learned throughout time ○ *With all our knowledge, we still haven't found a cure for the common cold.* **4.** INTERCOURSE sexual intercourse (*archaic*) [14thC. Origin uncertain: probably from obsolete *knowlechen* 'to acknowledge', ultimately from Old English *cnāwan* 'to know' + *-lǣcan*, from *-lāc*, noun suffix (source of English *wedlock*).]

── WORD KEY: SYNONYMS ──

knowledge, erudition, information, learning, scholarship, wisdom

CORE MEANING: what can be known

knowledge used to talk about what can be known by means of study as well as what can be known through observation, investigation, reasoning, and experience; **erudition** advanced academic learning, often of a specialized or difficult nature; **information** facts or data; **learning** what is known through formal study, especially when this is of quite an advanced nature; **scholarship** advanced academic learning, especially when this is specialized; **wisdom** knowledge or learning, but also the ability to use these prudently and to combine them with experience and good judgment.

---

knowledgeable /nóllijəb'l/, **knowledgable** *adj.* possessing or showing a great deal of knowledge, awareness, or intelligence —**knowledgeability** /nóllijə bílləti/ *n.* —**knowledgeableness** /nóllijəb'l nəss/ *n.* —**knowledgeably** /nóllijəbli/ *adv.*

knowledge base *n.* **1.** COMPUT DATA USED FOR PROBLEM SOLVING the computerized data in an expert system required for solving problems in a particular area **2.** NECESSARY FACTS FOR SOLVING PROBLEM the facts required for solving a problem or problems

knowledge industry *n.* businesses that specialise primarily in data processing or the development and use of information technology

knowledge worker *n.* sb working in an industry that produces information rather than goods, such as management consultancy and computer programming

known /nōn/ past participle of **know** ▪ *adj.* ESTABLISHED generally recognized as or proven to be sth ○ *a known criminal* ▪ *n.* CERTAINTY a fact or piece of information that is certain ○ *separate the knowns from the unknowns*

Knox /noks/, **John** (1513?–72) Scottish religious reformer. He helped to found the Presbyterian Church of Scotland (1560), and opposed the rule of the Roman Catholic Mary, Queen of Scots. He became chaplain to Edward VI of England. At Mary's accession he fled abroad.

KNP *symbol.* CHESS king's knight's pawn

Knt *abbr.* CHESS knight

knuckle /núk'l/ *n.* **1.** ANAT FINGER JOINT a joint of a finger, especially a joint connecting a finger to the hand **2.** ROUNDED PROJECTION WHEN A FIST IS MADE one of the rounded projections above a knuckle that appears on the back of a hand when a fist is made (*often used in the plural*) **3.** COOK PIECE OF MEAT NEAR THE KNEE a cut of meat consisting of the lower joint from the hind leg of a calf, pig, or lamb **4.** MECH ENG HINGE PIVOT the cylindrical part of a hinge through which the pin passes **5.** MECH ENG = **knuckle joint** *n.* **2** ▪ *v.* **(-les, -ling, -led) 1.** *vt.* APPLY KNUCKLES TO to rub, hit, or press sth with the knuckles ○ *knuckled her eyes in disbelief* **2.** *vi.* GAME HAVE KNUCKLES ON GROUND PLAYING MARBLES to have the knuckles on the ground when shooting a marble with the thumb pressed into the bent forefinger [14thC. From Middle Low German *knökel*, literally 'small bone', ultimately from a prehistoric Germanic word meaning 'small bone'.] —**knuckly** /núkli/ *adj.* ◇ **near the knuckle** rather indecent

knuckle down *vi.* to work hard and conscientiously at sth (*informal*)

knuckle under *vi.* to give in to force or pressure used against you

knucklebone /núk'l bōn/ *n.* any knobbly bone forming part of a joint in the human finger (*informal*)

knucklebones /núk'l bōnz/ *n.* = **jacks** (*takes a singular verb*)

knuckle-duster *n.* a piece of metal worn over the knuckles and used to make a punch inflict greater injury. US term **brass knuckles**

knucklehead /núk'l hed/ *n.* an offensive term referring to sb who is regarded as unintelligent or thoughtless (*slang insult*) —**knuckleheaded** *adj.*

knuckle joint *n.* **1.** ANAT FINGER JOINT a joint of the human finger **2.** MECH ENG HINGE FASTENING TWO RODS TOGETHER a hinge with a pin that fastens the ends of two rods together, allowing movement in one plane only

knuckle sandwich *n.* a blow with the fist to the mouth (*slang*)

knur /nur/, **knurr** *n.* a bump or knot on a tree trunk or in wood [15thC. Origin uncertain: perhaps a variant of KNAR.]

knurl /nurl/ *n.* **1.** BUMP OR KNOB a small hard knob or protuberance **2.** RIDGE USED FOR GRIPPING a ridge, especially one in a series that run along the edge of sth, e.g. those on a thumbscrew that make it easier to grip ▪ *vt.* **(knurls, knurling, knurled)** PUT RIDGES ON to give ridges to sth, especially to make it easier to grip [Early 17thC. Origin uncertain: probably literally 'small knur', formed from KNUR.] —**knurly** /núrli/ *adj.*

knurr *n.*, *vt.* = **knur**

KO *n.* (*plural* **KO's**) KNOCKOUT a knockout, especially in boxing (*informal*) ▪ *vt.* **(KO's, KO'ing, KO'd)** KNOCK SB OUT to knock sb out, especially in boxing (*informal*) [Early 20thC. From the initial letters of *knock out*.]

koa /kṓ ə/ (*plural* **koas** *or* **koa**) *n.* **1.** HAWAIIAN ACACIA TREE an acacia tree that is native to Hawaii and has spreading branches, grey bark, and hard wood valued as timber. Latin name: *Acacia koa.* **2.** WOOD OF THE KOA TREE the red or golden-brown hard wood of the koa tree, used to make furniture [Early 19thC. From Hawaiian.]

Koala

koala /kō áálə/, **koala bear** *n.* an Australian marsupial that resembles a small bear and has grey fur, a round face, and large ears. It lives in eucalyptus trees, feeding almost exclusively on their leaves. Latin name: *Phascolarctos cinereus.* [Late 18thC. From Dharuk (an Aboriginal language of southwestern Australia) *kūl(l)a.*]

koan /kṓ an/ (*plural* **-ans** *or* **-an**) *n.* a Zen Buddhist riddle used to focus the mind during meditation and to develop intuitive thinking [Mid-20thC. From Japanese *kōan*, from Chinese *gōngàn* 'official business'.]

kob /kob/ (*plural* **kobs** *or* **kob**) *n.* a large antelope of Central and West Africa with orange-brown fur. It lives in open grasslands near swamps or rivers. Latin name: *Kobus kob.* [Late 18thC. From Wolof *kooba.*]

Kobe /kṓbi/, **Kōbe** capital of Hyogo Prefecture, and port on Osaka Bay, southern Honshu Island, Japan. Population: 1,477,410 (1990).

Koblenz /kō blénts/ city in the Rhineland-Palatinate, west-central Germany, south of Bonn. Population: 109,600 (1994).

kobo /kṓ bō/ (*plural* **-bo** *or* **-bos**) *n.* **1.** NIGERIAN CURRENCY a subunit of currency in Nigeria, 100 of which are worth one naira. See table at **currency** **2.** COIN WORTH A KOBO a coin worth one kobo [Late 20thC. From Nigerian English, alteration of COPPER.]

kobold /kóbbōld/ *n.* in German folklore, a mischievous elf that lives in houses or a gnome that haunts underground places, especially mines [Mid-19thC. From German, variant of *Kobalt* (see COBALT).]

Kobuk Valley National Park /kṓ búk-/ national park located entirely north of the Arctic Circle in northwestern Alaska. Area: 708,498 hectares/1,750,737 acres.

Koch /kokh/, **Robert** (1843–1910) German bacteriologist. He discovered the tuberculosis bacillus (1882) and the cholera bacillus (1883). He was awarded the Nobel Prize for physiology or medicine (1905).

Kodak /kṓ dak/ *tdmk.* a trademark for a hand-held camera invented by George Eastman in 1888 and for photographic supplies such as film

Kodály /kṓd ῑ́/, **Zoltán** (1882–1967) Hungarian composer. His works are influenced by the folk songs he collected. He developed an influential system of music education for children.

Kodiak[1] /kṓdi ak/ (*plural* **-aks** *or* **-ak**), **Kodiak bear** *n.* a brown bear of the coastal areas and nearby islands of Alaska and British Columbia. Latin name: *Ursus middendorffi.* [Late 19thC. Named after KODIAK ISLAND.]

Kodiak[2] /kṓdi ak/ city in southern Alaska, on northeastern Kodiak Island, south of Anchorage. Population: 7,677 (1996).

Kodiak Island island in the Gulf of Alaska, southwestern Alaska, noted for its Kodiak bears and marine life. Area: 8,974 sq. km/3,465 sq. mi.

koeksister /kṓók sistər/ *n.* S Africa a twisted or plaited doughnut, deep-fried in oil and dipped into cold sugar syrup and sometimes desiccated coconut [Early 20thC. From Afrikaans, of uncertain origin: perhaps, literally, 'cake sizzle'.]

Koetsu Hon'Ami /ko áttsoo hōná ami/ (1558–1637) Japanese artist. A founder member of the revivalist Rimpa school, he was noted for his paintings, calligraphy, pottery, and patronage of the arts.

kofta /kóftə/ (*plural* **-tas**) *n.* S Asia an Indian dish consisting of minced meat, fish, or vegetables cooked in small balls [Late 19thC. From Urdu and Persian *koftah* 'pounded meat'.]

kohen *n.* = **cohen**

kohl /kōl/ *n.* a chemical preparation used by women, especially in Asia and the Middle East, to darken the rims of their eyelids. It usually consists of powdered antimony sulphide or lead sulphide. [Late 18thC. From Arabic *kuhl* (see ALCOHOL).]

Kohl /kōl/, **Helmut** (*b.* 1930) German statesman. As Christian Democratic chancellor (1982–98), he played the leading role in German reunification (1990).

Kohlrabi

kohlrabi /kōl raˈabi/ (*plural* **-bies**) *n.* **1.** CABBAGE PLANT WITH A THICK EDIBLE STEM a kind of cabbage with an edible swollen stem similar to a turnip and short leaf stalks sprouting vertically from it. Latin name: *Brassica oleracea caulorapa* and *Brassica oleracea gongylodes.* **2.** VEGETABLE RESEMBLING A TURNIP the thick stem of the kohlrabi plant that is eaten as a vegetable [Early 19thC. Via German from the plural of Italian *cavolo rapa*, from medieval Latin *caulorapa*, ultimately from Latin *caulis* 'cabbage' + *rapa* 'turnip'.]

Kohoutek /kə hóot ek/ *n.* a comet that passed around the sun in late 1973 and early 1974

koi /koy/ (*plural* **koi**), **koi carp** *n.* a carp native to Japan and the temperate regions of eastern Asia that is popular as an aquarium or ornamental pond fish because of its red-gold or white colouring. Latin name: *Cyprinus carpio*. [Early 18thC. From Japanese.]

koine /kóy nee/ *n.* **1.** = **lingua franca 2.** STANDARD DIALECT a dialect or regional variant of a language that becomes the standard language for a wider population of speakers [Late 19thC. From Greek *koinē*, a form of *koinos* 'common, ordinary'.]

Koine /kóy nee/ *n.* the form of Greek, derived primarily from the Attic dialect, that became the standard language for Greek-speaking people during the Hellenistic period

Koko Nor /kốkō nawr/ = **Qinghai Hu**

Kokoschka /ko kóshkə/, **Oskar** (1886–1980) Austrian-born painter and writer. He is best known for his expressionist portraits and landscapes. He lived in Britain (1938–53) before settling in Switzerland.

kola (*plural* **-las** *or* **-la**) *n.* = **cola**

kola nut *n.* = **cola nut**

Kola Peninsula /kốlə-/ peninsula in northwestern European Russia, between the Barents Sea and the White Sea. Area: 100,000 sq. km/40,000 sq. mi.

Kolar Gold Fields /kō laàr-/ city in southern Karnataka State, southern India, near Bangalore. Population: 156,398 (1991).

Kolhapur /kốl haa poŏr/ city in Maharashtra State, southwestern India. Population: 405,118 (1991).

kolinsky /kə línski/ (*plural* **-skies**) *n.* **1.** ZOOL WEASEL WITH TAWNY FUR a weasel of northern Europe and Asia that has dark tawny fur and is sometimes considered to be a subspecies of the European mink. Latin name: *Mustela sibirica*. **2.** TEXTILES KOLINSKY FUR the fur of the kolinsky weasel [Mid-19thC. From Russian *kolinskiĭ* 'of Kola', named after *Kola*, a port in northwestern Russia.]

kolkhoz /kól kóz, -káwz, -háwz/ (*plural* **kolkhozes** *or* **kolkhoz** *or* **kolkhozy** /-zi/), **kolkoz** (*plural* **-kozes** *or* **-koz** *or* **-kozy**) *n.* a collective farm in the former Soviet Union [Early 20thC. From Russian, from *kol(lektivnoe) khoz(yaĭstvo)* 'collective farm'.]

kolkhoznik /kól kóznik, -káwznik, -háwznik/ *n.* a worker on a collective farm in the former Soviet Union

Kol Nidre /kól níddray/ *n.* **1.** JEWISH PRAYER the prayer recited at the opening of the service on the eve of Yom Kippur. It asks that all unfulfilled vows to God be nullified and that all transgressions be forgiven. **2.** JEWISH RELIGIOUS SERVICE the service on the eve of Yom Kippur [Late 19thC. From Aramaic *kol nidrē*, literally 'all the vows', the opening words of the prayer.]

kolo /kốlō/ (*plural* **-los**) *n.* **1.** SERBIAN FOLK DANCE a Serbian folk dance in which one or more dancers perform in the centre of a circle of other dancers **2.** MUSIC FOR KOLO a piece of music for or in the style of a kolo [Late 18thC. From Serbo-Croat, 'wheel'.]

Kolyma Range /kə leèmə/ mountain range in northeastern Siberian Russia. Length: 2,100 km/1,300 mi.

komatik /kố matik/ *n.* an Inuit sledge with wooden crossbars tied to the runners with rawhide [Early 19thC. From Inuit *qamutik*.]

Kombi /kómbi/ *tdmk.* a trademark name for the Volkswagen camper van

kombu /kóm boo/ *n.* a type of kelp sold dried and used in Japanese cooking [Late 19thC. From Japanese.]

Komi /kốmi/ (*plural* **-mi** *or* **-mis**) *n.* **1.** MEMBER OF URALIC PEOPLE a member of a Uralic people who live in northeastern European Russia **2.** KOMI LANGUAGE the language of the Komi people. It belongs to the Finnic group of the Finno-Ugric branch of the Uralic family of languages. About 400,000 people speak Komi. [Late 19thC. From Komi.] —**Komi** *adj.*

Komodo dragon /kə mốdō-/, **Komodo lizard** *n.* a large monitor lizard found only on the island of Komodo, east of Java. It is the largest living lizard and can grow to a length of 3 m/10 ft. Latin name: *Varanus komodoensis*.

komondor /kómmən dawr/ *n.* a large dog with a long matted white coat, belonging to a Hungarian breed that is traditionally used for herding sheep or as a watchdog [Mid-20thC. From Hungarian.]

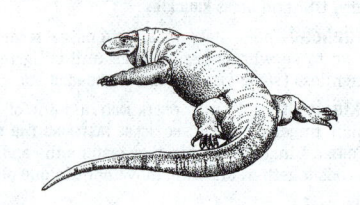

Komodo dragon

Komsomol /kómssə mol, kómssə mól/ *n.* a Communist organization for young people in the former Soviet Union [Mid-20thC. From Russian, coined from *Kommunisticheskiĭ Soyuz Molodёzhi* 'Communist Union of Youth'.]

Komsomolsk /kómssə molsk/ city in far eastern Russia, on the River Amur. Population: 318,600 (1992).

Kongo[1] (*plural* **-gos** *or* **-go**) *n.* **1.** PEOPLES MEMBER OF AN AFRICAN PEOPLE a member of a people who live along the lower part of the River Congo in west-central Africa **2.** LANG LANGUAGE OF KONGO PEOPLE the Bantu language spoken by the Kongo people, in southern Congo and northern Angola. There are about seven million native speakers of Kongo, with approximately two million more people using it as a common language. [Mid-19thC. From Kikongo.] —**Kongo** *adj.*

Kongo[2] /kóng gō/ former kingdom in central Africa that flourished from the 14th to 16th centuries in the area between present-day Gabon and northern Angola

Königsberg /kö́nigz burg/ former name for **Kaliningrad** (until 1946)

konimeter /kō nímmitər/ *n.* an instrument for measuring the amount of dust in the air [Early 20thC. Coined from Greek *konis* 'dust' + METER.]

koniology /kố ni ólləji/ *n.* the study of airborne dust and its effects on the environment [Formed from Greek *konis* 'dust']

Konkani /kóngkə nee/ *n.* a dialect of Marathi spoken in coastal Maharashtra in western India [Late 19thC. From Marathi *kōkṇi*.]

koodoo /koo doo/ *n.* = **kudu**

kook /kook/ *n.* US sb whose behaviour is considered unpleasantly eccentric (*informal insult*) [Mid-20thC. Origin uncertain: probably a shortening of CUCKOO.]

Kookaburra

kookaburra /kóŏkə burrə/ (*plural* **-ras** *or* **-ra**) *n.* a large kingfisher of Australia and nearby islands, known for its loud call that sounds like laughter. Latin name: *Dacelo novaeguineae* and *Dacelo leachii*. [Mid-19thC. From Wiradhuri *gugubarra*.]

kooky /kóŏki/ (**-ier, -iest**) *adj.* US considered to be unpleasantly eccentric (*informal insult*) —**kookily** *adv.* —**kookiness** *n.*

Kooning /kóoning/, **Willem de** (1904–97) Dutch-born US painter. Although he was a leading abstract expressionist, many of his works nevertheless include elements of the human form.

Koori /kóŏri/ (*plural* **Koories**), **koori** (*plural* **kooris**), **koorie** (*plural* **koories**) *n. Aus* an Aboriginal of southeastern Australia (*informal*) [Mid-18thC. From Awabakal *guri* 'man'.] —**Koori** *adj.*

Kootenay[1] /kóotə nay/, **Kootenai** river of the northwestern United States and southwestern Canada. It rises in the Rocky Mountains of southeastern British Columbia, flows into the United States, then reenters Canada through Kootenay Lake into the Columbia River. Length: 655 km/407 mi.

Kootenay[2], **Kootenai** *n.*, *n.* = **Kutenai**

kop /kop/ *n. S Africa* **1.** HILLTOP a prominent crest of a hill **2.** COMMON SENSE intelligence or common sense (*informal*) [Mid-19thC. Via Afrikaans from Dutch, 'head'.]

kopeck /kố pek/, **kopek, copeck** *n.* **1.** SUBUNIT OF RUSSIAN CURRENCY a subunit of currency in Russia and some other countries of the former Soviet Union, worth one hundredth of a rouble. See table at **currency 2.** COIN WORTH ONE KOPECK a coin worth one kopeck [Early 17thC. From Russian *kopeika*, literally 'little lance', from the figure of a tsar bearing a lance on the coins.]

koph /kof/, **qoph** *n.* the 19th letter of the Hebrew alphabet, represented in the English alphabet as 'q'. See table at **alphabet** [From Hebrew *qōph*]

kopje /kóppi/, **koppie** *n. S Africa* a small hill [Mid-19thC. Via Afrikaans from Dutch, literally 'small head', from *kop* 'head'.]

koppa /kóppə/ *n.* the 17th letter of the ancient Greek alphabet, represented in the English alphabet as 'q'. Though obsolete in Greek, it was later adopted by the Romans as the letter 'q'. [Late 19thC. From Greek.]

Kor. *abbr.* **1.** Korea **2.** Korean

kora /káwrə/ (*plural* **koras**) *n.* a type of West African 21-string lute that has a gourd resonator [Late 18thC. From a West African language.]

Koran /kaw raàn, kə-/, **Qur'an** the sacred text of Islam, believed by Muslims to record the revelations of God to Muhammad [Early 17thC. From Arabic *ḳur'ān* 'recitation, reading', from *ḳara'a* 'to read, recite'.] —**Koranic** /kaw ránnik, kə-/ *adj.*

Kordofan /kawr dō faàn/ former province in central Sudan

Kordofanian /káwrdō fáyni ən/ *n.* AFRICAN LANGUAGE GROUP a small group of languages spoken in southern Sudan that is considered either to be distinct from other African languages or to be a branch of the Niger-Congo family ■ *adj.* **1.** OF KORDOFANIAN LANGUAGES relating to the Kordofanian group of languages **2.** RELATING TO KORDOFAN relating to or typical of Kordofan [Named after the former province of KORDOFAN]

kore /káw ray/ (*plural* **korai** /-rī/) *n.* a Greek sculpture of a clothed, standing young woman dating from the period 650–480 BC. ◊ **kouros** [Early 20thC. From Greek *korē* 'maiden'.]

Korea, North /kə rée ə/ country in northeastern Asia that occupies the northern portion of the Korean Peninsula. Language: Korean. Currency: won. Capital: Pyongyang. Population: 23,904,124 (1996). Area: 120,538 sq. mi./46,540 sq. mi. Official name **Democratic People's Republic of Korea**

Korea, South country in northeastern Asia that occupies the southern portion of the Korean Peninsula. Language: Korean. Currency: won. Capital: Seoul. Population: 45,948,811 (1997). Area: 99,268 sq. km/38,328 sq. mi. Official name **Republic of Korea**

Korean /kə rée ən/ *n.* **1.** PEOPLES SB FROM NORTH OR SOUTH KOREA sb who was born or brought up in or is a citizen of North or South Korea **2.** LANG LANGUAGE OF NORTH AND SOUTH KOREA the official language of North and South Korea, also spoken in parts of China, Japan, and Asiatic Russia. It is often assigned to the Altaic family of languages. There are about 60 million native speakers of Korean, with a further 60 million using it as a second language. —**Korean** *adj.*

Korean War *n.* a war that lasted from 1950 to 1953 between North Korea, and its ally China, and South Korea, supported by United Nations troops, especially from the United States

korfball /káwrf bawl/ *n.* a game similar to basketball that is played by two teams of twelve players, each team having six men or boys and six women or girls [Early 20thC. From Dutch *korfbal*, literally 'basket ball'.]

korma /káwrmə/ (*plural* **-mas**), **qorma** (*plural* **-mas**) *n.* a mildly spiced, creamy Indian dish of meat, seafood, or vegetables cooked in a sauce that is enriched with yogurt or cream [Late 19thC. From Urdu *ḳormā*.]

Koror /kə ráwr/ island and administrative centre of the Republic of Palau, in the western Pacific Ocean. Population: 11,552 (1997). Area: 21 sq. km/8 sq. mi.

Korsakoffian /káwrsə kóffi ən/ *adj.* PSYCHIAT OF WENICKE-KORSAKOFF SYNDROME relating to the Wenicke-Korsakoff syndrome ■ *n.* PSYCHIAT SB WITH WENICKE-KORSAKOFF SYNDROME sb who is affected by the Wenicke-Korsakoff syndrome

Korsakoff's psychosis /káwrssə koffs-/, **Korsakoff's syndrome** *n.* ♦ **Wenicke-Korsakoff syndrome** [Early 20thC. Named after the Russian psychiatrist S. S. *Korsakoff* (1854–1900).]

koruna /ko roónə/ *n.* **1.** UNIT OF CZECH AND SLOVAK CURRENCY a unit of currency in the Czech Republic and Slovakia. See table at **currency 2.** COIN WORTH ONE KORUNA a coin worth a koruna [Early 20thC. From Czech, 'crown'.]

kos /kōss/ (*plural* **kos**) *n.* in India, a unit of measurement used for land distances that varies in length from region to region, ranging from 1.6 to 4.8 km/1 to 3 miles [Early 17thC. From Hindi, from Sanskrit *krośa*, literally 'cry, shout'.]

Kosciusko, Mount /kóssi úsk ō/ the highest mountain in Australia, located in the Snowy Mountains in southeastern New South Wales. Height: 2,228 m/7,310 ft.

Kościuszko /kóssi úsk ō/, **Tadeusz** (1746–1817) Polish national hero. He served with Washington in the American War of Independence, and in 1794 led a revolt for Polish independence.

kosher /kṓshər/ *adj.* **1.** JUDAISM RITUALLY PURE used to describe food that has been prepared so that it is fit and suitable under Jewish law **2.** JUDAISM PREPARING OR SELLING KOSHER FOOD preparing or selling foods that are fit and suitable under Jewish law **3.** REAL genuine, not false or fake (*informal*) **4.** LAWFUL OR PROPER allowed by law or regarded as correct or proper (*informal*) ○ *Something's not kosher about his handling of the situation.* ■ *vt.* (**-shers, -shering, -shered**) JUDAISM PREPARE KOSHER FOOD to prepare food in a way that is fit and suitable under Jewish Law [Mid-19thC. From Hebrew *kāšēr* 'fit, proper'.]

Kosovo /kóssəvo/ region in southwestern Serbia, in the Federal Republic of Yugoslavia. The administrative centre is Pristina. Population: 1,956,196 (1991). Area: 10,887 sq. km/4,203 sq. mi. —**Kosovan** *n., adj.* —**Kosovar** *n., adj.*

Kossuth /kósh oot/, **Lajos** (1802–94) Hungarian statesman. A leader of the Hungarian Revolution (1848), he was appointed provisional governor of Hungary (1849) but was deposed shortly after.

Kosygin /kə seégin/, **Alexey** (1904–80) Soviet statesman. He was chairman of the Council of Ministers of the Soviet Union, a position equivalent to that of premier, from 1964 to 1980. Full name **Alexey Nikolayevich Kosygin**

Kota Baharu /kṓtə baároo/ city on the northeastern coast of the Malay Peninsula, Malaysia, and capital of Kelantan State. Population: 220,000 (1991).

Kota Kinabalu /kṓtə kinəbə loó/ city in eastern Malaysia. It is the capital of Sabah State, on the South China Sea. Population: 55,997 (1993). Former name **Jesselton**

koto /kṓtō/ (*plural* **-tos**) *n.* a Japanese musical instrument similar to a zither, with 7 to 13 usually silk strings stretched over a convex wooden sounding board. It is plucked using three plectra worn on the thumb, index finger, and middle finger. [Late 18thC. From Japanese.]

kotuku /kṓtōō koo/ (*plural* **-kus**) *n.* NZ a white heron that is native to New Zealand. Latin name: *Egretta alba modesta*. [Mid-19thC. From Maori.]

koulibiac /koóli byák/, **koulibiaca** /-byákə/, **coulibiac**, **coulibiaca** *n.* a Russian-style fish pie, usually consisting of layers of cooked rice, fish, often salmon, and eggs encased in a crust of puff pastry or a brioche-type dough [Late 19thC. From Russian *kulebyaka*.]

koumiss, **koumis**, **koumyss** *n.* = **kumiss**

kouprey /koó pray/ (*plural* **-preys** *or* **-prey**) *n.* an endangered species of wild ox found in Cambodia and Vietnam that has a blackish-brown body with white markings on its back and feet. Latin name: *Bos sauveli*. [Mid-20thC. From Khmer.]

kouros /koór oss/ (*plural* **-roi** /koór oy/) *n.* a Greek sculpture of a naked, standing young man dating from the period 650–480 BC. ♢ **kore** [Early 20thC. From Greek, variant of *koros* 'boy'.]

Kowloon /kow loón/ town in Hong Kong Special Administrative Region, southeastern China, on the northern side of Hong Kong harbour. Population: 1,990,000 (1994).

kowtow /ków tów/ *vi.* (**-tows, -towing, -towed**) **1.** KNEEL TO SHOW RESPECT formerly, in China, to kneel and touch the forehead to the ground in order to show respect, awe, or submission **2.** BE SERVILE to behave in an extremely submissive way in order to please sb in a position of authority ■ *n.* **1.** ACT OF KNEELING TO SHOW RESPECT a show of respect or worship made by kneeling and touching the forehead to the ground **2.** SERVILE ACT an extremely submissive act aimed at pleasing sb in a position of authority [Early 19thC. From Chinese *kētóu* (Wade-Giles *kótóu*), literally 'strike head'.] —**kowtower** *n.*

KP[1] *symbol.* CHESS king's pawn

KP[2] *abbr.* Knight (of the Order) of St Patrick

kph *abbr.* kilometres per hour

Kr *symbol.* **1.** krona **2.** krone **3.** krypton

KR *symbol.* CHESS king's rook

kr. *abbr.* **1.** krona **2.** króna **3.** krone

kraal /kraal/ *n.* S Africa **1.** AFRICAN VILLAGE WITHIN STOCKADE a traditional rural village in Africa, usually consisting of a number of huts surrounded by a stockade (*sometimes considered offensive*) **2.** CATTLE PEN a pen or other enclosure for livestock, especially cattle [Mid-18thC. Via Afrikaans from Portuguese *curral*, from Nama.]

Krafft-Ebing /kráft áybing/, **Richard** (1840–1902) German neuropsychologist. He is known for his pioneering studies into sexual psychopathology. His main work is *Psychopathia Sexualis* (1886).

kraft /kraaft/, **kraft paper** *n.* a type of tough, usually brown, paper made from chemically treated wood pulp and used to make bags and wrapping paper [Early 20thC. From a shortening of Swedish *kraft-papper*, literally 'strength paper'.]

krait /krīt/ *n.* an extremely poisonous snake, native to Southeast Asia and nearby islands, that has brightly-coloured bands on its back. Genus: *Bungarus*. [Late 19thC. From Hindi *karait*.]

Krakatau /krakə tów/, **Krakatoa 1.** small volcanic island in southwestern Indonesia, in the Sunda Strait between Java and Sumatra. Area: 16 sq. km/6 sq. mi. **2.** volcano on the island of Krakatau, whose eruption in 1883 destroyed most of the island and caused thousands of deaths. Height: 813 m/2,667 ft.

kraken /kraákən/ *n.* in Norwegian folklore, a huge sea monster shaped like a giant squid. Norwegian fishermen have periodically reported sightings since the 16th century. [Mid-18thC. From Norwegian.]

krameria /krə meéri ə/ *n.* a genus of South American plants, the roots of some of which, e.g. rhatany, have medicinal uses and are used as dyes [Mid-19thC. Named after the Austrian botanist J. G. H. Kramer (d. 1742).]

krans /kraanss/ (*plural* **kranses**), **krantz** /kraants/ (*plural* **krantzes**) *n.* S Africa a sheer rock face, typically occurring in the form of a band of exposed rock around the summit of a mountain [Late 18thC. Via Afrikaans from Dutch, 'coronet, chaplet'.]

Krasnodar /krassnə daár/ city and port in southwestern Russia. It is the administrative centre of Krasnodar Territory. Population: 634,500 (1992). Former name **Yekaterinodar** (until 1922)

Krasnoyarsk /krəsnə yaásk/ city in southern Siberian Russia. It is the administrative centre of Krasnoyarsk Territory. Population: 925,000 (1992).

Krater

krater /kráytər/ *n.* US = **crater** [Mid-18thC. Via Latin *crater* from Greek *kratēr* 'mixing bowl', from *kerannunai* 'to mix' (source of English *idiosyncracy*).]

K ration *n.* an emergency food ration consisting of one prepared meal, supplied to US soldiers fighting in World War II [Mid-20thC. Named after the American physiologist Ancel Benjamin *Keyes* (born 1904).]

Kraut /krowt/ *n.* an offensive term referring to a German (*slang offensive*) [Early 20thC. From German, 'vegetable, cabbage'. From the stereotype of Germans as eaters of sauerkraut.] —**Kraut** *adj.*

Krebs /krebz/, **Sir Hans** (1900–81) German-born British biochemist. He discovered the citric acid cycle (Krebs cycle), for which he shared the Nobel Prize for physiology or medicine (1953). Full name **Sir Hans Adolf Krebs**

Krebs cycle /krébz-/ *n.* a sequence of biochemical reactions occurring in cell structures (**mitochondria**) of living organisms whereby energy is obtained from the oxidation of acetic acid and related compounds derived from food [Mid-20thC. Named after the British biochemist Sir Hans *Krebs*.]

kremlin /krémlin/ *n.* a fortress or citadel in any Russian city [Mid-17thC. Via French from Russian *kreml* 'citadel'.]

Kremlin /krémlin/ *n.* **1.** WALLED COMPOUND IN MOSCOW the walled citadel in Moscow in which cathedrals, palaces, and the offices of the Russian government are located. The outer walls date back to the 15th century. **2.** FORMER SOVIET GOVERNMENT the government of the former Soviet Union

Kremlinology /krémli nólləji/ *n.* the study of the government and policies of the former Soviet Union — **Kremlinological** /krémlinə lójjik'l/ *adj.* —**Kremlinologist** /krémli nóllǝjist/ *n.*

kreplach /krép laak, -laakh/ *npl.* a Jewish dish consisting of triangles or squares of pasta filled with liver or meat that are boiled and served in soup [Late 19thC. From Yiddish *kreplech*, the plural of *krepel*, from German dialect *Kräppel* 'fried pastry, fritter'.]

kreutzer /króytsər/, **kreuzer** *n.* a small silver or copper coin used in Germany, Austria, and Hungary from the 13th to the mid-19th centuries [Mid-16thC. From German *Kreuzer*, from *Kreuz* 'cross'; modelled on medieval Latin *denarius crucigerus*, literally 'cross-bearing penny'.]

krill /kril/ (*plural* **krill**) *n.* a tiny marine crustacean resembling a shrimp. It is the primary food of baleen whales and other animals that filter their food from seawater. Order: Euphausiacea. [Early 20thC. From Norwegian *kril* 'small fry of fish'.]

krimmer /krímmər/ *n.* whitish or pale grey fur that is made from the soft curly wool of lambs from the Crimean Peninsula [Mid-19thC. From German, where it was formed from *Krim* 'Crimea'.]

Krio /kreé ō/ (*plural* **-os**) *n.* **1.** LANG CREOLE LANGUAGE OF SIERRA LEONE a creole language spoken in Sierra Leone, especially in and around the capital, Freetown. It is based on English, with a strong Yoruba influence. About 50,000 people speak Krio as a first language, and a further 200,000 use it as a second language. **2.** PEOPLES SB WHO SPEAKS KRIO sb who speaks Krio [Mid-20thC. Origin uncertain: probably an alteration of CREOLE.] —**Krio** *adj.*

Kriol /krée ol/ *n. Aus* the English-based creole spoken by many Aboriginal people in northern Australia

kris /kreess, kriss/ *n.* a Malay and Indonesian dagger with a wavy two-edged blade [Late 16thC. From Malay *keris*.]

Krishna /kríshnə/ *n.* in Hindu religion, the eighth incarnation of the god Vishnu, often depicted as a young cowherd [From Sanskrit *kṛṣṇa*] —**Krishnaism** *n.*

Krivoy Rog /kri vóy rawk/, **Krivoi Rog** city and major iron-producing centre in south-central Ukraine. Population: 724,000 (1991).

KRL *n., abbr.* COMPUT knowledge representation language

kromesky /krə méski/ (*plural* **-kies**) *n.* **1.** FRIED STUFFED PANCAKE in Polish or Russian cooking, a thin pancake containing a savoury or sweet filling. The pancake is sometimes coated thinly in egg and breadcrumbs and then deep fried. **2.** SAVOURY FRITTER in Polish or Russian cooking, a small fritter or croquette of minced meat, chicken, or fish wrapped in bacon and fried in batter [Mid-19thC. From Polish *kromeczka* 'small slice'.]

krona /krốnə/ (*plural* **-nor** /-nawr/) *n.* **1.** UNIT OF SWEDISH CURRENCY the main unit of currency in Sweden, worth 100 öre. See table at **currency 2.** UNIT OF FAROESE CURRENCY the main unit of currency in the Faeroe Islands, worth 100 öre. See table at **currency 3.** COIN WORTH ONE KRONA a coin worth one krona [Late 19thC. From Swedish, 'crown'.]

króna /krốnə/ (*plural* **-nur** /krốnə/), **krona** (*plural* **-nur**) *n.* **1.** UNIT OF ICELANDIC CURRENCY the main unit of currency in Iceland, worth 100 aurar. See table at **currency 2.** COIN WORTH ONE KRÓNA a coin worth one króna [Late 19thC. From Icelandic, 'crown'.]

krone /krốnə/ (*plural* **-ner** /krốnə/) *n.* **1.** UNIT OF DANISH CURRENCY the main unit of currency in Denmark, worth 100 øre. See table at **currency 2.** UNIT OF NORWEGIAN CURRENCY the main unit of currency in Norway, worth 100 øre. See table at **currency 3.** COIN WORTH ONE KRONE a coin worth one krone **4.** (*plural* **-nen**) OLD GERMAN COIN a gold coin formerly used in Germany, equivalent to 10 marks **5.** OLD UNIT OF AUSTRIAN CURRENCY the main unit of currency in Austria from 1892 until 1925, or a coin representing it [Late 19thC. From Danish and German, 'crown'.]

Kronecker delta /krónnikər-/ *n.* a mathematical function of two variables that takes on only two values: 0 when the variables are unequal, and 1 when the variables are equal [Early 20thC. Named after the mathematician Leopold *Kronecker* (died 1891).]

kroner plural of **krone**

kronor plural of **krona**

Kronos *n.* = **Cronus**

Kronstadt /krónshtat/, **Kronshtadt** military port on Kotlin Island in the Gulf of Finland, in northwestern European Russia. Population: 44,400 (1994).

krónur plural of **króna**

kroon /kroon/ (*plural* **kroons** or **krooni** /króoni/) *n.* **1.** UNIT OF ESTONIAN CURRENCY the main unit of currency in Estonia, worth 100 sents. See table at **currency 2.** COIN WORTH ONE KROON a coin worth one kroon [Early 20thC. From Estonian 'crown'.]

Kropotkin /krə pótkin/, **Pyotr Alekseyevich, Prince** (1842–1921) Russian revolutionary. He was a leading theorist of the anarchist movement. Renouncing his title in 1871, he devoted himself to life as a revolutionary, advocating the abolition of governments and the founding of a society based on mutual trust.

KRP *symbol.* CHESS king's rook's pawn

Kruger /króogər/, **Paul** (1825–1904) South African statesman. President of the Transvaal (1883–1902), his discriminatory policies directed at non-Boers led to the Second Boer War (1899–1902). Full name **Stephanus Johannes Paulus Kruger**

Kruger National Park national park in northeastern South Africa, bordering Mozambique, established in 1928. Area: 19,485 sq. km/7,523 sq. mi.

Krugerrand /króogər rand/ *n.* a South African gold coin weighing one ounce, intended mostly to be purchased as an investment [Mid-20thC. From KRUGER + RAND.]

Krugersdorp /króogərz dawrp/ city in Gauteng Province, northeastern South Africa, near Johannesburg. Population: 93,000 (1991).

krumhorn *n.* = **crumhorn**

krummholz /króom hölts/ (*plural* **-holz**) *n.* the stunted trees that grow just above the timberline on a mountain, or the high-altitude zone in which they grow [Early 20thC. From German, 'elfin-wood', literally 'crooked wood'.]

krummhorn /krúm hawrn/ *n.* = **crumhorn**

Krupp /kroop/, **Alfried** (1812–87) German industrialist and arms manufacturer. He expanded his father's steel-manufacturing business into arms manufacture.

Krupp, Friedrich (1854–1902) German industrialist and arms manufacturer. He was the son of Alfried Krupp. Under his supervision the Krupp empire extended its dealings all over the world.

krypton /krípt on, kríptən/ *n.* a colourless inert gaseous chemical element found in small quantities naturally in the atmosphere and used in fluorescent lamps and lasers. Symbol **Kr** [Late 19thC. From Greek *krupton*, a form of *kruptos* 'hidden, concealed'.]

KS *abbr.* Kansas

KStJ *abbr.* Knight of the Order of St John

K selection *n.* a process of natural selection that leads to a lowering of the birthrate when the population of a species approaches the maximum number that the environment can sustain [From K, the constant for carrying capacity in the population growth equation]

Kshatriya /kshátri ə/ *n.* **1.** HINDU CASTE the second of the four Hindu castes, originally a royal and warrior caste. In modern times, its members are professionals, administrators, or military personnel. **2.** MEMBER OF KSHATRIYA CASTE a member of the Kshatriya caste [Late 18thC. From Sanskrit *kṣatriya*, from *kṣatra* 'rule'.]

kt *abbr.* PHYS kiloton

Kt *abbr.* knight

KT *abbr.* **1.** Knight Templar **2.** Knight (of the Order) of the Thistle

Kuala Lumpur /kwáalə lóompoor/ capital city of Malaysia, located on the southern Malay Peninsula. Population: 1,145,075 (1991).

Kubrick /kyóobrik/, **Stanley** (1928–99) US film director. His varied films include *Lolita* (1962), *Dr Strangelove* (1964), and *2001: A Space Odyssey* (1968).

kuccha /kúcha/ *n. S Asia* short trousers worn by Sikh men. ◊ **five Ks**

kuchen /kóohən/ (*plural* **-chen**) *n.* any cake that has been raised with yeast [Mid-19thC. From German, 'cake'.]

Kuching /kóo ching/ city in Malaysia. It is the capital of Sarawak State, on the island of Borneo. Population: 147,729 (1991).

kudos /kyóo doss/ *n.* praise, credit, or glory for an achievement (*takes a singular verb*) ○ *The president deservedly got the kudos for the success of the negotiations.* [Late 18thC. From Greek, 'praise, renown'.]

kudu /kóo doo/ (*plural* **-dus** or **-du**), **koodoo** (*plural* **-doos** or **-doo**) *n.* a large antelope native to Africa. The male has long spiralling horns. Latin name: *Tragelaphus strepsiceros* and *Tragelaphus imberbis.* [Late 18thC. Via Afrikaans *koedoe* from Xhosa *i-qudu*.]

kudzu /kóod zoo/ (*plural* **-zus**) *n.* a hardy vine from eastern Asia that has compound leaves, purplish flowers, and roots that contain a nourishing starch used medicinally. It was introduced into the United States to stop the erosion of the soil in the South, but now grows out of control. Latin name: *Pueraria lobata.* [Late 19thC. From Japanese *kuzu*.]

Kufic /kóofik, kyóofik/, **Cufic** *adj.* ANGULAR ARABIC ALPHABET an early angular style of Arabic writing used for Koranic manuscripts and inscriptions ■ *n.* KUFIC SCRIPT the Arabic alphabet written in Kufic script [Early 18thC. Named after the ancient city of *Kufa*,

south of Baghdad, because the script was attributed to the scholars there.]

kugel /kóog'l/ *n.* a savoury pudding in Jewish cuisine, often of noodles or potatoes [Mid-19thC. From Yiddish, 'ball', from Middle High German; probably from its traditional mound shape.]

Kuiper belt *n.* a ring of small celestial bodies orbiting through the outer solar system, beyond the farthest planets, Neptune and Pluto. It is believed that the Kuiper belt is a source of comets.

Ku Klux Klan /kóo kluks klán/ *n.* **1.** 19C US WHITE SUPREMACIST GROUP a terrorist secret society organized in the southern United States after the Civil War that used violence and murder to promote its white supremacist beliefs **2.** 20C US WHITE SUPREMACIST GROUP a white supremacist organization founded in Georgia in 1915. Its secret membership, supremacist views, and terrorist methods are similar to those of the 19th-century Ku Klux Klan. [Mid-19thC. Origin uncertain: perhaps from Greek *kuklos* 'circle' + a variant of CLAN.]

kukri /kóokri/ (*plural* **-ris**) *n.* a large knife with a sharp curved blade that gets broader towards the point, used by the Gurkhas in Nepal for hunting and fighting [Early 19thC. From Nepali *khukuri*.]

kukukuma /kóokŏŏ koomə/ (*plural* **-mas** or **-ma**) *n. NZ* ZOOL = **gurnard**

kulak /kóo lak/ *n.* a wealthy landowning peasant in Russia during the time between the emancipation of the serfs and the Russian Revolution [Late 19thC. Via Russian, literally 'fist, tight-fisted person', from Turkic *kol* 'hand'.]

kulfi /kóolfi/ (*plural* **-fis**) *n. S Asia* a rich Indian ice cream containing nuts

Kultur /kŏŏl tŏŏr/ *n.* HIST German culture, regarded as superior and used as a vehicle of German imperialism during the Hohenzollern and Nazi regimes [Early 20thC. Via German from Latin *cultura* or French *culture* 'culture'.]

Kulturkampf /kŏŏl tŏŏr kampf/ *n.* HIST the struggle between the German government under Bismarck and the Roman Catholic Church over control of education, marriage, and Church appointments. It lasted from 1871 to 1887 and ended in compromise. [Late 19thC. From German *Kultur* 'culture' + *Kampf* 'struggle'.]

Kumamoto /kŏŏma mŏtŏ/ capital city of Kumamoto Prefecture, on western Kyushu Island, Japan. Population: 579,306 (1990).

Kumasi /koo máassi/ capital of the Ashanti Region, central Ghana. It is situated northwest of Accra. Population: 399,300 (1990). Former name **Coomassie**

kumera /kóomərə/ (*plural* **-as**), **kumara** (*plural* **-as**) *n. ANZ* a sweet potato [Late 18thC. From Maori.]

kumiss /kóomiss/, **koumiss, koumis, koumyss** *n.* slightly alcoholic, fermented, and sour-tasting milk from a mare or camel, drunk by some of the peoples of western and Central Asia [Late 16thC. Via French *koumis*, German, Polish *kumys*, or Russian from Tartar *kumiz*.]

kumkum /kóom kŏŏm/ *n. S Asia* a red round decorative mark worn on the forehead by Hindu women and girls, but traditionally not by widows [Mid-20thC. From Sanskrit *kuṅkuma* 'saffron'.]

kümmel /kóomm'l/, **kummel** *n.* a colourless liqueur or cordial that is flavoured with cumin and caraway seeds and is made primarily in the Baltic region [Mid-19thC. From German, literally 'caraway seed', from Old High German *kumīn* 'cumin'.]

kumquat /kúm kwot/, **cumquat** *n.* **1.** FRUIT-BEARING TREE a Chinese evergreen shrub or small tree of the rue family, with small yellow edible fruit. Genus: *Fortunella.* **2.** EDIBLE FRUIT the sweet edible fruit of a kumquat shrub or tree. It is like a very small orange and is often used in preserves. [Late 17thC. From Chinese (Cantonese) *kam kwat*, literally 'gold orange'.]

Kun /koon/, **Béla** (1886–1939?) Hungarian communist leader. He set up a short-lived Soviet republic in Hungary (May–August 1919), and later died during Stalin's purges.

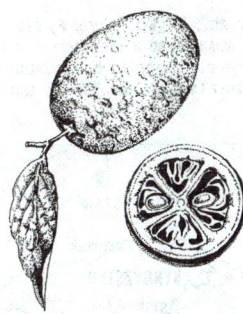

Kumquat

kundalini /koŏndə leeni/ *n.* vital energy that Hindus believe lies dormant at the base of the spine until it is called into action, e.g. through yoga, to be used in seeking enlightenment [Late 19thC. From Sanskrit *kundalinī*, literally 'snake', from the idea that it is like a coiled snake.]

Kundera /kúndərə/, **Milan** (*b.* 1929) Czech writer. His novels include *The Joke* (1967) and *The Unbearable Lightness of Being* (1984). He moved to France in 1957.

Kung fu: Bruce Lee

kung fu /kúng foó, koŏng-/ *n.* a Chinese form of self-defence in which fluid, circular movements of the arms and legs are used to attack an opponent [Late 19thC. From Chinese *gongfu*, literally 'merit-master'.]

Kunlun Mountains /koŏn loŏn-/ mountain range in western China. India claims territory in the western area. Height: 7,723 m/25,338 ft. Length: 2,400 km/1,500 mi.

Kunming /koŏn míng/ capital city of Yunnan Province and trade and transport centre of southwestern China. Population: 1,520,000 (1991).

Kununurra /kunə núrrə/ town in northeastern Western Australia, built in the 1960s to accommodate workers on nearby irrigation schemes. Population: 4,884 (1996).

kunzite /koŏnts īt/ *n.* a reddish-purple variety of the mineral spodumene, used as a gemstone [Early 20thC. Named after George F. *Kunz* (1856–1932), a US gem expert.]

Kuomintang /kwómin táng/ *n.* the political party that established China as a republic in 1911, ruled China from 1928 to 1947 until defeated by the Communists, and then withdrew to rule in Taiwan [Early 20thC. From Chinese *guómíndǎng*, literally 'national people's party'.]

Kura /koŏ raá/ river in the Transcaucasia Region. It flows through Turkey, Georgia, and Azerbaijan, and empties into the Caspian Sea. Length: 1,500 km/940 mi.

kurchatovium /kúrchə tóvi əm/ *n.* the name given to the element rutherfordium in the former Soviet Union [Mid-20thC. Named after I. V. *Kurchatov* (1903–60), a Russian nuclear physicist.]

Kurd /kurd/ *n.* a member of a largely Islamic people who live in an area straddling the borders of Iraq, Turkey, and Iran [Early 17thC. From Kurdish.]

kurdaitcha /kər díchə/, **kadaitcha** /kə díchə/ *n.* among Aboriginal peoples of central Australia, a sorcerer who was responsible for avenging the death of a kinsman [Late 19thC. From Aboriginal.]

Kurdish /kúrdish/ *n.* **LANGUAGE OF THE KURDS** an Iranian language spoken in parts of Turkey, Iraq, Iran, Armenia, and Syria. It belongs to the Indo-Iranian branch of the Indo-European family of languages. About 10 million people speak Kurdish. ■ *adj.* **OF KURDISH PEOPLE OR LANGUAGE** relating to the Kurds, their language, or their culture [Early 19thC]

Kurdistan

Kurdistan /kúrdi staán/, **Kurdistān** region in southwestern Asia, considered the homeland of the Kurdish people and encompassing parts of Turkey, Iraq, Iran, Armenia, and Syria. Population: 26,000,000 (early 1990s).

kurgan /koor gaán, -gán/ *n.* a burial mound built by a prehistoric culture of eastern Europe and northern Iran [Late 19thC. From Russian.]

Kurosawa /koŏrə saáwə/, **Akira** (1910–91) Japanese film director. He is known for such classic films as *Rashomon* (1950) and *The Seven Samurai* (1954).

Kuroshio /koŏ róshi ō/ warm current in the Pacific Ocean, flowing from the Philippines northeastwards along the eastern coast of Japan.

kurrajong /kúrrə jong/ *n.* a small or medium-sized tree that grows throughout eastern Australia, has yellowish or red bell-shaped flowers, and yields a tough fibre. Latin name: *Brachychiton populneum*. [Early 19thC. From Aboriginal.]

Kurri Kurri-Weston /kúrri kuri wéstən/ urban area in the Hunter Valley region of southeastern New South Wales, Australia. Population: 12,555 (1996).

Kursk /koorsk/ city in western Russia, the capital of Kursk Oblast, and a mining centre. Population: 430,000 (1990).

kurta /koórtə/ *n.* a long loose collarless shirt worn by Indian men [Early 20thC. From Urdu and Persian *kurtah*.]

kurtosis /kər tóssiss/ (*plural* **-ses** /-seez/) *n.* a measure of the extent to which a frequency distribution is concentrated about its mean [Early 20thC. From Greek *kurtōsis*, 'a bulging, curvature', from *kurtos* 'bulging, bent'.]

kuru /koŏroō/ *n.* a fatal degenerative disease of the central nervous system that affects some tribes in New Guinea. Similar to Creutzfeldt-Jakob disease, it is believed to derive from the practice of eating the brains of an ancestor. [Mid-20thC. From a name in New Guinea, literally 'trembling, shivering'.]

kurus /koŏ roŏsh, -roōsh/ (*plural* **-rus**) *n.* **1.** see table at **currency 2. COIN WORTH ONE KURUS** a coin worth one kurus [Late 19thC. From Turkish.]

Kush *n.* = Cush

Kuskokwim /kúskə kwim/ river in southwestern Alaska, rising in the Alaska Range and flowing into the Bering Sea. Length: 1,170 km/724 mi.

Kutch, Rann of /kuch/ region of mud flats and salt marshes in western India and southern Pakistan. Area: 21,000 sq. km/8,100 sq. mi.

Kutenai /koŏt'n ay, -ee/ (*plural* **-nai** *or* **-nais**), **Kootenai** (*plural* **-nai** *or* **-nais**), **Kootenay** (*plural* **-nay** *or* **-nays**) *n.* **1. PEOPLES MEMBER OF A NATIVE N AMERICAN PEOPLE** a member of a Native North American people living principally in Montana, Idaho, and British Columbia **2. LANG KUTENAI LANGUAGE** the language of the Kutenai people [Early 19thC. From Blackfoot *Kotonáai-*.] —**Kutenai** *adj.*

kutu /koŏ toō/ *n. NZ* a human louse (*slang*) [From Maori]

Kuwait

Kuwait /koŏ wáyt/ Islamic constitutional monarchy in southwestern Asia, located at the northwestern tip of the Persian Gulf. It is bordered by Iraq and Saudi Arabia. Language: Arabic. Currency: Kuwaiti dinar. Capital: Kuwait City. Population: 1,834,269 (1997). Area: 17,818 sq. km/6,880 sq. mi. Official name **State of Kuwait** —**Kuwaiti** *n.*, *adj.*

Kuwait City capital city of Kuwait, situated on the southern shore of Kuwait Bay in the Persian Gulf. Population: 31,241 (1993).

kV *abbr.* kilovolt

kvass /kvaass, kvass/, **kvas, quass** *n.* an alcoholic drink similar to beer, made in Russia and Eastern European countries from rye or barley or from stale bread [Mid-16thC. From Russian *kvas*.]

kvetch /kvech/ *vi.* (**kvetches, kvetching, kvetched**) **COMPLAIN INCESSANTLY** to grumble and complain about things all the time (*informal*) ■ *n.* (*informal*) **1. SB INCESSANTLY COMPLAINING** sb who is always grumbling and complaining about things **2. COMPLAINT** a complaint about sth [Mid-20thC. Via Yiddish *kvetsh* (noun) and *kvetshn* (verb) from German *Quetsche* 'crusher' and *quetschen* 'to crush, squeeze'.]

kW *abbr.* kilowatt

Kwa /kwaa/ *n.* a group of languages in the Niger-Congo family that are spoken in West Africa, and include Yoruba and Ibo [Mid-19thC. From Kwa.] —**Kwa** *adj.*

kwacha /kwaácha/ *n.* **1. UNIT OF ZAMBIAN CURRENCY** the main unit of currency in Zambia, worth 100 ngwee. See table at **currency 2. COIN OR NOTE WORTH ONE KWACHA** a coin or note worth one kwacha [Mid-20thC. From Bantu, 'dawn'.]

Kwakiutl /kwaáki oŏt'l/ (*plural* **-utl** *or* **-utls**) *n.* **1. PEOPLES MEMBER OF NATIVE N AMERICAN PEOPLE** a member of a Native North American people who live on Vancouver Island and parts of the adjacent coast of British Columbia **2. LANG LANGUAGE OF THE KWAKIUTL PEOPLE** the Wakashan language of the Kwakiutl people [Mid-19thC. From Kwakiutl *Kwáguł*.] —**Kwakiutl** *adj.*

Kwangju /kwung joó/ city in southwestern South Korea. It is the capital of South Cholla Province. Population: 1,257,504 (1995).

kwanza /kwánzə/ (*plural* **-zas** *or* **-za**) *n.* **1. UNIT OF ANGOLAN CURRENCY** the main unit of currency in Angola, worth 100 lwei. See table at **currency 2. COIN OR NOTE WORTH ONE KWANZA** a coin or note worth one kwanza [Late 20thC. Origin uncertain: perhaps from Swahili, literally 'first', or named after *Kwanza* (Cuanza), the name of a river in Angola.]

kwashiorkor /kwóshi áwr kawr, kwáshi-/ *n.* a type of malnutrition in children caused by inadequate intake of protein, common in African children weaned on to a traditional cornmeal diet [Mid-20thC. From a local name in Ghana, literally 'red boy' (from the symptomatic reddening of the hair).]

KwaZulu /kwaá zooloō/ former homeland in South Africa, part of the province of KwaZulu-Natal since 1994

KwaZulu-Natal province in southeastern South Africa, established in 1994. Capital: Pietermaritzburg. Population: 8,713,100 (1995). Area: 91,548 sq. km/35,348 sq. mi.

kwela /kwáylə/ *n. S Africa* a style of urban South African pop music [Mid-20thC. From Afrikaans, of uncertain origin: perhaps from Zulu *khwela* 'to climb, mount'.]

kWh *abbr.* kilowatt-hour

KWIC /kwik/ *abbr.* COMPUT key word in context

Kwinana /kwə naʹanə/ town in southwestern Western Australia, just south of Perth. Population: 15,674 (1996).

KWOC /kwok/ *abbr.* COMPUT key word out of context

KWT *abbr.* Kuwait (*international vehicle registration*)

Ky., KY *abbr.* Kentucky

kyanite /kíʹ ə nīt/, **cyanite** /síʹ ə-/ *n.* a bluish aluminosilicate mineral that is found as thin-bladed crystals or in masses in rocks that have been metamorphosed at high pressure, used as a gemstone and as a refractory [Late 18thC. Formed from Greek *kuan(e)os* 'dark blue'.]

kyanize /kíʹ ə nīz/ (**-nizes, -nizing, -nized**), **kyanise** (**-nises, -nising, -nised**) *vt.* to preserve wood against decay by treating it with a corrosive sublimate [Mid-19thC. Named after J. H. *Kyan* (1774–1850), the Irish inventor of the process.]

kyat /ki aʹat/ *n.* **1.** UNIT OF MYANMAR CURRENCY the main unit of currency in Myanmar, worth 100 pyas. See table at **currency 2.** COIN OR NOTE WORTH ONE KYAT a coin or note worth one kyat [Mid-20thC. From Burmese.]

Kyd /kid/, **Thomas** (1558–94) English playwright. His best known work is *The Spanish Tragedy* (1580?), which established the genre of revenge tragedy. He was imprisoned for atheism and died in poverty.

kyle /kīl/ *n. Scotland* a narrow passage of water between two areas of land [Mid-16thC. From Gaelic *caol*, from *caol* 'narrow'.]

Kyle of Tongue inlet of the sea on the northern coast of Scotland. It is designated a National Scenic Area.

Kyles of Bute stretch of water in the Firth of Clyde, western Scotland, separating the Island of Bute from the mainland. It is designated a National Scenic Area. Area: 119 sq. km/46 sq. mi.

kylie /kíli/, **kiley** (*plural* **-leys**) *n. Aus* a boomerang that has one convex and one flat side [Mid-19thC. From Aboriginal.]

kylix /kíliks, kílliks/ (*plural* **-lices** /-kees/) *n.* a shallow two-handled cup, often with a footed stem, used in ancient Greece [Mid-19thC. From Greek *kulix*.]

kymograph /kíʹmō graaf, -graf/ *n.* a device for recording variations in motion or pressure, e.g. of blood, consisting typically of a stylus and a rotating drum [Mid-19thC. Coined from Greek *kumo-* (from *kuma* 'wave') + -GRAPH.] —**kymographic** /kíʹmō gráffik/ *adj.* — **kymography** /kī móggrəfi/ *n.*

Kymry *npl.* = **Cymry**

Kyoto /ki ōʹtō/ manufacturing centre and capital of Kyoto Urban Prefecture, southern Honshu Island, Japan. Population: 1,461,000 (1990).

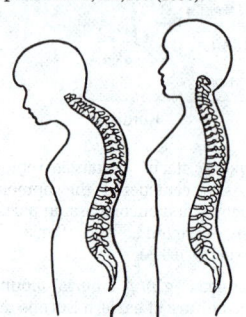

Kyphosis

kyphosis /kī fōʹssiss/ *n.* a permanent curving of the spine that makes sb look hunched over [Mid-19thC. From Greek *kuphōsis*, from *kuphos* 'bent, hunchbacked'.] — **kyphotic** /kī fóttik/ *adj.*

Kyprianou /kípri aʹan oo/, **Spyros** (*b.* 1932) Cypriot statesman. He succeeded Archbishop Makarios as president of Cyprus (1977–88).

Kyrgyz /kúr giz/, **Kirghiz** (*plural* **Kyrgyz** or **Kirghiz**) *n.* **1.** PEOPLES ASIAN NOMAD a member of a traditionally nomadic people living in Kyrgyzstan and Siberia **2.** LANG KYRGYZ LANGUAGE the Turkic language of the Kyrgyz

Kyrgyzstan

Kyrgyzstan /keʹergi staan/ republic in Central Asia, bordered by Kazakhstan, China, Tajikistan, and Uzbekistan. Language: Kyrgyz, Russian. Currency: som. Capital: Bishkek. Population: 4,512,809 (1997). Area: 198,500 sq. km/76,640 sq. mi. Official name **Kyrgyz Republic**

Kyrie /kírri ay, keʹeri-/, **Kyrie eleison** /-i láy son/ *n.* **1.** CHR FORM OF PRAYER a form of prayer that begins with the words 'Lord, have mercy', used in the Roman Catholic, Greek Orthodox, and Anglican Churches **2.** MUSIC MUSICAL SETTING FOR THE KYRIE a musical setting for the Kyrie, often forming part of a sung Mass [Via medieval Latin from Greek *Kuriē eleēson* 'Lord, have mercy']

Kyushu /kyoʹo shoo/, **Kyūshū** island of Japan, the most southerly of the four major Japanese islands. Population: 13,269,000 (1990). Area: 42,164 sq. km/16,279 sq. mi.

L L

l¹ /el/, **L** *n.* **1.** 12TH LETTER OF THE ALPHABET the 12th letter of the modern English alphabet **2.** SOUND OF THE LETTER 'l' the sound of a spoken letter 'L' **3.** STH SHAPED LIKE 'L' sth that has the same shape as a capital letter 'L'

l² *abbr.* latitude

L¹, l *n.* the Roman numeral for 50

L² *symbol.* **1.** PHYS angular momentum **2.** PHYS inductance *n.* 1. **3.** PHYS self-inductance **4.** PHYS latent heat **5.** PHYS luminance **6.** ASTRON luminosity

L³ *abbr.* **1.** Latin **2.** large **3.** CARS learner

l. *abbr.* **1.** law **2.** line **3.** left **4.** length **5.** MONEY lira **6.** ELEC live (*used on plugs*) **7.** AIR lift

L. *abbr.* **1.** MAPS Lake **2.** SPORTS League **3.** Liberal **4.** Licentiate

la¹ /laa, law/ *interj.* US used to show surprise or to emphasize what is being said [Late 16thC. Natural exclamation.]

la² /laa/, **lah, laa** *n.* MUSIC = **lah** [14thC. From medieval Latin, originally a syllable sung to this note in a hymn to St John the Baptist.]

La *symbol.* lanthanum

LA *abbr.* **1.** legislative assembly **2.** Library Association **3.** local agent **4.** Los Angeles **5.** LA, La. Louisiana

laager /láagər/, **lager** *n.* CAMP PROTECTED BY WAGONS a camp protected by a circle of wagons, used in the past by the Boers in South Africa ■ *vti.* (**-gers, -gering, -gered**) MAKE A PROTECTED CAMP to form wagons into a circle to make a protected camp [Mid-19thC. Alteration of obsolete Afrikaans *lager*, of uncertain origin: probably from German *Lager* 'camp, bed, storeroom' (source of English *lager¹*).]

La Argentina /la áarjən teénə/ (1888?–1936) Argentine dancer. She re-established Spanish dancing as a popular art form in the 20th century.

lab /lab/ *n.* a laboratory (*informal*) [Late 19thC. Shortening.]

Lab. *abbr.* **1.** POL Labour **2.** Labrador

Laban /láabən/, **Rudolf von** (1879–1958) Hungarian dancer and choreographer. He devised a method of notating dance movements and founded several dance schools, including the Laban Centre, London.

labanotation /láabə nō táysh'n/ *n.* a method of notating dance movements in detail, including the placement of the dancer's body, direction of movement, tempo, and dynamics [Mid-20thC. Named after Rudolf von LABAN who invented it, LABAN being blended with NOTATION.]

labarum /lábbərəm/ (*plural* **-ra** /-rə/) *n.* a military banner carried before Roman emperors, especially one with Christian symbols that was carried in front of Constantine the Great as a sign of his conversion to Christianity [Early 17thC. From late Latin, of unknown origin.]

labdanum /lábdənəm/, **ladanum** /láddənəm/ *n.* a bitter resinous gum extracted from various rockroses and used in flavourings and perfumes [Early 16thC. From medieval Latin, an alteration of Latin *ladanum*, from Greek *lēdanon*, from *lēdon* 'mastic'.]

label /láyb'l/ *n.* **1.** INFORMATIVE ITEM ATTACHED TO STH a piece of paper, fabric, or plastic attached to sth to give instructions about it or identify it **2.** DESCRIPTIVE WORD OR PHRASE a word or phrase used to describe a person or group **3.** RECORDING, COMM NAME OF A RECORD COMPANY the name of a record company, especially when displayed on a record, CD, or cassette **4.** COMPUT IDENTIFIER FOR PART OF A COMPUTER PROGRAM a number or word that acts as a unique identifier for a part of a computer program **5.** ARCHIT = **dripstone** *n.* 2 **6.** HERALDRY HERALDIC DESIGN a figure on a heraldic shield consisting of a horizontal band with pendants and identifying the person to whom it belongs as an eldest son **7.** CHEM STH USED TO IDENTIFY A CHEMICAL a substance, usually a radioactive isotope or dye, that can be traced to identify a compound as it undergoes a chemical reaction or assimilation ■ *vt.* (**-bels, -belling, -belled**) **1.** ATTACH A LABEL TO to attach a label to sth as identification or to give instructions **2.** USE A DESCRIPTIVE WORD FOR to describe sb or sth using a particular word or phrase ○ *resented being labelled as either liberal or progressive* **3.** CHEM ATTACH A CHEMICAL LABEL TO to make a chemical substance identifiable with a label such as a radioactive isotope or dye [13thC. From Old French, 'ribbon, fillet, fringe', of uncertain origin; probably ultimately from a prehistoric Germanic base that is also the ancestor of English *lap*.] —**labeller** *n.*

labellum /lə bélləm/ (*plural* **-la** /-lə/) *n.* **1.** BOT LARGE ORCHID PETAL the petal of an orchid that is its lowest and largest and forms a lip **2.** INSECTS INSECT'S FEEDING PART the lobe at the end of an insect's proboscis that it uses for feeding on liquids [Early 19thC. From Latin, 'small lip', from *labrum* 'lip' (source of English *labrum*).]

labia plural of **labium**

labial /láybi əl/ *adj.* **1.** ANAT INVOLVING LIPS OR LABIA in, on, close to, or involving the lips or the labia **2.** PHON WITH LIPS CLOSED pronounced with the lips closed or nearly closed as, e.g. in the sounds 'b' and 'p' **3.** MUSIC MOVING AIR ACROSS A LIPLIKE EDGE used to describe an instrument or organ pipe that produces sound by the movement of air across a sharp edge ■ *n.* **1.** PHON SOUND PRONOUNCED WITH LIPS CLOSED a speech sound pronounced with the lips closed or nearly closed as, e.g. in 'b' and 'p' **2.** MUSIC INSTRUMENT WITH A LIPLIKE EDGE an instrument or organ pipe in which sound is produced by the movement of air across a sharp liplike edge [Late 16thC. From medieval Latin *labialis*, from Latin *labia* 'lips'.] —**labially** *adv.*

labialize /láybi ə līz/ (**-izes, -izing, -ized**), **labialise** (**-ises, -ising, -ised**) *vt.* to pronounce a sound with the lips rounded —**labialization** /láybi ə līz záysh'n/ *n.*

labia majora /-mə jáwrə/ *npl.* the two thick outer folds of skin that surround the clitoris, the opening of the urethra, and the opening of the vagina of women and girls [From modern Latin, literally 'larger lips']

labia minora /-mi náwrə/ *npl.* the two small folds of skin that lie immediately inside the labia majora of women and girls and join at the front to form the hood of the clitoris [From modern Latin, literally 'smaller lips']

labiate /láybi ət, -ayt/ *adj.* **1.** WITH A DIVIDED SET OF PETALS used to describe a flower such as a snapdragon that has its set of petals (**corolla**) divided into two unequal and overlapping parts **2.** OF THE MINT FAMILY belonging to the mint family ■ *n.* PLANT OF THE MINT FAMILY any plant belonging to the mint family, which includes nettles, snapdragons, rosemary, and thyme. Labiates have square stems and aromatic leaves. Family: Labiatae. [Early 18thC. From modern Latin *labiatus*, from Latin *labium* 'lip'.]

labile /láy bīl, láyb'l/ *adj.* **1.** CHANGEABLE liable to change **2.** CHEM UNDERGOING FREQUENT CHANGE readily or frequently undergoing chemical or physical change ○ *a labile compound* [15thC. From late Latin *labilis* 'prone to slip', from Latin *labi* 'to fall, slip' (source of English *lapse*). The original English sense was 'prone to lapse'.]

labio- *prefix.* lips, labial ○ *labiodental* [From Latin *labium* (see LABIUM)]

labiodental /láybi ō dént'l/ *adj.* PHON WITH THE UPPER TEETH ON THE LOWER LIP pronounced with the upper teeth resting on the inside of the lower lip, as in the sounds 'f' and 'v' ■ *n.* PHON LABIODENTAL CONSONANT a labiodental speech sound

labionasal /láybi ō náyz'l/ *adj.* PHON PRONOUNCED LIKE 'M' pronounced with the lips closed and the air being pushed through the nose, as in the sound 'm' ■ *n.* PHON LABIONASAL CONSONANT a labionasal speech sound

labiovelar /láybi ō veélər/ *adj.* PHON PRONOUNCED LIKE 'KW' pronounced by constricting the back of the mouth and closing the lips, as in the sound 'kw' ■ *n.* PHON LABIOVELAR CONSONANT a labiovelar speech sound

labium /láybi əm/ (*plural* **-a** /-ə/) *n.* **1.** ANAT FOLD ROUND WOMEN'S GENITALIA any of the four folds, two inner (**labia minora**) and two outer (**labia majora**), that surround a woman's or girl's genital organs **2.** INSECTS INSECT MOUTHPART a mouthpart of some insects, formed from a fused pair of appendages **3.** BOT LIP OF A FLOWER the lower lip of the corolla of a labiate flower **4.** ANY LIP any part that looks or functions like a lip [Late 16thC. From Latin, 'lip'.]

lablab /láb lab/ *n.* BOT = **hyacinth bean** [Early 19thC. From Arabic *lablāb*.]

labor *n.*, *vti.* US = **labour**

laboratory /lə bórrətəri/ (*plural* **-ries**) *n.* **1.** ROOM FOR TEACHING SCIENCE a room or place with appropriate equipment for teaching science or doing scientific work **2.** PLACE FOR SCIENTIFIC RESEARCH a facility, or a room in a facility, where research and testing is carried out [Early 17thC. Via medieval Latin *laboratorium* 'place for work' from, ultimately, Latin *laborare* 'to work', from *labor* (see LABOUR).]

laborious /lə báwri əss/ *adj.* **1.** NEEDING EFFORT requiring a great deal of effort **2.** NOT FLUENT showing signs of effort or difficulty rather than naturalness or fluency, especially in speech or writing **3.** ENJOYING WORK happy or likely to work hard and long [14thC. Originally in the sense 'hard-working, industrious'.] —**laboriously** *adv.* —**laboriousness** *n.*

——— **WORD KEY: SYNONYMS** ———
See Synonyms at **hard**.

Laborite /láybə rīt/ *n.* a member or supporter of the Australian Labor Party

labor union *n.* US = **trade union**

labour /láybər/ *n.* **1.** PHYSICAL WORK work done using the strength of the body ○ *sentenced to two years' hard labour* **2.** WORKERS COLLECTIVELY the workers, especially manual workers, in a country, company, or industry considered as a group (*often used before a noun*) ○ *labour relations* **3.** SUPPLY OF WORK the supply of work or workers for a particular job, industry, or employer **4.** PARTICULAR PIECE OF WORK a particular piece of work, especially a difficult or long one (*often used in the plural*) ○ *the labours of Hercules* **5.** OBSTET **PROCESS OF CHILDBIRTH** the process of giving birth to a baby from when the contractions start to the baby's delivery, or the time taken for this process (*often used before a noun*) ○ *labour pains* ■ *v.* (**-bours, -bouring, -boured**) **1.** *vi.* **WORK HARD** to work hard, especially at physical work ○ *laboured all day in the hot sun* **2.** *vi.* **STRUGGLE TO DO STH** to struggle to do sth very difficult or very tiring ○ *laboured over the questions for several hours* **3.** *vi.* **OPERATE WITH DIFFICULTY** to have difficulty in running or functioning smoothly, e.g. because of being overloaded or defective (*refers to engines or machines*) **4.** *vi.* **MOVE WITH DIFFICULTY** to move with difficulty or great effort ○ *We laboured up to the summit.* **5.** *vi.* OBSTET **GIVE BIRTH** to be in the process of giving birth to a baby **6.** *vi.* NAUT **PITCH AND ROLL** to pitch and roll heavily at sea (*refers to ships*) **7.** *vt.* **OVEREMPHASIZE** to continue trying to express or emphasize sth when it is unnecessary ○ *There's no need to labour the point.* [14thC. Via Old French *labo(u)r* from Latin *labor* 'toil, pain' (source of English *elaborate*), perhaps literally 'stumbling under a burden'.] ◇ **labour of love** sth demanding or difficult that is done just for pleasure rather than for money

─────── **WORD KEY: SYNONYMS** ───────

See Synonyms at **work**.

labour under *vt.* to be at a disadvantage because of believing sth to be true that is not ○ *She had been labouring under the misconception that the problem was solved.*

Labour *n.* = **Labour Party** (*takes singular or plural verb*) ■ *adj.* **OF LABOUR PARTY** supporting, belonging to, or associated with a Labour Party, e.g. in the United Kingdom or Australia

labour camp *n.* a prison where the prisoners have to do hard physical work under a harsh, typically cruel, regime

Labour Day *n.* **1.** US AND CANADIAN PUBLIC HOLIDAY a national holiday observed in the United States and Canada on the first Monday in September in honour of working people **2.** = **May Day**

laboured /láybərd/ *adj.* done with obvious effort or difficulty rather than naturally or gracefully

labourer /láybərər/ *n.* sb who works in a job that requires physical strength and stamina

labour exchange *n.* *UK* a job centre (*dated*)

labour force *n.* = **workforce**

labour-intensive *adj.* involving a relatively high number of workers or greater costs for labour than for other areas such as materials, machines, or design ○ *a labour-intensive industry*

labourism /láybərizəm/ *n.* the political or social movement that upholds the rights of workers, or support for this movement

labourist /láybərist/ *n.* sb who supports the rights of workers

Labourite /láybə rīt/ *n.* a member or supporter of the Labour Party

Labour Party *n.* a British political party founded in 1900 to support the rights and interests of working people

labra plural of **labrum**

Labrador[1] /lábbrə dawr/ *n.* a large dog with a short thick black, brown, or yellow coat, originally bred to fetch killed or injured game during a shoot. Labradors were first bred in Newfoundland, Canada, and later imported into the UK. [Early 20thC. Named after LABRADOR, where the breed's stock originated.]

Labrador[2] /lábbrə dawr/ *n.* mainland portion of the eastern Canadian province of Newfoundland. It abuts Quebec to the west and south and the Atlantic Ocean on the east. Area: 296,860 sq. km/114,618 sq. mi.

Labrador Current cold ocean current that flows south past western Greenland and eastern Labrador and Newfoundland, Canada, to join the Gulf Stream

labradorite /lábbrə dawr īt/ *n.* a variety of plagioclase feldspar, the colour of which shifts between blue and green depending on the angle it is seen from [Named after LABRADOR, where it was found]

Labrador Peninsula large peninsula in eastern Canada. The region includes much of Quebec and the mainland portion of Newfoundland. Area: 1,619,000 sq. km/625,000 sq. mi.

Labrador retriever *n.* = **Labrador**[1]

Labrador Sea arm of the Atlantic Ocean that separates Labrador in eastern Canada from Greenland and the Atlantic Ocean

Labrador tea *n.* a low-growing evergreen shrub native to northern North America. It has bell-shaped flowers and leaves that are used in making a tea. Latin name: *Ledum groenlandicum.*

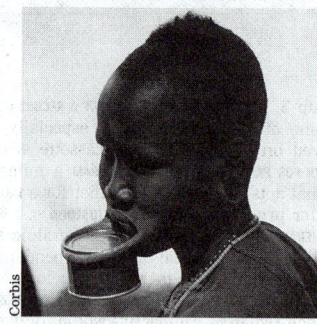

Labret

labret /láy bret/ *n.* an ornament made of bone, shell, or other materials that is worn pierced through the lip, especially by some peoples in East Africa and South America [Mid-19thC. Formed from Latin *labrum* 'lip' (source of English *labial*).]

labrid /lábbrid/ *n.* a fish belonging to the wrasse family, many species of which are colourful tropical coral reef fish. Family: Labridae. [From modern Latin *Labridae*, family name, from *Labrus*, genus name]

labrum /láybrəm, láb-/ (*plural* **-bra** /-brə/) *n.* a projecting upper mouthpart of some arthropods [Early 18thC. Via modern Latin from Latin, 'lip' (source of English *labial*).]

Labuan /lə bóoən, lábyōō ən/ island in Malaysia, situated off the northern coast of Borneo, northeast of Singapore. Capital: Victoria. Population: 54,307 (1991). Area: 100 sq. km/40 sq. mi.

Laburnum

laburnum /lə búrnəm/ *n.* a European or Asian tree or shrub with hanging sprays of bright yellow flowers and poisonous leaves, bark, and seeds. Genus: *Laburnum.* [Mid-16thC. From Latin, 'broad-leaved bean trefoil', of uncertain origin: perhaps from Etruscan.]

labyrinth /lábbərinth/ *n.* **1.** CONFUSING NETWORK a place with a lot of crisscrossing or complicated passages, tunnels, or paths in which it would be easy to become lost **2.** STH VERY COMPLICATED sth that is made up of many different parts that is complicated and hard to understand ○ *You need legal advice to guide you through the labyrinth of regulations.* **3.** ANAT INNER EAR a structure consisting of connected cavities or canals, especially the inside of the ear [14thC. Directly or via French from Latin *labyrinthus*, from Greek *laburinthos*, of uncertain origin: perhaps 'royal structure', formed from Lydian *labrus* 'two-edged axe', a symbol of royal power.]

Labyrinth *n.* in Greek mythology, the maze designed by Daedalus for King Minos of Crete to confine the Minotaur

labyrinth fish *n.* a fish with a specialized labyrinthine breathing organ that allows it to breathe air out of water. Family: Anabantidae.

labyrinthine /lábbə rín thīn/, **labyrinthian** /lábbə rínthiən/ *adj.* **1.** CONSISTING OF A CONFUSING NETWORK consisting of or resembling a labyrinth of passages or paths ○ *a labyrinthine maze of backstreets* **2.** EXTREMELY COMPLICATED extremely complicated and therefore difficult to understand

labyrinthitis /lábbərin thítiss/ *n.* an illness in which the inner ear becomes inflamed, causing a loss of balance and nausea

labyrinthodont /lábbə rínthə dont/ *n.* an extinct amphibian resembling the crocodile that lived in the Late Palaeozoic and Early Mesozoic eras. Order: Labyrinthodontia. [Mid-19thC. From modern Latin *Labyrinthodontia*, order name, literally 'labyrinth-toothed' (from the amphibians' labyrinthine dental structure), from Greek *laburinthos* (see LABYRINTH).]

lac[1] /lak/ *n.* a resinous substance secreted by an insect (**lac insect**), used in the past in the manufacture of shellac [15thC. Via Portuguese *lac(c)a* and medieval Latin *lac* from Persian *lāk* and Hindi *lākh*, from Sanskrit *lākṣā*, literally 'red dye' (source of English *lacquer*), an alteration of *rákṣā*.]

lac[2] *n.* = **lakh**

LAC *abbr.* leading aircraftman

laccolith /lákəlith/ *n.* a massive intrusion of igneous rock between beds of sedimentary rock, creating a dome-shaped structure [Late 19thC. Coined from Greek *lakkos* 'pond, pit, reservoir' + -LITH.] —**laccolithic** /lákə líthik/ *adj.* —**laccolitic** /-líttik/ *adj.*

Lace

lace /layss/ *n.* **1.** TEXTILES DELICATE FABRIC WITH PATTERNED HOLES a delicate fabric made by weaving cotton, silk, or a synthetic yarn in a pattern that leaves small holes between the threads (*often used before a noun*) ○ *a lace shawl* **2.** CLOTHES CORD USED TO TIE EDGES TOGETHER a long cord that is used to tie two parts of a garment, shoe, or boot together and is threaded through holes or around hooks **3.** MIL BRAID ON MILITARY UNIFORMS ornamental gold or silver braid used on military officers' uniforms and hats ■ *vt.* (**laces, lacing, laced**) **1.** FASTEN USING LACES to tie the edges of sth with holes or hooks together by threading laces through the holes or round the hooks, pulling the edges close, and knotting the laces **2.** THREAD A LACE THROUGH HOLES to thread a lace or cord through holes or around hooks **3.** DECORATE WITH LACE to decorate or trim sth with lace **4.** ADD ALCOHOL TO A DRINK to add a small amount of alcohol or a drug to a drink or to food ○ *eggnog laced with rum* **5.** ADD A SMALL AMOUNT TO to add an amount of sth to sth else to enhance it ○ *It was an intelligent article, laced with wit.* **6.** STREAK WITH A DIFFERENT COLOUR to mark sth with streaks of a different colour **7.** BEAT to beat or thrash sb (*informal*) **8.** INTERTWINE to intertwine sth with sth else, e.g. fingers [12thC. Via Old French *laz* 'net, string' (the original English senses) from assumed Vulgar Latin *lacium*, from Latin *laqueus* 'noose, snare' (source of English *lasso*).] —**lacelike** *adj.*

lace into *vt.* **1.** FASTEN INTO A GARMENT to fasten a corset or close-fitting garment around sb by lacing it up **2.** ATTACK VERBALLY OR PHYSICALLY to attack sb verbally or physically

lace up *vt.* to fasten or tighten the laces of sth such as a boot or corset

lacebark /láyss baark/ *n.* = ribbonwood

lace bug *n.* a small bug with a delicate lacy vein pattern on its wings. Family: Tingitidae.

Lacedaemonian /lássədi móni ən/ *adj.* relating to the ancient Greek city of Sparta [Mid-16thC. Formed from Latin *Lacedaemonius* or Greek *Lakedaimonios* 'of Lacedaemon (ancient name of an area including Sparta), Spartan'.] —**Lacedaemonian** *n.*

lacerate *vt.* /lássə rayt/ (-ates, -ating, -ated) 1. CUT JAGGEDLY to cut or gash the skin so that the wound is deep with irregular edges 2. DISTRESS DEEPLY to distress sb deeply or agonizingly ■ *adj.* /lássərət/ BOT WITH JAGGED EDGES used to describe leaves or petals that have jagged or irregular edges [15thC. From Latin *lacerat-*, the past participle stem of *lacerare* 'to tear to pieces', from *lacer* 'torn, mangled'.]

laceration /lássə ráysh'n/ *n.* 1. DEEP JAGGED CUT a deep and jagged cut in the flesh 2. STH THAT WOUNDS sth that is deeply wounding to the feelings

Lacerta /lə súrtə/ *n.* a small constellation in the northern hemisphere

lacertid /lə súrtid/ *n.* a lizard such as the common wall lizard or green lizard with rough irregular scales and bony plates on its skull. Family: Lacertidae. [Late 19thC. Formed from Latin *lacerta* 'lizard'.]

lace-up *n.* a shoe or boot that fastens with laces —**lace-up** *adj.*

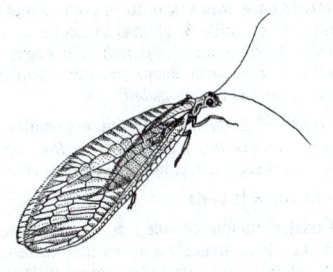

Lacewing

lacewing /láyss wing/ *n.* an insect with transparent wings and long antennae whose larvae feed on aphids and other insect pests. There are several species of lacewing, including the green lacewing and the brown lacewing. Superfamily: Hemerobioidea. [From the fine network of veins in its wings, likened to lace]

laches /láchiz, láy-/ *n.* LAW negligence or delay in doing sth, especially in pursuing a legal claim [14thC. Via Anglo-Norman *laches(se)* 'negligence', from Old French *lasche* 'lax, lazy', from, ultimately, Latin *laxus* 'wide, loose, relaxed' (source of English *lax* and *lease*).]

Lachesis /lákississ/ *n.* one of the three Fates in Greek mythology

Lachine /la sheen/ city on Montreal Island, southern Quebec Province, Canada, situated on the St Lawrence River 13 km/8 mi. southwest of Montreal. Population: 35,171 (1996).

Lachlan /laàk lən/ river in south-central New South Wales, Australia. Length: 1,480 km/920 mi.

lachrymal *adj.* 1. CRYING relating to tears or weeping (*literary*) 2. ANAT = lacrimal

lachrymation *n.* PHYSIOL = lacrimation

lachrymator *n.* = lacrimator

lachrymatory /lákrimətəri, lákri máytəri/ *n.* (*plural* -ries) BOTTLE FOR TEARS a small bottle of a kind found in ancient tombs, thought in the past to have contained the tears of mourners ■ *adj.* = lacrimatory

lachrymose /lákri mōss, -mōz/ *adj.* (*literary*) 1. CRYING crying, or tending to cry easily and often 2. SAD so sad as to make people cry [Early 18thC. From Latin *lacrimosus*, from *lacrima* 'tear'.] —**lachrymosely** *adv.* —**lachrymosity** /lákri mössəti/ *n.*

lacing /láyssing/ *n.* 1. ALCOHOL ADDED TO DRINK a small amount of alcohol or a drug added to a drink or to food 2. BEATING a beating or thrashing (*informal*)

laciniate /lə sínni ət, -ayt/, **laciniated** /lə sínni aytid/ *adj.* BOT, ZOOL having a fringed, jagged, or lobed border [Mid-17thC. Formed from Latin *lacinia* 'fringe, flap, edge'.] —**laciniation** /lə sínni áysh'n/ *n.*

lac insect *n.* a southern Asian insect, the female of which secretes a substance (**lac**) that was used in the past to make shellac. Latin name: *Laccifer lacca.*

lack /lak/ *n.* 1. SHORTAGE OR ABSENCE OF STH a shortage or complete absence of a particular thing ○ *Lack of sleep makes it difficult to concentrate.* 2. STH ABSENT sth that is needed but is in short supply or missing ○ *Courage is a lack in him.* ■ *vt.* (**lacks, lacking, lacked**) 1. NOT HAVE not to have sth that is needed ○ *the project lacked funding* 2. NOT HAVE ENOUGH to have too little of sth ○ *What he lacks in patience, he makes up for in drive.* [13thC. Origin uncertain: probably from assumed Old English *lac*, from a prehistoric Germanic base that also produced English *leak*.]

WORD KEY: SYNONYMS
lack, shortage, deficiency, deficit, want, dearth
CORE MEANING: an insufficiency or absence of sth
lack a general word used to talk about an insufficiency or total absence of sth; **shortage** a situation where there is less of sth than is needed; **deficiency** an insufficiency of a particular nutrient in the human body; **deficit** the amount by which sth falls short of a target amount or level; **want** a lack or absence of sth that is required or desirable; **dearth** the scarcity or rareness of sth, especially in a situation where more of that thing is desirable rather than necessary.

---

lackadaisical /lákə dáyzik'l/ *adj.* without much enthusiasm, energy, or effort [Mid-18thC. Formed from *lackadaisy* 'alas, alack', an alteration of LACKADAY.] —**lackadaisically** *adv.* —**lackadaisicalness** *n.*

lackaday /lákə day/ *interj.* used to express regret, disapproval, or dismay (*archaic*) [Late 17thC. Shortening of the phrase *alack-a-day* (from ALACK).]

lackey /láki/ *n.* (*plural* -eys) 1. OBEDIENT FOLLOWER sb excessively willing to obey another's orders 2. MAN SERVANT a man servant, especially a footman or valet who wears a uniform (*archaic*) ■ *vti.* (-eys, -eying, -eyed) ACT AS LACKEY to act as a servant, especially a footman [Early 16thC. From French *laquais*, of uncertain origin: perhaps ultimately from Arabic *al-kāḍī* 'the judge' (source of English *alcalde*).]

lackey moth *n.* a moth whose caterpillars are striped and live in a web on a tree or shrub. Latin name: *Malacosoma neustria.* [*Lackey* from its striped markings, which are reminiscent of a footman's livery]

lackluster *adj.* US = lacklustre

lacklustre /lák lustər/ *adj.* lacking energy, excitement, enthusiasm, or passion

Laconia /lə kóni ə/ region in Ancient Greece that occupied much of the Peloponnese. The capital city was Sparta.

laconic /lə kónnik/, **laconical** /lə kónnik'l/ *adj.* using very few words [Mid-16thC. Via Latin *Laconicus* 'of Laconia' from Greek *Lakōnikos*, from *Lakōn* (see LACONIA), whose inhabitants had a reputation for terseness.] —**laconically** *adv.*

laconism /lákənizəm/, **laconicism** /lə kónnissizem/ *n.* 1. BREVITY IN SPEECH the use of very few words 2. BRIEF BUT MEANINGFUL STATEMENT sth that is said in few words but is full of meaning [Late 16thC. From Greek *lakōnismos* 'imitation of Spartan manners', ultimately from *Lakōn* (see LACONIC).]

La Coruña /la ko rúnya/ city, port, and capital of La Coruña Province, in the autonomous region of Galicia, northwestern Spain. Population: 254,822 (1995).

lacquer /lákər/ *n.* 1. TYPE OF VARNISH a varnish made from the sap of an eastern Asian tree and used to give a protective surface, especially to wood 2. GLOSSY SYNTHETIC COATING a hard, glossy, clear or coloured coating made up of resins or cellulose derivatives and a plasticizer in a volatile solvent 3. = hair spray 4. ORNAMENTAL WOODEN OBJECTS ornamental objects made of wood and coated with lacquer ■ *vt.* (-quers, -quering, -quered) APPLY LACQUER TO to apply lacquer to or spray lacquer on sth [Late 16thC. From obsolete French *lacre* 'sealing wax', an alteration of Portuguese *la(c)ca* 'lac' (see LAC).]

lacquer tree *n.* a poisonous sumach tree of Southeast Asia whose sap is used to make lacquer. Latin name: *Rhus verniciflua.*

Lacquerware: Japanese lacquered box (1890)

lacquerware /lákər wair/, **lacquerwork** /lákər wurk/ *n.* ornamental objects, usually of wood, that have been coated with lacquer and sometimes inlaid

lacrimal /lákrim'l/, **lachrymal** *adj.* relating to, involving, or typical of tears, the glands that produce tears, or the ducts through which they drain [15thC. From medieval Latin *lacrimalis, lachrymalis*, from Latin *lacrima* 'tear'.]

lacrimal duct *n.* the passage carrying tears into the nose

lacrimal gland *n.* a gland in the outer corner of the eye that produces tears

lacrimation /lákri máysh'n/, **lachrymation** *n.* the production of tears in the eyes, especially excessive production as in crying or in reaction to a foreign body

lacrimator /lákri maytər/, **lachrymator** *n.* a substance such as tear gas that makes tears form in the eyes

lacrimatory /lákrimətəri, -máytəri/, **lachrymatory** *adj.* causing the eyes to produce tears

Lacrosse

lacrosse /lə króss/ *n.* a sport, originated by Native North Americans, in which two teams of ten players use sticks with a net pouch at one end (**crosse**) to throw and catch a small hard rubber ball. The aim is to score a goal by throwing the ball into the opposing team's goalnet. (*often used before a noun*) ○ *a lacrosse stick* [Early 18thC. From Canadian French *(jeu de) la crosse*, literally '(game of) the hooked stick', *crosse* 'hooked stick, crosier' ultimately from a prehistoric Germanic word that also produced English *crook*.]

lact- *prefix.* = lacto- (used before vowels)

lactalbumin /lak tálbyoomin/ *n.* a protein in milk and whey that contains all the amino acids needed in the human diet

lactase /lák tayss, -tayz/ *n.* an enzyme found in the intestines of young mammals and in yeasts that breaks down lactose into glucose and galactose [Late 19thC. Formed from LACTOSE.]

lactate[1] /lak táyt, lák tayt/ (-tates, -tating, -tated) *vi.* to produce milk in the body (*refers to female mammals*) [Late 19thC. Back-formation from LACTATION.]

lactate[2] /lák tayt/ *n.* a chemical compound that is a salt or ester of lactic acid [Late 18thC. Formed from LACTIC.]

lactation /lak táysh'n/ n. **1.** PRODUCTION OF MILK the production of milk by the mammary glands **2.** PERIOD OF MILK PRODUCTION the period during which milk is produced by the mammary glands [Mid-17thC. Directly or via French from, ultimately, Latin *lactare* 'to suckle', from *lact-*, the stem of *lac* 'milk' (see LACTO-).] —**lactational** *adj.*

lacteal /lákti əl/ adj. **1.** OF MILK relating to milk or milk production **2.** ANAT CARRYING MILKY FLUID carrying or containing a milky fluid (**chyle**) ◊ *a lacteal vessel* ■ *n.* ANAT LYMPHATIC VESSEL any lymphatic vessel that originates in the small intestine and carries a milky fluid (**chyle**) to the thoracic duct [Mid-17thC. Formed from Latin *lacteus* 'of milk', from *lact-*, the stem of *lac* 'milk' (see LACTO-).] —**lacteally** *adv.*

lactescent /lak téss'nt/ adj. **1.** BOT, ZOOL SECRETING A MILKY SUBSTANCE used to describe plants and insects that secrete a milky substance **2.** RESEMBLING MILK looking like milk, or becoming milky [Mid-17thC. From Latin *lactescent-*, the present participle stem of *lactescere* 'to turn to milk' from *lactere* 'to be milky', from *lact-*, the stem of *lac* 'milk' (see LACTO-).] —**lactescence** *n.*

lactic /láktik/ adj. relating to or derived from milk [Late 18thC]

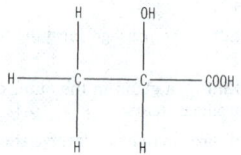
Lactic acid

lactic acid *n.* a colourless organic acid produced in muscles and found in sour milk. It is used as a preservative, in dyeing, and in making adhesives and pharmaceuticals. Formula: $C_3H_6O_3$.

lactiferous /lak tífferəss/ adj. **1.** ANAT CAPABLE OF PRODUCING MILK carrying or producing milk, or capable of producing milk ◊ *a lactiferous duct* **2.** BOT PRODUCING A MILKY JUICE used to describe a plant that produces a milky juice (**latex**) [Late 17thC. Coined from LACTO- + -IFEROUS.] —**lactiferousness** *n.*

lacto- prefix. **1.** milk ◊ *lactometer* **2.** lactic acid ◊ *lactate* **3.** lactose ◊ *lactase* [From Latin *lact-*, the stem of *lac* 'milk'; ultimately related to Greek *gala* (source of English *galaxy*)]

lactobacillus /láktō bə sílləss/ (*plural* **-li** /-sílī/) *n.* a rod-shaped bacterium that produces lactic acid through fermentation. Genus: *Lactobacillus*.

lactoflavin /láktō fláyvin/ *n.* BIOCHEM = **riboflavin**

lactogenic /láktō jénnik/ adj. causing the mammary glands to produce milk

lactoglobulin /láktō glóbbyo͝olin/ *n.* any one of a group of globular proteins that occur in milk

lactometer /lak tómmitər/ *n.* an instrument that is used to measure the density of milk. It is a kind of hydrometer.

lactone /láktōn/ *n.* any of several chemical compounds derived from hydroxy acids, often occurring as the odour-bearing component of a plant product —**lactonic** /lak tónnik/ *adj.*

lactoprotein /láktō prōt een/ *n.* any protein that is present in milk

lactose /lák tōss, -tōz/ *n.* **1.** SUGAR IN MILK a sugar (**disaccharide**) found in milk that breaks down into glucose and galactose and creates lactic acid through fermentation **2.** COMMERCIAL FORM OF LACTOSE a white crystalline form of lactose extracted from whey and used commercially in food products and pharmaceuticals

lactovegetarian /láktō véjjə táiri ən/ *n.* sb who eats vegetables, grains, fruit, nuts, and milk products but not meat or eggs

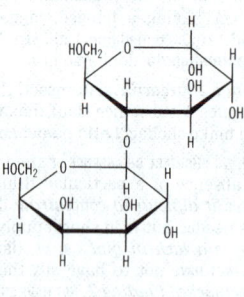
Lactose

lacuna /lə kyoónə/ (*plural* **-nae** /-nee/ *or* **-nas**) *n.* **1.** GAP a gap or place where sth is missing, e.g. in a manuscript or a line of argument (*literary*) **2.** ANAT SMALL PIT OR CAVITY a small pit or cavity, e.g. in bone or cartilage [Mid-17thC. From Latin, 'hole, pit', from *lacus* 'pond' (source of English *lagoon* and *lake*).] —**lacunal** *adj.*

lacunar /lə kyoónər/ *n.* **1.** CEILING WITH SUNKEN PANELS a ceiling that has sunken panels in it **2.** SUNKEN PANEL IN A CEILING a decorative sunken panel in a ceiling ■ *adj.* MED OF BODILY CAVITIES relating to pits or cavities in tissue, e.g. in bone or cartilage, especially ones that are abnormal [Late 17thC. From Latin, from *lacuna* (see LACUNA).]

lacustrine /lə kúss trīn/ adj. **1.** OF LAKES relating to lakes **2.** FOUND IN OR NEAR LAKES growing, living, or formed in or at the edge of a lake [Early 19thC. Formed either from French or Italian *lacustre* or from their source, Latin *lacus* 'lake' (see LACUNA) (on the model of Latin *palustris* 'marshy').]

LACW abbr. leading aircraftwoman

lacy /láyssi/ (**-ier, -iest**) adj. **1.** MADE OF LACE made of or decorated with lace **2.** LOOKING LIKE LACE having the appearance of lace ◊ *The sky was patterned with lacy clouds.* —**lacily** *adv.* —**laciness** *n.*

lad /lad/ *n.* **1.** YOUNG MAN a boy or young man **2.** MAN any man (*informal*) **3.** MAN WHO LOOKS AFTER HORSES a man whose job is to look after horses in a stable ◊ *The head lad accompanies the horses when they go racing.* ■ **lads** *npl.* MAN'S MALE FRIENDS the group of male friends or colleagues that a man socializes with [13thC. Origin uncertain: perhaps from a Scandinavian source originally meaning 'man of lowly status'.] ◊ **a bit of a lad** used in an affectionate way to describe a man who has a lively, even irresponsible, lifestyle

———— WORD KEY: CULTURAL NOTE ————
A Shropshire Lad, a collection of verse by poet A. E. Houseman (1896). Although they express a pessimistic world-view, these short poems about life in rural England are much loved for their sensitive handling of universal themes (the passing of time, the fleeting nature of existence, the trials and disappointments of life), as well as the poet's craftsmanship and musicality.

ladanum /láydənəm/ *n.* = **labdanum**

ladder /láddər/ *n.* **1.** DEVICE WITH RUNGS TO CLIMB ON a portable piece of equipment with rungs fixed to sides made of metal, wood, or rope, used for climbing up or down **2.** PATH TO ADVANCEMENT a series of hierarchical levels on which sb moves up or down within an organization or society ◊ *She joined the firm at a fairly low level but quickly moved up the ladder.* **3.** LINE OF MISSING STITCHES IN TIGHTS a vertical line of stitches that have come undone in tights, a stocking, or a knitted garment, leaving only the horizontal stitches in place **4.** SPORTS, GAME LIST OF RANKED PLAYERS a list of contestants in an ongoing sports or games competition, arranged according to ability ■ *vti.* (**-ders, -dering, -dered**) DAMAGE TIGHTS OR OTHER GARMENT to damage tights, a stocking, or knitted garment so that a line of vertical stitches have come undone, leaving only the horizontal stitches, or develop a ladder in this way [Old English *hlæd(d)er*. From, ultimately, an Indo-European base meaning 'to lean', which also produced English *incline*, *lid*, and *enclitic*.]

ladder-back *n.* **1.** CHAIR SHAPED LIKE A LADDER a chair with a back formed by horizontal slats between the two vertical parts that form the sides **2.** TALL CHAIR BACK a chair back formed by horizontal

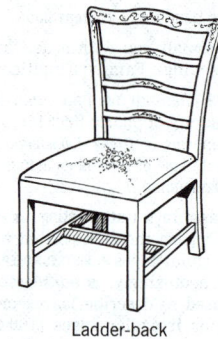
Ladder-back

slats between the two vertical parts that form the sides —**ladder-back** *adj.*

laddie /láddi/ *n.* a boy or young man (*informal*) ◊ *How old are you, laddie?*

laddish /láddish/ adj. relating to or traditionally considered typical of men whose behaviour conforms to a popular stereotype, featuring, e.g., absorbing interests in sport and drinking alcohol, and sexist attitudes towards women (*informal*) —**laddishly** *adv.* —**laddishness** *n.*

lade[1] /layd/ (**lades, lading, laded, laden** /láyd'n/ *or* **laded**) *v.* **1.** *vti.* LOAD UP A SHIP WITH CARGO to take on cargo or freight, or load up a ship with cargo or freight **2.** *vti.* REMOVE LIQUID WITH A LADLE to remove a measure of liquid using a ladle **3.** *vt.* LOAD to load sth, or place a heavy burden on sb (*dated*) [Old English *hladan* (source of English *ladle*), from a prehistoric Germanic base that also produced English *ballast*]

lade[2] /layd/ *n.* Scotland a stream, especially a millstream ◊ *A wee boy was fishing in the lade.* [Early 18thC. Origin uncertain: probably a variant of LEAD[1].]

la-de-da *adj.* = **la-di-da**

laden past participle of **lade**[1] ■ *adj.* **1.** HEAVILY LOADED carrying a load, usually a heavy load (*often used in combination*) ◊ *He was laden down with shopping bags.* ◊ *fruit-laden boughs* **2.** OPPRESSED BY STH weighed down by a problem or an unpleasant feeling such as doubt or unhappiness ◊ *laden with guilt*

la-di-da /laǎ dee daǎ/, **lah-di-dah, la-de-da** adj. speaking or behaving in a way that is affectedly upper-class (*informal*) [Late 19thC. An imitation of the sound of affectedly refined pronunciation.]

ladies /láydiz/ *n.* a women's public toilet (*informal; takes a singular verb*) ◊ *I think she went to the ladies.* US term **ladies room**

ladies' fingers *npl.* = **okra**

ladies' gallery *n.* an area of the public gallery of the House of Commons that is restricted to women only

ladies' man, **lady's man** *n.* a man who enjoys being with women and flirting with them

ladies room, **ladies' room** *n.* = **ladies**

ladies' tresses, **lady's tresses** *n.* an orchid with slender spiral spikes of small white flowers. Genus: *Spiranthes*. (*takes a singular or plural verb*)

ladified *adj.* = **ladyfied**

ladify *vt.* = **ladyfy**

Ladin /la deén/ *n.* a language spoken in some valleys in northern Italy, belonging to the Rhaeto-Romance subgroup of Romance languages. It has about 25,000 speakers. [Mid-19thC. Via Rhaeto-Romance from Latin *Latinus* 'Latin' (see LATIN).]

lading /láyding/ *n.* freight or cargo being transported from one place to another

Ladino /lə deénō/ (*plural* **-nos**) *n.* **1.** LANG SPANISH-HEBREW LANGUAGE a language based on Spanish with Hebrew elements, spoken by some Sephardic Jews. It is usually written in a form of Hebrew script. **2. Ladino, ladino** PEOPLES SPANISH-SPEAKING NATIVE CENTRAL AMERICAN sb of indigenous or partially Spanish ancestry in Central America who speaks Spanish [Late 19thC. Via Spanish from Latin *Latinus* 'Latin' (see LATIN). Recorded earlier (mid-19thC) of a vicious or unmanageable animal.]

ladino clover *n.* a large variety of white clover grown as forage in North America [Early 20thC. Via Italian from Latin *Latinus* 'Latin' (see LATIN).]

ladle /láyd'l/ *n.* LONG SPOON WITH A DEEP BOWL a spoon with a long handle and a deep bowl, used to serve soup and other liquids ■ *vt.* (**-dles, -dling, -dled**) SERVE USING A LADLE to serve food such as soup onto a plate using a ladle [Old English *hlædel*, from *hladan* 'to load' (see LADE).]

ladle out *vt.* to give out generous or overgenerous amounts of sth, especially sth intangible (*informal*) ○ *ladled out praise*

Ladoga, Lake /laá dəgə/ the largest lake in Europe, in northwestern Russia, northeast of St Petersburg. Its outlet is the River Neva, which connects it with the Gulf of Finland. Area: 18,390 sq. km/7,100 sq. mi.

lad's love *n.* PLANTS = southernwood

lady /láydi/ (*plural* **-dies**) *n.* **1.** WOMAN a woman, especially when addressed as part of a group ○ *Ladies and gentlemen, please take your seats.* **2.** ARISTOCRATIC WOMAN an upper-class woman **3.** POLITE DIGNIFIED WOMAN a woman who behaves very politely and with dignity **4.** WIFE OR USUAL WOMAN COMPANION a man's wife or usual woman companion (*informal*) **5.** WOMAN FEUDAL SUPERIOR a woman who, in medieval Europe, was a powerful land or property owner with authority over an area, castle, or community, e.g. a manor **6.** COCAINE the drug cocaine (*slang*) [Old English *hlæfdīge* 'woman in charge of a household, queen' (literally 'bread-kneader'), from *hlāf* 'bread' (source of English *loaf*) + a prehistoric Germanic base meaning 'to knead']

Lady *n.* **1.** TITLE FOR A WOMAN used as an alternative title for a marchioness, countess, viscountess, or baroness **2.** COURTESY TITLE FOR A WOMAN used as a courtesy title for the daughter of an earl, marquess, or duke **3.** FORM OF ADDRESS FOR A WOMAN used as a form of address for the wife of a viscount, earl, marquess, baron, baronet, or knight, and the daughter of a duke, marquess, or earl

ladybird /láydi burd/ *n.* a small round flying beetle that has red or orange outer wings with black spots. It eats aphids and other insects. Family: Coccinellidae. US term **ladybug**

lady bountiful *n.* a woman who makes generous and well-publicized charitable donations

ladybug /láydi bug/ *n. US* = ladybird

Lady Chapel, **lady chapel** *n.* a chapel dedicated to Mary, mother of Jesus Christ, that is inside a cathedral or church

Lady Day *n.* 25 March, celebrated in the Christian calendar as the feast of the Annunciation and used as a quarter day in England, Wales, and Ireland

ladyfied /láydi fīd/, **ladified** *adj.* affecting the manner or way of speaking of an upper-class woman

ladyfriend *n.* a man's regular woman companion, or a woman a man is seen with (*informal humorous; sometimes considered offensive*)

ladyfy /láydi fī/ *vt.* (**-fies, -fying, -fied**), **ladify** (**-fies, -fying, -fied**) to give a girl or woman the manner and way of speaking of an upper-class woman ○ *a finishing school that would ladyfy their daughter*

lady-in-waiting (*plural* **ladies-in-waiting**) *n.* a woman who is an attendant for a queen or princess

lady-killer *n.* a man who is extremely attractive to women

ladylike /láydi līk/ *adj.* behaving or done in the polite dignified way expected of an upper-class woman ○ *not a very ladylike thing to whine*

ladylove /láydi luv/ *n.* a woman that a man is in love with (*dated*)

lady luck, **Lady Luck** *n.* luck or good fortune personified as a woman (*literary; sometimes considered offensive*)

Lady Mayoress, **lady mayoress** *n.* the wife of a Lord Mayor

Lady Muck *n.* an ordinary woman who behaves as though she were very important (*informal*) ○ *Nothing's too good for Lady Muck next door, with her airs and graces.* ◊ **Lord Muck**

Lady of the Lake *n.* a supernatural woman who plays various roles in Arthurian legend, sometimes considered to be the same person as Vivian, the lover of Merlin

lady's bedstraw *n.* a plant of the bedstraw family that grows in Europe and Asia, with narrow leaves and clusters of small yellow flowers. Latin name: *Gallium verum.*

ladyship /láydi ship/, **Ladyship** *n.* a title used when addressing or referring to a woman with the title of 'Lady'

lady slipper *n.* PLANTS = lady's slipper

lady's maid *n.* a woman who works as a personal servant for another woman, looking after her and her clothes and accessories

lady's man *n.* = ladies' man

lady's mantle *n.* a low-growing plant of the rose family with clusters of small yellow-green flowers. Genus: *Alchemilla.* [From the round shape of its leaves]

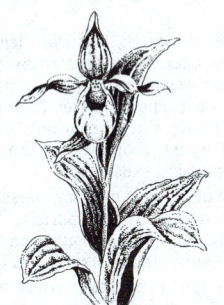

Lady's slipper

lady's slipper, **lady slipper** *n.* a North American orchid with reddish, purple, or yellow flowers that look like slippers. Genus: *Cypripedium.*

lady's smock *n.* = cuckooflower

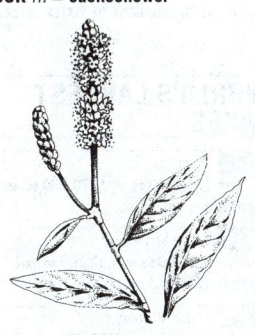

Lady's thumb

lady's thumb *n.* PLANTS = redshank

lady's tresses *n.* = ladies' tresses

Laënnec /la e nék/, **René** (1781–1826) French physician. He invented the stethoscope, and was a pioneer of thoracic medicine.

Laertes /lay úr teez/ *n.* in Greek mythology, the father of Odysseus

laetrile /láy ə trīl, -ətril, -trīl/ *n.* a drug extracted from peach stones that has been used in treating cancer but with no proven effectiveness

laevo- *prefix.* **1.** leftwards, anticlockwise ○ *laevorortation* **2.** laevorotatory ○ *laevulose* [Via French *lévo-* from Latin *laevus* 'left']

laevorotation /leévō rō táysh'n/ *n.* a rotation to the left or anticlockwise, especially of the plane of polarized light

laevorotatory /leévō rō táytəri, -rótətəri/ *adj.* **1.** WITH ANTICLOCKWISE MOTION turning or circling in a anticlockwise direction or to the left **2.** TURNING POLARIZED LIGHT ANTICLOCKWISE turning the plane of polarized light in an anticlockwise direction

laevulose /léevyoō lōss, -lōz/ *n.* = fructose [Late 19thC. Coined from LAEVO- + -ULE + -OSE.]

La Fayette /laá fī ét/, **Marie Madeleine, Comtesse de**

(1634–93) French novelist. She wrote the romances *Zaïde* (1670) and *La Princesse de Clèves* (1678).

laff /laaf/ *n.* a laugh (*slang; often used ironically*) ○ *a lot of tasteless laffs*

Laffer curve /láffər-/ *n.* a graph summarizing the fact that tax revenues are low for very high and for very low tax rates, thus demonstrating that raising tax rates beyond an optimum point will discourage investment and decrease tax revenues [Late 20thC. Named after Arthur B. *Laffer* (b. 1942), US economist.]

lag[1] /lag/ *vi.* (**lags, lagging, lagged**) **1.** FALL BEHIND COMPARED WITH OTHERS to go, develop, or progress more slowly than sb or sth similar so as to fall back or fall behind **2.** SLACKEN to decrease in strength or intensity ○ *Interest in the scandal has never lagged.* **3.** CUE GAMES DECIDE THE ORDER OF PLAY to decide who is to play first in billiards by having each player rebound a ball from the top cushion as close as possible to the hand rail ■ *n.* **1.** PERIOD BETWEEN EVENTS a period of time between one event and a related event **2.** POSITION OF HAVING FALLEN BEHIND the condition or an instance of having fallen behind **3.** CUE GAMES LAGGING IN BILLIARDS an act or instance of lagging in billiards [Early 16thC. Origin uncertain: perhaps from a Scandinavian source (compare Norwegian dialect *lagga* 'to go slowly').]

lag[2] /lag/ *vt.* (**lags, lagging, lagged**) INSULATE WITH LAGGING to insulate sth such as a pipe or hot water tank with lagging to prevent freezing or heat escaping ■ *n.* WOODEN STRIP a strip of wood such as a stave of a barrel or a lath [Late 17thC. Origin uncertain: probably from a Scandinavian source.]

lag[3] /lag/ *n.* (*slang*) **1.** PRISONER sb who is or has been in prison **2.** IMPRISONMENT a period of imprisonment ■ *vt.* (**lags, lagging, lagged**) ARREST OR IMPRISON to arrest sb or put sb in prison (*dated slang*) [Late 16thC. Origin unknown. The original sense was 'to steal'.]

lagan /lággən/, **ligan** /lígən/ *n.* cargo or wreckage lying on the sea bed, often with a buoy attached so that it can be recovered [Mid-16thC. From Old French, of uncertain origin: perhaps from Old Norse *lagn-*, the stem of *lögn* 'net' (related to English *lay*[1]).]

Lagan Valley /ləgán-/ region in southeastern Northern Ireland, near Belfast, and an Area of Outstanding Natural Beauty

lager[1] /laágər/ *n.* **1.** LIGHT-COLOURED BEER a type of light-coloured beer made with a low proportion of hops, usually stored for a period after brewing **2.** GLASS OF LAGER a drink of lager [Mid-19thC. Shortening of *lager beer*, a partial translation of German *Lager-Bier*, from *Lager* 'storehouse' + *Bier* 'beer'.]

lager[2] *n.* MIL = laager

Lagerkvist /laágər kvist/, **Pär Fabien** (1891–1974) Swedish novelist, poet, and playwright. In 1951 he won a Nobel Prize in literature for his novel *Barabbas* (1950).

Lagerlöf /laágər löf/, **Selma Ottiliana Louisa** (1858–1940) Swedish novelist. Writer of works based on Swedish folk tales, she was the first woman to be awarded a Nobel Prize in literature (1909).

lager lout *n.* a young man who gets drunk and behaves violently or disruptively (*informal insult*)

laggard /lággərd/ *n.* SB OR STH FALLING BEHIND sb who or sth that falls behind and does not keep up with others ■ *adj.* RELUCTANT slow or reluctant to do sth (*dated*) [Early 18thC. Formed from LAG[1].] —**laggardly** *adv., adj.* —**laggardness** *n.*

lagging /lágging/ *n.* **1.** INSULATION TO STOP HEAT ESCAPING insulating material used to keep heat from escaping, especially round a pipe or hot water tank **2.** BUILDING SUPPORTING FRAME a wooden frame used in building, especially to support an arch while it is being built

lagniappe /lán yap, lan yáp/ *n. Southern US* **1.** PRESENT GIVEN TO CUSTOMER a small present given by a shop to sb who has just purchased sth in the shop **2.** UNEXPECTED BONUS an unexpected bonus or extra [Mid-19thC. Via Louisiana French from American Spanish *la ñapa* 'the gift', from, ultimately, Quechua *yapay*, literally 'to give more'.]

lagomorph /lággə mawrf/ *n.* any plant-eating mammal with two pairs of incisors in the upper jaw specifically adapted for gnawing, e.g. the rabbit, hare, and pika. Order: Lagomorpha. [Late 19thC. From modern Latin *Lagomorpha*, order name, from, ultimately, Greek *lagōs* 'hare' + *morphē* 'shape, form'.] —**lagomorphic** /lággə máwrfik/ *adj.* —**lagomorphous** /-máwrfəss/ *adj.*

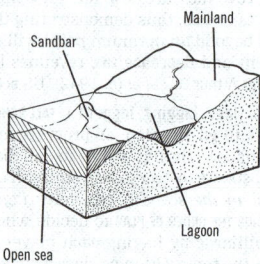

Lagoon

lagoon /lə góon/ *n.* **1. PARTLY ENCLOSED AREA OF SEA WATER** a coastal body of shallow water formed where low-lying rock, sand, or coral presents a partial barrier to the open sea **2. SMALL LAKE** a small lake adjoining a larger one [Early 17thC. Via Italian or Spanish *laguna* and French *lagune* from Latin *lacuna* 'hole, pit, pond' (see LACUNA).] —**lagoonal** *adj.*

Lagos /láygos/ the largest city, chief port, and former capital of Nigeria. Population: 1,347,000 (1992).

Lagrange /lə graáNzh/, **Joseph Louis, comte de l'Empire** (1736–1813) Italian-born French mathematician and astronomer. The author of *Méchanique analytique* (1788), he pioneered many concepts in mechanics, algebra, and number theory.

lah /laa/, **la** *n.* MUSIC the sixth note of a major scale in solfeggio. US term **la**[2] [Middle English, from medieval Latin]

lahar /laá haar/ *n.* a landslide or mudflow of volcanic debris, especially after a heavy rainfall [Early 20thC. From Javanese.]

lah-di-dah *adj.* = **la-di-da**

Lahnda /laándə/ *n.* a language spoken in Pakistan, related to Punjabi. It belongs to the Indic branch of the Indo-European family of languages. [Early 20thC. From Punjabi *lahandā*, literally 'western'.] —**Lahnda** *adj.*

Lahore /lə háwr/ city and capital of Punjab Province, northeastern Pakistan, about 257 km/160 mi. southeast of Islamabad. Population: 2,952,689 (1981).

Lahti /látti/ industrial city in southern Finland, north of Helsinki. Population: 95,119 (1995).

laic /láy ik/, **laical** /láy ik'l/ *adj.* relating to or involving followers of a religion who are not clergy [Mid-16thC. Via late Latin *laicus* from Greek *laikos* 'of the people', from *laos* 'people' (source of English *lay*).] —**laically** *adv.*

laicize /láy i sīz/ (**-cizes, -cizing, -cized**), **laicise** (**-cises, -cising, -cised**) *vt.* to remove sth from control or governance by the church or the clergy and give control of it to the lay community —**laicization** /láy isī záysh'n/ *n.*

laid past tense, past participle of **lay**[1]

laid-back *adj.* very relaxed, easygoing, and unworried (*informal*) —**laid-backness** *n.*

laid paper *n.* a paper with a watermark of fine lines on it that are produced in the manufacturing process

laid work *n.* a type of embroidery based on a lattice of threads that is used then decorated with filling stitches

laik /layk/ (**laiks, laiking, laiked**) *vti.* N England to play, or play at sth [14thC. From Old Norse *leika* 'to play'.]

━━━━━━━━ **WORD KEY: REGIONAL NOTE** ━━━━━━━━
In parts of England where Viking influence was strongest, many words of *laik* (Old Norse) origin persist. **Laik** means 'play', as in *There were children at bus stop laiking like*. In parts of Yorkshire, where this sentence comes from, it is estimated that about one third of the vocabulary is English, one third Viking (Old Norse), and the other third could be either English or Viking.

Lailat-ul-Qadr /láy lat ool kaádər/ *n.* an Islamic festival, the Night of Power, celebrating the sending

down of the Koran to Muhammad and occurring on the 27th of Ramadan

Laing /lang/, **R. D.** (1927–89) Scottish psychiatrist. His radical views on schizophrenia were set out in *The Divided Self* (1960). Other books include *The Politics of Experience* (1967) and *The Politics of the Family* (1971). Full name **Ronald David Laing**

lair /lair/ *n.* **1. WILD ANIMAL'S DEN** a place where a wild animal rests or sleeps **2. PLACE TO BE ALONE IN** a retreat or hideaway (*informal*) **3. CATTLE ENCLOSURE** an enclosure for livestock **4.** *Scotland* **GROUND FOR GRAVE** the ground for a single grave in a cemetery ■ *vti.* (**lairs, lairing, laired**) **GO TO A LAIR** to go to a lair, or be taken or made to go to a lair (*refers to an animal*) [Old English *leger* 'act of lying, bed, grave'. Ultimately from an Indo-European word that also produced English *lager*[1], *lay*[1], and *beleaguer*.]

lairage /láirij/ *n.* a place where livestock are kept temporarily, e.g. at docks or a market

laird /laird/ *n. Scotland* sb who owns land, especially a large estate ○ *the laird of Shaws* [14thC. Variant of LORD.]

laissez-faire /léssay fáir, láyssay-/, **laisser-faire** *n.* **1. PRINCIPLE OF NO REGULATION OF INDUSTRY** the principle that the economy works best if private industry is not regulated and markets are free **2. REFUSAL TO INTERFERE** refusal to interfere in other people's affairs, or the practice of letting people do as they please [From French, literally 'allow to do']

laissez-passer /léssay paá say, láyssay-/, **laisser-passer** *n.* a document that permits the holder to travel freely, especially one given in lieu of a passport [From French, literally 'allow to pass']

laity /láy əti/ *npl.* **1. LAY PEOPLE RATHER THAN CLERGY** the followers of a religion who are not clergy **2. PEOPLE NOT IN A PARTICULAR PROFESSION** all the people who are not members of a specific profession, as distinguished from those who are members [15thC. Formed from LAY[2].]

Laius /lí əss/ *n.* a king of Thebes in Greek mythology, mistakenly killed by his son Oedipus

lake[1] /layk/ *n.* **1. INLAND BODY OF WATER** a large body of

WORLD'S LARGEST LAKES		
1	Caspian Sea	
Area	[143,000 sq. mi. / 370,000 sq. km]	
Location	*Europe/Asia*	
2	Lake Superior	
Area	[31,700 sq. mi. / 82,100 sq. km]	
Location	*North America*	
3	Lake Victoria	
Area	[26,830 sq. mi. / 69,490 sq. km]	
Location	*Africa*	
4	Lake Huron	
Area	[23,000 sq. mi. / 59,600 sq. km]	
Location	*North America*	
5	Lake Michigan	
Area	[22,300 sq. mi. / 57,800 sq. km]	
Location	*North America*	
6	Lake Tanganyika	
Area	[12,700 sq. mi. / 32,900 sq. km]	
Location	*Africa*	
7	Great Bear Lake	
Area	[12,270 sq. mi. / 31,790 sq. km]	
Location	*North America*	
8	Lake Baikal	
Area	[12,200 sq. mi. / 31,500 sq. km]	
Location	*Asia*	
9	Aral Sea	
Area	[12,050 sq. mi. / 31,220 sq. km]	
Location	*Asia*	
10	Lake Nyasa	
Area	[8,683 sq. mi. /22,490 sq. km]	
Location	*Africa*	

water surrounded by land **2. SURPLUS OF LIQUID PRODUCT** a large surplus of a liquid product, such as milk or wine, that is stored and not sold in order to prevent prices from becoming too low, especially in the European Union (*informal; usually used in combination*) ◊ **mountain** *n.* 4 **3. POOL OF LIQUID** a large pool of liquid that has collected or spilled somewhere ○ *A lake of hot grease covered the floor by the cooker.* [Pre-12thC. Directly and via Old French *lac* from Latin *lacus* 'pond' (source of English *lacuna* and *lagoon*).]

━━━━━━━━ **WORD KEY: CULTURAL NOTE** ━━━━━━━━
The Lady of the Lake, a poem by Scottish writer Sir Walter Scott (1810). Set in early 16th-century Scotland, it describes the eventful courtship of Ellen, daughter of outlawed chieftain James of Douglas, who lives on Loch Katrine (the lake of the title). Regarded as one of Scott's finest works, it is admired for its satisfying plot, strong characterization, and charming songs.

lake[2] /layk/ *n.* **1. TRANSLUCENT PIGMENT** a bright translucent pigment that can be of different colours, made by combining an organic dye with a metallic hydroxide or other inorganic substance **2. RED PIGMENT** a red pigment made by combining cochineal with a metallic compound [Early 17thC. Variant of LAC.]

Lake District region of mountains and lakes in Cumbria, northwestern England. The district extends about 50 km/30 mi. from north to south and 40 km/25 mi. from east to west.

Lake District National Park national park in Cumbria, northwestern England, that includes all of the Lake District. It was established in 1951. Area: 2,243 sq. km/866 sq. mi.

lake herring *n.* a food fish related to the whitefish and found in the Great Lakes region of the United States. Latin name: *Coregonus artedii*.

Lakeland terrier

Lakeland terrier /láyklənd-/ *n.* a wire-haired terrier with a black and tan coat, originally bred for foxhunting [Early 20thC. Named after *Lakeland*, a name for the Lake District in northwestern England, where the breed originated.]

Lake Macquarie /layk mə kwáwri/ city in eastern New South Wales, Australia. Population: 162,026 (1991).

Lake of the Woods lake in central North America, on the border between the United States and Canada. It includes hundreds of wooded islands. Area: 4,390 sq. km/1,695 sq. mi.

Lake Poets *n.* the poets Wordsworth, Coleridge, and Southey, who lived in the Lake District in the early 19th century

laker /láykər/ *n.* **1.** SHIPPING **VESSEL SAILING ON LAKES** a boat or ship that is used on lakes rather than the sea **2.** ZOOL **FISH LIVING IN A LAKE** a fish living in a lake rather than the sea, e.g. a lake trout

lakeside /láyk sīd/ *n.* the land at the edge of a lake

lake trout *n.* = brown trout

lakh /laak/ (*plural* **lakhs** *or* **lakh**), **lac** (*plural* **lacs** *or* **lac**) *n.* S Asia the number 100,000, used especially for referring to sums of rupees [Early 17thC. Via Hindi *lākh* from Sanskrit *lakṣam* 'mark, token, 100,000'.]

Lakota /lə kṓtə/ *n.* (*plural* **-tas** *or* **-ta**), *adj.* PEOPLES = **Teton** [Mid-19thC. From Lakota *lakhóta*.]

laksa /láksə/ *n.* a Malaysian or Singaporean rice noodle, slightly thicker than spaghetti, often served in a spicy fish sauce or soup

Lakshmi /lákshmi/, **Laksmi** n. the Hindu goddess of prosperity, wealth, and royalty, and wife of the god Vishnu

laky /láyki/ adj. of a reddish or crimson colour similar to a red form of the pigment lake

Lala /laa laa/ n. S Asia a title equivalent to 'Mr', used in the Indian subcontinent before men's names [From Hindi]

lalang /laa laang/ n. a tall coarse tropical grass that grows in the Malay Archipelago. Latin name: *Imperata arundinacea*. [Late 18thC. From Malay.]

-lalia suffix. speech, speech disorder ○ *echolalia* [From Greek *lalia* 'talk', from *lalein* 'to talk']

Lalique glass /la léek-/ n. ornamental frosted glassware decorated with bas-relief figures, fruits, and flowers, designed by the French Art Nouveau craftsperson René Lalique

Lallans /lállənz/, **Lallan** /lállən/ n. Scotland LANGUAGE OF SCOTTISH LOWLANDS the form of Lowland Scots used in various revivals of Scots as a literary medium, especially in the 18th century and again in the 20th century ■ adj. TYPICAL OF LOWLAND SCOTS relating to or typical of the Lowlands of Scotland or any of the dialects of Scots spoken there [Early 18thC. Variant of *Lowlands*, LOWLAND.]

lallation /la láysh'n/ n. a mispronunciation of 'r', especially one that sounds like 'l' [Mid-17thC. From Latin *lallare* 'to sing lullaby'.]

Lalor /láylər/, **Peter** (1827–89) Irish-born Australian civil engineer and politician. He led protests that resulted in clashes between gold miners and the military at the Eureka Stockade in 1854. He subsequently became a state politician.

lam[1] /lam/ (**lams, lamming, lammed**) v. (informal) 1. vti. HIT HARD to hit sb or sth hard 2. vi. SPEAK ANGRILY to speak angrily to sb [Late 16thC. Origin uncertain: perhaps from Scandinavian.]

lam[2] /lam/ n. US, Can HASTY ESCAPE a hasty escape, especially to avoid arrest ■ vi. (**lams, lamming, lammed**) US, Can ESCAPE HASTILY to escape or run away, especially from the law (informal) [Late 19thC. From LAM[1]. The phrase *beat it* 'to run away' has a similar origin.] ◇ **on the lam** US, Can making a hasty escape, especially from the law (informal)

lam. abbr. laminated

Lam. abbr. BIBLE Lamentations

lama /laamə/ n. 1. BUDDHIST MONK a Tibetan or Mongolian Buddhist monk 2. TITLE FOR A REINCARNATED BUDDHIST a title used for those individuals who are believed to be the reincarnations of a Bodhisattva [Mid-17thC. Alteration of Tibetan *bla-ma*.]

Lamaism /laamə izəm/ n. a form of Mahayana Buddhism practised in Tibet and Mongolia that has non-Buddhist elements from India and from Bon, an older nature-worshipping religion. Lamaist monks, or lamas, are led by the Dalai Lama, a temporal as well as spiritual ruler. —**Lamaist** n., adj. —**Lamaistic** /laamə ístik/ adj.

La Mancha /laa maanchə/ barren plateau region in south-central Spain

Lamarck /lə maark/, **Jean Baptiste, Chevalier de** (1744–1829) French naturalist and evolutionist. His theory that evolution proceeded by the inheritance of acquired characteristics was superseded by Darwin's theory of natural selection. —**Lamarckian** adj., n.

Lamarckism /lə maarkizəm/ n. the evolutionary theory of the French naturalist Jean Baptiste Lamarck that holds that evolution proceeds through the inheritance of characteristics acquired by individual organisms, e.g. through intensive use —**Lamarckian** adj.

Lamartine /la maar teen/, **Alphonse Marie Louis Prat de** (1790–1869) French poet, historian, and statesman. A diplomat and government minister during the 1848 revolution, he was author of *Histoire des Girondins* (1847).

lamasery /laaməssəri/ (plural **-ies**) n. a Tibetan or Mongolian monastery of lamas [Mid-19thC. From French *lamaserie*, literally 'lama dwelling', from *lama* LAMA.]

Lamaze /lə maaz/ n. US, Can a method of natural childbirth by which a woman is physically and psychologically prepared through prenatal training. Lamaze encourages the use of controlled breathing and the participation of the woman's partner during the process of childbirth. [Mid-20thC. Named after the French physician Fernand Lamaze (1890–1957), its originator.]

lamb /lam/ n. 1. ZOOL YOUNG SHEEP an immature sheep, especially one under a year old and without permanent teeth 2. FOOD MEAT OF A LAMB the meat of an immature sheep that is under a year old 3. CLOTHES = lambskin 4. SB MEEK AND MILD sb who is gentle and innocent, especially a baby or small child 5. SB EASILY DECEIVED sb who is easily cheated, especially financially ■ vti. (**lambs, lambing, lambed**) AGRIC GIVE BIRTH TO A LAMB to give birth to a lamb [Old English, of prehistoric Germanic origin] ◇ **like a lamb to the slaughter** calmly and without resistance going to face sth unpleasant, difficult, or dangerous

Lamb n. = Lamb of God

Lamb /lam/, **Charles** (1775–1834) British essayist. He was a prose stylist of great clarity whose books include *Essays of Elia* (1823). Pseudonym **Elia**

Lamba /lámbə/ n. a language spoken in parts of Benin that belongs to the Gur branch of Niger-Congo languages. Lamba is spoken by about 29,000 people. [Early 20thC. From Bantu.] —**Lamba** adj.

lambada /lam baadə/ n. 1. DANCE LATIN AMERICAN DANCE an athletic erotic dance originating in Brazil, in which partners hold each other close and gyrate their hips in unison 2. MUSIC BRAZILIAN DANCE MUSIC the fast rhythmic music for the lambada [Late 20thC. From Brazilian Portuguese, literally 'a beating, a lashing'.]

Lambaréné /lámbə reeni, loNbə ráynay/ capital of Moyen-Ogooué Region, western Gabon. Population: 42,316 (1993).

lambaste /lam báyst/ (**-bastes, -basting, -basted**), **lambast** /lam bást/ (**-basts, -basting, -basted**) vt. 1. CRITICIZE STRONGLY to criticize sb or sth severely 2. WHIP to beat or whip sb (archaic) [Mid-17thC. From LAM[1] + BASTE 'to beat'.]

lambda /lámdə/ n. 1. 11TH LETTER OF GREEK ALPHABET the 11th letter of the Greek alphabet, represented in the English alphabet as 'l'. See table at **alphabet** 2. ANAT JUNCTION IN SKULL the point of junction at the centre of the back of the cranium between the rear plate of the cranium (**occipital bone**) and the two upper plates (**parietal bones**). This junction is said to resemble the Greek capital letter lambda. ◇ **lambdoid** [Early 17thC. From Greek.]

lambda calculus n. a descriptive theory of functions and the way they combine, used as the basis for certain high-level computer programming languages

lambdacism /lámdəssizəm/ n. the erroneous substitution of 'l' for 'r' in speech [Mid-17thC. Via late Latin from Greek *la(m)bdakismos*, from *la(m)bda* (see LAMBDA).]

lambda particle n. = lambda hyperon

lambdoid /lám doyd/, **lambdoidal** /lam dóyd'l/ adj. used to describe the suture that joins bones at the back of the skull, shaped like the Greek capitalized lambda

lambent /lámbənt/ adj. 1. GLEAMING softly gleaming or glowing (literary) 2. BRILLIANTLY LIGHT having a light but brilliant touch 3. PLAYING OVER A SURFACE flickering or playing as a flame over a surface without burning it (literary) [Mid-17thC. From Latin *lambent-*, the present participle stem of *lambere* 'to lick'. Ultimately from an Indo-European word that is also the ancestor of English *lap*[3].] —**lambency** n. —**lambently** adv.

lambert /lámbərt/ n. an SI unit of surface brightness (**luminance**) equivalent to one lumen per square centimetre [Late 19thC. Named after Johann Heinrich Lambert (1728–77), German scientist, in honour of his work on the measurement of light intensity and absorption.]

Lambeth walk /lámbəth-/, **Lambeth Walk** n. a lively ballroom dance originating and popularized in England during the 1930s [Mid-19thC. Named after a street in *Lambeth*, a South London borough.]

lamb fries npl. = lamb's fry

Lambic /loN bík/ n. a strong sour-tasting draught beer brewed in Belgium from aged hops [Late 19thC. From French *alambic* 'still'.]

lambing /lámming/ n. 1. BIRTH OF LAMBS the birth of lambs, or the season when they are born 2. DELIVERY OF BABY LAMBS the work of helping ewes give birth to lambs

lambkin /lámkin/ n. an infant lamb, sometimes used as a term of endearment for a baby or small child

Lamb of God n. Jesus Christ, seen as a sacrifice whose crucifixion and resurrection redeemed humankind

lambrequin /lámbrikin, lámbər-/ n. 1. HOUSEHOLD ORNAMENTAL HANGING a decorative strip of drapery, hung along the top of a doorway, window, shelf, or mantelpiece 2. HIST SCARF ATTACHED TO A KNIGHT'S HELMET a veil, scarf, or piece of drapery attached to a knight's helmet to protect it from heat and rust 3. HERALDRY = mantling 4. CERAMICS ORNAMENTAL BORDER ON A VASE a decorative border near the top of a vase [Early 18thC. Via French from assumed Dutch, literally 'small veil', from *lamper* 'veil'.]

Lambrusco /lam brōosk ō/ n. a sweet sparkling red or white wine from northern Italy [Mid-20thC. Via Italian from Latin *labruscum* 'fruit of the wild grape Vitis labrusca', from *labrusca*, the species name.]

lamb's ears n. a perennial plant of the mint family with small purple flowers that is often grown for its silvery woolly leaves. Latin name: *Stachys byzantina*. [From the resemblance of the leaves to a lamb's ears]

lamb's fry n. 1. lamb's testicles, traditionally sold skinned and ready for cooking by frying 2. lamb's offal [*Fry* from earlier English dialect *fry* 'internal part of an animal, usually eaten fried']

lambskin /lám skin/ n. 1. WOOLLY LAMB'S PELT the woolly pelt of a lamb, used for making or trimming winter clothing 2. LAMB'S HIDE the hide of a lamb, prepared as leather

lamb's lettuce n. BOT a lettuce with small rounded leaves and a slightly sweet, nutty flavour. US term **corn salad** [Translation of its old Latin name *lactuca agnina*]

lamb's lugs n. PLANTS = lamb's ears

lamb's tails npl. the drooping catkins of the hazel tree

lambswool /lámz wōol/, **lamb's wool** n. fine soft wool, especially the wool sheared from a year-old lamb, often used for knitwear

LAMDA /lámdə/ abbr. London Academy of Music and Dramatic Art

lame[1] /laym/ adj. (**lamer, lamest**) 1. OFFENSIVE TERM an offensive term meaning walking unevenly because of a leg injury or motion impairment (offensive when used of people) 2. OFFENSIVE TERM an offensive term meaning injured, or with impaired strength or motion (offensive when used of people) 3. UNCONVINCING inadequate, unconvincing, or unsatisfactory (offensive in some contexts) 4. INEFFECTIVE ineffectual or inept (offensive in some contexts) ■ vt. (**lames, laming, lamed**) OFFENSIVE TERM a term, often offensive, meaning to cause a person or animal to be unable to walk evenly because of injury or impairment (offensive when used of a person) [Old English *lama*, from prehistoric Germanic, 'weak-limbed' (source also of Dutch *lam* 'unable to move'). Ultimately from an Indo-European word meaning 'to break by hitting' (ancestor also of English *lambaste*).] —**lameness** n.

lame[2] /laym/ n. a thin plate of metal, especially one of the overlapping metal plates of which medieval armour was made from the mid-14th century [Late 16thC. Via French from Latin *lamina* (see LAMINA).]

lamé /laa may/ n. a fabric that has metallic threads, especially gold or silver, interwoven with silk, wool, or cotton [Early 20thC. From French, 'worked with silver and gold thread', from Old French *lame* 'thin metal plate', from Latin *lamina* (see LAMINA).]

lamebrain /láym brayn/ n. US an offensive term that deliberately insults sb's intelligence (informal insult) —**lamebrained** adj.

lamed /laamid/, **lamedh** /laa med/ n. the 12th letter of the Hebrew alphabet, represented in the English alphabet as 'l'. See table at **alphabet** [Mid-17thC. From Hebrew *lāmēdh*.]

lame duck *n.* **1.** SB OR STH WEAK sb who or sth that is weak, inadequate, or unfortunate, especially sb requiring special help **2.** *US* POL OFFICE-HOLDER UNABLE TO BE RE-ELECTED an elected official who either will not or may not legally run for another term in office and has reduced power or effectiveness **3.** *US* POL OUTGOING OFFICE-HOLDER WITH WEAKENED POWER an elected official or group left seemingly powerless after a successor has been elected but has not yet taken over

lamella /lə méllə/ (*plural* **-lae** /-lee/) *n.* **1.** ANAT THIN PIECE OF BONE any thin flat structure of bone or tissue **2.** FUNGI PART OF FUNGUS a gill of a fungus **3.** BOT CONNECTIVE LAYER a cementing layer between two plant cells **4.** CONSTR STRUCTURAL PART OF VAULT a structural part of wood, metal, or reinforced concrete that is criss-crossed to form a vault [Late 17thC. From Latin, literally 'small thin plate', from *lamina* (see LAMINA).] —**lamellar** *adj.* —**lamellarly** *adv.*

lamellate /lámmələt, lə méllət/ *adj.* arranged in, composed of, or resembling layers —**lamellated** /lámmə laytid/ *adj.* —**lamellation** /-láysh'n/ *n.*

lamelli- *prefix.* lamella ○ *lamelliform* [From LAMELLA]

lamellibranch /lə mélli brangk/ *n.* ZOOL = **bivalve** [Mid-19thC. From modern Latin *Lamellibranchia*, genus name, from Latin *lamella* (see LAMELLA) + Greek *bragkhia* 'gills'.] —**lamellibranchiate** /lə mélli brángki ət/ *adj., n.*

lamellicorn /lə mélli kawrn/ *adj.* WITH LAYERED SEGMENTED ANTENNAE used to describe a beetle such as the dung beetle, stag beetle, or chafer that has antennae composed of layered segments ■ *n.* LAMELLICORN BEETLE a beetle with layered antennae [Mid-19thC. From modern Latin *Lamellicornia*, former family name, from Latin *lamella* (see LAMELLA) + *cornu* 'horn'.]

lamelliform /lə mélli fawrm/ *adj.* shaped like a thin plate or scale [Early 19thC. Coined from LAMELLA + -FORM.]

lamely /láymli/ *adv.* inadequately, unconvincingly, or ineptly

lament /lə mént/ *vti.* (**-ments, -menting, -mented**) **1.** BE SAD ABOUT STH to express sorrow about sth **2.** EXPRESS DISAPPOINTED REGRET to express regret, annoyance, or disappointment ○ *She was lamenting the lack of funding for her project.* ■ *n.* **1.** EXPRESSION OF SADNESS an expression of grief or sorrow **2.** EXPRESSION OF REGRET an expression of regret or disappointment **3.** MUSIC, POETRY WORK LAMENTING A DEATH a song or poem of mourning [Mid-16thC. Directly or via French from Latin *lamentari*, from *lamenta* 'laments'. Ultimately from an Indo-European word, imitative of the sound of crying (ancestor also of English *lullaby*).] —**lamenter** *n.* —**lamentingly** *adv.*

lamentable /lámməntəb'l/ *adj.* **1.** DISAPPOINTINGLY BAD unsatisfactory, pitiful, or deplorable **2.** MOURNFUL sad and mournful (*literary*) —**lamentableness** *n.* —**lamentably** *adv.*

lamentation /lámmən táysh'n/ *n.* an act or expression of grief or sorrow [14thC. Directly or via French from, ultimately, Latin *lamentari* (see LAMENT).]

Lamentations /lámmən táysh'nz/ *n.* a book of the Bible written in the form of elegies, according to tradition, by Jeremiah (*takes a singular verb*) See table at **Bible**

lamented /lə méntid/ *adj.* dead or departed and grieved for —**lamentedly** *adv.*

lamia /láymi ə/ (*plural* **-as** *or* **-ae** /-ee/) *n.* in Greek and Roman mythology, a blood-sucking witch who takes the form of a serpent, used as a bogey with which to threaten children [14thC. Via Latin from Greek, 'mythical monster, carnivorous fish'. Ultimately from an Indo-European word meaning 'nocturnal spirits', which is also the ancestor of English *lemures*.]

lamina /lámminə/ (*plural* **-nae** /-nee/ *or* **-nas**) *n.* **1.** THIN LAYER a thin plate, layer, or flake **2.** BOT LEAF BLADE the blade or flat part of a leaf **3.** ZOOL PROTECTIVE PLATE INSIDE A HOOF in hoofed mammals, any of the parallel layers of sensitive tissue just inside the hard exterior of the hoof [Mid-17thC. From Latin, 'plate, leaf' (source of English *lamé* and *omelette*).]

laminal /lámmin'l/ *adj.* articulated using the blade or flat part of the tongue

laminar flow /lámminər-/ *n.* a type of flow in a liquid or gas in which neighbouring layers do not mix and flow at different velocities

laminaria /lámmi náiri ə/ *n.* a large brown seaweed (**kelp**) that has broad flat fronds. Genus: *Laminaria.* [Mid-19thC. From modern Latin *Laminaria*, genus name, from Latin *lamina* (see LAMINA), from the thin appendages.]

laminarin /lámmi naárrin/ *n.* a carbohydrate occurring in brown algae [Mid-20thC. Formed from modern Latin *Laminaria* (see LAMINARIA).]

laminate *v.* /lámmi nayt/ (**-nates, -nating, -nated**) **1.** *vt.* INDUST COVER STH WITH A THIN LAYER to cover sth with a thin sheet of protective material, e.g. plastic or metal **2.** *vt.* BOND LAYERS TOGETHER to bond sheets or layers together so as to produce a strong and durable composite material ○ *Wood veneers were laminated to produce a cheap and durable alternative to expensive hardwoods for furniture-making.* **3.** *vt.* METALL FORM METAL INTO THIN LAYERS to roll or beat metal into thin sheets **4.** *vti.* SEPARATE INTO LAYERS to split sth, or be split, into thin layers ■ *n.* /lámminət/ MATERIAL MADE UP OF BONDED LAYERS a product composed of layers or sheets bonded together —**laminable** /lámminəb'l/ *adj.* —**laminator** /lámmi naytər/ *n.*

laminated /lámmi naytid/ *adj.* **1.** MADE OF BONDED LAYERS composed of layers bonded together **2.** COVERED WITH A THIN LAYER covered with a thin layer of plastic or metal

lamination /lámmi náysh'n/ *n.* **1.** PROCESS OF BONDING LAYERS the bonding together of thin layers of materials to form a composite material **2.** FORMATION OF LAYERS the formation of layers in sth **3.** THIN LAYER a thin layer in sth (*technical*) **4.** THINLY-LAYERED STRUCTURE a structure composed of thin layers **5.** ELEC ENG THIN STEEL PLATE IN TRANSFORMER CORE one of a number of thin steel or iron plates that are held together to form a transformer core

laminectomy /lámmi néktəmi/ (*plural* **-mies**) *n.* a surgical operation to remove one or more sides of the rear arches of a spinal vertebra and gain access to the spinal cord or spinal nerve roots

lamington /lámmingtən/ *n. ANZ* a small square sponge cake covered in chocolate icing and desiccated coconut [Early 20thC. Originally used for 'Homburg hat', named after Lord *Lamington* (d. 1940), Governor of Queensland, Australia, 1895–1901.]

Lamington National Park national park in southeastern Queensland, Australia

Lamington Plateau high mountain plateau situated in the Macpherson Range, Lamington National Park, Queensland, Australia

laminitis /lámmi nítiss/ *n.* inflammation of the sensitive plates of tissue in a hoof, especially a horse's hoof, usually causing lameness. It is one of the most serious equine hoof diseases.

Lammas /lámməss/ *n.* **1.** CHR CHRISTIAN RELIGIOUS FEAST ON 1 AUGUST a Christian religious feast on 1 August to celebrate St Peter's deliverance from prison **2.** CALENDAR 1 AUGUST the first day of August, originally celebrated in England as a harvest festival. In Scotland, Lammas was formerly one of the quarter days. [Old English *hlāfmæsse*, from earlier forms of LOAF + MASS 'liturgy'; altered through folk etymology by association with LAMB]

Lammastide /lámməss tīd/ *n.* the season of Lammas (*archaic*) [From TIDE in the meaning of 'period of time']

lammergeier /lámmər gī ər/, **lammergeyer** *n.* a large rare vulture found in mountainous areas in southern Europe, Africa, and Asia, with dark wings and dark feathers that resemble a beard around its beak. Latin name: *Gypaetus barbatus.* [Early 19thC. From German *Lämmergeier*, literally 'lambs' vulture', because it can prey upon animals of that size.]

lamming /lámming/ *n.* a thorough whipping or beating (*informal*)

Lamont /lə mónt/, **Norman** (*b.* 1942) British statesman. A cabinet minister in the Thatcher government (1989), he became chancellor of the exchequer under John Major until replaced in 1993.

lamp /lamp/ *n.* **1.** DEVICE PRODUCING ELECTRIC LIGHT a device that produces electric light **2.** DEVICE PRODUCING LIGHT a device that burns oil, gas, or wax to produce light **3.** RADIATION SOURCE a device that supplies ultraviolet light or infrared heat radiation, especially for medical or cosmetic treatment ○ *sun lamp* **4.** SOURCE OF ENLIGHTENMENT a source of enlightenment or inspiration (*literary*) [12thC. Via French and Latin from Greek *lampas* 'burning torch', later 'oil lamp', from *lampein* 'to shine' (source of English *lantern*).]

lampas[1] /lámpəss/ *n.* an ornately patterned cloth resembling damask, especially one made of silk, that is used for upholstery [Mid-19thC. From French, of uncertain origin: perhaps from or related to obsolete Dutch *lampers* 'a kind of crape'.]

lampas[2] /lámpəss/ *n.* the swelling of the mucous membrane covering the roof of the mouth in horses, often due to tooth eruption and therefore transient [Early 16thC. From French, 'disease producing intense thirst', of uncertain origin: probably from French dialect *lāpā* 'throat' and *lāpé* 'gums'.]

lampblack /lámp blak/ *n.* a fine powdery form of carbon that is deposited when oils containing carbon are burned. It is used as a pigment, a printing ink, and in electrodes.

lampbrush chromosome /lámp brush-/ *n.* an enlarged chromosome covered with fine loops of chromatin, observed during cell division in many organisms [*Lampbrush* a loose translation of German *Lampencylinderputzer*, literally 'lamp-glass cleaner', coined by J. Rückert because it resembles a brush for the inside of a lampshade.]

lamp chimney *n.* a glass cover that is placed over the wick of an oil or kerosene lamp to protect and control the flame

lamper eel /lámpər-/ *n.* = **lamprey** [Early 16thC. *Lamper* probably from a variant of LAMPREY.]

lampern /lámpərn/ (*plural* **-perns** *or* **-pern**) *n.* a European river fish of the lamprey family that resembles an eel. Latin name: *Lampetra fluviatilis.* [14thC. From Old French *lampreion*, literally 'small lamprey', from *lampreie* (see LAMPREY).]

lamp glass *n.* = **lamp chimney**

lampion /lámpi ən/ *n.* a small oil lamp, usually with a tinted glass chimney, formerly popular as a carriage light [Mid-19thC. Via French from Italian *lampione*, literally 'large lamp', from *lampa* 'lamp', from French *lampe* (see LAMP).]

lamplight /lámp līt/ *n.* the light cast by a lamp —**lamplit** /lámp lit/ *adj.*

lamplighter /lámp lītər/ *n.* **1.** SB EMPLOYED TO LIGHT STREET LAMPS sb who was employed to light the gas lamps along a street in times before the introduction of electricity **2.** *US, Can* DEVICE FOR LIGHTING LAMPS a device used to light lamps

lamp oil *n.* oil suitable as lamp fuel

lampoon /lam poón/ *n.* SATIRICAL ATTACK IN WRITING OR VERSE a piece of satirical writing or verse ridiculing sb or sth ■ *vt.* (**-poons, -pooning, -pooned**) SATIRIZE WITH RIDICULE to use ridicule as a way of satirizing sb or sth in a piece of writing [Mid-17thC. From French *lampon*, of uncertain origin: perhaps from *lampons* 'let us drink!' (used as a refrain in songs), a form of *lamper* 'to gulp down'.] —**lampooner** *n.* —**lampoonery** *n.* —**lampoonist** *n.*

lamppost /lámp pōst/, **lamp post** *n.* a post or pillar that supports a streetlight

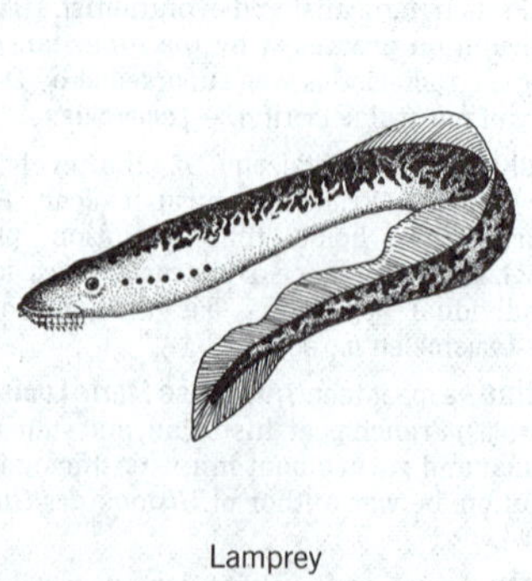

Lamprey

lamprey /lámpri/ (*plural* **-preys**) *n.* a freshwater jawless fish that has a round sucking mouth for attaching itself to other fish and, in the case of adults, feeding parasitically on their blood. Family: Petromyzontidae. [13thC. Via Old French *lampreie* from medieval Latin *lampreda* (source also of English *limpet*), perhaps from *lampetra*, literally 'stone-licker', because it clings to rocks with its mouth.]

lamprophyre /lámprə fīr/ *n.* an igneous rock that occurs mainly as an intrusion or dyke containing large crystals, especially of biotite and mica [Late 19thC. From German, literally 'shining porphyry'.]

lampshade /lámp shayd/ *n.* a cover, typically decorative, used to moderate and direct artificial light from a lamp

lamp shell *n.* = **brachiopod** [From its resemblance to an ancient oil lamp and its wick]

lamp standard *n.* = **lamppost**

lampworking /lámp wurking/ *n.* the process or technique of forming glass items made of rods and tubes by heating them with an oxygen-gas flame

Lamut /lə mo͞ot/ *n.* a language spoken in parts of eastern Siberia, belonging to the Manchu-Tungus branch of the Altaic languages. Lamut is spoken by about 12,000 people. [Early 18thC. Via Russian from Evenki, literally 'those living by the sea', from *lamu* 'sea'.] —**Lamut** *adj.*

lamziekte /lámsiktə/, **lamsiekte** *n.* S Africa botulism in cattle and sheep [Late 18thC. From Afrikaans, literally 'lame disease'.]

LAN /lan/ *abbr.* COMPUT local area network

lanai /lə nī/ (*plural* -**nais**) *n.* in Hawaii, an open roofed porch or verandah, often used as a living room [Early 19thC. From Hawaiian.]

Lanark /lánnərk/ town in central Scotland, in South Lanarkshire Council Area. Population: 8,877 (1991).

Lanarkshire /lánnərkshər/ former county in southern Scotland, until 1975

lanate /láy nayt/ *adj.* covered with or consisting of woolly hairs [Mid-18thC. From Latin *lanatus*, from *lana* 'wool' (source of English *lanolin*).]

lançado /lán sádō/ (*plural* -**dos**) *n.* a collection point in the interior of Africa for Portuguese trade, from the 16th century on, that linked African economies to the commercial centres on the Atlantic coast [From Portuguese, 'launching point']

Lancashire /lán kəshər/ coastal county of northwestern England. Population: 1,426,000 (1995). Area: 2,896 sq. km/1,183 sq. mi.

Lancaster[1] /láng kastər/ *n.* the branch of the Plantagenet dynasty that ruled England from 1399 to 1461. It was named after its founder, Henry duke of Lancaster (**Henry IV**).

Lancaster[2] /lán kastər/ historic city in the county of Lancashire, northwestern England. Population: 44,497 (1991).

Lancaster /láng kastər/, **Burt** (1913–94) US actor. His films include *From Here To Eternity* (1953), *Elmer Gantry* (1960), *The Swimmer* (1968), and *Local Hero* (1983).

Lancaster /lán kastər/, **Sir Osbert** (1908–86) British cartoonist and writer. He created Lady Maudie Littlehampton for the *Daily Express* (1939) and wrote many books on architecture.

Lancastrian /lang kástri ən/ *adj.* **1.** BELONGING TO LANCASHIRE belonging or relating to Lancashire or Lancaster **2.** HIST CONNECTED WITH THE LANCASTER ROYAL FAMILY belonging to or supporting the royal house of Lancaster, especially during the 15th-century Wars of the Roses ■ *n.* **1.** SB FROM LANCASHIRE sb who was born or brought up or who lives in Lancashire or Lancaster **2.** HIST PARTISAN OF THE LANCASTER ROYAL FAMILY sb who belonged to or supported the royal house of Lancaster, especially during the Wars of the Roses when the Yorkists and Lancastrians fought for the throne of England

lance /laanss/ *n.* **1.** ARMS LONG CAVALRY SPEAR a long weapon with a metal point carried by cavalry in battle **2.** HUNT HUNTING OR FISHING SPEAR a long pointed spear used in hunting or fishing **3.** METALL METAL-PIERCING DEVICE a thin metal tube or pipe through which a stream of oxygen is directed at a heated metal surface in order to pierce it **4.** SURG LANCET a lancet (*archaic*) ■ *vt.* (**lances, lancing, lanced**) MED PIERCE STH WITH A SHARP INSTRUMENT to pierce flesh with a

sharp instrument to let out pus [13thC. Via French from Latin *lancea* (source of English *launch*), of uncertain origin: probably from Celtic.]

lance corporal *n.* **1.** RANK OF NONCOMMISSIONED OFFICER the first rank above private soldier in the British army or the Royal Marines **2.** MARINE RANK a Marine in the US Marine Corps who ranks above private first class but below corporal [From obsolete *lancepesade* 'officer of lowest rank', via Old French from Old Italian *lancia spezzata*, literally 'broken lance', hence 'old soldier']

lancelet /laansslət/ *n.* a small slender translucent marine animal that is related to the ancestors of all vertebrate animals and lives buried in sand. Subphylum: Cephalochordata. [Mid-16thC. Originally used for 'lancet', it disappeared in the 17thC but was revived in the modern sense in the 19thC.]

Lanceley /laanssli/, **Colin** (b. 1938) New Zealand-born Australian painter and sculptor. His colourful assemblages combine painting with collages and found objects.

Lancelot /laansə lot/ in Arthurian legend, the most famous of King Arthur's knights and the lover of Queen Guinevere

lanceolate /laanssi ə layt/ *adj.* tapering to a point like the head of a lance ○ *lanceolate leaves* [Mid-18thC. From late Latin *lanceolatus*, from Latin *lanceola*, literally 'small lance', from *lancea* 'lance' (see LANCE).] —**lanceolately** *adv.*

lancer /laanssər/, **Lancer** *n.* a soldier on horseback armed with a lance

lance rest *n.* a support for a lance fitted to a medieval breastplate or saddle and used during a charge

lancers /laanssərz/ *n.* (*takes a singular verb*) **1.** DANCE SQUARE DANCE a square dance for 8 or 16 couples, originally a 19th-century quadrille **2.** MUSIC MUSIC FOR THE LANCERS the music for the lancers, a square dance

lance sergeant *n.* a corporal acting as a sergeant, usually temporarily and without extra pay

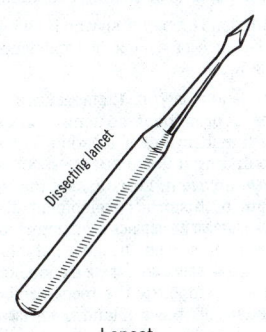

Dissecting lancet

Lancet

lancet /laanssit/ *n.* **1.** SURG SCALPEL a scalpel (*archaic*) **2.** ARCHIT = **lancet arch 3.** ARCHIT = **lancet window**

lancet arch *n.* a narrow arch that comes steeply to a point, typical in Gothic architecture

lanceted /laanssitid/ *adj.* **1.** WITH POINTED OPENINGS built with lancet arches or lancet windows, as in Gothic architecture **2.** WITH A POINTED TOP with an arched, steeply pointed top

lancet fish *n.* a long-bodied carnivorous deep-sea fish with a long dorsal fin and sharp teeth. Latin name: *Alepisauridae*. [From the sharpness of the fins]

Lancet window

lancet window *n.* a window formed as one or more slender pointed arches

lancewood /laanss wŏŏd/ (*plural* -**woods** *or* -**wood**) *n.* **1.** TREES TROPICAL TREE a tropical tree of the Americas, especially the West Indies, that yields a tough elastic wood. Latin name: *Oxandra lanceolata.* **2.** INDUST WOOD OF THE LANCEWOOD TREE the tough flexible wood of the lancewood tree, used for making fishing rods, bows, and in cabinetmaking [From the use of the wood in objects like fishing rods]

lanciform /laanssi fawrm/ *adj.* shaped like a lance

lancinate /laanssi nayt/ (-**nates**, -**nating**, -**nated**) *vt.* to stab or pierce sth (*archaic*) [Early 17thC. From Latin *lancinere* 'to tear'.] —**lancination** /laanssi n'ayshn/ *n.*

lancinating /laanssi nayting/ *adj.* producing a stabbing or piercing sensation (*formal*)

Lancs /langks/ *abbr.* Lancashire

land /land/ *n.* **1.** SOLID EARTH the solid part of the earth's surface not covered by a body of water **2.** EARTH FOR USE a part of the earth's surface of a particular kind or that is used for a particular purpose ○ *low-lying land* ○ *agricultural land* **3.** COUNTRYSIDE ground used for agriculture, or rural or agricultural areas as distinguished from villages, towns, or cities ○ *He had worked on the land all his life.* **4.** OWNED GROUND an area of ground that sb owns ○ *publicly owned land* ○ *What are you doing on my land?* **5.** HOMELAND a territory, country, or nation inhabited by those who regard it as their home ○ *her native land* **6.** AREA NOTABLE FOR STH an area, domain, or realm that is notable for sth ○ *She's living in the land of make-believe.* **7.** SMOOTH PARTS OF GROOVED AREA the unindented parts of a grooved surface, e.g. a ridge between grooves in the bore of a rifle **8.** AGRIC UNFURROWED SOIL the parts of the ground between furrows in a ploughed field **9.** *Scotland* TENEMENT a tenement house ■ *v.* (**lands, landing, landed**) **1.** *vi.* AIR ARRIVE FROM PLANE to arrive by aircraft ○ *We land at 8:43.* **2.** *vti.* AIR SET DOWN AIRCRAFT to come down, or bring an aircraft down, onto water or solid ground, especially at an airport ○ *The Luton plane landed five minutes ago.* **3.** *vti.* TRANSP GO OR PUT STH ASHORE to arrive on shore from a ship, or put sth ashore from a ship ○ *We decided to land and explore the port.* **4.** *vi.* COME DOWN THROUGH THE AIR to come down, or bring sb or sth down, from a height ○ *The ball shot up and landed on the roof.* **5.** *vt.* ANGLING CATCH AND BRING A FISH IN to catch a fish and get it onto a boat or solid ground **6.** *vt.* OBTAIN STH to win, obtain, secure, or be awarded sth desired ○ *He finally landed the job he wanted.* **7.** *vt.* HIT SB OR STH to succeed in hitting sb or sth ○ *She landed a blow on his head.* **8.** *vi.* APPEAR UNEXPECTEDLY to appear in an undesired and unexpected way ○ *One problem after another landed in our lap.* **9.** *vti.* END UP SOMEWHERE UNPLEASANT to end up or cause sb or sth to end up in an undesirable place or situation ○ *It could land him in jail.* [Old English, from a prehistoric Germanic word apparently meaning 'particular (enclosed) area', which is also the ancestor of English *lawn*]
◇ **be in the land of the living** to be alive (*humorous*)
◇ **see out how the land lies**, **find out how the land lies** to assess a situation before taking action
land in on *vt. Scotland* to visit sb unexpectedly (*informal*)
land up *vi. UK, Can* to finally get to a place or situation after a series of events or circumstances (*informal*) ○ *land up on the streets*
land with *vt. UK, Can* to give sb sth to do or deal with, especially because no one else wants to do it (*informal*) ○ *I was landed with the bill.*

land agent *n.* **1.** ESTATE MANAGER the manager or administrator of a landed estate **2.** AGENT FOR SALE OF LAND an agent for the buying and selling of land —**land agency** *n.*

land army *n.* **1.** HIST WOMEN FARM WORKERS IN WARTIME a collective unit of women recruited to do agricultural work in Britain during World War I and World War II **2.** ARMY GROUND FORCES ground forces (*dated*) ◇ **land forces**

landau /lán daw/ (*plural* -**daus**) *n.* a four-wheeled horse-drawn carriage with a top that may be let down or folded back and a raised seat for the driver [Mid-18thC. Named after *Landau*, a town in Bavaria, Germany, where it was first made.]

landaulet /lán daw lét/, **landaulette** *n.* **1.** SMALL HORSE-DRAWN CARRIAGE a small horse-drawn landau **2.** CAR WITH

A REAR FOLDING TOP a car that has a convertible top for the back seat, while the front seat is either roofed or open

land bank n. a bank that issues loans using the borrower's property as security

land bridge n. a tract of land that connects continents, permitting the passage of people and animals

land crab n. any crab that lives mainly on land and breeds in the sea

landed /lándid/ adj. 1. OWNING LAND possessing land, especially a large rural property 2. CONSISTING OF LAND consisting of a large area of land 3. Can OFFICIALLY A RESIDENT OF CANADA given official status as a resident in Canada prior to being granted citizenship

lander /lándər/ n. a spacecraft designed to land on the surface of the Moon or a planet

landfall /lánd fawl/ n. 1. ARRIVAL AT LAND an approach to, arrival on, or sighting of land, especially after a long journey by sea 2. FIRST LAND REACHED AFTER A JOURNEY the first land that sb reaches after a long journey, especially by sea

landfill /lánd fil/ n. 1. BURIAL OF WASTE MATERIAL the disposal of waste material or refuse by burying it in natural or excavated holes or depressions 2. AREA CONTAINING BURIED WASTE a site where waste material has been buried

land forces npl. armed forces serving exclusively on land. ◊ land army

landform /lánd fawrm/ n. a natural physical feature of the earth's surface, e.g. a valley, mountain, or plain

land girl n. a woman who did farm work as a member of the Land Army during World Wars I and II (sometimes considered offensive)

landgravate n. = landgraviate

landgrave /lánd grayv/ n. 1. COUNT WITH REGIONAL JURISDICTION in Germany, from the 13th century to 1806, a count who had jurisdiction over a region 2. TITLE OF SOME GERMAN PRINCES a title given to certain princes in central Germany after 1806 [Early 16thC. From Middle Low German, literally 'land count', from land 'land' + grave 'count, nobleman'.]

landgraviate /lánd gráyvi ət/, **landgravate** /lándgrə veit/ n. formerly, the office, jurisdiction, or territory presided over by a landgrave or landgravine [Early 17thC. From medieval Latin landgraviatus, from LANDGRAVE.]

landgravine /lándgrə veen/ n. 1. WOMAN LANDGRAVE a woman who held the rank of landgrave, a title given in central Germany after 1801 2. WIFE OF LANDGRAVE the wife or widow of a landgrave [Late 17thC. Via Dutch landgravin, the feminine of landgraaf 'landgrave', from Middle Low German landgrave (see LANDGRAVE).]

landholder /lánd hōldər/ n. the owner or occupant of a piece of land —**landholding** n., adj.

landing /lánding/ n. 1. ACT OF COMING TO THE GROUND the act of reaching, touching, or alighting on the ground, e.g. after a jump or fall 2. ARRIVAL ON LAND an arrival on the ground after having been in the air or at sea 3. PLACE FOR LOADING OR UNLOADING a place for loading or unloading passengers or goods, especially from a ship ○ There is a good landing at most of the villages along the coast. 4. BUILDING LEVEL AREA BETWEEN STAIRS a platform between flights of stairs or the floor at the top or foot of a flight of stairs

landing beacon n. a radio transmitter at an airfield that sends a beam to guide aircraft on landing

landing beam n. a radio beam emitted by a beacon at a landing field that enables incoming aircraft to make a landing

landing craft n. a low open flat-bottomed boat designed for landing troops and equipment on shore from a ship

landing field n. a place where aircraft can land and take off

landing gear n. the wheels or floats and related mechanisms that are used by an aircraft or spacecraft when taking off and landing

landing net n. a baglike net fitted on a frame that is used by anglers to scoop up a hooked fish

landing speed n. the minimum speed at which an aircraft has to be flying in order to land safely

landing stage n. a floating or fixed wooden platform, used for loading or unloading passengers and goods from a boat

landing strip n. = airstrip

landlady /lánd laydi/ (plural -dies) n. 1. WOMAN WHO RENTS OUT PROPERTY a woman who owns property that she rents to tenants 2. WOMAN WHO RENTS OUT LODGINGS a woman who owns or runs a place offering accommodation, e.g. a bed-and-breakfast, guesthouse, or lodging house 3. WOMAN RUNNING PUB a woman who manages a public house

ländler /léndlər/ (plural -ler) n. 1. DANCE SLOW GERMAN DANCE a dance of southern Germany and Austria in slow triple time, in which couples have to clap and whirl round. The ländler was a forerunner of the waltz. 2. MUSIC MUSIC FOR LÄNDLER a slow rustic waltz as the music for the ländler [Late 19thC. From German, literally 'sth connected with Landl', from Landl, a part of Austria, where the dance was first popular.]

landless /lándləss/ adj. without having the ownership of land —**landlessness** n.

landline /lánd līn/ n. a telecommunications cable laid overland

landlocked /lánd lokt/ adj. 1. GEOG SURROUNDED BY LAND closed in completely or almost completely by land 2. ZOOL LIVING WITH NO ACCESS TO SEA adapted to life in a freshwater environment, with no access to the sea, though being a species historically found in the ocean

landlord /lánd lawrd/ n. 1. MAN WHO RENTS OUT PROPERTY a man who owns property that he rents to tenants 2. MAN WHO RENTS OUT LODGINGS a man who owns or runs a place offering accommodation, e.g. a bed-and-breakfast, guesthouse, or lodging house 3. MAN RUNNING PUB a man who manages a public house

landlubber /lánd lubbər/ n. sb who is awkward aboard a ship because of a lack of experience at sea —**landlubberly** adj.

landmark /lánd maark/ n. 1. STH PROMINENT THAT IDENTIFIES A LOCATION a prominent structure or geographical feature that identifies a location and serves as a guide to finding it 2. STH THAT REPRESENTS IMPORTANT NEW DEVELOPMENT an event, place, or item that represents a significant or historic development 3. US STH PRESERVED FOR HISTORIC IMPORTANCE a structure or site identified and preserved because of its historical significance 4. BOUNDARY MARKER a conspicuous object, e.g. a tree or stone, that is recognized as marking the boundary of a piece of land ■ adj. HIGHLY SIGNIFICANT marking a significant change or turning point in sth, especially the law ○ a landmark ruling

landmass /lánd mass/ n. a very large unbroken area of land, e.g. a continent or large island

landmine /lánd mīn/ n. an explosive mine that is laid just under the surface of the ground and detonates if disturbed by pressure or the proximity of sth such as metal

land of milk and honey n. 1. BIBLE FERTILE LAND PROMISED TO ISRAELITES a land of prosperity and plenty promised by God to the Israelites 2. ANY FERTILE REGION a rich and fertile area, or region of plenty (literary)

landowner /lándōnər/ n. sb who owns land —**landownership** n. —**landowning** n., adj.

Landrace /lánd rayss/ (plural -drace or -draces) n. a northern European breed of pig, especially a white lean long-bodied variety developed in Denmark [Mid-20thC. From Danish, literally 'land breed, national breed'.]

landrail /lánd rayl/ n. = corncrake [From RAIL 'bird']

land reform n. the redistribution of agricultural land, especially by government measures, so that the landless receive some of it

Land Registry n. a government department in England and Wales at which land and its ownership is registered

land rights npl. ANZ the claim of aboriginal people to the ownership of an area of land, usually based on occupation before the arrival of immigrants

Land Rover tdmk. a trademark for a four-wheel-drive vehicle

landscape /lánd skayp/ n. 1. VISUALLY DISTINCT SCENERY an expanse of scenery of a particular type, especially as much as can be seen by the eye 2. ARTS PAINTING OF VIEW a painting, drawing, or photograph of scenery, especially rural scenery 3. ARTS THE PAINTING OR DRAWING OF SCENERY the branch of art dealing with the painting, drawing, or photography of scenery 4. GENERAL SITUATION OF ACTIVITY the general situation providing the background to a particular type of activity ○ the economic landscape 5. RANGE OF MENTAL CONCERNS any characteristic group of intellectual or imaginative features (literary) ■ adj. PRINTING PRINTED WITH LONG SIDES HORIZONTAL photographed or printed so that the long sides of a picture or the lines of text are parallel to the long sides of a rectangular page ○ It's best to print most tables in landscape. ◊ portrait ■ vt. (-scapes, -scaping, -scaped) ENVIRON MAKE LAND LOOK BETTER to enhance the appearance of land by altering its contours and planting trees and shrubs for aesthetic effect (often passive) ○ The property was beautifully landscaped. [Late 16thC. Anglicization of Dutch landschap, literally 'condition of being land', from land 'land'. Originally used in painting.]

landscape architect n. sb employed to plan and design an environment, especially with the aim of making new buildings, roads, and other structures compatible with their natural surroundings —**landscape architecture** n.

landscape gardener n. sb who designs and lays out grounds and gardens —**landscape gardening** n.

landscaper /lánd skaypər/ n. US sb who alters grounds or gardens for aesthetic effect

landscapist /lánd skaypist/ n. an artist who specializes in painting landscapes

Land's End /lándz énd/ cliff and promontory in Cornwall that forms the extreme southwestern tip of Great Britain

landshark /lánd shaark/ n. sb who profits by unethical dealings in land (informal insult)

landside /lánd sīd/ n. 1. AIR AIRPORT AREA FARTHEST FROM AIRCRAFT the part of an airport farthest from the aircraft 2. AGRIC PART OF PLOUGH the flat part of a plough that faces unbroken land as it moves

landsknecht /lándz knekt/ n. a mercenary foot soldier in Europe during the 16th century, especially a German pikeman [Early 17thC. From German, literally 'servant of the country'. By folk etymology 'lands' has often been misunderstood as 'lance'.]

landsleit plural of landsman

landslide /lánd slīd/ n. 1. SUDDEN COLLAPSE OF LAND the collapse of part of a mountainside or cliff so that it descends in a disintegrating mass of rocks and earth 2. MASS OF LOOSENED ROCK AND EARTH a disintegrating mass of rock and earth that suddenly descends from a mountainside or cliff 3. POL CONSPICUOUS TRIUMPH an overwhelming victory, especially in an election

landslip /lánd slip/ n. = landslide n. 1

Landsmål /laánts mawl/ n. an official form of the Norwegian language derived from the rural dialects of Norwegian spoken in the west and north of the country and standardized during the mid-19th century. ◊ Bokmål [Late 19thC. From Norwegian, literally 'country language'.]

landsman[1] /lándzmən/ (plural -men /-mən/) n. sb who lives and works on land rather than at sea

landsman[2] /lándzmən/ (plural -leit /-līt/) n. a fellow Jew from the same district or area, originally in Eastern Europe [Mid-20thC. Via Yiddish, from Middle High German lantsman, literally 'man from the (same) country', plural lantsliute.]

Landsturm /laánt shtoorm/ n. 1. MILITARY DRAFT in some European countries a general draft of people for conscription into the armed forces 2. CONSCRIPTED FORCE in some European countries, a military force of people drafted from the general population [Early 19thC. From German, literally 'land storm'.]

Landtag /laánt taak/ n. the legislative assembly of a German or Austrian state [Late 16thC. Via German, from, ultimately, Middle High German lanttac, literally 'land day'.]

land tax *n.* an annual tax levied on UK landed property, abolished in 1963

landward /lándwərd/ *adj.* facing towards the land

landwards /lándwərdz/ *adv.* in the direction of land

Landwehr /laánt vair/ *n.* in German-speaking countries, a reserve military force [Early 19thC. From German, literally 'national defence'.]

Landy /lándi/, **Michael John** (*b.* 1930) Australian athlete. A middle-distance runner, in 1954 he became the second person to run a mile in under four minutes.

land yacht *n.* a wind-driven vehicle resembling a boat with a mast, sails, and three wheels, for use on beaches or other hard surfaces

lane /layn/ *n.* **1.** NARROW STREET a narrow path, road or street, typically in older town areas or in the countryside, often enclosed by walls or hedges **2.** TRANSP **TRACK INTO WHICH ROAD IS DIVIDED** a division of a road, street, or motorway wide enough for a single line of motor vehicles **3.** SPORTS **TRACK ASSIGNED TO RACER** a track assigned to a competitive runner on a racing track or a swimmer in a swimming pool **4.** SHIPPING **SHIPPING ROUTE** a route assigned to a ship on a journey, especially through a congested area of sea **5.** AIR = **air lane 6.** BOWLS **STRIP OF FLOOR IN BOWLING ALLEY** the long strip of polished wooden flooring along which bowls are rolled in a bowling alley **7.** BASKETBALL **DIVISION OF BASKETBALL COURT** an area of a basketball court extending from the free-throw line to just below the basket [Old English, of unknown origin] ◇ **in the fast lane** at a fast, hectic, or stressful pace associated with success and achievement

Lane /layn/, **William** (1861–1917) English-born Australian journalist and political activist. He wrote *The Workingman's Paradise* (1892), and in 1893 founded an Australian socialist colony in Paraguay.

lane discipline *n.* the degree of care and restraint exercised by drivers when using busy multilane roads, avoiding constant lane changing, cutting-in, driving too close to vehicles in front, risk-taking, and opportunism

lang /lang/, **k.d.** (*b.* 1961) Canadian-born US singer. She is equally adept at country-and-western and popular songs. Full name **Kathryn Dawn Lang**

Fritz Lang

Lang /lang/, **Fritz** (1890–1976) German-born US film director. He made many Hollywood films, but is best known for the silent film *Metropolis* (1921) and the German-language *M* (1931).

lang. *abbr.* language

Lange /lóngi/, **David Russell** (*b.* 1942) New Zealand statesman. As prime minister of New Zealand (1984–89), he pursued a non-nuclear defence policy that led to a dispute with the United States.

Langi *n.* = **Lango**

langlauf /laáng lowf/ *n.* **1.** = **cross-country skiing 2.** **CROSS-COUNTRY SKIING CONTEST** a contest in cross-country skiing [Early 20thC. From German, literally 'long run', from *lang* 'long' + *Lauf* 'a run' (from, ultimately, a prehistoric Germanic word that is also the ancestor of English *leap*).] —**langlaufer** *n.*

langley /lángli/ (*plural* **-leys**) *n.* a unit of solar radiation equivalent to one calorie per square centimetre [Mid-20thC. Named after Samuel P. *Langley* (1834–1906), a US astronomer.]

Lango /láng gō/ (*plural* **-gos** *or* **-go**), **Langi** /láng gi/ (*plural* **-gis** *or* **-gi**) *n.* **1.** PEOPLES **MEMBER OF UGANDAN PEOPLE** a member of a Nilotic people who live in northern Uganda **2.** LANG **LANGO LANGUAGE** the language of the Lango people, belonging to the Chari-Nile branch of Nilo-Saharan languages. Lango is spoken by about half a million people. [Early 20thC. From Nilotic.] —**Lango** *adj.*

Langobard /láng gə baard/ *n.* = **Lombard** *n.* 2 [Late 18thC. From late Latin *Langobardus* (see LOMBARD).]

Langobardic /láng gə baárdik/ *n.* a dialect of Old High German spoken by the ancient Lombards

langouste /long goóst/ *n.* = **spiny lobster** [Mid-20thC. Via French from Old Provençal *lagosta*, from, ultimately, Latin *locusta* 'locust, crustacean' (source also of English *locust*).]

langoustine /lóng goō steén/ *n.* a large prawn or small lobster of the North Atlantic [Mid-20thC. Via French, from, ultimately, Latin *locusta* 'locust, crustacean'.]

langrage /láng grij/, **langridge** *n.* shot consisting of a case filled with fragments of iron, formerly used for tearing the sails and rigging of enemy ships [Mid-18thC. Origin unknown.]

Langrenus /láng grinəss/ *n.* a plain on the Moon with a complex central peak located on the eastern edge of the Mare Fecunditatis, 132 km/82 mi. in diameter

langsyne /láng sín/, **lang syne** *adv.* *Scotland* **LONG AGO** long ago (*literary*) ○ *It all happened lang syne.* ■ *n.* *Scotland* **TIME LONG AGO** a time long ago (*literary humorous*) ◊ **auld lang syne**

Langtry /lángtri/, **Lillie** (1853–1929) British actress. She was the first woman of high social standing to go on the stage in Great Britain. She became the mistress of the Prince of Wales (later Edward VII). Born **Emilie Charlotte Le Breton**

language /láng gwij/ *n.* **1.** **SPEECH OF GROUP** the speech of a country, region, or group of people, including its diction, syntax, and grammar **2.** **COMMUNICATION WITH WORDS** the human use of spoken or written words as a communication system **3.** **SYSTEM OF COMMUNICATION** a system of communication with its own set of conventions or special words **4.** **NONVERBAL COMMUNICATION BETWEEN ANIMALS** a nonverbal form of communication used by birds and animals **5.** **NONVERBAL COMMUNICATION BETWEEN HUMANS** the use of signs, gestures, or inarticulate sounds to communicate sth **6.** **SPECIALIST VOCABULARY** the characteristic forms of expression used by those in a specified group or sphere of activity **7.** **STYLE OF VERBAL EXPRESSION** the verbal style by which people express themselves ○ *the language of diplomacy* **8.** COMPUT = **programming language** [13thC. Via French *langage*, from *langue* 'tongue', from, ultimately, Latin *lingua*, literally 'tongue', hence 'language' (source of English *linguistics*).] ◇ **speak the same language** to have values and interests in common with sb so that it is possible to communicate effectively

WORD KEY: SYNONYMS

language, vocabulary, tongue, idiolect, dialect, slang, jargon, parlance, lingo, -speak, -ese

CORE MEANING: communication by words

language the way human beings communicate using words, whether written or spoken. It is also used for the particular system of communication prevailing in a specific country, nation, or community; **vocabulary** the body of words that make up a particular language. It can also be used to refer to the words used to talk about a particular subject; **tongue** the particular language used by a specific country, nation, or community; **idiolect** the particular language or speech habits of an individual; **dialect** the specific way a language is used in a particular area of a country or among those in a particular part of a community when this is distinct in some way from the language spoken generally in that nation or community; **slang** the words, expressions, and turns of phrase used by a particular group of people, especially when these are considered nonstandard; **jargon** the words associated with a particular specialized activity or group or used in a particular situation, especially in order to suggest that they are technical or difficult for an ordinary person to understand; **parlance** a formal and fairly old-fashioned word for the words and expressions usually associated with a particular group of people; **lingo** an informal word for the words or way of speaking associated with a particular, usually specialized, group of people; **-speak** a suffix added to nouns to describe the specific way words are used by a particular group of people or in a particular context. It is used especially to suggest that this way of speaking or writing is made deliberately hard for ordinary people to follow; **-ese** a suffix added to nouns to describe the words and speech patterns associated with a particular person or group of people, especially when the words have been coined or the speech is hard to understand, for example in the speech of journalists.

language laboratory *n.* a room equipped with audio or multimedia equipment for use in learning languages

langue /longg/ *n.* language regarded as a communication system and the common property of a speech community (*technical*) ◊ **parole** [14thC. Via French from Latin *lingua* (see LANGUAGE). The modern technical sense dates from the early 20thC.]

langue de chat /lóng də shaá/ (*plural* **langues de chat** /lóng də shaá/) *n.* a small narrow flat biscuit often coated with chocolate [From French, literally 'cat's tongue']

langue d'oc /lóngg dók/ *n.* the group of French dialects, usually thought of as including Provençal, spoken in southern parts of medieval France [From French, literally 'language of "oc" ', from the use of *oc* (from Latin *hoc*) for 'yes']

langue d'oïl /lóngg dóyl/ *n.* the group of French dialects spoken in the northern part of medieval France [From French, literally 'language of "oïl" ', from the use of *oïl* (from Latin *hoc ille*) for 'yes']

languet /láng gwet/ *n.* sth, e.g. a part in a machine or instrument, that is shaped like a tongue [14thC. From Old French *languete*, literally 'small tongue', from *langue* 'tongue', from Latin *lingua* (see LANGUAGE).]

languid /láng gwid/ *adj.* **1.** **WITHOUT ENERGY** lacking vigour and energy **2.** **SLUGGISH** sluggish or slow-moving **3.** **LISTLESS** listless and indifferent [Late 16thC. Directly or via French from Latin *languidus*, from *languere* (see LANGUISH).] —**languidly** *adv.* —**languidness** *n.*

languish /láng gwish/ (**-guishes, -guishing, -guished**) *vi.* **1.** **BE NEGLECTED OR DEPRIVED** to undergo hardship as a result of being deprived of sth, typically independence, freedom, or attention **2.** **BECOME LESS SUCCESSFUL** to decline steadily, becoming less vital, strong, or successful **3.** **PINE FOR STH** to long for sth that is being denied [14thC. From Old French *languiss-*, the stem of *languir*, from, ultimately, Latin *languere* 'to be weak or faint'.] —**languisher** *n.* —**languishing** *n., adj.* —**languishingly** *adv.* —**languishment** *n.*

languor /láng gər/ *n.* **1.** **TIREDNESS** a pleasant feeling of weariness or weakness **2.** **LISTLESSNESS IN SPEECH OR BEHAVIOUR** listlessness and indifference in speech or behaviour **3.** **HEAVINESS IN ATMOSPHERE** an oppressive heaviness or sultriness in the air [13thC. Via Old French from Latin, from *languere* (see LANGUISH).]

languorous /láng gərəss/ *adj.* **1.** **WEAK AND RELAXED** lazily or pleasantly lacking vigour and vitality **2.** **LISTLESS** listless and indifferent **3.** **SLUGGISH** slow-moving or sluggish —**languorously** *adv.* —**languorousness** *n.*

langur /láng gər, lang goór/ *n.* a slender, leaf-eating monkey of Southeast Asia with a long tail, bushy eyebrows, and a chin tuft. Genus: *Presbytis.* ◊ **leaf monkey** [Early 19thC. Via Hindi *langūr* from Sanskrit *lāngūla* 'having a tail'.]

laniard *n.* = **lanyard**

laniary /lánni əri/ *adj.* **FOR TEARING FOOD** adapted for tearing food ○ *laniary teeth* ■ *n.* **TOOTH FOR TEARING FOOD** a tooth adapted for tearing food [Early 19thC. From Latin *laniarius*, literally 'of a butcher', from *lanius* 'butcher', from *laniare* 'to tear'.]

laniferous /lə nífərəss/, **lanigerous** /lə níjjərəss/ *adj.* wool-bearing or wool-covered [Mid-17thC. Formed from Latin *lanifer*, from *lana* 'wool' (source of English *lanolin*).]

lank /langk/ *adj.* **1.** **LIMP** limp and straight ○ *lank hair* **2.** **ELONGATED** long and slender [Old English *hlanc* 'lean', from a prehistoric Germanic word meaning 'flexible' that is also the ancestor of English *flinch* and *link*] —**lankly** *adv.* —**lankness** *n.*

lanky /lángki/ (**-ier**, **-iest**) *adj.* tall and thin in a bony, ungracefully angular way —**lankily** *adv.* —**lankiness** *n.*

lanner /lánnər/ (*plural* **-ners** *or* **-ner**) *n.* a large falcon found in Africa, Southeast Asia, and the Mediterranean region, the female of which is used especially in falconry. Latin name: *Falco biarmicus.* [13thC. From French *lanier*, of uncertain origin: perhaps from Old French, 'cowardly', because it flies slowly and was therefore thought to lack courage.]

lanneret /lánnə ret/ (*plural* **-ets** *or* **-et**) *n.* a male lanner, smaller than the female and used in falconry.

lanolin /lánnəlin/, **lanoline** /lánnə leen/ *n.* a fat extracted from sheep's wool, often used as a base in ointments and skin medications [Late 19thC. Coined from Latin *lana* 'wool' (ultimately from an Indo-European word that is also the ancestor of English *wool*) + *oleum* 'oil' (source of English *oil*).]

lansfordite /lánzfərd īt/ *n.* a crystallized hydrate of magnesium carbonate occurring as stalactites [Late 19thC. Formed from *Lansford*, the name of a town in Pennsylvania, USA, where it was found.]

Lansing /lánsing/ **1.** village in northeastern Illinois, on the Illinois-Indiana border south of Calumet City. It is a southern suburb of Chicago. Population: 28,664 (1996). **2.** capital of Michigan, a manufacturing city in the south-central part of the state. Population: 127,812 (1994).

lantana /lan táynə, -taànə/ (*plural* **-nas** *or* **-na**) *n.* a shrub of the vervain family that is native to the tropical Americas and has bright aromatic spikes of yellow, orange, or blue and violet flowers. Genus: *Lantana.* [Late 18thC. Via modern Latin, genus name, from Italian dialect *lantana* 'wayfaring tree', which it resembles.]

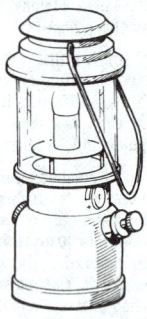

Lantern

lantern /lántərn/ *n.* **1.** PORTABLE LAMP a portable case with transparent or translucent sides that protects and holds a lamp **2.** LIGHTHOUSE ROOM a room containing the large lamp at the top of a lighthouse **3.** ARCHIT STRUCTURE WITH WINDOWS a structure with windows on all sides, resembling a lantern, e.g. one at the top of a dome **4.** ARTS STAGE LIGHT a light for illuminating a stage or part of a stage [13thC. Via French from, ultimately, Greek *lamptēr* 'torch, lamp', from *lampein* 'to shine' (source also of English *lamp*).]

lantern-eyed fish *n.* a marine fish with luminous organs under each eye that it can turn on and off at will. Family: Anomalopidae.

lantern fish *n.* a small bony deep-sea fish with rows of luminous spots along its body. Family: Myctophidae.

lantern fly *n.* a tropical insect with an elongated head that resembles a lantern and was formerly thought to emit light. Family: Fulgoridae.

lantern jaw *n.* a long bony lower jaw, typically projecting beyond the upper jaw —**lantern-jawed** *adj.*

lantern pinion *n.* a gearwheel used in clocks and watches that has two circular discs connected by cylindrical pins.

lantern slide *n.* a transparent slide, typically made of glass, for projection onto a screen by a slide projector or magic lantern.

lantern wheel *n.* = **lantern pinion**

lanthanide /lánthə nīd/ *n.* any of the chemical elements in the lanthanide series of rare earths [Early 20thC. Coined from LANTHANUM + -IDE.]

lanthanide series *n.* a group of the rare earths that range from lanthanum at atomic number 57 to lutetium at atomic number 71

lanthanum /lánthənəm/ *n.* a silvery ductile metallic element resembling aluminium that belongs to the rare earth series and is used in the manufacture of glass. Symbol **La** [Mid-19thC. Coined from Greek *lanthanein* 'to lie hidden' (because it was discovered hidden in cerium oxide).]

lanthorn /lánt hawrn, lántərn/ *n.* a lantern (*archaic*) [By folk etymology from LANTERN, by association with HORN, from which lanterns were formerly made.]

lanuginous /lə noójinəss/, **lanuginose** /-nōss, -nōz/ *adj.* covered with downy hairs [Late 16thC. Formed from Latin *lanuginosus*, from *lanugo* (see LANUGO).] —**lanuginousness** *n.*

lanugo /lə nyoógō/ (*plural* **-gos** *or* **-go**) *n.* a covering of soft downy hairs, especially those on a developing human foetus or newborn infant [15thC. From Latin, from *lana* 'wool' (source of English *lanolin*).]

Lanús /la noòs/ city in Buenos Aires Province, eastern Argentina, and a suburb of Buenos Aires. Population: 466,755 (1991).

lanyard /lányərd/, **laniard** *n.* **1.** MIL, SCOUTING CORD WORN ROUND THE NECK a cord worn round the neck by military and naval personnel or by Boy Scouts and Guides for carrying sth such as a whistle or penknife **2.** NAUT SHORT ROPE ABOARD SHIP a short rope or cord used to hold or fasten sth on a ship **3.** ARMS CORD FOR FIRING A CANNON a cord tied to the breech mechanism of a cannon and used to fire it [14thC. Anglicization (influenced by YARD 'spar') of French *lanière* 'strap', from, ultimately, *lasne*, of uncertain origin: perhaps a blend of *laz* 'string' (source of English *lace*) and *nasle* 'lace'.]

Lanzarote /lanzə ráwti/ the easternmost island of the Canary Islands, Las Palmas Province, Spain, situated northeast of Gran Canaria in the Atlantic Ocean. Population: 76,413 (1995). Area: 862 sq. km/335 sq. mi.

LAO *abbr.* Laos (*international vehicle registration*)

Laocoön /lay ókō on/, **Laocoon** *n.* a Trojan priest of Apollo who warned the Trojans about the Wooden Horse and was killed along with his two sons by sea serpents after he gave his warning

laodicean /láy ōdi seè ən/, **Laodicean** *adj.* UNCOMMITTED lacking in religious or political commitment ■ *n.* SB LACKING INTEREST sb who is lukewarm or indifferent, especially about religion or politics [Early 17thC. Formed from Latin *Laodicea*, modern-day western Turkey, whose Christians were rebuked for indifference (the Bible, *Revelation*, 3:16: '...you are lukewarm, and neither cold nor hot').]

Laos

Laos /láy oss/ independent state of Southeast Asia, bounded by China, Vietnam, Cambodia, Thailand, and Myanmar. It is the only landlocked nation in Southeast Asia. Language: Lao. Currency: new kip. Capital: Vientiane. Population: 5,116,959 (1997). Area: 236,800 sq. km/91,400 sq. mi. Official name **Lao People's Democratic Republic** —**Laotian** *n., adj.*

lap[1] /lap/ *n.* **1.** TOP OF SB'S THIGHS WHEN SITTING the level area provided by the upper surface of the thighs of sb who is seated **2.** CLOTHES PART OF CLOTHING RESTING ON THE THIGHS the part of a garment that hangs loosely across the thighs of sb seated **3.** GEOG VALLEY a hollow in the contours of land, especially the gap between hills ■ *vt.* WRAP STH to wrap sth (*regional informal*) ◇ *Lap that parcel up well.* [Old English *læppa* 'flap of a garment, lobe', from a prehistoric Germanic word that is perhaps also the ancestor of English *label*] —**lapful** *n.* ◇ **drop in** *or* **into your lap** to be given as sth welcome and unexpected ◇ **drop (sth) in sb's lap** to become or make sth sb's responsibility ◇ **in the lap of luxury** in great luxury and comfort ◇ **in the lap of the gods** beyond human control or influence

lap[2] /lap/ *n.* **1.** SPORTS ONE CIRCUIT OF A TRACK a single circuit of a racetrack or running track, or one length of a swimming pool **2.** STAGE IN STH a phase in an extended project, enterprise, or journey **3.** OVERLAPPING PART an overlapping part of sth **4.** LENGTH GOING ONCE ROUND A REEL a length of fabric, thread, or rope that goes once round a roller, drum, or reel **5.** POLISHING DISC a rotating disc for cutting or polishing sth such as glass or gemstones ■ *v.* (**laps**, **lapping**, **lapped**) **1.** *vt.* SPORTS PASS COMPETITORS BY A COMPLETE CIRCUIT to overtake a competitor on a racetrack or running track after having completed at least one circuit more than he or she has **2.** *vi.* SPORTS COMPLETE ONE TRACK CIRCUIT to run one complete circuit around a track **3.** *vt.* WRAP IN STH to enfold or enwrap sb in sth (*literary; often passive*) **4.** *vti.* OVERLAP to overlap sth (*literary*) **5.** *vt.* POLISH OR CUT HARD SURFACES to polish or cut sth hard such as glass, metal, or gemstones **6.** *vt.* FORM FIBRES INTO A BAND to arrange fibres so that they lie one against the other and form a band [14thC. From LAP[1], perhaps from the meaning 'folds of a garment'. The modern sense 'circuit of track' evolved from 'sth wrapped', via 'overlapping part'.] —**lapper** *n.*

lap[3] /lap/ *vti.* (**laps**, **lapping**, **lapped**) **1.** lap, lap up DRINK STH WITH THE TONGUE to drink a liquid by scooping it into the mouth with the tongue **2.** WASH GENTLY AGAINST A SURFACE to flow or splash gently against a surface ■ *n.* **1.** PROCESS OF DRINKING STH WITH TONGUE the action of drinking liquid by scooping small amounts of it into the mouth with the tongue **2.** SOUND OF MOVING LIQUID the sound of a liquid gently flowing or splashing against sth [Old English *lapian*, from, ultimately, a prehistoric Germanic word] —**lapper** *n.*

lap up *v.* **1.** *vti.* = **lap**[3] *v.* **1** **2.** *vt.* DRINK EAGERLY to drink or eat sth enthusiastically **3.** *vt.* ENJOY EAGERLY to enjoy sth eagerly and uncritically

La Palma /laa paálmə/ one of the Canary Islands, Spain, situated off the north coast of Africa. Population: 82,183 (1995). Area: 725 sq. km/280 sq. mi.

laparoscope /láppərə skōp/ *n.* an instrument in the shape of a tube that is inserted through the abdominal wall to give an examining doctor a view of the internal organs

laparoscopy /láppə róskəpi/ (*plural* **-pies**) *n.* examination of the internal organs of the abdomen using a laparoscope [Mid-19thC. Coined from Greek *lapara* 'flank' + -SCOPY.] —**laparoscopic** /láppərə skóppik/ *adj.* —**laparoscopist** *n.*

laparotomy /láppə róttəmi/ (*plural* **-mies**) *n.* a surgical incision through the abdominal wall made to allow investigation of an abdominal organ or diagnosis of an abdominal disorder [Mid-19thC. Coined from Greek *lapara* (see LAPAROSCOPY) + -TOMY.]

La Paz /la páz/ capital city of Bolivia, located in the western part of the country. Population: 711,036 (1992).

lap belt *n.* a safety belt that is fitted to the seat of a motor vehicle and fastens across the lap

lapboard /láp bawrd/ *n.* a thin flat board that is laid across the knees to serve as a table or writing surface

lap-chart *n.* a record of each lap made by a motor vehicle in a race, showing each vehicle's exact position

lap dancer *n.* a striptease artist who performs an erotic dance close to or in the lap of a customer —**lap dancing** *n.*

lapdog /láp dog/ *n.* **1.** SMALL PET DOG a small gentle-natured dog **2.** MINION sb who is willing to say or do anything at another's command, especially in an organization or institution

lapel /lə pél/ *n.* either of the two folded-back front edges of a jacket that are continuous with the collar [Mid-17thC. Diminutive of LAP[1] (in the earlier meaning 'part of a garment that projects and can be folded over').] —**lapelled** *adj.*

lapidary /láppidəri/ *adj.* **1.** ENGRAVED ON STONE engraved in stone or on a gemstone **2.** OF ENGRAVING GEMSTONES relating to the art of engraving gemstones **3.** DIGNIFIED AND ELEGANT careful, elegant, and dignified in style (*formal*) ■ *n.* (*plural* **-ies**) CUTTER OF PRECIOUS STONES sb who is expert at cutting, polishing, and engraving gemstones [14thC. From Latin *lapidarius* 'of stone', later 'stone-cutter', from *lapid-*, the stem of *lapis* 'stone' (source of English *lapis lazuli*), of uncertain origin; perhaps Mediterranean.]

lapidate /láppi dayt/ (**-dates, -dating, -dated**) *vt.* (*literary*) **1.** STONE SB to throw stones at sb **2.** STONE SB TO DEATH to stone sb to death, especially as a punishment for wrongdoing [Early 17thC. From Latin *lapidare*, from the stem *lapid-* (see LAPIDARY).] —**lapidation** /láppi dáysh'n/ *n.*

lapillus /lə pílləss/ (*plural* **-li** /-lī/) *n.* a small fragment of lava thrown from a volcano [Mid-18thC. From Latin, 'small stone', from *lapis* (see LAPIDARY).]

lapis lazuli /láppiss lázzyōō lī, -li/ *n.* BLUE GEMSTONE a deep blue semiprecious stone that is chiefly composed of lazurite and is used in making jewellery ■ *adj.* COLOURS DEEP BLUE of the same deep brilliant blue as lapis lazuli [Literally 'stone of lapis lazuli'; from Latin *lapis* 'stone' + medieval Latin *lazuli* 'of lapis lazuli', from, ultimately, Persian *lāžward* (source of English *azure*)]

Lapith /láppith/ (*plural* **-iths** *or* **-ithae** /-ith ee/) *n.* in Greek mythology, a member of a people of Thessaly who fought the drunken centaurs at the wedding of their king, Pirithous. The contest of the Lapiths and centaurs was a frequent theme in Greek sculpture and appeared notably in the metope frieze on the Parthenon at Athens. [Early 17thC. Via Latin *Lapithae* 'people of Thessaly', from Greek *Lapithai*.]

lap joint *n.* a joint made by overlapping the ends of two parts or pieces and fastening them together —**lap-jointed** *adj.*

Lapland /láplənd/ region largely within the Arctic Circle, extending across the northern parts of Norway, Sweden, Finland, and the Kola Peninsula of Russia —**Laplander** *n.*

La Plata /laa plaá tə/ city and capital of Buenos Aires Province, eastern Argentina. Population: 520,647 (1991).

lap of honour *n.* an extra lap round a racetrack or running track run by the winner of a race or game to acknowledge the presence and applause of spectators

Lapp /lap/ *n.* (*offensive*) **1.** PEOPLES OFFENSIVE TERM an offensive term for a member of the Sami people of northern Europe **2.** LANG OFFENSIVE TERM a name now considered offensive for the language of the Sami [Late 16thC. From Swedish, of uncertain origin.] —**Lapp** *adj.*

lapped joint *n.* = **lap joint**

lappet /láppit/ *n.* **1.** CLOTHES FOLD OR FLAP ON CLOTHING a loose fold or flap of fabric on a garment **2.** ZOOL LOOSE FLESHY PART a lobe or hanging flap of flesh such as a cow's dewlap or the wattle on a bird's head [15thC. Formed from LAP[1] + -ET.]

lappet moth *n.* a large purplish-brown moth whose furry larvae have flaps along their sides. Latin name: *Gastropacha quercifolia.*

lap pool *n. US* a pool designed for swimming laps, sometimes with a pump to create a current against which to swim

lap robe *n. US, Can* a small rug that wraps round the knees

Lapsang souchong /láp sang sōō shong/ *n.* a large-leafed type of Chinese tea with a smoky flavour

lapse /laps/ *n.* **1.** ERROR a momentary fault or failure in behaviour or morality **2.** GAP IN CONTINUITY a break in the continuity of sth **3.** PERIOD a passage of time **4.** LAW FAILURE TO ACT IN TIME a failure to exercise a right within a specified period of time, e.g. the failure to buy a property before the termination of an option to buy ■ *vi.* (**lapses, lapsing, lapsed**) **1.** GRADUALLY COME TO A STOP to gradually come to an end or stop doing sth **2.** DECLINE to decline in value, quality, or conduct ○ *Their standards have lapsed.* **3.** LOSE SIGNIFICANCE to decline gradually, becoming less important **4.** LAW BECOME VOID to become null and void through disuse, negligence, or death **5.** = **elapse** [14thC. From Latin *lapsus* 'falling, failure', from the past participle stem of *labi* 'to fall, slip' (source of English *collapse*).] —**lapsable** *adj.* —**lapser** *n.* ◇ **lapse from grace** a failure in moral conduct or religious belief

lapse into *vi.* **1.** SLIDE INTO A CONDITION to revert to a previous state, especially of quiet or inactivity **2.** RETURN TO PREVIOUS HABITS to revert to a previous habit or way of life, often an undesirable one

lapsed /lapst/ *adj.* **1.** NO LONGER FAITHFUL TO STH no longer committed to sth, especially religious faith or observance **2.** EXPIRED expired or terminated

lapse rate *n.* the rate at which the temperature of the atmosphere falls as altitude increases

lapstrake /láp strayk/ *adj.* = **clinker-built** ■ *n.* CLINKER-BUILT BOAT a boat built with overlapping planks [Late 18thC. From LAP[2] + STRAKE.]

Laptev Sea /láptef seé/ a section of the Arctic Ocean, situated off the northern coast of Siberian Russia

laptop /láp top/ *n.* a small portable personal computer, especially a battery operated one, usually consisting of a hinged outer case that opens to reveal a screen set in the upper part and a compact keyboard set in the lower part. ◊ **palmtop, notebook**

Laputan /lə pyōōt'n/ *adj.* concentrating on absurdly impractical ideas or projects, often to the exclusion of things that need to be done [Mid-19thC. Formed from *Laputa*, an island in Jonathan Swift's *Gulliver's Travels* where the inhabitants were given to unrealistic, fanciful hopes and plans.]

lapware /láp wair/ *n. US* software for children that includes simple text and animation for telling stories

lapwing /láp wing/ (*plural* **-wings** *or* **-wing**) *n.* a bird in the plover family that has a long crest and spurs and is noted for its shrill cry and erratic flight. Genus: *Vanellus.* [Old English *hleapewince* (altered by folk etymology), literally 'leaping from side to side', from LEAP + an assumed word that is also the ancestor of *wink*]

lar /laar/ (*plural* **lares** /laá reez/) *n.* a protective god or a statue of a protective god in an ancient Roman household [Late 16thC. From Latin.]

LAR *abbr.* Libya (*international vehicle registration*)

Lara /láwrə/, **Brian** (*b.* 1969) Trinidadian cricketer. His score of 375 for the West Indies against England (1994) set the record as the highest ever score in test cricket.

larboard /laárbərd/ *n.* the port or left side of a vessel (*archaic*) [Late 16thC. Alteration of *laddeborde*, literally 'loading side'.]

larceny /laárss'ni/ *n.* the unlawful taking and removal of another person's property (*dated*) [15thC. Via Anglo-Norman, from, ultimately, Latin *latrocinium*, 'theft, robbery', from *latro*, 'thief', from Greek *latron*, 'pay, wages'.] —**larcener** *n.* —**larcenist** *n.* —**larcenous** *adj.* —**larcenously** *adv.*

WORD KEY: SYNONYMS

See Synonyms at ***theft.***

larch /laarch/ (*plural* **larches** *or* **larch**) *n.* **1.** TREE OF PINE FAMILY a deciduous tree of the pine family that has clusters of leaves resembling needles and egg-shaped cones. Genus: *Larix.* **2.** LARCH WOOD the durable wood of the larch tree [Mid-16thC. Via Middle High German *larche*, from, ultimately, Latin *larix*.]

lard /laard/ *n.* WHITE COOKING FAT white, slightly soft, rendered pork used in cooking and baking, and as a base in some ointments and perfumes ■ *v.* (**lards, larding, larded**) **1.** *vti.* ADD LARD TO MEAT BEFORE COOKING to thread strips of fat or fatty bacon through holes made in a lean cut of meat to keep the meat moist while cooking **2.** *vt.* INCLUDE EXTRA WORDS to include an unnecessary or undesirable amount of additional material in a speech or piece of writing [14thC. From French *lard*, 'bacon', from Latin *lar(i)dum*.] —**lardy** *adj.*

larder /laárdər/ *n.* a cool place, especially a small room or large cupboard, used for storing food [13thC. Via Anglo-Norman from , ultimately, Latin *lar(i)dum* 'lard'.]

larder beetle *n.* a small beetle whose larvae eat dried meats, cheese, and other animal products. Genus: *Dermestes.*

larding-needle *n.* a long thick metal needle that grips one end of a strip of fat to allow it to be threaded through lean meat to keep it moist while cooking

lardy cake *n.* a small, sweet, usually square or oblong cake made with yeast dough folded and rolled with lard, fruit, and sugar

Laredo /la reédō/ city in southern Texas, on the border with Mexico. Population: 149,914 (1994).

laree /laári/ *n.* **1.** see table at **currency 2.** COIN WORTH ONE LAREE a coin worth one laree [Late 16thC. From Persian *lārī*, from *Lār*, the name of a town on the Persian Gulf.]

lares plural of **lar**

lares and penates *npl.* **1.** HOUSEHOLD GODS the household deities of the ancient Romans. The lares were believed to protect the household from danger, while the penates were believed to bring wealth. **2.** VALUABLES a family's treasured or valuable possessions (*dated*) [Late 16thC. From Latin.]

large /laarj/ (**larger, largest**) *adj.* **1.** VERY BIG comparatively big in size, number, or quantity, or bigger in size, number, or quantity than is usual or expected **2.** OF TALL HEAVY BUILD tall and well-built, heavy set, broad, or overweight **3.** SPACIOUS occupying a comparatively big space or a bigger space than is usual or expected ○ *a large house* **4.** IMPORTANT significant or general in scope, extent, or effect ○ *a large view of the subject* **5.** GENEROUS generous in spirit or attitude **6.** NAUT FAVOURABLE blowing in a favourable direction ○ *a large wind* **7.** VULGAR coarse or vulgar (*archaic*) [12thC. Via Old French from Latin *larga*, the feminine form of *largus*, 'large, copious'.] —**largeness** *n.* ◇ **at large 1.** as a widely based and general group of people **2.** escaped or free and possibly dangerous ◇ **by and large** speaking generally ◇ **large it, live large** to live or celebrate in an extravagant way (*informal*)

Large Black *n.* a lop-eared black-haired pig bred for pork and bacon

large calorie *n.* = **Calorie**

large copper *n.* a common European butterfly with black and orange markings on its wings. Latin name: *Lycaena dispar.*

large-handed *adj.* very generous or magnanimous —**large-handedness** *n.*

large-hearted *adj.* generous, kind, or understanding —**large-heartedness** *n.*

large intestine *n.* the end section of the alimentary canal reaching from ileum to anus, and consisting of the caecum, colon, and rectum. Its function is to extract water and form faeces.

largely /laárjli/ *adv.* **1.** PRINCIPALLY for the most part or mainly **2.** ON A GRAND SCALE on a big or grand scale

large-minded *adj.* characterized by a liberal attitude —**large-mindedly** *adv.* —**large-mindedness** *n.*

largen /laárjən/ (**largens, largening, largened**) *vt.* to enlarge sth (*literary*)

large-print *adj.* set in type that is bigger than normal for the benefit of partially sighted readers ○ *a large-print book*

larger-than-life *adj.* very confident, impressive, flamboyant, and likely to attract attention (*not hyphenated when used after a verb*)

large-scale *adj.* **1.** BIG AND DETAILED comparatively big in size and showing a lot of detail **2.** EXTENSIVE extensive in scope or scale

large-scale integration *n.* the process of integrating a large number of circuits, often several thousand, on a silicon chip

largesse /laar jéss/, **largess** *n.* **1.** GENEROSITY the generous giving of gifts, money, or favours **2.** GIFTS the gifts, money, or favours given as a result of sb's largesse **3.** LIBERALITY generosity or liberality, especially in spirit or attitude [13thC. Via French, from, ultimately, Latin *largus* (see LARGE).]

Large White *n.* a large white pig kept for meat

larghetto /laar géttō/ *adv.* MODERATELY SLOWLY at a fairly slow tempo, but slightly faster than largo (*used as a musical direction*) ■ *n.* (*plural* **-tos**) MUSIC PIECE OF LARGHETTO MUSIC a larghetto movement or musical piece [Early 18thC. From Italian, literally 'little largo', from *largo* (see LARGO).] —**larghetto** adj.

largish /laárjish/ adj. quite big, rather than enormous

largo /laárgō/ adv. FAIRLY SLOWLY at a fairly slow and broad tempo, more slowly than lento but faster than grave (*used as a musical direction*) ■ n. (*plural* **-gos**) PIECE OF LARGO MUSIC a largo movement or musical piece [Late 17thC. From Italian, literally 'broad'.] —**largo** adj.

lariat /lárri ət/ n. US, Can **1.** = LASSO **2.** ROPE FOR TETHERING AN ANIMAL a tethering rope, especially one used to hold a grazing animal in one place [Mid-19thC. From Spanish *la reata*, 'the rope', from *reatar*, 'to tie again', ultimately from Latin *aptare*, 'to adjust, fit' (source of English *apt*).]

Larissa /lə ríssə/ n. a small inner natural satellite of Neptune, discovered in 1989 by Voyager 2. It is irregular in shape having a maximum dimension of approximately 210 km.

Lark

lark[1] /laark/ n. a small songbird with brownish plumage, found worldwide and noted for its song. Family: Alaudidae. [Old English *laferce*, earlier *læwerce*, ultimately of unknown origin] ◇ **get up** or **rise** or **be up with the lark** to get up very early

lark[2] /laark/ n. **1.** MISCHIEVOUS ADVENTURE adventurous or risky fun **2.** INNOCENT FUN a carefree or harmless piece of fun **3.** AREA OF ACTIVITY an activity, pastime, or job referred to as though it is not being taken very seriously (*informal*) ■ vi. (**larks, larking, larked**) **1.** HAVE FUN to have fun, especially in a boisterous or good-humoured way **2.** ACT MISCHIEVOUSLY to behave in a mischievous, annoying, or irresponsible manner [Early 19thC. Origin uncertain: perhaps an alteration of LAIK 'to play'.] —**larker** n. —**larkiness** n. —**larkish** adj. —**larkishness** n. —**larky** adj.

lark about, **lark around** vi. to have fun in a playful, childish, or irresponsible way

Larkin /laárkin/, **Philip** (1922–85) British poet and novelist. He worked as a librarian at Hull University. His works include *The Whitsun Weddings* (1964) and *High Windows* (1974). Full name **Philip Arthur Larkin**

larkspur /laárk spur/ n. any delphinium plant with spikes of pink, white, or blue flowers. Genus: *Delphinium*. [From the resemblance of the spurred flowers to the unusually long hind claws of the lark]

Larne /laárn/ n. town in County Antrim, Northern Ireland. Population: 30,000 (1995).

La Rochelle /la ro shél/ seaport, tourist centre, and capital of Charente-Maritime Department, Poitou-Charentes region, western France. Population: 71,117 (1990).

Larousse /la roóss/, **Pierre** (1817–75) French lexicographer. He compiled the 15-volume *Grand Dictionnaire universel du XIXe siècle* (1865–76).

larrigan /lárrigən/ n. a knee-high boot with the leg part made of oiled leather, worn especially by lumberjacks, trappers, and woodsmen [Late 19thC. Origin uncertain: perhaps taken from the name of its first maker or wearer.]

larrikin /lárrikin/ n. ANZ **1.** SB UNCONVENTIONAL sb who is unconventional or nonconformist, especially someone in public life **2.** SB MISCHIEVOUS sb who is mischievous (*informal*) **3.** LOUT a hoodlum or lout (*dated informal*) [Mid-19thC. Origin uncertain: perhaps from an Irish pronunciation of *larking*, from LARK[2]; or from the name *Larry*.]

larrup /lárrəp/ vt. (**-rups, -ruping, -ruped**) BEAT SB to beat or flog a person or animal ■ n. THRASHING a blow, especially one delivered with a lot of force [Early 19thC. Origin uncertain.] —**larruper** n.

larum /lárrəm/ n. an alarm (*archaic*) [Mid-16thC. Variant of ALARM.]

larva /laárvə/ (*plural* **-vae** /-vee/) n. **1.** INSECTS IMMATURE INSECT the wingless immature worm-shaped form of many insects that develops into a pupa or chrysalis before becoming an adult insect **2.** ZOOL IMMATURE AMPHIBIAN OR FISH the immature, early-stage form of frogs and other animals that undergo marked changes during metamorphosis [Mid-17thC. From Latin, 'ghost, apparition, mask'.] —**larval** adj.

larvicide /laárvi sīd/ n. a chemical used to kill larvae —**larvicidal** /laárvi sīd'l/ adj.

Larwood /laár wŏŏd/, **Harold** (1904–95) British cricketer. A fast bowler, he was key to the 'bodyline' tactics in the 1932–33 England tour of Australia, which strained Anglo-Australian diplomatic relations.

laryng- prefix. = laryngo- (*used before vowels*)

laryngeal /lə rínjəl, -rínji əl, lárrin jee əl/ adj. **1.** ANAT RELATING TO THE LARYNX belonging to, relating to, situated in, or affecting the larynx **2.** PHON PRODUCED AT THE LARYNX used to describe a speech sound produced in the region of the larynx [Late 18thC. Formed from modern Latin *laryngeus*, from the stem *laryng-* (see LARYNX).] —**laryngeally** adv.

laryngectomy /lárrin jéktəmi/ (*plural* **-mies**) n. the surgical removal of all or part of the larynx

larynges plural of LARYNX

laryngitis /lárrin jítiss/ n. inflammation of the larynx, usually accompanied by hoarseness and coughing —**laryngitic** /lárrin jíttik/ adj.

laryngo- prefix. larynx ◇ *laryngotomy* [Via modern Latin from Greek *larugg-*, the stem of *larugx*]

laryngology /lárring gólləji/ n. a branch of medicine dealing with diseases and conditions of the larynx and vocal cords —**laryngologic** /lə ríng gə lójjik/ adj. —**laryngologically** /-lójjikli/ adv. —**laryngologist** /lárring gólləjist/ n.

laryngopharynx /lə ríng gō fárringks/ (*plural* **-pharynges** /-fə rín jeez/ or **-pharynxes**) n. the part of the throat immediately behind the voice box or larynx, and extending downwards to the top of the gullet or oesophagus

laryngoscope /lə ríng gə skōp/ n. a medical instrument consisting of a short metal or plastic tube fitted with a tiny light bulb, used when examining the larynx. Its commonest use is for viewing the entrance to the larynx when inserting a breathing tube during surgery.

laryngoscopy /lárring góskəpi/ (*plural* **-pies**) n. an examination of the entrance to, or interior of, the larynx, for the purpose of diagnosis or to facilitate the passage of a tube through the larynx —**laryngoscopic** /lə ríng gə skóppik/ adj. —**laryngoscopically** /-skóppikli/ adv. —**laryngoscopist** /lárring góskəpist/ n.

laryngotomy /lárring góttəmi/ (*plural* **-mies**) n. a surgical procedure in which an incision is made in the larynx

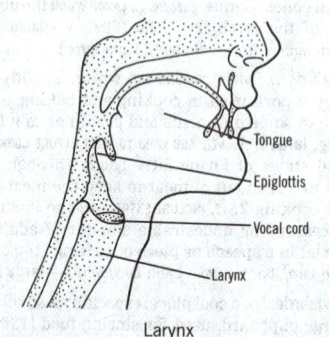

Tongue
Epiglottis
Vocal cord
Larynx

Larynx

larynx /lárringks/ (*plural* **larynges** /lə rín jeez/ or **larynxes**) n. the cartilaginous box-shaped part of the respiratory tract between the level of the root of the

tongue and the top of the trachea. In humans and certain other air-breathing vertebrates it is the organ of voice production, containing the vocal cords. [Late 16thC. Via modern Latin, from Greek *larugx*.]

lasagne /lə zánnyə, -sánn-, -zaán-/ (*plural* **-gnes** or **-gne**), **lasagna** (*plural* **-gnas** or **-gne**) n. **1.** SHEETS OF PASTA thin flat sheets of fresh or dried pasta, which are generally layered with sauces or other ingredients, then baked **2.** PASTA DISH a dish of Italian origin consisting of alternate layers of lasagne and filling, especially alternating pasta, a meat sauce, and a savoury white sauce, baked in the oven. Various fish, poultry, vegetable, or cheese sauces or fillings may also be used. [Mid-19thC. Via Italian, plural of *lasagna*, from, ultimately, Latin *lasanum*, 'cooking vessel'.]

La Salle /lə sál/ industrial city in La Salle County, north-central Illinois, 82 km/51 mi. northeast of Peoria. Population: 9,717 (1990).

lascar /láskər/, **Lascar** n. an Indian or Southeast Asian sailor, army servant, or artilleryman (*dated*) [Early 17thC. From Persian and Urdu *laškarī* 'soldier', from *laškar* 'army, camp'.]

Lascaux /láskō/ site of an underground cave, called Grotte de Lascaux, in southwestern France, that contains outstanding examples of Stone Age art

lascivious /lə sívvi əss/ adj. **1.** LEWD showing a desire for, or unseemly interest in, sex **2.** EROTIC provoking or exciting lust [15thC. From late Latin *lasciviosus*, from, ultimately, Latin *lascivus* 'lustful'.] —**lasciviously** adv. —**lasciviousness** n.

Lasdun /lázdən/, **Sir Denys** (b. 1914) British architect. His works include the National Theatre (1965–76) in London, and the University of East Anglia in Norwich (1962–68).

lase /layz/ (**lases, lasing, lased**) vi. to emit the type of single-wavelength radiation produced by a laser [Mid-20thC. Back-formation from LASER.]

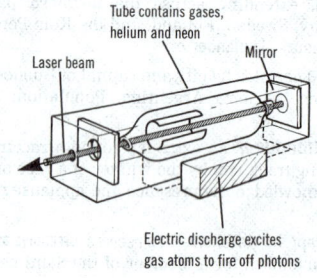

Tube contains gases, helium and neon
Laser beam
Mirror
Electric discharge excites gas atoms to fire off photons

Laser

laser /láyzər/ n. a device that utilizes the ability of certain substances to absorb electromagnetic energy and re-radiate it as a highly focused beam of synchronized single-wavelength radiation [Mid-20thC. Acronym formed from *Light Amplification by Stimulated Emission of Radiation*.]

laser card n. = smart card

laser disk n. = optical disk

laser printer n. a computer printer that uses a focused laser beam to place an image on a photosensitive drum, which uses an electrostatic charge to transfer the image to paper

laser ring gyro n. a navigation system for aircraft that uses measurement of laser light in a closed circuit

laser welding n. the process of using a laser to join tissues together in order to seal up wounds

lash[1] /lash/ n. **1.** STROKE WITH A WHIP a stroke with a whip or some other long flexible object, often one of several given as a punishment **2.** EYELASH an eyelash **3.** MOVEMENT LIKE A WHIP a movement like that of a whip being cracked ◇ *The lion gave a lash of its tail.* **4.** END OF A WHIP the flexible end of a whip **5.** SEVERE SCOLDING a severe reproof or verbal attack ◇ *He felt the full lash of his father's tongue.* **6.** IMPACT OF STH a strong or powerful, often continuous, impact of sth, especially a natural element, against a surface ◇ *the lash of waves onto the beach* ■ v. (**lashes, lashing, lashed**) **1.** vti. SMASH ONTO STH to have a strong or powerful, often continuous, impact on a surface ○ *Heavy seas lashed the shore.* **2.** *vti.* **CRITICIZE SB** to criticize sb or sth severely ○ *She lashed into her critics.* **3.** *vt.* **WHIP SB** to hit sb or sth with a whip or an object like a whip, often repeatedly as a form of punishment ○ *Prisoners were lashed severely.* **4.** *vti.* **FLICK TO AND FRO** to flick sth from side to side sharply so that it moves like a whip, or move in this way ○ *The cat lashed its tail angrily.* **5.** *vt.* **INCITE PEOPLE** to encourage strong emotion such as anger in others, especially in a crowd ○ *The fans had lashed themselves into a fever of enthusiasm.* [14thC. Origin uncertain: possibly an imitation of the sound made by a whip or rope swung through the air.] —**lasher** *n.*

lash out *vi.* **1. SUDDENLY ATTACK VERBALLY** to attack sb or sth verbally and suddenly **2. SUDDENLY ATTACK PHYSICALLY** to start suddenly to attack sb or sth with uncontrolled movements **3. SPEND A LOT OF MONEY** to spend money extravagantly on sth (*informal*)

lash[2] /lash/ **(lashes, lashing, lashed)** *vt.* to tie sth tightly or securely to another object [15thC. Origin uncertain; perhaps from Low German.] —**lasher** *n.*

lashing[1] /láshing/ *n.* **1. FLOGGING** a beating with a whip or sth resembling a whip **2. SEVERE SCOLDING** a severe rebuke or critical attack

lashing[2] /láshing/ *n.* rope, string, or cord used for securing things

lashings /láshingz/ *npl.* generous or plentiful amounts of sth

Lashkar /lásh kaar/ city in Madhya Pradesh, central India

lash-up *n.* sth hastily made or put together, especially in order to meet emergency needs

lasket /láskit/ *n.* a loop on a sail for fastening an extra sail [Early 18thC. Origin uncertain: perhaps an alteration of French *lacet*, 'lacing' (see LATCHET), modelled on GASKET.]

Las Palmas /las pálməss/ city, seaport, and capital of Las Palmas Province, northeastern Gran Canary Island, Spain. Population: 342,030 (1991).

La Spezia /la spétsi ə/ naval base, port city, and capital of La Spezia Province, Liguria Region, northwestern Italy. Population: 103,008 (1990).

lass /lass/ *n.* **1. YOUNG WOMAN** a girl or young woman (*sometimes considered offensive*) **2. GIRLFRIEND** a girlfriend or sweetheart **3.** *N England, Scotland* **WOMAN** a woman of any age [14thC. Origin uncertain: probably related to Old Norse *laskura* 'unmarried'.]

Lassa fever /lássə-/ *n.* an infectious, often fatal, viral disease of West Africa marked by high fever, muscle pain, ulcers of the mucous membranes, headaches, haemorrhaging, and heart and kidney failure [Late 20thC. Named after *Lassa*, Nigerian village where the disease first appeared.]

Lassalle /la sál/, **Ferdinand** (1825–64) German politician. A Socialist, he founded the Universal German Working Men's Association, which later became the Social Democratic party.

Lassen Volcanic National Park /lássən vol kánnik náshənəl paárk/ national park in northeastern California, established in 1907. Its main feature is the volcanic Lassen Peak, 3,187 m/10,457 ft high. Area: 43,049 hectares/106,372 acres.

Lasseter /lássətər/, **Harold Bell** (1880–1931) Australian prospector. His claim that an enormous reef of gold lay in northwestern Australia led to several expeditions to the area. Real name **Lewis Hubert Lasseter**

lassie /lássi/ *n. N England, Scotland* (*informal*) **1. WOMAN** a girl or young woman (*sometimes considered offensive*) **2. GIRLFRIEND** a girlfriend or sweetheart **3. DAUGHTER** a daughter

lassitude /lássi tyood/ *n.* a state of weariness accompanied by listlessness or apathy [15thC. Via French from Latin *lassitudo*, from *lassus* 'weary'.]

lasso /lə soó, la-, lássō/ *n.* (*plural* **-sos**) **ROPE WITH A SLIDING NOOSE** a long stiff piece of rope or cord with a sliding noose at one end, used especially for catching horses and cattle ■ *vt.* **(-sos, -soing, -soed) CAPTURE AN ANIMAL WITH A LASSO** to use a lasso or other length of rope to catch a horse, cow, or other animal [Mid-18thC. From the American English pronunciation of Spanish *lazo*, from Latin *laqueus* 'noose' (source of English *lace*).] —**lassoer** *n.*

last[1] /laast/ CORE MEANING: a grammatical word indicating that sth is the most recent or final of all ○ (adj) *She was married last April.* ○ (adj) *John turned and took a last look at the band.* ○ (adv) *Allow me to apologize for the uncomfortable circumstances under which we last met.* ○ (adv) *He got to the meeting last.* ○ (pron) *Her new album's even better than the last.*

1. *adj., pron.* **MOST RECENT** occurring most recently ○ (adj) *I saw him last Tuesday.* ○ (pron) *This flood may turn out to be even worse than the last.* **2.** *adj., pron.* **AFTER ALL THE OTHERS** being or occurring after all the others ○ (adj) *He is believed to be the last person to see her before she left.* ○ (pron) *Your first complaint may well be your last.* **3.** *adj., pron.* **ONLY REMAINING** the final or only person, thing, or part remaining ○ (adj) *This machine just ate my last pound coin!* ○ (pron) *Here – finish up the last of the cake.* **4.** *adj., pron.* **LEAST SUITABLE** least suitable, appropriate, or likely ○ (adj) *She's the last person we want on this project.* ○ (pron) *I am the last to criticize you in any way.* **5.** *adj.* **RELATING TO THE END** relating to the end of sb's life ○ *The priest performed the last rites.* **6.** *adv.* **MOST RECENTLY** on the most recent occasion ○ *When I last spoke to them they sounded fine.* **7.** *adv.* **AFTER ALL THE OTHERS** after all the others in a series or order **8.** *adv.* **FINALLY** as the final point ○ *Last, I'd like to mention all the people who helped to make this evening a success.* **9.** *n.* **FINAL MOMENT** the final moment, especially of life ○ *She remained cheerful to the last.* **10.** *adj.* **INFERIOR** inferior or unpleasant (*regional*) ○ *This food is last.* [Old English *latost* (adv.) 'after all the others', of prehistoric Germanic origin] ◇ **at last** finally or in the end ○ *I've found you at last – I've been looking everywhere.* ◇ **at long last** eventually, after a long delay or many difficulties ○ *They fought the case for years and at long last got some compensation.* ◇ **breathe your last** to die ○ *I was by her side when she breathed her last.* ◇ **every last** everything without exception ○ *They ate it up, every last piece of it.* ◇ **last but not least** the final thing to be mentioned but important nevertheless ○ *And of course, last but not least, we thank the staff of customer relations.* ◇ **the last of sb** *or* **sth 1.** the last remaining person, thing, or part of sth, or the last in a sequence ○ *That's the last of the bread – I'll get some more tomorrow.* **2.** sb's final contact with or news of sb or sth ○ *You haven't heard the last of this – I'm going to complain.*

WORD KEY: CULTURAL NOTE

The Last of the Mohicans, a novel by US writer James Fenimore Cooper (1826). The most popular of Cooper's evocative accounts of frontier life, it is set in mid-18th-century North America during the wars between Britain and France. It describes the attempts of frontiersman Hawkeye and his Mohican companions, Chingachook and Uncas, the last of their people, to protect a British family from the French and their Huron allies.

last[2] /laast/ **(lasts, lasting, lasted)** *vti.* **1. TO CONTINUE** to continue to exist or happen for a period of time ○ *The festival lasted for three hours.* ○ *The voyage lasted eight days.* **2. BE ABLE TO BE USED** to continue to be used or available for a period of time ○ *The provisions lasted for ten days.* ○ *The fruit lasted us a week.* [Old English *lǣstan* 'to last, follow'. The underlying idea is of following a track.]

last out *vt.* **1. BE SUFFICIENT FOR STH** to be an adequate supply for a particular length of time ○ *I think we've got enough food to last out the week.* **2. REMAIN ALIVE** to survive for a particular length of time ○ *The vet said she didn't think Prince would last out the night.*

last[3] /laast/ *n.* a wooden or metal block shaped like a human foot that a shoemaker or cobbler uses for making and repairing footwear [Old English *lǣste*, from *lāst* 'sole of the foot, footprint', from a prehistoric Germanic verb meaning 'to follow', which is also the ancestor of *last*[2]]

last[4] /laast/ *n.* a unit of measurement that has different values in different contexts including the values of 80 bushels and two tons [Old English *hlæst*, 'load']

last-born *adj.* **YOUNGEST** youngest in a particular family ■ *n.* **YOUNGEST CHILD** the youngest in a particular family

last call *n. US* a bartender's request for last drink orders before closing time (*informal*)

last-ditch *adj.* done or taken when all other options have been exhausted

last-gasp *adj.* done as a last measure when all other options have failed

last-in, first-out *n.* **1.** ACCT **ACCOUNTING METHOD FOR INVENTORIES** a method of accounting in which it is assumed that the most recently purchased items in an inventory are the first to be sold **2.** HR **DISMISSAL OF NEWEST STAFF** the dismissal of staff beginning with those who were employed most recently, used as a way of reducing personnel (*informal*)

lasting /laásting/ *adj.* **PERMANENT** continuing for a very long time or indefinitely ■ *n.* **SHOE MATERIAL** a strong durable twill fabric, mostly used for the uppers of shoes —**lastingly** *adv.* —**lastingness** *n.*

Last Judgment *n.* = **Judgment Day**

lastly /laástli/ *adv.* as the final thing at the end of a series

last minute *n.* the latest time that it is possible to do sth and still be in time —**last-minute** *adj.*

last name *n.* = **surname**

last orders *npl., interj.* the final opportunity to buy drinks before a pub, bar, or other place selling alcohol closes. US term **last call**

last post *n.* **1. SIGNAL FOR THE END OF THE DAY** a bugle call given to signal the end of the day at a British military establishment and the bringing down of the flag at last light **2. BUGLE CALL AT A FUNERAL** a bugle call that is given at a British military funeral

last resort *n.* sth tried or done when everything else has failed

last rites *npl.* **1. ROMAN CATHOLIC CEREMONY FOR SB DYING** in the Roman Catholic Church, religious rites performed for sb who is close to death **2. RELIGIOUS BURIAL RITES** in Christianity, religious rites accompanying a burial or funeral

last straw *n.* a minor annoyance that, because it comes at the end of a series of other misfortunes, turns out to be the thing that makes a situation unbearable [From the fable of the camel whose back was broken by the last straw added to its load]

Last Supper *n.* the last meal that Jesus Christ ate with his disciples before his crucifixion, commemorated by Christians in the Communion ceremony

last thing *adv.* immediately before going to bed for the night

last word *n.* **1. FINAL REMARK IN A DISCUSSION** the final thing to be said, especially at the end of an argument, disagreement, or discussion **2. ULTIMATE DECISION** the final decision on sth **3. BEST** the best of its kind ○ *the last word in convenience*

Las Vegas /laas váygəss/ city in southern Nevada, a centre for tourism and gambling. It is famous for the extravagant neon-lighted resort hotels, casinos, and bars that line its main street, known as 'The Strip'. Population: 327,878 (1994).

lat /lat/ *n.* a latissimus dorsi (*informal*) [Shortening]

lat. *abbr.* latitude

Lat. *abbr.* **1.** Latin **2.** Latvia **3.** Latvian

Latakia /lə táki ə/ city and seaport, capital of Latakia Governorate, northwestern Syria. Population: 303,000 (1994).

latch /lach/ *n.* **1. DEVICE FOR KEEPING DOORS SHUT** a device for holding a door, gate, or other opening closed consisting of a movable or liftable bar that drops into a hole or notch **2. DOOR LOCK** a door lock that needs a key to be opened from the outside but not the inside ■ *vt.* **(latches, latching, latched) LOCK STH WITH A LATCH** to close or lock sth with a latch [Old English *læccan*, 'to grasp, clasp, seize'. Ultimately from an Indo-European word that is also the ancestor of English *lasso*.]

latch on *vi.* to finally grasp sth or understand (*informal*)

latch onto *vt.* **1. REMAIN CONSTANTLY IN SB'S COMPANY** to remain constantly in sb's company even if the person would prefer other company or solitude **2.**

BECOME INTERESTED IN STH to become particularly interested in sth

latchet /láchit/ *n.* a leather thong for tying a shoe or sandal (*archaic*) [14thC. From Old French *lachet*, dialectal variant of *lacet*, literally 'little string', from *laz* 'string' (see LACE).]

latchkey /lách kee/ (*plural* **-keys**) *n.* a key for lifting a latch, especially one on an outside door or gate

latchkey child *n.* a child who returns from school to an empty home because the adults in the family are still at work

latchstring /lách string/ *n.* a string attached to a latch and passed through a hole in a door to allow sb to open it from the other side

late /layt/ *adj.* (**later, latest**) **1.** **AFTER AN EXPECTED TIME** happening or arriving after an expected or arranged time ○ *Hurry up or we'll be late!* **2.** **AFTER THE USUAL TIME** happening or done after the normal or usual time ○ *a late lunch* **3.** **NEAR THE END OF A PERIOD** near the end of a particular period of time ○ *The meeting is scheduled for late morning.* **4.** **INTO THE NIGHT** well into the evening or night ○ *It's late – time for bed.* **5.** **DEAD** having died, especially fairly recently ○ *my late grandfather* **6.** **UP UNTIL RECENTLY** having recently, but no longer, done sth, lived somewhere, or belonged to a group or organization ○ *That reporter, late of the European bureau, is now moving to Southeast Asia.* **7.** **DONE TOWARDS THE END OF A CAREER** produced near the end of sb's career or life ○ *a late Degas* ■ *adv.* (**later, latest**) **1.** **NOT ON TIME** at an expected or arranged time ○ *He arrived late.* **2.** **BEYOND THE USUAL TIME** after the usual or normal time ○ *She had to work late.* **3.** **NEAR THE END OF A PERIOD** towards the end of a period of time ○ *These birds tend to nest late in the year.* **4.** **WELL INTO EVENING** at or until a point well into the evening or night ○ *Their flight is due late on Friday.* **5.** **RECENTLY** relatively recently ○ *She didn't pack her bags until as late as yesterday.* [Old English *lǣt.* Ultimately from an Indo-European word meaning 'to let go', which is also the ancestor of English *let, liege,* and *lassitude.*] —**lateness** *n.* ◇ **of late** recently

late blight *n.* a disease of potatoes, caused by a fungus, in which both tubers and foliage decay

latecomer /láyt kummər/ *n.* **1.** **SB ARRIVING LATE** sb who arrives late for an event **2.** **RECENT CONVERT** sb who has participated in or started appreciating sth only recently

late developer *n.* a child whose potential in some or all aspects of school work develops later than is the case for the majority of his or her contemporaries

lateen /lə teen/ *adj.* used to describe a triangular sail hung on a yard attached to a small mast, or a ship with such a sail [Mid-16thC. From French (*voile*) *latine*, literally 'Latin (sail)', ultimately from Latin *latinus*, so called because it was used in the Mediterranean.]

lateen-rigged *adj.* using a lateen sail

late Greek *n.* the form of the Greek language used from around the 3rd to the 9th centuries AD

late Hebrew *n.* the form of the Hebrew language used from around the 12th to the 18th centuries AD

late Latin *n.* the written form of Latin used from around the 3rd to the 7th centuries AD

lately /láytli/ *adv.* within the last few days or weeks or not too long ago

laten /láyt'n/ (**-ens, -ening, -ened**) *vti.* to grow late, or make sth late

latency /láyt'nssi/ *n.* **1.** **STATE OF BEING LATENT** the state or condition of being latent **2.** **TIME TAKEN TO CROSS NETWORK** the time it takes for a data packet to move across a network connection. Latency and bandwidth are two factors that determine the speed of a network connection.

latency period *n.* = latent period

La Tène /la tén/ *adj.* ARCHAEOL relating to an Iron-Age culture that flourished in Europe from the fifth to the first century BC [Late 19thC. Named after *La Tène*, the district in Switzerland where the remains were first found.]

latent /láyt'nt/ *adj.* **1.** **HIDDEN** present or existing, but in an underdeveloped or unexpressed form **2.** BIOL **DORMANT** dormant or undeveloped but able to develop normally under suitable conditions **3.** PSYCHOANAL **PRESENT BUT UNEXPRESSED** present in the unconscious but not consciously expressed [Early 17thC. From Latin *latent-*, present participle stem of *latere*, 'to be hidden'.]

latent content *n.* the content of a dream that is hidden or repressed, and is represented in symbols

latent heat *n.* the heat that is absorbed or emitted when a substance undergoes a physical phase change but that does not make the substance change temperature. Symbol *L*

latent image *n.* the invisible image recorded on light-sensitive materials such as photographic film or paper but not yet developed

latent learning *n.* learning that is not apparent when it occurs, but that can be inferred later from improved performance

latent period *n.* **1.** PHYSIOL **TIME BETWEEN STIMULUS AND RESPONSE** the interval between the application of a stimulus and the start of a response **2.** MED **DISEASE INCUBATION PERIOD** the incubation period of a disease **3.** PSYCHOANAL **THEORETICAL CHILDHOOD DEVELOPMENTAL STAGE** in Freudian theory, a period between five or six years of age and adolescence when sexual interest is suppressed

latent print *n.* a fingerprint that is left at a crime scene and remains invisible until chemically treated

latent time *n.* PHYSIOL = latent period *n.* 1

later /láytər/ comparative of **late** ■ *adv.* **AFTER** after a particular period of time, the present time, or the time being discussed ■ *interj.* **SEE YOU LATER** used to say goodbye (*informal*)

lateral /láttərəl/ *adj.* **1.** **AT THE SIDE** belonging to, relating to, located at, or affecting the side **2.** **SIDEWAYS IN A CAREER, RATHER THAN UP** involving transfer to a different position in an organization or career, but without greater status or advancement **3.** **RELATING TO LATERAL THINKING** involving or relating to the use of lateral thinking **4.** PHON **PRODUCED WITH AN INCOMPLETE OBSTRUCTION OF AIR** produced with the tip of the tongue touching the alveolar ridge so that air moves around the outside of one or both sides of the tongue. The only lateral sound in English is /l/. ■ *n.* **1.** **PART AT THE SIDE** a part, appendage, movement, or object at the side of sth **2.** PHON **LATERAL SPEECH SOUND** a lateral speech sound such as /l/ in English [15thC. From Latin *lateralis*, from *later-*, stem of *latus* 'side'.] —**laterally** *adv.*

lateral bud *n.* a bud that develops in the angle between a leaf and a stem

lateralization /láttərə līZ záysh'n/, **lateralisation** *n.* the localization of the control centre for a particular function, e.g. speech, on the right or left side of the brain

lateral line *n.* a line of sensory pores along the head and sides of fish and some amphibians that detect pressure, current variations, and vibrations

lateral thinking *n.* a way of solving problems by unconventional or apparently illogical means rather than using a traditionally logical approach

laterite /láttə rīt/ *n.* a reddish mixture of clayey iron and aluminium oxides and hydroxides formed by the weathering of basalt under humid, tropical conditions. There are extensive deposits in India. [Early 19thC. Coined from Latin *later* 'brick' + -ITE.] —**lateritic** /láttə ríttik/ *adj.*

latest /láytist/ superlative of **late** ■ *adj.* **NEWEST** newest, most recent, or most up-to-date **2.** **MOST UP-TO-DATE VERSION** the newest, most recent, or most up-to-date news, fashion, or version of sth (*informal*)

late tackle *n.* in a game such as football, a foul resulting from an attempt to tackle an opposing player after the ball has been passed. This can be a bookable offence, especially if the player making the tackle comes into physical contact with the player who had possession of the ball.

latex /láy teks/ (*plural* **-texes** *or* **-tices** /láyti seez/) *n.* **1.** **PLANT SAP** a milky white liquid produced by some plants such as the rubber tree, whose sap is used to make rubber **2.** **MIXTURE OF PLASTIC PARTICLES IN WATER** a suspension of rubber or plastic (**polymer**) particles in water, used to make emulsion paints, adhesives, and other products [Mid-17thC. From Latin, 'liquid, watery fluid'.]

lath /laath, lath/ *n.* **1.** **THIN WOODEN STRIP USED IN A FRAMEWORK** one of the thin strips of wood used to form a framework to support plaster, tiles, or slates **2.** **SHEET OR WIRE SUPPORT FOR PLASTERING** a sheet of metal or a framework of wire mesh used as a support for plasterwork **3.** **THIN STRIP OF WOOD** a thin strip of wood, especially one used in the building trades ■ *vt.* (**laths, lathing, lathed**) **ATTACH LATHS TO A SURFACE** to attach or nail laths to a surface before plastering, tiling, or fixing slates [Old English *lætt*, of prehistoric Germanic origin]

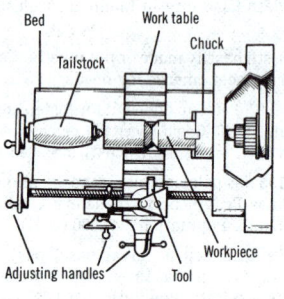

Lathe

lathe[1] /layth/ *n.* **TURNING TOOL** a machine for working wood or metal, in which the piece being worked is held and rotated while a cutting tool is applied to it ■ *vt.* (**lathes, lathing, lathed**) **SHAPE STH WITH A LATHE** to shape wood or metal using a lathe [14thC. Origin uncertain: probably from Old Danish *lad*, 'framework for supporting work'.]

lathe[2] /layth/ *n.* a former administrative division of the English county of Kent [Old English *læth*, from a prehistoric Germanic word meaning 'land']

lather /laáthər, láthər/ *n.* **1.** **SOAPY FROTH** foam that is produced by soap or detergent used with water **2.** **SWEATY FROTH** white foam produced during periods of extremely heavy sweating, especially by horses **3.** **AGITATED STATE** a state of agitation or nervous anxiety (*informal*) ■ *v.* (**-ers, -ering, -ered**) **1.** *vti.* **PRODUCE LATHER** to produce a lather using a soap or detergent **2.** *vt.* **COAT WITH LATHER** to coat sth with lather [Old English *læþor*. Ultimately from an Indo-European word meaning 'to wash', which is also the ancestor of English *lotion, latrine,* and *deluge*.] —**lathery** *adj.*

lathy /láythi/ *adj.* tall and skinny (*regional*) [Late 17thC. Literally 'like a lath'; formed from LATH.]

lathyrism /láthirizəm/ *n.* a neurological disease of humans and domestic animals, caused by eating certain legumes and characterized by lack of strength or in inability to move the legs. The legumes responsible for the disease are of the genus *Lathyrus*. [Late 19thC. Formed from modern Latin *Lathyrus*, genus name, from Greek *lathuros*, a species of vetch.]

latices plural of **latex**

laticifer /la tíssifər/ *n.* a duct that produces latex in some plants [Early 20thC. Formed from *latici-*, the stem of *latex*, 'liquid, watery fluid'.] —**laticiferous** /látti síffərəss/ *adj.*

latifundium /látti fúndi əm/ (*plural* **-a** /-ə/) *n.* in ancient Rome, an agricultural estate, especially one that was worked by enslaved labourers [Mid-17thC. From Latin, from *latus* 'broad' + *fundus* 'landed estate'.]

Latin /láttin/ *n.* **1.** LANG ANCIENT ROMAN LANGUAGE the extinct Indo-European language of ancient Rome and its empire, also adopted across medieval Europe as the language of education, government, law, the Church, the aristocracy, and cultured society. The Romance languages developed from Vulgar Latin, and its prominence during medieval times led to Latin-derived words entering the vocabularies of other European languages. **2.** PEOPLES SB FROM ANCIENT LATIUM sb who was born or lived in ancient Latium in western central Italy **3.** PEOPLES SB SPEAKING A ROMANCE LANGUAGE sb who speaks any of the languages derived from Latin, especially sb living in Latin America or southern Europe ■ *adj.* **1.** LANG OF THE LATIN LANGUAGE relating to the Latin language **2.** PEOPLES RELATING TO PEOPLE SPEAKING ROMANCE LANGUAGES relating to any of the peoples using languages derived from Latin, especially those people living in Latin America or in southern Europe **3.** CHR RELATING TO THE ROMAN CATHOLIC CHURCH belonging or relating to the Roman Catholic Church **4.** LANG WRITTEN IN THE ROMAN ALPHABET written in or relating to the Roman alphabet [Pre-12thC. From Latin *Latinus* 'of the people of Latium, Roman', from *Latium*, an ancient region of western central Italy.]

Latina /la teénə/ *n.* US a woman or girl of Latin American descent who was born in or is a citizen of the United States [Mid-20thC. From American Spanish, feminine of *Latino* (see LATINO).]

Latin alphabet *n.* = Roman alphabet

Latin America 1. the entire western hemisphere south of the United States **2.** those countries of the Americas that developed from the colonies of Spain, Portugal, and France

Latin American *adj.* relating to any of the countries of Latin America, or their peoples or cultures

Latin American *n.* **1.** SB FROM LATIN AMERICA sb who was born in or is a citizen of any of the countries of Latin America **2.** LATIN-AMERICAN LIVING IN US sb of Latin-American descent who was born in or is a citizen of the United States

Latinate /látti nayt/ *adj.* derived from, relating to, or characteristic of Latin

Latin Church *n.* = Roman Catholic Church

Latin cross *n.* an upright cross in which the lowest limb is longer than the other three, often associated with Christianity

Latinise *vt.* = Latinize

Latinism /láttinizəm/ *n.* a word or phrase e.g. 'ipso facto', that has been borrowed from Latin

Latinist /láttinist/ *n.* sb who is an expert in or student of the Latin language

Latinity /lə tínnəti/ *n.* a style or level of expertise in using Latin

Latinize /látti nīz/ (**-izes, -izing, -ized**), **Latinise** (**-ise, -ising, -ised**) *vt.* **1.** LANG TRANSLATE STH INTO LATIN to translate sth into Latin, or give a Latin form to sth such as a name **2.** LANG TRANSCRIBE STH INTO THE ROMAN ALPHABET to transcribe words into the Roman alphabet from another alphabet **3.** CHR MAKE STH LIKE THE ROMAN CATHOLIC CHURCH to adopt the practices of, or make practices more like those of, the Roman Catholic Church **4.** HIST MAKE PEOPLE MORE ROMAN to make people adapt to Roman customs and styles —**Latinization** /látti nī záysh'n/ *n.* —**Latinizer** /látti nīzər/ *n.*

Latin-Jazz *n.* a form of jazz music that is a mixture of both Afro-Cuban music and Fusion

Latino /la teénō/ (*plural* **-nos**) *n.* US **1.** SB FROM LATIN AMERICA sb who was born in or is a citizen of any of the countries of Latin America **2.** LATIN-AMERICAN LIVING IN US sb of Latin-American descent who was born in or is a citizen of the United States [Mid-20thC. From American Spanish, (perhaps via a shortening of *latino-americano*), from Spanish, 'Latin, a Latin', from Latin *Latinus* (see LATIN).]

Latin Quarter area in central Paris on the Left Bank of the River Seine, noted for educational and cultural pursuits

latish /láytish/ *adj.* FAIRLY LATE fairly late, or later than is desirable or expected ○ *a latish supper* ■ *adv.* AT

A FAIRLY LATE TIME at a fairly late time, or later than is desirable or expected ○ *They arrived latish.*

latissimus dorsi /la tíssiməss dáwr sī/ (*plural* **latissimi dorsi**) *n.* either of the two broad triangular muscles along the sides of the back [Shortening of modern Latin *musculus latissimus dorsi*, literally 'broadest muscle of the back']

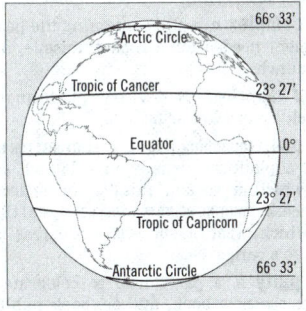

Latitude

latitude /látti tyood/ *n.* **1.** GEOG IMAGINARY LINE AROUND THE EARTH an imaginary line joining points on the Earth's surface that are all of equal distance north or south of the equator. ◊ **longitude 2.** GEOG AREA OF THE EARTH'S SURFACE a region of the Earth's surface near a particular latitude (*often plural*) ○ *snow showers in the northerly latitudes.* ◊ **longitude 3.** ROOM TO MANOEUVRE enough scope or leeway for some freedom of choice, action, or thinking ○ *It's a very creative job, allowing me a great deal of latitude.* **4.** PHOTOGRAPHY DEGREE OF TOLERANCE OF EXPOSURE ERROR the degree of over- or underexposure that light-sensitive material can accommodate and still provide an acceptable image [14thC. From Latin *latitudo*, 'breadth, width', from *latus* 'broad'.] —**latitudinal** /látti tyoódin'l/ *adj.* —**latitudinally** *adv.*

latitudinarian /látti tyoodi náiri ən/ *adj.* **1.** TOLERANT allowing some freedom in attitude, beliefs, behaviour, or interpretation, especially in religious matters **2.** HIST RELATING TO A 17C CHURCH MOVEMENT relating to a movement in the Church of England in the 17th century that accepted the authority of bishops but denied that this was divine in origin. The movement placed emphasis on reason and individual judgment rather than divine authority. ■ *n.* SB TOLERANT sb who believes in or advocates a latitudinarian approach, especially in religious matters [Mid-17thC. Formed from Latin *latitudin-*, stem of *latitudo* (see LATITUDE).]

latke /látkə/ *n.* a fried flat cake of grated potato made by moistening finely grated potato with beaten egg and frying it until golden brown on both sides. It is an Eastern European and particularly a Jewish speciality, traditionally served sprinkled with sugar, or as a savoury with a little grated onion added. [Early 20thC. From Yiddish, from, ultimately, Russian *latka*, 'earthenware cooking vessel, sth cooked in a latka'.]

Latona /lə tőnə/ *n.* MYTHOL in Roman mythology, the mother of Apollo and Diana by Jupiter. Greek equivalent **Leto**

latosol /láttə sol/ *n.* a soil variety that is common in tropical or subtropical regions and is rich in iron and aluminium [Mid-20thC. Coined from LATERITE + -SOL.]

latrine /lə treén/ *n.* a toilet, especially a communal one on a military base [13thC. From Latin *latrina*, contraction of *lavatrina* (see LAVATORY).]

-latry *suffix.* worship ○ *iconolatry* [From Greek *latreia* 'service, worship']

latte /láttay/ *n.* an espresso coffee with frothy steamed milk

latter /láttər/ *n.* SECOND OF TWO the second of two people or things that have been mentioned, or that are being considered or referred to ○ *She went out with Joe and Sam, eventually marrying the latter.* ◊ **former** ■ *adj.* **1.** CLOSING near the end of sth, or nearer to the end than the beginning ○ *spent the latter part of the day relaxing by the pool* **2.** LATER more recent or more advanced in time ○ *In his latter years he became*

very forgetful. [Old English *lætra* (adjective) and *lator* (adverb), comparatives of *læt*, an earlier form of LATE]

latter-day *adj.* resembling a particular person or type of person from the past ○ *thought of himself as a latter-day Roosevelt*

Latter-day Saint *n.* a member of the Church of Jesus Christ of Latter-day Saints, founded by Joseph Smith in 1830 in the United States and centred in Salt Lake City, Utah

latterly /láttərli/ *adv.* recently, or in the most recent period ○ *He was quite ill for a while, but latterly seems to have returned to normal.*

lattice /láttiss/ *n.* **1.** CRISS-CROSS FRAMEWORK an interwoven open-mesh frame made by criss-crossing strips of wood, metal, or plastic to form a pattern **2.** STH MADE FROM LATTICE sth such as a door, gate, or fence that is made from or consists of a lattice **3.** INTERWOVEN FORM a representation of a lattice framework, especially a heraldic one **4.** ARRANGEMENT OF POINTS a regular geometrical arrangement of points or objects, e.g. the atoms in a crystal ■ *vti.* (**-tices, -ticing, -ticed**) PROVIDE A LATTICE to make, decorate sth with, or provide a lattice [14thC. From Old French *lattis*, from *latte* 'lath', from a prehistoric Germanic word.]

latticework /láttiss wurk/ *n.* = **lattice** *n.* 1

Latvia

Latvia /látvi ə/ republic bordering the Baltic Sea in northeastern Europe. It is one of the Baltic States. Language: Latvian. Currency: lat. Capital: Riga. Population: 2,421,163 (1997). Area: 63,700 sq. km/24,600 sq. mi. Official name **Republic of Latvia**

Latvian /látvi ən/ *n.* **1.** PEOPLES SB FROM LATVIA sb who was born or brought up in, or who is a citizen of Latvia **2.** LANG OFFICIAL LANGUAGE OF LATVIA the official language of Latvia, also spoken in western parts of European Russia, belonging to the Balto-Slavonic branch of Indo-European languages. Latvian is spoken by about two million people. —**Latvian** *adj.*

laud /lawd/ *vt.* (**lauds, lauding, lauded**) PRAISE SB to glorify sb or praise sb highly ■ *n.* **1.** GREAT PRAISE high praise, acclaim, or glorification (*formal*) **2.** MUSIC SONG OF PRAISE a hymn of praise or glorification **3.** CHR MORNING PRAYER the first prayer of the day in some Christian churches, especially the Roman Catholic Church (*often used in the plural*) [14thC. From Old French *laude*, from Latin *laud-*, the stem of *laus*, 'praise'.] —**lauder** *n.*

Laud /lawd/, **William, Archbishop of Canterbury** (1573–1645) English clergyman. A close advisor to Charles I, he forwarded the king's desire to impose absolute monarchy in opposition to his Puritan Parliament and provoked the Bishops' War in Scotland (1639) by introducing the Anglican liturgy. He was impeached for treason and executed.

Lauda /lówdə/, **Niki** (*b.* 1949) Austrian racing car driver. He became Grand Prix world champion in 1975, 1977, and 1984, despite a near-fatal crash in 1976. Full name **Nikolas Andreas Lauda**

laudable /láwdəb'l/ *adj.* admirable and worthy of praise —**laudability** /láwdə bílləti/ *n.* —**laudableness** /láwdəb'lnəss/ *n.* —**laudably** /láwdəbli/ *adv.*

laudanum /láwd'nəm/ *n.* a solution of opium in alcohol, formerly used to treat pain [Mid-16thC. Origin uncertain: perhaps from Latin *ladanum*, 'juice of a shrub'.]

laudation /law dáysh'n/ *n.* great praise and acclaim, often in the form of a eulogy (*formal*)

laudatory /láwdətəri/, **laudative** /-tiv/ *adj.* expressing praise or admiration

laugh /laaf/ v. (laughs, laughing, laughed) 1. *vti.* MAKE SOUNDS EXPRESSING AMUSEMENT to make sounds from the throat while breathing out in short bursts or gasps as a way of expressing amusement 2. *vt.* BRING TO PARTICULAR STATE BY LAUGHING to cause sb or yourself to be in a particular state by laughing long and hard ○ *We both laughed ourselves silly.* 3. *vi.* MOCK to mock sb or sth 4. *vi.* SHOW CONTEMPT to express amusement, contempt, or disrespect for sth ○ *laugh in the face of adversity* 5. *vi.* ZOOL MAKE A NOISE LIKE LAUGHTER to make a noise that sounds like sb laughing (*refers to some birds and mammals*) ■ *n.* 1. SOUND MADE WHEN LAUGHING a series of sounds made when sb laughs 2. STH FUNNY OR ENJOYABLE a time of great fun and enjoyment, or sth that gives fun and enjoyment (*informal*) ○ *had a real laugh with Bob and Patty* 3. STH FUNNY sb who is funny or entertaining ○ *You'll like him; he's a good laugh.* [Old English *hlæhhan*] —**laugher** *n.* ◇ **have the last laugh** to be proved right or successful after being treated with disbelief, lack of confidence, or scorn **laugh down** *vt.* to reject sth with contemptuous laughter ○ *The entire committee laughed down the new design.*

laugh off *vt.* to trivialize or treat as amusing sth serious or important ○ *Later we laughed the incident off as just a silly mistake.*

laughable /laafəb'l/ *adj.* so inadequate as to cause laughter or ridicule —**laughably** *adv.*

laughing gas *n.* = nitrous oxide (*informal*)

laughing jackass *n.* = kookaburra (*dated*)

laughingly /laafingli/ *adv.* 1. BY LAUGHING with laughter that shows amusement or contempt at sth or sb funny or ridiculous ○ *She laughingly dismissed the idea and changed the subject.* 2. IN AN AMUSINGLY INAPPROPRIATE WAY in a form of words that is amusingly or contemptibly inappropriate ○ *what the brochure laughingly calls 'spacious accommodation'*

laughing stock *n.* sb whose behaviour has made him or her an object of ridicule or fun

laughter /laaftər/ *n.* 1. ACT OF LAUGHING the sound or an act of laughing 2. HAPPINESS EXPRESSED BY LAUGHING happiness or fun expressed by laughing [Old English *hleahtor*]

laugh track *n.* recorded laughter added to the soundtrack of a radio or television programme

launce /lawnss/ *n.* = sand eel [Early 17thC. A variant of LANCE, from its slender shape.]

Launceston /lawn stən/ historic town in Cornwall, southwestern England. Population: 6,800 (1994). ■ city and port in northern Tasmania, Australia, situated where the North Esk and South Esk rivers join to form the River Tamar. Population: 67,701 (1996).

launch[1] /lawnch/ *vt.* (launches, launching, launched) 1. SPACE TECH, MIL FIRE A ROCKET INTO THE AIR to send a rocket, missile, or spacecraft into the air or the upper atmosphere 2. NAUT PUT A CRAFT TO SEA to push or put a vessel into the water so that it is ready to sail 3. NAUT LAUNCH A SHIP FOR THE FIRST TIME to send a newly built vessel into the water for the first time, usually with a special ceremony 4. BEGIN A CAMPAIGN to begin an attack, campaign, investigation, or other carefully planned activity ○ *The police have launched an investigation.* 5. MARKETING PUT A PRODUCT ON SALE to put a new product on sale to the public and begin promoting it 6. THROW STH WITH GREAT FORCE to throw or propel sth, especially forcefully ■ *n.* 1. MARKETING START FOR A NEW PRODUCT an occasion such as a party at which a new product is launched ○ *the launch of her new book* 2. SPACE TECH, MIL TIME WHEN A ROCKET IS LAUNCHED the occasion when a rocket, missile, or spacecraft is launched 3. NAUT TIME WHEN A SHIP IS LAUNCHED the occasion when a boat or ship is launched, especially for the first time 4. START OF A CAMPAIGN the start of sth, especially a carefully planned activity such as a military offensive, an investigation, or a campaign [14thC. From Anglo-Norman *launcher*, a variant of Old French *lancier*, 'to wound with a lance, pierce', from *lance* (see LANCE).]

launch into *vt.* to begin a particular activity suddenly and enthusiastically ○ *The professor launched into yet another of his theories about how dinosaurs became extinct.*

launch out 1. START AFRESH to start doing sth new or

untried 2. BE EXTRAVAGANT to spend money extravagantly (*informal*)

launch[2] /lawnch/ *n.* 1. LARGE MOTORBOAT a large powerful motorboat 2. SMALL MOTORBOAT ON A LARGE SHIP a small motorboat carried on a large ship 3. LARGEST BOAT ON AN OLD WARSHIP the largest boat formerly carried by a man-of-war [Late 17thC. From Spanish *lancha*, 'pinnace', perhaps of Malay origin.]

launch complex *n.* a site containing the people and equipment needed for a rocket, missile, or spacecraft launch

launcher /lawnchər/ *n.* a device or platform for firing sth such as a rocket or missile

launch pad, **launching pad** *n.* 1. PLATFORM FOR LAUNCHING ROCKETS a platform, usually in a launch complex, from which a rocket, missile, or spacecraft is launched 2. STARTING POINT FOR SUCCESS a starting point from which great or successful progress is made, e.g. in sb's career

launch party *n.* a party held to celebrate and to introduce a new book, author, book publisher or retailer

launch shoe *n.* a device on an aircraft used for launching a missile

launch vehicle *n.* a rocket that is used to launch a spacecraft or satellite into space

launch window *n.* the restricted period during which a rocket or other projectile can be successfully launched

launder /lawndər/ *v.* (-ders, -dering, -dered) 1. *vt.* WASH AND IRON STH to wash dirty clothes or linen and, often, iron them as well 2. *vi.* BE WASHABLE to be able to be washed ○ *It's a beautiful fabric, but I doubt that it would launder well.* 3. *vt.* FIN MAKE MONEY APPEAR LEGAL to pass illegally acquired money through a legitimate business or bank account in order to disguise its illegal origins ■ *n.* MINING TROUGH USED FOR WASHING ORE a trough for washing ore [Late 16thC. From *launder* 'sb who washes linen', contraction of *lavender*, ultimately from Latin *lavare*, 'to wash' (see LAVATORY).] —**launderer** *n.*

launderette /lawndə rét, -drét/, **laundrette** *n.* UK a laundry, usually self-service, containing coin-operated washing and drying machines [Mid-20thC. Coined from LAUNDER + -ETTE.]

laundress /lawndrəss/ *n.* a woman who does washing and ironing, especially one who does other people's washing and ironing as a way of earning a living (*dated*) [Mid-16thC. Formed from *launder* 'sb who washes linen' (see LAUNDER).]

Laundromat /lawndrə mat/ *US, Can, Aus* a service mark for a self-service coin-operated commercial laundry

laundry /lawndri/ (*plural* -dries) *n.* 1. DIRTY WASHING dirty clothes or linen put aside to be washed and ironed 2. CLEAN WASHING freshly washed clothes or linen 3. WASHING AND IRONING PLACE a place, especially a commercial establishment or a communal room in a building, where clothes and linen can be washed and ironed [Early 16thC. Shortening of obsolete *lavendry*, ultimately from Latin *lavare*, 'to wash' (see LAVATORY).]

laundry list *n.* a lengthy list of items, usually things wanted or needed

Launfal /lawnfəl/ *n.* in the legend of King Arthur, one of the knights at the court

Laurasia /law ráyzi ə, -ráyshə/ the northern part of the ancient continent of Pangaea, a hypothetical ancient landmass that included what would become North America, Greenland, northern and central Europe, and most of Asia

laureate /láwri ət, lórr-/ *n.* 1. AWARD WINNER sb who has been awarded a prize or is recognized for outstanding achievement in the arts or sciences 2. = poet laureate ■ *adj.* 1. CROWNED WITH LAUREL crowned with laurel as a sign of honour (*literary*) 2. MADE OF LAUREL made of laurel leaves or branches [14thC. From Latin *laureatus*, from *laurea* 'laurel tree' from, ultimately, *laurus* (see LAUREL).] —**laureateship** *n.*

laurel /lórrəl/ *n.* 1. PLANTS MEDITERRANEAN EVERGREEN TREE a small evergreen tree that grows in southern Europe and has glossy aromatic leaves and dark purple or black berries. Latin name: *Laurus nobilis.* 2. PLANTS TREE OR SHRUB RESEMBLING LAUREL any tree or shrub whose

leaves, aroma, or berries are similar to those of the laurel, e.g. the mountain laurel and cherry laurel 3. HIST WREATH OF LEAVES the leaves of the laurel woven into a wreath and used as a mark of honour or victory in ancient times, e.g. to crown the winners of athletic events ■ **laurels** *npl.* HONOUR FOR ACHIEVEMENT honour won for an achievement ■ *vt.* (-rels, -relling, -relled) 1. CROWN WITH LAUREL to crown sb with laurel as a sign of honour (*literary*) 2. GIVE SB AWARD to honour sb with an award or prize [14thC. Via Old French *lorier* from Latin *laureola* 'small laurel branch', from *laurus* 'laurel tree'.] ◇ **look to your laurels** to watch out that you do not lose a successful or winning position because of a better performance by sb else ◇ **rest on your laurels** to be satisfied with your success and do nothing to improve on it

Laurel and Hardy

Laurel /lórrəl/, **Stan** (1890–1965) British-born US comedian. His partnership with Oliver Hardy was the first Hollywood film comedy duo. Laurel was the 'thin one' whose clumsiness was always getting them into trouble. Real name **Arthur Stanley Laurel Jefferson**

Laurentian Mountains /lo rénsh'n-/ range that runs north of the St Lawrence River in southern Quebec Province, Canada. Height: 1,190 m/3,905 ft.

lauric acid /láwrik-, lórrik-/ *n.* a crystalline fatty acid found mainly in coconut and laurel oils and used in making soaps, insecticides, cosmetics, and lauryl alcohol. Formula: $C_{12}H_{34}O_2$. [Late 19thC. *Lauric* formed from modern Latin *Laurus*, genus name, from Latin, 'laurel'.]

lauryl alcohol /láwrəl-, lórrəl-/ *n.* a crystalline solid that is insoluble in water and is used to make detergents. Formula: $C_{12}H_{27}O$. [Early 20thC. Coined from a shortening of *lauric* (see LAURIC ACID) + -YL.]

Lausanne /low zán/ capital of Vaud Canton, western Switzerland, on Lake Geneva. Population: 123,266 (1994).

LAUTRO /láw trō/, **Lautro** *abbr.* Life Assurance and Unit Trust Regulatory Organization

lav /lav/ *n.* a toilet (*informal*) [Early 20thC. Shortening of LAVATORY.]

lava /laavə/ *n.* 1. MOLTEN ROCK FLOWING FROM A VOLCANO molten rock that flows from a volcano or from a fissure on land or on the ocean floor. The molten rock originates in the Earth's mantle. 2. ROCK FULL OF SMALL AIR HOLES rock formed by the rapid cooling and hardening of lava. It usually has many small air holes caused by escaping volcanic gases. [Mid-18thC. Italian from Neapolitan dialect, of unknown origin.]

lavabo /lə vaabō, lə váy-/ (*plural* -boes) *n.* 1. lavabo, **Lavabo** CHR RELIGIOUS RITUAL a priest's ritual washing of the hands and reciting from the Psalms during the Communion service in some Christian churches 2. BASIN ATTACHED TO A WALL a basin with a water tank above attached to a wall, often used as a planter 3. WASHBASIN a washbasin or washstand 4. PLACE FOR WASHING IN A MONASTERY a place for washing in a monastery [Mid-18thC. From Latin, 'I will wash', a form of *lavare* (see LAVATORY).]

lavage /lávvij, la vaazh/ *n.* the washing out of a hollow body organ, e.g. the stomach, using a slow flow of water [Late 18thC. Formed from French *laver* 'to wash'.]

Laval /lə vaal/ 1. city in Île-Jésus County, southern Quebec, Canada, situated on Île-Jésus just north of Montreal. Population: 330,393 (1996). 2. capital of Mayenne Department, western France, situated 250 km/160 mi. southwest of Paris. Population: 50,473 (1990).

Laval /lə vál/, **Pierre** (1883–1945) French statesman. Three times prime minister of France (1931–32, 1936, 1942–44), he served as Pétain's deputy during the Vichy government, and was executed as a Nazi collaborator.

lava-lava /láavə láavə/ n. a rectangular piece of printed cotton worn wrapped around the waist by the people of Samoa and other parts of Polynesia [Late 19thC. From Samoan.]

lavaliere /lə válli áir/ n. a pendant on a chain worn around the neck [Late 19thC. Named after Louise de *la Valière*, lover of Louis XIV, with whose reign certain fashions were associated.]

lavatera /lávvə teérə, lə váttərə/ (*plural* -ras *or* -ra) n. a plant or shrub such as the tree mallow with pink, white, or purple flowers that is native to Europe but naturalized in California. Genus: *Lavatera*. [Mid-18thC. From modern Latin, genus name, named after the brothers *Lavater*, 17th and 18thC Swiss doctors and naturalists.]

lavation /lə váysh'n/ n. washing or cleansing (*formal*) [15thC. Formed from Latin *lavare* 'to wash' (source of English *lotion*, *dilute*, and *deluge*).]

lavatorial /lávvə táwri əl/ adj. **1.** CONTAINING REFERENCES TO EXCRETION containing childish references to faeces or urine (*disapproving*) **2.** OF PUBLIC LAVATORY relating to or suitable for a public lavatory

lavatory /lávvətri/ (*plural* -ries) n. **1.** TOILET a toilet or a small room or cubicle containing a toilet **2.** WASHROOM a room or building with washing and toilet facilities [14thC. From late Latin *lavatorium*, from Latin *lavare* (see LAVATION).]

lave[1] /layv/ (**laves, laving, laved**) vt. to wash or bathe sth (*archaic or literary*) [Pre-12thC. From Latin *lavare* 'to wash'.]

lave[2] /layv/ n. Scotland remainder [Old English *láf*, from a prehistoric Germanic word that is also the ancestor of English *leave*]

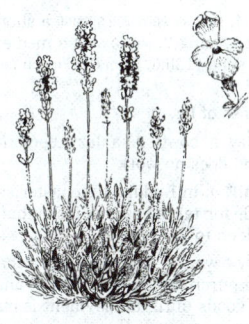
Lavender

lavender /lávvəndər/ n. **1.** PLANTS FRAGRANT PLANT a plant that has clusters of fragrant bluish-purple flowers that produce a fragrant oil. Latin name: *Lavendula officinalis*. **2.** HOUSEHOLD FLOWERS AND LEAVES the dried flowers and leaves of the lavender plant used to perfume clothes and linen **3.** COLOURS PALE PURPLE COLOUR a pale purple colour tinged with blue ■ adj. COLOURS PALE PURPLE a pale purple colour tinged with blue [14thC. Via Anglo-Norman *lavendre* from medieval Latin *lavendula*, of uncertain origin: perhaps formed from *lividus* 'bluish, livid'.]

lavender water n. perfume or toilet water made from the flowers of the lavender plant

laver[1] /láyvər/ n. **1.** JUDAISM JEWISH CEREMONIAL BASIN a large basin in the temple in Jerusalem and in modern synagogues used for ritual washing **2.** WASHBASIN a basin to wash in (*archaic*) [14thC. Via Old French *laveor* from late Latin *lavatorium* (see LAVATORY).]

laver[2] /láavər/ n. a dried edible seaweed of the red algae family. Genus: *Porphyra*. [12thC. From Latin.]

Laver /láyvər/, **Rod** (b. 1938) Australian tennis player. He is the only man to have won the tennis grand slam twice (1962 and 1969).

laver bread n. a Welsh dish made from boiled seaweed mixed with oatmeal, formed into cakes, and fried, traditionally in bacon fat. Sold as a dark

green puree, laver bread is also used in sauces or served plain, heated with butter.

laverock /lávvərək/ n. Scotland, N England a skylark (*archaic*) [Old English *láferce* (see LARK)]

lavish /lávvish/ adj. **1.** ABUNDANT given or produced in abundance or to excess **2.** GENEROUS giving or spending generously or to excess ■ vt. (-ishes, -ishing, -ished) BE EXTRAVAGANT WITH STH to give or spend sth generously or to excess [15thC. From Old French *lavasse* 'torrential rain', from *laver* 'to wash, pour'.] —**lavisher** n. —**lavishly** adv. —**lavishness** n.

Lavoisier /lə vwáazi ay/, **Antoine Laurent** (1743–94) French chemist. He disproved the phlogiston theory of combustion and published the first proper table of the chemical elements. He was guillotined during the Reign of Terror.

law /law/ n. **1.** BINDING OR ENFORCEABLE RULE a rule of conduct or procedure recognized by a community as binding or enforceable by authority **2.** PIECE OF LEGISLATION an act passed by a parliament or similar body **3.** LEGAL SYSTEM the body or system of rules recognized by a community that are enforceable by established process ○ *You are forbidden by law from entering the premises.* **4.** CONTROL OR AUTHORITY the control or authority resulting from the observance and enforcement of a community's system of rules ○ *Nobody is above the law.* **5.** BRANCH OF KNOWLEDGE the branch of knowledge or study concerned with the rules of a community and their enforcement ○ *went to university to study law* **6.** AREA OF LAW the body of law relating to a particular subject or area **7.** = **common law 8.** LAWYERS the legal profession **9.** LEGAL ACTION legal action or proceedings **10.** LAW ENFORCEMENT AGENT OR AGENCY a person or organization responsible for enforcing the law, especially the police **11.** SCI STATEMENT OF SCIENTIFIC TRUTH a statement of a scientific fact or phenomenon that is invariable under given conditions ○ *the laws of physics* **12.** MATH MATHEMATICAL PRINCIPLE a general relationship that is assumed or proved to exist between expressions **13.** GENERAL RULE OR PRINCIPLE a general rule or principle that is thought to be true or held to be binding [Pre-12thC. From Old Norse *lög* 'laws', from *lag* 'sth set down', from a prehistoric Germanic word meaning 'to put', which is also the ancestor of English *lay*.] ◇ **be a law unto yourself** to refuse to obey the rules, conventions, or suggestions made or upheld by others ◇ **lay down the law** to express an opinion in an overbearing or dogmatic way ◇ **take the law into your own hands** to try to obtain revenge or justice without involving the police, courts, or usual legal procedures

Law n. **1.** JUD-CHR DIVINE WILL the principles set out in the Bible, especially the Pentateuch, said to be the divine will. ◊ **Law of Moses, Mosaic Law 2.** JUDAISM = **Pentateuch**

law-abiding adj. voluntarily and habitually obeying the law

law agent n. Scotland a solicitor in England

law and order n. **1.** ENFORCEMENT OF LAW the strict enforcement of the law (*hyphenated before a noun*) ○ *law-and-order issues* **2.** SOCIAL STABILITY the stability created by the observance and enforcement of the law within a community

lawbreaker /láw braykər/ n. a person who breaks the law

law centre n. a place where citizens can obtain legal advice free of charge, paid for out of public funds

law court n. a court where legal cases are heard

lawful /láwf'l/ adj. **1.** PERMITTED BY LAW not forbidden by the law **2.** AUTHORIZED BY LAW authorized or recognized by the law **3.** OBEYING THE LAW obeying or conforming to the law —**lawfully** adv. —**lawfulness** n.

lawgiver /láw givvər/ n. **1.** SB WHO GIVES LAWS TO A COMMUNITY sb who gives a code of laws to a people, e.g. from a source considered to be divine **2.** = **lawmaker**

lawks /lawks/ interj. used to express surprise or concern (*regional dated*) [Mid-18thC. Variant of *lawk*, alteration of LORD.]

Lawler /láwlər/, **Ray** (b. 1921) Australian playwright. He wrote *The Summer of the Seventeenth Doll* (1955). Full name **Raymond Evenor Lawler**

lawless /láwləss/ adj. **1.** UNREGULATED uncontrolled or unregulated **2.** AGAINST THE LAW contrary to the law **3.** WITHOUT LAW having no laws —**lawlessly** adv. —**lawlessness** n.

Law Lords n. the members of the House of Lords qualified to take part in judicial business

lawmaker /láw maykər/ n. sb who drafts laws and causes them to be put into effect

lawman /láw man, -mən/ (*plural* -men /-mən/) n. US an officer responsible for enforcing the law, e.g. a sheriff

law merchant n. the principles and rules governing commercial transactions, which originated in English common law and are codified in US law

lawn[1] /lawn/ n. an area of closely mown grass, often part of a garden [Mid-16thC. Alteration of *laund*, from Old French *launde* 'wooded district, heath', from Celtic.]

lawn[2] /lawn/ n. a fine light fabric used for clothing and household linen. It is usually made of cotton, sometimes mixed with polyester. [15thC. Named after *Laon*, town in France known for linen manufacture.] —**lawny** adj.

lawn mower n. a machine, often power-operated, that cuts grass with rotating blades

lawn tennis n. a game for two or four players played on a hard or grass court of standard dimensions in which the players hit balls with rackets across a central net

law of averages n. **1.** PRINCIPLE ON EFFECT OF PROBABILITY LAWS the principle that over the long term laws of probability will influence all events that are subject to them **2.** PRINCIPLE THAT THINGS MUST EVEN OUT the unscientific but reasonable assumption that things are bound to change some time ○ *We have had bad weather for our holiday for the past six years, so by the law of averages we should get some sunshine this year.*

law of diminishing returns n. the principle that a continual increase in effort or investment does not lead to a continual increase in output or results

law of effect n. the theory that behaviour that is rewarded is more likely to be repeated than behaviour that is not rewarded. This theory was put forward by the US psychologist Edward Lee Thorndike.

law of large numbers n. the principle that a large sample is more likely than a smaller sample to have the characteristics of the whole

Law of Moses n. = Mosaic Law

law of nations n. = international law

law of nature n. a broadly applicable principle relating to natural phenomena

law of parsimony n. = Occam's razor

law of supply and demand n. the economic principle that the price charged for a product is determined by the level of demand and the quantity available

law of the jungle n. aggressive or competitive behaviour based on the principle that self-interest and survival are of prime importance

law of the sea n. the international rules that govern the use of the oceans, derived from custom, treaties, and judicial decisions

law of war n. a rule or body of rules that governs the rights and duties of those engaged in international war

Lawrence /lórrənss/, **Bruno** (1949–95) British-born New Zealand actor. Among his films are *Smash Palace* (1981) and *Spotswood* (1991).

Lawrence, D. H. (1885–1930) British writer. His novels include *Sons and Lovers* (1913), *Women in Love* (1921), and *Lady Chatterley's Lover* (1928). Full name **David Herbert Lawrence**

Lawrence, Gertrude (1898–1952) British actor. She starred in comedies and musical revues in London and New York, including *Blithe Spirit* (1945) and several other plays by her friend, Sir Noel Coward, as well as the film *The King and I* (1951). Born **Gertrud Alexandra Dagmar Lawrence Klasen**

Lawrence, Marjorie Florence (1908–79) Australian opera singer. She was soprano with many leading

AKG London

D. H. Lawrence

Barnaby's

Gertrude Lawrence

international companies, and continued to perform despite contracting poliomyelitis in 1941.

lawrencium /lə rénssi əm/ *n.* a short-lived radioactive metallic element that was first produced artificially from californium and later from other elements. The symbol Lw was used for lawrencium at first but in 1963 it was changed to Lr. Symbol **Lr** [Mid-20thC. Named after Ernest O. *Lawrence*, US physicist who first produced it.]

Lawson /láwss'n/, **Henry Hertzberg** (1867–1922) Australian writer. Amongst his poems and short stories the best-known book is the story collection *While the Billy Boils* (1896).

Lawson, Louisa (1848–1920) Australian writer, publisher, and feminist. In 1888 she founded *The Dawn*, Australia's first journal devoted to women's issues. She was the mother of Henry Lawson. Born **Louisa Albury**

Lawson, Nigel, Baron Lawson of Blaby (*b.* 1932) British politician. He was chancellor of the exchequer (1983–89) during Margaret Thatcher's administration.

Lawson, William (1774–1850) British-born Australian explorer. With Gregory Blaxland and William Wentworth he led the first crossing by Europeans of the Blue Mountains in New South Wales (1813).

lawsuit /láw soot, -syoot/ *n.* a legal action brought between two private parties in a court of law

lawyer /láwyər, lóyər/ *n.* sb who is professionally qualified to give legal advice to others and represent them in court

lax /laks/ *adj.* **1.** NOT STRICT not strict or careful enough **2.** NOT TENSE not tight or tense **3.** PHYSIOL WITH TENDENCY TO DIARRHOEA not easily controlled and producing loose faeces **4.** PHON PRONOUNCED WITH RELAXED MUSCLES pronounced with the muscles of the jaw relaxed rather than tense, as, e.g., is the 'a' in 'hat' [14thC. From Latin *laxus* 'loose'.] —**laxly** *adv.* —**laxness** *n.*

laxation /lak sáysh'n/ *n.* the action of making sth loose, or the process of becoming loose

laxative /láksətiv/ *n.* a drug or other substance that promotes bowel movements, either by irritating the lower colon or by bulking the stool [14thC. From Old French *laxatif*, from medieval Latin *laxativus* 'loosening', from Latin *laxare* 'to loosen', from *laxus* 'loose'.] —**laxative** *adj.*

laxity /láksəti/ *n.* the condition or fact of being not strict or careful enough

Laxness /laaks ness/, **Halldór** (*b.* 1902) Icelandic novelist and playwright. Author of *Salka Valka* (1934) and the Icelandic epic *Sjálfstaet Folk* (1934–35), he won a Nobel Prize in literature (1955).

lay[1] /lay/ *v.* (**lays, laying, laid**) **1.** *vt.* SET STH DOWN to put sth down, often carefully, in a horizontal position ○ *I laid the files on my desk.* **2.** *vt.* PUT IN RESTING POSITION to place sb or sth in a position of rest ○ *It was time to lay the baby down for a nap.* **3.** *vt.* BURY SB to bury sb or sth in the ground ○ *They laid him in the family plot.* **4.** *vt.* PLACE STH ON SURFACE to arrange, place, or spread sth on, over, or along a surface ○ *They are laying the carpet tomorrow.* **5.** *vt.* PRESS STH DOWN FLAT to smooth sth down, or make sth lie flat ○ *The cat laid back its ears.* **6.** *vt.* ARRANGE THINGS ON TABLE to prepare a table for a meal by setting out the required items **7.** *vt.* ARRANGE FUEL FOR FIRE to prepare a fire by arranging the fuel, usually in a grate **8.** *vti.* PRODUCE EGGS to produce or deposit eggs ○ *All the hens are laying.* **9.** *vti.* BETTING BET to place a bet with sb **10.** *vt.* IMPOSE STH to impose sth as a burden, duty, or penalty ○ *lay a tariff on imported products* **11.** *vt.* ATTRIBUTE to impute or attribute sth ○ *He laid the blame on me.* **12.** *vt.* BRING TO BEAR to bring sth to bear ○ *laid emphasis on the fact that we must study to excel* **13.** *vt.* CAUSE DECREASE to cause sth to decrease or subside ○ *Our discussion laid everyone's fears.* **14.** *vt.* DEVISE STH to devise, organize, or prepare sth **15.** *vt.* MAKE PREPARATIONS to prepare sth as a basis **16.** *vt.* BRING STH INTO CERTAIN STATE to bring sth into a particular state ○ *Their scheme was laid bare.* **17.** *vt.* OFFENSIVE TERM an offensive term meaning to have sexual intercourse with sb (*slang offensive*) **18.** *vt.* ARRANGE STRANDS OF ROPE to twist strands together to make a rope or cable **19.** *vt.* MIL PUT CANNON IN POSITION to establish the direction and elevation of a cannon or a battery of cannon **20.** *vt.* AGRIC TREAT HEDGE TO KEEP IT THICK to partially cut through some of the branches of a hedge, bending them over horizontally and pegging them to the ground to keep the hedge thick and dense ○ *hedge laying* **21.** *vi.* LIE DOWN to be in or adopt a lying position (*nonstandard*) ○ *Lay down on the sofa and have a rest.* **22.** *vi.* PUT EFFORT INTO STH to apply effort vigorously to a task ○ *The rowing team laid to their oars.* **23.** *vi.* NAUT BE IN OR GO TO POSITION to put a boat in a specified position, or move in a specified direction ■ *n.* **1.** WAY STH LIES the way or position in which sth lies ○ *wanted to inspect the lay of the property* **2.** OFFENSIVE TERM an offensive term for a partner in sexual intercourse (*slang offensive*) **3.** OFFENSIVE TERM an offensive term for sexual intercourse (*slang offensive*) **4.** TWIST OF ROPE OR CABLE STRANDS the arrangement of strands in a rope or cable, determined by the number, length, angle, and direction of twist **5.** FIN SHARE OF PROCEEDS a share in the proceeds of a whaling expedition [Old English *lecgan*, from a prehistoric Germanic word meaning 'to put', which is also the ancestor of English *lie* 'to rest horizontally'] ◇ **be laid low** to become ill or incapacitated ◇ **lay it on (thick)** to exaggerate greatly, especially in order to flatter sb ◇ **lay yourself open to sth** to put yourself in a position that will make you liable to be blamed, criticized, or attacked

lay about *vti.* to strike blows in all directions

lay aside *vt.* **1.** ABANDON STH to give up on or abandon sth ○ *'Be not the first by whom the new are tried, nor the last to lay the old aside'.* (Alexander Pope, *An Essay on Criticism*; 1711) **2.** SAVE STH to put sth away for the future

lay away *vt.* **1.** SAVE STH to put sth away for the future **2.** SET STH ASIDE to set merchandise aside for future delivery

lay before *vt.* to present sth for consideration by sb

lay by *vt.* **1.** SAVE STH to set sth aside for the future **2.** ANZ PAY FOR GOODS IN INSTALMENTS to purchase goods from a shop by placing a deposit then paying off the remainder in instalments, without interest. The shop retains the goods until full payment is received

lay down *v.* **1.** *vt.* SURRENDER STH to put down, surrender, or sacrifice sth **2.** *vt.* DECIDE ON RULE to formulate a rule or principle **3.** *vt.* STORE FOR FUTURE to acquire and store sth for future use **4.** *vt.* BETTING PLACE BET to place a bet **5.** *vt.* MIL DELIVER MILITARY FIRE to deliver a concentration of military fire **6.** *vi.* LIE DOWN to lie down in a horizontal position (*nonstandard*)

lay in *vt.* to acquire and store sth for future use

lay into *vt.* **1.** CRITICIZE SB to attack sb forcefully in words (*informal*) **2.** HIT SB to attack sb forcefully with blows

lay off *v.* **1.** *vt.* TERMINATE THE EMPLOYMENT OF SB to stop employing sb, often temporarily, when there is insufficient work to be done **2.** *vti.* STOP DOING STH to stop doing or using sth (*informal*) **3.** *vti.* STOP IRRITATING SB to stop bothering sb (*informal*) **4.** *vt.* MEASURE OR MARK STH OFF to measure off a distance, or mark out the boundaries of sth **5.** *vt.* BETTING REDUCE RISK ON BET to reduce risk as a bookmaker by placing all or part of a bet with another bookmaker

lay on *vt.* **1.** APPLY STH to apply sth by spreading it **2.** APPLY OR USE TO EXCESS to apply, administer, or use sth in an exaggerated manner **3.** PROVIDE STH SPECIAL to provide or arrange sth, often in an elaborate or extravagant manner **4.** INSTALL AN AMENITY to provide or install a supply of sth such as gas or electricity

lay out *v.* **1.** *vt.* SPREAD STH OUT FOR DISPLAY to arrange things, or spread things out for display **2.** *vt.* PLAN OR DESIGN STH to plan or design sth in detail **3.** *vt.* PREPARE SB FOR BURIAL to prepare a body for burial **4.** *vt.* KNOCK UNCONSCIOUS to knock sb unconscious (*informal*) **5.** *vt.* SPEND MONEY to spend money, especially in large quantities **6.** *vr.* MAKE AN EFFORT to make a considerable personal effort

lay over *vi. US, Can* to make a brief stop during a journey

lay to *vi.* to make a ship or boat stop, e.g. by turning a sailing vessel into the wind

lay up *vt.* **1.** STORE FOR FUTURE to store sth for future use **2.** CONFINE SB WITH INJURY OR ILLNESS to prevent sb from leading a normal active life, usually temporarily because of injury or illness **3.** STOP USING SHIP OR BOAT to take a ship or boat out of service, usually temporarily, e.g. by moving it to a dry dock for maintenance or repairs

lay[2] /lay/ *adj.* **1.** NOT BELONGING TO CLERGY belonging to or involving the people of a church who are not members of the clergy **2.** UNTRAINED without expertise or professional training in a particular field [14thC. Directly or via Old French *lai* from late Latin *laicus* 'secular' (see LAIC).]

lay[3] /lay/ *n.* **1.** POETRY POEM FOR SINGING a short narrative poem that is sung **2.** MUSIC SONG a medieval lyric or narrative song [13thC. From Old French *lai*, of unknown origin.]

lay[4] past tense of **lie**

layabout /láy ə bowt/ *n.* a lazy person who loafs around and does no work

lay attendant *n.* in Buddhist monasteries, sb who is responsible for taking care of tasks that the monks are forbidden to undertake

layaway /láy ə way/ *n.* a method of purchasing sth in which the purchaser pays a deposit and the seller keeps the goods until full payment is made

layback /láy bak/ *n.* a way of climbing a vertical crack in a rock by leaning back and pulling on one side of the crack and pushing against the other side with the feet

lay brother *n.* in a Christian religious order, a man who has taken vows, but does not take part in the full liturgical programme and serves as an ancillary or manual worker

lay-by (*plural* **lay-bys**) *n.* **1.** *UK* STOPPING PLACE AT EDGE OF ROAD a short strip of ground alongside a main road where vehicles can stop for a short time **2.** *ANZ* PAYING FOR GOODS IN INSTALMENTS a method of purchasing goods by placing a deposit and then paying off the full price in instalments, without interest, delivery of goods being made when full payment is received

lay days *npl.* the time allowed in port for a ship to load or unload its cargo without extra payment

lay-down *n. US* an easy target or victim (*slang*) ○ *I robbed ten lay-downs before being caught.*

layer /láyər/ *n.* **1.** FLAT COVERING OR SHEET-LIKE THICKNESS a single thickness of sth that lies over or under sth or between other similar thicknesses **2.** SB WHO LAYS STH sb whose work is laying sth such as tile or brick (*usually used in combination*) **3.** ZOOL LAYING HEN a hen that lays eggs **4.** GARDENING ROOTED PLANT SHOOT a branch or shoot that has been bent over and covered with soil to make it take root and grow into a new plant ■ *v.* (**-ers, -ering, -ered**) **1.** *vti.* MAKE LAYERS OF STH to apply or arrange things as separate thicknesses, or form into separate thicknesses **2.** *vt.* HAIR CUT HAIR IN DIFFERENT LENGTHS to cut sb's hair in overlapping sections of different lengths, usually in order to give shape to a hairstyle **3.** *vt.* GARDENING PROPAGATE PLANT BY ROOTING SHOOTS to bend a shoot over and cover it with soil to make it take root as a new plant, or take root as a result of this procedure

layer cake *n.* a sponge cake that consists of two or more layers sandwiched together with cream, jam, or other filling. The layers may be baked separately or cut horizontally.

layering /láyəring/ *n.* a method of propagating plants by covering a branch or shoot with soil so that it takes root while still attached to the parent plant

layette /lay ét/ *n.* a complete set of clothing and accessories for a newborn baby [Mid-19thC. From French, literally 'small drawer', from Old French *laie* 'drawer, box', from Middle Dutch *laege*, from a prehistoric Germanic word meaning 'load'.]

lay figure *n.* **1.** ARTIST'S DUMMY a jointed model of the human body used by artists **2.** COMPLIANT PERSON a submissive or insignificant person

laying on of hands *n.* placing the hands on sb's head in certain religious ceremonies or rituals, e.g. ordination and faith healing

Laylat al-Miraj /láy lat al mi raáj/ *n.* an Islamic festival, the Night of Ascent, celebrating the ascent of Muhammad to heaven and held on the 27th of Rajab [From Arabic, literally 'night of the ascent']

layman /láymən/ (*plural* **-men** /-mən/) *n.* **1.** SB WITHOUT SPECIALIST KNOWLEDGE sb who is not trained or expert in a particular area ○ *a law book for the layman* **2.** RELIG NONORDAINED PERSON sb who does not belong to the clergy

layoff /láy of/ *n.* **1.** DISMISSAL OF EMPLOYEES a dismissal of employees, usually temporary **2.** PERIOD OF UNEMPLOYMENT the time during which employees are out of work

lay of the land *n.* = lie of the land (*informal*)

layout /láy owt/ *n.* **1.** WAY THINGS ARE ARRANGED the way component parts or individual items are arranged **2.** DESIGN SHOWING RELATIVE POSITIONS a design or plan showing the way things are arranged **3.** DESIGN DESIGN OF PRINTED MATTER the design or arrangement of all the elements of printed material, e.g. an advertisement or the pages of a book **4.** DESIGN PAGE SHOWING DESIGN a page or pages showing the design for printed material **5.** DESIGN DESIGNING OF PRINTED MATERIAL the art of designing printed material **6.** US, Can LARGE ESTABLISHMENT a residence, business establishment, or other property, especially one that is large or elaborate ○ *a new high-tech manufacturing layout*

layover /láyōvər/ *n.* US, Can a brief stop during a journey

lay reader *n.* a lay member of a church, especially an Anglican church or the Roman Catholic Church, who is authorized to read some parts of the service

lay-up *n.* a basketball shot made close to the basket, usually made one-handed and by bouncing the ball off the backboard

laywoman /láy woomən/ (*plural* **-en** /-wimin/) *n.* **1.** WOMAN WITHOUT SPECIALIST KNOWLEDGE a woman who is not trained or expert in a particular area **2.** RELIG NONORDAINED WOMAN a woman who does not belong to the clergy

lazar /lázzər, láyzər/ *n.* a poor and sick person, especially sb affected by leprosy (*archaic*) [13thC. Via medieval Latin *lazarus* from Latin *Lazarus*, name of the beggar 'full of sores' described in Luke 16:20.]

lazaretto /lázzə réttō/ (*plural* **-tos**), **lazaret** /lázzə rét/, **lazarette** *n.* **1.** MED HOSPITAL FOR CONTAGIOUS DISEASES a hospital for the treatment of contagious diseases such as leprosy, especially in former times **2.** MED QUARANTINE FACILITY a building or ship used to hold people during a period of quarantine **3.** SHIPPING SHIP'S STORAGE SPACE a storage space below deck near the stern of a ship [Mid-16thC. Via Italian *lazzaretto*, blend of *lazzaro* 'leper' (see LAZAR) and Venetian dialect *nazareto*, hospital in Venice named after Santa Maria di *Nazaret* 'St Mary of Nazareth'.]

laze /layz/ (**lazes, lazing, lazed**) *v.* **1.** *vi.* TAKE IT EASY to relax and do no work ○ *I just lazed in the shade with a book.* **2.** *vt.* IDLE to pass time idly ○ *laze the day away* [Late 16thC. Back-formation from LAZY.]
laze around, laze about *vti.* to relax, doing nothing that requires effort

lazulite /lázzyoŏ līt/ *n.* a rare blue mineral, a phosphate of aluminium, iron, and magnesium, that has a glassy lustre and is used as a gem [Early 19thC. Coined from *(lapis) lazuli* + -ITE.]

lazurite /lázzyoŏ rīt/ *n.* a rare deep violet-blue or greenish-blue mineral, primarily a silicate of sodium and aluminium, that is the main constituent of the semiprecious gemstone lapis lazuli [Late 19thC. Via medieval Latin *lazur* from Arabic *lāzaward* '(lapis) lazuli'.]

lazy /láyzi/ (**-zier, -ziest**) *adj.* **1.** NOT WANTING TO WORK unwilling to do any work or make an effort **2.** CONDUCIVE TO IDLENESS contributing to an unwillingness to work or make an effort ○ *a lazy spring day* **3.** SLOW moving slowly ○ *a lazy river* **4.** AGRIC UPSIDE DOWN shown as a brand on livestock as a letter or number rotated through 90 degrees from an upright position ○ *a lazy H* [Mid-16thC. Origin uncertain: perhaps from Low German *lasich* 'feeble, tired'.] —**lazily** *adv.* —**laziness** *n.*

lazy bed *n. Scotland, Ireland* a bed about 2 m/6 ft wide where seed potatoes for cultivation are laid on the surface and covered with soil

lazybones /láyzi bōnz/ (*plural* **-bones**) *n.* sb who is lazy or without ambition (*informal*)

lazy daisy stitch *n.* a single unattached chain stitch in embroidery, often worked in a circle to resemble the petals of a flower

lazy eye *n.* **1.** IMPAIRED VISION an eye disorder in which vision is impaired for no apparent reason, or an eye affected by this disorder (*not used technically*) ♦ amblyopia **2.** CONVERGENT SQUINT a disorder in which the eyes appear to be looking in different directions, or an eye affected by this disorder

lazy Susan /-soŏz'n/ *n.* a revolving tray holding a selection of items such as cheeses or sauces, usually placed in the middle of a dining table

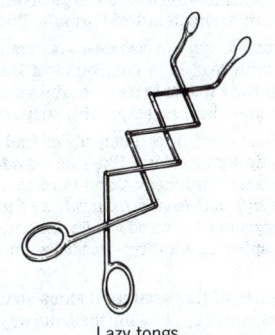

Lazy tongs

lazy tongs *npl.* tongs that can be used to grasp objects at a distance, usually by bringing together the handles to extend the jointed arms

lb *abbr.* **1.** pound or pounds **2.** CRICKET leg bye

LB *abbr.* Liberia (*international vehicle registration*)

L-band *n.* the range of frequencies of electromagnetic waves from 390 megahertz to 1550 megahertz used for radar. Other bands in the microwave spectrum used for radar are designated S, X, and K.

LBJ *abbr.* Lyndon Baines Johnson

LBO *abbr.* leveraged buyout

lbs *abbr.* pounds

LBV *abbr.* Late Bottled Vintage (*refers to port that is six years old*)

lbw *abbr.* leg before wicket

lc *abbr.* **1.** PRINTING lower case **2.** loco citato **3.** BANKING letter of credit **4.** THEATRE left centre (*of a stage*)

LC *abbr.* **1.** landing craft **2.** LC Library of Congress

L/C, l/c, lc *abbr.* letter of credit

LCC *abbr.* London Chamber of Commerce

LCD *abbr.* **1.** liquid-crystal display **2.** lcd MATH lowest common denominator

LCE *abbr.* London Commodity Exchange

l'chaim /lə khaá yim/, **lechayim** *interj.* GOOD HEALTH a word used to express good wishes just before drinking an alcoholic drink ■ *n.* SMALL DRINK OF ALCOHOL a small drink of alcohol used to toast sb or sth

LCL *abbr.* less-than-container load

LCM *abbr.* landing craft, mechanized ■ *n., abbr.* **lcm** MATH lowest common multiple

L/Cpl *abbr.* lance corporal

LCS *abbr.* landing craft, support

ld *abbr.* **1.** PRINTING lead **2.** load

Ld *abbr.* **1.** COMM Limited (company) **2.** Lord

LD *abbr.* **1.** EDUC learning disability **2.** EDUC learning-disabled **3.** PHARM lethal dose

LD50 *n.* a toxicological test in which the dose that kills 50% of a group of test animals is calculated. This test has been criticized by animal protection organizations and by many scientists, but it is still used.

LDC *abbr.* less-developed country

ldg *abbr.* **1.** landing **2.** loading

Ldg *abbr.* Leading

LDL *abbr.* low-density lipoprotein

L-dopa *n.* a natural substance that stimulates the production of dopamine in the brain and is used to treat Parkinson's disease [Mid-20thC. From the initial letters of *laevorotatory*, and of DI- + OXY- + PHENYL + ALANINE, the chemical names.]

L-driver *n.* sb who is learning to drive

LDS *abbr.* **1.** Latter-day Saints **2.** praise be to God forever **3.** Licentiate in Dental Surgery

lea /lee/ *n.* **1.** lea GRASSLAND a grassy field or meadow (*literary*) **2.** AGRIC SOWN GRASS a field sown with grass [Old English *lēah* 'meadow, clearing']

LEA *abbr.* Local Education Authority

lea. *abbr.* **1.** MEASURE league **2.** leather

leach /leech/ *v.* (**leaches, leaching, leached**) **1.** *vti.* DEPRIVE OR BE DEPRIVED OF STH to take sth away slowly, or be slowly taken away ○ *have the joy leached from life* **2.** *vt.* REMOVE STH BY DISSOLUTION to remove soluble components from a solid mixture by the use of a solvent **3.** *vi.* LOSE SOLUBLE MATERIAL to lose soluble material by dissolution ■ *n.* **1.** CONTAINER USED IN LEACHING a porous container used to hold a solid mixture through which a solvent is run in order to remove soluble components **2.** MIXTURE USED IN LEACHING a solid mixture through which a solvent is run in order to remove soluble components **3.** LIQUID CONTAINING LEACHED SUBSTANCE a solution containing a substance leached from a solid mixture [Old English *leccan*, from a prehistoric Germanic word that is also the ancestor of English *lake*] —**leachability** /leéchə bílləti/ *n.* —**leacher** /leéchər/ *n.*

Leach /leech/, **Bernard** (1887–1979) British potter. He revived the art of hand-made pottery in Britain, setting up the Leach pottery in St Ives, Cornwall (1920). Full name **Bernard Howell Leach**

leachate /leé chayt/ *n.* **1.** SOLUTION FORMED BY LEACHING a liquid containing soluble material removed from a solid mixture through which the liquid has passed **2.** LIQUID WASTE IN LANDFILL the liquid produced in a landfill from the decomposition of waste within the landfill

lead[1] /leed/ *v.* (**leads, leading, led** /led/) **1.** *vti.* GUIDE SB to show the way to others, usually by going ahead of them ○ *He led us down the mountain.* **2.** *vti.* BE THE WAY SOMEWHERE to be the route or direction that goes to a particular place or in a particular direction ○ *That street leads to the school.* **3.** *vt.* BRING SB OR STH to bring sb or sth along with physical guidance, e.g. by holding sb's hand or pulling a horse's reins **4.** *vt.* COMMAND OTHERS to control, direct, or command others ○ *He led an infantry division in Burma during the war.* **5.** *vt.* BE IN CHARGE OF STH to have a principal part or guiding role in sth **6.** *vt.* MUSIC BE PRINCIPAL MUSICIAN to be the principal performer of an orchestra or of a section of an orchestra **7.** *vt.* INFLUENCE SB TO DO STH to cause sb to think or act in a particular way ○ *I was led to believe the house had been sold.* **8.** *vi.* **RESULT IN STH** to bring about a particular outcome ○ *Her hard work ultimately led to widespread recognition.* **9.** *vt.* **LIVE LIFE** to go through life or spend time in a particular way ○ *We all lead very busy lives.* **10.** *vt.* **BE AT THE START** to be at the beginning or front of sth ○ *Your name leads the waiting list.* **11.** *vti.* **BE AHEAD OF OTHERS** to be ahead in a race or competition ○ *be leading in the election* **12.** *vt.* **BE MOST SUCCESSFUL** to be the most successful at sth and set an example to others ○ *They lead the world technologically.* **13.** *vti.* DANCE **GUIDE DANCE PARTNER** to guide a partner in a dance **14.** *vt.* LAW **ASK WITNESS LEADING QUESTION** to suggest to a witness an answer to a question by phrasing the question in a way that will elicit the desired response **15.** *vt.* **CHANNEL OR CONVEY STH** to guide sth through a passage such as a conduit or channel **16.** *vti.* CARDS **PUT DOWN FIRST CARD** to play the first card in a trick in a card game, often obliging others to play a card of the same suit if they can **17.** *vi.* BOXING **AIM THE FIRST BLOW** to direct the first of a series of punches **18.** *vi.* BASEBALL **LEAVE BASE EARLY** to leave a base as a runner before a pitch in baseball **19.** *vt.* **AIM AHEAD OF STH** to aim sth such as a missile or ball at a point in front of a moving target to allow for the time of flight ■ *n.* **1. FRONT POSITION OR PRINCIPAL ROLE** the front position, first place, or principal role **2. FORWARD POSITION** a position ahead of all competitors ○ *Portugal took the lead at the halfway stage.* **3. FRONT-RUNNER** sb or sth ahead of all competitors **4. DISTANCE BETWEEN FIRST AND SECOND** the margin by which sb or sth is ahead of all competitors ○ *She had a narrow lead as the runners entered the last lap.* **5.** ARTS **STAR ROLE IN PERFORMANCE** a principal role in a play, film, or show ○ *He will play the male lead in the film version.* **6.** ARTS **SB WITH STAR ROLE** sb who has a principal role in a play, film, or show **7. ROLE OF SB IN COMMAND** the role of sb who directs or guides others ○ *take the lead in a discussion* **8. PRECEDENT** an example or precedent ○ *follow his lead* **9. TIP OR CLUE** a piece of helpful or useful information ○ *The police are following up a number of leads.* **10.** PRESS **INTRODUCTION TO NEWS ITEM** an introduction to a news story **11.** PRESS **HEADLINE ITEM** the most important story in a newspaper or news broadcast ○ *The conflict should make the lead in all tomorrow's papers.* **12. LINE USED TO CONTROL ANIMAL** a strap, chain, or rope used to control the animal it is attached to, especially one used when walking a dog ○ *Dogs must be kept on a lead at all times.* **13.** ELEC **WIRE CONDUCTING ELECTRICITY** an insulated electrical conductor used to connect two points in a circuit, e.g. a cable connecting an appliance to a source of electricity **14.** GEOL **WATER CHANNEL THROUGH ICE** a water channel through an ice field **15.** NAUT **DIRECTION OF ROPE** the direction in which a rope runs **16.** CARDS **FIRST CARD PLAYED** the first card played in a trick in a game **17.** CARDS **RIGHT TO PUT DOWN FIRST CARD** the right to play a card first in a trick in a game **18.** BASEBALL **POSITION OF BASE RUNNER** a position taken by a runner off one base of a baseball diamond towards another **19.** BOXING **PUNCH** an attacking punch **20. DISTANCE AHEAD OF MOVING TARGET** the distance a missile, ball, or other projectile is aimed in front of a moving target to allow for the time of flight **21.** GEOL = **lode** [Old English *lǣdan*, from a prehistoric Germanic word that is also the ancestor of English *load*]

WORD KEY: SYNONYMS

See Synonyms at **guide**.

lead off *v.* **1.** *vi.* **BEGIN** to begin doing sth **2.** *vt.* BASEBALL **BE FIRST BATTER** to be the first batter in a baseball or softball lineup or innings

lead on *vt.* **1. ENTICE SB WITH FALSE PROMISE** to lure sb with an offer or promise that is later withdrawn **2. PERSUADE SB TO MISBEHAVE** to persuade sb to do sth foolish or wrong ○ *She doesn't let the older kids lead her on.*

lead up to *vt.* **1. PREPARE** to prepare the way for sth **2. APPROACH SUBJECT INDIRECTLY** to approach a subject gradually or indirectly

lead[2] /led/ *n.* **1.** CHEM ELEM **CHEMICAL ELEMENT** a heavy bluish-grey metallic chemical element that bends easily. It is used in car batteries, pipes, solder, and as a radiation shield. It usually occurs in the mineral galena. Symbol **Pb 2. DEVICE FOR MEASURING DEPTH** a weight on the end of a line used to measure the depth of water **3.** ANGLING **WEIGHT FOR FISHING LINE** a lead weight used on a fishing line **4.** ARMS **AMMUNITION FOR GUNS** bullets or shot for firearms **5. GRAPHITE IN A PENCIL** a long thin stick of graphite used in a pencil for writing or drawing **6.** PRINTING **STRIP BETWEEN LINES OF TYPE** in traditional hot-metal printing, a thin strip of metal between lines of type that creates the space between lines on the printed page ■ **leads** *npl.* **1.** CRAFT **LEAD STRIPS BETWEEN GLASS PANES** strips of lead used to hold the small glass panes in place in a decorative window or art object **2.** BUILDING **SHEETS OF LEAD** sheets of lead used to cover a roof **3.** BUILDING **ROOF COVERED WITH LEADS** a roof covered with lead sheets ■ *vt.* **(leads, leading, leaded) 1. COVER STH WITH LEAD** to cover, fill, or weight sth with lead **2.** PRINTING **INSERT STRIP BETWEEN LINES OF TYPE** to put a thin strip of metal between lines of type to create a space on the printed page **3.** CRAFT **SECURE GLASS USING LEADS** to hold small panes of glass together with strips of lead [Pre 12thC. Ultimately from a prehistoric Germanic word of uncertain origin: probably from Celtic, and originally meaning 'to flow' (referring to the metal's low melting point).] —**leady** *adj.* ◇ **swing the lead** to avoid work, often by feigning illness

lead acetate *n.* a poisonous crystalline compound used in making paints and varnishes and as a mordant in dyeing and printing cottons. Formula: $Pb(C_2H_3O_2)_2 \cdot 3H_2O$.

lead arsenate *n.* a poisonous crystalline compound used as an insecticide. Formula: $Pb_3(AsO_4)_2$.

lead azide *n.* a crystalline compound used as a detonator in explosives. Because of its sensitivity, lead azide must be submerged in water when transported. Formula: $Pb(N_3)_2$.

lead balloon *n.* a total failure ○ *went down like a lead balloon*

lead carbonate *n.* a poisonous white solid used as a pigment in paints. Formula: $PbCO_3$.

lead chromate *n.* a poisonous yellow crystalline substance used as a pigment. Formula: $PbCrO_4$.

lead crystal *n.* glass containing a high proportion of lead, used to make decorative items, especially tableware

lead dioxide *n.* a poisonous brown crystalline compound used in batteries and explosives, and as a mordant in dyeing textiles. Formula: PbO_2.

leaded /léddid/ *adj.* **1. CONTAINING LEAD** containing or treated with lead or a compound of lead **2.** CRAFT **WITH SMALL PANES SECURED BY LEAD** containing many small panes of glass held together with strips of lead

leaden /lédd'n/ *adj.* **1. OF LEAD** made of lead **2. DULL AND GREY** of a dull grey colour, like lead ○ *leaden skies* **3. TIRED AND HEAVY** tired, heavy, and hard to move ○ *My legs felt stiff and leaden from miles of walking.* **4. SLOW** sluggish or laboured ○ *a leaden pace* **5. LIFELESS** lacking spirit or vitality —**leadenly** *adv.* —**leadenness** *n.*

leader /leédər/ *n.* **1. SB WHOM PEOPLE FOLLOW** sb who guides or directs others by showing them the way or telling them how to behave **2. SB OR STH IN THE LEAD** sb or sth in front of all others, e.g. in a race or procession **3. SB IN CHARGE OF OTHERS** the head of a nation, political party, legislative body, or military unit **4.** MUSIC **PRINCIPAL MUSICIAN** the principal performer of an orchestra or of a section of an orchestra **5.** MUSIC **MUSICAL CONDUCTOR** a conductor of a band or group **6.** PRESS **NEWSPAPER ARTICLE EXPRESSING EDITOR'S OPINION** a newspaper article expressing the opinion of the editor. US term **editorial 7.** *US* MARKETING = **loss leader 8.** BOT **MAIN STEM** the main growing shoot of a tree or shrub **9.** RECORDING **BLANK END OF TAPE** a short strip of blank film or recording tape at the beginning or end of a reel, used for threading **10.** ANGLING **LINE CONNECTING HOOK** a short length of nylon or other material attached to a fishing line and used to connect the lure or hook **11.** ANGLING **LINE AT END OF FISHING LINE** a short length of heavy fishing line or wire tied to the end of the main line to prevent sharp-toothed fish from breaking off the hook ■ **leaders** *npl.* PRINTING **GUIDE IN PRINTED MATTER** dots or dashes in printed material used to guide the eye across a page

leadership /leédər ship/ *n.* **1. OFFICE OR POSITION OF LEADER** the office or position of the head of a political party or other body of people **2. ABILITY TO LEAD** the ability to guide, direct, or influence people **3. GUIDANCE** guidance or direction **4. LEADERS** a group of leaders (*takes a singular or plural verb*)

lead glass *n.* glass that contains a high proportion of lead oxide. It is used to make decorative objects and optical components.

lead-in *n.* **1. INTRODUCTORY REMARK** an introduction to sth such as an item on television or a topic for discussion **2.** BROADCAST **AERIAL WIRE** a wire that connects an outside aerial with a transmitter or receiver

leading[1] /leéding/ *adj.* **1. PROMINENT** most important or well known **2. AHEAD** ahead of all others, e.g. in a race or procession

leading[2] /lédding/ *n.* **1.** CRAFT **GLASS FRAMING** lead strips around small panes in windows or art objects ○ *The leading in the stained-glass window needs repair.* **2.** PRINTING **LINE SPACING** the spacing between lines of type in traditional hot-metal printing

leading aircraftman *n.* a man with the rank next above aircraftman in the Royal Air Force

leading aircraftwoman *n.* a woman with the rank next above aircraftwoman in the Royal Air Force

leading article *n.* PRESS = **leader** *n.* **6**

leading dog *n.* *NZ* a dog in New Zealand trained to run ahead of a flock of sheep and control them

leading economic indicator *n.* an economic variable that tends to show the direction of future economic activity

leading edge *n.* **1. MOST ADVANCED POSITION** the forefront of development in technology, science, or some other field (*hyphenated when used before a noun*) **2.** AIR **FRONT EDGE** the forward edge of an aircraft wing, propeller, or aerofoil **3.** HOUSEHOLD **INNER EDGE OF CURTAIN** the vertical edge of a curtain that faces the middle of the window

leading lady *n.* the actor who has the principal female role in a play or film (*dated*)

leading light *n.* sb who influences or sets an example to others

leading man *n.* the actor who has the principal male role in a play or film

leading note *n.* the seventh note of the diatonic scale. US term **leading tone**

leading question *n.* a question asked in a way that prompts the desired answer, e.g. 'Do you think the government should be wasting taxpayers' money on such a venture?'

leading rating *n.* a seaman in the Royal Navy with the rank next below petty officer

leading tone *n.* *US* = **leading note**

lead line *n.* a line, weighted at one end, used to measure the depth of water. The line is usually marked at intervals to make measurement easier.

lead monoxide *n.* a yellow or reddish-yellow poisonous lead compound used in making storage batteries, pottery, glass, and rubber, and as a pigment in paints. Formula: PbO.

lead poisoning *n.* poisoning from the absorption of lead into the body, the chronic form of which can cause damage to the nervous system, brain, liver, and gastrointestinal tract

lead replacement petrol *n.* lead-free petrol for compulsory use in vehicles that were designed to be used with leaded petrol, introduced as a way of improving air quality and protecting the environment

lead screw *n.* a threaded shaft that controls the movement of a machine part, e.g. the tool carriage of a lathe

leadsman /lédzmən/ (*plural* **-men** /-mən/) *n.* sb who uses a lead line to measure the depth of water

lead tetraethyl *n.* = **tetraethyl lead**

lead time *n.* **1. ADVANCE NOTICE** the length of time in advance of a deadline that sb must know or have sth **2. TIME TO COMPLETE PROCESS** the time needed to do sth measured from start to finish, e.g. from design to production or from placing an order to delivery of the goods ○ *How much lead time do you need?*

Leadville /léd vil/ city and county seat of Lake County, central Colorado, situated in the Rocky

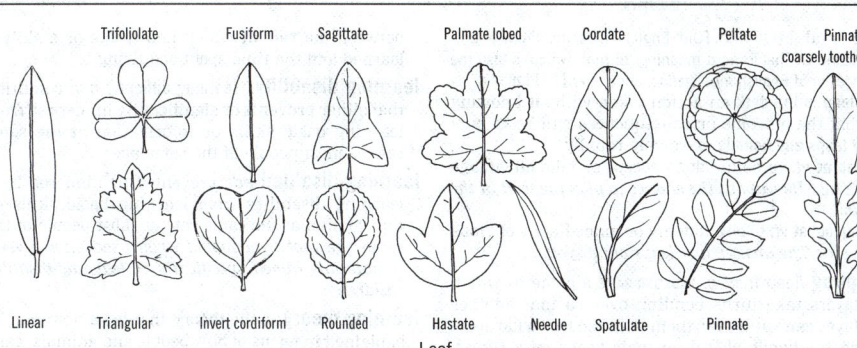

Trifoliolate — Fusiform — Sagittate — Palmate lobed — Cordate — Peltate — Pinnate/coarsely toothed

Linear — Triangular — Invert cordiform — Rounded — Hastate — Needle — Spatulate — Pinnate

Leaf

Mountains, southwest of Denver. Population: 2,629 (1990).

leadwort /léd wurt, -wawrt/ n. a tropical plant grown in gardens for its spikes of blue, white, or red flowers. Genus: *Plumbago*.

leaf /leef/ n. (plural **leaves** /leevz/) **1.** BOT PLANT PART FOR PHOTOSYNTHESIS any of the flat green parts that grow in various shapes from the stems or branches of plants and trees and whose main function is photosynthesis **2.** BOT FOLIAGE the foliage of a plant or tree, or the time when a plant or tree has leaves **3.** PUBL PAPER IN BOOK any of the sheets of paper that make up a book **4.** VERY THIN METAL FOIL a very thin sheet of metal such as gold or silver used, e.g. to decorate an art object **5.** FURNITURE PART OF TABLE TOP a hinged or removable section of a table top **6.** BUILDING PART OF DOOR a hinged or sliding section of a door, shutter, or gate **7.** PART OF SPRING IN VEHICLE one of the metal strips that form a spring in a vehicle suspension system (**leaf spring**) ■ vi. (**leafs**, **leafing**, **leafed**) BOT GROW LEAVES to put out new leaves [Old English *lēaf*, from a prehistoric Germanic word that is probably also the ancestor of English *lobby* and *lodge*] —**leafless** adj. ◇ **take a leaf out of sb's book** to follow sb's usually good example ◇ **turn over a new leaf** to start to behave in a more acceptable way

leaf through vt. to turn the pages of a book or magazine quickly and casually

leafage /leéfij/ n. leaves or foliage

leaf beetle n. a beetle, e.g. the Colorado beetle or the flea beetle, that feeds on the leaves of plants and can be destructive to cultivated crops. Family: Chrysomelidae.

leafbird /leéf burd/ n. a forest-dwelling bird of Southeast Asia with a long curved bill and bold black and green or yellow markings. Family: Aegithinidae.

leaf butterfly n. a butterfly of southern and southeastern Asia that resembles a leaf. Genus: *Kallima*.

leaf chafer n. a scarab beetle that eats the leaves of grape vines and many garden plants. Genus: *Macrodactylus*.

leaf curl n. a disease of plants that causes the leaves to curl

leafcutter ant /leéf kuttər-/ n. a tropical American ant that cuts leaves into pieces to use as fertilizer for the fungi it grows in its nest for food. Genus: *Atta*.

leafcutter bee n. a common solitary bee that usually nests in the ground or in a natural cavity and lines its nest with pieces of leaves. Family: Megachilidae.

leaf fat n. the dense layers of fat surrounding the kidneys, especially a pig's kidneys, often used for making lard

leaf fish n. a tropical freshwater fish that is laterally flat so that it appears like a floating dead leaf. Family: Nandidae.

leafhopper /leéf hoppər/ n. a slender spindle-shaped leaping insect found worldwide that sucks the sap from plants and spreads plant diseases. Family: Cicadellidae.

leaf insect n. an insect with a flat body that resembles a leaf in shape and colour, found mainly in southern Asia. Family: Phyllidae.

leaf lard n. a high-quality leaf lard made from the fat surrounding the kidneys of pigs (**leaf fat**)

leaflet /leéflət/ n. **1.** PUBL FREE PRINTED MATERIAL a sheet of printed paper, usually folded, that is distributed free as part of an advertising or information campaign **2.** BOT SMALL LEAF a small or young leaf **3.** BOT PART OF LEAF any of the divisions of a compound leaf ■ vti. (**-lets**, **-leting**, **-leted**) DISTRIBUTE LEAFLETS to hand out or distribute leaflets in a particular place or to a particular group of people

leafleteer /leéflə teér/, **leafleter** /leéflətər/ n. sb who writes or distributes leaflets

leaf miner n. any insect whose larvae tunnel into and feed on leaf tissue, including several species of very small moths and a particular species of fly. Family: Agromyzidae.

leaf monkey n. a leaf-eating Asian monkey related to the langurs. Genus: *Presbytis*. ◇ **langur**

leaf mould n. **1.** COMPOST OR SOIL nitrogen-rich compost or soil that consists mainly of decomposed leaves **2.** GROWTH ON LEAVES a fungal growth on leaves

leaf primordium n. a group of cells that develop into a leaf

leaf roll n. a viral disease of potatoes that is transmitted by aphids and causes the leaves to curl upwards

leaf roller n. a small moth whose larvae roll leaves to protect themselves while they eat them

leaf scar n. the mark left on a stem when a leaf falls

leaf sheath n. the part at the bottom of the leaf that surrounds the stem in grasses

leaf spot n. a fungal or bacterial plant disease that causes discoloured spots to develop on leaves

leaf spring n. a spring made of several curved metal strips of different lengths (**leaves**) bracketed together, used in motor vehicle suspension systems

leafstalk /leéf stawk/ n. a stalk by which a leaf is attached to a stem. Technical name **petiole**

leaf trace n. the structure that carries fluid between the main stem and the base of the leaf in plants

leaf tyer n. = leaf roller

leafy /leéfi/ (**-ier**, **-iest**) adj. **1.** WITH MANY LEAVES covered with or having many leaves **2.** WITH MANY TREES THAT HAVE LEAVES with many trees and therefore a lot of foliage **3.** PRODUCING LEAVES producing broad leaves as distinct from blades or needles **4.** WITH EDIBLE LEAVES having edible leaves ◇ *leafy vegetables* —**leafiness** n.

leafy spurge n. a tall perennial plant that is native to Europe but naturalized in the northern United States and Canada. It is found growing in patches along roadsides. Latin name: *Euphorbia esula*.

league[1] /leeg/ n. **1.** GROUP WITH COMMON GOALS an association of nations, states, organizations, or businesses with common interests or goals **2.** SPORTS GROUP OF SPORTS CLUBS an association of sports clubs or teams that compete with each other **3.** LEVEL OF SKILL a level of performance or skill ◇ *Her painting is not in the same league with yours.* **4.** Aus RUGBY LEAGUE rugby league (informal) ■ vti. (**leagues**, **leaguing**, **leagued**) FORM INTO LEAGUE to join with others for a common interest or goal, or bring people together for such a purpose [15thC. Via French *ligue* 'pact, agreement', from Italian *liga*, variant of *lega*, ultimately from Latin *ligare* 'to bind'; spelling later influenced by Italian *lega*.] ◇ **in league (with sb)** collaborating with sb, usually for a questionable purpose

league[2] /leeg/ n. a measure of distance of variable length, usually about 5 km/3 mi., no longer in general use [14thC. Directly or via French dialect *lega* (from Old French *legue*) from late Latin *leuca*, from late Greek *leugā*, ultimately from Gaulish.]

league football n. Aus rugby league (informal)

League of Nations n. an alliance of nations established in 1920 to promote world peace and co-operation that was replaced by the United Nations in 1946. It was first proposed by President Woodrow Wilson after World War I, though the United States never joined, and became increasingly ineffective in the 1930s.

leaguer[1] /leégər/ n. (archaic) **1.** SIEGE a siege **2.** BESIEGING ARMY CAMP the camp of a besieging army ■ vt. (**-ers**, **-ering**, **-ered**) BESIEGE to besiege a place (archaic) [Late 16thC. From Dutch *leger* 'camp'.]

leaguer[2] /leégər/ n. US, Can a member of a sports league

league table n. **1.** LIST OF SPORTS TEAMS OR PLAYERS a list of the members of a sports league arranged in order of rank **2.** LIST OF RANKING ORDER a comparison of performance in any area involving competition ■ npl. EDUC WRITTEN REPORT OF SCHOOLS EXAM RESULTS a comparison of schools' performance in National Curriculum tests and other public examinations (informal)

leak /leek/ n. **1.** HOLE OR CRACK an unintentional hole or crack that permits sth such as liquid, gas, or light to escape or enter **2.** ACCIDENTAL ESCAPE OR ENTRY the accidental escape or unwanted entry of sth, usually by way of an unintentional hole or crack **3.** ESCAPING LIQUID OR GAS sth that escapes through an unintentional hole or crack **4.** ELEC ACCIDENTAL ESCAPE OF ELECTRICITY a place through which an electric current escapes accidentally, or the resulting loss of electricity **5.** MEANS OF ESCAPE a means of escape, or the resulting loss ◇ *We need to plug the leak in our finances.* **6.** DISCLOSURE OF SECRETS an unofficial disclosure of confidential information, usually to the media **7.** ACT OF URINATION an act of urination (slang) ■ vti. (**leaks**, **leaking**, **leaked**) **1.** LET STH IN OR OUT to let sth escape or enter accidentally, or escape or enter in this way **2.** DISCLOSE SECRETS OR BE DISCLOSED to release confidential information unofficially or covertly, usually to the media, or become publicly known in such a way ◇ *She leaked the details of the deal to the press.* [15thC. Origin uncertain: perhaps via Old Norse *leka* or Middle Dutch *lek* from, ultimately, a prehistoric Germanic word meaning 'deficiency'.] —**leaker** n.

leak out vi. to become known unintentionally, or be disclosed unofficially

leakage /leékij/ n. **1.** ESCAPE OR ENTRANCE OF STH a gradual escape or entrance of sth such as oil, gas, or electric current by a leak **2.** STH THAT ESCAPES BY LEAKING an amount of sth that escapes or enters by leaking **3.** DISCLOSURE OF SECRETS the unofficial release of confidential information, usually to the media

Leakey /leéki/, **Louis** (1903–72) British archaeologist and paleontologist. He pioneered research into human ancestry at Olduvai Gorge in Tanzania, discovering several key hominid fossils. Full name **Louis Seymour Bazett Leakey**

Leakey, Richard (b. 1944) Kenyan-born British archaeologist and paleontologist. He continued his parents' research into human ancestry in Africa, becoming director of the Kenyan Wildlife and Conservation Management Service (1989). Full name **Richard Erskine Frere Leakey**

leakproof /leék proof/ adj. **1.** DESIGNED NOT TO LEAK designed to prevent any of the contents from escaping or anything unwanted from entering **2.** NOT DISCLOSING SECRETS not allowing breaches in secrecy or confidentiality

leaky /leéki/ (**-ier**, **-iest**) adj. **1.** LEAKING letting liquid or gas in or out accidentally through holes or cracks **2.** NOT SECURE allowing breaches in secrecy or confidentiality (informal) —**leakily** adv. —**leakiness** n.

leal /leel/ adj. Scotland loyal and true (literary) [14thC. Via Anglo Norman *leal* from Old French *leel* (see LOYAL).]

Leamington Spa /lémmingtən spaá/ elegant spa town in Warwickshire, central England, with mineral springs. Population: 42,304 (1991). Official name **Royal Leamington Spa**

lean[1] /leen/ *v.* (**leans, leaning, leant** /lent/ *or* **leaned**) **1.** *vi.* BEND OR INCLINE to be in or move to a position that is at an angle to the vertical **2.** *vti.* REST STH OR BE SUPPORTED to rest against sth for support, or rest sth against sth else **3.** *vi.* TEND TOWARDS STH to have a preference or inclination for a particular thing or course of action ■ *n.* TILTED POSITION a position that is at an angle to the vertical [Old English *hleonian*. Ultimately from an Indo-European word meaning 'slope', which is also the ancestor of English *decline*, *incline*, and *ladder*.]

lean on *vt.* **1.** DEPEND ON SB to be dependent on sb **2.** GET SUPPORT FROM SB to gain moral support from sb ○ *You can always lean on me.* **3.** INTIMIDATE SB INTO DOING STH to put pressure on sb to do sth (*informal*)

lean[2] /leen/ *adj.* **1.** WITHOUT EXCESS FAT having no excess fat **2.** NOT FATTY having little or no fat ○ *lean meat* **3.** NOT PRODUCTIVE not productive or profitable ○ *lean harvest* **4.** ECONOMICAL AND EFFICIENT not using any more resources than necessary ○ *He is able to compete because he runs a lean business.* **5.** MINING WITH FEW MINERALS low in mineral content ○ *lean ore* **6.** LOW IN COMBUSTIBLE MATERIAL used to describe a mixture of fuel and air that is low in combustible material ○ *lean fuel mixture* ■ *n.* MEAT WITHOUT FAT meat with little or no fat [Old English *hlǣne*, from prehistoric Germanic] —**leanly** *adv.*

WORD KEY: SYNONYMS

See Synonyms at ***thin***.

Lean /leen/, **Sir David** (1908–91) British film director. He won Academy Awards for *The Bridge on the River Kwai* (1957), and *Lawrence of Arabia* (1962).

lean-burn *adj.* designed to run on a mixture that has a high proportion of air to fuel in order to reduce air pollution ○ *a lean-burn engine*

leaning /léening/ *n.* an inclination or tendency towards sth such as a particular set of opinions

Leaning Tower of Pisa

Leaning Tower of Pisa the bell tower of Pisa Cathedral, Italy, built between 1173 and 1350 and well-known for its tilt. It is 55 m/180 ft high and leans more than 5 m/16 ft from the perpendicular.

leant past tense, past participle of **lean**[1]

lean-to (*plural* **lean-tos**) *n.* **1.** OUTBUILDING BUILT AGAINST WALL an outbuilding with a slanted roof that rests against the wall of a larger building **2.** SLOPE-ROOFED SHED a shed or shack with a roof that slopes in one direction

leap /leep/ *v.* (**leaps, leaping, leapt** /lept/ *or* **leaped**) **1.** *vi.* JUMP FORCEFULLY to make a jump with a long or high arc ○ *She leapt over the stream with ease.* **2.** *vi.* MOVE AS IF BY JUMPING to move abruptly, as if by jumping up or across sth ○ *The dog leapt into her arms.* **3.** *vi.* ABRUPTLY SWITCH TO STH to move abruptly to a new thought or action ○ *The reporters leapt to the conclusion that wrongdoing had occurred.* **4.** *vi.* GO UP SUBSTANTIALLY to increase suddenly and sizably ○ *Stock prices leaped to new highs.* **5.** *vt.* JUMP STH to jump over an obstacle ○ *didn't think he could leap the stream* **6.** *vt.* MAKE ANIMAL JUMP to cause an animal to jump over sth ■ *n.* **1.** ARCHING JUMP a long high jump **2.** DISTANCE OF JUMP the distance covered by a leap ○ *a leap of almost three metres* **3.** PLACE TO JUMP a place over or from which to leap **4.** LARGE INCREASE a sudden and sizable increase ○ *The market has made many leaps this quarter.* **5.** MUSIC MUSICAL INTERVAL a large interval in music [Old English *hlēapan*. From a prehistoric Germanic word meaning 'to run', which is also the ancestor of English *lope*, *gallop*, and *loafer*.] —**leaper** *n.* ◇ **a leap in the dark** an action taken without knowing what the outcome or consequences will be ◇ **in** *or* **by leaps and bounds** extremely rapidly

leap at *vt.* to be quick to accept or take advantage of sth ○ *He leapt at the chance to play the lead in the film.*

leap out at *vt.* to be suddenly or immediately obvious to sb ○ *The answer just leaps out at you.*

leapfrog /léep frog/ *n.* VAULTING GAME a game in which players take turns bending over so that another player can vault over them with the legs wide apart and the hands placed on their backs ■ *v.* (**-frogs, -frogging, -frogged**) **1.** *vti.* PLAY LEAPFROG to vault over sb in the game of leapfrog **2.** *vt.* VAULT OVER SB OR STH to vault over a person or obstacle in a style similar to that used in the game of leapfrog **3.** *vti.* PASS EACH OTHER ALTERNATELY to take turns overtaking each other ○ *The two drivers were leapfrogging down the racetrack.* **4.** *vi.* ADVANCE QUICKLY to advance quickly in status or position, usually bypassing competitors or colleagues ○ *She started the day in seventh place but soon leapfrogged into first.* **5.** *vt.* CIRCUMVENT STH to evade sth by passing around it [From the players' resemblance to jumping frogs]

leap second *n.* a second added at the end of June or December to a timekeeping system in order to keep measured time synchronized with the movement of the Earth around the Sun [Modelled on LEAP YEAR]

leapt past tense, past participle of **leap**

leap year *n.* a year with an extra day, 29 February, added to make up the difference between the 365-day calendar and the actual duration of the Earth's orbit of the Sun. Leap years occur every four years, except for years ending in '00' that are not divisible by 400. [Origin uncertain: probably so called because in such years any given date falls two days later than in the preceding year, instead of one as in a normal year]

Lear /leer/, **Edward** (1812–88) British writer and artist. His limericks and cartoons for children were first published in *A Book of Nonsense* (1846).

learn /lurn/ (**learns, learning, learned** *or* **learnt** /lurnt/) *v.* **1.** *vti.* COME TO KNOW STH to acquire knowledge of a subject or skill through education or experience ○ *I'm learning to play the piano.* **2.** *vti.* FIND OUT STH to gain information about sb or sth ○ *I just learned that Jim is arriving tomorrow.* **3.** *vt.* MEMORIZE STH to memorize sth, e.g. facts, a poem, a piece of music, or a dance ○ *I have to learn the periodic table for my exam.* **4.** *vt.* TEACH SB STH to teach a topic or skill to sb (*nonstandard*) [Old English *leornian*. Ultimately from an Indo-European word meaning 'track', which also produced English *lore* and *last*[2]. The underlying idea is 'to follow a course of instruction'.] —**learnable** *adj.*

learned /lúrnid/ *adj.* **1.** HIGHLY EDUCATED well-educated and very knowledgeable ○ *a learned professor* **2.** EDUC SCHOLARLY showing or requiring much education and knowledge **3.** LAW HONOURABLE used in addressing or referring to a lawyer in court ○ *my learned friend* **4.** PSYCHOL ACQUIRED, NOT INSTINCTUAL used to describe behaviour or knowledge that is acquired through training or experience rather than being instinctual [14thC. Originally the past participle of LEARN in the sense 'to teach'.] —**learnedly** *adv.* —**learnedness** *n.*

learned helplessness *n.* sb's failure to take action to make his or her life better, arising from a sense of not being in control

learner *n.* **1.** SB LEARNING sb who is learning a subject or skill **2. learner, learner driver** SB LEARNING TO DRIVE sb who is learning to drive a car

learner's permit *n.* US = **provisional licence**

learning /lúrning/ *n.* **1.** ACQUIRING OF KNOWLEDGE the acquisition of knowledge or skill **2.** EDUC ACQUIRED KNOWLEDGE knowledge or skill gained through education ○ *a man of great learning* **3.** PSYCHOL CHANGE IN KNOWLEDGE a relatively permanent change in, or acquisition of, knowledge, understanding, or behaviour

learning curve *n.* **1.** RATE OF LEARNING the rate at which a new subject or skill is learned ○ *the steep learning curve expected by the syllabus* **2.** EDUC GRAPH PLOTTING LEARNING OUTCOMES a graph that shows the relation between the rate at which knowledge or a skill is learned and the time spent acquiring it

learning disability, learning difficulty *n.* a condition that either prevents or significantly hinders sb from learning basic skills or information at the same rate as most people of the same age

learning-disabled *adj.* prevented or hindered by a learning disability from learning basic skills or information at the same rate as most people of the same age (*not hyphenated when used after a verb*) ○ *materials aimed specifically at learning-disabled children*

learning theory *n.* the theory that behaviour can be explained in terms of how people and animals learn to respond to a stimulus, e.g. learning by rewards and punishments (**operant conditioning**) and learning by association (**classical conditioning**)

learnt past tense, past participle of **learn**

leary /léeri/ *adj.* = **leery**

lease /leess/ *n.* **1.** RENTAL CONTRACT a legal contract allowing sb exclusive possession of another's property for a particular time in return for rent **2.** LENGTH OF LEASE the period of time covered by a lease ○ *Our lease is six months.* ■ *vt.* (**leases, leasing, leased**) **1.** RENT STH TO SB to rent property to sb under the terms of a lease **2.** RENT STH FROM SB to rent property from sb under the terms of a lease ○ *We've leased a cottage for the summer.* [14thC. From Anglo-Norman *les*, from *lesser* 'to lease', a variant of Old French *laissier* (see LEASH).] —**leasable** *adj.* —**leaser** *n.* ◇ **a new lease of life** renewed freshness or vigour, usually resulting from some minor change

WORD KEY: SYNONYMS

See Synonyms at ***hire***.

leaseback /léess bak/ *n.* an arrangement in which a property is sold and then leased to its former owner by its new owner

leasehold /léess hōld/ *n.* **1.** RENTING OF PROPERTY the holding of a property through a lease **2.** RENTED PROPERTY a property that is leased —**leaseholder** *n.*

leash /leesh/ *n.* **1.** = **lead**[1] *n.* 12 **2.** RESTRAINT sth that controls or restrains sb ○ *Our supervisor keeps us on a short leash.* **3.** THREE ANIMALS TOGETHER a set of three animals of one type, especially hounds ■ *vt.* (**leashes, leashing, leashed**) RESTRAIN STH to restrain your emotions or impulses or the emotions or impulses of sb under your control [13thC. From Old French *laisse*, from *laissier* 'to let go', from Latin *laxare*, literally 'to loosen', from *laxus* (see LAX).]

least /leest/ CORE MEANING: the smallest or lowest quantity or degree

1. *adj., adv., pron.* SMALLEST AMOUNT POSSIBLE a smaller amount than anything or anyone else ○ *He went up the steps without showing the least anxiety.* ○ *what I liked the least of all* ○ *The least said the soonest mended.* **2.** *adv.* LESS OF A QUALITY THAN OTHERS having less of a particular quality than most other people or things ○ *one of the least appealing films of the year* **3.** *adj.* EXTREMELY SMALL used to emphasize that sth is so small as to be virtually nonexistent ○ *She had not the least idea of what was going on with me.* **4.** *adv.* TO A SMALLER DEGREE indicates that sth happens or is true to a smaller degree than at any other time ○ *I had been appointed to take charge while I least expected anything of the sort.* **5.** *pron.* THE MINIMUM used to indicate the minimum that should be done in a situation ○ *The least you can do is to make yourself thoroughly acquainted with the procedure.* [Old English *lǣst*, a contraction of *lǣsest*, from *lǣs* 'less'] ◇ **at least 1.** not less than a particular amount ○ *It'll take at least two days to finish.* ○ *We travelled at least forty-five miles without a rest.* **2.** in any case and despite anything else ○ *At least you've got a job, which is more than I have.* **3.** indicates a correction or change ○ *The answer seemed right, or at least close enough.* ◇ **least of all** emphasizes that a negative applies to one case in particular ○ *No one must know of our discovery – least of all our competitors.* ◇ **not (in) the least** not in the slightest ○ *The only noteworthy point about him was of the negative sort – he was not in the least like his sister.* ○ *I'm not the least bit tired.* ◇ **not least** emphasizes sth particularly important ○ *It is too early to be sure, not* least because the weather may change. ◇ **to say the least** without exaggerating or overstating the case ○ *We were, to say the least, surprised at her rudeness.*

least common denominator *n.* = lowest common denominator *n.* 1

least common multiple *n.* = lowest common multiple

least squares *n.* a method of finding the best curve to fit a set of statistical data points. It involves squaring the distance that each point is from a given curve, summing the squares, and choosing the curve for which the sum has the minimum value.

leastways /leest wayz/ *adv.* in any case and despite anything else (*informal*)

leastwise /leest wīz/ *adv. US* leastways (*regional informal*)

leather /léthər/ *n.* **1.** TANNED AND DRESSED HIDE the processed hide of animals with the fur or feathers removed. It is used in making items such as shoes, saddles, luggage, and clothing. **2.** POLISHING CLOTH a piece of leather used for polishing sth **3.** MATERIAL LIKE LEATHER sth that is like leather in appearance or texture ○ *fruit leather* **4.** STH MADE OF LEATHER an item or part of an item that is made of leather **5.** ZOOL DOG'S EARFLAP the flap of a dog's ear ■ **leathers** *npl.* CLOTHES MOTORCYCLISTS' LEATHER CLOTHING the protective leather jacket, trousers, boots, and gloves worn by motorcyclists ■ *adj.* **1.** MADE OF LEATHER made of leather or a material that looks like leather **2.** INVOLVING SADOMASOCHISM OR FETISHISM wearing, or for people who wear, leather clothing as a symbol of interest in sadomasochism or as a fetish ■ *vt.* (**-ers, -ering, -ered**) **1.** COVER STH IN LEATHER to give sth a covering of leather **2.** PUNISH SB PHYSICALLY to beat a person or animal severely, especially by using a leather strap (*dated informal*) [Old English *lether-*. Ultimately from an Indo-European word that is also the ancestor of Irish *leathar* and Welsh *lledr.*]

Leatherback

leatherback /léthər bak/ *n.* the largest of the living sea turtles, which has a flexible shell ridged with bone and covered with leathery skin. Latin name: *Dermochelys coriacea.*

Leatherhead /léthər hed/ town in Surrey, southeastern England, on the River Mole. Population: 42,903 (1991).

leatherjacket /léthər jakit/ *n.* the tough-skinned larva of certain craneflies that is considered to be a pest because it destroys grass roots

leathern /léthərn/ *adj.* made of leather or a material that looks like leather (*archaic*)

leatherneck /léthər nek/ *n. US* a member of the United States Marine Corps (*slang*) [From the leather collar that was formerly part of the uniform]

leatherwood /léthər wŏŏd/ *n.* **1.** TREES TREE WITH YELLOW FLOWERS a small deciduous tree of eastern North America with pliable branches and bark and small yellow flowers. Latin name: *Dirca palustris.* **2.** PLANTS = titi[2] *n.* 2

leatherwork /léthər wurk/ *n.* **1.** DECORATING OF LEATHER the craft of sculpting, cutting, or burning designs into leather **2.** DECORATED LEATHER items made from leather, especially decorated leather —**leatherworker** *n.* —**leatherworking** *n.*

leathery /léthəri/ *adj.* looking or feeling like leather, especially having a grainy texture or a tough unyielding consistency —**leatheriness** *n.*

leave[1] /leev/ (**leaves, leaving, left** /left/) *v.* **1.** *vti.* DEPART to go away from a person or place ○ *I leave the office at five o'clock daily.* **2.** *vt.* LET SB CONTINUE DOING STH to go away from sb in order to allow that person to do sth ○ *You run along and leave me to my paperwork.* **3.** *vt.* CAUSE STH TO REMAIN to give sth to sb or put sth in a place before departing ○ *I left my number with Dan.* **4.** *vt.* LET STH REMAIN BEHIND ACCIDENTALLY to forget to bring sth away from a place ○ *I must have left my keys at the office.* **5.** *vt.* GIVE STH IN WILL to bequeath sth as a legacy ○ *He plans to leave all his money to charity.* **6.** *vt.* PRODUCE STH THAT REMAINS to cause a residue, trace, or mark to remain ○ *The snails left trails on the path.* **7.** *vt.* NOT CHANGE CONDITION OF STH to allow sth or sb to remain unchanged in a certain state ○ *I left my coat on.* ○ *Leave your sister alone.* **8.** *vt.* HAVE STH REMAINING to cause an amount to remain by removing some amount or part ○ *Six minus four leaves two.* **9.** *vt.* SET STH ASIDE to save or keep sth for sb's use ○ *I left some cake for you.* **10.** *vt.* DESERT SB OR STH to abandon a person or place ○ *She has left the city to live in the country.* **11.** *vt.* HAVE SB AS SURVIVOR to be survived by sb after death ○ *He leaves a wife and two young sons.* **12.** *vti.* GIVE UP POSITION IN STH to end participation in a group or activity ○ *She left that job for a better one.* **13.** *vt.* GIVE JOB TO ANOTHER to transfer control of or responsibility for sth to sb ○ *Leave the typing to me.* **14.** *vt.* REJECT STH to reject sth offered ○ *That's the best I can offer, take it or leave it.* [Old English *lǣfan.* Ultimately from an Indo-European word meaning 'to stick' and 'fatty substance', which is also the ancestor of English *life* and *liver.*] ◇ **leave go** *or* **hold of sb** *or* **sth 1.** to stop holding sb or sth (*nonstandard*) ○ *Leave go of my arm!* **2.** to stop bothering sb, or stop interfering in a situation ◇ **leave it at that** to do or say no more about sth ◇ **leave sb** *or* **sth alone** to avoid bothering or becoming involved with sb or sth ◇ **leave much to be desired** to be highly unsatisfactory ◇ **leave sb to himself** *or* **herself** to go away and allow sb to be alone (*often passive*) ◇ **leave well enough alone** to leave a situation as it is rather than risk making it worse

leave behind *vt.* **1.** PROGRESS FASTER THAN SB OR STH to move ahead of sb or sth proceeding at a slower pace (*often passive*) **2.** FORGET ABOUT STH to dismiss sth from the mind ○ *She left her worries behind as she headed for the Bahamas.*

leave off *v.* **1.** *vi.* CEASE to stop doing sth ○ *Leave off chatting and listen for a change!* **2.** *vt.* STOP USING STH to stop doing or making use of sth ○ *You can leave your coats since it's so warm.*

leave out *vt.* to fail to include sb or sth, whether by choice or accident ○ *I felt left out of the party.* ◇ **leave it out!** used to tell sb to stop saying or doing sth annoying (*informal*)

leave[2] /leev/ *n.* **1.** PERIOD OF PERMITTED ABSENCE time off from work or duty, with official permission ○ *He'll get a month's paternity leave.* **2.** PERMISSION permission to do sth (*formal*) ○ *He was given leave to present his proposal.* **3.** FAREWELL the act of saying goodbye to sb ○ *We took our leave of the host and went on to the next party.* [Old English *lēaf*, literally 'pleasure, approval'. Ultimately from an Indo-European word meaning 'to desire', which is also the ancestor of English *love, believe*, and *furlough.*] ◇ **take leave of your senses** to become entirely irrational or lose all sense of reality

leave[3] /leev/ (**leaves, leaving, leaved**) *vi.* to grow foliage ○ *The oak has started to leave.* [13thC. Formed from LEAF.]

leaven /lévv'n/ *n.* **leaven, leavening 1.** RAISING AGENT a substance used to make dough rise, especially yeast or other fermenting agents **2.** STH THAT ENLIVENS sth that lightens the weight or mood of sth (*literary*) ○ *with a leaven of wit* ■ *vt.* (**-ens, -ening, -ened**) **1.** MIX YEAST IN STH to add leaven to dough **2.** MAKE FOOD RISE to cause bread or cake to rise using leaven **3.** ENLIVEN STH to lighten the atmosphere or mood of sth (*literary*) ○ *His story leavened the mood of the gathering.* [14thC. Via Old French *levain* from assumed Vulgar Latin *levamen*, from Latin *levare* 'to raise'.]

Leavenworth /lévv'n wurth/ city in northeastern Kansas. It is home to Leavenworth Federal Penitentiary. Population: 39,431 (1996).

leave of absence *n.* **1.** PERMISSION TO BE ABSENT permission to have time off from work or another duty for a particular period ○ *I requested a leave of absence so that I could take a finance course.* **2.** TIME AWAY FROM WORK the time spent away from work or another duty while on leave of absence ○ *His leave of absence included the holidays.*

leaves plural of **leaf**

leave-taking *n.* a saying of goodbye before leaving sb (*literary*) ○ *After a tearful leave-taking, we set off.*

leavings /leevingz/ *npl.* sth that sb has left behind or that is left over from sth, usually of little value

Leavis /leeviss/, **F. R.** (1895–1978) British literary critic. He stressed the moral value of the study of literature. He edited the journal *Scrutiny* (1932–53), and wrote *The Great Tradition* (1948), as well as studies of Dickens and D. H. Lawrence. Full name **Frank Raymond Leavis**

Lebanese /lébbə neez/ (*plural* **-nese**) *n.* sb who was born or brought up in Lebanon, or who has Lebanese citizenship —**Lebanese** *adj.*

Lebanon

Lebanon /lébbənən/ republic on the eastern coast of the Mediterranean Sea, in southwestern Asia. Language: Arabic. Currency: Lebanese pound. Capital: Beirut. Population: 3,111,828 (1997). Area: 10,452 sq. km/4,036 sq. mi. Official name **Lebanese Republic**

Lebanon, Mount mountain in western Massachusetts, situated in Berkshire and Middlesex counties

lebensraum /láybənz rowm/ *n.* **1.** ADDITIONAL TERRITORY CLAIMED BY NAZIS additional land in Eastern Europe that the Nazi government claimed was necessary for the continued political and economic development of Germany **2.** SPACE FOR GROWTH adequate room for life or development [Early 20thC. From German, 'living space'.]

lebkuchen /láyb kookən/ (*plural* **-chen**) *n.* a rich decorated German gingerbread, traditionally baked in a wide variety of shapes and sizes for Christmas and other celebrations [Early 20thC. Via German from Middle High German *lebekuoche*, from *lebe* 'loaf' + *kuoche* 'cake'.]

Lebowa /lə bố ə/ former homeland in northern South Africa, created in 1969 for the northern Sotho people

Lebrun /lə brŏN/, **Albert** (1871–1950) French statesman. A left-winger, he became president of the Third Republic (1931) but retired to make way for Marshal Pétain in 1940.

Le Carré /lə kárray/, **John** (*b.* 1931) British novelist. His popular spy novels include *Tinker, Tailor, Soldier, Spy* (1974) and *Smiley's People* (1980). Real name **David John Moore Cornwell**

lech /lech/, **letch** *n.* (*informal*) **1.** LECHER a lecher **2.** INTENSE DESIRE a lustful desire for sb **3.** INSTANCE OF LECHERY an act or instance of lechery ■ *vi.* (**leches, leching, leched; letches, letching, letched**) BEHAVE LEWDLY to behave lewdly towards sb (*informal*) [Late 18thC. Origin uncertain: probably a back-formation from LECHER.]

Le Chatelier's principle /lə sha tél yayz-/ *n.* the principle that a change affecting a chemical equilibrium is offset by compensatory changes in other components of the equilibrium, thus producing little overall effect [Early 20thC. Named after the French chemist Henri Louis *Le Chatelier* (1850–1936), who formulated it.]

lechayim *interj., n.* = **l'chaim**

lecher /léchər/ *n.* a man who behaves lewdly and lustfully in a way regarded as distasteful (*disapproving*) [12thC. From Old French *lecheor*, from *lechier*, literally 'to lick'. Ultimately of Germanic origin.]

lecherous /léchərəss/ *adj.* expressing or displaying lewdness in a way regarded as distasteful —**lecherously** *adv.* —**lecherousness** *n.*

lechery /léchəri/ *n.* lustful behaviour especially by a man that is regarded as distasteful [12thC. From Old French *lecherie*, from *lecheor* (see LECHER).]

lechwe /láychwi/ *n.* **1.** S AFRICAN ANTELOPE an African antelope found mainly in marshes and by rivers in Botswana and Zambia. It has long narrow hooves and long backwards-pointing horns. Latin name: *Kobus leche*. **2.** NILE REGION ANTELOPE an African antelope with a white shoulder patch, found in the wetlands of the upper Nile valley. Latin name: *Kobus megaceros*. [Mid-19thC. Of uncertain origin: probably from Sesotho *lets'a*.]

lecithin /léssithin/ *n.* a waxy substance **(phospholipid)** that consists of choline and fatty acids and occurs widely in plants and animals. Lecithin is used as an emulsifier in foods and commercial products. [Mid-19thC. From French *lécithine*, from Greek *lekithos* 'egg yolk', of unknown origin.]

lecithinase /lə síthi nayss, -nayz/ *n.* = **phospholipase**

Le Corbusier

Le Corbusier /lə káwr bo`ozi ay/ (1887–1965) Swiss-born French architect and designer. His dictum that 'a house is a machine for living in' formed one of the bases of his own work and of functionalism. Pseudonym of **Charles-Édouard Jeanneret**

lect /lekt/ *n.* a variety within a language, having its own rules [Late 20thC. Back-formation from DIALECT.]

lect. *abbr.* **1.** lecture **2.** lecturer

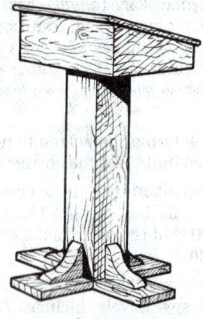

Lectern

lectern /léktərn/ *n.* **1.** READING STAND FOR SCRIPTURES a tall slender table with a slanted top on which an open book can rest, used in churches and synagogues for reading scriptures to the congregation **2.** READING STAND FOR SPEAKER a stand with a slanted top on which a book or lecture notes can rest before a standing speaker. It may be free-standing or be placed on a table or desk. [14thC. Via Old French *letrun* and medieval Latin *lectrinum* from late Latin *lectrum*, from *lect-*, the past participle stem of *legere* 'to read' (see LEGIBLE).]

lectin /léktin/ *n.* a plant protein that binds to particular sugars [Mid-20thC. Formed from *lect-*, the past participle stem of *legere* 'to choose, read' (see LEGIBLE).]

lection /léksh'n/ *n.* **1.** TEXTUAL VARIANT a variant reading of a text in a particular edition or translation **2.** CHR BIBLE READING a passage from Scripture that is set to be read on a particular day as part of the liturgy of a Christian service [Early 17thC. Via the Latin stem *lection-* 'reading', from, ultimately, *legere* (see LEGIBLE).]

lectionary /léksh'nəri/ *n.* (*plural* -ies) *n.* a schedule of scriptural readings to be read at church services over the course of the year

lector /lék tawr/ *n.* **1.** UNIV UNIVERSITY LECTURER a university teacher, especially a man who is a foreign language instructor at a European university. ◊ **lectrice 2.** CHR SCRIPTURE READER IN CHURCH sb who reads scriptural passages to the congregation at a religious service [14thC. From Latin, literally 'reader', from *lect-*, the past participle stem of *legere* (see LEGIBLE).]

lectrice /lek treéss/ *n.* a woman who is a university teacher, especially a woman who is a foreign language instructor at a university. ◊ **lector** *n.* 1 [Late 19thC. From French, feminine of *lecteur*, from Latin *lector* (see LECTOR).]

lecture /lékchər/ *n.* **1.** INSTRUCTIONAL SPEECH an educational speech on a particular subject made before an audience ○ *I missed the lecture on Shakespeare's use of irony.* **2.** TEACHING SESSION a class meeting at which a lecture is given ○ *The course involves two lectures and two lab sessions per week.* **3.** REPRIMAND a speech intended as a reprimand ○ *The teacher lectured the students on their tardiness.* ■ *v.* (-tures, -turing, -tured) **1.** *vti.* GIVE EDUCATIONAL SPEECH to deliver a speech before a group of people as a method of instruction ○ *He lectures on stress management all over the country.* **2.** *vi.* BE UNIVERSITY LECTURER to be employed as a lecturer at a university ○ *She lectures at the University.* **3.** *vt.* REPRIMAND SB to reprimand sb by making a speech about how a person should behave ○ *lecturing the congregation about church attendance* [13thC. Via French from medieval Latin *lectura*, literally 'reading', from Latin *lect-*, the past participle stem of *legere* (see LEGIBLE).]

lecturer /lékchərər/ *n.* **1.** UNIV UNIVERSITY TEACHER sb who works as a teacher in higher education in a British university and whose position is lower than that of a professor **2.** INFORMATIVE SPEAKER sb who gives an informative speech on a particular topic, especially as a profession ○ *a lecturer's tour*

lectureship /lékchər ship/ *n.* a post at the rank of lecturer in a British institution of higher education ○ *The University has three lectureships open.*

lecture theatre *n.* a large room with a stage for a speaker and desks and chairs for an audience, arranged so that the whole audience can see the speaker

LED *n.* a semiconductor that emits light when a current passes through it. LEDs are used as indicator lights on electronic equipment. They are commonly red or green in colour and very energy efficient. Full form **light-emitting diode**

Leda /léedə/ *n.* **1.** MYTHOL GREEK HEROINE in Greek mythology, a queen of Sparta. She was the mother of Helen of Troy and Pollux by Zeus, who wooed her in the shape of a swan. Her other children were Clytemnestra and Castor. **2.** ASTRON VERY SMALL MOON OF JUPITER a very small natural satellite of Jupiter discovered in 1974. It is approximately 10 km/6 mi. in diameter and occupies an intermediate orbit.

lederhosen /láydər hōz'n/ *npl.* a pair of Bavarian

Lederhosen

leather shorts, usually with braces, worn by men and boys [Mid-20thC. From German, 'leather trousers'.]

ledge /lej/ *n.* **1.** ARCHIT NARROW SHELF AGAINST WALL a narrow shelf or moulding fixed to a wall that serves a decorative or protective purpose **2.** GEOG FLAT SURFACE PROJECTING FROM ROCK FACE a narrow flat projecting rock shelf, e.g. on the vertical surface of a cliff **3.** OCEANOG UNDERWATER RAISED SURFACE a raised surface underwater such as a reef or ridge, especially one found near a shore **4.** MINING ROCK LAYER a layer of ore-bearing rock [Mid-16thC. Origin uncertain: possibly a variant of LAY[1]. The word's earliest meaning was 'crossbar'.] —**ledged** *adj.* —**ledgy** *adj.*

ledger /léjjər/ *n.* **1.** ACCT FINANCIAL RECORD BOOK a book or page with columns for debits and credits, on which to transcribe financial records **2.** HORIZONTAL GRAVESTONE a gravestone that lies flat on the ground **3.** CONSTR SCAFFOLDING BEAM a horizontal beam in a scaffolding that is attached to the uprights and supports the beams **(putlogs) 4.** ANGLING = **ledger-tackle** ■ *vi.* (-ers, -ering, -ered) FISH WITH LEDGER-TACKLE to fish using ledger-tackle [Early 16thC. Of uncertain origin: probably formed from *leggen*, an earlier form of LAY[1].]

ledger board *n.* **1.** HORIZONTAL RAIL a horizontal board, especially the top rail of a fence **2.** JOIST-SUPPORTING BOARD a narrow horizontal board attached to a row of studs to support joist ends

ledger line, **leger line** *n.* a short line added above or below a musical staff to accommodate notes that are higher or lower than those on the staff

ledger-tackle *n.* a fishing line with a weight attached near its end, in order to anchor the line so that the bait floats near the bottom of the water

Leduc /lədo`ok/ town in Alberta, Canada, situated 32 km/20 mi. south of Edmonton. Population: 13,970 (1991).

lee /lee/ *n.* **1.** NAUT SHIP SIDE AWAY FROM WIND the side of a ship away from the source of the wind **2.** PROTECTIVE COVER shelter from the elements when the wind is blowing ○ *in the lee of the wall* ■ *adj.* NAUT AWAY FROM WIND on or towards the side of a ship, natural feature, or object that is away from the wind [Old English *hlēo* 'shelter'. Ultimately from an Indo-European word meaning 'warm' that is also the ancestor of English *lukewarm*, *calorie*, and *chowder*.]

Lee /lee/, **Gypsy Rose** (1914–70) US entertainer and novelist. The musical *Gypsy* was in part based on her life as a striptease artist. Born **Louise Rose Hovick**

Lee, John A. (1891–1982) New Zealand politician and writer. As well as being active in the Labour Party, he wrote the novel *Children of the Poor* (1934). Full name **John Alfred Alexander Lee**

Robert E. Lee

Lee, Robert E. (1807–70) US general. He commanded the Confederate army during the last three years of the US Civil War, and surrendered to Ulysses S. Grant at Appomattox Courthouse. Full name **Robert Edward Lee**

leeboard /lee bawrd/ *n.* either of two movable wooden or metal shelves on the outside of a ship's hull that prevent sideways movement caused by the wind [So called because the board on the boat's leeward side is lowered into the water to prevent making leeway]

leech[1] /leech/ *n.* **1.** ZOOL BLOOD-SUCKING WORM a freshwater worm that sucks blood or eats flesh. One species has been used in medical treatments to bleed patients or to eat away putrid flesh from a wound. Class: Hirudinea. **2.** SB WHO EXPLOITS SB ELSE sb who clings to or takes advantage of sb else, e.g. for financial support **3.** DOCTOR a physician (*archaic informal*) ■ *v.* (**leeches, leeching, leeched**) **1.** *vt.* MED **BLEED SB USING LEECHES** to bleed a patient using leeches **2.** *vi.* **EXPLOIT SB** to cling to or take advantage of sb, e.g. for financial support (*informal*) [Old English *lǣce*, of uncertain origin: possibly identical with *lǣce* 'physician', originally perhaps 'speaker of spells', ultimately from an Indo-European base meaning 'to speak' that also produced English *lecture*]

leech[2] /leech/, **leach** *n.* **1. VERTICAL SAIL EDGE** a vertical edge of a square sail **2. EDGE OF SAIL AWAY FROM MAST** the edge of a fore-and-aft sail that is farthest from the mast or stay [15thC. Origin uncertain: possibly from Middle Low German *līk* 'leech line'. Ultimately from an Indo-European word meaning 'to bind' that is also the ancestor of English *rely* and *furl*.]

Leeds /leedz/ university city in Yorkshire, northern England. Population: 725,000 (1995).

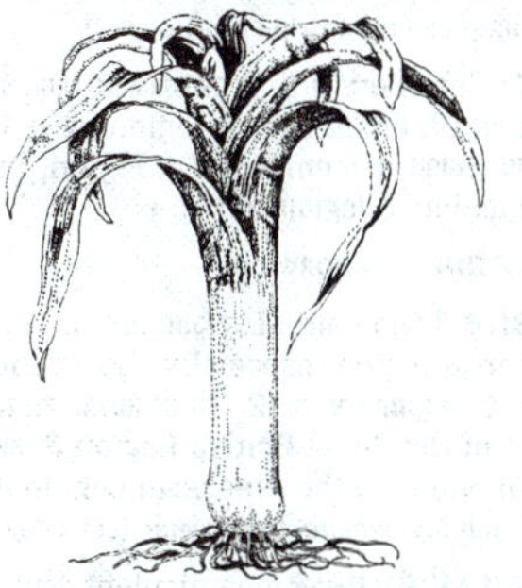

Leek

leek /leek/ *n.* an edible plant with dark green, coiled leaves rising from a close-set white base. It is related to the onion and has a flavour similar to it. The leek is one of the national symbols of Wales. Latin name: *Allium porrum*. [Old English *lēac* (source also of English *garlic*), of prehistoric Germanic origin)]

Leek /leek/ market town in Staffordshire, central England. Population: 18,167 (1991).

leer /leer/ *vi.* (**leers, leering, leered**) **LOOK LASCIVIOUSLY** to look or smile in a way that suggests unpleasantly lustful or malicious intent ■ *n.* **LASCIVIOUS LOOK** an unpleasantly lustful or malicious look or smile [Mid-16thC. Origin uncertain: probably from an obsolete word meaning 'cheek', from Old English *hlēor*.]

leery /leéri/ (**-ier, -iest**), **leary** (**-ier, -iest**) *adj.* **1. SUSPICIOUS** regarding sb or sth with suspicion (*informal*) ○ *I'm leery of anyone who approaches me on the street.* **2. HUNGRY** hungry (*regional informal*) [Early 18thC. Origin uncertain: probably formed from LEER in the obsolete meaning 'cheek, side of the face', with the underlying meaning 'looking sideways'.] —**leeriness** *n.*

lees /leez/ *npl.* sediment that settles in wine or other alcoholic beverage during fermentation [14thC. Via Old French *lie* from medieval Latin *lia*, probably of Celtic origin.]

lee shore *n.* a shore that is in the direction away from the wind, relative to a ship

leet[1] /leet/ *n.* a court formerly held at regular intervals by the lords of certain English manors [13thC. From Anglo-Norman *lete*, of unknown origin.]

leet[2] /leet/ *n. Scotland* a list of applicants or candidates for a post or office [15thC. Origin uncertain: possibly from Anglo-Norman *lite* 'list' (a variant of Old French *liste*; see LIST), or a variant of ELITE.]

Leeuwin, Cape /loǒ ən, kayp/ promontory in southwestern Western Australia, the most southwesterly point on the continent

leeward /leéwərd/; *nautical* /loǒ ərd/ *adj.* **AWAY FROM WIND** on or towards a location, especially the side of a ship, that is away or sheltered from the wind. ◊ **windward** ■ *n.* **PLACE AWAY FROM WIND** a place or direction away or sheltered from the wind. ◊ **windward**

Leeward Islands /leéwərd-/ chain of islands in the West Indies, between the Atlantic Ocean and the Caribbean Sea. The principal islands include Antigua, Guadeloupe, Montserrat, and St Kitts. Area: 3,297 sq. km/1,237 sq. mi.

leeway /leé way/ *n.* **1. LATITUDE FOR VARIATION** the permissible margin for variation or deviation from sth **2. FALLING BEHIND** falling behind in progress or performance ○ *He's got a lot of leeway to make up at work after his holiday.* **3.** SAILING, AEROSP **DEVIATION FROM COURSE** the sideways movement of a ship or aircraft from its course, caused by strong winds

Le Fanu /léffə nyoo/, **Sheridan** (1814–73) Irish novelist and journalist. His 14 novels include *Uncle Silas* (1864), and he also owned and edited the *Dublin University Magazine.* Full name **Joseph Sheridan Le Fanu**

left[1] /left/ *adj.* **1. WEST WHEN FACING NORTH** on or towards the west when sb or sth is facing north ○ *Her left leg is broken.* **2. left, Left** POL **ADVOCATING POLITICAL AND SOCIAL CHANGE** supporting liberal, socialist, or communist political and social changes or reform **3.** GEOG **ON LEFT WHEN LOOKING DOWNSTREAM** on the river bank to the left of sb facing downstream **4.** THEATRE **TO RIGHT OF AUDIENCE** on or relating to that part of a stage that is to the left of sb standing on it and facing the audience ○ *Exit stage left.* ■ *adv.* **ON LEFT SIDE** on or towards the left side of sb or sth ○ *The pole is leaning left a bit.* ■ *n.* **1. LEFT SIDE** the left side of sb or sth ○ *The house is on your left.* **2. left, Left** POL **LIBERALS, SOCIALISTS, AND COMMUNISTS** people who support liberal, socialist, or communist political and social changes or reform **3.** BOXING **LEFT-HANDED PUNCH** a blow delivered with the left hand ○ *took a hard left to the jaw* **4.** BOXING **LEFT-HANDED PUNCHING ABILITY** a boxer's left hand with respect to its ability to deliver a punch ○ *He's got a good left.* **5.** BASEBALL = **left field** [13thC. From Old English *lyft-* 'weak', of unknown origin.]

left[2] past tense, past participle of **leave**

left atrioventricular valve *n.* = **mitral valve**

Left Bank area in central Paris, south of the River Seine

left-brain *adj.* relating to or involving skills or knowledge such as analytical or linguistic ability that are believed to be associated with the left half of the cerebrum —**left brain** *n.*

left-footer *n.* offensive term for a Roman Catholic (*informal offensive*)

left-hand *adj.* **1. TO LEFT** on or towards the left **2. FOR LEFT HAND** intended for or done by the left hand

left-handed *adj., adv.* **1. USING LEFT HAND** using the left hand, rather than the right, for tasks such as writing and reaching for and manipulating objects. About ten per cent of the population is naturally left-handed. **2.** SPORTS **STARTING SWING FROM LEFT** swinging from the left to the right ■ *adj.* **1. DONE WITH LEFT HAND** done using the left hand **2. NOT SINCERE** ironic and insincere ○ *a left-handed compliment* **3. CLUMSY** lacking skill or grace **4. TURNING RIGHT TO LEFT** spiralling towards the left **5.** LAW = **morganatic** —**left-hander** *n.*

leftie *n.* = **lefty**

leftish /léftish/ *adj.* tending to be relatively left-wing in politics

leftism /léftizəm/ *n.* the advocating of liberal, socialist, or communist political and social change or reform —**leftist** *adj., n.*

left-luggage office *n.* a room in a railway or bus station where luggage can be temporarily deposited. US term **baggage check**

leftmost /léftmōst/ *adj.* in the position farthest to the left

leftover /léftōvər/ *adj.* **REMAINING UNUSED** remaining after the rest of sth has been used or eaten ■ *n.* **STH REMAINING** sth that remains from a previous period of time while everything else associated with that period has disappeared ■ **leftovers** *npl.* **SAVED FOOD** food remaining from a previous meal or meals, saved and served again or made into a new dish ○ *I made this soup from leftovers.*

leftward /léftwərd/ *adj.* **GOING OR BEING LEFT** moving towards or located on the left ■ *adv.* **leftward, leftwards TO OR AT LEFT** towards or on the left

left wing *n.* **1.** POL **MEMBERS OF ORGANIZATION MOST FAVOURING CHANGE** a subgroup of a larger organization that advocates greater political and social change or reform than the rest of the organization **2.** SPORTS **FIELD LEFT OF OPPONENT'S GOAL** the side of a playing field that is to the left of a player facing the opponent's goal **3.** SPORTS **SB PLAYING ON LEFT WING** a player whose position in a team is on the left wing —**left-wing** *adj.* —**left-winger** *n.*

lefty /léfti/ (*plural* **-ies**), **leftie** *n.* (*informal*) **1.** POL **LEFTIST** sb with left-wing beliefs **2.** *US, Can* **LEFT-HANDER** sb who is left-handed ○ *How many lefties are on the team?*

leg /leg/ *n.* **1.** ANAT **LOWER LIMB** any of the limbs that animals and people use for standing, walking, running, or jumping, either including or excluding the foot **2.** FURNITURE, BUILDING **SUPPORTING POLE** a part of an object that looks like a leg and is used to support it ○ *a table leg* **3.** FOOD **MEAT FROM ANIMAL'S OR FOWL'S LEG** the meat, including the bone, from the back hindquarter of a four-legged animal, or from the leg of a bird, that is cooked and eaten as food **4. BRANCH OF OBJECT** one of the extensions of a branched object **5.** CLOTHES **CLOTHING FOR LEG** the portion of a piece of clothing that covers all or part of the leg ○ *trouser leg* **6.** GEOM **RIGHT-ANGLE SIDE OF TRIANGLE** either of the two sides of a right-angled triangle that extends from the right angle **7. SECTION OF JOURNEY** a part of a journey that is separated from other parts by a period of rest, or by a change in direction or the manner of travel **8.** SAILING **SAILING COMPLETED ON ONE TACK** the distance travelled by a boat on a single tack **9.** SPORTS **RELAY RACE PORTION** one of the parts of a relay race that a single athlete completes **10.** SPORTS **PORTION OF SPORTS COMPETITION** one of stages, events, or games that is part of a larger competition but is treated independently of the other parts and has its own winner **11.** FOOTBALL **ONE OF TWO FOOTBALL GAMES** either of two games in a competition played between two football teams, one game being played at home, the other away. The aggregate score of the two games determines the overall winner of the round. **12.** CRICKET **LEFT-HAND PART OF CRICKET FIELD** in cricket, the part of the field that lies on the left of and behind a right-handed batsman as he or she stands in position to hit the ball [13thC. From Old Norse *leggr*, of unknown origin.] ◇ **get your leg over** to have sex (*slang*) ◇ **have legs** *US* to be of long or lasting duration ◇ **leg it 1.** to run away, especially in order to escape from sb or sth (*informal*) **2.** to walk or run (*informal*) ◇ **not have a leg to stand on** to have nothing to justify or support an attitude or position (*informal*) ◇ **on your last legs** on the verge of collapse or breakdown ◇ **pull sb's leg** to tell sb sth untrue as a tease or for fun (*informal*) ◇ **shake a leg 1.** to hurry up (*usually used as a command*) **2.** to dance (*dated informal*) ◇ **show a leg** to get out of bed in the morning (*dated informal*) (*usually used as a command*) ◇ **stretch your legs** to go for a walk after a period of being seated or stationary ◇ **talk the hind legs off a donkey** to talk a great deal

leg. *abbr.* **1.** legal **2.** legate **3.** MUSIC legato **4.** legislation **5.** legislative **6.** legislature

legacy /léggəssi/ *n.* (*plural* **-cies**) **1. BEQUEST MADE IN WILL** money or property that is left to sb in a will **2. STH FROM PAST** sth that is handed down or remains from a previous generation or time ■ *adj.* **OUTDATED OR DISCONTINUED** associated with sth that is outdated or discontinued [14thC. Via Old French *legacie* 'office of a delegate' from medieval Latin *legatia*, from Latin *legatus* (see LEGATE).]

legal /leég'l/ *adj.* **1. LAW-RELATED** relating to the law or to courts of law **2. OF OR FOR LAWYERS** relating to lawyers or to law as a profession **3. UNDER THE LAW** established under the law ○ *the legal age of consent* **4. PERMITTED BY LAW** allowed under the law ○ *Parking on the grass isn't legal.* **5. ESTABLISHED BY LAW COURT** recognized or established by a court of law, rather than a court of equity [15thC. Via French from Latin *legalis*, from *leg-*, the stem of *lex* 'law'.] —**legally** *adv.*

WORD KEY: SYNONYMS

legal, lawful, decriminalized, legalized, legitimate, licit

CORE MEANING: used to describe sth that is permitted, recognized, or required by law

legal permitted, recognized, or required by law; **lawful** a less commonly used word meaning the same as 'legal'; **decriminalized** no longer categorized as a criminal offence; **legalized** previously categorized as illegal and now declared legal; **legitimate** legally acceptable; **licit** a very formal and now rarely used word meaning the same as 'legal'.

WORD KEY: ORIGIN

The Latin stem *leg-*, from which ***legal*** is derived, is also the source of English *allegation, colleague, college, delegate, legacy, legislate, legitimate, loyal,* and *privilege.*

legal age *n.* the age established by law after which sb is considered to be an adult

legal aid *n.* **1.** FREE LAWYERS' SERVICES legal advice or representation that is provided by an organization at low or no cost to people who cannot afford to pay for legal services **2.** GOVERNMENT AID FOR LEGAL COSTS public funds used for legal advice and representation for people who cannot afford private lawyers ○ *Legal aid paid for his defence.*

legal eagle *n.* a lawyer, especially a skilful or successful one (*slang*) [Rhyming expression of uncertain origin, perhaps from the keenness of vision for which the eagle is known]

legalese /leégə leéz/ *n.* language that is typically used in legal documents and is generally considered by lay people to be difficult to understand

legal holiday *n. US* a day established as a holiday by law, when government offices, schools, and post offices are typically closed. Legal holidays usually commemorate an event or person and many businesses close as well.

legalise *vt.* = **legalize**

legalism /leégəlizzəm/ *n.* **1.** ADHERENCE TO LETTER OF LAW strict adherence to a literal interpretation of a law, rule, or religious or moral code **2.** LAW LAW TERM a word or phrase in legal jargon —**legalist** *n.* —**legalistic** /leégə lístik/ *adj.* —**legalistically** *adv.*

legality /li gálliti/ (*plural* **-ties**) *n.* **1.** CONFORMITY TO LAW the state of being in accordance with the law ○ *the legality of the corporation's activities* **2.** LEGAL REQUIREMENT sth required by law, especially when a technical detail (*often used in the plural*) ○ *We have to take care of certain legalities before opening the business.*

legalize /leégə līz/ (**-izes, -izing, -ized**), **legalise** (**-ises, -ising, -ised**) *vt.* to make an activity legal by making or changing a law —**legalization** /leégə lī záysh'n/ *n.*

legal separation *n.* separation of a married couple that is recognized by a court of law, or the court decree establishing such a separation. This is often required as a first step towards divorce.

legal tender *n.* the currency that is valid for the payment of a debt and must be accepted by a creditor

Legaspi /lə gásspi/, **Legazpi** city and capital of Albay Province, Philippines, situated at the head of Albay Gulf. Population: 121,120 (1990).

legate /léggət/ *n.* **1.** CHR POPE'S REPRESENTATIVE an emissary of the pope, especially one who represents the Vatican in other countries **2.** POL GOVERNMENT REPRESENTATIVE an official representative of a government, especially a diplomat [12thC. Via French from Latin *legatus*, from the past participle of *legare* 'to send as an envoy, bequeath' (source also of English *colleague, delegate,* and *relegate*).] —**legateship** *n.* —**legatine** /léggə tīn/ *adj.*

legatee /léggi teé/ *n.* sb who inherits a bequest under the terms of a will

legation /li gáysh'n/ *n.* **1.** DIPLOMAT'S RESIDENCE the official local residence of a senior diplomat assigned to a country. It ranks below an embassy in importance. **2.** DIPLOMATIC STAFF the staff of a legation **3.** DIPLOMATS ON MISSION a group of representatives sent on a mission, especially a diplomatic mission **4.** SENDING OF DIPLOMATIC REPRESENTATIVE the sending of a representative on a diplomatic mission **5.** DIPLOMATIC MISSION a mission performed by a diplomatic representative **6.** LEGATE'S POSITION the status or office of a legate [14thC. Directly or via French from, ultimately, Latin *legare* 'to send as an envoy' (source of English *legate*).]

legato /li gaátō/ *adv.* SMOOTHLY in a smooth, even manner, often indicated in a musical score by a curved line (**slur**) connecting the notes to be so played (*used as a musical direction*) ■ *n.* (*plural* **-tos**) LEGATO PIECE OF MUSIC a piece of music, or a section of a piece, played legato [Mid-18thC. From Italian, literally 'tied together'.] —**legato** *adj.*

legator /li gáytər/ *n.* sb who has made a will to pass on property to sb else

leg before wicket *adj.* HIT ON LEG BY BALL in cricket, forced to end an innings as a result of being hit on the leg by a ball, that would otherwise have hit the wicket ■ *n.* DISMISSAL BECAUSE BALL HITS LEG in cricket, the dismissal of a batsman as a result of being hit on the leg by a ball that would otherwise have hit the wicket

leg-break *n.* in cricket, a ball with a bounce that spins from the leg side to the off side

leg bye *n.* in cricket, a run scored after the ball hits some part of the batsman's body other than the hand, without touching the bat

legend /léjjənd/ *n.* **1.** OLD STORY a story that has been passed down for generations, especially one that is presented as history but is unlikely to be true **2.** OLD STORIES a group of stories presented as history but unlikely to be true **3.** MODERN MYTH a popular myth that has arisen in modern times **4.** CELEBRITY sb famous admired for a particular skill or talent **5.** INSCRIPTION an inscription on an object, especially a title or motto **6.** PUBL CAPTION a caption for an illustration **7.** MAPS MAP KEY an explanation of the symbols used on a map (*dated*) [14thC. Via French *légende* from medieval Latin *legenda*, literally 'things to be read', from Latin *legere* (see LEGIBLE).]

legendary /léjjəndəri/ *adj.* **1.** BELONGING TO LEGEND described or commemorated in a legend ○ *the legendary figure of Hercules* **2.** CONTAINING LEGENDS retold for generations as history but unlikely to be completely or even partially true ○ *the legendary tales of ancient warriors* **3.** LIKE STH IN LEGEND appropriate for a legend ○ *an organization of legendary proportions* **4.** FAMOUS very famous in contemporary society —**legendarily** *adv.*

legendry /léjjəndri/ (*plural* **-ries**) *n.* a collection or group of legends

Léger /láy zhay/, **Fernand** (1881–1955) French painter. One of the founders of the Cubist movement, he developed a personal style that used rounded and cylindrical forms.

legerdemain /léjjərdə máyn/ *n.* **1.** ARTS SLEIGHT OF HAND sleight of hand (*dated*) **2.** SHOW OF SKILL a display of skill or cleverness, especially for deceitful purposes ○ *a dazzling display of political legerdemain* [15thC. From French *léger de main*, literally 'light of hand'.]

leger line *n.* = **ledger line**

leges /leé jeez/ plural of **lex**

-legged *suffix.* with a particular number of legs ○ *four-legged*

legging /légging/ *n.* PROTECTIVE COVERING FOR LOWER LEG a protective covering made of a strong material that is wrapped around the lower leg by labourers and players in certain sports ■ **leggings** *npl.* **1.** CLOSE-FITTING TROUSERS women's trousers or footless tights made of stretchy material that fit very closely to the legs and hips **2.** PROTECTIVE OUTER TROUSERS waterproof or insulated outer trousers that are worn for protection from snow, rain, and cold

leggy /léggi/ (**-gier, -giest**) *adj.* **1.** WITH LONG LEGS having very long legs in relation to the rest of the body **2.** WITH SHAPELY LEGS having long good-looking legs ○ *a leggy supermodel* **3.** BOT SPINDLY IN GROWTH with long thin stems that have few and widely spaced leaves

leghorn /lég hawrn/ *n.* **1.** BLEACHED STRAW fine bleached straw made from a type of Italian wheat **2.** STRAW FABRIC a fabric made from plaited leghorn straw **3.** STRAW HAT a hat made from leghorn straw [Mid-18thC. Named after the city of *Leghorn* (Livorno) in Italy, where the wheat originated.]

Leghorn *n.* a small domestic fowl from the Mediterranean region that is noted for its rapid production of white eggs [Mid-18thC. Named after the city of *Leghorn* (Livorno) in Italy, where the bird originated.]

legible /léjjəb'l/ *adj.* **1.** ABLE TO BE READ clear enough to be read **2.** ABLE TO BE RECOGNIZED capable of being easily understood or recognized (*archaic*) [15thC. From late Latin *legibilis*, from *legere* 'to collect, read'. Ultimately from an Indo-European base meaning 'to gather, speak'.] —**legibility** /léjjə bílləti/ *n.* —**legibleness** /léjjəb'lnəss/ *n.*

WORD KEY: ORIGIN

The Latin word *legere*, from which ***legible*** is derived, is also the source of English *coil, collect, cull, elect, elegant, intelligent, lecture, legend, legion, lesson, neglect,* and *select.*

legion /leéjən/ *n.* **1.** HIST ROMAN ARMY DIVISION in ancient Rome, an army division of 3,000 to 6,000 soldiers, including cavalry **2.** MIL LARGE BODY OF SOLDIERS a large military unit, especially an army ○ *the French Foreign Legion* **3.** MIL ORGANIZATION OF EX-MILITARY PERSONNEL an association of ex-servicemen and ex-servicewomen ○ *the Royal British Legion* **4.** MULTITUDE a large number of people or things (*often used in the plural*) ○ *Their complicated affairs are managed by a legion of accountants.* ■ *adj.* MANY very numerous (*literary*) ○ *dissatisfied customers and their legion complaints* [12thC. Via Old French from the Latin stem *legion-*, from *legere* 'to gather, choose' (see LEGIBLE); the underlying meaning was 'picked troops'.]

legionary /leéjənəri/ *adj.* OF OR FORMING LEGION belonging to, typical of, or forming a legion ■ *n.* (*plural* **-ies**) SOLDIER IN LEGION a member of a legion, especially a Roman legion. ◊ **legionnaire** *n.* 1

legionary ant *n.* = **army ant**

legionnaire /leéjə náir/, **Legionnaire** *n.* **1.** SB IN LEGION a soldier in a legion, especially the French Foreign Legion. ◊ **legionary** *n.* **2.** SB IN ROYAL BRITISH LEGION a member of the Royal British Legion **3.** SB IN AMERICAN LEGION a member of the American Legion [Early 19thC. From French *légionnaire*, from *légion* (see LEGION).]

Legionnaires' disease *n.* a virulent and sometimes fatal form of pneumonia caused by a bacterium and spread mainly by the water droplets in air conditioning systems [From the first recognized occurrence of the disease at an American Legion convention in Philadelphia in 1976]

Legion of Honour *n.* a French order of merit awarded for illustrious military or civil service. It was established by Napoleon in 1802.

legis. *abbr.* **1.** legislation **2.** legislative **3.** legislature

legislate /léjji slayt/ (**-lates, -lating, -lated**) *v.* **1.** *vi.* MAKE LAWS to write and pass laws **2.** *vt.* BRING STH ABOUT BY MAKING LAWS to make laws or rules designed to bring about some action or condition ○ *Parliament can't legislate good manners.* [Early 18thC. Back-formation from LEGISLATOR.]

legislation /léjji sláysh'n/ *n.* **1.** MAKING OF LAWS the process of writing and passing laws **2.** LAW OR LAWS a law or laws passed by an official body

legislative /léjjislətiv/ *adj.* **1.** RELATING TO LAW-MAKING involved in the writing and passing of laws **2.** RELATING TO LAW-MAKING BODY relating to or part of a legislature **3.** ENACTED BY LAW created by governmental legislation ○ *There is no legislative solution to this problem.* —**legislatively** *adv.*

legislative assembly, **Legislative Assembly** *n.* **1.** US LAW-MAKING BODY the two-chamber legislature of some US states **2.** LOWER HOUSE OF COMMONWEALTH LEGISLATURE the lower house of a two-chamber state legislature in some Commonwealth countries, especially that of some Australian states **3.** SINGLE-CHAMBER COMMONWEALTH LEGISLATURE a single-chamber legislature, especially the legislature of most Canadian provinces and some Australian states **4.** GROUP WITH POWER TO PASS LAWS any official body with law- or rule-making powers

legislative council, **Legislative Council** *n.* **1.** COMMITTEE OF STATE SENATORS AND REPRESENTATIVES a permanent committee consisting of members of both houses of a two-chamber state legislature who discuss issues of common concern and plan a legislative programme for the next session **2.** UPPER HOUSE IN TWO-CHAMBER LEGISLATURE the upper house of the two-chamber legislature in some Commonwealth countries, e.g. in most Indian and Australian states **3.** LEGISLATURE IN FORMER BRITISH COLONY the single-chamber legislature of some former British colonies

legislator /léjji slaytər/ *n.* sb who writes and passes laws, especially as a member of a legislature [15thC. From Latin *legis lator* 'proposer of a law', from *lex* 'law' + *lat-*, the past participle stem of *ferre* 'to bring'.] —**legislato-**

rial /léjjislə táwri əl/ *adj.* —**legislatorship** /léjji sláytər ship/ *n.*

legislature /léjjislətʃər/ *n.* an official body, usually chosen by election, with the power to make, change, and repeal laws [Late 17thC. Formed from LEGISLATOR, on the model of JUDICATURE.]

legist /leéjist/ *n.* a specialist in law, especially classical law [15thC. Via French *légiste* from, ultimately, the Latin stem *leg*- (see LEGAL).]

legit /lə jít/ *adj.* **1.** LEGAL complying with the law (*slang*) **2.** HONEST AND TRUTHFUL telling the truth and not trying to deceive (*slang*) ○ *Is his story legit?* **3.** THEATRE PRESENTING SERIOUS DRAMAS performing professionally produced dramatic theatre that is considered to be serious art, in contrast to such forms as revues and musical comedy (*informal*) [Late 19thC. Shortening of LEGITIMATE.]

legitimate /lə jíttimət/ *adj.* **1.** LAW LEGAL complying with the law, or under the law ○ *legitimate tax deductions* **2.** CONFORMING TO ACKNOWLEDGED STANDARDS complying with recognized rules, standards, or traditions ○ *not a legitimate excuse for missing school* **3.** NOT SPURIOUS well-reasoned and sincere ○ *We have legitimate reasons for worrying about the quality of our water.* **4.** BORN IN WEDLOCK born of legally married parents **5.** POL, LAW WITH RIGHT OF INHERITANCE having the right to inherit sth, such as the throne in a monarchy **6.** THEATRE RELATING TO SERIOUS PROFESSIONAL DRAMA performing or involving professionally produced dramatic works that are considered to be serious art, in contrast to such forms as revues and musical comedy ■ *vt.* (-mates, -mating, -mated) **1.** LAW LEGALIZE STH to make sth lawful, by making, changing, or repealing laws or by decree **2.** PROVE STH TO BE LAWFUL to argue or prove that a claim or action is lawful or reasonable [15thC. Via medieval Latin *legitimatus*, the past participle of *legitimare* 'to make legal', from Latin *legitimus* 'lawful', from *lex* 'law' (see LEGAL).] —**legitimacy** *n.* —**legitimately** *adv.* —**legitimateness** *n.* —**legitimation** /lə jítti máysh'n/ *n.* —**legitimator** /lə jítti maytər/ *n.*

legitimatize /lə jíttimə tīz/ (-tizes, -tizing, -tized), **legitimatise** (-tises, -tising, -tised) *vt.* = legitimate *v.* 1, legitimate *v.* 2 —**legitimatization** /lə jíttimə tī záysh'n/ *n.*

legitimist /lə jíttimist/ *n.* **1.** MONARCHIST sb who believes in political rule by inheritance or in a particular person's claim to legitimate inheritance of a throne **2.** HIST BOURBON SUPPORTER a supporter of the Bourbon claimants to the French throne in the 19th century [Mid-19thC. From French *légitimiste*, from *legitime* 'legitimate', from Latin *legitimus* (see LEGITIMATE).] —**legitimism** /lə jíttimizəm/ *n.* —**legitimist** /li jíttimist/ *adj.*

legitimize /lə jítti mīz/ (-mizes, -mizing, -mized), **legitimise** (-mises, -mising, -mised) *vt.* = legitimate *v.* 1, legitimate *v.* 2 [Mid-19thC. Formed from Latin *legitimus* (see LEGITIMATE).] —**legitimization** /lə jítti mī záysh'n/ *n.* —**legitimizer** /li jítti mīzər/ *n.*

legless /léggləss/ *adj.* **1.** DRUNK extremely drunk, especially too drunk to stand (*informal*) **2.** WITHOUT LEGS having no legs

legman /lég man/ (*plural* -men /-mən/) *n.* US **1.** ERRAND RUNNER sb employed in an office to run errands and gather information **2.** COMMUNICATION NEWS REPORTER a reporter who gathers information for a story, especially from firsthand sources

Lego /léggō/ *tdmk.* a trademark for a toy consisting of plastic building blocks and other components

leg-of-mutton /lég ə mút'n/, **leg-o'-mutton** *adj.* shaped like a sharply tapered triangle

leg-pull /lég poŏl/ *n.* an amusing deception or practical joke (*informal*) [From the expression 'to pull sb's leg'] —**leg-puller** /lég poŏlər/ *n.*

legroom /lég roŏm, -roŏm/ *n.* space in front of a seat for sb's legs, especially enough space to stretch out and move the legs

legume /léggyoom/ *n.* **1.** PLANTS LEGUMINOUS PLANT a plant that has pods as fruits and roots that bear nodules containing nitrogen-fixing bacteria **2.** FOOD SEED OR POD OF LEGUMINOUS PLANT a seed, pod, or other part of a legume, used as food [Mid-17thC. Via French *légume* from Latin *legumen* 'bean', of uncertain origin.]

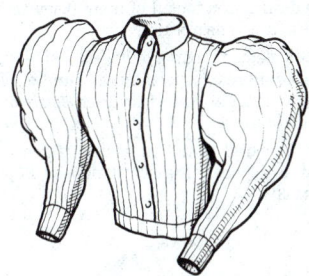

Leg-of-mutton

leguminous /li gyoŏminəss/ *adj.* **1.** OF LEGUME PLANT FAMILY belonging to or typical of the family of plants that has pods as fruits and roots that bear nodules containing nitrogen-fixing bacteria **2.** LIKE LEGUMES resembling a leguminous plant or its seed pods [Mid-17thC. From Latin *leguminosus*, from *legumin*-, the stem of *legumen* 'bean'.]

leg up *n.* (*informal*) **1.** UPWARDS BOOST help for sb to get up onto sth, e.g. a horse or a wall, by forming the open hands into a step and lifting the person's leg upwards **2.** CAREER HELP help for sb to move up in a hierarchy or a field of activity **3.** *US* POSITION OF SUPERIORITY an advantage that other people do not have in some activity

Legwarmer

legwarmer /lég wawrmər/ *n.* a knitted tube that covers the calf and sometimes also the top of the foot, and is typically worn by a dancer during practice (*usually used in the plural*)

legwork /lég wurk/ *n.* preparatory research for a project that is usually physically demanding or involves a lot of walking (*informal*)

Le Havre /lə haávrə/ city in Seine-Maritime Department, Haute-Normandie Region, northwestern France. Population: 197,219 (1990).

Lehrer /lairər/, **Tom** (*b.* 1928) US teacher and songwriter. A university professor, he became a successful entertainer in the 1960s with his humorous songs, many of them political satires.

lei[1] /layl/ (*plural* leis) *n.* a garland of flowers, especially one worn around the neck in Hawaii and other parts of Polynesia [Mid-19thC. From Hawaiian.]

lei[2] plural of **leu**

Leibniz /líb nits/, **Leibnitz, Gottfried Wilhelm von, Baron** (1646–1716) German philosopher and mathematician. The first president of the Prussian Academy of Sciences, he discovered calculus (independently of Newton) and contributed to the sciences of mechanics, optics, and logic, and to probability theory. —**Leibnizian** /líb nítsi ən/ *adj., n.*

Leicester /léstər/ industrial city in Leicestershire, central England. Population: 270,600 (1991).

Leicester, Robert Dudley, 1st Earl of (1532–88) English courtier. A favourite adviser to and unsuccessful suitor of Queen Elizabeth I, he helped involve England in the Protestant struggle against Philip II of Spain.

Leicestershire /léstərshər/ county in central England. Population: 592,700 (1995). Area: 2,553 sq. km/986 sq. mi.

Leichhardt /lík haart/, **Ludwig** (1813–48?) Prussian-born Australian naturalist and explorer. He led three major expeditions into the Australian interior, and he disappeared while attempting to cross the continent from east to west. Full name **Friedrich Wilhelm Ludwig Leichhardt**

Leics *abbr.* Leicestershire

Leiden /láydən/, **Leyden** university city in Zuid-Holland Province, western Netherlands. Population: 114,892 (1994).

Leif Ericson /leéf érrikss'n/ (975–1020) Icelandic explorer. He sailed from the Norse settlement in Greenland to become one of the first Europeans to reach North America. His story is told in the Icelandic *Eriks Saga.*

Leigh /lee/, **Mike** (*b.* 1943) British playwright and film director. His plays and films, notably *Abigail's Party* (1977), are developed with the actors in improvisation.

Vivien Leigh

Leigh, Vivien (1913–67) British actor. She won Academy Awards for her performances in *Gone with the Wind* (1939) and *A Streetcar Named Desire* (1951).

Leighton Buzzard /láytən búzzərd/ old market town in Bedfordshire, central England. Population: 32,610 (1991).

Leinster /línstər/ historic province in the eastern Republic of Ireland. Population: 1,921,835 (1996). Area: 19,633 sq. km/7,580 sq. mi.

Leipzig /lípsig/ city and cultural centre in east-central Germany, known for its international trade fairs. Population: 487,700 (1994).

leishmaniasis /leéshmə nī əssiss/ *n.* an infection such as kala-azar and some other skin diseases that are caused by a protozoan that is a parasite in the tissue of vertebrates [Early 20thC. Formed from modern Latin *Leishmania*, genus name, from the name of the Scottish pathologist Sir William Boog *Leishman* (1865–1926), who identified it.]

leister /leéstər/ *n.* THREE-PRONGED FISH SPEAR a stick with three prongs, used for spearing fish ■ *vt.* (-ters, -tering, -tered) CATCH FISH WITH LEISTER to catch fish using a three-pronged spear [Mid-16thC. From Old Norse *ljóstr*, from *ljósta* 'to strike', of unknown origin.]

leisure /lézhər/ *n.* time during which sb has no obligations or work responsibilities, and therefore is free to engage in enjoyable activities [13thC. Via Old French dialect *leisour* 'permission', literally 'to be allowed', a variant of *leisir*, from Latin *licere* (see LICENCE).] ◇ **at your leisure** at the time and pace that suits you ◇ **gentleman** *or* **lady of leisure** used to describe a man or woman who does not have to work for a living (*humorous*) ○ *a lady of leisure*

leisure centre *n.* a public establishment that provides the space and equipment for recreational activities such as sports, games, and hobbies

leisured /lézhərd/ *adj.* **1.** NOT HAVING TO WORK having a lot of free time, especially because of having enough money not to have to work for a living **2.** = leisurely

leisurely /lézhərli/ *adj.* leisurely, leisured SLOW AND RELAXED relaxed, unhurried, and enjoyable, usually because done during free time ○ *a leisurely stroll in the park* ■ *adv.* IN UNHURRIED WAY in a slow and relaxed manner —**leisureliness** *n.*

leisure society *n.* a society in which a greater proportion of people's time is spent at leisure than at work

leisurewear /lézhər wair/ *n.* comfortable informal clothing such as a tracksuit, appropriate for relaxation or play

Leith /leeth/ seaport of Edinburgh, Scotland, situated on the Firth of Forth

leitmotif /lítmō teef/, **leitmotiv** *n.* **1.** MUSIC **THEMATIC PASSAGE OF MUSIC** a musical theme that recurs in the course of a work to evoke a particular character or situation, especially typical of the operas of Richard Wagner **2.** MAIN RECURRING THEME a recurring theme, e.g. in literature or history [Late 19thC. From German, literally 'leading motif', from *leiten* 'to lead' + *Motiv* 'motif' (from French *motif*).]

Leitrim /léetrim/ county in Connacht Province, northern Republic of Ireland. The county town is Carrick-on-Shannon. Population: 25,032 (1996). Area: 1,525 sq. km/589 sq. mi.

Leizhou Peninsula /láy jṓ-/ peninsula in southwestern Guangdong Province, southeastern China

lek[1] /lek/ *n.* **1.** UNIT OF ALBANIAN CURRENCY the main currency unit of Albania, worth 100 qintars. See table at **currency 2.** COIN WORTH ONE LEK a coin worth one lek [Early 20thC. From Albanian, named after the Albanian lawgiver *Lek Dukagjin*.]

lek[2] /lek/ *n.* an area of ground that some birds such as the black grouse use as a stage for communal breeding displays and courtship during the mating season [Late 19thC. Origin uncertain: perhaps from Swedish *leka* 'to play'.]

lekker /lékər/ *adj.* S Africa enjoyable and pleasing (*informal*) [Early 20thC. Via Afrikaans from Middle Dutch. From a prehistoric Germanic word meaning 'to lick', which is also the ancestor of English *lick*.]

LEM /lem/ *abbr.* lunar excursion module

leman /lémmən, lēemən/ (*plural* **-mans**) *n.* sb loved, e.g. a sweetheart or lover (*archaic*) [12thC. Variant of *leofman*, literally 'beloved person', from LIEF + MAN.]

Le Mans /lə móN, lə mónz/ capital of Sarthe Department, Pays de la Loire Region, northern France. Population: 148,465 (1990).

lemma[1] /lémmə/ (*plural* **-mas** or **-mata** /-mətə/) *n.* **1.** LOGIC ASSUMPTION FOR THE SAKE OF ARGUMENT a proposition that is assumed to be true in order to test the validity of another proposition **2.** PUBL SUBJECT HEADING a heading that indicates the topic of a work or passage **3.** LING DICTIONARY HEADWORD the headword of a dictionary entry [Late 16thC. Via Latin from Greek *lēmma*, literally 'sth taken (for granted)'.]

lemma[2] /lémmə/ *n.* the lower of two bracts surrounding the flower of a grass [Mid-18thC. From Greek, 'husk', from the past participle of *lepein* 'to peel' (source of English *lepton*). Ultimately from an Indo-European word that is also the ancestor of English *leper*.]

lemmata plural of **lemma**[1]

Lemming

lemming /lémming/ *n.* **1.** ZOOL SUBARCTIC RODENT a rodent with a small thick furry body and furry feet that lives in subarctic regions. Lemmings are noted for their mass migrations in search of food during population explosions, which has given rise to the myth that they flock to the sea to drown themselves. Genus: *Lemmus* and *Dicrostonyx*. **2.** DOOMED CONFORMIST a member of a large group of people who blindly follow one another on a course of action that will lead to destruction for all of them [Early 18thC. From Norwegian, of uncertain origin.]

lemniscus /lem nískəss/ (*plural* **-ci** /-si, -kee/) *n.* a bundle of fibres, especially a bundle of nerve fibres [Mid-19thC. Via Latin from Greek *lēmniskos* 'ribbon', of unknown origin.]

Lemnos /lémnoss/ island in eastern Greece, in the Aegean Sea, near the Dardanelles. Population: 15,721 (1981).

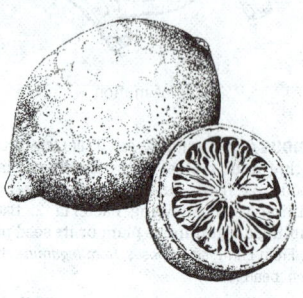

Lemon

lemon /lémmən/ *n.* **1.** FOOD YELLOW OR GREEN CITRUS FRUIT a yellow or, in some climates, green oval citrus fruit with a thick fragrant rind and sour juicy flesh **2.** TREES TREE THAT BEARS LEMONS the tree with glossy almond-shaped leaves and spiky branches that bears lemons. Latin name: *Citrus limon.* **3.** COLOURS PALE YELLOW COLOUR a pale yellow colour typical of the rind of a ripe lemon **4.** BEVERAGES LEMON DRINK a drink made from lemon juice **5.** DEFECTIVE PRODUCT sth that is defective or disappointing, especially a car that does not run properly (*informal*) **6.** SILLY PERSON a silly or thoughtless person (*informal*) ○ *I feel a right lemon now.* **7.** *Aus* OFFENSIVE TERM an offensive term for a lesbian (*slang offensive*) ■ *adj.* OF A PALE YELLOW COLOUR having the pale yellow colour typical of the rind of a ripe lemon [14thC. Via French *limon* from, ultimately, Arabic *līmūn*.]

lemonade /lémmə náyd/ *n.* **1.** FIZZY DRINK a sweet, fizzy, clear soft drink **2.** DRINK MADE FROM LEMONS a still soft drink made from fresh lemons, sugar, and water **3.** DRINK OF LEMONADE a drink of lemonade ○ *ordered a lemonade and two coffees*

lemon balm *n.* a widely-cultivated plant of the mint family native to southern Europe that has small white or pinkish flowers and lemon-scented leaves. It has long been used in food, as well as in herbal medicines to promote relaxation and sleep. Latin name: *Melissa officinalis.*

lemon curd, **lemon cheese** *n.* a thick sweet creamy-yellow spread made from lemons, sugar, eggs, and butter, usually eaten on bread

lemon drop *n.* a small lemon-flavoured boiled sweet

lemon grass *n.* a grass native to southern India that is cultivated in the tropics for a lemon-scented oil distilled from its leaves, and for use as a flavouring in cooking. Latin name: *Cymbopogon citratus.*

lemon sole *n.* an edible flatfish found in the northeastern Atlantic and the North Sea. Latin name: *Microstomus kitt.*

lemon-squeezer *n.* a device for extracting juice from lemons, usually consisting of a raised fluted cone onto which a halved lemon is pressed, set in a shallow bowl where juice collects. US term **reamer**

lemon verbena, **lemon vervain** *n.* a widely cultivated South American shrub with small lavender-coloured flowers and lance-shaped leaves that produce a lemony fragrance when crushed. The leaves and flower tops may be dried and used as a herbal tea. Latin name: *Lippia triphylla.*

lemony /lémməni/ *adj.* like a lemon in taste, smell, or colour

lemon yellow *n.* a pale yellow colour typical of the rind of a ripe lemon —**lemon-yellow** *adj.*

lempira /lem pēerə/ *n.* **1.** UNIT OF HONDURAN CURRENCY the main currency unit of Honduras, worth 100 centavos. See table at **currency 2.** NOTE WORTH ONE LEMPIRA a note worth one lempira [Mid-20thC. Named after *Lempira*, a 16th-century chieftain who fought against the Spanish conquerors of Honduras.]

Lemur

lemur /léemər/ *n.* a primate with a long snout, large ears, and a long tail, found only in Madagascar and nearby islands. Family: Lemuridae. ◊ **ring-tailed lemur** [Late 18thC. Via modern Latin from Latin *lemures* (see LEMURES), because it is nocturnal.]

lemures /lémmyŏŏ reez/ *npl.* in ancient Rome, the spirits of the dead (*literary*) [Mid-16thC. From Latin, literally 'shades of the dead'.]

Lena /léenə/ river in Siberian Russia that rises in southern Siberia and flows northwards before emptying into the Laptev Sea, an arm of the Arctic Ocean. Length: 4,313 km/2,680 mi.

lend /lend/ (**lends, lending, lent** /lent/) *v.* **1.** *vt.* LET SB BORROW STH to allow sb to take or use sth on the understanding that it will be returned later **2.** *vti.* GIVE SB MONEY FOR LIMITED TIME to allow a person or business to use a sum of money for a particular period of time, usually on condition that a charge (**interest**) is paid in return ○ *The bank lent us money at a good interest rate.* **3.** *vt.* ADD STH to give a certain quality or character to sth ○ *The candles lend an air of intimacy to the room.* [Old English *lǣnan.* Ultimately from a prehistoric Germanic word (ancestor also of English *loan*).] —**lendable** *adj.* —**lender** *n.* ◊ **lend itself to sth** to be suitable for a particular purpose or occasion

lending library *n.* a library or department of a library where the public can borrow books, and often audio tapes, video tapes, and CDs

lenes plural of **lenis**

Suzanne Lenglen: Photographed playing at Wimbledon (1922)

Lenglen /laaN glaàN/, **Suzanne** (1899–1938) French tennis player. The women's champion of France for several years (1920–23, 1925–26) and Olympic champion (1920), she also won several Wimbledon titles.

length /length/ *n.* **1.** DISTANCE FROM END TO END the distance along sth from end to end, or a measurement taken of this distance ○ *The length of the garden is 25 yards.* **2.** QUALITY OF LONGNESS the condition or state of being long ○ *The garden is designed to give a sense of length and openness.* **3.** HOW LONG STH TAKES the time sth lasts or takes from beginning to end ○ *The length of the second act is about 75 minutes.* **4.** HOW LONG STH IS how long sth is when measured from beginning to end ○ *The second volume is a massive 400 pages in length.* **5.** LONG PIECE OF STH a piece of sth long and narrow ○ *a length of copper piping* **6.** UNIT OF MEASUREMENT a piece of sth such as cloth that is measured or bought in units of a standard size ○ *bought three lengths of fabric* **7.** SWIMMING **END TO END IN SWIMMING POOL** the distance from one end of a swimming pool to the other **8.** SET DISTANCE a particular distance, e.g. between two points **9.** FASHION **HOW LONG GARMENT IS** how high the hem of a coat, skirt, or dress is above the ground or below the wearer's waist, or how much of the wearer's legs it shows **10.** SPORTS **WINNING DISTANCE** in sth such as a boat race or horse race, the distance between two competitors, measured according to how long a single boat or horse is ○ *two lengths ahead with only 100m to go* **11.** PHON **HOW LONG SOUND TAKES TO MAKE** the amount of time required to articulate a vowel or syllable **12.** CRICKET **DISTANCE BALL BOUNCES FROM BATSMAN** in cricket, the distance from the batsman at which the ball bounces [Old English *lengþ*, ultimately from a prehistoric Germanic word that is also the ancestor of English *long*] ◇ **at length 1.** in great detail and for a long time (*formal*) **2.** after some time or following a delay

-length *suffix*. extending all the way to a particular part of sth ○ *shoulder-length hair*

lengthen /léngth'n/ (**-ens, -ening, -ened**) *vti*. to make sth longer, or become longer ○ *The weeks lengthened into months and still no news came.* —**lengthener** *n*.

lengthways /léngth wayz/, **lengthwise** /-wīz/ *adv., adj.* in relation to sth's length from end to end ○ *attempting to force the suitcase into the boot lengthways*

lengthy /léngthi/ (**-ier, -iest**) *adj.* lasting for a long time, especially excessively long —**lengthily** *adv.* —**lengthiness** *n*.

leniency /leeeni ənssi/, **lenience** /-ənss/ *n*. **1.** LENIENT **TREATMENT** punishment, judgment, or action that is not too severe **2.** GENTLENESS OR TOLERANCE the personal characteristic or quality of being lenient

lenient /leeeni ənt/ *adj*. showing tolerance or mercy in dealing with crime or misbehaviour [Mid-17thC. From Latin *lenient-*, present participle stem of *lenire* 'to soothe', from *lenis* 'smooth'.] —**leniently** *adv*.

Vladimir Ilyich Lenin

Lenin /lénnin/, **Vladimir Ilyich** (1870–1924) Russian revolutionary leader. Founder of the Soviet Union, he led the Bolshevik revolution in October 1917. He was the first leader of the Soviet communist regime, but became less active after suffering a stroke in 1922. Born **Vladimir Ilyich Ulyanov**

Leninakhan /lénninə kaʹan/ former name for **Gyumri** (1924–90)

Leningrad /lénnin grad/ former name for **St Petersburg** (1924–90)

Leninism /lénninizəm/ *n*. the political, social, and economic theories of Lenin, which he developed from Marxist theory —**Leninist** *n., adj.*

Lenin Peak /lénnin-/ mountain in the Trans-Alai Range of the Pamirs, situated in Tajikistan. Height: 7,165 m/23,508 ft. Former name **Mount Kaufman**

lenis /leeeniss/ *adj.* PRONOUNCED USING LITTLE BREATH used to describe a consonant produced using little breath and muscle power ■ *n*. (*plural* **-nes** /-neez/) LENIS **CONSONANT** a consonant that is produced using little breath and muscle power [Early 20thC. From Latin, literally 'smooth'.]

lenition /li níshʹn/ *n*. the use of little breath and muscle power when articulating consonants [Early 20thC. From Latin *lenis* 'smooth'.]

lenity /lénnəti/ *n*. action or treatment that is lenient

(*formal*) [15thC. Directly or via Old French *lenite* from Latin *lenitas*, from *lenis* 'smooth'.]

Lennon /lénnən/, **John** (1940–80) British singer, songwriter, and musician. A member of the Beatles, he had a songwriting partnership with Paul McCartney that revolutionized popular music. His most distinctive solo recording was 'Imagine' (1971). He was murdered in 1980.

leno /leeenō/ (*plural* **-nos**) *n*. **1.** TYPE OF OPEN WEAVE a type of open weave created in textiles by twisting together pairs of warp threads to lock the weft threads in place **2.** FABRIC a fabric made using a leno weave [Late 18thC. From French *linon*, from *lin* 'flax', from Latin *linum*.]

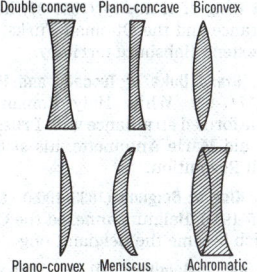

Double concave Plano-concave Biconvex

Plano-convex Meniscus Achromatic

Lens: Cross-sections of different lenses

lens /lenz/ *n*. **1.** OPTICS **TRANSPARENT PIECE OF GLASS FOR FOCUSING** a piece of curved and polished glass or other transparent material that forms an image by refracting and focusing light passing through it **2.** OPTICS **SYSTEM OF LENSES** a system of two or more lenses that is used in an optical instrument such as a telescope or camera **3.** OPHTHALMOL = **contact lens 4.** ANAT **LIGHT-FOCUSING PART OF THE EYE** the part of the eye that focuses light to produce an image on the light-sensitive cells of the retina. It is nearly spherical and convex on both sides, and sits behind the pupil. **5.** TECH **BEAM-FOCUSING DEVICE** a device that focuses a beam of electrons or radiation other than light [Late 17thC. From Latin, literally 'lentil' (so called because of its shape).]

lent past participle, past tense of **lend**

Lent /lent/ *n*. the period of 40 weekdays before Easter observed in some Christian churches as a period of prayer, penance, fasting, and self-denial. This period, starting on Ash Wednesday in Western churches, commemorates the 40 days that Jesus Christ spent fasting in the wilderness. [13thC. Shortening of LENTEN.]

Lenten /léntən/, **lenten** *adj*. happening in or suitable for Lent, especially in being meagre [Old English *lencten* 'spring' (in which Lent falls in the northern hemisphere). Ultimately from a prehistoric Germanic word (ancestor also of English *long*, referring to the lengthening days of spring).]

lentic /léntik/ *adj*. relating to or inhabiting still or slow-moving water [Mid-20thC. Formed from Latin *lentus* 'slow, calm'.]

lenticel /lénti sel/ *n*. a pore in the outer layer of a woody plant stem, through which gases pass from inside the stem to the atmosphere, or vice versa [Mid-19thC. From modern Latin *lenticella*, literally 'little lentil', from Latin *lens* 'lentil'.] —**lenticellate** /lénti séllət/ *adj*.

lenticular /len tíkyoōlər/ *adj*. **1.** LENS-SHAPED shaped like a biconvex lens in having two convex faces **2.** OF **LENSES** relating to a lens or lenses [15thC. From Latin *lenticularis*, from *lenticula* (see LENTIL).]

lentil /léntʹl/ *n*. **1.** PLANTS **PLANT WITH EDIBLE SEEDS** a plant of the pea family native to the Mediterranean area and to western Asia and grown for its edible seeds. Latin name: *Lens culinaris*. **2.** FOOD **SEED** a seed of the lentil plant that is lens-shaped, brown, grey, or black on the outside and yellow or orange inside, and rich in protein [14thC. Via French *lentille* from, ultimately, Latin *lenticula*, literally 'little lentil', from *lens* 'lentil'.]

lentisk /léntisk/ *n*. = **mastic tree** [14thC. From Latin *lentiscus*.]

lentissimo /len tíssimō/ *adv*. very slowly (*used as a musical direction*) [Early 20thC. From Italian, superlative of *lento* (see LENTO).] —**lentissimo** *adj*.

lentivirus /lénti vīrəss/ *n*. a retrovirus causing illness that characteristically does not produce symptoms until some time after infection [Late 20thC. Coined from Latin *lentus* 'slow' + -i- + VIRUS.]

lent lily *n*. a daffodil (*literary or dated*) [Because it often blooms during Lent]

lento /léntō/ *adv*. SLOWLY at a slow tempo (*used as a musical direction*) ■ *n*. (*plural* **-tos**) LENTO **PIECE OF MUSIC** a piece of music, or a section of a piece, to be played lento [Early 18thC. Via Italian from Latin *lentus* 'slow'.] —**lento** *adj*.

Lenya /lényə/, **Lotte** (1900–81) Austrian actress and cabaret singer. She played a leading role in several works by her husband Kurt Weill, including *The Threepenny Opera* (1928). Real name **Karoline Wilhelmine Blamauer**

Leo[1] /leee ō/ (*plural* **-os**) *n*. **1.** FIFTH SIGN OF THE ZODIAC the fifth sign of the zodiac, represented by the lion and lasting from approximately 23 July to 22 August. Leo is classified as a fire sign and is ruled by the sun. **2.** SB BORN UNDER LEO sb whose birthday falls between 23 July and 22 August [Pre-12thC. From Latin, literally 'lion'.] —**Leo** *adj*.

Leo[2] /leee ō/ *n*. a zodiacal constellation of the northern hemisphere lying between Cancer and Virgo

Leo I, St (400?–461) Pope. He summoned the Council of Chalcedon in 451 and was proclaimed a doctor of the church in 1574. Known as **Leo the Great**

Leo III, Emperor (680?–741) Byzantine monarch. He revitalized the Byzantine Empire, founded the Isaurian dynasty, and issued a legal code, the *Ecloga*.

Leo IX, St (1002–54) Pope. During his reforming reign (1049 –54), papal authority was strengthened, and this led to the Great Schism of 1054. Real name **Bruno of Egisheim**

Leo X, Pope (1475–1521). An important patron of the arts, as Pope (1513–21) he initiated the rebuilding of St Peter's Basilica, Rome. Real name **Giovanni de Medici**

Leo XIII, Pope (1810–1903). He upheld the authority of the papacy and promoted learning. His encyclical of 1896 declared Anglican orders invalid. Real name **Vincenzo Gioacchino Pecci**

Leo Minor *n*. a small inconspicuous constellation of the northern hemisphere between Ursa Major and Leo

Leominster /léminstər/ **1.** town in Herefordshire, England. Population: 9,543 (1991). **2.** city in central Massachusetts, southeast of Fitchburg and north of Worcester. Population: 39,263 (1996).

León /lay ón/ **1.** city and capital of León Province, in the Castile-Léon autonomous region of northwestern Spain. Population: 147,780 (1995). **2.** industrial city in central Mexico, founded in 1576. Population: 758,279 (1990).

Leonard /lénnərd/, **Sugar Ray** (*b.* 1956) US boxer. He won various boxing titles in five different weight categories, mainly in the 1980s. Real name **Ray Charles Leonard**

Leonardo da Vinci /leee ō naʹard ō də vínchi/ (1452–

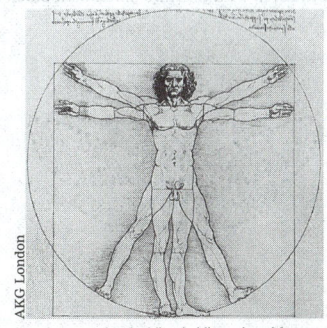

Leonardo da Vinci: Vitruvian Man (1490?)

1519) Italian painter, sculptor, architect, engineer, and scientist. One of the great masters of the High Renaissance, his works include the *Mona Lisa* (1503–06), and *The Last Supper* (1495–97).

Leoncavallo /láy ong ka vál ō/, **Ruggero** (1858–1919) Italian composer. An exponent of the 'verismo' style in opera, he composed *I Pagliacci* (1892).

leone /lee ón/ *n.* **1.** **UNIT OF SIERRA LEONEAN CURRENCY** the main currency unit of Sierra Leone, worth 100 cents. See table at **currency** **2.** **NOTE WORTH ONE LEONE** a note worth one leone [Mid-20thC. From the name of Sierra *Leone*.]

Leonian /lee óni ən/ *n.* ZODIAC = **Leo**[1] *n.* **2**

Leonidas /li ónni dass/, **King** (*d.* 480 BC) Spartan monarch. He withstood the Persian army of Xerxes I at the Battle of Thermopylae in 480 BC.

leonine /lee ə nīn/ *adj.* relating to or characteristic of a lion, e.g. in strength or appearance [14thC. Directly or via French from Latin *leoninus*, from *leo* 'lion'.]

Leopard

leopard /léppərd/ *n.* **1.** ZOOL **LARGE SPOTTED CAT** a large slender member of the cat family found in Africa and parts of Asia. It has a fawn to orange-red coat spotted with black rosettes. Leopards are generally solitary and nocturnal, living in scrub or forest and hunting a wide range of prey, including antelope, snakes, fish, and birds. Latin name: *Panthera pardus*. ◊ **panther, snow leopard, clouded leopard 2.** HERALDRY **HERALDIC FIGURE OF WALKING LION** an image of a lion viewed from the side facing left, with its head turned towards the viewer and one front leg raised [13thC. Via Old French from, ultimately, late Greek *leopardos*, from *leōn* (see LION) + *pardos* (see PARD).]

WORD KEY: CULTURAL NOTE

The Leopard, a novel by Italian writer Giuseppe Tomasi di Lampedusa (1958). Set in late 19th-century Sicily, it describes the social and political changes resulting from the unification of Italy from the point of view of a local nobleman, Prince Salina. In addition to its political and historical insights, the novel is admired for its evocative descriptions of the Sicilian landscape and its moving and poetic meditations on mortality.

leopard cat *n.* a small wild cat with spots like those of a leopard, found in southern and eastern Asia. Latin name: *Felis bengalensis*.

leopardess /léppərd ess/ *n.* a female leopard, usually an adult one

leopard lily *n.* a plant native to the southwestern United States that is cultivated for its attractive orange-red flowers with black-speckled petals. Latin name: *Lilium pardalinum*.

leopard moth *n.* a large white moth with black spots

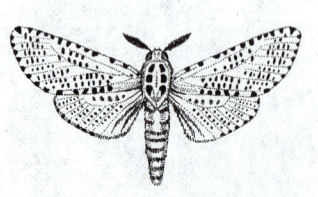

Leopard moth

that is found in Europe, Asia, North Africa, and North America. The caterpillars bore into trees, causing damage, and may be considered pests. Latin name: *Zeuzera pyrina*.

leopard's bane *n.* a European and Asian plant with clusters of yellow flowers resembling daisies on long stalks. Leopard's banes are cultivated as ornamentals and also grow wild. Genus: *Doronicum*.

leopard seal *n.* a seal with a spotted dark grey back and paler belly that lives as a solitary hunter in Antarctic waters, feeding mainly on penguins. Latin name: *Hydrurga leptonyx*.

Leopold I, **Holy Roman Emperor, King of Bohemia, and King of Hungary** (1640–1705). As Holy Roman Emperor (1658–1705), King of Bohemia (1656–1705), and King of Hungary (1655–87) he led wars against France and the Ottoman Turks, and made efforts to extend Habsburg territory.

Leopold II, **Grand Duke of Tuscany and Holy Roman Emperor** (1747–92). While Holy Roman Emperor (1790–92) he formed an alliance with Prussia against France to aid Marie Antoinette, his sister, during the French Revolution.

Leopold II, **King of Belgium** (1835–1909). During his reign (1865–1909), Belgium annexed the Congo Free State, which became the Belgian Congo.

Leopold III, **King of Belgium** (1901–83). He became king in 1934, but went into exile after the invasion by Germany during World War II. He abdicated in 1951.

Léopoldville /lee ə pōld víl/ former name for **Kinshasa** (until 1966)

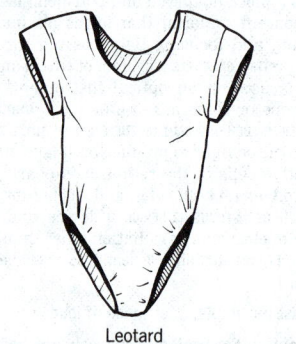

Leotard

leotard /lee ə taard/ *n.* a tight-fitting one-piece elastic garment that covers the torso and is worn especially by dancers, gymnasts, and acrobats [Late 19thC. Named after the French trapeze artist Jules *Léotard* (1830–70), its inventor.]

lep /lep/ *vi.* (**leps, lepping, lept** /lept/) Ireland **LEAP** to leap (*informal*) ■ *n.* N Ireland **ACT OF LEAPING** an act of leaping (*informal*) [Variant]

Lepcha /lépchə/ (*plural* **-chas** *or* **-cha**) *n.* **1.** PEOPLES **MEMBER OF PEOPLE OF INDIA** a member of a people who live in the northeastern Indian state of Sikkim **2.** LANG **LANGUAGE OF INDIA** a language spoken in the northeastern Indian state of Sikkim. It belongs to the Tibeto-Burman branch of Sino-Tibetan languages. Lepcha is spoken by about 65,000 people. [Early 19thC. From Nepali *lāpche*.] —**Lepcha** *adj.*

Le Pen /lə pén/, **Jean-Marie** (*b.* 1928) French politician, founder of the French National Front (1972), and presidential candidate (1988).

leper /léppər/ *n.* **1.** SB WITH LEPROSY sb affected with leprosy **2.** SB AVOIDED sb who is ignored or disliked by the rest of society [14thC. Via French *lèpra* from Latin *lepra* 'leprosy' (the original sense in English), from Greek *lepros* (see LEPROUS).]

lepido- *prefix.* flake, scale ◊ *lepidolite* [From Greek *lepid-*, the stem of *lepis, lepos* (source of English *leper*)]

lepidolite /li píddə līt, léppidə-/ *n.* a type of mica ranging in colour from pinkish purple to grey, used as an ore of lithium

lepidopteran /léppi dóptərən/ *n.* a butterfly or moth. Lepidopterans have four wings covered in tiny overlapping scales, and sucking mouthparts. Their larvae are caterpillars. Order: Lepidoptera. [Mid-

19thC. From modern Latin Lepidoptera, order name, from Greek *lepis* 'scale' + *pteron* 'wing'.]

lepidopterist /léppi dóptərist/ *n.* sb who studies or is an expert in butterflies and moths

lepidosiren /léppidō sīrən/ *n.* an eel-shaped South American freshwater fish that can breathe air using a pair of lungs that it has in addition to its gills. It spends the dry season lying dormant in a burrow. Latin name: *Lepidosiren paradoxa*.

lepidote /léppi dōt/ *adj.* covered in small scaly leaves [Mid-19thC. Via modern Latin *lepidotus* from Greek *lepidōtos*, from *lepis* 'scale'.]

leprechaun /léppri kawn/ *n.* in Irish folklore, a small man with magical powers, often dressed in green, who works as a shoemaker and is believed to know where treasure is hidden [Early 17thC. From Irish *le-ipreachán*, literally 'small body'.]

leprosarium /lépprə sáiri əm/ (*plural* **-a** /-ri ə/) *n.* a hospital for the treatment of patients with leprosy [Mid-19thC. From late Latin *leprosus* (see LEPROUS).]

leprose /léprōss/ *adj.* = **leprous** *adj.* **2** [Mid-19thC. Directly from or via late Latin *leprosus* (see LEPROUS).]

leprosy /léprəssi/ (*plural* **-sies**) *n.* a tropical disease that mainly affects the skin and nerves, and can cause tissue change. Leprosy is transmitted following close personal contact and has a long incubation period (1–30 years). It can now be cured if treated with a combination of drugs. [Mid-16thC. From LEPROUS (influenced by earlier *lepry* 'leprosy'), from LEPER.] —**leprotic** /le próttik/ *adj.*

leprosy gourd *n.* = **balsam pear**

leprous /léprəss/ *adj.* **1.** OF LEPROSY having or relating to leprosy **2.** WHITE AND SCALY resembling the physical symptoms of leprosy, especially in being pale or scaly ◊ *a leprous white deposit spreading across the cellar walls* [12thC. Via Old French *lepro(u)s* and late Latin *leprosus* from Greek *lepros* 'scaly', from *lepos* 'scale' (because of the white scales that form on the skin).]

-lepsy *suffix.* seizure ◊ *narcolepsy* [Via modern Latin *-lepsia* from Greek *lepsis*, from *lēp-*, the stem of *lambanein* 'to seize' (source also of English *astrolabe* and *syllable*)]

lept past tense, past participle of **lep**

lept- *prefix.* = **lepto-** (*used before vowels*)

lepta plural of **lepton**[1]

lepto- *prefix.* thin, slender ◊ *leptosome* [From Greek *leptos*, the past participle of *lepein* 'to peel' (see LEMMA)]

leptocephalus /léptō séffələss/ (*plural* **-li** /-lī/) *n.* the larva of some bony fishes such as the eel that has a markedly different appearance to that of the adult fish. The eel larva has a leaf-shaped, almost transparent body, in contrast to the long thin form of the adult eel. Genus: *Anguilla*. [Mid-18thC. From modern Latin, from Greek *leptos* 'fine, small' + *kephalē* 'head'.]

lepton[1] /lép ton/ (*plural* **-ta** /-tə/) *n.* **1.** GREEK MONETARY UNIT a monetary unit of Greece, used only in calculations **2.** OLD COIN WORTH ONE LEPTON an ancient Greek coin worth one lepton [Early 18thC. From Greek *leptos* 'small'.]

lepton[2] /lép ton/ *n.* a fundamental subatomic particle such as the electron, muon, neutrino, and their antiparticles that interacts only weakly with other particles [Mid-20thC. Coined from Greek *leptos* 'small' + -ON.] —**leptonic** /lep tónnik/ *adj.*

leptospirosis /léptō spī rṓssiss/ *n.* a disease affecting human beings and domestic animals caused by spiral-shaped bacteria (**spirochaetes**) of the genus *Leptospira*, sometimes with fever, jaundice, and kidney failure. In human beings a significant form of the disease is Weil's disease. [Early 20thC. Formed from modern Latin *Leptospira*, genus name, literally 'small coil'.]

Lepus /léppəss, leepəss/ *n.* a small constellation of the southern hemisphere located directly south of Orion

Lérida /lay reedə/ capital of Lérida Province in the autonomous region of Catalonia, northeastern Spain. Population: 114,367 (1995).

Lermontov /lyérməntəf/, **Mikhail Yuryevich** (1814–41) Russian poet and novelist. His works include *A*

Hero of our Time (1840) and *The Circassian Boy* (1840).

Lerwick /lúr wik/ seaport and largest town of the Shetland Islands, northern Scotland, on Mainland Island. Population: 7,336 (1991).

lesbian /lézbi ən/ *n.* HOMOSEXUAL WOMAN a woman who is sexually attracted to other women ■ *adj.* OF LESBIANS involving or relating to lesbians [From the poems of SAPPHO of *Lesbos*]

Lesbian *n.* SB FROM LESBOS sb who was born or brought up on the Greek island of Lesbos ■ *adj.* 1. OF LESBOS relating to the Greek island of Lesbos 2. OF THE POETRY OF SAPPHO relating to the writings of the poet Sappho of the 6th century BC, who was from Lesbos

lesbianism /lézbi ənizəm/ *n.* sexual attraction and sexual relations between women

Lesbos /léz boss/ island in eastern Greece, in the Aegean Sea, situated 10 km/6 mi. off the coast of Turkey. Population: 104,620 (1981). Area: 1,637 sq. km/632 sq. mi.

Les Cayes /lay káy/ town and seaport in southwestern Haiti, west of Port-au-Prince. Population: 36,000 (1994).

lese majesty /leéz májjəsti/, **lèse majesté** *n.* 1. DISRESPECT TO AUTHORITY disrespect towards the authority or dignity of sb or sth 2. ACT OF TREASON a criminal offence against a ruler or head of state [15thC. Via French from Latin *laesa majestas*, literally 'violated majesty'.]

lesion /leézh'n/ *n.* 1. CHANGE DUE TO ILLNESS OR INJURY a physical change in a body part that is the result of illness or injury 2. WOUND a wound, especially an area of skin that is broken or infected [15thC. Via French from the Latin stem *laesion-*, from the past participle stem of *laedere* 'to injure'.]

Lesotho

Lesotho /lə sōtō/ country in southern Africa, bordered on all sides by South Africa. It became independent from Britain in 1966. Language: English. Currency: loti. Capital: Maseru. Population: 2,049,275 (1997). Area: 30,355 sq. km/11,720 sq. mi. Official name **Kingdom of Lesotho**

lespedeza /léspə deézə/ (*plural* **-zas** *or* **-za**) *n.* = **bush clover** [Late 19thC. From modern Latin, genus name, from an alteration of the name of Vincente Manuel de Céspedes, 18th-C Spanish governor of eastern Florida.]

less /less/ CORE MEANING: a grammatical word used to indicate a smaller amount of sth

1. *det.*, *pron.* SMALLER AMOUNT a smaller amount or proportion of sth ○ *New cars tend to emit less air pollution.* ○ *Last month less of her salary was taken up with household expenses.* 2. *adv.* TO A SMALLER DEGREE to a smaller extent or degree ○ *Demanding? I've never known a less demanding patient!* ○ *I see her much less than I used to.* 3. *prep.* MINUS indicating that a number or amount is subtracted from a previously mentioned number or amount ○ *Total: £500, less £50 expenses.* ○ *I earned £45,000 last year, less tax and insurance.* [Old English *læssa*, ultimately of prehistoric Germanic origin] ◇ **less than** not having a particular quality ○ *Her whole attitude towards me has been less than pleasant.* ◇ **no less** expressing surprise or admiration at the importance of sb or sth ○ *He had borrowed money at Homburg from no less a person than Lord Montbarry.* ○ *The author says our whole universe, no less, is only one of many.* ◇ **much** *or* **still** *or* **even less** emphasizing that sth is done or happens to a smaller extent than sth

mentioned in the previous statement (*used after a negative statement*) ○ *She could not fix her attention on any object or feel sensations, much less have conscious thoughts.*

-less *suffix.* 1. without, lacking ○ *headless* ○ *restless* 2. unable to be ○ *fathomless* [From Old English *lēas* 'without'; related to *los* (see LOSS)]

lessee /le seé/ *n.* sb who is granted a lease for property [15thC. From Anglo-Norman, the past participle of *lesser* (see LEASE).]

lessen /léss'n/ (**-ens, -ening, -ened**) *vti.* to make sth less, or become less

Lesseps /lésseps/, **Ferdinand Marie, Vicomte de** (1805–94) French diplomat and engineer. While holding diplomatic posts he planned the cutting of the Suez Canal, and started work on the Panama Canal, which was eventually abandoned.

lesser /léssər/ *adj.*, *adv.* less significant, or smaller in size or amount

Lesser Bairam /-bī raám/ *n.* an Islamic festival held each year at the end of Ramadan

lesser carpenter bee *n.* a small usually black solitary bee that bores extensive nests out of solid wood. Family: Ceratinidae.

lesser celandine *n.* = **celandine**

lesser omentum *n.* ♦ **omentum**

Lesser Slave Lake /léssər slayv-/ lake in central Alberta, Canada, northwest of Edmonton. It empties through the Lesser Slave River into the Athabasca River. Area: 1,168 sq. km/451 sq. mi.

Doris Lessing

Lessing /léssing/, **Doris** (b. 1919) British novelist. Her works such as *The Grass is Singing* (1950), *Children of Violence* (1952–69), and *The Golden Notebook* (1962) explore political and social themes. Born **Doris May Tayler**

Lessing, Gotthold Ephraim (1729–81) German dramatist and critic. His plays and essays were highly influential in the development of the Enlightenment.

lesson /léss'n/ *n.* 1. INSTRUCTION PERIOD a period of time spent teaching or learning a subject ○ *I'm old enough to start taking driving lessons.* 2. MATERIAL TAUGHT material to be taught or studied 3. USEFUL EXPERIENCE sth that acts as an example, punishment, or warning by teaching sth not previously understood or accepted 4. NEW OR BETTER KNOWLEDGE some useful knowledge or sense that results from direct experience ○ *I think there's a lesson there for all of us – think ahead.* 5. **lesson, Lesson** CHR BIBLE PASSAGE a passage from the Bible that is read out to the congregation during a church service ○ *Today's lesson is from Matthew.* 6. REBUKE a strong criticism or telling-off, usually instructing or reminding sb how to behave correctly ○ *I need to give him a lesson in how to behave properly.* ■ *vt.* (**-sons, -soning, -soned**) (*archaic*) 1. INSTRUCT to teach sb 2. CRITICIZE FOR WRONGDOING to scold sb for doing sth wrong [12thC. Via French *leçon* from Latin *lectio* 'reading', formed from *legere* 'to read' (source also of English *lecture*). The underlying sense is 'sth to read or listen to'.]

lessor /le sáwr, léssawr/ *n.* sb who grants sb else a lease on property [14thC. From Anglo-Norman *lessour*, from *lesser* (see LEASE).]

lest /lest/ *conj.* in order to prevent sth happening, especially sth causing fear ○ *must stay out of sight*

lest we be discovered [Old English *þȳ læs þe*, literally 'by which less that']

let[1] /let/ *vt.* (**lets, letting, let**) 1. NOT PREVENT to allow sth to happen or sb to do sth ○ *You should let him explain what happened.* ○ *I won't let anything get in the way of us living a happy life together.* ○ *I never let myself worry about the future.* 2. PERMIT to give sb permission to do sth ○ *I want to go to the disco but Dad won't let me.* 3. EXPRESSING A SUGGESTION used to express a suggestion, an offer, or an order ○ *Let's eat – I'm starving.* ○ *Let me take that bag for you – you must be exhausted.* ○ *Let the show go on!* 4. MAKE STH PASS SOMEWHERE to allow or make sth pass from one place to another ○ *You need to let some air out of those tyres.* ○ *Open the window and let some fresh air in.* 5. EXPRESSING RESIGNATION used to indicate that you do not care what happens or what sb does, even though it may be unpleasant ○ *Let them do their worst.* ○ *If he wants to leave then let him – see if I care!* 6. MATH, LOGIC MAKE AS A MATHEMATICAL ASSUMPTION used to introduce an assumption or hypothesis ○ *Let the point P be on a line L.* 7. COMM LAW RENT OUT PROPERTY to allow people to use land, rooms, or a building in return for rent 8. *Ireland* UTTER to utter sth (*informal*) ■ *n.* 1. COMM LAW GRANT OF LEASE the granting of a lease 2. COMM, LAW RIGHT TO RENT STH permission to lease a building or piece of property [Old English *lǣtan* 'to leave behind, let alone, allow'. Ultimately from an Indo-European word meaning 'to let go', which is also the ancestor of English *late* and *let*.] ◇ **let alone** used to introduce sth that is even less likely or probable than what has just been mentioned ◇ **let go (of sth)** to stop holding sth ○ *She let go of her mother's hand and ran onto the playground.* ◇ **let yourself go 1.** to start acting in a much more relaxed or less inhibited way than usual **2.** to stop caring about your appearance

——— WORD KEY: SYNONYMS ———
See Synonyms at *hire*.

let down *vt.* 1. LOWER STH to move sth, or allow sth to move, to a lower position ○ *It was getting dark, so she let down the curtains.* 2. DISAPPOINT SB to disappoint sb by not meeting expectations ○ *Sorry to let you down, but I won't be able to make it tonight.* 3. MAKE AIR COME OUT OF STH to make the air come out of an inflated object until it goes flat 4. LENGTHEN GARMENT to lengthen clothing or part of a piece of clothing by shortening the hem ○ *let down the sleeves of the coat* 5. ALLOW HAIR TO HANG DOWN to undo long hair so that it falls to its full length

let in *vt.* 1. ALLOW SB ENTRANCE to allow sb to enter somewhere such as a building or a room ○ *They refused to let her in the house.* 2. ALLOW WATER OR AIR IN to allow water or air into sth that is meant to be sealed ○ *Their boat had hit a rock and was letting in water.*

let in for *vt.* to become involved in sth that turns out to be more difficult or complicated than expected (*informal*) ○ *didn't realize quite what I was letting myself in for*

let in on *vt.* to allow sb to know about sth

let into *vt.* 1. SHARE INFORMATION WITH SB to allow sb to know about sth 2. ALLOW TO ENTER to allow sb to enter somewhere 3. ALLOW TO JOIN A CLUB to allow sb to join an organization or club

let off *v.* 1. *vt.* EXCUSE SB FROM PUNISHMENT to allow sb to avoid sth such as an unpleasant task or a punishment ○ *I'll let you off this time, but you'd better behave from now on.* 2. *vt.* MAKE STH EXPLODE to fire shots from a gun, or make a firework or explosive blow up 3. *vt.* LET A PASSENGER GET OUT to allow sb to get off a vehicle such as a bus or train 4. *vti.* BREAK WIND to break wind (*informal*)

let on *v.* 1. *vi.* SHARE A SECRET to share a secret with sb ○ *He didn't let on that he was very rich.* 2. *vi.* PRETEND to make sb believe sth that is not true ○ *She let on that she was upset, but she wasn't really that bothered.* 3. *vt.* LET A PASSENGER GET ON to allow sb to board a vehicle such as a bus or train

let out *vt.* 1. MAKE A LOUD YELL to make a loud or piercing sound using the voice ○ *let out a scream* 2. RELEASE SB OR STH to set a person or animal free from being confined or trapped 3. RELEASE SB FROM PRISON to release sb from prison early or temporarily 4. ALLOW SB TO LEAVE to allow sb to leave a place such as a building or room 5. ENLARGE A GARMENT to make a piece of clothing, or a specific part of it, wider than it was before **6. SPREAD INFORMATION** to allow previously secret information to become more widely known **7. LET PROPERTY** to make a place available for letting ○ *They have recently let out a suite of rooms on the third floor.*

let through *vt.* to allow sb or sth to pass through a crowd ○ *Cars were pulling over to let an ambulance through.*

let up *vi.* **1. BECOME SLOWER** to become slower, calmer, or quieter ○ *Once the rain lets up a bit we'll have a look outside.* **2. RELAX** to stop working hard or being angry ○ *He never lets up, does he.*

let up on *vt.* to treat sb or sth in a more relaxed, gentle, or kind way

let[2] /let/ *n.* **1. REPLAYED SERVICE SHOT** in games such as tennis and squash, a service in which the ball is obstructed and the service has to be played again **2. REPLAYED POINT** the point that is replayed because of a let **3. DIFFICULTY OR OBSTACLE** sth that prevents sb doing sth, or makes it more difficult (*archaic*) [12thC. From Old English *lettan* 'to hinder or obstruct'. Ultimately from an Indo-European word that is also the ancestor of English *let*[1].]

-let *suffix.* **1.** small one ○ *wavelet* **2.** sth worn on ○ *anklet* [From Old French *-elet*, from *-el* 'small one' (from Latin *-ellus*) + *-et* (see -ET).]

letch *n., vi.* = **lech**

Letchworth /léch wurth/ town in Hertfordshire, south-eastern England. It was the first 'garden city' in the country. Population: 31,418 (1991).

letdown /lét down/ *n.* **1. DISAPPOINTMENT** an occasion when sb or sth disappoints expectations, or the feeling of disappointment that results ○ *After all the hype the concert was a bit of a letdown.* **2. AIR DESCENT OF AN AIRCRAFT** the descent of an aircraft in preparation for landing, before the actual landing approach

lethal /lééth'l/ *adj.* **1. DEADLY** causing or able to cause death **2. HARMFUL** causing disaster or destruction ○ *a move that was lethal to his career* [Late 16thC. From Latin *lethalis*, from *lethum*, an alteration of *letum* 'death', by association with Greek *lēthē* 'forgetfulness, oblivion'.] —**lethality** /lee thálləti/ *n.* —**lethally** /lééth'li/ *adv.*

── **WORD KEY: SYNONYMS** ──
See Synonyms at *deadly*.

lethal dose *n.* the amount of a drug or other substance that will cause death when administered. ◊ **median lethal dose**

lethargic /lə tháarjik/ *adj.* **1. TIRED** physically slow and mentally dull as a result of tiredness, disease, or drugs **2. CAUSING LETHARGY** causing a state of physical slowness and mental dullness —**lethargically** *adv.*

lethargy /léthərji/ *n.* **1. TIREDNESS** a state of physical slowness and mental dullness as a result of tiredness, disease, or drugs **2. LACK OF ENERGY** lack of energy, activity, or enthusiasm [14thC. Via Old French *litargia* from, ultimately, Greek *lēthargia*, from *lēthargos* 'forgetful', from *lēthē* 'forgetfulness, oblivion'.]

Lethbridge /léth brij/ city in southern Alberta, Canada. It is the cultural and economic centre of the surrounding agricultural area. Population: 63,053 (1996).

lethe /lééthi/ *n.* a dreamy state of forgetfulness or unconsciousness (*literary*) —**lethean** *adj.*

Lethe *n.* in Greek and Roman mythology, a river in Hades whose water made those who drank it forget their past [Mid-16thC. Via Latin from Greek *lēthē* 'forgetfulness, oblivion'.] —**Lethean** *adj.*

Leto /léétō/ *n.* in Greek mythology, the mother of Apollo and Artemis by Zeus. Roman equivalent **Latona**

let-out *n.* a way of freeing yourself from or avoiding sth you have committed yourself to

let's *contr.* let us ○ *Let's just wait and see what happens.*

Lett /let/ *n.* PEOPLES = **Latvian** *n.* **1** [Late 16thC. Via German *Lette* from Latvian *Latvi*.]

letter /léttər/ *n.* **1. MESSAGE SENT BY MAIL** a piece of handwritten, typed, or printed text addressed to a particular person or organization and typically sent by post **2. SYMBOL USED TO SPELL WORDS** each of a set of written or printed symbols representing a par-

ticular sound or set of sounds in a language and used for spelling words **3.** PRINTING FONT a typeface or font ■ *vt.* (**-ters, -tering, -tered**) WRITE ON STH. to write letters or words on sth such as a sign [13thC. Via French *lettre* from Latin *littera* 'letter of the alphabet', used in the plural to mean 'document, epistle, literature' (source of English *literature* and *obliterate*).]

letter bomb *n.* an envelope with an explosive device inside it, addressed and sent through the post and designed to blow up when it is opened

letterbox /léttər boks/ *n.* **1. SLOT FOR DELIVERING MAIL THROUGH A DOOR** a narrow opening in a door, through which letters and packages can be posted. Sometimes a basket or box is fitted on the inside of the door to catch anything that is delivered. US term **mailbox 2. BOX FOR LEAVING MAIL IN** a private box or other place to which mail for a specific person or organization is delivered. US term **maildrop**

letter card *n.* **1. LETTER ON FOLDED AND SEALED CARD** a card that is folded over and sealed before being posted, usually with perforations for tearing the sealed edges when opening it **2. LONG FOLDING LETTER WITH POST-CARD SCENES** a long folding letter with postcard scenes printed down the back, that can be folded, sealed, and then posted like a postcard

letter carrier *n.* sb who delivers letters or other mail (*dated formal*)

lettered /léttərd/ *adj.* **1. WITH LETTERS WRITTEN ON IT** marked with letters of the alphabet **2. EDUCATED** knowledgeable and cultured, especially in literary matters **3. LITERATE** able to read and write

letterform /léttər fawrm/ *n.* the shape of a letter of the alphabet

letterhead /léttər hed/ *n.* **1. PRINTED NAME AND ADDRESS ON STATIONERY** a printed heading for official stationery, usually containing a company's name, address, telephone and fax numbers, and often including a logo and other details **2. HEADED NOTEPAPER** a piece of writing paper with a printed letterhead ○ *Send in a letterhead along with your invoice details.*

lettering /léttəring/ *n.* **1. PIECE OF WRITING** letters of the alphabet written, printed, inscribed, or painted on sth **2. ACT OF WRITING** the physical process of forming letters, or the way sb forms letters

Letterman /léttərmən/, **David** (*b.* 1947) US television presenter. Host of US television programme *The Late Show with David Letterman* from 1993, he is known for his off-beat style.

letter of credit *n.* a letter from a bank, usually for presentation to another branch or bank, authorizing it to issue credit or money to the person named

letter of intent *n.* a signed statement outlining an intention to form an agreement or arrangement

letter of introduction *n.* a letter written by sb to introduce one person to another

letter-perfect *adj.* US = **word-perfect**

letterpress /léttər press/ *n.* **1. PRINTING BY USE OF PRESSURE** a printing technique that transfers ink by pressing raised type onto paper **2. PRINTED MATERIAL** material that is printed using the letterpress technique **3. TEXT** text as opposed to illustrations

letter-quality *adj.* of a quality high enough to be compared to conventional printing

letters /léttərz/ *n.* (*takes a singular or plural verb*) **1. LITERATURE** literature or literary culture **2. KNOWLEDGE** knowledge and education

letters credential *npl.* = **letters of credence**

letters of administration *npl.* an official court order appointing sb as the administrator of a deceased person's estate when no valid will exists

letters of credence *npl.* an official document presented to a government in order to authenticate the official status of a diplomatic representative of another country (*formal*)

letters of marque *npl.* **1. LICENCE TO SEIZE FOREIGN PROPERTY** a formal document issued by one country authorizing one of its private citizens to take possession of goods, or sometimes citizens, belonging to another country **2. LICENCE TO ARM A SHIP** an official document issued by one country authorizing one of

its citizens to fit a ship with weapons in order to attack or seize another country's ships and cargo

letters patent *npl.* an official document stating that sb has been granted the exclusive right to make and sell a new product. Letters patent are issued by the government and specify the length of time a patent will remain valid. (*formal*)

letters testamentary *npl.* an official document authorizing sb to assume the responsibilities and duties of executor of the will of a deceased person (*formal*)

letting /létting/ *n.* a property that is being let

Lettish /léttish/ *n.* LANG = **Latvian** *n.* **2** —**Lettish** *adj.*

lettre de cachet /léttrə də ká shay/ (*plural* **lettres de cachet** /léttrə-/) *n.* a letter sealed with the royal seal authorizing the arrest and indefinite imprisonment of sb who has offended the monarch (*archaic formal*) [Early 18thC. From French, literally 'letter of seal'.]

lettuce /léttiss/ *n.* a common plant that is widely grown for its edible leaves, which are usually eaten in salads. Genus: *Lactuca*. [13thC. Via Old French *letües* from Latin *lactuca*, from *lac* 'milk' (source of English *lactate*), from the milky sap of its stalk.]

let-up *n.* a pause, especially in sth unpleasant (*informal*) ○ *I can take criticism, but with her there's no let-up.*

leu /láy oo/ (*plural* **lei** /layl/) *n.* **1. ROMANIAN CURRENCY UNIT** the basic currency unit of Romania. See table at **currency 2. NOTE WORTH A LEU** a note worth a leu [Late 19thC. From Romanian, literally 'lion'.]

$$H_3C-CH-CH_2-CH-\overset{\displaystyle O}{\overset{\displaystyle \|}{C}}-OH$$
$$\quad\ \ |\qquad\qquad\quad\ |$$
$$\quad CH_3\qquad\qquad NH_2$$

Leucine

leucine /lóo seen/, **leucin** /lóossin/ *n.* a white crystalline essential amino acid that is one of the chemical constituents of proteins. Formula: $C_6H_{13}NO_2$. [Early 19thC. Formed from Greek *leukos* 'white'.]

Leucippus /loo síppəss/ (450?–370 BC) Greek philosopher. He is credited with founding the atomic theory of matter, later developed by Democritus. None of his writings survive.

leucite /lóo sīt/ *n.* a white or grey mineral consisting of a silicate of aluminium and potassium, found in igneous rocks and used as a source of aluminium and of potash for fertilizers [Late 18thC. Formed from Greek *leukos* 'white'.]

leuco- *prefix.* **1.** white, pale, colourless ○ *leucoplakia* **2.** leucocyte ○ *leucopenia* **3.** white matter of the brain ○ *leucodystrophy* [From Greek *leukos* 'white, clear'. Ultimately from an Indo-European base denoting lightness, which is also the ancestor of English *light*[1], *lucid*, and *lunar*.]

leucoblast /lóokō blaast/, **leukoblast** *n.* an immature white blood cell (**leucocyte**)

leucocyte /lóokə sīt/, **leukocyte** *n.* a white blood cell (*technical*) —**leucocytic** /lóokə síttik/ *adj.* —**leucocytoid** /-sī toyd/ *adj.*

leucocytosis /lóokə sī tóssiss/, **leukocytosis** *n.* a marked increase in the number of white blood cells (**leucocytes**), usually because of infection or disease —**leucocytotic** /lóokə sī tóttik/ *adj.*

leucoderma /lóokə dúrmə/, **leukoderma** *n.* = **vitiligo** [Late 19thC. Coined from LEUCO- + Greek *derma* 'skin'.]

leucodystrophy /lóokō dístrəfi/, **leukodystrophy** *n.* a degenerative disease of nerve fibres or white matter that impairs brain function, sight, and motion, leading to death, often at an early age. It involves progressive loss of the fatty myelin layer surrounding the nerve fibres.

leucoma /loo kṓmə/, **leukoma** *n.* a dense white scar on the cornea of the eye, caused by disease or injury [Early 18thC. Via modern Latin from Greek *leukōma* 'white tumour', from *leukos* 'white'.]

leucopenia /loòkō peéni ə/, **leukopenia** *n.* an abnormal reduction in the number of white blood cells (**leucocytes**) —**leucopenic** *adj.*

leucoplakia /loòkō pláyki ə, -plák-/, **leukoplakia** *n.* a pre-cancerous condition that is seen as small thickened white patches, usually inside the mouth or vulva. It requires expert management if cancer is to be avoided. Oral leucoplakia may be caused by smoking or by alcohol abuse. [Late 19thC. Coined from LEUCO- + Greek *plax* 'flat surface'.]

leucoplast /loòkō plast/, **leucoplastid** /loòkō plastid, loòkə plástid/ *n.* a common minute colourless body (**plastid**) found inside plant cells and used for storing food

leucorrhoea /loòkə reé ə/ *n.* thick whitish or yellowish discharge from the vagina —**leucorrhoeal** *adj.*

leucosis *n.* = leukosis

leucotomy /loo kóttəmi/ (*plural* **-mies**) *n.* a surgical operation that involves cutting nerve fibres, especially in the frontal lobes of the brain. It is now rarely performed, and only as a treatment for severe psychiatric disorders.

leucotriene /loòkə treen/, **leukotriene** *n.* a substance that functions as a powerful but short-range chemical messenger in various body systems, including the circulatory, nervous, and immune systems. Leukotrienes help regulate the state of blood vessels and airways, and influence the activities of certain white blood cells. [Late 20thC. Coined from LEUCO- + *triene* 'chemical compound containing three double bonds' (coined from TRI- + -ENE).]

leukaemia /loo keémi ə/ *n.* a type of cancer in which white blood cells displace normal blood. This leads to infection, shortage of red blood cells (**anaemia**), bleeding, and other disorders, and often proves fatal. Certain types of childhood leukaemias respond well to treatment, which includes drugs (**chemotherapy**) and radiotherapy. [Mid-19thC. Coined from LEUCO- + -AEMIA.] —**leukaemic** *adj.*

leukemia *n.* US = leukaemia

leuko- *prefix.* = leuco-

leukoblast *n.* = leucoblast

leukocyte *n.* = leucocyte

leukocytosis *n.* = leucocytosis

leukoderma *n.* = leucoderma

leukodystrophy *n.* = leucodystrophy

leukoma *n.* = leucoma

leukopenia *n.* = leucopenia

leukoplakia *n.* = leucoplakia

leukorrhea *n.* US = leucorrhoea

leukosis /loo kṓssiss/, **leucosis** *n.* any animal disease in which the blood contains an abnormally high number of white blood cells (**leucocytes**) [Early 18thC. From Greek *leukōsis*, from *leukon* 'to make white', from *leukos* 'white'.]

leukotomy *n.* US = leucotomy

leukotriene *n.* = leucotriene

Leunig /loònig/, **Michael** (*b.* 1945) Australian cartoonist. His wistful characters are prone to philosophical musings.

lev /lev/ (*plural* **leva** /lévvə/) *n.* **1.** BULGARIAN CURRENCY UNIT the basic unit of currency of Bulgaria. See table at **currency 2.** NOTE WORTH A LEV a note worth one lev [Late 19thC. From Bulgarian, a variant spelling of *lăv* 'lion', probably ultimately from Greek *leōn*.]

Lev. *abbr.* BIBLE Leviticus

lev- *prefix.* US = laev-

Levant /li vánt/ former name for the region in the eastern Mediterranean comprising modern-day Lebanon, Israel, and parts of Syria and Turkey [15thC. From French, literally 'rising' (referring to the point where the sun rises).] —**Levantine** /lévv'n tīn/ *n., adj.*

levanter /li vántər/ *n.* a strong easterly wind that blows in the western Mediterranean area, especially in the late summer

levantine /lévv'n tīn/ *n.* a type of rich heavy twilled cloth made from silk (*archaic*)

levator /lə váytər/ *n.* **1.** ANAT MUSCLE FOR LIFTING a muscle that helps to lift the body part to which it is attached **2.** SURG SURGICAL INSTRUMENT FOR LIFTING a surgical instrument used to lift up a body part, especially a bone or a tooth [Early 17thC. From Latin, literally 'lifter', from *levare* (see LEVER).]

levee[1] /lévvi, lévvay/ *n.* **1.** NATURAL EMBANKMENT BESIDE A RIVER a natural embankment alongside a river, formed by sediment during times of flooding **2.** ARTIFICIAL EMBANKMENT BESIDE A RIVER an artificial embankment alongside a river, built to prevent flooding of the surrounding land ■ *vt.* (**-ees, -eeing, -eed**) BUILD A LEVEE to provide a river with an embankment to prevent flooding [Late 17thC. From French *levé*, variant of *lever* 'rising', from *lever* 'to rise' (see LEVER).]

levee[2] /lévvi, lévvay/ *n.* **1.** MORNING VISITING TIME an occasion when a noble or royal receives visitors informally soon after getting up in the morning **2.** ROYAL RECEPTION FOR MEN a court reception at which a prince or sovereign receives men visitors. It is usually held in the early afternoon. [See LEVEE[1]]

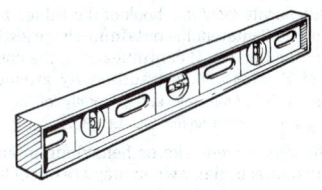

Level

level /lévv'l/ *n.* **1.** HEIGHT FOR MEASUREMENT a position, line, or flat surface according to which height is measured ○ *10,000 feet above sea level* **2.** HEIGHT OF A SURFACE FROM BOTTOM the height of a surface from the ground or from the bottom of its container ○ *The level of the river had fallen alarmingly during the summer.* **3.** STATED HEIGHT a particular height ○ *flying below the level of the tree tops* **4.** RANK OR SCALE a particular position in a range of relative scales or values ○ *playing tennis at the professional level* **5.** AMOUNT the amount or concentration of sth ○ *My job has a low stress level but few prospects.* **6.** ASPECT a quality or aspect of sth ○ *It's a film that works well on a number of different levels.* **7.** POSITION OF A PARTICULAR FLOOR the relative position of a particular floor or other plane in a structure, e.g. a building or bridge ○ *The storeroom is down on the second level.* **8.** HORIZONTAL SURFACE a horizontal surface or area of land **9.** CIV ENG SURVEYING INSTRUMENT an instrument used in surveying to measure the relative heights of different points in the landscape **10.** CIV ENG MEASUREMENT OF HEIGHT in surveying, a measurement taken of the relative heights of different points in a landscape **11.** CONSTR TOOL FOR DETERMINING LEVELNESS a calibrated glass tube containing liquid with an air bubble in it, mounted in a frame and used for measuring whether surfaces are horizontal **12.** MINING HORIZONTAL MINE TUNNEL a horizontal tunnel in a mine ■ *adj.* **1.** NOT SLOPING flat and horizontal, with an even surface or top **2.** EVEN smooth or even ○ *We wanted a house with a completely level lawn.* **3.** EQUAL equal to or even with another individual or group in rank, ability, or condition ○ *The two teams have drawn level after six games.* **4.** ALONGSIDE next to or alongside sb or sth else ○ *His car drew level as we approached the bend.* **5.** STEADY steady, consistent, or unchanging **6.** = level-headed **7.** OF A PARTICULAR LEVEL relating to or characteristic of a particular rank or condition (*usually used in combination*) ■ *v.* (**-els, -elling, -elled**) **1.** FLATTEN STH EVENLY to make sth even, flat, and horizontal ○ *We spent days levelling the ground before we could build anything.* **2.** *vt.* DEMOLISH AND FLATTEN STH to completely destroy a build-

ing, place, or area and leave it flattened ○ *The village had been levelled by the hurricane.* **3.** *vt.* KNOCK SB DOWN to knock sb to the ground, especially with a punch or blow (*informal*) ○ *levelled him with one punch* **4.** *vi.* BE HONEST WITH SB to speak frankly and honestly to sb (*informal*) ○ *I'd better level with you right now – I'm leaving the company and going it alone.* **5.** *vti.* MEASURE THE ELEVATION OF LAND in surveying, to measure the elevation of an area of land **6.** *vti.* MAKE OR BECOME EQUAL to make two things or people equal in position or of the same standard or value, or become equal in position, standard or value ○ *Another goal in the final few minutes levelled the scores again.* **7.** *vti.* AIM A GUN to aim or point a weapon ○ *He levelled his pistol at the target.* **8.** *vt.* DIRECT ATTENTION AT SB to direct criticism or an attack towards sb in a purposeful way ○ *Criticism has been levelled at a number of prominent politicians.* [14thC. Via Old French *livel* 'tool for determining levelness' (the earliest sense in English) from, ultimately, Latin *libra* 'balance, scales' (source of English *Libra*, the zodiac sign).] —**levelly** *adv.* —**levelness** *n.* ◇ **on the level** honest and trustworthy (*informal*)

level off *vti.* **1.** level off, level out FLY LEVEL WITH THE GROUND to make an aircraft fly level with the ground, especially after climbing or descending ○ *We passed through the clouds and eventually levelled off at about 10,000 feet.* **2.** BECOME STEADY to reach a level and become stable and unchanging ○ *Stock prices seem to have levelled off.*

level crossing *n.* a place where a road crosses a railway line, usually with a system of warning signals and barriers that close automatically when a train is approaching. US term **grade crossing**

leveler *n.* US = leveller

level-headed *adj.* remaining rational and fully in control in difficult situations or emergencies — **level-headedly** *adv.* —**levelheadedness** *n.*

leveller /lévvələr/ *n.* **1.** STH THAT MAKES SITUATIONS MORE EQUAL sth that makes situations or people more equal, especially by removing distinctions based on status or privilege ○ *Time is a great leveller; we all end up the same way in the end.* **2.** BELIEVER IN EQUALITY sb who wants to make everyone in society more equal

Leveller /lévvələr/ *n.* a member or supporter of a radical Parliamentarian movement during the Civil War, calling for religious tolerance, legal equality, a universal male vote, and the abolition of the monarchy. The movement was later suppressed by Cromwell.

levelling screw *n.* one of usually several screws on the bottom of sth such as a scientific instrument or a washing machine that can be adjusted to make the piece of equipment stand level

level of attainment *n.* the level that a child has reached on the eight-point scale by which the National Curriculum assesses pupils between the ages of 5 and 14. Pupils progress through the eight levels at different rates, although average pupils are expected to reach each level at a particular age.

level pegging *n.* in a game or competition, the same position, score, or level of achievement as sb else ○ *After four rounds we were both on level pegging.* ○ *It's level pegging at the moment though anything could happen in the next round.* [From the use of pegs stuck in parallel rows in a board to show the players' scores in card games]

Leven, Loch /leévən/ lake in east-central Scotland, north of the Firth of Forth. Area: 26 sq. km/10 sq. mi.

lever /leévər/ *n.* **1.** RIGID BAR USED FOR LEVERAGE a rigid bar that pivots about a point (**fulcrum**) and is used to move or lift a load at one end by applying force to the other end **2.** DEVICE OR MACHINE a mechanical device or machine that operates using leverage **3.** WAY OF ACHIEVING STH a device, tactic, or situation that can be used to advantage ■ *vt.* (**-ers, -ering, -ered**) MOVE WITH A LEVER to move sth using a lever [13thC. Via Anglo-Norman, literally 'sth that raises', from Old French *lever* 'to rise or raise', from Latin *levare*, from *levis* 'light' (source of English *levity*).]

Lever /leévər/, **William Hesketh, 1st Viscount Leverhulme** (1851–1925) British industrialist and philanthropist. Some of the fortune he made from manufacturing

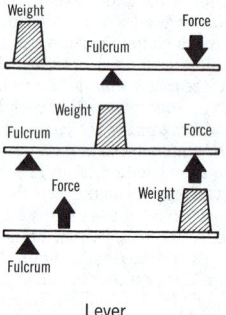

Lever

soap was used for the furtherance of higher education and for founding the industrial town of Port Sunlight.

leverage /léevərij/ *n.* **1. ACTION OF A LEVER** the action of a lever pivoting about a point **2. MECHANICAL ADVANTAGE** the mechanical advantage gained by using a lever **3. POWER TO GET THINGS DONE** power over other people, especially sth that gives an advantage but is not referred to openly ○ *He uses the leverage his age gives him with the more junior employees.* **4. FIN BORROWING OF MONEY TO PURCHASE COMPANY** the borrowing of money to purchase a company, relying on it making enough profit to cover the interest payable on the loan **5. FIN = gearing** ■ *vti.* **(-ages, -aging, -aged) FIN BORROW MONEY HOPING TO MAKE MORE** to borrow money in order to buy a company, relying on it making enough profit to cover the interest payable on the loan

leveraged buyout *n.* a takeover strategy in which a controlling proportion of a company's shares is bought using borrowed money, the collateral for which is assets belonging to the purchased company

leveret /lévvərət/ *n.* a young hare, especially one less than a year old [14thC. From Anglo-Norman, literally 'little hare', from *levre* 'hare', from Latin *lepus*.]

Leverrier /lə ver yáy/, **Urbain Jean Joseph** (1811–77) French astronomer. He predicted the existence of Neptune before it was discovered and improved the astronomical tables for Mercury.

Levi /léev ī/ *n.* in the Bible, the third son of Jacob and patriarch of the house of Levi (Genesis 29:34)

Levi /lévvi/, **Primo** (1919–87) Italian novelist, poet, and scientist. His book *If This Is a Man* (1959) recorded his experiences as a Jew during World War II.

leviable /lévvi əb'l/ *adj.* **1. ABLE TO BE TAXED** able to have a tax imposed **2. ABLE TO BE LEVIED** capable of being levied

leviathan /lə ví əth'n/ *n.* **1. Leviathan, leviathan MONSTER** in the Bible, a large beast or sea monster **2. STH HUGE** sth extremely large and powerful in comparison with others of its kind **3. WHALE** a whale or other large sea animal (*literary*) ○ *A leviathan from the icy deeps crashed ashore one night.* [14thC. Via late Latin from Hebrew *liwyāṯān*.]

— **WORD KEY: CULTURAL NOTE** —
Leviathan, a treatise by English philosopher Thomas Hobbes (1651). Hobbes's major work is a defence of the principle of absolute monarchy. It argues that human beings can only live in peace if they agree to subject themselves to a single, absolute ruler. Since this ruler should be answerable only to God, the church too must be subject to civil authority.

levigate /lévvi gayt/ **(-gates, -gating, -gated)** *v.* **1.** *vt.* **GRIND MINERAL INTO POWDER** to grind a mineral into a fine powder with water, forming a smooth paste or slurry **2.** *vt.* **SEPARATE PARTICLES IN LIQUID** to separate fine particles from coarser ones by suspending them in a liquid **3.** *vti.* **FORM A MIXTURE** to form a smooth uniform liquid mixture, e.g. a paste or gel [15thC. From Latin *levigat-*, the past participle stem of *levigare* 'to polish or make smooth'.] —**levigation** /lévvi gáysh'n/ *n.*

levirate /léevirət, lévvi-/ *n.* the practice or requirement of marriage of a widow to the brother of her deceased husband. This custom was practised in ancient Jewish society and is common in parts of

---

Africa today. [Early 18thC. From Latin *levir* 'husband's brother'.] —**leviratic** /léevi ráttik, lévvi-/ *adj.*

Levi-Strauss /lévvi strówss/, **Claude Gustave** (*b.* 1908) French social anthropologist. A proponent of structuralism, he originated the thesis that all cultures have a common framework.

Levit. *abbr.* Leviticus

levitate /lévvi tayt/ **(-tates, -tating, -tated)** *v.* **1.** *vti.* **RISE IN THE AIR** to rise and float in the air, or make sth rise and float in the air, seemingly in defiance of gravity **2.** *vt.* **MED SUPPORT A PATIENT ON AIR** to support a patient on a cushion of air during treatment for severe burns [Late 17thC. From Latin *levis* 'light', modelled on *gravitate*. Originally 'to make light'.] —**levitator** *n.*

levitation /lévvi táysh'n/ *n.* rising into the air or making sth float in the air without visible means of support —**levitational** *adj.*

Levite /lée vīt/ *n.* a member of the tribe of Levi, chosen to assist the priests of the Temple. The Levites were descended from Jacob's son Levi and constituted one of the twelve tribes of Israel. [14thC. Via ecclesiastical Latin *levita* from Greek *levitēs*, named after *Levi* 'Levi'.]

Levitical /lə víttik'l/ *adj.* **1. OF THE LEVITES** belonging or relating to the Levites **2. OF THE BOOK OF LEVITICUS** relating to the book of Leviticus, especially those portions containing laws relating to ritual or moral precepts

Leviticus /lə víttikəss/ *n.* a book of the Bible, the third book of the Pentateuch, containing the priestly tradition of the Levites. It continues from the end of the book of Exodus and is traditionally attributed to Moses. [14thC. From late Latin, literally 'of the Levites', ultimately from Greek *levitēs* (see LEVITE).]

levity /lévvəti/ *n.* remarks or behaviour intended to be amusing, especially when they are out of keeping with a serious occasion [Mid-16thC. From Latin *levitas*, from *levis* 'light'.]

levo- *n.* US = laevo-

levodopa /leévō dṓpə/ *n.* full form of **L-dopa** [Late 20thC. Coined from LEVO- + DOPA (see L-DOPA).]

levorotation[1] *n.* US = laevorotation

levorotation[2] *adj.* US = laevorotatory

levulose *n.* US = laevulose

levy /lévvi/ *v.* **(-ies, -ying, -ied) 1.** *vt.* **POL OFFICIALLY DEMAND TAX PAYMENTS** to use government authority to impose or collect a tax **2.** *vt.* **MIL RAISE AN ARMY** to enlist troops for military service, often by force **3.** *vt.* **DECLARE WAR** to declare war on sb **4.** *vi.* **LAW SEIZE PROPERTY TO FULFIL A JUDGMENT** to seize property in accordance with a legal ruling ■ *n.* (*plural* **-ies**) **1. TAX** money raised under government authority **2. THE RAISING OF TAX** the act of collecting taxes under government authority **3. MIL ARMY** a group of soldiers drafted under government authority **4. MIL CONSCRIPTION** the act of drafting soldiers under government authority [15thC. From French *lever* 'to raise or rise', from Latin *levare* (see LEVER).] —**levier** *n.*

lewd /lood, lyood/ *adj.* showing an inordinate interest in sex or sexual excitement (*disapproving*) [Old English *læw(e)de* 'lay, not in holy orders', of unknown origin. The current sense evolved via Middle English meanings 'not educated, ignorant' and 'crude, vulgar, vile'.] —**lewdly** *adv.* —**lewdness** *n.*

Lewes /loo əss/ county town of East Sussex, southeastern England. The ruined Norman castle makes it a popular tourist area. Population: 15,376 (1991).

lewis /loo iss/ *n.* an iron attachment consisting of linked pieces that fit into a dovetailed opening in a stone, used to grip heavy stones before lifting them [Mid-18thC. Origin uncertain: probably from French *lous*, plural of *lou(p)* 'kind of siege engine', literally 'wolf', from Latin *lupus* (see LUPUS).]

Lewis /loo iss/, **C. S.** (1898–1963) Irish-born British critic, scholar, and novelist. He wrote books on moral and religious issues, e.g. *The Screwtape Letters* (1942), and a children's book series known as *The Chronicles of Narnia* (1950–56). Full name **Clive Staples Lewis**

Lewis, Essington (1881–1961) Australian engineer and

---

company director. He was general manager of a mining company (1921–50).

Lewis, Jerry (*b.* 1926) US actor, screenwriter, film director, and film producer. He formed a comic duo with Dean Martin, with whom he made 18 films, and later starred in his own films. Real name **Joseph Levitch**

Lewis, Wally (*b.* 1959) Australian rugby league player. He played for Australia regularly from 1984 to 1989 and captained the team in 1984, 1986, and 1988.

Lewis, Wyndham (1882–1957) British painter, novelist, and critic. He was a noted portraitist, a war artist during World War I, the author of satirical novels, and founded the Vorticist movement.

Lewis acid *n.* a substance that can accept a pair of electrons from a base to form a covalent bond [Mid-20thC. Named after Gilbert Newton *Lewis*, who introduced the concept.]

Lewis gun *n.* a gas-powered machine gun with a circular magazine, first used in World War I [Early 20thC. Named after the US soldier Colonel Isaac Newton *Lewis* (1858–1931), who invented it.]

lewisite /loo i sīt/ *n.* a colourless or brownish oily poisonous liquid used in gaseous form in chemical warfare during World War I. Formula: $C_2H_2AsCl_3$. [Early 20thC. Named after the US chemist Winford Lee *Lewis* (1878–1943), who developed it.]

lewisson /loo iss'n/ *n.* = lewis

Lewis with Harris /loo iss with hárriss/ the largest and northernmost of the Outer Hebrides islands of Scotland. Population: 21,737 (1991). Area: 2,134 sq. km/824 sq. mi.

lex /leks/ (*plural* **leges** /lée jeez/) *n.* a named law or set of laws (*formal*) [Late 18thC. From Latin, literally 'law'.]

lex. *abbr.* lexicon

lexeme /léks eem/ *n.* a fundamental unit of the vocabulary of a language, e.g. 'make', which may exist in a number of different forms, e.g. 'make, makes, making, maker, made' [Mid-20thC. Coined from LEXICON + -EME.]

lexica plural of **lexicon**

lexical /léksik'l/ *adj.* **1. OF WORDS** relating to the individual words that make up the vocabulary of a language **2. OF A LEXICON** relating to a lexicon or lexicography [Mid-19thC. Formed from Greek *lexikos* (see LEXICON).] —**lexicality** /léksi kálləti/ *n.* —**lexically** /léksik'li/ *adv.*

lexicalization /léksikə lī záysh'n/, **lexicalisation** *n.* **1. MAKING A WORD FROM EXISTING WORDS** the creation of a single word out of existing words, usually in order to express sth previously conveyed by several words or a phrase, e.g. 'shoplifting' **2. WORD FORMED FROM EXISTING WORDS** a single word created by lexicalization

lexicalize /léksikə līz/ **(-izes, -izing, -ized)**, **lexicalise (-ises, -ising, -ised)** *vti.* to form a single word or be formed as a single word from existing words in order to express sth previously conveyed by several words or a phrase, e.g. 'shoplifting'

lexical meaning *n.* the meaning of the base word in the set of inflected forms (**paradigm**). In the paradigm 'throw, throws, throwing, threw, thrown', the lexical meaning is 'throw'.

lexicog. *abbr.* **1.** lexicography **2.** lexicographical

lexicography /léksi kóggrəfi/ *n.* the writing and editing of dictionaries [Mid-17thC. Coined from Greek *lexikos* (see LEXICON) + -GRAPHY.] —**lexicographer** *n.* —**lexicographic** /léksikə gráffik/ *adj.* —**lexicographically** *adv.*

lexicology /léksi kólləji/ *n.* the branch of linguistics dealing with the use and meanings of words and the relationships between items of vocabulary [Early 19thC. Coined from Greek *lexikos* (see LEXICON) + -LOGY.] —**lexicological** /léksikə lójjik'l/ *adj.* —**lexicologically** *adv.* —**lexicologist** /léksi kólləjist/ *n.*

lexicon /léksikən, -kon/ (*plural* **-cons** or **-ca** /-kə/) *n.* **1. DICTIONARY** a reference book with an alphabetized listing of words and their meanings, especially one dealing with an ancient language **2. VOCABULARY** the entire stock of words belonging to a branch of knowledge or known by sb [Early 17thC. Via modern

Latin from Greek *lexikon*, literally 'of words', from, ultimately, *lexis* 'word', from *legein* 'to speak'.]

lexigraphy /lek síggrəfi/ n. a system of writing in which each character stands for a word [Early 19thC. From Greek *lexis* (see LEXICON) + -GRAPHY.]

Lexington /léksingtən/ town in northeastern Massachusetts, northwest of Boston. It is the site of the first battle of the US War of Independence in 1775. Population: 29,484 (1996).

lexis /léksiss/ n. the entire stock of words in a language [Mid-20thC. From Greek (see LEXICON).]

lex talionis /-talli óniss/ n. the legal principle that proscribes retaliating in kind for crimes committed [From Latin, literally 'law of retaliation']

ley /lay, lee/ (plural **leys**) n. 1. AGRIC LAND PUT DOWN TO GRASS temporarily put down to grass 2. VERY OLD PATH any of many ancient paths in Britain that led from hilltop to hilltop and touched on water sources and places of worship

ley farming n. the practice of growing grass in fields normally planted with grain or other tilled crops in order to prevent the soil from becoming exhausted [*Ley* from assumed Old English *læge* 'fallow', related to English *lie*[1]]

ley line n. a straight line linking ancient landmarks and places of worship, believed to follow the course of former routes and popularly associated with mystical phenomena

Lezghian /lézgi ən/ n. a language spoken in an area around the Caspian Sea belonging to the Dagestanian branch of Caucasian languages. Lezghian is spoken by about 300,000 people. [Mid-19thC. From Russian *Lezgin*.] —**Lezghian** adj.

lf abbr. light face

LF abbr. 1. BASEBALL left field 2. BASEBALL left fielder 3. RADIO low frequency

L-form n. a bacterium that lacks cell walls [*L* from *Lister* Institute in London, where it was first isolated]

LG abbr. Low German

lg. abbr. large

lgth abbr. length

LGU abbr. Ladies' Golf Union

lh abbr. left hand

LH abbr. 1. luteinizing hormone 2. left hand

Lhasa /laássə/ city and capital of the autonomous region of Tibet, southwestern China. Population: 106,885 (1990).

Lhasa apso

Lhasa apso /laássə ápsō/ (plural **Lhasa apsos**) n. a small dog of a Tibetan breed with a long straight coat, hair that falls heavily over the eyes, and a fluffy tail that curls over the back [Early 20thC. From LHASA + *Apso*, the Tibetan name of the breed.]

lhd abbr. left-hand drive

LHD abbr. Litterarum Humaniorum Doctor

lherzolite /lúrzə līt/ n. a coarse-grained rock containing minerals high in iron and magnesium that is believed to originate in the Earth's mantle

LH-RH abbr. luteinizing hormone-releasing hormone

li /lee/ (plural **li**) n. a traditional Chinese unit of distance, now standardized at 500 m/547 yd [Late 16thC. From Chinese *li*.]

Li symbol. lithium

li. abbr. link

liability /lī ə bílləti/ n. (plural **-ties**) 1. LAW OBLIGATION UNDER THE LAW legal responsibility for sth, especially costs or damages 2. DEBT anything for which sb is responsible, especially a debt 3. DISADVANTAGE sth that holds sb back or causes trouble 4. SB WHO IS A BURDEN sb who prevents a successful outcome or causes social embarrassment 5. LIKELIHOOD OF STH likelihood or probability of sth happening ■ **liabilities** npl. ACCT MONEY OWED all debts and other financial obligations that appear on a balance sheet

liable /lī əb'l/ adj. 1. LAW RESPONSIBLE having legal responsibility for sth, especially costs or damages 2. LIKELY likely to experience or do sth, often sth unpleasant or hazardous [15thC. Origin uncertain: probably formed from French *lier* (see LIAISON).]

liaise /li áyz/ (-**aises**, -**aising**, -**aised**) vi. to establish or maintain close cooperation with sb [Early 20thC. Back-formation from LIAISON (originally military slang).]

liaison /li áyz'n, -zon/ n. 1. COORDINATION the exchange of information or the planning of joint efforts by separate groups or individuals, often of military units 2. COORDINATOR sb who is responsible for maintaining communication between one group or office and another 3. UNMARRIED LOVE AFFAIR a romantic and sexual relationship between people who are not married to each other 4. LING PRONOUNCED CONSONANT LINKING TWO WORDS in spoken French, the pronunciation of the usually silent final consonant of a word when it is followed by another word beginning with a vowel 5. FOOD STH USED TO THICKEN A LIQUID a thickening agent such as egg yolks or flour used in soups and sauces [Mid-17thC. From French, formed from *lier* 'to bind', from Latin *ligare* (source of English *ligature*).]

liana /li aánə/, **liane** n. a woody climbing tropical vine [Late 18thC. From French *liane*, originally 'clematis' of uncertain origin: perhaps formed from *lier* (see LIAISON).] —**lianoid** /li aá noyd/ adj.

Liao /lee ow/ river in northeastern China. Length: 1,125 km/700 mi.

Liaoning /lyów níng/ province in the historic region of Manchuria, northeastern China. Shenyang is the capital. Population: 40,670,000 (1994). Area: 151,000 sq. km/58,300 sq. mi.

Liaoyang /lee ow júng/, **Liao-yang** city in Liaoning Province, northeastern China, situated 56 km/35 mi. south of Shenyang. Population: 492,559 (1990).

liar /lī ər/ n. sb who tells lies

liard /li aárd/ n. a coin of small value formerly used in various European countries, including France [Mid-16thC. From French, of unknown origin.]

Liard /lee ərd/ river of western Canada, rising in the Yukon Territory and flowing through British Columbia and the Northwest Territories, where it joins the Mackenzie River. Length: 1,115 km/700 mi.

Liassic /lī ássik/ adj. belonging to or dating from the oldest division of the European Jurassic period, noted for its fossils of dinosaurs [Mid-19thC. From French *liassique*, from *Lias* 'series of strata forming the lowest division of the Jurassic system', from Old French *liais* 'hard limestone'.]

lib /lib/ n. a campaign to extend the rights of an oppressed group (*dated informal; usually used in combination*) [Mid-20thC. Shortening.] —**libber** n.

lib. abbr. 1. librarian 2. library

Lib. abbr. Liberal

libation /lī báysh'n/ n. 1. RELIG POURING OF LIQUID AS A RELIGIOUS OFFERING the pouring out of a liquid such as wine or oil as a sacrifice to a god or in honour of a dead person 2. RELIG STH POURED OUT AS A SACRIFICE a liquid such as wine or oil poured out as a religious offering 3. ALCOHOLIC DRINK an alcoholic drink (*humorous*) [14thC. From the Latin stem *libation-*, from *libare* 'to pour out'.] —**libational** /lī báyshən'l/ adj.

Lib Dem abbr. Liberal Democrat

libel /lī b'l/ n. 1. LAW DEFAMATION a false and malicious published statement that damages sb's reputation. Libel can include pictures and any other representations that have public or permanent form. 2. ATTACKING SB'S REPUTATION the making of false and damaging statements about sb 3. LAW WRITTEN STATEMENT the plaintiff's written statement in a case under admiralty law or in an ecclesiastical court ■ vt. (-**bels**, -**belling**, -**belled**) 1. DEFAME to publish false and malicious statements that damage sb's reputation 2. ATTACK to give a false and damaging account of sb 3. LAW BRING A SUIT FOR LIBEL to bring a suit for libel against sb under Admiralty law or in an ecclesiastical court [14thC. Via Old French from Latin *libellus* 'little book', diminutive of *liber* (see LIBRARY). Originally 'written declaration', later 'sth setting out the grounds for a lawsuit'.] —**libeller** n. —**libellist** n. —**libellous** adj. —**libellously** adv.

WORD KEY: SYNONYMS
See Synonyms at *malign*.

Liberace /líbbər aáchi/ (1919–87) US entertainer. A performer of popular piano pieces, he was distinguished by his flamboyant attire and lavish presentations. Real name **Wladziu Valentino Liberace**

liberal /líbbərəl/ adj. 1. BROAD-MINDED tolerant of different views and standards of behaviour in others 2. POL PROGRESSIVE POLITICALLY OR SOCIALLY favouring gradual reform, especially political reforms that extend democracy, distribute wealth more evenly, and protect the personal freedom of the individual 3. GENEROUS generous with money, time, or some other asset ○ *My great-aunt was liberal in her bequests.* 4. GENEROUS IN QUANTITY large in size or amount ○ *a liberal helping* 5. LANG NOT LITERAL not limited to the literal meaning in translation or interpretation 6. ARTS CULTURALLY ORIENTED concerned with general cultural matters and broadening of the mind rather than professional or technical study ○ *a liberal education* 7. JUDAISM OF BRANCH OF PROGRESSIVE JUDAISM used to describe or belonging to a branch of Progressive Judaism, characterized by radical revision of the liturgy and an emphasis on ethical teaching. Founded in England in the early 20th century by Claude Montefiore, it accepts patrilineal descent as a qualification for membership in the Jewish religious community. 8. HIST OF POLITICAL LIBERALISM relating to a political ideology of liberalism ■ n. LIBERAL PERSON sb who favours tolerance or reform [14thC. Via French from Latin *liberalis*, from *liber* 'free' (source of English *liberty*). The underlying sense is 'suitable for a free (later wellbred) person'.]

WORD KEY: SYNONYMS
See Synonyms at *generous*.

Liberal adj. OF A LIBERAL PARTY supporting, belonging to, or associated with a Liberal Party, e.g. in the United Kingdom, Canada, or Australia ■ n. MEMBER OF A LIBERAL PARTY sb who is a member of or supports a Liberal Party, e.g. in the United Kingdom, Canada, or Australia

liberal arts npl. 1. EDUCATION IN CULTURALLY ORIENTED SUBJECTS college and university subjects that are intended to provide students with general cultural knowledge, e.g. languages, literature, history, and philosophy 2. MEDIEVAL EDUCATION the medieval studies known as the trivium and quadrivium

liberal democracy n. a political system that has free elections, a multiplicity of political parties, political decision made through an independent legislature, and an independent judiciary, with a state monopoly on law enforcement

Liberal Democrat n. a member of the British Liberal and Social Democratic Party

liberalism /líbbərəlizəm/ n. 1. POL PROGRESSIVE VIEWS a belief in tolerance and gradual reform in moral, religious, or political matters 2. POL POLITICAL THEORY STRESSING INDIVIDUALISM a political ideology with its beginnings in western Europe that rejects authoritarian government and defends freedom of speech, association, and religion, and the right to own property 3. ECON FREE-MARKET ECONOMICS an economic theory in favour of free competition and minimal government regulation **4.** CHR **CHRISTIAN THEO-LOGICAL MOVEMENT** a movement in modern Protestantism stressing intellectual freedom and the moral content of Christianity over the doctrines of traditional theology —**liberalist** *n.* —**liberalistic** /líbbərə lístik/ *adj.*

liberality /líbbə rálləti/ *n.* **1.** GENEROSITY generous provision of money, time, or some other asset **2.** LARGENESS largeness in size or amount **3.** BROAD-MINDEDNESS tolerance of different views and standards of behaviour in others

liberalize /líbbərə līz/ (**-izes, -izing, -ized**), **liberalise** (**-ises, -ising, -ised**) *vti.* to reform and become less strict, or reform sth and make it less strict —**liberalization** /líbbərə līz záysh'n/ *n.* —**liberalizer** /líbbərə līzər/ *n.*

liberally /líbbərəli/ *adv.* **1.** GENEROUSLY giving money, time, or some other asset with generosity **2.** IN LARGE AMOUNTS in large quantities or amounts

liberalness /líbbərəlnəss/ *n.* = **liberality**

Liberal Party *n.* **1.** FORMER UK POLITICAL PARTY one of the main British political parties that evolved from the Whigs and eventually merged with the Social Democratic Party in 1988 to form the Social and Liberal Democratic Party. The Social and Liberal Democrats later became known as the Liberal Democrats. **2.** *Can* MAJOR CANADIAN POLITICAL PARTY a major Canadian political party at both the national and provincial levels that first came to power nationally in 1873

Liberal Party of Australia *n.* a conservative Australian political party founded in 1944 as an anti-socialist organization that, except for 1972–4, has always been in coalition with the National Party

liberal studies *n.* a combined arts subject intended to provide students with general cultural knowledge, provided as an element of a more specialized, technical, or vocational course at school or college. It may include, e.g., study of languages, literature, history, and philosophy. (*takes a singular verb*)

Liberal Unionist *n.* a member of the former Liberal Party who disagreed with Gladstone's policy on Irish Home Rule from 1886 onwards

liberate /líbbə rayt/ (**-ates, -ating, -ated**) *vt.* **1.** SET SB FREE PHYSICALLY to release an individual, group, population, or country from political or military control or from any severe physical constraint **2.** RELEASE SB FROM SOCIAL STEREOTYPING to set sb free from traditional socially imposed constraints such as those arising from stereotyping by sex or age **3.** STEAL to steal sth (*informal*) **4.** CHEM RELEASE GAS DURING A CHEMICAL REACTION to free sth such as a gas from combination in a chemical compound during a chemical reaction [Late 16thC. From Latin *liberare*, from *liber* 'free'.] —**liberation** /líbbə ráysh'n/ *n.*

liberation theology *n.* a movement in Roman Catholic religious teaching that argues that the Church should work actively together with socialists to combat social, political, and economic oppression. The movement is international but especially active in Latin America and bases its case on Jesus Christ's ministry to the poor and outcast in society. —**liberation theologian** *n.*

liberator /líbbə raytər/ *n.* sb who sets others free

Liberia

Liberia /lī beéri ə/ republic in western Africa, on the North Atlantic Ocean. Language: English. Currency: Liberian dollar. Capital: Monrovia. Popu-

lation: 2,602,068 (1997). Area: 99,067 sq. km/38,250 sq. mi. Official name **Republic of Liberia** —**Liberian** *adj., n.*

libero /leébərō/ (*plural* **-ros**) *n.* in football, a sweeper (*informal*) [Mid-20thC. From Italian, literally 'free', from Latin *liber.*]

libertarian /líbbər táiri ən/ *n.* **1.** PHILOS **ADVOCATE OF INDIVIDUAL RESPONSIBILITY** sb who believes in the doctrine of free will **2.** POL **ADVOCATE OF INDIVIDUAL FREEDOM** sb who believes that people should have complete freedom of thought and action and should not be subject to the authority of the state [Late 18thC. Formed from LIBERTY, modelled on words such as UNITARIAN.] —**libertarianism** *n.*

libertine /líbbər teen, -tīn/ *n.* sb, usually a man, who indulges in pleasures that are considered immoral and who has sexual relationships with many people [14thC. From Latin *libertinus*, from *libertus* 'sb freed from slavery', from *liber* 'free'. The underlying sense is of sb unrestrained.] —**libertinage** /líbbər teenij/ *n.* —**libertinism** /líbbər teenizəm, -tīnizəm/ *n.*

liberty /líbbərti/ (*plural* **-ties**) *n.* **1.** RIGHT TO CHOOSE the freedom to think or act without being constrained by necessity or force **2.** FREEDOM freedom from captivity or slavery **3.** POL BASIC RIGHT any of the political, social, and economic rights that belong to the citizens of a state or to all people (*often used in the plural*) ◊ **civil liberties 4.** BREACH OF ETIQUETTE an action or remark that violates the polite distance usually left between individuals and that may strike the person at whom it is directed as insultingly familiar [14thC. Via French *liberté* from Latin *libertas*, from *liber* 'free'.] ◊ **at liberty 1.** free or freed after a period of imprisonment or other constraint **2.** free or allowed to do sth ◊ **take liberties with 1.** behave inappropriately towards sb, especially by way of excessive familiarity or sometimes sexual harassment **2.** to be deliberately inaccurate when dealing with facts (*disapproving*) ◊ **take the liberty** be bold enough to do sth, sometimes without permission

— **WORD KEY: CULTURAL NOTE** —

Liberty Leading the People, a painting by French artist Eugène Delacroix (1830). Inspired by a scene witnessed by Delacroix during the 1830 uprisings in Paris, this mixture of allegory and realism shows a young woman leading a ragged band of rebels over razed barricades. Delacroix's declaration of solidarity with the revolutionary cause, it is also a powerful symbol of freedom and the struggle against oppression. The painting is sometimes called *Liberty on the Barricades*.

— **WORD KEY: CULTURAL NOTE** —

On Liberty, an essay by philosopher John Stuart Mill (1859). A work that has inspired civil libertarians around the world, it examines the relationship between the rights of the individual and the power of the state. Mill argues for freedom of thought and expression, asserting that the only valid restrictions on the rights of individuals are those that protect the rights of others.

liberty bodice *n.* a close-fitting sleeveless undergarment for the upper body made of thick soft cotton and worn by children, especially young girls. It was popular from the 1920s to the 1950s. [*Liberty* because it was less restrictive than a corset]

liberty cap *n.* a soft cone-shaped cap fitting tightly on the head and falling to one side, worn as a symbol of freedom by French revolutionaries and in the United States before 1800. It was first worn in ancient Rome, where it was given to people who were set free from slavery.

liberty hall, **Liberty Hall** *n.* a place where people can do whatever they want

liberty horse *n.* a horse that performs tricks in the circus in a group and without a rider

Liberty Island island in New York Bay, southeastern New York State. It is the site of the Statue of Liberty. Area: 5 hectares/12 acres. Formerly **Bedloe's Island** (until 1956)

liberty pole *n.* a tall flagpole to the top of which a liberty cap or the flag of a new republic is attached

liberty ship *n.* a type of cargo ship mass-produced in the United States during World War II

libidinous /li bíddinəss/ *adj.* having or expressing strong sexual desires (*formal*) [15thC. From Latin *libidinosus*, from *libido* 'desire, lust'.] —**libidinously** *adv.* —**libidinousness** *n.*

libido /li beédō/ (*plural* **-dos**) *n.* **1.** SEX DRIVE sexual drive **2.** PSYCHOANAL EMOTIONS THEORETICALLY LINKED TO SEXUALITY in some theories, the psychic and emotional energy in sb's psychological make-up that is related to the basic human instincts, especially the sex drive [Early 20thC. From Latin, literally 'desire, lust'.] —**libidinal** /li bíddin'l/ *adj.* —**libidinally** *adv.*

LIBOR /lī bawr/ *abbr.* London Inter-Bank Offered Rate

Libra /leébrə/ *n.* **1.** ASTRON CONSTELLATION IN THE SOUTHERN HEMISPHERE a small constellation in the southern hemisphere between Virgo and Scorpio **2.** ZODIAC SEVENTH SIGN OF THE ZODIAC the seventh sign of the zodiac represented by a pair of scales and lasting from approximately 23 September to 22 October. Libra is classified as an air sign and its ruling planet is Venus. **3.** SB BORN UNDER LIBRA sb whose birthday falls between 23 September and 22 October [Pre-12thC. From Latin, literally 'balance, scales'.] —**Libra** *adj.*

Libran /leébrən/ *n.* = **Libra** *n.* **3** —**Libran** *adj.*

librarian /lī bráiri ən/ *n.* sb who works in or is in charge of a library [Late 17thC. Formed from Latin *librarius* (see LIBRARY), literally 'of books', also 'scribe, sb concerned with books'.]

librarianship /lī bráiri ən ship/ *n.* the study of libraries and their administration, including techniques of research and principles of organization. US term **library science**

library /lī brəri, líbri/ (*plural* **-ies**) *n.* **1.** PLACE WHERE BOOKS ARE KEPT the room, building, or institution where a collection of books or other research materials is kept **2.** COLLECTION OF THINGS a collection of books, newspapers, records, tapes, or other materials that are valuable for research **3.** COMPUT COLLECTION OF SOFTWARE a collection of things for use on a computer, e.g. programs or diskettes, or a collection of routines or instructions used by a computer program [14thC. Via French *librairie*, from, ultimately, Latin *libraria* 'bookshop', literally 'of books', from, ultimately, *liber* 'book' (literally 'inner bark of a tree', once used as writing material).]

library edition *n.* a set of books, published in a series, that are either by a single author or on the same subject and are alike in size and format

Library of Congress *n.* the national library of the United States, located in Washington, D.C. and founded by an Act of Congress in 1800. It contains more than 28 million books and pamphlets as well as presidential papers, music, photographs, and recordings.

library science *n.* = **librarianship**

libration /lī bráysh'n/ *n.* a real or apparent oscillation in the orbit of one celestial body as seen from the one around which it orbits, especially as seen in the Moon from the Earth [Early 17thC. From the Latin stem *libration-*, from *librare* 'to balance', from *libra* 'balance, scales'.] —**librate** /lī brāyt/ *vi.* —**librational** *adj.*

libretti plural of **libretto**

librettist /li bréttist/ *n.* sb who writes the words of a dramatic musical work such as an opera or musical

libretto /li bréttō/ (*plural* **-tos** *or* **-ti**) *n.* the words of a dramatic musical work such as an opera, including both the spoken and the sung parts [Mid-18thC. From Italian, literally 'little book', from *libro* 'book', from Latin *liber* (see LIBRARY).]

Libreville /leébrə veél/ city, chief port, and capital of Gabon, on the Gulf of Guinea. Population: 365,650 (1993).

Librium /líbbri əm/ *tdmk.* a trademark for the long-acting benzodiazepine drug chlordiazepoxide, used to treat anxiety, alcohol withdrawal symptoms, and sometimes insomnia

Libya

Libya /líbbi ə/ country in northern Africa, south of the Mediterranean Sea. It became independent as a kingdom in 1951. Language: Arabic. Currency: Libyan dinar. Capital: Tripoli. Population: 5,484,202 (1997). Area: 1,757,000 sq. km/678,400 sq. mi. Official name **Socialist People's Libyan Arab Jamahiriyah**

Libyan /líbbi ən/ n. 1. PEOPLES SB FROM LIBYA sb who was born or brought up in Libya, or who is a citizen of Libya 2. LANG LANGUAGE OF ANCIENT LIBYA an extinct language formerly spoken in ancient Libya, belonging to the Nilo-Hamitic branch of Nilo-Saharan languages [15thC. Formed from Latin *Libya* 'Libya'.] —**Libyan** adj.

Libyan Desert /líbbi ən dézzərt/ desert, the northeastern section of the Sahara, extending from eastern Libya into southwestern Egypt and the extreme northwestern part of Sudan

lice plural of **louse**

licence /líss'nss/ n. 1. PERMIT a printed document that gives official permission to a specific person or group to own sth or do sth 2. LAW LEGAL AUTHORIZATION official permission to do sth, either from a government or under a law or regulation. US term **license** 3. CHANCE TO DO STH the opportunity to do sth, especially when this goes beyond normal limits ○ *a licence to print money* 4. PERMISSION TO BEND THE TRUTH the freedom of a writer or artist to rearrange the facts of ordinary life in order to make a more striking effect ○ *artistic licence* 5. LACK OF RESTRAINT excessive freedom in behaviour or speech that gives a bad name to liberty. US term **license** 6. *Scotland* CHR AUTHORITY TO PREACH a permission to enter the ministry of a Presbyterian church following a period of probation [14thC. Via French from Latin *licentia* 'freedom', later 'authority, permission', from *licere* 'to be allowed'.]

licence plate n. Can = **numberplate**

license /líss'nss/ (-censes, -censing, -censed) vt. to give official permission for sb to do sth or for an activity to take place (often passive) ○ *He was licensed to practise medicine in the United States.* [15thC. From LICENCE.] —**licensable** adj. —**licenser** n. —**licensor** n.

licensed premises npl. an establishment that is legally permitted to sell alcoholic drinks

licensee /líss'n seé/ n. sb who has been granted official permission to do sth, especially to sell alcohol

license plate n. US = **numberplate**

licentiate /lī sénshi ət/ n. 1. SB AUTHORIZED IN A PROFESSION sb who has been granted a licence to practise a particular profession or teach a particular skill 2. ACADEMIC DEGREE a degree awarded by some European universities that ranks one step below that of a doctorate 3. SB WITH A LICENTIATE DEGREE sb holding the degree of licentiate 4. CHR PRESBYTERIAN PREACHER sb licensed to preach but not perform the sacraments in a Presbyterian church, usually a trainee minister who has not yet been ordained [15thC. From medieval Latin *licentiatus*, past participle of *licentiare* 'to permit', from Latin *licentia* (see LICENCE).]

licentious /lī sénshəss/ adj. pursuing desires aggressively and selfishly, unchecked by morality, especially in sexual matters (formal disapproving) [15thC. From Latin *licentiosus*, from *licentia* (see LICENCE).] —**licentiously** adv. —**licentiousness** n.

lichee n. = **lychee**

lichen /líkən, líchən/ (plural -chen or -chens) n. a grey, green, or yellow plant appearing in often flat patches on rocks and other surfaces that is a complex organism consisting of fungi and algae growing together in symbiosis [Early 17thC. Via Latin from Greek *leikhēn*.] —**lichened** adj. —**licheniform** adj. —**lichenoid** adj. —**lichenous** adj.

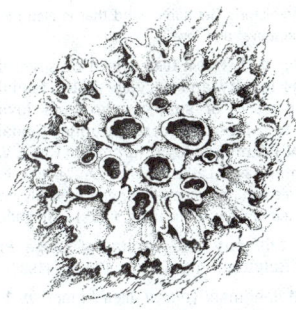

Lichen

lichen moth n. a moth found especially in Southeast Asia and Australia that has larvae that feed exclusively on lichen. It is sometimes included in the tiger moth family. Family: Lithosiidae.

lichenology /líkə nólləji/ n. the scientific study of lichens —**lichenologist** n.

Lichfield /lích feeld/ cathedral city in Staffordshire, central England. Population: 93,600 (1994).

lich-gate n. = **lych-gate**

Roy Lichtenstein

Lichtenstein /líktən stīn/, **Roy** (1923–97) US painter, graphic artist, and sculptor. A major figure in pop art, he is noted for his paintings featuring enlarged comic-strip images.

licit /líssit/ adj. allowed by law [15thC. From Latin *licitus*, past participle of *licere* 'to be allowed'.] —**licitly** adv. —**licitness** n.

—— **WORD KEY: SYNONYMS** ——
See Synonyms at **legal**.

lick /lik/ v. (**licks, licking, licked**) 1. vt. PASS THE TONGUE OVER STH to move the tongue across the surface of sth, either to wet or clean it or as a way to move sth into the mouth 2. vti. BRUSH AGAINST STH to touch or lightly move against sth 3. vt. BEAT SB to give sb a physical beating (informal) 4. vt. DEFEAT A COMPETITOR to defeat sb easily or thoroughly (informal) ■ n. 1. MOVEMENT OF THE TONGUE OVER STH a movement of the tongue across the surface of sth 2. QUICKLY APPLIED COATING a quick coat of sth, especially paint ○ *a lick of paint* 3. PUNCH a punch or blow (informal) 4. MUSIC BRIEF IMPROVISATION a distinctive few notes or short phrase in pop music or jazz, often improvised (informal) 5. NATURAL SALT LICKED BY ANIMALS an exposed natural deposit of salt that animals lick 6. VET MEDICINAL BLOCK FOR ANIMALS a block of salt or chemical material to be licked by domestic animals as medicine [Old English *liccian*, from a prehistoric Germanic word that is also the ancestor of English *lecher*] —**licker** n.

lickerish /líkərish/, **liquorish** adj. (archaic) 1. GREEDY taking an excessive or unfair amount, without concern for the needs of others 2. LECHEROUS continually thinking about sex or trying to make sexual contact with others [15thC. An alteration of *lickerous*,

from an Anglo-Norman variant of French *lecheros* 'lecherous' (see LECHEROUS).]

lickety-split /líkəti splít/ adv. US, Can very quickly (informal) [*Lickety* is a playful lengthening of LICK]

licking /líking/ n. (informal) 1. BEATING a beating or spanking 2. DEFEAT a severe defeat or setback

lickspittle /lík spitt'l/ n. UK sb who fawns on social superiors or powerful people (literary insult)

licorice n. US = **liquorice**

lictor /líktər/ n. one of a group of minor officials in ancient Rome whose duties included carrying the fasces as a symbol of authority and clearing the way for the chief magistrates [14thC. From Latin, of uncertain origin: perhaps formed from *ligare* 'to bind'.]

lid /lid/ n. 1. TOP FOR A CONTAINER a cover of a container that can be removed or raised on a hinge to open the container 2. = **eyelid** 3. RESTRAINT a restraint or control on sth that keeps it within acceptable bounds (informal) ○ *He promised to put a lid on manufacturing costs.* 4. BIOL = **operculum** n. 5. US DRUGS OUNCE OF MARIJUANA a quantity of marijuana, usually an ounce (slang) [Old English *hlid*. Ultimately from an Indo-European word meaning 'cover, sth that bends over', which is also the ancestor of English *lean*, *client*, and *climax*.]

lidar /lī daar/ n. a device, similar in operation to radar, that uses pulses of laser light to analyse atmospheric phenomena [Mid-20thC. Blend of LIGHT[1], DETECTION, and *ranging*.]

Liddell Hart /lídd'l haárt/, **Basil Henry** (1895–1970) British journalist and military strategist. As a writer and personal adviser to the minister of war, he advocated the need to modernize military equipment.

Lidice /líddichi, líddissi/ village in western Czechoslovakia, in what is now the Czech Republic. It was the scene of a retaliatory massacre of villagers by German forces during World War II.

lidless /líddləss/ adj. having no eyelids

lido /leé dō/ (plural -dos) n. an outdoor swimming pool, or a section of beach, that is open to the public [Late 17thC. From Italian *Lido*, a bathing beach near Venice.]

Lido /leé dō/ island reef in northeastern Italy, separating the Venice Lagoon from the Adriatic Sea. It is a beach resort.

lidocaine /lídə kayn/ n. = **lignocaine** [Mid-20thC. Coined from ACETANILIDE + -CAINE.]

lie[1] /lī/ vi. (**lies, lying, lay** /lay/, **lain** /layn/) 1. RECLINE to stretch out on a surface that is slanted or horizontal, ○ *She was lying on the sofa.* 2. BE PLACED FLAT ON A SURFACE to be positioned on and supported by a horizontal surface ○ *A book lay open on his bedside table.* 3. BE LOCATED SOMEWHERE to be located in a particular place ○ *Mexico lies south of the United States.* 4. BE BURIED to be buried in a particular place ○ *Here lies Martha, beloved daughter of John and Mary.* 5. BE IN A SPECIFIED POSITION IN A COMPETITION to be in a specified position in a race or a competition ○ *She's lying third in the overall ratings.* 6. BE IN A PARTICULAR STATE to be or continue to be in a particular condition or state ○ *It lay hidden for years.* 7. BE IN A PARTICULAR DIRECTION to extend or be in a particular direction ○ *The city lies beneath us, glittering with a thousand lights.* 8. BE IN STORE to be still to come ○ *A great deal of hard work lies ahead of us.* 9. STAY UNDISTURBED to remain undiscussed or undisturbed ○ *Let sleeping dogs lie.* 10. LAW BE ACCEPTABLE IN LAW to be acceptable as an assertion or as evidence in court ■ n. 1. ZOOL ANIMAL'S RESTING PLACE a place where an animal returns to rest or hide 2. GOLF POSITION OF A GOLF BALL the position of a golf ball after it comes to rest on a golf course or putting green ○ *The ball has quite a good lie, in spite of being in the rough.* [Old English *licgan*. Ultimately from an Indo-European word that is also the ancestor of English *ledge*, *lager*, and *litter*.]

lie around vti. 1. IDLE ABOUT to sit around doing nothing in particular (informal) 2. BE LEFT UNTIDIED to be left lying and not cleared away

lie back vi. to relax by stretching out flat on the back or reclining in a chair, especially one that tilts backwards

lie down vi. 1. LIE ON A SURFACE to stretch out flat 2. REST IN BED to rest, especially in bed ○ *I need to lie down* *for an hour or two.* **3. REMAIN PASSIVE** to do nothing or make no response ○ *I'm not going to take this lying down.*

lie in *vi.* to sleep or stay in bed later than usual in the morning (*informal*)

lie off *vti.* to stay close to the shore or to another ship

lie to *vi.* to remain motionless, facing the wind

lie with *v.* **1.** *vt.* **BE THE RESPONSIBILITY OF SB** to be the responsibility of a particular person or persons **2.** *vi.* **HAVE SEX WITH SB** to have sexual intercourse with sb (*archaic*)

lie² /līī/ *vi.* (**lies, lying, lied**) **1. DELIBERATELY SAY STH UNTRUE** to say sth that is not true in a conscious effort to deceive sb ○ *He lied about his age in order to get into the army.* **2. BE DECEPTIVE** to give a false impression ○ *Don't forget that appearances can lie.* ■ *n.* **1. FALSEHOOD** a false statement made deliberately ○ *She told me she wasn't seeing anyone else, but that was a lie.* **2. WRONG IMPRESSION** a false impression created deliberately ○ *I'm beginning to feel that my whole life is a lie.* [Old English *lēogan* 'to lie' and *lyge* 'a lie', both ultimately from a prehistoric Germanic word that is also the ancestor of English *warlock*]

--- **WORD KEY: SYNONYMS** ---

lie, untruth, falsehood, fabrication, fib, white lie
CORE MEANING: sth that is not true

lie used to describe a written or spoken statement that is not true; **untruth** a more formal word meaning the same as 'lie'; **falsehood** a formal or literary word meaning the same as 'lie'; **fabrication** a statement, story, or account devised with intent to deceive; **fib** an informal word for a minor or trivial lie, often used by or about children; **white lie** a minor harmless lie, usually told to avoid hurting sb's feelings.

Liebfraumilch /leéb frow milk, -milch/ *n.* a slightly sweet German white wine from the Rhine region [Mid-19thC. From German, from *lieb* 'dear' + *Frau* 'lady' (referring to the Virgin Mary, patroness of the convent where it was first produced) + *Milch* 'milk'.]

Liebig /leébig/, **Baron Justus von** (1803–73) German chemist. Noted for his contribution to organic analysis and biochemistry, he established the first chemical research laboratory.

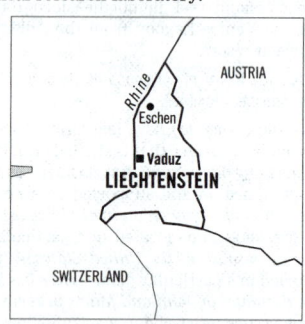

Liechtenstein

Liechtenstein /līkhtən shtīn/ small independent principality in central Europe, lying between Switzerland, with which it has close ties, and Austria. Language: German. Currency: Swiss franc. Capital: Vaduz. Population: 31,389 (1997). Area: 160 sq. km/62 sq. mi. Official name **Principality of Liechtenstein**

lied /leed/ (*plural* **lieder** /leédər/) *n.* a German folk or art song, especially an art song of the 19th century with a solo voice part and interwoven piano accompaniment of equal importance. Schubert, Brahms, and Schumann are major composers of lieder. (*usually used in the plural*) [Mid-19thC. From German, literally 'song'.]

lie detector *n.* a device for finding out whether sb is telling the truth during questioning. It has sensors that measure changes in blood pressure and pulse, which are supposed to reflect the uneasiness caused by lying.

lie-down *n.* a short rest, especially in bed (*informal*)

lief /leef/ *adv.* **WILLINGLY** readily or without reluctance (*archaic*) ■ *adj.* (*archaic*) **1. WILLING** ready or desirous **2. BELOVED** dear or treasured [Old English *lēof*. Ultimately

---

from a prehistoric Germanic word that is also the ancestor of English *leave²* and *love*.]

liege /leej/ *n.* **1. FEUDAL LORD** a lord or sovereign who deserves loyalty and service under feudal law **2. VASSAL** a vassal or subject who owes loyalty and service to a lord or sovereign under feudal law ■ *adj.* **LOYAL** faithful or loyal (*archaic*) [13thC. Via French *lige* from medieval Latin *leticus*, from *letus* 'colonist with limited freedom', of uncertain origin: probably from a prehistoric Germanic word meaning 'free'.] —**liegedom** *n.*

Liège /li éezh/ city and capital of Liège Province, eastern Belgium. Population: 190,525 (1996).

liegeman /leéj man/ (*plural* **-men** /-mən/) *n.* **1. =** **liege** *n.* 2 **2. LOYAL FOLLOWER** a faithful or loyal follower

lie-in *n.* a sleep or rest in bed until later than the usual time for getting up (*informal*)

lien /leen, leé ən/ *n.* the legal right to keep or sell sb else's property as security for a debt [Mid-16thC. Via French from, ultimately, Latin *ligamen* 'bond', from *ligare* 'to bind'.]

lie of the land *n.* the general appearance or state of an area or situation presenting itself to sb (*informal*) US term **lay of the land**

Lierne

lierne /li úrn/ *n.* a reinforcing rib in the vaulting of a Gothic cathedral or other roofed structure [Mid-19thC. From French, formed from *lier* 'to bind', from Latin *ligare*.]

lieu /lyoo, loo/ *n.* place or stead (*archaic*) [Mid-16thC. Via French from Latin *locus* 'place' (source of English *locate*).] ◇ **in lieu** instead of sth else already mentioned or that is usual in the current situation

Lieut *abbr.* Lieutenant

lieutenant /lef ténnənt/ *n.* **1. DEPUTY** sb who acts as an assistant to or in place of sb else **2. MIL ARMY OFFICER** the rank below captain in the British, Australian, and Canadian armies and in the United States Army, Marine Corps and Air Force. ◊ **first lieutenant, second lieutenant 3. NAVY NAVY OFFICER** the rank below lieutenant commander in the United States, British, Australian, and Canadian navies **4. EMERGENCIES POLICE OFFICER OR FIREFIGHTER** an officer in a United States or Canadian police department or a United States fire department ranking below a captain [14thC. From French, literally 'sb who holds a place', from *lieu* (see LIEU) + *tenant* (see TENANT).] —**lieutenancy** *n.*

lieutenant colonel *n.* an officer in the British and Australian armies and in the United States Army, Air Force, or Marine Corps ranking above a major and below a colonel

lieutenant commander *n.* an officer in the British navy and in the United States navy or coast guard ranking above a lieutenant and below a commander

lieutenant general *n.* an officer in the British and Australian armies and in the United States Army, Air Force, or Marine Corps ranking above a major general and below a general

lieutenant governor *n.* **1. US STATE OFFICIAL** an elected official in a United States state government ranking just below the governor **2. CANADIAN PROVINCIAL OFFICIAL** an official appointed by the Canadian federal government who acts for the Crown as the representative of the British monarch in a province — **lieutenant governorship** *n.*

Lifar /lyi faár/, **Serge** (1905–86) Russian-born French dancer and choreographer. Director of the Paris

---

Opéra Ballet, he created over 50 ballets, including *Prométhée* (1929) and *Icare* (1935).

life /līf/ (*plural* **lives** /līvz/) *n.* **1. EXISTENCE IN THE PHYSICAL WORLD** the quality that makes living animals and plants different from dead organisms and inorganic matter. Its functions include the ability to take in food, adapt to the environment, grow, and reproduce **2. LIVING INDIVIDUAL** a living being, especially a person, often used when referring to the number of people killed in an accident or a war (*usually used in the plural*) ○ *Two hundred lives were lost in the crash.* **3. LIVING THINGS CONSIDERED TOGETHER** a group of living things, usually of a particular kind ○ *She was an expert on plant life in the Amazon.* **4. WHOLE TIME SB IS ALIVE** the entire period during which sb is, has been, or will yet be alive ○ *All my life I've wanted to learn to fly.* **5. TIME WHEN STH FUNCTIONS** the period during which sth continues to function ○ *Cheap batteries usually have short lives.* **6. SOME PART OF SB'S LIFE** a particular aspect of sb's life ○ *social life* **7. HUMAN ACTIVITY** human existence or activity in general ○ *real life* **8. LIFE IMPRISONMENT** life imprisonment (*informal*) **9. WAY IN WHICH SB LIVES** the character or conditions of an individual's existence ○ *Most people in this city lead hard lives.* **10. CHARACTERISTIC WAY OF LIVING** a way of living that is characteristic of a particular place or group ○ *country life* **11. BIOGRAPHY** an account of a sb's life, usually in writing, but sometimes in other media such as film, video, or radio ○ *He was the author of 'The Life of Galileo'.* **12. VITALITY** animation and vitality, or sth that produces animation or vitality ○ *We liked him because he was so full of life.* **13. ARTIST'S SUBJECT** sth real used as a subject by an artist, especially human models, who are often nude ○ *She always insisted on painting from life.* [Old English *lif*, from a prehistoric Germanic word that is also the ancestor of English *live, delay,* and *liver*] ◇ **get a life** US to do sth to improve your situation or change your lifestyle for the better (*slang*)

--- **WORD KEY: CULTURAL NOTE** ---

The Life of Samuel Johnson, a biography by Scottish writer James Boswell (1791). Generally considered the finest biography in the English language, it is a rounded, revealing, and respectful portrait of one of the great scholars of the day. But its greatness also derives from its vivid descriptions of contemporary society and the candid revelations of its author.

---

life-and-death, **life-or-death** *adj.* extremely important or serious, especially when sb's life is at stake ○ *a life-and-death struggle*

life assurance *n.* a plan under which regular payments are made to a company during sb's lifetime, and in return the company pays a specified sum to the person's beneficiaries after the person's death. US term **life insurance**

life belt *n.* a belt or ring made of material that floats, worn to keep sb from sinking or drowning

lifeblood /līf blud/ *n.* **1. BLOOD NECESSARY FOR LIFE** blood when considered as necessary in maintaining life (*literary*) **2. STH VITAL TO A WHOLE** sth that is vitally important to the welfare of a larger entity ○ *Donations are the lifeblood of this organization.*

lifeboat /līf bōt/ *n.* **1. BOAT USED IN EMERGENCIES** any of a number of small boats kept on the deck or railings of a larger ship, for use if the ship has to be abandoned **2. RESCUE BOAT** a boat used for rescuing people from ships in trouble at sea

life buoy *n.* a float used in an emergency to keep sb's head and shoulders above water until help arrives

life crisis *n.* a major disruptive event that happens in sb's lifetime, e.g. bereavement or divorce

life cycle *n.* **1. STAGES OF DEVELOPMENT OF A LIVING ORGANISM** the series of changes of form and activity that a living organism undergoes from its beginning through its development to sexual maturity ○ *the life cycle of the snail* **2. ALL STAGES OF DEVELOPMENT** the complete process of change and development during sb's lifetime or the useful life of sth such as an organization, institution, or manufactured product

life estate *n.* property that belongs to a particular person but that cannot be sold or passed on to anyone until after the death of that person

---

a at; aa father; aw all; ay day; air hair; ə about, edible, item, common, circus; e egg; ee eel; hw when; i it, happy; ī ice; 'l apple; 'm rhythm; 'n fashion; o odd; ō open; oo good; oo pool; ow owl; oy oil; th thin; <u>th</u> this; u up; ur urge;

life expectancy *n.* the number of years that sb can be expected to live, according to statistics ○ *The rise in life expectancy can be traced to advances in nutrition and medical care.*

life force *n.* = élan vital

life form *n.* **1.** BIOL ADULT SPECIMEN the characteristic form of an organism at maturity **2.** STH ALIVE any living organism ○ *They scanned the surface of the planet for life forms.*

lifeguard /lÍf gaard/ *n.* sb trained in rescue techniques whose job is to watch over swimmers at a beach or swimming pool and save those in danger of drowning

Life Guards *n.* a cavalry regiment that, with the Horse Guards, forms the Household Cavalry responsible for guarding the sovereign, especially during public ceremonies

life history *n.* **1.** BIOL ENTIRE STAGES OF LIFE all the changes experienced by a living organism, from its conception to its death **2.** SB'S LIFE STORY the story of sb's life **3.** SOCIOL SB'S LIFE STORY USED FOR RESEARCH an account of the life of an individual derived from oral or documentary evidence and used in social research. It may shed light on issues of social concern or add to the sum of knowledge about society and social institutions.

life imprisonment *n.* a punishment in which sb convicted of a crime must remain in prison for the rest of his or her life. It may be shortened for good behaviour, but it normally remains a very lengthy period.

life insurance *n.* US = life assurance

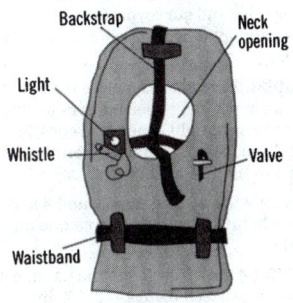

Life jacket

life jacket *n.* a sleeveless jacket made of light material or filled with air, used to keep sb afloat in water

lifeless /lÍfləss/ *adj.* **1.** DEAD dead, or seeming to be dead **2.** WITHOUT LIFE not capable of supporting life **3.** DULL lacking excitement or animation —**lifelessly** *adv.* —**lifelessness** *n.*

――――――――― **WORD KEY: SYNONYMS** ―――――――――
See Synonyms at *dead*.

lifelike /lÍf lÍk/ *adj.* looking alive, or representing real life accurately

lifeline /lÍf lÍn/ *n.* **1.** SHIPPING SAFETY CABLE a rope or cable used for safety in dangerous manoeuvres, especially at sea, e.g. attached to a diver's helmet or stretched along the deck of a boat **2.** VITAL LINK a means of communication or support that is extremely important to the survival of an isolated person or group

life list *n.* a bird-watcher's record of all the species of birds sighted in a lifetime

lifelong /lÍf long/ *adj.* lasting the whole of a lifetime

life mask *n.* a cast made of a living person's face, using plaster or another soft substance that hardens when it dries

life-or-death *adj.* = life-and-death

life partner *n.* the person with whom sb has decided to spend the rest of his or her life in a sexual and romantic relationship ○ *'...makes people believe that somewhere there really is the life partner who will provide the ecstatic happiness depicted in opera...'* (*The New York Times*; April 1999)

life peer *n.* sb who is given a title and place in the House of Lords that cannot be passed on to descendants. People are often made life peers when they have failed to be reelected to the House of Commons, in order to continue to work on behalf of their political party. —**life peerage** *n.*

life preserver *n.* US a life belt or life jacket

lifer /lÍfər/ *n.* sb sentenced to life imprisonment (*informal*)

life raft *n.* a raft usually made of inflatable plastic designed for use during an emergency at sea

lifesaver /lÍf sayvər/ *n.* **1.** ANZ LIFEGUARD a lifeguard **2.** RESCUER sb who or sth that provides help at a time of great need (*informal*)

lifesaving /lÍf sayving/ *adj.* RESCUING OR REVIVING used to rescue people or keep them alive ■ *n.* **1.** SWIMMING RESCUING OF PEOPLE techniques or efforts to rescue people from danger, especially from drowning **2.** ANZ SPORTS MULTI-ACTIVITY AUSTRALIAN WATER-BASED SPORT in Australia, the activities of a lifesaver or a team of lifesavers formalized as a multi-activity sport. This forms the basis of the Iron Man and Iron Woman contests.

lifesaving club *n.* = surf club *n.* 1

life science *n.* a principal branch of science concerned with plants, animals, and other living organisms and including biology, botany, and zoology (*often used in the plural*)

life sentence *n.* a court verdict that condemns a convicted felon to life in prison for the rest of his or her life. It may be shortened for good behaviour, but it normally remains a very lengthy sentence.

life-size *adj.* being the size of the original in life

life span *n.* **1.** EXPECTED LENGTH OF LIFE the length of time that a member of a particular species can be expected to remain alive **2.** LENGTH OF TIME STH LASTS the length of time that sth can be expected to last or function

life span psychology /lÍf span-/ *n.* a field of psychology that studies human development from birth to death

lifestyle /lÍf stÍl/ *n.* the way of life that is typical of a person, group, or culture

life-support *adj.* designed to keep sb alive in an environment such as space that does not support life or to maintain breathing, heartbeat, and other vital functions in sb who is seriously ill

life-support system *n.* **1.** TECHNICAL EQUIPMENT TAKING OVER BODY FUNCTION a piece of technical equipment that temporarily performs a vital body function, e.g., respiration, when sb's own organ cannot because of injury or disease **2.** TECHNICAL EQUIPMENT PROVIDING NORMAL LIVING CONDITIONS a piece of technical equipment that is designed to provide normal living conditions when these are not available, especially in space

life's work *n.* sth that is the product, result, or culmination of sb's working life. US term **lifework**

life table *n.* = mortality table

life-threatening *adj.* very dangerous or serious with the possibility of death as an outcome

lifetime /lÍf tÍm/ *n.* **1.** TIME REMAINING ALIVE the length of time that sb or sth remains alive **2.** TIME THAT STH REMAINS USEFUL the length of time that sth remains useful or in working order **3.** LONG TIME an extremely long time (*informal*)

lifework /lÍf wúrk/ *n.* US = life's work

LIFFE /lÍffi/ *abbr.* London International Financial Futures and Options Exchange

Liffey /lÍffi/ river in the eastern part of the Republic of Ireland. It rises in the Wicklow Mountains southwest of Dublin and empties into Dublin Bay. Length: 80 km/50 mi.

LIFO /lÍfō/ *abbr.* last in, first out

lift[1] /lift/ *v.* (**lifts, lifting, lifted**) **1.** *vt.* RAISE STH to carry or raise sth from one position to another, higher position **2.** *vi.* MOVE HIGHER to move to a higher level **3.** *vt.* MOVE STH UPWARDS to direct sth upwards ○ *lifting her eyes from the book* **4.** *vi.* GO UPWARD to move, especially mechanically, in an upward direction ○ *Just press the button, and the boot will lift auto-*

matically. **5.** *vt.* TAKE STH FROM A PLACE to take hold of sth and move it somewhere else ○ *She lifted the CD from the rack.* **6.** *vt.* CARRY IN AN AIRCRAFT to transport sb or sth in an aircraft ○ *The rescue helicopter lifted the stranded climbers to safety.* **7.** *vt.* MAKE STH INVALID to revoke sth or make sth no longer apply ○ *The government has decided to lift the trading restrictions.* **8.** *vti.* CHEER SB OR BECOME CHEERED to make sb happier or more cheerful, or become happier or more cheerful ○ *His low spirits lifted after a few songs.* **9.** *vi.* DIMINISH to clear, disappear, or become less severe ○ *I think we should wait until this fog lifts.* **10.** *vt.* RAISE SB OR STH'S STATUS to have the effect of raising sb or sth in terms of status, respect, or public or official estimation ○ *Her latest novel has lifted her into the league of best-selling authors.* **11.** *vt.* IMPROVE STH to raise the level of a performance, or enhance a skill **12.** *vt.* MAKE STH BE HEARD to make sth be heard, or make sth be heard more easily or clearly ○ *The choir lifted their voices in song.* **13.** *vt.* AGRIC, GARDENING HARVEST to dig up a plant for its edible underground tubers ○ *lift potatoes* **14.** *vt.* AGRIC, GARDENING DIG UP A PLANT FOR TRANSPLANTING to dig up a plant in order to transplant it **15.** *vt.* SURG REMOVE WRINKLES SURGICALLY to perform cosmetic surgery on a face to tighten the skin and so reduce wrinkling, or on a woman's breasts to reduce or eliminate sagging **16.** *vt.* STEAL STH to steal sth or take sth away without the owner's permission or knowledge (*informal*) ○ *OK! Who's lifted my pen this time?* **17.** *vt.* PLAGIARIZE SB'S WORK to take and use sb else's work without attributing it to its creator (*informal*) ○ *She was accused of lifting her first two paragraphs from a report on a Web page.* **18.** *vt.* ARREST to arrest sb (*informal*) ○ *Max got lifted for kerb-crawling.* **19.** *vt.* SPORTS HIT BALL HIGH INTO THE AIR to hit a cricket or golf ball high into the air **20.** *vt.* MIL STOP A MILITARY ASSAULT to cease the firing of artillery or naval guns during a combat operation or assault so as to allow ground personnel to move forwards ■ *n.* **1.** CAGE MOVING BETWEEN FLOORS OF A BUILDING a mechanically or electrically operated cage or platform, housed inside a shaft that runs vertically between the floors of a building or other construction, used for transporting people or things. ◊ elevator, chair lift, ski lift **2.** RIDE IN A VEHICLE a free ride as a passenger in sb else's motor vehicle (*informal*) ○ *Do you want a lift to the airport?* **3.** RISE IN SPIRITS a rise in spirits, mood, or emotions that can often be attributed to a specific cause ○ *audiences turning to feel-good movies to give themselves a lift* **4.** RAISING OF SB OR STH a placing of sb or sth in a higher position **5.** FORCE NEEDED TO RAISE STH the power or force available, necessary, or used for raising sth **6.** WEIGHT RAISED a weight or an amount of sth that is or can be raised **7.** DEGREE OF RISE the degree or distance by which sth rises ○ *a moderate lift in temperature* **8.** AEROSP UPWARD FORCE ACTING ON AN AIRCRAFT the combination of forces that act to cause an aircraft to leave the ground and stay in the air **9.** AEROSP FORCE MAKING A HOT-AIR BALLOON RISE the force, usually provided by heated air, that makes a hot-air balloon or airship rise into the sky **10.** ICE SKATING, DANCE RAISING A PARTNER IN THE AIR an act of raising a partner in pairs skating or ice dancing into the air as part of a choreographed sequence **11.** CLOTHES = heeltap *n.* 2 **12.** CLOTHES STH ADDED TO A SHOE a layer of sth that is put inside a shoe or added to the heel of a shoe to make the wearer appear taller (*dated*) **13.** MINING WATER PUMPS USED IN MINING a set of pumps used to pump water out of a mineshaft to the surface **14.** MINING AMOUNT OF EXTRACTED ORE the amount of ore extracted from a seam [12thC. From Old Norse *lypta*, from a prehistoric Germanic word that is also the ancestor of English *loft*.] —**liftable** *adj.* —**lifter** *n.*

――――――――― **WORD KEY: SYNONYMS** ―――――――――
See Synonyms at *raise*.

lift off *vi.* to leave a launching pad and head upwards into the atmosphere (*refers to spacecraft*)

lift[2] *n.* US a surgical operation to alter a part of the body for cosmetic effect (*informal*) ○ *Who did your lift?* [Shortening of FACE LIFT]

liftoff /lift of/ *n.* **1.** MOMENT WHEN A ROCKET LEAVES A LAUNCH PAD the time when a rocket or spacecraft leaves the launching pad **2.** INITIAL THRUST SENDING A ROCKET FROM THE GROUND the initial thrust that sends a rocket or

Labels on image: Backstrap, Neck opening, Light, Whistle, Valve, Waistband spacecraft upwards from the launching pad into the atmosphere

lig /lig/ (**ligs, ligging, ligged**) *vi.* (*informal*) **1. SPEND TIME LAZILY** to do nothing habitually, often abusing the generosity of others **2. GO ALONG SEEKING FREE TREATS** to associate with influential people, especially in the entertainment world, in order to benefit materially from the association, e.g., in the form of invitations to parties [Mid-20thC. Originally a northern English dialect verb meaning 'to lie about', a variant of LIE[1].]

ligament /líggəmənt/ *n.* **1. TOUGH TISSUE CONNECTING BODY PARTS** a sheet or band of tough fibrous tissue that connects bones or cartilages at a joint or supports an organ, muscle, or other body part **2. CONNECTOR** sth that forms a connection or bond [14thC. From Latin *ligamentum*, from *ligare* 'to bind'.] —**ligamental** /líggə mént'l/ *adj.* —**ligamentary** /-méntəri/ *adj.* —**ligamentous** /-méntəss/ *adj.*

WORD KEY: ORIGIN

The Latin word *ligare*, from which ***ligament*** is derived, is also the source of English *ally, liable, liaison, lien, oblige, religion,* and *rely.*

ligan *n.* **NAUT** = **lagan**

ligand /líggənd, lígənd/ *n.* an atom, molecule, group, or ion that is bound to a central atom of a molecule forming a complex [Mid-20thC. From Latin *ligandus*, from *ligare* 'to bind'.]

ligase /lí gayz, -gayss/ *n.* an enzyme that joins two molecules, especially in living organisms [Mid-20thC. From Latin *ligare* 'to bind' (see LIGAMENT).]

ligate /lí gayt, lì gáyt/ (**-gates, -gating, -gated**) *vt.* to bind sth or tie sth up (*formal or technical*) [Late 16thC. From Latin *ligare* 'to bind' (see LIGAMENT).] —**ligative** /líggətiv/ *adj.*

ligation /lī gáysh'n/ *n.* **1.** SURG **SURGICAL TYING** the tying of sth with a surgical ligature **2. STH USED FOR TYING** sth that is used for binding things or tying things up (*formal*)

ligature /líggəchər/ *n.* **1. STH USED FOR TYING** sth that is used for binding things or tying things up **2. TYING PROCESS** the process of binding sth or tying sth up **3. BOND** a unifying link or bond (*formal*) **4.** SURG **SURGICAL THREAD FOR TYING OFF A DUCT** a piece of surgical thread used to tie off a duct or blood vessel in order to cut off the supply of body fluid normally running through it **5.** PRINTING, LING **CHARACTER CONSISTING OF JOINED LETTERS** a character or piece of type, e.g. æ, that consists of two or more letters joined together **6.** MUSIC = **tie** *n.* 8 **7.** MUSIC **SYMBOL IN MEDIEVAL MUSIC** a symbol indicating a group of notes to be sung to one syllable in the notation of medieval music **8.** MUSIC **REED-HOLDER ON WOODWIND INSTRUMENT** on a woodwind instrument, a band, usually made of metal, that holds the reed to the mouthpiece [14thC. Via Old French from, ultimately, Latin *ligare* 'to bind' (see LIGAMENT).]

liger /lígər/ *n.* the offspring that results from breeding a male lion with a female tiger. ◊ **tigon** [Mid-20thC. Blend of LION and TIGER.]

Ligeti /líg eti/, **György** (*b.* 1923) Hungarian composer noted for his choral and orchestral works, which explore slowly moving colours and textures.

ligger /líggər/ *n.* (*informal*) **1. LAZY PERSON** sb who habitually does nothing, often abusing the generosity of others **2. HANGER-ON** sb who associates with influential people, especially in the entertainment world, in the hope of benefiting materially from the association, e.g., in the form of invitations to parties

light[1] /līt/ *n.* **1. ENERGY PRODUCING BRIGHTNESS** the energy producing a sensation of brightness that makes seeing possible **2. QUALITY OF LIGHT** a particular kind or quality of brightness ○ *We won't get good photographs in this fading light.* **3. ARTIFICIAL SOURCE OF LIGHT** an artificial source of illumination, e.g. an electric lamp or a candle ○ *switch the light on* **4.** PHYS **VISIBLE ELECTROMAGNETIC RADIATION** electromagnetic radiation in the range visible to the human eye, between approximately 4,000 and 7,700 angstroms **5.** PHYS **ELECTROMAGNETIC RADIATION** electromagnetic radiation that has wavelengths of any length **6. PATH THAT LIGHT TAKES** the path that light takes, or sb's share or access to light ○ *asked her to move out of my light* **7. DAYLIGHT** the condition of brightness created by the rays of the sun during the day ○ *keep filming while there's still some light left* **8. DAWN** the arrival of the sun's brightness at the beginning of the day ○ *get up before light to go running* **9.** ARTS **REPRESENTATION OF LIGHT IN ART** the representation of light or the effect it has in a work of art **10. TRAFFIC SIGNAL** a signal that controls the movement of traffic ○ *Turn right at the first set of lights.* **11. GENERAL NOTICE** general or public notice, attention, or knowledge ○ *facts that only recently came to light* **12. WAY STH IS VIEWED** the manner in which sb or sth is regarded, especially by the public ○ *These actions have shown the committee in a particularly bad light.* **13. STH THAT IGNITES STH** a source of fire, especially a match ○ *Have you got a light?* **14. GLEAM IN SB'S EYE** a glint in sb's eye that is taken to indicate a particular mood or expression ○ *had a mischievous light in her eye* **15. EYESIGHT** sb's general ability to see (*archaic*) **16.** BUILDING **WINDOW** a window or other opening in a building, designed to let sunlight in. ◊ **ancient lights** ■ *adj.* **1. FULL OF BRIGHTNESS** full of illumination, or relatively well lit ○ *a light airy room* **2. PALE** of a relatively pale shade ○ *decorated in light green* ■ *v.* (**lights, lighting, lit** /lit/ *or* **lighted, lit** *or* **lighted**) **1.** *vti.* **START BURNING** to begin to burn, or cause sth to begin to burn ○ *still trying to light the barbecue?* **2.** *vt.* **ILLUMINATE** to illuminate, brighten, or shine on sth ○ *Hundreds of stars lit the night sky.* **3.** *vt.* **GIVE STH AN ANIMATED LOOK** to give sb's eyes or face a happy or animated look ○ *A playful smile lit his face.* **4.** *vt.* **LEAD SB WITH A LIGHT** to lead or direct sb with a source of illumination such as a torch ○ *The usherette lit the way to our seats.* [Old English *lēoht*. Ultimately from an Indo-European word that is also the ancestor of English *lucid* and *illuminate*.] ◇ **bring sth to light** to reveal sth ◇ **come to light** to be revealed ◇ **go out like a light** to fall asleep very quickly and deeply (*informal*) ◇ **in the light of, in light of** taking into consideration what is known, or what has just been said or found out ◇ **the light of sb's life** the person sb cherishes the most ◇ **punch** *or* **put sb's lights out** to give sb a severe beating ◇ **see the light 1.** to have a sudden understanding or appreciation of sth **2.** to be converted to a faith, belief, or point of view ◇ **see the light of day** to be published or made publicly known ◇ **shed** *or* **throw** *or* **cast light on sth** make it possible or easier to understand sth ◇ **strike a light!** used to express surprise, shock, or disbelief (*dated informal*)

light into *vt.* to attack sb or sth either verbally or physically (*informal*)

light out *vi. US* to leave a place in a hurry (*informal*)

light up *v.* **1.** *vti.* **LIGHT A CIGARETTE OR PIPE** to light sth such as a cigarette, cigar, or pipe and begin smoking it **2.** *vt.* **ILLUMINATE STH** to cast light on sb or sth **3.** *vi.* **BEGIN SHINING** to start to shine **4.** *vti.* **MAKE OR BECOME CHEERFUL** to become, or cause sth or sb to become, animated or cheerful

light[2] /līt/ *adj.* **1. NOT HEAVY** weighing comparatively little **2. WEIGHING TOO LITTLE** weighing less than is correct or less than would be expected ○ *This sack is a couple of ounces light.* **3. LIGHTWEIGHT** made of thin fabric ○ *light summer apparel* **4. NOT DENSE** low in density or intensity ○ *only a light shower* **5. NOT FORCEFUL** performed with little physical force ○ *She felt a light tap on her shoulder.* **6. EASY TO DO** involving relatively little effort or exertion ○ *a little light weeding* **7. CONSUMING LITTLE OF STH** consuming sth in small quantities only ○ *a light eater* **8. LESS SEVERE THAN POSSIBLE** considered less severe or harsh than might have been the case ○ *a light sentence* **9. UNIMPORTANT** of relatively little importance or seriousness ○ *a light, throwaway remark* **10. NOT INTELLECTUALLY DEMANDING** not meant for serious study or contemplation ○ *some light holiday reading* **11. SHORT OF STH** lacking the usual or expected quantity of sth ○ *a nice flavour but a bit light on salt* **12. UNWORRIED** not burdened by worries or troubled ○ *a light heart* **13. DIZZY** slightly dizzy or not quite thinking clearly, e.g. because of fatigue, alcohol or drugs ○ *a light head* **14. NIMBLE** moving with grace, nimbleness, and agility ○ *She's very light on her feet.* **15. EASILY DIGESTED** easily digested or not very filling ○ *a light snack* **16. light, lite** FOOD **LOW IN CALORIES** low in calories, especially containing less than the usual amount of sugar or fat **17. light, lite** BEVERAGES **LOW IN ALCOHOL** having a very low alcohol content **18.** FOOD **FLUFFY AND WELL RISEN** of a light, flaky, fluffy, and well-risen consistency ○ *a very light pastry* **19.** WINE **DELICATELY FLAVOURED** having a fresh delicate flavour ○ *a light rosé* **20. EASILY WOKEN** easily woken or disturbed when asleep ○ *a light sleeper* **21.** AGRIC, GARDENING **EASILY WORKED** loose, well aerated, and therefore easily worked ○ *light soil* **22. CARRYING SMALL WEIGHTS** designed to carry sth that is relatively low in weight or relatively small in bulk ○ *a light delivery van* **23. NOT LOADED** not containing or carrying a full load **24. MANUFACTURING SMALL PRODUCTS** involved in the manufacture of comparatively small products, especially consumer goods made without the use of heavy machinery **25.** CHEM **WITH A LOW BOILING POINT** having a relatively low boiling point **26.** ARMY **NOT HEAVILY ARMED** carrying only hand-held weapons ○ *a light infantry brigade* **27.** PHON **UNSTRESSED** used to describe a syllable that is not stressed or accented **28.** BRIDGE **OF LOW VALUE** used to describe a bid in bridge that is made on a lower-than-normal number of points **29.** BRIDGE **WITH TOO FEW TRICKS** used to describe a bridge player who has taken too few tricks to make a contract **30. IMMORAL** with low moral standards, especially relating to sexual behaviour (*archaic*) ■ *adv.* **1. LENIENTLY** in a casual or lenient way **2. WITH LITTLE LUGGAGE** with only a small amount of luggage ○ *to travel light* ■ *vi.* (**lights, lighting, lighted** *or* **lit** /lit/, **lighted** *or* **lit**) **1. COME TO REST** to come to rest on a branch after flight (*refers to birds*) **2. GET DOWN FROM A VEHICLE** to get down from a horse, vehicle, or other form of transport (*dated*) [Old English *lēocht*. Ultimately from an Indo-European word that is also the ancestor of English *levity* and *lung*.] ◇ **make light of sth** to treat sth as unimportant

Light *n.* **1.** JUD-CHR **GOD** God as a source of spiritual illumination and strength **2.** CHR = **Inner Light**

Light /līt/, **William** (1786–1839) English-born Australian soldier and surveyor. In 1836 he selected the site for, and planned the layout of, the city of Adelaide.

light adaptation, **light adaption** *n.* the rapid changes that occur in the eye to permit vision when moving from darkness to light. The pupil constricts and the retina is bleached of visual pigment, making it less sensitive to light. —**light-adapted** *adj.*

light air *n.* a wind of between 1.6 and 4.8 km/1 and 3 miles per hour, classified as force one on the Beaufort scale

light aircraft *n.* an aircraft that has a takeoff weight that does not exceed 5,670 kg/12,500 lbs

light breeze *n.* a wind of between 6.4 and 11 km/4 and 7 mi. per hour, classified as force two on the Beaufort scale

light bulb *n.* a source of artificial light in the form of a near-spherical glass case containing a filament that emits light when an electric current is passed through it. The filament is usually made of tungsten and is surrounded by argon or neon.

light chain *n.* the shorter of the two main polypeptides that make up an antibody molecule. ◊ **heavy chain**

light-emitting diode *n.* full form of **LED**

lighten[1] /līt'n/ (**-ens, -ening, -ened**) *vti.* **1. MAKE OR BECOME LESS HEAVY** to become less heavy, or make sth less heavy **2. BECOME OR MAKE STH LESS BURDENSOME** to become, or cause sth to become, less of a burden or chore **3. BECOME OR MAKE STH MORE CHEERFUL** to become or make sb or sth become more relaxed or lively ○ *The mood of the gathering lightened a little.*

lighten up *vi.* to become less gloomy, serious, or angry (*informal*)

lighten[2] /līt'n/ (**-ens, -ening, -ened**) *v.* **1.** *vti.* **MAKE OR BECOME PALE** to become, or cause sth to become, pale or paler in colour **2.** *vi.* **GLOW** to give off shining or glowing illumination **3.** *vi.* **FLASH** to flash across the sky (*refers to lightning*) **4.** *vt.* **ENLIGHTEN** to enlighten (*archaic*)

lightening /līt'ning/ *n.* the process or time during late pregnancy when the foetal head begins to descend into the mother's pelvis resulting in a lessening of pressure on the diaphragm

lighter[1] /lītər/ *n.* **1. SMALL DEVICE FOR LIGHTING CIGARETTES** a small typically gas-filled container with a flint or other spark-producer that produces a flame used for lighting sth that is smoked such as a cigarette, cigar, or pipe **2.** SB OR STH THAT LIGHTS STH a person or device that lights, illuminates, or ignites sth (*usually used in combination*) ○ *a firelighter*

lighter[2] /lítər/ (**-ers, -ering, -ered**) *n.* a flat-bottomed open cargo boat or barge, used especially for taking goods to or from a larger vessel when it is being loaded or unloaded [14thC. Origin uncertain: possibly formed from LIGHT[2], or possibly from Dutch *lichter*, which was formed from *lichten* 'to lighten, unload'.]

lighter-than-air *adj.* WEIGHING LESS THAN AIR used to describe aircraft such as hot-air balloons and dirigibles that weigh less than the air they displace ■ *n.* AIRCRAFT WEIGHING LESS THAN AIR an aircraft, e.g. a hot-air balloon or a dirigible, that weighs less than the air it displaces

lightface /lít fayss/ *adj.* **lightface, light-faced** NOT BOLD having characters formed from relatively narrow lines (*refers to printed type*) ■ *n.* LIGHTFACE TYPE printed type that is lightface

lightfast /lít faast/ *adj.* used to describe a dye or dyed fabric whose shade or colour is unchanged by exposure to light, especially sunlight [Early 20thC. Modelled on COLOURFAST.] —**lightfastness** *n.*

light-fingered *adj.* **1.** LIKELY TO STEAL THINGS skilled at and likely to try shoplifting, pickpocketing, or petty stealing **2.** NIMBLE WITH THE FINGERS able to move the fingers quickly and nimbly, and therefore good at doing intricate jobs —**light-fingeredness** *n.*

light flyweight *n.* **1.** WEIGHT CATEGORY IN AMATEUR BOXING a weight category in amateur boxing for competitors whose weight does not exceed 48 kg/106 lbs **2.** LIGHT FLYWEIGHT BOXER an amateur boxer who competes at light flyweight level

light-footed *adj.* able to walk or run with light agile easy-flowing steps —**light-footedly** *adv.* —**light-footedness** *n.*

light globe *n.* ANZ a light bulb

lightheaded /lít héddid/ *adj.* **1.** DIZZY OR EUPHORIC slightly dizzy or euphoric, e.g. as an effect of caffeine, alcohol, or fatigue **2.** SILLY having a tendency to behave in a frivolous or immature way —**light-headedly** *adv.* —**lightheadedness** *n.*

lighthearted /lít haártid/ *adj.* **1.** HAPPY AND RELAXED not weighed down with worries or troubles **2.** ENJOYABLE entertaining in an amusing carefree way —**light-heartedly** *adv.* —**lightheartedness** *n.*

light heavyweight *n.* **1.** BOXING WEIGHT CATEGORY IN PROFESSIONAL BOXING a weight category in professional boxing for competitors who weigh between 72.5 and 79.5 kg/160 and 175 lbs **2.** BOXING WEIGHT CATEGORY IN AMATEUR BOXING a weight category in amateur boxing for competitors who weigh between 75 and 81 kg/165 and 179 lbs **3.** WRESTLING WEIGHT CATEGORY IN WRESTLING a weight category in wrestling for competitors who weigh between 87 and 97 kg/192 and 214 lbs. ◊ **heavyweight, middleweight 4.** BOXING BOXER COMPETING AT LIGHT HEAVYWEIGHT a professional or amateur boxer who competes at light heavyweight level **5.** WRESTLING WRESTLER COMPETING AT LIGHT HEAVYWEIGHT a wrestler who competes at light heavyweight level. ◊ **heavyweight, middleweight**

Lighthouse

lighthouse /lít howss/ (*plural* **-houses** /lít howziz/) *n.* a strategically placed coastal building, often a tall round tower, with a powerful flashing light, designed to guide sailors or warn them of dangers such as rocks

---

——————— WORD KEY: CULTURAL NOTE ———————
To the Lighthouse, a novel by writer Virginia Woolf (1927). Typical of Woolf's more experimental novels in its unusual structure and use of stream-of-consciousness narrative, it is set at the holiday home of the Ramsay family on a Scottish island. Through the relationship between Mrs Ramsay and a young painter, Lily Briscoe, Woolf explores the changing roles and attitudes of contemporary women.

light-independent reaction *n.* BOT = **dark reaction**

lighting /líting/ *n.* **1.** TYPE OF LIGHT light of a particular quality or type, or the equipment that produces it ○ *subdued lighting* **2.** EQUIPMENT FOR PROVIDING ARTIFICIAL LIGHT the equipment used for providing artificial light and light effects on a theatre stage or a television or film set **3.** EFFECT PRODUCED BY LIGHTS the overall effect produced by the lights used on a theatre stage or a television or film set **4.** QUALITY OF LIGHT IN ARTWORK the amount or type of light in a photograph, painting, or other artwork

lighting cameraman *n.* sb responsible for the lighting and camerawork for a film

lighting-up time *n.* the time, at night or in the late afternoon, when drivers of road vehicles are legally required to put their headlights on

lightly /lítli/ *adv.* **1.** WITH LITTLE FORCE without exerting much pressure, force, or weight **2.** WITH LEVITY without seriousness **3.** GRACEFULLY in an easy graceful way **4.** SPARINGLY in small or sparing amounts

light meter *n.* PHOTOGRAPHY = **exposure meter**

light middleweight *n.* ◊ **junior middleweight 1.** WEIGHT CATEGORY IN AMATEUR BOXING a weight category in amateur boxing for competitors who weigh between 67 and 71 kg/148 and 157 lbs **2.** AMATEUR BOXER COMPETING AT LIGHT MIDDLEWEIGHT an amateur boxer who competes at light middleweight level

light-minded *adj.* not capable of thinking seriously, or not likely to think about serious issues —**light-mindedly** *adv.* —**light-mindedness** *n.*

lightness[1] /lítnəss/ *n.* **1.** ILLUMINATION the illumination of sth relative to its surroundings **2.** OPTICS INTENSITY OF LIGHT OR COLOUR the attribute of an object or a colour that enables an observer to quantify the amount of light it appears to reflect

lightness[2] /lítnəss/ *n.* **1.** RELATIVE SLIGHTNESS OF WEIGHT the condition of sth that weighs relatively little **2.** RELATIVE SLIGHTNESS OF FORCE the condition of sth that has relatively little force ○ *lightness of touch* **3.** EASE OR DELICACY the ease or delicacy with which sth is done **4.** NIMBLENESS ease and rapidity of movement **5.** UNTROUBLED STATE total freedom from worry and trouble **6.** LEVITY lack of the seriousness that is required or expected

lightning /lítning/ *n.* FLASH OF LIGHT IN THE SKY flashes of light seen in the sky when there is a discharge of atmospheric electricity in the clouds or between clouds and the earth, usually occurring during a thunderstorm ■ *adj.* FAST very fast and often very sudden [14thC. Variant of *lightening*, formed from LIGHTEN[2].]

lightning arrester *n.* a device, often an aerial, that protects a piece of electrical equipment from damage by lightning or some other electrical surge by diverting the electricity to the ground

lightning chess *n.* a fast form of chess in which players either have a limited time to make each move or have to complete all their moves within a set time

lightning conductor *n.* a metal rod attached to the highest point of a building or other structure to protect it from lightning by conducting the lightning to the ground. US term **lightning rod**

lightning rod *n.* = **lightning conductor**

lightning strike *n.* an industrial strike that happens at short notice and often without union support

light opera *n.* = **operetta**

light organ *n.* ZOOL = **photophore**

light pen *n.* **1.** COMPUT PEN-SHAPED COMPUTER DEVICE a pen-shaped light-sensitive device used to manipulate

---

information on a computer screen by touching the screen directly **2.** COMM = **bar-code reader**

light pollution *n.* excessive artificial light, especially street lighting in towns and cities that prevents the night sky from being seen clearly

light railway *n.* a railway designed for light traffic, often with a narrower gauge or subject to lower-than-standard speed and weight limits

light reaction *n.* an initial stage in photosynthesis when light energy is absorbed by chlorophyll and converted into chemical energy that is stored as ATP (**adenosine triphosphate**). It also generates NADPH, a substance that, like ATP, is essential for subsequent stages of photosynthesis

light reflex *n.* the normal contracting of the pupil of the eye in response to increased light

lights[1] /líts/ *npl.* the lungs of domestic animals, especially those of pigs, sheep, or cattle when they are used in making pet food or, occasionally, food for people [Pre-12thC. From LIGHT[2], because the lungs are full of air and therefore light.]

lights[2] /líts/ *npl.* the ideas, theories, or principles peculiar to a particular person ○ *You must, in the end, act according to your lights.* [Early 16thC. From LIGHT[1]. The underlying sense is of mental illumination.]

light-sensitive *adj.* affected in some way by the presence of light, as are some materials such as photographic film or silicon sheets

lightship /lít ship/ *n.* a ship with a bright flashing light that functions as a lighthouse, especially one that is anchored in a place where a permanent structure would be impracticable

light show *n.* **1.** DISPLAY OF MOVING LIGHTS a spectacle in the form of a display of colourful moving lights, often a feature of a live pop or rock concert **2.** COLOURED LIGHTS SYNCHRONIZED WITH RECORDED MUSIC a form of entertainment in which moving coloured lights are synchronized with recorded music, usually synthesized instrumental music. ◊ **son et lumière**

lightsome[1] /lítsəm/ *adj.* (*archaic or literary*) **1.** HAPPY AND CAREFREE feeling and displaying happiness and freedom from worry **2.** FRIVOLOUS devoid of seriousness **3.** GRACEFUL with a graceful lightness of movement [15thC. Formed from LIGHT[2].] —**lightsomely** *adv.* —**lightsomeness** *n.*

lightsome[2] /lítsəm/ *adj.* (*archaic or literary*) **1.** EMITTING LIGHT producing plenty of light **2.** WELL LIT flooded with light [14thC. Formed from LIGHT[1].]

lights out *n.* **1.** TIME WHEN PEOPLE MUST SLEEP the time at night when people, especially those in the armed forces, prison, boarding schools, and other institutions, are supposed to go to sleep **2.** SIGNAL SOUNDED AT LIGHTS OUT a bugle call, gong, or other signal sounded at lights out

light stylus *n.* COMPUT = **light pen** *n.* 1

light water *n.* PHYS ordinary water, as opposed to heavy water

lightweight /lít wayt/ *adj.* **1.** NOT HEAVY IN WEIGHT OR TEXTURE relatively light in weight and in texture **2.** LACKING INTELLECTUAL DEPTH fairly frivolous or trivial and requiring little or no intellectual effort ■ *n.* **1.** INSIGNIFICANT PERSON OR THING sb or sth regarded as insignificant or without influence, often in a particular area ○ *a political lightweight* **2.** BOXING WEIGHT CATEGORY IN PROFESSIONAL BOXING a weight category in professional boxing for competitors who weigh between 59 and 61 kg/130 and 135 lbs **3.** BOXING WEIGHT CATEGORY IN AMATEUR BOXING a weight category in amateur boxing for competitors who weigh between 57 and 60 kg/126 and 132 lbs **4.** BOXING BOXER COMPETING AT LIGHTWEIGHT a boxer who competes at lightweight level **5.** WRESTLING WEIGHT CATEGORY IN WRESTLING a weight category in wrestling for competitors who weigh between 52 and 57 kg/115 and 126 lbs **6.** WRESTLING WRESTLER WHO COMPETES AT LIGHTWEIGHT a wrestler who competes at lightweight level

light welterweight *n.* **1.** WEIGHT CATEGORY IN AMATEUR BOXING a weight category in amateur boxing for competitors who weigh between 60 and 63.5 kg/132 and 140 lbs **2.** AMATEUR BOXER COMPETING AT LIGHT WELTERWEIGHT an amateur boxer who competes at light welterweight level

light-year *n.* UNIT OF DISTANCE IN ASTRONOMY a unit of distance in astronomy equal to the distance that light travels in a vacuum in one mean solar year, approximately 9.46 billion km/5.88 billion mi. ■ **light years** *npl.* LONG WAY a very long way in time, distance, or some other quantity or quality (*informal*)

lign- *prefix.* = **ligni-** (*used before vowels*)

ligneous /lígni əss/ *adj.* consisting of wood, or with the appearance or texture of wood [Early 17thC. From Latin *ligneus*, from *lignum* 'wood' (see LIGNI-).]

ligni- *prefix.* wood ○ *lignicole* [From Latin *lignum* 'wood, firewood', literally 'sth gathered'. Ultimately from an Indo-European base meaning 'to collect', which is also the ancestor of English *select* and *logic*.]

lignicole /lígni kōl/, **lignicolous** /lig níkələss/ *adj.* living or growing in or on wood [Mid-19thC. Coined from LIGNI- + Latin *colere* 'to inhabit'.]

lignify /lígni fī/ (**-fies, -fying, -fied**) *vti.* to become woody and relatively rigid as lignin is deposited in cell walls, or to make plant parts woody in this way [Early 19thC. Formed from Latin *lignum* 'wood' (see LIGNI-).] —**lignification** /lígnifi káysh'n/ *n.*

lignin /lígnin/ *n.* the complex polymer that is laid down in plant cell walls to give plant parts varying degrees of rigidity. It is the major component of wood, and enables, e.g. the trunk of a tree to support the weight of the crown. [Early 19thC. From Latin *lignum* 'wood'.]

lignite /líg nīt/ *n.* = **brown coal** [Early 19thC] —**lignitic** /lig níttik/ *adj.*

ligno- *prefix.* wood ○ *lignocellulose* [From Latin *lignum* 'wood' (see LIGNI-)]

lignocaine /lígnō kayn/ *n.* a strong local anaesthetic that can be applied externally to the gums, skin, or mucous membranes, or given by injection. It is commonly used in dentistry and minor surgery, and it can also be used to help stabilize an irregular heartbeat. Formula: $C_{14}H_{22}N_2O.HCl.H_2O$. US term **lidocaine** [Mid-20thC. Coined from Latin 'wood'.]

lignocellulose /lígnō séllyoō lōss, -lōz/ *n.* a substance that gives strength to the woody tissues of plants and is formed by the combination of lignin and cellulose

lignum vitae /lígnəm víti/ *n.* **1.** TREES TROPICAL AMERICAN TREE a tropical American tree that has purple or blue flowers and is grown commercially for its timber. Latin name: *Guaiacum officinale* and *Guaiacum sanctum*. **2.** INDUST WOOD OF THE LIGNUM VITAE TREE the valuable hard resinous heavy wood from the lignum vitae tree [Late 16thC. From Latin, literally 'wood of life' (from the medicinal uses of the wood and its resin).]

ligroin /líggrō in/ *n.* a solvent in the form of a flammable liquid mixture of hydrocarbons. It is obtained by the distillation of petroleum. [Late 19thC. Origin unknown.]

ligula /líggyoōlə/ (*plural* **-lae** /líggyoō lee/ *or* **-las**) *n.* **1.** INSECTS PART OF AN INSECT'S LIP the tip of the lower lip (**labium**) of an insect, which typically has four lobes **2.** BOT = **ligule** *n.* 1 [Mid-18thC. From Latin, 'strap', a variant of *lingula*, literally 'little tongue', from *lingua* 'tongue' (see LINGUA).] —**ligular** *adj.*

ligulate /líggyoōlət, -layt/ *adj.* **1.** STRAP-SHAPED shaped like a strap **2.** BOT WITH A LIGULE used to describe a plant that has a ligule, or to describe a plant part in the form of a ligule

ligule /líggyool/ *n.* **1. ligule, ligula** OUTGROWTH ON A LEAF IN GRASSES an outgrowth at the junction of the leaf sheath and leaf blade in a grass, typically a membranous or scaly flap but in some grasses a ring of hairs **2.** STRAP-SHAPED EXTENSION OF A FLORET the strap-shaped extension of florets found in the flower heads of some members of the daisy family and in some grasses [Early 19thC. From Latin *ligula* (see LIGULA).]

Ligurian Sea /li gōōri ən sée/ part of the Mediterranean Sea, bordering northwestern Italy

likable /líkəb'l/, **likeable** *adj.* pleasant and friendly and, therefore, easy to like —**likability** /līkə bílləti/ *n.* —**likableness** /líkəb'lnəss/ *n.*

Likasi /li káassi/ mining and industrial city in the southeastern part of the Democratic Republic of the Congo. Population: 299,118 (1994).

like[1] /līk/ CORE MEANING: a preposition indicating that two things or people are similar or share some of the same features, qualities, or characteristics; it also introduces an example of the set of things or people that have just been mentioned ○ *Vivid red phone booths, looking like London imports, stood nearby.*

1. *prep.* RESEMBLING having a resemblance to sb or sth ○ *She wrapped the towel like a turban on her head.* ○ *He looks like the hero type to me!* **2.** SUCH AS as a typical instance or example of ○ *She won't go to public places like cinemas.* ○ *I bought things like fishing tackle and waders.* **3.** INDICATES CHARACTERISTICS indicates qualities, characteristics, or features (*often used in questions*) ○ *What's it like, being a mother?* ○ *When you go on like this, you know what you sound like?* **4.** TYPICAL OF in a manner typical or characteristic of sb or sth (*often negative*) ○ *It's just like her to say catty things.* **5.** INCLINED TOWARDS having a tendency or desire for sth ○ *I felt like screaming when I found the kitchen floor flooded.* **6.** WITH A SUGGESTION OF as though sth might happen ○ *It looks like rain this morning.* **7.** *conj.* AS in the same way or manner as sth ○ *To ski like she does requires great athletic ability.* **8.** AS IF as though or as if (*nonstandard*) ○ *Butch hops out of the car like it was on fire.* ○ *Like I'd tell you a secret!* **9.** *adv.* IN A PARTICULAR WAY in a particular way or manner (*informal*) ○ *He fixed the chair like new.* **10.** USED AS FILLER OR FOR EMPHASIS used especially in conversation as a filler or for emphasis (*nonstandard*) ○ *You're, like, feeling stressed today, aren't you?* ○ *There were, like, hundreds of people there.* **11.** USED AS FINAL EMPHASIZER used in conversation, tacked on to the end of an adjective, adverb, phrase, or clause, to modify its force or as a filler (*regional nonstandard*) ○ *Can you lend me a fiver? Just till tomorrow, like.* **12.** INTRODUCES DIRECT SPEECH used informally to introduce what sb says (*nonstandard*) ○ *Susan is like 'It's not for me' and Brandon is like, 'You had me worried' and Susan is like, 'Don't worry, I'm not going anywhere'.* **13.** *n.* STH SIMILAR a thing or set of things similar to another ○ *window boxes, planters, flower pots, and the like* **14.** COUNTERPART one person or thing that is regarded as similar or almost identical to another ○ *Have you ever tasted the like of this cheesecake?* ○ *We won't see his like again in this decade.* **15.** *adj.* ALIKE having exactly the same or almost identical qualities or characteristics ○ *These two cats are as like as though they were of the same litter.* ○ *The new laws affect hospitals, nursing homes, clinics, and other like institutions.* [12thC. From Old Norse *líkr*, shortening of *glíkr*, from a prehistoric Germanic word that is also the ancestor of English *alike*, *each*, and *frolic*.] ◇ **like as not** to a probable or likely extent ○ *Like as not he'll show up very late.* ◇ **the likes of** people or things of the particular sort ○ *Such luxuries aren't for the likes of us.*

like[2] /līk/ *v.* (**likes, liking, liked**) **1.** *vt.* ENJOY to regard sth as enjoyable ○ *I like cross-country skiing.* ○ *Do you like prunes?* **2.** *vt.* CONSIDER PLEASANT to regard sb as pleasant and enjoy that person's company ○ *I like a man with a sense of humour.* ○ *Do you like your new teacher?* **3.** *vt.* WANT to want to have or do sth ○ *Would you like some coffee?* ○ *I'd like to meet your brother.* **4.** *vt.* REGARD IN A POSITIVE WAY to have a positive opinion about sth or sb ○ *How do you like her prose style?* **5.** *vi.* HAVE A PREFERENCE to have a specified or unspecified preference or inclination ○ *We can leave later than seven if you like.* ○ *If you like, I'll show you round the house.* ■ *n.* PREFERENCE sth that is preferred over others ○ *a full litany of her likes and dislikes* [Old English *lícian* 'to please'; related to Old Norse *líkr* (see LIKE[1])]

WORD KEY: CULTURAL NOTE

As You Like It, a play by dramatist William Shakespeare (1599?). Based on Thomas Lodge's romance ***Rosalynde*** (1590), it is one of Shakespeare's most charming romantic comedies. Its complex plot revolves around Rosalind, daughter of wicked Duke Ferdinand. Her love for a young knight, Orlando, results in her being banished to the forest, where she is eventually reunited with her lover. The oft-used expression 'All the world's a stage' comes from Act II, scene vii, line 139 of this play.

like[3] /līk/, **liked** /līkt/ *vi.* *Southern US* to be on the verge or point of doing or almost doing a particular thing (*informal*) ○ *I like to have died when I saw her in that getup.* [15thC. From LIKE[1]. Originally 'to make in a particular likeness, to pretend'.]

-like *suffix.* resembling or characteristic of ○ *workman-like* [From LIKE[1]]

likelihood /líkli hood/ *n.* **1.** DEGREE OF PROBABILITY the chance of sth happening **2.** PROBABLE EVENT sth that is likely to happen ◇ **in all likelihood** very probably

likely /líkli/ *adj.* (**-lier, -liest**) **1.** PROBABLE that will probably happen **2.** PLAUSIBLE fit to be believed (*often used ironically*) **3.** SUITABLE appropriate for a specified activity or purpose **4.** PROMISING with a good chance of success or victory ■ *adv.* PROBABLY to a probable degree or extent ○ *It will very likely snow tomorrow.* [14thC. From Old Norse *(g)líkligr*, from *líkr* (see LIKE[1]). The underlying sense is 'like the truth, apparently'.] ◇ **(as) likely as not** very probably

like-minded *adj.* sharing the same or similar views, opinions, tastes, values, or outlook —**like-mindedness** *n.*

liken /líkən/ (**-ens, -ening, -ened**) *vt.* to compare sth or sb to another, especially in order to point out the similarities

likeness /líknəss/ *n.* **1.** SIMILARITY similarity of appearance among or between people or things **2.** REPRESENTATION OF SB OR STH a representation of sb or sth, e.g. a painting or statue, often considered in terms of how accurately it represents the person or thing [Old English *(ge)līknes*, formed from the base that also produced *alike*]

Likert scale /líkert-/ *n.* PSYCHOL a scale measuring the degree to which people agree or disagree with a statement, usually on a 3-, 5-, or 7-point scale [Mid-20thC. Named after Rensis *Likert* (1903–81), US psychologist.]

likewise /līk wīz/ *adv.* **1.** IN THE SAME WAY in the same or a similar way **2.** ALSO used to state that the same applies in a second or subsequent case ○ *She works as a teacher; her brother likewise.* [15thC. Contraction of *in like wise* 'in like or similar manner'.]

liking /líking/ *n.* **1.** FONDNESS a feeling of enjoying sth or finding it pleasant **2.** PREFERENCE personal taste or choice [14thC. From LIKE[2].]

WORD KEY: SYNONYMS

See Synonyms at ***love***.

likuta /li kōōtə/ (*plural* **makuta** /ma-/) *n.* **1.** MINOR UNIT OF CURRENCY a subunit of currency of the Democratic Republic of Congo, 100 of which are worth one new zaire. See table at **currency 2.** LIKUTA COIN a coin worth one likuta [Mid-20thC. From Kikongo, literally 'the cloth' (a piece of cloth formerly being used as a unit of currency).]

lilac /lílək/ (*plural* **-lacs** *or* **-lac**) *n.* **1.** TREES FLOWERING TREE a European and Asian shrub or small tree with strongly perfumed sprays of white, pink, or pale purple flowers. It is a member of the olive family. Genus: *Syringa*. **2.** PLANTS BLOSSOM OF LILAC a pink, white, or pale purple blossom from the lilac tree or shrub **3.** COLOURS PALE PINKISH-PURPLE COLOUR a pale pinkish-purple colour with a tinge of blue [Early 17thC. Via French from, ultimately, Persian *līlak*, literally 'bluish'.] —**lilac** *adj.*

lilangeni /lée lang gáyni/ (*plural* **emalangeni** /émmə lang gáyni/) *n.* **1.** UNIT OF CURRENCY the basic unit of currency of Swaziland, worth 100 cents. See table at **currency 2.** LILANGENI COIN a coin worth one lilangeni [Late 20thC. From Bantu.]

Lilburn /líl burn/, **Douglas Gordon** (*b.* 1915) New Zealand composer. Among his best-known works is *Aotearoa Overture* (1940). His later work is more experimental and has included collaborations with leading poets.

Lilburne /líl burn/, **John** (c. 1614–57) English political agitator and pamphleteer. A prominent member of the Levellers, he was a parliamentary officer in the Civil War, and advocated political reform.

liliaceous /lílli áyshəss/ *adj.* used to describe plants that belong to the lily family [Mid-18thC. From late Latin *liliaceus*, from Latin *lilium* (see LILY).]

Lilienthal /lé̇eli ən taal/, **Otto** (1848–96) German inventor and aeronautical engineer. A pioneer of glider flight, his study of aerodynamics led to advances in the design of aircraft wings.

Lilith /líllith/ *n.* **1.** PREDECESSOR TO EVE in Hebrew Scripture, the first woman, believed to have been created before Eve **2.** JUDAISM EVIL SPIRIT OF A WOMAN in Jewish folklore, an evil spirit of a woman, believed to lurk in deserted places and attack children

Liliuokalani /lee lee ōō ō kaa láani/, **Queen of Hawaii** (1838–1917). She was the last native sovereign to govern Hawaii before its annexation by the United States, which she strongly opposed.

Lille /leel/ industrial city and capital of Nord Department, Nord-Pas-de-Calais Region, northern France. Population: 178,301 (1990).

Lillee /lílli/, **Dennis Keith** (*b.* 1949) Australian cricketer. A fast bowler, he had taken a world-record 355 test wickets at his retirement in 1984.

Lilliputian /lílli pyóosh'n/, **lilliputian** *n.* SMALL PERSON OR THING a person or thing that is unusually small in height ■ *adj.* **1.** TINY unusually small **2.** TRIVIAL OR PETTY of little or no importance or significance [Mid-18thC. From the name of the imaginary country of *Lilliput* in *Gulliver's Travels* (1726) by Jonathan Swift, whose people were only 15 cm./6 in. high.]

Lilo /lílō/ *tdmk.* a trademark for an inflatable bed for use in swimming-pools or on the sea

Lilongwe /li lóng wi/ capital and second largest city of Malawi. Population: 395,500 (1994).

lilt /lilt/ *n.* **1.** VARIATION IN VOICE PITCH a pleasant rising and falling variation in the pitch of a person's voice **2.** CHEERFUL PIECE OF MUSIC a cheerful song or piece of music, especially one that is easy to sing along with (*archaic*) **3.** BOUNCY STEP a light bouncy way of walking, often taken as an indication of a cheerful disposition ■ *v.* **(lilts, lilting, lilted) 1.** *vti.* SAY OR SING STH CHEERFULLY to say, sing, or play sth in a cheerful way, often with pleasant variations in pitch **2.** *vi.* WALK BOUNCILY to walk or move in a bouncy cheerful way [14thC. Origin uncertain. Originally 'to sound an alarm or raise your voice', later 'to strike up a song'.] —**lilting** *adj.*

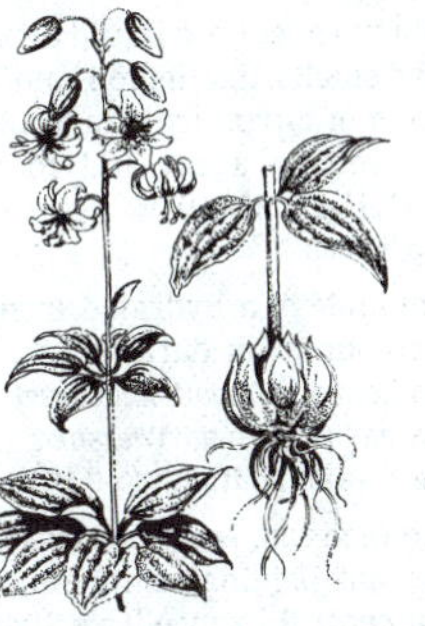

Lily

lily /lílli/ *n.* (*plural* **-ies**) **1.** PLANTS PERENNIAL PLANT a perennial plant that has layered bulbs, blade-shaped leaves, and single, large, sometimes trumpet-shaped flowers. The flowers often have spotted petals and conspicuous protruding stamens. Genus: *Lilium.* **2.** PLANTS PLANT RESEMBLING A LILY a plant that resembles the lily but is not necessarily related to it, e.g., the lily of the valley, the arum lily, or the water lily **3.** PLANTS FLOWER OF THE LILY PLANT a flower of any of the lily plants ○ *Julia chose lilies for her wedding bouquet.* **4.** HERALDRY = **fleur-de-lis** *n.* 1 **5.** WHITE OR PURE THING sb or sth that is particularly white or pure (*dated*) ■ *adj.* PALE unusually pale in colour or shade [Pre-12thC. From Latin *lilium*, of uncertain origin: probably ultimately from a pre-Indo-European Mediterranean language.] ◇ **gild the lily** to try to improve sth that is good or beautiful enough

lily iron *n.* a harpoon that has a detachable head with barbs on it, used especially in swordfishing [From its shape, thought to resemble the leaves of a lily]

lily-livered *adj.* lacking in courage (*literary*) [From the idea that a cowardly person's liver is pale through lack of bile, once thought to engender courage]

lily of the valley (*plural* **lilies of the valley** *or* **lily of the valley**) *n.* a small ornamental flowering plant with two long, oval, dark green leaves and small, white or pale pink, sweet-scented, bell-shaped drooping flowers growing from a single spike. All parts of the plant, which is grown throughout North America, Europe, and Asia, are poisonous, including the bright red berries. Genus: *Convallaria.* [Translation of Latin *lilium convallium*, name of an unidentified plant in the Bible]

lily pad *n.* a floating leaf of a water lily

lily-white *adj.* **1.** PALE AND UNBLEMISHED unusually pale in tone and free from blemishes **2.** UNMIXED characterized by complete or extreme absence of admixture

Lima[1] /lé̇emə/ *n.* COMMUNICATION the NATO phonetic alphabet code word for the letter 'L', used in international radio communications

Lima[2] /lé̇emə/ capital city of Peru, situated in the west-central part of the country, on the Pacific Ocean and adjacent to the River Rimac in an arid coastal region. Population: 6,400,000 (1991).

lima bean /límə-/ *n.* **1.** PLANTS PLANT OF THE BEAN FAMILY a plant of the bean family, originally native to tropical America but now widely grown throughout the United States for its edible seeds that develop inside flat pods. Latin name: *Phaseolus limensis* and *Phaseolus lunatus.* **2.** FOOD SEED OF THE LIMA BEAN the pale green edible seed produced by the lima bean plant. ◊ **butter bean** [Mid-18thC. Named after LIMA[1], the capital of Peru.]

limacine /límmə sīn, -sin, límə-, -l *adj.* **1.** OF THE SLUG FAMILY belonging or relating to the slug family of invertebrate terrestrial molluscs **2.** LIKE A SLUG resembling a slug in appearance or movement [Late 19thC. Formed from the Latin stem *limac-* 'slug, snail'.]

limaçon /límmə son/ *n.* a heart-shaped mathematical curve that is generated by a point on a line that intersects with a circle and rotates about a point on the circle [Late 19thC. From French, literally 'snail shell', ultimately from the Latin stem *limac-* 'slug, snail'.]

Limassol /límasol/ city and port in southern Cyprus. It is the capital of Limassol District. Population: 143,400 (1994).

Limavady /límmə váddi/ town in County Londonderry, Northern Ireland. Population: 10,764 (1991).

limb[1] /lim/ **(limbs, limbing, limbed)** *n.* **1.** BODY PART an arm, leg, or similar appendage, e.g. a wing or flipper **2.** LARGE BRANCH any of the major branches of a tree **3.** ASSOCIATED PERSON OR ORGANIZATION sb or sth that is affiliated with a larger group or organization **4.** PART STICKING OUT a part that sticks out, e.g. on a building or a mountain range [Old English *lim*] —**limbed** *adj.* —**limbless** *adj.* ◇ **go out on a limb** to express a viewpoint that risks being controversial ◇ **out on a limb** in an isolated position, without support

limb[2] /lim/ *n.* **1.** ASTRON RIM OF A PLANET the illuminated edge of the Sun, the Moon, or a planet **2.** MATH ARC-SHAPED SCALE ON A MEASURING DEVICE an arc-shaped scale on an instrument such as a sextant that measures angles **3.** BOT END OF A PLANT PART the expanded end of a plant part, especially of a sepal, petal, or leaf **4.** BOT RIM OF A FLOWER the flared outer rim of a bell- or trumpet-shaped flower **5.** ARCHERY PART OF A BOW either of the two halves of a bow used in archery [14thC. Directly or via French *limbe* from Latin *limbus* (see LIMBUS).]

limbate /lím bayt/ *adj.* used to describe flowers that are a different colour at the edges ○ *limbate carnations* [Early 19thC. From late Latin *limbatus*, from Latin *limbus* 'limbus' (see LIMBUS).]

limber[1] /límbər/ *adj.* **1.** SUPPLE AND AGILE able to move with elastic ease and nimble quickness **2.** FLEXIBLE able to be bent easily ■ *vti.* **(-bers, -bering, -bered)** MAKE OR BECOME FLEXIBLE to become, or cause sth to become, flexible or supple [Mid-16thC. Origin uncertain: probably from LIMBER[2], from its ease of movement.] —**limberness** *n.*

limber up *vi.* to do gentle physical exercises to loosen and warm the muscles prior to taking part in more strenuous physical activity

limber[2] /límbər/ *n.* VEHICLE FOR TRANSPORTING A LARGE GUN a two-wheeled vehicle that forms the detachable front part of a gun carriage. It was also used for transporting ammunition and other supplies on the battlefield. ■ *vt.* **(-bers, -bering, -bered)** ATTACH TO A LIMBER to attach a gun or other piece of field equipment to a limber [Early 17thC. Origin uncertain: perhaps via French *limon* 'shaft of a cart' from Celtic or a prehistoric Germanic word that is also the ancestor of *limb.*]

limbi plural of **limbus**

limbic /límbik/ *adj.* ANAT **1.** OF OR NEAR A LIMBUS belonging to a limbus or situated in or near a limbus **2.** OF THE LIMBIC SYSTEM belonging to or situated in the limbic system [Late 19thC. From French *limbique*, ultimately from Latin *limbus* (see LIMBUS).]

limbic system *n.* an interconnected system of brain nuclei associated with basic needs and emotions, e.g. hunger, pain, pleasure, satisfaction, sex, and instinctive motivation. The most primitive part of the brain, it is situated close to the inner wall of each cerebral hemisphere and includes the brain system concerned with the sense of smell.

limbo[1] /límbō/ *n.* **1. Limbo, limbo** CHR PLACE FOR SOULS OF UNBAPTIZED CHILDREN in Roman Catholic theology, the place that is believed to be home to the souls of children who have died before baptism, and the souls of the righteous who died before Jesus Christ. Although they are barred from entry to heaven, they are not condemned to the eternal suffering of hell. **2.** STATE OF OBLIVION a state in which sb or sth is neglected or is simply left in oblivion **3.** PRISON a place for the confinement of prisoners (*archaic*) [14thC. From Latin, literally 'on the border (of hell)', where limbo was thought to be, a form of *limbus* (see LIMBUS).] ◇ **in limbo** in a state of uncertainty or of being kept waiting

limbo[2] /límbō/ (*plural* **-bos**) *n.* a West Indian dance that involves bending the body backwards from the knees and moving under a horizontal bar or rope that is put into progressively lower positions (*often used before a noun*) ○ *a limbo dancer* [Mid-20thC. Alteration of LIMBER[1].]

Limburger /lím burgər/, **Limburger cheese, Limburg cheese** /lím burg-/ *n.* a soft white Belgian cheese noted for its characteristically strong smell and taste [Mid-19thC. From Dutch or German, literally 'from Limburg', a province of northwestern Belgium, where it was first made.]

limbus /límbəss/ (*plural* **-bi** /-bī/) *n.* the edge of various organs or body parts, e.g. the area in the eyeball where the cornea and sclera meet [15thC. From Latin, literally 'edge, border'.]

lime[1] /līm/ *n.* **1.** CHEM CALCIUM OXIDE the chemical calcium oxide **2.** AGRIC, GARDENING CALCIUM USED FOR IMPROVING SOIL any of several forms of calcium, especially calcium hydroxide, used for improving soil that has a low calcium content **3.** HUNT BIRDLIME the substance birdlime ■ *vt.* **(limes, liming, limed) 1.** AGRIC, GARDENING SPREAD CALCIUM ON to spread calcium, often in the form of ground limestone, on soil in order to reduce its acidity **2.** BUILDING PAINT WITH WHITEWASH to cover a surface with whitewash **3.** HUNT SMEAR WITH BIRDLIME to smear twigs or branches with birdlime in order to catch small birds **4.** HOUSEHOLD BLEACH WOOD to treat wood with lime so that it has a pale bleached appearance ○ *kitchen cabinets of limed ash* **5.** HUNT CATCH BIRDS OR ANIMALS USING BIRDLIME to catch small birds or animals using birdlime or some other sticky substance [Old English *līm*, from a prehistoric Germanic word that is also the ancestor of English *slime, loam*, and *slippery*] —**limy** *adj.*

lime[2] /līm/ *n.* **1.** TREES EVERGREEN TREE a small evergreen citrus tree, originally native to Asia, but now widely grown for its small green fruits. Latin name: *Citrus aurantifolia.* **2.** FOOD SMALL GREEN FRUIT the small acid-tasting citrus fruit of the lime tree that has a thin green rind and pale green juicy flesh (*often used before a noun*) ○ *lime juice* **3.** BEVERAGES NON-ALCOHOLIC DRINK a non-alcoholic drink made from or tasting of the juice of limes ■ *adj.* COLOURS LIME-GREEN lime-green [Mid-17thC. Via French from, ultimately, Arabic *līma* 'citrus fruit' (source of English *lemon*).]

lime[3] /līm/ *n.* **1. lime, lime tree** TREES DECIDUOUS TREE WITH HEART-SHAPED LEAVES a deciduous tree with heart-shaped leaves, clusters of fragrant yellow flowers, and wide-spreading shady branches, often planted as an ornamental tree in gardens and streets. Genus: *Tilia.* US term **linden 2.** INDUST **WOOD** the wood of the lime tree [Early 17thC. Alteration of *line,* ultimately from Old English *linde* (probable source of English *linden*).]

lime[4] /līm/ (**limes, liming, limed**) *vi. Carib* to spend time lazily (*slang*) [Late 20thC. Back-formation from offensive *limey* 'low-class white person'.]

limeade /līm áyd/ *n.* a non-alcoholic, usually carbonated drink made from or tasting of lime juice

lime-green *adj.* having the pale green colour of a lime

limekiln /līm kiln/ *n.* an oven that is used for heating limestone to produce quicklime

limelight /līm līt/ *n.* **1. FOCUS OF ATTENTION** the focus of attention or public interest **2.** THEATRE **LAMP IN WHICH QUICKLIME IS HEATED** a type of lamp in which quicklime is heated to produce a brilliant light. It was used in theatres as an early form of stage lighting. **3. LIGHT PRODUCED BY LIMELIGHT** the light that a limelight lamp produces

limerick /límmərik/ *n.* a five-line humorous poem with regular metre and rhyme patterns, often dealing with a risqué subject and typically opening with a line such as 'There was a young lady called Jenny'. Lines one, two, and five rhyme with each other and have three metrical feet, and lines two and four rhyme with each other and have two metrical feet, giving the poem a catchy bouncy rhythm. [Early 19thC. Said to derive from the Victorian custom of singing nonsense songs with this rhyme scheme, with the refrain 'will you come up to LIMERICK'.]

Limerick /límmərik/ **1.** port and chief city of Limerick County, southwestern Republic of Ireland. Population: 75,436 (1991). **2.** county in the southwestern Republic of Ireland, in Munster Province. Population: 112,975 (1996). Area: 2,686 sq. km/1,039 sq. mi.

limes /lī meez/ (*plural* **limites** /límmi teez/) *n.* a boundary or boundary wall, especially one that marked the outskirts of territory held by the ancient Romans [Mid-16thC. From Latin (see LIMIT).]

limestone /līm stōn/ *n.* sedimentary rock formed from the skeletons and shells of marine organisms that consists chiefly of calcium carbonate and is used widely in construction and in making lime and cement

lime tree *n.* = **lime**[3] *n.* 1

limewater /līm wawtər/ *n.* **1.** CHEM **CALCIUM HYDROXIDE IN WATER** a clear alkaline solution of calcium hydroxide in water, used in skin lotions and as an antacid **2.** GEOL **WATER CONTAINING CALCIUM SALTS** water that is naturally high in dissolved calcium carbonate or calcium sulphate

limey /līmi/ *n. US, Can, ANZ* (*sometimes considered offensive*) **1. BRITISH PERSON** a name, sometimes considered offensive, for a British person, originally a British sailor (*slang offensive*) **2. BRITISH SHIP** a name, sometimes considered offensive, for a British commercial or naval vessel (*slang*) ■ *adj. US, Can, ANZ* **BRITISH** a term, sometimes considered offensive, meaning belonging or relating to the United Kingdom (*slang offensive*) [Late 19thC. Shortening of *lime-juicer* (because sailors in the British Navy were made to drink lime juice to prevent scurvy).]

liminal /límmin'l/ *adj.* belonging to the point of conscious awareness below which sth cannot be experienced or felt [Late 19thC. Formed from Latin *limin-,* stem of *limen* 'threshold'.]

limit /límmit/ *n.* **1. FURTHEST POINT, DEGREE, OR AMOUNT** the furthest point, degree, amount, or boundary, especially one that cannot or should not be passed or exceeded ○ *impose a spending limit* **2. MAXIMUM OR MINIMUM AMOUNT ALLOWED** the maximum or minimum amount, or the largest or lowest quantity, that is available or allowed ○ *an upper age limit of 12 years* **3. BOUNDARY OF AN AREA** the boundary or edge of an area, or sth that marks a boundary or edge (*often used in the plural*) ○ *the city limits* **4. RESTRICTION** a feature or circumstance that restricts what can be done ○ *a time limit* **5.** GAMBLING **MAXIMUM MONEY ALLOWED IN BETTING** the maximum amount of money that can be staked at any one time in various games of chance **6.** MATH **MAXIMUM OF A MATHEMATICAL FUNCTION** a numerical value approached by a mathematical function as the independent variable of the function approaches infinity or some specified value **7.** MATH **VALUE SPECIFYING AN INTEGRAL'S RANGE** one of the two given values specifying the range over which a definite integral is evaluated ■ *vt.* (**-its, -iting, -ited**) **1. RESTRICT** to restrict sth or sb in number or quantity, or restrict sth to a specified group ○ *had to limit the number of guests because of space problems* **2. BE BOUNDARY TO** to be or act as a boundary to a specified area [14thC. From Latin *limit-,* stem of *limes,* literally 'ridge of land separating fields', later 'boundary'.] —**limitable** *adj.* ◇ **be the limit** to be so bad as to be almost beyond what sb is able or prepared to tolerate ◇ **over the limit 1.** with more alcohol in the bloodstream than the driver of a vehicle is legally permitted to have **2.** driving at a speed beyond the maximum legal speed limit

limitary /límmitəri/ *adj.* (*archaic*) **1. RESTRICTED** on which limits are imposed **2. RESTRICTIVE** imposing limits of some kind

limitation /límmi táysh'n/ *n.* **1. RESTRICTION** an imposed restriction that cannot be exceeded or sidestepped ○ *limitations on the height of vehicles* **2. RESTRICTING FLAW** a disadvantage or weakness in a person or thing (*often used in the plural*) ○ *One of the limitations of the program is the amount of memory it requires.* **3. SETTING OF A LIMIT** the act of limiting sth ○ *damage limitation* **4.** LAW **MAXIMUM DELAY ALLOWED** a stated period of time within which a legal action must start **5.** LAW **LEGAL RESTRICTION** a legal restriction on the powers that sb has

limit down *n.* FIN under futures exchange rules, the point reached by a commodity price that has fallen by the maximum amount allowed in a single day's trading

limited /límmitid/ *adj.* **1. WITH A LIMIT IMPOSED** on which some form of limit or restriction is imposed ○ *We have limited space available.* **2. LACKING FULL SCOPE** existing at below the full degree or extent, usually far below ○ *limited powers* **3. OF RELATIVELY LITTLE TALENT** with talents or skills that fall short of what is expected or required **4.** POL **LACKING FULL AUTHORITY** lacking a full range of powers, especially because of constitutional or legal limitations **5. limited, Limited** COMM **WITH RESTRICTED SHAREHOLDER LIABILITY** used to describe a company or other business enterprise whose shareholders' liability for any debts or losses is restricted **6.** *US, Can* TRANSP **STOPPING AT ONLY A FEW PLACES** used to describe a passenger train or bus that stops at only a few places along a route ■ *n. US, Can* TRANSP **BUS OR TRAIN MAKING FEW STOPS** a bus or train that stops at only a few places on its route —**limitedly** *adv.* —**limitedness** *n.*

limited company *n.* a company in which the shareholders' liability for any debts or losses is restricted

limited edition *n.* an edition, especially of a book or an art print, of which only a set number of copies have been made. This has the effect of increasing the item's exclusivity value. (*hyphenated before a noun*) ○ *limited-edition prints*

limited liability *n.* an investor's liability for no greater a proportion of a company's debt than is represented by the value of his or her financial stake in the business

limited partner *n.* a business partner who has no management responsibility and whose liability for company debts is limited to his or her financial stake —**limited partnership** *n.*

limited war *n.* a war in which it is not the aim of the participants to defeat or destroy the enemy totally, especially a war in which nuclear weapons are available but are not used

limiter /límmitər/ *n.* **1.** ELECTRON ENG **CIRCUIT THAT LIMITS OUTPUT** an electronic circuit that limits the amplitude of an output wave to a specified value **2. STH IMPOSING A LIMIT** sb or sth that has a restricting effect

limites plural of **limes**

limiting /límmiting/ *adj.* **1. IMPOSING RESTRICTIONS** imposing limits of some kind, especially limits on the scope for development, progress, or improvement ○ *a limiting factor* **2.** GRAM **IDENTIFYING, NOT DESCRIBING** identifying rather than describing the referent of a noun, as the possessive adjective 'your' does in the phrase 'your house'. The term 'limiting adjective' is now rarely used, having been superseded by the term 'determiner'.

limitless /límmitləss/ *adj.* very great in amount, extent, or degree ○ *limitless resources* —**limitlessly** *adv.* —**limitlessness** *n.*

limit order *n.* FIN an order instructing an investment broker to buy or sell sth at a set price or better within a certain period of time

limit point *n.* MATH a point in a set of mathematical points, such that for every neighbourhood around the point at least one other point in the set is contained in the neighbourhood

limitrophe /límmi trōf/ *adj.* on or close to the border of a country or region (*formal*) [Late 16thC. Via French from late Latin *limitrophus,* literally 'supporting a boundary', from the Latin stem *limit-* 'boundary'.]

limit up *n.* FIN under futures exchange rules, the point reached by a commodity price that has risen by the maximum amount allowed in a single day's trading

limn /lim/ (**limns, limning, limned**) *vt.* (*literary*) **1. DRAW OR PAINT** to draw or paint a picture of sb or sth, especially in outline **2. DESCRIBE** to describe sth in words [15thC. Alteration of *lumine* 'to illustrate a manuscript', from Old French *luminer,* ultimately from Latin *luminare* 'to illumine', from *lumin-* 'light'.] —**limner** *n.*

limnetic /lim néttik/ *adj.* relating to or living in the deep open water of a freshwater pond or lake [Late 19thC. Formed from Greek *limnētēs* 'living in marshes', from *limnē* 'marshy lake'.]

limnology /lim nólləji/ *n.* the scientific study of lakes and other bodies of fresh water, including their physical and biological features [Late 19thC. Coined from Greek *limnē* 'marshy lake' + -LOGY.] —**limnological** /límnə lójjik'l/ *adj.* —**limnologically** /-lójjikli/ *adv.* —**limnologist** /lim nólləjist/ *n.*

limo /límmō/ (*plural* **-os**) *n.* a limousine (*informal*) [Mid-20thC. Shortening.]

Limoges[1] /li mōzh/ *n.* a fine porcelain made in the town of Limoges, France, since the 19th century [Mid-19thC. From *French.*]

Limoges[2] /li mōzh/ town and capital of Haute-Vienne Department and Limousin Region, central France. Population: 136,407 (1990).

limonene /límmə neen/ *n.* a liquid unsaturated hydrocarbon that smells like lemon and is found in the essential oils of citrus fruits and peppermint. It is used as a wetting agent and in making resins. Formula: $C_{10}H_{16}$. [Mid-19thC. From German *Limonen,* from *Limone* 'lemon'.]

limonite /līmə nīt/ *n.* a hydrated iron oxide ore that varies in colour from dark brown to yellow [Early 19thC. From German *Limonit,* from Greek *leimōn* 'meadow', modelled on earlier German *Wiesenerz* 'limonite', literally 'meadow ore'.] —**limonitic** /līmə níttik/ *adj.*

Limousin /límmoo zan, -záN/ *n.* a breed of large hardy beef cattle that originated in Limousin, a former province of central France [Late 20thC. From French.]

limousine /límmə zeen, -zeen/ *n.* **1. LARGE CAR** a large luxurious car, usually chauffeur-driven, with a partition between the chauffeur and passengers **2.** *US* **TRANSPORTATION TO AIRPORT** a vehicle used to transport passengers to and from an airport, usually between a hotel and airport [Early 20thC. From French, feminine of *Limousin,* 'caped cloak worn by cart drivers of the Limousin area', hence 'vehicle with roofed passenger compartment'.]

limp[1] /limp/ *vi.* (**limps, limping, limped**) **1. WALK UNEVENLY** to walk with an uneven step, usually because of having an injured leg **2. PROCEED WITH DIFFICULTY** to move or continue with great difficulty ○ *The business limped through the recession.* ■ *n.* **IMPAIRED GAIT** a way of walking or running that involves a motion impairment, either slight or more extensive (*offensive in some contexts*) [Late 16thC. Origin uncertain: possibly a back-formation from obsolete *limphalt* 'motion impaired', from Old English *lempheal t,* from *lemp* (of uncertain origin) + HALT 'motion impaired'.] —**limper** *n.*

limp[2] /limp/ *adj.* **1. FLEXIBLE** without stiffness or rigidity **2. WEAK** without strength, power, or firmness ○ *a limp handshake* **3. LACKING FORCE** without energy, vitality, or enthusiasm **4. LACKING VOLUME OR SUBSTANCE** without a firm or substantial feel or texture **5.** PUBL

NOT STIFFENED BY BOARDS used to describe a book cover that is not stiffened by boards but is made of more durable material than a paperback **6. UNCONVINCING** not very convincing [Early 18thC. Origin uncertain: possibly related to Middle High German *lampen* 'to hang down'.] —**limply** *adv.* —**limpness** *n.*

limpet /límpit/ (*plural* **-pets** *or* **-pet**) *n.* a marine gastropod mollusc that has a low rough conical shell and clings to rocks [Pre-12thC. Via medieval Latin *lampreda* from late Latin *lampetra* (source also of English *lamprey*), of uncertain origin: probably literally 'lick-rock'.]

limpet mine *n.* an explosive device that can be attached to the hull of a ship

limpid /límpid/ *adj.* **1. CLEAR** clear and transparent **2. LUCID** expressing sth in a way that is clear and easy to understand ○ *limpid prose* **3. UNWORRIED** emotionally calm and composed [Early 17thC. Directly or via French *limpide* from Latin *limpidus* 'clear', of uncertain origin.] —**limpidity** /lim píddəti/ *n.* —**limpidly** /límpidli/ *adv.* —**limpidness** /límpidnəss/ *n.*

limpkin /límpkin/ (*plural* **-kins** *or* **-kin**) *n.* a wading bird with a long neck, a long curved bill, long legs, and short rounded wings. It lives in marshes in South America and southeastern North America. Latin name: *Aramus guarauna*. [Late 19thC. Coined from LIMP + -KIN, from the bird's limping walk.]

Limpopo /lim pópō/ river in southeastern Africa. Length: 1,800 km/1,100 mi.

limp-wristed *adj.* an offensive term meaning effeminate (*insult*) [From the stereotypic attitude offensively associated with effeminate or gay men, with hands relaxed from raised wrists]

limulus /límmyōoləss/ (*plural* **-li** /-lī/ *or* **-lus**) *n.* a member of a group of arthropods that includes the horseshoe crab. Genus: *Limulus*. [Mid-19thC. Via modern Latin from Latin, 'somewhat sidelong', from *limus* 'sidelong, oblique'; from the crab's sideways motion.]

limy /lími/ (**-ier**, **-iest**) *adj.* **1. COVERED WITH BIRDLIME** smeared with birdlime **2. OF LIME** consisting of, containing, or similar to lime

lin. *abbr.* **1.** lineal **2.** linear

linac /línnak/ *n.* PHYS = **linear accelerator** [Mid-20thC. Shortening.]

Linacre /línnəkər/, **Thomas** (c. 1460–1524) English humanist and physician. He was an advocate of the New Learning, translated Galen, and founded the Royal College of Physicians.

linage /línij/, **lineage** *n.* **1. NUMBER OF PRINTED LINES** the number of lines in a printed text **2. PAYMENT BY THE LINE** a fixed payment per line of printed text made to the author

Linalool

linalool /li nállo ol/, **linalol** /línnə lol/ *n.* a colourless liquid with a pleasant smell that is found in many essential plant oils. It is used in making perfumes. [Late 19thC. Coined from Mexican Spanish *linaloë* 'lignaloes' + -OL.]

linchpin /línch pin/, **lynchpin** *n.* **1. PIN TO STOP A WHEEL COMING OFF** a pin placed crosswise through an axle to prevent a wheel from coming off **2. ESSENTIAL ELEMENT** sb or sth that is an essential element in the success of sth such as a team or a plan [14thC. From obsolete *linch* 'linchpin', from Old English *lynis*, + PIN.]

Lincoln[1] /língkən/ *n.* a heavy-fleeced sheep of a breed originally developed in Lincolnshire and raised mainly for its meat

Abraham Lincoln

Lincoln[2] /língkən/ historic cathedral city in eastern England. Population: 84,300 (1995).

Lincoln, Abraham (1809–65) US statesman and 16th president of the United States. He led the North to victory in the US Civil War and abolished slavery. He was assassinated while attending a theatre performance.

Lincoln green *adj.* of a bright green colour [Early 16thC. Named after the city of LINCOLN, where cloth of this colour was originally manufactured.] —**Lincoln green** *n.*

Lincolnshire /língkənshər/ county in eastern England, bordering the North Sea and its inlet the Wash. Population: 611,800 (1995). Area: 5,885 sq. km/2,272 sq. mi.

Lincolnshire Wolds /-wóldz/ region of chalk hills in the northern and western parts of Lincolnshire, England

Lincs. /lingks/ *abbr.* Lincolnshire

linctus /língktəss/ (*plural* **-tuses**) *n.* a medicinal syrup given to relieve coughs and soothe sore throats [Late 17thC. From medieval Latin, '(medicine) for licking', from Latin *lingere* 'to lick'.]

Lind /lind/, **Jenny** (1820–87) Swedish soprano. The best known singer of her day, she established the Mendelssohn Scholarships and various charities. Known as **The Swedish Nightingale**

lindane /lín dayn/ *n.* a white poisonous crystalline powder that biodegrades very slowly, used to kill insects and weeds. Formula: $C_6H_6Cl_6$. [Mid-20thC. Named after Dutch chemist Teunis van der *Linden*.]

Charles Augustus Lindbergh and Anne Lindbergh

Lindbergh /línd burg/, **Charles Augustus** (1902–74) US aviator and engineer. In 1927 he became the first person to fly solo across the Atlantic, which he described in *The Spirit of St Louis* (1953). Known as **Lucky Lindy**

linden /líndən/ (*plural* **-dens** *or* **-den**) *n.* = **lime** [Late 16thC. Origin uncertain: perhaps from *linden* 'made of limewood', from *lind* 'lime tree'.]

Lindisfarne /líndiss faarn/ an island off the northeastern coast of England, separated from the shore by tidal waters. It is the site of a 7th century monastery founded by St Aidan. Area: 5.2 sq. km/2 sq. mi.

Lindrum /líndrəm/, **Walter Albert** (1898–1960) Australian billiards player. He was world champion (1933–34) and made a world-record break of 4317 (1932).

Lindsay /líndzi/, **Jack** (1900–90) Australian writer and historian. The eldest son of Norman Lindsay, he gained an international reputation for his writings on philosophy and art history. He also published novels, including *Rising Tide* (1953).

Lindsay, Norman Alfred William (1879–1969) Australian artist and writer. He was noted for his paintings, drawings, and etchings of classical and erotic scenes, and for his children's story *The Magic Pudding* (1919).

Lindsay, Vachel (1879–1931) US poet. He wrote *General Booth Enters into Heaven* (1913) and *The Congo* (1914). Full name **Nicholas Vachel Lindsay**

lindy /líndi/, **lindy hop** *n.* a lively dance for couples that is a kind of jitterbug [Early 20thC. From *Lindy*, nickname of Charles Augustus LINDBERGH.]

line[1] /līn/ *n.* **1. LONG NARROW MARK** a long narrow mark or stroke made on or in a surface **2. FACIAL MARK** a wrinkle or crease in the skin of the face (*often used in the plural*) **3. TRACED PATH OF POINT** an imaginary path that has length but not width, traced by a moving point **4. GEOM ONE-DIMENSIONAL ELEMENT** a straight geometrical element that has length but not width or thickness and whose identity is determined by two points **5. BORDER** a boundary or division between two properties, jurisdictions, or political units **6. SPORTS CONFINING BOUNDARY** a long narrow mark that shows the boundary of any of the divisions of a playing area or race track **7. TRANSP ROUTE** a rail, sea, or air route served by a transport organization **8. RAIL TRACK** the track on which a railway train runs **9. RAIL FIXED RAILWAY ROUTE** a particular part of a railway network **10. TRANSP TRANSPORT COMPANY** a company that runs a regular service of buses, ships, or aircraft on a route **11. THIN ROPE** a length of rope or wire **12. ELEC ELECTRIC CABLE** a cable used for transmitting electric power or electronic messages **13. COMMUNICATION CONNECTION** a telephone connection **14. MUSIC PART OF STAVE** any of the five horizontal marks that make up a stave **15. MUSIC MELODY** the notes that make up a melody **16. SERIES** a series of people, usually in the same family, who follow one another in the same job or role ○ *the last in a long line of musicians* **17. COMM TYPE OF MERCHANDISE** a particular type of product or merchandise **18. PRINTING ROW OF PRINT** a row of words or numbers on a page or other surface ○ *a few lines of doggerel* **19. MIL POSITIONED FORMATION** a formation of troops, ships, weapons, or fortifications positioned in a place (*often used in the plural*) ○ *behind enemy lines* **20. MIL FIGHTING FORCE** the military or naval units of a country that actually go into battle **21. ELECTRON ENG NARROW BAND OF FREQUENCIES** a narrow band of frequencies in an electromagnetic spectrum **22. AMERICAN FOOTBALL AMERICAN FOOTBALL PLAYERS** either of the two rows of opposing players facing each other on either side of the line of scrimmage in American football **23. LIMIT** any limit or division ○ *a thin line between happiness and misery* **24. US ODDS** odds for wagering **25. SHAPE** the characteristic shape or contour of sth (*often used in the plural*) **26. DIRECTION** a path or direction of movement **27. APPROACH** a course or approach followed in doing sth ○ *must decide what line to take before the meeting* **28. POLICY** a policy, a way of thinking, or a version of sth ○ *What's the government line on this?* **29. SPECIALIZED FIELD** a particular area of interest, work, activity, or expertise **30. THEATRE ACTOR'S WORDS** the words spoken that make up an actor's part (*often used in the plural*) **31. USEFUL INFORMATION** useful information or an insight into sth **32. BRIEF MESSAGE** a short written message ○ *Why not drop me a line?* **33. GEOG EQUATOR** the equator (*dated*) **34. ROW** a row of people or things **35. US** = **queue 36. TV PART OF TELEVISION PICTURE** any of the horizontal scans that make up the picture on a television screen **37. DECEIVING TALK** sth said to deceive, impress, or attract sb (*informal*) ○ *gave me that old line about the dog eating his report card* **38. DRUGS AMOUNT OF A DRUG** a portion of a drug, such as cocaine, scraped into a long thin row to be inhaled (*slang*) **39. Ireland ROAD** a road, especially a new road **40. Scotland NOTE OF AUTHORIZATION** a note of authorization, especially a medical certificate issued by a doctor (*informal*) ■ **lines** *npl.* **1. CERTIFICATE** a certificate, especially a marriage certificate **2. SCHOOL PUNISHMENT** a phrase or sentence that a school pupil is made to write out a specified number of times as a punishment, or the material that is actually written out ■ *vt.* **(lines, lining, lined) 1.** MARK A LINE ON STH to mark sth with lines **2.** ARRANGE ALONG AN EDGE to arrange or be arranged along the edge or length of sth [Pre-12thC. Directly or via Old French *ligne* from Latin *linea* 'linen string, line', a form of *lineus* 'made of linen', from *linum* 'flax, linen'.] —**linable** *adj.* ◇ **all along the line** throughout or at every stage in sth ◇ **draw the line** to restrict or set limits at a particular point ◇ **hold the line 1.** to keep a telephone connection open while waiting to speak to sb **2.** MIL to resist a military attack without giving ground or allowing a formation to be broken ◇ **in line 1.** arranged in an orderly row **2.** in keeping with a policy or obedient to a set of rules ◇ **in line for** likely to receive sth such as a promotion or position ◇ **in line with** in agreement or conformity with sth ◇ **lay it on the line** to speak about sth frankly (*informal*) ◇ **lay** *or* **put sth on the line** to risk by some action the loss of sth valuable (*informal*) ◇ **off line** temporarily not connected in an electronic communications system ◇ **on line** connected in an electronic communications or other system ◇ **out of line 1.** *US* rude and disrespectful (*informal*) **2.** *US* unruly or out of control (*informal*) ◇ **read between the lines** to deduce sth that is not made explicit (*informal*) ◇ **toe the line** to comply with what is expected

line up *v.* **1.** *vti.* FORM A ROW to form a row or form people or things into a row **2.** *vi.* FORM A QUEUE to form a queue to wait for a turn **3.** *vt.* PROVIDE to organize, provide, or make sth available to sb ○ *had lined up a programme of entertainments for us* **4.** *vti.* ALIGN THINGS to align two or more things or be in alignment

line[2] /līn/ **(lines, lining, lined)** *vt.* **1.** REINFORCE to cover or reinforce the inside or unexposed surface of sth ○ *a jacket lined with silk* **2.** COVER to completely cover sth with sth else ○ *The walls were lined with books.* **3.** FILL to fill or supply sth with sth else ○ *a good hot meal to line your stomach* [14thC. From obsolete *line* 'spun or woven flax', from Old English *līn*, from or related to Latin *linum* 'flax' (source of LINE[1]); from the frequent use of linen to line garments.]

lineage[1] /línni ij/ *n.* **1.** LINE OF DESCENT the line of descent from an ancestor to a person or family **2.** RELATED GROUP OF PEOPLE a group of people related by descent from a common ancestor [14thC. From French *lignage*, from *ligne* 'line', (see LINE[1]).]

lineage[2] /línij/ *n.* = **linage**

lineal /línni əl/ *adj.* in or from a direct line from an ancestor —**lineally** *adv.*

lineament /línni əmənt/ *n.* **1.** FACIAL FEATURE a feature or contour of a face (*literary*) **2.** CHARACTERISTIC FEATURE a characteristic feature, especially of sth immaterial (*literary*) **3.** GEOL FEATURE OF LAND a major topographical feature, such as a long fault plane, that reveals sth about its subsurface [15thC. From Latin *lineamentum* 'line', from *lineare* 'to make straight', from *linea* 'line'.]

linear /línni ər/ *adj.* **1.** RELATING TO LINES relating to, consisting of, or using lines **2.** RELATING TO A STRAIGHT LINE relating to a straight line or capable of being represented by a straight line **3.** CHANGING PROPORTIONALLY changing proportionally and representable on a graph as a straight line (*refers to variables*) ○ *There's no linear relation between mortality and size.* **4.** ARTS WITH CLEARLY DEFINED LINES dominated by clearly defined lines rather than relying on the effects of colour **5.** MATH OF THE FIRST DEGREE about or in the first degree relative to a mathematical variable **6.** ELECTRON ENG WITH OUTPUT VARYING AS INPUT DOES with an output that varies directly with the input **7.** BOT LONG AND NARROW used to describe a leaf that is long and narrow —**linearity** /línni árrəti/ *n.* —**linearly** /-ərli/ *adv.*

Linear A /línni ər-/ *n.* an undeciphered writing system, dating from about 1500 BC and found on clay remains in Crete

linear accelerator *n.* a device that propels charged particles in straight paths by using alternating high-frequency voltages

linear algebra *n.* a branch of algebra dealing with linear transformations, vector spaces, matrices, and determinants

Linear B *n.* an early form of Greek that dates from about 1400 BC, found on clay remains in Crete and the Greek mainland, and deciphered about 1952

linear equation *n.* an equation with no variable raised to a power

linear function *n.* = **linear transformation**

linear induction motor *n.* = **linear motor**

linearize /línni ə rīz/ **(-izes, -izing, -ized)**, **linearise (-ises, -ising, -ised)** *vt.* to form or project sth into a line —**linearization** /línni ə rī záysh'n/ *n.*

linear measure *n.* any system or unit used to measure length

linear motor *n.* an electric motor in which the motion between the rotor and stator is linear so that thrust is produced along a straight line

linear perspective *n.* a form of perspective in which drawings or paintings are given apparent depth by showing parallel lines as converging on the horizon

linear programming *n.* MATH a method of finding the maximum and minimum values of a linear transformation using variables that are subject to constraints

linear transformation *n.* a mathematical transformation in which the resulting variables are neither multiplied together nor raised to any power

lineation /línni áysh'n/ *n.* **1.** ARRANGEMENT OF LINES division into or arrangement of lines **2.** OUTLINE the outline of an image

linebacker /lín bakər/ *n.* a player in American football who takes a position near and behind the defensive line —**linebacking** *n.*

line breeding *n.* the deliberate mating of closely related individuals in order to retain characteristics of a common ancestor

line cut *n.* a photoengraving made from a line drawing

line dancing *n.* a style of dancing to country-and-western music, in which dancers follow the same steps in rows rather than as couples —**line dance** *n., vi.* —**line dancer** *n.*

line drawing *n.* a drawing done entirely in lines, with tones shown by the thickness or closeness of the lines

line engraving *n.* an engraving in which lines are cut by hand into a metal plate from which the print is made

line item *n.* an item of important financial data presented on a separate line, such as in a ledger or an annual report

line judge *n.* = **linesman** *n.* 2

Lineker /línnəkər/, **Gary** (*b.* 1960) British footballer. Noted for his skill as a goal scorer, he was top scorer in the 1986 World Cup. Full name **Gary Winston Lineker**

lineman /línmən/ (*plural* **-men** /-mən/) *n.* **1.** *US* COMMUNICATION = **linesman** *n.* 3 **2.** AMERICAN FOOTBALL AMERICAN FOOTBALL PLAYER in American football, a player on the forward line, especially a center, guard, tackle, or tight end **3.** TRANSP SURVEYOR'S ASSISTANT sb who assists a surveyor by marking points or positions

line management *n.* the managers in a company that are involved in production or the central part of the business, as opposed to managers of service sectors

line manager *n.* a manager in a company who is involved in production or the central part of the business and to whom a nonmanagement-level employee is directly answerable

linen /línnin/ (*plural* **-en** *or* **-ens**) *n.* **1.** FABRIC MADE FROM FLAX a thread or durable fabric made from the spun fibres of flax **2.** THINGS MADE FROM LINEN clothes, table coverings, undergarments, or bedclothes made from linen or cotton (*often used in the plural*) [Old English *līnen* 'made of flax', from *līn* 'flax' (source of English *linseed*). Ultimately from an Indo-European word that is also the ancestor of English *line* and English *lingerie*.]

linen paper *n.* fine paper that is made from flax fibres, or given a finish to resemble linen

line of credit *n.* the amount of credit that a customer is allowed to draw on. US term **credit line**

line officer *n.* an officer who serves in combat

line of fire *n.* **1.** PATH OF FIRED PROJECTILE the path taken by a bullet or missile fired from a weapon **2.** EXPOSED POSITION a position exposed to a threat, attack, or criticism

line of force *n.* an imaginary curve whose tangent at any point is that of the electric or magnetic field that is operating there

line of sight *n.* **1.** LINE FROM EYE TO OBJECT an imaginary line from an observer to a distant object **2.** OPTICS = **line of vision 3.** TELECOM UNOBSTRUCTED TRANSMITTING PATH a straight path, unobstructed by the horizon, between a transmitting and receiving aerial

line-out *n.* a restart of play in Rugby Union. After the ball goes out of bounds it is thrown from the touchline for two lines of opposing forwards to jump and catch.

line printer *n.* a printing device that prints a line at a time rather than one character at a time

liner[1] /línər/ *n.* **1.** TRANSP PASSENGER SHIP OR PLANE a passenger ship or aeroplane run by a shipping line or airline **2.** COSMETICS = **eyeliner**

liner[2] /línər/ *n.* **1.** LINING sth used as a lining or padding **2.** ENG PROTECTIVE SLEEVE FOR COMPONENT a protective sleeve, usually made of metal, fitted inside or outside a cylindrical component

liner notes *npl.* *US* = **sleeve notes**

linesman /línzmən/ (*plural* **-men** /-mən/) *n.* **1.** SPORTS REFEREE'S ASSISTANT in football, tennis, and ice hockey, an official who assists the head official, referee, or umpire, e.g. by deciding whether or not the ball has gone out of play **2.** AMERICAN FOOTBALL AMERICAN FOOTBALL OFFICIAL an official in American football who watches for infringements, marks the downs, and places the ball in position **3.** COMMUNICATION SB MAINTAINING PHONE OR POWER LINES sb who installs or repairs telephone or power lines. US term **lineman** *n.* 1

line squall *n.* a strong storm advancing along a weather front

lineup /lín up/, **line-up** *n.* **1.** SPORTS LIST OF PLAYERS a list of players in a team together with the positions they play in **2.** TV TELEVISION SCHEDULE a programming schedule of a television network **3.** *US* CRIMINOL = **identification parade 4.** GROUP UNITED IN A PURPOSE a group of people or organizations recruited for a cause or common purpose such as raising funds for a charity

ling[1] /ling/ (*plural* **ling** *or* **lings**) *n.* an edible fish that is related to the cod and is found off the coasts of Greenland and northern Europe. Genus: *Molva.* [13thC. Origin uncertain.]

ling[2] /ling/ *n.* = **heather** *n.* 1 [Old English *lyng*, of unknown origin]

-ling[1] *suffix.* **1.** one connected with or resembling ○ *hatchling* **2.** small one ○ *princeling* ○ *spiderling* [Old English]

-ling[2] *suffix.* in a particular manner or condition ○ *darkling* [Old English]

Lingala /ling gaálə/ *n.* a language belonging to the Bantu group of Benue-Congo languages and used as a lingua franca in the Democratic Republic of Congo. More than 10 million speakers use Lingala as a second language. [Early 20thC. From Bantu.]

lingam /líng gəm/ *n.* **1.** PHALLIC SYMBOL a stylized phallus, used to represent the Hindu god Shiva **2.** PENIS a penis **3.** SANSKRIT MASCULINE GENDER the masculine gender in Sanskrit grammar [Early 18thC. From Sanskrit *liṅga* 'mark, phallus'.]

lingcod /líng kod/ (*plural* **-cod** *or* **-cods**) *n.* a spiny-finned large-mouthed fish that lives in the North Pacific Ocean and is caught for food and sport. Latin name: *Ophidion elongatus.* [Mid-20thC. From LING + COD.]

linger /líng gər/ **(-gers, -gering, -gered)** *vi.* **1.** DELAY LEAVING to put off leaving a place because you are reluctant to go **2.** WAIT AROUND to wait around or move about a place slowly and idly **3.** BE BARELY ALIVE to remain alive, although very weak, while gradually dying **4.** TAKE TIME TO DO STH to take longer than is usual to do sth, e.g. to complete a task or look at sb or sth, usually because you are enjoying yourself ○ *Her eyes lingered on the letter.* **5.** PERSIST to remain fixed in the mind or noticed by the senses for a long time [13thC. Literally 'to delay repeatedly', formed from Middle English *lengen* 'to delay', from, ultimately, Old Norse *lengja* 'to lengthen'.] —**lingerer** *n.*

lingerie /lánzhəri, lónzhəri, láNzhəri/ *n.* women's underwear and nightdresses [Early 19thC. From French, literally 'things made of linen', from *linge* 'linen', from Latin *lineus* 'made of flax'.]

lingering /líng gəring/ *adj.* **1.** DRAWN-OUT long and drawn-out, especially with pain **2.** SLOW done slowly in order to prolong sth as long as possible **3.** PERSISTING IN THE MIND remaining for some time in the thoughts or mind —**lingeringly** *adv.*

lingo /líng gō/ (*plural* **-goes**) *n.* a language that is not the speaker's native language or a specialized set of terms requiring to be learned (*informal*) [Mid-17thC. Origin uncertain: perhaps an alteration of *lingua* in LINGUA FRANCA; or via Portuguese *lingoa* or Provençal *lingo* from, ultimately, Latin *lingua* 'tongue'.]

lingua /líng gwə/ (*plural* **-guae** /-gwee/) *n.* the tongue or a part resembling one [Late 17thC. From Latin, 'tongue'.]

lingua franca /-frángkə/ (*plural* **lingua francas** or **linguae francae** /-kee/) *n.* **1.** LANGUAGE USED FOR CONVENIENCE a language or mixture of languages used for communication by people who speak different first languages **2.** TRADERS' LANGUAGE IN MEDITERRANEAN the mixed language used chiefly by merchants throughout the Mediterranean ports until the 18th century, consisting mainly of Italian with elements of French, Spanish, Greek, Arabic, and Turkish [Late 17thC. From Italian, literally 'Frankish tongue'.]

lingual /líng gwəl/ *adj.* relating to, using, or similar to the tongue [Mid-17thC. From medieval Latin *lingualis*, from Latin *lingua* 'tongue, language'.] —**lingually** *adv.*

linguine /ling gwéeni, **linguini** *n.* a type of pasta consisting of long narrow flat strips [Mid-20thC. From Italian *linguine*, plural of *linguina*, literally 'little tongue', from *lingua* 'tongue', from Latin.]

linguist /líng gwist/ *n.* **1.** SPEAKER OF SEVERAL LANGUAGES sb who speaks several languages or finds it easy to learn languages **2.** STUDENT OF LINGUISTICS sb who studies linguistics [Late 16thC. Formed from Latin *lingua* 'tongue, language'.]

linguistic /ling gwístik/ *adj.* **1.** OF LANGUAGE relating to language or languages **2.** OF LINGUISTICS relating to linguistics —**linguistically** *adv.*

linguistic atlas *n.* a collection of maps showing the distribution of varying language features in a region

linguistic form *n.* an identifiable unit of speech such as a word, prefix, phrase, or sentence

linguistic geography *n.* the study of regional variation in speech —**linguistic geographer** *n.*

linguistic philosophy *n.* a form of philosophy prevalent during the 20th century, asserting that the function of philosophy is to clarify philosophical expressions by analysing and explaining them

linguistics /ling gwístiks/ *n.* the systematic study of language (*takes a singular verb*)

lingulate /líng gyŏŏlət, -layt/, **lingulated** /-layted/ *adj.* shaped like a tongue [Mid-19thC. From Latin *lingulatus*, from *lingula*, literally 'little tongue', from *lingua* 'tongue'.]

liniment /línnəmənt/ *n.* a liquid such as one containing alcohol and camphor, rubbed into the skin to relieve aches or pain [15thC. From late Latin *linimentum*, from Latin *linire* 'to smear'.]

linin /línin/ *n.* a connective material in a cell nucleus [Mid-19thC. Coined from Greek *linon* 'thread' + -IN.]

lining /líning/ *n.* a layer or a material used to cover, protect, or insulate the inner or unexposed surface of sth [14thC. Formed from LINE².]

link¹ /lingk/ *n.* **1.** PART OF A CHAIN any of the connected rings or loops that make up a chain, or sth resembling a loop in a chain **2.** CONNECTION sth that ties, connects, or relates two or more things **3.** TRANSP ROUTE any part of a transport system, especially a connection between major routes **4.** COMMUNICATION

UNIT FOR COMMUNICATING BROADCASTS a broadcasting unit or system used to relay radio or television signals, e.g. a transmitter, receiver, or relay station **5.** MEASURE SURVEYOR'S UNIT OF LENGTH a unit of length used in surveying equal to 20.12 cm/7.92 in, and one hundredth of a chain ▪ *vti.* (**links, linking, linked**) CONNECT to connect, join, or associate sb or sth with another or to become joined with another [14thC. From Old Norse *hlekkr* 'link', from a prehistoric Germanic word meaning 'bending'.] —**linker** *n.*

link up (**links up, linking up, linked up**) *v.* **1.** *vti.* CONNECT THINGS OR PEOPLE to join, connect, or unite sb or sth with another or to become joined with another **2.** *vi.* JOIN to meet and join with sb or sth else

link² /lingk/ *n.* a burning torch used in the past to give light [Mid-16thC. Origin uncertain: perhaps from medieval Latin *linchinus* 'candle', alteration of Latin *lichinus* 'wick', from Greek *lukhnos* 'light'.]

linkage /língkij/ *n.* **1.** LINK a link or connection or the fact of being connected **2.** DIPLOMATIC PROCEDURE a procedure in diplomacy that requires progress towards an overall objective to depend on concessions made by the various parties on other related issues **3.** TECH SYSTEM OF INTERCONNECTED PARTS a system of interconnected rods, springs, or levers that transmit motion in a mechanism **4.** GENETICS ASSOCIATED GENES the proximity of two or more genes on a chromosome, which tends to cause them to be inherited together

linkage group *n.* two or more genes on a chromosome that tend to be inherited together as a group

Linklater /língklətər/, **Eric Robert Russell** (1899–1974) British writer, journalist, and broadcaster. He wrote novels, plays, books for children, histories, and memoirs, which include *Fanfare for a Tin Hat* (1970).

linkman /língk man, -mən/ (*plural* **-men** /-men/) *n.* = anchorman *n.* 2

Linköping /líng chúrping/ industrial city and capital of Östergötland County, southeastern Sweden. Population: 131,370 (1995).

links /lingks/ *n.* (*takes a singular or plural verb*) **1.** GOLF COURSE a golf course, especially one near the sea **2.** *Scotland* UNDULATING SANDY AREA an area of gently undulating sandy ground near a seashore [Old English *hlincas*, plural of *hlinc* 'ridge', of uncertain origin: possibly formed from *hlinian* 'to lean']

linkup /língk up/ *n.* a connection or association between two or more things or people

Linlithgow /lin líthgō/ town in West Lothian, eastern Scotland. Population: 12,453 (1994).

linn /lin/ *n.* a waterfall or a pool at the foot of a waterfall (*regional*) [Old English *hlynn* 'torrent', of uncertain origin]

Linnaean /li náy ən, -née-/ *adj.* relating to the system devised by Linnaeus for classifying plants and animals under two names, one referring to the genus and one to the species [Mid-18thC. From Carolus LINNAEUS, who devised the system.]

Linnaeus /li née əss/, **Carolus** (1707–78) Swedish naturalist. A pioneer of taxonomy, he devised the standard system of binomial nomenclature for plants and animals. Real name **Carl von Linné**

linnet /línnit/ (*plural* **-nets** or **-net**) *n.* a small brownish songbird of the finch family that lives in Europe, Africa, and Asia. The male has a red breast and forehead. Latin name: *Carduelis cannabina.* [Early 16thC. From Old French *linette*, from *lin* 'flax', from Latin *linum*; from the bird's diet of flaxseed.]

Linnhe, Loch /línni-/ inlet of the sea in western Scotland, at the southern end of the Great Glen. Length: 50 km/31 mi.

lino /líno/ *n.* linoleum (*informal*) [Early 20thC. Shortening.]

linocut /líno kut/ *n.* a print made from a design that has been cut in relief into a piece of linoleum and mounted on a block of wood, or the design itself

linoleate /li nóli ayt/ *n.* any salt or ester of linoleic acid [Mid-19thC. Coined from *linoleic* (see LINOLEIC ACID) + -ATE.]

linoleic acid /línnō lée ik-/ *n.* a colourless liquid, essential to human nutrition, found in linseed and other natural oils and used in making soaps, emulsifiers, and quick-drying oils. Formula: $C_{18}H_{32}O_2$. [*Linoleic* coined from Latin *linum* 'flax' + OLEIC]

linolenic acid /línnō lée′enik-/ *n.* a colourless liquid found in linseed and other natural oils, essential to human nutrition, and used in making paints and synthetic resins. Formula: $C_{18}H_{30}O_2$. [Translation of German *Linolensäure*, coined from *Linolsäure* 'linoleic acid', with insertion of *-en*, equivalent to -ENE]

linoleum /li nóli əm/ *n.* a tough washable floor covering, made from canvas or other material coated under heat and pressure with powdered cork, rosin, and linseed oil [Late 19thC. Originally a trademark, from Latin *linum* 'flax' + *oleum* 'oil'.]

linsang /lín sang/ (*plural* **-sangs** or **-sang**) *n.* **1.** ASIAN ANIMAL LIKE A GENET a carnivorous mammal related to and resembling the civet and genet that lives in forests in southern Asia and has spotted or banded fur and a long tail. Genus: *Prionodon.* **2.** AFRICAN ANIMAL an animal similar to the Asian linsang that lives in forests in West Africa. Genus: *Poiana.* [Early 19thC. From Javanese *lingsang*.]

linseed /lín seed/ *n.* = flaxseed [Old English *līnsæd*, from *līn* 'flax' (see LINEN) + *sæd*, an earlier form of SEED]

linseed oil *n.* oil pressed from flaxseed, used in making linoleum and in paints and inks to help them dry more quickly

linsey-woolsey /línzi wŏŏlzi/ *n.* a coarse cloth made from linen interwoven with wool or cotton [15thC. Origin uncertain: possibly from *lyn*, from Old English *līn* 'flax' (see LINSEED) + *wolle*, an earlier form of WOOL, with *-sey* for a rhyme.]

linstock /lín stok/ *n.* a long staff with a forked end designed to hold a lighted match, used in the past to fire cannons [Mid-16thC. From Dutch *lontstok*, from *lont* 'match' (altered perhaps by association with *lint*) + *stok* 'stick'.]

lint /lint/ *n.* **1.** MATERIAL FOR COVERING WOUNDS a soft absorbent material made from cotton or linen, used to dress wounds **2.** THREAD OR FLUFF little pieces of thread or fluff **3.** COTTON FIBRES the fibres that surround unprocessed cotton seeds [14thC. Origin uncertain: perhaps from Old French *linette*, literally 'small flax', from *lin* 'flax', from Latin *linum* (see LINE¹).] —**linty** *adj.*

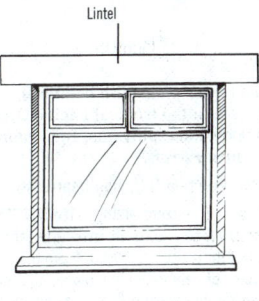

Lintel

lintel /línt′l/ *n.* a horizontal beam that supports the weight of the wall above a window or door [14thC. From Old French, from Latin *limitaris* 'relating to a boundary', from the stem *limit-* 'boundary' (confused with popular Latin *liminaris* 'of a threshold').]

lintie /línti/ *n. Scotland* a linnet [Late 18thC. From Scots *lintwhite* 'linnet', from Old English, from *līn* 'flax' (see LINEN) + *-twige* 'plucker'.]

linum /línəm/ (*plural* **-num** or **-nums**) *n.* any plant of a family that includes flax, especially cultivated varieties grown for their yellow, purple, red, or blue funnel-shaped flowers. Genus: *Linum.* [Mid-19thC. From modern Latin, genus name, from Latin *linum* 'flax'.]

Linz /lints/ capital of Upper Austria Province, northern Austria. Population: 203,044 (1991).

Lion

lion /líf ən/ *n.* **1.** ZOOL BIG WILD PREDATORY CAT a large wild member of the cat family that lives in Africa and India in extended family groups and hunts co-operatively for prey. It has a tawny yellow coat and the males have a shaggy mane. Latin name: *Panthera leo.* **2.** HERALDIC SYMBOL the lion used as a symbol in heraldry, varieties of which are national emblems of Great Britain and of Scotland **3.** SB BRAVE AND STRONG sb who is very brave, strong, or fierce **4.** CELEBRITY sb who is admired and celebrated [13thC. Via Anglo-Norman *liun* and the Latin stem *leon-* from Greek *leōn*, of uncertain origin: probably from a Semitic language.]

Lion *n.* **1.** ASTRON, ZODIAC = **Leo 2.** CHARITY CLUB MEMBER a member of a Lions Club

Lion, Gulf of /líf ən/ gulf in the Mediterranean Sea. It extends eastwards from the border between Spain and France to the French islands, Îles d'Hyères.

lion dance *n.* a traditional Chinese ritual performed to bring good luck, especially at Chinese New Year, in which two men dance costumed in a large ornamental artificial lion head and body

lioness /líf ə ness/ *n.* a female lion

Lionfish

lionfish /líf ən fish/ (*plural* **-fish** *or* **-fishes**) *n.* a scorpion fish that lives in the tropical Pacific Ocean and has a striped body, long spiny fins, and venomous dorsal spines. Genus: *Pterois.*

lionhearted /líf ən haártid/, **lion-hearted** *adj.* very brave

lionize /líf ə nīz/ (**-izes, -izing, -ized**), **lionise** (**-ises, -ising, -ised**) *vt.* to make sb into a celebrity or treat sb like a celebrity [Early 19thC. From the notion of a lion as sth unusual or celebrated in a place, and therefore worth going to see.] —**lionization** /líf ə nī záysh'n/ *n.* —**lionizer** /líf ə nīzər/ *n.*

Lion Rampant *n.* a heraldic image of a red lion standing up on its hind legs, one of the national emblems of Scotland

Lions Club *n.* any club belonging to the International Association of Lions Clubs, an organization founded in the United States in 1917 to promote fellowship and service in local communities

lion's share *n.* the largest part or share of sth [Late 18thC. From Aesop's story in which a lion joins a hunt with other animals and by means of spurious reasoning and intimidation gets the whole kill for himself.]

lip /lip/ *n.* **1.** ANAT PART OF MOUTH either of two fleshy folds around the mouth that help control eating, drinking, and the production of sounds by the mouth **2.** STH LIKE A LIP sth like a lip, especially an edge or rim of sth hollow **3.** LANGUAGE IMPERTINENCE impudent or disrespectful talk (*slang*) **4.** ANAT PART OF

VULVA any of the two sets of folds of skin (**labia**) at the opening of the vulva ■ *vt.* (**lips, lipping, lipped**) **1.** TOUCH WITH LIPS to touch sth with the lips **2.** FORM LIP OF to form or be a lip of sth [Old English *lippa.* Ultimately from an Indo-European word meaning 'lip' that is also the ancestor of English *labial.*] ◇ **bite your lip 1.** to stop yourself from saying sth you feel moved to say (*informal*) **2.** to show that you are angry (*informal*) ◇ **button your lip** to stop speaking, not begin speaking, or to keep a secret (*slang*) ◇ **stiff upper lip** a brave and composed bearing, with no giving way to emotion (*informal*)

lipaemia /li peémi ə/ *n.* the presence of excessive fat in the blood

Lipari Islands /líppəri-/ group of volcanic islands off the northern coast of Sicily in the Tyrrhenian Sea. Area: 44 sq. km/114 sq. mi.

lipase /lí payss, líppayss, lí payz, líppayz/ *n.* an enzyme produced by the liver, pancreas, or stomach, or by plant seeds, that breaks down fats

lip balm *n.* US = **lip salve**

lipectomy /li péktəmi, lī-/ (*plural* **-mies**) *n.* the surgical removal of fatty tissue from beneath the skin

Li Peng /lí peng/ (b. 1928) Chinese statesman. Having become prime minister in 1987, he crushed the prodemocracy movement that had occupied Tiananmen Square (1989).

lip gloss *n.* a cosmetic used on the lips to make them look shiny

lipid /líppid/, **lipide** *n.* any of a group of organic compounds consisting of fats, oils, and related substances that, along with proteins and carbohydrates, are the structural components of living cells. In addition to fats the group includes waxes, oils, sterols, triglycerides, phosphatides, and phospholipids. [Early 20thC. From French *lipide*, which was coined from Greek *lipos* 'fat' (see LIPO-) + French *-ide*, equivalent to -ID.] —**lipidic** /li píddik/ *adj.*

Lipizzaner /líppit sáanər/, **Lippizaner** *n.* a compact, usually white or grey horse, belonging to a breed often used in equestrian displays [Early 20thC. From German, literally 'of Lipizza', named after *Lipizza*, a place near Trieste in Italy where the stud producing these horses was located.]

lip liner *n.* a cosmetic, usually in soft pencil form, used to outline the lips before lipstick is applied

lip microphone *n.* a microphone designed to be held close to the user's mouth so that too much background noise is not picked up

lipo- *prefix.* fat, fatty tissue ○ *lipolysis* [From Greek *lipos* 'fat'. Ultimately from an Indo-European base meaning 'to stick' that is also the ancestor of English *live*[1] and *liver*[1].]

lipogenesis /líppō jénnəsiss, lípō-/ *n.* the formation of fatty acids in the body

lipoic acid /li pố ik-/ *n.* a fatty acid that contains sulphur, metabolizes carbohydrates in the body, and, as part of the vitamin B complex, contributes to growth

lipoid /lípp oyd, lí poyd/ *adj.* FATTY containing or resembling fat ■ *n.* SUBSTANCE LIKE FAT a substance such as wax that is similar to fat —**lipoidal** *adj.*

lipolysis /li pólləsiss, lī-/ *n.* the breakdown of fats into other compounds —**lipolytic** /líppō líttik, lípō-/ *adj.*

lipoma /li pốmə, lī-/ (*plural* **-mas** *or* **-mata** /-mətə/) *n.* a benign tumour made up of fatty tissue —**lipomatous** /li pómmətəss, lī-, lī pốmətəss, lī-/ *adj.*

lipophilic /líppō fíllik, lípō-/ *adj.* with a chemical affinity for lipids

lipopolysaccharide /líppō pólli sákə rīd, lípō-/ *n.* a carbohydrate consisting of a sugar chemically linked to a lipid

lipoprotein /líppō prố teen, lípō-/ *n.* a protein that contains a lipid molecule and carries lipids in the bloodstream

liposome /líppō sốm, lípō-/ *n.* a tiny artificial sac formed from one or more layers of lipid, used medicinally to carry a drug, vaccine, or enzyme to targeted cells in the body

liposuction /líppō suksh'n, lípō-/ *n.* cosmetic surgery in which fat is removed from under the skin by vacuum suction

lipotropic /líppō trốpik, lípō-, -tróppik/ *adj.* preventing or reducing the accumulation of fat in the liver

lipotropin /líppō trốpin, lípō-/ *n.* either of two hormones produced in the pituitary gland that play a part in using up fat reserves in the body and are a source of endorphins

-lipped *suffix.* having a particular kind of lip or lips

lippie *n.* = **lippy**

Lippizaner *n.* = **Lipizzaner**

lippy /líppi/ *adj.* (**-pier, -piest**) IMPUDENT tending to say impudent things (*informal*) ■ *n.* **lippy, lippie** LIPSTICK lipstick (*informal*)

lip-read (**lip-reads, lip-reading, lip-read** /-red/) *vti.* to understand what is said by watching how sb's lips move rather than by listening —**lip-reader** *n.*

lip-reading *n.* understanding spoken words by watching lip movements, rather than by listening

lip salve *n.* an ointment used on the lips, often in stick form, especially to relieve chapping or dryness. US term **lip balm**

Lipscomb /lípskəm/, **William Nunn, Jr.** (b. 1919) US chemist. He conducted pioneering research on the molecular structure and chemical bonding of boron compounds.

lip service *n.* support or agreement that does not appear to be sincere because the words spoken are not followed up by appropriate action or behaviour

lipstick /líp stik/ *n.* an oily cosmetic in stick form, in a plastic or metal tube, used to colour the lips

lip-synch /-singk/ (**lip-synchs, lip-synching, lip-synched**), **lip-sync** (**lip-syncs, lip-syncing, lip-synced**) *vti.* to pretend to sing or speak by moving lips in synchronization with a recorded song or speech, or to perform a song or speech in this way

lipuria /li pyoóri ə/ *n.* the abnormal presence of fat in the urine [Late 19thC. From modern Latin, from Greek *lipos* 'fat' + *ouron* 'urine'.]

liq. *abbr.* **1.** liquid **2.** liquor

liquate /li kwáyt/ (**-quates, -quating, -quated**) *vt.* to heat an alloy or ore to a temperature high enough to separate the constituents with the lowest melting point from the rest [Mid-17thC. From Latin *liquat-*, past participle stem of *liquare* 'to liquefy'.] —**liquation** /li kwáysh'n/ *n.*

liquefacient /líkwi fáysh'nt/ *n.* STH THAT TURNS STH TO LIQUID sth that liquifies or helps to liquify sth else ■ *adj.* TURNING STH TO LIQUID capable of liquifying or helping to liquify sth [Mid-19thC. From Latin *liquefacient-*, present participle stem of *liquefacere* (see LIQUEFY).]

liquefaction /líkwi fáksh'n/ *n.* the process of liquifying sth or the state of having been liquified [14thC. From the late Latin stem *liquefaction-*, from Latin *liquefacere* (see LIQUEFY).]

liquefied natural gas *n.* a gas refined as a byproduct of petroleum or natural gas, liquefied under pressure, and used as a fuel for heating, cooking, and transportation

liquefied petroleum gas *n.* a mixture of petroleum gases liquefied under pressure and mainly used as heating or engine fuel

liquefy /líkwi fī/ (**-fies, -fying, -fied**) *vti.* to become or cause sth to become liquid [14thC. Via French *liquéfier* from Latin *liquefacere*, from *lique-*, stem of *liquere* 'to be liquid' (source of English *liquid* and *liquor*) + *facere* 'to make, render'.] —**liquefiable** *adj.* —**liquefier** *n.*

liquescent /li kwéss'nt/ *adj.* becoming or tending to become liquid [Early 18thC. From Latin *liquescent-*, present-participle stem of *liquescere* 'to become liquid', from *liquere* 'to be liquid'.] —**liquescence** *n.* —**liquescency** *n.*

liqueur /li kyoór/ *n.* a sweet flavoured alcoholic drink usually considered an after-meal beverage [Mid-18thC. Via French from Latin *liquor* 'fluid'.]

liquid /líkwid/ *n.* **1.** SCI FLOWING SUBSTANCE a substance in a condition in which it flows, that is a fluid at room temperature and atmospheric pressure, and whose shape but not volume can be changed **2.** LING FRIC-

TIONLESS CONSONANT a consonant that is pronounced without friction and is capable of being prolonged like a vowel. In modern English, 'l' and 'r' are liquids. ■ *adj.* 1. CONSISTING OF A LIQUID relating to, characteristic of, or consisting of a liquid or liquids 2. SMOOTH AND FLUENT moving or produced in a smooth and fluent way 3. FIN CONVERTIBLE TO CASH easily converted into cash 4. CLEAR clear and shining 5. LING ARTICULATED WITHOUT FRICTION used to describe a consonant that is articulated without friction and capable of being prolonged like a vowel [14thC. Via Old French *liquide* from Latin *liquidus* 'fluid', from *liquere* 'to be fluid'.] —**liquidly** *adv.* —**liquidness** *n.*

liquid air *n.* a pale blue mixture of gases, mainly oxygen and nitrogen, that has been cooled and liquefied to be used in manufacturing pure gases and as a refrigerant

liquidambar /líkwid ámbər/ (*plural* **-bars** *or* **-bar**) *n.* a tree of North and Central America and Asia that exudes a yellowish aromatic balsam. Genus: *Liquidambar.* [Late 16thC. From modern Latin, genus name, irregularly formed from Latin *liquidus* (see LIQUID) + medieval Latin *ambar* 'amber'.]

liquidate /líkwi dayt/ (**-dates, -dating, -dated**) *v.* 1. *vti.* FIN PAY DEBT to pay a debt or other financial obligation 2. *vti.* COMM WIND UP A BUSINESS to wind up a business, paying off its liabilities from its assets, or to cease trading as a business in this way 3. *vt.* FIN CASH ASSETS to turn assets into cash 4. *vt.* KILL to kill or dispose of sb [Mid-16thC. From late Latin *liquidat-*, past participle stem of *liquidare* 'to melt, make clear', ultimately from Latin *liquere* 'to be liquid or clear'.] —**liquidation** /líkwi dáysh'n/ *n.*

liquidator /líkwi daytər/ *n.* sb appointed to oversee the liquidation of a business

liquid crystal *n.* a liquid that changes between being clear and cloudy depending on variations in temperature or applied voltage and is used in some types of display unit

liquid-crystal display *n.* a display of numbers or letters in a calculator, watch, or other electronic device, created by applying electricity to cells made of liquid crystal to make some of them look darker

liquid glass *n.* = **water glass** *n.* 2

liquidise *vti.* = **liquidize**

liquidiser *n.* = **liquidizer**

liquidity /li kwíddəti/ *n.* 1. STATE OF BEING LIQUID the state or quality of being liquid 2. FIN ASSETS CONVERTING EASILY TO CASH assets that can easily be converted into cash

liquidize /líkwi dīz/ (**-izes, -izing, -ized**), **liquidise** (**-uidises, -uidising, -uidised**) *v.* 1. *vti.* TURN TO LIQUID to become liquid or cause sth to become liquid 2. *vt.* TURN TO LIQUID IN LIQUIDIZER to make sth solid into a liquid using a liquidizer

liquidizer /líkwi dīzər/, **liquidiser** *n.* = **blender** *n.* 1

liquid measure *n.* any unit or system of units for measuring liquid volume or capacity

liquid paraffin *n.* a clear oil distilled from petroleum and used as a laxative and skin softener. US term **mineral oil**

liquor /líkər/ *n.* 1. BEVERAGES ALCOHOLIC BEVERAGE an alcoholic drink, especially of the type produced by distillation, e.g. whisky, rather than of the type produced by fermentation, e.g. wine or beer 2. COOK COOKING LIQUID a reduced liquid or juice left after cooking food, used as a sauce or as a basis for sauces 3. PHARM SOLUTION OF DRUG a concentrated solution of a drug in a liquid, usually water 4. BEVERAGES, FOOD TECH WATER IN WHICH MALT IS STEEPED warm water added to malt in order to produce wort in the brewing process ■ *vti.* (**-uors, -uoring, -uored**) BEVERAGES, FOOD TECH STEEP MALT IN WATER to steep malt in warm water in order to form wort in the brewing of beer [13thC. Via Old French from Latin.]

liquored up *adj. US* drunk (*informal*)

liquorice /líkərish, -iss/ (*plural* **-rice**) *n.* 1. PLANTS PLANT WITH A SWEET ROOT a perennial plant growing near the Mediterranean that has spiked blue feathery leaves and a root with a sweet flavour. Latin name: *Glycyrrhiza glabra.* 2. FOOD KIND OF SWEET a dense rubbery sweet that is usually made in black or red strips and flavoured with the root of the liquorice plant 3. ROOT OF THE LIQUORICE PLANT the dried black root of the liquorice plant or an extract made from it, used as a laxative and in confectionery and brewing [12thC. Via Anglo-Norman *lycorys* from, ultimately, Greek *glukurrhiza*, from *glukus* 'sweet' + *rhiza* 'root' (source of English *rhizome*).]

liquorish *adj.* = **lickerish**

liquor store *n. US* a store that sells alcoholic beverages for consumption off the premises

lira /léərə/ (*plural* **-re** /léerə, -r ay/) *n.* 1. ITALIAN UNIT OF CURRENCY the standard unit of currency of Italy, worth 100 centesimi. See table at **currency** 2. TURKISH UNIT OF CURRENCY the standard unit of currency of Turkey, worth 100 kurus 3. COIN WORTH ONE LIRA a coin worth one lira [Early 17thC. Via Italian from, ultimately, Latin *libra*, a measure of weight.]

Lisbon /lízbən/ capital and largest city of Portugal. Population: 681,063 (1991).

Lisburn /líz burn/ town near Belfast in eastern Northern Ireland. Population: 42,110 (1991).

lisle /līl/ *n.* a strong smooth fine cotton thread or fabric used for making gloves and stockings [Mid-16thC. Named after the town of *Lisle* (Lille) in northern France, where it was originally made.]

Lismore /lísmawr/ city in northeastern New South Wales, Australia, that is a dairy farming and educational centre. Population: 28,380 (1996).

lisp /lisp/ *n.* 1. SPEECH DEFECT a minor speech defect in which the sounds 's' and 'z' are pronounced like the soft 'th' sound in 'third' or 'thick'. Small children whose front teeth have not come through yet often have a temporary lisp. 2. SPEECH SOUND the sound produced when 's' and 'z' are pronounced like the soft 'th' sound in 'third' or 'thick' ■ *vti.* (**lisps, lisping, lisped**) 1. PRONOUNCE 'S' LIKE 'TH' to pronounce sth or speak so that 's' and 'z' are pronounced like the soft 'th' sound in 'third' or 'thick' 2. SPEAK LIKE A CHILD to speak in a childish or halting way [Old English *wlyspian*, of prehistoric Germanic origin; ultimately an imitation of the sound] —**lisper** *n.* —**lisping** *adj., n.* —**lispingly** *adv.*

LISP /lisp/ *n.* a high-level computer programming language, widely used in artificial intelligence research, that converts data into lists [Mid-20thC. Contraction of *List Processing (language)*.]

lissom /líssəm/, **lissome** *adj.* 1. GRACEFULLY FLEXIBLE slender and able to bend easily and gracefully 2. QUICK AND GRACEFUL IN MOVING quick, light, and graceful in movement [Late 18thC. Alteration of LITHESOME.] —**lissomly** *adv.* —**lissomness** *n.*

list[1] /list/ *n.* 1. ORDERED SERIES a series of related words, names, numbers, or other items that are arranged in order, one after the other ○ *a list of people to call* 2. COMPUT SET OF DATA an ordered set of data ■ *v.* (**lists, listing, listed**) 1. *vt.* ARRANGE ITEMS AS ORDERED SERIES to arrange a series of related words, names, numbers, or other items one after the other ○ *She listed the things she intended to get done that afternoon.* 2. *vt.* INCLUDE IN ORDERED SERIES to include sb or sth in a series of words, numbers, or other items arranged one after the other ○ *He's listed among the founding members in the club brochure.* 3. *vt.* CATEGORIZE SB to place sb in a category or classification ○ *She lists herself as a club member but never attends meetings.* 4. *vt.* STOCK EXCH ADMIT SECURITY TO EXCHANGE to admit a security for trading on an exchange 5. *vt.* BUILDING OFFICIALLY PROTECT BUILDING to state officially that a building is one of a specified group that cannot be demolished or altered without government permission because they are of special architectural or historical importance 6. *vti.* ENLIST to enlist or enlist sb (*archaic*) [Late 16thC. From French *liste*, ultimately of prehistoric Germanic origin.]

list[2] /list/ *n.* 1. ARCHIT = **fillet** *n.* 3 2. AGRIC FURROWS FORMING RIDGE a ridge of earth formed by two furrows ploughed side by side 3. TRIMMED STRIP OF WOOD a narrow strip of wood, especially sapwood, trimmed from a board or plank (*archaic*) 4. STRIP OF MATERIAL a band or strip of cloth or other material, especially one forming a border (*archaic*) 5. TEXTILES SELVAGE a selvage (*archaic*) ■ **lists** *npl.* HIST, MIL FENCED AREA IN TOURNAMENT an area of combat in a medieval tournament enclosed by a fence of high stakes ■ *vt.* (**lists, listing, listed**) 1. COVER STH WITH STRIP OF MATERIAL to cover or border sth with a band or strip of cloth or other material 2. CUT STRIP OF WOOD to cut a narrow strip of wood, especially sapwood, from a board or plank (*archaic*) 3. AGRIC FORM RIDGE FROM FURROWS to plough together two furrows of earth to form a ridge [Old English *līste*. From a prehistoric Germanic word meaning 'band, strip' that is also the ancestor of English *list*[1].] ◇ **enter the lists** to begin to take part in a fight or argument

list[3] /list/ *vti.* (**lists, listing, listed**) LEAN TO ONE SIDE to lean or make a ship lean to one side ■ *n.* SIDEWAYS TILT an inclination to one side, especially one developed by a ship [Mid-17thC. Origin unknown.]

list[4] /list/ *vt.* (**lists, listing, listed**) (*archaic*) 1. WISH STH to choose, wish, or like sth 2. PLEASE SB to give pleasure to sb ■ *n.* DESIRE a choice, wish, or liking (*archaic*) [Old English *lystan*. Ultimately from an Indo-European base meaning 'to be eager' that is also the ancestor of English *lust* and *lascivious*.]

list[5] /list/ (**lists, listing, listed**) *vti.* to listen (*archaic*) [Old English *hlystan*]

listed /lístid/ *adj.* 1. INCLUDED IN LIST included in a list, catalogue, or directory ○ *a listed phone number* 2. BUILDING OFFICIALLY PROTECTED placed on an official list of buildings that cannot be demolished or altered without government permission because they are of special architectural or historical importance 3. STOCK EXCH TRADABLE ON EXCHANGE placed on a list of securities that may be traded on an exchange [Formed from LIST[1]]

listed building *n.* a building on an official list of structures that cannot be demolished or altered without government permission because they are of special architectural or historical importance

listed company *n.* a business whose securities may be traded on an exchange

listed security *n.* a security that may be traded on an exchange

listel /líst'l/ *n.* ARCHIT = **fillet** *n.* 3 [Late 16thC. From Italian *listello*, literally 'small border', from *lista* 'border'; ultimately of the same prehistoric Germanic origin as English *list*[3].]

listen /líss'n/ *vi.* (**-tens, -tening, -tened**) 1. MAKE CONSCIOUS EFFORT TO HEAR to concentrate on hearing sb or sth ○ *We listened for the sound of the geese overhead.* 2. PAY ATTENTION to pay attention to sth and take it into account ○ *She wouldn't listen to my advice.* ■ *n.* ACT OF HEARING an act of making an effort to hear sth (*informal*) ○ *Why not give their new CD a listen?* [Old English *hlysnan* (influenced by LIST[5]). Ultimately from an Indo-European word meaning 'to hear' that is also the ancestor of English *list*[5] and *loud*.]

listen in *vi.* 1. EAVESDROP to listen to other people, sometimes without their knowing it 2. LISTEN TO RADIO to listen to a radio broadcast 3. MONITOR TELECOMMUNICATIONS to monitor radio or telephone communications

listen up *vi.* to pay attention or listen carefully (*informal*)

listenable /líss'nəb'l/ *adj.* pleasant to listen to or suitable for listening to —**listenability** /líss'nə bílləti/ *n.*

listener /líss'nər/ *n.* sb who listens, especially sb who tunes in to a radio broadcast

listenership /líss'nər ship/ *n.* the number or kind of people who listen to a radio broadcast, programme, or station (*takes a singular or plural verb*)

listening post *n.* 1. FORWARD POSITION an advanced position near enemy lines from which troops can detect the enemy's movements 2. MONITORING PLACE a post or area where information or intelligence is gathered

lister /lístər/ *n. US, Can* a plough that heaps earth on both sides of a furrow [Late 17thC. Formed from LIST[2].]

Lister /lístər/, **Joseph, 1st Baron** (1827–1912) British surgeon. His discoveries in antisepsis, which led to the use of carbolic acid during operations, greatly reduced surgical mortality.

listeria /li stéeri ə/ *n.* a rod-shaped aerobic parasitic bacterium that causes disease, especially listeriosis. Genus: *Listeria.* [Mid-20thC. From modern Latin, genus name, formed from the name of Joseph LISTER.]

listeriosis /li stéeri óssiss/ *n.* a disease of the nervous system of mammals, birds, and occasionally

humans that can cause fever, meningitis, miscarriage, or premature birth and is spread by eating food contaminated with listeria [Mid-20thC]

listing /lísting/ *n.* **1. STH ENTERED IN LIST** an entry in a list, catalogue, or directory **2. LIST** a list, catalogue, or directory **3.** COMPUT **PRINTOUT** a printout of a computer file or program **4.** STOCK EXCH **PLACE ON OFFICIAL LIST OF SECURITIES** a place on an official list of securities that can be traded on an exchange ■ **listings** *npl.* ARTS, COMMUNICATION **LISTS OF EVENTS** published lists of films, plays, or other cultural events, containing information such as times, locations, and ticket prices [Mid-17thC. Formed from LIST[1].]

listless /lístləss/ *adj.* lacking energy, interest, or the willingness to make an effort [15thC. Formed from LIST[4], literally 'without pleasure'.] —**listlessly** *adv.* —**listlessness** *n.*

Liston /lístən/, **Sonny** (1917?–70) US boxer. As world heavyweight champion (1962–64), he was noted for his power and physical stature. Real name **Charles Liston**

list price *n.* a published or advertised retail price of sth that can often be discounted by the seller

listserv *n.* a free service available on the Internet that is like a forum that allows users to discuss a subject via e-mail

Franz Liszt

Liszt /list/, **Franz** (1811–86) Hungarian pianist, composer, and conductor. His compositions, including *A Faust Symphony* (1857), arrangements, and transcriptions for piano, influenced other composers. He was a brilliant virtuoso pianist.

lit past participle of **light**[1] *v.* 2. past tense of **light**[1] *v.* 1

lit. *abbr.* **1.** litre **2.** literal **3.** literally **4.** literary **5.** literature

litany /líttəni/ (*plural* **-nies**) *n.* **1.** CHR **PRAYERS DURING WORSHIP** a series of sung or spoken liturgical prayers or requests for the blessing of God, including invocations from a priest or minister and responses from a congregation **2. LONG REPETITIOUS LIST** a long and repetitious list of things such as complaints or problems ○ *recited a litany of complaints about the system* [13thC. Via Old French *letanie* from, ultimately, Greek *litaneia* 'prayer', from *litanos* 'entreating', from *litē* 'supplication', of unknown origin.]

LitB = **LittB**

litchi *n.* = **lychee**

lit. crit. *abbr.* literary criticism

LitD, **LittD** = **LittD** [Shortening of Latin *Litterarum Doctor*]

lite /līt/ *adj.* low in alcohol, calories, sugar, or fat (*used especially in labelling or advertising foods and beverages*) [Mid-20thC. Variant of LIGHT.]

-lite *suffix.* mineral, rock, fossil ○ *halite* ○ *coprolite* [Via French from, ultimately, Greek *lithos* 'stone']

liter *n.* US = **litre**

literacy /líttərəssi/ *n.* **1. READING AND WRITING ABILITY** the ability to read and write at a conventionally accepted level **2. SKILL IN PARTICULAR SUBJECT** knowledge of or training in a particular subject or area of activity ○ *computer literacy*

literal /líttərəl/ *adj.* **1. FOLLOWING BASIC MEANING** adhering strictly to the basic meaning of an original word or text without further elaboration or interpretation ○ *a literal reading of the story of Noah* **2. WORD FOR WORD** exactly following the order or meaning of an original word or text **3. USED TO EMPHASIZE TRUTH OF STH** a word used to emphasize that sth is true ○ *That's the literal truth.* **4. TAKING THINGS AT FACE VALUE** understanding words, behaviour, and situations in a simple factual way that ignores context or implications **5. FACTUAL AND UNIMAGINATIVE** simple in a clear unimaginative way that sticks to the facts and avoids embellishment ○ *a literal account of the incident for the court* **6. USING ALPHABETICAL LETTERS** involving or expressed by letters of the alphabet ■ *n.* **PRINTING ERROR** a misprint, especially involving a single alphabetical letter [14thC. Via Old French from Latin *literalis*, from *littera* 'letter' (source of English *letter*).] —**literalness** *n.*

literalism /líttərə lìzzəm/ *n.* **1. FAITHFULNESS TO EXPLICIT MEANING** strict adherence to the basic or primary meaning of a word or text **2. REALISM** the realistic representation of sth in art or literature —**literalist** *n.* —**literalistic** /líttərə lístik/ *adj.* —**literalistically** /-lístikli/ *adv.*

literally /líttərəli/ *adv.* **1. STRICTLY ADHERING TO BASIC MEANING** in a way based on the explicit meaning of a word or text **2. USED TO EMPHASIZE** a word used to emphasize another word or a phrase (*informal*) ○ *I was literally freezing.*

literary /líttərəri/ *adj.* **1. RELATING TO LITERATURE** relating to literature, writing, or the study of literature **2. FORMALLY EXPRESSED** typical of literature rather than everyday speech **3. PROFESSIONALLY INVOLVED WITH LITERATURE** involved with literature or writing as a profession **4. KNOWLEDGEABLE ABOUT LITERATURE** well-read or knowledgeable about literature [Mid-17thC. From Latin *literarius* 'having to do with letters', from *littera* 'letter' (source of English *letter*).] —**literarily** *adv.* —**literariness** *n.*

literary agent *n.* sb whose job is to negotiate business contracts on behalf of an author

literary executor *n.* sb who is appointed to manage literary property on behalf of an author's estate

literate /líttərət/ *adj.* **1. ABLE TO READ AND WRITE** having the ability to read and write **2. KNOWLEDGEABLE** having a good understanding of a particular subject **3. WELL-EDUCATED AND WELL-READ** well-educated and cultured, particularly with respect to literature or writing **4. SKILFULLY WRITTEN** showing skill in the techniques of writing ○ *a literate account of the voyage* ■ *n.* **1. SB CAPABLE OF READING AND WRITING** sb who is able to read and write **2. SB WITH EXTENSIVE EDUCATION** sb who is well-educated, learned, or cultured [15thC. From Latin *litteratus* 'lettered, acquainted with literature', from *littera* 'letter' (source of English *letter* and *literature*).] —**literately** *adv.* —**literateness** *n.*

literati /líttə ràa tee/ *npl.* (*formal*) **1. HIGHLY EDUCATED PEOPLE** intellectuals or the educated class **2. PEOPLE DEEPLY INVOLVED IN LITERATURE** authors and other people closely or professionally involved with literature and the arts [Early 17thC. Directly or via Italian from Latin *litterati*, literally 'lettered people', from *littera* 'letter'.]

literatim /líttə ràatim/ *adv.* word for word (*formal*) [Mid-17thC. From medieval Latin, 'by the letter'.]

literation /líttə ráysh'n/ *n.* the representation of sounds or words by means of alphabetical letters [Early 20thC. Formed from Latin *littera* 'letter' (source of English *letter*).]

literator /líttə raytər/ *n.* a littérateur (*archaic*) [Mid-17thC. From Latin, 'teacher of letters', from *littera* 'letter'.]

literature /líttərəchər/ *n.* **1. WRITTEN WORKS WITH ARTISTIC VALUE** written works such as fiction, poetry, drama, and criticism that are recognized as having important or permanent artistic value **2. BODY OF WRITTEN WORKS** the body of written works of a culture, language, people, or period of time ○ *Russian literature* **3. WRITINGS ON SPECIFIC SUBJECT** the body of published work concerned with a particular subject ○ *scientific literature* **4. PRINTED INFORMATION** printed matter that gives information, in the form of, e.g. brochures or leaflets **5. PRODUCTION OF LITERARY WORKS** the creation of literary work, especially as an art or occupation [14thC. Via Old French from Latin *litteratura*, from *litteratus* 'lettered' (see LITERATE).]

lith. *abbr.* **1.** lithograph **2.** lithography

Lith. *abbr.* **1.** Lithuania **2.** Lithuanian

lith- *prefix.* = **litho-** (*used before vowels*)

-lith *suffix.* **1.** mineral, rock, stone ○ *batholith* **2.** stone structure or implement ○ *megalith* ○ *microlith* **3.** calculus, concretion ○ *otolith* [Via modern Latin *-lithus* from Greek *lithos* 'stone', of unknown origin]

litharge /líth aarj/ *n.* = **lead monoxide** [14thC. Via Old French *litarge* from, ultimately, Greek *litharguros*, literally 'stone-silver', from *lithos* 'stone' + *arguros* 'silver'.]

lithe /līth/ (**lither, lithest**) *adj.* able to move or bend the body lightly and gracefully ○ *a lithe gymnast* [Old English *līþe* 'gentle'. Ultimately from an Indo-European word meaning 'flexible', which is also the ancestor of English *linden* and *relent*.] —**lithely** *adv.* —**litheness** *n.*

lithesome /līthsəm/ *adj.* lithe (*archaic or literary*)

Lithgow /líthgō/ town in southeastern New South Wales, Australia, a centre of coal mining and light industry. Population: 11,441 (1996).

lithia /líthi ə/ *n.* = **lithium oxide** [Early 19thC. Alteration of earlier *lithion* (on the model of words such as SODA, from Greek *lithos* 'stone'.]

lithiasis /li thī́ əssiss/ *n.* the formation or presence of stones formed by mineral concretions in the body, e.g. in the kidney, gall bladder, pancreas, or salivary glands [Mid-17thC. Via modern Latin from Greek, from *lithos* 'stone'.]

lithic[1] /líthik/ *adj.* **1.** GEOL **MADE OF STONE** consisting of stone **2.** MED **RELATING TO STONES IN BODY** relating to undesirable mineral concretions in the body, e.g. kidney stones [Late 18thC. From Greek *lithikos*, from *lithos* 'stone'.]

lithic[2] /líthik/ *adj.* CHEM relating to lithium [Early 19thC. Formed from LITHIUM.]

-lithic *suffix.* of a particular stage in human beings' use of stone implements ○ *Neolithic* [Formed from Greek *lithos* 'stone']

lithify /líthi fī/ (**-fies, -fying, -fied**) *vti.* to change, or change sth, from loose sediments into solid rock [Late 19thC. Formed from Greek *lithos* 'stone'.] —**lithification** /líthifi káysh'n/ *n.*

lithium /líthi əm/ *n.* a soft silver-white chemical element that is the lightest metal known, used in alloys, ceramics, and batteries, and in compounds as a medical treatment for manic-depressive disorders. Symbol **Li** [Early 19thC. Coined from LITHIA + -IUM.]

lithium carbonate *n.* a white crystalline salt used in ceramics and glass and medicinally to treat manic-depressive disorders. Formula: Li_2CO_3.

lithium fluoride *n.* a white, slightly water-soluble powder used in making ceramics. Formula: LiF.

lithium oxide *n.* a white alkaline solid that absorbs carbon dioxide and water vapour and is used in ceramics and glass. Formula: Li_2O.

litho., **lithog.** *abbr.* **1.** lithograph **2.** lithography

litho- *prefix.* **1.** stone ○ *lithosphere* **2.** calculus, concretion ○ *lithotomy* [From Greek *lithos* 'stone', of unknown origin]

lithogenous /li thójjənəss/ *adj.* secreting stony deposits (*refers to organisms such as coral*)

lithograph /líth ə graaf, -graf/ *n.* **LITHOGRAPHIC PRINT** a print made by lithography ■ *vti.* (**-graphs, -graphing, -graphed**) **MAKE PRINT USING LITHOGRAPHY** to make a print using the lithography process [Early 19thC. Back-formation from LITHOGRAPHY.]

lithography /li thóggrəfi/ *n.* a printing process using a plate on which only the image to be printed takes up ink. The non-printing area is treated to repel ink. [Early 19thC. From German *Lithographie*, from Greek *lithos* 'stone' + *graphein* 'to write'; so called because the printing plate was originally a porous stone.] —**lithographer** *n.* —**lithographic** /líthə gráffik/ *adj.* —**lithographically** *adv.*

lithoid /líth oyd/, **lithoidal** /li thóyd'l/ *adj.* consisting of or resembling stone [Mid-19thC. From Greek *lithoeidēs*, from *lithos* 'stone'.]

lithology /li thólləji/ *n.* **1. STUDY OF ROCKS** the scientific study of rocks **2. CHARACTERISTICS OF ROCKS** the physical characteristics of a rock or a rock formation —**lithological** /líthə lójjik'l/ *adj.* —**lithologically** /-lójjikli/ *adv.* —**lithologist** /li thólləjist/ *n.*

lithophyte /líthə fīt/ n. **1.** PLANT GROWING ON ROCK a plant that grows on rock and absorbs nutrients from the atmosphere **2.** STONY ORGANISM an organism such as a coral that is composed in part of stony material —**lithophytic** /líthə fíttik/ adj.

lithopone /líthə pōn/ n. a white pigment that is a mixture of barium sulphate and zinc sulphide and is used in making paints and linoleum [Late 19thC. Coined from Greek litho- + ponos 'product'.]

lithosphere /líthə sfeer/ n. the solid outer layer of the Earth above the asthenosphere, consisting of the crust and upper mantle —**lithospheric** /líthə sférrik/ adj.

lithotomy /li thóttəmi/ (plural -mies) n. the surgical removal of a stone from an organ or duct of the body, especially the urinary tract or bladder —**lithotomic** /líthə tómmik/ adj. —**lithotomist** /li thóttəmist/ n.

lithotripsy /líthō tripsi/ n. the fragmentation of a stone in the urinary system or gall bladder, e.g. with ultrasound shock waves, so that the gravel can be passed naturally [Mid-19thC. Coined from LITHO- + Greek tripsis 'rubbing, crushing'.]

lithotripter /líthə triptər/ n. a device that breaks up kidney stones using ultrasound shock waves [Early 19thC. Alteration of earlier lithotriptor, from, ultimately, Greek lithon thruptika 'capable of pulverizing stones', from lithos 'stone' + thruptein 'to crush'.]

Lithuania

Lithuania /líthyoʻo áyni ə/ republic bordering the Baltic Sea in northeastern Europe. Language: Lithuanian. Currency: litas. Capital: Vilnius. Population: 3,617,104 (1997). Area: 65,300 sq. km/25,200 sq. mi. Official name **Republic of Lithuania**

Lithuanian /líthyoʻo áyni ən/ n. **1.** PEOPLES SB FROM LITHUANIA sb who was born or lives in Lithuania **2.** LANG OFFICIAL LANGUAGE OF LITHUANIA the official language of Lithuania, also spoken in western parts of European Russia, belonging to the Balto-Slavonic branch of Indo-European languages. Lithuanian is spoken by about four million people. —**Lithuanian** adj.

litigable /líttigəb'l/ adj. able to be pursued in court

litigant /líttigənt/ n. sb engaged in a lawsuit —**litigant** adj.

litigate /lítti gayt/ (-gates, -gating, -gated) vti. to contest or be involved in a lawsuit [Early 17thC. From Latin litigat-, past participle stem of litigare, from lit-, the stem of lis 'lawsuit' + agere 'to drive, pursue'.] —**litigator** n.

litigation /lítti gáysh'n/ n. **1.** EXISTENCE OF LAWSUIT the act or process of bringing or contesting a lawsuit ○ The matter is in litigation. **2.** LAWSUIT a lawsuit (technical)

litigious /li tíjjəss/ adj. **1.** INCLINED TO GO TO LAW tending or wanting to take legal action ○ a litigious person **2.** RELATING TO LEGAL ACTION relating to litigation **3.** QUARRELSOME inclined to quarrel or argue (formal) [14thC. From French litigieux, from, ultimately, Latin litigium 'litigation', from litigare 'to quarrel' (see LITIGATE).] —**litigiously** adv. —**litigiousness** n.

litmus /lítməss/ n. a powdery substance obtained from lichens that is used to indicate whether sth is an acid or a base, turning red in acids and blue in bases [14thC. From Old Norse litmosi, from litr 'dye' + mosi 'moss'.]

litmus paper n. a strip of paper treated with litmus, used to find out if sth is an acid or a base

litmus test n. **1.** TEST TO IDENTIFY ACID OR BASE a test in which litmus is used to find out if sth is an acid or a base **2.** TEST DETERMINED BY SINGLE FACTOR a test in which a single factor determines the outcome ○ The candidate's stance on free trade was a litmus for the nomination.

litotes /líto teez, lī tót eez/ (plural -tes) n. a deliberate understatement, such as an affirmative statement formed by a negation of the contrary, as in the sentence 'I am not unmindful of your devotion' [Late 16thC. Via late Latin from Greek litotes, from litos 'simple, plain'.]

litre /leétər/ n. a unit of volume equal to 1 cubic decimetre or 1.056 liquid quarts [Late 18thC. Via French litre from, ultimately, Greek litra, a unit of measure.]

LittB, **LitB** abbr. **1.** Bachelor of Letters **2.** Bachelor of Literature [From Latin Litterarum Baccalaureus]

LittD, **LitD** abbr. **1.** Doctor of Letters **2.** Doctor of Literature [From latin Litterarum Doctor]

litter /líttər/ n. **1.** SCATTERED RUBBISH pieces of rubbish that have been carelessly left on the ground, especially in a public place or the outdoors **2.** MESSY STATE OR PLACE a large number of objects that have been scattered around untidily or a place that is in an untidy state ○ I found her working away in the litter of her study. **3.** ZOOL ANIMAL OFFSPRING a group of young animals born at the same time from the same mother **4.** AGRIC BEDDING FOR ANIMALS material such as hay or straw that is used as bedding for animals **5.** MATERIAL FOR PET'S TOILET TRAY a dry absorbent substance, often in the form of granules, that is spread in a shallow container where a pet, especially a cat, can urinate or defecate when indoors **6.** GROUND SURFACE OF FOREST the surface layer of a forest floor, consisting of partly decomposed leaves and twigs **7.** STRETCHER WITH LONG SHAFTS a piece of cloth stretched between two long poles on either side that is used to carry a sick person or a dead body (dated) **8.** HIST COUCH FOR CARRYING PASSENGER a couch with poles on either side, used to transport a single passenger on people's shoulders or on animals. It is often enclosed with curtains. ■ v. (-ters, -tering, -tered) **1.** vti. MAKE PLACE UNTIDY to make a place, especially a public place or the outdoors, untidy by leaving or scattering rubbish **2.** vt. COVER PLACE WITH SCATTERED OBJECTS to put a place in disorder by leaving scattered objects in it ○ Toys littered the playroom floor. **3.** vt. FILL WITH THINGS to fill sth with or contain many examples of a particular thing ○ an essay littered with spelling mistakes **4.** vti. ZOOL HAVE YOUNG to give birth to young (refers to animals) **5.** vt. AGRIC SUPPLY ANIMAL WITH BEDDING to provide an animal with hay or straw for bedding [14thC. Via Anglo-Norman litere from medieval Latin lectaria, from Latin lectus 'bed'. Ultimately from an Indo-European word meaning 'to lie', which is also the ancestor of English lie[1].] —**litterer** n.

littérateur /líttərə túr/ n. sb closely involved with literature, especially a professional writer (archaic) [Early 19thC. Via French from Latin litterator, from littera 'letter'.]

litterbug /líttər bug/ n. = litter lout (informal)

litter lout n. sb who leaves litter in public places or outdoors (informal disapproving)

littermate /líttər mayt/ n. one of several animal young born or reared in the same litter

little /lítt'l/ (-tler, -tlest) CORE MEANING: an adjective meaning 'small' or 'young', or a grammatical word indicating that sth exists in small quantities ○ (adj) It was only a very little mistake! ○ (adj) He was helping the little boy put on his boots. ○ (adj) I'll bring my little sister with me. ○ (det) There was a little food left. ○ (det) There was little chance of winning.

1. adj. SMALL small or of less than average size ○ He gave her a little Christmas tree ornament. **2.** adj. YOUNG young ○ I met her when she was just a little girl. **3.** adj. YOUNGER refers to a younger sister or brother ○ My little sister is always causing problems. **4.** adj. SMALL AND PLEASANT small in a pleasant or good looking way ○ a cute little button nose ○ one of his sweet little habits **5.** adj. SHORT short or quick ○ Wait a little while. ○ He turned and gave them a little nod. **6.** adj. TRIVIAL of no importance ○ It's the little things that count when you're sharing a house with some-body. **7.** det., pron. A SMALL AMOUNT a small amount of sth (used after 'a') ○ She was given a little alimony and a little child support. ○ We paid only a little for it. ○ A little of what you fancy does you good. **8.** det., pron. NOT MUCH only a very small amount ○ The cleanups had little or no effect on the environment. ○ She would eat very little. ○ Little of what was said meant much to me. **9.** adv. HARDLY hardly or not at all ○ He little knew what was in store for him. **10.** adv. NOT OFTEN on rare occasions ○ We visit him very little these days. [Old English lýtel. From a prehistoric Germanic base meaning 'small', which is also the ancestor of English lout.] ◇ **little by little** gradually; by small degrees ○ Little by little I grew too drowsy to think – then too lazy to go on walking. ◇ **no little** considerable ○ They commenced eating with no little appetite. ◇ **not a little** a lot ○ I was rather shocked and not a little embarrassed. ◇ **quite a little** to a considerable degree or extent ○ The rest of the evening was quite a little triumph for her. ◇ **think little of** to have a low opinion of ○ I have learned not to think little of anyone else's beliefs.

little auk n. a small squat northern seabird of the auk family with a strong bill. Its dark-coloured throat and breast change to white in winter. Latin name: Alle alle. US term **dovekie**

Little Barrier Island /lítt'l bárri ər-/ uninhabited island in the Hauraki Gulf, off the northeastern coast of the North Island, New Zealand. It is a nature reserve. Area: 28 sq. km/11 sq. mi.

Little Bear n. = Ursa Minor

Little Dipper n. US, Can = Ursa Minor

little end n. the part of a connecting rod that attaches to the gudgeon pin in an internal-combustion engine or reciprocal pump

Little Englander n. sb who emphasized the interests of Britain itself rather than those of the British Empire, especially in the 19th century

little finger n. the smallest finger of the human hand, located furthest from the thumb

little folk npl. = little people npl.

Little grebe

little grebe n. a small diving bird with brown plumage, the smallest European grebe. Latin name: Tachybaptus ruficollis.

little green man n. an imaginary person from outer space (humorous)

little hours, **Little Hours** npl. the hours of prime, terce, sext, and nones in the divine office to be recited every day by members of Roman Catholic orders

Little John n. in English legend, a particularly tall and strong member of Robin Hood's band of men

little magazine n. a literary magazine primarily made up of work by writers who have yet to become established, usually having a limited circulation and a small format

little man n. **1.** = little guy **2.** UNIMPORTANT PERSON an average person, as opposed to an important or wealthy one **3.** SMALL BUSINESS PERSON OR INVESTOR sb who operates a small business or invests on a small scale

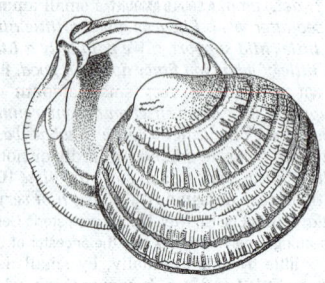

Littleneck

littleneck, littleneck clam *n. US* a small young quahog clam, often eaten raw [Mid-19thC. Named after *Little Neck* Bay, Long Island, New York, in the US, where the clams were once plentiful.]

little office, Little Office *n.* CHR a Roman Catholic office similar to but shorter than a divine office, especially a liturgical service of psalms and prayers to the Virgin Mary

little owl *n.* a small owl, native to Europe, Africa, and Asia, that eats insects and small rodents and has speckled brown feathers, a broad head, and a low forehead. Genus: *Athene noctua.*

little people *npl.* tiny imaginary or mythological beings such as fairies, elves, and leprechauns

Little Richard /lítt'l ríchərd/ (b. 1935) US pianist and singer. A pioneer of rock-and-roll, his performance of songs such as 'Tutti Frutti' and 'Good Golly Miss Molly' made them classics of the genre. Real name **Richard Wayne Penniman**

Little Rock capital of Arkansas State and port in central Arkansas, on the Arkansas River. Population: 175,752 (1996).

Little Russia former area that included Carpathian Ruthenia, eastern Poland, Ukraine, and the western shores of the Black Sea

little slam *n.* the winning of 12 out of the 13 tricks in a deal in the game of bridge

little theater *n.* **1.** *US, Can* SMALL EXPERIMENTAL THEATRE a small, usually noncommercial theatre that produces experimental drama **2.** *US* EXPERIMENTAL NON-COMMERCIAL DRAMA a form of noncommercial drama emphasizing experimental work

little toe *n.* the fifth and smallest toe of the human foot, located furthest from the big toe

little woman *n.* an offensive term for a wife (*dated offensive*)

Littlewood /lítt'l wood/, **Joan** (b. 1914) British theatre director. She founded the left-wing Theatre Workshop, for whom she helped devise *Oh, What a Lovely War* (1963). Full name **Maudie Joan Littlewood**

littlie /lítt'li/ *n. Aus* a young child (*informal*) [Late 19thC. Formed from LITTLE.]

littoral /líttərəl/ *adj.* **1.** ON OR NEAR A SHORE on or near a shore, especially the zone between the high and low tide marks **2.** SHORE-LIVING living on or near a shore ■ *n.* SHORE a shore or coastal region [Mid-17thC. From Latin *littoralis*, from *litor-*, the stem of *litus* 'shore'.]

lit up *adj.* drunk (*slang*)

liturgical /li túrjik'l/, **liturgic** /-jik/ *adj.* **1.** OF LITURGY relating to liturgy **2.** RELATING TO WORSHIP relating to religious worship or to a service of worship, especially the Communion —**liturgically** *adv.*

liturgics /li túrjiks/ *npl.* the study of public worship or liturgies (*takes a singular verb*)

liturgiology /li túrji ólləji/ *n.* = liturgics —**liturgiologist** /-/ *n.*

liturgist /líttərjist/ *n.* **1.** SB WHO STUDIES LITURGIES sb who studies or compiles liturgies **2.** PRACTITIONER OF LITURGY sb who practises the liturgy **3.** SUPPORTER OF LITURGIES sb who favours using liturgies —**liturgism** *n.* —**liturgistic** /líttər jístik/ *adj.*

liturgy /líttərji/ (*plural* -gies) *n.* a form and arrangement of public worship laid down by a church or religion [Mid-16thC. Via Old French *liturgie* from, ul-

timately, Greek *leitourgia* 'public worship service', from *lei-tourgos* 'public servant', from *leitos* 'public' + *ergon* 'work'.]

Liturgy /líttərji/ (*plural* -gies), **liturgy** (*plural* -gies) *n.* the form of service used to celebrate Communion in a Christian denomination, especially the Eucharist in Eastern churches

Litvinov /lit veen óf/, **Maksim** (1876–1951) Russian revolutionary and diplomat. A member of the Bolshevik Party, he worked for international recognition of the Soviet Union. He was ambassador to the United States (1941–43). Full name **Maksim Maksimovich Litvinov**. Real name **Meier Wallach**

livable /lívvəb'l/, **liveable** *adj.* **1.** COMFORTABLE comfortable or suitable for living in ○ *a very livable flat* **2.** WORTH LIVING endurable and worthwhile ○ *It's very tense at home, but still livable.* **3.** ENJOYABLE AS LIVING COMPANION enjoyable to live with —**livableness** *n.* —**livability** /lívvə bílləti/ *n.*

live[1] /liv/ (**lives, living, lived**) *v.* **1.** *vi.* BE ALIVE to be alive or have life **2.** *vi.* STAY ALIVE to remain alive or to continue living ○ *lived through a serious illness last year* **3.** *vi.* MAKE A HOME to reside in a particular place or way ○ *He lived in Bangkok for two years.* ○ *She lives alone.* **4.** *vti.* LEAD CERTAIN TYPE OF EXISTENCE to have a particular kind of life ○ *live comfortably* **5.** *vi.* MAKE A LIVING to earn or make a living ○ *She wants to be an actor but lives by waiting on tables.* **6.** *vti.* FULLY ENJOY LIFE to enjoy life to the fullest ○ *He really knows how to live.* **7.** *vi.* CONTINUE to persist or continue ○ *Her fame lives on.* **8.** *vt.* EXPERIENCE to experience or go through sth ○ *earthquake survivors living a nightmare* **9.** *vti.* MAKE LIFE CONFORM to make your life conform to sth such as a philosophy or religion ○ *lived her faith* ○ *lived by strict rules* **10.** *vi.* BE KEPT SOMEWHERE to be found or kept in a particular place (*informal*) ○ *The spare car keys live in this drawer.* [Old English *libban, lifian.* Ultimately from an Indo-European word meaning 'fat, to stick', which is also the ancestor of English *lipo-*, in prehistoric Germanic it developed the sense 'to continue, live'.] ◊ **live and let live** to be tolerant of others ◊ **live it up** to live or celebrate in an extravagant way (*informal*)

live down *vt.* to live in a blameless or commendable way long enough for sth shameful to be forgotten

live in *vi.* to live at your place of work

live off, live on *vt.* to depend on sb or sth as a source of financial support or for a livelihood ○ *He lived off his parents.* ○ *They live on a small private income.*

live on *vt.* **1.** = **live off** **2.** EAT TO SURVIVE to eat a certain type of food in order to survive or thrive ○ *The koala lives on eucalyptus leaves.*

live out *v.* **1.** *vt.* DO STH PREVIOUSLY IMAGINED to do in reality what had previously only been imagined or fantasized about ○ *live out a dream* **2.** *vt.* LIVE UNTIL END OF PERIOD to spend the rest of your life or a period of time in a certain manner or place **3.** *vi.* LIVE SOMEWHERE OTHER THAN WORKPLACE to live away from the place where you work

live through *vt.* to experience and survive sth difficult or dangerous

live together *vi.* to share the same home and have a sexual relationship without being married

live up to *vt.* to meet sb's expectations or desires, or match sb's good example

live with *vt.* **1.** PUT UP WITH to accept or tolerate sth difficult or unpleasant ○ *The house is tiny, but we'll just have to live with it.* **2.** COPE WITH to cope with or match sb or sth (*slang*)

live[2] /līv/ *adj.* **1.** LIVING alive or living **2.** BROADCAST AS IT HAPPENS broadcast while an event is happening ○ *Tonight's show is live from Paris.* **3.** IN PERSON appearing or performing in front of an audience or in person, rather than recorded or filmed ○ *I'd rather dance to live music.* **4.** RECORDED DURING PERFORMANCE recorded while a performance is happening ○ *live footage of the concert* **5.** RELEVANT TO CURRENT CONCERNS relevant to current interests or concerns ○ *a live topic* **6.** ELEC CONNECTED TO POWER SOURCE connected to an electrical power source ○ *a live wire* **7.** CHARGED WITH EXPLOSIVE containing an explosive and able to be used ○ *live ammunition* **8.** BURNING burning or glowing ○ *live coals* **9.** WITH LIVING BACTERIA made using living bacteria ○ *live yoghurt cultures* **10.** BRIGHT OR VIVID bright or brilliant, especially in terms of colour **11.** GEOL ACTIVE used to describe a volcano that is still active **12.** HIGHLY RESONANT with highly resonant or

reverberant acoustics **13.** SPORTS IN PLAY in play (*informal*) **14.** GEOL FOUND AS ORIGINAL ROCK used to describe a rock or mineral that is found free and not mined or quarried ■ *adv.* **1.** IN PERSON in front of an audience or in person ○ *performing live here tomorrow night* **2.** BROADCAST WHILE EVENT HAPPENS broadcast at exactly the same time as a performance or event happens ○ *a live transmission* [Mid-16thC. Shortening of ALIVE.]

live-bearer /līv-/ *n.* a fish that gives birth to living young, rather than producing eggs —**live-bearing** *adj.*

live birth /līv-/ *n.* the birth of a living infant —**live-born** *adj.*

lived-in /līvd-/ *adj.* **1.** SLIGHTLY UNTIDY BUT HOMELY with a comfortable but slightly worn or untidy look that is consistent with actual or current occupation **2.** CAREWORN showing the effects of life's experiences

livedo /li veedō/ (*plural* -dos) *n.* a bluish-black patch of discoloured skin caused by the settling of blood, especially after death [From modern Latin, formed from Latin *livere* (see LIVID), on the model of COMEDO]

live-forever /līv-/ *n.* **1.** = **houseleek** **2.** = **orpine** [So called because it lives for a long time]

live-in /līv-/ *adj.* **1.** LIVING AT PLACE OF WORK living in your place of employment ○ *a live-in nanny* **2.** SHARING HOME sharing a home with a sexual partner

livelihood /lívlihood/ *n.* work done to earn a living, or whatever provides a source of income [13thC. Alteration (influenced by LIVELY and -HOOD) of Old English *līflād* 'way of living', from *līf* 'life' + *lād* 'way'.]

live load *n.* the variable load or weight borne by a structure such as a bridge, in addition to its own weight

livelong[1] /lív long/ *adj.* used to emphasize how long a period of time seems to last or how tedious it feels (*literary*) [14thC. From LIEF + LONG, literally 'dearly long', influenced by LIVE[1].]

livelong[2] /līv long/ *n.* PLANTS = **orpine** [Late 16thC. From LIVE[1] + LONG; from its longevity]

lively /lívli/ (-lier, -liest) *adj.* **1.** FULL OF ENERGY full of life and energy ○ *two lively children* **2.** ANIMATED animated, exciting, or intellectually stimulating ○ *A lively discussion ensued.* **3.** ENTHUSIASTIC active and enthusiastic ○ *Pat takes a lively interest in local politics.* **4.** FULL OF MOVEMENT full of activity or movement ○ *a lively dance* **5.** VIVID clear, distinct, and vivid ○ *possessed a lively recollection of the events of that summer* **6.** BRILLIANT IN COLOUR bright and colourful in a good looking way **7.** REFRESHING stimulating or refreshing ○ *a lively little breeze* **8.** SPRINGY bouncy or springy ○ *a lively ball* **9.** SAILING RESPONSIVE very responsive to the helm [Old English *līflīc* 'life-like'] —**livelily** *adv.* —**liveliness** *n.* ◊ **look lively, step lively** to hurry up and get going

liven /lív'n/ (-vens, -vening, -vened) *vti.* to become, or make sb or sth, lively or cheerful ○ *What can we do to liven up the party?* ○ *At the sound of its trainer's voice, the sick horse livened considerably.* [Early 18thC. Formed from LIFE.] —**livener** *n.*

live oak *n.* **1.** EVERGREEN OAK OF SOUTHERN UNITED STATES an evergreen oak of Mexico and the southern United States that has a short broad trunk and shiny leaves. Latin name: *Quercus virginianus.* **2.** WOOD OF LIVE OAK the hard strong wood of the live oak tree [From LIVE[2]; from its being evergreen]

liver[1] /lívvər/ *n.* **1.** ANAT LARGE VITAL ORGAN a vascular

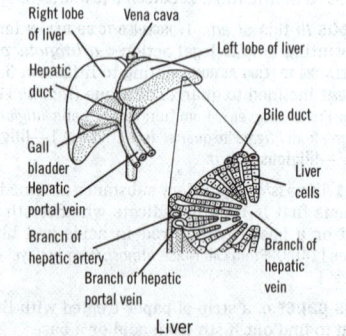

Liver

glandular organ in vertebrates that secretes bile, stores and filters blood, and takes part in many metabolic functions, e.g. the conversion of sugars into glycogen. The liver is reddish-brown, multi-lobed, and in humans is located in the upper right part of the abdominal cavity. **2. INVERTEBRATE ORGAN** any of various glandular organs of invertebrates that are involved with digestion and metabolism **3. LIVER CONSIDERED AS FOOD** the liver of an animal or fish eaten as food or taken as medicine **4. COLOURS DARK BROWN COLOUR** a dark brown colour with a tinge of red or grey ■ adj. COLOURS OF DARK BROWN COLOUR of a dark brown colour with a tinge of red or grey [Old English *lifer*. Ultimately from an Indo-European word meaning 'fat, to stick', later 'to continue', hence 'life'; the liver was once thought to be the organ that made blood.]

liver² /lívvər/ n. sb who lives in a specified way ○ *a fast liver* [14thC. Formed from LIVE¹.]

liver-coloured adj. of a reddish-brown colour, like liver

liver fluke n. a parasitic worm that infests the liver of mammals, including humans. Latin name: *Fasciola hepatica.*

liveried /lívvərid/ adj. wearing a livery ○ *the monarch's liveried attendants*

liverish /lívvərish/, **livery** /lívvəri/ adj. **1. WITH LIVER DIS-ORDER** affected by a liver disorder **2. IRRITABLE** bad-tempered or irritable **3. LIKE LIVER** resembling liver, especially in colour (*informal*) —**liverishness** n.

Liverpool /lívvər pool/ port and university city in northwestern England, on the River Mersey. Population: 470,800 (1995).

Liverpool Plains rich agricultural region of eastern New South Wales, Australia

Liverpool Range mountain range in eastern New South Wales, Australia. The highest peak is Oxleys Peak. Height: 1,372 m/4,500 ft.

Liverpudlian /lívvər púddli ən/ n. sb who lives in or comes from Liverpool [Mid-19thC. Formed from an alteration of LIVERPOOL, substituting *puddle* for *pool*.] —**Liverpudlian** adj.

liver salts n. a solution of mineral salts taken to relieve indigestion (*takes a singular or plural verb*)

liver sausage n. a sausage containing cooked minced liver, usually eaten cold as a spread. US term **liverwurst**

liver spot n. a usually dark brown patch of pigmentation on the skin, usually occurring later in life. It is caused by an aggregation of cells containing melanin. [From its colour]

liverwort /lívvər wurt/ n. a small dense green plant that grows on moist surfaces and resembles moss. Class: Hepaticae. [Old English *liferwyrt*, a translation of medieval Latin *hepatica*. So called from its lobed shape, thought to resemble the liver.]

liverwurst /lívvər wurst/ n. US = **liver sausage** [Mid-19thC. Partial translation of German *Leberwurst* 'liver sausage'.]

livery¹ /lívvəri/ (plural -ies) n. **1. UNIFORM** an identifying uniform worn by members of a group or trade, especially men and boys who are servants of a household or feudal retainers **2. UNIFORMED GROUP** the members of a group or trade who wear a livery (*archaic*) **3. EMBLEM OR DESIGN** a distinctive colour scheme or design used by a company to make its property and vehicles easily identifiable **4. CHARACTERISTIC APPEARANCE** a distinctive colouring, marking, dress, or outward appearance (*literary*) **5. PROFESSIONAL CARE OF HORSES** the care, feeding, and stabling of horses for money **6. HIRING OF HORSES** the business of hiring out horses [14thC. From Old French *livree* 'delivery', from, ultimately, Latin *liberare* 'to liberate', from *liber* 'free' (see LIBERAL).]

livery² adj. = **liverish** (*informal*)

livery company n. one of several chartered companies of the City of London entitled to wear an identifying uniform. They started as craft guilds in the 14th century.

liveryman /lívvərimən/ (plural -men /-mən/) n. **1. MEMBER OF A LIVERY COMPANY** a member of a livery company. Members are freemen of the City of London and are entitled to certain privileges. **2. OWNER OR EMPLOYEE**

OF LIVERY STABLE sb who owns or works in a livery stable

livery stable n. **1. STABLE THAT HIRES OUT HORSES** a stable where horses and carriages are kept for hire **2. PLACE THAT STABLES HORSES** a stable that accommodates and looks after horses for their owners

livestock /lív stok/ n. animals raised for food or other products, or kept for use, especially farm animals such as meat and dairy cattle, pigs, and poultry

live trap /lív-/ n. a trap designed to catch a wild animal without injuring it

live wire /lív-/ n. **1. ELEC WIRE CONNECTED TO POWER SOURCE** a wire connected to a source of voltage **2. ENERGETIC PERSON** sb who is keen and energetic (*informal*)

livid /lívvid/ adj. **1. FURIOUS** very angry **2. WITH BLUISH BRUISED COLOUR** bluish or discoloured as a result of bruising **3. ASHEN** very pale, especially when this is not natural **4. GREYISH** tinged with grey [15thC. Directly or via Old French from Latin *lividus*, from *livere* 'to be bluish in colour'. Ultimately from an Indo-European word that is also the ancestor of English *sloe*.] —**lividity** /li víddəti/ n. —**lividly** /lívvidli/ adv.

living /lívving/ adj. **1. ALIVE** alive, not dead **2. LIKE THE REAL THING** realistic or true to life ○ *a living likeness* **3. INTERESTING AND RELEVANT** interesting in a way that is relevant and useful ○ *make history a living subject* **4. SUITABLE FOR DOMESTIC LIVING** designed for living in, especially for social and recreational activities ○ *lots of living space in the home* **5. STILL USED** still used or in existence ○ *a living language* **6. NATURAL** in a natural condition or place ○ *living water* ■ n. **1. MONEY OR MEANS OF EARNING** a means of earning money to live on, or the money sb earns to live on ○ *What do you do for a living?* **2. MAINTENANCE OF WAY OF LIFE** a means of sustaining or maintaining a way of life ○ *improve your standard of living* **3. MANNER OF LIFE** quality of life or the way in which it is lived ○ *likes country living* ■ npl. THOSE WHO ARE ALIVE people who are alive (*takes a plural verb*) ■ n. = benefice

WORD KEY: SYNONYMS

living, alive, animate, extant
CORE MEANING: having life or existence
living used to indicate that a person is not dead. It can also be used to describe sth such as a language or way of life that has not died out; **alive** used to indicate that a person, animal, or plant is not dead. It can also be used to indicate that a feeling of vitality is strong in a person; **animate** a formal word used to indicate that sth is alive. It is also used to describe things such as animals and plants that live, as opposed to things such as rocks, water, or buildings that do not; **extant** a formal word emphasizing the continuing existence or survival of sth.

living death n. a life or period of time that is full of misery or pain

living fossil n. an organism that is virtually unchanged from early geological time and belongs to a group whose other members are extinct. Gingko trees and coelacanths are living fossils.

living picture n. = **tableau vivant**

living room n. a room in a house where people usually relax or entertain guests

living standard n. = **standard of living**

Livingston /lívvingstən/ town in West Lothian, Scotland. Population: 41,647 (1991).

Livingstone /lívvingstən/ city and tourist centre in southern Zambia, north of the Victoria Falls. Population: 82,218 (1990).

Livingstone, David, Dr (1813–73) British doctor, missionary, and explorer. One of the most important explorers of the African interior, he was the first European to visit many areas of the continent.

Livingstone daisy n. a species of mesembryanthemum grown as a garden plant for its brightly coloured flowers that are like large daisies. Latin name: *Mesembryanthemum criniflorum*. [Mid-20thC. *Livingstone* is a proper name of unknown origin.]

living wage n. a wage that will allow a worker to support a family in reasonable comfort

living will n. a document, typically signed in advance while in good health, in which sb declines to be

kept alive artificially by life-support systems in case of a terminal illness

Livonia /li vóni ə/ ancient Baltic region, comprising most of present-day Estonia and Latvia. Russia annexed it in 1721. —**Livonian** /lə vóni ən/ adj., n.

Livorno /li váwrnō/ port and industrial city in the Tuscany region, central Italy. Population: 166,394 (1992). English **Leghorn**

livre /léevrə/ n. an old unit of French currency, equivalent to a pound of silver [Mid-16thC. Via French from Latin *libra* 'pound'.]

Livy /lívvi/ (59 BC–AD 17) Roman historian. His *History of Rome*, ranging from the foundation of the city in 753 BC to 9 BC, was the basis for the Western tradition of historical writing, and remained the primary source of information about Rome until the 18th century. Full name **Titus Livius**

lixiviate /lik sívvi ayt/ (-ates, -ating, -ated) vti. CHEM to leach (*dated*) [Mid-17thC. From late Latin *lixiviare*, from Latin *lixivius* (see LIXIVIUM).] —**lixivial** adj. —**lixiviation** /lik sívvi áysh'n/ n.

lixivium /lik sívvi əm/ (plural -ums or -a /-ívvi ə/) n. a solution, e.g. lye, obtained by leaching [Mid-17thC. From late Latin, from Latin *lixivius* 'made into ashes or lye', from *lix* 'lye'.]

Lizard

lizard /lízzərd/ n. **1. FOUR-LEGGED REPTILE** a reptile with a long scaly body, movable eyelids, a long tapering tail, and four legs, typically living in hot dry regions. Lizards include the gecko, iguana, chameleon, and horned toad. Suborder: Sauria. **2. LARGE REPTILE RESEMBLING LIZARD** any large reptile with four legs and a tapering tail that resembles the lizard, e.g. the alligator, crocodile, or certain dinosaurs **3. LEATHER MADE FROM LIZARD SKIN** leather made from the skin of a lizard [14thC. Via Old French *lesard* from Latin *lacertus* 'lizard', of unknown origin.]

Lizard, The /lízzərd/ peninsula in southwestern Cornwall, England. Its tip, Lizard Head or Lizard Point, is the southernmost part of England.

lizard fish n. a slender, large-mouthed, predatory marine fish that has a head shaped like that of a lizard. Family: Synodontidae.

Lizard Island /lízzərd-/ island off the coast of Queensland, Australia

LJ abbr. Lord Justice

Ljubljana /lyoŏ bli áanə/ capital of Slovenia, in the central part of the country, near Trieste. Population: 269,972 (1994).

'll after a pronoun /l/; after a vowel /əl/; after a consonant /'l/ contr. **1. WILL** will **2. SHALL** shall

LL abbr. **1.** late Latin **2.** Lord Lieutenant **3.** Low Latin

ll. abbr. lines

llama /láamə/ n. **1. SHAGGY-COATED LONG-NECKED MAMMAL** a shaggy-coated long-necked cud-chewing South American mammal related to the camel, kept to carry loads. It yields wool, leather, milk, and meat, and is believed to be a domesticated variety of the guanaco. Genus: *Llama*. **2. WOOL** the shaggy wool of a llama **3. CLOTH FROM LLAMA WOOL** cloth made from the wool of a llama [Early 17thC. Via Spanish from Quechua.]

Llandaff /hlan dáf/ suburb of Cardiff, home of the ancient cathedral of Saints Dyfrig and Teilo

Llandrindod Wells /hlan drin dod wélz/ spa town in Powys, eastern Wales. Its mineral springs make it a popular tourist area. Population: 4,900 (1993).

Llama

David Lloyd George

Llandudno /hlan dúdnō/ town and seaside resort in Conwy, northern Wales. Population: 18,573 (1991).

Llanelli /hla néthli/ market town and port in Carmarthenshire, Wales, on the Burry Inlet of Carmarthen Bay. Population: 44,953 (1991).

Llanfair /hlan vír/ village in southeastern Anglesey Island, northwestern Wales. Population: 3,101 (1991).

Llangefni /hlaan gév ni/ town in central Anglesey, Wales. It is the island's administrative centre. Population: 4,643 (1991).

Llangollen /hlan góthlən/ town in Denbighshire, Wales, that is host to an International Musical Eisteddfod. Population: 3,253 (1991).

llano /laáanō/ (plural **-nos**) n. a large open grassy plain, especially in Latin America and the southwestern United States [Early 17thC. Via Spanish from, ultimately, Latin planus 'flat, level' (see PLAIN.)]

LLB abbr. Bachelor of Laws [Shortening of Latin Legum Baccalaureus]

LLD abbr. Doctor of Laws [Shortening of Latin Legum Doctor]

Llewellyn /lə wéllin, thlə-/, **Richard** (1907–83) British author. His best-selling novel How Green Was My Valley (1939), the story of a Welsh mining family, was also turned into a successful film. Pseudonym **Richard Doyle Vivian Llewellyn Lloyd**

Llewelyn ap Gruffudd /lə wéllin ap grífith, thlə-/, **Prince of Gwynned** (d. 1282) Welsh monarch. Grandson of Llewelyn ap Iorweth, in 1258 he won recognition as Prince of Wales, and rebelled unsuccessfully against the English.

Llewelyn ap Iorweth /lə wéllin ap yáwr wurth, thlə-/, **Prince of Gwynedd** (d. 1240) Welsh monarch. He extended his sovereignty over almost all of Wales and successfully fought against the English. Known as **Llewelyn the Great**

Lleyn Peninsula /hlīn pə nínshələ/ peninsula in Wales, lying between Cardigan Bay and Caernarvon Bay. Length: 45 km/28 mi.

LLM abbr. Master of Laws [Shortening of Latin Legum Magister]

Lloyd /loyd/, **Clive** (b. 1944) West Indian cricketer. A fine batsman and fielder, he was captain of the West Indies and Lancashire cricket teams. Full name **Clive Hubert Lloyd**

Lloyd, Marie (1870–1922) British music-hall entertainer. Her Cockney songs won her great popularity. She performed in Britain, the United States, South Africa, and Australia. Born **Matilda Alice Victoria Wood**

Lloyd George /lóyd jáwrj/, **David, 1st Earl of Dwyfor** (1863–1945) British statesman. As the last Liberal prime minister of the United Kingdom (1916–22), he was a strong wartime leader during World War I. He granted home rule to Ireland (1920).

Lloyd Webber /lóyd wébbər/, **Andrew, Lord Lloyd Webber of Sydmonton** (b. 1948) British composer. His popular stage musicals include Jesus Christ Superstar (1971), Cats (1981), and Phantom of the Opera (1986).

lm symbol. lumen

LMVD abbr. NZ Licensed Motor Vehicle Dealer

ln symbol. natural logarithm

LNG abbr. liquefied natural gas

lo /lō/ interj. used to draw attention to sth (archaic or literary) [Old English lā]

loach /lōch/ n. a freshwater fish of Europe and Asia. It is related to the carp and has a long slender body with barbels around its mouth. Family: Cobitidae. [14thC. From Old French locke, of uncertain origin: perhaps ultimately from Celtic.]

load /lōd/ n. 1. STH CARRIED OR TRANSPORTED sth that is carried by an animal, person, or vehicle, especially sth heavy or bulky 2. AMOUNT CARRIED IN ONE TRIP the amount of material, goods, or people that are carried in one journey (often used in combination) ○ delivered a boatload of passengers to the island 3. WORK DEMANDED OF SB OR STH the amount of work that a person or machine is required to do ○ unhappy about his teaching load this term 4. MENTAL BURDEN sth that makes sb feel mentally weighed down, e.g. responsibility, worry, or guilt ○ carrying around a load of guilt 5. QUANTITY THAT MACHINE CAN COPE WITH the amount that can be handled by a machine at one time, especially the amount of clothes that can be handled by a washing machine 6. ARMS SINGLE CHARGE FOR GUN a single charge of ammunition for a firearm 7. ELEC AMOUNT OF DRAWN ELECTRICAL POWER the amount of electrical power that is drawn from a line or source 8. ELEC DEVICE DRAWING ELECTRICAL POWER any device to which electrical power is delivered 9. MECH ENG FORCE AND WEIGHT ON STRUCTURE the total force and weight that a structure, e.g. a bridge, is designed to withstand. For a bridge this includes the dynamic loads of traffic, wind, snow, and ice and the static load of the bridge's own weight. 10. MECH ENG WORK REQUIRED OF MECHANICAL DEVICE the work required of or placed on an engine or machine, measured in kilowatts or horsepower ■ loads npl. LARGE AMOUNT OR NUMBER a large amount or a lot of (informal) ○ We had loads of guests at the party. ■ adv. loads VERY MUCH very much or a great deal (informal) ○ feeling loads better ■ v. (loads, loading, loaded) 1. vti. TRANSP PUT STH ON VEHICLE to put cargo or passengers on a vehicle, ship, or aircraft or to have cargo or passengers put on ○ The aircraft is now loading. 2. vt. PUT STH ON PERSON OR ANIMAL to put a load on an animal or give a load to a person so that it can be carried 3. vt. COMPUT PUT DISK IN DRIVE ON COMPUTER to put a disk or tape in a drive on a computer 4. vti. ARMS PUT ROUNDS IN GUN to put ammunition into a firearm ○ loaded the rifle 5. vt. COMPUT PUT PROGRAM IN COMPUTER to transfer data or a program to the main memory of a computer 6. vt. PUT STH IN MACHINE to put into a machine the items that it will work on, e.g. clothes for washing 7. vti. PHOTOGRAPHY, TECH PUT STH IN CAMERA to put a film, plate, or tape in a camera or to take in a film, plate, or tape 8. vt. GAMBLING WEIGHT ONE SIDE OF DICE to weight one side of a dice or roulette wheel so that it has a bias towards certain numbers 9. vt. FIN ADD EXTRA CHARGE TO INSURANCE PREMIUM to add an extra charge to an insurance premium, e.g. because of an increased risk 10. vt. ELEC INCREASE ELECTRIC OUTPUT OF GENERATOR to increase the output produced by or drawn from a circuit or generator 11. vt. MECH ENG INCREASE WORK REQUIRED OF ENGINE to increase the work required from an engine or motor [Old English lād 'course, way, carrying'. Ultimately from an Indo-European word meaning 'to go ahead', which is also the ancestor of lead[1] and lode.] ◇ **a load of** used to say emphatically that sth is ridiculous or nonsensical (informal) ○ a load of nonsense ◇ **get a load of** to look at or listen to sth or sb (slang) ◇ **load the dice 1.** GAMBLING to add weight to a dice so that it always falls on a particular side (informal) **2.** to arrange things in advance to create an unfair bias in favour of or against sb (informal)

loaded /lōdid/ adj. **1.** WITH FULL LOAD carrying a full load **2.** ARMS CONTAINING AMMUNITION containing bullets or other ammunition and ready to fire **3.** WITH HIDDEN IMPLICATION with a hidden or secondary implication designed to trick sb into making an admission or commitment ○ That is a loaded question. **4.** RICH extremely rich (slang) ○ Her parents are loaded. **5.** US DRUNK very drunk (slang) **6.** US INTOXICATED BY DRUGS under the influence of drugs (slang) **7.** GAMBLING WEIGHTED UNFAIRLY with one side weighted to prevent dice or a roulette wheel from operating randomly

Loader /lōdər/, **Danyon Joseph** (b. 1975) New Zealand swimmer. He won a silver medal in the 200 metres butterfly at the 1992 Olympics and two gold medals in the 200 metres and 400 metres freestyle at the 1996 Olympics.

load factor n. **1.** AIRCRAFT PAYLOAD the payload of an aircraft for a particular flight, expressed as a percentage of the maximum allowable payload **2.** LOAD DIVIDED BY WEIGHT OF AIRCRAFT an external load divided by the weight of an aircraft

loading /lōding/ n. **1.** WEIGHT CARRIED a load or weight carried **2.** INDUST FILLER material added to sth to improve certain properties or add weight **3.** INSUR ADDITIONAL INSURANCE PREMIUM an additional insurance premium or higher rating incurred by items that are more valuable or at greater risk **4.** ELEC ADDITION OF INDUCTANCE the addition of inductance to a transmission line to improve its performance over a given frequency band **5.** Aus ADDITIONAL WAGE a payment made to workers over and above the basic wage in recognition of special skills or unfavourable conditions such as overtime or weekend work

loading gauge n. the height and width limits that apply to trains, including external loads, on particular railways

load line n. = Plimsoll line

loadmaster /lōd maastər/ n. sb who is in charge of loading cargo on a military or commercial transport aircraft

load shedding n. a temporary reduction in a supply of electricity as a method of reducing the demand on the generator

loadstar n. = lodestar

loadstone n. = lodestone

loaf[1] /lōf/ (plural **loaves** /lōvz/) n. **1.** QUANTITY OF BREAD a quantity of bread, shaped and baked as a whole, to be cut into slices for eating **2.** BLOCK OF FOOD SHAPED LIKE LOAF a quantity of food baked in a loaf tin or shaped to form a rectangular block and baked (used in combination) **3.** BRAIN common sense or intelligence (slang) ○ Use your loaf! [Old English hlāf]

loaf[2] /lōf/ (loafs, loafing, loafed) vi. to do very little and spend time in a lazy, rather wasteful way [Mid-19thC. Origin uncertain: probably a back-formation from LOAFER.]

loafer /lōfər/ n. **1.** CLOTHES CASUAL SHOE a casual leather slip-on shoe **2.** LAZY PERSON a lazy person who avoids work and wastes time [Mid-19thC. Origin uncertain: perhaps from German Landläufer 'vagabond', from Land 'country' + laufen 'to run'.]

loaf sugar n. sugar in the form of a large solid cone, formed using 19th-century methods of processing and purifying using large clay moulds

loam /lōm/ n. **1.** GARDENING FERTILE WORKABLE SOIL an easily-worked fertile soil consisting of a mixture of clay, sand, and silt and sometimes also organic matter **2.** BUILDING CLAY AND SAND MIXED FOR BUILDING a mixture of moist clay and sand used for making bricks and in plastering ■ vt. (loams, loaming, loamed) BUILDING USE LOAM IN BUILDING JOB to use loam in the process of covering, filling, or coating sth [Old English lām 'clay, earth'. Ultimately from an Indo-European base meaning 'slippery', which is also the ancestor of English slime and slip.] —**loamy** adj.

loan[1] /lōn/ *n.* **1.** MONEY LENT an amount of money given to sb on the condition that it will be paid back later **2.** LENDING the act of letting sb use sth temporarily **3.** LING = **loanword** ■ *vt.* **(loans, loaning, loaned)** LEND to allow sb to borrow sth on the condition that it is returned ○ *Loan me five pounds, will you?* [12thC. From Old Norse *lán*. Ultimately from an Indo-European word meaning 'to leave', which is also the ancestor of English *lend* and *relinquish*.] ◇ **on loan 1.** being lent or borrowed **2.** working at a temporary location because additional help or expertise is needed there

WORD KEY: USAGE

loan or **lend** sb sth? If you are letting someone else temporarily use physical property or money of yours, it is quite acceptable to use the verb *loan*, as in *I loaned him some lunch money.* This verb, however, can be used only with reference to the temporary lending of physical property or assets in a physical, nonfigurative transaction. But if the context is figurative or nonphysical, **lend** is the only choice: *The evidence lends credence to the witness's prior testimony. Lend me your ears, for I have much to tell. The subtle use of strings lends fluidity to the composition.*

loan[2] /lōn/ *n.* **1.** *Scotland* PATHWAY a rural pathway or grassy cattletrack **2.** MILKING AREA an open area used for milking cows [14thC. Variant of LANE.]

loanback /lōn bak/ *n.* the opportunity for sb to borrow from his or her own pension fund

Loan Council *n.* an Australian federal body set up in 1924 to monitor borrowing by state governments

loan shark *n.* sb who lends money at excessively high rates of interest

loansharking /lōn shaarking/ *n.* the activity or business of lending money at excessively high rates of interest

loan translation *n.* a word or expression that enters a language as a direct translation from another [Translation of German *Lehnübersetzung*]

loanword /lōn wurd/, **loan word** *n.* a word from one language that has become part of everyday usage in another, often with slight modification [Late 19thC. Translation of German *Lehnwort*.]

loath /lōth/, **loth** *adj.* unwilling or reluctant to do sth [Old English *lāþ* 'loathsome']

WORD KEY: SYNONYMS

See Synonyms at ***unwilling***.

loathe /lōth/ **(loathes, loathing, loathed)** *vti.* to dislike sb or sth intensely [Old English *lāþian*. Ultimately from an Indo-European base meaning 'to despise'.] —**loather** *n.*

loathing /lōthing/ *n.* intense dislike of sb or sth —**loathingly** *adv.*

WORD KEY: SYNONYMS

See Synonyms at ***dislike***.

loathly[1] /lōthli/ *adv.* reluctantly or unwillingly (*archaic*) [Old English *lāþlice*]

loathly[2] /lōthli/ *adj.* loathsome (*archaic*) [Old English *lāþlic*]

loathsome /lōthsəm/ *adj.* arousing intense dislike and disgust —**loathsomeness** *n.*

loaves plural of **loaf**[1]

lob /lob/ *v.* **(lobs, lobbing, lobbed) 1.** *vti.* SPORTS HIT BALL IN HIGH ARC to hit or throw a ball in a high curving trajectory **2.** *vt.* THROW CASUALLY to throw sth in a casual careless way **3.** *vi.* MOVE SLOWLY to move slowly or heavily ■ *n.* **1.** SPORTS HIGH ARCHING SHOT a ball hit or thrown in a high curving path **2.** TENNIS BALL OVER TENNIS PLAYER'S HEAD a ball that travels over the head of a tennis player [Late 16thC. Origin uncertain: probably from Low German.] —**lobber** *n.*

lob in *vi. Aus* to arrive or turn up (*informal*)

Lobachevsky /lóbə chéfski/, **Nikolay Ivanovich** (1793–1856) Russian mathematician. His system of non-Euclidian geometry undermined various previously held theories.

lobar /lóbər/ *adj.* ANAT relating to or affecting a lobe, e.g. in the lungs

lobate /ló bayt/, **lobated** /lō báytid/ *adj.* **1.** BIRDS HAVING LOBED TOES having toes with rounded flaps on either side, as grebes have **2.** BOT, ZOOL WITH OR LIKE LOBES having or resembling a lobe or lobes —**lobately** *adv.*

lobby /lóbbi/ *n.* (*plural* **-bies**) **1.** ARCHIT ENTRANCE AREA IN PUBLIC BUILDING a large entrance hall or foyer immediately inside the door of a hotel, theatre, or other public building **2.** POL PUBLIC AREA IN LEGISLATIVE BUILDING a public area in or near a legislative building where people can meet and petition their political representatives **3.** POL VOTING CORRIDOR either of the two rooms in Parliament where members of both houses of Parliament vote for or against bills and proposals **4.** POL GROUP TRYING TO INFLUENCE POLICY a group of campaigners and representatives of particular interests who try to influence political policy on a particular issue (*takes a singular or plural verb*) ○ *the environmental lobby* **5.** POL ATTEMPT TO INFLUENCE POLICY a visit to a legislative building to petition political representatives, organized by a campaign group as a protest or in an attempt to influence policy ■ *v.* **(-bies, -bying, -bied)** POL **1.** *vti.* PETITION POLITICIANS OR INFLUENTIAL PEOPLE to attempt to persuade a political representative or influential person to support or fight a particular cause **2.** *vt.* CAMPAIGN ABOUT LEGISLATION to campaign for or against a particular piece of legislation by attempting to influence politicians [Mid-16thC. From medieval Latin *lobia* 'cloister, covered walk'. Ultimately from a prehistoric Germanic word denoting a roof made of bark, which is also the ancestor of English *lodge*.] —**lobbyer** *n.*

lobbyist /lóbbi ist/ *n.* sb who is paid to lobby political representatives on a particular issue —**lobbyism** *n.*

lobby system *n.* the system of employing professional lobbyists to influence political policy

lobe /lōb/ *n.* **1.** ANAT EARLOBE an earlobe **2.** ANAT ROUNDED BODY PART a rounded division or projection of an organ or part in the body, especially in the lungs, brain, or liver **3.** ROUNDED PROJECTING PART a rounded part that projects from the main body of sth **4.** BOT ROUNDED PLANT PART a rounded segment on a leaf that is not divided all the way to the midrib [15thC. Via late Latin *lobus* from Greek *lobos* 'lobe, pod'.]

lobectomy /lō béktəmi/ (*plural* **-mies**) *n.* the surgical removal of a lobe, e.g. of the lungs, liver, or thyroid

lobefin /lōbfin/ *n.* ZOOL = **crossopterygian** —**lobefinned** *adj.*

lobelia /lō béeli ə/ *n.* a plant that is widely grown for its two-lipped blue, red, or white flowers. Some varieties of lobelia are low-growing or trailing annuals, while others are tall perennials with lance-shaped leaves. Genus: *Lobelia*. [Mid-18thC. Named after Matthias de *Lobel* 1538–1616, Flemish botanist and physician to James I.]

Lobito /loo béetoo/ city and port in western Angola. Population: 150,000 (1983).

Lobito Bay arm of the Atlantic Ocean, western Angola

loblolly boy /lób loli-/, **loblolly man** *n.* in former times, a junior sailor acting as a medical assistant on board ship [From 'thick gruel' *loblolly* (see LOBLOLLY PINE), used as a shipboard remedy]

loblolly pine /lób loli-/, **loblolly** *n.* a pine found in the southeastern United States that has reddish brown flaky bark, long needles grouped in threes, and oblong cones. Genus: *Pinus taeda*. [From earlier *lobololly* 'thick gruel', of uncertain origin (perhaps from dialect *lob* 'to bubble while boiling', an invitation of the sound + dialect *lolly* 'soup'); possibly from its growing where the ground is swampy or muddy, or perhaps from the consistency of its pulp when cooked to make paper]

lobola /lō bólə/, **lobolo** /lō bólō/ *n.* a payment, often in cattle, made by a groom's family to his bride's family before their wedding in some parts of southern and eastern Africa [Mid-19thC. Of Bantu origin.]

lobotomize /lə bóttə mīz/ **(-mizes, -mizing, -mized)**, **lobotomise (-mises, -mising, -mised)** *vt.* **1.** PERFORM BRAIN SURGERY to carry out a surgical operation in which nerves to the prefrontal lobe of the brain are severed **2.** CAUSE TO FEEL APATHETIC OR SLUGGISH to make sb feel sluggish, mentally numb, or lacking in energy or vitality (*informal*)

lobotomy /lə bóttəmi/ (*plural* **-mies**) *n.* a prefrontal lobotomy (*dated*) [Mid-20thC. Coined from LOBE + -TOMY.]

lobscouse /lób skowss/ *n.* a stew of meat and vegetables thickened with ship's biscuits, traditionally eaten by sailors [Early 18thC. Origin uncertain.]

lobster /lóbstər/ *n.* **1.** ZOOL EDIBLE SEA CREATURE a hard-shelled edible marine crustacean that has a pair of large pincers, five pairs of limbs, eyes on stalks, and long antennae. Family: Homaridae. **2.** ZOOL SPINY LOBSTER a crustacean that is similar in appearance to the true lobster but without the two large pincers, especially the spiny lobster. Family: Palinuridae. **3.** LOBSTER'S FLESH AS FOOD the flesh of a lobster as food. The tail meat and meat extracted from the claws is particularly valued for its fine, slightly sweet flavour. ■ *vi.* **(-sters, -stering, -stered)** CATCH LOBSTERS to fish for lobsters [Old English *loppestre*, of uncertain origin: probably an alteration of Latin *locusta* 'locust, crustacean', influenced by *loppe* 'spider' and nouns ending in *-ster*]

lobsterman /lóbstərmən/ (*plural* **-men** /-mən/) *n.* **1.** CATCHER OF LOBSTERS sb who catches lobsters for a living **2.** LOBSTERING BOAT a boat designed for catching lobsters

lobster Newburg /-nyoo burg/ *n.* lobster meat cooked in a rich sherry sauce with butter and cream and usually served on small pieces of toast or croutons or in a pastry shell [Early 20thC. Origin uncertain, possibly from *Newburgh*, city in New York state.]

lobster pot *n.* a trap in the form of a basket, used for catching lobsters

lobster thermidor /-thúrmi dawr/ *n.* cooked lobster with a wine and cream sauce served in the shell with a topping of melted cheese [Late 19thC. *Thermidor* from *Thermidor* (1891), play by the French dramatist Victorien Sardou (1831–1908).]

lobulate /lóbbyoolət/ *adj.* having or made up of small lobes ○ *a lobulate organ* —**lobulation** /lóbbyoo láysh'n/ *n.*

lobule /lóbbyool/ *n.* **1.** SMALL LOBE a small lobe **2.** SECTION OF LOBE a section or division of a lobe [Late 17thC. Formed from LOBE, on the model of GLOBULE.] —**lobular** /lóbbyoolər/ *adj.* —**lobulate** /lóbbyoolət/ *adj.* —**lobulose** /lóbbyoolōss/ *adj.* —**lobularly** /lóbbyoolərli/ *adv.*

lobworm /lób wurm/ *n.* **1.** = **lugworm 2.** EARTHWORM a large earthworm used by anglers as bait [Mid-17thC. *Lob* from obsolete sense 'sth hanging', (see LOB).]

local /lók'l/ *adj.* **1.** IN NEARBY AREA relating to, situated in, or providing a service for a particular area, especially the area near home or work ○ *the local school* **2.** TYPICAL OF PARTICULAR AREA typical of, or only found in, a particular area ○ *the local dialect* **3.** NOT WIDESPREAD not covering a wide area or the whole country ○ *There have been local outbreaks of the disease.* **4.** POL RELATING TO GOVERNMENTAL REGION relating to a comparatively small region that controls some aspects of practical government such as housing or education ○ *local elections* **5.** MED AFFECTING SMALL PART affecting only a specific part of the body ○ *local infection* **6.** TRANSP STOPPING EVERYWHERE stopping at all the stations or bus stops on a route ○ *a local train* **7.** TELECOM TO A PHONE NUMBER NEARBY made to a phone number within a fairly small radius and therefore charged at a lower rate than long-distance calls ○ *a phone for local calls only* ■ *n.* **1.** SB WHO COMES FROM PARTICULAR AREA sb who lives in a particular area, was born there, or has lived there for a long time **2.** NEIGHBOURHOOD PUB a pub close to where sb lives that the person visits regularly (*informal*) ○ *I called in at the local on the way home from work.* **3.** TRANSP STOPPING TRAIN OR BUS a train or bus that stops at all the stations or stops on the route **4.** MED LOCAL ANAESTHETIC a local anaesthetic (*informal*) **5.** *US, Can* POL BRANCH OF ORGANIZATION a local branch or office, especially of a labour union [14thC. Via French from late Latin *localis*, from Latin *locus* 'place'.] —**locally** *adv.* —**localness** *n.*

local anaesthetic *n.* a drug, usually given by injection, that eliminates pain, though not necessarily all sensation, in a particular area of the body without affecting consciousness

local area network *n.* a network of personal computers and peripheral devices linked by cable and able to share resources

local authority *n.* the body that has political and administrative powers to control a particular city or region. US term **local government**

local colour *n.* unusual or traditional features of a particular place that make it interesting

locale /lō kaál/ *n.* the place in which sth happens or in which the action in a book or film takes place [Late 18thC. Alteration of French *local* 'local', on the model of MORALE.]

local examination *n.* an examination, e.g. the GCSE, set by a national examination board but held at local schools and colleges around the country

local government *n.* **1.** GOVERNMENT OF LOCAL AREA the government of a town, city, or region at a local level by locally elected politicians ○ *worked in local government all his life* **2.** *US* = local authority

localise *vti.* = localize

localism /lōkəlizəm/ *n.* **1.** LOCAL IDIOM OR TRADITION a phrase, expression, or custom peculiar to the people in a particular area **2.** INTEREST NARROWED TO LOCAL AFFAIRS interest in local matters and customs rather than in national or global issues, sometimes resulting in a limited perspective —**localist** *n.*

locality /lō kálləti/ (*plural* **-ties**) *n.* **1.** PARTICULAR PLACE a particular place, district, or neighbourhood **2.** SETTING FOR EVENT the place or setting where sth happens **3.** SITUATION IN SPACE OR TIME the fact of being situated at a particular point in space or time

localize /lōkə līz/ (**-izes, -izing, -ized**), **localise** (**-ises, -ising, -ised**) *v.* **1.** *vti.* CONFINE OR BE CONFINED TO PLACE to become confined to or restrict sth to a particular area **2.** *vt.* FIND LOCATION OF to find the source or location of sth **3.** *vt.* DECENTRALIZE CONTROL OF to transfer power or control from a central authority to local bodies —**localizable** *adj.* —**localization** /lōkə līz záysh'n/ *n.*

local option *n.* the power granted to a local government to decide whether to implement a particular policy, especially with regard to the sale of alcohol

Locarno /lo kaárnō/ town and resort in Ticino Canton, southern Switzerland. Population: 14,765 (1992).

locate /lō káyt/ (**-cates, -cating, -cated**) *v.* **1.** *vt.* FIND to discover where sth is **2.** *vi.* ESTABLISH BUSINESS IN PLACE to establish a residence or business in a particular place **3.** *vt.* POSITION to put sth in a particular place [Early 16thC. From Latin *locat-*, past participle stem of *locare*, from *locus* 'place'.] —**locatable** *adj.* —**locater** *n.*

located /lō káytid/ ◇ **be located** to exist or be found in a particular place

location /lō káysh'n/ *n.* **1.** POSITION the site or position of sth **2.** CINEMA FILM SETTING a place away from a studio where scenes for a film are shot ○ *The film was shot on location in Scotland.* **3.** DISCOVERY the discovery of sth ○ *A metal detector is an essential aid in the location of buried treasure.* **4.** POSITIONING OF STH the positioning or siting of sth or sb in a particular place **5.** *S Africa* S AFRICAN TOWNSHIP a small township in South Africa for people classed by the apartheid system as Black or Coloured **6.** *Scotland* LAW HIRING STH OUT a contractual state under Scots law in which sb has agreed to hire out either an object or his or her services —**locational** *adj.*

locative /lōkətiv/ *adj.* INDICATING PLACE OR DIRECTION with the grammatical ending or form that indicates place or direction ■ *n.* **1.** GRAMMATICAL CASE the grammatical case indicating place or direction **2.** WORD IN LOCATIVE CASE a word or expression in the locative case [Early 19thC. Coined from LOCATE, on the model of NOMINATIVE and ACCUSATIVE.]

loc. cit., in loc. cit. *adv.* in the place cited. Full form **loco citato**

loch /lokh, lok/ *n. Scotland* **1.** LAKE a lake **2.** ARM OF SEA a narrow arm of the sea stretching inland [14thC. From Scottish Gaelic. Ultimately from an Indo-European word denoting a body of water, which is the ancestor of English *lake*.]

lochan /lókhən, lókən/ *n. Scotland* a small lake or pool [Late 17thC. From Scottish Gaelic, literally 'small loch'.]

Lochgilphead /lokh gílp hed/ town in Argyll and Bute Council Area, west-central Scotland. It is the administrative centre. Population: 2,521 (1991).

lochia /lóki ə/ *n.* the normal vaginal discharge of cell debris and blood after childbirth [Late 17thC. From Greek *lokhia*, from *lokhos* 'childbirth'. Ultimately from an Indo-European base meaning 'to lie', which is also the ancestor of English *lie* and *lay*.] —**lochial** *adj.*

Loch na Keal /lókh na keˊel/ sea loch classified as a National Scenic Area of Scotland, on the island of Mull

Loch Rannoch and Glen Lyon /lokh ránnəkh ənd glen lī ən/ a National Scenic Area in central Scotland

loci plural of **locus**

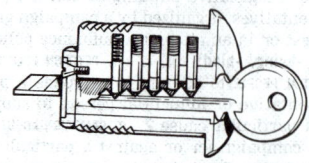

Lock: Cross-section of a key-operated lock

lock¹ /lok/ *n.* **1.** FASTENING MECHANISM a mechanism used to fasten or secure a door, window, or lid, especially one operated by a key **2.** TRANSP GATED SECTION OF CANAL a short section of a canal or river with gates at each end and a mechanism for letting water in and out. Boats enter the lock and are raised or lowered as the water level is altered and then exit to a higher or lower section of the waterway. **3.** CARS DEGREE OF WHEEL TURN the degree to which the wheels of a vehicle pivot as the car turns. A good lock means that the wheels can be turned a long way, making it easier to turn the vehicle in a small space. **4.** WRESTLING WRESTLING HOLD a wrestling hold in which a wrestler twists or puts pressure on part of the other wrestler's body **5.** ARMS GUN PART the part of a gun that makes the charge explode **6.** BLOCKING DEVICE a device, e.g. one operated by a password, that prevents an unauthorized person from using sth **7.** RUGBY PLAYER IN A RUGBY SCRUM either of the two players in the second row in a rugby scrum **8.** ENG AIRLOCK an airlock ■ *v.* (**locks, locking, locked**) **1.** *vti.* FASTEN USING LOCK to fasten sth or become fastened using a lock **2.** *vt.* PUT IN A SECURE PLACE to put sth into a safe place or container that can be locked ○ *Her diamonds are locked in a safe deposit box.* **3.** *vt.* SECURE PLACE to make a building or vehicle secure by locking the doors and windows **4.** *vt.* COMPUT PREVENT UNAUTHORIZED USE OF to prevent sth from being used by an unauthorized person, e.g. via software **5.** *vti.* FIX OR BE FIXED IN PLACE to become fixed in one position, or fix sth in one position, so that it cannot move normally **6.** *vt.* HOLD FIRMLY to hold sb tightly ○ *locked in a passionate embrace* **7.** *vt.* TRAP IN A DIFFICULT SITUATION to put sb in a situation or conflict from which it is difficult to escape ○ *locked into a lengthy argument* **8.** *vt.* TRANSP PUT LOCKS ON WATERWAY to put locks on a stretch of canal or river **9.** *vi.* TRANSP GO THROUGH CANAL LOCKS to go through a series of locks on a boat, or take a boat through a series of locks **10.** *vt.* PRINTING SECURE TYPE IN PRESS to secure metal type in a press **11.** *vt.* FIN = **lock up** *v.* 4 [Old English *loc*] —**lockable** *adj.* ◇ **lock, stock, and barrel** completely

lock away *vt.* = lock up *v.* 1, lock up *v.* 2

lock in *vt.* to prevent sb from leaving a room or building by locking the door

lock on *vti.* MIL to find a target and track it automatically, or to make a radar or missile find and track a target

lock out *vt.* **1.** PREVENT FROM ENTERING to prevent sb from entering a place by locking the door **2.** DENY ACCESS TO WORKPLACE to prevent workers from entering their workplace, usually as a strategy in an industrial dispute

lock up *v.* **1.** *vt.* IMPRISON to put sb into prison, a secure hospital, or other institution that deprives him or her of freedom **2.** *vt.* STORE IN A SECURE PLACE to put valuables in a secure locked place **3.** *vti.* SECURE

BUILDING to make a building secure by locking all the doors and windows **4.** *vt.* FIN INVEST IN LONG-TERM PLAN to put money into a form of savings or investment that does not allow easy access to the funds

lock² /lok/ *n.* **1.** PIECE OF HAIR a group of hairs that hang together, on sb's head or cut off **2.** TEXTILES WISP OF FIBRE a small bunch of wool, cotton, or other fibre ■ **locks** *npl.* HAIR sb's hair (*literary*) [Old English *locc*]

lockage /lókij/ *n.* **1.** PASSAGE THROUGH LOCK the passage of a boat through a canal or river lock **2.** FEE a fee paid by a boat to pass through a lock **3.** LOCKS a number of locks on a canal or river

Locke /lok/, John (1632–1704) English philosopher. He developed the doctrine of empiricism according to which knowledge was acquired by experience, not by intuition.

locker /lókər/ *n.* **1.** LOCKABLE COMPARTMENT a small lockable cupboard or compartment where personal belongings can be left, e.g. at a swimming pool, gym, school, or workplace **2.** TRUNK a trunk or low chest, used for storage **3.** SB OR STH THAT LOCKS a person who or device that locks sth

Lockerbie /lókərbi/ town in Dumfries and Galloway, southwestern Scotland. In 1988 an airliner was destroyed over the town by a terrorist bomb, killing all the passengers and crew and 11 of the town's residents. Population: 3,982 (1991).

locker room *n.* a room containing lockers, where people change their clothes for sports or swimming

locker-room *adj.* typical of or suitable only for a men's locker room ○ *telling locker-room jokes*

locket /lókit/ *n.* a small decorative metal case with a hinged cover containing a picture or memento, worn on a neck chain or bracelet [14thC. From Old French *locquet*, literally 'small latch', from *loc* 'latch', ultimately of prehistoric Germanic origin.]

lockfast /lók faast/ *adj. Scotland* fastened with a lock and consequently the subject of a more serious offence if burgled

lock forward *n.* RUGBY = **lock¹** *n.* 7

lock-in *n.* a session of after-hours drinking inside a pub (*informal*)

lockjaw /lók jaw/ *n.* **1.** = trismus **2.** = tetanus [Early 19thC. From the muscle spasms in the jaw that affect sufferers.]

lockkeeper /lók keepər/ *n.* sb employed to look after or control a lock on a waterway and collect any fees payable. Traditionally, the lockkeeper lives in a house close to the lock.

locknut /lók nut/ *n.* **1.** SECOND NUT TIGHTENED ON A FIRST a second nut tightened on a first to prevent it from loosening **2.** SELF-LOCKING NUT a nut designed to lock itself in place once tightened

lock-on *n.* MIL the point at which a radar or missile locates and starts to track a target

lockout /lók owt/ *n.* the preventing of workers from entering their workplace, a tactic sometimes used by management in an industrial dispute

lockram /lókrəm/ *n.* a coarse linen fabric [15thC. From French *locrenan*, an alteration of *Locronan*, a village in Brittany where the cloth was made.]

locksmith /lók smith/ *n.* sb who makes or sells locks and keys and repairs and installs locks. A locksmith can also open a lock when the owner has lost the key or has become locked out. —**locksmithing** *n.*

lock stitch *n.* the usual stitch made by a sewing machine, formed by the thread above the fabric interlocking with the bobbin thread

lockup /lók up/ *n.* **1.** PLACE WITH PRISON CELLS a small prison, a block of cells at a police station, or a similar place where prisoners are kept for a short time **2.** GARAGE a garage, usually one of several grouped together, that can be rented (*often used before a noun*) ○ *a lockup garage* **3.** COMM SHOP a small shop with no accommodation attached to it (*often used before a noun*) ○ *a lockup shop* **4.** SECURING OF BUILDING the securing of a building by locking it **5.** TIME FOR LOCKING BUILDING the time at which a building is locked

loco[1] /lṓkō/ *n.* a railway locomotive (*informal*) [Mid-19thC. Shortening of LOCOMOTIVE.]

loco[2] /lṓkō/ *adj.* **WILDLY IRRATIONAL** wildly irrational (*informal*) ▪ *vt.* (-cos, -coing, -coed) AGRIC **POISON ANIMAL** to poison an animal with locoweed [Late 19thC. From Spanish, 'irrational', of uncertain origin: perhaps from Arabic *laqwā* 'thoughtless'.]

loco[3] /lṓkō/ *adj.* indicating that the performer should return to playing notes in the original register, negating a previous direction that they should be played an octave higher [Early 19thC. From Italian, literally 'at the place'.] —**loco** *adv.*

loco citato /lṓkō si tāátō/ *adv.* full form of **loc. cit.** [From Latin, 'in the place cited']

loco disease *n.* a disease of cattle, sheep, and horses in the western United States and Canada, caused by eating locoweed. It affects the animals' nervous systems, with symptoms of weakness, trembling, and inability to move.

locoman /lṓkōmən/ (*plural* **-men** /-mən/) *n.* a train's engine driver or other engine crew (*informal*) [Mid-20thC. From LOCO[1] + MAN.]

locomotion /lṓkə mṓsh'n/ *n.* movement or the power to move from one place to another [Mid-17thC. From Latin *loco* 'from a place' + MOTION.]

Locomotive

locomotive /lṓkə mṓtiv/ *n.* RAIL **RAIL ENGINE** a railway engine ▪ *adj.* **1.** MOVABLE able to move about freely **2.** RELATING TO LOCOMOTION relating to, allowing, or aiding in the ability to move ○ *locomotive organs* [Early 17thC. From modern Latin *locomotivus*, from Latin *loco* 'from a place' + late Latin *motivus* 'moving' (see MOTIVE).]

locomotor /lṓkə mṓtər/ *adj.* relating to or aiding in locomotion ○ *locomotor hyperactivity* [Late 19thC. From Latin *loco* 'from a place' + MOTOR.]

locomotor ataxia *n.* MED = **tabes dorsalis**

locomotory /lṓkə mṓtəri/ *adj.* able to move independently

locoweed /lṓkō weed/ *n.* a perennial plant of the pea family, found in western North America. Animals that eat it can contract loco disease. Genera: *Oxytropis* and *Astragalus.* [Late 19thC. From LOCO[2] + WEED.]

locular /lṓkyōōlər/, **loculate** /-yōōlət/ *adj.* separated into small chambers or cavities that are divided by membranes —**loculation** /lṓkyōō láysh'n/ *n.*

locule /lṓkyōol/, **loculus** /lṓkyōōləss/ (*plural* **-li** /-lī/) *n.* a small cavity, chamber, or cell in a plant or animal [Late 19thC. Via French from Latin *loculus,* literally 'small place', from *locus* 'place'.]

locum /lṓkəm/, **locum tenens** /-tënnenz/ (*plural* **locum tenentes** /-te nén teez/) *n.* sb, especially a doctor or a member of the clergy, who stands in to do the job of another who is away or unwell [Mid-17thC. From medieval Latin *locum tenens* 'one holding the place', from Latin *locus* 'place' + *tenere* 'to hold'.]

locus /lṓkəss/ (*plural* **-ci** /lṓ sī/) *n.* **1.** PLACE a place where sth happens **2.** MATH **SET OF POINTS** a set of points, the positions of which satisfy a set of algebraic conditions **3.** GENETICS **GENE POSITION** the position of a gene in a chromosome [Early 18thC. From Latin, 'place' (source of English *local* and *locate*), of unknown origin.]

locus classicus /-klássikəss/ (*plural* **loci classici** /lṓ sī klássi sī/) *n.* a much-quoted passage from an authoritative text [From Latin, 'classical place']

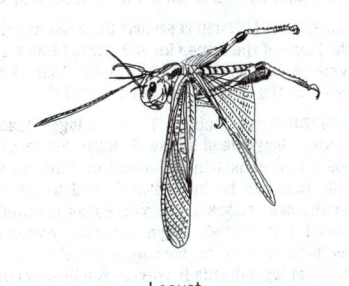

Locust

locust /lṓkəst/ *n.* **1.** INSECTS **SWARMING GRASSHOPPER** a grasshopper found in warm regions that often swarms and devours crops and vegetation. Family: Acrididae. **2.** INSECTS = **seventeen-year locust 3.** TREES **POD-BEARING TREE** a pod-bearing tree of the pea family, including honey locust, swamp locust, and carob **4.** TREES = **false acacia 5.** INDUST **HARD WOOD** the hard yellowish wood of a locust tree [14thC. Via French from Latin *locusta* 'locust' (source also of English *lobster*); in sense 3, from the supposed resemblance of the pod to a locust.]

locution /lə kyōosh'n/ *n.* **1.** PHRASE a phrase or expression typically used by a group of people **2.** STYLE OF SPEECH the way in which sb speaks [15thC. Directly or via French from, ultimately, Latin *locut-*, the past participle stem of *loqui* 'to speak'.]

Lod /lod/ city in Israel, situated 37 km/23 mi. northwest of Jerusalem. Population: 45,500 (1992).

lode /lōd/ *n.* **1.** GEOL **DEPOSIT OF ORE** a deposit or vein of ore **2.** GEOG **FENS WATERWAY** a waterway that acts as a drain off the land in an area of fenland [Old English *lād,* literally 'sth that leads' (see LOAD).]

loden /lṓd'n/ *n.* **1.** TEXTILES **THICK WATERPROOF WOOLLEN CLOTH** a thick waterproof woollen cloth used for coats and jackets **2.** COLOURS **DARK GREEN** the dark-green colour of loden cloth [Early 20thC. From German.] —**loden** *adj.*

lodestar /lṓd staar/, **loadstar** *n.* **1.** THE NORTH STAR the North Star (**Polaris**), used for navigation or as a reference position in astronomy **2.** GUIDING PRINCIPLE sth that sb uses as a model or principle to guide behaviour (*literary*) [14thC. From LODE in the obsolete sense 'course, leading' + STAR.]

lodestone /lṓd stōn/, **loadstone** *n.* **1.** GEOL **MAGNETITE** magnetite or a piece of magnetite with magnetic properties **2.** ATTRACTION sb or sth that attracts others like a magnet [Early 16thC. From LODE in the obsolete sense 'way, leading', from the use of the stone's magnetic properties as a guide + STONE.]

lodge /loj/ *n.* **1.** SMALL GATEKEEPER'S HOUSE a small house in the grounds of a large country house, usually near the main gate, traditionally occupied by a gatekeeper, gardener, or estate worker **2.** LEISURE **COUNTRY BUILDING** a cabin or other building in the country providing temporary accommodation, e.g. as a holiday home or a temporary shelter for campers, walkers, skiers, or hunters **3.** LEISURE **INN OR HOTEL** a large house or hotel **4.** EDUC **PORTER'S ROOM** a room or set of rooms at the entrance to a university college for use by the college porter or caretaker **5.** BRANCH OF UNION OR SOCIETY a local branch or chapter of a society such as the Freemasons, or an organization such as a trade union **6.** MEETING HALL a hall or other meeting place used by a branch of a society **7.** NATIVE N AMERICAN DWELLING a dwelling traditionally used by Native North American people, e.g. a wigwam, hogan, or longhouse **8.** ZOOL **BEAVER'S DEN** the den of certain animals, especially the dome-shaped structure built by a beaver ▪ *v.* (**lodges, lodging, lodged**) **1.** *vt.* REGISTER COMPLAINT OR APPEAL to make a formal complaint, accusation, or appeal by handing the documents to the appropriate authority **2.** *vt.* DEPOSIT STH IN SAFE PLACE to put sth somewhere or give it to sb for safekeeping **3.** *vti.* STICK OR GET STUCK to become jammed or embedded somewhere, or to jam or embed sth somewhere ○ *His head was lodged between the railings.* **4.** *vt.* LIVE IN SB'S HOUSE to live in sb's house, free or as a paying guest (*dated*) ○ *She is lodging with her sister.* **5.** *vt.* PUT IN ACCOMMODATION

to place sb in temporary accommodation ○ *They were evacuated and lodged in a nearby school overnight.* **6.** *vt.* GIVE SB POWER TO ACT to invest sb with the power or authority to do sth ○ *powers that are lodged with the cabinet* **7.** *vti.* AGRIC **BEAT CROPS FLAT** to flatten crops, or be flattened by the wind and rain [13thC. From Old French *loge* 'hut'. Ultimately from a prehistoric Germanic word denoting a roof made of bark, which is also the ancestor of English *lobby*.]

Lodge /loj/ *n. Aus* the official residence of the Australian prime minister in Canberra

Lodge /loj/, **David John** (*b.* 1935) British novelist, critic, and scholar. Many of his novels, such as *Small World* (1984), are autobiographical, describing university life.

lodgement *n.* = **lodgment**

lodger /lṓjər/ *n.* sb who rents a room in another person's house, sharing the accommodation with the owner ○ *'...the small kitchen in which she cooked the food for her lodgers'* (Jack London, *The People of the Abyss*; 1905)

lodging /lṓjjing/ *n.* ACCOMMODATION somewhere to stay temporarily ○ *We asked where we could find lodging for the night.* ▪ **lodgings** *npl.* RENTED ROOM a room or rooms in a boarding house or private home available for rent (*dated*)

lodging house *n.* a private home or boarding house offering accommodation for rent (*dated*) US term **rooming house**

lodgment /lṓjmənt/, **lodgement** *n.* **1.** PLACING OF SB IN ACCOMMODATION the accommodation of sb in a particular place (*formal*) **2.** PLACE TO STAY a temporary place to stay (*formal*) **3.** ACCUMULATION OR BLOCKAGE a build-up of sth, especially when this causes a blockage **4.** MIL FOOTHOLD IN ENEMY TERRITORY a small area of land that has been captured and held on the edge of enemy territory

lodicule /lṓddi kyōol/ *n.* any of the tiny scales at the base of the ovary of the flower of certain grasses [Mid-19thC. From Latin *lodicula,* literally 'small coverlet', from *lodix* 'blanket', of uncertain origin.]

Lodz /wooch/, **Łódź** industrial city in central Poland, situated about 121 km/75 mi. southwest of Warsaw. Population: 825,600 (1995).

Loeb /lōb/, **Jacques** (1859–1924) German-born US physiologist. He produced pioneering work in artificial parthenogenesis, and conducted important research in physiology and psychology.

loess /lṓ ess, löss/ *n.* a fine-grained yellowish-brown deposit of soil left by the wind. The loess deposited by winds from Central Asia provided the basis for productive farming in early China. [Mid-19thC. From German *Löss,* from, ultimately, Swiss German *lösch* 'loose'.]

Loewi /lṓ i/, **Otto** (1873–1961) German pharmacologist. He shared a Nobel Prize in chemistry (1936) for his work on the chemical transmission of nerve impulses.

Lofoten Islands /lṓ fótən-/ chain of two groups of rock islands, northwestern Norway, in the Norwegian Sea. The southernmost group is the Lofoten, and the Vesterålen are to the north. Population: 26,241 (1970). Area: 4,044 sq. km/1,600 sq. mi.

loft /loft/ *n.* **1.** ROOF SPACE the area between the ceiling of the top floor of a building and the roof (*often used before a noun*) ○ *We've got so much junk in the loft!* ○ *loft conversions* ○ *loft ladder* **2.** UPPER FLOOR OF BARN the upper floor of a barn or stable, used for storing hay ○ *a hay loft* **3.** GALLERY a gallery or balcony, especially the gallery where the organ is situated in a church ○ *the organ loft* **4.** US BUILDING **UPPER FLOOR OF WAREHOUSE OR FACTORY** an upper floor of a commercial building such as a factory or warehouse, typically converted to residential or studio use **5.** PIGEON COOP a shelter in which domesticated pigeons are kept ○ *a pigeon loft* **6.** GOLF SLANTING ANGLE ON GOLF CLUB the angle of the face of a golf club designed to drive the ball high into the air **7.** TEXTILES **THICKNESS OF FABRIC** the thickness and fluffiness of fabric, especially as an indication of its warmth ▪ *vt.* (**lofts, lofting, lofted**) **1.** SPORTS HIT BALL HIGH to hit a ball in a high arching path in golf or cricket **2.** KEEP IN LOFT to store sth in a loft [Pre-12thC. From Old Norse *lopt* 'air, upstairs room'. Ultimately from a prehistoric Germanic word meaning 'air, sky', which is also the ancestor of English *lift*.]

lofty /lófti/ (**-ier, -iest**) *adj.* **1. HAUGHTY** behaving in a falsely superior or haughty manner **2. EXALTED** exalted and refined **3. HIGH-RANKING** of the highest rank or status **4. VERY HIGH** very high or tall ○ *lofty peaks*

log[1] /log/ *n.* **1. PIECE CUT FROM TREE** a section of the trunk or a thick branch of a tree that has been cut for fuel or building material **2. TRANSP RECORD OF JOURNEY** a record of a journey made by a ship or aircraft, detailing all events, or the book in which it is kept **3. RECORD OF EVENTS** any detailed record of events **4. NAUT DEVICE FOR MEASURING SPEED** a float attached to a ship by a line, formerly used for measuring the ship's speed ■ *v.* (**logs, logging, logged**) **1.** *vt.* **TRANSP RECORD EVENT IN LOG** to record information or an event in a log ○ *The computer will log all these transactions automatically.* **2.** *vti.* **FELL TREES** to cut down the trees growing on a particular area of land **3.** *vti.* **CUT UP TREE FOR LOGS** to cut up a tree to produce logs for fuel or building **4.** *vt.* **TRAVEL PARTICULAR DISTANCE OR SPEED** to travel a particular distance, time, or speed that is then recorded in a log ○ *These checks are made routinely once the aircraft has logged 100,000 miles.* [14thC. Origin unknown.] ◇ **sleep like a log** to sleep very soundly

log in *vti.* = **log on**

log off, log out *vi.* COMPUT to end a session on a computer by typing in the appropriate command

log on, log in *vti.* COMPUT to gain access to a computer system by entering a name and password or other appropriate commands

log out *vi.* = **log off**

log[2] /log/ *n.* a logarithm (*informal*) [Mid-17thC. Shortening.]

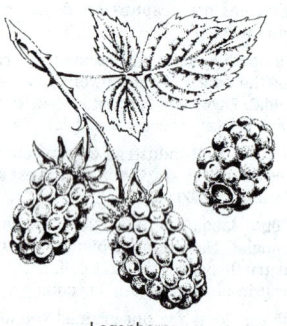

Loganberry

loganberry /lṓgənbəri/ (*plural* **-ries**) *n.* **1. PLANTS PLANT WITH EDIBLE FRUIT** a prickly trailing hybrid plant native to the western United States and northwest Mexico, cultivated for its edible fruit. Latin name: *Rubus ursinus loganobaccus.* **2. PURPLISH-RED FRUIT** the purplish-red fruit obtained from the loganberry, similar to a large raspberry [Late 19thC. Named after James H. *Logan* (1841–1928), US horticulturist who first cultivated the plant.]

logaoedic /lògġə eédik/ *adj.* used to describe a poem or line of verse in which different metrical feet are mixed to give an effect like speech or prose [Mid-19thC. Via Late Latin from Greek *logaoidikos*, from *logos* 'speech' + *aoidē* 'song'.]

logarithm /lógġə rithəm/ *n.* the power to which a base must be raised to equal a given number. For example, the logarithm of 8 to the base 2 is 3, since $2^3 = 8$. [Early 17thC. From modern Latin *logarithmus*, from Greek *logos* 'word, proportion' (see LOGOS) + *arithmos* 'number' (see ARITHMETIC).] —**logarithmic** /lògġə ríthmik/ *adj.* —**logarithmically** /-ríthmikli/ *adv.*

logbook /lóg boòk/ *n.* **1. BOOK CONTAINING RECORD OF JOURNEY** a book containing a record of a journey made by a ship or aircraft **2. VEHICLE REGISTRATION DOCUMENT** a document issued formerly in the UK giving details of a vehicle and its owners. This has now been replaced by the registration document, which some people still refer to informally as the logbook. [Late 17thC. So called because it recorded all *loggings*, measurements of the ship's speed.]

log cabin *n.* **1. LOG HOUSE** a simple house made with logs **2. SEW PATCHWORK DESIGN** a patchwork design

formed from blocks that are made up of strips of fabric attached round each side of a central square

loge /lōzh/ *n.* **1.** *US* **FRONT OF BALCONY** the area in a theatre at the front of the upper level **2. BOX IN THEATRE** a small private enclosure or box in a theatre [Mid-18thC. Via French from Old French, 'hut' (see LODGE).]

loggerhead /lógġər hed/ *n.* **1.** ZOOL = **loggerhead turtle 2.** BIRDS = **loggerhead shrike 3.** MECH ENG **TOOL FOR HOT LIQUIDS** a tool consisting of a ball or bulb on a long handle that can be heated and used to melt pitch **4. UNINTELLIGENT PERSON** sb perceived as unintelligent (*archaic*) [Late 16thC. Origin uncertain: probably from *logger* 'block of wood for hobbling a horse' (from LOG[1]) + HEAD.] ◇ **at loggerheads** involved in a quarrel or feud

loggerhead shrike *n.* BIRDS a North American shrike that has grey plumage, black and white wings and tail, a black facial mask, and a hooked beak. Latin name: *Lanius ludovicianus.*

loggerhead turtle *n.* a large flesh-eating sea turtle that lives in warm waters and has a large head and rounded shell. Latin name: *Caretta caretta.*

Loggia

loggia /lójji ə, lṓ-/ (*plural* **-gias** or **-gie** /-jay, -/) *n.* **1. COVERED BALCONY AND WALKWAY** a covered open-sided walkway, often with arches, along one side of a building **2. THEATRE BALCONY** a balcony in a theatre [Mid-18thC. Via Italian from Old French *loge* (see LODGE).]

logging /lógging/ *n.* the job of felling, trimming, and transporting trees

logia plural of **logion**

logic /lójjik/ *n.* **1.** PHILOSOPHY **THEORY OF REASONING** the branch of philosophy that deals with the theory of deductive and inductive arguments and aims to distinguish good from bad reasoning **2. SYSTEM OF REASONING** any system of or an instance of reasoning and inference **3. SENSIBLE ARGUMENT AND THOUGHT** sensible rational thought and argument rather than ideas that are influenced by emotion or whim **4. REASONING OF PARTICULAR FIELD** the principles of reasoning relevant to a particular field **5. INESCAPABLE RELATIONSHIP AND PATTERN OF EVENTS** the relationship between certain events, situations, or objects, and the inevitable consequences of their interaction **6.** COMPUT **CIRCUIT DESIGN** the circuit design and principles used by a computer in its operation [14thC. Via French *logique* from, ultimately, Greek *logikē (tekhnē)* '(art) of reason', from *logos* (see LOGOS).]

logical /lójjik'l/ *adj.* **1. SENSIBLE AND BASED ON FACTS** based on facts, clear rational thought, and sensible reasoning **2. ABLE TO THINK RATIONALLY** able to think sensibly and come to a rational conclusion based on facts rather than emotion **3.** PHILOSOPHY **OF PHILOSOPHICAL LOGIC** relating to philosophical logic —**logicality** /lójji kálləti/ *n.* —**logicalness** /lójjik'lnəss/ *n.*

logical atomism *n.* the philosophical theories of Bertrand Russell and Ludwig Wittgenstein's early period that analyse a proposition in terms of its relation to certain philosophically basic propositions

logical consequence *n.* a proposition that is implied by valid reasoning from true propositions

logical constant *n.* a connective expression such as 'not', 'or', 'if … then', or 'if and only if' that is used in formal logic

logically /lójjikli/ *adv.* **1. WITH REGARD TO REASON** in a rational well-reasoned way ○ *consider something*

logically **2. USING REASON** using good or rational reasoning ○ *Your conclusion follows logically.*

logical positivism *n.* a theory in linguistic philosophy that holds that in order for a sentence to be cognitively meaningful, it has to be verifiable

logical truth *n.* a proposition that is necessarily true

logic bomb *n.* a piece of software that interferes with the proper working of the computer's operating system

logic circuit *n.* a computer switching circuit that performs operations on input signals

logician /lə jísh'n/ *n.* sb whose special training is in philosophical logic

logicism /lójjisizəm/ *n.* the theory at the base of mathematics that mathematics is reducible to logic broadly construed to include set theory

login *n.* = **logon**

logion /lóggi on/ (*plural* **-a** /-gi ə/) *n.* a saying attributed to Jesus Christ that is not in the New Testament [Late 19thC. From Greek, 'oracle', from *logos* (see LOGOS).]

logistic[1] /lə jístik/ *adj.* relating to an uninterpreted calculus or system of symbolic logic [Early 17thC. From medieval Latin *logisticus*, from, ultimately, Greek *logos* 'reckoning, calculation' (see LOGOS).] —**logistician** /lójji stísh'n/ *n.*

logistic[2] /lə jístik/, **logistical** /-tik'l/ *adj.* **1. RELATING TO TRANSPORTING OF THINGS** involving the planning and management of how things are moved, especially military forces or industrial goods **2. INVOLVING COMPLICATED ORGANIZATION** involving the planning and management of any complex task [Mid-20thC. From French *logistique* (see LOGISTICS).] —**logistically** *adv.*

logistics /lə jístiks/ *n.* (*takes a singular or plural verb*) **1. ORGANIZATION OF COMPLEX TASK** the planning and implementation of a complex task **2. MOVEMENT MANAGEMENT** the planning and control of the flow of goods and materials through an organization or manufacturing process **3.** MIL **ORGANIZATION OF TROOP MOVEMENTS** the planning and organization of the movement of troops, their equipment, and supplies [Late 19thC. Formed from French *logistique*, from *loger* 'to lodge', from Old French *loge* (see LODGE).]

logjam /lóg jam/ *n.* **1. DEADLOCK** a situation where sth is blocked or at a standstill and is unable to progress **2.** *US, Can* **RIVER BLOCKAGE** a blockage caused by floating logs in a river

log line *n.* a line from a ship trailing a floating log to determine the ship's speed

logo /lṓgō/ (*plural* **-gos**) *n.* a design used by an organization on its letterhead, advertising material, and signs as an emblem by which the organization can easily be recognized [Mid-20thC. Shortening of LOGOGRAM and LOGOTYPE.]

logo- *prefix.* word, thought, speech ○ *logotype* [From Greek *logos* (see LOGOS).]

log of claims *n.* *Aus* a list of claims regarding pay and working conditions presented to an employer by a group of employees or a trade union

logogram /lóggə gram/, **logograph** /lóggə graf, -graf/ *n.* a symbol that represents the meaning of a whole word or phrase, e.g. the symbols used in shorthand, or the symbol '&' used instead of the word 'and' —**logogrammatic** /lóggəgrə máttik/ *adj.* —**logogrammatically** /-máttikli/ *adv.*

logograph /lóggō grif/ *n.* a word puzzle, especially an anagram [Late 16thC. From French *logographe*, from Greek *logos* (see LOGOS) + *griphos* 'fishing-basket', hence 'anything intricate, riddle'.]

logomachy /lo gómməki/ (*plural* **-chies**) *n.* an argument about the use or meaning of words [Mid-16thC. From Greek *logomakhia*, from *logomakhein* 'to fight with words', from *logos* 'word' (see LOGOS) + *makhē* 'battle'.]

logon /lóggon/, **login** /lóggin/ *n.* **1. ACT OF LOGGING ON** the act of logging on to a computer **2. PASSWORD FOR LOGGING ON** a name and password or other appropriate commands used for logging on to a computer

logorrhoea /lóggə reè ə/ *n.* excessive talkativeness, especially when the words are uncontrolled or incoherent, as is seen in certain psychiatric illnesses —**logorrhoeic** *adj.*

Logos /lóggoss/ *n.* **1.** CHR **JESUS CHRIST AS DIVINE WISDOM** Jesus Christ, so named in St John's Gospel, as the word of God, the personification of the wisdom of God and divine wisdom as the means for human salvation **2.** JUDAISM **WORD OF GOD** the divine wisdom of the word of God [Late 16thC. From Greek, 'word, reason'. Ultimately from an Indo-European base meaning 'to collect' and 'to speak', which is also the ancestor of English *collect*, *lecture*, and *lexicon*.]

logotype /lóggō tīp/ *n.* **1.** PRINTING **TYPE WITH DIFFERENT CHARACTERS** a single piece of type that has different unconnected characters on it **2.** COMM **LOGO** a logo

logroll /lóg rōl/ (**-rolls, -rolling, -rolled**) *vti.* *US* to trade votes with political colleagues to support one another's interests [Mid-19thC. Back-formation from LOGROLLING.]

logrolling /lóg rōling/ *n.* *US* POL the striking of a deal between colleagues in a legislature whereby support is given to a piece of legislation on the understanding that the favour will be returned at a later date ○ *'The national interest will lose out to the logrolling tradeoffs of Congressional business'.* (National Public Telecomputing Network, *Bush speeches in campaign '92*; 1992) [Early 19thC. From the former custom especially in the United States of neighbours helping each other to clear land by rolling logs to burn them.]

-logue *suffix.* speech ○ *monologue* [Via French from Greek *-logos* 'speaking', from *logos* 'word' (see LOGOS)]

logwood /lóg wŏŏd/ *n.* **1.** **SPINY TREE THAT GIVES DYE** a spiny tree of the pea family that grows in the West Indies and Central America and yields a dye from the heart of the wood. Latin name: *Haematoxylon campechianum.* **2.** INDUST **WOOD GIVING DYE** the wood of the logwood from which a purplish-red dye is obtained [Late 16thC. So called because the tree's wood was imported in log form.]

-logy *suffix.* **1.** speech, expression ○ *haplology* **2.** science, study ○ *musicology* [Directly and via French from, ultimately, Greek *-logia*, from *logos* 'word, reason' and from *-logos* 'speaking' (see LOGOS)]

loin /loyn/ *n.* **1.** ANAT **BACK BETWEEN RIBS AND HIPS** the area on each side of the backbone of a human or animal between the ribs and hips **2.** FOOD **MEAT CUT FROM LOIN OF ANIMAL** a prime cut of tender meat taken from the backbone and rib area of a pig, lamb, or calf. The meat is sold either as joints or cut into chops. ■ **loins** *npl.* **AREA BELOW WAIST** the hips and the front of the body below the waist, considered as the part of the body that should be covered and as the site of the sexual organs (*literary*) [14thC. Via Old French *loigne* from, ultimately, Latin *lumbus* (source of English *lumbar*, *sirloin*, and *lumbago*).] ◇ **gird (up) your loins** to prepare yourself to do sth difficult and challenging

loincloth /lóyn kloth/ *n.* a cloth covering the hips and the genital area

Loire /lwaar/ the longest river in France, rising in the Cévennes mountains, southeastern France. Length: 1,020 km/634 mi.

loiter /lóytər/ (**-ters, -tering, -tered**) *vi.* **1.** **STAND AROUND IDLY** to stand around without any obvious purpose (*disapproving*) **2.** **PROCEED SLOWLY** to do sth in a slow lazy way, often stopping to rest [15thC. Origin uncertain: possibly from Middle Dutch *loteren* 'to totter, linger'.] — **loiterer** *n.*

Loki /lṓki/ *n.* MYTHOL in Norse mythology, a handsome giant god who was the embodiment of evil

Lok Sabha /lṓk súbbə/ *n.* the lower chamber of the Indian Parliament [From Hindi, 'people's assembly']

LOL *abbr.* laughing out loud (*used in e-mail messages*)

Lolita /lo léetə/ *n.* a young teenage girl regarded or depicted as the object of sexual desire [Mid-20thC. From the name of the main character in *Lolita* (1958), a novel by Vladimir Nabokov.]

loll /lol/ (**lolls, lolling, lolled**) *vi.* **1.** **LOUNGE IN A RELAXED WAY** to relax in a reclining or leaning position **2.** **DROOP** to droop or hang down in a loose floppy way [14thC. Origin uncertain: possibly from Middle Dutch *lollen* 'to doze'.]

Lolland /lólland/ island of southeastern Denmark, situated in the Baltic Sea. Population: 72,026 (1994). Area: 1,241 sq. km/479 sq. mi.

lollipop /lólli pop/ *n.* a large boiled sweet fixed onto a stick [Late 18thC. Origin uncertain: perhaps from dialect *lolly* 'tongue' (formed from LOLL) + POP.]

lollipop lady *n.* a woman employed to stop traffic to allow schoolchildren to cross a road (*informal*) ◊ **school crossing patrol** [From the shape of the sign used to stop traffic]

lollipop man *n.* a man employed to stop traffic to allow schoolchildren to cross a road (*informal*) ◊ **school crossing patrol** [From the shape of the sign used to stop traffic]

lollop /lólləp/ (**-lops, -loping, -loped**) *vi.* **1.** **MOVE IN BOUNCY UNCONTROLLED WAY** to move along in a bouncy relaxed clumsy way **2.** **LOUNGE ABOUT** to loll or lounge about [Mid-18thC. Formed from LOLL, under the influence of GALLOP.] —**lollopy** *adj.*

lollo rosso /lóllō róssō/ *n.* a variety of lettuce with curly red-tipped leaves

lolly /lólli/ (*plural* **-lies**) *n.* **1.** **LOLLIPOP** a lollipop (*informal*) **2.** *UK* **ICE LOLLY** an ice lolly (*informal*) **3.** **MONEY** money (*informal*) **4.** *Aus* **SWEET** a sweet made from boiled sugar [Mid-19thC. Shortening of LOLLIPOP.]

Lomax /lṓm aks/, **Alan** (*b.* 1915) US ethnomusicologist. He was noted for his work in the collection of American folk songs, in collaboration with his father John Lomax.

Lomax, John (1867–1948) US ethnomusicologist. He was noted for his work in the collection of American folk songs, in collaboration with his son Alan Lomax.

Lombard /lómbərd, -baard/ *n.* **1.** **SB FROM LOMBARDY** sb who was born in or who lives in Lombardy in Italy **2.** **ANCIENT ITALIAN** a member of an ancient Germanic people who settled in northern Italy during the 6th century AD, where they soon became the dominant people

Lombardy /lómbərdi/ region in northern-central Italy, a major commercial and industrial centre —**Lombardic** /lom báardik/ *adj.*

Lombardy poplar *n.* a variety of poplar that has upright branches and a tall, narrow shape. Latin name: *Populus nigra italica.*

Lombok /lómbok/ island of the Lesser Sunda Islands, West Nusa Tenggara Province, southern Indonesia, situated east of Bali. Population: 2,403,399 (1990). Area: 5,180 sq. km/2,000 sq. mi.

Lomé /lṓ may/ capital and largest city of Togo, situated on the Bight of Benin, close to the Ghana border. Population: 450,000 (1990).

loment /lṓ ment/, **lomentum** /lō méntəm/ (*plural* **-menta**) *n.* a pod or fruit of certain plants that splits and separates at maturity into one-seeded segments [Mid-19thC. From Latin *lomentum* 'cosmetic made of bean-meal', from *lavare* 'to wash'.]

Lomond, Loch /lṓmənd, lokh/ the largest lake in Scotland, located in the Highlands north of Glasgow. Area: 70 sq. km/27 sq. mi.

London /lúndən/ **1.** capital city of the United Kingdom of Great Britain and Northern Ireland. It is one of the world's leading financial, industrial, and cultural centres. Population: 6,967,000 (1994). Area: 1,580 sq. km/610 sq. mi. **2.** city in Middlesex County, southwestern Ontario, Canada, on the Thames River. Population: 325,646 (1996). —**Londoner** *n.*

Londonderry /lúndən deri/ **1.** city in northwestern Northern Ireland, officially called Derry until it was fortified by people from London, England, in 1613. Population: 72,334 (1991). **2.** former county of Northern Ireland

London pride *n.* a variety of saxifrage with rosettes of fleshy leaves and clusters of pale pink flowers on long stems. Latin name: *Saxifraga urbium.*

lone /lōn/ *adj.* **1.** **SOLITARY** having no one else around **2.** **ONLY** only or sole **3.** **ISOLATED** situated in an isolated position **4.** **SINGLE** without a husband, wife, or partner **5.** **LONELY** lonely and having no companions (*literary*) [14thC. Shortening of ALONE by mistaken division of *al one* 'all by yourself' as *a lone*.]

lone hand *n.* **1.** CARDS **HAND PLAYED WITHOUT PARTNER** a hand played in some card games without help from a partner, or a player without a partner **2.** **SB OPERATING ALONE** sb who lives or works alone

lonely /lṓnli/ (**-lier, -liest**) *adj.* **1.** **FEELING ALONE** having or causing a feeling of being alone and sad **2.** **ISOLATED** isolated and rarely visited **3.** **LACKING SUPPORT** lacking companionship, aid, or encouragement **4.** **SOLITARY** having no one or nothing else around (*literary*) — **loneliness** *n.*

lonely hearts *adj.* relating to people who are looking for a partner for a romantic relationship

lone pair *n.* a pair of unshared electrons in a molecule that are not involved in bonding in that molecule

loner /lṓnər/ *n.* sb who prefers to be alone

lonesome /lṓnssəm/ *adj.* *US* **1.** **SAD FROM BEING ALONE** feeling sad, or causing a feeling of sadness, because of being alone **2.** **DESOLATE** isolated from human habitation **3.** **ALONE** having no one or nothing else around —**lonesomely** *adv.* —**lonesomeness** *n.*

lone wolf *n.* sb who prefers to be alone

long[1] /long/ *adj.* **1.** **EXTENDING CONSIDERABLE DISTANCE** extending a relatively great length or height **2.** **GOING ON FOR LENGTHY PERIOD** lasting for an extended period of time **3.** **HAVING MANY ITEMS** containing a relatively large number of parts or individual items **4.** **OF SPECIFIED LENGTH** of a specified length, height, total, number, or duration ○ *a book 300 pages long* **5.** **LONGER THAN IT IS WIDE** with a greater length than width ○ *Look in the long box, not the square one.* **6.** **BEYOND WHAT IS WANTED** extending in time or space beyond what is considered normal, reasonable, or desirable **7.** **MORE DISTANT OR LENGTHY** the more or most distant or lengthy of two or more things ○ *the long way home* **8.** **ABLE TO REACH CONSIDERABLE DISTANCE** capable of reaching or travelling far ○ *to have a long reach* **9.** **SEEMING TO LAST FOREVER** appearing to be or take more time than is really the case ○ *a long hour waiting* **10.** **GOING FAR BACK IN TIME** extending back in time ○ *a long memory* **11.** **CONTAINING MUCH LIQUID** containing a large quantity of liquid to drink, especially of a thirst-quenching kind ○ *a long cold drink on a hot day* **12.** **EXTENSIVE** exhaustive and critical ○ *Take a good long look at yourself.* **13.** **RISKY** with an uncertain outcome **14.** **HAVING PLENTY OF STH** possessing enough or more than enough of sth (*informal*) ○ *a politician who is long on rhetoric* **15.** FIN **HOLDING STOCK IN ANTICIPATION OF RISE** used to describe shares and other securities or commodities that are held with the expectation that prices will rise **16.** PHON **DRAWN OUT IN PRONUNCIATION** used to describe a speech sound that is relatively drawn out **17.** PHON **DESCENDED FROM LONG VOWEL** used to describe an English vowel sound that is historically descended from vowels that were drawn out in pronunciation, e.g. the ones in English 'beet' and 'bite' **18.** POETRY **ACCENTED** used to describe a syllable in accentual verse that is stressed **19.** POETRY **OF GREATER METRICAL DURATION** used to describe a syllable in quantitative verse that is the one of the two types that is of greater duration ■ *adv.* **1.** **FOR LONG TIME** for or during a lengthy period of time ○ *Have you been here long?* **2.** **FAR** at or to a great distance ○ *hit the ball long* **3.** **FOR CERTAIN TIME** for or during a particular length of time ○ *work all day long* **4.** **AT ANOTHER TIME** at a time much later or earlier than the time specified ○ *long after he left* **5.** STOCK EXCH **IN LONG STOCK POSITION** in a long position in securities or commodities ■ *n.* **1.** **A LONG TIME** a lengthy period of time ○ *Will you be visiting for long?* **2.** PHON **LONG SOUND** a long syllable or sound **3.** CLOTHES **SIZE FOR TALL PEOPLE** a garment or garment size designed for sb tall ■ **longs** *npl.* **1.** CLOTHES **LONG TROUSERS** trousers with full-length legs (*informal*) **2.** FIN **LONG-DATED GILT-EDGED SECURITIES** gilt-edged securities with more than 15 years to run before redemption **3.** FIN **SECURITIES HELD UNTIL PRICES RISE** securities or commodities that are held with the expectation that prices will rise [Old English, from a prehistoric Germanic base that is also the ancestor of English *linger*, *Lent*, *lunge*, and *long*[2]] ◇ **any longer** for any further time ◇ **as** *or* **so long as 1.** during the time that **2.** because of the fact that **3.** on the condition that ◇ **before long** before much time passes ◇ **no longer** as until the present but not for any further time ◇ **not long for** sth with little time remaining for sth ◇ **so long** good-bye (*informal*) ◇ **the long and the short of it** the basic idea or facts

long² /long/ (**longs, longing, longed**) *vi.* to have a strong desire or yearning for sb or sth, especially sb or sth unattainable or not within immediate reach [Old English *langian*, from a prehistoric Germanic base that is also the ancestor of English *long*¹. The meaning 'yearn' developed from 'grow long' via 'seem long'.]

———— **WORD KEY: SYNONYMS** ————
See Synonyms at *want*.

long. *abbr.* longitude

long-ago *adj.* relating to or in the distant past ○ *long-ago civilizations*

longan /lóngən/, **lungan** /lúngən/ *n.* **1. EVERGREEN TREE** an evergreen tree of tropical and subtropical Asia that has small yellowish-white flowers and small white-fleshed fruits. Latin name: *Euphoria longan*. **2. FRUIT** a small juicy fruit with a yellowish brown exterior, white juicy flesh, and a large black seed. The dried fruit is often used as a Chinese health food or cooked with herbal medicine. [Mid-18thC. From Chinese *lóngyan*, literally 'dragon's eye' (which the fruit is thought to resemble).]

long-awaited *adj.* hoped for and expected for a considerable time

Long Beach 1. city in Los Angeles County, southwestern California, situated on San Pedro Bay. Population: 433,852 (1994). **2.** city in Nassau County, southeastern New York, situated off the southern shore of Long Island 34 km/21 mi. southeast of New York City. Population: 33,510 (1990).

long black *n.* ANZ a half-strength espresso in a standard-size cup. ♭ **short black**

longboat /lóng bōt/ *n.* **1. LONGEST BOAT CARRIED BY SAILING SHIP** the longest boat, usually a seaworthy rowing boat, carried on board a sailing ship, especially a merchant ship **2.** = **longship**

long bone *n.* any long cylindrical limb bone in vertebrates that contains marrow and ends in an enlarged head that unites to form a joint with another bone

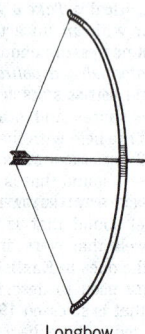
Longbow

longbow /lóngbō/ *n.* a large powerful hand-drawn bow made from a long piece of slightly curved wood and a bowstring, used, especially in medieval England, for hunting and in warfare

longbowman /lóngbō mən/ (*plural* **-men** /-men/) *n.* an archer who used a longbow, especially in medieval England

longcase clock /lóng kayss-/ *n.* = **grandfather clock**

long-chain *adj.* used to describe a molecule or substance that has a relatively long chain of atoms, especially carbon atoms

long-dated *adj.* used to describe a gilt-edged security that has more than 15 years to run before redemption

long-day *adj.* requiring long periods of daylight, usually more than 12 hours, followed by short nights in order to mature and flower

long-distance *adj.* **1. FOR LONG WAY** travelling or extending a relatively long way **2.** TELECOM **BETWEEN DISTANT PHONES** relating to or providing telephone service between places that are far apart **3.** **BETWEEN DISTANT PLACES** occurring between places that are far apart ○ *a long-distance romance* ■ *adv.* TELECOM **USING LONG-DISTANCE LINE** using a long-distance telephone line

$$58 \overline{\smash{)}\begin{array}{r} 71.3 \\ 4135.4 \\ -406 \\ \hline 75 \\ -58 \\ \hline 174 \\ 174 \\ \hline 0 \end{array}}$$
Long division

long division *n.* a method or instance of dividing one number by another in which each step is written out in full

long dozen *n.* a set of 13 items

long-drawn-out *adj.* going on for an undesirably long period of time

long-eared owl *n.* a medium-sized owl with distinctive pointed ear tufts that lives in coniferous forests in Europe, Asia, and North America. Latin name: *Asio otus*.

Long Eaton /long éetən/ town in Derbyshire, central England, situated 11 km/7 mi. southwest of Nottingham. Population: 32,895 (1981).

longeron /lónjərən/ *n.* a main structural component of an aeroplane's fuselage that runs from one end of the aeroplane to the other [Early 20thC. From French, literally 'beam', ultimately from Latin *longus* 'long'.]

longevity /lon jévvəti/ (*plural* **-ties**) *n.* **1. LONG LIFE** long duration of life **2. DURATION OF LIFE** the length of a person's or animal's life **3. CAREER SPAN** the length of sb's employment or career [Early 17thC. From late Latin *longaevitas*, from Latin *longaevus*, literally 'of a long age', from *aevum* 'age'.] —**longevous** /lon jévvəss/ *adj.*

long face *n.* a facial expression showing unhappiness, disappointment, or seriousness —**long-faced** *adj.*

long finger *n. Ireland* a state of being postponed for a long time (*informal*)

Longford /lóngfərd/ county in Leinster Province, central Republic of Ireland. Population: 30,296 (1991). Area: 1,044 sq. km/403 sq. mi.

Longford /lóngfərd/, **Frank, 7th Earl** (*b.* 1908) British politician. Once a Conservative, he later held ministerial posts with the Labour Party. He was an advocate of penal reform.

Longford /lóngfərd/, **Raymond Hollis** (1878–1959) Australian actor and director. His silent films include *The Sentimental Bloke* (1919).

longhair /lóng hair/ *n.* **1.** ZOOL **CAT WITH LONG FUR** a domestic cat with long fur **2.** US **LONGHAIRED MAN** sb with long hair, especially a hippie man (*dated informal disapproving*) —**longhaired** *adj.*

longhand /lóng hand/ *n.* words and letters written by hand in full, rather than in shorthand

long haul *n.* (*informal*) **1.** US **LENGTHY PERIOD** a long period of time **2. LOT OF WORK** a long-lasting job or ordeal **3. LONG DISTANCE** an extensive distance

long-haul *adj.* relating to travel or transportation over long distances

long-headed /lóng héddid/ *adj.* perceptive and wise (*archaic or literary*) [From the belief that a long head indicated wisdom]

long hop *n.* a short delivery in cricket that is very easy to hit

longhorn /lóng hawrn/ (*plural* **-horns** or **-horn**) *n.* **1.** US **RED COW WITH LONG HORNS** a red or variegated cow with long horns, belonging to a breed of beef cattle of Spanish origin that was once very common in the southwestern United States **2. COW WITH LONG HORNS** a cow belonging to a breed that has long horns

long-horned beetle *n.* US = **longicorn**

long-horned grasshopper *n.* a large, usually green grasshopper with long antennae and often a characteristic song. Family: Tettigoniidae.

long house *n.* **1.** *US, Can* **COMMUNAL DWELLING OF NATIVE N AMERICANS** a long bark-covered communal dwelling place built by some Native North American peoples, especially the Iroquois. It had compartments for families around central meeting areas. **2. COMMUNAL DWELLING** a communal dwelling housing entire extended families and found, e.g. in Borneo or Sarawak

long hundredweight *n.* = **hundredweight** *n.* 1

longicorn /lónji kawrn/ *n.* **BEETLE WITH LONG ANTENNAE** a beetle with long antennae, long legs, and a narrow, often brightly coloured body. The larvae of many species are wood borers. Family: Cerambycidae. US term **long-horned beetle** ■ *adj.* **WITH LONG ANTENNAE** having long antennae [Mid-19thC. From modern Latin *Longicornia*, literally 'long-horned ones', former scientific name, from Latin *cornu* 'horn'.]

longing /lónging/ *n.* **YEARNING** a persistent and strong desire, usually for sb or sth unattainable or not within immediate reach ■ *adj.* **SHOWING YEARNING** expressing yearning or desire —**longingly** *adv.*

Long Island the largest island in the continental United States, southeastern New York State. Queens and Brooklyn, two boroughs of New York City, are situated here. Population: 6,861,474 (1990). Area: 4,356 sq. km/1,682 sq. mi.

Long Island Sound body of salt water situated between the southern shore of Connecticut and the northern shore of Long Island, New York. Area: 3,364 sq. km/1,299 sq. mi.

longitude /lónji tyood, lónggi-/ *n.* ◊ **latitude 1. ANGULAR DISTANCE FROM PRIME MERIDIAN** the angular distance east or west of the prime meridian that stretches from the North Pole to the South Pole and passes through Greenwich, England. Longitude is measured in degrees, minutes, and seconds. **2. AREA OF EARTH'S SURFACE** a region near a particular longitude [14thC. From Latin *longitudo* 'length' (the original sense in English), from *longus* 'long'.]

longitudinal /lónji tyóodin'l, lónggi-/ *adj.* **1. GOING FROM TOP TO BOTTOM** extending from the top to the bottom of sth **2. OVER TIME** relating to development over a period of time **3. OF LONGITUDE** relating to longitude or length —**longitudinally** *adv.*

longitudinal wave *n.* a wave, e.g. a sound wave that is propagated in the same direction in which the particles of the medium vibrate

long jenny /-jenni/ *n.* a shot in billiards in which the ball goes into a far pocket after striking another ball [*Jenny* from JENNY in the sense 'a losing hazard in billiards made with the object-ball near a cushion']

long johns /-jonz/ *npl.* underpants with full-length legs, or one-piece underwear covering the torso, arms, and legs [*Johns* from the name *John*]

long jump *n.* a field event in which competitors jump for distance, usually from a running start into a sand pit

long-lasting *adj.* continuing for a long time

longleaf pine /lóng leef-/ *n.* **1. TREES** US **PINE TREE** a pine tree native to the southeastern United States, that has long needles grouped in threes, long cones, heavy resinous wood, and orange-brown bark. It is highly valued as a source of timber, pulp, and turpentine. Latin name: *Pinus palustris*. **2.** INDUST **WOOD FROM LONGLEAF PINE** the wood of the longleaf pine, used for timber

long lease *n.* in England and Wales, a lease for a period of more than 21 years on a house that is the occupants' main residence

long leg *n.* a position in cricket on the leg side behind the batsman's wicket and close to the boundary, or a fielder occupying this position

long-legged /-léggid/ *adj.* **1. WITH LONG LEGS** having long legs **2. ABLE TO RUN FAST** capable of running quickly

long-life *adj.* specially treated to last for a long time ○ *long-life milk*

long-lived *adj.* living, lasting, or enduring for a long time

long-lost *adj.* not seen for a long period of time (*humorous*)

a at; aa father; aw all; ay day; air hair; ə about, edible, item, common, circus; e egg; ee eel; hw when; i it, happy; ī ice; 'l apple; 'm rhythm; 'n fashion; o odd; ō open; oo good; oo pool; ow owl; oy oil; th thin; th this; u up; ur urge;

long measure *n.* **1.** MEASURE = **linear measure 2.** = **long metre**

long metre *n.* POETRY a four-line stanza in which the second and fourth lines always rhyme and the first and third sometimes rhyme. It is often used for hymns.

long moss *n.* = **Spanish moss**

long-off *n.* a position in cricket on the off side, behind the bowler and close to the boundary, or a fielder occupying this position

long-on *n.* a position in cricket on the leg side, behind the bowler and close to the boundary, or a fielder occupying this position

long pig *n.* human flesh as eaten by cannibals [Translation of a Polynesian name]

long-playing record *n.* full form of **LP**

long purse *n.* a great deal of money (*dated informal*)

long-range *adj.* **1.** EXTENDING WELL INTO THE FUTURE extending a long time into the future **2.** TRAVELLING LONG DISTANCES able to travel long distances **3.** ARMS ABLE TO HIT DISTANT TARGET relating to weapons that are capable of hitting a target a considerable distance away

Longreach /lòng reech/ town in central Queensland, Australia, a cattle grazing centre. Population: 3,766 (1996).

long-service leave *n.* *ANZ* extended paid leave awarded in some places of employment, especially the public service, in recognition of long service

longship /lóng ship/ *n.* a narrow wooden ship with oars and a large square sail used by the Vikings

longshore /lóng shawr/ *adj.* living, working, or situated on the coast [Early 19thC. Shortening of ALONGSHORE.]

longshoreman /lóng shawrmən/ (*plural* **-men** /-mən/) *n.* *US* = **docker**

long shot *n.* **1.** SB OR STH UNLIKELY TO WIN sb or sth that is unlikely to win a race or competition **2.** GAMBLING BET UNLIKELY TO WIN a bet on sb or sth that is unlikely to win a race or competition **3.** VENTURE UNLIKELY TO SUCCEED a venture, guess, or possibility that has little chance of success, although, if successful, it would be very profitable or rewarding **4.** PHOTOGRAPHY CAMERA SHOT OF DISTANT OBJECT a camera shot taken some distance from the object or scene [Originally in the meaning of 'shot fired at a distance'] ◇ **(not) by a long shot** (not) in any way at all (*informal*)

long-sighted *adj.* US term **farsighted 1.** UNABLE TO SEE NEARBY OBJECTS CLEARLY able to see distant objects more easily than near objects, which can be seen clearly only by strongly focusing the eyes **2.** TAKING FUTURE NEEDS INTO CONSIDERATION taking future problems or needs into consideration —**long-sightedly** *adv.* —**long-sightedness** *n.*

Longs Peak /longz peek/ mountain in Boulder County, northern Colorado, and the highest peak in Rocky Mountain National Park. Height: 4,345 m/14,255 ft.

longspur /lóng spur/ (*plural* **-spurs** *or* **-spur**) *n.* a bunting native to the northern United States, Canada, and the Arctic that has brownish plumage and long-clawed hind toes. Genera: *Calcarius* and *Rhyncophanes.*

long-standing *adj.* having existed or been going on for a long period of time

long-suffering *adj.* PATIENTLY ENDURING patient and enduring in the face of suffering or difficulty ■ *n.* PATIENT ENDURANCE patience and endurance in the face of suffering or difficulty —**long-sufferingly** *adv.*

long suit *n.* **1.** CARDS SUIT OF MOST CARDS the suit to which the majority of cards in a player's hand belongs **2.** FINEST QUALITY sb's strongest quality or talent (*informal*)

long-tailed duck *n.* a long-tailed duck common in Arctic seas that has a black back and wings, a white breast, and a brown-and-white head. Latin name: *Clangula hyemalis.* US term **oldsquaw**

long-tailed tit *n.* a small black, white, and pink tit of Europe and Asia that has a distinctive call. Latin name: *Aegithalos caudatus.*

long term *n.* the period of time continuing from now long into the future

long-term *adj.* **1.** IN FUTURE relating to or affecting a time long into the future **2.** ACCT WITH LONGER ACCOUNTING PERIOD with or relating to an accounting period of longer than one year **3.** FIN MATURING IN NUMBER OF YEARS maturing only after a long time, usually a number of years **4.** LONG-LASTING continuing for a long period of time

longtime /lóng tīm/ *adj.* having continued in existence for a long period of time

long tin *n.* an oblong loaf of bread with a risen rounded crusty top, made in a long baking tin (*dated*)

long tom /-tóm/ *n.* **1.** LONG-BARRELLED CANNON USED BY NAVY a swivelling cannon with a long barrel, used in the past by the navy **2.** LONG-RANGE CANNON USED BY ARMY a long-range cannon used by the army **3.** AUTOMATIC ANTIAIRCRAFT GUN a large-calibre automatic antiaircraft gun (*slang*)

long ton *n.* = **ton**[1] *n.* 2

Longueuil /lóng gayl, loN gōyi/ city in southern Québec Province, Canada, situated on the St Lawrence River. Population: 127,977 (1996).

longueur /long gúr/ *n.* a period of boredom, e.g. a boring passage in a book or a boring scene in a dramatic work (*literary*) [Late 18thC. From French, literally 'length', from *long* 'long', from Latin *longus*.]

long vacation, long vac *n.* a period of roughly three months in the summer when law courts and universities are shut for the holidays

long view *n.* the consideration of how events or circumstances are likely to develop in the long term

long wave *n.* the broadcasting or receiving of radio waves of 1000 m or more in length (*hyphenated when used before a noun*)

longways /lóng wayz/ *adj., adv.* = **lengthways**

long-winded /-wíndid/ *adj.* **1.** USING TOO MANY WORDS tediously wordy in speech or writing **2.** NOT EASILY BECOMING SHORT OF BREATH capable of doing physical exercise for a relatively long period of time without getting short of breath —**long-windedly** *adv.* —**long-windedness** *n.*

WORD KEY: SYNONYMS

See Synonyms at ***wordy***.

longwise /lóng wīz/ *adj., adv. US, Can* = **lengthways**

Longyearbyen /lóng yeer byen/ town in the Svalbard archipelago of Norway, north of the Arctic Circle

loo[1] /loo/ (*plural* **loos**) *n.* a lavatory or toilet (*informal*) [Mid-20thC. Origin uncertain.]

WORD KEY: ORIGIN

The most widely claimed source of ***loo*** is *gardy loo* (based on pseudo-French *gare de l'eau* 'mind the water'), used in 18th-century Edinburgh to warn passers-by when a chamber pot was about to be emptied into the street below. However, this is chronologically unlikely, as there is no evidence of ***loo*** being used for 'lavatory' before the 1930s. Other possible candidates include *Waterloo* (the link with 'water' gives this some plausibility) and *louvre*, from the use of slatted screens for a makeshift lavatory. The likeliest source is perhaps French *lieux d'aisances*, literally 'places of ease', hence 'lavatory', possibly picked up by British service personnel in France during World War I.

loo[2] /loo/ (*plural* **loos**) *n.* **1.** CARDS GAMBLING CARD GAME a gambling card game in which players place the money they are betting in a pool **2.** GAMBLING BET IN POOL AT LOO a bet placed in the pool in a game of loo [Late 17thC. From French *lantur(e)lu*, the meaningless refrain of a popular song, later the name of the card game.]

looby /lóobi/ (*plural* **-bies**) *n.* an unintelligent or lazy person (*archaic*) [14thC. Origin uncertain.]

loofah /lóofə/ *n.* **1.** NATURAL SPONGE a sponge made from the dried fibrous interior of an oblong fruit of a tropical gourd **2.** TROPICAL VINE a tropical vine of the gourd family that bears the large oblong fruits from which loofah sponges are made. Genus: *Luffa.* [Late 19thC. From Arabic *lūfa*.]

look /lòok/ *v.* (**looks, looking, looked**) **1.** *vti.* DIRECT EYES to turn the eyes towards or on sth **2.** *vi.* USE EYES TO SEARCH to use the eyes to examine, watch, or find sb or sth ○ *We looked everywhere.* **3.** *vi.* SEEM AS SPECIFIED to appear in a specified way ○ *He looks tired.* **4.** *vi.* CONSIDER STH to direct the attention towards sth in order to consider it ○ *Let's look at the entire situation.* **5.** *vt.* FIT STH BY APPEARANCE to have an appearance that is in accordance with sth ○ *He looks his age.* **6.** *vi.* USE EYES IN SPECIFIED WAY to use the eyes in a specified way ○ *He looked intently at the ball.* **7.** *vi.* FACE SPECIFIED WAY to face a specified direction or have a specified view ○ *The room looks over the lake* **8.** *vt.* EXPRESS STH to communicate sth by an expression ○ *She looked her anger at all of us.* **9.** *vi.* PAY ATTENTION used to tell sb to pay attention or see sth ○ *Look, why don't we split the difference?* ○ *Look! There he goes!* ■ *n.* **1.** ACT OR INSTANCE OF LOOKING an act or instance of looking, e.g. to examine, watch, or find sth ○ *Take a look at this.* **2.** WAY SB OR STH APPEARS an impression conveyed by a manner or quality ○ *He has the look of someone enjoying himself.* **3.** EXPRESSION a facial expression that communicates sth ○ *a meaningful look* **4.** FASHION an appearance, style, or fashion, especially of dress or hairstyle ■ **looks** *npl.* OUTWARD APPEARANCE sb's outward physical appearance, especially if it is pleasing ○ *good looks* [Old English *lōcian*, from prehistoric Germanic]

look after *vt.* to care for or be responsible for sb or sth

look ahead *vi.* to think about or plan for the future

look back *vi.* **1.** THINK ABOUT PAST to think about the past or past experiences **2.** REVISIT to visit again later on (*informal*)

look down on, look down upon *vt.* to regard or treat sb or sth as inferior or with contempt

look for *vt.* **1.** SEARCH FOR to try to find sb or sth **2.** EXPECT to hope for or anticipate sth ○ *We're looking for a successful year.*

look forward to *vt.* to anticipate a future event with excitement or pleasure

look in *vi.* to pay a short visit (*informal*)

look into *vt.* to carry out a careful investigation of sth such as a possibility, problem, or crime

look on *v.* **1.** *vi.* WATCH to be a spectator or witness **2.** *vt.* REGARD SB OR STH to regard sb or sth in a particular way

look out *v.* **1.** *vi.* BE CAREFUL to be take care to avoid danger **2.** *vt.* SEARCH FOR AND FIND STH to search for and find sth among a number of things, especially personal belongings

look out for *vt.* **1.** KEEP WATCH FOR SB OR STH to watch for sb or sth to appear (*informal*) **2.** TAKE CARE OF SB OR STH to take particular care of sb or sth

look over *vt.* **1.** INSPECT PROPERTY to inspect a property by visiting it and walking round it **2.** EXAMINE SB OR STH to inspect or examine sb or sth either quickly or carefully

look through *vt.* to fail to acknowledge sb's presence, either intentionally or unintentionally

look to *vt.* **1.** EXPECT SB TO DO STH to hope or expect that sb or sth will do or provide sth **2.** WANT OR HOPE to want or hope to do sth (*informal*) ○ *if you're looking to upgrade your computer*

look up *v.* **1.** *vt.* SEARCH FOR IN REFERENCE BOOK to search for information, e.g. by consulting a reference book **2.** *vi.* IMPROVE to become better **3.** *vt.* VISIT SB to locate sb, especially for a visit

look upon *vt.* = **look on** *v.* 2

look up to *vt.* to have respect and admiration for sb

lookalike /lòokə līk/ *n.* sb or sth that looks like sb or sth else (*informal*)

looker /lòokər/ *n.* **1.** SB WHO WATCHES sb who watches, especially an observer or spectator **2.** SB GOOD-LOOKING a good-looking person, especially a girl or woman (*informal; sometimes considered offensive*)

looker-on (*plural* **lookers-on**) *n.* = **onlooker**

look-in *n.* (*informal*) **1.** CHANCE TO PARTICIPATE an opportunity to participate in sth or be considered for sth **2.** BRIEF VISIT a visit of short duration

looking glass *n.* a mirror (*archaic*)

WORD KEY: CULTURAL NOTE

Through the Looking-Glass and What Alice Found There, a children's story by English writer Lewis Carroll (1871). In this inspired sequel to ***Alice's Adventures in Won-***

derland, Alice climbs through a mirror into a magical world where chess pieces come alive, and flowers, insects, and animals all talk. The story features bizarre characters such as Tweedledum and Tweedledee and Humpty Dumpty, and the well-known poems 'Jabberwocky' and 'The Walrus and the Carpenter'.

---

looking-glass *adj.* characterized by the complete reversal of everything normal (*literary*) [From *Through the Looking Glass* (1871) by Lewis Carroll]

lookout /lo͝ok owt/ *n.* **1.** CAREFUL WATCH an act of watching carefully for sb or sth **2.** SB WATCHING FOR DANGER sb who watches carefully for any signs of attack or danger **3.** PLACE GIVING GOOD VIEW a place or structure that affords a good view for observation **4.** PROBLEM a problem or concern (*informal*) ○ *That's your lookout.* **5.** PROSPECT a prospect or outlook (*informal*)

lookover /lo͝okōvər/ *n.* a quick inspection or examination

look-see *n.* a brief look or inspection (*informal*)

look-up *n.* a computer procedure in which a term or value is matched against a table of stored information

loom[1] /loom/ *vi.* (**looms, looming, loomed**) **1.** BE SEEN AS LARGE SHAPE to appear as a large or indistinct, and sometimes menacing, shape **2.** BE ABOUT TO HAPPEN to be imminent, often in a threatening way ■ *n.* APPEARANCE OF STH LARGE an appearance of sth, usually sth large and threatening (*literary*) [Mid-16thC. Origin uncertain: perhaps from Low Dutch, or from a Scandinavian language.]

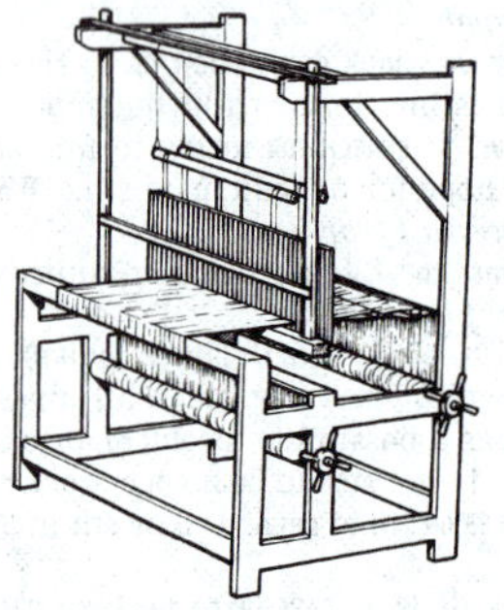

Loom

loom[2] /loom/ *n.* **1.** INDUST WEAVING APPARATUS a hand-operated or machine-operated device for weaving thread or yarn into cloth **2.** NAUT MIDDLE PART OF OAR the middle part of an oar between the blade and the handle [Old English *gelōma* 'implement, tool' (source of English *heirloom*), of unknown origin]

loon[1] /loon/ *n.* *US* = **diver** [Mid-17thC. Origin uncertain: perhaps ultimately from Old Norse *lómr* 'loon', also a name for several other diving birds.]

loon[2] /loon/ *n.* **1.** OFFENSIVE TERM an offensive term that deliberately insults sb's mental condition or intelligence (*informal*) **2.** *Scotland* BOY a boy or young man [15thC. Origin unknown. In the first sense, influenced by LOON[1] (because of the bird's call), or by LOONY.]

loonie /lo͞oni/, **loon** *n. Can* a Canadian one-dollar coin with an image of a loon on the back (*informal*) [Late 20thC. Formed from LOON[1].]

loony /lo͞oni/, **looney, luny** *adj.* (**-ier, -iest**) **1.** OFFENSIVE TERM an offensive term meaning irrational (*informal offensive*) **2.** SILLY silly, thoughtless or strange (*informal*) ○ *loony ideas* ■ *n.* (*plural* **-ies**; *plural* **-eys**) **1.** OFFENSIVE TERM an offensive term that deliberately insults sb's intelligence and ability to act rationally (*informal insult*) **2.** SB SILLY sb who behaves in an eccentric or thoughtless way (*informal; often considered offensive*) [Mid-19thC. Shortening and alteration of LUNATIC.] —**loonily** *adv.* —**looniness** *n.*

loony bin *n.* a highly offensive term for a hospital for people who have psychiatric disorders (*informal offensive*)

loop[1] /loop/ *n.* **1.** CIRCLE OR OVAL MADE WITH STRING a circular or oval shape formed by a line or sth such as a piece of string that curves back over itself **2.** CIRCLE OR OVAL FOR FASTENING OR HOLDING sth that has a closed or nearly closed circular or oval shape and is often used to carry or fasten sth **3.** CONTRACEPTIVE DEVICE a contraceptive device in the shape of a loop of plastic or metal that is placed in a woman's womb **4.** ELEC CLOSED CIRCUIT a closed electric circuit **5.** COMPUT SET OF COMMANDS IN COMPUTER PROGRAM a set of instructions in a computer program that is repeated a certain number of times or until a certain objective has been achieved **6.** AIR FLIGHT MANOEUVRE a flight manoeuvre in which a plane flies vertically in a circle ○ *to loop the loop* **7.** RAILWAY BRANCH LINE a railway branch line that leaves the main line and then joins it again later on **8.** CINEMA PIECE OF FILM OR TAPE a piece of film or tape joined at both ends to allow repeated use of images or sound, especially in dubbing procedures **9.** ELEC = **loop aerial** **10.** CRIMINOL COMMON FINGERPRINT PATTERN the commonest pattern of a human fingerprint formed by U-shaped ridges **11.** ICE SKATING SKATING JUMP AND TURN a jump in which a skater takes off from the outer back edge of a blade, turns in the air, and lands again on the same blade's outer back edge ■ *v.* (**loops, looping, looped**) **1.** *vti.* MAKE LOOP to form or make sth form the shape of a loop **2.** *vt.* to fasten, join, or arrange sth using a loop **3.** *vi.* CURVE to move in a curved path [14thC. Origin uncertain: perhaps from Irish *lúb* 'loop, bend'.] ◇ **in** *or* **out of the loop** *US* belonging or not belonging to the people who are decision-makers or are fully informed (*informal*) ◇ **knock** *or* **throw sb for a loop** *US* to surprise, shock, or upset sb (*informal*)

loop[2] /loop/ *n.* a loophole in a wall (*archaic*) [14thC. Origin uncertain.]

loop aerial *n.* an aerial consisting of a coil of wire wound around a frame

looped /loopt/ *adj.* formed into a circular or oval shape

looper /lo͞opər/ *n.* **1.** SB OR STH THAT LOOPS sb who or sth that makes loops **2.** = **measuring worm**

loophole /lo͞op hōl/ *n.* **1.** GAP IN LAW a small mistake or omission in a rule or law that allows it to be circumvented **2.** MIL SLIT IN WALL a small slit or hole in a wall, especially one in a fortified wall for firing guns or other weapons through ■ *vt.* (**-holes, -holing, -holed**) MAKE LOOPHOLES IN WALL to provide a wall with loopholes [Formed from LOOP[2]]

loop knot *n.* a square knot that leaves a single loop hanging free

loop line *n.* = **loop**[1] *n.* 7

loop of Henle /-hénli/ *n.* the part of the kidney tubule in birds and mammals that forms a loop between the cortex and medulla [Mid-19thC. Named after the German anatomist and pathologist Friedrich Gustav *Henle* (1801–85).]

loopy /lo͞opi/ (**-ier, -iest**) *adj.* **1.** HAVING LOOPS consisting of loops **2.** OFFENSIVE TERM an offensive term for sb considered to be irrational (*offensive*)

Loos /looss/, **Adolf** (1870–1933) Austrian architect. A pioneer of functionalism in architecture, his Steiner House (1910) was a landmark of modernism and the use of concrete.

loose /looss/ *adj.* **1.** NOT FIRMLY FIXED not firmly fastened or fixed in place ○ *a loose floorboard* **2.** SLACK not fastened or pulled tight ○ *a loose knot* **3.** NOT TIGHT-FITTING baggy and not fitting closely **4.** FREE allowed to move around freely without any restraint **5.** NOT PACKAGED not enclosed in a container or bound together ○ *loose tea* **6.** NOT FIRMLY PACKED not compact or dense in texture or arrangement ○ *loose soil* **7.** IMPRECISE not exact, literal, or precise ○ *a loose translation* **8.** FLEXIBLE not strictly controlled or organized ○ *a loose arrangement* **9.** AVAILABLE not earmarked for a particular purpose ○ *loose funds* **10.** RELAXED relaxed or free from tension (*informal*) **11.** IRRESPONSIBLE lacking restraint or a sense of propriety (*dated*) ○ *loose talk* **12.** PROMISCUOUS having many sexual partners (*dated*) **13.** TOO FLUID too fluid in consistency ○ *loose stools* **14.** ACCOMPANIED BY PHLEGM accompanied by the production of phlegm or mucus ○ *a loose cough* ■ *adv.* FREELY freely or without restraint ■ *v.* (**looses, loosing, loosed**) **1.** *vt.* SET FREE to release a person or animal from restraint or confinement **2.** *vt.* UNTIE KNOT to undo, untie, or unfasten sth **3.** *vti.* MAKE STH LESS TIGHT to make sth less tight, or be made less tight **4.** *vti.* FIRE MISSILE to fire an arrow, bullet, or other missile (*literary*) **5.** *vt.* RELEASE FROM OBLIGATION to release sb from an obligation or pressure ■ *n.* RUGBY PLAY any part of the play in rugby other than scrums, line-outs, or set kicks [12thC. From Old Norse *lauss*, from a prehistoric Germanic word that is also the ancestor of English *-less*.] —**loosely** *adv.* —**looseness** *n.* ◇ **be on the loose 1.** to be free from confinement, e.g. a prison **2.** to be free from responsibilities and having a good time (*informal*) ◇ **let loose** *US* to obtain relief from tension or worry

loosebox /lo͞oss boks/ *n.* an enclosed compartment forming part of a stable in which the horse is not tied up but can move around. US term **box stall**

loose cannon *n.* sb who behaves unpredictably or indiscreetly, often causing trouble for colleagues or associates (*slang*)

loose cover *n.* a fitted cover for a sofa or an armchair that can be easily removed. US term **slipcover**

loose end *n.* a small part of sth, e.g. a project or a story, that has not been completed or fully explained (*informal; often used in the plural*) [Literally referring to the loose end of a string left hanging] ◇ **at a loose end** restless and a little bored because of having nothing to do (*informal*)

loose head *n.* the rugby prop forward occupying the position to the left of the hooker in the front row of a scrum

loose-jointed *adj.* **1.** AGILE agile and supple in movement **2.** WITH MOBILE JOINTS having joints that fit loosely or that are very mobile —**loose-jointedness** *n.*

loose-leaf *adj.* with pages that can be removed and replaced easily

loose-limbed /-límd/ *adj.* having supple legs and arms

loose man *n. Aus* a player in Australian Rules football who is not being marked by an opposing player

loosen /lo͞oss'n/ (**-ens, -ening, -ened**) *v.* **1.** *vti.* BECOME OR MAKE LESS TIGHT to become or make sth become less tight or fixed **2.** *vt.* UNTIE HAIR OR KNOT to untie sth such as hair or a knot **3.** *vt.* RELAX CONTROL OVER SB OR STH to lessen control, pressure, or strictness **4.** *vt.* MAKE BOWELS MORE REGULAR to make sb's bowel movements more fluid or regular

loosen up *v.* **1.** *vti.* WARM UP to do exercises or exercise muscles or joints in order to become more limber, e.g. prior to strenuous activity **2.** *vi.* RELAX to become less tense, strict, or serious

loose smut *n.* a disease of cereal grasses in which powdery spore masses replace the grain head

loosestrife /lo͞oss strīf/ (*plural* **-strifes** *or* **-strife**) *n.* **1.** PLANT WITH YELLOW FLOWERS a plant of the primrose family with clusters of yellow flowers. Genus: *Lysimachia.* **2.** PLANT WITH PURPLE FLOWERS a plant with spikes of purple flowers. Genus: *Lythrum.* [Mid-16thC. Literal translation of Latin *lysimachia* (as if from Greek *lusis* 'loosening' ['ending'] + *makhē* 'battle'), named after *Lysimachus*, Greek physician and discoverer of the plant.]

loose-tongued *adj.* liable to gossip or reveal information that should not be told (*informal*)

loot /loot/ *n.* **1.** MIL SPOILS OF WAR OR RIOT money or goods that have been pillaged during wartime or a riot **2.** CRIMINOL STOLEN GOODS money or goods that have been stolen or obtained illegally **3.** MONEY money (*informal*) **4.** LOT OF PRESENTS OR PURCHASES a large amount of goods that have been bought or given on one occasion (*informal*) ■ *vti.* (**loots, looting, looted**) STEAL LOOT FROM to steal valuables from a place during wartime or a riot [Mid-19thC. From Hindi *lūṭ*.] —**looter** *n.*

lop[1] /lop/ *vt.* (**lops, lopping, lopped**) **1.** CUT BRANCH OFF TREE to cut a branch off a tree cleanly **2.** CUT OFF STH to cut off sth, e.g. hair or a limb, with one stroke **3.** GET RID OF SB OR STH to eliminate sb or sth as superfluous **4.** TAKE AMOUNT OFF PRICE to deduct an amount from a price ■ *n.* CUT-OFF BRANCH a branch that has been cut off [Early 16thC. From or related to archaic *lop* 'smaller branches and twigs of a tree', of uncertain origin: perhaps literally 'things stripped off'.] —**lopper** *n.*

lop[2] /lop/ (**lops, lopping, lopped**) *v.* **1.** *vti.* DROOP to hang or allow sth to hang loosely **2.** *vi.* MOVE AWKWARDLY to move with an awkward slouching posture [Late 16thC. Thought to suggest the action of flopping about.]

lope /lōp/ v. (lopes, loping, loped) 1. vi. RUN IN LONG EASY STRIDES to run in a relaxed and easy way, taking long strides 2. vti. CANTER to canter or to make a horse canter with a long easy stride ■ n. LONG-STRIDING GAIT a relaxed and easy gait with long strides [13thC. Ultimately from Old Norse *hlaupa* 'to leap'.] —**loper** n.

lop-eared /-ee'rd/ adj. used to describe domestic rabbits, dogs, and goats that have loosely hanging ears

lophophore /lóffō fawr/ n. a circular or horseshoe-shaped structure of tentacles round the mouth of a bryozoan or brachiopod that is used for capturing food [Mid-19thC. Coined from Greek *lophos* 'crest' + -PHORE.]

lopolith /lóppō lith/ n. a basin-shaped body of igneous rock formed by the penetration of magma between existing layers of rock [Early 20thC. Coined from Greek *lopas* 'basin' + -LITH.]

lopsided /lop sídid/ adj. 1. SLOPING leaning or drooping to one side 2. UNBALANCED unevenly balanced because one side is larger, stronger, or heavier than the other [Early 18thC. 'Lop' from LOP².]

loquacious /lo kwáyshəss/ adj. tending to talk a great deal (formal) [Mid-17thC. Formed from Latin *loquaci-*, stem of *loquax*, from *loqui* 'to speak' (source of English *ventriloquist*).]

WORD KEY: SYNONYMS

See Synonyms at *talkative*.

---

loquat /lố kwot, -kwət/ (plural -quats or -quat) n. 1. ORNAMENTAL ORIENTAL TREE a small ornamental evergreen tree native to China and Japan with reddish woolly branches, sweet-smelling white flowers, and edible fruit. Latin name: *Eriobotrya japonica*. 2. FRUIT OF LOQUAT TREE the small pear-shaped orange-yellow sweet but slightly tangy fruit of the loquat tree, eaten raw or used in cooking [Early 19thC. From Chinese *luh kwat*, literally 'rush orange'.]

loran /láwrən/ n. a long-distance radio navigation system by which a ship or aircraft determines its position using radio signals sent out by two ground stations [Mid-20thC. Acronym formed from 'long-range navigation'.]

Federico García Lorca

Lorca /láwrkə/, **Federico García** (1898–1936) Spanish poet and playwright. A popular poet and powerful dramatist, he was assassinated by Nationalists during the Spanish Civil War. His works include *Blood Wedding* (1933) and *The House of Bernard Alba* (1936).

lord /lawrd/ n. 1. ARISTOCRAT a man who is a member of the nobility, especially in Great Britain 2. FEUDAL SUPERIOR in medieval Europe, a powerful land- or property-owner, with authority over an area, castle, or community, e.g. the lord of a manor 3. POWERFUL MAN a man who has considerable power, authority, or influence over others, e.g. a business tycoon ■ vti. (lords, lording, lorded) ACT IN A SUPERIOR WAY to act in a superior, masterful, or bullying way towards others [Old English *hláford*, contraction of *hláfweard*, literally 'loaf-guardian', from *hláf*, an earlier form of LOAF (source of English *lady*)] ◇ **lord it (over sb)** to act in a superior, masterful, or bullying way towards other people (disapproving)

Lord n. 1. CHRISTIAN GOD a title Christians give to God or specifically to Jesus Christ 2. JEWISH GOD a title that Jews give to God 3. TITLE FOR A MAN used as an alternative title for a marquess, earl, viscount, or baron 4. COURTESY TITLE FOR A MAN used as a courtesy title for the younger son or sons of a marquess, or duke 5. FORM OF ADDRESS FOR A MAN used as a form of address for an earl, viscount, or baron, and for the younger son of a duke or marquess 6. TITLE OF HIGH-RANKING OFFICIAL a title given to some high-ranking British officials ■ interj. EXPRESSING SURPRISE used to express surprise, concern, or annoyance about sth (informal) ■ **Lords** npl. HOUSE OF LORDS the House of Lords [Old English]

Lord Advocate n. the chief law officer in Scotland, responsible for the public prosecution service and the administration of the criminal justice system

Lord Chamberlain n. the official in charge of the British royal household

Lord Chancellor n. the cabinet minister in the British government who is the Speaker in the House of Lords and the official in charge of the judiciary in England and Wales

Lord Chief Justice n. in England, a judge who is the Lord Chancellor's deputy and president of the Queen's Bench Division of the High Court of Justice

Lord High Chancellor n. = Lord Chancellor

Lord Howe Island /lawrd how íland/ island in the South Pacific Ocean, 700 km/435 mi. northeast of Sydney, Australia. Population: 369 (1996). Area: 145 sq. km/56 sq. mi.

lording /láwrding/ n. (archaic) 1. MEMBER OF NOBILITY a gentleman or member of the nobility 2. YOUNG LORD a young lord [Old English]

Lord Justice of Appeal (plural **Lord Justices of Appeal**) n. in England, a judge in the Court of Appeal

Lord Lieutenant n. the representative of the sovereign in a British county

lordling /láwrdling/ n. a young lord

lordly /láwrdli/ adj. (-lier, -liest) 1. ARROGANT arrogant, aloof, and behaving in a superior way 2. IMPRESSIVE very grand, magnificent, and suitable for a lord ■ adv. IN GRAND MANNER in the manner of a lord (archaic) —**lordliness** n.

Lord Mayor n. the mayor of the City of London and some other large British boroughs and cities, e.g. York

Lord Muck n. an ordinary man who behaves as though he were very important. ◇ **Lady Muck**

Lord of Appeal n. a British judge who assists the House of Lords in hearing appeals

Lord of Hosts n. the Christian God

Lord of Misrule n. in Europe in the 15th and 16th centuries, sb appointed to organize celebrations and sporting events, especially at Christmas

Lord of the Flies n. = Beelzebub [Literal translation of Hebrew *ba'al zebūb* (see BEELZEBUB)]

lordosis /lawr dóssiss/ (plural -doses /-seez/) n. 1. MED CURVATURE OF BACK an unusual inward curving of the spine in the lower part of the back, which may be medically significant 2. ZOOL ARCHING OF BACK DURING SEX an inward arching of the back of female mammals during sexual stimulation [Early 18thC. Via modern Latin from Greek *lordōsis*, from *lordos* 'bent backwards'.] —**lordotic** /lawr dóttik/ adj.

Lord President of the Council (plural **Lord Presidents of the Council**) n. the cabinet minister in the British government who presides over meetings of the Privy Council

Lord Privy Seal (plural **Lords Privy Seal**) n. the senior cabinet minister in the British government with no specific portfolio

Lord Protector n. = Protector

Lord Provost n. the chairman and head of the local authority in one of the five major Scottish cities, Edinburgh, Glasgow, Aberdeen, Perth, and Dundee

lords-and-ladies n. = cuckoopint (takes a singular verb) [Said to be because some plants have dark spadices (the 'lords') and some light (the 'ladies')]

Lord's Day n. the Christian Sabbath

lordship /láwrd ship/ n. the position held by, land owned by, or period of tenure of, a lord (formal)

Lordship /láwrd ship/ n. a respectful way to refer to or address a judge, bishop, or some nobles

Lord's Prayer n. the most important prayer in Christianity, which Jesus Christ taught to his disciples according to the Gospels of Luke and Matthew

Lords Spiritual npl. the Anglican Archbishops of Canterbury and York and the 24 most senior bishops of England and Wales, who are entitled to sit in the House of Lords

Lord's Supper n. = Holy Communion [So called because Holy Communion commemorates the LAST SUPPER of Jesus Christ and his disciples]

Lord's Table n. 1. HOLY COMMUNION Holy Communion in the Protestant Church 2. ALTAR OR COMMUNION TABLE the altar or communion table in a Protestant church

Lords Temporal npl. the British peers sitting in the House of Lords who are not archbishops or bishops

lordy /láwrdi/ interj. US used to express surprise, shock, or disappointment (dated informal)

lore[1] /lawr/ n. 1. KNOWLEDGE HANDED DOWN VERBALLY acquired knowledge or wisdom on a particular subject, e.g. local traditions, handed down by word of mouth and usually in the form of stories or historical anecdotes 2. KNOWLEDGE FROM TEACHING OR EXPERIENCE knowledge that has been acquired through teaching or experience 3. TEACHING teaching, or sth that has been taught (archaic) [Old English *lār* 'teaching, learning', from a prehistoric Germanic word that is also the ancestor of English *learn*]

lore[2] /lawr/ n. 1. BIRDS PART BETWEEN BIRD'S EYES AND BEAK the part on either side of a bird's head between its eyes and the base of the bill 2. ZOOL AREA ON SNAKE'S OR FISH'S FACE the area on a snake's or a fish's face between its eyes and its mouth [Early 17thC. From Latin *lorum* 'strap, thong' (the original sense in English). The underlying meaning is 'flat surface'.]

Lorelei[1] /lórrə lī, láwrə-/ n. a legendary beautiful woman said to live on a rock near the Rhine and lure sailors onto the rocks with enchanting songs

Lorelei[2] /lórrə lī, láwrə-/ jutting cliff overlooking the River Rhine, between Mainz and Koblenz, western-central Germany. Height: 120 m/390 ft.

Loren /láwr en, law rén/, **Sophia** (b. 1934) Italian actor. Her film career includes both Italian comedies, often with Marcello Mastroianni, and work in Hollywood. Real name **Sofia Scicolone**

Lorentz-Fitzgerald contraction /lórrənts fits jérrəld-/ n. the consequence of relativity that causes a reduction in length of an object travelling at a speed approaching that of light

Lorenz /láw rents/, **Konrad** (1903–89) Austrian zoologist and ethologist. He founded the science of ethology, and his research on animal behaviour included work on imprinting in birds and on human and animal aggression. He shared the Nobel Prize in physiology or medicine in 1973. Full name **Konrad Zacharias Lorenz**

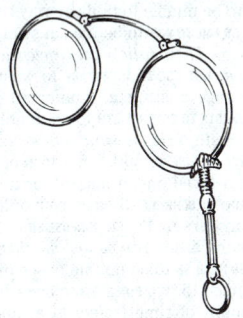
Lorgnette

lorgnette /lawr nyét/ n. a pair of glasses or opera glasses with a short handle at the side [Early 19thC. From French, formed from *lorgner* 'to squint, peer at', ultimately from a prehistoric Germanic word.]

lorica /lórrikə/ (plural -cae /-kee/) n. 1. BIOL PROTECTIVE SHELL a lightweight loose-fitting external shell that protects ciliated or flagellated protozoans 2. HIST, ARMS PIECE OF ROMAN ARMOUR a protective metal or leather garment covering the chest and back, worn by the ancient Romans [Early 18thC. From Latin, literally 'breastplate', formed from *lorum* 'strap, thong'.]

lorikeet /lórri keet, lórri keét/ (*plural* **-keets** *or* **-keet**) *n.* a small brightly-coloured long-necked parrot native to Australia and other Pacific Islands that has a bristle-tipped tongue for extracting nectar and pollen from flowers. Genera: *Trichoglosus* and *Glossopsitta.* [Late 18thC. Formed from LORY, modelled on *parakeet*.]

lorimer /lórrimər/, **loriner** /lórrinər/ *n.* a craftsman who in the past made small metal accessories for horses, e.g. bits and spurs [13thC. From Old French *lorenier*, from *lorain* 'harness-strap', from Latin *lorum* 'strap, thong'.]

loris /láwriss/ (*plural* **-ris**) *n.* a small slow-moving nocturnal tree-dwelling primate native to tropical regions of southern Asia that has large eyes, dense woolly fur, a vestigial index finger, and no tail [Late 18thC. From French, of uncertain origin: perhaps from obsolete Dutch *loeris* 'clown, fool', ultimately from Latin *lurid* 'pale' (source of English *lurid*.)]

lorn /lawrn/ *adj.* forsaken or forlorn (*archaic literary*) [13thC. Past participle of *lese* 'to lose', from Old English *-lēosan* (source of English *forlorn*).]

Lorrain /lə ráyn/, **Claude** (1600–82) French painter. He was unsurpassed in his mastery of light effects in his idealized landscape paintings, often based on classical or biblical themes. Real name **Claude Gellée**

lorry /lórri/ (*plural* **-ries**) *n.* a large vehicle for transporting goods by road. ◊ **truck** [Mid-19thC. Origin uncertain: perhaps from the name *Laurie*; or from northern English dialect *lurry* 'to haul', of unknown origin.]

lory /láwri/ (*plural* **-ries** *or* **-ry**) *n.* a small brightly-coloured parrot native to Australia and Indonesia that has a bristle-tipped tongue for extracting nectar and pollen from flowers. It has a heavier build than the lorikeet. Subfamily: Loriidae. [Late 17thC. From Malay *lori*.]

Los Alamos /los állə moss/ city in Los Alamos County, central New Mexico, situated approximately 55 km/35 mi. northwest of Santa Fe. Population: 11,455 (1990).

Los Angeles /los ánjələss, -leez/ city and county seat of Los Angeles County, southwestern California. Located on the Pacific Ocean, it is the second most populous city in the United States. Population: 3,448,613 (1994).

lose /looz/ (**loses, losing, lost** /lost/, **lost**) *v.* **1.** *vti.* FAIL TO WIN to fail to win a victory, e.g. in a contest, argument, war, game, or in court **2.** *vt.* MISLAY to be unable to find sth, often only temporarily **3.** *vt.* HAVE STH TAKEN AWAY to cease to possess or have sth, e.g. a job or home **4.** *vt.* CEASE HAVING QUALITY to cease having a quality, belief, attitude, or characteristic ○ *He's lost the will to live.* **5.** *vt.* CEASE HAVING ABILITY OR SENSE to cease having a particular ability or sense, e.g. through illness or an accident ○ *He lost his sight in the war.* **6.** *vt.* EXPERIENCE REDUCTION IN STH to experience a reduction in sth, e.g. weight or heat **7.** *vt.* BE UNABLE TO FIND WAY to be unable to find the way ○ *lost his way* **8.** *vt.* MAKE SB FAIL TO WIN to be the cause of sb's failure to win sth ○ *The goalie's inexperience lost us the match.* **9.** *vt.* NOT USE TO ADVANTAGE to waste or fail to take advantage of sth, e.g. time or an opportunity **10.** *vt.* BE UNABLE TO CONTROL STH to be unable to control or maintain sth ○ *He loses his composure easily.* **11.** *vt.* HAVE LOVED ONE DIE to suffer the loss of sb through death, e.g. a loved one, a patient, or a baby **12.** *vt.* LEAVE SB FOLLOWING BEHIND to escape from or leave behind sb who is in pursuit **13.** *vt.* CONFUSE SB to fail to make sb understand sth ○ *You've lost me there.* **14.** *vt.* NO LONGER SEE OR HEAR SB to be unable to see or hear sb or sth any longer **15.** *vti.* RUN SLOW to be or become slow by an amount of time (*refers to a timepiece*) [Old English *losian* 'to perish, destroy, or lose', formed from *los* (see LOSS)] —**losable** *adj.* —**losableness** *n.* ◇ **lose it 1.** to become removed from reality (*informal*) **2.** to be unable to maintain emotional control or composure (*informal*)

lose out *vi.* to fail to win or obtain sth in a competition or rivalry (*informal*)

loser /loózər/ *n.* **1.** SB WHO HAS NOT WON a person or team that has failed to win a particular contest **2.** SB UNSUCCESSFUL OR UNLUCKY sb who is unsuccessful or unlucky and seems destined to fail repeatedly

Losey /lózi/, **Joseph** (1909–84) US film director. His works explored social issues and criticized American society. In 1951 he was blacklisted as left wing and moved to Europe. Full name **Joseph Walton Losey**

losings /loózingz/ *npl.* money or possessions that are lost, especially through gambling

loss /loss/ *n.* **1.** FACT OF NO LONGER HAVING STH the fact of no longer having sth or of having less of sth **2.** DEATH the death of sb **3.** SB OR STH LOST sb or sth that has been lost **4.** MONEY SPENT IN EXCESS OF INCOME the amount of money by which a company's expenses exceed income (*often used in the plural*) **5.** SAD FEELING a feeling of sadness, loneliness, or emptiness at the absence of sb or sth **6.** REDUCTION a reduction in the level of sth, especially in the body ○ *weight loss* **7.** INSTANCE OF LOSING CONTEST an instance of losing a competition, race, or contest **8.** ELEC DROP IN POWER CAUSED BY RESISTANCE a drop in power caused by resistance in an electric circuit **9.** INSTANCE OR AMOUNT OF CLAIM an instance or the amount of a claim made by an insurance policyholder [Old English *los* 'ruin, destruction', from a prehistoric Germanic word that is also the ancestor of English *lease*, *lorn*, and *loose*. In later use a back-formation from LOST.] ◇ **at a loss** uncertain what to say or do ◇ **cut your losses** to withdraw from a situation in which there is no possibility of winning

loss adjuster *n.* sb employed by an insurance company to assess the financial losses incurred through, e.g. accident, theft, fire, or natural disaster, and determine the amount of compensation. US term **adjuster**

loss leader *n.* an item sold at a price below its cost in the hope that customers who buy it will also buy other things

lossmaker /lóss maykər/ *n.* a business, organization, or industry that does not make a profit —**lossmaking** *adj.*

loss ratio *n.* the ratio of the losses paid out in a year by an insurance company against the income from premiums

lost /lost/ *v.* past tense, past participle of **lose** ■ *adj.* **1.** MISLAID unable to be found for the moment **2.** UNABLE TO FIND THE WAY unable to find the way to a place **3.** NOT USED PROPERLY wasted or not taken advantage of **4.** UNAPPRECIATED not understood or appreciated by sb **5.** LACKING CONFIDENCE unable to cope with a job or situation, usually because of inexperience or lack of confidence **6.** GONE no longer in existence or use **7.** PREOCCUPIED completely absorbed or involved in sth **8.** CONFUSED BY STH COMPLICATED confused or bewildered by sth complicated or poorly explained **9.** DESTROYED destroyed or killed **10.** LACKING MORALS morally or spiritually past hoping for (*formal*) ◇ **get lost** used to tell sb in a blunt and rude way to go away (*slang*)

lost and found *n. US* = **lost property**

lost cause *n.* sb who cannot be influenced to change, or sth that cannot succeed

Lost Generation, lost generation *n.* **1.** MEN KILLED IN WORLD WAR I the large numbers of young men who were killed in World War I **2.** AUTHORS WRITING AFTER WORLD WAR I the group of authors, including Ernest Hemingway and F. Scott Fitzgerald, who came to prominence shortly after World War I.

lost property *n.* **1.** THINGS ACCIDENTALLY LEFT BEHIND personal possessions that have been accidentally left in a public place, e.g. in a cinema or on a train **2.** **lost property office** PLACE WHERE LOST PROPERTY IS KEPT a place in a public building, e.g. a theatre or railway station, where personal possessions that have accidentally been left behind are kept for reclaiming by their owners. US term **lost and found**

lost tribes *n.* the ten Hebrew tribes that separated from the other two to create a kingdom in northern Israel after Solomon's death. They were defeated by the Assyrians in 721 BC and may have become assimilated, but legend predicts their return.

lost wax *n.* a method of casting metal in which a wax model is coated with a material with a high melting point. The wax is melted and replaced by the molten metal.

lot /lot/ *pron.* MANY a large number of people or things ■ *n.* **1.** A SET a set or group of things or people **2.** ITEMS IN AUCTION an item or group of items on sale at an auction ○ *I bought the silver as one lot.* **3.** GROUP a particular group of people (*informal*) ○ *Don't expect any help from that lot.* **4.** DESTINY the things sb has or experiences in life ○ *our lot in life* **5.** *US* PIECE OF LAND a small area of land that has fixed boundaries ○ *a vacant lot* **6.** CINEMA FILM STUDIO a film studio together with the land that belongs to it ■ **lots** *npl.* LARGE NUMBERS OR LARGE AMOUNT large numbers of people or things, or a large amount ○ *Lots of us went.* ○ *I've got lots left.* ■ *adv.* **1.** TO A GREAT EXTENT to a great extent or degree ○ *Fishing has changed a lot in the last century.* **2.** OFTEN often or much of the time ○ *We went out to restaurants a lot.* **3.** **lots** MUCH a great deal (*informal*) ○ *I'm feeling lots better, thanks.* [Old English *hlot* 'one of a set of objects used to make decisions by chance', also 'share assigned by lot', hence 'sb's destiny decided by fate'] ◇ **a bad lot** an unpleasant or disreputable person ○ *Don't have anything to do with him: he's a bad lot.* ◇ **draw lots, cast lots** to choose sth at random, e.g. a straw or piece of paper, to determine an outcome ○ *We cast lots to decide who should go first.* ◇ **the lot** everything, or everything considered as one ○ *Personality, looks, brains...she's got the lot.*

WORD KEY: USAGE

a lot or **alot**? The superficial similarity of ***a lot*** to adjectives and adverbs like *alone* and *aloud* gives rise to a temptation to treat the expression as one word. This is substandard usage. Even in informal English ***lot*** should be treated as a noun, which may be used either in the plural (*I have lots of ideas*) or as a singular after the indefinite article ***a*** (*Thanks a lot*).

Lot /lot/ in the biblical Book of Genesis, the son of Haran, brother of Abraham. He is mentioned as Lut in the Koran.

Lot 1. department in Midi-Pyrénées Region, southwestern France, known for its scenic beauty. Population: 155,816 (1990). Area: 5,217 sq. km/2,014 sq. mi. **2.** river in southwestern France. Length: 483 km/300 mi.

lota /lṓtə/, **lotah** *n.* a small round water container, usually made of brass or copper, used in the Indian subcontinent [Early 19thC. From Hindi *loṭā*.]

loth /lōth/ *adj.* = **loath**

Lothair II /lō tháir/, **King of Germany and Holy Roman Emperor** (1075–1137). His election as king of Germany (1125) led to a war between two rival families, the Guelphs and the Ghibellines.

Lothario /lō thaári ō, -thaíri ō/ (*plural* **-os**), **lothario** *n.* a man who attempts to persuade women to enter sexual affairs with him (*literary*) [Mid-18thC. The name of such a character in *The Fair Penitent* (1703), a tragedy by Nicholas Rowe.]

Lothian /lṓthi ən/ former region of southeastern Scotland, approximately equivalent to the modern-day council areas of East Lothian, Midlothian, West Lothian, and the City of Edinburgh

loti /lṓti/ (*plural* **maloti** /maa lṓti/) *n.* **1.** AFRICAN MONETARY UNIT the basic unit of currency in Lesotho. See table at **currency 2.** NOTE WORTH A LOTI a note worth a loti [Late 20thC. From Sesotho, named after the *Maloti* mountains in Lesotho.]

lotic /lṓtik/ *adj.* used to describe ecological communities that live in swift-flowing water [Early 20thC. Formed from Latin *lotus*, past participle of *lavare* 'to wash'.]

lotion /lṓsh'n/ *n.* a thick liquid preparation that is applied to the skin for cosmetic or medical reasons [14thC. Directly or via French from the Latin stem *lotion-*, from *lot-*, past participle stem of *lavare* 'to wash'.]

lottery /lóttəri/ (*plural* **-ies**) *n.* **1.** GAMBLING GAMBLING GAME a large-scale gambling game, usually organized to raise money for a public cause, in which numbered tickets are sold and a draw is held to select the winning numbers **2.** SITUATION WHERE OUTCOME DEPENDS ON CHANCE an activity, situation, or enterprise with an outcome dependent on chance [Mid-16thC. Origin uncertain: probably ultimately from Dutch *loterij*, from *lot* 'lot'.]

lotto /lóttō/ (*plural* **-tos**) *n.* **1.** GAME RESEMBLING BINGO a game resembling bingo, in which numbers are called at random and players try to be the first to cover all the corresponding numbers on their cards **2.** **lotto, Lotto** STATE-RUN LOTTERY a state-run lottery in Australia and some other countries, and in some US states, in which players buy tickets bearing combinations of numbers. Periodically a combination of numbers is selected at random and people with matching tickets win cash prizes. [Late 18thC. Directly or via French *loto* from Italian *lotto*, ultimately from assumed Frankish *lot* 'lot'.]

Lotus

lotus /lótəss/ (*plural* **-tuses** *or* **-tus**) *n.* **1.** MYTHOLOGICAL FRUIT CAUSING DROWSINESS a fruit in Greek mythology that made people who ate it feel a pleasant drowsiness **2.** MYTHOLOGICAL PLANT BEARING LOTUS FRUIT a plant in Greek mythology that bore the lotus fruit, thought to be the date or jujube **3.** SACRED WATER LILY a white water lily, native to tropical Africa and Asia, that was sacred to the ancient Egyptians. Latin name: *Nymphaea lotus*. **4.** SACRED PINK WATER LILY a water lily native to Asia and Australia with large leaves and fragrant pink flowers, regarded as sacred in India, China, and Tibet. Latin name: *Nelumbo nucifera*. **5.** PLANT OF PEA FAMILY a plant of the pea family with yellow, pink, or white flowers. Genus: *Lotus*. **6.** RELIG, ARTS LOTUS FLOWER IN SACRED ART a representation of the flower of either of the sacred lotus plants, common in ancient Egyptian, Hindu, and Buddhist sacred art [15thC. Via Latin from Greek *lōtos*, applied by ancient writers to a variety of plants.]

lotus-eater *n.* **1.** LAZY AND INDULGENT PERSON sb who leads a lazy and self-indulgent life **2.** MYTHOL SB STUPEFIED BY EATING LOTUS sb who, in the *Odyssey*, lived in a state of idle stupor after feeding on the legendary lotus

Lotus position: Seated *Buddha*, Uttar Pradesh, northern India

lotus position *n.* a sitting position, used especially in yoga and meditation, in which the legs are crossed in such a way that each foot rests on top of the other leg's thigh [*Lotus* from the supposed resemblance of the position to a lotus blossom]

Louangphrabang /loo áng prə báng/ city in northern Laos, on the Mekong River. Population: 68,399 (1985).

louche /loosh/ *adj.* disreputable or of doubtful morality [Early 19thC. Via French, 'cross-eyed, shady', from Latin *luscus* 'one-eyed', of unknown origin.]

loud /lowd/ *adj.* **1.** HIGH IN VOLUME high in volume of sound **2.** EXPRESSING STH NOISILY expressing sth forcefully and frequently ○ *loud protests* **3.** VISUALLY SHOCKING shockingly bright in colour or bold in design ○ *a loud shirt* **4.** OFFENSIVE noisy, coarse, and offensive ■ *adv.* LOUDLY in a loud way [Old English *hlūd*. Ultimately from an Indo-European word meaning 'to hear', which also produced English *listen* and *leer*. The underlying idea is of sth that is heard.] —**loudly** *adv.*

louden /lówd'n/ (**-ens**, **-ening**, **-ened**) *vti.* to become louder, or to make a sound louder

loudhailer /lówd háylər/ *n.* a portable device for amplifying the voice consisting of a loudspeaker with an integrated amplifier and microphone. US term **bullhorn**

loudmouth /lówd mowth/ (*plural* **-mouths** /-mowthz, -mowths/) *n.* sb who talks a lot and loudly, especially gossiping or boasting (*informal*) —**loudmouthed** /lówd mowthd, -mowtht/ *adj.*

loudness /lówdnəss/ *n.* **1.** DEGREE OF SOUND VOLUME the degree of volume of sound **2.** PHYS VOLUME PERCEIVED BY EAR the magnitude of the physiological effect produced when a sound stimulates the ear

loud pedal *n.* = **sustaining pedal**

loudspeaker /lówd spéekər/ *n.* an electronic or electromagnetic device used to convert electrical energy into sound energy, providing the audible sound in equipment such as televisions, radios, CD players, and public-address systems

loudspeaker van *n.* a van or other vehicle provided with a loudspeaker so that political or other messages can be delivered to people in the streets and adjacent houses. US term **sound truck**

Lou Gehrig's disease /loő gérrigz-/ *n.* = amyotrophic lateral sclerosis [Mid-20thC. Named after Henry *Lou*is *Gehrig* (1903–41), US baseball player who died from the disease.]

lough /lokh, lok/ *n. Ireland* **1.** LAKE a lake **2.** LONG NARROW INLET a long inlet of the sea [13thC. Origin uncertain: probably ultimately from Old Irish *loch* 'lake', perhaps via obsolete Welsh *llwch*.]

Loughborough /lúfbərə/ industrial and university town in Leicestershire, England. Population: 47,600 (1994).

louis *n.* = **louis d'or**

Louis XIV /loő i/, King of France (1638–1715). He was a strong military leader and patron of the arts whose long reign (1642–1715) saw a great strengthening of the monarchy. Known as **the Sun King**

Louis XV, King of France (1710–74). His weak leadership and despotic rule (1715–74) contributed to the crisis that led to the French Revolution.

Louis XVI, King of France (1754–93). Coming to the throne (1774) when France was impoverished, he was deposed during the French Revolution and executed.

Louis /loő iss/, Joe (1914–81) US boxer. He was the world heavyweight champion from 1937 to 1942. Known as **the Brown Bomber**

louis d'or /loő i dáwr/ (*plural* **louis d'or**), **louis** (*plural* **-is**) *n.* **1.** OLD FRENCH COIN a gold coin of France used from the 17th century to the Revolution **2.** FRENCH POST-REVOLUTION COIN a former gold coin worth 20 francs used in France after the Revolution [Mid-17thC. From French, *louis d'or*, literally 'louis of gold', named for *Louis* XIII of France, during whose reign the coin was first issued.]

Louisiana

Louisiana /loő eézi áanə/ state in the southern United States bordering the Gulf of Mexico, Texas, Arkansas, and Mississippi. Capital: Baton Rouge. Population: 4,351,769 (1997). Area: 128,595 sq. km/49,651 sq. mi. —**Louisianan** *n.*, *adj.*

Louis Philippe /loő i fee leép/, King of the French (1773–1850). Proclaimed king after the July Revolution

(1830), he ruled as a constitutional monarch until the Revolution of 1848. Known as **the Citizen King**

Louisville /loő i vil/ city in northern Kentucky, on the Ohio River at Kentucky's border with Indiana. The largest city in the state, it is the site of Churchill Downs, home of the Kentucky Derby, a thoroughbred horse race run each May. Population: 260,689 (1996).

lounge /lownj/ *n.* **1.** SITTING ROOM IN HOUSE a sitting or living room in a house **2.** PUBLIC ROOM FOR RELAXING a room in a public building or vehicle, e.g. a hotel, airport, or ship, in which people may relax or wait **3.** LOUNGE BAR a lounge bar **4.** *US, Can* = cocktail lounge **5.** *Aus* SOFA a sofa or couch **6.** FURNITURE BACKLESS COUCH WITH HEADREST a couch without a back but with a headrest at one end **7.** PERIOD OF LOUNGING a period of relaxation, laziness, or inactivity ○ *having a lounge on the sofa after lunch* ■ *v.* (**lounges**, **lounging**, **lounged**) **1.** *vi.* LIE OR SIT LAZILY to sit or act in a casual, relaxed way **2.** *vti.* PASS TIME LAZILY to pass time in a relaxed or lazy way ○ *lounged the afternoon away* [Early 16thC. Origin uncertain: perhaps from obsolete *lungis* 'gangling foolish fellow, slow person', from French *longis*, from Latin *Longinus*, apocryphal name of the Roman centurion who pierced Jesus Christ's side.]

lounge bar, **lounge** *n.* a more comfortable and expensive bar in a pub or hotel

lounge lizard *n.* **1.** MAN FREQUENTING CLASSY VENUES a man who goes to places or events attended by the rich and famous, especially in order to approach wealthy women (*slang insult*) **2.** *US* LOUNGE FREQUENTER a frequent patron of cocktail lounges (*slang*) [Origin uncertain: probably an alliterative formation based on the negative associations of reptiles]

lounger /lównjər/ *n.* **1.** FURNITURE COMFORTABLE CHAIR OR COUCH an extendable chair or a lightweight, usually adjustable, couch designed to be comfortable for the user **2.** SB WHO LOUNGES ABOUT sb who typically sits or walks in an especially casual relaxed way

lounge suit *n.* a man's suit consisting of a jacket and trousers, occasionally also including a waistcoat, all made from the same cloth, worn as formal daywear

lounge suite *n. Aus* a three-piece suite

loungewear /lównj wair/ *n.* clothing designed to be worn when relaxing, usually at home

loup /lowp/, **lowp** *vti.* (**loups**, **louping**, **louped**; **lowps**, **lowping**, **lowped**) *Scotland* LEAP to leap or jump ■ *n. Scotland* LEAP a leap or a jump [14thC. From Old Norse *hlaupa* (see LEAP).]

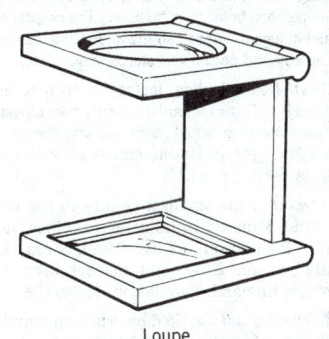

Loupe

loupe /loop/ *n.* a magnifying glass used especially by jewellers and watchmakers [Late 19thC. From French, 'flawed gem', of uncertain origin: probably from prehistoric Germanic.]

loup-garou /loő ga roő/ (*plural* **loups-garous**) *n. US* a werewolf (*dated*) [Late 16thC. From French, from Old French *leu* 'wolf' (from Latin *lupus*) + *garoul* 'werewolf', from a prehistoric Germanic word meaning literally 'man-wolf'.]

louping ill /lówping-/ *n.* a serious viral disease spread by ticks that damages the central nervous system, causing tremors and difficulty in mobility. It affects many animals, including sheep, cattle, goats, and pigs. ['Louping' 'leaping' from Scottish and northern English *loup* 'to leap', from Old Norse *hlaupa* (source of English *lope*). From the jumps that the disease often causes.]

lour /lowr/ *vi.*, *n.* = **lower**[2]

Lourdes /loordz/ town and place of pilgrimage in Hautes-Pyrénées Department, Provence-Alpes-Côte-d'Azur Region, southwestern France. Population: 16,301 (1990).

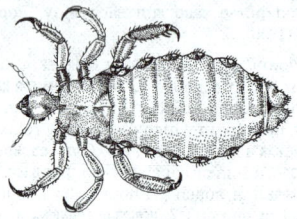

Louse

louse /lowss/ n. (plural **lice** /līss/) **1.** PARASITIC INSECT a small wingless insect that lives as a parasite on humans and other animals.There are sucking lice, e.g. head and body lice, and biting lice, e.g. bird lice. **2.** SMALL INVERTEBRATE ANIMAL a small invertebrate animal, e.g. a wood louse (often used in combination) **3.** (plural **louses**) OFFENSIVE TERM an offensive term that deliberately insults sb's behaviour and attitude towards others (informal insult) ■ vt. (**louses, lousing, loused**) MED = **delouse** [Old English lūs. Ultimately from an Indo-European word meaning 'louse'. Celtic languages also have words meaning 'louse' from this ancestor.]
louse up vti. to mishandle a situation or task so that it is ruined (informal)

lousewort /lówss wurt/ n. a plant of the snapdragon family that is native to northern regions and has feathery leaves and spikes of white, yellow, or pinkish-purple flowers. Genus: Pedicularis. ◊ **wood betony** [From the belief that sheep feeding on it became infested with lice]

lousy /lówzi/ (**-ier, -iest**) adj. **1.** INFERIOR inferior or second-rate (informal) **2.** UNPLEASANT unpleasant or unacceptable (informal) ○ a lousy way to treat somebody **3.** ILL painful or in bad health (informal) **4.** US HAVING A LOT OF STH having a large amount of sth (informal) ○ His parents are lousy with money. **5.** LOUSE-INFESTED infested with lice —**lousily** adv. —**lousiness** n.

lout[1] /lowt/ n. an offensive term that deliberately insults the behaviour and attitude of sb, especially a young man (informal insult) [Mid-16thC. Origin uncertain: perhaps from LOUT[2] 'to bend'. The original meaning was 'unintelligent person', so the underlying idea seems to be of an awkward person who stoops or slouches.]

lout[2] /lowt/ (**louts, louting, louted**) vi. to bow or bend (archaic) [Old English lūtan. Ultimately from an Indo-European word meaning 'small', which is also the ancestor of English little. The underlying idea is of making yourself smaller by bending down.]

Louth /lowth/ **1.** the smallest county in the Republic of Ireland, situated in Leinster Province, north of Dublin. Population: 92,163 (1996). Area: 821 sq. km/317 sq. mi. **2.** ancient market town in Lincolnshire, England. Population: 14,248 (1991).

loutish /lówtish/ adj. marked by crude and unpleasant behaviour —**loutishly** adv. —**loutishness** n.

Louvain /loo váN/ town in central Belgium, near Brussels, famous for its old buildings and churches. Population: 87,132 (1996).

louvar /loó vaar/ (plural **-vars** or **-var**) n. a large deep-sea fish that lives in tropical waters and has a blunt head, silvery-pink body, and bright red fins. Latin name: Luvarus imperialis. [Late 20thC. Origin uncertain: probably from modern Latin Luvarus, scientific name of the genus, from Italian dialect (Sicilian) luvaru, perhaps ultimately from Latin ruber 'red'.]

louvre /loóvər/, **louver** n. **1.** FRAME WITH HORIZONTAL SLATS a frame on a door or window supporting spaced horizontal slats angled to admit air and light but not rain ○ a set of louvre doors **2.** SLAT IN LOUVRE an individual slat in a louvre **3.** ANY SLATTED OPENING any slatted opening, generally for ventilation or cooling **4.** ROOF STRUCTURE RELEASING SMOKE a structure such as a

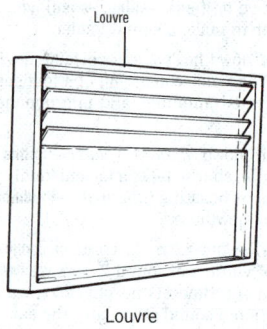

Louvre

lantern or turret on the roof of a building, especially a medieval building, that allows smoke to escape [14thC. From Old French lover 'skylight', of uncertain origin: probably from prehistoric Germanic.] —**louvred** adj.

Louvre /loóvrə/ n. a museum in Paris that contains the national art collection, including such famous works as the Mona Lisa and Venus de Milo. Located in the former palace of the kings of France, the museum opened to the public in 1793.

lovable /lúvvəb'l/, **loveable** adj. attracting or worthy of love or affection —**lovability** /lúvvə bílləti/ n. —**lovableness** /lúvvəb'lnəss/ n. —**lovably** adv.

lovage /lúvvij/ n. a perennial herb, native to the Mediterranean, with greenish flowers. It is cultivated for its small aromatic fruit used in seasoning. Latin name: Levisticum officinale. [14thC. Alteration (by folk etymology from LOVE and obsolete ache 'parsley') of Old French levesche, from late Latin levisticum (apium) 'Ligurian (parsley)', variant of ligusticum 'of Liguria', region in Italy.]

lovat /lúvvət/ n. a colour that is a muted dusty mixture of green and yellow or green and blue [Early 20thC. Origin uncertain: probably named after Thomas Alexander Fraser, Lord Lovat (1802–75), Scottish nobleman who popularized tweeds in muted colours as hunters' dress.]

love /luv/ v. (**loves, loving, loved**) **1.** vti. FEEL TENDER AFFECTION FOR to feel tender affection for sb, e.g. a close relative or friend, or for sth such as a place, an ideal, or an animal **2.** vti. FEEL DESIRE FOR to feel romantic and sexual desire and longing for sb **3.** vt. LIKE VERY MUCH to like sth or like doing sth very much ○ I love watching old movies on TV. **4.** vt. SHOW KINDNESS TO to feel and show kindness and charity to sb ○ love one another and love your neighbour **5.** vt. VENERATE to worship and venerate God **6.** vt. HAVE SEXUAL INTERCOURSE WITH to have sexual intercourse with sb (dated) ■ n. **1.** VERY STRONG AFFECTION an intense feeling of tender affection and compassion ○ Young children need unconditional love. **2.** PASSIONATE ATTRACTION AND DESIRE a passionate feeling of romantic desire and sexual attraction **3.** KIND PERSON sb who is kind or pleasant (informal) ○ Be a love and pour me a cup of tea. **4.** SB MUCH LOVED sb who is loved romantically ○ He was her first real love. **5.** ROMANTIC AFFAIR a romantic affair, possibly sexual **6.** STRONG LIKING strong liking for or pleasure gained from sth ○ his love of music **7.** STH ELICITING ENTHUSIASM sth that elicits deep interest and enthusiasm in sb ○ Music was his greatest love but he also liked ballet. **8.** BELOVED used as an affectionate word to sb loved **9.** TERM OF FRIENDLY ADDRESS used as a friendly term of address, usually to a woman (informal) ○ Here's your change, love. **10.** SPORTS, GAME SCORE OF ZERO a score of zero in sports and games, e.g. tennis, squash, and whist **11.** CHR GOD'S LOVE FOR HUMANITY the mercy, grace, and charity shown by God to humanity **12.** CHR WORSHIP OF GOD the worship and adoration of God [Old English lufian, from lufu 'love' (source of the noun). Ultimately from an Indo-European word meaning 'to love', which is also the ancestor of English libido, belief, and leave 'absence'.]

——— WORD KEY: SYNONYMS ———
love, liking, affection, fondness, passion, infatuation, crush
CORE MEANING: a strong positive feeling towards sb or sth **love** used to describe a very strong, positive feeling towards sb or sth. It is used especially to talk about strong romantic or sexual feelings between people; **liking** used to talk about positive feelings towards sb or sth.

These feelings are not as strong as those suggested by 'love'; **affection** used to describe warm friendly caring feelings between people. It can also be used to talk about a liking for sth such as a place; **fondness** used in a similar way to 'affection' to talk about feelings between people. It can also be used to describe a strong liking or preference for sth; **passion** used to describe an exceptionally intense love for sb, usually of a strong sexual nature. It can also be used to refer to a strong liking or enthusiasm for sth, sometimes of an excessive nature; **infatuation** used to describe an intense but short-lived and often unrealistic love for sb, usually of a romantic or sexual nature; **crush** used to describe sb's strong feeling of attraction towards a person with whom he or she is not having a relationship. It is used especially to talk about teenagers and young people.

love affair n. **1.** SEXUAL OR ROMANTIC RELATIONSHIP a sexual or romantic relationship between people who are not married to one another or who do not live together in a permanent relationship **2.** INTENSE LIKING FOR STH an intense liking or enthusiasm for sth ○ his love affair with the cinema

love apple n. = **tomato** [Translation of French pomme d'amour and German Liebesapfel, perhaps from the reputed aphrodisiac properties of the tomato]

love beads npl. a necklace of coloured beads, first popular with hippies in the 1960s

lovebird /lúv burd/ n. **1.** BIRDS SMALL PARROT a small greenish short-tailed African parrot, noted for close bonding and mutual preening between mates. They are popular as cage birds. Genus: Agapornis. **2.** LOVER a lover, especially one who is publicly affectionate (usually used in the plural) [From the fact that the pairs display very affectionate behaviour]

lovebite /lúv bīt/ n. a small patch of bruised skin, often on the neck, caused by a partner's sucking kiss. US term **hickey**

love child n. the child of parents who are not married to each other

love feast n. **1.** CHR SYMBOLIC CHRISTIAN MEAL a symbolic meal shared among Christians as a symbol of love and charity **2.** GOODWILL MEAL a meal held with the intention of stimulating goodwill

love game n. a game in tennis and some other sports in which the loser scores no points [From LOVE 'zero']

love handles npl. two regions of fat located at either side of the back just above the pelvis (humorous informal)

love-in n. a relatively large gathering in which participants experience feelings of love and mutual support (dated)

love-in-a-mist n. an erect Mediterranean annual plant with white or pale blue flowers surrounded by very fine bracts, giving the flowers a delicate appearance. Latin name: Nigella damascena. [Mist from the mass of threadlike bracts that surrounds the flower]

love knot n. a knot or bow of ribbon used to symbolize love

Lovelace /lúv layss/, **Richard** (1618–57) English poet. An ardent Royalist, he was one of the writers known as the Cavalier poets.

loveless /lúvləss/ adj. **1.** EMPTY OF LOVE devoid of love ○ a loveless marriage **2.** NOT SHOWING LOVE not exhibiting or giving love ○ a loveless glance **3.** UNLOVED not receiving love ○ a loveless child

love-lies-bleeding n. a tropical Indian plant with drooping clusters of small red flowers. Latin name: Amaranthus candatus. [From the resemblance of the flowers to a flow of blood]

love life n. the romantic or sexual relationships in a person's life

Lovell /lúvv'l/, **Sir Bernard** (b. 1913) British astronomer. Director of Jodrell Bank Experimental Station (1951–81), he was a pioneer of radio astronomy. Full name **Alfred Charles Bernard Lovell**

lovelock /lúv lok/ n. a long lock of hair separated from the rest by a ribbon, worn forward over the shoulder in the 16th century, or worn on the forehead in later periods

Lovelock /lúv lok/, **Jack** (1910–49) New Zealand athlete. He won the 1,500 metres at the 1936 Olympics in a world-record time of 3 minutes 47.8 seconds.

lovelorn /lúv lawrn/ adj. terribly unhappy because of unrequited love or difficulties with love —**lovelornness** n.

lovely /lúvli/ adj. (**-lier, -liest**) **1. BEAUTIFUL AND PLEASING** beautiful and pleasing, especially in a harmonious way **2. DELIGHTFUL** very enjoyable or pleasant **3. CARING** loving or friendly and caring **4. ATTRACTING LOVE** attracting or inspiring love in others ■ n. (plural **-lies**) **SB OR STH GOOD-LOOKING** sb who or sth that is very good-looking, especially a woman (often used in the plural; sometimes considered offensive) ○ Farewell, my lovely! [Old English luflic. The word originally meant 'affectionate' and 'lovable'; the modern sense 'beautiful' did not develop until the late 13thC.] —**loveliness** n.

—————— WORD KEY: SYNONYMS ——————
See Synonyms at *goodlooking*.

lovemaking /lúv mayking/ n. **1. SEXUAL ACTIVITY** sexual activity between lovers, especially sexual intercourse **2. COURTSHIP** courtship or wooing (dated)

love nest n. a place, such as a small flat or secluded house, where lovers can be together

love potion n. a magical drink intended to stimulate sexual desire in the person who consumes it, for the person who gives it

lover /lúvvər/ n. **1. SEXUAL PARTNER** sb's sexual partner, especially if the two are not married to each other **2. SB HAVING LOVE AFFAIR** either of two people involved in a love affair (often used in the plural) **3. SB DEVOTED TO PARTICULAR THING** sb who is devoted to or very much likes a particular thing (often used in combination) ○ opera-lovers

—————— WORD KEY: CULTURAL NOTE ——————
Lady Chatterley's Lover, a novel by English writer D. H. Lawrence (1928). Lawrence's last novel, it describes an aristocratic woman's search for love and sexual satisfaction after her husband is crippled in war. The novel's notoriety, and the fact that the publishers of the first unexpurgated British edition were prosecuted for obscenity in 1960, has obscured its many qualities, including its insightful analysis of contemporary social and political values.

lover's knot n. = love knot

love seat n. a small sofa that seats two people

lovesick /lúv sik/ adj. listless or distracted because of love —**lovesickness** n.

lovey-dovey /lúvvi dúvvi/ adj. showing affection in an excessive or excessively sentimental way (informal) [From pet-forms of LOVE and DOVE]

loving /lúvving/ adj. **1. SHOWING AFFECTION** showing or feeling affection **2. DONE WITH CAREFUL ATTENTION** done with enjoyment and careful attention —**lovingly** adv. —**lovingness** n.

Loving cup

loving cup n. **1. TWO-HANDLED DRINKING VESSEL** a large drinking vessel with two or more handles, sometimes passed between people at a banquet **2. SPORTS ORNAMENTAL VESSEL** an ornamental vessel with two handles awarded to the winner of a sports contest [From the former use of the vessel in ceremonial drinking at banquets. Two people always stood up together, one to drink and the other to 'defend' the drinker.]

low[1] /lō/ adj. **1. WITHOUT GREAT HEIGHT** relatively little in height between the top and bottom ○ a low fence **2. CLOSE TO THE GROUND** located close or closer than usual to the ground or the base of sth ○ The sinking sun was low in the sky. **3. BELOW AVERAGE** below the average or expected degree, amount, or intensity ○ The lowest rainfall in fourteen years. **4. CONTAINING SMALL AMOUNT** having or containing a relatively small amount ○ low in calories **5. WITH LITTLE MONETARY VALUE** small in monetary value ○ low prices **6. LACKING MONEY** lacking resources, especially money (informal) ○ Can you lend me some cash, I'm a bit low. **7. OF BAD QUALITY** bad in quality or having little value ○ low standards **8. OF LITTLE IMPORTANCE** having little importance or urgency ○ low priority **9. NEAR DEPLETION** approaching or near depletion ○ We're low on supplies. **10. TURNED DOWN OR DIMMED** adjusted so that there is less of sth ○ low lighting **11. QUIET** at a quiet, soft, or hushed level ○ a low murmur **12. MUSIC DEEP IN PITCH** with a relative pitch that is closer to bass than soprano sounds ○ Her singing voice was a low soprano **13. SMALL** small or relatively small ○ a low risk **14. NEAR BOTTOM OF SCALE** near the beginning or bottom of sth measured on a scale ○ The temperature was in the low 80s. **15. DISPIRITED** melancholy, hopeless, or dispirited ○ in low spirits **16. LACKING PHYSICAL STRENGTH** lacking in physical strength or vitality ○ feeling low after a dose of flu **17. CLOTHES SHOWING NECK AND CHEST** cut to show more than usual of the wearer's neck and bosom ○ a low neckline **18. AUTOMOT PROVIDING SLOW SPEED** providing a relatively slow speed ○ a low gear **19. LACKING STATUS** lacking status or rank, or closer to the bottom of a class system **20. UNCOMPLIMENTARY** unfavourable or uncomplimentary ○ a low opinion of someone **21. UNPRINCIPLED** without principles or morals **22. VULGAR** full of vulgarity or coarseness **23. GEOG NEAR EQUATOR** near to the equator **24. BIOL NOT COMPLEX** simple in organic structure **25. PHON PRONOUNCED WITH LOW TONGUE** pronounced with the tongue lying low on the bottom of the mouth ○ a low vowel ■ adv. **1. IN LOW POSITION** in or to a low position, state, degree, or level ○ Turn the gas down low. **2. NEAR GROUND** near or nearer to the ground ○ flew low over the trees **3. WITH A DEEP PITCH** with a low or deep pitch ○ Play it a semitone lower. **4. QUIETLY** in a soft or quiet way **5. AT SMALL PRICE** at a low or small price ■ n. **1. STH LOW** sth such as a position or degree that is low ○ Sales dropped to an all-time low. **2. METEOROL BAD WEATHER REGION** a region of low barometric pressure that results in bad weather **3. UNHAPPY PERIOD** an unhappy or unfortunate experience or period of sb's life [12thC. From Old Norse lágr. Ultimately from an Indo-European word meaning 'to lie', which also produced English lie[1], lager[1], and fellow. The underlying idea is of lying flat.] —**lowness** n.

—————— WORD KEY: SYNONYMS ——————
See Synonyms at *mean*.

low[2] /lō/ n. **MOOING SOUND OF COW** a characteristic mooing sound made by a cow or similar animal ■ vti. (**lows, lowing, lowed**) **MOO** to make a mooing sound [Old English hlōwan 'to bellow' (used of cows). Ultimately from an Indo-European word meaning 'to shout', which also produced English clamour and declare.]

lowball /lō bawl/ (**-balls, -balling, -balled**) vti. US to deliberately quote a price or estimate that is lower than the eventual cost [From the card game lowball, a game of draw poker in which the player with the lowest-ranking hand wins the pot]

low blow n. an unfair comment or blow (informal) [From boxing, where it is prohibited to strike the opponent anywhere other than on the upper body or head]

lowborn /lō báwrn/, **lowbred** /-bréd/ adj. being of common rather than aristocratic parentage

lowbred /lō bréd/ adj. **1. COARSE** with a rude and vulgar manner (insult) **2.** = lowborn

lowbrow /lō brow/ adj. **UNSOPHISTICATED** unsophisticated or trivial and not requiring intellectual effort to be understood or appreciated (disapproving) ■ n. **UNSOPHISTICATED PERSON** sb who has unsophisticated or unintellectual tastes [Early 20thC. Modelled on HIGHBROW.]

low-cal /-kál/ adj. with few calories or fewer calories than usual

low camp n. a style of affectation or effeminacy expressed in an unsophisticated or coarse way

Low Church n. a branch of the Church of England that favours less ritual and ceremony and prefers an evangelical approach to services

low comedy n. comedy based on slapstick and coarse actions rather than more sophisticated forms of humour

Low Countries region in northwestern Europe, made up of Belgium, the Netherlands, and Luxembourg. Population: 26,016,000 (1995). Area: 73,943 sq. km/28,550 sq. mi.

low-density adj. having a low concentration of sth in an area

low-density lipoprotein n. a blood-plasma lipoprotein that is high in cholesterol and low in protein content, and that carries cholesterol to cells and tissue. High levels are associated with the development of atherosclerosis.

lowdown /lō down/ n. significant information about sb or sth, especially information that is not widely known (informal) ○ waiting for someone to give us the lowdown [Early 20thC. Origin uncertain: from either low down 'very low' or low-down 'contemptible'; perhaps because it was considered improper to impart such information.]

low-down adj. mean and contemptible (informal)

low earth orbit n. an orbit that is nearer to the Earth than a geostationary orbit. Satellites in such an orbit are usually part of a global mobile telephone system.

Amy Lawrence Lowell

Lowell /lō əl/, **Amy Lawrence** (1874–1925) US poet and critic. A leader of the imagist school, she wrote poems that exhibit a terseness of style and a use of free verse.

low-end adj. inexpensive compared to a group of similar products

lower[1] /lō ər/ adj. **1. BELOW STH** physically below another thing, especially one of the same type ○ the lower lip **2. REDUCED OR LESS** reduced or less in amount ○ agreed to work for lower wages **3. CLOSER TO BOTTOM** closer to the bottom or base of sth ○ camped on the lower slopes of the mountain **4. OF LESS IMPORTANCE** of less importance or inferior status ○ lower rank **5. GEOL EARLIER IN GEOLOGICAL PERIOD** relating to the earlier part of a geological period or system **6. ZOOL LESS ADVANCED** less advanced in terms of development or complexity **7. FARTHER FROM SOURCE** indicating that part of a river that is farthest away from the source ○ the lower Rio Grande ■ v. (**-ers, -ering, -ered**) **1.** vt. **BRING TO LOWER LEVEL** to move sth down to a lower level or to move sth downwards ○ lower the flag **2.** vti. **REDUCE OR FALL** to reduce sth or fall in quantity, quality, or value ○ Interest rates have been lowered by the Bank of England. **3.** vt. **REDUCE IN DEGREE** to reduce sth in degree **4.** vt. **LOOK DOWNWARDS** to move the head or eyes downwards ○ She lowered her eyes. **5.** vr. **HUMILIATE YOURSELF** to reduce your dignity or the respect in which you are held ○ I wouldn't lower myself to discuss it. **6.** vt. **REDUCE VOLUME OF SOUND** to reduce the volume of sound that sth produces ○ lower your voice **7.** vt. **MUSIC REDUCE SOUND PITCH** to bring a sound to a lower pitch **8.** vt. **PHON MODIFY VOWEL SOUND** to change the sound of a vowel by pushing the tongue to the bottom of the mouth ■ n. **STH LOWER** sth that is the lower of two or more things [12thC. Comparative of LOW[1], literally 'more low'.]

lower[2] /lów ər/, **lour** /lowr/ vi. (**-ers, -ering, -ered**) **lours, louring, loured**) **1.** BE OVERCAST to be overcast and threatening storms or heavy rain **2.** LOOK ANGRY to look angry or sullen ■ n. SCOWL a scowl or miserable look [13thC. Origin uncertain.] —**lowering** adj. —**loweringly** adv.

lower bound n. a number that is less than or equal to all the members of a set

Lower California /ló ər kálli fáwrni ə/ = **Baja California**

Lower Canada /ló ər kánnidə/ southern portion of present-day Quebec. It was a British province separate from Upper Canada from 1791 to 1840.

Lower Carboniferous n. = **Mississippian**. **2**

lower case adj. NOT CAPITAL written in small rather than capital form (hyphenated when used before a noun) ○ written with a lower-case 'p' ■ n. SMALL LETTERS NOT CAPITALS the small rather than capital form of letters ○ printed in lower case [Late 17thC. From compositors' practice of keeping types for small letters in the lower of a pair of type cases.]

lower chamber n. = **lower house**

lower class n. the social group considered to occupy the lowest position in a hierarchical society, typically composed of manual workers and their families

lower deck n. **1.** DECK ABOVE THE HOLD the next deck in a ship above the hold **2.** NAVY SAILORS NOT COMMISSIONED OFFICERS a ship's ordinary seamen and petty officers considered as a group (informal)

lower house, **lower chamber** n. one of two legislative houses, generally more directly representative and larger than the other house

Lower Hutt /ló ər hút/ city in the south of the North Island, New Zealand, now a suburb of Wellington. Population: 98,300 (1996).

Lower Lakes /ló ər láyks/ part of the Upper and Lower Lakes Management Area, St Lawrence County, New York, situated 6 km/4 mi. outside of Canton. Area: 3,513 hectares/8,782 acres.

lowermost /ló ər mōst/ adj. very lowest

lower school n. the younger pupils in a secondary school, usually the pupils in the first three or four years

lower world n. the dwelling place of the dead, often considered to be beneath the ground

lowest common denominator n. **1.** LOWEST MULTIPLE FOR ALL DENOMINATORS the lowest multiple shared by all the denominators in a set of fractions **2.** UNDISCERNING PUBLIC the mass of ordinary people, particularly when considered to have low critical standards and to lack taste

lowest common multiple n. the lowest whole number that is divisible without a remainder by all of the members of a set of numbers

Lowestoft /ló stoft/ seaside resort and fishing port in Waveney District, Suffolk, eastern England. Population: 62,907 (1991).

low-fat adj. prepared with a reduced amount of fat

low frequency n. a radio frequency ranging from 30 to 300 kilohertz

Low German n. the German dialects that are spoken in northern regions of Germany. Low German dialects differ in their development from the High German dialects that gave rise to standard German and are generally regarded as forming a separate language. ◊ **Middle Low German** ['Low' from the fact that the language is spoken in the low-lying part of Germany near the sea-shore]

low-grade adj. **1.** INFERIOR IN QUALITY bad or inferior in quality or grade **2.** MED MILD used to describe a medical condition, especially a fever, that is mild and not serious

low-impact adj. US **1.** NOT STRENUOUS not requiring a lot of energy or effort **2.** CAUSING LITTLE DAMAGE TO THE ENVIRONMENT causing little or no damage to the surrounding environment

low-income adj. having a relatively small income or used by people on a relatively small income ○ low-income families ○ low-income housing

lowing n. = **low**[2]

low-key, **low-keyed** adj. **1.** RESTRAINED restrained and understated in character ○ a relatively low-key campaign **2.** SUBDUED IN COLOUR subdued or of low intensity, particularly in colour **3.** PHOTOGRAPHY, PAINTING DARK-TONED used to describe a photograph or painting made up of dark tones and containing few highlights

lowland /lóland/ n. land that is relatively flatter or lower than adjacent land —**lowland** adj.

Lowlands /lólandz/ area of Scotland lying below the Highlands, south of a line drawn between Dumbarton and Stonehaven —**Lowlander** n.

low-level adj. **1.** LOW DOWN situated or done at a low or lower than usual level **2.** LOW IN STATUS relatively low in terms of importance, status, expertise, or intensity

low-level language n. COMPUT any computer-oriented programming language such as assembly language, in which the instructions are written in a code closer to machine code than to human language

lowlife /ló lìf/ n. **1.** CRIMINAL OR ASSOCIATE a criminal or sb who associates with criminals (informal) **2.** SB IMMORAL sb who is disreputable and immoral (insult) **3.** CRIMINAL OR IMMORAL PEOPLE people with criminal tendencies or extremely low morals, regarded as a group (informal insult) —**lowlife** adj.

low-loader n. a truck or railway carriage built with a low platform so as to make it easier to load and unload heavy goods

lowly /lóli/ adj. (**-lier, -liest**) **1.** LOW IN STATUS low in rank, status, or importance **2.** MEEK with a meek and humble way of behaving **3.** SIMPLE AND MODEST simple, plain, and modest in character ■ adv. (**-lier, -liest**) **1.** IN MEEK WAY in a humble or meek way **2.** AT LOW VOLUME at a subdued pitch or volume —**lowliness** n.

low-lying adj. at a lower level or closer to sea level than neighbouring ground

low-maintenance adj. US requiring only a little attention or effort to maintain (informal) ◊ **high-maintenance**

Low Mass, **low mass** n. a plain Mass celebrated in a Roman Catholic or Anglican church that is recited, not sung

low-minded adj. thinking or behaving in a coarse vulgar way —**low-mindedly** adv. —**low-mindedness** n.

low-necked adj. cut to have a low neckline

low-pass filter n. an electronic filter that blocks signals above a specified cut-off frequency but allows those below it to pass through unchanged

low-pitched adj. **1.** LOW IN PITCH low in pitch or tonal range ○ a low-pitched hum **2.** SHALLOW IN SLOPE with a shallow slope ○ a low-pitched roof

low-pressure adj. **1.** PHYS NEEDING LITTLE PRESSURE having, exerting, or working under little pressure **2.** RELAXED relaxed, easygoing, or presenting little stress

low profile n. a way of behaving in which sb deliberately seeks to avoid attention or publicity ○ keep a low profile

low-profile adj. **1.** AVOIDING ATTENTION deliberately avoiding attention or publicity **2.** AUTOMOT WIDE RELATIVE TO HEIGHT having a wide tread relative to its radial height ○ low-profile tyres

low relief n. = **bas-relief** [Translation of French bas-relief]

low-res adj. low-resolution [Shortening]

low-resolution adj. relating to a device, such as a computer screen or printer, in which the text or pictures are not sharply defined. The relatively large blocks of colour that are used cause the text or pictures to take on an angular appearance.

low rise n. a building consisting of only a few storeys (Modelled on HIGH-RISE) —**low-rise** adj.

Lowry /lówri/, **L. S.** (1887–1976) British painter. His stylized depictions of the industrial north of England were deliberately executed in a childlike manner. Full name **Laurence Stephen Lowry**

low-slung adj. closer to the ground or the floor than usual

low spirits npl. a state of unhappiness, hopelessness or despondency ○ The search party was in low spirits after three days. —**low-spirited** adj. —**low-spiritedly** adv. —**low-spiritedness** n.

Low Sunday n. the Sunday after Easter [Origin uncertain: 'Low' probably in contrast to the 'high' feast of Easter Sunday]

low tech n. low technology [Shortening of LOW TECHNOLOGY] —**low-tech** adj.

low technology n. simple technology, especially that used to make basic items or perform basic tasks

low-tension adj. capable of carrying low voltage or operating under low-voltage conditions

low tide n. **1.** LOWEST TIDE LEVEL a tide at its lowest level, or the time of day when this occurs **2.** WORST POINT a lowest or worst point

Lowveld /ló felt/ n. = **Bushveld**

low water n. **1.** = **low tide**. **1** **2.** DIFFICULT SITUATION a very difficult situation or point

low-water mark n. **1.** LOWEST LEVEL OF WATER the lowest level reached by a body of tidal or fresh water **2.** LINE MARKING LOW-WATER MARK a natural or artificial line marking a low-water mark **3.** LOWEST POINT a lowest or most difficult point

lox[1] /loks/ n. smoked salmon [Mid-20thC. Via Yiddish laks from Middle High German Lachs 'salmon'. Ultimately from an Indo-European word meaning 'salmon'.]

lox[2] /loks/ n. liquid oxygen, especially when used as an oxidizer for rocket fuel [Early 20thC. From l(iquid) o(xygen) (e)x(plosive); later misinterpreted by folk etymology as from l(iquid) ox(ygen).]

loxodrome /lóksə drōm/ n. = **rhumb line** [Late 19thC. Back-formation from LOXODROMIC.]

loxodromic /lóksə drómmik/, **loxodromical** /lóksə drómmik'l/ adj. relating to a map in which the rhumb lines appear straight, or to the rhumb lines on such a map [Late 17thC. From French loxodromique, from Greek loxos 'oblique', of unknown origin, + dromos 'course' (source of English -drome).] —**loxodromically** adv.

loxodromic curve n. = **rhumb line**

loyal /lóyəl/ adj. **1.** FAITHFUL remaining faithful to a country, person, ruler, government, or ideal **2.** EX-PRESSING LOYALTY expressing or relating to loyalty [Mid-16thC. Via French from Old French loial, variant of leial, from Latin legalis 'legal' (see LEGAL). The underlying idea is of faithfully carrying out legal obligations.] —**loyally** adv. —**loyalness** n.

loyalist /lóyəlist/ n. sb who firmly supports a country, ruler, or government —**loyalism** /lóy əlizəm/ n.

Loyalist /lóyəlist/ n. **1.** POL SUPPORTER OF ULSTER UNION WITH BRITAIN a Northern Ireland Protestant who wishes to continue Northern Ireland's political union with Britain **2.** AMERICAN WHO SUPPORTED BRITISH an American who supported the British during the American Revolution **3.** SPANISH CIVIL WAR SUPPORTER OF GOVERNMENT a supporter of the republican government during the Spanish Civil War

loyalty /lóyəlti/ (plural **-ties**) n. **1.** STATE OF BEING LOYAL the quality or state of being loyal **2.** FEELING OF DUTY a feeling of devotion, duty, or attachment to sb or sth (often used in the plural) [14thC. From Old French loialté, from loial 'loyal' (see LOYAL).]

lozenge /lózzinj/ n. **1.** PHARM MEDICATED TABLET a medicated tablet or sweet that is dissolved in the mouth, especially to soothe the throat **2.** MATH DIAMOND SHAPE a diamond-shaped figure **3.** HERALDRY DIAMOND-SHAPED IMAGE a diamond-shaped design or device on heraldic arms [14thC. From Old French losenge 'windowpane, small square cake', of uncertain origin: perhaps related to Spanish losa 'slab' and ultimately from Gaulish or Iberian.] —**lozenged** adj.

Lozi /lózi/ (plural **-zis** or **-zi**) n. a language of western Zambia, related to Sotho. About 450,000 people speak Lozi. [Mid-20thC. From Bantu.] —**Lozi** adj.

LP n. LONG-PLAYING RECORD a long-playing gramophone record that turns at 33⅓ revolutions per minute

LP abbr. **1.** Lord Provost **2.** low pressure

LPG abbr. liquefied petroleum gas

LPGA abbr. Ladies Professional Golf Association

L-plate (plural **L-plates**) n. a small square sign consisting of a red letter 'L' on a white background to indicate that a driver has not yet passed the driving test. By law, such a sign must be displayed on the front and rear of any vehicle driven by a learner until that person has passed the driving test. ['L' shortening of *learner*]

LPM, **lpm** abbr. lines per minute (*refers to a computer printer*)

LPS abbr. **1.** lipopolysaccharide **2.** Lord Privy Seal

Lr symbol. lawrencium

LR abbr. **1.** living room (*in advertisements*) **2.** INSUR Lloyd's Register (of Shipping)

LRAM abbr. Licentiate of the Royal Academy of Music

LRP abbr. UK lead replacement petrol

LRV abbr. light rail vehicle

l.s. abbr. locus sigilli (*on documents*) [Latin, 'the place of the seal']

LSD n. a hallucinogenic drug made from lysergic acid that was used experimentally as a medicine and is taken as an illegal drug [From German L(yserg)s(äure)-D(iäthylamid) 'lysergic acid diethylamide']

L.S.D, **l.s.d.** abbr. pounds, shillings, pence [Latin, librae, solidi, denarii]

LSE abbr. London School of Economics

LSI abbr. ELECTRON ENG large-scale integration

LSO abbr. London Symphony Orchestra

LSZ abbr. NZ limited speed zone

lt abbr. light

Lt abbr. Lieutenant

LT abbr. ELEC ENG low tension

l.t. abbr. local time

LTA abbr. Lawn Tennis Association

Lt Cdr abbr. Lieutenant Commander

Lt Col abbr. Lieutenant Colonel

Ltd, **ltd** abbr. limited (liability) (*used after the name of a British company*)

Lt Gen abbr. Lieutenant General

Lt Gov abbr. Lieutenant Governor

LTOM abbr. London Traded Options Market (*part of London Stock Exchange*)

Lu symbol. lutetium

Lualaba /loo ə laábə/ headstream of the River Congo in southeastern Democratic Republic of the Congo. Length: 1,800 km/1,100 mi.

Luanda /loo ándə/ seaport and capital of Angola, situated in the northwestern part of the country, on the Atlantic Ocean. Population: 2,250,000 (1995).

Luba /loóbə/ (plural **-bas** /loóbəz/ or **-ba**) n. Luba, Luba-Lulua a group of languages or dialects of southern Congo, around Kinshasa. Luba has about 8 million speakers and belongs to the Bantu group of Benue-Congo languages. [Late 19thC. From Bantu.] —**Luba** adj.

lubber /lúbbər/ n. **1.** CLUMSY OR UNINTELLIGENT PERSON a big person who is clumsy or unintelligent (*insult*) **2.** LANDLUBBER a landlubber [14thC. Origin uncertain: perhaps from *lob* 'lout', from Low Dutch; or from Old French *lobeor* 'swindler, parasite', from *lober* 'to deceive', perhaps from Frankish *lobon* 'to praise'.] —**lubberly** adj., adv.

lubber line, **lubber's line** n. a mark on a ship's compass that indicates the vessel's heading [*Lubber* from the fact that the line made steering easier for the inexperienced helmsman]

lubber's hole n. a space in a platform around a mast, allowing a sailor to climb through the space and stand on the platform [*Lubber's* from the idea that the hole was for inexperienced sailors who were too frightened to climb by way of the ropes at the edge of the platform]

lubber's line n. = lubber line

lube /loob/ n. US, Aus LUBRICANT a lubricant (*informal*) ■ vt. (**lubes**, **lubing**, **lubed**) US, Aus LUBRICATE to apply lubricant to sth (*informal*)

Lübeck /loó bek/ port and city in Schleswig-Holstein State, north-central Germany. Population: 217,300 (1994).

Lubitsch /loóbich/, **Ernst** (1892–1947) German-born US actor and film director. He started making films in Germany, then moved to Hollywood as a director of comedies and costume epics.

Lublin /loóblin/ city in southeastern Poland, situated about 153 km/95 mi. southeast of Warsaw. Population: 353,300 (1995).

lubricant /loóbrikənt/ n. **1.** FRICTION-REDUCING SUBSTANCE a substance, typically oil or grease, applied to a surface to reduce friction between moving parts **2.** ELEMENT EASING DIFFICULT SITUATION sb or sth that eases or facilitates a solution to a potentially difficult or awkward situation —**lubricant** adj.

lubricate /loóbri kayt/ (**-cates**, **-cating**, **-cated**) v. **1.** vti. APPLY LUBRICANT to apply an oily or greasy substance to sth in order to reduce friction to moving parts **2.** vt. MAKE SLIPPERY to make sth slippery **3.** vt. MAKE STH RUN SMOOTHLY to make sth run smoothly and without problems [Early 17thC. From Latin *lubricare*, from *lubricus* 'slippery' (source of English *lubricious*). Ultimately from an Indo-European word meaning 'to slide', which also produced English *sleeve*.] —**lubrication** /loóbri káysh'n/ n. —**lubricational** /-káysh'nəl/ adj. —**lubricative** /loóbri kaytiv, loóbrikətiv/ adj.

lubricator /loóbri kaytər/ n. **1.** DEVICE FOR APPLYING LUBRICANT a device for applying a lubricant to moving parts **2.** SB WHO EASES SITUATION sb who is diplomatic and able to ease a difficult situation

lubricious /loo bríshəss/, **lubricous** /loóbrikəss/ adj. (*literary*) **1.** LEWD OR OBSCENE lewd, obscene, or intended to be sexually exciting **2.** SLIPPERY slippery or oily [Late 16thC. Formed from Latin *lubricus* 'slippery' (see LUBRICATE). Former meanings of the word include 'slippery' and 'fickle'.] —**lubriciously** adv.

lubricity /loo bríssəti/ n. behaviour that is obscene or unchaste (*literary*) [15thC. Directly or via French from late Latin *lubricitas*, from Latin *lubricus* 'slippery' (see LUBRICATE).]

lubricous adj. = lubricious

Lubumbashi /loóbo͞om báshi/ industrial city and mining centre in Katanga Region, southeastern Democratic Republic of the Congo. Population: 851,381 (1994). Former name **Elizabethville**

Lucania, Mount /loo káyni ə/ mountain in the Saint Elias Range, southwestern Yukon Territory, Canada, near the Alaskan border. Height: 5,226 m/17,147 ft.

lucarne /loo kaárn/ n. a dormer window [Mid-16thC. Via French from Provençal *lucana*, of uncertain origin: perhaps from prehistoric Germanic.]

Lucas van Leyden /loókəss van líd'n/ (1494–1533) Dutch painter and engraver. One of the earliest painters of genre scenes, he also produced engravings of religious and allegorical subjects.

Lucca /loókə/ historic town and capital of Lucca Province, Tuscany Region, north-central Italy. Population: 100,508 (1992).

lucent /loóss'nt/ adj. **1.** LUMINOUS shining with a glowing light **2.** TRANSLUCENT translucent or clear [15thC. From Latin, the present participle stem of *lucere* 'to shine' (see LUCID).] —**lucency** n. —**lucently** adv.

lucerne /loo súrn/ n. = alfalfa [Mid-17thC. Via French from modern Provençal *luzerno*, originally 'glowworm', from Latin *lucerna* 'lamp', from *lucere* 'to shine' (see LUCID). Perhaps from the plant's shiny seeds.]

Lucerne /loo súrn/ city and capital of Lucerne Canton, central Switzerland. It is a tourist centre. Population: 61,656 (1994).

Lucerne, Lake of lake and popular tourist region in central Switzerland. Area: 114 sq. km/44 sq. mi.

lucid /loóssid/ adj. **1.** EASILY UNDERSTOOD clear and easily understood ○ *a lucid explanation* **2.** RATIONAL rational, and mentally clear, especially only for a period between episodes of delirium or psychosis **3.** SHINING emitting light [Late 16thC. From Latin *lucidus*, from *lucere* 'to shine', from the stem *luc-* 'light' (source of English *elucidate* and *translucent*). Ultimately from an Indo-European word that also produced English *lunar*.] —**lucidity** /loo síddəti/ n. —**lucidness** /loóssidnəss/ n. —**lucidly** adv.

lucifer /loóssifər/ n. a friction match (*dated*) [Mid-19thC. From *lucifer match*, originally a trade name.]

Lucifer /loóssifər/ n. **1.** SATAN a rebellious archangel who is held to be the same as Satan **2.** THE MORNING STAR the planet Venus appearing before sunrise as the morning star [Pre-12thC. From Latin, 'the planet Venus', literally 'light-bearing', from the stem *luc-* 'light' (see LUCID).]

luciferase /loóssifər ayz, -ayss/ n. an enzyme that aids the oxidation of luciferin in the cells of organisms that emit light

luciferin /loo síffərin/ n. a substance found in the cells of bioluminescent organisms, e.g. glowworms and fireflies, that on oxidation emits bluish-green light with very little heat

luciferous /loo síffərəss/ adj. bringing or emitting light

lucifugous /loo síffyo͞ogəss/ adj. ZOOL shunning or a-voiding light [Mid-17thC. Formed from Latin *lucifugus*, literally 'light-fleeing', from the stem *luc-* 'light' (see LUCID) + *fugere* 'to flee'.]

Lucina /loo sínə/ n. in Roman mythology, Juno in her capacity as goddess of childbirth

Lucite /loó sīt/ tdmk. a trademark for polymethyl methacrylate

luck /luk/ n. **1.** GOOD FORTUNE good fortune ○ *a stroke of luck* **2.** CHANCE the arbitrary distribution of events or outcomes ○ *a game of luck* **3.** FORTUNATE OR UN-FORTUNATE EVENT sth fortunate or unfortunate that happens to sb, or a series of such events ○ *Just my luck!* **4.** STH BEARING LUCK an event, action, or object regarded as bringing good or bad luck ○ *It's said to be bad luck to walk under ladders.* [15thC. Origin uncertain: probably from Low German *luk*. The word was most likely borrowed as a gambling term.]

luck into vt. US to obtain sth desirable or experience sth pleasurable by chance

luck out vi. US to be lucky enough to succeed by chance (*informal*)

luckenbooth /lúkən booth/ n. a Scottish brooch design, in the shape of a silver heart, given in the past as a token of love or betrothal [15thC. Literally 'booth that can be locked' (where such brooches were sold); *lucken*, past participle of obsolete *louk* 'to lock', from Old English *lūcan*, related to English *lock*[1].]

luckily /lúkili/ adv. as a result of or the occasion for good luck

luckless /lúkləss/ adj. without success or fortune — **lucklessly** adv. —**lucklessness** n.

Lucknow /lúk now/ capital of Uttar Pradesh State, northern India, situated in the Ganges valley, about 64 km/40 mi. northeast of Kanpur. Population: 1,592,010 (1991).

luckpenny /lúk peni/ (plural **-nies**) n. **1.** COIN BRINGING GOOD FORTUNE a coin kept or given to bring good fortune **2.** Scotland TOKEN SUM TRADITIONALLY RETURNED a small sum of money returned to a buyer for luck (*archaic*)

lucky /lúki/ (**-ier**, **-iest**) adj. **1.** FORTUNATE having good fortune ○ *You were lucky not to be seriously injured.* **2.** BRINGING GOOD FORTUNE producing or bringing good fortune ○ *lucky charm* **3.** RESULTING FROM GOOD LUCK as a result of good luck ○ *lucky escape* —**luckiness** n.

—— **WORD KEY: SYNONYMS** ——

lucky, fortunate, happy, providential

CORE MEANING: relating to advantage or good fortune

lucky used to describe sth that brings success or advantage. It can also be used to describe the person who gains the success or advantage, especially when this seems to happen by chance; **fortunate** used to describe sth that brings success or advantage, or the person who gains the success or advantage, especially when this is a greater degree than was expected or deserved; **happy** an old-fashioned or literary word used in the same way as 'lucky' or 'fortunate'; **providential** used to describe sth that happens at a favourable time, for example because it presents an opportunity or the means to do sth.

—— **WORD KEY: CULTURAL NOTE** ——

Lucky Jim, a novel by English writer Kingsley Amis (1954). The protagonist of this satire on academic life, Jim Dixon, is a junior lecturer at a provincial university and the plot revolves around his problematic relationships with his employers, colleagues, and girlfriend. While some critics condemned the book's amorality, many regarded Jim as a symbol of social protest.

Lucky Country *n. Aus* Australia seen as a comfortable country whose people can enjoy a pleasant life, particularly during the boom era of the 1960s and early 1970s

lucky dip *n.* **1.** GAME OF MYSTERY PRIZES a game in which sb takes a prize out of a container which is filled with soft material such as sawdust or shredded paper and within which prizes are hidden. US term **grab bag** **2.** SITUATION DEPENDING ON BLIND CHOICE a situation or venture with a large element of chance (*informal*)

lucrative /lóokrətiv/ *adj.* producing profit or wealth [15thC. From Latin *lucrativus*, from *lucrari* 'to gain', from *lucrum* 'gain' (see LUCRE). The word once also meant 'covetous'.] —**lucratively** *adv.* —**lucrativeness** *n.*

lucre /lóokər/ *n.* money, wealth, or profit (*dated or humorous*) ○ *filthy lucre* [14thC. Directly or via French from Latin *lucrum* 'gain' (source of English *lucrative*). Ultimately from an Indo-European word that also produced English *guerdon* and *galore*.]

Lucretia /loo kréeshə/ (*fl.* 6th century BC) Roman matron. After being raped by Tarquinius Superbus, she committed suicide, and the Tarquins were expelled from Rome.

Lucretius /loo kréeshəss/ (99?–55 BC) Roman poet and philosopher. His *De Rerum Natura*, based on the theories of Democritus and Epicurus, expounds his materialist philosophy. Full name **Titus Lucretius Carus**

lucubration /lóokyoo bráysh'n/ *n.* **1.** PIECE OF LEARNED WRITING a written work resulting from prolonged study, often having a scholarly or pedantic style (*usually used in the plural*) **2.** LONG STUDY long hard study, especially at night [Late 16thC. From the Latin stem *lucubration-*, ultimately from *lucubrare* 'to compose at night', from the stem *luc-* 'light' (see LUCID). The underlying idea is of working by lamplight.] —**lucubrate** /lóokyoo brayt/ *vi.*

luculent /lóokyoolənt/ *adj.* **1.** UNDERSTANDABLE easy to understand **2.** GLOWING shining or glowing [15thC. From Latin *luculentus*, from the stem *luc-* 'light' (see LUCID).]

Lucullan /loo kúllən/ *adj.* lavish or overindulgent, especially with regard to food [Mid-19thC. From Latin *Lucullanus*, from (Licinius) *Lucullus*, a Roman general of the 1stC BC famous for his lavish banquets.]

Lucullus /loo kúlləss/, **Lucius Licinus** (110?–56 BC) Roman general. A distinguished public career brought him great wealth. He was also a patron of artists and writers.

lud /lud/ *n.* used to address a judge in court, either as 'm'lud' or 'my lud' [Early 18thC. A hurried form of LORD.]

Luddite /lúddīt/ *n.* **1.** OPPONENT OF NEW TECHNOLOGY sb who opposes technological or industrial innovation **2.** HIST 19TH-CENTURY PROTESTER AGAINST TECHNOLOGY a worker involved in protests in Britain in the 1810s against new factory methods of production and in favour of traditional methods of work [Early 19thC. Origin uncertain: according to tradition, named after Ned *Ludd*, an 18th-century Leicestershire farm worker, who destroyed two stocking frames in a fit of rage.] —**Luddite** *adj.* —**Luddism** *n.*

Lüderitz /lóodərits/ port on the southern coast of Namibia, situated about 482 km/300 mi. southwest of Windhoek. Population: 6,000 (1990).

ludic /lóodik/ *adj.* playful in a way that is spontaneous and without any particular purpose (*literary*) [Mid-20thC. From French *ludique*, from Latin *ludere* 'to play', from *ludus* 'game' (see LUDICROUS).]

ludicrous /lóodikrəss/ *adj.* utterly ridiculous because of being absurd, incongruous, impractical, or unsuitable [Early 17thC. Formed from Latin *ludicrus*, from *ludus* 'play'.] —**ludicrously** *adv.* —**ludicrousness** *n.*

WORD KEY: ORIGIN

The Latin word *ludus*, from which **ludicrous** is derived, is also the source of English *allude, collude, delude, elude,* and *illusion*.

Ludlow /lúdlō/ ancient market town in Shropshire, England. It was a Roman settlement, and later a Saxon town, and now part of the Ludlow rural district.

ludo /lóodō/ *n.* a board game in which counters progress according to a player's dice throw [Late 19thC. From Latin, 'I play', a form of *ludere* 'to play', from *ludus* 'game'.]

Ludwigshafen /lóodvigs hafən/ port in Rhineland-Palatinate State, southwestern Germany, situated on the western bank of the River Rhine, opposite Mannheim. Population: 168,100 (1994).

lues /lóo eez/ *n.* syphilis [Mid-17thC. From Latin, 'plague'. Ultimately from an Indo-European word meaning 'to loosen', which also produced English *loose, forlorn,* and *dissolve*.]

luff /luf/ *v.* (**luffs, luffing, luffed**) **1.** *vt.* SAIL TOO CLOSE TO WIND to bring a boat closer in to the wind, or to sail too close to the wind, so that the sails flap **2.** *vi.* FLAP to flap when a boat is in a position too close to the wind (*refers to a sail*) ■ *n.* FRONT EDGE OF SAIL the front edge of a sail [12thC. From Old French *lof*, of uncertain origin: probably from Low German *lōf* or Dutch *loef* 'windward side of a ship'.]

Luftwaffe /lóoft vaffə/ *n.* the German Air Force [Mid-20thC. From German, literally 'air weapon'.]

lug[1] /lug/ *n.* **1.** PROJECTING PART a projecting part, especially one by which sth can be moved, rotated, or supported **2.** PROJECTION FOR ELECTRICAL CONTACT a small metal projection to which an electrical conductor or wire may be attached, usually by soldering or using mechanical pressure **3.** SMALL PROJECTION IMPROVING TRACTION a small projection on a tyre or boot that helps provide traction **4.** FRUIT OR VEGETABLE BOX a box for vegetables or fruit **5.** EAR an ear, especially the external ear (*informal*) **6.** CLUMSY MAN a man, especially one who is unintelligent or clumsy (*informal insult*) [14thC. Origin uncertain: probably from a Scandinavian language.]

WORD KEY: REGIONAL NOTE

A **lug** was originally a lock of hair or sth that could be pulled. It is uncertain when 'ear-pulling' became fashionable, but **lug** is still widely used as a word for 'ear': *Little jugs have big lugs* (Little children often hear more than they should).

lug[2] /lug/ *vt.* (**lugs, lugging, lugged**) **1.** PULL STH WITH EFFORT to carry or pull sth that is heavy or bulky, using great effort **2.** INTRODUCE IRRELEVANTLY INTO DISCUSSION to introduce irrelevant material into a discussion or conversation ■ *n.* ACT OF PULLING A LOAD the effort or action of pulling sth very heavy [15thC. Origin uncertain: probably from a Scandinavian language.The underlying idea would be of sth that can be pulled or grasped.]

lug[3] /lug/ *n.* = **lugsail** [Mid-19thC. Shortening of LUGSAIL.]

lug[4] /lug/ *n.* = **lugworm** *n.* 1 [Early 17thC. Origin unknown.]

Luganda /loo gándə/ *n.* = **Ganda** [Late 19thC. From Bantu.]

Lugano /loo gaánō/ town and tourist centre in Ticino Canton, southern Switzerland. Population: 26,025 (1992).

Lugano, Lake lake in southern Switzerland and northern Italy. Area: 49 sq. km/19 sq. mi.

luge /loozh/ *n.* RACING TOBOGGAN a racing toboggan on which the riders lie on their backs with their feet pointing forwards ■ *vi.* (**luges, luging, luged**) RACE ON LUGE to race on a luge [Late 19thC. Via Swiss French from medieval Latin *sludia*, of uncertain origin: perhaps from Gaulish, and ultimately from an Indo-European word that also produced English *sled*.] —**luger** *n.*

Luger /lóogər/ *tdmk.* a trademark for a German automatic pistol

luggage /lúggij/ *n.* suitcases, bags, and other items for carrying sb's belongings during a journey [Late 16thC. Formed from LUG[2] 'to carry', on the model of BAGGAGE. The original meaning was 'inconveniently heavy baggage'.]

luggage rack *n.* **1.** *US* = **roof rack** **2.** OVERHEAD FRAME FOR LUGGAGE an overhead frame in a train, bus etc. for passengers to keep small items of luggage.

lugger /lúggər/ *n.* a small boat for fishing or pleasure sailing that is rigged with a lugsail [Mid-18thC. Origin uncertain: perhaps formed from *lug-* in LUGSAIL, or possibly from Dutch *logger*, from *loggen* 'to fish with a drag-net'.]

lughole /lúg hōl/ *n.* an ear, especially the hole of the ear (*informal*)

lug nut *n.* a large nut that screws onto a heavy bolt, especially one used to attach a wheel to a motor vehicle

Lugosi /loo gṓssi/, **Bela** (1884–1956) Hungarian-born US actor. He starred in numerous horror films, and was especially closely identified with the title role in *Dracula* (1931). Real name **Bela Ferenc Denzso Blasko**

lugsail /lúg sayl, lúgss'l/ *n.* a four-sided sail bent on a yard that crosses the mast at an angle [Late 17thC. Origin uncertain: 'lug' probably from LUG[1].]

lugubrious /lə góobri əss/ *adj.* extremely mournful, sad, or gloomy [Early 17thC. Formed from Latin *lugubris*, from *lugere* 'to mourn'. Ultimately from an Indo-European word meaning 'to break'. The underlying idea seems to be of breaking down emotionally.] —**lugubriously** *adv.* —**lugubriousness** *n.*

lugworm /lúg wurm/ *n.* **1.** MARINE WORM a segmented marine worm that burrows in sandy shores, has rows of tufted gills, and is often used as angling bait. Genus: *Arenicola*. **2.** = **fanworm** [Early 19thC. 'Lug' from LUG[4].]

Luhansk /loo hánsk/, **Luhans'k** industrial city in eastern Ukraine. Population: 504,000 (1991).

Luhrmann /lúrmən/, **Baz** (*b.* 1962) Australian film and theatre director. His films include *Strictly Ballroom* (1992) and *Romeo and Juliet* (1997).

Lukács /lóok ach/, **György** (1885–1971) Hungarian philosopher, critic, and politician. Marxist in thought, his work *History and Class Consciousness* (1923) attempts to combine socialism and humanism.

Luke /look/ *n.* the third book of the New Testament in which the life and teachings of Jesus Christ are described. It is believed to have been written by St Luke. See table at **Bible**

Luke /look/, **St** (*fl.* 1st century AD) evangelist companion to St Paul. Perhaps a physician, he was by tradition author of the biblical Acts of the Apostles and the third Gospel.

lukewarm /look wáwrm/ *adj.* **1.** WARM just slightly warm, especially of food or drink that is expected to be hot (*disapproving*) **2.** SHOWING LITTLE ENTHUSIASM showing or having little enthusiasm, interest, support, or conviction [14thC. 'Luke' from obsolete *luke* 'lukewarm', of uncertain origin: perhaps a variant of dialect *lew* 'lukewarm', from Old English *hlēo* 'warm', of unknown origin.] —**lukewarmly** *adv.* —**lukewarmness** *n.*

Luleå /lóolə ō, lóoli-/ seaport at the head of the Gulf of Bothnia, northern Sweden. Population: 71,106 (1995).

lull /lul/ *v.* (**lulls, lulling, lulled**) **1.** *vt.* SOOTHE OR CALM SB to soothe or calm a person or animal, especially by using gentle sounds or motions **2.** *vt.* MAKE SB FEEL SAFE to give sb a false sense of security so that an unpleasant situation takes the person by surprise ○ *They lulled us into thinking we still had time.* **3.** *vi.* BECOME CALM to become calm or calmer ■ *n.* PERIOD OF CALM a brief interval of calm or decreased activity [14thC. Origin uncertain: probably an imitation of the sounds used to sing a child to sleep.]

lullaby /lúllə bī/ *n.* (*plural* **-bies**) **1.** GENTLE SONG a gentle song for soothing a child, especially into sleep **2.** MUSIC FOR LULLABY instrumental music in the style of a lullaby ■ *vt.* (**-bies, -bying, -bied**) SOOTHE CHILD WITH LULLABY to soothe a child with a lullaby [Mid-16thC. From obsolete *lulla* 'lullaby', an imitation of the sounds used to sing a child to sleep + *-by*, as in BYE-BYE.]

Lully /loo lee/, **Jean-Baptiste** (1633–87) Italian-born French composer. He wrote ballets and other musical entertainments for the court of Louis XIV.

lulu /lóo loo/ *n.* a remarkable or outstanding person, object, or idea (*slang*) [Late 19thC. Alteration (perhaps with influence from *Lulu*, pet-form of the name *Louise*, female name) of earlier *looly*, of unknown origin, used in the admiring phrase 'looliest looly of the loolies'.]

Luluabourg /loo lóo ə boorg/ former name for **Kananga**

lum /lum/ *n. Scotland* a chimney or chimney-stack (*informal*)

lumbago /lum báygō/ *n.* pain in the lower or lumbar region of the back [Late 17thC. From Latin, where it was formed from *lumbus* 'loin'.]

lumbar /lúmbər/ *adj.* relating to or situated in the loins or the small of the back [Mid-17thC. From medieval Latin *lumbaris*, from Latin *lumbus* 'loin' (source of English *loin* and *sirloin*).]

lumbar puncture *n.* the insertion of a needle between two lumbar vertebrae into the spinal cord in order to obtain a sample of cerebrospinal fluid for diagnosis or to introduce medication

lumber[1] /lúmbər/ *n.* **1.** *US* = **timber 2.** UNWANTED OBJECTS large objects that are not being used and are stored out of sight ■ *v.* (**-bers, -bering, -bered**) **1.** *vt.* BURDEN SB WITH TASK to burden sb with sth unpleasant or unwanted, especially a responsibility or a task (*informal*) **2.** *vti. US, Can* TURN TREES INTO TIMBER to cut down the trees in a region and convert them into saleable timber **3.** *vt.* PILE THINGS TOGETHER to pile things together haphazardly [Mid-16thC. Originally 'disused articles of furniture', of uncertain origin: perhaps literally 'things that impede movement', from LUMBER[2], influenced by obsolete *lumber* 'pawnbroking establishment' (filled with disused property), variant of LOMBARD.] —**lumberer** *n.*

lumber[2] /lúmbər/ (**-bers, -bering, -bered**) *vi.* to move clumsily or heavily [14thC. Origin uncertain: perhaps from a Scandinavian language.]

lumberjack /lúmbər jak/ *n.* **1.** *US, Can* FELLER OF TREES sb who cuts down trees and transports the timber **2.** *US* CLOTHES = **lumberjacket** [Mid-19thC. *Jack* from JACK 'man, labourer'.]

lumberjacket /lúmbər jakit/ *n.* a work jacket made from thick, warm material, usually brightly coloured with a checked pattern [Mid-20thC. From its being of a type worn by lumberjacks.]

lumberyard /lúmbər yaard/ *n. US* = **timberyard**

lumen /lóomin/ (*plural* **-mens** *or* **-mina** /-minə/) *n.* **1.** PHYS, MEASURE UNIT OF LUMINOUS FLUX the SI unit of luminous flux, equal to the amount of light crossing a unit area at a unit distance from a light source of luminous intensity of one candela. Symbol **lm 2.** ANAT SPACE WITHIN TUBE the space inside any tubular structure in the body, e.g. an intestine, artery, or vein **3.** BOT CAVITY IN PLANT the cavity within a plant cell wall [Late 19thC. From Latin, 'light, opening' (see LUMINOUS).]

Lumet /loo mét/, **Sidney** (*b.* 1924) US actor, director, and screenwriter. Among his greatest successes are *Murder on the Orient Express* (1974), *Dog Day Afternoon* (1975), and *Network* (1976).

Lumière /lóomi air/, **Auguste** (1864–1948) French inventor. He and his brother Louis invented the cinema camera and projector, and made the first film, *La sortie des usines Lumière* (1895).

Lumière, Louis (1862–1954) French inventor. He and his brother Auguste invented the cinema camera and projector, and made the first film, *La sortie des usines Lumières* (1895).

luminaire /lóomi náir/ *n.* a tungsten or fluorescent light fitting [Early 20thC. From French, from Old French *luminarie* (see LUMINARY).]

luminance /lóominənss/ *n.* **1.** QUALITY OF BEING LUMINOUS the condition or quality of emitting or reflecting light. Symbol *L* **2.** MEASURE MEASURE OF BRIGHTNESS a measure of the brightness of a surface equal to to the amount of luminous flux arriving at, passing through, or leaving a unit area of surface. It is measured in candelas per square metre. [Late 19thC. Formed from *luminant* 'luminous', from Latin *luminant-*, the present participle stem of *luminare* 'to illuminate', from the stem *lumin-* 'light' (see LUMINOUS).]

luminary /lóominəri/ *n.* (*plural* **-ies**) **1.** EMINENT PERSON an eminent or famous person **2.** SUN, MOON, OR STAR an object, especially a celestial body, that emits light (*literary*) ■ *adj.* CHARACTERIZED BY LIGHT relating to or characterized by light [15thC. Directly or via Old French *luminarie* from late Latin *luminarium*, from the Latin stem *lumin-* 'light' (see LUMINOUS).]

luminesce /lóomi néss/ (**-nesces, -nescing, -nesced**) *vi.* to emit light by phosphorescence, fluorescence, or bioluminescence [Late 19thC. Back-formation from *luminescent* (see LUMINESCENCE).]

luminescence /lóomi néss'nss/ *n.* **1.** LIGHT EMISSION WITHOUT HEAT the emission of light produced by means other than heat (**incandescence**), e.g. phosphorescence, fluorescence, or bioluminescence **2.** LIGHT FROM LUMINESCENCE the light emitted by luminescence [Late 19thC. From *luminescent*, which was coined from the Latin stem *lumin-* 'light' (see LUMINOUS) + -ESCENT.] —**luminescent** *adj.*

luminiferous /lóomi níffərəss/ *adj.* generating or giving off light [Early 19thC. Coined from the Latin stem *lumin-* 'light' (see LUMINOUS) + -FEROUS.]

luminosity /lóomi nóssəti/ (*plural* **luminosities**) *n.* **1.** STATE OF BEING LUMINOUS the state or quality of being luminous **2.** ASTRON ENERGY RADIATED BY CELESTIAL OBJECT the energy radiated per second by a celestial body. Symbol *L* **3.** PHYS STRENGTH OF LIGHT EMITTED the visual perception of the extent to which an object emits light **4.** STH LUMINOUS sth that emits light

luminous /lóominəss/ *adj.* **1.** LIGHT-EMITTING emitting or reflecting light **2.** BRIGHT startlingly bright ○ *luminous orange* **3.** ILLUMINATED brightly illuminated **4.** UNDERSTANDABLE clear and easy to understand **5.** INSPIRING enlightened and inspiring **6.** PHYS RELATING TO LIGHT evaluated on the basis of the visual sensation produced in an observer rather than energy measurements [15thC. Directly or via French from Latin *luminosus*, from the stem *lumin-* 'light, opening' (source of English *lumen* and *illuminate*).] —**luminously** *adv.* —**luminousness** *n.*

luminous energy *n.* the total amount of light emitted by a source. Symbol Q_v

luminous flux *n.* the rate of emission of light evaluated by the visual sensation it produces. Symbol Φ_v

luminous intensity *n.* the amount of light emitted by a source in a particular direction. Symbol I_v

lumme /lúmmi/, **lummy** *interj.* used to express surprise or shock [Late 19thC. Representing a casual pronunciation of *(Lord) love me.*]

lummox /lúmməks/ *n.* sb who is clumsy or unintelligent (*informal insult*) [Early 19thC. Origin unknown.]

lump[1] /lump/ *n.* **1.** SOLID CHUNK a small irregularly shaped solid mass or piece **2.** TUMOUR a tumour or other swelling in the body **3.** SUGAR CUBE a small cube of solid sugar **4.** LARGE AND CLUMSY PERSON sb who is large and unintelligent or clumsy (*informal insult*) **5.** CASUAL CONSTRUCTION WORKERS a collective term for workers in the building trade who are casual and do not belong to a union (*informal*) **6.** *Scotland* a big, fleshy, slow-moving person (*informal*) ■ **lumps** *npl. US* HARDSHIP harsh, often undeserved, criticism, punishment, or hardship (*informal*) ○ *You have to take your lumps like everyone else.* ■ *v.* (**lumps, lumping, lumped**) **1.** *vt.* GROUP THINGS TOGETHER CARELESSLY to consider people, ideas, or objects as a single group, often without good reason ○ *All the students were lumped together as lazy.* **2.** *vi.* MOVE HEAVILY to move in a heavy and clumsy manner ○ *He lumped along.* ■ *adj.* IN LUMPS in small cubes or lumps ○ *lump sugar* [14thC. Origin uncertain. The underlying idea seems to be of sth coarse or shapeless.]

lump[2] /lump/ (**lumps, lumping, lumped**) *vt.* to endure sth unpleasant that cannot be changed (*informal*) ○ *like it or lump it* [Late 16thC. Origin unknown. The original sense was 'to look sulky'; the meaning 'to tolerate' dates from the mid-19thC.]

lumpectomy /lum péktəmi/ (*plural* **-mies**) *n.* a surgical operation for breast cancer in which the surgery is limited to the removal of the visible and palpable tumour only [Late 20thC. Coined from LUMP, on the model of MASTECTOMY.]

lumpen /lúmpən, lóom-/ *adj.* (*disapproving*) **1.** MARGINALIZED living, or regarded as living, on the margins of society **2.** NOT EDUCATED OR ENLIGHTENED stupidly content with a life regarded as intellectually empty and socially inferior ■ *npl.* LUMPEN PEOPLE people regarded by others as lumpen (*disapproving; takes a plural verb*) [Mid-20thC. Back-formation from LUMPENPROLETARIAT, with the meaning influenced by LUMP.]

lumpenproletariat /lúmpən prōlə táiri ət, lóom-/ *n.* (*takes a singular or plural verb*) **1.** POL PERMANENT UNDERCLASS in Marxist analysis, people regarded as living on the margins of society, particularly criminals, homeless people, and the long-term unemployed **2.** LOWER-CLASS PEOPLE people from the lowest social class who are regarded as too content with a life supposedly intellectually empty and socially inferior (*disapproving*) [Early 20thC. From German, formed from *Lumpen*, plural of *Lump* 'ragamuffin' + French *prolétariat*(see PROLETARIAT).]

lumpfish /lúmpfish/ (*plural* **-fishes** *or* **-fish**) *n.* a marine fish of northern waters that has a short scaleless body covered with rows of thorny lumps. Its roe is eaten as a cheaper alternative to caviar. Family: Cyclopteridae. [Early 17thC. *Lump*, from Middle Dutch *lumpe* 'cod', of uncertain origin: perhaps ultimately the same word as LUMP[1], referring to the fish's lumpy shape.]

lumpish /lúmpish/ *adj.* **1.** MOVING AWKWARDLY tending to move awkwardly or slowly and heavily **2.** UNINTELLIGENT AND LETHARGIC with no intelligence, energy, or enthusiasm (*insult*) —**lumpishly** *adv.* —**lumpishness** *n.*

lumpsucker /lúmp sukər/ *n.* = **lumpfish** [Mid-18thC. From obsolete *lump* 'lumpfish' + SUCKER.]

lump sum *n.* an amount of money that is given in a single payment, rather than being divided into smaller periodic payments

lumpy /lúmpi/ (**-ier, -iest**) *adj.* **1.** WITH LUMPS having or filled with lumps, especially when lumps are unwanted, e.g. in the upholstery of a chair or the mattress of a bed **2.** LACKING SMOOTHNESS OF TEXTURE used to describe semiliquid foods, e.g. sauces and soups, that lack the normal appetizing smoothness of texture **3.** CUMBERSOME with a cumbersome quality or appearance **4.** CHOPPY having or exhibiting short choppy waves —**lumpily** /lúmpili/ *adv.* —**lumpiness** *n.*

lumpy jaw *n.* = **actinomycosis**

Lumumba /loo móombə/, **Patrice** (1925–61) Congolese statesman. The first prime minister of the Republic of the Congo (1960–61), his tenure was marked by civil war.

Luna /lóonə/ *n.* **1.** MYTHOL ROMAN MOON GODDESS the goddess of the Moon in Roman mythology. Greek equivalent **Selene 2.** CHEM SILVER the element silver in alchemy (*archaic*) [14thC. From Latin, 'moon' (see LUNAR).]

lunacy /lóonəssi/ (*plural* **lunacies**) *n.* **1.** THOUGHTLESSNESS unintelligent, inconsiderate, or misguided behaviour, or an example of it **2.** OFFENSIVE TERM an offensive former term for any psychiatric disorder that rendered patients legally incompetent and required them to be taken into care. This obsolete term has never been used by physicians in medical or psychiatric contexts. (*archaic offensive*) [Mid-16thC. Formed from LUNATIC.]

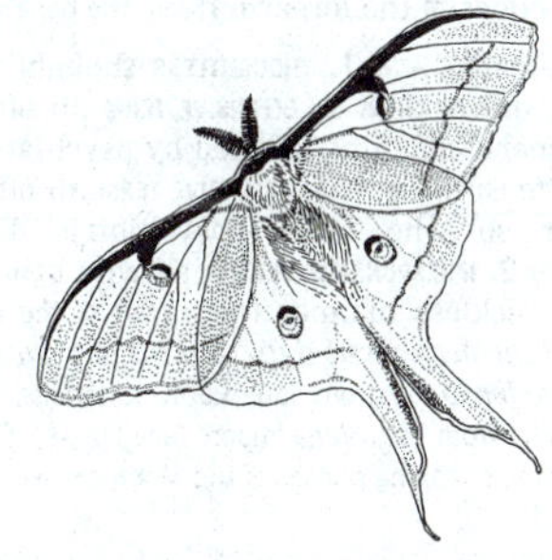

Luna moth

luna moth /lóonə-/ *n.* a large North American moth that has spotted light-green wings with long thin extensions at the back that look like tails. Latin name: *Actias luna.* [From Latin, 'moon' (see LUNAR); so called because of the crescent-shaped spots on the moth's wings]

lunar /lóonər/ *adj.* **1.** ASTRON RELATING TO MOON relating to a moon or its movement around a planet, especially the Moon in relation to the Earth **2.** SPACE TECH USED FOR TRAVEL TO THE MOON for use in space travel to or on the Moon **3.** CRESCENT-SHAPED in the shape of a crescent moon **4.** PALE pale and cold-looking, as the Moon is compared to the Sun [15thC. From Latin *lunaris*, from *luna* 'moon' (source of English *lunatic*). Ultimately from an Indo-European word meaning 'light', which is also the ancestor of English *light*, *luminous*, and *lucid*.]

Lunar: A lunar rover used by astronaut James Irwin on the Moon (1971)

lunar caustic *n.* silver nitrate, especially when formed into small sticks (*archaic*)

lunar cycle *n.* a principal means of establishing a calendar, based on the cycles of the Moon. The Muslim calendar is based on the lunar cycle.

lunar eclipse *n.* an eclipse of the Moon caused by the Earth passing between the Sun and the Moon and casting its shadow on the Moon

lunar excursion module *n.* = lunar module

lunarian /loo náiri ən/ *n.* in mythology and science fiction, an inhabitant of the Moon [Early 18thC. Formed from Latin *lunaris* (see LUNAR).]

lunar module *n.* a small spacecraft used to travel from an orbiting command module to the surface of the Moon and back

lunar month *n.* **1. PERIOD BETWEEN NEW MOONS** the time between one new moon and the next, a period of about 29.5 days. It is the time the Moon takes to make one complete orbit of the Earth. **2. 28-DAY PERIOD** a period of four weeks

Lunar New Year *n.* the Chinese New Year, which usually occurs at a point between late January and mid-February

lunarscape /loonər skayp/ *n.* a rugged barren landscape of strange rock formations, similar to the surface of the Moon

lunar year *n.* a period of 12 lunar months

lunate /loon ayt/ *adj.* **lunate, lunated** CRESCENT-SHAPED shaped like a crescent moon ■ *n.* ANAT = **lunate bone** [Late 18thC. From Latin *lunatus*, from *luna* 'moon' (see LUNAR).]

lunate bone *n.* a bone of the wrist that articulates with the bones of the forearm [From the bone's shape]

lunatic /loonətik/ *adj.* **1. THOUGHTLESS** thoughtless, ridiculous, or reckless **2. OFFENSIVE TERM** an offensive term formerly meaning affected by psychiatric disorder (*offensive*) ■ *n.* **1. OFFENSIVE TERM** an offensive term for sb who has a psychiatric disorder (*offensive*) **2. IRRESPONSIBLE PERSON** sb who behaves in a wildly reckless manner (*informal*) ○ *the lunatic who went through a red light and hit our car* [13thC. Via French *lunatique* from late Latin *lunaticus*, literally 'moonstruck', from Latin *luna* 'moon' (see LUNAR). From the belief that the changing phases of the Moon caused periodic symptoms.]

lunatic fringe *n.* people whose views are regarded as eccentrically radical (*insult*)

lunation /loo náysh'n/ *n.* = lunar month *n.* 1 [14thC. From the medieval Latin stem *lunation-*, from Latin *luna* 'moon' (see LUNAR).]

lunch /lunch/ *n.* **1. MIDDAY MEAL** a meal eaten in the middle of the day, especially a light meal that is not the main meal of the day (*often used before a noun*) **2. FOOD EATEN AT MIDDAY** the food prepared and eaten at the midday meal ○ *Our lunch was soup and salad.* **3.** Carib **AFTERNOON TEA** mid-afternoon tea, or an afternoon snack (*dated*) ■ *vi.* (**lunches, lunching, lunched**) EAT LUNCH to eat lunch, especially a specified kind of lunch eaten somewhere other than at home [Early 19thC. Shortening of LUNCHEON.] ◇ **out to lunch** displaying thoughtlessness or unusual behaviour that suggests a loss of touch with reality (*slang insult*)

━━ **WORD KEY: USAGE** ━━
See Usage note at *dinner*.

━━ **WORD KEY: CULTURAL NOTE** ━━
The Naked Lunch, a novel by US writer William Burroughs (1959). This controversial portrayal of drug abuse was written by Burroughs in Tunisia as he attempted to free himself of his own addiction. It consists of a series of surreal episodes linked by themes and characters and described in language that is by turns clinical, hallucinatory, poetic, and scatological.

lunchbox /lunch boks/ *n.* **1. SANDWICH CONTAINER** a container for sandwiches or other foods carried somewhere, e.g. to work, to eat for lunch **2. MAN'S GENITALS** a man's genitals when they are visible through tight-fitting clothes, e.g. sportswear (*slang; offensive in some contexts*)

luncheon /lunchən/ *n.* (*formal*) **1. LUNCH** lunch **2. MIDDAY GATHERING WITH FOOD** an organized gathering in the middle of the day, with invited guests being served a meal and often offered some form of entertainment, e.g., a guest speaker [Mid-17thC. Origin uncertain: probably an alteration of earlier *nuncheon* 'snack', from NOON + obsolete *schench* 'drink', under the influence of obsolete *lunch* 'piece of bread'.]

luncheon meat *n.* processed meat, e.g. ham mixed with cereal, sold in a tin or sliced, and usually eaten cold

luncheon voucher *n.* a voucher that can be exchanged for food in participating restaurants, sandwich bars, and other food establishments at lunchtime. Luncheon vouchers are offered by some firms to their employees as a bonus or incentive.

lunchroom /lunch room, -room/ *n.* US a room in a school or office where people can buy lunch or eat a packed lunch

lunchtime /lunch tīm/ *n.* the time, around the middle of the day, when lunch is usually eaten (*often used before a noun*)

Lund /loond/ historic city in southern Sweden, situated about 18 km/11 mi. northeast of Malmö. Population: 96,557 (1995).

Lunda /loondə/ *n.* a Bantu language spoken in western parts of Central Africa, especially in Zaïre. It belongs to the Benue-Congo branch of Niger-Congo languages. Lunda is spoken by about 82,000 people. [Late 19thC. From Bantu.] —**Lunda** *adj.*

Lundy /lúndi/ *n.* island in the Bristol Channel, England, off the Devon coast. Area: 4 sq. km/1.6 sq. mi.

lune /loon/ *n.* **1.** GEOM **CRESCENT AREA ON PLANE OR SPHERE** a crescent-shaped area on the surface of a plane or sphere defined by two semicircles whose common end points are diametrically opposed **2.** CHR = **lunette** *n.* 6 [Early 18thC. Via French from Latin *luna* 'moon' (see LUNAR); so called because its shape resembles a crescent moon.]

Lüneburg /loonə burg/ *n.* town in Lower Saxony State, north-central Germany. Population: 60,100 (1989).

lunette /loo nét/ *n.* **1. CRESCENT-SHAPED OBJECT** any object that has a crescent shape **2.** ARCHIT **WINDOW IN DOMED CEILING** an arch-shaped window at the height of a domed ceiling **3.** ARCHIT **SEMICIRCULAR PANEL** a semicircular panel on a wall, containing a window, painting, or frieze **4. VEHICLE'S TOWING RING** a metal ring on a vehicle to which a rope can be attached for towing **5.** GEOG **CRESCENT-SHAPED MOUND OF SILT** a crescent-shaped mound of fine silt or clay similar in form to a sand dune, found especially near the edge of a temporary lake **6.** CHR **CONTAINER USED IN ROMAN CATHOLIC MASS** in the Roman Catholic Church, a crescent-shaped container in which the consecrated bread is placed during a Mass [Late 16thC. Via French, literally 'little moon', from, ultimately, Latin *luna* (see LUNAR).]

lung /lung/ *n.* **1. RESPIRATORY ORGAN IN VERTEBRATES** in air-breathing vertebrate animals, either of the paired spongy respiratory organs, situated inside the ribcage, that transfer oxygen into the blood and remove carbon dioxide from it (*often used before a noun*) **2. RESPIRATORY ORGAN IN INVERTEBRATES** any of various respiratory organs found in invertebrate animals, especially the highly vascular region of the mantle cavity in some terrestrial snails [Old English. Ultimately, from an Indo-European base meaning

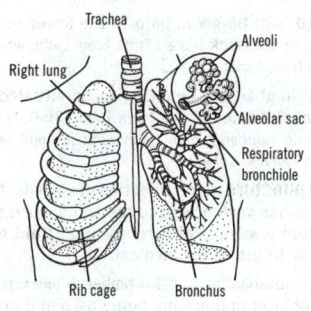

Lung

'light', which is also the ancestor of English *light* [2].] ◇ **at the top of your lungs** extremely loudly (*informal*)

lungan *n.* = longan

lunge [1] /lunj/ *n.* **1. SUDDEN FORWARD MOVEMENT** a sudden strong attacking movement forwards **2.** FENCING **QUICK THRUST** a sudden thrust made at an opponent ■ *vi.* (**lunges, lunging, lunged**) **1. MOVE SUDDENLY FORWARDS THREATENINGLY** to make a sudden attacking movement, thrusting forwards **2.** FENCING **MAKE A QUICK THRUST** to execute a sudden thrust at an opponent, especially with the sword or épée extended parallel to the floor [Mid-18thC. Alteration of French *allonger*, via Old French *alongier* 'to lengthen' from, ultimately, Latin *longus* 'long'. The underlying meaning is 'to lengthen one's reach'.]

lunge [2] /lunj/, **longe** /lunj, lonj/ *n.* **1. HORSE-TRAINING ROPE** a long rope used to hold a horse while it is being trained **2. HORSE-TRAINING AREA** an enclosed circular area where young horses are trained ■ *vt.* (**lunges, lunging, lunged; longes, longing, longed**) TRAIN USING LUNGE to train a horse using a lunge [Early 18thC. Via French *longe* 'cord' from, ultimately, Old French *alongier* 'to lengthen' (see LUNGE [1]).]

lungfish /lung fish/ (*plural* **-fishes** *or* **-fish**) *n.* any of various bony fishes of Australia, Africa, and South America that inhabit freshwater swamps and pools and have one or two lungs for breathing air as well as gills. They often become inactive and cocoon themselves in mud during the dry season. Order: Dipneusti.

lungi /loong gi/, **lungyi** *n.* a long piece of cloth, often brightly coloured, traditionally worn by men as a loincloth in the Indian subcontinent and like a skirt by men and women in Myanmar [Early 17thC. Via Hindi *lungī* from Persian.]

lungworm /lung wurm/ *n.* a parasitic nematode worm that inhabits the lungs of mammals and birds, sometimes causing coughs or respiratory distress

lungwort /lung wurt/ *n.* **1. WOODLAND PLANT** any of various perennial woodland plants native to Europe and Asia that have clusters of purple or blue tubular flowers, often pink as buds. They were used in the past to treat respiratory disorders. Genus: *Pulmonaria*. **2. PLANT OF BORAGE FAMILY** any of various plants belonging to the borage family that have dangling clusters of blue flowers. They are found in northern temperate regions. Genus: *Mertensia*. **3. LICHEN RESEMBLING LUNG TISSUE** a lichen that bears a superficial resemblance to lung tissue. It is dark green when wet and pale greenish-brown when dry. It was used in the past to treat lung diseases. Latin name: *Lobaria pulmonaria*. [Old English *lungenwyrt*. So called from the belief that such plants cured lung disorders.]

lungyi *n.* = lungi

lunisolar /looni sólər/ *adj.* relating to both the Sun and the Moon, especially to the gravitational pull of both the Sun and the Moon

lunitidal interval /looni tíd'l-/ *n.* the time between the moon's passing a given point and the next high tide at that point

lunula /loonyoolə/ (*plural* **-lae** /-lee/), **lunule** /loo nyool/ *n.* ANAT a semicircular mark, especially the white crescent-shaped area at the base of the fingernail (*technical*) [Late 16thC. From Latin, literally 'small moon', from *luna* (see LUNAR).] —**lunular** *adj.* —**lunulate** *adj.*

Luo /loo ó/ (*plural* **-o** *or* **-os**) *n.* **1.** PEOPLES **MEMBER OF AFRICAN PEOPLE** a member of an African people who migrated from the Upper Nile Valley, establishing a dynasty among the Bantu-speaking people in the lake region of eastern Africa, around Bunyoro **2.** LANG **LANGUAGE SPOKEN IN KENYA AND TANZANIA** a language spoken in parts of Kenya and Tanzania that belongs to the Nilotic branch of Nilo-Saharan languages. Luo is spoken by about six million people. [Early 20thC. From Luo.] —**Luo** *adj.*

Luoyang /lṓ yáng/ city in Henan Province, northern China, situated on the River Luo. It alternated with Xian as the capital of ancient China, and after 1948 became a major industrial centre. Population: 1,190,000 (1991).

lupin /lóopin/ *n.* any of various annual or perennial plants that have tall spikes of flowers and seeds in pods. They are native to the northern hemisphere. Genus: *Lupinus.* [14thC. From Latin *lupinus* 'wolflike' (see LUPIN).]

lupine[1] /lóo pīn/ *adj.* **1. RELATING TO A WOLF** relating to wolves, or resembling a wolf **2. RAVENOUS** wildly hungry or greedy in behaviour or character [Mid-17thC. From Latin *lupinus*, from *lupus* 'wolf'. Ultimately, from the Indo-European word for 'wolf', which is also the ancestor of English *wolf* and *lycanthrope*.]

lupine[2] *n.* US = **lupin**

lupulin /lóopyōolin/ *n.* a sticky yellow powder found in hop cones and containing the resins and essential oils that give beer its bitter taste. It was formerly used as a sedative. [Early 19thC. Formed from modern Latin *lupulus*, species name, from Latin, 'hop plant', literally 'little wolf', from *lupus* 'wolf'.]

lupus /lóopəss/ *n.* **1.** = **lupus erythematosus 2.** = **lupus vulgaris** [Late 16thC. From Latin, 'wolf'. So called because people having the disease were thought to look as if they had been attacked by a wolf.]

Lupus /lóopəss/ *n.* a constellation of the southern hemisphere lying in the Milky Way, located between Scorpius and Centaurus

lupus erythematosus /-érri theemə tṓssəss/ *n.* either of two inflammatory diseases affecting connective tissue. One **(discoid lupus erythematosus)** is largely confined to the skin, the other **(systemic lupus erythematosus)** affects the joints and internal organs. [*Erythematosus* via modern Latin from Greek *eruthēma* (see ERYTHEMA)]

lupus vulgaris /-vul gáiriss/ *n.* tuberculosis of the skin in which reddish-brown patches develop on the face, leading to tissue destruction and scarring [From modern Latin, 'common lupus']

lurch[1] /lurch/ *vi.* **(lurches, lurching, lurched) 1. MOVE VIOLENTLY** to lean or pitch suddenly to one side **2. MOVE UNSTEADILY** to move along unsteadily, swaying from side to side ■ *n.* **SUDDEN SIDEWAYS MOVEMENT** a sudden unbalanced movement to the side [Late 17thC. Origin unknown.] —**lurchingly** *adv.*

lurch[2] /lurch/ *n.* in the card game cribbage, the state of being left with less than 30 points or half the winner's score at the end of a game [14thC. Origin uncertain: perhaps a back-formation from *lurching* 'decisive defeat at "lorche"' (a game resembling backgammon), from obsolete French *lourche*, of uncertain origin.] ◇ **leave sb in the lurch** to leave sb in a difficult or embarrassing situation and offer no help

lurcher /lúrchər/ *n.* a long-limbed crossbred dog that has predominant greyhound features, especially one used by poachers for catching rabbits [Early 16thC. From *lurch* 'to lurk', of uncertain origin: probably a variant of LURK.]

lure /lyoor, loor/ *vt.* **(lures, luring, lured) 1. ENTICE** to persuade sb to go so somewhere or do sth by offering sth tempting **2. RECALL FALCON** to persuade a falcon to return by swinging a device in the air to attract its attention ■ *n.* **1. STH THAT ENTICES** sth that attracts or entices sb to do sth or go somewhere **2. ATTRACTION** the attractive or tempting quality that sth has **3. DEVICE ATTRACTING FISH** a device attached to a fishing line to attract fish **4. DEVICE FOR RECALLING FALCON** a device swung through the air to attract or recall a falcon, usually a leather bag attached to the end of a line [13thC. From Old French *luere*, of Germanic origin.] —**lurer** *n.*

Lurex /lyóor eks, lóor-/ *tdmk.* a trademark for a plastic-coated metallic thread or fabric made from this

lurgy /lúrgi/ *n.* any illness or infection (*informal*) [Mid-20thC. Origin uncertain: perhaps an alteration of ALLERGY. Popularized by the radio comedy series 'The Goon Show'.]

lurid /lyóorid, lóor-/ *adj.* **1. HORRIFYING OR SHOCKING** sensational and shocking, with graphic details of horror, devastation, or violence **2. UNATTRACTIVELY BRIGHT** of a sickeningly intense brightness or boldness of colour ○ *a lurid green* **3. GLOWING UNNATURALLY** glowing with an unnaturally vivid brightness **4. PALLID** with a pale sickly complexion [Mid-17thC. From Latin *luridus* 'pale yellow, ghastly', of unknown origin.] —**luridly** *adv.* —**luridness** *n.*

Lurie /lóori/, **Alison** (*b.* 1926) US novelist and scholar. Many of her novels deal with middle-class discontent. She won the Pulitzer Prize for fiction (1985).

lurk /lurk/ *vi.* **(lurks, lurking, lurked) 1. MOVE OR WAIT FURTIVELY** to move about furtively, or wait in a concealed position or a shadowy corner, especially with the intention of doing sth wrong ○ *a figure lurking in the bushes* **2. EXIST UNSUSPECTED** to exist as an unsuspected threat or danger **3.** COMPUT **READ BUT NOT SEND MESSAGES** to read messages sent to an online discussion forum without contributing (*slang*) ■ *n.* *ANZ* **SCAM** a sly or underhanded scheme (*informal*) [13thC. Origin uncertain: probably of Low German or Scandinavian origin.] —**lurker** *n.* —**lurking** *adj.*

Lurlei = **Lorelei**

Lusaka /loo saákə, -zaákə/ capital city of Zambia, situated in the southern-central part of the country, about 145 km/90 mi. northeast of Kariba Dam, on the Zimbabwe border. Population: 982,362 (1989).

luscious /lúshəss/ *adj.* **1. SWEET AND JUICY** with a rich, sweet, and juicy taste **2. ROMANTIC AND EMOTIONAL** written in a dramatic and romantic style with a strong appeal to the emotions and senses **3. DESIRABLE** very desirable physically, especially with a strong and direct sexual presence (*informal*) [14thC. Alteration of earlier *licious*, of uncertain origin: possibly a shortening of DELICIOUS.] —**lusciously** *adv.* —**lusciousness** *n.*

lush[1] /lush/ *adj.* **1. GROWING VIGOROUSLY** producing a lot of vigorous rich young growth **2. WITH RICH TASTE** tasting rich, sweet, and juicy **3. LUXURIOUS** with luxurious decoration and furnishings **4. IN A DRAMATIC STYLE** written in a dramatic style that is intended to produce an emotional response **5. SEXY** voluptuously sensual in appearance or behaviour (*informal*) [15thC. Origin uncertain: probably an alteration of *lache* 'loose, weak', via Old French, 'soft', from, ultimately, Latin *laxus* 'loose'.] —**lushly** *adv.* —**lushness** *n.*

lush[2] /lush/ *n.* *US* **1. HEAVY DRINKER** sb who regularly drinks too much alcohol (*slang disapproving*) **2. ALCOHOL** alcoholic drink (*slang*) ■ *vi.* **(lushes, lushing, lushed)** *US* **DRINK HEAVILY** to drink too much alcohol regularly (*slang disapproving*) [Late 18thC. Origin unknown.]

Lushun /lóo shóon/, **Lü-shun** town and seaport in Liaoning Province, northeastern China, situated opposite the northern coast of Shandong. Former name **Port Arthur**

Lusitania /lóossi táyni ə/ ancient region and Roman province, corresponding approximately to present-day Portugal and the Spanish provinces of Salamanca and Cáceres —**Lusitanian** *adj., n.*

lust /lust/ *n.* **1. SEXUAL DESIRE** the strong physical desire to have sex with sb, usually without associated feelings of love or affection **2. EAGERNESS** great eagerness or enthusiasm for sth ○ *the lust for power* ■ *vi.* **(lusts, lusting, lusted) 1. DESIRE SEXUALLY** to feel a strong desire to have sex with sb **2. BE EAGER FOR STH** to have a very strong desire to obtain sth [Old English, 'pleasure, desire'. Ultimately, from an Indo-European word meaning 'to be eager', which is also the ancestor of English *lascivious*.]

luster *n., vt.* US = **lustre**

lustful /lústf'l/ *adj.* with strong feelings of sexual desire —**lustfully** *adv.* —**lustfulness** *n.*

lustra plural of **lustrum**

lustral /lústrəl/ *adj.* **1.** RELIG **SPIRITUALLY PURIFYING** serving to purify the spirit, or relating to ceremonies of religious purification **2.** TIME **HAPPENING FIVE-YEARLY** taking place once every five years [Mid-16thC. From Latin *lustralis*, from *lustrum* (see LUSTRUM).]

lustrate /lu stráyt, lús trayt/ **(-trates, -trating, -trated)** *vt.* to make sb or sth spiritually pure by means of a special religious ceremony [Early 17thC. From Latin *lustrare* 'to purify by lustral rites', from *lustrum* (see LUSTRUM).] —**lustration** /lu stráysh'n/ *n.* —**lustrative** /lústrətiv/ *adj.*

lustre /lústər/ *n.* **1. SOFT SHEEN** a soft sheen of reflected light, especially from metal that has been polished gently **2. SHININESS** a bright and shiny condition or tone **3. SPLENDOUR** the glory and magnificence of a great achievement **4. POLISH** polish or wax used to give sth a shiny finish **5. CHANDELIER** a chandelier or candelabrum made of cut glass, designed to reflect the light **6. GLASS PENDANT ON CHANDELIER** any of the decorative pieces of cut glass hanging from a chandelier **7.** CERAMICS **GLAZE ON POTTERY** an opalescent metallic glaze on pottery, especially porcelain **8.** MINERALS **LIGHT REFLECTED BY A MINERAL** the quality and amount of light reflected from the surface of a mineral. This is one of the ways in which a mineral is defined, the highest degree of lustre being splendent. **9.** TEXTILES **GLOSSY FABRIC** fabric with a sheen or glossy surface **10.** TIME = **lustrum** *n.* 1 ■ *vt.* **(-tres, -tring, -tred) 1. IMPART GLOSSY FINISH TO** to impart a glossy finish or coating to sth **2. GLORIFY** to give sth a glorious or magnificent quality [Early 16thC. Via French from, ultimately, Latin *lustrare* 'to brighten', from *lustrum* 'purification' (see LUSTRUM).]

lustrous /lústrəss/ *adj.* with a soft shine or gloss —**lustrously** *adv.* —**lustrousness** *n.*

lustrum /lústrəm/ (*plural* **-trums** *or* **-tra** /-trə/) *n.* (*formal*) **1.** TIME **FIVE-YEAR PERIOD** a period of five years **2.** HIST **ROMAN PURIFICATION** purification of the entire ancient Roman people, taking place every five years after the census [Late 16thC. From Latin, 'purification'. Probably ultimately from an Indo-European word meaning 'light, bright'.]

lusty /lústi/ **(-ier, -iest)** *adj.* **1. STRONG AND HEALTHY** in extremely good physical health, especially possessing great stamina and strength **2. ENERGETIC** full of energy, vitality, and enthusiasm **3. LUSTFUL** strongly desiring sex —**lustily** *adv.* —**lustiness** *n.*

lusus naturae /lóossəss nə tyóor ee/ (*plural* **lusus naturae** *or* **lususes naturae**) *n.* sth that has developed abnormally (*literary*) [From Latin, literally 'sport of nature']

Lute

lute[1] /loot/ *n.* a plucked musical instrument that is similar to the guitar but has a pear-shaped body with a flat front. It was popular from the 14th to the 17th century. [13thC. Via Old French *lut* from, ultimately, Arabic *al-'ūd*.]

lute[2] /loot/ *n.* **1.** BUILDING **SEALANT USED IN THE BUILDING TRADE** any substance, e.g. clay or cement, used for sealing apertures, joints, or porous surfaces in the building trade **2.** COOK **FLOUR AND WATER PASTE** a paste of flour and water used in cooking as a seal, e.g. to keep a casserole lid on tight **3.** DENT **PASTE USED IN DENTISTRY** a paste used in dentistry to attach a crown or cap onto a tooth ■ *vt.* **(lutes, luting, luted) SEAL WITH LUTE** to seal, pack, or coat sth using lute [14thC. Directly or via French from medieval Latin *lutum*, from Latin, 'mud, potter's clay'. Ultimately from an Indo-European word meaning 'dirt', which is also the ancestor of English *pollute*.]

luteal /lóoti əl/ *adj.* relating to the stage of the menstrual cycle between the formation of a yellow mass of tissue **(corpus luteum)** after the release of an ovum and the start of the next period [Early 20thC. Coined from Latin *luteus* 'yellow' + -AL.]

lutein /loʻoti in/ *n.* **1. YELLOW PIGMENT IN EGG YOLK** the yellowish pigment found in egg yolk, some algae, and many plants, as well as in the tissue (**corpus luteum**) formed following the release of an ovum **2. DRIED TISSUE** a powdered preparation of the tissue (**corpus luteum**) formed following the release of an ovum [Mid-19thC. Formed from Latin *luteus* 'yellow'.]

luteinizing hormone /loʻoti inˈzing-/, **luteinising hormone** *n.* a hormone produced by the pituitary gland. It causes the ovary to produce one or more eggs, to secrete the hormone progesterone, and to form the corpus luteum. In the male, the luteinizing hormone promotes the secretion of male sex hormones by the testes.

luteinizing hormone-releasing hormone, luteinising hormone-releasing hormone, luteinizing hormone-releasing factor, luteinising hormone-releasing factor *n.* a hormone, released by the hypothalamus, that triggers the secretion of luteinizing hormone by the anterior lobe of the pituitary gland. It is now known to be identical with gonadotropin-releasing hormone.

lutenist /loʻotənist/ *n.* sb who plays the lute [Early 17thC. From medieval Latin *lutanista*, from *lutana* 'lute', of uncertain origin: probably from Old French *lut* (see LUTE1).]

luteolin /loʻoti ōlin/ *n.* a yellow pigment that is found in some plants, e.g. dyer's rocket. It is a tetrahydroxyflavone compound. [Mid-19thC. Via French from modern Latin *luteola*, species name of dyer's rocket, from Latin *luteolus* 'yellowish', from *luteus* 'yellow'.]

lutetium /loo teeshəm, -shi əm/ *n.* a silvery-white metallic chemical element that belongs to the rare-earth series. It is used as a catalyst in the nuclear industries. Symbol **Lu** [Early 20thC. Formed from Latin *Lutetia*, an ancient name for Paris, the native city of the French chemist Georges Urbains (1872–1938), who discovered the element.]

Luther /loʻothər/, **Martin** (1483–1546) German theologian and religious reformer. His 95 theses against papal indulgences (1517) launched the Protestant Reformation.

Lutheran /loʻothərən/ *n.* **ADHERENT OF LUTHERANISM** a Christian who is a member of the Protestant church established by Martin Luther (**Lutheran Church**) ■ *adj.* **RELATING TO LUTHERANISM** relating or belonging to Lutheranism

Lutheranism /loʻothərənizəm/ *n.* the first form of Protestantism, founded by Martin Luther in 16th-century Germany. It focuses on the teachings of Jesus Christ and stresses individual faith over collective church authority. Spreading first through northern Europe, particularly Scandinavia, it now has adherents worldwide.

luthier /loʻoti ər/ *n.* sb who makes and repairs violins and other stringed instruments [Late 19thC. From French, formed from *luth* 'lute', from Old French *lut* (see LUTE1).]

Luthuli /loo toʻoli/, **Albert** (1899–1967) South African political leader. As the president-general of the African National Congress (1952–67), he campaigned against apartheid and won the Nobel Peace Prize (1960) for his steadfast opposition to violence. Full name **Albert John Mvumbi Luthuli**

Luton /loʻot'n/ town in Bedfordshire, central England. Population: 167,300 (1991).

Lutosławski /loʻot ō slávski/, **Witold** (1913–94) Polish composer and conductor. His use of the 12-tone system and of chance elements in his compositions produced works of considerable variety.

Lutyens /lútyənz/, **Sir Edwin Landseer** (1869–1944) British architect. A designer of houses, gardens, and furniture, his most monumental work is the layout and design of new public buildings for New Delhi (1913–30).

lutz /luts/ *n.* a figure-skating jump from the back edge of one skate, landing on the back edge of the other, with one or more full rotations [Mid-20thC. Origin uncertain: possibly an alteration of the name of the Swiss figure skater Gustave *Lussi* (born 1898), who introduced the jump.]

Lützen /loʻotsən/ site of a battle in what is now Saxony-Anhalt state, east-central Germany

luv /luv/ *n.* an informal way of spelling 'love', especially when sb is being addressed (*informal*)

luvvie /lúvvi/, **luvvy** (*plural* **-vies**) *n.* an actor, or sb whose behaviour conforms to a stereotype of actors (*informal humorous or disapproving; often used before a noun*) [Late 20thC. Variant of *lovey*, a form of address seen as typical of the acting profession.] —**luvviedom** *n.* —**luvviness** *n.*

Luwian /loʻoi ən/ *n.* an extinct Anatolian language belonging to the Indo-European group of languages [Early 20thC. Translation of German *Luwisch*, from *Luwia* 'Luvia', the name of an ancient region of Asia Minor where the language was used.] —**Luwian** *adj.*

lux /luks/ (*plural* **lux** or **luces** /loʻo seez/) *n.* the SI unit of illumination, equal to one lumen per square metre. Symbol **lx** [Late 19thC. From Latin *lux* 'light' (source of English *lucid*).]

Lux. *abbr.* Luxembourg

luxate /luk sáyt, lúk sayt/ (**-ates, -ating, -ated**) *vt.* to displace the bones of a joint (*technical*) [Early 17thC. From Latin *luxare*, from *luxus* 'dislocated'. Ultimately from an Indo-European word meaning 'to turn away', which is also the ancestor of English *lock*, *luxury*, and *leek*.] —**luxation** /luk sáysh'n/ *n.*

Luxembourg

Luxembourg /lúksəm burg/ **1.** country in western Europe bordered by Belgium, Germany, and France. Language: Luxembourgish. Currency: Luxembourg franc. Capital: Luxembourg (City). Population: 420,415 (1997). Area: 2,586 sq. km/998 sq. mi. Official name **Grand Duchy of Luxembourg 2.** the largest and southernmost province of Belgium. Population: 241,339 (1996). Area: 4,440 sq. km/1,714 sq. mi. —**Luxembourger** *n.*

Luxembourg City capital of Luxembourg, situated in the southern-central part of the country. Population: 76,446 (1995).

Luxembourgish /lúksəm burg ish/ *n.* the official language of Luxembourg, a form of German with many French elements —**Luxembourgish** *adj.*

Rosa Luxemburg

Luxemburg /lúksəm burg/, **Rosa** (1871–1919) Polish-born German political activist. With Karl Liebknecht she founded the Spartacus League (1916), which became the German Communist Party. She was murdered by German soldiers.

Luxor /loʻok sawr, lúk-/ town on the eastern bank of the River Nile, eastern-central Egypt. Population: 146,000 (1992).

luxulyanite /luk soʻolyə nīt/ *n.* a rare type of granite that contains needles of tourmaline in quartz and feldspar [Late 19thC. Named after the village of *Luxullian* in Cornwall, where it was first found.]

luxuriant /lug zyoʻori ənt, luk syoʻori-, lug zhoʻori-/ *adj.* **1. LUSH** with a lot of young rich healthy growth ○ *luxuriant ground cover* **2. GROWING PROFUSELY** growing thickly and profusely ○ *a luxuriant mane of dark curly hair* **3. ELABORATE** written in an elaborate, showy, and dramatic style **4. PRODUCTIVE** producing vast quantities of sth [Mid-16thC. From Latin *luxuriant-*, the present participle stem of *luxuriare* (see LUXURIATE).] —**luxuriance** *n.* —**luxuriantly** *adv.*

luxuriate /lug zyoʻori ayt, luk syoʻori-, lug zhoʻori-/ (**-ates, -ating, -ated**) *vi.* **1. DERIVE GREAT ENJOYMENT** to enjoy sth in a self-indulgent way, taking great pleasure from the luxury and comfort that it offers **2. GROW VIGOROUSLY** to grow vigorously and successfully [Early 17thC. From Latin *luxuriat-*, the past participle stem of *luxuriare*, from *luxuria* 'profusion, excess'.]

luxurious /lug zyoʻori əss, luk syoʻori-, lug zhoʻori-/ *adj.* **1. COMFORTABLE AND EXPENSIVE** very comfortable, with high-quality expensive fittings or fabrics **2. ENJOYING LUXURY** with a liking for luxury, or used to living in luxury —**luxuriously** *adv.* —**luxuriousness** *n.*

luxury /lúkshəri/ (*plural* **luxuries**) *n.* **1. PLEASURABLE SELF-INDULGENT ACTIVITY** an activity that gives great pleasure, especially one only rarely indulged in **2. NONESSENTIAL ITEM** an item that is desirable but not essential, and often expensive or hard to get (*often used before a noun*) **3. GREAT COMFORT** expensive high-quality surroundings, and the great comfort that they provide (*often used before a noun*) [14thC. Via Old French *luxurie* from Latin *luxuria* 'profusion, excess', from *luxus* 'dislocated'.]

Luzon /loo zón/ the largest island in the Philippines, situated in the northern part of the country. Population: 30,759,000 (1990). Area: 104,687 sq. km/40,420 sq. mi.

Lv *abbr.* lev

LV *abbr.* (*plural* **LVs**) luncheon voucher

lv. *abbr.* MIL leave

Lv. *abbr.* BIBLE Leviticus

Lviv /lə víf/, **L'viv, Lvov** industrial city in western Ukraine, capital of L'viv Oblast. Population: 806,000 (1995).

LW *abbr.* **1.** RADIO long wave **2.** low water

lwei /lə wáy/ (*plural* **lweis** or **lwei**) *n.* **1. ANGOLAN CURRENCY UNIT** a subunit of currency in Angola. See table at **currency 2. COIN WORTH LWEI** a coin worth one lwei [Late 20thC. Of Bantu origin.]

LWM, lwm *abbr.* low water mark

lx *symbol.* lux

-ly *suffix.* **1.** like, having the characteristics of ○ *brotherly* ○ *kindly* **2.** in a particular manner ○ *briefly* **3.** recurring at a particular interval of time ○ *monthly-* [The adjective is from Old English *-līc*; the adverb from Old English *-līce*. Both ultimately from an Indo-European word meaning 'body, form', which is also the ancestor of English *like* and *alike*.]

lyase /lī ayz, -ayss/ *n.* any of a group of enzymes that catalyse either the formation of a double bond within a chemical compound, or the addition of a chemical group at a double bond [Mid-20thC. Coined from Greek *luein* 'to loosen' (see LYSIS).]

lycanthrope /līkənthrōp, lī kán-/ *n.* a werewolf (*literary*) [Early 17thC. Via modern Latin from Greek *lukanthrōpos*, from *lukos* 'wolf' + *anthrōpos* 'human being'.]

lycanthropy /lī kánthrəpi/ *n.* in horror stories and legends, the transformation of a person into a wolf

lyceum /lī see əm/ *n.* **1. BUILDING FOR PUBLIC EVENTS** a building where concerts, lectures, and other public events take place (*usually used in names of buildings*) **2. US SPONSOR** an organization that arranges or sponsors public events and entertainment [Late 16thC. Via Latin from Greek *Lukeion* (*gymnasion*), name of the school near Athens where Aristotle taught, which was named after the nearby temple of Apollo *Lukeios*.]

lychee /lī chee, lī chee/, **litchi, lichee** *n.* **1. FOOD CHINESE FRUIT** a small round sweet and juicy Chinese fruit with whitish translucent pulp and a red heart-shaped crust **2. TREES CHINESE TREE** the tree that lychees grow on. Latin name: *Litchi chinensis*. [Late 16thC. From Mandarin Chinese *lìzhī*.]

lych-gate /lích-/, **lich-gate** *n.* a covered gateway into a churchyard. Traditionally, coffin-bearers would rest the coffin there before carrying it into the church. [15thC. From Old English *līc* 'body, corpse' + GATE.]

Lycian /líssi ən/ *n.* **1.** PEOPLES **SB FROM LYCIA** sb from the ancient region of Lycia, in Asia Minor **2.** LANG **EXTINCT LANGUAGE OF LYCIANS** an extinct language spoken by the ancient Lycians, belonging to the Anatolian group of languages [Late 16thC. Formed from Latin *Lycia* 'Lycia', from Greek *Lukia*.] —**Lycian** *adj.*

lycopodium /líkə pṓdi əm/ *n.* **1.** MOSS WITH BRANCHING STEMS a plant that is a kind of club moss, with long branching stems covered in small leaves. It has small spore-carrying cones. Genus: *Lycopodium.* **2.** FLAMMABLE POWDER a flammable powder, composed of spores of lycopodium and other club mosses, used in the past as a coating for pills and suppositories, in fireworks, and in foundry work [Early 18thC. From modern Latin, genus name, from Greek *lukos* 'wolf' + the stem *pod-* 'foot'; so called because of the plant's claw-like foot.]

Lycra /líkrə/ *tdmk.* a trademark for a lightweight stretchy polyurethane fabric that is widely used in the manufacture of clothing, particularly sportswear and swimwear

lyddite /líddīt/ *n.* a powerful explosive consisting mainly of picric acid mixed with 10 per cent nitrobenzene and 3 per cent petroleum jelly. It is used in shells. [Late 19thC. Named after the town of *Lydd* in Kent, SE England, where the explosive was first tested.]

Lydgate /líd gayt/, **John** (1370?–1450?) English monk and poet. He wrote *The Troy Book* (1412–20), *The Siege of Thebes* (1420–22), and *Fall of Princes* (1430–38).

Lydia /líddi ə/ ancient country in the northwestern part of present-day Turkey, on the Aegean Sea. It reached its peak of wealth in the 7th and 6th centuries BC before being conquered by Cyrus the Great of Persia about 546 BC.

Lydian /líddi ən/ *n.* **1.** PEOPLES **SB FROM LYDIA** sb from the ancient region of Lydia **2.** LANG **EXTINCT LANGUAGE OF LYDIANS** an extinct language spoken by the Lydians, belonging to the Anatolian group of languages ■ *adj.* RELATING TO LYDIA relating to ancient Lydia, or to its people, culture, or langauge [15thC. Formed from Latin *Lydius*, from Greek *Ludios* 'Lydia'.]

lye /lī/ *n.* a strong solution of sodium hydroxide or potassium hydroxide in water, used in industrial drain and oven cleaners [Old English *lēag*. Ultimately from an Indo-European word meaning 'to wash', which is also the ancestor of English *lather*, *lotion*, and *deluge*.]

Lye /lī/, **Len** (1901–80) New Zealand artist. He pioneered experimental films and kinetic sculpture.

Lyele /lyéllay/ *n.* a language spoken in parts of Burkina Faso, belonging to the Gur branch of Niger-Congo languages. Lyele is spoken by about 60,000 people. —**Lyele** *adj.*

Lyell /lī əl/, **Sir Charles** (1797–1875) British geologist. His theories and research influenced the development of modern geology.

lygus bug /lígəss/ *n.* a plant-eating insect that is especially common in North America, where it is a pest of cotton and other crops. Genus: *Lygus.* [[*Lygus*], modern Latin, genus name, of uncertain origin: probably from Greek *lugos* 'chaste-tree, withy']

lying present participle of **lie**[1], **lie**[2]

lying-in (*plural* **lyings-in**) *n.* the period of time leading up to and immediately following childbirth, during which women used to be confined to bed (*archaic; often used before a noun*)

lyke-wake /līk-/ *n.* a vigil held over a dead body, often accompanied by festivities [14thC. Formed from Old English *līc* 'body, corpse' + WAKE.]

Lyme disease /līm-/ *n.* an infectious bacterial disease transmitted by ticks, in which skin rash, fever, and headache precede arthritis and nervous disorder [Late 20thC. Named after the town of *Lyme*, Connecticut, USA, where it was first reported.]

lyme grass /līm-/ *n.* a perennial grass with broad bluish-green leaves that is found on sand dunes in northern temperate regions. It is sometimes planted to help stabilize shifting dunes. Latin name: *Elymus arenarius.* [Origin of *lyme* uncertain: perhaps from LIME, from the plant's binding properties]

Lyme Regis /līm reéjiss/ seaside resort in Dorset, southern England. Population: 3,851 (1991).

Lymington /límmingtən/ ancient town and seaport in Hampshire, England, on the edge of the New Forest. Population: 13,508 (1991).

lymph /limf/ *n.* a fluid containing white cells, chiefly lymphocytes, that is drained from tissue spaces by the vessels of the lymphatic system. It can transport bacteria, viruses, and cancer cells. Colourless in hue, lymph draining the intestines can turn opalescent from fatty globules absorbed from a meal. [Late 17thC. Directly or via French from Latin *lympha* 'water', of uncertain origin: probably an alteration of Greek *numphē* 'bride, nymph'.]

lymph- *prefix.* = **lympho-** (*used before vowels*)

lymphadenopathy /lim fáddi nóppəthi, lím fadi-/ (*plural* **-thies**) *n.* any disease, disorder, or enlargement of the lymph nodes [Early 20thC. Coined from LYMPHO- + ADENO- + -PATHY, literally 'lymph gland disease'.]

lymphatic /lim fáttik/ *adj.* **1.** PHYSIOL **RELATING TO THE LYMPH SYSTEM** relating to lymph or the lymphatic system **2.** SLUGGISH without any energy or enthusiasm ■ *n.* PHYSIOL **VESSEL TRANSPORTING LYMPH** a vessel that transports or contains lymph

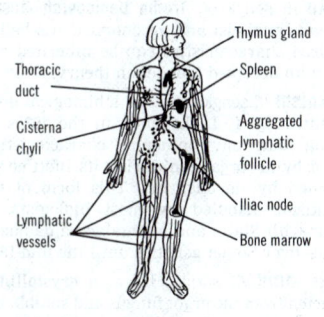

Thymus gland

Thoracic duct

Spleen

Cisterna chyli

Aggregated lymphatic follicle

Iliac node

Lymphatic vessels

Bone marrow

Lymphatic system

lymphatic system *n.* a network of vessels that transport fluid, fats, proteins, and lymphocytes to the bloodstream as lymph, and remove microorganisms and other debris from tissues

lymph gland *n.* a popular but inaccurate term for a lymph node

lymph node *n.* any of numerous oval bodies, distributed throughout the lymphatic system, that produce and house lymphocytes and filter microorganisms and other particles from lymph. The function of these nodes is to reduce the risk of infection.

lympho- *prefix.* lymph, lymphocyte, lymphatic system ○ *lymphocytosis* [From LYMPH]

lymphoblast /límfō blast/ *n.* an immature cell that develops into a lymphocyte

lymphoblastic /límfō blástik/ *adj.* relating to the production of lymphocytes

lymphoblastic leukaemia *n.* a disease in which there is great overproduction of immature lymphocytes

lymphocyte /límfō sīt/ *n.* an important cell class in the immune system that produces antibodies to attack infected and cancerous cells, and is responsible for rejecting foreign tissue. It is a kind of white blood cell.

lymphocytosis /límfō sī tóssiss/ *n.* an abnormal increase in the number of lymphocytes in the bloodstream. It occurs in some chronic infections, some forms of leukaemia, and other diseases.

lymphogranuloma venereum /límfō grányōo lṓmə və neéri əm/ *n.* a sexually transmitted disease caused by a bacterial infection, in which there is swelling of the genital lymph nodes and, especially in men,

a genital ulcer. It occurs mainly in tropical and subtropical regions. [From modern Latin, literally 'venereal granuloma of the lymph nodes']

lymphoid /límf oyd/ *adj.* relating to lymph, lymphatic tissue, or the lymphatic system

lymphokine /límfō kīn/ *n.* any of various soluble substances released by lymphocytes during an immune response that influence the behaviour of other immune cells. Lymphokines are now included in the more general class of cytokines. (*dated*) [Mid-20thC. Coined from LYMPHO- + Greek *kinein* 'to move' (see KINETIC).]

lymphoma /lim fṓmə/ (*plural* **-mas** or **-mata** /-mətə/) *n.* a malignant tumour originating in a lymph node, e.g. Hodgkin's disease or any of the range of cancers known as non-Hodgkin's lymphomas

lymphopoiesis /límfō poy eéssiss/ *n.* the production of lymphocytes, which occurs mainly in the bone marrow, thymus, lymph nodes, spleen, and tonsils —**lymphopoietic** /-poy éttik/ *adj.*

Lynbrook /lín brŏok/ village in Nassau County, New York, situated on the southern shore of Long Island, 29 km/18 mi. east of New York City. Population: 19,208 (1990).

lynch /linch/ (**lynches, lynching, lynched**) *vt.* to seize sb believed to have committed a crime and put him or her to death immediately and without trial, usually by hanging [Early 19thC. From LYNCH LAW.] —**lyncher** *n.* —**lynching** *n.*

Lynch /linch/, **David** (*b.* 1946) US film director. His distinctively bizarre and surreal work includes the films *Eraserhead* (1977) and *Blue Velvet* (1986) and the cult television series *Twin Peaks* (1989–90).

Lynch, Jack (*b.* 1917) Irish statesman. Leader of the Fianna Fáil Party (1966–79) he was twice prime minister (1966–73, 1977–79). He was also a noted Gaelic footballer. Real name **John Lynch**

lynch law *n.* the condemnation and punishment of sb by a mob or self-appointed group without a legal trial [Early 19thC. Named after Capt. William *Lynch* (1724–1820), a planter and justice of the peace who organized an extralegal tribunal in Virginia, in the United States, in 1780.]

lynch mob *n.* a group of people who capture and hang sb without legal arrest and trial, because they think the person has committed a crime

Lynn /lin/, **Dame Vera** (*b.* 1917) British singer. For many people, her shows and radio broadcasts for servicemen during World War II stood for the fight for freedom. Known as **the Forces' Sweetheart**

Lynx

lynx /lingks/ (*plural* **lynx** or **lynxes**) *n.* a short-tailed cat found in northern coniferous forests, with a lightly mottled yellowish- to reddish-brown coat and tufted ears. Genus: *Lynx.* ◊ **bobcat, caracal** [14thC. Via Latin from Greek *lugx*, of uncertain origin. Perhaps, ultimately, from an Indo-European word meaning 'light', referring to the animal's shining eyes.]

Lynx /links/ *n.* a faint northern constellation of stars between Ursa Major and Auriga

lynx-eyed *adj.* with very good eyesight

lyo- *prefix.* dissolution, dispersion ○ *lyophobic* [From Greek *luein* 'to loosen, dissolve' (see LYSIS)]

lyolysis /lī ólləssiss/ *n.* the reaction of a salt with a solvent to form an acid and a base

Lyon = **Lyons**

Lyonnais /lee əN áy/ historic region of France, comprising the present-day Loire and Rhône departments

lyonnaise /leè ə náyz/ adj. cooked with onions, or containing fried onions [Early 19thC. From French (à la) lyonnaise 'in the manner of Lyons'.]

Lyons /lee óN/, **Lyon** capital of the Rhône Department and the Rhône-Alpes Region, eastern-central France. Population: 422,444 (1990).

Lyons /lī́ ənz/, **Dame Enid Muriel** (1897–1981) Australian politician. In 1943 she became one of the first two women to be elected to the federal parliament. She was the wife of Joseph Aloysius Lyons. Born **Enid Muriel Burnell**

Lyons, Sir Joseph (1848–1917) British businessman. He was a cofounder of a teashop that grew into a major catering firm.

Lyons, Joseph Aloysius (1879–1939) Australian statesman. After founding the United Australian Party in 1931, he became prime minister (1932–39).

lyophilic /lī́ ō fíllik/ adj. used to describe a finely dispersed solid (**colloid**) that forms a stable dispersion

lyophilize /lī́ óffi līz/ (**-lizes, -lizing, -lized**), **lyophilise** (**lyophilises, lyophilising, lyophilised**) vt. to freeze-dry sth (technical) —**lyophilization** /lī́ óffi līzáysh'n/ n. — **lyophilizer** /lī́ óffi līzər/ n.

lyophobic /lī́ ō fóbik/ adj. used to describe a finely dispersed solid (**colloid**) that forms an unstable dispersion

Lyra /lī́rə/ n. a small prominent constellation of the northern hemisphere between Cygnus and Hercules. It contains a very bright star (**Vega**) and a planetary nebula (**Ring Nebula**).

lyrate /lī́rət, -ayt/ adj. 1. LYRE-SHAPED in the shape of a lyre 2. BOT WITH ROUNDED APEX used to describe a leaf that has a broad rounded apex and small lateral lobes at the base [Mid-18thC. Formed from Latin lyra (see LYRE).]

Lyre

lyre /lī́r/ n. a plucked string instrument associated with ancient Greece and consisting of a U-shaped frame from which the strings stretch down to the soundbox [12thC. Via Old French from, ultimately, Greek lura, of unknown origin.]

lyrebird /lī́r burd/ n. either of two ground-dwelling birds found in the mountain forests of southeastern Australia. The males have long tail feathers that form into a lyre shape during courtship. Family: Menuridae.

lyric /lírrik/ adj. 1. POETRY EXPRESSING PERSONAL FEELINGS relating to poetry that often has a musical quality and expresses personal emotions or thoughts ○ a lyric poet 2. MUSIC WITH LIGHTNESS OF VOICE singing with a voice that has a light quality and a vocally undramatic delivery 3. MUSIC WITH LIGHTNESS OF MUSICAL QUALITY having or played with a light smooth nondramatic quality that suggests singing 4. MUSIC RELATING TO THE LYRE relating to or written for the lyre, or for accompaniment by the lyre ■ n. 1. MUSIC SONG WORDS the words of a song, especially a popular song (often used in the plural) 2. POETRY SHORT PERSONAL POEM a short poem expressing personal feelings or thoughts [Late 16thC. Via French from, ultimately, Greek lurikos 'singing to the lyre', from lura 'lyre'.]

lyrical /lírrik'l/ adj. 1. POETRY, MUSIC = lyric adj. 1, lyric adj. 2, lyric adj. 3 2. GUSHINGLY COMPLIMENTARY wildly enthusiastic and emotional about sth ○ critics waxing lyrical about the new exhibition —**lyrically** adv. —**lyricalness** n.

lyricism /lírrisizəm/ n. 1. POETRY, MUSIC LYRIC STYLE a lyric style in poetry or music 2. ENTHUSIASTICALLY EMOTIONAL EXPRESSION emotional and enthusiastic expressions of feelings or opinions

lyricist /lírrissist/ n. 1. MUSIC SONGWRITER sb who writes words for songs, especially popular songs 2. POETRY LYRIC POET a writer of lyric poems

lys- prefix. = lyso- (used before vowels)

lyse /līss/ /līz/ (**lyses, lysing, lysed**) vti. to undergo, or cause cells to undergo, destruction by disruption of the bounding membrane (**lysis**) [Early 20thC. Back-formation from LYSIS, on the model of analyse.]

Lysenko /li séngk ō/, **Trofim Denisovich** (1898–1976) Russian geneticist and agronomist. His belief that acquired characteristics can be inherited were at odds with accepted Mendelian theory.

Lysenkoism /lī séngkō izəm/ n. a biological doctrine, presented by T. D. Lysenko in the 1930s, maintaining that environmental characteristics acquired by an organism during its lifetime can be inherited by its offspring. This form of neo-Lamarckism, disputed by most biologists, found favour with Stalin and maintained a damaging influence over Soviet genetics until the mid-1960s.

lysergic acid /lī súrjik-, li-/ n. a crystalline acid extracted from the ergot fungus and soluble in most organic solvents. Formula: $C_{16}H_{16}N_2O_2$. [Coined from LYSO- + ERGOT + -IC]

lysergic acid diethylamide n. full form of LSD

lysin /lī́ssin/ n. an agent, e.g. an enzyme or antibody, that is able to destroy cells by disruption of the bounding membrane (**lysis**) [Early 20thC. Formed from LYSIS.]

lysine /lī́ seen/ n. an amino acid that occurs in nature

$$CH_2 - CH_2 - CH_2 - CH_2 - CH - \overset{O}{\overset{\|}{C}} - OH$$
$$\underset{NH_2}{|} \qquad\qquad\qquad \underset{NH_2}{|}$$

Lysine

as a component of proteins. It is an essential nutrient in the diet of people and animals. [Late 19thC. From German Lysin, from Greek lusis 'loosening' (see LYSIS).]

lysis /lī́ssiss/ (plural **lyses** /lī́ seez/) n. 1. BIOL DESTRUCTIVE DISRUPTION OF CELLS the destruction of cells by disruption of the bounding membrane, allowing the cell contents to escape 2. MED GRADUAL REDUCTION OF DISEASE SYMPTOMS a gradual reduction in severity of a patient's signs and symptoms during the course of a disease [Mid-16thC. Via Latin, 'loosening', from Greek lusis, from luein 'to loosen'.]

-lysis suffix. 1. dissolution, decomposition, disintegration ○ thermolysis 2. hydrolysis ○ proteolysis [Via modern Latin from Greek lusis (see LUSIS)]

Lysithea /lī sī́thi ə/ n. a very small natural satellite of Jupiter, discovered in 1938. It is approximately 35 km in diameter and occupies an intermediate orbit.

lyso- prefix. lysis ○ lysosome [From LYSIS]

lysogen /lī́ssəjən/ n. 1. VIRUS-RELEASING BACTERIUM a bacterium that is capable of releasing a bacterium-destroying virus (**bacteriophage**) 2. ANTIGEN STIMULATING CELL-DESTROYING AGENTS an agent, particularly an antigen, that provokes the production of cell-destroying agents (**lysins**) by cells of the immune system

lysogenic /lī́ssə jénnik/ adj. used to describe a bacterium that is capable of producing and releasing a bacterium-destroying virus (**bacteriophage**) in response to certain stimuli

lysogenize /lī sójjə nīz/ (**-nizes, -nizing, -nized**), **lysogenise** (**-nises, -nising, -nised**) vt. to convert a bacterium to a lysogenic state by infection with a bacterium-destroying virus (**bacteriophage**)

lysogeny /lī sójjəni/ n. the ability of a bacterial cell to produce and release a bacterium-destroying virus (**bacteriophage**) in response to certain stimuli

lysosome /lī́ssōssōm/ n. a membrane-bound cavity in living cells that contains enzymes that are responsible for degrading and recycling molecules. They can deal with material both originating within the cell and entering from outside, and are especially important in the immune cells that ingest and degrade bacteria. —**lysosomal** /lī́ssō sṓm'l/ adj.

lysozyme /lī́ssō zīm/ n. an enzyme, found in tears, saliva, other body fluids, and egg white, that weakens the cell walls of some bacteria and thus contributes to their ultimate destruction. It was the first enzyme to have its three-dimensional structure determined. [Early 20thC. Coined from LYSO- + ENZYME.]

-lyte suffix. a substance that can be decomposed by a particular process ○ electrolyte [From Greek lutos 'soluble', from the past participle of luein (see LYSIS)] —**-lytic** suffix.

Lytham St Anne's /lī́thəm saynt ánz/ popular seaside resort in western Lancashire, on the northwestern coast of England. Population: 40,866 (1991).

lytic /líttik/ adj. relating to, resulting from, or causing the destruction of cells by disruption of the bounding membrane (**lysis**) [Late 19thC. From Greek lutikos 'able to loosen', from luein 'to loosen'.]

Lyttleton /lítt'ltən/, **Humphrey** (b. 1921) British jazz trumpeter, bandleader, broadcaster, and author. He formed his own band in 1948 that initially played traditional jazz, but then moved to include modern jazz.

-lyze suffix. to cause or undergo lysis ○ plasmolyze [Back-formation from -LYSIS]

LZ abbr. MIL landing zone

m[1] /em/ (*plural* m's), **M** (*plural* M's *or* Ms) *n.* **1.** 13TH LETTER OF ENGLISH ALPHABET the 13th letter of the modern English alphabet **2.** SPEECH SOUND CORRESPONDING TO LETTER 'M' the speech sound that corresponds to the letter 'M' **3.** LETTER 'M' WRITTEN a written representation of the letter 'M'

m[2] *symbol.* **1.** magnetic moment **2.** MEASURE metre **3.** TIME minute *or* minutes **4.** PHYS mass **5.** milli- **6.** million **7.** PHYS mutual inductance

m[3] *abbr.* PHYS modulus

M[1], **m** *n.* the Roman numeral for 1000

M[2] *abbr.* **1.** CHEM mass **2.** Master **3.** CLOTHES medium (*used of clothes size*) **4.** mega- **5.** Member **6.** LOGIC middle term **7.** million **8.** CHEM molar **9.** motorway

m. *abbr.* **1.** M. male **2.** married **3.** GRAM masculine **4.** medium **5.** mile **6.** TIME minute **7.** CALENDAR month **8.** CRICKET maiden (over)

MO *n.* an assessment of the amount of money in public circulation, the money represented by banks' balances, and the money held in banks' tills (**narrow money**)

M1 *n.* an assessment of the amount of money in coins, notes, and current and deposit accounts

M-1 rifle *n.* a .30 calibre rifle invented by John C. Garand and adopted by the US Army in 1936.

M2 *n.* an assessment of the amount of money in coins, currency, current and deposit accounts, savings accounts, and deposits

M3 *n.* an assessment of the amount of money in M1, M2, and also large denomination repurchase agreements, institutional money market accounts, and certain Eurodollar time deposits

ma /maa/ (*plural* **mas**) *n.* **1.** MOTHER a word used to refer to a mother or to address your own mother (*informal*) **2.** WOMAN PAST MIDDLE AGE a way of addressing or referring to a woman past middle age (*often considered offensive*) [Early 19thC. Shortening of MAMMA.]

mA *symbol.* milliampere(s)

MA, **M.A.** *abbr.* **1.** PSYCHOL mental age **2.** Military Academy **3.** Master of Arts **4.** Massachusetts

ma'am /mam, maam, məm/ *n.* **1.** FORMAL FORM OF ADDRESS used when addressing royal women or other women of high status (*formal*) **2.** RESPECTFUL FORM OF ADDRESS used when addressing a woman in a polite and respectful way (*dated*) [Mid-17thC. Contraction of MADAM.]

maar /maar/ (*plural* **maars** *or* **maare** /máari/) *n.* a broad flat volcanic crater formed by a single explosive eruption and often filled with water [Early 19thC. Via German dialect, 'crater lake', from, ultimately, Latin *mare* 'sea'.]

Ma'ariv /maariv/, **Maariv** *n.* in Judaism, the evening service of prayer [Late 20thC. From Hebrew *ma'ărībh* 'evening prayer'.]

Maasai *n., adj.* = Masai

Maastricht /maastrikht/, **Maestricht** capital of Limburg Province, in the southeastern Netherlands. Population: 118,102 (1994).

Maastricht Treaty /maastrikt-, -strikht-/ *n.* a treaty signed in Maastricht in late 1991 by heads of the 12 member states of the European Community that set out a framework for increased political and economic integration. It was ratified in 1993.

Maat /maat/ *n.* in Egyptian mythology, the goddess of the underworld who tests the value of a person's soul after death by weighing the heart on an ostrich feather

maatjes herring *n.* = matjes herring

Mab /mab/ *n.* in Celtic mythology, the god of light, who mediates between humankind and the divine

mabe pearl /máyb-, máybi-/ *n.* a cultured pearl with a flat base and a rounded top [Origin unknown]

Mabinogion /mábbi nóggi on/ *n.* a collection of ancient Welsh stories of magic and mythology, including stories about King Arthur [From Welsh, plural of *mabinogi* 'youthful career', from *mab* 'youth, son', from Old Welsh *map*, from a Celtic word meaning 'son']

Mabo /máybō/ *n.* ANZ a 1992 landmark Australian legal case relating to the land rights of indigenous peoples. The ruling was that native claim was not extinguished by European settlement.

Mabo /mábbō, maábō, máybō/, **Ernie Koiki** (1936–92) Australian Torres Strait Islander elder. He was leader of a group of Islanders whose land rights claim led to an Australian High Court ruling in 1992 that European settlement did not extinguish native title.

mac /mak/, **mack** *n.* a mackintosh (*informal*) [Early 20thC. Shortening.]

Mac /mak/ *n.* US, Scotland used as an informal way of addressing a man whose name is not known (*informal*) [Mid-20thC. From the Scottish name element MAC- = Mac or Mc.]

MAC /mak/ *n.* a system for transmitting pictures to colour televisions using satellites. Full form **multiplexed analogue component**

Mac. *abbr.* BIBLE Maccabees

macabre /mə kaábrə, -bə/ *adj.* including gruesome and horrific details of death and decay [15thC. From French (*danse*) *macabre*, a dance in which Death lured people to dance until they dropped dead. Of uncertain origin: probably an alteration of *danse Macabé*, a translation of medieval Latin *chorea Machabaeorum* 'dance of the Maccabees', originally probably a representation of the slaughter of the Maccabees in a medieval mystery play.]

macaco /mə kaákō/ (*plural* -**cos**) *n.* a lemur, especially a species of lemur in which the male is black and the female brown [Mid-18thC. From French *mococo*, of uncertain origin: perhaps from Malagasy *maka* 'lemur'.]

macadam /mə káddəm/ *n.* a smooth hard road surface made from small pieces of stone, usually mixed with tar or asphalt, in compressed layers [Early 19thC. Named after the Scottish civil engineer John Loudon McAdam (1756–1836), who developed the system.]

macadamia /máka dáymi ə/ *n.* an evergreen tree found in Australia and Southeast Asia that has clusters of white flowers and is cultivated for its edible nuts. Genus: *Macadamia*. [Early 20thC. From modern Latin, named after the Scottish-born Australian chemist John *Macadam* (1827–65).]

macadamia nut, **macadamia** *n.* an edible, round, hard-shelled, waxy nut with a mild creamy flavour, produced by the macadamia tree

macadamize /mə káddə mīz/ (-**izes**, -**izing**, -**ized**), **macadamise** (-**ises**, -**ising**, -**ised**) *vt.* to build or surface a road with macadam —**macadamization** /mə káddə mī záysh'n/ *n.* —**macadamizer** /mə káddə mīzər/ *n.*

Macaque

macaque /mə kaák, -kák/ (*plural* -**caques** *or* -**caque**) *n.* a short-tailed, sturdily built monkey that inhabits wooded or rocky areas of Asia and northern Africa. Genus: *Macaca*. [Late 17thC. Via French from, ultimately, Bantu *makaku*, literally 'some monkeys'.]

macaroni /máka rőni/ *n.* **1.** SMALL PASTA TUBES hollow tubular pasta, usually produced in short lengths **2.** (*plural* -**nis** *or* -**nies**) WELL-TRAVELLED DANDY an affected, foppish young man of 18th-century Britain who adopted the fashions, manners, and customs of the other countries he had visited [Late 16thC. From Italian dialect *maccarone* 'macaroni, dumpling', of uncertain origin; probably from Greek *makaria* 'food made from barley'.]

macaronic /máka rónnik/ *adj.* **1.** MIXING LANGUAGES IN VERSE used to describe verse containing words and phrases from everyday language mixed with Latin or other foreign words and phrases, or with vernacular terms with Latinate endings added, usually for comic effect **2.** RELATING TO A MIXTURE OF LANGUAGES relating to or involving a combination of two or more languages ■ *n.* MACARONIC VERSE a macaronic poem or macaronic poetry in general [Early 17thC. Via modern Latin from MACARONI.] —**macaronically** *adv.*

macaroni cheese *n.* boiled macaroni in a cheese sauce, baked or grilled until golden

macaroon /máka roőn/ *n.* a biscuit made from sugar and egg whites, with ground almonds or pieces of dried coconut folded in [Late 16thC. Via French *macaron* from Italian dialect *maccarone* (see MACARONI).]

Macarthur /mək aárthər/, **John** (1767–1834) English-born Australian pioneer and wool merchant. He was a ringleader in the Rum Rebellion (1808–10), and as a pioneer of sheep-breeding established New South Wales as a wool exporting region.

MacArthur /mək aárthər/, **Douglas, General** (1880–1964) US soldier. He played a key role in US military affairs in Japan and the Philippines during World War II, and in Korea (1950–51).

Macassar /mə kássər/, **Macassar oil** *n.* an oily substance formerly used to make the hair smooth and shiny [Early 19thC. Named after MAKASSAR, from where the ingredients for the hair oil were claimed to have come.]

Macau /mə ków/, **Macao** Portuguese territory in southern China, on the South China Sea, west of Hong Kong. Population: 497,000 (1996). Area: 17.4 sq. km/6.7 sq. mi.

macaw /mə káw/ (*plural* -**caws** *or* -**caw**) *n.* a large parrot with a long tail and brilliant plumage found in Central and South America. Genus: *Anodorhyn-*

chus. [Early 17thC. From Portuguese *macao,* of unknown origin.]

Macbeth /mək béth/, **King of Scotland** (c. 1005–57). After murdering Duncan I in 1040, he held the throne until he was killed by Duncan's son, Malcolm III, in 1057.

Macc. *abbr.* BIBLE Maccabees

Maccabees /máka beez/ *npl.* **1.** FOLLOWERS OF JUDAS MAC-CABEUS the followers of Judas Maccabeus, who led the revolt of the Jews against Syria in 168 BC. The victory of the Maccabees is celebrated at Hannukah. **2.** BOOKS OF JEWISH HISTORY four books of Jewish history. The first two of these are included in the Apocrypha. [14thC. Via Latin *Maccabaeus* from Greek *Makkabaios,* a name given to Judas, perhaps from the Hebrew *maqqebet* 'hammer'.] —**Maccabean** /-bee ən/ *adj.*

maccaboy /máka boy/ *n.* rose-scented snuff from Martinique

Macclesfield /mák'lzfeeld/ manufacturing town in Cheshire, northeastern England. Population: 49,900 (1994).

MacDiarmid /mək dúrmid/, **Hugh** (1892–1978) British poet, editor, and critic. A pioneer in the Scottish literary renaissance and active in reviving literary Scots, he was a founder of the Scottish National Party. Pseudonym of **Christopher Murray Grieve**

Macdonald /mək dónn'ld/, **Flora** (1722–90) Scottish Jacobite. She helped Charles Edward Stewart, pretender to the English throne, escape to Skye after the uprising of 1745.

MacDonald /mək dónn'ld/, **Ramsay** (1866–1937) British statesman. He was a founder-member of the Labour Party and the United Kingdom's first Labour prime minister (1924 and 1929–31). Full name **James Ramsay MacDonald**

Macdonnell Ranges /mək dónnəl ráynjəz/ mountain ranges in central Australia, in the southern Northern Territory. The highest point in the range is Mount Zeil, 1,510 m/4,953 ft.

Mace

mace[1] /mayss/ *n.* **1.** CEREMONIAL STAFF OF OFFICE a stick or rod, usually with an ornamental head, carried by certain officials on ceremonial occasions as a symbol of authority **2.** SPIKED METAL CLUB a medieval weapon in the form of a heavy club with a round spiked metal head **3.** = **macebearer 4.** EARLY BILLIARD CUE an early form of the modern billiard cue [13thC. Via Old French from, ultimately, Latin *mateola* 'mallet'.]

mace[2] /mayss/ *n.* a spice made from the covering of the nutmeg seed, used in the form of dried blades or as a yellow-orange powder [13thC. Via Anglo-Norman *macis* from Latin *macir,* the name of an oriental spice. The term 'macis' was understood as a plural, and a new supposedly singular form made.]

Mace *tdmk.* a trademark for Chemical Mace, an aerosol used to immobilize an attacker for a brief time

macebearer /máyss bairər/ *n.* an official who carries a mace on ceremonial occasions

Maced. *abbr.* **1.** Macedonia **2.** Macedonian

macédoine /mássə dwaăn/, **macedoine** *n.* **1.** MIXED CHOPPED VEGETABLES a mixture of diced vegetables served hot or cold as a garnish, appetizer, or side dish **2.** MIXED CHOPPED FRUITS a salad of small diced pieces of fruit, often in syrup or jelly **3.** MEDLEY a mixed-up jumble or medley (*literary*) [Early 19thC. From French *Macédoine* 'Macedonia', the underlying idea

being of a mixture of the different peoples ruled by ALEXANDER the Great of Macedonia.]

Macedon /mássə don/ = **Macedonia 2**

Macedonia /mássə dốni ə/ **1.** republic in the Balkan region of southeastern Europe. Formerly part of the Federal People's Republic of Yugoslavia, it became independent in 1991. Language: Macedonian. Currency: dinar. Capital: Skopje. Population: 1,980,000 (1996). Area: 25,713 sq. km/9,928 sq. mi. **2.** **Macedonia, Macedon** ancient kingdom in northern Greece, centralized under Philip II, who, with his son, Alexander the Great, created a vast empire in the 4th century BC **3.** region in modern Greece, situated in the northeastern part of the country ■ *n.* BULGARIAN DISTRICT a district in southwestern Bulgaria

Macedonian /mássə dốni ən/ *n.* **1.** SB FROM THE REPUBLIC OF MACEDONIA sb who was born in or is a citizen of the Republic of Macedonia **2.** SB FROM MODERN GREEK MACEDONIA sb who was born in or is a citizen of the modern Greek region of Macedonia **3.** SB FROM ANCIENT MACEDONIA sb who was born in or was a citizen of the ancient kingdom of Macedonia **4.** LANGUAGE OF REPUBLIC OF MACEDONIA the official language of the Republic of Macedonia, also spoken in Albania, Bulgaria, and Greece. It belongs to the Balto-Slavonic branch of Indo-European languages and is spoken by about two million people. **5.** LANGUAGE OF ANCIENT MACEDONIA an extinct language formerly spoken in ancient Macedonia. Its relationship with other European languages remains unclear. [Mid-16thC] —**Macedonian** *adj.*

macerate /mássə rayt/ *vti.* (-ates, -ating, -ated) **1.** SOFTEN BY SOAKING to soften sth by soaking it in liquid or to become soft by soaking in liquid **2.** SEPARATE BY SOAKING to make sth break up into pieces or into its various parts by soaking it in liquid, or to break up in this way **3.** MAKE STH THIN OR WASTE AWAY to make sb or sth thin or lean, or to become thin or lean, especially by starvation or fasting ■ *n.* STH PRODUCED BY SOAKING sth prepared by soaking in a liquid [Mid-16thC. From Latin *macerat-,* the past participle stem of *macere* 'to soften.'] —**macerater** *n.* —**macerative** /mássərətiv/ *adj.* —**maceration** /mássə ráysh'n/ *n.*

Macgillicuddy's Reeks /mə gílli kudiz reéks/ mountain range in County Kerry, southwestern Ireland. Its highest peak is Carrantuohill, 1,041 m/3,415 ft.

MacGuffin /mə gúffin/ *n.* in a film, play, or book, sth that starts or drives the action of the plot but later turns out to be unimportant [Mid-20thC. Coined by Alfred HITCHCOCK.]

Mach /maak, mak/ *n.* = **Mach number**

Mach /makh/, **Ernst** (1838–1916) Austrian physicist and philosopher. He was noted for his pioneering work in ballistics. The Mach number and Mach angle are named after him.

mach. *abbr.* **1.** machine **2.** machinery **3.** machinist

Machado de Assis /ma sháddoo də ə seéss/, **Joachim Maria** (1839–1908) Brazilian novelist, poet, and critic. Author of *Dom Casmurro* (1899), he founded the Brazilian Academy of Letters (1896).

machair /mákər, mákhər/ *n.* Scotland a strip of grassland on a sandy shore, chiefly used for grazing livestock [Late 17thC. From Scottish Gaelic.]

machan /mə chaăn/ *n.* a raised platform, often in a tree, used to watch for tigers and other game in India [Late 19thC. From Hindi.]

mache /maash/, **mâche** *n.* = **lamb's lettuce** [Late 17thC. From French.]

Machel /mə shél/, **Samora Moïses** (1933–86) Mozambican statesman. He fought for the independence of Mozambique and became the country's first president (1975–86).

machete /mə shétti, -chétti/ *n.* a large heavy broad-bladed knife used as a weapon or as a tool for cutting a way through vegetation, especially in Central and South America and the West Indies [Late 16thC. From Spanish, literally 'little sledgehammer', from *macho* 'sledge hammer', ultimately from Latin *mateola* 'mallet' (source of English MACE[1]).]

Machiavelli /mə vélli, má kyə vélli/, **Niccolò** (1469–1527) Italian historian, statesman, and philosopher. He wrote several works on statecraft, of which *The*

Machete

Prince (1532) had a huge influence in his own time and later.

Machiavellian /máki ə vélli ən/ *adj.* **1.** CUNNING AND UNSCRUPULOUS using clever trickery, amoral methods, and expediency to achieve a desired goal, especially in politics (*disapproving*) **2.** RELATING TO MACHIAVELLI relating to or characteristic of the statesman and political philosopher Niccolò Machiavelli [Mid-16thC. From the advice in the writings of Niccolò MACHIAVELLI.] —**Machiavellian** *n.* —**Machiavellianism** *n.* —**Machiavellist** *n.,* *adj.*

Machiavellian intelligence *n.* in psychology, social intelligence, especially the intelligence that involves deception and the formation of coalitions

machicolate /mə chíkō layt/ (-lates, -lating, -lated) *vt.* to provide a castle wall with projecting galleries along its top [Late 18thC. Via Anglo-Latin, from, ultimately, Provençal *machacol,* literally 'neck-crusher', presumably because of the effect on those underneath.]

Machicolation

machicolation /mə chíkō láysh'n/ *n.* **1.** GALLERY ON TOP OF CASTLE WALL a projecting gallery on top of a castle wall, supported by a row of arches and containing openings through which rocks and boiling oil could be dropped on attackers **2.** OPENING IN MACHICOLATION an opening in the floor of a machicolation **3.** ROW OF ARCHES an ornamental row of supported arches that project from a building

machinate /máki nayt, máshi-/ (-nates, -nating, -nated) *vti.* to devise secret, cunning, or complicated plans and schemes to achieve a goal or to cause harm to others [Late 16thC. From Latin *machinat-,* past participle stem of *machinari,* from *machina* (see MACHINE).] —**machinator** *n.*

machination /máki náysh'n, máshi-/ *n.* **1.** PLOTTING OR INTRIGUE the devising of secret, cunning, or complicated plans and schemes **2.** PLOT OR INTRIGUE a secret, cunning, or complicated plan or scheme designed to achieve a particular end

machine /mə sheén/ *n.* **1.** MECH ENG MECHANICAL DEVICE a device with moving parts, often powered by electricity, used to perform a task, especially one that would otherwise be done by hand ○ *a washing machine* **2.** MECH ENG SIMPLE UNPOWERED DEVICE a simple device used to overcome resistance at one point by applying force at another point, e.g. a lever, pulley, or an inclined plane **3.** POWERED FORM OF TRANSPORT an engine-driven means of transport, e.g. an aircraft, car, or motorcycle **4.** POL GROUP OF PEOPLE IN CONTROL an organized group of people that controls or directs sth, especially a political group ○ *the party machine* **5.** COMPLEX SYSTEM a complex system structured so as to accomplish a specific goal ○ *the war machine* **6. SB WHO BEHAVES MECHANICALLY** sb who acts or works like a mechanical device, e.g. sb who is very efficient or who shows no emotion or initiative ○ *an editing machine* **7. THEATRE DEVICE TO PRODUCE STAGE EFFECTS** a mechanical device used in the theatre, especially in classical drama, to create special effects such as the entrance of a supernatural being **8. LITERAT LITERARY DEVICE** sb or sth introduced into a work of literature to produce an effect or to resolve the plot ■ *v.* (**-chines, -chining, -chined**) **1.** *vti.* **WORK WITH POWER-DRIVEN TOOL** to cut, shape, or finish a piece of work using a power-driven tool such as a lathe or drilling device, or to be cut, shaped, or finished in this way **2.** *vt.* **USE MACHINE ON STH** to make or do sth using a machine [Mid-16thC. Via Old French from Latin *machina*, 'device, engine, contrivance' from, ultimately, Greek *mēkhanē* (source of English *mechanic*), from Greek *mēkhos* 'contrivance, means'.] —**machinability** /mə shēēnə bílləti/ *n.* —**machinable** /mə shēēnəb'l/ *adj.* —**machineless** /mə shēēnləss/ *adj.* —**machine-like** *adj.*

machine bolt *n.* a bolt with a square or hexagonal head, usually of heavy duty construction for use in aircraft and automobiles

machine code *n.* = **machine language**

machine finish *n.* = **mill finish**

machine gun *n.* an automatic weapon that fires rapidly and repeatedly without requiring separate squeezes on the trigger each time

machine-gun *vt.* (**machine-guns, machine-gunning, machine-gunned**) **1. SHOOT SB WITH MACHINE GUN** to shoot or kill sb with a machine gun, or to fire a machine gun at sb or sth **2. ADDRESS SB RAPIDLY** to speak rapidly to sb (*informal*) ■ *adj.* **STACCATO** rapid, abrupt, and staccato in delivery —**machine-gunner** *n.*

machine language *n.* instructions, usually written in binary code, telling a computer how to process data

machine pistol *n.* a light automatic or semi-automatic submachine gun that can be discharged using only one hand

machine-readable *adj.* in a form that is able to be used directly by a computer

machinery /mə shēēnəri/ *n.* **1. MECH ENG MECHANICAL PARTS** the aggregate parts that make up a machine or group of machines **2. MECH ENG MACHINES** machines collectively or in general **3. SYSTEM OF MACHINES** a system of machines working together **4. SET OF PROCEDURES** an interconnected series of processes that works like a mechanical system to produce a particular result **5. LITERARY DEVICES** literary devices used for effect, especially in poetry, or to resolve the plot of a play or book

machine screw *n.* a slotted or hexagonal-headed screw with a standardized thread used to connect machine parts together

machine shop *n.* a workshop where various materials, especially metals, are cut, shaped and worked, often to tight specifications using machine tools

machine tool *n.* a machine such as a lathe or grinder, used for shaping and finishing metals and other solid materials —**machine-tooled** *adj.*

machine translation *n.* the translation of text from one language to another by computer

machine-wash (**machine-washes, machine-washing, machine-washed**) *vt.* to wash sth in a washing machine

machine-washable *adj.* able to be washed in a washing machine without being damaged

machinist /mə shēēnist/ *n.* **1. SB WHO MACHINES STH** sb whose job involves machining sth or operating a machine or machine tool, especially in a factory **2. MACHINE MAKER OR REPAIRER** sb who makes or repairs machines **3. THEATRE OPERATOR OF MECHANICAL STAGE EFFECTS** sb who is in charge of the machinery used to create theatrical effects (*archaic*)

machismo /mə chízmō/ *n.* an exaggerated sense or display of masculinity, emphasizing characteristics that are conventionally regarded as typically male, usually physical strength and courage, aggressiveness, and lack of emotional response [Mid-

20thC. From Mexican Spanish, formed from *macho* (see MACHO).]

Machmeter /maak meetər, mák-/ *n.* an instrument for measuring the Mach number of an aircraft

Mach number *n.* the speed of an object relative to the speed of sound. An aircraft travelling at twice the speed of sound has a Mach number of 2. [Early 20thC. Named after Ernst MACH, because of his work in aerodynamics.]

macho /máchō/ *adj.* **STEREOTYPICALLY MASCULINE** having or showing characteristics conventionally regarded as typically male, especially physical strength and courage, aggressiveness, and lack of emotional response ■ *n.* (*plural* **-chos**) **STEREOTYPICALLY MASCULINE MALE** a male who displays conventionally typical masculine characteristics [Early 20thC. From Mexican Spanish *macho* 'male plant or animal, masculine, vigorous' from Spanish 'male, masculine', from Latin *masculus* (source of English *masculine* and *male*).] —**machoism** *n.*

machree /mə kreé/ *interj. Ireland* used as an endearment [Early 19thC. From Irish *mo chroidhe* 'of my heart'.]

Barnaby's

Machu Picchu

Machu Picchu /maachoo pichoo/ *n.* the ruins of a large ancient Inca city in the Andes in southern Peru, discovered in 1911. It is well known for its architecture and system of terraces.

machzor /maak záwr, maakh záwr/ (*plural* **-zorim** /maakh záwrim, maàakh zaw reém/), **mahzor** (*plural* **-zorim** *or* **-zors**) *n.* a Jewish prayer book that details the rituals prescribed for festivals and holidays [Mid-19thC. From Hebrew *mahzōr*.]

macintosh *n.* = **mackintosh**

mack *n.* = **mac**

Mackellar /mə kéllər/, **Dorothea** (1885–1968) Australian poet. She was author of *My Country* (1908). Full name **Isobel Marion Dorothea Mackellar**

Mackenzie /mə kénzi/ river in the Northwest Territories, Canada. Its main stream originates in Great Slave Lake. Length: 1,705 km/1,060 mi.

Mackenzie, Sir Compton (1883–1972) British novelist and playwright. He was author of many works including *Carnival* (1912) and *Whisky Galore* (1947). During World War I, he served in the intelligence service. Full name **Sir Edward Montague Compton Mackenzie**

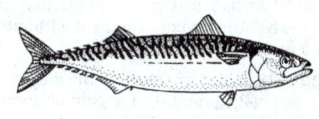

Mackerel

mackerel /mákrəl/ (*plural* **-els** *or* **-el**) *n.* **1. OILY FOOD FISH OF NORTHERN ATLANTIC** a bony oily food fish of northern Atlantic coastal waters that has a greenish-blue body with dark blue bars and a forked tail. Latin name: *Scomber scombrus*. **2. RELATED FISH** any fish

that is related to the mackerel, e.g. the Spanish mackerel. Family: Scombridae. [13thC. From Anglo-Norman, of unknown origin.]

mackerel breeze *n.* a breeze strong enough to disturb the surface of the water

mackerel shark *n.* a large fierce shark with a pointed snout, related to the great white shark, mako shark, and porbeagle. Family: Lamnidae.

mackerel sky *n.* a sky covered with cirrocumulus or altocumulus clouds in a pattern that resembles the markings on a mackerel (*regional*)

Mackerras /mə kérrəss/, **Sir Charles** (b. 1925) US-born Australian conductor and musical director. He has been holder of various posts, notably in the United Kingdom. He is also an authority on Leos Janáček. Full name **Sir Alan Charles Mackerras**

Mackillop /mə kílləp/, **Mary Helen** (1842–1909) Australian nun. She founded the Sisters of St Joseph of the Sacred Heart in 1866. She was canonized, making her Australia's first saint. Known as **Mother Mary of the Cross**

mackinaw /máki naw/ *n. US, Can* **1. HEAVY WOOLLEN FABRIC** a thick heavy woollen cloth, usually with a plaid design **2. SHORT HEAVY COAT** a short double-breasted coat made from mackinaw or a similar fabric [Early 19thC. Named after the fort, once an important trading post, which once stood on the site of Mackinaw City, northern Michigan, USA.]

Mackinder /mə kíndər/, **Sir Halford John** (1861–1947) British geographer and politician. He established geography as an academic discipline and in 1919 expounded the geopolitical idea of the Eurasian heartland.

Mackinnon /mə kínnən/, **Catherine** (b. 1946) US legal scholar. A pioneer in changing the legal attitude towards sex discrimination, she wrote the influential *Sexual Harassment of Working Women* (1979).

mackintosh /mákin tosh/, **macintosh** *n.* **1. RAINCOAT** a waterproof coat worn for protection against the rain, originally one made from rubberized fabric (*dated*) **2. WATERPROOF FABRIC** a waterproof fabric, especially rubberized cotton [Mid-19thC. Named after the Scottish inventor Charles *Macintosh* (1766–1843), who patented a waterproof rubberized cloth.]

AKG London

Charles Rennie Mackintosh

Mackintosh /mákin tosh/, **Charles Rennie** (1868–1928) British architect and interior designer. Noted for his art nouveau designs, he worked primarily on buildings and interiors in and around Glasgow.

mackle /mák'l/ *n.* **PRINTING ERROR** a blurred or double impression caused by the movement of paper or type during the printing process ■ *vti.* **BLUR IMAGE** to cause a printed impression to blur, or to appear blurred [Late 16thC. Either directly or via French from Latin *macula* 'spot, stain'.]

MacLaine /mə kláyn/, **Shirley** (b. 1934) US film actress. Sister of Warren Beatty, she has appeared in many films, including *Terms of Endearment* (1983), and has worked in television. Real name **Shirley MacLean Beatty**

Maclaurin /mə kláwrin/, **Richard Cockburn** (1870–1920) Scottish-born New Zealand academic. A professor of mathematics and law, he was the president of the Massachusetts Institute of Technology (MIT) (1909–20).

macle /mák'l/ n. **1.** MINERALS = **chiastolite 2.** CRYSTALS TWINNED CRYSTAL a crystal that is twinned **3.** DISCOLOURED SPOT IN CRYSTAL a discoloured spot within a crystal [Early 19thC. Via French from Latin *macula* 'spot, mesh'.]

Maclean /mə kláyn/, **Alistair** (1922–87) British novelist. Many of his adventure stories, set in different parts of the world, were made into films.

Maclean /mə kláyn/, **Donald Duart** (1913–83) British spy. He worked for the KGB while holding posts in the foreign office. He defected to Russia in 1951.

Macleod /mə klówd/, **John James Rickard** (1876–1935) British physiologist. He discovered insulin with Sir Frederick Grant Banting and Charles Best, for which he shared the Nobel Prize.

Harold Macmillan

Macmillan /mək míllən/, **Harold, 1st Earl of Stockton** (1894–1986) British statesman. He became prime minister of the United Kingdom (1957–63). His two successful terms of office were marred by the John Profumo scandal (1963). Full name **Maurice Harold Macmillan**

MacMillan /mək míllən/, **Sir Kenneth** (1929–92) British choreographer. He was the holder of various posts in Europe and the United States, including the directorship of the Royal Ballet (1970–77).

MacNaughten Rules /mək náwt'n-/, **MacNaghten Rules** npl. in English law, judges' rules determining the conditions on which a defendant may escape conviction on the grounds of legal insanity [Late 19thC. Named after Daniel M'Naughten, who was acquitted of murder in 1843. The rules were drawn up as a result of the House of Lords' decision on his case.]

MacNeice /mək neéss/, **Louis** (1907–63) British poet and playwright. His poetry, incorporating assonance and internal rhyme, shows great technical skill. He also wrote documentaries and plays for radio, notably *The Dark Tower* (1947).

macon /maá koN, má k-/, **Macon, Mâcon** n. a red or white wine from the Mâcon area in central France

Macon /máykən/ city in central Georgia. It is the seat of Bibb county. Population: 109,191 (1994).

Mâcon /máykən/ capital of Saône-et-Loire Department, in Burgundy, east-central France. Population: 106,612 (1990).

Macquarie, Lake /mə kwórri/ coastal lake in New South Wales, Australia. It is bordered by residential areas as well as centres of energy production and tourism. Area: 110 sq. km/43 sq. mi.

Macquarie, Lachlan (1762–1824) Australian colonial administrator. As governor of New South Wales (1810–21), he turned the settlement into a prosperous colony and was noted for his progressive attitude towards convict rehabilitation.

Macquarie Harbour large natural harbour in western Tasmania, Australia. Area: 285 sq. km/110 sq. mi.

Macquarie Island uninhabited Australian island located in the Southern Ocean, 1,300 km/835 mi. southeast of Tasmania. Area: 128 sq. km/50 sq. mi.

macr- prefix. = **macro-** (used before vowels)

macramé /mə kraámi, -may/ n. pieces of string or cord knotted together to form a coarse ornamental lacy pattern, or sth made using this method [Mid-19thC. Via Turkish *makrama* 'towel, handkerchief, tablecloth', from

Arabic *mikrama* 'bed cover'. Macramé work was first mainly used to make fringes on items such as towels.]

Macready /mə kreédi/, **William Charles** (1793–1873) British actor. A leading actor of his day, he was noted for his stage theory and productions of Shakespearean tragedies.

macro /mákrō/ (plural **-ros**) n. a single computer instruction that initiates a series of additional instructions for a computer to perform [Mid-20thC. From MACRO-.]

macro- prefix. **1.** large, inclusive ◦ *macrocyte* ◦ *macroclimate* **2.** long ◦ *macrobiotics* [From Greek *makros*. Ultimately from an Indo-European base meaning 'long, thin', which is also the ancestor of English *meager* and *emaciate*.]

macrobiotics /mákrō bī óttiks/ n. a vegan diet of seeds, grains, and organically grown fruit and vegetables, said to prolong life and balance the body's systems by adjusting the amount and kind of food eaten (takes a singular verb) [Late 18thC. From Greek *makrobiotos*, literally 'long life'.] —**macrobiotic** adj.

macrocarpa /mákrō kaárpə/ n. a large evergreen tree native to New Zealand that is used as a windbreak on farms. Latin name: *Cupressus macrocarpa*. [Early 20thC. From modern Latin, formed from Grek *makro-* (see MACRO-) + *karpos* 'fruit'.]

macrocephaly /mákrō séffəli/, **macrocephalia** /mákrō sə fáyli ə/ n. the condition of having a head that is excessively large [Mid-19thC. Formed from MACRO and -CEPHALY.] —**macrocephalic** /mákrō si fállik/ adj. —**macrocephalous** /-séffələss/ adj.

macroclimate /mákrō klímət/ n. the general climate of a large region such as a continent —**macroclimatic** /mákrō klī máttik/ adj. —**macroclimatically** /-máttikli/ adv.

macrocosm /mákrō kozəm/ n. a complex structure such as the world or the universe considered as a single entity that contains numerous similar smaller-scale structures [Early 17thC. From medieval Latin *macrocosmus*, from Greek *makro-* (see MACRO-) + *kosmos* 'world'.] —**macrocosmic** /mákrō kózmik/ adj. —**macrocosmically** /-kózmikli/ adv.

macrocyte /mákrō sīt/ n. an unusually large red blood cell that commonly occurs in cases of anaemia [Late 19thC. Coined from MACRO- + -CYTE.] —**macrocytic** /mákrō síttik/ adj.

macrocytosis /mákrō sī tóssiss/ n. the presence of abnormally large red cells in the blood —**macrocytotic** /-sī tóttik/ adj.

macroeconomics /mákrō eekə nómmiks, -ekə-/ n. a branch of economics that focuses on the general features and processes that make up a national economy and the ways in which different segments of the economy are connected (takes a singular verb) —**macroeconomic** adj. —**macroeconomist** /mákrō i kónnəmist/ n.

macroeconomy /mákrō ikónnəmi/ n. the economy viewed as a whole and in terms of all those factors that control its overall performance ◦ *Employment rates did not respond to the macroeconomy as expected.* [Combination of MACRO + ECONOMY]

macroevolution /mákrō eévə loósh'n/ n. evolution theorized to occur over a long period of time, producing major changes in species and other taxonomic groups —**macroevolutionary** adj.

macrofossil /mákrō foss'l/ n. a fossil that is large enough to be observed or examined without the aid of a microscope

macrogamete /mákrō gámmeet/ n. the larger, usually female sex cell (**gamete**) in a pair of conjugating cells of a heterogamous species

macroglobulin /mákrō glóbbyoolin/ n. **1.** SOLUBLE PROTEIN WITH HIGH MOLECULAR WEIGHT a soluble protein in the blood with a high molecular weight, typically seen in some diseases **2.** SOLUBLE PROTEIN WITH NORMAL MOLECULAR WEIGHT a soluble protein in the blood with a normal molecular weight

macroglobulinaemia /mákrō glóbbyooli neémi ə/ n. a condition marked by an increase of macroglobulins in the blood

macroglobulinemia n. US = **macroglobulinaemia**

macrograph /mákrō graaf, -graf/ n. a drawing, photograph, or other representation in which sth appears at its actual size or larger [Late 19thC. Coined from MACRO- + -GRAPH.] —**macrographic** /mákrō gráffik/ adj. —**macrography** /ma króggrəfi/ n.

macroinstruction /mákrō in strúksh'n/ n. COMPUT = **macro**

macro lens n. a lens used for close-up photography that produces a life-size or larger image on film, with a minimum of 1:1 object-to-image ratio

macromere /mákrō meer/ n. a large yolk-filled cell formed from the unequal splitting of a fertilized egg [Late 19thC. Coined from MACRO- + BLASTOMERE.]

macromolecule /mákrō mólli kyool/ n. a large molecule, e.g. that of a protein or polymer, made up of smaller elements connected to one another —**macromolecular** /mákrō mə lékyoolər/ adj.

macron /mák ron/ n. **1.** PHON MARK INDICATING LONG SOUND a short horizontal line placed over a vowel sound to indicate that it is long or stressed. Macrons are used in some languages, some phonetic transcription systems, and in the study or analysis of poetic metre. **2.** POETRY LONG OR STRESSED SYLLABLE a stressed syllable in a foot of verse, marked with a macron [Mid-19thC. From Greek literally 'long thing', from *makros* 'long'.]

macronucleus /mákrō nyoókli əss/ (plural **-i** /-kli ī/) n. the larger of two nuclei in most ciliate protozoans, involved in nonreproductive functions such as feeding and metabolism —**macronuclear** adj.

macronutrient /mákrō nyoótri ənt/ n. a chemical element, e.g. nitrogen, carbon, or potassium, needed in large amounts by plants for normal growth and development

macrophage /mákrō fayj/ n. a large cell that is present in blood, lymph, and connective tissues, removing waste products, harmful micro-organisms, and foreign material from the bloodstream [Late 19thC. Coined from MACRO +-PHAGE.] —**macrophagic** /mákrō fájjik/ adj.

macrophotography /mákrō fə tóggrəfi/ n. close-up photography that produces images on the film that are life-size or larger than life

macrophysics /mákrō físsiks/ n. a branch of physics that studies systems and objects large enough to be easily observed (takes a singular verb)

macrophyte /mákrō fīt/ n. a plant large enough to be studied and observed using the unaided eye, especially an aquatic plant [Early 20thC. Coined from MACRO- + -PHYTE.] —**macrophytic** /mákrō fíttik/ adj.

macropsia /mə krópsi ə/ n. a condition in which everything perceived by the eye appears to be larger than it really is, often as a result of a retinal disease or a brain disorder [Late 19thC. Coined from MACRO- + Greek *opsia* 'seeing'.]

macroscopic /mákrō skóppik/, **macroscopical** /-skóppik'l/ adj. **1.** VISIBLE TO NAKED EYE large enough to be seen and examined without the aid of magnifying equipment **2.** COMPREHENSIVE relating to or concerned with large units [Late 19thC. From MACRO-, modelled on MICROSCOPIC.] —**macroscopically** adv.

macroscopic anatomy n. = **gross anatomy**

macrosociology /mákrō sóssi óllǝji/ n. the branch of sociology concerned with the study and analysis of societies in their entirety —**macrosociological** /-sóssi ə lójjik'l/ adj.

macrosporangium /mákrōspə ránji əm/ (plural **-a** /-ji ə/) n. BIOL = **megasporangium** [Late 19thC. From modern Latin, formed from MACRO- + Greek *spora* 'spore' + *aggeion* 'vessel'.]

macrospore /mákrō spawr/ n. BIOL = **megaspore**

macrostructure /mákrō strukchər/ n. a structure, e.g. that of a metal, large enough to be seen or examined with little or no magnification —**macrostructural** /mákrō strúkchərəl/ adj.

macula /mákyoolə/ (plural **-lae** /-lee/) n. **1.** PHYSIOL SMALL SPOT ON SKIN a small pigmented spot on the skin that is neither raised nor depressed **2.** OPHTHALMOL YELLOW SPOT NEAR RETINA a small yellowish spot in the middle of the retina that provides the greatest visual acuity and colour perception **3.** ASTRON SUNSPOT a sunspot (*technical*) [14thC. From Latin, 'spot, stain'.] —**macular** *adj.*

macula lutea /-lŏoti ə/ (*plural* **maculae luteae** /-ti ee/) *n.* = **macula** *n.* 2 ['Lutea' from Latin *luteus* 'yellow']

maculate /mákyŏŏ layt/ *vt.* (-**lates**, -**lating**, -**lated**) (*archaic or literary*) **1.** STAIN SB OR STH to mark sb or sth with a spot, blotch, or blemish **2.** MAKE SB OR STH IMPURE to defile or pollute sb or sth ■ *adj.* **maculate, maculated** (*archaic or literary*) **1.** STAINED marked with spots, blotches, or blemishes **2.** IMPURE defiled, polluted, or impure [15thC. From Latin *maculat-*, past participle stem of *maculare*, from *macula* 'spot'.]

maculation /mákyŏŏ láysh'n/ *n.* **1.** SPOTTED MARKINGS the pattern of spots on some animals and plants **2.** STAINING OR BEING STAINED the act of marking sth with a spot, blotch, or blemish, or the state of being marked in this way (*archaic or literary*)

macule[1] /mákyool/ *n.* = **macula** *n.* 1 [Mid-19thC. Either directly or via French from Latin *macula* 'spot, stain'.]

macule[2] /mákyool/ *n.* PRINTING = **mackle**

mad /mad/ *adj.* (**madder, maddest**) **1.** VERY ANGRY affected by great displeasure or anger **2.** OFFENSIVE TERM an offensive term meaning affected with psychiatric disorder (*offensive*) **3.** VERY UNWISE OR RASH lacking common sense and not reasoning logically (*insult*) (*offensive in some contexts*) **4.** WILDLY EXCITED completely unrestrained and out of control (*offensive in some contexts*) **5.** FRANTIC done with great haste, excitement, or confusion (*offensive in some contexts*) **6.** EXCITING very exciting or boisterous (*offensive in some contexts*) **7.** SEIZED BY UNCONTROLLABLE EMOTION overcome with a violent emotion (*offensive in some contexts*) **8.** PASSIONATE ABOUT STH very fond of, enthusiastic about, or interested in sth, often to the exclusion of everything else (*often used in combination; offensive in some contexts*) ○ *football mad* **9.** ABNORMALLY AGGRESSIVE used to describe an animal that is abnormally aggressive or ferocious (*disapproving; offensive in some contexts*) **10.** RABID having rabies ■ *adv.* UK EXTREMELY used for emphasis (*informal*) ○ *She's not mad keen on the idea.* [Old English *gemǣd* 'deprived of reason', that was formed from *gemād* 'irrational', from, ultimately, an Indo-European ancestor meaning 'change' (source of English *mutate*)] —**maddish** *adj.* ◇ **like mad** with great speed or energy (*offensive in some contexts*)

MAD /mad/ *abbr.* **1.** PSYCHIAT major affective disorder **2.** *US* MIL mutual assured destruction

Madag. *abbr.* Madagascar

Madagascar

Madagascar /máddə gáskər/ island republic separated from southeastern mainland Africa by the Mozambique Channel. Language: Malagasy, French. Currency: Malagasy franc. Capital: Antananarivo. Population: 13,671,000 (1996). Area: 587,041 sq. km/226,658 sq. mi. Official name **Democratic Republic of Madagascar**. Former name **Malagasy Republic** —**Madagascan** *adj., n.*

Madagascar aquamarine *n.* a type of blue beryl found in Madagascar, used as a gemstone

Madagascar periwinkle *n.* a perennial plant of India and Madagascar that is poisonous to domestic animals. It has white or pink flowers and produces various substances used to treat cancer. Latin name: *Catharanthus roseus.*

madam /máddəm/ *n.* **1.** (*plural* **mesdames**) USED TO ADDRESS A WOMAN a polite term of address for a woman, especially a customer in a shop, restaurant, or hotel (*formal*) **2.** WOMAN RUNNING A BROTHEL a woman who manages a brothel **3.** PRECOCIOUS GIRL a petulant or self-willed girl who expects everybody to do as she says (*informal disapproving*) [13thC. From Old French *ma dame* 'my lady', from, ultimately, Latin *mea domina* (source of English *Madonna*).]

Madam /máddəm/ *n.* (*plural* **Mesdames** /máy dam/ or **Madams**) *n.* **1.** USED TO ADDRESS WOMAN IN LETTER used at the beginning of a formal letter to a woman, especially one whose name is not known (*formal*) **2.** USED TO ADDRESS WOMAN OFFICIAL used before the name of a woman's official position as a term of address ○ *Madam President*

Madame /máddəm/ *n.* (*plural* **Mesdames** /máy dam/), **madame** (*plural* **mesdames**) *n.* the title of a Frenchwoman or French-speaking woman, especially if married, used before her name or as a polite term of address

—— **WORD KEY: CULTURAL NOTE** ——
Madame Bovary, a novel by French writer Gustave Flaubert (1857). It tells the story of Emma Bovary, a young married woman who seeks refuge from the mundanity of her provincial life in a series of reckless affairs. The novel's frank depiction of middle-class society and its almost scientific analysis of human behaviour made it a pioneering work of modern realism.

madcap /mád kap/ *adj.* acting or behaving without caring or stopping to think about possible consequences [Late 16thC. 'Cap' used to represent the head.] —**madcap** *n.*

mad cow disease *n.* VET = **BSE**

madden /mádd'n/ *n.* (-**dens**, -**dening**, -**dened**) *vti.* **1.** MAKE OR BECOME ANGRY to make a person or animal extremely angry, or to become extremely angry (*usually passive*) **2.** MAKE OR BECOME IRRATIONAL OR FURIOUS to make sb irrational or furious, or to become irrational or furious

maddening /mádd'ning/ *adj.* **1.** CAUSING ANGER causing anger, impatience, or frustration **2.** CAUSING INTENSE ANNOYANCE AND DISTRESS causing intense annoyance and distress —**maddeningly** *adv.* —**maddeningness** *n.*

madder[1] comparative of **mad**

madder[2] /máddər/ *n.* **1.** HERB WITH RED ROOT a perennial Eurasian herb that has open clusters of small yellow flowers and a red fleshy root. Latin name: *Rubia tinctorum.* **2.** ROOT YIELDING DYE the root of the madder plant, formerly used for obtaining a red dye by fermentation **3.** RED DYE a red dye formerly obtained from the root of the madder plant **4.** RED PIGMENT a red pigment obtained from alizarin, used in dyes, inks, and paints **5.** COLOURS REDDISH-PURPLE a deep reddish-purple colour ■ *adj.* COLOURS OF REDDISH-PURPLE deep reddish-purple in colour [Old English *mædere*, ultimately from a prehistoric Germanic word]

maddest /máddəst/ superlative of **mad**

madding /mádding/ *adj.* acting in a way that suggests or reveals the presence of a psychiatric disorder (*archaic*)

—— **WORD KEY: CULTURAL NOTE** ——
Far from the Madding Crowd, a novel by Thomas Hardy (1874). The first of Thomas Hardy's *Wessex Novels*, it is the story of a capricious, forceful young woman, Bathsheba Everdene, and her attempts to improve her social position through marriage. It was made into a film by John Schlesinger in 1967.

mad-dog skullcap *n.* a North American perennial plant that has clusters of two-lipped blue or white flowers and is used as an antispasmodic. Latin name: *Scutellaria lateriflora.*

made *v.* **1.** past tense of **make 2.** past participle of **make** ■ *adj.* **1.** ARTIFICIALLY PRODUCED produced by artificial means **2.** SUCCESSFUL certain of achieving success ◇ **have it made** to be in a position to succeed at sth without obstacles or serious problems (*informal*)

Madeira /mə deérə/ *n.* a sweet or dry wine fortified with brandy, made on the island of Madeira and usually served as a dessert wine or after a meal

Madeira cake *n.* a fine-textured plain cake, similar to a creamed sponge cake, made with fat, butter, and flour and served without filling or icing

Madeira Islands /mə deérə/ group of islands with many resorts in the eastern North Atlantic Ocean. Population: 256,000 (1992). Area: 741 sq. km/286 sq. mi.

Madeira vine *n.* a tropical South American ornamental vine with small fragrant flowers. Latin name: *Anredera cordifolia.*

madeleine /mádd'lin, máddə layn/ *n.* **1.** SMALL PLAIN SPONGE CAKE a small light whisked sponge cake baked in an individual shell-shaped tin **2.** SPONGE CAKE WITH JAM AND COCONUT a sponge cake that is cooked in a small cup-shaped mould, coated in raspberry jam, rolled in desiccated coconut, and topped with a glacé cherry [Mid-19thC. Probably named after the 19th-century French pastry cook Madeleine Paulmier.]

mademoiselle /máddəmwə zél/ (*plural* **mesdemoiselles** /máydə-/ or **mademoiselles**) *n.* **1.** **Mademoiselle, mademoiselle** TITLE OF FRENCHWOMAN the title of a French woman or French-speaking young or unmarried woman, used before her name or as a polite term of address (*sometimes considered offensive*) **2.** FRENCHWOMAN a young Frenchwoman or French-speaking woman **3.** WOMAN FRENCH TEACHER a woman French teacher or French governess (*dated*) **4.** ZOOL = **silver perch** [15thC. From Old French *ma demoiselle* 'my damsel'.]

made-to-measure *adj.* made by a tailor to fit a particular person

made-to-order *adj.* **1.** *US* CUSTOM-MADE made in accordance with a customer's specifications or requirements **2.** PERFECTLY SUITABLE perfectly suitable or exactly as required

made-up *adj.* **1.** UNTRUE lacking any basis in fact or reality **2.** WEARING COSMETICS having applied cosmetics to the face **3.** ASSEMBLED completely put together and prepared

madhouse /mád howss/ (*plural* -**houses** /-howziz/) *n.* **1.** OFFENSIVE TERM an offensive term for hospital or residential facility for people who have psychiatric disorders (*offensive*) **2.** SCENE OF CHAOS OR CONFUSION a place where there is much noise and activity and little order or control (*informal; sometimes considered offensive*)

Madison /máddissən/ **1.** capital city of Wisconsin, situated in the south-central part of the state. Population: 194,586 (1994). **2.** town in southern Connecticut. Population: 15,485 (1990). **3.** city in northern New Jersey. Population: 15,763 (1994).

James Madison

Madison, James (1751–1836) US statesman and fourth president of the United States. He played a leading role in the Constitutional Convention (1787), and enjoyed two terms as president (1809–17).

Madison Avenue /máddiss'n-/ *n.* the centre of the US advertising and public-relations industries, or the US advertising industry itself [Named after the street in New York that is the centre of the advertising industry]

madly /máddli/ *adv.* **1.** WILDLY in a wild and uncontrolled way **2.** TO NO PURPOSE with great haste or activity but without accomplishing much **3.** RASHLY in a rash or thoughtless way **4.** WILDLY wildly and with intense emotion **5.** WITH SIGNS OF MENTAL DISTRESS like sb who is affected by a psychiatric disorder **6.** INTENSELY with an extraordinary degree of intensity or devotion

madman /mádmən/ (*plural* -**men** /-mən/) *n.* an offensive term for a man with a psychiatric disorder (*offensive*)

madness /mádnəss/ *n.* **1. OFFENSIVE TERM** offensive term for psychiatric disorder (*offensive*) **2. RASHNESS** rash or thoughtless behaviour **3. ANGER** great anger or fury **4. EXCITEMENT** great enthusiasm or excitement

Madonna: Byzantine mosaic, Athens, Greece

Madonna /mə dónnə/ *n.* **1. VIRGIN MARY** the Virgin Mary, mother of Jesus Christ **2. Madonna, madonna IMAGE OF VIRGIN MARY** a picture, statue, or other artistic representation of the Virgin Mary [Late 16thC. From obsolete Italian *ma donna* 'my lady' from Latin *mea domina* (source of Madam).]

Madonna

Madonna /mə dónnə/ (*b.* 1959) US pop singer and actor. Her career, which started in the early 1980s, shows an ability to change her style and image ahead of current trends. Full name **Madonna Louise Veronica Ciccone**

Madonna lily *n.* an eastern Mediterranean plant widely cultivated for its white trumpet-shaped flowers that produce an oil used in the making of perfume. Latin name: *Lilium candidum.* [Traditionally regarded as a symbol of purity, and often included in pictures of the Madonna]

madras /mə drááss, -dráss/ *n.* **1. STRONG FINE CLOTH** a strong fine fabric of cotton or silk, often with a woven striped or checked design **2. LIGHT CLOTH** a light cotton or rayon fabric used to make curtains **3. BRIGHTLY COLOURED SCARF** a scarf, handkerchief, or other article made from brightly coloured cotton or silk **4. FAIRLY HOT CURRY** a fairly hot curried dish made with meat, spices, chillies, and lentils [Late 19thC. Named after MADRAS in southeastern India, where the products were made.]

Madras /mə drááss/ former name for **Chennai**

madrasa /mə drássə/ *n.* a school for the study of Islamic religion and thought, especially the Koran [Mid-17thC. From Arabic, literally 'place to study'.]

madrepore /máddri pawr/ *n.* a reef-building coral that lives in tropical waters. Genus: *Madreporaria.* [Mid-18thC. Via French or modern Latin from Italian *madrepora,* from *madre* 'mother' and either *poro* 'pore, tufa' (from late Latin *porus* 'passageway, pore') or Latin *porus* 'calcerous stone' (from Greek *poros*).] —**madreporal** /máddri páwrəl/ *adj.* —**madreporian** *adj.* —**madreporic** *adj.* —**madreporitic** /-pə ríttik/ *adj.*

madreporite /máddri páw rīt/ *n.* a porous plate in an echinoderm that takes in water to the vascular system [Early 19thC. From MADREPORE.]

Madrid /mə dríd/ capital and largest city of Spain, located in the centre of the country. Population: 3,029,734 (1995).

madrigal /máddrig'l/ *n.* **1. MUSIC ENGLISH PART SONG** a song with parts for several usually unaccompanied voices that was popular in England in the 16th and 17th centuries **2. MUSIC MEDIEVAL ITALIAN SONG** a secular Italian song of the 13th and 14th centuries, written for two or three unaccompanied voices singing in harmony **3. POETRY LYRIC POEM** a short pastoral or love poem suitable for singing as a madrigal [Late 16thC. Via *Italian* from Latin *matricalis* literally 'of the mother', but used in late Latin to mean 'uncomplicated', from *matrix* (see MATRIX). A madrigal was originally a simple unaccompanied song or poem.] —**madrigalesque** /máddrigə lésk/ *adj.* —**madrigalian** /máddri gálli ən, -gáyli-/ *adj.* —**madrigalist** /máddri gə'list/ *n.*

madrilène /máddri lén, -láyn/, **madrilene** *n.* a clear soup flavoured with tomato, usually served cold [Early 20thC. Via French from Spanish *madrileño* 'of Madrid'.]

madroña /mə drónyə/, **madroño** /-nyō/ (*plural* **-ños**) *n.* a North American evergreen tree of the heath family, with smooth bark, shiny leathery leaves, white flowers, edible red berries, and wood often used to make furniture. Latin name: *Arbutus menziestii.* [Mid-19thC. From Spanish.]

mad tom *n.* a small North American freshwater catfish that has poisonous pectoral spines, a long adipose fin, and a rounded dorsal fin. It is common in the east central United States. Genus: *Noturus.* [Short for 'mad tom cat', since the fish inflicts nasty wounds with its poisonous spines]

Madura /mə doŏrə/ island in southwestern Indonesia, off the northeastern coast of Java. Population: 2,832,900 (1989). Area: 5,290 sq. km/2,042 sq. mi.

Madurai /mád yoŏrī/ historic city and pilgrimage centre in southern India. Population: 951,696 (1991).

maduro /mə doŏrō/ (*plural* **-ros**) *n.* a dark strong cigar [Late 19thC. From Spanish 'ripe, mature'.]

madwoman /mád woŏmən/ (*plural* **-en** /-wimin/) *n.* an offensive term for a woman with a psychiatric disorder (*offensive*)

madwort /mád wurt/ (*plural* **-worts** *or* **-wort**) *n.* a low-growing Eurasian herb of the borage family that has small blue flowers. Latin name: *Asperugo procumbens.* [Late 16thC. A translation of the modern Latin ALYSSUM 'removing rabies' because the plant was believed to cure the bites of rabid dogs.]

Maecenas /mī seé nass/ (*plural* **-nas**) *n.* a rich patron of the arts (*literary*)

Maecenas /mī seén ass, mee-/, **Gaius** (74?–8 BC) Roman statesman. He was an adviser to Augustus and generous patron of artists and writers, notably Horace and Virgil.

maelstrom /máyl strom/ *n.* **1. WHIRLPOOL** an exceptionally large or violent whirlpool **2. TURBULENT OR VIOLENT SITUATION** a situation marked by confusion, turbulence, strong feelings, violence, or destruction [Late 17thC. From early modern Dutch, formed from *maalen* 'to grind, whirl round' + *stroom* 'stream'.]

Maelstrom /máyl strəm/ marine whirlpool in northwestern Norway between two islands of the Lofoten Islands

maenad /meé nad/ *n.* **1. WOMAN MEMBER OF DIONYSIAN CULT** in ancient Greece, a woman who belonged to the cult of Dionysus and took part in orgiastic rites **2. WILDLY EXCITED WOMAN** a woman affected by wild, uncontrollable emotion [Late 16thC. Via Latin from Greek *Mainad-,* stem of *Mainas,* from *mainesthai* 'to rave'.] —**maenadic** /mee náddik/ *adj.* —**maenadically** /-náddikli/ *adv.* —**maenadism** /mee nadizəm/ *n.*

maestoso /mī stóssō/ *adv.* **AT STATELY TEMPO** in a dignified or majestic manner (*used as a musical direction*) ■ *n.* (*plural* **-sos**) **MAESTOSO PIECE OF MUSIC** a section of a piece of music played maestoso [Early 18thC. Via Italian, literally 'majestic', ultimately from Latin *majestas* 'majesty' (see MAJESTY).] —**maestoso** *adj.*

maestro /mIstrō/ (*plural* **-tros** *or* **-tri** /mIstri/) *n.* sb who is regarded as an expert in an art or skill, especially a skilled or distinguished musician, conductor, composer, or music teacher [Early 18thC. Via Italian,

literally 'master', from Latin *magister* (source of English *magistrate*).]

maestro di cappella /-di kə péllə/ (*plural* **maestri di cappella** /mīstri-/) *n.* formerly, sb in charge of a group of musicians, especially a chapel choir or the private orchestra of a royal court or noble household, especially in 17th-century Italy ['di capella' Italian 'of the chapel'.]

Maeterlinck /máytərlingk/, **Count Maurice Polydore Marie Bernard** (1862–1949) Belgian poet and playwright. He was an exponent of symbolism, exemplified by his play *Pelléas and Mélisande* (1892) and a volume of poetry, *Hothouses* (1889).

Mae West /máy wést/, **mae west** *n.* (*informal*) **1. INFLATABLE LIFE JACKET** an inflatable life jacket, especially one issued to US pilots during World War II **2. PARACHUTE MALFUNCTION** a parachute malfunction in which a suspension line goes over the top of the canopy, creating what appears to be a huge brassiere [Mid-20thC. So called because the shape of the inflated jacket reminded airmen of the large bosom of Mae WEST.]

MAFF /maf/ *n., abbr.* Ministry of Agriculture, Fisheries, and Food

mafficking /máffiking/ *n.* a boisterous and extravagant public celebration (*archaic*) [Early 20thC. A playful coinage based on MAFEKING, following the wild celebrations when news of the relief of the town, which had been beseiged during the Boer War, reached London in 1900 (see MAFIKENG).] —**maffick** *vi.* —**mafficker** *n.*

Mafia /máffi ə/ *n.* **1. CRIMINAL ORGANIZATION** a secret criminal organization originating in Sicily that spread to mainland Italy and the United States and is involved in international drug-dealing, racketeering, gambling, and prostitution **2. mafia, Mafia MUTUALLY SUPPORTIVE CLIQUE** a close-knit or influential group of people who work together and protect one another's interests or the interests of a particular person [Mid-19thC. From the Sicilian dialect of Italian, 'bragging, blustering, boldness' especially of the type shown by the Mafia.]

mafic /máffik/ *adj.* relating to or being a dark-coloured igneous group of minerals that have a high magnesium and iron content [Early 20thC. Coined from MAGNESIUM + FERRIC.]

Mafikeng /máffi keng/ town in north-central South Africa, formerly known as Mafeking. Population: 6,900 (1994).

Mafioso /máffi óssō, -ózō/ (*plural* **-si** /-ōsee, -ee/ *or* **-sos**), **mafioso** *n.* a member of the Mafia [Late 19thC. From Italian, formed from *mafia* (see MAFIA).]

mag /mag/ *n.* PUBL = **magazine** *n.* **1** (*informal*) [Early 19thC. Shortening.]

mag. *abbr.* **1.** PUBL magazine **2.** magnesium **3.** magnet **4.** magnetic **5.** magnetism **6.** magnitude **7.** magnum

magazine /mággə zeén/ *n.* **1.** PUBL **PERIODICAL PUBLICATION** a publication issued at regular intervals, usually weekly or monthly, containing articles, stories, photographs, advertisements, and other features, with a page size that is usually smaller than that of a newspaper but larger than that of a book **2.** BROADCAST, TV **PROGRAMME CONTAINING ASSORTED ITEMS** a television or radio programme made up of an assortment of short factual items, often of interest to a particular group of people **3.** ARMS **BULLET OR CARTRIDGE HOLDER** a detachable container for cartridges or bullets that can be quickly inserted or removed from a gun **4.** MIL **STOREHOUSE FOR MILITARY SUPPLIES** a structure on land or a part of a ship where weapons, ammunition, explosives, and other military equipment or supplies are stored **5.** ARMS **STOCK OF AMMUNITION** a stock of ammunition or other supplies kept in a storehouse **6.** PHOTOGRAPHY **SLIDE HOLDER** a container designed to hold a number of photographic slides and feed them automatically through a projector **7.** PHOTOGRAPHY **LIGHT-TIGHT FILM CONTAINER** a container that is used for loading film into a camera without exposing it to light **8.** SUPPLY DEVICE a device or container attached to a machine that holds or supplies necessary material [Late 16thC. Via French *magazin* from Italian *magazzino,* from Arabic *makzan* 'storehouse'. The sense 'periodical publication' developed by way of the idea of a storehouse of information.]

magdalen /mágdələn/, **magdalene** /mágdə leéni, mágdə leen/ n. (*literary*) **1.** FORMER PROSTITUTE a reformed prostitute **2.** PROSTITUTES' REFUGE OR REFORMATORY a refuge for reformed prostitutes or an institution where prostitutes are sent to be reformed [14thC. From *Mary Magdalen*, a reformed sinner, in the Bible.]

Magdalena /mágdə láynə/ major river of Colombia. It flows north from the Andes into the Caribbean Sea. Length: 1,540 km/960 mi.

Magdalene n. = **Mary Magdalene**

Magdeburg /mágdə burg/ capital of Madgeburg District, Saxony-Anhalt State, north-central Germany. Population: 269,500 (1994).

mage /mayj/ n. a magician or magus (*archaic*) [14thC. An anglicization of MAGUS.]

Magellan, Strait of /mə géllən-/ channel between the southernmost tip of the South American mainland and the island of Tierra del Fuego

Magellan /mə géllən/, **Ferdinand** (1480?–1521) Portuguese explorer. He was the first person to circumnavigate the earth, and the first European to cross the Pacific Ocean.

Magellanic Cloud /mággi lánnik-, májji-/ n. either of two small galaxies near the south celestial pole that are irregularly shaped and closest to the Milky Way [Early 17thC. Named after Ferdinand MAGELLAN, whose crew discovered them during the first voyage round the world.]

Magen David /máwgən dáyvid/, **Mogen Dovid** n. = **Star of David** [From Hebrew literally 'shield of David']

magenta /mə jéntə/ n. **1.** COLOURS PURPLISH-PINK a brilliant purplish-pink colour that, together with cyan and yellow, is one of the three primary colours used in printing and photographic processing **2.** CHEM = **fuchsin** ■ adj. COLOURS OF PURPLISH-PINK brilliant purplish-pink in colour [Mid-19thC. Named after Magenta in Northern Italy where a major battle was fought shortly before the discovery of the dye.]

maggid /máagid/ (*plural* -**gidim** /-dim/) n. a popular teacher travelling among the Ashkenazi Jewish communities of Eastern Europe [Late 19thC. From Hebrew maggīd 'narrator'.]

maggiore /ma jáw ray/ n. a section of a fugue or set of variations in the major mode that occurs especially after a section in a minor [Late 19thC. From Italian, 'major'.]

Maggiore, Lake /ma jáw ray/ lake that lies partly in the Ticino Canton, Switzerland, and partly in the Lombardy Region of northern Italy. Area: 212 sq. km/82 sq. mi.

maggot /mággət/ n. **1.** INSECT LARVA the worm-shaped larva of any of various members of the fly family, e.g. the housefly, found in decaying matter and used as bait in fishing **2.** FANCY a fanciful notion or idea (*archaic*) [14thC. Possibly from earlier maddock 'worm, maggot', ultimately from a prehistoric Germanic word.]

maggoty /mággəti/ (-**ier**, -**iest**) adj. **1.** FULL OF MAGGOTS full of or containing maggots **2.** DRUNK extremely intoxicated by alcohol (*slang*) **3.** Aus ANGRY extremely angry or irritated (*slang*)

Magha n. INDIAN RELIG in the Hindu calendar, the 11th month of the year, made up of 29 or 30 days and falling in approximately January to February [Late 20thC. From Hindi.]

Magherafelt /mákərə félt/ town in County Londonderry, Northern Ireland. Linen is made there. Population: 7,143 (1991).

Maghreb /múgrəb/, **Maghrib** loosely defined region in northwestern Africa, centred on Algeria, Morocco, and Tunisia

magi plural of **magus**

Magi /máy jī/ npl. in the Bible, the three wise men, known as Caspar, Melchior, and Balthazar, who came to Bethlehem from the east to celebrate the birth of Jesus Christ. (Matthew 2: 1–12). [Plural of MAGUS] —**Magian** /máyji ən/ adj., n. —**Magianism** /-ji ənizəm/ n.

magic /májjik/ n. **1.** SUPPOSED SUPERNATURAL POWER a supposed supernatural power that makes impossible things happen, or that gives sb control over the forces of nature. Magic is used in many cultures for healing, keeping away evil, seeking the truth, and for vengeful purposes. **2.** PRACTICE OF MAGIC the use of supposed supernatural power to make impossible things happen **3.** CONJURING TRICKS conjuring tricks and illusions that make apparently impossible things seem to happen, usually performed as entertainment **4.** INEXPLICABLE THINGS a special, mysterious, or inexplicable quality, talent, or skill ○ watched the dancer's feet work their magic ■ adj. **1.** OF OR FOR MAGIC relating to magic or used in the working of magic ○ a magic potion **2.** PARTICULARLY IMPORTANT particularly important or desirable ○ reach the magic figure of 100 points **3.** EXCELLENT very good or enjoyable (*informal*) ○ a great film and a magic dinner ■ vt. (-**ics**, -**icking**, -**icked**) SUBJECT STH TO MAGIC to make sb or sth seem to appear, disappear, change, or move by using magic [14thC. Via Old French magique from, ultimately, Greek magikē, which in turn was formed, ultimately, from magos (see MAGUS).] ◇ **like magic 1.** rapidly **2.** without obstacles or difficulties

---
WORD KEY: CULTURAL NOTE

The Magic Mountain, a novel by German writer Thomas Mann (1924). It describes young engineer Hans Castorp's lengthy stay in a Swiss TB clinic. The clinic is a microcosm of European society at the time of World War I, with a cosmopolitan group of patients reflecting a range of contemporary political, philosophical, and scientific viewpoints.

---

magical /májjik'l/ adj. **1.** APPARENTLY PRODUCED BY MAGIC made or created by or as if by magic **2.** WONDERFUL so beautiful or pleasing as to seem supernaturally created —**magically** adv.

magical realism n. = **magic realism**

magic bullet n. **1.** MIRACLE DRUG a drug that cures a serious disease with no undesirable side effects on the patient **2.** EASY SOLUTION a quick and easy solution for a difficult problem, or a means of accomplishing the impossible

magic carpet n. in fairy stories, a carpet that flies through the air and is used as a form of transportation

magic eye n. a tiny cathode-ray tube used in a radio receiver to help tuning

magician /mə jísh'n/ n. **1.** CONJURER OR ILLUSIONIST an entertainer who performs conjuring tricks and illusions **2.** SB WHO SUPPOSEDLY PRACTISES SORCERY sb who uses supposed supernatural powers to perform magic **3.** SB WITH EXCEPTIONAL ABILITY sb who has extraordinary skill, power, or ability

Magic Marker tdmk. a trademark for a highlighting pen that comes in various colours of ink

magic mushroom n. a fungus that contains a hallucinogenic substance (*informal*)

magic number n. any of the numbers 2, 8, 20, 28, 50, 82, and 126 that represent the number of protons or neutrons in the nucleus of very stable atomic nuclei

magic realism, **magical realism** n. a style of art or literature that depicts fantastic or mythological subjects in a realistic manner —**magic realist** n.

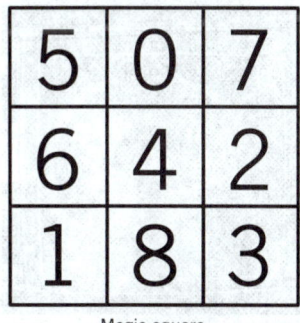

Magic square

magic square n. a square containing rows and columns of numbers arranged in such a way that each horizontal, vertical, and diagonal line has the same sum

magic wand n. **1.** STICK USED BY MAGICIAN a small thin stick used by a sorcerer or conjurer to perform magic **2.** STH ABLE TO WORK WONDERS sth fanciful or make-believe that would, if it existed, be able to solve a difficult or impossible problem immediately

Maginot line /mázhi nō-/ n. **1.** FORTIFIED FRANCO-GERMAN BORDER a line of fortifications constructed by the French along the border between France and Germany before World War II to stop the German army from invading **2.** INEFFECTIVE DEFENCE an ineffective defensive strategy that is relied on with unthinking confidence [Mid-20thC. Named after André Maginot (1877–1932) who was French Minister of War when it was built.]

magisterial /májji steéri əl/ adj. **1.** DIGNIFIED showing great authority and dignity **2.** DOMINEERING behaving in an overbearing or dictatorial way **3.** MASTERLY AND AUTHORITATIVE produced by or characteristic of a teacher, scholar, or expert **4.** OF MAGISTRATE relating to or characteristic of a magistrate [Early 17thC] —**magisterially** adv. —**magisterialness** n.

magisterium /májji steéri əm/ n. the authority of the church in the Roman Catholic tradition to teach religious doctrine [Late 16thC. From Latin, formed from magister 'master' (source of English magistrate).]

magistracy /májjistrəssi/ (*plural* -**cies**), **magistrature** /-strəchər/ n. **1.** OFFICE OF MAGISTRATE the position or function of a magistrate **2.** MAGISTRATE'S TERM OF OFFICE the term of office of a magistrate **3.** AREA OF MAGISTRATE'S JURISDICTION the district over which a magistrate has the power and authority to administer justice **4.** MAGISTRATES COLLECTIVELY magistrates considered as a group

magistral /májjistrəl/ adj. **1.** OF MAGISTRATE relating to or characteristic of a magistrate **2.** OF EXPERT relating to or characteristic of an expert or scholar **3.** PRINCIPAL OR DETERMINING used to describe a line of fortifications that determines the position of other lines ■ n. MAGISTRAL LINE OF FORTIFICATIONS a line of fortifications that determines the position of other lines —**magistrality** /májji strálləti/ n. —**magistrally** /májjistrəli/ adv.

magistrate /májji strayt, -strət/ n. **1.** LOWER COURT JUDGE a judge in a lower court whose jurisdiction is limited to the trial of misdemeanours and the conduct of preliminary hearings on more serious charges **2.** LOCAL LAW OFFICER a minor law officer or member of a local judiciary with extremely limited powers, e.g. a justice of the peace who deals with moving vehicular violations **3.** Aus JUDGE OF AUSTRALIAN LOWER COURT a judicial officer appointed by the executive government to hear civil and criminal cases in a court of summary jurisdiction [14thC. From Latin magistratus, formed in turn from magister 'master' (source of English mister and master).] —**magistrateship** n.

magistrates' court n. **1.** ENGLISH COURT FOR PRELIMINARY HEARINGS in England, a summary court presided over by a magistrate or two or more justices of the peace who make decisions about minor crimes, some civil actions, and preliminary hearings **2.** Aus AUSTRALIAN LOWER COURT a court of summary jurisdiction in the Australian states of Victoria and Queensland

maglev /mág lev/ n. an electrically operated high-speed train that glides above a track by means of a magnetic field (**magnetic levitation**) [Late 20thC. A blend of MAGNETIC and LEVITATION.]

magma /mágmə/ (*plural* -**mas** or -**mata** /-mətə/) n. **1.** GEOL MOLTEN ROCK molten rock deep within the earth from which igneous rock is formed by solidification at or near the earth's surface **2.** CHEM PASTE OR SUSPENSION a soft paste or thick suspension made from fine solid particles mixed with liquid [15thC. Via Latin from Greek, formed from massein 'to knead'; the underlying idea being of a mixture kneaded together.] —**magmatic** /mag máttik/ adj.

magma chamber n. an underground cavity that contains magma, often located below a volcano

Magna Carta /mágnə kaártə/, **Magna Charta** n. **1.** CHARTER SIGNED AT RUNNYMEDE charter establishing the rights of English barons and free citizens, granted by King John at Runnymede in 1215 and regarded as the basis of civil and political liberty in England **2.** DOCUMENT ACKNOWLEDGING RIGHTS a document that recognizes or guarantees rights, privileges, or liberties [From Latin literally 'great charter']

magna cum laude /mágnə kóom lów day, -di/ adv., adj. at the second of three levels of commendation for those who achieve excellent grades in coursework, especially graduates of North American universities and colleges that have honours programmes involving theses. ◊ **cum laude, summa cum laude** [From Latin, literally 'with great praise']

Magna Graecia /mágnə greéssi ə, -greéshə/ *n.* in ancient times, the parts of southern Italy and Sicily that contained numerous Greek colonies [From Latin, literally 'great Greece']

magnanimity /mágnə nímməti/ (*plural* **-ties**) *n.* **1.** NOBLE-SPIRITEDNESS great generosity or noble-spiritedness **2.** NOBLE-SPIRITED ACT a generous or noble-spirited act [14thC. Via French *magnanimité* from Latin *magnanimitas*, from *magnanimus* (see MAGNANIMOUS).]

magnanimous /mag nánniməss/ *adj.* very generous, kind, or forgiving [Late 16thC. From Latin *magnanimus*, formed from *magnus* 'great' and *animus* 'mind'.] —**magnanimously** *adv.* —**magnanimousness** *n.*

—————— **WORD KEY: SYNONYMS** ——————
See Synonyms at *generous*.

magnate /mág nayt, -nət/ *n.* **1.** SB RICH AND POWERFUL sb who has a lot of wealth and power, especially sb in business or industry **2.** SENIOR NOBLE a high-ranking member of the nobility [15thC. From late Latin *magnat-*, stem of *magnas*, from Latin *magnus* 'great'.] —**magnateship** *n.*

magnesia /mag neésha, -neézhə/ *n.* CHEM = **magnesium oxide** [14thC. Via medieval Latin from Greek *magnēsia* 'mineral from Magnesia' in Asia Minor (source of English *magnet*).] —**magnesial** *adj.* —**magnesian** *adj.* —**magnesic** /-neéssik/ *adj.*

magnesite /mágni sīt/ *n.* a white or colourless magnesium carbonate that occurs naturally and is used in making refractories and as a source of magnesium oxide [Early 19thC. From MAGNESIA.]

magnesium /mag neézi əm/ *n.* a light silver-white metallic element that occurs naturally in compounds and is used in alloys, metallurgy, photography, and fireworks. Symbol **Mg** [Early 19thC. From MAGNESIA.]

magnesium carbonate *n.* a white crystalline salt found naturally as dolomite and magnesite and used in antacids, glass, and refractories. Formula: $MgCO_3$.

magnesium hydroxide *n.* a white crystalline powder used as an antacid and laxative. Formula: $Mg(OH)_2$.

magnesium oxide *n.* a white powder found naturally as periclase and used as an antacid and laxative and in refractories, cements, electrical insulation, and fertilizers. Formula: MgO.

magnesium sulphate *n.* a colourless crystalline salt used in medicine, fertilizers, and various manufacturing processes. Formula: $MgSO_4$.

magnet /mágnət/ *n.* **1.** PIECE OF METAL THAT ATTRACTS METAL a piece of metal, often bar-shaped or U-shaped, that has the power to draw iron or steel objects towards it and to hold or move them **2.** ELECTROMAGNET an electromagnet **3.** SOURCE OF GREAT ATTRACTION sb or sth that has a great power of attraction over people [15thC. Directly or via Old French *magnete*, from Latin *magnes*, from Greek *Magnēs lithis* 'stone from Magnesia', an ancient city in Asia Minor at which magnetic stone was mined.]

magnetic /mag néttik/ *adj.* **1.** HAVING POWER OF MAGNET able to attract iron or steel objects **2.** ABLE TO BE MAGNETIZED able to be magnetized, or able to be attracted by a magnet **3.** RELATING TO MAGNETISM relating to, involving, or produced by magnetism **4.** USING MAGNET OR MAGNETISM containing or using a magnet or magnetism **5.** OF EARTH'S MAGNETISM relating to the Earth's magnetism **6.** POWERFULLY CHARMING having a great power of attraction over people ◊ *a magnetic personality* —**magnetically** *adv.*

magnetic bottle *n.* a strong magnetic field used to confine plasma in nuclear fusion experiments

magnetic bubble *n.* a small movable magnetic region in a thin film of magnetic material, used to store data in computer memory

magnetic compass *n.* an instrument used to indicate magnetic north and other directions, containing a magnetic needle that swings horizontally

around a circle marked in degrees or with the points of the compass

magnetic declination *n.* the angle between magnetic north and true north at a particular point on the Earth's surface

magnetic disk *n.* COMPUT a computer disk consisting of one or more thin magnetically etched plates

magnetic epoch *n.* a long period of geological time between reversals of the earth's magnetic field

magnetic equator *n.* an imaginary line that lies near the geographical equator and passes through all points where a magnetic needle has no dip

magnetic field *n.* a region of space surrounding a magnetized body or current-carrying circuit in which the resulting magnetic force can be detected

magnetic flux *n.* the strength of a magnetic field represented by lines of force. Symbol ϕ

magnetic flux density *n.* the strength of a magnetic field multiplied by the porosity of a medium, measured in teslas or gauss. Symbol B

magnetic head *n.* an electromagnetic device to read, write, or erase data on a magnetic medium

magnetic induction *n.* = **magnetic flux density**

magnetic levitation *n.* a system of high speed rail travel using magnetism both to suspend and to propel trains above and along the track. ◊ **maglev**

magnetic meridian *n.* an imaginary line around the Earth's surface that passes through both magnetic poles

magnetic mine *n.* an underwater mine equipped with magnetic sensors that cause it to detonate when a large metal object, usually a ship, passes into its magnetic field

magnetic mirror *n.* = **magnetic bottle**

magnetic moment *n.* a vector quantity representing the torque experienced by a magnetic system in a magnetic field. Symbol m

magnetic needle *n.* thin bar of magnetized metal used in navigational instruments, mounted or suspended so that it swings freely in a horizontal circle and indicates the direction of the Earth's magnetic poles

magnetic north *n.* the direction of the north magnetic pole, indicated by the needle of a magnetic compass

magnetic pole *n.* **1.** END OF A MAGNET either of the two points at the end of a magnet where the magnet's field is most intense **2.** REGION NEAR A GEOGRAPHIC POLE either of the two regions on the Earth's surface near the geographic poles where the Earth's magnetic field is most intense

magnetic recording *n.* **1.** STORING DATA ON A MAGNETIZED MEDIUM the storage of analogue or digital data on a magnetized medium, e.g. audio, video, or computer data on tape, disk, or cards **2.** SURFACE CONTAINING A MAGNETIC RECORDING a surface on which information has been magnetically recorded

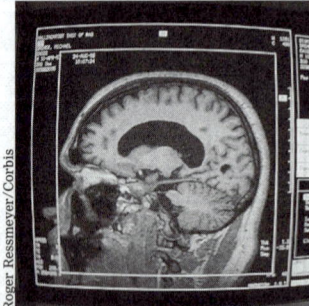

Magnetic resonance imaging of human head

magnetic resonance imaging *n.* an imaging technique, useful in diagnosing certain diseases, that uses electromagnetic radiation to obtain images of the body's soft tissues, e.g. the brain and spinal cord. The body is subjected to a powerful magnetic field, allowing tiny signals from atomic nuclei to be

detected and then processed and converted into images by a computer.

magnetic storm *n.* a disturbance in the Earth's magnetic field associated with charged particles from solar flares and sunspot activity

magnetic stripe, **magnetic strip** *n.* a strip of magnetic medium on a plastic card such as a credit card, encoded with information

magnetic susceptibility *n.* a number that characterizes the magnetization of a substance when it is subjected to a magnetic field

magnetic tape *n.* a thin ribbon of material, usually plastic, coated with iron oxide and used to record sounds, images, or data. It is the tape used in audio and video cassettes, and on computers with tape drives.

magnetic transition temperature *n.* = **Curie point**

magnetic variation *n.* = **magnetic declination**

magnetise *vti.* = **magnetize**

magnetism /mágnətizzəm/ *n.* **1.** PHYS ATTRACTION OF MAGNETS FOR IRON the phenomenon of physical attraction for iron, inherent in magnets or induced by a moving electric charge or current **2.** PHYS MAGNETIC FIELD FORCE the force exerted by a magnetic field **3.** ATTRACTION the strong attractiveness of sth, e.g. the power of sb's personality to influence others ◊ '*He was a born boon companion, with a magnetism which drew good humour from all around him.*' (Arthur Conan Doyle, *The Valley of Fear*; 1915)

magnetite /mágnə tīt/ *n.* a common black magnetic mineral consisting of iron oxide. It is an important ore of iron. Formula: Fe_3O_4.

magnetize /mágnə tīz/ (**-tizes**, **-izing**, **-ized**), **magnetise** (**-ises**, **-ising**, **-ised**) *v.* **1.** *vti.* PHYS MAKE OR BECOME MAGNETIC to become magnetic, or to make an object or material magnetic **2.** *vt.* ATTRACT SB STRONGLY to hold a strong attraction for sb ◊ *prospectors magnetized by the possibility of finding gold in the hills* —**magnetizable** *adj.* —**magnetization** /mágnə tī záysh'n/ *n.* —**magnetizer** /mágnə tīzər/ *n.*

magneto /mag neétō/ (*plural* **-tos**) *n.* a small alternator that uses permanent magnets to generate a spark in an internal-combustion engine, especially in marine and aircraft engines [Late 19thC. Shortening of *magneto-electric machine*.]

magneto- *prefix.* magnetic field ◊ *magnetograph* [From MAGNET]

magnetograph /mag neétō graaf, -graf/ *n.* an instrument used to record variations in a magnetic field, usually that of the Earth

magnetohydrodynamics /mag neétō hīdrō dī námmiks/ *n.* the study of magnetic and electric fields in relation to the movement of electrically conducting fluids, e.g. plasmas and molten metal (*takes a singular verb*) —**magnetohydrodynamic** *adj.*

magnetometer /mágnə tómmitər/ *n.* a device for measuring the direction and intensity of a magnetic field

magnetomotive force /mag neétō mótiv-/ *n.* a force that produces magnetic flux. Symbol F_m

magneton /mágnə ton/ *n.* a unit that expresses the combined force and direction of a magnetic field (**magnetic moment**), e.g. the magnetic field of an atom or elementary particle [Early 20thC. Coined from MAGNETIC + -ON.]

magnetopause /mag neétō pawz/ *n.* the region between the magnetosphere and outer space

magnetosphere /mag neétō sfeer/ *n.* the region surrounding a celestial body, e.g. the Earth, in which charged particles are trapped and affected by the body's magnetic field —**magnetospheric** /mag neétō sférrik/ *adj.*

magnetron /mágnə tron/ *n.* an electronic valve in which the flow of electrons is manipulated by electric and magnetic fields to generate microwaves. The microwave radiation produced is either pulsed, for use in radar applications, or continuous, as required for microwave cooking. [Early 20thC]

magnet school *n.* US a state school specializing in a particular area, e.g. languages or technology, in addition to providing general education. It draws students from inside and outside the local area, and serves as a way of integrating the student population and of providing innovative or alternative education.

magnific /mag níffik/, **magnifical** /-níffik'l/ *adj.* (*archaic*) **1.** MAGNIFICENT magnificent **2.** USING IMPRESSIVE WORDS using high-sounding vocabulary, often for effect [15thC. Directly, or via Old French *magnifique*, from Latin *magnificus*, literally 'performing great actions', from *magnus* 'great' (see MAGNIFY).] —**magnifically** *adv.*

Magnificat /mag níffi kat/ *n.* **1.** HYMN OF THE VIRGIN MARY the Virgin Mary's hymn of praise to God, taken from and sung or chanted in church **2.** HYMN OF PRAISE any hymn of praise sung or chanted in church [12thC. From Latin, literally '(my soul) magnifies', a form of *magnificare* (see MAGNIFY), from the opening word of the Latin version.]

magnification /mágnifi káysh'n/ *n.* **1.** OPTICS INCREASING OF APPARENT SIZE the process of causing an object or image to appear larger than it really is, especially by using a lens or microscope **2.** INCREASING OF ACTUAL SIZE the process of increasing the size or magnitude of sth **3.** GROWTH IN IMPORTANCE the increasing of the importance attributed to sb or sth **4.** OPTICS DEGREE OF ENLARGEMENT the amount by which an image is made bigger **5.** ENLARGED COPY OF STH a copy of a map, photograph, or other image that has been made larger than the original **6.** RATIO the size of the image of an object, expressed as a ratio of its actual size

magnificence /mag níffiss'nss/ *n.* **1.** GREAT BEAUTY the impressive beauty or grandeur of sb or sth ○ *the magnificence of the palace and its formal gardens* **2.** RICHNESS OF APPEARANCE the great richness and splendour of sb or sth, usually indicating great wealth ○ *the magnificence of a royal wedding* [14thC. Directly, or via Old French, from Latin *magnificentia*, from the stem *magnificent-* (see MAGNIFICENT).]

magnificent /mag níffiss'nt/ *adj.* **1.** BEAUTIFUL beautiful, impressive, and splendid in appearance ○ *a magnificent view of Rome from our balcony* **2.** EXCEPTIONAL exceptionally good of its kind ○ *The caterers had laid out a magnificent spread.* **3.** VERY GOOD excellent (*informal*) ○ *The response to the appeal has been magnificent.* [15thC. Directly, or via Old French, from Latin *magnificent-*, stem of *magnificus*, literally 'performing great actions', from *magnus* 'great' (see MAGNIFY).] —**magnificently** *adv.*

— WORD KEY: CULTURAL NOTE —
The Magnificent Ambersons, a film by US director Orson Welles (1942). Based on a novel by Booth Tarkington, it is set in the midwestern United States during the industrial revolution and contrasts the declining fortunes of the upper-class Amberson family with the rise of a young entrepreneur. Despite suffering savage cuts at the hands of the studio, it is regarded as one of Welles's masterpieces.

magnifico /mag níffikō/ (*plural* **-coes**) *n.* **1.** MAGNATE a rich or powerful person **2.** HIST VENETIAN NOBLEMAN a nobleman of the Venetian Republic [Late 16thC. From Italian, literally 'magnificent'.]

magnify /mágni fī/ (**-fies, -fying, -fied**) *v.* **1.** *vt.* OPTICS INCREASE THE APPARENT SIZE OF STH to cause sth to appear larger than it is, especially by using a microscope or lens ○ *a virus magnified 50,000 times* **2.** *vt.* INCREASE THE ACTUAL SIZE OF STH to increase the size or magnitude of sth **3.** *vt.* INCREASE THE IMPORTANCE OF STH to increase the importance attributed to sb or sth ○ *The complexities of today's medicine only magnify the need for better hospital management.* **4.** *vt.* OVERSTATE THE IMPORTANCE OF SB OR STH to cause sb or sth to appear more important than is in fact the case ○ *He tried to magnify his plight by complaining to the media about unfair stories.* **5.** *vi.* HAVE AN ENLARGING ABILITY to have the ability to increase the size or magnitude of sth **6.** *vt.* RELIG PRAISE GOD to give praise or thanks to God (*formal*) ○ *'my heart doth magnify his holy name'* (*The Book of Mormon [part 1]*) [14thC. Directly, or via Old French *magnifier*, from Latin *magnificare*, literally 'to make greater', ultimately from *magnus* 'great' (source of English *major* and *maxim*).] —**magnifiable** *adj.* —**magnifier** *n.*

magnifying glass *n.* a convex lens in a frame with a handle, used to make objects viewed through it appear larger

magniloquent /mag níllǝkwǝnt/ *adj.* employing impressive words and an exaggerated solemn and dignified style [Mid-17thC. Formed from Latin *magniloquus*, which in turn was coined from *magnus* 'great' + *-loquus* 'speaking'.] —**magniloquently** *adv.* —**magniloquence** *n.*

Magnitogorsk /mágnitǝ gáwrsk/ city in southwestern Siberian Russia, on the River Ural. Population: 427,000 (1995).

magnitude /mágni tyood/ *n.* **1.** GREATNESS OF SIZE greatness of size, volume, or extent ○ *computing the magnitude of heavenly bodies* **2.** IMPORTANCE the importance or significance of sth ○ *the magnitude of the discovery* **3.** STATUS great personal importance or status ○ *a person of her magnitude* **4.** GEOL MEASURE OF EARTHQUAKE SIZE a measure of the energy of an earthquake, specified on the Richter scale **5.** MATH NUMBER ASSIGNED TO A MATHEMATICAL QUANTITY a numerical value that describes the amount of sth, usually expressed in terms of a multiple of standard units, or the item measured in this way **6.** ASTRON BRIGHTNESS OF A CELESTIAL BODY a numerical measure of the apparent brightness of a celestial body, on a scale in which a lower number represents greater brightness [14thC. From Latin *magnitudo*, from *magnus* 'great' (see MAGNIFY).] —**magnitudinous** /mágni tyoódinǝss/ *adj.*

magnolia /mag nóli ǝ/ (*plural* **magnolia** *or* **magnolias**) *n.* **1.** FLOWERING TREE any one of a group of evergreen or deciduous trees or shrubs that typically have large simple leaves and showy yellow, white, pink, or green flowers. Native to North America and Asia, they are widely cultivated as ornamentals. Magnolias were among the first plants to have flowers, some 100 million years ago. Genus: *Magnolia*. **2.** FLOWER the flower of a magnolia **3.** COLOURS BEIGE a creamy-white colour [Mid-18thC. Named in honour of the French professor of botany Pierre *Magnol* (1638–1715).] —**magnolia** *adj.*

Magnox /mág noks/ *tdmk.* a trademark for an alloy of magnesium and other metals, used to make casings for fuel in nuclear reactors

magnum[1] /mágnǝm/ (*plural* **-nums**) *n.* **1.** LARGE WINE BOTTLE a wine bottle that holds approximately 1.5 litres, the equivalent of two normal bottles **2.** CONTENTS OF MAGNUM the volume of liquid contained in a magnum [Late 18thC. From Latin, a form of *magnus* 'large'.]

— WORD KEY: ORIGIN —
The Latin word *magnus*, from which **magnum** is derived, is also the source of English *magnanimous*, *magnate*, *magnificent*, *magnify*, and *magnitude*.

magnum[2] /mágnǝm/ *adj.* WITH A LARGER CHARGE used to describe firearms cartridges that have a larger charge and casing and are thus more high-powered than other gun cartridges of the same calibre ▪ *n.* POWERFUL GUN a gun capable of shooting magnum cartridges

magnum opus *n.* a great work of art or literature, especially the finest work produced by one individual [From Latin, 'great work']

Magog *n.* ♦ Gog and Magog

magot /ma gō, mággǝt/ *n.* **1.** ZOOL BARBARY APE a Barbary ape **2.** SCULPTURE CROUCHING FIGURINE a crouching, often grotesque figurine in the Japanese or Chinese style [Early 17thC. From Old French *magos*, a kind of monkey, from *Magog* 'Magog' (see GOG AND MAGOG), the biblical giant used as an emblem of ugliness in medieval romance.]

magpie /mág pī/ *n.* **1.** BIRDS CHATTERING BLACK-AND-WHITE BIRD a gregarious bird of the crow family with vivid black-and-white plumage, a long wedge-shaped tail, and a chattering call. Genus: *Pica*. **2.** BIRDS AUSTRALIAN BIRD a large, widely distributed, black-and-white Australian bird with a melodious song. Latin name: *Gymnorhina tibicen*. **3.** TALKATIVE PERSON an incurable chatterer (*informal*) **4.** AVID COLLECTOR an enthusiastic or compulsive collector, especially of small objects (*informal*) **5.** DARTS RING ON A TARGET the outermost but one ring on a dartboard **6.** DARTS HIT ON MAGPIE a hit on the magpie of a target [Late 16thC. From *Mag*, a shortening of the name *Margaret* + PIE. It is not known why the 'mag' part was added.]

Magpie

MAgr *abbr.* Master of Agriculture

Magritte /ma greét/, **René** (1898–1967) Belgian painter. A leading member of the Belgian surrealists, his work consists of strange juxtapositions of ordinary objects and parodies of famous paintings. Full name **René François Gislain Magritte**

mag tape *n.* magnetic tape (*informal*)

maguey /mǝ gáy, mág way/ *n.* **1.** TROPICAL PLANT any one of various plants cultivated in Mexico and other tropical regions for their fibre or as a source of an alcoholic drink called pulque. Genus: *Agave*. **2.** FIBRE fibre from the stalks of maguey plants [Mid-16thC. Via Spanish from Taino.]

magus /máygǝss/ (*plural* **-gi** /máy jī/) *n.* **1.** ZOROASTRIAN PRIEST a priest in the ancient Persian religion of Zoroastrianism **2.** MAN WITH MAGICAL POWERS a man with supernatural or magical powers, especially in ancient times [Early 17thC. Via Latin from Greek *magos*, from Old Persian *magūs*.] —**magian** /máyji ǝn/ *adj.* —**magianism** /-ji ǝnizǝm/ *n.*

— WORD KEY: CULTURAL NOTE —
The Magus, a novel by English writer John Fowles (1966). The plot concerns a young teacher, Nicholas Urfe, who takes a job on a Greek island and finds himself lured into an elaborate fiction staged by a wealthy resident, Maurice Conchis. Fowles uses this enigmatic story to explore the nature of individual identity and freedom of choice.

Magus (*plural* **-gi** /máy jī/) *n.* BIBLE in the Bible, one of the men, traditionally three in number, who followed a star to Bethlehem to worship the baby Jesus Christ. They are often called the Three Wise Men or the Three Kings. (*literary*) ◊ **Caspar, Melchior, Balthazar**

Magyar /mág yaar/ (*plural* **-yars** *or* **-yar**) *n.* **1.** PEOPLES MEMBER OF A HUNGARIAN PEOPLE a member of the Hungarian people that forms the largest population group of Hungary **2.** LANG = **Hungarian** [Late 18thC. From Hungarian.] —**Magyar** *adj.*

Mahabharata /mǝ haa báárǝtǝ/ *n.* one of India's two great national epic poems, written in Sanskrit from about 300 BC. It tells of the great war in northern India between the Pandava and Kaurava families. The 'Bhagavad-Gita' is the most important section of the Mahabharata. [Late 18thC. From Sanskrit, literally 'the great history of the Bharata dynasty'.]

Mahajanga /maa zhaángǝ/ port on the northwestern coast of Madagascar. Population: 100,807 (1993).

mahaleb /máahǝ leb/ *n.* a tree whose seeds are used in Middle Eastern cookery. It belongs to the rose family and is used as a grafting stock in the United States. Latin name: *Prunus mahaleb*. [Mid-16thC. Via French from Arabic *mahaleb*.]

Mahallat al Kubra /mǝ háálǝ el kōbrǝ/ industrial city in the central Nile delta, northern Egypt. Population: 408,000 (1992).

maharajah /máahǝ ráájǝ/, **maharaja** *n.* an Indian prince, higher in rank than a rajah, especially the ruler of one of the former Native States of India [Late 17thC. From Sanskrit, formed from *mahā* 'great' + *rājan* 'raja' (see RAJ).]

maharani /máahǝ raáni/ *n.* **1.** MAHARAJAH'S WIFE the wife of a maharajah **2.** INDIAN PRINCESS an Indian princess, higher in rank than a rani, especially the ruler of one of the former Native States of India [Mid-19thC. From Hindi, formed from Sanskrit *mahā* 'great' + *rājñī*.]

Maharashtra /maá hə ráshtrə/ state in western India, situated in the northwestern part of the Deccan plateau. Capital: Mumbai. Population: 85,865,000 (1994). Area: 307,690 sq. km/118,799 sq. mi.

maharishi /maáhə ríshi/ *n.* a Hindu religious teacher [Late 18thC. From Sanskrit *maharṣi* from *mahā* 'great' + *ṛṣi* 'inspired sage'.]

mahatma /mə haátmə, -hát-/ *n.* in India, a title bestowed on sb who is deeply revered for wisdom and virtue [Late 19thC. From Sanskrit *mahātman*, formed from *mahā* 'great' + *ātman* 'soul'.]

Mahavira /maá hə veérə/ (599?–527 BC) Indian founder of Jainism. He was thought to be last in a line of 24 great teachers.

Mahayana /maáhə yaánə/ *n.* the branch of Buddhism that includes Tibetan, Chinese, and Zen Buddhism, developed around AD 1. It stresses compassion for all sentient beings and universal salvation. [Mid-19thC. From Sanskrit, formed from *mahā* 'great' + *yana* 'vehicle'.]

Mahdi /maádi/ *n.* **1.** ISLAMIC MESSIAH in Islamic belief, a prophet or messiah who is expected to appear in the world sometime before it ends **2.** ISLAMIC LEADER sb fulfilling a messianic role [Early 19thC. From Arabic *al-mahdī*, literally 'he who is rightly guided', from *hadā* 'to lead in the right way'.] —**Mahdism** *n.* —**Mahdist** *n.*

Mahdi /maádi/ (1843–85) Sudanese religious leader. Claiming to be the Islamic spiritual saviour, he led a revolt in 1883, wresting control of Egyptian Sudan from General Charles Gordon. Real name **Mohammad Ahmad**

Mahé /moháy/ the largest island in the Republic of Seychelles, in the western Indian Ocean. Population: 59,500 (1987). Area: 148 sq. km/57 sq. mi.

Mahfouz /maa foóz/, **Naguib** (*b.* 1911) Egyptian novelist and screenwriter. He is author of *The Cairo Trilogy* (1956–57) and other works that explore Egyptian society and culture.

Mahican /mə heékən/, **Mohican** /mō heékən, mṓ ikən/ *n.* **1.** PEOPLES MEMBER OF A NATIVE N AMERICAN CONFEDERACY a member of a Native North American confederacy of peoples formerly living in the upper Hudson River Valley from the Catskill Mountains north to Lake Champlain. Their descendants live in Wisconsin and Oklahoma. **2.** LANGUAGE MAHICAN LANGUAGE the Algonquian language spoken by the Mahican people, belonging to the Algonquian-Wakashan group of Native North American languages [Early 17thC. From Mahican *muhheakunneuw*, literally 'people of the tidal water'.] —**Mahican** *adj.*

mahi-mahi /maáhi maáhi/ *n.* an edible marine tropical fish that has a bright blue body and long dorsal fin. Latin name: *Coryphaena hippurus.* [From Hawaiian]

mahjongg /maá jóng/, **mahjong** *n.* a game of Chinese origin using 144 small tiles bearing various designs, played by four people around a square table. The winning player is the first one who completes a particular pattern using 13 tiles. [Early 20thC. From Chinese dialect *ma jiang*, literally 'sparrows'.]

Mahler /maálər/, **Gustav** (1860–1911) Czech-born Austrian composer and conductor. He is best known for his songs and large-scale orchestral works, many of them involving voices, as in *Das Lied von der Erde* (1908).

mahogany /mə hóggəni/ (*plural* **-nies**) *n.* **1.** TROPICAL HARDWOOD TREE any one of several evergreen hardwood trees native to tropical America but widely cultivated for their red-brown wood. Genus: *Swietenia.* **2.** REDDISH-BROWN HARDWOOD the hard reddish-brown wood of any mahogany tree, used in the building industry and for making furniture **3.** COLOURS REDDISH-BROWN a dark reddish-brown colour [Mid-17thC. From obsolete Spanish *mahogani*, of uncertain origin: perhaps a Mayan language.] —**mahogany** *adj.*

mahonia /mə hṓni ə/ *n.* any one of various evergreen shrubs native to America and Asia that typically have spiny leaflets and clusters of small yellow flowers and are widely cultivated as ornamentals. Genus: *Mahonia.* ◊ **Oregon grape** [Early 19thC. Named after the US botanist Bernard *McMahon* (1775–1816).]

mahout /mə hówt/ *n.* in South and Southeast Asia, sb who trains, drives, and looks after elephants [Mid-17thC. Via Hindi *mahāut* from Sanskrit *mahāmātra* 'high official, elephant-keeper', from *mahā* 'great' + *mātra* 'measure'.]

Mahratta *n.* = **Maratha**

Mahratti *n.* = **Marathi**

Mahy /máy i/, **Margaret** (*b.* 1936) New Zealand writer. A children's author, her books include *The Changeover* (1984).

maid /mayd/ *n.* **1.** WOMAN SERVANT a woman servant, e.g. one working in a hotel **2.** YOUNG UNMARRIED WOMAN a young unmarried woman (*archaic or literary*) (*sometimes considered offensive*) **3.** UNMARRIED WOMAN an unmarried woman past middle age (*often considered offensive*) **4.** VIRGIN a woman who has never had sexual intercourse (*archaic or literary*) [12thC. Shortening of MAIDEN.]

maiden /máyd'n/ *n.* **1.** YOUNG UNMARRIED WOMAN a young unmarried woman (*sometimes considered offensive*) **2.** VIRGIN a woman who has never had sexual intercourse (*archaic or literary*) **3.** HIST GUILLOTINE in 16th and 17th-century Scotland, a guillotine used to execute criminals **4.** *N England* FRAME FOR DRYING CLOTHES a frame on which wet laundry is hung to dry **5.** HORSERACING HORSE YET TO WIN a horse that has never won a race **6.** CRICKET = **maiden over** ■ *adj.* **1.** FIRST done for the very first time (*offensive in some contexts*) ○ *a maiden voyage* **2.** UNTOUCHED still in its original, unused, untouched, or unexplored condition (*literary*) (*offensive in some contexts*) **3.** HORSERACING FOR HORSES YET TO WIN for horses that have never won a race [Old English *mægden* from a prehistoric Germanic ancestor meaning 'young woman']

maidenhair fern /máyd'n hair-/ *n.* any one of various ferns with slender dark stems and delicate fronds of numerous leaflets. Native to warm moist regions worldwide, they are widely cultivated as ornamentals. Genus: *Adiantum.*

maidenhair tree *n.* = **ginkgo**

maidenhead /máyd'n hed/ *n.* (*literary*) **1.** HYMEN the hymen **2.** VIRGINITY a woman's virginity [13thC. Coined from MAIDEN + *-head*, a variant of HOOD.]

Maidenhead /máyd'n hed/ town and boating centre on the River Thames in southeastern England. Population: 49,000 (1992).

maidenhood /máyd'n hood/, **maidhood** /máyd hood/ *n.* the period of a woman's life before marriage or before becoming sexually active (*literary*) (*sometimes considered offensive*) [Old English]

maidenly /máyd'nli/ *adj.* of, like, or thought suitable for a maiden —**maidenliness** *n.*

maiden name *n.* the former surname of a woman who has assumed her husband's surname

maiden over *n.* in cricket, an over in which no runs are scored

maidhood *n.* = **maidenhood** [Old English]

maid-in-waiting (*plural* **maids-in-waiting**) *n.* a young, usually unmarried lady-in-waiting

Maid Marian /-márri ən/ *n.* **1.** ROBIN HOOD'S BELOVED in English legend, the beautiful young noblewoman loved by Robin Hood **2.** DANCING CHARACTER IN MORRIS DANCING a character in morris dancing, played by a man dressed as a woman

maid of all work (*plural* **maids of all work**) *n.* a maid who does all kinds of domestic work

maid of honour *n.* **1.** ROYAL ATTENDANT an unmarried woman of noble birth who attends a queen or princess **2.** COOK INDIVIDUAL SPONGE CAKE a small individual cake with a base of short crust pastry topped with sponge cake and baked until golden **3.** *US, Can* BRIDE'S ATTENDANT in the United States and Canada, the chief bridesmaid

maidservant /máyd survənt/ *n.* a woman servant, especially one working in a large private house (*archaic*)

Maidstone /máydstən/ town in Kent, southeastern England, on the River Medway. Population: 71,800 (1993).

Maiduguri /máydo goóri/ city in Borno State, northeastern Nigeria. Population: 289,100 (1992).

maieutic /may yoótik, mī-/, **maieutical** /may oótik'l/ *adj.* PHILOS Socratic (*technical*) [Mid-17thC. From Greek *maieutikos*, literally 'acting as midwife', ultimately, from *maia* 'midwife'.]

maigre /máygər/ *adj.* CHR **1.** CONTAINING NO FLESH containing no meat and therefore suitable for eating on days when abstinence from meat is prescribed by the Roman Catholic Church **2.** PRESCRIBED FOR ABSTINENCE FROM MEAT used to describe a day when abstinence from meat is prescribed by the Roman Catholic Church [Late 17thC. From French, literally 'lean'.]

maihem *n.* = **mayhem**

mail[1] /mayl/ *n.* **1.** ITEMS SENT the letters, cards, periodicals, and packages that are handled and distributed in a postal system ○ *Is there any mail for me?* **2.** POSTAL SYSTEM the system that handles the collection and delivery of post (*often used before a noun*) ○ *send it by mail* **3.** SPECIFIC MAIL COLLECTION OR DELIVERY a particular collection or delivery of letters, cards, periodicals, and packages ○ *It came in yesterday's mail.* **4.** VEHICLE DELIVERING MAIL a car, train, ship, aircraft, or other vehicle used to collect and deliver mail **5.** COMPUT = **e-mail** ■ *vt.* (**mails, mailing, mailed**) *US, Can, Aus* SEND STH BY MAIL to send a letter, card, periodical, or package by mail [13thC. Via Old French *male* 'bag, trunk' from a prehistoric Germanic word meaning 'bag, wallet'. Originally in the meaning of 'bag', hence 'letters carried in a bag'.]

mail[2] /mayl/ *n.* **1.** HIST ARMOUR a kind of flexible armour made of interlocking metal rings or overlapping plates **2.** ZOOL HARD BODY COVERING the hard protective body covering of some animals, e.g. turtles and crabs ■ *vt.* (**mails, mailing, mailed**) COVER THE BODY WITH MAIL to cover or protect the body with mail ○ *a mailed torso* [13thC. Via French *maille* 'mesh' from Latin *macula* 'spot, holes in a net' (source of English *immaculate*).]

mailbag /máyl bag/ *n.* **1.** BAG FOR TRANSPORTING MAIL a bag used for transporting mail, typically a sack made of coarse material **2.** = **postbag** [Early 19thC. From MAIL[1].]

mailbox /máyl boks/ *n.* **1.** *US* = **postbox 2.** *US, ANZ* BOX FOR RECEIVING MAIL a container into which mail is delivered **3.** COMPUT MESSAGE STORAGE FILE an area of computer memory designated for messages, especially those sent by e-mail ○ *Your online mailbox is empty.* [Early 19thC. From MAIL[1].]

maildrop /máyl drop/ *n. US* **1.** CONTAINER FOR MAIL a container into which delivered mail is placed **2.** DELIVERY PLACE a place where messages or packages can be left for later pickup by sb else, often secretly and prearranged

mailed fist *n. US* the threat of military force (*literary*) [*Mailed* from MAIL[2]]

mailer /máylər/ *n.* **1.** MAIL CONTAINER a packet or tube for sending objects of a particular kind through the post **2.** SB WHO PREPARES MAIL sb whose job it is to address, stamp, weigh, and sort items for mailing [Late 19thC. Formed from MAIL[1].]

mailing /máyling/ *adj. US* suitable for or associated with mail ○ *a mailing label* ○ *mailing costs* [Late 19thC. Formed from MAIL[1].]

mailing list *n.* a list, typically computerized, of names and addresses to which advertising material or information can be posted

maillot /mī ṓ/ *n.* **1.** TEXTILES STRETCHY FABRIC a soft stretchable jersey fabric **2.** CLOTHES LEOTARD OR TIGHTS a leotard or a pair of tights made of maillot, worn for dancing or gymnastics **3.** CLOTHES SWIMSUIT a woman's one-piece bathing suit made of stretchy fabric, especially one with a high-cut leg **4.** CLOSE-FITTING TOP a tight-fitting knitted top or jersey [Late 19thC. From French, from Old French, 'swaddling clothes', from *maille* 'mesh' (see MAIL[2]).]

mail merge *n.* the process of creating a series of individual documents on a computer by combining a list of different names and addresses with a single body of text

mail order *n.* **1.** SELLING BY POST a method of buying and selling goods by post (*hyphenated before a noun*) ○ *a mail-order catalogue* **2.** PURCHASE ORDER an order for goods to be sent by post

mailroom /máyl room, -ro͝om/ *n.* a room in an organization where mail is sorted, prepared, and distributed [Late 19thC. From MAIL[1].]

mailshot /máyl shot/ *n.* a letter, advertisement, brochure, or other item sent unsolicited to a large number of people at one time [Mid-20thC. From MAIL[1].]

mail slot *n. US* = **letterbox** [Mid-20thC. From MAIL[1].]

maim /maym/ (**maims, maiming, maimed**) *vt.* to inflict a severe and permanent wound on a person or animal, especially one that renders a limb unable to move ○ *maimed by a land mine* [14thC. From Old French *mahaignier* (source of English *mangle* and *mayhem*), of uncertain origin: perhaps, ultimately, from Germanic.]

main /mayn/ *adj.* 1. PRINCIPAL greatest in size or importance ○ *the main reason we're here* 2. UTMOST exerted to the full or the utmost ○ *main force* 3. NAUT OF A MAINMAST on or relating to a sailing ship's mainmast ■ *n.* 1. LARGE PIPE OR CABLE a large and important pipe or line for the distribution of water, gas, or electricity ○ *a ruptured water main* 2. SEA the open sea (*archaic or literary*) 3. MAINLAND the mainland (*archaic*) [Old English *mægen*, influenced by Old Norse *magn*, from a prehistoric Germanic word meaning 'to have power', which is also the ancestor of English *may* and *might*] ◇ **in the main** largely or in general

Main /mīn, mayn/ river in south-central Germany. Length: 494 km/307 mi.

main chance *n.* sb's chief opportunity or best interest ○ *have an eye to the main chance*

main course *n.* the most substantial dish eaten at a meal with several courses

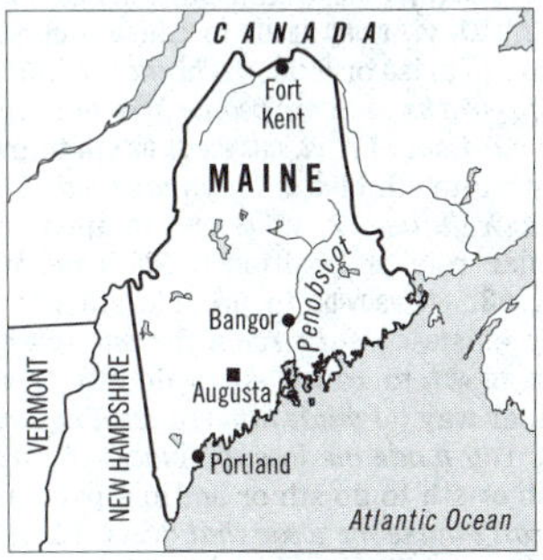

Maine

Maine /mayn/ state in the northeastern United States, bordered by New Hampshire, Quebec and New Brunswick Provinces, Canada, and the Atlantic Ocean. Capital: Augusta. Population: 1,242,051 (1997). Area: 85,802 sq. km/33,128 sq. mi.

Maine coon, Maine coon cat *n.* a large, long-haired North American cat of a breed with a bold striped pattern, usually brown with black stripes

mainframe /máyn fraym/ *n.* a fast powerful computer with a large storage capacity that has a number of terminals for individual users connected to it

mainland /máynlənd, -land/ *n.* a continent's or country's principal landmass, as distinct from its islands and sometimes excluding peninsulas (*often used before a noun*) ○ *a ferry from the mainland* —**mainlander** *n.*

Mainland /máynlənd/ 1. the largest of the Orkney Islands, northeastern Scotland. Population: 15,123 (1991). Area: 500 sq. km/195 sq. mi. 2. the largest of the Shetland Islands, northeastern Scotland. Fishing is the main occupation. Population: 17,562 (1991). Area: 1,053 sq. km/406 sq. mi.

main line *n.* 1. RAIL PRINCIPAL RAIL ROUTE a major rail route between two cities, often joined by branch lines along its length 2. DRUGS PRINCIPAL VEIN a major vein in the arm or leg into which drugs may be injected (*slang*)

mainline /máyn līn/ *vti.* (**-lines, -lining, -lined**) (*slang*) 1. DRUGS TAKE DRUGS INTRAVENOUSLY to inject an illicit drug, especially heroin or cocaine, intravenously 2. *US* CONSUME EXCESSIVELY to consume or be affected by sth excessively ■ *adj.* RAIL OF A MAIN RAIL LINE situated on or relating to a main rail line ○ *a mainline station* —**mainliner** *n.* —**mainlining** *n.*

mainly /máynli/ *adv.* to a large extent or in most cases ○ *bacteria that live mainly in the small intestine*

mainmast /máyn maast/ *n.* the principal mast on a sailing ship with more than one mast, usually either the foremost mast or the second from the bow

main memory *n.* the random access memory of a computer, which executes instructions in real time

mains /maynz/ *npl.* the central network of pipes or cables that distribute water, gas, or electricity from a local station to individual buildings in an area (*often used before a noun*) ○ *connected to a mains supply* [Early 17thC. Plural of MAIN.]

mainsail /máyn sayl, máynss'l/ *n.* the largest and most important sail on a sailing ship

main sequence *n.* a grouping of stars that consists of most of the known stars in the universe, represented on a graph of luminosity (**Hertzsprung-Russell diagram**) as a diagonal band

mainspring /máyn spring/ *n.* 1. SPRING IN A WATCH OR CLOCK the largest and most important spring in the mechanism of a watch or clock 2. CHIEF REASON FOR ACTION the driving or motive force behind sth such as a course of action

mainstay /máyn stay/ *n.* 1. CHIEF SUPPORT sb or sth that plays the most important role in a particular group, place, or situation ○ *Tourism is the mainstay of the country's economy.* 2. SAILING ROPE SECURING SHIP'S MAINMAST the strong rope that secures the mainmast on a sailing ship

main stem *n.* the principal waterway of a river, excluding its tributaries

mainstream /máyn streem/ *n.* MAIN CURRENT OF THOUGHT OR BEHAVIOUR the ideas, actions, and values that are most widely accepted by a group or society ○ *views well outside those of the mainstream* ■ *adj.* REFLECTING THE NORM reflecting the most widely accepted views of a nation or culture and therefore not exceptional, extreme, or avant-garde ○ *The scandal, previously ignored by the mainstream media, is now on the front pages.* ■ *vti.* (**-streams, -streaming, -streamed**) EDUC ENROL SPECIAL STUDENTS IN GENERAL CLASSES to enrol students with physical disabilities or learning difficulties in general school classes —**mainstreamer** *n.*

mainstreaming /máyn streeming/ *n.* EDUC the practice of educating children with physical or developmental disabilities in regular classes

main street *n.* the most important street in a small town

Main Street *n. US* people living in small towns, considered as a group and often described as conservative and unsophisticated (*hyphenated when used before a noun*) ○ *Main Street will never accept those fashions.*

maintain /mayn táyn, mən-/ (**-tains, -taining, -tained**) *v.* 1. *vt.* MAKE STH CONTINUE to make a situation or course of action continue in the same way as before ○ *maintained a semblance of normal procedures even with half the staff out sick* 2. *vt.* KEEP STH IN WORKING ORDER to ensure that sth continues to work properly by checking it regularly and making repairs and adjustments if required ○ *gives years of service if maintained properly* 3. *vt.* PROVIDE SB WITH FINANCIAL SUPPORT to provide sb with the money required for a reasonable standard of living ○ *She maintains a big family on a tight budget.* 4. *vt.* KEEP SB ALIVE to keep a person or animal alive by providing food and other basic necessities ○ *maintained the injured animal in a cage over the winter* 5. *vt.* DECLARE STH TO BE TRUE to insist on the truth of sth in the face of challenge or disbelief ○ *He maintains that she knew all along.* 6. *vt.* SPEAK IN FAVOUR OF STH to defend an opinion, idea, or argument against criticism ○ *The governor continues to maintain his position on cleaning up the environment.* 7. *vt.* MIL DEFEND A PLACE to defend a place against physical attack ○ *The unit maintained its position in spite of heavy enemy shelling.* 8. *vi. US* KEEP GOING to continue in the present state or situation without losing control (*informal*) ○ *Until the reorganization is complete, we're maintaining, and that's about it.* [13thC. Via Old French *maintener*, from assumed late Latin *manutenere*, literally 'to hold in the hand', from Latin *manus* 'hand' (source of English *manual*).] —**maintainability** /mayn táynə bílləti, mən-/ *n.* —**maintainable** /mayn táynəb'l/ *adj.* —**maintainer** *n.*

maintenance /máyntənənss/ *n.* 1. CONTINUING REPAIR WORK work that is done regularly to keep a machine, building, or piece of equipment in good condition and working order (*often used before a noun*) ○ *We take the car in for maintenance every six months.* 2. CONDITION working order ○ *a car in a poor state of maintenance* 3. MAINTAINING OF STH the continuation or preservation of sth ○ *behaviour that threatens the maintenance of our security* 4. PROVISION OF FINANCIAL SUPPORT the provision of enough money to enable the things necessary for a decent lifestyle, e.g. clothes, food, and a place to live ○ *responsible for the maintenance of two retired parents* 5. MEANS OF SUPPORT the money that sb has to pay for necessities, e.g. food, clothing, and a place to live ○ *Family maintenance takes a big bite out of our budget.* 6. MONEY PAID TO SUPPORT EX-SPOUSE a sum of money paid regularly or in a lump sum by a divorced person, usually as part of a divorce settlement, to maintain the normal standard of living of the ex-spouse and any children 7. LAW INTERFERENCE IN LEGAL ACTION improper or unlawful meddling in a lawsuit by a party typically with no legal standing in the matter

Mainz /mīnts/ historic city and river port in southwestern Germany, on the River Rhine. Population: 185,300 (1994).

maiolica *n.* = **majolica**

maisonette /máyzə nét/, **maisonnette** *n.* living accommodation with its own entrance, arranged on two floors of a larger house [Late 18thC. From French, literally 'little house', formed from *maison* 'house'.]

Maistre /méstrə/, **Roy de** (1894–1968) Australian painter. He was the pioneer of post-impressionism, synchronism, and cubism in Australia. Full name **Leroy Leveson Laurent de Maistre**

Maitland /máytlənd/ city in eastern New South Wales, Australia, a centre of coal mining, light industry, and agriculture. Population: 50,108 (1996).

maitre d' /méttrə dée/ *n.* a maitre d'hotel (*informal*)

maitre d'hotel /méttrə dō tél/ (*plural* **maitres d'hotel** /méttrə dō-/) *n.* 1. HEAD-WAITER a head-waiter in a restaurant or a hotel dining room 2. HEAD MAN SERVANT the senior man servant in a large household, e.g. a royal palace [Mid-16thC. From French, literally 'master of house'.]

maize /mayz/ *n.* US term **corn** 1. STAPLE CEREAL CROP an annual cereal grass that yields densely packed ears (**cobs**) of yellow grains. Native to Central and South America, it has been cultivated as a food crop since ancient times. The grains are a staple food for both humans and livestock in many countries, and the entire plant is sometimes used for silage. Latin name: *Zea mays.* 2. GRAIN the grain of the maize plant. It is used as a vegetable and a livestock feed, ground for flour, and processed to produce cooking oil. (*often used before a noun*) ○ *maize oil* [Mid-16thC. Directly, or via French *maïs*, from Spanish *maís*, from Taino *mahis*.]

Maj. *abbr.* Major

majestic /mə jéstik/ *adj.* 1. IMPRESSIVE greatly impressive in appearance ○ *a majestic seascape showing the masts of twenty tall ships under full sail* 2. DIGNIFIED showing great dignity and grandeur ○ *a majestic inclination of the head* —**majestically** *adv.*

majesty /májjəsti/ *n.* 1. DIGNITY a deeply impressive dignified quality ○ *a duchess whose majesty was clearly present in her every move* 2. POWER supreme authority and power ○ *The full majesty of the Crown was brought to bear during the diplomatic mission.* 3. SPLENDOUR awesomely large size or splendour ○ *the majesty of the Rocky Mountain peaks* 4. ROYALTY royal status (*archaic*) [13thC. Via Old French *majesté* from Latin *majestas*, from the stem of *major* (see MAJOR).]

Majesty (*plural* **-ties**) *n.* the title used to address or refer to a king or queen ○ *Her Majesty the Queen*

Maj. Gen. *abbr.* Major General

majlis /májjliss/ *n.* an assembly or parliament in various countries in North Africa and the Middle East [Early 19thC. From Arabic, 'place of session', from *jalasa* 'to be seated'.]

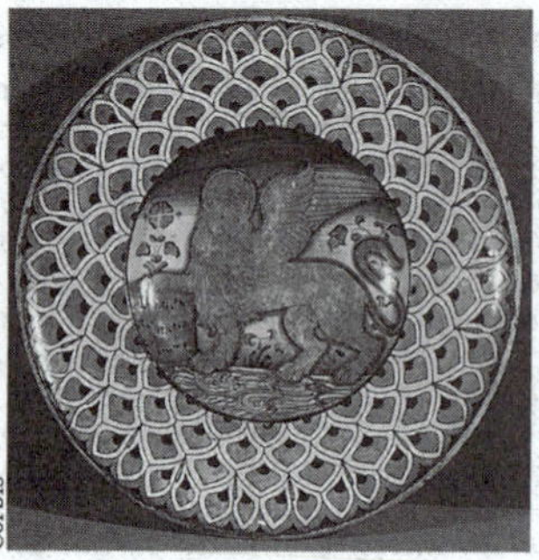

Majolica

majolica /mə jóllikə, -yólli-/, **maiolica** /mə yóllikə/ *n.* Italian earthenware that is coated with a tin oxide glaze and highly decorated [Mid-16thC. From Italian, an old form of the name of the island of *Majorca*.]

major /máyjər/ *n.* **1.** MIL **MILITARY RANK** a military rank immediately below that of lieutenant colonel in many armed forces around the world, including the British and United States armies and the United States Air Force and Marine Corps **2.** MIL **OFFICER** sb who holds the rank of major **3.** LAW **SB OF LEGAL AGE** sb who has reached the age at which a person is deemed fully responsible for his or her actions **4.** *US, Can, ANZ* EDUC **MAIN SUBJECT** the field of study in which a college or university student chooses to specialize ○ *a major in philosophy* **5.** *US, Can, ANZ* EDUC **STUDENT IN A SPECIALISM** a student studying a particular academic specialism ○ *a math major* **6.** MUSIC **MUSICAL KEY OR HARMONY** a key or harmony based on a musical scale that has intervals of a semitone between the third and fourth and the seventh and eighth notes (**major scale**) **7.** FOOTBALL **GOAL** in Australian Rules football, a goal ■ *adj.* **1. OF HIGH STANDING** greater in importance than most others ○ *a major recording artist* **2. SIGNIFICANT** of considerable degree or significance ○ *major bridge repairs ahead* **3. SERIOUS** of great severity ○ *a major illness* **4. LARGE** great in number or proportion ○ *A major part of the meeting was devoted to agreeing on our report.* **5.** LAW **AT THE AGE OF MAJORITY** of the age at which a person is deemed fully responsible for his or her actions **6.** EDUC **OF A PRINCIPAL SUBJECT** relating to a subject studied as a specialism **7.** MUSIC **DESCRIBING A MUSICAL SCALE** used to describe a musical scale that has intervals of a semitone between the third and fourth and the seventh and eighth notes **8.** MUSIC **DESCRIBING A MUSICAL INTERVAL** used to describe the interval between the keynote of a major scale and any other note in it, excluding the perfect intervals ○ *a major sixth* **9.** MUSIC **DESCRIBING A KEY** used to describe a key that is based on a major scale ○ *in B major* **10. THE ELDER** in British public schools, used after the surname to refer to the older of two brothers (*dated*) ○ *Hobbs major* ■ *vi.* (**-jors, -joring, -jored**) *US, Can, ANZ* EDUC **STUDY STH AS A MAIN SUBJECT** to make a particular subject the main field of study ○ *She majored in economics.* [13thC. From Latin, 'greater', from *magnus* 'great' (source of English *mayor* and *majesty*).]

Major /máyjər/, **John** (*b.* 1943) British statesman. As Conservative prime minister (1990–97), he worked towards peace talks with Northern Ireland but was troubled by party splits on the issue of closer European integration.

Major, Dame Malvina Lorraine (*b.* 1943) New Zealand opera singer. A soprano, she has performed with numerous international companies.

Majorca /mə yáwrkə/ largest of the Balearic Islands, an autonomous region of Spain, in the western Mediterranean Sea. Population: 736,885 (1994). Area: 3,640 sq. km/1,405 sq. mi. —**Majorcan** *n., adj.*

major-domo /-dṓmō/ (*plural* **major-domos**) *n.* **1. CHIEF MAN SERVANT** the chief man servant in a large household, especially a royal or noble household, responsible for managing domestic affairs **2. MAKER OF ARRANGEMENTS** sb responsible for managing the affairs of others, and making arrangements for others (*humorous*) [Late 16thC. Via French, Italian, and Spanish from medieval Latin *major domus* literally 'chief of the house', from Latin *magnus* (see MAJOR) and *domus* 'house' (source of English *domestic*).]

majorette /máyjə rét/ *n. US* a girl or young woman who marches in front of a marching band, twirling a baton

major general (*plural* **major generals**) *n.* **1. HIGH MILITARY RANK** a military rank immediately below that of lieutenant general in many armed forces around the world, including the British and United States Armies, and the United States Air Force and Marine Corps **2. MILITARY OFFICER** a military officer holding the rank of major general

major histocompatibility complex *n.* a cluster of genes occurring in humans and other animals that determines the recognizable pattern on the surface of the body's cells. This determines the extent to which an individual's immune system will accept or reject tissue from another individual.

majority /mə jórrəti/ (*plural* **-ties**) *n.* **1. GREATER NUMBER OF PEOPLE OR THINGS** most of the people or things in a large group (*takes a singular or plural verb*) ○ *The majority of women now work.* **2. DIFFERENCE IN NUMBER OF VOTES** the number of votes by which the winning party or group beats the opposition ○ *swept to power with an overwhelming majority* **3. GROUP IN POWER** the most powerful party or group voting together in a legislature **4.** LAW **AGE OF LEGAL RESPONSIBILITY** the age, generally either 18 or 21, at which sb is legally responsible and can assume civil duties and rights such as serving on a jury or voting **5.** MIL **RANK OF MAJOR** the military rank of major **6. PRE-EMINENCE** superior position or status (*archaic*)

majority leader *n. US* the head of the majority party in a legislature

majority minority *n. US* a majority of people in a particular area who belong to a minority group overall ○ *a majority minority district*

majority rule *n.* control of an organization or institution according to the wishes or votes of the majority of its members

major league *n.* **1.** BASEBALL **MAIN BASEBALL LEAGUE** either of the two main professional baseball leagues in the United States **2.** SPORTS **TOP SPORTS LEAGUE** a top league of professional football, ice hockey, and basketball teams in the United States

major-league *adj.* **1. OF MAJOR SPORTS LEAGUE** relating to or being a team member of a major sports league in the United States ○ *major-league ice hockey* **2.** *US* **OF HIGHEST LEVEL** being at the top of any field of activity (*informal*) ○ *a major-league law firm* —**major-leaguer** *n.*

majorly /máyjərli/ *adv.* in a large degree or to a great extent (*informal*) ○ *an account that was majorly overdrawn*

major order *n.* in the Roman Catholic Church, one of the higher holy orders of bishop, priest, deacon, or subdeacon

major penalty *n.* in sports such as ice hockey and lacrosse, a player's removal from the game for five minutes for a serious violation of the rules

major scale *n.* a musical scale with intervals of a semitone between the third and fourth notes and the seventh and eighth notes and whole tones between all other consecutive notes. Major scales potentially have a bright and joyful quality. ◊ **minor scale**

major suit *n.* in bridge and some other card games, spades or hearts, owing to their greater scoring potential

Majuba Hill /mə jŏobə-/ hill in eastern South Africa, the site of a battle in 1881 when a Boer force defeated the British

Majuro /mə jŏorō/ atoll, capital island of the Marshall Islands, in Micronesia, in the central North Pacific Ocean. Population: 19,664 (1988). Area: 10 sq. km/4 sq. mi.

majuscule /májjə skyool/ *n.* a large letter used in writing or printing, e.g. a capital letter or any of the large rounded letters (**uncials**) used in ancient manuscripts [Early 18thC. Via French from Latin *majuscula (littera)*, literally 'somewhat larger (letters)', from *major* (see MAJOR).] —**majuscular** /mə júskyŏolər/ *adj.*

Makalu /múkəloo/ mountain in the Himalayas, on the Nepal-China border, estimated to be the fourth or fifth highest in the world. Height: 8,481 m/27,824 ft.

makar /mákər/ *n. Scotland* a writer, especially a poet (*archaic or literary*) [14thC. Originally a variant of MAKER.]

Makarios /mə kaári oss/, **Archbishop** (1913–77) Cypriot cleric and statesman. Orthodox archbishop of Cyprus (1950–74) and first president of Cyprus (1959–77), he was noted for his efforts to unify Greek and Turkish Cypriots. Real name **Mihail Christodolou Mouskos**

Makassar /mə kássər/ former name for **Ujungpandang**

make /mayk/ *v.* (**makes, making, made** /mayd/) **1.** *vt.* **DO** used with a range of nouns to describe an action, where 'make' is used rather than a more specific verb ○ *She made no effort whatsoever to pass her exams.* **2.** *vt.* **SAY** to say or deliver a statement or speech ○ *He made an emotional speech about his parents' struggle to get ahead in a new country* **3.** *vt.* **CONSTRUCT** to assemble sth from constituent parts ○ *The exhibit contains items made out of recyclable materials.* **4.** *vt.* INDUST **MANUFACTURE** to manufacture sth as a business ○ *The company makes surgical instruments.* **5.** *vt.* COOK **PRODUCE BY COMBINING INGREDIENTS** to prepare food or drink by mixing and usually cooking a number of ingredients ○ *Let's make soup.* **6.** *vt.* **FORM WITH MOTION** to form sth by performing the movements that it requires ○ *She made the signs for 'I'll see you later'.* ○ *He made a circular motion with his hands.* **7.** *vt.* **FORMULATE** to form sth in the mind ○ *These politicians have made a tacit commitment to try to solve the problem.* **8.** *vt.* **UNDERSTAND** to comprehend the meaning or truth of sth ○ *I couldn't make anything of her last remark.* **9.** *vt.* **RECKON** to reckon or estimate sth ○ *What time do you make it?* **10.** *vt.* **BRING ABOUT** to cause a condition or situation to arise or exist ○ *The state made it illegal to sell fireworks.* ○ *Some people here have made this a personal issue.* **11.** *vt.* **CHANGE SB OR STH** to transform sb or sth into sth else ○ *They made old clothes into patchwork quilts.* **12.** *vt.* **APPOINT** to appoint sb to a particular role or position ○ *She's made me her deputy.* **13.** *vt.* **PROVIDE** to provide sth out of what already exists ○ *Make room for one more.* **14.** *vt.* **CAUSE SB TO ACT** to cause sb to do sth or act in a particular way ○ *I made him realize how wrong he'd been.* ○ *You made me lose my place.* **15.** *vt.* **FORCE** to force sb or sth to do sth or act in a particular way ○ *You can't make me wear that dress.* **16.** *vt.* **CAUSE TO EXIST FOR REASON** to cause sb or sth to exist for a particular reason (*usually passive*) ○ *She was made to be a star.* **17.** *vt.* **EARN** to earn or be paid a specified sum of money ○ *He makes fifty thousand a year.* **18.** *vt.* **CAUSE SOUND TO BE HEARD** to produce or give rise to a sound ○ *She made a choking noise in her throat.* **19.** *vt.* **ARRANGE FOR USE** to arrange sth properly for later use ○ *He made the bed carefully.* **20.** *vt.* **SCHEDULE MEETING** to fix a meeting or time ○ *Let's make a date for Friday.* **21.** *vt.* **REPRESENT STH** to count as one in a series ○ *That makes the third time he's lied to me.* **22.** *vt.* **AMOUNT TO** to amount to a total ○ *Five and three make eight.* **23.** *vt.* **HAVE NECESSARY QUALITIES FOR STH** to have the qualities required to be sth ○ *She'll make a very good doctor.* **24.** *vt.* **DEVELOP RELATIONSHIP** to acquire a friend, enemy, or acquaintance ○ *They made friends straightaway.* **25.** *vt.* **CAUSE TO SUCCEED** to cause sb to be successful, or cause sth to seem successful ○ *the novel that made her career* **26.** *vt.* **REACH A PLACE** to reach or arrive at a place ○ *I'm not sure we can make the island in this boat.* **27.** *vt.* **BE IN TIME FOR** to be in time to do sth or for sth to happen ○ *We can make the 10:05 if we hurry.* **28.** *vt.* **COVER DISTANCE** to travel a particular distance ○ *They made only five miles a day on the ascent.* **29.** *vt.* **BE INCLUDED IN** to succeed in being included or mentioned in sth ○ *stories that never make the national news* **30.** *vi.* **SIGNAL INTENTIONS** to act so as to indicate what is coming ○ *They made as if to leave.* **31.** *vt.* **ACHIEVE SEX WITH SB** to succeed in having sex with sb (*dated slang*) **32.** *vt.* BRIDGE **FULFIL BRIDGE CONTRACT** to fulfil a contract in a game of bridge by winning the required number of tricks **33.** *vt.* CARDS **WIN TRICK IN CARDS** to win a trick in a card game **34.** *vt.* ELECTRON ENG **CLOSE A CIRCUIT** to close an electrical circuit **35.** *vi.* AGRIC **MATURE** to dry and mature (*refers to hay*) ■ *n.* **1. BRAND** a brand of sth, e.g. an appliance, car, or machine ○ *Specify the make and model of the car.* **2. PROCESS AND OUTPUT** the process of making sth, or the amount or number made **3.** BUILD OR APPEARANCE the way that sth has been made, or the size or shape it naturally has (*literary*) ○ *a woodland cabin of rustic make* **4.** SORT a type with reference to character (*archaic or literary*) ○ *What make of man is he?* **5.** IDENTIFICATION the identification of sb or sth, usually made with the help of police records or information (*slang*) ○ *The police got a make on him from their records.* [Old English *macian.* Ultimately, from an Indo-European word meaning 'kneading', which is also the source of English *magma* and *match.*] —**makable** *adj.* ◇ **make believe** to pretend ◇ **make certain, make sure** to do what is necessary to ensure sth ○ *Make sure the door is locked.* ◇ **make do (with sth)** to use sth that is an unsatisfactory substitute or temporary alternative for the real thing ◇ **make it 1.** to be successful (*informal*) ○ *You'll never make it as an actor.* **2.** to succeed in getting somewhere ○ *We finally made it to the top of the hill.* **3.** to be able to attend ○ *I can't make it to the party tonight.* ◇ **make like** to imitate (*informal*) ○ *She made like she was doing the breaststroke.* ◇ **on the make 1.** trying hard to gain a profit or advantage, especially using underhand or dishonest means (*informal*) **2.** looking for or making efforts to persuade sb to be a sexual partner (*slang*)

WORD KEY: SYNONYMS

make, produce, create, fashion, manufacture

CORE MEANING: to bring sth into existence

make to bring sth into existence; **produce** to make sth in large quantities or in a commercial setting; **create** to make sth using imagination and artistic skill or to cause sth such as a job or opportunity to exist; **fashion** to make sth by shaping and working raw materials, especially when using only the hands or hand-held tools; **manufacture** to make sth in large numbers, usually in a factory using machinery, or, showing disapproval, to make sth quickly and cynically, especially sth that normally requires time and artistic skill.

---

make after *vt.* to chase after sb or sth

make away *vi.* = **make off**

make away with *vt.* **1.** STEAL to steal sth and abscond with it ○ *They made away with the week's takings.* **2.** ABDUCT to carry sb off by force **3.** GET RID OF to destroy or get rid of sth incriminating ○ *We think someone's made away with the DNA evidence.* **4.** KILL to kill sb (*dated*)

make for *vt.* **1.** MOVE TOWARDS to move quickly in the direction of sb or sth ○ *The reporters made for the courtroom.* **2.** HAVE AS RESULT to result in a particular situation ○ *This plan will make for a successful product launch.*

make off *vi.* to leave a place quickly, usually with good reason

make off with *vt.* = **make away with**

make out *v.* **1.** *vt.* SEE OR HEAR INDISTINCTLY to see or hear sb or sth but not clearly ○ *I could just make out her profile in the darkness.* **2.** *vt.* COMPREHEND to identify or understand sth ○ *I can't make out the suspect's motive.* **3.** *vt.* COMPLETE IN WRITING to write necessary information such as the date and the recipient's name on a bill or similar document ○ *The deed is made out in my spouse's name.* **4.** *vt.* SUGGEST to suggest or imply sth that may not be true ○ *The kids make him out to be a real tyrant.* **5.** *vt.* ARGUE IN SUPPORT OF to try to prove sth is true or valid by giving good reasons ○ *made out a case for keeping the work in-house* **6.** *vi.* MANAGE to perform in a situation (*informal*) ○ *How did you make out on the test?* **7.** *vi. US* ENGAGE IN SEXUAL ACTIVITIES WITHOUT INTERCOURSE to kiss and caress sb as an expression of sexual desire (*slang*) **8.** *vi. US* HAVE SEX to have sexual intercourse (*slang*)

make over *vt.* **1.** LAW MAKE SB ELSE OWNER OF STH to transfer the ownership of money or property to sb, usually in a legal document ○ *half of her estate was made over to her cousin* **2.** *US* SEW REFASHION GARMENT to alter or remodel a garment **3.** CHANGE APPEARANCE OF SB OR STH to make major changes to the way sb or sth looks

make up *v.* **1.** *vt.* MAKE READY to get sth ready, especially by putting a number of items together ○ *I've made up a packed lunch.* **2.** *vt.* JOIN TO FORM STH to combine with other people or objects to form a whole ○ *a group made up of four men and six women* **3.** *vt.* CONSTITUTE to form part of sth ○ *Women make up more than half the country's workforce.* **4.** *vt.* INVENT to invent an excuse, fact, or story ○ *made the whole story up to shock her parents* **5.** *vti.* THEATRE PREPARE FOR PERFORMANCE to prepare sb or yourself for an acting performance by applying cosmetics and fitting other accessories, e.g. false hair, necessary for assuming a given role ○ *It takes her two hours to make up for the role.* **6.** *vt.* COSMETICS PUT ON FACIAL COSMETICS to apply cosmetics to your own face or sb else's face **7.** *vt.* COMPLETE to make a number or amount complete ○ *You three pay £10 each and I'll make up the rest.* **8.** *vti.* RESOLVE A QUARREL to become friends again after a quarrel ○ *Haven't you two made up yet?* **9.** *vt.* APPLY SURFACE TO ROAD to surface a road, e.g. with tarmac, concrete, or bitumen **10.** *vt.* PRINTING ARRANGE LAYOUT OF PAGE to arrange columns of print and illustrations on a page **11.** *vi.* COMPENSATE to compensate for a failing such as a disappointment, deficiency, or shortcoming ○ *I'll buy lunch to make up for being late.*

make up to *vt.* **1.** TRY TO GAIN SB'S FAVOUR to try to gain sb's favour by behaving in a flattering and attentive way ○ *making up to the general manager's assistant* **2.** BEHAVE FLIRTATIOUSLY to flirt with sb

make with *vt. US* to start doing, using, or producing sth (*dated slang*) ○ *Hey, let's make with the party, huh?*

Makeba /mə káybə/, **Miriam** (*b.* 1932) South African-born US jazz and folk singer. The first internationally famous Black South African singer, she introduced African song to western audiences. Real name **Sensile Makeba**

make-believe *n.* imaginary situations or events that sb, especially a child playing, pretends are true (*often used before a noun*) ○ *watching them in their make-believe world*

make-do *n.* (*plural* **make-dos**) *US* SUBSTITUTE a substitute, often an inferior one ■ *adj.* SUBSTITUTING temporarily substituting for sth else ○ *a make-do dinner service in a furnished flat*

makefast /máyk faast/ *n.* a strong ring, post, or buoy to which a boat or ship is moored

make-or-break *adj.* likely to result in either complete success or complete failure

makeover /máykōvər/ *n.* **1.** CHANGE OF PHYSICAL APPEARANCE an alteration of the way sb looks, usually including changes in hairstyle and in style of make-up and clothes **2.** REMODELLING a remodelling of sth that completely changes the way it looks

maker /máykər/ *n.* **1.** CREATOR OR CAUSE sb who creates sth or is the source or cause of it (*often used in combination*) ○ *a maker of mischief* **2.** PRODUCER OF GOODS a person or organization that produces goods (*often used in combination*) ○ *a maker of mid-priced textiles* **3.** LAW SIGNER OF DOCUMENT sb who signs a legal document, especially a promissory note

Maker *n.* God, regarded as the creator of everything (*literary*)

makeshift /máyk shift/ *adj.* SUBSTITUTING providing a temporary and usually inferior substitute ■ *n.* SUBSTITUTE a temporary and usually inferior substitute [Mid-16thC. From *to make shift* 'to try all means'.]

makeup /máyk up/, **make-up** *n.* **1.** COSMETICS cosmetic products, especially for the face, e.g. lipstick and mascara (*often used before a noun*) ○ *Slap on a bit of makeup and you'll feel better.* **2.** THEATRE THEATRICAL COSMETICS the cosmetics and other accessories, e.g. false hair, that actors wear to alter their appearance on stage (*often used before a noun*) ○ *makeup department* **3.** THEATRE APPLYING ACTORS' COSMETICS the application of actors' cosmetics and other appearance-altering accessories, e.g. false hair (*often used before a noun*) ○ *working in makeup* **4.** COMBINATION OF PARTS OR QUALITIES the way parts or qualities combine or are arranged, especially in sb's personality ○ *Self-deprecation is an intrinsic part of her makeup.* **5.** PRINTING ARRANGEMENT OF TYPE the arrangement of typographic elements on a page

makeweight /máyk wayt/ *n.* **1.** ADDITIONAL WEIGHT sth placed on a scale to bring a weight up to a required level **2.** EXTRA PERSON OR OBJECT an extra person or object of no intrinsic importance introduced into a situation for the sole purpose of making up the required numbers ○ *invited her cousin along as a makeweight*

makimono /máki mṓnō/ (*plural* **-nos**) *n.* a horizontal Japanese scroll decorated with paintings or calligraphy [Late 19thC. From Japanese, 'a scroll', literally 'sth rolled up'.]

making /máyking/ *n.* **1.** CREATIVE ACTIVITY the activity of sb who makes sth ○ *during the making of the film* **2.** CAUSE OF SUCCESS sth that causes sb's success or progress ○ *a book that was the making of her career* ◇ **in the making** in the process of being made, formed, or developed

makings /máykingz/ *npl.* **1.** REQUIRED INGREDIENTS the things required to make sth, especially a dish of food **2.** POTENTIAL the qualities required to become a particular thing ○ *has the makings of a good lawyer*

mako shark /maákō-/ *n.* a slender blue-grey shark with a sharp nose and ferocious teeth, found in southern oceans. It can exceed 4 m/13 ft in length and is prized as a game fish. Genus: *Isurus.* [*Mako* from Maori]

makuta plural of **likuta**

Mal. *abbr.* **1.** BIBLE Malachi **2.** Malay **3.** Malayan **4.** Malaysia **5.** Malaysian

mal- /mə láy/ *prefix.* **1.** bad, badly ○ *malpractice* **2.** abnormal or inadequate ○ *malnutrition* [Via Old French from Latin *malus* 'bad' (source of English *malice, malady, malaria,* and *dismal*) and *male* 'badly']

Malabar Coast /mállәbaar-/ region on the south-western coast of India, that stretches from Goa southwards and includes most of Kerala State

malabsorption /mál əb sáwrpsh'n, -záwrpsh'n/ *n.* the inadequate absorption of nutrients from digested food in the alimentary canal, especially by the small intestine in coeliac disease

malac- *prefix.* = **malaco-** (*used before vowels*)

malacca /mə lákə/, **malacca cane** *n.* **1.** RATTAN PALM STEM the stem of the rattan palm, used to make walking sticks **2.** RATTAN WALKING STICK a walking stick made from the stem of the rattan palm [Mid-19thC. Named after MALACCA.]

Malacca former name for **Melaka**

Malacca, Strait of strait in southeastern Asia connecting the Andaman Sea with the South China Sea. Length: 800 km/500 mi.

Malachi /mállə kī/ *n.* **1.** HEBREW PROPHET an unidentified Hebrew prophet who wrote in the 5th century BC, usually referred to by this name **2.** BOOK OF THE BIBLE a book of the Bible containing writings by Malachi. See table at **Bible**

malachite /mállə kīt/ *n.* a green naturally-occurring carbonate of copper, used as a decorative stone and a source of copper. Formula: $Cu_2CO_3(OH)_2$. [14thC. Via Old French *melochite* from, ultimately, Greek *molokhitis,* a stone similar in colour to the mallow leaf, from *malakhē* 'mallow'.]

malacia /mə láyshi ə/ *n.* the abnormal softening of a tissue or organ of the body, e.g. the bones or kidneys, caused by a disease (*often used in combination*) [Early 18thC. Formed from Greek *malakos* 'soft' (see MALACO-).]

malaco- *prefix.* soft ○ *malacophyllous* [From Greek *malakos.* Ultimately from an Indo-European word that is also the ancestor of English *mild, melt,* and *mulch.*]

malacology /mállə kólləji/ *n.* the branch of zoology that involves the study of molluscs [Mid-19thC. Via French from, ultimately, modern Latin *Malacozoa* 'soft-bodied creatures', from Greek *malakos* (see MALACO-).] —**malacological** /mállәkә lójjik'l/ *adj.* —**malacologist** /mállə kólləjist/ *n.*

malacostracan /mállə kóstrəkən/ *n.* a member of a common group of crustaceans that usually have stalked eyes, a carapace, and a tail fan formed from the rear limbs. The group includes the lobster, crab, woodlouse, and krill. Subclass: Malacostraca. [Mid-19thC. Formed from modern Latin *Malacostraca,* order name, from Greek *malakos* 'soft' + *ostrakon* 'shell'.] —**malacostracan** *adj.*

maladaptation /mál adap táysh'n/ *n.* unsuitable or ineffective adaptation to a particular situation, function, or purpose

maladapted /mállə dáptid/ *adj.* unsuitable for or

poorly adapted to a particular situation, function, or purpose

maladaptive /málla dáptiv/ adj. **1. BADLY OR INCOMPLETELY ADAPTED** unsuitable for or poorly adapted to a particular situation, function, or purpose **2. NOT CONDUCIVE TO ADAPTATION** not facilitating or encouraging adaptation —**maladaptively** adv.

maladjusted /málla jústid/ adj. **1. BEHAVING AWKWARDLY IN SOCIAL SETTINGS** unable to cope with everyday social situations and personal relationships **2. ENG NOT PROPERLY ADJUSTED** needing to be correctly adjusted —**maladjustment** n.

maladministration /málləd minni stráysh'n/ n. incompetent or dishonest management or administration, especially in public affairs —**maladministrator** /málləd mínni straytər/ n. —**maladminister** /-mínnistər/ vt.

maladroit /málla dróyt/ adj. clumsy or insensitive in speech or behaviour (formal) [Late 17thC. From French, literally 'not adept', from adroit (see ADROIT).] —**maladroitly** adv. —**maladroitness** n.

malady /málladi/ (plural -**dies**) n. **1. ILLNESS** a physical or psychological disorder or disease (dated or humorous) **2. PROBLEM** a condition or situation that is problematic and requires a remedy [13thC. Via French maladie from, ultimately, Latin male habitus 'in bad condition'.]

mala fide /málla fídi/ adj., adv. done insincerely or dishonestly (formal) [Early 17thC. From Latin.]

Málaga /málləgə/ city, seaport, and holiday resort in southern Spain, on the Mediterranean Sea. It is the centre of the Costa del Sol, a major tourist region. Population: 532,425 (1995).

Malagasy /málla gássi/ n. (plural -**y** or -**ies**) **1. PEOPLES SB FROM MADAGASCAR** sb who was born on or is a citizen of Madagascar **2. LANG OFFICIAL LANGUAGE OF MADAGASCAR** one of the official languages of Madagascar, belonging to the Western branch of Austronesian languages. Malagasy is spoken by about 12 million people. ■ adj. **OF MADAGASCAR** relating to Madagascar, or its people, language, or culture [Mid-19thC. Variant of MADAGASCAR.] —**Malagasy** adj.

Malagasy Republic former name for **Madagascar** (1958–75)

malagueña /málla gáynyə/ n. **1. DANCE SPANISH DANCE** a Spanish dance that is similar to the fandango **2. MUSIC SPANISH TUNE** a Spanish folk song or tune similar to a fandango [Late 19thC. From Spanish, literally from MALAGA, a city in southern Spain.]

malaise /ma láyz/ n. **1. MED FEELING OF ILLNESS** a general feeling of illness or sickness without any specific diagnostic significance **2. GENERAL FEELING OF DISCONTENT** a general feeling of worry, discontent, or dissatisfaction, often resulting in lethargy [Mid-18thC. From French, literally 'ill ease', from aise (see EASE).]

malamute /málla moot, málla myoot/, **malemute** n. an Alaskan dog with a thick grey, black, or white coat, used especially for pulling sledges [Late 19thC. From Inupiaq malimiut, the name of an Alaskan people who developed the breed.]

Malang /mállang/ city in southwestern Indonesia, on the island of Java. Population: 548,193 (1989).

malapert /málla purt/ adj. **SAUCY OR BRAZEN** impudent or bold in speech or behaviour (archaic or literary) ■ n. **SAUCY OR BRAZEN PERSON** sb who is impudent or bold in speech or behaviour (archaic or literary) [15thC. Via Old French, literally 'not experienced', from, ultimately, Latin expertus (see EXPERT). The meaning was influenced in Old French by association with apert 'saucy'.] —**malapertly** adv. —**malapertness** n.

malaprop /málla prop/ n. = **malapropism** n. 2

malapropism /málla propizəm/ n. **1. UNINTENTIONAL USE OF WRONG WORD** the misuse of a word through confusion with another word that sounds similar, especially when the effect is ridiculous **2. EXAMPLE OF MALAPROPISM** an instance of using malapropism [Early 19thC. Formed from the name of Mrs Malaprop (from MALAPROPOS), a character in Richard Sheridan's play The Rivals, who often confused words in this way.] —**malapropist** n.

malapropos /mál apprə pó/ adj. **OUT OF PLACE** not appropriate to the situation in which sth is done or

said (formal) ■ adv. **INAPPROPRIATELY OR INOPPORTUNELY** in an inappropriate way or at an inopportune moment (formal) ■ n. **INAPT OR UNTIMELY SPEECH OR ACTION** sth that is done or said in an inappropriate way or at an inopportune moment (formal) [Mid-17thC. From French mal à propos 'ill-suited to the purpose'.]

malar /máylər/, **malar bone** adj. **OF THE CHEEK OR CHEEKBONE** relating to the cheek, the cheekbone, or the side of the head ■ n. **CHEEKBONE** the cheekbone [Late 18thC. From modern Latin malaris, from Latin mala 'jaw, cheekbone', of unknown origin.]

Mälaren /mélərən/ lake in southeastern Sweden. Stockholm lies on its eastern shore. Area: 1,140 sq. km/440 sq. mi.

malaria /mə láiri ə/ n. an infectious disease caused by a parasite that is transmitted by the bite of infected mosquitoes. Common in hot countries, the disease is characterized by recurring chills and fever. [Mid-18thC. From Italian malaria 'bad air', which was once thought to be the cause of the disease.] —**malarial** adj. —**malarian** adj. —**malarious** adj.

malariology /mə láiri ólləji/ n. the scientific study of malaria —**malariologist** n.

malarkey /mə láarki/, **malarky** n. nonsense or rubbish, especially insincere talk (informal) [Early 20thC. Origin unknown.]

malate /mállayt, máy layt/ n. a chemical compound that is a salt or ester of malic acid

malathion /málla thí on/ n. a colourless solid organophosphorus insecticide. Formula: $C_{10}H_{19}O_6PS_2$. [Mid-20thC. Coined from MALATE + THIO- + -ON.]

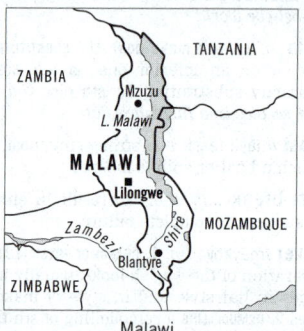

Malawi

Malawi /mələáawi/ republic in southeastern Africa. Language: English. Currency: kwacha. Capital: Lilongwe. Population: 9,453,000 (1996). Area: 118,484 sq. km/45,747 sq. mi. Official name **Republic of Malawi**. Former name **Nyasaland** —**Malawian** n., adj.

Malawi, Lake = **Nyasa, Lake**

Malay /mə láy/ n. **1. PEOPLES MEMBER OF SE ASIAN ETHNIC GROUP** a member of an ethnic group that inhabits the Malay Peninsula, Indonesia, and other islands of the Malay Archipelago and the Philippines **2. LANG LANGUAGE OF MALAYSIA** a language spoken in Malaysia, also spoken in parts of Singapore, Borneo, Sumatra, Java, and surrounding areas. It belongs to the Western branch of Austronesian languages. Malay is the native tongue of about 22 million speakers, with approximately 100 million people using it as a second language. ■ adj. **1. PEOPLES OF MALAYS** relating to the Malay people, or their language or culture **2. GEOG OF MALAYSIA** relating to the Malay Peninsula,

Malaysia, or the Malay Archipelago **3. PEOPLES** relating to the Malay people or their culture [Late 16thC. From Malay malayu, melayu.] —**Malayan** n., adj.

Malaya, Federation of /mə láy ə/ former state in the Malay Peninsula. It was incorporated into the Federation of Malaysia in 1963.

Malayalam /málli áaləm, mállay áaləm/, **Malayalaam** n. a Dravidian language that is the official language of the Indian state of Kerala. Malayalam is spoken by about 30 million people. [Early 19thC. From Malayalam Malayālam, literally 'mountain man'.] —**Malayalam** adj.

Malayan /mə láyən/ adj. **PEOPLES** relating to Malaya, or its people or culture

Malay Archipelago the world's largest system of island groups, comprising over 20,000 islands, mainly in Indonesia and the Philippines. Area: 2.8 million sq. km/1.1 million sq. mi.

Malay Peninsula peninsula in southeastern Asia that includes parts of Myanmar, Thailand, and Malaysia

Malaysia /mə láyzi ə, mə láyzhə/ constitutional monarchy in southeastern Asia, on the South China Sea, comprising the southern portion of the Malay Peninsula and parts of the Island of Borneo. Language: Bahasa Malaysia. Currency: ringgit. Capital: Kuala Lumpur. Population: 17,566,982 (1991). Area: 329,758 sq. km/127,320 sq. mi. Official name **Federation of Malaysia** —**Malaysian** n., adj.

Malaysian English n. a variety of English spoken in Malaysia

--- **WORD KEY: WORLD ENGLISH** ---

Malaysian English is the English language as used in Malaysia since the formation of the nation-state in 1963. Prior to independence from Britain the term *Anglo-Malay* was used, indicating the influence of the Malay language. From the earlier period come such general English words of Malay origin as *amok*, *durian*, *kampong*, *mango*, *orang-utan*, *sago*, and *sarong*. Malaysian English is 'rhotic' (i.e., 'r' is pronounced in such words as *art*, *door*, and *worker*). There is a tendency towards full vowels in all syllables (e.g. *7* pronounced 'seh-ven', not 'sevn') and a reduction in consonant clusters at the ends of words ('muss' for *must*, 'bes' for *best*, 'liv' *lived*, 'relac' *relax*). In grammar, reflexive pronouns are used for emphasis, often without the verb *to be*, as in 'Himself sick', and certain general-purpose particles are used, such as *lah*, indicating informality and intimacy, as in 'Can do it lah?' ('Can you do it?'). There is considerable hybridization between Malay and English, as in: 'She wanted to beli some barang-barang' ('She wanted to buy some things'). See ANGLO-HYBRID, SINGAPOREAN ENGLISH.

Malcolm III /málkəm/, **King of Scotland** (c. 1031–93). He became king after killing Macbeth in 1057 and ruled until his death. He made peace with the King of England, William I (the Conqueror), in 1072.

Malcolm X (1925–65) US political activist. He was a prominent member of the Black Muslims and founder of the Organization of Afro-American Unity (1964). After moderating his views on Black separatism, he was assassinated. Born **Malcolm Little**

malcontent /mál kən tent/ n. **DISCONTENTED PERSON** sb who is discontented or dissatisfied with a particular state of affairs, e.g. a political system, or with things in general ■ adj. **NOT CONTENT** discontented or dis-

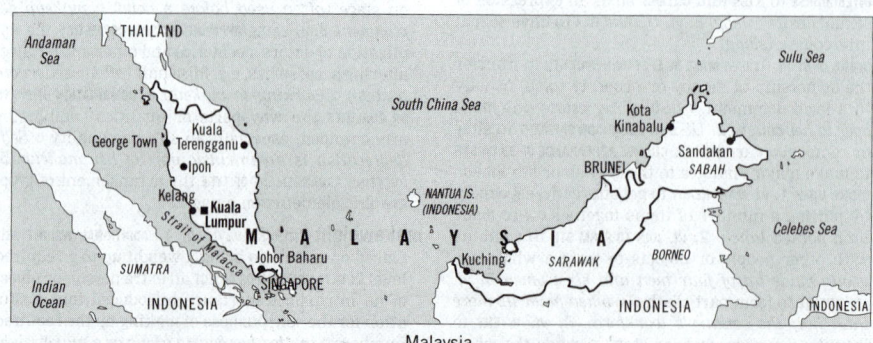

Malaysia

Malcolm X

satisfied with sth, especially a political system [Late 16thC. From French, literally 'ill contented', from *content* (see CONTENT).] —**malcontented** /málkən téntid/ *adj.* —**malcontentedly** *adv.* —**malcontentedness** *n.*

mal de mer /mál də máir/ *n.* = **seasickness** [Late 18thC. From French, literally 'sea sickness'.]

maldistribution /mál distri byóosh'n/ *n.* unequal and unfair distribution of sth, especially resources or wealth

Maldivan /máwl dīv'n, -divv'n/ *adj.* PEOPLES relating to the Maldives, or their people or culture

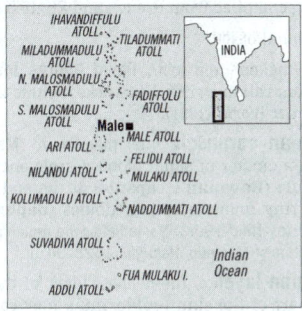

Maldives

Maldives /máwl divz, mál dīvz/ island republic in southern Asia, located southwest of the southern tip of India. Language: Divehi. Currency: rufiyaa. Capital: Male. Population: 270,758 (1996). Area: 298 sq. km/115 sq. mi. Official name **Republic of the Maldives** —**Maldivan** *n., adj.*

Maldon /máwldən/ historic town, river port, and local government district in Essex, England. Population: 15,841 (1991).

male /mayl/ *adj.* **1.** ZOOL PRODUCING SPERM relating or belonging to the sex that produces sperm to fertilize female eggs **2.** RELATING TO MEN OR BOYS relating to, involving, or traditionally characteristic of men or boys. ◊ **masculine 3.** BIOL FERTILIZING FEMALE SEX CELL capable of fertilizing a female reproductive cell (**gamete**) during sexual reproduction **4.** BOT BEARING ONLY STAMENS used to describe a flower or plant that bears stamens but not pistils and does not produce fruit or seeds **5.** ENG MACHINE PART OR FITTING used to describe a projecting part such as a bolt or plug that is designed to fit into a hollow part or socket that is the female counterpart ■ *n.* **1.** BIOL MALE PERSON OR ANIMAL a person or animal belonging to the sex that produces sperm **2.** BOT PLANT WITH MALE FLOWERS ONLY a plant that has only male flowers [14thC. Via Old French from Latin *masculus* (source of English *masculine*), from *mas* 'male person', of unknown origin.] —**maleness** *n.*

Male /maá lay/ **1.** atoll in the Maldives in the northern Indian Ocean **2.** capital city of the Maldives, on the Male atoll. Population: 62,973 (1995).

male alto (*plural* **male altos**) *n.* = **countertenor**

maleate /málli ayt/ *n.* any salt or ester of maleic acid

Malebo Pool /mə láybō-/ broad section of the River Congo. Area: 450 sq. km/174 sq. mi. Former name **Stanley Pool**

male chauvinist *n.* a man who believes in the innate superiority of men over women (*disapproving*) — **male chauvinism** *n.*

male chauvinist pig *n.* an offensive term for a man who believes that men are innately superior to women, especially one who expresses his opinions in an aggressive or offensive way (*slang insult*)

Malecite /málla sīt/ (*plural* **-cites** *or* **-cite**), **Maliseet** /-seet/ (*plural* **-seets** *or* **-seet**) *n.* **1.** PEOPLES NATIVE N AMERICAN PEOPLE a member of a Native North American people who live in New Brunswick, Quebec, and Maine. The Malecites joined the Abenaki confederacy and fought against both the Iroquois confederacy and the British. **2.** LANG LANGUAGE OF THE MALECITES the language of the Malecites, belonging to the Algonquian branch of Algonquian-Wakashan languages [Mid-19thC. From Micmac *malisiit*, literally 'sb who speaks an incomprehensible language'.] —**Malecite** *adj.*

maledict /málli dict/ *vti.* (**-dicts, -dicting, -dicted**) CURSE SB OR STH to utter a curse against sb or sth (*literary*) ■ *adj.* ACCURSED cursed or deserving to be cursed (*archaic*) [Early 17thC. From Latin *maledicere* (see MALEDICTION).]

malediction /málli díksh'n/ *n.* (*formal*) **1.** CURSE a curse **2.** SLANDER slander or evil talk about sb [14thC. From the Latin stem *maledicere-*, from *maledicere* 'to speak ill of', from *dicere*.] —**maledictive** *adj.*

malefactor /málli faktər/ *n.* sb who does wrong, especially a criminal (*formal*) [15thC. From Latin, formed from *male facere* 'to do evil'.] —**malefaction** /málli fáksh'n/ *n.*

male fern *n.* a fern whose rhizomes and scaly stalks are used to make a resin that expels tapeworms. Latin name: *Dryopteris filix-mas*.

malefic /mə léffik/ *adj.* having a harmful or evil effect or influence (*formal*) [Mid-17thC. From Latin *maleficus*, literally 'evil-doing', from *male* 'badly'.]

maleficent /mə léffiss'nt/ *adj.* causing harm or doing evil intentionally, or capable of such acts [Mid-17thC. Back-formation from earlier *maleficence*, from Latin *maleficentia*, literally 'evil doing', from *male* 'badly'.] —**maleficence** *n.*

maleic acid /mə láyik-/ *n.* a colourless crystalline solid used in the manufacture of polymers. Formula: $C_4H_4O_4$. [*Maleic* from French *maléique*, an alteration of *malique* (see MALIC)]

male menopause *n.* a period in middle age when some men experience feelings of insecurity and anxiety about physical decline, sometimes compared to the effects of the menopause in women

malemute *n.* = **malamute**

Malevich /mállivich/, **Kasimir** (1878–1935) Russian painter. He formulated an approach he called suprematism and contributed to the development of geometrical abstraction.

malevolent /mə lévvələnt/ *adj.* **1.** WANTING TO CAUSE HARM having or showing a desire to harm others **2.** HARMFUL OR EVIL having a harmful or evil effect or influence [Early 16thC. Directly or via Old French from the Latin stem *malevolent-*, from *male* 'badly' + *volens*, the present participle of *velle* 'to wish'.] —**malevolence** *n.* —**malevolently** *adv.*

malfeasance /mal feéz'nss/ *n.* (*formal*) **1.** MISCONDUCT wrong or illegal conduct, especially in politics or the civil service. ◊ **misfeasance, nonfeasance 2.** UNLAWFUL ACT an unlawful act, especially one committed by a politician or civil servant [Late 17thC. From Anglo-Norman *malfaisance*, from Old French *malfaire* 'to do ill', from Latin *malefacere*.] —**malfeasant** *adj., n.*

malformation /mál fawr máysh'n/ *n.* abnormality in the shape or structure of sth

malformed /mál fáwrmd/ *adj.* abnormal in shape or structure

malfunction /mal fúngksh'n/ *vi.* (**-tions, -tioning, -tioned**) FAIL TO WORK NORMALLY to fail to function in the correct or normal way, or stop working altogether, usually because of a fault or bad design ■ *n.* FAILURE TO WORK NORMALLY a breakdown or failure to function in the correct or normal way, usually because of a fault or bad design

Mali

Mali /maáli/ landlocked republic in western Africa. A former French colony, it gained independence in 1960. Language: French. Currency: CFA franc. Capital: Bamako. Population: 9,204,000 (1996). Area: 1,240,192 sq. km/478,841 sq. mi. Official name **Republic of Mali**

malic /mállik, máylik/ *adj.* relating to or derived from malic acid [Late 18thC. Directly or via French *malique* from, ultimately, Latin *malum* 'apple'.]

$$HO-\overset{O}{\underset{H}{\overset{||}{C}}}-\overset{H}{\underset{OH}{\overset{|}{C}}}-\overset{H}{\underset{H}{\overset{|}{C}}}-\overset{O}{\overset{||}{C}}-OH$$

Malic acid

malic acid *n.* a colourless crystalline solid found in fruits such as apples. Formula: $C_4H_6O_5$.

malice /málliss/ *n.* **1.** WISH TO HARM OTHERS the desire to cause harm to another or others, or to see sb in pain **2.** LAW INTENT TO HARM OTHERS the intention to commit an unlawful act that will result in harm to others and does not have excusable cause [Via French from Latin *malitia*, from *malus* (see MAL-)]

malicious /mə líshəss/ *adj.* motivated by or resulting from a desire to cause harm or pain to others — **maliciously** *adv.* —**maliciousness** *n.*

malign /mə lín/ *vt.* (**-ligns, -ligning, -ligned**) DEFAME OR SPEAK BADLY OF SB to say or write bad or unpleasant things about sb or sth, especially things that are potentially damaging and may not be true ■ *adj.* HARMFUL OR EVIL harmful or evil in nature, effect, or intention [15thC. Via French from, ultimately, Latin *malignus*, literally 'of evil kind'.] —**maligner** *n.* —**malignly** *adv.*

—————— WORD KEY: SYNONYMS ——————
malign, cast aspersions, defame, slander, libel, vilify
CORE MEANING: to say or write sth damaging about sb
malign to criticize sb in a spiteful and false or misleading way; **cast aspersions** to make remarks or comments that challenge sb's reputation; **defame** to make an attack on sb's good name or reputation with a view to damaging or destroying it; **slander** in legal terms, to make spoken false damaging accusations about sb injurious to the person's reputation; **libel** in legal terms, to make false damaging accusations about sb in writing, signs, or pictures; **vilify** to make viciously defamatory statements about sb.

malignancy /mə lígnənssi/ (*plural* **-cies**) *n.* **1.** **malignity, malignance** STATE OF BEING MALIGNANT the condition or quality of being malignant **2.** MED CANCEROUS GROWTH a tumour that invades surrounding tissue and may spread to distant parts of the body by way of the lymphatic system or the circulation of the blood

malignant /mə lígnənt/ *adj.* **1.** WANTING TO DO EVIL full of hate and showing a desire to harm others **2.** HARMFUL likely to cause harm **3.** MED LIKELY TO GROW OR SPREAD used to describe a tumour that invades the tissue around it and may spread to other parts of the body **4.** MED LIKELY TO CAUSE DEATH used to describe a disease or condition that is liable to cause death or serious disablement unless effectively treated [Mid-16thC. From late Latin *malignare* 'to plot against', from Latin *malignus*, literally 'of evil kind'.] —**malignantly** adv.

malignity /mə lígnəti/ (plural **-ties**) n. **1.** DESIRE TO DO EVIL intense hatred and a strong desire to harm others **2.** INTENTIONALLY HARMFUL ACT an intentionally harmful or evil act **3.** HARMFUL POTENTIAL potential to cause harm or death

malines /mə leén/ n. **1.** NETTING USED IN DRESSMAKING thin stiff net with hexagonal holes that is used in dressmaking **2.** = **Mechlin** [Mid-19thC. From French, named after the city of *Malines* (Mechlin) in Belgium.]

malinger /mə líng gər/ (**-gers, -gering, -gered**) vi. to pretend to be ill, especially in order to avoid work (*disapproving*) [Late 18thC. From French *malingre* 'sickly', of unknown origin.] —**malingerer** n.

Malinke /mə língki/ (plural **-ke** or **-kes**) n. **1.** PEOPLES MEMBER OF W AFRICAN PEOPLE a member of a people who live in parts of West Africa, especially in the Côte d'Ivoire, Mali, Senegal, and Gambia. The Malinke have traditionally used cowry shells as a medium of exchange. **2.** LANG LANGUAGE OF THE MALINKE the language of the Malinke, belonging to the Mande branch of Niger-Congo languages. Malinke is spoken by about four million people. [Late 19thC. From Malinke.] —**Malinke** adj.

Malinowski /málli nófski/, **Bronislaw Kasper** (1884–1942) Polish-born British social anthropologist. He is regarded as the founder of the functional school of anthropology and was noted for his research into the formation of human culture.

Maliseet n., adj. = **Malecite**

malison /málliss'n, málliz'n/ n. a curse (*archaic*) [13thC. Via Old French *maleiçon* from the Latin stem *malediction-* (see MALEDICTION).]

malkin /máwlkin, máwkin, málkin/ n. a cat (*regional archaic*) [Late 17thC. Formed from *Malde*, an early variant of the name 'Maude'.]

mall /mawl, mal/ n. **1.** US = **shopping centre 2.** SHADY AVENUE a sheltered and shady avenue or promenade **3.** GAME, HIST PALL-MALL ALLEY in former times, an alley used for playing the game of pall-mall [Mid-17thC. Shortening of PALL-MALL, formerly a popular game. The sense 'shopping complex' comes from the name of *The Mall* in London, a former pall-mall alley that became a fashionable promenade.]

Mallard

mallard /máll aard, mállərd/ (plural **-lards** or **-lard**) n. a wild duck found in most parts of the northern hemisphere. The male has a dark green head with a white ring round the neck. Latin name: *Anas platyrhynchos*. [14thC. From Old French, of uncertain origin: perhaps formed from *male* (see MALE).]

Mallarmé /mál aar may/, **Stéphane** (1842–98) French poet. The author of *L'après-midi d'un faune* (1876) and an originator of the symbolist movement, his work is characterized by obscurity and allusion.

mall crawl n. US the act of going to a large number of different shops in a shopping centre (*informal*)

malleable /málli əb'l/ adj. **1.** ABLE TO BE SHAPED AND BENT used to describe a metal or other substance that can be shaped or bent without breaking **2.** EASILY INFLUENCED easily persuaded or influenced by

others [14thC. Via Old French from, ultimately, Latin *malleus* 'hammer' (see MALLEUS).] —**malleability** /málli ə bílləti/ n. —**malleableness** /málli əb'lnəss/ n. — **malleably** adv.

—— **WORD KEY: SYNONYMS** ——
See Synonyms at *pliable*.

mallee /mállee/ n. **1.** SHRUBBY EUCALYPTUS a low-growing eucalyptus tree that flourishes in desert regions of Australia. Genus: *Eucalyptus*. **2.** THICKET OF MALLEE TREES a group of mallee trees growing closely together **3.** **mallee, Mallee** *Aus* AREA WITH MANY MALLEE TREES an area of land in southern Australia where mallee trees are the predominant vegetation [Mid-19thC. From an Australian Aboriginal language.]

Mallee /málli/ region in Australia, in northwestern Victoria State, situated between the rivers Murray and Wimmera. Area: 41,000 sq. km/16,000 sq. mi.

mallee root n. the thick underground stem (**rhizome**) of a mallee tree, often used as fuel

mallemuck /málli muk/ n. a sea bird such as the fulmar, petrel, or albatross [Late 17thC. From Dutch *mallemok*, literally 'stupid gull'.]

malleolus /mə leé ələss/ (plural **-li** /-lī/) n. either of the hammer-shaped bony protuberances at the sides of the ankle joint that project from the lower end of the tibia and fibula [Early 17thC. From Latin, literally 'little hammer', from *malleus* (see MALLEUS).] —**malleolar** /mə leé ələr, málli-/ adj.

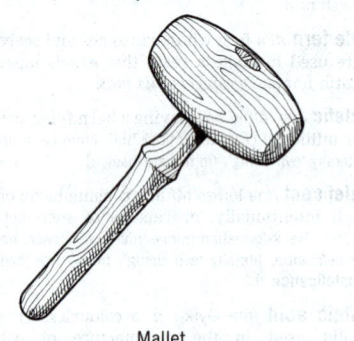

Mallet

mallet /mállət/ n. **1.** TOOL SIMILAR TO HAMMER a tool with a large usually wooden or metal head that is used for driving another tool such as a chisel, or for striking or moulding a material **2.** SPORTS STICK USED IN CROQUET OR POLO a long stick with a cylindrical head, used to hit the ball in the games of croquet and polo **3.** MUSIC HAMMER USED TO PLAY PERCUSSION INSTRUMENT a small hammer often with a padded head used for playing musical instruments such as the marimba, xylophone, drums, and chimes [15thC. From French *maillet*, literally 'small hammer', from *mail* (see MAUL).]

malleus /málli əss/ (plural **-i** /-ī/) n. a hammer-shaped bone, the outermost of three small bones in the middle ear that transmit sound waves from the eardrum to the inner ear. ◊ **incus, stapes** [Mid-17thC. From Latin, 'hammer' (source of English *mallet* and *malleable*). Ultimately from an Indo-European word meaning 'to crush', which is also the ancestor of English *meal*[1] and *molar*[1].]

mallow /mállō/ (plural **-lows** or **-low**) n. **1.** FLOWERING PLANT a wild or cultivated plant with pink, purple, or white flowers, fine hairs on its stem and leaves, and disc-shaped fruit. Genus: *Malva*. **2.** PLANT RELATED TO MALLOW a plant resembling or related to the true mallow. ◊ **rose mallow, marsh mallow** [Pre-12thC. From Latin *malva*.]

malm /maam/ n. **1.** GEOL TYPE OF LIMESTONE a limestone that is greyish in colour and crumbles easily **2.** GEOL CHALKY SOIL a chalky soil produced by the crumbling of malm **3.** BUILDING MIXTURE OF CLAY AND CHALK a mixture of clay and chalk used to make bricks [Old English *mealm*. Ultimately from an Indo-European base meaning 'to pound, grind', which is also the ancestor of English *meal*[1].]

Malmesbury /maalmz bəri/ ancient market town on the River Avon in Wiltshire, southwestern England. Population: 4,439 (1991).

Malmö /málmō/ industrial city and port in southwestern Sweden, opposite Copenhagen on the

Danish side of the Øresund. Population: 245,699 (1996).

malmsey /maámzi/ n. a dark fortified wine produced in Madeira, the sweetest type of Madeira wine [14thC. Via Middle Dutch from medieval Latin *malmasia*, named after the town of *Monemvasia* in southern Greece, where it was originally made.]

malnourished /mal núrrisht/ adj. having a diet that leads to physical harm through inadequacy, inappropriateness, or excess —**malnourishment** n.

malnutrition /mál nyoo trísh'n/ n. a lack of healthy foods in the diet or an excessive intake of unhealthy foods, leading to physical harm

malocclusion /mállə kloózh'n/ n. an undesirable relative positioning of the upper and lower teeth when the jaw is closed —**maloccluded** adj.

malodorous /mal ōdərəss/ adj. smelling unpleasant or offensive —**malodorously** adv. —**malodorousness** n.

malonic acid /mə lónik ássid, mə lónnik-/ n. a colourless crystalline solid obtained from sugar beet. It is used in the manufacture of pharmaceuticals. Formula: $C_3H_4O_4$. [From French *malonique*, an alteration of *malique* (see MALIC).]

Malory /málləri/, **Sir Thomas** (d. 1471) English writer and translator. He wrote *Le Morte d'Arthur* (1469–70), a retelling of the legends surrounding King Arthur, compiled from French and English sources.

maloti plural of **loti**

Malouf /málloof, mə loóf/, **David George Joseph** (b. 1934) Australian writer. His works include the novel *The Great World* (1991).

Malpighian corpuscle /mal píggi ən-/, **Malpighian body** n. a cluster of small blood vessels enclosed in a capsule (**Bowman's capsule**) at the end of each of the tiny urine-secreting tubules (**nephrons**) of the kidney [Mid-19thC. Named after the Italian physician and anatomist Marcello *Malpighi* (1628–94).]

Malpighian layer n. the deepest layer of the outermost part of the skin (**epidermis**), now called the basal cell layer (*dated*) [See MALPIGHIAN CORPUSCLE]

Malpighian tubule, **Malpighian tube** n. a narrow tube in the body of an insect that serves as an organ of excretion [See MALPIGHIAN CORPUSCLE]

malposition /málpə zísh'n/ n. the undesirable position of sth, especially a part of the body or a fetus in the womb —**malposed** /mal pōzd/ adj.

malpractice /mal práktiss/ n. **1.** WRONG OR NEGLIGENT CONDUCT OF PROFESSIONAL illegal, unethical, negligent, or immoral behaviour by sb in a professional or official position, resulting in a failure to fulfil the duties or responsibilities associated with that position **2.** MED MEDICAL MISCONDUCT unethical, illegal, negligent, or immoral behaviour by a physician, resulting in a failure to fulfill the duties and responsibilities required of a physician **3.** EXAMPLE OF MALPRACTICE an act or instance of malpractice —**malpractitioner** /mál prak tísh'nər/ n.

Malraux /mal rō/, **André** (1901–76) French novelist, art theorist, archaeologist, and public servant. Although known chiefly for his novels, his writings reflect the many fields in which he worked.

malt /mawlt, molt/ n. **1.** GRAIN USED TO MAKE ALCOHOLIC DRINKS grain such as barley that has begun germination by being soaked in water. It is used chiefly in brewing and distilling to make beer and whisky. **2.** = **malt whisky 3.** = **malt liquor 4.** US = **malted milk** n. **2** ■ adj. CONTAINING MALT made from or containing malt ■ v. (**malts, malting, malted**) **1.** vti. CHANGE GRAIN INTO MALT to make cereal grain into malt by soaking it in water to start germination and then drying it in a kiln, or undergo this process **2.** vt. MAKE OR MIX STH WITH MALT to make sth with malt, or add malt to sth [Old English *mealt*, of prehistoric Germanic origin]

Malta /máwltə/ republic consisting of two main islands and nearby islets in the central Mediterranean Sea. It became independent from Britain in 1964. Language: Maltese, English. Currency: Maltese lira. Capital: Valletta. Population: 373,000 (1996). Area: 316 sq. km/122 sq. mi. Official name **Republic of Malta**

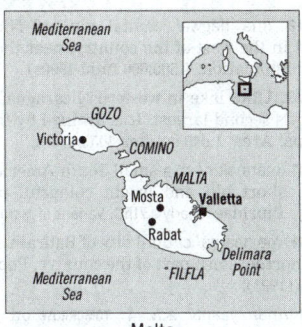

Malta

Malta fever *n.* = **brucellosis** [Named after MALTA, because the disease was once common in the Mediterranean area]

maltase /máwl tayz, -tayss, mol-, -/ *n.* an enzyme that breaks down maltose into glucose

malted milk, malted *n.* **1. POWDER USED TO MAKE DRINK** a soluble powder made from dried milk and malted grain **2. DRINK MADE FROM MALTED MILK** a drink made from malted milk, whole milk, ice cream, and flavouring

Maltese /máwl teéz, mól-/ *n.* (*plural* -tese) **1. PEOPLES SB FROM MALTA** sb who was born on or is a citizen of Malta **2. LANG LANGUAGE OF MALTA** one of the official languages of Malta, belonging to the Semitic branch of Afro-Asiatic languages and featuring a large number of words adopted from Italian. Maltese is spoken by about 300,000 people. **3. ZOOL MALTESE DOG OR CAT** a Maltese dog or Maltese cat ■ *adj.* **PEOPLES** relating to Malta, or its people or culture —**Maltese** *adj.*

Maltese cross *n.* a cross with four arms resembling arrowheads that taper towards the centre

malt extract *n.* a sweet sticky substance produced from malt and used as an additive in cooking or brewing

maltha /máltha/ *n.* a black viscous bitumen that is a naturally-occurring mixture of hydrocarbons [Early 17thC. Via Latin from Greek, a mixture of pitch and wax.]

Malthus /málthəss/, **Thomas Robert** (1766–1834) British economist. His theory of population growth led to fears that the rising number of living people would produce widespread famine. He advocated birth control as a means of combating poverty. —**Malthusian** /mal thyoózi ən/ *adj., n.* —**Malthusianism** /mal thyoózi ənizəm/ *n.*

malt liquor *n.* an alcoholic drink that is brewed from malt, especially one having a higher alcohol content than most beer or ale

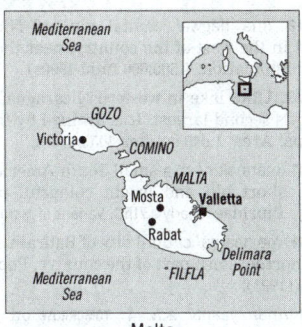

Maltose

maltose /máwl tōz, -tōss, mól-, -/ *n.* a white crystalline sugar formed from starch by enzymes and used as a sweetener and nutrient. Formula: $C_{12}H_{22}O_{11}$. [Mid-19thC. Formed from MALT.]

maltreat /mal treét/ (-treats, -treating, -treated) *vt.* to treat sb or sth badly or cruelly, usually through neglect or abuse [Early 18thC. From French *maltraiter*, literally 'to treat badly', from *traiter* (see TREAT).] —**maltreater** *n.* —**maltreatment** *n.*

————— WORD KEY: SYNONYMS —————
See Synonyms at *misuse*.

maltster /máwltstər, mólt-/ *n.* sb whose job involves producing or selling malt

malt sugar *n.* = **maltose**

malt whisky *n.* **1. WHISKY MADE FROM MALTED BARLEY** a whisky distilled from malted barley, often one designated single-malt **2. PORTION OF MALT WHISKY** a drink or measure of malt whisky

malvasia /málvə seé ə/ *n.* the variety of grape that is used to make malmsey wine [Mid-19thC. Via Italian from medieval Latin, a variant of *malmasia* (see MALMSEY).] —**malvasian** *adj.*

Malvern Hills /máwlvərn hílz/ range of hills in west-central England. The highest point is the Worcestershire Beacon, 425 m/1,395 ft. Population: 91,700 (1995).

malversation /málvər sáysh'n/ *n.* dishonest or unethical conduct by sb in a professional position or public office, often involving bribery, extortion, or embezzlement (*formal*) [Mid-16thC. Via French from, ultimately, Latin *male versari* 'to behave badly'.]

mam /mam/ *n.* mother (*regional informal*) [Late 16thC. Origin uncertain: probably an imitation of a child's first attempts at speech.]

mama /maámə, mə maá/, **mamma** *n.* **1. MOTHER** mother (*dated informal*) **2.** *US* **WOMAN OR WIFE** a woman, especially sb's girlfriend or wife (*slang*) (*sometimes considered offensive*) [Late 16thC. From children's first attempts at speech.]

mamba /mámbə/ *n.* a large venomous snake found in tropical Africa, especially a green or black snake that lives in trees. Genus: *Dendroaspis*. [Mid-19thC. From Zulu *imamba*.]

mambo /mámbō/ *n.* (*plural* -bos) **1. DANCE DANCE RESEMBLING RUMBA** a modern Latin American dance originating in Cuba, similar to the rumba **2. MUSIC MUSIC FOR MAMBO** the music for the mambo. It is in 4/4 time and has strong accents on the backbeats. ■ *vi.* (-bos, -boing, -boed) **DANCE THE MAMBO** to dance the mambo [Mid-20thC. From American Spanish, of uncertain origin.]

Mameluke /mámmi look/ *n.* a member of a former military caste, originally comprising enslaved Turks, that ruled Egypt from the 13th century to the 16th, remaining powerful until the early 19th century [Early 16thC. Via French from Arabic *mamlūk* 'enslaved person', from *malaka* 'to possess'.]

Mamet /mámmit/, **David** (*b.* 1947) US playwright, and film director. His work, e.g. the film *Glengarry Glen Ross*, often focuses on the alienation of lower middle-class life.

mamey /ma meé/ (*plural* -meys) *n.* **1. TREES W INDIAN TREE** a tree that grows in the West Indies, bears large edible fruit, and has white fragrant flowers. Latin name: *Mammea americana*. **2. FOOD RED-SKINNED FRUIT** the edible fruit of the mamey tree that has red skin, yellow flesh, and poisonous seeds [Late 16thC. Via American Spanish *mamei* from Taino.]

mamilla /ma míllə/ (*plural* **mamillae** /ma míllee/) *n.* **1. NIPPLE** a nipple or teat **2. PART RESEMBLING NIPPLE** a protuberance or organ that resembles a nipple or teat [Late 17thC. From Latin, literally 'little breast', from *mamma* (see MAMMA[1]).] —**mamillary** /mámmiləri/ *adj.*

mamillate /mámmi layt/, **mamillated** /-laytid/ *adj.* **1. HAVING NIPPLES** having nipples or protrusions that resemble nipples **2. LIKE A NIPPLE** resembling a nipple in shape or function

mamm- *prefix.* = **mammo-** (*used before vowels*)

mamma[1] /mámmə/ (*plural* -mae /-mee/) *n.* the milk-secreting organ of female mammals, e.g. a woman's breast or a cow's udder. It includes the mammary gland and associated exterior structures such as the nipple or teat. (*technical*) [Pre-12thC. From Latin. Ultimately from an Indo-European word meaning 'mother', ultimately from children's first attempts at speaking.] —**mammate** *adj.* —**mammiform** *adj.*

mamma[2] *n.* = **mama** (*informal*)

mammae plural of **mamma**[1]

mammal /mámm'l/ *n.* a class of warm-blooded vertebrate animals that have, in the female, milk-secreting organs for feeding the young. The class includes human beings, apes, many four-legged animals, whales, dolphins, and bats. [Early 19thC. From modern Latin *Mammalia*, class name, from Latin *mamma* (see MAMMA[1]).] —**mammalian** /mə máyli ən/ *adj.*

mammalogy /ma mállaji/ *n.* the branch of zoology that deals with the study of mammals —**mammalogical** /mámmə lójjik'l/ *adj.* —**mammalogist** /ma mállajist/ *n.*

mammaplasty *n.* = **mammoplasty**

mammary /mámməri/ *adj.* relating or belonging to the milk-secreting organ of a female mammal, e.g. the breast or udder [Late 17thC. Formed from MAMMA[1].]

mammary gland *n.* a large milk-producing gland in female mammals that consists of a network of ducts and cavities leading to a nipple or teat. Mammary glands usually occur in pairs.

mammee /ma meé/ *n.* = **mamey** **1** [Variant of MAMEY]

mammee apple *n.* = **mamey** *n.* **2**

mammiferous /ma mífferəss/ *adj.* having mammary glands [Early 19thC. Coined from MAMMA[1] + -FEROUS.]

mammilla *n.* US = **mamilla**

mammillate *adj.* US = **mamillate**

mammo- *prefix.* breast ○ *mammogram* [From Latin *mamma* (see MAMMA[1])]

mammock /mámmək/ *n.* **SMALL PIECE** a small piece of sth (*regional archaic*) ■ *vt.* (-mocks, -mocking, -mocked) **TEAR STH UP** to tear sth to shreds (*regional archaic*) [Early 16thC. Origin unknown.]

mammogram /mámmə gram/ *n.* the procedure of taking an X-ray of all or part of the breast [Mid-20thC. Coined from Latin *mamma* 'breast' + -GRAM.]

mammography /ma móggrəfi/ *n.* X-ray examination of the breast, used for the early detection of developing tumours, especially cancerous ones —**mammographic** /mámmə gráffik/ *adj.*

mammon /mámmən/ *n.* wealth and riches considered as an evil and corrupt influence (*disapproving*) [14thC. Via late Latin from, ultimately, Aramaic *māmōnā* 'riches'.] —**mammonish** *adj.* —**mammonism** *n.* —**mammonist** *n.*

Mammon *n.* the personification of wealth portrayed as a false god in the Bible

mammoplasty /mámmə plasti/ (*plural* -ties), **mammaplasty** (*plural* -ties) *n.* plastic surgery performed on a woman's breast to alter the shape or size, e.g. as reconstruction following a mastectomy or as cosmetic surgery

mammoth /mámməth/ *n.* (*plural* -moths *or* -moth) **1. EXTINCT ELEPHANT** a large extinct elephant that had long curved tusks and was covered with hair. It existed mainly in the northern hemisphere and died out more than 10,000 years ago. Genus: *Mammuthus*. **2. STH ENORMOUS** sth that is a particularly large example of its kind ■ *adj.* **VERY LARGE** of very great size or extent [Early 18thC. From obsolete Russian *mámot*, ultimately from a Siberian language.]

————— WORD KEY: ORIGIN —————
In its original Siberian language (possibly Ostyak) *mammoth* meant literally 'earth, soil': the first remains of *mammoths* to be found were dug out of the frozen soil of Siberia, and it came to be believed that the animals burrowed in the earth. The adjectival use of *mammoth* for 'huge' dates from the early 19th century.

mammy /mámmi/ (*plural* -mies) *n.* mammy, mammie mother (*informal; usually used by or to children*) [Early 16thC. Variant of MAMMA[2].]

mammy wagon *n.* in West Africa, a bus with open sides that is used to carry both passengers and goods [Origin unknown]

Mamoré /maa móray/ river in northern Bolivia, flowing northwards into the River Madeira on the Brazilian border. Length: 1,900 km/1,200 mi.

mamzer /mámzər/ (*plural* -erim /-ərim/) *n.* in Jewish religious law, a child born of an adulterous or incestuous relationship [Mid-16thC. Via late Latin from Hebrew *mamzēr*.]

man /man/ *n.* (*plural* **men** /men/) **1. ADULT MALE HUMAN** an adult male human being **2. PERSON** a person, regardless of sex or age (*often considered offensive*) ○ *a six-man crew* **3. PARTICULAR TYPE OF MAN** an adult male human being with a particular occupation, responsibility, background, or nationality (*usually used in combination*) ○ *the TV repair man* ○ *I'm not a dogs man.* **4. HUMAN RACE** the human race in general (*often considered offensive*) **5. ZOOL MODERN OR EARLIER**

HUMAN BEING a member of the group that comprises modern humans and their ancestors. Genus: *Homo*. (*sometimes considered offensive*) **6. EMPLOYEE OR WORKER** an employee or worker of either sex (*often considered offensive*) **7.** MIL **MALE MEMBER OF ARMED FORCES** a male member of the armed forces, especially one who is not an officer (*usually used in the plural*) **8. SERVANT** a man who is a servant (*dated*) **9. VIRILE PERSON** the personification of qualities traditionally associated with the male sex, including courage, strength, and aggression, or sb with such qualities **10. HUSBAND OR MAN COMPANION** a husband, or a man who is a woman's companion or lover (*slang*) **11. TERM OF ADDRESS** a term of address to a person of either sex (*slang; sometimes considered offensive*) ○ *Cool it, man!* **12. man, Man** *US* **AUTHORITY FIGURE** sb in a position of authority, or a group that is seen as having an unfair advantage or undue power over others (*slang; sometimes considered offensive*) ○ *in trouble with the Man* **13.** GAME **PIECE USED IN BOARD GAMES** a piece used in playing board games such as draughts **14.** HIST **MEDIEVAL VASSAL** in feudal societies of the early Middle Ages, an adult male human who swore allegiance to a lord in return for help and protection **15.** NAUT **SHIP** a ship, especially one of a particular kind (*used in combination*) ○ *man-of-war* ■ *vt.* (**mans, manning, manned**) (*often considered offensive*) **1. SUPPLY STH WITH WORKERS** to provide sth with workers, operators, or military personnel **2. BE READY FOR ACTION** to be ready to operate or defend sth ■ *interj.* **USED FOR EMPHASIS** used to add emphasis (*slang; sometimes considered offensive*) ○ *Man, that was exciting!* [Old English *man(n)*. Ultimately from an Indo-European word meaning 'person, man', which is also the ancestor of English *manikin, mensch,* and *muzhik*.] ◇ **as a man, as one man** unanimously or without exception (*often considered offensive*) ◇ **man and boy** throughout sb's life ○ *He's lived in this house for 60 years, man and boy.* ◇ **be your own man** to have the resources or confidence to be responsible for yourself or your actions (*often considered offensive*) ◇ **to a man** everyone, without any exceptions (*often considered offensive*)

WORD KEY: USAGE

See Usage note at ***person***.

WORD KEY: ORIGIN

The etymologically primary sense of ***man*** is 'human being, person', and that is what it generally meant in Old English: the sexes were usually distinguished by *wer* 'man' (which survives probably in WEREWOLF) and *wif* (source of modern English WIFE) or *cwene* 'woman'. But during the Middle English and early modern English periods 'male person' gradually came to the fore, and today ***man*** is decidedly on the decline (helped on its way by those who feel that the usage discriminates against women).

WORD KEY: REGIONAL NOTE

The use of address terms is both culture-specific and socially revealing. In the United Kingdom, there are a number of generic terms, all of which provide covert information on region or gender or ethnic origins. **Man** as in 'Are you coming, man?' is now occasionally addressed to females, as is 'you guys'. Terms such as *bo* and *mate* are still male and indicate a degree of friendship, whereas *Jimmy, Paddy, Mac(k),* or *Taf(fy)* can be condescending or offensive. Terms such as *kid* and *love* are addressed to all ages and both sexes, whereas *hen* and *cock* are gender specific.

Man, Isle of self-governing Crown dependency of the United Kingdom, located in the Irish Sea about midway between Northern Ireland and England. Language: English, Manx. Capital: Douglas. Population: 69,788 (1991). Area: 572 sq. km/221 sq. mi.

MAN *abbr.* metropolitan area network

man. *abbr.* manual

Man. *abbr.* PAPER Manila *or* Manila paper ■ *abbr.* Manitoba

mana /maánə/ *n. NZ* a life force associated with ritual power and high social status, especially in Polynesia and Melanesia [Mid-19thC. From Maori.]

man about town (*plural* **men about town**) *n.* a sophisticated and cultured man who socializes in fashionable circles (*dated*)

manacle /mánnək'l/ *n.* **RING AROUND PRISONER'S WRIST** either of a pair of metal rings joined by a chain and fastened around the wrists of a prisoner to be restrained (*usually used in the plural*) ■ *vt.* (**-cles, -cling, -cled**) **PUT MANACLES ON SB** to restrain sb using manacles [14thC. Via French *manicle* 'handcuff' from Latin *manicula*, from *manus* 'hand'.]

manage /mánnij/ (**-ages, -aging, -aged**) *v.* **1.** *vti.* **ACHIEVE STH WITH DIFFICULTY** to succeed in doing sth, especially sth that seems difficult or impossible ○ *I finally managed to open the door.* **2.** *vt.* **HAVE ENOUGH ROOM FOR STH** to have enough time or space for sth ○ *couldn't manage a whole steak by himself* **3.** *vi.* **COPE IN DIFFICULT SITUATION** to survive or continue despite difficulties, especially a lack of resources ○ *He manages with very little money.* **4.** *vti.* BUSINESS **ADMINISTER OR RUN STH** to be in charge of sth such as a shop, department, or project and be responsible for its smooth running and for any personnel employed ○ *manages a department of 25 people* **5.** *vt.* **HANDLE AND CONTROL STH** to handle and keep control of sth such as a weapon or tool ○ *could manage a computer without difficulty* **6.** *vt.* **DISCIPLINE OR CONTROL PERSON OR ANIMAL** to keep control of a person or animal, or a number of people or animals, especially when they are wild or unruly **7.** *vt.* BUSINESS **BE SB'S MANAGER** to guide the career and control the business affairs of sb such as a professional entertainer or athlete [Mid-16thC. Via Italian *maneggiare* 'to train a horse' from, ultimately, Latin *manus* 'hand'.]

manageable /mánnijəb'l/ *adj.* able to be handled or controlled without much difficulty —**manageability** /mánnijə bílləti/ *n.* —**manageableness** /mánnijəb'lnəss/ *n.* —**manageably** *adv.*

management /mánnijmənt/ *n.* **1. ADMINISTRATION OF BUSINESS** the organizing and controlling of the affairs of a business or a particular sector of a business **2. MANAGERS AS A GROUP** managers and employers considered collectively, especially the directors and executives of a business or organization **3. HANDLING OF STH SUCCESSFULLY** the act of handling or controlling sth successfully **4. SKILL IN HANDLING OR USING STH** the skilful handling or use of sth such as resources —**managemental** /mánnij mént'l/ *adj.*

management accounting *n.* = **cost accounting**

management information system *n.* a system for gathering the financial, production, and other information that managers need to operate a business, especially a system that is computerized

manager /mánnijər/ *n.* **1. SB WHO MANAGES BUSINESS** sb who is responsible for directing and controlling the work and personnel of a business, or of a particular department within a business **2. SB WHO CONTROLS SB'S BUSINESS AFFAIRS** sb who organizes and controls sb's business affairs, especially those of a professional actor, singer, or other entertainer **3. SB ORGANIZING AFFAIRS OF ATHLETE** sb who organizes and controls the training of an individual athlete or of a team **4.** LAW **SB APPOINTED BY COURT** sb who is appointed by a court to manage a business or organization that has been taken into receivership **5.** POL **SB ORGANIZING PARLIAMENTARY AFFAIRS** in Britain, a member of the House of Commons or the House of Lords appointed to organize matters of concern to both Houses of Parliament **6. SB WHO MANAGES STH WELL** sb who handles or controls sth such as resources, especially one who does so with skill **7. PROGRAM FOR BASIC COMPUTER OPERATIONS** a computer program designed to carry out the basic functions of a computer's operations —**managership** *n.*

managerial /mánni jéeri əl/ *adj.* involving or characteristic of a manager or management, especially in business —**managerially** *adv.*

managerialism /mánni jéeri əlizzəm/ *n.* the application of the techniques of managing a commercial business to the running of some other organization such as local government or public services —**managerialist** *n.*

managing director *n.* sb, usually the head of a board of directors, who has administrative control over a large company or other commercial organization

managing editor *n.* an editor of books, newspapers, or other publications who is responsible for the administration of the editorial process

Managua /mə nágwə/ capital city of Nicaragua, located in the west of the country, near the Pacific Ocean. Population: 1,500,000 (mid-1990s).

Managua, Lake lake in western Nicaragua, and the country's second largest. It is drained by the River Tipitapa. Area: 1,049 sq. km/405 sq. mi.

manakin /mánnəkin/ *n.* a small South American bird with a short bill and bright colourful plumage. Family: Pipridae. [Early 17thC. Variant of MANIKIN.]

Manama /mə naámə/ capital city of Bahrain, situated in the northeastern part of the country. Population: 136,999 (1991).

mañana /man yaánə/ *adv.* **1. TOMORROW** on the day following the present day **2. LATER** at some unspecified time in the future [Mid-19thC. Via Spanish, 'morning, tomorrow', from, ultimately, Latin *mane* 'in the morning'.]

Manapouri, Lake /mánnə póori/ lake in the southwestern part of the South Island, New Zealand. At 444 m/1,455 ft deep, it is the deepest lake in New Zealand. Area: 142 sq. km/55 sq. mi.

man-at-arms (*plural* **men-at-arms**) *n.* a soldier, especially a medieval mounted soldier who was heavily armed

manatee /mánnə tée/ *n.* a large plant-eating mammal found in warm Atlantic coastal waters. It has front flippers and a broad flattened tail. Genus: *Trichechus*. [Mid-16thC. Via Spanish *manatí* from Carib *manáti* 'breast'.]

Manaus /mə nówss/ city and river port in northwestern Brazil. It is the capital of Amazonas State. Population: 1,078,277 (1993).

Manawatu-Wanganui /mánnə waá too wong gə nóoi/ administrative region of New Zealand, situated in the southwestern part of the North Island. Population: 229,989 (1996). Area: 25,317 sq. km/9,775 sq. mi.

manche /maaNsh/ *n.* HERALDRY a sleeve (*technical*) [14thC. Via French from Latin *manicae* '(long) sleeves', from *manus* 'hand'.]

manchester /mánchistər/ *n. ANZ* household linen or cotton goods such as sheets and towels [Mid-16thC. From MANCHESTER, an important textile-manufacturing city.]

Manchester /mán chestər/ **1.** city in northwestern England. Population: 432,600 (1995). **2.** historic town in central Connecticut. Population: 52,208 (1994).

Manchester terrier *n.* a small terrier with a short-haired coat that is mainly black with tan patches [Named after the city of MANCHESTER, where the breed originated]

man-child (*plural* **men-children**) *n.* a male child (*literary*)

manchineel /mánchi néel/ (*plural* **-neels** *or* **-neel**) *n.* a tropical American tree of the spurge family that has poisonous apple-shaped fruit and milky sap that causes blistering. Latin name: *Hippomane mancinella*. [Mid-17thC. Via French *mancenille* from Spanish *manzanilla*, literally 'little apple', from *manzana* 'apple', ultimately from Latin *matiana*, a kind of apple, named after *Matia*, a Roman gens.]

Manchu /mán chóo/ *n.* (*plural* **-chus** *or* **-chu**) **1.** PEOPLES **MANCHURIAN INVADERS OF CHINA** a member of a people who originally came from Manchuria and invaded China in the 17th century, establishing a powerful dynasty that lasted until the beginning of the 20th century **2.** LANG **LANGUAGE SPOKEN IN CHINA** a language spoken in northeastern parts of the People's Republic of China. It belongs to the Manchu-Tungus branch of Altaic languages. Manchu is spoken by about 20,000 people. ■ *adj.* PEOPLES relating to the Manchu people, or their culture or dynasty [Late 17thC. From Manchu, literally 'pure'.] —**Manchu** *adj.*

Manchuria /man chóoree ə/ historic mountainous region of northeastern China comprising the modern-day provinces of Heilongjiang, Jilin, and Liaoning —**Manchurian** *n., adj.*

Manchu-Tungus *n.* = **Tungusic**

manciple /mánssip'l/ *n.* sb responsible for buying food and other supplies for a college, Inn of Court, or monastery [13thC. Via Anglo-Norman from, ultimately, Latin *mancipium* 'purchase, enslaved person'.]

Mancunian /man kyŏoni ən/ *n.* **SB FROM MANCHESTER** sb who was born in, or who lives in, the city of Manchester ■ *adj.* **PEOPLES** relating to Manchester, a city in NW England, or its people or culture [Early 20thC. Formed from Latin *Mancunium* 'Manchester'.] —**Mancunian** *adj.*

-mancy *suffix.* divination ○ *geomancy* [Via Old French *-mancie* from, ultimately, Greek *mantis* (see **MANTIC**)]

Mandaean /man dĕé ən/, **Mandean** *n.* **1.** **RELIG WORSHIPPER OF JOHN THE BAPTIST** a member of a Gnostic religious group who believe themselves to be descendants of John the Baptist. The group originated in Jordan and still exists in Iraq and Iran. **2.** **LANG LANGUAGE OF MANDAEAN TEXTS** a form of Aramaic used in Mandaean sacred writings ■ *adj.* **RELATING TO MANDAEANS** relating to the Mandaeans or their language [Late 18thC. Formed from Mandaean *mandaia* 'having knowledge', from *manda* 'knowledge'.] —**Mandaean** *adj.* —**Mandaeanism** *n.*

Mandala

mandala /mándələ, man daálə/ *n.* **1.** **INDIAN RELIG BUDDHIST OR HINDU SYMBOL** a geometric or pictorial design usually enclosed in a circle, representing the entire universe. It is used in meditation and ritual in Buddhism and Hinduism. **2.** **PSYCHOANAL SYMBOL REPRESENTING SELF** in Jungian psychology, a symbol representing the self and harmony within the individual [Mid-19thC. From Sanskrit *maṇḍalam* 'circle'.] —**mandalic** /man daálik/ *adj.*

Mandalay /mándə láy/ city and transportation centre on the River Irrawaddy in central Myanmar. Population: 532,949 (1983).

mandamus /man dáyməss/ (*plural* **-muses**) *n.* an order from a high court to a lower court or to an authority instructing it to perform a specific action or duty [Mid-16thC. From Latin, literally 'we command'.]

Mandan /mán dan, mándən/ (*plural* **-dan** *or* **-dans**) *n.* **1.** **PEOPLES MEMBER OF NATIVE AMERICAN PEOPLE** a member of a Native American people of North Dakota who originally occupied lands along the Missouri River and who now mainly live on the Fort Berthold Reservation near Lake Sakakawea **2.** **LANG MANDAN LANGUAGE** the language of the Mandan, belonging to the Siouan branch of Hokan-Siouan languages. Mandan is spoken by about 1,200 people. [Late 18thC. From North American French *Mandane*, of uncertain origin: probably from Dakota *mawátana*.]

mandarin[1] /mándərin/ *n.* **1.** **FORMER HIGH-RANKING CHINESE OFFICIAL** in the Chinese Empire, a member of any of the nine highest ranks of public officials, attained by examinations **2.** **HIGH-RANKING CIVIL SERVANT** a high-ranking civil servant or bureaucrat with wide-ranging powers **3.** **INFLUENTIAL MEMBER OF ELITE GROUP** an influential member of an elite group, especially a literary or intellectual group [Late 16thC. Via Spanish *mandarín* and Portuguese *mandarim* from, ultimately, the Sanskrit stem *mantrin-* 'counsellor', from *mantraḥ* 'counsel' (see **MANTRA**).] —**mandarinate** *n.* —**mandarinic** /mándə rínnik/ *adj.* —**mandarinism** /mándərinizəm/ *n.*

mandarin[2] /mándərin/ *n.* **1.** **CITRUS FRUIT RESEMBLING A SMALL ORANGE** a small citrus fruit, similar in size to a tangerine but with a loose orange skin that is easy to peel, especially a variety with a yellow-orange skin. The segments are commonly sold as tinned fruit. **2.** **SMALL CITRUS TREE** a small citrus tree that originated in China and is cultivated for its edible fruit. Latin name: *Citrus reticulata*. [Late 18thC. Via French *mandarine* from, ultimately, Spanish *mandarín* (see

MANDARIN[1]), so called because of its colour, likened to that of mandarins' yellow robes.]

Mandarin, **Mandarin Chinese** *n.* the official language of the People's Republic of China, also spoken by people of Chinese descent in various parts of the world. It belongs to the Chinese branch of Sino-Tibetan languages. Mandarin Chinese is spoken by about 800 million people as a first language and one hundred million people as a second language. —**Mandarin Chinese** *adj.*

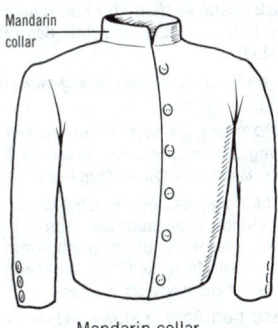

Mandarin collar

Mandarin collar

mandarin collar *n.* a narrow collar that stands up from a close-fitting neckline and opens at the front

Mandarin duck

mandarin duck *n.* an Asian duck with a crested head and colourful plumage. The male has one enlarged showy orange feather on each wing, which it uses in displays. Latin name: *Aix galericulata*.

mandarin orange *n.* = **mandarin**[2] *n.* 1

mandatary /mándətəri/ (*plural* **-ies**) *n.* a person or state that has been given a mandate

mandate /mán dayt/ *n.* **1.** **AUTHORITATIVE ORDER** an official command or instruction from an authority **2.** **POL SUPPORT FOR GOVERNMENT FROM ELECTORATE** the authority bestowed on a government or other body by an electoral victory, effectively authorizing it to carry out the policies for which it campaigned ○ *The party in power has a clear mandate for reform.* **3.** **LAW AGREEMENT FOR FREE SERVICE** a contract by which sb agrees to perform a service without payment **4.** **LAW INSTRUCTION FROM SUPERIOR COURT OR OFFICIAL** an order from a superior court or official to a lower one **5.** **BANKING INSTRUCTION FOR REGULAR TRANSFER OF FUNDS** an instruction to a bank or building society to arrange for a regular payment such as a salary to be made into a customer's account **6.** **HIST REGION RULED BY OUTSIDE POWER** any of the territories that were placed by the League of Nations under the administration of one of its European member states after World War I **7.** **HIST COMMISSION TO ADMINISTER STATE** the power conferred by the League of Nations on a member state to administer a region ■ *vt.* (**-dates**, **-dating**, **-dated**) **1.** **INTERNAT LAW ASSIGN COLONY TO A NATION** to assign a territory or region to a particular nation under a mandate **2.** **DELEGATE AUTHORITY** to delegate authority to sb or require sb to do sth through use of a mandate **3.** **US MAKE STH MANDATORY** to require or order sth by making it mandatory ○ *The law mandates systematic tracking and reporting of hazardous wastes.* [Early 16thC. From Latin *mandatum*, from the past participle of *mandare*, literally 'to give into sb's hand', ultimately from the Indo-European word for 'hand'.] —**mandator** *n.*

mandated territory *n.* = **mandate** *n.* 6

mandatory /mándətəri/ *adj.* **1.** **COMPULSORY** needing to be done, followed, or complied with, usually because of being officially required **2.** **WITH POWER OF MANDATE** resembling or having the power of a mandate **3.** **INTERNAT LAW AUTHORIZED TO ADMINISTER TERRITORY** having a mandate to administer a region or territory ■ *n.* = **mandatary** —**mandatorily** *adv.*

man-day *n.* the work done by one person in one day

Mande /máan day, mán-/ (*plural* **-de** *or* **-des**) *n.* **1.** **GROUP OF WEST AFRICAN LANGUAGES** a group of around 20 languages spoken in western Africa, especially in Sierra Leone, Mali, Guinea, and the Côte d'Ivoire. It is a branch of the Niger-Congo family of languages. About nine million people speak one of the Mande languages. **2.** **MANDE SPEAKER** a member of any of the West African groups that speak a Mande language [Late 19thC. From Mande, literally 'little mother'.] —**Mande** *adj.*

Mandean *n., adj.* = **Mandaean**

Nelson Mandela

Mandela /man déllə, -dáylə/, **Nelson** (*b.* 1918) South African statesman. After a long incarceration as a political prisoner (1964–90), in 1994 he became the first Black president of the Republic of South Africa.

Mandela, **Winnie** (*b.* 1934) South African political activist. She married Nelson Mandela in 1958 (divorced 1996), and continued his work after his imprisonment. She was convicted of a kidnapping charge in 1991. Born Nkosikazi Nomzamo Madikizela

Mandelstam /mánd'l stam/, **Osip Yemilyevich** (1891?–1938?) Russian poet. A critic of Joseph Stalin, he was arrested in 1934 and is believed to have died in a labour camp.

mandible /mándib'l/ *n.* **1.** **ANAT LOWER JAW OF VERTEBRATE** the lower jaw of a person or animal, usually containing a single bone (*technical*) **2.** **BIRDS BIRD'S BEAK** the upper or lower part of a bird's beak **3.** **ZOOL INSECT'S MOUTHPART** either of a pair of parts in insects and similar animals used for biting and cutting food [Mid-16thC. Directly or via Old French from late Latin *mandibula*, from Latin *mandere* 'to chew' (source of English *manger* and *mange*).] —**mandibular** /man díbbyŏolər/ *adj.* —**mandibulate** /man díbbyŏolit, -layt/ *adj., n.*

Mandingo /man díng gō/ (*plural* **-gos** *or* **-goes** *or* **-go**) *n.* **1.** **PEOPLES A MEMBER OF A WEST AFRICAN PEOPLE** a member of any of several peoples that live in parts of western Africa, especially along the Niger River valley **2.** **LANG WEST AFRICAN LANGUAGE GROUP** a group of languages spoken in parts of western Africa, especially along the Niger River valley. It forms a sub-group of the Mande branch of Niger-Congo languages. About six million people speak one of the Mandingo languages. [Early 17thC. From Mandingo, from Mande *mandi* (see **MANDE**).] —**Mandingo** *adj.*

mandir /mún deer/ *n.* **S Asia** a Hindu temple [Via Hindi from Sanskrit *mandiram* 'dwelling, mansion']

mandolin /mándə lín/, **mandoline** *n.* a stringed instrument of the lute family with a pear-shaped body and four or more pairs of strings, usually played with a plectrum [Early 18thC. Via French from Italian *mandolino*, literally 'small lute', from *mandola* 'mandola'.] —**mandolinist** *n.*

mandorla /man dáwrlə/ *n.* an oval area or panel in painting or sculpture, e.g. the area of light surrounding a representation of Jesus Christ after the resurrection [Late 19thC. Via Italian, 'almond', from medieval Latin *amandula* (see **ALMOND**).]

mandragora /man drággərə/ n. = mandrake 1

mandrake /mán drayk/ n. **1.** PLANT OF NIGHTSHADE FAMILY a plant of Europe and Asia that has yellow or purplish flowers and a forked root resembling a human body. It was formerly believed to have magical powers and a drug was prepared from the root. Latin name: *Mandragora officinarum*. **2.** = May apple n. 2 [14thC. Alteration of medieval Latin *mandragora*, under the influence of MAN (from the shape of the plant's root) and DRAKE 'dragon' (from its emetic and narcotic properties).]

mandrel /mándrəl/, **mandril** n. **1.** TAPERED SHAFT FOR SECURING WORK TO a tapered shaft or arbor to which work is secured during machining or turning, e.g. on a lathe **2.** CORE ROD a rod around which materials such as metal or glass are moulded, forged, or shaped **3.** SHAFT FOR MOUNTING TOOL a shaft on which a tool such as a dentist's drill or machining tool is mounted **4.** MINING a miner's pick [Early 16thC. Origin uncertain.]

mandrill /mándril/ n. a large baboon of western Africa with a beard, mane, and crest. The male also has a brilliant ribbed blue, white, and scarlet muzzle. Latin name: *Mandrillus sphinx*. [Mid-18thC. Said to be coined from MAN and DRILL[4].]

manducate /mándyoŏ kayt/ (**-cates, -cating, -cated**) vt. to chew or eat sth (*literary*) [Early 17thC. Formed from late Latin *manducare* 'to chew'.] —**manduction** /mándyoŏ káysh'n/ n. —**manducatory** /mándyoŏkətəri, -kaytəri/ adj.

Mandurah /•mán dyoorə•/ coastal town in southwestern Western Australia, on the Peel Inlet south of Perth. Population: 35,945 (1996).

mane /mayn/ n. **1.** ZOOL HAIR ON ANIMAL'S NECK long hair on the head and neck of an animal such as a lion or horse **2.** PERSON'S LONG HAIR a large amount of thick long hair on sb's head (*literary or informal*) [Old English *manu*] —**maned** adj.

man-eater n. **1.** ZOOL MAN-EATING ANIMAL an animal such as a tiger or great white shark that eats or is thought to eat human flesh **2.** CANNIBAL sb who eats human flesh **3.** OFFENSIVE TERM an offensive term for a woman who pursues men in order to make them her lovers and then discards them (*offensive*) —**man-eating** adj.

manège /ma náyzh, -nézh/, **manege** n. **1.** ART OF RIDING the art of riding or training horses **2.** TRAINED HORSE'S MOVEMENTS the movements that a horse has been trained to make **3.** RIDING SCHOOL a school where people are taught to ride and horses trained [Mid-17thC. From French, from Italian *maneggio*, from *maneggiare* (see MANAGE).]

manes /máa nayz/, **Manes** n. HONOURED GHOST the revered spirit of a dead person (*literary; takes a singular verb*) ■ npl. SPIRITS OF ANCESTORS in ancient Roman religious belief, the divine spirits of the dead (*takes a plural verb*) [14thC. From Latin, literally 'good ones', from *manus* 'good'.]

Édouard Manet: Portrait drawing by Edgar Degas

Manet /mán ay/, **Édouard** (1832–83) French painter. His innovative work such as *The Bar at the Folies-Bergère* (1882) contributed to the development of impressionism.

man Friday (*plural* **man Fridays** *or* **men Friday**) n. a man acting as an assistant or servant who is loyal and able to do many things [Named after the loyal servant of the title character in the 1719 novel *Robinson Crusoe* by Daniel Defoe]

manful /mánf'l/ adj. brave, strong, and resolute, as a man is conventionally supposed to be —**manfully** adv. —**manfulness** n.

manga /máng gə/ n. a Japanese style of comic books or animated cartoons, often very violent or erotic

mangabey /máng gə bay/ (*plural* **-beys**) n. a large agile African monkey with a long tail, slender body, and white eyelids. Genus: *Cercocebus*. [Late 18thC. Named after the *Mangabey* region in Madagascar, to which monkeys of this genus were wrongly believed to be native.]

Mangalore /máng gə láwr/ city and seaport in southwestern India, on the Arabian Sea. Population: 272,819 (1991).

mangan- prefix. manganese ○ *manganous* [From MANGANESE]

manganate /máng gə nayt/ n. any mixed-metal salt containing manganese and oxygen in the form of an anion [Mid-19thC. Coined from MANGANESE + -ATE.]

manganese /máng gə neez/ n. a brittle greyish-white metallic chemical element found in pyrolusite and rhodonite and used in strengthening steel and alloys. Symbol **Mn** [Late 17thC. Via French and Italian from medieval Latin *magnesia* 'magnesia'.]

manganese nodule n. a stony nodule rich in manganese, found on the ocean floor

manganese steel n. steel containing 11 to 14 per cent manganese, used to make drills and crushing blades and tools

manganic /man gánnik/ adj. containing or derived from manganese, especially with a valency of three or six [Mid-19thC. Formed from MANGANESE.]

manganite /máng gə nīt/ n. a greyish crystalline mineral consisting of a hydroxide of manganese [Early 19thC. Coined from MANGANESE + -ITE.]

manganous /máng gənəss, man gánnəss/ adj. containing or derived from manganese, especially with a valency of two

mange /maynj/ n. an infectious skin disease of animals and sometimes humans that is caused by mites and results in hair loss, scabs, and itching [15thC. From French *manjue* 'itch', from Old French *mangier* 'to eat', from Latin *manducare* (see MANGER).]

mangel /máng g'l/, **mangel-wurzel** /-wurz'l/, **mangold** /máng gōld/, **mangold-wurzel** n. a large yellow or reddish variety of beet that is grown as food for livestock. ◊ **beet** [Late 18thC. From German *Mangold-wurzel* 'beet root'.]

manger /máynjər/ n. a trough from which livestock eat [14thC. From Old French *mangeoire*, from *mangier* 'to eat', from Latin *manducare* 'to chew', from, ultimately, *mandere* (source of English *mange* and *mandible*).]

Lata Mangeshkar

Mangeshkar /man gésh kaar/, **Lata** (b. 1929) Indian singer. She provided playback singing voices in Hindi films for more than 30 years, making over 30,000 recordings before retiring in 1984. Full name **Lata Dinanath Mangeshkar**

mangetout /mónj too, móNzh-/, **mangetout pea** n. UK a variety of pea in which the whole pod is eaten. ◊ **snow pea** [Early 19thC. From French, literally 'eat-all'.]

mangey adj. = mangy

mangle[1] /máng g'l/ (**-gles, -gling, -gled**) vt. **1.** DESTROY SB OR STH BY CRUSHING to mutilate or disfigure sb or sth by violent tearing, cutting, or crushing **2.** RUIN STH to spoil or ruin sth through carelessness or in-

eptitude ○ *a reading that mangled the rhythm of the poem* [14thC. From Anglo-Norman *mahangler*, of uncertain origin: perhaps literally 'to maim repeatedly', from Old French *mahaigner* 'to maim', from, ultimately, assumed Vulgar Latin *mahagnare* 'to wound'.] —**mangler** n.

mangle[2] /máng g'l/ n. CLOTHES WRINGER a machine for squeezing water out of wet clothes after washing by means of two rotating cylinders between which the clothes are drawn. US term **wringer** ■ vt. (**-gles, -gling, -gled**) PUT STH THROUGH A MANGLE to put washing through a mangle in order to squeeze out water [Late 17thC. From Dutch *mangelstok* 'mangling roller', of uncertain origin: ultimately perhaps from Greek *magganon* 'war engine' (see MANGONEL) or assumed Vulgar Latin *mahagnare* 'to wound' (see MANGLE[1]).]

Mango

mango /máng gō/ (*plural* **-goes** *or* **-gos**) n. **1.** TROPICAL ASIAN EVERGREEN TREE a tropical Asian evergreen tree of the cashew family, grown for its edible fruit. Latin name: *Magifera indica*. **2.** SWEET RED FRUIT the mango tree's red or green fruit with juicy, sweet, orange-yellow pulp [Late 16thC. Via Portuguese *manga* and Malay *mangga* from Tamil *mānkāy* 'mango -tree fruit'.]

mangold, **mangold-wurzel** n. = mangel

mangonel /máng gənəl, máng gə nəl/ n. a medieval military machine used for hurling stones at an enemy [13thC. Via Old French *mangonel(le)* from medieval Latin *manganellus* 'little war-engine', ultimately from Greek *magganon* 'war engine, axis of pulley'.]

mangosteen /máng gō steen/ n. **1.** EVERGREEN TREE OF SOUTHEAST ASIA an evergreen tree native to Southeast Asia that has leathery leaves and large edible fruit. Latin name: *Garcinia mangostana*. **2.** REDDISH-BROWN FRUIT the fruit with a hard reddish-brown rind and sweet juicy pulp that the mangosteen tree produces [Late 16thC. From Malay *manggustan*, an alteration of *manggis*.]

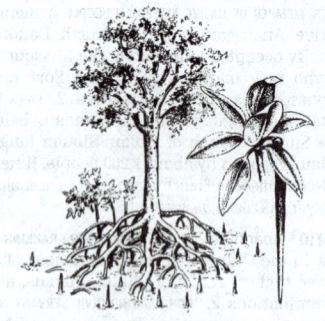

Mangrove

mangrove /máng grōv/ n. a tropical evergreen tree or shrub with intertwined roots and stems resembling stilts that grows in dense groves along tidal coasts. Genus: *Rhizophora*. [Early 17thC. Blend of Portuguese *mangue* or Spanish *mangle*, from Taino, and GROVE.]

mangy /máynji/, **mangey** (**-ier, -iest**) adj. **1.** HAVING MANGE affected by or caused by mange **2.** SCRUFFY having a dirty or shabby appearance (*informal*) **3.** Ireland MISERLY reluctant to spend or give money (*informal*) —**mangily** adv. —**manginess** n.

manhandle /mán hand'l, man hánd'l/ (**-dles, -dling, -dled**) vt. **1.** HANDLE SB OR STH ROUGHLY to pull or push sb or sth around roughly **2.** MOVE STH BY HAND to move sth using human strength alone rather than machinery

Manhattan[1] /man hátt'n/, **manhattan** *n.* a cocktail made from vermouth, whisky, and a dash of bitters [Late 19thC. Named after MANHATTAN, where it was invented.]

Manhattan[2] /man hátt'n/ **1.** borough and main economic centre of New York City, occupying Manhattan Island at the northern end of New York Bay together with several adjacent areas. Population: 1,487,536 (1990). Area: 80 sq. km/31 sq. mi. **2.** city in northeastern Kansas, northeast of Junction City and northwest of Topeka. Population: 42,117 (1996).

Manhattan Project *n.* the top-secret research and development in several places in the United States that led to the successful construction and detonation of the first atomic bombs [Mid-20thC. From *Manhattan District*, the codename that was given to the research project.]

manhole /mán hōl/ *n.* an opening with a detachable cover that gives access to an enclosed area, especially a sewer, drain, or tank

manhood /mán ho͝od/ *n.* **1.** STATE OF BEING A MAN the state of being an adult male human **2.** TRADITIONAL MANLINESS the qualities and attributes conventionally thought to be appropriate to a man, especially physical strength, courage, and determination **3.** MEN men considered collectively ○ *the nation's manhood* **4.** PENIS a man's penis (*literary or humorous*)

manhood suffrage *n.* the right to vote given to all adult men

man-hour *n.* the amount of work that can be done by one person in one hour, used as a means of assessing requirements, production, and performance ○ *the number of man-hours lost through sickness*

manhunt /mán hunt/ *n.* an organized search, especially by the police, for an escaped criminal or other wanted person —**manhunter** *n.*

mania /máyni ə/ *n.* **1.** OBSESSION an excessive and intense interest in or enthusiasm for sth **2.** PSYCHIATRIC DISORDER psychiatric disorder characterized by excessive physical activity, rapidly changing ideas, and impulsive behaviour [14thC. Via late Latin from Greek *mania* 'loss of reason', from *mainesthai* 'to rage'. Ultimately from an Indo-European word meaning 'think'.]

-mania *suffix.* excessive enthusiasm for or attachment to ○ *pyromania* [From MANIA]

maniac /máyni ak/ *n.* **1.** OFFENSIVE TERM an offensive term for sb who behaves in such an uncontrolled manner as to appear to be affected by mania (*offensive*) **2.** ENTHUSIAST sb who has an excessive and intense interest in or enthusiasm for a particular thing **3.** OFFENSIVE TERM an offensive term for sb affected by mania (*offensive*) ■ *adj.* = **maniacal** [Late 16thC. Via late Latin *maniacus* from late Greek *maniakos*, from *mania* (see MANIA).]

maniacal /mə nī ək'l/ *adj.* (*offensive*) **1.** OFFENSIVE TERM an offensive term meaning so uncontrolled as to appear to be affected by mania **2.** OFFENSIVE TERM an offensive term meaning or indicative of mania —**maniacally** *adv.*

manic /mánnik/ *adj.* **1.** RELATING TO MANIA relating to or affected by mania **2.** HECTIC extremely or excessively busy (*informal; sometimes considered offensive*) **3.** OVEREXCITED in a state of abnormally high excitement, especially because of tension (*informal*) [Early 20thC. Coined from MANIA + -IC.] —**manically** *adv.*

manic-depressive *n.* PERSON WITH BIPOLAR DISORDER sb affected by bipolar disorder ■ *adj.* CHARACTERISTIC OF BIPOLAR DISORDER typical of or affected by bipolar disorder

manic-depressive disorder, **manic-depressive illness** *n.* = **bipolar disorder**

Manichaeism /mánni kee izəm/, **Manicheism** *n.* **1.** RELIG ANCIENT DUALIST BELIEF SYSTEM a religious doctrine based on the separation of matter and spirit and of good and evil that originated in 3rd-century Persia and combined elements of Zoroastrianism, Buddhism, Christianity, and Gnosticism **2.** CHR CHRISTIAN RELIGIOUS DUALISM a heretical Christian belief in the separate nature of matter and spirit [Early 17thC. Formed from late Latin *Manichaeus*, from, ultimately, *Manes*, (216?–276?), name of the Persian founder of this belief system.] —**Manichaean** *adj.* —**Manichee** /mánni kee/ *n.*

manicotti /mánni kótti/ *n.* a dish of large pasta tubes that are usually stuffed with a ricotta or meat filling and then baked [Mid-20thC. From Italian, literally 'sleeves'.]

manicure /mánni kyoor/ *n.* COSMETICS HAND AND NAIL COSMETIC TREATMENT a cosmetic treatment for the hands and nails that usually involves shaping and polishing the fingernails, pushing back the cuticles, and treating rough skin ■ *vt.* (**-cures, -curing, -cured**) **1.** TREAT HANDS AND NAILS to treat the hands and fingernails by cutting, shaping, and polishing the nails, and softening the hands **2.** CUT AND SHAPE STH CAREFULLY to cut and shape sth with great care and precision [Late 19thC. Via French from Latin *manus cura* 'hand care'.]

manicurist /mánnikyoorist/ *n.* sb whose job is to give people manicures

manifest /mánni fest/ *adj.* OBVIOUS clear to see or understand ■ *v.* (**-fests, -festing, -fested**) **1.** *vt.* SHOW STH CLEARLY to make sth evident by showing or demonstrating it very clearly **2.** *vi.* APPEAR to appear or be revealed **3.** *vt.* INCLUDE STH IN CARGO LIST to include sth in a ship's cargo list ■ *n.* **1.** SHIP'S CARGO LIST a list giving details of a ship's cargo, its destination, and other particulars for customs purposes **2.** PLANE OR TRAIN'S CARGO LIST a list of cargo or passengers on a plane or train [14thC. Directly or via Old French from Latin *manifestus* 'apprehensible' (literally 'seized by hand'), from *manus* 'hand' and *festus* 'seizable'.] —**manifestable** *adj.* —**manifestly** *adv.* —**manifestness** *n.*

manifestation /mánni fe stáysh'n/ *n.* **1.** ACT OF SHOWING STH an act of showing or demonstrating sth **2.** STATE OF BEING MANIFESTED the state or condition of being shown or perceptible **3.** SIGN an indication that sth is present, real, or exists ○ *one of the first manifestations of the disease* **4.** PUBLIC DEMONSTRATION a public demonstration, usually over a political issue **5.** MATERIALIZATION a supposed appearance in visible form by a spiritual being **6.** VISIBLE FORM OF DIVINE BEING a visible form in which a divine being, idea, or person is believed to be revealed or expressed —**manifestational** *adj.*

manifest content *n.* in dream analysis, the overt meaning of a dream remembered by the dreamer on waking that requires analysis to interpret its latent content or real meaning

Manifest Destiny *n.* the 19th-century doctrine according to which the United States was believed to have the God-given right to expand into and possess the whole of the North American continent

manifesto /mánni féstō/ (*plural* **-toes** *or* **-tos**) *n.* a public written declaration of principles, policies, and objectives, especially one issued by a political movement or candidate [Mid-17thC. From Italian, where it was formed from *manifestare* 'to make evident', ultimately from Latin *manifestus* (see MANIFEST).]

manifold /mánni fōld/ *adj.* **1.** MANY AND VARIOUS of many different kinds ○ *The reasons for the crisis are manifold.* **2.** HAVING MANY FORMS having many parts, forms, or applications ○ *a manifold political system* ■ *n.* **1.** ENG CHAMBER WITH PORTS a chamber or pipe with several openings for receiving or distributing a fluid or gas, such as the intake or exhaust manifolds of an internal-combustion engine **2.** MATH TOPOLOGICAL SPACE a topological space or surface satisfying specific conditions ■ *vt.* (**-folds, -folding, -folded**) **1.** MULTIPLY to multiply sth **2.** MAKE COPIES OF STH to make several copies of a book or page [Old English *manigfeald*, from earlier forms of MANY + FOLD] —**manifolder** *n.* —**manifoldly** *adv.* —**manifoldness** *n.*

manikin /mánnikin/, **mannikin** *n.* **1.** CLOTHES = **mannequin** *n.* 1 **2.** ANATOMICAL MODEL OF HUMAN BODY an anatomical model of the human body, used in teaching art or medicine **3.** OFFENSIVE TERM an offensive term for a very short man (*offensive*) [Mid-16thC. From Dutch *manneken* 'little man', from *man* 'man'.]

manila /mə nílla/, **Manila** *adj.* MADE OF MANILA PAPER made of manila paper ○ *a manila envelope* ■ *n.* **1.** CIGAR a cigar made in Manila **2.** = **Manila hemp 3.** = **Manila paper** [Late 17thC. Named after the port of *Manila*, the capital of the Philippines.]

Manila /mə nílla/ capital city of the Philippines, located on the coast of Luzon Island. Population: 1,601,234 (1990).

Manila Bay bay of the South China Sea in the northern Philippines, on Luzon Island. Area: 2,000 sq. km/770 sq. mi. Length: 60 km/37 mi.

Manila hemp, **Manilla hemp** *n.* a strong fibre obtained from the Philippine abaca plant and used in making rope and paper [Mid-19thC. Named after MANILA.]

Manila paper, **Manilla paper** *n.* a strong pale-brown paper with a smooth surface, made from Manila hemp and used for wrapping or for envelopes [Late 19thC. Named after MANILA, where it was originally made.]

manille /mə níl/ *n.* CARDS the second-best trump in the card games ombre and quadrille [Late 17thC. Via French from Spanish *malilla* 'little bad (card)'.]

man in the moon *n.* the imaginary being behind the apparent face on the moon when it is full

man in the street *n.* the average person, as opposed to an expert, celebrity, or prominent person

manioc /mánni ok/, **manioca** /mánni ṓkə/ *n.* = **cassava** [Mid-16thC. From Tupi *mandioca* (influenced by French *manihot*), from Guarani *mandio*.]

maniple /mánnip'l/ *n.* **1.** HIST PART OF ROMAN LEGION in the ancient Roman army, a subdivision of a legion, containing 60 or 120 men **2.** CHR FORMER ECCLESIASTICAL ADORNMENT a silk band or folded napkin formerly worn on the left arm of sb administering the Eucharist [Late 16thC. From Latin *manipulus* 'handful', from *manus* 'hand'.]

manipular /mə níppyo͝olər/ *adj.* **1.** HIST OF ROMAN MANIPLE relating to an ancient Roman maniple **2.** OF MANIPULATION relating to or constituting manipulation

manipulate /mə níppyoo layt/ (**-lates, -lating, -lated**) *vt.* **1.** OPERATE STH to operate, use, or handle sth ○ *manipulating the crane into position* **2.** CONTROL SB OR STH DEVIOUSLY to control or influence sb or sth in a clever or devious way **3.** FALSIFY STH to change or present sth in a way that is false but personally advantageous **4.** COMPUT HANDLE NUMBERS to work with data on a computer **5.** MED TREAT BODY PART USING HANDS ONLY to treat a part of the body, or to move a part such as a joint during examination, using the hands only [Early 19thC. Back-formation from *manipulation*, from French, where it was formed from *manipule*, literally 'handful', from Latin *manipulus* (see MANIPLE). Originally 'digging for silver ore', hence 'skilful handling'.] —**manipulability** /mə níppyo͝olə bílləti/ *n.* —**manipulable** /-yo͝oləb'l/ *adj.* —**manipulatable** /-laytəb'l/ *adj.* —**manipulation** /mə níppyo͝o láysh'n/ *n.* —**manipulator** /mə níppyo͝o laytər/ *n.* —**manipulatory** /-lətəri/ *adj.*

manipulative /mə níppyo͝olətiv/ *adj.* **1.** DEVIOUS using clever, devious ways to control or influence sb or sth ○ *a manipulative personality* **2.** OF MANIPULATION relating to or involved in manipulation ○ *a manipulative technique* —**manipulatively** *adv.* —**manipulativeness** *n.*

Manitoba

Manitoba /mánni tṓbə/ province in south-central Canada, the easternmost of Canada's three Prairie provinces. Capital: Winnipeg. Population: 1,145,200 (1997). Area: 649,950 sq. km/250,947 sq. mi. —**Manitoban** /mánni tṓbən/ *adj.*, *n.*

Manitoba, Lake lake in southern Manitoba, Canada. It discharges through the Dauphin River to Lake Winnipeg. Area: 4,659 sq. km/1,798 sq. mi.

manitou /mánni too/, **manitu, manito** /-tō/ (*plural* **-tos**) *n.* a supernatural force or spirit believed by Algonquian peoples to suffuse various living things and inanimate objects [Late 16thC. From Narragansett *manittówock*.]

Manitoulin Islands /mánni tōolin-/ archipelago on the border between the United States and Canada, in northern Lake Huron. They include Manitoulin Island, the world's largest freshwater island.

Manizales /mánni thaálayss/ city in western Colombia. It is the capital of Caldas Department, in the Andes mountains. Population: 329,844 (1993).

man jack n. a single individual (*informal; often considered offensive*)

mankind /man kínd/ n. **1.** ALL HUMAN BEINGS human beings considered collectively (*often considered offensive*) **2.** MEN, NOT WOMEN men considered collectively, as distinct from women (*dated*)

manky /mángki/ (**-kier, -kiest**) adj. dirty, disgusting, or otherwise unpleasant (*informal*) ○ *that manky old sweater of his* [Mid-20thC. From Scots dialect *mank* 'mutilated, defective', via Old French *manc* 'maimed' from Latin *mancus*.]

─────── **WORD KEY: REGIONAL NOTE** ───────

Manky is one of the many dialect words that come from French. It would appear that many dialect speakers took the adage 'Cleanliness is next to Godliness' seriously, for the dialects abound in words meaning 'dirty'. These include *boggin*, *clarty*, *clabbery*, *cloggy*, *mucky*, and *smalmy*.

manly /mánnli/ (**-lier, -liest**) adj. **1.** CONVENTIONALLY TYPICAL OF A MAN having or showing qualities conventionally thought to be typical of or appropriate to a man, especially physical strength or courage **2.** CONSIDERED APPROPRIATE FOR A MAN considered suitable or appropriate for a man —**manliness** n.

man-made, **manmade** adj. made by human beings and not occurring naturally (*often considered offensive*)

Mann /man/, **Heinrich** (1871–1950) German novelist writer. Brother of the writer Thomas Mann, his book *Professor Unrat* (1904) was made into a film, *The Blue Angel* (1930).

Mann, Thomas (1875–1955) German-born US novelist and critic. His work, much of which explores the relationship between society and the creative artist, earned him the Nobel Prize in literature (1929).

manna /mánnə/ n. **1.** BIBLE DIVINELY PROVIDED SUSTENANCE in the Bible, food provided miraculously to feed the Israelites in the wilderness **2.** UNEXPECTED BENEFIT sth very welcome or of great benefit that comes unexpectedly **3.** TREES SWEET SUBSTANCE FROM ASH TREE a sweet substance, used in the past as a laxative, exuded by the European ash tree **4.** INSECTS SWEET INSECT SUBSTANCE a sweet substance excreted by a scale insect that feeds on the tamarisk and eaten by ants [Pre-12thC. Via late Latin from, ultimately, Hebrew *mān*.]

mannan /mán an, mánnən/ n. a complex carbohydrate found in the cell walls of some plants such as the ivory nut and carob bean [Late 19thC. Coined from MANNOSE + -AN.]

Mannar, Gulf of /ma naár/ arm of the Indian Ocean between the southern tip of India and western Sri Lanka

manned /mand/ adj. (*often considered offensive*) **1.** HAVING PEOPLE ABOARD having a human crew **2.** HAVING STAFF operated or attended by staff

mannequin /mánnikin/ n. **1.** CLOTHES DUMMY FOR DISPLAYING CLOTHES a usually life-size model of the human body used to display or fit clothes **2.** FASHION MODEL a model (*dated*) **3.** ARTS = lay figure [Mid-18thC. Via French from Dutch *manneken* (see MANIKIN).]

manner /mánnər/ n. **1.** WAY STH IS DONE the way in which sth is done or happens ○ *His manner of doing things is often a little unconventional.* **2.** WAY OF BEING the characteristic way in which sb behaves ○ *had a capricious manner about him* **3.** TYPE a type or kind ○ *What manner of insect makes this hole?* **4.** STYLE OF WORK OF ART the style in which a work of art is executed ○ *painted in the manner of Vermeer* ■ **manners** npl. **1.** SOCIAL BEHAVIOUR social behaviour, especially in terms of what is considered correct or unacceptable **2.** CUSTOMS AND PRACTICES the customs and practices of a particular society or period in time ○ *18th-century manners* [12thC. Via Anglo-Norman

manere 'way of handling', from Latin *manuarius* 'of the hand', from *manus* 'hand'.] ◇ **in a manner of speaking** in some ways, though not exactly or not in all ways ◇ **to the manner born** naturally adapted to sth as though accustomed to it from birth

mannered /mánnərd/ adj. **1.** AFFECTED characterized by affected mannerisms ○ *her mannered tones* **2.** BEHAVING IN PARTICULAR WAY behaving in a particular way or having manners of a particular kind (*usually used in combination*) ○ *an ill-mannered child*

Mannerheim /mánnər hīm/, **Baron Carl Gustaf Emil** (1867–1951) Finnish army officer and statesman. He ruled Finland as regent from 1918 to 1919 and as president from 1944 to 1946. He was commander-in-chief of the Finnish army in the Russo-Finnish War (1939–40).

mannerism /mánnərizəm/ n. **1.** IDIOSYNCRASY a particular gesture, habit, or way of doing sth ○ *one of his odd little mannerisms* **2.** AFFECTED BEHAVIOUR affected or exaggerated speech, behaviour, or writing —**manneristic** /mánnə rístik/ adj. —**manneristically** /-rístikli/ adv.

Mannerism, **mannerism** n. a style of art and architecture, predominant in Italy in the late 16th century, characterized by stylized and elongated forms and the pursuit of a representation of idealized beauty —**Mannerist** adj., n.

mannerless /mánnərləss/ adj. having or showing bad manners —**mannerlessness** n.

mannerly /mánnərli/ adj. POLITE well-mannered or polite ■ adv. POLITELY in a well-mannered or polite way (*archaic*) ○ *'A child should always say what's true, And speak when he is spoken to, And behave mannerly at table; At least as far as he is able.'* (Robert Louis Stevenson, *A Child's Garden of Verse*; 1885) —**mannerliness** n.

Mannheim /mán hīm/ city and riverport in south-western Germany, on the River Rhine. Population: 317,300 (1994).

Mannheim /mánn hīm/, **Karl** (1893–1947) Hungarian-born German sociologist. His main work was in the sociology of knowledge.

Mannheim school /mánn hīm-/ n. a style of orchestral and string playing associated with the rise of the Classical period, developed at the court of Mannheim in the 18th century [Named after MANNHEIM]

mannikin n. = manikin

Manning /mánning/ river in eastern New South Wales, Australia. Length: 225 km/140 mi.

Manning, Frederic (1892–1935) Australian-born British writer. He was author of *Her Privates We* (1930), a novel based on his experience of World War I.

Manning, Henry, Cardinal (1808–92) British clergyman. He converted from the Anglican Church to Roman Catholicism in 1851 and was made a cardinal in 1875.

mannish /mánnish/ adj. **1.** LIKE OR FOR A MAN resembling or suitable for a man instead of a woman (*often considered offensive*) **2.** TYPICAL OF A MAN considered characteristic of a man [Old English] —**mannishly** adv. —**mannishness** n.

mannitol /mánni tol/, **mannite** /mánnīt/ n. a sweet white crystalline alcohol found in some plants and used as a sweetener, dietary supplement, diuretic, and in kidney testing. Formula: $C_6H_{14}O_6$. [Late 19thC. Formed from MANNA.] —**mannitic** /ma níttik/ adj.

Mannix /mánniks/, **Daniel** (1864–1963) Irish-born Australian clergyman. He was archbishop of Melbourne (1917–63). His involvement in politics led to the founding of the Catholic Social Movement and the anti-communist Democratic Labour Party.

mannose /mánnōss, -nōz/ n. a plant sugar obtained from manna and mannitol. Formula: $C_6H_{12}O_6$. [Late 19thC. Coined from MANNITE + -OSE.]

manoeuvre /mə nóovər/ n. **1.** SKILLED MOVEMENT a movement or action that requires skill or dexterity **2.** MIL MILITARY MOVEMENT a planned movement of one or several military or naval units **3.** DEVIOUS ACT an action, especially a devious or deceptive one, done to gain advantage ○ *one of his little manoeuvres to try to stay in total control* **4.** TRANSP CHANGE OF COURSE a

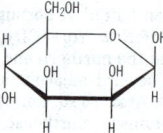

Mannose

controlled change of course of a vehicle or vessel ■ **manoeuvres** npl. MIL MILITARY EXERCISES large-scale military exercises used for training or practice ■ v. (**-vres, -vring, -vred**) **1.** vti. MOVE SKILFULLY to move or cause sth to move skilfully **2.** vti. MIL DO MILITARY EXERCISES to perform or cause sb or sth to perform military manoeuvres **3.** vt. MANIPULATE SB OR STH to manipulate sb or sth to gain advantage ○ *trying to manoeuvre her into agreeing* **4.** vi. BEHAVE DEVIOUSLY to use devious means in order to gain advantage ○ *the various parties manoeuvring for the leadership* [15thC. Via French *manoeuvre* 'manipulation' from Old French *maneuvre* 'manual labour', from medieval Latin *manuoperare* 'to work with the hands', from Latin *manus* 'hand'.] —**manoeuvrability** /mə noóvərə bílləti/ n. —**manoeuvrable** /-noóvərəb'l/ adj. —**manoeuvrer** /-vərər/ n.

man of God n. **1.** CLERGYMAN a man who is a member of the clergy **2.** SAINT a saint or godly man

man of letters n. a man who is a writer or scholar (*literary*)

man of straw n. US term **straw man** **1.** UNIMPORTANT ISSUE OR PERSON an issue or person of little importance or relevance, brought up to be shown as an easily defeatable idea or adversary **2.** FRONT FOR SB sb who acts as a front for sb else's questionable or illegal activities

man of the cloth (*plural* **men of the cloth**) n. a man who is a member of the clergy

man-of-war /mán əv wáwr/ (*plural* **men-of-war**), **man o'war** /mánnə wáwr/ (*plural* **men o'war** /ménnə-/) n. **1.** WARSHIP a warship (*archaic*) **2.** MARINE BIOL = Portuguese man-of-war

man-of-war bird, **man-o'-war bird** n. = frigate bird

manometer /mə nómmitər/ n. an instrument used to measure the pressure of a gas [Mid-18thC. From French *manomètre*, from Greek *manos* 'thin, rare' + an equivalent French form of METER.] —**manometric** /mánnə méttrik/ adj. —**manometrically** /-méttrikli/ adv. —**manometry** /mə nómmitri/ n.

manor /mánnər/ n. **1.** NOBLE'S HOUSE AND LAND a house and the land surrounding it, owned by a medieval noble **2.** POLICE DISTRICT the area for which a particular local police station is responsible (*slang*) **3.** PERSONAL TERRITORY sb's own local area or territory (*slang*) **4.** = manor house [13thC. Via Anglo-Norman *maner* from Old French *maneir* 'dwelling-place', ultimately from Latin *manere*, 'to remain, stay'.] —**manorial** /mə náwri əl/ adj.

─────── **WORD KEY: ORIGIN** ───────

The Latin word *manere*, from which *manor* is derived, is also the source of English *maisonette*, *manse*, *mansion*, *menagerie*, *permanent*, and *remain*.

manor house n. the residence of the lord or lady of a manor

manpower /mán powər/ n. power in terms of the number of people available or needed to do sth

manqué /móngk ay, maaN káy/ adj. having wanted unsuccessfully to be or do sth ○ *an artist manqué* [Late 18thC. From French, past participle of *manquer* 'to fail, lack'.]

mansard /mán saard, -ərd/ n. the part of a building enclosed by a mansard roof [Mid-18thC. From French, named after François *Mansard* (1598–1666), the architect credited with designing buildings with roofs of this type.] —**mansarded** adj.

Mansard roof

mansard roof *n.* a roof that slopes on all four sides, with each side divided into a gentle upper slope and a steeper lower slope

manse /manss/ *n.* a house provided for a church minister by some Christian denominations [Late 15thC. From medieval Latin *mansus* 'unit of land', from Latin *manere* (see MANOR).]

Mansell /mánss'l/, **Nigel** (b. 1953) British motor racing driver. He won the World Grand Prix Formula One Championship (1992) and then started racing in the United States, where he won the Indy Car Championship (1993).

manservant /mán survənt/ (*plural* **menservants** /mén survənts/) *n.* a man who is a servant, especially sb's valet

Mansfield /mánss feeld/ town in Nottinghamshire, east-central England. Population: 71,858 (1991).

Mansfield, Jayne (1933–67) US film actor. As a film comedienne she played leading roles in *The Girl Can't Help It* (1956) and *Will Success Spoil Rock Hunter?* (1957). Real name **Vera Jayne Palmer**

Mansfield, Katherine (1888–1923) New Zealand-born British writer. She was a major figure in the development of the short-story form. Pseudonym of **Katherine Mansfield Beauchamp**

mansion /mánsh'n/ *n.* **1.** LARGE HOUSE a large and stately house **2.** ZODIAC DIVISION OF ZODIAC any one of the 28 divisions of the zodiac through which the Moon passes successively each month ■ **mansions** *npl.* LARGE BUILDING DIVIDED INTO FLATS a large building that is divided up into separate flats (*often used in names of buildings*) [14thC. Via Old French, 'dwelling-place', from Latin *manere* 'to remain, stay' (source of English *manor* and *remain*).]

mansion house *n.* = mansion *n.* 1

Mansion House *n.* the official residence of the Lord Mayor of London

man-sized, **man-size** *adj.* **1.** LARGE larger than the ordinary size ○ *a man-sized appetite* **2.** BIG ENOUGH FOR MAN the same size as or big enough for a man ○ *a man-sized hole in the fence*

manslaughter /mán slawtər/ *n.* the unlawful killing of one human being by another without advance planning (**malice aforethought**)

man's man (*plural* **men's men**) *n.* a man who prefers the company of other men to that of women (*informal*)

Manson /mánssən/, **Charles** (b. 1934) US cult leader and murderer. Founder of the 'Manson Family', he was sentenced to death for ritual murders carried out in California in 1969, but his sentence was later commuted to life imprisonment by a Supreme Court ruling.

mansuetude /mánsswi tyood/ *n.* a meek or gentle attitude or behaviour (*archaic*) [14thC. Via Old French or directly from Latin *mansuetus*, from *mansuetus* 'tame', literally 'accustomed to the hand', from *suescere* 'to accustom'.]

manta /mántə/ *n.* **1.** ZOOL = manta ray **2.** *Southwest US* TEXTILES SQUARE OF ROUGH CLOTH a square piece of rough cloth, used as a cape, shawl, or horse blanket [Late 17thC. From Spanish, literally 'blanket, mantle' (because the ray is traditionally caught in a blanket-like fish-trap).]

manta ray *n.* a large warm-water ray with wide pectoral fins, a long tail, and two fins resembling

horns that project from the head. Family: Mobulidae. US term **manta** *n.* 1

Mantegna /man ténnyə/, **Andrea** (1431–1506) Italian painter. He was a master of illusionistic perspective and foreshortening. His chief patrons were the Gonzaga family of Mantua.

mantel /mánt'l/ *n.* an ornamental frame around a fireplace, usually made of stone or wood [15thC. From MANTLE.]

mantelet /mántələt/, **mantlet** *n.* a short cape worn by women in the 19th century

mantelpiece /mánt'l peess/, **mantlepiece** *n.* the mantel of a fireplace, especially its projecting top

mantelshelf /mánt'l shelf/ (*plural* **-shelves** /-shelvz/), **mantleshelf** (*plural* **-shelves**) *n.* the projecting top of the mantel of a fireplace, used as a shelf

manteltree /mánt'l tree/, **mantletree** *n.* a stone or beam that acts as a support for the masonry above a fireplace

mantic /mántik/ *adj.* relating to or having powers of divination or prophecy [Mid-19thC. From Greek *mantikos*, from *mantis* 'prophet', from *mainesthai* 'to rage' (see MANIA).] —**mantically** *adv.*

mantid, **mantis** *n.* = mantis

mantilla /man tíllə/ *n.* **1.** LACE HEADSCARF a lace scarf that covers the head and shoulders, often worn by women in church, especially in Spain and Latin America **2.** SHORT CLOAK a short light cape [Early 18thC. From Spanish, 'little mantle'.]

mantis /mántiss/ (*plural* **-tises** *or* **-tes** /-teez/) *n.* a large, usually green insect that feeds on other insects and has a long body, large eyes, and strong grasping front legs that it holds up at rest. Family: Mantidae. [Mid-17thC. Via modern Latin from Greek, literally 'prophet' (see MANTIC). From the insect's forelegs, the position of which suggests an attitude of prayer.]

mantis crab *n.* = squilla

mantissa /man tíssə/ *n.* the fractional part of a logarithm, to the right of the decimal point [Mid-17thC. From Latin, 'makeweight', of ultimately unknown origin, perhaps from Etruscan.]

mantis shrimp *n.* = squilla

mantle /mánt'l/ *n.* **1.** CLOTHES SLEEVELESS CLOAK a loose sleeveless cloak **2.** COVERING sth that envelops or covers sth else (*literary*) ○ *a mantle of snow* **3.** TRANSFERRED OR INHERITED POSITION a role or position, especially one that can be passed from one person to another (*formal*) ○ *assumed the mantle of the Presidency* **4.** WIRE MESH FOR GAS LIGHT a small circle of wire mesh in a gas or oil lamp that gives out incandescent light when heated by the flame it surrounds **5.** ZOOL SHELL-PRODUCING GLAND a layer of epidermis in a mollusc or brachiopod with glands that secrete a shell-producing substance **6.** BIRDS FEATHERS the back, inner-wing, and shoulder-area (**scapular**) plumage of a bird **7.** GEOL CENTRAL PART OF EARTH the part of the Earth or another planet that lies between the crust and core **8.** = mantel ■ *v.* (**-tles**, **-tling**, **-tled**) **1.** *vt.* COVER STH to cover sth with a mantle or with sth resembling a mantle ○ *hilltops mantled with snow* **2.** *vi.* FLUSH to become flushed (*refers to sb's face*) ○ *His puffy face mantled in angry red blotches.* [Pre-12thC. Via Old French *mantel* from Latin *mantellum* 'cloak' (source of English *mantelpiece* and *dismantle*), of uncertain origin: perhaps ultimately from Celtic.]

mantlepiece /mánt'l peess/ *n.* = mantelpiece

mantleshelf *n.* = mantelshelf

mantlet /mántlit/ *n.* = mantelet

mantletree *n.* = manteltree

mantling /mántling/ *n.* ornamental drapery round a shield on a coat of arms

man-to-man *adj.* **1.** HONEST AND INTIMATE honest and intimate and treating sb as an equal ○ *a man-to-man talk* **2.** SPORTS PAIRING PLAYERS in sports such as soccer, hockey, or basketball, having each defender of one team mark a corresponding attacker of the other team (*sometimes considered offensive*) ○ *man-to-man marking* —**man-to-man** *adv.*

Mantoux test /mán too-/ *n.* a test to determine whether sb has ever had the tuberculosis infection and so has a measure of immunity to the

disease [Mid-20thC. Named after the French physician Charles *Mantoux* (1877–1947), its inventor.]

mantra /mántrə/ *n.* **1.** RELIG HOLY WORD IN MEDITATION a sacred word, chant, or sound that is repeated during meditation to facilitate spiritual power and transformation of consciousness **2.** OFTEN REPEATED EXPRESSION OR IDEA an expression or idea that is repeated, often without thinking about it, and closely associated with sth ○ *the mantra of marketing being 'new, improved'* [Late 18thC. From Sanskrit, literally 'thought', from *man* 'to think'.]

mantrap /mán trap/ *n.* an illegal trap set to catch poachers or trespassers on private land, usually in the form of a metal device that snaps shut onto sb's leg

mantua /mántyoo ə/ *n.* a woman's gown, fitted above the waist, with an open front and draped skirt to show the underskirt, worn in Europe in the late 17th and 18th centuries [Late 17thC. Alteration of *manteau*, modelled on MANTUA, which was famous for fabric production.]

Mantua /mán choo ə/ historic city in northern Italy, a tourist and agricultural centre. Population: 52,205 (1993).

manual /mánnyoo əl/ *adj.* **1.** USING HANDS relating to, done with, or involving the hands ○ *manual dexterity* **2.** PHYSICAL involving physical rather than mental exertion ○ *manual tasks* **3.** OPERATED BY PERSON operated by human effort rather than by a machine, computer, or type of power ○ *switching to manual control* ■ *n.* **1.** HANDBOOK a book that contains information and instructions about the operation of a machine or how to do sth **2.** MUSIC KEYBOARD PLAYED WITH HANDS an organ or harpsichord keyboard that is played with the hands alone **3.** ARMS RIFLE DRILL a drill or exercise in the use of a hand-held weapon ○ *cadets practising the manual of arms* [15thC. Via French *manuel* or directly from Latin *manualis* 'of the hand', from *manus* 'hand'.] —**manually** *adv.*

─── **WORD KEY: ORIGIN** ───

The Latin word *manus*, from which **manual** derives, is also the source of English *amanuensis*, *command*, *demand*, *emancipate*, *manacle*, *manage*, *mandate*, *manifest*, *manipulate*, *manner*, *manoeuvre*, *manufacture*, *manure*, *mastiff*, *maundy*, and *remand*.

manual alphabet *n.* an alphabet in which various finger movements and positions stand for letters, used with other hand signs by hearing-impaired people

manual transmission *n.* a vehicle transmission that requires the driver to shift gears using a clutch

manubrium /mə nyoóbri əm/ (*plural* **-nubria** /-ri ə/ *or* **-nubriums**) *n.* a handle-shaped anatomical part, e.g. the upper part of the sternum or part of the inner ear [Mid-17thC. From Latin, 'handle', from *manus* 'hand'.] —**manubrial** *adj.*

manuf., **manufac.** *abbr.* **1.** manufacture **2.** manufactured **3.** manufacturer

manufactory /mánnyoo fáktəri/ (*plural* **-ries**) *n.* a factory (*archaic*) [Early 17thC. Formed from MANUFACTURE, modelled on FACTORY.]

manufacture /mánnyoo fákchər/ *v.* (**-tures**, **-turing**, **-tured**) **1.** *vti.* INDUST TO PRODUCE STH INDUSTRIALLY to make sth into a finished product using raw materials, especially on a large industrial scale ○ *built up a business manufacturing lightweight metal goods* **2.** *vt.* BIOCHEM MAKE BODY CHEMICAL to produce a substance needed by the body ○ *Bile is manufactured in the liver.* **3.** *vt.* PRODUCE MECHANICALLY to produce sth in the manner of a machine, without creativity **4.** *vt.* INVENT to invent or make sth up ○ *manufactured an excuse to get out of the meeting* ■ *n.* **1.** INDUST PRODUCTION OF GOODS the production of finished goods from raw materials, especially on a large industrial scale ○ *engaged in the manufacture of arms for the military* **2.** COMM PRODUCT sth that has been produced from raw materials, especially on a large industrial scale **3.** BIOCHEM MAKING OF BODY CHEMICAL the production of a substance needed by the body [Mid-16thC. Via French from Italian *manifattura* 'sth made by hand', from Latin *manu factum* 'made by hand', from *manus* 'hand' + *facere* 'to make'.] —**manufacturable** *adj.* —**manufactural** *adj.*

——— WORD KEY: SYNONYMS ———

See Synonyms at **make**.

manufacturer /mánnyŏŏ fákchərər/ n. a factory, individual, or organization that produces finished goods from raw materials, especially on a large industrial scale

Manukau City /mánnə kow-/ city in the northwestern part of the North Island, New Zealand, near Auckland. Population: 254,577 (1997).

Manukau Harbour /mánnə kow-/ bay on the northwestern coast of the North Island, New Zealand. The city of Auckland lies on its northern shore. Area: 350 sq. km/150 sq. mi.

manumit /mánnyŏŏ mít/ (**-mits, -mitting, -mitted**) vt. to free sb from slavery (formal) [14thC. From Latin manumittere, from manu emittere, literally 'to send out from your hand'.] —**manumission** /mánnyŏŏ mísh'n/ n. —**manumitter** n.

manure /mə nyoór/ n. **1.** FERTILIZER MADE FROM DUNG animal excrement, often mixed with straw, used as fertilizer for soil **2.** FERTILIZER any fertilizer or compost ■ vt. (**-nures, -nuring, -nured**) FERTILIZE WITH MANURE to spread manure on land or soil to fertilize it [14thC. Via Anglo-Norman from Old French manouver 'to work with the hands', from medieval Latin manuoperare (see MANOEUVRE). Originally 'to cultivate, manage land'.] —**manurer** n.

——— WORD KEY: ORIGIN ———

When English originally took the word *manure* over from Anglo-Norman, its connotations of manual labour had been channelled into the management of land, and in particular the cultivation of land. It was not until the middle of the 16th century that the noun *manure* came to denote 'dung spread in cultivating the land'. The related MANOEUVRE, reborrowed from French in the 18th century, has remained in more refined use.

manus /máynəss/ (plural **-nus**) n. the wrist and hand of humans or the carpus and forefoot of other vertebrates (technical) [Early 16thC. From Latin, 'hand'.]

manuscript /mánnyŏŏskript/ n. **1.** HANDWRITTEN BOOK a book or other text written by hand, especially one written before the invention of printing ○ rare medieval manuscripts **2.** AUTHOR'S ORIGINAL TEXT an author's text for a book, article, or other piece of written work as it is submitted for publication **3.** HANDWRITING handwriting as opposed to the printed word ○ a manuscript version of the text [Late 16thC. From medieval Latin manuscriptus 'written by hand', from scribere 'to write' (source of English inscription and scribble).]

Manx /mangks/ adj. OF ISLE OF MAN relating to the Isle of Man, its people, language, or culture ■ n. OLD ISLE OF MAN LANGUAGE a language formerly spoken on the Isle of Man, belonging to the Goidelic group of the Celtic branch of Indo-European languages. The last native speaker died in the 1970s, but it survives especially in legal documents and is kept alive as the second language of the island by the Manx Society. ■ npl. MANX PEOPLE the people of the Isle of Man [Early 16thC. Alteration of assumed Old Norse manskr, from Old Irish Manu 'Isle of Man'.]

Manx cat, **manx cat** n. a short-haired, tailless, domestic cat [From the origin of the breed in the Isle of Man]

Manxman /mángksmən/ (plural **-men** /-mən/) n. a man who comes from or lives on the Isle of Man

Manx shearwater n. an Atlantic seabird with black plumage on its upper parts and white plumage on its underparts that nests in burrows on rocky islands. Latin name: *Puffinus puffinus*.

Manxwoman /mángkswŏŏmən/ (plural **-en** /-wimin/) n. a woman who comes from or lives on the Isle of Man

many /ménni/ CORE MEANING: a considerable number of people or things ○ (det) Many people own their homes. ○ (det) Not many people know about this. ○ (pron) Many believe that the matter will never come to trial. ○ (pron) Many of you may have heard this. ○ (adj) He was among the many visitors to this town. **1.** det., pron., adj. A CONSIDERABLE NUMBER a considerable number of people or things ○ (det) Many children are in the park today. ○ (pron) He is a friend to many. ○ (pron) Many of us agree with you. ○ (adj)

Among his many faults is self-importance. **2.** det., pron. A LARGE NUMBER a large number of people or things (used after 'so', 'too', 'not', 'as', or 'that') ○ (det) She has so many clocks, she can't be sure exactly what time it is. ○ (det) I've just seen too many government studies that don't move quickly enough. ○ (det) There aren't that many people who would agree with you. ○ (pron) Help yourself – you can have as many as you like. **3.** det. EACH OF A CONSIDERABLE NUMBER each of a considerable number (used before 'a', 'an', or 'another') ○ The situation has caused them many a sleepless night. ○ We did better than many another regiment. **4.** pron. THE MAJORITY the majority of people ○ All these advantages should be available to the many – not just the few. [Old English manig. Ultimately from an Indo-European word meaning 'many, often'.]

manyplies /ménni plīz/ (plural **-plies**) n. = omasum [Late 18thC. From MANY + PLY, because of the organ's many folds.]

many-sided adj. having a large number of sides, aspects, or abilities —**many-sidedness** n.

many-valued logic n. a system of logic in which propositions may have values in addition to true or false

manzanilla /mánzə níllə/ n. a pale dry Spanish sherry [Mid-19thC. From Spanish, literally 'camomile', because its smell resembles camomile.]

Manzoni /man zŏ́ni, -dzŏ́ni/, **Alessandro Francesco Tommaso Antonio** (1785–1873) Italian novelist, poet, and playwright. His historical novel *The Betrothed* (1825–27), with its colloquial language, laid the basis for modern Italian fiction.

Maoism /mów izəm/ n. the Marxist-Leninist doctrines, teachings, and policies of the former Chinese Communist leader Mao Zedong —**Maoist** n., adj.

Mao jacket /mów-/ n. a plain tunic-style jacket with a stand-up collar worn by Chairman Mao Zedong and the Chinese people under his regime

Maori /mówri/ (plural **-ri**) n. **1.** PEOPLES MEMBER OF NEW ZEALAND PEOPLE a member of a people living in New Zealand and on the Cook Islands. The Maori are believed to have originated on various Polynesian islands and to have migrated to New Zealand using canoes before the 14th century AD. **2.** LANG MAORI LANGUAGE the language of the Maori people, belonging to the Eastern branch of Austronesian languages. Maori is spoken by about 300,000 people. [Mid-19thC. From Maori.] —**Maori** adj.

Maoridom /mówridəm/ n. NZ the world of the Maori people, including their culture, society, and language

Maoriland /mówri land/ n. New Zealand (archaic) [From the fact that the Maoris were the land's original inhabitants] —**Maorilander** n.

Maori oven n. NZ = hangi

Maori rat n. a small rat native to New Zealand. Latin name: *Rattus exulans*.

Mao suit n. a style of suit consisting of plain loose-fitting trousers and a tunic-style jacket with a stand-up collar worn by Chairman Mao Zedong and the Chinese people under his regime

Mao Zedong

Mao Zedong /mów tsay tŏ́ong/, **Mao Tse-tung** (1893–1976) Chinese statesman. Leader of the Long March in the Chinese Civil War (1934), he became the first president of Communist China (1949–67).

map /map/ n. **1.** GEOGRAPHICAL DIAGRAM a visual representation that shows all or part of the Earth's surface with geographical features, urban areas, roads, and other details **2.** DIAGRAM OF STARS a representation of the stars or the surface of a planet, usually in the form of a diagrammatical drawing **3.** DRAWING SHOWING ROUTE OR LOCATION a diagrammatical drawing of sth such as a route or area made to show the location of a place or how to get there **4.** MATH = function n. 6 ■ vt. (**maps, mapping, mapped**) **1.** CREATE MAP OF STH to represent a geographical or other defined area on a map ○ mapping the heavens **2.** DISCOVER AND SHOW to discover sth and create a visual representation of it **3.** BIOL NOTE GENE SEQUENCE to determine and record the sequence of encoded information on a gene or chromosome **4.** MATH MATCH SET ELEMENTS to assign an element in one set to an element in another through a mathematical correspondence [Early 16thC. From medieval Latin mappa (mundi), literally 'sheet (of the world)', from Latin mappa 'towel, sheet' (source of English napkin and apron).] —**mappable** adj. —**mapper** n. ◇ on the map so as to be famous or important (informal) ◇ off the map so as to be no longer famous or important (informal) **map out** vt. to construct sth such as a plan in detail

Map /map/, **Mapes** /máy peez/, **Walter** (1140?–1210) English clergyman and writer. He was a clerk to Henry II and author of *De Nugis Curialium* (1181–93), a book of satirical anecdotes and reflections.

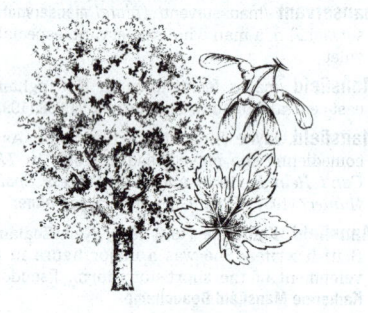

Maple

maple /máyp'l/ n. **1.** TREES DECIDUOUS TREE WITH WINGED SEEDS a deciduous tree of northern temperate regions with divided leaves that have attractive autumn colours and winged seeds occurring in pairs. Genus: *Acer*. **2.** INDUST WOOD FROM MAPLE the hard wood from the maple tree, used to make furniture and flooring **3.** FOOD SUGAR MAPLE FLAVOUR the flavour of the processed sap of the sugar maple [Old English mapul-]

Maple Leaf n. the Canadian flag, showing a stylized red maple leaf on a white background between vertical red bars

maple sugar n. a sugar made by boiling down the sap of the sugar maple

maple syrup n. a sweet syrup made from the sap of the sugar maple, or from various other sugars and artificially flavoured with maple

mapmaker /máp maykər/ n. sb who makes maps —**mapmaking** n.

mapping /mápping/ n. **1.** MAKING OF MAPS the act or process of making maps **2.** MATH = function n. 6

Mapplethorpe /máyp'l thawrp/, **Robert** (1946–89) US photographer. Acclaimed for his elegant photographic technique and experimentation with printing, light, and colour, he was controversial for the sexually explicit content of his work.

map projection n. a representation of or way of representing a three-dimensional object on a two-dimensional surface

Mapuche /ma pŏ́ochi/ (plural **-che** or **-ches**) n. **1.** PEOPLES MEMBER OF NATIVE S AMERICAN PEOPLE a member of a subgroup of the Araucanian people of central Chile and western Argentina, known for their resistance to Spanish and Chilean rule **2.** LANG MAPUCHE LANGUAGE the language of the Mapuche people, belonging to the Araucanian family. About 400,000 people speak Mapuche. —**Mapuche** adj.

Maputo /mə pŏŏtŏ/ capital city of Mozambique, situ-

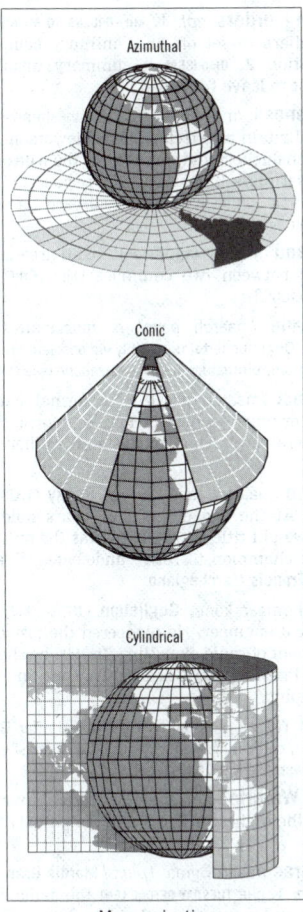

Map projection

Marabou

Via French from Arabic *murābit* 'holy man', because the stork was considered holy by Muslims.]

marabout /márrə boo/ *n.* **1.** MUSLIM HERMIT OR MONK a Muslim hermit, monk, or holy man, especially in North Africa **2.** TOMB OF MARABOUT the tomb or a shrine of a marabout that is often a destination for pilgrims [Early 17thC. Via French and Portuguese from Arabic *murābit*, from *ribāt* 'frontier post', because hermits would go to such places to gain merit.]

Maracas

maraca /mə rákə/ *n.* a percussion instrument usually shaken in pairs as an accompaniment to Latin American music and consisting of a hollow rattle filled with small pebbles or beans [Early 17thC. Via Portuguese *maracà* from Tupi *maráka*.]

Maracaibo, Lake /márə kī́bō-/ large shallow lake in northwestern Venezuela. It is the largest lake in South America. Area: 13,300 sq. km/5,140 sq. mi.

Maracay /márrə káy/ city in northern Venezuela, and capital of the state of Aragua, in the central highlands. Population: 538,616 (1990).

Maradona /marrə dónnə/, **Diego** (*b.* 1960) Argentinian football player. An outstanding midfielder and goalscorer, he captained Argentina to World Cup victory in 1986.

marae /mə rí́/ (*plural* **-rae**) *n.* NZ a meeting-place for Maoris [Late 18thC. From Polynesian.]

maraging steel /maá rayjing-/ *n.* a strong, low-carbon, martensitic steel formed by ageing and heating and containing up to 25 per cent nickel with lesser amounts of titanium, aluminium, and niobium [*Maraging* from a blend of MARTENSITE and AGE]

Marajó /márra zhṓ/ island in Brazil, in Para State, in the delta of the Amazon River. Area: 40,100 sq. km/15,500 sq. mi.

Marañón /márra nyṓn/ river in South America, flowing northwards from the Andes into the Amazon River. Length: 1,415 km/879 mi.

maranta /mə rántə/ *n.* a tropical American plant, widely cultivated for its variegated thin leaves. Genus: *Maranta*. [Late 19thC. From modern Latin *Maranta*, named after Bartolomeo *Maranta*, an Italian herbalist of the 16thC.]

marasca /mə ráskə/ *n.* a cultivated variety of the sour cherry tree that produces the fruit used to make maraschino. Latin name: *Prunus cerasus*. [Mid-19thC. From Italian, alteration of *amarasca*, from *amaro* 'bitter'.]

maraschino /márrə skéenō, -shéenō/ (*plural* **-nos**) *n.* a sweet liqueur distilled from marasca cherries [Late

18thC. From Italian, where it was formed from *marasca* (see MARASCA).]

maraschino cherry *n.* a bright red cherry preserved in a sweet syrup flavoured with maraschino or an imitation of this, used especially as an addition to cocktails or to decorate cakes

marasmus /mə rázməss/ *n.* a gradual wasting away of the body, generally associated with severe malnutrition or inadequate absorption of food and occurring mainly in young children [Mid-17thC. From modern Latin, from Greek *marasmos* 'wasting, decay', from *marainein* 'to waste away'.] —**marasmic** *adj.*

Marat /má raa/, **Jean-Paul** (1743–93) French journalist and politician. He was a radical leader of the French Revolution, and was murdered in his bath by Charlotte Corday.

Maratha /mə ráatə/, **Maratta, Mahratta** *n.* a member of a people living mainly in the Deccan plateau in the Indian state of Maharashtra [Mid-18thC. From Marathi *marāthā*, or Hindi *marhattā*, from Sanskrit *Mahārāṣṭra* 'great kingdom'.]

Marathi /mə ráati/, **Mahratti** *n.* LANGUAGE SPOKEN IN MAHARASHTRA a language belonging to the Indo-Iranian branch of Indo-European languages and spoken mainly in the Indian state of Maharashtra, where it is the state language. Marathi is spoken by about 70 million people. ■ *adj.* OF MAHARASHTRA relating to the Indian state of Maharashtra, its people, language, or culture [Late 17thC. From Marathi *marāṭhī*, from Sanskrit *Mahārāṣṭrī*, from *Mahārāṣṭra* (see MARATHA).]

marathon /márrəth'n, -thon/ *n.* **1.** LONG-DISTANCE RACE a long-distance footrace run over a distance of 42.195 km/26 mi. 385 yds **2.** LENGTHY AND DIFFICULT TASK a lengthy and difficult task, event, or activity **3.** ENDURANCE TEST a test of endurance, especially in a competition ○ *a dance marathon* [Late 19thC. Named after MARATHON in Greece. In 490 BC, a messenger ran from there to Athens, bearing news of a victory against Persian invaders.] —**marathoner** *n.*

━━━━ **WORD KEY: ORIGIN** ━━━━

According to tradition, when the Greek army defeated the Persians at *Marathon*, on the northeastern coast of Attica, in 490 BC, the runner Pheidippides was dispatched to bring the good news to Athens (in fact there is no contemporary evidence for the story, which is not recorded until 700 years after the event). When the modern Olympic Games were first held, in Athens in 1896, a long-distance race was introduced to commemorate the ancient feat, run over a course supposedly equal in distance to the journey from *Marathon* to Athens (about 35 km/22 mi.). The present distance was established at the 1948 London Olympics.

Marathon /márrə thon/ plain in Attica, northeast of Athens, Greece. It was the site of an important Greek victory over the Persians in 490 BC.

Maratta *n.* = Maratha

maraud /mə ráwd/ (**-rauds, -rauding, -rauded**) *vti.* to rove around carrying out violent attacks or looking for plunder, or to raid a place in search of plunder [Late 17thC. From French *marauder*, from *maraud* 'rogue, vagabond'.] —**marauder** *n.*

marauding /mə ráwding/ *adj.* roving around carrying out violent attacks or looking for plunder ○ *marauding pirates cruising the high seas*

marble /maárb'l/ *n.* **1.** INDUST DENSE CRYSTALLIZED ROCK a form of limestone transformed through the heat and pressure of metamorphism into a dense, variously coloured, crystallized rock used in building, sculpture, and monuments **2.** SCULPTURE MARBLE SCULPTURE a sculpture made from marble ○ *the Elgin Marbles* **3.** STH RESEMBLING MARBLE sth that resembles marble in being cold, hard, smooth, or white (*literary*) **4.** GAME SMALL GLASS BALL a small hard ball, usually made of glass, used in the game of marbles ■ **marbles** *npl.* **1.** GAME WITH GLASS BALLS a game, played mainly by children, in which small hard balls are rolled on the ground with the aim of hitting the opponent's ball (*takes a singular verb*) **2.** WITS mental abilities or sense of reality (*informal*) ■ *vt.* (**-bles, -bling, -bled**) COLOUR STH WITH MOTTLED STREAKS to colour sth, usually paper, with mottled streaks to give the appearance of marble ○ *an 18th-century volume with marbled endpapers* [12thC. Via Old French *marbre* and Latin

ated on Delagoa Bay in the southeastern part of the country. Population: 1,098,000 (1991).

maquette /ma két/ *n.* a small model of a planned sculpture or architectural work [Early 20thC. Via French from Italian *macchietta* 'little spot', from Latin *maculare* 'to spot, stain' (source of English *immaculate*).]

maquillage /máki aázh/ *n.* make-up, or the art of applying make-up [Late 19thC. From French, from *maquiller* 'to make up face', from Old French *masquiller* 'to stain'.]

maquis /ma kée/ (*plural* **-quis**) *n.* **1.** DENSE COASTAL VEGETATION dense shrubby vegetation of Mediterranean coastal regions **2.** maquis, Maquis HIST FRENCH RESISTANCE the underground French Resistance movement that fought against the German occupying forces during World War II **3.** maquis, Maquis HIST FRENCH RESISTANCE FIGHTER a member of the World War II French Resistance movement [Mid-19thC. Via French from Italian *macchia*, literally 'spot', from Latin *macula* (from the vegetation's resemblance to spots). 'French Resistance' from the use of the maquis countryside for hiding.]

mar /maar/ (**mars, marring, marred**) *vt.* to spoil or detract from sth [Old English *merran* 'to waste, spoil', from prehistoric Germanic]

mar. *abbr.* **1.** maritime **2.** married

Mar. *abbr.* March

mara /mə ráa/ *n.* a large long-legged member of the cavy family that resembles a hare and is native to the Argentine pampas. Latin name: *Dolichotis patagonum*. [Mid-19thC. From American Spanish *mará*.]

Mara /maárə/ *n.* in Buddhism, a force of evil, sometimes conceived of as a being [Late 19thC. From Sanskrit *Māra* 'death', from the stem *mr̥-* 'to die'.]

marabou /márrə boo/, **marabout** *n.* **1.** LARGE AFRICAN STORK a large African carrion stork that has dark-grey plumage and a short naked neck with a pink pouch at the front. Latin name: *Leptoptilos crumeniferus*. **2.** MARABOU FEATHERS down taken from the tail of the marabou and used as trimming for clothes **3.** TEXTILES RAW SILK a fine white raw silk [Early 19thC.

marmor from Greek *marmaros*, 'hard, shiny stone' (influenced by *marmairein* 'to shine').] —**marbly** *adj.*

Marble Bar /maábəl baár/ mining town in north-western Western Australia. It has the highest average monthly temperatures in Australia. Population: 318 (1996).

marble cake *n.* a type of cake made with two different flavours of sponge, often chocolate and plain, dropped into the same tin and very lightly mixed before baking

Marblehead /maárb'l hed/ resort town in north-eastern Massachusetts, on the northern shore of Massachusetts Bay, southwest of Gloucester. Population: 19,973 (1996).

marblewood /maárb'l wood/ *n.* **1.** TREES MALAYSIAN TREE a Malaysian tree with mottled black-banded wood. Latin name: *Diospyros marmorata.* **2.** INDUST WOOD FROM MARBLEWOOD TREE the wood of the marblewood tree, used in cabinet-making

marbling /maárbling/ *n.* **1.** COLOURING LIKE MARBLE colouring or mottling that looks like marble **2.** CREATION OF MARBLED EFFECT the process of applying mottled streaks of colour to paper or other material to create the appearance of marble **3.** STREAKS OF FAT IN MEAT streaks of fat in lean meat

Marburg disease /maár burg-/ *n.* a severe viral infection causing high fever, haemorrhaging, rashes, vomiting, and often death. The source of human infection has been traced to green monkeys imported from Africa for use in laboratory experiments. [Mid-20thC. Named after the city of *Marburg* in Germany, where the first major outbreak occurred.]

marc /maark/ *n.* **1.** SKINS AND PULP OF PRESSED FRUIT the skins and pulp remaining after grapes, apples, or other fruit have had their juice pressed out, e.g. for wine-making **2.** WINE BRANDY FROM FRUIT SKINS AND PULP brandy made from the skins and pulp that remain when grapes and other fruit have had their juice pressed out [Early 17thC. From French, formed from *marcher*, in an earlier sense 'to tread or trample' (see MARCH[1]).]

Marc /maark/, **Franz** (1880–1916) German painter. He was a founder of the expressionist group Der Blaue Reiter (The Blue Rider). Semi-abstract paintings of horses and deer are typical of his style.

marcasite /maárkə sīt, -zeét/ *n.* **1.** MINERALS YELLOW MINERAL a yellowish mineral consisting of iron sulphide, used in jewellery. Marcasite is chemically identical to iron pyrites, but has a different crystalline structure. Formula: FeS$_2$. **2.** ACCESSORIES DECORATIVE PIECE OF POLISHED METAL polished steel or other white metal cut with facets and used in jewellery, or sth made from this [15thC. Via medieval Latin *marcasita* from Arabic *markašīta*, of Persian or Aramaic origin.] —**marcasitical** /maárkə síttik'l/ *adj.*

marcato /maar kaátō/ *adv.* with a heavy accentuation of individual notes that are often also played in a detached style (*used as a musical direction*) [Mid-19thC. From Italian, literally 'marked, accented'.] —**marcato** *adj.*

marc brandy *n.* = marc *n.* 2

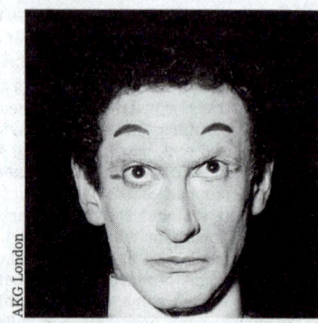
Marcel Marceau

Marceau /maar sṓ/, **Marcel** (b. 1923) French mime artist. His white-faced character, Bip, became for a time synonymous with mime.

marcel /maar sél/ *n.* **marcel, marcel wave** WAVY HAIRSTYLE a women's hairstyle, popular in the 1920s, con-

sisting of regular, deep waves created with curling tongs ■ *vt.* (-**cels, -celling, -celled**) STYLE HAIR IN A MARCEL to style sb's hair in a marcel [Late 19thC. Named after the French hairdresser François *Marcel* Grateau (1852–1936), who devised the method.] —**marcelled** *adj.* —**marceller** *n.*

marcescent /maar séss'nt/ *adj.* remaining attached to a plant when withered [Early 18thC. From Latin *marcescent-*, the present participle stem of *marcescere*, literally 'to begin to wither', from *marcere* 'to wither, decay'.]

march[1] /maarch/ *v.* (**marches, marching, marched**) **1.** *vi.* WALK IN MILITARY FASHION to walk with regular formalized movements of the arms and legs at a steady rhythmic pace, often in a military formation **2.** *vti.* MOVE IN MILITARY-STYLE FORMATION to proceed somewhere, or direct a body of people or troops to proceed somewhere, on foot, in a disciplined military or military-style formation ○ *marched the troops off to battle* **3.** *vi.* MIL SET OFF to set off, usually on foot, on a military campaign or expedition ○ *Our orders are to march at daybreak.* **4.** *vi.* WALK WITH DETERMINATION to walk quickly and with an air of determination ○ *She marched into the shop and demanded to see the manager.* **5.** *vt.* FORCE SB TO GO SOMEWHERE to force sb to go along with you somewhere, usually by physically taking hold of the person ○ *She grabbed hold of the boys and marched them into the house.* **6.** *vi.* WALK TO PROTEST OR PUBLICIZE STH to take part in a protest march or demonstration ○ *A huge crowd marched in support of the needy.* **7.** *vi.* PASS STEADILY to pass steadily or inexorably ○ *Time marches on.* ■ *n.* **1.** ACT OR EXTENT OF MARCHING a journey on foot, especially under military discipline or in a military formation ○ *After a four-hour march, they arrived back at the camp.* **2.** MARCHING SPEED a particular speed or style of marching ○ *The funeral procession advanced at a slow march.* **3.** WALK FOR PROTEST OR PUBLICITY a political demonstration or protest, in the form of an organized walk in procession by a group of people to a place in support of a particular cause ○ *Police estimated that about 20,000 people took part in yesterday's march against world hunger.* **4.** MOVEMENT FORWARDS a steady forwards movement or progression ○ *the march of time* **5.** MUSIC MUSIC IN MARCHING RHYTHM a piece of music especially written or suitable to accompany marching, usually with a regular emphatic beat and in a military style [14thC. From Old French *marchier*, ultimately from a prehistoric Germanic word meaning 'to measure off, mark out' that is also the ancestor of English *mark* and *margin*.] —**marcher** *n.* ◇ **on the march 1.** proceeding somewhere on foot, especially purposefully and in a military or military-style formation **2.** advancing or making progress ◇ **steal a march on sb** to do or achieve sth before sb else, thereby gaining an advantage over the person

march[2] /maarch/ *n.* **1.** BORDER AREA BETWEEN TWO COUNTRIES an area along the border between two countries, especially an outlying area that is subject to territorial disputes and hostile incursions **2.** BORDER a border between countries or territories ■ *vi.* (**marches, marching, marched**) SHARE BORDER to share a border with a country or territory (*formal*) [13thC. From Old French *marche*, ultimately from a prehistoric Germanic word that is also the ancestor of English *mark*. The underlying sense is of territory marked out.]

March *n.* in the Gregorian calendar, the third month of the year, made up of 31 days [Via Anglo-Norman from Latin *Martius (mensis)* '(month) of Mars']

MArch *n.*, *abbr.* Master of Architecture

March. *abbr.* Marchioness

Marches, The historical name for the borderlands between England and Scotland (also called the Borders), and England and Wales

marchesa /maar káyzə/ (*plural* -**se** /-zay/) *n.* an Italian marchioness, holding the title either in her own right or as the wife or widow of a marchese [Late 18thC. From Italian, feminine of *marchese* (see MARCHESE).]

marchese /maar káy zay/ (*plural* **marchesi** /-zi/) *n.* an Italian marquess, a nobleman of a rank between a prince and a count [Early 16thC. Via Italian from medieval Latin *(comes) marcensis* 'count of the border', from *marca* 'border', of prehistoric Germanic origin; ultimately related to English *mark*[1].]

marching orders *npl.* **1.** MIL ORDERS TO MARCH orders to soldiers to set off on a military campaign or expedition **2.** DISMISSAL a summary dismissal or request to leave (*informal*)

marchioness /maársh néss, maár shənəss/ *n.* in Great Britain and Ireland, a noblewoman ranking between duchess and countess, or the wife or widow of a marquess [Late 16thC. Via medieval Latin *marchionissa* from, ultimately, *marca* 'borderland', of prehistoric Germanic origin.]

marchland /maárch land, -lənd/ *n.* an area along the border between two countries [Mid-16thC. Formed from MARCH[2].]

marchpane /maárch payn/ *n.* marzipan (*archaic*) [15thC. Origin uncertain: possibly via obsolete French *marcepain* from, ultimately, Italian *marzapane* (see MARZIPAN).]

marchpast /maárch paast/ *n.* a formal parade by troops or other people who march in formation past sb who reviews them from a stand or other vantage point

Marciano /maárssi aánō, -ánnō/, **Rocky** (1923–69) US boxer. At the end of his four years holding the heavyweight title (1952–56), he was the only heavyweight champion to retire undefeated. Real name **Rocco Francis Marchegiano**

Marconi /maar kṓni/, **Guglielmo** (1874–1937) Italian electrical engineer. He pioneered the practical development of radio signalling. In 1909 he shared the Nobel Prize in physics for his work in wireless telegraphy.

Marconi rig *n.* = **Bermuda rig** [Named after Guglielmo MARCONI, comparing the rig's unusually tall mast with early radio towers] —**Marconi-rigged** *adj.*

Mardal Waterfall /maárdəl-/ waterfall in Norway, one of the highest in the world. Height: 517 m/1,696 ft.

Mardi Gras /maárdi graá/ (*plural* **Mardis Gras** /maárdi graá/) *n.* **1.** CHR TUESDAY BEFORE LENT the name given in France and many other places to Shrove Tuesday, the last day before the beginning of Lent in the Christian calendar **2.** LEISURE CARNIVAL BEFORE LENT in some places, a carnival held or ending on the day before the beginning of Lent, in the Christian calendar, often celebrated with costumes, parades, balls, and other festivities [From French, literally 'fat Tuesday' (the day on which rich foods were used up before Lent)]

Marduk /maárdook/ *n.* in Babylonian mythology, the god who defeated the great goddess Tiamat and created humankind

mare[1] /mair/ *n.* an adult female horse, or adult female of a species closely related to the horse such as the zebra [Old English *mearh*. Ultimately from an Indo-European word meaning 'horse'.]

mare[2] /maá ray, -ri/ (*plural* -**ria** /-ri ə/) *n.* any of the large dark plains on the surface of the Moon, or any similar area on Mars [Mid-19thC. From Latin, 'sea' (source of English *marine*). Ultimately from an Indo-European word that is also the ancestor of English *mere*, *marsh*, *morass*, and *meerschaum*.]

mare clausum /maá ray klówssoōm/ *n.* a sea or other area of water that is under the jurisdiction of one country and closed to all others [From Latin, literally 'closed sea', the title of a work (1635) by John Selden defending the right of a single nation to control parts of the sea]

Mare Crisium /maá ray kríssi əm/ *n.* a lunar lowland plain surrounded by high mountains, approximately 435 × 565 km/270 × 350 mi. Visible with the unaided eye as a dark area near the Moon's eastern edge.

Mare Fecunditatis /maá ray fe kúndi taátiss/ *n.* a lunar lowland region of irregular shape. It is visible with the unaided eye as a dark area southeast of Mare Tranquillitatis.

Mare Frigoris /maá ray fri gáwriss/ *n.* a long narrow lunar lowland region near to the north pole. It is just visible as a dark area north of Mare Imbrium and Mare Serenitatis.

Mare Humorum /maá ray hyoo máwrəm/ *n.* a lunar lowland plain, approximately 420 km/260 mi.

a at; aa father; aw all; ay day; air hair; ə about, edible, item, common, circus; e egg; ee eel; hw when; i it, happy; ī ice; 'l apple; 'm rhythm; 'n fashion; o odd; ō open; oō good; oo pool; ow owl; oy oil; th thin; <u>th</u> this; u up; ur urge;

across. It is just visible with the unaided eye as a dark area near the Moon's southwestern edge.

Mare Imbrium /maá ray ímbri əm/ n. a large round lunar lowland plain, approximately 1250 km/775 mi. across. It is easily visible with the unaided eye as a large dark area in the Moon's northwest quadrant.

mare liberum /maá ray léebərŏŏm/ n. an area of sea that is open to the ships of all countries [Mid-17thC. From Latin, literally 'free sea', the title of a treatise (1609) by the Dutch jurist Hugo Grotius, defending free access to the ocean by all nations.]

maremma /mə rémmə/ (plural -me /-mee/) n. an area of marshy ground near the sea, especially in Italy [Mid-19thC. Via Italian from, ultimately, Latin maritimus, from mare 'sea'.]

Mare Nectaris /maá ray nek taáriss/ n. a rounded lunar lowland plain, approximately 400 km/250 mi. across. It is visible with the unaided eye as a dark area south of Mare Tranquillitatis.

Marengo /mə réng gō/ adj. browned in oil and cooked in a sauce of tomatoes, mushrooms, garlic, onion, and white wine ○ chicken Marengo [Mid-19thC. Named after the village of Marengo in northern Italy, where such a dish is said to have been served to Napoleon in 1800.]

mare nostrum /maá ray nóstrŏŏm/ n. an area of sea that is under the jurisdiction of one country or shared by two or more countries [From Latin, literally 'our sea' (the Roman name of the Mediterranean)]

Mare Nubium /maá ray nyŏŏbi əm/ n. a lunar lowland region that is irregularly shaped. It is visible with the unaided eye as a dark area near the centre of the Moon's southwest quadrant.

Mare Orientale /maá ray áwri en taáli/ n. a round lunar lowland region on the side of the Moon that is furthest from the Earth

Mare Serenitatis /maá ray sə rénni taátiss/ n. a large rounded lunar lowland plane where Apollo 17 landed. It is approximately 580 × 680 km/360 × 425 mi. and easily visible in the Moon's northeast quadrant.

mare's nest n. **1.** DISCOVERY FOUND TO BE VALUELESS a discovery at first thought to be important or valuable but subsequently found to be an illusion, a hoax, or valueless **2.** COMPLICATED SITUATION a complicated or muddled situation [Late 16thC]

mare's-tail n. **1.** METEOROL STRAND OF CLOUD a long wispy strand of cloud (usually used in the plural) **2.** PLANTS WATER PLANT a water plant that has erect, partially submerged stems with narrow leaves and insignificant flowers. Latin name: Hippuris vulgaris.

Mare Tranquillitatis /maá ray trang kwílli taátiss/ n. a large irregularly-shaped lunar lowland plain, approximately 650 × 900 km/405 × 560 mi., where Apollo 11 made the first manned lunar landing in 1969

Mareva injunction /mə réevə-/ n. an injunction allowing a court to freeze a defendant's assets to prevent them being transferred abroad

Marfan syndrome /maár fan-/, **Marfan's syndrome** /maár fans-/ n. a hereditary disorder that affects the body's connective tissues [Mid-20thC. Named after the French paediatrician A. B. J. Marfan (1858–1942).]

marg /maarj/ n. margarine (informal) [Mid-20thC. Shortening.]

marg. abbr. **1.** margin **2.** marginal

Margaret /maárgrət, -ərət/, **St, Queen of Scotland** (1046?–93). Sister of Edgar (the Aetheling) and wife of Malcolm Canmore, she instigated reforms in the Celtic Church.

Margaret (of Anjou) (1430?–82) Queen of England. She was the wife of Henry VI of England, and led the Lancastrians in the Wars of the Roses.

Margaret, Princess, Countess of Snowdon (b. 1930). The younger sister of Elizabeth II, Queen of the United Kingdom, she was the first president of the Royal Ballet.

margaric /maar gárrik/, **margaritic** /maárgə ríttik/ adj. resembling a pearl or pearls (formal) [Early 19thC. Via French margarique from, ultimately, Greek margaron 'pearl'.]

margarine /maárjə reén, maárgə-/ n. a yellow fat for spreading and cooking that usually consists of a blend of vegetable oils or animal fats mixed with water, vitamins, colouring, flavouring, and other ingredients. Originally produced as a substitute for butter and considered inferior to it in all uses, it is now a food in its own right. [Late 19thC. From French.]

margarita /maárgə reétə/ n. a cocktail made with tequila, lemon or lime juice, and an orange-flavoured liqueur, typically served in a chilled glass whose rim has been dipped into salt [Early 20thC. From Spanish, from the name Margarita.]

Margarita /maár gə reétə/ island in northern Venezuela, in Nueva Esparta State, in the Caribbean Sea. Population: 117,700 (1979). Area: 1,072 sq. km/414 sq. mi.

margaritic adj. = margaric

Margasirsa /maárgə seérsə/ n. in the Hindu calendar, the ninth month of the year, made up of 29 or 30 days and occurring about the same time as November to December

Margate /maár gayt/ seaside resort in northeastern Kent, southeastern England. Population: 56,734 (1991).

margay /maár gay/ n. a wild cat not much bigger than a domestic cat with colouring and markings similar to those of a leopard, found in the rainforests of Central and South America. Latin name: Felis wiedi. [Late 18thC. Via French from Portuguese maracaj'a, from Tupi marakaya.]

marge /maarj/ n. margarine (informal) [Early 20thC. Shortening.]

margent /maárjənt/ n. a margin or edge (archaic or literary)

margin /maárjin/ n. **1.** BLANK SPACE AT SIDE OF PAGE a blank space on the left or right edge, or the top or bottom, of a written or printed page ○ comments scribbled in the margin **2.** LINE DOWN SIDE OF PAGE a straight line drawn down the left- or right-hand side of a page to separate a narrow section off from the main part ○ Draw a margin about one inch from the edge of the paper. **3.** OUTER EDGE the edge of sth, especially the outer edge, or the area close to it ○ dark-green leaves with reddish margins **4.** PART FURTHEST FROM CENTRE that part of anything, e.g. a society or organization, that is least integrated with its centre, least often considered, least typical, or most vulnerable (often used in the plural) ○ people living on the margins of society **5.** LIMIT a boundary indicating the limit beyond which sth should not go or below which sth should not fall (often used in the plural) ○ beyond the margins of good taste **6.** DIFFERENCE BETWEEN ONE AMOUNT AND ANOTHER the difference between two amounts or scores ○ She won by a margin of only 270 votes. **7.** ADDITIONAL AMOUNT an amount over and above what is strictly necessary, included, e.g. for safety reasons or to allow for mistakes or delays ○ They left no margin for error. **8.** COMM PROFIT the profit on a transaction, or the amount by which the price of sth exceeds its cost ○ We've cut our margins to the absolute bare minimum. **9.** ECON LOWEST VIABLE PROFIT the minimum profit that a business must make in order to remain viable **10.** FIN DIFFERENCE BETWEEN LOAN AND COLLATERAL VALUES the difference between the face value of a loan and the value of the collateral given to secure the loan **11.** FIN BROKER'S LOSS COVER the amount deposited with a stockbroker by a client to cover possible losses on transactions made on account **12.** Aus HR SUPPLEMENT TO WAGES OR SALARY an additional payment made to a worker in recognition of specific skills or to compensate for extra responsibilities ■ vt. (-gins, -gining, -gined) **1.** CREATE MARGIN AROUND to create a margin around sth **2.** FIN PLACE AS DEPOSIT WITH BROKER to place sth such as collateral with a broker as a deposit [14thC. From Latin margin-, the stem of margo. Ultimately from an Indo-European word meaning 'boundary, border' that is also the ancestor of English mark[1] and march[1].]

marginal /maárjinəl/ adj. **1.** IN A MARGIN written in a margin **2.** SMALL IN SCALE very small in scale or importance ○ You can ignore any marginal discrepancies you find. **3.** IRRELEVANT not of central importance or relevance ○ In what follows, I have ignored everything that is marginal to my main

thesis. **4.** ON THE FRINGE operating or existing on the fringes of a group or movement ○ a marginal group with no political base **5.** VERY LOW at or close to the lowest acceptable or viable limit ○ a marginal standard of living **6.** POL WON BY SMALL MAJORITY won by only a small majority at a previous election and therefore likely to provide a closely fought contest in any subsequent election ○ a marginal constituency **7.** ECON BARELY COVERING COSTS barely able to cover the costs of production when sold or when producing goods for sale **8.** AGRIC DIFFICULT TO CULTIVATE difficult to cultivate and therefore only brought into use if profits are high enough to make it worth the effort ○ marginal land ■ n. POL MARGINAL SEAT a marginal political constituency —**marginality** /maárji nálləti/ n.

marginal cost n. the additional cost of producing one more item

marginalia /maárji náyli ə/ npl. notes written in a margin

marginalize /maárjinə līz/ (-izes, -izing, -ized), **marginalise** (-ises, -ising, -ised) vt. to take or keep sb or sth away from the centre of attention, influence, or power —**marginalization** /maárjinə līzáysh'n/ n.

marginally /maárjinəli/ adv. **1.** SLIGHTLY very slightly **2.** BARELY only just or barely

marginal utility n. ECON the increase in utility prompted by one extra unit of a given service or product

marginate /maárji nayt/ vt. (-ates, -ating, -ated) ADD MARGIN TO to add a margin to sth, or provide sth with a margin ■ adj. **marginate, marginated** BIOL WITH DIFFERENT EDGE with a border or edge of a different colour or pattern ○ a marginate leaf —**margination** /maárji náysh'n/ n.

margin of safety n. the difference between budgeted output level and the break-even output level

margravate /maárgrəvət, -vayt/, **margraviate** /maar gráyvi ət, -ayt/ n. **1.** MARGRAVE'S TERRITORY the territory ruled by a margrave or margravine **2.** RANK OF MARGRAVE the rank or position of a margrave or margravine

margrave /maár grayv/ n. in the past, a German nobleman of a rank equivalent to a British marquess [Mid-16thC. From Middle Dutch markgrave, literally 'count of the border'.] —**margravial** /maar gráyvi əl/ adj.

margraviate n. = margravate

margravine /maárgrə veen/ n. in the past, a German noblewoman, equal in rank to a British marchioness, who is the wife or widow of a margrave or who holds the rank in her own right [Late 17thC. From Dutch markgravin, feminine of markgraaf 'margrave'.]

marguerite /maárgə reét/ n. a widely cultivated garden plant from the Canary Islands that has a flower resembling a daisy with narrow white or pale yellow petals radiating from a yellow centre. Latin name: Chrysanthemum frutescens. [Early 17thC. From French, from the female name Marguerite.]

maria plural of mare[2]

mariachi /maári aáchi, márri-/ (plural -chis) n. **1.** MEXICAN STREET BAND a Mexican street band usually consisting of stringed instruments, especially violins and guitars, but sometimes also including brass instruments and singers **2.** MARIACHI BAND MEMBER a member of a mariachi band **3.** MARIACHI MUSIC traditional Mexican folk music as played by a mariachi band [Mid-20thC. From Mexican Spanish, of uncertain origin: perhaps from French mariage 'wedding', because such bands probably played at weddings.]

mariage blanc /márri aazh blaán, maárri-/ (plural mariages blancs) n. a marriage that has not been consummated [From French, literally 'white marriage']

mariage de convenance /márri aazh də koNvə naáNss, maárri-/ (plural mariages de convenance) n. = marriage of convenience [From French, 'marriage for expediency or propriety']

Marian /máiri ən/ adj. **1.** CHR OF VIRGIN MARY relating to, characteristic of, or devoted to Mary, the mother of Jesus Christ **2.** HIST OF MARY relating to any Mary other than the Virgin Mary, especially Mary Queen of Scots or Queen Mary I of England ■ n. CHR DEVOTEE

OF VIRGIN MARY sb who is especially devoted to Mary, the mother of Jesus Christ

Mariana Islands /márri a̅a̅nə-/ island group in the western Pacific Ocean, south of Japan and east of the Philippines. It comprises the island of Guam and the Commonwealth of the Northern Mariana Islands. Area: 958 sq. km/370 sq. mi.

Marianao /ma̅a̅rja na̅a̅ õ/ city in western Cuba, on the northern coast, in City of Havana Province. Population: 133,016 (1989).

Mariana Trench /márri a̅a̅nə trénch/ the deepest ocean trench, in the western Pacific Ocean, stretching from northwest of the Mariana Islands to southwest of Guam. Length: 2,500 km/1,554 mi.

Marianne /márri án/ n. an image of a woman personifying the French republic, e.g. on French coins, usually depicted in a light flowing robe and wearing the Phrygian cap of liberty [Late 19thC. From French.]

Maria Theresa /mə ree̅ ə tə ráyzə/, **Archduchess of Austria and Queen of Hungary and Bohemia** (1717–80). Her succession as ruler of the Hapsburg dominions led to the War of the Austrian Succession (1740–48) and the Seven Years' War (1756–63).

Maria Theresa dollar n. a silver coin minted in 1780 and used in the Middle East [Named after MARIA THERESA, whose image appears on it]

mariculture /márri kulchər/ n. the cultivation of sea animals and plants in their usual habitats, generally for commercial purposes [Early 20thC. Coined from Latin mari- (stem of mare 'sea') + CULTURE.] —**maricultural** adj. —**mariculturist** n.

Marie Antoinette /márri antwə nét/, **Queen of France** (1755–93). The wife of Louis XVI, she was unpopular for promoting the interests of her native Austria and for her extravagance. She was captured after attempting to escape the French Revolution, imprisoned, and guillotined.

Marie Byrd Land /ma̅a̅ri búrd land/ unclaimed ice-covered region in Antarctica, on the Amundsen Sea, in the southern Pacific Ocean

Marie de Médicis /mə ree̅ də méddi chee/, **Queen of France** (1573–1642). As widow of Henry IV of France, she became regent during Louis XIII's minority. Political intrigue resulted in her exile in 1630.

Marie Galante /maa ree̅ gaa lóNt/ island in the French West Indies, in the Caribbean Sea. It is a dependency of Guadeloupe. Population: 3,757 (1982). Area: 158 sq. km/61 sq. mi.

Marie-Louise (of Austria) /mə ree̅ loo ee̅z əv óstri ə/, **Empress of France** (1791–1847). She was Napoleon Bonaparte's second wife.

Marigold

marigold /márri gōld/ n. a common garden plant, native to tropical America, with scented stems and strikingly rich yellow or orange flowers. Genus: *Tagetes*. [14thC. From the name *Mary* (referring to the Virgin Mary) + Old English *golde*, corn marigold'; so called because of its medicinal properties.]

marigram /márri gram/ n. a printed record of tide levels at a particular place [Late 19thC. Coined from Latin mari-, stem of mare 'sea' (+-GRAM).]

marigraph /márri graaf, -graf/ n. an instrument for recording tide levels [Mid-19thC. Coined from Latin mari-, the stem of mare 'sea' (+-GRAPH).]

marijuana /márri wa̅a̅nə, -hwa̅a̅nə/, **marihuana** n. 1. DRUGS DRUG FROM HEMP the dried flowers and leaves of the Indian hemp plant, smoked or eaten as a drug 2. PLANTS HEMP PLANT the Indian hemp plant that is the source of the drugs marijuana and cannabis. Latin name: *Cannabis sativa*. [Late 19thC. From Mexican Spanish *mariguana*, *marihuana*, of unknown origin.]

marimba /mə rímbə/ n. a large musical instrument like a xylophone, with resonators made from metal or hollow gourds beneath the bars, used especially in African and Latin American music [Early 18thC. From Portuguese, of Bantu origin.] —**marimbist** n.

marina /mə ree̅nə/ n. a harbour specially designed to cater for pleasure boats and their owners [Early 19thC. Via Italian or Spanish, 'seashore', from, ultimately, Latin *marinus*, from *mare* 'sea'.]

marinade /márri náyd, -nayd/ n. FLAVOURINGS FOR FOOD BEFORE COOKING a liquid or paste made with ingredients such as vinegar, wine, oil, spices, and herbs, in which food is soaked or allowed to stand to give extra flavour and tenderness before cooking ■ vti. (-nades, -nading, -naded) = **marinate** [Early 18thC. Via French from, ultimately, Italian *marinare* or Spanish *marinar* (see MARINATE).]

marinara /márri na̅a̅rə/ adj. 1. MADE WITH TOMATOES AND GARLIC made with tomatoes and garlic, often with other ingredients such as onions, parsley, capers, or olives, to serve on pasta or as a pizza topping ○ *marinara sauce* 2. WITH MARINARA SAUCE served with marinara sauce ○ *spaghetti marinara* [Mid-20thC. From Italian *alla marinara* 'in sailor style', from *marinaro* 'sailor', from *marino* 'marine', from Latin *marinus*, from *mare* 'sea'.] —**marinara** n.

marinate /márri nayt/ (-nates, -nating, -nated) vti. to soak or stand, or leave food to soak or stand, in a marinade before cooking [Mid-17thC. From Italian *marinare* or Spanish *marinar* 'to pickle in brine', both from Latin *(aqua) marina* 'sea (water), brine', feminine of *marinus*, from *mare* 'sea'.] —**marination** /márri náysh'n/ n.

Marinduque /márrən do̅o̅ki/ island in the Philippines, south of Luzon Island. Its provincial capital is Boac. Population: 173,715 (1980).

marine /mə ree̅n/ adj. 1. OF THE SEA relating to, found in, or living in the sea 2. NAUT NAUTICAL relating to ships or sailing 3. MIL OF SEAGOING SOLDIERS relating to soldiers who serve at sea as well as on land ■ n. 1. **marine, Marine** MIL SEAGOING SOLDIER a soldier who serves at sea as well as in the air and on land, e.g. a member of the Royal Marines 2. SHIPPING NATION'S COMMERCIAL FLEET a nation's fleet of merchant or naval ships and their crews (formal) 3. PAINTING SEA SCENE a painting or photograph of a seascape, ship, or scene at sea [14thC. Via French from Latin *marinus*, from *mare* 'sea' (see MARE[2].] ◇ **tell that to the marines** used to express disbelief (slang)

marine architect n. sb specially trained to design ships —**marine architecture** n.

marine biology n. the branch of biology that deals with the plants and animals of the oceans —**marine biologist** n.

Marine Corps n. a branch of the United States armed forces, trained to operate on land, at sea, and in the air, and especially in amphibious assaults

marine engineer n. sb who attends to the engines and other heavy machinery on board a ship or any other offshore structure

mariner /márrinər/ n. sb who sails or navigates vessels [13thC. Via Anglo-Norman or French *marinier* from Latin *marinarius*, from *marinus*, from *mare* 'sea'.]

■ WORD KEY: CULTURAL NOTE ■

The Rime of the Ancient Mariner, a poem by the writer Samuel Taylor Coleridge (1798). A cautionary tale of sin and redemption, it describes a curse placed on a sailor after he kills an albatross that has led his ship out of danger. The vessel is becalmed and the rest of the crew die of thirst. After his rescue, the sailor is compelled to repeat his story for the remainder of his days. The expressions 'Water, water, every where/ Nor any drop to drink' and 'He prayest best who loveth best/ All things both great and small' come from Part II, stanza 9, and Part VII, stanza 23 respectively, of this poem.

Marinetti /márri nétti/, **Filippo Tommaso Emilio** (1876–1944) Italian writer and political activist. His writings reflect the tenets of futurism, which he founded in 1909. In 1919 he joined the Fascist Party.

marinière /márrini áir/ adj. cooked with a little wine, herbs, and chopped onion or shallot, in a closed pan, so that the main ingredient, which is usually mussels, is partly poached and partly steamed ○ *mussels marinière* [From French, literally 'sailor-style', possibly a translation of Italian *marinara* (see MARINARA)]

Mariolatry /máiri óllətri, márri-/ n. extreme devotion to Mary, the mother of Jesus Christ [Early 17thC. Coined from Latin *Maria* 'Mary' + -LATRY.] —**Mariolater** n. —**Mariolatrous** adj.

Mariology /máiri ólləji, márri-/ n. the study of the doctrines and beliefs concerning Mary, the mother of Jesus Christ [Mid-19thC. Coined from Latin *Maria* 'Mary' + -LOGY.] —**Mariological** /máiri ə lójjik'l, márri-/ adj. —**Mariologist** /máiri ólləjist, márri-/ n.

marionette /márri ə nét/ n. a puppet operated by means of strings attached to its hands, legs, head, and body [Early 17thC. From French, literally 'little Mary', from *Marion*, of the same meaning.]

mariposa /márri pōzə, -póssə/ n. a western North American plant of the lily family that grows from a bulb and bears brightly coloured flowers resembling tulips. Genus: *Calochortus*. [Mid-19thC. From Spanish, literally 'butterfly' (because of its brightly-coloured flowers).]

Marist /máirist/ n. 1. CHR MEMBER OF ROMAN CATHOLIC ORDER a member of either of two Roman Catholic orders, the Society of Mary or Marist Fathers, and the Little Brothers of Mary or Marist Brothers 2. NZ EDUC TEACHER OR PUPIL IN MARIST SCHOOL a teacher or pupil in a school run by the Marist Brothers [Late 19thC. From French *mariste*, from *Marie* 'Mary'.] —**Marist** adj.

maritage /márritij/ n. 1. RIGHT OF LORD TO ARRANGE MARRIAGE the right of a feudal lord to choose the husband or wife of a vassal's heir 2. FINE PAID TO FEUDAL LORD money paid to a feudal lord in return for his not exercising his right to choose the husband or wife of a vassal's heir [Early 16thC. From medieval Latin *maritagium*, a Latinized form of French *mariage*, from *marier* (see MARRY).]

Maritain /márri téN, -táyn/, **Jacques** (1882–1973) French philosopher. An exponent of neo-scholasticism, his greatest work was in epistemology, political philosophy, and aesthetics.

marital /márrit'l/ adj. 1. OF MARRIAGE relating to marriage or the marriage of a particular couple 2. OF HUSBANDS relating to a husband or husbands (formal) [15thC. From Latin *maritalis*, from *maritus* 'married' (source also of English *marry*).] —**maritally** adv.

maritime /márri tīm/ adj. 1. SHIPPING OF THE SEA relating to the sea, shipping, sailing in ships, or living and working at sea 2. CLOSE TO THE SEA situated or living close to the sea 3. METEOROL INFLUENCED BY THE SEA influenced by the sea, and therefore generally temperate and with relatively small variations in seasonal temperatures [Mid-16thC. Directly or via French from Latin *maritimus*, from *mare* 'sea' (see MARE[2]).]

Maritime Provinces, Maritimes collective name for the eastern Canadian provinces of New Brunswick, Nova Scotia, and Prince Edward Island —**Maritimer** /márri tīmər/ n.

Maritsa /mə ree̅tsə/ river in southeastern Europe, in the Balkan Peninsula. Length: 480 km/300 mi.

Mariupol /məri óopəl/ city in southeastern Ukraine, on the Sea of Azov. Population: 510,000 (1996).

Marius /márri əss, máiri-/, **Gaius** (157?–86 BC) Roman general and statesman. His political rivalry with Lucius Sulla led to the civil war of 88–86 BC, in which Marius was victorious.

Marivaux /márri vō, márri vó/, **Pierre Carlet de Chamblain de** (1688–1763) French playwright and novelist. His romantic comedies and novels portray 18th-century middle-class life.

marjoram /ma̅a̅rjərəm/ n. a Mediterranean herb that has small purple or white flowers and aromatic leaves, often used as a seasoning in cookery and salads. Latin name: *Origanum majorana*. [14thC. Via Old French *marjorane*, from medieval Latin *majorana*, of unknown origin.]

mark[1] /maark/ n. 1. SPOT, SCRATCH, OR DIRT a coloured, discoloured, or dirty patch, a scratch, dent, or impression, either deliberately or accidentally made, that makes a usually small area of a surface visibly different from the rest ○ *The hot plate left a mark on the table.* **2.** SYMBOL a recognizable sign or symbol used, e.g. to indicate ownership, the quality or origin of goods, or punctuation in a piece of writing (*often used in combination*) ○ *a question mark* **3.** SUBSTITUTE FOR SIGNATURE a cross or other symbol used in place of a signature by sb who cannot write **4.** INDICATION OF FEELING an action, gesture, or other outward sign of sb's feeling or attitude ○ *a mark of respect* **5.** SIGN OF INFLUENCE OR INVOLVEMENT sth that is evidence of sb's or sth's influence on or involvement in sth ○ *He left his mark on the firm.* **6.** IDENTIFYING FEATURE OR CHARACTERISTIC a distinctive and identifying feature or characteristic ○ *That perfect finish is the mark of the true professional.* **7.** INDICATION OF CORRECTNESS OR QUALITY a number, letter, or percentage indicating sb's assessment of sth, e.g. the correctness or quality of answers to examination questions or sb's performance in a gymnastic or ice-skating contest ○ *She always gets top marks in English.* **8.** INDICATOR OF POSITION OR EXTENT any object, sign, or line used to indicate the position, extent, or amount of sth ○ *the high-water mark* **9.** AMOUNT the amount, distance, or level reached by sth ○ *The temperature is way above the 80 degree mark.* **10.** STANDARD the desired or required standard for sth ○ *Your work is simply not up to the mark these days.* **11.** TYPE a model or variety, e.g., of a car, aircraft, or weapon, usually distinguished from earlier or later models by a number **12.** ARMS TARGET a target, or sth that sb aims at with a weapon ○ *He missed the mark.* **13.** GOAL a goal or standard that sb wishes to achieve **14.** CRIMINOL VICTIM OF CRIME the victim or intended victim of a theft or swindle (*slang*) ○ *a soft mark* **15.** NAVIG GUIDE TO POSITION OR DIRECTION a conspicuous object or another point of reference that serves as a visual guide to sb when proceeding in a particular direction or carrying out an action **16.** ATHLETICS STARTING LINE the starting line for a race **17.** RUGBY UNION INSTANCE OF PLAYER SHOUTING MARK in a game of rugby, an instance of a player within his or her 22 m line shouting 'mark' when intercepting the ball from an opponent's kick, entitling him or her to a free kick **18.** FOOTBALL CATCH OF THE BALL in Australian Rules football, a catch made after an opponent kicks the ball at least 9 m/10 yds without it touching the ground or another player. This entitles the catcher to a free kick. **19.** BOXING MIDDLE OF STOMACH the middle of an opponent's stomach **20.** SPORTS = **jack**[1] *n.* 5 **21.** SAILING STH THAT INDICATES DEPTH OF WATER a knot or other marker used to indicate intervals of fathoms on a sounding line **22.** HIST COMMON LAND in medieval Germany and England, land held in common by the members of a community ■ **marks** *npl.* ATHLETICS RUNNER'S STARTING POSITION a runner's individual starting position for a race ■ *v.* (**marks, marking, marked**) **1.** *vti.* MAKE OR GET SPOTS OR SCRATCHES to make or get a coloured or discoloured patch, dent, scratch, or other mark on sth, either accidentally or deliberately ○ *The mugs have marked the table.* **2.** *vt.* PUT MARK OR SYMBOL ON STH to put a recognizable sign or symbol or write on sth, e.g. to show ownership, to indicate price, or to give a warning or instruction ○ *All items of clothing must be clearly marked with the student's name.* **3.** *vt.* MAKE CLEARLY IDENTIFIABLE to make sth clearly visible, recognizable, or traceable by putting a mark on it ○ *I've marked on the map where our house is.* **4.** *vt.* INDICATE WHERE STH IS OR HAPPENED to be an indicator showing where sth is situated, how far it extends, or where an event took place ○ *This monument marks their last resting place.* **5.** *vt.* BE OR INDICATE POINT OF CHANGE to indicate that a significant point in time or in a process has been reached ○ *It marks the end of an era in British theatre.* **6.** *vt.* GIVE PROMINENCE TO EVENT to do sth to celebrate or give prominence to a particular event ○ *We should do something really special to mark their 50th anniversary.* **7.** *vt.* SELECT FOR SPECIAL ATTENTION to select or destine sb or sth for particular attention or treatment ○ *He was always marked out for success.* **8.** *vt.* CHARACTERIZE to characterize, distinguish, or set sb or sth apart in some way ○ *The originality of her approach marks her as a candidate of real distinction.* **9.** *vt.* ASSESS AND INDICATE QUALITY OR CORRECTNESS to assess the quality or correctness of sth and indicate the assessment by means of a mark such as a tick or cross, a letter, number, or percentage ○ *marking exam papers* **10.** *vt.* ASSESS THE WORK OF SB to assess the quality or correctness of the work or performance of sb and indicate the assessment by means of a mark ○ *marked him high on the test* **11.** *vt.* TAKE NOTICE OF to pay attention to sth or sb (*often used as a command*) ○ *Mark my words, this'll make them sit up and take notice.* **12.** *vt.* SEE STH to see or notice sth (*archaic*) **13.** *vt.* SPORTS STAY CLOSE TO PLAYER in games such as football and hockey, to stay close to an attacking player in the opposing team to prevent the player from receiving the ball or scoring **14.** *vti.* SPORTS KEEP SCORE to keep a note of the score **15.** *vt.* FOOTBALL MAKE A MARK in Australian Rules football, to catch the ball after it has been kicked at least 9 m/10 yds without having touched the ground or another player **16.** *vt. ANZ* AGRIC CASTRATE to castrate a lamb ■ *interj.* RUGBY SHOUT FROM RUGBY PLAYER in a game of Rugby Union, the shout made by a player who catches the ball within his or her own 22 m line in order to gain a free kick [Old English *mearc* 'boundary, marker'. Ultimately from an Indo-European word meaning 'boundary', which is also the ancestor of English *march* and *margin*.] ◇ **mark time 1.** to continue marching in rhythm without moving forwards **2.** to do sth that makes no contribution towards achieving a goal or ambition while awaiting an opportunity to make progress ◇ **make your mark** to achieve recognition or success, usually in a particular field ◇ **mark you** used to call sb's attention to a point or remark that you are making ◇ **on your marks** used as a command to runners to take up their starting positions ready for the start of a race ◇ **quick off the mark, slow off the mark** quick or slow to begin, react to, or understand sth ◇ **up to the mark** of an acceptable standard or quality, or at an acceptable level ◇ **wide of the mark, off the mark** inaccurate or incorrect

mark down *vt.* **1.** MAKE WRITTEN NOTE to make a written note of sth somewhere **2.** COMM LOWER PRICE to lower the price of sth **3.** EDUC GIVE LOWER MARK to reduce the mark given to sth or sb in a test, examination, or contest, as a result of a mistake or inadequacy ○ *You get marked down for bad spelling.* **4.** CHARACTERIZE to form an opinion as to the character or likely behaviour of sb

mark off *vt.* **1.** SEPARATE ONE AREA FROM ANOTHER to separate one area from another by means of a boundary line or barrier **2.** MAKE DIFFERENT to make sb or sth different from others ○ *Her mathematical ability marks her off from the rest of her class.* **3.** PUT A MARK ON STH to put a mark such as a tick, cross, or line beside, through, or around sth, to show that it has been dealt with or to highlight it

mark out *vt.* **1.** INDICATE BOUNDARIES AND DIVISIONS OF STH to draw lines or use some other method to indicate the boundaries and divisions of sth, especially the playing area for a game or a racecourse **2.** MAKE NOTICEABLY DIFFERENT to make sb or sth noticeably different from and often superior to others

mark up *vt.* **1.** BUSINESS INCREASE PRICE to increase the price of sth, especially to provide the seller with a profit **2.** EDUC INCREASE MARKS AWARDED to increase the marks awarded to sb in a test, examination, or contest **3.** PUBL MARK CORRECTIONS AND INSTRUCTIONS ON TEXT to prepare a piece of written work for printing or rekeying by making corrections to it or adding instructions to the typesetters or keyboarders

mark[2] /maark/ *n.* **1.** MONEY = **Deutschmark 2.** MONEY OLD COIN IN ENGLAND AND SCOTLAND a former unit of currency in England and Scotland that was worth 13 shillings and 4 pence, or two thirds of a pound **3.** MEASURE UNIT OF WEIGHT formerly, a unit of weight equivalent to 227 gr/8 oz that was used for weighing gold and silver [Old English *marc*, a unit of weight. From a prehistoric Germanic word (ancestor also of English *mark*[1]). In the sense 'Deutschmark': late 19thC, from German.]

Mark *n.* the second of the gospels in the Bible in which the life and teachings of Jesus Christ are described. It is thought to have been written by St Mark. See table at **Bible**

Mark /maark/, **St** (*fl.* 1st century) apostle. A disciple of St Peter and one of the apostles of Jesus Christ, he is credited with writing the New Testament Gospel of Mark.

Marka /múrkə/ town and seaport in southeastern Somalia. Population: 100,000 (1987).

markdown /maárk down/ *n.* a reduction in price

marked /maarkt/ *adj.* **1.** NOTICEABLE very noticeable ○ *a marked contrast* **2.** SINGLED OUT singled out for surveillance, suspicion, hostility, or an unpleasant fate ○ *a marked man* **3.** CARDS WITH MARK ON BACK having a concealed identifying mark that makes it easier to use when cheating in card games or performing conjuring tricks ○ *marked cards* **4.** LING WITH DISTINCTIVE LINGUISTIC FEATURE having an extra or less usual distinctive linguistic feature —**markedness** /maárkidnəss/ *n.*

markedly /maárkidli/ *adv.* to a significant extent

marker /maárkər/ *n.* **1.** INDICATOR OF POSITION, PRESENCE, OR ROUTE an object or sign that indicates the position or presence of sth or the direction in which sb is to go **2.** STH THAT MAKES MARKS sth used to make marks, especially a felt-tip pen **3.** EDUC SB WHO ASSESSES STUDENTS' ANSWERS sb who marks examination papers or student exercises **4.** SPORTS SCORER sb who keeps a note of the score in certain games, e.g. snooker and billiards, or sth that shows the score **5.** SPORTS PLAYER MARKING ANOTHER in games such as football and hockey, a player who stays close to an attacking player in the opposing team to prevent the player from receiving the ball or scoring

market /maárkit/ *n.* **1.** COMM GATHERING FOR BUYING AND SELLING a gathering of people who sell things, especially food or animals, in a place open to the public or other buyers, especially a gathering that is held regularly ○ *a cattle market* **2.** MARKET BUILDING OR PLACE a building or open space where a market is regularly held **3.** COMM COLLECTION OF SHOPS OR STALLS a number of small shops or stalls, housed in the same building and sometimes all selling the same type of goods, belonging to different, independent traders **4.** COMM SHOP a shop, especially one that sells goods or food of a particular type **5.** FIN SUPPLY AND DEMAND the whole area of economic activity where buyers are in contact with sellers and in which the laws of supply and demand operate. Besides being considered as the arena for buying and selling, the market is often thought of as a controlling or regulatory force affecting both economic and political affairs. ○ *market forces* **6.** FIN BUYING AND SELLING OF PARTICULAR COMMODITY the trade in, or buying and selling of, a particular commodity ○ *the futures market* **7.** COMM REGION OR GROUP CONSIDERED AS CUSTOMERS a geographical area or a section of the population, considered from the point of view of the amount of goods that can be sold to it ○ *the teenage market* **8.** COMM DEMAND the demand for a particular type of goods or service being offered for sale ○ *You've got to go out and create a market if you want to succeed.* **9.** ECON TOTAL AMOUNT OF PRODUCT SOLD the total amount of a particular product sold within a particular geographical area or over a particular period of time **10.** STOCK EXCH = **stock market** ○ *Prices rose on the New York and Chicago markets this morning* **11.** FIN TRADING IN STOCKS trading in stocks, shares, and commodities ○ *The market was very slow this morning but picked up later.* **12.** FIN PRICES OR EXCHANGE RATES the prices or rates of exchange offered for stocks, shares, or commodities ○ *The market fell this morning but rallied later.* ■ *vt.* (**-kets, -keting, -keted**) MARKETING OFFER FOR SALE to offer sth for sale, or sell sth, especially by using advertising and other techniques to attract buyers ○ *If this is marketed in the right way, it'll sell very well.* [Pre-12thC. Via Old French dialect from, ultimately, Latin *mercatus*, from the past participle of *mercari* 'to buy', from *merx* 'goods' (source of English *merchant* and *commerce*).] —**marketer** *n.* ◇ **come onto the market** to become available for customers to buy ◇ **in the market (for sth)** interested in buying or ready to buy sth ◇ **on the market** available for customers to buy ◇ **on the open market** where goods are freely available and prices are subject mainly to the law of supply and demand ◇ **put sth on the market** to offer sth for sale

marketable /maárkitəb'l/ *adj.* **1.** COMM SUITABLE FOR SELLING fit to be sold ○ *a highly marketable property* **2.** IN DEMAND in demand and therefore relatively easy to sell ○ *skills that are readily marketable* **3.** FIN CONVERTIBLE INTO CASH able to be converted into cash quickly, but at a price that is determined by the market in that commodity ○ *marketable value* — **marketability** /máarkitə bílləti/ *n.* —**marketableness** /-əb'lnəss/ *n.* —**marketably** *adv.*

market economy *n.* an economy where prices and wages are determined mainly by the market and the laws of supply and demand, rather than being regulated by a government

marketeer /máarki teér/ *n.* **1.** COMM SB WHO TRADES AT MARKET sb who buys or sells things either at a market or in ordinary trade **2.** POL SUPPORTER OF TYPE OF MARKET sb who advocates or supports a particular type of market (*usually used in combination*) ○ *a free marketeer*

market garden *n.* a plot of ground or small farm where fruit, vegetables, and sometimes flowers are grown for sale rather than for the grower's own use —**market gardener** *n.* —**market gardening** *n.*

marketing /máarkiting/ *n.* the business activity of presenting products or services to potential customers in such a way as to make them eager to buy. Marketing includes such matters as the pricing and packaging of the product and the creation of demand by advertising and sales campaigns.

marketing board *n.* Can, UK an organization set up by a government to promote and regulate the sale of a particular agricultural product, e.g. grain, dairy products, or poultry

marketing mix *n.* the particular mixture of marketing techniques, e.g. pricing, packaging, and advertising, used to promote the sale of a product

market leader *n.* a company or brand that has a very large, or the largest, share of the market for a particular product

market maker *n.* a dealer who buys and sells securities such as shares

market order *n.* an order instructing a broker to buy or sell an asset immediately at the best prevailing price

marketplace /máarkit playss/ *n.* **1.** OPEN SPACE FOR MARKET an open space where a market is held **2.** COMM SPHERE OF TRADING the commercial sphere where buying and selling takes place and the laws of supply and demand operate **3.** SET-UP WHERE IDEAS CAN BE DISCUSSED a forum in which ideas are exchanged, discussed, and compete for recognition

market price *n.* the price at which sth is currently being bought by the majority of customers

market research *n.* the gathering and analysis of information about what people want or like, or what they actually buy —**market researcher** *n.*

market share *n.* the proportion of the total sales of a product secured by one particular company or brand

market town *n.* a town in which a market is held regularly, usually the chief town of a farming area

market value *n.* the amount that a seller could expect to obtain for property or goods sold on the open market

markhor /máar kawr/ (*plural* **-khors** *or* **-khor**) *n.* the largest wild goat, which has a reddish-brown coat, spiral horns, and a shaggy beard on the male, and is found in the Himalayas. Latin name: *Capra falconeri.* [Mid-19thC. From Persian *mār-ḵwār*, literally 'serpent-eater'.]

marking /máarking/ *n.* **1.** ZOOL MARK OR MARKS a mark or pattern of marks that occurs naturally, e.g. on an animal's coat (*often used in the plural*) **2.** AIR AIRCRAFT IDENTIFYING MARK an identifying mark, usually a coloured symbol, on an aircraft (*often used in the plural*) **3.** EDUC ASSESSMENT AND GRADING OF WRITTEN WORK a teacher's correction and assessment of students' written work **4.** EDUC WRITTEN WORK TO BE MARKED a quantity of written work that has to be corrected and assessed

marking ink *n.* a type of ink used for writing on such things as clothes and bed linen because it does not wash out

markka /máar kaa, máarkə/ (*plural* **-kaa** /-kaa/) *n.* **1.** UNIT OF FINNISH CURRENCY the main unit of currency in Finland, worth 100 pennia. See table at **currency 2.**

COIN WORTH A MARKKA a coin worth one markka [Early 20thC. Via Finnish from Swedish *marka*.]

Dame Alicia Markova: In *Mr Puppet* with Anton Dolin

Markova /maar kṓvə/, **Dame Alicia** (*b.* 1910) British ballerina. She was a cofounder of the London Festival Ballet (1950) and director of the Metropolitan Opera Ballet (1963–69). Real name **Lillian Alicia Marks**

Markov chain /maár kof-/ *n.* a random process in which events are discrete rather than continuous and the future development of each event is independent of all historical events or dependent only on the immediately preceding event [See MARKOV PROCESS]

Markov process /maárkof-/ *n.* a continuous random process in which the probability of occurrence of each random event in a series is independent of all historical events or dependent only on the immediately preceding event [Named after the Russian mathematician A. A. *Markov*, who developed it.]

Marks /maarks/, **Simon, 1st Baron Marks of Broughton** (1888–1964) British retailing magnate. He was the son of Michael Marks, founder of Marks and Spencer. With Israel Seiff he transformed the company into a successful retailing chain.

marksman /maárksmən/ (*plural* **-men** /-mən/) *n.* **1.** SB SKILLED IN SHOOTING sb who is able or trained to shoot accurately, especially with a firearm **2.** SB CONSIDERED GOOD OR BAD SHOT sb considered from the point of view of his or her ability to shoot accurately —**marksmanship** *n.*

markswoman /maárkswoõmən/ (*plural* **-men** /-wimin/) *n.* **1.** WOMAN SKILLED IN SHOOTING a woman who is able or trained to shoot accurately, especially with a firearm **2.** WOMAN CONSIDERED GOOD OR BAD SHOT a woman considered from the point of view of her ability to shoot accurately

mark-up *n.* COMM the difference between the manufacturing cost or wholesale price of an item and its selling price, that is, the amount added to provide the seller with a profit

marl /maarl/ *n.* GEOL MIXTURE OF CLAY AND LIME a naturally occurring fine crumbly mixture of clay and limestone, often containing shell fragments and sometimes other minerals. Marls are used as fertilizer and to soften water. ■ *vt.* (**marls, marling, marled**) AGRIC FERTILIZE WITH MARL to add marl to soil as a fertilizer [14thC. Via Old French *marle* from medieval Latin *margila*, from Latin *marga* 'marl', on the model of *argilla* 'white clay'.] —**marlacious** /maar láyshəss/ *adj.* —**marly** /maárli/ *adj.*

marl[2] /maarl/ (**marls, marling, marled**) *vt.* to bind sth with a light two-stranded rope [Early 18thC. From Dutch *marlen*, literally 'to keep binding', from Middle Dutch *marren* 'to bind' (source of English *marline*).]

Marlborough /maárl bərə/ **1.** market town in Wiltshire, south-central England. Population: 17,771 (1991). **2.** administrative region of New Zealand, occupying the northeastern corner of the South Island. It is chiefly an agricultural district. Population: 40,242 (1996).

Marlborough, John Churchill, 1st Duke of (1650–1722) English general. He won a string of brilliant victories as commander-in-chief of English forces during the War of the Spanish Succession (1701–14).

Marley /maárli/, **Bob** (1945–81) Jamaican musician. His music, much of which he wrote himself, es-

tablished reggae internationally as an important part of pop music.

marlin[1] /maárlin/ (*plural* **-lins** *or* **-lin**) *n.* a large food and game fish found in warm and tropical regions of the Atlantic and Pacific oceans that has a very long thin upper jaw, like a spear. It can reach 4.5 m/14 ft in length and 680 kg/1,500 lb in weight. Family: Istiophoridae. [Early 20thC. Shortened from *marlinspike*, from the shape of its upper jaw.]

marlin[2] *n.* = **marline**

marline /maárlin/, **marlin** *n.* a light two-stranded rope, used especially for binding around larger ropes to prevent them from fraying [15thC. Via Dutch *marlijn*, literally 'binding line', and *marling* 'binding', both ultimately from Middle Dutch *marren* 'to bind']

marlinespike /maárlin spīk/, **marlinspike** *n.* a pointed metal tool used to separate strands of rope that are being spliced [Early 17thC. Alteration (under the influence of MARLINE) of earlier *marlingspike*, from MARL[2] + SPIKE.]

marlite /maár līt/ *n.* a rock with the same composition as marl but with a harder, more resistant texture [Late 18thC. Formed from MARL[1].] —**marlitic** /maar líttik/ *adj.*

Marlowe /maár lō/, **Christopher** (1564–93) English playwright. Often considered the first great English playwright, he wrote tragedies including *The Tragical History of Doctor Faustus* (1588?) and *Edward II* (1594).

marlstone /maárl stōn/ *n.* = **marlite**

marmalade /maármə layd/ *n.* FOOD CITRUS FRUIT PRESERVE a clear or thick preserve made with citrus fruits, usually containing the shredded rind of the fruit, and traditionally made with bitter Seville oranges ■ *adj.* ZOOL WITH ORANGE FUR used to describe cats with orange fur, or orange fur streaked with yellow or brown [15thC. Via French *marmelade* 'quince jam', from Portuguese *marmelada*, from *marmelo* 'quince', from, ultimately, Greek *melimēlon*, literally 'honey-apple', denoting a kind of apple grafted onto the quince.]

marmalade plum *n.* the edible brownish fruit of the marmalade tree, with sweet, slightly spicy, reddish flesh

marmalade tree *n.* a tree found in Central America, Mexico, and the southern United States, with brownish edible fruit (**marmalade plums**). Latin name: *Calocarpum sapota.*

Marmara, Sea of /maármərə, seé əv/, **Marmora, Sea of** inland sea in northwestern Turkey, separating Asiatic and European regions. It forms part of the passage between the Black Sea and the Mediterranean Sea. Area: 11,350 sq. km/4,382 sq. mi. Length: 280 km/175 mi.

marmite /maár mīt/ *n.* a deep earthenware or metal cooking pot with a close-fitting lid, used for making soups, stews, or stock [Early 19thC. Via French from Old French, literally 'hypocritical' (perhaps because the food is concealed), from *marmouser* 'to murmur' + *mite* 'cat', both imitations of sounds.]

Marmite /maár mīt/ *tdmk.* a trademark for a sticky dark brown mixture of yeast and vegetable extracts, used as a spread and for flavouring

marmoreal /maar máwri əl/ *adj.* made of marble, or like marble, especially in being white, cold, or aloof and impressive (*formal*) [Late 18thC. Formed from Latin *marmoreus*, from *marmor* (see MARBLE).] —**marmoreally** *adv.*

marmoset /maármə zét, -zet/ (*plural* **-sets** *or* **-set**) *n.* a small monkey that lives in Central and South America and has soft thick fur, tufts of fur around its head and ears, a long tail, and clawed digits. Family: Callithricidae. [14thC. From French *marmouset* 'grotesque figure', of uncertain origin.]

marmot /maármət/ (*plural* **-mots** *or* **-mot**) *n.* a large brownish stout-bodied rodent of the squirrel family that lives on the ground and in burrows, and is found throughout North America, Europe, and northern Asia. One species of American marmot is known as the woodchuck or groundhog. Genus: *Marmota.* [Early 17thC. From French *marmotte*, of uncertain origin.]

Marne /maarn/ river in northern France. Length: 523 km/325 mi.

marocain /márrə kayn, -káyn/ n. a ribbed crepe fabric [Early 20thC. From French, literally 'Moroccan'.]

Maronite /márrə nīt/ adj. belonging or relating to the Christian Uniat Church of the Lebanon, an Eastern Catholic church [Early 16thC. From medieval Latin *Maronita*, from the name of the 4thC Syrian hermit *Maro*, who founded the group.] —**Maronite** n.

Maroochydore /maroóchee dawr/ coastal town in southeastern Queensland, Australia, located at the mouth of the River Maroochy. Population: 36,406 (1996).

maroon[1] /mə roón/ adj. COLOURS DEEP PURPLISH-RED of a deep purplish-red colour with a tinge of brown ■ n. 1. COLOURS DEEP PURPLISH-RED COLOUR a deep purplish-red colour tinged with brown 2. COMMUNICATION EXPLOSIVE SIGNALLING DEVICE a small explosive device that makes a loud noise and is used for giving distress or warning signals [Late 18thC. Via French *marron* 'large sweet chestnut' from, ultimately, medieval Greek *maraon*. So called because of the colour of the nut's inner skin.]

maroon[2] /mə roón/ vt. (**-roons, -rooning, -rooned**) 1. NAUT LEAVE IN LONELY PLACE to put sb ashore on a lonely island or coast and leave the person there with no means of escape 2. LEAVE SB ISOLATED to leave sb somewhere with no means of getting away ■ n. 1. **maroon, Maroon** PEOPLES DESCENDANT OF PEOPLE ESCAPED FROM SLAVERY a descendant of people escaped from slavery in Guyana and the remoter parts of the West Indies 2. MAROONED PERSON sb who has been marooned, especially on a desert island [Mid-17thC. From French *marron* 'fugitive from slavery', shortening of American Spanish *cimarrón* 'wild, untamed', probably from *cima* 'peak'.]

maroquin /márrə keen, -kin, -kwin/ n. morocco leather, used especially for bookbindings and shoes [Early 16thC. From French, formed from *Maroc* 'Morocco', probably under the influence of Spanish *marroquin* 'Moroccan, morocco leather'.]

Marq. abbr. 1. Marquess 2. Marquis

marque /maark/ n. a brand or make of product, especially a make of luxury or high-performance items [Early 20thC. From French, formed from *marquer* 'to mark or brand', ultimately of prehistoric Germanic origin.]

marquee /maar keé/ n. 1. LARGE TENT a very large tent with straight sides that can be rolled up or removed, used for large gatherings such as parties, meetings, sales, and exhibitions 2. US, Can COVERING LIKE ROOF a permanent canopy, often of metal and glass, projecting out over the entrance to a large building such as a hotel or theatre [Late 17thC. Alteration of French *marquise* (see MARQUISE), which also denoted a canopy erected over the tent of a nobleman or officer to distinguish it from others.]

Marquesas Islands /maar káyssəss-/ group of volcanic islands in French Polynesia, 1,200 km/740 mi. north of Tahiti, in the Pacific Ocean. Population: 7,538 (1988). Area: 1,274 sq. km/492 sq. mi.

marquess /máarkwiss/ n. in Great Britain and Northern Ireland, a nobleman ranking between a duke and an earl [15thC. From Old French *marchis*, from *marche* 'border land' (see MARCH[2]).] —**marquessate** n.

Marquetry

marquetry /máarkitri/, **marqueterie** n. 1. DECORATIVE DESIGNS MADE OF INLAID MATERIALS designs or pictures made of thin pieces of wood, metal, shell, or other materials, inlaid in a wood veneer and often applied as decoration to pieces of furniture 2. CRAFT OF MAKING MARQUETRY the craft of making marquetry designs

or pictures [Mid-16thC. From French *marqueterie*, from *marqueter* 'to variegate', from *marquer* 'to mark or brand'.]

Márquez /maar kez/, **Gabriel García** (b. 1928) Colombian writer. In novels such as *100 Years of Solitude* (1967) and *Love in the Time of Cholera* (1985), he developed a distinctive style of fantasy blended with realism. He won the Nobel Prize in literature in 1982.

marquis /máarkwiss, -keé/ (plural **-quises** or **-quis** /maar keéz/) n. 1. NOBLEMAN in various European countries, a nobleman ranking above a count 2. = **marquess** [14thC. From Old French, an alteration of Old French *marchis* (see MARQUESS).] —**marquisate** /máarkwizit, -zayt/ n.

marquise /maar keéz/ n. 1. POL NOBLEWOMAN in various European countries, a noblewoman ranking above a countess, or the wife or widow of a marquis 2. CRAFT POINTED OVAL GEM a gem cut into the shape of a pointed oval and usually faceted 3. ACCESSORIES RING WITH POINTED OVAL a ring set with a pointed oval gem, or a cluster of stones arranged in a pointed oval shape [Early 17thC. From French, feminine of MARQUIS.]

marquisette /máarki zét, máarkwi-/ n. a fine woven fabric, often made of cotton or silk, that is used for making curtains and mosquito nets [Early 20thC. From French, literally 'little marquise'.]

Marrakesh /márrə késh/, **Marrakech** city in western Morocco, on the fertile Haouz Plain, at the foot of the High Atlas Mountains. Population: 602,000 (1994).

marram /márrəm/, **marram grass** n. a variety of grass that grows on sandy shores and is often planted to prevent erosion of sand dunes. Genus: *Ammophila*. [Mid-17thC. From Old Norse *marálmr* 'sea haulm'.]

Marrano /mə raánō/ (plural **-nos**) n. in the Middle Ages, a Jew from Spain or Portugal who converted to Christianity under duress and without conviction, and who continued to practise Judaism in secret [Late 16thC. From Spanish, literally 'pig' (because of the Jewish prohibition against pork), of uncertain origin: probably from Arabic *maḥram* 'sth forbidden' (because of the Islamic prohibition against pork).]

marriage /márrij/ n. 1. LEGAL RELATIONSHIP BETWEEN SPOUSES a legally recognized relationship, established by a civil or religious ceremony, between two people who intend to live together as sexual and domestic partners 2. PARTICULAR MARRIAGE RELATIONSHIP a married relationship between two people, or an individual's relationship with an individual spouse 3. JOINING IN MARRIAGE the joining together in marriage of two people 4. MARRIAGE CEREMONY the ceremony in which two people are joined together formally in marriage 5. UNION OF TWO THINGS a close union, blend, or mixture of two things ○ *Civilization is based on the marriage of tradition and innovation.* 6. CARDS KING AND QUEEN OF SAME SUIT a combination of the king and queen of the same suit, in card games such as pinochle and bezique [13thC. From French *mariage*, from *marier* (see MARRY).]

marriageable /márrijəb'l/ adj. suitable or ready for marriage, or old enough to be married —**marriageability** /márrijə bílləti/ n. —**marriageableness** /-əb'lnəss/ n.

marriage bureau n. an organization that sets up introductions and meetings between single people who are looking for sb to marry

marriage counselling, **marriage guidance** n. advice given by professionals to help married couples who are having difficulties in their relationship to solve their problems

marriage lines npl. record of legal marriage, with the names of those marrying, the time and place, and other details (informal)

marriage of convenience n. a marriage between two people that is intended to serve a practical, financial, or political purpose and is not based on their love for each other [Translation of French *mariage de convenance*, literally 'marriage for expediency']

married /márrid/ adj. 1. HAVING A SPOUSE having a wife or husband ○ *married people* 2. JOINED IN MARRIAGE joined together in marriage ○ *get married* 3. RELATING TO MARRIAGE arising out of or connected with marriage

○ *her married name* 4. COMPLETELY DEDICATED TO STH completely dedicated to sth and devoting a lot of time and effort to it ○ *married to her job* ■ **marrieds** npl. MARRIED PEOPLE people who are married ○ *young marrieds*

marron glacé /márron glássay, márroN-/ (plural **marrons glacés** /márron glássay, márroN-/) n. a chestnut cooked and preserved in sugar syrup, drained and then coated with a sugar glaze finish [From French, literally 'iced chestnut']

marrow /márrō/ n. 1. FOOD LARGE LONG GREEN VEGETABLE a large long cylindrical vegetable with a tough green or green and yellow rind, creamy-white flesh, and a core of seeds that is usually scraped out before it is eaten. US term **marrow squash** 2. (plural **-rows** or **-row**) PLANTS MARROW PLANT a plant in the cucumber family that produces marrows as fruit. Latin name: *Cucurbita pepo*. US term **marrow squash** 3. ANAT SOFT TISSUE IN BONES soft red or yellow fatty tissue that fills the central cavities of bones. Red marrow is the site of blood cell production. 4. ESSENCE the essence, core, or key part of sth (literary) 5. VITALITY vigour or vitality (archaic) [Old English *mærh*. Ultimately from an Indo-European word meaning 'marrow'.] ◇ **to the marrow (of your bones)** used to emphasize how intensely or deeply sb is affected by sth, especially the cold or an unpleasant experience ○ *I was chilled to the marrow.*

marrowbone /márrō bōn/ n. a hollow bone that contains edible marrow, traditionally considered to be a culinary delicacy

marrowfat /márrō fat/, **marrowfat pea** n. a particularly large type of pea, or the variety of pea plant on which it grows [Mid-18thC. From an earlier sense denoting a substance like tallow, obtained by boiling down marrow, which the pea's texture resembles.]

marrow pea n. = marrowfat

marrow squash n. US FOOD = marrow n. 1, marrow n. 2

marry[1] /márri/ (**-ries, -rying, -ried**) v. 1. vti. TAKE SB IN MARRIAGE to commit yourself to sb, or yourselves to each other, formally in marriage 2. vt. LAW, RELIG JOIN IN MARRIAGE to officiate at sb's marriage ceremony and give legal sanction or a religious blessing to the marriage 3. vt. LAW GIVE IN MARRIAGE to give sb, usually a child or ward, to sb in marriage, or bring about his or her marriage to sb 4. vt. ACQUIRE BY MARRIAGE to acquire sth, especially money, by marrying sb who has it ○ *wanted to marry wealth and power, and got both* 5. vti. COMBINE SUCCESSFULLY to combine successfully, or match things with each other that combine successfully ○ *The meat and the spices marry well.* 6. vti. = marry up 7. vt. NAUT MATCH TWO PIECES OF ROPE TOGETHER to match two pieces of rope together, especially before splicing them together [13thC. Via French *marier* from Latin *maritare*, from *maritus* 'married person, husband', literally 'sb who has a wife'.] —**marrier** n.

marry into vt. to become part of sth, or gain sth, through marriage

marry off vt. to find a husband or wife for sb, especially a child of yours, often to serve your own ends or to free yourself from responsibility for the person

marry up vti. to fit and join together, or make two things fit and join together

marry[2] /márri/ interj. used to add emphasis to a statement, or to convey surprise or indignation (archaic) [Late 16thC. Alteration of *Mary* the mother of Jesus Christ.]

marrying /márri ing/ adj. likely or inclined to get married

Mars /maarz/ n. 1. MYTHOL ROMAN GOD OF WAR in Roman mythology, the god of war and the father of Romulus, the founder of Rome. Greek equivalent **Ares** 2. ASTRON PLANET 4TH FROM THE SUN the third smallest planet in the solar system and the fourth planet from the Sun. Mars has two small satellites and its surface is a reddish-orange colour.

Marsala /maar saálə/ n. a sweet or dry dark red fortified wine from Sicily [Early 19thC. Named after the Sicilian port of *Marsala*, from which it was exported.]

Marsalis /maar saáliss/, **Wynton** (b. 1961) US musician and bandleader. His skill on the trumpet has won him renown in jazz and classical music.

Mars: View of the surface of Mars from the Sojourner rover (1997)

Wynton Marsalis

Marsden /maárzdən/, **Samuel** (1765–1838) British-born Australian clergyman and magistrate. Renowned as a harsh magistrate, he was also a leading figure in the development of agriculture in the colony of New South Wales.

Marseillaise /maár say éz, -áyz, maárssə láyz/ n. the French national anthem, written in Strasbourg in 1792 by Claude-Joseph Rouget de Lisle, a captain in the French revolutionary army. Originally called 'War Song of the Army of the Rhine', its present name derives from its popularity with army units from Marseilles, the first to sing it in Paris.

marseille /maar sáy/, **marseilles** /maar sáy, -sáylz/ n. a heavy cotton fabric with a raised pattern, used for such things as bedspreads [Mid-18thC. Named after MARSEILLES, from which it was exported.]

Marseilles /maar sáy/, **Marseille** the leading port and capital of Bouches-du-Rhône Department, Provence-Alpes-Côtes d'Azur Region, southern France. Population: 1,230,936 (1990).

marsh /maarsh/ n. an area of low-lying waterlogged land, often beside water, that is poorly drained and liable to flood, difficult to cross on foot, and unfit for agriculture or building [Old English merisc. From a prehistoric Germanic word that is also the ancestor of English mere, morass, meerschaum, and mermaid; ultimately from an Indo-European word that also produced English marine.]

Marsh /maarsh/, **Graham** (b. 1944) Australian golfer. The brother of cricketer Rodney Marsh, he was winner of the 1977 World Matchplay Championship.

Marsh, Dame Ngaio (1899–1982) New Zealand writer and theatre director. She wrote more than 30 crime novels, and played an important part in the development of live theatre in New Zealand. Full name **Dame Edith Ngaio Marsh**

Marsh, Rodney (b. 1947) Australian cricketer. He was a Test wicket-keeper and batsman. At his retirement in 1984, he was holder of a wicket-keeping world record of 355 Test dismissals.

marshal /maarsh'l/ n. **1.** MIL HIGH RANK OR HIGH-RANKING OFFICER an officer of the highest rank in some armies and air forces **2.** SB IN CHARGE OF EVENT sb in charge of or controlling an event or gathering such as a parade, ceremony, race meeting, or sports competition **3.** LAW CIRCUIT JUDGE'S ASSISTANT a trained lawyer who acts as assistant to a judge on circuit and performs secretarial and other duties **4.** HIST HIGH ROYAL COURT OFFICIAL a high official in a royal court who was formerly a military adviser and commander for the monarch. The duties of present-day mar-

shals are usually ceremonial or concerned with protocol. **5.** LAW US FEDERAL LAW ENFORCEMENT OFFICER a US federal law enforcement officer who carries out court orders in a given federal judicial district **6.** LAW CITY LAW OFFICER a municipal law enforcement officer in some US cities ○ The city marshal's office delivered the subpoenas. **7.** PUBLIC ADMIN SENIOR FIRE OR POLICE OFFICER the head of the fire or police service in some US cities ■ v. (-shals, -shalling, -shalled) **1.** vt. ARRANGE to arrange things in an appropriate order so that they can be used effectively ○ marshal your thoughts **2.** vti. MIL GATHER AND ORGANIZE TROOPS to gather troops together and organize them, or gather together and organize, before embarking on a military campaign or expedition **3.** vt. GATHER TOGETHER to gather people together and organize them into an effective body ○ marshal your supporters **4.** vt. GUIDE OR LEAD to guide or lead sb carefully or in an obsequious or ceremonious way **5.** vti. ACT AS MARSHAL to act as a marshal at sth such as a ceremony, parade, or sports event [13thC. From Old French mareschal 'royal court official'; ultimately from a prehistoric Germanic word meaning 'groom', literally 'horse-servant'.] —**marshalcy** n. —**marshaller** n. —**marshalship** n.

Marshall /maársh'l/, **George C.** (1880–1959) US military commander and politician. As secretary of state he initiated the Marshall Plan (1948) to coordinate European economic recovery after World War II. Full name **George Catlett Marshall**

Marshall, Sir John Ross (1912–88) New Zealand statesman. He was a National Party politician and prime minister of New Zealand (1972).

marshalling yard n. an area occupied by many parallel railway tracks, where railway wagons are made up into trains

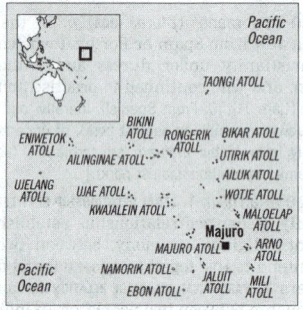

Marshall Islands

Marshall Islands republic consisting of 34 islands in the central North Pacific Ocean. Population: 60,652 (1997). Area: 181 sq. km/70 sq. mi. Official name **Republic of the Marshall Islands**

Marshall Plan /maársh'l-/ n. a programme of loans and other economic assistance provided by the US government between 1947 and 1952 to help western European nations rebuild after World War II [Mid-20thC. Named after George C. MARSHALL, who proposed it.]

Marshal of the Royal Air Force n. the highest rank in the Royal Air Force, or an officer of that rank

marsh andromeda n. a low-growing evergreen shrub, related to the rhododendron, heather, and azalea, that has pink flowers and grows in marshy areas. Latin name: Andromeda polifolia.

marsh elder n. a coarse shrubby composite plant with unisexual flowers and greenish flower heads, found growing in marshy areas of eastern and central North America, especially in salt marshes. Genus: Iva.

marsh fever n. = malaria

marsh gas n. a gas, consisting mostly of methane, formed by the decomposition of plant matter in the absence of air, e.g. in marshes. Spontaneous combustion of marsh gas is usually supposed to be the cause of the phenomenon known as a will-o'-the-wisp or ignis fatuus.

marsh harrier n. a long-winged long-tailed hawk, the largest of the harriers, found mainly in Europe and Asia, almost always in marshland and reed-beds. Latin name: Circus aeruginosus.

marsh hen n. a wading bird that inhabits marshy areas and belongs to the family of birds that includes the rail, coot, and moorhen. Family: Rallidae.

marshland /maársh land, -lənd/ n. marshy ground, or an area or expanse of it

marsh mallow n. a perennial shrubby European plant that grows in marshes and has pink flowers and sticky roots that were used in confections and medicine. Latin name: Althaea officinalis.

marshmallow /maarsh mállō/ n. a soft spongy sweet made from sugar syrup, starch, gelatine, egg whites, flavouring, and setting agents, formerly made from the root of the marsh mallow plant —**marshmallowy** adj.

marsh marigold n. a plant of the buttercup family that grows in swampy areas of Europe and North America and has round or kidney-shaped leaves and bright yellow flowers. Latin name: Caltha palustris.

marsh tit n. a small European bird belonging to the tit family that has brownish-grey wings and a black cap and is found in wooded, but not necessarily marshy, areas. Latin name: Parus palustris.

marsh treader n. a slender aquatic insect with an elongated head that crawls on floating vegetation and the surface of water, preying on mosquito larvae and tiny crustaceans. Family: Hydrometridae.

marshy /maárshi/ (-ier, -iest) adj. wet, soft, and muddy underfoot, or consisting of marshland —**marshiness** n.

Marston /maárstən/, **John** (c. 1575–1634) English playwright, and satirist. He is best known for his comedies such as The Malcontent (1604). He later became a clergyman.

marsupial /maar syoópi əl, -soó-/ n. a mammal, e.g. a kangaroo, wombat, opossum, or koala, having no placenta and bearing immature young that are developed in a pouch on the mother's abdomen. Order: Marsupialia. [Late 17thC. From modern Latin marsupialis, from marsupium (see MARSUPIUM).] —**marsupialian** /maar syoópi áyli ən, -soó-/ adj. —**marsupian** /-syoópi ən, -soó-/ adj.

marsupial frog n. any one of several species of tree frog in which the female carries the eggs in a pouch on her back

marsupium /maar syoópi əm, -soópi-/ (plural **-a** /-pi ə, -/) n. a pouch on the abdomen of most marsupials that encloses the mammary glands and in which the animal's newly born offspring complete their development [Mid-17thC. Via Latin from Greek marsupion, 'pouch', literally 'little purse', from marsippos 'purse', perhaps of Iranian origin.]

mart /maart/ n. a market, saleroom, or large shop [15thC. Via Dutch, an obsolete variant of markt, from Latin mercatus (see MARKET).]

Martaban, Gulf of /maártə baán, gulf əv/ inlet of the Andaman Sea, east of the Irrawaddy delta, southeastern Myanmar

martagon /maártəgən/, **martagon lily** n. a lily native to Europe and Asia with mottled pinkish-purple flowers. Latin name: Lilium martagon. [15thC. Via French from, ultimately, Turkish martağan, a kind of turban, which the flower is thought to resemble.]

martelé /maártə lay/, **martellato** /maártə laátō/ adv. with the strings played in a strongly accented way (used as a musical direction) [Late 19thC. From French, literally 'hammered'.]

Martello /maar téllō/ (plural **-los**), **Martello tower** n. a fort in the form of a small circular tower, especially one built on the coast for defence against invasion during the Napoleonic Wars [Early 19thC. An alteration, influenced by Italian martello 'hammer', of Cape Mortella in Corsica, where such a tower was captured with great difficulty by the British fleet in 1794.]

marten /maártin/ (plural **-tens** or **-ten**) n. a short-legged bushy-tailed mammal with a long slender body that lives in trees, is carnivorous, and is found in northern forests. It is related to the weasel. Genus: Martes. [13thC. Via Middle Dutch martren from, ultimately, Old French martre, ultimately from a prehistoric Germanic word.]

Martens /maártinz, maar ténz/, **Conrad** (1801–74) British-born Australian painter. One of the first professional artists in Australia, his works include many paintings of the New South Wales landscape.

martensite /maártin zīt/ n. the hard solid solution of iron and carbon used in making hardened steel tools [Late 19thC. Named after the German metallurgist Adolf Martens (1850–1914).]

Martha /maárthə/ n. in the Bible, the sister of Mary and Lazarus, and friend of Jesus Christ (Luke 10: 38–42)

martial /maársh'l/ adj. **1.** OF SOLDIERS AND WAR typical of or suitable for soldiers, the military life, or war **2.** WARLIKE warlike and fierce [14thC. Directly or via French from Latin martialis, from Mars, the god of war.] —**martialism** n. —**martialist** n. —**martially** adv. —**martialness** n.

martial art n. a system of combat and self-defence, e.g. judo or karate, developed especially in Japan and Korea and now usually practised as a sport

martial law n. the control and policing of a civilian population by military forces and according to military rules, imposed, e.g. in wartime or when the civilian government no longer functions

Martian /maársh'n/ adj. OF THE PLANET MARS found on, typical of, or originating from the planet Mars ■ n. INHABITANT OF MARS a supposed inhabitant of the planet Mars [14thC. Directly or via Old French martien from Latin Martianus, from Mart-, the stem of Mars 'Mars'.]

martin /maártin/ n. a bird of the swallow genus with a notched or square tail, e.g. the house martin or the purple martin [15thC. Origin uncertain: possibly referring to St Martin of Tours, perhaps because the birds migrate around the time of his feast day in mid-November.]

Martin /maártin/, **St** (316?–397?) Roman monk. The bishop of Tours, he spread Christianity throughout Gaul, establishing monasticism in the country, and became the patron saint of France.

Martin V /maártin thə fífth/, **Pope** (1368–1431). His election in 1417, at the Council of Constance, ended the Great Schism. He reunified the Western Church and the Papal States.

Martin /maártin/, **Archer** (b. 1910) British biochemist. In 1952 he shared the Nobel Prize in chemistry for his study of protein structure and later developed chromatography for protein analysis. Full name **Archer John Porter Martin**

martinet /maárti nét/ n. **1.** MILITARY DISCIPLINARIAN a military officer who demands absolute adherence to military rules and behaviour by subordinates and peers **2.** RIGID DISCIPLINARIAN sb who imposes strict discipline on others [Late 17thC. Named after Jean Martinet (died 1672), who introduced drills into the French army.] —**martinettish** adj. —**martinetism** n.

martingale /maártin gayl/, **martingal** n. **1.** EQU PART OF A HORSE'S HARNESS a strap of a horse's harness connecting the girth to the reins to keep the horse from throwing its head back **2.** **martingale**, **martingale shroud** NAUT PART OF A SAILING SHIP'S RIGGING a rope or cable that supports the forward-projecting spar (**bowsprit**) on some sailing ships **3.** GAMBLING **GAMBLING SYSTEM** gambling in which the stakes are doubled after each loss [Late 16thC. From French, of uncertain origin: perhaps from modern Provençal marte(n)gal 'inhabitant of Martiques (in Provence)' or an alteration of Spanish almártaga 'rein'.]

martini /maar téeni/ n. a cocktail made of gin or vodka with vermouth [Late 19thC. From Italian Martini, the surname of a winemaker.]

Martini tdmk. a trademark for an Italian variety of vermouth

Martinique /maárti neek/ island in the eastern Caribbean Sea, an overseas department of France. Population: 363,031 (1990). Area: 1,102 sq. km/425 sq. mi.

Martinmas /maártinməss, -mass/ n. the eleventh of November, one of the Scottish quarter days [13thC. Formed from St Martin + MASS.]

Martinů /maárti noo/, **Bohuslav Jan** (1890–1959) Czech composer. His music, ranging from operas to piano pieces, often combines a vibrant dissonance with elements of Czech folk music.

martlet /maártlət/ n. **1.** BIRDS **HOUSE MARTIN** a house martin (archaic or literary) **2.** HERALDRY **BIRD SYMBOL ON A COAT OF ARMS** on coats of arms, a footless bird used to represent a fourth son [Early 16thC. From French martlet, alteration of martinet, pet form of the male name Martin.]

martyr /maártər/ n. **1.** SB PUT TO DEATH sb who chooses to die rather than deny religious or political beliefs **2.** SB WHO MAKES SACRIFICES sb who makes sacrifices or suffers greatly in order to advance a cause or principle **3.** SB IN PAIN sb who experiences frequent or constant pain as a result of sth **4.** SB SEEKING ATTENTION sb who complains a great deal in order to get sympathy from others ■ v. (-tyrs, -tyring, -tyred) **1.** vt. KILL SB FOR HOLDING BELIEFS to kill sb for refusing to deny religious or political beliefs **2.** vr. MAKE SACRIFICES FOR STH to make sacrifices or endure hardship for sth [Pre-12thC. Via ecclesiastical Latin from Greek martur 'witness'.]

martyrdom /maártərdəm/ n. **1.** BEING A MARTYR the state of having been killed for refusing to deny religious or political beliefs **2.** DEMISE OF A MARTYR the actual death of a martyr **3.** SACRIFICES AND ENDURANCE the hardship and endurance involved in making sacrifices for a cause

marvel /maárv'l/ n. **1.** WONDERFUL THING sth that inspires awe, amazement, or admiration ○ one of the marvels of the Ancient World **2.** SB SKILFUL OR HELPFUL sb who is very good at sth, often sb who gives much-needed help ■ vt. (-vels, -velling, -velled) BE AMAZED to be very impressed, surprised, or bewildered ○ I could only marvel at her stamina. [13thC. Via French merveille from Latin mirabilis 'wonderful', from mirari 'to wonder at sth' (see MIRACLE).]

Marvell /maárvəl/, **Andrew** (1621–78) English poet and politician. A metaphysical poet, he also wrote verse satires vigorously opposing the post-Restoration government.

marvellous /maárvələss/ adj. **1.** AMAZINGLY IMPRESSIVE extraordinarily wonderful ○ a marvellous example of Baroque architecture **2.** EXTREMELY GOOD very good or pleasing ○ It was marvellous to see them all again. —**marvellously** adv. —**marvellousness** n.

marvelous adj. US = **marvellous**

marvelously adv. US = **marvellously**

Karl Marx

Marx /maarks/, **Karl** (1818–83) German philosopher. His books, especially the Communist Manifesto (1848) and Das Kapital (1867, 1885, 1894), were the basis of Communism.

Marx Brothers /maárks bruthərz/ US comedians. Chico (born Leonard, 1891–1961), Groucho (born Julius Henry, 1895–1977), and Harpo (born Adolph, 1888–1964), the three most prominent of the brothers, appeared in comedy films such as A Night at the Opera (1935) and were known for their anarchic verbal and visual humour. Groucho later hosted the television game show You Bet Your Life (1950–61). Two other brothers, Gummo (born Milton, 1893–1977) and Zeppo (born Herbert, 1901–79), appeared in some of the Marx Brothers' early work.

Marxian /maárksi ən/ adj. = **Marxist** adj.

Marxism /maárks izəm/ n. **1.** MARX'S THEORIES the political and economic theories of Karl Marx and Friedrich Engels, in which class struggle is a central element in the analysis of social change in Western societies **2.** POLITICS BASED ON MARX'S THEORIES political ideology based on the theories of Karl Marx and Friedrich Engels

Marxism-Leninism n. Marxism with the inclusion of Lenin's idea that imperialism is the final stage of capitalism, and Lenin's shifting of the focus of class struggle from industrialized to non-industrialized societies. ◊ **Leninism** —**Marxist-Leninist** n., adj.

Marxist /maárksist/ n. FOLLOWER OF MARXISM sb who supports or practises Marxism ■ adj. OF OR SUPPORTING MARXISM relating to, supporting, or implementing Marxism

Mary /máiri/, **St** Mother of Jesus Christ. Christians believe that she conceived Jesus Christ, without human contact, through the direct intervention of God. In Islam she is venerated as Maryan.

Mary, Queen of the United Kingdom (1867–1953). A great-granddaughter of George III, she was the queen consort of George V and the mother of Edward VIII and George VI. She is remembered especially for her charitable and relief work during World War II. Known as **Mary of Teck**

Mary I /máiri thə fúrst/, **Queen of England and Ireland** (1516–58). She was the daughter of Henry VIII and Catherine of Aragon. As queen (1553–58) she tried to restore Roman Catholicism in England, and to cement union with Spain by marrying Philip II (1554).

Mary II /máiri/, **Queen of England, Scotland, and Ireland** (1662–94). After the Glorious Revolution (1688) she was made coregent with her husband William III (Prince of Orange), during whose absences she governed as regent.

Mary (Queen of Scots): Anonymous 16th-century portrait

Mary (Queen of Scots) (1542–87). The daughter of James V of Scotland, she was dowager queen of France when her marriage to Lord Darnley (1565) gave her a claim to the English throne. Elizabeth I imprisoned her in England after 1568 and signed the warrant under which she was executed for treason in 1587. Born **Mary Stuart**

Maryborough /máiri bərə/ city and seaport in south-eastern Queensland, Australia, an industrial and service centre. Population: 21,286 (1996).

Mary Jane /-jáyn/ n. US marijuana (slang) [Early 20thC. Origin uncertain: possibly from Spanish Maria Juana, by folk etymology from mariguana (see MARIJUANA).]

Mary Janes /máiri jáynz/ tdmk. a trademark for shoes and boots, especially low-cut patent-leather shoes for girls with a strap fastening near the ankle at the side

Maryland /máirilənd/ state in the eastern United States, bordered by Delaware, the District of Columbia, Pennsylvania, Virginia, West Virginia, and the Atlantic Ocean. Capital: Annapolis. Population: 5,094,289 (1997). Area: 27,089 sq. km/10,455 sq. mi. —**Marylander** n.

Mary Magdalene n. in the Bible, a follower of Jesus Christ, who cured her of evil spirits (Luke 8:2)

marzipan /maárzi pan, -pán/ n. ALMOND PASTE a sweet paste made of ground almonds and sugar, often with egg whites or yolks, used as a layer in cakes or moulded into ornamental shapes ■ adj. HR OF UPPER-MIDDLE MANAGEMENT relating or belonging to the upper-middle levels of the management hierarchy in an organization, just below the top ex-

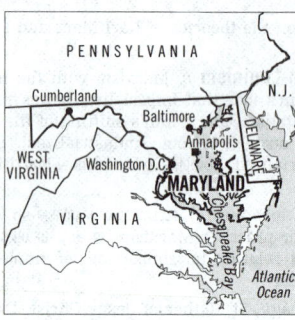

Maryland

ecutives [15thC. Via German from Italian *marzapane* 'type of box', originally for sweets or coins. Ultimately from Arabic *mawtabān*, literally 'enthroned king'.]

───── **WORD KEY: ORIGIN** ─────

Arabic *mawtabān* meant literally 'enthroned king'. It was used by the Saracens as the name of a medieval Venetian coin that had a figure of the seated Jesus Christ on it. In the Italian dialect of Venice the word became *matapan*, and eventually, in general Italian, *marzapane*; and its meaning supposedly progressed from the 'coin' via 'measure of weight or capacity', 'box of such capacity', and 'such a box containing confectionery' to 'the contents of such a box'. After English originally acquired the word (possibly via French) it became anglicized to *marchpane*, and that remained the standard form until the 19th century. Around this time ***marzipan*** was borrowed from German. This was an alteration of Italian *marzapane*, based on the misconception that it came from Latin *marci panis* 'St Mark's bread'.

Masada /mə saádə/ ancient ruined fortress in Israel, on a mountaintop 48.3 km/30 mi. southeast of Jerusalem, southwest of the Dead Sea

Masai /maá sī, maa sí, mássí/ (*plural* **-sai** *or* **-sais**), **Maasai** (*plural* **-sai** *or* **-sais**) *n.* **1.** PEOPLES **MEMBER OF AN E AFRICAN PEOPLE** a member of a people who live in East Africa, mainly in Kenya and Tanzania. Characteristically tall and slender, the Masai are a pastoral people with strong warrior traditions. **2.** LANG **LANGUAGE OF THE MASAI** the Nilotic language of the Masai, from the Nilo-Saharan family of languages. About 700,000 people speak Masai. —**Masai** *adj.*

masala /mə saálə, maa-/ *n.* **1.** FOOD **SPICY PASTE** a mixture of spices ground into a paste, used to flavour Indian dishes, or a dish flavoured with such a paste **2.** S Asia GOSSIP casual conversation (*informal*) ■ *adj.* S Asia CINEMA **DESCRIBING INDIAN FILMS** used to describe Indian popular films (*informal*) [Late 18thC. From Urdu *maṣālah*.]

Masbate /maas baáti/ island in the central Philippines, in Masbate Province. Area: 4,046 sq. km/1,562 sq. mi.

masc. *abbr.* GRAM masculine

Mascagni /mass kánnyi/, **Pietro** (1863–1945) Italian composer. His opera *Cavalleria Rusticana* (1890) is his best-known work. It exemplifies Roman verismo, a style of opera that dealt with stories of ordinary people.

mascara /ma skaárə, mə-/ *n.* EYELASH COSMETIC thick coloured paste applied to the eyelashes with a fine brush to darken them and give the appearance of greater length and thickness ■ *vt.* (**-as, -aing, -aed**) **PUT ON MASCARA** to apply mascara to eyelashes [Late 19thC. Origin uncertain: probably from Spanish or Italian *maschera* (see MASK).]

Mascarene Islands /máskə reén-/ group of islands east of Madagascar in the Indian Ocean, including Réunion, Mauritius, and Rodrigues. Population: 1,798,000 (1996).

mascarpone /maáskər póni, máskaar-/ *n.* a rich fatty unsalted Italian cream cheese with a spreadable texture [Mid-20thC. From Italian, literally 'rich whey cheese'.]

mascle /másk'l/ *n.* a design on coats of arms in the form of a lozenge with a lozenge-shaped hole in the middle [13thC. Via Anglo-Norman from, ultimately, Latin *macula* 'mesh'.]

mascon /máss kon/ *n.* an area of higher-than-normal gravity on the surface of the Moon [Mid-20thC. Contraction of *mass concentration*.]

mascot /más kot, máskət/ *n.* a person, animal, or thing that is believed to bring good luck, usually one that becomes the symbol of a particular group, especially a team [Late 19thC. Via French *mascotte* from modern Provençal *mascoto* 'little witch'.]

masculine /máskyŏolin/ *adj.* **1.** OF MEN AND BOYS relating or belonging to men and boys rather than women and girls **2.** OF TRADITIONAL MANLY CHARACTER traditionally associated with men or boys rather than women or girls **3.** GRAM OF GRAMMATICAL GENDER relating to one of the classes that words and grammatical forms are divided into in some languages **4.** MUSIC CONCLUDING ON AN ACCENTED BEAT ending on a beat that is accented ■ *n.* GRAM MASCULINE GENDER the masculine gender, or a word or form in the masculine gender [14thC. Via French from, ultimately, Latin *masculinus*, from *masculus*.] —**masculinely** *adv.* —**masculineness** *n.*

masculine cadence *n.* MUSIC a closing section of music (**cadence**) that ends on a strong beat

masculine ending *n.* **1.** POETRY STRESSED LINE-ENDING a stressed syllable that ends a line of poetry **2.** GRAM ENDING MARKING MASCULINE GENDER an ending that marks a word as belonging to the masculine gender in some languages

masculine rhyme *n.* POETRY a rhyme between two monosyllabic words, e.g. 'gab' and 'blab', or between the final stressed syllables of polysyllabic words, e.g. 'connive' and 'survive'

masculinise *vt.* = masculinize

masculinity /máskyŏo línnəti/ *n.* **1.** CONDITION OF MALE HUMAN the state of being a man or boy **2.** TRADITIONAL MANLY QUALITIES those qualities conventionally supposed to make a man a typical or excellent specimen of manhood, traditionally physical strength and courage

masculinize /máskyŏolin īz/ (**-izes, -izing, -ized**), **masculinise** (**-ises, -ising, -ised**) *vt.* **1.** MAKE STH SEEM MALE to give sth or sb features conventionally associated with maleness **2.** PRODUCE MALE CHARACTERISTICS IN FEMALE to cause a female animal or a plant to acquire male sexual characteristics, e.g. as a result of administering steroids —**masculinization** /máskyŏolin ī záysh'n/ *n.*

Masefield /máyss feeld/, **John** (1878–1967) British poet. The author of vigorous narrative verse, collected in *Salt Water Ballads* (1902) and other volumes, he was named poet laureate in 1930.

maser /máyzər/ *n.* a device used in radar and radio astronomy to boost the strength of microwaves [Mid-20thC. Acronym formed from *Microwave Amplification by Stimulated Emission of Radiation*.]

Maseru /mə sáiroo/ capital of Lesotho, situated on the River Caledon, near the border with South Africa. Population: 130,000 (1992).

mash /mash/ *n.* **1.** BEVERAGES GRAIN AND WATER MIX a fermentable mixture of hot water and grain, usually barley or wheat, from which alcohol is brewed or distilled **2.** AGRIC ANIMAL FOOD a mixture of ground feeds for livestock or poultry **3.** PULPY MASS the consistency of a soft pulp **4.** COOK MASHED POTATOES potatoes that have been reduced to a pulp or puree (*informal*) ■ *v.* (**mashes, mashing, mashed**) **1.** *vt.* MAKE PULP OF to squash sth into a pulpy mass **2.** *vt.* SOAK GRAIN to soak grain in hot water to make a mash for brewing or for feeding to animals **3.** *vt.* CRUSH STH to crush or grind sth (*informal*) **4.** *vti.* BREW TEA to soak tea leaves in hot water until the tea is ready to drink, or infuse in this way (*regional*) [Old English *masc* 'mash for brewing', ultimately from an Indo-European word that is also the ancestor of English *mix* and *promiscuous*] —**masher** *n.*

MASH /mash/, **M.A.S.H.** *abbr.* mobile army surgical hospital

───── **WORD KEY: CULTURAL NOTE** ─────

*M*A*S*H*, a film by US director Robert Altman (1970). Set in a Mobile Army Surgical Hospital during the Korean War, this dark satire focuses on a group of eccentric medics who combat the horrors of war with cynicism, ribald humour, and practical jokes. The film

gave rise to a long-running television series that made household names of characters such as Hawkeye Pierce, Hot Lips Houlihan, and Major Frank Burns.

mashgiah /mash geé akh/ (*plural* **-him** /-khim/), **mashgiach** (*plural* **-chim**) *n.* an Orthodox rabbi, or a man appointed or approved by such a rabbi, who inspects slaughterhouses, meat markets, and restaurants to check that kosher food has been properly prepared and served [Mid-20thC. From Hebrew *maṣgīaḥ* 'supervisor'.]

mashie /máshi/ *n.* an obsolete golf club similar to the modern five-iron [Late 19thC. Origin uncertain: perhaps via French *massue* 'club' from, ultimately, late Latin *mattea* 'mace'.]

mashie niblick *n.* an obsolete golf club similar to the modern six-iron

Mashona /mə shónə/ *n., adj.* = Shona

mask /maask/ *n.* **1.** COVERING FOR THE FACE a covering for the eyes, mouth, or whole face **2.** CONCEALING THING sth that conceals or disguises sth else, e.g. true motives or feelings **3.** FACE-LIKE ORNAMENT a representation of a face used as an ornament or decoration **4.** ZOOL ANIMAL'S FACE MARKINGS the face or facial markings of some animals, e.g. foxes and racoons **5.** MIL CONCEALMENT FOR TROOPS a natural or artificial feature that hides military troops and installations from an enemy **6.** ELECTRON ENG TEMPLATE FOR ELECTRONIC CHIPS a template used to control the pattern of conducting material deposited or etched onto a semiconductor chip **7.** COSMETICS BEAUTY TREATMENT a facial preparation used to tighten the skin and remove impurities, applied to the skin as a paste and allowed to dry before being removed **8.** PHOTOGRAPHY PHOTOGRAPHIC GUARD a guard, often a sheet of paper, placed over areas of unexposed photographic film to stop light hitting it ■ *vt.* (**masks, masking, masked**) **1.** HIDE STH to conceal or disguise sth, e.g. an unpleasant smell or a true intention **2.** PHOTOGRAPHY SHIELD PART OF STH to cover part of a surface using masking tape before painting or spraying **3.** PHOTOGRAPHY SHIELD PHOTOGRAPHIC FILM FROM LIGHT to prevent stray or unwanted light from reaching areas of unexposed photographic film, either using hands or a special shield **4.** CHEM STOP CHEMICAL REACTING to prevent a chemical substance from reacting by the addition of another chemical [Early 16thC. Via French *masque* from late Latin *masca* 'ghost, mask', of uncertain origin: perhaps from Arabic *maskara* 'buffoon'.] —**maskable** *adj.*

masked /maaskt/ *adj.* **1.** WEARING A MASK with the face covered in order to prevent recognition **2.** MED NOT DETECTABLE used to describe diseases and symptoms that are present but not yet perceptible **3.** BOT = personate **4.** ZOOL WITH MARKINGS LIKE A MASK with markings on the head or around the eyes that resemble a mask

masked ball *n.* a ball at which people wear masks

masked hunter *n.* a central European insect, belonging to the assassin bug family, introduced to the southern United States, that usually preys on household insects, but occasionally bites humans. Latin name: *Reduvius personatus*.

masker /maáskər/ *n.* sb who wears a mask at a masked ball

masking /maásking/ *n.* **1.** PHYSIOL COVERING ONE SENSE WITH ANOTHER the hiding or screening of one sensory process, e.g. hearing, by another, e.g. sight **2.** THEATRE SCENERY HIDING STAGE scenery that is used to hide a part of the stage from the audience

masking tape *n.* easy-to-remove adhesive tape used to cover parts of a surface that are not meant to be painted

masochism /mássəkizəm/ *n.* **1.** SEXUAL PLEASURE DERIVED FROM HUMILIATION sexual gratification achieved by humiliation and the acceptance of physical and verbal abuse **2.** NEED FOR PAIN the psychological disorder in which sb needs to be emotionally or physically abused in order to be sexually satisfied **3.** SEARCH FOR ABUSIVE SEXUAL PARTNERS the active seeking out of sexual partners who will dominate, humiliate, and physically and verbally abuse **4.** ENJOYMENT OF HARDSHIP the tendency to invite and enjoy misery of any kind, especially in order to be pitied by others or perhaps admired for forbearance [Late 19thC. Named after the

Austrian novelist Leopold von Sacher-Masoch (1836–95), who described such sexual practices.] —**masochist** n.

masochistic /mássə kístik/ adj. **1.** OF OR FEELING MASOCHISM relating to or experiencing the desire to be humiliated and abused by others in order to feel sexually fulfilled **2.** LIKING AND INVITING MISERY tending to invite and enjoy misery —**masochistically** adv.

mason /máyss'n/ n. SB WORKING WITH STONE sb who makes things out of stone, e.g. buildings or statues, or who prepares stone for builders to use ■ vt. (-sons, -soning, -soned) BUILD USING STONE to build or strengthen sth using stone [12thC. From Old Norman French machun or Old French masson, of uncertain origin: probably from a prehistoric Germanic word that is also the ancestor of English make.]

Mason /máyss'n/ n. = **Freemason**

Mason /máyss'n/, **Bruce** (1921–84) New Zealand playwright. He wrote the one-man show *The End of the Golden Weather* (1963).

mason bee n. any solitary bee that builds nests of sand or clay held together with saliva

Mason-Dixon Line /máyss'n díks'n-/ n. the boundary that separated Pennsylvania from Maryland and Virginia, regarded as the dividing line between free and slave states before the American Civil War [Named after the 18thC surveyors Charles *Mason* and Jeremiah *Dixon*]

masonic /mə sónnik/ adj. relating to stonemasons or their work —**masonically** adv.

Masonic /mə sónik/ adj. relating to Freemasons or Freemasonry

Masonite /máyssə nīt/ tdmk. a trademark for hardboard products used as insulation, panelling, and partitions in buildings

masonry /máyss'nri/ n. **1.** MASON'S TRADE the trade of a mason **2.** STONEWORK the stone or brick parts of a building or other structure

Masonry /máyss'nri/ n. Freemasonry

mason wasp n. a solitary wasp that builds mud nests or digs out nests in old mortar. Genus: *Odynerus*.

Masorete /mássə reet/, **Masorite** /-rīt/ n. one of the scholars who produced the traditional text of the Hebrew Bible (**Masoretic text**) [Late 16thC. Via French or modern Latin *Massoreta* from a misuse of Hebrew *māsōreṭ*).]

Masoretic /mássə réttik/ adj. used to describe or relating to the traditional text of the Hebrew Bible

Masoretic text n. the traditional text of the Hebrew Bible, revised and annotated by Jewish scholars between the 6th and 10th centuries AD

Masorite n. = **Masorete**

masque /maask/ n. **1.** PERFORMANCE a dramatic entertainment similar to opera, popular in England in the 16th and 17th centuries, in which masked performers represented mythological or allegorical characters **2.** TEXT OF MASQUE the music and words written for a masque **3.** = **masquerade** n. 1 [Early 16thC. From French (see MASK).]

masquer /maaskər/ n. = **masker**

masquerade /maaskə ráyd/ n. **1.** PARTY WITH MASKS a party at which masks and costumes are worn, whether an informal gathering of friends or a formal ball **2.** DISGUISING COSTUME a costume worn to a masquerade **3.** DISGUISING PRETENCE a pretence or disguise ■ vi. (-ades, -ading, -aded) **1.** PRETEND to be sb or sth else **2.** WEAR A COSTUME to wear a particular costume to a party [Late 16thC. Via French *mascarade* from Italian *mascherata*, from *maschera* MASK.] —**masquerader** n.

mass /mass/ n. **1.** LUMP a body of matter that forms a whole but has no definable shape **2.** COLLECTION a collection of many individual parts ○ *The garden is a mass of weeds.* **3.** GREAT UNSPECIFIED QUANTITY a large but unspecified number or quantity ○ *I have masses of work to do.* **4.** MAJOR PART the greater part or majority ○ *The mass of respondents oppose the legislation.* **5.** PHYS PHYSICAL QUANTITY the property of an object that is a measure of its inertia, the amount of matter it contains, and its influence in a gravitational field. Symbol *m* **6.** PAINTING AREA OF PAINTING a large area of a painting where the light, shade, or

colour is uniform **7.** PHARM MIXTURE CONTAINING DRUGS a thick paste containing drugs that is made into pills **8.** MINING DEPOSIT OF ORE an irregular deposit of ore that does not occur in veins ■ vti. (**masses, massing, massed**) COLLECT to gather or be gathered in a mass ○ *Troops are massing on the border.* ■ adj. **1.** OF A LARGE NUMBER made up of or containing a large number ○ *a mass demonstration* **2.** GENERAL broadly general, in scope or effect ○ *The mass effect is rather disappointing.* [14thC. Via French *masse* and Latin *massa* from Greek *maza* 'barley cake'.] ◇ **in the mass** considered as a whole, not as separate entities

mass in vt. to fill in areas of colour or shade in a drawing or painting

Mass, mass n. **1.** CHRISTIAN CEREMONY in the Roman Catholic Church and some Protestant churches, the religious ceremony of the Communion **2.** MUSICAL SETTING OF MASS a part of the text of a Roman Catholic Mass set to music, to be sung by a choir [Pre-12thC. Via ecclesiastical Latin *missa* from, ultimately, Latin *mittere* 'send away'.]

Mass. abbr. Massachusetts

Massachuset /mássə chóosit/ (plural **-set** or **-sets**), **Massachusett** (plural **-sett** or **-setts**) n. **1.** PEOPLES MEMBER OF NATIVE N AMERICAN PEOPLE a member of a Native North American people who used to live in the Massachusetts Bay area **2.** LANG EXTINCT N AMERICAN LANGUAGE an extinct Native North American language formerly spoken in an area around Massachusetts Bay and belonging to the Algonquian branch of Algonquian-Wakashan languages. It died out in the 17th century when disease wiped out the entire population of its speakers. —**Massachuset** adj.

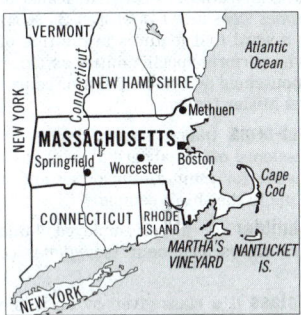

Massachusetts

Massachusetts /mássə chóossəts/ state in the northeastern United States, bordered by Connecticut, New Hampshire, New York, Rhode Island, Vermont, and the Atlantic Ocean. Capital: Boston. Population: 6,117,520 (1997). Area: 21,399 sq. km/8,262 sq. mi. Official name **Commonwealth of Massachusetts**

massacre /mássəkər/ n. **1.** KILLING OF MANY PEOPLE the vicious killing of large numbers of people or animals **2.** BAD DEFEAT a contest in which one side is badly beaten (informal) ■ vt. (-cres, -cring, -cred) **1.** KILL IN LARGE NUMBERS to kill large numbers of people or animals **2.** DEFEAT SB COMPLETELY to defeat sb completely, especially in a sporting contest (informal) [Late 16thC. From French, 'butchery', of unknown origin.] —**massacrer** n.

massage /mássaazh, -aaj/ n. RUBBING OF THE BODY a treatment that involves rubbing or kneading the muscles, either for medical or therapeutic purposes or simply as an aid to relaxation ■ vt. (-sages, -saging, -saged) **1.** RUB SB'S MUSCLES to rub or knead sb's muscles **2.** MANIPULATE DECEPTIVELY to manipulate statistics or other information in order to create a more suitable or falsely impressive result ○ *They massaged the figures.* **3.** ENHANCE to give sth a boost with kind or uplifting treatment, especially sb's ego with flattery [Late 19thC. From French, from *masser* 'to massage', of uncertain origin: perhaps from Arabic *masaha* 'to stroke' or Portuguese *amassar* 'to knead'.] —**massager** n.

massage parlour n. **1.** PLACE FOR MASSAGE a place that provides massages to paying customers **2.** BROTHEL a place that offers sex services for money, including sexual massages

massasauga /mássə sáwgə/ n. a small North American rattlesnake that has variable colouring. Latin

name: *Sistrurus catenatus*. [Mid-19thC. Alteration of *Mississagi*, a river in southeastern Ontario, Canada.]

mass balance n. a mathematical equation, table, or quantitative chart showing the mass inputs and outputs of a process, plant, or machine, the principle being that what goes in must come out

mass communication, mass communications n. communication by means of broadcasting and newspapers, that reaches all or most people in society

masscult /máss kult/ n. culture as it is presented and interpreted by the mass media (informal) [Shortening of *mass culture*]

mass defect n. the difference between the mass of an isotope and the element's mass number

massé /mássi/ n. a shot in cue games in which the cue is held almost vertically to strike the cue ball off-centre, making it curve round one ball to hit another [Late 19thC. From French, from *masse* (see MACE[1]).]

Masséna /máss ay naa/, **André, Prince of Essling and Duke of Rivoli** (1758–1817) French soldier. He was a marshal of the Napoleonic empire, noted for his military victories, but switched loyalty to the Bourbons after the Restoration.

mass-energy equivalence n. the principle in the theory of relativity that mass and energy are equivalent and interchangeable according to the equation $E = mc^2$

Massenet /mássə nay/, **Jules Emile Frédéric** (1842–1912) French composer. Famous for his opera *Manon* (1884), he also wrote oratorios, cantatas, and orchestral pieces.

masses /mássiz, mássəz/ npl. **1.** ORDINARY PEOPLE ordinary people in society, as distinct from political leaders, aristocracy, or educated people **2.** LOTS large amounts or large numbers (informal)

masseter /ma séetər/ n. a muscle in the cheek that moves the jaws during chewing [Late 16thC. From Greek *masētēr*, from *masasthai* 'to chew'.] —**masseteric** /mássi térrik/ adj.

masseur /ma súr/ n. a man who gives massages professionally [Late 19thC. From French, from *masser* (see MASSAGE).]

masseuse /ma sőz/ n. a woman who gives massages professionally [Late 19thC. From French, feminine of *masseur* (see MASSAGE).]

Massey /mássi/, **William Ferguson** (1856–1925) Irish-born New Zealand statesman. He was a Reform Party politician and prime minister of New Zealand (1912–25).

massicot /mássi kot/ n. a yellow mineral consisting of lead oxide, or a powdered form of it used as a pigment [15thC. From French, of uncertain origin: probably from Italian *marzacotto* 'potter's glaze', perhaps ultimately of Arabic or Greek origin.]

massif /másseef/ n. **1.** MOUNTAINS a large mountain mass, or a group of connected mountains that form a mountain range **2.** EARTH'S CRUST a part of the Earth's crust that is surrounded by faults and may be shifted or displaced by tectonic movements [Early 16thC. From French (see MASSIVE).]

Massif Central /mássif sen traál/ highland region in south-central France

massive /mássiv/ adj. **1.** BULKY large, solid, and heavy **2.** LARGE-SCALE extremely large in amount, degree, or scope **3.** UNUSUALLY LARGE large in comparison to what is typical or usual ○ *gained a massive amount of weight* **4.** MINERALS DEVOID OF VISIBLE CRYSTALS with no visible crystalline structure **5.** GEOL HOMOGENOUS used to describe rock that is of the same composition throughout, as distinct from being layered [15thC. Via French *massif* and Old French *massiz* from, ultimately, Latin *massa* (see MASS).] —**massiveness** n.

massively /mássivli/ adv. to a very great extent or by a very large amount (informal)

mass leisure n. the everyday leisure pursuits of the majority of a population, an aspect of popular culture. It is shaped by and shapes the values, behaviours, and economics of societies and cultures.

massless /mássləss/ adj. with a mass of zero

mass-market adj. designed for sale to as wide a range of people as possible, rather than to a particular group in society

mass media n. all of the communications media that reach a large audience, especially television, radio, and newspapers (takes a singular or plural verb)

mass noun n. a noun representing sth that cannot be counted, e.g. 'water', or sth that can only be counted if the meaning is a single type or serving, e.g. 'coffee'

mass number n. CHEM the number of protons and neutrons in the nucleus of an atom of a particular substance. Symbol A

mass observation n. a method of observing how people act in social contexts by collating the subjects' own reports, diaries, and responses to questionnaires

mass-produce vt. to manufacture a product in very large quantities in factories, especially using mechanization and assembly-line methods —**mass producer** n.

mass production n. the manufacturing of products on a large scale in factories, especially using mechanization and assembly-line methods

mass society n. a society in which the national or global nature of the influences on life, e.g. mass production and the mass media, has stripped the population of its diversity

mass spectrograph n. CHEM an instrument that separates atoms and molecules according to their mass and that records the resulting mass spectrum

mass spectrum n. CHEM a record of the chemical constituents of a substance separated according to their mass and presented as a spectrum

mast[1] /maast/ n. **1.** NAUT VERTICAL SUPPORT a vertical spar that supports sails, rigging, or flags on a ship **2.** UPRIGHT POLE a vertical pole **3.** BROADCAST BROADCAST TOWER a tall broadcasting aerial **4.** NAVY = captain's mast ■ vti. (**masts, masting, masted**) NAVY SUBJECT TO CAPTAIN'S MAST to subject sb charged with a usually shipboard or on-base crime or infringement to a disciplinary hearing (**captain's mast**), or undergo such a hearing [Old English mæst, ultimately via Indo-European] ◇ **at half mast 1.** partway down a flagpole, usually as a sign of respect following a death ○ flags flying at half mast **2.** partway up or down from the usual position at which sth is worn (informal humorous) ○ trousers at half mast ◇ **before the mast** serving as an ordinary sailor or apprentice seaman

mast[2] /maast/ n. AGRIC the nuts of certain trees, such as beech, oak, and chestnut, especially when used as food for pigs [Old English mæst 'fodder'. Ultimately from a prehistoric Germanic word meaning 'meat'.]

mast- prefix. breast, nipple, mammary gland ○ mastitis [From Greek mastos, of unknown origin]

mastaba /mástəbə/, **mastabah** n. an ancient Egyptian mudbrick tomb built with a flat base, sloping sides, and a flat roof. Its design inspired the pyramids. [Early 17thC. From Arabic maṣṭaba.]

mastalgia /ma stáljə/ n. pain in the breast

mast cell n. a large cell in connective tissue consisting of granules that release histamine and heparin during allergic reactions [From German Mast 'fattening, feeding']

mastectomy /ma stéktəmi/ (plural -mies) n. the surgical removal of one or both breasts, usually as a treatment for breast cancer [Early 20thC. Coined from Greek mastos 'breast' + -ECTOMY.]

master /máastər/ n. **1.** BOSS a man in a position of authority, e.g. over a business, servants, or an animal **2.** SB HIGHLY SKILLED sb who has great skill in a particular area **3.** SB IN CONTROL sb or sth controlling or influencing events or other things (sometimes considered offensive) **4.** ABSTRACT CONTROL an abstract idea or force that is thought of as having control or influence (sometimes considered offensive) **5.** INDUST SKILLED WORKER sb who is highly skilled in a trade or craft and is qualified to teach apprentices (usually used in combination) **6.** ORIGINAL COPY an original copy of sth such as a recording tape or a stencil, from which other copies can be made **7.** GAME PLAYER AT HIGH LEVEL sb who has reached a level of excellence in some games, especially chess or bridge, reckoned by number of games or points won in major tournaments. ♦ **International Master 8.** EDUC MAN TEACHER a man teacher (dated) **9.** LEADER sb whose philosophy or religious belief has attracted followers (sometimes considered offensive) **10.** NAUT SHIP'S OFFICER the captain of a merchant ship **11.** LAW LAW COURT OFFICER a man who serves as officer in the Supreme Court of Judicature, subordinate to a judge **12.** VICTOR sb who defeats another (literary) **13.** COMPUT, MECH ENG CONTROLLING MACHINE a device or computer that controls the operation of one or more other connected devices or computers (sometimes considered offensive) ■ adj. (sometimes considered offensive) **1.** MAIN devised to operate on the broadest level ○ a master plan for flood evacuations **2.** CONTROLLING controlling the operation of everything or of all others **3.** PRINCIPAL biggest or primary among several ○ redecorated the master bedroom ■ vt. (**-ters, -tering, -tered**) **1.** LEARN STH to become highly skilled in sth, or acquire a complete understanding of it **2.** CONTROL STH to learn to control feelings or behaviour (sometimes considered offensive) **3.** CONTROL SB to break the will of a person or animal (sometimes considered offensive) **4.** RECORDING MAKE MASTER RECORDING to produce a master recording [Pre-12thC. Via Old English mægister and Old French maistre from Latin magister 'chief' (source of English magistrate), from magis 'more'.] —**masterless** adj.

Master n. **1.** PREFIX TO BOY'S NAME a title sometimes prefixed to a boy's surname in formal circumstances **2.** RELIG RELIGIOUS TEACHER a title used to address a man who is a religious leader or teacher (sometimes considered offensive) **3.** SB APPOINTED BY ROYALTY a word that features in the title of various men who perform specific duties as officers in the royal household or who hold senior court positions **4.** MISTER Mister (archaic)

master-at-arms n. (plural **masters-at-arms**) a noncommissioned officer aboard a naval vessel who is responsible for maintaining order and enforcing discipline in the ship's company

master-builder n. a self-employed builder who employs others as labour (sometimes considered offensive)

master class n. a class given by an acknowledged expert in a particular field (sometimes considered offensive)

master corporal n. a noncommissioned officer in the Canadian armed forces, senior to a corporal and junior to a sergeant

masterful /máastərf'l/ adj. **1.** EXPERT demonstrating exceptional skill or ability in a specific area (sometimes considered offensive) **2.** SHOWING LEADERSHIP showing the ability or tendency to lead others —**masterfully** adv. —**masterfulness** n.

master key n. a key that will open all the locks in a particular set or place

masterly /máastərli/ adj. demonstrating outstanding skill —**masterliness** n.

master mariner n. = master

mastermind /máastər mīnd/ n. CHIEF PLANNER sb who plans, organizes, and oversees a complex operation ■ vt. (**-minds, -minding, -minded**) OVERSEE OPERATION to plan, organize, and oversee a complex operation

Master of Arts n. a degree in a nonscience subject, usually awarded after one or two years of postgraduate study, but sometimes awarded as a first degree in place of a bachelor's degree

Master of ceremonies n. sb who performs the duties of a host at a formal event, making the opening speech and introducing other speakers or performers (sometimes considered offensive)

Master of Science n. a degree in a science subject, usually awarded after one or two years of postgraduate study, but sometimes awarded as a first degree in place of a bachelor's degree

Master of the Rolls n. the senior judge in England, who sits in the Court of Appeal and also has the official title of Keeper of the Records at the Public Record Office

masterpiece /máastər peess/ n. **1.** GREAT ARTISTIC WORK an exceptionally good piece of creative work, e.g. a book, film, or performance **2.** ARTIST'S BEST WORK the best piece of work by a particular artist or craftsperson [Early 17thC. Formed on the model of Dutch meesterstuk or German Meisterstück.]

master race n. a group of people who consider themselves a race superior to all others, especially the Aryans in the ideology of Nazi Germany (offensive in some contexts)

Master's degree n. a university degree with the title Master, usually awarded after one or two years of postgraduate study

mastersinger /máastər singər/ n. = Meistersinger [Early 19thC. An Anglicization of MEISTERSINGER.]

masterstroke /máastər strōk/ n. a brilliant idea or very clever tactic

Masterton /máastərtən/ town in the south of the North Island, New Zealand. Population: 19,954 (1996).

masterwork /máastər wurk/ n. = masterpiece n. 1, masterpiece n. 2

mastery /máastəri/ n. **1.** EXPERT SKILL expert knowledge or outstanding ability **2.** COMPLETE CONTROL total control over sb or sth (sometimes considered offensive)

masthead /máast hed/ n. **1.** SAILING MAST'S TOP the top of a mast **2.** PRESS NEWSPAPER'S TITLE AS DISPLAYED the name of a newspaper or magazine as it appears in large letters on the front cover **3.** PRESS NEWSPAPER INFORMATION the list that provides information about staff, owners, and circulation in a newspaper or magazine, usually printed on the first page

mastic /mástik/ n. **1.** RESIN an aromatic resin produced by a Mediterranean tree, used to make lacquer, varnish, adhesives, and condiments **2.** INDUST CEMENT a flexible cement used as a filler, adhesive, or sealant in woodwork, plaster, or brickwork **3.** BEVERAGES LIQUOR a liquor in which mastic gum is used as a flavouring **4.** TREES = mastic tree n. [14thC. Via French from, ultimately, Greek mastikhan 'to grind the teeth'. So called because the resin of the mastic tree can be chewed.]

masticate /másti kayt/ (**-cates, -cating, -cated**) v. **1.** vti. CHEW FOOD to grind and pulverize food inside the mouth, using the teeth and jaws **2.** vt. GRIND TO A PULP to grind or crush sth until it turns to pulp [Mid-17thC. Via the past participle stem of Latin masticare from Greek mastikhan 'to grind the teeth'.] —**masticable** adj. —**mastication** /másti káysh'n/ n. —**masticator** /másti kaytər/ n.

masticatory /mástikətəri/ adj. OF CHEWING relating to chewing ■ n. (plural **-ries**) MED MEDICINE a medicine made to be chewed in order to increase the production of saliva

mastic tree n. a small Mediterranean evergreen shrub belonging to the cashew family, grown for its resin. Latin name: Pistachia lentiscus.

Mastiff

mastiff /mástif/ n. a breed of large powerful smooth-haired dog, often fawn or greyish with a dark face [14thC. Via Old French mastin from, ultimately, Latin mansuetus literally 'used to the hand', from manus 'hand'.]

mastiff bat n. a snub-nosed bat found in most of the warm regions of the world. It has narrow wings and brown, grey, or black fur. Family: Molossidae.

mastigure /másti gyoor/ *n.* a lizard of northern Africa and the Middle East that blocks its burrow with its very spiny tail. Genus: *Uromastix.* [Mid-19thC. Coined via modern Latin from Greek *mastix* 'whip' + *oura* 'tail'.]

mastitis /ma stítiss/ *n.* inflammation of a woman's breast or an animal's udder, usually as a result of bacterial infection [Mid-19thC. Coined from MASTO- + -ITIS.] —**mastitic** /ma stíttik/ *adj.*

mastodon /mástə don, -dən/ *n.* a large extinct mammal that resembled an elephant, with shaggy hair and two sets of tusks. Genus: *Mastodon.* [Early 19thC. Coined from MASTO- + Greek *odōn* 'tooth'. So called because it had nipple-shaped tubercles on its molars.] —**mastodonic** /mástə dónnik/ *adj.* —**mastodontic** /-dóntik/ *adj.*

mastoid /máss toyd/ *adj.* **1. NIPPLE-SHAPED** shaped like a nipple or breast **2. OF MASTOID PROCESS** relating to the mastoid process ■ *n.* ANAT = **mastoid process** [Mid-18thC. Via French *mastoïde* or modern Latin *mastoides* from Greek *mastoeidēs*, from *mastos* 'breast'.]

mastoid bone *n.* = **mastoid process**

mastoid cell *n.* an air-filled space in the mastoid process

mastoidectomy /máss toyd éktəmi/ (*plural* **-mies**) *n.* a surgical operation to remove part of an infected mastoid process to allow pus to drain off and prevent infection from spreading to the meninges

mastoiditis /máss toyd ítiss/ *n.* inflammation of the mastoid process and mastoid cells

mastoid process *n.* a bony protuberance on the skull, found behind the ear in many vertebrates, including humans

Mastroianni /mást roy yánni/, **Marcello** (1924–96) Italian film actor. Specializing in romantic or bitter-sweet comedy, he worked with many of the great Italian directors, including Federico Fellini in *La Dolce Vita* (1960).

masturbate /mástər bayt/ (**-bates, -bating, -bated**) *vti.* to give oneself or sb else sexual pleasure by stroking the genitals, usually to orgasm [Mid-19thC. From the past participle of *masturbari*, of uncertain origin: perhaps from *manu stuprare* 'to defile with the hand'.] —**masturbator** *n.*

masturbation /mástər báysh'n/ *n.* the stroking of genitals for sexual pleasure, usually to orgasm

masturbatory /mástər baytəri/ *adj.* relating to or for the purpose of masturbation

masurium /mə sóori əm/ *n.* the metallic element technetium (*dated*) [Early 20thC. From German, named after *Masuria*, a region of northeastern Poland.]

mat[1] /mat/ *n.* **1. PIECE OF CARPET** flat material placed on a floor for decoration or protection or for wiping the feet **2.** SPORTS, LEISURE **PIECE OF PADDED MATERIAL** a piece of padded material placed on the floor for use in some sports and activities, e.g. to absorb the impact of falling in judo **3.** HOUSEHOLD **PROTECTIVE COVER** a piece of fabric or board that protects tables and other surfaces from damage by heat or scratching, e.g. placed under hot dinner plates or ornaments **4. THICK MASS** any thick or interwoven mass, e.g. a tangle of hair ■ *vti.* (**mats, matting, matted**) **FORM TANGLED MASS** to make sth into or become a thick tangled mass [Pre-12thC. From Latin *matta*, of uncertain origin: probably from a Phoenician word.]

mat[2] *n., adj.* = **matt**

mat., **mat** *abbr.* matinée

Matabeleland /máttə béeli land/ region in southern Zimbabwe

Matadi /mə taádi/ capital of Bas-Congo Region, western Democratic Republic of the Congo. Population: 172,730 (1994).

matador /máttə dawr/ *n.* **1. BULLFIGHTER** the main bullfighter, whose job is to kill the bull **2.** CARDS **HIGH CARD** one of the highest playing cards in some games such as skat **3.** GAME **DOMINO GAME** a variety of the game of dominoes in which the dots on adjacent halves must total seven [Late 17thC. From Spanish, from *matar* 'to kill', of uncertain origin: perhaps from late Latin *mattare* 'to beat senseless' or Persian *māt* 'dead'.]

matagouri /máttə góori/ (*plural* **-ris**) *n.* a thorny bush that forms thickets in open areas of New Zealand. Latin name: *Discaria toumatou.* [Mid-19thC. Alteration of Maori *tumatakuru*.]

Mata Hari /maátə haári/ *n.* a valuable food fish in the tropical Pacific and Indian oceans that looks like a snapper with a scaleless head. Latin name: *Lethrinus nebulosis.* [From MATA HARI, formed from Malay *mata* 'eye' + *hari* 'day']

Mata Hari /maátə haári/ (1876–1917) Dutch dancer and spy. Through her liaisons with high-ranking officers, she gathered intelligence for the Germans during World War I. She was executed by the French. Real name **Margaretha Geertruida Zelle**

matai /maá tī/ (*plural* **-ais**) *n.* a cone-bearing evergreen tree found in New Zealand with bluish bark and small narrow leaves that grow in two rows. Its wood is often used for flooring. Latin name: *Podocarpus spicatus.* [Mid-19thC. From Maori.]

Matamoros /máttə máwrəss/ city and port in northeastern Mexico, near the mouth of the Rio Grande and across the river from Brownsville, Texas. Population: 266,065 (1990).

Mataura /mə tówrə/ river in the southern part of the South Island, New Zealand, that rises in the Eyre Mountains south of Lake Wakatipu and flows into the Foveaux Strait east of Bluff. Length: 240 km/149 mi.

match[1] /mach/ *n.* **1. CONTEST** a contest between opponents, especially a sporting contest **2. STH SIMILAR** sb who or sth that resembles another in certain qualities **3. AN EQUAL** sb or sth capable of competing equally with another **4. GOOD COMBINER** sth that combines well with sth else **5. MARITAL PARTNERSHIP** a partnership in wedlock **6. POTENTIAL PARTNER** sb who is thought to be a suitable marriage or romantic partner **7. COUNTERPART** sb who or sth that is identical to another or is one half of a pair ■ *v.* (**matches, matching, matched**) **1.** *vt.* **BE ALIKE** to be similar or identical to sb or sth **2.** *vt.* **COMPETE EQUALLY** to be as good, or sometimes as bad, as sb or sth else **3.** *vti.* **COMBINE WELL** to make a suitable or pleasing combination, or put things together to make such a combination **4.** *vt.* **FIND STH THAT COMBINES** to find sth that makes a suitable accompaniment **5.** *vti.* **JOIN CLEANLY** to fit or join sth smoothly **6.** *vt.* **PLACE IN OPPOSITION** to provide sb or sth with an opponent **7.** *vti. US* **TOSS COINS** to toss coins to see which sides land face up in order to determine a choice or decision **8.** *vt.* **MARRY SB** to give or join sb in marriage (*archaic*) [Old English *gemæcca* 'spouse, lover'. Ultimately from a prehistoric Germanic word that is also the ancestor of English *make*.] —**matchability** /máchə bíllәti/ *n.* —**matchable** /máchəb'l/ *adj.* —**matcher** *n.*

match[2] /mach/ *n.* **1. STICK PRODUCING FIRE** a thin stick of wood whose tip is coated with a combustible material that ignites when scraped against a rough surface, used to light a fire, candle, or gas appliance **2.** ARMS **EXPLOSIVES FUSE** a slow-burning fuse used in cannons and explosives [14thC. Via Old French *meiche* from, ultimately, Greek *muxa* 'lampwick' (original sense in English).]

matchboard /mách bawrd/ *n.* a board that has a tongue along one edge and a groove along the other so that it can be fitted together with other boards

matchbook /mách book/ *n.* a small cardboard folder with safety matches inside and a striking surface usually on the outside

matchbox /mách boks/ *n.* a small cardboard box for matches, with a striking surface along one or both sides

matchless /máchləss/ *adj.* so outstandingly great as to have no rival —**matchlessly** *adv.* —**matchlessness** *n.*

matchlock /mách lok/ *n.* **1. TRIGGER** an old trigger mechanism in guns that ignited the powder with a slow-burning fuse **2. GUN** a gun fitted with a matchlock

matchmaker /mách maykər/ *n.* sb who tries to arrange romantic partnerships or marriages, either professionally or informally

match play *n.* a method of golf scoring in which the number of holes won is counted rather than the number of strokes taken —**match player** *n.*

match point *n.* **1.** SPORTS **FINAL POINT** the final point needed to win a match, especially in tennis and other racket games **2.** BRIDGE **SCORING UNIT** a unit used for scoring in bridge tournaments

matchstick /mách stik/ *n.* **STEM OF MATCH** the wooden part of a match ■ *adj.* **1. MADE FROM MATCHES** built of matchsticks **2. LIKE STICKS IN THINNESS** in the form of thin strips or simple lines

mate[1] /mayt/ *n.* **1. FRIEND** a friend, also used as a friendly, or sometimes hostile, form of address to a man **2. BREEDING PARTNER** either of a pair of animals that breed together **3. PARTNER IN SEX OR WEDLOCK** a sexual or marriage partner (*informal or humorous*) **4. SKILLED WORKER'S HELPER** an assistant to a skilled worker ○ *a plumber's mate* **5.** SHIPPING **DECK OFFICER** a deck officer ranking below the master on a merchant ship, or the rank the officer holds **6.** *US* NAVY **PETTY OFFICER** a petty officer in the US Navy who is assistant to a warrant officer, or the rank the officer holds **7. STH THAT MATCHES** one of a pair of things that belong together ■ *v.* (**mates, mating, mated**) **1.** *vti.* **BREED** to come together or be brought together to breed **2.** *vi.* **HAVE SEX** to engage in sex **3.** *vt.* **CONNECT TWO OBJECTS** to combine or connect two things **4.** *vti.* **MARRY** to join or become joined in marriage (*informal or humorous*) [14thC. From Middle Low German *gemate*. Ultimately from a prehistoric Germanic word that is also the ancestor of English *meat*. The underlying sense is 'sb you share food with'.] —**mateless** *adj.*

mate[2] *n., vt.* (**mates, mating, mated**) CHESS = **checkmate** [14thC. (See CHECKMATE).]

maté /maá tay, máttay/ *n.* **1.** TREES **EVERGREEN TREE** a South American evergreen tree widely grown for its leaves that are used to make a tea. Latin name: *Ilex paraguariensis.* **2.** BEVERAGES **STIMULATING DRINK** a popular South American milky drink containing caffeine that is made from the dried leaves of the maté tree [Early 18thC. Via Spanish from Quechua *mati*.]

matelote /mátt'lōt/ *n.* a chunky fish stew made with wine [Early 18thC. Via French, 'sailor', from Middle Dutch *mattenoot* 'bed companion'.]

mater /máytər/ *n.* mother (*dated informal or humorous*) [Late 16thC. From Latin (see MOTHER).]

WORD KEY: ORIGIN

The Latin word from which ***mater*** derives is also the source of English *madrigal, material, maternal, matriculate, matrimony, matrix, matron,* and *matter.* Its ultimate Indo-European ancestor also produced English *metropolis* and *mother.*

materfamilias /máytər fə mílli ass/ (*plural* **-tresfamilias** /máy trayz-/) *n.* a woman described in her role as head of a household or as the mother of her children (*literary*) [Mid-18thC. From Latin, literally 'mother of the family'.]

material /mə téeri əl/ *n.* **1. STH USED IN MAKING ITEMS** the substance used to make things **2. INFORMATION** information such as facts, notes, and research, used in the making of a book, film, or other work **3.** TEXTILES **FABRIC** woven flat cloth or fabric **4. SB SUITABLE** sb regarded in terms of his or her suitability to perform a certain job or do a task ○ *She's certainly executive material.* ■ **materials** *npl.* **EQUIPMENT** the tools and other things needed to perform a particular task ■ *adj.* **1. PHYSICAL** relating to or consisting of solid physical matter ○ *the material universe* **2. WORLDLY** relating to physical wellbeing rather than emotional or spiritual wellbeing ○ *material comforts* **3. PERTINENT** relevant or important **4.** LAW **IMPORTANT IN COURT** important to a case that is being tried in court ○ *testimony that is material to the case* **5.** PHILOSOPHY **OF CONTENT NOT FORM** relating to the substance of reasoning rather than the form it takes [14thC. Via French *matériel* from late Latin *materialis*, from Latin *materia* (see MATTER).] —**materiality** /mə téeri állәti/ *n.* —**materialness** /mə téeri əlnəss/ *n.*

materialise *vti.* = **materialize**

materialism /mə téeri əlizəm/ *n.* **1.** PHILOSOPHY **THEORY OF THE PHYSICAL** the theory that physical matter is the only reality and that psychological states such as emotions, reason, thought, and desire will eventually be explained as physical functions **2. FOCUS ON POSSESSIONS** devotion to material wealth and possessions at the expense of spiritual or intellectual values

materialist /mə teeri əlist/ *n.* **1.** SB CONCERNED ABOUT POSSESSIONS sb who is concerned with material wealth and possessions at the expense of spiritual and intellectual values **2.** PHILOSOPHY SUPPORTER OF PHILOSOPHICAL MATERIALISM sb who supports the view that physical matter is the only reality and that psychological states will eventually be explained as physical functions ■ *adj.* = **materialistic**

materialistic /mə teeri ə listik/ *adj.* concerned with material wealth and possessions at the expense of spiritual and intellectual values —**materialistically** /mə teeri ə listikli/ *adv.*

materialize /mə teeri ə līz/ (-izes, -izing, -ized), **materialise** (-alises, -alising, -alised) *v.* **1.** *vi.* BECOME REAL to become real or become fact **2.** *vti.* ASSUME PHYSICAL FORM to assume, or cause a ghost or spirit to assume, a physical form **3.** *vi.* APPEAR to appear suddenly, as if out of nowhere —**materialization** /mə teeri ə lī záysh'n/ *n.*

materially /mə teeri əli/ *adv.* **1.** MUCH in a real sense or to a significant degree **2.** PHYSICALLY in terms of material wealth and possessions

materials science *n.* the study of the features and applications of the different materials used in science and technology such as metals, plastics, and ceramics

matériel /mə teeri él/, **materiel** *n.* the supplies, weapons, and equipment associated with a military force [Early 19thC. From French (see MATERIAL).]

maternal /mə túrn'l/ *adj.* **1.** OF OR LIKE A MOTHER belonging or relating to motherhood, a mother, or mothers in general ○ *maternal pride* **2.** CARING kind, caring, and protective in a motherly way ○ *a very maternal person* **3.** ON OR FROM THE MOTHER'S SIDE relating to or inherited from the mother or the mother's side of a family ○ *Her maternal grandfather was Polish.* [15thC. Via French *maternel* from assumed Vulgar Latin *maternalis*, from Latin *maternus*, from *mater* (see MATTER).] —**maternalism** /mə túrnə listik/ *adj.* —**maternally** /mə túrn'li/ *adv.*

maternity /mə túrnəti/ *n.* **1.** MOTHERHOOD the condition of being a mother ○ *Maternity did not affect the progress of her career.* **2.** MOTHERLY CHARACTERISTICS the characteristics and emotions traditionally associated with being a mother such as loving kindness and protectiveness **3.** HOSPITAL SECTION CARING FOR NEWBORNS a ward, floor, or other section of a hospital where mothers and newborn babies are cared for ■ *adj.* OF OR FOR PREGNANCY OR BIRTH relating to or provided for pregnancy, pregnant women, or women who have just given birth ○ *maternity clothes* [Early 17thC. Via French *maternité* from, ultimately, Latin *maternus* (see MATERNAL).]

maternity benefit, **maternity allowance** *n.* a series of regular payments made by the state to a woman who has a baby, usually covering the eighteen weeks around the child's birth

maternity leave *n.* paid or unpaid leave from work that a woman is entitled to take before, at, and after the time that she has a child

maternity ward *n.* a hospital ward for the care of newly delivered babies and their mothers, often also with beds for pregnant women who need medical attention before having their babies

mateship /máyt ship/ *n.* friendship, especially between two men or within a group of men, on terms of equality and mutual support

matey /máyti/, **maty** *adj.* (-ier, -iest) FRIENDLY friendly, especially in a way that is familiar or seems insincere ○ *Those two have been very matey lately.* ■ *n.* (*informal*) **1.** TERM OF ADDRESS FOR UNKNOWN MAN used by a man to address another man he does not know **2.** FRIEND a man who is another man's friend and companion —**matily** *adv.* —**matiness** *n.*

matgrass /mát graass/, **mat grass** *n.* a common European grass that grows in dense tufted clumps on peaty moorland. Latin name: *Nardus stricta*. [Late 18thC. From its being likened to thick matting.]

math /math/ *n. US* = **maths** [Late 19thC. Shortening.]

math. *abbr.* **1.** mathematical **2.** mathematically **3.** mathematician **4.** mathematics

mathematic /máthə máttik/ *adj.* MATHEMATICAL mathematical (*archaic or literary*) ■ *n.* MATHS mathematics (*archaic*) [14thC. Directly or via French *mathématique* from Latin *mathematicus*, from, ultimately, the Greek stem *mathēmat-* 'sth learned', related to *manthanein* 'to learn'.]

mathematical /máthə máttik'l/ *adj.* **1.** OF MATHEMATICS belonging to, relating to, or used in mathematics **2.** ACCURATE as accurate as if calculated by mathematics ○ *crafted the strategy with mathematical precision* **3.** WORKED OUT BY MATHEMATICS calculated or proved by mathematics ○ *It's a mathematical certainty that two numbers in the set will be the same.* **4.** GOOD AT MATHEMATICS skilled in mathematics ○ *more artistic than mathematical* [15thC. Formed from French *mathématique* or its source Latin *mathematicus* (see MATHEMATIC).] —**mathematically** *adv.*

mathematical expectation *n.* = **expected value**

mathematical induction *n.* = **induction** *n.* 9

mathematician /máthəmə tísh'n/ *n.* a student or expert in mathematics, or sb whose job involves mathematics

mathematics /máthə máttiks/ *n.* **1.** MATH STUDY OF RELATIONSHIPS USING NUMBERS the study of the relationships among numbers, shapes, and quantities. It uses signs, symbols, and proofs and includes arithmetic, algebra, calculus, geometry, and trigonometry. (*takes a singular verb*) **2.** CALCULATIONS the calculations involved in a process, estimate, or plan (*takes a plural verb*) ○ *I like the idea, but the mathematics of it are beyond me.* [Late 16thC. Formed from MATHEMATIC, probably modelled on French (*les*) *mathématiques*, a rendering of Latin *mathematica*, from, ultimately, Greek *mathēmat-* (see MATHEMATIC).]

mathematize /máthəmə tīz/ (-tizes, -tizing, -tized), **mathematise** (-tises, -tising, -tised) *vt.* to consider sth in, or reduce it to, purely mathematical terms —**mathematization** /máthəmə tī záysh'n/ *n.*

Mather /máythər, máth-/, **Cotton** (1663–1728) US puritan minister and theologian. He published 469 works on witchcraft, ethics, religion, natural history, medicine and science, and championed inoculations against smallpox.

maths /maths/ *n.* mathematics (*informal*) US term **math** [Early 20thC. Contraction.]

Mathura /mu thoorə/ capital city of Mathura District, Uttar Pradesh State, northern India. Population: 226,850 (1991).

Matilda /mə tíldə/ (1102–67) English princess. Though she was the daughter and acknowledged heir of Henry I of England, the throne was seized by Stephen and she was never crowned queen.

matilija poppy /mə tílli haa-/ *n.* a perennial Californian and Mexican plant of the poppy family that produces a single large white flower. Latin name: *Romneya coulteri*. [Named after *Matilija* Canyon in California]

matin /máttin/, **mattin**, **matinal** /máttinəl/ *adj.* belonging or relating to matins, or taking place during matins [13thC. From French *matines* (see MATINS).]

matinée /mátti nay/, **matinee** *n.* **1.** AFTERNOON PERFORMANCE a performance of a play, concert, or film that is given during the day, especially in the afternoon, often with cheaper seats than the evening performance **2.** MIDDAY OR AFTERNOON EVENT an event or social occasion taking place at midday or in the afternoon ○ *The Senior Centre holds a matinée dance on the first Saturday of each month.* [Mid-19thC. From French, literally 'morning', because it takes place in the daytime, from *matin* (see MATINS).]

matinée coat, **matinée jacket** *n.* a flared top for a baby. It is usually long-sleeved and knitted and comes down to just on or below the level of the nappy.

matinée idol *n.* an actor, especially a good-looking man actor of the 1930s and 1940s, who was attractive to matinée audiences formed mostly of women (*dated*)

matinée jacket *n.* = **matinée coat** (*dated*)

matins /máttinz/, **mattins** *n.* **1.** CHR MORNING LITURGY in the Roman Catholic Church, the morning hours of the Divine Office **2.** CHR MORNING PRAYER in the Church of England, the ceremony of morning prayer **3.** CHR HOURS BEFORE VIGIL in some Roman Catholic monastic communities, the hours before a Vigil **4.** DAWN CHORUS a morning song, especially one sung by birds (*literary*) [13thC. Via French *matines* from, ultimately, Latin *matutinus* 'of the morning', from *Matuta* 'goddess of dawn' (related to *maturus*, source of English *mature*).]

Henri Matisse: Photographed in 1948 working on his paper cut-outs

Matisse /mə teess/, **Henri** (1869–1954) French artist. A leader of the fauve group from 1904, and an influential 20th-century artist, he used bold colour to create rhythmical forms and a flat perspective, later working with brightly coloured cut-out paper on canvas. Full name **Henri Émile Benoît Matisse**

matjes herring /máttyəz-/, **maatjes herring** *n.* a fillet or fillets of herring, especially of a young herring that has not spawned, that is lightly salted, usually sweetened with sugar and flavoured with spice, and eaten raw with onions [Partial translation of Dutch *maatjesharing*, literally 'maiden's herring', from *maatjes* 'maiden's', from its use for young herring, + *haring* 'herring']

matlo /máttlō/ (*plural* **matlos**), **matlow** *n.* a sailor (*dated slang*) [Early 20thC. Representing a pronunciation of French *matelot*, 'sailor'.]

Matlock /mát lok/ town in Derbyshire in the Peak District of central England. Population: 14,680 (1991).

Mato Grosso /máttō gróssō/ state in southwestern Brazil. Population: 2,020,581 (1991). Area: 881,000 sq. km/340,000 sq. mi.

matoke /mə tóki/ *n.* banana or plantain flesh boiled and mashed and used in Uganda as a staple food [Mid-20thC. From Bantu.]

Matopo Hills /mə tōpə hilz/ region of granite hills in southwestern Zimbabwe. Area: 3,240 sq. km/1,250 sq. mi.

matrass /máttrəss/, **mattrass** *n.* a flask with a long neck and rounded body, formerly used in distillation (*archaic*)

matri- *prefix.* mother, maternal ○ *matrilineal* ○ *matriarchy* [From Latin *matr-*, the stem of *mater* (see MATER)]

matriarch /máytri aark/ *n.* **1.** WOMAN HEAD OF A FAMILY OR GROUP a woman who is recognized as being the head of a family, community, or people **2.** STRONG SENIOR WOMAN a woman, usually a grandmother, who is highly respected by her family and to whom the family turn for advice and help **3.** WOMAN IN A POWERFUL POSITION a woman who holds a position of dominance, authority, or respect [Early 17thC. Formed from Latin *matri-* (see MATRI-), on the model of *patriarch*.] —**matriarchic** /máytri aárkik/ *adj.*

matriarchal /máytri aárk'l/ *adj.* **1.** IN WHICH WOMEN HOLD POWER used to describe a society in which power and property are held by women and handed down through matrilineal descent **2.** CONTROLLED BY WOMEN controlled or dominated by women **3.** WITH THE TRADITIONAL QUALITIES OF A STRONG WOMAN showing strength and assurance as the most respected woman in a group ○ *My grandmother was a powerful, matriarchal figure.* **4.** OF MATRIARCHS relating to a matriarch or to matriarchs in general —**matriarchalism** *n.*

matriarchate *n.* = **matriarchy** *n.* 2 [Late 19thC. Formed from MATRIARCH on the model of *patriarchate*.]

matriarchy /máytri aarki/ (*plural* **-chies**) *n.* **1.** SOCIAL ORDER WHERE WOMEN HAVE POWER a form of social order where women are in charge and are recognized as the heads of families, with power, lineage, and inheritance passing, where possible, from mothers to daughters **2.** COMMUNITY WHERE WOMEN HAVE POWER any community, society, or social group that is based on matriarchy **3.** ORGANIZATION WHERE WOMEN HAVE POWER any form of organization or government where women have power [Late 19thC. Modelled on PATRIARCHY.]

matric /mə trík/ *abbr.* matriculation (*dated informal*) [Late 19thC. Shortening.]

matrices plural of **matrix**

matricide /máytri sīd, máttri-/ *n.* **1.** KILLING OF OWN MOTHER the act of murdering your own mother **2.** KILLER OF OWN MOTHER sb who has murdered his or her own mother [Late 16thC. Directly or via French from Latin *matricidium*, from *matr-* (see MATRI-).] —**matricidal** /máytri sīd'l, máttri-/ *adj.*

matriclinous /máttri klīnəss/, **matroclinous** /máttrō-/, **matroclinal** /-klīn'l/ *adj.* having obvious characteristics that are inherited predominantly from the woman parent

matriculant /mə tríkyŏŏlənt/ *n.* = **matriculate** *n.* [Mid-19thC. From medieval Latin *matriculant-*, the present participle stem of *matriculare* (see MATRICULATE).]

matriculate /mə tríkyŏŏ layt/ *v.* (**-lates, -lating, -lated**) **1.** *vt.* ADMIT SB AS STUDENT to admit a student to membership of a college or university **2.** *vi.* BE ENROLLED AS A STUDENT to be enrolled at a college or university, after meeting the academic standard required to be accepted for a course of further education ■ *n.* SB ENROLLED sb who has matriculated [Late 16thC. From assumed medieval Latin *matriculare*, from *matricula*, literally 'little list', from *matrix* (see MATRIX).] —**matriculator** /mə tríkyoo laytər/ *n.*

matriculation /mə tríkyŏŏ láysh'n/ *n.* **1.** MATRICULATING PROCESS the act or process of matriculating at a college or university **2.** SCHOOL-LEAVING EXAM an examination formerly taken in Britain as a school-leaving qualification ○ *matriculation card*

matrilineage /máttri línni ij/ *n.* **1.** LINE OF DESCENT THROUGH MOTHERS the line of genealogical relationship or descent that follows the women's side of a family **2.** PEOPLE RELATED THROUGH MOTHERS a group of people related by descent through mothers

matrilineal /máttri línni əl/ *adj.* **1.** FOLLOWING THE FEMALE LINE used to describe the line of genealogical relationship or descent that follows the female side of a family **2.** RELATED THROUGH MOTHERS used to describe a group that is related by descent through mothers **3.** COMING THROUGH THE WOMEN'S LINE inherited or traced through the women's line of descent —**matrilineally** *adv.*

matrilocal /máttri lōk'l/ *adj.* **1.** INVOLVING A MOVE TO A WIFE'S FAMILY HOME used to describe a form of marriage in which, after the wedding, the bridegroom moves to his new wife's family home **2.** INVOLVING LIVING WITH A WIFE'S FAMILY used to describe a culture in which young men live with their brides' families after marriage —**matrilocality** /máttri lō kálləti/ *n.* —**matrilocally** /máttri lōk'li/ *adv.*

matrimonial /máttri mṓni əl/ *adj.* belonging or relating to marriage or to a particular marriage [15thC. Directly or via French from Latin *matrimonialis*, from *matrimonium* (see MATRIMONY).] —**matrimonially** *adv.*

matrimony /máttriməni/ *n.* **1.** MARRIED STATE the state or condition of being married **2.** MARRIAGE CEREMONY the religious ceremony of marriage **3.** CARDS CARD GAME a type of card game in which players try to hold a king and queen [13thC. Directly or via Anglo-Norman *matrimonie* from Latin *matrimonium*, literally 'state of motherhood' (because of the association of marriage with parenthood), from *matri-* (see MATRI-).]

matrimony vine *n.* any one of several shrubs cultivated for their bright berries and purple flowers. Genus: *Lycium.*

matrix /máytriks/ (*plural* **-trices** /máytri seez/ *or* **-trixes**) *n.* **1.** SUBSTANCE THAT CONTAINS STH a substance in which sth is embedded or enclosed **2.** SITUATION IN WHICH STH DEVELOPS a situation or set of circumstances that allows or encourages the origin, development, or growth of sth ○ *The matrix of video and computers is producing new forms of art.* **3.** BIOL TISSUE-FORMING SUBSTANCE the substance that exists between cells and from which tissue, e.g. cartilage and bone, develops **4.** PHYSIOL TISSUE AT THE BASE OF THE NAIL the thickened tissue at the base of a fingernail, toenail, or tooth from which a new nail or tooth grows **5.** GEOL SOIL OR ROCK CONTAINING STH the soil or rock in which sth such as a fossil, crystal, or mineral is embedded. ◊ **gangue 6.** METALL MAIN PART OF AN ALLOY the main metal component in an alloy **7.** MATH ARRAY OF MATHEMATICAL ELEMENTS a rectangular array of mathematical elements, e.g. the coefficients of linear equations, whose rows and columns can be combined with those of other arrays to solve problems **8.** COMPUT NETWORK OF CIRCUIT ELEMENTS a network of circuit elements, e.g. transistors and resistors **9.** PRINTING METAL TYPE MOULD a metal mould from which type is cast in the hot-metal process **10.** MANUF MOULD MADE FROM A RAISED SURFACE a mould made by taking the impression of a raised surface in a substance such as plastic, used in stereotyping or electrotyping **11.** RECORDING GRAMOPHONE RECORD MOULD a mould used in the production of gramophone records **12.** MECH ENG BED OR SURROUND OF MATERIAL a bed or surround of material that gives protection or absorbs a force **13.** WOMB the womb (*archaic*) [14thC. Directly or via French *matrice* from Latin *matrix* 'womb' (the original sense in English), later 'list', from, ultimately, *mater* 'mother'. The underlying idea is of sth growing.]

matrix sentence *n.* the main clause in a complex sentence

matro- *prefix.* = **matri-**

matroclinal *adj.* = **matriclinous**

matroclinous *adj.* = **matriclinous**

matron /máytrən/ *n.* **1.** MATURE WOMAN a woman, especially a married woman of middle age or later, who has had children and is thought of as being mature, sensible, and of good social standing **2.** SUPERVISOR a woman in charge of the medical and housekeeping arrangements in an institution, e.g. a British boarding school **3.** HEAD NURSE a woman who is head of the nursing staff in a hospital, nursing home, or other medical institution, now called the senior nursing officer (*no longer used technically*) **4.** *US* WOMAN WARDEN a woman who is a warden in a women's correctional institution [14thC. Directly or via French *matrone* from Latin *matrona*, from *matr-* (see MATRI-).] —**matronal** *adj.* —**matronhood** /máy trən hŏŏd/ *n.* —**matronship** *n.*

matronage /máytrənij/ *n.* the duties performed by a matron

matronly /máytrənli/ *adj.* **1.** LIKE A MATRON having qualities associated with a matron, especially dignity and placidity **2.** MATURE AND FULL-FIGURED mature and plump, especially with a large bosom **3.** OF A MATRON relating to or typical of a matron ○ *matronly duties* —**matronliness** *n.*

matron of honour *n.* a married woman who acts as chief bridesmaid at the wedding of a woman friend or relative

matronymic /máttrə nímmik/, **metronymic** /méttrə nímmik/ *adj.* a name derived from a mother or a matrilineal ancestor [Late 18thC. Formed from Latin *matr-* (see MATRI-).]

Matsu Islands /mat sṓo-/ island group in Taiwan, close to the Chinese mainland

matsutake /mátsoo táaki/, **matsutake mushroom** *n.* an edible dark brown mushroom with a cinnamon fragrance, native to Japan. Latin name: *Tricholoma matsutake.* [From Japanese, literally 'pine mushroom']

Matsuyama /mát sŏŏ yaámə/ industrial city in southwestern Japan, on the island of Shikoku. Population: 443,322 (1990).

matt /mat/, **matte, mat** *n.* NONGLOSS FINISH a dull or nonglossy finish, e.g. on paintwork or photographic prints ■ *adj.* WITH A MATT FINISH having a matt finish [Mid-17thC. From French, 'dull'.]

mattamore /máttə mawr/ *n.* an underground chamber, room, or storage place [Late 17thC. Via French *matamore* from Arabic *maṭmūra*, from *ṭamara* 'to bury'.]

matte[1] /mat/ *n.* **1.** MIXTURE OF METAL SULPHIDES a mixture of metal sulphides formed during the smelting of sulphide ores, e.g. ores of copper or nickel **2.** DEVICE OBSCURING PART OF IMAGE a mask used for obscuring part of an image so that another image can be put on top of the original. ◊ **matte shot** [Mid-19thC. From French (see MAT), used as a noun.]

matte[2] *n., adj.* = **matt**

matted /máttid/ *adj.* **1.** TANGLED forming a thick tangled mass ○ *Long-haired cats need lots of brushing to prevent their coats becoming matted.* **2.** WITH MATS covered with mats or matting

matter /máttər/ *n.* **1.** STH UNDER CONSIDERATION sth that is being considered or needs to be dealt with ○ *This is a matter for serious thought.* **2.** SUBSTANCE a substance or material of a particular kind ○ *reading matter* **3.** PHYS MATERIAL SUBSTANCE the material substance of the universe that has mass, occupies space, and is convertible to energy **4.** PRINTED TEXT text or other material that is printed ○ *cheaper rates for printed matter* **5.** SUBJECT OF SPEECH OR WRITING the subject that is dealt with in speech or writing, as opposed to its presentation ○ *The subject matter was well presented.* **6.** PHILOSOPHY WHAT IS PERCEIVED BY THE MIND in Cartesian philosophy, sth that is extended in space and persists through time, and is contrasted with mind **7.** *US* LAW STH TO BE PROVED a case to be proved or resolved in a court of law ○ *Who is the defendant in this matter?* **8.** MED BODILY DISCHARGE sth such as pus that is discharged from the body ■ **matters** *npl.* CIRCUMSTANCES the current situation or circumstances ○ *We were both under a lot of stress, which didn't improve matters.* ■ *vi.* (**-ters, -tering, -tered**) **1.** HAVE IMPORTANCE to be important ○ *The only thing that matters is for you to get better.* **2.** MAKE DIFFERENCE to make a difference ○ *It doesn't matter how you tell her, just make sure she knows.* **3.** MED PRODUCE PUS to form or discharge pus [12thC. Directly or via Anglo-Norman *mater(i)e* and French *matière*, from Latin *materia* 'timber, stuff of which sth is made', later 'subject, topic', from *mater* 'mother'.] ◇ **for that matter** as far as that is concerned ◇ **a matter of opinion** a subject about which there are varying views ◇ **sth** *or* **nothing is** *or* **nothing the matter** sth is wrong ○ *What's the matter with the toaster?*

WORD KEY: SYNONYMS

See Synonyms at ***subject***.

Matterhorn

Matterhorn /máttər hawrn/ steep pyramid-shaped peak in southwestern Switzerland, near the Italian border. Height: 4,478 m/14,692 ft.

matter of fact *n.* **1.** ACTUAL FACT sth that is true and that cannot be denied ○ *Very few people here have jobs – it's a matter of fact.* **2.** LAW STH TO BE PROVED OR DISPROVED a question to be decided by a court of law that involves deciding on the truth of a statement, rather than interpreting a point of law or forming an opinion. ◊ **matter of law** ◇ **as a matter of fact 1.** used to add a statement that completes what you are saying or emphasizes its truth **2.** used to contradict what sb has said or express disagreement

matter-of-fact *adj.* **1.** RATIONAL straightforward and not fanciful or emotional ○ *I admired her matter-of-fact approach to life.* **2.** FACTUAL dealing with facts and not emotions or opinions ○ *The report gave a very matter-of-fact account of the incident.* —**matter-of-factly** *adv.* —**matter-of-factness** *n.*

matter of law *n.* a question to be decided by a court of law that involves the interpretation of a point of law

mattery /máttəri/ *adj.* secreting or discharging pus

matte shot *n.* in film-making, a visual effect that is achieved by masking out part of an image using a matte and superimposing another image so that it combines with the rest of the original

Matthew *n.* the first of the gospels of the Bible in which the life and teachings of Jesus Christ are described. It is thought to have been written by St Matthew. See table at **Bible**

Matthew /máthyoo/, **St** (*fl.* 1st century) Arabian apostle. He is credited with writing the Gospel According to Matthew.

Matthews /máthyooz/, **Sir Stanley** (*b.* 1915) British footballer. Noted for his skill as a dribbler, he played for Blackpool (1947–61) and for England, winning 54 international caps.

Matthew Walker /máth yoo wáwkər/ *n.* a type of knot made in the strands at the end of a rope [Mid-19thC. Probably the name of the person who invented or introduced it.]

Matthias /mə thī́ əss/ *n.* in the Bible, the disciple chosen to replace Judas as one of the 12 apostles of Jesus Christ (Acts 1:15–26)

Matthias Corvinus /mə thī́ əss kawr vī́nəss/, **King of Hungary** (1443–90). His acquisition of Austria and various provinces made him a powerful ruler. He was also a patron of the arts.

mattin *adj.* = **matin**

matting[1] /mátting/ *n.* **1. MATERIAL WOVEN FROM NATURAL FIBRES** a coarse material woven from natural fibres such as hemp or grass and used especially to make mats or other coverings ○ *coconut matting* **2. MATS** mats, taken collectively ○ *Matting is integral to Japanese interior design.* **3. LAYER OF NATURAL MATERIALS** a bed or layer formed by natural materials, e.g. by fallen leaves in a forest ○ *We walked through the pines on a matting of needles.* **4. MAKING MATS** the process of making a mat or mats

matting[2] /mátting/ *n.* **1. DULL SURFACE** a surface that is dull or without sheen **2. DULLING OF SURFACE** the process of giving a surface, especially a metallic one, a dull finish

mattins *n.* = **matins**

mattock /máttək/ *n.* a tool like a pickaxe with one end of its blade flattened at right angles to its handle and used for loosening soil and cutting through roots [Pre-12thC. Origin uncertain: perhaps from assumed Vulgar Latin *matteuca* 'club'.]

mattrass *n.* = **matrass**

mattress /máttrəss/ *n.* **1. PAD FOR SLEEPING ON** a large pad on which to sleep, usually containing springs or a material such as foam rubber, flock, horsehair, or straw. Some modern mattresses have electronic controls that allow them to tilt into different positions. **2. INFLATABLE PAD** a large pad that can be filled with air or water and used as a bed or for floating on, e.g. in a pool **3.** CONSTR **FOUNDATION** a slab or platform used as a foundation for a building **4. INTERNAL METAL FRAMEWORK** a metal framework inside reinforced concrete **5.** CIV ENG = **blinding 6. SHIELD FOR EMBANKMENTS** a closely woven structure made from brushwood and poles and used for protecting dykes, embankments, dams, and other susceptible slopes from erosion [13thC. Via Old French *materas*, from, ultimately, Arabic *al-matraḥ* 'carpet, cushion, bed', from the practice of sleeping on cushions, copied by Europeans from Arabs during the Crusades.]

maturate /máttyoo͝ rayt, máchoo͝-/ (**-rates, -rating, -rated**) *vti.* to mature, ripen, or develop, or develop or ripen sth [Mid-16thC. Origin uncertain: either from Latin *maturare* (see MATURE) or a back-formation from MATURATION.] —**maturative** /mə tyoo͝rə tiv/ *adj.*

maturation /máttyoo͝ ráysh'n, máchoo͝-/ *n.* **1. PROGRESS TO MATURITY** the process of becoming mature, ripe, or more developed **2. PROCESS OF MAKING STH MORE MATURE** the process of ripening or developing sth, or of making it more mature **3.** BIOL **PROCESS OF CELL DEVELOPMENT** the process in which immature cells in the ovary and testes develop into ova and spermatozoa [14thC. Directly or via French from the medieval Latin stem *maturation-*, from, ultimately, *maturare* (see MATURE).] —**maturational** *adj.*

maturation division *n.* the process of cell division by which the ova and spermatozoa are developed

mature /mə tyo͝or, mə cho͝or/ *adj.* **1. ACTING OR SEEMING LIKE AN ADULT** showing mental, emotional, or physical characteristics that are typical of a fully developed adult person ○ *Philip is only 12 but he's very tall and already quite mature.* **2. EXPERIENCED** showing qualities gained by development and experience ○ *in the author's mature writings* **3. ADULT** adult or fully grown ○ *a mature animal capable of breeding* **4.** BIOL **FULLY DEVELOPED** fully developed to a complete or final stage **5.** FOOD, WINE **OLD AND OF GOOD FLAVOUR** old enough to have acquired the maximum flavour ○ *mature Orkney cheddar* **6. IN LATER LIFE** no longer young ○ *the wisdom shown by the mature dramatist* **7. INVOLVING SERIOUS THOUGHT** involving or reached by a period of serious thought ○ *On mature reflection, I feel it would be wiser to sell.* **8.** FIN **DUE FOR PAYMENT** used to describe a financial arrangement that has reached a previously set or mutually agreed-on time limit and is therefore due for payment or repayment ○ *mature bonds* **9.** COMM **NOT SUBJECT TO MAJOR CHANGE** no longer subject to the instability of early development or expansion ○ *Hydroelectric power is a mature industry in the region.* **10.** GEOL **IN THE MIDDLE OF AN EROSION CYCLE** used to describe a natural feature or landform that is in the middle stages of an erosion cycle ■ *v.* (**-tures, -turing, -tured**) **1.** *vti.* **DEVELOP** to go through, or make sth or sb go through, a developmental process ○ *Children begin to mature at different ages.* **2.** *vi.* FIN **FALL DUE FOR PAYMENT** to reach a previously set or mutually agreed-on time limit and therefore fall due for payment or repayment (*refers to a financial arrangement*) **3.** *vti.* **DEVELOP INTO STH FINISHED** to become fully worked out, or work sth out fully, especially through long consideration ○ *The plan had matured over the intervening months.* [14thC. Directly or via French from Latin *maturus* 'ripe, mature, timely, early' (source also of Old French *mur*, which produced English *demure*). The underlying idea is of 'earliness, calmness'.] —**maturely** *adv.* —**matureness** *n.*

mature student *n.* a student aged 25 or over who has gone into higher or further education later than is usual, especially after working or raising a family

maturity /mə tyo͝orəti, mə cho͝orəti/ *n.* **1. FULL GROWTH OR DEVELOPMENT** the state or condition of being fully grown or developed ○ *Girls tend to reach maturity earlier than boys.* **2.** FIN **TIME FOR REPAYMENT** the time when a financial arrangement falls due for payment or repayment **3.** FIN **READINESS FOR REPAYMENT** the state of a financial arrangement when it falls due for payment or repayment **4. MATURE STATE** the condition of being ripe, fully aged, or fully grown, especially mentally or emotionally ○ *I'm amazed at the maturity shown by these young people.* **5.** GEOL **MATURE STATE OF A LANDFORM** the stage in the development of a landform at which there is maximum relief and drainage is well developed [15thC. Directly or via French *maturité* from Latin *maturitas*, from *maturus* (see MATURE).]

maturity-onset diabetes *n.* = **noninsulin-dependent diabetes**

matutinal /máttyoo͝ tī́n'l/ *adj.* relating to or happening in the morning or in the early part of the day (*formal*) [Mid-16thC. From late Latin *matutinalis*, from *Matuta*, goddess of the dawn.] —**matutinally** *adv.*

MATV *abbr.* master antenna television

maty *adj., n.* = **matey**

matzo /mótsə/, **matzoh** *n.* (*plural* **-zos** *or* **-zoth**; *plural* **-zohs** *or* **-zoth**) **UNLEAVENED BREAD** unleavened bread that is traditionally eaten during Passover in commemoration of the unleavened bread eaten by Hebrews escaping from slavery in Egypt ■ *adj.* **OF OR FOR MATZO** made from or like matzo, or used to make matzo ○ *matzo meal* ○ *matzo balls* [Mid-19thC. Via Yiddish *matse* from Hebrew *maṣṣāh*.]

matzoon /maat so͞on/, **madzoon** /maad zo͞on/ *n.* a food similar to yoghurt and made from fermented milk [From Armenian *madzun*]

matzoth plural of **matzo**

mauby /máwbi/ *n.* *Carib* a drink made from the bark of a tree of the buckthorn family [Late 18thC. From Carib *mabi* 'sweet potato (drink)'.]

maudlin /máwdlin/ *adj.* tearfully or excessively sentimental, especially because affected by alcohol [Early 16thC. Via French *Madeleine* 'Madeleine', from, ultimately, Greek *Mariaē Magdalēnē* 'Mary Magdalene', because she was commonly represented in medieval art weeping in repentance.] —**maudlinism** *n.* —**maudlinly** *adv.* —**maudlinness** *n.*

Mauger /máyjər/, **Ivan Gerald** (*b.* 1939) New Zealand speedway rider. He won the world championship a record six times (1968–70, 1972, 1977, 1979).

maugre /máwgər/, **mauger** *prep.* in spite of (*archaic*) [13thC. From French *maugré*, literally 'bad pleasure'.]

Maui /mówi/ the second largest island of Hawaii, consisting of two oval peninsulas connected by an isthmus. Population: 100,374 (1990). Area: 1,884 sq. km/727 sq. mi.

maul /mawl/ *vt.* (**mauls, mauling, mauled**) **1. ASSAULT OR ATTACK SB** to beat, batter, or tear at a person or animal ○ *He got mauled in the ring by a better boxer.* **2. HANDLE SB OR STH ROUGHLY** to handle sb or sth too roughly or clumsily ○ *Children may need to be taught not to maul their pets.* **3. CRITICIZE SB OR STH FIERCELY** to criticize sb or sth severely or mercilessly ○ *Despite being a box-office success, her new film was mauled by the critics.* ■ *n.* **1.** RUGBY **MOVING SCRUM** a type of loose scrum that members of both teams form around the player holding the ball or trying to run with the ball. ◊ **ruck 2. CROWD** a crowd of people who are pushing, struggling, or fighting ○ *'The maul of medics holding bags and cords around the stretcher'* (Mark Lawson, *Idlewild*; 1995) **3.** CONSTR **PILE-DRIVING HAMMER** a large heavy hammer, usually with a wooden head, that is used for driving in piles, stakes, or wedges **4. LOG-SPLITTING HAMMER** a heavy hammer that has one side of the head shaped like a wedge, making it suitable for splitting logs or wood [13thC. Via Old French *mail* 'hammer' (source of English *mallet*) from Latin *malleus* (source of English *malleable* and *mall* 'shopping precinct'). Originally in the sense 'to strike with a hammer'.] —**mauler** *n.*

Maulana /maw láanə/ *n.* a title given to a man who is learned in Persian and Arabic [Mid-19thC. From Arabic *mawlānā* 'our master'.]

maulers /máwlərz/ *npl.* the hands (*archaic slang*)

Mau Mau /mów mow/ *npl.* a secret Kenyan organization set up in 1952 with the aim of forcing European settlers from the land and ending British rule in Kenya [Mid-20thC. From Kikuyu.]

mau-mau /mów mow/ (**mau-maus, mau-mauing, mau-maued**) *vt.* **mau-mau** (**mau-maus, mau-mauing**) *US* to confront sb, e.g. a public official or bureaucrat, with the intent of gaining concessions, benefits, or advantage through intimidation (*slang*)

maumet /máw mit/ *n.* a doll [13thC. Via Old French *mahomet* from, ultimately, Arabic *Muḥammad* (see MUHAMMAD), because medieval Christians believed that his followers worshipped images of him.] —**maumetry** /máw mitri/ *n.*

maun *v.* **maun, man, mun** *Scotland* must (*nonstandard*) ○ *I maun get to the shops afore they shut.* [13thC. From Old Norse *man*, a present tense form of *munu* 'to intend to'.]

Mauna Kea /máwnə kée ə/ dormant volcano in Hawaii, on northern Hawaii Island. It is the highest point in the state, 4,205 m/13,796 ft.

Mauna Loa /máwnə lṓ ə, mówna-/ active volcano on Hawaii Island. It is one of the world's largest volcanoes. Height: 4,170 m/13,680 ft.

maund *n.* a unit of weight used in the Indian subcontinent, with a value that varies from place to place but is often equal to 37 kg/82 lb [Late 16thC. From Arabic *mann*.]

maunder /máwn dər/ (**maunders, maundering, maundered**) *v.* **1.** *vti.* **SAY STH VAGUE OR INCOHERENT** to talk or say sth in a vague, rambling, or incoherent way **2.** *vi.* **MOVE OR ACT WITHOUT PURPOSE** to move or act in a vague, aimless, or directionless way [Early 17thC. Origin uncertain: perhaps formed from earlier *maund* 'to beg' in the literal sense of 'to keep on begging', or perhaps an imitation of the sound of muttering.] —**maunderer** /máwn dər ər/ n.

maundy /máwn di/ n. a ceremony held in some Christian churches on Maundy Thursday that involves an actual or symbolic washing of people's feet in commemoration of Jesus Christ's washing of his disciples' feet (John 13:3–34) [13thC. Via Old French *mandé* from Latin *mandatum* 'commandment' (source also of English *mandate*), in *mandatum novum* 'new commandment', the first words of an antiphon sung in the ceremony.]

Maundy /máwn di/ n. the distribution of Maundy money by the British sovereign

Maundy money n. specially minted silver coins that the British sovereign distributes in a church ceremony on Maundy Thursday

Maundy Thursday n. the Thursday before Easter Sunday, observed in Christian belief in commemoration of the Last Supper. ◊ **Holy Thursday**

Guy de Maupassant

Maupassant /mố pass oN, mố pass aáN/, **Guy de** (1850–93) French novelist and short-story writer. His short stories have been particularly influential and are written with a direct realism, portraying ordinary people in extraordinary situations. Full name **Henri René Albert Guy de Maupassant**

Mauriac /máwr yak/, **François** (1885–1970) French poet, novelist, and playwright. Much of his work, coloured by his adherence to Roman Catholicism, centres on moral conflict and psychological analysis.

Maurist /máwrist/ n. a member of a group of French Benedictine monks, founded in 1618 and dissolved during the French Revolution, who were renowned for their great scholarship, especially in hagiography [Late 18thC. Named after St *Maur*, a 6th-century disciple of St Benedict.]

Mauritania

Mauritania /máw ri táyni ə/ republic in northwestern Africa. It became independent from France in 1960. Language: Arabic, French. Currency: ouguiya. Capital: Nouakchott. Population: 2,333,000 (1996). Area: 1,030,700 sq. km/397,955 sq. mi. Official name **Islamic Republic of Mauritania** —**Mauritanian** /mórri táyni ən/ n., adj.

Mauritius /mə ríshəss/ island republic in the western Indian Ocean consisting of the islands of Mauritius and Rodrigues and some islets. Language: English. Currency: Mauritian rupee. Population: 1,141,000 (1996). Area: 2,045 sq. km/790 sq. mi. Official name **Republic of Mauritius** —**Mauritian** n., adj.

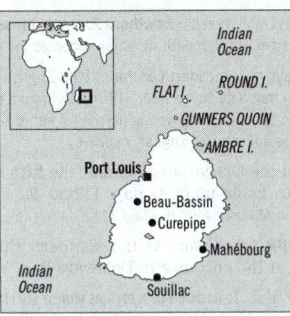
Mauritius

Maurya /mówri ə/ n. an Indian dynasty established in the 4th century BC after invasions by Alexander the Great, members of which included the emperor Ashoka [Late 19thC. From Sanskrit, named after Candragupta *Maurya*, its founder.]

Mauser /mówzər/ tdmk. a trademark for a repeating rifle and other firearms

mausoleum /máwssə leé əm, máwzə-/ (plural **-ums** or **-a**) n. **1.** TOMB a large tomb, especially one that is ornately decorated or made from expensive stone **2.** BUILDING CONTAINING TOMBS a building, often a highly decorated or elaborate one, that houses a tomb or several tombs **3.** GLOOMY INTERIOR a large gloomy oppressive room or building ○ *I can't study in the library; it's a mausoleum.* [15thC. Via Latin from Greek *Mausōleion* 'tomb of Mausolus' (a 4th-century BC king of Caria in Asia Minor), built in 353 BC at Halicarnassus (now Bodrum in Turkey).] —**mausolean** adj.

mauve /mōv/ n. a pale colour between purple and blue or pink [Mid-19thC. Via French from Latin *malva* 'mallow plant' (source of English *mallow*); from the colour of its flowers.] —**mauve** adj.

maven /máyvən/, **mavin** n. sb who is an expert or knowledgeable enthusiast in a particular field [Mid-20thC. Via Yiddish *meyvn* from Hebrew *mēḇīn*, literally 'sb who understands'.]

maverick /mávvərik/ n. **1.** INDEPENDENT PERSON sb who holds independent views and who refuses to conform to the accepted or orthodox thinking on a subject **2.** AGRIC UNBRANDED ANIMAL an unbranded animal, especially a calf that has become separated from its mother and herd. By convention, it can become the property of whoever finds it and brands it. [Mid-19thC. Origin uncertain: probably named after Samuel Augustus *Maverick* (1803–70), a Texas cattle owner who did not brand some of his calves.]

mavin n. = maven

mavis /máyviss/ n. a songthrush (literary) [14thC. From French *mauvis*, of uncertain origin: probably formed from *mauve* 'gull', from Old English *mǣw* (source of English *mew*).]

mavourneen /mə voór neen/, **mavournin** n. Ireland my darling [Early 19thC. From Irish *mo mhuirnín*, literally 'my little love'.]

maw /maw/ n. **1.** ANIMAL'S MOUTH the mouth, jaws, throat, or stomach of an animal, especially a carnivorous animal that devours food greedily **2.** GREEDY PERSON'S MOUTH the mouth, throat, or stomach of a greedy person (informal) **3.** GAPING HOLE anything that seems like a gaping hole that devours things or people ○ *the ravenous maw of readers' expectations* [Old English *maga* 'stomach'. From a prehistoric Germanic word that is also the ancestor of Welsh *megin* 'bellows' and Lithuanian *makas* 'purse', the underlying idea being 'bag'.]

mawkin /máwkin/ n. **1.** SCARECROW a scarecrow (regional archaic) **2.** OFFENSIVE TERM an offensive term that deliberately insults a woman's care for her appearance or a woman's decency of speech and behaviour (regional insult offensive) [13thC. Formed from the name *Matilda* or *Maud*, in the literal sense of 'little Matilda' or 'little Maud'.]

mawkish /máwkish/ adj. **1.** SENTIMENTAL sentimental, especially in a contrived or off-putting way **2.** BLAND OR UNPLEASANT bland or unappetizing in taste or smell [Mid-17thC. Formed from earlier *mawk* 'maggot', from Old Norse *maðkr*. Originally in the sense 'nauseated, lacking appetite'.] —**mawkishly** adv. —**mawkishness** n.

Mawlid al-Nabi /máwlid al naábi/ n. in Islam, the celebrations held in honour of the prophet Muhammad's birthday, which falls on the 12th day of the month of Rabi I [From Arabic, literally 'birthday of the prophet']

Mawson /máwss'n/, **Sir Douglas** (1882–1958) British-born Australian geologist and explorer. He was a member of the first party to reach the South Magnetic Pole (1909) and was head of the Australasian Antarctic Expedition (1911–14).

max /maks/ n. MAXIMUM the maximum limit or amount of sth (informal) ○ *I could lend you 50 quid, but that's my max.* ■ adj. MOST most or highest (slang) ○ *Turn up the volume to get the max effect.* ■ adv. AT THE MOST as a maximum (slang) ○ *We were offered £100 max.* [Mid-19thC. Shortening of MAXIMUM.]

max. abbr. maximum

maxi /máksi/ n. ANKLE-LENGTH PIECE OF CLOTHING an ankle-length coat, skirt, or dress ■ adj. **1.** ANKLE-LENGTH used to describe an article of clothing that is ankle-length. ◊ **mini 2.** ABNORMALLY LARGE larger than normal ○ *maxi tubs of ice cream* [Mid-20thC. From MAXIMUM.]

maxilla /mak síllə/ (plural **-lae** /-lee/) n. **1.** UPPER JAW OF VERTEBRATES either of a pair of bones that are fused at the midline and together form the upper jawbone in vertebrates **2.** MOUTHPART OF ARTHROPODS a mouthpart that is one of one or two pairs behind the mandibles of arthropods [Late 17thC. Directly and via Old French *maxille* from Latin *maxilla*, literally 'little jaw', from *mala* 'jaw'.] —**maxillar** adj. —**maxillary** adj.

maxilliped /mak sílli ped/ n. one of the six specialized feeding appendages arranged in pairs and located just behind the maxillae on the heads of crustaceans [Mid-19thC. Coined from MAXILLA + -I- + -PED.] —**maxillipedary** /mak sílli peédəri/ adj.

maxillofacial /mak síllō fáysh'l/ adj. relating to, located in, or affecting the face in the region of the upper jaw [Early 20thC. From MAXILLA + FACIAL.]

maxim /máksim/ n. **1.** SAYING a succinct or pithy saying that has some proven truth to it **2.** GENERAL RULE a general rule, principle, or truth [15thC. Via French from medieval Latin *maxima*, literally 'largest', used as a noun (a shortening of *maxima propositio* 'largest proposition', hence 'fundamental axiom'), a form of *maximus* (see MAXIMUM).]

Maxim n. = Maxim gun

Maxim /máksim/, **Sir Hiram** (1840–1916) US-born British engineer and inventor. He is best known for inventing the Maxim gun, an automatic machine gun.

maxima plural of **maximum**

maximal /máksim'l/ adj. **1.** CONSTITUTING A MAXIMUM relating to or constituting a maximum **2.** BEST POSSIBLE the best or greatest possible —**maximally** adv.

maximalist /máksiməlist/ n. sb who is determined to achieve a political aim, by direct action or intervention if necessary, and is unwilling to compromise [Early 20thC. Formed from MAXIMAL on the model of Russian *maksimalist*.] —**maximalist** adj.

Maximalist n. a member of a Russian group that, in the early 20th century, advocated terrorist action to get rid of the tsar and the setting up of a temporary proletarian dictatorship

Maxim gun /máksim-/ n. an early single-barrelled machine gun that was cooled by an outer casing containing water [Late 19thC. Named after Sir Hiram MAXIM who invented it.]

Maximilian /máksi mílli ən/, **Archduke of Austria** (1832–67). He was made Emperor of Mexico by Napoleon III of France in 1863, but was executed by Mexican republicans.

Maximilian I /máksi mílli ən thə fúrst/, **Holy Roman Emperor** (1459–1519). He made the Hapsburg Dynasty a major power through diplomacy and marriage policy.

maximin /máksimin/ n. **1.** MATH LARGEST OF A SET the largest of a set of minimum values **2.** STRATEGY OF INCREASING SMALLEST ADVANTAGE in game theory, a strategy of attempting to maximize the smallest possible advantage [Mid-20thC. Blend of MAXIMUM and MINIMUM; modelled on MINIMAX.]

maximize /máksi mīz/ (-mizes, -mizing, -mized), **maximise** (-mises, -mising, -mised) *vt.* **1.** INCREASE STH TO THE MAXIMUM to make sth as large as possible ○ *You can maximise the picture by clicking on this button.* **2.** REGARD STH AS MOST IMPORTANT to attach the greatest importance to sth ○ *Historians maximize the treaty's benefits to trade and tend not to mention its political costs.* **3.** MATH FIND A FUNCTION'S LARGEST VALUE to find or work out the largest value of a function —**maximization** /máksi mī záysh'n/ *n.* —**maximizer** /-mīzər/ *n.*

maximum /máksiməm/ *n.* (*plural* **-mums** *or* **-ma** /-mə/) **1.** GREATEST POSSIBLE AMOUNT the largest or greatest amount, number, extent, or degree possible or allowed ○ *The stadium seats a maximum of 60,000.* **2.** HIGHEST AMOUNT OR LEVEL REACHED the largest amount, level, or value that sth variable can reach or reaches during a period ○ *Even at its maximum, the noise did not exceed legal levels.* **3.** MATH LARGEST NUMBER the largest number in a set **4.** MATH FUNCTION'S GREATEST VALUE the greatest value that a continuous function can attain over a specific interval **5.** ASTRON TIME OF A STAR'S GREATEST BRIGHTNESS the interval during which a variable star is most luminous **6.** ASTRON VARIABLE STAR'S MAGNITUDE the magnitude of a variable star at its greatest ■ *adj.* GREATEST POSSIBLE of the greatest possible or permitted amount or value ○ *visual effects with maximum impact* ○ *Maximum occupancy in this building is 235.* ■ *adv.* AT THE MAXIMUM at the maximum extent ○ *The hall seats 400 maximum.* [Mid-16thC. Directly or via French from modern Latin, a form of Latin *maximus* 'greatest' (used as a noun), from *magnus* 'great' (source of English *magnify*).]

maximum-minimum thermometer *n.* a special type of thermometer that logs the highest and lowest temperatures recorded during the period since it was last set

maximum-security *adj.* protected or made secure by the most extensive and elaborate security arrangements that are available or in current use ○ *a maximum-security jail*

maxixe /mə shéesh, mak séeks/ *n.* **1.** DANCE BRAZILIAN DANCE a Brazilian dance performed in duple time **2.** MUSIC MUSIC FOR MAXIXE music suitable for a maxixe [Early 20thC. From Brazilian Portuguese.]

maxwell /máks wel/ *n.* the centimetre-gram-second unit of magnetic flux, equal to the flux over one square centimetre perpendicular to a magnetic field of one gauss. Symbol **Mx** [Late 19thC. Named after James Clerk *Maxwell* (1831–79), a Scottish physicist.]

Maxwell /máks wel, mákswəl/, **James Clerk** (1831–79) British physicist. He did revolutionary work on electromagnetic fields and the electromagnetic theory of light.

may[1] /may/ (**may, might** /mīt/) CORE MEANING: a modal verb indicating that sth could be true, or could have happened, or will possibly happen in the future ○ *I may not be able to meet you.* ○ *He may have been working too hard.* ○ *A verdict may be announced today.*
v. **1.** INDICATES POSSIBILITY indicates that sth is possibly true ○ *I may have left my book on the bus.* **2.** INDICATES THAT STH COULD HAPPEN indicates that sth could have happened, or could happen in the future ○ *The crash may well have been caused by faulty brakes.* ○ *The comet may be remembered best for its nonscientific impact.* **3.** INDICATES PERMISSION indicates that sb is asking sb for permission or giving sb permission to do sth (*formal*) ○ *'May I leave the table'? 'No, you may not'.* **4.** INDICATES A RIGHT indicates that sb has a legal or moral right to do sth ○ *You may withdraw money from this account at any time.* **5.** INDICATES REQUESTS OR SUGGESTIONS indicates polite requests, suggestions, or offers ○ *May I remind you of our earlier agreement?* ○ *May I help you with that bag?* **6.** INDICATES A WISH indicates that sb wishes for sth very strongly (*formal*) ○ *May God bless us, every one.* [Old English *mæg*, a form of *magan* 'to be able'. Ultimately from an Indo-European base that is also the source of English *machine* and *magic*.] ◇ **come what may** whatever happens ○ *He swore that, come what may, he would never let her out of his sight again.*

— WORD KEY: USAGE —
See Usage note at **can**.

may[2] /may/ *n.* **1.** TREES = hawthorn **2.** = **may blossom** [From MAY, this being the month in which it comes into flower]

may[3] /may/ *n.* a maiden (*archaic*) [Old English *mæg*, and later also from Old Norse *mær*. Ultimately from a prehistoric Germanic base meaning 'young person (of either sex)', which is also the ancestor of English *maiden*.]

May *n.* in the Gregorian calendar, the fifth month of the year, made up of 31 days [12thC. Via French *mai* from Latin *Maius*, a form of *Maia* 'Maia' (a fertility goddess).]

May, Cape /may/ cape at the southern tip of New Jersey, at the entrance to Delaware Bay

maya /mí ə/ *n.* **1.** ILLUSION OF MATERIAL WORLD in Hinduism, the material world, considered in reality to be an illusion **2.** ABILITY TO CREATE ILLUSION in Hinduism, the ability to create illusion through supernatural, magical, or sacred power [Late 18thC. From Sanskrit *māyā*.] —**mayan** *adj.*

Maya[1] /mí ə/ (*plural* **-ya** *or* **-yas**) *n.* **1.** PEOPLES MEMBER OF A CENTRAL AMERICAN PEOPLE a member of a Native American people of Central America and southern Mexico whose classical culture featured highly developed mathematics, religion, writing, and monumental architecture. It flourished from the 4th to the 8th centuryAD, and was in decline by the 12th century. **2.** LANG NATIVE AMERICAN LANGUAGE a Mayan language spoken in parts of Mexico, Guatemala, and Belize. Maya is spoken by about half a million people. [Early 19thC. Via Spanish from Maya.] —**Maya** *adj.*

Maya[2] /mí ə/ *n.* the mother of the Buddha, by a miraculous virgin birth

Vladimir Mayakovsky

Mayakovsky /mí ə kófski/, **Vladimir** (1893–1930) Russian poet and propagandist. He wrote propaganda for the Bolsheviks after the Russian Revolution, but later fell from favour and committed suicide. Full name **Vladimir Vladimirovich Mayakovsky**

Mayan /mí ən/ *adj.* OF THE MAYA relating to the Maya, their classical culture, or their language ■ *n.* **1.** PEOPLES MEMBER OF THE MAYA a member of the Maya people **2.** LANG GROUP OF CENTRAL AMERICAN LANGUAGES a group of Native Middle American languages spoken in parts of Mexico, Guatemala, and Belize. It forms a branch of the Penutian family of languages.

Mayapán /mí ə pán/ ruined ancient Mayan city in southeastern Mexico, in Yucatan State

May apple *n.* **1.** PLANT WITH A SINGLE YELLOW FRUIT a plant of the barberry family that grows in eastern North America. It has a single white flower that produces an oval yellowish fruit with edible pulp. Other parts of the plant, notably the roots, leaves, and seeds, are poisonous. Latin name: *Podophyllum peltatum.* **2.** FRUIT OF MAY APPLE PLANT the edible fruit of the May apple plant [Because the fruit is produced in the month of May]

maybe /máybi, máy bee/ *adv.* **1.** PERHAPS expresses uncertainty ○ *I'm being too optimistic, but I really think we can get the best players.* **2.** NEITHER YES NOR NO used to give a response that is neither yes nor no ○ *'So do you want to come with us or not?' 'Well, maybe'.* **3.** INTRODUCES SUGGESTIONS used to introduce advice or suggestions ○ *Maybe you should ask her what she means before you jump to conclusions.* **4.** APPROXIMATELY indicates an approximate estimation, e.g. of frequency or a number ○ *The coastal glacier gives off large icebergs maybe every three or four years.* ○ *The forests in this region are no more*

than 60, maybe 70, years old. [14thC. From the phrase (*it*) *may be.*]

May beetle *n.* **1.** = cockchafer **2.** = June bug [Because they appear in late spring]

may blossom *n.* the flower of the hawthorn

May bug *n.* **1.** = cockchafer **2.** = June bug [See MAY BEETLE]

mayday /máy day/ *n.* the internationally recognized communications distress call, used especially by ships and aircraft [Early 20thC. Representing the pronunciation of French *m'aider* in *venez m'aider* 'come and help me'!]

May Day *n.* **1.** SPRING FESTIVAL the first of May, traditionally a time for celebrating the coming of spring, often with dancing round a maypole, sports, and other festivities **2.** HOLIDAY IN RECOGNITION OF WORKERS the first of May, a national holiday in some countries in recognition of the importance of workers, a time when workers march and demonstrate to show their solidarity. It is called Labour Day in many countries, but in the United States Labor Day is in early September.

Mayer /mí ər/, **Sir Robert** (1879–1985) German-born British businessman and philanthropist. He founded the London Philharmonic Orchestra (1923) with Sir Thomas Beecham and promoted concerts for young people.

mayest *v.* = mayst

mayflower /máy flowər/ (*plural* **-ers** *or* **-er**) *n.* **1.** PLANT THAT FLOWERS IN MAY any of various plants that flower in May, including the cowslip and marsh marigold **2.** HAWTHORN FLOWER the flower of the hawthorn

mayfly /máy flī/ (*plural* **-flies**) *n.* **1.** INSECTS SHORT-LIVED INSECT any one of various insects that live as adults for only a few days, typically having two or four pairs of flimsy wings and two or three long slender tail appendages. The female lays her eggs in fresh water, where the larvae develop without a chrysalis stage. Order: Ephemeroptera. **2.** ANGLING FISHING FLY a fishing fly that looks like a mayfly [Mid-17thC. From a mistaken belief that they appear only in May.]

mayhap /máy hap/ *adv.* perhaps (*archaic*) [Mid-16thC. From the phrase *it may hap* 'it may happen (by chance)'.]

mayhem /máy hem/, **maihem** *n.* **1.** CHAOS absolute chaos or severe disruption (*informal*) ○ *Whenever the teacher left the room, it was mayhem.* **2.** LAW DISABLING OF SB under old common law, the disabling or deprivation of a limb or other body part, with the result that the victim is unable to offer any defence or fight his or her adversary (*archaic*) [15thC. Via Anglo-Norman *mahem* and Old French *mahaing* 'mutilating injury' (the original sense in English), from, ultimately, assumed Vulgar Latin *mahagnare* 'to injure' (source also of English *maim*).]

Mayhew /máy hyoo/, **Henry** (1812–87) British writer and editor. His book *London Labour and the London Poor* (1851–62) influenced social policy.

maying /máying/, **Maying** *n.* May Day celebrations, or participation in them

mayn't /maynt, máyənt/ *contr.* may not

mayo /máyō/ (*plural* **-os**) *n.* mayonnaise (*informal*) [Mid-20thC. Shortening.]

Mayo /máy yō/ county in Connacht Province, northwestern Republic of Ireland. Castlebar is the county town. Population: 111,395 (1996). Area: 5,398 sq. km/2,084 sq. mi.

mayonnaise /máy ə náyz/ *n.* a rich creamy sauce or dressing made from egg yolks, vegetable oil, vinegar, lemon juice, and spices, and served with salads, sandwiches, and other foods [Early 19thC. Origin uncertain: probably from French.]

— WORD KEY: ORIGIN —
There are several conflicting theories about the origin of *mayonnaise*, among them that it is an alteration of *bayonnaise*, as if the sauce originated in Bayonne, in southwestern France; that it was derived from the French verb *manier* 'to stir'; and that it goes back to Old French *mayou* 'egg yolk'. But the early variant spelling *mahonnaise* suggests that it originally meant literally 'of Mahon', and that the sauce was so named to commemorate the taking of Port Mahon, the capital of the island of Minorca, by the duc de Richelieu in 1756.

Mayon Volcano /ma yŏn̄-/ active volcano in the northeastern Philippines, on Luzon Island, beside the city of Legaspi. Height: 2,421 m/7,943 ft.

mayor /mair/ *n.* the person elected to be head of government in a city, town, or borough in many countries including the United States, and in the United Kingdom except for Scotland [13thC. Via French *maire* from Latin *major*, literally 'more great' (source also of English *major*), from *magnus* 'great' (source of English *maximum*).] —**mayoral** *adj.* —**mayorship** *n.*

—— **WORD KEY: CULTURAL NOTE** ——
The Mayor of Casterbridge, a novel by writer Thomas Hardy (1886). It is the tragic story of Michael Henchard, a labourer whose success in business raises him to the position of mayor of his home town, but who then loses his fortune as a result of a petty dispute with his assistant. An instructive character study, it is also a revealing portrait of contemporary rural mores.

mayoralty /máirəlti/ (*plural* **-ties**) *n.* **1.** MAYOR'S OFFICIAL POSITION the official position held by a mayor **2.** MAYOR'S PERIOD IN OFFICE the length of time that a mayor holds office ○ *a five-year mayoralty*

mayoress /máir ress/ *n.* **1.** HEAD OF CITY OR TOWN GOVERNMENT a woman elected to be head of government in a city, town, or borough in many countries including the United States, and in the United Kingdom except for Scotland (*dated*) **2.** WIFE OF A MAYOR the wife of a mayor or a woman chosen to assist an unmarried mayor at a social function

Mayotte /ma yáwt/ island in the western Indian Ocean near Madagascar, an overseas dependency of France. One of the Comoros islands, it stayed under French control when the remaining islands declared independence in 1975. Language: French. Currency: French franc. Capital: Mamoudzou. Population: 108,000 (1996). Area: 373 sq. km/144 sq. mi.

maypole /máy pōl/ *n.* a tall pole that is traditionally erected for May Day celebrations, usually decorated with flowers and with long coloured ribbons attached at the top. Dancers each take hold of the end of a ribbon and dance round the pole so that the ribbons become wrapped around the pole, forming coloured patterns.

May queen *n.* a young woman chosen, often for her beauty and charm, to reign over a May Day celebration

mayst /mayst/, **mayest** /máyist/ *v.* 2nd person present singular of **may**[1] (*archaic*)

may tree *n.* = hawthorn

mayweed /máy weed/ *n.* a straggly weed of the daisy family that has foul-smelling leaves and white flowers resembling daisies. Latin name: *Anthemis cotula*. [Mid-16thC. *May* an alteration of earlier *maythe* 'mayweed, camomile', from Old English *magope*.]

mazaltov, mazal tov *interj.* = mazeltov

Mazarin /mázərin/, **Jules, Cardinal** (1602–61) Italian-born French clergyman and statesman. He virtually governed France during the minority of Louis XIV, when his absolutist policies resulted in the anti-royalist rebellions known as the Fronde (1648–53). He negotiated the Peace of Westphalia (1648) and the Treaty of the Pyrenees (1659), ending major European wars. Born **Giulio Raimondo Mazzarino**

Mazatlán /máthat lán/ city, seaport, and tourist resort in western Mexico. Population: 314,345 (1990).

Mazdaism /mázdə izəm/, **Mazdeism** *n.* RELIG = Zoroastrianism [Late 19thC. Formed from Avestan *mazdā*, from *Ahura Mazda*, the name of the supreme god of ancient Persian religion.]

maze /mayz/ *n.* **1.** PUZZLE MADE OF CONNECTING PATHS an area of interconnected weaving paths that it is difficult to find a way through, especially one in a garden with hedges between the paths or one designed for laboratory animals **2.** ROUTE TRACING PUZZLE a diagrammatic version of a maze, where the object is to arrive at a specific point by tracing a route with a pen or pencil **3.** CONFUSING NETWORK OF PATHS a network, especially of paths, streets, or passageways, that a walker or driver might easily become lost in ○ *a maze of narrow cobbled streets* **4.** CONFUSING MUDDLE any confusing tangle or muddle, e.g. of regulations or procedures, that is difficult to negotiate ○ *a maze of official rules* ■ *vt.* (**mazes, mazing, mazed**) *Southern US, UK* ASTONISH SB to astonish, stun, or stupefy sb (*regional*) [13thC. Shortening of AMAZE, originally in the sense 'to stupefy, daze'.]

mazeltov /mázz'l tov/, **mazel tov, mazaltov, mazal tov** *interj.* used to express good wishes or congratulations [Mid-19thC. From modern Hebrew *mazzāl tŏb*, literally 'good star'.]

Mazer

mazer /máyzər/ *n.* a large drinking cup or bowl, usually made from hardwood or metal (*archaic*) [13thC. Via Old French *masere* 'kind of hardwood, maple', and perhaps reinforced by Middle Dutch *maeser* 'maple', from prehistoric Germanic. Originally, 'hardwood (such as maple) for making cups'.]

mazourka *n.* = mazurka

mazuma /mə zoomə/ *n.* money, especially cash or loose change (*informal*) [20th C. From Yiddish.]

mazurka /mə zúrkə/, **mazourka** *n.* **1.** DANCE LIVELY POLISH DANCE a Polish national dance, similar to the polka **2.** MUSIC MUSIC FOR A MAZURKA a piece of music composed for or suitable for the mazurka, usually in three-four time and having several repeated sections [Early 19thC. Origin uncertain: probably via Russian from Polish *mazurek* 'dance of an inhabitant of Mazovia (an ancient part of Poland)', from *mazur* 'inhabitant of Mazovia'.]

mazy /máyzi/ (**-ier, -iest**) *adj.* **1.** LIKE A MAZE tangled and interwoven like a maze **2.** CONFUSING confusing or complicated **3.** GIDDY giddy or confused (*archaic or literary*) —**mazily** *adv.* —**maziness** *n.*

mazzard /mázzərd/ *n.* **1.** TREES WILD CHERRY TREE a wild sweet cherry tree that fruit growers often use as grafting stock for cultivated varieties of cherry. Latin name: *Prunus avium*. **2.** HOUSEHOLD = mazer (*archaic*) [Late 16thC. Origin uncertain.]

mb *abbr.* millibar

MB *abbr.* **1.** Bachelor of Medicine **2.** COMPUT megabyte **3.** Medal of Bravery

MBA *abbr.* Master of Business Administration

Mbabane /əmba báani/ town and capital of Swaziland, located in the western part of the country near the border with South Africa. Population: 42,000 (1992).

mbaqanga /əm baa káng gə/ *n. S Africa* a rhythmical type of southern African popular music [Origin uncertain: perhaps from Zulu *umbaqanga* 'mixture']

MBE *abbr.* Member of the Order of the British Empire

mbira /əm beérə/ *n.* an African musical instrument that has a resonating box which is often a hollow gourd, with tuned strips of wood or metal attached to it that are plucked using the thumbs [Late 19thC. From Bantu.]

MBO *abbr.* **1.** management by objectives **2.** management buyout

Mbps *abbr.* megabytes per second

Mbuji-Mayi /əmboójə mī i/ town in south-central Democratic Republic of the Congo, the capital of Kasai-Oriental Region. Population: 806,475 (1994).

Mbyte /ém bīt/ *abbr.* COMPUT megabyte

mc *abbr.* millicurie

MC *abbr.* **1.** master of ceremonies **2.** Medical Corps **3.** Midheaven **4.** Military Cross

McAdam /mə káddəm/, **John Loudon** (1756–1836) British inventor and engineer. He developed an innovative method of road construction known as macadamization, in which foundations were raised to effect drainage.

McBride /mək brīd/, **Willie John** (*b.* 1940) Irish rugby union player. He became captain of Ireland and of the British Lions, and manager of the British Lions in 1983.

MCC *abbr.* Marylebone Cricket Club

McCahon /mə káa ən/, **Colin John** (1919–87) New Zealand painter. He produced works whose subjects include religious paintings, expressionistic landscapes, and 'word paintings' incorporating biblical and Maori texts.

McCarthy /mə káothi/, **Joseph R.** (1908–57) US politician. A Republican US senator (1947–57), he instigated highly publicized Senate hearings in the early 1950s into Communist subversion of the US government. His often unsubstantiated charges and extreme methods led to a Senate censure, and the period is often referred to as 'the McCarthy era'. Full name **Joseph Raymond McCarthy**

McCarthyism /mə káarthi izəm/ *n.* **1.** PUBLIC ACCUSATION OF COMMUNIST SYMPATHIES the practice of publicly accusing sb, especially sb in government or the media, of subversive or Communist activities or sympathies, especially without real evidence to substantiate this **2.** UNFAIR ACCUSATION OR INVESTIGATION OF PEOPLE the practice of using unsubstantiated accusations or unfair methods of investigation to discredit people [Mid-20thC. Named after Joseph R. McCARTHY, who pursued this policy.] —**McCarthyist** *n.*, *adj.* —**McCarthyite** *n.*, *adj.*

McCartney /mə káartni/, **Sir Paul** (*b.* 1942) British singer and songwriter. He was a founder member, singer, and bass guitarist of the *Beatles* (1959–70), cowriting most of their songs with John Lennon. He later formed the band Wings (1971–81) with his wife, Linda. Full name **Sir James Paul McCartney**

McColgan /mə kólgən/, **Liz** (*b.* 1964) British cross-country and marathon runner. An Olympic medallist, winning the New York (1991) and Tokyo (1992) marathons, she set a world indoor record for 5,000 m (1992). Born **Elizabeth Lynch**

McCoy /mə kóy/ [Early 20thC. Origin uncertain: perhaps an alteration of *Mackay*, as the title of the chief of a branch of the Mackay clan, whose leadership was regularly disputed.] ◇ **the real McCoy** sb or sth that is genuine (*informal*)

—— **WORD KEY: ORIGIN** ——
Among the suggested origins of the phrase **the real McCoy** are that it may be an alteration of *the Reay Mackay*, a title applied to Lord *Reay*, the name of the chief of the northern branch of the Scots *Mackay* clan, the leadership of which was disputed by various branch factions; that it may be from Mackay, a whisky named after its makers A. and M. *Mackay* of Glasgow (once referred to as *the clear McCoy*); and that it may be from the professional name of the US welterweight boxing champion Kid *McCoy* (real name Norman Selby (1873–1940), so named to distinguish himself from another boxer of the same name.

McCubbin /mə kúbbin/, **Frederick** (1855–1917) Australian painter. He was one of the founders of the impressionist Heidelberg School. Many of his works, such as *The Pioneer* (1904), depict the lives of early settlers in Australia.

McCullough /mə kúllək, -əkh/, **Colleen Margaretta** (*b.* 1937) Australian novelist. Her novel *The Thorn Birds* (1977) was an international best-seller.

McEnroe /mákənrō/, **John** (*b.* 1959) US tennis player. He was four times winner of the US Open (1979, 1980, 1981, and 1984) and won the Wimbledon men's singles title three times (1981, 1983, and 1984). Full name **John Patrick McEnroe, Jr.**

McEwen /mə kyoó ən/, **Sir John** (1900–80) Australian statesman. A Country Party politician, he was deputy prime minister (1958–71), and caretaker prime minister of Australia (1967–68).

MCG *abbr.* Melbourne Cricket Ground

McGrath /mə graáth, -gráth/, **John** (*b.* 1935) British playwright. Founder of the 7:84 company (1971), he distanced himself from the theatrical establishment by his political stance.

McGraw /mə gráw/, **John Joseph** (1873–1934) US baseball manager. He led the New York Giants (1902–32) to three World Series titles (1905, 1921–22). Known as **Little Napoleon**

MCh *abbr.* Master of Surgery [Latin, *Magister chirurgiae*]

McIndoe /mákindō/, **Sir Archibald Hector** (1900–60) New Zealand plastic surgeon. He was renowned for his pioneering work on injured airmen during the Battle of Britain. His patients were known as the Guinea Pig Club.

McKay /mə kí/, **Heather Pamela** (b. 1941) Australian squash player. She was winner of the women's world championship in 1975 and 1979.

McKenna /mə kénnə/, **Siobhan** (1923–86) Irish stage and film actress. She was noted for her interpretation of the title role in *St Joan* by George Bernard Shaw. She also worked in film and television.

McKenzie /mə kénzi/, **Sir John** (1838–1901) Scottish-born New Zealand politician. Minister of lands and agriculture (1891–1900), he was a prominent defender of the rights of small farmers and promoter of scientific agricultural methods.

Mount McKinley

McKinley, Mount /mə kínnli/ the highest mountain in North America, in Denali National Park and Preserve, south-central Alaska. Height: 6,194 m/20,320 ft.

William McKinley

McKinley, William (1843–1901) US statesman and 25th president of the United States (1897–1901). Shortly after election to his second term he was assassinated by anarchist Leon Czolgosz.

McLaren /mə klárrən/, **Bruce Leslie** (1937–70) New Zealand motor racing driver. Runner-up in the 1960 Formula 1 world championship, he founded the McLaren Grand Prix racing team (1963).

McLuhan /mə klóoən/, **Marshall** (1911–80) Canadian-born US critic and theorist. His writings dealt with the effects of media technology on the public. Full name **Herbert Marshall McLuhan**

McMahon /mək maá ən/, **Sir William** (1908–88) Australian statesman. He was a Liberal Party politician and prime minister of Australia (1971–72).

McMurdo Sound /mək mÚrdō/ bay in eastern Antarctica, in the southern Ross Sea. It is in the south of the Pacific Ocean.

McNaughten Rules /mək náwtən-/ *npl.* in English law, a legal ruling establishing that a defence of insanity depends on proving that the defendant was unaware or unable to understand that wrong was being done [Mid-19thC. Named after McNaughten, in the case Regina vs McNaughten, on which the rules are based.]

MCom *abbr.* Master of Commerce

MCP *abbr.* male chauvinist pig (*informal insult*)

McQueen /mə kweén/, **Steve** (1930–80) US actor. He achieved his greatest success in tough-guy and loner roles in films such as *The Magnificent Seven* (1960) and *Bullitt* (1968). Full name **Terence Steven McQueen**

Md *symbol.* mendelevium

MD *abbr.* **1.** managing director **2.** Doctor of Medicine **3.** BANKING memorandum of deposit **4.** muscular dystrophy **5.** musical director

Md. *abbr.* Maryland

m/d, M/d *abbr.* months after date

M/d *abbr.* COMM months after date

MDF *abbr.* medium density fibreboard

MDiv *abbr.* Master of Divinity

Mdm *abbr.* Madam

MDMA *n.* the drug Ecstasy. Full form **methylenedioxymethamphetamine**

MDS *abbr.* Master of Dental Surgery

mdse *abbr.* merchandise

me[1] *(stressed)* /meé/; *(unstressed)* /mi/ *pron.* **1.** THE SPEAKER OR WRITER used to refer to the speaker or writer ○ *asked her to do me a big favour* ○ *Listen to me!* ○ *Was it me?* **2.** PERSONALITY OF THE SPEAKER OR WRITER used to refer to the personality of the speaker or writer, or sth that may express it (*informal*) ○ *I don't think I like this hat; it isn't really me.* **3.** US MYSELF myself (*informal*) ○ *I'll get me a new boyfriend– see if I don't.* [Old English mē, me. Ultimately from an Indo-European word that is also the ancestor of English *mine*, French *me*, Greek *me*, *emé*, Welsh and Irish *mi*, and German *mich*.]

me[2] *n.* MUSIC = **mi**

Me *symbol.* methyl

ME *n.* ILLNESS INVOLVING EXHAUSTION AND WEAKNESS an illness without a known cause that is characterized by long-term exhaustion, muscle weakness, depression, and sleep disturbances, possibly as a reaction to a viral infection in sb already debilitated. Full form **myalgic encephalomyelitis** ■ *abbr.* **1.** Middle English **2.** mechanical engineer **3.** Methodist Episcopal **4.** mining engineer **5.** Most Excellent

Me. *abbr.* Maine

mea culpa /máy ə kóolpə/ *interj.* EXPRESSING GUILT OR FAULT used to express an admission of your own guilt (*formal or humorous*) ■ *n.* FORMAL APOLOGY a formal apology or acknowledgment of responsibility or guilt ○ *His grudging mea culpa failed to soothe feelings.* [From Latin, literally '(through) my fault', these words being taken from the prayer of confession in the Roman Catholic Church's Latin liturgy]

mead[1] /meed/ *n.* an alcoholic drink made by fermenting honey with water, often with added spices [Old English me(o)du. Ultimately from an Indo-European word meaning 'honey, sweet drink', which is also the ancestor of Greek *methu* 'wine' (source of English *amethyst*).]

mead[2] /meed/ *n.* a meadow (*archaic or literary*) [Old English mæd (see MEADOW)]

Margaret Mead

Mead /meed/, **Margaret** (1901–78) US anthropologist. In such influential books as *Coming of Age in Samoa* (1928) she formalized her field work research on child care, adolescence, and sexual behaviour in North American society and nonindustrial societies.

Meade /meed/, **George Gordon** (1815–72) US Union general. He commanded the Army of the Potomac (1863–65) in the American Civil War.

Meade, James Edward (b. 1907) British economist. His writings on international economic policy were very influential. He won a Nobel Prize in economics (1977).

meadow /méddō/ *n.* **1.** GRASSY FIELD a grassy field used for producing hay or for grazing domestic livestock **2.** GRASSY AREA an area of low-lying grassland, especially a marshy one near a river [Old English mædwe, a form of mæd, from, ultimately, an Indo-European base meaning 'to cut grass with a scythe', which is also the ancestor of English *mow*] —**meadowy** *adj.*

meadow brown *n.* a very common brown butterfly that lives in grassy places throughout Europe. The female has an orange tinge to the underside of her wings. Latin name: *Maniola jurtina*.

meadow fern *n.* = **sweet gale**

meadow fescue *n.* a perennial grass that grows throughout Europe and Asia and has shiny leaves and stem bases that are surrounded by brown sheaths. Latin name: *Festuca pratensis*.

meadow grasshopper *n.* a large green grasshopper with delicate wings that look like leaves and help it to remain concealed among foliage. Latin name: *Tettigonia viridissima*.

meadowland /méddō land/ *n.* a large area of land that is made up of meadows

meadowlark /méddō laark/ (*plural* **-larks** *or* **-lark**) *n.* either of two related North American songbirds of the blackbird family that have brown speckled feathers, a yellow breast, and a black crescent-shaped mark just under the bill. Genus: *Sturnella*.

meadow mouse *n.* a field mouse or vole

meadow mushroom *n.* an edible mushroom that grows in European grassland. It has a white cap, a white stem, and pink gills that turn to brown as it matures. Latin name: *Agaricus campestris*.

meadow nematode *n.* any of several parasitic nematode worms that infest and destroy the roots of plants. Genus: *Pratylenchus*.

meadow pipit *n.* a common small songbird related to the wagtails, with brown speckled feathers. It lives in a wide variety of habitats from Greenland to central Asia and builds a concealed, cup-shaped, woven grass nest on the ground. Latin name: *Anthus pratensis*.

meadow rue *n.* any of several plants related to the buttercup, with small yellow flowers. They grow in Northern temperate zones. Genus: *Thalictrum*.

meadow saffron *n.* = **colchicum**

meadowsweet /méddō sweet/ (*plural* **-sweets** *or* **-sweet**) *n.* **1.** EUROPEAN PLANT WITH CREAMY-WHITE FLOWERS a tall European perennial plant of the rose family that grows in damp and marshy places and has clusters of tiny creamy-white flowers with a sweet smell. Latin name: *Filipendula ulmaria.* ◊ dropwort **2.** N AMERICAN PLANT any of several North American plants of the rose family that have clusters of small white flowers. Genus: *Spiraea*.

Meads /meedz/, **Colin** (b. 1936) New Zealand rugby union player. His 15-year career set a record as the longest of any member of the All Blacks.

meager *adj.* US = **meagre**

meagre /meégər/ *adj.* **1.** UNSATISFACTORILY SMALL unsatisfactory in quantity, substance, or size ○ *a company that is notorious for paying meagre salaries* **2.** OF BAD QUALITY bad and unsatisfying in quality, strength, or effectiveness ○ *The street outside my window furnished meagre entertainment.* **3.** THIN very thin, especially through malnutrition or illness [14thC. Via Anglo-Norman *megre*, French *maigre* 'lean, thin', from Latin *macr*-, the stem of *macer* (source of English *emaciate*).]

meal[1] /meel/ *n.* **1.** FOOD EATEN AT ONE TIME a substantial amount of food, often more than one course, that is provided and eaten at one time **2.** TIME FOR EATING FOOD any of the usual occasions, e.g. breakfast or lunch, when a substantial amount of food is provided and eaten [Old English *mæl* 'measure, mealtime'. Ultimately from a prehistoric Germanic word, ancestor also of German *mal* 'time, occasion'.] ◇ **make a meal of sth 1.** to put more time or effort into sth than is usual or necessary (*informal*) **2.** to exaggerate the importance, intensity, or severity of sth (*informal*)

meal² /meel/ *n.* **1.** GROUND GRAIN the edible part of a cereal crop that has been ground to a powder **2.** GROUND-UP SUBSTANCE any substance ground to a fine or coarse powder ○ *fish meal* **3.** *Scotland* GROUND OATS ground oats, especially when used to make porridge [Old English *melu*. Ultimately from an Indo-European base meaning 'to crush, grind', which is also the ancestor of English *maul*, *mill*, and *molar*.]

mealie /meeli/ *n. S Africa* an ear of maize. ◇ **mealies** [Early 19thC. Via Afrikaans *mielie* from, ultimately, Latin *milium* (see MILLET).]

mealie pap *n. S Africa* a type of porridge made from ground maize [*Pap* via Afrikaans *pap* 'porridge', from, ultimately, Latin *papa* (see PAP).]

mealie pudding *n. Scotland* = **white pudding** [Because it is made from oatmeal]

meals on wheels *n.* a service, usually provided by a social work department or charity, whereby hot meals are brought to senior citizens, disabled people, or housebound people (*takes a singular verb*)

meal ticket *n.* **1.** DEPENDABLE SOURCE OF MONEY OR SUPPORT sb who or sth that can be counted on, or is exploited for financial gain or support (*informal*) **2.** VOUCHER FOR MEAL a voucher that entitles the holder to a meal

mealtime /meel tīm/ *n.* the time when a meal is usually or regularly served

mealworm /meel wurm/ (*plural* **-worms** *or* **-worm**) *n.* the larva of various beetles that feeds on stored grain or flour and can cause severe damage and loss. Genus: *Tenebrio*.

mealy /meeli/ (**-ier**, **-iest**) *adj.* **1.** LIKE MEAL powdery or granular, like meal or grain ○ *mealy potatoes* **2.** MADE OF MEAL containing, made of, or covered with meal **3.** DAPPLED with a spotted or dappled hide or coat **4.** PALE exceptionally pale, especially through malnutrition or illness —**mealiness** *n.*

mealy bug *n.* any of various scale insects that are covered with a white powdery secretion and feed on plants, often causing significant damage to citrus crops and greenhouse plants. Family: Pseudococcidae.

mealy-mouthed *adj.* wary of speaking plainly or openly, especially of admitting unpleasant truths (*disapproving*)

mean¹ /meen/ (**means**, **meaning**, **meant** /ment/) *vt.* ◇ MEANS **1.** HAVE A PARTICULAR SENSE to indicate or represent a particular sense ○ *I don't know what half these words mean.* ○ *When he raises his hand, it means he's making a bid.* **2.** INTEND TO EXPRESS STH to intend or be intended to express a particular idea in speech or writing ○ *That's not quite what I meant.* ○ *Just what's that supposed to mean?* **3.** INTEND TO DO STH to have an intention to do sth ○ *I didn't mean to upset you.* ○ *I've been meaning to call you for weeks.* **4.** EXPRESS AN OPINION OR INTENTION to be expressing a definite opinion or intention in what you say ○ *She says she's resigning, and I think this time she means it.* **5.** BE A CAUSE OR SIGN OF STH to be a cause or indication of sth ○ *The strike will mean a hard winter for many families.* ○ *A red sunset means fine weather.* **6.** GO WITH STH to accompany or be associated with sth ○ *For Sam, summer meant golf.* [Old English *mænan*. Ultimately from an Indo-European base that is also the ancestor of English *mind*.]

mean² /meen/ *adj.* **1.** UNKIND unkind or malicious ○ *You hurt her feelings – that was a mean thing to do.* **2.** NOT GENEROUS unwilling to spend money on other people ○ *the meanest person I know* **3.** US CRUEL cruel and bad-tempered ○ *He can be pretty mean at times.* **4.** SHABBY shabby and poor-looking ○ *streets full of small mean houses* **5.** US EXCELLENT excellent or skilful (*informal*) ○ *He plays a mean sax.* **6.** HUMBLE of low social position (*archaic*) ○ *living among the poor and mean* **7.** UNCOMFORTABLE uncomfortable or disagreeable ○ *This is the meanest climate I've ever lived in.* [Old

English *mæne*, from *gemæne* 'shared by everyone'. Ultimately from a prehistoric Germanic word (ancestor also of German *gemein*). The modern sense evolved via 'inferior'.]

mean³ /meen/ *n.* ◇ **means 1.** MATH INTERMEDIATE VALUE a value that is intermediate between other values, e.g. an average or expected value **2.** MATH MEDIUM TERM OF A PROPORTION either the second or third term of a proportion **3.** MIDDLE WAY a medium or moderate alternative or course of action, in the middle of a range of possibilities ○ *We need to find the mean between these extremes.* ■ *adj.* ◇ **means 1.** MEDIUM medium or intermediate in size, strength, or quality **2.** IN AN INTERMEDIATE POSITION occupying an intermediate position in a range ○ *Speech was achieved in 74.3% of patients within a mean time interval of 63 days.* [14thC. Via Old French *meien* from Latin *medianus* (see MEDIAN).]

Meander

meander /mi ándər/ *vi.* (**-ders**, **-dering**, **-dered**) **1.** FOLLOW A TWISTING ROUTE to follow an indirect route or course, especially one with a series of twists and turns ○ *The river meanders to the sea.* **2.** WANDER SLOWLY AND AIMLESSLY to move in a leisurely way, especially for pleasure or because of a lack of motivation ○ *meandering through the park* ■ *n.* **1.** RELAXED WALK a slow leisurely walk or journey ○ *We went for a meander in the woods.* **2.** TWIST OR BEND a twist or bend in sth, especially a river, path, or street **3.** TWISTING ROUTE an indirect course or route, especially one that twists and turns ○ *We followed the meanders of the path.* **4.** ARTS ORNAMENTAL DESIGN an ornamental design, popular in ancient Greek art and architecture, made by a continuous line that forms square shapes by doubling back on itself [Late 16thC. Directly or via French from Latin, 'winding course', from Greek *maiandros*, from the name of a river (now called the Büyük Menderes) in Turkey.] —**meanderer** *n.* —**meanderingly** *adv.* —**meandrous** /mi ándrəss/ *adj.*

mean deviation *n.* in statistics, the mean of the absolute values of the differences between individual values and the mean or median, used as a measure of dispersion

mean distance *n.* the average distance between an orbiting celestial object and the object it is orbiting

mean free path *n.* the average distance a gas molecule travels before it collides with another molecule or the containing vessel. Symbol λ

meanie /meeni/, **meany** (*plural* **-ies**) *n.* an ungenerous or miserly person (*informal*)

meaning /meening/ *n.* **1.** WHAT STH MEANS what a word, sign, or symbol means ○ *Do you know the meaning*

of this word? **2.** WHAT SB WANTS TO EXPRESS what sb intends to express ○ *I want to make my meaning very clear.* **3.** WHAT STH SIGNIFIES what sth signifies or indicates ○ *I could not fathom the meaning of their glances.* **4.** INNER IMPORTANCE psychological or moral sense, purpose, or significance ○ *an empty life without meaning* ■ *adj.* SIGNIFICANT conveying a significance that is not directly expressed ○ *A meaning silence followed these words.*

meaningful /meeningf'l/ *adj.* **1.** WITH MEANING having a discernible meaning ○ *To me, that is not a meaningful expression.* **2.** SIGNIFICANT conveying a meaning or significance that is not directly expressed ○ *She gave me a meaningful glance.* **3.** ADDING VALUE TO LIFE adding significance, meaning, or purpose to sb's life ○ *I'm not claiming that we have a deep and meaningful relationship, but we do have fun.* —**meaningfully** *adv.* —**meaningfulness** *n.*

meaningless /meeningləss/ *adj.* **1.** WITHOUT MEANING having no discernible meaning ○ *a meaningless scrawl* **2.** WITHOUT PURPOSE lacking purpose or significance ○ *Offering to help now could be a meaningless gesture.* —**meaninglessly** *adv.* —**meaninglessness** *n.*

mean lethal dose *n.* SCI = **median lethal dose**

means /meenz/ *n.* STH ENABLING SB TO DO STH sth that is available and makes it possible for sb to do sth (*takes a singular or plural verb*) ○ *You can't live out there alone with no means of transport* ■ *npl.* AVAILABLE MONEY the money and other resources that sb has to live on ○ *It'll be impossible to find a house in this area that's within their means.* [From MEAN³] ◇ **by all means** used as a polite way to give permission ◇ **by no means** used to emphasize a negative ○ *You were by no means the worst player.*

mean sea level *n.* the sea level determined and used in mapmaking by the Ordnance Survey

means of production *npl.* in Marxism, the raw materials, tools, machinery, and other necessities required in the manufacturing process

mean solar day *n.* the constant interval between two successive transits of the mean sun across the meridian

mean-spirited *adj.* malicious or bad-tempered —**mean-spiritedly** *adv.* —**mean-spiritedness** *n.*

mean square *n.* the mean of the squares of a set of values

means test *n.* an examination of sb's income and savings, carried out in order to determine whether the criteria for a benefit or financial aid are met —**means testing** *n.*

mean sun *n.* in timekeeping, an imaginary sun that moves uniformly in the celestial equator taking the same time to complete a circuit as the real sun takes in the ecliptic

meant past participle, past tense of **mean¹**

mean time *n.* time measured with reference to the mean sun crossing a given meridian

meantime /meen tīm/ *n.* the intervening period of time between two events, or from now until sth else happens ○ *I'll start dinner now and in the meantime you can have an apple.* ○ *I'll come as soon as I can; just wait there for the meantime.* ○ *Repairs will be done tomorrow and meantime please don't use the sink.*

meanwhile /meen wīl/ *adv.* **1.** DURING A PERIOD during the period of time between two events ○ *I'll meet you later; meanwhile I'll leave you to your food.* **2.** WHILE STH IS HAPPENING at the same time as sth is happening ○ *I tried to keep everybody calm, meanwhile struggling to open the car door.*

meany *n.* = **meanie**

meas. *abbr.* **1.** measure **2.** measurement

measles /meez'lz/ *n.* **1.** CONTAGIOUS VIRAL DISEASE a very contagious acute viral disease with symptoms that include a high temperature, sore throat, and a bright red rash of small spots that spread to cover the whole body. The presence of small white spots, known as Koplik's spots, in the mouth on the inside of the cheeks a few days before the rash appears is often used as a diagnostic symptom of the disease. (*takes a singular or plural verb*) **2.** MEASLES SPOTS the spots that are characteristic of measles [14thC. Origin uncertain: probably from Middle Low German *masele* or Middle Dutch *masel* 'spot, blemish', and by folk etymology from earlier *mesel* 'leper'.]

measly /meézli/ (**-slier, -sliest**) *adj.* **1.** VERY LITTLE AND POINTLESS ridiculously or disappointingly small or inadequate (*informal*) ○ *He tipped me a measly 5p.* **2.** HAVING MEASLES infected with measles [The sense 'inadequate' evolved from 'infected with measles' via 'spotty']

measurable /mézhərəb'l/ *adj.* capable of being measured or perceived [13thC. Via French *mesurable* from late Latin *mensurabilis* (source of English *mensurable*), from, ultimately, Latin *mensura* (see MEASURE).] —**measurability** /mézhərə bílləti/ *n.* —**measurableness** /mézhərəb'l nəss/ *n.* —**measurably** *adv.*

measure /mézhər/ *n.* **1.** SIZE the size or extent of sth, especially in comparison with a known standard **2.** SYSTEM FOR DETERMINING SIZE a particular system used to determine the dimensions, area, volume, or weight of sth **3.** WAY OF EVALUATING a way of evaluating sth, or a standard against which sth can be compared **4.** ACTION TAKEN an action taken to make sth happen or prevent sth (*often used in the plural*) ○ *to take precautionary measures* **5.** UNIT IN A SYSTEM a unit in a system that is used to determine the dimensions, area, volume, or weight of sth (*often used in the plural*) **6.** STANDARD AMOUNT OF STH a standard amount of sth, e.g. of a spirit poured into a glass for drinking **7.** STH USED TO DETERMINE QUANTITY sth used to determine a quantity, e.g. a ruler, or a spoon or small container that holds a known volume **8.** STANDARD USED FOR DETERMINING SIZE a standard used for determining the dimensions, area, volume, or weight of sth **9.** DEGREE OF STH an extent or amount that is limited, appropriate, or has its size specified ○ *Their help contributed in no small measure to our success.* **10.** LIMITS a limit or limits, especially one that is reasonable or appropriate ○ *His rage had no measure.* **11.** LAW LAW a bill to be enacted into law, or a law that has been enacted **12.** POETRY POETIC METRE the rhythm or metre of a piece of poetry **13.** POETRY METRICAL FOOT a foot or unit of metre in poetry **14.** PRINTING WIDTH OF TYPE AREA the width of the type area on a page or in a column ○ *In unjustified typesetting, not all lines extend to the full measure.* **15.** DANCE a dance (*archaic*) ■ **measures** *npl.* MINING, GEOL ROCK LAYERS strata of rock, especially when they contain a particular material ■ *v.* (**-ures, -uring, -ured**) **1.** *vt.* FIND SIZE, LENGTH, QUANTITY, OR RATE to find out the size, length, quantity, or rate of sth using a suitable instrument or device **2.** *vt.* ASSESS EFFECT OR QUALITY to assess the effect or quality of sth, often against a standard ○ *You can't measure a hospital just by its facilities.* **3.** *vt.* BE A PARTICULAR SIZE, LENGTH, QUANTITY to be a particular size, length, quantity, or rate **4.** *vt.* DETERMINE SB'S SIZE FOR CLOTHES to determine sb's size in order to make a garment or garments that will fit ○ *She was being measured for her wedding dress.* **5.** *vt.* COMPARE SIZE OR QUALITY to compare the size, effect, or quality of sth with another thing ○ *The champion needs to measure his skill against a worthy challenger.* **6.** *vt.* ADJUST FOR EFFECT to adjust sth so that it is suitable or effective ○ *He measured his punch exactly to catch his opponent on the jaw.* **7.** *vi.* JOURNEY to travel a particular distance (*archaic*) [12thC. Via French *mesure* from Latin *mensura*, from *mens-* the past participle stem of *metiri* 'to measure'.] —**measurer** *n.* ◇ **beyond measure** very greatly, or to an enormous extent ◇ **for good measure** as sth extra to the amount required, especially to make sure of sth ◇ **get** or **have sb's measure** to arrive at an accurate assessment of sb's qualities or abilities

WORD KEY: ORIGIN

The Latin stem *mens-*, from which *measure* derives, is also the source of English *commensurate, dimension,* and *immense.*

WORD KEY: CULTURAL NOTE

Measure for Measure, a play by William Shakespeare (1604). Set in the court of the Duke of Vienna, this tragicomedy tells of a sister's attempts to win clemency for her brother, who has been condemned to death for the relatively minor crime of permissive behaviour. It deals broadly with morality and the nature of justice.

measure off *vt.* **1.** MEASURE A LENGTH FOR CUTTING to de-

termine a particular length of sth so that this amount may be cut off **2.** MARK OFF AN AREA to find or mark the limits of an area

measure out *vt.* **1.** MEASURE AN AMOUNT FOR USE to take a particular amount from a larger amount of sth for use **2.** MARK OFF AREA to find or mark the limits of an area

measure up *v.* **1.** *vi.* BE GOOD ENOUGH to be good enough to meet a standard ○ *Her new play didn't measure up to expectations.* **2.** *vt.* to find out the various dimensions of sth using a suitable instrument or device

measured /mézhərd/ *adj.* **1.** UNHURRIED OR REASONABLE slow, deliberate, or carefully considered ○ *spoke in measured tones* **2.** ADJUSTED FOR EFFECT adjusted to be suitable or effective ○ *a measured response to the criticism* **3.** BY MEASUREMENT determined as a result of measuring ○ *a measured mile* —**measuredly** *adv.* —**measuredness** *n.*

measureless /mézhərləss/ *adj.* too great to be measured (*literary*) ○ *'Through caverns measureless to man'* (Samuel Taylor Coleridge, *Kubla Khan;* 1816) —**measurelessly** *adv.* —**measurelessness** *n.*

measurement /mézhərmənt/ *n.* **1.** SIZE OF STH MEASURED the size, length, quantity, or rate of sth that has been measured **2.** BODY DIMENSION MEASURED FOR CLOTHING the size of a part of sb's body, especially used to fit or make clothing (*often used in the plural*) **3.** MEASURING OF STH an act of measuring sth

measuring worm *n.* the larva of a geometrid moth that has legs only at each end of its body and moves by bringing its rear forward, forming a loop, then moving its front. US term **inchworm**

meat /meet/ *n.* **1.** EDIBLE ANIMAL FLESH the flesh of an animal that is considered edible, especially a mammal or bird **2.** EDIBLE PART the edible part of anything, e.g. a coconut **3.** IMPORTANT PART the essence or important part of sth ○ *the meat of the argument* **4.** MATERIAL FOR THOUGHT material that is interesting or stimulates thought ○ *There is plenty of meat in the book.* **5.** FOOD food or a meal (*archaic or literary*) [Old English *mete* 'food'. Ultimately from an Indo-European word meaning 'measure', which is also the ancestor of English *measure*, the underlying idea being 'measured portion of food'.] —**meatless** *adj.* ◇ **meat and drink** sth that sb particularly enjoys

WORD KEY: ORIGIN

The sense of *meat* as 'animal flesh (eaten as food)' developed in the 13th century, but the original English sense 'food' still survives in phrases such as *meat and drink* and 'one man's meat is another man's poison' (and is also seen in the word's relatives Danish *mad*, Icelandic *matur*, and Swedish *mat*).

meatball /meét bawl/ *n.* **1.** MINCED MEAT IN BALL SHAPE minced meat that is shaped into a small round ball, usually with seasonings and a binding ingredient such as breadcrumbs or egg, and then cooked **2.** *US, Can* OFFENSIVE TERM an offensive term that deliberately insults sb's intelligence or energy (*slang insult*)

Meath /meeth/ county in Leinster Province, northeast of Dublin in eastern Republic of Ireland. The county town is Navan. Population: 109,371 (1996). Area: 2,336 sq. km/902 sq. mi.

meat hook *n.* a large hook used for hanging carcasses of meat

meat loaf *n.* a mixture of minced meat and other ingredients, usually cooked in a loaf tin and served hot or cold

meatus /mi áytəss/ (*plural* **-tuses** or **-tus**) *n.* a body opening, e.g. the passage in the ear that leads to the eardrum [15thC. From Latin, 'passage, channel', the past participle of *meare* 'to go, pass' (source of English *permeate*).]

meaty /meéti/ (**-ier, -iest**) *adj.* **1.** CONTAINING OR TASTING OF MEAT containing a high proportion of meat or tasting strongly of meat **2.** INTERESTING AND THOUGHT-PROVOKING full of interesting and thought-provoking material ○ *a meaty role* **3.** FLESHY OR MUSCLED big and fleshy or muscular —**meatiness** *n.*

mecca /mékə/ *n.* a place that is an important centre for a particular activity or that is visited by a great many people

Mecca /mékə/ city in western Saudi Arabia, the birthplace of Muhammad. It is considered by Muslims the most sacred of the holy cities of Islam. Population: 1,500,000 (1994).

Meccano /mi kaánō/ *tdmk.* a trademark for a children's construction system of metal or plastic pieces that can be used to build mechanical models

mech. *abbr.* **1.** mechanical **2.** mechanics **3.** mechanism

mechan- *prefix.* = mechano- (*used before vowels*)

mechanic /mi kánnik/ *n.* **1.** SB WHO REPAIRS MACHINERY a skilled worker who is employed to repair or operate machinery or engines **2.** UNSKILLED WORKER an unskilled worker or labourer (*archaic*) [Mid-16thC. Directly or via French *mechanique* from Latin *mechanicus*, from, ultimately, Greek *mēkhanē* (see MACHINE).]

mechanical /mi kánni k'l/ *adj.* **1.** MACHINE-OPERATED operated by or using a machine or mechanism **2.** INVOLVING A MACHINE OR ENGINE involving or located in or on a machine or engine ○ *mechanical failure* **3.** DONE AS IF BY MACHINE done automatically or as if by a machine instead of a human being ○ *His playing was mechanical.* **4.** UNDERSTANDING MACHINES having an aptitude for using or understanding machines ○ *I'm not very mechanical* **5.** INVOLVING PHYSICAL FORCES relating to, involving, or done by physical forces ○ *mechanical erosion* **6.** PHYS OF MECHANICS relating to, involving, or typical of the science of mechanics ○ *mechanical energy* ■ *n.* = mechanic *n.* 2 (*archaic*) —**mechanically** *adv.* —**mechanicalness** *n.*

mechanical drawing *n.* **1.** DRAWING OF MACHINERY TO SCALE a drawing done to scale using specialized instruments, e.g. a sketch showing machinery or an architectural plan **2.** PROCESS OF DRAWING the process of making mechanical drawings

mechanical engineering *n.* the branch of engineering that deals with the design, production, and use of machinery and tools, as well as the generation and transmission of heat and mechanical power —**mechanical engineer** *n.*

mechanical pencil *n. US* = propelling pencil

mechanical weathering *n.* the breakdown of rocks and minerals by physical agents such as frost, wind, and tree roots, with no chemical alteration

mechanician /mékə nísh'n/ *n.* sb who makes machines or tools

mechanics /mi kánniks/ *n.* **1.** STUDY OF ENERGY AND FORCES the branch of physics and mathematics that deals with the effect of energy and forces on systems (*takes a singular verb*) **2.** MAKING AND RUNNING OF MACHINES the application of the science of mechanics to the design, making, and operating of machines (*takes a singular or plural verb*) ■ *npl.* HOW STH WORKS OR IS DONE the details of how sth works or the way it is done ○ *She's a strategic player who really understands the mechanics of the game.*

mechanise *vt.* = mechanize

mechanism /mékənizəm/ *n.* **1.** TECH MACHINE PART a machine or part of a machine that performs a particular task **2.** STH LIKE A MACHINE sth that is not a machine but is like one or is studied as if it were one ○ *the fragile mechanism of the planet's ecology* **3.** METHOD OR MEANS a method or means of doing sth ○ *Interest rates are only one mechanism for controlling inflation.* **4.** WAY THAT STH WORKS the methods, procedures, or processes involved in how sth works or is done ○ *the mechanism of international diplomacy* **5.** PSYCHOL INSTINCTIVE BEHAVIOURAL REACTION a natural unconscious reaction or type of behaviour that comes into action when sb is faced with a particular situation ○ *defence mechanisms* **6.** PHILOS PHILOSOPHICAL THEORY the philosophical theory that all natural phenomena, including human behaviour, can be explained by physical causes and processes [Mid-17thC. From modern Latin *mechanismus*, from Greek *mēkhanē* (see MACHINE).]

mechanist /mékənist/ *n.* **1.** PHILOS SB BELIEVING IN PHILOSOPHICAL MECHANISM sb who believes that all natural phenomena, including human behaviour, can be explained by physical causes and processes **2.** = mechanician [Early 17thC. Formed from MECHANIC.]

MEASUREMENTS

SI Metric System

The SI (Système Internationale d'Unités) is founded on seven base units that can be multiplied or divided by each other to yield derived units. Values of the base and derived units can be increased or decreased by using SI prefixes indicating decimal multiplication factors. Units and prefixes are assigned internationally accepted symbols.

Base Units

Name	Physical Quantity	Symbol
metre	length	m
kilogram	mass	kg
second	time	s
ampere	electric current	A
kelvin	thermodynamic temperature	K
mole	amount of substance	mol
candela	luminous intensity	cd

Derived Units With Special Names and Symbols

Name	Physical Quantity	Symbol
becquerel	radioactivity	Bq
coulomb	electric charge	C
degree Celsius	temperature	°C
farad	electric capacitance	F
gray	absorbed radiation dose	Gy
henry	inductance	H
hertz	frequency	Hz
joule	energy, work	J
lumen	luminous flux	lm
lux	illumination	lx
newton	force	N
ohm	electric resistance	Ω
pascal	pressure, stress	Pa
radian	plane angle	rad
siemens	electric conductance	S
sievert	radiation dose equivalent	Sv
steradian	solid angle	sr
tesla	magnetic flux density	T
volt	electric potential difference	V
watt	power	W
weber	magnetic flux	Wb

Some Derived Units Without Special Names and Symbols

Name	Physical Quantity	Symbol
ampere per metre	magnetic field strength	A/m
cubic metre	volume	m^3
henry per metre	permeability	H/m
joule per kelvin	heat capacity, entropy	J/K
kilogram per cubic metre	mass density	kg/m^3
metre per second	linear speed	m/s
metre per second squared	linear acceleration	m/s^2
mole per cubic metre	concentration of substance	mol/m^3
newton metre	moment of force, torque	N·m
radian per second	angular speed	rad/s
square metre	area	m^2
volt per metre	electric field strength	V/m
watt per metre kelvin	thermal conductivity	W/(m·K)
watt per steradian	radiant intensity	W/sr

Prefixes

Multiplication Factor		Name	Symbol
1 000 000 000 000 000 000	or 10^{18}	exa-	E
1 000 000 000 000 000	or 10^{15}	peta-	P
1 000 000 000 000	or 10^{12}	tera-	T
1 000 000 000	or 10^9	giga-	G
1 000 000	or 10^6	mega-	M
1 000	or 10^3	kilo-	k
100	or 10^2	hecto-	h
10	or 10^1	deca- or deka-	da
0.1	or 10^{-1}	deci-	d
0.01	or 10^{-2}	centi-	c
0.001	or 10^{-3}	milli-	m
0.000 001	or 10^{-6}	micro-	μ
0.000 000 001	or 10^{-9}	nano-	n
0.000 000 000 001	or 10^{-12}	pico-	p
0.000 000 000 000 001	or 10^{-15}	femto-	f
0.000 000 000 000 000 001	or 10^{-18}	atto-	a

Other Units Used With the SI

Some units technically outside of the SI are nevertheless employed with it due to their practical or special significance or because they are already in wide use. Excepting the electronvolt, litre, tex, and tonne, prefixes are not used with these units. The tonne does not take prefixes indicating a multiplication factor of less than ten.

Name	Symbol	Quantity	SI Equivalent
astro-nomical unit	–	length	$\approx 1.4960 \times 10^{11}$ m
barn	b	area	$= 10^{-28}$ m^2
day, mean solar	d	time	= 86 400 s
degree	°	plane angle	$= (\Pi/180)$ rad
electronvolt	eV	energy	$\approx 1.60\,22 \times 10^{-19}$ J
hectare	ha	area	= 10 000 m^2
hour, mean solar	h	time	= 3600 s
knot	kn	linear speed	= 1852 m/h
litre	L or l	volume	≈ 1 dm^3 or 1000 cm^3
millibar	mbar	pressure	= 100 Pa
minute, mean solar	min	time	= 60 s
minute	'	plane angle	$= (\Pi/10\,800)$ rad
nautical mile	M	length	= 1852 m
parsec	pc	length	$\approx 3.0857 \times 10^{16}$ m
revolution	r	plane angle	$= 2\Pi$ rad
second	"	plane angle	$= (\Pi/648\,000)$ rad
tex	tex	linear density	= 1 mg/m
tonne	t	mass	= 1000 kg
unified atomic mass unit	u	mass	$\approx 1.6605 \times 10^{-27}$ kg
year	a	time	= 3.1536×10^7 s (calendar)
			= 3.155693×10^7 s (solar)
			= 3.155815×10^7 s (sidereal)

Conversion of Common SI Units

Conversions for some common SI units or those used with the SI to Imperial or US Customary units are given below.

SI Unit	Conversion
length	
micrometre	= 0.000 039 37 inches
millimetre	= 0.039 37 inches
centimetre	= 0.3937 inches
metre	$= 39.37$ inches or ≈ 1.094 yards
kilometre	≈ 0.621 miles
area	
square millimetre	= 0.001 55 square inches
square centimetre	= 0.155 square inches
square metre	≈ 1.196 square yards or 10.76 square feet
hectare	≈ 2.471 acres
square kilometre	≈ 0.386 square miles
volume or capacity	
cubic millimetre	= 0.000 061 cubic inches
cubic centimetre or millilitre	= 0.0610 cubic inches, 0.0352 Imp. fl.ounces, or 0.0338 US fl. ounces
cubic decimetre or litre	= 61.0 cubic inches, 0.880 Imp. quarts, 1.057 US liquid quarts, or 0.908 US dry quarts
cubic metre	≈ 1.308 cubic yards
mass	
gram	≈ 0.0353 ou. avoirdupois or 0.0322 ou. troy
kilogram	≈ 2.205 pounds avoirdupois
tonne	≈ 2205 pounds avoirdupois
temperature	
degree Celsius	(°C × 1.8) + 32 = degrees Fahrenheit

Foot-Pound-Second and Troy Systems

The Imperial and US Customary systems are the last foot-pound-second systems still used nationally in everyday trade and commerce, while the troy system of weights continues to find use in the precious metals market, chiefly in North America. All have been supplanted by the SI in scientific and technical work and in nearly all international trade.

Imperial and US Customary System Units

Units of the Imperial and US Customary systems are equal except for some units of volume and capacity.

Unit	Relation	Conversion
length		
inch	–	= 25.4 mm
foot	12 inches	= 0.3048 m
yard	3 feet, 36 inches	= 0.9144 m
rod	$5\frac{1}{2}$ yards, $16\frac{1}{2}$ feet	= 5.0292 m
furlong	220 yards, $\frac{1}{8}$ mile	≈ 0.201 km
mile (statute)	1760 yards, 5280 feet	≈ 1.609 km
area		
square inch	–	= 645.16 mm^2
square foot	144 sq. inches	= 929.0304 cm^2
square yard	9 sq. feet	≈ 0.836 m^2
acre	4840 sq. yards	≈ 0.405 ha
volume or capacity		
cubic inch	–	≈ 16.387 cm^3
cubic foot	1728 cubic inches	≈ 28.316 dm^3
cubic yard	27 cubic feet	≈ 0.765 m^3
(Imperial)		
fluid ounce	–	≈ 28.413 cm^3
pint	20 Imp. fl. ou.	≈ 0.568 dm^3
quart	2 Imp. pints	≈ 1.136 dm^3
gallon	4 Imp. quarts	≈ 4.546 dm^3
peck	8 Imp. quarts	≈ 9.092 dm^3
bushel	4 Imp. pecks	≈ 36.369 dm^3
barrel	36 Imp. gallons	≈ 163.7 dm^3
(US, liquid)		
fluid ounce	–	≈ 29.573 cm^3
pint	16 US fl. ou.	≈ 0.473 dm^3
quart	2 US fl. pints	≈ 0.946 dm^3
gallon	4 US fl. quarts	≈ 3.785 dm^3
barrel, wine	$31\frac{1}{2}$ US gallons	≈ 119.2 dm^3
barrel, oil	42 US gallons	≈ 0.159 m^3
(US, dry)		
pint	–	≈ 0.551 dm^3
quart	2 US dry pints	≈ 1.101 dm^3
peck	8 US dry quarts	≈ 8.810 dm^3
bushel	4 pecks	≈ 35.239 dm^3
weight or mass		
ounce	–	≈ 28.349 g
pound	16 ounces	≈ 0.454 kg
(avoirdupois)		
stone (UK)	14 pounds	≈ 6.350 kg
hundred-weight(UK)	112 pounds	≈ 50.80 kg
(long) ton (UK)	2240 pounds	$\approx 1.016 \times 10^3$ kg
(short) ton (US)	2000 pounds	$\approx 0.907 \times 10^3$ kg
(troy)		
ounce	–	≈ 31.103 g
pound	12 ou. troy	≈ 373.242 g
temperature		
degree Fahrenheit	(°F – 32) ÷ 1.8 = degrees Celsius	

Some Volumetric Measurement Comparisons

Imperial Units	In US Units	In SI Units
1 UK fluid ounce	≈ 0.961 US fluid ounce	≈ 28.413 cm^3
1 UK pint	≈ 1.201 US liquid pint	≈ 0.568 dm^3
1 UK pint	≈ 1.032 US dry pint	≈ 0.568 dm^3
1 UK gallon	≈ 1.201 US gallon	≈ 4.546 dm^3

US Units	In Imperial Units	In SI Units
1 US fluid ounce	≈ 1.041 UK fluid ounce	≈ 29.573 cm^3
1 US liquid pint	≈ 0.833 UK pint	≈ 0.473 dm^3
1 US gallon	≈ 0.833 UK gallon	≈ 3.785 dm^3
1 US dry pint	≈ 0.969 UK pint	≈ 0.551 dm^3

mechanistic /mékə nístik/ *adj.* **1.** PHILOS EXPLAINING BEHAVIOUR MECHANICALLY explaining human behaviour or other natural processes in terms of physical causes and processes **2.** LIKE A MACHINE typical of a machine rather than a thinking and feeling human being **3.** PHYS OF THE SCIENCE OF MECHANICS relating to, involving, or typical of the science of mechanics —**mechanistically** *adv.*

mechanize /mékə nīz/ (**-nizes, -nizing, -nized**), **mechanise** (**-nises, -nising, -nised**) *vt.* **1.** USE MACHINERY TO DO STH to change a process so that it is performed by machinery rather than human or animal labour **2.** EQUIP WITH MACHINERY to equip a place of work or a workforce with machines to do work previously done by human or animal labour **3.** MIL EQUIP AN ARMY WITH TRACKED VEHICLES to equip an armed force with tracked armoured vehicles [Late 17thC. Formed from MECHANIC.] —**mechanization** *n.* —**mechanized** /mékə nīzd/ *adj.* —**mechanizer** *n.*

mechano- *prefix.* **1.** mechanical ○ *mechanoreceptor* **2.** machinery ○ *mechanize* [From Greek *mēkhanē* (see MACHINE).]

mechanochemistry /mékənō kémmistri/ *n.* the branch of chemistry concerned with the conversion of chemical energy into mechanical work —**mechanochemical** *adj.*

mechanoreceptor /mékənōri séptər/ *n.* a sensory receptor of a nerve that responds to pressure, vibration, or some other mechanical stimulus —**mechanoreception** *n.* —**mechanoreceptive** /-séptiv/ *adj.*

mechanotherapy /mékənō thérrəpi/ *n.* the treatment of injuries through mechanical means such as massage and exercise machines —**mechanotherapist** *n.*

Mechlin /méklin/, **Mechlin lace** *n.* a type of bobbin lace made at Mechlin, Belgium [15thC. Named after *Mechlin*, the former English name of the Belgian city *Mechelen*, where it was first made.]

MEcon *abbr.* Master of Economics

meconium /mi kóni əm/ *n.* the dark greenish faeces that have collected in the intestines of an unborn baby and are released shortly after birth [Early 17thC. Via Latin, 'poppy juice', hence 'newborn baby's faeces' (because of the similarity in colour), from Greek *mēkōnion* 'poppy juice', from *mēkōn* 'poppy'.]

mecopteran /mi kóptərən/ *n.* an insect with long legs and wings and a structure resembling a beak at the front of the head, e.g. the scorpion fly. Order: Mecoptera. [Formed from modern Latin *Mecoptera*, order name, from Greek *mēkos* 'length' + *ptera* 'wings'] —**mecopterous** *adj.*

Med /med/ *n.* the Mediterranean Sea (*informal*)

MEd *abbr.* Master of Education

med. *abbr.* **1.** medical **2.** medicine **3.** medieval **4.** medium

médaillon /méddī yón/ *n.* = medallion n. 3 (*often used in the plural*) [Early 20thC. From French, plural of *medaillon* (see MEDALLION).]

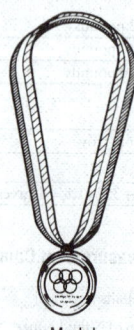
Medal

medal /médd'l/ *n.* **1.** PIECE OF METAL GIVEN AS AN AWARD a small flat piece of metal, usually shaped like a coin and stamped with an inscription or design, awarded to sb for outstanding achievement or bravery or to commemorate sth **2.** RELIGIOUS IMAGE WORN AS ACCESSORY a cut and shaped piece of metal on which a religious image is often stamped, worn as a brooch or on a chain ■ *v.* (**-als, -alling, -alled**) **1.** *vi.* US WIN A MEDAL to win a medal in a competition ○ *She medalled in the javelin throw.* **2.** *vt.* GIVE MEDAL to award sb a medal (*archaic*) [Late 16thC. Via French from, ultimately, assumed Vulgar Latin *medalia* 'coins worth half the value of a denarius', from, ultimately, late Latin *medialis* 'medial' (source of English *middle*).] —**medallic** /mi dállik/ *adj.*

medalist *n.* US = medallist

medallion /mə dálli ən/ *n.* **1.** MEDAL a large medal **2.** LARGE DECORATIVE METAL DISC a large metal disc worn as an ornament, usually on a chain round the neck **3.** COOK ROUND THIN FOOD SLICE a round thin slice or portion of meat or another food **4.** ARTS ROUND DECORATION ON STH a round or oval decoration on sth, e.g. a building, vase, or piece of material [Mid-17thC. Via French *medaillon* from Italian *medaglione*, literally 'large medal', from *medaglia* (see MEDAL).]

medallist /médd'list/ *n.* **1.** SB AWARDED A MEDAL sb who has been awarded a medal, especially in a sports competition **2.** MEDAL DESIGNER, MAKER, OR COLLECTOR sb who designs, makes, collects, or is an expert on medals **3.** GOLF WINNER OF A STROKE PLAY TOURNAMENT a golfer who wins a stroke play tournament

Medal of Honor *n.* = Congressional Medal of Honor

medal play *n.* GOLF = stroke play

Medan /máy daan/ industrial city in western Indonesia on the island of northern Sumatra. Population: 1,730,052 (1990).

Medawar /méddəwər/, **Sir Peter** (1915–87) Brazilian-born UK zoologist and immunologist. He shared a Nobel Prize in physiology or medicine (1960) for his work on immunology in organ transplants and skin grafts. Full name **Sir Peter Brian Medawar**

meddle /médd'l/ (**-dles, -dling, -dled**) *vi.* to interfere or become involved in sb else's concerns or with sth that is sb else's property (*disapproving*) ○ *I don't mean to meddle, only to offer advice.* ○ *Who's been meddling with the settings on my computer?* [13thC. Via Old French *me(s)dler* (variant of *mesler*), from assumed Vulgar Latin *misculare* 'to mix thoroughly'.] —**meddler** *n.*

meddlesome /médd'lsəm/ *adj.* tending to interfere in other people's business (*disapproving*) —**meddlesomely** *adv.* —**meddlesomeness** *n.*

Mede /meed/ *n.* a member of an Indo-European people who ruled an empire northwest of Persia in ancient times [Via Latin *Medi*, plural of *Medus*]

Medea /mə dée ə/ *n.* in Greek mythology, a woman with magical powers who was the daughter of the king of Colchis. She helped Jason steal the Golden Fleece and, when he deserted her, killed their children in revenge.

Medellín /méddə yeén/ major city and capital of Antioquia Department in west-central Colombia. Population: 1,621,356 (1995).

medevac /méddi vak/ *n.* **1.** MEDICAL EVACUATION OF INJURED the removal of injured people, especially military casualties, from the scene of their injury to the nearest hospital or place of treatment **2.** US HELICOPTER USED TO EVACUATE INJURED an aircraft, especially a helicopter, used to take injured people, especially military casualties, from the scene of their injury to the nearest hospital or place of treatment ■ *vt.* (**-vacs, -vacing, -vaced**) EVACUATE AN INJURED PERSON to evacuate sb who is injured in order to take them to a hospital or place of treatment [Mid-20thC. Blend of MEDICAL and EVACUATION.]

media[1] /méedi ə/ *n.* TELEVISION, NEWSPAPERS, AND RADIO COLLECTIVELY the various means of mass communication thought of as a whole, including television, radio, magazines, and newspapers, together with the people involved in their production (*takes a singular or plural verb*) ■ plural of MEDIUM [Early 20thC. Plural of MEDIUM.]

media[2] /méedi ə/ (*plural* **-ae** /-ee/) *n.* **1.** ANAT LAYER OF A BLOOD VESSEL the middle, muscular layer of the wall of a blood or lymph vessel **2.** INSECTS VEIN IN AN INSECT'S WING a primary vein in an insect's wing [Mid-19thC. From Latin, 'middle', the feminine of *medius* (see MEDIUM).]

media circus *n.* a situation in which members of the media vie with each other in covering an event so that the coverage overwhelms the event and distorts its importance (*informal disapproving*)

mediacy /méedi əssi/ *n.* the condition of being intermediate or of having an intermediate effect [Mid-19thC. Formed from MEDIATE.]

mediae plural of **media**

mediaeval *adj.* = medieval

mediaevalism *n.* = medievalism

mediaevalist *n.* = medievalist

media event *n.* sth that attracts great attention from the mass media, often arranged specifically for that purpose

mediagenic /méedi ə jénnik/ *adj.* US appealing or attractive when covered by the media and thus highly suitable for media exposure

medial /méedi əl/ *adj.* **1.** AT THE MIDDLE situated in or towards the middle **2.** ORDINARY not extreme or exceptional but average **3.** STATS = median *adj.* 2 **4.** ZOOL NEAR THE MEDIAN PLANE near the median plane of an organism or body part **5.** LING IN THE MIDDLE OF A LANGUAGE UNIT occurring between the first and last positions in a word or linguistic unit (**morpheme**) ■ *n.* PHON SOUND BETWEEN STRONG AND SOFT a speech sound midway between a strong sound (**fortis**) and a soft sound (**lenis**) [Late 16thC. From late Latin *medialis*, from Latin *medius* (see MEDIUM).] —**medially** *adv.*

median /méedi ən/ *n.* **1.** MIDDLE POINT a point, line, part, or plane that is in the middle **2.** STATS MIDDLE OF ORDERED VALUES the middle value in a set of statistical values that are arranged in ascending or descending order **3.** STATS MIDPOINT IN A FREQUENCY DISTRIBUTION the value in a frequency distribution above and below which values with equal total frequencies appear **4.** GEOM LINE DIVIDING A TRIANGLE a line connecting a vertex of a triangle and the midpoint of the opposite side **5.** GEOM LINE DIVIDING A TRAPEZOID a line connecting the midpoints of the nonparallel sides of a trapezoid ■ *adj.* **1.** IN, TO, OR THROUGH THE MIDDLE in, towards, or passing through the middle **2.** STATS OF OR AS A STATISTICAL MEDIAN relating to, involving, or constituting a statistical median **3.** ZOOL IN THE MIDDLE OF A BILATERAL ANIMAL lying in the plane that divides a bilaterally symmetrical animal into right and left halves [14thC. Directly or via French (*veine*) *médiane* 'median (vein)' (the original sense in English), from Latin *medianus* 'median', from *medius* (see MEDIUM).] —**medianly** *adv.*

median plane *n.* a vertical plane that divides a bilaterally symmetrical animal into right and left halves

median strip *n.* US, Aus a strip of land down the centre of a road that separates lanes of traffic travelling in opposite directions

mediant /méedi ənt/ *n.* the third note of a major or minor musical scale, and the harmony built upon this note [Mid-18thC. Via French *médiante* from, ultimately, late Latin *mediare* 'to be in the middle' (source of English *mediate*), from Latin *medius* (see MEDIUM).]

mediastinum /méedi ə stínəm/ (*plural* **-na** /-nə/) *n.* in mammals, the region of the chest between the lungs that contains the heart, trachea, and other organs [15thC. Via medieval Latin, 'medial', the neuter form of *mediastinus*, from Latin, 'common servant', from *medius* (see MEDIUM).] —**mediastinal** *adj.*

media studies *n.* a field of academic work that examines the role and operation of the mass media (*takes a singular or plural verb*)

mediate /méedi ayt/ *v.* (**-ates, -ating, -ated**) **1.** *vi.* INTERVENE TO RESOLVE CONFLICT to work with both sides in a dispute in an attempt to help them reach an agreement ○ *mediating between the government and the rebels* **2.** *vt.* OVERSEE ATTEMPTS TO SOLVE A DISPUTE to oversee an attempt to solve a dispute by working with both sides to help them reach an agreement ○ *appointed to mediate the talks* **3.** *vt.* ACHIEVE AGREEMENT BETWEEN DISPUTING GROUPS to achieve a solution, settlement, or agreement by working with both sides in a dispute ○ *negotiators have mediated a ceasefire* **4.** *vt.* PHYSIOL TRANSFER to act as a medium that transfers sth from one place to another **5.** *vi.* BE BETWEEN to be between two stages, ideas, times, or things ■ *adj.* DEPENDING ON INTERMEDIATE ACTION involving or depending on an intermediary or an intermediate action [15thC. Partly from late Latin *mediare* 'to halve, be in the middle, mediate', from Latin *medius* (see MEDIUM), and partly by back-formation from MEDIATION.] —**mediately** *adv.* —**mediateness** *n.* —**mediative** *adj.*

mediation /meēdi áysh'n/ *n.* **1.** INTERVENTION TO SETTLE A DISPUTE the intervention by a third party between two sides in a dispute in an attempt to help them reach an agreement **2.** PHYSIOL ACTION AS MEDIUM the action a medium that transfers sth from one place to another [14thC. Directly or via Old French *mediacion* from the late Latin stem *mediation-*, from, ultimately, Latin *mediare* (see MEDIATE).]

mediatize /meēdi ə tīz/ (**-tizes, -tizing, -tized**), **mediatise** (**-atises, -atising, -atised**) *vt.* to take control of another country but allow its ruler to retain his or her title and have some role in governing the country [Early 19thC. Via French *médiatiser* from, ultimately, late Latin *mediare* (see MEDIATE).] —**mediatization** /meēdi ə tī záysh'n/ *n.*

mediator /meēdi aytər/ *n.* **1.** SB HELPING END A DISPUTE sb who works with both sides in a dispute in an attempt to help them reach an agreement **2.** PHYSIOL SUBSTANCE ACTING AS A MEDIUM a substance that acts as a medium in transferring sth from one place to another in the body [14thC. Directly or via French *médiateur* from ecclesiastical Latin *mediator*, from late Latin *mediare* (see MEDIATE).] —**mediatorial** /meēdi ə táwri əl/ *adj.* —**mediatorially** /-táwri əli/ *adv.*

medic[1] /méddik/ *n.* **1.** DOCTOR a doctor or medical student (*informal*) **2.** *US* MIL MEMBER OF AN ARMY MEDICAL CORPS an enlisted or noncommissioned member of a military medical corps [Mid-17thC. From Latin *medicus* (see MEDICINE). Perhaps also by back-formation from MEDICAL.]

medic[2] /méddik/ *n.* PLANTS a plant of the pea family, some types of which are used for fodder and green manure. Genus: *Medicago.* US = **medick**

Medicaid /méddi kayd/ *n.* a programme funded by the US and state governments that pays the medical expenses of people who are unable to pay some or all of their own expenses. ◊ **Medicare** [Mid-20thC. Blend of MEDICAL and AID.]

medical /méddik'l/ *adj.* INVOLVING MEDICINE relating to, involving, or used in medicine or treatment given by doctors ■ *n.* PHYSICAL EXAMINATION TO DETERMINE HEALTH a physical examination by a doctor to check a patient's state of health [Mid-17thC. Directly or via French from medieval Latin *medicalis*, from Latin *medicus* (see MEDICINE).]

medical certificate *n.* a document signed by a doctor giving a judgment on sb's state of health, especially certifying the person's fitness or unfitness for work

medical jurisprudence *n.* = **forensic medicine**

medicament /mə díkəmənt/ *n.* a substance used to treat an illness [15thC. Directly or via French from Latin *medicamentum*, from *medicari* (see MEDICATE).]

Medicare /méddi kair/ *n.* **1.** US PUBLIC HEALTH CARE FOR SENIOR CITIZENS a health insurance programme in the United States under which medical care and hospital treatment for people over 65 is partially paid by the government **2.** AUSTRALIAN HEALTH INSURANCE SCHEME in Australia, the national health insurance scheme, which is funded by a tax levy [Mid-20thC. Blend of MEDICAL and CARE.]

medicate /méddi kayt/ (**-cates, -cating, -cated**) *vt.* **1.** MED GIVE MEDICINE TO SB to treat a patient with a drug (*often passive*) **2.** PHARM ADD A DRUG TO STH to add a drug to sth, e.g. an antibacterial agent to a soap, or an anaesthetic to a throat lozenge [Early 17thC. Origin uncertain: either from Latin *medicari* 'to heal, cure', later 'to treat', from *medicus* (see MEDICINE); or by back-formation from MEDICATION.] —**medicated** *adj.* —**medicative** /-kətiv/ *adj.*

medication /méddi káysh'n/ *n.* **1.** DRUG a drug used to treat an illness **2.** TREATMENT WITH MEDICINE treatment of an illness using drugs [15thC. Directly or via French from, ultimately, Latin *medicari* (see MEDICATE).]

Medicean /méddi seēən/ *adj.* relating to the Medici family and the period of their rule over Florence and Tuscany

Medici /méddichi, mə deēchi/, **Cosimo de'** (1389–1464) Italian banker and statesman. He established the Medici as virtual rulers of Florence without holding public office himself, and was a patron of the arts and learning. Known as **Cosimo the Elder**

Medici, Cosimo I de', 1st Grand Duke of Tuscany (1519–74). He became the sovereign ruler of Florence (1570) and established firm autocratic control over Florence and Tuscany.

Medici, Lorenzo de' (1449–92) Italian statesman. He was the virtual ruler of the Florentine Republic, a poet, and a patron of the arts. Known as **Lorenzo the Magnificent**

medicinal /mə díss'nəl/ *adj.* **1.** CAPABLE OF TREATING ILLNESS having properties that can be used to treat illness ○ *a medicinal plant* **2.** INTENDED TO IMPROVE SB'S WELLBEING intended to improve sb's physical or emotional wellbeing in the way a medicine does ○ *a drink taken for medicinal purposes* **3.** LIKE MEDICINE like medicine, especially in having a bitter taste [14thC. Directly or via French from Latin *medicinalis*, from *medicina* (see MEDICINE).] —**medicinally** *adv.*

medicinal leech *n.* a large European freshwater leech that lives on blood. In the past doctors used it in bloodletting, and it is still occasionally used to prevent coagulation. Latin name: *Hirudo medicinalis.*

medicine /méddss'n, méddiss'n/ *n.* **1.** DRUG FOR TREATING ILLNESS a drug or remedy used for treating illness, especially in liquid form ○ *cough medicine* **2.** TREATMENT OF ILLNESS the diagnosis and treatment of illnesses, wounds, and injuries **3.** TREATMENT USING DRUGS the treatment of illness or injury using drugs rather than surgery **4.** MEDICAL PROFESSION the profession of treating illness as a doctor **5.** ANTHROP RITUAL PRACTICE OR SACRED OBJECT a ritual practice or sacred object believed, especially by Native Americans, to control supernatural powers or work as a preventive or remedy of illness [12thC. Directly or via Old French from Latin *medicina* 'practice of medicine', formed from *medicus* 'doctor', from *mederi* 'to heal'.]

medicine ball *n.* a large heavy ball that people throw to one another as a strength-building exercise

medicine chest *n.* a small cupboard or chest where medicines, bandages, and other things used in treating illness or injury are stored

medicine dance *n.* a ceremonial religious dance performed by an aboriginal group or individual to obtain supernatural assistance for sth, e.g. to cure illness

medicine lodge *n.* a wooden building used by some Native North American peoples for rituals, e.g. ceremonial curing

medicine man *n.* sb who is believed to heal others by using supernatural powers, especially among Native North American peoples

medick /méddik/ *n.* a plant of the pea family that has three-lobed leaves and is often used as fodder. Genus: *Medicago.* [14thC. Via Latin *medica* from Greek *Mēdikē (poa)*, literally 'Median (poppy)', *Media* being the name of an ancient southwestern Asian country (present-day northwestern Iran).]

medick *n.* PLANTS = **medic**[2]

medico /méddikō/ (*plural* **-cos**) *n.* a doctor or medical student (*informal*) [Late 17thC. Via Italian from Latin *medicus* (see MEDICINE).]

medieval /méddi eēv'l/, **mediaeval** *adj.* **1.** OF THE MIDDLE AGES relating to, involving, belonging to, or typical of the Middle Ages **2.** OLD-FASHIONED old-fashioned, especially because lacking in modern enlightened attitudes ○ *Some of the working practices in the industry were positively medieval.* [Early 19thC. Formed from modern Latin *medium aevum* 'middle age'.] —**medievally** *adv.*

medieval Greek *n.* the form of Greek used between the 7th and 13th centuries —**Medieval Greek** *adj.*

medievalism /méddi eēv'lizəm/, **mediaevalism** *n.* **1.** CUSTOMS AND BELIEFS OF THE MIDDLE AGES the customs, practices, or beliefs of the Middle Ages **2.** DEVOTION TO THE MIDDLE AGES devotion to the spirit or beliefs of the Middle Ages **3.** STH FROM THE MIDDLE AGES a belief, custom, or style from or like one from the Middle Ages

medievalist /méddi eēv'list/, **mediaevalist** *n.* sb who studies, teaches the history of, or has special knowledge of the Middle Ages

medieval Latin *n.* the form of Latin used in Europe during the Middle Ages —**Medieval Latin** *adj.*

medina /me deēnə/, **Medina** *n.* the oldest part of many North African cities [Early 20thC. From Arabic, literally 'town'.]

Medina /me deēnə/ city in western Saudi Arabia, the site of the Mosque of the Prophet that houses the tomb of Muhammad. Population: 500,000 (1990).

mediocre /meēdi ṓkər/ *adj.* adequate but not very good [Late 16thC. Directly or via French from Latin *mediocris*, literally 'middle of a rugged mountain', hence 'in a middle state', from *medius* 'middle' + *ocris* 'rugged mountain'.]

mediocrity /meēdi ókrəti/ (*plural* **-ties**) *n.* **1.** AVERAGENESS a quality that is acceptable but not very good ○ *His poetry seldom rises above the level of mediocrity.* **2.** MEDIOCRE PERSON sb who is not particularly good at anything [15thC. Directly or via French *médiocrité* from Latin *mediocritas*, from *mediocris* (see MEDIOCRE).]

Medit. *abbr.* Mediterranean

meditate /méddi tayt/ (**-tates, -tating, -tated**) *v.* **1.** *vi.* EMPTY OR CONCENTRATE THE MIND to empty the mind of thoughts, or concentrate the mind on one thing, in order to develop the mind or spirit, aid contemplation, or relax **2.** *vi.* THINK CAREFULLY ABOUT STH to think about sth calmly, seriously, and for some time **3.** *vt.* PLAN STH to plan or consider doing sth [Mid-16thC. Origin uncertain: either from Latin *meditare*, literally 'to keep on measuring', related to *mederi* 'to cure' (source of English *remedy*); or by back-formation from MEDITATION.] —**meditator** *n.*

meditation /méddi táysh'n/ *n.* **1.** EMPTYING OR CONCENTRATION OF THE MIND the emptying of the mind of thoughts, or concentration of the mind on just one thing, in order to aid mental or spiritual development, contemplation, or relaxation **2.** PONDERING OF STH the act of thinking about sth deeply and carefully, or an instance of such thinking **3.** SERIOUS STUDY OF A TOPIC an extended and serious study of a particular topic [15thC. Directly or via French from the Latin stem *meditation-*, from, ultimately, *meditari* (see MEDITATE).] —**meditational** *adj.* —**meditative** /médditətiv/ *adj.* —**meditatively** *adv.* —**meditativeness** *n.*

Mediterranean /méddi tə ráy ni ən/ *n.* **1.** MEDITERRANEAN SEA OR SURROUNDING AREA the Mediterranean Sea or the lands bordering it ○ *holidaying in the Mediterranean* **2.** SB FROM THE AREA OF THE MEDITERRANEAN SEA sb who lives in or comes from a region bordering the Mediterranean Sea ■ *adj.* **1.** IN OR NEAR THE MEDITERRANEAN SEA in the Mediterranean Sea, or in a region that borders it **2.** TYPICAL OF MEDITERRANEANS typical of the people living in a region that borders the Mediterranean Sea **3.** METEOROL WITH HOT SUMMERS AND WARM WINTERS having hot summers and warm winters, with most of the rainfall occurring in the winter **4.** ANTHROP WITH DARK HAIR AND OLIVE SKIN resembling people from countries around the Mediterranean Sea, who often have dark hair and olive complexions

Mediterranean fever *n.* = **brucellosis** [Because it is commonly contracted in that region]

Mediterranean flour moth *n.* a small grey moth, common worldwide, whose larvae feed on grain and grain products. Latin name: *Anagasta kuehniella.*

Mediterranean fruit fly *n.* a black-and-white two-winged fly that spread worldwide from the Mediterranean region. It lays its eggs in citrus and other types of fruit, which the maggots then destroy. Latin name: *Ceratitis capitata.*

Mediterranean Sea inland sea of Europe, Asia, and Africa, linked to the Atlantic Ocean at its western end by the Strait of Gibraltar. Area: 2,510,000 sq. km/969,000 sq. mi.

medium /meēdi əm/ *adj.* **1.** NEITHER LARGE NOR SMALL of middling size or dimensions, neither large nor small ○ *a man of medium build* **2.** NEITHER DARK NOR LIGHT not particularly dark or particularly light as a shade of the specified colour **3.** COOK BETWEEN RARE AND WELL-DONE cooked so that the meat is brown on the outside but slightly pink and moist inside ■ *n.* (*plural* **-dia** /meēdi ə/ *or* **-diums**) **1.** STATE BETWEEN EXTREMES an intermediate state or condition halfway between two extremes **2.** MEANS OF MASS COMMUNICATION one of the means of mass communication such as television, radio, or newspapers **3. VEHICLE FOR IDEAS** a means of conveying ideas or information ○ *French is the medium of instruction in all subjects.* **4. SUBSTANCE CONVEYING STH** a substance through which sth is carried or transmitted **5. MEANS OF ACHIEVING STH** the means by which sth is carried out or achieved **6. COMPUT MATERIAL HOLDING DATA** any form of material on which data is stored or printed, e.g. paper, tape, or disk **7. BIOL PRESERVING SUBSTANCE** a substance in which specimens of animals and plants are preserved or mounted **8. PARANORMAL PERSON SUPPOSEDLY RECEIVING MESSAGES FROM DEAD** sb who is supposedly able to convey messages between the spirits of the dead and living people **9. BIOL = culture medium 10. BIOL NATURAL ENVIRONMENT** a substance or the environment in which an organism naturally lives or grows **11. ARTS TYPE OF ART** a method that an artist uses or a category such as sculpture in which an artist works **12. ARTS ARTIST'S MATERIALS** the materials that an artist uses in creating a work **13. INDUST SOLVENT** a solvent mixed with a pigment or paint to make it thinner **14. PAPER PAPER SIZE** any of several similar sizes of paper, especially 47 cm by 58.5 cm/18.5 in by 23 in ■ **mediums** *npl.* **FIN GILT-EDGED SECURITIES** securities that are very safe as an investment [Late 16thC. From Latin, the neuter of *medius* 'middle'.]

──── **WORD KEY: ORIGIN** ────

The Latin word *medius*, from which **medium** is derived, is also the source of English *immediate, intermezzo, mean, media, mediate, medieval, mediocre, meridian, mezzanine, mitten,* and *moiety.*

medium-dated *adj.* used to describe gilt-edged securities redeemable after a period of between five and fifteen years

medium frequency *n.* a radio frequency lying between 300 and 3,000 kilohertz

medium of exchange *n.* sth commonly recognized in a country or community as a standard of value and used in the same way as money, e.g. gold

medium shot *n.* a filmed view, midway between long shot and close-up, that shows a standing person from the waist up or the full body of a sitting person ○ *a medium shot of the two characters in conversation*

medium wave *n.* a radio wave with a wavelength that lies between 100 and 1,000 metres

medlar /méddlər/ *n.* **1. TREES TREE WITH APPLE-SHAPED FRUIT** a small tree of the rose family, native to Europe and Asia, that has white flowers, long oblong leaves, and small apple-shaped fruit. Latin name: *Mespilus germanica.* **2. FOOD FRUIT OF THE MEDLAR TREE** the small apple-shaped fruit of the medlar tree. It can be eaten raw when overripe but is more often used to make preserves. [14thC. Via Old French *medler,* from *medle* 'medlar fruit' (a variant of *mesle*), from, ultimately, Greek *mespilē*.]

medley /méddli/ (*plural* **-leys**) *n.* **1. MIXTURE OF THINGS** a mixture or assortment of various things **2. MUSIC MUSICAL SEQUENCE OF DIFFERENT SONGS** a continuous piece of music consisting of two or more different tunes or songs played one after the other **3. medley, medley relay SWIMMING SWIMMING RACE USING DIFFERENT STROKES** a relay swimming race in which each team member must use a different stroke **4. medley, medley relay SPORTS RELAY RACE WITH DIFFERENT LENGTHS** a relay race in which each member of a team runs a different length [14thC. Via Old French *medlee* (variant of *meslee* 'mêlée', source of English *melee*), ultimately from medieval Latin *misculare* 'to mix thoroughly'.]

medulla /mi dúllə/ (*plural* **-lae** /-lee/ *or* **-las**) *n.* **1. BIOL INNERMOST STRUCTURE** the innermost area of a part or organ of an animal or plant ○ *the adrenal medulla* **2. ANAT = medulla oblongata 3. BOT = pith** *n.* 2 [14thC. From Latin, 'pith, marrow', of uncertain origin: perhaps formed from *medius* (see MEDIUM).] —**medullar** *adj.*

medulla oblongata /-ób long gaátə/ (*plural* **medullae oblongatae** /mi dúllee ób long gaá tee/ *or* **medulla oblongatas**) *n.* the lowermost part of the brain in vertebrates. It is continuous with the spinal cord and controls involuntary vital functions such as those involved with the heart and lungs. [From Latin, literally 'prolonged marrow']

medullary ray /mi dúlləri-, médd'ləri-/ *n.* any one of the bands or sheets of connective tissue that radiate between the pith and bark in the stems of some higher woody plants

medullary sheath *n.* ANAT = **myelin sheath**

medullated /méddə laytid, mi dúllaytid/ *adj.* **1. ANAT = myelinated 2. BIOL WITH MEDULLA** having a medulla ○ *medullated fibres*

medulloblastoma /mi dúllō bla stṓmə/ (*plural* **-mas** *or* **-mata** /-mətə/) *n.* a rapidly growing malignant tumour of the central nervous system arising in the brain. It occurs especially in children. [Early 20thC. Coined from MEDULLA + BLASTO- + -OMA.]

medusa /mə dyoózə/ (*plural* **-as** *or* **-ae** /-zee/) *n.* **1. REPRODUCTIVE STAGE OF JELLYFISH** the free-swimming reproductive stage of an animal such as a jellyfish, during which it has a transparent umbrella-shaped body with tentacles **2. = jellyfish** [Mid-18thC. Via modern Latin, the genus name, from, ultimately, Greek *Medousa* 'Medusa', from the resemblance of the tentacles to the snakes on Medusa's head.] —**medusan** *adj.*

Medusa: Ancient Roman mosaic, Sousse, France

Medusa /mə dyoózə/ *n.* in Greek mythology, a Gorgon who could turn to stone anyone who looked at her. She was killed by Perseus. —**Medusan** *adj.*

medusoid /mə dyoó zoyd/ *adj.* **LIKE A MEDUSA** relating to, typical of, or like a medusa ■ *n.* = **medusa** *n.* 1 [Mid-19thC. Coined from MEDUSA + -OID.]

Medway /méd way/ river in southeastern England, flowing through Kent to the Thames Estuary. Length: 112 km/70 mi.

meed /meed/ *n.* sth given as a reward or compensation (*archaic or literary*) [Old English *mēd* 'price, bribe, compensation', of prehistoric Germanic origin]

meek /meek/ *adj.* **1. MILD** showing mildness or quietness of nature **2. COWED** showing submissiveness and lack of initiative or will [12thC. From Old Norse *mjúkr* 'soft, pliant'. Ultimately from a prehistoric Germanic stem meaning 'soft', which is also the ancestor of English *muck*.] —**meekly** *adv.* —**meekness** *n.*

Meerkat

meerkat /meér kat/ *n.* a burrowing South African mongoose with four-toed feet and a greyish coat with faint black markings. Meerkats live in colonies and often stand erect near their burrows. Latin name: *Suricata suricatta.* [Early 19thC. Via Afrikaans from, ultimately, Middle Low German *meerkatte,* literally 'sea-cat', from *meer* 'sea' + *katte* 'cat', of uncertain origin: perhaps an alteration of an Asian word.]

meerschaum /meérshəm/ *n.* **1. MINERAL RESEMBLING CLAY** a fine whitish mineral, hydrous magnesium silicate, that resembles clay and is found in the Mediterranean region **2. meerschaum, meerschaum pipe PIPE WITH A MEERSCHAUM BOWL** a tobacco pipe with a bowl made of meerschaum [Late 18thC. From German, literally 'sea-foam', from *Meer* 'sea' + *Schaum* 'foam', a translation of Persian *kef-i-daryā* 'sea-foam', from its frothy appearance.]

meet[1] /meet/ *v.* (**meets, meeting, met** /met/) **1. vti. COME ACROSS SB** to encounter sb without having arranged to do so beforehand ○ *Guess who I met in the supermarket?* **2. vti. GET TOGETHER** to get together with sb by arrangement ○ *We could meet for lunch tomorrow.* **3. vti. ENCOUNTER SB FOR FIRST TIME** to encounter sb or be introduced for the first time ○ *It's exactly a year since they met.* **4. vt. GREET SB** to go somewhere to greet or fetch sb who is arriving there ○ *I'll come and meet you at the airport.* **5. vi. GATHER FOR DISCUSSION** to gather in a place to discuss sth ○ *The committee meets monthly.* **6. vti. JOIN STH** to join, cross, or be adjacent to sth or each other ○ *where the two roads meet* **7. vti. TOUCH STH** to come into contact with sth, or bring two objects into contact ○ *I can't get the two ropes to meet.* **8. vti. EXPERIENCE STH** to experience sth, e.g. a difficulty, challenge, or success ○ *All our attempts met with failure.* **9. vt. SATISFY STH** to cope with, satisfy, or fulfil what is required **10. vt. AGREE** to come to an agreement on sth ○ *I think we can meet you on that price.* **11. vti. LOOK AT STH** to look at or confront sth, or look at or confront each other ○ *Their glances met.* **12. vti. COMPETE OR FIGHT WITH SB** to come together to compete or fight with sb else ○ *The two teams have already met this year.* **13. vt. RESPOND IN A PARTICULAR WAY** to respond to a situation with a particular type of behaviour ○ *He met success and failure with equal indifference.* **14. vi. OCCUR TOGETHER** to happen or come together in the same place or person ○ *The extremes of creativity and irresponsibility meet in this genius.* ■ *n.* **1. SPORTS SPORTING OCCASION** an occasion at which numbers of competitors and spectators come together **2. HUNT GATHERING BEFORE HUNT** the period before a hunt when the riders and hounds gather together [Old English *mētan* 'to come upon, fall in with, find, find out'. Ultimately from a prehistoric Germanic base meaning 'meeting', which is also the ancestor of English *moot*.] —**meeter** *n.*

meet up *vi.* to get together with sb

meet[2] /meet/ *adj.* suitable or fitting for a particular situation (*archaic*) [Old English *gemǣte*. Ultimately from a prehistoric Germanic base meaning 'to measure', which is also the ancestor of English *mete out*. Originally also, 'having the correct dimensions'.] —**meetly** *adv.*

meeting /meéting/ *n.* **1. GATHERING OF PEOPLE FOR DISCUSSION** an occasion when people gather together to discuss sth **2. GROUP AT A MEETING** the people attending a meeting ○ *The chairman stood up to address the meeting.* **3. OCCASION WHEN SB MEETS SB ELSE** an occasion when sb encounters sb else, either accidentally or by arrangement **4. SPORTS SPORTING OCCASION** an occasion when people get together for a sporting competition, e.g. a number of horse races **5. CHR OCCASION FOR WORSHIP** a regular occasion when a group of people, especially Quakers, gather for worship

meeting house *n.* a room or building where some religious groups, especially Quakers, meet to worship

meg /meg/ *n.* a megabyte (*informal*)

meg- *prefix.* = **mega-** (used before vowels)

mega[1] /méggə/ *adj.* extremely enjoyable, impressive, excellent, or large (*informal*) [Late 20thC. From MEGA-.]

mega[2] /méggə/ *adj.* extremely good or successful (*slang*) ○ *This is going to be mega!*

mega- *prefix.* **1.** one million (10^6) ○ *megavolt.* Symbol **M 2.** COMPUT a binary million (2^{20}) ○ *megabyte* **3.** very large ○ *megadose* **4.** very great or excellent (*slang*) ○ *megastar* **5.** to a great extent (*slang*) ○ *megarich* [From Greek *megas* 'great'. Ultimately from an Indo-European word meaning 'large', which is also the ancestor of English *much, magnitude, major,* and *maharajah*.]

megabar /méggə baar/ *n.* a unit of pressure equal to one million bars

megabit /méggə bit/ *n.* **1.** 1,048,576 BITS 2^{20} (= 1,048,576) bits **2.** COMPUT MILLION BITS one million bits

megabuck /méggə buk/ *n.* US, Can **MILLION DOLLARS** a million dollars (*slang*) ▪ **megabucks** *npl.* US, Can **LARGE AMOUNT OF MONEY** a large unspecified amount of money (*slang*) ○ *an actor earning megabucks in Hollywood*

megabyte /méggə bīt/ *n.* **1. 1,048,576 BYTES** a unit of computer memory or disk storage space equal to 1,048,576 bytes **2. MILLION BYTES** one million bytes

megacephaly /méggə séffəli/ *n.* = **macrocephaly** — **megacephalic** /méggəsi fállik/ *adj.* —**megacephalous** /méggə séffə ləss/ *adj.*

megadeath /méggə deth/ *n.* one million deaths, used as a unit for recording deaths in a nuclear war

megadose /méggədōss/ *n.* a very large dose of a medical drug or food supplement

Megaera /mə jeérə/ *n.* in Greek mythology, one of the Furies. ◊ **Alecto, Tisiphone**

megafauna /méggə fawnə/ *n.* all the animals in a certain place that are larger than microscopic size —**megafaunal** *adj.*

megagamete /méggə ga meet/ *n.* = **macrogamete**

megahertz /méggə hurts/ (*plural* -**hertz**) *n.* one million hertz. Symbol **MHz**

megakaryocyte /méggə kárri ō sīt/ *n.* a large cell in bone marrow that fragments to produce blood platelets

megal- *prefix.* = **megalo-** (*used before vowels*)

megalith /méggə lith/ *n.* an enormous stone, usually standing upright or forming part of a prehistoric structure —**megalithic** /méggə líthik/ *adj.*

megalo- *prefix.* exceptionally large ○ *megalocardia* [From Greek *megal-*, the stem of *megas* (see MEGA-)]

megaloblast /méggələ blast/ *n.* an abnormally large red blood cell that has failed to mature properly, found especially in people affected by anaemia

megaloblastic anaemia /méggələ blástik-/ *n.* a form of anaemia in which the red blood cells are abnormally large because they fail to mature properly. It includes the type formerly known as pernicious anaemia. [*Megaloblastic* formed from MEGALOBLAST]

megalocardia /méggələ kaárdi ə/ *n.* = **cardiomegaly**

megalomania /méggələ máyni ə/ *n.* **1. GREED FOR POWER** the enjoyment of having power over other people and the craving for more of it (*disapproving*) **2.** PSYCHIAT **PSYCHIATRIC DISORDER WITH DELUSIONS OF POWER** a psychiatric disorder in which the patient experiences delusions of great power and importance —**megalomaniac** *n., adj.* —**megalomaniacal** /méggələ mə ní ək'l/ *adj.* —**megalomaniacally** /-ək'li/ *adv.*

megalopolis /méggə lóppə liss/ *n.* **1. AREA CONTAINING LARGE CITIES** an area in which there are several large cities whose suburbs meet or nearly meet **2. VERY LARGE CITY** an extremely large and populous city [Mid-19thC. Coined from MEGALO- + Greek *polis* 'city'.] —**megalopolistic** /méggə lóppə lísstik/ *adj.* —**megalopolitan** /méggə lə póllitən/ *adj.*

megalosaur /méggələ sawr/ *n.* a very large carnivorous dinosaur of the Jurassic and early Cretaceous periods. Genus: *Megalosaurus*. [Mid-19thC. Anglicization of modern Latin *megalosaurus*, from MEGALO- + Greek *sauros* 'lizard' (source of English *dinosaur*).] —**megalosaurian** /méggələ sáwri ən/ *adj.*

-megaly *suffix.* abnormal enlargement ○ *hepatomegaly* [From modern Latin *-megalia*, from Greek *megal-* (see MEGALO-) + *-ia* (see -Y¹)]

megaphone /méggə fōn/ *n.* a device shaped like a funnel, used to channel the voice in a certain direction and increase its volume —**megaphonic** /méggə fónnik/ *adj.* —**megaphonically** *adv.*

megaplex /méggə pléks/ *n.* a large cinema complex housing at least fifteen screens, often with the same film playing simultaneously in three or four of the theatres

megapode /méggə pōd/ *n.* a large Australasian ground-dwelling bird that builds a large mound of earth in which to incubate its eggs. Family: Megapodiidae. [Mid-19thC. From modern Latin *Megapodius*, genus name, from MEGA- + modern Latin *-podius*, masculine form of *-podium* '-pod'.]

Megara /méggərə/ historic town in southern Greece. It once rivalled ancient Athens in power. Population: 26,562 (1991).

megaron /méggə ron/ (*plural* -**ra** /-rə/) *n.* the largest room in a house built during the Mycenaean period of ancient Greek civilization [Late 19thC. From Greek, 'large room, hall, sanctuary, shrine'.]

megascopic /méggə skóppik/ *adj.* = **macroscopic** — **megascopically** *adv.*

megasporangium /méggə spaw ránji əm/ (*plural* -**a** /-ə/) *n.* an organ in seed plants and ferns that produces large spores (**megaspores**) that give rise to female gametophytes

megaspore /méggə spawr/ *n.* the larger of two kinds of spore produced by seed plants and some ferns that develops into a female gametophyte. ◊ **microspore**

megastar /méggə staar/ *n.* sb who is very famous, especially an entertainer who is extremely popular

megathere /méggə theer/ *n.* a large extinct American ground sloth that lived in the Miocene and Pleistocene epochs. Family: Megatheriidae. [Mid-19thC. Anglicization of modern Latin *Megatherium*, the genus name, from Greek *mega-* 'large' + *thērion* 'animal'.] — **megatherian** /méggə theéri ən/ *adj.*

megaton /méggə tun/ *n.* **1. UNIT OF EXPLOSIVE POWER** a unit of explosive power, e.g. in a nuclear weapon, that is equivalent to one million tons of TNT **2. MILLION TONS** one million tons —**megatonic** /méggə tónnik/ *adj.* —**megatonnage** /-tunnij/ *n.*

megavitamin /méggə víttəmin, -vítəmin/ *n.* a dose of a vitamin or vitamins that is much higher than the normal dose —**megavitamin** *adj.*

megavolt /méggə vōlt/ *n.* one million volts

megawatt /méggə wot/ *n.* one million watts

Megiddo /mə geédō/ ruined ancient city in northern Israel, thought to be the predicted site of the battle of Armageddon described in the Bible

megillah /mə gíllə/ (*plural* -**lahs** or -**loth** /məgi lóth/) *n.* **1.** JUDAISM **HEBREW SCROLL** a scroll containing part of the Hebrew Bible, especially the scroll containing the Book of Esther **2. OVERELABORATE ACCOUNT** an overelaborate and unnecessarily lengthy account of sth [Mid-17thC. From Hebrew, literally 'roll, scroll', from *gālal* 'roll'.]

megilp /mə gílp/, **magilp** *n.* a mixture of linseed oil and mastic varnish or turpentine, used as a solvent for oil paints [Mid-18thC. Origin unknown.]

megrim¹ /meégrim/ (*plural* -**grims** or -**grim**) *n.* a flatfish related to the turbot caught for food in European seas. Latin name: *Lepidorhombus whiffiagonis.* [Mid-19thC. Origin unknown.]

megrim² /meégrim/ *n.* (*archaic*) **1.** MED **MIGRAINE** a migraine headache **2. WHIM** a sudden change of mind, or sth about which sb is briefly enthusiastic ▪ **megrims** *npl.* **MELANCHOLY** a spell of melancholy or low spirits (*archaic*) [15thC. Variant of MIGRAINE.]

Mehmet Ali /mi hémmit aáli/ (1769–1849) Albanian-born Egyptian monarch. He became Pasha of Egypt (1805–49), extending his dominions as far as the Persian Gulf. His descendants ruled Egypt until 1952. Alternative name **Muhammad Ali**

meibomian cyst /mī bốmi ən-/ *n.* a painless swelling in the eyelid, somewhat like a pea, caused by blockage of the outlet duct of a meibomian gland and the resulting accumulation of fatty secretion [See MEIBOMIAN GLAND]

meibomian gland *n.* any of the sebaceous glands in the eyelid [Early 19thC. Named after Heinrich *Meibom* (1638–1700), a German anatomist who discovered it.]

Meiji /máy jee, -jeé/ *n.* the reign of the Japanese emperor Meiji Tenno (1867–1912), a period of extensive reform, including the abolition of feudalism [Late 19thC. From Japanese, literally 'enlightened government']

meiny /máy ni/ (*plural* **meinies**), **meinie** *n.* **1.** Scotland **CROWD** a crowd of people or a rabble **2. RETINUE** a group of people who are attached to a household or work for an individual (*archaic*) [13thC. Via Old French *meinee*, *mesnée* from, ultimately, Latin *mansion-* (see MANSION).]

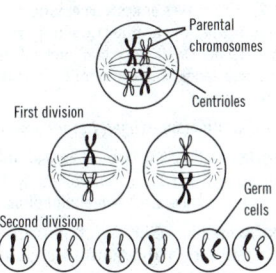

Meiosis

meiosis /mī ṓssiss/ *n.* **1.** CELL BIOL **PROCESS OF CELL DIVISION** in organisms that reproduce sexually, a process of cell division during which the nucleus divides into four nuclei, each of which contains half the usual number of chromosomes **2.** LITERAT = **litotes** [Mid-16thC. Via modern Latin from, ultimately, Greek *meiōn* 'less'. Originally meaning 'litotes'.]

Golda Meir

Meir /may eér/, **Golda** (1898–1978) Russian-born national leader of Israel. She entered the Labour government of Israel in 1949 and served as prime minister from 1969 until 1974, when she resigned after the Yom Kippur War (1973).

Meissen¹ /míss'n/ *n.* = **Dresden china**

Meissen² /míssən/ town in east-central Germany, famous for its porcelain manufacture. Population: 36,800 (1989).

Meissner's corpuscle /mīsnərz-/ *n.* = **tactile corpuscle**

Meistersinger /místər singər/ (*plural* -**ers** or -**er**) *n.* sb who belonged to one of the German guilds for poets and musicians in the 14th, 15th, and 16th centuries. A Meistersinger had completed an apprenticeship and composed original work. [Mid-19thC. From German, literally 'master-singer'.]

Meknés /mek nész/ city and former capital of Morocco, located in the north of the country. Population: 401,000 (1993).

Mekong /mee kóng/ major river in southeastern Asia, flowing through a number of countries before emptying into the South China Sea. Length: 4,200 km/2,600 mi.

melaena /mə leénə/ *n.* a condition characterized by the production of black stools that are caused by bleeding into the bowel and the subsequent chemical changes in the blood effected by the bowel fluids [Early 19thC. Via modern Latin from Greek *melaina*, feminine of *melas* 'black' (source of English *melancholy* and *melano-*).]

melaena *n.* = **melena**

Melaka /mə lákə/ city and seaport in Malaysia, on the southern coast of the Malay Peninsula. Population: 295,999 (1991). Former name **Malacca**

melaleuca /méllə lốokə/ *n.* a tree or shrub of the myrtle family that is native to Australia and grows especially in swampy areas and along rivers. One species has naturalized in California and Florida and has become a pest plant in the Everglades. Genus: *Melaleuca.*

melamine /méllə meen/ *n.* **1.** CHEM **COMPOUND USED IN RESINS** a white crystalline solid used in making synthetic resins and in leather tanning. Formula:

$C_3H_6N_6$. **2.** INDUST TYPE OF RESIN OR PLASTIC a resin made from melamine, or a plastic made from such a resin [Mid-19thC. Origin uncertain: probably from German *Melamin*, a substance obtained from the distillation of ammonium thiocyanate.]

melan- *prefix.* = **melano-** (*used before vowels*)

melancholia /méllən kṓli ə/ *n.* depression as a form of psychiatric disorder (*archaic*) [Early 17thC. From late Latin (see MELANCHOLY).] —**melancholiac** *n., adj.*

melancholic /méllən kóllik/ *adj.* **1.** PENSIVELY SAD feeling or tending to feel a thoughtful or gentle sadness (*literary*) **2.** DEPRESSED experiencing psychiatric depression (*archaic*) ■ *n.* DEPRESSED PERSON sb who has psychiatric depression (*archaic*) [14thC. Origin uncertain: either formed from MELANCHOLY, or via French *mélancolique* from, ultimately, Greek *melankholikos*, from *melankholia* (see MELANCHOLY).] —**melancholically** *adv.*

melancholy /méllənkəli/ *adj.* FEELING OR CAUSING PENSIVE SADNESS feeling or making sb feel a thoughtful or gentle sadness ■ *n.* **1.** PENSIVE SADNESS thoughtful or gentle sadness **2.** GLOOMY CHARACTER the gloomy character of sb said to have an excess of black bile, one of the four bodily humours that were once thought to determine people's health and emotional state (*archaic*) **3.** = black bile (*archaic*) [14thC. Directly or via French *mélancholie* from late Latin *melancholia*, from Greek *melankholia*, literally 'black bile', from *melan-*, the stem of *melas* 'black' + *kholē* 'bile'.] —**melancholily** /-kolili/ *adv.* —**melancholiness** *n.*

Melanchthon /mə lángkthən, me lánkh ton/, **Philipp** (1497–1560) German religious reformer. Working in association with Martin Luther, he produced some of the most important theological works of the Protestant Reformation, including *Commonplaces of Theology* (1521) and the Augsburg Confession (1530). Real name **Philipp Schwartzert**

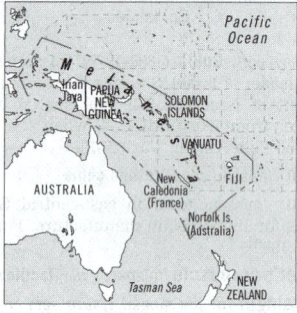

Melanesia

Melanesia /méllə néezi ə, -néezhə/ ethnographic region in Oceania, encompassing a number of island groups in the western Pacific Ocean, south of the equator

Melanesian /méllə néezi ən, -néezhən/ *adj.* OF MELANESIA relating to Melanesia, or its peoples, cultures, or languages ■ *n.* **1.** LANG GROUP OF PACIFIC ISLAND LANGUAGES a group of languages, including Fijian, spoken in Melanesia, a subgroup of the Eastern branch of the Austronesian family of languages. About 300,000 people speak a Melanesian language. **2.** PEOPLES SB FROM MELANESIA a member of any of the peoples living on the islands of Melanesia

melange /may lóNzh, -laánzh/, **mélange** *n.* **1.** MIXTURE OF THINGS a collection of things of different kinds (*literary or formal*) **2.** GEOL MIXTURE OF ROCKS a region of rock that consists of a mixture of dissimilar rocky materials [Mid-17thC. From French *mélange*, from *mêler* 'to mix', ultimately from Latin *miscere* (see MIXED).]

melanin /méllənin/ *n.* a dark brown or black pigment that is naturally present to varying degrees in the skin, hair, eyes, fur, or feathers of people and animals as well as in plants —**melanoid** *adj.*

melanism /méllənizzəm/ *n.* **1.** BIOL DARK PIGMENTATION dark pigmentation of the skin, hair, fur, or feathers in a human being, animal, or plant, resulting from the presence of melanin **2.** MED = melanosis —**melanic** /mə lánnik/ *adj.* —**melanistic** /méllə nístik/ *adj.*

melanite /méllə nīt/ *n.* a black form of andradite garnet containing titanium —**melanitic** /-níttik/ *adj.*

melano- *prefix.* black, dark ○ *melanocyte* [From Greek *melan-*, the stem of *melas* 'black' (source of English *melancholy*)]

melanoblast /méllənō blast/ *n.* a cell that gives rise to either a melanocyte or melanophore, which produces the black or dark brown pigment melanin —**melanoblastic** /méllə nō blástik/ *adj.*

melanocyte /méllənō sīt/ *n.* a cell in the epidermal layer of the skin that produces the black or dark brown pigment melanin

melanocyte-stimulating hormone *n.* either of two hormones in vertebrates produced in the pituitary gland that darken the skin by regulating melanin dispersal

melanoma /méllə nṓmə/ (*plural* -**mas** *or* -**mata** /-mətə/) *n.* a malignant tumour, most often on the skin, that contains dark pigment and develops from a melanin-producing cell (**melanocyte**)

melanophore /méllənō fawr/ *n.* a cell in fishes, amphibians, and reptiles that contains the black to dark brown pigment melanin

melanosis /méllə nṓssiss/ *n.* an unexpected presence of dark pigmentation in the tissues [Early 19thC. From modern Latin, from the Greek stem *melan-* (see MELANCHOLY).] —**melanic** /mə lánnik/ *adj.* —**melanoid** /méllə noyd/ *adj.* —**melanotic** /méllə nóttik/ *adj.*

melanous /méllənəss/ *adj.* having a dark complexion and dark hair [Mid-19thC. Formed from the Greek stem *melan-* (see MELANCHOLY).] —**melanosity** /méllə nóssəti/ *n.*

melatonin /méllə tṓnin/ *n.* a hormone derived from serotonin and secreted by the pineal gland that produces changes in the skin colour of vertebrates, reptiles, and amphibians and is important in regulating biorhythms [Mid-20thC. Blend of MELANO- + SEROTONIN.]

Melba /mélbə/ ◇ **do a Melba** ANZ to announce your retirement from a job or occupation repeatedly without actually doing so

Dame Nellie Melba

Melba /mélbə/, **Dame Nellie** (1861–1931) Australian opera singer. She was a soprano who won international acclaim for her performances in roles such as Mimi in *La Bohème*. Real name **Helen Porter Mitchell**

Melba sauce *n.* a sauce consisting of puréed sweetened raspberries, served especially with poached peaches and ice cream in peach Melba [Early 20thC. Named after Nellie MELBA, in whose honour peach Melba was created.]

Melba toast *n.* very thin slices of bread toasted on both sides, sliced horizontally to expose two untoasted sides of bread that are then toasted too, causing the bread to curl [Early 20thC. Named after Nellie MELBA, because it was part of her diet during an illness in 1897.]

Melbourne /mél burn/ city in southeastern Australia, the capital of the state of Victoria. Population: 2,865,329 (1996).

Melbourne, William Lamb, 2nd Viscount (1779–1848) British statesman and prime minister. A Whig MP after 1806, he was prime minister (1834, 1835–41) during the early years of Queen Victoria's reign, and was her political mentor.

Melbourne Cup /mélbərn-/ *n.* the best-known horse race in Australia, which takes place each year on

the first Tuesday in November. The first race was held in 1861.

Melchite /mél kīt/, **Melkite** *n.* a member of any of several Christian churches in the Middle East that use the Greek Orthodox liturgy but acknowledge the authority of the Roman Catholic Pope [Early 17thC. Via ecclesiastical Latin from Byzantine Greek *Melkhitai* 'Melkites', from Syriac *malkāyē*, literally 'royalists', from *malkā* 'king'.]

Melchizedek /mel kízzə dek/ *n.* in the Bible, a priest and king of Salem who blessed Abraham

meld[1] /meld/ *vti.* (**melds, melding, melded**) COMBINE to cause various things to combine or blend and become one thing or substance, or be combined or blended in this way ■ *n.* COMBINATION a combination or blend of various things [Mid-20thC. Origin uncertain: perhaps from the past participle of a dialect word *mell* 'to mix', from Old French *mesler* (see MELEE).]

meld[2] /meld/ *vti.* (**melds, melding, melded**) SHOW A HAND OF CARDS to show or declare some or all of a hand of cards in order to score points in games such as canasta or pinochle ■ *n.* HAND OF SHOWN OR DECLARED CARDS a hand of cards that are shown or declared in order to score points in games such as canasta or pinochle, or an act of showing or declaring these cards [Late 19thC. From German *melden* 'to announce'.]

Meldrum /méldrəm/, **Max** (1875–1955) British-born Australian painter. He was a proponent of a scientific, realist approach to painting.

Meleager /mélli áygər/ *n.* in Greek mythology, a prince who killed the Calydonian boar

melee /méllay/, **mêlée** *n.* **1.** FIGHT a noisy confused fight **2.** CONFUSED MINGLING a confused, often noisy mixing of people or things, usually in a public place [Mid-17thC. Via French *mêlée* from Old French *meslee*, the past participle of *mesler* 'to mix', via assumed Vulgar Latin *misculare* from Latin *miscere*.]

melena *n.* US = **melaena**

melic /méllik/ *adj.* used to describe an ancient Greek lyric poem that is meant to be sung rather than recited [Late 17thC. Via Latin from Greek *melikos*, from *melos* 'song' (source of English *melody* and *melodrama*).]

Méliès /máyl yess/, **Georges** (1861–1938) French film director. A pioneer of cinematography, he built the first film studio, devising trick effects, and created his own production company.

Melilla /mə líllə/ Spanish enclave and port on the Mediterranean coast of Morocco. Population: 64,727 (1995). Area: 14 sq. km/55 sq. mi.

melilot /mélli lot/ *n.* a plant belonging to the pea family that has compound leaves consisting of three oval leaflets, and spikes of small flared yellow or white flowers. Genus: *Melilotus*. [14thC. Via French from, ultimately, Greek *melilōtos*, from *meli* 'honey' + *lōtos* 'lotus, clover'.]

melinite /mélli nīt/ *n.* an explosive made from picric acid [Late 19thC. From French, formed from Greek *mēlinos* 'quince-coloured', from *mēlon* 'apple, quince' (source of English *melon*); so called because of its yellow colour.]

meliorate /méeli ə rayt/ (-**rates, -rating, -rated**) *vti.* to become better, or make sth better [Mid-16thC. From late Latin *meliorare*, from Latin *melior* 'better'.] —**meliorable** /méeli ərəb'l/ *adj.* —**melioration** /méeli ə ráysh'n/ *n.* —**meliorative** /méeli ə rətiv/ *adj.* —**meliorator** /-raytər/ *n.*

meliorism /méeli ərizəm/ *n.* the belief that human society has a natural tendency to improve and that people can consciously assist this process [Mid-19thC. Formed from Latin *melior* 'better'.] —**meliorist** *n.* —**melioristic** /méeli ə rístik/ *adj.*

melisma /mə lízmə/ (*plural* -**mata** /-mətə/ *or* -**mas**) *n.* **1.** SEVERAL NOTES SUNG ON ONE SYLLABLE a decorative phrase or passage in vocal music, especially one in which one syllable of a plainsong text is sung to a melodic sequence of several notes **2.** EMBELLISHMENT OF MELODY an embellishment or decoration of a melody **3.** = cadenza [Late 19thC. Via modern Latin from Greek, 'tune', from *melizein* 'to sing', from *melos* 'song' (source of English *melody*).] —**melismatic** /mélli máttik/ *adj.*

Melkite *n.* = **Melchite**

melli- prefix. honey ○ melliphagous [From Latin mel (source of English molasses). Ultimately from the Indo-European for 'honey', which is also the ancestor of marmalade and mildew.]

melliferous /mə líffərəss/, **mellific** /mə líffik/ adj. producing or bearing large quantities of honey [Mid-17thC. Formed from Latin mellifer 'honey-bearing', from mel 'honey'.]

mellifluous /mə líffloo əss/, **mellifluent** /mə lífloo ənt/ adj. pleasant and soothing to listen to, and sweet or rich in tone [15thC. Formed from late Latin mellifluus, literally 'flowing like honey', from mel 'honey' (see MELLI-) + fluere 'to flow' (see FLUENT).] —**mellifluously** adv. —**mellifluousness** n.

melliphagous /mə líffəgəss/, **mellivorous** /mə lívvərəss/ adj. feeding on honey

mellophone /méllə fōn/ n. a portable brass musical instrument similar in tone to a French horn, used mainly in brass bands and marching bands [Early 20thC. Coined from MELLOW + -PHONE.]

mellow /méllō/ adj. 1. SOFT IN COLOUR OR TONE comfortingly soft, warm, and rich in colour or tone and lacking any harsh, brash, or jarring quality 2. SMOOTH AND RICH IN TASTE matured to a long-lasting smooth, rich taste 3. FULLY RIPE soft, juicy, fully ripened, and sweet 4. EASY-GOING good-humoured, tolerant, and approachable, especially as a result of long experience or a relaxed atmosphere 5. MILDLY INTOXICATED mildly intoxicated by drink or drugs 6. AGRIC MOIST AND RICH IN TEXTURE having a moist, rich, loamy texture ■ vti. (-lows, -lowing, -lowed) 1. BECOME MORE EASY-GOING to become or make sb more good-humoured, tolerant, and approachable, especially as a result of long experience or a relaxed atmosphere 2. BECOME OR MAKE RICHER IN QUALITY to become or make sth richer, smoother, or softer in taste, colour, tone, or atmosphere [15thC. Origin uncertain: perhaps an adjectival use of Old English melu 'meal, flour', the underlying sense being 'soft and rich like flour'.] —**mellowly** adv. —**mellowness** n.

mellow out vti. US (slang) 1. RELAX to become or make sb more relaxed and friendly 2. CALM DOWN to become calm, or make sb calm

melodeon /mə lṓdi ən/ n. 1. SMALL REED ORGAN a small reed organ, similar to a harmonium, that uses suction bellows to draw air through its reeds 2. SMALL ACCORDION a small accordion, used especially by German folk musicians [Mid-19thC. Origin uncertain: probably an alteration of melodium 'small reed organ', from MELODY on the model of HARMONIUM.]

melodic /mə lóddik/ adj. 1. CONSISTING OF MELODY consisting of the melody of a piece of music ○ the melodic line 2. RELATING TO MELODY relating to or characteristic of melody or the composition of melodies 3. = melodious —**melodically** adv.

melodic minor scale n. a scale with the sixth and seventh notes raised a semitone when played in ascending order but in the natural minor pitch when played in descending order

melodious /mə lṓdi əss/ adj. 1. PLEASING TO HEAR tuneful or varied and interesting in tone 2. CHARACTERIZED BY MELODY having the character of a melody —**melodiously** adv. —**melodiousness** n.

melodise vti. = melodize

melodist /méllə dist/ n. 1. COMPOSER OF MELODIES sb who composes melodies, especially beautiful or memorable melodies for song lyrics 2. SINGER sb who sings sweetly

melodize /méllə dīz/ (-dizes, -dizing, -dized), **melodise** (-dises, -dising, -dised) v. 1. vti. COMPOSE MELODIES to compose a melody or melodies, or compose a melody to which lyrics can be sung 2. vt. MAKE STH MELODIOUS to make sth tuneful and pleasing to hear —**melodizer** n.

melodrama /méllə draamə/ n. 1. SENSATIONALIZED DRAMATIC OR LITERARY WORK a dramatic or other literary work characterized by the use of stereotyped characters, exaggerated emotions and language, simplistic morality, and conflict 2. DRAMATIC OR LITERARY GENRE melodramas collectively considered as a dramatic or literary genre 3. HISTRIONIC BEHAVIOUR exaggerated behaviour or emotional displays, like those characteristic of a melodrama 4. DRAMA INTERSPERSED WITH MUSIC formerly, a play with a sensational or romantic plot that is interspersed with musical numbers and often has music accompanying the action 5. SPOKEN WORDS WITH MUSICAL ACCOMPANIMENT a piece of poetry or a scene in a dramatic or operatic work in which the text is recited to a musical accompaniment [Early 19thC. From French mélodrame 'drama with songs', from Greek melos 'song' + French drame (see DRAMA).]

melodramatic /mélladrə máttik/ adj. 1. EXAGGERATEDLY THEATRICAL behaving, speaking, done, or said in a way that is more dramatic, shocking, or highly emotional than the situation demands 2. RELATING TO MELODRAMA relating to or typical of melodrama [Early 19thC. Formed from MELODRAMA, on the model of DRAMATIC.] —**melodramatically** adv.

melodramatics /mélladrə máttiks/ npl. exaggeratedly theatrical behaviour, speech, or writing

melodramatize /méllə drámmə tīz/ (-tizes, -tizing, -tized), **melodramatise** (-tises, -tising, -tised) vti. to treat or react to sth in an exaggeratedly theatrical way [Early 19thC. Formed from MELODRAMA, on the model of DRAMATIZE.] —**melodramatization** /méllə drámmə tī záysh'n/ n.

melody /mélladi/ (plural -dies) n. 1. TUNE a series of musical notes that form a distinct unit, are recognizable as a phrase, and usually have a distinctive rhythm 2. LINEAR MUSICAL STRUCTURE the linear structure of a piece of music in which single notes follow one another 3. MAIN TUNE the primary and most recognizable part in a harmonic piece of music 4. MUSICALLY EXPRESSIVE QUALITY the musically expressive quality of sth, especially poetry 5. MUSICAL LYRIC a poem that lends itself easily to being set to music or sung [12thC. Via French mélodie from, ultimately, Greek melōidia 'choral song', from melos 'tune' + aoidē 'song' (see ODE).]

meloid /mélloyd/ n. any beetle with a flexible body, e.g. the blister beetle or the oil beetle. Family: Meloidae. [Late 19thC. From modern Latin Meloidae, family name, from Meloë, genus name, of uncertain origin.]

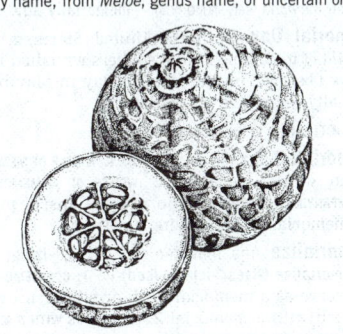

Melon

melon /méllən/ n. 1. FOOD ROUND JUICY GOURD FRUIT the round edible fruit of vines belonging to the gourd family, with a tough rind and sweet juicy flesh ranging in colour from pale yellow to deep orange 2. PLANTS PLANT THAT BEARS MELONS a vine of the gourd family widely grown for its edible fruit. Latin name: Cucumis melo and Citrullus lanatus. 3. ZOOL SOUND ORGAN IN SEA MAMMAL'S HEAD a rounded waxy mass found in the head of some dolphins and toothed whales that is thought to play a part in the focusing of sound signals 4. OFFENSIVE TERM an offensive term for a woman's large breast (offensive) [14thC. Via French from, ultimately, Greek mēlopepōn, a kind of gourd, from mēlon 'apple' + pepōn 'gourd'.]

Melos /méelos loss/, **Mílos** island in southeastern Greece, one of the Cyclades. Population: 4,554 (1981). Area: 150 sq. km/58 sq. mi.

Melpomene /mel pómməni/ n. in Greek mythology, the muse of tragedy

Melrose /mél rōz/ 1. historic market town on the River Tweed in southeastern Scotland. Population: 2,270 (1991). 2. city in northeastern Massachusetts, north of Malden, a northern suburb of Boston. Population: 27,426 (1996).

melt[1] /melt/ v. 1. vti. CHANGE FROM A SOLID TO A LIQUID STATE to change a substance from a solid to a liquid state by heating it, or be changed in this way 2. vti. DISSOLVE to dissolve sth, e.g. sugar, in a liquid or be dissolved in a liquid 3. vi. DISAPPEAR to disappear gradually and inconspicuously 4. vi. MERGE INTO to change into, or blend with, sth in such a way that the actual point of change or blending is almost imperceptible 5. vti. BE MOVED EMOTIONALLY to cause sb to be moved emotionally so as to become gentler and more sympathetic, or be moved in this way 6. vi. FEEL HOT to feel uncomfortably hot (informal) ■ n. 1. MASS OF MELTED MATERIAL a mass or an amount of melted material, especially metal, produced in a single operation or during a specific period of time 2. MOLTEN MATERIAL a material such as metal or glass in a molten state 3. MELTING OF STH the process of melting sth 4. LIQUEFACTION the state or condition of being liquefied 5. FOOD TOASTED CHEESE-TOPPED OPEN SANDWICH an open toasted sandwich, usually with cheese melted on top —**meltability** n. —**meltable** adj. —**melter** n.

melt down vti. to liquefy metal or glass by heating in order to reuse it, or to be liquefied in this way

melt[2] /melt/ n. the spleen of a slaughtered animal, used mainly for animal food (often used in the plural) [Late 16thC. Variant of MILT.]

meltage /méltij/ n. 1. MELTING OF STH the process of melting sth 2. SUBSTANCE PRODUCED BY MELTING a liquefied substance produced by a heating process, or an amount of such a substance

meltdown /mélt down/ n. 1. PHYS MELTING OF NUCLEAR REACTOR FUEL RODS the melting of fuel rods in a nuclear reactor because of overheating that results in the escape of radioactive materials or radiation 2. COMPLETE COLLAPSE OF AN ORGANIZATION a situation of complete collapse of an organization or institution (informal) 3. EXTREMELY ANGRY STATE a loss of composure, especially an extremely angry response to sth (informal) 4. PERSONAL BREAKDOWN a loss of coherence, rationality, or awareness of reality (informal)

melting /mélting/ adj. full of or causing sweet and tender or sentimental emotion —**meltingly** adv. —**meltingness** n.

melting point n. PHYS the temperature at which a substance changes from a solid to a liquid form

melting pot n. 1. METALL CONTAINER FOR MELTING AND MIXING a container in which substances, especially metals, are placed to be liquefied and mixed together 2. SOC SCI SOCIETY COMPOSED OF MANY DIFFERENT CULTURES a place where people of different ethnic groups are brought together and can assimilate, especially a country that takes immigrants from many different ethnic backgrounds 3. PROCESS THAT CREATES STH NEW a process of mixture and integration of different elements that can produce sth new

melton /méltən/ n. a type of smooth heavy wool cloth, used primarily to make overcoats [Mid-19thC. Named after the town of Melton Mowbray in Leicestershire, where it was made.]

Melton Mowbray /méltən mṓbray/ ancient market town in Leicestershire, central England. It is famous for its pork pies. Population: 24,348 (1991).

meltwater /mélt wawtər/ n. water formed by the melting of ice or snow, especially from a glacier

Melville Island /mélvil-/ island located in the Timor Sea, off the northern coast of the Northern Territory of Australia. Population: 2,033 (1996). Area: 5,700 sq. km/2,200 sq. mi.

Melville Peninsula peninsula in Nunavut, northern Canada. Foxe Basin lies to its west, and Committee Bay to its east. Area: 65,000 sq. km/25,100 sq. mi.

mem /mem/ n. the 13th letter of the Hebrew alphabet, represented in the English alphabet as 'm' [Early 19thC. From Hebrew mēm, literally 'water'.]

mem. abbr. 1. member 2. memoir 3. memorandum 4. memorial

member /mémbər/ n. 1. SB BELONGING TO PARTICULAR GROUP sb who belongs to and participates in a particular group by birth, e.g. a family, species, or social class, or by choice, e.g. a club, church, or organization 2. member, Member POL POLITICAL REPRESENTATIVE sb elected to a legislative body such as the British Parliament or the US Congress 3. LIMB a part or organ of a plant or animal body, especially a limb 4. PENIS a penis (formal or humorous) 5. INDIVIDUAL PART OF A WHOLE a separate and distinct part of a whole, e.g. an object belonging to a mathematical set, a clause in a sentence, or a proposition in a syllogism **6.** CONSTR **STRUCTURAL UNIT IN BUILDING** a beam, wall, or similar structural unit in a building or other construction **7.** MATH **ELEMENT IN A MATHEMATICAL EQUATION** either of the expressions in a mathematical equation linked by an equals sign [14thC. Via French *membre* from Latin *membrum* 'limb, part' (source also of English *membrane*).] —**memberless** *adj.*

member firm *n.* a company trading in securities that belongs to an organized exchange

Member of Congress *n.* sb elected to the US Congress, especially to the House of Representatives

Member of Parliament *n.* sb who has been elected to a parliament

membership /mémbərship/ *n.* **1. BEING A MEMBER OF STH** the state or condition belonging to a particular group, e.g. a species, social class, team, club, or political party **2. MEMBERS OF AN ORGANIZATION** the members of a group, e.g. a species, social class, organization, or mathematical set, considered collectively (*takes a singular or plural verb*)

membrane /mém brayn/ *n.* **1.** BIOL **THIN LAYER OF TISSUE** a thin flexible sheet of tissue connecting, covering, lining, or separating various parts or organs in animal and plant bodies, or forming the external wall of a cell **2.** CHEM **THIN POROUS SHEET** a thin, pliable, and often porous sheet of any natural or artificial material **3. PIECE OF PARCHMENT** a piece of parchment forming part of a roll [15thC. Directly or via French from Latin *membrana* 'skin (covering part of the body)', from *membrum* 'limb, part' (source of English *member*).] —**membranaceous** /mémbrə náyshəss/ *adj.* —**membranal** /mémbrən'l/ *adj.* —**membraned** /mém braynd/ *adj.*

membrane bone *n.* a bone that develops directly out of membranous connective tissue rather than from cartilage, e.g. the clavicle and some cranial bones

membrane transport *n.* the process by which substances in solution pass through a biological membrane

membranous /mémbrənəss/ *adj.* **1.** BIOL **RELATING TO A MEMBRANE** relating to or similar to a membrane, especially in being thin, pliable, and often translucent **2.** PHYSIOL **RESULTING IN THE FORMATION OF A MEMBRANE** resulting in the formation of a membrane or of a thin layer similar to a membrane —**membranously** *adv.*

membranous labyrinth *n.* the structure of fluid-filled sacs in the inner ear that are vital to hearing and balance

memento /mə méntō, mi-/ (*plural* **-tos** *or* **-toes**) *n.* an object given or kept as a reminder of or in memory of sb or sth [Mid-18thC. From Latin, 'remember' (originally the first word in prayers for the dead), from *meminisse* 'to remember'.]

memento mori /-máw ree/ (*plural* **memento mori**) *n.* **1. REMINDER OF DEATH** an object, especially a skull, intended as a reminder of the fact that humans die **2. REMINDER OF HUMAN ERROR** a reminder of the fact that humans fail and make mistakes (*literary*) [From Latin, 'remember (that you have) to die']

Memling /mémmling/, **Hans** (1435?–94) Flemish painter. He chose mainly religious subjects, imbued with delicacy, harmony, and repose, and also painted idealized portraits.

Memnon /mém non/ *n.* in Greek mythology, the Ethiopian king who fought for the Trojans in the siege of Troy and was killed by Achilles

memo /mémmō/ (*plural* **-os**) *n.* **1. WRITTEN COMMUNICATION** a written communication similar to a letter but without the formal address blocks at the beginning, especially one that is circulated to people within an office or organization **2.** = **memorandum** *n.* 2 [Early 18thC. Shortening of MEMORANDUM.]

memoir /mém waar/ *n.* **1. BIOGRAPHY OR HISTORICAL ACCOUNT** a biography or an account of historical events, especially one written from personal knowledge **2. ESSAY ON A SCHOLARLY SUBJECT** a short essay, article, or report on a scholarly subject, usually one in which the writer is a recognized specialist ■ **memoirs** *npl.* **1. AUTOBIOGRAPHY** sb's written account of his or her own life, or of events in which he or she took part **2. PROCEEDINGS** the records of the business and discussions of a learned society [Mid-17thC. Via French *mémoire* 'memory, recollection' from Old French *memorie* (see MEMORY).]

memorabilia /mémmərə bílli ə/ *npl.* **1. OBJECTS CONNECTED WITH A FAMOUS PERSON** objects associated with a famous person or event, especially considered as collectors' items **2. PERSONAL SOUVENIRS** objects collected as souvenirs of important personal events or experiences [Late 18thC. From Latin, literally 'memorable things', formed from *memorabilis* (see MEMORABLE).]

memorable /mémmərəb'l/ *adj.* **1. WORTH REMEMBERING** sufficiently interesting, exciting, or unusual to be worth remembering or likely to be remembered **2. EASILY REMEMBERED** easy to remember [15thC. Via French from Latin *memorabilis*, from *memorare* 'to bring to mind' (source of English *commemorate*), from *memor* 'mindful' (see MEMORY).] —**memorability** /mémmərə bílləti/ *n.* —**memorableness** /mémmərəb'lnəss/ *n.* —**memorably** *adv.*

memorandum /mémmə rándəm/ (*plural* **-dums** *or* **-da** /-də/) *n.* **1.** COMM = **memo** *n.* 1 **2. REMINDER** a note to serve as a reminder of sth **3.** POL **BRIEF DIPLOMATIC COMMUNICATION** a brief, often unsigned communication circulated among diplomats, especially one that summarizes a country's position on a particular issue **4.** LAW **SUMMARY OF A LEGAL AGREEMENT** a written statement summarizing the terms of a contract or a similar legal transaction **5.** TRANSP **CONSIGNOR'S STATEMENT** a consignor's brief statement about a shipment of returnable goods [15thC. From Latin, literally 'thing to be remembered', from *memorare* 'to bring to mind', from *memor* 'mindful' (see MEMORY).]

memorial /mə máwri əl/ *n.* **1. COMMEMORATIVE OBJECT** sth that is intended to remind people of a person who has died or an event in which people died, e.g. a statue, speech, or special ceremony **2. STATEMENT OF FACTS ACCOMPANYING A PETITION** a written statement of facts accompanying a petition presented to sb in authority ■ *adj.* **COMMEMORATIVE** intended as a reminder of a person or event or as a celebration of sb's life and work [14thC. Via French from, ultimately, Latin *memoria* (see MEMORY).] —**memorially** *adv.*

Memorial Day *n.* in the United States, a public holiday to commemorate soldiers who died in war, now observed on the last Monday in May but originally celebrated on 30 May

memorialise *vt.* = **memorialize**

memorialist /mə máwri əlist/ *n.* **1. WRITER OF MEMOIRS** sb who writes memoirs **2. WRITER OF A MEMORIAL ACCOMPANYING A PETITION** sb who writes, signs, or presents a memorial accompanying a petition

memorialize /mə máwri ə līz/ (**-izes, -izing, -ized**), **memorialise** (**-ises, -ising, -ised**) *vt.* **1. COMMEMORATE STH** to serve as a memorial to sb or sth, or provide sb or sth with a memorial **2. PRESENT SB WITH A MEMORIAL ACCOMPANYING A PETITION** to present a written memorial accompanying a petition to sb or a group in power —**memorialization** /mə máwri ə lī záysh'n/ *n.* —**memorializer** *n.*

memoria technica /mə máwri ə téknikə, mi-/ (*plural* **memoria technicas**) *n.* a means or device that aids the memory (*formal*) [From modern Latin, 'artificial memory']

memorize /mémmə rīz/ (**-rizes, -rizing, -rized**), **memorise** (**-rises, -rising, -rised**) *vt.* to commit sth to memory —**memorizable** *adj.* —**memorization** /mémmə rī záysh'n/ *n.* —**memorizer** /mémmə rīzər/ *n.*

memory /mémməri/ (*plural* **-ries**) *n.* **1. ABILITY TO RETAIN KNOWLEDGE** the ability of the mind or of an individual or organism to retain learned information and knowledge of past events and experiences and to retrieve it **2. SB'S STOCK OF RETAINED KNOWLEDGE** an individual's stock of retained knowledge and experience ○ *has a good memory for faces* **3. RETAINED IMPRESSION OF PARTICULAR EVENT** the knowledge or impression that sb retains of a particular person, event, period, or subject ○ *memories of a happy childhood* **4. RECOLLECTION** the act or a specific instance of remembering **5. PRESERVATION OF KNOWLEDGE** the preservation of knowledge of and, usually, celebration of a deceased person or past event ○ *a poem in memory of her father* **6. POSTHUMOUS IMPRESSION** the knowledge or impression of sb retained by other people after that person's death **7. TEMPORAL EXTENT OF RECOLLECTION** the period of past time that a person or group is able to remember ○ *within living memory* **8.** COMPUT **DATA STORAGE UNIT IN COMPUTER** the part of a computer in which data is stored **9.** COMPUT **COMPUTER'S DATA STORAGE CAPACITY** the data storage capacity of a computer **10. ABILITY TO RETURN TO ORIGINAL SHAPE** the ability of some materials, e.g. plastics and metals, to return to their original shape after being subject to deformation [13thC. Via Old French *memorie* from Latin *memoria*, from *memor* 'mindful'. Ultimately from an Indo-European base meaning 'to remember', which is also the ancestor of English *remember* and *mourn*.]

memory bank *n.* COMPUT = **memory** *n.* 8

memory lane *n.* the past, especially the past shared and remembered by a group of people, thought of as a path that can be travelled along to visit specific former times

memory span *n.* a measure of sb's memory, often for units of information such as nonsense syllables or sequences of random numbers, over a short period of time

memory trace *n.* PSYCHOL = **engram**

Memphian /mémfi ən/ *n.* **1. SB FROM MEMPHIS, EGYPT** sb who was born in or lived in the ancient Egyptian city of Memphis **2. SB FROM MEMPHIS, TENNESSEE** sb who was born or brought up in, or who lives in the city of Memphis, Tennessee —**Memphian** *adj.*

Memphis /mém fiss/ **1.** ruined city and capital of ancient Egypt, located at the head of the Nile delta in the north of the country **2.** the largest city in Tennessee, located in the southwestern corner of the state. Population: 614,289 (1994).

Memphremagog, Lake /mémfrə máygog/ lake in Quebec, Canada, and Vermont. It is the second largest lake in Vermont. Length: 43 km/27 mi.

memsahib /mém saab, mém saab/ *n. S Asia* a respectful form of address formerly used by Indians to a European married woman [Mid-19thC. From MA'AM + SAHIB.]

men plural of **man**

men- *prefix.* = **meno-** (*used before vowels*)

menace /ménnəss/ *n.* **1. POSSIBLE SOURCE OF DANGER** sb who or sth that is a possible source of danger or harm to sb or sth else **2. NUISANCE** sb who or sth that is a constant source of trouble and annoyance (*informal*) **3. THREATENING QUALITY** a threatening quality, feeling, or tone **4. THREATENING ACT** a threatening act, gesture, or speech ○ *demanding money with menaces* ■ *v.* (**-aces, -acing, -aced**) **1.** *vt.* **BE DANGEROUS TO SB OR STH** to be a possible or actual source of danger or harm to sb or sth **2.** *vti.* **MAKE A THREAT AGAINST SB** to behave towards or speak to sb in a way that threatens injury or harm (*often passive*) [14thC. Via French from, ultimately, Latin *minax* 'threatening', from *minari* 'to threaten', from *minae* 'threats', literally 'projecting points'.] —**menacer** *n.* —**menacing** *adj.* —**menacingly** *adv.*

menadione /ménnə dī ōn/ *n.* a yellow crystalline solid used as a fungicide and as a vitamin K supplement in medicines and animal feedstuffs. Formula: $C_{11}H_8O_2$. [Mid-20thC. Contraction of METHYL + NAPHTHALENE + DI- + -ONE.]

ménage /máy naazh/ *n.* (*formal*) **1. HOUSEHOLD** a group of people living together as a household **2. MANAGEMENT OF A HOUSE** the running of a household [Late 17thC. Via French from, ultimately, Latin *manere* 'to dwell, stay' (see REMAIN).]

ménage à trois /máy naazh aa trwaá/ (*plural* **ménages à trois** /máy naazh-/) *n.* a sexual relationship involving three people [From French, literally 'household for three']

menagerie *n.* **1. WILD ANIMAL EXHIBIT** a collection of wild animals kept in captivity for the curiosity and entertainment of the public, sometimes as part of a travelling show such as a circus **2. WILD ANIMAL ENCLOSURE** an enclosure in which wild animals are kept for public exhibition **3. DIVERSE OR EXOTIC GROUP** a diverse, exotic, or peculiar group of people or things

Menai Strait /ménī stráyt/ narrow arm of the sea in northwestern Wales, separating the island of Anglesey from the mainland

menaquinone /ménnə kwínnōn/ *n.* a form of vitamin K, produced by bacteria in the large intestine, that plays an essential part in the blood-clotting process [Mid-20thC. Contraction of METHYL + NAPHTHALENE + QUINONE.]

menarche /me na´arki/ *n.* the first time that a girl or young woman menstruates (*formal*) [Early 20thC. Coined from MENO- + Greek *arkhē* 'beginning' (see ARCHAIC).] —**menarcheal** *adj.*

menazon /ménnə zon/ *n.* a colourless crystalline solid used to kill aphids. Formula: $C_6H_8N_5O_2PS_2$. [Mid-20thC. Contraction of METHYL + AMINO- + AZO- + THIONATE.]

MENCAP /mén kap/ *n., abbr.* Royal Society for Mentally Handicapped Children and Adults [Contraction of *mental handicap* or *mentally handicapped*]

Mencius /ménshi əss, -shəss/ (371?–289BC) Chinese philosopher. The successor of Confucius, he argued that humans are born good and are made better or worse by their environment. Born **Meng-tzu**

Mencken /méngkən/**, H. L.** (1880–1956) US journalist and critic. An authority on the American language, he was also an effective satirist. Full name **Henry Louis Mencken**

mend /mend/ *v.* (**mends, mending, mended**) **1.** *vti.* RESTORE STH TO SATISFACTORY CONDITION to work on sth that is damaged or defective and return it to its original or a satisfactory condition **2.** *vt.* REMOVE A HOLE to fill, cover, or otherwise remove damage such as a hole or break **3.** *vti.* IMPROVE STH to improve sth or make it more acceptable, or be improved or made more acceptable ○ *You'd better mend your ways.* **4.** *vi.* RECOVER OR HEAL to heal or return to a healthy state after illness or injury ■ *n.* REPAIR an instance of repair work or a repaired place on a damaged object, especially a darn on a piece of clothing [12thC. Partly a shortening of AMEND, and partly from Anglo-Norman *mender* (a shortening of *amender*; see AMEND).] —**mendable** *adj.* —**mender** *n.* ◇ **on the mend** recovering or healing after illness or injury

mendacious /men dáyshəss/ *adj.* **1.** TELLING LIES having lied in the past, or prone to lying at any time **2.** FALSE deliberately untrue [Early 17thC. Formed from Latin *mendac-*, the stem of *mendax* 'lying'.] —**mendaciously** *adv.* —**mendaciousness** *n.*

mendacity /men dássəti/ (*plural* **-ties**) *n.* **1.** TELLING OF LIES deliberate untruthfulness **2.** LIE a lie or falsehood [Mid-17thC. Via French *mendacité* from, ultimately, Latin *mendax* 'lying'.]

Mende /méndi/ (*plural* **-de** *or* **-des**) *n.* **1.** PEOPLES MEMBER OF A SIERRA LEONE ETHNIC GROUP a member of one of several ethnic groups living in Sierra Leone **2.** LANGUAGE NIGER-CONGO LANGUAGE a language of the Niger-Congo language group, spoken by the Mende of Sierra Leone. Over one million people speak Mende. [Mid-18thC. From Mende.]

Mendel /ménd'l/**, Gregor Johann** (1822–84) Austrian monk and scientist. Through his experiments he developed the principles of heredity, and so laid the basis of modern genetics. —**Mendelian** /men deélian/ *adj.*

mendelevium /méndə leévi əm/ *n.* a synthetic short-lived radioactive chemical element produced by bombarding einsteinium atoms with helium particles. Symbol **Md** [Mid-20thC. Named in honour of the Russian chemist Dmitri Ivanovich MENDELEYEV.]

Mendeleyev /méndə láyef/**, Dmitri Ivanovich** (1834–1907) Russian chemist. He formulated the periodic law of elements and devised the periodic table (1869), using it to predict the existence of several then-unknown elements. He wrote a classic text, *Principles of Chemistry* (1868–70).

Mendelism /méndəlizəm/**, Mendelianism** /men deéli ənizəm/ *n.* the theory of heredity formulated by Mendel, which explains how certain characteristics are passed on from one generation to the next through genes

Mendel's Laws /mend'lz-/ *npl.* the laws of heredity formulated by Mendel to explain the transmission of characteristics from one generation to the next. There are two laws, the Law of Segregation and the Law of Independent Assortment.

Menderes /méndə ress/ river in southwestern Turkey, flowing west from the Anatolian Plateau into the Aegean Sea. Length: 584 km/363 mi.

mendicant /méndikənt/ *adj.* LIVING ON ALMS begging for and living on alms ■ *n.* **1.** BEGGAR sb who begs for money, usually in the street (*formal*) **2.** FRIAR BEGGING FOR ALMS a member of a religious order, e.g. the Franciscans, Dominicans, Carmelites, or Augustinians, that forbids the ownership of property and encourages working or begging for a living [14thC. From Latin *mendicare* 'to beg', from *mendicus* 'beggar', from *mendum* 'defect' (source of English *amend, mend*).]

mending /ménding/ *n.* articles, especially clothes, to be mended

Mendip Hills /méndip-/ range of limestone hills in southwestern England. The highest point is Black Down, 326 m/1,068 ft.

Mendoza /men dózə/ city in western Argentina, the capital of Mendoza Province. Population: 121,696 (1991).

meneer /mə neér/ *n.* S Africa a title in Afrikaans equivalent to 'Mr' or a respectful form of address equivalent to 'sir' [Mid-17thC. Via Afrikaans from Dutch *mijnheer*, literally 'my lord'.]

Menelaus /ménni láyəss/ *n.* in Greek mythology, the king of Sparta and husband of Helen of Troy. Her abduction by the Trojan prince Paris led to the Trojan War.

Menelik II /ménnilik thə sékənd/**, Emperor of Ethiopia** (1844–1913). He formed a united Ethiopian empire, resisting incursions by Italy and embarking on a programme of colonial expansion.

menfolk /mén fōk/ *npl.* (*takes a plural verb*) **1.** MEN ASSOCIATED WITH A FAMILY OR GROUP the men associated with a particular family or group **2.** MEN IN GENERAL men in general or considered collectively

MEng /em éng/ *abbr.* Master of Engineering

Mengistu Haile Mariam /meng gístoo híli maári əm/ (b. 1937) Ethiopian statesman. As president (1987–91), he made Ethiopia a communist state but was forced to flee the country in 1991.

menhaden /men háyd'n/ (*plural* **-dens** *or* **-den**) *n.* a North American marine fish belonging to the herring family, used mainly as a source of oil, fertilizer, and bait. Latin name: *Brevoortia tyrannus.* [Mid-17thC. Origin uncertain: possibly an alteration of Narragansett *munnawhattea*, literally 'they fertilize' (from the fish's use as fertilizer by Native Americans), influenced by US English dialect *poghaden* 'menhaden' (of Algonquian origin).]

Menhir: Le Grand Menhir Dol, Brittany, France

menhir /mén heer/ *n.* a large single upright stone, erected by prehistoric people and thought to have been used for astronomical observations, found in the British Isles and northern France [Mid-19thC. Directly or via French from Breton *maen-hir*, literally 'long stone', from *men* 'stone' (source of English *dolmen*) + *hir* 'long'.]

menial /meéni əl/ *adj.* **1.** UNSKILLED relating to or involving work that requires little skill or training, is not interesting, and confers low social status on the person doing it **2.** RELATING TO SERVANTS suitable, typical of, or relating to a servant or servants ■ *n.* **1.** DOMESTIC SERVANT a domestic servant, especially one of low status **2.** SB WHO DOES MENIAL WORK sb employed to do work that requires no skill or training (*formal*) [14thC. Via Anglo-Norman, 'of a household' from, ultimately, Latin *mansio* 'house' (SEE MANSION).] —**menially** *adv.*

Ménière's disease /máyn yairz-/, **Ménière's syndrome** *n.* a disorder caused by an accumulation of fluid in the labyrinths of the inner ear. Symptoms include vertigo, persistent ringing in the ears, and some loss of hearing. [Late 19thC. Named after the French physician Prosper *Ménière* (1799–1862), who described it.]

menilite /ménni lit/ *n.* a liver opal, especially a brown or grey one [Early 19thC. From French, named after *Ménilmontant*, a quarter of Paris where such stones were found.]

Menindee Lakes /mə níndi-/ group of reservoirs in southeastern Australia, in New South Wales

mening- *prefix.* = **meningo-**

meninges /mə nín jeez/ *npl.* the three membranes that surround and protect the brain and the spinal cord, called the dura mater, the arachnoid mater, and the pia mater [Early 17thC. Via modern Latin from Greek *mēnigg-*, the stem of *mēnigx* 'membrane'.] —**meningeal** /mə nínji əl/ *adj.*

meningi- *prefix.* = **meningo-**

meningioma /mə nínji ómə/ (*plural* **-mas** *or* **-mata** /-mətə/) *n.* a slow-growing benign tumour that affects the meninges of the brain or spinal cord and may cause serious damage by compression [Early 20thC. Shortening of *meningothelioma*, from MENINGO- + ENDOTHELIOMA.]

meningitis /ménnin jítiss/ *n.* a serious, sometimes fatal illness in which a viral or bacterial infection inflames the meninges, causing symptoms such as severe headaches, vomiting, stiff neck, and high fever —**meningitic** /ménnin jíttik/ *adj.*

meningo- *prefix.* meninges ○ *meningocele* [From Greek *mēnigg-*, the stem of *mēnigx* 'membrane']

meningocele /mə níng gō seel/ *n.* the protrusion of the meninges through a defect in the skull or backbone to form a cyst

meningococcus /mə níng gō kókəss/ (*plural* **-ci** /-sī/) *n.* a bacterium that causes cerebrospinal meningitis. Latin name: *Neisseria meningitidis.* —**meningococcal** *adj.* —**meningococcic** /-kóksik/ *adj.*

meningoencephalitis /mə níng gō en kéffə lítiss, -séffə-/ *n.* an inflammation of the brain and the meninges —**meningoencephalitic** /-kéffə líttik, -séffə líttik/ *adj.*

meniscus /mə nískus/ (*plural* **-ci** /-níssī/ *or* **-cuses**) *n.* **1.** PHYS UPPER SURFACE OF LIQUID the curved upper surface of a still liquid in a tube, concave if the liquid wets the walls of the container, convex if it does not, caused by surface tension **2.** ANAT CARTILAGE DISC a crescent-shaped cartilage disc cushioning the end of a bone where it meets another bone in a joint, especially in the knee **3.** OPTICS CONCAVO-CONVEX LENS a lens that is convex on one side and concave on the other **4.** CRESCENT SHAPE a crescent-shaped body or figure [Late 17thC. Via modern Latin from Greek *mēniskos*, literally 'little moon', from *mēnē* 'moon' (see MENO-).] —**meniscal** *adj.* —**meniscate** *adj.* —**meniscoid** *adj.* —**meniscoidal** /ménniss kóyd'l/ *adj.*

Mennonite /ménnə nīt/ *n.* a member of a Protestant denomination emphasizing adult baptism and pacifism and rejecting church organization and, in many cases, the holding of public office and the taking of oaths. There are many different bodies of Mennonites throughout the world, with especially large communities in the United States and Canada. [Mid-16thC. From German *Mennonit*, from the name of *Menno* Simons (1496–1561), an early Frisian leader of the group.] —**Mennonitism** *n.*

meno /ménnō/ *adv.* used with a musical direction to mean less quickly or softly [Late 19thC. From Italian, 'less'.]

meno- *prefix.* menstruation ○ *menopause* [Formed from Greek *mēn(ē)* 'month'. Ultimately from an Indo-European word that is also the ancestor of English *moon, month*, and *menses*, from a base meaning 'to measure'.]

menology /mi nólləji/ (*plural* **-gies**) *n.* a church calendar of the months, especially in the Eastern Orthodox Church, that shows saints' days and gives biographies of the saints [Early 17thC. Via modern Latin from ecclesiastical Greek *mēnologion*, literally 'month-reckoning', from *mēn* 'month' + *logos* 'account'.]

Menominee /mə nómminee/ (*plural* **-nee** *or* **-nees**), **Menomini** (*plural* **-ni** *or* **-nis**) *n.* **1.** PEOPLES **MEMBER OF A NATIVE AMERICAN PEOPLE** a member of a Native American people who used to live along the shores of the Menominee River, some of whom now live in northeastern Wisconsin **2.** LANG **ALGONQUIAN LANGUAGE** an Algonquian language spoken in parts of Wisconsin, belonging to the Algonquian-Wakashan languages [Mid-18thC. From Ojibwa *manōmīnī*, literally 'wild-rice person'.] —**Menominee** *adj.*

meno mosso /ménnō mɔ́ssō/ *adv.* at a slower speed (*used as a musical direction*) [From Italian, literally 'less agitated']

Menon /ménnən/, **V. K. Krishna** (1896–1974) Indian politician. He was a leading member of the Indian nationalist movement in the 1920s and 1930s. He was forced to resign as India's defence minister (1957–62) after a border war with China. Full name **Vengalil Krishnan Krishna Menon**

menopause /ménnō pawz/ *n.* the time in a woman's life when menstruation diminishes and ceases, usually between the ages of 45 and 50 [Late 19thC. Coined from MENO- + Greek *pausis* (see PAUSE).] —**menopausal** /ménnō páwz'l/ *adj.* —**menopausic** *adj.*

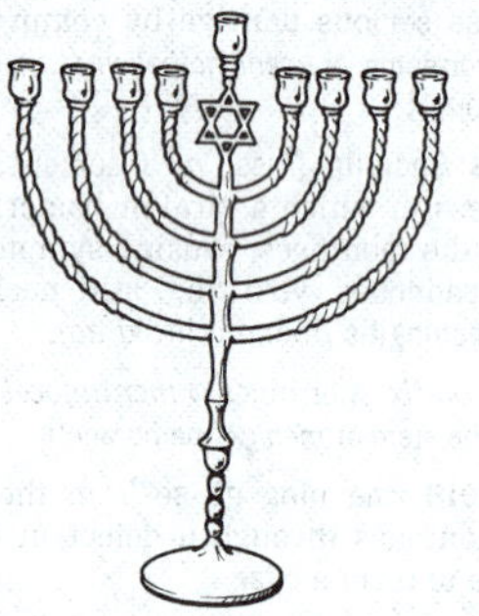

Menorah

menorah /mə náwrə/ *n.* **1.** **7-BRANCHED CEREMONIAL CANDLEHOLDER** a ceremonial candleholder consisting of a central stem surrounded by six curved branches, used in the Jewish Temple and as an emblem of Judaism and the state of Israel **2.** **8-BRANCHED HANUKKAH CANDLEHOLDER** an eight-branched candleholder, lit during the festival of Hanukkah [Late 19thC. From Hebrew *mĕnōrāh*, literally 'candlestick'.]

menorrhagia /ménnə ráyji ə/ *n.* abnormally heavy or prolonged bleeding during menstruation — **menorrhagic** *adj.*

menorrhea *n.* US = **menorrhoea**

menorrhoea /ménnə reé ə/ *n.* normal bleeding during menstruation [Mid-19thC. Back-formation from AMENORRHOEA.]

Mensa /ménssə/ *n.* **1.** **CONSTELLATION IN THE SOUTHERN HEMISPHERE** a faint constellation, found between Hydrus and Volans in the southern hemisphere, that forms part of the Large Magellanic Cloud **2.** **HIGH-IQ ORGANIZATION** an international organization for people with a very high IQ. Members are admitted after passing an IQ test. [Mid-20thC. From Latin, 'table'.]

mensal[1] /ménss'l/ *adj.* occurring monthly [Mid-19thC. Formed from Latin *mensis* 'month'. Ultimately from an Indo-European word that is also the ancestor of English *moon* and *month*, from a base meaning 'to measure'.]

mensal[2] /ménss'l/ *adj.* used or done at the meal table, or connected with eating meals [15thC. From late Latin *mensalis*, from Latin *mensa* 'table', of unknown origin.]

mensch /mensh/ (*plural* **menschen** /ménsh'n/ *or* **mensches**), **mensh** (*plural* **menshen** *or* **menshes**) *n. US* sb good, kind, decent, and honourable (*informal*) [Mid-20thC. Via Yiddish from, ultimately, Old High German *mennisco* 'manly, human'. Ultimately from an Indo-European word meaning 'person, man' that is also the ancestor of English *man*.]

menses /mén seez/ *n.* (*technical*) (*takes a singular or plural verb*) **1.** **MENSTRUATION** menstruation, or the period of time that it lasts **2.** **MENSTRUAL DISCHARGE** the blood and other matter discharged from the womb during menstruation [Late 16thC. From Latin, plural of *mensis* 'month' (see MENSAL[1]).]

Menshevik /ménshəvik/ (*plural* **-viks** *or* **-viki** /-víki/) *n.* a member of the moderate minority faction of the Marxist Social Democratic Party in pre-revolutionary Russia that advocated a gradual approach to social reform, in contrast to the Bolsheviks [Early 20thC. From Russian *men'shevik*, from *men'she* 'less'; so called because they favoured less extreme Socialist reform than the Bolsheviks.] —**Menshevism** *n.* —**Menshevist** *n.*

mens rea /ménz ráyə/ *n.* prior intention to commit a criminal act, without necessarily knowing that the act is a crime. For all but some minor statutory offences, mens rea is basic to establishing the actual guilt of sb alleged to have committed a crime. [From modern Latin, 'guilty mind']

men's room *n. US* = **gents**

mens sana in corpore sano /ménz saánə in káwpəri saánō/ *n.* a healthy mind in a healthy body, as an ideal in living (*formal*) [From Latin]

menstrual /mén stroo əl/ *adj.* occurring during, or connected with, menstruation

menstruate /mén stroo ayt/ (**-ates, -ating, -ated**) *vi.* to discharge blood and other matter from the womb as part of the menstrual cycle [Early 19thC. Via late Latin *menstruare* from, ultimately, Latin *menstruus* 'monthly, menstrual', from *mensis* 'month' (see MENSAL[1]).]

menstruation /mén stroo áysh'n/ *n.* the monthly process of discharging blood and other matter from the womb that occurs between puberty and menopause in women and female primates who are not pregnant

menstruous /mén stroo əss/ *adj.* = **menstrual**

menstruum /mén stroo əm/ (*plural* **-ums** *or* **-a** /-ə/) *n.* a solvent, especially one used to extract compounds from plant or animal tissue or in the preparation of drugs [Early 17thC. Via medieval Latin, literally 'menstruation', singular of Latin *menstrua* (see MENSTRUATE). By analogy between the alchemical use of solvents and the menses' supposed function in nurturing unborn babies.]

mensurable /ménshərəb'l/ *adj.* **1.** MATH **ABLE TO BE MEASURED** capable of being measured **2.** MUSIC = **mensural** *adj.* 2 [Late 16thC. Via late Latin *mensurabilis* from, ultimately, Latin *mensura* 'measure' (see MEASURE).] —**mensurability** /ménshərə bílləti/ *n.* —**mensurableness** /ménshərəb'lnəss/ *n.*

mensural /ménshərəl/ *adj.* **1.** **RELATING TO MEASUREMENT** relating to or involving measurement or measurable values **2.** MUSIC **USING NOTES WITH FIXED VALUES** used to describe or relating to notes, particularly in medieval music, that have a fixed length or time value relative to one another [Late 16thC. From Latin *mensuralis*, from *mensura* (see MEASURE).]

mensuration /ménshə ráysh'n/ *n.* **1.** MATH **WORKING OUT GEOMETRIC QUANTITIES** the calculation of geometric quantities such as length, area, and volume from dimensions and angles that are already known **2.** **MEASUREMENT** the act, process, or skill of measuring sth (*formal*) [Late 16thC. Via late Latin from, ultimately, Latin *mensura* (see MEASURE).] —**mensurational** *adj.* —**mensurative** /ménshərətiv/ *adj.*

menswear /ménz wair/ *n.* **1.** **MEN'S CLOTHING** clothing designed to be worn by men **2.** **MENSWEAR DEPARTMENT** the department in a shop that sells menswear

-ment *suffix.* **1.** action, process ○ *arraignment* ○ *betterment* **2.** result of, or condition resulting from an action ○ *bewilderment* **3.** instrument or agent of an action ○ *refreshment* **4.** place ○ *emplacement* ○ *escarpment* [Directly and via French from Latin *-mentum*]

mental /mént'l/ *adj.* **1.** **RELATING TO THE MIND** relating to, found in, or occurring in the mind ○ *mental stimulation* **2.** **CARRIED OUT IN THE MIND** carried out in the mind without any physical action or the use of any physical aid ○ *mental arithmetic* **3.** **PRODUCED BY THE MIND** produced by the mind and visible only in the mind ○ *mental imagery* **4.** **EXPERIENCING EXTREME EMOTION** affected by extreme distress, anxiety, anger, or other emotional reaction to sb or sth (*informal offensive*) **5.** **OFFENSIVE TERM** an offensive term meaning having a psychiatric disorder (*offensive*) **6.** **UNINTELLIGENT** extremely unintelligent or silly (*informal insult*) [15thC. Via French from Latin *ment-*, the stem of *mens* 'mind'. Ultimately from an Indo-European word meaning 'to think', also the ancestor of English *mind, mania, demented*, and *amnesia*.] —**mentally** *adv.* ◇ **chuck** *or* **throw a mental** *Aus* to become very angry or upset (*informal*)

mental age *n.* a measure of intellectual development developed by the French psychologist Binet, who devised norms against which children could be compared with other children of the same chronological age ○ *a four-year-old with a mental age of seven*

mental block *n.* an inability to carry out a mental task such as remembering sth, especially when caused by subconscious emotional factors

mental cruelty *n.* the infliction of psychological pain on sb

mental disorder *n.* in English law, a psychiatric disorder or impairment of mental faculties

mental handicap *n.* an offensive term for an intellectual impairment (*offensive*)

mental hospital *n.* = **psychiatric hospital**

mental illness *n.* any psychiatric disorder of the mind that causes untypical behaviour

mental impairment *n.* in English law, a state of mental development that negatively affects sb's intellectual capacity and ability to function

mentalism /mént'lizəm/ *n.* the belief that all objects of knowledge, including the physical universe, ultimately have no existence except as creations of the mind —**mentalist** *n.* —**mentalistic** /-lístik/ *adj.* —**mentalistically** /-lístik'li/ *adv.*

mentality /men tálləti/ (*plural* **-ties**) *n.* **1.** **PERCEPTUAL FRAMEWORK** a habitual way of thinking or interpreting events peculiar to an individual or type of person, especially with reference to the behaviour that it produces **2.** **INTELLECTUAL ABILITY** sb's intellectual ability

mental lexicon *n.* the words of a language that sb knows the meanings of, can use, or uses habitually

mentally challenged *adj.* affected by a condition that limits the ability to learn and to function independently, as a result of congenital causes, brain injury, or disease

mental reservation *n.* a tacit qualification of a statement or oath made when it would be unwise or disadvantageous to express doubt or disagreement openly

mental retardation *n.* an offensive term for difficulty in learning or in daily functions (*dated offensive*)

mentation /men táysh'n/ *n.* (*formal*) **1.** **THINKING** mental activity, especially thinking **2.** **STATE OF MIND** sb's state of mind or general attitude [Mid-19thC. Formed from Latin *ment-*, the stem of *mens* 'mind' (see MENTAL).]

menthol /mén thol/ *n.* an organic compound extracted from peppermint oil that has a cool minty taste and is used as a flavouring and as a mild anaesthetic. Formula: $CH_3C_6H_9(C_3H_7)OH$. [Late 19thC. From German, literally 'mint-oil', formed from Latin *mentha* (see MINT).]

mentholated /ménthə laytid/ *adj.* flavoured with or containing menthol

mention /ménsh'n/ *v.* (**-tions, -tioning, -tioned**) **1.** *vti.* **SAY A PARTICULAR WORD OR THING** to use a particular word or name when speaking or writing, often in a casual way ○ *I happened to mention your name to her.* **2.** *vt.* MIL **CITE SB FOR BRAVERY** to refer to sb by name in an official report as a way of acknowledging exceptional conduct, especially during a military action ■ *n.* **1.** **SPECIFIC REFERENCE** the use of a particular word or name, or a reference to a particular person or thing **2.** MIL **ACKNOWLEDGMENT OF SB'S EXCEPTIONAL CONDUCT** an acknowledgment, especially in an official report, of sb's exceptional conduct **3.** LOGIC **LINGUISTIC SELF-REFERENCE** the use of a word to refer to itself instead of to perform its usual linguistic function [14thC. Via French from Latin *mention-*, the stem of *mentio* 'calling to mind'.] —**mentionable** *adj.* —**mentioner** *n.* ◇ **don't mention it** used in reply to an expression of thanks as a polite way of saying that none are necessary ◇ **not to mention** used to emphasize a point by introducing sb who or sth that needs to be taken into consideration and is even more significant than what has been spoken of before

mentor /mén tawr/ *n.* **EXPERIENCED ADVISER AND SUPPORTER** sb, usually older and more experienced, who provides advice and support to, and watches over and fosters the progress of, a younger, less experienced person ■ *vt.* (**-tors, -toring, -tored**) **BE A MENTOR TO SB** to act as a mentor to sb, especially a junior colleague [Mid-18thC. Via French from, ultimately, Greek *Mentōr* (see MENTOR).]

Mentor /mén tawr/ *n.* in Homer's *Odyssey*, the friend whom Odysseus left in charge of the household while he was at Troy and who was the teacher and protector of Telemachus, Odysseus' son

mentoring /méntəring/ *n.* the task of acting as a mentor to sb, especially a junior colleague, or the system of appointing mentors

menu /mén yoo/ *n.* **1.** FOOD **LIST OF DISHES AVAILABLE** a list of the dishes that can be ordered in a restaurant or that are to be served at a formal meal **2.** COMPUT **LIST OF PROGRAM OPTIONS** a list on a computer screen of the various options available to the user of a program or function **3. LIST OR COLLECTION** a list of things available, or a collection of things from which a selection can be made [Mid-19thC. Via French, 'minute, detailed', from Latin *minutus* 'small' (see MINUTE[2]); the underlying meaning is 'detailed list'.]

menu-driven *adj.* COMPUT operated by selecting options from menus

Menuhin /ményoo in/, **Yehudi, Baron Menuhin of Stoke d'Abernon** (1916–99) US-born British violinist. He was known as much for mentoring younger players as for his own virtuoso performances.

Menzies /ménziz, míng iss/, **Sir Robert** (1894–1978) Australian politician. As prime minister of Australia (1939–41, 1949–66), he pursued close political ties with Great Britain and firmly aligned Australia economically and militarily with the United States. Full name **Sir Robert Gordon Menzies**

meow /mi ów/ *n., vi.* = **miaow**

MEP *abbr.* **1.** Member of the European Parliament **2.** Master of Engineering Physics

meperidine /mə pérri deen/ *n.* = **pethidine** [Mid-20thC. Blend of METHYL and PIPERIDINE.]

Mephistopheles /méffi stóffə leez/, **Mephisto** /mə fístō/ *n.* in medieval mythology, a subordinate to the Devil, one of the seven archangels cast out of heaven, to whom Faust sold his soul —**Mephistophelean** /méffistə féeli ən/ *adj.*

mephitic /mi fíttik/, **mephitical** /-tik'l/ *adj.* relating to or resembling a poisonous or foul smell (*literary*) [Early 17thC. From late Latin *mephiticus* 'pestilential', from Latin *mephitis* (see MEPHITIS).] —**mephitically** *adv.*

mephitis /mi fítiss/ *n.* **1.** GEOL **FOUL-SMELLING GAS** a foul-smelling or poisonous vapour coming out of the earth **2. STENCH** a foul smell (*literary*) [Early 18thC. From Latin, of unknown origin.]

meprobamate /mə prṓbə mayt, mépprō bámmayt/ *n.* a bitter white powder used as a tranquillizer and muscle relaxant. Formula: $C_9H_{18}N_2O_4$. [Mid-20thC. Blend of METHYL, PROPYL, and CARBAMATE.]

mer. *abbr.* meridian

mer- *prefix.* = **mero-**

-mer *suffix.* polymer ○ *oligomer* [Back-formation from -MERISM]

Merano /mə raánō/ city and health resort in Bolzano Province, Trentino-Alto Adige Region, northeastern Italy. Population: 33,638 (1993).

meranti /mi rántí/ *n.* a hardwood, white, yellow, or red in colour, obtained from some Malaysian and Indonesian trees. Genus: *Shorea.* [Late 18thC. From Malay.]

merbromin /mər brṓmin/ *n.* a green crystalline solid that forms a red solution when dissolved in water, mainly used as an antiseptic. Formula: $C_{20}H_8Br_2HgNa_2O_6$. [Mid-20thC. Coined from MERCURIC + BROM- + -IN.]

Mercalli scale /mur kálli-/ *n.* a scale for measuring the intensity of earthquakes, ranging from 1 to 12, in which 1 denotes a weak earthquake and 12 one that causes complete destruction. ◊ **Richter scale** [Early 20thC. Named after Giuseppe *Mercalli* (1850–1914), the Italian geologist who devised it.]

mercantile /múrkən tīl/ *adj.* **1. RELATING TO MERCHANTS OR TRADING** used for trade or by merchants, or characteristic of merchants or trading **2. RELATING TO MERCANTILISM** relating to or typical of mercantilism [Mid-17thC. Via French from, ultimately, Italian *mercante* 'merchant', from Latin *mercari* 'to trade' (see MERCHANT).]

mercantilism /múrkəntilizəm, múrkən tīlizəm/ *n.* **1. ECONOMIC THEORY AND SYSTEM** an early modern European economic theory and system that actively supported the establishment of colonies that would supply materials and markets and relieve home nations of dependence on other nations **2. COMMERCIALISM** the principles and methods of commerce —**mercantilist** *n.* —**mercantilistic** /múrkənti lístik, -tī-/ *adj.*

mercaptan /mur káp tan/ *n.* = **thiol** [Mid-19thC. Formed from modern Latin *(corpus) mercurium captans*, literally '(substance) that seizes mercury'.]

mercaptopurine /mur káptō pyóor een/ *n.* a drug used in the treatment of leukaemia. Formula: $C_5H_4N_4S$. [Mid-20thC. Coined from MERCAPTO- + PURINE.]

Mercator /mur káytər/, **Gerardus** (1512–94) Flemish geographer, cartographer, and mathematician. His map projection allowed compass courses to be plotted as straight lines, and is widely used in navigation. Born **Gerhard Kremer**

Mercator Projection *n.* a method of making a map of the globe on a flat surface in which the meridians and latitudes are shown as straight lines that cross at right angles [Mid-17thC. Named after Gerardus MERCATOR, who invented it.]

mercenary /múrss'nəri/ *n.* (*plural* **-ies**) **1.** MIL **PROFESSIONAL SOLDIER** a professional soldier paid to fight for an army other than that of his or her country **2. SB INTERESTED ONLY IN PROFIT** sb who works or serves only for personal profit ■ *adj.* **1. MOTIVATED ONLY BY MONEY** motivated solely by a desire for money **2. RELATING TO MERCENARIES** paid to serve in a foreign army, or consisting of mercenaries [14thC. Directly or via French *mercenaire* from Latin *mercen(n)arius* 'hireling', from *merces* 'wages' (source of English *mercy*).] —**mercenarily** *adv.* —**mercenariness** *n.*

mercer /múrssər/ *n.* a dealer in fabrics, especially in silks and other fine cloth, especially formerly [13thC. Via Anglo-Norman from, ultimately, Latin *merc-*, the stem of *merx* 'merchandise' (see MERCHANT).]

Mercer Island /mÚrsər-/ island in Mississippi, in Adams County. Population: 21,522 (1995).

mercerize /múrssə rīz/ (**-izes, -izing, -ized**), **mercerise** (**-ises, -ising, -ised**) *vt.* to treat cotton fabric or thread with an alkali to strengthen it and make it more lustrous and more receptive to dyes [Mid-19thC. Named after John Mercer (1791–1866), the English calico printer who is said to have discovered the process.] —**mercerization** /múrssə rī záysh'n/ *n.*

merchandise /múrchən dīz/ *n.* **GOODS** goods bought and sold for profit ■ *v.* (**-dises, -dising, -dised**) **1.** *vti.* **TRADE COMMERCIALLY** to trade in or buy and sell products for profit **2.** *vt.* **MARKET PRODUCTS** to promote a product by developing strategies for packaging, display, and publicity [13thC. From French *marchandise* 'goods', from Old French *marchant* (see MERCHANT).] —**merchandisable** *adj.* —**merchandiser** *n.*

merchandising /múrchən dīzing/ *n.* **1. MARKETING** the promotion of a product by developing strategies for packaging, displaying, and publicizing it **2. SPIN-OFF PRODUCTS** commercial products that are developed as spin-offs from the success of a film, TV programme, sports team, or event

merchant /múrchənt/ *n.* **1. DEALER IN WHOLESALE GOODS** sb who buys and sells goods, especially as a wholesaler or on the international market **2. RETAILER** sb who sells products at retail, especially in a shop or other outlet **3. SB NOTED FOR SOME ACTIVITY** sb who is noted for a particular activity or characteristic (*informal; usually used in combination*) ○ *a speed merchant in a souped-up car* ■ *adj.* **1. RELATING TO TRADE OR MERCHANTS** used for or relating to commerce, wholesalers, or retailers **2.** SHIPPING **OF A MERCHANT NAVY** relating to, belonging to, or involving a merchant navy ■ *vt.* (**-chants, -chanting, -chanted**) **DEAL IN STH** to trade or deal in products [12thC. Via Old French *marchant* from, ultimately, Latin *mercari* 'to trade', from *merc-*, the stem of *merx* 'merchandise' (source of English *merchandise* and *market*).]

WORD KEY: CULTURAL NOTE

The Merchant of Venice, a play by William Shakespeare (1596–97). The story revolves around a loan made by Jewish usurer Shylock to Venetian merchant Antonio, and Shylock's subsequent attempts to claim the pound of flesh he has stipulated as security. Among the more serious issues raised in this blend of comedy, romance, and realism are the correct administration of justice and the power conferred by wealth. The well-known saying 'It is a wise father that knows his own child' comes from Act II, scene ii, line 83 of this play.

Merchant /múrchənt/, **Ismail** (*b.* 1936) Indian film producer and director. In partnership with James Ivory, he produced films set in India and created adaptations of European literary classics.

merchantable /múrchəntəb'l/ *adj.* suitable or of a sufficiently high quality for buying and selling —**merchantability** /múrchəntə bílləti/ *n.*

merchant bank *n.* a bank that provides financial services mainly for companies and large-scale investors —**merchant banker** *n.* —**merchant banking** *n.*

merchantman /múrchəntmən/ (*plural* **-men** /-mən/) *n.* = **merchant ship**

merchant marine *n.* *US* = **merchant navy**

merchant navy *n.* a country's fleet of merchant ships, or the sailors who serve in them. US term **merchant marine**

merchant prince *n.* an extremely wealthy, powerful, and prestigious merchant, especially in Renaissance Italy

merchant ship *n.* a seagoing ship designed to carry goods, especially for international trade

merchet /múrchət/ *n.* in feudal times, a sum of money paid by a tenant to his lord so that his daughter could marry [13thC. Via Anglo-Norman from, ultimately, Latin *merc-*, the stem of *merx* 'merchandise' (see MERCHANT).]

Mercia /múrshi ə, múrssi ə/ ancient Anglo-Saxon kingdom of central England

Mercian /múrssi ən/ *n.* **DIALECT OF OLD ENGLISH** a dialect of Old English spoken in the Anglo-Saxon kingdom of Mercia, in central and southern England ■ *adj.* **OF MERCIA** relating to the Anglo-Saxon kingdom of Mercia, its people, its language, or its culture

merciful /múrssif'l/ *adj.* **1. SHOWING MERCY** showing mercy or compassion to sb **2. WELCOME** welcome because putting an end to sth unpleasant or distressing —**mercifulness** *n.*

mercifully /múrssifəli/ *adv.* **1. SO AS TO SHOW MERCY** so as to show mercy or compassion **2. FORTUNATELY** fortunately or luckily

merciless /múrssiləss/ *adj.* **1. LACKING MERCY** showing no mercy or compassion towards sb or sth **2. STRICT AND INTOLERANT** very strict or harsh in the treatment of other people and extremely intolerant of their weaknesses or mistakes **3. RELENTLESS** continuing at a high level of violence or unpleasantness without pause or relief —**mercilessly** *adv.* —**mercilessness** *n.*

Merckx /murks/, **Eddy** (*b.* 1945) Belgian bicycle racer. Winner of five Tours de France (1969–74) and numerous other races, he also broke the world hour record (1972).

mercur- *prefix.* mercury ○ *mercurous* [From MERCURY]

mercurate /múr kyoo rayt/ (**-rates, -rating, -rated**) *vt.* to treat or combine sth with mercury —**mercuration** /múr kyoo ráysh'n/ *n.*

mercurial /mur kyóori əl/ *adj.* **1. LIVELY AND UNPREDICTABLE** lively, witty, fast-talking, and likely to do the unexpected **2.** CHEM **CONTAINING MERCURY** containing or caused by mercury ■ *n.* MED **MEDICINE CONTAINING MERCURY** formerly, a drug or chemical preparation containing mercury [14thC. Directly and via French *mercuriel* from Latin *mercurialis*, from *Mercurius* 'Mercury'.] —**mercuriality** /mur kyoori álləti/ *n.* —**mercurially** /mur kyóori əli/ *adv.* —**mercurialness** /-əlnəss/ *n.*

Mercurial /mur kyóori əl/ *adj.* **1.** MYTHOL **OF THE GOD MERCURY** relating to the Roman god Mercury **2.** ASTRON **OF THE PLANET MERCURY** relating to the planet Mercury

mercurialise *vt.* = **mercurialize**

mercurialism /mur kyóori əlizəm/ n. poisoning caused by ingesting mercury

mercurialize (-izes, -izing, -ized), **mercurialise** (-ises, -ising, -ised) vt. to treat sb or sth with mercury or with a compound containing mercury —**mercurialization** /mur kyóori ə līt záysh'n/ n.

mercuric /mur kyóorik/ adj. relating to or containing mercury with a valency of 2

mercuric chloride n. a white crystalline solid that is poisonous, soluble, and used mainly as an insecticide, fungicide, or wood preservative or in photography. Formula: HgCl₂.

mercuric oxide n. a poisonous orange-yellow solid used as a pigment. Formula: HgO.

mercuric sulphide n. a poisonous compound existing as a red or a black solid, both forms being used as pigments. Formula: HgS.

Mercurochrome /mur kyóorə krōm/ tdmk. a trademark for a liquid antiseptic

mercurous /múrkyóorəss/ adj. relating to or containing mercury with a valency of 1

mercurous chloride n. a white poisonous insoluble powder used as a fungicide and, formerly, widely used in medicines for various purposes. Formula: Hg₂Cl₂.

mercury /múrkyóori/ (plural -ries) n. 1. CHEM ELEM LIQUID METALLIC ELEMENT a poisonous heavy silver-white metallic chemical element that is liquid at room temperature. It is obtained chiefly from the mineral cinnabar and is used in thermometers, barometers, pharmaceuticals, dental amalgams, and lamps. Symbol **Hg** 2. METEOROL TEMPERATURE OR PRESSURE the mercury in a weather thermometer or barometer, or the air temperature or pressure it indicates ○ The mercury rose steadily throughout the early part of the day. 3. PLANTS WEEDY PLANT a weedy plant of the spurge family. Genus: Mercurialis. [14thC. From Latin Mercurius (see MERCURY).]

Mercury /múrkyóori/ n. 1. MYTHOL ROMAN GOD the Roman god of commerce and rhetoric, who also acted as a messenger between humans and gods. His symbol is the caduceus, a staff with two snakes entwined around it. 2. ASTRON PLANET NEAREST THE SUN the smallest planet in the solar system and the one nearest the Sun [12thC. From Latin Mercurius, from merc-, the stem of merx 'merchandise' (source of English merchant).]

mercury chloride n. CHEM = mercuric chloride

mercury-vapour lamp n. an electric lamp whose light is generated when electricity is passed through a vapour of low-pressure mercury. Its bright bluish-green light has a strong ultraviolet component, and these rays are used for cosmetic and therapeutic treatment.

mercy /múrssi/ (plural -cies) n. 1. COMPASSION kindness or forgiveness shown to an offender or to a person who has power over ○ The judge showed mercy and imposed the shortest sentence he could. 2. COMPASSIONATE DISPOSITION a disposition to be compassionate or forgiving of others ○ a killer completely without mercy 3. STH TO BE THANKFUL FOR a welcome event or situation that provides relief or prevents sth unpleasant from happening ○ It was a mercy that no one was hurt in the accident. 4. EASING OF DISTRESS the easing of distress or pain ○ The supply convoy was on a mission of mercy. [12thC. Via French merci 'thank you', from Latin merces 'reward, wages' (source of English mercenary).] ◇ **at the mercy of sb** or **sth** completely unprotected against whatever sb or sth does

mercy killing n. 1. EUTHANASIA euthanasia regarded as motivated by compassion 2. ACT OF EUTHANASIA an act of killing sb out of compassion, often at that person's request, in order to end his or her pain or distress

mercy seat n. 1. JUDAISM COVERING FOR THE ARK OF THE COVENANT the gold covering on the Ark of the Covenant, regarded as God's resting place 2. CHR GOD'S THRONE the throne of God in heaven [Modelled on late Latin propitiatorium, literally 'sth atoning', and German Gnadenstuhle, literally 'mercy seat']

mere¹ /meer/ (superlative **merest**) adj. 1. UTTER just what is specified and nothing more ○ She was no mere journalist. 2. BY ITSELF by itself and without anything

more ○ The mere mention of his ex's name would make him upset. [14thC. Directly or via Anglo-Norman meer, Old French mier, from Latin merus 'pure, unmixed' (especially of wine), the original meaning in English.]

mere² /meer/ n. a body of standing fresh water, especially a lake (archaic or literary; often used in placenames) [Old English, originally used for 'sea' (source also of English mermaid). Ultimately from an Indo-European word that is also the ancestor of Latin mare (source of English marine).]

mere³ /meer/ n. a boundary, or sth that marks a boundary (archaic) [Old English (ge)mære. Ultimately from an Indo-European word meaning 'to fix, build fences', which is also the ancestor of English mural and ammunition.]

mere⁴ /mérri/ n. a short flat curved club used as a weapon by Maoris [Early 19thC. From Maori.]

-mere suffix. part, segment ○ centromere [Via French from Greek meros (see MERO-)]

Meredith /mérrə dith/, **George** (1828–1909) British novelist and poet. His novels are noted for their psychological analysis and distinctive style. They include The Egoist (1879) and Diana of the Crossways (1885).

merely /meerli/ adv. only as described and nothing more ○ merely silly ○ merely a temporary setback

merengue /mə réng gay/ n. 1. BALLROOM DANCE a ballroom dance, originally from Dominica and Haiti, characterized by a shuffling step 2. MUSIC MUSIC FOR MERENGUE a piece of music for the merengue [Mid-20thC. Via American Spanish from Haitian creole méringue, literally 'meringue', from French (see MERINGUE).]

meretricious /mérrə tríshəss/ adj. 1. SUPERFICIALLY ATTRACTIVE attractive in a superficial or vulgar manner but without real value (formal) ○ meretricious extras that don't really add to the car's value 2. MISLEADINGLY PLAUSIBLE seemingly plausible or significant, but actually insincere or false ○ Don't be swayed by this meretricious argument in the project's favour. 3. OF PROSTITUTES relating to or like a prostitute (archaic) [Early 17thC. Formed from Latin meretricius, from, ultimately, meretrix 'prostitute', from mereri (see MERIT).] —**meretriciously** adv. —**meretriciousness** n.

Merganser

merganser /mur gánssər/ (plural -sers or -ser) n. a fish-eating diving duck with a crested head and a long bill notched like the blade of a saw. Genus: Mergus. [Mid-17thC. From modern Latin, literally 'diver goose', from Latin mergus 'diver' + anser 'goose'.]

merge /murj/ (merges, merging, merged) vti. 1. COMBINE to combine or unite with sth to form a single entity, or make two or more things do this ○ Two of the country's largest banks have decided to merge. 2. BLEND to blend or make two or more things blend together gradually ○ The sky and sea seem to merge at the horizon. [Mid-17thC. From Latin mergere 'to plunge, dip' (source also of English submerge and immerse), the original sense in English.] —**mergence** n. —**merging** n.

merger /múrjər/ n. 1. BUSINESS COMBINING OF COMPANIES the joining together of two or more companies or organizations ○ a merger between two of the country's leading manufacturers 2. UNION a blending, combining, or joining of sth with sth else, or the state of being blended, combined, or joined together [Early 18thC. From Anglo-Norman, literally 'to drown', from, ultimately, Latin mergere (see MERGE).]

Mérida /may réedə/ 1. city in western Spain, in Badajoz Province. Population: 52,200 (1987). 2. city in southeastern Mexico, the capital of Yucatán

State. It was founded by the Spanish on a Mayan site in 1542. Population: 523,422 (1990).

meridian /mə ríddi ən/ n. 1. GEOG LINE OF LONGITUDE an imaginary line between the North and South poles that crosses the equator at right angles. A meridian is designated by the degrees of longitude that it is west or east of the prime meridian. 2. GEOG HALF OF A CIRCLE BETWEEN POLES either half of the circle of the meridian, from pole to pole 3. ASTRON CELESTIAL GREAT CIRCLE a great circle of the celestial sphere that passes through the celestial poles and the zenith of the observer 4. HIGHEST POINT the peak or a high point, e.g. of development or success (literary) ○ the decade when the empire's power reached its meridian 5. ALTERN MED LINE OF ACUPUNCTURE POINTS in acupuncture, one of the pathways in the body along which the body's energy is believed to flow and along which acupuncture points are located 6. TIME NOON the hour of midday (archaic) [14thC. Via Old French from Latin meridianus, from meridies 'midday', an alteration of medidies, literally 'middle day' from medius 'middle' + dies 'day'.]

meridian circle n. = transit circle

meridional /mə ríddi ən'l/ adj. 1. OF A MERIDIAN along, belonging to, relating to, or like a meridian 2. GEOG OF SOUTHERN REGIONS typical of or located in the south, especially southern Europe 3. OF SOUTHERN PEOPLES typical of people who live in the south, especially southern Europe ■ n. PEOPLES SOUTHERN PERSON sb born or living in the south, especially the south of France [14thC. Via French from late Latin meridionalis, from Latin meridies (see MERIDIAN) on the model of septentrionalis 'northern'.] —**meridionally** adv.

Mérimée /mérri may/, **Prosper** (1803–70) French writer. His works include the novella Carmen (1845), the basis of Bizet's opera. He was also a historian.

meringue /mə ráng/ n. 1. WHIPPED EGG WHITES a mixture of egg whites and sugar beaten until stiff, cooked, and used as a topping for tarts or to make biscuits and shells 2. MERINGUE CAKE OR SHELL a cake, biscuit, or shell made of meringue, often with a cream filling [Early 18thC. From French, of uncertain origin: perhaps via French dialect maringue 'shepherd's loaf', from Latin merenda 'snack', from a form of merere 'to earn'.]

merino /mə réenō/ n. (plural -nos) 1. merino, merino sheep ZOOL SHEEP BRED FOR WOOL a sheep of a breed originally from Spain that is bred for its wool in many parts of the world, especially Australia 2. WOOL the long fine white wool of the merino sheep 3. TEXTILES YARN OR FABRIC a fine yarn or fabric made from the wool of the merino sheep, often mixed with cotton ■ adj. TEXTILES OF MERINO WOOL made of merino wool ○ a merino shawl [Late 18thC. Via Spanish from Arabic (banū) marīn, the name of a Berber people who raised the breed.]

-merism suffix. denoting a relationship between chemical constituents ○ isomerism [Coined from Greek meros 'part' + -ISM]

meristem /mérri stem/ n. embryonic plant tissue that is actively dividing, such as is found at the tip of stems and roots [Late 19thC. From Greek meristos 'divided', from merizein 'to divide', from meros 'part' (see -MERE).] —**meristematic** /mérristə máttik/ adj. —**meristematically** /-máttikli/ adv.

meristic /mə rístik/ adj. BIOL 1. SEGMENTED divided into or having segments 2. WITH CHANGING BODY PARTS involving a change in the number or arrangement of body parts or segments [Late 19thC. Formed from Greek meris, meros 'part'.] —**meristically** adv.

merit /mérrit/ n. 1. VALUE value that deserves respect and acknowledgment ○ The film is a work of considerable technical as well as artistic merit. 2. GOOD QUALITY a good or praiseworthy characteristic that sb or sth has (often used in the plural) 3. ABILITY proven ability or accomplishment ○ She got her promotion based on merit. 4. RELIG SPIRITUAL CREDIT spiritual worthiness achieved by doing good works ■ **merits** npl. FACTS OF A CASE the facts of a matter considered without regard for emotional, procedural, or other issues ○ to consider a proposal on its merits ■ vt. (-its, -iting, -ited) DESERVE to be worthy of or earn sth ○ Some people feel the award wasn't merited. [12thC. Via French mérite from Latin meritum 'price, value', a form of the past participle of *merere* 'to earn' (source of English *emeritus*), used as a noun.]

meritocracy /mérri tókrəssi/ (*plural* **-cies**) *n.* **1.** SYSTEM BASED ON ABILITY a social system that gives opportunities and advantages to people on the basis of their ability rather than, e.g., wealth or seniority **2.** ELITE GROUP an elite group of people who achieved their positions on the basis of ability and accomplishment **3.** LEADERSHIP BY ELITE leadership by an elite group of people who are chosen on the basis of their abilities and accomplishments [Mid-20thC. Coined from MERIT + -CRACY.] —**meritocratic** /mérritō kráttik/ *adj.*

meritorious /mérri táwri əss/ *adj.* deserving honour and recognition (*formal*) ○ *She was awarded a medal for meritorious service.* [15thC. Formed from Latin *meritorius*, from *merere* 'to earn'.] —**meritoriously** *adv.* —**meritoriousness** *n.*

merle /murl/, **merl** *n.* a blackbird (*archaic or literary*) [15thC. Via French from Latin *merula*, of uncertain origin: probably ultimately from an Indo-European word that is also the ancestor of English *ouzel*.]

Merleau-Ponty /múrlō pónti/, **Maurice** (1908–61) French philosopher. An existentialist, he was noted for his critical writings on behaviourism and the phenomenology of perception.

Merlin

merlin /múrlin/ *n.* a small dark falcon found throughout the northern hemisphere that has a broad black band on the end of its tail. Latin name: *Falco columbarius*. [14thC. Via Anglo-Norman *merilun*, an alteration of Old French *esmirillon*, literally 'large merlin', from *esmiril* 'merlin', of uncertain origin.]

Merlin *n.* a legendary magician and adviser to King Arthur

merlon /múr lon/ *n.* a solid part between two openings (**crenels**) in a battlement, e.g. on a castle [Early 18thC. Via French from Italian *merlone*, literally 'large battlement', from *merlo* 'battlement'.]

merlot /múrlō/, **Merlot** *n.* **1.** WINE a red wine made from a variety of black grape **2.** WINE GRAPE a variety of black grape used in winemaking, originally grown in France and now raised in many wine-growing regions worldwide [Early 19thC. From French, literally 'small blackbird', from *merle* 'blackbird' (source of English *merle*), probably from the colour of the grape.]

mermaid /múr mayd/ *n.* a mythical sea creature with the head and upper body of a woman and the tail of a fish instead of legs [14thC. From MERE[2] + MAID.]

mermaid's purse *n.* MARINE BIOL = sea purse

merman /múr man/ (*plural* **-men** /-men/) *n.* a mythical sea creature with the head and upper body of a man and the tail of a fish instead of legs [Early 17thC. Coined from MERE[2] + MAN.]

mero- *prefix.* part, partial ○ *merozoite* ○ *meroplankton* [From Greek *meros* 'part']

meroblastic /mérrō blástik/ *adj.* used to describe an egg undergoing only partial division after being fertilized, with the undivided cells becoming the yolk —**meroblastically** *adv.*

merocrine /mérrō krīn/ *adj.* relating to or produced by glands that make secretions without cell damage or disintegration [Early 20thC. Coined from MERO- + Greek *krinein* 'to separate'.]

Meroë /mérrō i/ **1.** ruined city in northern Sudan, on the River Nile **2.** ancient kingdom ruled from the city of Meroë

meroplankton /mérrō plángktən/ (*plural* **-tons** *or* **-ton**) *n.* organisms that are plankton only for part of their life cycle, usually during the larval stage —**meroplanktonic** /mérrō plangk tónnik/ *adj.*

-merous *suffix.* having a particular number or kind of parts ○ *tetramerous* ○ *heteromerous* [Formed from Greek *meros* 'part']

Merovingian /mérrō vínji ən/ *adj.* OF A FRANKISH DYNASTY belonging or relating to a dynasty of Frankish kings that was founded by Clovis I and reigned in Gaul and Germany from about AD 500 to 751 ■ *n.* MEROVINGIAN KING a member of the Merovingian dynasty [Late 17thC. Via French *mérovingien* from, ultimately, Latin *Meroveus* 'Merowig' (d. 458), the grandfather of Clovis.]

merozoite /mérrō zō īt/ *n.* any of the protozoan cells produced by the fission of a schizont, e.g. that of the malaria protozoan

Merrick /mérrik/ hill in southwestern Scotland, in the Southern Uplands. It is the highest peak in the south of Scotland. Height: 842 m/2,766 ft.

merriment /mérrimənt/ *n.* fun and enjoyment marked by noise and laughter

merry /mérri/ (**-rier, -riest**) *adj.* **1.** LIVELY AND CHEERFUL full of or showing lively cheerfulness or enjoyment ○ *a merry laugh* **2.** TIPSY mildly drunk (*informal*) **3.** FUNNY very funny or amusing (*dated*) ○ *a merry quip* **4.** DELIGHTFUL tending to produce cheerfulness or happiness in people (*archaic*) ○ *the merry month of May* [Old English *myrige* 'pleasant'. Ultimately from a prehistoric Germanic base meaning 'short', which is also the ancestor of English *mirth*. The underlying idea is of making time seem short.] —**merrily** *adv.* —**merriness** *n.* ◇ **make merry** to be amused, or take part in a celebration or festivity

——— **WORD KEY: CULTURAL NOTE** ———
The Merry Wives of Windsor, a play by William Shakespeare (1600–01). Shakespeare's only play in prose was written to exploit the popularity of Falstaff, a comic character in *Henry IV*. It tells of Falstaff's attempts to woo two married women in order to gain access to their wealth, the wives' discovery of his plan, and their imaginative revenge. The adjective *Falstaffian*, convivially jovial, derives from the character in both of the plays.

merry-andrew /-ándroo/ *n.* a buffoon, clown, or jester (*archaic*) [*Andrew* the forename, used in the sense of 'any man']

merry bone *n.* N England a wishbone

merry-go-round *n.* **1.** FAIRGROUND RIDE a fairground or amusement park ride with a rotating circular platform fitted with seats that are usually shaped like animals such as horses and move up and down to music **2.** US = roundabout *n.* **1 3.** WHIRL OF ACTIVITY a busy or continuous cycle of fast-paced activities or events ○ *a merry-go-round of press interviews and promotional events*

merrymaking /mérri mayking/ *n.* lively celebration, fun, or enjoyment —**merrymaker** *n.*

merry men *npl.* sb's followers (*humorous*)

merrythought /mérri thawt/ *n.* a wishbone (*dated*)

merse /murss/ *n.* Scotland an area of flat, often marshy, alluvial land near a river or estuary [Early 19thC. From Old English *mersc* (source of English *marsh*).]

Merse /murss/ a rich agricultural area of the Scottish Borders, formerly called March

Mersey /múrzi/ river of northwestern England. Liverpool lies on its estuary. Length: 113 km/70 mi.

Mersey beat /múrzi-/, **Mersey sound** *n.* a type of pop music of the 1960s that originated in the Merseyside area, especially Liverpool, and was performed by groups such as the Beatles

Merthyr Tydfil /múrthər tídfil/ town in southern Wales, formerly a centre of ironworking. Population: 39,482 (1991).

mes- *prefix.* = meso- (*used before vowels*)

Mesa: Devil's Tower, Wyoming, United States

mesa /máyssə/ *n.* a relatively flat elevated area with steep sides that is less extensive than a plateau, found especially in the southwestern United States. ◊ **butte** [Mid-18thC. From Spanish, literally 'table', from Latin *mensa*.]

mésalliance /me zálli ənss/ *n.* a marriage with sb of a lower social position, regarded as a bad match [Late 18thC. From French, literally 'bad alliance', from *alliance* 'alliance', from Old French *aliance*.]

mesarch /méssaark, méz-/ *adj.* ECOL used to describe a succession of plant or animal communities (**sere**) that originates in a moist habitat [Late 19thC. Coined from MESO- + Greek *arkhē* 'beginning, origin'.]

Mesa Verde National Park /máyssə vúrdi náshənəl paárk/ national park in southwestern Colorado, established in 1906. It is noted for its well-preserved ancient cliff dwellings. Area: 21,093 hectares/52,122 acres.

mescal /més kal/ (*plural* **-cals** *or* **-cal**) *n.* **1.** ALCOHOLIC BEVERAGE a colourless Mexican spirit distilled from the fermented sap of some species of agave plant. It is often sold with an agave worm in the bottle. ◊ **tequila 2.** = peyote [Early 18thC. Via Spanish *mezcal* from Nahuatl *mexcalli* 'mescal liquor'.]

Mescalero /méskə láirō/ (*plural* **-ro** *or* **-ros**) *n.* a member of a Native North American people who originally occupied lands in Mexico, New Mexico, and Texas, and whose members now live mainly in southern New Mexico [Mid-19thC. From Spanish, from *mezcal* (see MESCAL).]

mescaline /méskəlin, -leen/, **mescalin** /-lin/ *n.* a hallucinogenic drug that is extracted from the button-shaped nodules on the stem of the peyote cactus [Late 19thC. From German *Mezcalin*, from Spanish *mezcal* (see MESCAL).]

mescla /mésklə/ *n.* DRUGS a drug made from the residue of processing cocaine, which is mixed with marijuana and smoked

mesclun /mésskln/ *n.* a green salad made from several types of young leaves, typically including rocket, dandelion, radicchio, and endive [From Provençal *mesclar* 'to mix', from Old French *mescler*, ultimately from Latin *miscere*]

Mesdames /máy dam/ **1.** plural of **Madame 2.** plural of **Madam 3.** plural of **Mrs** [Late 16thC. From French, plural of *Madame*.]

mesdemoiselles plural of **mademoiselle**

meseems /mi seémz/ (**-seemed**) *vi.* it seems to me (*archaic*) [14thC. From an earlier form of the phrase *it seems to me*.]

mesembryanthemum /mi zémbri ánthiməm/ (*plural* **-mums** *or* **-mum**) *n.* a southern African succulent plant that has thick fleshy leaves and is widely grown for its colourful flowers. Genus: *Mesembryanthemum*. [Late 18thC. Via modern Latin, genus name, from, ultimately, Greek *mesēmbria* 'noon' + *anthemon* 'flower'.]

mesencephalon /méss en séffə lon/ *n.* the midbrain (*technical*) —**mesencephalic** /méss enssi fállik/ *adj.*

mesenchyme /méss eng kīm/ *n.* the cells within the embryo that develop into connective tissue, bone, cartilage, blood, and the lymphatic system [Late 19thC. Anglicization of *mesenchyma*, literally 'middle infusion', from Greek *mesos* 'middle' + *egkhuma* 'infusion'.] —**mesenchymal** /mi séngkim'l/ *adj.* — **mesenchymatous** /-kímmətəss/ *adj.*

mesenteritis /me séntə rítiss/ *n.* inflammation of the mesentery of the peritoneum

mesenteron /me séntə ron/ (*plural* **-a** /-ə/) *n.* the middle section of the embryonic intestine, which develops into the stomach, small intestine, and most of the large intestine —**mesenteronic** /me séntə rónnik/ *adj.*

mesentery /méss'ntəri/ (*plural* **-ies**) *n.* **1.** ANAT **SUPPORTING MEMBRANE** a membrane that supports an organ or body part, especially the double-layered membrane of the peritoneum attached to the back wall of the abdominal cavity that supports the small intestine **2.** ZOOL **MEMBRANE IN INVERTEBRATES** a supportive membrane surrounding and giving structure to the inner organs of invertebrates [15thC. Via modern Latin *mesenterium* from Greek *mesenterion*, literally 'middle intestine', from *enteron* 'intestine' (source of English *enteron*).] —**mesenteric** /méss'n térrik/ *adj.*

mesh /mesh/ *n.* **1. NETLIKE MATERIAL** material or a piece of material made of plastic, thread, or wire woven together like a net ○ *wire mesh* **2. OPENING IN A NET** the open space between the threads or wires of a net **3. STRANDS OF NET** the threads or wires that make up a net **4. TRAP** sth that holds or entangles like a net or a trap (*often used in the plural*) ○ *caught in the meshes of the criminal underworld* **5. STH INTERWOVEN** an interwoven or interlinked arrangement or construction ○ *the mesh of the girders against the sky* **6. INTERLOCKING METAL LINKS** a material consisting of interlocking metal links, used in jewellery **7.** MECH ENG **ENGAGEMENT OF GEARS** engagement of the teeth on gear wheels **8. OPENING IN A SCREEN** a measure of the number of openings in a screen for sorting things into different sizes, usually per inch. A 20-mesh screen has 20 openings per inch. ■ *vti.* (**meshes, meshing, meshed**) **1. FIT TOGETHER** to fit or work closely or well together, or make things work closely or well together ○ *Her vision of the company's future meshes perfectly with ours.* **2. CATCH OR ENTANGLE** to catch or entangle sb or sth, or become caught or entangled, in a mesh **3.** MECH ENG **ENGAGE GEARS** to make gear teeth engage together, or become engaged [14thC. Origin uncertain: probably from Middle Dutch *maesche*, and ultimately from an Indo-European word meaning 'knot' or 'to knit'.] —**meshy** *adj.*

meshuga /mə shóoggə/, **meshugah** *adj.* totally unreasonable or thoughtless (*slang insult*) [Late 19thC. Via Yiddish *meshuge* from Hebrew *mĕshuggā*.]

meshuggener /mə shóoggənər/, **meshugana** *n.* sb who is totally unreasonable or thoughtless (*slang insult*) [Early 20thC. Variant of MESHUGA.]

mesial /meézi əl/ *adj.* DENT relating to or occurring along the dental arch near the middle of the front of the jaw [Early 19thC. Formed from Greek *mesos* 'middle'.] —**mesially** *adv.*

mesic[1] /meézik/ *adj.* ECOL growing in or characterized by moderate moisture [Early 20thC. Formed from Greek *mesos* 'middle'.] —**mesically** *adv.*

mesic[2] /meézik/ *adj.* PHYS relating to a meson [Mid-20thC. Formed from MESON.]

mesmeric /mez mérrik/ *adj.* completely absorbing sb's attention [Early 19thC. Formed from *Mesmer* (see MESMERIZE).] —**mesmerically** *adv.*

mesmerise *vt.* = **mesmerize**

mesmerism /mézmərizəm/ *n.* **1. FASCINATING POWER** the power to fascinate sb in a way that is almost hypnotic **2.** HIST **HYPNOTISM** hypnotism, formerly believed to involve animal magnetism [Late 18thC. Formed from *Mesmer* (see MESMERIZE).] —**mesmerist** *n.*

mesmerize /mézmə rīz/ (**-izes, -izing, -ized**), **mesmerise** (**-ises, -ising, -ised**) *vt.* **1. ABSORB SB'S ATTENTION** to fascinate sb or absorb all of sb's attention ○ *The speaker mesmerized the audience with his dramatic tale.* **2. HYPNOTIZE** to hypnotize sb, especially formerly in a way believed to involve animal magnetism [Early 19thC. Formed from the name of F. A. *Mesmer* (1734–1815), an Austrian physician who conducted experiments in which he induced trance-like states in his subjects.] —**mesmerization** /mézmə rī záysh'n/ *n.* —**mesmerizer** /mézmə rīzər/ *n.*

mesne /meen/ *adj.* LAW happening or appearing between two other things, especially assignments of property [Mid-16thC. From legal French, a variant of Anglo-Norman *meen* 'middle'.]

mesne profits *npl.* intermediate profits received by a tenant who is in wrongful possession of an estate, which the landlord is entitled to recover

meso- *prefix.* middle, intermediate ○ *mesopelagic* [From Greek *mesos*. Ultimately from an Indo-European word that is also the ancestor of English *middle* and *medial*.]

Mesoamerica /méssō ə mérrikə/ *n.* a region of Central America and southern North America that was occupied by several civilizations, especially the Mayan, in pre-Columbian times —**Mesoamerican** *adj.*, *n.*

mesoblast /méssō blast/ *n.* CELL BIOL = **mesoderm**

mesocarp /méssō kaarp/ *n.* the middle layer of a fruit wall (**pericarp**), e.g. the fleshy part of some fruits

mesocratic /méssō krátik/ *adj.* used to describe igneous rock containing as much as 60 per cent of heavy dark ferromagnesium minerals in its composition

mesoderm /méssō durm/ *n.* the middle of the three cell layers in an embryo, from which connective tissue, muscle, blood, dermis, and bone develop —**mesodermal** /méssō dúrm'l/ *adj.* —**mesodermic** *adj.*

mesoglea /méssō gleé ə/, **mesogloea** *n.* a layer of gelatinous substance separating the inner and outer walls of a coelenterate such as a jellyfish [Late 19thC. From modern Latin, literally 'middle glue', from Greek *glia* 'glue' (source of English *glia*).] —**mesogleal** *adj.*

Mesolithic /méssō líthik/, **mesolithic** *n.* the middle period of the Stone Age, between the Palaeolithic and Neolithic —**Mesolithic** *adj.*

mesomorph /méssō mawrf/ *n.* a large muscular body, or sb who has such a body. ◊ **ectomorph, endomorph**

meson /meé zon/ *n.* an elementary particle, e.g. a pion or kaon, that has a rest mass between that of an electron and proton and participates in the strong interaction. Mesons consist of a quark and antiquark, and have a spin that is zero or an integer. —**mesonic** /mi zónnik/ *adj.*

mesopause /méssō pawz/ *n.* the upper boundary of the mesosphere, approximately 80 km/50 mi. above the Earth's surface

mesopelagic /méssōpə lájjik/ *adj.* found in or relating to the intermediate oceanic depths between approximately 100 and 1,000 m/300 and 3,300 ft

mesophyll /méssōfil/ *n.* the soft tissue (**parenchyma**) containing chlorophyll between the epidermal layers of a plant leaf —**mesophyllic** /méssō fíllik/ *adj.* —**mesophyllous** /-fílləss/ *adj.*

mesophyte /méssō fīt/ *n.* a land plant that needs moderate amounts of moisture for growth —**mesophytic** /méssō fíttik/ *adj.*

Mesopotamia /méssəpə táymi ə/ ancient region located between the rivers Tigris and Euphrates in modern Iraq and Syria. It was the site of several early urban civilizations, including Babylonia. —**Mesopotamian** *n.*

mesosome /méssō sōm/ *n.* an indentation in the cell membrane of some bacteria

mesosphere /méssō sfeer/ *n.* the layer of the Earth's atmosphere in which temperature decreases rapidly, located between the stratosphere and thermosphere —**mesospheric** /méssō sférrik/ *adj.*

mesothelium /méssō theéli əm/ (*plural* **mesotheliums** *or* **mesothelia** /-ə/) *n.* a cell layer derived from mesoderm that lines the body cavity of a vertebrate embryo and develops into epithelia and muscle tissue —**mesothelial** *adj.*

mesothorax /méssō tháwraks/ (*plural* **-raxes** *or* **-races** /-rə seez/) *n.* the middle of the three segments of an insect's thorax, from which the middle pair of legs and first pair of wings grow —**mesothoracic** /méssō thaw rássik/ *adj.*

Mesozoic /méssō zṓ ik/ *adj.* **BELONGING TO PREHISTORIC ERA** belonging to or dating from an era of geological time 250 to 65 million years ago, between the Permian and Tertiary eras, when dinosaurs, birds, and flowering plants first appeared ■ *n.* **MESOZOIC ERA** the Mesozoic era

mesquite /me skeét/ (*plural* **-quite** *or* **-quites**) *n.* **1.** TREES **SMALL SPINY TREE** a small spiny tree or shrub of the legume family that grows in the southwestern United States and has pods that are used as fodder. Genus: *Prosopis*. **2.** INDUST **MESQUITE WOOD** the wood of a mesquite tree or shrub, often burned in a barbecue to flavour food [Mid-18thC. Via Mexican Spanish *mezquite* from Nahuatl *mizquitl*.]

mess /mess/ *n.* **1. UNTIDY CONDITION** a dirty or untidy state ○ *The flat was left in a terrible mess after the party.* **2. CHAOTIC STATE** a chaotic, confused, or troublesome state or situation ○ *Their business affairs were in a complete mess.* **3. UNTIDY PERSON OR THING** sb or sth in a confused, dirty, or untidy state (*informal insult*) **4. EXCREMENT** animal excrement (*informal*) ○ *Someone had tramped dog mess on the front steps.* **5. PLACE FOR COMMUNAL MEALS** a place where a group of people, especially members of the armed forces, have meals together **6. PEOPLE WHO EAT TOGETHER** a group of people, especially members of the armed forces, who have meals together (*takes a singular or plural verb*) **7. COMMUNAL MEAL** a meal eaten together by a group of people, especially members of the armed forces **8. QUANTITY OF FOOD** a serving or quantity of food, especially of soft or soggy food (*archaic*) ■ *v.* (**messes, messing, messed**) **1.** *vti.* **MAKE STH DIRTY** to make sth dirty, muddled, or disordered ○ *She messed her jacket while checking the oil.* **2.** *vi.* **MEDDLE** to interfere or meddle in sth ○ *Don't mess in their business.* **3.** *vi.* **USE STH CARELESSLY** to use sth carelessly, causing a problem or damage as a result ○ *Who's been messing with my computer?* **4.** *vi.* **EAT TOGETHER** to take meals along with a particular group of people, especially members of the armed forces ○ *I used to mess with the three of them.* [13thC. From Old French, 'portion of food', the original sense in English, from, ultimately, Latin *mittere* 'to send, put', the underlying idea being 'placing (as if on the table)'.]

mess around, mess about *v.* **1.** *vi.* **WASTE TIME** to waste time in an unproductive or aimless manner (*informal*) **2.** *vi.* **RELAX** to spend time in a leisurely and pleasant manner (*informal*) **3.** *vti.* **INTERFERE** to interfere or meddle in sth (*informal*) **4.** *vi.* **ASSOCIATE WITH SB** to associate with sb, especially sb who is seen as undesirable (*informal*) ○ *She started messing around with that crowd last summer.* **5.** *vi.* **BEHAVE IN UNSERIOUS WAY** to joke or behave playfully (*informal*) ○ *I thought he was just messing around.* **6.** *vt.* **TREAT SB BADLY** to treat sb badly or unfairly, e.g. by continual changes of mind or lack of honesty (*informal*) ○ *Neil felt that he was being messed around by his manager.* **7.** *vi.* **BE SEXUALLY UNFAITHFUL** to have sexual activity with sb other than a spouse or regular partner (*slang*)

mess up *v.* (*informal*) **1.** *vti.* **RUIN STH** to spoil or bungle sth, or make a mistake ○ *The rain messed up our plans to go for a picnic.* **2.** *vt.* **MAKE STH MESSY** to make sth dirty or disordered **3.** *vt.* **UPSET SB** to confuse or upset sb

message /méssij/ *n.* **1. COMMUNICATION** a communication in speech, writing, or signals **2. MEANING** a lesson, moral, or important idea that sb wants to communicate, e.g. in a work of art **3. ERRAND** the mission or errand of a messenger (*dated*) ○ *sent on a message to her grandmother's* **4.** US **ADVERTISEMENT** an advertisement, especially one on television, paid for by the sponsors of a programme or event ○ *and now a message from our sponsor* ■ **messages** *npl.* *Scotland* **SHOPPING** shopping, especially the everyday necessities ○ *I'm away to get the messages.* ■ *vt.* (**-sages, -saging, -saged**) **1. COMMUNICATE WITH SB** to send a message to sb ○ *Can you message me about that?* **2. COMMUNICATE STH TO SB** to send sth as a message ○ *to message the news to your boss* [13thC. Via French from, ultimately, Latin *missus*, the past participle of *mittere* 'to send' (source of English *mission*, *transmit*, and *promise*).] ◇ **get the message** to take sth in and understand it (*informal*)

message board *n.* COMPUT = **bulletin board**

Messager /méssazhər/, **André Charles Prosper** (1853–1929) French composer. He was noted chiefly for his operettas such as *Véronique* (1898).

messaging /méssijing/ *n.* **1. SYSTEM FOR MESSAGES** a system for sending messages to people, e.g. by computer, telephone, or pager **2. SENDING OF MESSAGES** the process of sending a message using a messaging system

messaline /méssə leén/ n. a soft shiny lightweight silk fabric, used for making dresses [Early 20thC. From French, from the name of Valeria *Messalina*, adulterous wife of the Roman emperor Claudius; perhaps because the fabric was considered sensuous.]

Messeigneurs plural of **Monseigneur**

messenger /méss'njər/ n. 1. SB CARRYING MESSAGE sb who carries a message or messages between people 2. PAID COURIER sb who is employed to carry messages, especially an employee of a courier or telegram delivery service or a government courier 3. SB RUNNING ERRAND sb who runs an errand 4. HERALD a herald or forerunner of sth (*archaic*) 5. messenger, messenger line NAUT LIGHT ROPE a lightweight rope that is used to haul a heavier one, e.g. from one ship to another [12thC. From French *messager*, from *message* 'a MESSAGE'.]

Messenger /méss'njər/, **Dally** (1883–1959) Australian rugby league player. He scored a record-breaking 155 points during the first Australian Rugby League tour of England in 1908. Real name **Herbert Henry Messenger**

messenger RNA n. a form of RNA that is transcribed from a strand of DNA and translated into a protein sequence at a cell ribosome

Messerschmitt /méssər shmit/ n. a fighter aircraft, especially the Me-109 or the Me-262, used by the German air force in World War II [Mid-20thC]

Messerschmitt /méssərshmit/, **Willy** (1898–1978) German aircraft designer. His Me 109 set a world speed record (1939), and his Me 262, used by the Luftwaffe, was the first jet fighter plane. Real name **Wilhelm Messerschmitt**

mess hall n. a building or room where a group of people, especially members of the armed forces, eat their meals together

Messiaen /méss yoN, -yaan/, **Olivier Eugène Prosper Charles** (1908–92) French composer and organist. His works for organ, piano, voice, chamber ensemble, and orchestra have a mystic quality, with a unique harmonic language.

messiah /mə sí ə/ n. sb regarded as or claiming to be a saviour or liberator of a country, people, or the world —**messiahship** n.

Messiah /mə sí ə/ n. 1. CHR JESUS CHRIST in Christianity, Jesus Christ regarded as the Messiah prophesied in the Hebrew Bible 2. JUDAISM KING OF THE JEWS in the Hebrew Bible, an anointed king who will lead the Jews back to the land of Israel and establish justice in the world [12thC. Via French *Messie* from, ultimately, Greek *Messias*, from Aramaic *měshīhā* and Hebrew *māshīāh*, literally 'anointed', from *māshah* 'to anoint'.] —**Messiahship** n.

—— **WORD KEY: CULTURAL NOTE** ——

The Messiah, an oratorio by German composer George Frederick Handel (1742). Consisting of biblical scriptures selected by Charles Jennens set to music by Handel, this enduringly popular work is noted for the power of its (distinctively Anglican) religious expression. For a time in the 19th century, it became fashionable to perform the work with an enormous orchestra and chorus.

messianic /méssi ánnik/ adj. 1. messianic, Messianic JUD-CHR RELATING TO THE MESSIAH belonging or relating to the Messiah 2. JUDAISM OF JUDAIC GOLDEN AGE relating to, belonging to, or constituting a Judaic golden age of peace, truth, and happiness 3. OF A LIBERATOR relating or belonging to an inspirational leader, especially one claiming to be or regarded as a saviour or liberator 4. INVOLVING GREAT ENTHUSIASM done with or showing great enthusiasm or devotion ○ *preaching with messianic fervour* —**messianically** adv.

messianism /mə sí ənizəm/, **Messianism** n. belief in the coming of the Messiah or a messiah or messianic age

Messidor /méssi dawr/ n. the tenth month of the year in the French Revolutionary calendar, corresponding to 20 June to 19 July in the Gregorian calendar [Mid-19thC. From French, literally 'harvest gift', from Latin *messis* 'harvest' + Greek *dōron* 'gift'.]

Messieurs plural of **Monsieur**

Messina /messéena/ historic Italian city and seaport in northeastern Sicily. Population: 234,000 (1994).

Messina, Strait of strait between Sicily and the Italian mainland, linking the Ionian and Tyrrhenian seas. Length: 32 km/20 mi.

mess jacket n. a waist-length jacket, worn as part of a military uniform, especially on formal occasions

mess kit n. 1. COOKING AND EATING UTENSILS a compact set of cooking and eating utensils, usually made of metal, used especially by soldiers or campers 2. MIL FORMAL MILITARY UNIFORM a dress uniform worn by officers and senior noncommissioned officers at formal dinners

messmate /méss mayt/ n. sb with whom sb regularly eats, especially in a military mess

Messrs plural of **Mr**

messuage /mésswij/ n. a dwelling with its outbuildings and the surrounding land that is used by the dwelling's occupants [14thC. From Anglo-Norman, of uncertain origin: probably from a misreading of *mesnage*, from Old French (see MÉNAGE).]

messy /méssi/ (-ier, -iest) adj. 1. DIRTY OR DISORDERED involving, producing, or marked by dirt or disorder ○ *Repairing a car can be a messy business.* 2. DIFFICULT TO SORT OUT complicated and unpleasant to resolve or deal with 3. CARELESS showing a lack of carefulness or precision ○ *an erroneous conclusion resulting from messy reasoning* —**messily** adv. —**messiness** n.

mestiza /mess teézə/ n. a woman who has parents or ancestors of different racial origins, especially a woman in Latin America of both Native American and European ancestry [Late 16thC. From Spanish, the feminine of MESTIZO.]

mestizo /mess teézō/ (*plural* -**zos** *or* -**zoes**) n. sb who has parents or ancestors of different racial origins, especially sb in Latin America of both Native American and European ancestry. Mestizos form the largest population group in many Latin American countries. [Late 16thC. Via Spanish, from Latin *mixtus*, the past participle of *miscere* 'to mix' (source of English *mix* and *meddle*).]

mestranol /méstrə nol/ n. a synthetic oestrogen used in oral contraceptives. Formula: $C_{21}H_{26}O_2$. [Mid-20thC. Coined from METHYL + OESTRADIOL + -OL.]

met past tense, past participle of **meet**

Met /met/ n., *abbr.* Meteorological Office ■ *abbr.* Metropolitan Opera House (in New York) ■ n., *abbr.* Metropolitan Police

met. *abbr.* 1. metallurgy 2. metaphor 3. metaphysics 4. meteorological 5. meteorology 6. metropolitan

met- *prefix.* = **meta-** (*used before vowels*)

meta- *prefix.* 1. later, behind ○ *metaphase* ○ *metathorax* 2. beyond, transcending, encompassing ○ *metagalaxy* ○ *metalanguage* 3. change, transformation ○ *metaplasia* 4. higher, more developed ○ *metaxylem* 5. used in chemical names ○ *metaphosphate* [From Greek *meta* 'beside, after'. Ultimately from an Indo-European base meaning 'between' that is also the ancestor of English *midwife*.]

metabolic /méttə bóllik/ adj. relating to or typical of metabolism [Mid-19thC. From Greek *metabolikos* 'changeable', from *metabolē* (see METABOLISM).] —**metabolically** adv.

metabolise vti. = **metabolize**

metabolism /mə tábbəlizəm/ n. 1. LIFE-SUSTAINING CHEMICAL ACTIVITY the ongoing interrelated series of chemical interactions taking place in living organisms that provide the energy and nutrients needed to sustain life 2. CHEMICAL ACTIVITY INVOLVING PARTICULAR SUBSTANCE the chemical activity involving a particular substance in a living organism [Late 19thC. Formed from Greek *metabolē* 'change', from *metaballein*, literally 'throw differently', from *ballein* 'to throw' (source of English *ballistic*).]

metabolite /mə tábbə līt/ n. a substance that is involved in or is a by-product of metabolism

metabolize /mə tábbə līz/ (-lizes, -lizing, -lized), **metabolise** (-lises, -lising, -lised) vti. to subject sth to the biochemical processes of metabolism, or to undergo

metabolism [Late 19thC. Formed from Greek *metabolē* (see METABOLISM).] —**metabolizable** adj.

metacarpal /méttə ka̱arp'l/ n. HAND OR FOREFOOT BONES any of the bones in the human hand between the wrist and digits, or the similar bones in a vertebrate animal's forefoot ■ *adj.* OF HAND OR FOREFOOT BONES relating or belonging to the metacarpals —**metacarpally** adv.

metacarpus /méttə ka̱arpəss/ (*plural* -**pi** /-pī/) n. 1. ANAT BONES IN HUMAN HAND the set of five long bones in the human hand between the wrist and fingers 2. ZOOL FOREFOOT REGION the region between the wrist and digits of the forefoot or hand of a vertebrate animal

metacentre /méttə sentər/ n. the intersection of the vertical line through the centre of buoyancy of an object at equilibrium with the vertical line through the centre of buoyancy when the object is tilted

metacentric /méttə séntrik/ adj. 1. OF METACENTRE relating or belonging to a metacentre 2. GENETICS HAVING CENTROMERE IN MIDDLE used to describe a chromosome whose centromere is located at or near the middle. ◊ **acentric, telocentric**

metachromatic /méttəkrō máttik/ adj. 1. TAKING ON DIFFERENT COLOUR taking on a colour atypical of the staining solution 2. PRODUCING DIFFERENT SHADES able to produce a colour in different shades in tissue or cells [Late 19thC. Coined from META- + Greek *khrōmat-* (see CHROMAT-) + -IC.]

metachromatism /méttə krṓmətizəm/ n. a change in colour caused by a change in physical conditions such as temperature

metacognition /méttə kog nísh'n/ n. knowledge about your own thoughts and the factors that influence your thinking —**metacognitive** /méttə kógnətiv/ adj.

meta-ethics /méttə-/ n. the branch of linguistic philosophy that analyses and seeks to clarify the meaning and use of ethical expressions such as 'good' and 'ought' (*takes a singular verb*) —**meta-ethical** adj.

metafemale /méttə feé mayl/ n. a female organism with an extra female chromosome

metafiction /méttə fiksh'n/ n. 1. FICTION ABOUT NATURE OF LITERATURE fiction that emphasizes the nature of fiction, the techniques and conventions used to write it, and the role of the author 2. PIECE OF META-FICTION a work of metafiction —**metafictional** /méttə fiksh'nəl/ adj. —**metafictionist** /-fiksh'nist/ n.

metagalaxy /méttə gallaksi/ n. the total of all galaxies making up the universe —**metagalactic** /méttəgə láktik/ adj.

metage /meétij/ n. 1. OFFICIAL MEASUREMENT the official measurement of the contents or weight of a load, e.g. of coal or grain 2. CHARGE a charge for making an official measurement of the contents or weight of a load [Early 16thC. Formed from METE 'to measure'.]

metagnathous /mə tágnəthəss/ adj. used to describe a bird that has the tips of its bill crossed —**metagnathism** n.

metal /métt'l/ n. 1. METALL TYPE OF CHEMICAL ELEMENT a chemical element such as copper or iron that is usually solid in form, is usually a good conductor of heat and electricity, is malleable and ductile, and has a characteristic lustre 2. METALL MIXTURE OF METALS a mixture (**alloy**) of one or more metals 3. MUSIC HEAVY METAL heavy metal (*informal*) 4. PRINTING PRINTING TYPE printer's type made of metal 5. CRAFT MOLTEN GLASS molten glass for use in glassmaking 6. HERALDRY GOLD OR SILVER gold or silver when used in heraldry 7. NAVY WEIGHT FIRED IN BROADSIDE the collective weight of the projectiles a warship can fire in a broadside 8. TRANSP = **road metal** ■ **metals** *npl.* RAIL RAILS the rails of a railway track ■ *vt.* (-**als**, -**alling**, -**alled**) 1. FIT WITH METAL to cover, fit, or provide sth with metal 2. MAKE OR MEND ROAD to make or repair a road with broken stones (**road metal**) [13thC. Directly or via French from Latin *metallum* 'mine, metal', from Greek *metallon*, of unknown origin.]

metal. *abbr.* 1. metallurgical 2. metallurgy

metalanguage /méttə lang gwij/ n. a language or system of symbols used to describe or analyse another language or system of symbols

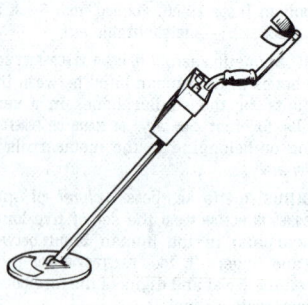

Metal detector

Metallophone

metal detector n. **1.** DEVICE FOR DETECTING BURIED METAL a portable electronic device with a search head that is swept over the ground and used to detect buried metal objects such as coins **2.** DEVICE FOR DETECTING WEAPONS an electronic device for detecting metal weapons, and e.g. to screen passengers at an airport **3.** FOOD TECH DEVICE FOR DETECTING METAL IN FOOD an electronic device used in the food industry to check for the presence of pieces of metal that might have accidentally got into food during processing

metalinguistic /méttə ling gwístik/ adj. relating to a metalanguage or to metalinguistics

metalinguistics /méttə ling gwístiks/ n. (takes a singular verb) **1.** STUDY OF METALANGUAGES the branch of linguistics that deals with the study of metalanguages **2.** STUDY OF LANGUAGE AND CULTURE the branch of linguistics that deals with the relation between a language and other aspects of a particular culture

metalize vt. US = metallize

metall. abbr. **1.** metallurgical **2.** metallurgy

metall- prefix. = metallo- (used before vowels)

metallic /mə tállik/ adj. **1.** CONTAINING OR BEING METAL made of, containing, or constituting metal or a metal **2.** OF METAL typical of a metal **3.** SHINY shiny and highly reflective ○ a sports car with a metallic finish **4.** TASTING OF METAL sharp and bitter to the taste ○ This water has a slightly metallic taste. **5.** SOUNDING LIKE HIT METAL like the sound of a metal object hitting or knocking against sth **6.** HARSH-SOUNDING harsh and unpleasant in tone ○ speaking with a metallic edge to her voice —**metallically** adv.

metallic bond n. a chemical bond characteristic of metals, in which electrons are shared between atoms and move about in the crystal

metalliferous /méttə lífferəss/ adj. containing or yielding metal

metalline /méttə līn/ adj. **1.** LIKE METAL resembling a metal **2.** WITH METAL IONS containing metal ions

metalling /métt'ling/ n. **1.** = road metal **2.** MAKING OR REPAIRING ROADS the process of making or repairing roads with broken stones or other material

metallize /méttə līz/ (-lizes, -lizing, -lized) vt. to coat or cover sth with metal

metallo- prefix. metal ○ metallophone [From Latin metallum (see METAL).]

metallography /méttə lóggrəfi/ n. the study of the composition and microscopic structure of metals —**metallographer** n. —**metallographic** /mə tállə gráffik/ adj. —**metallographically** adv. —**metallographist** /méttə lóggrəfist/ n.

metalloid /méttə loyd/ n. NONMETALLIC ELEMENT WITH METAL PROPERTIES a nonmetallic element such as silicon that has properties between those of a metal and nonmetal ■ adj. metalloid, metalloidal **1.** OF METALLOID relating to or having the characteristics of a metalloid **2.** LIKE METAL resembling a metal

metallophone /me tállə fōn/ n. a musical instrument, similar to a xylophone, with tuned metal bars that are struck with mallets

metallurgy /mə tállurji/ n. the study of the structure and properties of metals, their extraction from the ground, and the procedures for refining, alloying, and making things from them —**metallurgic** /méttə lúrjik/ adj. —**metallurgical** adj. —**metallurgically** adv. —**metallurgist** /mə tállərjist/ n.

metalwork /métt'l wurk/ n. **1.** MAKING OF METAL OBJECTS the craft of making objects out of metal **2.** METAL THINGS objects made of metal **3.** METAL PART OF STH the metal part of an object —**metalworker** n.

metalworking /métt'l wurking/ n. the process or technique of making or shaping objects out of metal

metamale /méttə mayl/ n. a male organism with an extra male chromosome

metamere /méttə meer/ n. any of the series of similar segments into which the bodies of animals such as worms or lobsters are divided

metameric /méttə mérrik/ adj. **1.** HAVING METAMERES with a body divided into a series of similar segments (**metameres**) **2.** OF METAMERISM relating to or typical of metamerism —**metamerically** adv.

metamerism /mə támmərizəm/ n. the condition of having the body divided into a series of similar segments (**metameres**), or an embryonic stage in which the body is divided in this way

metamorphic /méttə máwrfik/, **metamorphous** /-máwrfəss/ adj. **1.** GEOL BY OR FROM METAMORPHISM relating to or having undergone metamorphism **2.** OF METAMORPHOSIS relating to or involving a change in physical form, appearance, or character —**metamorphically** adv.

metamorphism /méttə máwrfizəm/ n. **1.** GEOL CHANGE IN ROCK STRUCTURE a change in the physical structure of rock that results from long-term heat and pressure, especially a change that increases the rock's hardness and crystalline structure **2.** METAMORPHOSIS metamorphosis (archaic)

metamorphose /méttə máwrfōz/ (-phoses, -phosing, -phosed) v. **1.** vti. CHANGE PHYSICAL FORM to undergo or make sb or sth undergo a complete or marked change of physical form, structure, or substance ○ The water had metamorphosed into ice. **2.** vti. CHANGE APPEARANCE OR CHARACTER to undergo or make sb or sth undergo a complete or marked change in appearance, character, or condition **3.** vti. CHANGE SUPPOSEDLY BY MAGIC to undergo or make sb or sth undergo a transformation supposedly by magic **4.** vi. ZOOL UNDERGO BODILY CHANGES DURING GROWTH to undergo a complete or marked change of bodily form while developing into an adult animal ○ The tadpole has metamorphosed into a frog. **5.** vti. GEOL CHANGE ROCK STRUCTURE to undergo or make a rock undergo metamorphism [Late 16thC. From French métamorphoser, from métamorphose 'metamorphosis', from Latin metamorphosis (see METAMORPHOSIS).]

metamorphosis /méttə máwrfəssiss/ (plural **-ses** /-seez/) n. **1.** CHANGE OF PHYSICAL FORM a complete or marked change of physical form, structure, or substance ○ the overnight metamorphosis of the pond water into ice **2.** CHANGE OF APPEARANCE OR CHARACTER a complete or marked change in appearance, character, or condition **3.** SUPPOSED SUPERNATURAL TRANSFORMATION a transformation caused by supposed supernatural powers **4.** TRANSFORMED PERSON OR THING sb or sth that has gone through a complete or marked change **5.** ZOOL CHANGE IN ANIMAL FORM a complete or marked change in the form of an animal as it develops into an adult, e.g. the change from tadpole to frog or from caterpillar to butterfly [Mid-16thC. Via Latin from Greek metamorphōsis, from metamorphoun 'to transform', literally 'to form differently', from morphē 'form' (see MORPH-).]

WORD KEY: CULTURAL NOTE

Metamorphoses, a poem by the Roman poet Ovid (AD 8). This long narrative work consists of a series of tales in which characters undergo some kind of transformation. The stories were based on Greek myths and legends and are presented in chronological order, but much of their liveliness derives from events, characters, and details invented by the poet.

WORD KEY: CULTURAL NOTE

The Metamorphosis, a short novel by Czech writer Franz Kafka (1915). The protagonist of this bizarre tale, Gregor Samsa, awakens to find himself transformed into an insect, then dies as a result of his family's neglect and his own failure to act. Gregor's metamorphosis can be read as both a portrayal of the author's troubled family life and a metaphor for the artist's power to transform life into art.

metanephros /méttə néffross/ (plural **-roi** /-néffroy/) n. an embryonic organ of excretion in reptiles, birds, and mammals that develops into the kidney [Late 19thC. Coined from META- + Greek nephros 'kidney' (see NEPHR-).]

metaphase /méttə fayz/ n. the second stage of cell division, during which chromosomes line up in preparation for separation. ◊ anaphase, prophase, telophase

metaphase plate n. the equatorial plane along which chromosomes line up during the second stage of cell division in preparation for separation

metaphor /méttəfər, -fawr/ n. **1.** IMPLICIT COMPARISON the application of a word or phrase to sb or sth that is not meant literally but to make a comparison, e.g. saying that sb is a snake. ◊ mixed metaphor, simile **2.** FIGURATIVE LANGUAGE all language that involves figures of speech or symbolism and does not literally represent real things **3.** SYMBOL one thing used or considered to represent another [15thC. From, ultimately, Greek metaphora, from metapherein 'to transfer', literally 'to carry between', from pherein 'to carry' (see -PHORE).] —**metaphoric** /méttə fórrik/ adj. —**metaphorical** adj. —**metaphorically** adv.

metaphosphate /méttə fóss fayt/ n. any salt or ester of metaphosphoric acid

metaphosphoric acid /méttə foss fórrik-/ n. a glassy solid containing linked phosphate groups and used as a drying agent and in dental cements. Formula: HPO_3.

metaphrase /méttə frayz/ n. LITERAL TRANSLATION a word-for-word translation of sth ■ vt. (-phrases, -phrasing, -phrased) **1.** TRANSLATE STH LITERALLY to translate sth, especially word for word **2.** CHANGE WORDING OF to change the wording of a text [Mid-16thC. From, ultimately, Greek metaphrasis, from metaphrazein 'to translate', literally 'to tell differently', from phrazein 'to tell'.]

metaphrast /méttə frast/ n. sb who changes the form of a text, e.g. from prose into verse [Early 17thC. From Greek metaphrastēs, from metaphrazein 'to translate' (see METAPHRASE).] —**metaphrastic** /méttə frástik/ adj. —**metaphrastical** adj. —**metaphrastically** adv.

metaphysic n. = metaphysics

metaphysical /méttə fízzik'l/ adj. **1.** RELATING TO METAPHYSICS relating to the philosophical study of the nature of being and beings or a philosophical system resulting from such study **2.** SPECULATIVE based on speculative reasoning and unexamined assumptions that have not been logically examined or confirmed by observation ○ a metaphysical system whose claim to truth is undermined by contradictions **3.** ABSTRACT extremely abstract or theoretical ○ metaphysical subjects removed from everyday life **4.** INCORPOREAL without material form or substance ○ the metaphysical realm of pure thought **5.** SUPERNATURAL originating not in the physical world but somewhere outside it ○ a metaphysical explanation of beauty and goodness —**metaphysically** adv.

Metaphysical /méttə fízzik'l/, **metaphysical** adj. OF EARLY 17C POETRY relating to the poetic style of John Donne, George Herbert, and other early 17th-century English poets who used consciously intellectual language and elaborate metaphors that compared dissimilar things ■ n. METAPHYSICAL POET a poet of the Metaphysical group

a at; aa father; aw all; ay day; air hair; ə about, edible, item, common, circus; e egg; ee eel; hw when; i it, happy; ī ice; 'l apple; 'm rhythm; 'n fashion; o odd; ō open; ōo good; oo pool; ow owl; oy oil; th thin; th this; u up; ur urge;

metaphysics /méttə fízziks/, **metaphysic** /-ik/ n. (takes a singular verb) **1.** PHILOSOPHY OF BEING the branch of philosophy concerned with the study of the nature of being and beings, existence, time and space, and causality **2.** UNDERLYING PRINCIPLES the ultimate underlying principles or theories that form the basis of a particular field of knowledge ○ Symmetry is part of the metaphysics of quantum mechanics. **3.** ABSTRACT THINKING abstract discussion or thinking [Mid-16thC. From medieval Latin metaphysica (plural), from medieval Greek (ta) metaphusika '(the) metaphysics', from ta meta ta phusika 'the (works of Aristotle) after the "Physics"' (see PHYSICS).]

metaplasia /méttə pláyzi ə/ n. the transformation of one kind of tissue into another undesirable type, e.g. in tumour formation [Late 19thC. From Greek metaplassein 'to mould into a new form', from plassein 'to mould' (see -PLASIA).] —**metaplastic** /méttə plástik/ adj.

metapsychology /méttə sī kólləji/ n. the philosophical study of those aspects of psychology that cannot be examined experimentally —**metapsychological** /méttə sīkə lójjik'l/ adj.

metasomatism /méttə sṓmətizəm/, **metasomatosis** /-sṓmə tṓssiss/ n. the gradual change in rock structure caused by the natural replacement of chemicals through interaction with liquids or gases [Late 19thC. Coined from META- + the Greek stem sōmat- 'body' (see SOMATIC) + -ISM.] —**metasomatic** /méttəsō máttik/ adj. —**metasomatically** /-máttikli/ adv.

metastable /méttə stáyb'l/ adj. **1.** IN APPARENT EQUILIBRIUM in an apparent state of equilibrium, but likely to change to a more truly stable state if conditions change **2.** IN EXCITED STATE remaining in an excited physical state for a relatively long time —**metastability** /méttəstə bílləti/ n.

metastasis /me tástəssiss/ (plural **-ses** /-seez/) n. **1.** SPREAD OF CANCER the spread of a cancer from the original tumour to other parts of the body by means of tiny clumps of cells transported by the blood or lymph **2.** MALIGNANT TUMOUR a malignant tumour that has developed in the body as a result of the spread of cancer cells from the original tumour [Late 16thC. From, ultimately, Greek, 'removal, change', from methistanai 'to remove', literally 'to place differently', from histanai 'to place' (see APOSTASY).] —**metastatic** /méttə státtik/ adj. —**metastatically** /-státtikli/ adv.

metastasize /me tástə sīz/ (**-sizes, -sizing, -sized**), **metastasise** (**-sises, -sising, -sised**) vi. to spread in the body from the site of the original tumour by means of tiny cells transported by the blood or lymph (refers to a cancer)

metatarsal /méttə taárss'l/ adj. OF FOOT BONES belonging or relating to the bones between the toes and ankle ■ n. FOOT BONE any of the set of bones between the toes and ankle —**metatarsally** adv.

metatarsus /méttə társsəss/ (plural **-si** /-ssī/) n. **1.** ANAT BONES OF HUMAN FOOT the set of five long bones in the human foot between the toes and ankle **2.** ZOOL PART OF VERTEBRATE HIND FOOT the region between the ankle and toes of the hind foot in vertebrates

metatherian /méttə theeri ən/ adj. OF MARSUPIALS relating or belonging to marsupials ■ n. MARSUPIAL a marsupial [Late 19thC. Formed from modern Latin Metatheria, group name, literally 'wild animals between', from Greek thēria 'wild animals', plural of thērion 'wild animal'.]

metathesis /me táthəssiss/ (plural **-ses** /-seez/) n. **1.** LING TRANSPOSITION OF SOUNDS a reversal of the order of two sounds or letters in a word, either as a mispronunciation or as a historical development **2.** CHEM = **double decomposition** [Late 16thC. From, ultimately, Greek, from metatithenai 'to transpose', literally 'to place differently', from tithenai 'to place' (see THESIS).] —**metathetic** /méttə théttik/ adj. —**metathetical** /-théttik'l/ adj. —**metathetically** /-théttikli/ adv.

metathesize /me táthə sīz/ (**-sizes, -sizing, -sized**), **metathesise** (**-sises, -sising, -sised**) vti. LING to change or make a word change by metathesis

metathorax /méttə tháw raks/ (plural **-raxes** or **-races** /-rə seez/) n. the last segment of an insect's thorax, where the hind legs and hind wings are located —**metathoracic** /méttə thaw rássik/ adj.

metaxylem /méttə zíləm/ n. the rigid thick-walled tissue of plant parts that have matured

metazoan /méttə zṓ ən/ n. an animal whose body consists of cells that are separated into different parts such as tissues and organs. All animals except for sponges and protozoans are classified as metazoans. Group: Metazoa. [Late 19thC. Formed from modern Latin Metazoa, division name, from Greek meta- 'beside, after' + zoion 'animal'.] —**metazoan** adj.

mete out vt. to give out sth such as punishment or justice, especially in a way that seems harsh or unfair [Mete from Old English metan 'to measure'. Ultimately from an Indo-European word that is also the ancestor of English meet[2], moderate, and meditate.]

metempsychosis /méttem sī kṓssiss/ n. the passage of sb's soul after death into the body of another person or an animal [Late 16thC. Via late Latin from Greek metempsukhōsis, from meta 'after' + empsukhos 'having a soul within'.]

metencephalon /métten séffə lon/ (plural **-lons** or **-la** /-lə/) n. the part of an embryo's brain that develops into the cerebellum and the pons —**metencephalic** /métten si fállik/ adj.

meteor /meéti ə, -awr/ n. **1.** FIERY MASS OF ROCK FROM SPACE a mass of rock from space that burns up after entering the Earth's atmosphere. ♦ meteoroid, meteorite **2.** LIGHT FROM METEOR the brief streak of light that a meteor creates, visible in the night sky [Late 16thC. Via modern Latin meteorum 'atmospheric phenomenon' from Greek meteōron, literally 'sth raised up', from meta 'up' + -aoros 'lifted'.]

meteor. abbr. meteorology

meteoric /meéti órrik/ adj. **1.** RELATING TO METEORS relating to or resembling meteors **2.** VERY FAST OR BRILLIANT characterized by great speed or brilliance —**meteorically** adv.

meteorite /meéti ə rīt/ n. a piece of rock that has reached the Earth from outer space. ♦ meteor, meteoroid [Early 19thC. Formed from METEOR.]

meteoritics /meéti ə ríttiks/ n. the scientific study of meteors and meteorites —**meteoriticist** n.

meteoroid /meéti ə royd/ n. a mass of rock in space, often a remnant of a comet, that becomes a meteor when it enters the earth's atmosphere and a meteorite when it falls to earth. ♦ meteor, meteorite [Mid-19thC. Formed from METEOR.] —**meteoroidal** adj.

meteorol. abbr. meteorology

meteorology /meéti ə rólləji/ n. the scientific study of the Earth's atmosphere, especially its patterns of climate and weather [Early 17thC. From Greek meteōrologia, from meteōron (see METEOR).] —**meteorological** /meéti ərə lójjik'l/ adj. —**meteorologically** /-lójjikli/ adv. —**meteorologist** /meéti ə rólləjist/ n.

meteor shower n. a number of meteors seen at regular intervals in a particular area of the sky when a large group of meteors passes through the Earth's atmosphere

meter[1] /meétər/ n. **1.** DEVICE FOR MEASURING AMOUNT OR FLOW a device that measures and records the quantity or flow of sth such as electricity, gas, water, distance, or time **2.** = **parking meter** ■ vt. (**-ters, -tering, -tered**) MEASURE AMOUNT OR FLOW OF STH to measure the amount or flow of sth such as electricity or water, using a meter [Early 19thC. Origin uncertain: perhaps originally formed from METE 'to measure out', later influenced by -METER.]

meter[2] n. US = metre

-meter suffix. measuring device ○ heliometer [Via French -mètre from Greek metron 'measure' (see METRE[2])]

metered mail n. mail that is franked privately by a machine licensed from the postal service

meter maid n. a woman employed to report traffic violations (dated informal)

Meth. abbr. Methodist

meth- prefix. methyl ○ methicillin [Shortening]

methacrylate /meth ákri layt/ n. an ester derived from methacrylic acid

methacrylic acid /méthə kríllik-/ n. a synthetic, colourless liquid used to make plastic. Formula: $C_4H_6O_2$. [Coined from METH- + ACRYLIC]

methadone /méthə dōn/, **methadon** /-don/ n. a synthetic narcotic drug similar in its painkilling effect to morphine and often prescribed as a substitute for heroin in the treatment of addiction. Formula: $C_{21}H_{27}NO$. [Mid-20thC. Coined from METH- + AMINO + DI- + -ONE.]

methaemoglobin /met heemə glóbin, me theemə/ n. an abnormally altered form of haemoglobin that can occur as a result of poisoning with certain drugs or as a genetic disorder [Late 19thC. Coined from META- + HAEMOGLOBIN.]

methaemoglobinaemia /met heemə glóbi neemi ə, me theemə-/ n. the presence in the blood of methaemoglobin

methanal /méthə nal/ n. = formaldehyde [Late 19thC. Formed from METHANE.]

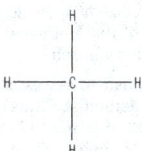

Methane

methane /meé thayn/ n. a colourless, odourless, flammable gas that is the main constituent of natural gas and is used as a fuel. Formula: CH_4. [Mid-19thC. Formed from METHYL.]

methanoic acid /méthənō ik-/ n. = formic acid [Formed from METHANE]

methanol /méthə nol/ n. a colourless, volatile, poisonous, water-soluble liquid that is used as a solvent, a fuel, and in antifreeze for motor vehicles. Formula: CH_3OH. [Late 19thC. Formed from METHANE.]

methaqualone /méthə kwáylōn/ n. a drug that is used to induce sleep and is also taken illegally. Formula: $C_{16}H_{14}N_2O$. [Mid-20thC. Coined from METH- + a contraction of quinazolinon, a derivative of quinoline.]

methemoglobin n. US = methaemoglobin

methenamine /me theénə meen, -mīn/ n. = hexamethylenetetramine [Early 20thC. Contraction of METHYLENE + AMINE.]

methicillin /méthə síllin/ n. an antibiotic used against infections that are resistant to penicillin. Formula: $C_{17}H_{19}N_2NaO_6S$. [Mid-20thC. Coined from METH- + PENICILLIN.]

methinks /mi thíngks/ (**-thought** /mi tháwt/, **-thought**) vi. it seems to me (humorous or archaic) [Old English mē þyncþ 'it seems to me', from þyncan 'to seem'. Ultimately from an Indo-European base that is also the ancestor of English think, thought, and thank.]

$$H_3C—S—CH_2—CH_2—CH—\overset{\overset{\textstyle O}{\textstyle \|}}{C}—OH$$
$$\underset{NH_2}{|}$$

Methionine

methionine /me thí ə neen, -nīn/ n. a sulphur-containing amino acid that occurs in proteins or can be prepared synthetically [Early 20thC. Coined from METH- + THIO- + -INE.]

metho /méthō/ (plural **methos**) n. Aus **1.** METHYLATED

SPIRITS methylated spirits (*informal*) **2. METHYLATED SPIRITS DRINKER** sb who drinks methylated spirits

method /méthəd/ *n.* **1. WAY OF DOING STH** a way of doing sth or carrying sth out, especially according to a plan **2. ORDERLINESS** orderly thought, action, or technique ○ *There is no method whatsoever in his approach to business.* **3. BODY OF SCIENTIFIC TECHNIQUES** the body of systematic techniques used by a particular discipline, especially a scientific one [15thC. Via Latin from Greek *methodos* 'pursuit, way', from *meta-* 'after' + *hodos* 'journey'.]

Method *n.* a theory and system of acting that involves the actor identifying strongly with the internal motivation of the character being portrayed. It is based on the teachings of Konstantin Stanislavsky.

methodical /mə thóddik'l/, **methodic** /-dik/ *adj.* systematic or painstaking —**methodically** *adv.* —**methodicalness** *n.*

methodise *vt.* = **methodize**

Methodism /méthədizəm/ *n.* the doctrines, principles, or organization of the Methodist church, or a specific feature of this Church

Methodist /méthədist/ *n.* **MEMBER OF METHODIST CHURCH** a member of the Methodist Church ■ *adj.* **RELATING TO THE METHODIST CHURCH** relating to Methodism or membership of the Methodist Church [Mid-18thC. Originally applied to members of a society founded at Oxford, from the methodical habits of life and worship it promoted.] —**Methodistic** /méthə dístik/ *adj.* —**Methodistically** *adv.*

Methodist Church *n.* a group of Nonconformist Protestant denominations founded in 18th century England by John Wesley and his followers. The Methodist Church came out of the evangelical revivalist movement, and is rooted in personal faith, the singing of hymns, and praying.

methodize /méthə dīz/ (**-izes**, **-izing**, **-ized**), **methodise** (**-ises**, **-ising**, **-ised**) *vt.* to reduce or arrange sth according to a method —**methodization** /méthə dī záysh'n/ *n.* —**methodizer** /méthə dīzər/ *n.*

methodology /méthə dólləji/ (*plural* **-gies**) *n.* **1. ORGANIZING SYSTEM** the methods or organizing principles underlying a particular art, science, or other area of study **2. PHILOS STUDY OF ORGANIZING PRINCIPLES** in philosophy, the study of organizing principles and underlying rules **3. STUDY OF RESEARCH METHODS** the study of methods of research —**methodological** /méthədə lójjik'l/ *adj.* —**methodologically** /-llójjikli/ *adv.* —**methodologist** /méthə dólləjist/ *n.*

methotrexate /métho trék sayt, meétho-/ *n.* a drug that inhibits cellular reproduction and is used to treat cancer. Formula: $C_{20}H_{22}N_8O_5$. [Mid-20thC. Coined from METH- + *-trex-*, of unknown origin.]

methought past participle, past tense of **methinks**

methoxide /meth óksīd/ *n.* any chemical derivative of methanol that has some features of a salt, e.g. sodium methoxide. Formula: $NaOCH_3$. [Late 19thC. Coined from METH- + OXY- + -IDE.]

methoxychlor /me thóksi klaw/ *n.* a white crystalline compound used as an insecticide. Formula: $C_{16}H_{15}Cl_3O_2$. [Mid-20thC. Coined from METH- + OXY- + CHLORINE.]

meths /meths/ *n. UK* methylated spirit (*informal*) [Mid-20thC. Contraction.]

Methuselah /mə thyoózələ/ *n.* **1. BIBLICAL FIGURE** a man in the Bible who was an ancestor of Noah and is said to have lived 969 years. (Gen 5: 21–27). **2. LARGE WINE BOTTLE** a wine or champagne bottle that holds the equivalent of eight normal bottles, approximately 6 1/208 fl oz

methyl /meéthīl, méth'l/ *adj.* containing the group of atoms CH_3 [Mid-19thC. From French *méthyl*, a back-formation from *méthylène* (see METHYLENE).] —**methylic** /mə thíllik/ *adj.*

methyl acetate *n.* a fragrant colourless liquid used as a solvent in paint removers. Formula: $C_3H_6O_2$.

methylal /méthi lal/ *n.* a colourless flammable liquid used as a solvent and in making perfumes and adhesives. Formula: $C_3H_8O_2$.

methyl alcohol *n.* = methanol

methylamine /me thílə meen, mee-/ *n.* any of three colourless flammable derivatives of ammonia, especially used in dyes, drugs, and herbicides. Formula: CH_5N.

methylate /méthi layt/ *n.* = methoxide ■ *vt.* (**-ates**, **-ating**, **-ated**) **1. REPLACE HYDROGEN ATOM WITH METHYL GROUP** to replace one or more hydrogen atoms in a molecule with the methyl group **2. MIX WITH METHANOL** to mix sth with methanol —**methylation** /méthi láysh'n/ *n.* —**methylator** /méthi laytər/ *n.*

methylated spirit, **methylated spirits** *n.* ethanol with methanol added, to make it undrinkable, and coloured with a violet dye, used as a fuel and in solvents

methylbenzene /meéthīl bén zeen/ *n.* = toluene

methyl bromide *n.* a poisonous colourless gas or liquid used as a solvent, fumigant, and refrigerant. Formula: CH_3Br.

methylcellulose /meéthīl séllyoō lōss/ *n.* a greyish-white powder derived from cellulose that swells up in water and is used as a food additive and in making paints and cosmetics

methyl chloride *n.* a colourless poisonous gas used as a refrigerant and local anaesthetic. Formula: CH_3Cl.

methyldopa /meé thīl dópə/ *n.* a white powder used as a drug to treat hypertension. Formula: $C_{10}H_{13}NO_4$.

methylene /méthə leen/ *n.* **METHANE DERIVATIVE** a bivalent group of atoms derived from methane. Formula: CH_2. ■ *adj.* **CONTAINING METHYLENE GROUP OF ATOMS** containing or relating to the group of atoms derived from methane containing one carbon atom and two hydrogen atoms. Formula: CH_2. [Mid-19thC. From French *méthylène*, from Greek *methu* 'wine' + *hulē* 'wood, substance'.]

methylene blue *n.* a crystalline compound that turns blue when dissolved in water and is used as a dye, an antiseptic, an antidote for cyanide poisoning, and a stain in laboratories. Formula: $C_{16}H_{18}ClN_3S$.

methyl isocyanate *n.* a flammable, colourless, extremely toxic liquid that is used in making herbicides. Formula: CH_3NCO.

methylmercury /meéthīl múrkyoori/ *n.* an extremely toxic compound formed from metallic mercury by the action of microorganisms and used as a seed disinfectant. Mercury compounds such as this can enter the food chain and are toxic to living organisms.

methyl methacrylate *n.* a colourless flammable liquid that can be converted into clear plastic resins

methylnaphthalene /meéthīl náptha leen/ *n.* either of two forms of naphthalene, a liquid used in making diesel fuels, or a solid used in making insecticides. Formula: $C_{11}H_{10}$.

Methyl orange

methyl orange *n.* an alkaline dye that is used as a chemical indicator. It turns yellow when neutral and pink when acid.

methylphenidate /meéthīl fénni dayt/ *n.* a stimulant of the central nervous system used to treat narcolepsy and attention deficit disorder. Formula: $C_{14}H_{19}NO_2$. [Mid-20thC. Contraction of METHYL + PHENYL + PIPERIDINE + ACETATE.]

metical /méttik'l/ (*plural* **-cais** /métti kísh/ *or* **-cals**) *n.* **1. UNIT OF CURRENCY IN MOZAMBIQUE** the standard unit of currency in Mozambique, worth 100 centavos. See table at **currency 2. NOTE WORTH ONE METICAL** a note worth a metical [Late 20thC. Via Portuguese *matical* from Arabic *miṯkāl*, a unit of weight, from *ṯakala* 'to weigh'.]

meticulous /mə tíkyooləss/ *adj.* extremely careful and precise [Early 19thC. From Latin *meticulosus* 'fearful, timid', from *metus* 'fear', of unknown origin.] —**meticulously** *adv.* —**meticulousness** *n.*

— WORD KEY: SYNONYMS —
See Synonyms at **careful**.

métier /métti ay/, **metier** *n.* **1. OCCUPATION** sb's occupation or trade **2. FORTE** an activity that sb is particularly good at [Late 18thC. Via French from assumed Vulgar Latin *misterium*, alteration of Latin *ministerium* (see MINISTRY).]

Metis /meétiss/ *n.* the innermost known natural satellite of Jupiter, discovered in 1979. It is irregularly shaped and approximately 40 km in diameter.

metol /meé tol/ *n.* a colourless soluble salt used in developing photographs. Formula: $C_{14}H_{20}N_2O_6S$. [Late 19thC. Arbitrarily coined by its inventor.]

Metonic cycle /mi tónnik-/ *n.* a cycle of 235 lunar months, after which the phases of the moon occur on the same days of the month as they did at the start of the cycle [Late 17thC. Named after the Athenian astronomer *Metōn* of the 5thC BC, who discovered it.]

metonym /méttənim/ *n.* a word or phrase used in a figure of speech in which an attribute of sth is used to stand for the thing itself [Late 16thC. Back-formation from METONYMY.] —**metonymic** /méttə nímmik/ *adj.* —**metonymically** /-nímmikli/ *adv.*

metonymy /me tónnəmi/ *n.* a figure of speech in which an attribute of sth is used to stand for the thing itself, such as 'laurels' when it stands for 'glory' or 'brass' when it stands for 'military officers' [Mid-16thC. Via late Latin from Greek *metōnumia*, literally 'change of name', from *meta-* 'beside, different' + *onuma* 'name'.]

me-too *adj.* using products, methods, or policies copied from sb else (*informal*) —**me-tooer** *n.* —**me-tooism** *n.*

metope /méttōp, méttəpi/ *n.* in a Doric frieze, a square space between two sets of three vertical grooves (**triglyphs**) [Mid-16thC. From Greek *metopē*, from *meta-* 'between' + *opē* 'hole'.]

metopic /me tóppik/ *adj.* relating to the forehead [Late 19thC. Formed from Greek *metōpon* 'forehead', from *meta-* 'between' + *ōps* 'eye'.]

metralgia /mi trálji ə/ *n.* pain in the womb

metre¹ /meétər/ *n.* the basic SI unit of length, equivalent to approximately 1.094 yd or 39.37 in. Originally based on a metre-long platinum-iridium bar kept in Paris, France, it is now defined as the distance travelled by light in vacuum in 1/299,792,458 seconds. Symbol **m** [Late 18thC. Via French from Greek *metron* (see METRE²).]

metre² /meétər/ *n.* **1. PATTERN IN VERSE** an arranged pattern of rhythm in a line of verse **2. PATTERN OF RHYTHM IN MUSIC** the pattern of beats that combines to form musical rhythm [Pre-12thC. Directly and via French from Latin *metrum*, from Greek *metron* 'measure' (see METRE²).]

metre-kilogram-second *adj.* using or based on the metre, kilogram, and second as the measuring units of length, mass, and time

metric /méttrik/ *adj.* **1. MEASURE RELATING TO METRIC SYSTEM** relating to or using the metric system of measurement **2.** = metrical ■ *n.* **MATH MATHEMATICAL FUNCTION** a mathematical function defined for a coordinates system that associates properties to each pair of elements that are analogous to distance between points on a line

metrical /méttrik'l/ *adj.* relating to or using poetic metre —**metrically** *adv.*

metricate /méttri kayt/ (**-cates**, **-cating**, **-cated**) *vt.* to convert sth from nonmetric to metric units of measurement —**metrication** /méttri káysh'n/ *n.*

metric hundredweight *n.* a unit of weight equal to 50 kg

metricize /méttri sīz/ (**-cizes**, **-cizing**, **-cized**), **metricise** (**-cises**, **-cising**, **-cised**) *vt.* to express a measurement in metric units or change it into metric units

metrics /méttriks/ *n.* the art of using metre in poetry (*takes a singular verb*)

metric system *n.* a decimal system of weights and measures based on units such as the kilogram and metre

metric ton *n.* a unit of weight equal to 1000 kg

metrify /méttri fī/ (**-fies, -fying, -fied**) *vt.* to put prose into verse or metre —**metrifier** *n.*

metrist /méttrist/ *n.* sb who is skilled in using poetic metre

metritis /mi trítiss/ *n.* inflammation of the womb

metro /méttrō/ (*plural* **-ros**) *n.* **1.** metro, Metro SUBWAY an undergound railway system in a town or city **2.** Can LOCAL GOVERNMENT the metropolitan area or government of a large city [Mid-20thC. Shortening of METROPOLITAN.]

metro- *prefix.* uterus ○ *metrorrhagia* [From Greek *mētra*, related to *mētēr* 'mother'. Ultimately from the Indo-European word for 'mother', that is also the ancestor of English *mother* and *maternal*.]

metrology /mi trólləji/ (*plural* **-gies**) *n.* **1.** STUDY OF MEASUREMENT the scientific study of units of measurement **2.** MEASUREMENT SYSTEM a system of measurement [Early 19thC. Via French from Greek *metrologie*, from *metron* 'measure' (see METRE²).] —**metrologic** /méttrə lójjik/ *adj.* —**metrologically** /-lójjikli/ *adv.* —**metrologist** /mi tróllǝjist/ *n.*

metronidazole /méttrō nídəzōl/ *n.* a yellow crystalline compound used in treating infections, especially vaginal infections. Formula: $C_6H_9N_3O_3$. [Mid-20thC. Contraction of METHYL + NITRO- + IMIDAZOLE, elements of its chemical name.]

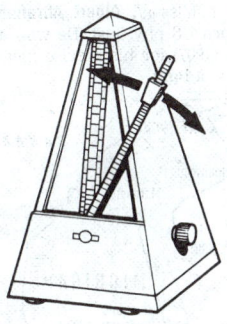

Metronome

metronome /méttrənōm/ *n.* a device used to indicate a given tempo by means of an aural or visual signal produced electronically or by an adjustable pendulum [Early 19thC. From Greek *metron* 'measure', metre' + *nomos* 'rule, division'.] —**metronomic** /méttrə nómmik/ *adj.* —**metronomically** /-nómmikli/ *adv.*

metronymic *adj.* = matronymic

metropolis /mə tróppəliss/ *n.* **1.** GEOG LARGE CITY a very large city, often the capital or chief urban centre of a country, state, or region **2.** CENTRE OF AN ACTIVITY the centre or principal place for a particular activity **3.** CHR MAIN DIOCESE in Christianity, the principal diocese or see in an ecclesiastical province [Mid-16thC. Via late Latin from Greek *mētropolis*, literally 'mother city', from *mētēr* 'mother' + *polis* 'city'.]

——— **WORD KEY: SYNONYMS** ———
See Synonyms at **city**.

metropolitan /méttrə póllitən/ *adj.* **1.** GEOG TYPICAL OF A METROPOLIS typical of a metropolis in scale, variety, or sophistication **2.** GEOG FORMING LARGE CITY constituting a large urban area, usually including a city and its suburbs and outlying areas **3.** GEOG DOMESTIC AND INTERNAL relating to the home territory of a country rather than its territories elsewhere **4.** CHR RELATING TO ECCLESIASTICAL METROPOLIS relating to or constituting an ecclesiastical metropolis ■ *n.* **1.** GEOG METROPOLIS INHABITANT sb who lives in a metropolis **2.** CHR HIGH-RANKING CHURCH OFFICIAL in Christianity, a high-ranking church dignitary such as an archbishop or head of an ecclesiastical metropolis ■ CHR HEAD OF RUSSIAN ORTHODOX CHURCH the head of the Russian Orthodox Church, based in Moscow

metropolitan county *n.* in England, any of the six large urban administrative units in the system of local government between 1974 and 1986

metropolitan district *n.* in England, any of the districts that used to be metropolitan counties. They are the principal units of local government, each with an elected council.

metrorrhagia /meetrō ráyji ə/ *n.* excessive discharge of blood from the womb —**metrorrhagic** *adj.*

-metry *suffix.* measuring ○ *cephalometry* [From Greek *-metria*, which was formed from *metron* 'measure' (see METRE²)]

Metternich /méta nikh/, **Klemens, Prince of** (1773–1859) German-born Austrian statesman. An Austrian diplomat and chancellor of the Hapsburg Empire (1821–48), he was the most powerful political figure in Europe between 1814 and 1848. He was driven from office in the Revolution of 1848. Full name **Klemens Wenzel Nepomuk Lothar von Metternich**

mettle /métt'l/ *n.* **1.** STRENGTH OF CHARACTER courage, spirit, or strength of character **2.** INHERENT TEMPERAMENT the particular mental and emotional character unique to an individual [Mid-16thC. Variant of METAL. The underlying meaning is 'the substance sb is made of'.]

——— **WORD KEY: SYNONYMS** ———
See Synonyms at **courage**.

mettlesome /métt'lsəm/ *adj.* spirited and courageous

Metz /mets/ capital of Moselle Department, Lorraine region, eastern France. Population: 119,594 (1990).

meunière /mŏni áir/ *adj.* dredged in flour, fried in butter, and sprinkled with lemon juice and chopped parsley ○ *sole meunière* [Mid-19thC. From French *à la meunière*, literally 'in the way of a miller's wife'.]

Meursault /múrsō/ *n.* a dry white wine from the Burgundy region of northeastern France [Mid-19thC. From French, name of a commune in the Côte de Beaune.]

Meuse /mŏz/ river that flows through northeastern France, Belgium, and the Netherlands. Length: 900 km/560 mi.

MeV, **Mev**, **mev** *symbol.* million electron volts

mevrou /mə frŏ/ *n. S Africa* a title in Afrikaans equivalent to Mrs or a respectful form of address equivalent to Madam [Via Afrikaans from Dutch]

mew¹ /myoo/ *n.* any common seagull, especially the common gull [Old English *mæw*]

mew² /myoo/ *vi.* (**mews, mewing, mewed**) MAKE HIGH-PITCHED CRY to give out a high-pitched cry (*refers to cats and kittens*) ■ *n.* HIGH-PITCHED CRY the high-pitched sound a cat or kitten makes [14thC. An imitation of the sound.]

mew³ /myoo/ *n.* CAGE FOR HAWKS a cage for keeping hawks in ■ *v.* (**mews, mewing, mewed**) **1.** *vt.* CONFINE HAWK OR FALCON to confine a hawk or falcon, especially by tying it to a perch **2.** *vi.* MOULT to shed feathers [14thC. From French *mue*, from *muer* 'to moult', from Latin *mutare* 'to change' (see MUTATION).]

mewl /myool/ (**mewls, mewling, mewled**) *vi.* to whimper or cry weakly [Early 17thC. Origin uncertain: possibly an imitation of the sound.] —**mewler** *n.*

mews /myooz/ *n.* a street that originally had stables built on it but has now been converted into housing, or the houses themselves (*takes a singular or plural verb*) [Early 19thC. From MEW³.]

——— **WORD KEY: ORIGIN** ———
In the latter part of the 14th century the Royal Mews were built in London on the site of what is now Trafalgar Square, to house the royal hawks. By Henry VII's time they were being used as stables, and from at least the early 17th century the term *mews* was used for 'stabling around an open yard'. The modern application to a 'street of former stables converted to human dwellings' dates from the early 19th century.

MEX *abbr.* Mexico (*international vehicle registration*)

Mex. *abbr.* **1.** Mexican **2.** Mexico

Mexican /méksikən/ *adj.* PEOPLES relating to Mexico, or its people or culture

Mexican hairless *n.* a tiny, mainly hairless dog, belonging to a breed originating in Mexico

Mexican ivy vine *n.* = cup-and-saucer plant

Mexican jumping bean *n.* = jumping bean

Mexican Spanish *n.* the form of the Spanish language used in Mexico —**Mexican Spanish** *adj.*

Mexican standoff *n.* a dispute or argument that cannot be won (*informal*)

Mexican War *n.* a war between Mexico and the United States that lasted from 1846 to 1848, during which the United States won territory that now constitutes most of the states of the Southwest

Mexican wave *n.* the rippling effect produced by rows of spectators at a sporting or musical event standing up, raising their arms, and then sitting down again in sequence. US term **wave** [So called because it was first used at the World Cup soccer finals in Mexico in 1986]

Mexico

Mexico /méksikō/ federal republic in North America, south of the United States. Language: Spanish. Currency: peso. Capital: Mexico City. Population: 96,807,451 (1997). Area: 1,964,382 sq. km/758,452 sq. mi. Official name **United Mexican States**

Mexico, Gulf of arm of the Atlantic Ocean, bordered on the north by the United States, on the east by Cuba, and on the south and west by Mexico. Area: 1,812,990 sq. km/700,000 sq. mi.

Mexico City /méksikō sítti/ capital city of Mexico and of the Federal District, located in the south-central part of the country. It the most populous urban area in the world. Population: 8,236,960 (1990).

Meyerhof /míyər hof, -hōf/, **Otto Fritz** (1884–1951) German-born US biochemist. He worked on the metabolism of muscles, for which he was joint winner of the 1922 Nobel Prize in physiology or medicine.

Meynell /mə nél/, **Alice** (1847–1922) British poet and literary critic. Her essay collections include *The Colour of Life* (1896) and *Hearts of Controversy* (1917).

meze /mézzay/ (*plural* **-zes** or **-ze**) *n.* an assortment of snacks served with drinks as an appetizer or a light meal in Greece and the Near East and usually consisting of simple foods such as olives, cheese, cucumber, stuffed vine leaves, small pastries, or grilled sausages [Early 20thC. Via Turkish from Persian *maza* 'to taste, relish'.]

mezereon /mə zéeri ən/ *n.* a poisonous shrub of Europe and Asia that has clusters of fragrant purplish flowers and bark that was once used to treat blisters and arthritis. Latin name: *Daphne mezereum*. [15thC. Via medieval Latin from Arabic *māzaryūn*.]

mezuzah /mə zŏŏzə, -zŏŏ-/ (*plural* **-zahs** or **-zoth** /-zōt/) *n.* a scroll with biblical passages on one side and a name of God on the other, inserted in a small case attached by religious Jews to doorposts in the home [Mid-17thC. From Hebrew *mĕzūzāh*, literally 'doorpost'.]

mezzanine /mézzə neen/ *n.* **1.** mezzanine, mezzanine floor INTERMEDIATE STOREY a low storey, especially one between the ground floor and the first floor in a building **2.** US THEATRE'S LOWEST BALCONY the lowest balcony in a theatre **3.** AREA UNDER STAGE a floor or room beneath the stage in a theatre ■ *adj.* FIN WITHIN INTERMEDIATE RANGE OF INVESTMENT constituting an intermediate range of funding or investment, such as certain unsecured high-yielding loans [Early 18thC. Via French from Italian *mezzanino*, literally 'small one in the middle', from *mezzano* 'middle', from Latin *medianus* (see MEDIAN).]

mezza voce /métsa vőchi, -vő chay/ *adv.* with moderate volume from the voice or instrument (*used as a musical direction*) [From Italian, literally 'half voice'] —**mezza voce** *adj.*

mezzo /métsō/ *adv.* MODERATELY moderately (*used as a musical direction*) ■ *n.* (*plural* **-zos**) = **mezzo-soprano** [Mid-18thC. Via Italian, literally 'middle, half', from Latin *medius* (see MEDIUM).]

mezzo forte *adv.* moderately loud (*used as a musical direction*) —**mezzo forte** *adj.*

mezzo piano *adv.* moderately soft (*used as a musical direction*) [From Italian] —**mezzo piano** *adj.*

mezzo-relievo /-ri leěvō, -ri lyáy/ (*plural* **mezzo-relievos**) *n.* a carving in which the depth of the relief is midway between high relief and bas relief [From Italian, literally 'half-relief']

mezzo-soprano *n.* a woman whose singing voice is between a soprano and a contralto in range [From Italian, literally 'half soprano']

mezzotint /métsō tint/ *n.* **1.** ENGRAVING PROCESS an engraving process that involves scraping and burnishing the roughened surface of a copper plate **2.** MEZZOTINT PRINT a print produced by the mezzotint process ■ *vt.* (**-zotints**, **-zotinting**, **-zotinted**) ENGRAVE PLATE USING MEZZOTINT to engrave a copper plate by using the mezzotint process [Mid-18thC. Anglicization of Italian *mezzotinto*, literally 'half-tint'.] —**mezzotinter** *n.*

mf *abbr.* mezzo forte

mF *abbr.* millifarad

MF *abbr.* **1.** medium frequency **2.** Middle French

M/F, **m/f** *abbr.* male or female (*in advertisements*)

MFA *abbr.* Master of Fine Arts

mfd *abbr.* manufactured

mfecane /əm fe kaáni/ *n.* a series of wars in 19th-century southern Africa caused by Zulu expansion under Shaka, which revolutionized political organization in the area [Mid-20thC. Origin uncertain: perhaps from Bantu.]

mfg *abbr.* manufacturing

mfr *abbr.* **1.** manufacture **2.** manufacturer

mg *symbol.* milligram

Mg *symbol.* magnesium

MG *abbr.* **1.** machine gun **2.** Major General

MGB *n.* the secret police of the former Soviet Union from 1946 to 1954. Abbr of **Ministerstvo Gosudarstvennoi Bezopasnosti** [Mid-20th C. Shortening of Russian 'Ministry of State Security'.]

mgmt *abbr.* management

mgr *abbr.* manager

Mgr *abbr.* **1.** Monseigneur **2.** Monsignor

mgt *abbr.* management

mH *symbol.* millihenry

MH *abbr.* mental health

MHA *abbr.* Member of the House of Assembly

MHC *n.* a group of genes in mammals located next or near to one another that serve to make cells separate and distinguishable from those of other organisms. Abbr of **major histocompatibility complex**

MHD *abbr.* magnetohydrodynamics

MHG *abbr.* Middle High German

MHL *abbr.* Master of Hebrew Literature

MHR *abbr.* Member of the House of Representatives

MHz *symbol.* megahertz

mi /mee/, **me** *n.* MUSIC a syllable that represents the third note in a scale, used for singing solfège. In fixed solfège it represents the note E, the third note in the scale of C, while in solfège with movable soh, it is used to represent the third note of the key being sung. [15thC. From medieval Latin.]

MI *abbr.* **1.** Military Intelligence **2.** myocardial infarction

mi. *abbr.* mile

MI5 /ém ī fív/ *n.* a former official and current popular

name for Military Intelligence, section five, the British security and counterintelligence service

MI6 /ém ī síks/ *n.* a former official and current popular name for Military Intelligence, section six, the British secret intelligence and espionage service

MIA *n.* a soldier who is reported missing during a military mission. Full form **missing in action**

Miami /mī ámmi/ city and seaport in southeastern Florida. Population: 373,024 (1994).

Miami Beach city and tourist resort in southeastern Florida. Population: 90,153 (1994).

Miao /myow/ *n.*, *adj.* = **Hmong** [Early 20thC. From Chinese *Miáo*, literally 'people'.]

miaow /mi ów/, **meow** *n.* CHARACTERISTIC CRY OF A CAT the characteristic cry made by a domestic cat ■ *vi.* (**-aows**, **-aowing**, **-aowed**, **-ows**, **-owing**, **-owed**) UTTER MIAOW to utter a miaow ■ *interj.* DESIGNATING A SPITEFUL OR MEAN COMMENT used to indicate that you think sb's comment is spiteful or malicious (*informal*) [Late 16thC. An imitation of the sound.]

Miao-Yao /myów yow/ *n.* a group of languages, including Hmong and Yao, spoken in parts of the People's Republic of China, Vietnam, Laos, and Thailand. About six million people speak one of the Miao-Yao languages. —**Miao-Yao** *adj.*

miasma /mi ázmə, mī-/ (*plural* **-mata** /-mətə, -/ *or* **-mas**) *n.* **1.** HARMFUL FUMES a harmful or poisonous emanation, especially one caused by burning or decaying organic matter **2.** UNWHOLESOME ATMOSPHERE an unwholesome or menacing atmosphere [Mid-17thC. Directly or via French *miasme* from Greek *miasma* 'defilement, pollution', from *miainein* 'to pollute'.] —**miasmal** *adj.* —**miasmatic** /meě əz máttik/ *adj.*

Mic. *abbr.* BIBLE Micah

mica /míkə/ *n.* any of several shiny silica minerals that occur in igneous and metamorphic rocks. They split easily and are used as electrical insulators and in heating elements because of their resistance to electricity and heat. [Early 18thC. From Latin, 'grain, crumb'. Ultimately from an Indo-European word that is also the ancestor of Greek *mikros* 'small' (source of English *micro-*).]

Micah[1] /míkə/ *n.* in the Bible, a prophet who lived during the 8th century BC. He was a contemporary of Isaiah.

Micah[2] *n.* one of the 12 prophetic books of the Bible known as the Minor Prophets, containing both threats of doom and the prophecy of an age of universal peace. It is traditionally attributed to the prophet Micah. See table at **Bible**

Micawber /mi káwbər/ *n.* sb who is poor and idle but expects a better life to come along someday [Mid-19thC. Named after Wilkins *Micawber*, a character in *David Copperfield* (1850) by Charles Dickens.] —**Micawberish** *adj.*

Miccosukee *n.* (*plural* **-kees** *or* **-kee**), *adj.* = **Mikasuki**

mice plural of **mouse**

—————— **WORD KEY: CULTURAL NOTE** ——————

Of Mice and Men, a novella by US author John Steinbeck (1937). With great compassion and realism, Steinbeck recounts the tragic tale of two itinerant labourers, George Milton and Lennie Small. When Lennie, a mentally ill giant, accidentally kills a girl, George shoots his friend rather than surrender him to a lynch mob. It was made into a film by Lewis Milestone in 1939.

micelle /mi sél/ *n.* an electrically charged particle formed by an aggregate of ions or molecules in soaps, detergents, and other suspensions [Late 19thC. From modern Latin *micella*, literally 'small crumb', from Latin *mica* (see MICA).] —**micellar** *adj.*

Mich. *abbr.* **1.** Michaelmas **2.** Michigan

Michael /míkʼl/, **King of Romania** (b. 1921). He held the throne from 1927 to 1930 and from 1940 to 1947, when he abdicated and went into exile.

Michaelmas /míkʼlməss/ *n.* a Christian holy day on September 29 celebrating the feast of St Michael the Archangel [Pre-12thC. Contraction of *Michael's mass*.]

Michaelmas daisy *n.* a common aster that has small purple, pink, or white flowers and blooms in the autumn

Michaelmas term *n.* the name used for the autumn term at Oxford and Cambridge Universities, the Inns of Court, and some other educational institutions

Michelangelo: Engraving after a 16th-century portrait by Giuliano Bugiardini

Michelangelo /mík'l ánjəlō/ (1475–1564) Italian sculptor, painter, architect, and poet. One of the great masters of the High Renaissance, his major works, such as the ceiling of the Sistine Chapel in the Vatican, were executed for patrons in Florence and Rome. Full name **Michelangelo di Lodovico Buonarroti Simoni**

Michelin /meéshəlin, meéshə leN/, **André** (1853–1931) French tyre manufacturer. He established the Michelin Tyre company with his brother Edouard in 1888, and initiated a series of road maps and influential guide books.

Michelson /mík'lssən/, **Albert Abraham** (1852–1931) German-born US physicist. He won a Nobel Prize in physics (1907) for his precise measurements of the velocity of light.

Michigan

Michigan[1] /míshigən/ state in the northern United States, consisting of two peninsulas situated among four of the Great Lakes. It has a border with Canada, and the US states of Ohio, Indiana, Illinois, Wisconsin, and Minnesota. Capital: Lansing. Population: 9,773,892 (1997). Area: 151,549 sq. km/58,513 sq. mi. —**Michigander** /míshi gándər/ *n.* —**Michiganite** /míshigə nīt/ *n.*, *adj.*

Michigan[2] /míshigən/ *n.* US CARDS = **Newmarket** [Early 20thC. Named after the state of MICHIGAN.]

Michigan, Lake lake in the northern United States. It is the only one of the Great Lakes that lies entirely in the United States. Area: 57,800 sq. km/22,300 sq. mi.

Mick /mik/ *n.* a highly offensive term that deliberately insults sb's Irish origin or Roman Catholic faith or an Irish person or a Roman Catholic (*offensive*) [Mid-19thC. From Mick, nickname for *Michael*.]

mickey /míki/ (*plural* **-eys**) *n.* (*informal*) **1.** = **Mickey Finn 2.** Can BOTTLE OF LIQUOR a bottle of liquor, formerly a pint, now 375 ml, shaped to fit in a pocket [Early 20thC] ◊ **take the mickey** to tease sb (*informal*)

Mickey Finn /míki fín/ *n.* an alcoholic drink to which a strong sedative has been added to make the drinker unconscious (*informal*) [Early 20thC. Origin uncertain: perhaps the name of an unidentified individual.]

Mickiewicz /mits kyévvich/, **Adam** (1798–1855) Polish poet. A major figure in Polish Romanticism, he also campaigned for his country's independence from Russia.

mickle /mík'l/ adj. Scotland ABUNDANT abundant or much ■ adv. Scotland GREATLY greatly or much [Old English micel (source also of much), later reinforced by Old Norse mikill, both ultimately from an Indo-European base that is also the ancestor of English magnify, major, maximum, and mega-]

Micmac /mík mak/ (plural -macs or -mac) n. a Native North American language belonging to the Algonquian branch of Algonquian-Wakashan languages, spoken in eastern parts of Canada. Micmac is spoken by about three thousand people. [Early 18thC. Via French from Micmac migmac, literally 'allies'.] —**Micmac** adj.

micr- prefix. = micro- (sometimes used before vowels)

micro /míkrō/ adj. SMALL very small ■ n. (plural -cros) (informal) 1. MICROPROCESSOR a microprocessor 2. MICROWAVE OVEN a microwave oven 3. MICROCOMPUTER a microcomputer [Mid-19thC. From MICRO-.]

micro- prefix. 1. small, minute ○ microseism. 2. using a microscope or requiring magnification ○ microanatomy 3. one millionth (10^{-6}) Symbol μ ○ microcurie. 4. of a small area or on a small scale ○ microhabitat ○ microteaching 5. microfilm, microphotography ○ microform 6. abnormally small ○ microdont [From Greek mikros 'small' (source of English micron and omicron)]

microampere /míkrō ám pair/ n. one millionth part of an ampere

microanalysis /míkrō ə nálləssiss/ (plural -ses) n. 1. ANALYSIS OF A TINY SAMPLE the chemical analysis of tiny samples of a substance 2. DETAILED ANALYSIS any extremely detailed analysis of sth —**microanalyst** /míkrō ánnəlist/ n. —**microanalytical** /míkrō anə líttik'l/ adj.

microbalance /míkrō balənss/ n. a balance for precisely weighing extremely small quantities up to 0.1 gm

microbar /míkrō baar/ n. a unit of pressure equal to one millionth of a bar

microbarograph /míkrō bárrə graaf, -graf/ n. a barograph that records tiny changes in atmospheric pressure

microbe /míkrōb/ n. a microscopic organism, especially one that transmits a disease [Late 19thC. From French, from Greek mikros 'small' + bios 'life'.] —**microbial** /mī krôbi əl/ adj.

microbiology /míkrō bī ólləji/ n. the scientific study of microscopic organisms and their effects —**microbiological** /míkrōbī ə lójjik'l/ adj. —**microbiologically** /-lójjikli/ adv.

microbrewery /míkrō broo əri/ (plural -ries) n. a small, usually independently owned brewery that produces limited quantities of specialized beers, often selling them on the premises —**microbrewer** n. —**microbrewing** n.

microburst /míkrō burst/ n. a strong localized air current that hits the ground and spreads, causing wind to rapidly change direction and speed

microcapsule /míkrō kap syool/ n. a tiny capsule used to release a drug, flavour, or chemical

microcassette /míkrō kə sét/ n. a small audiotape cassette designed to fit into a pocket-size tape recorder or dictation machine

microcephaly /míkrō séffəli/, **microcephalia** /-sə fáyli ə/ n. the condition of having a small head or having reduced space for the brain in the skull. This is often associated with learning difficulties. —**microcephalic** /míkrō sə fállik/ adj.

microchemistry /míkrō kémmistri/ n. the scientific study of extremely small quantities of substances —**microchemical** adj. —**microchemist** n.

microchip /míkrō chip/ n. = chip

microcircuit /míkrō surkit/ n. = integrated circuit —**microcircuitry** /míkrō súrkitri/ n.

microclimate /míkrō klímət/ n. the climate of a confined space or small geographical area —**microclimatic** /míkrō klī máttik/ adj. —**microclimatically** /-klī máttikli/ adv.

microclimatology /míkrō klímə tólləji/ n. the scientific study of microclimates —**microclimatologic** /míkrō klímətə lójjik/ adj. —**microclimatologist** /míkrō klímə tólləjist/ n.

microcline /míkrō klīn/ n. a mineral of the feldspar group used in manufacturing glass and porcelain. Formula: $KAlSi_3O_8$. [Mid-19thC. From German Mikroklin, from Greek mikros 'small' + klinein 'to lean'; so called because its angle of cleavage differs only slightly from 90°.]

micrococcus /míkrō kókəss/ (plural -ci -kóksī/) n. any mainly harmless spherical bacterium, such as the one that ferments milk. Genus: Micrococcus. —**micrococcal** adj.

microcomputer /míkrō kəm pyootər/ n. a small computer in which the central processing unit is a single silicon chip (**microprocessor**) [Late 20thC. Modelled on MINICOMPUTER.]

microcopy /míkrō kopi/ (plural -ies) n. a photographic reproduction of sth on microfilm or microfiche

microcosm /míkrō kozəm/ n. a miniature copy of sth, especially when it represents or stands for a larger whole ○ Our classroom was a microcosm of the university. [12thC. Via French microcosme from, ultimately, Greek mikros kosmos 'little world'.] —**microcosmic** /míkrō kózmik/ adj. —**microcosmically** /-kózmikli/ adv.

microcosmic salt n. a colourless odourless salt obtained from human urine and used to test metallic salts and oxides

microcosmos /míkrō kózmoss/ n. = microcosm

microcrystal /míkrō krist'l/ n. a crystal that can only be seen under a microscope —**microcrystalline** /míkrō krístə līn/ adj.

microcurie /míkrō kyoori/ n. a unit of radioactivity that is equal to a millionth of a curie

microcyte /míkrō sīt/ n. an unusually small red blood cell —**microcytic** /míkrō síttik/ adj.

microdissection /míkrō di séksh'n/ n. dissection carried out using a microscope

microdot /míkrō dot/ n. 1. TINY PHOTOGRAPH a tiny photographic reproduction of sth, about the size of a dot or a pinhead 2. DOSE OF LSD a dose of LSD in a tiny tablet (informal)

microeconomics /míkrō eekə nómmiks, -ekə-/ n. the study of specific or localized aspects of an economy (takes a singular verb) —**microeconomic** adj.

microelectronics /míkrō ilek trónniks, -elek-/ n. the technology and techniques involved in the design, development, and construction of extremely small electronic circuits, e.g. computers on a single silicon chip (takes a singular verb) —**microelectronic** adj. —**microelectronically** adv.

microelement /míkrō eləmənt/ n. = trace element

microencapsulate /míkrō in kápsyoo layt/ (-lates, -lating, -lated) vt. to enclose a substance in microcapsules —**microencapsulation** /míkrō in kápsyoo láysh'n/ n.

microevolution /míkrō eevə loósh'n, -evə-/ n. minor change within a species or small group of organisms, usually within a short period of time —**microevolutionary** adj.

microfarad /míkrō farəd, -rad/ n. one millionth part of a farad

microfauna /míkrō fawnə/ npl. animals so small that they can only be seen under a microscope —**microfaunal** adj.

microfibril /míkrō fíbril/ n. in cells, any extremely fine structure resembling a thread

microfiche /míkrō feesh/ n. a sheet of microfilm containing information laid out in a grid pattern [Mid-20thC. From French, from Greek mikros 'small' + French fiche 'slip of paper'.]

microfilament /míkrō fílləmənt/ n. a very thin cellular filament that contains protein, found in muscle and the cytoplasm of other cells —**microfilamentous** /míkrō filə méntəss/ adj.

microfilaria /míkrō fi láiri ə/ (plural -ae /-láiri ī/) n. the early larval stage of a parasitic nematode worm (**filaria**), a cause of heartworm in dogs and elephantiasis in humans —**microfilarial** adj.

microfilm /míkrō film/ n. TINY PHOTOGRAPHS a strip of photographic film on which highly miniaturized reproductions have been recorded ■ vti. (-films, -filming, -filmed) PHOTOGRAPH ON MICROFILM to photograph sth on microfilm

microflora /míkrō flawrə/ npl. plants that can only be seen under a microscope —**microfloral** adj.

microform /míkrō fawrm/ n. film or paper that contains miniature reproductions, as microfilm and microfiche do

microfossil /míkrō foss'l/ n. a fossil that can only be studied with a microscope, e.g. a bacterium fossil

microfungus /míkrō fung gəss/ (plural -gi /-fung gī/ or -guses) n. any fungus that has tiny or unobservable reproductive organs

microgram /míkrō gram/ n. one millionth part of a gram

micrograph /míkrō graaf, -graf/ n. 1. PICTURE AS SEEN THROUGH MICROSCOPE a photograph or drawing of sth as seen through a microscope 2. DEVICE FOR PRODUCING FINE ENGRAVINGS a device that can produce engraving or writing using very fine lines —**micrographic** /míkrō gráffik/ adj. —**micrographically** /-gráffikli/ adv.

microgravity /míkrō gravəti/ n. a force of gravity so low that weightlessness occurs, e.g. during space travel

microgroove /míkrō groov/ n. the narrow spiral groove on a gramophone record

microhabitat /míkrō hábbi tat/ n. an environment that has a unique set of ecological conditions within a larger habitat and supports distinct flora and fauna. For example wood lice are found beneath the bark of rotting wood in a deciduous woodland microhabitat.

microinch /míkrō inch/ n. a unit of linear measurement equivalent to one millionth of an inch. Symbol μin

microinjection /míkrō in jeksh'n/ n. the injection of a very small amount of liquid into individual cells, using a specialized instrument and a microscope for observation —**microinject** vti.

microinstruction /míkrō in struksh'n/ n. a single instruction in a low-level computer program

microlepidopteran /míkrō léppi dóptərən/ (plural -a /-tərə/) n. a small or medium-sized moth, e.g. a leaf miner, that is of little interest to a collector

microlight /míkrō līt/, **microlight aircraft**, **microlite**, **microlite aircraft** n. a small low-speed lightweight aircraft, often with an open fuselage, that can carry one or two people and is used for flying for pleasure or reconnaissance

microlith /míkrō lith/ n. a tiny flint tool, usually triangular, found in Mesolithic sites in Europe and dating from 12,000 to 3,000 BC —**microlithic** /míkrō líthik/ adj.

micromanage /míkrō mannij/ (-ages, -aging, -aged) vt. to manage a business or organization by paying extreme attention to small details —**micromanagement** n. —**micromanager** n.

micromanipulator /míkrō mə níppyoo laytər/ n. a device consisting of geared controls for the manipulation of extremely small dissecting tools or miniature surgical instruments under a microscope —**micromanipulation** /míkrō mə níppyoo láysh'n/ n. —**micromanipulative** /míkrō mə níppyoolətiv/ adj.

micromere /míkrō meer/ n. either of the small cells (**blastomeres**) formed by the division of a fertilized egg

micrometeorite /míkrō meéti ə rīt/ n. a particle of cosmic dust that falls to Earth or onto the Moon's surface. Micrometeorites originate in space where they are called micrometeoroids. —**micrometeoritic** /míkrō meéti ə ríttik/ adj.

micrometeoroid /míkrō meéti ə royd/ n. an extremely small dust particle found in space that may land on Earth or the Moon as a micrometeorite

micrometeorology /míkrō meéti ə rólləji/ n. the study of weather conditions in the air immediately above ground level, especially in small areas such as the area around a tree trunk or above a puddle —

micrometeorological /-mèeti ərə lójjik'l/ *adj.* **—micrometeorologist** /-mèeti ə róllǝjist/ *n.*

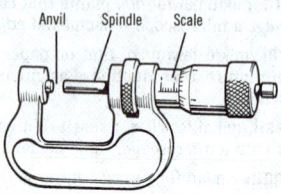

Micrometer

micrometer[1] /mī krómmitər/ *n.* a device for measuring small diameters, thicknesses, distances, or angles to a high degree of accuracy. The gap between the two measuring faces of the instrument is measured by the movement of one face that has a finely threaded screw marked with calibrated divisions. [Late 17thC. From French *micromètre*.] **—micrometric** /mīkrō méttrik/ *adj.* **—micrometrically** /-méttrikli/ *adv.* **—micrometry** /mī krómətri/ *n.*

micrometer[2] *n.* US = **micrometre**

micrometre /mīkrō meetər/ *n.* (*plural* **-tres**) *n.* a unit of linear measurement equivalent to one millionth of a metre. Symbol μm

microminiaturization /mīkrō mínnichə rī záysh'n/, **microminiaturisation** *n.* the production and use of extremely small electronic components, especially semiconductors **—microminiaturize** /mīkrō mínnichə rīz/ *vt.* **—microminiaturized** /-rīzd/ *adj.*

micromole /mīkrō mōl/ *n.* a molecular weight expressed in grams that is equivalent to one millionth of a mole. Symbol μmol **—micromolar** /mīkrə mólər/ *adj.*

micromorphology /mīkrō mawr fólləji/ *n.* the study of the fine detail in the external form and structure of organisms, or of other objects such as metal surfaces **—micromorphological** /mīkrə mawrfə lójjik'l/ *adj.*

micron /mī kron/ *n.* a unit of linear measurement equivalent to one millionth of a metre [Late 19thC. Coined from Greek *mikros* 'small' + -ON.]

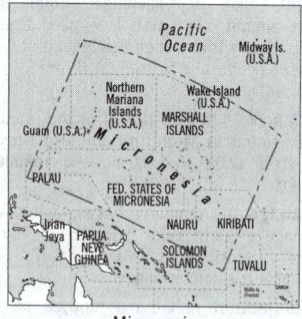

Micronesia

Micronesia[1] /mīkrə neezi ə/ one of the three major divisions of the Pacific Islands, comprising over 2,000 small islands in the western Pacific Ocean, mainly north of the equator

Micronesia[2] country in the western Pacific Ocean, comprising more than 600 islands, about 60 of which are inhabited. Language: English. Currency: US dollar. Capital: Palikir. Population: 127,616 (1997). Area: 702 sq. km/271 sq. mi. Official name **Federated States of Micronesia**

Micronesian /mīkrə neezi ən/ *adj.* **OF MICRONESIA** relating to Micronesia or its people or culture ■ *n.* **1.** **INHABITANT OF MICRONESIA** a member of any of the groups of people native to Micronesia **2.** **GROUP OF LANGUAGES SPOKEN IN MICRONESIA** a group of languages, including Gilbertese and Marshallese, spoken in Micronesia. It forms a subgroup of the Eastern branch of Malayo-Polynesian languages. About 200,000 people speak a Micronesian language.

micronize /mīkrə nīz/ (**-izes**, **-izing**, **-ized**), **micronise** (**-ises**, **-ising**, **-ised**) *vt.* to reduce the particle size of a powder down to a few millionths of a metre [Mid-20thC. Origin uncertain: perhaps formed from MICRON.]

micronucleus /mīkrō nyoókli əss/ (*plural* **-i** /-kli ī/ *or* **-uses**) *n.* the smaller of the two nuclei in the cells of ciliate protozoans. It contains genetic material and is involved in sexual reproduction. **—micronuclear** *adj.*

micronutrient /mīkrō nyoótri ənt/ *n.* a substance such as a vitamin or mineral that an organism requires for normal growth and development but only in very small quantities

microorganism /mīkrō áwrgənizəm/ *n.* a tiny organism such as a virus, protozoan, or bacterium that can only be seen under a microscope

micropalaeontology /mīkrō pálli on tólləji/ *n.* a branch of palaeontology that studies the microorganisms preserved as fossils in sedimentary rocks **—micropalaeontological** /mīkrō pálli ontə lójjik'l/ *adj.* **—micropalaeontologist** /mīkrō pálli on tólləjist/ *n.*

micropaleontology *n.* US = **micropalaeontology**

microparasite /mīkrō párrə sīt/ *n.* a microorganism that lives as a parasite on other organisms **—microparasitic** /mīkrō párrə síttik/ *adj.*

microphagous /mī króffəgəss/ *adj.* feeding on food in the form of microscopic particles, e.g. marine organisms

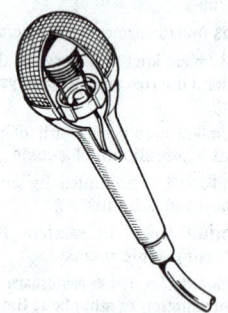

Microphone: Cutaway view

microphone /mīkrəfōn/ *n.* a device that converts sounds to electrical signals by means of a vibrating diaphragm. The signals can then be amplified, transmitted for broadcasting, or used for recording the sounds. [Late 17thC. The word originally denoted a device for making faint sounds louder.] **—microphonic** /mīkrə fónnik/ *adj.*

microphonics /mīkrə fónniks/ *n.* the sound heard from an electronic device, especially a loudspeaker, caused by the vibration of some mechanical part (*takes a plural verb*)

microphotograph /mīkrō fótə graaf, -graf/ *n.* **1.** **TINY PHOTOGRAPHIC IMAGE** a photographic image, e.g. on microfilm, that is so small that it has to be magnified in order to be viewed **2.** **PHOTOGRAPH OF MICROSCOPE IMAGE** a photograph of an object viewed through a microscope **—microphotographer** /mīkrōfə tóggrəfər/ *n.* **—microphotographic** /mīkrō fótə gráffik/ *adj.* **—microphotography** /mīkrōfə tóggrəfi/ *n.*

microphysics /mīkrō fízziks/ *n.* the branch of physics that studies objects and systems such as molecules, atoms, and elementary particles that are observable only microscopically or indirectly (*takes a singular verb*) **—microphysical** *adj.* **—microphysically** *adv.* **—microphysicist** *n.*

microphyte /mīkrō fīt/ *n.* a plant observable only under a microscope, especially one that is parasitic **—microphytic** /mīkrō fíttik/ *adj.*

micropipette /mīkrōpi pet/ *n.* a very slender graduated tube that is used to measure, transfer, or remove minute amounts of sth

microprint /mīkrō print/ *n.* printed text, e.g. on microfilm, that is so small that it has to be magnified in order to be viewed

microprism /mīkrō prizəm/ *n.* a small prism that is part of the focusing screen of many single-lens reflex cameras. When the image is in focus, the prism prevents it from shimmering.

microprocessor /mīkrō pró sessər/ *n.* the central processing unit that performs the basic operations in a microcomputer. It consists of an integrated circuit contained on a single chip.

microprogram /mīkrō prō gram/ *n.* a built-in program used within a microprocessor, consisting of a series of arithmetical and logical steps that enable basic instructions to be carried out

microprogramming /mīkrō prō gramming/ *n.* a means of programming the central processing unit of a computer by breaking down instructions into a series of small steps

micropsia /mī krópsi ə/ *n.* a vision defect in which the cones of the retina are abnormally separated by local swelling, making objects appear smaller than they really are [Mid-19thC. Coined from MICRO- + Greek *opsis* 'sight' + -IA.]

micropyle /mīkrō pīl/ *n.* **1.** **SMALL OPENING IN PLANT OVULE** a small opening in the covering of the ovule of a plant through which the pollen tube passes prior to fertilization. After fertilization, the ovule becomes a seed and water is absorbed through the opening. **2.** **SMALL PORE OF INSECT EGG** a small pore in the membrane of an insect egg that allows sperm to enter and fertilize the egg [Early 19thC. From French, from *micro-* 'micro-' + Greek *pulē* 'gate' (source of English *pylon*).] **—micropylar** /mīkrō pīlər/ *adj.*

microreader /mīkrō reedər/ *n.* a device that projects enlarged images and text from microfilm and microfiche onto a screen for easy reading

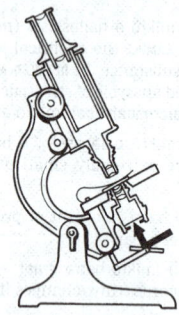

Microscope

microscope /mīkrə skōp/ *n.* a device that uses a lens or system of lenses to produce a greatly magnified image of an object. An optical microscope uses transmitted or reflected light to obtain the image. An electron microscope uses a beam of electrons and a system of electron-focusing lenses to obtain images.

microscopic /mīkrə skóppik/ *adj.* **1.** **VERY SMALL** extremely small **2.** **THOROUGH AND DETAILED** very thorough and meticulous **3.** **microscopic, microscopical INVISIBLE WITHOUT MICROSCOPE** invisible without the use of a microscope **4.** **microscopic, microscopical INVOLVING MICROSCOPE** using or involving a microscope **—microscopically** *adv.*

Microscopium /mīkrō skópi əm/ *n.* a small inconspicuous constellation in the skies of the southern hemisphere near Sagittarius

microscopy /mī króskəpi/ (*plural* **-pies**) *n.* **1.** **STUDY OF MICROSCOPES** the study and design of microscopes **2.** **EXPERIMENT USING MICROSCOPE** an investigation, observation, or experiment that involves the use of a microscope **—microscopist** *n.*

microsecond /mīkrō sekənd/ *n.* a measurement of time equivalent to one millionth of a second. Symbol μs

microseism /mīkrō sīzəm/ *n.* a recurrent low-level earth tremor caused by phenomena such as the force of crashing waves rather than by movement of rock masses **—microseismic** /mīkrō sízmik/ *adj.* **—microseismicity** /mīkrō sīz míssəti/ *n.*

microsmatic /mī kroz máttik/ *adj.* having poorly developed olfactory organs [Late 19thC. Coined from MICRO- + Greek *osmē* 'smell' + -atic (related form of -ATE).]

microsociology /mīkrō sōssi ólləji/ *n.* the branch of sociology that studies small groups and units within a larger society

microsome /míkrōsōm/ *n.* a small particle obtained after isolating a cell using centrifugal action, typically consisting of ribosomes associated with fragments of endoplasmic reticulum. Microsomes are filled with enzymes and may be involved in the synthesis of proteins. —**microsomal** /míkrō sṓm'l/ *adj.*

microsporangium /míkrō spaw ránji əm/ (*plural* **-a** /-ji ə/) *n.* a part of the reproductive structure of certain plants, especially ferns, that produces microspores. ◊ **sporangium** —**microsporangiate** /-ji ət/ *adj.*

microspore /míkrō spawr/ *n.* the smaller of two kinds of spore produced by seed plants and some ferns that develops into a male gametophyte

microspore mother cell *n.* = **microsporocyte**

microsporocyte /míkrō spáwrə sīt/ *n.* a plant cell that divides to produce four microspores

microsporophyll /míkrō spáwrəfil/ *n.* a leaf that bears a structure by which microspores are formed. In ferns, these are normal foliage leaves, the equivalent of the stamen of a flowering plant.

microstructure /míkrō strukchər/ *n.* the fine structure of a material, usually only visible through a microscope and sometimes after some form of surface preparation, e.g. the etching of metal alloys —**microstructural** /míkrō strúkchərəl/ *adj.*

microsurgery /míkrō súrjəri/ *n.* surgery performed with the aid of miniaturized precision instruments, including scalpels, needles, and a specially designed optical microscope. Microsurgery is used to perform almost all eye operations, in surgery on the middle and inner ear, and to reattach limbs. —**microsurgical** *adj.*

microswitch /míkrō swich/ *n.* a very small sensitive switch that acts by the movement of a small lever and is used where rapid precise movements are required, especially in keyboards and automatic control devices

microteaching /míkrō teeching/ *n.* a training exercise used in teacher training in which a student or student teacher is videotaped during a class. The videotape is then played back for analysis and evaluation.

microtome /míkrōtōm/ *n.* an instrument that uses a steel blade to cut biological tissues into very thin transparent slices a few millionths of a metre thick for microscopic examination

microtomy /mī króttəmi/ *n.* the process of preparing thin slices of biological tissues using a microtome, so that they can be observed under a microscope —**microtomic** /míkrō tómmik/ *adj.* —**microtomist** /mī króttəmist/ *n.*

microtone /míkrōtōn/ *n.* a musical interval smaller than a semitone, especially a quartertone —**microtonal** /míkrō tṓn'l/ *adj.* —**microtonality** /míkrōtō nálləti/ *n.* —**microtonally** /míkrō tṓn'li/ *adv.*

microtubule /míkrō tyoób yool/ *n.* a hollow tubular structure composed of the protein tubulin that helps to maintain the shape and movement of a living cell and the transport of material within it. ◊ **tubule** —**microtubular** /míkrō tyoóbyoōlər/ *adj.*

microvasculature /míkrō váskyoōləchər/ *n.* a part of the circulatory system made up of the smallest vessels such as capillaries, arterioles, and venules —**microvascular** *adj.*

microvillus /míkrō vílləs/ (*plural* **-li** /-lī/) *n.* a microscopic hair-shaped cell that projects from the surface of the lining of the small intestine, increasing the surface area available for the absorption of nutrients. ◊ **epithelium** —**microvillar** *adj.*

microvolt /míkrōvōlt/ *n.* a unit of electric potential or electromotive force equivalent to one millionth of a volt. Symbol **μV**

microwatt /míkrō wot/ *n.* a measurement of power equivalent to one millionth of a watt. Symbol **μW**

microwave /míkrə wayv/ *n.* **1.** HIGH-FREQUENCY ELECTROMAGNETIC WAVE a type of electromagnetic wave whose wavelength ranges from 1.0 mm to 30 cm, used in radar, to carry radio transmissions, and in cooking or heating devices **2.** OVEN USING ELECTROMAGNETIC RADIATION an oven that cooks or heats up food or beverages relatively quickly using high-frequency electromagnetic radiation ■ *vt.* (**-waves, -waving, -waved**) HEAT OR COOK IN A MICROWAVE to heat or cook food or beverages using an oven that uses high-frequency electromagnetic radiation —**microwavable** *adj.*

microwave oven *n.* = **microwave** *n.* 2

micturate /míktyoō rayt/ (**-rates, -rating, -rated**) *vi.* to urinate (*technical*) [Mid-19thC. Back-formation from *micturition* 'urination', from Latin *micturire*, literally 'to want to urinate', from *mict-*, the past participle stem of *meiere* 'to urinate'.] —**micturation** /míktyoō ráysh'n/ *n.*

mid /mid/ *adj.* **1.** OCCUPYING MIDDLE OR CENTRAL POSITION being in the centre or halfway through sth **2.** DONE WITH TONGUE IN MIDDLE POSITION produced as a vowel with the tongue halfway between the high and low positions, e.g. in the words 'but' or 'bet' [Old English *midd.* Ultimately from an Indo-European word that is also the ancestor of English *medium* and *meso-*.]

'mid /mid/, **mid** *prep.* among a group [15thC. Shortening of AMID.]

mid. *abbr.* middle

Mid. *abbr.* Midshipman

mid- *prefix.* middle ○ *midrange* ○ *midmost* [From MID]

midafternoon /mid áaftər noón/ *n.* the part of the afternoon midway between noon and sunset —**midafternoon** *adj.*

midair /mid áir/ *n.* POINT IN AIR ABOVE SURFACE a point in the air above the ground or another surface ■ *adj.* OCCURRING IN AIR ABOVE SURFACE occurring or located at a point in the air above the ground or another surface

Midas /mídəss/ *n.* in Greek mythology, a Phrygian king who had befriended Silenus, a follower of Dionysus, and was rewarded by Dionysus with the gift of making everything he touched turn into gold

Midas touch *n.* the ability to make large amounts of money, often with very little apparent effort

mid-Atlantic *adj.* influenced by both North America and Great Britain, especially in behaviour or speech

Mid-Atlantic Ridge *n.* submarine mountain ridge that runs north-south through the Atlantic Ocean

Mid-Atlantic States *npl.* = **Middle Atlantic States**

midbrain /míd brayn/ *n.* the middle part of the three main divisions of either the embryonic or the adult brain in vertebrates. Technical name **mesencephalon**

midcourse /míd káwrss/ *n.* MISSILE'S FLIGHT BETWEEN LAUNCH AND RE-ENTRY the part of a missile's flight between the end of its launch and the beginning of its re-entry ■ *adj.* HAPPENING PARTWAY THROUGH STH present or occurring partway through a course or course of action

midday /mid dáy/ *n.* twelve o'clock noon or the period around the middle of the day

midden /mídd'n/ *n.* **1.** DUNGHILL a pile of dung or refuse (*archaic*) **2.** = **kitchen midden 3.** *N England* EARTH CLOSET an earth closet [14thC. Of Scandinavian origin.]

middle /mídd'l/ *n.* **1.** MIDWAY PART OR POSITION the part or position furthest from the sides, edges, or ends of sth ○ *sitting in the middle of the row* **2.** PART BETWEEN BEGINNING AND END the part between or halfway between the beginning and end of a period of time or an event ○ *in the middle of June* **3.** POSITION BETWEEN HIGHEST AND LOWEST the position or rank midway between the highest and lowest **4.** INSIDE PART the interior or central part of sth **5.** CENTRAL PART OF BODY the waist, stomach, or central area of the human body (*informal*) **6.** GRAM VOICE EXPRESSING REFLEXIVE ACTION the voice of verbs in some languages such as ancient Greek and Sanskrit that expresses the action of a subject on or for itself ■ *adj.* **1.** CENTRAL AND EQUIDISTANT FROM LIMITS equidistant from the sides, edges, or ends of sth **2.** BEING HALFWAY BETWEEN BEGINNING AND END occurring or located halfway between the start and finish of a period of time, an event, or a series **3.** OCCUPYING INTERMEDIATE POSITION situated in an intermediate position, e.g. in age or status **4.** BEING MIDWAY BETWEEN EXTREMES lying between two extremes or opposites and, consequently, usually moderate **5.** GRAM CONCERNING VOICE EXPRESSING REFLEXIVE ACTION relating to the voice of verbs in some languages such as ancient Greek and Sanskrit that expresses the action of a subject on or for itself ■ *v.* (**-dles, -dling, -dled**) **1.** *vti.* PUT STH IN MIDDLE to place sth equidistant from the sides, edges, or ends of sth **2.** *vti.* SAILING FOLD SAIL IN HALF to fold a sail in half or to be folded in half **3.** *vt.* CRICKET HIT BALL WITH MIDDLE OF BAT to hit a cricket ball firmly with the middle of the bat [Old English *middel*]

Middle *adj.* relating to a language or literature between its early and later stages of development

middle age *n.* the period in sb's life when that person is no longer considered young, usually between 40 and 60

middle-aged *adj.* **1.** NO LONGER YOUNG no longer considered young, but not yet considered old **2.** TYPICAL OF SB MIDDLE-AGED characterized by the behaviour, attitudes, lifestyle, or interests considered typical of middle age, especially staidness, conventionality, or old-fashionedness

middle-aged spread *n.* the excess fat sometimes accumulated around the waist during middle age (*humorous*)

Middle Ages *n.* the period in European history between antiquity and the Italian Renaissance, often considered to be between the end of the Roman Empire in the 5th century and the early 15th century

Middle America *n.* **1.** SOCIALLY TRADITIONAL US MIDDLE CLASS a section of the middle class in the United States considered to be politically conservative and to hold traditional social and moral values **2.** = **Midwest 3.** *US* MEXICO AND CENTRAL AMERICA the area to the south of the United States and the north of South America that includes Mexico, Central America, and sometimes the West Indies —**Middle American** *adj.*, *n.*

Middle Atlantic States, **Mid-Atlantic States** *npl. US* the states midway along the Atlantic coast of the United States, consisting of New York, New Jersey, and Pennsylvania, and usually Delaware and Maryland

Middleback Ranges /mídd'l bak-/ *npl.* range of hills in South Australia. It is the eastern section of the Gawler Ranges.

middlebreaker /mídd'l braykər/, **middlebuster** /-bustər/ *n.* = **lister**

middlebrow /mídd'l brow/ *n.* sb who is conventional and moderately inclined in cultural tastes and interests (*informal*) ◊ **highbrow, lowbrow** [Early 20thC. Modelled on HIGHBROW and LOWBROW.] —**middlebrow** *adj.*

middle C *n.* a note roughly in the middle of a piano keyboard, written in musical notation on the first ledger line below the treble staff or above the bass staff

middle class *n.* the section of society between the poor and the wealthy, including many business and professional people and skilled workers —**middle-class** *adj.*

middle common room *n.* a room in some colleges and universities where postgraduate students can meet and relax

middle distance *n.* the portion of space that is further away from a viewer than the foreground but nearer than the background, especially in a landscape painting or photograph

middle-distance *adj.* relating to foot races between 400 m/440 yards and 1500 m/one mile long

Middle Dutch *n.* the form of the Dutch language spoken and written from about the 12th to the beginning of the 16th centuries AD

middle ear *n.* the narrow air-filled space between the ear drum and the outer wall of the inner ear that contains the three tiny bones that transmit sound vibrations

Middle Earth *n.* = **Midgard**

Middle East *n.* **1.** REGION STRETCHING FROM EGYPT TO IRAN the region stretching from the eastern Mediterranean to the western side of the Indian subcontinent, including Egypt, the Arabian Peninsula, Israel, Jordan, Lebanon, Syria, Turkey, Iran, and Iraq **2.** HISTORICAL AREA FROM IRAN TO MYANMAR formerly, the area extending from Iran to Myanmar, including Afghanistan, India, and Tibet. —**Middle Eastern** *adj.* —**Middle Easterner** *n.*

Middle England *n.* a section of the middle class in

England considered to be politically conservative and to hold traditional social and moral values

Middle English *n.* the form of the English language spoken and written from about the 12th to the beginning of the 16th centuries AD. The leading dialects of this period were Kentish, West Saxon, West Midland, East Midland, and Northern. ◊ **Old English, Modern English**

Middle French *n.* the form of the French language spoken and written from about the 14th to the beginning of the 17th centuries AD. ◊ **Old French**

middle game *n.* the middle part of a game of chess, after the opening moves and before the endgame

Middle Greek *n., adj.* = **Medieval Greek**

middle ground *n.* **1.** = **middle distance 2.** POSITION BETWEEN EXTREMES an intermediate position between two opposing views or factions ○ *The two parties were unable to find any middle ground.*

Middle High German *n.* the form of High German spoken and written from about the 12th to the beginning of the 16th centuries AD

middle-income *adj.* earning a wage or salary that is roughly the same as the average for a population

Middle Irish *n.* the form of Irish Gaelic spoken and written from about the 11th to the beginning of the 15th centuries AD

Middle Kingdom *n.* **1.** PERIOD OF ANCIENT EGYPTIAN HISTORY a period of Egyptian history from the late 11th dynasty, approximately 2040 BC, to the 13th dynasty, 1670 BC **2.** FORMER CHINESE EMPIRE the former Chinese Empire, so called because it was supposedly at the centre of the earth **3.** CENTRAL TERRITORY OF CHINESE EMPIRE the central territory held by most Chinese Empires, including the Huang and Yangtze river valleys, and eventually the eighteen inner provinces of China

middle lamella (*plural* **middle lamellae**) *n.* a thin membrane, composed of pectin and other polysaccharides, that cements the walls of two adjacent plant cells together

Middle Low German *n.* the form of Low German spoken and written from about the 12th to the beginning of the 16th centuries AD

middleman /mídd'l man/ (*plural* **-men** /-men/) *n.* **1.** SB WHO BUYS AND SELLS GOODS a trader who buys goods from a producer and then sells them to retailers or consumers **2.** GO-BETWEEN sb who acts as a negotiator or intermediary

middle management *n.* managers who are responsible for relatively small numbers of staff and are involved in the details of running an organization rather than in taking major decisions or setting policy —**middle manager** *n.*

middlemost /mídd'l mōst/ *adj.* = **midmost**

middle name *n.* the name between a first name and a surname ◇ **be sb's middle name** to possess a great deal of a quality, attribute, or characteristic (*informal*) ○ *Tact's my middle name.*

middle-of-the-road *adj.* **1.** OCCUPYING INTERMEDIATE POSITION taking a course of action or adopting a point of view that is midway between two extremes **2.** MUSIC INTENDED TO HAVE BROAD MUSIC APPEAL intended to be musically appealing to many people and avoiding stylistic extremes ■ *n.* MUSIC MUSIC AIMING FOR BROAD APPEAL music intended to appeal to many people and avoiding stylistic extremes —**middle-of-the-roader** *n.*

Middle Palaeolithic *n.* the period between the Lower and Upper Palaeolithic ages, from about 70 000 BC to 32 000 BC

middle passage *n.* the journey from western Africa across the Atlantic to the West Indies or the Americas, undertaken by many slave ships

Middlesbrough /mídd'lzbərə/ industrial town and port in northeastern England. Population: 147,500 (1995).

middle school *n.* **1.** BRITISH INTERMEDIATE SCHOOL in Great Britain, a state-run school for children between the ages of about 8 and 13 years. The age range depends upon the local authority in which the school is situated. **2.** US SCHOOL FOR PRETEENS in the United States, a school for children between the ages of about 11

and 14 years, depending on the school's location. ◊ **junior high**

Middle Scots *n.* the form of the Scots language written and spoken between the late 15th and the early 17th centuries

Middlesex /mídd'l seks/ former county in southeastern England. In 1965 most of the county became part of Greater London.

Middle Temple *n.* in England, one of four London legal societies of the Inns of Court

middle term *n.* LOGIC a term that appears in both premises of a syllogism but not in the conclusion

middleware /mídd'l wair/ *n.* COMPUT software that manages the connection between a client and a database

middle watch *n.* NAUT the watch from midnight until 4:00 AM aboard a vessel

middleweight /mídd'l wayt/ *n.* **1.** BOXING PROFESSIONAL BOXER LIGHTER THAN LIGHT HEAVYWEIGHT a professional boxer weighing between 66.5 and 72.5 kg/147 and 160 lb, heavier than a welterweight but lighter than a light heavyweight **2.** BOXING AMATEUR BOXER LIGHTER THAN LIGHT HEAVYWEIGHT an amateur boxer weighing between 71 and 75 kg/157 and 165 lb **3.** SPORTS, WRESTLING WRESTLER OF INTERMEDIATE WEIGHT a contestant in various sports, such as wrestling, of approximately the same weight as a middleweight boxer

Middle Welsh *n.* the form of the Welsh language written and spoken from about the 12th to the beginning of the 15th centuries AD

Middle West *n.* US = **Midwest** —**Middle Western** *adj.* — **Middle Westerner** *n.*

middling /míddling/ *adj.* **1.** MEDIUM, MODERATE, OR AVERAGE of average size, quantity, quality, or position **2.** ORDINARY AND UNEXCEPTIONAL neither good nor bad, especially in health or mood ■ *adv.* MODERATELY AND UNEXCEPTIONALLY in a moderate and unremarkable way (*informal*) ■ **middlings** *npl.* **1.** COMM THINGS OF AVERAGE QUALITY commodities or resources, such as ore or petrol, that are of average quality, grade, or price **2.** FOOD POOR-QUALITY FLOUR poor-quality flour made from coarsely ground wheat and bran (*takes a singular or plural verb*) [Late 16thC. Formed from MID + -LING.] — **middlingly** *adv.*

Middx *abbr.* Middlesex

middy /míddi/ (*plural* **-dies**) *n.* **1.** NAVY MIDSHIPMAN a midshipman (*informal*) **2.** CLOTHES middy blouse CLOTHES BLOUSE WITH SAILOR COLLAR a loose blouse with a sailor collar worn by women and children **3.** Aus FOOD HALF A PINT OF BEER a medium-sized beer glass, holding seven to ten ounces

Mideast /míd eést/ *n.* US the Middle East —**Mideastern** *adj.* —**Mideasterner** *n.*

midfield /míd feeld/ *n.* **1.** CENTRAL AREA OF PITCH the middle portion of a sports pitch, especially the area midway between the two penalty areas **2.** PLAYERS IN CENTRAL AREA OF PITCH the group of players who contest control of the central area of the pitch between the two penalty areas (*takes a singular or plural verb*) — **midfielder** *n.*

Midgard /míd gaard/, **Midgarth** /-gaarth/, **Midgarthr** /-gaarthər/ *n.* in Norse mythology, the home of humankind, midway between Asgard and the underworld, encircled by a huge serpent, and formed from the body of the giant Ymir

midge /mij/ *n.* **1.** INSECTS TINY SWARMING FLY a small slender flying insect that occurs globally, particularly in swarms near bodies of standing water, or a related biting insect that can transmit blood-borne diseases. Family: Chironomidae and Ceratopogonidae. **2.** PERSON OF SMALL STATURE a person or animal of small stature [Old English *mycg*. Ultimately from an Indo-European base, probably originally an imitation of the sound of humming, that is also the ancestor of English *mosquito*, *musket*, and *myiasis*.]

midget /míjjit/ *n.* **1.** OFFENSIVE TERM an offensive term for a very short person whose skeleton and features are of normal proportions (*offensive*) **2.** VERY SMALL VERSION OF STH a very small version of sth, such as a car or boat ■ *adj.* MINIATURE OR SMALLER THAN USUAL miniaturized or belonging to a class smaller than

the ordinary size [Mid-19thC. Formed from MIDGE, literally 'little midge'.]

midgut /míd gut/ *n.* **1.** BIOL PART OF DIGESTIVE TRACT the central section of the digestive tract of a vertebrate, in which the processes of digestion and absorption take place **2.** BIOL PART OF INVERTEBRATE ALIMENTARY CANAL the middle section of the alimentary canal of an invertebrate **3.** EMBRYOL PART OF EMBRYO the middle portion of the gut of an embryo that develops into most of the small intestine and part of the large intestine

Midheaven /míd hévv'n/ *n.* the point on the apparent annual path of the sun in the celestial sphere where the meridian is crossed, or the sign of the zodiac that contains it

midi /míddi/ (*plural* **-is**) *n.* a skirt or coat that comes down to just below the knee or halfway down the calf [Mid-20thC. From *midi-* 'medium-sized', a combining form formed from MID on the model of MINI- and MAXI-.]

Midi /meédi/ name for the south of France

Midi, Canal du /meédi kə nál doo/ canal that links the Bay of Biscay to the Mediterranean Sea

MIDI /míddi/ *n.* the interface between an electronic musical instrument and a computer, used in composing and editing music to allow the computer to control an instrument or one instrument to control others. Abbr of **musical instrument digital interface**

midiron /míd ī ərn/ *n.* in golf, a number 5, 6, 7, or 8 iron, used to give the ball a medium amount of lift

midi system *n.* a compact hi-fi system, usually consisting of a CD-player, tuner, cassette deck, and amplifier, designed as a single unit with separate speakers

midland /mídlənd/ *n.* INTERIOR PART OF COUNTRY the middle, inland, or interior part of a country ■ *adj.* OF MIDDLE OF COUNTRY relating to or being in the middle or interior of a country

Midland /mídlənd/ *n.* **1.** FORM OF BRITISH ENGLISH a variety of British English spoken in the Midlands of England, divided into East Midland and West Midland **2.** US FORM OF AMERICAN ENGLISH a variety of American English spoken in parts of states south from New Jersey to Georgia, especially in the Appalachian and Piedmont mountains and in the Shenandoah Valley

Midlands /mídləndz/ central, largely industrialized part of England, centred on Birmingham (*takes a singular or plural verb*) —**Midlander** *n.*

midlife /míd líff/ *n.* = **middle age**

midlife crisis (*plural* **midlife crises**) *n.* feelings of self-doubt and a lack of confidence experienced by some people when they become middle-aged

Midlothian /mid lṓthi ən/ a council area in southeastern Scotland, on the Firth of Forth

midmorning /míd máwrning/ *n.* the middle part of the morning —**midmorning** *adj.*

midmost /mídmōst/ *adj.* LOCATED AT OR NEAREST CENTRE situated at or nearest the centre of sth ■ *adv.* IN MIDDLE in the middle or midst of sth [Old English *midmest*]

midnight /míd nīt/ *n.* **1.** MIDPOINT OF NIGHT twelve o'clock at night or the period around the middle of the night **2.** TIME OF GREAT DARKNESS a period of intense darkness or gloom (*literary*) —**midnightly** *adj., adv.*

midnight blue *adj.* of a dark blue colour verging on black, like the sky on a clear night —**midnight blue** *n.*

midnight sun *n.* the sun when it is visible from within the Arctic or Antarctic circles at midnight during their respective summer months

mid-ocean ridge *n.* a long underwater mountain range of the Atlantic, Indian, or South Pacific Oceans formed from volcanic rock released during the movement of tectonic plates

midpoint /míd poynt/ *n.* **1.** POINT HALFWAY BETWEEN BEGINNING AND END the point on a line, journey, or distance that is halfway between the beginning and end **2.** POINT OF TIME HALFWAY THROUGH STH the point of time halfway between the beginning and end of an event, course of action, or period of time

midrange /míd raynj/ *adj.* **1.** OCCURRING IN MIDDLE OF SERIES occurring in the middle of a series, array, or range **2.** COVERING MEDIUM DISTANCE covering a distance midway between a short-range and long-range trajectory

midrash /míd rash/ (*plural* **-rashim**) *n.* the technique of interpreting or commenting on the Hebrew Scriptures

Midrash (*plural* **-rashim**) *n.* a body of Rabbinic literature consisting of commentary on and clarification of biblical texts, first compiled before 500 AD [Early 17thC. From Hebrew *midraš*, from *dāraš* 'to expound'.] —**midrashic** /mi dráshik/ *adj.*

midrib /míd rib/ *n.* the thick central vein that runs from the base of a leaf to its apex

midriff /mídrif/ *n.* **1.** MIDDLE FRONT AREA OF HUMAN BODY the area of the human body between the chest and the waist **2.** ANAT DIAPHRAGM the diaphragm (*dated*) **3.** CLOTHES CLOTHING EXPOSING STOMACH AREA an article of clothing that exposes the stomach area [Old English *midhrif* 'diaphragm', from *midd* (see MID) + *hrif* 'belly' (ultimately from an Indo-European word meaning 'body' that is also the ancestor of English *corpse*).]

mid-rise *adj.* US MODERATELY HIGH relating to or consisting of buildings that are of moderate height, about five to ten storeys ■ *n.* US MODERATELY HIGH BUILDING a building of moderate height, about five to ten storeys

midsagittal /míd sájjit'l/ *adj.* relating to or situated along an imaginary plane that passes through the midline of the body or an organ

midsection /míd seksh'n/ *n.* the middle part of sth, especially the area of the human body between the chest and waist

midship /míd ship/ *adj.* RELATING TO MIDDLE SECTION OF SHIP relating to or located in the middle section of a ship or vessel ■ *n.* CENTRAL SECTION OF SHIP the middle section of a ship or vessel

midshipman /míd shipmən/ (*plural* **-men** /-mən/) *n.* **1.** BRITISH NAVAL OFFICER an officer in the British or other navies who holds a rank just above a naval cadet and below a sub-lieutenant **2.** US STUDENT TRAINING TO BE NAVAL OFFICER a student who is training to be a naval officer, especially one at a naval academy. ◊ **cadet** [Late 17thC. Alteration of earlier *midshipsman*, so called because such officers were originally stationed amidships.]

midships /míd ships/ *adv., adj.* = amidships [Mid-19thC. Shortening.]

midsize /míd síz/, **midsized** /míd sízd/ *adj.* with a size midway between large and small

midst /midst/ *n.* CENTRE the middle or central part of sth ■ *prep.* AMID amid sb or sth (*literary*) [15thC. Alteration of earlier *middes*, from MID.] ◊ **in the midst of** in the middle of a situation, place, event, or period of time ◊ **in our midst** among us

midstream /míd streem/ *n.* **1.** MIDDLE PART OF RIVER the middle part of a river or stream where the current is often very strong **2.** POINT HALFWAY THROUGH STH a point after the beginning and before the end of sth such as a speech or course of action —**midstream** *adv.*

midsummer /míd súmmər/ *n.* **1.** MIDDLE OF SUMMER the period of time in the middle of summer **2.** = summer solstice

Midsummer Day, **Midsummer's Day** *n.* the day of 24 June, celebrated by Christians as the feast of St. John the Baptist. It is one of the quarter days in England, Wales, and Ireland.

midsummer madness *n.* eccentric, foolish, or frivolous behaviour that is traditionally supposed to occur around the middle of the summer

midsummer-men *n.* = rose-root [Perhaps from young women's use of similar plants on Midsummer Eve to divine whether their young men would stay faithful to them]

midterm /míd túrm/ *n.* **1.** EDUC, POL MIDPOINT OF TERM the middle of an academic term or a term of office **2.** OBSTET PERIOD MIDWAY THROUGH PREGNANCY the period halfway through a pregnancy **3.** US, Can EDUC EXAM HALFWAY THROUGH ACADEMIC TERM an exam sat halfway through an academic term in North American colleges and universities (*often used in the plural*) ■ *adj.* IN MIDDLE OF TERM OF OFFICE occurring in the middle

of a term of office, especially the term of a president of the United States ◦ *midterm elections*

midtown /míd town/ *n.* US the central area of a city between the uptown and downtown areas especially in Manhattan

midway /míd wáy/ *adv., adj.* **1.** HALF OF THE WAY halfway between two points, parts, or places **2.** HALFWAY THROUGH STH halfway through an event, course of action, or period of time ■ *n.* US, Can AREA OF SIDESHOWS AT FAIR an area in a fair, carnival, or circus for sideshows and other amusements [Old English *midweg*]

midweek /míd week/ *n.* MIDDLE OF WEEK the period of time in the middle of a week ■ *adj., adv.* IN MIDDLE OF WEEK on a day in the middle of the week —**midweekly** *adj., adv.*

Midweek /míd week/ *n.* the day of Wednesday, so called by members of the Society of Friends

Midwest /míd wést/ *n.* the northern region of the central United States east of the Rocky Mountains, generally including the states of Illinois, Indiana, Iowa, Kansas, Michigan, Minnesota, Missouri, Nebraska, Ohio, and Wisconsin —**Midwestern** *adj.* —**Midwesterner** *n.*

mid-wicket *n.* in cricket, the fielder or fielding position located between square leg and mid-on, usually on the batsman's left

midwife /míd wíf/ *n.* (*plural* **-wives** /míd wívz/) **1.** MED SB TRAINED TO DELIVER BABIES sb trained to help deliver babies and offer support and advice to pregnant women **2.** SB HELPING TO CREATE STH sb who or sth that helps create or produce sth new ■ *vt.* (**-wifes, -wifing** *or* **-wiving** /-wíving/, **-wifed** *or* **-wived** /-wívd/) US ASSIST IN BIRTH OF BABY to assist in the delivery of a baby [13thC. Origin uncertain: probably from obsolete *mid* 'with' + WIFE in the obsolete sense 'woman'.]

midwifery /míd wíffəri/ *n.* the technique or practice of helping to deliver babies and offering advice and support to pregnant women

midwife toad *n.* a European toad that mates on land. The male carries a band of fertilized eggs wrapped round his back legs until they are ready to hatch. Latin name: *Alytes obstetricans*.

midwinter /míd wíntər/ *n.* **1.** MIDDLE OF WINTER the period in the middle of winter **2.** = winter solstice

midyear /míd yeér/ *n.* the period in the middle of the academic, calendar, or fiscal year

mien /meen/ *n.* sb's appearance, bearing, or posture, especially facial expressions, as an indication of mood or character (*literary*) [Early 16thC. Origin uncertain: probably a shortening of obsolete *demeine* 'demeanour' (from Old French, from *demener*; see DEMEAN); subsequently influenced by French *mine* 'facial appearance'.]

AKG London

Ludwig Mies van der Rohe

Mies van der Rohe /meéz van dər rő ə/, **Ludwig** (1886–1969) German-born US architect and designer. He was a pioneer in the design of glass-walled skyscrapers, in particular the Seagram Building, New York City (1958), on which he collaborated with Philip Johnson. His architecture and furniture are characterized by austere forms, elegant materials such as marble and chrome, and subtle proportion and detailing.

mifepristone /mi féppri stōn/ *n.* a drug used to abort a foetus in the first nine weeks following conception. It acts by blocking the hormone pro-

gesterone which is essential for maintaining a pregnancy. [Late 20thC. Contraction of *aminophenol* + *propyne* + *oestradiol* (elements of the drug's chemical name) + -ONE.]

miff /mif/ *vt.* (**miffs, miffing, miffed**) ANNOY OR OFFEND to annoy or anger sb (*informal*) ■ *n.* ILL HUMOUR an angry mood or sulk (*informal*) [Early 17thC. Origin uncertain: perhaps an imitation of an exclamation of disgust.]

miffed /mift/ *adj.* annoyed or offended (*informal*)

miffy /míffi/ (**-fier, -fiest**) *adj.* **1.** TOUCHY AND EASILY OFFENDED easily upset or offended (*informal disapproving*) **2.** BOT HARD TO GROW difficult to propagate because very specific environmental conditions are required (refers to a plant) —**miffily** *adv.* —**miffiness** *n.*

MiG /mig/ *n.* a type of high-speed high-altitude fighter aircraft built in Russia [Mid-20thC. Acronym formed from the names of A. I. *Mikoyan* and M. I. *Gurevich*, the aircraft's designers.]

MIG *abbr.* mortgage indemnity guarantee

might[1] /mīt/ CORE MEANING: a modal verb indicating the possibility that sth is true or will happen in the future ◦ *She said that John might be living abroad now.* ◦ *The meeting might be next week.*

vi. **1.** GIVING ADVICE used as a polite way of making suggestions and giving advice ◦ *I thought we might go out tonight.* ◦ *You might want to give him a ring first.* **2.** EXPRESSING OBLIGATION used to indicate that sb ought to do sth, often when you are annoyed that the person has not done it ◦ *You might at least have told me!* [Old English *mihte, meahte*, the past tense of *magan* (see MAY)]

might[2] /mīt/ *n.* **1.** GREAT POWER great power or influence ◦ *up against the might of a huge organization* **2.** PHYSICAL STRENGTH physical strength and determination ◦ *We must push with all our might.* [Old English *miht*. Ultimately from an Indo-European base meaning 'to be able' that is also the ancestor of English *may*, *main*, and *mechanism*.]

might-have-been *n.* an event or outcome that could have occurred but did not

mightily /mítili/ *adv.* **1.** VERY to a great extent or degree (*dated*) ◦ *mightily relieved* **2.** WITH MUCH PHYSICAL POWER with considerable physical strength and effort

mightn't /mítn't/ *contr.* a spoken form of 'might not'

mighty /míti/ (**-ier, -iest**) *adj.* **1.** STRONG AND POWERFUL of great strength and power **2.** BIG AND IMPRESSIVE very impressive in size, scope, or extent **3.** US VERY MUCH so extremely or to a great degree (*regional informal*) ◦ *mighty fine* [Old English *mihtig*, from *miht* (see MIGHT[2])] —**mightiness** *n.*

migmatite /mígmə tīt/ (*plural* **-tites** *or* **-tite**) *n.* a coarsely crystalline rock composed of a mixture of bands of metamorphic and igneous rocks and found in areas where high-grade metamorphic rocks are partly melted to form igneous rock [Early 20thC. Coined from Greek *migmat-*, the stem of *migma* 'mixture' + -ITE.]

mignon /mín yon/ *adj.* SMALL AND PRETTY very delicate and pretty (*literary*) ■ *n.* SMALL BEEF PORTION a small portion of prime beef, especially filet mignon [Mid-16thC. From French, an alteration of Old French *mignot*, of uncertain origin.]

mignonette /mínyə nét/ (*plural* **-ettes** *or* **-ette**) *n.* a Mediterranean plant with small fragrant greenish-white flowers and spiky leaves. Genus: *Reseda*. [Early 18thC. From French, *mignon* 'dainty' (see MIGNON).]

migraine /meé grayn, mī-/ *n.* a recurrent, throbbing, very painful headache, often affecting one side of the head and sometimes accompanied by vomiting or by distinct warning signs including visual disturbances [14thC. Via French from, ultimately, Greek *hēmikrania* 'half of the skull', from *hēmi-* 'half' + *kranion* 'skull' (see CRANIUM).] —**migrainous** *adj.*

migrant /mígrənt/ *n.* **1.** SOC SCI SB MOVING FROM PLACE TO PLACE sb who moves from one region or country to another, often in search of work or other economic opportunities **2.** ZOOL MIGRATORY ANIMAL an animal, especially a bird, that moves from one region to another, often at specific times of the year in order to breed or avoid unsuitable weather conditions **3.** *Aus* RECENT IMMIGRANT an immigrant, especially one who has entered the country recently ■ *adj.* MOVING FROM PLACE TO PLACE moving from one region or country to another [Late 17thC. From Latin *migrant-*, the present participle stem of *migrare* (see MIGRATE).]

migrate /mī gráyt/ (**-grates, -grating, -grated**) *v.* **1.** *vi.* SOC SCI **MOVE FROM PLACE TO PLACE** to move from one region or country to another, often to seek work or other economic opportunities **2.** *vi.* ZOOL **MOVE BETWEEN HABITATS** to move from one habitat or environment to another in response to seasonal changes and variations in food supply **3.** *vi.* **MOVE POSITION WITHIN ORGANISM** to move within an organism or substance as, e.g., cells do during the growth of an embryo **4.** *vt.* COMPUT **MOVE BETWEEN SYSTEMS** to transfer a file from one system to another [Early 17thC. From Latin *migrat-*, the past participle stem of *migrare*. Ultimately from an Indo-European base meaning 'to move, change' that is also the ancestor of English *mutate* and *amoeba*.] —**migrator** *n.*

migration /mī gráysh'n/ *n.* **1.** SOC SCI **MOVEMENT FROM ONE PLACE TO ANOTHER** the act or process of moving from one region or country to another **2.** SOC SCI **PEOPLE OR ANIMALS MIGRATING TOGETHER** a group of people or animals that are moving together from one region or country to another **3. SHIFT OF IONS** the movement of ions under the influence of an electric field **4.** CHEM **MOVEMENT OF ATOMS** the movement of an atom or a group of atoms or double bonds, from one part of a molecule to another —**migrational** *adj.*

migratory /mígrətəri, mī gráytəri/, **migrative** /mígrətiv/ *adj.* **1.** ZOOL **MOVING TO ANOTHER REGION EVERY YEAR** moving as part of a bird, fish, or other animal population from one region to another every year, usually at specific times in order to breed or avoid unsuitable weather conditions **2.** SOC SCI **RELATING TO MOVEMENT FROM PLACE TO PLACE** relating to the movement of people or animals from one place to another in order to achieve better living conditions **3. NOT SETTLING DOWN** tending to wander from one region or country to another without settling down in one place for any length of time

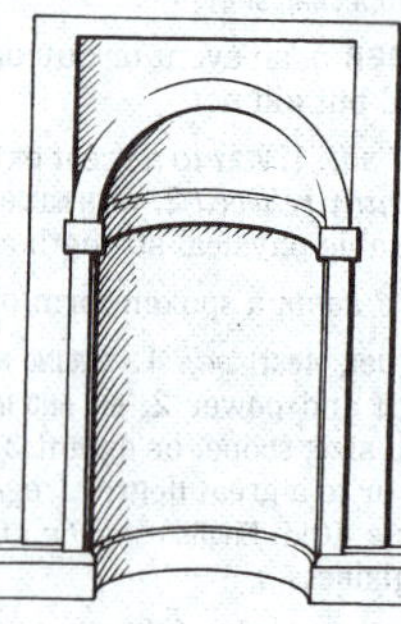

Mihrab

mihrab /meé rab, meérəb/ *n.* **1. NICHE IN MOSQUE POINTING TOWARDS MECCA** a small niche in a mosque that indicates the direction of Mecca **2. RECTANGULAR SPACE IN PRAYER RUG** a blank rectangular space in the middle of a prayer rug that faces Mecca during prayer [Early 19thC. From Arabic *mihrāb*.]

mikado /mi káad ō/ (*plural* **-dos**) *n.* formerly a title of the Japanese emperor [Early 18thC. From Japanese, literally 'honourable gate'.]

Mikasuki /míkə sóoki/ (*plural* **-ki** *or* **-kis**), **Miccosuki** (*plural* **-ki** *or* **-kis**), **Miccosukee** (*plural* **-kee** *or* **-kees**) *n.* a member of a Native N American people from Florida [Mid-20thC. From the Mikasuki language, the name of a lake in northern Florida where they first settled.] —**Mikasuki** *adj.*

mike /mīk/ *n.* **MICROPHONE** a microphone (*informal*) ■ *vt.* (**mikes, miking, miked**) **FIT WITH MICROPHONE** to supply sb with or transmit sth through a microphone (*informal*) [Early 20thC. Shortening.]

Mike /mīk/, **mike** *n.* the NATO phonetic alphabet code word used to represent the letter 'm' in international radio communications

mikvah /mik vaá, míkvə/, **mikveh, mikve** *n.* among Orthodox Jews, a ritual bath for cleansing or purification, especially before the Sabbath or following menstruation, childbirth, or contact with a dead body [Mid-19thC. Via Yiddish *mikve* from Hebrew *miqweh*, literally 'mass (of water)'.]

mil /mil/ *n.* **1. ONE THOUSANDTH OF INCH** a unit of linear measurement equivalent to 0.0254 mm/one thousandth of an inch, often used in measuring the diameter of wires **2. UNIT OF ANGULAR MEASUREMENT FOR ARTILLERY** a unit of measurement in the military that is the equivalent to the angle subtended by 1/6400th of a circumference. It is used in aiming artillery. **3. ONE MILLILITRE** a unit of volume equivalent to one millilitre or a cubic centimetre [Early 18thC. Shortening of Latin *millesimus* 'thousandth', from *mille* thousand.]

mil. *abbr.* 1. military 2. militia

milady /mi láydi/ (*plural* **-dies**), **miladi** (*plural* **-dies**) *n.* (*archaic*) **1. ARISTOCRATIC BRITISH WOMAN** a British gentlewoman or a woman member of the aristocracy **2. FORM OF ADDRESS FOR GENTLEWOMAN** a form of address for a gentlewoman or female member of the aristocracy [Late 18thC. Via French from English *my lady*.]

milage *n.* = **mileage**

Milan /mi lán/ capital of Milan Province and Lombardy Region, northern Italy. Population: 1,334,171 (1993).

Milanese /míllə neéz/ (*plural* **-nese**) *n.* **1. SB FROM MILAN** sb who was born in or is a resident of the Italian city of Milan **2. MILANESE DIALECT** the dialect of Italian spoken in and around Milan **3. KNITTED FABRIC USED FOR WOMEN'S CLOTHES** a knitted fabric of silk, rayon, or nylon, usually used in making women's clothing —**Milanese** *adj.*

milch cow /mílch-/ *n.* US term **milk cow 1. COW GIVING MILK** a cow that produces milk (*dated*) **2. SOURCE OF EASY INCOME** a source of easily gained income (*informal*) [*Milch* from Old English *-milce* 'a milking', from the same prehistoric Germanic base as *milk*]

mild /mīld/ *adj.* **1. SLIGHT OR NOT HARSH** not strict, severe, or strong ○ *a mild earth tremor* **2. GENTLE AND AMIABLE** gentle, easy-going, and slow to get angry **3.** METEOROL **PLEASANT AND TEMPERATE** pleasant and temperate and not excessively hot or cold ○ *one of the mildest winters on record* **4.** FOOD **LIGHTLY FLAVOURED** lightly flavoured and not strong, hot, spicy, or bitter in taste ○ *a mild sauce* **5. NOT CONTAINING HARMFUL CHEMICALS** feeling soft and gentle and not containing any chemicals that might harm the skin or clothes ○ *mild soap* ■ *n.* BEVERAGES **DRAUGHT BEER** a dark-brown draught beer with a blander taste than bitter [Old English *milde*. Ultimately from an Indo-European base meaning 'soft' that is also the ancestor of English *melt* and *mollify*.] —**mildly** *adv.* —**mildness** *n.*

milden /mīldən/ (**-ens, -ening, -ened**) *vti.* to become or make sb or sth mild or milder (*literary*)

mildew /míl dyoo/ *n.* **1. FUNGAL DISEASE OF PLANTS** a plant disease in which the parasitic fungus is visible as white or grey powdery deposits on the leaves or fruit **2. GREY OR WHITE FUNGUS** a grey or white fungus that grows on walls, paper, leather, and other similar materials in damp conditions ■ *vti.* (**-dews, -dewing, -dewed**) **AFFECT OR BE AFFECTED BY FUNGUS** to become affected or to affect sth with a grey or white fungus [Old English *mildēaw* 'honeydew, nectar'. Ultimately from an Indo-European base meaning 'honey' (source also of English *mellifluous* + an earlier form of DEW). The sense 'kind of fungus' developed as a result of its appearance.] —**mildewed** *adj.* —**mildewy** *adj.*

mild-mannered *adj.* polite and of a gentle disposition

mild steel *n.* a strong steel containing a low proportion of carbon [From its being easily worked]

mile /mīl/ *n.* **1.** MEASURE **UNIT OF DISTANCE** a unit of linear measurement on land, used in English-speaking countries, equivalent to 5,280 ft or 1,760 yd or 1.6 km **2.** MEASURE = **nautical mile 3.** MEASURE **UNIT OF MEASUREMENT COMPARABLE TO MILE** a unit of distance or length used in different historical periods or in non-English-speaking countries, e.g. the Roman mile **4.** ATHLETICS **RACE OVER ONE MILE** a foot race that is a mile long ■ **miles** *npl.* **A LONG WAY** a considerable distance (*informal*) ○ *We're miles from anywhere.* ■ *adv.* **miles EMPHASIZING DEGREE OR EXTENT OF STH** emphasizing how much better, longer, farther, or more difficult sth is (*informal*) ○ *His car's miles better.* [Old English *mīl*, from, ultimately, Latin *milia (passuum)* 'a thousand (paces)', from *mille* 'thousand']

mileage /mílij/, **milage** *n.* **1. DISTANCE IN MILES** a distance or length measured in miles **2. NUMBER OF MILES VEHICLE HAS TRAVELLED** the total number of miles a vehicle has travelled **3. MILES VEHICLE TRAVELS ON FUEL** the total number of miles a vehicle can travel on a specified amount of fuel, such as a gallon or a litre **4. TRAVEL ALLOWANCE AT FIXED RATE** a travel allowance, usually set and paid per mile by sb's employer **5. ADVANTAGE OR USEFULNESS OF STH** the amount of use, advantage, profit, or service that may be obtained from sth (*informal*)

mileometer /mī lómmitər/, **milometer** *n.* a device built into the dashboard of a vehicle that records distance travelled. US term **odometer**

milepost /mīl pōst/ *n.* **1. POST ONE MILE FROM RACE FINISH** a post on a racecourse one mile from the finishing line **2.** *US, Can* **POST SHOWING DISTANCE TO PLACE** a post by the side of a road indicating the number of miles to a certain place, or placed a mile from a similar post

miler /mīlər/ *n.* an athlete or horse that competes in a one-mile race

Miles /mīlz/, **Bernard, Baron** (1907–91) British stage actor and director. He was a member of the Old Vic company and founded the Mermaid Theatre, London, in 1951.

miles gloriosus /meé layz gláwri ṓssəss/ (*plural* **milites gloriosi** /meéli tayz gláwri ō sī/) *n.* an arrogant, bragging, and often cowardly soldier, especially one who appears as a stock character in comedies (*literary*) [From Latin, literally 'boastful soldier', the title of a comedy by Plautus]

Milesian[1] /mī leézi ən/ *n.* **SB FROM MILETUS** sb who was born in or was a citizen of the ancient Ionian city of Miletus ■ *adj.* **OF MILETUS** relating to the ancient Ionian city of Miletus, its people, or its culture [Mid-16thC. Formed from Latin *Milesius*, from Greek *Milēsios*, from *Milētos* 'Miletus'.]

Milesian[2] /mī leézi ən/ *n.* in Irish mythology, a member of a group of people from a royal Spanish family who invaded Ireland about 1300 BC and became the ancestors of the modern Irish [Late 16thC. Named after *Milesius*, the legendary head of the family.]

milestone /mīl stōn/ *n.* **1. STONE SHOWING DISTANCE TO PLACE** a stone by the side of a road indicating the number of miles to a certain place **2. IMPORTANT EVENT** a significant or important event, e.g. in the history of a country or in sb's life

milfoil /míl foyl/ (*plural* **-foils** *or* **-foil**) *n.* **1.** = **yarrow 2.** = **water milfoil** [13thC. Via Old French from Latin *mil(l)efolium*, literally 'thousand-leaf', a translation of Greek *muriophullon*; from the plant's feathery leaves.]

Milford Haven /mílfərd-/ seaport in Pembrokeshire, southwestern Wales. Population: 13,194 (1991).

Milford Sound deep coastal inlet in the southwestern part of the South Island, New Zealand

Milhaud /meé ō/, **Darius** (1892–1974) French composer and teacher. A member of Les Six, his work was marked by polytonality and elements of jazz.

miliaria /mílli áiri ə/ *n.* prickly heat (*technical*) [Early 19thC. Via modern Latin from, ultimately, Latin *miliarius* (see MILIARY).] —**miliarial** *adj.*

miliary /mílli əri/ *adj.* **1. LIKE MILLET SEEDS** resembling millet seeds **2.** DERMAT **HAVING SMALL NODULES OR LESIONS** consisting of or characterized by small nodules or lesions resembling millet seeds [Late 17thC. From Latin *miliarius*, from *milium* 'millet' (source also of English *millet*).]

miliary fever *n.* a highly infectious illness characterized by a high fever, excessive sweating, and a rash of small fluid-filled spots

miliary tuberculosis *n.* an acute form of tuberculosis in which lesions resembling millet seeds occur in the affected organs after bacilli are spread by the blood from one point of infection

milieu /meél yō, meel yṓ/ (*plural* **-lieus** *or* **-lieux**) *n.* the surroundings or environment that sb lives in and is influenced by (*formal*) [Mid-19thC. From French, literally 'middle-place', from *mi* 'mid' (from Latin *medius*) + *lieu* 'place'.]

milit. *abbr.* military

militant /míllitənt/ *adj.* 1. AGGRESSIVE extremely active in the defence or support of a cause, often in ways that other people find unacceptable 2. INVOLVED IN FIGHTING engaged in fighting or warfare ■ *n.* SB AGGRESSIVELY SUPPORTING CAUSE sb who is active in the defence or support of a cause, often using methods that other people find unacceptable [15thC. Directly or via French from Latin *militant-*, the present participle stem of *militare* 'to be a soldier', from the stem *milit-* (see MILITARY).] —**militancy** /míllitənsi/ *n.* —**militantly** *adv.*

Militant Tendency *n.* a former Trotskyite faction of the Labour Party, active in the 1970s and 1980s

militaria /mílli táiri ə/ *n.* military objects such as weapons, medals, and uniforms that are collected as a hobby or for historical interest [Mid-20thC. Formed from MILITARY.]

militarise *vt.* = **militarize**

militarism /míllitərizəm/ *n.* 1. PURSUIT OF MILITARY AIMS the pursuit or celebration of military ideals 2. STRONG INFLUENCE OF MILITARY ON GOVERNMENT a high level of influence by military personnel and ideals in the government or policies of a country or state 3. GOVERNMENT POLICY OF INVESTING IN MILITARY a government policy of investing heavily in and strengthening the armed forces

militarist /míllitərist/ *n.* 1. SUPPORTER OF MILITARISM sb who zealously supports and promotes military ideals 2. STUDENT OF MILITARY HISTORY a student of military history and strategy —**militaristic** /míllitə rístik/ *adj.* —**militaristically** /-rístikli/ *adv.*

militarize /míllitə rīz/ (**-rizes, -rizing, -rized, -rized**), **militarise** (**-rises, -rising, -rised, -rised**) *vt.* 1. EQUIP OR TRAIN FOR WAR to equip or train a person or group of people for war 2. CONVERT FOR MILITARY USE to convert sth such as a piece of land or a building for military use 3. PERSUADE TO SUPPORT MILITARISM to persuade sb to support a policy of aiding and promoting the military —**militarization** /míllitə rī záysh'n/ *n.*

military /míllitəri/ *adj.* 1. OF WAR OR ARMED FORCES relating to matters of war or the armed forces 2. OF ARMY relating to the army, especially as distinguished from the navy or air force 3. TYPICAL OF SOLDIER characteristic of a soldier or the armed forces ■ *n.* ARMED FORCES OR ITS HIGH-RANKING OFFICERS the armed forces or high-ranking members of the armed forces [15thC. Directly or via French *militaire* from Latin *militaris*, from *milit-*, the stem of *miles* 'soldier', of uncertain origin.] —**militarily** *adv.* —**militariness** *n.*

military academy *n.* a secondary school or college that prepares students to enter the military at officer level, and that typically emphasizes rigorous discipline

military attaché *n.* an officer in the armed forces who has been assigned to the official staff of an ambassador in order to gather military intelligence

military honours *npl.* ceremonies or ceremonial duties performed by the armed forces on special occasions such as a royal event or a soldier's funeral

military-industrial complex *n.* *US* the military and the defence industries considered as a combined influence on US foreign and economic policy

military intelligence *n.* information gathered about another country's military equipment and capabilities by means of observation, exchange of information, surveillance, or spying

military law *n.* the legal system, including statutes, regulations, and procedures, that applies to military personnel

military pace *n.* the length of a single marching step, taken to be 76 cm/30 inches in quick time

military police *n.* a police force within the armed forces

militate /mílli tayt/ (**-tates, -tating, -tated**) *vi.* to have an influence, especially a negative one, on sth [Late 16thC. From Latin *militat-*, the past participle stem of *militare* 'to be a soldier, wage war', from the stem *milit-* (see MILITARY).]

militia /mə líshə/ *n.* 1. SOLDIERS WHO ARE ALSO CIVILIANS an army of soldiers who are civilians but take military training and can serve full-time during emergencies 2. RESERVE MILITARY FORCE a reserve army that is not part of the regular armed forces but that can be called up in an emergency 3. UNAUTHORIZED QUASI-MILITARY GROUP an unauthorized group of people who arm themselves and conduct quasi-military training [Late 16thC. From Latin, 'military service, body of soldiers', from the stem *milit-* (see MILITARY).]

militiaman /mə líshəmən/ (*plural* **-men** /-mən/) *n.* a man who serves in a militia

militiawoman /mə líshəwoŏmən/ (*plural* **-en** /-wimmən/) *n.* a woman who serves in a militia

milium /mílli əm/ (*plural* **-a** /-li ə/) *n.* a whitehead (*technical*) [Mid-19thC. From Latin, 'millet' (source of English *millet*); so called from the nodule's size and shape.]

milk /milk/ *n.* 1. BIOL NUTRITIOUS FLUID PRODUCED BY MAMMALS a nutritious white fluid that women and other female mammals produce to feed their young immediately after birth. It is rich in protein, fats, lactose, and vitamins. 2. FOOD DAIRY PRODUCT an opaque white fluid produced by mammals and used by human beings as a food and for other purposes. Milk, especially that produced by cows and goats, is widely used as a beverage, as a cooking ingredient, and to make other dairy products, e.g. butter, cheese, yogurt, and cream. 3. BOT PLANT SAP a white or off-white liquid from a plant, such as the liquid inside a coconut or the sap of certain trees 4. COSMETICS COSMETIC OR PHARMACEUTICAL PRODUCT a cosmetic or pharmaceutical product that is thick and white ○ *cleansing milk* ■ *v.* (**milks, milking, milked**) 1. *vti.* TAKE MILK FROM COW to draw milk for use as a dairy product from the udder of a cow, goat, sheep, or similar mammal manually or by using a special machine 2. *vi.* PRODUCE MILK to yield or supply milk (*refers to a dairy animal*) 3. *vt.* REMOVE VENOM OR SAP FROM to remove the venom from a snake or drain the sap from a tree 4. *vt.* STEAL MONEY IN SLOW STEADY AMOUNTS to steal money from sth such as a fund or an account, in small quantities over a period of time (*informal*) 5. *vt.* EXPLOIT to get as much money or benefit from sth as possible, often in a dishonest or unscrupulous way (*informal disapproving*) [Old English *milc*. Ultimately from an Indo-European base meaning 'to rub, milk' that is also the ancestor of English *emulsion*.]

WORD KEY: CULTURAL NOTE

Under Milk Wood, a play by Welsh poet Dylan Thomas (1953). This play for voices was originally written for radio but is occasionally presented as a stage play. It describes a day in the life of a Welsh fishing village and is noted for its poetic prose, rich humour, and vivid characterization.

Milk /milk/ river that originates in Montana and flows into Alberta, Canada, before joining the Missouri River. Length: 1,006 km/625 mi.

milk-and-water *adj.* weak or bland, especially in expression or sentiment [From the idea of dilution]

milk bar *n.* a café or snack bar that specializes in milkshakes and other milk drinks

milk chocolate *n.* chocolate that has been made with milk and has a sweet creamy taste

milker /mílkər/ *n.* 1. MILK-YIELDING ANIMAL an animal that produces milk used for human consumption, especially a cow 2. PERSON OR MACHINE THAT MILKS ANIMALS a milking machine, or sb who milks animals, especially cows

milk fever *n.* 1. FEVER FOLLOWING CHILDBIRTH mild fever that some new mothers have around the time that they begin to produce breast milk 2. ANIMAL DISEASE a disease in cows, sheep, and goats that have recently given birth, caused by mineral depletion due to milk production. Symptoms include temporary loss of consciousness or ability to move.

milkfish /mílk fish/ (*plural* **-fishes** *or* **-fish**) *n.* a large toothless silver fish that lives in warm parts of the Pacific and Indian oceans and grows up to 1.5 m/5 ft long. It is related to the herring and the salmon. Latin name: *Chanos chanos*. [Early 20thC. *Milk* from its colour.]

milk float *n.* a small, often electrically powered vehicle used for door-to-door deliveries of milk and other dairy products

milk glass *n.* white or translucent whitish glass used in decorative glasswork

milking parlour, **milking shed** *n.* a building with equipment for milking cows, usually part of a farm

milking stool *n.* a short simple three-legged stool of a style used in the past when milking cows

milk leg *n.* painful leg swelling that some women have following childbirth, caused by inflammation and clotting in the femoral vein

milkmaid /mílk mayd/ *n.* a woman or girl who milks cows or does other jobs in a dairy

milkman /mílkmən/ (*plural* **-men** /-mən/) *n.* a man who delivers or sells milk door to door

Milk of Magnesia *tdmk.* a trademark for a milky mixture of magnesium hydroxide and water, used as a laxative and antacid

milk pudding *n.* a dessert consisting of a sweetened boiled or baked mixture of milk and grain, usually rice, semolina, tapioca, or sago

milk punch *n.* a drink consisting of alcoholic spirit, milk, and sometimes sugar or spices

milk round *n.* 1. MILKMAN'S ROUTE a regular route for door-to-door milk deliveries 2. TOUR WITH MANY STOPS a regular tour with frequent stops along the way, especially a tour of universities made by companies looking to recruit graduates

milk run *n.* a routine trip, especially an airline's regular flight or an uneventful sortie made by a military aircraft (*informal*) [From the routine early-morning trips of milk trains]

milk shake, **milkshake** *n.* a cold drink made by whisking or blending milk and flavouring

milk sickness *n.* 1. MED ILLNESS FROM POISONED MILK a now uncommon disease caused by eating dairy products or meat from a cow that has eaten white snakeroot. The symptoms include shaking, weakness, vomiting, and constipation. 2. VET = **trembles**

milk snake *n.* a white or tan nonpoisonous king snake of North America with red, yellow, brown, or black markings. Genus: *Lampropeltis*. [*Milk* from its colour]

milksop /mílk sop/ *n.* a weak-willed or ineffectual man (*dated insult*) [14thC. The original meaning was 'bread soaked in milk'.]

milk stout *n.* a type of sweet dark beer that contains lactose and has no bitter aftertaste

milk sugar *n.* = **lactose**

milk thistle *n.* = **sow thistle** [*Milk* from its milky juice]

milk tooth *n.* a tooth in young mammals including humans that falls out in early life to be replaced by the adult tooth

milk vetch *n.* a plant with yellow, white, or purple flowers and seeds in pods. It is thought by some to increase milk production in goats. Genus: *Astragalus*.

milkweed /mílk weed/ *n.* a flowering plant that secretes a milky latex. The seed pods burst open to release seeds with a tuft of silky hair. Genus: *Asclepias*.

milkweed bug *n.* a black crawling insect with red markings that feeds on the juice of the milkweed and is often used in scientific research. Latin name: *Oncopeltus fasciatus*.

milkwort /mílk wurt/ *n.* a plant with blue, pink, or white flowers with winged petals that in the past was believed to increase milk production in nursing mothers. Genus: *Polygala*.

milky /mílki/ (**-ier, -iest**) *adj.* 1. MILK-COLOURED like milk in colour or consistency 2. CONTAINING MILK full of or containing milk 3. OPAQUE cloudy or translucent, as if milk had been added 4. LACKING COURAGE lacking courage, strength, or steadfastness (*dated*) —**milkily** *adv.* —**milkiness** *n.*

Milky Way *n.* the spiral galaxy to which the Earth and its solar system belong, some of which appears as a faint band of light in the night sky [14thC. A translation of Latin *via lactea* (compare GALAXY).]

mill[1] /mil/ *n.* 1. INDUST FLOUR-MAKING FACTORY a building or group of buildings in which cereal grains are ground to make meal or flour. In previous times this place would have been a windmill or a water mill. 2. INDUST PROCESSING PLANT a building or group of

MILITARY RANKS

Military ranks of the United Kingdom, Australia, and New Zealand

Royal Navy	Royal Marines	British Army	Royal Air Force
Admiral of the Fleet	[1]	Field Marshal	Marshal of the Royal Air Force
Admiral	General	General	Air Chief Marshal
Vice Admiral	Lieutenant General	Lieutenant General	Air Marshal
Rear Admiral	Major General	Major General	Air Vice Marshal
Commodore	Brigadier	Brigadier	Air Commodore
Captain	Colonel	Colonel	Group Captain
Commander	Lieutenant Colonel	Lieutenant Colonel	Wing Commander
Lieutenant Commander	Major	Major	Squadron Leader
Lieutenant	Captain	Captain	Flight Lieutenant
Sub Lieutenant	Lieutenant	Lieutenant	Flying Officer
	Second Lieutenant	Second Lieutenant	Pilot Officer
Midshipman			
*			
Warrant Officer	Warrant Officer (1st, 2nd Class)	Warrant Officer (1st, 2nd Class)	Warrant Officer
Chief Petty Officer	Colour/Staff Sergeant	Colour/Staff Sergeant	Flight Sergeant
			Chief Technician
Petty Officer	Sergeant	Sergeant	Sergeant
Leading Rate[2]	Corporal	Corporal	Corporal
	Lance Corporal	Lance Corporal	
Able Rate[3]	Marine 1st Class	Private	Junior Technician/Senior Aircraftman
Ordinary Rate[4]	Marine 2nd Class		Leading Aircraftman/Aircraftman

Notes

NB Ranks shown are not comparative between United Kingdom, Australia, New Zealand and the United States and Canada

* Indicates the end of officer rank

1 Marine service not applicable for Australia and New Zealand.

2 Leading Rate: also called 'Leading Seaman' in some forces.

3 Able Rate: also called 'Able Seaman' in some forces.

4 Ordinary Rate: also called 'Seaman' in some forces.

Military ranks of the United States and Canada

United States Navy	United States Marine Corps	United States Army	United States Air Force
Fleet Admiral		General of the Army	General of the Air Force
Admiral	General	General	General
Vice Admiral	Lieutenant General	Lieutenant General	Lieutenant General
Rear Admiral Upper Half	Major General	Major General	Major General
Rear Admiral Lower Half	Brigadier General	Brigadier General	Brigadier General
Captain	Colonel	Colonel	Colonel
Commander	Lieutenant Colonel	Lieutenant Colonel	Lieutenant Colonel
Lieutenant Commander	Major	Major	Major
Lieutenant	Captain	Captain	Captain
Lieutenant Junior Grade	Lieutenant	Lieutenant	Lieutenant
Ensign	Second Lieutenant	Second Lieutenant	Second Lieutenant
*			
	Chief Warrant Officer 5	Chief Warrant Officer 5	
Warrant Officer 4	Chief Warrant Officer 4	Chief Warrant Officer 4	
Warrant Officer 3	Chief Warrant Officer 3	Chief Warrant Officer 3	
Warrant Officer 2	Chief Warrant Officer 2	Chief Warrant Officer 2	
	Warrant Officer 1	Warrant Officer 1	
Master Chief Petty Officer of the Navy	Sergeant Major of the Marine Corps	Sergeant Major of the Army	Chief Master Sergeant of the Air Force
Master Chief Petty Officer	Master Gunnery Sergeant	Command Sergeant Major	Chief First Sergeant
	Sergeant Major	Sergeant Major	Chief Master Sergeant
Senior Chief Petty Officer	First Sergeant	First Sergeant	Senior First Sergeant
	Master Sergeant	Master Sergeant	Senior Master Sergeant
Chief Petty Officer	Gunnery Sergeant	Sergeant First Class	First Sergeant
			Master Sergeant
Petty Officer 1st Class	Staff Sergeant	Staff Sergeant	Technical Sergeant
Petty Officer 2nd Class	Sergeant	Sergeant	Staff Sergeant
Petty Officer 3rd Class	Corporal	Corporal	Senior Airman
Seaman	Lance Corporal	Private First Class	Airman First Class
Apprentice	Private First Class	Private	Airman
Recruit	Private	Recruit	Airman Basic

Milkweed

buildings used for processing raw materials and manufacturing a product such as paper, fabric, or steel **3.** INDUST **ROTARY PROCESSING MACHINE** a machine that processes materials, especially one that grinds, presses, or pulverizes raw materials using a rotary motion **4.** SMALL DEVICE FOR GRINDING GRAINS a small device for grinding sth such as coffee, pepper, or salt into granules **5.** INDUST **PROCESSING MACHINE** a machine that repeats a simple manufacturing procedure, e.g. one that stamps or cuts metal **6.** METAL ROLLER a metal roller used for impressing a design on sth such as textiles or bank notes **7.** INDUST = **milling cutter 8.** = **milling machine 9.** STH WORKING REPETITIVELY OR UNTHINKINGLY an institution, person, or process that operates in the same automatic, repetitive, or productive manner as a factory (*disapproving*) ○ *Our family is a regular rumour mill.* **10.** TEDIOUS PROCESS a slow, unpleasant, or tedious process ○ *Getting the book through the editorial mill could take months.* **11.** BOXING FIGHT a boxing match or other fist fight (*archaic slang*) ■ *v.* (**mills, milling, milled**) **1.** *vt.* GRIND GRAIN BY MACHINE to grind grain or seed by machine **2.** *vt.* INDUST MANUFACTURE BY MACHINE to manufacture a product such as paper or fabric from raw materials by machine **3.** *vt.* INDUST PROCESS MATERIALS USING ROTARY MACHINERY to process materials using machinery that grinds, presses, or pulverizes raw materials using a rotary motion **4.** *vt.* INDUST SHAPE METAL BY MACHINE to use a milling cutter or milling machine to cut, shape, or finish metals **5.** *vt.* INDUST PUT RIDGES ON COIN EDGE to cut ridges or grooves into sth metal, especially the edge of a coin **6.** *vt.* MAKE CREAM FROTHY to whisk or shake sth, e.g. cream or chocolate, until it is foamy **7.** *vi.* FIGHT WITH FISTS to fight using the fists (*archaic slang*) [Pre-12thC. From late Latin *molina*, from, ultimately, Latin *molere* 'to grind' (source of English *molar*). Ultimately from an Indo-European base that is also the ancestor of English *meal*.] —**millable** *adj.* ◇ **put sb through the mill** to subject sb to a difficult or unpleasant ordeal (*informal*)

─── **WORD KEY: CULTURAL NOTE** ───
The Mill on the Floss, a novel by writer George Eliot (1860). Set in eastern England in the early 19th century, it describes the intellectual and emotional development of Maggie Tulliver, the daughter of a miller. By contrasting Maggie's inquisitiveness and independent spirit with the dreary conservatism of most of her family and acquaintances, Eliot highlights the obstacles faced by women in English society at the time.

mill about, mill around *vi.* to wander about aimlessly, restlessly, or in confusion

mill² /mil/ *n.* a million pounds, or some other currency (*informal*) ○ *got over two mill from a bank job in London* [Mid-20thC. Shortening of MILLION.]

mill³ /mil/ *n.* a millimetre (*informal*)

mill⁴ /mil/ *n.* a millilitre (*informal*)

Mill /mil/, **James** (1773–1836) British philosopher and economist. Father of John Stuart Mill and an associate of Jeremy Bentham, he was one of the founders of utilitarianism.

Mill, John Stuart (1806–73) British philosopher and economist. The son of James Mill, he was one of the leading intellectuals of his day, and a major proponent of utilitarianism. His most important works include *A System of Logic* (1843) and the essay 'On Liberty' (1859).

Millais /míl ay, mi láy/, **Sir John Everett** (1829–96) British painter. A leading member of the Pre-Raphaelite movement, he painted many historical scenes and worked as a portraitist.

millboard /míl bawrd/ *n.* thick paperboard used in binding books [Early 18thC. Alteration of *milled board*.]

milldam /míl dam/ *n.* a dam built near a mill in order to raise the water level of a stream so that the flow is strong enough to turn a millwheel

milled /mild/ *adj.* **1.** INDUST **PROCESSED OR GROUND IN MILL** processed or ground in a mill especially in an industrial context **2.** RIDGED with grooves or ridges cut by machine **3.** INDUST **PRESSED FLAT** pressed flat by rollers **4.** INDUST **POLISHED** polished by a machine (*archaic*)

millefeuille /meel fő i, meel fő i/ (*plural* **-feuilles**) *n.* a dessert or pastry consisting of several layers of puff pastry with a filling of cream and jam, topped with icing sugar or icing [Late 19thC. From French, literally 'a thousand leaves'.]

millefiori /mílli fi áwri/ *n.* decorative glassware made by cutting and arranging cross sections of fused glass rods of varied colour and thickness [Mid-19thC. From Italian, literally 'a thousand flowers'.]

millefleurs /meel flúr/ *adj.* covered with a design of small flowers or plants [Early 20thC. From French, literally 'a thousand flowers'.]

millenarian /mílli náiri ən/, **millenary** /mi lénnəri, míllinəri/ (*plural* **-ies**) *adj.* **1.** CHR **RELATING TO JESUS CHRIST'S SECOND COMING** relating to or believing in Jesus Christ's Second Coming, a final conflict between good and evil, the end of the world, or similar doctrines, especially based on the book of Revelation **2.** RELATING TO FUTURE UTOPIA relating to or expressing belief in the coming of some future utopian age **3.** RELATING TO END OF WORLD relating to or suggesting the end of the world **4.** RELATING TO 1,000 relating to units of 1,000, especially 1,000 years [Mid-17thC. Formed from Latin *millenarius*, from, ultimately, Latin *mille* 'thousand'.] —**millenarian** *n.* —**millenarianism** *n.*

millenarianism /mílli náiri ənizəm/ *n.* **1.** CHR **BELIEF IN JESUS CHRIST'S SECOND COMING** belief in Jesus Christ's Second Coming, a final conflict between good and evil, the end of the world, or similar doctrines, especially based on the book of Revelation **2.** BELIEF IN COMING UTOPIA belief in a future utopian age, especially one created through revolution **3.** BELIEF IN END OF WORLD belief that the end of the world is near

millenary /mi lénnəri, míllinəri/ *adj.* = millenarian ■ *n.* **1.** (*plural* **-ies**) = millennium *n.* **1 2.** = millenarian [Mid-16thC. From Latin *millenarius* (see MILLENARIAN).] —**millenarism** /míllinərizəm/ *n.*

mill end *n.* either end of a roll of fabric or carpet that is finished, rather than cut

millennium /mi lénni əm/ (*plural* **-ums** *or* **-a** /-ni ə/) *n.* **1.** 1,000 YEARS a period of 1,000 years, especially a period that begins or ends in a year that is a multiple of 1000 **2.** CHR **PROPHESIED RULE BY JESUS CHRIST** the thousand-year period of peace on earth that, according to one interpretation of prophecies in the book of Revelation, will follow the Second Coming of Jesus Christ **3.** HOPED-FOR UTOPIAN AGE an imagined future utopian period of joy, peace, and justice, especially one created through revolution **4.** THOUSANDTH ANNIVERSARY a thousand-year anniversary, especially the one in the year 2000 [Mid-17thC. From modern Latin, formed from Latin *mille* 'thousand' + *annus* 'year' (see ANNUAL).] —**millennial** *adj.* —**millennialism** *n.* —**millennialist** *n.* —**millennially** *adv.*

─── **WORD KEY: USAGE** ───
See Usage note at **century**.

millennium bug *n.* the problem posed by the year 2000 for computer software coding dates using only the last two digits of each year (*informal*)

Millennium Dome *n.* a large structure by the River Thames in Greenwich, London, designed by Richard Rogers Partnership to celebrate the year 2000. The world's largest dome, more than 1 km/half a mile in circumference, it houses commercial and educational facilities.

millepore /mílli pawr/ *n.* a kind of coral that forms white or yellow reefs [Mid-18thC. From modern Latin

Millennium Dome: Model by Richard Rogers Partnership

Millepora, genus name, from Latin *mille* 'thousand' + *porus* 'pore' (see PORE).]

miller /míllər/ *n.* **1.** MILL-OPERATOR sb who owns, manages, or operates a mill **2.** MACHINE THAT MILLS a machine that mills materials **3.** MOTH WITH POWDERY WINGS any of various moths whose wings have a powdery appearance

Arthur Miller

Miller /míllər/, **Arthur** (*b.* 1915) US playwright. He won a Pulitzer Prize for his tragedy *Death of a Salesman* (1949). His play *The Crucible* (1953) was a veiled critique of the House Un-American Activities committee. His second wife was the film actor Marilyn Monroe.

Miller, George (*b.* 1945) Australian film director. His greatest successes included the *Mad Max* series of films (1979, 1981, 1985), and *The Witches of Eastwick* (1987).

Miller, Glenn (1904–44) US bandleader and composer. Leader of a big-band orchestra of the late 1930s and early 1940s, he was noted for swing music such as 'In the Mood' (1939). Full name **Alton Glenn Miller**

Miller, Harry M. (*b.* 1934) New Zealand-born Australian entrepreneur. He was a producer of musicals and concerts, and a consultant to media personalities. Full name **Harry Maurice Miller**

Henry Miller: Photographed in 1932 by Brassaï

Miller, Henry (1891–1980) US writer. His novels *Tropic of Cancer* (1934) and *Tropic of Capricorn* (1939) are sexually explicit and were banned in the United States. Full name **Henry Valentine Miller**

Miller, Hugh (1802–56) British geologist. He was the author of *The Old Red Sandstone* (1841) and *Footprints of the Creator* (1849), which stimulated popular interest in geology.

millerite /mílla rīt/ *n.* nickel sulphide in the form of long wiry crystals. It is one of the sources of nickel. Formula: NiS. [Mid-19thC. Named after W. H. *Miller* (1801–80), English mineralogist.]

miller's thumb *n.* a small, flat, spiny fish found in European and North American fresh waters. Genus: *Cottus*. [From the shape of its body, alluding to the proverbial distrust of millers' methods of measurement]

millesimal /mi léssim'l/ *adj.* RELATING TO THOUSANDTHS divided by one thousand or relating to thousandths ■ *n.* THOUSANDTH PART a thousandth part of sth [Early 18thC. Formed from Latin *millesimus* 'thousandth', from *mille* 'thousand'.] —**millesimally** *adv.*

millet /míllit/ *n.* **1.** CEREAL PLANT a fast-growing annual cereal plant grown for its seed and used for hay. Latin name: *Panicum miliaceum*. **2.** GRAIN the pale shiny grain of the millet plant, used for food and as birdseed **3.** GRASS PLANT a grass that is similar or related to millet and is grown for its grain, e.g. pearl millet [15thC. Via Old French from, ultimately, Latin *milium*.]

Millet /mée ay/, **Jean-François** (1814–75) French painter. Strong draughtsmanship and mellow colours characterize his realistic scenes of rural life.

mill finish *n.* a particularly smooth surface on paper, made by a machine

milli- *prefix.* one thousandth (10 −3) ○ *milliroentgen*. Symbol **m** [From Latin, formed from *mille* 'thousand']

milliampere /mílli ám peer, -ám pair/ *n.* a unit of electric current equal to one thousandth of an ampere

milliard /mílli aard/ *n.* an obsolete word for one thousand million, now called a billion (*dated*) [Late 18thC. Via French from Old French *miliart*, from *milion* (see MILLION).]

milliary /mílli əri/ *adj.* indicating or marking a distance of one Roman mile, measured as one thousand paces [Mid-17thC. From Latin *milliarius*, from *mille* 'thousand' (see MILE).]

millibar /mílli baar/ *n.* a unit of atmospheric pressure equal to one thousandth of a bar

millicurie /mílli kyoori/ *n.* a unit of radioactivity equal to one thousandth of a curie

millieme /meel yém/ *n.* **1.** MINOR UNIT OF EGYPTIAN AND SUDANESE CURRENCY minor unit of currency in Egypt and Sudan equal to one thousandth of a pound. See table at **currency 2.** = **millime** [Early 20thC. From French *millième* (see MILLIME).]

millifarad /mílli fərəd, -fa rad/ *n.* a unit of electrical capacitance equal to one thousandth of a farad

milligram /mílli gram/ *n.* a unit of mass and weight equal to one thousandth of a gram

millihenry /mílli henri/ (*plural* **-ries**) *n.* a unit of electrical inductance equal to one thousandth of a henry

millilambert /mílli lambərt/ *n.* a unit of luminance equal to one thousandth of a lambert

milliliter *n.* US = **millilitre**

millilitre /mílli leetər/ *n.* a unit of volume equal to one thousandth of a litre

millime /mee leém, milleem/, **millieme** /meel yém/ *n.* a minor unit of currency in Tunisia equal to one thousandth of a dinar. See table at **currency** [Mid-20thC. Via French *millième* 'thousandth' from Latin *millesimus*, from *mille* 'thousand'.]

millimeter *n.* US = **millimetre**

millimetre /mílli meetər/ *n.* a unit of length equal to one thousandth of a metre

millimicron /mílli mī kron/ *n.* an obsolete name for a unit of length equal to one millionth of a millimetre, now called a nanometre (*dated*)

millimole /mílli mōl/ *n.* a unit used to measure the amount of a chemical substance, equal to one thousandth of a mole —**millimolar** *adj.*

milline /míl līn, mil lín/ *n.* **1.** UNIT OF ADVERTISING COPY a unit of advertising copy equal to one column line in agate type in one million copies of a newspaper or magazine **2.** = **milline rate** [Late 20thC. Blend of MILLION and LINE.]

milliner /míllinər/ *n.* sb who designs, makes, or sells hats for women [Mid-16thC. Alteration of earlier *Milaner* 'importer of fancy fabrics and wares from Milan, Italy'.]

milline rate *n.* the cost per unit of advertising copy

millinery /míllinəri/ *n.* **1.** WOMEN'S HATS hats and other accessories for women, sold by a milliner **2.** HAT BUSINESS the design, manufacture, or sale of women's hats

milling /mílling/ *n.* the ridged edge of a coin

milling cutter *n.* a rotary tool used for cutting, shaping, and finishing metal objects

milling machine *n.* a machine fitted with milling cutters to cut, shape, or finish metal objects

million /míllyən/ *n.* **1.** THOUSAND THOUSAND a thousand thousand (10⁶) **2.** LARGE NUMBER a very large number (*often used in the plural*) **3.** MILLION UNITS OF A CURRENCY a million units of a currency, especially dollars or pounds **4.** FIFTH DIGIT TO LEFT OF DECIMAL the fifth digit to the left of the decimal point in the decimal number system ○ *In the number 54321, the 5 is in the millions place.* ■ **millions** *npl.* ORDINARY PEOPLE ordinary people, considered collectively ○ *entertainment for the millions* [14thC. Via French from obsolete Italian *millione*, literally 'great thousand', from *mille* 'thousand' (source of English *mile* and *milli-*).] —**million** *adj.*

millionaire /míllyə náir/ *n.* sb whose net worth or income is more than one million pounds, or other unit of currency (*often used before a noun*) [Early 19thC. From French, where it was formed from *million* (see MILLION).]

millionairess /míllyə náirəss, míllyə náir ess/ *n.* a wealthy woman whose net worth or income is more than one million dollars, pounds, or other unit of currency

millionth /míllyənth/ *n.* one of a million equal parts of sth —**millionth** *adj.*

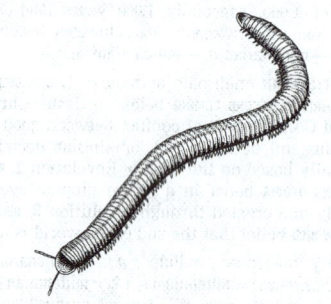

Millipede

millipede /mílli peed/, **millepede** *n.* a small plant-eating arthropod with a tubular body made up of segments. Most segments have two pairs of legs. Class: Diplopoda. [Early 17thC. From Latin *millipeda* 'woodlouse', literally 'with a thousand feet', from the stem *ped-* 'foot' (see PEDAL).]

millisecond /mílli sekənd/ *n.* a unit of time equal to one thousandth of a second

millivolt /mílli vōlt/ *n.* a unit of electrical voltage or potential difference equal to one thousandth of a volt. Symbol **mV**

milliwatt /mílli wot/ *n.* a unit of electrical power equal to one thousandth of a watt. Symbol **mW**

millpond /míl pond/ *n.* a pond created by damming a stream in order to create a flow of water to turn a millwheel

millrace /míll rayss/ *n.* **1.** WATER IN MILLWHEEL the stream of water that flows through a millwheel, making it turn **2.** CHANNEL PROVIDING WATER FOR MILLWHEEL a channel that directs water to and from a millwheel

millrun /míll run/ *n.* **1.** TEST OF MINERAL a test to determine the quality of a mineral or the mineral content of an ore **2.** MINERAL FROM TEST a quantity or quality of mineral yielded from a millrun test **3.** = **millrace**

Mills /milz/, **Sir John** (*b.* 1908) British actor. His early roles were those of military or naval servicemen. He went on to play a great diversity of characters.

Mills and Boon /milz ənd boón/ *n.* a romantic novel published by, or of the kind typically published by,

the firm of Mills and Boon, publishers of popular romantic fiction

Mills bomb *n.* an oval hand grenade [Early 20thC. Named after the English engineer Sir William *Mills* (1856–1932), who invented it.]

millstone /míl stōn/ *n.* **1.** GRAIN-GRINDING STONE either of two large circular stones used to grind grain in a mill **2.** BURDENSOME RESPONSIBILITY a great burden or responsibility

millstream /míl streem/ *n.* **1.** STREAM SUPPLYING MILL a stream from which the water turns a millwheel **2.** = **millrace** *n.* 1

millwheel /míl weel/ *n.* a wheel that powers a mill, typically turned by a flow of water

millwright /míl rīt/ *n.* sb who designs, builds, or maintains mills or mill machinery

Milne /miln/, **A. A.** (1882–1956) British writer. He created the character Winnie the Pooh to amuse his son Christopher Robin, and wrote four much-loved collections of children's poems and stories, including *Now We Are Six* (1927) and *The House at Pooh Corner* (1928). Full name **Alan Alexander Milne**

milo /mílō/ (*plural* **-los**) *n.* a variety of sorghum grain that resembles millet, known for growing early and resisting drought [Late 19thC. Origin uncertain: possibly from Sesotho *maili*.]

milometer *n.* = **mileometer**

milord /mi láwrd/ *n.* **1.** BRITISH ARISTOCRAT a British gentleman or member of the aristocracy **2.** FORM OF ADDRESS FOR A GENTLEMAN a form of address for a gentleman or member of the aristocracy [Late 16thC. Via French, from English *my lord*.]

Milošević /mi lóssəvich/, **Slobodan** (*b.* 1941) Yugoslavian national leader. After the breakup of the former Yugoslavia, he became president of Serbia (1989–97) and the Federal Republic of Yugoslavia (1997).

Miłosz /mée losh, mée wosh/, **Czeslaw** (*b.* 1911) Lithuanian-born US writer. He defected from communist Poland to the West in 1951, and wrote poetry, fiction, translations, and essays, often treating the relationship between culture, morality, and politics. He won the Nobel Prize in literature in 1980.

milreis /míl rayss, mil ráysh/ (*plural* **-reis**) *n.* an obsolete Portuguese and Brazilian unit of currency and coin equal to one thousand reis [Late 16thC. From Portuguese, formed from *mil* 'thousand' + *real* 'real' (a unit of currency).]

milt /milt/ *n.* **1.** FISH SEMEN the semen and seminal fluid of a fish **2.** FISH TESTIS the testis or sperm duct of a fish [Old English *milte* 'spleen', later reinforced by Middle Dutch *milte* 'milt']

milter /míltər/ *n.* a fertile male fish during the mating season

Milton /míltən/, **John** (1608–74) English poet. His poems rank among the greatest treasures of English literature, and include the epic narrative of Adam and Eve's banishment from Paradise, *Paradise Lost* (1667). During the Civil Wars, he wrote powerful polemics that championed religious and civil liberty. —**Miltonian** /mil tóni ən/ *adj.* —**Miltonic** /mil tónnik/ *adj.*

Milton Keynes /míltən keénz/ town in Buckinghamshire, England, designated a New Town in 1967. Population: 192,900 (1995).

Milwaukee /mil wáwki/ the largest city in Wisconsin, located in the southeastern corner of the state. Population: 617,044 (1994). —**Milwaukeean** *adv., n.*

mim /mim/ *adj.* Scotland excessively or affectedly shy or prim [Late 16thC. An imitation of the gesture of pursing one's lips.]

Mimas /mí mass, mímass/ *n.* one of the satellites of Saturn, the nearest to the planet

mime /mīm/ *n.* **1.** ACTING USING ONLY GESTURE AND ACTION a style of performance in which people act out situations or portray characters using only gesture and action (*often used before a noun*) **2.** PERFORMER WHO USES MIME a performer who relies on gesture, facial expression, and action rather than using the voice **3.** THEATRICAL PERFORMANCE IN MIME a theatrical piece performed with gesture, facial expression, and action rather than with words **4. ANCIENT FARCE** in ancient Greek and Roman theatre, a lewd comedy including dialogue, dance, and gesture ■ *vti.* **(mimes, miming, mimed) 1. EXPRESS STH IN MIME** to express sth or act it out using gestures and facial expressions only **2. MOUTH WORDS** to mouth the words to a song silently [Early 17thC. Via Latin *mimus* from Greek *mimos* 'imitator, mimic' (source of English *mimic*).] —**mimer** *n.*

mimeograph /mímmi ə graaf, -graf/ *n.* **1. mimeograph, Mimeograph COPYING MACHINE** a machine that prints copies onto paper from an inked stencil that is rotated on a cylinder across the pages **2. mimeograph, Mimeograph MIMEOGRAPHED COPY** a copy made on a mimeograph ■ *vt.* **(-graphs, -graphing, -graphed) MAKE COPIES USING MIMEOGRAPH** to make a copy of a document using a mimeograph [Late 19thC. Originally a trademark, coined from Greek *mimeisthai* (see MIMESIS) + -GRAPH.]

mimesis /mi méessiss, mī-/ *n.* **1. ART'S IMITATION OF LIFE** the imitation of life or nature in the techniques and subject matter of art and literature **2.** BIOL = **mimicry** *n.* 2 **3.** MED **DISEASE SYMPTOMS IN HEALTHY PERSON** the occurrence of a disease's symptoms in sb who does not have the disease, often psychosomatically caused **4. RHETORICAL DEVICE** the rhetorical use of what sb else might have said [Mid-16thC. From Greek *mimēsis*, from *mimeisthai* 'to imitate', from *mimos* 'mime'.]

mimetic /mi méttik, mī-/, **mimetical** /-méttik'l, -/ *adj.* **1. IMITATING STH** imitating sth, or relating to imitation, e.g. in artistic or literary mimesis **2.** BIOL, MED **RELATING TO BIOLOGICAL MIMICRY** relating to mimicry in animals and plants [Mid-17thC. From Greek *mimētikos*, from *mimēsis* (see MIMESIS).] —**mimetically** *adv.*

mimic /mímmik/ *vt.* **(-ics, -icking, -icked) 1. MOCK SB THROUGH IMITATION** to make fun of sb by imitating him or her in an exaggerated way **2. IMITATE SB** to imitate sb, or copy sb's voice, gestures, or appearance **3. COPY STH** to resemble sth in a way that seems like a deliberate copy ○ *houses with façades that mimic the Tudor style* **4.** BIOL **RESEMBLE OTHER SPECIES** to take on the appearance of another plant or animal, e.g. when a harmless animal evolves to look like a poisonous one to discourage predators ■ *n.* **SB WHO IMITATES OTHERS** sb who imitates others, especially for comic effect ■ *adj.* **1. RELATING TO MIMICRY** relating to mime, mimicry, or imitation **2. SIMULATED** simulated or pretend (*literary*) **3. RESEMBLING STH** imitating or resembling sth (*literary*) [Late 16thC. Via Latin *mimicus* from Greek *mimikos*, from *mimos* (see MIME).] —**mimicker** *n.*

WORD KEY: SYNONYMS

See Synonyms at *imitate*.

mimicry /mímmikri/ *n.* **1. ART OF IMITATION** the imitating of other people's voices, gestures, or appearance, often for comic effect **2.** BIOL **SIMILARITY OF APPEARANCE IN NATURE** a plant's or animal's resemblance to another species or to a feature of its natural surroundings, evolved as protection from predators **3.** BIRDS **BIRDS' IMITATION OF OTHERS' CALLS** the ability of some birds to imitate the songs of other species and incorporate them into their own repertoire, especially developed in the mockingbird family

miminy-piminy *adj.* = **niminy-piminy** [Early 19thC. Alteration of NIMINY-PIMINY, perhaps modelled on MIM.]

Mimir /mée meer/ *n.* in Norse mythology, the god of wisdom, a giant water demon who was said to reside at and drink from the well of wisdom at Yggdrasil

mimosa /mi mṓzə, mi mṓssə/ *n.* **1. FLOWERING TREE WITH SENSITIVE LEAVES** a tree or shrub that grows in warm climates and has round clusters of white, yellow, or pink flowers and leaves that are sensitive to touch. Genus: *Mimosa.* **2.** = **silk tree** [Mid-18thC. From modern Latin, genus name, from Latin *mimus* 'imitator' (see MIME), because its leaves seem to flinch when touched, mimicking a recoiling animal.]

mimulus /mímmyŏoləss/ (*plural* **-lus**) *n.* a plant that grows in temperate climates in a number of varieties with yellow or red flowers. Genus: *Mimulus.* US term **monkey flower** [Mid-18thC. From modern Latin, genus name, literally 'little mime', from Latin *mimus* (see MIME); perhaps from its mask-like flowers.]

min /min/ *n.* a minute or a short while (*informal*) [Late 19thC. Shortening of MINUTE.]

min. *abbr.* **1.** mineralogical **2.** mineralogy **3.** MEASURE minim **4.** minimum **5.** *US* minister **6.** minor **7.** minute

Min. *abbr.* **1.** Minister **2.** Ministry

mina /mínə/ (*plural* **-nae** /-nee/ *or* **-nas**) *n.* a unit of weight and money used in ancient Greece and Asia, usually equal to one sixtieth of a talent [Late 16thC. Via Latin and Greek from Akkadian.]

minacious /mi náyshəss/ *adj.* menacing or threatening (*literary*) [Mid-17thC. Formed from the Latin stem *minac-*, from *minari* 'to threaten' (see MENACE).] —**minaciously** *adv.* —**minaciousness** *n.* —**minacity** /mi nássəti/ *n.*

Minamata disease /mìnnə maátə-/ *n.* a severe degenerative disease of the nervous system caused by mercury contamination, especially through eating mercury-tainted seafood [Mid-20thC. Named after *Minamata*, a town in Japan.]

Minaret

minaret /mínnə ret, mínnə rét/ *n.* a tall slender tower attached to a mosque, from which the muezzin calls the faithful to prayer [Late 17thC. Via French and Turkish from Arabic *manāra* 'lighthouse, minaret'.]

Minas Basin /mínəss-/ tidal inlet on the coast of Nova Scotia, southeastern Canada. It is connected by the Bay of Fundy. Length: 80 km/50 mi.

Minas Gerais /méenaz zhay ráyəss/ inland state in eastern Brazil. Much of its terrain is mountainous. Capital: Belo Horizonte. Population: 15,731,961 (1991). Area: 586,624 sq. km/226,497 sq. mi.

minatory /mínnətəri/, **minatorial** /mínnə táwri əl/ *adj.* menacing or threatening (*literary*) [Mid-16thC. From late Latin *minatorius*, from Latin *minari* 'to threaten' (see MENACE).] —**minatorially** /mínnə táwri əli/ *adv.* —**minatorily** /mínnə táwrəli/ *adv.*

mince /minss/ *v.* **(minces, mincing, minced) 1.** *vt.* **SHRED FOOD** to chop or grind meat or other food into very small pieces. US term **grind 2.** *vt.* **USE TACT** to use words or deal with matters delicately, so as not to offend or upset others ○ *She did not mince her words.* **3.** *vti.* **WALK DAINTILY** to walk with small light steps in an affectedly dainty way **4.** *vti.* **SPEAK DAINTILY** to speak, or say sth, in an affectedly dainty way ■ *n.* **FINELY SHREDDED MEAT** finely shredded or ground meat, especially beef [14thC. Via Old French *mincier* from assumed Vulgar Latin *minutiare*, from *minutus* 'very small' (see MINUTE).] —**mincer** *n.*

mincemeat /minss meet/ *n.* **1. FRUIT AND SPICE MIXTURE** a mixture of spiced and finely chopped fruits, such as apples and raisins, usually cooked in pies **2. MINCED MEAT** minced meat [Mid-17thC. Alteration of *minced meat.*] ◇ **make mincemeat of sb** *or* **sth** to defeat sb or sth thoroughly (*informal*)

mince pie *n.* an individual pie filled with mincemeat and served hot or cold, especially as a Christmas speciality

Minch, The /minch/, **Minches, The** /mínchiz/ sea channel in northwestern Scotland, separating the Outer Hebrides from the Inner Hebrides and the mainland. It is divided into the North Minch and the Little Minch.

Mincha /mínkhə, min khaa/, **Minchah** *n.* a daily Jewish prayer said in the afternoon [Early 19thC. From Hebrew *minḥāh*, literally 'offering'.]

mincing /mínssing/ *adj.* affectedly dainty or prim —**mincingly** *adv.*

mind /mīnd/ *n.* **1. SEAT OF THOUGHT AND MEMORY** the centre of consciousness that generates thoughts, feelings, ideas, and perceptions and stores knowledge and memories **2. THINKING CAPACITY** the capacity to think, understand, and reason (*often used in combination*) **3. CONCENTRATION** concentration, or the ability to concentrate ○ *My mind was wandering.* **4. WAY OF THINKING** an opinion or personal way of thinking about sth ○ *I've changed my mind about going with you.* **5. STATE OF THOUGHT OR FEELING** the state of thought or feeling that is regarded as normal **6. DESIRE** the desire or intention to act or behave in a specified way ○ *After such insults, I had a mind to leave right then.* **7. INTELLECTUAL PERSON** sb considered in terms of his or her intellect or intelligence ○ *Einstein was among the greatest minds of the modern era.* **8. GENERAL TYPE OF PERSON** a pattern of thinking or feeling that is typical of a particular group ○ *Who knows what goes through the criminal mind?* **9.** PHILOS **NONMATERIAL THINGS** in the philosophy of Descartes, all things that are not matter ■ *v.* **(minds, minding, minded) 1.** *vt.* **PAY ATTENTION TO** to pay attention to sth, especially so as to avoid danger or an accident ○ *Mind your step!* **2.** *vt.* **CONTROL** to remain aware of the need to control sth **3.** *vti.* **OBJECT TO** to object to sb or sth ○ *Do you mind if we leave early?* **4.** *vt.* **TEMPORARILY WATCH OVER** to watch over and look after sb or sth, usually for a short time ○ *Will you mind the dog over the weekend?* **5.** *vt.* **OBEY** to listen to and obey sb ○ *Be sure to mind your father while I'm away.* **6.** *vt.* **REMEMBER** to remember sth (*regional*) ○ *Mind what I told you.* **7.** *vt. Scotland, US* **REMIND** to remind sb of sth (*regional*) **8.** *vt. US* **TAKE NOTE OF STH** to notice or perceive sth (*regional*) ○ *Mind the new detour signs or you'll get lost.* **9.** *vt. Scotland* **REMIND SB** to remind sb about sth ○ *That minds me of what we came here for in the first place.* [Old English *gemynd*. Ultimately from an Indo-European base meaning 'to think', which is also the ancestor of English *mental, amnesia, mania,* and *monitor.*] ◇ **do you mind?** used to show that you object to sth sb is doing (*informal*) ◇ **mind you** used to qualify sth you have just said (*informal*)

mind out *vi.* to avoid sth by keeping watch or being careful

mind-altering *adj.* changing perceptions, moods, or thought patterns

Mindanao /mində nów/ island in the southern Philippines, the largest after Luzon. Population: 14,536,000 (1990). Area: 94,630 sq. km/36,537 sq. mi.

mind-bending *adj.* **1. OVERWHELMING** mentally overwhelming, e.g. because of great size or complexity (*informal*) **2. ALTERING PERCEPTIONS** changing perceptions, moods, or thought patterns (*dated informal*) —**mind-bendingly** *adv.*

mind-blowing *adj.* (*informal*) **1. EXTREMELY EXCITING** extremely exciting, surprising, or shocking **2. ALTERING PERCEPTIONS** changing perceptions, moods, or thought patterns —**mind-blower** *n.*

mind-body problem *n.* the philosophical question of whether the mind is part of the body or separate from it, first formulated as a problem by the French philosopher René Descartes

mind-boggling *adj.* mentally overwhelming, e.g. because of great size or complexity (*informal*) —**mind-bogglingly** *adv.*

mind candy *n. US* sth that is entertaining but not intellectually demanding (*slang*) [Late 20thC]

minded /míndid/ *adj.* inclined to do a particular thing or act in a particular way (*formal*)

minder /míndər/ *n.* **1. CHILD MINDER** a child minder **2. BODYGUARD** a bodyguard or assistant who accompanies and protects a public figure, celebrity, or criminal (*informal*) **3. ASSISTANT** a public-relations assistant to someone in public life (*informal*)

mind-expanding *adj.* **1. ALTERING PERCEPTIONS** changing perceptions, moods, or thought patterns **2. EXPANDING KNOWLEDGE** expanding knowledge and awareness

mindful /míndf'l/ *adj.* paying attention or taking care —**mindfully** *adv.* —**mindfulness** *n.*

WORD KEY: SYNONYMS

See Synonyms at *aware*.

mind game *n.* a psychologically manipulative and deceptive practice intended to deceive or confuse sb (*informal*)

mindless /mīndləss/ *adj.* **1. UNINTELLIGENT** requiring or displaying very little intelligence **2. PURPOSELESS** having no apparent purpose or rational cause **3. UNCONCERNED** not careful or concerned —**mindlessly** *adv.* —**mindlessness** *n.*

mind-numbing *adj.* inspiring no interest or thought, especially because of dullness or repetitiveness —**mind-numbingly** *adv.*

Mindoro Island /min dáwrō īlənd/ island in the western Philippines. Area: 9,738 sq. km/3,760 sq. mi.

mind reader *n.* sb who can sense the thoughts of others without being told what they are

mindset /mīnd set/ *n.* a set of beliefs or a way of thinking that determine sb's behaviour and outlook

mind's eye *n.* the mind as a place where visual images are conjured up from memory or imagination

mine[1] /mīn/ *n.* **1. HOLE IN EARTH FOR EXTRACTING MINERALS** an excavated area from which minerals, often in the form of ore, are extracted **2. MINERAL-EXCAVATING BUSINESS** the industrial and commercial buildings, machinery, and personnel used to work a mine **3. MINERAL DEPOSIT** an area within or on the surface of the earth where there is a deposit of ore, minerals, or precious stones **4. SOURCE** a rich source of sth, especially information **5.** ARMS **HIDDEN EXPLOSIVE** an explosive device that is concealed underground or underwater to be detonated by nearby people or vehicles **6.** MIL **TUNNEL UNDER ENEMY TERRITORY** a tunnel dug under enemy territory in order to gain entry, undermine fortifications, or lay explosives **7.** ZOOL **INSECT BURROW** a tunnel made by a burrowing insect or larva, especially in a plant leaf ■ *v.* **(mines, mining, mined) 1.** *vti.* MINING **REMOVE MINERALS** to extract minerals from the earth **2.** *vt.* ARMS **LAY EXPLOSIVE MINES IN** to place mines throughout an area of ground or water **3.** *vt.* **DIG TUNNEL BENEATH** to dig a tunnel under the surface of the earth **4.** *vt.* **MAKE USE OF RESOURCE** to make use of a particular resource ○ *Generations of scholars mined the archives.* **5.** *vt.* **UNDERMINE** to undermine (*archaic*) [14thC. Via Old French from assumed Vulgar Latin *mina*, of uncertain origin: probably from Celtic.] —**minable** *adj.*

mine[2] /mīn/ *pron.* **INDICATES POSSESSION** refers to sth that belongs or relates to the speaker or writer ○ *He put on his coat, and told me to put mine on.* ○ *She was a friend of mine.* ■ *det.* **MY** belonging to or associated with me (*archaic; used before a vowel*) ○ *By mine eyes and by mine ears I swear.* [Old English *min*. Ultimately from an Indo-European word meaning 'me', which is also the ancestor of English *me* and *my*.]

mine detector *n.* an instrument used for finding explosive mines hidden under the ground or in water

mine dump *n. S Africa* a hill-like heap of waste material from mines, especially gold mines

minefield /mīn feeld/ *n.* **1. AREA CONTAINING EXPLOSIVE MINES** an area of land or sea in which explosive mines have been placed **2. HAZARDOUS SITUATION** a situation in which great care is needed to avoid the many hazards that exist

minelayer /mīn layər/ *n.* a ship fitted with equipment for laying explosive mines under water

miner /mīnər/ *n.* **1. SB WORKING IN MINE** sb who works in a mine digging for minerals, especially coal **2. MINERAL-EXTRACTING MACHINE** a machine that extracts minerals, especially coal, from the ground **3.** INSECTS = **leaf miner 4.** *Aus* BIRDS **HONEY-EATER BIRD** any of several birds in the honey-eater family. Genus: *Manorina*. **5. SB LAYING EXPLOSIVE MINES** sb whose task is to place and set explosive mines

mineral /mínnərəl/ *n.* **1. INORGANIC SUBSTANCE IN NATURE** an inorganic solid substance that occurs naturally in rocks and in the ground and has its own characteristic appearance and chemical composition **2. MINED SUBSTANCE** any naturally occurring substance that is mined or extracted from the ground **3. MATTER NOT ANIMAL OR VEGETABLE** non-technically anything that is not made of animal or vegetable matter **4. INORGANIC NUTRITIVE SUBSTANCE** an inorganic substance that must be ingested by animals or plants in order to remain healthy **5.** BEVERAGES **SOFT DRINK** a soft drink (*dated; usually used in plural*) ■ *adj.* **CONTAINING MINERALS** made of or containing minerals [15thC. Via medieval Latin *minerale* from, ultimately, Old French *miniere* 'mine', from *mine* (see MINE[1]).]

mineralize /mínnərə līz/ **(-izes, -izing, -ized), mineralise (-ises, -ising, -ised)** *v.* **1.** *vt.* **IMPREGNATE STH WITH MINERALS** to impregnate sth, e.g. water or organic matter, with minerals **2.** *vti.* **MAKE OR BECOME MINERAL** to transform organic matter into a mineral, as happens in petrification, or to be transformed in this way —**mineralizable** *adj.* —**mineralization** /mínnərə lī záysh'n/ *n.*

mineralocorticoid /mínnərəlō káwrti koyd/ *n.* a hormone **(corticosteroid)**, e.g. aldosterone, that controls electrolyte and fluid balance in the body and is secreted by the adrenal cortex [Mid-20thC. Coined from MINERAL + CORTICOSTEROID.]

mineralogy /mínnə rálləji/ (*plural* **-gies**) *n.* **1. STUDY OF MINERALS** the scientific study of minerals and how to classify, distinguish, and locate them **2. AREA'S MINERAL DEPOSITS** a profile of an area's mineral deposits —**mineralogical** /mínnərə lójjik'l/ *adj.* —**mineralogically** *adv.* —**mineralogist** /mínnə rálləjist/ *n.*

mineral oil *n.* **1.** *US* = **liquid paraffin 2. OIL FROM MINERALS** any oil obtained from minerals, especially from petroleum

mineral spring *n.* a spring whose water has high mineral or gas content

mineral tar *n.* = **maltha**

mineral water *n.* drinkable water with a high mineral salt or gas content, either obtained from a mineral spring or with minerals added. It is usually sold in bottles.

mineral wax *n.* wax made from a mineral, especially a hydrocarbon wax **(ozocerite)** found in veins in sandstone

mineral wool *n.* a lightweight fibrous material made from slag or glass, used for insulation, packing material, and filters

Minerva /mi núrvə/ *n.* in Roman mythology, the goddess of wisdom and patron of arts, trade, and the art of war, who was born fully armed from the head of Jupiter

mineshaft /mīn shaaft/ *n.* a nearly vertical passageway that provides access or ventilation to an underground mine

minestrone /mínni strṓni/ *n.* an Italian soup made with vegetables, pasta, beans, and herbs. It is often served sprinkled with Parmesan cheese. [Late 19thC. From Italian, from, ultimately, Latin *ministrare* 'to serve', from *minister* 'servant' (see MINISTER).]

minesweeper /mīn sweepər/ *n.* a ship fitted with equipment for detecting and clearing underwater explosive mines

mineworker /mīn wurkər/ *n.* sb who works in a mine

Ming /ming/ *n.* the Chinese dynasty that ruled from 1364 to 1644, under which arts, trade, and scholarship were greatly developed (*often used before a noun*) [Late 18thC. From Chinese, literally 'bright, clear'.]

minge /minj/ *n.* (*taboo offensive*) **1. TABOO OFFENSIVE TERM** taboo offensive term for a woman's genitals **2. TABOO OFFENSIVE TERM** a taboo offensive term for women collectively [Late 19thC. Origin unknown.]

mingle /míng g'l/ **(-gles, -gling, -gled)** *v.* **1.** *vti.* **MIX GENTLY** to mix, or mix ingredients, together gently or gradually ○ *Heat gently to allow the flavours to mingle.* **2.** *vi.* **SPEAK TO PEOPLE** to circulate among a group of people, e.g. guests at a party [15thC. Alteration of obsolete *menglen*, literally 'to keep mixing', from Old English *mengan* 'to mix'.]

Mingrel /míng grəl/, **Mingrelian** /ming greéli ən/ *n.* a language spoken in the mountainous region to the northeast of the Black Sea. It belongs to the southern branch of Caucasian languages and is closely related to Georgian.

ming tree *n.* **1. BONSAI TREE** an evergreen tree used for bonsai, usually in a flat-topped asymmetrical arrangement **2. ARTIFICIAL BONSAI** an artificial bonsai tree [*Ming* of uncertain origin: perhaps from MING]

Mingus /míng gəss/, **Charles** (1922–79) US double bassist and composer. He played in various jazz bands, establishing the double bass as a principal jazz instrument.

mingy /mínji/ **(-gier, -giest)** *adj.* (*informal*) **1. STINGY** mean or stingy **2. INSUFFICIENT** extremely small, ungenerous, or stingy [Early 20thC. Origin uncertain; perhaps a blend of MEAN and STINGY.]

mini /mínni/ *n.* sth that is small compared to other things of its type, especially a minicomputer or a miniskirt (*informal*) [Mid-20thC. From MINI-.]

mini- *prefix.* small, short, miniature ○ *ministroke* [Shortening of MINIATURE]

miniature /mínnichər/ *n.* **1. SMALLER VERSION** a smaller-than-usual version of sth, e.g. a very small model or a smaller version of a particular breed of animal **2.** ARTS **TINY PAINTING** a very small, detailed, and well-finished painting, especially a portrait made to fit inside a locket or other piece of jewellery **3.** PAINTING **PAINTING OF MINIATURES** the art of painting miniatures **4.** BEVERAGES **SMALL BOTTLE OF SPIRITS** a small bottle of alcoholic spirits, containing one or two measures only **5. ILLUMINATED MANUSCRIPT ILLUSTRATION** a small picture or decorative initial in an illuminated manuscript ■ *adj.* **SMALLER THAN USUAL** smaller in size or scale than others of its type [Late 16thC. Via Italian *miniatura* 'illumination', from, ultimately, Latin *minium* 'red lead'.] ◇ **in miniature** on a small scale

WORD KEY: ORIGIN

Red lead was used in ancient and medieval times for making a sort of red ink with which manuscripts were decorated, and so the medieval Latin verb *miniare* was coined from *minium*, 'red lead', meaning 'to illuminate a manuscript'. Italian took this over and derived *miniatura* 'painting, illumination' from it. It referred particularly to the small paintings in manuscripts, and, after English acquired it, it was soon broadened out to refer to any 'small image'. Association with *minute, minimum*, etc. led by the early 18th century to its adjectival use for 'small'.

miniaturize /mínnichə rīz/ **(-izes, -izing, -ized), miniaturise (-ises, -ising, -ised)** *vt.* to make a version of sth in a much smaller size or on a greatly reduced scale —**miniaturization** /mínnichə rī záysh'n/ *n.*

minibar /mínni baar/ *n.* a small refrigerator in a hotel room stocked with alcoholic beverages and often also with soft drinks and snacks

mini-blind *n. US* a venetian blind with narrow slits

minibreak /mínni brayk/ *n.* a point won against the serve in a tie-break in a tennis match (*informal*)

minibus /mínni buss/ *n.* a small bus for carrying around 10 to 15 passengers, usually on short journeys

minicab /mínni kab/ *n.* an ordinary car used as a taxi, responding to telephone calls but not generally cruising the streets for business

minicompact /mínni kóm pakt/ *n.* a passenger vehicle smaller than a subcompact in size

minicomputer /mínni kəm pyootər/ *n.* a computer of a size, speed, and capacity intermediate between a standard personal computer and a mainframe

Miniconjou /mínni kón joo/ (*plural* **-jous** *or* **-jou**), **Minneconjou** *n.* a member of a Native North American people who originally occupied lands from the Black Hills to the Platte River, and whose members now live mainly in South Dakota

MiniDisc /mínni disk/ *tdmk.* a trademark for a small recordable compact disc housed in a rectangular plastic case. It measures 5 cm/2 in in diameter.

minidress /mínni dress/ *n.* a dress with a hemline above the knee

Minié ball /mínni ay-/ *n.* a bullet with a cone-shaped head and a hollow base that expands when fired, used in muzzle-loading rifles of the 19th century [Mid-19thC. Named after the French army officer Claude-Étienne *Minié* (1804–79), who invented it.]

minify /mínnifī/ (**-fies, -fying, -fied**) *vt.* to understate or reduce the size or importance of sth [Late 17thC. Formed from Latin *minimus* 'least' (see MINIMUM), on the model of MAGNIFY.] —**minification** /mínnifi káysh'n/ *n.*

minikin /mínnikin/ *n.* TINY CREATURE a tiny or dainty creature (*archaic*) ■ *adj.* DELICATE small and delicate (*archaic*) [Mid-16thC. From Dutch *minneken* 'darling', from *minne* 'love'.]

minim /mínnim/ *n.* **1.** MUSIC MUSICAL NOTE a note with the time value of half a semibreve or two crotchets. US term **half note 2.** MEASURE UNIT OF FLUID MEASURE a unit of fluid measure equal to one sixtieth of a fluid drachm, 0.0616 millilitres, or approximately one drop **3.** PEN-STROKE a downward vertical stroke of the pen in handwriting [15thC. Via medieval Latin *minimus* 'least' from Latin (see MINIMUM).]

minima *n.* plural of **minimum**

minimal /mínnim'l/ *adj.* **1.** VERY SMALL very small in amount or extent **2.** SMALLEST POSSIBLE smallest possible in amount or least possible in extent **3.** minimal, Minimal RELATING TO MINIMALISM relating to or displaying attributes associated with minimalism [Mid-17thC. Formed from Latin *minimus* 'least' (see MINIMUM).] —**minimality** /mínni mállǝti/ *n.* —**minimally** /mínniməli/ *adv.*

——— **WORD KEY: USAGE** ———
Extensions of meaning: Strictly speaking, *minimal* means 'the least possible', just as *minimize* means 'to reduce to a minimum; to reduce to the least possible amount'. Often, however, these words are not used strictly: *a minimal amount of noise* is unlikely to mean none at all but may simply be the least amount of noise conveniently possible to make. If the word is to retain any sense of being a superlative (like *least*), it should not be used with modifiers such as *rather*, *somewhat*, and *slightly*. *Small*, *limited*, *reduced*, and *as little as possible* are all suitable alternatives to overextending *minimal*; and *diminish*, *lessen*, and *reduce* do the job that *minimize* is sometimes improperly asked to do.

minimal art *n.* **1.** = **minimalism** *n.* **2.** MINIMALIST ART WORKS minimalist works of art —**minimal artist** *n.*

minimalise *vt.* = **minimalize**

minimalism /mínnimə līzəm/, **Minimalism** *n.* **1.** minimalism, Minimalism ARTISTIC MOVEMENT a movement of abstract artists who produce uncluttered paintings and sculptures that make use of basic colours and geometric shapes in impersonal arrangements. The movement originated in New York in the 1960s. **2.** SIMPLICITY OF STYLE simplicity in artwork, design, interior design, or literature, achieved by using a few very simple elements to maximum effect **3.** MUSIC MOVEMENT FOR SIMPLICITY IN MUSIC a trend in music towards simplicity of rhythm and tone, including sustained or repeated rhythmic and melodic patterns resulting in a hypnotic effect

minimalist /mínniməlist/, **Minimalist** *n.* **1.** minimalist, Minimalist PRACTITIONER OF ARTISTIC MINIMALISM sb whose works of art, literature, or music display the simplicity associated with minimalism **2.** ADVOCATE OF SMALLER ROLE FOR GOVERNMENT sb who advocates restricting the power and goals of an organization, especially sb who wishes to restrict government involvement in nongovernmental matters [Early 20thC. Translation of Russian *men'shevik*.]

Minimalist /mínnəmälist/ *n.* = **Menshevik** [Early 20thC. Translation of Russian *men'shevik*.]

minimalize /mínnimə līz/ (**-izes, -izing, -ized**), **minimalise** (**-ises, -ising, -ised**) *vt.* to reduce sth to the minimum —**minimalization** /mínnimə līz záysh'n/ *n.*

minimal pair *n.* in linguistics, a pair of words or other linguistic expressions that are the same except for one sound, e.g. 'bit' and 'pit'

minimax /mínnimaks/ *n.* MATH LOWEST MAXIMUM the lowest of a set of maximum values ■ *adj.* DESIGNED TO MINIMIZE LOSS used to describe options or strategies designed to minimize the risk of sustaining maximum loss in any situation that involves conflict or competition. ◊ **game theory** [Mid-20thC. Coined from MINIMUM + MAXIMUM.]

minimize /mínni mīz/ (**-mizes, -mizing, -mized**), **minimise** (**-mises, -mising, -mised**) *vt.* **1.** REDUCE STH TO MINIMUM to reduce sth to the lowest possible amount or degree **2.** UNDERRATE STH to play down the extent or

seriousness of sth —**minimization** /mínni mī záysh'n/ *n.* —**minimizer** /mínni mīzər/ *n.*

——— **WORD KEY: USAGE** ———
See Usage note at *minimal*.

minimum /mínniməm/ *n.* (*plural* **-mums** *or* **-ma** /-mə/) **1.** LOWEST POSSIBLE DEGREE the lowest possible amount or degree of sth **2.** LOWEST RECORDED DEGREE the lowest recorded amount or degree of sth **3.** LOWEST PERMISSIBLE DEGREE the lowest amount or degree of sth permitted by law, e.g. the lowest speed on a road or the youngest age at which sth can be done legally **4.** MATH LOWEST NUMBER the lowest number in a finite set **5.** MATH FUNCTION'S LOWEST VALUE the smallest value of a continuous function over a particular interval ■ *adj.* LOWEST ALLOWED lowest possible, recorded, or allowed [Mid-17thC. From Latin, from *minimus* 'least'. Ultimately from an Indo-European base denoting 'small', which is also the ancestor of English *minor*, *minute*, *diminish*, and *minister*.]

minimum lending rate *n.* the official lowest interest rate at which the Bank of England lent in the past to discount houses, replaced by the base rate in 1981

minimum-security *adj.* with security measures appropriate to inmates or patients who are not considered dangerous or who are not likely to try to escape

minimum wage *n.* the lowest rate of pay allowed by law or contract, either in general or for a certain type of work

minimus /mínnimǝss/ *n.* (*plural* **-mi** /-mī/) INSIGNIFICANT PERSON a very small or insignificant person (*literary*) ■ *adj.* YOUNGEST WITH THAT NAME a word sometimes placed after the surname of the youngest of several school pupils with the same surname, especially in public schools in the past (*dated*) ◊ **minor** [Late 16thC. From Latin, 'least' (see MINIMUM).]

mining /mīning/ *n.* **1.** REMOVING MINERALS FROM EARTH the process or business of removing minerals from the earth (*often used before a noun*) **2.** ARMS LAYING EXPLOSIVES the process of laying explosive mines

minion /mínnyən/ *n.* **1.** ASSISTANT a servile or slavish follower of sb generally regarded as important **2.** SERVANT a servant or enslaved person (*archaic or literary*) **3.** FAVOURITE a favoured person (*archaic*) [Early 16thC. From French *mignon* 'darling' (see MIGNON).]

minipill /mínni pil/ *n.* an oral contraceptive that contains progesterone but not oestrogen

mini roundabout *n.* a small traffic roundabout at junctions on lesser roads, often no more than a white disc painted on the road surface

miniseries /mínni seeriz/ (*plural* **-ries**) *n.* a short series of television programmes, often a serialized fictional story, usually broadcast on consecutive nights

miniskirt /mínni skurt/ *n.* a skirt with a hemline well above the knee

minister /mínnistər/ *n.* **1.** CHR MEMBER OF CLERGY a member of the clergy of a Christian, especially Protestant, church **2.** POL SENIOR POLITICIAN a senior politician who heads a government department, especially in the parliamentary system of government **3.** INTERNAT REL DIPLOMAT RANKED UNDER AMBASSADOR a diplomat representing a country, especially in the rank below ambassador **4.** CHR HEAD OF ROMAN CATHOLIC ORDER the superior in some orders in the Roman Catholic Church **5.** RELIG SPIRITUAL ADVISER a person who sees to the spiritual needs of others **6.** BUSINESS REPRESENTATIVE sb's agent or representative (*formal or literary*) ■ *v.* (**-ters, -tering, -tered**) **1.** *vi.* GIVE HELP to give help to sb in need (*formal*) **2.** *vi.* CHR DO RELIGIOUS MINISTER'S WORK to perform the duties of a member of the clergy **3.** *vt.* GIVE STH to administer sth, e.g. aid, medicine, or a sacrament (*archaic*) [13thC. Via Old French from Latin, 'servant'.] —**ministership** *n.*

ministerial /mínni steéri əl/ *adj.* **1.** RELATING TO CLERGY relating to a religious minister **2.** RELATING TO GOVERNMENT MINISTER relating to a government minister or the minister's department **3.** LAW REQUIRING FOLLOWING OF INSTRUCTIONS allowing no personal discretion, only the strict following of law **4.** INSTRUMENTAL playing an important part in achieving sth (*formal*) **5.** min-

isterial, Ministerial WITH GOVERNMENT supporting the government rather than the opposition —**ministerially** *adv.*

ministerialist /mínni steéri əlist/, **Ministerialist** *n.* a person who sides with the government against the opposition

Minister of State *n.* an assistant minister in a government department, who is usually not a member of the Cabinet

Minister of the Crown *n.* a senior minister who is head of a government department and a member of the Cabinet

minister plenipotentiary (*plural* **ministers plenipotentiary**) *n.* a diplomat who ranks below an ambassador but who has full power and authority to represent a government

minister resident (*plural* **ministers resident**) *n.* a diplomat who is ranked below a minister plenipotentiary

minister without portfolio *n.* a senior government minister who is a member of the Cabinet but has no direct responsibility for a government department

ministrant /mínnistrənt/ *n.* AID GIVER sb who gives aid to others (*literary*) ■ *adj.* HELPING giving aid or serving others (*archaic*) [Mid-16thC. From Latin *ministrant-*, the present participle stem of *ministrare* 'to serve', from *minister* 'servant' (see MINISTER).]

ministration /mínni stráysh'n/ *n.* **1.** TREATMENT help, treatment, or service (*formal; often used in the plural*) **2.** RELIGIOUS MINISTER'S WORK the service provided by a religious minister **3.** ACT OF SUPPLYING the supplying or administering of sth (*archaic*) [14thC. From the Latin stem *ministration-*, from *ministrare* (see MINISTRANT).]

ministroke /mínni strōk/ *n.* a temporary blockage of blood circulation in some part of the brain, causing short-term stroke symptoms, e.g. dizziness, inability to speak or move, or loss of senses

ministry /mínnistri/ (*plural* **-tries**) *n.* **1.** ministry, Ministry POL GOVERNMENT DEPARTMENT a government department headed by a minister **2.** POL GOVERNMENT BUILDING the building in which a government department is housed **3.** CHR WORK OF RELIGIOUS MINISTER the profession and services of a religious minister **4.** CHR PERIOD OF SERVICE a religious minister's career or period of service **5.** CHR MINISTERS ministers collectively, especially religious ministers (*takes a singular or plural verb*) **6.** POL PRIME MINISTER'S SERVICE the period of government under a prime minister [14thC. Via Old French from Latin *ministerium*, from *minister* 'servant' (see MINISTER).]

Minitrack /mínni trak/ *tdmk.* a trademark for an electronic system that tracks artificial satellites by sending and receiving radio signals from ground stations

minium /mínni əm/ *n.* = **red lead** [Mid-17thC. From Latin.]

minivan /mínni van/ *n.* a small van, often with seats that can be removed or rearranged to accommodate cargo

miniver /mínnivər/ *n.* white or light grey fur used as trim on ceremonial costumes [Late 16thC. From Old French *menu vair* 'small vair'.]

Mink

mink /mingk/ *n.* **1.** (*plural* **minks** *or* **mink**) WEB-TOED MEMBER OF WEASEL FAMILY either of two species of semiaquatic carnivorous members of the weasel family with webbed toes, a bushy tail, and thick dark brown fur. One is found in Europe and Asia, the other in North America. Genus: *Mustela*. **2.** MINK FUR the highly-valued, thick, shiny brown fur of the mink (often used before a noun) **3.** MINK FUR GARMENT a coat, stole, or other garment made of mink fur [15thC. From Swedish.]

minke whale /míngkə-, -ki-/ *n.* a small grey and white whale with a pointed snout. It is the smallest of the rorqual family, the family that includes the blue whale, and grows up to 10 m/30 ft long. Latin name: *Balaenoptera acutorostrata*. [Mid-20thC. *Minke* from Norwegian, of uncertain origin: possibly named after *Meincke*, a gunner on a 19thC whaling crew.]

Minn. *abbr.* Minnesota

Minna /mínnə/ city in west-central Nigeria, the capital of Niger State, situated about 80 km/50 mi. northwest of Abuja. Population: 134,000 (1995).

Minneapolis /mínni áppəliss/ the largest city in Minnesota, in the southeastern part of the state, close to the city of St Paul. Population: 368,383 (1990).

minneola /mínni ṓlə/ *n.* an orange coloured citrus fruit that is a cross between a tangerine and a grapefruit [Mid-20thC. Named after the town of *Minneola* in Florida, where it was developed.]

Minnesota

Minnesota /mínnə sṓtə/ state in the north-central United States, bordered by Iowa, North Dakota, South Dakota, Wisconsin, the Manitoba and Ontario Provinces of Canada, and Lake Superior. Capital: St Paul. Population: 4,685,549 (1997). Area: 218,588 sq. km/84,397 sq. mi. —**Minnesotan** /mínni sṓt'n/ *adj., n.*

Minnesota Multiphasic Personality Inventory *n.* a standardized test that uses true-false questions to assess sb's psychological and social adjustment. It is widely used in recruitment and screening. [Named after the University of MINNESOTA, where it was developed]

minnow /mínnō/ *n.* **1.** BAIT FISH any small freshwater fish of the carp family, commonly used as fishing bait. Family: *Cyprinidae*. **2.** SMALL FISH any small silvery freshwater fish **3.** INSIGNIFICANT PERSON OR THING a person or organization of relatively low status or little importance [15thC. Origin uncertain: probably related to Old English *myne* 'minnow' and perhaps influenced by French *menu* 'small'.]

Minoan /mi nṓ ən/ *adj.* RELATING TO ANCIENT CRETE relating or belonging to the Bronze Age civilization that flourished on Crete from around 3000 to 1100 BC ■ *n.* NATIVE OF ANCIENT CRETE sb who was born on or was a citizen of the island of Crete during ancient times, especially when the Minoan Bronze Age civilization flourished [Late 19thC. Named after *Minos*, legendary king of Crete associated with the great palace at Knossos.]

minor /mínər/ *adj.* **1.** SMALL relatively small in quantity, size, or degree **2.** LOW IN RANK relatively low in rank or importance **3.** LOW IN SEVERITY relatively low in severity or danger **4.** MUSIC DESCRIBING MUSICAL SCALE used to describe a scale that has a semitone interval between the second and third, fifth and sixth, and sometimes seventh and eighth notes **5.** MUSIC DESCRIBING MUSICAL INTERVAL used to describe an interval that is a semitone less than a major interval **6.** MUSIC DESCRIBING A KEY used to describe a key that is based on a minor scale ○ *in B minor* **7.** LAW NOT LEGALLY ADULT younger than the legal age of adulthood **8.** US EDUC RELATING TO SECONDARY SPECIALIZATION secondary to the major course of study **9.** YOUNGER WITH SAME NAME a word sometimes placed after the surname of the

younger of two school pupils with the same surname, especially in public schools in the past (dated) ■ *n.* **1.** LAW SB NOT LEGALLY ADULT sb who has not reached the legal age of adulthood **2.** MUSIC MUSICAL KEY OR HARMONY a key or harmony based on a musical scale whose third and, usually, sixth and seventh notes are lower by a semitone than those in the major scale ■ *vi.* (**-nors, -noring, -nored**) US STUDY AS SECONDARY SUBJECT to have as a second specialization in higher education, in addition to a major specialization [13thC. From Latin, 'lesser'.]

minor axis *n.* the shorter axis of an ellipse

Minorca[1] /mi náwrkə/ Spanish island in the western Mediterranean Sea, the second largest of the Balearic Islands. Population: 66,900 (1989). Area: 702 sq. km/271 sq. mi. —**Minorcan** /mi náwrkən/ *adj., n.*

Minorca[2] /mi náwrkə/ *n.* a white and black domestic chicken from the Mediterranean region [Mid-19thC. Named after MINORCA.]

minor element *n.* = **trace element** *n.* 2

minoritarianism /mī nórri tári ənizem/ *n.* advocacy or political action on behalf of a minority

Minorite /mínə rīt/ *n.* a friar of the Franciscan order [Mid-16thC. From *Minor Friars*, a translation of medieval Latin *Fratres Minores*, literally 'lesser brethren', because the Franciscan order stressed the virtue of humility.]

minority /mī nórrəti, mi-/ *n.* (plural **-ties**) **1.** SMALL GROUP a group of people or things that is a small part of a much larger group **2.** GROUP WITH INSUFFICIENT VOTES TO WIN a group that has fewer votes in an organization than another group or groups **3.** SMALLER SOCIALLY-DEFINED GROUP a group of people, within a society, whose members have different ethnic, racial, national, religious, sexual, political, linguistic, or other characteristics from the rest of society **4.** LAW NONADULTHOOD the state or period of being younger than the legal age of adulthood ■ *adj.* OF A MINORITY relating to or constituting a minority

minor key *n.* a key based on a minor scale

minor league *n.* in the United States, a league of professional baseball, football, ice hockey, and basketball teams that do not belong to the major leagues

minor-league *adj.* **1.** OF MINOR SPORTS LEAGUE relating to or being a team member of a minor sports league in the United States **2.** US MEDIOCRE mediocre in quality or position (informal)

minor scale *n.* a scale whose third and, usually, sixth and seventh notes are lower by a semitone than those in the major scale, giving it a less bright, more emotionally suggestive quality. ◊ **major scale**

minor suit *n.* either clubs or diamonds, which in bridge and similar games are ranked below hearts and spades

Minos /mín oss/ *n.* in Greek mythology, the son of Zeus and the king of Crete, who kept a monster (**Minotaur**) in a labyrinth

Minotaur /mínə tawr/ *n.* in Greek mythology, a monster with the body of a man and head of a bull that lived in the Cretan labyrinth and was fed human sacrifices until it was killed by Theseus

Minsk /minsk/ capital city of Belarus, situated in the north of the country. It is a major industrial city. Population: 1,700,000 (1996).

minster /mínstər/ *n.* a large or important cathedral or church, usually one originally connected with a monastery [Old English *mynster*, from, ultimately, late Latin *monasterium* (see MONASTERY)]

minstrel /mínstrəl/ *n.* **1.** MEDIEVAL TRAVELLING MUSICIAN a medieval singer, musician, or reciter of poetry who travelled around from place to place giving performances **2.** BLACKFACE ENTERTAINER IN VARIETY SHOW one of a group of entertainers who wore blackface make-up and sang and performed in variety shows (a form of entertainment now usually considered racist and highly offensive) [13thC. Via Old French *menestral* 'entertainer, handicraftsman', from, ultimately, late Latin *ministerialis* 'official', from *ministerium* (see MINISTRY).]

minstrelsy /mínstrəlssi/ (plural **-sies**) *n.* **1.** MINSTREL'S ART a minstrel's art or performance, or the profession of a minstrel **2.** MINSTRELS' POEMS AND SONGS the poems and songs written and performed by minstrels or

by a particular minstrel **3.** MINSTREL TROUPE a troupe of medieval minstrels [14thC. From Old French *menestralsie*, from *menestrel* (see MINSTREL).]

Mint

mint[1] /mint/ *n.* **1.** PLANT USED FOR FLAVOURING a plant with aromatic leaves that grows in northern temperate regions. Some types, like peppermint and spearmint, are used for flavouring. Genus: *Mentha*. **2.** MINT-FLAVOURED SWEET a mint-flavoured sweet [Old English *minte*. Via prehistoric Germanic from Latin *mentha*, from Greek *minthē*, of unknown origin.] —**minty** *adj.*

mint[2] /mint/ *n.* **1.** PLACE COINING MONEY a place where the coins used in a currency are manufactured under government control **2.** MUCH MONEY a large amount of money (informal) ■ *vt.* (**mints, minting, minted**) **1.** MAKE COINS to make coins by stamping metal **2.** INVENT to create or invent sth, especially a word or phrase, that is new ■ *adj.* IN PERFECT CONDITION in perfect condition as when first made [Old English *mynet*. Via prehistoric Germanic from Latin *moneta* 'mint money' (see MONEY).] —**minter** *n.* ◊ **in mint condition** in perfect condition, as if brand-new

mintage /míntij/ *n.* **1.** MINTING COINS the minting of coins **2.** COINS FROM MINT coins made in a mint, especially a quantity of coins minted at the same time **3.** FEE FOR MINTING a fee paid to a mint by a government for minting its coins

mint julep *n.* a drink made by pouring spirits, usually bourbon whiskey, and sugar, over crushed ice and flavouring or garnishing with mint

mintmark /mínt maark/ *n.* a letter or symbol stamped on a coin that identifies the mint where it was made

Mintoff /mínt of/, **Dom** (b. 1916) Maltese statesman. Twice prime minister of Malta (1955–58, and 1971–84), in his second term he followed a policy of severing ties with Britain. Full name **Dominic Mintoff**

mint sauce *n.* a sauce made from mint, sugar, and vinegar, and traditionally served with roast lamb

minuend /mínnyoo end/ *n.* the number from which another number (**subtrahend**) is to be subtracted [Early 18thC. From Latin *minuendus* 'to be made smaller', from *minuere* 'to diminish'.]

minuet /mínnyoo ét/ *n.* **1.** STATELY COURT DANCE a slow stately court dance in triple time that originated in France in the 17th century **2.** MUSIC FOR MINUET a piece of music in slow triple time written for or in the style of a minuet, often forming part of a Baroque dance suite or classical sonata or symphony [Late 17thC. From French, noun use of *menuet* 'small, dainty', from, ultimately, Latin *minutus* (source of English *minute*) from the steps taken in the dance.]

minus /mínəss/ *prep.* **1.** MATH LESS reduced by the subtraction of a number ○ *Seven minus four is three.* **2.** WITHOUT lacking in or deprived of sth ○ *Minus the tools, he cannot do the work required.* ■ *adj.* **1.** MATH SHOWING SUBTRACTION relating to or showing subtraction ○ *a minus sign* **2.** MATH LESS THAN ZERO relating to or showing a value less than zero ○ *Temperatures hovered near minus 20 degrees* ○ *a minus amount* **3.** HAVING DETRIMENTAL EFFECT having a negative or detrimental effect ○ *a minus factor in our assessment* **4.** SLIGHTLY BELOW STANDARD LEVEL used in marking or assessing sth to show that it is slightly below the average standard indicated by a particular symbol ○ *a grade of C minus* ■ *n.* **1.** = **minus sign** ○ *The minus shows that it's a subtraction* **2.** NEGATIVE QUANTITY a quantity below zero ○ *If we take that away we're left with a minus.* **3.** DISADVANTAGE sth that is detrimental or disadvantageous ○ *The power problem may prove to be a minus.* [15thC. From Latin, from *minor* 'less' (source of English *minor*).]

minuscule /mínnəss kyool/ *adj.* **1. EXTREMELY SMALL** extremely small or completely insignificant **2. LOWERCASE** lowercase, or printed in lowercase letters ■ *n.* **1. PRINTING SMALL LETTER** a lowercase letter **2. PRINTING MEDIEVAL WRITING STYLE** a small cursive style of writing used in certain medieval manuscripts **3. LETTER WRITTEN IN MINUSCULE** a letter of the alphabet written in minuscule style [Early 18thC. Via French from Latin *minusculus* 'rather small', from *minus* 'less' (see MINUS).] — **minuscular** /mi núskyōōlər/ *adj.*

minus sign, **minus** *n.* a symbol, (-), used to indicate subtraction or a negative quantity

minute[1] /mínnit/ *n.* **1. 60 SECONDS** a period of 60 seconds, or a 60th part of an hour **2. VERY SHORT TIME** a very short period of time ○ *I'll only be gone a minute.* **3. MOMENT** a particular moment ○ *The minute we got there the show began.* **4. SHORT DISTANCE** a distance that can be travelled in a minute ○ *The villa is only a couple of minutes from the beach.* **5. UNIT OF ANGULAR MEASURE** one 60th of a degree, a unit used in measuring angles **6. BRIEF NOTE** a brief note or memorandum ■ **minutes** *npl.* **RECORD OF A MEETING'S PROCEEDINGS** an official record of what is said or done during a meeting ■ *vt.* (**-utes, -uting, -uted**) **WRITE DOWN MEETING'S PROCEEDINGS** to record or summarize officially what happens during a meeting, or make a note in the minutes of a particular thing that is said or done [14thC. Directly or via Old French from Latin *minuta*, from *minutus*, the past participle of *minuere* 'to make small' (source of English *diminish*. From medieval Latin *pars minuta prima* 'first minute (i.e. small) part', referring to one sixtieth of a unit.] ◇ **up to the minute** aware of, taking account of, or reporting the very latest developments

minute[2] /mī nyoot/ (**-nuter, -nutest**) *adj.* **1. VERY SMALL** extremely small in size or scope **2. INSIGNIFICANT** so very small as not to matter **3. CONCERNED WITH EVERY DETAIL** extremely or laboriously thorough and painstaking, and concerned with every detail [Early 17thC. From Latin *minutus* (see MINUTE[1]).] — **minuteness** *n.*

minute gun /mínnit-/ *n.* a gun fired every minute as a distress signal or sign of mourning

minute hand /mínnit-/ *n.* the longer pointer on a watch or clock that indicates the minutes

minutely /mī nyoōtli/ *adv.* **1. IN GREAT DETAIL** very thoroughly, carefully, and in great detail **2. TO SMALL EXTENT** to a very small extent **3. INTO STH VERY SMALL** into a very small shape or very small pieces

minuteman /mínnit man/ (*plural* **-men** /-men/) *n.* an armed fighter in the American War of Independence pledged to be ready to fight for the American cause at a minute's notice

Minuteman (*plural* **-men**), **minuteman** (*plural* **-men**) *n.* an intercontinental ballistic missile of the United States armed forces

minute steak /mínnit-/ *n.* a piece of frying steak sliced so thinly that it can be cooked very quickly

minutiae /mī nyoōshi ee/ *npl.* small or trivial details [Mid-18thC. From Latin, literally 'small things', from *minutus* (see MINUTE[1]).]

minx /mingks/ *n.* an offensive term that insults a woman or girl as being impertinent or flirtatious (*offensive*) [Mid-16thC. Origin uncertain: perhaps from Middle Dutch *minnekijn* 'darling'.] — **minxish** *adj.*

Minya, Al- /mínyə/ city and trading centre in the Nile valley, eastern Egypt. Population: 208,000 (1992).

minyan /mínnyən/ (*plural* **-yanim** /mínnyə ním/ *or* **-yans**) *n.* the minimum number, ten, of adult Jewish men required to be present for an orthodox religious service [Mid-18thC. From Hebrew, 'count, reckoning'.]

Miocene /mī ə seen/ *n.* the epoch of geological time when the great mountain ranges of Europe, Asia, and the Americas were created and the mastodon first appeared, 23.3 to 5.2 million years ago [Mid-19thC. From Greek *meiōn* 'less' + *kainos* 'recent', from the remains of fewer modern species than in the PLIOCENE.] — **Miocene** *adj.*

miosis /mī ōssiss/ (*plural* **-ses** /-seez/), **myosis** (*plural* **-ses**) *n.* a contraction of the pupil of the eye, caused

e.g. by a reaction to a drug [Early 19thC. Coined from Greek *muein* 'to shut the eyes' + -OSIS.] — **miotic, myotic** /mī óttik/ *adj.*

MIP *abbr.* **1.** marine insurance policy **2.** monthly investment plan

MIPS /mips/, **mips** *abbr.* COMPUT million instructions per second

Miquelon Island ♦ St Pierre and Miquelon

mir /meer/ *n.* a peasant commune in tsarist Russia [Late 19thC. From Russian.]

Mir: Photographed from the space shuttle Atlantis (1997)

Mir *n.* a space station launched by the former Soviet Union in 1986, designed to be permanently crewed

mirabile dictu /mi rábbi lay dík too/ *interj.* used to introduce the announcement of sth the speaker, genuinely or ironically, considers to be amazing [From Latin, 'amazing to relate', literally 'amazing in the saying']

miracidium /mírə síddi əm/ (*plural* **-a** /-di ə/) *n.* the free-swimming first-stage larva of a trematode worm that hatches from an egg and then reproduces asexually [Late 19thC. From modern Latin, from Greek *meirakidion* 'little boy'.] — **miracidial** *adj.*

miracle /mírrək'l/ *n.* **1. ACT OF GOD** an event that appears to be contrary to the laws of nature and is regarded as an act of God **2. AMAZING EVENT** an event or action that is totally amazing, extraordinary, or unexpected ○ *It'll be a miracle if we get there on time.* **3. MARVELLOUS EXAMPLE OF SKILL** sth admired as a marvellous creation or example of a particular type of science or skill ○ *a miracle of modern engineering* [12thC. Via Old French from Latin *miraculum* 'object of wonder', from *mirari* 'to wonder at', from *mirus* 'wonderful'.]

miracle drug *n.* a drug, usually a new one, that is extraordinarily effective and seems to represent a breakthrough in the treatment of disease

miracle play *n.* a medieval play broadly depicting miracles taken from the life of a saint or a story from the Bible

miraculous /mə rákyooləss/ *adj.* **1. REGARDED AS CAUSED BY SUPERNATURAL INTERVENTION** apparently contrary to the laws of nature and caused by a supernatural power **2. EXTRAORDINARY** totally unexpected, extraordinary, and marvellous **3. ABLE TO PERFORM MIRACLES** having the power to perform miracles [15thC. Directly or via French *miraculeux*, from, ultimately, medieval Latin *miraculum* (see MIRACLE).] — **miraculously** *adv.* — **miraculousness** *n.*

mirador /mírrə dáwr/ *n.* a window, balcony, or turret designed to command a wide view [Late 17thC. From Spanish, from *mirar* 'to look', from Latin *mirare* (see MIRAGE).]

Miraflores, Lake /meérə fláwrayz/ lake in Panama, through which the Panama Canal passes

mirage /mírraazh, mə raázh/ *n.* **1. OPTICAL ILLUSION** an optical illusion of a sheet of water appearing in the desert or on a hot road, caused by light being distorted by alternate layers of hot and cool air **2. STH ILLUSORY** sth that is unreal or merely imagined [Early 19thC. From French, from *mirer* 'to look at', from Latin *mirare* 'to wonder at', variant of *mirari* (see MIRACLE).]

Miranda /mi rándə/ *n.* one of the satellites of Uranus

Barnaby's

Carmen Miranda

Miranda /mi rándə/, **Carmen** (1909–55) Portuguese dancer and singer. Star of Brazilian and Hollywood musicals, she is remembered particularly for her elaborate costumes and head-dresses made from tropical fruit. Born **Carmo Miranda da Cunha**

MIRAS /mírəss/ *abbr.* mortgage interest relief at source

mire /mīr/ *n.* **1. BOG** an area of very marshy ground or deep slushy mud **2. THICK MUD** thick slimy mud **3. DIFFICULT SITUATION** a troublesome or oppressive situation or state that is very difficult to escape from ■ *v.* (**mires, miring, mired**) **1.** *vti.* **GET STH STUCK IN MUD** to sink into mud, or make sth sink into mud, and become stuck **2.** *vt.* **MAKE MUDDY** to make sth muddy or dirty **3.** *vt.* **ENTANGLE** to involve or entangle sb or sth in difficulties [13thC. From Old Norse *myrr* 'bog'.] — **miriness** *n.* — **miry** *adj.*

Miró /meérō, mee ró/, **Joan** (1893–1983) Spanish painter, sculptor, and printmaker. A leading surrealist, he developed a form of abstraction, that produced his dreamlike, ethereal compositions.

mirror /mírrər/ *n.* **1. HIGHLY REFLECTIVE SURFACE** a surface such as glass or polished metal that reflects light without diffusing it so that it will give back a clear image of anything placed in front of it **2. GLASS FOR REFLECTING AN IMAGE** a piece of reflective material, especially glass coated on one side with metal, mounted in a frame for use, e.g. in the home or a vehicle **3. STH ACCURATELY REPRODUCING STH ELSE** sth that accurately reproduces, describes, or conveys sth else **4. EXAMPLE TO OTHERS** sth or sb that serves as an example to others (*archaic*) ■ *vt.* (**-rors, -roring, -rored**) **1. REFLECT IN SURFACE** to reflect sth clearly in a surface (*often passive*) ○ *The mountains were mirrored in the lake.* **2. BE SIMILAR TO** to be very similar to or correspond closely with sth else, or to reproduce it accurately ○ *These developments are now mirrored on the other side of the world.* [13thC. From Old French *mirour*, from, ultimately, an assumed Vulgar Latin form of Latin *mirari* 'to wonder at' (see MIRACLE).]

mirror carp *n.* a carp with very small scales that give its body a smooth shiny appearance. Latin name: *Cyprinus carpio*.

mirror image *n.* sth that, like a reflection in a mirror, is identical to sth else but reversed

mirth /murth/ *n.* happiness or enjoyment, especially accompanied by laughter [Old English *myrgzz*. Ultimately from a prehistoric Germanic word meaning 'pleasant, joyful', which is also the ancestor of English *merry*.]

mirthful /múrthf'l/ *adj.* full of gaiety, laughter, or amusing things — **mirthfully** *adv.* — **mirthfulness** *n.*

mirthless /múrthləss/ *adj.* without, or not expressing, amusement, good humour, or gladness — **mirthlessly** *adv.* — **mirthlessness** *n.*

MIRV /murv/ *abbr.* multiple independently targeted re-entry vehicle

Mirza /múrzə/ *n.* an Iranian title of respect signifying a learned man or official when placed before a name, or formerly a royal prince when placed after a name [Early 17thC. From Persian.]

MIS *abbr.* COMPUT management information system

mis- *prefix.* **1.** badly, wrongly ○ *mishandle* **2.** bad, wrong ○ *misdeed* **3.** opposite, lack, failure ○ *mislike* [Partly Old English, and partly via Old French *mes-* from a prehistoric Germanic word meaning 'to go wrong', which is also the ancestor of English *miss* and *amiss*]

misaddress /míssə dréss/ (-dresses, -dressing, -dressed) vt. to put an incorrect address on an item of mail

misadventure /míssəd vénchər/ n. 1. UNFORTUNATE EVENT an unfortunate event, especially sth untoward, unlucky, or amusing that happens to sb 2. ACCIDENTAL DEATH an accidental cause of death, not involving a crime or negligence on the part of sb else [13thC. From Old French mesaventure, from mesavenir 'to turn out badly', from avenir 'to happen', from Latin advenire 'to come to'.]

misalliance /míssə lí ənss/ n. an unsuitable alliance, especially a marriage between mismatched partners

misandry /miss ándri/ n. hatred of men as a sexually defined group [Early 20thC. Coined from the Greek stem andr- 'man', on the model of MISOGYNY.] —**misandrist** n. —**misandrous** adj.

misanthrope /míss'n thrōp/, **misanthropist** /miss ánthrəpist/ n. sb who hates humankind in general, or dislikes and distrusts other people and tends to avoid their company [Mid-16thC. Via French from Greek misanthrōpos, from MISEIN 'to hate' + anthrōpos 'man'.] —**misanthropic** /miss 'n thróppik/ adj. —**misanthropically** /-li/ adv. —**misanthropy** /miss ánthrəpi/ n.

misapprehend /míss apri hénd/ (-hends, -hending, -hended) vt. to fail to understand (formal)

misapprehension /míss apri hénsh'n/ n. a false impression or incorrect understanding, especially of the nature of a situation or sb's intentions —**misapprehensive** adj. —**misapprehensively** adv. —**misapprehensiveness** n.

misappropriate /míssə própri ayt/ (-ates, -ating, -ated) vt. to take sth, especially money, dishonestly, or in order to use it for an improper or illegal purpose —**misappropriation** /míssə própri áysh'n/ n.

—— **WORD KEY: SYNONYMS** ——
See Synonyms at **steal**.

misbecome /míssbi kúm/ (-comes, -coming, -came, -come) vt. to be unsuitable for or detrimental to sb, or unfitting for an event or occasion (formal)

misbegotten /míssbi gótt'n/ adj. 1. ILL-CONCEIVED AND GENERALLY BAD from a bad source, badly planned, badly thought out, or generally deplorable from start to finish 2. DISHONESTLY OBTAINED obtained by dishonest means 3. ILLEGITIMATE born to parents who are not married to each other

misbehave /míssbi háyv/ (-haves, -having, -haved) vi. 1. BE NAUGHTY AND TROUBLESOME to be naughty and troublesome, or otherwise behave in an unacceptable way 2. NOT FUNCTION PROPERLY to function badly or not at all, or to cause problems (informal) —**misbehaver** n.

misbehaved /míssbi háyvd/ adj. naughty, disobedient, or troublesome (disapproving)

misbehavior n. US = misbehaviour

misbehaviour /míssbi háyvyər/ n. unacceptable behaviour, especially naughtiness, disobedience, or troublesomeness on the part of children

misbelief /míssbi leéf/ n. a belief that is or is considered to be false or unorthodox

misbelieve /míssbi leév/ (-lieves, -lieving, -lieved) vi. to hold beliefs that are or are considered to be false or unorthodox, especially on religious matters (disapproving) —**misbeliever** n.

misc. abbr. 1. miscellaneous 2. miscellany

miscalculate /míss kálkyoŏ layt/ (-lates, -lating, -lated) vti. 1. CALCULATE WRONGLY to calculate sth incorrectly 2. MAKE WRONG ASSESSMENT to judge or assess sth incorrectly, or form false expectations as to the consequences of an action —**miscalculation** /míss kalkyoŏ láysh'n/ n. —**miscalculator** /míss kálkyoŏ laytər/ n.

miscall /míss káwl/ (-calls, -calling, -called) vt. to use the wrong or an inappropriate name for sb or sth —**miscaller** n.

miscarriage /miss kárrij, míss karij/ n. 1. PREMATURE EXPULSION OF FOETUS an involuntary ending of a pregnancy through the discharge of the foetus from the womb at too early a stage in its development for it to survive. Technical name **abortion** 2. FAILURE OF UNDERTAKING the mishandling or failure of sth, such as a plan or project (formal)

miscarriage of justice n. a failure of the legal system to come to a just decision

miscarry /miss kárri/ (-ries, -rying, -ried) vi. 1. HAVE SPONTANEOUS ABORTION to lose a foetus, especially a human foetus, through a miscarriage 2. BE SPONTANEOUSLY ABORTED to be expelled from the womb at too early a stage in development to be able to survive 3. FAIL to result in failure (formal) 4. BE LOST IN TRANSIT to be lost or go astray before reaching an intended destination

miscast /míss kaást/ (-casts, -casting, -cast) vt. (often passive) 1. GIVE ACTOR UNSUITABLE PART to choose sb to play a stage or film part to which he or she is unsuited 2. CHOOSE WRONG ACTORS FOR to choose unsuitable actors for the roles in a play or film, or an unsuitable actor for a particular role

miscegenation /míssijə náysh'n/ n. (offensive when used disapprovingly, as often formerly) 1. SEXUAL RELATIONS BETWEEN RACES sexual relations between people of different races, especially of different skin colours, leading to the birth of children 2. INTERMARRIAGE BETWEEN RACES marriage or cohabitation between people of different races [Mid-19thC. Coined from Latin miscere 'to mix' + genus 'race' + -ATION.] —**miscegenational** adj.

miscellanea /míssə láyni ə/ npl. miscellaneous things, especially pieces of writing, brought together as a collection [Late 16thC. From Latin, from miscellaneus (see MISCELLANEOUS).]

miscellaneous /míssə láyni əss/ adj. 1. COMPOSED OF VARIED THINGS made up of many different things or kinds of things that have no necessary connection with each other 2. EACH BEING DIFFERENT each being different or having different abilities or qualities from the others ○ a task force of miscellaneous specialists [Early 17thC. From Latin miscellaneus, from, ultimately, miscere 'to mix' (source of English mix).] —**miscellaneously** adv. —**miscellaneousness** n.

miscellanist /mi séllənist/ n. sb who compiles or writes miscellanies

miscellany /mi sélləni/ (plural -nies) n. 1. MISCELLANEOUS COLLECTION a miscellaneous collection of things 2. COLLECTED MISCELLANEOUS WRITINGS a collection of miscellaneous pieces of writing in one volume, often by different authors on various subjects and in different genres [Late 16thC. Via French miscellanées from Latin miscellanea (see MISCELLANEA).]

mischance /míss cháanss/ n. 1. MISFORTUNE the occurrence of unfortunate events by chance 2. PIECE OF BAD LUCK sth that happens through bad luck [14thC. From Old French mescheance (see CHANCE).]

mischief /mísschif/ n. 1. NAUGHTY BEHAVIOUR behaviour, especially by children, that is undesirable or troublesome without being wicked 2. TENDENCY TO NAUGHTY BEHAVIOUR a tendency to mildly troublesome or undesirable behaviour such as teasing or practical jokes 3. INJURY OR DAMAGE injury or damage caused by the actions of sb or sth 4. HARMLESS TROUBLEMAKER sb who causes or enjoys causing harmless trouble 5. SOURCE OF HARM OR TROUBLE sth or sb that causes serious harm or trouble to sb [13thC. From Old French meschef, from meschever 'to meet with misfortune', from chever 'to come to an end', from chef 'head'.]

mischief-maker n. sb who deliberately causes trouble and sets people against each other, especially by spreading malicious gossip

mischievous /mísschivəss/ adj. 1. PLAYFULLY NAUGHTY OR TROUBLESOME behaving or likely to behave in a naughty or troublesome way, but in fun and not meaning serious harm 2. TROUBLESOME OR IRRITATING intended to tease or cause trouble, though usually in fun or without much malice 3. FULL OF MISCHIEF expressing sb's intention or inclination to have fun by teasing, playing tricks, or causing trouble 4. DAMAGING causing or meant to cause serious trouble, damage, or hurt (formal) —**mischievously** adv. —**mischievousness** n.

—— **WORD KEY: SYNONYMS** ——
See Synonyms at **bad**.

misch metal /mish-/ n. an alloy of cerium and rare earth metals used, e.g., in the flints of cigarette lighters [Early 20thC. From German Mischmetall, literally 'mix-metal'.]

miscible /míssəb'l/ adj. used to describe two or more liquids that can be mixed together [Late 16thC. From medieval Latin miscibilis, from miscere 'to mix' (source of English MIX).]

miscommunication /mísskə myoöni káysh'n/ n. 1. FAILURE TO COMMUNICATE STH CLEARLY failure to communicate sth clearly or correctly 2. UNCLEAR COMMUNICATION a communication that is unclear or likely to be misinterpreted

misconceive /mísskən seév/ (-ceives, -ceiving, -ceived) vt. to fail to understand sth correctly, or to form a false conception of sth

misconceived /mísskən seévd/ adj. resulting from a wrong or faulty understanding or idea of sth and consequently doomed to failure

misconception /mísskən sépsh'n/ n. a mistaken idea or view resulting from a misunderstanding of sth

misconduct n. /miss kóndukt/ 1. IMMORAL, UNETHICAL, OR UNPROFESSIONAL BEHAVIOUR behaviour that is not in accordance with accepted moral or professional standards (disapproving) 2. INCOMPETENCE incompetent or dishonest management of sth, especially on behalf of others ■ v. /mísskən dúkt/ (-ducts, -ducting, -ducted) 1. vr. ACT IMMORALLY to act in an immoral or improper way 2. vt. MANAGE INCOMPETENTLY to manage sth in an incompetent or dishonest way ○ guilty of misconducting the whole affair

misconstruction /mísskən strúksh'n/ n. GRAM 1. FAULTY UNDERSTANDING a faulty understanding or interpretation of sth 2. FAULTY GRAMMAR a faulty grammatical construction

misconstrue /mísskən stroö/ (-strues, -struing, -strued) vt. to understand or interpret sth incorrectly

miscount vti. /míss kównt/ (-counts, -counting, -counted) COUNT INCORRECTLY to make a mistake when counting sth ■ n. /míss kownt/ INCORRECT COUNT an incorrect count or calculation

miscreant /mísskri ənt/ n. 1. SB WHO DOES WRONG a villain, wrongdoer, or generally wicked and contemptible person (literary) 2. INFIDEL an infidel or heretic (archaic insult) [13thC. From Old French, present participle of mescroire 'to disbelieve', from, ultimately, Latin credere 'to believe' (source of English creed).]

miscue /míss kyoö/ n. 1. CUE GAMES FAULTY SHOT IN BILLIARDS in billiards or snooker, a shot that fails because the cue does not strike the cue ball properly 2. MISTAKE a mistake, especially one that involves giving sb the wrong cue to say or begin sth or giving a cue at the wrong time (informal) ■ v. (-cues, -cuing, -cued) 1. vti. CUE GAMES MAKE FAULTY SHOT in billiards or snooker, to fail to strike the cue ball properly, or to play a miscue 2. vti. MISS A CUE to fail to respond to a cue, to give the wrong cue for sth, or to give a cue at the wrong time 3. vi. ERR to make a mistake (informal)

misdeal /míss deél/ vti. (-deals, -dealing, -dealt) DEAL CARDS WRONGLY to deal playing cards incorrectly ■ n. MISTAKE IN DEALING CARDS a mistake in the way playing cards are dealt, or an incorrectly dealt hand —**misdealer** n.

misdeed /míss deéd/ n. a wicked, blameworthy, or unlawful act (formal)

misdemeanant /míssdi meénənt/ n. LAW sb convicted of a misdemeanour

misdemeanor n. US = misdemeanour

misdemeanour /míssdi meénər/ n. 1. LESS SERIOUS CRIME in the US and before 1967 in England and Wales, a crime less serious than a felony and resulting in a less severe punishment 2. MINOR MISDEED a relatively minor misdeed

misdial /miss dí əl/ (-als, -aling, -alled) vti. to dial a telephone number incorrectly —**misdial** /míss dī əl/ n.

misdirect /míssdə rékt/ (-rects, -recting, -rected) vt. 1. GIVE WRONG DIRECTIONS to give sb wrong directions or instructions 2. WRONGLY ADDRESS MAIL to put a wrong address on an item of mail 3. AIM INACCURATELY to aim sth, e.g. a punch or bullet, inaccurately, or direct sth, e.g. a comment or insult, at the wrong person

misdoubt /miss dówt/ (**-doubts, -doubting, -doubted**) *vt.* to doubt or suspect sb or sth (*archaic*)

mise en scène /meéz on sáyn/ (*plural* **mises en scène**) *n.* **1.** CINEMA, THEATRE **ARRANGEMENT OF ACTORS, SCENERY, ETC** the positioning of actors, scenery, and properties on a stage or film set for a particular scene or particular production **2. SETTING FOR STH** the physical environment in which an event takes place [From French, literally 'putting on stage']

miser /mízər/ *n.* (*disapproving*) **1. SB WHO HOARDS MONEY** sb who hoards money, hates spending it, and as a result, though rich, lives as if he or she were poor **2. UNGENEROUS OR SELFISH PERSON** sb who is mean and ungenerous, or selfish and greedy [Mid-16thC. From Latin, 'unfortunate'.]

miserable /mízzərəb'l/ *adj.* **1. VERY UNHAPPY** experiencing a serious lack of contentment or happiness ○ *feeling a bit miserable* **2. VERY UNPLEASANT** causing or accompanied by discomfort, unpleasantness, or unhappiness **3. CONTEMPTIBLE** deserving contempt or condemnation **4. INADEQUATE** inadequate, often insultingly or embarrassingly inadequate, in quantity or quality **5. DIRTY OR SQUALID** dirty, squalid, and lacking any comfort **6.** *Scotland, ANZ* **STINGY** mean or stingy [15thC. Via Old French from Latin *miserabilis* 'pitiable', from, ultimately, *miser* 'unfortunate'.] —**miserableness** *n.* —**miserably** *adv.*

WORD KEY: CULTURAL NOTE

Les Misérables, a novel by French writer Victor Hugo (1862). Set in mid-19th century France, it tells the story of Jean Valjean, whose attempts to escape his criminal past are dogged by guilt, fate, and persistent police inspector Javert. This epic tale is noted for its gripping plot and vivid descriptions of events such as the battle of Waterloo. The noun *javert*, meaning a persistent, bloodhound-like pursuing detective or prosecutor, derives directly from the name of the detective in this novel. The novel was successfully adapted as a stage musical.

---

misère /mi záir/ *n.* **1. CALL IN SOLO WHIST** a call in certain card games, especially solo whist, indicating that a hand is expected to win no tricks **2. HAND WINNING NO TRICKS** a hand that is expected to win no tricks [Early 19thC. From French, literally 'poverty, misery'.]

miserere /mízzə ráiri/ *n.* = **misericord** [Late 18thC. From Latin, 'have mercy!', from *misereri* 'to have mercy', from *miser* 'unfortunate'.]

Miserere /mízzə ráiri/ *n.* **1.** BIBLE **50TH OR 51ST PSALM** the 50th or 51st Psalm, depending on the version of the Bible **2.** MUSIC **MUSICAL MISERERE** a musical setting of the Miserere [13thC. From the first word of the Latin text, beginning MISERERE MEI, DEUS 'have mercy on me, O God' (see MISERERE).]

misericord /mi zérri kawrd/ *n.* a projecting ledge often with elaborate carving on the underside of a seat in a church stall that, when the seat is turned up, gives a standing person sth to rest against [14thC. Via Old French from, ultimately, Latin *misericors* 'merciful, compassionate', from *miser* 'unfortunate' + *cor* 'heart'.]

miserly /mízərli/ *adj.* **1. AVARICIOUS** greedy for money and unwilling to share or to spend it **2. EXTREMELY SMALL** so small as to be insufficient or inadequate —**miserliness** *n.*

misery /mízzəri/ (*plural* **-ies**) *n.* **1. GREAT UNHAPPINESS** a serious lack of contentment or happiness **2. SOURCE OF GREAT UNHAPPINESS** sth that causes great unhappiness **3. POVERTY** a state of extreme poverty and squalor **4. GLOOMY PERSON** sb who is always gloomy or brooding (*informal*) [14thC. Directly or via Anglo-Norman *miserie*, from Latin *miseria*, from Latin *miser* 'unfortunate'.] ◇ **put sb out of his** *or* **her misery** to put an end to sb's suspense or anxiety, especially by revealing sth that he or she is desperate to know (*humorous*) ◇ **put sth out of its misery** to kill an animal in order to prevent it suffering further pain

misfeasance /missfeéz'nss/ *n.* LAW acting improperly or illegally in performing an action that is in itself lawful. ◊ **malfeasance, nonfeasance** [Early 17thC. From Anglo-Norman *mesfaisance*, from *mesfaire* 'to misdo', from *mes-* 'wrongly' + *faire* 'to do', from Latin *facere*.] —**misfeasor** *n.*

misfire *vi.* /miss fír/ (**-fires, -firing, -fired**) **1. NOT FIRE PROPERLY** to fail to shoot a bullet or shell when fired **2. FAIL TO OPERATE PROPERLY** to fail to ignite the fuel mixture in the cylinder or to ignite it at the wrong time (*refers to an internal-combustion engine*) **3. GO WRONG** to fail to achieve a planned result ○ *the plot misfired* ■ *n.* /míss fīr/ **MALFUNCTION IN FIRING** a failure to fire or function properly

misfit /míss fit/ *n.* **1. SB WHO DOES NOT BELONG** sb who is out of place in a particular situation or environment **2. STH ILL-FITTING** sth that does not fit properly

misfortune /miss fáwrchən/ *n.* **1. ILL LUCK** bad luck **2. UNHAPPY EVENT** an undesirable or unhappy event or circumstance

misgive /miss gív/ (**-gives, -giving, -gave** /-gáyv/, **-given** /-gívv'n/) *vt.* to feel apprehensive, or to cause a feeling of apprehension or foreboding in sb (*literary*) [Early 16thC. Formed from GIVE in the obsolete sense 'to suggest'.]

misgiving /miss gívving/ *n.* a feeling of doubt or apprehension, especially about undertaking a course of action (*often used in the plural*) ○ *I had misgivings about the plan from the beginning.*

misguide /miss gíd/ (**-guides, -guiding, -guided**) *vt.* to lead sb in a wrong direction or into making a mistake —**misguidance** *n.* —**misguider** *n.*

misguided /miss gídid/ *adj.* motivated by or based on ideas that are mistaken, heedless, or inappropriate (*disapproving*) —**misguidedly** *adv.* —**misguidedness** *n.*

mishandle /miss hánd'l/ (**-dles, -dling, -dled**) *vt.* **1. DEAL WITH INCOMPETENTLY** to deal with sth or sb in an incompetent or ineffective way **2. TREAT ROUGHLY** to treat sth or sb roughly

mishap /míss hap/ *n.* **1. ACCIDENT** an unfortunate accident or piece of bad luck **2. BAD LUCK** an unfortunate circumstance or set of circumstances (*formal*)

mishear /miss heér/ (**-hears, -hearing, -heard** /-húrd/) *vti.* to fail to hear sb or sth correctly

Mishima /míshimə/, **Yukio** (1925–70) Japanese novelist. He celebrated Japan's nationalist and imperialist history, deploring the sterility of contemporary life, and committed ritual suicide. His novels include the tetralogy *The Sea of Fertility* (1965–70). Pseudonym of **Hiraoka Kimitake**

mishit /miss hít/ (**-hits, -hitting, -hit**) *vt.* to hit sth badly, e.g. a ball or puck, so that it does not go in the desired direction or has insufficient force behind it —**mishit** /míss hit/ *n.*

mishmash /mísh mash/ *n.* a disorderly collection or confused mixture of things [15thC. Formed from the repetition of MASH.]

Mishmi /míshmi/ (*plural* **-mi** *or* **-mis**) *n.* **1. MEMBER OF PEOPLE IN ASSAM** a member of a people living in a mountainous region of Assam in northeast India **2. MISHMI LANGUAGE** the Tibeto-Burman language spoken by the Mishmi people —**Mishmi** *adj.*

Mishnah /míshnə/, **Mishna** *n.* **1. JEWISH LAW** the primary body of Jewish civil and religious law, forming the first part of the Talmud. These laws were handed down orally until written down around AD 200. **2. JEWISH ORAL LAW** Jewish law from the oral tradition, as distinguished from law derived from the scriptures **3. JEWISH LEGAL TEACHING** the teaching of an authority on Jewish law [Early 17thC. From Hebrew *mišnāh* 'repetition, teaching'.] —**Mishnaic** /mish náy ik/ *adj.*

misinform /míssin fáwrm/ (**-forms, -forming, -formed**) *vt.* to give incorrect information to sb —**misinformant** *n.* —**misinformation** *n.* —**misinformer** *n.*

misinterpret /míssin túrprit/ (**-prets, -preting, -preted**) *vt.* to understand or explain the meaning of sth incorrectly —**misinterpreter** *n.*

misjoinder /miss jóyndər/ *n.* an improper combining of plaintiffs, defendants, or causes of action in a single lawsuit

misjudge /miss júj/ (**-judges, -judging, -judged**) *v.* **1.** *vti.* **MAKE A BAD JUDGMENT** to make a mistake when judging or assessing sth, or when attempting to do sth that requires accurate judgment **2.** *vt.* **FORM INCORRECT OPINION** to form an incorrect opinion about sb or sth, especially to attribute bad qualities to sb unjustly or mistakenly —**misjudger** *n.* —**misjudgment** *n.*

Miskito /mi skeét ō/ (*plural* **-to** *or* **-tos**) *n.* **1. MEMBER OF NATIVE CENTRAL AMERICAN PEOPLE** a member of a Native Central American people living along the Caribbean coasts of Nicaragua and Honduras **2. MISKITO LANGUAGE** the language of the Miskito people [Late 18thC. From *miskito*.] —**Miskito** *adj.*

Miskolc /meésh koolts/ historic and industrial city in northeastern Hungary. Population: 182,000 (1995).

mislay /miss láy/ (**-lays, -laying, -laid** /-láyd/) *vt.* to lose sth temporarily, especially by forgetting where it was put —**mislayer** *n.*

mislead /miss leéd/ (**-leads, -leading, -led**) *vt.* **1. INFORM FALSELY** to cause sb to make a mistake or form a false opinion or belief, either by employing deliberate deception or by supplying incorrect information ○ *The defendant is trying to mislead the jury.* **2. LEAD INTO BAD ACTIONS** to be responsible for making sb, especially sb younger, do wrong or adopt bad habits **3. LEAD IN WRONG DIRECTION** to lead sb in a wrong direction —**misleader** *n.*

misleading /miss leéding/ *adj.* likely or deliberately intended to confuse people or give them a false idea of sth —**misleadingly** *adv.*

misled past participle, past tense of **mislead**

mislike /miss lík/ (**-likes, -liking, -liked**) *vt.* (*archaic*) **1. DISLIKE** to dislike sb or sth **2. DISPLEASE** to displease sb

mismanage /miss mánnij/ (**-ages, -aging, -aged**) *vt.* to run, organize, or deal with sth incompetently —**mismanagement** *n.*

mismatch *n.* /míss mach/ **UNLIKELY OR ILL-SUITED PAIR** a pairing or combination of people or things that are incompatible with or apparently ill-suited to each other ■ *vt.* /míss mách/ (**-matches, -matching, -matched**) **FAIL TO MATCH WELL** to fail to match or pair suitably (*usually passive*) ○ *They'd been mismatched from the start.*

misnomer /miss nṓmər/ *n.* **1. UNSUITABLE NAME** a wrong or unsuitable name or term for sth or sb **2. CALLING STH BY A WRONG NAME** a use of a wrong or unsuitable name or term to describe sth or sb [15thC. From Old French, from *mes-* 'wrongly' + *nommer* 'to name', from Latin *nominare*.]

miso /meéssō/ *n.* Japanese fermented soya bean paste used mainly in vegetarian cooking [Early 18thC. From Japanese.]

misogamy /mi sóggəmi/ *n.* an aversion to marriage and the married state [Mid-17thC. From modern Latin *misogamia*, which was coined from Greek *misein* 'to hate' + *gamos* 'marriage'.] —**misogamic** /míssə gámmik/ *adj.* —**misogamist** /mi sóggəmist/ *n.*

misogyny /mi sójjəni/ *n.* the hatred of women, as a sexually defined group [Mid-17thC. From Greek *misogunia*, from *misein* 'to hate' + *gunē* 'woman'.] —**misogynic** /míssə jínnik/ *adj.* —**misogynist** /mi sójjənist/ *n.* —**misogynistic** /mi sójjə nístik/ *adj.* —**misogynistically** *adv.*

misology /mi sólləji/ *n.* the hatred of reason, logical argument, or enlightenment [Early 19thC. From Greek *misologia*, from *misein* 'to hate' + *-logia* -LOGY.] —**misologist** *n.*

misoneism /míssō neé izəm/ *n.* the hatred of new things or change [Late 19thC. From Italian *misoneismo*, which was coined from Greek *misein* 'to hate' + *neos* 'new' + Italian *-ismo* '-ism'.] —**misoneist** *n.* —**misoneistic** /míssō nee ístik/ *adj.*

mispickel /míss pik'l/ *n.* = **arsenopyrite** [Late 17thC. From German, variant of earlier Mispūtl, of unknown origin.]

misplace /miss pláyss/ (**-places, -placing, -placed**) *vt.* **1. PUT IN WRONG PLACE** to put sth in a wrong place or position **2. MISLAY** to lose sth, especially temporarily, through forgetting where it was put **3. RELY ON SB OR STH INAPPROPRIATE** to put confidence, faith, or trust in sb or sth unsuitable or unworthy —**misplacement** *n.*

misplaced modifier *n.* a phrase positioned so that it is unclear what exactly it refers to, e.g. *lying in the gutter* in 'Lying in the gutter, we saw a dead rat'

misplay /míss pláy/ (**-plays, -playing, -played**) *vt.* **MAKE BAD MOVE** to play or move sth such as a ball or game piece badly or carelessly ■ *n.* **MISTAKE MADE IN GAME** a bad or unintended play in sport or a game

misplead /miss pleéd/ (**-pleads, -pleading, -pleaded, -plead** *or* **-pled** /-pléd/) *vt.* to make or answer an allegation in a lawsuit in a manner not in accordance with procedure or the law

mispleading /miss pleéding/ *n.* an error made or contained in the pleading in a lawsuit

misprint *n.* /miss print/ MISTAKE IN PRINTED COPY OR PRINTING an error in the printed copy of a text resulting from a mistake made when the text was being printed ■ *vt.* /miss prínt/ (**-prints, -printing, -printed**) PRINT INCORRECTLY to print sth wrongly

misprise *vt.* = **misprize**

misprision[1] /miss prízh'n/ *n.* **1.** HIDING A CRIME the failure of sb who knows of but is not involved in a felony or treason to report it to the authorities **2.** *US* WRONGDOING IN OFFICIAL DUTIES neglect or wrong done by a public official in the performance of the duties of his or her office [15thC. From Anglo-Norman *mesprisioun* 'error', from Old French *mesprendre* 'to make a mistake'.]

misprision[2] /miss prízh'n/ *n.* (*archaic*) **1.** CONTEMPT disdain for sth or sb considered of little value **2.** FAILURE TO UNDERSTAND OR SEE VALUE a misunderstanding of sth, especially a failure to appreciate the true worth of sb or sth [Late 16thC. Formed from MISPRIZE + -ION on the model of MISPRISION[1].]

misprize /miss príz/ (**-prizes, -prizing, -prized**), **misprise** (**-prises, -prising, -prised**) *vt.* (*formal*) **1.** UNDERVALUE to fail to appreciate the true worth of sth or sb **2.** CONSIDER CONTEMPTIBLE to consider sb or sth unworthy of respect or admiration [14thC. From Old French *mesprisier*, literally 'to misestimate value', from *prisier* (see PRIZE).] —**misprizer** *n.*

mispronounce /míssprə nówns/ (**-nounces, -nouncing, -nounced**) *vti.* to pronounce sth incorrectly —**mispronunciation** /míssprə n/ *n.*

misquote /miss kwót/ (**-quotes, -quoting, -quoted**) *vti.* to quote sb or sth inaccurately —**misquoter** *n.*

misread /miss reéd/ (**-reads, -reading, -read** /-réd/) *vt.* **1.** READ WRONGLY to make a mistake in reading sth, e.g. reading aloud inaccurately, mistaking one word for another, or misunderstanding the sense of what is written **2.** MISINTERPRET to fail to understand the true meaning or nature of sth

misrepresent /míss repri zént/ (**-sents, -senting, -sented**) *vt.* **1.** GIVE FALSE ACCOUNT OF to give an inaccurate or deliberately false account of the nature of sb or sth **2.** NOT REPRESENT TRULY not to be truly or typically representative of sb or sth —**misrepresentation** /míss repri zen táysh'n/ *n.* —**misrepresentative** /míss repri zéntətiv/ *adj.* —**misrepresenter** *n.*

misrule /miss ról/ *vti.* (**-rules, -ruling, -ruled**) RULE BADLY to govern a people or place unjustly or inefficiently ■ *n.* **1.** BAD GOVERNMENT unjust or inefficient government of a people or place **2.** PUBLIC DISORDER a state of public disorder or anarchy

miss[1] /miss/ *v.* (**misses, missing, missed**) **1.** *vti.* NOT HIT TARGET to fail to hit, reach, or make contact with sb or sth that is being aimed at **2.** *vt.* NOT ATTEND OR CATCH to fail to be present or on time for sth, or to fail to meet or be on time for sb **3.** *vt.* NOT HEAR, SEE, OR UNDERSTAND to fail to hear, see, or understand sth, e.g. through inattention or being distracted **4.** *vt.* NOT TAKE ADVANTAGE OF CHANCE to fail to take advantage of a chance or opportunity **5.** *vti.* FAIL TO ACHIEVE to fail to achieve a set target or goal **6.** *vt.* AVOID to escape or avoid sb or sth, especially being hurt or being involved in a dangerous or unpleasant situation **7.** *vt.* OMIT to leave sth out **8.** *vt.* DESIRE SB'S PRESENCE to feel sorry that sb or sth is absent ○ *missed her a lot while she was away* **9.** *vt.* DISCOVER ABSENCE OF to realize that sb or sth is not there, at a time when or in a place where sb would expect him, her, or it to be present ○ *He was halfway home before he missed his wallet.* **10.** *vi.* MISFIRE to fail to ignite the fuel mixture in the cylinder (*refers to an internal-combustion engine*) ■ *n.* **1.** FAILURE TO HIT a failure to hit, reach, or make contact with sb or sth aimed at **2.** A FAILURE sth that does not succeed or fails to impress [Old English *missan*. Ultimately from a prehistoric Germanic word meaning 'to go wrong', which is also the ancestor of English *mis-*.] —**missable** *adj.* ◇ **give sth a miss** to choose not to do sth or attend sth (*informal*) ◇ **miss the boat** *or* **bus** to fail to take advantage of an opportunity

miss out *v.* **1.** *vt.* OMIT to omit or overlook sth ○ *You missed out the best bit of the whole story.* **2.** *vi.* LOSE OPPORTUNITY to lose an opportunity of doing sth

miss[2] /miss/ *n.* **1.** WAY OF ADDRESSING A YOUNG WOMAN a term of address for a girl or young woman, sometimes used in place of her name (*dated*) **2.** YOUNG WOMAN a girl or young woman [Mid-17thC. Shortening of MISTRESS.]

Miss *n.* **1.** TITLE PRECEDING A NAME a title placed before the name of a girl or unmarried woman **2.** WINNER'S TITLE used together with a place name or another word in the winner's title awarded in a beauty contest or similar event ○ *Miss Panama* **3.** WAY OF ADDRESSING A WOMAN TEACHER a term of address for or way of referring to a woman teacher

Miss. *abbr.* **1.** mission **2.** missionary **3.** Mississippi

missal /míss'l/ *n.* a book that contains all the prayers, responses, and hymns used in the Roman Catholic Mass [13thC. From medieval Latin *missale*, from, ultimately, late Latin *missa* (see MASS).]

missel thrush *n.* = **mistle thrush**

missense /míss senss/ *n.* a genetic mutation in which a genetic coding sequence (**codon**) for one amino acid is changed to one that codes for another

misshapen /miss sháypən/, **misshaped** /-sháypt/ *adj.* having an undesirably unusual shape —**misshapenly** *adv.* —**misshapenness** *n.*

missile /míssīl/ *n.* **1.** ROCKET-PROPELLED WEAPON a weapon consisting of a warhead propelled by a rocket **2.** PROJECTILE any object thrown or launched as a weapon, e.g. a stone or bullet [Early 17thC. From Latin *missilis*, from, ultimately, *mittere* 'to send' (source of English *mission*).]

missilery /míssīlri/, **missilry** *n.* **1.** MISSILES COLLECTIVELY missiles, considered collectively **2.** OPERATING OF MISSILES the designing, building, or operating of missiles

missing /míssing/ *adj.* **1.** ABSENT not present in an expected place, absent, or lost ○ *There's a page missing from the book.* **2.** DISAPPEARED not yet traced and not known for certain to be alive, but not confirmed as dead ○ *missing persons* ◇ **go missing** to disappear or become lost, untraceable, or unaccounted for ◇ **missing in action** absent after combat and not known to be captured, injured, or dead

missing link *n.* **1.** ANIMAL LINKING APES TO HUMANS an animal theorized or sought as a transitional evolutionary stage between apes and humans **2.** STH REQUIRED FOR COMPLETION sth that is absent from a sequence or series and is needed to connect up its various parts and complete it

missiology /míssi ólləji/ *n.* the study of Christian missionary work [Mid-20thC. Coined from MISSION + -OLOGY.]

mission /mísh'n/ *n.* **1.** ASSIGNED TASK a particular task given to a person or group to carry out **2.** CALLING an aim or task that sb believes it is his or her duty to carry out or to which he or she attaches special importance and devotes special care **3.** AEROSP SPACE VEHICLE'S TRIP a single flight or voyage of a military aircraft or a spacecraft **4.** GROUP OF REPRESENTATIVES a group of people sent to a country to represent their government, a business, or other organization **5.** *US* POL REPRESENTATION ABROAD a permanent diplomatic delegation in another country **6.** CHR GROUP OF CHURCH WORKERS a body of people sent by a church to another part of the country or to a foreign country to spread their faith or do medical and social work **7.** CHR CHURCH WORK IN THE COMMUNITY a campaign of religious work, often including community aid at home or abroad, carried out by a church **8.** CHR COMMUNICATION OF BELIEFS the vocation or work of a church or other religious organization or of individuals in communicating their faith in a variety of ways to the wider community **9.** CHR HOUSING USED BY MISSIONARIES a building or group of buildings belonging to a missionary organization **10.** CHR MISSIONARY'S TERRITORY an area assigned to a missionary or missionary group **11.** CHR PLACE THAT HELPS THE NEEDY a centre run by a religious or charitable organization offering food, shelter, aid, and spiritual comfort to needy people **12.** CHR MINOR CHURCH a church that has no permanent clergy and is supported by a larger church ■ *adj.* **mission, Mission** IN SPANISH MISSION STYLE relating to or similar to a style of architecture or heavy dark oak furniture used in early Spanish missions in the southwestern United States ■ *vt.* (**-sions, -sioning, -sioned**) **1.** SEND ON A MISSION to send sb on or give sb a mission **2.** OPERATE A MISSION to establish or conduct a religious mission in a place or among a people [Late 16thC. Directly or via French from the Latin stem *mission-*, from, ultimately, *mittere* 'to send off'.]

WORD KEY: ORIGIN

The Latin word *mittere*, from which **mission** is derived, is also the source of English *admit, commit, mess, message, missile, missive, permit, promise, remit, submit*, and *transmit*.

missionary /mísh'nəri/ *n.* (*plural* **-ies**) **1.** SB WHO DOES A CHURCH'S WORK ABROAD sb sent to another country by a church to spread its faith or to do social and medical work **2.** PERSUADER sb who tries to persuade others to accept or join sth such as a belief, cause, or movement ■ *adj.* OF OR LIKE A MISSIONARY relating to or typical of a missionary

missionary position *n.* a position for sexual intercourse in which the woman lies on her back and the man lies on top of and facing her [Because missionaries held it to be least reprehensible]

missioner /mísh'nər/ *n.* **1.** = **missionary 2.** HEAD OF PARISH MISSION a person in charge of a mission church in a parish

mission statement *n.* a formal document that states the aims of a company or organization

missis /míssiz/, **missus** *n.* (*informal*) **1.** WAY OF ADDRESSING A WOMAN used as a term of address for a woman, sometimes in place of her name **2.** WIFE used to refer to a man's wife or woman partner, usually either by the man himself or by another man (*sometimes considered offensive*) [Late 18thC. Alteration of MISTRESS.]

Mississauga /míssi sáwgə/ city in southern Ontario, Canada, on the shore of Lake Ontario. Population: 544,383 (1996).

Mississippi

Mississippi /míssi síppi/ **1.** state in the southeastern United States, bordered by Tennessee, Alabama, Louisiana, and Arkansas, and northwest of the Gulf of Mexico. Capital: Jackson. Population: 2,730,501 (1997). Area: 123,530 sq. km/47,695 sq. mi. **2.** major river in the United States, flowing between Minnesota and Louisiana, with a basin of 3,100,000 sq. km/1,200,000 sq. mi. Length: 3,782 km/2,350 mi.

Mississippian /míssi síppi ən/ *n.* **1.** SB FROM MISSISSIPPI sb who lives in or was born or brought up in the US state of Mississippi **2.** GEOL GEOLOGICAL EPOCH the epoch of geological time in North America when large land masses were submerged underwater, 362.5 to 320 million years ago. It is the first of two epochs of the Carboniferous Period used by North American geologists. —**Mississippian** *adj.*

missive /míssiv/ *n.* a letter or written communication [Early 16thC. Via medieval Latin *missivus* from, ultimately, Latin *mittere* 'to send' (source of English *mission*).]

Missouri[1] /mi zóori/ state in the north-central United States, bordered by Iowa, Illinois, Kentucky, Tennessee, Arkansas, Oklahoma, Kansas, and Nebraska. Capital: Jefferson City. Population: 5,402,058 (1997). Area: 180,545 sq. km/69,709 sq. mi. —**Missourian** *n.*, *adj.*

Missouri

Missouri[2] the longest river in the United States, flowing from Montana into the Mississippi River in Missouri. Length: 4,128 km/2,565 mi.

misspell /míss spél/ (-**spells**, -**spelling**, -**spelt** /-spélt/ *or* -**spelled**) *vt.* to spell a word incorrectly

misspelling /míss spélling/ *n.* an incorrect spelling of a word

misspelt past participle, past tense of **misspell**

misspend /míss spénd/ (-**spends**, -**spending**, -**spent** /-spént/) *vt.* to spend money or time badly or wastefully —**misspender** *n.*

misstate /míss stáyt/ (-**states**, -**stating**, -**stated**) *vt.* to state sth incorrectly, e.g. by giving false information or mispronouncing sth —**misstatement** *n.*

misstep /míss stép/ *n.* **1. WRONG STEP** a bad or awkward step, or a step in a wrong direction **2. FAUX PAS** an error in judgment or conduct

missus *n.* = **missis**

missy /míssi/ (*plural* -**ies**) *n.* used as a term of address for a girl or young woman, often expressing affection or reprimand (*informal; sometimes considered offensive*)

mist /mist/ *n.* **1. METEOROL THIN FOG** a thin grey cloud of water droplets that condenses in the atmosphere just above the ground, limiting the view and making objects appear indistinct **2. CONDENSED WATER VAPOUR** a film of water vapour that has condensed on a surface **3. FINE SPRAY** a fine spray of liquid, e.g. from an atomizer or aerosol **4. LIQUID SUSPENSION IN GAS** a suspension of liquid in a gas **5. OBSCURING THING** sth that makes it difficult to see or understand sth ■ *v.* (**mists**, **misting**, **misted**) **1.** *vti.* **FILM OVER** to cover or obscure sth in a mist, or to become covered in or obscured by mist **2.** *vi.* **BECOME BLURRED BY TEARS** to become blurred by tears **3.** *vt.* **SPRAY STH** to apply a fine liquid spray to sth [Old English. Ultimately from an Indo-European word meaning 'urinate', which is also the ancestor of English *micturate*.]

mistake /mi stáyk/ *n.* **1. INCORRECT ACT OR DECISION** an incorrect, unwise, or unfortunate act or decision caused by bad judgment or a lack of information or care ○ *It's an easy mistake to make.* **2. ERROR** sth in a piece of work that is incorrect, e.g. a misspelling or a misprint **3. MISUNDERSTANDING** a misunderstanding of sth ○ *There must be some mistake, I didn't order this.* ■ *vt.* (-**takes**, -**taking**, -**took** /-stóók/, -**taken** /-stáykən/) **1. MISUNDERSTAND STH** to misunderstand or misinterpret sth ○ *I mistook the meaning of the phrase.* **2. IDENTIFY SB OR STH INCORRECTLY** to identify sb or sth incorrectly or fail to recognize sb or sth ○ *We tend to mistake infatuation for real love.* **3. CHOOSE STH INCORRECTLY** to choose sth incorrectly or injudiciously [14thC. From Old Norse *mistaka* 'to take in error'.] —**mistakable** *adj.* —**mistakably** *adv.* —**mistaker** *n.* ◇ **by mistake** accidentally, without wishing or intending to do sth

— WORD KEY: SYNONYMS —
mistake, error, inaccuracy, slip, blunder, faux pas
CORE MEANING: sth incorrect or improper
mistake a general word used to talk about sth incorrect, inappropriate, or unwise; **error** sth that deviates from a recognized standard or guide. It is also used as a more formal word for *mistake*; **inaccuracy** sth that is incorrect because it has been measured, calculated, or copied incorrectly; **slip** a fairly informal word for a minor mistake, especially one caused by carelessness; **blunder**

an obvious and usually serious mistake, especially one that seems to be a result of ignorance or ineptitude; **faux pas** a fairly formal term for a mistake in behaviour or speech that constitutes a breach of etiquette.

mistaken /mi stáykən/ *adj.* **1. WRONG IN YOUR OPINION** wrong or incorrect in, e.g. an assumption, belief, or your understanding of sth ○ *If you think that'll work, then you're sadly mistaken.* **2. BASED ON INCORRECT INFORMATION** based on incorrect information or values ○ *a mistaken sense of loyalty* —**mistakenly** *adv.* —**mistakenness** *n.*

Mistassini, Lake /místə séeni/ lake in central Canada, the largest in Quebec Province. Area: 2,200 sq. km/840 sq. mi.

mister /místər/ *n.* **1. WAY TO ADDRESS A MAN** used as a term of address for a man, usually in place of his name (*dated*) **2. HUSBAND** used to refer to a woman's husband or man partner, either by the woman or by another woman (*informal; sometimes considered offensive*) [Mid-16thC. Alteration of MASTER.]

Mister *n.* **1. FORM OF 'MR'** used as the full form of the courtesy title 'Mr' **2. MIL WAY TO ADDRESS JUNIOR OFFICERS** used as the official term of address for men junior officers or warrant officers **3. SURG WAY TO ADDRESS SURGEON** used as the usual title for a surgeon **4. SHIPPING WAY TO ADDRESS MERCHANT NAVY OFFICER** used as the official term of address for any man officer in the merchant navy except the captain of a ship [Mid-18thC. From MISTER.]

misterm /miss túrm/ (-**terms**, -**terming**, -**termed**) *vt.* to call sth by a wrong or inappropriate name

Misti, Volcán /méesti-/ dormant volcano in southern Peru, in the Andes mountains, northeast of Arequipa city. Height: 5,822 m/19,101 ft.

mistime /miss tím/ (-**times**, -**timing**, -**timed**) *vt.* to time sth wrongly, usually by missing the precise point of time at which sth should be done to be successful [Old English *mistimian*, from *timian* 'to time']

mistle thrush /míss'l-/, **missel thrush** *n.* a large European thrush with a spotted breast and greyish back that feeds on berries, especially those of mistletoe. Latin name: *Turdus viscivorus.*

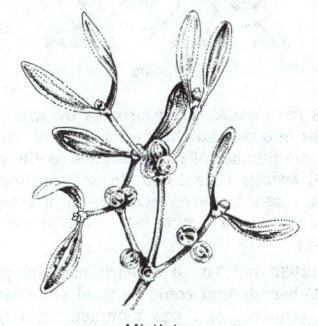

Mistletoe

mistletoe /míss'l tō/ *n.* **1. PARASITIC SHRUB** an evergreen shrub of Europe and Asia that grows as a parasite on trees such as apple and oak, has leaves in horseshoe-shaped pairs, and bears white berries in winter. Latin name: *Viscum album.* **2. PLANT RESEMBLING MISTLETOE** a North American shrub that resembles the true mistletoe. Latin name: *Phoradendron flavescens.* **3. CHRISTMAS DECORATION** a sprig of mistletoe traditionally used as a decoration and for kissing under at Christmas [Old English *misteltan.* Ultimately from a prehistoric Germanic word meaning 'urine' (because it is propagated by the droppings of the mistle thrush).]

mistook past tense of **mistake**

mistral /místrəl/ *n.* a powerful cold dry northeasterly wind that blows in the south of France [Early 17thC. Via French from, ultimately, Latin *magistralis* 'dominant', from its power.]

mistreat /miss tréet/ (-**treats**, -**treating**, -**treated**) *vt.* to treat sb or sth badly or roughly

— WORD KEY: SYNONYMS —
See Synonyms at *misuse.*

mistress /místrəss/ *n.* **1. EXTRAMARITAL LOVER** a woman with whom a man has a usually long-term extramarital sexual relationship and for whom he often provides financial support **2. WOMAN OWNER OF A PET** the woman owner of a pet animal **3. ABLE WOMAN** a woman who is highly skilled in a particular activity ○ *a mistress of the art of negotiation* **4. WOMAN TEACHER** a woman teacher (*dated*) **5. PERSONIFICATION AS WOMAN** sth that rules or controls, personified as a woman ○ *Venice, once mistress of the seas* **6. WOMAN OWNER OR CONTROLLER OF STH** a woman who owns or controls sth, e.g. a woman owner of an estate, head of a household, or employer of servants **7. LOVED WOMAN** a woman with whom a man is in love (*archaic*) [13thC. From Old French *maistresse*, feminine of *maistre* (see MASTER).]

Mistress /místrəss/ *n.* used as a courtesy title to address a married woman, usually in front of the surname (*archaic*)

mistress of ceremonies *n.* a woman in charge of the proceedings at an event or entertainment

mistrial /miss trí əl/ *n.* **1. INVALID TRIAL** a trial that is invalid because a mistake such as an error in procedure has been made **2. US INCONCLUSIVE TRIAL** a trial that does not come to a proper conclusion, e.g. because the jury cannot agree on a verdict

mistrust /miss trúst/ *n.* **1. SUSPICION** suspicion about or lack of confidence in sb or sth ■ *vt.* (-**trusts**, -**trusting**, -**trusted**) **BE SUSPICIOUS OF SB OR STH** to be suspicious of and unable to trust or rely on sb or sth —**mistruster** *n.* —**mistrustful** *adj.* —**mistrustfully** *adv.* —**mistrustfulness** *n.*

misty /místi/ (-**ier**, -**iest**) *adj.* **1. METEOROL COVERED IN MIST** with a lot of mist in the air or surrounded or covered by mist ○ *a misty mountain* ○ *a misty morning* **2. LIKE MIST** like mist, especially in being in a cloud or spray of fine drops **3. DIM AND INDISTINCT** rather dim and indistinct, as if veiled by mist [Old English *mistig*, from *mist* (see MIST)] —**mistily** *adv.* —**mistiness** *n.*

misty-eyed *adj.* **1. WITH TEARS IN THE EYES** with a film of tears in the eyes **2. SENTIMENTAL** sentimental or dreamlike

misunderstand /miss undər stánd/ (-**stands**, -**standing**, -**stood** /-stóod/) *vti.* to fail to realize the real or intended meaning of sth, the true nature of sth, or what sb is really like

misunderstanding /míss undər stánding/ *n.* **1. LACK OF COMPREHENSION** a failure to understand or interpret sth correctly **2. MINOR DISPUTE** a minor disagreement or dispute

misunderstood past participle, past tense of **misunderstand** ■ *adj.* **NOT CORRECTLY UNDERSTOOD** not correctly understood, or not properly and sympathetically appreciated ○ *a misunderstood teenager*

misusage /miss yóossij, miss yóozij/ *n.* **1. LANG INAPPROPRIATE USE OF LANGUAGE** a wrong or inappropriate use of language **2.** = **misuse n. 1**

misuse *n.* /míss yóoss/ **1. WRONG USE** the incorrect or improper use of sth **2. CRUEL TREATMENT** cruel treatment of a person or animal ■ *vt.* /miss yóoz/ (-**uses**, -**using**, -**used**) **1. USE STH WRONGLY** to use sth in an incorrect or improper way or for a dishonest purpose **2. TREAT SB CRUELLY** to treat a person or animal cruelly (*archaic*) —**misused** *adj.*

— WORD KEY: SYNONYMS —
misuse, abuse, ill-treat, maltreat, mistreat
CORE MEANING: wrong or bad use or treatment of sb or sth
misuse a neutral word meaning to put sth to an inappropriate use or purpose. It can be used in more formal contexts to talk about treating a person or animal badly or harshly; **abuse** a stronger word than *misuse*, used to emphasize that the way sth is being used is wrong or inappropriate, especially sth that should be used responsibly such as power or privilege or a substance that should be used with caution such as alcohol or a drug. It is also used to refer to cruel or violent treatment of a person or animal, especially on a regular or habitual basis; **ill-treat** used to talk about treating a person or animal badly or wrongly. It suggests a more severe degree of bad treatment than 'mistreat'; **maltreat** a more formal word meaning the same as *ill-treat*; **mistreat** to treat a person badly, inconsiderately, or unfairly,

not necessarily in a way that involves cruelty, physical abuse, or the desire to harm. It can also be used to mean treating an animal badly.

misuser /míss yóozər/ *n.* the illegal use of a right, privilege, or position of authority [Mid-16thC]

MIT *abbr.* Massachusetts Institute of Technology

mitch /mich/ (**mitches, mitching, mitched**) *vi. UK, Ireland* to stay away from school without permission (*regional informal*) [14thC. Probably from Old French *muchier* 'to hide, lurk' (probable source of English *mooch*).]

Mitchell /míchəl/ river in northern Queensland, Australia, that rises in the Atherton Tableland and flows west to the Gulf of Carpentaria. Length: 560 km/348 mi.

Mitchell, Joni (*b.* 1943) Canadian singer and songwriter. Her albums include *Clouds* (1969), *Blue* (1971), and *Wild Things Run Fast* (1982). Real name **Roberta Joan Anderson**

Mitchell, Reginald Joseph (1895–1937) British aircraft designer. As chief designer at the Vickers Armstrong Supermarine Company, he developed seaplanes and created the Spitfire fighter.

Mitchell, Sir Thomas Livingstone (1792–1855) British-born Australian explorer and surveyor. He was leader of four major expeditions to the interior of eastern Australia.

Mitchum /míchəm/, **Robert** (1917–86) US film actor. His many films include *Night of the Hunter* (1955), *Cape Fear* (1961), and *Farewell My Lovely* (1975).

mite[1] /mīt/ *n.* INSECTS a tiny eight-legged creature related to spiders and ticks. Some mites live freely and some as parasites that can carry disease, attack plants, and cause human allergies. Order: Acarina. [Old English *mīte*, from a prehistoric Germanic base meaning 'cut' (which probably also produced English *mite*[2]), via the meaning 'sth cut up small']

mite[2] /mīt/ *n.* **1.** SMALL CHILD a small child or animal, especially one that inspires pity (*informal*) **2.** SMALL AMOUNT a small piece or small amount (*dated*) **3.** SMALL COIN a small coin of little value (*archaic*) [14thC. From Middle Low German and Middle Dutch *mīte*, a small Flemish coin, also 'tiny animal'.]

miter *n., vt. US* = **mitre**

Mitford /mítfərd/, **Jessica** (1917–97) British-born US writer. Her best-known book is *The American Way of Death* (1965). *Hons and Rebels* (1960) gives an account of her eccentric family, including her sister Nancy Mitford.

Mitford, Nancy (1904–73) British writer. Author of *Love in a Cold Climate* (1949) and *The Blessing* (1951), she was the sister of Jessica Mitford.

mither /mīthər/ (**mithers, mithering, mithered**) *v.* (*regional*) **1.** *vt.* PESTER SB to pester or annoy sb **2.** *vi.* FUSS to worry or fuss [Late 17thC. Variant of MOITHER; of unknown origin.]

Mithraism /míth ray izəm/ *n.* a religion originating in Persia and involving worship of the god Mithras. It became popular among the Roman military in the Late Roman Empire. [Early 19thC] —**Mithraic** /mith ráy ik/ *adj.* —**Mithraist** /míth rayist/ *n.*

Mithras /míth rass/ *n.* the god of light, truth, and goodness in the Zoroastrian tradition and Persian mythology. He is often shown with a bull, which he is said to have slain before fertilizing the world with its blood. [Mid-16thC. Via Latin *Mithras* from, ultimately, Old Persian and Avestan *Mithra*.]

mithridate /míthri dayt/ *n.* a substance believed in ancient medicine and folklore to be an antidote to every poison and a cure for every disease [Early 16thC. Via medieval Latin *mithridatum*, from, ultimately, late Latin *mithridatius* 'relating to Mithridates'. Named after Mithridates VI, king of Pontus (died 63 BC), who was reputedly immune to poisons.] —**mithridatic** /mithri dáttik/ *adj.* —**mithridatism** /míthri day tizəm/ *n.*

miticide /mítti sīd/ *n.* a substance that kills mites —**miticidal** /mítti sīd'l/ *adj.*

mitigate /mítti gayt/ (**-gates, -gating, -gated**) *vt.* **1.** PARTLY EXCUSE A CRIME to make an offence or crime less serious or more excusable **2.** LESSEN STH to make sth less harsh, severe, or violent [15thC. From Latin *mitigatus*, past participle of *mitigare* 'to make mild', from assumed *mitigus* 'making mild', ultimately from *mitis* 'gentle, soft' + *agere* 'to make'.] —**mitigable** /míttigəb'l/ *adj.* —**mitigation** /mítti gáysh'n/ *n.*

mitigating /mítti gayting/ *adj.* making an offence or a crime seem less serious, or partly excusing it ○ *mitigating circumstances*

mitis /mítiss, meétiss/, **mitis metal** *n.* a form of iron made malleable by having a small amount of aluminium added to it [Late 19thC. Named by the inventor of the process, P. Östberg of Stockholm, apparently from Latin *mitis* 'mild' used in the sense found in 'mild steel'.]

Mitnagged /mít naa géd/ (*plural* **-dim** /mít naag dím/), **Mitnaged** (*plural* **-nagdim**), **Misnaged** /míss naa géd/ (*plural* **-dim** /míss naag dím/) *n.* in the 18th and 19th centuries, a Jew in central and eastern Europe who believed in rationalism and opposed Hassidism [Early 20thC. From Hebrew *mitnaggēd* 'opponent'.]

mitochondrion /mītō kóndri ən/ (*plural* **-a** /mītō kóndri ə/) *n.* a small round or rod-shaped body that is found in the cytoplasm of most cells and produces enzymes for the metabolic conversion of food to energy [Early 20thC. From Greek *mitos* 'thread' + *khondrion*, from *khondros* 'granule, lump (of salt)'.] —**mitochondrial** /mītō kóndri əl/ *adj.*

mitogen /mītəjən/ *n.* PHYSIOL a substance or agent that induces mitosis [Mid-20thC. Formed from MITOSIS + -GEN.]

mitomycin /mītō míssin/ *n.* any of a group of antibiotics produced by a soil bacterium that inhibit DNA synthesis and are used against tumours [Mid-20thC. Coined from *mito-* (perhaps from Greek *mitos* 'thread', MITOSIS, or MITOCHONDRION) + -MYCIN.]

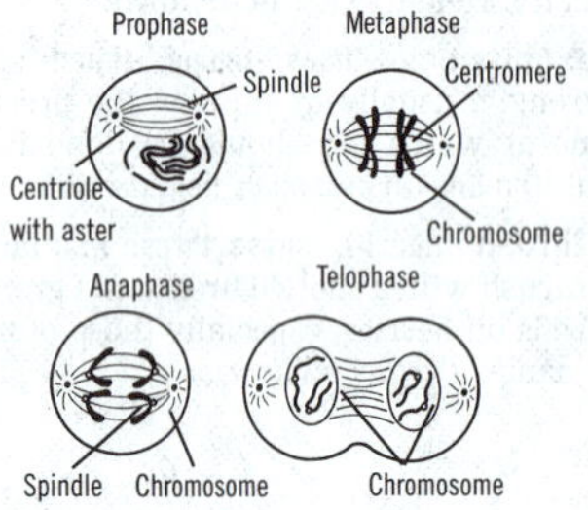

Prophase
Metaphase
Spindle
Centromere
Centriole with aster
Chromosome
Anaphase
Telophase
Spindle
Chromosome
Chromosome

Mitosis

mitosis /mī tóssiss/ *n.* the process by which a cell divides into two daughter cells, each of which has the same number of chromosomes as the original cell. ◊ **meiosis** [Late 19thC. Coined from Greek *mitos* 'thread' + -OSIS. So named because in the first stage of the process the chromatin of the cell nucleus appears as long threads.]

mitrailleuse /mítrī óz/ *n.* an early machine gun that had 35 barrels that could be fired simultaneously or in sequence and was mounted on a carriage drawn by four horses. The gun was developed in France and first used in the Franco-Prussian War of 1870. [Late 19thC. Ultimately from French *mitrailler* 'to fire mitraille', from *mitraille* 'small money, pieces of metal', alteration of Old French *mitaille*, from *mite*.]

mitral /mītrəl/ *adj.* relating to a bishop's mitre or like it in shape, especially in having separate front and back sections [Early 17thC. Via modern Latin *mitralis* from Latin *mitra* (see MITRE).]

mitral stenosis *n.* the narrowing of the heart's mitral valve as the result of disease

mitral valve *n.* the one-way valve between the upper and lower chambers, or atrium and ventricle, on the left side of the heart [Named after its shape]

mitre /mītər/ *n.* **1.** CHR BISHOP'S HAT the ceremonial head-dress of a Christian bishop or abbot, consisting of a tall pointed hat creased across the top, with two ribbons hanging down the back **2.** WOODWORK = **mitre joint 3.** WOODWORK SURFACES OF A MITRE JOINT either of the surfaces that are joined together to form a mitre joint **4.** SEW DIAGONAL JOIN AT THE CORNER BETWEEN HEMS in sewing, a diagonal join between the edges of two hems that meet at a corner of a piece of fabric ■ *vt.* (**mitres, mitreing, mitred**) **1.** WOODWORK JOIN PIECES OF WOOD to join pieces of wood using a mitre joint **2.** WOODWORK SHAPE WOOD FOR JOINT to shape the end of a piece of wood, especially by cutting it off at an angle of 45° when making a corner or mitre joint **3.** SEW DIAGONALLY JOIN HEMS AT THE CORNER in sewing, to make a diagonal join at a corner between two hems **4.** CHR GIVE A MITRE TO SB to confer a mitre on sb, indicating promotion to the rank of bishop [14thC. Via Old French from Latin *mitra*, from Greek, 'belt, turban', of uncertain origin: perhaps from an Asian language.] —**mitrer** *n.*

mitre block *n.* a block with slots cut in it to guide a handsaw at the appropriate angle when cutting a mitre joint

mitre box *n.* a box with open ends that is used to hold wood and guide a handsaw at the appropriate angle when cutting a mitre joint

mitre joint *n.* a corner joint in woodwork, usually made by cutting two ends to be joined at 45° angles and gluing or nailing them together into a right angle

mitre square *n.* a tool used in cutting wood at an angle that has a bevelled arm either fixed at an angle of 45° or adjustable to any angle

mitrewort /mītər wurt/ (*plural* **mitreworts** *or* **mitrewort**) *n.* an Asian and North American plant of the saxifrage family with clusters of small white flowers and seed pods that look a little like a bishop's mitre. Genus: *Mitella*. [Mid-19thC. From the shape of its capsule.]

Mits'twa /mi tseéwə/ town and seaport in northern Eritrea, on the Red Sea. Population: 19,400 (1989).

mitt /mit/ *n.* **1.** MITTEN a mitten, especially a child's mitten (*informal*) **2.** HAND COVERING a covering for the hand and fingers, especially one shaped like a mitten ○ *an oven mitt* **3.** HAND a hand, especially when large, clumsy, or dirty (*slang*) **4.** BASEBALL BASEBALL PLAYER'S PADDED GLOVE in baseball, a large fingerless padded glove worn by the catcher or the first baseman **5.** GLOVE WITHOUT FINGERS a woman's glove, popular in the 19th century, that left the fingers uncovered [Mid-18thC. Shortening of MITTEN.]

mitten /mítt'n/ *n.* a glove with one covering for the thumb and one covering for the four fingers [14thC. From French *mitaine*, of uncertain origin: perhaps originally denoting 'glove cut off at the middle', ultimately from Latin *medietas* 'half' (source of English *moiety*).]

Mitterrand /meétə roN/, **François** (1916–96) French statesman. A Socialist, as president (1981–95) he worked to strengthen France's position in the European Union.

mittimus /míttiməss/ (*plural* **-muses**) *n.* an official order to send sb to prison [15thC. From Latin, literally 'we send', the first word of this order in Latin.]

mitzvah /mítsvə/ (*plural* **-vahs** *or* **-voth** /míts vōt/) *n.* **1.** RELIGIOUS DUTY a Jewish religious duty or obligation, especially one of the commandments of Jewish religious law **2.** GOOD DEED an act of kindness performed by or to a Jewish person [Mid-17thC. From Hebrew *miṣwāh* 'commandment'.]

mix /miks/ *v.* (**mixes, mixing, mixed**) **1.** *vt.* COMBINE INGREDIENTS to combine ingredients by putting them together or blending them to make a single new substance ○ *Mix the flour and dried fruit together.* **2.** *vi.* BE COMBINED to become combined, or be capable of becoming combined ○ *Oil and water don't mix.* **3.** *vti.* MAKE STH BY COMBINING to form or create sth by combining separate ingredients ○ *Would you mix me a cocktail?* **4.** *vt.* ADD STH EXTRA to add sth as an extra or later ingredient ○ *Mix the fruit into the batter.* **5.** *vt.* COMBINE THINGS to do sth at the same time as sth else, or to arrange things next to or alongside each other ○ *mixing browns and golds to create a sense of warmth* **6.** *vi.* GO TOGETHER to go well together ○ *Reds and greens just don't mix.* **7.** *vi.* MEET PEOPLE to meet other people socially, or enjoy being with other people in social situations **8.** *vt.* CONSUME THINGS TOGETHER to consume different drinks or foods on a single occasion **9.** *vti.* RECORDING BLEND MUSICAL SOUNDS to adjust and blend sounds from prerecorded tracks or live performers to create the desired combination of musical sounds. The process is done either by using a mixing deck or a multitrack tape machine. **10.** *vt.* BIOL CROSSBREED PLANTS OR ANIMALS to breed one variety of a plant or animal with a different variety in order to create a new variety ■ *n.* **1.** ACT OF MIXING STH an act of mixing sth, or an occasion on which it is done ○ *Give all the ingredients a good mix.* **2. COMBINATION** a combination or blend of things ○ *There's an intriguing mix of styles on her latest CD.* **3. SUBSTANCE USED TO PREPARE STH** a substance, especially a number of dried ingredients in powder form, from which sth is prepared ○ *cake mix* **4. RECORDING MUSICAL BLEND** a balanced blend of live or prerecorded musical sound ○ *He thinks the drums are too low in the mix.* **5. RECORDING VERSION OF A RECORDING** a version of a musical recording that has been changed in some way to give it a different type of sound ○ *Their last hit has been rereleased in a disco mix.* **6. BUILDING RATIO OF MORTAR INGREDIENTS** the ratio of sand and cement in mortar, or of sand, cement, and gravel in concrete [15thC. Formed from MIXED.] —**mixable** *adj.*

mix down *vt.* to create a final finished sound recording by blending elements that have been recorded separately

mix up *v.* **1.** *vt.* **MISTAKE THE IDENTITY OF THINGS** to confuse things or people and mistakenly identify one as the other ○ *People always mix her up with her sister.* **2.** *vt.* **CHANGE THE ORDER OF THINGS** to change the usual or previous order of things, either deliberately or by accident ○ *The pages got mixed up on the way to the printer's.* **3.** *vti.* **BECOME INVOLVED IN STH** to involve yourself with a particular group of people or activity, especially sth wrong or illegal **4.** *vt.* **MAKE STH FROM INGREDIENTS** to prepare or make sth by mixing different ingredients **5.** *vt.* **MAKE SB CONFUSED** to make sb confused and unsure of sth ○ *He got mixed up because the street names sounded so similar.*

mixdown /míks down/ *n.* **1. MIXING OF A RECORDING** the process of converting a multitrack recording, usually a master tape recorded in a studio, into a stereo recording, usually for public release **2. NEW RECORDING** a new recording produced by a mixdown

mixed /míkst/ *adj.* **1. WITH DIFFERENT THINGS COMBINED** consisting of different elements or different kinds of things combined **2. INVOLVING BOTH SEXES** intended for, used by, or done by people of both sexes together **3. INVOLVING DIFFERENT RACES** intended for, used by, or done by people of different races together **4. WITH INCONSISTENT ELEMENTS** consisting of inconsistent or conflicting elements ○ *The play has had mixed reviews.* [15thC. Ultimately via Old French from Latin *mixtus* (source of English *mustang*), past participle of *miscere* 'to mix' (source of English *meddle, miscellaneous,* and *promiscuous*).] —**mixedly** /míksidli/ *adv.* —**mixedness** /-nəss/ *n.*

mixed bag *n.* a group of people or things of widely differing kinds

mixed blessing *n.* sth that has both advantages and disadvantages or good points and bad points

mixed doubles *n.* a tennis, table tennis, or badminton match played by two pairs, each consisting of a man and a woman (*takes a singular verb*)

mixed economy *n.* an economy in which some industries and businesses are state-owned and some are privately owned

mixed farming *n.* farming that combines growing crops and rearing livestock on the one farm

mixed grill *n.* a dish consisting of a grilled meat chop or steak, kidneys, sausage, bacon, mushrooms, and tomatoes

mixed marriage *n.* a marriage between people of different racial or religious backgrounds

mixed media *n.* **1. USING DIFFERENT ARTISTIC MEDIA** the use of different artistic media, e.g. painting combined with photography or collage, in a single composition or work **2. USING DIFFERENT ADVERTISING METHODS** the use of different advertising media together, e.g. billboards, TV, and radio

mixed metaphor *n.* a combination of two or more metaphors that together evoke a strange or incongruous image, e.g. 'This thorn in my side has finally bitten the dust'

mixed nerve *n.* a nerve that has both motor and sensory fibres, and thus has nerve impulses passing in both directions

mixed number *n.* a figure that consists of a whole number and a fraction, such as the figure $2\frac{3}{4}$

mixed-up *adj.* (*informal*) **1. BADLY ORGANIZED** in a disorganized state **2. CONFUSED** in a state of emotional or psychological confusion

mixed-use *adj.* US combining commercial and residential elements in a single property, e.g. a block of flats with offices or shops

mixer /míksər/ *n.* **1. MIXING DEVICE** a machine or device for mixing food, cement, or some other substance **2. BEVERAGES NONALCOHOLIC DRINK OFTEN MIXED WITH ALCOHOL** a nonalcoholic drink, e.g. fruit juice or soda water, that is often mixed with alcoholic drinks **3. SOCIABLE PERSON** a person considered in terms of whether he or she is good at socializing (*usually used in combination*) ○ *She's a good mixer.* **4. TROUBLEMAKER** sb who constantly creates trouble, especially by gossiping or spreading rumours (*informal*) **5. RECORDING ELECTRONIC DEVICE FOR MIXING SOUNDS** an electronic device used to adjust and combine various inputs, e.g. performed or broadcast sounds, to create a single output **6. BROADCAST, CINEMA SB CREATING SOUND FOR FILM** sb who combines various sound recordings to create the final soundtrack of a film

mixer tap *n.* a tap with separate controls for hot and cold water and a single outlet that combines both flows

mixte /míksti/, **mixte frame** *adj.* used to describe a frame for bicycles designed for women, consisting of two horizontal tubes connecting to the back axle without a crossbar [Late 20thC. 'Mixte' from French, 'mixed'.]

Mixtec /méess tek/ (*plural* **-tecs** *or* **-tec**), **Mixtecan** /meess téc ən/ (*plural* **-ans** *or* **-an**) *n.* **1. PEOPLES MEMBER OF A NATIVE MIDDLE AMERICAN PEOPLE** a member of a Native Middle American people that originally lived in southern Mexico and are now spread throughout Mexico. The Mixtec are noted for their artistic and architectural skills. **2. LANG NATIVE MIDDLE AMERICAN LANGUAGE** a Native Middle American language spoken in parts of Mexico, belonging to the Oto-Manguean family of languages. Mixtec is spoken by about 400,000 people. [Late 18thC. Via Spanish from Nahuatl *mixtecah* 'person from a cloudy place'.] —**Mixtec** *adj.*

mixter-maxter /míkstər mákstər/ *adj.* Scotland **DISORGANIZED** in a disorganized or confused state (*informal*) ■ *n.* Scotland **DISORGANIZED MESS** a confused or disorganized collection of things (*informal*) [Late 18thC. From a reduplication of *mixt*, a variant of MIXED.]

mixture /míkschər/ *n.* **1. BLEND OF INGREDIENTS** a substance containing several ingredients combined or blended together ○ *cough mixture* **2. DIFFERENT THINGS COMBINED** a number of different elements brought or existing together ○ *an interesting mixture of people* ○ *a mixture of old and new styles* **3. PHARM LIQUID MEDICINE** a liquid medicine consisting of an insoluble solid suspended in a liquid, often with flavouring and colouring **4. CHEM SUBSTANCE FORMED WITHOUT CHEMICAL REACTION** a substance consisting of two or more substances that have been combined without chemical bonding taking place **5. ENG FUEL AND AIR MIX** the combination of petrol vapour and air in an internal-combustion engine **6. ACT OF MIXING** the combining or mixing of different ingredients or elements (*formal*) [15thC. Directly or via French from Latin *mixtura*, from *mixt-*, the past participle stem of *miscere* (see MIXED).]

— **WORD KEY: SYNONYMS** —

mixture, blend, combination, compound, alloy, amalgam
CORE MEANING: sth formed by mixing materials

mixture a general word used to talk about sth formed by mixing two or more things. It does not necessarily suggest that the materials involved have bonded together to form a new whole; **blend** sth formed by putting together two or more things, especially in a skilled or scientific way, in order to form a new whole in which the original constituents are bonded irreversibly; **combination** sth formed by mixing two or more things, usually in a skilled or careful way, especially when the result is pleasing or successful. It is usually used to describe a process in which the original constituents retain their separate identities; **compound** a technical word for a chemical formed from two or more elements. It is also used generally to describe a combination of two or more things and in particular a word that is made up of two or more existing words; **alloy** a technical word for a metal such as steel that is formed by combining two or more different metallic elements; **amalgam** a technical word

for an alloy formed by combining mercury with another metal. It can also be used in a general context to describe sth that is a mixture of two or more things.

mix-up *n.* a state of confusion, or an error resulting from confusion ○ *an administrative mix-up*

Mizar /mī zaar/ *n.* a four-component multiple star in the constellation Ursa Major [From Arabic *Mi'zar* 'cloak', Mizar.]

mizzen /mízz'n/ *n.* **1. SAIL ON A MIZZENMAST** a sail on a mizzenmast **2.** = **mizzenmast** ■ *adj.* **OF A MIZZENMAST** relating to, or used on, a mizzenmast or its sail [15thC. From French *misaine* 'foresail, foremast', either from or influenced by Italian *mezzana* 'middle', with both forms ultimately from Latin *medianus* 'of the middle, median'.]

mizzenmast /mízz'n maast/ *n.* **1. 3RD MAST** on a ship with three or more masts, the third mast from the front **2. REAR MAST** on a boat such as a ketch or yawl, the mast nearest the back

mizzle[1] /mízz'l/ *n.* **DRIZZLE** very fine rain (*regional*) ■ *vi.* (**-zles, -zling, -zled**) **DRIZZLE** to rain lightly in fine drops (*regional*) [15thC. Origin uncertain: perhaps from Low German *miseln*.] —**mizzling** *adj.* —**mizzly** *adj.*

mizzle[2] /mízz'l/ (**-zles, -zling, -zled**) *vi.* to leave suddenly or quickly (*dated slang*) [Late 18thC. Origin unknown.]

mk *abbr.* FIN **1.** mark **2.** markka

Mk *abbr.* **1.** BIBLE Mark **2.** CARS mark

mks, MKS *abbr.* metre-kilogram-second

mksA *abbr.* metre-kilogram-second-ampere

mks units *npl.* the metric system of measurement, which has the metre, the kilogram, and the second as its basic units of length, mass, and time

mkt *abbr.* market

mktg *abbr.* marketing

ml *symbol.* **1.** mile ■ *abbr.* **2.** millilitre

mL *symbol.* **1.** millilambert **2.** millilitre

MLA *abbr.* **1.** Master of Landscape Architecture **2.** Member of the Legislative Assembly **3.** Modern Language Association

MLD *abbr.* MED minimum lethal dose

MLF *abbr.* multilateral (nuclear) force

MLG *abbr.* Middle Low German

MLitt /em lít/ *abbr.* Master of Letters [Latin, *Magister Litterarum*]

Mlle *abbr.* Mademoiselle

Mlles *abbr.* Mesdemoiselles

MLR *abbr.* minimum lending rate

mm *abbr.* millimetre

MM *abbr.* **1.** Messieurs **2.** Military Medal

m.m. *abbr.* mutatis mutandis

MMC *abbr.* Monopolies and Mergers Commission

MMDS *abbr.* RADIO multipoint microwave distribution system

Mme *abbr.* Madame

Mmes *abbr.* Mesdames

mmf *abbr.* PHYS magnetomotive force

mmHg *n.* a unit for measuring atmospheric pressure. Full form **millimetre of mercury**

MMM *abbr.* Member of the Order of Military Merit

MMP *abbr.* NZ Mixed Member Proportional

MMPI *abbr.* PSYCHOL Minnesota Multiphasic Personality Inventory

MMR vaccine *n.* a vaccine that is routinely given to small children to protect them against measles, mumps, and rubella

MMus *abbr.* Master of Music

Mn *symbol.* manganese

MN *abbr.* **1.** GEOG magnetic north **2.** NAVY Merchant Navy

MNA *abbr.* Member of the National Assembly (of Quebec)

MNC *abbr.* multinational company

mnemonic /ni mónnik/ *n.* **MEMORY AID** a short rhyme, phrase, or other mental technique for making information easier to memorize ■ *adj.* **1. ACTING AS A MNEMONIC** acting as a memory aid **2. RELATING TO MNEMONICS** relating to the practice of improving the memory, or to systems designed to improve the memory [Mid-18thC. Either formed from MNEMONICS or, perhaps via medieval Latin, from Greek *mnēmonikos* 'relating to memory', from the stem *mnēmon-* 'mindful'.]

mnemonics /ni mónniks/ *n.* the practice of improving or helping the memory, or the systems used to achieve this (*takes a singular verb*) [Early 18thC. From Greek *mnēmonika*, neuter plural of *mnēmonikos* (see MNEMONIC).]

Mnemosyne /nee mózzini, -móssini/ *n.* in Greek mythology, the goddess of memory and mother of the Muses [Via Latin from Greek *Mnēmosunē*]

mngr *abbr.* manager

mo /mō/ (*plural* **mos**) *n.* a moment or short while (*informal*) ○ *I'll be there in half a mo.* [Late 19thC. Shortening, in the sense 'short while', of MOMENT.]

Mo *symbol.* molybdenum

MO *abbr.* **1.** m.o. mail order **2.** Medical Officer **3.** Missouri **4.** m.o. money order **5.** COMPUT magneto-optical

mo. *abbr.* month

Mo. *abbr.* Missouri

m.o. = MO

M.O., m.o. *abbr.* modus operandi

-mo *suffix.* used after numerals to indicate the number of pages made by folding a sheet of paper ○ *16mo* [From *12mo*, an abbreviation of Latin *(in) duodecimo* '(in) a twelfth'; *duodecimus* (see DUODECIMAL)]

moa /mō ə/ *n.* a large extinct flightless bird of New Zealand similar to the ostrich that existed in a number of varieties and died out at the end of the 18th century. Family: Dinornithidae. [Mid-19thC. From Maori.]

Moab[1] /mō ab/ *n.* the son of Lot and his eldest daughter, whose descendants were the enemies of Israel

Moab[2] /mō ab/ ancient kingdom situated on a plateau to the east of the Dead Sea in modern-day Jordan — **Moabite** /mō ə bīt/ *n., adj.*

moan /mōn/ *v.* (**moaning, moaned, moans, moaned**) **1.** *vi.* **MAKE A LOW SOUND EXPRESSING PAIN** to make a long low sound that expresses pain or misery **2.** *vti.* **COMPLAIN** to complain about sth, especially unreasonably or needlessly (*informal*) ○ *What's he moaning on about?* **3.** *vt.* **SAY STH IN A PAINED VOICE** to say sth in a voice that expresses pain or misery ○ *'Oh no!', she moaned* **4.** *vi.* **MAKE A NOISE LIKE SB IN PAIN** to make a long low noise that sounds like sb expressing pain or misery ○ *the wind moaning in the trees* ■ *n.* **1. SOUND OF PAIN** a long, low sound made by sb expressing pain or misery **2. SOUND LIKE MOAN** a long, low sound that resembles an expression of pain or misery, made by sth such as the wind **3. COMPLAINING SESSION** a period of time during which sb has an opportunity to complain about a particular thing or about things in general (*informal*) ○ *had a good moan* **4. COMPLAINT** a complaint, especially one that is unreasonable or trivial (*informal*) [12thC. Via assumed Old English *mān* 'complaint' from a prehistoric Germanic base that is also the ancestor of English *bemoan* and *mean*[1].] **—moaner** *n.* **—moanful** *adj.*

moat /mōt/ *n.* **1. DITCH AROUND A CASTLE** a wide water-filled ditch around a castle or fort, dug to give protection from invaders **2. DITCH ACTING AS A BARRIER** a water-filled ditch dug to prevent access or escape, e.g. to confine animals in a zoo **3.** *Ireland* = motte ■ *vt.* (**moats, moating, moated**) **PUT A MOAT AROUND A CASTLE** to surround a castle or other fortified place with a moat [14thC. From Old French *mote* 'mound' (source of English *motte*) or medieval Latin *mota*, perhaps of Gaulish origin. The sense 'ditch around a castle' developed from 'mound', which it surrounded.]

mob /mob/ *n.* **1. NOISY CROWD** a large and unruly crowd of people **2. GROUP OF PEOPLE** a particular group of people (*informal*) **3. ORDINARY PEOPLE** ordinary people, especially when thought of collectively as unintelligent or irrational (*informal*) ■ *vt.* (**mobs, mobbing, mobbed**) **1. CROWD ROUND SB** to crowd round sb or sth noisily and excitedly **2. CROWD INTO A PLACE** to crowd into and fill a place **3. ATTACK SB** to attack sb in a large group **4.** ZOOL **ATTACK A PREDATOR** among animals that are preyed upon, to surround and harass a potential predator [Late 17thC. Shortening of archaic *mobile*, from Latin *mobile (vulgus)*, literally 'excitable (crowd)', a form of *mobilis* (source of English *mobile*).] **—mobber** *n.* **—mobbish** *adj.*

Mob *n.* a group of people who are involved in organized crime, or the world of organized crime (*informal*)

mobbed *adj.* crowded with people (*informal*)

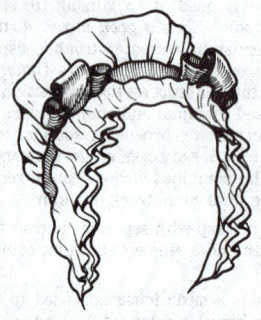
Mobcap

mobcap /mób kap/ *n.* **1. WOMAN'S INDOOR CAP** a loose-fitting frilly cap women often wore indoors in the 18th and early 19th centuries **2. HAT SHAPED LIKE A MOBCAP** a soft hat that is shaped like a mobcap and worn especially by small children and babies [Mid-18thC. *Mob* from obsolete *mob* 'prostitute, negligé', variant of *mab* 'promiscuous woman', of unknown origin.]

mob-handed *adj.* in a large, often threatening, group of people (*informal*)

mobile /mō bīl/ *adj.* **1. EASY TO MOVE** able to move freely or easily ○ *She's mobile again after her skiing accident.* **2. OPERATING FROM A VEHICLE** operating from or set up in a vehicle that travels from place to place **3. CHANGING EXPRESSION** changing expressions quickly and easily ○ *a mobile face* **4. PREPARED FOR CHANGE** able or willing to change job, move home, or alter other arrangements at short notice if necessary **5. CHANGING SOCIALLY** moving or able to move from one social or professional class or group to another, e.g. by changing jobs or moving to a new neighbourhood **6. WITH OWN TRANSPORT** able to go somewhere because you have transport available (*informal*) ○ *He's got his wife's car for the evening, so we're mobile.* ■ *n.* **1. HANGING DECORATION** a hanging sculpture or decoration whose parts are balanced to move in response to air currents **2. MOBILE TELEPHONE** a mobile phone (*informal*) [15thC. Via French from Latin *mobilis* 'movable', shortening of assumed *movibilis*, from *movere* 'to move' (source of English *move*).]

Mobile /mō béel/ city and port in southwestern Alabama, on the northwestern shore of Mobile Bay. Population: 202,581 (1996).

-mobile *suffix.* automobile, vehicle ○ *bloodmobile* ○ *snowmobile* [From AUTOMOBILE]

mobile home *n.* a large caravan that can be transported on the back of a lorry but is usually connected to utilities and left on a single site

mobile library *n.* a library operating from a bus or van and travelling from place to place, e.g. in rural areas

mobile phone *n.* a portable telephone that works using a series of locally based cellular radio networks

mobility /mō bílləti/ *n.* **1. ABILITY TO MOVE** the ability to physically move about, especially to do work or take exercise **2. MOVEMENT TO ANOTHER SOCIAL GROUP** the ability of people to move from one social group or class to another **3. BEING MOBILE** the quality of being mobile [15thC]

mobility housing *n.* housing built or adapted for people who use wheelchairs for whom walking requires effort

mobilize /mōbə līz/ (**-lizes, -lizing, -lized**), **mobilise** (**-lises, -lising, -lised**) *vti.* to organize people or re-

sources to be ready for action, or to take action, especially in a military or civil emergency [Mid-19thC. From French *mobiliser*, from *mobile* 'movable', from Latin *mobilis* (see MOBILE).] **—mobilizable** *adj.* **—mobilization** /mōbə līzáysh'n/ *n.*

Möbius strip /móbi ess-/ *n.* a continuous single-sided surface formed by rotating one end of a strip through 180° and joining it to the other end [Early 20thC. Named after the German mathematician August Ferdinand *Möbius* (1790–1868).]

mobocracy /mo bókrəssi/ (*plural* **-cies**) *n.* **1. CONTROL BY A MOB** political control exercised by a mob (*disapproving*) **2. PLACE RUN BY A MOB** a place where a mob has political control **3. MOB THAT RULES** a mob that rules in a mobocracy **—mobocrat** /móbbə krat/ *n.* **—mobocratic** /-krátttik/ *adj.* **—mobocratical** *adj.*

mobster /móbstər/ *n.* US sb who is involved in organized crime (*informal*) [Early 20thC. Formed from MOB (sense 4) + *-ster*, on the model of GANGSTER.]

Mobutu, Lake /mə bōōtōō, layk/ lake on the Zaïre-Uganda border, in the north of the Rift Valley system. Area: 5,600 sq. km/2,160 sq. mi. Length: 160 m/100 mi.

Mobutu Sese Seko /mə bōōtoo séss e sékō/ (1930–97) Zaïrean soldier and statesman. He was president of Zaïre (Democratic Republic of the Congo) from 1965 until he was forced into exile in 1997. Born **Joseph Désiré Mobutu**

MoC *abbr.* mother of the chapel

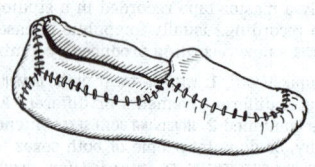
Moccasin

moccasin /mókəssin/ *n.* **1.** CLOTHES **NATIVE N AMERICAN SHOE** a Native North American heelless shoe made of deerskin or other soft leather wrapped around over the foot and stitched on top **2.** CLOTHES **LEATHER SHOE** a low-heeled leather shoe whose side panels are joined to the upper panel using prominent stitching to form a raised puckered seam **3.** ZOOL = **water moccasin** *n.* **1** [Early 17thC. From Virginia Algonquian *mockasin*; in sense 3 there may be a different, unknown, origin.]

moccasin telegraph *n.* Can the exchange of news or information through social networks, especially by casual conversation (*informal; sometimes considered offensive*) [So named because such information was originally transmitted by a Native North American runner]

mocha /mókə/ *n.* **1.** BEVERAGES **STRONG ARABIAN COFFEE** a dark-brown strong-tasting coffee from Yemen and some other countries on the Arabian peninsula **2.** FOOD **FLAVOURING** a flavouring made by mixing coffee and cocoa, used in baking **3.** INDUST **LEATHER** soft suede leather made from sheepskin or goatskin, originally from Africa ■ *adj.* COLOURS **DARK BROWN** of a dark brown colour, like mocha coffee [Late 18thC. Named after MOCHA, from where these goods were originally exported.]

Mocha /mókə, mókə/ town and seaport in southwestern Yemen, on the Red Sea, historically a coffee-exporting centre. Population: 1,163 (1977 estimate).

Moche /mō chay/ *adj.* **OF THE MOCHICA PEOPLE** relating to the Mochica people or their culture ■ *n.* = **Mochica** [From *Moche*, an archaeological site and valley on the northwestern coast of Peru]

Mochica /mō chéeka/ (*plural* **-cas** or **-ca**), **Moche** /mō chay/ (*plural* **-ches** or **-che**) *n.* a member of an ancient Native South American people that lived along the northern coast of Peru, where their civilization flourished between the sixth century BC and the second century BC. The Mochica are particularly noted for their pottery, which was decorated with realistic paintings of human and animal forms. [Mid-19thC. Via Spanish from a Native American word.]

mock /mok/ *v.* (**mocks, mocking, mocked**) **1.** *vti.* **TREAT STH WITH SCORN** to treat sb or sth with scorn or contempt **2.** *vt.* **MIMIC SB** to imitate people in a way that is intended to make them appear silly or ridiculous **3.** *vt.* **PREVENT STH** to prevent sth from succeeding in a way that causes frustration or humiliation ○ *the wind mocking his efforts to light a fire* ■ *adj.* **1. IMITATION** made to appear like sth else, usually sth older or more expensive ○ *mock leather* **2. PRETEND** done as an act, especially in order to amuse people ○ *frowned in mock disapproval* **3. PRACTICE** done as practice for the real thing ○ *mock exams* ■ *n.* **1. AN IMITATION** sth made as an imitation **2. OBJECT OF SCORN** sth or sb ridiculed by others (*dated*) ■ **mocks** *npl.* EDUC **PRACTICE EXAMINATION** the practice examinations given to school pupils in England and Wales to prepare them for examinations such as GCSEs and A-Levels [15thC. From Old French *mocquer,* perhaps from assumed Vulgar Latin *muccare* 'to wipe the nose', and perhaps of imitative origin.] —**mockable** *adj.* —**mocker** *n.* —**mocking** *adj.* —**mockingly** *adv.*

WORD KEY: SYNONYMS

See Synonyms at ***ridicule***.

mock up *vt.* to make a full-scale model of sth, e.g. a working model of a machine to undergo testing

mockernut /mókər nut/ *n.* **1. N AMERICAN HICKORY TREE** a North American hickory tree with smooth bark and fragrant leaves that turn bright yellow in the autumn. Latin name: *Carya tomentosa.* **2. NUT OF THE MOCKERNUT TREE** the large nut produced by the mockernut tree

mockery /mókəri/ (*plural* **-ies**) *n.* **1. SCORN** words or behaviour intended to make sth or sb look silly or ridiculous **2. STH INADEQUATE** sth that is ridiculously inadequate or wholly unsuccessful ○ *the survey was a mockery from start to finish* **3. OBJECT OF SCORN** sb or sth that is treated with scorn or contempt and made to look silly or ridiculous [15thC]

mock-heroic *adj.* **COMIC IN HEROIC STYLE** used to describe poetry that satirizes the heroic style by using it to describe sth trivial. Traditionally, heroic and mock-heroic poetry used classical forms such as the iambic pentameter (**heroic couplet**) or the hexameter (**alexandrine**). ■ *n.* **MOCK-HEROIC VERSE** verse written in the mock-heroic style

mockingbird /móking burd/ *n.* a long-tailed greyish North American bird that incorporates the songs and calls of other birds into its own song. Latin name: *Mimus polyglottus.*

WORD KEY: CULTURAL NOTE

To Kill a Mockingbird, a novel by US writer Harper Lee (1960). Set in the southern United States, it tells the story of a white lawyer who agrees to defend an African American man wrongly accused of the rape of a white girl. The events are narrated from the point of view of the lawyer's six-year-old daughter, Scout. It was made into a film by Robert Mulligan in 1962.

mock moon *n.* ASTRON = **paraselene**

mock orange *n.* **1. TREE WITH FLOWERS LIKE THE ORANGE TREE** a shrub or tree that bears fragrant white flowers like the flowers of an orange tree. Genus: *Philadelphus.* **2. TREE SIMILAR TO THE MOCK ORANGE** a shrub or tree that resembles the mock orange

mock sun *n.* ASTRON = **parhelion**

mock turtle soup *n.* an old-fashioned soup made in imitation of turtle soup, using meat from a calf's head to replace the flesh of the green turtle. This soup was popular in Victorian times.

mock-up *n.* **1. FULL-SCALE MODEL** a full-sized model of sth, built to scale and with working parts, used especially for testing or research **2.** PUBL **LAYOUT** a preliminary layout of a newspaper, magazine, or other publication, showing the size and arrangement of material to be included

mod /mod/, **Mod** *n.* a festival of Gaelic music and poetry held annually in Scotland, usually in the Highlands [Late 19thC. Via Gaelic *mòd* 'assembly, court' from Old Norse *mót.*]

Mod /mod/, **mod** *n.* **mod, Mod** a member of a youth group in 1960s Britain remembered especially for their fashionable dress, motor scooters, and fights with motorcycle gangs (**rockers**) [Mid-20thC. Shortening of MODERN or MODERNISM.]

MoD *abbr.* Ministry of Defence

mod. *abbr.* **1.** moderate **2.** moderato **3.** modern

modal /mṓd'l/ *adj.* **1.** GRAM **EXPRESSING GRAMMATICAL MOOD** used to describe verbs and auxiliary verbs expressing a grammatical mood, e.g. possibility or necessity. ◊ **modal auxiliary 2.** MUSIC **RELATING TO MUSICAL MODES** relating to or using a mode, especially instead of a major or minor scale **3.** PHILOS **DESCRIBING LOGICAL MODALITIES** used to describe propositions involving necessity or probability, and those relating to knowledge, belief, and obligation [Mid-16thC. Directly or via French from medieval Latin *modalis,* from Latin *modus* (see MODE).] —**modally** /mṓdəli/ *adv.*

modal auxiliary *n.* a verb used with other verbs to express such ideas as permission, possibility, and necessity. The modal auxiliaries in English grammar are 'can', 'could', 'may', 'might', 'must', 'ought to', 'shall', 'should', 'will', and 'would'. Some classifications also include 'dare', 'need', and 'used'.

modality /mō dálləti/ (*plural* **-ties**) *n.* **1.** GRAM **WHAT A MODAL VERB EXPRESSES** the idea or concept that a modal auxiliary verb expresses **2.** PHILOS **PROPOSITIONS OF NECESSITY OR POSSIBILITY** the purely logical classification of propositions that relate to necessity or possibility **3.** MED **TREATMENT** sth used in the treatment of a disorder, e.g. surgery or chemotherapy [Early 17thC. Directly or via French *modalité* from Medieval Latin *modalitas,* from *modalis* (source of English *modal*), in turn formed from Latin *modus* (see MODE).]

modal logic *n.* the branch of logic that studies the relations between modal propositions

mod cons /mód kónz/ *npl.* the facilities that make modern life easier and more comfortable such as central heating, hot water, telecommunications, and household appliances (*informal*) [Mid-20thC. Plural of 'mod con', shortened from 'modern convenience'.]

mode /mōd/ *n.* **1. MANNER OR FORM** a way, manner, or form, e.g. a way of doing sth, or the form in which sth exists **2. STYLE OR FASHION** a style or fashion, e.g. in art or in dress **3. MACHINE SETTING** a setting or function on a machine such as a computer **4. TYPE OF AUTOMATIC BEHAVIOUR** a way of behaving, especially one that is instinctive, familiar, or habitual (*informal humorous*) **5.** MUSIC **MUSICAL SCALE** a musical scale that is one of the seven patterns of notes that can be played over an octave using only the white notes of the piano keyboard. Some modes were widely used in European religious, folk, and art music until around 1600, after which they were largely replaced by keys, while others were used in ancient Greece, although their exact nature remains unknown. **6.** MATH, STATS **MOST FREQUENT VALUE** the value that has the highest frequency within a statistical range **7.** LOGIC **MODAL STATUS OF A PROPOSITION** the modal status of a proposition, e.g. its being necessary or merely possible **8.** PHYS **RADIO FREQUENCY** one of the radio frequencies characteristic of a given resonator or oscillator **9.** PHILOS **COMBINATION OF IDEAS** a combination of ideas that cannot be worked out merely by analysis of its components [14thC. From Latin *modus* 'measure, rhythm, song, manner'; in the sense 'fashion', from French *mode.*]

model /módd'l/ *n.* **1. COPY OF AN OBJECT** a copy of an object, especially one made on a smaller scale than the original (*often used before a noun*) **2.** MANUF **PARTICULAR VERSION OF MANUFACTURED ARTICLE** a particular version of a manufactured article ○ *had traded in her car for the latest model* **3. STH COPIED** sth that is copied or used as the basis for a related idea, process, or system **4.** FASHION **SB PAID TO WEAR CLOTHES** sb who is paid to wear clothes and demonstrate merchandise as a profession, e.g. in fashion shows and photographs for magazines and catalogues **5. SIMPLIFIED VERSION** a simplified version of sth complex used, e.g. to analyse and solve problems or make predictions ○ *a financial model* **6. PERFECT EXAMPLE** an excellent example that deserves to be imitated **7.** PAINTING **ARTIST'S SUBJECT** sb who poses for a painter, sculptor, photographer, or other artist **8.** SCULPTURE **SMALL VERSION OF SCULPTURE** a small version of a sculpture, from which a finished work is copied **9.** ZOOL **ANIMAL COPIED BY ANOTHER ANIMAL** an animal species repellent to predators which another animal mimics for protection **10.** LOGIC **INTERPRETATION** an interpretation of a theory arrived at by assigning referents in such a way as to make the theory true **11.** FASHION **EXCLUSIVE GARMENT** the first sewn example of a couturier's or clothing manufacturer's design, from which a new line of garments is produced ■ *v.* (**-els, -elling, -elled**) **1.** *vti.* **WORK AS FASHION MODEL** to work as a fashion model, wearing clothes, make-up, and other items in order to display them to others **2.** *vi.* **BE AN ARTIST'S MODEL** to sit as a model for sb such as a painter or photographer **3.** *vt.* **BASE STH ON STH ELSE** to base sth, especially sb's appearance or behaviour, on sb or sth else ○ *She modelled herself on her older sister.* **4.** *vt.* **SHAPE STH** to make sth by shaping a substance or material, e.g. clay or wood **5.** *vti.* **MAKE SIMPLIFIED VERSION OF PROCESS** to make a model of a process or system as a way of analysing and solving problems or making predictions [Late 16thC. Via French *modèle* from Italian *modello* 'model', from, ultimately, Latin *modulus* 'measure' (source of English *module*), from *modus* (see MODE).] —**modeller** *n.*

model home *n.* = **show house** [19thC]

modeling *n.* US = **modelling**

modelling /móddl-/ *n.* **1. FASHION MODEL'S WORK** the work of a fashion model **2. MAKING MODELS** the activity or hobby of making models **3.** PSYCHOL **DEMONSTRATION OF BEHAVIOUR** the demonstration of a way of behaving to sb, especially a child, in order for that behaviour to be imitated

model theory *n.* the branch of logic that deals with providing models for theories —**model-theoretic** *adj.*

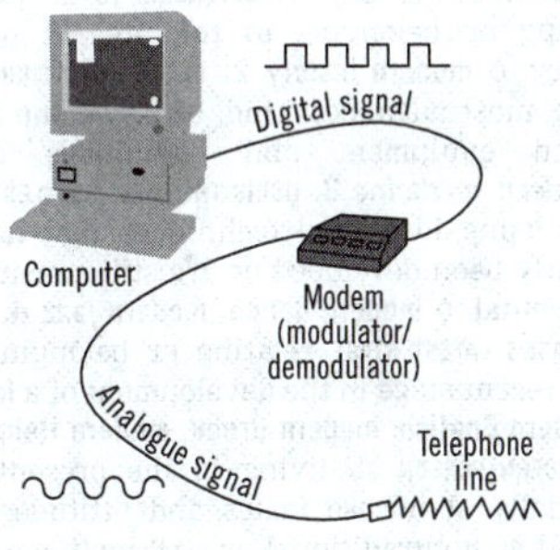

Modem

modem /mṓ dem/ *n.* an electronic device that connects computers via a telephone line, allowing the exchange of information. It consists of a modulator to convert computer information into a telephone signal and a demodulator to convert it back again. [Mid-20thC. Blend of MODULATE and DEMODULATE.]

Modena /mo deénə/ historic city in northern Italy. It is an agricultural and industrial centre. Population: 176,972 (1992).

moderate *adj.* /móddərət/ **1. SMALL OR SLIGHT** not large, great, or severe ○ *a moderate portion* **2. REASONABLE** not excessive or unreasonable ○ *a moderate eater* **3. MIDDLE-OF-THE-ROAD** not extreme or radical ○ *moderate views* **4. AVERAGE** neither particularly good nor particularly bad ○ *moderate results* ■ *n.* **SB WITH MODERATE VIEWS** sb who holds views, especially political views, that are not extreme ■ *vti.* /móddə rayt/ (**-ates, -ating, -ated**) **1. MAKE OR BECOME LESS EXTREME** to become, or make sth become, less great, extreme, violent, or severe **2. PRESIDE OVER STH** to chair or preside over sth such as a meeting or discussion **3. ACT AS EXAM MODERATOR** to act as a moderator in school examinations **4.** *Scotland* **PRESIDE OVER CHURCH ASSEMBLY** in the Presbyterian denominations of the Christian Church, to preside over a formal meeting or assembly [14thC. From Latin *moderat-,* past participle stem of *moderari* 'regulate', from a prehistoric pre-Latin stem that is also the source of English *modest.*] —**moderately** /móddərətli/ *adv.* —**moderateness** /-rətnəss/ *n.*

moderate breeze *n.* a wind that measures force four

on the Beaufort scale, with a speed of between 13 and 18 mph or 20.9 and 29 kph

moderate gale *n.* a wind that measures force seven on the Beaufort scale, with a speed of between 32 and 38 mph or 51.5 and 61.2 kph

moderation /móddə ráysh'n/ *n.* **1.** BEING MODERATE the state in which sth remains moderate rather than becoming extreme or excessive ○ *moderation in all things* **2.** MAKING STH MODERATE the limiting, controlling, or restricting of sth so that it becomes or remains moderate **3.** ACTING AS MODERATOR the position or function of moderating sth [15thC] ◇ **in moderation** within reasonable limits, and never to excess

Moderations /móddə ráysh'nz/ *npl.* EDUC = **Honour Moderations** [Mid-19thC]

moderato /móddə raátō/ *adv.* at a moderate tempo (*used as a musical direction*) [Early 18thC. Via Italian from Latin *moderat-* (see MODERATE).]

moderator /móddə raytər/ *n.* **1.** SB IN CHARGE OF DISCUSSIONS sb who presides over an assembly, especially a legislative assembly, or who acts as a mediator in discussions or negotiations **2.** CHR PRESIDING MINISTER in the Presbyterian denominations of the Christian church, a minister presiding over a church court or other assembly **3.** *Scotland* CHR PRESIDING MINISTER IN CHURCH OF SCOTLAND in the Church of Scotland, the minister chosen to preside for one year over the General Assembly of the Church of Scotland and perform ceremonial duties **4.** NUCLEAR PHYS NEUTRON ABSORBER a substance, e.g. graphite or beryllium, that slows neutrons in a nuclear reactor so that they can bring about the fission of uranium **5.** EDUC EXTERNAL EXAMINER an official responsible for making sure that standards of marking in public examinations are consistent from region to region —**moderatorship** *n.*

modern /módd'n/ *adj.* **1.** BELONGING TO THE PRESENT DAY relating or belonging to the present period in history. ◊ **modern history 2.** OF THE LATEST KIND of the latest, most advanced kind, or using the most advanced equipment and techniques available ○ *modern medicine* **3.** USING THE LATEST STYLES relating to or using ideas and techniques that have only recently been developed or are still considered experimental. ◊ **modern dance, modern jazz 4.** LING OF A LANGUAGE'S LATEST STAGE relating or belonging to the most recent stage in the development of a language. ◊ **modern English, modern Greek, modern Hebrew** ■ *n.* **1.** MODERN PERSON sb living in the present period, especially sb whose tastes and attitudes are regarded as nontraditional or strikingly new **2.** PRINTING TYPEFACE a typeface with heavy vertical strokes and straight serifs [Early 16thC. Directly or via French *moderne* from Latin *modernus*, from *modo* 'just now, in a (certain) manner', from *modus* (see MODE).] —**modernly** *adv.* —**modernness** *n.*

WORD KEY: SYNONYMS

See Synonyms at ***new***.

Modern Apprenticeship *n.* work-based training for 16 to 17 year olds, intended to include the achieving of an NVQ (National Vocational Qualification) at level 3 within three years

modern dance *n.* a free unrestricted style of theatrical dancing that developed in the early 20th century as a reaction against the conventions of ballet

moderne /mə dáirn/ *adj.* used to describe a style of architecture and design popular in the 1920s and 1930s and characterized by streamlined and curved forms [Mid-20thC. From French *moderne* (see MODERN).]

modern English *n.* the English language from about 1500, when it began to develop a more standardized form compared with the many dialects of Middle English. Modern English developed mainly from the East Midland dialect, and the standardization process was accelerated by the introduction of the printing press during the 1470s. ◊ **Old English, Middle English —modern English** *adj.*

modern Greek *n.* the form of Greek spoken since around 1453, the year of the fall of Byzantium —**modern Greek** *adj.*

modern Hebrew *n.* the form of the Hebrew language that is the official language of the state of Israel. It is a revival of the ancient form of the language. —**modern Hebrew** *adj.*

modern history *n.* the study of the period of history that extends from the end of the Middle Ages in Europe, around the middle of the 15th century, to the present day. In the United States this term refers to European history after 1789.

modernism /módd'nizəm/ *n.* **1.** LATEST THINGS the latest styles, tastes, attitudes, or practices **2.** ARTS MODERN STYLES IN ART the revolutionary ideas and styles in art, architecture, and literature that developed in the early 20th century as a reaction to traditional forms **3.** CHR MOVEMENT WITHIN ROMAN CATHOLICISM a movement in European Roman Catholicism in which scholars and theologians attempt to accommodate the contemporary world view within Roman Catholic theology and doctrine —**modernist** /módd'n ist/ *n., adj.* —**modernistic** /-ístik/ *adj.* —**modernistically** /-ístikli/ *adv.*

modernity /mo dúrnəti/ (*plural* **-nities**) *n.* **1.** QUALITY OF BEING MODERN the quality of being modern or up-to-date **2.** STH MODERN a modern thing **3.** SOC SCI PERIOD SINCE ENLIGHTENMENT the historical period from Enlightenment to the present day, associated with the search for rational explanation of the universe and all things in it

modernize /módd'n īz/ (**-izes, -izing, -ized**), **modernise** (**-ises, -ising, -ised**) *vti.* to change sth in order to make it conform to modern tastes, attitudes, or standards [Mid-18thC] —**modernizer** *n.* —**modernization** /módd'n ī záysh'n/ *n.*

modern jazz *n.* a style of jazz that developed in the early 1940s, with rhythms and harmonies much more complex than those of traditional jazz

modern pentathlon *n.* an athletics competition consisting of the five events of swimming, horse riding and jumping, cross-country running, fencing, and pistol shooting

modest /móddist/ *adj.* **1.** HUMBLE not having or expressing a high opinion of your own achievements or abilities **2.** SHY not confident or assertive, and tending to be easily embarrassed in company **3.** REASONABLE not large, extreme, or excessive ○ *a modest income* **4.** SIMPLE not showy, elaborate, or pretentious ○ *a modest dwelling* **5.** NOT OVERTLY SEXUAL not drawing attention to or discussing sexuality, and so unlikely to offend or arouse others [Mid-16thC. Perhaps both a back-formation from MODESTY and via French *modeste* from Latin *modestus* 'kept within due measure' (from the same source as English *moderate*).] —**modestly** *adv.*

modesty /móddisti/ *n.* **1.** HUMILITY unwillingness to draw attention to your own achievements or abilities **2.** SEXUAL RESERVE reserve about nudity or sexual matters, especially a preference for clothes that keep much of the body covered **3.** SHYNESS lack of confidence when speaking to others or stating opinions, and the tendency to be uneasy or embarrassed in company **4.** SIMPLICITY lack of grandeur or ostentation **5.** MODERATION moderation in size, scale, or extent [Mid-16thC]

modicum /móddikəm/ *n.* a small amount, especially of sth abstract, such as a particular quality ○ *It only requires a modicum of common sense.* [Late 15thC. From Latin, 'little way, short time', a form of *modicus* 'moderate', from *modus* (see MODE).]

modif. *abbr.* **1.** modification **2.** GRAM modifier

modification /móddifi káysh'n/ *n.* **1.** CHANGE a slight change or alteration made to improve sth or make it more suitable ○ *made a few modifications to the original design* **2.** ACT OF MODIFYING the act or process of modifying sth, or the condition of having been modified ○ *in need of modification* **3.** STH MODIFIED sth that has been modified ○ *The new version is a modification and is based on existing software.* **4.** GRAM GRAMMATICAL RELATIONSHIP WITH A MODIFIER in grammar, the relationship between a modifier and what it modifies [15thC. Directly or via French from Latin *modificatio(n)-*, past participle stem of *modificare* (see MODIFY).] —**modificative** /móddifi kaytiv/ *adj.* —**modificator** *n.* —**modificatory** *adj.*

modifier /móddi fī ər/ *n.* GRAM **1.** SB OR STH THAT MODIFIES STH sb or sth that makes slight changes to sth, especially to improve it **2.** WORD QUALIFYING ANOTHER a word or phrase that affects the meaning of another, usually describing or restricting its meaning. 'Pink' in the phrase 'the pink ribbon', 'fire' in the compound 'fire alarm', and 'in the morning' in the sentence 'She always goes jogging in the morning' are modifiers.

modify /móddi fī/ (**-fies, -fying, -fied**) *v.* **1.** *vti.* MAKE CHANGES TO STH to make a slight change or alteration to sth, or to change slightly **2.** *vt.* LESSEN STH to make sth less extensive, severe, or extreme **3.** *vt.* GRAM AFFECT A WORD'S MEANING to affect the meaning of a word, usually by describing or limiting it, by adding an adjective, noun, or phrase **4.** *vt.* LING CHANGE A VOWEL SOUND to change the sound of a vowel by adding an umlaut [14thC. Via French *modifier* from Latin *modificare* 'to limit', ultimately from *modus* 'measure' (source of English *mode*) + the base of *facere* 'to make' (source of English *fact*).] —**modifiability** /móddi fī ə bíllәti/ *n.* —**modifiable** /-fī əb'l/ *adj.* —**modifiableness** /móddi fī əb'lnəss/ *n.*

WORD KEY: SYNONYMS

See Synonyms at ***change***.

Modigliani /móddil yaáni/, **Amedeo** (1884–1920) Italian painter and sculptor. His distinctive style, seen to best effect in his portraits, is characterized by graceful, elongated proportions.

modillion /mə díllyən/ *n.* ARCHIT a small curved ornamental bracket under the corona of a Corinthian or Composite column [Mid-16thC. Via French *modillion* from Italian *modiglione*, from, ultimately, Latin *mutulus* 'mutule' (source of English *mutule*), perhaps of Etruscan origin.]

modiolus /mō dí ələss/ (*plural* **-li** /-ə lī/) *n.* the bony central pillar of the cochlea in the inner ear [Late 17thC. From Latin 'nave of a wheel', originally 'small measure', from *modius* 'a measure'.]

modish /módish/ *adj.* in, or conforming to the very latest fashions or styles, especially those considered extreme or outrageous —**modishly** *adv.* —**modishness** *n.*

modiste /mō deést/ *n.* a designer, maker, or seller of fashionable women's clothes, especially in the late 18th and early 19th century (*dated*) [Mid-19thC. From French, from *mode* 'fashion' (source of English *mode* in the sense 'fashion').]

Modred /módrid/, **Mordred** /máwdrid/ *n.* in Arthurian legend, a knight of the Round Table who killed his uncle, King Arthur

Mods /modz/ *npl.* = **Honour Moderations** [Mid-19thC. Shortening of MODERATIONS.]

modular /móddyŏŏlər/ *adj.* **1.** INVOLVING MODULES made up of separate modules that can be rearranged, replaced, or interchanged easily ○ *modular construction techniques* **2.** INVOLVING MODULI relating to or resembling a modulus, or made up of moduli ○ *modular construction techniques* [Late 18thC. From modern Latin *modularis*, from Latin *modulus* (see MODULUS).] —**modularity** /móddyŏŏ lárrəti/ *n.* —**modularly** /móddyŏŏlərli/ *adv.*

modular arithmetic *n.* a branch of arithmetic that deals with the remainders of whole numbers after the numbers have been divided by a modulus

modularized /móddyŏŏlə rīzd/, **modularised** *adj.* made up of separate parts or modules that can be rearranged, replaced, or interchanged easily

modulate /móddyŏŏ layt/ (**-lates, -lating, -lated**) *v.* **1.** *vt.* CHANGE SOUND to change the tone, pitch, or volume of sound or sth that produces sound, e.g. a musical instrument or the human voice, usually by lowering or softening it **2.** *vt.* ALTER STH to make alterations in sth to make it less strong, forceful, or severe **3.** *vti.* MUSIC CHANGE KEY in tonal music, to change from one key to another through a harmonic progression **4.** *vt.* PHYS VARY WAVE CHARACTERISTICS to vary the frequency, amplitude, or other characteristic of a radio wave or some other carrier wave in order to transmit information [Mid-16thC. Perhaps both a back-formation from MODULATION and from Latin *modulat-*, past participle stem of *modulari* 'to measure, adjust to rhythm', from *modulus* (see MODULUS).] —**modulable** /-yŏŏləb'l/ *adj.* —

a at; aa father; aw all; ay day; air hair; ə about, edible, item, common, circus; e egg; ee eel; hw when; i it, happy; ī ice; 'l apple; 'm rhythm; 'n fashion; o odd; ō open; ŏŏ good; oo pool; ow owl; oy oil; th thin; th this; u up; ur urge;

modulability /móddyŏŏlə bílləti/ *n.* —**modulative** *adj.* —**modulator** *n.* —**modulatory** /-lətəri/ *adj.*

modulation /móddyŏŏ láysh'n/ *n.* **1.** ADJUSTMENT OF SOUND adjustment of the tone, pitch, or volume of sound, or of sth that produces sound, e.g. a musical instrument or the human voice **2.** SLIGHT ALTERATION slight alteration that makes sth less strong, forceful, or severe **3.** PHYS PROCESS OF MODULATING CARRIER WAVE the process of changing the amplitude or frequency of a wave, used in radio broadcasting to superimpose a sound signal on a continuously transmitted carrier wave

module /móddyool/ *n.* **1.** INDEPENDENT INTERCHANGEABLE UNIT a unit that is combined with others to form a larger structure or system and is self-contained enough to be easily rearranged, replaced, or interchanged to form different structures or systems **2.** EDUC SHORT COURSE OF STUDY a short course of study that forms part of a larger academic course or training programme, e.g. any of the elements that form part of a degree course **3.** SPACE TECH PART OF A SPACE VEHICLE one of the self-contained units or craft that make up a space vehicle **4.** ARCHIT UNIT OF MEASUREMENT a unit of measurement or a standard, used especially in measuring architectural features [Late 16thC. Directly or via French from Latin *modulus* (see MODULUS). The current sense of 'independent part' evolved from 'allotted measure'.]

modulo /móddyŏŏlō/ *prep.* MATH with respect to a particular modulus ○ *9 and 30 are congruent modulo 7 because both leave the same remainder if they are divided by 7.* [Late 19thC. From Latin, ablative singular of *modulus* (see MODULUS).]

modulus /móddyŏŏləss/ (*plural* **-li** /-lī/) *n.* **1.** PHYS CO-EFFICIENT a coefficient expressing the degree to which a substance exhibits a particular property **2.** MATH LOGARITHM FACTOR the factor by which a logarithm of one base must be multiplied to become the logarithm of another base **3.** MATH ABSOLUTE VALUE the absolute value of a complex number **4.** MATH DIVISION NUMBER a number by which two other numbers can be divided so that both give the same remainder [Mid-16thC. From Latin, 'small measure', from *modus* 'measure' (source of English *mode*).]

modus operandi /módəss óppə rán dee, -dī/ (*plural* **modi operandi** /mŏ dee óppə rán dee, mŏ dī óppə rán dī/) *n.* a particular way of doing things [From Latin, 'mode of operating']

modus vivendi /módəss vi vén dee, -dī/ (*plural* **modi vivendi** /mŏ dee vi vén dee, mŏ dī vi vén dī/) *n.* **1.** COMPROMISE a practical arrangement that allows conflicting people, groups, or ideas to coexist **2.** WAY OF LIFE the way that a particular person or group of people lives [From Latin, 'mode of living']

mofette /mŏ fét/ *n.* a fumarole (*archaic*) [Early 19thC. Via French from Neapolitan Italian *mofetta*, from *muffa* 'mould, mouldy smell', probably of Germanic origin.]

mog /mog/ *n.* a cat (*informal*) [Early 20thC. Shortening of MOGGY.]

Mogadishu /mogə díshŏŏ/ capital city and chief port of Somalia, situated in the southeast of the country. Population: 1,200,000 (1990).

Mogadon /móggə don/ *tdmk.* a trademark for the long-acting benzodiazepine drug nitrazepam, a potentially addictive drug used for the short-term treatment of insomnia [Mid-20thC]

Mogen David /mŏgən-/ *n.* = Star of David [From Hebrew, literally 'shield of David']

moggy /móggi/ (*plural* **-gies**) *n.* a cat (*slang*) [Late 17thC. Variant of *Maggie*, from *Mag*, shortening of *Margaret*.]

Moghul *n.* = Mogul

Mogollon /mŏgə yŏn/ (*plural* **-lons** *or* **-lon**) *n.* a member of a Native North American people whose civilization flourished in parts of Arizona and New Mexico from around the 2nd century BC to the 13th century AD. The Mogollon are particularly noted for their attractive pottery, traditionally decorated with black and white designs. [From the *Mogollon* Rim, Arizona, and the *Mogollon* Mountains, New Mexico, both named after Juan Ignacio Flores *Mogollon*, governor of New Mexico 1712–15]

mogul[1] /mŏg'l/ *n.* an important or powerful person, especially sb working in the media [Late 17thC. From MOGUL.]

mogul[2] /mŏg'l/ *n.* a mound of hard compacted snow formed as an obstacle on a ski slope [Mid-20thC. Origin uncertain: perhaps from southern German dialect *Mugel* or a Scandinavian word.]

Mogul /mŏg'l/, **Moghul, Mughal** /mŏŏg'l/ *n.* **1.** MEMBER OF AN INDIAN MUSLIM DYNASTY a member of the Muslim dynasty of Mongol origin that ruled large parts of India from 1526 to 1857 **2.** MOGUL EMPEROR the Mogul emperor of Delhi [Late 16thC. Via Urdu *mug̲al* from Persian and Urdu *mug̲ul* 'Mongol'.]

mohair /mŏ hair/ *n.* **1.** WOOL the soft silky wool of the Angora goat. ◊ **angora** **2.** YARN the silky yarn made from mohair [Late 16thC. By folk etymology (from HAIR) from earlier *mocayre*, ultimately from Arabic *mukayyar* 'cloth of goat's hair', literally 'select, choice', past participle of k̲ayyara 'to prefer'.]

Mohammed = Muhammad

Mohammed Ali /mŏ hámmid áali/ (1769–1849) Albanian-born Egyptian monarch. He became viceroy of Egypt (1805–49), extending his dominions as far as the Persian Gulf. His descendants ruled Egypt until 1952.

Moharram *n.* = Muharram

Mohave /mŏ haávi/ (*plural* **-haves** *or* **-have**), **Mojave** (*plural* **-ves** *or* **-ve**) *n.* **1.** PEOPLES MEMBER OF A NATIVE N AMERICAN PEOPLE a member of a Native North American people that originally occupied lands along the Colorado River valley on the border between California and Arizona **2.** LANG NATIVE N AMERICAN LANGUAGE a Native North American language spoken along parts of the Colorado River valley. It belongs to the Yuman branch of Hokan-Siouan languages. [Mid-19thC. From Mohave *hàmakhá:v.*] —**Mohave** *adj.*

Mohawk /mŏ hawk/ (*plural* **-hawks** *or* **-hawk**) *n.* **1.** PEOPLES MEMBER OF A NATIVE N AMERICAN PEOPLE a member of a Native North American people that originally occupied lands along the Mohawk and Hudson rivers, and whose members now live mainly in Ontario and New York State. The Mohawk were one of the five peoples who formed the Iroquois Confederacy, which later became known as the Six Nations. **2.** LANG NATIVE N AMERICAN LANGUAGE a Native North American language spoken in Quebec, Ontario, and northern New York State, belonging to the Iroquoian language family. About 3,000 people speak Mohawk. [Mid-17thC. From Narragansett *mohowawog*, literally 'man-eaters'.]

Mohegan /mŏ heegən/ (*plural* **-gans** *or* **-gan**) *n.* **1.** PEOPLES MEMBER OF A NATIVE N AMERICAN PEOPLE a member of a Native North American people that originally occupied lands in eastern Connecticut, and whose members now live mainly in southeastern Connecticut and Wisconsin **2.** LANG NATIVE N AMERICAN LANGUAGE an Algonquian language spoken in Connecticut and Wisconsin that belongs to the Algonquian-Wakashan languages. Mohegan is spoken by around one thousand people. [Variant of MOHICAN.] —**Mohegan** *adj.*

mohel /mŏ hel, -el/ (*plural* **-helim** /-he leem/) *n.* sb who is qualified under Jewish religious law to carry out circumcisions [Mid-17thC. From Hebrew *môhēl*.]

Mohenjo-daro /məhen jō daárō/ ruined Bronze Age city in southern Pakistan. It formed part of the Indus Valley civilization.

mohican /mŏ heekən, mŏ ikən/ *n.* a hairstyle in which the sides of the head are shaved and the remaining hair is worn sticking up. It became associated with the punk movement and was often brightly coloured. [Mid-20thC. From the deer-hide topknots worn by Native American men in *Last of the Mohicans* (1826), a novel by John Fenimore Cooper (1789–1851).]

Mohican (*plural* **-cans** *or* **-can**) *n.* a Mahican or Mahican language (*archaic*) —**Mohican** *adj.*

Moho /mŏhō/ *n.* GEOG = Mohorovicic discontinuity [Mid-20thC. Shortening.]

Mohock /mŏ hok/ *n.* a member of a gang of ruffians from the upper classes who terrorized people in the streets of London in the early 18th century [Mid-17thC. Originally a variant of MOHAWK.]

László Moholy-Nagy

Moholy-Nagy /mō hŏli nój/, **László** (1895–1946) Hungarian-born US artist. He was codirector, with Walter Gropius, of Chicago's American School of Design (1937–39), and was known for his artistic experiments involving modern technology.

Mohorovicic discontinuity /mŏhə rŏvichich-/ *n.* the boundary between the Earth's crust and the mantle, occurring on average at 8 km/5 mi. under the oceans to 35 km/22 mi. under the continents [Mid-20thC. Named after A. *Mohorovičić* (1857–1936), Yugoslav seismologist.]

Mohs scale /mŏz-/ *n.* a scale ranging from zero to ten used to measure the hardness of minerals, with talc at the bottom end and diamond at the top end. Each mineral on the scale is hard enough to scratch the one below it in the scale. [Late 19thC. Named after Friedrich *Mohs* (1773–1839), German mineralogist.]

mohur /mŏ hər/ *n.* a gold coin worth 15 rupees used in British India in the 19th and early 20th centuries [Late 17thC. From Persian and Urdu *muhr* 'seal'.]

MOI *abbr.* Ministry of Information (*dated*)

moidore /móy dáwr/ *n.* an obsolete Portuguese or Brazilian gold coin [Early 18thC. From Portuguese *moeda d'ouro* 'coin of gold'.]

moiety /móy əti/ (*plural* **-ties**) *n.* **1.** ONE OF TWO PARTS either of the two parts, not necessarily equal, into which sth is divided (*formal*) **2.** ANTHROP SOCIAL GROUP among Native South Americans and Aboriginal Australians, one of two halves into which society is divided for ritual and marriage purposes. Marriages are forbidden within the same moiety. [15thC. Via French *moitié* 'half' from late Latin *medietas*, from *medius* 'middle'.]

moil /moyl/ *n.* (*regional archaic*) **1.** DRUDGERY hard work **2.** MUD sticky, slimy dirt or mud **3.** TURMOIL a state of agitation or confusion ■ *v.* (**moils, moiling, moiled**) **1.** *vi.* WORK HARD to work very hard ○ *toiling and moiling* **2.** *vt.* MAKE STH DIRTY to dirty sth, especially with soil or mud (*regional archaic*) [14thC. Via Old French *moillier* 'to moisten, paddle in mud' from, ultimately, Latin *mollire* 'to soften', from *mollis* 'soft'.] —**moiler** /móylər/ *n.*

Moirai /móy ree/ *npl.* = Fates *npl.* [From Greek]

moire /mwaar/, **moiré** /mwaá ray/ *n.* a moiré fabric, especially silk but also, in the past, mohair [Mid-17thC. From French, a later form of *mouaire* 'mohair'.]

moiré /mwaá ray/ *adj.* TEXTILES WITH A WAVY PATTERN used to describe fabric with a shiny or wavy pattern on the surface ■ *n.* **1.** TEXTILES WAVY PATTERN ON FABRIC a shiny finish and wavy pattern on fabric, especially silk, created by using engraved rollers **2.** WAVY PATTERN the wavy or blurred effect created by superimposing one geometric pattern on a similar or identical pattern that is slightly out of alignment with the first [Early 19thC. From French *moiré*, the past participle of *moirer* 'to water', from *moire* 'moiré fabric', probably an alteration of MOHAIR.]

moiré effect *n.* = moiré

moiré pattern *n.* = moiré *n.* 2

moist /moyst/ *adj.* **1.** DAMP slightly wet or damp **2.** FRESH pleasantly fresh, rather than dry or stale ○ *a rich, moist fruitcake* **3.** TEARFUL full of tears ○ *moist eyes* **4.** RAINY humid or rainy, especially with light rain or drizzle [14thC. Via Old French *moiste* from, ultimately, Latin *mucidus* 'mouldy', from *mucus* 'slime' (source of

English *mucus*), apparently influenced by *musteus* 'new'.] —**moistly** adv. —**moistness** n.

—————— **WORD KEY: SYNONYMS** ——————
See Synonyms at **wet**.

moisten /móyss'n/ (**-tens, -tening, -tened**) vti. to make sth moist or to become moist ◊ *Moisten the mixture with a little beaten egg.* —**moistener** n.

moisture /móysschər/ n. wetness, especially droplets of condensed or absorbed liquid, or in a vapour [14thC. From Old French *moistour*, from *moiste* (see MOIST).]

moisturize /móysschə rīz/ (**-izes, -izing, -ized**), **moisturise** (**-ises, -ising, -ised**) v. **1.** vti. USE CREAM ON FACE to apply a cosmetic cream or lotion to the skin, especially on the face, to help prevent the skin drying out **2.** vt. MAKE STH MOIST to make sth moist or more moist

moisturizer /móysschər īzər/ n. a cosmetic cream or lotion used to make the skin, especially on the face, feel less dry

moither /móythər/ (**moithers, moithering, moithered**) v. (*regional*) **1.** vt. WORRY SB to worry, bother, or confuse sb **2.** vi. RAMBLE to talk in an aimless or confused way [Variant of MITHER]

mojarra /mō haárə/ (*plural* **-ras** *or* **-ra**) n. a small silvery sea fish found mainly in shallow tropical American waters, with mouthparts that can be thrust outward. Family: Gerridae. [Mid-19thC. From American Spanish.]

Mojave n., adj. PEOPLES, LANG = **Mohave**

Mojave Desert /mō haávi-/ arid region in southern California, part of the Great Basin region. Area: 39,000 sq. km/15,000 sq. mi.

mojo /mójō/ (*plural* **-joes** *or* **-jos**) n. US (*slang*) **1.** MAGIC witchcraft or magic, or some powerful influence **2.** MAGIC CHARM an object believed to have magical powers, especially the power to keep away evil spirits [Early 20thC. Probably of African origin.]

moke /mōk/ n. a donkey (*slang*) [Mid-19thC. Probably from a personal name.]

moko /mókō/ (*plural* **-kos**) n. NZ **1.** MAORI FACE TATTOOING tattooing practised by Maoris, especially on the face **2.** MAORI TATTOO PATTERN a Maori tattoo pattern [Mid-19thC. From Maori.]

moksha /mókshə/ n. in Hinduism, the spiritual goal of release from reincarnation [Late 18thC. From Sanskrit *mokṣa*, from *muc* 'to set free, release'.]

mol CHEM symbol **mole**

mol. abbr. **1.** molecular **2.** molecule

mola /mólə/ (*plural* **-las** *or* **-la**) n. = **sunfish** n. **1** [Late 17thC. From French *mole*.]

molal /móləl/ adj. used to describe a solution consisting of one mole of dissolved substance (**solute**) per 1,000 grams of solution

molality /mo lálləti/ (*plural* **-ties**) n. the concentration of a solution, expressed as the number of moles of a dissolved substance (**solute**) that can be found in 1,000 grams of solvent

molar[1] /mólər/ n. a large back tooth in humans and other mammals, used for chewing and grinding. Human beings have twelve molars. ◊ **incisor**, **canine**, **premolar** [14thC. From Latin *molaris* 'of a mill; grindstone, molar tooth', from *mola* 'mill'.]

molar[2] /mólər/ adj. **1.** CHEM RELATING TO A MOLE used to describe sth that relates to or is a mole of a substance ◊ *the molar volume of hydrogen* **2.** CHEM CONTAINING ONE MOLE PER LITRE containing one mole of substance per litre of solution **3.** PHYS RELATING TO A WHOLE RATHER THAN PARTS relating to a body of matter rather than the properties of its molecules or atoms [In the chemical senses: Mid-19thC, formed from MOLE. In the sense 'relating to a whole': Early 20thC, formed from Latin *moles* 'mass'.] —**molarity** /mə lárrəti/ n.

molasses /mō lássiz/ n. **1.** RESIDUE OF SUGAR REFINING the thick dark bitter residue produced at the end of the sugar refining process **2.** US = **treacle** [Late 16thC. Via Portuguese *melaço* from late Latin *mellaceum* 'new wine, must', from, ultimately, Latin *mel* 'honey'.]

mold n., vt. US = **mould**

Mold /mōld/ market town and administrative centre of Flintshire, Wales. Population: 9,168 (1991).

Moldavia /mol dáyvi ə/ former principality, located in what is now Romania and Moldova —**Moldavian** n., adj.

moldboard n. US = **mouldboard**

molder vi. US = **moulder**

molding n. US = **moulding**

Moldova

Moldova /mol dóvə/ independent republic in south-eastern Europe. It was a republic of the Soviet Union until 1991. Language: Romanian. Currency: leu. Capital: Chisinau. Population: 4,372,000 (1996). Area: 33,008 sq. km/13,012 sq. mi. Official name **Republic of Modova** —**Moldovan** n., adj.

moldy adj. US = **mouldy**

mole[1] /mōl/ n. **1.** ZOOL BURROWING MAMMAL a small mammal that usually lives underground and has large forelimbs for digging, no external ears, minute eyes, and dense velvety fur. Family: Talpidae. **2.** SPY sb employed by a group or organization such as a government ministry who discloses sensitive information while keeping his or her own identity secret **3.** CONSTR TUNNELLING MACHINE a machine designed for boring through hard materials such as rock [14thC. Probably from Middle Dutch *mol*, of unknown origin.]

mole[2] /mōl/ n. a small dark, sometimes raised, growth on the human skin, sometimes with a hair or hairs growing from it [Old English *māl* 'discoloured mark'. Ultimately from a prehistoric Germanic base meaning 'spot, mark', which is also the ancestor of German *malen* 'paint'.]

mole[3] /mōl/ n. **1.** SEA WALL a massive wall, usually made of stone, that extends into the sea and encloses or protects a harbour **2.** HARBOUR a harbour enclosed or protected by a mole [Mid-16thC. Via French *môle* and medieval Greek *molos* from Latin *moles* 'mass, massive structure', the original sense in English.]

mole[4] /mōl/ n. the basic SI unit of amount of substance equal to the amount containing the same number of elementary units as the number of atoms in 12 grams of carbon-12. Symbol **mol** [Early 20thC. From German *Mol*, a shortening of *Molekul* 'molecule'.]

mole[5] /móli/ n. a spicy Mexican sauce made with unsweetened chocolate and a variety of chillies and spices, used especially for cooking poultry [Mid-20thC. Via Mexican Spanish from Nahuatl *molli* 'sauce, stew'.]

Molech n. BIBLE = **Moloch**

mole cricket n. a cricket with a heavy body and short wings that burrows in the ground using front legs that are adapted for digging. It feeds primarily on plant roots. Family: Gryllotalpidae.

molecular /mə lékyoolər/ adj. **1.** SCI RELATING TO MOLECULES relating to or made up of molecules **2.** LOGIC MADE UP OF SIMPLER PARTS relating to or organized from simpler parts —**molecularity** /mə lekyoo lárrəti/ n. —**molecularly** /mə lékyoolərli/ adv.

molecular biology n. the branch of biology concerned with the nature and function, at the molecular level, of biological phenomena, such as RNA and DNA, proteins, and other macromolecules

molecular distillation n. a technique of vacuum distillation in which the molecules of the distilled

substance reach the condenser before colliding with each other

molecular film n. SCI = **monolayer**

molecular formula n. a chemical formula that specifies which atoms and how many of each atom there are in a molecule of a compound

molecular genetics n. the branch of genetics that studies genes, chromosomes, and the transmission of hereditary characteristics at the molecular level (*takes a singular verb*)

molecular sieve n. a crystalline compound with molecule-sized pores that can be used in separating larger molecules from smaller ones

molecular volume n. the volume occupied by one mole of a substance when in the form of a gas

molecular weight n. = **relative molecular mass**

molecule /mólli kyool/ n. **1.** CHEM SMALLEST PART OF A CHEMICAL COMPOUND the smallest physical unit of a substance that can exist independently, consisting of one or more atoms held together by chemical forces **2.** TINY AMOUNT a very small amount of sth [Late 18thC. Via French *molécule* from modern Latin *molecula*, literally 'small mass', from Latin *moles* 'mass'.]

molehill n. a small mound of earth on the surface of the ground dug up by a burrowing mole

mole rat n. **1.** EUROPEAN AND MIDDLE EASTERN RODENT a tailless rodent found in eastern Europe and the Middle East that digs burrows with its enlarged incisors and powerful head. Genus: *Spalax*. **2.** AFRICAN RODENT a rodent found in Africa south of the Sahara that has large protruding incisors for digging burrows. Family: Bathyergidae.

mole run n. a part of a network of tunnels and underground rooms built to provide shelter during a nuclear war (*informal*)

moleskin /mól skin/ n. **1.** ZOOL FUR OF THE MOLE the short dense soft fur of a mole **2.** TEXTILES CLOTHING FABRIC a strong heavy cotton fabric used for clothing ■ **moleskins** npl. CLOTHES MOLESKIN CLOTHING clothing, especially trousers, made of moleskin fabric

molest /mə lést/ (**-lests, -lesting, -lested**) vt. **1.** LAW ABUSE SB SEXUALLY to force unwanted sexual attentions on sb, especially a child or physically weaker adult (*disapproving*) **2.** ANNOY SB to pester, bother, or disturb a person or animal [14thC. Directly or via Old French *molester* from Latin *molestare*, from *molestus* 'troublesome'.] —**molestation** /mō le stáysh'n/ n. —**molester** /mə léstər/ n.

Molière /mólli air/ (1622–73) French dramatist. He satirized contemporary society in a series of witty plays such as *Tartuffe* (1664). He also wrote *Le Bourgeois Gentilhomme* (1670) and *Le Malade imaginaire* (1673). Pseudonym of **Jean-Baptiste Poquelin**

moline /mō leén/ adj. HERALDRY used to describe a heraldic cross that has arms of equal length that broaden at the ends by forking and curving backwards [Mid-16thC. Origin uncertain: probably via Anglo-Norman, from *molin* 'mill', from late Latin *molinum*.]

Molinism /mólənizəm/ n. the doctrine in Christianity formulated by Luis Molina, that a person has a choice in accepting divine grace [Mid-17thC. Named after the Spanish Jesuit, Luis Molina, who formulated it.] —**Molinist** n.

Molinos /mō leén oss/, **Miguel de** (1628–96) Spanish clergyman and mystic. The founder of quietism, he was accused of heresy and immorality and in 1687 was sentenced to life imprisonment.

moll /mol/ n. (*slang*) **1.** GANGSTER'S WOMAN COMPANION the woman companion of a gangster **2.** PROSTITUTE a woman prostitute [Early 17thC. Shortening of the forename *Molly*, a petform of *Mary*.]

mollie n. ZOOL = **molly**

mollify /mólli fī/ (**-fies, -fying, -fied**) vt. **1.** PACIFY SB to calm or soothe sb who is angry or upset **2.** TEMPER STH to make sth less intense or severe **3.** SOFTEN STH to make sth less hard, rigid, or stiff [15thC. Directly or via French *mollifier* 'mollify'.] —**mollifiable** adj. —**mollification** /mólli fī káysh'n/ n. —**mollifier** /mólli fī ər/ n. —**mollifyingly** /-fī ingli/ adv.

Mollusc

mollusc *n.* an invertebrate with a soft unsegmented body, usually protected by a shell in one, two, or three pieces. The molluscs include clams, snails, slugs, squid, and octopuses. Most molluscs are aquatic. Phylum: Mollusca. [Late 18thC. Via French *mollusque* from, ultimately, Latin *molluscus* 'thin-shelled nut', from *mollis* (see MOLLIFY).] —**molluscan** *adj.*, *n.*

molluscicide /mə lúski sīd/ *n.* a chemical that kills molluscs —**molluscicidal** /mə lúski síd'l/ *adj.*

molluscum contagiosum /mə lúskəm kən táyji óssəm/ *n.* a benign viral skin infection characterized by numerous small round dimpled pearly-white nodules [Early 19thC. From modern Latin, literally 'contagious fungus'.]

mollusk *n.* US = mollusc

Mollweide projection /mól vīdə-/ *n.* a projection of a map of the world showing lines of latitude as straight lines and lines of longitude as elliptical lines, used to show the distribution of land masses and oceans. This projection distorts shape but gives an indication of the relative size of countries and oceans. [Early 20thC. Named after the German mathematician Karl B. *Mollweide* (1774–1825).]

molly /mólli/ (*plural* -lies), **mollie** *n.* a tropical and subtropical fish native to Central and South America that bears live young and is popular as an aquarium fish. Genera: *Poecilia* and *Mollienesia*. [Mid-20thC. Shortening of modern Latin *Mollienisia*, the name of the genus, named after the French statesman Count F. N. *Mollien* (1758–1850).]

mollycoddle /mólli kod'l/ *vt.* (-dles, -dling, -dled) PAMPER AND SPOIL SB to treat sb in an overprotective and overindulgent way ■ *n.* OVERPROTECTED BOY a child, especially a boy, who is spoilt and over-protected [Mid-19thC. From the name *Molly* (used for an effeminate boy or man) + CODDLE.] —**mollycoddler** *n.*

Molly Maguire /mólli mə gwír/ *n.* **1.** IRISH FIGHTER AGAINST GOVERNMENT EVICTIONS a member of a secret organization founded in Ireland in 1843 that used violent methods to stop evictions by the government **2.** IRISH-AMERICAN MINER FIGHTING FOR BETTER CONDITIONS a member of a secret Irish-American organization, active in the coal-mining districts of Pennsylvania from about 1865 to 1877, that used violent methods to try to get improved working conditions [Mid-19thC. From the common Irish name, because members of the original society disguised themselves as women.]

Molnár /mól naar, mől-/, **Ferenc** (1878–1952) Hungarian playwright and novelist. His plays and short stories about fashionable society are underpinned by a concern for social justice.

moloch /mő lok/ (*plural* -lochs) *n.* a lizard found in the

plains and deserts of central and southern Australia that has large spiny scales covering its head and back. Latin name: *Moloch horridus*. [Mid-19thC. Via late Latin from Greek *Molokh* from Hebrew *Mōlek* 'a Canaanite idol'.]

Moloch /mő lok/, **Molech** /mő lek/ *n.* **1.** BIBLE BIBLICAL DEITY GIVEN CHILD SACRIFICES in the Bible, a Semitic deity to whom children were sacrificed **2.** STH REQUIRING COSTLY SACRIFICES sb or sth that requires a costly and painful sacrifice [Early 17thC. Via late Latin from Greek *Molokh*, from Hebrew *mōlek*.]

Molotov /móllə táwf/, **Vyacheslav Mikhailovich** (1890–1986) Soviet statesman. He was a close associate and advisor of Joseph Stalin as premier (1930–41) and foreign minister (1939–49, 1953–56) of the Soviet Union. He negotiated the German-Soviet non-aggression pact in 1939. Born **Vyacheslav Mikhailovich Scriabin**

Molotov cocktail /móllə tof-/ *n.* = **petrol bomb** (*dated*) [Mid-20thC. Named after Vyacheslav Mikhailovich MOLOTOV, who ordered their large-scale production after the Nazi invasion of Russia.]

molt *vi.*, *n.* US = moult

molten /mőltən/ *adj.* **1.** MELTED changed into liquid form by heat **2.** MOULDED produced by melting a material and then shaping it in a mould **3.** GLOWING glowing with great heat [13thC. Originally the past participle of MELT.]

Moltke /mőltkə/, **Helmuth Johannes Ludwig, Count** (1848–1916) German military commander. As chief of staff, he led Germany's unsuccessful invasion of France at the beginning of World War I.

molto /mőltō/ *adv.* used for emphasis before or after a musical direction derived from Italian [Early 19thC. Via Italian from Latin *multus* 'much' (source of English *multitude*).]

Moluccas /mə lúkəz/ group of islands in eastern Indonesia, part of the Malay Archipelago. Population: 1,741,800 (1998). Area: 74,500 sq. km/28,800 sq. mi. —**Moluccan** *n.*, *adj.*

mol. wt. *abbr.* molecular weight

moly /mőli/ (*plural* -lies) *n.* **1.** MYTHOL MAGIC HERB in Homers' 'Odyssey', a magic herb with milky-white flowers and black roots that Hermes gave to Odysseus to protect him from Circe's spells **2.** PLANTS EUROPEAN PLANT WITH YELLOW FLOWERS a plant of the garlic family that has yellow flowers and is native to southern Europe. Latin name: *Allium moly*. [Mid-16thC. Via Latin from Greek *mōlu*.]

molybdate /mə líb dayt/ *n.* any salt of molybdenum [Late 18thC. Formed from MOLYBDIC.]

molybdenite /mə líbdə nīt/ *n.* a greyish mineral, consisting of molybdenum sulphide, that is the main ore of molybdenum. Formula: MoS_2. [Late 18thC. Formed from modern Latin *molybdenum* (see MOLYBDENUM).]

molybdenous /mə líbdənəss/ *adj.* relating to or containing molybdenum, especially with a valency of 2 [Late 18thC. Formed from modern Latin *molybdenum* (see MOLYBDENUM).]

molybdenum /mə líbdənəm/ *n.* a very hard, silver-coloured metallic chemical element, used to strengthen steel alloys and found as a trace element in plants and animals. Symbol **Mo** [Early 19thC. Via modern Latin from, ultimately, Greek *molubdaina* 'piece of lead', from *molubdos* 'lead'.]

molybdenum sulphide, **molybdenum disulphide** *n.* a black crystalline powder that is insoluble in water and is used as a lubricant. Formula: MoS_2.

molybdic /mə líbdik/ *adj.* relating to or containing molybdenum, especially with a valency of 6 [Late 18thC. Formed from modern Latin *molybdenum* (see MOLYBDENUM).]

molybdous /mə líbdəss/ *adj.* relating to or containing molybdenum, especially with a valency lower than 6 [Late 18thC. Formed from modern Latin *molybdenum* (see MOLYBDENUM).]

mom /mom/ *n.* US = mum (*informal*) [Late 19thC. Shortening of MOMMA.]

mom-and-pop, **ma-and-pa** *adj.* US used to describe a

business that is owned and operated by a family, especially by a husband and wife

Mombasa /mom bássə/ city and chief seaport of Kenya, in the southeast of the country on the Indian Ocean. It is also a tourist centre. Population: 600,000 (1991).

moment /mőmənt/ *n.* **1.** UNSPECIFIED SHORT TIME a very short period of time ○ *Wait a moment.* **2.** SPECIFIC INSTANT a specific instant in time ○ *At that moment she walked in the door.* **3.** PRESENT the present time ○ *busy at the moment* **4.** SIGNIFICANT PERIOD an important or significant time or occasion ○ *great moments in world history* **5.** SHORT PERIOD OF EXCELLENCE a brief period of excellence or interest (*often used in the plural*) ○ *It's not a great opera, but it has its moments.* **6.** IMPORTANCE special importance or significance (*formal*) ○ *a decision of great moment* **7.** PHILOS SPECIFIC STAGE a specific stage or aspect of sth **8.** PHILOS MOMENTUM a momentum (*dated*) **9.** PHYS TENDENCY TO PRODUCE ROTATION a tendency to cause motion, especially rotation **10.** PHYS PRODUCT OF FORCE TIMES DISTANCE the product of a quantity, e.g. force, multiplied by its perpendicular distance from a given point **11.** STATS MEAN IN FREQUENCY DISTRIBUTION the expected value of the deviations of a variable, compared to a fixed value, raised to a given power [14thC. Via French from Latin *momentum*, literally 'movement', later 'instant, moment' (from the notion of a tiny movement), hence 'importance', from, ultimately, *movere* 'to move' (source of English *move*).]

momentarily /mőməntərəli/ *adv.* **1.** BRIEFLY for a brief period of time **2.** US, Can VERY SOON within a very short period of time ○ *He'll be here momentarily.* **3.** PROGRESSIVELY with every passing moment

momentary /mőməntəri/ *adj.* **1.** VERY BRIEF lasting for a very short time **2.** CONSTANT present or happening at every moment **3.** WITH SHORT LIFE living or continuing for only a relatively short time —**momentariness** *n.*

momently /mőməntli/ *adv.* US **1.** PROGRESSIVELY with every passing moment ○ *to grow momently more uneasy* **2.** VERY SOON within a very short period of time **3.** FOR AN INSTANT for a very short period of time

moment of inertia *n.* PHYS a measure of resistance to changes in angular speed, calculated as the sum of the products of the component masses of an object multiplied by the square of their distance from the axis. Symbol *I*

moment of truth *n.* **1.** DECISIVE POINT a point in time when a crucial decision has to be taken or when sb or sth is put to an important test **2.** MOMENT OF BULLFIGHTER'S KILLING BLOW in a bullfight, the point at which the bull is about to be killed with the final blow

momentous /mő méntəss/ *adj.* extremely important or crucial, especially in its effect on the future course of events —**momentously** *adv.* —**momentousness** *n.*

momentum /mő méntəm/ (*plural* -ta /-méntə/ *or* -tums) *n.* **1.** CAPACITY FOR PROGRESSIVE DEVELOPMENT the power to increase or develop at an ever-growing pace ○ *The project was in danger of losing momentum.* **2.** FORWARD MOVEMENT the speed or force of forward movement of an object ○ *the momentum gained on the downhill stretches of the course* **3.** PHYS MEASURE OF MOVEMENT a quantity that expresses the motion of a body and its resistance to slowing down. It is equal to the product of the body's mass and velocity. Symbol *p* **4.** PHILOS BASIC ELEMENT an essential part of a whole [Early 17thC. From Latin *momentum* (see MOMENT).]

MOMI /mőmi/ *abbr.* Museum of the Moving Image (London)

momma /mómmə/ *n.* US, Can sb's mother (*informal*) [Early 19thC. Alteration of MAMMA.]

Mommsen /mómzən/, **Theodor** (1817–1903) German historian. A specialist in Roman history, he was awarded a Nobel Prize in literature (1902). He was of outstanding importance in the foundation of modern Latin epigraphy.

mommy /mómmi/ (*plural* -mies) *n.* US = mummy[2] (*informal*) [Early 20thC. Alteration of MAMMY.]

mommy track *n.* US a career route taken by a woman whereby she risks reducing her chances of career advancement by working flexitime or fewer hours

Moloch

in order to look after a child or children (*informal*)
◊ **daddy track**

Momus /mṓməs/ *n.* the god of fault-finding and
mockery in Greek mythology. He is a son of
Night. [Late 16thC. Via Latin from Greek *Mṓmos*.]

Mon /mōn/ (*plural* **Mon** or **Mons**) *n.* **1.** PEOPLES SB FROM
THE THAILAND AND MYANMAR BORDER a member of a people
that lives in adjacent parts of Thailand and
Myanmar (Burma) **2.** LANG LANGUAGE OF THE THAILAND AND
MYANMAR BORDER Mon-Khmer language belonging to
the Austro-Asiatic languages that is spoken in adjacent parts of Thailand and Myanmar (Burma).
Mon is spoken by about 700 thousand people. [Late
18thC. From Mon.] —**Mon** *adj.*

mon. *abbr.* **1.** monastery **2.** monetary

Mon. *abbr.* Monday

mon- *prefix.* = **mono-** (*used before vowels*)

mona /mṓnə/ *n.* a West African monkey that has a
dark back and white or yellow front and is capable
of moving at speed through the trees. Latin name:
Cercopithecus mona. [Late 18thC. Via Spanish from Portuguese from Italian *monna* 'monkey'.]

Monacan /mónnəkən, mə náakən/ *n., adj.* = **Mone-
gasque**

monachal /mónnək'l/ *adj.* relating to a monastery
or monks, or resembling monastic life [Late 16thC.
Directly or via French *monacal* from ecclesiastical Latin
monachalis, from late Latin *monachus* (see MONK).] —
monachism *n.* —**monachist** *adj., n.*

monacid *n.* = monoacid ■ *adj.* = monoacidic

monacidic *adj.* = monoacidic

Monaco

Monaco /mə nákō, mónnəkō/ small independent prin-
cipality of Europe, bordered by France and the
Mediterranean Sea. Language: French. Currency:
French franc. Capital: Monaco. Population: 31,719
(1996). Area: 1.95 sq. km/0.75 sq. mi. Official name
Principality of Monaco —**Monacan** *n., adj.*

monad /mónnad/ *n.* **1.** PHILOS BASIC ENTITY IN THE METAPHYSICS
OF LEIBNITZ in the metaphysics of Leibnitz, an indivisible indestructible unit that is the basic
element of reality and a microcosm of it **2.** BIOL SINGLE-
CELLED MICROORGANISM a microorganism consisting of
just one cell, especially a flagellate protozoan.
Genus: *Monas*. **3.** CHEM ATOM WITH VALENCY OF ONE an atom
or chemical group that has a valency of one [Mid-
16thC. Directly or via French *monade* from the late Latin
stem *monad-*, from, ultimately, Greek *monos* (see
MONO-).] —**monadic** /mo náddik/ *adj.* —**monadical**
/-náddik'l/ *adj.* —**monadically** /-náddikli/ *adv.* —**mo-
nadism** /mónnadizəm/ *n.*

monadelphous /mónnə délfəss/ *adj.* **1.** WITH FILAMENTS
IN A TUBE SHAPE used to describe stamens that have all
the filaments united to form a single bundle in the
shape of a tube **2.** WITH MONADELPHOUS STAMENS used to
describe a flower that has monadelphous
stamens [Early 19thC. Coined from MONO- + Greek *adelphos* 'brother'.]

monadnock /mə nád nok/ *n.* an isolated mountain or
rock that has resisted the process of erosion and
stands alone in an otherwise flat area [Late 19thC.
Named after such a peak in New Hampshire US.]

Monaghan /mónnəhən/ county in the northeast of the
Republic of Ireland. Population: 51,266 (1996). Area:
1,291 sq. km/498 sq. mi.

monandrous /mo nándrəss/ *adj.* **1.** WITH ONE MALE LOVER
having a sexual relationship with only one man
during a period of time **2.** BOT WITH ONE STAMEN used to
describe a flower that has a single stamen **3.** BOT
WITH MONANDROUS FLOWERS used to describe a plant that
has monandrous flowers

monandry /mo nándri/ *n.* **1.** ANTHROP MARRIAGE TO ONE
HUSBAND the practice of having only one husband at
a time **2.** TAKING OF ONE LOVER the practice of having a
sexual relationship with only one man during a
period of time

monanthous /mo nánthəss/ *adj.* producing a single
flower [Mid-19thC. Coined from MONO- + Greek *anthos*
'flower'.]

Mona Passage /mṓnə pássij/ area of sea separating
the islands of Hispaniola and Puerto Rico, linking
the Atlantic Ocean to the Caribbean Sea

monarch /mónnərk/ *n.* **1.** SUPREME RULER SB, especially a
king or queen, who rules a state or territory, usually
for life and by hereditary right **2.** EXCEPTIONALLY POWER-
FUL PERSON sb who possesses exceptional power or
influence in a given sphere of activity (*literary*) **3.**
STH OUTSTANDING OR PREDOMINANT sth that occupies a pre-
eminent or predominant position (*literary*) **4.** =
monarch butterfly [15thC. Directly or via French *monarque*
from late Latin *monarcha* from Greek *monarkhos*, literally
'to rule alone', from MONO- 'alone' + *arkhein* 'to rule'.] —
monarchal /mə náark'l/ *adj.* —**monarchally** /-kəli/ *adv.*

monarch butterfly *n.* a large migrating orange and
black North American butterfly whose caterpillars
feed on milkweed plants. Latin name: *Danaus plex-
ippus*.

monarchic /mə náarkik/, **monarchical** /mə náarkik'l/
adj. relating to a monarch or monarchy —**mo-
narchically** *adv.*

monarchism /mónnərkizəm/ *n.* **1.** SUPPORT FOR MONARCHY
belief in or support for monarchy as a system of
government **2.** GOVERNMENT BY MONARCHY the system of
government in which a monarch rules

monarchist /mónnərkist/ *n.* SUPPORTER OF MONARCHY sb
who favours or supports the system of monarchy
■ *adj.* SUPPORTING MONARCHY favouring or supporting
the system of monarchy

monarchy /mónnərki/ (*plural* **-chies**) *n.* **1.** SYSTEM OF RULE
BY MONARCHS a political system in which a state is
ruled by a monarch **2.** ROYAL FAMILY a monarch and
his or her family **3.** STATE RULED BY A MONARCH a country
ruled by a monarch

monarda /mə náardə/ *n.* a North American aromatic
plant of the mint family. Genus: *Monarda*. [Late
18thC. From modern Latin, the name of the genus. Named
after the Spanish botanist Nicolas *Monardes* (1493–1588).]

Monash /món ash, món-/, **Sir John** (1865–1931) Australian soldier, engineer, and administrator. He was
commander of the Australian forces in France
(1918–19).

monastery /mónnəstəri/ (*plural* **-ies**) *n.* **1.** MONKS' RESI-
DENCE a building or buildings with grounds in which
a group of people observing religious vows, especially monks, live together **2.** COMMUNITY OF MONKS a
group of people, especially monks, living together
and observing religious vows [14thC. Via ecclesiastical
Latin *monasterium* from, ultimately, Greek *monazein* 'to live
alone', from *monos* (see MONO-).] —**monasterial** /mónnə
stéeri əl/ *adj.*

monastic /mə nástik/ *adj.* **monastic, monastical 1.** RELIG
OF MONKS, NUNS, OR MONASTERIES relating to monks, nuns,
or their way of life or the buildings in which they
live ○ *monastic rule* **2.** RECLUSIVE OR AUSTERE characteristic of the life of a monk, especially in being
reclusive, self-denying, or austere ■ *n.* RELIG MONK
sb, especially a monk, who lives with others in
a monastery and observes religious vows [15thC.
Directly or via French *monastique* from late Latin *monasticus*
(source of English *minister*), from, ultimately, Greek *monazein* (see MONASTERY).] —**monastically** *adv.*

monasticism /mə nástissizəm/ *n.* the way of life
typical of monks or nuns, in which they withdraw
entirely or in part from society to devote themselves
to prayer, solitude, and contemplation

monatomic /mónnə tómmik/, **monoatomic** /mónnō ə
tómmik/ *adj.* **1.** WITH ONE ATOM having only one atom
in the molecule **2.** WITH ONE REPLACEABLE ATOM OR GROUP

with one atom or chemical group that can be replaced during a chemical reaction **3.** = **monovalent** —
monatomically *adv.*

monaural /mo náwrəl/ *adj.* **1.** MED HEARING WITH JUST ONE
EAR relating to or involving the hearing of sound by
one ear **2.** ELECTRON ENG = **monophonic** —**monaurally** *adv.*

monaxial /mon áksi əl/ *adj.* CRYSTALS = **uniaxial**

monazite /mónnə zīt/ *n.* a reddish-brown mineral
that is a phosphate of cerium and lanthanum and
contains some thorium [Mid-19thC. Formed from Greek
monazein 'to be alone', from *monos* (see MONO-), because
of its rare occurrence.]

Monck /mungk/, **George, 1st Duke of Albemarle** (1609–
70) English soldier. Initially a Royalist in the Civil
War, he later served under Oliver Cromwell, but
regained favour after the Restoration.

Moncton /múngktən/ city in southeastern New Brunswick, Canada. It is a transport centre for the country's Maritime Provinces. Population: 159,313 (1996).

mondain /mon dáyn, moN dáN/ *n.* MAN BELONGING TO
FASHIONABLE SOCIETY a man who belongs to fashionable
society ■ *adj.* = **mondaine** [Late 19thC. From French
(see MUNDANE).]

mondaine /mon dáyn, moN dén/ *n.* WOMAN BELONGING TO
FASHIONABLE SOCIETY a woman who belongs to fashionable society ■ *adj.* **mondaine, mondain** FASHIONABLE
typical of, or relating to fashionable society, especially in being worldly or sophisticated [Late
19thC. From French, the feminine of *mondain* (see
MUNDANE).]

Monday /mún day, -di/ *n.* the first day of the traditional working week, coming after Sunday and
before Tuesday [Old English *mōnandæg*. Ultimately from
a prehistoric Germanic translation of Latin *lunae dies* 'day
of the moon', which also produced German *montag*.]

Monday Club *n.* a club for right-wing Conservatives,
founded in 1961. Their first meetings were over
lunch on Mondays.

Mondayize /mún day īz/ (**-izes, -izing, -ized**) *vt. NZ* to
move a statutory holiday to the Monday falling
closest to it so as to make a long weekend —
Mondayization /mún day ī záysh'n/ *n.*

Mondays /mún dayz, -diz/ *adv.* every Monday

mondial /móndi əl/ *adj.* relating to or involving the
entire world [Early 20thC. Via French, formed from *monde*
'world', from Latin *mundus* (see MUNDANE).]

Mondrian /móndri áan, móndri aan/, **Piet** (1872–1944)
Dutch painter. Founder of the magazine *De Stijl*,
he formulated neo-plasticism, a form of geometric
abstraction with flat planes and straight lines. Born
Pieter Cornelis Mondriaan

monecious *adj.* BOT, ZOOL = **monoecious**

Monégasque /mónnə gásk/ *n.* SB FROM MONACO sb who
was born in or who lives in Monaco ■ *adj.* RELATING
TO MONACO relating to or typical of Monaco, or its
people or culture [Late 19thC. Via French from, ultimately, *Mounegue* 'Monaco'.]

Monel /mō nél/ *tdmk.* a trademark for a corrosion-
resistant alloy of nickel and copper with some iron,
manganese, and aluminium

monestrous *adj.* US = **monoestrous**

Monet /món ay/, **Claude** (1840–1926) French painter.
A leading figure of the impressionist movement, he
is noted for his studies of the effects of light on
scenes and subjects in nature. Full name **Claude
Oscar Monet**

monetarism /múnnitərizəm/ *n.* **1.** MONEY SUPPLY THEORY
the theory that inflation and other economic variations are caused by changes in the money supply
2. CONTROL OF THE MONEY SUPPLY the policy of controlling
an economic system by increasing or decreasing the
money supply, especially in a gradual manner —
monetarist *n., adj.*

monetary /múnnitəri/ *adj.* **1.** RELATING TO MONEY relating
to or involving money **2.** RELATING TO CURRENCY relating
to a national currency ○ *The monetary unit of the
US is the dollar.* [Early 19thC. Directly or via French
monétaire from late Latin *monetarius*, from Latin *moneta*
(see MONEY).] —**monetarily** *adv.*

monetary unit *n.* the standard unit in a nation's currency system, e.g. the pound in the United Kingdom or the dollar in the United States

monetize /múnni tīz/ (**-tizes, -tizing, -tized**), **monetise** (**-tises, -tising, -tised**) *vt.* **1.** MAKE STH LEGAL TENDER to make sth the legal tender of a country **2.** COIN METAL to convert a metal into coins **3.** CONVERT DEBT INTO AVAILABLE MONEY to convert a government debt into available currency, especially by issuing securities [Late 19thC. Formed from Latin *moneta* (see MONEY).] —**monetization** /múnni tīzáysh'n/ *n.*

money /múnni/ *n.* **1.** SB'S COINS AND BANKNOTES the amount of coins and banknotes in sb's possession at any one time **2.** SAVINGS OR CREDIT the amount of money held in a bank account or available on credit to sb **3.** WAGES OR SALARY the amount sb is paid for working **4.** CONVERTIBLE ASSETS assets or property that can be converted into cash **5.** NATIONAL CURRENCY the official currency of a country **6.** OFFICIAL MEDIUM OF EXCHANGE a commodity, usually gold, that is an official medium of exchange and a measure of value **7.** UNOFFICIAL MEDIUM OF EXCHANGE a medium of exchange that can be used to purchase goods and services **8.** RICH PEOPLE a rich individual, family, or class ○ *She married money.* ■ **monies** *npl.* SUMS OF MONEY specific individual sums of money (*formal*) ○ *all monies payable* [13thC. Via Old French *monie* from Latin *moneta* 'mint, money' (source also of English *mint*), from *Moneta* (epithet of the goddess Juno, in whose temple coins were minted).] ◇ **for sb's money** in sb's opinion ◇ **in the money** having a lot of money ◇ **on the money** *US* correct or accurate ◇ **put your money where your mouth is** to take action to show that you truly mean what you have said (*informal*)

money-back *adj.* refunding money paid for sth if the product or service is unsatisfactory ○ *It comes with a money-back guarantee.*

moneybags /múnni bagz/ (*plural* **-bags**) *n.* sb who is rich, especially sb who makes a show of being wealthy (*informal; takes a singular verb*)

moneychanger /múnni chaynjər/ *n.* sb who exchanges currencies of different countries, usually for a fee

moneyed /múnnid/, **monied** *adj.* **1.** RICH possessing a great deal of money **2.** CONSISTING OF MONEY consisting of or resulting from money

moneygrubber /múnni grubbər/ *n.* sb bent on making money from every possible opportunity (*disapproving*) —**moneygrubbing** *adj., n.*

moneylender /múnni lendər/ *n.* sb whose business is lending money in exchange for interest on the amount borrowed

moneymaker /múnni maykər/ *n.* **1.** SB GOOD AT MAKING MONEY sb who is very good at making money **2.** STH THAT MAKES MUCH MONEY a business, product, or project that makes a lot of money —**moneymaking** *n., adj.*

moneyman /múnni man/ (*plural* **-men**) *n.* *US* sb who is an expert on finance and economics (*informal*)

money market *n.* the trade in low-risk securities that have a life of one year or less

money of account *n.* a monetary unit that is used to keep accounts. It does not necessarily correspond to an actual currency unit.

money order *n.* *US, Can* = postal order

money shell *n.* the shell of the butter clam, formerly used as money by Native Americans on the western coast of North America

money spider *n.* a tiny brownish spider. Family: Linyphiidae. [From the folk belief that money will come to those on whom it crawls]

money-spinner *n.* = moneymaker (*informal*)

money supply *n.* the total amount of money available in a given economy. The money supply may be measured in various ways, e.g. as the total amount of currency in circulation combined with the money available in bank deposits.

money wages *npl.* wages considered only in terms of how much money is paid and not in terms of what that money can buy

moneywort /múnni wurt/ *n.* = creeping Jennie

mong /mung/ *n.* *Aus* **1.** MONGREL a dog, especially a mongrel (*informal*) **2.** an offensive term for an un-

intelligent person (*slang offensive*) [Mid-20thC. Shortening.]

-monger *suffix.* seller, dealer, promoter ○ *fashionmonger* [Old English *mangere*, via prehistoric Germanic from, ultimately, Latin *mango* 'peddler, swindler']

mongo /móng gō/ (*plural* **-go** *or* **-gos**) *n.* a Mongolian sub-unit of currency equal to one hundredth of a tugrik. See table at **currency** [Mid-20thC. From Mongolian *möngö* 'silver'.]

mongol /móng g'l/ *n.* a highly offensive term for sb who is affected by Down's syndrome (*dated offensive*)

Mongol /móng g'l, -gol/ *adj.* **1.** PEOPLES OF MONGOLIA relating to Mongolia, its people, or its culture **2.** LANG RELATING TO MONGOLIAN LANGUAGE relating to the Mongolian language (*dated*) ■ *n.* **1.** PEOPLES SB FROM MONGOLIA a member of the originally nomadic peoples who inhabit Mongolia and established the Mongol Empire in the 13th century **2.** LANG = **Mongolian** *n.* 2 [Late 17thC. From Mongolian.]

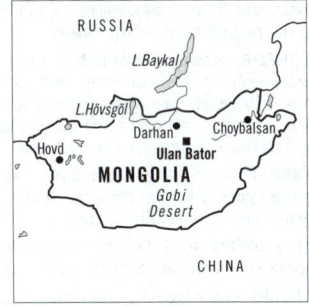

Mongolia

Mongolia /mong gṓli ə/ nation in eastern Asia, bounded on the north by Russia and on the east, south, and west by China. Language: Mongolian. Currency: tughrik. Capital: Ulan Batar. Population: 2,538,211 (1997). Area: 1,566,500 sq. km/604,830 sq. mi.

Mongolian /mon gṓli ən/ *n.* **1.** PEOPLES SB FROM MONGOLIA sb who was born in or lives in Mongolia **2.** LANG LANGUAGE OF MONGOLIA a group of languages or dialects of the Altaic family spoken in Mongolia, in the Chinese region of Inner Mongolia, in the Buryat Republic of Russia, and elsewhere in Central Asia. About 6 million people speak one of the varieties of Mongolian. —**Mongolian** *adj.*

Mongolic /mon gṓllik/ *n.* LANG GROUP OF ALTAIC LANGUAGES a group of languages belonging to the Altaic family that includes Mongolian, Buryat, and Santa ■ *adj.* **1.** ANTHROP RELATING TO MONGOLOID RACIAL GROUP belonging or relating to Mongoloid racial group (*dated*) **2.** LANG RELATING TO MONGOLIC LANGUAGE relating to the Mongolic languages

mongolism /móng gəlizəm/ *n.* a highly offensive term for Down's syndrome (*dated offensive*)

mongoloid /móng gə loyd/ *adj.* a highly offensive term for Down's syndrome (*dated offensive*)

Mongoloid /móng gə loyd/ *adj.* relating to or belonging to the racial group that includes the peoples of eastern Asia, the Inuit, and the Native Americans (*no longer used technically*) —**Mongoloid** *n.*

mongoose /móng gooss/ (*plural* **-gooses**) *n.* a small

Mongoose

short-legged carnivorous mammal that resembles a ferret and is native to India, noted for its ability to kill poisonous snakes. Genus: *Herpestes*. [Late 17thC. From Marathi *maṅgūs*.]

mongrel /múng grəl/ *n.* **1.** ZOOL DOG OF MIXED BREED a dog that is a mixture of different breeds **2.** BIOL ANIMAL OR PLANT OF MIXED BREED an animal or plant that is a mixture of different breeds or strains **3.** OFFENSIVE TERM an offensive term for sb who is of mixed racial ancestry (*offensive*) **4.** STRANGE MIXTURE a combination or mixture of different people or things, especially one that seems particularly strange **5.** *Aus* OBNOXIOUS PERSON sb who is considered to be obnoxious (*insult*) ■ *adj.* MIXED IN ORIGIN OR CHARACTER of mixed breed, descent, type, or character [15thC. Origin uncertain: probably from, ultimately, a prehistoric Germanic base meaning 'to mix' (source of English *among* and *mingle*), the underlying idea being 'mixture'.] —**mongrelism** *n.* —**mongrelly** *adj.*

mongrelize /múng grə līz/ (**-izes, -izing, -ized**), **mongrelise** (**-ises, -ising, -ised**) *vt.* to make sth or sb become mongrel or mixed in character, type, or race (*offensive when used of a person*) —**mongrelization** *n.*

'mongst /mungst/ *prep.* amongst (*literary*) [Late 16thC. Variant of *amongst*, a variant of AMONG.]

Monicagate /mónikə gáyt/ *n.* *US* the 1998–99 sex scandal involving US President William Jefferson Clinton and a former White House intern, culminating in his impeachment and subsequent acquittal (*slang*) [From, *Monica* S. Lewinsky, the name of the intern + -GATE.]

monicker *n.* = moniker (*dated slang*)

monied *adj.* = moneyed

monies plural of money (*formal*)

moniker /mónnikər/, **monicker** *n.* sb's name or nickname (*dated slang*) [Mid-19thC. Origin unknown.]

moniliform /mə nílli fawrm/ *adj.* used to describe a plant root or insect antenna that resembles a string of beads [Early 19thC. Directly or via French *moniliforme* from modern Latin *moniliformis*.] —**moniliformly** *adv.*

monism /mónnizəm/ *n.* **1.** PHILOS THEORY OF REALITY AS A SINGLE ENTITY the theory that reality is a unified whole and is grounded in a single basic substance or principle **2.** SINGLE EXPLANATION FOR EVERYTHING a theory or point of view that attempts to explain everything in terms of a single principle —**monist** *n., adj.* —**monistic** /mo nístik/ *adj.* —**monistically** /-nístikli/ *adv.*

monition /mə nísh'n/ *n.* **1.** WARNING OF DANGER a warning, especially a warning of danger **2.** EXHORTATION TO CAUTION a piece of advice counselling caution **3.** LAW SUMMONS an order to appear in court **4.** CHR WARNING FROM A BISHOP an official warning from a bishop to refrain from doing sth [14thC. Via French from, ultimately, Latin *monit-*, the past participle stem of *monere* 'to warn'.]

monitor /mónnitər/ *n.* **1.** TV CLOSED-CIRCUIT TELEVISION SET a receiving device used in a closed-circuit television or video system **2.** COMPUT VDU a video device that displays data or images generated by a computer or terminal **3.** ARTS STAGE LOUDSPEAKER a loudspeaker on a stage during a concert used to let performers hear what they are playing ○ *playing a guitar solo with one foot up on the monitor* **4.** SB WHO CHECKS FOREIGN BROADCASTS sb who listens to and checks broadcasts from other countries for information useful to the government or organization he or she works for **5.** SB ENSURING PROPER CONDUCT sb who checks for incorrect or unfair conduct **6.** EDUC PUPIL GIVEN SPECIAL DUTY a pupil who helps a teacher by being given a particular responsibility or special duty (*dated*) **7.** BROADCAST VIEWING DEVICE IN A STUDIO a receiver in a studio that enables the audience to watch the recorded portions of a show or performers to view parts of a programme **8.** ZOOL LARGE LIZARD a large tropical carnivorous lizard, found in Asia, Africa, and Australia. Family: Varanidae. US term **monitor lizard 9.** COMPUT COMPUTER PROGRAM a computer program that observes and controls other programs in a system **10.** NOZZLE a jointed device with a rotating nozzle that controls and aims a jet of water **11.** NAVY WARSHIP a warship used to bombard coastlines **12.** HISTORY 19THC WARSHIP a heavily armoured warship with gun turrets used in the 19th century in coastal manoeuvres ■ *vt.* (**-tors, -toring, -tored**) **1.** CHECK REGULARLY

FOR DEVELOPMENTS to check sth at regular intervals in order to find out how it is progressing or developing **2.** LISTEN TO BROADCASTS OR TELEPHONE CONVERSATIONS to use an electronic receiver to listen in on broadcasts or telephone conversations, especially in order to discover secret or illegal plans and activities **3.** BROADCAST **CHECK THE QUALITY OF TRANSMITTED SIGNALS** to use an electronic receiver to check the quality of transmitted audio or visual signals **4.** WATCH OVER TO CHECK CONDUCT to watch over sb or sth, especially in order to ensure that good order or proper conduct is maintained [Early 16thC. From Latin, from *monit-*, the past participle stem of *monere* (see MONITION).] —**monitorial** /mónni táwri əl/ *adj.* —**monitorially** /-táwri əli/ *adv.* —**monitorship** /mónnitər ship/ *n.*

WORD KEY: ORIGIN

The Latin word *monere*, from which **monitor** is derived, is also the source of English *admonish*, *demonstrate*, *monster*, *monument*, *muster*, *premonition*, *remonstrate*, and *summon*.

---

monitor lizard *n.* = **monitor** [From the belief that they warn of the proximity of crocodiles]

monitory /mónnitəri/ *adj.* WARNING communicating a warning ▪ *n.* (*plural* **-ries**) CHR WARNING LETTER a letter, usually from a bishop, that warns sb to refrain from doing sth

monk /mungk/ *n.* a man who withdraws entirely or in part from society and goes to live in a religious community to devote himself to prayer, solitude, and contemplation [Old English *munuc*. Ultimately from a prehistoric Germanic word, from late Latin *monachus*, from, ultimately, Greek *monos* 'alone' (source of English *mono-*).]

Thelonious Monk

Monk /mungk/, **Thelonious** (1917–82) US pianist and composer. An influential modern jazz musician, he was known for his compositions in the bop style. Full name **Thelonious Sphere Monk**

monkery /múngkəri/ (*plural* **-ies**) *n.* (*disapproving*) **1.** MONASTIC WAY OF LIFE the way of life led by monks in a monastery **2.** MONKS monks as a group

monkey /múngki/ *n.* (*plural* **-keys**) **1.** ZOOL NONHUMAN PRIMATE a medium-sized primate found mostly in tropical areas. Monkeys include baboons, marmosets, capuchins, macaques, guenons, and tamarins, but exclude apes, lemurs, and tarsiers. **2.** MISCHIEVOUS CHILD sb, usually a child, who behaves badly, annoyingly, or high-spiritedly (*informal*) ○ *Did you hear what that cheeky monkey said?* **3.** CONSTR PILE DRIVER RAM the ram of a pile driver **4.** DUPE sb who has been made to look foolish or ridiculous (*informal*) ○ *Nobody makes a monkey out of me.* **5.** BETTING £500 the sum of £500, especially in betting (*slang*) ▪ *vt.* (**-keys**, **-keying**, **-keyed**) MIMIC to copy or imitate sb or sth (*archaic*) [Mid-16thC. Origin uncertain: perhaps from, ultimately, Arabic *maimūn*, the probable source of Spanish *mono* and Old Italian *monno*.] ◇ **have a monkey on your back** *US* to have an addiction to drugs (*slang*) ◇ **I'll be a monkey's uncle** used to express surprise (*dated informal*) ◇ **not give a monkey's (about)** not to care at all about sb or sth (*informal*)

monkey around, **monkey about** *vi.* to behave in a silly, casual, or careless way

monkey with *vt.* to touch or move sth casually or carelessly

monkey bread *n.* **1.** GOURD-SHAPED FRUIT the gourd-shaped fruit of the baobab tree. Its pulp is eaten by monkeys. **2. monkey bread, monkey bread tree** = baobab tree

monkey business *n.* (*informal*) **1.** TRICKS silly or mischievous behaviour **2.** DUBIOUS ACTIVITY illegal, dishonest, or dubious activity

monkey flower *n.* = **mimulus** [Because spots on the flowers form a pattern that is reminiscent of a monkey's face]

monkey jacket *n.* a tight-fitting waist-length jacket, especially one worn by a sailor or as part of a military dress uniform [Because it resembles the kind worn by an organ grinder's monkey]

monkey nut *n.* a peanut while still in its shell (*informal*)

monkey orchid *n.* a European orchid with white and pink flowers. Latin name: *Orchis simia*. [Because the shape of the lip of the flower is reminiscent of a monkey]

monkeypot /múngki pot/ *n.* **1.** TREES TROPICAL AMERICAN TREE WITH LARGE PODS a tropical American tree that bears large pods. Genus: *Lecythis*. **2.** TREES POD OF THE MONKEYPOT TREE a large bulbous woody pod of the monkeypot tree **3.** CRAFT GLASSMAKING POT a melting pot used in the manufacture of flint glass

monkey puzzle, **monkey puzzle tree** *n.* a large, cone-bearing, evergreen Chilean tree with spreading branches, stiff sharp dark-green leaves, and edible nuts. Latin name: *Araucaria araucana*. [Apparently because of its long intertwining limbs and leaves]

monkey suit *n.* (*dated slang*) **1.** DINNER SUIT a suit worn by a man as part of formal evening wear **2.** UNIFORM a uniform, especially a military one

monkey's wedding *n.* *S Africa* a simultaneous occurrence of sunshine and a light shower (*informal*)

monkey tricks *npl.* silly or mischievous behaviour (*slang*) US term **monkeyshine**

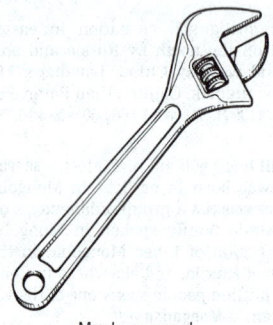

Monkey wrench

monkey wrench *n.* a spanner with a jaw that can be adjusted so that it can be used to turn nuts of different sizes

monkfish /múnk fish/ (*plural* **-fish** *or* **-fishes**) *n.* **1.** LARGE EDIBLE ANGLERFISH a large grotesque bottom-dwelling edible anglerfish of European and African Atlantic waters. Latin name: *Lophius piscatorius*. **2.** = angel shark [Early 17thC. *Monk* perhaps because its head slightly resembles a cowl.]

Mon-Khmer /mōn kmér/ *n.* a group of languages of the Austro-Asiatic family that includes Mon and Khmer, spoken in parts of Southeast Asia —**Mon-Khmer** *adj.*

monkish /múngkish/ *adj.* **1.** RELIG RELATING TO MONKS relating to monks or their way of life **2.** RECLUSIVE OR AUSTERE characteristic of the life of a monk, especially in being reclusive, self-denying, or austere —**monkishly** *adv.* —**monkishness** *n.*

monk's cloth *n.* a heavy cotton fabric with a basket weave, used primarily to make curtains or bedcovers

monk seal *n.* a small dark brown subtropical seal that inhabits the waters of the Hawaiian Islands and the Mediterranean and is now endangered. Genus: *Monachus*. [Perhaps from the colour of its coat, which is like that of a monk's robe]

monkshood /múngks hŏŏd/ (*plural* **-hood** *or* **-hoods**) *n.* **1.** POISONOUS N EUROPEAN PLANT a poisonous perennial plant native to northern Europe that has purplish flowers. Latin name: *Aconitum napellus*. **2.** = aconite [Late 16thC. From the hooded shape of its flowers.]

Monmouth /món məth/ market town in Monmouthshire, southeastern Wales. Population: 7,246 (1991).

Monmouthshire /món məthshər/ county in southeastern Wales, known as Gwent from 1974 to 1996. The name is now applied to an administrative region that is only a part of the historic county. Population: 85,600 (1995). Area: 1,375 sq. km/530 sq. mi.

Monnet /món ay/, **Jean** (1888–1979) French diplomat and financier. He was the first deputy secretary of the League of Nations (1919–23) and founder of the Action Committee for a United States of Europe (1955).

mono /mónnō/ *n.* monophonic sound reproduction [Mid-20thC. Shortening.]

mono- *prefix.* **1.** one, single, alone ○ *monoculture* **2.** containing a single atom, radical, or group ○ *monoxide* **3.** monomolecular ○ *monolayer* [Via Old French and Latin from Greek *monos* (source of English *monad* and *monk*)]

monoacid /mónnō-/, **monacid** /mon-/ *n.* an acid that has only one replaceable hydrogen atom

monoacidic /mónnō ə síddik/, **monacidic** /mónnə síddik/, **monacid** /mónnō ássid/ *adj.* used to describe a chemical base or alcohol that has only one hydroxyl group that can react with an acid

monoamine /mónnō áy meen/ *n.* an amine compound that contains one amino group, especially a compound such as adrenaline or serotonin that transmits nerve impulses

monoamine oxidase *n.* an enzyme in cell tissue that breaks down monoamines

monoamine oxidase inhibitor *n.* an antidepressant drug that works by blocking the breakdown of monoamines by monoamine oxidase in the brain, thus allowing monoamines to build up

monoatomic *adj.* = monatomic

monobasic /mónnō báyssik/ *adj.* used to describe an acid that has only one replaceable hydrogen atom in each molecule

monocarboxylic /mónnō káar bok síllik/ *adj.* used to describe an acid that has only one carboxyl group

monocarp /mónnō kaarp/ *n.* a plant that flowers and bears fruit only once before dying

monocarpellary /mónnō káarpiləri/, **monocarpous** /mónnō káarpəss/ *adj.* **1.** WITH ONLY ONE CARPEL used to describe a flower that has only one carpel **2.** CONSISTING OF ONLY ONE CARPEL used to describe a plant gynoecium that consists of only one carpel

monocarpic /mónnō káarpik/, **monocarpous** /mónnō káarpəss/ *adj.* used to describe a plant that flowers and bears fruit only once before dying

monocarpous *adj.* BOT **1.** = monocarpic **2.** = monocarpellary

monocephalic /mónnō sə fállik/, **monocephalous** /mónnō séffələss/ *adj.* used to describe a plant, e.g. a tulip or dandelion, with a stalk that bears a single flower head

Monoceros /mə nóssərəss/ *n.* the Unicorn, a constellation lying across the celestial equator near Canis Major, Canis Minor, and Orion [Late 18thC. Via French from, ultimately, Greek *monokerōs* 'having one horn'.]

monochasium /mónnō káyziə m/ (*plural* **-a** /-zi ə/) *n.* a flower cluster in which each branch bears one other branch and ends in a single flower [Late 19thC. Coined from MONO- + DICHASIUM.] —**monochasial** *adj.*

monochlamydeous /mónnōklə míddi əss/ *adj.* used to describe a flower that does not have a separate calyx and corolla [Mid-19thC. Coined from MONO- + the Greek stem *khlamud-* 'cloak'.]

monochord /mónnə kawrd/ *n.* an ancient acoustical device consisting of a single string stretched over an oblong sounding box, used to determine mathematical intervals between musical tones

monochromat /mónnō krŏ mat/, **monochromate** /-krŏ mayt/ *n.* sb who is unable to perceive any colours and sees only shades of grey [Early 20thC. Back-formation from MONOCHROMATIC.]

monochromatic /mónnōkrō máttik/ *adj.* **1.** COLOURS WITH ONLY ONE COLOUR having, or perceived as having, only one colour **2.** PHYS WITH ONLY ONE WAVELENGTH consisting of radiation that has only one wavelength, like the light of a laser **3.** IN ONE COLOUR painted, decorated, or printed in a single colour **4.** MED RELATING TO TOTAL COLOUR BLINDNESS relating to or having total colour blindness (**monochromatism**) [Early 19thC] —**monochromatically** *adv.* —**monochromaticity** /mónnōkrōmə tíssəti/ *n.*

monochromatism /mónnō krōmətizəm/ *n.* a defect of vision in which the retina cannot distinguish any colours and a person sees only shades of grey

monochrome /mónnə krōm/ *adj.* **1.** COLOURS IN SHADES OF ONE COLOUR photographed in, using, or displaying only shades of one colour or black and white **2.** COLOURS CONSISTING OF ONE COLOUR painted or drawn in different shades of a single colour **3.** DULL dull, insipid, and lacking interest or distinctiveness ■ *n.* **1.** PHOTOGRAPHY BLACK-AND-WHITE IMAGE a black-and-white photograph or transparency **2.** COLOURS BLACK-AND-WHITE COLORATION the condition of being only in black and white **3.** ARTS ARTWORK IN ONE COLOUR a painting, drawing, or print done in different shades of a single colour **4.** PAINTING, DRAWING ART TECHNIQUE USING ONE COLOUR the art of painting or drawing using different shades of a single colour **5.** ARTS STATE OF HAVING ONE COLOUR the condition of being painted, drawn, or printed in shades of a single colour [Mid-17thC. Via medieval Latin *monochroma* from Greek *monokhrōmatos* 'of one colour', from *khrōma* 'colour'.] —**monochromic** /mónnə krōmik/ *adj.* —**monochromist** /-krōmist/ *n.*

Monocle

monocle /mónnək'l/ *n.* a lens for correcting the vision of one eye, held in position by the muscles around the eye socket [Mid-19thC. Via French from late Latin *monoculus* 'single-eyed', from Greek *mono-* 'single' + Latin *oculus* 'eye'.]

monocline /mónnō klīn/ *n.* GEOL a rock structure in which all the strata slope in one direction [Late 19thC. Coined from MONO- + Greek *klinein* 'to lean'. Ultimately from an Indo-European word that is also the ancestor of English *lean* and *lid*.] —**monoclinal** /mónnō klīn'l/ *adj.* —**monoclinally** /-klīn'li/ *adv.*

monoclinic /mónnō klínnik/ *adj.* used to describe a type of crystal that has three unequal axes, with one pair not at right angles [Mid-19thC. Formed from Greek *klinein* (see MONOCLINE).]

monoclinous /mónnō klīnəss/ *adj.* used to describe a flower that has both pistils and stamens [Early 19thC. Directly or via French *monocline* from modern Latin *monoclinus*, literally 'in a single bed', from Greek *klinē* 'bed' (source of English *clinic*).]

monoclonal /mónnō klōn'l/ *adj.* used to describe cells or products of cells that are formed or derived from a single clone

monoclonal antibody *n.* a highly specific antibody produced in large quantities by clones of an artificially created cell

monocoque /mónnō kok/ *n.* **1.** METAL OUTER SHELL the metal outer shell of an aircraft, boat, or rocket that absorbs most of the stresses to which the craft is subjected **2.** INTEGRATED CAR DESIGN a type of motor vehicle design in which the body and frame are integrated [Early 20thC. From French, literally 'having a single shell', from *coque* 'shell'.]

monocot /mónnō kot/ *n.* a monocotyledon (*informal*)

monocotyledon /mónnō kotə leéd'n/ *n.* a flowering plant that has a single leaf in the seed and floral parts in multiples of three. Monocotyledons include grasses and lilies. Class: Monocotyledones. —**monocotyledonous** *adj.*

monocracy /mo nókrəssi/ (*plural* **-cies**) *n.* a form of government in which one person alone rules — **monocrat** /mónnə krat/ *n.* —**monocratic** *adj.*

monocular /mo nókyōōlər/ *adj.* RELATING TO ONE EYE relating to, affecting, or having only one eye ■ *n.* OPTICAL DEVICE FOR ONE EYE an optical device such as a field glass or a microscope designed for use with one eye only [Mid-17thC. Formed from late Latin *monoculus* (see MONOCLE).] —**monocularly** *adv.*

monoculture /mónnō kulchər/ *n.* the practice of growing a single crop plant in a field or a larger area, e.g. a cereal crop such as wheat —**monocultural** /mónnō kúlchərəl/ *adj.*

monocycle /mónnə sīk'l/ *n.* = **unicycle**

monocyclic /mónnō síklik/ *adj.* **1.** CHEM WITH A SINGLE-RING MOLECULAR STRUCTURE used to describe a chemical compound that has a molecular structure in which there is only one ring **2.** BIOL FORMING ONE WHORL forming a single whorl as, e.g. the petals of a flower do **3.** BOT LIVING DURING ONE YEAR used to describe a plant that completes its life cycle within a single year

monocyte /mónnō sīt/ *n.* a large circulating white blood cell, formed in the bone marrow and in the spleen, that has a single well-defined nucleus and consumes large foreign particles and cell debris — **monocytic** /mónnō síttik/ *adj.* —**monocytoid** /mónnō sī toyd/ *adj.*

monocytosis /mónnō sī tóssiss/ *n.* an abnormal increase in the numbers of a type of white blood cell (**monocyte**)

monodisperse *adj.* used to describe a colloid that contains particles that are all of a uniform size

monodrama /mónnō draamə/ *n.* a dramatic piece written for one actor —**monodramatic** /mónnōdrə máttik/ *adj.*

monody /mónnədi/ (*plural* **-dies**) *n.* **1.** THEATRE ODE SUNG BY ONE ACTOR in Greek tragedy, an ode for one actor to sing alone **2.** POETRY ELEGY a poem that mourns sb's death **3.** MUSIC 17C ITALIAN VOCAL MUSIC a type of Italian vocal music of the 17th century for solo voice with instrumental accompaniment **4.** MUSIC MUSIC WITH A SINGLE MELODIC LINE a piece of music that has a single melodic line [Early 17thC. Via late Latin *monodia* from, ultimately, Greek *monōdos* 'singing alone', from *ōdē* 'song' (source of English *ode*).] —**monodic** /mə nóddik/ *adj.* —**monodically** /-dikli/ *adv.* —**monodist** /mónnədist/ *n.*

monoecious /mo neéshəss/, **monecious**, **monoicous** /mo nóykəss/ *adj.* used to describe a plant that has separate male and female flowers on the same plant [Mid-18thC. Formed from modern Latin *Monoecia*, the class name, literally 'single house' (perhaps from the idea of males and females co-habiting), from Greek *oikos* 'house'.] —**monoeciously** *adv.*

monoestrous /mon éestrəss/ *adj.* used to describe mammals that have only one oestrous cycle in a year or breeding season

monofilament /mónnə fílləmənt/ *n.* an untwisted and continuous single strand of natural or artificial fibre such as nylon, often used for fishing line

monogamy /mə nóggəmi/ *n.* **1.** PRACTICE OF HAVING ONE SEXUAL PARTNER the practice of having a sexual relationship with only one partner during a period of time **2.** ANTHROP MARRIAGE TO ONE PERSON the practice of being married to only one person at a time. ◊ **monandry, monogyny 3.** ZOOL PRACTICE OF HAVING ONE MATE the practice of having only one mate at a time or during a lifetime [Early 17thC. Via French *monogamie* from, ultimately, Greek *monogamos* (see MONOGAMIST).] —**monogamist** *n.* —**monogamous** *adj.* —**monogamously** *adv.*

monogenean /mónnə jeéni ən/ *n.* a parasitic flatworm that spends its entire life cycle on the outside of the same fish. Order: Monogenea. [Mid-20thC. Formed from modern Latin *Monogenea*, the order name, literally 'single generation', from Greek *genea* 'generation' (source of English *genealogy*).]

monogenesis /mónnō jénnəssiss/ *n.* BIOL **1.** DESCENT FROM A SINGLE CELL the theory that all living organisms are ultimately descended from a single cell **2.** ASEXUAL REPRODUCTION reproduction that does not involve the fusion of male and female gametes. = **asexual reproduction** —**monogenous** /mə nójjənəs/ *adj.*

monogenetic /mónnōjə néttik/ *adj.* **1.** BIOL RELATING TO MONOGENESIS relating to or involving monogenesis **2.** MARINE BIOL LIVING AS A PARASITE ON ONE FISH used to describe a nematode that spends its entire life cycle as a parasite on the outside of the same fish

monogenic /mónnə jénnik/ *adj.* GENETICS **1.** CONTROLLED BY ONE GENE used to describe a characteristic that is controlled by one gene or one pair of genes **2.** HAVING ONE SEX OF OFFSPRING producing offspring that are all of the same sex —**monogenically** *adv.*

monoglot /mónnō glot/ *n.* SB SPEAKING ONLY ONE LANGUAGE sb who is able to speak only one language ■ *adj.* SPEAKING ONLY ONE LANGUAGE able to speak only one language [Mid-19thC. From Greek *monoglōttos*, literally 'one tongue', from *glōtta* 'tongue'.]

monoglyceride /mónnō glíssə rīd/ *n.* any ester derived from glycerol in which only one hydroxyl group has combined with an acid

monogram /mónnə gram/ *n.* a design of one or more letters, usually the initials of a name, used to decorate or identify an object —**monogram** *vt.* —**monogrammatic** /mónnəgrə máttik/ *adj.*

monogrammed /mónnə gramd/ *adj.* bearing one or more initials as a decoration or an identifying mark

monograph /mónnə graaf, -graf/ *n.* a scholarly article, paper, or book on a single topic —**monographer** /mə nóggrəfər/ *n.* —**monographic** /mónnə gráffik/ *adj.* —**monographically** /-gráffikli/ *adv.*

monogyny /mə nójjəni/ *n.* **1.** ANTHROP PRACTICE OF HAVING ONE WIFE the practice of having only one wife at a time. ◊ **monogamy 2.** PRACTICE OF HAVING ONE FEMALE LOVER the practice of having a sexual relationship with only one woman during a period of time. ◊ **monandry, monogamy** —**monogynist** *n.* —**monogynous** *adj.*

monohull /mónnō hul/ *n.* a boat that has a single hull

monohybrid /mónnō híbrid/ *n.* a hybrid from parents that are different only with respect to a single gene pair

monohydrate /mónnō hī drayt/ *n.* a salt that is combined with one molecule of water

monohydric /mónnō hídrik/ *adj.* used to describe an alcohol that contains one replaceable atom of hydrogen

monohydroxy /mónnō hī dróksi/ *adj.* used to describe a compound that contains one hydroxyl group

monoicous *adj.* BOT = **monoecious**

monolatry /mə nóllətri/ *n.* the practice of worshipping only one god without, however, denying the existence of other gods —**monolater** *n.* —**monolatrous** *adj.*

monolayer /mónnō layər/ *n.* **1.** SCI LAYER ONE MOLECULE IN THICKNESS a film or or other coating of a compound that is one molecule thick **2.** BIOL LAYER ONE CELL IN THICKNESS a cultured layer of cells that is one cell thick

monolingual /mónnō língwəl/ *adj.* **1.** SPEAKING ONLY ONE LANGUAGE able to speak only one language **2.** USING ONLY ONE LANGUAGE written, spoken, or produced in only one language —**monolingualism** *n.*

monolith /mónnə lith/ *n.* **1.** PILLAR OF ROCK a tall block of solid stone standing by itself, whether a natural rock feature or a stone column shaped and erected by people, e.g. as a monument **2.** CONSTR LARGE BLOCK OF BUILDING MATERIAL a large uniform block of a single building material such as concrete placed together with others to form a building or other structure **3.** STH LARGE AND IMMOVABLE sth massive and unchanging, especially a large and long-established organization that is slow to change, uniform in character, and difficult to deal with on a human level

monolithic /mónnō líthik/ *adj.* **1.** IN THE FORM OF A LARGE STONE BLOCK consisting of or formed into a tall column of solid stone **2.** BUILT USING LARGE BLOCKS constructed using massive stones or solid blocks of material **3.**

LARGE AND UNCHANGING massive, uniform in character, and slow to change —**monolithically** adv.

monolithic technology n. a technology in electronic manufacturing in which all circuit components, e.g. resistors, capacitors, and diodes, are mounted on a single uniform piece of material

monologue /mónnə log/ n. 1. THEATRE ACTOR'S LONG SPEECH a long passage in a play or film spoken by one actor, or an entire play for one actor only 2. SB'S LONG UNINTERRUPTED SPEECH a long tedious uninterrupted speech during a conversation 3. ARTS PERFORMANCE BY COMEDIAN a set of jokes or humorous stories following one another without a break, told by a solo entertainer —**monologic** /mónnə lójjik/ adj. —**monologist** /mónnə logist, mə nóllajist/ n. —**monologize** /mə nóllə jīz/ vti.

monomania /mónnō máyni ə/ n. an obsessive interest in a single thing or a preoccupation with a single idea or thought —**monomaniac** n. —**monomaniacally** /mónnō mə nī əkli/ adv.

monomark /mónnə maark/ n. ID MARK an identifying set of numbers or letters marked on an individual item, especially by a retailer ■ vt. (-marks, -marking, -marked) LABEL WITH MONOMARK to put a monomark on sth

monomer /mónnəmər/ n. a relatively light, simple organic molecule that can join in long chains with other molecules to form a more complex molecule or polymer —**monomeric** /mónnə mérrik/ adj.

monometallic /mónnō mə tállik/ adj. 1. ECON USING ONE METAL AS A MONETARY STANDARD used to describe a currency or monetary system that uses one type of metal, especially gold or silver, as a monetary standard 2. MADE OF SINGLE METAL made of one type of metal only

monometallism /mónnō métt'lizəm/ n. ECON the use of just one metal, especially gold or silver, as a basic monetary standard

monomial /mo nómi əl/ n. 1. MATH ALGEBRAIC EXPRESSION an expression in algebra consisting of a single term, e.g. 3y, as distinct from one that contains two or more terms, e.g. 3x + 5y 2. BIOL SCIENTIFIC NAME WITH ONE ELEMENT a scientific name that consists of one element only, as do the names of most families of plants and animals [Early 18thC. Formed from MONO- on the model of binomial (see BINOMIAL).] —**monomial** adj.

monomolecular /mónnō mə lékyoolər/ adj. 1. RELATING TO A SINGLE MOLECULE relating to or involving single molecules 2. WITH THE THICKNESS OF A SINGLE MOLECULE used to describe a surface film that has a thickness of only one molecule. Monomolecular layers of alcohols or acids are used to retard water evaporation. —**monomolecularly** adv.

monomorphic /mónnō máwrfik/, **monomorphous** /-máwrfəss/ adj. 1. BIOL WITH A SINGLE DISCRETE FORM used to describe an organism or species that exists in a single discrete form, as distinct from one that changes form, as a caterpillar does when it becomes a butterfly 2. CHEM WITH ONE CRYSTALLINE FORM exhibiting only one crystalline form —**monomorphism** n.

Monongahela /mə nóng gə heélə/ river in the east-central United States. It flows north through West Virginia and Pennsylvania. Length: 206 km/128 mi.

mononuclear /mónnō nyookli ər/ adj. 1. BIOL WITH A SINGLE NUCLEUS used to describe a cell that has a single nucleus 2. CHEM WITH ONE RING OF ATOMS used to describe an organic compound with a molecular structure containing only one ring of atoms

mononucleosis /mónnō nyookli óssiss/ n. 1. ABNORMAL PRESENCE OF LYMPHOCYTES a significant rise in the number of atypical lymphocytes in the blood 2. = infectious mononucleosis

mononucleotide /mónnō nyookli ə tīd/ n. a nucleotide that contains one molecule each of phosphoric acid, a sugar, and a nitrogenous base

monophagous /mo nóffəgəss/ adj. feeding on a single type of plant or animal —**monophagy** /mo nóffəji, mə-/ n.

monophonic /mónnō fónnik/ adj. using only one channel to carry sound from the source to the loudspeaker, as distinct from, e.g. stereophonic sound that transmits across multiple channels to

give some auditory perspective —**monophonically** adv.

monophthong /mónnəf thong, mónnəp-/ n. a vowel sound that keeps the same quality for the whole syllable [Early 17thC. From Greek monophthoggos, from phthoggos 'sound'.] —**monophthongal** /mónnəf thóng g'l, mónnəp-/ adj.

monophyletic /mónnō fī léttik/ adj. used to describe a group of plants or animals that are descended from a single stock or ancestral form —**monophyletically** adv. —**monophyletism** /mónnō fíləti zəm/ n.

Monophysite /mo nóffi sīt/ n. sb who believes that Jesus Christ has a single inseparable nature that is both human and divine. This belief is held by the Coptic and Armenian churches amongst others. [Late 17thC. Via ecclesiastical Latin Monophysita from ecclesiastical Greek monophusitēs, from phusis 'nature' (see PHYSIC).] —**Monophysitic** /mónnō fi síttik, mə nóffə síttik/ adj. —**Monophysitism** /mo nóffissitizəm/ n.

Monoplane

monoplane /mónnō playn/ n. an aeroplane that has just one pair of wings

monoplegia /mónnō pleéji ə/ n. inability to move a single limb or a single group of muscles —**monoplegic** adj.

monopod /mónnə pod/ adj. CONSISTING OF ONE-LEGGED STRUCTURE used to describe a structure whose only support is one central pillar. Such designs are used in drilling rigs in the Arctic where the shifting ice could damage conventional supports. ■ n. ONE-LEGGED CAMERA SUPPORT a single-legged adjustable support used to steady a camera

monopode /mónnə pōd/ n. 1. BOT = monopodium 2. ONE-FOOTED ANIMAL a person or animal with a single foot, especially a member of a mythical African race of one-legged people [Early 19thC. From late Latin monopodius (see MONOPODIUM).] —**monopodially** /mónnə pódi əli/ adv.

monopodium /mónnə pódi əm/ (plural -a /-di ə/) n. the main axis of some plants such as the pine tree that extends to the tip of the plant and produces lateral branches

monopole /mónnə pōl/ n. 1. PHYS SINGULAR MAGNETIC POLE OR ELECTRIC CHARGE an electric charge or hypothetical magnetic pole isolated from its opposite charge or pole 2. PHYS HYPOTHETICAL MAGNETICALLY CHARGED ELEMENTARY PARTICLE a theoretical elementary particle that has only one magnetic pole, instead of the two present in ordinary magnetic bodies 3. RADIO RADIO ANTENNA a radio antenna made of an electrically charged conducting rod with an electrical connection at one end

monopolise vt. = monopolize

monopolist /mə nóppə list/ n. 1. CONTROLLER OF A MONOPOLY sb who controls a monopoly 2. SUPPORTER OF MONOPOLY a supporter of monopolistic policies —**monopolistic** /mə nóppə lístik/ adj. —**monopolistically** /-lístikli/ adv.

monopolize /mə nóppə līz/ (-lizes, -lizing, -lized), **monopolise** (-lises, -lising, -lised) vt. 1. BUSINESS HAVE EXCLUSIVE COMMERCIAL CONTROL OF to have complete control of an industry or service and prevent other companies or people from participating or competing in it 2. DOMINATE SELFISHLY to demand or take all of sth such as sb's time, attention, or affections, in a selfish way —**monopolization** /mə nóppə lī záysh'n/ n. —**monopolizer** n.

monopoly /mə nóppəli/ (plural -lies) n. 1. ECON CONTROL OF MARKET SUPPLY a situation in which one company controls an industry or is the only provider of a product or service 2. COMM BUSINESS CORPORATION WITH EXCLUSIVE CONTROL a company with a commercial monopoly 3. ECON EXCLUSIVE COMMODITY OR AREA OF CONTROL a product or service whose supply is controlled by only one company 4. LAW LEGAL RIGHT GRANTED TO SB a legal right to the exclusive control of an industry or service, as granted by a government 5. PERSONAL AND EXCLUSIVE POSSESSION an exclusive right to have or do sth ○ He seems to think he has a monopoly on common sense. [Mid-16thC. Via Latin monopolium from Greek monopōlion, from pōlein 'to sell'.] —**monopolism** n.

Monopoly /mə nóppəli/ tdmk. a trademark for a property trading board game

monopsony /mə nópsəni/ (plural -nies) n. a situation in which a particular type of product or service is only being bought or used by one customer [Mid-20thC. Coined from MONO + Greek opsōnein 'to purchase provisions'.] —**monopsonist** n. —**monopsonistic** adj.

monopteros /mo nóptə ross/ (plural -oi /-roy/), **monopteron** /mo nóptə ron/ (plural -a /-rə/) n. a circular classical temple surrounded by a single ring of columns [Late 17thC. Via Latin from Greek 'having one wing', formed from pteron 'wing'.] —**monopteral** adj.

monorail /mónnō ráyl/ n. a passenger transport system in which the carriages straddle or are suspended from a single beam

monosaccharide /mónnō sákə rīd, -rid/ n. a simple sugar such as glucose or fructose that cannot be broken down into simpler sugars

monosemy /mo nóssəmi, mónnō seemi/ n. LING the linguistic feature or fact of having only one meaning [Mid-20thC. Formed from MONO-, on the model of POLYSEMY.]

monoski /mónnō skee/ n. a broad single ski on which a skier stands with both feet —**monoskier** n. —**monoskiing** n.

$$HO-\overset{\overset{\displaystyle O}{\|}}{C}-CH_2-CH_2-\underset{\underset{\displaystyle NH_2}{|}}{C}H-\overset{\overset{\displaystyle O}{\|}}{C}-O^-Na^+$$

Monosodium glutamate

monosodium glutamate /mónnə sódi əm glootə mayt/ n. the crystalline sodium salt of glutamic acid, used in cooking primarily to enhance the flavour of food. Some people are sensitive to it and react with headaches or vomiting.

monosome /mónnə sōm/ n. 1. UNPAIRED CHROMOSOME a chromosome that abnormally exists on its own, without its usual pair, especially an unpaired X-chromosome 2. SINGLE RIBOSOME a single protein-manufacturing particle (**ribosome**) combined with messenger RNA [Early 20thC. Formed from -SOME.] —**monosomic** /mónnə sómik/ adj. —**monosomy** /-sōmi/ n.

monospermous /mónnō spúrməss/ adj. used to describe a plant that produces only one seed

monosyllabic /mónnō si lábbik/ adj. 1. BRIEF AND UNHELPFUL saying very little, often in a way that gives an impression of unfriendliness or unintelligence 2. CONTAINING ONLY ONE SYLLABLE consisting of one syllable only —**monosyllabically** adv. —**monosyllabicity** /mónnō silə bíssəti/ n.

monosyllable /mónnō silləb'l/ n. a word or sentence consisting of only one syllable, e.g. 'Yes' or 'me'

monotheism /mónnə thee izəm/ n. the belief that there is only one God. This belief is found, e.g. in Judaism, Christianity, and Islam. —**monotheist** n., adj. —**monotheistic** /mónnə thi ístik/ adj. —**monotheistically** /-ístikli/ adv.

monotint /mónnə tint/ *n.* DRAWING, PAINTING = **monochrome**

monotone /mónnə tōn/ *n.* **1.** ONE UNCHANGING SOUND TONE a sound, especially a speech sound, that does not rise and fall in pitch, but stays on the same tone all the time **2.** SERIES OF IDENTICAL SOUNDS a sequence of sounds, such as a piece of speech, singing, or music, that stays at exactly the same pitch throughout **3.** UNVARYING QUALITY complete lack of variety in colour, expression, or style **4.** MUSIC SINGER WITH NO SENSE OF PITCH sb who cannot produce, or distinguish between, sounds of varying pitches when singing ■ *adj.* **1.** WITH UNVARYING QUALITY lacking variety in pitch, colour, or another quality **2.** monotone, monotonic MATH ASCENDING OR DESCENDING IN SEQUENCE used to describe a function or a sequence of real numbers that steadily increases or decreases —**monotonicity** /mónnə to níssəti/ *n.*

monotonous /mə nóttənəs/ *adj.* **1.** REPETITIOUS AND UNINTERESTING uninteresting or boring as a result of being repetitive and unvaried **2.** UTTERED IN UNVARIED TONE uttered or performed in one unvaried tone — **monotonously** *adv.* —**monotonousness** *n.*

——— **WORD KEY: SYNONYMS** ———
See Synonyms at *boring*.

monotony /mə nóttəni/ *n.* **1.** TEDIOUS LACK OF VARIETY boredom or dullness arising from the fact that nothing different ever happens **2.** UNVARYING CONDITION repetitiousness or lack of variation in pitch or tone, especially in relation to music or speech

monotype /mónnə tīp/ *n.* **1.** BIOL SOLE MEMBER OF A BIOLOGICAL GROUP a plant or animal that is the only member of the taxonomic category to which it belongs **2.** ART UNIQUE PRINTED IMAGE an artwork created by pressing on paper laid on an inked metal plate or sheet of glass. Although similar prints can be made, each one will be unique. —**monotypic** /mónnə típpik/ *adj.*

Monotype /mónnə tīp/ *tdmk.* a trademark for a typesetting machine that is run from a keyboard activating a unit that sets type by individual characters

monounsaturated /mónnō un sáchə raytid/ *adj.* used to describe vegetable oils and fatty acids whose molecular structure includes only one double carbon bond

monovalent /mónnō váylənt/ *adj.* **1.** CHEM WITH A VALENCY OF ONE used to describe a chemical element or isotope that has a valency of one **2.** IMMUNOL WITH ONE KIND OF ANTIBODY containing only one type of antibody — **monovalence** *n.* —**monovalency** /-váylənsee/ *n.*

monoxide /mo nók sīd/ *n.* a chemical compound with molecules that consist of one atom of oxygen and one or more atoms of another element

monozygotic /mónnō zī góttik/ *adj.* used to describe twins that are derived from a single fertilized egg. In humans, identical twins are monozygotic.

James Monroe

Monroe /mən rố/, **James** (1758–1821) US statesman and 5th President of the United States. He held numerous state and national offices in nearly fifty years of public service, and was a popular president (1817–25).

Monroe, Marilyn (1926–62) US actor. She starred in films such as *Bus Stop* (1956), *Some Like It Hot* (1959), and *The Misfits* (1961). She was married to the baseball player Joe DiMaggio and later the

Marilyn Monroe

playwright Arthur Miller. Real name **Norma Jean Mortenson**

Monroe doctrine *n.* the political principle, as stated by President James Monroe in 1823, that Europe should no longer involve itself in the American continent. The policy was part of the US recognition of the independence of several Latin American countries. [Mid-19thC. Named after James MONROE, during whose presidency the principle was first advocated.]

Monrovia /mon róvi ə/ capital city and chief seaport of Liberia, situated in the west of the country. Population: 490,000 (1992).

mons /monz/ (*plural* **montes** /món teez/) *n.* a fleshy body part that sticks out, especially the one formed by a pad of flesh at the juncture of the pubic bones. ◊ **mons pubis** [Mid-20thC. Shortening of MONS PUBIS.]

Mons /moNs/ historic city in southwestern Belgium, situated about 48 km/30 mi. southwest of Brussels. Population: 92,260 (1996).

Monseigneur /móN see nyúr, -say-/ (*plural* **Messeigneurs** /máy see-, -say-/) *n.* a title given to some dignitaries, especially bishops and princes, in France and French-speaking countries [Early 17thC. From French, from *mon* 'my' + *seigneur* 'lord' (see SEIGNEUR).]

Monsieur /mə syúr/ (*plural* **Messieurs** /may syúr/), **monsieur** (*plural* **messieurs**) *n.* **1.** FRENCH FOR 'MR' a title for a man in France or a French-speaking country, if he has no other special title **2.** FRENCH WORD USED TO ADDRESS MAN a form of address used when speaking or referring to a French or French-speaking man whose name is not known [Early 16thC. From French, from *mon* 'my' + *sieur* 'lord', from, ultimately, Latin *senior* 'older' (see SENIOR).]

Monsignor /mon seényər, -nyawr/ (*plural* **-gnors** or **-gnori** /món see nyáwri/) *n.* a title used when speaking or referring to certain clerics of the Roman Catholic Church, especially bishops and officials of the papal court [Late 16thC. Via Italian from French *monseigneur* (see MONSEIGNEUR).] —**Monsignorial** /món see nyáwri əl/ *adj.*

monsoon /mon soón/ *n.* **1.** WINDS THAT REVERSE DIRECTION SEASONALLY a large-scale wind system that seasonally blows in opposite directions and determines the climate of large regions. The reversal of wind direction is caused by the greater annual temperature differences over large land masses than over the adjacent waters. **2.** RAINY SEASON, ESPECIALLY IN INDIA any period of heavy rainfall, especially during the summer over Southeast Asia and India **3.** HEAVY RAINFALL a very heavy fall of rain (*informal*) [Late 16thC. Via obsolete Dutch *monssoen* from Portuguese *monção*, from Arabic *mawsim* 'season'.] —**monsoonal** *adj.*

mons pubis /-pyoóbiss/ (*plural* **montes pubis** /món teez-/) *n.* a prominence caused by the pad of fat that overlies the junction of the pubic bones in women and girls [Late 19thC. From Latin, literally 'mount of the pubes'.]

monster /mónstər/ *n.* **1.** UGLY TERRIFYING CREATURE any large, ugly, terrifying animal or person found in mythology or created by the imagination, especially sth fierce that kills people. Monsters often feature in folklore and fairytales as evil creatures resembling a mixture of different animals. **2.** EVIL PERSON sb whose inhumanity or vicious behaviour terrifies and disgusts people **3.** HUGE THING sth extraordinarily or unusually large (*informal; often used*

before a noun) **4.** PATHOL IMPROPERLY FORMED FOETUS a foetus that is markedly improperly formed, especially one that cannot live outside the uterus **5.** SB OR STH UNDESIRABLY FORMED a person, animal, or plant that is undesirably formed (*archaic offensive*) [13thC. Via French *monstre* from Latin *monstrum* 'monster, divine omen', from *monere* 'to warn, remind' (source of English *muster* and *monument*).]

Monstrance

monstrance /mónstrənss/ *n.* CHR a large gold or silver container in which the Host is placed and then shown to the congregation for adoration in a Roman Catholic Mass [13thC. Via medieval Latin *monstrantia* from, ultimately, Latin *monstrare* 'to show', from *monstrum* (see MONSTER).]

monstrosity /mon stróssəti/ (*plural* **-ties**) *n.* **1.** VERY UGLY THING an object, animal, or person that is very unpleasant or frightening to look at, often because it is large and strangely shaped **2.** MONSTROUSNESS frightening size, shape, and ugliness ○ *a figure of overwhelming monstrosity* [Mid-16thC. From late Latin *monstrositas*, from Latin *monstruosus* (see MONSTROUS).]

monstrous /mónstrəss/ *adj.* **1.** SHOCKING AND MORALLY UNACCEPTABLE wicked, cruel, or unpleasant to an extent that is morally unacceptable **2.** EXTREMELY LARGE extremely large, often in a way that seems ugly and frightening **3.** LIKE A MONSTER resembling a monster of the type found in folklore and fairytales **4.** EXTREMELY UNUSUAL greatly different from the norm (*archaic*) [14thC. Via Old French *monstreux* from Latin *monstruosus*, from *monstrum* (see MONSTER).] —**monstrousness** *n.*

monstrously /mónstrəssli/ *adv.* in a way or to an extent that shocks or offends other people

mons veneris /-vénnəriss/ (*plural* **montes veneris** /món teez-/) *n.* = mons pubis [Early 17thC. From Latin, literally 'the mount of Venus', goddess of love.]

Mont. *abbr.* Montana

montage /mon taázh/ *n.* **1.** ARTS ARTWORK CREATED FROM MANY SMALL PIECES a picture or other work of art composed by assembling, overlaying, and overlapping many different materials or pieces collected from different sources, e.g. photographs, magazines, and other pictures **2.** ARTS CREATION OF IMAGE FROM COLLECTED BITS the technique of creating a montage **3.** CINEMA SEQUENCE OF OVERLAPPING FILM CLIPS a film sequence consisting of a series of dissolves, superimpositions, or cuts used to condense time or to suggest memories or hallucinations **4.** CINEMA FILM-MAKING STYLE a style of film-making that makes extensive use of cuts, camera movements, and changes of camera position, particularly to set up new meanings not conveyed by the filmed action itself [Early 20thC. From French, formed from *monter* 'to mount' (see MOUNT).]

Montagnais /móntə nyáy/ (*plural* **-nais**) *n.* **1.** PEOPLES MEMBER OF NATIVE AMERICAN PEOPLE a member of a Native American people who live in parts of Quebec and Labrador **2.** LANG MONTAGNAIS LANGUAGE the Algonquian language of the Montagnais people. Montagnais is spoken by about four thousand people. [Early 18thC. From French, formed from *montagne* 'mountain.'] —**Montagnais** *adj.*

Montagnard /mónta nyaárd, -nyaàr/ (*plural* **-gnard** or **-gnards**) *n.* a member of a people who live in the mountainous border region between Vietnam, Laos, and Cambodia [Mid-19thC. From French, 'mountaineer', from *montagne* 'mountain'.]

Montaigne /mon táyn, mon tényə/, **Michel de Eyquem** (1533–92) French essayist. He invented the essay form in his *Essays* (1572–80,1588), original pieces on the ideas and personalities of his time.

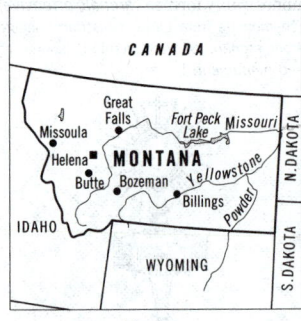
Montana

Montana /mon taánə/ state in the northwestern United States, bordered by Canada, and the US states of North Dakota, South Dakota, Wyoming, and Idaho. Capital: Helena. Population: 878,810 (1997). Area: 380,849 sq. km/147,046 sq. mi. —**Montanan** *n.*, *adj.*

montane /món tayn/ *adj.* growing or living in mountainous regions [Mid-19thC. From Latin *montanus*, from the stem *mont-* 'mountain' (see MOUNTAIN).]

montan wax /món tan-/ *n.* a brittle, white to dark brown wax extracted from lignite and substituted in polishes and candles for carnauba and beeswax [Early 20thC. From Latin *montanus* 'montane' (see MONTANE), because it is extracted from lignite, a mountain ore.]

Montauk /món tawk/ (*plural* **-tauk** *or* **-tauks**) *n.* a member of a Native North American people that originally occupied lands in the eastern part of New York's Long Island [Mid-19thC. From *Montauk*, a local place name.]

Mont Blanc /móN blaáN/ the highest mountain in western Europe, in the western Alps on the border of France and Italy. Height: 4,807 m/15,771 ft.

monte /mónti/ *n.* **1.** CARDS BETTING GAME PLAYED WITH CARDS a game in which a player chooses between two cards and bets on being dealt a card of that same suit before being dealt a card of the other suit **2.** Aus A CERTAINTY sth that is sure to happen or sure to be had or achieved [Early 19thC. Via Spanish from, ultimately, the Latin stem *mont-* 'mountain' (see MOUNTAIN); from the mountain or heap of cards present on the table.]

Monte Carlo /mónti kaárlō/ tourist resort with a famous casino in Monaco, on the Mediterranean Sea. Population: 13,154 (1982).

Montego Bay /mon teégō báy/ **1.** inlet of the Caribbean Sea in northwestern Jamaica **2.** city, seaport and tourist resort in Jamaica, located on the bay of the same name. Population: 83,446 (1991).

monteith /mon teéth/ *n.* a silver or pewter basin with notches around the edge, made to hold punch, or to cool punch glasses by resting their bases over the scalloped edge [Late 17thC. Said to be named after a Scotsman *Monteith*, known for his capes with scalloped hems.]

Montélimar /món tay li maár/ town in Drôme Department, central France, situated about 129 km/80 mi. south of Lyon. Population: 31,386 (1990).

Montenegro /móntə neégrō/ constituent republic of the Federal Republic of Yugoslavia, along with Serbia. Until 1991 it was part of the larger state of Yugoslavia. Capital: Podgorica. Population: 635,442 (1996). Area: 13,812 sq. km/5,333 sq. mi. —**Montenegrin** *n.*, *adj.*

Monterey /móntə ráy/ city and port in western California, on Monterey Bay. Population: 29,812 (1994).

Monterey Jack /móntə ráy-/ *n.* a semihard cheese that is mild when young and becomes stronger and drier as it ages [Mid-20thC. Named after Monterey County, California, US, where it was first made.]

Monterey pine *n.* a pine tree that is native to the Monterey Peninsula of California and is now widely planted throughout the world for timber. Latin name: *Pinus radiata*.

Monte Rosa /mónti rōzə/ mountain in the Pennine Alps, on the Swiss-Italian border, south of Zermatt. Height: 4,633 m/15,200 ft.

Monterrey /móntə ráy/ an industrial city in northeastern Mexico, capital of Nuevo Leon State. Population: 1,064,197 (1990).

Montes Alpes /món tayz ál páyz/ *n.* an extensive range of mountains on the Moon arching around the northeast of Mare Imbrium

Montes Apenninus /món tayz áppa nínəss/ extensive range of mountains on the Moon surrounding the southeastern edge of Mare Imbrium

Montes Jura /món tayz joórə/ range of lunar mountains north of Mare Imbrium. Height: 4,500 m/15,000 ft.

Montesquieu /món təskyə, -təskyoó/, **Charles Louis de Secondat, Baron de la Brède et de** (1689–1755) French jurist and writer. His works, including his seminal comparative political study *The Spirit of Laws* (1748), contributed to the European Enlightenment and helped create the political climate that led to the French Revolution.

Maria Montessori

Montessori /móntə sáwri/, **Maria** (1870–1952) Italian physician and educationalist. She devised a system for educating young children.

Montessori method /móntə sáwri-/ *n.* a system of educating young children that was initiated by Maria Montessori in 1952 and aims to develop the child's natural interests and activities rather than use formal teaching methods

Monteverdi /mónti váirdi/, **Claudio** (1567–1643) Italian composer. His secular and sacred choral works and his operas mark the transition from Renaissance to Baroque music. Full name **Claudio Giovanni Antonio Monteverdi**

Montevideo /móntivi dáyō/ capital city of Uruguay, located on the Atlantic Ocean in the south of the country. Population: 1,251,647 (1985).

Montez /mon téz/, **Lola, Baroness Rosenthal and Countess of Lansfield** (1818–61) Irish dancer. She enjoyed an international career and in 1847 became the mistress of Louis I of Bavaria, who ennobled her. Pseudonym of **Marie Dolores Eliza Rosanna Gilbert**

Montezuma II /mónti zoómə/ (1466–1520) Aztec emperor. His empire was brought down by Spanish invaders (1520).

Montezuma's revenge /mónti zoóməz-/ *n.* an offensive term for diarrhoea and sickness experienced when visiting a foreign country, originally Mexico, and eating unfamiliar food (*informal offensive*) [Mid-20thC. Named after the last Aztec emperor of Mexico, MONTEZUMA II, as if the malady were his revenge for the loss of his empire to the Spanish.]

Montfort /móntfərt/, **Simon de, Earl of Leicester** (1200?–65) English aristocrat and soldier. Having captured Henry III of England, in 1264 he set up a short-lived parliamentary-style assembly.

Montgolfier /mont gólfi ər, moN gólfyər/, **Jacques Etienne** (1745–99) French industrialist and inventor. His development, with his brother Joseph (1740–1810), of the hot-air balloon, led to the first manned balloon flight, launched from Paris (1873).

Montgomery /mənt gómməri/ **1.** market town in Powys, Wales. Population: 1,035 (1981). **2.** capital city of Alabama, in the centre of the state. It is a port on the Alabama River. Population: 196,363 (1996).

Montgomery, Bernard Law, 1st Viscount Montgomery of Alamein (1887–1976) British soldier. In World War II, he commanded the Eighth Army in northern Africa defeating Rommel, and became chief of the land forces in the Normandy invasion. After the war, he was deputy supreme commander of NATO forces (1951–58).

Montgomeryshire /mənt gómmərishər/ former county in central Wales, now part of Powys

month /munth/ *n.* **1.** CALENDAR MAJOR DIVISION OF YEAR any of the major named divisions of the year in various calendar systems. In the Gregorian calendar, there are 12 months, varying in length from 28 to 31 days. **2.** CALENDAR FOUR WEEKS OR 30 DAYS a period of time equivalent to about four weeks or 30 days **3.** INTERVAL BETWEEN DATES IN CONSECUTIVE MONTHS a time lasting from a specified date in one calendar month until the same date in the next calendar month **4.** ASTRON **5.** solar month **6.** ASTRON = lunar month **6.** ASTRON = sidereal month ■ **months** *npl.* LONG PERIOD OF TIME a long time, often an excessively or unacceptably long time [Old English *mōnap*. Ultimately 'sth measured by the revolutions of the moon', from an Indo-European word meaning 'to measure' that is also the ancestor of English *moon*.] ◇ **a month of Sundays** a long time, or one that is apparently unending (*informal*)

monthly /múnthli/ *adj.* **1.** HAPPENING EACH MONTH done, held, or arranged once every month ○ *a monthly meeting* **2.** PRODUCED EVERY MONTH published or issued once a month ○ *a monthly periodical* **3.** LASTING A MONTH valid for one month ○ *a monthly pass* ■ *adv.* ONCE A MONTH at intervals of one month ■ *n.* (*plural* **-lies**) **1.** PUBL MAGAZINE ISSUED EVERY MONTH a publication or periodical that is produced once a month **2.** WOMAN'S MENSTRUAL PERIOD a woman's monthly menstruation (*informal; usually plural*)

monticule /mónti kyool/ *n.* **1.** SECONDARY VOLCANIC CONE a subordinate volcanic cone **2.** MOUND any mound or small hill [Late 18thC. Via French from late Latin *monticulus*, a diminutive of the Latin stem *mont-* 'mountain' (see MOUNTAIN).]

Montmorency /móntmə rénssi/ river in southern Quebec, Canada. It flows south to join the St Lawrence River. Length: 97 km/60 mi.

Montmorency Falls the highest waterfall in Quebec, Canada. They are located east of Quebec City where the Montmorency River empties into the St Lawrence River. Height: 84 m/275 ft.

montmorillonite /móntmə rílla nīt, -reè ə nīt/ *n.* a soft clayey mineral that is composed of hydrous aluminium silicate. It is the major component of bentonite clay deposits. [Mid-19thC. Named after *Montmorillon*, the French town where it was discovered.] —**montmorillonitic** /móntmə rílla níttik, -reè ə-/ *adj.*

Montpellier /moN pə lyáy/ city in southern France, capital of the Hérault Department and administrative and commercial centre of the Languedoc-Roussillon Region. Population: 207,996 (1990).

Montreal /móntri áwl/ the second largest city in Canada, situated on Montreal Island in the St Lawrence River, Quebec. Population: 3,326,510 (1996).

Montreux /mon trō/ major resort area in western Switzerland, on the northeastern shore of Lake Geneva. Population: 20,060 (1990).

Montserrat /móntsə rát/ island in the eastern Caribbean Sea, a dependency of the United Kingdom. It was economically devastated by volcanic eruptions in 1997. Population: 12,771 (1996). Area: 102 sq. mi./39 sq. mi.

monument /mónnyooment/ *n.* **1.** LARGE STONE STATUE OR CARVING sth designed and built as a lasting public tribute to a person, a group of people, or an event **2.** FAMOUS PLACE OR BUILDING a site or structure that is preserved because of its historical, cultural, or aesthetic importance **3.** CARVED HEADSTONE a tombstone, plaque, or ornamental stone structure placed on sb's grave. A monument in a cemetery is usually inscribed with the name and dates of birth and death of the deceased person, and often a religious quotation or verse. **4. WORTHY REMINDER OF STH** sth that remains as a reminder of sth, especially sth fine or distinguished **5. MEMORIAL TRIBUTE** a memorial to sb in the form of a written or spoken tribute **6. BOUNDARY MARKER** an object such as a stone that marks a boundary [13thC. Via French from Latin *monumentum*, from *monere* 'to remind'.]

monumental /mónnyŏŏ mént'l/ *adj.* **1. LARGE** huge in size, importance, or intensity **2. DESERVING SPECIAL ADMIRATION** so important or enduring that people cannot fail to notice or be impressed **3. MAKING CARVED HEADSTONES** related to or involved in the making of tombstones and memorial items to go in cemeteries and churches **4. OF MONUMENTS** relating to monuments or taking the form of a monument —**monumentality** /mónnyŏŏ men tálləti/ *n.* —**monumentally** /mónnyŏŏ mént'li/ *adv.*

Monument Valley

Monument Valley /mónnyŏŏmənt válli/ region in northeastern Arizona and southeastern Utah, notable for its scenic rock formations

monuron /mónnyŏŏ ron/ *n.* a herbicide that is particularly effective against broad-leaved weeds, in the form of a white crystalline odourless solid [Mid-20thC. Blend of MONO- and UREA and -ON.]

Monza /mŏntsa, mónzə/ city in northern Italy, situated about 13 km/8 mi. northeast of Milan. Population: 120,054 (1992).

monzonite /mónzə nīt/ *n.* a visibly crystalline, granular igneous rock composed chiefly of equal amounts of two feldspar minerals, plagioclase and orthoclase, and small amounts of a variety of coloured minerals [Late 19thC. Named after Mount *Monzoni* in the Tyrol.] —**monzonitic** /mónzə níttik/ *adj.*

moo /moo/ *vi.* (**moos, mooing, mooed**) **MAKE NOISE LIKE COW** to produce the deep drawn-out sound that a cow makes ■ *n.* (*plural* **moos**) **1. NOISE THAT COW MAKES** a deep drawn-out sound made by a cow, or by sb imitating this sound **2. OFFENSIVE TERM** an offensive term that deliberately insults a woman's intelligence and usefulness (*offensive*) [Mid-16thC. An imitation of the sound.]

mooch /mooch/ (**mooches, mooching, mooched**) *v.* **1.** *vti.* **GET THINGS FOR NOTHING FROM OTHERS** to get sth for nothing from sb by asking directly for it, without making any personal effort for it (*informal*) ○ *He's always mooching off friends.* **2.** *vi.* **WANDER AIMLESSLY** to wander or linger in an aimless way (*slang*) ○ *just mooching about* **3.** *vi.* **US SNEAK AROUND SUSPICIOUSLY** to move around or wait somewhere quietly and secretly, trying not to be noticed (*slang*) [15thC. From Old French *muchier* 'to hide', of unknown origin.] —**moocher** *n.*

mood[1] /mood/ *n.* **1. STATE OF MIND** a state of mind that sb experiences at a particular time ○ *a good mood* **2. GENERAL FEELING OF GROUP** the way a group of people think and feel about sth at a particular time ○ *The mood of the country after the war was generally optimistic.* **3. BAD TEMPER** a feeling or display of sullen anger or irritability, especially one that begins suddenly or lasts a relatively short time ○ *He's in a mood.* [Old English *mōd* 'mind, courage', from a prehistoric Germanic word] ◇ **in the mood** in the right or best state of mind for a particular activity or experience

mood[2] /mood/ *n.* **1. GRAM SET OF VERB FORMS** a group of verb forms expressing a particular attitude. English has the indicative mood, expressing factual state-

ments, the imperative mood, expressing commands, and the subjunctive mood, expressing possibilities and wishes. **2. LOGIC = mode** *n.* **7** [Mid-16thC. Alteration of MODE.]

moody /moódi/ (**-ier, -iest**) *adj.* **1. UNPREDICTABLY GRUMPY OR GLOOMY** tending to change mood unpredictably from cheerful to bad-tempered **2. CHANGEABLE** unusually changeable or difficult to predict **3. DISPLAYING PARTICULAR MOOD** displaying particular emotions, especially unhappiness or anger, clearly and intensely [Old English] —**moodily** *adv.* —**moodiness** *n.*

Moody /moódi/, **Dwight Lyman** (1837–99) US evangelist. He founded Northfield Seminary girls' school (1879) and Mount Hermon School for boys (1881).

moola /moólə, moo laa/, **moolah** *n.* US money (*slang dated*) [Mid-20thC. Origin unknown.]

mooli /moóli/ (*plural* **-lis** *or* **-li**) *n.* a large long white radish that can be eaten raw, cooked, or pickled and is typically used in Japanese, Chinese, and other Asian cuisines. US term **daikon** [Mid-20thC. From Hindi *mūlī*.]

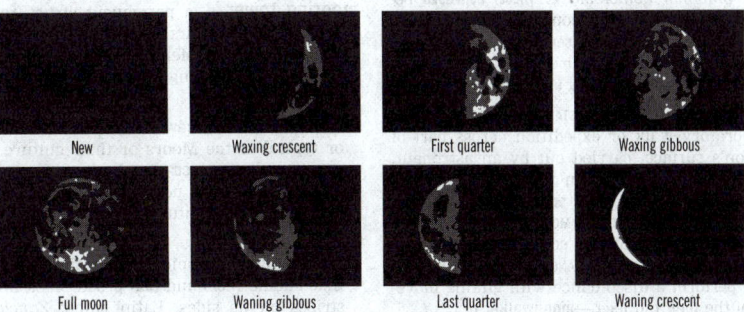

Moon: Phases of the moon

[New] [Waxing crescent] [First quarter] [Waxing gibbous] [Full moon] [Waning gibbous] [Last quarter] [Waning crescent]

moon /moon/ *n.* **1. moon, Moon** ASTRON **ONLY NATURAL SATELLITE OF EARTH** the Earth's only natural satellite. It is the astronomical body nearest to the Earth, except for some artificial satellites and occasional meteors. **2. ASTRON PLANET'S NATURAL SATELLITE** any natural satellite revolving around a planet. Mars, Jupiter, Saturn, Uranus, and Neptune each have more than one moon. **3. MOON'S SHAPE AS SEEN FROM EARTH** a form or view of the Moon, called its phase, at a specific point in the lunar cycle. Since it shines only by reflected sunlight, the phases of the Moon depend on its position relative to the Earth and the Sun. **4. SYMBOLIC REPRESENTATION OF MOON** a simple or stylized representation of the Moon, usually in the form of a circle or crescent **5. PERIOD OF TIME** a month, either as a rough estimate of time or as the time it takes for the Moon to complete its cycle of the Earth (*archaic or literary*) **6. MOONLIGHT** light given out by the Moon ■ *v.* (**moons, mooning, mooned**) **1.** *vi.* **WANDER AIMLESSLY** to wander around in a dreamy or listless state, unable to concentrate on anything **2.** *vi.* **YEARN FOR LOVED ONE** to be stricken with longing for an absent loved one, and rendered listless and dreamy as a result (*literary or humorous*) **3.** *vti.* **BARE THE BUTTOCKS** to bend over and deliberately expose the bare buttocks to sb, either as a rude joke or as an act of defiance and disrespect (*informal*) [Old English *mōna*, from a prehistoric Germanic word that is also the ancestor of English *month* (see MONTH)]

Moon /moon/, **William** (1818–94) British inventor. In 1845 he developed a system of embossed line type, based on Roman letters, designed to be read by blind people.

moonbeam /moón beem/ *n.* a pale, milky, or iridescent beam of light reflected to the Earth by the Moon at night

moon blindness *n.* periodic episodes of impaired vision in horses that often lead to permanent loss of sight

mooncalf /moón kaaf/ (*plural* **-calves** /-kaavz/) *n.* **1. THOUGHTLESS PERSON** an unintelligent or thoughtless person (*archaic insult*) **2. STH BADLY FORMED** sth that is badly formed, especially a stillborn human or animal baby (*archaic*) [Mid-16thC. From MOON + CALF; originally in the meaning of 'shapeless fleshy mass in the womb', thought to be caused by the influence of the moon.]

moon dog *n.* ASTRON = **paraselene**

mooneye /moón ī/ *n.* a silvery freshwater fish found in North America that looks like a herring with very large eyes. Latin name: *Hiodon tergisus.*

moon-faced *adj.* with a large round face

moonflower /moón flowər/ *n.* a name given to various plants whose flowers open at night, especially climbing plants related to the morning glories

Moonie /moóni/ *n.* sb who belongs to the Unification Church founded by Sun Myung Moon (*informal; often considered offensive*)

moonlight /moón līt/ *n.* **LIGHT FROM THE MOON** the pale cool light that shines from the Moon on a clear night, often considered eerie or romantic. Moonlight is light from the Sun reflected from the Moon's surface. ■ *vi.* (**-lights, -lighting, -lighted**) **WORK AT SECOND JOB** to have a second job in addition to a main job, often done at night and kept secret for purposes of tax evasion (*informal*) —**moonlighting** *n.*

moonlight flit *n.* an act of secretly abandoning a rented house during the night, in order to avoid paying rent that is owed

moonlit /moón lit/ *adj.* brightened or illuminated by light from the Moon

Moonlite /moón līt/, **Captain** (1842–80) Irish-born Australian bushranger. A former preacher turned thief, he was captured by police and hanged. Real name **Andrew George Scott**

moon pool *n.* INDUST an open shaft in a deep-sea drilling vessel, usually located in the centre of the hull, through which the drilling takes place

moonraker /moón raykər/ *n.* a small sail sometimes set above the skysail on a square-rigged ship [Early 19thC. Origin uncertain: probably from its great height (compare SKYSCRAPER).]

moonrise /moón rīz/ *n.* **1. MOMENT WHEN MOON APPEARS** the time of day when the Moon rises over the horizon **2. MOON'S APPEARANCE IN SKY** the Moon's rising in the sky over the horizon [Early 18thC. Formed from MOON on the model of *sunrise*.]

moonscape /moón skayp/ *n.* **1. VIEW OF THE MOON'S SURFACE** the general appearance of the surface of the Moon as seen or portrayed **2. BARE DESERTED LANDSCAPE** a view or place that looks as rough, grey, and bleak as the surface of the Moon

moonseed /moón seed/ *n.* a name given to various climbing plants that have tiny greenish flowers and red or black fruit with crescent-shaped seeds. Genera: *Menispermum* and *Cocculus.* [Mid-18thC. From the crescent shape of their seeds.]

moonset /moón set/ *n.* **1. MOMENT WHEN MOON GOES DOWN** the time of day when the Moon disappears below the horizon **2. MOON'S LEAVING THE SKY** the disappearance of the Moon below the horizon [Mid-19thC. Formed from MOON on the model of *sunset*.]

moonshine /mo͞on shīn/ *n.* **1.** **ILLEGALLY MADE ALCOHOL** whisky or other strong spirits produced and sold illegally (*informal dated or humorous*) **2.** **NONSENSE** talk, opinions, or ideas dismissed as senseless (*informal*) **3.** **MOONLIGHT** moonlight —**moonshiner** *n.*

moonshot /mo͞on shot/ *n.* the launch of a crewed or uncrewed spacecraft to orbit or land on the Moon

moonstone /mo͞on stōn/ *n.* a translucent variety of the mineral feldspar that has a bluish-white lustre and is used as a gemstone

WORD KEY: CULTURAL NOTE

The Moonstone, a novel by the writer Wilkie Collins (1868). The first English detective novel, it involves the disappearance of a priceless Indian diamond and a subsequent puzzling murder. All the classic elements of the whodunit genre are present, including red herrings, alibis, and sufficient clues for the reader to solve the crime ahead of its hero, Sergeant Cuff of Scotland Yard.

moonstruck /mo͞on struk/ *adj.* **1.** **IN A DAZE** acting in a rather irrational, dreamy, confused way, often out of love (*informal humorous*) **2.** **WILDLY CONFUSED** behaving in a wild or confused way (*dated literary*) [Late 17thC. The two senses of the word came from the romantic associations of moonlight and the popular belief that the Moon has an effect upon mental stability.]

moonwalk /mo͞on wawk/ *n.* **INSTANCE OF WALKING ON MOON** an exploratory walk or expedition across part of the Moon's surface, carried out by an astronaut. The first person to walk on the Moon was Neil Armstrong on 20 July, 1969. ■ *vi.* (**-walks, -walking, -walked**) **1.** **GO ON FOOT ACROSS MOON'S SURFACE** to walk away from a spacecraft for some distance across the surface of the Moon **2.** DANCE **PERFORM GLIDING DISCO DANCE** to perform a disco dance with gliding movements of the feet and legs —**moonwalker** *n.*

moony /mo͞oni/ (**-ier, -iest**) *adj.* **1.** **DREAMY** in a distracted or dreamy state, with little energy or concentration (*informal*) **2.** **RELATING TO MOON** relating to or resembling the Moon —**moonily** *adv.* —**mooniness** *n.*

moor[1] /moor, mawr/ *n.* a large uncultivated treeless stretch of land covered with bracken, heather, coarse grasses, or moss (*often used in the plural*) [Old English *mōr*, from prehistoric Germanic]

moor[2] /moor, mawr/ (**moors, mooring, moored**) *vti.* to fix a boat, ship, or aircraft to one place with cables, chains, or an anchor, or to be secured in this way [15thC. Origin uncertain: probably from Middle Low German *mōren*.]

Moor /moor, mawr/ *n.* a member of a nomadic people of Arab and Berber descent who originally occupied lands in various parts of North Africa, and whose members continue to live there. Their civilization flourished from the 8th to the 15th centuries, during which time they also settled in Spain. [14thC. Via Old French *More* from Latin *Maurus*, from Greek *Mauros* (source of English *morris dance*), of uncertain origin: probably from a North African language.]

moorage /mo͞orij, máwrij/ *n.* **1.** = **mooring** *n.* 1 **2.** **MOORING FEE** the fee charged for mooring somewhere

Moore /mo͞o o͞o ray/ *n., adj.* LANG, PEOPLES = **Mossi**

Moore /moor, mawr/, **Bobby** (1941–93) British footballer. A skilled defensive player and team captain, he captained England to victory in the 1966 World Cup. Full name **Robert Frederick Moore**

Moore, Dudley (*b.* 1935) British actor, comedian, and pianist. After working in partnership with comedian Peter Cook, he appeared in Hollywood film comedies.

Moore, G.E. (1873–1958) British philosopher. Author of *Principia Ethica* (1903), he is noted for his contribution to ethical theory and modern philosophical realism. Full name **George Edward Moore**

Moore, Gerald (1899–1987) British pianist. He was a leading accompanist of singers and instrumentalists.

Moore, Henry (1898–1986) British sculptor, and printmaker. He is noted for his large-scale, stylized representations of the human body, many made for outdoor locations.

Moore, Michael Kenneth (*b.* 1949) New Zealand statesman. He was a Labour Party politician and prime minister of New Zealand for two months in 1990.

Moore, Patrick (*b.* 1923) British astronomer. He popularized astronomy with his regular television programme *The Sky at Night* and in books and lectures.

moorhen /moor hen, máwr-/ *n.* a medium-sized water bird found in marshy areas throughout the world. It has black plumage and a red bill. Latin name: *Gallinula chloropus.*

Moorhouse /moor howss, máwr-/, **Frank Thomas** (*b.* 1938) Australian writer. His short story collections include *The Americans, Baby* (1972) and his novels *Grand Days* (1994).

mooring /mooring, máwr-/ *n.* **1.** NAUT, AIR **PLACE FOR SECURING WATERCRAFT OR AIRCRAFT** a place where a boat, ship, or aircraft can be moored **2.** NAUT, AIR **CABLE SECURING WATERCRAFT OR AIRCRAFT** a rope, cable, or chain used to stop a watercraft or aircraft from drifting away **3.** **PHYSICAL OR EMOTIONAL TIE** sth such as a family bond that gives a feeling of emotional or physical security (*usually used in the plural*)

mooring tower *n.* a permanent structure built as a place to moor airships. The structure provides facilities for transferring passengers, crew, and freight, for refuelling, and for replenishing ballast and lifting gas.

Moorish /moorish, máwr-/ *adj.* **1.** **OF MOORS** relating to or typical of the Moors or their culture **2.** ARCHIT **WITH ORNATE CURVED DECORATION** built or designed in an architectural style popular in Spain between the 8th and the 16th century, noted for its use of ornate, curving decoration

Moorish idol *n.* a tropical marine fish that lives near Indo-Pacific reefs and has broad black and yellow stripes on its sides. Latin name: *Zanclus canescens.* [Because its markings resemble those found in Moorish art]

moorland /moorlənd, máwr-/ *n.* countryside, or a piece of countryside, consisting of a moor [Old English]

moose /mooss/ (*plural* **moose**) *n. US* = **elk** [Early 17thC. From Abenaki *mos*.]

moot /moot/ *adj.* **ARGUABLE** open to argument ○ *a moot point* ■ *v.* (**moots, mooting, mooted**) **1.** *vt.* **SUGGEST FORMALLY** to offer an idea for consideration or a topic for discussion (*usually passive*) **2.** *vi.* **HAVE FORMAL ARGUMENT** to take part in a debate, especially one organized as an academic exercise, e.g. among law students (*formal*) ■ *n.* **1.** **DEBATE ON HYPOTHETICAL ISSUE** an academic discussion in which people such as law students argue hypothetically or plead a hypothetical legal case **2.** HIST **ANGLO-SAXON LOCAL COURT** in Anglo-Saxon England, a formal gathering for settling legal and administrative matters [Old English *mōt* 'assembly, meeting, litigation', from a prehistoric Germanic word meaning 'meeting' that is also the ancestor of English *meet*]

moot court *n.* a court in which imaginary legal cases are conducted and tried by law students as part of their training

mop /mop/ *n.* **1.** **FLOOR-WASHING TOOL** a long-handled tool for washing floors, with a washing head consisting of a large sponge or a thick mass of absorbent threads or fabric strips **2.** **WASHING-UP TOOL** a short-handled washing-up tool with a washing head consisting of a mass of twisted cotton threads **3.** **UNTIDY MASS** a thick or scruffy-looking tangle of hair ■ *vt.* (**mops, mopping, mopped**) **1.** **WASH WITH A MOP** to use a mop to wipe a floor surface clean, usually using warm, soapy water **2.** **WIPE TO REMOVE PERSPIRATION** to wipe perspiration from a part of the body, e.g. with a handkerchief [15thC. Origin uncertain: perhaps directly or via French dialect from Latin *mappa* 'napkin, towel'. Originally in the meaning of 'bundle of cloth for caulking a ship'.]

mop up *v.* **1.** *vti.* **GET RID OF LIQUID WITH CLOTH** to wipe or rub a piece of material over a liquid to soak it up **2.** *vt.* MIL **DEAL WITH REMAINING ENEMY FORCES** to capture or kill remaining enemy troops in order to secure an area after a decisive victory **3.** *vt.* **FINISH OFF** to complete or carry out the final details of a task (*informal*) [Early 18thC. From MOP.]

mope /mōp/ *vi.* (**mopes, moping, moped**) **1.** **BE MISERABLE** to be full of self-pity or sulky unhappiness and lose interest in everything else **2.** **WANDER ABOUT SADLY** to show self-pity and sulky unhappiness, especially by listless or aimless lingering or with a self-consciously slumping gait ■ *n.* **mope** **MISERABLE PERSON** sb who tends to mope and who depresses others as a result (*informal*) ■ **mopes** *npl.* **GLOOMY MOOD** a bout of melancholy or sulkiness (*informal*) [Mid-16thC. Origin uncertain: perhaps from a Scandinavian language.] —**moper** *n.* —**mopy** *adj.*

moped /mō ped/ *n.* a lightweight pedalled motorcycle with an engine of less than 50cc. Mopeds generally need pedals to start them up and to supply extra power, e.g. when going uphill. [Mid-20thC. Blend of MOTOR and PEDAL.]

moppet /móppit/ *n.* a small child, or a term of endearment for a child (*informal*) [Early 17thC. Literally 'small "mop"', formed from obsolete *mop* 'baby, doll', earlier 'fool', of uncertain origin.]

moquette /mo két, mō két/ *n.* thick fabric with a velvety texture, used as carpeting or for upholstery [Mid-19thC. From French, of unknown origin.]

MOR *abbr.* MUSIC middle-of-the-road (*used especially in radio programming*)

mor. *abbr.* morocco

Mor. *abbr.* **1.** Morocco **2.** Moroccan

moraine /mə ráyn/ *n.* a mass of earth and rock debris carried by an advancing glacier and left at its front and side edges as it retreats [Late 18thC. Via French from French dialect *morena* 'mound', from, ultimately, an unassumed Vulgar Latin word.] —**morainal** *adj.* —**morainic** *adj.*

moral /mórrəl/ *adj.* **1.** **INVOLVING RIGHT AND WRONG** relating to issues of right and wrong and to how individuals should behave **2.** **DERIVED FROM PERSONAL CONSCIENCE** based on what sb's conscience suggests is right or wrong, rather than on what the law says should be done **3.** **IN TERMS OF NATURAL JUSTICE** regarded in terms of what is known to be right or just, as opposed to what is officially or outwardly declared to be right or just ○ *a moral victory.* **4.** **ENCOURAGING GOODNESS AND RESPECTABILITY** giving guidance on how to behave decently and honourably **5.** **GOOD BY ACCEPTED STANDARDS** good or right, when judged by the standards of the average person or society at large **6.** **TELLING RIGHT FROM WRONG** able to distinguish right from wrong and to make decisions based on that knowledge **7.** **BASED ON CONVICTION** based on an inner conviction, in the absence of physical proof ■ *n.* **1.** **VALUABLE LESSON IN BEHAVIOUR** a conclusion about how to behave or proceed drawn from a story or event **2.** **FINAL SENTENCE OF STORY GIVING ADVICE** a short, precise rule, usually written in a rather literary style as the conclusion to a story, used to help people remember the best or most sensible way to behave ■ **morals** *npl.* **STANDARDS OF BEHAVIOUR** principles of right and wrong as they govern standards of general or sexual behaviour [14thC. From Latin *moralis*, from *mor-*, stem of *mos* 'custom', in plural 'morals' (source of English *morale* and *morose*).] —**morally** *adv.*

morale /mə ráal/ *n.* the general level of confidence or optimism felt by a person or group of people, especially as it affects discipline and willingness [Mid-18thC. Via French *moral* from Latin *moralis* (see MORAL). The spelling was altered in English to indicate syllable to be stressed.]

moralism /mórrəlizəm/ *n.* **1.** **PIECE OF MORAL ADVICE** a conventional moral maxim or saying **2.** **MORAL BEHAVIOUR** behaviour conforming to a system of moral standards that do not depend on religion **3.** **MORALIZING** criticism of other people's moral standards (*formal or dated*)

moralist /mórrəlist/ *n.* **1.** **SB GIVING ADVICE ON MORAL STANDARDS** sb who criticizes or lectures other people about their standards of morality, or who tries to teach them better moral standards **2.** **SB WITH HIGH MORAL STANDARDS** sb who follows a strict, personal, moral code **3.** **SPECIALIST WHO STUDIES MORALITY** sb who studies or teaches morals as an academic discipline —**moralistic** /mórrə lístik/ *adj.* —**moralistically** /-lístikli/ *adv.*

morality /mə rálləti/ (*plural* **-ties**) *n.* **1.** **ACCEPTED MORAL STANDARDS** standards of conduct that are accepted as right or proper **2.** **HOW RIGHT OR WRONG STH IS** the rightness or wrongness of sth as judged by accepted moral standards 3. MORAL LESSON a lesson in moral behaviour

morality play *n.* a play intended to teach a moral lesson, in which the characters embody human virtues and vices, e.g. Mercy and Lust, especially a medieval play written in verse. Morality plays were popular in Europe from the 15th century to the 17th century, the later plays featuring some humour and satire.

moralize /mórrə līz/ (-izes, -izing, -ized), **moralise** (-ises, -ising, -ised) *v.* 1. *vi.* CRITICIZE THE MORALS OF OTHERS to criticize other people's conduct or standards of behaviour or give advice on how general moral standards should be improved 2. *vt.* ANALYSE IN TERMS OF MORALITY to consider and explain sth in terms of its moral significance 3. *vt.* MAKE MORE MORAL to change sth to make it conform, or conform better, with society's ideas of what is good, right, or decent —**moralization** /mórrə lī záysh'n/ *n.* —**moralizer** /mórrə līzər/ *n.*

moralizing /mórrə līzing/, **moralising** *n.* lecturing others on their low moral standards or pronouncing on how general standards of behaviour should be improved

moral philosophy *n.* = **ethics** *n.* 1

moral theology *n.* the academic study of moral and ethical questions from a Christian viewpoint

Morant /mə ránt/, **Breaker** (1864?–1902) British-born Australian soldier and poet. He was court-martialled and executed by the British army in South Africa, an act which aroused protest and indignation in Australia. Pseudonym of **Harry Harbord Morant**

morass /mə ráss/ *n.* 1. AREA OF SOGGY GROUND an area of low-lying ground that is soft and wet to a great depth and therefore difficult to walk on 2. STH THAT OVERWHELMS, CONFUSES, OR IMPEDES a frustrating, confusing, or unmanageable situation that makes any kind of progress extremely slow [Mid-17thC. Via Dutch *moeras* from, ultimately, French *marais*, of uncertain origin: probably from a prehistoric Germanic word that is also the ancestor of English *marsh*.]

moratorium /mórrə táwri əm/ (*plural* -ums or -a /-ri ə/) *n.* 1. AGREED PERIOD OF DELAY a formally agreed period during which a specific activity is halted or a planned activity is postponed 2. ALLOWED DELAY IN MEETING OBLIGATION a period during which a person, usually a debtor, has the right to postpone meeting an obligation [Late 19thC. From modern Latin, formed from late Latin *moratorius* 'delaying' (see MORATORY).]

moratory /mórrətəri/ *adj.* giving sb the right to delay making payments on a debt [Late 19thC. From late Latin *moratorius* 'delaying', from Latin *morat-*, the past participle stem of *morari* 'to delay', from *mora* 'delay'.]

Morava /mə raávə/ river in Serbia, in the Federal Republic of Yugoslavia. It flows northwards to join the River Danube. Length: 160 km/100 mi.

Moravia /mə ráyvi ə/ region occupying the eastern part of the Czech Republic. Major cities include Brno and Ostrava.

Moravian /mə ráyvi ən/ *n.* 1. PEOPLES SB FROM MORAVIA sb who was born or brought up in Moravia 2. CHR MORAVIAN CHURCH MEMBER a member of the Moravian Church 3. LANG DIALECT OF CZECH the dialect of the Czech language spoken in Moravia —**Moravian** *adj.*

Moravian Church *n.* a Protestant church founded in Moravia in 1722 whose members place a strong emphasis on evangelism, ecumenism, and the authority of the Bible

moray /mórr ay, mo ráy/, **moray eel** *n.* a brightly coloured sharp-toothed voracious eel that lives in rocky crevices of tropical coastal waters or reefs. Family: Muraenidae. [Early 17thC. Via Portuguese *moréia* from Latin *murena*, from, ultimately, Greek *muros* 'sea eel'.]

Moray /múrri/ council area in northeastern Scotland. The administrative centre is in Elgin. Population: 87,600 (1995).

Moray Firth /múrri fúrth/ arm of the North Sea, on the northeastern coast of Scotland

morbid /máwrbid/ *adj.* 1. INTERESTED IN GRUESOME SUBJECTS showing a strong interest in unpleasant or gloomy subjects such as death, murder, or accidents 2. GRISLY inspiring disgust or horror 3. MED RELATING TO DISEASE relating to or resulting in illness [Early 17thC. From Latin *morbidus* 'diseased', from *morbus* 'sickness'.] —**morbidly** *adv.* —**morbidness** *n.*

morbidity /mawr bíddəti/ *n.* 1. DISEASED STATE the presence of illness or disease 2. MED OCCURRENCE OF A DISEASE the relative frequency of occurrence of a particular disease in a particular area (*often used before a noun*)

morceau /máwr sō, mawr sṓ/ (*plural* -ceaux /máwr sō, mawr sṓ/) *n.* 1. SHORT COMPOSITION a short musical or literary composition 2. SMALL PIECE a tiny piece, e.g. a small mouthful of food [Mid-18thC. Via French from Old French *morsel* MORSEL.]

mordacious /mawr dáyshəss/ *adj.* 1. SHARPLY SARCASTIC deliberately bitter or critical, and intended to hurt sb's feelings 2. BITING capable of biting or tending to bite (*archaic or literary*) [Mid-17thC. From the Latin stem *mordac-* 'biting', from *mordere* 'to bite'.] —**mordaciously** *adv.* —**mordaciousness** *n.* —**mordacity** /mawr dássəti/ *n.*

mordant /máwrd'nt/ *adj.* 1. SARCASTIC sharply sarcastic or bitingly critical 2. CORROSIVE having a corrosive effect ■ *n.* INDUST 1. SUBSTANCE THAT FIXES DYES a substance that fixes a dye in and on textiles and leather by combining with the dye to form a stable insoluble compound (**lake**). Some dyes assume different colours depending on the mordant used. 2. ACID USED IN ETCHING a corrosive substance used to etch treated areas on a metal plate ■ *vt.* (-dants, -danting, -danted) TEXTILES APPLY MORDANT TO to apply a mordant to fabric in order to fix a dye [15thC. Via French from, ultimately, a Vulgar Latin variant of Latin *mordere* 'to bite' (source of English *morsel* and *remorse*).] —**mordancy** *n.*

mordantly /máwrd'ntli/ *adv.* in a cruelly sarcastic or bitingly critical way

mordent /máwrd'nt/ *n.* a musical embellishment, similar to a short trill, in which either the note above or the note below the written note is played as well as the principal note [Early 19thC. Via German from Italian *mordente*, from *mordere* 'to bite', from, ultimately, Latin.]

Mordvin /máwrdvin/ (*plural* -vin or -vins) *n.* 1. PEOPLES MEMBER OF FINNISH PEOPLE a member of a Finnish people who live mainly in the middle of the Volga region of western Russia 2. LANG MORDVIN LANGUAGE the Finno-Ugric language of the Mordvin people. Mordvin is spoken by about one million people. [Mid-18thC. From Russian.] —**Mordvin** *adj.*

more /mawr/ CORE MEANING: a grammatical word, the comparative of 'much' and 'many', used to indicate a greater number of sth, either a greater number than before, than average, or than sth else ○ (det) *a need for more adult education programs* ○ (pron) *As benefits go, this job offers me more.*

1. *adv.* TO A GREATER EXTENT having a larger amount or a greater extent of a particular quality (*forming the comparative of some adjectives and adverbs*) ○ (adv-attrib) *This problem is more complex than the other one.* 2. *adv.* FOR A LONGER TIME doing sth or happening for a longer time ○ *We chatted a bit more.* 3. *adv., pron.* WITH GREATER FREQUENCY OR INTENSITY used as the comparative of 'much' to mean 'with greater frequency or intensity' ○ (adv-degree) *We go out more than we used to.* ○ (adv-degree) *It inspires me more now than ever.* ○ (pron) *The more you listen, the more you hear.* 4. *det., pron.* ADDITIONAL additional or further (*Pronoun takes a singular or plural verb*) ○ (det) *I need more light.* ○ (pron) *There aren't any more of these.* ○ (pron) *No more is expected.* [Old English *māra*, from a prehistoric Germanic base that is also the ancestor of English *most*] ◇ **more or less** 1. approximately 2. essentially or basically ◇ **more so, all the more so** to an even greater extent or degree ◇ **no** *or* **neither more nor less (than)** simply, or exactly ◇ **what is more** moreover, or furthermore ◇ **the more Ireland** although (*nonstandard*)

More /mawr/, **Sir Thomas, St** (1478–1535) English statesman and scholar. He resigned as Henry VIII's Lord Chancellor (1529–32) in protest against the King's break with the Roman Catholic Church, and was executed after refusing to recognize Henry as the head of the English Church. His literary works include *Utopia* (1516).

Moreau /mo rṓ/, **Gustave** (1826–98) French painter. He is noted for his literary, mythological, and biblical scenes, which he depicted in a colourful symbolist style.

Morecambe /máwrkəm/ popular seaside resort on Morecambe Bay, Lancashire, northwestern England. Population: 46,657 (1991).

Moree /maw reé/ town in northern New South Wales, a major cotton-growing centre. Population: 9,270 (1996).

moreen /mo reén/ *n.* a thick, ribbed curtain material made of wool, cotton, or a mixture of both [Mid-17thC. Origin unknown.]

moreish /máwrish/, **morish** *adj.* so good to eat or drink that you keep wanting more of it (*informal*)

morel /mo rél/ *n.* an edible mushroom with a brown pitted spongy cap. Genus: *Morchella*. [Late 17thC. From French *morille*, of uncertain origin: perhaps ultimately from Latin *Maurus* 'Moor' (see MOOR).]

morello /mə réllō/ (*plural* -los) *n.* a small sour cultivated cherry with dark red skin [Mid-17thC. Origin uncertain: perhaps from Italian *amarello* 'amarelle' (influenced by Italian *morello* 'blackish'), from, ultimately, Latin *Maurus* 'Moor' (see MOOR).]

morendo /mə réndō/ *adv.* growing continuously softer and sometimes slower (*used as a musical direction*) [Early 19thC. From Italian, literally 'dying', a form of *morire* 'to die'.] —**morendo** *adj.*

moreover /mawr ṓvər/ *adv.* used to add a further piece of information that supports a previous statement

mores /máwr ayz, máwr eez/ *npl.* the customs and habitual practices, especially as they reflect moral standards, that a particular group of people accept and follow [Late 19thC. From Latin, plural of *mos* 'manner, custom' (see MORAL).]

Moresco /mə réskō/ *adj.* Moorish (*archaic*) [Mid-16thC. From Italian, formed from *Moro* 'Moor', from Latin *Maurus* (see MOOR).]

Moresque /maw résk/ *adj.* ARCHIT Moorish (*dated*) [Early 17thC. Via French, from Italian *moresco* (see MORESCO).]

Moreton Bay /máwrt'n báy/ bay in southeastern Queensland, Australia, bounded in the east by Moreton and North Stradbroke, two large islands. Area: 800 sq. km/310 sq. mi.

Moreton Bay chestnut /máwrtən-/ *n.* = **black bean** *n.* 3

Moreton Bay fig *n.* a large fig tree with glossy leaves that is native to eastern Australia. It has massive buttresses at the foot of its trunk and huge spreading roots. Latin name: *Ficus macrophylla*.

Moreton Island /máwrt'n īlənd/ island in Moreton Bay, off the coast of Queensland, Australia. Population: 455 (1996). Area: 170 sq. km/66 sq. mi.

morgan /máwrgən/ *n.* unit of chromosome length [Early 20thC. Named after Thomas Hunt Morgan, 1866–1945, American geneticist and zoologist.]

Morgan /máwrgən/ *n.* a black, bay, brown, or chestnut horse with a full mane and tail, short deep body, and slender legs, belonging to a US breed popular for hunting, jumping, and recreation [Mid-19thC. Named after Justin *Morgan* (1747–98), US schoolteacher and owner of a stallion from which the breed descends.]

Morgan /máwrgən/, **Sir Henry** (1635?–88) Welsh buccaneer. He carried out attacks on Spanish settlements and vessels from a base in Jamaica. He later became lieutenant-governor of Jamaica.

morganatic /máwrgə náttik/ *adj.* used to describe a marriage in which neither the spouse of lower social rank nor any children of the marriage may inherit the title or possessions of the higher-ranking spouse [Late 16thC. Directly or via French or German from medieval Latin (*matrimonium ad*) *morganaticam* '(marriage for the) morning-gift' (the bridegroom's gift to the bride, which relieved him of further responsibility).] —**morganatically** *adv.*

morganite /máwrgə nīt/ *n.* a pink gemstone that is a variety of beryl [Early 20thC. Named after John Pierpont MORGAN.]

Morgan le Fay /máwrgən lə fáy/ *n.* in Arthurian legend, an evil sorceress who was the half-sister and enemy of King Arthur

morgen /máwrgən/ *n.* a unit of measurement for land area formerly used in various parts of the world and still in use in South Africa. It is equal in South Africa to just over 0.85 hectare/2 acres. [Early 17thC. From Dutch and German, with the sense 'area of land that can be ploughed in a morning'.]

morgue /mawrg/ *n.* **1.** PLACE FOR DEAD BODIES a room or building in which dead bodies are kept until a post mortem has been carried out or until they are buried or cremated **2.** PRESS COLLECTION OF INFORMATION a room or file in a newspaper office containing miscellaneous pieces of information kept for future reference, e.g. for writing obituaries **3.** DISMAL PLACE a gloomy place that lacks warmth or cheer (*informal*) [Mid-19thC. From French *Morgue*, a building in Paris used as a morgue, perhaps from *morgue* 'room in a prison where new prisoners were examined', perhaps ultimately from *morgue* 'haughtiness'.]

——————— WORD KEY: CULTURAL NOTE ———————
The Murders in the Rue Morgue, a novel by US writer Edgar Allan Poe (1841). Regarded as the world's first detective story, it begins with the brutal murder of an old woman and her daughter, a crime that perplexes the police since the women's apartment is sealed from the inside. Amateur sleuth C. Auguste Dupin comes to their aid, providing an explanation based on a brilliant analysis of scattered clues.

MORI /máwri, mórri/, **Mori** *abbr.* Market and Opinion Research Institute

moribund /mórri bund/ *adj.* **1.** DYING nearly dead **2.** STAGNANT having lost all sense of purpose or vitality **3.** OBSOLESCENT becoming obsolete [Early 18thC. From Latin *moribundus*, from *mori* 'to die' (source of English *mortuary*).] —**moribundity** /mórri búndəti/ *n.* —**moribundly** /-bundli/ *adv.*

Moriori /mórri áwri/ (*plural* **-i** *or* **-is**) *n.* **1.** PEOPLES MEMBER OF EXTINCT NEW ZEALAND PEOPLE a member of a now extinct indigenous people that lived in New Zealand, especially on the Chatham Islands **2.** LANG MORIORI LANGUAGE the extinct language of the Moriori people. It belongs to the Eastern branch of Malayo-Polynesian languages. [Mid-19thC. From Polynesian.] —**Moriori** *adj.*

Morisco /mə rískō/ (*plural* **-cos** *or* **-coes**), **Moresco** /mə réskō/ (*plural* **-cos** *or* **-coes**) *n.* **1.** RELIG MUSLIM CONVERT TO CHRISTIANITY a Muslim of medieval Spain who was forcibly converted to Christianity and often continued the surreptitious practice of Islam, or a descendant of such a person **2.** DANCE MORRIS DANCE OR DANCER a morris dance or morris dancer [Mid-16thC. From Spanish, from *Moro* 'Moor'.] —**Morisco** *adj.*

Berthe Morisot: Portrait by Marcellin Desboutin

Morisot /mórri sō/, **Berthe** (1841–95) French painter. Her paintings, in a subtle and delicate impressionistic style, often depict landscapes or women and children.

Morley /máwrli/, **Thomas** (1557–1603) English composer. Noted for his madrigals, lute songs, and instrumental music, he helped to establish the madrigal in England as a distinctive musical form.

Mormon /máwrmən/ *adj.* relating to the Church of Jesus Christ of Latter-day Saints, its members, or its doctrines and beliefs [Mid-19thC. Named after the prophet believed to be the author of the *Book of Mormon*, a sacred history of the Americas.] —**Mormonism** *n.*

morn /mawrn/ *n.* **1.** MORNING a morning (*literary*) **2.** *Scotland* TOMORROW tomorrow [Old English *morgen*, from prehistoric Germanic]

mornay /máwr nay/ *adj.* served in a white sauce containing grated cheese ◊ *eggs/cod mornay* [Early 20thC. Perhaps named after Philippe de *Mornay* (1549–1623), a French Huguenot writer.]

morning /máwrning/ *n.* **1.** EARLY PART OF DAY the early part of the day, from dawn until noon or lunchtime **2.** MIDNIGHT TO MIDDAY the part of the day between midnight and midday **3.** DAWN dawn or daybreak **4.** EARLY PART the beginning of sth ■ *interj.* GOOD MORNING good morning (*informal*) [13thC. Coined from MORN + -ING, modelled on EVENING.]

morning-after pill *n.* a contraceptive pill designed to be taken after sexual intercourse

morning coat *n.* a man's jacket, usually black, cut away at the front below the waist and with a long divided tail, worn on formal occasions as part of morning dress

morning dress *n.* a man's suit worn to formal daytime events such as weddings, consisting of a black morning coat, striped black trousers, usually a waistcoat, and sometimes a top hat

morning glory *n.* a climbing plant of the bindweed family, widely cultivated for its trumpet-shaped blue, purple, pink, or white flowers that close towards evening. Genus: *Ipomoea.*

morning line *n.* a list of entrants and their odds for a race, estimated by a bookmaker and posted before betting begins, usually on the morning of the race

Morning Prayer *n.* the morning service of worship in the Anglican Church

morning roll *n. Scotland* a plain bread roll made from white flour

mornings /máwrningz/ *adv.* during the morning or every morning (*informal*)

morning sickness *n.* nausea and vomiting experienced by many pregnant women, usually in the morning and during the early months of pregnancy

Morningside /máwrning sīd/ *n. Scotland* an old-fashioned anglicized accent of Scottish English, widely perceived as affected. ◊ **Kelvinside** [Late 19thC. Named after *Morningside*, a district of Edinburgh, where it originated.]

morning star *n.* a planet, especially Venus, seen in the eastern sky around dawn

morning tea *n. ANZ* a mid-morning snack or drink

morning watch *n.* the period of watch between four o'clock and eight o'clock in the morning

Moro /máwrō/, **Aldo** (1916–78) Italian statesman. He was prime minister of Italy twice (1963–68 and 1974–76). In 1978 he was kidnapped and murdered by the Red Brigades.

morocco /mə ró kō/, **morocco leather** *n.* INDUST a soft leather made from goatskin, used especially for covering books and for shoes, or any similar leather made in imitation of it from sheepskin or calfskin [Mid-17thC. Named after MOROCCO, where it was first made.]

Morocco

Morocco /mə rókō/ monarchy in northwestern Africa. Formerly ruled by France and Spain, it became an independent kingdom in 1956. Language: Arabic. Currency: dirham. Capital: Rabat. Population: 27,020,000 (1996). Area: 446,550 sq. km/172,414 sq. mi. Official name **Kingdom of Morocco** —**Moroccan** *n., adj.*

moron /máwr on/ *n.* **1.** OFFENSIVE TERM an offensive term that deliberately insults sb's intelligence (*offensive insult*) **2.** PSYCHOL OFFENSIVE TERM an offensive term for sb with very significant learning difficulties and difficulty in carrying out usual social functions (*offensive*) [Early 20thC. From Greek *mōron*, neuter of *mōros* 'unintelligent, thoughtless'.] —**moronic** /mə rónnik/ *adj.* —**moronically** /-li/ *adv.* —**moronism** /máwr on izəm/ *n.* —**moronity** /mə rónnəti/ *n.*

Moroni /mə róni/ capital city of the Comoros. Population: 22,000 (1992).

morose /mə róss/ *adj.* having a withdrawn gloomy personality [Mid-16thC. From Latin *morosus* 'peevish', from, ultimately, *mos* 'manner, disposition', which also produced English *moral*.] —**morosely** *adv.* —**moroseness** *n.* —**morosity** /mə róssəti/ *n.*

Morpeth /máwrpəth/ market town in Northumberland, northeastern England. Population: 14,500 (1992).

morph[1] /mawrf/ *n.* an element of speech or writing that represents and expresses one or more morphemes [Mid-20thC. Shortening of MORPHEME.]

morph[2] /mawrf/ *n.* one of two or more variant forms of an animal or plant [Mid-20thC. From Greek *morphē* 'form'.]

morph[3] /mawrf/ (**morphs, morphing, morphed**) *vti.* **1.** TRANSFORM FROM ONE IMAGE TO ANOTHER to transform one graphic image on screen into another or others, through the use of sophisticated computer software, or to be transformed in this way **2.** TRANSFORM QUICKLY to cause sth to change its outward appearance completely and instantaneously, or to undergo this process [Late 20thC. From METAMORPHOSIS.]

morph. *abbr.* **1.** morphological **2.** morphology

-morph *suffix.* sth that has a particular form, shape, or structure ◊ *mesomorph* [From Greek *morphē* (see MORPHO-)] —**-morphic** *suffix.* —**-morphism** *suffix.* —**-morphous** *suffix.* —**-morphy** *suffix.*

morphactin /mawrf áktin/ *n.* a chemical that disrupts various aspects of plant development and induces dwarfing [Mid-20thC. Origin uncertain: probably coined from MORPH- + ACTIVE + -IN.]

morphallaxis /mawrfə láksiss/ *n.* the process whereby an organism regenerates body parts by the reorganization and transformation of existing tissue, rather than by the formation of new tissue [Late 19thC. Formed from Greek *morphē* 'form' + *allaxis* 'exchange'.]

morpheme /máwr feem/ *n.* the smallest meaningful element of speech or writing [Late 19thC. Via French, from Greek *morphē* 'form', modelled on English *phoneme*.] —**morphemic** /mawr feémik/ *adj.* —**morphemically** /mawr feémik-/ *adv.*

morphemics /mawr feémiks/ *n.* (*takes a singular verb*) **1.** MORPHEME COMBINATION PROCESS the way in which morphemes combine to form words in a language **2.** STUDY OF MORPHEME COMBINATION the study and description of the ways in which morphemes combine in languages

Morpheus /máwr fi əss, -fyooss/ *n.* in Greek mythology, the god of dreams and sleep, and son of Hypnos [14thC. From Latin.] —**Morphean** /máwrfi ən/ *adj.*

morphia /máwrfi ə/ *n.* morphine (*archaic*) [Early 19thC. Formed from MORPHEUS.]

morphine /máwr feen/ *n.* an alkaloid drug derived from opium and used in medicine to relieve severe pain. Prolonged non-medical use may lead to addiction. [Early 19thC. Via French, from *Morphée*, from Latin *Morpheus* (see MORPHEUS).]

morphinism /máwrfinizəm/ *n.* addiction to morphine and the related health problems of such addiction (*dated*) —**morphinist** /máwr feenist, máwrfinist/ *n.*

morpho /máwrfō/ (*plural* **-phos**) *n.* a large tropical American butterfly with iridescent blue wings. Genus: *Morpho.* [Mid-19thC. Via modern Latin, from Greek *Morphō*, an epithet of APHRODITE.]

morpho- *prefix.* form, shape, structure ◊ *morphogenesis* [From Greek *morphē*, of unkown origin]

morphogen /máwrfəjən, máwrfə jen/ *n.* a substance produced in an embryo that influences the differentiation and development of the embryonic cells [Mid-20thC. Coined from MORPHO- + -GEN.]

morphogenesis /máwrfō jénnəssiss/ *n.* **1.** DEVELOPMENT OF INDIVIDUAL ORGANISM the origin and development of an organism or of some part of one, as it grows from embryo to adult **2.** DEVELOPMENT OF SPECIES OF ORGANISM the development of an organism or of some part of one, as it changes as a species [Late 19thC. Coined from MORPHO- + -GENESIS.] —**morphogenetic** /máwrfōjə néttik/ *adj.* —**morphogenetically** /-li/ *adv.* —**morphogenic** /-jénnik/ *adj.*

morphol. *abbr.* **1.** morphological **2.** morphology

morphology /mawr fólləji/ (*plural* -gies) *n.* **1.** BIOL STRUCTURE OF ORGANISM the form and structure of an organism or of any part of an organism **2.** BIOL STUDY OF STRUCTURE OF ORGANISMS the study of the form and structure of organisms **3.** LING STRUCTURE OF WORDS the structure of words in a language, including patterns of inflections and derivation **4.** LING STUDY OF WORD FORMATION the study of the structure of words in a language **5.** STRUCTURE OF STH the structure of sth, or the study of the structure of sth [Mid-19thC. Coined from MORPHO- + -LOGY.] —**morphologic** /máwrfə lójjik/ *adj.* —**morphological** /-lójjik'l/ *adj.* —**morphologically** /-lójjikli/ *adv.* —**morphologist** /mawr fólləjist/ *n.*

morphometry /mawr fómmətri/ *n.* the measurement of the outside of sth [Mid-19thC. Coined from MORPHO- + -METRY.] —**morphometric** /máwrfə méttrik/ *adj.* —**morphometrically** /-méttrikli/ *adv.*

morphosis /mawr fóssiss/ (*plural* -ses /-seez/) *n.* a variation in the pattern of development (**morphogenesis**) of an organism as a result of changes in the external environment [Late 17thC. From Greek *morphōsis* 'a shaping', from, ultimately, *morphē* 'form'.] —**morphotic** /mawr fóttik/ *adj.*

morris /mórriss/ *n.* = morris dance [15thC. From Old French *morois* 'Moorish', from *More* 'Moor', because it is perhaps of Moorish origin.]

Morris /mórriss/, **William** (1834–96) British artist, poet, and social activist. His decorations and furnishings drew on medieval tradition and his love of craftsmanship, and laid the foundations for the Arts and Crafts movement and art nouveau. His poetry included classical translations, some published in fine editions by Kelmscott Press, which he founded in 1890.

Morris chair *n.* a light carved wooden armchair with removable cushions and a reclining back that can be set at varying angles [Named after William MORRIS]

morris dance *n.* a lively English folk dance, traditionally performed by men, usually in white costumes and using small bells, sticks, and handkerchiefs. US term **morris** —**morris dancer** *n.* —**morris dancing** *n.*

Morrison /mórriss'n/, **Herbert Stanley, Baron Morrison of Lambeth** (1888–1965) British Labour Party politician. He held various senior government posts, including that of deputy prime minister, in the first Labour government after World War II (1945–51).

Morrison, James (*b.* 1962) Australian jazz musician. A performer on several instruments, he is known both for his solo and ensemble work.

Morrison, Jim (1943–71) US rock singer and songwriter. He was the lead singer of the Doors and attracted a cult following after his death. Full name **James Douglas Morrison**

Morrison, Toni (*b.* 1931) US writer. Her novels deal with the experience of being an African American. She received the Nobel Prize in literature in 1993. Pseudonym of **Chloe Anthony Wofford**

Morrison, Van (*b.* 1945) British singer and songwriter. Born in Northern Ireland, he is noted for a repertoire ranging from rhythm and blues to folk and jazz, and including elements of Celtic music. Real name **George Ivan Morrison**

morro /mórrō/ (*plural* -ros) *n.* a hill or headland with a rounded outline [From Spanish]

morrow /mórrō/ *n.* **1.** NEXT DAY the day after today or after a particular day (*archaic or literary*) **2.** FOLLOWING PERIOD OF TIME the period of time following an event

Toni Morrison

or occurrence (*literary*) [13thC. Variant of earlier form of MORN.]

Mors /mawrz/ *n.* in Roman mythology, the god of death. Greek equivalent **Thanatos** [From Latin, literally 'death']

Morse /mawrss/, **Morse code** *n.* a system for representing letters and numbers by signs consisting of one or more short or long signals of sound or light that are printed out as dots and dashes [Mid-19thC. Named after Samuel F. B. MORSE.]

Morse /mawrss/, **Helen** (*b.* 1946) British-born Australian actor. A frequent stage performer, her work also includes roles in films such as *Caddie* (1976).

Morse, Samuel F. B. (1791–1872) US inventor and artist. He invented the electric telegraph (1837) and the Morse code. Full name **Samuel Finley Breese Morse**

morsel /máwrss'l/ *n.* **1.** SMALL PIECE OF FOOD a small piece of sth, especially of food **2.** SMALL AMOUNT a small amount of sth [13thC. From Old French, 'little bite', from *mors* 'bite', from, ultimately, the past participle of Latin *mordere* 'to bite'.]

Mort /mawrt/, **Thomas Sutcliffe** (1816–78) British-born Australian merchant and shipbuilder. He was a pioneer of the use of refrigerated containers for shipping frozen meat.

mortadella /máwrtə déllə/ *n.* a smoked, fried, or steamed Italian sausage consisting of pork and beef flavoured with wine, garlic, and pepper [Early 17thC. Via Italian, from Latin *murtatum* '(sausage) seasoned with myrtle berries'.]

mortal /máwrt'l/ *adj.* **1.** EVENTUALLY DYING certain to die eventually **2.** HUMAN relating to human beings **3.** FATAL causing death ○ *a mortal blow* **4.** CONTINUING UNTIL SB DIES continuing, or intended to continue, until sb dies ○ *mortal combat* **5.** OF DEATH relating to or accompanying death ○ *in mortal agony* **6.** SHOWING HATRED showing great and unrelenting hatred ○ *his mortal enemy* **7.** INTENSE intensely felt ○ *mortal fear* **8.** CONCEIVABLE being within the bounds of what is imaginable or possible ○ *What mortal reason could there be for him to leave like that?* **9.** BORING tedious and dull (*slang*) ■ *adj., adv.* USED FOR EMPHASIS used for emphasis, and sometimes indicating that the speaker is frustrated or annoyed (*dated*) ■ *n.* **1.** HUMAN BEING a human being, who will eventually die **2.** PERSON a person (*informal*) [14thC. Directly or via Old French, from Latin *mortalis*, from, ultimately, *mors* 'death' (which also produced English *mortify*).]

——— **WORD KEY: SYNONYMS** ———
See Synonyms at *deadly*.

mortality /mawr tálləti/ *n.* **1.** CERTAINTY TO DIE the state of being certain to die eventually **2.** NUMBER OF DEATHS the number of deaths that occur at a given time, in a given group, or from a given cause **3.** MANY DEATHS great loss of life **4.** RATE OF FAILURE the rate of failure of sth, such as businesses or farms **5.** HUMAN BEINGS the human race **6.** DEATH death (*archaic*) [14thC]

mortality rate *n.* the number of deaths in a particular place or group compared with the total number of residents in that place or members of that group

mortality table *n.* a table listing the life expectancy and death rate for various ages or occupations and based on mortality statistics over the course of a number of years

mortally /máwrt'li/ *adv.* **1.** FATALLY so badly that death follows **2.** VERY in an extreme or intense way

mortal sin *n.* CHR in the Roman Catholic Church, a sin considered to be so wicked that it causes a complete loss of grace and leads to damnation unless it is absolved. ◊ **venial sin**

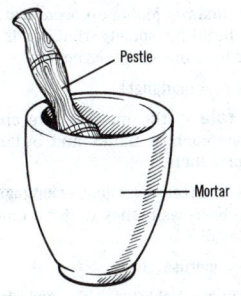
Pestle
Mortar
Mortar and pestle

mortar /máwrtər/ *n.* **1.** BUILDING CEMENT, SAND, AND WATER a mixture of sand, water, and cement or lime that becomes hard like stone and is used in building to join and hold bricks and stones together **2.** ARMS CANNON a cannon with a relatively short and wide barrel, used for firing shells at a high angle over a short distance. Formerly, mortars were heavy cannons operated by the artillery, but they are now light guns used by the infantry. **3.** GUN FIRING A LIFELINE a gun for firing sth other than a bullet, e.g. a rope to sb in need of rescue **4.** COOK BOWL USED FOR GRINDING a hard, heavy bowl in which substances are ground into small pieces or powder by means of a club-shaped tool (**pestle**) **5.** MINING BOWL FOR CRUSHING ORE a cast-iron bowl in which ore is crushed ■ *vt.* (-tars, -taring, -tared) **1.** ARMS FIRE AT SB OR STH to fire at sb or sth with a mortar **2.** BUILDING FIX STH WITH MORTAR to hold stones and bricks together with mortar [Pre-12thC. Via Old English *mortere* and French *mortier*, 'bowl for mixing', from Latin *mortarium* 'bowl, substance prepared in it'. In the sense 'cannon', via French *mortier* in that sense.]

Mortarboard

mortarboard /máwrtər bawrd/ *n.* **1.** EDUC ACADEMIC HAT a hat often worn on formal academic occasions, consisting of a round cap with a hard, square, flat top and usually a tassel **2.** BUILDING BOARD FOR CARRYING MORTAR a square board with a handle in the centre of the underside, used by bricklayers for carrying mortar

mortgage /máwrgij/ *n.* **1.** LOAN AGREEMENT FOR PROPERTY an agreement by which sb borrows money from an organization and gives that organization the right to take possession of property given as security if the loan is not repaid. It is the main means by which people purchase homes. **2.** CONTRACT BETWEEN BORROWER AND LENDER a written contract describing the agreement between a borrower and a lender by which a loan is given against security **3.** TOTAL MONEY BORROWED the total amount of money lent to a borrower by a money-lending organization, with some of the borrower's property being given as security **4.** LOAN INSTALMENT TO BE REPAID the money paid by a borrower, usually monthly, to a bank or building society until the entire sum borrowed by a mortgage agreement has been repaid ■ *vt.* (-gages, -gaging, -gaged) **1.** GRANT CLAIM TO OWNERSHIP OF PROPERTY to give a claim to legal possession of property to a money-lending organization such as a bank or building society as security for a loan **2. PLEDGE RISKILY** to pledge sth when risk is involved (*informal*) [14thC. From Old French, from *mort* 'dead' + *gage* 'pledge', because property pledged as security is lost to a mortgagor who fails to repay the loan.] —**mortgageable** *adj.*

mortgagee /máwrgi jeé/ *n.* an organization such as a bank or building society that lends money to a borrower by a mortgage agreement

mortgager *n.* = mortgagor

mortgage rate *n.* the interest rate charged by organizations such as banks and building societies on mortgage loans

mortgagor /máwrgi jáwr, -jər/, **mortgager** /máwrgijər/ *n.* sb who borrows money under a mortgage agreement [Late 16thC]

mortice *n.* = mortise

mortician /mawr tísh'n/ *n.* US = undertaker *n.* 1 [Late 19thC. Formed from the stem of Latin *mors* 'death' + ENGLISH -ICIAN.]

mortification /máwrtifi káysh'n/ *n.* **1. SHAME** deep shame and humiliation **2. STH CAUSING MORTIFICATION** sth that causes a feeling of shame and humiliation **3.** RELIG **SELF-IMPOSED HARDSHIP** the use of self-imposed discipline, hardship, abstinence from pleasure, and especially self-inflicted pain in an attempt to control or put an end to desires and passions, especially for religious purposes **4.** MED **DEATH AND DECAY OF LIVING TISSUE** the death and decaying of a part of a living body, e.g. because the blood supply to it has been cut off (*archaic*) [14thC. Directly and via Old French, from late Latin *mortificatio(n-)* 'destruction', from the past participle stem of *mortificare* (see MORTIFY).]

mortify /máwrti fī/ (**-fies, -fying, -fied**) *v.* **1.** *vt.* **SHAME SB** to make sb feel ashamed and humiliated **2.** *vt.* RELIG **IMPOSE HARDSHIP ON** to use self-imposed discipline, hardship, abstinence from pleasure, and especially self-inflicted pain in an attempt to control or put an end to desires and passions, especially for religious purposes **3.** *vi.* MED **DECAY** to decay and die (*archaic*) (*refers to living tissue*) [14thC. Via Old French *mortifier*, from Latin *mortificare* 'kill', from the stem of *mors* 'death'. The main modern meaning developed via the sense 'subdue by discipline'.] —**mortifier** *n.* —**mortifying** *adj.* —**mortifyingly** *adv.*

Mortimer /máwrtimər/, **Roger de, 8th Baron of Wigmore, 1st Earl of March** (1287?–1330) English aristocrat. In 1327, following the deposition of Edward II, he became virtual ruler of England. He was executed by Edward III.

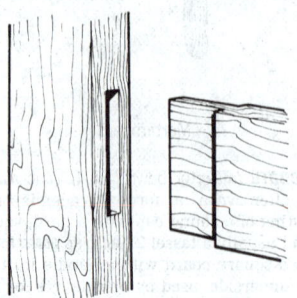

Mortise-and-tenon joint

mortise /máwrtiss/, **mortice** *n.* **1.** FURNITURE, BUILDING **HOLE CUT TO HOLD OTHER PART** a hole or slot cut into a piece of wood, stone, or other material, for a projecting part (**tenon**) to be inserted into it, in order to form a tight joint **2.** PRINTING **HOLE IN PRINTING PLATE** a hole cut in a printing plate to receive type or another plate ■ *vt.* (**-tises, -tising, -tised; -tices, -ticing, -ticed**) **1.** FURNITURE, BUILDING **CUT MORTISE IN** to cut a mortise in sth **2.** FURNITURE, BUILDING **JOIN BY MORTISE AND TENON** to join two things or parts by means of a mortise and tenon **3.** PRINTING **CUT HOLE IN PRINTING PLATE** to cut a hole in a printing plate [14thC. From Old French, probably from Arabic *murtaj* 'locked'.] —**mortiser** *n.*

mortise lock *n.* a lock inserted into a hole (**mortise**)

cut into the side edge of a door so that when the door is closed the lock cannot be seen or removed

mortmain /máwrt mayn/ *n.* the perpetual, non-transferable, and nonsaleable ownership of property by organizations such as churches [13thC. Via Anglo-Norman and Old French from medieval Latin *mortua manus* 'dead hand', from, ultimately, Latin *mortuus* 'dead' + *manus* 'hand', as a metaphor for impersonal ownership.]

mortuary /máwrchoŏ əri/ *n.* (*plural* **-ies**) **PLACE FOR DEAD BODIES** a room or building in which dead bodies are kept until a post mortem has been carried out or until they are buried or cremated ■ *adj.* **RELATING TO DEATH** relating to death or funerals [14thC. Directly or via Anglo-Norman, from, ultimately, Latin *mortuus* 'dead', the past participle of *mori* 'to die' (source of English *moribund*).]

morula /máwryoŏlə/ (*plural* **-las** or **-lae** /-lee/) *n.* an early stage in the development of an animal embryo, consisting of a solid ball of cells derived by cleavage of the fertilized egg (**zygote**). It precedes the blastocyst. [Mid-19thC. From an obsolete sense 'growth (or disease causing growths) that resembles a berry', because of the segmentation, from modern Latin, 'little mulberry', from *morum* 'mulberry'.] —**morular** *adj.* —**morulation** /máwryoŏ láysh'n/ *n.*

Morwell /máwrwəl/ town in southeastern Victoria, Australia, a mining and dairy farming centre. Population: 13,823 (1996).

morwong /máwr wong/ (*plural* **-wongs** or **-wong**) *n.* a large Australasian marine food fish with a thick-lipped head, sharply tapering body, and extended dorsal fin. Family: Cheilodactylidae. [Late 19thC. Probably from an Aboriginal language.]

MOS abbr. metal oxide semiconductor

mos. abbr. months

Barnaby's

Mosaic: Detail of mosaic floor at the Roman settlement of Verulamium, St Albans, England

mosaic /mō záy ik/ *n.* **1.** ARTS **PICTURE MADE WITH SMALL COLOURED PIECES** a picture or design made with small pieces of coloured material such as glass or tile stuck onto a surface **2.** ARTS **MAKING OF MOSAICS** the art of making mosaics **3.** STH CONSISTING OF VARIETY OF ELEMENTS sth consisting of a number of things of different types, forms, or colours **4.** TV **LIGHT-SENSITIVE SURFACE IN TV CAMERA** a light-sensitive surface on a television camera tube, consisting of a thin sheet covered by particles that convert incoming light into an electric charge for scanning by an electron beam **5.** BOT **VIRAL PLANT DISEASE** a plant disease, often caused by a virus, in which the foliage develops irregular patches of discoloration. Tobacco, maize, and sugar cane are among the crops that can be seriously affected. **6.** BOT **PLANT DISCOLORATION** a pattern of light-green or yellowish mottling on the foliage of a plant, usually caused by a viral infection **7.** GENETICS = chimera *n.* 2 ■ *vt.* (**-ics, -icking, -icked**) **DECORATE WITH MOSAIC** to make sth into, or decorate sth with, a mosaic [14thC. Via Old French, from, ultimately, Latin *Musa* 'Muse', from the decorations of medieval shrines dedicated to the Muses.]

Mosaic /-ik'l/, **Mosaical** *adj.* relating to the biblical figure Moses [Mid-17thC. Directly or via French, from, ultimately, Latin *Moses* 'Moses', from Hebrew *Mōsheh*.]

mosaic disease *n.* = mosaic

mosaic gold *n.* **1.** TIN DISULPHIDE tin disulphide used in gilding **2.** ALLOY RESEMBLING GOLD IN APPEARANCE an alloy of copper and either zinc or tin that looks like gold

and is used to decorate such things as furniture and jewellery

mosaicism /mō záy issizəm/ *n.* the occurrence of genetically distinct cells within tissue or an individual organism

Mosaic Law *n.* the ancient code of law of the Hebrews, beginning with the Ten Commandments, believed to have been set down by Moses and contained in the Pentateuch

mosasaur /móssə sawr/, **mosasaurus** /-sáwrəss/ (*plural* **-sauri** /-sáw rī/) *n.* an extinct marine lizard that had a long slender body with limbs resembling paddles for steering, and a long flexible tail for propulsion. Family: Mosasauridae. [Mid-19thC. From modern Latin *Mosasaurus*, the genus name, from Latin *Mosa*, the River Meuse, where the first remains were found.]

moschatel /móskə tél/ (*plural* **-tels** or **-tel**) *n.* a low-growing plant found in moist locations in northern temperate regions and bearing clusters of small yellowish-green flowers arranged like the faces of a cube. Latin name: *Adoxa moschatellina*. [Mid-18thC. Via French, from, ultimately, Italian *moscato* 'musk', from the scent of the flowers.]

Moscow /móss kō/ **1.** capital city of Russia, located in the west-central European part of the country. It was also the capital of the Soviet Union from 1922 to 1991. Population: 8,300,000 (1994). **2.** city in north-western Idaho, on the border with Washington, north of Lewiston. Population: 20,101 (1996).

Moseley /mózli/, **Henry Gwyn-Jeffreys** (1887–1915) British physicist. Using X-ray diffraction, he showed that a chemical element's position in the periodic table is related to its nuclear electric charge.

Moselle[1] /mō zél/ *n.* a light dry to sweet white wine from the Moselle valley in Germany

Moselle[2] /mō zél/ river in France and Germany. Length: 515 km/320 mi.

Moses /móziz/ *n.* in the Bible, a Hebrew prophet and the brother of Aaron who led the Israelites from slavery in Egypt to the Promised Land. He is believed to have written down the Ten Commandments (Exodus 20).

Popperfoto

Grandma Moses

Moses, Grandma (1860–1961) US artist. She is known for her primitivist paintings of US rural life, which she began in her late seventies. Real name **Anna Mary Robertson Moses**

Moses basket *n.* a portable wicker or straw cot for a baby [Because Moses was placed in such a basket (Exodus 2)]

mosey /mózi/ (**-seys, -seying, -seyed**) *vi.* to walk somewhere at a leisurely unhurried pace (*informal*) [Early 19thC. Origin uncertain: perhaps a shortening and alteration of Spanish *vamos* 'let's go', or an alteration of dialectal English *mose about* 'to go about in a purposeless manner'.]

mosh (**moshes, moshing, moshed**) *vt.* to dance to rock music in a frenzied violent way (*informal*) [Late 20thC. Origin uncertain: probably thought to suggest the action.]

moshav /mō sháav/ (*plural* **-shavim** /-shaa vém/) *n.* in Israel, a cooperative settlement consisting of independent small farms, or land farmed by the whole community with each family having its own house and garden [Mid-20thC. From modern Hebrew *mōšāb* 'dwelling, colony'.]

mosh pit *n.* an area in front of the stage at a rock concert where people dance in an unrestrained way (*informal*)

Moslem /mózləm, moózləm/ *n.* (*plural* **-lems** *or* **-lem**), *adj.* a Muslim (*dated offensive*) [Variant] —**Moslemic** /moz lémmik, moóz-/ *adj.* —**Moslemism** /mózləm izzəm, moózləm-/ *n.*

Mosley /mózli/, **Sir Oswald Ernald** (1896–1980) British politician. He founded the British Union of Fascists in 1932.

Mosque: Delhi, India

mosque /mosk/ *n.* a building in which Muslims worship [15thC. Via French, from, ultimately, Arabic *masjid* 'place of worship', from *sajada* 'bow down'.]

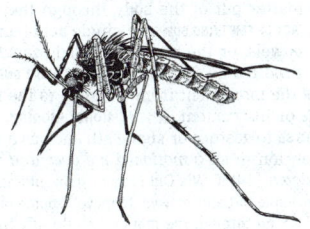

Mosquito

mosquito /mə skeét ō, mo-/ (*plural* **-toes** *or* **-tos**) *n.* a small slender fly found worldwide, especially in the tropics, that feeds on the blood of mammals, including humans, and transmits diseases such as malaria, yellow fever, and dengue. Typically, only females are blood-feeders, the males feeding on plant juices. Family: Culicidae. [Late 16thC. Via Spanish, 'little fly', from *mosca* 'fly', from Latin *musca*. Ultimately from an Indo-European base, imitative of humming, that is also the ancestor of English *midge*.]

mosquito boat *n.* = **motor torpedo boat**

mosquito coil *n.* incense in the form of a coil that is lit at night to repel mosquitoes

mosquito fern *n.* a small floating fern that has branched stems with small leaves resembling scales and is found on freshwater ponds and lakes, especially in warmer regions. The leaves harbour a nitrogen-fixing cyanobacterium and the fern is grown in rice paddies to enhance fertility. Genus: *Azolla*.

mosquito net *n.* a curtain of fine netting hung over a bed or across a window as a protection against mosquitoes

moss /moss/ *n.* **1.** PLANTS SIMPLE NONFLOWERING PLANT a simple nonflowering plant (**bryophyte**) that has short stems bearing small spirally arranged leaves resembling scales and inhabits moist shady sites worldwide. Certain mosses, notably sphagnums, flourish in bogs, where their remains can accumulate to form peat. Class: Musci. **2.** PLANTS PLANT RESEMBLING MOSS a plant that in some way resembles a true moss, e.g. a variety of seaweed known as Irish moss **3.** GEOG MARSHY AREA in Scotland and Northern England, an area of marshy ground or moorland, especially a peat bog (*often used in placenames*) [Old English *mos* 'swamp' (of which moss is the characteristic plant), from a prehistoric Germanic word that is also the ancestor of English *mire*]

Moss /moss/, **Stirling** (1929–98) British racing driver. He was winner of the British Grand Prix (1955, 1957) and the Mille Miglia (1955). An accident in 1962 ended his career. Full name **Stirling Crauford Moss**

Mossad /móssad/ *n.* the intelligence service of Israel, established in 1951 (*takes a singular or plural verb*) [Mid-20thC. From Hebrew *mosad* 'institution'.]

moss agate *n.* a whitish agate with dark-green patterns resembling moss or ferns in it

moss animal *n.* a minute colony-forming animal, found mainly in the sea attached to rocks or seaweeds. The colonies have rigid or gelatinous walls and often resemble mosses. Phylum: Bryozoa.

mossback /móss bak/ (*plural* **-backs** *or* **-back**) *n.* **1.** US, Can OLD TURTLE, SHELLFISH, OR FISH an old turtle, shellfish, or fish with algae growing on its back **2.** US SB CONSERVATIVE sb who is very old-fashioned or conservative (*insult*)

mossbunker /móss bungkər/ *n.* US = **menhaden** [Late 18thC. From Dutch *marsbanker*.]

moss campion *n.* a plant of the pink family found in cool alpine regions that forms tufts of leaves resembling moss and bears solitary pink flowers. Latin name: *Silene acaulis*.

moss green *adj.* of a dull green colour tinged with yellow —**moss green** *n.*

mossgrown /móss grōn/ *adj.* **1.** MOSS-COVERED covered with moss **2.** OLD-FASHIONED old-fashioned or out-of-date

Mossi /móssi/ (*plural* **-si** *or* **-sis**) *n.* **1.** PEOPLES MEMBER OF W AFRICAN PEOPLE a member of a people living in West Africa, especially in Burkina Faso **2.** LANG MOSSI LANGUAGE the language of the Mossi people. It belongs to the Gur branch of Niger-Congo languages. Mossi is spoken by about six million people. [Mid-19thC. An African name.]

mossie[1] /móssi/ *n.* = **mozzie** (*informal*)

mossie[2] /mózzi/ *n.* S *Africa* a Cape sparrow [Late 19thC. Via Afrikaans, from Dutch *musje* 'little sparrow', from *mus* 'sparrow'.]

mosso /móssō/ *adv.* in a quick and lively way (*used as a musical direction*) ◊ **meno mosso** [Late 19thC. From Italian, the past participle of *muovere* 'move'.]

moss pink, **moss phlox** *n.* a plant of the pink family native to eastern North America but widely grown ornamentally that produces spreading mats of tiny leaves and lavender, pink, or white flowers. Latin name: *Phlox subulata*.

moss rose *n.* a rose with a mossy surface to the calyx and flower stalk, and fragrant pink flowers. Latin name: *Rosa centifolia muscosa*.

moss stitch *n.* a basic knitting stitch consisting of alternating knit and purl stitches in one row, then alternating purl and knit stitches in the next row, producing a regular raised design

moss-trooper *n.* in the 17th century, sb involved in raiding, especially cattle-raiding, in the area around the Scottish-English border [From MOSS 'marshy area', a characteristic of the border-land]

mossy /móssi/ (**-ier**, **-iest**) *adj.* **1.** COVERED WITH MOSS covered or overgrown with moss **2.** RESEMBLING MOSS similar to moss, e.g. in texture or colour **3.** OLD-FASHIONED old-fashioned or out-of-date (*informal*) —**mossiness** *n.*

mossy zinc *n.* a form of zinc with a grainy texture made by pouring melted zinc into water

most /mōst/ CORE MEANING: a grammatical word indicating nearly all or the majority of the people or things mentioned ◊ *Most people enjoy watching a good film.* ◊ *We'd finished off most of the work by lunchtime.*
1. *det.*, *pron.* GREATEST greatest in number, amount, extent, or degree ◊ (*det*) *He won the most seats in the election.* ◊ (*pron*) *The most I can lend you is 50 pounds.* **2.** *adv.* TO THE GREATEST EXTENT in or to the greatest extent (*used to form the superlative of adjectives and adverbs*) ◊ *the most expensive suit I'd ever bought* ◊ *What I like most effectively if you heat it gently first.* **3.** *adv.* SUPERLATIVE OF 'MUCH' the superlative of 'much' ◊ *What I like most about him is his*

easygoing attitude. **4.** *adv.* VERY in a high degree ◊ *a most enjoyable day* **5.** *adv.* US, Can ALMOST nearly but not entirely ◊ *Most everyone was invited.* [Old English *mæst*. Ultimately, from an Indo-European word meaning 'big'.] ◊ **at (the) most** at the maximum ◊ *It'll take you two hours at the most.* ◊ **the most** the best of all (*slang*) ◊ *That song is the most!* ◊ **for the most part** in the majority of cases ◊ **make the most of sth** to take full advantage of sth

-most *suffix.* **1.** nearest to or toward ◊ *endmost* **2.** most ◊ *nethermost* [Old English *-mest*, which was formed from *-mo*, *-ma*]

Mostaganem /mə stággə ném/ fishing port on the Mediterranean Sea coast in northwestern Algeria. Population: 114,037 (1987).

Mostar /móss taar/ city in Herzegovina, southern Bosnia-Herzegovina. Population: 126,000 (1991).

most favoured nation *n.* a nation accorded the most favourable trading terms by another nation

Most Honourable *adj.* in the United Kingdom, a title given to marquesses and marchionesses, and to members of the Order of the Bath

mostly /móstli/ *adv.* **1.** MAINLY almost entirely ◊ *The audience was mostly made up of younger fans.* **2.** USUALLY on most occasions ◊ *I swim mostly at weekends.*

Most Reverend *adj.* a title given to Anglican and Roman Catholic archbishops, to Irish Roman Catholic bishops, to the Anglican Bishop of Meath, and to the Primus of the Episcopal Church in Scotland

mot /mot/ *n.* Ireland a girl or young woman, especially a regular woman companion (*slang*) [Mid-16thC. Origin unknown.]

MOT *n.* **MOT, MOT certificate** a certificate of roadworthiness awarded to a vehicle that has passed its MOT test. Full form **Ministry of Transport** ■ *vt.* (**MOTs, MOTing, MOTed**) CARRY OUT MOT ON A VEHICLE to carry out an MOT test on a vehicle [Late 20thC. Abbreviation of *Ministry of Transport*, which administers the test.]

mote /mōt/ *n.* a tiny speck or particle [Old English *mot*, of unknown origin]

motel /mō tél/ *n.* a hotel intended to provide short-term accommodation for travelling motorists, usually situated close to a main road and having rooms accessible from the parking area [Early 20thC. Blend of MOTOR and HOTEL.]

motet /mō tét/ *n.* a vocal composition with parts for different voices, usually based on a sacred text [14thC. Via Old French 'little word', from, ultimately, Latin *muttire* 'to murmur'.]

Moth

moth /moth/ *n.* an insect resembling a butterfly, typically with a duller colour and differently shaped antennae, active at night. Order: Lepidoptera. [Old English *moppe*, of uncertain origin]

mothball /móth bawl/ *n.* MOTH-REPELLENT CHEMICAL BALL a small ball of a strong-smelling chemical such as camphor or naphthalene, used for keeping clothes moths away from clothing and other materials ■ *vt.* (**-balls**, **-balling**, **-balled**) **1.** PUT STH OFF INDEFINITELY to postpone work or discussion on sth for an indefinite time ◊ *We'll mothball the expansion plans until we have the financing.* **2.** INDUST TAKE A FACTORY OUT OF OPERATION to take a factory out of operation but protect the equipment in it so that it can be used again at some time in the future **3.** INSUR, AEROSP SEAL A CRAFT UP FOR STORAGE to seal all the openings in a ship or aircraft in order to protect it from corrosion while it is not in use ◇ **in mothballs** put aside or stored and not in use

moth bean *n.* **1.** AGRIC **PLANT GROWN TO BOOST SOIL FERTILITY** a plant of the pea family grown in tropical regions, especially India, to provide forage, to boost soil fertility, and for its seeds. It has hairy foliage and small yellow flowers. Latin name: *Phaseolus aconitifolius.* **2.** FOOD **SEED OF THE MOTH BEAN PLANT** the yellowish-brown seed of the moth bean plant that is used for food

moth-eaten *adj.* **1. EATEN BY MOTH LARVAE** damaged by clothes moth caterpillars **2. WORN-OUT** old and worn-out from use **3. OUTDATED** no longer usable or appropriate (*informal*)

mother[1] /múthər/ *n.* **1. FEMALE PARENT** a woman who has a child or a female animal that has produced young **2. WOMAN ACTING AS PARENT** a woman who acts as the parent of a child to whom she has not given birth **3. CHARACTERISTICS OF A MOTHER** the qualities or feelings that are traditionally associated with being a mother ○ *brought out the mother in her* **4. ORIGINATOR** a woman regarded as the creator, instigator, or founder of sth **5. ORIGIN OF STH** the cause, source, or origin of sth ○ *Necessity is the mother of invention* **6. PROTECTOR** sth that protects and nourishes like a mother **7. Mother, mother TITLE OF RESPECT** used as a title of respect for a woman past middle age (*archaic*) (*sometimes considered as offensive*) **8. GOOD OR BAD EXAMPLE OF STH** sth very big, good, bad, or extreme, or particularly noteworthy in some other way (*slang*) (*sometimes considered offensive*) ○ *a real mother of a headache* **9.** *US* **OFFENSIVE TERM** a highly offensive term referring to sb regarded as despicable or contemptible (*taboo offensive*) ■ *vt.* (**-ers, -ering, -ered**) **1. LOOK AFTER SB WITH CARE** to look after sb with great care and affection, sometimes to an excessive degree **2. GIVE BIRTH TO A BABY** to give birth to and bring up a baby **3. BRING STH ABOUT** to give rise to sth [Old English *modor.* Ultimately from an Indo-European word with descendants in most modern European languages, based on the baby-talk form *ma*, that also produced English *mammal.*] ◇ **at your mother's knee** in early childhood ◇ **be mother** to pour out tea from a teapot for those present (*humorous*) ◇ **every mother's son** every man or boy (*dated*)

mother[2] /múthər/ *n.* a slimy mass of bacteria and yeast cells that forms on the surface of alcohol being converted into acetic acid [Mid-16thC. Origin uncertain: probably by folk etymology from obsolete Dutch *moeder*, from Middle Dutch *moeder* 'female parent', from its part in the production of vinegar.]

Mother *n.* used as a title or form of address for a senior nun in a religious community

motherboard /múthər bawrd/ *n.* a circuit board in a minicomputer or microcomputer through which all signals are directed

Mother Carey's chicken /-káiriz-/ *n.* a storm petrel (*dated*) [Probably a translation and alteration of medieval Latin *mater cara* 'Virgin Mary']

mother cell *n.* a cell that gives rise to other cells by cell division

mother church *n.* a church from which other churches derive their authority

mother country *n.* **1. COUNTRY COLONISTS HAVE LEFT** the country of origin of people who have left to found a colony or colonies elsewhere **2. COUNTRY OF BIRTH** the country that sb was born and grew up in

mother figure *n.* a woman who embodies the qualities traditionally associated with a mother, especially support, advice, and affection

motherfucker /múthər fukər/ *n. US* a highly offensive term referring to sb regarded as despicable or contemptible (*insult offensive*)

Mother Goddess *n.* = **Earth Goddess**

Mother Goose *n.* the supposed author of a collection of nursery rhymes first published in the 18th century

mother hen *n.* sb who is too protective towards other people and who fusses over them

motherhood /múthər hòod/ *n.* **1. STATE OF BEING A MOTHER** the status of a mother or the state of being a mother **2. QUALITIES TRADITIONALLY CHARACTERISTIC OF MOTHERS** the qualities traditionally associated with mothers

motherhouse /múthər howss/ *n.* a monastery or convent from which monks or nuns have gone out to found new monasteries and convents

Mother Hubbard /-húbbərd/ *n.* a long loose-fitting shapeless dress [Late 16thC. Named after a nursery rhyme character who was depicted wearing such a dress.]

Mothering Sunday *n.* Mother's Day (*dated*)

mother-in-law (*plural* **mothers-in-law**) *n.* the mother of your spouse

mother-in-law apartment *n. US* = **granny flat**

mother-in-law's tongue *n.* PLANTS = **sansevieria** [From its long pointed leaves]

motherland /múthər land/ *n.* the country that sb was born and grew up in

motherless /múthərləss/ *adj.* **WITHOUT A MOTHER** without a mother or having lost a mother through bereavement ■ *adv. Australian* **USED FOR EMPHASIS** completely or thoroughly ○ *motherless broke* [Old English *modorleas*]

mother lode *n.* **1.** MINING **MAIN VEIN OF ORE** the main vein of ore in a mine **2. GOOD SUPPLY** a plentiful supply of sth

motherly /múthərli/ *adj.* having or showing qualities traditionally considered to be typical of a mother, especially kindness and protectiveness [Old English] —**motherliness** *n.*

Mother Nature *n.* the forces of nature conceived of as a wilful being

Mother of God *n., interj.* a title given to Mary, the mother of Jesus Christ, especially by Catholics

Mother of Parliaments *n.* the British parliament, thought of as the model for the parliaments of many other countries

mother-of-pearl *n.* the hard pearly internal layer of the shells of some molluscs such as oysters and clams, used, e.g. as a gemstone and as a decorative inlay [Early 16thC. Translation of obsolete French *mère perle.*]

mother of the chapel (*plural* **mothers of the chapel**) *n.* in trade unions in the printing and publishing industries, the woman head of a workplace section (**chapel**) of a union

mother-of-thousands (*plural* **mothers-of-thousands** *or* **mother-of-thousands**) *n.* a creeping or trailing plant that produces masses of small flowers, especially the ivy-leaved toadflax or the strawberry geranium

mother of vinegar *n.* = **mother**[2]

Mother's Day *n.* the fourth Sunday in Lent, when people traditionally give cards and presents to their mothers

mother ship *n.* a ship or spaceship that provides services and supplies for a number of other, usually smaller ships

mother superior (*plural* **mother superiors** *or* **mothers superior**) *n.* the head of a convent or community of Christian nuns

mother-to-be (*plural* **mothers-to-be**) *n.* a woman who is expecting a baby

mother tongue *n.* **1. FIRST LANGUAGE** the first language sb learns as a child at home **2. ORIGINAL LANGUAGE** a language from which other languages have developed

Motherwell /múthərwel/ town in North Lanarkshire, Scotland. Population: 30,717 (1991).

mother wit *n.* natural intelligence or good sense

motherwort /múthər wurt/ (*plural* **-worts** *or* **-wort**) *n.* a plant of Europe and Asia with deeply lobed leaves and white or pink purple-spotted flowers that was traditionally used as a medicinal herb during childbirth. Latin name: *Leonarus cardiaca.* [14thC. From obsolete sense of *mother* 'womb'.]

moth fly *n.* a tiny insect with wings covered with hairs that resembles an extremely small moth. Family: Psychodidae.

mothproof /móth proof/ *adj.* **PROTECTED AGAINST CLOTHES MOTHS** treated with a substance designed to prevent damage by clothes moths ■ *vt.* (**-proofs, -proofing, -proofed**) **PROTECT AGAINST CLOTHES MOTHS** to treat sth such as clothing with a substance designed to protect it from damage by clothes moths —**mothproofer** *n.*

mothy /móthi/ (**-ier, -iest**) *adj.* **1. DAMAGED BY MOTHS** damaged by the action of clothes moths **2. FULL OF MOTHS** full of or infested by moths

motif /mō tēef/ *n.* **1.** ARCHIT, DESIGN **REPEATED DESIGN** a repeated design, shape, or pattern **2.** CRAFT **SEWN OR PRINTED DECORATION** a decorative repetitive design sewn into or printed on sth such as a piece of clothing, or a single example of the pattern **3.** LITERAT **THEME IN A WORK OF LITERATURE** an important and sometimes recurring theme or idea in a work of literature **4.** MUSIC **PROMINENT SEQUENCE OF NOTES** a short prominent sequence of notes forming the basis for development in a piece of music **5. CAR DECORATION** a decoration on a car that serves to identify the manufacturer [Mid-19thC. Via French, from Old French (see MOTIVE).]

motile /mōt īl/ *adj.* capable of or demonstrating movement by independent means [Mid-19thC. Formed from Latin *motus* 'motion', from the past participle of *movere* 'to move'.] —**motility** /mō tílləti/ *n.*

motion /mósh'n/ *n.* **1. ACT OF MOVING** the act or process of moving or the way in which sb or sth moves ○ *walked with a swaying motion* **2. A MOVEMENT** a movement, action, or gesture ○ *made a quick motion of the wrist* **3. POWER OF MOVEMENT** the power or ability to move sth **4. PROPOSAL** a proposal put forward for discussion at a meeting **5.** LAW **APPLICATION TO A JUDGE OR COURT** an application made to a court or judge for an order or ruling in a legal proceeding **6.** PHYSIOL **PASSING OF SOLID WASTE FROM THE BODY** the passing of solid waste matter out of the body through the anus **7.** PHYSIOL **ACT OF EMPTYING BOWELS** a single act of emptying of the bowels, or the matter emptied (*dated*) (*often used in the plural*) **8.** MUSIC **MOVEMENT FROM ONE NOTE TO ANOTHER** the movement from one note to the next by a voice or instrument ■ *vti.* (**-tions, -tioning, -tioned**) **SIGNAL TO SB** to gesture or signal sth such as a request or intention to sb ○ *motioned me over and told me to sit down* [14thC. Via Old French, from, ultimately, the past participle of Latin *movere* 'to move' (source of English *move*).] ◇ **go through the motions** to do sth in a perfunctory or mechanical way, without enthusiasm or commitment ◇ **put** *or* **set sth in motion** to cause sth to start moving, functioning, or happening

motionless /mósh'nləss/ *adj.* not moving —**motionlessly** *adv.* —**motionlessness** *n.*

motion picture *n. US, Can* a film (*formal or technical*)

motion sickness *n.* = **travel sickness**

motion study *n.* = **time and motion study**

motivate /mōti vayt/ (**-vates, -vating, -vated**) *v.* **1.** *vt.* **GIVE SB AN INCENTIVE** to give sb a reason or incentive to do sth **2. MAKE SB WILLING** to make sb feel enthusiastic, interested, and committed to sth **3.** *vt.* **CAUSE SB'S BEHAVIOUR** to be the cause or driving force behind sth that sb does ○ *motivated purely by greed* [Mid-19thC. Formed from MOTIVE, modelled on French *motiver* 'to motivate'.] —**motivator** *n.*

motivated /mōti vaytid/ *adj.* **1. INTERESTED OR ENTHUSIASTIC** having enough interest or incentive to do sth **2. HAVING STH AS A MOTIVE** having sth such as an emotion or a belief as a motive

motivation /mōti váysh'n/ *n.* **1. GIVING OF A REASON TO ACT** the act of giving sb a reason or incentive to do sth **2. ENTHUSIASM** a feeling of interest or enthusiasm that makes sb want to do sth, or sth that causes such a feeling **3. REASON** a reason for doing sth or behaving in some way **4.** PSYCHOL **FORCES DETERMINING BEHAVIOUR** the biological, emotional, cognitive, or social forces that activate and direct behaviour —**motivative** /mōti vaytiv/ *adj.* —**motivational** /mōti váysh'nəl/ *adj.* —**motivationally** /-nəli/ *adv.*

motivational research, **motivation research** *n.* the study of the motivation of consumers in their buying practices, used to plan marketing and sales

motive /mōtiv/ *n.* **1. REASON** the reason for doing sth or behaving in a particular way **2.** ARTS = **motif** *n.* 1, **motif** *n.* 3 ■ *adj.* **1. CAUSING MOTION** capable of causing or producing motion **2. DRIVING SB TO DO STH** tending to make sb want or be willing to do sth ■ *vt.* (**-tives, -tiving, -tived**) **MOTIVATE SB** to make sb want or be willing to do sth [14thC. Via Old French *motif*, from, ultimately, the past participle of Latin *movere* 'to move' (source of English *mobile*).]

WORD KEY: SYNONYMS
---
motive, incentive, inducement, spur, goad

CORE MEANING: sth that prompts action

motive the emotion or intention that an action is driven by, e.g. love, revenge, or ambition; **incentive** sth external that inspires extra enthusiasm or effort, often suggesting some kind of reward; **inducement** sth external that persuades or attracts sb to a course of action; **spur** sth external or internal that increases effort or energy without necessarily involving reward; **goad** similar to *spur* but often used to suggest that force is used on an unwilling subject.

motive power *n.* **1.** ENG ENERGY OR A SOURCE OF ENERGY the power or energy that drives a piece of machinery, or the source of that power or energy **2.** MOTIVATING FORCE the driving force behind an action or activity

motivic /mō tívvik/ *adj.* relating to a musical motif or motifs

motivity /mō tívvəti/ *n.* the power to move or to make sth move

mot juste /mó zhoōst/ (*plural* **mots justes**) *n.* exactly the right word or words to express sth [From French]

motley /mótli/ *adj.* (**-lier, -liest**) **1.** MADE UP OF DIFFERENT TYPES consisting of people or things that are very different from one another and do not seem to belong together **2.** OF VARIED COLOURS made up of different colours ■ *n.* (*plural* **-lies**) **1.** CLOTHES JESTER'S COSTUME the multicoloured clothing worn by medieval jesters **2.** VARIED GROUP a group of people or things that are very different from one another and do not seem to belong together [14thC. Origin uncertain: perhaps via Anglo-Norman, from earlier English *mot* 'speck' (source of English *mote*).]

motmot /mót mot/ *n.* a Central and South American bird with a broad downward-curved bill, long tail, and usually greenish plumage with a black patch on the chest. Family: Momotidae. [Mid-19thC. From American Spanish, of imitative origin.]

motocross /mṓtō kross/ *n.* a motorcycle race, or the sport of racing motorcycles, over a rough course with steep hills, wet or muddy areas, and turns of varying difficulty. ◊ **autocross** [Mid-20thC. From French, from *moto* 'motorcycle' + English CROSS(-COUNTRY).]

motoneuron /mṓtō nyoŏr on/ *n.* = **motor neuron** [Early 20thC. Coined from MOTOR + NEURON.] —**motoneuronal** /mṓtō nyoŏrənəl/ *adj.*

motor /mṓtər/ *n.* **1.** ENG MACHINE THAT CREATES MOTION a machine that converts energy into motion and can be used as a power source, e.g. to drive another machine or to move some form of transport **2.** CAR a vehicle, especially a car, powered by a motor (*dated or informal*) ■ *adj.* **1.** AUTOMOT OF VEHICLES relating to vehicles, especially cars, powered by a motor **2.** AUTOMOT MOTOR-DRIVEN powered by a motor **3.** CAUSING MOTION causing or producing motion **4.** PHYSIOL OF MUSCLE ACTIVITY relating to muscle activity, especially voluntary muscle activity, and the consequent body movements ■ *vi.* (**-tors, -toring, -tored**) **1.** DRIVE IN A CAR to travel by car or some other form of private vehicle, especially for pleasure (*dated*) **2.** MOVE FAST to move or progress at a fast pace (*informal*) **3.** PROCEED SMOOTHLY to be moving towards an objective, e.g. in work, with the desired degree of speed and momentum (*slang*) ○ *Now we're really motoring!* [15thC. From Latin, 'mover', from *movere* 'to move' (source of English *momentum*).]

motorable /mṓtərəb'l/ *adj.* suitable for driving motor vehicles on

motorbicycle /mṓtər bīssik'l/ *n.* a motorcycle or moped

motorbike /mṓtər bīk/ *n.* = **motorcycle**

motorboat /mṓtər bōt/ *n.* a small boat powered by an engine —**motorboater** *n.* —**motorboating** *n.*

motorbus /mṓtər buss/ *n.* a passenger bus (*dated*)

motorcade /mṓtər kayd/ *n.* a procession of cars or other vehicles, especially one forming an escort for sb important [Early 20thC. Coined from MOTOR + CAVALCADE.]

motor camp *n.* NZ a drive-in campsite for motorists with tents or caravans

motor car *n.* a car (*dated or formal*)

motor caravan *n.* a vehicle with cooking, living, and sleeping facilities like those of a caravan. US term **motor home**

motor cortex *n.* the region of the outer surface of the brain (**cortex**) where nervous impulses controlling voluntary muscle activity are initiated. The motor cortex in the right hemisphere of the brain is responsible for controlling muscles in the left side of the body, and vice versa for the left hemisphere.

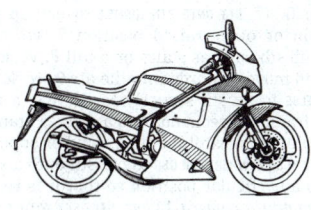

Motorcycle

motorcycle /mótər sīk'l/ *n.* 2-WHEELED MOTOR-POWERED VEHICLE a two-wheeled road vehicle powered by an engine ■ *vi.* (**-cles, -cling, -cled**) RIDE ON A MOTORCYCLE to ride or travel on a motorcycle —**motorcyclist** *n.*

motor drive *n.* a motorized mechanism to advance film in a camera

motor home *n.* US = **motor caravan**

motoric /mō tórrik/ *adj.* relating to voluntary muscle movement —**motorically** *adv.*

motorist /mṓtərist/ *n.* sb who owns and drives a car

motorize /mṓtə rīz/ (**-izes, -izing, -ized**), **motorise** (**-ises, -ising, -ised**) *vt.* **1.** FIT STH WITH A MOTOR to fit sth with a motor **2.** GIVE TROOPS VEHICLES to provide troops with motor vehicles —**motorization** /mṓtə rī záysh'n/ *n.*

motorman /mṓtərmən/ (*plural* **-men** /-mən/) *n.* the driver of a tramcar or electric train

motormouth /mṓtər mowth/ (*plural* **-mouths** /-mowthz/) *n.* sb who talks too much or too fast (*informal insult*)

motor neuron, motor neurone *n.* a nerve cell (**neuron**) that conveys nerve impulses from the spinal cord or brainstem away from the central nervous system towards a muscle or gland

motor neuron disease *n.* a progressive degenerative disease involving the motor neurons and causing weakness and wasting of the muscles

motor park *n.* in West Africa, a car park

motor racing *n.* racing in motor vehicles, especially in cars that are specially designed to travel at high speeds. US term **auto racing**

motor rhythm *n.* a rhythmic motif in a piece of music maintaining a constant pulse, usually at a fast tempo, for an extended period

motorsailer /mṓtər saylər/ *n.* a sailing boat equipped with a motor

motor scooter *n.* a light motorcycle with small wheels, an enclosed engine, and a framework that includes a protective front plate and support for the rider's feet

motor ship *n.* a ship powered by an engine

motor torpedo boat *n.* a highly manoeuvrable vessel, 18 to 30 m/60 to 100 ft in length, carrying light armament and used to torpedo enemy shipping. US term **PT boat**

motor unit *n.* a motor neuron and the muscle fibres it acts on

motor vehicle *n.* a car, lorry, or other road vehicle powered by an engine

motor vessel *n.* a ship powered by an engine

motorway /mṓtər way/ *n.* UK a limited-access road usually consisting of three lanes for vehicles moving in both directions, intended for travelling relatively fast over long distances

Motown /mṓ town/ *tdmk.* a trademark for a music company based in Detroit whose music, consisting of elements of pop, soul, and gospel, was especially popular during the 1960s and 1970s [From the nickname for Detroit, itself a shortening of *Motor Town*, from the association of the city with the car industry]

motser /mótsər/, **motza** /mótsə/ *n.* Aus a large sum of money, especially a gambling win (*informal*) [20thC. Origin uncertain: perhaps from Yiddish *matzo* 'bread'.]

motte /mot/ *n.* a mound on which a castle was built [Late 19thC. Via French, 'mound', from Old French *mote* (source also of English *moat*).]

motte and bailey (*plural* **mottes and baileys**) *n.* a castle consisting of a fortified courtyard (**bailey**) overlooked by a wooden castle built on a mound of earth (**motte**). Such castles were built by the Normans in the 11th and 12th centuries.

MOT test *n.* = **MOT**

mottle /mótt'l/ *vt.* (**-tles, -tling, -tled**) MARK STH WITH DIFFERENT COLOURS to mark sth with an irregular pattern of patches or spots of different colours ■ *n.* **1.** IRREGULAR PATTERN OF COLOURS an irregular pattern of patches or spots of different colours **2.** PATCH OF COLOUR a patch or spot of colour that forms part of an irregular pattern [Late 17thC. Probably a back-formation from MOTLEY.]

mottled enamel *n.* tooth enamel that is mottled as a result of swallowing excessive amounts of fluoride at the age when teeth harden

motto /móttō/ (*plural* **-toes** *or* **-tos**) *n.* **1.** RULE TO LIVE BY a short saying that expresses a rule to live by ○ '*I heartily accept the motto, "That government is best which governs least"; and I should like to see it acted up to more rapidly and systematically.*' (Henry David Thoreau, *Civil Disobedience*; 1849) **2.** HERALDRY SAYING ON A COAT OF ARMS a short saying that forms part of a coat of arms and expresses sth about the family or place whose coat of arms it is **3.** SAYING OR QUOTATION a saying or quotation printed on a small piece of paper, generally one of the contents of a cracker **4.** QUOTATION AT BEGINNING OF WRITING a short quotation at the beginning of a piece of writing, e.g. a book, a chapter of a book, or a poem, related in some way to its contents **5.** MUSIC = **motif** *n.* 4 [Late 16thC. From Italian, probably from an assumed Vulgar Latin word meaning 'word'.]

motu proprio /mṓ too prṓpri ō/ (*plural* **motu proprios**) *n.* a decree issued by a pope acting independently and on his own initiative [From Latin, literally 'on your own initiative']

motza *n.* Aus = **motser** (*informal*)

moue /moo/ *n.* a look of discontent with the lips pressed together and forward [Mid-19thC. From French. Ultimately of Germanic origin.]

mouflon /moó flon/ *n.* a reddish-brown wild sheep belonging to a Sardinian and Corsican breed. The males have prominent curved horns and a white patch on the back and on the rump. Latin name: *Ovis musimon*. [Late 18thC. Via French, from Italian *muflone*.]

mouillé /mweé ay/ *adj.* PHON used to describe a consonant pronounced with the tongue touching the palate [Mid-19thC. From French, the past participle of *mouiller* 'to wet, moisten'.]

moulage /moo laázh/ *n.* **1.** MAKING OF A CAST OF STH AS EVIDENCE the process of making of a mould or cast of sth, e.g. a footprint, in the course of a criminal investigation **2.** MOULD OR CAST a mould or cast made in the course of a criminal investigation [Early 20thC. Via French, 'moulding, moulded copy', from, ultimately, Old French *mouler* 'to mould'.]

mould[1] /mōld/ *n.* **1.** CONTAINER FOR MAKING A SHAPE a container that gives a shape to a molten or liquid substance poured into it to harden **2.** FRAME a frame on which sth is formed or built **3.** OBJECT MADE IN A MOULD an object that was formed using a mould **4.** DISTINCTIVE TYPE a particular type that has a distinctive character or nature ○ *a leader in the heroic mould* **5.** SET OF ASSUMPTIONS a fixed pattern or framework of assumptions, especially when regarded as restricting ○ *negotiators who break out of the trad-*

itional diplomatic mould **6.** = **moulding** *n.* **1** ■ *v.* **(moulds, moulding, moulded) 1.** *vt.* **MAKE STH IN MOULD** to shape or form sth in a mould **2.** *vt.* **GIVE STH SHAPE** to shape or give form to sth **3.** *vt.* **INFLUENCE SB'S CHARACTER** to guide or influence the growth or development of sb or sth ○ *the childhood experience that helped mould her personality* **4.** *vti.* **FIT THE CONTOURS OF STH** to fit closely by following the contours or acquiring the shape of sth **5.** *vt.* **METALL MAKE A MOULD FROM STH** to make a material into a mould to be used in casting metal **6.** *vt.* **ARCHIT PUT MOULDING ON STH** to decorate sth with a moulding [12thC. Via Old French *modle* from Latin *modulus*, literally 'little measure', from *modus* 'measure' (source of English *mode*).] —**mouldable** *adj.*

mould[2] /mōld/ *n.* **1.** **FUNGUS** a fungus that causes organic matter to decay **2.** **GROWTH OF MOULD** a growth of mould on the surface of sth, or the discoloration caused by the growth of mould ■ *vi.* **(moulds, moulding, moulded) BECOME COVERED WITH MOULD** to become covered with or affected by mould [15thC. From earlier English *moul* 'to go mouldy', from assumed Old Norse *mugla*.]

mould[3] /mōld/ *n.* **1.** **SOIL RICH IN HUMUS** soil that is rich in humus and easily worked or crumbled **2.** **EARTH** the earth or ground (*literary*) **3.** **THE GROUND** the ground, especially the earth of the grave (*literary*) [Old English. Ultimately from an Indo-European base meaning 'to grind', which is also the ancestor of English *meal*[1] and *mill*[1].]

mouldboard /mōld bawrd/ *n.* **1.** **BLADE OF A PLOUGH** the curved metal blade of a plough that turns over the soil **2.** **BLADE OF A BULLDOZER OR SNOWPLOUGH** the large curved blade on the front of a bulldozer or snowplough that pushes the soil or snow **3.** **CONSTR SIDE OF A CONCRETE MOULD** a board that forms one side or one surface of a concrete mould

moulder[1] /mōldər/ **(-ers, -ering, -ered)** *vti.* to crumble or decay because of natural processes, or to make sth crumble or decay [Mid-16thC. From *mold* 'loose soil', from, ultimately, a prehistoric Germanic word meaning 'to grind'.]

moulder[2] /mōldər/ *n.* sb who makes moulds or who moulds things

moulding *n.* **1.** **ARCHIT, WOODWORK DECORATIVE STRIP** a strip of wood or some other material that is used to decorate or finish a surface of a wall or a piece of furniture **2.** **STH MADE IN A MOULD** sth that is produced using a mould

mouldy /mōldi/ **(-ier, -iest)** *adj.* **1.** **WITH MOULD** with mould growing on or inside it **2.** **STALE FROM AGE OR ROT** stale and unpleasant from old age, neglect, or fungal growth **3.** **OLD** old-fashioned or out-of-date (*informal*) **4.** **BORING** dull, boring, or contemptible (*informal*) —**mouldiness** *n.*

moules marinières /mool mari nyér/ *npl.* a dish of mussels cooked and served in their shells with a wine sauce [French]

moulin /moolin/ *n.* an almost vertical shaft in a glacier, created by meltwater and debris boring into a crack in the surface of the ice [Mid-19thC. Via French 'mill', from, ultimately, late Latin *molinum* (source of English *mill*).]

moult /mōlt/ *vti.* **(moults, moulting, moulted) LOSE FEATHERS, FUR, OR SKIN** to shed feathers, hair, or skin periodically, especially seasonally, to allow replacement of what is lost with new growth ■ *n.* **1.** **LOSS OF FEATHERS, FUR, OR SKIN** the process or time during which a bird or animal casts off all or part of its feathers, fur, or skin **2.** **SHED FEATHERS, FUR, HAIR, OR SKIN** the material shed during moulting [Pre-12thC. From Latin *mutare* 'to change' (which also produced English *mutate*).] —**moulter** *n.*

mound /mownd/ *n.* **1.** **SMALL HILL** a small hill **2.** **CONSTRUCTED PILE OF STH** a pile of earth, stones, or other material built up for some purpose, e.g. to provide shelter, defence, or concealment **3.** **PILE OF OBJECTS** an untidy heap or pile of objects ○ *a mound of dirty laundry on the floor* **4.** **LARGE AMOUNT** a large amount of sth ○ *a mound of mashed potatoes* ■ *vt.* **(mounds, mounding, mounded) PUT STH INTO A MOUND** to form sth into a mound [Early 16thC. Origin uncertain.]

moundbird /mownd burd/ *n.* = **megapode** [Mid-19thC. From its custom of depositing its eggs in a mound.]

Mound Builder *n.* a member of an early Native North American people who built burial mounds and earthwork fortifications in what is now the Midwest and Southeast of the United States

mound-builder *n.* = **megapode** [See MOUNDBIRD]

mount[1] /mownt/ *v.* **(mounts, mounting, mounted) 1.** *vt.* **BEGIN A COURSE OF ACTION** to put into operation a course of action such as a campaign, rescue, or attack **2.** *vt.* **ORGANIZE AN ARTS PRODUCTION** to organize sth such as an exhibition or production of a play **3.** *vi.* **INCREASE** to become greater, stronger, or more intense ○ *tension was mounting* **4.** *vti.* **GET ONTO OR IN STH** to get onto an animal or a form of transport such as a bicycle **5.** *vt.* **PUT SB ON A FORM OF TRANSPORT** to put sb onto an animal or a form of transport such as a bicycle **6.** *vt.* **GET ONTO STH HIGHER** to get up onto a platform or other raised position **7.** *vti.* **CLIMB** to climb up sth such as stairs or a hill **8.** *vi.* **GO UP INTO THE AIR** to move upwards into the air **9.** *vt.* **SECURE STH TO STH ELSE** to fix sth securely to sth, e.g. a picture into a frame, a specimen onto a slide, a stamp into an album, or an exhibit onto a stand or support **10.** *vt.* **PUT STH SOMEWHERE FOR USE** to put sth onto a support or into a particular position so that it is ready for use ○ *mount a camera* **11.** *vt.* **HAVE SEX WITH** to climb onto an animal or person, especially from behind, in order to copulate (*technical or offensive*) ■ *n.* **1.** **STH FOR FIXING STH IN PLACE** sth such as a stand, support, frame, or backing on which or with which sth can be mounted **2.** **ANIMAL FOR RIDING** an animal, e.g. a horse, used for riding **3.** **STAMPS STH FOR MOUNTING A STAMP** an envelope or card on which to mount a stamp [13thC. Via Old French *monter* 'to go up', from, ultimately, Latin *mons* 'mountain' (see MOUNTAIN).] —**mountable** *adj.* —**mounter** *n.*

mount[2] /mownt/ *n.* = **mountain** (*often used in placenames*) [Pre-12thC. Via Old English *mount* and Old French *mont* from Latin *mons* 'mountain' (see MOUNTAIN).]

mountain /mówntin/ *n.* **1.** **HIGH POINT OF LAND** a high and often rocky area of a land mass with steep or sloping sides ○ *a plateau surrounded by mountains* **2.** **LARGE PILE** a large pile or heap of sth ○ *a mountain of books* **3.** **mountain, mountains LARGE AMOUNT** a large amount of sth (*informal*) ○ *a mountain of work* **4.** **SURPLUS** a large surplus of a particular commodity (*informal*) (*usually used in combination*) ○ *a butter mountain*. ◊ **lake**[1] *n.* **2** [13thC. Via Old French *montaigne* from, ultimately, Latin *mont-*, stem of *mons*. Ultimately from an Indo-European word meaning 'to project', which is also the ancestor of English *prominent*.] ◊ **make a mountain out of a molehill** treat sth that is not important as if it were

mountain ash *n.* TREES = **rowan** *n.* **1**

mountain avens *n.* a small trailing plant of the rose family that grows in temperate mountainous and arctic areas and has white flowers. Latin name: *Dryas octopetala*.

mountain beaver *n.* a large thick-set rodent that lives in colonies made up of extensive burrows in northwestern North America. Latin name: *Aplodontia rufa*.

mountain bike *n.* a bicycle built for rough terrain with wide thick tyres, straight handlebars, a strong frame, and more gears than a standard bicycle

mountain cat *n.* any of various feline animals that live in mountainous areas, e.g. the lynx and puma

mountain chain *n.* a range of mountains or a string of adjacent mountain peaks

mountain devil *n.* Aus ZOOL = **moloch**

mountaineer /mównti néer/ *n.* **1.** **MOUNTAIN CLIMBER** sb who climbs mountains for sport **2.** **MOUNTAIN INHABITANT** sb who lives in a mountainous area (*archaic*) ■ *vi.* **(-eers, -eering, -eered) CLIMB MOUNTAINS** to climb mountains for sport

mountaineering /mównti néering/ *n.* the sport or pastime of climbing mountains

mountain everlasting *n.* PLANTS = **cat's-foot**

mountain goat *n.* a large white wild North American goat with a woolly coat that lives above the timberline in mountains from Alaska to Colorado. Latin name: *Oreamnus americanus*.

mountain gorilla *n.* a gorilla that lives in forests in the mountainous regions of east central Africa. Latin name: *Gorilla gorilla beringei*.

mountain hare *n.* = **arctic hare** *n.* **2**

mountain laurel *n.* an evergreen shrub of the heath family that grows in eastern North America and has white or pink flowers and shiny poisonous leaves. It is the state flower of Pennsylvania and Connecticut. Latin name: *Kalmia latifolia*.

mountain lion *n.* = **puma**

mountainous /mówntinəss/ *adj.* **1.** **HAVING MOUNTAINS** characterized by many mountains **2.** **VERY LARGE** very large in height, shape, or size ○ *The ship was battered by mountainous waves.* —**mountainousness** *n.*

mountain range *n.* a series of adjacent or interconnected mountains forming a distinct group and usually dating from the same geological period

mountain rescue *n.* an organization of experienced climbers who go to the aid of people who get into difficulties in a mountainous place

mountain sheep *n.* any of several kinds of wild sheep that live in mountainous areas, e.g. the bighorn

mountain sickness *n.* = altitude sickness

Mountain Standard Time, **Mountain Time** *n.* the standard time in the time zone centred on longitude 105° W, which includes the Rocky Mountains region of North America. It is seven hours earlier than Universal Coordinated Time.

mountainy /mówntini/ *adj.* having many mountains or forming part of a mountainous area

Mount Aspiring National Park /-ə spíring-/ national park in the southwestern part of the South Island, New Zealand. Situated in forested, mountainous terrain, the park was established in 1964 and expanded in 1989. Area: 3,167 sq. km/1,223 sq. mi.

Mountbatten /mownt bátt'n/, **Louis, 1st Earl Mountbatten of Burma** (1900–79) British naval officer and diplomat. After service in World War II he became the last viceroy of India in 1947. He was killed by an IRA bomb.

Mount Cook lily *n.* a large white buttercup that grows in the mountains of the South Island of New Zealand. Latin name: *Ranunculus lyallii*.

mountebank /mównti bangk/ *n.* (*literary*) **1.** DECEIVER sb who deceives other people **2.** FAKE HEALER in the past, sb who sold ineffective medicines in public places [Late 16thC. From Italian *montambanco*, from *monta in banco* (command) 'get up onto the bench', from the quack's practice of hocking goods from a platform.] —**mountebankery** *n.*

mounted /mówntid/ *adj.* **1.** ON HORSEBACK riding on a horse ○ *mounted policemen* **2.** FIXED IN PLACE fixed onto sth for use or display

Mount Gambier /-gámbi ər/ town in southeastern South Australia, built on the slopes of an extinct volcano. Population: 22,037 (1996).

Mountie /mównti/, **Mounty** (*plural* -ies) *n.* a member of the Royal Canadian Mounted Police (*informal*) [Early 20thC. Formed from MOUNTED.]

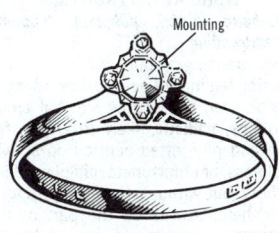
Mounting

mounting /mównting/ *n.* SUPPORTING DEVICE a support onto which another thing is fixed ■ *adj.* BECOMING GREATER becoming greater in size, number, or intensity ○ *We listened to the news with mounting alarm.*

mounting block, **mounting-block** *n.* a block of stone on which sb stands to get onto a horse (*archaic*)

Mount Isa /-ízə/ city in western Queensland, Australia. Population: 21,751 (1996).

Mount Lofty Ranges range of hills in South Australia, situated east of Adelaide. It forms part of the Flinders Range. Length: 320 km/200 mi.

Mount Rainier National Park /-ráyni ər-/ national park in western Washington State, established in 1899 and centred around Mount Rainier and its glacier system. Area: 95,349 hectares/235,613 acres.

Mount Rushmore National Memorial national memorial in South Dakota, featuring the heads of four US presidents carved onto the face of Mount Rushmore, each approximately 20 m/60 ft tall. Area: 517 hectares/1,278 acres.

Mount Vernon /-vúrnən/ city in southeastern New York State, on the Bronx River. It is a northern suburb of New York City. Population: 67,112 (1996).

mourn /mawrn/ (**mourns, mourning, mourned**) *v.* **1.** *vti.* EXPRESS SADNESS AT SB'S DEATH to feel and show sadness because sb has died ○ *mourning the loss of his father* **2.** *vti.* WEAR MOURNING CLOTHES to wear mourning clothes or other things that indicate grief over a death **3.** *vi.* EXPRESS SADNESS AT STH LOST to feel and show sadness because sth has been lost or no longer exists ○ *She mourned the loss of her independence.* [Old English *murnan*. Ultimately from an Indo-European base meaning 'to remember', which is also the ancestor of English *remember* and *memory*.] —**mourner** *n.*

Mourne Mountains /máwrn-/ granite mountain range in southern County Down, Northern Ireland. The highest point is Slieve Donard, 852 m/2,796 ft.

mournful /máwrnf'l/ *adj.* **1.** FEELING SAD expressing or feeling deep sadness ○ *a youth with a mournful face* **2.** CAUSING SADNESS causing or suggesting deep sadness ○ *a mournful anniversary* —**mournfully** *adv.* —**mournfulness** *n.*

mourning /máwrning/ *n.* **1.** SHOW OF SADNESS the feeling or showing of deep sadness following the death of sb ○ *was still in mourning over the death of her mother* **2.** CLOTHING FOR SB WHO IS MOURNING clothing of a particular style, fabric, or colour, e.g. black in Christian cultures, worn as a sign of sorrow following sb's death ○ *wore mourning for a year* **3.** PERIOD OF SADNESS the period during which the death of sb is mourned ○ *The family observed a period of 40 days' mourning.* [Old English] —**mourningly** *adv.*

─── WORD KEY: CULTURAL NOTE ───
Mourning Becomes Electra, a play by US dramatist Eugene O'Neill (1931). This 13-act drama, lasting six hours, is a somewhat Freudian reworking of the *Oresteia* trilogy by Greek author Aeschylus. Set in New England during the American Civil War (O'Neill's equivalent of the Trojan Wars), it portrays Lavinia Brant's attempts to avenge her mother's infidelity by turning the rest of the family against her.

mourning cloak *n.* US ZOOL = Camberwell beauty

mourning dove *n.* a common North American dove with greyish-brown feathers, a long pointed tail, and a mournful call. Latin name: *Zenaida macroura*. [*Mourning* from the bird's mournful call]

mouse[1] /mowss/ *abbr.* MIL minimum orbital unmanned satellite of the earth

mouse[2] /mowss/ *n.* (*plural* **mice** /mīss/) **1.** SMALL RODENT a small rodent found all over the world that has a brown or greyish-brown coat and a long mostly hairless tail. Family: Muridae and Cricetidae. **2.** COWARD sb who is thought to be timid or cowardly (*insult*) **3.** (*plural* **mouses** or **mice**) COMPUTER CONTROLLING DEVICE a hand-held device for controlling a computer. A pointer on the screen (**cursor**) is controlled by moving the device, which has one or more pushbuttons that transmit instructions to the computer. **4.** BLACK EYE a dark swelling under the eye that is caused by a blow (*dated slang*) ■ *vi.* (**mouses, mousing, moused**) HUNT MICE to hunt for and kill mice [Old English *mūs*. Ultimately from an Indo-European word meaning 'mouse', which is also the ancestor of English *muscle* and *murine*.]

mousebird /mówss burd/ *n.* = coly [Early 19thC. *Mouse* from the bird's soft hairlike plumage.]

mouse button *n.* a pushbutton, typically one of two or three, on a computer mouse that transmits instructions to the computer

mouse-coloured *adj.* COLOURS of a dull nondescript brown or grey colour

mouse deer *n.* = chevrotain [From the animal's small size and its similarity in form to a deer]

mouse-ear, **mouse-ear chickweed** *n.* a variety of chickweed or hawkweed with short hairy leaves resembling mouse ears. Genus: *Cerastium*.

mouse mat, **mouse pad** *n.* a piece of foam-backed material for a computer mouse to move on while being used

mouse potato *n.* sb who spends a great deal of time sitting at a computer (*slang*) [Late 20thC. Modelled on COUCH POTATO.]

mouser /mówssər/ *n.* a domestic animal such as a dog or cat that catches mice

mousetail /mówss tayl/ *n.* a plant that grows in temperate regions and has long flower spikes resembling tails. Genus: *Myosurus*.

mousetrap /mówss trap/ *n.* a trap for catching and often killing mice

mousey *adj.* = mousy

mousing /mówssing/ *n.* NAUT a cord or bar across the opening of a hook to prevent its load from slipping

moussaka /moo sa'akə/ *n.* a Greek baked dish with alternating layers of aubergine and minced meat in a tomato sauce, topped with a savoury white sauce [Mid-20thC. Via Turkish *musakka* from Arabic *musakka*.]

mousse /mooss/ *n.* (*plural* **mousses**) **1.** LIGHT FOOD a light rich dish consisting mostly of whipped cream, eggs, or gelatin that is sweetened to serve as dessert, or flavoured with vegetables, meat, or fish **2.** FOAMY HAIR PRODUCT a foamy substance used to set or style hair ■ *vt.* (**mousses, moussing, moussed**) STYLE HAIR to apply mousse to hair in order to style it [Mid-19thC. From French, 'moss, foam', of Germanic origin.]

mousseline /moóss leén/ *n.* **1.** TEXTILES LOOSELY WOVEN FABRIC a loosely woven fine fabric of natural or synthetic fibres, resembling muslin **2.** CRAFT GLASS a type of delicate blown glass **3.** COOK = mousseline sauce [Late 17thC. Via French from Italian *mussolina*, named after *Mosul*, a city of Iraq where the fabric was once manufactured.]

mousseline de laine /-də lén/ *n.* a thin lightweight woollen fabric, often with a printed pattern [From French, literally, 'muslin of wool']

mousseline de soie /-də swaá/ *n.* a thin plain-woven fabric of rayon or silk [From French, literally, 'muslin of silk']

mousseline sauce *n.* hollandaise sauce to which whisked egg white or whipped cream has been added

moustache /mə staásh/ *n.* **1.** HAIR ON UPPER LIP facial hair allowed to grow on sb's upper lip and often down the sides of the mouth or onto the cheeks **2.** HAIR ON ANIMAL'S FACE hair, bristles, or feathers around the mouth or beak of an animal [Late 16thC. Via French from Italian *mostaccio*, ultimately from Greek *mustak-*, stem of *mustax* 'upper lip, moustache'.] —**moustached** *adj.*

moustache cup *n.* an old-fashioned cup with a partial cover to prevent the contents from getting onto a drinker's moustache

Mousterian /moo steéri ən/ *n.* a prehistoric culture of the Palaeolithic period in Europe, North Africa, and the Middle East associated with the Neanderthals and marked by the use of flint tools [Late 19thC. From French *moustérien*, named after *Le Moustier*, a cave in southwestern France where remains from this period were discovered.]

mousy /mówssi/ (**-ier, -iest**), **mousey** (**-ier, -iest**) *adj.* **1.** DULL BROWN dull brown in colour **2.** TIMID shy or uncommunicative, especially boringly or irritatingly so **3.** FULL OF MICE overrun with mice **4.** RESEMBLING MOUSE having features that resemble a mouse, e.g. big front teeth or a pointed nose —**mousily** *adv.* —**mousiness** *n.*

mouth *n.* /mowth/ (*plural* **mouths** /mowthz/) **1.** ANAT FOOD AND VOICE ORGAN in people and animals, the opening in the head and its surrounding lips, gums, tongue, and teeth, through which food is taken in and through which sounds come out **2.** ANAT FACE FEATURE the part of the mouth visible to others, including the lips and the opening between them ○ *She kissed him on the mouth.* **3.** SPEECH ORGAN the mouth regarded as the organ of speech ○ *You wouldn't believe some of the things that came out of his mouth.* **4.** WAY OF SPEAKING a particular way of using language that other people think is inappropriate or offensive (*disapproving*) ○ *a foul mouth* **5.** BACK TALK a response that refuses to respond to a question or an order and is impudent or sarcastic (*informal*) ○ *All I got from them was a lot of mouth.* **6.** WATER JUNCTION the place where a stream or river enters a sea or lake **7.** OPENING IN THE EARTH an opening to a cave, tunnel, mineshaft, or volcano **8.** CONTAINER OPENING the opening of a container such as a jar, tube, or bottle **9.** OPENING BETWEEN PARTS OF A TOOL the opening between the two sides of a device that can be closed to hold sth, e.g.

in a vice or clamp **10. GRIMACE** a facial expression that shows displeasure, distaste, or sulkiness (*dated*) ○ *She made a mouth at him and quickly turned away.* **11.** MUSIC **PIPE OPENING** the slit in the pipe of a pipe organ **12.** *vti.* MUSIC **FLUTE OPENING** the hole in a flute that the player blows into ■ *vt.* /mowth/ **(mouths, mouthing, mouthed) 1. SAY STH INSINCERELY** to speak or say sth in a loud, affected, or insincere way ○ *How can you get up there and mouth such clichés?* **2. FORM WORDS** to form words with the tongue and lips without making a sound, usually in order to prevent being heard or to pretend to speak or sing sth **3. PUT STH IN THE MOUTH** to put and hold sth in the mouth as babies and young animals do **4. CARESS STH WITH THE MOUTH** to touch or caress sth with the mouth **5. TRAIN A HORSE** to train a horse to get used to a bit and bridle [Old English *mūþ*. Ultimately from an Indo-European base meaning 'to project', which is also the ancestor of English *eminent* and *mountain*.] ◇ **a mouth to feed** sb who must be provided for, especially fed ◇ **be all mouth** to boast about doing sth but never actually do it (*informal*) ◇ **down in the mouth** looking sad or gloomy (*informal*) ◇ **give mouth to** to express sth in speech or writing

mouthbreeder /mówth breedər/, **mouthbrooder** /-broodər/ *n.* a freshwater fish that carries its eggs and young in its mouth, especially an African fish of the cichlid family. Genus: *Haplochromis* and *Tilapia*.

-mouthed *suffix.* **1.** with a particular kind of mouth ○ *wide-mouthed* **2.** speaking in a particular way ○ *foul-mouthed*

mouthful /mówthfŏŏl/ (*plural* **-fuls**) *n.* **1. QUANTITY OF FOOD** the amount of food that can comfortably be chewed in the mouth at one time **2. SMALL AMOUNT OF FOOD** only a very little amount to eat ○ *You can't go all day on a mouthful of food like that.* **3. HARD-TO-PRONOUNCE WORD OR PHRASE** a word or phrase that is hard to pronounce because of its unfamiliar sound combinations ○ *Her last name's a mouthful!* **4. OFFENSIVE SPEECH** sth said that is offensive or cheeky (*disapproving*) ○ *If you complain about the noise you only get a mouthful from them.*

mouth guard *n.* *US* = **gumshield**

mouth organ *n.* = **harmonica**

mouthpart /mówth paart/ *n.* a body part near the mouth of an insect or other arthropod that it uses to gather or chew food

mouthpiece /mówth peess/ *n.* **1. PART HELD TO THE MOUTH** a part of a musical instrument, telephone, or other device that is held to or in the mouth **2. CONDUIT FOR VIEWS** a person or publication that expresses the views of an organization ○ *He is the mouthpiece for big business in this city.* **3.** *US* = **gumshield**

mouth-to-mouth, mouth-to-mouth resuscitation *n.* a method of reviving sb who is not breathing in which the rescuer places his or her mouth over the mouth of the person not breathing and inflates the lungs with air

mouthwash /mówth wosh/ (*plural* **-washes**) *n.* a medicated liquid that is gargled and swilled around the mouth to cleanse it and to freshen the breath

mouthwatering /mówth wawtəring/ *adj.* stimulating the appetite by having a delicious smell or appearance —**mouthwateringly** *adv.*

mouthy /mówthi, mówthi/ (**-ier, -iest**) *adj.* tending to talk rudely, loudly, or too much (*informal*) —**mouthiness** *n.*

mouton /mŏŏ ton/ *n.* sheepskin processed to resemble a fur such as seal or beaver [Mid-20thC. From French (see MUTTON).]

movable /mŏŏvəb'l/, **moveable** *adj.* **1. EASILY MOVED** able to move or be moved easily **2. CHANGING DATE FROM YEAR TO YEAR** falling on a different date from year to year ■ *n.* LAW **PROPERTY** sth that can be easily moved from one place to another, especially personal property such as an item of furniture (*often used in the plural*) —**movability** /mŏŏvə bíllәti/ *n.* —**movableness** /mŏŏvәb'lnәss/ *n.* —**movably** *adv.*

movable feast *n.* a religious festival that is not fixed but falls on a different day from year to year, as does Easter in the Christian calendar

move /moov/ *v.* **(moves, moving, moved) 1.** *vti.* **CHANGE POSITION** to change position or location, or to change the position or location of sth ○ *Something moved behind that tree.* **2.** *vti.* **CHANGE YOUR RESIDENCE, JOB, OR SCHOOL** to change your place of residence, work, or study, or make sb change ○ *move to the other side of town* **3.** *vti.* **TAKE ACTION** to take action, or make sb act ○ *It's due next week so we need to move quickly.* **4.** *vti.* **CHANGE YOUR VIEW** to change a view or opinion or cause sb to do so ○ *She has moved to a more moderate position.* **5.** *vti.* **IMPROVE OR PROGRESS** to make progress or start to go in the desired direction ○ *Finally things have started moving.* **6.** *vi.* **ASSOCIATE WITH A GROUP** to associate with a particular group ○ *She moves among the yachting set.* **7.** *vi.* **PROPOSE ACTION** to propose formally that sth should happen or be done ○ *I move that the meeting be adjourned.* **8.** *vt.* **STIR SB'S EMOTIONS** to make sb feel sth, especially tender feelings ○ *Her performance moved all of us.* **9.** *vti.* BOARD GAMES **TAKE A TURN IN A GAME** to take a turn in a board game ○ *Have you moved yet?* **10.** *vti.* **SELL STH** to sell well or effectively, or sell sth well or effectively ○ *The souvenir mugs aren't really moving.* **11.** *vti.* **EMPTY THE BOWELS** to empty the bowels ■ *n.* **1. ACT OF MOVING** an act or instance of moving ○ *One false move and we're done for.* **2. STEP IN SERIES** an action considered as one of a series ○ *Keep your rivals guessing what your next move will be.* **3.** BOARD GAMES **SB'S TURN TO PLAY** sb's turn in a board game ○ *It's your move.* **4. CHANGE OF LOCATION** a change of residence or location ○ *I'm considering a move across town.* **5. MANOEUVRE** a manoeuvre or particular way of doing sth ○ *If you're interested in martial arts, I could show you a few moves.* [13thC. Via Anglo-Norman *mover* from Latin *movere*.] ◇ **get a move on** start doing sth right away, or do sth faster (*informal*) ◇ **make a move on sb** to proposition sb sexually (*slang*) ◇ **on the move 1.** going from one place to another **2.** busy doing one thing after another **3.** going forward, or making progress

WORD KEY: ORIGIN

The Latin word *movere*, from which ***move*** is derived, is also the source of English *commotion, emotion, mobile, moment, motif, motive, motor, mutiny, promote,* and *remote*.

---

move in *v.* **1.** *vti.* **START LIVING OR WORKING SOMEWHERE** to begin living or doing business in a place **2.** *vi.* **GET CLOSER** to approach closer to sb or sth, especially to make an attack ○ *move in for the kill*

move in on *vt.* **1.** *US* **INTRUDE ON SB** to intrude on sb **2. ATTEMPT TO TAKE CONTROL** to attempt to take control of sb or sth, or take over from sb ○ *He's trying to move in on our department* **3. APPROACH TO ATTACK** to approach closer to sb or sth, especially to make an attack ○ *The guards are moving in on the intruders.*

move into *vt.* **1. SET UP HOME** to begin living in a particular place ○ *move into a new flat* **2. START DEALING WITH STH** to begin dealing with sth or doing business in a particular field ○ *The company is set to move into home banking.*

move on *vi.* **1. LEAVE FOR ELSEWHERE** to leave a place and go somewhere else ○ *I think I'll be moving on.* **2. DO STH ELSE** to stop doing or dealing with sth and start doing sth else ○ *Let's move on to the next item in the agenda.*

move out *vi.* to leave a place of residence or business, or help sb do this

move over *vti.* to move to one side in order to make room, or to help or make sb do this ○ *If you move over I'll be able to sit down.*

movement /mŏŏvmənt/ *n.* **1. ACT OF MOVING** an act of changing location or position ○ *an instrument to detect subtle movements* **2. WAY OF MOVING** the way in which sb or sth moves ○ *the awkward movement of an injured arm* **3. EFFORT BY MANY TO ACHIEVE STH** a collective effort by a large number of people to try to achieve sth, especially a political or social reform ○ *the civil rights movement* **4. PEOPLE ORGANIZED TO EFFECT CHANGE** the people who organize themselves in order to achieve some political or social reform **5. MOVING PARTS** the parts of a clock or watch mechanism that drive and regulate it **6.** STOCK EXCH **CHANGE IN PRICE** a change in the prices of traded securities ○ *upward movement before the close of trading* **7.** LITERAT **PLOT EVENTS** developments in the plot of a literary work ○ *no movement in the plot for three chapters* **8.** ARTS **SUGGESTED MOTION** the illusion or suggestion of motion in a work of art, e.g. a sculpture or painting **9.** MUSIC **SECTION OF MUSICAL WORK** one of several self-contained sections that make up a large-scale musical work, often differentiated from one another by different tempos and characters ○ *the concerto's third movement* **10.** MIL **TACTICAL CHANGE OF POSITION** a tactical change in the position or location of a military unit **11.** POETRY **RHYTHM** the cadence or rhythm of a piece of poetry **12.** *US* PHYSIOL = **motion** *n.* **6, motion** *n.* **7** ■ **movements** *npl.* **ACTIVITIES AND LOCATION** what sb does and where he or she goes, noted over a period of time ○ *The accused was asked to describe his movements on the day in question.*

mover /mŏŏvər/ *n.* **1. SB OR STH THAT CAUSES MOTION** sb or sth that causes movement or accomplishes sth ○ *She's the prime mover behind the project.* **2.** *US* **MOVING COMPANY** a company or individual whose work is to transport the personal property of households or businesses from one location to another **3. SB WHO MAKES A MOTION** sb who formally proposes sth during a meeting ○ *Does the mover of the motion consent to the amendment?*

movers and shakers *npl.* people in society who are powerful or influential ○ *one of the industry's movers and shakers*

movie /mŏŏvi/ *n.* *US* = **film** ■ **movies** *npl.* *US* **1. FILM INDUSTRY** the film industry, treated as a whole **2. FILM SHOWING** the showing of a film in a cinema [Early 20thC. Shortening and alteration of *moving picture*.]

movie camera *n.* *US* = **cine camera**

movie film *n.* *US* = **cine film**

moviegoer /mŏŏvi gō ər/ *n.* *US* = **filmgoer**

movie star *n.* = **film star**

Movietone /mŏŏvi tōn/ *tdmk.* a trademark for a technique of adding a soundtrack to a film

moving /mŏŏving/ *adj.* **1. MAKING PEOPLE FEEL EMOTION** making people feel deep emotions, especially sadness or compassion ○ *After such a moving speech we were all in tears.* **2. MOVABLE** able to move ○ *moving parts* **3. IN MOTION** in a state of movement (*usually used in combination*) ○ *slow-moving* **4. CAUSED BY CHANGING PLACES** involved in or caused by a change of residence or business location

WORD KEY: SYNONYMS

moving, pathetic, pitiful, poignant, touching, heartwarming, heartrending

CORE MEANING: arousing emotion

moving causing feelings of deep sadness or compassion. It can also be used to describe sth that arouses other strong emotions; **pathetic** likely to arouse feelings of compassion and pity, often centred on sb who is vulnerable, helpless, or unfortunate; **pitiful** used in a similar way to *pathetic* but without necessarily suggesting vulnerability or helplessness on the part of the person pitied; **poignant** causing strong, often bitter-sweet feelings of sadness or regret; **touching** causing feelings of warmth and tenderness; **heartwarming** making people feel happy and more positive or optimistic because it involves people doing good things or behaving kindly to one another; **heartrending** arousing feelings of intense sadness or pity, especially because it involves suffering or tragic events.

---

movingly /mŏŏvingli/ *adv.* in a way that makes people feel deep emotions, especially tender ones ○ *She spoke movingly about their plight.*

moving pavement *n.* an endlessly circulating motor-driven belt that conveys people over a flat expanse of ground, e.g. in an airport. US term **moving sidewalk**

moving picture *n.* a cinematographic film (*dated*)

moving sidewalk *n.* *US* = **moving pavement**

moving spirit *n.* sb who works hard to bring sth about and inspires others to do the same ○ *She was one of the moving spirits behind the campaign.*

moving staircase *n.* = **escalator** *n.*

Moviola /mŏŏvi ṓlə/ *tdmk.* a trademark for a film editing machine

mow[1] /mō/ **(mows, mowing, mowed, mown** /mōn/ *or* **mowed)** *v.* **1.** *vti.* **CUT DOWN TALL GROWTH** to cut tall grass, hay, or grain with a scythe or machine **2.** *vt.* **CUT GRASS** to cut the grass, hay, or grain growing in a particular place ○ *Mow the front lawn today, please.* [Old English *māwan*. From a prehistoric Germanic base that is also the ancestor of English *meadow* and *aftermath*.]

mow down *vt.* **1. KILL MANY PEOPLE QUICKLY** to kill people quickly and in large numbers **2. KNOCK SB DOWN** to knock sb or sth down by force

mow[2] /mō/ *n.* **1. STORAGE PLACE FOR HAY** the part of a barn where hay or grain is stored when it has been harvested **2. STORED HAY** a pile of hay or grain, especially in a barn [Old English *mūga*, of unknown origin]

MOW *abbr.* Ministry of Works

mown past participle of **mow**

MOX /moks/ *n.* reactor fuel made from plutonium that has been separated from spent nuclear fuel by chemical reprocessing and mixed with natural or depleted uranium [Blend of MIXED and OXIDE]

moxie /móksi/ *n. US* courage combined with inventiveness (*slang dated*) [Mid-20thC. Named after a brand of soft drink that was originally marketed as a 'nerve tonic', said to restore virility and intelligence.]

Moynihan /móynihən/, **Daniel Patrick** (*b.* 1927) US academic and politician. He was ambassador to India (1973–74), and won a seat in the Senate (1976).

Moz. *abbr.* Mozambique

Mozambique

Mozambique /mṓ zam beék/ republic in southeastern Africa. It became independent from Portugal in 1975. Language: Portuguese. Currency: metical. Capital: Maputo. Population: 18,028,000 (1996). Area: 801,590 sq. km/309,496 sq. mi. Official name **Republic of Mozambique** —**Mozambican** *n., adj.*

Mozarab /mō zárrəb/ *n.* a Christian living in Moorish Spain who adopted some Arab customs without converting to Islam [Early 17thC. Via Spanish *mozárabe* from Arabic *musta'rib* 'becoming an Arab'.] —**Mozarabic** *adj.*

Mozart /mōts aart/, **Wolfgang Amadeus** (1756–91) Austrian composer. A figure of key importance in Western music, his compositions, in almost every musical genre, epitomize the classical style.

mozetta *n.* CHR = **mozzetta**

mozzarella /mótsə réllə/ *n.* a rubbery white unsalted Italian cheese used in salads, cooking, and especially on pizza [Early 20thC. From Italian, literally 'little mozza', from *mozza*, type of cheese (literally 'a cut'), from *mozzare* 'to cut off'.]

mozzetta /mō zéttə/, **mozetta** *n.* a short hooded cape worn by the pope and other senior Roman Catholic clergymen [Late 18thC. Via Italian from, ultimately, medieval Latin *almutia* (also the source of English *amice*), of unknown origin.]

mozzie /mózzi/ *n.* a mosquito (*informal*) [Mid-20thC. Shortening and alteration.]

mp *abbr.* **1.** melting point **2.** MUSIC mezzo piano

MP *abbr.* **1.** Member of Parliament **2.** Metropolitan Police **3.** military police **4.** mounted police

mpg *abbr.* miles per gallon

mph *abbr.* miles per hour

MPhil /ém fíl/ *abbr.* Master of Philosophy

Mpumalanga /əm poòmə láng gə/ province in northeastern South Africa, bordering Swaziland and Mozambique. Capital: Nelspruit. Population: 3,007,100 (1995). Area: 78,370 sq. km/30,259 sq. mi. Former name **Eastern Transvaal**

Mr /místər/ *n.* **1. MAN'S TITLE** the customary title of courtesy used before the name or names of a man ○ *Mr Smith* **2. JOB OR FUNCTION TITLE** a courtesy title used for a man before the name of his position or function ○ *Mr President* **3. DESCRIPTIVE TITLE** a humorous title used for a man before a place, name, thing, or description that he is supposed to typify or represent ○ *He's not exactly Mr Personality, is he?* **4. SURGEON'S TITLE** a title used instead of a surgeon's surname, rather than 'Dr' **5. JUNIOR OFFICER'S TITLE** a title used in addressing an officer in the navy below the rank of commander, a warrant officer in the army, or a cadet in a service academy [15thC. Contraction of *maister*, an earlier form of MASTER.]

MR *abbr.* Master of the Rolls

Mr Big *n. US* a powerful or important man, e.g. the chief of a criminal organization (*slang*)

MRBM *abbr.* medium-range ballistic missile

MRC *abbr.* Medical Research Council

MRCA *abbr.* multirole combat aircraft

Mr Clean *n. US* sb, especially a public figure, who is seen as being admirably upright, honest, and moral (*informal*) [Mid-20thC. Named after a cleaning solution trademark.]

MRCS *abbr.* Member of the Royal College of Surgeons

MRCVS *abbr.* Member of the Royal College of Veterinary Surgeons

MRI *abbr.* MED magnetic resonance imaging

MRIA *abbr.* Member of the Royal Irish Academy

mridanga /mri dúng gə/, **mridang** /mri dúng/, **mridangam** /-gəm/ *n.* an Indian drum that is shaped like a barrel and is made in various sizes [Late 19thC. From Tamil.]

mRNA *abbr.* messenger RNA

MRP *abbr.* manufacturer's recommended price

Mr Right *n.* sb seen as being a perfect partner for sb else (*informal*) ○ *One day Mr Right will come along.*

Mrs /míssiz/ *n.* a customary title of courtesy for a married or widowed woman, used before her name or names ○ *Mrs Wright* [Early 17thC. Contraction of MISTRESS.]

MRSA *n.* a strain of bacteria that has become resistant to antibiotic drugs and is therefore a hazard in places such as hospitals. Full form **multiply resistant Staphylococcus aureus**

MRSC *abbr.* Member of the Royal Society of Chemistry

Mrs Grundy /-grúndi/ *n.* a very narrow-minded and prudish person (*informal*) [Late 18thC. Named after a character in the play *Speed the Plough*, by Thomas Morton (1764–1838).]

Mrs Mop /-móp/ (*plural* **Mrs Mops**), **Mrs Mopp** (*plural* **Mrs Mopps**) *n.* a woman employed to do domestic cleaning (*dated informal*)

ms *abbr.* millisecond

Ms /məz, miz/ *n.* **1. WOMAN'S TITLE** a customary title of courtesy used before the name or names of a woman without making a distinction between married and unmarried status ○ *Ms Bennett* **2. WOMAN'S DESCRIPTIVE TITLE** a title used for a woman before a place, thing, or description that she is supposed to typify or represent ○ *Ms Efficiency* [Mid-20thC. Blend of MISS and MRS.]

MS *abbr.* **1.** mail steamer **2.** Master of Surgery **3.** sacred to the memory of (*on gravestones*) **4.** motor ship **5.** multiple sclerosis

ms. *abbr.* ms., MS. manuscript

MSB *abbr.* COMPUT most significant bit

MSc *abbr.* Master of Science [From Latin *Magister Scientiae*]

MS-DOS /ém ess dóss/ *tdmk.* a trademark for a widely used computer operating system

msec *abbr.* millisecond

Mses plural of **Ms**

MSF *abbr.* Manufacturing, Science, and Finance (Union)

MSG *abbr.* monosodium glutamate

Msgr *abbr.* **1.** Monseigneur **2.** Monsignor

MSI *abbr.* ELECTRON ENG medium scale integration

MSP *abbr.* POL Member of the Scottish Parliament

Ms Right *n.* sb seen as being the perfect romantic partner for sb else ○ *tired of waiting for Ms Right to come along*

mss., **MSS** *abbr.* manuscripts

mt *abbr.* **1.** mount **2.** mountain **3.** Mountain Time

Mt *abbr.* **1.** BIBLE Matthew **2.** Mount **3.** Mountain

MT *abbr.* **1.** megaton **2.** Mountain Time

mt. *abbr.* **1.** megaton **2.** mount **3.** mountain

m.t. *abbr.* metric ton

Mtarazi Waterfall /əm təráatsi/ waterfall in Zimbabwe, south-eastern Africa, one of the highest in the world. Height: 762 m/2,500 ft.

MTB *abbr.* motor torpedo boat

MTBE *n.* a lead-free antiknock petrol additive. Abbr of **methyl tertiary-butyl ethyl**

MTBF *abbr.* COMPUT mean time between failures

MTech /ém ték/ *abbr.* Master of Technology

mtg *abbr.* meeting

mtg. *abbr.* mortgage

mtge *abbr.* mortgage

Mt Rev. *abbr.* Most Reverend

mu /myoo/ *n.* the 12th letter of the Greek alphabet, represented in the English alphabet as 'm' [Late 19thC. From Greek.]

MU *abbr.* **1.** Mothers' Union **2.** Musicians' Union

Mu'awiya /moó ə weè ə/ *n.* a leader of the Umayyad clan who became the first Umayyad caliph following civil war with Ali. He died in AD 680.

Mubarak /moo baárək, moo baárək/, **Hosni** (*b.* 1928) Egyptian statesman. He succeeded Anwar Sadat as president of Egypt in 1981. He continued Sadat's foreign policy of peace with Israel while mending strained relations with the Arab League. Full name **Muhammad Hosni Said Mubarak**

muc- *prefix.* = **muco-** [See MUCO-]

much /much/ *adv.* **1. LARGELY** used to indicate that sth exists or is true to a great extent, intensity, or degree ○ *She hasn't changed much over the years.* ○ *It's a much more difficult game than the other.* **2. OFTEN** happening often or frequently ○ *I don't get out much these days.* ○ *Do you see your children much over the holidays?* **3. NEARLY** nearly or practically ○ *One day is much like the next when you're ill.* ○ *It's much the same problem all over again.* ■ *pron., det.* **LARGE AMOUNT** a large amount or degree ○ (det) *He doesn't have much free time due to the demands of work.* ○ (pron) *Much remains to be done.* ○ (pron) *She does much of her writing at home.* ■ *pron.* **IMPRESSIVE** sth impressive, important, or unusual ○ *The house isn't much to look at, but it's very comfortable.* [13thC. Shortening of Old English *mycel*. Ultimately from an Indo-European base meaning 'great', which is also the ancestor of English *major* and *mickle*.] ◇ **a bit much** excessive or unacceptable (*informal*) ◇ **as much** precisely that ○ *I wasn't surprised when she said she'd taken the money, as I'd suspected as much from the start.* ◇ **(as) much as** although, or even though ○ *As much as I'd like to join you, I'm afraid I can't.* ◇ **much as** to almost the same degree, or in a similar manner ○ *You cook it much as you would a potato.* ◇ **not much of a** not particularly good at sth or not a very good example of sth ○ *It's not been much of a celebration, has it?* ◇ **not up to much** **1.** of a low standard (*informal*) **2.** *US* not very active

muchness /múchnəss/ *n.* greatness in quantity, extent, or degree (*archaic*) ◇ **much of a muchness** amounting to or being practically the same (*informal*)

muci- *prefix.* = **muco-**

$$HO-\underset{\underset{O}{\|}}{C}-\underset{\underset{OH}{|}}{C}H-\underset{\underset{}{|}}{C}H-\underset{\underset{OH}{|}}{C}H-\underset{\underset{}{|}}{C}H-\underset{\underset{O}{\|}}{C}-OH$$

Mucic acid

mucic acid /myoóssik-/ *n.* a colourless crystalline solid obtained from lactose. It is used in the manufacture of other chemicals. Formula: $C_4H_4(OH)_4(COOH)_2$.

muciferous /myoo sífferəss/ *adj.* producing or containing a lot of mucus

mucigen /myoóssijən/ *n.* a substance in mucous cells that is converted into mucin

mucilage /myoóssilij/ *n.* **1.** GLUE a thick water-based solution used as an adhesive **2.** STICKY PLANT PRODUCT a gummy substance secreted by some plants such as seaweed that contains protein and carbohydrates [14thC. Via French from late Latin *mucillago* 'mouldy juice', from Latin *mucus* (see MUCUS).]

mucilaginous /myoóssi lájjinəss/ *adj.* **1.** PRODUCING MUCILAGE relating to or producing mucilage **2.** MOIST AND STICKY moist and sticky like glue —**mucilaginously** *adv.* —**mucilaginousness** *n.*

mucin /myoóssin/ *n.* a complex protein found in the substances secreted by mucous membranes —**mucinous** *adj.*

muck /muk/ *n.* **1.** STICKY DIRT soft moist dirt or filth (*informal*) **2.** MANURE moist manure or compost, especially when used to fertilize land **3.** RUBBISH sth that is distasteful, disgusting, or of very poor quality (*informal*) ○ *don't know how they can publish such muck* **4.** MINE WASTE waste material from mining, e.g. earth or rubble ■ *vt.* (**mucks, mucking, mucked**) **1.** FERTILIZE LAND to fertilize land with manure or compost (*informal*) **2.** CLEAN OUT A PLACE to clean the muck out of a place such as a stable or barn **3.** MAKE STH DIRTY to pollute sth or make sth dirty (*informal*) [13thC. From Scandinavian, ultimately from a prehistoric Germanic base meaning 'soft'. Originally 'excrement'; the more general 'dirt' is a 14thC development.]

muck about *v.* **1.** *vi.* WASTE TIME to waste time instead of doing sth useful or important (*informal*) ○ *We'd get this job finished sooner if you two stopped mucking about.* **2.** *vt.* WASTE SB'S TIME to waste sb's time or fail to deal with sb in a serious way ○ *The car people keep mucking me about.*

muck in *vi.* to share sth, especially work or accommodation, with other people (*informal*) ○ *It won't take long if everyone mucks in.* ○ *The house is a little overcrowded but we all just muck in together.*

muck up *v.* **1.** *vt.* DAMAGE STH to ruin or make a mess of sth (*informal*) ○ *She's really mucked up her chances now.* **2.** *vt.* MAKE STH DIRTY to soil or stain sth (*informal*) ○ *He fell in the mud and mucked up his trousers.* **3.** *vi.* *Aus* ACT INAPPROPRIATELY to misbehave ○ *The kids have been mucking up all day.*

muckamuck *n.* *US* = high-muck-a-muck (*informal*)

mucker /múkər/ *n.* **1.** FRIEND a friend (*dated slang*) ○ *This is my old mucker Charlie.* **2.** WASTE REMOVER sb whose job is to remove rocky mine waste

muckle /múk'l/ *adj.* *Scotland* LARGE very big or great ○ *a muckle stone* ■ *adv.* *Scotland* MUCH much or greatly ○ *not muckle clever* ■ *n.* *Scotland* A LOT a large amount of sth ○ *Many a mickle makes a muckle.* [Old English *mycel* (see MUCH)]

muckluck *n.* CLOTHES = mukluk

muckrake /múk rayk/ *vi.* (**-rakes, -raking, -raked**) EXPOSE SCANDAL to seek out and publicize misconduct by prominent people ■ *n.* RAKE FOR MANURE a rake used to spread manure or compost [Late 17thC. From MUCK + RAKE.] —**muckraker** *n.* —**muckraking** *n.*

mucksweat /múk swet/ *n.* heavy sweating, or a condition in which sb does this (*informal*) ○ *I've been in a mucksweat over that lost file.*

muck-up day *n.* *Aus* the last day of school before exams, on which pupils play practical jokes (*informal*)

muckworm /múk wurm/ *n.* an insect larva that lives in mud or manure

mucky /múki/ (**-ier, -iest**) *adj.* **1.** FILTHY very dirty or covered with muck (*informal*) **2.** RUDE rude or obscene **3.** RAINY rainy or stormy —**muckily** *adv.* —**muckiness** *n.*

muco-, muc-, muci- *prefix.* mucus, mucous membrane ○ *mucocutaneous* [Formed from Latin *mucus* (see MUCUS)]

mucocutaneous /myoóko kyoo táyni əss/ *adj.* involving both skin and mucous membrane

mucoid /myoo koyd/, **mucoidal** *adj.* resembling mucus in appearance, consistency, or function

mucolytic /myoóko líttik/ *adj.* able to break down substances that contain mucus

mucopeptide /myoóko pép tīd/ *n.* = peptidoglycan

mucopolysaccharide /myoóko pólli sákə rīd/ *n.* a polysaccharide that forms complexes with proteins and contains an amino group

mucoprotein /myoóko pró teen/ *n.* a complex protein that is found in body fluids and tissues

mucopurulent /myoóko pyoórələnt/ *adj.* containing both mucus and pus

mucosa /myoo kóssə/ (*plural* **-sae** /-see/) *n.* = mucous membrane [Late 19thC. From modern Latin (*membrana*) *mucosa* 'mucous membrane', from the feminine of Latin *mucosus* (see MUCOUS).]

mucous /myoókəss/ *adj.* containing, secreting, resembling, or covered with mucus [Mid-17thC. From Latin *mucosus*, from *mucus* (see MUCUS).]

mucous membrane *n.* a moist lining in the body passages of all mammals that contains mucus-secreting cells and is open directly or indirectly to the external environment

mucro /myoókrō/ (*plural* **-cros**) *n.* a sharp point projecting from an organ or plant part [Mid-17thC. From Latin, 'sharp point, sword'.]

mucronate /myoókrə nayt/, **mucronated** /myoókrə naytid/ *adj.* BOT, ZOOL ending in a sharp point —**mucronation** /myoókrə náysh'n/ *n.*

mucus /myoókəss/ *n.* the clear slimy lubricating substance consisting mostly of mucins and water that coats and protects mucous membranes [Mid-17thC. From Latin. Ultimately from an Indo-European word meaning 'slimy', which is also the ancestor of English *meek* and *moist*.]

mud /mud/ *n.* **1.** WET SOIL earth that is very wet, soft, and gummy **2.** DEFAMATORY MATERIAL defamatory things said or written about sb [14thC. Origin uncertain: probably from Middle Low German *mudde*.] ◇ **(as) clear as mud** not clear or understandable at all (*informal*) ◇ **here's mud in your eye!** used as a drinking toast (*informal*) ◇ **sling** or **throw mud at** make defamatory statements about sb or sth (*informal*)

mudbath /múd baath/ (*plural* **-baths** /-baathz/) *n.* **1.** BEAUTY TREATMENT a bath in heated mud, thought to tone the skin and organs **2.** ACTIVITY IN A MUDDY PLACE sth such as a football game that takes place outdoors in very muddy conditions (*informal*)

mud dauber *n.* a wasp that builds multicellular nests with mud. Family: Sphecidae. US term **mud wasp**

muddle /múdd'l/ *v.* (**-dles, -dling, -dled**) **1.** *vt.* MIX THINGS TOGETHER IN DISORDER to mix things together in a confused or disordered way ○ *The disks have been carefully filed, so don't muddle them.* **2.** *vt.* CONFUSE THINGS to confuse things in the mind (*often passive*) ○ *They look so alike that it's easy to muddle them up.* **3.** *vti.* CONFUSE OR BE CONFUSED to be confused or bemused or to cause sb to be so ○ *Tell me again slowly – you're muddling me.* ■ *n.* **1.** CONFUSED STATE sth that is in such a confused condition that it is hard to organize or understand ○ *How did our records get into such a muddle?* **2.** MIXUP a misunderstanding arising from or causing a confused situation or state ○ *There's been a muddle over the bookings.* [Mid-16thC. Origin uncertain: possibly from

Middle Dutch *moddelen* 'to make muddy', from *modde* 'mud'.] —**muddler** *n.* —**muddly** *adj.*

muddle through *vi.* to succeed or manage to keep going despite being disorganized ○ *I expect we'll muddle through somehow.*

muddled /múdd'ld/ *adj.* being in a condition of disorder or confusion

muddleheaded /múdd'l héddid/ *adj.* **1.** CONFUSED unable to think clearly **2.** INEPT not clearly thought out —**muddleheadedly** *adv.* —**muddleheadedness** *n.*

muddy /múddi/ *adj.* (**-dier, -diest**) **1.** MARKED WITH MUD full of, covered in, or dirtied with mud **2.** RESEMBLING MUD like mud in being cloudy or thick **3.** LACKING CLARITY lacking clarity, brightness, or transparency ○ *a muddy colour* **4.** CONFUSED hard to understand or lacking in logical reasoning ■ *vt.* (**-dies, -dying, -died**) **1.** MAKE STH MUDDY to make sth muddy **2.** MAKE STH UNCLEAR to make sth confused and unclear —**muddily** *adv.* —**muddiness** *n.*

Mudéjar /moo dáy haar/ *n.* (*plural* **-jares** /-haa ress/) SPANISH MOOR a Moor who was allowed to stay in a part of Spain after it had been recaptured by the Christians ■ *adj.* OF THE SPANISH MOORS belonging to or typical of the Mudéjares, especially their style of architecture [Mid-19thC. From Spanish, from Arabic *mudajjan*, the past participle of *dajjana* 'to permit to stay'.]

mudfish /múd fish/ (*plural* **-fish** or **-fishes**) *n.* *US* a fish that lives in muddy waters, especially the bowfin

mud flap *n.* a flap attached behind the wheel of a vehicle to prevent mud and water from splashing up onto the vehicle, or to the vehicles following. US term **splashguard**

mudflat /múd flat/, **mud flat** *n.* an area of low muddy land that is underwater only at high tide, especially one near an estuary

mudflow /múd flō/ *n.* a fast-moving downhill flow of mud and soil loosened by rainfall or melting snow

mudguard /múd gaard/ *n.* a curved rigid arch above the wheel of a bicycle or motorcycle designed to cut down the amount of water or mud thrown up by the wheel. US term **fender**

mudlark /múd laark/ *n.* a child who lives on the streets and makes money by selling objects found in tidal mud (*archaic*) [Late 18thC. Humorous formation from MUD + LARK.]

mudpack /múd pak/ *n.* a beauty treatment for the face made of fuller's earth and additives that is allowed to dry before being removed

mud pie *n.* a mass of mud shaped by children as a game

mud puppy /múd puppi/, **mudpuppy** (*plural* **-pies**) *n.* an eastern North American salamander that lives on muddy banks and has dark red external gills. Genus: *Necturus*.

mudra /mə draa/ (*plural* **-dras**) *n.* any of the various symbolic positions in which the hands are held in Indian dancing and ritual [Early 19thC. From Sanskrit *mudrā* 'seal, sign'.]

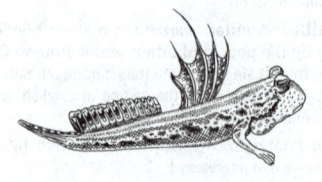

Mudskipper

mudskipper /múd skipər/ *n.* an Asian or African tropical fish of the goby family that can manoeuvre on land or climb roots on its pectoral fins to feed. Genera: *Periophthalmus* and *Boleophthalmus*.

mudslide /múd slīd/ *n.* a slow-moving and often destructive mass of mud flowing down a slope

mudslinging /múd slinging/ *n.* the making of defamatory remarks about sb, especially a political opponent or other competitor ○ *The level of debate in this election has seldom risen above petty mudslinging.* —**mudslinger** *n.*

mudstone /múd stōn/ *n.* a grey sedimentary rock formed from mud, similar to shale but with less developed lamination

mud turtle *n.* a small North and Central American freshwater turtle that lives at the bottom of muddy ponds and streams. Genus: *Kinosternon*.

mud volcano *n.* a conical mound of mud that forms around a hot spring or geyser

mud wasp *n. US* = **mud dauber**

Mueller /múllər, mülər/, **Sir Ferdinand Jakob Heinrich von, Baron** (1825–96) German-born Australian botanist and explorer. He was the author, with George Bentham, of *Flora Australiensis* (1863–78), and introduced the blue gum tree to Europe, North America, and Africa.

Muenster /múnstər, mo͞onstər/, **muenster, Munster, munster** *n.* a white to yellow semisoft mildly flavoured cheese that typically has an orange edible rind [Early 20thC. Named after the town of *Munster* in northeastern France, known for production of this cheese.]

muesli /myoŏzli/ *n.* an originally Swiss mixture of cereal flakes and rolled oats with dried fruit and nuts, eaten with milk for breakfast [Mid-20thC. From Swiss German, literally 'little purée', from German *Mus* 'purée'.]

muezzin /moo ézzin, myoo-/ *n.* a mosque official who calls Muslims to prayer from a minaret five times a day [Late 16thC. From a dialect variant of Arabic *mu'addin*, active participle of *'addana* 'to call to prayer', from *'udn* 'ear'.]

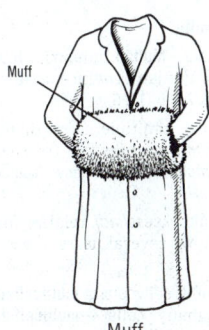

Muff

muff[1] /muf/ *n.* **1.** CLOTHES **FURRY CYLINDER** an open-ended cylinder of fur or cloth used for keeping hands warm, one hand going in at each end **2.** BIRDS **FOWL FEATHERS** either of the tufts of feathers on each side of the face of some fowl [Late 16thC. From Dutch *mof*, a shortening of Middle Dutch *moffel*, from medieval Latin *muffula* 'glove', of unknown origin.]

muff[2] /muf/ *vt.* (**muffs, muffing, muffed**) **1.** FAIL TO CATCH STH to fail to catch a ball or make a shot ○ *He got right under the ball and still muffed it.* **2.** DO STH BADLY to do sth badly or awkwardly ○ *The play got off to a bad start when the actors muffed the opening lines.* ■ *n.* **1.** FAILED ACTION a badly performed catch, shot, or action **2.** BUNGLER sb who is clumsy or bungles sth [Mid-19thC. Origin unknown.]

muffin /múffin/ *n.* **1.** SMALL BREAD ROLL a small round thick savoury cake (**griddle cake**) made from yeasted batter and usually served split, toasted, and buttered. US term **English muffin 2.** SMALL CAKE a small round cake for one person made from a thick batter and often containing fruit or nuts [Early 18thC. Origin uncertain: perhaps from Low German *muffen*, plural of *muffe* 'small cake'.]

muffle[1] /múff'l/ *vt.* (**-fles, -fling, -fled**) **1.** WRAP STH TO STIFLE SOUND to wrap or pad sth with material in order to deaden the sound it makes **2.** MAKE STH LESS LOUD to make a sound less loud ○ *He put his hands over his ears to muffle the noise of the sirens.* **3.** PREVENT STH BEING EXPRESSED to prevent sth from being said or written ○ *a government that sought to muffle all opposition* **4.** KEEP SB WARM to wrap sb or a part of sb's body in a garment or cloth for warmth ○ *She muffled*

herself up in a thick shawl. ■ *n.* **1.** STH MUFFLING A SOUND sth used to muffle a sound **2.** TYPE OF KILN a kiln in which objects being fired are protected from direct contact with the flames [15thC. Origin uncertain: possibly via Old French *moufler* from, ultimately, medieval Latin *muffula* 'glove', of unknown origin.]

muffle[2] /múff'l/ *n.* the moist fleshy hairless upper lip of some rodents and ruminants [Early 17thC. From French *mufle*, of unknown origin.]

muffled /múff'ld/ *adj.* **1.** NOT HEARD CLEARLY unable to be heard clearly because of being deadened or stifled ○ *There was a muffled cheer from the back of the audience.* **2.** WRAPPED TO STIFLE SOUND wrapped or padded with material in order to deaden the sound it is making ○ *The soldiers in the funeral procession marched to the beat of muffled drums.* [Late 16thC. Formed from MUFFLE[1].]

muffler /múfflər/ *n.* **1.** SCARF a scarf worn around the neck for warmth **2.** *US, ANZ* CAR PART a device attached to a car's exhaust pipe to reduce the amount of noise made by the engine **3.** = **muffle**[1] *n.* 1 [Mid-16thC. Formed from MUFFLE[1].]

mufti /múfti/ *n.* ordinary clothes when worn by sb who is normally in uniform [Early 19thC. Origin uncertain: perhaps a humorous use of MUFTI 'Muslim jurist'.]

Mufti /múfti, moŏfti/ *n.* an expert on Islamic religious law [Late 16thC. From Arabic *muftī*, past participle of *aftā* 'to decide a legal point'.]

mufti day *n.* a day on which school students are permitted to wear casual clothes rather than uniform, as a fundraising exercise

mug[1] /mug/ (**mugs, mugging, mugged**) *n.* **1.** DRINKING CUP a large round straight-sided cup typically made of earthenware and having a handle **2.** CONTENTS OF A MUG what a mug has in it, or the amount of liquid it can hold ○ *a mug of hot soup* [Early 16thC. Origin uncertain: possibly from Scandinavian.]

mug[2] /mug/ *n.* **1.** SB'S FACE sb's face or mouth (*informal*) **2.** UNINTELLIGENT PERSON sb who is unintelligent or easily deceived (*slang*) ■ *v.* (**mug, mugging, mugged**) **1.** *vt.* ROB SB to attack and rob sb, especially a pedestrian in a public place **2.** *vi.* MAKE FACES to make exaggerated facial expressions when performing or posing for a camera ○ *The actors were playing it for laughs, mugging in every scene.* ◇ **a mug's game** sth only gullible people would take part in (*informal*)

Robert Mugabe

Mugabe /moŏ gaábi/, **Robert** (b. 1924) Zimbabwean politician. After leading the struggle against the white government of Rhodesia, he became the first prime minister of Zimbabwe (1980–87) and president (1987–). Abandoning attempts to form a one-party state, he held multi-party elections in 1990. Full name **Robert Gabriel Mugabe**

mugful *n.* = **mug**[1] *n.* 2

mugger[1] /múggər/ *n.* sb who attacks and robs another in a public place

mugger[2] /múggər/, **muggar, muggur** *n.* a freshwater crocodile of India and Sri Lanka. Latin name: *Crocodylus palustris*. [Mid-19thC. From Hindi *magar*.]

mugging /múgging/ *n.* the crime of attacking and robbing sb

—— **WORD KEY: SYNONYMS** ——
See Synonyms at **theft**.

muggins /múgginz/ *n.* GULLIBLE PERSON a gullible person (*humorous insult*) ■ *pron.* NAME FOR GULLIBLE PERSON a

title people use to refer to themselves when they believe they are acting gullibly (*informal humorous*) ○ *I suppose muggins will have to come and pick you up?* [Mid-19thC. Origin uncertain: perhaps from the proper name *Muggins* in association with MUG in the sense 'gullible person'.]

muggy /múggi/ (**-gier, -giest**) *adj.* unpleasantly hot and humid [Mid-18thC. Ultimately from the obsolete and dialect form *mug* 'to rain lightly', of Scandinavian origin.] —**muggily** *adv.* —**mugginess** *n.*

Mughal *n.* HIST = **Mogul**

mug shot, mugshot *n.* a photograph of sb's face, especially one of a suspected criminal's face or profile taken by police

mug up *vti.* to study hard at a particular subject, especially in preparation for an exam (*informal*)

mugwort /múg wurt/ *n.* a herbaceous perennial wormwood that grows in temperate regions in the northern hemisphere and has aromatic leaves and small pale green flowers. Latin name: *Artemisia vulgaris*. [Old English *mucgwyrt*, from earlier forms of MIDGE + WORT]

mugwump /múg wump/ *n. US* sb who takes an independent or neutral stance, especially in politics [Mid-19thC. From Massachuset *mugquomp* 'war leader'.] —**mugwumpery** *n.* —**mugwumpish** *adj.* —**mugwumpism** *n.*

Muhammad /mə húmmid/, **Mohammed** (570?–632) Arabian founder of Islam. According to Islamic tradition he received his first command from Allah in 610. In 628 he made Mecca the religious capital of Islam. He recorded his visions and teachings in the Koran.

Muharram /moo hárrəm/, **Moharram** /mō-/ *n.* the first month of the Islamic calendar, made up of 30 days and falling around the same time as September to October [Early 19thC. From Arabic *muharram* 'inviolable', the past participle of *harrama* 'to forbid'.]

Muir /myoor/, **Edwin** (1887–1959) British poet, translator, and critic. His work reflected his interest in psychoanalysis and his native Scotland. He was important as a translator of Franz Kafka.

Muir, Jean Elizabeth (1933–96) British fashion designer. She was noted for the classic cut and fluid shape of her designs.

Muir Glacier /myoor-/ glacier in southeastern Alaska. It reaches the sea at Glacier Bay.

mujaheddin /moŏjəhə deén/, **mujahedeen, mujahideen, mujahidin** *npl.* Islamic guerrillas based in Iran and Pakistan who fought holy war (**jihad**) against the Soviet forces occupying Afghanistan in the late 1970s and the 1980s [Mid-20thC. From Persian or Arabic *mujāhidīn*, the plural of *mujāhid* 'one who fights a jihad'.]

mukluk /múk luk/, **muckluck** *n.* **1.** *US* LARGE BOOT a waterproof boot made of animal skin or canvas that is large enough to be worn over shoes or several pairs of socks **2.** INUIT SEALSKIN BOOT a sealskin boot originally worn by the Inuit [Mid-19thC. From Yupik *maklak* 'bearded seal', misunderstood as meaning 'sealskin' and then used as the name of the boot made of this material.]

mulatto /myoŏ láttō, moŏ-/ (*plural* **-tos** *or* **-toes**) *n.* (*dated offensive*) **1.** OFFENSIVE TERM REFERRING TO PARENTS' RACES an offensive term for sb who has one Black and one Caucasian parent **2.** REFERRING TO ANCESTORS' RACES an offensive term for sb who has both Black and Caucasian ancestors [Late 16thC. From Spanish *mulato* 'young mule', from *mulo* 'mule', from Latin *mulus* (source of English *mule*).]

mulberry /múlbəri/ *n.* (*plural* **-ries**) **1.** TREES TREE WITH EDIBLE PURPLE FRUIT a deciduous tree that grows in temperate regions with purplish edible fruit and leaves that are fed to silkworms. Genus: *Morus*. **2.** PURPLE FRUIT the fruit of the mulberry **3.** COLOURS PURPLE COLOUR a dark purple colour with a tinge of red or grey ■ *adj.* COLOURS OF DARK PURPLE of a dark purple colour tinged with red or grey [Old English *mōrberie*, from *mōr-*, from Latin *morum* 'mulberry', + BERRY]

Mulberry Harbour *n.* either of two preconstructed floating harbours that were towed across the English Channel to France as part of the Allied invasion in 1944

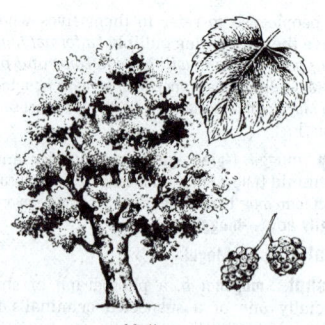

Mulberry

mulch /mulch/ *n.* SOIL COVERING a protective covering of organic material laid over the soil around plants to prevent erosion, retain moisture, and sometimes enrich the soil ■ *vti.* (**mulches, mulching, mulched**) COVER SOIL WITH MULCH to cover soil with mulch ○ *mulch with newspaper* [Mid-17thC. Origin uncertain: perhaps from Old English *melsc* 'soft'; ultimately from an Indo-European base meaning 'soft', which is also the ancestor of English *melt* and *mollify*.]

mulct /mulkt/ *vt.* (**mulcts, mulcting, mulcted**) (*archaic*) **1.** FINE SB to fine sb as a penalty **2.** CHEAT SB to cheat sb out of sth ■ *n.* PENALTY a fine or penalty (*archaic*) [15thC. From Latin *mulctare*, from *mulcta* 'fine'.]

Muldoon /mul doʻon/, **Sir Robert David** (*b.* 1921) New Zealand statesman. He was a National Party leader and prime minister of New Zealand (1975–84).

Mule

mule[1] /myool/ *n.* **1.** CROSS BETWEEN A HORSE AND DONKEY the offspring of a female horse and a male donkey **2.** HYBRID PLANT OR ANIMAL the sterile offspring of two closely related species of animal or plant **3.** STUBBORN PERSON sb who is very stubborn (*informal*) **4.** DRUG COURIER sb who transports illegal drugs for a dealer (*slang*) **5.** SPINNING MACHINE a machine that draws and spins cotton fibres into yarn and winds it onto spindles [Old English *mūl*, of uncertain origin: perhaps ultimately via Latin *mulus* from a pre-Latin language of the Mediterranean]

mule[2] /myool/ *n.* a backless slipper or shoe [Mid-16thC. Via French from Latin *mulleus (calceus)* 'reddish-purple (shoe)'. Ultimately from an Indo-European base meaning 'having dark colour', which is also the ancestor of English *mullet* and *melano-*.]

mule deer *n.* a large deer of western North America that has a greyish-brown coat, some white underparts, a black tail, and long ears. Latin name: *Odocoileus hemionus.*

muleta /myoo léttə/ (*plural* **-tas**) *n.* a short red cape attached to a stick that a matador uses instead of the full cape in the final stages of a bullfight [Mid-19thC. From Spanish, a diminutive of *mula* 'female mule', from, ultimately, Latin *mulus* 'mule' (see MULE[1]).]

muleteer /myoolə teʻer/ *n.* sb whose occupation is driving mules [Mid-16thC. From French *muletier*, from *mulet*, a diminutive of Old French *mul* 'mule', from Latin *mulus* (see MULE[1]).]

muley /myooli/ *adj.* HORNLESS having no horns ■ *n.* (*plural* **-leys**) HORNLESS ANIMAL an animal that does not have horns [Late 16thC. Origin uncertain: probably from Irish *maol* or Welsh *moel* 'bald'; ultimately from an Indo-European base meaning 'to cut', which is also the ancestor of English *mite*.]

mulga /múlgə/ *n.* **1.** AUSTRALIAN ACACIA an acacia tree that grows in arid regions of Australia **2.** *Aus* ARID AREA an arid part of Australia where mulga trees are the most common vegetation ○ *His car broke down out in the mulga.* [Mid-19thC. From Aboriginal.]

mulga snake *n.* a large aggressive brown or tan snake found throughout the Australian interior. Latin name: *Pseudechis australis.*

Mulhacen /moʻola tháyn/ the highest peak on the Spanish mainland, situated in the Sierra Nevada, about 32 km/20 mi. southeast of Granada. Height: 3,478 m/11,411 ft.

Mulhouse /mü looz/ industrial city in Haut-Rhin Department, Alsace Region, northeastern France. Population: 108,357 (1990).

muliebrity /myooli ébbriti/ *n.* (*literary*) **1.** BEING A WOMAN the condition of being a woman **2.** CONVENTIONALLY WOMANLY QUALITIES the qualities conventionally associated with women [Late 16thC. From Latin *muliebritas*, from, ultimately, *mulier* 'woman'.]

mulish /myoʻolish/ *adj.* obstinate and unwilling to cooperate or listen to suggestions [Mid-18thC. Formed from MULE[1].] —**mulishly** *adv.* —**mulishness** *n.*

mull[1] /mul/ *n.* a period of deep thought [Mid-19thC. Origin uncertain: perhaps from obsolete and dialect *mull* 'to pulverize'; ultimately from an Indo-European base meaning 'to crush', which is also the ancestor of English *meal*.] **mull over** *vti.* to consider sth thoroughly

mull[2] /mul/ (**mulls, mulling, mulled**) *vt.* to heat, sweeten, and flavour wine, beer, or cider [Early 17thC. Origin unknown.]

mull[3] /mul/ *n.* soft cotton muslin used in dresses [Late 17thC. Shortening of Hindi *malmal*.]

mull[4] /mul/ *n.* nonacidic humus on a forest floor that eventually integrates into the soil beneath it [Early 20thC. From Danish *muld* 'mould'.]

mull[5] /mul/ *n.* Scotland GEOG a promontory (*often used in placenames*) [14thC]

Mull /mul/ island in the Inner Hebrides, western Scotland. Population: 2,078 (1991). Area: 925 sq. km/353 sq. mi.

mullah /múllə, moolə/ *n.* **1.** MUSLIM SCHOLAR in Iran and Central Asia, a Muslim cleric who specializes in the interpretation of Islamic religious law **2.** MAN'S TITLE used in Iran and Central Asia as a term of respect for a Muslim man who is thought to be very wise [Early 17thC. Via Persian or Urdu *mullā* from, ultimately, Arabic *mawlā*.]

mullein /múllin/ *n.* a tall plant that grows in Europe and Asia and has spikes of yellow, lavender, or white flowers and hairy leaves. Genus: *Verbascum.* [15thC. From Old French *moleine*, of uncertain origin: perhaps from a prehistoric Celtic word meaning 'yellow'.]

muller /múllər/ *n.* a heavy smooth object made of stone, metal, wood, or glass, used for grinding paints or drugs on a flat surface [14thC. Origin uncertain: perhaps from Anglo-Norman *moldre* 'to grind', from, ultimately, Latin *molere* (see MOLAR).]

Müller /múllər, myoʻolər/, **Paul Hermann** (1899–1965) Swiss chemist. He demonstrated the insecticidal properties of DDT, which was widely used from the 1940s to the 1970s.

Müllerian mimicry /moo leʻeri ən–/ *n.* mimicry in which two or more animals that are inedible or harmful assume one another's appearance so that predators will leave them alone [Late 19thC. Named after J. F. T. Müller (1821–97), the German-born Brazilian zoologist who described the phenomenon.]

Müller-Lyer illusion /moʻolər lí̄ ər–/ *n.* an optical illusion in which a line with inward-pointing arrows is seen as longer than one of equal length with outward-pointing arrows [Late 19thC. *Müller-Lyer* after Franz Carl Müller-Lyer (1857–1916), German sociologist and philosopher.]

mullet /múllit/ *n.* **1.** (*plural* **-lets** *or* **-let**) EDIBLE FISH an edible spiny small-mouthed fish that lives in fresh water or salt water and is found all over the world. Family: Mugilidae and Mullidae. **2.** LONG HAIRSTYLE a hairstyle that is long at the back and short at the front and sides [15thC. From Old French *mulet*, from

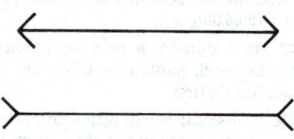

Müller-Lyer illusion

mul, from Latin *mullus* 'red mullet', from Greek *mullos* 'a sea-fish'.]

mulligatawny /múlligə táwni/ (*plural* **-nies**) *n.* a spicy meat and vegetable soup originally from eastern India [Late 18thC. From Tamil *milaku-tanni,* literally 'pepper-water'.]

Mullingar /múlling gaʻar/ town in Westmeath, central Republic of Ireland, situated about 74 km/46 mi. west of Dublin. Population: 8,003 (1991).

mullion /múllyən/ *n.* a vertical piece of stone, metal, or wood that divides the panes of a window or the panels of a screen [Mid-16thC. Variant (through the exchange of letters) of obsolete *monial* 'mullion', from Anglo-Norman *moinel,* literally 'middle (part)', from *moien* 'in the middle, median'.] —**mullioned** *adj.*

mullite /múllīt/ *n.* a colourless mineral consisting of crystalline aluminium silicate, able to withstand corrosion and very high temperatures [Early 20thC. Coined from MULL, where the mineral was first identified + -ITE.]

mult- *prefix.* = **multi-**

Multan /moʻol taʻan/, **Multān** industrial town, district, and division of Punjab Province, eastern Pakistan. Population: 1,257,000 (1995).

multi- *prefix.* many, multiple, more than one or two ○ *multilevel* ○ *multiparous* [Via Old French from, ultimately, Latin *multus* 'much, many' (source of English *multitude*)]

multiaccess /múlti áksess/ *adj.* relating to a computer system that allows several users to access it at the same time

multicellular /múlti séllyoolər/, **multicelled** /-séld/ *adj.* consisting of many cells —**multicellularity** /múlti séllyoo lárrəti/ *n.*

multichannel communication /múlti chánn'l–/ *n.* the existence or use of two or more communication channels over the same path, e.g. in radio transmission or within a communication cable

multicolour /múlti kulər/, **multicoloured** /-kulərd/ *adj.* of many different colours

multicultural /múlti kúlchərəl/ *adj.* **1.** OF MORE THAN ONE CULTURE relating to, consisting of, or participating in the cultures of different countries, ethnic groups, or religions **2.** SUPPORTING INTEGRATION advocating or encouraging the integration of people of different countries, ethnic groups, and religions into all areas of society —**multiculturalism** *n.* —**multiculturalist** *n.*

multidimensional /múlti di ménsh'nəl, -dī–/ *adj.* **1.** WITH MORE THAN THREE DIMENSIONS relating to or having more than three dimensions **2.** WITH MANY DIFFERENT ASPECTS having several different aims, qualities, or aspects —**multidimensionality** /múlti di mensh'nə nálləti, -dī–/ *n.*

multidirectional /múltidi réksh'nəl, -dī–/ *adj.* **1.** WITH SEVERAL AIMS OR CONCERNS having several aims or covering several aspects of a situation **2.** ELEC ENG CO-VERING SEVERAL DIFFERENT DIRECTIONS going, operating, or pointing in several different directions

multidisciplinary /múlti díssə plinəri/, **multidiscipline** /-plin/ *adj.* studying or using several specialized subjects or skills

multiethnic /múlti éthnik/ *adj.* relating to or including several different ethnic groups

multifaceted /múlti fássitid/ *adj.* **1.** WITH DIVERSE QUALITIES with many different talents, qualities, or features

2. WITH MANY FACETS having many facets or cut surfaces

multifactorial /múlti fak táwri əl/, **multifactor** /múlti fáktər/ *adj.* **1. WITH MULTIPLE FACTORS** involving several different factors or elements **2. DEPENDING ON MULTIPLE GENES** relating to or used to describe inheritance depending on more than one gene. Height and weight are examples of characters determined by multifactorial inheritance. —**multifactorially** *adv.*

multifarious /múlti fáiri əss/ *adj.* including parts, things, or people of many different kinds [Late 16thC. From Latin *multifarius* 'varied, diverse', from *multi-* 'many' + the suffix *-farius* 'doing', a relative of *facere* 'to do'.] —**multifariously** *adv.* —**multifariousness** *n.*

multifid /múltifid/, **multifidous** /mul tíffidəss/ *adj.* having many lobe-shaped segments

multiflora rose /múlti fláwrə-/ *n.* a wild climbing rose, native to Asia, that has clusters of small fragrant flowers. It is the origin of many cultivated roses. Latin name: *Rosa multiflora.*

multifoil /múlti foyl/ *n.* in architecture, a flat shape, opening, or decorative design with many lobes or scallops at its edges

multigrain /múlti grayn/ *adj.* used to describe bread that is made from several different types of grain

multigravida /múlti grávvidə/ *n.* a pregnant woman who has had at least one previous pregnancy. ◊ **primigravida**

multigym /múlti jim/ *n.* an exercise apparatus with a range of weights, used for muscle toning [Late 20thC]

multihull /múlti hul/ *n.* a sailing vessel with two or more hulls

multilateral /múlti láttərəl/ *adj.* **1. INVOLVING SEVERAL PARTIES** involving more than two parties or countries **2.** GEOM **MANY-SIDED** having many sides [Late 17thC. From medieval Latin *multilateralis*, from Latin *multi-* 'many' + *lateralis* 'belonging to the side' (see LATERAL).] —**multilaterally** *adv.*

multilateralism /múlti láttərə lizəm/ *n.* the principle or belief that several nations should be cooperatively involved in the process of achieving sth, especially nuclear disarmament [Early 20thC] —**multilateralist** *n., adj.*

multilingual /múlti líng gwəl/ *adj.* **1. SPEAKING SEVERAL LANGUAGES** able to speak more than two languages fluently **2. INVOLVING SEVERAL LANGUAGES** written in, expressed in, or using more than two languages —**multilingualism** *n.* —**multilingually** *adv.*

multimedia /múlti meédi ə/ *n.* **1.** COMPUT **SOUND AND VIDEO ON COMPUTERS** programs, software, and hardware capable of using a wide variety of media such as film, video, and music as well as text and numbers **2.** ARTS **USE OF VARIOUS MATERIALS AND MEDIA** the use in art, especially the plastic arts, of different kinds of materials and media such as television, sound, and text (*often used before a noun*) **3.** MARKETING **USE OF ALL COMMUNICATIONS MEDIA** the use in advertising of a combination of media such as television, radio, and the press (*often used before a noun*) **4.** EDUC **USE OF MEDIA IN TEACHING** the use of film, video, and music in addition to more traditional teaching materials and methods (*often used before a noun*)

multimeter /múlti meetər/ *n.* an instrument that reads and measures the values of several different electrical parameters such as current, voltage, and resistance

multimillionaire /múlti míllyə náir/ *n.* sb with money or assets worth several million dollars or pounds

multinational /múlti násh'nəl/ *adj.* **1. OPERATING IN SEVERAL COUNTRIES** operating or having investments in several countries **2. INVOLVING PEOPLE FROM SEVERAL COUNTRIES** relating to or including people from more than two countries ■ *n.* **LARGE COMPANY OPERATING IN SEVERAL COUNTRIES** a large company that operates or has investments in several different countries —**multinationalism** *n.*

multinomial /múlti nṓmi əl/ *n., adj.* MATH = **polynomial**

multinuclear /múlti nyoókli ər/, **multinucleate** /-ət/ *adj.* having more than two nuclei

multipack /múlti pak/ *n.* a packet that contains more than two of a particular item of consumer goods, e.g. batteries, and is sold at a reduced price

multipara /mul típpərə/ (*plural* **-rae** /-ree/) *n.* a woman who has borne a live child from each of two or more pregnancies [Mid-19thC. From the feminine form of modern Latin *multiparus* (see MULTIPAROUS).]

multiparous /mul típpərəss/ *adj.* **1.** BIOL **PRODUCING SEVERAL YOUNG AT ONE TIME** used to describe an animal, especially a mammal, that normally gives birth to two or more offspring at one time **2.** MED **HAVING BORNE AT LEAST TWO CHILDREN** used to describe a woman who has borne a child from each of two or more pregnancies, each pregnancy lasting for at least 20 weeks [Mid-17thC. From modern Latin *multiparus*, from Latin *multi-* 'many' + *-parus* '-bearing' (see -PAROUS).] —**multiparity** /múlti párrəti/ *n.*

multipartite /múlti paár tīt/ *adj.* **1. WITH MANY SECTIONS** divided into many sections **2.** POL **INVOLVING SEVERAL PARTIES** involving more than two parties or countries

multipath /múlti paath/ *adj.* relating to or used to describe television or radio signals that use more than one route from the transmitter to the receiver, causing picture or sound distortion

multiphase /múlti fayz/ *adj.* = **polyphase** —**multiphasic** /múlti fáyzik/ *adj.*

multiplane /múlti playn/ *n.* an aircraft with more than one pair of wings

multiple /múltip'l/ *adj.* **INVOLVING SEVERAL THINGS** involving or including several things, people, or parts ■ *n.* **1.** MATH **NUMBER DIVISIBLE BY ANOTHER** a number that can be divided exactly by a particular smaller number **2.** TELECOM **SYSTEM WITH MANY POSSIBLE ACCESS POINTS** a system of wiring so arranged that a group of communication lines are accessible at a number of points **3.** = **multiple store** [Mid-17thC. Via French from late Latin *multiplus*, an alteration of Latin *multiplex* (see MULTIPLEX).]

multiple alleles *npl.* three or more different forms of a gene. Any two of these forms can be present in a normal diploid cell or organism.

multiple-choice *adj.* requiring the choice of the correct answer or answers out of several possible suggested answers ○ *a multiple-choice question*

multiple factor *n.* a polygene (*dated*)

multiple fission *n.* a form of asexual reproduction occurring in some single-celled organisms such as malaria parasites in which a single parent cell breaks up to yield numerous daughter cells. The nucleus of the parental cell divides to form many daughter nuclei, then the cytoplasm divides to form the daughter cells.

multiple fruit *n.* a fruit such as a pineapple or fig that is produced from the ovaries of several flowers that merge to form a single structure

multiple myeloma, multiple myelomatosis *n.* a form of cancer of the bone marrow characterized by swellings, deformities, and fractures of various bones and accompanied by pain, anaemia, and weight loss. It affects the plasma cells that produce antibodies and can be diagnosed by the presence of abnormal proteins in the blood.

multiple personality *n.* a very rare psychological disorder in which sb appears to have two or more distinct, independent, and often complex personalities that are present at different times and dominate behaviour. It is a form of dissociative disorder.

multiple sclerosis *n.* a serious progressive disease of the central nervous system, occurring mainly in young adults and thought to be caused by a malfunction of the immune system. It leads to the loss of myelin in the brain or spinal cord and causes muscle weakness, poor eyesight, slow speech, and some inability to move.

multiple shop *n.* = **multiple store**

multiple star *n.* a group of three or more stars, usually with the same gravitational centre, that appears as one star to the naked eye

multiple store, multiple shop, multiple *n.* any of several retail outlets that are owned or managed by the same person or team. = **chain store**

multiplet /múlti plet/ *n.* **1. SPECTRAL LINE** a line in a spectrum made up of two or more component lines, caused by slight variations in atomic or molecular energy levels **2. GROUP OF RELATED ELEMENTARY PARTICLES** a group of elementary particles such as nucleons that have a different electric charge but have otherwise similar properties [Early 20thC. Coined from MULTIPLE, on the model of 'doublet', 'triplet'.]

multiple unit *n.* a passenger train with engines or motors in or beneath the coaches that require no separate locomotive

multiple voting *n.* the practice of voting in more than one constituency in an election

multiplex /múlti pleks/ *n.* **1.** CINEMA **CINEMA COMPLEX** a large cinema complex that has several separate units with screens as well as other facilities such as a restaurant or bar **2.** ELECTRON ENG **MULTIPLE TRANSMISSION** the simultaneous transmission of two or more signals along one communications channel **3.** ELECTRON ENG **SYSTEM FOR SIMULTANEOUS TRANSMISSION** a transmission system that carries two or more individual channels over a single communication path ■ *adj.* **COMPLEX** involving or including several different things, parts, or factors ■ *vti.* (**-plexes, -plexing, -plexed**) ELECTRON ENG **SEND BY MULTIPLEX** to send two or more messages or signals along one communications channel at the same time [Mid-16thC. From Latin, formed from *multi-* 'many' + *-plex* '-fold' (see -PLEX).]

multiplexer /múlti pleksər/, **multiplexor** *n.* **1.** COMPUT **DEVICE FOR ROUTING DATA** a device for sending several different data streams down a single communications line and for splitting a received multiple stream into component parts **2.** VIDEO **FILM-TO-VIDEO SYSTEM** a device for transferring projected film to video

multiplicand /múltipli kánd/ *n.* a number that is multiplied by another number (**multiplier**). The number 2 is the multiplicand in the statement 2 × 4 = 8. [Late 16thC. From medieval Latin *multiplicandus*, the gerundive of Latin *multiplicare* (see MULTIPLY).]

multiplicate /múltipli kayt/ *adj.* containing many elements or parts [15thC. From Latin *multiplicat-*, the past participle stem of *multiplicare* (see MULTIPLY).]

multiplication /múltipli káysh'n/ *n.* **1.** MATH **ARITHMETIC OPERATION** a mathematical operation, symbolized by ×, that for integers is equivalent to adding a number to itself a particular number of times **2.** MATH **MATHEMATICAL OPERATION** a mathematical operation equivalent to multiplication extended to expressions that are not numbers, e.g. functions or matrices **3. INCREASE** a marked increase in the number or amount of sth ○ *a multiplication of claims* **4.** BIOL **REPRODUCTION** the act or process of reproduction in animals, plants, or people —**multiplicational** *adj.*

multiplication sign *n.* the symbol × or ·, used to indicate that one number is to be multiplied by another

multiplicative /múlti plíkətiv/ *adj.* **1. INCREASING** likely to increase, or capable of increasing **2.** MATH **INVOLVING MULTIPLICATION** involving or relating to multiplication —**multiplicatively** *adv.*

multiplicity /múlti plíssəti/ (*plural* **-ties**) *n.* **1. GREAT VARIETY** a considerable number or variety ○ *Her style was shaped by a multiplicity of influences.* **2. COMPLEXITY** the state of being multiple or varied **3.** PHYS **NUMBER OF MOLECULAR ENERGY LEVELS** the number of energy levels of a molecule, atom, or nucleus that result from interactions between angular momenta **4.** PHYS **PARTICLES IN A MULTIPLET** the number of elementary particles that form a multiplet [15thC. From late Latin *multiplicatus*, from Latin *multiplic-*, the stem of *multiplex* (see MULTIPLEX).]

multiplier /múlti plī ər/ *n.* **1. SB OR STH THAT MULTIPLIES** sb who or sth that multiplies or increases **2.** MATH **MULTIPLYING NUMBER** the number by which another number (**multiplicand**) is multiplied, e.g. the number 4 is the multiplier in the statement 2 × 4 = 8 **3.** PHYS = **photomultiplier**

multiply[1] /múlti plī/ (**-plies, -plying, -plied**) *v.* **1.** *vti.* MATH **PERFORM MULTIPLICATION** to perform the mathematical operation of multiplication **2.** *vti.* **INCREASE IN AMOUNT** to increase or make sth increase by a considerable number, amount, or degree **3.** *vi.* BIOL **BREED** to increase in number by breeding [12thC. Via French *multiplier* from Latin *multiplicare*, from the stem *multiplic-*

(see MULTIPLICITY).] —**multipliable** adj. —**multiplicable** /múlti plikəb'l/ adj.

multiply² /múltipli/ adv. many times or in many different ways

multipolar /múlti pólər/ adj. **1.** ANAT WITH MANY CONNECTIONS used to describe a nerve cell with more than two of the connecting fibres that carry impulses into the cell body **2.** WITH MULTIPLE POLES having several poles —**multipolarity** /múlti pō lárrəti/ n.

multiport /múlti pawrt/ adj. used to describe a computer network with more than one point of access or connection

multipotent /mul típpətənt/, **multipotential** /múltipə ténsh'l/ adj. capable of developing into various types of cell, depending on the surrounding conditions

multiprocessing /múlti pró sessing/ n. the operation of a computer in which two or more processing units work on separate parts of the same program or set of instructions in order to reduce processing time

multiprocessor /múlti pró sessər/ n. a system of linked central processing units on which two or more programs can be run simultaneously by parallel processing

multipronged /múlti próngd/ adj. **1.** WITH MULTIPLE ELEMENTS involving several different approaches or elements **2.** WITH MULTIPLE PRONGS having several prongs

multipurpose /múlti púrpəss/ adj. designed or able to be used for several different purposes

multiracial /múlti ráysh'l/ adj. relating to, made up of, or involving people from several races ○ a multiracial society —**multiracially** adv.

multiracialism /múlti ráysh'l izəm/ n. the principle or practice of ensuring that people of various races are fully integrated into a society —**multiracialist** adj.

multirole /múlti rōl/ adj. having several roles or functions

multiscreen /múlti skreen/ adj. with several screens for showing films, videos, or slides

multisense /múlti senss/ adj. having many different meanings

multisensory /múlti sénssəri/ adj. relating to or involving two or more of the senses

multistage /múlti stayj/ adj. **1.** IN SEVERAL STAGES divided into or taking place in several separate stages **2.** WITH SEVERAL SOURCES OF MOTION having several propulsion units, each of which operates sequentially ○ a multistage rocket

multistage rocket n. a rocket with two or more propulsion units that are used and discarded in succession

multistorey /múlti stáwri/ adj. WITH SEVERAL LEVELS having several storeys ■ n. (plural -storeys) A MULTISTOREY CAR PARK a car park on several levels (informal)

multitasking /múlti taasking/ n. the simultaneous management of two or more distinct tasks by a computer

multitrack /múlti trak/ adj. using, capable of, or produced by the separate recording of several different tracks

multitude /múlti tyood/ n. **1.** CROWD a large crowd of people **2.** LARGE NUMBER a very large number of things or people (often used in the plural) **3.** MAJORITY the majority of ordinary people [14thC. Via French from Latin multitudo, from multus 'much, many' (see MULTI-).]

multitudinous /múlti tyoódinəss/ adj. **1.** VERY NUMEROUS very great in number **2.** FULL OF VARIETY with many parts, great in number, or existing in many varieties **3.** CROWDED crowded with people (archaic) [Early 17thC. Formed from Latin multitudin-, the stem of multitudo (see MULTITUDE).] —**multitudinously** adv. —**multitudinousness** n.

multiuser /múlti yoózər/ adj. capable of being used by several people at the same time

multivalent /múlti váylənt/ adj. **1.** = **polyvalent** adj. 1 **2.** WITH MULTIPLE MEANINGS with several meanings or values —**multivalence** n.

multivariate /múlti váiri ət/, **multivariable** /-váiri əb'l/ adj. used to describe or relating to a statistical distribution that involves a number of random but often related variables

multivibrator /múlti vī bráytər/ n. an oscillating electronic circuit consisting of pairs of tubes, transistors, or other components, whose oscillation is sustained by coupling the output of one to the input of the other

multivocal /múlti vók'l/ adj. with many different and valid meanings or interpretations (formal)

multivolume /múlti vóllyoom/ adj. published in several volumes

multum in parvo /móoltoom in paárvō/ n. the quality or fact of containing, implying, or expressing much in a little space or time [From Latin, 'much in little']

mum¹ /mum/ n. mother (informal) US term **mom** [Mid-17thC. Partly (especially in early use) a variant of MAM and partly a shortening of MUMMY.]

mum² /mum/ adj. saying nothing, especially about a sensitive piece of information (informal) [15thC. An imitation of the sound made when the lips are closed.]

mum³ /mum/ (**mums, mumming, mummed**), **mumm** (**mumms, mumming, mummed**) vi. **1.** ACT IN A PLAY to act in a masked folk play or mime **2.** CELEBRATE IN DISGUISE to participate in festivities wearing a mask or disguise [Mid-16thC. From French momer 'to act in a mime' (see MUMMER).]

mum⁴ /mum/ n. a strong beer of German origin (archaic) [Early 17thC. From German Mumme.]

Mumbai /móom bī/ capital of Maharashtra State and the largest city in India, situated on the Arabian Sea. Population: 9,925,891 (1991). Former name **Bombay**

mumble /múmb'l/ vti (**-bles, -bling, -bled**) **1.** MUTTER to speak or utter sth quietly and unclearly without opening the mouth very much **2.** CHEW WITH DIFFICULTY to chew food with difficulty ■ n. INDISTINCT SPEECH an indistinct and quiet utterance [14thC. Formed from earlier English mum 'to make an indistinct sound with closed lips'. Also, probably thought to be imitative of the sound of mumbling.] —**mumbler** n. —**mumbling** adj. —**mumblingly** adv.

mumbo jumbo /múmbō júmbō/ n. **1.** CONFUSING LANGUAGE complicated and confusing language, especially technical jargon, that is difficult to understand (informal) **2.** WORTHLESS RELIGIOUS BELIEF OR RITUAL religious beliefs, language, or rituals that appear pointless or meaningless to the speaker (disapproving) (offensive in some contexts) **3.** OBJECT BELIEVED SUPERNATURAL an object or effigy that is believed to hold supernatural powers [Mid-18thC. Origin uncertain: perhaps from Mande mama 'ancestor' + dyumbo 'pompomwearer'; originally applied to a masked figure worshipped by the Mande peoples of West Africa.]

mumchance /múm chaanss/ adj. not speaking, or unable to speak (archaic) [Early 16thC. From Middle Low German mummenschanze 'game of dice, masked serenade', from mummen 'mask' + Old French chëance 'chance'. 'Silent' came from the idea of acting in mime.]

mu meson n. = **muon**

mumm vt. = **mum³**

mummer /múmmər/ n. **1.** ACTOR one of a group of actors in a pantomime, folk play, or mime show **2.** SB WHO CELEBRATES IN DISGUISE sb who participates in festivities wearing a mask or disguise **3.** MIME ARTIST an artist who performs in mimes **4.** ACTOR an actor (humorous) [15thC. From Old French momeur, from momer 'to act in a mime', perhaps ultimately of prehistoric Germanic origin.]

Mummerset /múmmər set/ n. a stereotypical West Country accent used in drama [Mid-20thC. Probably a blend of MUMMER and Somerset, a county in the west of England.]

mummery /múmməri/ (plural **-ies**) n. **1.** PERFORMANCE BY MUMMERS a performance by a group of mummers **2.** SHOWY CEREMONY a showy or hypocritical ceremony (disapproving)

mummify /múmmi fī/ (**-fies, -fying, -fied**) v. **1.** vt. PRESERVE CORPSE FOR BURIAL to preserve the corpse of a person or animal for burial by embalming it and wrapping it in cloth **2.** vti. SHRIVEL to dry out and shrivel, or cause sth to dry out and shrivel **3.** vt. PRESERVE AGAINST NATURAL TENDENCY to preserve sth such as an old custom

or an institution just for the sake of it and without making any effort to keep it alive [Early 17thC. Formed from MUMMY¹ on the model of French momifier.] —**mummification** /múmmifi káysh'n/ n.

Mummy: Detail of wall painting in the tomb of Sennudjem, Deir-el-Medinah, near Luxor, Egypt (1295–1186BC)

mummy¹ /múmmi/ (plural **-mies**) n. **1.** PRESERVED BODY the body of a person or animal that has been embalmed and wrapped in cloth, especially as was the custom in ancient Egypt **2.** NATURALLY PRESERVED BODY the body of an organism preserved by natural processes, e.g. by burial in peat or ice [Early 17thC. Via Old French momie from, ultimately, Arabic mūmiyā 'embalmed body', perhaps formed from Persian mūm 'wax'.]

mummy² /múmmi/ (plural **-mies**) n. mother (usually used by or to children) US term **mommy** [Late 18thC. Dialectal variant of MAMMY.]

mummy's boy n. a boy or man who is considered to be weak and cowardly (insult) US term **mama's boy**

mumps /mumps/ n. an acute contagious disease, usually affecting children, that causes a fever with swelling of the salivary glands, sometimes also affecting the pancreas and ovaries or testes. It is caused by a virus and can be prevented through vaccination. It may cause sterility if contracted by a man. (takes a singular or plural verb) [Late 16thC. Plural of the obsolete noun mump 'grimace', an imitation of the sounds made with a closed mouth.]

mums and dads /múmz ən dádz/ npl. Aus the uninformed general public, especially investors who know nothing about the stock market (informal)

mumsy /múmzi/ (**-sier, -siest**) adj. **1.** DOWDY unfashionable and dowdy (informal) **2.** MOTHERLY kind and motherly in a gentle sweet-natured way [Late 19thC. Formed from MUM¹; 'dowdy' from the stereotype of the drab-looking housewife.]

mumu n. = **muumuu**

munch /munch/ (**munches, munching, munched**) vti. to chew food purposefully, usually with visible movements of the jaw and sometimes with a crunching sound [14thC. Origin uncertain: perhaps via Old French mangier 'to eat' from Latin manducare 'to chew'.] —**muncher** n.

Edvard Munch

Munch /moongk/, **Edvard** (1863–1944) Norwegian painter. His work, suffused with melancholy and anguish, most famously in The Scream (1893), anticipates expressionism.

Münchausen /múnch owz'n/ n. **1.** TALL STORY a fantastic story full of exaggeration, told to impress people **2.** FANTASIST sb who makes up fantastic stories in order to impress others [Mid-19thC. Named after the eponymous hero, Baron *Münchausen*, of a book of impossible adventures (1785) written in English by the German author Rudolf Eric Raspe.]

Münchausen syndrome /mún chowz'n-/ *n.* a psychological disorder in which sb pretends to have a serious illness in order to undergo testing or treatment or be admitted to hospital. In Münchausen syndrome by proxy, medical attention is sought for sb else, who is sometimes harmed by attempts to create an illness to warrant such attention. [From Baron *Münchausen*, hero of exaggerated traveller's tales in a book (1785) by R. E. Raspe.]

munchies /múnchiz/ *npl.* a craving for snack food (*informal*)

munchkin /múnchkin/ *n. US* (*informal*) 1. CHILD a small child 2. INSIGNIFICANT PERSON an insignificant person who keeps busy with trivial matters [Late 20thC. From the name of creatures invented by L. Frank Baum in *The Wizard of Oz* (1900).]

Muncie /múnssi/ city in eastern Indiana, on the White River, southwest of Fort Wayne and northeast of Indianapolis. Population: 69,058 (1996).

Munda /móŏndə/ *n.* 1. LANG INDIAN LANGUAGE GROUP one of the four major Indian language groups spoken throughout the Indian subcontinent. Over 5 million people speak a Munda language. 2. PEOPLES SPEAKER OF MUNDA sb who speaks Munda as a native language [Mid-19thC. From Munda *Muṇḍā*.] —**Munda** *adj.*

mundane /mun dáyn/ *adj.* 1. ORDINARY commonplace, not unusual, and often boring 2. OF THIS WORLD relating to matters of this world [15thC. Via French *mondain* from late Latin *mundanus*, from Latin *mundus* 'world'.] —**mundanely** *adv.* —**mundaneness** *n.*

munga /múng gə/ *n. ANZ* an army canteen (*informal*) [Early 20thC. Origin uncertain: perhaps from French *manger* 'to eat' or the Italian imperative *mangia* 'eat!'.]

mung bean /múng-/ *n.* 1. FOOD GREEN OR YELLOW BEAN a small green or yellow bean that is dried, sometimes split, and used in Indian cookery. It is also germinated to produce bean sprouts. 2. PLANTS BEAN PLANT a bean plant native to eastern Asia that produces mung beans and is used as food for livestock. Latin name: *Vigna radiata*. [*Mung* from Hindi *mūng*]

mungo /múng gō/ (*plural* **-gos** *or* **-goes**), **mongo** (*plural* **-gos** *or* **-goes**), **mongoe** *n.* a cheap fabric made from waste wool and rags [Mid-19thC. Origin uncertain: perhaps formed from dialectal *mong* 'mixture', possibly on the model of the Scottish forename *Mungo*.]

Mungo, Lake /múng gō/ dry lake in western New South Wales, Australia. It is part of Mungo National Park.

Munich /myóŏnikh/ capital and largest city in the state of Bavaria, southeastern Germany. Population: 1,251,100 (1994).

Munich Conference *n.* a meeting concerning Germany's occupation of Czechoslovakia in 1938, at which Western leaders agreed to the division of Czechoslovakia after receiving Hitler's assurances that he would take no more land

municipal /myoŏ níssip'l/ *adj.* relating to a town, city, or region that has its own local government [Mid-16thC. Directly or via French from Latin *municipalis*, from the stem *municip-* 'holder of a civic office', from *munus* 'gift, service, duty' (see MUNIFICENT) + *capere* 'to take' (see CAPABLE).] —**municipalism** *n.* —**municipalist** *n.* —**municipally** *adv.*

municipalise *vt.* = municipalize

municipality /myoŏ níssi pálləti/ (*plural* **-ties**) *n.* 1. PLACE WITH OWN LOCAL GOVERNMENT a city, town, or other region that has its own local government 2. MEMBERS OF LOCAL GOVERNMENT the appointed or elected members of a local government

— WORD KEY: SYNONYMS —
See Synonyms at *city*.

municipalize /myoŏ níssipə līz/ (**-izes**, **-izing**, **-ized**), **municipalise** (**-ises**, **-ising**, **-ised**) *vt.* 1. BRING STH UNDER MUNICIPAL CONTROL to bring sth such as a public service or area of land under the ownership or control of a city, town, or region with its own local government 2. MAKE PLACE A MUNICIPALITY to grant a city, town, or

---

region powers of government on local matters — **municipalization** /myoŏ níssipə līt záysh'n/ *n.*

munificent /myoŏ níffiss'nt/ *adj.* 1. VERY GENEROUS very generous in giving 2. AMPLE characterized by generosity ○ *a munificent award* [Late 16thC. From Latin, formed from *munificus* 'generous', from *munus* 'gift, service, duty' (source also of English *municipal* and *remunerate*).] —**munificence** *n.* —**munificently** *adv.*

— WORD KEY: SYNONYMS —
See Synonyms at *generous*.

muniment /myoŏnímənt/ *n.* MIL PROTECTION sth providing defence or protection (*archaic*) ■ **muniments** *npl.* LAW DOCUMENTS THAT SUPPORT A CLAIM documents by which a claim to property or rights is supported, e.g. the title deeds to land [15thC. From Latin *munimentum* 'fortification', from *munire* 'to fortify' (see MUNITION). The meaning 'title deeds' developed in medieval Latin.]

munition /myoŏ nísh'n/ *vt.* (**-tions**, **-tioning**, **-tioned**) SUPPLY WITH WEAPONS to supply sb or a group with arms and ammunition ■ **munitions** *npl.* MILITARY SUPPLIES military supplies such as weapons and ammunition [Early 16thC. Via French from the Latin stem *munition-*, from *munire* 'to fortify', from *moenia* 'defensive walls'.] —**munitioner** *n.*

Munnings /múnningz/, **Sir Alfred James** (1878–1959) British painter. He was a conservative stylist, noted for his equestrian scenes. He served as a war artist during World War I.

munnion /múnnyən/ *n.* a mullion between panes of glass in a window (*archaic*) [Late 16thC. Alteration of obsolete *monial* (see MULLION).]

Munro /mən rō/ (*plural* **-ros**) *n.* a mountain peak over 3,000 ft high, either in Scotland only or in any part of the British Isles [Early 20thC. Named after Sir H. T. Munro, who compiled a list of Scottish mountains for the Journal of the Scottish Mountaineering Club in 1891.]

Munster[1] *n.* = Muenster

Munster[2] /múnstər/ historic province in southwestern Republic of Ireland. Population: 1,033,045 (1996). Area: 24,127 sq. km/9,315 sq. mi.

Münster /múnstər/ inland port on the Dortmund-Ems Canal, North Rhine-Westphalia State, northwestern Germany. Population: 265,500 (1994).

munt /moŏnt/ *n. S Africa* an offensive term for a Black African (*dated slang offensive*) [Mid-20thC. From Bantu *umuntu* 'person', the singular of *abantu* (source of English Bantu).]

muntin /múntin/ *n.* a strip of wood or metal that separates and holds in place the panes of a window [Early 17thC. Alteration of Old French *montant* 'upright', from the present participle of *monter* (see MOUNT).]

muntjac /múnt jak/ (*plural* **-jacs** *or* **-jac**), **muntjak** (*plural* **-jaks** *or* **-jak**) *n.* a small deer, native to Southeast Asia, that has a reddish-brown coat, a cry like a dog's bark, and small antlers. Genus: *Muntiacus*. [Late 18thC. From Sundanese (an Austronesian language of western Java) *minchek* and Malay *menjangan* 'deer'.]

Muntz metal /múnts-/ *n.* a type of brass containing two parts of zinc to three parts of copper, used in casting and extrusion [Mid-19thC. Named after the English metallurgist George Frederick *Muntz* (1794–1857).]

muon /myoŏ on/ *n.* an elementary particle with a mass about 200 times that of an electron. It is a lepton with a negative charge and a half-life of two-millionths of a second. [Mid-20thC. Contraction of MU MESON.] —**muonic** /myoo ónnik/ *adj.*

muon neutrino *n.* a lepton that exists in association with a muon. It has zero rest mass and no charge.

mural /myoŏrəl/ *n.* PAINTING PAINTING ON WALL a usually large picture painted directly onto an interior or exterior wall ■ *adj.* OF WALLS applied to or relating to a wall [Mid-16thC. Via French from Latin *muralis*, from *murus* 'wall' (source also of English *immure*).] —**muralist** *n.*

muramic acid /myoŏ rámmik-/ *n.* an amino sugar found in the cell walls of blue-green algae. Formula: $C_9H_{17}NO_7$. [*Muramic* coined from Latin *murus* 'wall' + AMINE + -IC]

Murat /myoor a, mü rá/, **Joachim, King of Naples** (1767–1815) French military commander. Brother-in-law of Napoleon, he served under Napoleon in several campaigns and was awarded the monarchy of Naples by him in 1808.

Murchison /múrchəssən/ river in Western Australia that rises in the Robinson Range and flows into the Indian Ocean near the town of Kalbarri. Length: 800 km/500 mi.

Murchison /múrchiss'n/, **Sir Roderick Impey** (1792–1871) British geologist. His study of early Palaeozoic rock strata and their fossils led to his formulation of the Silurian rock system.

Murcia /múrssi ə/ capital of Murcia Province and Murcia Region, southeastern Spain. Population: 344,904 (1995).

murder /múrdər/ *n.* LAW CRIME OF KILLING SB the crime of killing another person deliberately and not in self-defence or with any other extenuating circumstance recognized by law ■ *v.* (**-ders**, **-dering**, **-dered**) 1. *vti.* LAW KILL SB ILLEGALLY to kill another person deliberately and not in self-defence or with any other extenuating circumstance recognized by law 2. *vt.* DESTROY to put an end to or destroy sth (*informal*) ○ *The fire murdered their chances of selling the house.* 3. *vt.* SPOIL to spoil sth such as a song or a piece of writing by performing it badly or changing it (*informal*) 4. *vt.* SPORTS DEFEAT COMPLETELY to defeat a person or team completely, especially in a sporting contest (*informal*) 5. *vt.* PUNISH to punish or be very angry with sb (*informal*) ○ *My mother will murder me if I'm not on time.* [Old English *morþor*. Ultimately from an Indo-European word that is also the ancestor of English *mortal*, *moribund*, and *ambrosia*. Later reinforced by Old French *murdre*, from prehistoric Germanic.] —**murderer** *n.* —**murderess** *n.* ◇ **get away with murder** to escape punishment for or detection of wrongdoing ◇ **sth is murder** sth is very difficult or unpleasant, requiring great effort or hardship (*informal*) ○ *Driving in this morning was murder.*

— WORD KEY: SYNONYMS —
See Synonyms at *kill*.

murderee /múrdə reé/ *n.* a victim of murder

murderous /múrdərəss/ *adj.* 1. LIKELY TO MURDER capable of, guilty of, or likely to commit murder 2. LIKELY TO CAUSE DEATH violent and likely to result in bloodshed or murder 3. DIFFICULT very difficult, unpleasant, or dangerous (*informal*) —**murderously** *adv.* —**murderousness** *n.*

Dame Iris Murdoch

Murdoch /múr dok/, **Dame Iris** (1919–99) Irish-born British novelist and philosopher. Her many novels are noted for their thoughtful exploration of moral and philosophical problems. She is the author of *A Severed Head* (1961) and the Booker Prize-winning *The Sea, the Sea* (1978). Full name **Dame Jean Iris Murdoch**

Murdoch, Sir Keith Arthur (1885–1952) Australian journalist and newspaper proprietor. He was chairman of an organization that owned several Australian newspapers.

Murdoch, Rupert (*b.* 1931) Australian-born US media proprietor. He extended his family newspaper empire to control a global network of media organizations. Full name **Keith Rupert Murdoch**

mure /myoor/ (**mures**, **muring**, **mured**) *vt.* to enclose sb or sth within walls (*archaic or literary*) [14thC. Via

Rupert Murdoch

French *murer* from late Latin *murare* 'to provide with walls', from Latin *murus* 'wall' (see MURAL).]

murein /myoór een/ *n.* = **peptidoglycan** [Mid-20thC. Coined from Latin *murus* 'wall' (see MURAL) on the model of PROTEIN; from its forming the walls of cells.]

murex /myoór eks/ (*plural* **-rices** /-ri seez/) *n.* a gastropod marine shellfish that lives mainly in tropical waters and typically has a spiny shell. One species yields a purple dye. Genus: *Murex*. [Late 16thC. From Latin.]

muriatic acid /myoóri áttik-/ *n.* = **hydrochloric acid** [*Muriatic* from Latin *muriaticus* 'pickled in brine', from *muria* 'brine']

muricate /myoórikət/, **muricated** /-kaytid/ *adj.* covered in short spines or points [Mid-17thC. From Latin *muricatus* 'shaped like a murex', from *murex* (see MUREX).]

murid /myoórid/ *n.* an animal such as a mouse or rat that belongs to the rodent family. Family: Muridae. [Early 20thC. Shortening of modern Latin *Muridae*, family name, from *mur-*, the stem of *mus* (see MOUSE).]

Murillo /myoo rílló/, **Bartolomé Esteban** (1617–82) Spanish painter. He is noted for his religious subjects and genre scenes.

murine /myoór īn/ *adj.* **1.** OF MOUSE AND RAT FAMILY relating to or belonging to the family of long-tailed rodents that includes rats and mice. Family: Muridae. **2.** LIKE A RODENT like a mouse or a rat **3.** SPREAD BY RODENTS caused or transmitted by mice or rats [Early 17thC. From Latin *murinus*, from *mur-*, the stem of *mus* 'mouse'. Ultimately from the same Indo-European word as produced English *mouse*.]

murine typhus *n.* a relatively mild form of typhus that is transmitted from rats to humans by fleas or lice. Symptoms include fever, headaches, and muscular pain, and recovery is usually rapid. It is caused by the microorganism *Rickettsia typhi*.

murk /murk/, **mirk** *n.* **1.** GLOOMY DARKNESS gloomy darkness caused by mist, smoke, or cloud **2.** *N England* MIST a mist or thin fog (*informal*) ■ *adj.* MURKY murky (*archaic or literary*) [Old English *mirce*, *myrce*. Supplemented in Middle English by the related Old Norse *myrkr*.]

murky /múrki/ (**-ier**, **-iest**), **mirky** (**-ier**, **-iest**) *adj.* **1.** GLOOMY dark and gloomy **2.** HARD TO SEE THROUGH thick with fog, cloud, smoke, or dirt, and difficult to see through **3.** OBSCURE unclear and difficult to understand ○ *offered several murky excuses* **4.** DISHONEST involving dishonesty or illegal activities —**murkily** *adv.* —**murkiness** *n.*

Murmansk /mur mánsk/ city in northwestern Russia, on the Kola Inlet, an arm of the Barents Sea. Population: 472,000 (1990).

murmur /múrmər/ *n.* **1.** CONTINUOUS HUM a continuous low sound that often seems to be coming from some distance away **2.** STH SAID QUIETLY sth said that is either very quiet or sounds indistinct **3.** COMPLAINT a complaint, especially one that is not made openly **4.** MED SYMPTOMATIC SOUND IN THE CHEST a soft blowing or fluttering sound, usually heard via a stethoscope, that originates from the heart, lungs, or arteries and may indicate disease or structural concerns. It is caused by turbulent blood flow. ■ *v.* (**-murs**, **-muring**, **-mured**) **1.** *vti.* SAY STH SOFTLY to say sth very softly so that it can hardly be heard **2.** *vi.* COMPLAIN DISCREETLY to complain in a discreet or secretive way **3.** *vi.* MAKE A CONTINUOUS LOW SOUND to make a continuous

low sound, as if from a distance [14thC. Via French *murmurer* from Latin *murmurare*. Probably an imitation of the sound (compare Greek *mormurein* and German *murmeln*, which have a similar meaning).] —**murmurer** *n.* —**murmuringly** *adv.* —**murmurous** *adj.* —**murmurously** *adv.*

murmurings /múrməringz/ *npl.* quiet and unforceful expressions of discontent

murphy /múrfi/ (*plural* **-phies**) *n.* a potato (*dated informal*) [Early 19thC. From the Irish surname *Murphy*; from the stereotypical prominence of the potato in the Irish diet.]

Murphy /múrfi/, **Graeme** (*b.* 1950) Australian dancer and choreographer. He became artistic director of the Sydney Dance Company in 1976.

Murphy's Law /múrfiz-/ *n.* = **Sod's law** (*informal*) [Mid-20thC. Named after the American engineer Edward *Murphy* (b. 1917), who enunciated it.]

murragh /múrrə/ (*plural* **-raghs** or **-ragh**) *n.* a type of caddis fly to which trout are particularly attracted. Latin name: *Phryganea grandis*. [Origin uncertain: perhaps from MURREY]

murrain /múrrin/ *n.* (*archaic*) **1.** CATTLE DISEASE an infectious disease such as anthrax that affects cattle **2.** PLAGUE an infectious and fast-spreading disease [14thC. From Anglo-Norman *moryn* and French *morine*, from *mourir* 'to die', from, ultimately, Latin *mori* (source of English *mortgage* and *mortuary*).]

Murray /múrri/ major river in southeastern Australia. Length: 2,520 km/1,566 mi.

Murray, Gilbert (1866–1957) British scholar. He was a classicist noted for his translations of Greek plays and for his critical editions of the works of Euripides and Aeschylus. Full name **George Gilbert Aimé Murray**

Murray, Sir James Augustus Henry (1837–1915) British philologist and lexicographer. He laid the foundations of what became the *Oxford English Dictionary* and edited half of the first edition.

Murray, Les (*b.* 1938) Australian poet and critic. He was author of *Subhuman Redneck Poems* (1996) and winner of the 1997 T.S. Eliot Prize for Poetry. Full name **Leslie Alan Murray**

Murray Bridge town in southeastern South Australia, an agricultural centre located on the River Murray. Population: 12,831 (1996).

Murray cod /múrri-/ *n.* a large freshwater fish found in Australian inland waterways. Latin name: *Maccullochella peeli*.

murrelet /múrlit/ (*plural* **-lets** or **-let**) *n.* a small diving bird that is related to and resembles an auk. Genera: *Brachyramphus* and *Synthliboramphus*.

murrey /múrri/ *adj.* of the purplish-red colour mulberry (*archaic*) [15thC. Via Old French *moré* from medieval Latin *moratus*, from Latin *morum* 'mulberry'.]

murrhine /múr īn/, **murrine** *n.* a substance, possibly fluorite, that the ancient Romans used to make vases, cups, and other similar objects [Late 16thC. From Latin *murr(h)inus*, from *murra*, denoting this substance.]

murrhine glass *n.* a type of Eastern glassware made from fluorspar and decorated with flecks of metal

Murrumbidgee /múrrəm bíji/ river in southeastern Australia. Length: 1,690 km/1,050 mi.

Murry /múrri/, **John Middleton** (1889–1957) British writer and literary critic. He was editor of several periodicals, author of critical studies of British authors, and biographer of his wife, Katherine Mansfield.

murther /múrthər/ *n.* murder, or a murder (*archaic*)[14thC. Variant of MURDER.]

mus. *abbr.* **1.** museum **2.** music **3.** musical **4.** musician

Musaf /moo sáf/ *n.* in Judaism, a group of additional prayers that is included in morning services on Sabbaths, festivals, and Rosh Chodesh [From Hebrew, literally 'addition']

MusB, **MusBac** *abbr.* Bachelor of Music [Latin *Musicae Baccalaureus*]

Musca /múskə/ *n.* a small constellation in the southern hemisphere between the Southern Cross and Chamaeleon

muscadel, **muscadelle** *n.* = muscatel

Muscadet /múskə day/ *n.* a dry white wine from the Loire Valley in France [Early 20thC. From French, name of the grape from which this wine is made, from *muscade* 'nutmeg', from *musc* 'musk' (see MUSK).]

muscadine /múskə dīn/ *n.* **1.** WILD GRAPEVINE a grapevine, native to the southeastern United States, that is the ancestor of cultivated varieties used for winemaking. Latin name: *Vitis rotundifolia*. **2.** PURPLE GRAPE a purple grape from the muscadine vine with a thick skin and musky smell, used for making wine [Mid-16thC. Probably a variant of MUSCATEL.]

muscae volitantes /múski vólli tán teez/ *npl.* MED specks that appear to float before the eyes (*technical*) [Mid-18thC. From Latin, literally 'flies flying about'.]

muscarine /múskərin/ *n.* a toxic substance, found in fly agaric and certain other fungi, that when ingested affects the nervous system. Among other effects it dilates blood vessels, slows heart rate, constricts the airways, and stimulates the gut. [Late 19thC. Formed from modern Latin *Muscaria*, species name of the fly agaric, from Latin *musca* 'fly'.] —**muscarinic** /múskə rínnik/ *adj.*

muscat /múskət/ *n.* **1.** PLANTS WHITE GRAPEVINE a grapevine with sweet white grapes that are used for winemaking and are dried as raisins **2.** WINE = **muscatel** *n.* 1 [Mid-16thC. Via French from Provençal, formed from *musc* (see MUSK).]

Muscat /mús kat/, **Masqat** /máss gat/ capital city of Oman, on the northeastern coast of the country, on the Gulf of Oman. Population: 622,506 (1993).

muscatel /múskə tél/, **muscadel** /-dél/, **muscadelle** *n.* **1.** SWEET WHITE WINE a sweet white wine made from muscat grapes **2.** WHITE GRAPE OR RAISIN a grape or raisin from the muscat vine [Mid-16thC. Via Old French from Provençal, literally 'little muscat', formed from *muscat* (see MUSCAT).]

muscid /mússid/ *n.* any fly of the family that includes the housefly and the stable fly. Family: Muscidae. [Late 19thC. Back-formation from modern Latin *Muscidae*, family name, from Latin *musca* 'fly'.] —**muscid** *adj.*

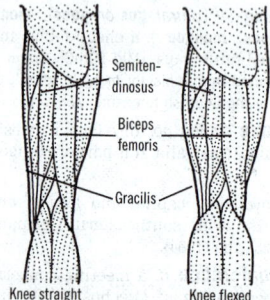

Muscle: Muscles of the human knee

Semitendinosus
Biceps femoris
Gracilis
Knee straight
Knee flexed

muscle /múss'l/ *n.* **1.** BODY TISSUE PRODUCING MOVEMENT a tissue that is specialized to undergo repeated contraction and relaxation, thereby producing movement of body parts, maintaining tension, or pumping fluids within the body. There are three types: voluntary (**striped muscle**), involuntary (**smooth muscle**), and branched or heart muscle. **2.** ORGAN COMPOSED OF MUSCLE TISSUE an organ composed of bundles or sheets of muscle tissue, bound together with connective tissue and with tendons by which the contracting part is attached to the bones that it moves **3.** INFLUENCE power and influence, especially in the realm of politics, finance, or the military **4.** STRENGTH physical strength (*informal*) ○ *put some muscle into it* ■ *vti.* (**-cles**, **-cling**, **-cled**) MOVE BY USING STRENGTH to move, or make sb or sth move, using strength and force or effort (*informal*) [14thC. Via French from Latin *musculus*, literally 'small mouse', from *mus* 'mouse'; from the resemblance of certain muscles to mice moving under the skin.] —**muscly** *adj.*

muscle in *vi.* to become involved in or interfere in sth by disregarding other people's wishes or by using strength, power, or influence (*informal*)

muscle-bound *adj.* **1.** WITH OVERDEVELOPED MUSCLES with muscles so bulky that they restrict movement **2.** RIGID AND INFLEXIBLE too large, powerful, or over-developed to be capable of flexibility or a swift response

muscle fibre *n.* a basic contracting unit of striated muscle, as found, e.g., in arm and leg muscles. Each is a microscopic thread-like structure, formed from several fused cells. It contains numerous cylindrical structures (**myofibrils**) that contract when stimulated.

muscleman /múss'l man/ (*plural* -**men** /-men/) *n.* **1.** STRONG MAN a man with highly developed muscles who is very strong **2.** BODYGUARD a strong man hired by a criminal or gangster for protection and to intimidate enemies

muscle mary (*plural* **muscle marys**) *n.* an offensive term for a gay man with a very muscular physique (*slang offensive*)

muscle sense *n.* = kinaesthesia

muscovado /múskə vaádō/, **muscavado** *n.* a raw or unrefined sugar made by evaporating the molasses from sugar-cane juice [Early 17thC. From Portuguese *mascabado* 'made badly', referring to the quality of refinement.]

muscovite /múskə vīt/ *n.* the most common of the mica group of minerals, consisting of potassium aluminium silicate and found in plutonic and sedimentary rocks [Mid-19thC. Coined from *Muscovy glass* 'mica' (from its being obtained from Russia) + -ITE.]

Muscovite /múskə vīt/ *n.* SB FROM MOSCOW sb who lives in or comes from Moscow, the capital of Russia ■ *adj.* RUSSIAN Russian (*archaic*) [Mid-16thC. Formed from modern Latin *Muscovia*, from Russian *Moskva* 'Moscow'.]

Muscovy /múskəvi/ former principality in western Russia, centred on Moscow

Muscovy duck /múskəvi-/ *n.* a large duck, native to Central America but widely domesticated, valued for its succulent flesh. It has greenish-black plumage with white markings and heavy red wattles. Latin name: *Cairina moschata*. [Alteration (by association with archaic *Muscovy* 'of Moscow') of MUSK DUCK]

muscular /múskyŏŏlər/ *adj.* **1.** OF THE MUSCLES consisting of, relating to, or affecting muscles **2.** STRONG physically strong and with well-developed muscles **3.** VIGOROUS having considerable power or strength but sometimes lacking subtlety [Late 17thC. Alteration of obsolete *musculous*, which came directly or via French *musculeaux* from Latin *musculosus*, from *musculus* (see MUSCLE).] —**muscularity** /múskyŏŏ lárrəti/ *n.* —**muscularly** /múskyŏŏlərli/ *adv.*

muscular dystrophy *n.* a medical condition in which there is gradual wasting and weakening of skeletal muscles. There are several forms in humans, generally linked to genetic defects and showing characteristic patterns of inheritance, the most common being Duchenne muscular dystrophy.

musculature /múskŏŏləchər/ *n.* **1.** ARRANGEMENT OF MUSCLES the way a person's or animal's muscles are arranged in a limb or organ **2.** MUSCULAR SYSTEM an organism's entire muscular system [Late 19thC. From French, formed from Latin *musculus* (see MUSCLE).]

musculo- *prefix.* muscle, muscular ○ *musculocutaneous* [From Latin *musculus* (see MUSCLE).]

musculocutaneous /múskyŏŏlō kyŏŏ táyni əss/ *adj.* relating to or supplying the muscles and skin

musculoskeletal /múskyŏŏlō skéllit'l/ *adj.* relating to or involving the muscles and the skeleton

MusD, MusDoc *abbr.* Doctor of Music [Latin *Musicae Doctor*]

muse[1] /myooz/ *v.* (**muses, musing, mused**) **1.** *vti.* THINK ABOUT STH to think about sth in a deep and serious or dreamy and abstracted way **2.** *vti.* SAY STH THOUGHTFULLY to say sth in a thoughtful or questioning way (*literary*) **3.** *vi.* GAZE THOUGHTFULLY to gaze at sb or sth thoughtfully or abstractedly (*literary*) ■ *n.* THOUGHTFUL STATE a state of deep thought (*literary*) [14thC. From Old French *muser* 'to meditate', perhaps literally 'to go around with your nose in the air', from *muse* 'muzzle, snout', from medieval Latin *musum* (source of English *muzzle*).] —**museful** *adj.* —**musefully** *adv.* —**muser** *n.*

muse[2] /myooz/ *n.* **1.** SB WHO INSPIRES AN ARTIST sb who is a source of inspiration for an artist, especially a poet **2.** ARTIST'S INSPIRATION the inspiration that supposedly visits, leaves, and suggests things to an artist, especially a poet **3.** ARTIST'S PARTICULAR TALENT the particular gift or talent of an artist, especially a poet ○ *'With Donne, whose muse on dromedary trots, Wreathe iron pokers into true-love knots'* (Samuel Taylor Coleridge, *On Donne's Poetry*; 1818) [14thC. Directly or via French from Latin *musa*, from Greek *mousa*.]

Muse *n.* in Greek mythology, one of the nine daughters of Zeus and Mnemosyne, goddess of memory. The Muses inspired and presided over the different creative arts. They are Calliope (the muse of epic poetry), Clio (history), Erato (love poetry), Euterpe (lyric poetry), Melpomene (tragedy), Polyhymnia (sacred song), Terpsichore (dance), Thalia (comedy), and Urania (astronomy).

museology /myoózi ólləji/ *n.* the study of how museums are designed, organized, and managed —**museological** /myoózi ə lójjik'l/ *adj.* —**museologically** *adv.* —**museologist** /myoózi ólləjist/ *n.*

musette /myoo zét/ *n.* MUSIC **1.** FRENCH BAGPIPE a French bagpipe that makes a relatively soft sound. It was popular in the 17th, 18th, and 19th centuries. **2.** PASTORAL DANCE MUSIC a piece of pastoral dance music that imitates the sound of a bagpipe or has a bagpipe playing the bass line [14thC. From French, literally 'little bagpipe', formed from *muse* 'bagpipe'.]

museum /myoo zée əm/ *n.* a building or institution where objects of artistic, historical, or scientific importance and value are kept, studied, and put on display [Early 17thC. Via Latin, 'library, academy', from Greek *mouseion* 'place of the Muses', from *mousa* 'muse' (see MUSE[2]).]

museum piece *n.* **1.** VALUABLE AND INTERESTING OBJECT an object that is so valuable, interesting, or old that it could be in a museum **2.** SB OR STH OLD-FASHIONED sb or sth considered very old-fashioned (*informal*)

Musgrave Ranges /múss grayv-/ mountain range in central Australia, on the border between the Northern Territory and South Australia

mush[1] /mush/ *n.* **1.** PULP a soft pulpy mass **2.** SENTIMENTAL STUFF overly romantic and sentimental words or ideas, e.g. in a book or film **3.** RADIO INTERFERENCE radio interference, especially a hissing noise **4.** *US* FOOD PORRIDGE a thick mixture made from cornmeal and milk or water ■ *vt.* (**mushes, mushing, mushed**) *US* MASH STH to mash sth into a soft pulpy mass [Late 17thC. Origin uncertain: probably a variant of MASH.]

mush[2] /mush/ *interj. US, Can* COMMAND TO SLED DOGS used to make sled dogs start pulling or moving faster ■ *n. US, Can* DOGSLED JOURNEY a journey on a dogsled ■ *vti.* (**mushes, mushing, mushed**) *US, Can* TRAVEL BY DOGSLED to travel on a dogsled, or drive a dogsled or team of dogs [Mid-19thC. From North American *Mush on!*, perhaps a variant of French *marchons* 'let us march', from *marcher* 'to march' (source of English *march*).] —**musher** *n.*

mush[3] /mŏŏsh/ *n.* sb's face or mouth (*dated slang*) [Mid-20thC. Origin uncertain: perhaps an alteration of MOUSTACHE.]

mush[4] /mŏŏsh/ *n.* a familiar or disrespectful way of addressing sb, usually a man (*slang*) [Mid-20thC. Origin unknown.]

mush area *n.* a region where two or more radio signals overlap, causing interference

mushroom /músh room, -rŏŏm/ *n.* **1.** UMBRELLA-SHAPED FUNGUS the typically umbrella-shaped spore-producing body of a fungus that consists of a usually fleshy cap on a stalk. Class: Basidiomycetes. **2.** EDIBLE FUNGUS an edible mushroom, especially the field mushroom that grows very fast ■ *vi.* (-**rooms, -rooming, -roomed**) **1.** GROW QUICKLY to grow or develop very rapidly **2.** BECOME MUSHROOM-SHAPED to swell into a shape like a mushroom **3.** PICK MUSHROOMS to go mushroom picking [15thC. Via French *mousseron* from the late Latin stem *mussirion-* 'type of mushroom', of unknown origin.] —**mushroomy** *adj.*

Mushroom cloud

mushroom cloud *n.* the large mushroom-shaped cloud of dust and debris caused by an explosion, especially a nuclear explosion

mushy /múshi/ (-**ier, -iest**) *adj.* **1.** PULPY forming a thick soft pulp **2.** TOO SENTIMENTAL overly romantic or sentimental —**mushily** *adv.* —**mushiness** *n.*

music /myoózik/ *n.* **1.** SOUNDS THAT PRODUCE EFFECT sounds, usually produced by instruments or voices, that are arranged or played in order to create a pleasing or stimulating effect **2.** ART OF ARRANGING SOUNDS the art of arranging or making sounds, usually those of musical instruments or voices, in groups and patterns that create a pleasing or stimulating effect **3.** TYPE OF MUSIC music of a particular type, e.g. of a particular place or time, for a particular instrument, of a particular style, or appealing to a particular group ○ *rock-and-roll music* **4.** WRITTEN MUSIC written notation on paper indicating the pitch, duration, rhythm, and tone of notes to be played **5.** PLEASING SOUND any sound or group of sounds that is pleasing or stimulating ○ *the music of the wind in the trees* **6.** GROUP a group of musicians (*archaic*) [13thC. Via French *musique* from, ultimately, Greek *mousikē* 'art of the Muse, music', from *mousikos* 'of a Muse', from *mousa* 'muse' (see MUSE[2]).] ◇ **face the music** to deal with a pressing and difficult situation arising from sth done previously

musical /myoózik'l/ *adj.* **1.** OF OR FOR MUSIC relating to or producing music **2.** PLEASANT-SOUNDING sounding pleasant and melodious **3.** GOOD AT MUSIC having a talent for or a keen interest in music **4.** WITH MUSIC set to, consisting of, or involving music ■ *n.* FILM OR PLAY WITH SONGS a light-hearted film or play that has singing, music, and often dancing in it as important elements in developing the story and portraying the emotions of the characters —**musically** *adv.* —**musicalness** *n.*

musical box *n.* a box that contains a mechanical device that plays music. US term **music box**

musicale /myoózi kaál/ *n. US* a social occasion in which music is the featured entertainment

music box *n. US* = musical box

music centre *n.* a one-piece hi-fi unit that has a turntable, amplifier, cassette deck, radio, and speakers (*dated*)

music drama *n.* a type of opera, first composed by Richard Wagner in the late 19th century, in which the dramatic and musical content are intended to be of equal importance

music hall *n.* **1.** POPULAR ENTERTAINMENT a type of entertainment, popular in the late 19th and early 20th centuries, that consisted of a variety of singing, dancing, and comic acts. US term **vaudeville 2.** THEATRE a theatre in which music hall shows were staged

musician /myoo zísh'n/ *n.* sb who plays, performs, conducts, or composes music, either as a hobby or a profession —**musicianly** *adj.*

musicianship /myoo zísh'n ship/ *n.* skill in playing or performing music

music of the spheres *n.* the perfect but inaudible music that Pythagoras and other later philosophers believed was created by the movement of the celestial bodies

musicology /myoózi kólləji/ *n.* the academic study of music and its history —**musicological** /myoózikə

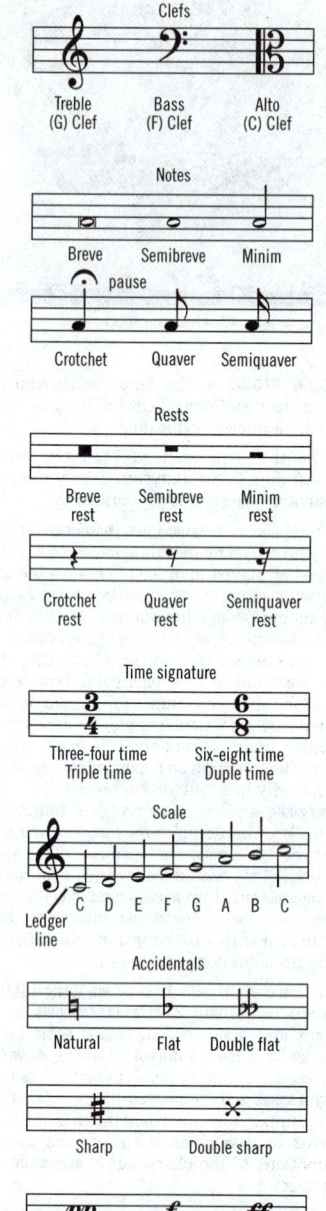

Clefs

Treble (G) Clef   Bass (F) Clef   Alto (C) Clef

Notes

Breve   Semibreve   Minim

pause

Crotchet   Quaver   Semiquaver

Rests

Breve rest   Semibreve rest   Minim rest

Crotchet rest   Quaver rest   Semiquaver rest

Time signature

Three-four time / Triple time   Six-eight time / Duple time

Scale

C D E F G A B C

Ledger line

Accidentals

Natural   Flat   Double flat

Sharp   Double sharp

Pianissimo   Forte   Fortissimo

Music: Musical notation

lójjik'l/ *adj.* —**musicologically** *adv.* —**musicologist** /myoʻozi kólləjist/ *n.*

music paper *n.* paper with staves printed on it that is used for writing down music

music roll *n.* a roll of paper with carefully positioned holes in it, used for controlling a mechanical instrument such as a player piano

music stand *n.* a height-adjustable frame for holding printed music that is being performed

music video *n.* a short video or film made to accompany a song or piece of popular music, often as a cinematic or dramatic interpretation of it

Musil /moʻozil/, **Robert** (1880–1942) Austrian novelist. Much of his work was biographical, drawing on personal experiences and often reflecting Austrian culture.

musings /myoʻozingz/ *npl.* thoughts, especially when aimless and unsystematic ○ *philosophical musings*

musique concrète /myoo zeʻek kong krét/ *n.* recorded music composed by electronically combining and enhancing natural and musical sounds [Mid-20thC. From French, literally 'concrete music'.]

musk /musk/ *n.* **1.** GLANDULAR SECRETION OF DEER a pungent and greasy secretion from a gland in the male musk deer, used in the manufacture of perfumes **2.** SUBSTANCE LIKE MUSK a secretion similar to musk from other animals such as the civet or otter, or a synthetic substance with similar properties **3.** PLANTS PLANT WITH MUSKY SCENT a plant that has a musky scent **4.** SMELL OF MUSK the smell of musk, or a similar smell [14thC. Ultimately from Latin *muscus*, from Persian *mušk*, perhaps from Sanskrit *muṣka* 'scrotum' (from the shape of the musk gland of the musk deer, literally 'little mouse', from *mūṣ* 'mouse'.]

musk deer *n.* a small mountain-dwelling deer native to central and northeastern Asia. The males lack antlers but possess long canine teeth and secrete musk from an abdominal gland. Latin name: *Moschus moschiferus.*

musk duck *n.* = Muscovy duck [From its smell]

muskeg /músk eg/ *n.* **1.** US, Can BOGGY LAND an area of swamp or boggy land covered in sphagnum moss, leaves, and a mass of dead plant matter resembling peat **2.** DEAD PLANT MATTER the dead plant matter resembling peat that covers areas of muskeg [Early 19thC. From Cree *maske:k*.]

musket /múskit/ *n.* a shoulder gun with a long barrel and a smooth bore. It was used between the 16th and 18th centuries, before rifling was invented. [Late 16thC. Via French *mousquet* from Italian *moschetto* 'crossbow bolt', from *mosca* 'fly', from Latin *musca*.]

─────── **WORD KEY: ORIGIN** ───────

Early **muskets** could fire crossbow bolts as well as bullets. The name was probably reinforced by Italian *moschetto* 'sparrow hawk' (from its fly-like markings), early guns being often named after birds of prey (e.g. 'falconet', a type of small cannon).

musketeer /múskə teér/ *n.* **1.** INFANTRYMAN an infantryman armed with a musket **2.** ROYAL BODYGUARD a member of a company of musketeers in the French royal household's personal troops in the 17th and 18th centuries

─────── **WORD KEY: CULTURAL NOTE** ───────

The Three Musketeers, a novel by French writer Alexandre Dumas (1844). Set in France during the reign of Louis XIII, this historical romance tells the story of a young adventurer, D'Artagnan, who is taken under the wing of three musketeers, Athos, Porthos, and Aramis. The four become embroiled in a series of adventures involving love, politics, swordsmanship, and the machinations of the evil Cardinal Richelieu.

musketry /múskitri/ *n.* **1.** MUSKETS OR MUSKETEERS a group of muskets or musketeers **2.** FIRING OF SMALL GUNS the technique or practice of using small arms

musk mallow *n.* **1.** MALLOW WITH PINK FLOWERS a plant of the mallow family, native to Europe and northern Africa, with a hairy and often purple-spotted stem, pink flowers, and a slight musky scent. Latin name: *Malva moschata.* **2.** = abelmosk

muskmelon /músk mellən/ *n.* **1.** PLANTS MELON PLANT a trailing vine that bears melons with a ridged skin such as the cantaloupe. Latin name: *Cucumis melo.* **2.** FOOD MELON FRUIT the fruit of a muskmelon plant, having a ribbed or rough rind and white, yellow, or green flesh with a sweet full flavour and a pleasant slightly musky smell

Muskogean /mu skōgi ən/, **Muskhogean** *n.* a branch of Native North American languages from the Hokan-Siouan family. It includes Chickasaw, Choctaw, and Creek. —**Muskogean** *adj.*

Muskogee /mu skōgi/ (*plural* **-gee** *or* **-gees**) *n.* a member of a Native North American people who inhabited the southeastern part of North America and formed part of the confederacy that included the Creek [Late 18thC. From Creek *ma:skó:ki*.]

musk orchid *n.* a small orchid, native to Europe and Asia, that has dense spikes of musk-scented greenish-yellow flowers. Latin name: *Herminium monorchis.*

musk ox (*plural* **musk oxen**) *n.* a large wild ox, native to the arctic tundra of northern Canada and Greenland, with a black or brown shaggy coat and flat downward-curving horns. Males emit a strong musky smell during the breeding season. Latin name: *Ovibos moschatus.*

Muskrat

muskrat /músk rat/ (*plural* **-rats** *or* **-rat**) *n.* **1.** LARGE RODENT a large amphibious rodent, native to North America and widespread in Europe, closely related to the vole and the lemming, with a thick brown coat and musk glands. Latin name: *Ondatra zibethica.* **2.** MUSKRAT FUR the fur of the muskrat [Early 17thC. By folk etymology from Algonquian *muscascus*, literally 'it is red' (from the animal's colour), by association with MUSK and RAT.]

musk rose *n.* a rose, native to the Mediterranean, that is widely cultivated for its musk-scented flowers. Latin name: *Rosa moschata.*

musk thistle *n.* a thistle, native to temperate regions of Europe and Asia, that has leaves divided into narrow spine-tipped lobes and single drooping reddish-purple flowers. Latin name: *Carduus nutans.*

musk turtle *n.* a small freshwater turtle native to the eastern United States and Canada that gives off a pungent smell. Genus: *Sternotherus.*

musky /múski/ (**-ier, -iest**) *adj.* with a sweet pungent smell similar to that of musk —**muskily** *adv.* —**muskiness** *n.*

Muslim /móozləm/ *n.* FOLLOWER OF ISLAM sb who believes in and practises Islam ■ *adj.* FOLLOWERS OF ISLAM relating to the followers of Islam or to areas, cultures, or activities in which followers of Islam are especially numerous [Early 17thC. From Arabic, literally 'sb who surrenders (to God)', the active participle of *'aslama* (see ISLAM).] —**Muslimism** *n.*

Muslim Brotherhood *n.* an Egyptian nationalist movement founded by Hasan al-Bannah in 1928 that is committed to the Islamic fundamentalist cause and opposes Western influence. The Muslim Brotherhood is active in several other countries throughout the Middle East, North Africa, South Asia, and Southeast Asia.

Muslim League *n.* an organization founded in 1906 to support the demands of Muslims for separate electorates and legislative seats in Hindu-dominated India. It caused a division within the Indian nationalist movement.

muslin /múzlin/ *n.* a thin plain-weave cotton cloth used for curtains, sheets, and dresses [Early 17thC. Via French *mousseline* MOUSSELINE and Italian *mussolina* from Arabic *mawsiliy* 'of Mosul', the Iraqi city where the fabric was made.]

MusM *abbr.* Master of Music [Latin *Musicae Magister*]

muso /myoʻozō/ (*plural* **-sos**) *n.* (*informal*) **1.** UNINSPIRED POP MUSICIAN a musician, especially in a pop group, who pays too much attention to technique and not enough to musicianship and artistry **2.** Aus MUSICIAN a musician [Mid-20thC. Shortening of MUSICIAN.]

musquash /múss kwosh/ *n.* = muskrat [Early 17thC. From Western Abnaki *mòskwas*.]

muss /muss/ *vt.* (**musses, mussing, mussed**) US MESS UP to make sth, especially sb's hair or clothes, untidy or ruffled (*informal*) ■ *n.* US MESS a state of untidiness or disorder (*informal*) [Mid-19thC. Probably a variant of MESS.]

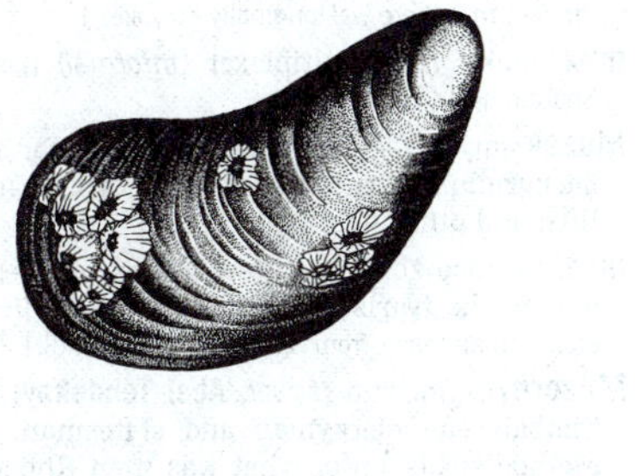

Mussel

mussel /múss'l/ *n.* **1.** EDIBLE MARINE MOLLUSC an edible marine bivalve mollusc with a blue-black shell that lives attached to objects in the sea. Genus: *Mytilus.* **2.** FRESHWATER MOLLUSC a freshwater bivalve mollusc whose shell is a source of mother of pearl. Genera: *Anodonta* and *Unio.* [Pre-12thC. From assumed Vulgar Latin *muscula*, an alteration of Latin *musculus*, literally 'small mouse' (see MUSCLE); from the mussel's supposed resemblance in shape and colour to a mouse.]

Mussolini /mòossə lééni/, **Benito** (1883–1945) Italian statesman. He founded the Italian fascist party in 1919 and served as prime minister from 1922 and dictator (1925–43). After forming an alliance with Germany in 1939, he brought Italy into World War II (1940). Overthrown three years later, he was assassinated by the Italian Resistance. Full name **Benito Amilcaro Andrea Mussolini**. Known as **Il Duce**

Mussulman /múss'lmən/ (*plural* **-men** /-mən/ *or* **-mans**) *n.* a Muslim (*archaic literary*) [Late 16thC. From Persian *musulmān* 'Muslim' (adjective), from Arabic *muslim* 'Muslim' (see MUSLIM).]

mussy /mússi/ (**mussier, mussiest**) *adj. US* not tidy or in an orderly state (*informal*) —**mussily** *adv.* —**mussiness** *n.*

must[1] (*stressed*) /must/; (*unstressed*) /məst, məss/ (**must**) CORE MEANING: a modal indicating that sb is compelled to do sth because of a rule or law, or that it is necessary or advisable to do sth ○ *Accidents causing injury must be reported immediately.* ○ *Employment decisions must be based on ability.* ○ *We must improve our schools.* ○ *You must give him a chance to state his case.*

1. *v.* BE COMPELLED to be compelled to do sth because of a rule or law ○ *You must stop when the light is red.* ○ *All guests must vacate their rooms by 12 noon.* **2.** *v.* BE NECESSARY to be important or necessary to do sth ○ *Henceforth, he said, the central organizing principle of all governments must be the environment.* ○ *Health care insurance must be affordable.* **3.** *v.* BE CERTAIN indicates that sb is sure that sth is the case ○ *This must seem strange to you.* ○ *Those must be your footprints in the garden.* **4.** *v.* INDICATES BELIEF indicates that sb concludes that sth is the case, based on the available evidence ○ *Palaeontologists know that primates must have immigrated to South America sometime before 28 million years ago.* **5.** *v.* INTEND to intend or be determined to do sth ○ *I must be going.* ○ *I must telephone my brother.* **6.** *v.* USED TO MAKE SUGGESTIONS used to make suggestions or invitations, or to give advice ○ *You must see a doctor.* ○ *You must come round for dinner one evening.* **7.** *vi.* BE OBLIGED TO GO to be obliged to go (*archaic*) ○ *We must away ere nightfall.* **8.** *n.* STH ESSENTIAL sth that is essential or obligatory ○ *Formal attire is a must at a state dinner.* **9.** *prefix.* ABSOLUTELY NECESSARY absolutely necessary for sb or highly recommended for sb (*informal; added to a verb to form a noun or adjective*) ○ *a must-see film* ○ *a must-have fashion* [Old English *mōste*, past tense of assumed *mōtan* 'to have to, be able to']

must[2] /must/ *n.* the juice from grapes or other fruit that is to be fermented into wine [Pre-12thC. From Latin *mustum*, a form of *mustus* 'new, fresh' (source of English *mustard*).]

must[3] /must/ *n.* the condition of being musty or mouldy [Early 17thC. Back-formation from MUSTY.]

must[4] *n.* = **musth**

mustache *n.* US = **moustache**

mustachio /mə stááshi ō/ (*plural* **-chios**) *n.* a moustache that is thick or trimmed into a fancy shape (*archaic or humorous; often used in the plural*) [Mid-16thC. Blend of Spanish *mostacho* and its source Italian *mostaccio* (see MOUSTACHE).] —**mustachioed** *adj.*

mustang /mús tang/ *n.* a small hardy wild horse, living on the plains of North America, descended from Arab horses brought to the continent by Spanish soldiers [Early 19thC. Via Mexican Spanish *mestengo* from Spanish, 'ownerless', literally 'mixed (with ranchers' herds)', from *mesta* 'ranchers who appropriated wild cattle', from Latin *mixta*, a form of *mixtus* 'mixed'.]

mustard /mústərd/ *n.* **1.** PLANTS PLANT WITH PUNGENT SEEDS a plant with small yellow flowers and long thin seedpods containing small pungent seeds. Genus: *Brassica.* **2.** FOOD SPICY CONDIMENT powdered mustard seeds, or a hot spicy paste made from powdered, or sometimes whole, mustard seeds, water, and other ingredients, eaten in small quantities as a condiment **3.** *US* ENTHUSIASM enthusiasm or zest (*informal*) **4.** COLOURS DARK YELLOW COLOUR a dark yellow colour tinged with brown, like that of mustard ■ *adj.* COLOURS OF DARK YELLOW COLOUR of a dark yellow colour tinged with brown, like that of mustard [12thC. Via Old French *mo(u)starde* from, ultimately, Latin *mustum* 'must, new wine' (the condiment originally having been made by mixing crushed seeds with MUST[2].] —**mustardy** *adj.* ◇ **cut the mustard** to be up to the desired standard of performance, ability, or quality (*informal*)

mustard and cress *n.* a salad of seedlings of white mustard and garden cress, cultivated indoors in small containers

mustard gas *n.* an oily liquid, made from ethene and disulphur dichloride, that evaporates to a poison gas. Used in chemical warfare, it burns the skin and causes often fatal respiratory damage. Formula: $(ClCH_2CH_2)_2$. [*Mustard* from its smell, which resembles mustard]

mustard oil *n.* an oil obtained from mustard seeds that is used in making soap

mustard plaster *n.* a paste made from black mustard seeds, formerly applied to the skin to stimulate blood flow. It was a folk remedy used to aid healing and counter inflammation.

musteline /músti līn, -lin/ *adj.* belonging to, relating to, or typical of the group of mammals that includes weasels, otters, badgers, and skunks. Family: Mustelidae. [Mid-17thC. From Latin *mustelinus*, from *mustel* 'weasel', of uncertain origin: probably formed from *mus* 'mouse' (source of English *muscle*) + *-tela*, an element of unknown origin.]

muster /mústər/ *v.* (**-ters, -tering, -tered**) **1.** *vti.* MIL ASSEMBLE PEOPLE to bring together a group of soldiers or the members of a crew for a particular reason, e.g. inspection, or assemble in this way **2.** *vt.* GATHER PEOPLE OR THINGS to gather people or things together for a particular reason **3.** *vt.* CALL UP STH to summon up sth such as strength or courage that will help in doing sth **4.** *vt. ANZ* AGRIC ROUND UP LIVESTOCK to round up animals, especially cattle or sheep ■ *n.* **1.** MIL MILITARY ASSEMBLY a gathering of soldiers or a crew for a particular reason, e.g. inspection **2.** MIL = **muster roll 3.** *ANZ* AGRIC ROUNDUP OF ANIMALS a roundup of animals, especially cattle or sheep **4.** GATHERING OR COLLECTION any gathering of people or collection of things [14thC. Via Old French *mo(u)strer* 'to show' and *moustre* 'showing' from Latin *monstrare*, from *monstrum* '(evil) omen, sign' (source of English *monster*).] ◇ **pass muster** to measure up to set standards or to expectations

muster in *vti. US* to enrol sb or be enrolled for military service

muster out *vti. US* to discharge sb, or be discharged, from military service

muster roll *n.* a list of the members of a military or naval unit

musth /must/, **must** *n.* a state of increased sexual activity, accompanied by aggression, in large male land mammals, especially male elephants, lasting 2–3 months. At this time, testosterone levels are high, and an additional hormone, temporin, is excreted from a gland between the eye and the ear. [Late 19thC. Via Urdu *mast* from Persian, literally 'drunk, intoxicated'.]

must-have *n.* sth that is considered to be essential ○ *a list of this year's must-have accessories*

Mustique /mu stéék, mōō-/ island in the eastern Caribbean Sea. It is part of St Vincent and the Grenadines.

mustn't /múss'nt/ *contr.* must not ○ *You mustn't worry.*

musty /músti/ (**-ier, -iest**) *adj.* **1.** WITH OLD DAMP SMELL smelling old, damp, and stale because of not having been used or exposed to fresh air for a long time **2.** STALE tasting old, stale, and mouldy **3.** OUTDATED AND UNINTERESTING no longer relevant or interesting because of being old-fashioned [Early 16thC. Origin uncertain: perhaps an alteration of obsolete *moisty* 'moist, damp', from MOIST.] —**mustily** *adv.* —**mustiness** *n.*

Muswellbrook /mússəl brŏŏk/ town in eastern New South Wales, Australia, a coal mining and agricultural centre. Population: 10,541 (1996).

mutable /myōōtəb'l/ *adj.* **1.** CHANGEABLE tending or likely to change **2.** CAPABLE OF CHANGE capable of changing, or subject to change **3.** BIOL TENDING TO UNDERGO MUTATION used to describe a gene or organism that has a tendency to undergo mutation **4.** ZODIAC OF GEMINI, VIRGO, SAGITTARIUS, AND PISCES used to describe the signs of the zodiac Gemini, Virgo, Sagittarius, and Pisces, thought to be characterized by adaptability. ◊ **cardinal, fixed** [14thC. From Latin *mutabilis*, from *mutare* 'to change' (source of English *mew, moult*, and *mutant*).] —**mutability** /myōōtə bíllәti/ *n.* —**mutableness** /myōōtəb'lness/ *n.* —**mutably** /myōōtəbli/ *adv.*

mutagen /myōōtəjən/ *n.* an external agent, e.g. radiation or some chemicals or viruses, that increases the rate of mutation of cells or organisms [Mid-20thC. Coined from MUTATION + -GEN.] —**mutagenic** /myōōtə jénnik/ *adj.* —**mutagenically** /-jénnikli/ *adv.* —**mutagenicity** /myōōtəjə níssəti/ *n.*

mutagenesis /myōōtə jénnəssiss/ *n.* the process of mutation in a cell or organism [Mid-20thC. Formed from MUTATION + -GENESIS.]

mutant /myōōt'nt/ *n.* **1.** BIOL STH THAT HAS MUTATED an animal, organism, cell, or gene that has mutated **2.** STH ODD-LOOKING sb who or sth that has a strange appearance, unlike others of a similar type (*slang*) ■ *adj.* **1.** BIOL RESULTING FROM MUTATION undergoing or resulting from mutation **2.** RESEMBLING GENETIC MUTANT with an odd appearance or other qualities comparable to those of a genetic mutant (*slang*) [Early 20thC. From Latin *mutant-*, the present participle stem of *mutare* 'to change' (see MUTABLE).]

Mutare /moo tàári/ resort town and capital of Manicaland Province in eastern Zimbabwe, close to the Mozambique border. Population: 131,808 (1992).

mutase /myōō tayz/ *n.* an enzyme that promotes change in the arrangement of molecules in a substance, especially the movement of a phosphate group from one carbon to another [Early 20thC. Formed from Latin *mutare* 'to change' (see MUTABLE) + -ASE.]

mutate /myoo táyt/ (**-tates, -tating, -tated**) *vti.* to undergo or make sth undergo mutation [Mid-18thC. Partly a back-formation from MUTATION; partly from Latin *mutatus*, the past participle of *mutare* 'to change' (see MUTABLE).] —**mutative** /myōōtətiv, -aytiv/ *adj.*

mutation /myoo táysh'n/ *n.* **1.** BIOL CHANGE IN GENETIC MATERIAL a random change in a gene or chromosome resulting in a new trait or characteristic that can be inherited. Mutation can be a source of beneficial genetic variation, or it can be neutral or harmful in effect. **2.** BIOL = **mutant** *n.* 1 **3.** ALTERATION the action or process of changing sth or of being changed **4.** PHON = **umlaut 5.** PHON PHONETIC CHANGE a phonetic change found in Celtic languages in which the initial consonant of a word changes according to the preceding word —**mutational** *adj.* —**mutationally** *adv.*

mutation stop *n.* a stop that controls a set of organ pipes that do not play the tones of the written notes but usually a fifth or third above them

mutatis mutandis /moo tàátiss moo tándiss/ *adv.* with the necessary changes having been made (*formal*) [From Latin, literally 'with things being changed that have to be changed']

mute /myoot/ *adj.* **1.** UNABLE TO SPEAK unable or unwilling to speak **2.** MAKING NO SOUND saying nothing, or making no sound **3.** NOT EXPRESSED IN WORDS felt or expressed without speech **4.** LAW REFUSING TO ANSWER CHARGE refusing to answer a charge brought in a court of law **5.** PHON = plosive *adj.* **6.** PHON NOT PRONOUNCED not pronounced, like the final 'e' in 'cheese' ■ *n.* **1.** OFFENSIVE TERM an offensive term for sb who is unable or unwilling to speak (*offensive*) **2.** LAW SB REFUSING TO ANSWER CHARGE sb who refuses to answer a charge in a court of law **3.** PHON = plosive **4.** PHON SILENT LETTER a letter that is not pronounced **5.** MUSIC DEVICE TO ALTER INSTRUMENT'S TONE a pad, clip, or other device used to reduce or alter in some way the tone of a brass or stringed instrument **6.** HIST HIRED MOURNER sb who is paid to act as a mourner at a funeral ■ *vt.* (mutes, muting, muted) **1.** TURN DOWN SOUND to moderate the volume of a sound **2.** MAKE STH LESS BRIGHT to make a colour or light less bright or harsh **3.** MUSIC ALTER INSTRUMENT'S TONE to reduce or alter in some way the tone of a brass or stringed instrument using a pad, clip, or other device [14thC. From French *muet*, literally 'slightly mute', from Old French *mu*, from Latin *mutus*.] —**mutely** *adv.* —**muteness** *n.*

——— WORD KEY: SYNONYMS ———
See Synonyms at **silent**.

muted /myootid/ *adj.* **1.** NOT BRIGHT OR INTENSE not bright, intense, or harsh in colour or tone **2.** NOT LOUD not loud or distinct enough to be heard clearly **3.** UNDERSTATED subdued and understated rather than forceful or enthusiastic **4.** MUSIC MADE BY INSTRUMENT FITTED WITH MUTE fitted with a mute, or produced by an instrument fitted with a mute

mute swan *n.* a large white swan with an orange bill, common in Europe and Asia and introduced to other regions. Latin name: *Cygnus olor.*

mutilate /myooti layt/ (-lates, -lating, -lated) *vt.* **1.** REMOVE OR DESTROY BODY PART to inflict serious injury on a person or animal or part of sb or sth's body by removing or destroying parts of it **2.** RUIN STH BY REMOVING PARTS to damage or spoil sth such as a piece of writing or a film by removing important parts of it **3.** DAMAGE STH SERIOUSLY to inflict serious damage on sth [Mid-16thC. Partly from Latin *mutilat-*, the past participle stem of *mutilare* 'to cut or lop off', from *mutilus* 'maimed'; partly from earlier *mutilate* 'mutilated', of the same origin.] —**mutilative** /myootilativ, -laytiv/ *adj.* —**mutilator** *n.*

mutilation /myootil laysh'n/ *n.* an act, the process, or the result of inflicting serious injury on a person or animal or part of sb or sth's body by removing or destroying parts of it

mutineer /myooti neer/ *n.* sb who rebels against the legal authority of others, especially a soldier or sailor [Early 17thC. From French *mutinier*, from Old French *mutin* 'rebellious' (see MUTINY).]

mutinous /myootinəss/ *adj.* **1.** INVOLVING MUTINY plotting, participating in, or typical of a mutiny **2.** REFUSING TO OBEY refusing to obey or submit to control, especially military control [Late 16thC. Either from Old French *mutineus*, from *mutin* 'rebellious' (see MUTINY), or formed from English *mutine* 'mutiny', ultimately of the same origin.] —**mutinously** *adv.* —**mutinousness** *n.*

mutiny /myootəni/ *n.* (*plural* -nies) REBELLION AGAINST LEGAL AUTHORITY a rebellion against legal authority, especially by soldiers or sailors refusing to obey orders and, often, attacking their officers ■ *vi.* (-nies, -nying, -nied) PARTICIPATE IN MUTINY to take part in a rebellion against legal authority [Mid-16thC. Via obsolete *mutine* 'to revolt' from French *mutiner*, from Old French *mutin* 'rebellious', from *muete* 'revolt' (literally 'movement'), via assumed Vulgar Latin *movitus* from Latin *motus* 'moved' (see MOTION).]

mutism /myootizəm/ *n.* **1.** OFFENSIVE TERM an offensive term for the inability to speak (*offensive*) **2.** REFUSAL TO SPEAK a refusal to speak either at all times or at some, which may indicate trauma or stress

muton /myoot on/ *n.* the smallest known unit of DNA in which mutation can take place, either spontaneously or caused by an external agent [Mid-20thC. Formed from MUTATION + -ON.]

mutt /mut/ *n.* **1.** MONGREL DOG a dog that is of mixed or unknown breed (*slang*) **2.** OFFENSIVE TERM an offensive

term that deliberately insults sb's intelligence or knowledge (*offensive insult*) [Late 19thC. Shortening of MUTTONHEAD.]

mutter /múttər/ *v.* (-ters, -tering, -tered) **1.** *vti.* SAY STH QUIETLY to speak or say sth quietly and indistinctly **2.** *vi.* GRUMBLE to say sth in a quiet voice, especially as a complaint or in annoyance ■ *n.* STH SAID QUIETLY an act of saying sth quietly and indistinctly, or sth said in this way [14thC. Origin uncertain: perhaps from Latin *muttire*.]

mutton /mútt'n/ *n.* the flesh of a fully grown sheep, eaten as food [13thC. Directly or via Old French *molton* 'ram, wether, sheep' from medieval Latin *multon-*, the stem of *multo*, of uncertain origin: probably ultimately from assumed Gaulish *multo*.] —**muttony** *adj.* ◇ **mutton dressed as lamb** an older woman who dresses or behaves in a way more suitable to a younger one (*disapproving*)

mutton bird *n.* an Australasian sea bird of the shearwater family. Mutton birds are traditionally hunted by the Maori for food. [*Mutton* from the taste of its cooked flesh, which is said to resemble mutton]

mutton-birder *n. NZ* sb who hunts mutton birds

muttonchops /mútt'n chops/ *npl.* facial hair trimmed into a narrow strip beside each ear, broadening out along the lower cheek and stopping at the side of the chin, which is kept bare [From the shape]

muttonhead /mútt'n hed/ *n.* an offensive term that deliberately insults sb's intelligence or knowledge (*offensive insult*) —**muttonheaded** *adj.*

mutual /myóochoo əl/ *adj.* **1.** FELT AND EXPRESSED BY EACH done, felt, or expressed by each towards or with regard to the other **2.** WITH SAME FEELINGS OR RELATIONSHIP with the same feelings, or in the same relationship to each other **3.** SHARED BY TWO PEOPLE OR GROUPS shared by or common to two or more people or groups **4.** INSUR OF MUTUAL INSURANCE relating to mutual insurance [15thC. From French *mutuel*, from Latin *mutuus* 'borrowed, reciprocal, done in exchange'.] —**mutuality** /myoochoo álləti/ *n.* —**mutually** /myoochoo əli/ *adv.* —**mutualness** /myoochoo əl nəss/ *n.*

mutual assured destruction *n.* the enormous reciprocal damage that the superpowers and their allies would inflict on each other in the event of a nuclear war

mutual fund *n. US* = unit trust

mutual inductance *n.* a measure of the change in the electromotive force of a circuit caused by a change in the current flowing through an associated circuit. It is given as the ratio of the electromotive force induced to the rate of current change producing it. Symbol M

mutual induction *n.* the production of an electromotive force in a circuit resulting from a change in the current flowing through another circuit to which it is magnetically linked

mutual insurance *n.* a method of insurance in which the customers buying policies own the company, pay premiums into a common fund to cover claims, and share in the profits

mutualise *vti.* = mutualize

mutualism /myoochoo əlizəm/ *n.* a relationship between two organisms of different species that benefits both and harms neither. For example, lichens are a fungus and an alga living in mutualism: the fungus provides a protective structure, and the alga produces a carbohydrate as food for the fungus. ◇ **symbiosis** —**mutualist** *n.* —**mutualistic** /myoochoo ə listik/ *adj.*

mutualize /myoochoo ə līz/ (-izes, -izing, -ized), **mutualise** (-ises, -ising, -ised) *vti.* to become mutual, or make sth mutual —**mutualization** /myoochoo ə līzáysh'n/ *n.*

mutual savings bank *n.* a bank without shareholders in which the depositors are technically the owners

mutule /myoo tyool/ *n.* a projecting block that holds a gutta under a Doric cornice [Mid-17thC. Via French from Latin *mutulus.*]

muumuu /moo moo/ (*plural* -muus), **mumu** (*plural* -mus) *n.* a loose shapeless dress made of brightly coloured fabric worn especially by women in Hawaii [Early

20thC. From Hawaiian *mu'u mu'u*, literally 'cut off' (from the fact that there was originally no yoke).]

mux /muks/ *n.* a multiplexer (*informal*) [Late 20thC. Shortening.]

Muzak /myóo zak/ *tdmk.* a trademark for recorded background music played in shops, restaurants, lifts, and other public places

muzhik /moo zhík/ *n.* a Russian peasant, especially during the tsarist era [Mid-16thC. From Russian, literally 'small man', from *muzh* 'man, husband'.]

Muzorewa /móozzə ráywə/, **Abel Tendekayi** (*b.* 1925) Zimbabwean clergyman and statesman. He was Methodist bishop of what was then Rhodesia and prime minister (1979–80) during its transition to becoming the state of Zimbabwe.

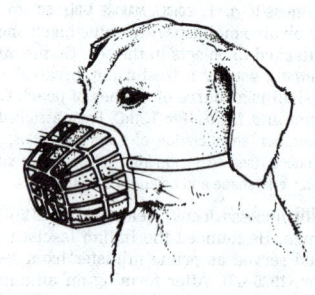

Muzzle

muzzle /múzz'l/ *n.* **1.** ZOOL ANIMAL'S NOSE AND JAWS the projecting part of an animal's face, made up of its nose and jaws **2.** RESTRAINING DEVICE FOR ANIMAL a device that is strapped over the nose and jaws of an animal to prevent it from opening its mouth, e.g. to bite, bark, or eat **3.** ARMS END OF GUN BARREL the front open end of the barrel of a firearm **4.** STH THAT PREVENTS FREE EXPRESSION sth that is meant to prevent free expression ■ *vt.* (-zles, -zling, -zled) **1.** PUT MUZZLE ON ANIMAL to put a muzzle over the nose and jaws of an animal **2.** PREVENT SB'S FREE EXPRESSION to prevent a person or group from publicly expressing particular views or opinions **3.** SAILING TAKE IN A SAIL to roll up and secure a sail [14thC. From Old French *musel*, literally 'small muzzle', from *muse* 'muzzle', from assumed Gallo-Romance *musa* 'snout', of unknown origin.] —**muzzler** *n.*

muzzleloader /múzz'l lōdər/ *n.* a firearm that is loaded through its muzzle

muzzle velocity *n.* the speed of a bullet or other projectile as it leaves the muzzle of a firearm

muzzy /múzzi/ (-zier, -ziest) *adj.* **1.** NOT THINKING CLEARLY thinking in a confused way, especially as a result of illness or drinking alcohol **2.** VAGUE vague and confused [Early 18thC. Origin uncertain: perhaps a blend of MUDDLED and FUZZY.] —**muzzily** *adv.* —**muzziness** *n.*

mv *abbr.* mezza voce

mV *abbr.* millivolt

MV *abbr.* **1.** MEASURE megavolt **2.** SHIPPING merchant vessel **3.** SHIPPING motor vessel **4.** ARMS muzzle velocity

m.v. *abbr.* **1.** COMM market value **2.** STATS mean variation

MVD *n.* the Ministry for Internal Affairs in the former Soviet Union from 1946 to 1960, acting as secret police. Full form **Ministerstvo vnutrennikh del**

MVO *abbr.* Member of the Royal Victorian Order

MVS *abbr.* Master of Veterinary Surgery

MVSc *abbr.* Master of Veterinary Science

mW *abbr.* milliwatt

MW *abbr.* **1.** RADIO medium wave **2.** CHEM molecular weight **3.** MEASURE megawatt **4.** CARS Malawi (*international vehicle registration*)

Mx *abbr.* maxwell

MX *abbr.* motocross

mxd *abbr.* mixed

my[1] /mī/ *det.* BELONGING TO ME belonging or relating to the speaker (*first person possessive determiner*) ○ *You can borrow my car.* ○ *I always keep my promises.* ■ *interj.* USED TO EXPRESS SUDDEN EMOTION used to express sudden emotion such as surprise, fright, concern, or pleasure ○ *My! What a mess!* [12thC. Shortening of MINE originally found only before consonants other than 'h'.]

my² *abbr.* million years

MY *abbr.* motor yacht

my- *prefix.* = myo- (*used before vowels*)

myalgia /mī álji ə/ *n.* pain or tenderness in a muscle or group of muscles [Mid-19thC. From modern Latin, from my- MY- + Greek *-algia* (see -ALGIA).] —**myalgic** *adj.*

myalgic encephalomyelitis *n.* full form **ME**.

myalism /mí əlizəm/ *n.* a type of witchcraft practised in the West Indies [Mid-19thC. Formed from *myal*, of uncertain origin: perhaps from Hausa *maye* 'sorcerer'.] —**myalist** *n.*

Myall Lake /mí əl-/ coastal lake in eastern New South Wales, north of Port Stephens. Area: 310 sq. km/120 sq. mi.

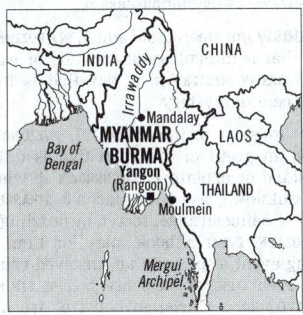
Myanmar

Myanmar /mée ən maar/ republic in southeastern Asia. It became independent from Britain as the Union of Burma in 1948. Language: Burmese. Currency: kyat. Capital: Yangon. Population: 45,570,000 (1996). Area: 676,552 sq. km/261,218 sq. mi. Official name **Union of Myanmar**. Former name **Burma**

myasthenia /mí əss theeni ə/ *n.* chronic condition of muscle weakness. Myasthenia is an autoimmune disease. [Mid-19thC. From modern Latin, from my- MY- + *asthenia* (see ASTHENIA).] —**myasthenic** /mí əss thénnik/ *adj.*

mycelium /mī seeli əm/ (*plural* **-a** /-li ə/) *n.* a loose network of the delicate filaments (**hyphae**) that form the body of a fungus, consisting of the feeding and reproducing hyphae [Mid-19thC. From modern Latin, from Greek *mukēs* 'fungus' on the model of modern Latin *epithelium* (see EPITHELIUM).] —**mycelial** *adj.* —**myceloid** /mísse loyd/ *adj.*

Mycenae /mì seè nee/ *n.* an ancient Greek city in the Peloponnese that was a centre of Bronze Age culture until its destruction around 1100 BC —**Mycenaean** *n., adj.*

mycet- *prefix.* = myceto- (*used before vowels*)

-mycete *suffix.* a fungus [Via modern Latin *-mycetes* from Greek *mukētes*, the plural of *mukēs* 'fungus' (source of English *mycelium*)]

myceto- *prefix.* fungus, fungi ○ *mycetophagous* [Via modern Latin from Greek *mukēt*, the stem of *mukēs* (see MYCO-)]

mycetoma /míssi tṓmə/ (*plural* **-mas** or **-mata** /-mətə/) *n.* an inflammation of tissues caused by a fungal or bacterial infection, usually of the feet or legs, which swell and develop pus-discharging nodules [Late 19thC. From modern Latin, from Greek *mukēt-*, the stem of *mukēs* 'fungus'.] —**mycetomatous** /míssi tómmətəss/ *adj.*

mycetophagous /míssi tóffəgəss/ *adj.* feeding on fungi

-mycin *suffix.* a substance derived from a bacterium ○ *streptomycin* [Coined from MYCO- + -IN; so called because the bacteria were originally thought to be fungi]

myco- *prefix.* fungus, fungi ○ *mycotoxin* [From Greek *mukēs*. Ultimately from an Indo-European word meaning 'slimy', which is also the ancestor of English *mucus*.]

mycobacterium /míkō bak teèri əm/ (*plural* **-a** /-ri ə/) *n.* a rodlike Gram-positive aerobic bacterium that can form branching structures resembling filaments. Some cause diseases in humans, e.g. tu-

berculosis or leprosy. Genus: *Mycobacterium*. —**mycobacterial** *adj.*

mycology /mī kóllǝji/ *n.* **1.** BOT STUDY OF FUNGI a branch of botany that specializes in the scientific study of fungi **2.** FUNGI FUNGI OF PARTICULAR AREA the fungi that live in a particular area **3.** FUNGI CHARACTERISTICS OF INDIVIDUAL FUNGUS the characteristics of a particular fungus [Mid-19thC. From modern Latin *mycologia*, from *myco-* MYCO- + Latin *-logia* (see -LOGY).] —**mycologic** /míkǝ lójjik/ *adj.* —**mycologically** *adv.* —**mycologist** /mī kóllǝji/ *n.*

mycophagist /mī kóffǝjist/ *n.* an animal that eats fungi [Mid-19thC. Formed from *mycophagy*, from MYCO- + -PHAGY.]

mycophagous /mī kóffǝgǝss/ *adj.* feeding on fungi —**mycophagy** /-kóffǝji/ *n.*

mycoplasma /míkō plázmǝ/ *n.* a microorganism of a genus considered to be the smallest known living cells. Some species cause respiratory diseases in animals and human being. Regarded by some as primitive bacteria, they need sterols such as cholesterol for growth. Genus: *Mycoplasma*. —**mycoplasmal** *adj.*

mycorrhiza /míkō rízǝ/ (*plural* **-zas** or **-zae** /-rí zee/), **mycorhiza** (*plural* **-zas** or **-zae**) *n.* a mutually beneficial association of a fungus and the roots of a plant such as a conifer or an orchid, in which the plant's mineral absorption is enhanced and the fungus obtains nutrients [Late 19thC. From modern Latin, from *myco-* (See MYCO-) + Greek *rhiza* 'root'.] —**mycorrhizal** *adj.*

mycosis /mī kṓssiss/ (*plural* **-ses** /-seez/) *n.* any disease or infection of human beings or animals caused by a fungus

mycotoxin /míkō tóksin/ *n.* a poisonous substance produced by a fungus. Mycotoxins may affect foods such as peanuts.

mycotrophic /míkō trṓffik, -tróffik/ *adj.* used to describe a plant that lives in association with a fungus, as do various orchids in which the fungus lives on the roots

mydriasis /mī drí əssiss, mi-/ *n.* excessive dilation of the pupils of the eye, usually caused by prolonged drug therapy, coma, or injury to the eye [Early 19thC. Via Latin from Greek *mudriasis*.]

myel- *prefix.* = myelo- (*used before vowels*)

myelencephalon /mí ə len séffǝ lon/ *n.* a part of the embryonic hindbrain formed by an extension of the spinal cord into the skull. It is the major pathway for nerve impulses leaving and entering the brain. [Mid-19thC. From modern Latin, from *myel-* MYEL- + *encephalon* (see ENCEPHALON).] —**myelencephalic** /mí ə len sə fállik/ *adj.*

myelin /mí əlin/ *n.* a whitish material made up of protein and fats that surrounds some nerve cells in concentric sheaths, insulating adjacent nerve fibres and enabling transmission of nerve impulses [Late 19thC. Coined from MYEL- + -IN.]

myelinated /mí əli naytid/ *adj.* used to describe nerve fibres that are surrounded by a sheath of myelin

myelin sheath /mí əlin/ *n.* a layer of myelin that insulates some nerve cells. In multiple sclerosis, the myelin sheath is damaged and the nerve impulse is impaired.

myelitis /mí ə lítiss/ *n.* inflammation of the spinal cord or bone marrow

myelo- *prefix.* **1.** bone marrow ○ *myelofibrosis* **2.** spinal cord, spinal column ○ *myelencephalon* [Via modern Latin from Greek *muelos* 'marrow', of uncertain origin: probably formed from *mus* 'muscle' (see MYO-)]

myeloblast /mí əlō blast/ *n.* a cell that develops into a type of white blood cell (**granulocyte**) and that is normally seen only in the bone marrow where blood is formed. In some diseases, e.g. leukaemia, myeloblasts may appear in the blood. —**myeloblastic** /mí əlō blástik/ *adj.*

myelocyte /mí əlō sīt/ *n.* an immature form of a type of white blood cell (**granulocyte**), normally found in the blood-forming tissue of the bone marrow —**myelocytic** /mí əlō síttik/ *adj.*

myelofibrosis /mí əlō fī bróssiss/ *n.* a progressive disease in which the cells of the bone marrow that

produce fibre rather than blood cells proliferate, leading to anaemia and enlargement of the spleen and liver —**myelofibrotic** /mí əlō fī bróttik/ *adj.*

myelogenous /mí ə lójjənəss/, **myelogenic** /mí əlō jénnik/ *adj.* originating in or produced by the bone marrow

myelogenous leukaemia *n.* = myeloid leukaemia

myelogram /mí əlō gram, mī éllō-/ *n.* a radiographic image created by injecting an X-ray/opaque liquid into the spinal cord, to diagnose disorders of the spine including slipped discs or tumours —**myelography** /mí ə lóggrəfi/ *n.*

myeloid /mí ə loyd/ *adj.* relating to, involving, or derived from bone marrow or the spinal cord

myeloid leukaemia *n.* a variety of leukaemia in which some types of white blood cells, originating in the myeloid tissue of the bone marrow, proliferate abnormally, suppressing healthy red and white blood cells

myeloma /mí ə lṓmə/ (*plural* **-mas** or **-mata** /-mətə/) *n.* a malignant tumour that develops in the blood-cell-producing cells of the bone marrow —**myelomatoid** *adj.*

Myer /mí ər/, **Sidney Baevski** (1878–1934) Russian-born Australian retailer. He was founder of the Myer's chain of department stores. Real name **Simcha Baevski Myer**

myiasis /mí əssiss/ (*plural* **-ses** /-seez/) *n.* an infestation of living tissue or an organism by maggots such as fly larvae. It can affect the skin, eyes, digestive tract, or open wounds. [Mid-19thC. From modern Latin, from Greek *muia* 'fly'.]

My Lai /mí lī/ village in Vietnam that was the site of a massacre of civilians by US troops during the Vietnam War (1968)

mylonite /mílǝ nīt, míllǝ-/ *n.* a fine-grained layered metamorphic rock, formed where the movement of rocks against each other causes crushing and grinding. It is found in fault zones. [Late 19thC. Formed from Greek *mulōn* 'mill' (source of English *amyl*).]

mynah /mínǝ/, **mynah bird**, **myna** *n.* a medium-sized bird of the starling family, native to southeastern Asia and Australia. Some varieties are known for their ability to mimic human speech. Genera: *Acridotheres* and *Gracula*. [Mid-18thC. From Hindi *mainā*.]

Mynheer /mǝ neèr/ *n.* **1.** TITLE FOR DUTCH MAN a title used to address a Dutch man, equivalent to 'Mr' when used before a surname and to 'sir' when used alone **2.** **Mynheer, mynheer** DUTCHMAN a Dutchman (*informal*) [Mid-17thC. From Dutch *mijnheer*, literally 'my lord', from *heer* 'lord, master'.]

myo- *prefix.* muscle ○ *myofibril* [Via modern Latin from Greek *mus*. Ultimately from an Indo-European word meaning 'mouse', which is also the ancestor of English *mouse* and *muscle*.]

myocardial /mí ō kaárdi əl/ *adj.* relating to or affecting the thick muscular wall of the heart. ♦ **myocardium**

myocardial infarction *n.* the death of a segment of heart muscle, caused by a blood clot in the coronary artery interrupting blood supply

myocarditis /mí ō kaar dítiss/ *n.* acute or chronic inflammation of the heart muscle

myocardium /mí ō kaárdi əm/ (*plural* **-a** /-di ə/) *n.* the thick muscular wall of the heart. The myocardium is thickest around the left ventricle where the pressure generated by the heart is greatest. [Late 19thC. From modern Latin, from *myo-* MYO- + Greek *kardia* 'heart'.]

myoclonus /mī óklənəss/ *n.* a sudden muscular contraction, or a series of these, which if persistent usually indicates a disorder of the nervous system. It is normal to experience these contractions when falling asleep. —**myoclonic** /mí ō klónnik/ *adj.*

myoelectric /mí ō i léktrik/, **myoelectrical** /-trik'l/ *adj.* **1.** OF ELECTRICAL PROPERTIES OF MUSCLE relating to or involving the electrical properties of muscle **2.** USING ELECTRICAL PROPERTIES OF MUSCLE using the detection of electrical impulses in muscle to activate a bionic part such as an artificial limb

myofibril /mí ō fíbril/ *n.* structure resembling a thread running through a muscle cell that enables the muscle to contract

myofilament /mī ō fíllәmәnt/ *n.* one of the filaments that make up a myofibril, either the thicker filaments composed of the protein myosin or the thinner filaments composed of the proteins actin or troponin

myogenic /mī ō jénnik/ *adj.* originating in or able to form in muscle cells, as are the contractions of heart muscle fibres that are spontaneous and do not depend on nerve stimulation

myoglobin /mī ō glṓbin/ *n.* an iron-containing protein resembling haemoglobin, found in muscle cells. It takes oxygen from the blood, releasing it to the muscles during strenuous exercise. The three-dimensional structure of myoglobin and the alpha and beta chains of haemoglobin are almost identical.

myograph /mī ә graaf, -graf/ *n.* an instrument that produces a tracing corresponding to muscle contractions —**myographic** /mī ә gráffik/ *adj.* —**myographically** /-gráffikli/ *adv.*

myology /mī óllәji/ *n.* the study of the structure, function, and diseases of muscle [Mid-17thC. Directly or via French *myologie* from modern Latin *myologia*, from *myo-* (See MYO-) + *-logia* (see -LOGY).] —**myologic** /mī ә lójjik/ *adj.* —**myologist** /mī óllәjist/ *n.*

myoma /mī ṓmә/ (*plural* **-mas** *or* **-mata** /-mәtә/) *n.* a benign tumour of the muscle tissue —**myomatous** *adj.*

myoneural /mī ō nyóorәl/ *adj.* relating to or involving both muscles and nerves

myopathy /mī óppәthi/ (*plural* **-thies**) *n.* any disease of the muscles or muscle tissues, either inherited such as muscular dystrophy or acquired such as polio. All myopathies are characterized by muscle weakness and wasting with pain and tenderness. —**myopathic** /mī ә páthik/ *adj.*

myope /mī ōp/ *n.* sb affected by myopia [Early 18thC. Via French from Latin *myop-*, the stem of *myops* 'short-sighted', from Greek *muōps* (see MYOPIA).]

myopia /mī ṓpi ә/ *n.* **1.** MED **SHORTNESS OF SIGHT** a common condition in which light entering the eye is focused in front of the retina and distant objects cannot be seen sharply. In high myopia the eyeball is unusually long, whereas in physiological myopia the eyeball length is normal but the power of the cornea is too great for the axial length. **2. LACK OF FORESIGHT** lack of foresight or long-term planning [Early 18thC. Via modern Latin from late Greek *muōpia*, from Greek *muōps* 'short-sighted', from *muein* 'to blink' (source of English *mystery*[1]).]

myopic /mī óppik/ *adj.* **1.** MED **HAVING MYOPIA** affected by myopia **2. LACKING IN FORESIGHT** showing a lack of foresight or long-term planning —**myopically** *adv.*

myosin /mī ә ssin/ *n.* a protein that is present in the filaments of muscles and is responsible for the contraction of muscle cells [Mid-19thC. Coined from MY- + -OSE + -IN.]

myosis *n.* = **miosis**

myositis /mī ә sītiss/ *n.* muscle inflammation and soreness [Early 19thC. From modern Latin, from Greek *muos* 'of a muscle', a form of *mus* 'mouse, muscle'.]

myosotis /mī ә sṓtiss/ (*plural* **-tes**), **myosote** /mī ә sōt/ *n.* a plant of the borage family with hairy leaves and stems and small flowers that may be pink at first and then blue. The forget-me-not is one variety of myosotis. Genus: *Myosotis.* [Early 17thC. Via modern Latin, genus name, from Latin, 'mouse-ear (a plant)', from Greek *muosōtis*, from, ultimately, *mus* 'mouse, muscle' + *ous* 'ear' (source of English *otic*).]

myotome /mī ә tōm/ *n.* **1.** BIOL **TYPE OF EMBRYONIC CELL** any of the cells in early embryos that give rise to all the muscles in the body **2.** ANAT **TYPE OF MUSCLE** a muscle that is supplied by a nerve of the spine

myotonia /mī ә tṓni ә/ *n.* a muscle condition that results in the muscles maintaining contractions for much longer than normal and having difficulty in relaxing [Late 19thC. From modern Latin, from *myo-* (See MYO-) + Greek *tonos* 'tone'.] —**myotonic** /mī ә tónnik/ *adj.*

myriad /mírri әd/ *adj.* **1. TOO NUMEROUS TO COUNT** so many that they cannot be counted **2. OF MANY DIFFERENT ELEMENTS** made up of many different elements ■ *n.* **1. LARGE NUMBER** a huge number **2. TEN THOUSAND** ten thousand (*archaic*) [Mid-16thC. Directly or via Old French from the late Latin stem *myriad-*, from Greek *muriad-*, from, ultimately, *murios* 'countless' (plural *murioi* 'ten thousand').]

myriapod /mírri ә pod/ *n.* an arthropod such as a centipede or millipede with a head, a long segmented body, and at least nine pairs of legs. Class: Myriapoda. [Early 19thC. From modern Latin *Myriapoda*, class name, literally 'with a myriad of feet', from, ultimately, Greek *murias* 'myriad'.]

myrica /mi rīkә/ *n.* a tonic and anti-diarrhoea agent extracted from the root bark of the wax myrtle tree [Early 18thC. Via Latin, 'tamarisk', from Greek *murikē*.]

myristic acid /mi rístik-/ *n.* an acid found in the fats of plants and animals and used in making soaps, flavourings, cosmetics, and perfumes. Formula: $C_{14}H_{28}O_2$. [*Myristic* from modern Latin *Myristica* (name of a genus of trees), from medieval Latin *(nux) myristica* 'nutmeg', from Greek *murizein* 'to anoint']

myrmecology /múrmi kóllәji/ *n.* the scientific study of ants [Late 19thC. Formed from Greek *murmēko-*, from *murmēx* 'ant'.] —**myrmecologic** /múrmikә lójjik/ *adj.* —**myrmecologist** /múrmi kóllәjist/ *n.*

myrmidon /múrmidәn, -don/ *n.* a faithful follower who obeys orders unquestioningly [Mid-17thC. See MYRMIDON.]

Myrmidon *n.* in Greek mythology, a member of a people who lived in Thessaly and were led by Achilles to the Trojan War [15thC. Via Latin *Myrmidones* (plural) from Greek *Murmidones* from *murmēkes* (according to legend, from 'ants', from which they were created according to legend.]

myrobalan /mī róbbәlәn, mi-/ *n.* **1. FRUIT USED IN DYEING** the dried fruit of a tropical shrub that resembles a plum and is used in dyeing and in making ink **2.** = **cherry plum** [Mid-16thC. Directly or via French from Latin *myrobalanum*, from Greek *murobalanon*, from *muron* 'balsam, ointment' + *balanos* 'acorn'.]

myrrh /mur/ *n.* **1. AROMATIC RESIN** an aromatic resinous gum obtained from various trees and shrubs that are native to Africa and southern Asia, used in perfume, incense, and medicinal preparations **2.** BOT = **sweet cicely** [Pre-12thC. From Latin *myrrha*, from Greek *murra*, of Semitic origin (source of English *myrtle*).]

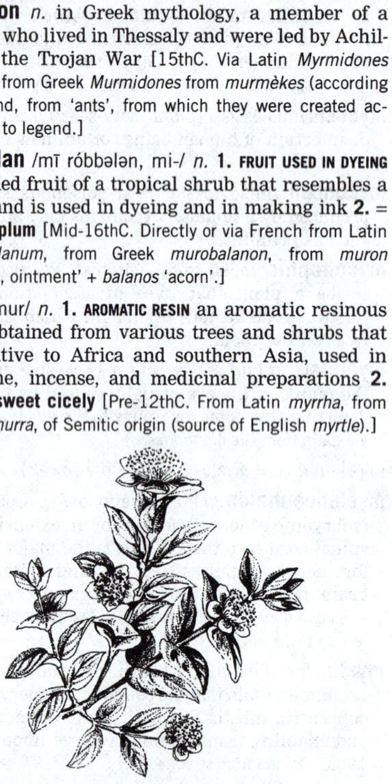

Myrtle

myrtle /múrt'l/ *n.* TREES an evergreen tree or shrub, native to the Mediterranean region and western Asia, with white or pink flowers and edible blue-black fruit. Family: Myrtaceae. [14thC. Directly or via Old French from medieval Latin *myrtilla*, literally 'small myrtle tree', from Latin *myrtus* 'myrtle tree', from Greek *murtos*, of Semitic origin.]

Myrtle Beach /múrt'l-/ city and tourist resort in eastern South Carolina, on the Atlantic Ocean, southeast of Florence. Population: 25,456 (1996).

myself /mī sélf/ *pron.* **1. REFERS BACK TO SPEAKER** used to refer to the speaker or writer (*first person reflexive pronoun, used when the object of a verb or preposition refers to the same person as the subject of the verb*) ○ *I didn't enjoy myself very much.* ○ *Of all the people I am hard on, I am hardest on myself.* **2. REFERS EMPHATICALLY TO SPEAKER** refers emphatically to the speaker or writer ○ *I'm curious about that myself.* ○ *I can't expect you to be able to read my writing; I myself can't read it.* **3. MY NORMAL SELF** my normal or usual self ○ *I haven't been myself since the accident.* [Old English *mēseolf*, literally 'me self' (*self* in the obsolete sense of 'same')]

Mysore /mī sáwr/ city in the Mysore District, south-central Karnataka State, southern India. Population: 480,006 (1991).

mystagogue /místә gog/ *n.* **1. INSTRUCTOR OF INITIATES** sb who instructs candidates for initiation into sacred mysteries **2. SB SPREADING MYSTICAL DOCTRINES** sb who believes in and disseminates mystical doctrines [Mid-16thC. Directly or via French from Latin *mystagogus*, from Greek *mustagōgos*, literally 'leader of candidates for initiation', from *mustēs* 'initiated person' (see MYSTERY[1]).] —**mystagogic** /místә gójjik/ *adj.* —**mystagogically** /-gójjikli/ *adv.* —**mystagogy** /místә goji/ *n.*

mysterious /mi stéeri әss/ *adj.* **1. ABOUT WHICH LITTLE IS KNOWN** about whom or which little is known or explained **2. DIFFICULT TO UNDERSTAND** difficult to understand or explain **3. FULL OF MYSTERY** full of or suggesting mystery [Late 16thC. Formed from French *mystérieux*, from *mystère* 'mystery', via Old French from Latin *mysterium* (see MYSTERY[1]).] —**mysteriousness** *n.*

mysteriously /mi stéeri әssli/ *adv.* **1. IN A PUZZLING WAY** in a way that is difficult to understand or explain **2. IN A WAY FULL OF MYSTERY** in a way that is full of or reminiscent of mystery

mystery[1] /místәri/ *n.* (*plural* **-ies**) **1. PUZZLING EVENT OR SITUATION** an event or situation that is difficult to understand or explain **2. SB UNKNOWN** sb who or sth that is unknown, secret, or hidden **3. STRANGENESS** the quality of being strange, secret, or puzzling **4. STORY ABOUT PUZZLING EVENT** a book, play, or film about a puzzling event, especially an unsolved crime, that makes great use of suspense **5.** CHR **STH KNOWN BY DIVINE REVELATION** a Christian belief or truth that is considered to be beyond human understanding and can be made known only by divine revelation **6.** CHR **INCIDENT FROM LIFE OF JESUS CHRIST** an incident in the life of Jesus Christ that Christians believe to have particular spiritual significance, especially, in Roman Catholicism, one of 15 events including the Annunciation and the Crucifixion **7.** CHR **CHRISTIAN SACRAMENT** one of the Christian sacraments, especially Communion **8.** RELIG **RELIGIOUS GROUP** a religious group having secret rites, especially one of the ancient Mediterranean religions, e.g. of the Romans **9.** RELIG **RELIGIOUS RITE** a secret rite or ceremony performed by a religious group, especially belonging to one of the ancient Mediterranean religions (*often used in the plural*) **10.** ARTS = **mystery play** ■ **mysteries** *npl.* **1. SECRET KNOWLEDGE** special knowledge known only to people skilled or involved in a particular activity, group, or subject **2.** CHR **CONSECRATED BREAD AND WINE** in Christianity, the consecrated bread and wine used in the sacrament of Communion [14thC. Directly or via assumed Anglo-Norman from Latin *mysterium*, from Greek *mustērion* 'secret rite', from *mustēs* 'initiated person', from *muein* 'to close the eyes or lips, initiate'.]

WORD KEY: SYNONYMS

See Synonyms at ***problem***.

mystery[2] /místәri/ (*plural* **-ies**) *n.* (*archaic*) **1. GUILD** a guild of merchants or craftsmen **2. CRAFT** a handicraft or trade [13thC. From medieval Latin *misterium* 'service, office', a contraction (influenced by Latin *mysterium* 'mystery') of Latin *ministerium*, from *minister* 'servant' (see MINISTER).]

mystery play *n.* a medieval drama staged by a craft guild and often based on stories from the Bible such as the Flood or incidents from the life of Jesus Christ

mystery tour *n.* a pleasure trip, especially by bus, to a destination that is not made known to the passengers beforehand

mystic /místik/ *n.* RELIG **FOLLOWER OF MYSTICISM** sb who practises or believes in mysticism ■ *adj.* = **mystical** [14thC. Directly or via French *mystique* (adjective) from Latin *mysticus*, from Greek *mustikos*, from *mustēs* 'initiated person' (see MYSTERY[1]).]

mystical /místik'l/ *adj.* **1.** RELIG **WITH DIVINE MEANING** with a divine meaning beyond human understanding **2.** RELIG **OF MYSTICISM** relating to, involving, or typical of mysticism or mystics **3.** PARANORMAL **WITH SUPERNATURAL SIGNIFICANCE** with supernatural or spiritual significance or power **4. MYSTERIOUS** mysterious or difficult to understand —**mystically** adv. —**mystical-ness** n.

mysticism /místissizəm/ n. **1.** RELIG **BELIEF IN INTUITIVE SPIRITUAL REVELATION** the belief that personal communication or union with the divine is achieved through intuition, faith, ecstasy, or sudden insight rather than through rational thought **2.** RELIG **SPIRITUAL SYSTEM** a system of religious belief or practice that people follow to achieve personal communication or union with the divine **3.** CONFUSED AND VAGUE IDEAS vague or unsubstantiated thought or speculation about sth

mystify /místi fī/ (**-fies, -fying, -fied**) vt. **1.** PUZZLE SB to put sb in a position of being unable to understand or explain sth **2.** MAKE STH MYSTERIOUS to make sth mysterious or unclear [Early 19thC. From French mystifier, from mystère 'mystery' (ultimately from Latin mysterium; see MYSTERY[1]) or mystique 'mystic' (see MYSTIC).] —**mystification** /místifi káysh'n/ n. —**mystifier** /místi fī ər/ n.

mystifying /místi fī ing/ adj. difficult to understand or explain —**mystifyingly** adv.

mystique /mi steék/ n. a special quality or air that makes sb or sth appear mysterious, powerful, or desirable [Late 19thC. Via French (source of English mystic) from, ultimately, Greek mustikos, from mustēs 'initiated person' (see MYSTERY[1]).]

myth /mith/ n. **1.** MYTHOL **ANCIENT STORY** a traditional story about heroes or supernatural beings, often explaining the origins of natural phenomena or aspects of human behaviour **2.** LITERAT, MYTHOL **MYTHS COLLECTIVELY** myths considered as a group or a type of story **3.** SOC SCI **SYMBOLIC CHARACTER OR STORY** a character, story, theme, or object that embodies a particular idea or aspect of a culture **4.** SB OR STH FICTITIOUS sb or sth whose existence is or was widely believed in, but who is fictitious **5.** ALLEGORY OR PARABLE a story that has a hidden meaning, especially one that is meant to teach a lesson [Mid-19thC. Directly or via French mythe from modern Latin mythus, from Greek muthos 'speech, myth' (source of English mythos).]

myth. abbr. **1.** mythological **2.** mythology

mythical /míthik'l/, **mythic** /míthik/ adj. **1.** TYPICAL OF MYTH relating to, appearing in, based on, or typical of myth **2.** IMAGINARY not true or real, but existing only in sb's imagination **3.** LIKE MYTH like a myth, especially in being widely known or considered wonderful —**mythically** adv.

mythicize /míthi sīz/ (**-cizes, -cizing, -cized**), **mythicise** (**-cises, -cising, -cised**) vt. **1.** MAKE INTO MYTH to make sb or sth into a myth **2.** TREAT AS MYTH to see or explain an event or person as a myth —**mythicization** /míthi sī záysh'n/ n. —**mythicizer** /míthi sīzər/ n.

mythmaker /míth maykər/ n. sb who creates myths —**mythmaking** n.

mythography /mi thógrəfi/ (plural **-phies**) n. **1.** LITERAT **VOLUME OF MYTHS** a collection of myths **2.** ARTS **ARTISTIC REPRESENTATION** the representation of a mythical subject in a work of art

mythoi plural of **mythos**

mythol abbr. **1.** mythological **2.** mythology

mythological /míthə lójjik'l/, **mythologic** /-ik/ adj. **1.** MYTHOL IN MYTHS relating to, typical of, or appearing in myth **2.** IMAGINARY not real, but existing only in the imagination —**mythologically** adv.

mythologise vti. = **mythologize**

mythologist /mi thólləjist/ n. **1.** WRITER OF MYTHS sb who writes or collects myths **2.** STUDENT OF MYTHS sb who studies or is an expert on myths

mythologize /mi thóllə jīz/ (**-gizes, -gizing, -gized**), **mythologise** (**-gises, -gising, -gised**) v. **1.** vt. MAKE INTO MYTH to make sb or sth into a myth **2.** vti. EXPLAIN OR MAKE UP MYTHS to explain or relate myths **3.** vi. CREATE MYTHS to create or make up myths —**mythologization** /mi thóllə jī záysh'n/ n. —**mythologizer** /mi thóllə jīzər/ n.

mythology /mi thólləji/ (plural **-gies**) n. **1.** MYTHOL **BODY OF MYTHS** a group of myths that belong to a particular people or culture and tell about their ancestors, heroes, gods and other supernatural beings, and history **2.** BODY OF STORIES a body of stories, ideas, or beliefs that are not necessarily true about a particular place or individual **3.** MYTHOL **MYTHS COLLECTIVELY** myths considered as a group **4.** MYTHOL **STUDY OF MYTHS** the study of myths, or the branch of knowledge that deals with myths [15thC. Directly or via French from late Latin mythologia, from Greek muthologia, literally 'science of myths', from muthos (see MYTH).] —**mythologer** n.

mythomania /míthō máyni ə/ n. a very strong tendency to tell lies or exaggerate, which may be symptom of a disorder —**mythomaniac** /-máyni ak/ n.

mythopoeia /míthō peé ə/, **mythopoesis** /-pō eéssiss/ n. the creating of myths [Mid-19thC. Directly or via late Latin from Greek muthopoiia, from muthos (see MYTH) + poiein 'to make' (source of English poem).] —**mythopoeist** n.

mythopoeic /míthō peé ik/ adj. relating to, involving, or engaged in the production of myths [Mid-19thC. Formed from Greek muthopoios, from muthos (see MYTH) + poiein 'to make'.]

mythos /mī thoss, mí-/ (plural **-thoi**) n. **1.** SET OF ATTITUDES the interrelated set of beliefs, attitudes, and values held by a society or cultural group **2.** MYTH OR MYTHOLOGY a myth or mythology [Mid-18thC. From Greek muthos 'speech, myth' (source of English myth).]

myx- prefix. = **myxo-** (used before vowels)

myxo- prefix. mucus ○ myxomycete [Via modern Latin from Greek muxa 'slime, mucus' (source of English match)]

myxoedema /míksə deémə/ n. **1.** THYROID DISEASE a disease caused by an underactive or atrophied thyroid gland, characterized by sluggishness and weight gain. It can be treated with artificial thyroid hormone. **2.** SKIN SWELLING dry swelling of the skin and subcutaneous tissues, associated with an underactive thyroid gland —**myxoedematous** /míksə démmətəss, -deé-/ adj. —**myxoedemic** /míksi démmik/ adj.

myxoma /mik sōmə/ (plural **-mas** or **-mata** /-mətə/) n. a benign tumour composed of mucus and gelatinous material embedded in connective tissue, typically in the heart where it can obstruct blood flow and lead to sudden unconsciousness —**myxomatous** /mik sómmətəss/ adj.

myxomatosis /míksəmə tóssiss/ n. a highly infectious disease of rabbits caused by a virus, leading to swelling of the mucous membranes and the formation of tumours similar to myxomas [Early 20thC. From modern Latin, from myxomat-, the stem of myxoma (see MYXOMA).]

myxomycete /míksō mī seét/ n. = **slime mould** [Late 19thC. From modern Latin Myxomycetes, class name, from myxo- MYXO- + Greek mukētes, the plural of mukēs 'fungus'.]

myxovirus /míksō vīrəss/ n. any of a group of RNA-containing viruses, including those that cause diseases of the respiratory tract such as influenza, and those that cause measles and mumps (**paramyxoviruses**)

mzungu /mə zoóng goo/ n. in eastern Africa, sb who is white [From Swahili]

N n

n¹ /en/ (*plural* **n's**), **N** (*plural* **N's** *or* **Ns**) *n.* **1.** 14TH LETTER OF ENGLISH ALPHABET the 14th letter of the modern English alphabet **2.** SPEECH SOUND CORRESPONDING TO LETTER 'N' the speech sound that corresponds to the letter 'N' **3.** LETTER 'N' WRITTEN a written representation of the letter 'N'

n² /en/ *n.* an indefinite whole number

n³ *symbol.* **1.** amount of substance **2.** n, N PRINTING en dash **3.** MEASURE nano- **4.** PHYS neutron **5.** PHYS, OPTICS refractive index

n⁴, **n.**, **N**, **N.** *abbr.* **1.** north **2.** northern

n' /ən/, **'n** *conj.* and

N¹ *symbol.* **1.** PHYS Avogadro's number **2.** PHYS, MEASURE newton **3.** CHEM ELEM nitrogen

N² *abbr.* **1.** CHESS knight **2.** CARS neutral (*used on gear sticks*) **3.** November

n. *abbr.* **1.** COMM net **2.** GRAM neuter **3.** GRAM nominative **4.** noon **5.** note **6.** GRAM noun **7.** number

N. *abbr.* **1.** GEOG New (*in place names*) **2.** LANG Norse

n- *prefix.* normal

Na *symbol.* sodium [Shortening of modern Latin *natrium*, from, ultimately, Greek *nitron* 'nitre']

NA *abbr.* North America

n/a *abbr.* **1.** not applicable **2.** not available

NAACP *abbr.* National Association for the Advancement of Colored People

NAAFI /náffi/, **Naafi** *n.* **1.** an organization that provides canteens and shops for people who work in the armed forces. Full form **Navy, Army, and Air Force Institutes 2.** (*plural* **NAAFIs** *or* **Naafis**) a canteen or shop provided by the NAAFI

naan /naan/, **naan bread** *n.* = **nan¹** *n.*

naartje /naárchi/ *n.* S Africa = **nartjie**

Naas /nayss/ town in County Kildare in the eastern Republic of Ireland, 32 km/20 mi. southwest of Dublin. Population: 11,141 (1991).

nab /nab/ *n.* (**nabs, nabbing, nabbed**) *vt.* **1.** GRAB STH to seize, snatch, or take sth suddenly **2.** CATCH SB to catch and arrest a criminal or fugitive (*informal*) [Late 17thC. Origin uncertain: probably a variant of earlier *nap*, from Scandinavian.]

— WORD KEY: SYNONYMS —
See Synonyms at *catch*.

Nabataean /nábbə teé ən/, **Nabatean** *n.* **1.** PEOPLES MEMBER OF AN ARAB PEOPLE a member of an Arab people who in Roman times lived in part of modern Jordan, and whose capital city was Petra **2.** LANG EXTINCT NABATAEAN LANGUAGE the now extinct language spoken by the Nabataeans, a dialect of Aramaic [Early 17thC. Formed from Latin *Nabat(h)aeus.*] —**Nabataean** *adj.*

Nabis /naábi/ *npl.* a group of 19th-century French artists, including Bonnard, who embraced symbolism rather than the naturalism of the impressionist painters [Mid-20thC. Plural of *nabi* 'member of the Nabis', from Hebrew *nābī* 'prophet'.]

Nablus /nábləss/= **Nabulus**

nabob /náy bob/ *n.* **1.** SB RICH sb who is very rich or powerful (*informal*) **2.** HIST PERSON MADE RICH IN EAST a person from Europe who, in the past, made a fortune in the East, especially in India **3.** HIST =

nawab *n.* **1** [Early 17thC. Via Portuguese *nababo* or Spanish *nabab* from Urdu *nawwāb* 'deputy governor'.]

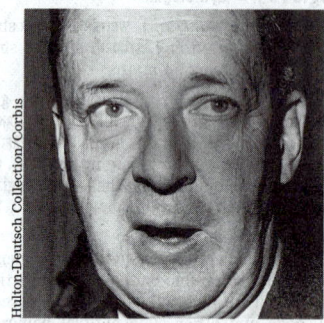

Vladimir Nabokov

Hutton-Deutsch Collection/Corbis

Nabokov /nə bŏk of, -bók-, nábbə kof/, **Vladimir** (1899–1977) Russian-born US writer. He is known for the stylish word-play of his novels, especially the controversial *Lolita* (1955). Full name **Vladimir Vladimirovich Nabokov**

Nabulus /nábbəlŏoss/, **Nablus, Nābulus** city in the West Bank Region, 48 km/30 mi. north of Jerusalem. Population: 106,944 (1987).

NAC *abbr.* National Advisory Council

nacelle /nə sél/ *n.* a separate streamlined enclosure on an aircraft for crew, cargo, or engines [Early 20thC. Via French, 'dinghy, gondola', from late Latin *navicella* 'boat' (literally 'small ship'), from Latin *navis* 'ship' (source of English *navy*).]

nachos /náchōz/ *npl.* a hot dish of tortilla chips covered with melted cheese, chili sauce, or another savoury topping, usually served as a snack or a starter [Mid-20thC. Plural of *nacho*, of uncertain origin: perhaps from Mexican Spanish, pet-form of *Ignacio*, the name of the chef who is said to have created it.]

NACODS /náy kodz/ *abbr.* National Association of Colliery Overmen, Deputies, and Shotfirers

nacre /náykər/ *n.* = **mother-of-pearl** [Late 16thC. Via French from Italian *naccaro*, from Arabic *nāqūr* 'hunting horn', from the similarity in shape to a mollusc.]

nacreous /náykri əss/ *adj.* **1.** OF MOTHER-OF-PEARL relating to, typical of, or made of mother-of-pearl **2.** LIKE MOTHER-OF-PEARL with the iridescent quality of mother-of-pearl

nacreous cloud *n.* an iridescent cloud that looks like a cirrus and appears especially in the winter at high latitudes

NACRO /nákrō/, **Nacro** *abbr.* National Association for the Care and Resettlement of Offenders

NAD *n.* a coenzyme acting as a hydrogen acceptor in many biochemical reactions, e.g. in the electron transport chain, where it is vital in the production of energy. Full form **nicotinamide adenine dinucleotide**

Na-Dene /naá dáyni, nə deén/ *n.* a language group of over 30 Native North American languages spoken in parts of Alaska, Canada, and the southwestern United States. About 200,000 people speak a Na-Dene language. [From Athapaskan *na* + North Athapaskan *dene* 'people'] —**Na-Dene** *adj.*

NADH *n.* the chemically reduced form of NAD that reverts to NAD in a process that initiates the gen-

eration of cellular energy [Mid-20thC. From NAD + *H* 'hydrogen'.]

nadir /náy deer, nád-/ *n.* **1.** LOWEST POINT the lowest possible point ○ *the nadir of despair* **2.** ASTRON POINT ON CELESTIAL SPHERE the point on the celestial sphere directly below the observer and opposite the zenith [14thC. Via French and medieval Latin from Arabic *naẓīr (as-samt)*, literally 'opposite (the zenith)'.]

NADP *n.* a coenzyme in living cells that is similar to NAD but with an extra phosphate group. It tends to participate in biochemical syntheses rather than energy-yielding reactions. Formula: $C_{21}H_{28}N_7O_{17}P_3$. Full form **nicotinamide adenine dinucleotide phosphate**

nae /nay/ *adv.* Scotland **1.** NO no **2.** NOT not

naevus /neévəss/ (*plural* **-vi** /-vī/) *n.* a birthmark, mole, or any other kind of growth or mark on the skin that a person is born with. US term **nevus**

naff /naf/ *adj.* lacking real or fashionable stylishness and appearing boring, tasteless, or unattractive (*informal*)

naff off (**naffs off, naffing off, naffed off**) *vi.* used as a rude way of telling sb to go away (*informal*)

NAFTA /náftə/ *n.* a free trade agreement signed between the United States and Canada in 1989, and extended to include Mexico in 1994. Full form **North American Free Trade Agreement**

nag¹ /nag/ *v.* (**nags, nagging, nagged**) **1.** *vti.* ASK REPEATEDLY to ask or urge sb persistently and annoyingly to do sth ○ *He keeps nagging me to go and see the doctor.* **2.** *vti.* KEEP CRITICIZING to complain repeatedly to sb in an irritating way, e.g. about some aspect of their behaviour or appearance **3.** *vi.* BE PERSISTENTLY PAINFUL OR BOTHERSOME to be a persistent cause of discomfort, anxiety, or unease ○ *My conscience had been nagging me all week.* ○ *a nagging pain* ■ *n.* SB WHO NAGS sb, especially a woman, who tends to nag (*insult*) [Early 19thC. Originally 'to gnaw, nibble', of uncertain origin: probably from Old Norse *gnaga* 'to bite' or Low German *(g)naggen* 'to irritate'.] —**nagger** *n.* —**nagging** *n.* —**naggingly** *adv.*

— WORD KEY: SYNONYMS —
See Synonyms at *complain*.

nag² /nag/ *n.* **1.** OLD HORSE an old horse, especially one that is worn out **2.** RACEHORSE a horse, especially a racehorse (*slang*) **3.** SMALL HORSE a small horse for riding (*archaic*) [15thC. Origin uncertain.]

Naga /naágə/ (*plural* **-ga** *or* **-gas**) *n.* **1.** PEOPLES MEMBER OF SOUTH ASIAN PEOPLE a member of a South Asian people who live in northeastern India and western Myanmar. They were head-hunters until the 20th century and still maintain a traditional style of life. **2.** LANG NAGA LANGUAGE the Tibeto-Burman language of the Naga people. It is spoken by about 120,000 people. [Mid-19thC. Origin uncertain: perhaps from Sanskrit *nagna* 'naked' or *naga* 'mountain'.] —**Naga** *adj.*

Nagaland /naágə land/ state in northeastern India, bordering Myanmar. Area: 16,579 sq. km/6,400 sq. mi. Population: 1,410,000 (1994).

Naga-Mikir *n.* LANG = **Naga**

nagana /nə gaánə/, **n'gana** *n.* an often fatal disease caused by trypanosome protozoan parasites that affects hoofed animals such as cattle, horses, and goats in tropical Africa and is transmitted by the tsetse fly. It is related to sleeping sickness. [Late 19thC. From Zulu *nakane*.]

Nagano /nə gaánō/ city and port in Japan, on Honshu Island. It is the commercial centre and capital of Nagano Prefecture. Population: 347,036 (1990).

Nagari /náagəri/ *n.* **1.** SET OF INDIAN ALPHABETS a set of alphabets used for several languages of the Indian subcontinent, including Sanskrit and Hindi **2.** = **Devanagari** [Late 18thC. From Sanskrit *nagari*, literally 'script of the city'.]

Nagarjuna /nág aar jóonə/ (*fl.* mid-2nd or 3rd century AD) Indian philosopher. One of the greatest Buddhist thinkers, he founded the Madhyamika (Middle Path) school of Mahayana Buddhism.

Nagasaki /nágge saáki/ city and port in southern Japan, on Kyushu Island, and capital of Nagasaki Prefecture. It was destroyed by an atomic bomb in 1945. Population: 445,000 (1990).

Nagoya /na góy yə/ city in Japan, on Honshu Island. It is the capital city and industrial centre of Aichi Prefecture. Population: 2,091,000 (1994).

Nagpur /nag poór/ city in central India, in Maharashtra State, on the River Nag. Population: 1,622,225 (1991).

Imre Nagy

Nagy /nóddyə/, **Imre** (1896–1958) Hungarian statesman. Prime minister of communist Hungary (1953–55 and 1956), he led the Hungarian uprising (1956) and was later executed.

nah /na, naa/ *interj.* no (*nonstandard*) [Early 20thC. Alteration of NO.]

Nah. *abbr.* BIBLE Nahum

Nahanni National Park /nə haáni-/ national park and preserve in northern Canada, in southwestern Northwest Territories, on the South Nahanni River. It is a World Heritage Site. Area: 4,766 sq. km/1,840 sq. mi.

NAHT *abbr.* National Association of Headteachers

Nahuatl /naá waat'l/, naa waát'l/ (*plural* **-tl** *or* **-tls**), **Nahua** /naá waa, naa waá/ (*plural* **-hua** *or* **-huas**) *n.* **1.** PEOPLES MEMBER OF NATIVE CENTRAL AMERICAN PEOPLE a member of a Native Central American people who live in southern Mexico and Central America. The Nahuatl include the ancient Aztecs. **2.** **Nahuatl, Nahua, Nahuatlan** LANG NAHUATL LANGUAGE the language of the Nahuatl people. It belongs to the Uto-Aztecan family of languages, and is spoken by over one million people. [Early 19thC. Via Spanish from Nahuatl, singular of *Nahua* 'the Nahuatl people'. English words of Nahuatl origin include: avocado, Aztec, cacao, chili, chocolate, coyote, guacamole, mesquite, peyote, tamale, tomato.] —**Nahuatl** *adj.*

Nahum /náyhəm/ *n.* **1.** BIBLICAL HEBREW PROPHET a Hebrew prophet who lived in the 7th century BC. He was one of the minor prophets. **2.** BOOK OF THE BIBLE a book of the Bible that records the prophecies of Nahum, including the prophecy foretelling the siege and sack of the Assyrian capital of Nineveh in 612 BC. See table at **Bible**

NAI *abbr.* nonaccidental injury

naiad /níı ad/ (*plural* **-ads** *or* **-ades** /níı ədeez/) *n.* **1.** MYTHOL GREEK WATER NYMPH in Greek mythology, a nymph of lakes, rivers, springs, and fountains. The naiads were skilled in music and dancing, and were supposed to have healing powers. **2.** INSECTS AQUATIC LARVA the immature water-dwelling form (**larva**) of a dragonfly, damselfly, mayfly, or stonefly **3.** BOT AQUATIC PLANT a plant that grows under water and has narrow leaves and small white flowers. Genus:

Najas. [14thC. Via the Latin stem *naiad-* from the Greek stem *naiad-* 'water nymph', from *naein* 'to flow'.]

Naiad /níı ad/ *n.* the innermost known natural satellite of Neptune, discovered in 1989 by Voyager 2. It is approximately 58 km/36 mi. in diameter.

naïf *adj.* naive [Late 16thC. From French *naïf* (see NAIVE).]

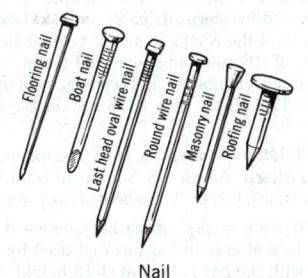

Nail

nail /nayl/ *n.* **1.** SHORT POINTED METAL ROD a strong metal pin with a flat round head and a pointed end that is hammered into wood or masonry and used to fasten objects together or hang sth on **2.** STH LIKE NAIL sth that is like a nail in its shape, in being sharp, or in the way it is used **3.** ANAT, ZOOL HARD AREA ON FINGER OR TOE in humans and other primates, the thin horny covering that grows on the upper surface of the end of each finger and toe **4.** ZOOL CLAW the claw of a bird, mammal, or reptile **5.** MEASURE UNIT OF MEASURE an old unit of measure for cloth that was equal to 5.7 cm/2¼ in ■ *vt.* (**nails, nailing, nailed**) **1.** ATTACH WITH NAILS to fasten, attach, or secure sth using nails **2.** FIX STEADILY to keep sth fixed or focussed on sth ○ *His gaze was nailed to the astonishing scene.* **3.** CATCH OR CONVICT GUILTY PERSON to catch sb who is guilty of an offence, prove the person's guilt, or have the person convicted (*informal*) ○ *It took them five years to nail him for insider trading.* **4.** EXPOSE UNTRUTH to prove that sth is not true or valid and so stop others from believing it (*informal*) **5.** HIT WITH BULLET OR PROJECTILE to hit or bring down sb or sth with a bullet or a projectile **6.** STOP to stop sb and speak to him or her (*informal*) ○ *nailed me in the corridor and demanded a raise.* **7.** US DO PRECISELY OR WELL to catch, hit, seize, or execute sth adroitly or precisely (*informal*) **8.** US PIN DOWN to identify sb or establish sth precisely (*informal*) ○ *I nailed him as a fraud as soon as he started talking about his wealthy background.* [Old English *nægl*. Ultimately from an Indo-European word denoting a fingernail or toenail that is also the ancestor of English *onyx* and *ungulate*. The meaning 'fastener' evolved in prehistoric Germanic.] —**nailable** *adj.* —**nailer** *n.* ◇ **hit the nail on the head** to be absolutely correct or accurate ◇ **a nail in sb's coffin** an event or action that further weakens the position of sb or sth already in decline ◇ **on the nail** immediately, or paid immediately

nail down *v.* **1.** *vt.* PIN DOWN to make sb be definite about sth **2.** ESTABLISH DEFINITIVELY to establish sth clearly and conclusively ○ *an investigation that will attempt to nail down what really happened here*

nail bed *n.* the layer of tissue at the base of a fingernail or toenail from which new nail material develops

nail-biter *n.* **1.** SB WHO BITES NAILS sb who has the habit of biting off the ends of his or her fingernails **2.** CAUSE OF TENSION a situation or contest that is extremely tense and exciting because its outcome remains uncertain until the end (*informal*) [From the stereotype of nail-biting as a sign of anxiety]

nail-biting *n.* HABIT OF BITING FINGERNAILS the habit of biting off the ends of the fingernails, especially out of anxiety, tension, or boredom ■ *adj.* TENSE extremely tense and exciting because the outcome is uncertain [See NAIL-BITER]

nail bomb *n.* a bomb packed with nails to cause widespread injuries among people who are near it when it goes off

nailbrush /náyl brush/ *n.* a small brush used for cleaning the fingernails, with short stiff bristles on one or both sides

nail clippers *npl.* a small pair of clippers used for trimming fingernails and toenails

nail enamel *n.* = nail polish

nail file *n.* a small file used for smoothing and shaping the ends of the fingernails

nailhead /náyl hed/ *n.* a decorative design that resembles the round head of a nail, used on furniture and leather

nail polish *n.* a fast-drying coloured or transparent varnish, often worn by women on their fingernails or toenails

nail punch, **nail set** *n.* CONSTR a tool that pushes a nail level with or lower than the surrounding surface

nail scissors *npl.* small scissors, sometimes with curved blades, used for trimming fingernails or toenails

nail varnish *n.* = nail polish

nainsook /náynssóok, nán-/ *n.* a lightweight cotton fabric used for babywear and lingerie, originally from India [Late 18thC. From Hindi *nainsukh*, literally 'pleasure to the eye'.]

Naipaul /níı pawl/, **V. S.** (*b.* 1932) West-Indian born British novelist. His novels include *A House for Mr Biswas* (1961) and the Booker Prize-winning *In a Free State* (1971). Full name **Sir Vidiadhar Surajprasad Naipaul**

naira /nírə/ *n.* **1.** UNIT OF CURRENCY IN NIGERIA the standard unit of currency in Nigeria, worth 100 kobo. See table at **currency 2.** NOTE WORTH ONE NAIRA a note worth one naira [Late 20thC. From Nigerian English, alteration of NIGERIA.]

Nairnshire /náirnshər/ former county of northern Scotland, abolished in 1975, and incorporated into Highland Region

Nairobi /níı rôbi/ capital city of Kenya, situated in the south-central part of the country. Population: 1,673,000 (1993).

Nairobi National Park national park in south-central Kenya, near the capital city. It was established in 1946. Area: 115 sq. km/44 sq. mi.

NAIRU *abbr.* nonaccelerating inflation rate of unemployment

naissant /náyss'nt/ *adj.* used in heraldry to describe a beast figure shown in the top half of a shield with only the upper part of its body visible [Late 16thC. From French, present participle of *naître* 'to be born' (source of English *Renaissance*). The underlying idea is of the animal emerging as if being born.]

naive /níı eev/, **naïve** *adj.* **1.** EXTREMELY SIMPLE AND TRUSTING having or showing an excessively simple and trusting view of the world and human nature, often as a result of youth and inexperience **2.** NOT SHREWD OR SOPHISTICATED showing a lack of sophistication and subtlety or of critical judgment and analysis ○ *a politically naive statement* **3.** ARTLESS admirably straightforward and uncomplicated or refreshingly innocent and unaffected **4.** ARTS REJECTING SOPHISTICATED TECHNIQUES IN ART not using the conventional styles and techniques of trained artists, e.g. in the treatment of perspective or light and shade **5.** SCI NOT PREVIOUSLY EXPERIMENTED ON not previously used in any scientific tests or experiments or not having previously used a particular drug ○ *naive laboratory mice* [Mid-17thC. From French *naïve*, feminine of *naïf*, from Latin *nativus* 'born' (source of English *native*). The underlying idea is of the innocence or gullibility of the newborn.] —**naively** *adv.* —**naiveness** *n.*

naive realism *n.* the theory of perception that holds that when we look at an object what we see is the actual object, not a mental representation of it

naiveté /níı éeva tay/, **naïveté, naivety** /níı éevəti/ (*plural* **naiveties**) *n.* **1.** NAIVENESS a naive quality or naive behaviour **2.** NAIVE ACTION a naive action or remark

Najd /najd, nejd/ region in central Saudi Arabia. Area: 1,158,000 sq. km/447,000 sq. mi.

NAK /nak/, **nak** *n.* TELECOM an ASCII control code used to indicate to the sender that a transmitted message has not been properly received. Full form **negative acknowledgment**

naked /náykid/ *adj.* **1. WITH NO CLOTHES ON** not covered by clothing, especially having no clothing on any part of the body **2. LACKING COVERING** without the usual covering or protection ○ *a naked flame* ○ *a naked light bulb* **3. NOT CONCEALED** openly displayed or expressed and often threatening or disturbing ○ *naked aggression* **4. UNADORNED** plain and lacking any decoration or embellishment ○ *the naked truth* **5. UNARMED** unarmed and defenceless ○ *'If you carry this resolution you will send Britain's Foreign Secretary naked into the conference chamber.'* (Aneurin Bevan; 1957) **6. DEVOID OF STH** without or unaccompanied by a particular quality or thing ○ *naked of all pretensions to grandeur* **7. WITHOUT NATURAL COVERING** without any natural covering in the form of earth, vegetation, or foliage **8.** ZOOL **WITHOUT HAIR, FUR, OR FEATHERS** without hair, fur, scales, shell, or feathers **9.** BOT **WITH NO GROWTH** without a covering of leaves or hairs ○ *naked stems* **10.** BOT **NOT ENCLOSED IN OVARY** used to describe conifer seeds that are not enclosed in an ovary **11.** BOT **WITHOUT SEPALS OR PETALS** used to describe flowers that have no sepals or petals [Old English *nacod*. Ultimately from an Indo-European word that is also the ancestor of English *nude*.] —**nakedness** *n.*

— **WORD KEY: SYNONYMS** —

naked, bare, nude, undressed, unclothed

CORE MEANING: devoid of clothes or covering

naked the most general word used to describe sb who is not wearing any clothes. It can also be used to describe an object that is uncovered or undecorated, especially when this is not what is usual or desirable; **bare** used to describe a part of sb's body that is uncovered. It can also be used to describe objects or surfaces that are not decorated or covered; **nude** used to describe sb who is not wearing any clothes at all, especially in an artistic context; **undressed** a general word used to describe sb who is not wearing any clothes at all, especially in a situation where clothes have just been removed. It can also be used to describe sb who has not finished putting on or taking off his or her clothes; **unclothed** a fairly formal word used to describe sb who is not wearing any clothes.

— **WORD KEY: CULTURAL NOTE** —

The Naked and the Dead, a novel by US writer Norman Mailer (1948). Set on a Pacific island during World War II, it is both a powerful account of the experience of war and, through its description of the conflicting political and philosophical views of the principal characters, a portrayal of some of the tensions in contemporary American society. It was made into a film by Raoul Walsh in 1958.

naked eye *n.* human sight without the aid of a microscope, telescope, or other optical instrument

naked ladies (*plural* **naked ladies**) *n.* = autumn crocus (*takes a singular verb*) [From its leafless flower stems]

nakedly /náykidli/ *adv.* without any attempt at disguise or concealment ○ *a description of the state as a nakedly repressive machine*

naked option *n.* a stock or commodity option sold by sb who does not own the underlying asset, and who is exposed to considerable risk if the price of the underlying asset changes adversely

Nakuru /nə kóo roo/ city in west-central Kenya. It is the capital of Rift Valley Province. Population: 124,200 (1994).

Nakuru, Lake lake in west-central Kenya, noted for its flamingos and other birds. Area: 62 sq. km/24 sq. mi.

nalbuphine /nal béw feen/ *n.* a painkilling drug similar to morphine that is used for moderate to severe pain. Formula: $C_{21}H_{27}NO_4$. [Mid-20thC. Blend of NALORPHINE and BUTYL.]

NALGO /nálgō/, **Nalgo** *abbr.* National Association of Local Government Officers

nalidixic acid /náyli díkssik-/ *n.* an antibacterial drug used to treat bacterial infections of the urinary tract. Formula: $C_{12}H_{12}N_2O_3$. ['Nalidixic' coined from NAPHTHALENE + DI + *carboxylic*]

naloxone /nə lóksōn/ *n.* a drug resembling morphine that is used to diagnose narcotics addiction and to reverse the effects of narcotics poisoning by blocking morphine receptor cells, thereby preventing the morphine from acting. Formula: $C_{19}H_{21}NO_4$. [Mid-

20thC. Contraction of N-ALLYLNOROXYMORPHONE, coined from N- + ALLYL + NOR- + OXY- + MORPHINE + -ONE.]

Nam /nam, naam/ *n.* US a name for Vietnam, used particularly by veterans of the war there during the 1960s and 1970s (*informal*) [Mid-20thC. Shortening.]

N. Am. *abbr.* **1.** North America **2.** North American

Nama /naama/ (*plural* **-ma** or **-mas**), **Namaqua** /nə maákwə/ (*plural* **-qua** or **-quas**) *n.* **1.** PEOPLES **MEMBER OF AFRICAN PEOPLE** a member of a Khoikhoi people who live in southwestern Africa **2.** LANG **NAMA LANGUAGE** the language of the Nama people. It belongs to the San branch of Khoisan languages and features the use of click consonants. Nama is spoken by about 25,000 people. [Mid-19thC. From the Khoikhoin language.] —**Nama** *adj.*

Namaqualand /nə maákwə land/ coastal region in southwestern Africa, in southern Namibia and South Africa. It is the homeland of the Nama people.

namaste /númmə stay/, **namaskar** /nummə skaàr/ *n.* a polite bow of greeting or farewell used by Hindus, made with the hands held at chest height and both palms pressed together [Mid-20thC. From Hindi, literally 'bowing to you'.]

Namatjira /nám at jeèrə/, **Albert** (1902–59) Australian Aboriginal painter. His watercolours of Australia's heartland were much sought after from the 1930s.

Nambour /nám boŏr/ town in southeastern Queensland, northeastern Australia. Population: 12,205 (1996).

namby-pamby /námbi pámbi/ *adj.* (*informal*) **1.** WEAK feeble, childish, and weak **2.** SILLY silly, sentimental, or overly sensitive ■ *n.* (*plural* **namby-pambies**) NAMBY-PAMBY PERSON sb who is considered weak or silly (*informal*) [Mid-16thC. Originally a mocking nickname for the English poet Ambrose Philips (1674–1749), who wrote feebly sentimental pastorals; based on *Amb(rose)*.]

name /naym/ *n.* **1. WHAT SB OR STH IS CALLED** a word, term, or phrase by which sb or sth is known and distinguished from other people or things **2. UN-COMPLIMENTARY WORD ABOUT SB** a usually uncomplimentary or abusive word or phrase used to describe sb's character ○ *called him names behind his back* **3. REPUTATION** the reputation or standing of sb or sth ○ *She's made quite a name for herself in the music world.* **4. FAMOUS PERSON** sb who is famous ○ *All the big Hollywood names were there.* **5. MEMBER OF LLOYD'S** a member of Lloyd's, the London insurance house, who provides capital for a syndicate but is not involved in how it is run ■ *adj.* RESPECTED having an established and good reputation ○ *name brands at discount prices* ■ *vt.* (**names, naming, named**) **1.** GIVE A NAME TO to give sb or sth a name ○ *They named the dog Sport.* **2.** IDENTIFY BY NAME to identify sb or sth by giving his, her, or its name ○ *He says he can name all fifty state capitals.* **3.** DECIDE ON STH to decide upon or specify sth, such as a date, time, or price ○ *would not name a figure* **4.** APPOINT TO OFFICE to choose sb for a particular office or honour ○ *They haven't yet named her successor.* **5.** BAN MP FROM COMMONS to refer formally by name to a Member of Parliament who has behaved in an unparliamentary manner, thereby temporarily banishing that MP from the House of Commons [Old English *nama*. Ultimately from an Indo-European word.] —**namable** *adj.* —**namer** *n.* ◇ **in name only** supposedly or officially, but not in any real sense ◇ **in the name of 1.** by the authority of **2.** for the sake of sth ◇ **name names** to mention the names of specific people in order to blame or accuse them of sth ◇ **sb's name is mud** sb is in trouble or the object of sb else's disapproval ◇ **to sb's name** belonging to sb ○ *hasn't got a penny to his name* ◇ **the name of the game** what sth is all about, its most important element or the kind of thing that most commonly happens in it ◇ **you name it** used to suggest that an enormous number of things are involved or an enormous number of options are possible (*informal*)

— **WORD KEY: ORIGIN** —

The Indo-European ancestor of *name* is also the ultimate source of English *anonymous, nomenclature, nominate, noun, renown, pseudonym,* and *synonym.*

name and shame *vti.* to reveal the name of a person, company, or organization that has done sth illegal

or immoral in order to embarrass them and shame them into not doing it again [Late 20thC]

name-calling *n.* verbal abuse, especially as a substitute for reasoned argument in a dispute

name-dropping *n.* the practice of frequently mentioning the names of famous or influential people as friends or acquaintances in order to impress people —**name-drop** *vi.* —**name-dropper** *n.*

nameless /náymləss/ *adj.* **1.** LACKING A NAME not having a name **2.** ANONYMOUS having a name that is unknown or not revealed **3.** INDESCRIBABLE unable to be accurately described ○ *a nameless fear* **4.** DISTRESSING BEYOND WORDS too unpleasant or disgusting to be described or mentioned **5.** ILLEGITIMATE illegitimate or not legally entitled to a name

namely /náymli/ *adv.* used to introduce a specific description or explanation of sth just referred to in a more general way ○ *She was given a new post, namely that of head of department.*

nameplate /náym playt/ *n.* a plate or plaque, e.g. on a door, bearing a name and associating the named person with the place or thing that the plate is attached to

namesake /náym sayk/ *n.* sb or sth with the same name as sb or sth else [Mid-17thC. Origin uncertain: probably ultimately from *for one's name's sake*.]

name tag *n.* a small piece of metal or plastic with your name on, attached to your clothing for purposes of identification at work or social functions

name tape *n.* a small strip of cloth with sb's name on, sewn onto the inside of his or her clothing as proof of ownership

Namib Desert /nə míb-/ desert in southwestern Africa, mostly in Namibia. Length: 1,930 km/1,200 mi.

Namibe /na meéb/ city and port in southwestern Angola. It is the capital of Namibe Province. Population: 77,000 (1987). Former name **Moçâmedes** (until 1982)

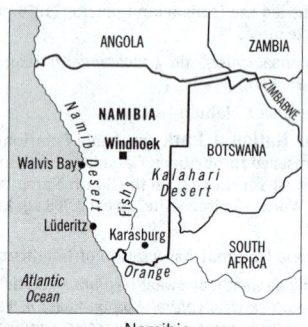

Namibia

Namibia /nə míbbi ə/ republic in southwestern Africa, with its western coast on the Atlantic Ocean, directly north of South Africa. Language: English, German, Afrikaans. Currency: Namibian dollar. Capital: Windhoek. Population: 1,709,000 (1996). Area: 824,268 sq. km/318,252 sq. mi. Official name **Republic of Namibia** —**Namibian** *n., adj.*

Namoi /nám oy/ river in northeastern New South Wales, southeastern Australia. Length: 845 km/525 mi.

Nampa /námpə/ city in southwestern Idaho, west of Boise and east of the Oregon border. Population: 37,558 (1996).

nam pla /nám plaà/ *n.* a thin sauce of fermented fish with a strong flavour and smell and a salty taste, widely used in Southeast Asian cookery [From Thai]

Namur /nə moór-/ city in southeastern Belgium. It is the capital city of Namur Province. Population: 105,059 (1996).

nan[1] /naan, nan/, **naan** *n.* a flat round or oval bread served with Indian food [Early 20thC. From Persian and Urdu *nān*.]

nan[2] *n.* = nana (*informal*)

nana /nánnə/, **nanna, nan** /nan/ *n.* sb's grandmother (*informal*)

Nanaimo /nə nímō/ city in southwestern Canada, on Vancouver Island, on the Strait of Georgia. Population: 85,585 (1996).

Nanak /naanək/ (1469–1539) Indian religious leader. He founded the Sikh religion, and his teachings were collected as the *Adi Granth*, the Sikh scriptures. Known as **Guru Nanak**

Nanchang /nan chúng/ city in eastern China. It is the capital of Jiangxi Province. Population: 1,350,000 (1991).

nancy /nánssi/ (*plural* **nancies**), **nancy boy, nance** (*plural* **nances**) *n.* a highly offensive term for an effeminate man or a homosexual man (*slang offensive*)

Nancy /noN seé/ city in northeastern France, in Lorraine Region. It is the capital of Meurthe-et-Moselle Department. Population: 102,410 (1990).

NAND /nand/ (*plural* **NANDs**), **NAND gate** *n.* a logic operator used in computing that produces an output signal only if at least one of its inputs has no signal, thus being the inverse of an AND operator [Mid-20thC. Blend of NOT and AND.]

Nanda Devi /núndə deévi/ the second highest mountain in India after Kangchenjunga. It is in the extreme northwest of the country, in the Himalayas, near the Tibetan border. Height: 7,817 m/25,645 ft.

Nanga Parbat /núng gə paár baat/ mountain in northeastern Pakistan, in the Himalayas. Height: 8,126 m/26,660 ft.

Nanjing /nán jíng/ city in eastern China, on the Yangtze River. It is the capital of Jiangsu Province. Population: 2,090,204 (1990). Former name **Nanking**

nankeen /nan keén/ *n.* a durable yellowish-brown cotton fabric [Mid-18thC. Named after *Nanking* (Nanjing), city in China, because it was originally made there.]

nankeen kestrel *n.* a small falcon with reddish-brown upper parts and cream-coloured underparts, common throughout Australia and New Guinea. Latin name: *Falco cenchroides*. [Because it is the colour of nankeen cloth]

Nanking /nan kíng/ former name for **Nanjing**

nanna *n.* = nana (*informal*)

Nanning /nan níng/ city and capital of Guangxi Zhuangzu Autonomous Region, southeastern China, situated approximately 530 km/330 mi. west of Guangzhou. Population: 721,877 (1990).

nannofossil *n.* = nanofossil

nannoplankton *n.* = nanoplankton

nanny /nánni/, **nannie** *n.* (*plural* **-nies**) **1.** SB EMPLOYED TO WATCH A FAMILY'S CHILDREN sb who is employed full-time to take care of one or more children in a family home, often living in the family home **2.** GRANDMOTHER sb's grandmother (*informal*) ■ *vt.* (**-nies, -nying, -nied**) BE FUSSY AND OVERPROTECTIVE to behave in an overprotective and patronizing way towards others, not allowing them to make their own decisions (*disapproving*) [Early 18thC. Pet-form of name Ann(e).]

nanny goat *n.* a female domestic goat [*Nanny* a former variant of the name *Anne*]

nanny state *n.* a government that brings in legislation that it considers is in the people's best interests but that is regarded by some as interfering and patronizing

nano- *prefix*. Symbol **n 1.** extremely small ○ *nanofossil* ○ *nanotechnology* **2.** one thousand millionth (10⁻⁹) ○ *nanosecond* [Via Greek *nan(n)os* 'dwarf, little old man']

nanobot /nánnō bot/ *n.* US a robot of microscopic proportions built using nanotechnology (*informal*) [Combination of prefix nano- + ROBOT]

nanofossil /nánnō foss'l/, **nannofossil** *n.* a very small fossil, especially of nanoplankton

nanogram /nánnō gram/ *n.* one billionth (one thousand-millionth) of a gram

nanometre /nánnō meetər/ *n.* one billionth (one thousand-millionth) of a metre

nanoplankton /nánnō plangktən/, **nannoplankton** *n.* very small plankton including bacteria, algae, and protozoa. They are usually in the size range 5–60 micrometres.

nanosecond /nánnō sekənd/ *n.* one billionth (one thousand-millionth) of a second

nanotechnology /nánnō tek nólləji/ (*plural* **-gies**) *n.* the art of manipulating materials on a very small scale in order to build microscopic machinery

Nansen /nánss'n/, **Fridtjof** (1861–1930) Norwegian explorer and statesman. He led several expeditions to the Arctic and was also involved in humanitarian projects, for which he won the Nobel Peace Prize in 1922.

Nantong /nan toóng/ city and seaport in eastern China, in southeastern Jiangsu Province. Population: 343,341 (1990).

Nantucket /nan túkət/ island in southeastern Massachusetts, in the Atlantic Ocean, south of Cape Cod. Population: 6,012 (1990). Area: 148 sq. km/57 sq. mi.

Nantwich /nántwich/ market town in northwestern England, in Cheshire. Population: 11,695 (1991).

Nanuet /nánnyoŏ ət/ city in New York State, in Rockland County. Population: 14,065 (1990).

Naomi /náyəmi/ *n.* in the Bible, the mother-in-law of Ruth (Ruth 1: 2)

naos /náyoss/ (*plural* **-oi** /-oy/) *n.* ARCHIT = **cella** [Late 18thC. From Greek, 'temple'.]

nap[1] /nap/ *n.* SHORT SLEEP a period of short light sleep, especially during the day ■ *vi.* (**naps, napping, napped**) **1.** SLEEP LIGHTLY to have a short period of light sleep **2.** BE OFF GUARD to be inattentive or off guard [Old English *hnappian*]

nap[2] /nap/ *n.* PILE the small soft fibres that stick up slightly from the surface of a fabric such as velvet and that usually all lie in one direction only ■ *vt.* (**naps, napping, napped**) RAISE PILE OF FABRIC to raise the nap of a fabric by brushing it [15thC. From Middle Low German and Middle Dutch *noppe*, from a prehistoric Germanic word perhaps meaning 'to pluck', that may also be the ancestor of English *nip*.]

nap[3] /nap/ *n.* **1.** CARDS CARD GAME a card game similar to whist, played with hands of five cards, in which players bid for the number of tricks they will take. Full form **napoleon 2.** CARDS BID IN NAP a bid to win all five tricks in the game of nap. Full form **napoleon 3.** HORSERACING A GOOD TIP IN RACING in horse racing, a tip for a horse that is very likely to win ■ *vt.* (**naps, napping, napped**) HORSERACING NAME LIKELY WINNER to name a horse as a likely winner of a race [Early 19thC. Shortening of NAPOLEON.]

Napa /náppə/ city in west-central Florida. It is the administrative seat of Napa County. Population: 61,842 (1990).

napalm /náy paam, náp-/ *n.* **1.** JELLY USED FOR FIRE BOMBS a highly flammable jelly, produced by mixing a thickening agent with petrol, and used in flame-throwers and fire bombs **2.** CHEM THICKENING AGENT FOR JELLIED PETROL a thickening agent, consisting of aluminium soap, that can be used for making jellied petrol ■ *vt.* (**-palms, -palming, -palmed**) ATTACK WITH NAPALM to attack or destroy sth with napalm [Mid-20thC. Blend of NAPHTHENE and PALMITATE.]

nape /nayp/ *n.* the back part of the neck [13thC. Origin unknown.]

Naperville /náypərvil/ city in northeastern Illinois, southeast of Aurora, and west of Chicago. Population: 85,351 (1990).

napery /náypəri/ *n.* tablecloths and napkins, collectively (*archaic*) [14thC. From Old French *naperie*, from *nappe* 'tablecloth' (see NAPKIN).]

nap hand *n.* a situation that appears to be favourable for taking risks

Naphtali /náftə lī/ *n.* in the Bible, the son of Jacob and Rachel's handmaid, Bilhah (Genesis 30: 7–8)

naphtha /náfthə, náphə/ *n.* a clear colourless flammable mixture of light hydrocarbons obtained from petroleum. It boils at between 45°C and 155°C and is used as a raw material for many petrochemicals and plastics. [Late 16thC. Via Latin from Greek, originally 'inflammable liquid come from earth', from Iranian.]

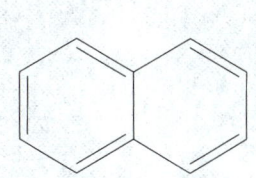

Naphthalene

naphthalene /náfthə leen, nápth-/ *n.* a white crystalline hydrocarbon derived from coal tar and used as a moth repellent, in solvents, and in the manufacture of dyes, resins, plasticizers, polyesters, and explosives. Formula: $C_{10}H_8$. [Early 19thC. Coined from NAPHTHA + -AL³ + -ENE.] —**napthalenic** /náfthə lénnik, nápthə-/ *adj.*

naphthene /náf theen, nápth-/ *n.* a cycloalkane obtained from petroleum [Late 19thC. Coined from NAPHTHA + -ENE.] —**naphthenic** *adj.*

naphthol /náfthol, nápth-/ *n.* either of two derivatives of naphthalene that are isomers, and are used as antiseptics and in manufacturing. Formula: $C_{10}H_7OH$. [Mid-19thC. Formed from NAPHTHA.]

Napier /náypi ər/ city in New Zealand, situated on the eastern coast of the North Island. Devastated by an earthquake in 1931, it was rebuilt in a distinctive art-deco style. Population: 55,044 (1996).

Napier, John (1550–1617) Scottish mathematician. He invented logarithms and a calculating device called Napier's bones.

Napier, Robert Cornelis, 1st Baron Napier of Magdala (1810–90) British field marshal. He served in the Sikh Wars and Indian Mutiny, and captured Magdala during an expedition to Ethiopia (1868).

Napierian logarithm /nə peéri ən-/ *n.* = natural logarithm [Early 19thC. Named after John NAPIER.]

Napier's bones /náypi ərz-/ *npl.* a set of graduated rods based upon the principles of logarithms, formerly used to perform multiplication and division but now used primarily for educational purposes [Mid-17thC. Named after John NAPIER.]

napiform /náypi fawrm/ *adj.* shaped like a turnip in being conical at one end and spherical at the other [Mid-19thC. Coined from Latin *napus* 'turnip' + -FORM.]

napkin /nápkin/ *n.* **1.** PIECE OF CLOTH FOR WIPING MOUTH a usually square piece of cloth or tissue paper used at mealtimes to protect clothes and wipe the mouth **2.** full form of **nappy** (*formal*) [14thC. Formed from French *nap(p)e* 'tablecloth', from Latin *mappa* 'napkin, cloth' (source of English *map*), from Carthaginian or Phoenician.]

Naples /náyp'lz/ **1.** city in southern Italy. It is the capital of Campania Region and of Napoli Province and an important seaport. Population: 1,061,583 (1993). **2.** city in southwestern Florida, in Collier County, on the Gulf of Mexico. Population: 19,505 (1990).

NAPO *abbr.* National Association of Prison Officers

napoleon /nə póli ən/ *n.* **1.** MONEY OLD FRENCH COIN a gold coin formerly used in France, equivalent to 20 francs **2.** CARDS full form of **nap**³ [Early 19thC. Named after NAPOLEON I; because the coin was issued in his reign.]

Napoleon I, Emperor of the French (1769–1821). He made his name as a general, was appointed first consul of France in 1799, and took the title of emperor in 1804. After conquering most of Europe, he was exiled after defeat at the battle of Waterloo (1815). Real name **Napoleon Bonaparte** —**Napoleonic** /nə póli ónnik/ *adj.*

nappa /náppə/ *n.* a soft leather made from sheep or kid's skin [Late 19thC. Named for *Nappa*, a county, town, and valley in California, USA.]

nappe /nap/ *n.* **1.** SHEET OF WATER a sheet of water flowing over a dam or a weir **2.** GEOL SHEET OF ROCK a large arch-shaped sheet of rock that has been forced over

Napoleon I, Emperor of the French:
Portrait (1807) by Andrea Appiani

underlying rocks by internal stresses **3.** GEOM PART OF CONE either of the two parts, or sheets, of a conical or pyramidal surface that are separated by a line through the vertex [Late 19thC. From French, literally 'tablecloth' (see NAPKIN).]

napper /náppər/ n. a person's head (dated informal) [Late 18thC. Origin unknown.]

nappy /náppi/ (plural -pies) n. a piece of soft absorbent material, usually made of paper or cloth, that is wrapped around a baby's bottom and between its legs to absorb urine and excrement. US term **diaper** [Early 20thC. Shortening and alteration of NAPKIN.]

nappy rash n. a sensitive red area on a baby's skin around the genitals and buttocks caused by irritation from urine or faeces. US term **diaper rash**

Nara /náarə/ city in Japan, on southern Honshu Island. It is the capital of Nara Prefecture. Population: 349,349 (1990).

Naracoorte /nárrə kawrt/ agricultural town in southern South Australia. Population: 4,674 (1996).

Narayan /nə ríyən/, **Jayaprakash** (1902–79) Indian politician. He was the uniting force in the Janata Party, which defeated the government of Indira Gandhi in 1977.

Narayan, R. K. (b. 1906) Indian writer. Many of his gentle novels are set in the fictional southern Indian town of Malgudi. They include The Vendor of Sweets (1967) and The World of Nagaraj (1990). Full name **Rasipuram Krishnaswamy Narayan**

narc /naark/ (narcs, narcing, narced) vi. = **nark** v. 3 (slang) [Mid-19thC. From Romany nāk 'nose'.]

narcissism /náarssissizəm/ n. **1.** SELF-ADMIRATION excessive self-admiration and self-centredness **2.** PERSONALITY DISORDER in psychiatry, a personality disorder characterized by the patient's overestimation of his or her own appearance and abilities and an excessive need for admiration. In psychoanalytic theory, emphasis is placed on the element of self-directed sexual desire in the condition. [Early 19thC. Named after NARCISSUS.] —**narcissist** n. —**narcissistic** /náarssi sístik/ adj.

narcissus /naar síssəss/ (plural -suses or -si /-síssī/) n. a spring-blooming plant that grows from a bulb and has narrow leaves and showy yellow or white flowers with a cup-shaped centre. Genus: Narcissus. [Mid-16thC. Via Latin from Greek narkissos, from narkē 'numbness' (source of English narcotic); in reference to its narcotic properties.]

Narcissus n. in Greek mythology, a youth who was punished for repulsing Echo's love by being made to fall in love with his own reflection in a pool. He died gazing at his own image, and was turned into a flower.

narco-[1] prefix. sleep, stupor ○ narcolepsy [From Greek narkoun 'to make numb', from narkē 'numbness']

narco-[2] prefix. relating to illicit narcotics and the narcotics trade (informal)

narcoanalysis /náarkō ə nálləssiss/ n. psychoanalysis using drugs to induce a state akin to sleep [Mid-20thC. Coined from NARCO- + ANALYSIS.]

narcolepsy /náarkō lepsi/ n. a condition characterized by frequent, brief, and uncontrollable bouts of deep sleep, sometimes accompanied by hallucinations and inability to move [Late 19thC. Coined from NARCO-

+ -LEPSY, on the model of EPILEPSY.] —**narcoleptic** /náarkō léptik/ adj., n.

narcosis /naar kṓssiss/ n. a state of unconsciousness or stupor caused by a narcotic or other drug [Late 17thC. From Greek narkōsis, from narkoun (see NARCOTIC).]

narcotic /naar kóttik/ n. **1.** PHARM DRUG a drug, especially one derived from opium, that has effects ranging from mild dulling of the senses, pain relief, and sleep, to stupor, coma, and convulsions. Most narcotics are addictive. **2.** US DRUGS ILLEGAL DRUG a drug whose use is illegal, whether or not it is an addictive narcotic **3.** SOOTHING THING sth that soothes, induces sleep, relieves pain or stress, or causes a sensation of mental numbness ■ adj. **1.** CAUSING SLEEP able to induce drowsiness, sleep, or stupor, or alter mental states through its chemical properties **2.** SOOTHING having a generally soothing, numbing, or soporific effect **3.** PHARM OF NARCOTICS relating to narcotic drugs and their use **4.** DRUGS OF ADDICTS relating to people addicted to narcotics [14thC. Via French narcotique and medieval Latin from Greek narkōtikos 'numbing', from narkoun 'to make numb', from narkē 'numbness'.] —**narcotically** adv.

narcotization /náarkə tī záysh'n/ n. US the process by which a society falls under the control of drugs, drug traffickers, and the illegal drug business (informal)

narcotize /náarkə tīz/ (-tizes, -tizing, -tized), **narcotise** (-tises, -tising, -tised) vt. **1.** TREAT WITH NARCOTIC to treat sb with a narcotic **2.** PUT INTO STUPOR to induce stupor in sb, especially by administering a narcotic drug

nard /naard/ n. = **spikenard** [14thC. Via Latin nardus from Greek nardos, probably ultimately from Sanskrit naladam 'Indian spikenard'.]

nares /náir eez/ npl. openings or passages leading out of the nose or naval cavity. Most vertebrate animals have paired external nares, the nostrils, and a pair of internal nares opening into the mouth. [Late 17thC. From Latin, plural of naris 'nostril'.]

narghile /náargə lay/, **nargileh** n. = **hookah** [Mid-18thC. From (partly via French and Turkish) Persian nārgīl 'coconut, hookah', from Sanskrit nārikela 'coconut'.]

Narita /nə reétə/ city in Japan, on southeastern Honshu Island, in Chiba Prefecture. Population: 86,708 (1990).

nark /naark/ v. (narks, narking, narked) **1.** vt. ANNOY to irritate, offend, or annoy sb (informal) **2.** vi. COMPLAIN to complain in an irritating way (informal) **3.** vi. ACT AS INFORMER to act as an informer, especially for the police (slang) US term **narc** ■ n. POLICE INFORMER a person who acts as a decoy or informer, especially an ex-criminal who is working for the police (slang) [Mid-19thC. From Romany nāk 'nose'.]

Narrabri /nárrə brī/ town in northeastern New South Wales, southeastern Australia. Population: 14,653 (1991).

Narraganset /nárrə gánssət/ (plural -sets or -set), **Narragansett** (plural -setts or -sett) n. **1.** PEOPLES MEMBER OF NATIVE N AMERICAN PEOPLE a member of a Native North American people who originally lived in a broad territory centred on the western edge of present-day Rhode Island. The Narragansets were among the largest and strongest of the northeastern Native American peoples until large numbers of them were killed in a war against the New England colonists in the late 17th century. **2.** LANG NARRAGANSET LANGUAGE the now extinct Iroquoian language of the Narragansett people [Early 17thC. From Narraganset.] — **Narraganset** adj.

Narragansett /nárrə gánssət/ town and summer resort in southern Rhode Island State, Washington County. Population: 14,985 (1990).

Narragansett Bay /nárrə gánssət-/ inlet of the Atlantic Ocean in eastern Rhode Island State. Length: 42 km/26 mi.

narrate /nə ráyt/ (-rates, -rating, -rated) vt. **1.** TELL THE STORY OF STH to be the teller of a story, or to give an account of sth in detail **2.** BROADCAST SPEAK ON FILM to provide the narration for a film or television programme [Mid-17thC. From Latin, past participle stem of narrare, from gnarus 'knowing'.] —**narratable** adj.

narration /nə ráysh'n/ n. **1.** ACT OF NARRATING the act of telling a story or giving an account of sth **2.** STH NARRATED a narrative or story **3.** BROADCAST, CINEMA SOUNDTRACK VOICED BY ACTOR the voiced soundtrack of a broadcast or film when given by an actor or commentator who does not appear —**narrational** adj.

narrative /nárrətiv/ n. **1.** STORY a story or an account of a sequence of events in the order in which they happened **2.** PROCESS OF NARRATING the art or process of telling a story or giving an account of sth **3.** LITERAT STORY IN LITERARY WORK the part of a literary work that is concerned with telling the story ■ adj. **1.** TELLING A STORY having the aim or purpose of telling a story ○ narrative poetry **2.** RELATING TO NARRATION relating to or involving the art of storytelling —**narratively** adv.

narrator /nə ráytər/ n. **1.** STORYTELLER sb who tells a story or gives an account of sth **2.** LITERAT TALKING CHARACTER a character in a work of fiction who is presented as telling the story and who refers to himself or herself as 'I' **3.** CINEMA, BROADCAST COMMENTATOR sb who provides the narration for a film or television programme

narrow /nárrō/ adj. **1.** SMALL IN WIDTH having a small width, especially in comparison to height or length ○ a narrow gap **2.** LIMITED IN SIZE limited or restricted in size or scope ○ a narrow range of options **3.** NARROW-MINDED limited and usually inflexible in outlook ○ a narrow view of events **4.** JUST ENOUGH FOR SUCCESS only just sufficient for success ○ a narrow victory ○ a narrow escape **5.** NOT GENEROUS mean and stingy **6.** THOROUGH close and thorough, leaving nothing uninvestigated **7.** MEAGRE small or limited in quantity ○ a narrow provision **8.** PHON = **tense**[1] adj. 4 **9.** AGRIC HIGH IN PROTEIN used to describe animal feed that is very rich in protein ■ n. A NARROW PASSAGE a narrow place or passage. ◊ **narrows** ■ vti. (-rows, -rowing, -rowed) **1.** MAKE OR BECOME NARROW to make sth, or to become, narrow or narrower **2.** CONTRACT OR BE CONTRACTED to restrict or limit the scope or extent of sth, or to become restricted or limited in scope or extent ○ narrowed the focus of their investigation to two individuals [Old English nearu, from prehistoric Germanic] —**narrowness** n.

narrowband /nárrō band/ adj. functioning within a narrow band of broadcasting frequencies

narrow boat n. a long canal barge with a width not exceeding 2.1 m/7 ft

narrowcast /nárrō kaast/ (-casts, -casting, -cast or -casted) vt. to aim a radio or television transmission at a limited group of people such as cable subscribers or a particular target audience

narrow gauge n. **1.** REDUCED DISTANCE BETWEEN RAILS a distance between the two rails of a railway track that is less than the 143.5 cm/4 ft 8½ in distance of the standard gauge railways **2.** TRACK OR VEHICLE WITH NARROW GAUGE a railway line with track of a narrow gauge, or a carriage or locomotive designed to run on one —**narrow-gauge** adj.

narrowly /nárrōli/ adv. **1.** BY SMALL MARGIN by a very small margin or distance ○ narrowly avoided capture **2.** INTENTLY in a very concentrated, searching, or detailed way ○ eyed him narrowly **3.** WITHIN NARROW LIMITS in a way that allows little freedom or scope ○ narrowly circumscribed

narrow-minded /-míndid/ adj. having or showing a limited and often prejudiced or intolerant outlook —**narrow-mindedly** adv. —**narrow-mindedness** n.

narrows /nárrōz/ n. a narrow section of a river, or a narrow stretch of sea usually between two larger bodies of water (takes a singular or plural verb) ◊ **narrow**

narthex /naar theks/ n. **1.** ENTRANCE HALL OF CHURCH an entrance hall at the west end of a Christian church between the porch and the nave **2.** SCREENED AREA AT END OF NAVE an area at the west end of the nave of an early Christian church separated off by a screen or railing behind which women, catechumens, or penitents were admitted [Late 17thC. Via late Greek narthēx 'giant fennel', later 'casket' (because the plant was used to make boxes). The modern meaning evolved via the idea of an enclosed space.]

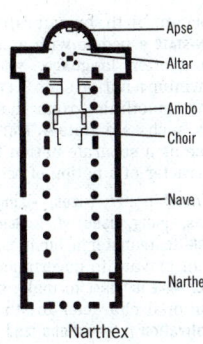

Narthex

nartjie /naártshi/, **naartje** /naárki/ *n. S Africa* a small sweet tangerine [Late 18thC. Via Afrikaans from Tamil *nārattai* 'citrus'.]

Narwhal

narwhal /naár wayl/ (*plural* **-whal** *or* **-whals**), **narwal** (*plural* **-wal** *or* **-wals**), **narwhale** (*plural* **-whale** *or* **-whales**) *n.* a small arctic whale, about 6 m/20 ft long, with a spotted body, short flippers, and, in the male, a long twisted ivory tusk. It was formerly hunted for oil and ivory. Latin name: *Monodon monoceros*. [Mid-17thC. From Danish or Norwegian *narhval*, of uncertain origin: perhaps from Old Norse *náhvalr*, literally 'corpse-whale', from *nár* 'corpse' (in allusion to its pale skin).]

NAS *abbr.* naval air station

NASA /nássə/ *n.* the US government agency responsible for nonmilitary programmes in the exploration and scientific study of space. Full form **National Aeronautics and Space Administration**

nasal /náyz'l/ *adj.* **1.** OF THE NOSE forming part of or relating to the nose **2.** PHON PRONOUNCED THROUGH NOSE pronounced with breath escaping mainly through the nose rather than the mouth **3.** WITH NASAL SOUNDS characterized by nasal sounds ○ *a nasal accent* ■ *n.* **1.** PHON NASAL SOUND a nasal sound or a letter that represents it **2.** HELMET PART the nosepiece of a helmet [Mid-17thC. Directly or via French from medieval Latin *nasalis*, from Latin *nasus* 'nose'.] **—nasality** /nay zálləti/ *n.* **—nasally** /náyzə li/ *adv.*

nasalize /náyzə līz/ (**-izes, -izing, -ized**), **nasalise** (**-ises, -ising, -ised**) *vti.* to make a sound nasal by lowering the soft palate so that air flows through the nose — **nasalization** *n.*

nascence /náss'nss, náyss-/, **nascency** /náss'nssi, náyss-/ *n.* the beginning or coming into being of sth (*literary*)

nascent /náss'nt, náyss-/ *adj.* **1.** JUST BEGINNING TO DEVELOP in the process of emerging, being born, or starting to develop **2.** CHEM PRODUCED IN REACTION MEDIUM in the process of being created in a reaction medium, often in a highly active form [Early 17thC. From Latin *nascent-*, present participle stem of *nasci* 'to be born' (source of English *nation* and *nature*).]

naseberry /náyz berri/ (*plural* **-ries**), **neesberry** /neéz berri/ (*plural* **-ries**) *n.* TREES = **sapodilla** [Late 17thC. By folk etymology from Spanish *nispero* or Portuguese *nespera*, from Latin *mespilus* 'medlar', by association with BERRY.]

Nash /nash/, **John** (1752–1835) English architect. His designs include the Neo-Classical Regent Street in London (begun 1812) and the fantastical Royal Pavilion in Brighton (1815–23).

Nash, Paul (1889–1946) English painter. His landscapes reflect the influence of surrealism, and he worked as an official war artist during World Wars I and II.

Nash, Sir Walter (1882–1968) British-born New Zealand statesman. He was Labour prime minister of New Zealand (1957–60).

Nashua /náshoo ə/ city in southern New Hampshire. It is the administrative seat of Hillsborough County. Population: 79,662 (1990).

Nashville /násh vil/ capital city of Tennessee, situated in the north-central part of the state. It is a major centre for country-and-western music. Population: 504,505 (1994).

nasi goreng /naássi gə réng/ *n.* a Malaysian dish of fried rice with other ingredients, usually including meat or fish [From Malay, literally 'fried rice']

nasion /náyzi ən/ *n.* the point where the bridge of the nose meets the forehead [Late 19thC. From French, formed from *nasal* 'nasal', on the model of INION.] **—nasial** /náyzi əl/ *adj.*

naso- *prefix.* nose, nasal ○ *nasogastric* [From Latin *nasus* (source also of English *nasturtium*. Ultimately from the Indo-European word for 'nose' that is also the ancestor of *nose* and *ness*.]

nasofrontal /náyzō frúnt'l/ *adj.* relating to the nasal and the frontal bones jointly

nasogastric /náyzō gástrik/ *adj.* passing through the nose to the stomach

nasolacrimal /náyzō lákrim'l/, **nasolachrymal** *adj.* relating to or connecting the nose and the tear-producing sacs

nasopharyngeal /náyzō fə rínji əl/ *adj.* relating to the nose and pharynx or to the nasopharynx

nasopharynx /náyzō fárringks/ (*plural* **-pharynges** /-fə rínjeez/ *or* **-pharynxes**) *n.* the upper part of the pharynx, behind and above the soft palate, continuous with the nasal passages

Nasruddin /názroo deen/ *n.* a trickster who appears in Muslim folklore. He first appeared in stories used by Sufis to teach their students. [Mid-20thC. From Turkish.]

Nassau /nássaw/ capital city and principal port of the Bahamas, situated on the northeastern coast of New Providence Island. Population: 171,542 (1990).

AKG London

Gamel Abdel Nasser

Nasser /nássər/, **Gamel Abdel** (1918–70) Egyptian statesman. Originally a soldier, he became prime minister in 1954 and president two years later.

Nastase /nə stássi/, **Ilie** (*b.* 1946) Romanian tennis player. He won the US Open (1972) and French Open (1973), and many doubles titles.

nastic /nástik/ *adj.* BOT relating to the movement of the parts of a plant in response to external stimuli such as the opening of a crocus flower in response to temperature [Early 20thC. Formed from Greek *nastos* 'pressed together', from *nassein* 'to press'.]

nasturtium /nə stúrshəm/ *n.* a plant with shield-shaped pungent leaves and showy long-spurred yellow, orange, or red irregular flowers. Its leaves, flowers, and seeds are edible. Genus: *Tropaeolum*. [12thC. From Latin, of uncertain origin: probably an alteration of assumed *nasitortium*, literally 'nose-twister'. From its pungent odour.]

Nasturtium

nasty /naásti/ *adj.* (**-tier, -tiest**) **1.** SPITEFUL showing spitefulness, malice, or ill-nature ○ *a nasty trick to play on someone* **2.** REPUGNANT TO SENSES repugnant or disgusting to the senses ○ *a nasty smell* **3.** UNPLEASANT generally disagreeable, unpleasant, or causing discomfort ○ *The weather turned nasty.* **4.** SERIOUS likely to cause harm or to be painful ○ *a nasty accident* ○ *a nasty bump on the head* **5.** MORALLY OFFENSIVE morally offensive or obscene (*informal*) **6.** DIFFICULT difficult to solve or deal with (*informal*) ■ *n.* (*plural* **-ties**) UNPLEASANT PERSON OR THING sb or sth that is very disagreeable, harmful, or offensive (*informal*) [14thC. Origin uncertain: perhaps from a Scandinavian word meaning 'dirty'.] **—nastily** *adv.* **—nastiness** *n.*

── **WORD KEY: SYNONYMS** ──

See Synonyms at **mean**.

-nasty *suffix.* nastic response ○ *thermonasty* [Formed from Greek *nastos* (see NASTIC)]

NAS/UWT *abbr.* National Association of Schoolmasters/Union of Women Teachers

Nat /nat/ *n.* ANZ, S Africa a member of the National Party in Australia, New Zealand, or South Africa, or a Member of Parliament belonging to the National Party (*informal*) Full form **Nationalist** [Mid-20thC. Shortening.]

nat. *abbr.* **1.** national **2.** natural **3.** native

natal[1] /náyt'l/ *adj.* **1.** OF BIRTH relating to birth or to the time and place of birth **2.** NATIVE native (*literary*) [14thC. Via Latin *natalis* (source of English *noel*) from, ultimately, *nasci* 'to be born' (see NATION).]

natal[2] /náyt'l/ *adj.* relating to the buttocks [Late 19thC. Formed from Latin *natis* (see NATES).]

Natal /nə taál/ **1.** city and seaport in northeastern Brazil. It is the capital of Rio Grande do Norte State. Population: 606,541 (1991). **2.** former province of eastern South Africa, merged in 1994 with KwaZulu to form KwaZulu-Natal

natality /nay tálləti, nə-/ *n.* **birthrate**

natant /náyt'nt/ *adj.* ZOOL floating or swimming in water (*technical*) [15thC. From Latin *natant-*, the present participle stem of *natare* (see NATATORY).]

Nataraja /naátə raàjə/ *n.* the Hindu god Shiva when represented as a dancing figure with several arms and legs [Early 20thC. From Hindi, literally 'prince of dancers'.]

natation /nə táysh'n/ *n.* the action or skill of swimming (*formal*) [Mid-16thC. From the Latin stem *natation-*, ultimately from *natare* (see NATATORY).] **—natational** *adj.*

natatory /nə táytəri/, **natatorial** /náttə táwri əl/ *adj.* relating to or adapted for swimming (*formal*) [Late 18thC. Via late Latin *natatorius* from Latin *natator* 'swimmer', from *natare* 'to keep on swimming', from *nare* 'to swim, float'.]

natch /nach/ *adv.* naturally or of course (*informal*) [Mid-20thC. Shortening of NATURALLY.]

Natchitoches /nákə tosh/ city in western Louisiana, just west of the Red River. Population: 17,267 (1996).

nates /náy teez/ *npl.* the buttocks [Late 17thC. From Latin, the plural of *natis* 'buttock, rump'.]

NATFHE *abbr.* National Association of Teachers in Further and Higher Education

Nathan *n.* in the Bible, a prophet at David's court (2 Samuel 7:1–17, 12:1–15)

Natick /náttik/ town in eastern Massachusetts, east of Framingham and southwest of Boston. Population: 31,310 (1996).

nation /náysh'n/ n. **1. PEOPLE IN LAND UNDER SINGLE GOVERNMENT** a community of people or peoples who live in a defined territory and are organized under a single government **2. PEOPLE OF SAME ETHNICITY** a community of people who share a common ethnic origin, culture, historical tradition, and, frequently, language, whether or not they live together in one territory or have their own government **3. NATIVE AMERICAN PEOPLE OR FEDERATION** a Native American people or a federation of peoples ○ the Apache nation **4. LAND OF NATIVE AMERICAN NATION** a territory occupied by a Native American nation **5. GROUP WITH COMMON INTEREST** a group of people united by a common interest ○ the hip-hop nation [13thC. Via French from the Latin stem nation-'birth, race, nation', from nat-, past participle stem of nasci 'to be born' (source of English innate).] —**nationhood** n.

Nation /náysh'n/, **Carry** (1846–1911) US temperance leader. She believed that she had a divine calling to carry out violent anti-alcohol attacks on saloons, armed with a hatchet. Full name **Carry Amelia Moore Nation**

national /násh'nəl/ adj. **1. OF A NATION** relating or belonging to, or representing a nation, especially a nation as a whole rather than any particular part of it or section of its territory ○ the national team **2. FOR WHOLE NATION** relating or applicable to, or representing a whole nation ○ the chairman of a national search committee **3. CHARACTERISTIC OF PEOPLE OF PARTICULAR NATION** relating to or characteristic of the people of a particular nation ○ the British national character **4. OWNED OR CONTROLLED BY CENTRAL GOVERNMENT** owned, maintained, or controlled by the central government of a nation ○ a national film museum **5. REFERRING TO COALITION GOVERNMENT** used to describe a coalition government consisting of members of all the major political parties ■ n. **1. CITIZEN OF PARTICULAR NATION** a citizen of a particular nation, especially when living in another country **2. PRESS** = **national newspaper 3.** SPORTS **COMPETITION INVOLVING CONTESTANTS FROM WHOLE COUNTRY** a sports contest involving participants from every part of a country (often used in the plural)

National n. the Grand National (informal)

national anthem n. a nation's official hymn or song, expressing patriotic sentiments and played or sung on public occasions

national assembly n. a legislative body consisting of the elected representatives of a particular nation or country

National Assembly n. the first legislative assembly set up during the French Revolution and ruling from 1789 to 1791

national bank n. **1. BANK ACTING FOR GOVERNMENT** a bank that acts as banker to a government and performs duties relating to national finances, especially the country's fiscal and monetary policy **2.** US **PRIVATE BANK UNDER FEDERAL CHARTER** a bank in a system of privately owned commercial banks in the United States, operating under federal charter and legally required to be a member of the Federal Reserve System

National City /náshənəl sítti/ city in southwestern California, in San Diego County, south of San Diego. Population: 54,249 (1990).

national code n. Aus = Australian Rules Football

national colours n. the colours of a country's flag

national consciousness n. the ideas, beliefs, and attitudes regarded as characteristic of a nation

national costume n. = national dress

National Curriculum n. the curriculum for pupils aged 5–16 taught in state schools in England and Wales following the Education Reform Act of 1988. It is divided into three 'core' subjects of English, maths, and science, and seven 'foundation' subjects comprising art, design and technology, geography, history, music, physical education, and a foreign language.

national debt n. the total amount of money owed by a nation's central government as a result of borrowing

national dress n. clothes of a distinctive design that are, or were, typical of the people of a particular country

national emblem n. an object that a country has adopted as its symbol, e.g. Canada's maple leaf or Scotland's thistle

National Gallery n. a museum in Trafalgar Square, London, that contains more than 2,000 paintings from the national collection. Founded in 1824, it opened in its present building in 1838.

National Gallery of Art n. a museum in Washington, D.C. that contains the national collection of paintings, prints, drawings, sculptures, photographs, and other works of art. It was founded in 1937 with the gift to the nation of the art collection of the financier Andrew W. Mellon.

National Gallery of Australia n. a museum in Canberra that contains the national collection of Aboriginal, modern Australian, and world art. The collection was begun in 1911, and is housed in a building dating from 1982. Formerly called **Australian National Gallery**

National Gallery of Canada n. a museum in Ottawa that contains the national collection of Canadian and European art. It was created by an Act of Parliament in 1913.

national grid n. **1.** UTIL **NETWORK OF POWER LINES** a network of high-voltage electric power lines linking major power stations throughout the United Kingdom **2.** MAPS **COORDINATES USED FOR MAP-READING** a system of metric coordinates, shown as vertical and horizontal lines on maps, used for map reference purposes by the Ordnance Survey and other map-producing organizations

national guard n. a military organization that operates as a national defence or police force

National Guard n. in the United States, the military reserve units controlled by individual states and equipped by the federal government that can be called into service by either federal or state governments

National Health Service n. in the United Kingdom, the state system for providing free or subsidized medical care, established in 1948 and financed mainly by taxation and national insurance

National Hunt racing, **national hunt racing** n. horseracing over distances up to 6.5 km/4½ mi in which horses jump over movable hurdles or fixed fences, as opposed to flat racing

national income n. the total money earned or gained by all residents of a country over a particular period of time, including income from rent, profits, interest, government benefits, salaries, and wages

National Insurance n. in Britain, a state system based on compulsory contributions from employees and employers that provides medical and financial assistance, including pensions, to people who are ill, retired, or unemployed

National Insurance Number n. in Britain, a unique reference number assigned to everyone within the National Insurance system. It remains the same throughout each person's working life. Abbreviation **NI number**. US term **Social Security Number**

national interest n. whatever will benefit a nation, or a nation's concern for its own survival and prosperity

nationalism /násh'nəlizəm/ n. **1. DESIRE FOR POLITICAL INDEPENDENCE** the desire to achieve political independence, especially by a country under foreign control or by a people with a separate identity and culture but no state of their own **2. PATRIOTISM** proud loyalty and devotion to a nation **3. EXCESSIVE DEVOTION TO NATION** excessive or fanatical devotion to a nation and its interests, often associated with a belief that one country is superior to all others —**nationalist** n., adj.

nationalistic /násh'nə lístik/ adj. relating to or supporting nationalism, especially the kind that emphasizes fervent devotion to one nation and its interests above all others —**nationalistically** adv.

nationality /náshə nálləti/ n. (plural **-ties**) n. **1. CITIZENSHIP OF PARTICULAR NATION** the status of belonging to a specific nation by origin, birth, or naturalization **2. PEOPLE FORMING NATION-STATE** a people with a common origin, tradition, and often language, who form or are capable of forming a nation-state **3. ETHNIC GROUP WITHIN A LARGER ENTITY** an ethnic group that is part of a larger entity such as a state **4. NATIONHOOD** political independence as a separate nation **5. NATIONAL CHARACTER** the character of a nation of people

nationalize /násh'nəlīz/ (-izes, -izing, -ized), **nationalise** (-ises, -ising, -ised) vt. **1. TRANSFER BUSINESS TO STATE OWNERSHIP** to transfer a business, property, or industry from private to governmental control or ownership **2. MAKE NATIONAL** to make sth national or to give a national character to sth **3.** = **naturalize** v. 1 —**nationalization** n. —**nationalized** adj. —**nationalizer** n.

National Liberation Front n. radical nationalist movement in Algeria which launched a guerilla war against France in the 1950s that led to Algeria's independence in 1958

National Library of Australia n. the national library of Australia, in Canberra, established as an independent institution by an Act of Parliament in 1960. It was founded in 1901 as part of the Commonwealth Parliamentary Library.

National Library of Canada n. the national library of Canada, founded in Ottawa in 1953

National Library of New Zealand n. the national library of New Zealand, in Wellington, created in 1966 by combining the collections of the General Assembly Library, the Alexander Turnbull Library, and the National Library Service

nationally /násh'nəli/ adv. in, to, or throughout an entire nation

national monument n. a structure or site of scenic, historical, or scientific significance that is protected and maintained by a national government

national newspaper n. a newspaper that is distributed to and sold in all parts of a country

national park n. a large area of public land chosen by a government for its scenic, recreational, scientific, or historical importance and usually given special protection

National Party n. **1.** Aus **AUSTRALIAN POLITICAL PARTY** in Australia, a conservative political party that has strong support in rural areas and has usually formed a coalition with the Liberal Party of Australia **2.** NZ **NEW ZEALAND POLITICAL PARTY** in New Zealand, a conservative political party **3. SOUTH AFRICAN POLITICAL PARTY** in South Africa, a conservative political party that developed from the Afrikaner nationalist movement, came to power in 1948, was largely responsible for instituting apartheid, and relinquished power in 1994

national press n. the national newspapers of a country collectively

national product n. the total value of all goods and services produced by a nation during a specified, usually annual, period

National Record of Achievement (plural **National Records of Achievement**) n. a record of a young person's achievements that, together with portfolios of evidence, will help in making a decision about the young person's future education, training, or employment

National Savings n. in the United Kingdom, a savings bank that operates through local post offices and offers a variety of government-backed savings and investment schemes (takes a singular verb)

national security n. the protection of a nation from attack or other danger by maintaining adequate armed forces and guarding state secrets

national service n. compulsory service in the armed forces or in a civilian role, as prescribed in some countries

national socialism, **National Socialism** n. the ideology and practices of the Nazi Party, in Germany's Third Reich, which included national expansion, state control of the economy, the totalitarian principle of government, and antisemitism —**national socialist** n., adj.

WORLD'S LARGEST NATIONAL PARKS

Wood Buffalo *Canada*
Area [17,298 sq. mi. / 44,802 sq. km] est. 1922

Ellesmere Island *Canada*
Area [14,585 sq. mi. / 37,775 sq. km] est. 1988

Gates of the Arctic *United States*
Area [11,756 sq. mi. / 30,448 sq. km] est. 1980

Death Valley *United States*
Area [8,554 sq. mi. / 13,765 sq. km] est. 1994

Etosha *Namibia*
Area [8,000 sq. mi. / 20,700 sq. km] est. 1958

Tsavo *Kenya*
Area [8,000 sq. mi. / 20,700 sq. km] est. 1948

Kakadu *Australia*
Area [7,770 sq. mi. / 20,000 sq. km] est. 1979

Kruger *South Africa*
Area [7,523 sq. mi. / 19,485 sq. km] est. 1926

Serengeti *Tanzania*
Area [5,700 sq. mi. / 14,760 sq. km] est. 1941

Hwange *Zimbabwe*
Area [5,657 sq. mi. / 14,651 sq. km] est. 1929

Fiordland *New Zealand*
Area [4,678 sq. mi. / 12,116 sq. km] est. 1952

Kalahari Gemsbok *Botswana/Namibia*
Area [3,703 sq. mi. / 9,591 sq. km] est. 1933

Yellowstone *United States*
Area [3,468 sq. mi. / 8,983 sq. km] est. 1872

Daintree *Australia*
Area [2,734 sq. mi. / 7,000 sq. km] est. 1962

Everglades *United States*
Area [2,354 sq. mi. / 6,096 sq. km] est. 1947

Grand Canyon *United States*
Area [1,904 sq. mi. / 4,930 sq. km] est. 1919

Mount Aspiring *New Zealand*
Area [1,109 sq. mi. / 2,873 sq. km] est. 1964

Lake District *England*
Area [866 sq. mi. / 2,243 sq. km] est. 1951

Snowdonia *Wales*
Area [840 sq. mi. / 2,171 sq. km] est. 1951

Dartmoor *England*
Area [368 sq. mi. / 954 sq. km] est. 1951

National Trust *n.* **1.** CHARITY PRESERVING HISTORIC SITES a charitable organization in England, Wales, and Northern Ireland, concerned with the preservation of areas of great natural beauty, historic buildings and monuments for the benefit of the public **2.** *Aus* AUSTRALIAN CHARITY PRESERVING BEAUTIFUL AREAS an organization in Australia concerned with the preservation of areas of natural beauty and historic monuments

National Trust for Scotland *n.* a Scottish charitable organization, established in 1931, concerned with the preservation of areas of natural beauty, historic buildings and monuments for the benefit of the public

National Vocational Qualification *n.* full form of NVQ

Nation of Islam *n.* a movement of African Americans founded in 1930 whose members follow Islamic religious practice, because of a belief that Black Americans have Muslim origins. Malcolm X was a leading spokesman for the organization until he left it in 1964.

nation-state *n.* an independent state recognized by and able to interact with other states, especially one composed of people who are of one, as opposed to several, nationalities

nationwide /náysh'n wíd/ *adj.* EVERYWHERE IN NATION applying to, happening in, or found in all parts of a nation ○ *a nationwide advertising campaign* ■ *adv.* THROUGHOUT NATION covering the whole nation or throughout the nation

native /náytiv/ *adj.* **1.** INBORN existing in or belonging to someone by nature ○ *her native intelligence* **2.** BORN OR ORIGINATING SOMEWHERE born or originating in a particular place **3.** RELATING TO SB BECAUSE OF BIRTH relating or belonging to sb or sth because of the place or circumstances of birth **4.** INDIGENOUS originating, produced, growing, or living naturally in a place **5.** LOCAL, ESPECIALLY ABORIGINAL, INHABITANTS characteristic of, belonging to, or relating to, the indigenous inhabitants of a particular place, particularly those with an aboriginal culture **6.** NOT EXTERNALLY AFFECTED unaffected by artificial or outside influences **7.** CHEM ELEM OCCURRING NATURALLY found in nature, especially in a pure or unadulterated form ○ *native copper* **8.** AGRIC RAISED IN BRITISH WATERS used to describe oysters raised in British waters, especially in artificial beds **9.** COMPUT FOR PARTICULAR COMPUTER SYSTEM designed exclusively for a particular computer operating system ■ *n.* **1.** SOMEONE BORN IN PARTICULAR PLACE someone born or brought up in a particular place ○ *a native of Birmingham* **2.** INDIGENOUS INHABITANT an original indigenous inhabitant of a place **3.** OFFENSIVE TERM an offensive term for an original inhabitant of a place belonging to an indigenous non-white people with a traditional culture, as distinct from a colonial settler and immigrant (*dated offensive*) **4.** S Africa OFFENSIVE TERM an offensive term for a black South African (*dated offensive*) **5.** LONG-TERM LOCAL RESIDENT an established permanent local resident as opposed to a visitor, temporary resident, or newcomer (*humorous*) **6.** BOT, ZOOL INDIGENOUS PLANT OR ANIMAL SPECIES a plant or animal species that originates from a particular area **7.** AGRIC OYSTER RAISED IN BRITISH WATERS an oyster raised in British waters, especially in an artificial bed [14thC. Directly or via French *natif* from Latin *nativus* 'born' (source of English *naive*), from, ultimately, *nasci* 'to be born' (see NATION).] —**natively** *adv.* —**nativeness** *n.* ◇ **go native** to take up the customs and culture of the foreign place where you have settled (*humorous*)

——— **WORD KEY: SYNONYMS** ———

native, *aboriginal*, *indigenous*, *autochthonous*
CORE MEANING: originating in a particular place
native used to describe sb or sth born or originating in a particular place; **aboriginal** used to describe the people who are the earliest known inhabitants of a particular region; **indigenous** a fairly formal word used to describe species that occur naturally in a particular place and were not introduced from elsewhere; **autochthonous** a technical word used to refer to rocks and minerals that were formed in their present position.

——— **WORD KEY: ORIGIN** ———
The Latin word *nasci*, from which **native** is derived, and its past participle *natus* are also the source of English *cognate*, *impregnate*, *innate*, *naive*, *nascent*, *nation*, *nature*, *noel*, *pregnant*, *puny*, and *renaissance*.

Native American *n.* ABORIGINAL AMERICAN a member of any of the indigenous peoples of North, South, or Central America, belonging to the Mongoloid group of peoples ■ *adj.* RELATING TO INDIGENOUS AMERICAN PEOPLES relating to any of the indigenous American peoples, their languages, or their cultures

——— **WORD KEY: USAGE** ———
See Usage note at **Indian.**

native-born *adj.* belonging to a place by birth

native land *n.* the land to which sb belongs by birth

native speaker *n.* sb who has learned to speak a particular language as a first language

native title *n.* ANZ a right to an area of land claimed by native people whose ancestors were the original inhabitants before European settlement and who can prove a continuous association with that land

native tongue *n.* the first language that sb learns to speak

native wit *n.* practical intelligence that is inborn rather than acquired

nativism /náytivizəm/ *n.* **1.** POL POLICY OF FAVOURING NATIVE INHABITANTS a policy, especially in the United States, of favouring the interests of the native inhabitants of a country over those of immigrants **2.** ANTHROP POLICY OF REAFFIRMING INDIGENOUS CULTURE a policy of protecting and celebrating traditional cultures **3.** PHILOS DOCTRINE OF INNATE IDEAS the belief that the mind possesses some ideas that are inborn and not derived from external sources **4.** PSYCHOL THEORY CLAIMING PERSONALITY IS INNATELY DETERMINED a theory claiming that personality and behaviour are determined from within, not externally —**nativist** *n.*, *adj.* —**nativistic** /náyti vístik/ *adj.*

nativity /nə tívvəti/ (*plural* -**ties**) *n.* **1.** BIRTH OR ORIGIN birth or origin, especially the place, process, or circumstances of being born **2.** HOROSCOPE a horoscope based on the time of sb's birth [14thC. Via Old French from Latin *nativitas*, from *nativus* (see NATIVE).]

Nativity /nə tívvəti/ (*plural* -**ties**) *n.* **1.** BIRTH OF JESUS CHRIST the birth of Jesus Christ, which is celebrated by Christians at Christmas **2.** REPRESENTATION OF JESUS CHRIST'S BIRTH an artistic representation, especially a painting, of the events surrounding the birth of Jesus Christ **3.** CHRISTMAS the festival of Christmas, which commemorates the birth of Jesus Christ

nativity play *n.* a play, usually performed by children at Christmas time, that tells the story of the birth of Jesus Christ

natl *abbr.* national

NATO /náytō/, **Nato** *n.* an international organization established in 1949 to promote mutual defence and collective security that was the primary Western alliance during the Cold War. Full form **North Atlantic Treaty Organization**

natrium /náytri əm/ *n.* the Latin name for sodium, which gave it its chemical symbol of Na [Mid-19thC. Formed from NATRON.]

natriuresis /náytriyoo reessiss/ *n.* the excretion of sodium in urine, especially in excessive amounts [Mid-20thC. Formed from NATRIUM + Greek *ourēsis* 'urination'.] —**natriuretic** /náytriyoo réttik/ *adj.*

natrolite /náttrə līt/ *n.* a white hydrous silicate of sodium and aluminium related to zeolite [Early 19thC. Coined from NATRON + -LITE.]

natron /náytrən, -tron/ *n.* a white, yellow, or grey mineral consisting of hydrous sodium carbonate, found in saline residues, and once used in embalming [Late 17thC. Via French, Spanish, and Arabic *natrūn* from Greek *nitron* (see NITER).]

natter /náttər/ *vi.* (-**ters**, -**tering**, -**tered**) CHAT to talk about not very serious matters, often rapidly and at length and sometimes in an irritating way (*informal*) ■ *n.* NON-SERIOUS CONVERSATION a trivial or gossipy conversation (*informal*) [Early 19thC. Variant of earlier *gnatter* 'to chat, grumble, gnaw', of uncertain origin: probably an imitation of the sound made when talking rapidly.]

natterjack /náttər jak/ *n.* a rare West European toad that inhabits sandy areas and has short hind legs and a skin colour ranging from yellow-green to olive-grey. It moves by running rather than hopping, inflates its body when alarmed, and has the loudest croak of all European toads. Latin name: *Bufo calamita*. [Mid-18thC. Origin uncertain: perhaps from NATTER (because of its loud croak) + JACK (meaning 'newt, fly' in some English dialects).]

natty /nátti/ (-**tier**, -**tiest**) *adj.* neat and smart in appearance or dress [Late 18thC. Origin uncertain: perhaps a variant of earlier *netty* 'neat', from *net* 'clean, tidy' (see NEAT).] —**nattily** *adv.* —**nattiness** *n.*

natural /náchərəl/ *adj.* **1.** OF NATURE relating to nature **2.** CONFORMING WITH NATURE in accordance with the usual course of nature ○ *natural symptoms of aging* **3.** PRODUCED BY NATURE present in or produced by nature, rather than being artificial or created by people ○ *a natural sapphire* **4.** OF PHYSICAL WORLD relating to the physical rather than the spiritual world **5.** LIKE HUMAN

NATURE in accordance with human nature ○ *It's only natural that they should want to be independent.* **6.** **INNATE** inborn, rather than acquired ○ *lots of natural charm* **7.** **BEING STH BY NATURE** having a particular character by nature ○ *a natural leader* **8.** **NOT AFFECTED** behaving in a sincere and unaffected way and not affected or adopted for a particular purpose **9.** **NOT ARTIFICIAL** not artificially coloured or treated **10.** **LIKE REAL LIFE** representing sth in a way that seems true to life **11.** **ILLEGITIMATE** illegitimate (*archaic*) ○ *a natural child* **12.** **BIOLOGICAL** related by blood, rather than adoption ○ *her natural mother* **13.** MUSIC **NOT SHARP OR FLAT** used to describe a note in music that is neither sharp nor flat **14.** MUSIC **WITHOUT SHARPS OR FLATS** used to describe a musical key or scale containing no sharps or flats **15.** CARDS **WITHOUT JOKER OR WILD CARD** not made using a joker or a wild card ○ *a natural flush* ■ *n.* **1.** **SB WITH NATURAL SKILLS OR ABILITIES** sb who has seemingly innate skills or abilities ○ *a natural at bowling* **2.** MUSIC **MUSICAL SIGN CANCELLING SHARP OR FLAT** a sign placed before a musical note in order to cancel a previous sharp or flat **3.** MUSIC **NOTE AFFECTED BY NATURAL SIGN** a musical note affected by a natural sign **4.** CARDS, GAMBLING **STAKE-WINNING RESULT OR COMBINATION** a result or combination in certain card and dice games such as craps and pontoon, that immediately wins the stake **5.** COLOURS **LIGHT COLOUR** a nearly white colour with tints of grey, yellow, or brown, like that of undyed fibres or yarn [13thC. Via French from Latin *naturalis*, from *natura* (see NATURE).] **—naturalness** *n.*

natural childbirth *n.* childbirth with little or no medication or medical intervention. The mother uses special techniques and exercises in order to minimize pain and assist in the delivery.

natural death *n.* death caused by disease or old age rather than by an act of violence or an accident

natural disaster *n.* a disaster such as an earthquake caused by natural forces rather than by human action

natural fibre *n.* a fibre such as cotton, wool, or silk that forms naturally

natural gas *n.* a mixture of combustible hydrocarbon gases, mostly methane and ethane, found trapped in the pore spaces of certain sedimentary rocks, often along with petroleum deposits

natural history *n.* **1.** **STUDY AND DESCRIPTION OF NATURE** the study and description of living things, especially their behaviour and how they relate to one another **2.** **NATURAL PHENOMENA OF TIME OR PLACE** the natural phenomena, especially plants and animals, of a particular time or place **3.** **NATURAL DEVELOPMENT OF STH** the natural development of sth such as an organism or a disease over a period of time ○ *the natural history of the leech* **4.** **WRITTEN ACCOUNT OF ASPECT OF NATURE** a written account of a particular aspect of the natural world

naturalism /náchərəlizəm/ *n.* **1.** ARTS, LITERAT **MOVEMENT OR SCHOOL ADVOCATING REALISTIC DESCRIPTION** in art or literature, a movement or school advocating factual or realistic description of life including its less pleasant aspects. In literature, it is applied especially to Zola, Maupassant, and other 19th-century French writers. In the visual arts, it refers to the practice of faithfully representing subjects. **2.** RELIG **BELIEF IN RELIGIOUS TRUTH FROM NATURE** a belief that all religious truth is derived from nature and natural causes, and not from revelation **3.** PHILOS **DOCTRINE REJECTING SPIRITUAL EXPLANATIONS OF WORLD** a system of thought that rejects all spiritual and supernatural explanations of the world and holds that science is the sole basis of what can be known

naturalist /náchərəlist/ *n.* **1.** BIOL **SB STUDYING NATURAL HISTORY** sb who studies or is interested in natural history, especially botany or zoology. The term is particularly used to describe a field biologist. **2.** ARTS, PHILOS **ADVOCATE OF NATURALISM** sb who believes in or practises naturalism, especially in the arts ■ *adj.* **RELATING TO BELIEFS OF NATURALISM** relating to or in accordance with the beliefs of naturalism

naturalistic /náchərə lístik/ *adj.* **1.** **REPRODUCING EFFECTS OF NATURE** imitating or reproducing nature or perceived reality in a very exact and faithful way **2.** **RELATING TO BELIEFS OF NATURALISM** relating to, characteristic of, or in accordance with the tenets of naturalism, especially in art or literature **3.** **OF NATURALISTS** relating to naturalists or natural history **—naturalistically** *adv.*

naturalize /náchərə līz/ (**-izes, -izing, -ized**), **naturalise** (**-ises, -ising, -ised**) *v.* **1.** *vti.* **GRANT CITIZENSHIP TO** to grant citizenship to sb of foreign birth, or to acquire citizenship in an adopted country **2.** *vt.* **INTRODUCE STH FOREIGN INTO GENERAL USE** to introduce sth foreign such as a word or custom into general use or into the language of a community **3.** *vti.* BOT, ZOOL **ACCLIMATIZE PLANT OR ANIMAL** to cause a plant or animal from another region to become established in a new environment or to adapt successfully to new environmental conditions **4.** *vt.* **EXPLAIN IN NATURAL TERMS** to explain a phenomenon in terms of natural as opposed to supernatural causes **5.** *vt.* **MAKE NATURAL** to make sth natural or lifelike **—naturalization** *n.* **—naturalized** *adj.* **—naturalizer** *n.*

natural killer cell *n.* a white blood cell (**lymphocyte**) that can recognize microbes and tumour cells as 'foreign', without requiring prior exposure to them, and destroy them

natural language *n.* **1.** **NATURALLY EVOLVED HUMAN LANGUAGE** a naturally evolved human language as opposed to a created language such as a computer language **2.** **NATURALLY EVOLVED HUMAN LANGUAGES** naturally evolved human languages considered collectively

natural language processing *n.* the branch of computational linguistics concerned with the use of artificial intelligence to process natural languages as, e.g., in machine translation

natural law *n.* **1.** **LAW OF MORALITY** a law of morality believed to be derived from human beings' inherent sense of right and wrong, rather than from revelation or the legislation produced by society **2.** **LAW OF NATURE** a law that governs the behaviour of natural phenomena **3.** PHILOS **BELIEF IN UNIVERSAL JUSTICE SYSTEM** the belief that general laws of nature can be applied as a system of justice for all societies, regardless of their individual culture or customs

natural light *n.* light from a natural source, usually the sun, as opposed to artificial light

natural logarithm *n.* a logarithm with the irrational number *e* as a base

naturally /náchərəli/ *adv.* **1.** **AS EXPECTED** as might be expected ○ *They naturally objected to being treated in this way.* **2.** **OF COURSE** without any question or doubt ○ *'You'll go then?' 'Naturally'.* **3.** **BY NATURE** as a result of a natural feature, talent, or quality that sb possesses ○ *a naturally gifted player* **4.** **IN NORMAL WAY** in a normal and unaffected manner ○ *People seldom act naturally when being filmed.* **5.** **WITHOUT ARTIFICIAL AID OR TREATMENT** occurring as a natural feature or quality without artificial aid **6.** **REALISTICALLY** in a manner that faithfully represents nature

natural medicine *n.* = **naturopathy**

natural number *n.* any whole number greater than zero

natural philosophy *n.* the study of nature and natural phenomena (*archaic*)

natural resource *n.* a naturally occurring material such as coal or wood that can be exploited by people

natural scale *n.* a musical scale without sharps or flats

natural science *n.* any of the sciences such as biology, chemistry, and physics that deal with phenomena observable in nature **—natural scientist** *n.*

natural selection *n.* the process, according to Darwin, by which organisms best suited to survival in a particular environment achieve greater reproductive success, thereby passing advantageous genetic characteristics on to future generations. ◊ **artificial selection**

natural theology *n.* a theology that holds that knowledge of God can be derived by human reason alone, not requiring divine revelation

natural virtue *n.* in theology, one of the four virtues of which people are capable without direct assistance from God, specifically fortitude, justice, prudence, and temperance

natural wastage *n.* a gradual reduction in the workforce of an organization achieved by not replacing staff who leave through retirement or resignation

natural world *n.* natural phenomena collectively, as opposed to supernatural or paranormal phenomena or those created by human activity

nature /náychər/ *n.* **1.** **PHYSICAL WORLD** the physical world including all natural phenomena and living things **2.** **nature, Nature** **FORCES CONTROLLING PHYSICAL WORLD** the forces and processes collectively that control the phenomena of the physical world independently of human volition or intervention, sometimes personified as a woman called 'Mother Nature' **3.** **COUNTRYSIDE** the countryside or the environment in a condition relatively unaffected by human activity or as the home of living creatures other than human beings **4.** **TYPE** a type or sort of thing ○ *a detective novel or something of that nature* **5.** **INTRINSIC CHARACTER OF PERSON OR THING** the intrinsic or essential character of sb or sth **6.** **TEMPERAMENT** disposition or temperament in a person ○ *It's just not part of his nature to act unkindly.* **7.** **REAL APPEARANCE OR ASPECT** the appearance or aspect of a person, place, or thing that is considered to reflect reality ○ *The portrait was remarkably true to nature.* **8.** **PRIMITIVE EXISTENCE** a basic state of existence, untouched and uninfluenced by civilization **9.** RELIG **NATURAL STATE OF HUMANKIND** the natural and original condition of humankind, as distinguished from a state of grace **10.** **UNIVERSAL HUMAN BEHAVIOUR** the patterns of behaviour or the moral standards that are considered to be universally found and recognized among human beings **11.** **GENETIC MATERIAL AFFECTING ORGANISM** the inherited genetic material that partly determines the behaviour, character, and structure of an organism, as opposed to what is learnt from experience or the environment ○ *nature versus nurture* [13thC. Via Old French from Latin *natura* 'birth, innate qualities, nature' from, ultimately, *nasci* 'to be born' (see NATION).] ◇ **by nature** as a part of his, her, or its essential character ◇ **call of nature** the need to urinate or defecate (*humorous*) ◇ **in the nature of sb** *or* **sth** **1.** characteristic of sb *or* sth **2.** in the category of sth

-natured *adj.* having or showing a particular nature or disposition (*often used in combination*) ○ *good-natured* [Formed from NATURE]

nature reserve, nature preserve *n.* a managed and protected area of land usually containing rare or endangered plants or animals

nature strip *n. Aus* a strip of vegetation, such as trees, grass, or other plants, along the edge of a pavement or between the lanes of a main road or highway

nature trail *n.* a route through a natural area that is specially designed to draw attention to interesting natural features

naturism /náychərizəm/ *n.* **1.** **WEARING NO CLOTHES AS A CUSTOM** the practice of going without clothes, usually in a communal setting or in designated areas, in the belief that nudity is a healthy natural state **2.** RELIG **NATURE WORSHIP** worship of nature in general, or of objects of nature such as trees and mountains **—naturist** *n.* **—naturistic** /naychə rístik/ *adj.* **—naturistically** /-rístikli/ *adv.*

naturopathy /náychə róppəthi/ *n.* a system of medicine founded on the belief that diet, mental state, exercise, breathing, and other natural factors are central to the origin and treatment of disease **—naturopath** /náychərō path/ *n.* **—naturopathic** /-páthik/ *adj.* **—naturopathically** /-páthikli/ *adv.*

Naugatuck /náwgə tuk/ **1.** river in western Connecticut. Length: 105 km/65 mi. **2.** town in southern Connecticut, in New Haven County, south of Waterbury. Population: 30,625 (1990).

naught /nawt/, **nought** *n.* **1.** *US* = **nought** *n.* 1 **2.** **NOTHING** nothing at all (*archaic or literary*) ○ *Their efforts were all for naught.* [Old English *nāwiht*. From *nā* NO + *wiht* 'thing, being'.]

naughty /náwti/ *adj.* (**-tier, -tiest**) **1.** **BADLY BEHAVED** badly behaved, especially by being mischievous or disobedient **2.** **MILDLY INDECENT** mildly indecent or improper (*humorous*) ○ *standing with his hands over his naughty parts* ○ *a naughty smile* **3.** **SINFUL** mildly sinful (*humorous*) ○ *Would it be naughty of me to* have another chocolate? ■ *n.* (*plural* **-ties**) ANZ ACT OF HAVING SEX an act of sexual intercourse (*slang*) ○ *They were upstairs having a quick naughty.* [14thC. The current meaning evolved from 'having naught, poor' via 'bad'.] —**naughtily** *adv.* —**naughtiness** *n.*

WORD KEY: SYNONYMS

See Synonyms at **bad**.

nauplius /náwpli əss/ (*plural* **-i** /-pli ī/) *n.* a free-swimming larva that is produced by many different crustaceans, with an unsegmented body, three pairs of limbs, and a single eye [Mid-19thC. Via Latin, 'kind of shellfish', from Greek *nauplios*.]

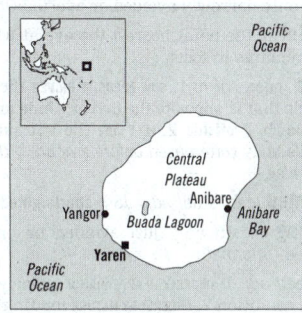

Nauru

Nauru /na roŏ/ island republic in Micronesia, in the central Pacific Ocean, northeast of Australia. Language: English, Nauruan Currency: Australian dollar. Capital: Yaren. Population: 10,273 (1996). Area: 21 sq. km/8.1 sq. mi. Official name **Republic of Nauru**. Former name **Pleasant Island** —**Nauruan** *n., adj.*

nausea /náwzi ə, -si ə/ *n.* **1.** SICKNESS OF THE STOMACH the unsettling feeling in the stomach that accompanies the urge to vomit **2.** DISGUST deep disgust (*literary*) [15thC. Via Latin and Greek *nausia* from, ultimately, *naus* (see NAUTICAL). The underlying idea is of seasickness.]

nauseate /náwzi ayt, -si ayt/ (**-ates, -ating, -ated**) *vti.* **1.** MAKE OR BECOME SICK to have, or make sb have, the unsettling feeling in the stomach that accompanies the urge to vomit **2.** DISGUST OR BECOME DISGUSTED to feel, or make sb feel, deep disgust

nauseating /náwzi ayting, -si ayting/ *adj.* **1.** CAUSING SICKNESS IN STOMACH producing the unsettling feeling in the stomach that accompanies the urge to vomit **2.** DISGUSTING deeply disgusting —**nauseatingly** *adv.*

nauseous /náwzi əss, -si əss/ *adj.* **1.** SICK IN THE STOMACH suffering from the unsettling feeling in the stomach that accompanies the urge to vomit **2.** CAUSING SICKNESS IN STOMACH producing the unsettling feeling in the stomach that accompanies the urge to vomit —**nauseously** *adv.* —**nauseousness** *n.*

naut. *abbr.* nautical

nautch /nawch/ *n.* a professional performance of traditional Indian dancing [Early 19thC. Via Hindi *nāc* from, ultimately, Sanskrit *nṛt* 'to dance'.]

nautical /náwtik'l/ *adj.* relating to sailors, ships, or seafaring [Mid-16thC. Via Latin from Greek *nautikos*, from *nautēs* 'sailor', from *naus* 'ship' (source of English *astronaut*, *nausea*, and *noise*).] —**nautically** *adv.*

nautical mile *n.* **1.** INTERNATIONAL SEA MEASURE an international unit of measurement of distance at sea equal to 1.852 kilometres **2.** UK MEASUREMENT AT SEA a measurement of distance at sea used in the UK and taken to be equal to 1.8532 kilometres or about 6076 ft

nautiloid /náwti loyd/ *n.* a mollusc that belongs to the group that includes the nautiluses and many fossil species. The group includes species with chambered, straight, and coiled shells. Subclass: Nautiloidea. [Mid-19thC. Formed from NAUTILUS.]

nautilus /náwtiləss/ (*plural* **-luses** or **-li** /-ti lī/) *n.* **1.** SEA CREATURE WITH A COILED SHELL a mollusc with numerous tentacles, a horny beak, and a spiral shell with gas-filled chambers for buoyancy. It is found in the South Pacific and Indian Oceans. Genus: *Nautilus*. **2.** = **paper nautilus** [Early 17thC. Via Latin from Greek *nautilos* 'sailor, nautilus', from *nautēs* (see NAUTICAL).]

NAV *abbr.* FIN net asset value

nav. *abbr.* **1.** naval **2.** navigable **3.** navigation

Navajo /návvəhō/, **Navaho** *n.* (*plural* **-jo** or **-jos** or **-joes**; *plural* **-ho** or **-hos** or **-hoes**) **1.** PEOPLES MEMBER OF A NATIVE N AMERICAN PEOPLE a member of a Native North American people living mainly in northern New Mexico and Arizona. They are the most populous of all US Native American peoples. **2.** PEOPLES MEMBER OF NAVAJO a member of the Navajo people **3.** LANG LANGUAGE OF THE NAVAJO a Native North American language spoken in parts of Arizona, New Mexico, and Utah. It belongs to the Athabaskan branch of Na-Déné languages and is spoken by about 225,000 people. ■ *adj.* OF THE NAVAJOS produced by or belonging to the Navajo ○ *a Navajo rug* [Late 18thC. Via Spanish (*Apaches de*) *Navajó*, literally '(Apaches of) Navajó', from extinct Tewa (a Tanoan language) *navahū* 'fields adjoining a ravine'.]

naval /náyv'l/ *adj.* relating or belonging to a navy or to warships —**navally** *adv.*

naval architect *n.* sb who designs ships —**naval architecture** *n.*

naval dockyard *n.* a navy-owned shipyard where warships are built and repaired. US term **navy yard**

Navarre /nə vaár/ autonomous region in northeastern Spain, between the Basque Country and Catalonia. Capital: Pamplona. Population: 519,227 (1991). Area: 10,421 sq. km/4,024 sq. mi.

nave[1] /nayv/ *n.* the long central hall of a cross-shaped church, often with pillars on each side, where the congregation sits [Late 17thC. Via medieval Latin from Latin *navis* (see NAVY). Perhaps from its resemblance in shape to or from the idea of the church as a ship.]

nave[2] /nayv/ *n.* the hub of a wheel [Old English *nafu*. Ultimately from a prehistoric Germanic word that is also the ancestor of English *navel*.]

navel /náyv'l/ *n.* a small rounded hollow on the surface of the human stomach, where the end of the umbilical cord was tied after being cut. Technical name **umbilicus** [Old English *nafela*. Ultimately from an Indo-European word that also produced English *nave* and Latin *umbilicus* (source of English *umbilical*).] ◇ **examine** or **contemplate your navel** to spend too much time in pointless self-analysis (*informal humorous*)

navel-gazing *n.* pointless self-analysis as opposed to considering broader issues or making a decision

navel orange *n.* a sweet seedless orange with a small navel-shaped depression or bump at its blossom end enclosing a smaller secondary fruit. Latin name: *Citrus sinensis*.

navelwort /náyv'l wurt/ *n.* = **pennywort** [15thC. From the navel-shaped indentation on its leaves.]

navicular /nə víkyoŏlər/ *n.* ANAT = **navicular bone** ■ *adj.* **1.** BOAT-SHAPED shaped like a boat (*formal*) **2.** MED OF THE NAVICULAR BONE relating to a navicular bone [15thC. From late Latin *navicularis*, from Latin *navicula*, literally 'a small ship', from *navis* (see NAVY).]

navicular bone *n.* **1.** ANAT HUMAN BONE a small boat-shaped bone in the human wrist or ankle **2.** VET HORSE BONE a small bone in a horse's hoof. It is prone to disease (**navicular disease**), causing lameness.

navigable /návvigəb'l/ *adj.* **1.** PASSABLE BY SHIP passable by ship or boat, especially deep enough and wide enough to allow ships or boats to sail through **2.** STEERABLE able to be steered or otherwise controlled —**navigability** /návvigə bílləti/ *n.* —**navigably** /návvigəbli/ *adv.*

navigate /návvi gayt/ (**-gates, -gating, -gated**) *v.* **1.** *vti.* FIND A ROUTE to find a way through a place, or direct the course of sth, especially a ship or aircraft, using a route-finding system ○ *navigating by the stars* **2.** *vt.* PASS THROUGH A PLACE to follow a correct or satisfactory course along a route ○ *Even a champion paddler would have difficulty navigating those rapids.* **3.** *vi.* KEEP A CAR ON THE RIGHT ROUTE to have responsibility for keeping a car on the right route, e.g. by following a map and giving the driver instructions **4.** *vt.* FIND YOUR WAY to find a way to a place, usually with difficulty (*informal*) ○ *managed to navigate his way through the fog* [Late 16thC. From the past participle stem of Latin *navigare* 'to sail', from *navis* (see NAVY) + *agere* 'to drive'.]

navigation /návvi gáysh'n/ *n.* **1.** SCIENCE OF NAVIGATING the science of plotting and following a course from one place to another and of determining the position of a moving ship, aircraft, or other vehicle **2.** DIRECTING OF A VEHICLE'S COURSE the plotting and directing of the course of a ship, aircraft, or other vehicle **3.** MOVEMENT THROUGH A PLACE the act or task of moving through a place or along a route, e.g. along a river or through a range of mountains —**navigational** *adj.* —**navigationally** *adv.*

navigation light *n.* any one of a number of lights on the outside of a ship or aircraft that alert others to its position and direction

navigation satellite *n.* an artificial satellite, used as an aid to navigation, that follows a fixed orbit made known to navigators on ships and aircraft

navigator /návvi gaytər/ *n.* **1.** SB IN CHARGE OF NAVIGATION sb who is qualified in navigation, especially sb responsible for navigating a ship or aircraft **2.** DRIVER'S ROUTE INSTRUCTOR sb who gives information on the route ahead to the driver of a car

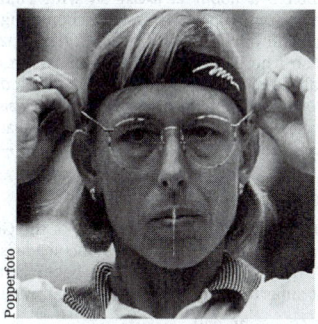

Martina Navratilova

Navratilova /na vrátti lóvə/, **Martina** (*b.* 1956) Czech-born US tennis player. She holds the women's record of 167 singles championships (1974–94), including nine Wimbledon titles.

NAVSAT /náv sat/ *abbr.* navigation satellite (*informal*)

navvy /návvi/ *n.* (*plural* **-vies**) LABOURER an unskilled labourer, especially sb who does the heavy digging work involved in the building of roads, railways, and canals (*dated*) ■ *vi.* (**-vies, -vying, -vied**) WORK AS NAVVY to work as a navvy [Early 19thC. Shortening of NAVIGATOR (in its earlier meaning 'canal labourer').]

navy /náyvi/ *n.* (*plural* **-vies**) **1.** SEAGOING MILITARY FORCE the branch of a country's armed forces that crews, maintains, and fights on warships **2.** FLEET OF SHIPS a fleet of ships, especially one belonging to a country **3.** COLOURS = **navy blue** ■ *adj.* COLOURS = **navy blue** [14thC. Via Old French *navie* 'fleet', from, ultimately, Latin *navis* 'ship'.]

navy blue, **navy** *n.* DARK BLUE a dark blue colour ■ *adj.* COLOURS DARK BLUE IN COLOUR of a dark blue colour (*hyphenated before a noun*) ○ *a navy-blue dress* [From the colour of the British naval uniform]

navy cut *n.* tobacco that has been cut into fine slices from a large block

nawab /nə waáb/ *n.* **1.** INDIAN NOBLEMAN a title used for a local nobleman in India during the Mogul empire **2.** DISTINGUISHED PAKISTANI MAN a distinguished Muslim man in Pakistan [Mid-18thC. Via Urdu *nawāb* from, ultimately, Arabic *nā'ib* 'deputy'.]

nay /nay/ *n.* **1.** NO VOTE a vote of no or sb who votes no ■ *adv.* INTRODUCING CORRECTION used to introduce a phrase that corrects sth just said, often a phrase that states the truth in stronger terms (*archaic or literary*) ○ *It was a disappointing, nay, humiliating, outcome.* ■ *interj.* NO no (*archaic*) [12thC. From Old Norse *nei*, from *ne* 'not' + *ei* 'ever' (source of English *aye*).]

naysay /náy say/ (**-says, -saying, -said**) *vt.* US to refuse, oppose, or criticize a proposal (*literary*)

naysayer /náy sayər/ *n.* US sb who votes no or who speaks against sth (*literary*)

Nazarene /názzə reén/ *n.* **1.** SB FROM NAZARETH sb who was born or brought up in Nazareth **2.** MEMBER OF PROTESTANT CHURCH a member of the Church of the Nazarene, a modern Protestant denomination **3.** JESUS CHRIST Jesus Christ, as connected with Nazareth (*literary*) [13thC. Via late Latin from Greek *Nazarēnos*, from *Nazaret* 'Nazareth'.]

Nazareth /názzərəth/ town in northern Israel, in Galilee, situated southeast of Haifa. It is believed to be where Jesus Christ lived during his childhood. Population: 49,800 (1992).

Nazarite /názzə rīt/, **Nazirite** *n.* a member of a Jewish religious group in biblical times whose members made various vows of abstinence, including a vow not to drink wine or cut their hair [Mid-16thC. Formed from late Latin *Nazaraeus*, from Greek *Nazōraios*, from *Nazaret* 'Nazareth'.]

Nazca Lines *n.* a group of large-scale figures carved into the desert near Nazca, southern Peru, in pre-Inca times. They consist of long straight lines representing birds, fish, animals, or geometrical figures and are only visible from the air.

Nazi /náatsi/ *n.* **1.** FOLLOWER OF HITLER a member of the German National Socialist Party that came to power under the leadership of Adolf Hitler in 1933 (*often used before a noun*) **2.** RACIST sb with right-wing political views, especially sb with right-wing views on race and immigration (*insult*) **3.** Nazi, nazi BOSSY PERSON sb who behaves in an authoritarian or dictatorial manner (*insult; offensive in some contexts*) [Mid-20thC. From German, a shortening of *Nationalsozialist* 'national socialist' or *Nationalsozialismus* 'national socialism'.] —**Nazification** /náatsifi káysh'n/ *n.* —**Nazify** /náatsi fī/ *vt.*

Nazirite *n.* = **Nazarite**

Nazism /náatsizəm/ *n.* the philosophy of the German National Socialist Party under the leadership of Adolf Hitler. Central to it was a belief in the inherent superiority of a supposed Aryan race.

nb *abbr.* CRICKET no ball

Nb *symbol.* niobium

NB, **N.B.** *abbr.* New Brunswick

n.b., **nb** used to draw sb's attention to sth particularly important, usually an addition to or qualification of a previous statement. Full form **nota bene** [Latin, *nota bene* 'note well']

NBA *abbr.* **1.** National Boxing Association **2.** Net Book Agreement **3.** National Basketball Association

NBC *abbr.* **1.** National Broadcasting Company **2.** INDUST nuclear, biological, and chemical (*used of weapons or warfare*)

NbE *abbr.* north by east

NBG, **nbg** *abbr.* no bloody good (*informal*)

NBL *abbr.* National Book League

NBV *abbr.* ACCT, COMM net book value

NbW *abbr.* north by west

NC *abbr.* **1.** no charge **2.** NC, N.C. North Carolina **3.** NC, N.C. National Curriculum

n/c *abbr.* no charge

NCC *abbr.* **1.** National Consumer Council **2.** National Curriculum Council **3.** Nature Conservancy Council

NCCL *abbr.* National Council for Civil Liberties (*dated*)

NCO *abbr.* noncommissioned officer

NCT *abbr.* National Childbirth Trust

NCU *abbr.* National Communications Union

Nd *symbol.* neodymium

ND, **N.D.** *abbr.* North Dakota

n.d., **ND** *abbr.* no date

N. Dak. *abbr.* North Dakota

NDE *abbr.* near-death experience

NDP *abbr.* net domestic product

Ne *symbol.* neon

NE *abbr.* **1.** Nebraska **2.** NE, N.E. New England **3.** COMPASS northeast **4.** COMPASS northeastern

NEA *abbr.* National Education Association

Neagh, Lough /nay/ inland lake in central Northern Ireland, and the largest lake in the British Isles. Area: 396 sq. km/153 sq. mi.

Neandertal /ni ándər taal/, **Neanderthal** /ni ándər thaal/ *adj.* **1.** RELATING TO NEANDERTAL MAN relating to Neandertal man or the culture **2.** Neandertal, neandertal OFFENSIVE TERM an offensive term used to describe sb displaying the lack of intellect, lack of sensitivity, and boorishness traditionally associated with cavemen (*insult*) **3.** Neandertal, neandertal OLD-FASHIONED very old-fashioned or conservative (*insult*) ■ *n.* **Neandertal, neandertal** OFFENSIVE TERM an offensive term for sb who is crude, primitive, or excessively old-fashioned (*insult*) [Mid-19thC. Named after a valley in western Germany where evidence of Neandertal man was first found.]

Neandertal man *n.* an extinct subspecies of human beings that populated Europe, northern Africa, and western Asia in the early Stone Age. Physical characteristics include a sloping forehead and large brow ridges.

neap /neep/ *n.* = **neap tide** ■ *adj.* RELATING TO NEAP TIDE relating to or associated with a neap tide [15thC. From Old English *nēp-*, of uncertain origin.]

Neapolitan /nee ə póllitən/ *adj.* OF NAPLES relating to the Italian city of Naples, or its people or culture ■ *n.* SB FROM NAPLES sb who was born or brought up or who lives in Naples [15thC. Via Latin *Neapolitanus* from, ultimately, Greek *Neapolis*, literally 'new town', 'Naples'.]

Neapolitan ice cream *n.* ice cream made in differently coloured and flavoured layers, usually served in a slice

neap tide *n.* a tide that shows the least range between high and low and occurs twice a month between the first and third quarters of the moon

near /neer/ (**nears, nearing, neared**) CORE MEANING: at or to a point that is not far away in space ○ (prep) *The art exhibition is near here.* ○ (adv) *He took a step nearer to the water.* ○ (adv) *as the car drew nearer* ○ (adj) *There must be a restaurant nearer than that.* ○ (adj) *Can you tell me where the nearest telephone is?* **1.** *adv., prep., adj.* SHORT TIME AWAY at or to a time not far away ○ (adv) *as the time for her to leave drew near* ○ (prep) *He should arrive near the end of the week* ○ (adj) *We shall be moving in the very near future.* **2.** *adv., adj.* CLOSE at a point that is not far away in state, resemblance, or number ○ (adv) *It was nearer two hours before he got through customs.* ○ (adv) *He felt a sensation that was near to fear.* ○ (adj) *the nearest thing to a champion this country has ever had* **3.** *adv., adj.* ALMOST almost the state or situation mentioned ○ (adv) *I damn near fainted.* ○ (adv) *near total failure* ○ living in near poverty **4.** *adj., n.* ON THE LEFT on the left side, especially of an animal or a horse-drawn vehicle ○ *the near foreleg.* ◊ **nearside 5.** *adj.* CLOSELY RELATED closely related to sb **6.** *adj.* MISERLY reluctant to give or spend money (*archaic*) **7.** *vti.* APPROACH to approach, or approach a particular place, time, or state ○ *The project is nearing completion.* ○ *With the big event nearing, everyone was working hard.* [12thC. From Old Norse *nær* 'nearer', from *ná* 'near'.] —**nearness** *n.* ◊ **near the bone** *or* **knuckle** rather vulgar or indecent (*informal*)

nearby /neer bī/ *adj., adv.* in, at, or to a place a short distance away ○ *a nearby grocer* ○ *His mother was waiting nearby.*

Nearctic /ni áarktik/ *adj.* related to or located in the region of plant and animal life in the Arctic and temperate areas of Greenland and North America [Mid-19thC. Coined from NEO- + ARCTIC.]

near-death experience *n.* a sensation that people on the brink of death have described as leaving their own bodies and observing them as though they were bystanders

Near East *n.* **1.** = **Middle East** *n.* ↑ **2.** THE BALKANS the countries on the Balkan peninsula, comprising Greece, Albania, Romania, Bulgaria, the states of the former Yugoslavia, and the European part of Turkey (*dated*)

near gale *n.* = **moderate gale**

near hand *adj., adv.* = **near about**

near letter quality *adj.* used to describe the printing quality of a computer printer that produces printed characters as clear as a typewriter's

nearly /neerli/ *adv.* **1.** ALMOST almost but not quite the case ○ *We waited for nearly an hour.* **2.** CLOSELY closely, in time, proximity, or relationship ○ *'Brennan described to the police the man he saw in the window and then identified Oswald as the person who most nearly resembled the man he saw '.* (Earl Warren et al, *The Report of the Warren Commission*; 1964) ◊ **not nearly** used to emphasize that sth stated, implied, or assumed is very far from being the case ○ *not nearly enough time to answer all the questions*

near miss *n.* **1.** SHOT NEAR TARGET a shot or strike that comes very close to a target but does not quite hit it **2.** NEAR COLLISION a situation in which two vehicles only narrowly avoid colliding with each other **3.** BARELY AVERTED DISASTER sth, especially sth undesirable, that is only narrowly avoided or averted (*informal*)

near point *n.* the point nearest the eye at which an object remains in focus

nearside /neer sīd/ *n.* **1.** SIDE OPPOSITE DRIVER the side of a vehicle that is opposite the driver's side and close to the kerb. ◊ **offside 2.** LEFT SIDE the left side of an animal's body (*often used before a noun*) ○ *the nearside foreleg*

nearsighted /neer sītid/ *adj.* US = **shortsighted**

near thing *n.* sth only just avoided or only just achieved (*informal*)

neat[1] /neet/ *adj.* **1.** ORDERLY IN APPEARANCE orderly and in a clean condition **2.** ORDERLY BY NATURE tending to keep things in an orderly and clean condition ○ *My husband's very neat in the kitchen.* **3.** UNDILUTED not diluted with water, ice cubes, or a mixer **4.** ELEGANT simple, effective, and elegant ○ *a neat solution to a complex problem* **5.** SKILFULLY PERFORMED performed with skill, ingenuity, and apparent ease ○ *a neat pirouette* **6.** COMPACT appealingly regular or compact ○ *She stood admiring her own neat little figure in the mirror.* **7.** US EXCELLENT used as a general term of approval (*informal*) ○ *Her parents are really neat.* [Mid-16thC. Via French *net* from Latin *nitidus* 'shiny', from *nitere* 'to shine' (source of English *net*).] —**neatness** *n.*

neat[2] /neet/ (*plural* **neats** *or* **neat**) *n.* an animal in the cattle family, e.g. a cow or ox (*archaic*) [Old English *nēat*. Ultimately from a prehistoric Germanic word meaning 'to use'.]

neaten /neet'n/ (**-ens, -ening, -ened**) *vt.* to make sth neat or orderly

neath /neeth/, **'neath** *prep.* beneath (*literary*) [Late 18thC. Shortening of BENEATH.]

Neath /neeth/ industrial town in southern Wales. Population: 45,965 (1991).

neatly /neetli/ *adv.* **1.** CAREFULLY with care, order, and some precision ○ *a pile of clothes neatly folded* **2.** ELEGANTLY simply, effectively, and elegantly **3.** SKILFULLY with skill, ingenuity, and apparent ease

neat's-foot oil *n.* a pale yellow oil made from the feet and shinbones of cattle, used to treat leather [From NEAT]

neb /neb/ *n.* **1.** Scotland *or* N England SB'S NOSE sb's nose (*informal or humorous*) ○ *told him to keep his neb out of my business* **2.** N England ANIMAL'S NOSE an animal's bill, beak, nose, or snout (*informal*) **3.** POINT OR PROJECTION sth that sticks out, e.g. an overhanging rock or peak (*archaic*) [Old English *nebb*]

NEB *abbr.* **1.** National Enterprise Board **2.** New English Bible

nebbish /nébbish/ *n.* an offensive term that deliberately insults sb's courage, personality, and initiative (*informal insult*) [Late 19thC. Via Yiddish *nebekh* 'poor thing' from, ultimately, assumed Common Slavic *ne-bogŭ* 'poor'.]

NEbE *abbr.* northeast by east

NEbN *abbr.* northeast by north

Nebr. *abbr.* Nebraska

Nebraska /nə bráskə/ state in the central United States, bordered by South Dakota, Iowa, Missouri, Kansas, Colorado, and Wyoming. Capital: Lincoln. Population: 1,656,870 (1997). Area: 200,359 sq. km/77,359 sq. mi. —**Nebraskan** *n., adj.*

Nebuchadnezzar II /nébbyŏŏkəd nézzər/ (*fl.* 6th century BC) Babylonian king. He conquered and destroyed Jerusalem in 586 BC, consigning its in-

Nebraska

habitants to captivity. He is thought to have created the Hanging Gardens of Babylon.

Nebula: Eagle Nebula, photographed by the Hubble Space Telescope (1995)

nebula /nébbyŏŏlə/ (*plural* **-lae** /-lee/ *or* **-las**) *n.* **1.** ASTRON **SPACE DUST** a region or cloud of interstellar dust and gas appearing variously as a hazy bright or dark patch **2.** MED **FLAW ON EYEBALL** a faint cloudy area or scar on the cornea **3.** MED **CLOUDY URINE** cloudiness in the urine **4.** MED **LIQUID FOR SPRAYING** liquid prepared for use in any kind of atomizing sprayer, especially a nebulizer [Mid-17thC. From Latin, 'mist, vapour'.] — **nebular** *adj.*

nebular hypothesis *n.* a now largely rejected theory that the solar system evolved from a hot rotating flattened gaseous nebula. The theory states that as the nebula cooled, the Sun condensed at the centre and planets and their moons formed from contracting concentric rings at the rim.

nebulize /nébbyŏŏ līz/ (**-lizes, -lizing, -lized**), **nebulise** (**-lises, -lising, -lised**) *vt.* to reduce a liquid to a fine spray for medical use —**nebulization** /nébbyŏŏ līzáysh'n/ *n.*

nebulizer /nébbyŏŏ līzər/, **nebuliser** *n.* a device, with a face mask attached, for administering a medicinal liquid in the form of a fine spray that is breathed in through the mouth or nose

nebulosity /nébbyŏŏ lóssəti/ (*plural* **-ties**) *n.* = **nebula** *n.* 1

nebulous /nébbyŏŏləss/ *adj.* **1.** UNCLEAR not clear, distinct, or definite **2.** ASTRON **RELATING TO NEBULAS** relating to or resembling a nebula —**nebulously** *adv.* —**nebulousness** *n.*

NEC *n., abbr.* **1.** National Exhibition Centre (Birmingham) **2.** National Executive Committee

necessarily /néssəssərəli, néssə sérrəli/ *adv.* **1.** INEVITABLY inevitably, or in every case ○ *This route isn't necessarily the best one.* **2.** UNAVOIDABLY following as an unavoidable result or consequence ○ *Voting was a necessarily slow and complex process.*

necessary /néssəssəri/ *adj.* **1.** REQUIRED needed, essential, or required by authority or convention ○ *Is it really necessary to contact the police?* **2.** FOLLOWING INEVITABLY inevitable given what has happened previously ○ *No doubt they will draw the necessary conclusion.* **3.** LOGIC **LOGICALLY TRUE** logically true because of being impossible to be false ■ *n.* (*informal*) **1.** (*plural* **-ies**) STH ESSENTIAL an essential item ○ *I've packed the necessaries.* **2.** STH NEEDED sth that is needed, especially a sum of money or a particular action ○ *Tell him to do the necessary.*

[14thC. Via Anglo-Norman from Latin *necessarius*, from *necesse*, literally 'unyielding', from *cess-*, the stem of *cedere* (see CEDE).]

─── **WORD KEY: SYNONYMS** ───

necessary, essential, vital, indispensable, requisite, needed

CORE MEANING: used to describe sth that is required

necessary used to describe sth that must be done or provided, or to indicate that sb's presence is required; **essential** used to emphasize that sth is necessary, for example because a process could not take place without it; **vital** a very emphatic word used to stress that sth is urgently necessary; **indispensable** literally suggesting sb who or sth that cannot be done without, but also often used simply to indicate that sth is desirable or useful; **requisite** a formal word used especially to suggest that sth has been made necessary by a particular circumstance; **needed** used to describe sth that is required or desired but implying less urgency than the other words in the group.

necessary condition *n.* sth that must happen or exist in order for sth else to happen or exist

necessary evil *n.* sth that is unpleasant or undesirable but is needed to achieve a desired result

necessitarian /ni séssi táiri ən/ *n.* sb who believes that there is no free will and that all events are determined by previous causes —**necessitarianism** *n.*

necessitate /nə séssi tayt/ (**-tates, -tating, -tated**) *v.* **1.** *vti.* MAKE STH NECESSARY to make sth necessary or inescapable ○ *a dry climate that necessitates water conservation* **2.** *vt.* OBLIGE SB to force or oblige sb to do sth (*formal*) —**necessitation** /nə séssi táysh'n/ *n.* —**necessitative** /nə séssitətiv/ *adj.*

necessitous /nə séssitəss/ *adj.* **1.** POOR in a state of poverty (*literary*) ○ '*grew necessitous, pawn'd his cloaths, and wanted bread*' (Benjamin Franklin, *The Autobiography of Benjamin Franklin*; 1788) **2.** NECESSARY pressingly necessary (*old*) —**necessitously** *adv.* —**necessitousness** *n.*

necessity /nə séssəti/ (*plural* **-ties**) *n.* **1.** STH ESSENTIAL sth that is essential, especially a basic requirement ○ *food, shelter, and the other necessities of life* **2.** COMPELLING CIRCUMSTANCES circumstances that create a need or an obligation ○ *The decision was taken out of necessity.* **3.** NEED the condition of being needed or required ○ *We'll hire new staff when the necessity arises.* **4.** PHILOS **NECESSARY QUALITY** the quality of being necessary or of not being able to be otherwise [14thC. Via French *nécessité* from Latin *necessitas*, from *necesse* (see NECESSARY).]

neck /nek/ *n.* **1.** ANAT **PART BETWEEN HEAD AND BODY** the part of the body that joins the head to the rest of the body **2.** CLOTHES **GARMENT PART ROUND NECK** the part of a garment that goes round or lies below the wearer's neck **3.** FOOD **CUT OF MEAT** a cut of meat from the neck of an animal, especially a sheep **4.** LONG OPENING a long narrow opening ○ *a bottle with a long neck* **5.** GEOG **STRIP OF LAND OR WATER** a long narrow strip of land or stretch of water **6.** MUSIC **LONG NARROW FINGERBOARD** the long narrow fingerboard that projects out of the body or sound box of a hand-held string instrument such as a guitar or violin **7.** HORSERACING **WINNING MARGIN** in horseracing, a narrow winning margin equal to the distance between a horse's nose and its shoulder **8.** STH IMPORTANT RISKED OR SAVED sb's life, job, reputation, or other important asset that has been placed at risk or saved from danger (*informal*) ○ *I'm not going to lie to save your neck again.* **9.** CHEEK impudence or cheek (*informal*) ○ *had the neck to ask another favour* **10.** GEOL **SOLIDIFIED LAVA** a plug of solidified lava or igneous rock filling the vent of an extinct or dormant volcano **11.** MARINE BIOL = **siphon** *n.* 3 **12.** ARCHIT **BAND AROUND PILLAR** a narrow band around the top of a pillar ■ *v.* (**necks, necking, necked**) **1.** *vi.* KISS AND CUDDLE to kiss and embrace sexually, usually sitting or lying with clothes on (*dated informal*) ○ *teenagers necking in the car* **2.** *vt.* COOK KILL POULTRY to kill a bird to be cooked by breaking its neck or chopping its head off (*informal*) [Old English *hnecca* 'nape'. Ultimately from an Indo-European word meaning 'high point, ridge', which also produced German *Nacken* 'nape'.] ◇ **be breathing down sb's neck 1.** to be close behind sb **2.** to be putting pressure on sb to do sth

more quickly ◇ **be in sth up to your neck** to be very much involved in sth, often sth dishonest or illegal ◇ **break your neck** to try very hard to achieve sth (*informal*) ◇ **get it in the neck** to be punished or scolded severely (*informal*) ◇ **neck and neck** level in a competition and with an equal chance of winning (*informal*) ◇ **neck of the woods** a particular area or part of the country (*informal*) ◇ **neck or nothing** risking everything, or prepared to risk everything (*informal*) ◇ **stick your neck out** to take a risk by saying or doing sth that could bring blame or censure (*informal*)

neckband /nék band/ *n.* the part of a garment that fits or wraps round the neck

neckcloth /nék kloth/, **neck-cloth** *n.* a cravat or scarf worn round the neck rather than round the collar by men between the 17th and mid-19th centuries

necked *adj.* with a particular kind of neck (*used in combination*) ○ *long-necked*

neckerchief /nékər chif, -cheef/ (*plural* **-chiefs** *or* **-chieves** /nékər cheevz/) *n.* a square of cloth worn tied round the neck as a scarf (*dated*) [14thC. From NECK + KERCHIEF.]

necking /néking/ *n.* **1.** KISSING AND CUDDLING kissing and embracing sexually while sitting or lying with clothes on (*dated informal*) **2.** ARCHIT **PART AT TOP OF PILLAR** a moulding at the top of a pillar, below the capital

necklace /nékləss/ *n.* a decorative chain or string of jewels worn around the neck [From *lace*, 'cord, string']

necklet /néklət/ *n.* a small plain necklace

neckline /nék līn/ *n.* the line formed by the edge of a garment at or under the neck, especially at the front

neckpiece /nék peess/ *n.* a garment like a scarf, especially one made of fur

neck ring *n.* a rigid necklace or ornamental band that fits snugly round the neck

necktie /nék tī/ *n.* US a tie

neckwear /nék wair/ *n.* garments or fashion accessories worn round the neck, e.g. ties, cravats, and scarves

necr- *prefix.* = **necro-** (used before vowels)

necro- *prefix.* death, the dead, dead body ○ *necrophobia* [From Greek *nekros* 'corpse'. Ultimately from an Indo-European base that is also the ancestor of English *pernicious*, *noxious*, *innocent*, and *nectar*.]

necrobiosis /nékrō bī óssiss/ *n.* the degeneration and death of the body's cells from natural processes. ◊ **necrosis** —**necrobiotic** /-bī óttik/ *adj.*

necrolatry /ne króllətri/ *n.* the worshipping of the dead —**necrolatrous** *adj.*

necrology /ne królləji/ (*plural* **-gies**) *n.* (*formal*) **1.** LIST OF THE DEAD a list of people who have died recently or during a particular period **2.** OBITUARY a notice of sb's death —**necrological** /nékrə lójjik'l/ *adj.* —**necrologist** /ne królləjist/ *n.*

necromancy /nékrō manssi/ *n.* **1.** PREDICTION USING SPIRITS the practice of attempting to communicate with the spirits of the dead in order to predict or influence the future **2.** WITCHCRAFT witchcraft or sorcery in general (*literary*) [13thC. Alteration of earlier *nigromancie*, via Old French, from medieval Latin *nigromantia* from late Latin *necromantia* (influenced by Latin *niger* 'black') from Greek *nekromanteia*, from *nekros* 'corpse' + *manteia* 'divination'.] —**necromancer** *n.* —**necromantic** /nékrō mántik/ *adj.* —**necromantically** *adv.*

necrophagous /nə króffəgəss/ *adj.* feeding on the flesh of dead animals (**carrion**)

necrophilia /nékrō filli ə/ *n.* sexual feelings for or sexual acts with dead bodies —**necrophiliac** *n.* —**necrophilic** *adj.*

necrophobia /nékrō fōbi ə/ *n.* an irrational fear of death or of dead bodies —**necrophobe** /nékrō fōb/ *n.* —**necrophobic** /nékrō fōbik/ *adj.*

necropolis /nə króppəlis/ (*plural* **-lises** *or* **-leis** /nə króppə layss/) *n.* a cemetery, especially a large, elaborate, or ancient one [Early 19thC. From Greek, from *nekros* (see NECRO-) + *polis* 'city'.]

necropsy /nékropsi/ (*plural* **-sies**) *n.* = **autopsy** [Mid-19thC. Coined from NECRO- + AUTOPSY.]

necrosis /ne krṓssiss/ (*plural* **-ses** /ne krṓ seez/) *n.* the death of cells in a tissue or organ caused by disease or injury. ◊ **necrobiosis** [Mid-17thC. From modern Latin, formed from Greek *nekrōsis* 'deadness', from, ultimately, *nekros* (see NECRO-).] —**necrotic** /ne króttik/ *adj.*

necrotizing /nékrō tīzing/, **necrotising** *adj.* causing or undergoing the death of cells (**necrosis**) ○ *necrotizing bacteria* [Late 19thC. Formed from *necrotize* 'to become affected with necrosis', from *necrotic* (formed from Greek *nekroun* 'to kill').]

necrotizing faciitis /nékrō tīzing fáshi ítiss/, **necrotising faciitis** *n.* a severe bacterial infection that causes cell tissue to decay rapidly. This is the 'flesh-eating bug' sometimes referred to in the media.

nectar /néktər/ *n.* 1. BOT **PLANT LIQUID** the sweet liquid that flowering plants produce as a way of attracting the insects and small birds that assist in pollination 2. MYTHOL **DRINK OF THE GODS** in Greek and Roman mythology, the drink of the gods that sustained their beauty and immortality 3. **ENJOYABLE DRINK** an enjoyable or much appreciated drink (*informal*) 4. *US* BEVERAGES **PULPY JUICE** a thick drink made from pureed fruit ○ *mango nectar* [Mid-16thC. Via Latin from Greek *nektar* 'drink of the gods'.] —**nectarous** *adj.*

nectarine /nékta reen/ *n.* 1. FOOD **SMOOTH-SKINNED PEACH** a variety of peach that has a smooth skin 2. TREES **PEACH TREE** the tree that nectarines grow on. Latin name: *Prunus persica*.

nectary /néktəri/ (*plural* **-ries**) *n.* the nectar-producing organ of a flowering plant —**nectarial** /nek táiri əl/ *adj.* —**nectaried** /néktərid/ *adj.*

neddy /néddi/ (*plural* **-dies**) *n.* 1. a child's name for a donkey (*babytalk informal*) 2. *Aus* **RACEHORSE** a horse, particularly a racehorse (*informal*) [Mid-16thC. Formed from *Ned*, a nickname for the male name *Edward*.]

née /nay/, **nee** *adj.* used to introduce a married woman's maiden name ○ *Jane Smith née Jones* [Mid-18thC. From French, the feminine form of the past participle of *naître* 'to be born', from Latin *nasci* (see NATURE).]

need /need/ *v.* (**needs, needing, needed**) 1. vti. **REQUIRE** used to indicate that sth is required in order to have success or achieve sth ○ *Do you need any money?* ○ *He told me that I didn't need to know.* 2. vi. **BE UNNECESSARY** used to indicate that a course of action is not desirable or not necessary (*used in negative statements*) ○ *You don't need to thank me; I'm happy to help whenever I can.* ○ *Studying medicine need not mean you can't study architecture later.* 3. vti. **DESERVE** to deserve a particular, usually punishing treatment (*informal*) ○ *That little boy needs to be given a good talking to.* ○ *Those troops need to be shown who's boss.* 4. vi. **TO BE ESSENTIAL** essential or necessary to sth (*archaic*) ○ *'I think that we are all agreed in this matter, and therefore there needs no more words about it'.* (John Bunyan, *Pilgrim's Progress*; 1678) ■ *n.* **REQUIREMENT** sth that is a requirement or is wanted ○ *an economic system that recognizes the need for financial security* ○ *His needs are small.* [Old English *nē(o)d.* Ultimately from an Indo-European word that is also the ancestor of German *Not* 'need, misery'.] ◊ **in need** 1. not having enough of things essential for an adequate standard of living ○ *children in need* 2. needing sth ◊ **no need to** *or* **for** no reason or justification for sth

— **WORD KEY: SYNONYMS** —
See Synonyms at *necessary*.

needful /néedf'l/ *adj.* 1. **REQUIRING** lacking or requiring (*formal*) ○ *a situation needful of common sense* 2. **REQUIRED** necessary or required (*formal or archaic*) ○ *'erection of forts, magazines, arsenals, dockyards, and other needful buildings'* (Constitution of the Confederate States; 1860–61) 3. **POOR** poverty-stricken (*archaic*) ■ *n.* **STH NEEDED** sth that is needed, especially the sum of money required or the action that needs to be taken (*informal*) ○ *Make sure you bring the needful.* —**needfully** *adv.* —**needfulness** *n.*

needle /néed'l/ *n.* 1. SEW **SEWING TOOL** a small sharp metal pin used for sewing, with a hole at the blunt end for holding thread 2. CRAFT **KNITTING TOOL** a pointed rod used in knitting 3. HOUSEHOLD **STYLUS** the stylus on a record player 4. MEASURE **POINTER** a pointed indicator on a dial, scale, or scientific instrument such as a compass or a car's speedometer 5. MED

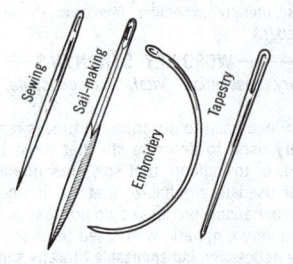

Needle

SYRINGE a hypodermic syringe, or its hollow pointed end 6. ALTERN MED **ACUPUNCTURE TOOL** a small sharp metal pin used in acupuncture to stimulate points on the body 7. BOT **CONIFER LEAF** a small pointed leaf of a conifer tree ○ *pine needles* 8. BIOL **POINTED PART** a long thin pointed part of an animal's body, e.g. a porcupine quill or a sea urchin spine 9. CRYSTALS **POINTED CRYSTAL** a long thin pointed crystal 10. ARCHIT **OBELISK** a tall stone pillar 11. CRAFT **ENGRAVING TOOL** a sharp tool used in engraving 12. BUILDING **SUPPORTING BEAM** a beam that passes through a wall as a temporary support 13. ENMITY a feeling of antagonism or hostility (*informal*) ■ *vt.* (**-dles, -dling, -dled**) 1. **PROVOKE** to tease or provoke sb, especially repeatedly in an indirect way (*informal*) 2. CRAFT **USE A NEEDLE ON STH** to sew, prick, or pierce sth with a needle [Old English *nǣdl.* Ultimately from an Indo-European base meaning 'to sew', which is also the ancestor of English *nerve* and *neural*.] —**needler** *n.*

needlecord /néed'l kawrd/ *n.* corduroy fabric with very fine ribs

needlecraft /néed'l kraaft/ *n.* sewing as a skill or craft

needle exchange *n.* a public health programme that allows drug addicts to exchange used hypodermic needles for new ones in an effort to stop the spread of disease and infection

needlefish /néed'l fish/ *n.* 1. **LONG MARINE FISH** a carnivorous marine fish found in tropical and subtropical waters that has a very long slender body and long jaws with sharp teeth. Family: Belonidae. 2. = pipefish

needle match *n.* a bitterly fought contest between two competitors or teams who bear each other a grudge (*informal*)

needlepoint /néed'l poynt/ *n.* (*often used before a noun*) 1. **EMBROIDERY ON CANVAS** embroidery done with thick coloured threads on canvas or plain cloth, usually in uniform diagonal stitches. US term **tapestry** 2. **LACE** a kind of lace made with a needle and a paper pattern

Needles, The /néed'lz/ group of three chalk rocks in southern England, off the western tip of the Isle of Wight. Height: 30 m/100 ft.

needless /néedləss/ *adj.* without reason or justification —**needlessly** *adv.* —**needlessness** *n.*

needle time *n.* the amount of time that a radio station spends playing music [From the use of a record player]

needle valve *n.* a valve in which the flow of a fluid or gas is precisely controlled by a needle-shaped insert in a conical seat

needlewoman /néed'l wŏŏmən/ (*plural* **-en** /-wimin/) *n.* = seamstress

needlework /néed'l wurk/ *n.* 1. **CRAFTS USING NEEDLES** a craft such as sewing, needlepoint, embroidery, quilting, crochet, or knitting, that involves the use of a needle 2. **PIECE OF SEWING OR EMBROIDERY** an example or piece of work done with a needle in a craft such as sewing, needlepoint, embroidery, quilting, crochet, or knitting —**needleworker** *n.*

needn't /néed'nt/ *contr.* need not [Mid-19thC. Contraction.]

needs /needz/ *adv.* (*archaic*) 1. **EMPHASIZING NECESSITY** used before or after 'must' to reinforce necessity, urgency, or inevitability ○ *'any abstract ideas that are once true must needs be eternal'* (John Locke, *An Essay Concerning Human Understanding*; 1690) 2.

EMPHASIZING DETERMINATION used after 'will' or 'would' to emphasize determination or resolve ○ *'these men, who will needs have all knowledge'* (John Locke, *An Essay Concerning Human Understanding*; 1690)

needy /néedi/ (**-ier, -iest**) *adj.* 1. **POOR** living in poverty (*dated*) ○ *gifts for needy children* 2. **NEEDING AFFECTION** feeling or showing a strong need for affection, love, or other emotional support —**needily** *adv.* —**neediness** *n.*

neem /neem/ *n.* a tall evergreen tree native to India, grown for its bark, resin, and seed oil. Latin name: *Azadirachta indica*. [Early 19thC. Via Hindi *nīm* from Sanskrit *nimba*.]

neep /neep/ *n. Scotland, N England* a turnip [Pre-12thC. From Latin *napus* (source of English *napiform*).]

ne'er /nair/ *adv.* never (*archaic or literary*) [13thC. Contraction.]

Ne'erday /náir day/ *n. Scotland* New Year's Day [Mid-19thC. Contraction of NEW YEAR'S DAY.]

ne'er-do-well *n.* **LAZY PERSON** a lazy and irresponsible person (*dated*) ■ *adj.* **LAZY** lazy and irresponsible (*dated*)

nefarious /ni fáiri əss/ *adj.* utterly immoral or wicked [Early 17thC. Formed from Latin *nefarius*, from *nefas* 'sin', from *ne* 'not' + *fas* 'divine law'.] —**nefariously** *adv.* —**nefariousness** *n.*

Nefertiti /néffər téeti/, **Queen of ancient Egypt** (*fl.* 14th century BC) As the chief wife of King Akhenaton, she supported his religious and cultural reforms. Her carved and painted image is a famous surviving Egyptian artwork.

neg. *abbr.* negative

negate /ni gáyt/ (**-gates, -gating, -gated**) *vt.* (*formal*) 1. **PROVE STH IS FALSE** to deny the truth of sth, or prove sth to be false ○ *a theory that negates all previous research* 2. **INVALIDATE STH** to officially declare sth to be invalid or render it invalid ○ *Failure to disclose such a change of circumstances would automatically negate the policy.* [Early 17thC. From the past participle stem of Latin *negare* 'to deny'.] —**negator** *n.*

— **WORD KEY: SYNONYMS** —
See Synonyms at *nullify*.

negation /ni gáysh'n/ *n.* 1. **DENIAL OR ANNULMENT** the denying, disproving, or nullifying of sth 2. LOGIC **LOGICAL DENIAL** a statement of denial or contradiction, especially an assertion that a particular proposition is false 3. **NEGATIVE OF STH** the opposite of sth regarded as positive, or the absence of such a thing ○ *The existence of happiness implies its negation.*

negative /néggətiv/ *adj.* 1. **MEANING 'NO'** meaning 'no', or refusing or denying sth ○ *a negative response* 2. **BAD** unhappy, discouraging, angry, or otherwise detracting from a happy situation ○ *You're having very negative feelings towards him.* 3. **PESSIMISTIC** pessimistic, or tending to have a pessimistic outlook ○ *Don't be so negative, cheer up!* 4. MED **SHOWING THAT STH IS NOT PRESENT** not showing the presence of a particular disease or condition that is being tested for ○ *The test came back negative.* 5. MED = Rh negative 6. MATH **LESS THAN ZERO** indicating a quantity that is less than zero ○ *a negative number* 7. MATH **OPPOSITE TO POSITIVE** used to describe sth, e.g. a quantity or angle, of the same magnitude as, but opposite to, sth considered positive 8. PHYS **HAVING SAME CHARGE AS ELECTRON** with the same electric charge as that of an electron, shown by the symbol − 9. PHYS **SHOWING DIRECTION OF CURRENT** indicating the direction toward which current flows in an external circuit 10. PHOTOGRAPHY **WITH TONES AND COLOURS REVERSED** used to describe photographic film that has been exposed to light, used as a basis for preparing final prints. Black and white tones are reversed and colours are complementary. 11. LOGIC **OPPOSING** denying or contradicting a statement, proof, or argument 12. BIOL **MOVING AWAY** moving or growing away from a source of stimulation, e.g. heat or light ○ *negative tropism* ■ *n.* 1. PHOTOGRAPHY **PHOTOGRAPHIC IMAGE** a photographic image, or the film containing it, that shows black and white tones reversed and colours as complementary. It is used to make prints. 2. **ANSWER OF 'NO'** an answer meaning 'no' ○ *The general answered in the negative.* 3. GRAM **WORD IMPLYING 'NO'** any word that expresses the idea 'no', e.g. the words 'not', 'nothing', and 'never' **4.** LOGIC **NEGATING PROPOSITION** a statement that contradicts, denies, or disproves sth **5.** ELEC **DESTINATION OF ELECTRONS** the part of an electric circuit to which the electrons flow, e.g. a terminal or the cathode where negative ions are formed in electrolytic applications **6.** STH OR SB **UNDESIRABLE** sth that or sb who is bad, undesirable, discouraging, or otherwise detracts from a pleasant situation (*informal*) ○ *The area's harsh winters will be a negative for anyone who doesn't like snow.* **7.** MATH **QUANTITY OPPOSITE TO POSITIVE** a number or quantity, e.g. speed, angle, or direction, that is less than zero or considered to be the opposite of positive ■ *interj.* NO used to say 'no' to sth or sb (*formal*) ■ *vt.* (**-tives, -tiving, -tived**) **1.** SAY 'NO' to refuse, reject, deny, cancel, or forbid sth (*formal*) ○ *'a polite request that Elizabeth would lead the way, which the other politely and more earnestly negatived'* (Jane Austen, *Pride And Prejudice*; 1813) **2.** LOGIC **DISPROVE PROPOSITION** to contradict or invalidate a proposition (*informal*) —**negativeness** *n.* —**negativity** /néggə tívvəti/ *n.*

negative equity *n.* a situation in which, as a result of falling prices, a piece of property is worth less than the amount of money that was borrowed to buy it

negative feedback *n.* in an electronic or mechanical system, the redirecting of part of the output back to the input as a way of improving the quality of the output

negatively /néggətivli/ *adv.* **1.** SAYING 'NO' in a way that means 'no' **2.** ADVERSELY in an adverse way ○ *patients reacting negatively to the medication* **3.** PESSIMISTICALLY in a pessimistic or defeatist way **4.** PHYS WITH NEGATIVE ELECTRICAL CHARGE with the same electric charge as that of one or more electrons, shown by the symbol –

negative reinforcement *n.* encouragement of a desired response by giving an unpleasant stimulus when the response is absent, or discouragement of an undesired response by an unpleasant stimulus when the response is present. An unpleasant stimulus is sth such as pain or disapproval.

negative staining *n.* staining of an area around a biological subject, rather than the subject itself, so that the subject can be clearly seen against it

negativism /néggətivizəm/ *n.* **1.** HABITUAL SCEPTICISM a strong tendency to be pessimistic, to assess situations in the worst light, or to be unreasonably sceptical about generally accepted beliefs **2.** PSYCHOL PERSISTENT UNREASONABLE DEFIANCE persistent defiance of authority and refusal to obey instructions —**negativist** *n.* —**negativistic** /néggəti vístik/ *adj.* —**negativistically** *adv.*

Negeri Sembilan /négri sem beelən/ state in southwestern Malaysia. Population: 691,150 (1991). Area: 6,500 sq. km/2,510 sq. mi.

Negev /néggev/, **Negeb** /néggeb/ triangular desert region in southern Israel. Area: 12,950 sq. km/5,000 sq. mi.

neglect /ni glékt/ *vt.* (**-glects, -glecting, -glected**) **1.** NOT CARE FOR STH PROPERLY to fail to give the proper or required care and attention to sb or sth **2.** FAIL TO DO STH to fail to do sth, especially because of carelessness or forgetfulness ○ *I neglected to tell you that I won't be here next week.* ■ *n.* **1.** WITHHOLDING OF PROPER CARE the failure to give proper care or attention to sb or sth ○ *parents charged with criminal neglect* **2.** LACK OF CARE lack of proper care or attention ○ *Soon the business began to suffer from neglect.* [Early 16thC. From the past participle stem of Latin *neglegere*, from *legere* 'to choose' (source of English *collect*, *legion*, and *lecture*).] —**neglecter** *n.*

——— WORD KEY: SYNONYMS ———
neglect, forget, omit, overlook
CORE MEANING: to fail to do sth

neglect to fail to act in a situation where it is obligatory or important to do so, especially as a result of carelessness or indifference; **forget** to fail to remember to do sth; **omit** to fail to do sth either deliberately or as a result of carelessness or haste; **overlook** to fail to notice or check sth as a result of inattention, preoccupation, or haste.

neglectful /ni gléktfʹl/ *adj.* tending to ignore or forget

responsibilities —**neglectfully** *adv.* —**neglectfulness** *n.*

negligée /néggli zhay/, **negligé** /négli zhay/ *n.* **1.** LONG SILKY NIGHTDRESS a woman's long nightdress made of thin silky often see-through fabric **2.** CASUAL DRESS informal dress (*dated formal*) [Mid-18thC. From French *négligé*, the past participle of *négliger* 'to neglect', from Latin *neglegere* (see NEGLECT). The underlying idea is of having failed to get fully dressed.]

negligence /négglijənss/ *n.* **1.** CONDITION OF BEING NEGLIGENT the condition or quality of being negligent **2.** LAW CIVIL WRONG CAUSING INJURY OR HARM a civil wrong (**tort**) causing injury or harm to another person or to property as the result of doing sth or failing to provide a proper or reasonable level of care. ◊ **contributory negligence 3.** CASUALNESS casualness in matters of dress or general appearance, whether regarded as stylish or slovenly (*dated formal*) ○ *'clad in an artist's velvet, but with none of an artist's negligence'* (G. K. Chesterton, *The Wisdom of Father Brown*; 1914)

negligent /négglijənt/ *adj.* **1.** HABITUALLY CARELESS habitually careless or irresponsible **2.** LAW GUILTY OF NEGLIGENCE guilty of failing to provide a proper or reasonable level of care **3.** CASUAL IN APPEARANCE casual in matters of dress or general appearance, whether considered stylish or slovenly (*dated formal*) [14thC. Via French from Latin *negligent-*, the present participle stem of *negligere*, a variant of *neglegere* (see NEGLECT).] —**negligently** *adv.*

negligible /négglijəbʹl/ *adj.* too small or unimportant to be worth considering [Early 19thC. From obsolete French *négligible*, from *négliger* 'to neglect', from Latin *neglegere* (see NEGLECT).] —**negligibility** /négglijə bílləti/ *n.* —**negligibleness** /négglijəbʹlnəss/ *n.* —**negligibly** *adv.*

negotiable /ni gṓshəbʹl, -gṓshi əbʹl/ *adj.* **1.** OPEN TO DISCUSSION not fixed but able to be established or changed through discussion and compromise ○ *Salary is negotiable, according to age and experience.* **2.** FIN EXCHANGEABLE FOR MONEY used to describe financial instruments, e.g. cheques and securities, that can be transferred to another person in exchange for money **3.** NAVIGABLE able to be crossed, passed, or successfully dealt with —**negotiability** /ni gṓshə bílləti, -gṓshi ə-/ *n.* —**negotiably** /ni gṓshəbli, -gṓshi əbli/ *adv.*

negotiant /ni gṓshi ənt/ *n.* = negotiator (*formal*)

negotiate /ni gṓshi ayt/ (**-ates, -ating, -ated**) *v.* **1.** *vti.* DISCUSS TERMS OF AGREEMENT to attempt to come to an agreement on sth through discussion and compromise **2.** *vt.* FIN SELL STH to transfer ownership of a financial instrument, e.g. a cheque or security, to sb else in exchange for money **3.** *vt.* NAVIGATE STH SUCCESSFULLY to manage to get past or deal with sth that constitutes a hazard or obstacle ○ *A canoe can negotiate these waters when the wind is calm.* [Late 16thC. From the past participle stem of Latin *negotiari* 'to do business', from *negotium* 'business', from *neg-* 'not' + *otium* 'leisure' (source of English *otiose*).]

negotiation /ni gṓshi áysh'n/ *n.* **1.** RESOLVING OF DISAGREEMENTS the reaching of agreement through discussion and compromise **2.** NAVIGATION the tackling of a hazard or problem (*formal*) ■ **negotiations** *npl.* DISCUSSION SESSIONS one or more meetings at which attempts are made to reach agreement through discussion and compromise ○ *Negotiations are already under way between the opposing factions.*

negotiator /ni gṓshi aytər/ *n.* sb who negotiates, especially in a political or diplomatic context

Negress /néegress, -grəss/ *n.* a highly offensive term for a Black woman

Negrillo /ni gríllō/ (*plural* **-los** *or* **-loes**) *n.* a member of any of a number of peoples of central and southern Africa [Mid-19thC. From Spanish, literally 'a small Negro', from *negro* (see NEGRO).]

Negrito /ni greétō/ (*plural* **-tos** *or* **-toes**) *n.* a member of any of a number of Asian peoples, including the Eta of the Philippines, the Semang of the Malay Peninsula, and the people of the Andaman Islands of India [Early 19thC. From Spanish, literally 'a small Negro', from *negro* (see NEGRO).]

negritude /néggri tyood/ *n.* identity as a Black person, especially awareness of a distinct Black history and culture as sth to be proud of (*dated*)

Negro /née grō/ (*plural* **-groes**) *n.* a highly offensive term for a Black person (*offensive*) [Mid-16thC. Via Spanish and Portuguese from the Latin stem *nigr-* 'black' (source of English *denigrate* and *niello*).]

Negro, Río /néggrō/ **1.** river in northwestern South America that rises in Colombia, flows along the Colombia-Venezuela border, and empties into the Amazon at Manaus, Brazil. Length: 2,253 km/1,400 mi. **2.** river in central Argentina that empties into the Atlantic Ocean near Viedma. Length: 644 km/400 mi.

Negroid /née groyd/ *adj.* an offensive term referring to a division of humankind that originated in Africa (*offensive*)

negrophile /née grō fīl/ *n.* an offensive term for a person who favours the interests of Black people (*offensive*) —**negrophilia** /néegrō fílli ə/ *n.* —**negrophilism** /-ffilizəm/ *n.*

negrophobe /née grō fōb/ *n.* sb prejudiced against Black people or with an irrational fear of Black people (*dated*) —**negrophobia** *n.*

Negro spiritual *n.* = spiritual

negus /néegəss/ *n.* a hot drink made of port or sherry with water, sugar, lemon juice, and spices [Mid-18thC. Named after the English colonel Francis *Negus* (died 1732), who reputedly invented the drink.]

Negus /née gəss/ *n.* a title used in the past for the king or emperor of Ethiopia [Late 16thC. From Amharic *n'gus* 'kinged, king'.]

Neh. *abbr.* BIBLE Nehemiah

Nehemiah[1] /née i mí ə/ *n.* in the Bible, a Jewish leader and governor of Judea. He was responsible for rebuilding Jerusalem in 444 BC.

Nehemiah[2] *n.* a book of the Bible, recounting the rebuilding of Jerusalem in the 5th century BC and the reforms undertaken after its completion. It is traditionally attributed to Nehemiah. See table at **Bible**

Nehru /náir oo/, **Jawaharlal** (1889–1964). The first prime minister of independent India (1947–64). He abandoned his legal career to follow Gandhi in 1929 and was elected president of the Indian National Congress. He was the father of Indira Gandhi.

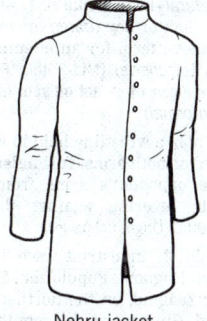
Nehru jacket

Nehru jacket *n.* a long narrow jacket with a high stand-up collar [Mid-20thC. Named after Jawaharlal NEHRU, who often wore jackets of this style.]

neigh /nay/ *n.* HORSE SOUND the long high-pitched sound that a horse makes ■ *vi.* (**neighs, neighing, neighed**) MAKE SOUND OF HORSE to make the high-pitched sound characteristic of a horse [Old English *hnægan*, of uncertain origin: probably an imitation of the sound]

neighbor *n.*, *vt.* US = neighbour

neighborhood *n.* US = neighbourhood

neighboring *adj.* US = neighbouring

neighborly *adj.* US = neighbourly

neighbour /náybər/ *n.* **1.** SB LIVING NEARBY sb who lives or is located very close by, e.g. on the same street or in the same village **2.** STH OR SB NEARBY a person, place, or thing located next to another or very nearby (*often used before a noun*) ○ *the Spanish and their Portuguese neighbours* **3.** FELLOW HUMAN a fellow human being (*archaic or literary*) ■ *vti.* (**-bours, -bouring, -boured**) BE CLOSE TO STH OR SB to be very close to sth or sb [Old English *nēahgebūr*, from *nēah* 'near' (source of English *nigh*) + *gebūr* 'dweller']

neighbourhood /náybər hŏŏd/ *n.* **1.** COMMUNITY a local community with characteristics that distinguish it from the areas around it **2.** APPROXIMATION OF AMOUNT an approximate amount, size, or range (*informal*) ○ *expenses in the neighbourhood of £175,000* **3.** MATH SURROUNDING POINTS the set of all points within a given distance from a specified point

neighbourhood watch *n.* a nationwide scheme to raise awareness of crime and crime prevention within local communities, with members taking part in various initiatives, including keeping watch on one another's homes

neighbouring /náybəring/ *adj.* situated or located nearby

neighbourly /náybərli/ *adj.* friendly, helpful, and kind, especially to a neighbour —**neighbourliness** *n.*

Neill /neel/, **Sam** (*b.* 1948) New Zealand actor. His films include *Jurassic Park* (1993) and *The Piano* (1993). Real name **Nigel Neill**

neither /nī́thər/ CORE MEANING: a grammatical word used to indicate that each of two things or people is included when making a negative statement ○ (*det*) *Neither shirt looks good on you.* ○ (*pron*) *Neither of the boys wants to go.* ○ (*pron*) 'Would you like pork or fish?' 'Neither, thank you'.
1. *conj.* NOT used preceding two alternatives joined by 'nor' to indicate that both did not happen or are not true ○ *Neither my boss nor his wife can cook.* ◊ **nor, either 2.** *adv.* ALSO NOT used to indicate people or things that can also be included in a statement just made (*used in response to no, not, or another negative*) ○ *'We've never been to Paris'. 'Neither have I'.* ○ *She doesn't want to go? Me neither!* ○ *She can't play today, and neither can her brother.* ◊ **either, nor** [12thC. Alteration (influenced by EITHER) of Old English *nawþer*, a contraction of *nāhwæþer*, from *nā* 'not' + *hwæþer* 'which of two' (source of *whether*).] ◇ **neither here nor there** not relevant and therefore not important

nekton /nék ton/ *n.* a creature that lives in water and can actively swim against currents, e.g. a fish, reptile, mammal, or seabird, as opposed to microorganisms that are simply carried along [Late 19thC. From Greek *nēkton*, a form of *nēktos* 'swimming', from *nēkhein* 'to swim'.] —**nektonic** /nek tónnik/ *adj.*

nelly /nélli/ (*plural* **-lies**), **nellie** *n.* **1.** WEAK MAN a weak or cowardly man or boy (*dated informal*) **2.** OFFENSIVE TERM an offensive term for an effeminate or homosexual man (*offensive*) [Mid-20thC. Formed from the name *Helen* or *Eleanor*.] ◇ **not on your nelly** absolutely not (*dated informal*)

nelson /nélss'n/ *n.* a wrestling hold in which one arm (**half nelson**) or both arms (**full nelson**) are passed through the opponent's arms from behind and pulled back, levering against the opponent's back [Late 19thC. Origin unknown.]

Nelson /nélss'n/ **1.** industrial town in Lancashire, northwestern England. Population: 29,120 (1991). **2.** city in New Zealand, on the northern coast of the South Island. Situated at the mouth of the River Matai, it is an agricultural and tourist centre. Population: 50,692 (1996). **3.** region of New Zealand, located in the north of the South Island. It is the site of Kahurangi, Nelson Lakes, and Abel Tasman national parks. Population: 42,073 (1996). Area: 1,114 sq. km/430 sq. mi.

Nelson, Horatio, Viscount (1758–1805) English admiral. He defeated the French at Trafalgar (1805), but was killed during the battle. His affair with Lady Hamilton caused a considerable scandal.

nemat- *prefix.* = **nemato-** (*used before vowels*)

nematic /ni máttik/ *adj.* used to describe a phase of liquid crystals in which the axes of the molecules become parallel in response to a magnetic field [Early 20thC. Formed from the Greek stem *nēmat-* (see NEMATO-).]

nemato- *prefix.* **1.** thread, threadlike ○ *nematocyst* **2.** nematode ○ *nematocide* [From Greek *nēmat-*, the stem of *nēma* 'thread'. Ultimately from an Indo-European base meaning 'to spin', which is also the ancestor of English *needle*.]

nematocide /ne mátto sīd/, **nematicide** *n.* a substance that destroys nematodes —**nematocidal** /ne mátto sīd'l/ *adj.*

nematocyst /némmə tō sist/ *n.* a sting found in animals of the jellyfish family. It comprises a fluid-filled sac within which is a coiled hollow thread that is rapidly turned outwards (**everted**) to capture food or for defence.

nematode /némmə tōd/ *n.* a worm, often microscopic, with a cylindrical unsegmented body protected by a tough outer skin (**cuticle**). Some nematodes are parasites of plants and animals, e.g. pinworms and hookworms. Phylum: Nematoda. [Mid-19thC. From modern Latin, coined from NEMATO- + modern Latin -*ōda* (an alteration of Greek -*oeidēs* (see -OID).]

nematology /némmə tólləji/ *n.* the branch of zoology that is concerned with the study of nematodes —**nematological** /-lójjik'l/ *adj.* —**nematologically** *adv.* —**nematologist** /némmə tólləjist/ *n.*

Nembutal /némbyŏŏ tal/ *tdmk.* a trademark for the sodium salt of pentobarbitone, a barbiturate used as a sedative and an anticonvulsant

nem. con. /ném kón/ *adv.* without opposition ○ *The motion was carried nem. con.* [From Latin, shortening of *nemine contradicente* 'with no one contradicting']

Nemean lion /ni mee an-/ *n.* in Greek mythology, the huge lion that Hercules killed as the first of his twelve labours [Late 16thC. Named after *Nemea*, a district in ancient Greece, where it was killed.]

nemertean /ni múrti ən/ *n.* a burrowing marine worm with a long flat unsegmented body. Phylum: Nemertia. [Mid-19thC. Formed from modern Latin *Nemertes*, genus name, from Greek *Nēmertēs* 'Nereid'.]

nemesis /némməssiss/ (*plural* **nemeses** /-seez/) *n.* (*literary*) **1.** AVENGER a person or force that inflicts punishment or revenge **2.** DESERVED PUNISHMENT punishment that is deserved, especially when it results in sb's downfall [Late 16thC. From Greek, 'Nemesis, righteous indignation', from *nemein* 'to distribute what is due'.]

Nemesis /némməssis/ *n.* the ancient Greek goddess of just punishment or vengeance

nene /náy nay/ *n.* a rare wild goose with a greyish-brown body and a black face that is found in the Hawaiian Islands. Latin name: *Branta sandvicensis*. [Early 20thC. From Hawaiian.]

neo- *prefix.* new, recent ○ *neotype* ○ *neo-Darwinism* [From Greek *neos*. Ultimately from the Indo-European word for 'new', which is also the ancestor of English *new* and *novel*.]

Neoclassical: Front porch of Monticello, Charlottesville, Virginia (begun 1770)

neoclassical /nee ō klássik'l/, **neoclassic** /-klássik/ *n.* ARTS OF REVIVAL OF CLASSICISM IN ART an 18th- and 19th-century revival in art and architecture of the simple symmetrical styles of ancient Greece and Rome, or created in this style ■ *adj.* **1.** LITERAT OF CLASSICAL REVIVAL relating to or typical of the European revival of Greek and Roman literary form **2.** MUSIC OF PRE-ROMANTIC STYLE relating to a movement in the late 19th and early 20th centuries that favoured the more formal style of composers before the Romantic movement **3.** ECON OF MACROECONOMIC MONETARIST THEORY related to macroeconomic monetarist theories that emphasize the need for the free operation of market forces —**neoclassicism** /nee ō klássisizəm/ *n.* —**neoclassicist** *n.*

neocolonialism /nee ō kə lṓni əlizəm/ *n.* the domination by a powerful, usually Western nation of another nation that is politically independent but has a weak economy greatly dependent on trade with the powerful nation —**neocolonial** *adj.* —**neocolonialist** *n.*

neoconservative /nee ō kən súrvətiv/ *n.* SUPPORTER OF RETURN TO CONSERVATIVE VALUES sb who, during the mid-1980s, began to support conservatism in society, and in politics in particular, as a reaction to the social freedoms sought throughout the 1960s and early 1970s ■ *adj.* RELATING TO SHIFT TOWARDS CONSERVATISM relating to or forming part of the shift during the mid-1980s towards social and political conservatism that occurred after the freedom movement of the 1960s and early 1970s —**neoconservatism** *n.*

neocortex /nee ō káwr teks/ (*plural* **-tices** /-káwrt seez/ *or* **-texes**) *n.* the roof of the cerebral cortex that forms the part of the mammalian brain that has evolved most recently and makes possible higher brain functions such as learning —**neocortical** /-káwrtik'l/ *adj.*

Neo-Darwinism *n.* a theory of evolution that combines Darwin's theory and modern genetics, especially with regard to variations in populations as a result of genetic mutations —**neo-Darwinian** *adj.* —**neo-Darwinist** *n.*, *adj.*

neodymium /nee ō dímmi əm/ *n.* a silvery-white or yellowish metallic chemical element used in lasers and glass that is one of the lanthanide series or rare-earth elements. Symbol **Nd** [Late 19thC. Coined from NEO- + DIDYMIUM, because didymium was found to consist of two elements (neodymium and praseodymium).]

neo-expressionism *n.* a 20th-century art movement, begun in Germany, Italy, and the United States, and based on expressionism, that focuses on the artist's inner experiences and often produces violent or erotic paintings —**neo-Expressionist** *n.*, *adj.*

neofascism /nee ō fáshizəm/ *n.* **1.** MODERN SUPPORT FOR FASCISM the modern-day revival of Fascist beliefs of the 1930s and 1940s, which assume that a supposed Aryan race is superior to all others and justify genocide **2.** RACIST BELIEFS the views or actions of any modern-day Caucasian group or movement that holds racist views, especially anyone involved in the violent intimidation of people of colour —**neofascist** *adj.*, *n.*

neo-Freudianism *n.* a theory of psychoanalysis that modifies Freudian theory by emphasizing social and cultural influences on personality development —**neo-Freudian** *adj.*, *n.*

neogenesis /nee ō jénnəssiss/ *n.* the regrowth of living tissue —**neogenetic** /nee ō jə néttik/ *adj.* —**neogenetically** *adv.*

neo-Gothic *adj.* BASED ON THE GOTHIC REVIVAL based on a reintroduction of the Gothic style of architecture, popular in the 18th and 19th centuries ■ *n.* GOTHIC REVIVAL the Gothic Revival style

neoimpressionism /nee ō im présh'nizəm/ *n.* the 19th-century movement in painting, led by the pointillist Georges Seurat, that favoured stricter and more formal techniques of composition —**neoimpressionist** *adj.*, *n.*

Neo-Latin *n.*, *adj.* = New Latin ■ *adj.* OF ROMANCE LANGUAGES relating to a language that has developed from Latin

neoliberalism /nee ō líbbərəlizəm/ *n.* the political view, arising in the 1960s, that emphasizes the importance of economic growth and asserts that social justice is best maintained by minimal government interference and free market forces —**neoliberal** *adj.*, *n.*

neolith /nee ō lith/ *n.* a stone tool from the Neolithic period

Neolithic /nee ō líthik/ *n.* NEW STONE AGE the latest period of the Stone Age, between about 8000 BC and 5000 BC, characterized by the development of settled agriculture and the use of polished stone tools and weapons ■ *adj.* RELATING TO NEOLITHIC relating to or characteristic of the Neolithic [Mid-19thC. Coined from NEO- + -LITH + -IC by Sir John Lubbock in his work *Prehistoric Times*.] —**Neolithic** *adj.*

neologism /ni óllǝjizǝm/, **neology** /ni óllǝji/ (*plural* **-gies**) *n*. **1. NEW WORD OR MEANING** a recently coined word or phrase, or a recently extended meaning of an existing word or phrase **2. COINAGE OF NEW WORDS** the practice or process of coining new words or phrases, or of extending the meaning of existing words or phrases [Early 19thC. From French *néologisme*, from *néo-*.] —**neologist** *n*. —**neologistic** /-/ *adj*. —**neologistically** *adv*.

neologize /ni óllǝ jīz/ (**-gizes, -gizing, -gized**), **neologise** (**-gises, -gised**) *vi*. to coin new words or phrases, or extend the meaning of existing words or phrases

neology *n*. = **neologism**

neo-Melanesian *n*. a creole language based on English with borrowings from other languages that is widely used in the island groups of the south-western Pacific

neomycin /nee ō míssin/ *n*. an antibiotic used to treat a wide variety of bacterial infections, especially skin and eye infections, and obtained from the bacterium *Streptomyces fradiae*

neon /née on, -ǝn/ (*plural* **-ons** *or* **-on**) *n*. **1. CHEM ELEM GAS THAT GLOWS ORANGE** a colourless odourless gaseous chemical element that occurs in very small quantities in the air and glows orange when electricity is passed through it. Symbol **Ne 2. ZOOL** = **neon tetra** [Late 19thC. From Greek, a form of *neos* 'new'. Coined by the British chemists Sir William Ramsay and Morris Travers, who discovered the gas.]

neonate /née ō nayt/ *n*. a newborn child, especially one less than one month old [Early 20thC. Coined from NEO- + Latin *natus* 'born' (see NATAL).] —**neonatal** /née ō nàytl/ *adj*.

neonatology /née ō nay tóllǝji/ *n*. the branch of medicine that deals with the care and development of newborn babies and the treatment of their diseases —**neonatological** /née ō náytǝ tóllǝji/ *adj*. —**neonatologist** /-nay tóllǝjist/ *n*.

neophilia /née ō fílli ǝ/ *n*. a liking for new things, change for the sake of change, or novelty —**neophile** /née ō fīl/ *n*. —**neophiliac** /-fílli ak/ *n*., *adj*.

neophyte /née ō fīt/ *n*. **1. BEGINNER** a beginner or novice at some task, work, or endeavour **2. RECENT CONVERT** sb who has recently converted to a particular religion **3. RELIGIOUS NOVICE** sb who has recently joined a religious community but has not yet taken vows and is therefore not yet part of the order [14thC. Via late Latin *neophytus* from Greek *neophutos*, literally 'newly planted', from, ultimately, *phuein* 'to plant, cause to grow'.] —**neophytic** /née ō fíttik/ *adj*.

neoplasia /née ō pláyzi ǝ/ *n*. the formation or existence of tumours

neo-Nazi *n*. **1. MODERN-DAY ADVOCATE OF NAZISM** a member of a modern-day movement that promotes the idea that a supposed race of Aryans is superior to all others, and that genocide is justifiable **2. CAUCASIAN RACIST** a member of any modern-day group or movement of Caucasians who hold racist views, especially those involved in violent attacks on people of colour —**neo-Nazism** *n*.

neon tetra *n*. a small iridescent blue and red freshwater fish found in the River Amazon and often kept in aquariums. Latin name: *Hyphessobrycon innesi*. [From its bright colours like that of neon glowing]

neoorthodoxy /née ō ówrtha dóksi/ *n*. an early 20th-century Protestant movement connected with the theology of Karl Barth that emphasizes ethics and the teachings of the Bible —**neoorthodox** *adj*.

neoplasm /née ō plazm/ *n*. a tumour or tissue containing an abnormal growth [Late 19thC. Coined from NEO- + Greek *plasma* 'formation', from *plassein* 'to form, mould'.]

neoplasticism /née ō plástissizǝm/ *n*. a style of abstract painting, as found in the work of Mondrian, using black, grey, white, and the primary colours and horizontal and vertical lines and planes —**neoplastic** /née ō plástik/ *adj*.

neoplasty /née ō plasti/ *n*. the surgical construction of new tissue, or the repair of damaged tissue —**neoplastic** /née ō plástik/ *adj*.

neoprene /née ō preen/ *n*. a synthetic material resembling rubber that does not perish as quickly as rubber and is more resistant to oil, used in the manufacture of equipment for which waterproofing is important [Mid-20thC. Coined from NEO- + PRENE.]

neorealism /née ō rée alizǝm/ *n*. a style of cinema developed in Italy in the 1940s by directors such as Rossellini, De Sica, and Visconti, dealing typically with the problems of ordinary working-class life —**neorealist** *n*., *adj*. —**neorealistic** /née ō rée a listik/ *adj*.

neo-Scholasticism *n*. a late 19th-century Roman Catholic movement that used the writings of the early Scholasticists such as Albert the Great and Anselm as the basis for its teachings —**neo-Scholastic** *adj*.

neostigmine /née ō stíg meen/ *n*. a white crystalline compound used in the treatment of myasthenia [Mid-20thC. Coined from NEO- + PHYSOSTIGMINE.]

neoteny /ni óttani/ *n*. the existence of juvenile features in an adult animal, e.g. the retention of gills in certain salamanders [Late 19thC. Coined from NEO- + Greek *teinein* 'to stretch, extend'.]

neoteric /née ō térrik/ *adj*. having a contemporary origin [Late 16thC. Via Latin from Greek *neōterikos* 'youthful'.]

neotype /née ō tīp/ *n*. a specimen of a plant or animal selected to replace an original representative example used in classification (**holotype**) that has been lost or destroyed —**neotypical** (**holotype**) *adj*.

neo-Platonism /née ō pláytǝnizǝm/, **Neoplatonism** *n*. a philosophical system combining Platonism with mysticism and Judaic and Christian ideas and positing one source for all existence, developed by Plotinus and his followers in the 3rd century AD —**neo-Platonic** *adj*. —**neo-Platonist** *n*.

neper *n*. a unit for comparing two currents, voltages, or related quantities, equal to the natural logarithm of the ratio of the quantities. Symbol **Np**

nepenthe /ni pénthi/ *n*. **1. ANCIENT DRUG INDUCING FORGETFULNESS** a supposed substance that people took in ancient times to forget their sadness or troubles, or the plant that produced the substance **2. DISTRACTION** sth that eases pain or makes people forget their troubles (*literary*) ○ *'respite and nepenthe from thy memories of Lenore'* (Edgar Allan Poe, *The Raven*; 1845) [Late 16thC. Alteration (modelled on Italian *nepente*) of Greek *nepenthes*, literally 'banishing pain', from *nē* 'not' + *penthos* 'grief'.] —**nepenthean** *adj*.

nepheline /néffǝlin, -leen/, **nephelite** /-līt/ *n*. a white aluminosilicate of potassium and sodium found in igneous rock and used in the manufacture of glass and ceramics [Early 19thC. Via French from Greek *nephelē* 'cloud'. The underlying idea is that the crystals become cloudy when immersed in nitric acid.]

nephelinite /néffali nīt/ *n*. a fine-grained igneous rock that has nepheline and pyroxene as its main mineral ingredients

nephelometer /néffa lómmitar/ *n*. **1. CHEM INSTRUMENT MEASURING PARTICLE SIZE OR DENSITY** an instrument that uses reflected light to measure the size or density of solid particles present in a liquid **2. METEOROL DEVICE MEASURING CLOUDINESS OF SKY** an instrument used to measure the degree of cloudiness in the sky [Late 19thC. Coined from Greek *nephelē* 'cloud' + -METER.] —**nephelometric** /néffalō méttrik/ *adj*. —**nephelometry** /néffa lómmatri/ *n*.

nephew /néffyoo, névvyoo/ *n*. the son of sb's brother, sister, brother-in-law, or sister-in-law [13thC. Via French *neveu* from the Latin stem *nepot-* 'sister's son, grandson, descendant' (source of English *nepotism*).]

nephogram /néffō gram/ *n*. a photograph of a cloud [Late 19thC. Coined from Greek *nephos* 'cloud' + -GRAM.]

nephograph /néffō graaf, -graf/ *n*. a device for taking photographs of clouds [Late 19thC. Coined from Greek *nephos* 'cloud' + -GRAPH.]

nephology /ne fóllǝji/ *n*. the branch of meteorology concerned with the study of clouds [Late 19thC. Coined from Greek *nephos* 'cloud' + -LOGY.] —**nephological** /néffō lójik'l/ *adj*. —**nephologist** /ne fóllǝjist/ *n*.

nephoscope /néffǝ skōp/ *n*. an instrument for measuring the altitude, speed, and direction of movement of clouds [Late 19thC. Coined from Greek *nephos* 'cloud' + -SCOPE.]

nephr- *prefix*. = **nephro-** (*used before vowels*)

nephralgia /ni frálja/ *n*. pain in the kidneys

nephrectomy /ni fréktami/ (*plural* **-mies**) *n*. the surgical removal of a kidney

nephric /néfrik/ *adj*. relating to or affecting the kidneys

nephridium /ni friddi em/ (*plural* **-a** /-ǝ/) *n*. **1. EXCRETORY ORGAN** a simple tube-shaped organ in earthworms and many other invertebrate organisms for releasing waste matter into the gut or out of the body **2. EMBRYONIC KIDNEY** the organ that develops into the kidney in a vertebrate animal's embryo [Late 19thC. Coined from NEPHRO- 'small kidney' + modern Latin *-idium* 'small one' (from Greek *-idion*).] —**nephridial** *adj*.

nephrite /néf rīt/ *n*. a variety of jade that ranges in colour from white to dark green and is made up primarily of iron, calcium, and magnesium in monoclinic crystalline form

nephritic /ni frittik/ *adj*. **1. RELATING TO NEPHRITIS** relating to or affected by nephritis **2. OF THE KIDNEYS** relating to or affecting the kidneys

nephritis /ni frítiss/ *n*. severe inflammation of the kidney, caused by infection, degenerative disease, or disease of the blood vessels

nephro- *prefix*. kidney ○ *nephrotoxic* [From Greek *nephros*]

nephrogenous /ni frójanass/, **nephrogenic** /néffrō jénnik/ *adj*. **1. FOUND IN KIDNEY** located in or moving into a kidney **2. DEVELOPING INTO KIDNEY TISSUE** capable of developing into kidney tissue

nephrology /ni fróllǝji/ *n*. the branch of medicine concerned with the study and treatment of diseases of the kidneys —**nephrological** /néffrō lójik'l/ *adj*. —**nephrologist** /ni fróllǝjist/ *n*.

nephron /néf ron/ *n*. any of the numerous fine tubules

Nepal /nǝ páwl/ monarchy in southern Asia, north-east of India, in a mountainous region. Language: Nepali. Currency: rupee. Capital: Katmandu. Population: 22,090,000 (1996). Area: 140,797 sq. km/54,362 sq. mi. Official name **Kingdom of Nepal**

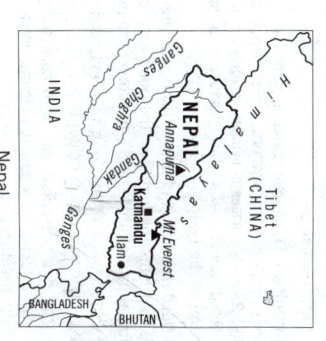

Nepal

Nepalese /néppa leez/ (*plural* **-ese**) *n*. **1. LANG DIALECT OF NEPAL** any of the several dialects, sometimes considered as separate languages, of Nepali spoken throughout Nepal and in some parts of adjacent countries **2. PEOPLES** = **Nepali** (n. 2) —**Nepalese** *adj*.

Nepali /ni páwli/ (*plural* **-i** *or* **-is**) *n*. **1. LANG LANGUAGE OF NEPAL** the official language of Nepal, also spoken in parts of Bhutan and northeastern India. It belongs to the Indic group of the Indo-Iranian branch of Indo-European languages. Nepali is spoken by about 16 million people. **2. PEOPLES sb FROM NEPAL** sb who was born, brought up, or lives in Nepal —**Nepali** *adj*.

in the kidneys of vertebrates that filter and excrete waste materials from the blood and produce urine

nephropathy /ni fróppathi/ (*plural* **-thies**) *n.* a disease or medical disorder of the kidney —**nephropathic** /néffrō páthik/ *adj.*

nephroscope /néffrō skōp/ *n.* a tube-shaped instrument inserted into an incision in the body wall in order to examine a patient's kidneys

nephrosis /ni fróssiss/ *n.* a disease that causes the kidneys to degenerate without inflaming them, especially one that affects the nephrons —**nephrotic** /ni fróttik/ *adj.*

nephrostome /néffrō stōm/ *n.* the funnel-shaped inner opening of a nephridium that is lined with cilia and allows water and waste to enter from the body cavity [Late 19thC. From NEPHRO- + Greek *stoma* 'mouth'.]

nephrotomy /ni fróttami/ (*plural* **-mies**) *n.* a surgical incision into a kidney

ne plus ultra /náy plóoss ōól traa, neē pluss úl tra/ *n.* the highest level of excellence, or sth that reaches it (*formal*) [Late 17thC. From Latin, literally 'not farther beyond', supposed to have been inscribed on the Pillars of Hercules (the Strait of Gibraltar) as a warning to ships.]

nepotism /néppatizam/ *n.* favouritism shown by sb in power to relatives and friends, especially in appointing them to good positions [Mid-17thC. Via French *nepotisme* from, ultimately, the Latin stem *nepot-* 'grandson, descendant, sister's son' (source of English *nephew*).] —**nepotist** *n.* —**nepotistic** /néppe tistik/ *adj.* —**nepotistically** *adv.*

Neptune /néptyoon/ *n.* **1.** ASTRON EIGHTH PLANET the eighth planet from the Sun in our solar system **2.** MYTHOL ROMAN GOD OF SEA in Roman mythology, the god of the sea, son of Saturn, brother of Jupiter and Pluto. Greek equivalent **Poseidon** [15thC. Directly or via French from Latin *Neptunus*.]

neptunium /nep tyōoni am/ *n.* a silvery radioactive metallic chemical element found in small amounts in uranium ores. It is artificially produced in nuclear reactors as a by-product of plutonium production. Symbol **Np** [Late 19thC. Coined by R. Hermann as the next chemical element discovered after uranium; the sequence of names follows the order of the planets (Uranus, Neptune).]

NERC *abbr.* Natural Environment Research Council

nerd /nurd/ *n.* (*slang insult*) **1.** OFFENSIVE TERM an offensive term that deliberately insults sb's, especially a man's or boy's, social skills or intelligence **2.** SINGLE-MINDED ENTHUSIAST an enthusiast whose interest is regarded as too technical or scientific and who seems obsessively wrapped up in it (*often used in combination*) [Mid-20thC. Origin uncertain: perhaps created by US children's author Dr. Seuss (Theodore Seuss Geisel, 1904–91) in *If I Ran the Zoo* (1950).] —**nerdish** *adj.* —**nerdy** *adj.*

Nereid[1] /neeri id/ (*plural* **-ides** /na reē a deez/) *n.* in Greek mythology, a sea nymph, one of the 50 daughters of Nereus [Late 17thC. Via Latin from the Greek stem *Nereid-*, from Greek *Nereus*, name of a Greek sea god.]

Nereid[2] /neeri id/ *n.* ASTRON the outermost known natural satellite of Neptune, discovered in 1949. It is 340 km in diameter.

nereis /neeri iss/ (*plural* **-ides** /na reē a deez/ or **-ises**) *n.* a large segmented worm usually found living in saltwater, e.g. the ragworm. Genus: *Nereis*. [Mid-18thC. Via modern Latin, genus name, from Latin (see NEREID).]

neritic /na rittik/ *adj.* relating to or found in shallow coastal waters [Late 19thC. Formed from Latin *nerita*, type of shellfish of shallow seas, from, ultimately, Greek *Nereus* (see NEREID).]

Nernst /nurnst/, **Walther Hermann** (1864–1941) German physical chemist. He developed the third law of thermodynamics and won a *Nobel Prize in Chemistry* (1920).

Nero /neérō/ (AD 37–68) Roman emperor. He succeeded Claudius (AD 54), but his tyrannical and neglectful rule led to his deposition, and he committed suicide. Born **Lucius Domitius Ahenobarbus**. Full name **Claudius Caesar Drusus Germanicus Nero**

nerol /neer ol, neer-/ *n.* a colourless alcohol obtained from neroli and other essential oils, used in perfumes [Early 20thC. Coined from NEROLI + -OL.]

neroli /neérali/, **neroli oil** *n.* an oil distilled from the flowers of orange trees, especially the Seville orange, used in aromatherapy, in perfumes, and as a flavouring in food [Late 17thC. Via French from Italian, from the name of an Italian princess who supposedly discovered the oil.]

Nerva /núrva/, **Marcus Cocceius** (AD 35?–98) Roman emperor. He succeeded Domitian in 96, and introduced measures to help the poor. He was succeeded by his son Trajan.

nerve /nurv/ *n.* **1.** FIBRES COMMUNICATING BETWEEN BRAIN AND BODY a bundle of fibres forming a network that transmits messages, in the form of impulses, between the brain or spinal cord and the body's organs. Motor nerves carry impulses outwards to the muscles and glands, while sensory nerves carry inbound information about the body's movements and sensations. Mixed nerves perform both functions. **2.** SENSITIVE PULP IN TOOTH the sensitive tissue inside the roots of a tooth **3.** COURAGE courage or self-assurance ○ *lost his nerve* **4.** BOLDNESS boldness or impudence ○ *You've got a nerve!* **5.** BOT LEAF VEIN a vein in a leaf **6.** INSECTS VEIN IN INSECT'S WING a thin rib visible inside an insect's wing ■ **nerves** *npl.* **1.** STRESS THRESHOLD sb's ability to tolerate emotional stress or excitement ○ *My nerves are shattered.* **2.** NERVOUSNESS a state of emotional agitation (*informal*) ○ *He's a bundle of nerves before every performance.* ■ *vt.* (**nerves, nerving, nerved**) STEEL YOURSELF to gather all your courage or self-control in preparation for dealing with sth difficult, stressful, or frightening [14thC. Directly or via Old French *nerf* 'sinew, tendon' from Latin *nervus* 'nerve, sinew, tendon'.]

WORD KEY: SYNONYMS
See Synonyms at *courage*.

nerve block *n.* use of a local anaesthetic to numb a part of the body, thereby preventing the transmission of pain messages to the brain

nerve cell *n.* = neuron

nerve centre *n.* **1.** CONTROL CENTRE a place from which a large organization, system, or network is controlled **2.** PHYSIOL GROUP OF NEURONS a cluster of interconnected nerve cells that performs a specific function in the body

nerve cord *n.* a strand of nerve tissue, e.g. the spinal cord, that runs the length of the body and forms a principal part of an animal's nervous system

nerve fibre *n.* one of the long thin extensions of a neuron such as an axon or dendrite

nerve gas *n.* a poisonous gas used as a weapon of war that attacks the central nervous system and stops the breathing

nerve impulse *n.* a rapid and momentary change in electrical activity that passes along a nerve fibre to other neurons, muscles, or other body organs and signals instructions or information

nerveless /núrvlass/ *adj.* **1.** NUMB having no sensation or strength **2.** FEARLESS showing calmness, courage, or confidence, especially in a dangerous situation **3.** COWARDLY lacking courage or determination —**nervelessly** *adv.* —**nervelessness** *n.*

nerve net *n.* a simple nervous system, found in some invertebrates such as jellyfish, consisting of interconnecting nerve cells but lacking a control centre such as a brain

nerve-racking, **nerve-wracking** *adj.* causing great anxiety or distress

nerve trunk *n.* a bundle of nerve fibres surrounded by a sheath of connective tissue that forms the main stem of a nerve

Nervi /núrvi/, **Pier Luigi** (1891–1979) Italian architect and engineer. His designs for large-scale public buildings, in Europe and in North and South America, make use of reinforced concrete.

nervous /núrvass/ *adj.* **1.** UNEASY having a feeling of dread or apprehension ○ *feeling nervous about* meeting his parents **2.** TIMID easily worried or frightened ○ *people of a nervous disposition* **3.** AFFECTING THE NERVES relating to sb's ability to tolerate anxiety and stress ○ *a nervous illness* **4.** OF NERVES relating to or located in nerves, or the nervous system ○ *nervous tissue* [14thC. Originally in the sense 'sinewy'; its most important meanings today, of fear and worry, date from the 18thC.] —**nervosity** /nur vóssiti/ *n.* —**nervously** /núrvassli/ *adv.* —**nervousness** *n.*

nervous breakdown *n.* a psychiatric disorder, usually caused by intense stress or anxiety, in which sb becomes incapable of coping with daily life and exhibits low self-esteem or depression

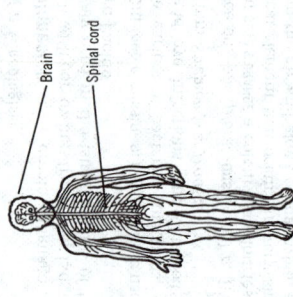
Nervous system

nervous system *n.* the network of nerve cells and nerve fibres in most animals that conveys sensations to the brain and motor impulses to organs and muscles

nervous tic *n.* an involuntary twitch of a muscle, especially of the face, that is sometimes a symptom of nervousness or a nervous disease

nervure /núr vyoor/ *n.* **1.** INSECTS STRUCTURE IN INSECT'S WING a supporting structure resembling a rod that is visible inside an insect's wing **2.** BOT = **vein** *n.* **3.** [Early 19thC. Via French, literally 'strap', from, ultimately, Latin *nervus* (see NERVE).]

Nesbit /nézbit/, **E.** (1858–1924) British novelist and poet. Her children's books include *Five Children and It* (1902), *The Phoenix and the Carpet* (1904), and *The Railway Children* (1906). Full name **Edith Nesbit**

nescience /néssi anss/ *n.* lack of knowledge or experience (*formal*) [Early 17thC. From Late Latin *nescientia*, from Latin *nescient-*, present participle stem of *nescire* 'not to know', from *scire* 'to know' (see SCIENCE).] —**nescient** *adj.* —**nesciently** *adv.*

nesh /nesh/ *adj.* (*regional*) **1.** SENSITIVE TO COLD very sensitive to cold temperatures **2.** TIMID lacking courage or self-confidence [Old English *hnesce*, ultimately of unknown origin]

ness /ness/ *n.* a section of coastline that projects into the sea (*often used in placenames*) [Old English *naes(s)*. Ultimately from an Indo-European word that is also the ancestor of *nose*. The underlying idea is of a nose-shaped projection from the mainland.]

Ness, Loch /ness/ long narrow lake in northern Scotland, forming part of the Caledonian Canal. It is believed by some people to be the home of an ancient monster. Length: 39 km/24 mi.

-ness *suffix.* state, condition, quality ○ *callousness* [Old English *-nes*]

nesselrode /néss'l rōd/, **Nesselrode** *n.* a creamy frozen dessert containing puréed chestnuts, candied fruit, and usually a sweet wine or liqueur [Mid-19thC. Named after the Russian statesman Karl-Robert Nesselrode (1780–1862), whose chef invented it.]

nest /nest/ *n.* **1.** BIRD OR ANIMAL'S DWELLING a structure that birds and other animals such as mice build to shelter themselves and their young, using available natural materials such as grass, twigs, and mud **2.** COMMUNITY OF ANIMALS the community of animals living in a nest **3.** STH SHAPED LIKE BIRD'S NEST sth shaped more or less like a bird's nest, especially sth that encloses or contains things ○ *a meringue nest* **4.** COSY PLACE a

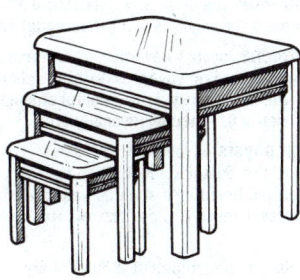

Nest: Nest of tables

cosy, protected, or secluded place **5. BAD PLACE** a place where sth bad, such as crime or treason, flourishes ○ *a nest of vice* **6. CRIMINALS' SECRET PLACE** a hideaway for criminals, or a group of criminals hiding away there ○ *a nest of thieves* **7. SET OF THINGS** a set of things such as tables or wooden eggs that fit one inside the other **8. GUN EMPLACEMENT** a protected or camouflaged place from which a gun or other weapon is fired ■ *v.* (**nests, nesting, nested**) **1.** *vi.* **BUILD NEST** to make or live in a nest, especially in preparation for giving birth to young **2.** *vi.* **MAKE PLACE MORE HOME-LIKE** to make a place more comfortable and home-like (*informal*) **3.** *vt.* **PUT THINGS TOGETHER** to put one thing inside another, or group things together into a single unit such as items in a reference book into a single entry or under a main heading **4.** *vi.* **LOOK FOR BIRDS' NESTS** to go looking for birds' nests in order to take the eggs [Old English. Ultimately from an Indo-European word meaning 'place where a bird sits down'.]

nest box, **nesting box** *n.* a box of the appropriate size, depending on the species, placed in a park, forest, or other place for wild birds to use for breeding

nest-building *n.* **1. BIRD'S BUILDING OF NEST** a bird's construction of a nest in preparation for having young **2. MAKING PLACE MORE HOME-LIKE** the process of making a place more comfortable and home-like, often for an expected baby (*informal*)

nest egg *n.* **1. SAVINGS** a sum of money put aside for future expenses or emergencies **2. EGG TO ENCOURAGE LAYING** a real or artificial egg that is put in a hen's nest to encourage it to continue laying after the other eggs have been removed

nesting box *n.* = **nest box**

nestle /néss'l/ (**nestles, nestling, nestled**) *v.* **1.** *vti.* **SETTLE INTO COMFORTABLE POSITION** to settle into a position that feels comfortable, warm, and safe, or lay a part of the body in such a position **2.** *vt.* **CUSHION STH WITH SOFT MATERIAL** to put sth such as delicate china or glassware in a protected cushion of soft material **3.** *vi.* **BE SECLUDED** to be in a sheltered or secluded place [Old English *nestlian*. From a prehistoric Germanic word that was formed from the ancestor of English *nest*.] —**nestler** *n.*

nestling /néstling/ *n.* a young bird that does not yet have its flight feathers, and is therefore not yet able to leave the nest [Late 14thC. Origin uncertain: formed from NEST or NESTLE, perhaps on the model of Dutch *nesteling*.]

Nestorian /ne stáwri ən/ *adj.* **RELATING TO ASIAN CHRISTIAN GROUP** relating to an Asian Christian denomination that believes that two distinct persons, one divine and the other human, existed in Jesus Christ. This doctrine was declared heresy in AD 431. ■ *n.* **MEMBER OF NESTORIAN GROUP** a member of the Nestorian denomination [15thC. From late Latin *Nestorianus*, named after *Nestorius* (AD 428–31), patriarch of Constantinople, who originated the doctrine.]

net[1] /net/ *n.* **1. MESH** material made from threads or wires knotted, twisted, or woven to form a regular pattern with spaces between the threads **2. MESHWORK BAG** a piece of meshwork fabric in a shape resembling a bag that is used for holding, carrying, trapping, or confining sth ○ *a fishing net* **3. LIGHT MESHWORK FABRIC** a fine light fabric with an open weave, usually made of cotton or synthetic yarn ○ *net curtains* **4. SELECTING OR RESTRICTING SYSTEM** a plan or system designed to select or restrict sb or sth ○ *those who slip through the net* **5. SPORTS STRIP**

OF MATERIAL ACROSS PLAYING AREA a strip of meshwork material that divides a court into halves in some sports, e.g. tennis and volleyball, and over which the players must hit a ball or shuttlecock **6. SPORTS GOAL IN SOME SPORTS** a goal in some sports, e.g. soccer and water polo, with a backing made of meshwork material **7. BASKETBALL PART OF BASKETBALL NET** an open-bottomed piece of meshwork material attached to the hoop of the basket in basketball **8. CRICKET PRACTICE CRICKET PITCH** in cricket, an indoor or outdoor practice pitch surrounded on three sides by nets that contain the ball after it has been hit (*often used in the plural*) **9. CRICKET CRICKET PRACTICE SESSION** in cricket, a session on a practice pitch (*often used in the plural*) **10. BROADCAST NETWORK** a network **11. COMPUT, BROADCAST NETWORK** telecommunications or computer network ■ *v.* (**nets, netting, netted**) **1.** *vt.* **TRAP IN NET** to catch or snare sth in a net **2.** *vt.* **GET STH** to manage to obtain or achieve sth (*informal*) ○ *We may net ourselves several new clients this way.* **3.** *vt.* **PROTECT WITH NET** to cover sth with a net in order to keep sth out or away ○ *Net the cherry trees to keep birds out.* **4.** *vi.* **MAKE NET** to make a net by knotting, twisting, or weaving threads or wires together **5.** *vt.* **SPORTS HIT BALL INTO NET TO SCORE** to score by hitting the ball into the net in games such as soccer and hockey **6.** *vt.* **SPORTS SERVE BALL INTO NET** to lose a serve, and sometimes a point, by hitting the ball into the net in games such as tennis and volleyball [Old English. Ultimately from an Indo-European word meaning 'to bind, tie', which is also the ancestor of English *nettle*, *node*, and *connect*.] —**netless** *adj.* —**netlessly** *adv.*

net[2] /net/, **nett** *adj.* **1. FIN LEFT AFTER DEDUCTIONS** remaining from an amount, especially of money, after all necessary deductions have been made **2. RELATING TO CONTENTS** relating to contents only, excluding the container or the packaging **3. HAVING ALL THINGS CONSIDERED** general or overall when positive and negative features have been weighed against each other ■ *vt.* (**nets, netting, netted; netts, netting, netted**) **FIN EARN PROFIT** to earn or provide a sum of money as pure profit after all necessary deductions have been made ■ *n.* **1. NET AMOUNT** a net profit or weight **2. GOLF GOLFER'S SCORE** a player's final score after his or her handicap has been deducted [15thC. Via Italian *netto* from Latin *nitidus* 'gleaming, clean, elegant' (see NEAT).]

Net, **net** *n.* the Internet (*informal*) [Late 20thC. Shortening.]

Netanyahu /nétt'n yaáhoo/, **Benjamin** (*b.* 1949) Israeli statesman. He was elected Likud prime minister in 1996. He was criticized for failing to press for the implementation of the peace agreements with the Palestinians.

net asset value *n.* the value of the securities owned by a mutual fund, calculated as the total value of assets minus the total amount of liabilities divided by the number of shares issued

netball /nét bawl/ *n.* an indoor or outdoor game similar to basketball, usually played by girls or women, who can hand or throw the ball to each other but not run with it

Net Book Agreement *n.* an agreement in the British book trade, ended in 1995, that prevented booksellers from selling books at prices lower than those fixed by the publishers

net cord *n.* **1. TENNIS SHOT TOUCHING NET** a tennis shot, especially a serve, that touches the net before landing on the opponent's side. In the case of a serve, the server retakes the shot. **2. WIRE SUPPORTING TENNIS NET** the wire that holds up the net on a tennis court

net domestic product *n.* the gross sum of domestic production minus the cost of depreciation of capital goods

Neth. *abbr.* Netherlands

nether /néthər/ *adj.* located in a low or lower position or under sth (*formal*) [Old English *neopera*. Ultimately from an Indo-European word meaning 'down', which is also one of the ancestors of English *nest*.]

Netherlands /néthər ləndz/ monarchy in northwestern Europe, west of Germany, on the North Sea. Language: Dutch. Currency: guilder. Capital: Amsterdam. Population: 15,451,000 (1995). Area: 41,526 sq. km/16,033 sq. mi. Official name **Kingdom of**

Netherlands

the Netherlands —**Netherlander** *n.* —**Netherlandish** *adj.*

Netherlands Antilles /néthər ləndz an tíl leez/ two Dutch island groups in the western Caribbean Sea, part of the Lesser Antilles. Population: 202,244 (1994). Area: 996 sq. km/390 sq. mi.

Netherlands Guiana /néthər ləndz gee aán ə/ former name for **Suriname**

nethermost /néthərmōst/ *adj.* lowest or farthest down (*formal*)

nether world *n.* **1. RELIG HELL** hell, or the place where evil spirits live in the belief system of some cultures (*formal*) **2. MYTHOL ABODE OF DEAD SOULS** in Greek and Roman mythology, the place below the earth's surface where the souls of the dead live **3. CRIMINAL UNDERWORLD** the world of organized crime, or the people involved in it (*literary*)

netiquette /nétti ket, -kət/ *n.* a set of empirically derived rules for getting along harmoniously in the electronic communication environment (*informal*) [Late 20thC. Blend of NET and ETIQUETTE.]

Netizen /néttizən/ *n.* sb who has access to and uses the Internet frequently (*informal*) [Late 20thC. Blend of NET and CITIZEN.]

net national product *n.* the amount left after subtracting a depreciation allowance for capital goods from the gross national product

net present value *n.* the value of an investment project found by adding the present value of expected future cash flows and the cost of the initial investment

net profit *n.* gross profit minus all the costs incurred by a business

net realizable value, **net realisable value** *n.* the value an asset would have if sold, allowing for the costs of bringing it to a condition for sale and making the sale

netsuke /nétski, -kay, nétsoōki, -kay/ *n.* a carved wooden or ivory ornamental toggle worn at the end of a cord that holds a kimono closed, originally used to fasten a purse or pouch [Late 19thC. From Japanese.]

Net surfing *n.* browsing through the information and sites available on the Internet, especially casually

nett *adj.* = **net**[2]

netter /néttər/ *n.* sb with an Internet address (*slang*)

netting /nétting/ *n.* fabric made from threads or wires knotted, twisted, or woven to form a regular pattern with spaces between the threads

nettle /nétt'l/ *n.* **1. PLANT WITH STINGING LEAVES** a wild plant with serrated-edged leaves that are covered with fine hairs or spines that sting when touched. Genus: *Urtica*. **2. NONSTINGING PLANT RESEMBLING NETTLE** a wild plant with serrated leaves like a stinging nettle, but without the stinging hairs, especially a deadnettle. Genus: *Lamium*. ■ *vt.* (**-tles, -tling, -tled**) **1. IRRITATE SB** to irritate or annoy sb (*informal*) **2. STING** to sting sb [Old English *netele*. Ultimately from an Indo-European word meaning 'to tie', which also produced English *net*. Nettles were often used as a source of fibre for making cords.]

nettle rash *n.* = **urticaria**

net ton *n.* = **ton**[1] *n.* 1 [From NET[2]]

net weight *n.* the weight of the contents only, excluding the weight of the container or packaging [From NET[2]]

net-winged *adj.* used to describe the wings of beetles and midges that have a network of veins

network /nét wurk/ *n.* **1.** SYSTEM OF INTERCONNECTED LINES a pattern or system that looks like a series of branching or interconnecting lines **2.** COORDINATED SYSTEM OF PEOPLE OR THINGS a large and widely distributed group of people or things such as shops, colleges, or churches, that communicate with one another and work together as a unit or system **3.** BROADCAST GROUP OF BROADCASTING CHANNELS a group of radio or television channels with a core of programmes that they all broadcast at the same time, with local or regional variations at other times **4.** ELEC SYSTEM OF ELECTRICAL CIRCUITS a system of interconnected electrical circuits or components **5.** COMPUT SYSTEM OF LINKED COMPUTERS a system of two or more computers, terminals, and communications devices linked by wires, cables, or a telecommunications system in order to exchange information. The network may be limited to a group of users in a local area (**local area network**), or be global in scope, as the Internet is. **6.** NETTING net or netting ■ *v.* (**-works, -working, -worked**) **1.** *vi.* MAINTAIN RELATIONSHIPS WITH PEOPLE to build up or maintain informal relationships, especially with people whose friendship could bring advantages such as job or business opportunities **2.** *vt.* COMPUT LINK COMPUTERS to link a group of computers or their users so that information can be mutually accessed or exchanged **3.** *vt.* BROADCAST BROADCAST STH SIMULTANEOUSLY to broadcast a programme simultaneously on all the channels that form a network

networking /nét wurking/ *n.* **1.** COMPUT LINKING OF COMPUTERS the linking of computers so that users can exchange information or share access to a central store of information **2.** GATHERING OF ACQUAINTANCES OR CONTACTS the building up or maintaining of informal relationships, especially with people whose friendship could bring advantages such as job or business opportunities —**networker** *n.*

neume /nyoom/, **neum** *n.* during the Middle Ages in Europe, an early kind of musical notation that sometimes indicated only the approximate shape of a melody [15thC. Via French from, ultimately, Greek *pneuma* 'breath'. The modern usage is a 19thC revival.] —**neumatic** /nyoo máttik/ *adj.*

neur- *prefix.* = **neuro-** (used before vowels)

neural /nyóorəl/ *adj.* relating to or located in a nerve or the nervous system —**neurally** *adv.*

neural arch *n.* a bony or cartilaginous arch enclosing the spinal cord on the outward-facing side of a vertebra

neural computer *n.* = **neurocomputer**

neural crest *n.* a ridge of cells in the ectoderm of the vertebrate embryo that develops into cranial, spinal, and autonomic ganglia

neuralgia /nyoo ráljə/ *n.* intermittent and often severe pain in a part of the body that a particular nerve runs through, especially when there is no physical change in the nerve itself —**neuralgic** *adj.*

neural net *n.* a system of electrical circuits designed to perform like the human nervous system, especially a computer system mimicking the human brain

neural network *n.* **1.** ANAT SYSTEM OF NEURONS an interconnecting system of nerve cells such as the system that makes the brain function **2.** COMPUT = **neural net**

neural spine *n.* a projection that points backwards from the neural arch of a vertebra

neural tube *n.* the hollow tube of tissue in the embryo of humans and other vertebrates that develops into the spinal cord and brain

neural tube defect *n.* a congenital disorder such as spina bifida caused by failure of the neural tube to close completely and resulting in loss of muscle function and various medical disorders

neurasthenia /nyóorəss theeni ə/ *n.* a condition marked by chronic mental and physical fatigue and depression (*dated*) —**neurasthenic** /-thénnik/ *adj.* —**neurasthenically** *adv.*

neurectomy /nyoo réktəmi/ (*plural* **-mies**) *n.* the removal of part of a nerve using surgery, e.g. as a treatment for neuralgia

neurilemma /nyóori lémmə/, **neurolemma** /nyoōrō-/ *n.* the outermost layer of the myelin sheath that surrounds the axon of a myelinated nerve cell [Early 19thC. Coined from NEUR- + Greek *eilēma* 'covering'.] —**neurilemmal** *adj.* —**neurilemmally** *adv.*

neurilemmoma /nyóori le mómə/ (*plural* **-mas** *or* **-mata** /-mətə/) *n.* = **neurofibroma** [Mid-20thC. Coined from NEURILEMMA + -OMA.]

neurinoma /nyóori nómə/ (*plural* **-mas** *or* **-mata** /-mətə/) *n.* MED = **neurofibroma** [Early 20thC. Coined from NEURO- + INO- + -OMA.]

neuritis /nyoo rítiss/ *n.* inflammation of a nerve, accompanied by pain, loss of reflexes, and muscle shrinkage —**neuritic** /-ríttik/ *adj.*

neuro- *prefix.* nerve, neural ○ *neurosurgery* [From Greek *neuron* (see NEURON)]

neuroactive /nyóorō áktiv/ *adj.* having an effect on neural tissue or the nervous system

neuroanatomy /nyóorō ə náttəmi/ *n.* **1.** STRUCTURE OF NERVOUS SYSTEM the structure of the nervous system **2.** BRANCH OF ANATOMY the branch of anatomy that studies the structure of the nervous system —**neuroanatomical** /-ánnə tómmik'l/ *adj.* —**neuroanatomically** *adv.* —**neuroanatomist** /-ə náttəmist/ *n.*

neurobiology /nyóorō bī ólləji/ *n.* = **neuroscience** —**neurobiological** /-bī ə lójjik'l/ *adj.* —**neurobiologically** *adv.* —**neurobiologist** /-bī ólləjist/ *n.*

neuroblast /nyóorō blast/ *n.* an embryonic cell that develops into a nerve cell

neuroblastoma /nyóorō bla stómə/ (*plural* **-mas** *or* **-mata** /-mətə/) *n.* a malignant tumour of embryonic nerve cells (**neuroblasts**)

neurochemistry /nyóorō kémmistri/ *n.* the study of the chemical composition and reactions within the nervous system —**neurochemical** *adj.* —**neurochemically** *adv.* —**neurochemist** *n.*

neurocomputer /nyóorō kəm pyootər/ *n.* a computer designed to imitate the human brain's ability to identify patterns, learn by trial and error, and find relationships in information. It is used in artificial intelligence research and to perform such tasks as machine translation, process control, handwriting recognition, and weather forecasting. —**neurocomputing** *n.* —**neurocomputational** /nyóorō kómpyoo táysh'nəl/ *adj.*

neuroendocrine /nyóorō éndō krīn, -krin/ *adj.* relating to or involving a nerve cell that releases a chemical messenger, especially a neurohormone, directly into the bloodstream

neuroendocrinology /nyóorō éndōkri nólləji/ *n.* the study of the interrelationships between the nervous system, the endocrine system, and hormones —**neuroendocrinological** /-krínnə lójjik'l/ *adj.* —**neuroendocrinologically** *adv.* —**neuroendocrinologist** /-éndōkri nólləjist/ *n.*

neurofibril /nyóorō fíbril/ *n.* a microscopic thin strand that occurs inside the cell body, axon, and dendrites of a nerve cell —**neurofibrillary** /nyóorófi brílləri/ *adj.*

neurofibroma /nyóorō fī brómə/ (*plural* **-mas** *or* **-mata** /-mətə/) *n.* a usually benign tumour arising from the sheath of a nerve

neurofibromatosis /nyóorō fī brómə tóssiss/ *n.* an inherited disorder marked by coffee-coloured patches on the skin and neurofibromas formed along nerves, causing visual and hearing defects, other nervous disorders, and sometimes major deformities

neurogenesis /nyóorō jénnəssiss/ *n.* the formation and development of nerve cells —**neurogenetic** /nyóorō jə néttik/ *adj.* —**neurogenetically** /-jə néttikli/ *adv.*

neurogenetics /nyóorō jə néttiks/ *n.* the branch of medicine that studies the genetic influences involved in neurological disorders (*takes a singular verb*) —**neurogeneticist** /-néttissist/ *n.*

neurogenic /nyóorō jénnik/ *adj.* **1.** CAUSING GROWTH OF NERVE TISSUE causing or relating to the growth of nerve tissue **2.** OF NERVOUS SYSTEM arising in or stimulated by nerve tissue or the nervous system —**neurogenically** *adv.*

neuroglia /nyoo róggli ə/ *n.* = **glia** [Mid-19thC. Coined from NEURO- + Greek *glia* 'glue'.] —**neuroglial** *adj.*

neurohormone /nyóorō háwrmōn/ *n.* a hormone such as noradrenaline or vasopressin that acts on nerve cells or the nervous system —**neurohormonal** /nyóorō hawr mónəl/ *adj.* —**neurohormonally** *adv.*

neurohypophysis /nyóorō hī póffississ/ (*plural* **-ses** /-seez/) *n.* the posterior lobe of the pituitary gland that secretes hormones such as vasopressin —**neurohypophyseal** /nyóorō hīpō fízzi əl, -hī póffi seē əl/ *adj.*

neurol. *abbr.* **1.** neurological **2.** neurology

neurolemma *n.* = **neurilemma**

neuroleptic /nyóorō léptik/ *adj.* TRANQUILLIZING reducing nerve activity and producing a tranquillizing effect ■ *n.* TRANQUILLIZER a drug used in the treatment of conditions such as delirium and behavioural disturbances that has a tranquillizing effect by reducing nerve activity [Mid-20thC. Coined from NEURO- + Greek *lēptikos* 'seizing', from, ultimately, *lambanein* 'to seize, take'.] —**neuroleptically** *adv.*

neurolinguistic programming /nyóorō ling gwístik-/ *n.* **1.** RELATIONSHIP BETWEEN COMMUNICATION AND BEHAVIOUR a theory and model of human behaviour and communication based on linguistic insights into how people avoid change and how to assist them in changing **2.** GOAL-ORIENTATED THERAPY a system of therapy in which the brain is viewed as a computer that can be reprogrammed to think and feel in a way that helps people achieve specific goals

neurolinguistics /nyóorō ling gwístiks/ *n.* the branch of linguistics that explores how the brain encodes language (*takes a singular verb*) —**neurolinguist** /nyóorō líng gwist/ *n.* —**neurolinguistic** /-ling gwístik/ *adj.* —**neurolinguistically** /-ling gwístikli/ *adv.*

neurology /nyoo rólləji/ *n.* the branch of medicine that deals with the structure and function of the nervous system and the treatment of the diseases and disorders that affect it —**neurological** /nyóorə lójjik'l/ *adj.* —**neurologically** *adv.* —**neurologist** /nyoo róllə jist/ *n.*

neuroma /nyoo rómə/ (*plural* **-mata** /-mətə/ *or* **-mas**) *n.* MED = **neurofibroma** [Mid-19thC. Coined from NEUR- + -OMA.]

neuromuscular /nyóorō múskyoōlər/ *adj.* **1.** OF NERVE AND MUSCLE TISSUE relating to or affecting both nerve and muscle tissue **2.** IN BOTH NERVE AND MUSCLE TISSUES having features common to both nerve and muscle tissue —**neuromuscularly** *adv.*

neuromuscular junction *n.* the connection between a nerve cell and a muscle, where nerve impulses are transmitted to initiate contraction of the muscle

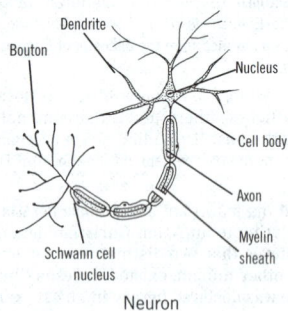

Neuron

neuron /nyóor on/, **neurone** /nyóor ōn/ *n.* a cell, typically consisting of a cell body, axon, and dendrites, that transmits nerve impulses and is the basic functional unit of the nervous system [Late 19thC. Via German from Greek *neuron* 'sinew, cord, nerve'.] —**neuronal** /nyóorō rón'l/ *adj.* —**neuronally** /-rón'li/ *adv.*

neuropath /nyóorō path/ *n.* sb affected by a disorder of the nervous system

neuropathology /nyóorō pə thólləji/ *n.* the branch of medicine that studies diseases and disorders of the nervous system —**neuropathological** /nyóorō páthə lójjik'l/ *adj.* —**neuropathologically** /-lójjikli/ *adv.* —**neuropathologist** /-pə thólləjist/ *n.*

neuropathy /nyoo͝ róppəthi/ (*plural* **-thies**) *n.* a disease or disorder, especially a degenerative one, that affects the nervous system —**neuropathic** /nyo͝orō páthik/ *adj.* —**neuropathically** /-páthikli/ *adv.*

neuropeptide /nyo͝orō pép tīd/ *n.* a peptide that has the properties of a hormone or other neurotransmitter and is released into the blood stream by a nerve cell, not by endocrine tissue

neurophysiology /nyo͝orō fízzi ólləji/ *n.* the branch of physiology that studies how the nervous system functions —**neurophysiological** /nyo͝orō fízzi ə lójjik'l/ *adj.* —**neurophysiologically** /-lójjikli/ *adv.* —**neurophysiologist** /-fízzi ólləjist/ *n.*

neuropsychiatry /nyo͝orō sī kí ətri/ *n.* the study of the neurological aspects of psychiatric disorders —**neuropsychiatric** /nyo͝orō sīki áttrik/ *adj.* —**neuropsychiatrically** *adv.* —**neuropsychiatrist** /-sī kí ətrist/ *n.*

neuropsychology /nyo͝orō sī kólləji/ *n.* the branch of neurology that studies behaviour, especially in disorders such as epilepsy, memory loss, or speech impairment —**neuropsychological** /nyo͝orō sīkə lójjik'l/ *adj.* —**neuropsychologically** /-sīkə lójjikli/ *adv.* —**neuropsychologist** /-sī kólləjist/ *n.*

neuropteran /nyoo͝ róptərən/, **neuropteron** (*plural* **-tera** /-tərə/) *n.* an insect such as the antlion or lacewing that has two large pairs of veined wings and mouthparts adapted for chewing. Order: Neuroptera. —**neuropterous** *adj.*

neuroscience /nyo͝orō sī ənss/ *n.* **1.** SCIENTIFIC STUDY OF NERVOUS SYSTEM a scientific discipline such as neuroanatomy and neurophysiology that studies nerve cells or the nervous system or all such disciplines collectively **2.** MOLECULAR AND CELLULAR NEUROLOGY the scientific study of the molecular and cellular levels of the nervous system, of systems within the brain such as vision and hearing, and behaviour produced by the brain —**neuroscientific** /nyo͝orō sī ən tíffik/ *adj.* —**neuroscientifically** /-tíffikli/ *adv.* —**neuroscientist** /nyo͝orō sí əntist/ *n.*

neurosensory /nyo͝orō sénssəri/ *adj.* relating to the sensory activity of nerve cells or the nervous system —**neurosensorily** *adv.*

neurosis /nyoo͝ róssiss/ (*plural* **-ses** /nyoo͝ ró seez/) *n.* a mild psychiatric disorder characterized by anxiety, depression, and hypochondria (*dated*)

neurosurgery /nyo͝orō súrjəri/ *n.* surgery on any part of the nervous system, including the brain —**neurosurgeon** /nyo͝orō súrjən/ *n.* —**neurosurgical** /-súrjik'l/ *adj.* —**neurosurgically** /-súrjikli/ *adv.*

neurotic /nyoo róttik/ *adj.* PSYCHIAT **1.** AFFECTED BY NEUROSIS relating to, involving, affected by, or typical of a mild mental disorder characterized by depression, anxiety, and hypochondria (*dated*) **2.** OVERANXIOUS OR OBSESSIVE overanxious, oversensitive, or obsessive about everyday things (*informal; often considered offensive*) ■ *n.* **1.** PSYCHIAT SB AFFECTED BY NEUROSIS sb diagnosed as affected by neurosis (*dated*) **2.** SB WHO IS EXTREMELY SENSITIVE sb who is overanxious, oversensitive, or obsessive (*informal; often considered offensive*) [Mid-17thC. Formed from Greek *neuron* (see NEURO-).] —**neurotically** /nyoo͝ róttikli/ *adv.* —**neuroticism** /nyoo͝ rótti sizəm/ *n.*

neurotomy /nyoo͝ róttəmi/ (*plural* **-mies**) *n.* a surgical operation to cut a nerve, especially in order to relieve pain

neurotoxin /nyo͝or ō tóksin/ *n.* a substance that damages, destroys, or impairs the functioning of nerve tissue —**neurotoxic** *adj.* —**neurotoxically** *adv.* —**neurotoxicity** /nyo͝orō tok síssəti/ *n.*

neurotransmitter /nyo͝or ō tranz míttər/ *n.* a chemical that carries messages between different nerve cells or between nerve cells and muscles, e.g. usually to trigger or prevent an impulse in the receiving cell. Excitatory neurotransmitters trigger a nerve impulse in the receiving cell while inhibitory neurotransmitters act to prevent further transmission of an impulse.

neurotropic /nyo͝or ō tróppik/ *adj.* affecting or having an affinity with nerve tissue —**neurotropically** *adv.* —**neurotropism** /nyoo͝ róttrəpizəm, nyo͝orə trṓpizəm/ *n.*

neurula /nyo͝oryo͝olə/ (*plural* **-rulae** /-lee/ *or* **-ralas**) *n.* a vertebrate embryo in an early stage during which the nervous system begins to develop [Late 19thC. Coined from NEURO- + Latin *-ula* 'small' on the model of BLASTULA and SCROFULA.] —**neurulation** /nyo͝oryo͝o láysh'n/ *n.*

neuston /nyo͞ost'n/ *n.* minute organisms that float or swim on the surface of water [Early 20thC. From German, from a form of Greek *neustos* 'swimming', from *nein* 'to swim'.]

neut. *abbr.* neuter

neuter /nyo͞otər/ *vt.* (**-ters, -tering, -tered**) VET REMOVE TESTICLES OR OVARIES to remove the testicles or ovaries of an animal ■ *adj.* **1.** PHYSIOL WITHOUT SEX ORGANS with undeveloped, nonfunctioning, or no sexual organs **2.** NOT INDICATING SEX OR OTHER CHARACTERISTICS not indicating the sex of a person, the qualities of a thing, or an attitude towards sb or sth **3.** GRAM GRAMMATICALLY NEITHER MASCULINE NOR FEMININE used to describe nouns and adjectives in languages such as Latin or German belonging to a separate gender that is neither masculine nor feminine **4.** GRAM INTRANSITIVE used to describe a verb that is neither active nor passive **5.** NEUTRAL supporting or belonging to neither side in a dispute (*archaic*) ■ *n.* **1.** VET CASTRATED OR SPAYED ANIMAL an animal that has been castrated or spayed **2.** GRAM GRAMMATICALLY NEUTER WORD a grammatically neuter noun, adjective, or verb **3.** INSECTS INSECT WITH UNDEVELOPED SEXUAL ORGANS an insect with undeveloped sexual organs, e.g., a worker bee **4.** BOT FLOWER WITHOUT STAMEN OR PISTIL an asexual flower without a stamen or pistil [14thC. From Latin *ne* 'not' + *uter* 'which of two', thus meaning 'neither one thing nor the other' (compare English *neither*).]

neutral /nyo͞otrəl/ *adj.* **1.** NOT TAKING SIDES not belonging to, favouring, or assisting any side in a war, dispute, contest, or controversy **2.** WITHOUT DISTINCTIVE QUALITIES not possessing any particular quality or revealing a particular attitude or feeling ○ *She was careful to explain the problem in neutral terms.* **3.** COLOURS WITHOUT HUE used to describe a colour such as white, black, or grey that does not belong in the spectrum **4.** COLOURS NOT STRONGLY COLOURED AND BLENDABLE not strongly or strikingly coloured and thus relatively inconspicuous and able to blend easily with other colours **5.** PHYSIOL = **neuter** *adj.* 1 **6.** CHEM NOT ACID NOT ALKALINE neither acidic nor alkaline **7.** PHYS WITH ZERO ELECTRIC CHARGE with zero electric charge or potential **8.** MECH ENG WITH NO MOTION TRANSMITTED in which no motion is transmitted **9.** PHON PRONOUNCED WITH TONGUE MIDWAY used to describe a vowel articulated with the tongue relaxed and in the mid-central position, as, e.g., in the first syllable of 'away' ■ *n.* **1.** POL SB OR STH NONALIGNED sb who or a country that remains neutral in a war, dispute, contest, or controversy **2.** AUTOMOT GEAR WITH NO MOTION TRANSMITTED a gear in which no power is transmitted from the engine to the moving parts [15thC. From Latin *neutralis* 'of neuter gender', from *neuter* (see NEUTER).] —**neutrally** *adv.*

neutral corner *n.* either of the two corners of a boxing ring that are not used by boxers between rounds. If one boxer is knocked down during a round, the other must go to a neutral corner.

neutralism /nyo͞otrəlizəm/ *n.* the policy of remaining neutral in wars and other disputes, or support for this policy —**neutralist** /nyo͞otrəlist/ *n., adj.* —**neutralistic** /nyo͞otrə lístik/ *adj.* —**neutralistically** *adv.*

neutrality /nyoo trálləti/ *n.* the state of being neutral, especially as regards noninvolvement in wars and disputes, not taking sides, and not joining alliances

neutralize /nyo͞otrə līz/ (**-izes, -izing, -ized**), **neutralise** (**-ises, -ising, -ised**) *vt.* **1.** RENDER STH INEFFECTIVE to make sth ineffective, especially by removing its ability to act as a threat or obstacle **2.** POL MAKE A PLACE NONALIGNED to make or declare a country unaligned in an international dispute or war **3.** CHEM MAKE STH NEITHER ACID NOR ALKALINE to render a substance neither acid nor alkaline **4.** PHYS GIVE ZERO CHARGE TO STH to make the electric charge or potential of sth zero —**neutralization** /nyo͞otrə lī záysh'n/ *n.* —**neutralizer** /nyo͞otrə līzər/ *n.*

neutral spirits *n.* US alcohol distilled at or above 190 proof, often used in blending alcoholic drinks (*takes a singular or plural verb*)

neutrino /nyoo tréen ō/ (*plural* **-nos**) *n.* any of three stable neutral elementary particles of the lepton family with a zero rest mass and no charge. Neutrinos have a spin of 1/2. [Mid-20thC. Coined from NEUTRAL + Italian *-ino* 'small'.]

neutron /nyo͞o tron/ *n.* a neutral elementary particle of the baryon family with a zero electrical charge and a mass approximately equal to that of a proton [Early 20thC. Coined from NEUTRAL + -ON.] —**neutronic** /nyoo trónnik/ *adj.*

neutron bomb *n.* a nuclear bomb designed to kill all life by a heavy bombardment with neutrons but to cause little blast damage and leave relatively low radioactive contamination

neutron star *n.* a celestial body consisting entirely of a very dense compact mass of neutrons, the remnant of a star that has collapsed under its own gravity

neutrophil /nyo͞otrə fil/ *adj.* STAINABLE ONLY WITH NEUTRAL DYES used to describe cells or tissues, e.g. white blood cells, that are readily stainable only with chemically neutral dyes ■ *n.* **neutrophil, neutrophile** COMMON WHITE BLOOD CELL the most common type of white blood cell in vertebrates, responsible for protecting the body against infection and stainable with neutral dyes [Late 19thC. Coined from Latin *neutr-*, stem of *neuter* (see NEUTER), + -PHIL.] —**neutrophilic** *adj.*

Nev. *abbr.* Nevada

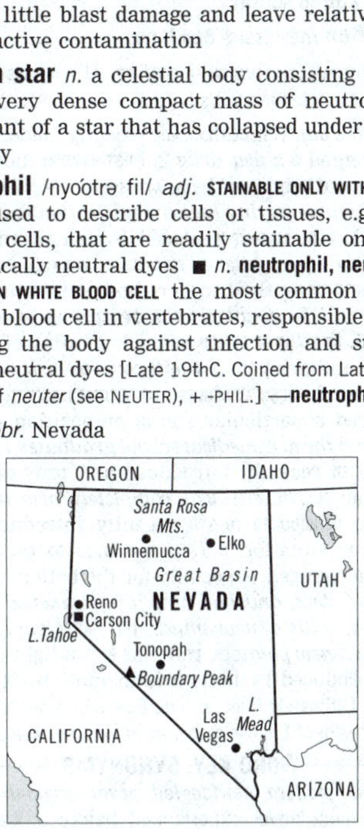

Nevada

Nevada /nə vaádə/ state in the western United States, bordered by Oregon, Idaho, Utah, Arizona, and California. Capital: Carson City. Population: 1,676,809 (1997). Area: 286,367 sq. km/110,567 sq. mi. —**Nevadan** *n., adj.*

névé /névvay/ (*plural* **-vés**) *n.* **1.** SNOW AT GLACIER TOP compact granular snow, found at the top of a glacier, that has not yet become ice **2.** FIELD OF COMPACTED SNOW ON GLACIER a field of compacted granular snow at the top of a glacier [Mid-19thC. From Swiss French, ultimately from Latin *nivatus* 'snow-cooled', from the stem *niv-* 'snow'.]

never /névvər/ CORE MEANING: an adverb indicating that sth will not happen at any time, or that sb will definitely not do sth ○ *The details will never be known.* ○ *I would never do anything to harm or hurt her.*

1. *adv.* AT NO TIME at no time in the past or the future ○ *The bird has never been seen in Iceland before. It may never appear there again.* **2.** *adv.* CERTAINLY NOT not in any circumstances at all ○ *I would never turn my back on them.* **3.** *interj.* EXCLAMATION OF SURPRISE an exclamation indicating surprise or shock ○ *'She's come top again'.'Never!'* [Old English, from *ne* 'not' + an earlier form of EVER] ◇ **never ever** an emphatic expression for 'never' (*informal*) ◇ **sth will** *or* **would never do** indicates that sth is not appropriate or suitable in the circumstances ◇ **well I never!** an exclamation of surprise or shock ○ *Well I never! You've done it again!*

never-ending *adj.* continuing on and on and seeming unlikely ever to stop

nevermore /névvər máwr/ *adv.* never again (*literary*)

never-never *n.* **1.** HIRE PURCHASE hire purchase (*dated informal*) ○ *They bought a three-piece suite on the never-never.* **2.** *Aus* CENTRAL AUSTRALIAN DESERT the remote arid parts of central Australia

never-never land *n.* an unreal or imaginary place, especially one where wonderful things happen ○ *The Opposition's budget policy springs from the* same never-never land as their employment policy. [From *Never Never Land* in J. M. Barrie's *Peter Pan* (1904).]

nevertheless /névvərthə léss/ *adv.* despite a situation or comment

Nevin /névvin/, **Robyn Anne** (*b.* 1942) Australian actor. She is a stage and screen performer. Her films include *The Chant of Jimmie Blacksmith* (1978).

Nevis /névviss/ island in St Kitts and Nevis, in the eastern West Indies. It is one of the Leeward Islands. Capital: Charlestown. Population: 8,794 (1991). Area: 93 sq. km/36 sq. mi.

Nevis, Ben /névviss/ ♦ Ben Nevis

nevus /néevəss/ (*plural* **-i** /-vī/) *n.* US = **naevus** [Mid-19thC. From Latin *naevus*.]

new /nyoo/ *adj.* **1. RECENTLY MADE** recently made, created, or invented ○ *a new drug* **2. FIRST-HAND** indicates that sth has not been used by anyone else ○ *And motorists will continue paying higher registration fees for new cars.* **3. REPLACEMENT** replaced by sth recent or innovative ○ *new rules to enhance security* **4. RECENTLY DISCOVERED** recently discovered or noticed ○ *The new comet will be visible at the beginning of July this year.* **5. AT START OF PERIOD** at the beginning of another day, month, or year ○ *I will come to visit you in the new year.* **6. RECENTLY ACQUIRED OR BECOME** having recently acquired a particular status or position ○ *a new mother* ○ *the new medical school graduates* **7. RECENTLY INTRODUCED** recently introduced and previously unfamiliar ○ *The city was completely new to me.* **8. RECENTLY INTRODUCED TO STH** recently introduced to a place or situation ○ *He's not new to this city.* **9. CHANGED** changed, especially for the better ○ *I felt as if I had slept, and had now just awakened – a new woman, with a new mind.* **10. EARLY** early in the season ○ *new potatoes* ■ *n. Aus* **BEER** a light-coloured beer produced by bottom fermentation [Old English *nēowe*. Ultimately from an Indo-European word that is also the ancestor of English *novel*, *neon*, and *renovate*.]

─── **WORD KEY: SYNONYMS** ───

new, fresh, modern, newfangled, novel, original

CORE MEANING: never experienced before or having recently come into being

new a general word used to describe sth that has just been invented, discovered, made, bought or experienced. It can also be used to describe sb or sth not previously known or encountered, for example a new friend or a new doctor; **fresh** used to describe sth new and different, especially when it involves a reexamination or reappraisal of sb or sth. It can also be used to describe sth that seems interesting or exciting because it has not been tried or experienced before; **modern** used to describe sth that is the result of or is characterized by up-to-date ideas, techniques, design, and equipment; **newfangled** used informally to show disapproval of sth such as a machine or a system that is new or different, especially because it seems gimmicky or over-complicated; **novel** used to describe sth that is new and inventive; **original** used to describe sth that is new and unique.

NEW *abbr.* nonexplosive warfare [This term was coined in 1988 by Richard Danzig who later became Secretary of the Navy in the Clinton Administration. It refers to two kinds of viruses—biological and and high-tech—that terrorists and rogue nations can use against a nation's military and civilian infrastructure, creating illness, death, and communication chaos.]

New Age *adj.* **OF MODERN MOVEMENT EMPHASIZING SPIRITUALITY** relating to a cultural movement dating from the 1980s that emphasizes spiritual consciousness, and often involves belief in reincarnation and astrology and the practice of meditation, vegetarianism, and holistic medicine ■ *n.* **New Age, New Age music** **MUSIC INDUCING SERENITY** a style of instrumental music with simple repetitive melodies, often synthesized or reproducing natural sounds, that is intended to promote mental tranquillity —**New Ager** *n.*

New Age traveller *n.* sb who belongs to the New Age cultural movement and lives a nomadic life, travelling the country, often in a group, to gather at places believed to be spiritually significant

Newark **1.** city in northeastern New Jersey. It is the county seat of Essex County, situated 14 km/9 mi.

west of New York City. Population: 258,751 (1994). **2.** city in Alameda County, western California, east of San Francisco. Population: 37,861 (1990). **3.** city in northern Delaware, in New Castle County, situated 19 km/12 mi. southwest of Wilmington. Population: 25,098 (1990).

Newark-on-Trent historic market town in central England, in Nottinghamshire, on an arm of the River Trent. Population: 35,129 (1991).

new arrival *n.* **1. MOST RECENT ARRIVAL** sb who or sth that is the latest to arrive ○ *She's a new arrival at the firm.* **2. BABY** a recently born baby (*informal*) ○ *I hear there's been a new arrival in the family.*

New Bedford city and port in southeastern Massachusetts, on Buzzards Bay, southeast of Taunton. It was a major whaling centre during the 1800s. Population: 96,903 (1996).

newbie /nyoóbi/, **Newbie** *n.* a new user of on-line computer services, especially the Internet ○ *most users welcome newbies*

new blood *n.* a person or group bringing fresh ideas and enthusiasm to a place, situation, or organization

newborn /nyoó bawrn/ *adj.* **1. BORN RECENTLY** born very recently **2. NEWLY DISCOVERED OR RECOVERED** recently discovered or recovered afresh ○ *newborn faith* ■ *n.* **NEW BABY** a newborn child

New Britain **1.** the largest island in Papua New Guinea, and in the Bismarck Archipelago. It is divided into two districts: East New Britain and West New Britain. Population: 311,955 (1990). Area: 36,520 sq. km/14,100 sq. mi. **2.** city in Hartford County, central Connecticut, situated 14 km/9 mi. southwest of the city of Hartford. Population: 75,491 (1990).

new broom *n.* sb who has recently arrived in a place or organization and is keen to make improvements [From the phrase *new brooms sweep clean*]

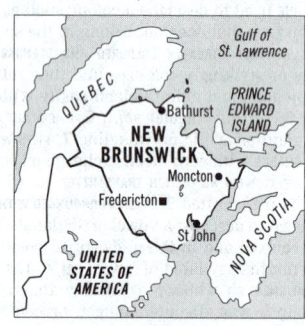

New Brunswick

New Brunswick region in eastern Canada, the largest of the Maritime Provinces. Capital: Fredericton. Population: 738,133 (1996). Area: 73,440 sq. km/28,355 sq. mi.

Newburg /nyoó burg/ *adj.* cooked and served with a rich sauce of cream, butter, sherry, and egg yolks ○ *lobster Newburg* [Early 20thC. Origin unknown.]

Newbury /nyoóbəri/ town in southern England, in Berkshire. Population: 33,273 (1991).

New Caledonia island and overseas territory of France in the southwestern Pacific Ocean, east of Australia. Capital: Nouméa. Population: 183,200 (1994). Area: 19,103 sq. km/7,374 sq. mi.

Newcastle /nyoó kaassəl/ city in eastern New South Wales, southeastern Australia, located at the mouth of the Hunter River. Population: 427,703 (1991).

Newcastle /nyoó kaass'l/, **Thomas Pelham-Holles, 1st Duke of** (1693–1768) British statesman. He was Whig prime minister of Great Britain (1754–56 and 1757–62). His second ministry was a coalition with William Pitt the Elder. Born **Thomas Pelham**

Newcastle disease *n.* a highly infectious viral disease that affects poultry and other birds, attacking the lungs and nervous system [Early 20thC. Named after NEWCASTLE UPON TYNE, where it was first recorded.]

Newcastle upon Tyne /nyoó kaassəl ə pon tín/ city and port on the River Tyne, northeastern England. It is situated at one end of Hadrian's Wall, and the Romans built a bridge over the river there. Population: 283,600 (1994).

Newcombe /nyoókəm/, **John** (*b.* 1944) Australian tennis player. He was singles champion at Wimbledon in 1967, 1970, and 1971. Full name **John David Newcombe**

Newcomen /nyoó kumən/, **Thomas** (1663–1729) English inventor. He developed a steam engine that was used for pumping water from coal mines throughout Europe and North America.

newcomer /nyoó kummər/ *n.* sb who has recently arrived in a place, situation, or organization, or sth that has recently appeared or been introduced

New Country *n.* a form of country-and-western music, originating in the 1980s, that typically features bland lyrics and smooth arrangements and is designed to appeal to an urban audience

New Deal *n.* **1. ROOSEVELT REFORM POLICIES** the policies of social and economic reform introduced in the United States in the 1930s under the presidency of Franklin D. Roosevelt. **2. PERIOD OF ROOSEVELT REFORMS** the period during which Franklin D. Roosevelt's policies of social and economic reform were implemented. [From the likening of the policies to a new deal in a card game] —**New Dealer** *n.*

New Delhi capital city of India, situated in the northern part of the country adjacent to Delhi. It was built between 1912 and 1929 and inaugurated as the capital in 1931. Population: 294,149 (1991).

New Economic Policy *n.* a programme implemented in the Soviet Union between 1921 and 1928 that permitted some private enterprise although the state retained overall economic control

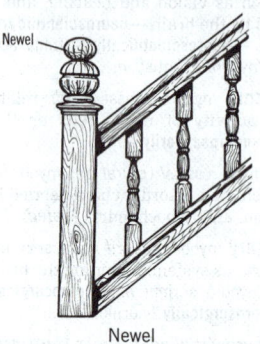

newel /nyoó əl/ *n.* **1. SUPPORT FOR STAIRCASE** a vertical pillar to which the steps of a spiral staircase are attached **2. newel, newel post** **POST FOR HANDRAIL** a post supporting the handrail of a staircase at the top or bottom or on a landing [14thC. Via French *novel* 'knob', from assumed Vulgar Latin *nodellus* 'little knot'.]

New Eng. *abbr.* New England

New England region in the northeastern United States, comprising the states of Maine, New Hampshire, Vermont, Massachusetts, Rhode Island, and Connecticut —**New Englander** *n.*

New England Range mountain range in southeastern Australia, in northeastern New South Wales. Its highest peak is Ben Lomond, 1,550 m/5,100 ft.

New English Bible *n.* a version of the Bible in modern English translated by British scholars from various denominations and published in 1970

Newf. *abbr.* Newfoundland

newfangled /nyoó fáng g'ld/ *adj.* puzzlingly or suspiciously new or novel [15thC. *-Fangled* from the past participle of Old English *fōn* 'to capture'.] —**new-fangledness** *n.*

─── **WORD KEY: SYNONYMS** ───
See Synonyms at *new*.

new-fashioned *adj.* up-to-date or modern (*informal*) [Modelled on OLD-FASHIONED]

Newfie /nyoʹofi/ n. Can sb who comes from New-foundland (*informal*) [Mid-20thC. Shortening and alteration of *Newfoundland*.]

New Forest designated area of heathland, marsh, and forest in Hampshire, southern England. Area: 580 sq. km/225 sq. mi.

New Forest pony (*plural* **New Forest ponies**) n. a hardy pony with a short neck and sturdy body belonging to a breed originating from the New Forest area of England

newfound /nyoʹo fownd/ adj. recently discovered or met

Newfoundland /nyoʹofəndlənd/ n. a large sturdy dog with a long straight back and a dense, usually black, coat, belonging to a breed formerly used in water rescues

Newfoundland

Newfoundland, Island of /nyoo fówndlənd, nyoo fəndlənd/ island in the Atlantic Ocean. Along with Labrador, it comprises the province of New-foundland. Area: 93,830 sq. km/36,900 sq. mi. —**Newfoundlander** n.

Newfoundland and Labrador the easternmost province in Canada, comprising the island of New-foundland and Labrador on the mainland. Capital: St John's. Population: 551,792 (1996). Area: 405,720 sq. km/156,649 sq. mi. —**Newfoundlander** n.

New Georgia islands in the central Solomon Islands

New Granada former Spanish colony in north-western South America that included present-day Colombia, Ecuador, Venezuela, and Panama

New Guinea the second largest island in the world, in the western Pacific Ocean, off the northern coast of Australia. It is divided between the Indonesian province of Irian Jaya in the west and Papua New Guinea in the east. Area: 808,510 sq. km/312,170 sq. mi. —**New Guinean** n., adj.

New Hampshire

New Hampshire state in the northeastern United States, bordered by Canada, Maine, the Atlantic Ocean, Massachusetts, and Vermont. Capital: Concord. Population: 1,172,709 (1997). Area: 24,043 sq. km/9,283 sq. mi.

New Harmony town in Posey County, southwestern Indiana, situated 37 km/23 mi. northwest of Evansville. The Harmony Society and Robert Owen both established utopian communities here in the 19th century. Population: 846 (1990).

Newhaven town and seaport in southeastern England, in East Sussex, with regular cross-Channel ferry services to Dieppe, France. Population: 11,208 (1991).

New Haven city in New Haven County, southern Connecticut, situated 58 km/36 mi. southwest of Hartford. Population: 119,604 (1994).

New Hebrides former name for **Vanuatu** (until 1980)

New Ireland island in the Bismarck Archipelago, northeastern Papua New Guinea, in the south-western Pacific Ocean. Population: 87,194 (1990). Area: 8,650 sq. km/3,340 sq. mi.

New Jersey

New Jersey state on the eastern coast of the United States, bordered by New York State, the Atlantic Ocean, Delaware, and Pennsylvania. Capital: Trenton. Population: 8,052,849 (1997). Area: 21,277 sq. km/8,215 sq. mi. —**New Jerseyan** n., adj. —**New Jerseyite** n.

New Kingdom n. a period in the history of ancient Egypt, from the 18th to the 20th dynasty (circa 1580 to 1090 BC)

Newlands /nyoʹoləndz/, **John** (1837–98) British chemist. By listing the elements according to atomic weight, he established the law of octaves, which led to the periodic table. Full name **John Alexander Reina Newlands**

New Latin n. the form of the Latin language used since about the beginning of the 16th century AD especially for scientific and taxonomic classification

New Left n. a political movement, chiefly among students and intellectuals in the United States and Europe during the 1960s and 1970s, that sought radical social and economic change —**New Leftist** n.

new look n. a radical change in appearance, design, or style —**new-look** adj.

New Look n. a style in women's clothes introduced in 1947 by the designer Christian Dior that featured broad shoulders, narrow waists, and long full skirts

newly /nyoʹoli/ adv. **1.** LATELY recently or lately **2.** AGAIN again or once more **3.** DIFFERENTLY in a different or novel way

newlywed /nyoʹoli wed/ n. sb who has recently been married —**newlywed** adj.

Newman /myoʹomən/, **John Henry, Cardinal** (1801–90) English theologian. After converting in 1845, he became the leading British Roman Catholic and was made a cardinal in 1879.

New Man (*plural* **New Men**) n. a late-20th-century man characterized by emotional sensitivity, recognition of women as equals, and a desire to share in domestic chores and the work associated with child rearing

Newmarket[1] /nyoʹo maarkit/ n. **1.** CARDS CARD GAME a card game in which players win by playing cards that match those already on the table. US term **Michigan 2.** CLOSE-FITTING JACKET WITH FULL SKIRT a long double-breasted close-fitting jacket with a full skirt worn in the 19th century as a riding coat or overcoat [Late 17thC. Named after NEWMARKET[2].]

Newmarket[2] /nyoʹo maarkət/ market town in Suffolk, famous for its horseracing since the early 1600s. Population: 16,498 (1991).

new maths n. a method of teaching mathematics, devised in the 1960s, in which children are introduced to elementary set theory at an early stage

New Mexico

New Mexico state in the southwestern United States, bordered by Colorado, Oklahoma, Texas, Mexico, and Arizona. Capital: Santa Fe. Population: 1,729,751 (1997). Area: 314,937 sq. km/121,598 sq. mi. —**New Mexican** n., adj.

new money n. recently acquired wealth or people who have it ○ *It's largely new money that's buying this kind of property these days.*

new moon n. **1.** MOON AS NARROW CRESCENT the Moon at the beginning of its cycle, when it is invisible from Earth or when only a narrow crescent on the right-hand side of its surface is visible **2.** MOON PERIOD the period during which there is a new moon **3.** PHASE OF MOON one of the four phases of the Moon, during which it is directly between Earth and the Sun and invisible or seen only as a narrow crescent

New Netherland Dutch colony in North America between 1613 and 1664, when it was conquered by the English and divided into the states of New York and New Jersey

New Orleans /nyoo áwrleenz, -áwrlinz/ city in south-eastern Louisiana, on the eastern bank of the Mississippi River. The largest city in the state, it is known for its annual Mardi Gras festival. Population: 476,625 (1996).

New Plymouth city in New Zealand, on the south-western coast of the North Island. It is a centre for dairy farming and oil and gas production. Population: 48,871 (1996).

Newport /nyoʹo pawrt/ **1.** town on the River Usk in southeastern Wales. Population: 137,200 (1996). **2.** town in southern England. It is the county town of the Isle of Wight. Population: 25,033 (1991). **3.** city in southeastern Rhode Island State, on Rhode Island itself, connected to the mainland by bridges. Population: 24,295 (1996).

Newquay /nyoʹo kee/ town and seaside resort in Cornwall, England. Population: 17,390 (1991).

New Quebec district in northern and eastern Quebec, Canada. Area: 777,000 sq. km/300,000 sq. mi.

New Right n. a conservative political movement that arose in the United States during the late 1960s and affirmed a commitment to established religion, patriotism and smaller, less interventionist government

Newry /nyoʹori/ town and port in Newry and Mourne District, County Down, Northern Ireland. Population: 22,975 (1991).

Newry and Mourne /nyoʹori ənd mawrn/ local government district in Northern Ireland, in counties Armagh and Down. Population: 83,500 (1995).

news /nyooz/ n. **1.** RECENT INFORMATION information about recent events or developments ○ *I phoned the hospital, and the news is good.* **2.** CURRENT EVENTS information about current events printed in newspapers or broadcast by the media ○ *She has been in the news a lot lately.* **3.** PROGRAMME a radio or television broadcast presenting the important events or developments that have taken place on a particular day ○ *I heard about it on the radio news.* **4.** SB OR STH INTERESTING sb or sth considered as being of interest to people in general ○ *The reporters considered that the Royal Family were always news.* **5.** STH PREVIOUSLY UNKNOWN sth previously unknown to sb that he or she is surprised to hear about [15thC. Plural of NEW.]

news agency *n.* an organization that gathers information about current events and supplies it to the media

newsagent /nyoʻoz ayjənt/ *n.* sb who keeps a shop or stall selling newspapers and magazines, often together with confectionery, tobacco, and other items. US term **newsdealer**

newsboy /nyoʻoz boy/ *n.* a boy who sells newspapers in the street or delivers them to houses

newscast /nyoʻoz kaast/ *n.* a television or radio broadcast consisting of news

newscaster /nyoʻoz kaastər/ *n.* sb who reads or presents the news on a television or radio broadcast

news conference *n.* = **press conference**

news desk *n.* an area of a newspaper office or a radio or television studio where news is prepared for publication or broadcasting

news flash *n.* a brief item of urgent news, often broadcast at short notice interrupting a scheduled programme

newsgirl /nyoʻoz gurl/ *n.* a girl who sells newspapers in the street or delivers them to houses

newsgroup /nyoʻoz groop/ *n.* a discussion group maintained on a computer network such as the Internet in which people leave messages on topics of mutual interest for other participants to read

newshawk /nyoʻoz hawk/, **newshound** /nyoʻoz hownd/ *n.* US, Can a newspaper reporter (*informal*)

New Siberian Islands island group in northeastern Russia, in the Arctic Ocean, between the Laptev Sea and the East Siberian Sea. The islands are uninhabited apart from the workers on research stations in the area. Area: 38,000 sq. km/14,700 sq. mi.

newsletter /nyoʻoz letər/ *n.* a printed report or letter containing news of interest to a particular group, e.g. the members of a society or employees of an organization, and circulated to them periodically

news magazine *n. US* **1.** PRESS WEEKLY NEWS MAGAZINE a magazine, usually published weekly, containing news and news analysis from the preceding week **2.** BROADCAST WEEKLY RADIO OR TV PROGRAMME a weekly radio or television programme of interviews, investigative reportage, features, and commentary on the news

newsman /nyoʻozmən, -man/ (*plural* -**men** /-mən, -men/) *n.* a man journalist or broadcaster who reports news

newsmonger /nyoʻoz mung gər/ *n.* sb who gathers and spreads gossip —**newsmongering** *n.*

New South Wales state in southeastern Australia. Capital: Sydney. Population: 6,204,000 (1996). Area: 801,600 sq. km/309,500 sq. mi.

newspaper /nyoʻoss paypər, nyoʻoz-/ *n.* **1.** PRINTED ACCOUNT OF NEWS a publication, usually appearing daily or weekly, containing news and comment on current events, together with features and advertisements, and printed on large sheets of paper that are folded together **2.** ORGANIZATION an organization that produces a newspaper **3.** PAPER FROM A NEWSPAPER a sheet or sheets of the printed paper from a newspaper when used for a purpose other than reading

newspaperman /nyoʻoss paypər man, nyoʻoz-/ (*plural* -**men** /-men, -/) *n.* **1.** MAN NEWS JOURNALIST a man who writes or edits for a newspaper ○ *Although he eventually built up a global media empire he remained a newspaperman at heart.* **2.** NEWSPAPER OWNER a man who owns or publishes a newspaper

newspaperwoman /nyoʻoss paypər wŏomən, nyoʻoz-/ (*plural* -**en** /-wimin, -/) *n.* **1.** WOMAN NEWS JOURNALIST a woman who writes or edits for a newspaper **2.** WOMAN NEWSPAPER OWNER a woman who owns or publishes a newspaper

newspeak /nyoʻo speek/ *n.* language that is ambiguous and designed to conceal the truth, especially that sometimes used by bureaucrats and propagandists ○ *She said that to call sacking workers 'rationalization' was typical of modern newspeak.* [Named with reference to the propagandist language given official recognition in *Nineteen Eighty-Four*, by British novelist George Orwell, 1949]

newsperson /nyoʻoz purss'n/ (*plural* -**persons** *or* -**people** /-peep'l/) *n. US* a journalist or broadcaster who reports news

newsprint /nyoʻoz print/ *n.* a relatively cheap and low-quality paper made from recycled materials or wood pulp and used for printing newspapers

newsreader /nyoʻoz reedər/ *n.* sb who reads the news on a television or radio broadcast. US term **anchor**

newsreel /nyoʻoz reel/ *n.* a short cinema film about recent news events, formerly often shown before a feature film

news release *n.* = **press release**

newsroom /nyoʻoz room, -rŏom/ *n.* a room in a radio or television studio or newspaper office where news is prepared for publication or broadcasting

news service *n.* = **news agency**

newssheet /nyoʻoz sheet/ *n.* = **newsletter**

newsstand /nyoʻoz stand/ *n.* a stall or booth where newspapers and magazines are sold

New Style *n.* the reckoning of dates by the Gregorian calendar, in use since 1582

newsvendor /nyoʻoz vendər/ *n. UK, Can* sb who sells newspapers

newswoman /nyoʻoz wŏomən/ (*plural* -**en** /-wimin/) *n.* a woman journalist or broadcaster who reports news

newsworthy /nyoʻoz wurthi/ (-**thier**, -**thiest**) *adj.* interesting or important enough to be reported in the media —**newsworthily** *adv.* —**newsworthiness** *n.*

newsy /nyoʻozi/ (-**ier**, -**iest**) *adj.* filled with news and gossip —**newsily** *adv.* —**newsiness** *n.*

Newt

newt /nyoot/ *n.* a small amphibian of the salamander family with short legs and a well-developed tail. Family: Salamandridae. [15thC. From the mistaken division of *an ewte*, *ewte* being a variant of Middle English *evete* 'eft'.]

——————— **WORD KEY: REGIONAL NOTE** ———————
Newts were originally *ewts* or *efts*, a name they retain in many British dialects. The opening *n*- is the result of 'an ewt' being interpreted incorrectly as 'a newt'. The reverse phenomenon occurred when 'a norange' (from Spanish *naranja*) became 'an orange' and 'a napron' (from Old French *naperon*) became 'an apron'.

New Territories former region of Hong Kong that was leased to Great Britain by China

New Testament *n.* the second section of the Christian Bible dealing with the life and teachings of Jesus Christ, containing the Gospels, the Acts of the Apostles, the Epistles, and the Book of Revelations

newton /nyoʻot'n/ *n.* an SI unit of force equivalent to the force that produces an acceleration of one metre per second on a mass of one kilogram. Symbol **N** [Early 20thC. Named after Sir Isaac NEWTON.]

Newton /nyoʻot'n/, **Sir Isaac** (1642–1727) English scientist. He discovered gravitation, invented calculus, and formulated the laws of motion. He recognized that white light is a mixture of coloured lights, and wrote *Mathematical Principles of Natural Philosophy* (1687) and *Opticks* (1704).

Newtonian /nyoo tŏni ən/ *adj.* relating to, involving, derived from, or typical of the work and theories of Sir Isaac Newton ○ *Newtonian physics*

Newtonian telescope *n.* a type of reflecting telescope in which mirrors transfer an image to an eyepiece in the side of the telescope's body

Newton-John /nyoʻot'n jón/, **Olivia** (*b.* 1948) Australian singer and actor. She has starred in several films including *Grease* (1978).

Newton's cradle /nyoʻot'nz-/ *n.* a toy consisting of five metal balls hanging side by side in a frame. Swinging one ball transmits force along the line so the other end ball swings away. [Named after Sir Isaac NEWTON]

Newton's rings *n.* a pattern of light interference created by the contact of a convex lens with a glass plate, appearing as a series of alternating bright and dark rings [Named after Sir Isaac NEWTON, who discovered the pattern]

new town *n.* a complete self-contained town with all the usual facilities, created with government funding on an open site, usually to accommodate excess population from existing urban areas

Newtown /nyoʻo town/ new town on the River Severn in Powys, Wales. It was designated in 1967. Population: 10,548 (1991).

Newtownabbey /nyoʻotən ábbi/ town in northeastern Northern Ireland, in CountyAntrim. Population: 57,103 (1991).

Newtownards /nyoʻotənərdz/ industrial town in County Down, Northern Ireland, at the head of Strangford Lough. Population: 8,737 (1991).

new towns term for towns built in one phase by the United Kingdom government, mostly during the period 1946–69, to resettle city dwellers. There are 32 of them, mostly based on existing towns or villages.

Newtown St Boswells /nyoʻo town sənt bózwelz/ town in Roxburghshire, Scotland. It is the administrative headquarters of Scottish Borders Council. Population: 1,102 (1991).

new university *n.* one of the former British polytechnics or colleges of higher education designated as a university in the 1990s

new wave *n.* **1.** ARTS INNOVATIVE ARTS MOVEMENT any new and innovative movement in the arts **2.** MUSIC POST-PUNK ROCK MUSIC rock music made in the late 1970s after the punk rock era **3.** CINEMA FORM OF FRENCH CINEMA a form of film-making originating in France during the 1950s that emphasized spontaneity, unconventionality, and the individual styles of directors

New World *n.* North and South America as considered by Europeans following Columbus's discovery of the Americas (*dated*) ▷ **Old World**

new year *n.* the year following the current year, especially the early part of it ○ *We hoped that things would be better in the new year.*

New Year *n.* the first day or first few days of a calendar year

New Year's Day *n.* 1 January, the first day of the year in the Gregorian calendar, widely celebrated as a public holiday

New Year's Eve *n.* 31 December, the last day of the year in the Gregorian calendar, or the evening of 31 December

New Year's resolution *n.* a decision to do or stop doing sth, made or announced at the New Year, which is traditionally considered a time for a fresh start

New York 1. New York, New York City city and major

New York

port in southeastern New York State. It is the most populous city in the United States. It comprises Manhattan, Bronx, Brooklyn, Queens, and Staten Island boroughs. Population: 7,380,906 (1996). **2.** state in the eastern United States, bordering the Atlantic Ocean, New Jersey, Pennsylvania, Ontario and Quebec in Canada, Vermont, Massachusetts, and Connecticut. Capital: Albany. Population: 18,137,226 (1997). Area: 139,831 sq. km/53,989 sq. mi. —**New Yorker** n.

New York Bay inlet of the Atlantic Ocean situated at the mouth of the Hudson River, in southeastern New York State

New York English n. a variety of English spoken in New York

———— WORD KEY: WORLD ENGLISH ————

New York English is the English language as used in New York City, whose idiom has been influenced by waves of immigration, especially from Central Europe (notably Jewish and Italian immigrants) and from Latin America (notably Puerto Rican immigrants). Local pronunciation is largely 'non-rhotic' (that is, 'r' is not pronounced in such words as *art*, *door*, and *worker*). There is a distinctive 'o'-sound in such words as *coffee* ('kawfee') and *ought* ('awght'). Although 'broad New York' tends to have low prestige in the United States (including among its own speakers), its everyday usage has had a marked influence nationwide and abroad, notably in Yiddish-derived words like *bagel*, *chutzpah*, *klutz*, *maven*, *s(c)hmaltz*, and *s(c)hlock*, and the humorously or ironically dismissive repeated element *s(c)h-* as in 'fancy-s(c)hmancy' (too fancy to be acceptable). New York English is also called New Yorkese.

new zaire (*plural* **new zaire** *or* **new zaires**) n. = zaire

New Zealand /nyoo zeéland/ country in the southwestern Pacific Ocean, consisting of two large islands, the North Island and the South Island, and numerous smaller islands. Its Maori name is Aotearoa, meaning 'Land of the Long White Cloud'. Language: English. Currency: New Zealand dollar.

Capital: Wellington. Population: 3,681,546 (1996). Area: 270,534 sq. km/104,454 sq. mi. —**New Zealander** n.

New Zealand English n. a variety of English spoken in New Zealand

———— WORD KEY: WORLD ENGLISH ————

New Zealand English is the English language as it has been used in New Zealand for over 200 years. It has much in common with Australian English, but differs from it in co-existing with, and influencing and being influenced by, Maori and other Polynesian languages. Some phoneticians identify three varieties of pronunciation: (1) Cultivated New Zealand, similar to Received Pronunciation in the UK; (2) Broad New Zealand, with low prestige; (3) General New Zealand, occupying the social middle ground. New Zealand English is predominantly 'non-rhotic' (that is, 'r' is not pronounced in words such as *art*, *door*, and *worker*). Distinctive pronunciations include the vowels in words like *ham* and *pen*, and a short *i* in a phrase like 'fish and chips', these being heard by outsiders as 'hem', 'pin', and 'fush and chups', respectively. In addition, final *y* as in *city* and *tidy*, may be lengthened, becoming 'citee' and 'tidee'. There is little distinctiveness in grammar, but New Zealand English vocabulary has three special features, the first being adoptions from Maori – e.g., *Pakeha* (a European, also a common name for caucasian New Zealanders generally), *haere mai* (a term of greeting), *hongi* (to press noses, the Maori greeting), *kiwi* (a flightless bird unique to New Zealand and by extension a New Zealander), and *rahui* (a sign warning against trespass). The second major vocabulary feature involves words shared with and borrowed from Australia, such as *larrikin* for *hooligan*, *ocker* for *boor*, *shanghai* for *catapult*, and *truckie* for *truck-driver*. Compare AUSTRALIAN ENGLISH.

New Zealand Time n. the standard time in the time zone with an eastern border of 180° longitude (**the International Date Line**), that includes New Zealand. It is twelve hours later than universal time.

New Zealand

New Zild /nyoó zíld/ n. NZ New Zealand or New Zealand English (*humorous slang*)

next /nekst/ CORE MEANING: a grammatical word indicating that sth is close to sth else, e.g. in space or time ○ (adj) *He lives next door to me.* ○ (adj) *When I returned, my next patient was waiting.* ○ (adv) *Which patient do you want to see next?*

1. *adj., adv.* IMMEDIATELY FOLLOWING following immediately after the present or previous one ○ (adj) *Our next meeting is on April 2nd.* ○ (adv) *Are you wondering what to do next?* **2.** *det.* THE ONE AFTER THIS ONE the day, month, or year following this one ○ *The case is scheduled for trial next month.* ○ *There is no way of predicting whether this might happen next year or in 300 years.* **3.** *adj.* ADJOINING the one that is nearest ○ *My colleague in the next office called.* **4.** *adj.* CLOSEST TO closest to in degree ○ *It's 40 times heavier than the next heaviest quark.* [Old English *nēhsta*, literally 'most near', from a prehistoric Germanic word meaning 'near', which is also the ancestor of English *nigh*] ◇ **next to 1.** adjacent to or beside sth or sb ○ *Come and sit next to me.* **2.** closest to, in comparison with sth else ○ *Cleanliness, he said, was next to godliness.* **3.** almost, but not completely (*used with a negative*) ○ *I have spent many days trying to figure out a good alternative, and it's next to impossible.*

next door *adv.* **1.** IN NEXT HOUSE OR ROOM in or into the house or room next to the one sb is in ○ *Go next door and see if their phone's working.* **2.** VERY CLOSE a very short distance away ■ *adj.* IMMEDIATELY ADJACENT situated immediately beside or very close to the one sb is in or at, or living in the adjoining house or flat (*hyphenated when used before a noun*) ◇ **next door to** almost, or virtually the same thing as

next friend n. sb who acts for a person who is not legally allowed to act independently, e.g. a child

next of kin n. sb's nearest relative or relatives

nexus /néksəss/ (*plural* **-us** *or* **-uses**) n. **1.** CONNECTION a connection or link associating two or more people or things **2.** CONNECTED GROUP a group or series of connected individuals or things **3.** CENTRE the centre or focus of sth **4.** BIOL SPECIALIZED PART OF CELL MEMBRANE a specialized area of the cellular membrane that helps cells to communicate or adhere [Mid-17thC. Formed from Latin *nex-*, past participle stem of *nectere* 'to bind'.]

———— WORD KEY: ORIGIN ————

The Latin word *nectere*, from which **nexus** is derived, is also the source of English *connect*.

Nez Percé /nez púrss, -páir say/ (*plural* **Nez Percés** *or* **Nez Percé**) n. **1.** PEOPLES MEMBER OF NATIVE N AMERICAN PEOPLE a member of a Native North American people that originally occupied lands along the Snake River, and whose members now live mainly in western Idaho and northeastern Washington state **2.** LANG NATIVE N AMERICAN LANGUAGE a Native North American language, spoken in parts of Idaho and Washington, belonging to the Sahaptin-Chinook branch of Penutian languages. Nez Percé is spoken by about 5,000 people. [From French, literally 'pierced nose']

NF abbr. **1.** National Front **2.** Newfoundland **3.** **NF, N/F** BANKING no funds **4.** LANG Norman French

N/F abbr. no funds

NFER abbr. National Foundation for Educational Research

NFL abbr. US National Football League

Nfld abbr. Newfoundland

NFS abbr. **1.** National Fire Service **2.** network file service **3.** network file system **4.** not for sale

NFT abbr. National Film Theatre

NFU abbr. National Farmers' Union

NFWI abbr. National Federation of Women's Institutes

ng abbr. NG no good

ngaio /ní ō/ (*plural* **ngaios**) n. a small New Zealand evergreen tree with white wood and leaves dotted with oil glands. Latin name: *Myoporum laetum*. [Mid-19thC. From Maori.]

Ngata /náatə, 'ng gáatə/, **Sir Apirana Turupa** (1874–1950) New Zealand Maori leader and politician. He did much to promote Maori culture and welfare, and was minister of native affairs (1928–34).

Ngo Dinh Diem /'ng gố din deém/ (1901–63) South Vietnamese statesman. During his presidency (1955–63), communist insurgence from North Vietnam became frequent and disruptive. He was assassinated in a coup.

ngultrum /əng goŏltrəm/ *n.* **1.** BHUTANESE CURRENCY UNIT the main unit of currency in Bhutan. See table at **currency 2.** COIN OR NOTE WORTH A NGULTRUM a coin or note worth one ngultrum [Late 20thC. From Tibetan.]

ngwee /əng gwáy/ (*plural* **ngwee**) *n.* **1.** MINOR UNIT OF ZAMBIAN CURRENCY a minor currency unit of Zambia. See table at **currency 2.** COIN WORTH ONE NGWEE a coin worth a ngwee, 100 of which are worth one kwacha [Mid-20thC. From Bantu.]

NH, N.H. *abbr.* New Hampshire

NHI *abbr.* National Health Insurance

NHS *abbr.* National Health Service

Ni *symbol.* nickel

NI *abbr.* **1.** National Insurance **2.** Northern Ireland **3.** *NZ* North Island

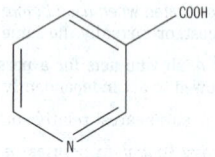

Niacin

niacin /ní əssin/ *n.* a vitamin of the B complex, found in wheat, meat, and dairy products, and used to prevent and treat pellagra. Formula: $C_6H_5NO_2$. [Mid-20thC. Coined from NICOTINE + ACID + -IN.]

niacinamide /ní ə sínnə mīd/ *n.* a compound of the vitamin B complex that is an amide of niacin and is important in the human diet. Formula: $C_6H_6N_2O$.

Niagara /nī ággərə/ river in east-central North America, in New York State and Ontario, flowing between Lake Erie and Lake Ontario via the Niagara Falls. Length: 55 km/34 mi.

Niagara Falls

Niagara Falls two waterfalls in North America, on the United States-Canada border, on the Niagara River. Height: 49 m/161 ft and 51 m/167 ft.

Niamey /nyaa máy/ capital city of Niger, situated on the River Niger in the southwestern part of the country. Population: 495,000 (1995).

Niarchos /ni áark oss/, **Stavros Spyros** (1909–96) Greek ship owner. He was a pioneer in the construction of super-tankers and the owner of a large independent fleet.

nib /nib/ *n.* **1.** METAL WRITING TIP OF PEN a shaped detachable metal tip on the end of a pen such as a fountain pen, by means of which the ink is transferred to the paper **2.** SHARP POINT a sharp point or tip, especially the sharpened end of a quill pen **3.** BIRDS BEAK a bird's beak [Late 16thC. Originally a Scottish variant of Old English *nebb* 'beak, bill', from a prehistoric Germanic word meaning 'beak'.]

nibble /níbb'l/ *v.* (**-bles, -bling, -bled**) **1.** *vti.* TAKE SMALL QUICK BITES to take a series of small quick bites at sth, or eat sth in a series of small quick bites ○ *She nibbled an apple while she read.* **2.** *vti.* EAT STH DAINTILY OR CAUTIOUSLY to take dainty, cautious, or reluctant little bites of sth or eat sth in this way taking a very small amount at a time ○ *The mouse had nibbled the cheese.* **3.** *vti.* BITE PLAYFULLY AND CARESSINGLY to take gentle playful little bites at part of sb's body as a form of caress ○ *The lion cubs nibbled at each other playfully.* **4.** *vi.* REDUCE GRADUALLY to reduce or wear away sth gradually by taking a small amount at a time ○ *These day-to-day expenses nibble away at our funds.* **5.** *vi.* SHOW MILD INTEREST to show a tentative interest in sth ○ *Lower the price a little and the buyers will start to nibble.* ■ *n.* **1.** ACT OF NIBBLING a series of small quick or gentle bites at sth **2.** TINY AMOUNT OF FOOD a tiny amount of some type of food (*informal*) **3.** EXPRESSION OF MILD INTEREST an expression of tentative interest ○ *I've been trying to make a sale all day but not a nibble so far.* ■ **nibbles** *npl.* SMALL THINGS TO EAT small pieces of food intended as appetizers, snacks, or party food, e.g. nuts or canapés ○ *Help yourself to some nibbles while I put away your coat.* [Early 16thC. Origin uncertain: perhaps from Low German *nibbeln* 'to nibble, gnaw'.] —**nibbler** *n.*

Nibelung /neébəloŏng/ *n.* in German mythology, a member of a race of dwarfs who owned a hoard of treasure that was captured by the heroic prince Siegfried [Mid-19thC. From German.]

niblick /níbblik/ *n.* a golf club that has a short iron head with a steeply sloping face, used to give extra lift, e.g. when playing out of a bunker (*dated*) [Mid-19thC. Origin unknown.]

nibs /nibz/ *n.* used as a kind of mock title when referring to an important or self-important person (*informal*) ○ *His nibs will doubtless be expecting the red carpet treatment.* [Early 19thC. Origin unknown.]

Nic. *abbr.* Nicaragua

nicad /ní kad/, **nicad battery** *n.* a dry cell battery with electrodes of nickel and cadmium in an alkaline electrolyte [Mid-20thC. From NICKEL + CADMIUM.]

Nicaea /nī seé ə/ ancient city in Asia Minor, in present-day Turkey, which flourished under the Romans

Nicaragua

Nicaragua /ní kə rággyoŏ ə/ republic and largest nation in Central America, situated between the North Pacific Ocean and the Caribbean Sea. Language: Spanish. Currency: córdoba. Capital: Managua. Population: 4,272,000 (1996). Area: 131,812 sq. km/50,893 sq. mi. Official name **Republic of Nicaragua** —**Nicaraguan** *n.*, *adj.*

niccolite /níkə līt/ *n.* a copper-coloured mineral that is a source of nickel. Formula: NiAs. [Mid-19thC. Formed from modern Latin *niccolum* 'nickel'.]

nice /nīss/ (**nicer, nicest**) *adj.* **1.** PLEASANT pleasant or enjoyable **2.** KIND kind, or showing courtesy, friendliness, or consideration ○ *It was a nice gesture to return the money.* **3.** RESPECTABLE respectable, or of an

acceptable social or moral standard ○ *She's made some nice friends at work.* **4.** GOOD-LOOKING good-looking or pleasing to look at ○ *What a nice hat you're wearing!* **5.** ACCOMPLISHED skilful and accomplished **6.** SUBTLE subtle and involving delicacy or fine discrimination **7.** FASTIDIOUS AND FUSSY very concerned and careful about choosing, or being seen to do, the right thing ○ *You can't be too nice about your methods if you want to get the job done.* [13thC. Via Old French from, ultimately, Latin *nescius* 'ignorant'. The meanings 'minutely discriminating' and 'pleasant' developed by way of 'shy', 'fastidious', and 'refined'.] —**nicely** *adv.* —**niceness** *n.* ◇ **nice and** sufficiently or pleasingly ○ *It's nice and warm by the fire.*

Nicene creed /ní seen-/ *n.* a formal statement of Christian beliefs formulated at the first Nicene Council, held in Nicaea in AD 325, subsequently altered and expanded, and still in use in most Christian churches

nice-nelly *adj.* *US* **1.** PRUDISH prudish or excessively modest **2.** FULL OF EUPHEMISMS using or including a great many euphemisms (*disapproving*) [From the name *Nelly*] —**nice-nellyism** *n.*

nicety /níssəti/ (*plural* **-ties**) *n.* **1.** REFINEMENT OR DETAIL a subtle distinction or point, or a small detail, especially of proper procedure or social etiquette (*often used in the plural*) **2.** REFINED FEATURE a feature that makes sth particularly refined and pleasurable (*often used in the plural*) **3.** SUBTLETY a subtle, delicate, or fastidious quality, especially in sb's feelings or taste **4.** PRECISION the ability to be precise and accurate and make fine distinctions ○ *the nicety of his powers of judgment* ◇ **to a nicety** with great precision or exactness

niche /neesh, nich/ *n.* **1.** ARCHIT WALL RECESS a recess in a wall, especially one made to hold a statue **2.** GEOL RECESS IN ROCK any recess or hollow, such as in a rock formation **3.** SUITABLE PLACE FOR SB a position or activity that particularly suits sb's talents and personality or that sb can make his or her own ○ *She carved out her own niche in the industry.* **4.** COMM SPECIALIZED MARKET an area of the market specializing in a particular type of product ○ *designed to undercut the competition in the same niche* ○ *'Thanks to the Internet, small niche companies can reach mass markets in a heartbeat.'* (*Forbes Global Business and Finance*; November 1998) **5.** ECOL PLACE IN NATURE the role of an organism within its natural environment that determines its relations with other organisms and ensures its survival ■ *vt.* (**niches, niching, niched**) PUT STH IN NICHE to place sth in a niche [Early 17thC. Via Old French *nichier* 'to build a nest, nestle', from Latin *nidus* 'nest' (see NEST).]

Nicholas I /níkələss/, **Tsar of Russia** (1796–1855). Tsar from 1825, his attempts to take Constantinople led to the Crimean War (1853–56).

Nicholas II, Tsar of Russia (1868–1918). The last tsar of Russia (1894–1917), he was overthrown in the Russian Revolution and executed with his family.

Nicholas of Cusa /níkələss əv kyoŏzə/ (1401–64) German cardinal and scholar. He opposed Scholasticism, suggested a reform of the calendar, and posited a theory on the rotation of the earth.

Nicholson /ník'lssən/, **Ben** (1894–1982) English painter and sculptor. After experimenting with cubism, he evolved a more personal abstract style.

nick /nik/ *n.* **1.** NOTCH a small V-shaped cut or indentation in an edge or surface **2.** SMALL CUT a small cut on the skin **3.** PRINTING GROOVE ON TYPE a groove on the side of a piece of metal printing type, used to identify and orient it **4.** POLICE STATION a police station (*slang*) **5.** PRISON prison (*slang*) ○ *He spent ten years in the nick.* **6.** CONDITION the particular condition of sth or sb (*slang*) ○ *What kind of nick is your motor in?* ■ *vt.* (**nicks, nicking, nicked**) **1.** NOTCH OR CUT SLIGHTLY to make a notch, indentation, or small cut in sth ○ *The scythe blade had been nicked by a stone.* **2.** STEAL STH to steal sth (*slang*) ○ *Somebody's nicked my bike.* **3.** ARREST SB to place sb under arrest (*slang*) ○ *A copper's job is to nick villains.* **4.** *US* CHEAT to cheat or defraud sb (*slang*) **5.** VET INCISE HORSE'S TAIL to make a cut in the tendons at the root of a horse's tail to make the tail stick up [15thC. Origin uncertain.] ◇ **in the nick of time** at the critical or last possible moment

nickel /ník'l/ *n.* **1.** SILVERY WHITE METALLIC ELEMENT a hard silvery-white metallic element that is resistant to corrosion and used in alloys, batteries, electroplating, and as a catalyst. Symbol **Ni 2.** *US, Can* FIVE-CENT COIN a coin worth five cents ■ *vt.* (**-ells, -elling, -elled**) COAT STH WITH NICKEL to plate sth with nickel [Mid-18thC. Shortening of German *Kupfernickel* 'copper nickel': 'nickel' from *nickel* 'mischievous demon', because the ore yielded no copper.]

nickel-and-dime *adj. US* **1.** LOW-PAID paying or involving only a small amount of money (*slang*) **2.** MINOR small-scale or of little importance (*informal*) ■ *vt.* (**nickel-and-dimes, nickel-and-diming, nickel-and-dimed**) *US* **1.** IMPOVERISH THROUGH SMALL EXPENSES to get sb or sth into financial trouble by accumulating many small costs and expenses (*slang*) **2.** BOTHER SB IN MANY SMALL WAYS to hinder or harass sb with trivialities and insignificant matters

nickel-cadmium battery *n.* = nicad battery

nickelic /ni kéllik/ *adj.* containing nickel, especially nickel with a valency of three

nickeliferous /níkə líffərəss/ *adj.* containing or yielding nickel

nickelodeon /níkə lódi ən/ *n. US* **1.** EARLY JUKEBOX an early variety of coin-operated jukebox **2.** FIVE-CENT CINEMA an early 20th-century cinema, charging five cents for admission **3.** COIN-OPERATED PLAYER PIANO an early variety of player piano operated by inserting coins [Early 20thC. From NICKEL + shortening of MELODEON.]

nickelous /níkələss/ *adj.* containing nickel, especially nickel with a valency of two

nickel plate *n.* a thin coating of nickel applied to sth, usually by electrolysis —**nickel-plated** *adj.* —**nickel-plating** *n.*

nickel silver *n.* a hard durable white alloy of copper, zinc, and nickel, used, e.g. in making cutlery and wire

nicker[1] /níkər/ (**-ers, -ering, -ered**) *vi.* to make a soft neighing sound ○ *The pony nickered and shook its head.* [Late 16thC. An imitation of the sound.] —**nicker** *n.*

nicker[2] /níkər/ (*plural* **-er**) *n.* a pound sterling (*slang*) [Early 20thC. Origin unknown.]

Jack Nicklaus

Nicklaus /ník lowss/, **Jack** (*b.* 1940) US golfer. He dominated professional golf in the 1960s and 1970s, winning a record 20 championship titles. Known as **Golden Bear**. Full name **Jack William Nicklaus**

nick-nack *n.* = knick-knack

nickname /ník naym/ *n.* **1.** INVENTED NAME an invented name for sb or sth, used humorously or affectionately instead of the real name and usually based on a conspicuous characteristic of the person or thing involved **2.** SHORT NAME a shortened or altered form of a name, such as 'Billy' for 'William' or 'Peggy' for 'Margaret' ■ *vt.* (**-names, -naming, -named**) CALL BY NICKNAME to give a nickname to sb or sth ○ *They nicknamed him 'Spuds' because of his fondness for potatoes.* [15thC. Mistaken division of *an eke name* 'an additional name'.] —**nicknamer** *n.*

Nicobar Islands /níkə baar-/ southern part of the Indian union territory of the Andaman and Nicobar Islands, situated between the Bay of Bengal and the Andaman Sea. The Nicobar Islands consist of 19

islands. Population: 39,022 (1991). Area: 1,841 sq. km/711 sq. mi.

Nicosia /níkə see ə/ capital city of Cyprus, situated on the Pedhieos River in the northern part of the island. In 1974 it was partitioned into Turkish and Greek Cypriot sectors. Population: 228,215 (1994).

nicotiana /ni kóshi áanə, níkəti áanə/ (*plural* **-as** or **-a**) *n.* a perennial or annual flowering plant with fragrant white, yellow, or purple flowers, of a genus that includes the tobacco plant and belongs to the nightshade family. Genus: *Nicotiana*. [Early 17thC. Named after French courtier Jacques *Nicot* (1530–1604), ambassador to Lisbon, who introduced tobacco to France.]

nicotinamide /níkə tínnə mīd/ *n.* = niacinamide

nicotinamide adenine dinucleotide *n.* full form of NAD

nicotinamide adenine dinucleotide phosphate *n.* full form of NADP

nicotine /níkə teen/ *n.* **1.** POISONOUS ALKALOID a toxic alkaloid found in tobacco and also used in liquid form as an insecticide. Formula: $C_{10}H_{14}N_2$. **2.** TOBACCO tobacco products, or the smoking of them (*informal*) [Early 19thC. Shortening of NICOTIANA + chemical suffix -INE.] —**nicotinic** /níkə tínnik/ *adj.*

nicotine gum *n.* chewing gum containing nicotine, used as a substitute for tobacco by people who are trying to give up smoking

nicotine patch *n.* a small patch that when placed on the skin releases nicotine directly into the bloodstream, used by people who are trying to give up smoking

nicotinic acid /níkə tínnik-/ *n.* = niacin

nicotinism /níkə tee nizəm/ *n.* poisoning caused by an excessive intake of nicotine through smoking

nictitate /níkti tayt/ (**-tates, -tating, -tated**), **nictate** /nik táyt, níkt ayt/ (**-tates, -tating, -tated**) *vti.* to blink or wink (*technical*) [Early 19thC. Ultimately from medieval Latin *nictitat-*, past participle stem of *nictitare*, literally 'to wink repeatedly', from Latin *nictare* 'to wink'.] —**nictation** *n.* —**nictitation** /níkti táysh'n/ *n.*

nictitating membrane /níkti tayting-/ *n.* a thin transparent layer of skin underneath the eyelid that can cover the eye surface of birds, reptiles, and some mammals to moisten and protect it

NIDA /nídə/, **Nida** *abbr. Aus* National Institute of the Dramatic Arts

Nidderdale /níddər dayl/ region in northern England, in West Yorkshire, in the valley of the River Nidd, designated as an Area of Outstanding Natural Beauty. Area: 603 sq. km/233 sq. mi.

nide /nīd/ *n.* a brood of pheasants or a pheasant's nest [Late 17thC. Via French *nid*, from Latin *nidus* 'nest'.]

nidi plural of nidus

nidicolous /ni díkələss/ *adj.* used to describe young birds that remain in the nest for some time after hatching [Early 20thC. Literally 'frequenting a nest', formed from Latin *nidus* 'nest'.]

nidificate *vi.* = nidify [Early 19thC. From the Latin stem *nidificat-*, past participle stem of *nidificare* (see NIDIFY).]

nidifugous /ni díffyoŏgəss/ *adj.* used to describe young birds that leave the nest a short time after hatching [Early 20thC. Formed from Latin *nidus* 'nest' (see NEST) + *fugere* 'to flee'.]

nidify /níddi fī/ (**-fies, -fying, -fied**), **nidificate** /níddifi kayt/ (**-cates, -cating, -cated**) *vi.* to build a nest [Mid-17thC. From Latin *nidificare* 'to build a nest', from *nidus* 'nest' (see NEST).] —**nidification** /níddifi káysh'n/ *n.*

nidus /nídəss/ (*plural* **-duses** or **-di** /nī dī/) *n.* **1.** ZOOL SPIDER OR INSECT NEST a nest in which spiders or insects deposit eggs **2.** MED FOCUS OF INFECTION a site in the body at which an infection develops **3.** BOT SPORE-DEVELOPING PLANT PART a place in a plant where its spores develop [Early 18thC. From Latin, 'nest' (see NEST).]

niece /neess/ *n.* a daughter of sb's brother, brother-in-law, sister, or sister-in-law [13thC. Via Old French, from Latin *neptis* 'granddaughter, niece'. Ultimately from an Indo-European base that is also the ancestor of English *nephew* and *nepotism*.]

niello /ni éllō/ *n.* (*plural* **-li** /-élli/ or **-los**) **1.** BLACK ALLOY USED AS INLAY a deep black alloy of sulphur and silver,

lead, or copper, used to fill lines inlaid as decoration on a metal surface **2.** USE OF NIELLO the process of using niello to decorate a metal surface **3.** STH DECORATED WITH NIELLO sth decorated with niello as an inlay ■ *vt.* (**-los, -loing, -loed**) DECORATE STH WITH NIELLO to decorate sth using niello as an inlay [Early 19thC. Via Italian from Latin *nigellus* 'blackish', diminutive of *niger* 'black'.] —**niellist** *n.*

nielsbohrium /neelz báwri əm/ *n.* an artificially produced radioactive chemical element with the atomic number 105 [Late 20thC. Named in honour of *Niels Bohr* (1885–1962), Danish physicist.]

AKG London

Friedrich Wilhelm Nietzsche

Nietzsche /neétshə/, **Friedrich Wilhelm** (1844–1900) German philosopher. Author of *Thus Spake Zarathustra* (1883–85) and one of the most influential thinkers of the 19th century, he founded his philosophy on the will-to-power and rejected religion. —**Nietzschean** *n., adj.* —**Nietzscheanism** *n.*

nieve /neev/ *n. Scotland* a fist [13thC. From Old Norse *hnefi*, of unknown origin.]

nifedipine /nī féddi peen/ *n.* a drug that stops the heart muscles from taking up calcium and is used to treat high blood pressure and angina pectoris. Formula: $C_{17}H_{18}N_2O_6$. [Late 20thC. Coined from NITRO- + *fe* (shortening and alteration of PHENYL) + DI- 'twice' + *pine* (contraction of PYRIDINE).]

niff /nif/ *n.* UNPLEASANT SMELL an unpleasant smell or odour (*slang*) ■ *vi.* (**niffs, niffing, niffed**) SMELL UNPLEASANT to have an unpleasant or strong smell (*slang*) [Early 20thC. Origin uncertain: perhaps a shortening of SNIFF.] —**niffiness** *n.* —**niffy** *adj.*

nifty /níftī/ (**-tier, -tiest**) *adj.* (*informal*) **1.** AGILE good, quick, and clever at doing sth or using sth **2.** STYLISH AND GOOD-LOOKING fashionable and good-looking **3.** VERY GOOD very good or effective [Mid-19thC. Origin unknown.] —**niftily** *adv.* —**niftiness** *n.*

Nig. *abbr.* **1.** Nigeria **2.** Nigerian

nigella /nī jéllə/ *n.* a flowering plant of the buttercup family native to the Mediterranean region and western Asia, with white, blue, or yellow flowers. Love-in-a-mist is the best-known variety. Genus: *Nigella*. [14thC. From modern Latin, genus name, feminine of *nigellus* 'small black (thing)' (see NIELLO).]

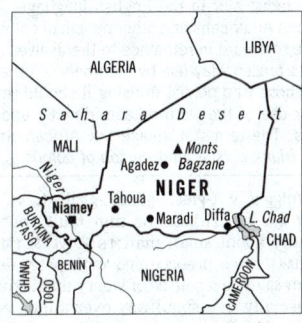

Niger

Niger[1] /nījər/ republic in northwestern Africa, north of Nigeria and south of Libya. Language: French. Currency: CFA franc. Capital: Niamey. Population: 9,465,000 (1996). Area: 1,267,000 sq. km/489,191 sq. mi. Official name **Republic of Niger**

Niger[2] /nījər/ river in northern West Africa. The third longest river in Africa, it rises in southern Guinea, and flows northwards through Mali, then southwest into the Gulf of Guinea, through Niger and Nigeria. Length: 4,180 km/2,600 mi.

Niger-Congo *n.* a family of over one thousand languages spoken in central and southern parts of Africa, the major branches of which are Adamawa-Eastern, Benue-Congo, Gur, Kwa, Mande, and West Atlantic. Well over 200 million people speak one of the Niger-Congo languages. —**Niger-Congo** *adj.*

Nigeria /nī jeˈeri ə/ republic in western Africa, on the Gulf of Guinea, south of Niger. Language: English. Currency: kobo. Capital: Abuja. Population: 103,912,000 (1996). Area: 923,773 sq. km/356,669 sq. mi. Official name **Federal Republic of Nigeria** —**Nigerian** *n., adj.*

Nigerian English *n.* a variety of English spoken in Nigeria

---WORD KEY: WORLD ENGLISH---

Nigerian English is the English language as it has been used in the region of the Niger, West Africa, for purposes of trade since at least the 18th century, at missions since the 19th century, and increasingly in education, administration, the media, and the 20th-century workplace, especially since the formation by the British of a unified Nigeria in 1914. The existence of a single Nigerian English continues to be debated and disputed within the country, in which there is a spectrum of usage from West African Pidgin English through varieties influenced by local languages such as Hausa, Igbo, and Yoruba, to a standardizing general usage similar to other English-speaking West African countries. All varieties are 'non-rhotic' (that is, 'r' is not pronounced in such words as *art*, *door*, and *worker*). There is a tendency towards full vowels in all syllables (e.g. *7* pronounced *seh-ven*, not *sevn*). There is often no distinction between words like *chip* and *cheap* and ones like *caught*, *cot*, and *court*. In grammar, there is a tendency towards countability in nouns (as in *I gave them some advices*) and the reflexive pronoun *themselves* is often used instead of *one another* (as in *That couple really love themselves*). Distinctive vocabulary includes borrowings and loan translations from local languages, such as *danshiki* from *Hausa* ('a gown worn by men') and *to throw water* ('to offer a bribe'). See AFRICAN ENGLISH.

niggard /níggərd/ *n.* sb who is stingy or miserly [14thC. Alteration of *nigon*, of uncertain origin: possibly formed from *nig* 'stingy', from Scandinavian.]

niggardly /níggərdli/ *adj.* (**-lier, -liest**) **1.** NOT GENEROUS very reluctant to give or spend anything **2.** SMALL OR INADEQUATE very small or inadequate in quantity ■ *adv.* IN A STINGY WAY in a miserly or stingy way — **niggardliness** *n.*

nigger /níggər/ *n.* (*taboo*) **1.** TABOO OFFENSIVE TERM a highly offensive taboo term for a Black person **2.** TABOO OFFENSIVE TERM a highly offensive taboo term for a dark-skinned person [Late 17thC. Via Spanish *negro* from Latin *niger* 'black'.]

---WORD KEY: USAGE---

Racism trap : This term is arguably the single most offensive racist slur in the English language. The fact that African Americans and other people of colour sometimes use this word in reference to themselves does not excuse its present-day use by members of other ethnic groups. Those who persist in using it should remember that their use of the word reflects directly upon them, the users. The terms of choice are *African American*, *Black* or *Black person*, and *person of colour*.

niggle /nígˈl/ *v.* (**-gles, -gling, -gled**) **1.** *vi.* CRITICIZE IN PETTY WAY to criticize or find fault continually, especially about small matters **2.** *vi.* BE PREOCCUPIED WITH DETAILS to be preoccupied with petty details **3.** *vt.* WORRY SB to be a source of worry and irritation to sb, especially in a small way over a long period of time ■ *n.* UK, Can **1.** PETTY CRITICISM a petty or carping criticism ○ *Once we have a broad agreement, we can sort out these niggles.* **2.** NAGGING WORRY a small but continuing source of annoyance or worry [Early 17thC. Origin uncertain: possibly from Scandinavian.] — **niggler** *n.*

niggling /nígling/ *adj.* **1.** TOO PREOCCUPIED WITH DETAIL petty or too preoccupied with details **2.** IRRITATING irritating, painful, or worrying, especially in a small but persistent way —**niggling** *n.* —**nigglingly** *adv.*

nigh /nī/ *adv., adj.* NEAR near in place or time (*literary*) ○ (adv) *Daybreak drew nigh.* ○ (adj) *Morning was nigh.* ■ *adv.* ALMOST nearly ○ *We talked for nigh on two hours.* [Old English *nēah*, from a prehistoric Germanic word that is also the ancestor of English *near* and *next*]

night /nīt/ *n.* **1.** DAILY PERIOD OF DARKNESS the period of darkness occurring each day in most parts of the world, or the entire period between sunset and sunrise **2.** TIME BETWEEN BEDTIME AND WAKING the time between sb's going to sleep in the evening and waking the next morning **3.** PERIOD OF EVENING ACTIVITIES the period between sunset and bedtime, especially when spent in entertainment or some other activity ○ *We had a great night at her birthday party.* **4.** **night, Night** EVENING DEVOTED TO SPECIAL ACTIVITY any period after sunset devoted to a special activity, function, or observance ○ *Tomorrow night is Burns Night.* **5.** NIGHTFALL the period of time just after the sun goes down, when it gets dark **6.** DARK OR DARKENED STATE a dark or darkened state, or an absence of light, consciousness, or enlightenment (*literary*) **7.** SAD OR BAD PERIOD a period marked by grief, gloom, ignorance, or obscurity ○ *Europe slipped into the long night of the Dark Ages.* ■ *adj.* **1.** OCCURRING AT NIGHT occurring, appearing, or visible at night ○ *night terrors* **2.** USED AT NIGHT used chiefly at night ○ *Use the night entrance.* **3.** WORKING AT NIGHT working at night in a job also done during the day ○ *the night porter* **4.** ACTIVE AT NIGHT awake or active at night ○ *night feeders* ■ *interj.* GOODNIGHT goodnight (*informal*) [Old English *niht*. Ultimately from an Indo-European word that is also the ancestor of English *nocturnal* and *equinox*.]

night blindness *n.* an inability to see clearly in dim light while having normal vision in clear light. Technical name **nyctalopia** —**night-blind** *adj.*

night-blooming cereus *n.* a cactus whose large fragrant flowers open at night. Genera: *Hylocereus, Peniocereus, Nyctocereus, Selenicereus.*

nightcap /nít kap/ *n.* **1.** BEVERAGES DRINK BEFORE SLEEP a drink, often alcoholic, taken before going to bed **2.** CLOTHES CAP USED AS NIGHTWEAR a soft cap worn in bed to keep the head warm, in use mainly until the late 19th century **3.** US SPORTS LAST EVENT the last event of a day of sports, especially the second game of a baseball double-header

nightclothes /nít klōthz/ *npl.* any clothes designed to be worn in bed

nightclub /nít klub/ *n.* a place of entertainment open late at night, offering music, dancing, and drinks, and sometimes serving food and providing a floor show

nightclubbing /nít klubing/ *n.* = **clubbing** *n.* 1

night depository *n.* US = **night safe**

nightdress /nít dress/ *n.* a loose dress of light material worn in bed by women and girls. US term **nightgown**

nightfall /nít fawl/ *n.* the time of evening at which it becomes dark and night begins ○ *Be home by nightfall.*

night fighter *n.* a fighter aircraft designed to fly at night

nightglow /nít glō/ *n.* a dim light from the upper atmosphere seen at night

nightgown /nít gown/ *n.* **1.** = **nightdress 2.** = **nightshirt**

nighthawk /nít hawk/ *n.* **1.** INSECT-FEEDING NIGHTJAR a North American nightjar that feeds on flying insects after dark and has long pointed wings and black, white, and buff plumage. Genus: *Chordeiles.* **2.** = **night owl** (*informal*)

night heron *n.* a stocky heron with short legs and a thick bill that is active at night or twilight. Genus: *Nycticorax.*

nightie /níti/, **nighty** (*plural* **-ies**) *n.* a nightdress (*informal*) [Late 19thC. Shortening and alteration.]

nightingale /níting gayl/ *n.* a migratory songbird of the thrush family with brownish plumage. The male is known for its melodious song, especially noticeable at night during the breeding season. Latin name: *Luscinia megarhynchos.* [13thC. Alteration of Old English *nihtegala*, from a prehistoric Germanic compound meaning 'night-singer', from the ancestors of English *night* and *yell*.]

Nightingale

---WORD KEY: CULTURAL NOTE---

Ode to a Nightingale, a poem (1819) by John Keats. The poet recounts how on hearing the joyful song of the nightingale he is filled with an intense joy that provides an escape from his woes. But, as he considers the fact that the bird's song has been an inspiration throughout history, the sound fades and he is suddenly returned to reality.

AKG London

Florence Nightingale

Nightingale /níting gayl/, **Florence** (1820–1910) British nurse. She worked in the Crimean War, becoming known as 'The Lady with the Lamp'. Later she founded the Nightingale School of Nurses at St Thomas's Hospital, London.

nightjar /nít jaar/ *n.* a bird with a short bill, large gaping mouth, and dark plumage that is active at night and twilight and feeds on insects caught in flight. Family: Caprimulgidae. [*Jar* from JAR² with the sense 'quivering sound']

night latch *n.* a door lock operated from inside by a knob and from outside by a key

nightlife /nít līf/ *n.* the entertainment or social life that goes on in a place in the evenings ○ *Let's go out and check out the local nightlife.*

nightlight /nít līt/ *n.* a small lamp or candle lit to give a dim light during the night, especially in a child's bedroom

nightlong /nít lóng/ *adj.* lasting or occurring throughout the entire night —**nightlong** *adv.*

nightly /nítli/ *adj.* **1.** OCCURRING AT NIGHT typically occurring at night **2.** HAPPENING EVERY NIGHT taking place every night ■ *adv.* EVERY NIGHT on or during each and every night ○ *The band is playing nightly this week.*

nightmare /nít mair/ *n.* **1.** BAD DREAM a frightening or upsetting dream **2.** TRAUMATIC EXPERIENCE a traumatic, very upsetting, or extremely difficult and troublesome experience or situation **3.** DREADED EVENT a situation or event that sb particularly fears **4.** PARANORMAL EVIL SPIRIT a malign spirit formerly believed to suffocate or haunt people during sleep ■ *adj.* EXTREMELY FRIGHTENING OR DIFFICULT extremely frightening, upsetting, or difficult to deal with [13thC. Literally 'night goblin'; *mare* from Old English, from prehistoric Germanic.] —**nightmarish** *adj.* —**nightmarishly** *adv.*

night owl *n.* sb who stays up late at night, especially to work or socialize (*informal*)

nightrider /nít rīdər/ *n.* a member of a group of masked horsemen who at night terrorized or intimidated African Americans and their sympathizers in the southern United States in the period after the Civil War

nights /nīts/ *adv.* during the night or every night ○ *They work nights.*

night safe *n.* a safe in the wall of a bank that can be opened from outside to allow people to deposit money at times that the bank is closed. US term **night depository**

night school *n.* a school or college that holds classes in the evening, especially for people who are at work during the day

nightscope /nít skōp/ *n.* an optical device, e.g. using infrared radiation, that gives better vision in the dark ○ *The police surveillance team used a nightscope after dark.*

nightshade /nít shayd/ *n.* a wild plant, related to potatoes, tomatoes, and aubergines, with flowers that have five petals, and small berries. Some are poisonous, e.g. deadly nightshade. Family: Solanaceae. [Said to be so called with reference to its poisonous properties]

nightshirt /nít shurt/ *n.* a long loose shirt-like garment worn in bed by men

nightside /nít sīd/ *n.* the side of a planet or moon that is not lit by the sun

night sight *n.* an infrared sight on a rifle used for taking aim in darkness

night soil *n.* human excrement collected at night from toilets or cesspools, especially for use as fertilizer

nightspot /nít spot/ *n.* = **nightclub**

nightstick /nít stik/ *n. US* a club carried by a police officer [*Night* because the club was traditionally carried especially at night]

night table *n. US, Can* a bedside table or stand

night terror *n.* a sudden awakening from sleep in a condition of extreme fear that is not associated with a dream or nightmare

nighttime /nít tīm/ *n.* the period of each day when it is dark, or the time between sunset and sunrise

night vision *n.* sb's ability to see in the dark ○ *They say eating carrots improves your night vision.*

night watch *n.* **1.** GUARD KEPT AT NIGHT a guard or watch kept during the night ○ *I'm on night watch this week.* **2.** = **night watchman** *n.* 1

night watchman *n.* **1.** SB GUARDING AT NIGHT sb who keeps watch over or guards a building or a place such as a building site or factory at night **2.** CRICKET LOWER-ORDER BATSMAN PLAYING OUT TIME a lower-order batsman who is sent in out of order if a wicket falls near the end of a day's play, to play defensively and prevent the loss of another more important wicket

nightwear /nít wair/ *n.* clothes for people to wear while sleeping. US term **sleepwear**

nighty *n.* = **nightie**

nigrescence /nī gréss'nss/ *n.* the process of becoming black or dark (*formal*) [Mid-19thC. Formed from Latin *nigrescent-*, present participle stem of *nigrescere* 'to grow black', from *niger* 'black'.] —**nigrescent** *adj.* —**nigrescently** /-s'ntli/ *adv.*

nigrosine /nígrə seen, -sin/, **nigrosin** /-sin/ *n.* a black aniline pigment or dye used in making ink and polish and in dyeing textiles [Late 19thC. Coined from Latin *niger* 'black' (see NEGRO) + -OSE + -INE.]

NIHE *abbr.* National Institute for Higher Education

nihilism /ní i lizəm, nîhi-/ *n.* **1.** TOTAL REJECTION OF SOCIAL MORES the general rejection of established social conventions and beliefs, especially of morality and religion **2.** BELIEF THAT NOTHING IS WORTHWHILE a belief that life is pointless and human values are worthless **3.** DISBELIEF IN OBJECTIVE TRUTH the belief that there is no objective basis for truth **4.** BELIEF IN DESTRUCTION OF AUTHORITY the belief that all established authority is corrupt and must be destroyed in order to rebuild a just society [Early 19thC. From German *Nihilismus*, from Latin *nihil* 'nothing'.] —**nihilist** *n.* —**nihilistic** /ní i lístik, nîhi-/ *adj.* —**nihilistically** *adv.*

Nihilism *n.* a political movement in late 19th-century Russia that sought to bring about a just new society by destroying the existing one through acts of terrorism and assassination

nihility /nī hílləti, nee-/ *n.* the condition of being nothing [Late 17thC. From medieval Latin *nihilitas*, from Latin *nihil* 'nothing'.]

nihil obstat /nîhil ób stat, nîhil-/ *n.* **1.** CHR LACK OF OBJECTION TO PUBLICATION a statement by a Roman Catholic Church official that a publication is not offensive to religion or morals **2.** STATEMENT OF NONOPPOSITION any official statement of nonopposition [Mid-20thC. From Latin, literally 'nothing hinders'.]

NII *abbr.* Nuclear Installations Inspectorate

Niigata /nyi ə ga̅ata̅/ city and port in Japan, on northern Honshu. It is the capital city of Niigata Prefecture. Population: 486,097 (1990).

Vaslav Nijinsky: Performing in *Le Spectre de la Rose* (1911)

Nijinsky /ni jínski/, **Vaslav** (1890–1950) Russian ballet dancer. The leading dancer of the original Ballets Russes, he choreographed several innovative ballets, such as *The Rite of Spring* (1913).

-nik *suffix.* sb associated with or characterized by ○ *peacenik* [Directly and via Yiddish from Russian]

Nikko /neékō/ city in Japan, in Tochigi Prefecture, central Honshu, 145 km/90 mi. north of Tokyo. Population: 20,128 (1990).

nil /nil/ *n.* nothing or zero , often used in the scores of games or to indicate that sth is nonexistent or at the lowest possible level ○ *Our team won two-nil.* [Early 19thC. Contraction of Latin *nihil* 'nothing'.]

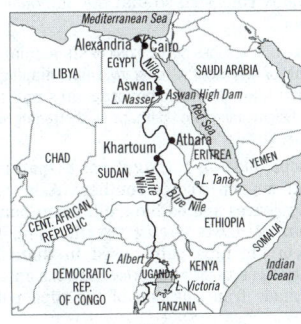

Nile

Nile /nīl/ river in northeastern Africa. It is the longest river in the world. Rising in east-central Africa near Lake Victoria, it flows 5,584 km/3,470 mi. northwards through Uganda, Sudan, and Egypt before emptying into the Mediterranean Sea.

Nile blue *adj.* of a pale greenish-blue colour —**Nile blue** *n.*

Nile green *adj.* of a yellowish-green colour —**Nile green** *n.*

nilgai /níl gī/ (*plural* **-gai** *or* **-gais**), **nilgau** /-gaw/ (*plural* **-gau** *or* **-gaus**), **nilghau** (*plural* **-ghau** *or* **-ghaus**) *n.* a large antelope of India, the male of which is bluish-grey and horned, the female brownish and hornless. Latin name: *Boselaphus tragocamelus*. [Late 18thC. From Hindi *nīlgāe*, from Sanskrit *nīla* 'blue' + -*gāvī* 'cow'.]

Nilo-Saharan /nīlō-/ *n.* a family of around 100 languages spoken in some central parts of Africa, the major branches of which are Chari-Nile, Nilotic,

and Saharan. About 15 million people speak one of the Nilo-Saharan languages. —**Nilo-Saharan** *adj.*

Nilotic /nī lóttik/ *adj.* **1.** RELATING TO THE NILE relating to, involving, or living beside the River Nile **2.** OF NILOTIC PEOPLE OR LANGUAGE relating to a Nilotic people or language ■ *n.* NILE VALLEY LANGUAGE GROUP a group of languages spoken in parts of the Nile valley, mainly in Uganda and Sudan and forming a branch of the Nilo-Saharan family of languages. About three million people speak a Nilotic language. [Mid-17thC. Formed from Greek *Neilos* 'Nile'.]

nim /nim/ *n.* a game in which players remove small, differently arranged items from piles, the winner being the player who takes, or sometimes does not take, the final item [Early 20thC. Origin uncertain, perhaps from German *nimm*, imperative form of *nehmen* 'to take'.]

nimble /nímb'l/ (**-bler**, **-blest**) *adj.* **1.** FAST AND AGILE agile, fast, and light in movement **2.** QUICK-THINKING able to think quickly and cleverly [Alteration (modelled on BRAMBLE and THIMBLE) of Old English *n_æmel* and *numol* 'quick at grasping', from *niman* 'to take'] —**nimbleness** *n.* —**nimbly** *adv.*

nimbostratus /nímbō stráytəss, -stra̅atəss/ (*plural* **-ti** /-tī/) *n.* a low dark layer of rain-bearing cloud covering all of the sky. ◊ *stratus* [Late 19thC. See NIMBUS.]

nimbus /nímbəss/ (*plural* **-buses** *or* **-bi** /-bī/) *n.* **1.** METEOROL DARK RAIN-BEARING CLOUD a dense, dark rain-bearing cloud **2.** RELIG CLOUD OF LIGHT AROUND DEITY a cloud of light believed to surround a god or goddess while on earth or a saint or holy person **3.** PAINTING IMAGE OF HALO a bright halo or disc around the head of a deity, saint, or sovereign in a painting, icon, or medal **4.** AURA OF SPLENDOUR an aura or atmosphere of splendour surrounding sb or sth [Early 17thC. From Latin, 'cloud, rain, corona'.] —**nimbused** *adj.*

NIMBY /nímbi/ (*plural* **-BYs**), **Nimby** (*plural* **-bys**) *n.* **1.** SB OBJECTING TO LOCATION OF STH sb who objects to sth unpleasant or dangerous being located near his or her home but is perfectly happy to see it located elsewhere (*informal*) **2.** NIMBY ATTITUDE the attitude of a NIMBY [Late 20thC. Acronym from *not in my backyard.*] —**nimbyism** *n.*

nimiety /ni mí əti/ (*plural* **-ties**) *n.* an excess or overabundance of sth (*formal*) [Mid-16thC. Formed from Latin *nimis* 'too much'.]

niminy-piminy /nímməni pímməni/ (**niminy-piminier**, **niminy-piminiest**), **miminy-piminy** /mímməni-/ (**miminy-piminier**, **miminy-piminiest**) *adj.* affected and mincing [Late 18thC. Whimsical formation based on NAMBY-PAMBY.]

nimrod /ním rod/ *n.* any skilful or enthusiastic hunter (*literary*) [Mid-16thC. From the tradition of *Nimrod* as a 'mighty hunter' (Genesis 10:9).]

Anaïs Nin

Nin /nin/, **Anaïs** (1903–77) French writer. She is best known for her passionate and self-revelatory *Journals* (1966–83).

nincompoop /níngkəm poop/ *n.* an offensive term that deliberately insults sb's intelligence or competence (*informal insult*) [Late 17thC. Alteration of *nicompoop*, of uncertain origin, possibly from French *nicodême* 'simpleton' + *poop* with sense 'clown'.] —**nincompoopery** *n.* —**nincompoopish** *adj.*

nine /nīn/ *n.* **1.** NUMBER 9 the cardinal number 9 **2.** STH WITH VALUE OF 9 sth in a numbered series, e.g. a playing card, with a value of 9 ○ *a nine of clubs* ○ *to play the nine* **3.** GROUP OF NINE a group of nine objects or people

4. BASEBALL **BASEBALL TEAM** a team of nine baseball players **5.** GOLF **HALF OF GOLF COURSE** half of the total number of holes on a golf course, usually specified as the front nine or the back nine [Old English *nigon.* Ultimately from an Indo-European word.] —**nine** *adj.* —**nine** *pron.* ◇ **dressed (up) to the nines** very elaborately or formally dressed

ninebark /nīn baark/ *n.* a shrub of the rose family native to eastern North America with bark that separates into many layers. Genus: *Physocarpus.*

nine days' wonder, **nine day wonder** *n.* sth that, or sb who, briefly arouses great interest or excitement but is soon forgotten again [Named with reference to Lady Jane Grey (1537–54), who was proclaimed Queen of England in 1553 but was deposed after only nine days and subsequently beheaded]

ninefold /nīn fōld/ *adj.* **1. BY NINE TIMES** of nine times the original figure ○ *a ninefold rise* **2. WITH NINE PARTS** made up of nine parts ○ *The problem is ninefold.* ■ *adv.* **BY NINE TIMES AS MUCH** by nine times as much or as many ○ *The numbers increased ninefold.*

ninepin /nīn pin/ *n. US* = **skittle**

ninepins *n.* = **skittles**

nineteen /nīn te͞en/ *n.* **1. NUMBER 19** the cardinal number 19 **2. STH WITH VALUE OF 19** sth in a numbered series with a value of 19 **3. GROUP OF 19** a group of 19 objects or people [Old English *nigontȳne*, from a prehistoric Germanic compound meaning 'nine-ten'] —**nineteen** *adj.* —**nineteen** *pron.*

nineteenth /nīn te͞enth/ *n.* one of 19 equal parts of sth ○ *My share came to three-nineteenths.* —**nineteenth** *adj.* —**nineteenth** *pron.*

nineteenth hole *n.* a place, especially the bar of a clubhouse, where players can drink and socialize after a round of golf (*slang*) [Named as the hole after the conventional 18 holes on a golf course]

nineteenth man *n.* in an Australian Rules football team, the first of two substitutes that can be used during a regular match

ninetieth /nīnti əth/ *n.* one of 90 equal parts of sth ○ *a ninetieth of the whole* —**ninetieth** *adj.* —**ninetieth** *pron.*

nine-to-five *adj.* requiring regular attendance, e.g. at an office job, especially between 9 a.m. and 5 p.m. (*informal*) ○ *without the self-discipline to hold down a nine-to-five job*

nine-to-fiver *n. US* sb who works regular hours, especially from 9 a.m. to 5 p.m. (*informal*) ○ *She took the morning train with the rest of the nine-to-fivers.*

ninety /nīnti/ *n.* (*plural* **-ties**) **NUMBER 90** the cardinal number 90 ■ *npl.* **1. nineties NUMBERS BETWEEN 90 AND 99** the numbers between 90 and 99, particularly as a range of Fahrenheit temperature **2. YEARS 90 TO 99** the years in a century from 90 to 99 **3. PERIOD FROM AGE 90 TO 99** the period of sb's life from the age of 90 to 99 —**ninety** *adj.* —**ninety** *pron.*

Nineveh /nínnəvə/ ancient capital of the Assyrian Empire, situated on the River Tigris in northern Iraq. At the height of its importance from about 705 BC, it was destroyed by the Babylonians and Medes in 612 BC.

Ningbo /ning bṓ/ city in northeastern Zhejiang Province, eastern China, situated approximately 145 km/90 mi. southeast of Hangzhou. Population: 552,540 (1990).

Ninian /nínni ən/, **St** (360?–432?) Scottish bishop and missionary. He was the earliest known Christian missionary in Scotland.

ninja /nínjə/ (*plural* **-jas** *or* **-ja**) *n.* a member of a group of mercenaries in feudal Japan who were trained in stealth and the martial arts and employed as spies, saboteurs, or assassins [Mid-20thC. From Japanese, 'spy'.]

ninjitsu /nin jít soo/ *n.* a Japanese martial art that emphasizes stealth in movement and camouflage [Mid-20thC. From Japanese, literally 'stealth art'.]

ninny /nínni/ (*plural* **-nies**) *n.* an offensive term that deliberately insults sb's intelligence, common sense, or effectiveness (*informal insult*) [Late 16thC. Origin uncertain, perhaps from a misdivision and shortening of *an inno(cent).*] —**ninnyish** *adj.*

ninon /ne͞e non, nī-/ *n.* a sturdy sheer fabric made of silk or synthetic material [Early 20thC. From French.]

ninth /nīnth/ *n.* **1. ONE OF 9 PARTS** one of 9 equal parts of sth ○ *A ninth of the total is still a considerable sum.* **2.** MUSIC **MUSICAL TONE OR INTERVAL** a musical tone separated from another by an interval of an octave and a second, or the interval of this tone —**ninth** *adj.* —**ninth** *pron.*

ninth chord *n.* a musical chord containing four thirds, including the ninth, added above the root

niobic /nī ṓbik/ *adj.* concerning or containing niobium with a valency of five

niobite /nī ə bīt/ *n.* = **columbite**

niobium /nī ṓbi əm/ *n.* a lustrous light grey ductile metallic chemical element, a superconductor that resembles tantalum chemically and is used in steel alloys. Symbol **Nb** [Mid-19thC. From the association of the element with tantalum, *Tantalus* being the father of *Niobe.*]

niobous /nī ṓbəss/ *adj.* concerning or containing niobium with a valency less than five

nip[1] /nip/ *v.* (**nips, nipping, nipped**) **1.** *vt.* **PINCH STH** to take hold of sth and squeeze or compress it, often painfully, between two surfaces, e.g. to pinch skin between a forefinger and thumb **2.** *vti.* **TAKE BRIEF BITE AT STH** to bite sth briefly, often painfully, but without doing much damage **3.** *vt.* **SEVER STH** to remove sth by pinching, biting, or clipping ○ *She nipped off the growing point of the plant to encourage bushiness.* **4.** *vt.* **AFFECT SB WITH COLD** to sting or chill a person or part of the body painfully with cold ○ *As she struggled with the car door the frost began to nip her fingers.* **5.** *vt.* **INJURE GROWTH OF STH** to halt or destroy the growth of sth **6.** *vt.* **MAKE STH NARROWER** to make sth narrower or tighter ○ *The dress is nipped in at the waist.* **7.** *vt. US* **STEAL STH** to steal or snatch sth (*informal*) **8.** *vi.* **GO QUICKLY** to go somewhere quickly or briefly (*informal*) ○ *She nipped down to the shop for bread.* ■ *n.* **1. SHARP SQUEEZE** a sharp or painful squeeze with the fingers or between two surfaces **2. SMALL BRIEF BITE** a small bite with the teeth that may be painful but does not do much damage ○ *The dog tried to give my ankle a nip as I passed.* **3. SMALL CUT-OUT PIECE** a small piece cut from sth **4. CHILL** a chilly feeling caused by a marked drop in temperature ○ *There's a nip in the air tonight.* **5. SHARP FLAVOUR** a sharp or pungent flavour [14thC. From Middle Low German *nipen* 'to nip'.] ◇ **nip and tuck** *US* very closely and evenly contested so that the outcome remains in doubt

nip[2] /nip/ *n.* BEVERAGES **SMALL DRINK OF STH** a small portion or drink of sth alcoholic ■ *vti.* (**nips, nipping, nipped**) **SIP** to drink an alcoholic beverage in small sips [Late 18thC. Origin uncertain: perhaps a shortening of archaic *nipperkin*, literally 'small sip'.]

nipa /ne͞epə, nīpə/ *n.* **1.** (*plural* **-pas** *or* **-pa**) TREES **ASIAN PALM TREE** a palm tree of southern Asia with long feathery leaves and edible fruit. Latin name: *Nipa fruticans.* **2. LEAVES OF PALM TREE** the long feathery leaves of the nipa palm, used in thatching and basketry **3.** BEVERAGES **DRINK FROM PALM SAP** an alcoholic drink made from the sap of the nipa palm [Late 16thC. From Malay *nipah.*]

Nipigon, Lake /níppi gon/ lake in Canada, in west-central Ontario. It drains into Lake Superior via the Nipigon River. Area: 4,848 sq. km/1,872 sq. mi. Depth: 165 m/540 ft.

Nipissing, Lake /níppə sing/ lake in southeastern Ontario, Canada. It empties via the French River into Georgian Bay. Area: 832 sq. km/321 sq. mi.

nipper /níppər/ *n.* **1.** ZOOL **PINCER** a large claw of a crustacean, especially a lobster or crab **2. CHILD** a small child (*informal*) ■ **nippers** *npl.* **PLIERS** a tool, such as pliers, used to squeeze or clip sth [Mid-16thC. 'Small child' probably from an earlier sense of 'costermonger's boy', because he nipped off to run errands.]

nipping /nípping/ *adj.* **1. SHARP AND COLD** very cold and biting **2. SARCASTIC** bitingly sarcastic —**nippingly** *adv.*

nipple /nípp'l/ *n.* **1.** ANAT **TIP OF MAMMARY GLAND** a small knob in the centre of the breast that in females is the outlet for the ducts that provide young mammals with milk. In humans it is also an erogenous zone. **2.** *US* = **teat 3. SMALL OUTLET** a small knob on a device that is the outlet for fluid such as oil or grease [Mid-16thC. Origin uncertain: perhaps literally 'little neb', formed from NEB.]

nipplewort /nípp'l wurt/ (*plural* **-worts** *or* **-wort**) *n.* a European annual plant, now naturalized in eastern North America, that has small yellow flowers and a milky juice. It was once used as a herbal remedy for breast tumours. Latin name: *Lapsana communis.*

Nippon /níppon/ the Japanese name for Japan —**Nipponese** /níppə ne͞ez/ *adj.*

nippy /níppi/ (**-pier, -piest**) *adj.* **1. CHILLY** rather chilly **2. SMALL AND FAST** small, quick, and easy to manoeuvre **3. TENDING TO BITE** inclined to attempt to bite people or animals —**nippily** *adv.* —**nippiness** *n.*

NIRC *abbr.* National Industrial Relations Court

N. Ire. *abbr.* Northern Ireland

NIREX /nī reks/ *abbr.* Nuclear Industry Radioactive Waste Executive

nirvana /neer vaánə, nur-/ *n.* **1. nirvana, Nirvana** RELIG **SPIRITUAL ENLIGHTENMENT** in Hinduism, Buddhism, and Jainism, the attainment of enlightenment and freeing of the spiritual self from attachment to worldly things, ending the cycle of birth and rebirth **2. COMPLETELY ENJOYABLE EXPERIENCE** an ultimate experience of some pleasurable emotion such as harmony or joy [Mid-19thC. From Sanskrit, from *nirvā-* 'to be extinguished', from *nis-* 'out' + *vā-* 'to blow'.]

Nisan /ne͞e saan/, **Nissan** *n.* in the Jewish calendar, the seventh month of the religious year and first of the civil year. It is 30 days long and occurs around March or April.

nisi /nī sī, ne͞essi/ *adj.* scheduled to take effect on a specified date unless some cause can be shown for cancelling or changing the date [Mid-19thC. From Latin, 'unless'.]

Nissan *n.* = **Nisan**

Nissen hut /níss'n-/ *n.* a temporary shelter made of corrugated steel in the shape of a half cylinder that was first used by the British during World War I [Early 20thC. Named after its inventor Lt-Col. Peter Norman *Nissen* (1871–1930).]

nisus /níssəss/ (*plural* **-sus**) *n.* an attempt or effort to accomplish an aim or goal (*formal*) [Late 17thC. From Latin, from *niti* 'to strive'.]

nit /nit/ *n.* **1. EGG OF A LOUSE** the egg or larva of a parasitic insect, especially a louse **2. OFFENSIVE TERM** an offensive term that deliberately insults sb's common sense or intelligence (*informal insult*) [Old English *hnitu*, ultimately from Indo-European. Partly a shortening of NITWIT.] —**nitty** *adj.*

niter *n.* US = **nitre**

Niterói /nee te róy/ city and capital of Rio de Janeiro State, southeastern Brazil, situated on the south-eastern shore of Guanabara Bay, opposite the city of Rio de Janeiro. Population: 416,123 (1991).

nitpick /nít pik/ (**-picks, -picking, -picked**) *vti.* to find fault, often unjustifiably, with insignificant details of sth —**nitpicker** *n.* —**nitpicky** *adj.*

WORD KEY: SYNONYMS

See Synonyms at ***criticize.***

nitpicking /nít piking/ *n.* trivial, unnecessary, detailed, and often unjustified faultfinding

nitr- *prefix.* = **nitro-** (*used before vowels*)

nitrate /nī trayt/ *n.* **1.** CHEM **CHEMICAL RADICAL** a univalent radical or a compound such as a salt or an ester of nitric acid that contains the radical NO_3 **2.** AGRIC **FERTILIZER** a fertilizer that consists of sodium nitrate, potassium nitrate, or ammonium nitrate ■ *vt.* (**-trates, -trating, -trated**) CHEM, INDUST **USE NITRATE ON STH** to treat sth with a nitrate or nitric acid, usually in order to change an organic compound into a nitrate [Late 18thC. From French, formed from *nitre* 'nitre'.] —**nitration** /nī tráysh'n/ *n.*

nitrazepam /nī trázzi pam/ *n.* a type of tranquillizer used in some sleeping pills. Formula: $C_{15}H_{11}N_3O_3$. [Mid-20thC. Coined from NITRO + AZO- + -EPINE + AMIDE.]

nitre /nītər/ *n.* **1.** = **potassium nitrate 2.** = **sodium nitrate** [14thC. Via Old French, from Latin *nitrum*, from Greek *nitron*, of uncertain origin: perhaps from Semitic, or Egyptian *ntrj*.]

nitric /ní trik/ *adj.* made from or containing nitrogen, especially in a high valency state

nitric acid *n.* a transparent fuming corrosive colourless or yellowish liquid that is a highly reactive oxidizing agent. It has many industrial uses, including the making of explosives, fertilizers, and rocket fuels, and is also used in various metallurgical processes. Formula: HNO_3.

nitric oxide *n.* a colourless poisonous gas that is a stage in the production of nitric acid from ammonia or atmospheric nitrogen. Formula: NO.

nitride /ní trīd/ *n.* a compound made up of nitrogen and another more electropositive element such as phosphorus or a metal [Mid-19thC. Coined from NITROGEN + -IDE.]

nitrify /nítri fī/ (-**fies**, -**fying**, -**fied**) *vt.* **1.** CHEM TREAT WITH NITROGEN to treat or combine sth with nitrogen or nitrogen compounds **2.** AGRIC FERTILIZE SOIL to introduce nitrogen or nitrogen compounds into the soil in order to increase fertility **3.** BIOCHEM OXIDIZE AMMONIA ION to oxidize ammonia ions into nitrite or nitrate ions, as nitrobacteria do [Early 19thC. From French *nitrifier*, from *nitre* NITRE.] —**nitrification** /nítrifi káysh'n/ *n.* —**nitrifier** /nítri fī ər/ *n.*

nitrifying bacterium *n.* a bacterium found in the soil that converts ammonia compounds to nitrites, or nitrites to nitrates, thus making nitrogen available to plants

nitrile /nítrəl, -trīl/ *n.* an organic cyanide

nitrite /ní trīt/ *n.* a salt or ester of nitrous acid

nitro /ní trō/ *n.* nitroglycerine (*informal*) [Early 20thC. Shortening.]

nitro- *prefix.* **1.** nitrogen ○ *nitrify* **2.** nitre, nitrate ○ *nitrogen* **3.** containing a univalent NO_2 group ○ *nitroparaffin* [From Latin *nitrum* (see NITRE)]

nitrobenzene /nítrō bén zeen/ *n.* a poisonous organic compound that occurs either as bright yellow crystals or an oily liquid that smells like almonds. It is used to make polishes and insulating compounds. Formula: $C_6H_5NO_2$.

nitrocellulose /nítrō séllyoō lóss, -lōz/ *n.* a chemical compound produced by the reaction of nitric and sulphuric acids on cellulose, used in the manufacture of plastics, explosives, and lacquers. ◊ **guncotton**

nitrochloroform /nítrō klórrə fawrm/ *n.* = **chloropicrin**

nitrogen /nítrəjən/ *n.* a nonmetallic chemical element that occurs as a colourless odourless almost inert gas and makes up four-fifths of the Earth's atmosphere by volume. It is important in the making of ammonia, explosives, and fertilizers. Symbol **N** [Late 18thC. From French *nitrogène* from *nitre* NITRE and -*gène* -GEN.] —**nitrogenous** /nī trójjənəss/ *adj.*

nitrogenase /nī trójjə nayz, -nayss/ *n.* an enzyme found in nitrogen-fixing bacteria that catalyses the conversion of nitrogen to ammonia. It is a key component of the nitrogen cycle, providing nitrogen compounds for plants.

nitrogen balance *n.* **1.** PHYSIOL NITROGEN INTAKE AND EXCRETION the difference between the amount of nitrogen taken into the body and the amount excreted **2.** AGRIC NITROGEN ABSORBED AND LOST BY SOIL the difference between the amount of nitrogen absorbed by the soil and the amount lost

nitrogen cycle *n.* the series of processes by which

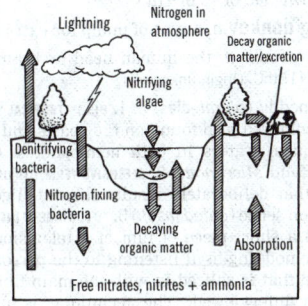

Nitrogen cycle

nitrogen is converted from a gas in the atmosphere to nitrogen-containing substances in soil and living organisms, then reconverted to a gas. The main chemical transformations are performed by microorganisms and include nitrogen fixation, nitrification, and denitrification.

nitrogen dioxide *n.* a highly poisonous brown gas used to make nitric and sulphuric acids. It is often found in smog and in the exhaust from vehicles that lack pollution control devices. Formula: NO_2.

nitrogen fixation *n.* **1.** BIOL NATURAL NITROGEN CONVERSION the conversion of atmospheric nitrogen by certain bacteria found in the nodules of legumes into compounds in the soil that plants and other organisms can use **2.** INDUST INDUSTRIAL NITROGEN CONVERSION a process in which nitrogen from the atmosphere is changed into compounds such as ammonia by either chemical or bacterial agents —**nitrogen-fixer** *n.* —**nitrogen-fixing** *adj.*

nitrogenize /nī trójjə nīz/ (-**izes**, -**izing**, -**ized**), **nitrogenise** (-**ises**, -**ising**, -**ised**) *vt.* to combine or treat sth with nitrogen or one of its compounds —**nitrogenization** /nī trójjə nī záysh'n/ *n.*

nitrogen mustard *n.* a poisonous substance similar to mustard gas but containing nitrogen instead of sulphur. Such compounds have been used to treat leukaemia and other cancers.

nitrogen narcosis *n.* light-headedness, confusion, or exhilaration caused by increased nitrogen in the blood. This occurs in deep-sea divers exposed to pressures several times that of the atmosphere.

nitroglycerine /nítrō glíssərin, -reen/, **nitroglycerin** /-rin/ *n.* a colourless thick oily flammable and explosive liquid used to manufacture explosives and in medicine to dilate veins in the treatment of angina pectoris. Formula: $C_3H_5N_3O_9$.

nitrohydrochloric acid /nítrō hídrō klórrik-/ *n.* = **aqua regia**

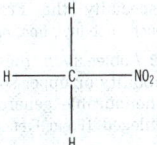

Nitromethane

nitromethane /nítrō mee-/ *n.* a poisonous colourless oily slightly water-soluble liquid used to make dyes, resins, and rocket fuels, and as a solvent and petrol additive. Formula: CH_3NO_2.

nitroparaffin /nítrō párrəfin/ *n.* a colourless simple hydrocarbon containing the chemical group NO_2

nitrosamine /nī trōzə meen/ *n.* an organic carcinogenic compound found in various foods. Formula: R_2NNO. [Late 19thC. Coined from Latin *nitrosus* 'nitrous' + AMINE.]

nitrous /nítrəss/ *adj.* made from or containing nitrogen, especially in a low valency state

nitrous acid *n.* a weak inorganic acid found only in solution or in the form of its salts. Formula: HNO_2.

nitrous oxide *n.* a colourless nonflammable sweet-smelling, sweet-tasting gas used as an anaesthetic in dentistry and surgery. Formula: N_2O.

nitty-gritty /nítti grítti/ *n.* BASICS the basic and most important details of sth (*informal*) ■ *adj.* (*informal*) **1.** BASIC AND IMPORTANT concerning or involving the most important aspects of a subject **2.** PRACTICAL useful and direct in a practical down-to-earth way ○ *a nitty-gritty approach to teaching* [Mid-20thC. Origin unknown.]

nitwit /nít wit/ *n.* sb thought to be silly or unintelligent (*insult*) [Early 20thC. Origin uncertain: perhaps from German dialect *nit* 'not' + WIT.]

Niue /nyoó ay/ island territory in free association with New Zealand. It is in the central Pacific Ocean, situated 563 km/350 mi. southeast of Samoa. Population: 2,244 (1991). Area: 260 sq. km/100 sq. mi.

nival /nív'l/ *adj.* growing in or under the snow [Mid-17thC. From Latin *nivalis*, from *niv-*, stem of *nix* 'snow'.]

Nivôse /ni vōz/ *n.* the fourth month of the year in the French Revolutionary calendar, corresponding to 22 December to 20 January in the Gregorian calendar

nix[1] /niks/ *n.* US NOTHING nothing (*dated slang*) ■ *vt.* (**nixes, nixing, nixed**) US SAY NO TO STH to refuse, forbid, or veto sth (*slang*) [Late 18thC. From German, dialectal and colloquial variant of *nichts* 'nothing'.]

nix[2] /niks/ *n.* = **nixie** [Mid-19thC. From German.]

nixie /níksi/ *n.* in German mythology, a female water spirit that can appear in human form or as half-human, half-fish [Early 19thC. From German *Nixe*, feminine of *Nix* (see NIX[2]).]

Richard Nixon

Nixon /níks'n/, **Richard Milhous** (1913–94) US statesman and 37th president of the United States. President from 1969 until 1974, he was forced to resign after the Watergate scandal (1974). He was responsible for ending the US commitment in Vietnam.

Nizhny Tagil /nízhni taa gíl/ city in western Siberian Russia, in Sverdlovsk Oblast, situated 129 km/80 mi. north of Yekaterinburg. Population: 437,000 (1992).

NJ, N.J. *abbr.* New Jersey

Nkomo /'ng kōmō/, **Joshua** (*b.* 1917) Zimbabwean statesman. He led the Zimbabwe African People's Union in the struggle against white rule, and after independence held various government posts.

Nkrumah /'n króomə, 'ng króomə/, **Kwame** (1909–72) Ghanaian statesman. He was the first prime minister (1957–60) and president (1960–66) of Ghana, and a strong supporter of pan-Africanism.

NKVD *n.* the Soviet secret police from 1934 to 1946. Full form **Narodny Kommissariat Vnutrennikh Del** [Russian, 'People's Commissariat of Internal Affairs']

nl *abbr.* PRINTING new line

NL, N.L. *abbr.* **1.** Netherlands (*international vehicle registration*) **2.** New Latin

NLF *abbr.* National Liberation Front

NLP *abbr.* **1.** neurolinguistic programming **2.** natural language processing

nm *abbr.* **1.** nanometre **2.** nautical mile **3.** nuclear magneton

NM *abbr.* **1.** New Mexico **2.** nautical mile

N.Mex. *abbr.* New Mexico

NMR *abbr.* nuclear magnetic resonance

NNE *abbr.* north-northeast

NNP *abbr.* net national product

NNW *abbr.* north-northwest

no[1] /nō/ *interj.* **1.** an interjection used to indicate a negative response in order to refuse, deny, or disagree with sth ○ '*Will you be taking the car?*' – '*No, not today.*' '*Would you like a coffee?*' – '*No, I'm fine, thanks*'. **2.** ACKNOWLEDGING A NEGATIVE STATEMENT used to acknowledge a negative statement, by expressing acceptance or understanding of sth ○ '*Nobody seems to have the time to really listen these days.*' – '*No, they don't.*' **3.** INDICATING DISBELIEF used to indicate shock, disbelief, or disappointment at sth sb has said ○ *'The car's going to be in the garage for another week.' – 'Oh no!'* ■ *n.* **1.** (*plural* **noes** *or* **nos**) ANSWER OR VOTE an answer or vote of 'no' ○ *They all gave resounding noes to the proposition.* **2.** SB VOTING 'NO' sb who answers 'no' to a question or votes against sth [Old English *nā*, from *ne* 'not' + *ā* 'ever' (see AYE)] ◇ **the noes have it** used to indicate that the majority have voted against sth

no² /nō/ CORE MEANING: a determiner used to indicate that there is not any or not one person or thing ○ *There is nothing within walking distance: no post office, no bank.* ○ *I had no choice in the matter.* ○ *They pay no attention to me.*

det. **1.** NOT AT ALL used to indicate that sb or sth does not have any of the characteristic or identity mentioned ○ *She's no fool.* **2.** NOT not exceeding a particular amount or quality (*used with comparative adjectives and adverbs*) ○ *The issue was no less important to us than you.* [12thC. Shortening of NONE.]

No¹ /nō/, **Noh** *n.* a form of Japanese drama that presents a story in a highly stylized fashion, using music, dance, and elaborate costumes. It flourished in the 14th and 15th centuries, and its development was influenced by Zen Buddhism. [Late 19thC. From Japanese *nō* 'talent, ability'.]

No² *symbol.* nobelium

no., **No.** *abbr.* **1.** north **2.** northern **3.** number

n.o. *abbr.* not out

Noachian /nō áyki ən/, **Noachic** /-áykik/, **Noachical** /-áykik'l/ *adj.* **1.** OF NOAH typical of or relating to Noah or his time **2.** ANTIQUATED long out-of-date [Late 19thC. Formed from *Noach*, a form of *Noah*.]

Noah /nṓ ə/ *n.* in the Bible, at God's command, Noah built an ark and saved himself, his family, and a pair of every kind of animal from the Flood (Genesis 6–9)

Noah's ark *n.* = **ark** *n.* 1

nob¹ /nob/ *n.* sb who is rich or socially powerful (*informal*) [Late 17thC. Origin unknown.]

nob² /nob/ *n.* **1.** HEAD the human head (*slang*) **2.** CARDS JACK OF SUIT TURNED UP in cribbage, the jack of the suit that the dealer turns up, which scores one point for the player who holds it [Late 17thC. Origin uncertain: perhaps from KNOB.]

no ball *n.* in cricket, a ball that has been bowled in a way not permitted by the rules of the game

nobble /nóbb'l/ (**-bles, -bling, -bled**) *vt.* (*informal*) **1.** FIND AND PERSUADE SB to make contact with sb, especially in order to persuade that person to do sth **2.** WIN SB OVER to get sb to do sth using lies, threats, or bribes **3.** DISABLE A RACEHORSE to prevent a racehorse from winning a race by drugging or disabling it **4.** CHEAT to swindle or defraud sb **5.** STEAL to steal sth **6.** SEIZE to seize hold of sb **7.** KIDNAP to kidnap sb [Mid-19thC. Perhaps from obsolete *knobble*, literally 'to hit with the knuckles repeatedly', from *knub*, an imitation of the sound.] —**nobbler** *n.*

nobbut /nóbbət/ *adv.* *N England* just or only [14thC. From NO + BUT.]

Nobel /nō bél/, **Alfred** (1833–96) Swedish chemist. His development of dynamite brought him great wealth, which was used after his death to set up the Nobel Prizes. Full name **Alfred Bernhard Nobel**

Nobelist /nō béllist/ *n.* sb who has been awarded a Nobel Prize

nobelium /nō béeli əm/ *n.* an artificial chemical element produced from curium. Symbol **No** [Mid-20thC. Named after the *Nobel* Institute for Physics, and named after Alfred *Nobel* (see NOBEL PRIZE).]

Nobel Prize /nṓ bel-/ *n.* any of six international awards made annually for outstanding achievement in the fields of chemistry, literature, physics, physiology or medicine, economics, and for promoting world peace [Early 20thC. Named after the Swedish inventor of dynamite, Alfred *Nobel* who established the original five prizes.] —**Nobel prizewinner** *n.* —**Nobel-prize-winning** *adj.*

nobiliary /nō bílli əri/ *adj.* relating to the nobility

nobiliary particle *n.* a preposition, such as 'de' in French or 'von' in German, used before a title or surname as a mark of rank

nobility /nō bílləti/ (*plural* **-ties**) *n.* **1.** ARISTOCRATS a noble class or people of noble rank in a country **2.** NOBLE RANK aristocratic social position or rank **3.** NOBLE CHARACTER high ideals or excellent moral character **4.** MAGNIFICENCE impressiveness or magnificence [14thC. Directly or via French *nobilité* from Latin *nobilis*, from *nobilis* (see NOBLE).]

noble /nṓb'l/ *adj.* (**-bler, -blest**) **1.** HAVING EXCELLENT MORAL CHARACTER possessing high ideals or excellent moral character **2.** RELATING TO HIGH MORAL PRINCIPLES based on high ideals or revealing excellent moral character **3.** MAGNIFICENT impressive in quality or appearance **4.** ARISTOCRATIC belonging or relating to an aristocratic social or political class **5.** CHEM NONREACTIVE chemically inactive or inert ■ *n.* **1.** ARISTOCRAT sb who belongs to a titled aristocracy **2.** MONEY FORMER ENGLISH COIN a gold coin worth half a mark, formerly used in England [13thC. Via French, from Latin *(g)nobilis* (source of English *ignoble*). Ultimately from an Indo-European word that is also the ancestor of English *know*.] —**nobleness** *n.* —**nobly** *adv.*

noble gas *n.* a chemically inert rare gas belonging to group 18 of the periodic table, including helium, neon, argon, krypton, xenon, and radon

nobleman /nṓb'lmən/ (*plural* **-men** /-mən/) *n.* a man who belongs to a titled aristocracy

noble metal *n.* a metal, such as gold, silver, or platinum that is resistant to oxidation

noble rot *n.* a parasitic fungus that shrivels ripe grapes, increasing the proportion of sugar to liquid in them. It is desirable in the making of certain wines such as French Sauternes. Latin name: *Botrytis cinerea.*

noble savage *n.* sb belonging to a nontechnological culture whose life is, according to an idea popularized by *Rousseau*, purer because it is closer to nature (*offensive in some contexts*)

noblesse /nō bléss/ *n.* **1.** NOBLE RANK aristocratic social position or rank **2.** ARISTOCRATS the members of an aristocracy, especially the French aristocracy [13thC. From French, 'nobility', from *noble* (see NOBLE).]

noblesse oblige /-ōbléezh/ *n.* the idea that people born into the nobility or upper social classes must behave in an honourable generous way towards those less privileged [From French, literally 'nobility obliges']

noblewoman /nṓb'l wòomən/ (*plural* **-en** /-wimin/) *n.* a woman who belongs to a titled aristocracy

nobody /nṓbədi, -bodi/ *pron.* NOT ONE PERSON not one single person ○ *Nobody can order the attack except the general.* ■ *n.* (*plural* **-ies**) SB UNIMPORTANT sb who feels or is regarded as unimportant or insignificant ○ *I felt like a nobody among so many important scientists*

nocent /nṓss'nt/ *adj.* causing harm, injury, or damage [15thC. From Latin *nocent-*, present participle stem of *nocere* 'to hurt, harm' (source of English *noxious*).] —**nocently** *adv.*

nociceptive /nṓssi séptiv/ *adj.* **1.** CAUSING PAIN used to describe a stimulus that causes pain **2.** IN RESPONSE TO PAIN caused by or reacting to pain [Early 20thC. Coined from Latin *nocere* 'to hurt, harm' (source of English *noxious*) + RECEPTIVE.] —**nociceptively** *adv.*

nock /nok/ *n.* **1.** GROOVE ON BOW one of the grooves at either end of a bow that holds the bowstring **2.** NOTCH ON ARROW the notch at the end of an arrow that holds it on the bowstring ■ *vt.* (**nocks, nocking, nocked**) **1.** PREPARE TO FIRE ARROW to place an arrow on a bowstring **2.** CUT NOTCH IN BOW OR ARROW to put a notch in a bow or an arrow [14thC. Origin uncertain: probably from Middle Dutch *nocke* 'projection, tip'.]

no claims bonus, **no claim bonus, no claims discount** *n.* a discount or reduction on an insurance premium, especially for a car, applied when the insured has not made a claim on the insurance during a specified period of time

noct- *prefix.* = **nocti-** (*used before vowels*)

nocti- *prefix.* night, at night ○ *noctilucent* [From Latin *noct-*, the stem of *nox* 'night' (source of English *equinox*). Ultimately from an Indo-European word that is also the ancestor of *night*.]

noctiluca /nókti lóokə/ (*plural* **-cae** /-kī/) *n.* a plankton that produces light. When present in large groups they make the sea appear to glow. Genus: *Noctiluca.* [Mid-19thC. From Latin, 'moon, lantern'.]

noctilucent /nókti lóoss'nt/ *adj.* used to describe high clouds that are visible at night [Late 19thC. Coined from NOCTI- + Latin *lucere* 'to shine'.]

noctuid /nóktyoo id/ *n.* a dull-coloured moth whose larvae, called army worms and cutworms, are destructive to young plants. Family: Noctuidae. [Late 19thC. Formed from Latin *noctua* 'night-owl'.] —**noctuid** *adj.*

noctule /nók tyool/ *n.* a large reddish-brown bat, common in Europe and Asia, that eats insects. Latin name: *Nyctalus noctula.* [Late 18thC. Via French from Italian *nottola* 'bat'.]

nocturn /nók turn/ *n.* one of the three divisions of the Roman Catholic service of matins, the first service of the day, previously held at midnight but now usually at daybreak [14thC. Directly or via French *nocturne*, from ecclesiastical Latin *nocturnus*, from Latin 'of the night', from *noct-*, stem of *nox* 'night'.]

nocturnal /nok túrn'l/ *adj.* ◊ **diurnal 1.** AT NIGHT occurring at night, as opposed to during the day **2.** ZOOL ACTIVE AT NIGHT used to describe animals that are active at night rather than during the day **3.** BOT FLOWERING AT NIGHT used to describe flowers that open at night and close during the day —**nocturnally** *adv.*

nocturne /nók turn/ *n.* **1.** MUSIC DREAMY MUSIC a musical composition, especially for the piano, that suggests a tranquil, dreamy mood. It evolved during the early 19th century, and Chopin was the most famous composer of nocturnes. **2.** PAINTING NIGHT SCENE a painting of a night scene [Mid-19thC. From French (see NOCTURN).]

nocuous /nókyoo əss/ *adj.* likely to cause injury or damage [Mid-17thC. From Latin *nocuus*, from *nocere* 'to hurt'.] —**nocuously** *adv.* —**nocuousness** *n.*

nod /nod/ *v.* (**nods, nodding, nodded**) **1.** *vti.* MOVE HEAD IN AGREEMENT to lower and then raise the head quickly in order to show agreement or recognition **2.** *vi.* DOZE to let the head fall forward because of sleepiness **3.** *vi.* LOSE CONCENTRATION to be momentarily careless or negligent **4.** *vi.* MOVE IN WIND to droop, bend, or sway in a breeze ■ *n.* **1.** MOVEMENT OF HEAD TO SHOW AGREEMENT a quick lowering and raising of the head in order to show agreement or recognition **2.** APPROVAL OF STH an indication of approval or agreement **3.** PERMISSION permission to do sth (*informal*) [14thC. Origin uncertain: perhaps from Low German.] —**nodder** *n.* ◇ **a nod's as good as a wink (to a blind horse)** used to indicate that sth expressed indirectly has been understood and that no further explanation is required ◇ **be on nodding terms (with sb)** to know sb slightly ◇ **on the nod** agreed without formal discussion or procedures (*informal*)

nod off *vi.* to fall asleep unintentionally or go into a drug-induced state of semiconsciousness

nod through *vt.* **1.** PASS STH ON THE NOD to approve sth without discussing it and voting on it **2.** CONSIDER MP TO HAVE VOTED to consider an MP as having voted in the House of Commons when he or she is unable to do so

nodal /nṓd'l/ *adj.* resembling, constituting, or found at or near a node —**nodally** *adv.*

nodding acquaintance *n.* a slight familiarity with or knowledge of sb or sth

nodding donkey *n.* a type of pump for extracting oil

noddle /nódd'l/ *n.* the human head or brain (*dated slang*) [15thC. Origin unknown.]

noddy /nóddi/ (*plural* **-dies**) *n.* **1.** BIRDS TROPICAL SEABIRD a dark-coloured tern found on the coasts and islands of tropical waters in both hemispheres. Genera: *Anous* and *Micranous.* **2.** OFFENSIVE TERM an offensive term that deliberately insults sb's intelligence or common sense (*dated insult*) **3.** TV FOOTAGE OF INTERVIEWER NODDING a short piece of film of a television interviewer nodding as if listening to the person interviewed that is spliced in with the main film of the person interviewed. The technique is used especially when only one camera is available.

(*informal*) [Early 16thC. Origin uncertain: perhaps formed from NOD.]

node /nōd/ *n.* **1.** ANAT BULGE OR SWELLING a knob, knot, or other kind of swelling that sticks out **2.** BOT POINT ON PLANT STEM the place on a plant stem where a leaf is attached or has been attached **3.** PHYS POINT ON WAVE in physics, a place in a standing wave that has little or no amplitude **4.** GEOM POINT WHERE PARTS OF CURVE INTERSECT in geometry, a place on a curve where it crosses itself **5.** MATH POINT OF INTERSECTION a point where lines meet or intersect in a diagram or graph **6.** ASTRON POINT WHERE ORBIT INTERSECTS ECLIPTIC either of the two points where an orbit, e.g. that of a planet, crosses the ecliptic plane **7.** COMPUT TERMINAL OR POINT IN NETWORK a terminal or other point in a computer network where a message can be created, received, or repeated **8.** LING POINT IN SENTENCE STRUCTURE in transformational grammars, a point in a sentence diagram where a category label, indicating the part of speech, appears and from which further branches may lead off [14thC. From Latin *nodus* 'knot'.]

node of Ranvier /-raánvi ay/ *n.* a short gap in the myelin sheath that occurs at intervals along the length of a nerve fibre [Named after the French histologist Louis Antoine *Ranvier* (1835–1922), who described them in 1878]

nodose /nṓd ōss, nō dṓss/ *adj.* having many points at which leaves join the stem —**nodosity** /nō dóssəti/ *n.*

nodule /nóddyool/ *n.* **1.** SMALL LUMP a small protruding knob, lump, or swelling on sth **2.** BOT ROOT PROTUBERANCE a swelling or knob on the roots of legumes that contains bacteria **3.** ANAT CELL OR TISSUE MASS a small mass of cells or tissue, which may be a normal part of the body or a growth such as a tumour **4.** GEOL LARGE ROUNDED MINERAL FORM a form of a mineral that is massive with a rounded outer surface [15thC. From Latin *nodulus* 'small knot', from *nodus* (see NODE).] —**nodular** /nóddyōōlər/ *adj.* —**nodulose** /nóddyōō lṓss/ *adj.*

noel /nō éll/, **noël** *n.* a Christmas carol (*archaic or literary*) [12thC. From French, from *nael*, from Latin (*dies*) *natalis* 'birth (day)', ultimately from *nasci* 'to be born' (source of English *nascent*).]

Noel /nō éll/, **Noël** *n.* Christmas, especially in carols or greetings

noetic /nō éttik/ *adj.* typical of, coming from, or understood by the human mind [Mid-17thC. From Greek *noētikos*, ultimately from *noein* 'to think', from *nous* 'mind' (source of English *nous*).] —**noetically** *adv.*

no-fly-zone *n.* **1.** AREA FORBIDDEN TO AIRCRAFT an area over which aircraft, especially those of another country, are forbidden to fly, and in which they will be attacked if they enter it **2.** *US* FORBIDDEN TOPIC a topic of questioning or conversation that is off-limits (*slang*) ○ *The press secretary declared that issue to be a no-fly-zone for reporters.*

no-frills *adj.* relating to a kind of service or establishment that does not offer extra or special treatment (*informal*)

nog[1] /nog/ (**nogs, nogging, nogged**) *n.* **1.** BUILDING WOODEN BLOCK FOR NAILING a block of wood inserted into masonry or brickwork so that sth can be nailed to it **2.** JOINERY PEG a wooden peg or pin [Early 17thC. Origin unknown.]

nog[2] /nog/ *n.* **1.** = eggnog **2.** TYPE OF ENGLISH BEER a strong ale once brewed in Norfolk [Early 17thC. Origin unknown.]

noggin /nóggin/ *n.* **1.** MEASURE ONE-FOURTH OF PINT a measure of spirits equivalent to 0.148 litres/¼ of a pint (*dated*) **2.** CUP a small cup or mug (*dated*) **3.** HEAD the human head (*dated informal*) [Mid-17thC. Origin unknown.]

—— WORD KEY: REGIONAL NOTE ——
Many of the items used in the past would now be considered politically incorrect. Among such terms are those for supposed stupidity. We find *addle-headed, barmy, bull-skulled, daft, dozy, dummel-headed,* and supposedly stupid people may be *noggin-heads, noodle-noggins, num(b)skulls,* or *staups.* Like many terms of abuse, they could be used affectionately: *You wee pet, you! You dummel-headed wee darling!*

nogging /nógging/ *n.* **1.** MASONRY BETWEEN STUDS small stones, bricks, or bits of masonry used to fill the spaces between studs in a wall or partition **2.** WOODEN PIECE BETWEEN TIMBERS one of the pieces of wood that are inserted between the main timbers of a half-timbered wall

no-go *n.* STH THAT WILL NOT HAPPEN an event or situation that is not going to occur because of adverse conditions (*informal*) ■ *adj.* CANCELLED no longer going to happen or scheduled to occur

no-go area *n.* **1.** DANGEROUS PART OF CITY a district where people are frightened or unable to go because of the violence and crime there **2.** RESTRICTED AREA an area in which unauthorized people are forbidden to go

no-good *adj.* GOOD-FOR-NOTHING lacking merit, virtue, worth, or morals (*insult*) ■ *n.* SB OR STH WORTHLESS sb or sth considered to lack merit, virtue, worth, or morals (*insult*)

Isamu Noguchi

Noguchi /naw goóchi/, **Isamu** (1904–88) US sculptor. He is known for his abstract sculptures and his sculpture gardens.

Noh *n.* THEATRE = No[1]

no-holds-barred *adj.* happening, or engaged in sth, without restraint or control, like a wrestling match in which any hold is permitted (*informal*)

no-hoper *n.* an offensive term that deliberately insults sb's achievements and likelihood of future success (*informal*)

nohow /nṓ how/ *adv.* not in any way (*nonstandard*)

Nol *abbr.* Nation of Islam

noil /noyl/ *n.* short fibres separated during combing from the long fibres of cotton, wool, or another material [Early 17thC. Origin uncertain: probably from Old French *noel*, from medieval Latin *nodellus* 'small knot', from Latin *nodus* 'knot' (source of English *node*).]

noise /noyz/ *n.* **1.** UNPLEASANT SOUND a loud, surprising, irritating, or unwanted sound **2.** ANY SOUND any sound or combination of sounds **3.** OUTCRY a loud clamour or commotion concerning sth **4.** COMPLAINT a complaint or protest about sth (*informal*) **5.** RUMOUR idle talk, rumour, or gossip (*informal*) **6.** PHYS ELECTRIC DISTURBANCE a random disturbance in an electric circuit that makes clear reception of a signal difficult **7.** COMPUT MEANINGLESS DATA unwanted or meaningless data intermixed with the relevant information in the output from a computer ■ *vt.* (**noises, noising, noised**) SPREAD GOSSIP to spread a rumour or gossip ○ *an ugly story that was being noised about in newsrooms* [13thC. Via French, 'uproar, brawl', from assumed late Latin *nausea* 'discomfort', from Latin, 'seasickness', ultimately from Greek *naus* 'ship' (source of English *nausea*).] ◇ **make noises** to do or say sth intended to attract attention or indicate an intention ○ *He's making noises about a career change.*

noiseless /nóyzləss/ *adj.* not making any noise —**noiselessly** *adv.* —**noiselessness** *n.*

noisemaker /nóyz maykər/ *n. US* a device such as a rattle or horn used to make noise at a party or a celebration

noise pollution *n.* irritating, distracting, or physically dangerous noise to which people are exposed in their environment and over which they usually have no control

noisette /nwaa zét/ *n.* a piece of boned and rolled meat, especially the neck or loin of lamb [Late 19thC. From French, literally 'little nut', from its shape.]

noisome /nóyssəm/ *adj.* **1.** FOUL so offensive, especially to the senses, as to arouse feelings of disgust or repulsion **2.** DANGEROUS extremely harmful [14thC. From obsolete *noy*, a shortening of ANNOY, + -SOME.] —**noisomely** *adv.* —**noisomeness** *n.*

noisy /nóyzi/ (**-ier, -iest**) *adj.* **1.** MAKING NOISE making a loud and annoying racket **2.** CONTAINING MUCH NOISE full of or characterized by loud sounds —**noisily** *adv.* —**noisiness** *n.*

noisy miner *n.* an Australian honey-eating bird that has grey and brown plumage with a black facial mask, yellow beak and legs, and is noted for its strident calls. Latin name: *Manorina melanocephala.* [*Miner* a variant of MYNAH]

Nok /nok/ *n.* a civilization located in the forests of central Nigeria that flourished between 500 BC and AD 300. It is known for its highly developed art style.

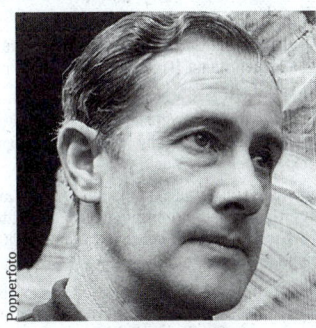

Sir Sidney Nolan

Nolan /nṓlən/, **Sir Sidney Robert** (1917–92) Australian painter. His colourful figurative works, often based on Australian folk history, include the *Ned Kelly* series.

nolens volens /nṓ lenz vṓ lenz/ *adv.* whether willing or not willing [From Latin, literally 'unwilling willing']

noli-me-tangere /nṓli may táng gəri, -tánjəri/ *n.* **1.** PROHIBITION AGAINST TOUCHING a warning not to touch or interfere with sb or sth **2.** SB OR STH NOT FOR TOUCHING sb who or sth that must not be touched or interfered with **3.** PAINTING PAINTING OF JESUS CHRIST AND MARY MAGDALENE a depiction in art of Jesus Christ appearing to Mary Magdalene after his resurrection [From Latin, literally 'do not touch me', from Jesus Christ's words to Mary Magdalene in the *Bible*, John 20:17]

nolle prosequi /nólli próssi kwī/ *n.* an entry made in a court record when a plaintiff or a prosecutor decides not to proceed further with a case or action [From Latin, literally 'to be unwilling to pursue']

nolo contendere /nṓlō kon téndəri/ *n. US* in law, a plea entered by a defendant that does not explicitly admit guilt, but subjects the defendant to punishment, while allowing denial of the alleged facts in other proceedings [From Latin, literally 'I do not wish to contend']

no-lose *adj.* certain to result in success or be beneficial, regardless of the outcome ○ *a no-lose proposition*

nol. pros. /nól próss/ *abbr.* nolle prosequi

nom. *abbr.* nominative

noma /nṓmə/ *n.* a severe gangrenous inflammation of the mouth or genitals, usually occurring in children who are malnourished or otherwise debilitated [Mid-19thC. From a modern Latin alteration of Latin *nome*, ultimately from Greek *nom-*, stem of *nemein* 'to feed'.]

nomad /nṓ mad/ *n.* **1.** ANTHROP MEMBER OF ITINERANT PEOPLE sb who belongs to a group of people who move from place to place seasonally in search of pasture for their herds or food and water **2.** WANDERER sb who wanders from one place to another [Late 16thC. From French *nomade*, ultimately from Greek *nomas* 'wandering about to find pasture', from *nemein* 'to pasture'.] —**nomadic** /nō máddik/ *adj.* —**nomadically** /-li/ *adv.* —**nomadism** /nṓ madizəm/ *n.*

no-man's-land *n.* **1.** MIL **TERRITORY BETWEEN OPPOSING FORCES** the area of land that lies between two opposing armies and is held by neither side **2. UNCLAIMED TERRITORY** any area of land that no one has established a claim to **3.** RACKET GAMES **BAD POSITION ON TENNIS COURT** in tennis and other court games, an area on a court in which a player is tactically at a disadvantage **4. AMBIGUOUS AREA** any indefinite or ambiguous situation in which boundaries, rules, or authority are unclear or unfamiliar

nomarchy /nóm aarki/ (*plural* **-chies**) *n.* any of the administrative provinces into which modern Greece is divided [Mid-17thC. From Greek *nomarkhia*, from *nomos* 'district' (see NOME) + *-arkhia* 'government'.]

nombril /nómbril/, **nombril point** *n.* in heraldry, the midpoint of the lower half of an escutcheon, halfway between the fess point and the base point [Mid-16thC. From French, literally 'navel'.]

nom de guerre /nóm də gáir/ (*plural* **noms de guerre** /nóm-/) *n.* an assumed name that sb uses in certain situations, e.g. when fighting [From French, literally 'name of war']

nom de plume /nóm də plōom/ (*plural* **noms de plume** /nóm-/) *n.* = **pen name** [From French, literally 'name of pen']

nome /nōm/ *n.* **1.** HIST **EGYPTIAN PROVINCE** a province of ancient Egypt **2.** = **nomarchy** [Early 18thC. From Greek *nomos*, from *nemein* 'to divide'.]

nomen /nṓ men/ (*plural* **nomina** /nó minə/) *n.* in ancient Rome, a citizen's second name, which indicated the clan to which he or she belonged [Early 18thC. From Latin, 'name'.]

nomenclator /nṓ men klaytər/ *n.* sb who assigns names to objects or items in a scientific classification system (**taxonomy**) [Mid-16thC. From Latin, from *nomen* 'name' + *calare* 'to call'.]

nomenclature /nō méngkləchər, nṓmən klaychər, -kláychər/ *n.* **1. ASSIGNING OF NAMES** the assigning of names to organisms in a scientific classification system (**taxonomy**) **2. NAME SYSTEM** a system of names assigned to objects or items in a particular science or art [Early 17thC. Via French from Latin *nomenclatura*, formed from *nomen* 'name' + *calare* 'to call'.] —**nomenclatural** /nō mĕngklə chóorəl/ *adj.*

nomenklatura /nṓ men klə tóorə/ *n.* **1. ELITE COMMUNIST CLASS** in Communist governments, the elite, privileged class consisting of the people holding positions of authority in the bureaucracy (*takes a plural verb*) **2. COMMUNIST PATRONAGE SYSTEM** the system in the former Soviet Union and other Communist countries, controlled by committees in the Communist Party, for assigning senior positions in the bureaucracy (*takes a singular verb*) [Mid-20thC. From Russian, from Latin *nomenclatura* NOMENCLATURE.]

nomina plural of **nomen**

nominal /nómmin'l/ *adj.* **1. SO-CALLED** acting or being sth in name only, but not in reality **2. VERY LOW IN COST** representing very little cost when compared with the actual value received **3.** ACCT **RELATING TO CURRENT PRICES** considered in terms of the stated or original value only, and ignoring changes due to inflation and other factors **4.** GRAM **OF NOUN** relating to a noun or a group of words that functions as a noun **5. BEARING SB'S NAME** assigned to a named person, and bearing that person's name **6. OF NAMES** relating to or consisting of a name or names ■ *n.* GRAM **NOUN OR NOUN GROUP** a word or group of words that functions as a noun [15thC. Either directly or via French from Latin *nominalis*, from *nomen* 'name'.] —**nominally** *adv.*

nominalise *vt.* = **nominalize**

nominalism /nómminəlizəm/ *n.* the philosophical doctrine that there are no realities other than concrete individual objects —**nominalist** /nómminəlist/ *n.*, *adj.* —**nominalistic** *adj.* —**nominalistically** *adv.*

nominalize /nómminə līz/ (**-izes, -izing, -ized**), **nominalise** (**-ises, -ising, -ised**) *vt.* **1. FORM NOUN FROM WORD** to change a part of speech into a noun by the addition of a suffix **2. FORM NOUN GROUP FROM CLAUSE** to change an underlying clause by a syntactic process or series of rules so that it functions like a noun —**nominalization** /nómminə lī záysh'n/ *n.*

nominal value *n.* = **par value**

nominal wages *npl.* = **money wages**

nominate /nómmi nayt/ (**-nates, -nating, -nated**) *vt.* **1. PROPOSE SB** to suggest sb for appointment or election to a position or for an honour or award **2. APPOINT SB** to appoint sb to a position, or make sb responsible for a duty **3.** HORSERACING **ENTER HORSE FOR RACE** to enter a horse in a race [Mid-16thC. From Latin *nominat-*, past participle stem of *nominare* 'to name', from *nomin-*, stem of *nomen* 'name'.] —**nominator** *n.*

nomination /nómmi náysh'n/ *n.* **1. PROPOSAL** a suggestion of sb for appointment or election to a position or for receiving an honour or award **2. SB OR STH PROPOSED** sb or sth suggested for appointment or election to a position or for receiving an honour or award **3. APPOINTMENT** the appointment of sb to a position, or assignment of sb to a duty

nominative /nómminətiv/ *adj.* **1.** GRAM **OF THE SUBJECT CASE** relating or belonging to the case used in some languages to designate a noun or pronoun that is functioning as the subject of a clause or sentence. Other words such as adjectives may have a nominative form in agreement with a noun. **2. APPOINTED TO OR PROPOSED FOR OFFICE** appointed or suggested for election to an office or position **3. WITH OWNER'S NAME** having the name of the owner specified on it ■ *n.* GRAM **1. SUBJECT NOUN CASE** the grammatical case in some languages of a noun functioning as a subject of a sentence or clause, and of some other words agreeing with the noun **2. NOUN IN SUBJECT CASE** a form of a noun used in some languages when the noun functions as the subject of a sentence or clause, or when another word agrees with such a noun [14thC. Either directly or via French *nominatif* from Latin *nominativus (casus)* 'nominative (case)', from *nominat-* (see NOMINATE).]

nominee /nómmi neé/ *n.* **1. SB PROPOSED** sb who has been suggested for a position, honour, or award, or as a candidate for office **2.** BUSINESS **NOMINAL OWNER** a person or group that holds title to a security or property but is not actually the holder or owner [Mid-17thC. Formed from NOMINATE.]

nomograph /nómmə graaf, nṓmə-, -graf/, **nomogram** /-gram/ *n.* **1. GRAPH WITH THREE SCALES** a graph with three lines graduated so a straight line intersecting any two of the lines at their known values intersects the third at the value of the related variable. To show the relationship of the variables in more complicated expressions, nomographs often have to resort to nonuniform and even curved scales. **2. GRAPH** any graph that represents numerical relationships [Mid-18thC. Coined from Greek *nomos* 'law, custom' + -GRAPH.] —**nomographic** /nómmə gráffik, nṓmə-/ *adj.* —**nomography** /no móggrəfi, nō-/ *n.*

nomothetic /nómmə théttik, nṓmə-/, **nomothetical** /-théttik'l/ *adj.* **1.** POL **LEGISLATIVE** relating to the enactment of laws **2.** PSYCHOL **RELATING TO DISCOVERY OF GENERAL LAWS** relating to the discovery of universal laws, e.g. those principles that explain how some aspects of personality affect behaviour [Early 17thC. From Greek *nomothetikos*, from *nomothetēs* 'lawgiver', from *nomos* 'law'.] —**nomothetically** /nómmə théttikli, nṓmə-/ *adv.*

-nomy *suffix.* system of rules, laws, or knowledge about a particular field ○ *gastronomy* [From Greek *-nomia*, from *nomos* 'law, custom'] —**-nomic** *suffix.* —**-nomical** *suffix.* —**-nomically** *suffix.*

non *prefix.* = **nona-** (*used before vowels*)

-non *prefix.* non ○ *nonconducting* ○ *nondiscrimination* [Via Old French from Latin *non*. Ultimately from an Indo-European base that is also the ancestor of English *no*, *un-*, and *in-*.]

non-A, non-B hepatitis *n.* an acute chronic viral disease of the liver, similar to hepatitis B but caused by neither the hepatitis A nor the hepatitis B virus. Among the several new hepatitis viruses discovered relatively recently, non-A, non-B hepatitis, in most cases, is thought to be due to the hepatitis C virus.

nona- *prefix.* nine ○ *nonagon* [From Latin *nonus* 'ninth' (source of English *noon*). Ultimately from the Indo-European word for 'nine', which is also the ancestor of *nine*, *November*, and *ennead*.]

nonacademic /nón akə démmik/ *adj.* **1. NOT TEACHING** working at a university or college but not involved in teaching or research **2. NOT STUDIOUS** lacking an aptitude for studying **3. VOCATIONAL** practical or vocational in content

nonage /nṓnij, nón-/ *n.* **1.** LAW **NOT BEING OF LEGAL AGE** the status of being under the requisite age for some legal entitlement (*formal*) **2. TIME BEFORE MATURITY** any time of immaturity [14thC. From Anglo-Norman *nounage*, a variant of Old French *nonage*, literally 'not (the full) age', from *age* (see AGE).]

nonagenarian /nṓnəjə náiri ən, nón-/ *n.* **SB 90 TO 99 YEARS OLD** sb 90 years of age or between 90 and 100 years old ■ *adj.* **90 TO 99 YEARS OLD** 90 years of age or between 90 and 100 years old [Early 19thC. Formed from Latin *nonagenarius* 'consisting of ninety', from, ultimately, *nonaginta* 'ninety', from *nonus* (see NOON).]

nonaggression /nónnə grésh'n/ *n.* a policy of not attacking other countries ○ *The two countries have signed a nonaggression pact.*

nonagon /nónnə gon, nṓn-/ *n.* a plane geometric figure with nine angles and sides [Mid-17thC. Coined from NONA- + -GON.] —**nonagonal** /no nággən'l, nō-/ *adj.*

nonalcoholic /nón álkə hóllik/ *adj.* containing no alcohol, or an extremely low amount of alcohol

nonaligned /nónnə līnd/ *adj.* not allied with any major world power —**nonalignment** *n.*

nonanoic acid /nónnə nṓ ik-/ *n.* a colourless to yellow oil obtained from beet and potatoes, used in plastics, pharmaceuticals, synthetic flavours, and as an additive in petrol. Formula: $CH_3(CH_2)_7COOH$. [*Nonanoic* formed from *nonane* 'straight chain hydrocarbon containing nine carbon atoms', from NONA- + -ANE]

nonappearance /nónnə peéranss/ *n.* failure to appear or attend, especially the failure of an accused person or witness to turn up for a court appearance

nonassessable /nónnə séssəb'l/ *adj.* impossible to estimate or determine ○ *nonassessable losses*

nonbeliever /nónbi leévər/ *n.* sb who has no religious faith or beliefs

nonbook /nón bŏŏk/ *adj.* kept in a permanent form other than as books, e.g. as video-tapes ○ *the library's nonbook holdings*

nonbreaking /nón bráyking/ *adj.* designed so as not to break ○ *a nonbreaking windscreen*

nonbreeding /nón breéding/ *adj.* not kept for breeding purposes

nonbusiness /nón bíznəss/ *adj.* personal and not relating to business ○ *details of nonbusiness expenditure*

nonce[1] /nonss/ *n.* the present time [12thC. Alteration resulting from misdivision of *for then anes* 'for the one (occasion)', from *for* + *then*, a form of THE + *anes*, an obsolete form of ONE.] ◇ **for the nonce 1.** for the present occasion **2.** for the time being

nonce[2] /nonss/ *n.* sb who has committed a sexual offence against a child, especially a prisoner convicted of such an offence (*slang insult*) [Late 20thC. Origin unknown.]

nonce word *n.* a word that is coined for a single occasion

nonchalance /nónshələnss/ *n.* the quality of appearing calm and unconcerned

nonchalant /nónshələnt/ *adj.* calm and unconcerned about things [Mid-18thC. From French, literally 'not being concerned', from *chalant*, present participle of *chaloir* 'to be concerned', from, ultimately, Latin *calere* 'to be hot or roused'.] —**nonchalantly** *adv.*

noncling /nón klíng/ *adj.* made of a material that prevents the garment clinging to the wearer's body

nonclinical /nón klínnik'l/ *adj.* not relating to or involved in the medical care of patients

noncollegiate /nónkə leéji ət/ *adj.* **1. NOT CONSISTING OF COLLEGES** used to describe a university that does not consist of colleges **2. NOT BELONGING TO COLLEGE** not associated with or belonging to a particular college within a university

noncom /nón kom/ *n.* a noncommissioned officer (*informal*) [Late 19thC. Shortening.]

noncombatant /non kómbətənt/ *n.* **1.** CIVILIAN IN WARTIME sb who is not in the armed forces during a war **2.** NONFIGHTING MEMBER OF ARMED FORCES a chaplain, medical officer, or other member of the armed forces who does not take part in battle

noncommissioned officer /nónkə mísh'nd-/ *n.* a subordinate officer in any of the armed forces, e.g. a sergeant or corporal, who, instead of being given a commission, has been appointed from the lower ranks

noncommittal /nónkə mítt'l/ *adj.* not making clear any personal opinions or feelings about sth —**noncommittally** *adv.*

noncompetitive /nónkəm péttətiv/ *adj.* **1.** COMM WITHOUT BUSINESS RIVALRY not characterized by competition between rival businesses or organizations **2.** COMM UNABLE TO COMPETE COMMERCIALLY unable to compete commercially against rival businesses or organizations **3.** COMM NEITHER CHEAP NOR GOOD ENOUGH neither low enough in price nor high enough in quality to compete in the marketplace **4.** UNAMBITIOUS not having the type of personality that makes sb want to compete against and beat other people **5.** SPORTS NOT INVOLVING COMPETING SPORTSPEOPLE not involving competition between athletes, players, or teams

noncompliance /nónkəm plí ənss/ *n.* a refusal or failure to obey a law, rule, contractual agreement, or a doctor's order for medicine-taking —**noncompliant** *adj.*

non compos mentis /nón kómpəss méntiss/ *adj.* in law, not mentally competent to understand what is happening and to make important decisions [From Latin, literally 'not having control of (your) mind']

nonconductor /nónkən dúktər/ *n.* a substance that does not conduct heat, electricity, or sound —**nonconducting** *adj.*

nonconformist /nónkən fáwrmist/ *adj.* UNCONVENTIONAL not conforming to an established pattern of behaviour ■ *n.* **1.** UNCONVENTIONAL PERSON sb who does not conform to an accepted pattern of behaviour **2.** **nonconformist, Nonconformist** CHR MEMBER OF DISSENTING PROTESTANT CHURCH a member of a Protestant church not adhering to the doctrines or usage of a national or established church —**nonconformism** *n.*

nonconformity /nónkən fáwrməti/ *n.* **1.** UNCONVENTIONALITY the practice of not conforming to an established pattern of behaviour **2.** LACK OF AGREEMENT the state of being in disagreement with sth

noncontributory /nónkən tríbbyŏōtəri/ *adj.* **1.** NOT REQUIRING CONTRIBUTIONS used to describe a health insurance or pension scheme that does not require contributions from an employee or member **2.** NOT CONTRIBUTING not contributing to a health insurance or pension scheme

noncooperation /nónkō óppə ráysh'n/ *n.* **1.** REFUSAL TO COOPERATE refusal or failure to cooperate **2.** POL CIVIL DISOBEDIENCE the practice of refusing to pay taxes or otherwise obey government decrees, as a means of protest —**noncooperative** /nónkō ópparətiv/ *adj.*

noncustodial /nón ku stódi əl/ *adj.* LAW not involving imprisonment or detention in custody

nondairy /nón dáiri/ *adj.* used to describe ingredients or foods that contain no dairy products and can be substituted for them, e.g. some kinds of margarine

nondeductible /nóndi dúktəb'l/ *adj.* not allowed to be deducted, especially as an allowance against income taxes

nondegradable /nóndi gráydəb'l/ *adj.* not subject to decomposition by biological or chemical means

nondenominational /nóndi nómmi náysh'nəl/ *adj.* not associated with or restricted to a particular religious denomination

nondescript /nóndiskript/ *adj.* UNREMARKABLE with no interesting or remarkable characteristics ■ *n.* UNREMARKABLE PERSON sb with no interesting or remarkable characteristics [Late 17thC. Formed from Latin *descriptus*, past participle of *describere* (see DESCRIBE).]

nondestructive testing /nóndi strúktiv-/ *n.* any technique used to test for flaws in materials, components, and joints without causing damage or destruction

nondirective /nóndə réktiv, -dī-/ *adj.* used to describe a form of psychotherapy or counselling in which the patient is encouraged to speak freely with minimal input from the therapist

nondiscrimination /nóndi skrímmi náysh'n/ *n.* **1.** FAIR AND EQUAL TREATMENT FOR ALL the practice of treating different people or groups fairly, equally, and without prejudice **2.** NO DISCRIMINATION the absence of discrimination —**nondiscriminatory** /nóndi skrímminətəri/ *adj.*

nondisjunction /nóndiss júngksh'n/ *n.* a failure of paired chromosomes or sister chromatids to separate during cell division —**nondisjunctional** *adj.* —**nondisjunctionally** *adv.*

nondistinctive /nóndi stíngktiv/ *adj.* used to describe features of speech sounds that do not distinguish meanings

non dit /nón dee/ *n.* US a taboo subject or fact that remains unspoken or is not discussed ○ *His absence was a non dit.* [Late 20thC. From French *le non-dit*, 'what is left unsaid'.]

nondrinker /nón drínkər/ *n.* sb who does not drink alcohol —**nondrinking** *adj.*

nondrip /nón dríp/ *adj.* not likely to drip while being applied

none /nun/ *pron.* **1.** NOBODY not one person ○ *Wealth that is free for all is valued by none.* ○ *None of us wanted the situation to continue.* **2.** NOT ANY not any of sth, or any part of sth ○ *None of it seemed to matter any more.* ○ *We wrote last week demanding some answers, but so far have received none.* ■ *det.* NOT ANY OF not any of (*archaic*) (*used before vowels*) [Old English *nān*, literally 'not one', from *ne* 'not' + *ān*, an earlier form of ONE] ◇ **have none of sth** to refuse to tolerate sth (*informal*) ○ *We asked him to explain himself, but he would have none of it.* ◇ **none the** in no degree (*used in front of comparative adjectives*) ○ *I'm still none the wiser.* ◇ **none too** not very

nonelected /nónni léktid/ *adj.* holding a position or office without having been elected to it

nonelectrolyte /nónni léktrə līt/ *n.* a substance that does not ionize readily in solution or in the molten state and is therefore a bad conductor of electricity

nonentity /no néntəti/ *n.* (*plural* **-ties**) *n.* **1.** INSIGNIFICANT PERSON sb who has no importance, influence, or significance **2.** STH NONEXISTENT sth that does not exist in reality **3.** NOT EXISTING the state of being nonexistent [Late 16thC. From medieval Latin *nonentitas*, from *entitas* 'existence' (see ENTITY).]

nonequivalence /nónni kwívvələnss/ *n.* **1.** NOT BEING EQUAL the state of not being equal or equivalent **2.** LOGIC DIFFERENCE IN TRUTH VALUES a situation in which two propositions can have different truth values —**nonequivalent** *adj.*

nones /nónz/ *n.* (*takes a singular or plural verb*) **1.** CALENDAR, HIST DAY IN ROMAN CALENDAR the ninth day before the ides of each month in the ancient Roman calendar **2.** CHR TIME FOR AFTERNOON PRAYER the fifth canonical hour of prayer, originally held at the ninth hour after sunrise [15thC. '9th day' via French from Latin *nonas*, plural of *nonus* 'ninth'. 'Prayer hour' plural of *none*, ultimately from Latin *nona*, feminine of *nonus* (see NOON).]

nonessential /nónni sénsh'l/ *adj.* **1.** NOT NECESSARY not absolutely necessary **2.** BIOCHEM NOT NECESSARY TO THE DIET manufactured by the body and therefore not essential in the diet ■ *n.* NONESSENTIAL PERSON OR THING sb who or sth that is not absolutely necessary

nonesuch /nún such/, **nonsuch** *n.* sb who or sth that has no equal (*archaic*) [Late 16thC. From NONE + SUCH.]

nonet /no nét/ *n.* **1.** COMPOSITION FOR NINE VOICES OR INSTRUMENTS a piece of music composed for nine voices or instruments **2.** GROUP OF NINE MUSICIANS a group of nine singers or instrumentalists [Mid-19thC. From Italian *nonetto*, literally 'small ninth', from *nono* 'ninth', from Latin *nonus* (see NOON).]

nonetheless /núnthə léss/ *adv.* = **nevertheless**

non-Euclidean *adj.* used to describe or relating to any branch of geometry not based on the postulates of Euclid

nonevent /nón i vént/ *n.* an occasion that is disappointingly unexciting

nonexecutive director /nón ig zékyŏōtiv-/ *n.* a director of a business organization who is not a full member of staff but whose duty is to advise the other directors

nonexistent /nónnig zístənt/ *adj.* not in existence —**nonexistence** *n.*

nonfat /nón fát/ *adj.* without fat solids, or with the fat content removed

nonfeasance /nón feéz'nss/ *n.* failure to do sth that is legally obligatory. ◊ **malfeasance, misfeasance** [Early 17thC. Formed from obsolete *feasance* 'doing', from Anglo-Norman *fesa(u)nce* and French *faisance*, from *fais-*, present stem of *faire* 'to do', from Latin *facere*.]

nonferrous /nón férrəss/ *adj.* **1.** CONTAINING NO IRON not composed of or containing iron **2.** NOT IRON being a metal other than iron

nonfiction /nón fíksh'n/ *n.* prose literature that consists of factual information rather than works of the imagination ○ *her first nonfiction work* —**nonfictional** *adj.*

nonfigurative /nón fíggərətiv/ *adj.* **1.** = **literal 2.** ARTS = **nonrepresentational**

nonflammable /nón flámməb'l/ *adj.* difficult to burn or ignite

nonfood /nón fóod/ *adj.* used to describe sth that is sold in a supermarket that is not for eating or drinking

nongonococcal urethritis /nón gonō kók'l-/ *n.* = **nonspecific urethritis**

nongraded /nón gráydid/ *adj.* not sorted into different sizes ○ *nongraded rocks*

non grata /nón gra̋atə/ *adj.* not welcome [Extracted from PERSONA NON GRATA]

non-Hodgkin's lymphoma *n.* a cancer of the lymph nodes that is not Hodgkin's disease

nonidentical /nón T déntik'l/ *adj.* **1.** DIFFERENT not the same **2.** BIOL = **fraternal** *adj.* 4 ○ *nonidentical twins*

nonillion /nō níllyən/ *n.* the number equal to 10^{54}, written as 1 followed by 54 zeros [Late 17thC. From French, coined from Latin *nonus* 'ninth' + *-illion* as in MILLION.] —**nonillionth** *adj., n.*

nonimmigrant /non ímmigrənt/ *n.* **1.** TEMPORARY NON-CITIZEN RESIDENT sb who enters a country of which he or she is not a national for a temporary stay **2.** RETURNING NATIONAL sb who returns to his or her own country after a period of time spent in another country

noninflammable /nónin flámməb'l/ *adj.* = **nonflammable**

non-insulin-dependent diabetes *n.* a type of diabetes mellitus that does not require insulin for its treatment

nonintervention /nón intər vénsh'n/ *n.* the policy and practice of a nation's abstaining from involvement in the affairs of another state or population group —**noninterventionist** *n., adj.*

noninvasive /nón in váyssiv/ *adj.* **1.** NOT ENTERING INTO THE BODY not involving cutting into the body or entry into a body cavity, e.g. the colon or stomach **2.** LOCALLY CONFINED not spreading or likely to spread to other parts of the body

noninvolvement /nón in vólvmənt/ *n.* the practice of not participating in sth or not being associated with sth

noniron /nón Í ərn/ *adj.* not needing to be ironed because it is crease-resistant

nonissue /nón íssyoo, -íshyoo/ *n.* sth that is so unimportant that it is not worth considering or discussing

nonjoinder /non jóyndər/ *n.* failure to include a party in a lawsuit who should have been included

nonjudgmental /nón juj mént'l/, **nonjudgemental** *adj.* not making or involving moral judgments —**nonjudgmentally** *adv.*

nonjuror /nón jŏōrər/ *n.* sb who refuses to take an oath, especially a member of the Church of England clergy who refused to take an oath of allegiance to William and Mary in 1689 —**nonjuring** adj.

nonjury /nón joòri/ adj. used to describe a trial where the verdict is not the responsibility of a jury but of a judge

nonlinear /nón línni ər/ adj. 1. NOT IN A LINE not lying on the same straight line 2. NOT PREDICTABLE FROM PAST varying markedly as a result of individual factors or circumstances and so difficult to anticipate or likely to depart from previous patterns 3. ALGEBRA NOT IN DIRECT PROPORTION used to describe a relationship or function that is not strictly proportional

nonmetal /nón métt'l/ n. a chemical element that does not have the chemical and physical properties of a metal, e.g. carbon or oxygen

nonmoral /nón mórrəl/ adj. 1. INDEPENDENT OF MORAL CONSIDERATIONS neither immoral nor moral, but unrelated to moral or ethical considerations 2. WITHOUT MORALS not having or showing moral principles

nonnegative /nón néggətiv/ adj. in mathematics, relating to or being a real quantity that is positive or zero

nonnegotiable /nón ni góshəb'l, -shi əb'l/ adj. 1. NOT OPEN TO NEGOTIATION not open to negotiation or arbitration 2. NOT MARKETABLE not legally transferable from one owner to another

nonnuclear /nón nyoòkl ər/ adj. not using nuclear power or weapons

no-no /nónō/ (plural **no-nos**) n. sth that is not allowed or is disapproved of (informal)

nonobjective /nónnəb jéktiv/ adj. 1. NOT IMPARTIAL based on sb's opinions or feelings, rather than on facts or evidence 2. ARTS = **nonrepresentational** —**nonobjectivity** /nón ob jek tívvəti/ n.

nonobservance /nónnəb zúrv'nss/ n. a failure to comply with sth such as a law or practice, especially a religious practice —**nonobservant** adj.

no-nonsense adj. 1. BUSINESSLIKE direct and practical in dealing with things or people 2. BASIC AND UNADORNED basic and offering no extras, frills, or luxuries

nonparametric /nón parrə méttrik/ adj. used to describe or relating to statistical methods that do not require assumptions about the form of the underlying distribution

nonpareil /nónpə ráy'l/ n. 1. SB OR STH UNPARALLELED sb who or sth that has no equal 2. PRINTING SIX-POINT TYPE a size of printers' type equivalent to six point (dated) ■ adj. PEERLESS having no equal [15thC. From French, literally 'not (having) equal', from pareil 'equal', from popular Latin pariculus, diminutive of Latin par 'equal' (see PAIR).]

nonpartisan /nón paárti zán/, **nonpartizan** adj. NOT SUPPORTING ANY POLITICAL PARTY not belonging to, supporting, or biased in favour of any political party ■ n. SB NOT SUPPORTING ANY POLITICAL PARTY sb who does not belong to, support, or show bias in favour of any political party

nonpayment /non páymənt/ n. a refusal or failure to pay money owed

nonpenetrative /nón pénnitrətiv/ adj. not involving penetration of the vagina or anus by the penis

nonpersistent /nónpər sístənt/ adj. used to describe chemicals, especially pesticides, that tend to decompose within a short time after application and are used with a view to limiting environmental damage

nonperson /nón púrss'n/ n. 1. SB IGNORED BY A REGIME sb who is ignored by a government and the news media it controls, usually because the person's political or ideological views are disapproved of by the government 2. INSIGNIFICANT PERSON sb of no importance or significance

nonplaying /nón pláy ing/ adj. not playing in a game or competition, but usually having a coaching or advisory role

nonplus /non plúss/ vt. (-plusses, -plussing, -plussed) CONFUSE SB to make sb feel confused and unable to decide what to do ■ n. STATE OF CONFUSION a state of confusion and nervousness (dated) [Late 16thC. From Latin non plus 'no more'; from being a state in which 'no more' can be done.] —**nonplussed** adj.

nonprescription /nónpri skrípsh'n/ adj. PHARM = **over-the-counter** adj. 1

nonproductive /nónprə dúktiv/ adj. 1. NOT PRODUCING GOOD RESULTS not producing adequate or satisfactory results 2. ECON NOT INVOLVED IN PRODUCING GOODS not directly involved in producing goods 3. NOT YIELDING STH not producing crops or a natural resource 4. MED NOT PRODUCTIVE OF PHLEGM used to describe a cough that does not produce phlegm —**nonproductively** adv. —**nonproductiveness** n.

nonprofessional /nónprə fésh'nəl/ n. SB WHO IS NOT PROFESSIONAL sb who does not have professional status ■ adj. NOT PROFESSIONAL not having professional status

nonprofit /nón próffit/ adj. US = **non-profitmaking**

nonprofitmaking /nón próffit mayking/ adj. not operated with the primary aim of making a profit. US term **nonprofit**

nonproliferation /nónprə líffə ráysh'n/ n. the practice of limiting the production or spread of sth, especially nuclear weapons (often used before a noun) ○ nonproliferation agreements

nonpros /nón prós/ n. (plural **-prosses**) = **non prosequitur** (informal) ■ vt. (-prosses, -prossing, -prossed) JUDGE AGAINST PLAINTIFF IN DEFAULT to enter a judgment against a plaintiff who fails to appear in court (informal) [Late 17thC. Shortening.]

non prosequitur /nónprō sékwitər/ n. a judgment in the defendant's favour when the plaintiff fails to appear in court [From Latin, 'he or she does not prosecute']

nonreader /non reédər/ n. sb who does not or is unable to read, especially a child who has difficulty in learning to read

nonrecombinant /nón ri kómbinənt/ adj. not produced by artificially manipulating genetic material

nonrelativistic /nón rélləti vístik/ adj. not affected by the effects of relativity —**nonrelativistically** adv.

nonrepresentational /nón réppri zen táysh'nəl/ adj. not aiming to depict an object but composed with the focus on internal structure and form —**nonrepresentationalism** n. —**nonrepresentationally** adv.

nonresident /nón rézzidənt/ adj. 1. NOT RESIDING IN A PLACE not living or staying in a particular place 2. NOT INVOLVING LIVING AT WORKPLACE not involving living at the place of work ■ n. SB NOT RESIDING IN PLACE sb who is not living or staying in a particular place or at a workplace —**nonresidence** n. —**nonresidency** n. —**nonresidential** /nón rezzi dénsh'l/ adj.

nonresistant /nónri zístənt/ adj. 1. SUSCEPTIBLE TO STH unable to withstand sth, especially a disease 2. PASSIVELY OBEDIENT exhibiting passive obedience to people in authority —**nonresistance** n.

nonrestrictive /nón ri stríktiv/ adj. with few or no restrictions

nonrestrictive clause n. a relative clause that gives additional information about a noun or pronoun in the main clause but that is not essential to the understanding of the main clause. A nonrestrictive clause is usually separated from the rest of the sentence by commas, e.g. 'My partner, who is an artist, comes from Edinburgh'.

nonreturnable /nón ri túrnəb'l/ adj. not able to be returned to the place of purchase for refund of a deposit

nonreturn valve /nón ri túrn-/ n. a valve that allows flow in only one direction

nonrigid /nón ríjid/ adj. 1. FLEXIBLE not stiff 2. AIR WITH A FLEXIBLE GAS CONTAINER used to describe airships such as balloons or dirigibles that have a flexible gas container held in shape by the internal gas pressure

nonrun /non rún/ adj. designed not to ladder easily ○ nonrun tights

nonscheduled /nón shéddyoold/ adj. 1. UNPLANNED not planned to happen as part of a schedule 2. TRANSP OPERATING WITHOUT PUBLISHED SCHEDULE operating according to demand, rather than on a published schedule

nonsectarian /nón sek táiri ən/ adj. 1. NOT RELATING TO RELIGIOUS SUBGROUP not relating to a group or denomination within a wider religion or disputes between such groups 2. NOT RESTRICTED TO ONE DE-

NOMINATION not restricted to members of one religious denomination, but open to all

nonsense /nónssənss/ n. 1. MEANINGLESS LANGUAGE OR BEHAVIOUR pointless or meaningless language or behaviour 2. POINTLESS ACT OR UTTERANCE an instance of pointless or meaningless language or behaviour ○ To pay more than the price would be a nonsense. 3. IRRITATING BEHAVIOUR disrespectful, obnoxious, or irritating behaviour ○ the kind of judge who won't stand for any nonsense from barristers 4. = **nonsense verse** 5. **nonsense, nonsense codon** GENETICS DNA SECTION PRODUCING NO AMINO ACID a triplet of nucleotides, or codon, in a DNA molecule that does not code for any amino acid. These codons are believed to signal the beginning and end of the synthesis of particular protein molecules. ■ interj. EXPRESSION OF CONTRADICTION used to contradict what sb has said or written [Early 17thC. Coined from NON- + SENSE.] ◇ **make (a) nonsense of sth** to make sth seem pointless or absurd

— **WORD KEY: CULTURAL NOTE** —

A Book of Nonsense, a collection of poems by English writer Edward Lear (1846). Written for the grandchildren of the Earl of Derby, these songs, verses, and limericks, illustrated with Lear's own line drawings, conjure up a bizarre world where strange beings participate in surreal adventures. Although comic and fantastic, the verses are also tinged with a melancholy thought to reflect the author's depressive personality.

nonsense verse n. poetry that is written in deliberately absurd language for humorous effect, mainly for children

nonsense word n. a word with no meaning, usually created for humorous effect

nonsensical /non sénssik'l/ adj. 1. MEANINGLESS having no sense or meaning 2. LAUGHABLE deserving ridicule —**nonsensically** adv. —**nonsensicalness** n.

non sequitur /nón sékwitər/ n. 1. INCONGRUOUS STATEMENT a statement that appears unrelated to a statement that it follows 2. UNWARRANTED CONCLUSION a conclusion that does not follow from its premises [From Latin, literally 'it does not follow']

nonsexist /nón séksist/ adj. avoiding or not involving discrimination, limitation, or stereotypes based on gender

nonshrink /nón shríngk/ adj. resistant to shrinking when washed

nonskid /nón skíd/ adj. designed to prevent or lessen skidding

nonslip /nón slíp/ adj. designed to prevent people from slipping

nonsmoker /non smókər/ n. 1. SB WHO DOES NOT SMOKE sb who does not smoke cigarettes, cigars, or a pipe 2. RAIL COMPARTMENT WHERE NO SMOKING IS ALLOWED a carriage or compartment in a train in which smoking is not allowed

nonsmoking /nón smóking/ adj. 1. RESTRICTED TO NON-SMOKERS reserved for people who do not want to smoke cigarettes, cigars, or pipes 2. NOT SMOKING not smoking cigarettes, cigars, or a pipe ■ n. AREA WHERE SMOKING IS FORBIDDEN an area of, e.g., a restaurant or an aircraft, where smoking is not permitted ○ Do you want smoking or nonsmoking?

nonspecific urethritis /nónspə síffik-/ n. inflammation of the urethra not caused by any identified infection. It is sexually transmitted but is not caused by gonorrhoeal organisms

nonstandard /nón stándərd/ adj. 1. NOT OF ACCEPTED STANDARD not conforming to an accepted standard 2. LANGUAGE NOT USED IN STANDARD LANGUAGE not conforming to a standard accepted as grammatically correct by educated native speakers, or not used by educated native speakers

nonstarter /nón staártər/ n. 1. STH OR SB UNLIKELY TO SUCCEED sth that or sb who is obviously going to be unsuccessful right from the beginning (informal) 2. HORSERACING HORSE THAT DOES NOT COMPETE a horse that does not run in a race in which it has been entered 3. SPORTS COMPETITOR WHO WITHDRAWS BEFORE START a competitor who does not start a race, event, or competition in which he or she has been entered

Non-Status Indian /nón stáytəss-/, **non-status Indian** *n. Can* a member of an indigenous people whom the federal government do not recognize as having special rights and privileges, especially the right to live on a reserve

nonsteroid /nón stéer oyd, -stér-/ *n.* DRUG WITHOUT STEROID a drug that does not contain a steroid ■ *adj.* **nonsteroid, nonsteroidal** NOT STEROID not containing or being a steroid

nonstick /nón stík/ *adj.* with a coating or surface that prevents food sticking during cooking

nonstop /nón stóp/ *adj., adv.* **1.** WITHOUT STOP continuing without a stop ○ *a nonstop flight* **2.** WITHOUT INTERRUPTION continuing without interruption or rest ○ *a weekend of nonstop partying*

nonsuch *n.* = **nonesuch**

nonsuit /nón sóot, -syóot/ *n.* the dismissal of a suit by a judge when the plaintiff fails to make out a legal case or to produce adequate evidence

nonsupport /nón sə páwrt/ *n.* failure or refusal to supply legally required financial support, usually for a child or ex-spouse

nontarget /nón taargit/ *adj.* used to describe cells, tissues, or organisms that are not intended for treatment, e.g. by drugs or radiation, but may be affected by such treatment aimed elsewhere

nontitle /nón tít'l/ *adj.* not competed in to win a sports title or championship ○ *a nontitle fight*

non-treaty Indian /nón tréeti-/ *n. Can* = **Non-Status Indian**

non troppo /non tróppō/ *adv., adj.* not too much (*used as a musical direction*) [From Italian]

non-U /nón yóo/ *adj.* not belonging to or characteristic of the upper classes (*dated informal*) ○ *a non-U word for 'napkin'* [*U* abbreviation of *upper (class)*]

nonunion /nón yóonyən/ *adj.* **1.** NOT IN UNION not belonging to a trade union **2.** NOT USING UNION MEMBERS not employing trade-union members **3.** NOT MADE BY UNION MEMBERS not produced by trade-union members —**nonunionized** *adj.*

nonuser /non yóozər/ *n.* sb who does not use sth, especially sb who does not take addictive drugs

nonverbal /nón vúrb'l/ *adj.* not using or involving words

nonverbal communication *n.* methods of communicating other than by using words, e.g. facial expressions, hand gestures, and tone of voice

nonviable /nón ví əb'l/ *adj.* **1.** BIOL NOT ABLE TO DEVELOP ALONE incapable of growing and developing independently **2.** NOT ABLE TO SUCCEED not capable of succeeding

nonvintage /nón víntij/ *adj.* not belonging to an especially good year for a wine and not identified by year

nonviolence /nón ví ələnss/ *n.* **1.** PRINCIPLE OF REFRAINING FROM USING VIOLENCE the principle of refraining from using violence, especially as a means of protest **2.** ABSENCE OF VIOLENCE the absence of or freedom from violence —**nonviolent** *adj.* —**nonviolently** *adv.*

nonvoter /non vṓtər/ *n.* sb who does not vote or is not entitled to vote

nonvoting /nón vṓting/ *adj.* used to describe a share that does not give the holder the right to vote at company meetings

nonwoven /nón wṓv'n/ *adj.* made of fibres that have been bonded or interlocked by mechanical, chemical, thermal, or solvent methods

nonzero /nón zéerō/ *adj.* greater or less than zero in value or quantity

noodle[1] /nóod'l/ *n.* a long thin strip of pasta. Noodles are a staple of Italian and Chinese cookery. (*often used in the plural*) [Late 18thC. From German *Nudel*, of uncertain origin: perhaps a variant of *Knödel* 'dumpling'.]

noodle[2] /nóod'l/ *n.* **1.** *US* HEAD the head or mind (*slang*) **2.** SB UNINTELLIGENT a term that deliberately, though perhaps affectionately, insults sb's intelligence or common sense (*dated informal*) [Mid-18thC. Origin uncertain: perhaps an alteration of NODDLE or NODDY.]

noodle[3] /nóod'l/ (**-dles, -dling, -dled**) *vti.* to improvise on a musical instrument in a random, meandering fashion, often for the purpose of warming up (*slang*) [Mid-19thC. Origin uncertain: probably from likening such playing to the disorganized, convoluted appearance of a dish of noodles.]

nook /nóok/ *n.* **1.** PRIVATE PLACE a quiet private place **2.** SMALL CORNER OR RECESS a corner or small recess in a room [13thC. Origin uncertain: probably from Old Norse.] ◇ **every nook and cranny** every tiny part of a place

nookie /nóoki/, **nooky** *n.* sexual intercourse (*slang*) (*sometimes considered offensive*) [Early 20thC. Origin uncertain: perhaps formed from NOOK (from sex taking place in a private place).]

noon /noon/ *n.* **1.** 12 O'CLOCK MIDDAY 12 o'clock in the middle of the day **2.** MOST IMPORTANT PERIOD the most important period of sth (*literary*) [Pre-12thC. From Latin *nona (hora)* 'ninth (hour) (of the Roman day, counted from sunrise)', feminine of *nonus* 'ninth' (source of English *nonagenarian*). Originally about 3 p.m.]

noonday /nóon day/ *adj.* RELATING TO MIDDAY relating to or happening at midday ■ *n.* MIDDAY the middle of the day (*dated or literary*)

no one *pron.* no person at all

noontide /nóon tīd/ *n.* the middle of the day (*literary*)

noontime /nóon tīm/ *n.* the middle of the day, around 12 o'clock

Noonuccal /nṓ ō núk'l/, **Oodgeroo** (1920–93) Australian poet. Her collections include *We Are Going* (1964), the first book of poems published by an Aboriginal writer. Born **Kath Walker**

noose /nooss/ *n.* **1.** LOOP IN ROPE a loop, tied with a knot, at the end of a rope that permits tightening and slackening, and is used for trapping animals or hanging people **2.** STH THAT TRAPS SB sth that traps sb in an unpleasant or unwanted situation ■ *vt.* (**nooses, noosing, noosed**) **1.** CATCH WITH A NOOSE to catch sb or sth with a noose **2.** TIE IN A NOOSE to tie a rope or cord in a noose [15thC. Origin uncertain: probably via Old French *nos* (singular) and *nous* (plural) from Latin *nodus* 'knot' (source of English *denouement* and *node*).]

Nootka /nóotkə, nóot-/ (*plural* **-kas** *or* **-ka**) *n.* **1.** PEOPLES MEMBER OF NATIVE N AMERICAN PEOPLE a member of a Native North American people of the western coast of Vancouver Island, British Columbia, and Cape Flattery, on the Olympic Peninsula in Washington State **2.** LANGUAGE LANGUAGE OF NOOTKA the language of the Nootka, belonging to the Wakashan family of languages. Few people now speak Nootka. [Early 19thC. Named after *Nootka* Sound, an inlet on the coast of Vancouver Island, British Columbia, Canada.] —**Nootka** *adj.*

nopal /nóp'l/ (*plural* **-pals** *or* **-pal**) *n.* **1.** PLANTS AMERICAN CACTUS an American cactus that has red flowers and long stamens and is a host plant to the cochineal insect. Latin name: *Nopalea cochinellifera.* **2.** FOOD FRUIT OF NOPAL the edible fruit of a nopal cactus, used in Mexican cookery [Mid-18thC. Via French from, ultimately, Nahuatl *nopalli*, literally 'cactus'.]

no-par, **no-par-value** *adj.* used to describe a security without a par or face value

nope /nōp/ *interj.* used to indicate a negative response in order to refuse, deny, or disagree with sth (*slang*) [Late 19thC. Alteration of NO[1] (probably reflecting the sound of the lips' closure after an emphatic pronunciation of the word).]

nor /nawr/ *conj.* **1.** AND NOT used to introduce an alternative, after a first alternative that is preceded by 'neither' (*used in negative statements*) ○ *Neither he nor his wife had profited in any way from the crime.* **2.** AND NOT EITHER used to indicate that what has just been said also applies to sb or sth else, or to add extra information to what has just been said (*used after negative statements and followed by 'have', 'do', or 'be'*) ○ *He doesn't want to move to another town, and nor do I.* ○ *No surrounding tissue was damaged, nor did the infection spread.* ■ *prep.* THAN than (*nonstandard*) ■ *conj.* NEITHER neither (*literary*) [13thC. Contraction of obsolete *nouther* 'neither, nor' (see NEITHER).]

NOR /nawr/ *n.* a logical operator with two arguments that returns true if, and only if, both arguments are false [Mid-20thC. Blend of NOT and OR.]

Nor. *abbr.* **1.** North **2.** Norway **3.** Norwegian **4.** Norman

nor- *prefix.* an unaltered parent compound ○ *nornicotine* [Shortening of NORMAL]

noradrenaline /náwrə drénnəlin/, **noradrenalin** *n.* MED a hormone, secreted by the adrenal gland and similar to adrenaline, that is also the principal neurotransmitter of sympathetic nerve endings supplying the major organs and skin. It increases blood pressure and rate and depth of breathing, raises the level of blood sugar, and decreases the activity of the intestines. US term **norepinephrine**

noradrenergic /náwr adrə núrjik/ *adj.* releasing or involving noradrenaline in the transmission of nerve impulses

NOR circuit *n.* a computer circuit with two inputs and one output where the output is on only when both inputs are off

Nordic /náwrdik/ *adj.* **1.** SCANDINAVIAN relating to the countries of northwestern Europe, especially the Scandinavian countries and Iceland **2.** ANTHROP TALL, FAIR, AND BLUE-EYED tall, blonde, fair-skinned and blue-eyed, in a way that is considered to be typical of people from Scandinavian countries **3.** **Nordic, nordic** SKIING INVOLVING CROSS-COUNTRY SKIING OR JUMPING used to describe or relating to ski events involving either cross-country racing or ski jumping or both ■ *n.* SB NORDIC sb from a Nordic country or of Nordic appearance [Late 19thC. From French *nordique*, from *nord* 'north', ultimately from a prehistoric Germanic word that is also the ancestor of English *north*.]

Nord-Ostsee-Kanal /náwrt óst zay kə nál/ = **Kiel Canal**

nor'easter /náwr éestər/ *n.* METEOROL = **northeaster** [Mid-19thC. Alteration.]

norepinephrine /náwr eppi néffrin/ *n. US* MED = **noradrenaline**

norethisterone /náwr e thístərōn/ *n.* a progestogen drug used in oral contraceptives and hormone replacement therapy and to treat premenstrual syndrome, menstrual disorders, endometriosis, and cancer

Norf. *abbr.* Norfolk

Norfolk /náwrfək/ county in eastern England, with a coastline on the Wash and the North Sea. Population: 772,400 (1995). Area: 5,360 sq. km/2,069 sq. mi.

Norfolk Island island dependency of Australia in the southwestern Pacific Ocean, 1,676 km/1,042 mi. northeast of Sydney. Population: 2,756 (1995). Area: 34 sq. km/13 sq. mi.

Norfolk Island pine *n.* a tall symmetrical pine tree, native to Norfolk Island, but now found in many parts of Australia, especially lining the promenades of eastern coastal towns. Latin name: *Araucaria heterophylla.*

Norfolk jacket *n.* a loose jacket with a belt and box pleats, first worn by men and later adapted to women's fashions [Named after NORFOLK]

Norfolk terrier *n.* a small wire-haired breed of terrier with a short tail and drop ears [Named after NORFOLK]

norg /nawrg/, **nork** /nawrk/ *n. Aus* a woman's breast (*slang offensive; often used in the plural*) [Mid-20thC. Origin uncertain: perhaps from *Norco* butter, whose packaging shows a cow's udder.]

NOR gate *n.* = **NOR circuit**

nori /náwri/ *n.* an edible preparation of dried pressed seaweed, often used to wrap sushi [Late 19thC. From Japanese.]

noria /náwri ə/ *n.* a series of buckets on a water wheel, used for raising water from a stream [Late 18thC. Via Spanish from Arabic *nā'ūra*.]

norite /náwr īt/ *n.* a coarse-grained igneous rock containing mainly plagioclase and orthopyroxene [Late 19thC. Formed from NORWAY + -ITE.] —**noritic** /naw ríttik/ *adj.*

norm /nawrm/ *n.* **1.** STANDARD PATTERN OF BEHAVIOUR a standard pattern of behaviour that is considered normal in a particular society **2.** USUAL SITUATION the usual situation or circumstances **3.** REQUIRED ACHIEVEMENT LEVEL a required level of achievement **4.** PSYCHOL EXPECTED RANGE OF FUNCTIONING the range of functioning that can be expected of members of a particular population, e.g. babies of nine months or ten-year-old children. Psychologists use this to determine whether individuals functioning outside the expected range may need specialist help or support. **5.** MATH **REAL-VALUED FUNCTION** the magnitude of a vector expressed as the square root of the sum of the squares of the absolute values of the components of the vector **6.** MATH **= mode** *n.* 6 [Early 19thC. Anglicization of Latin *norma* 'carpenter's square, rule', of uncertain origin; perhaps ultimately from Greek *gnōmōn*. Subsequently influenced by NORMAL.]

Norm /nawrm/ *n. Aus* a stereotype of an Australian male who enjoys watching sport on television while consuming large quantities of beer (*slang*) ○ *It's Grand Final weekend so your average Norm will be glued to the box.* [From the male forename *Norm* short for *Norman,* influenced by NORM, NORMAL]

norm. *abbr.* GEOM normal

Norm. *abbr.* Norman

Norma /náwrmə/ *n.* a small faint constellation of the southern hemisphere lying in the Milky Way, located between Ara and Lupus

normal /náwrm'l/ *adj.* **1.** USUAL conforming to the usual standard, type, or custom **2.** HEALTHY physically, mentally, and emotionally healthy **3.** OCCURRING NATURALLY maintained or occurring in a natural state **4.** MEASURE **ONE GRAM EQUIVALENT WEIGHT PER LITRE** containing an equivalent weight of solute in grams per litre of solution **5.** CHEM **UNBRANCHED** used to describe aliphatic hydrocarbons with unbranched chains of carbon atoms **6.** GEOM **= perpendicular** *adj.* 3 ■ *n.* **1.** USUAL STANDARD the usual standard, type, or custom **2.** GEOM **PERPENDICULAR LINE OR PLANE** a line or plane that is perpendicular to another line or plane [15thC. Directly or via French from Latin *normalis* 'made according to the square', from *norma* (see NORM).]

normal curve *n.* the symmetrical bell-shaped curve of a normal distribution

normalcy /náwrm'lssi/ *n. US* **= normality**

normal distribution *n.* a probability frequency distribution for a random variable that theoretically takes on a bell shape symmetrical about the mean

normalise *vti.* **= normalize**

normality /nawr málləti/ *n.* the way things are under normal circumstances

normalize /náwrmə līz/ (-**izes, -izing, -ized**), **normalise** (-**ises, -ising, -ised**) *v.* **1.** *vti.* MAKE OR BECOME NORMAL to make sth normal or return sth to normal, or become or return to normal **2.** *vt.* MAKE CONFORM to make sth or sb conform to a standard **3.** *vt.* METALL HEAT STEEL to heat steel above a particular temperature and then cool it in order to reduce internal stress —**normalization** /náwrmə līt záysh'n/ *n.*

normally /náwrm'li/ *adv.* **1.** ORDINARILY as a custom or habit ○ *Normally, we go swimming on Sundays.* **2.** IN USUAL WAY in the usual or standard way ○ *The trains are running normally again.*

normal school *n.* a school or college for training teachers, especially in France and, in the past, in England, the United States, and Canada (*dated*) [Mid-19thC. Modelled on French *école normale;* from the first French school so named being considered a model for others.]

Norman /náwrmən/ *n.* **1.** HIST **MEDIEVAL INHABITANT OF NORMANDY OR ENGLAND** a member of a Viking people who raided and then settled in the French province subsequently known as Normandy and who later successfully invaded England in 1066 **2.** PEOPLES **SB FROM NORMANDY** a person who was born or brought up in the French region of Normandy **3.** LANG **= Norman French** *n.* **1 4.** ARCHIT **STYLE OF MEDIEVAL ARCHITECTURE** a style of Romanesque architecture developed by the Normans in the Middle Ages, characterized by groined vaults, heavy walls, and deeply recessed portals [13thC. From Old French *Normans,* plural of *Normant,* from Old Norse *Norðmaðr* (*Norðmenn* in plural), literally 'northman', from *norð* 'north'.] —**Norman** *adj.*

Norman /náwrmən/, **Greg** (b. 1955) Australian golfer. He was the winner of the British Open (1986, 1993), and the World Match Play Championship (1980, 1983, and 1986). Full name **Gregory John Norman.** Known as **Great White Shark**

Norman Conquest *n.* the invasion and conquest of England by the Normans, led by William the Conqueror, in 1066

Normandy /náwrməndi/ region in northwestern France, on the English Channel. Capital: Rouen.

Norman French *n.* **1.** FRENCH SPOKEN BY MEDIEVAL NORMANS a variety of French spoken by the Normans in the Middle Ages **2.** FRENCH DIALECT OF MODERN NORMANDY the French dialect spoken in modern Normandy

normative /náwrmətiv/ *adj.* (*formal*) **1.** OF STANDARDS relating to standards **2.** CREATING STANDARDS tending to create or prescribe standards [Late 19thC. From French, from Latin *norma* (see NORM).] —**normatively** *adv.* —**normativeness** *n.*

norming /náwrming/ *n. US* the practice of adjusting the scores on standardized tests in order to compensate for the possible effects that ethnic and cultural differences may have on the test results

normotensive /náwrmō ténssiv/ *adj.* WITH NORMAL BLOOD PRESSURE having or indicating normal blood pressure ■ *n.* SB WITH NORMAL BLOOD PRESSURE sb who has normal blood pressure [Mid-20thC. From NORM or NORMAL + TENSIVE.]

normothermia /náwrmō thúrmi ə/ *n.* the state of having a normal body temperature —**normothermic** *adj.*

norm-referenced *adj.* using a comparison of a pupil's performance in a test with the performance of other children in the same test

norm-referencing *n.* the comparing of a pupil's performance in a test with the performance of other children in the same test

Norse /nawrss/ *adj.* **1.** HIST OF OLD SCANDINAVIA relating to ancient or medieval Scandinavia, or its people or culture **2.** OF NORWAY relating to Norway, or its people or culture **3.** LANG OF N GERMANIC LANGUAGES relating to the North Germanic languages ■ *npl.* **1.** HIST VIKINGS the Viking people of medieval Scandinavia **2.** PEOPLES NORWEGIANS the people of Norway **3.** PEOPLES SCANDINAVIANS the people of Scandinavia **4.** LANG, PEOPLES N GERMANIC NATIVE SPEAKERS the people who speak one of the North Germanic languages as their native language ■ *n.* LANG N GERMANIC LANGUAGE a language belonging to the North Germanic branch of Indo-European, especially Danish, Icelandic, or Norwegian in their earlier forms. ◊ **Old Norse, Proto-Norse** [Late 16thC. Via Dutch *Noorsch* from *noordsch* 'northern'.]

Norseman /náwrssmən/ (*plural* **-men** /-mən/) *n.* a member of one of the medieval Scandinavian groups, especially a Viking

north /nawrth/ *n.* **1.** DIRECTION the direction that lies directly to the left of sb facing the rising sun or that is located towards the top of a conventional map of the world **2.** COMPASS POINT one of the cardinal points on a compass. North is 90 degrees anti-clockwise from east. **3.** north, North AREA IN THE NORTH the part of an area, region, or country that is situated in or towards the north **4.** CHR LEFT-HAND SIDE OF CHURCH the left-hand side of a church as you face the altar from the central section of the building **5.** north, North POSITION EQUIVALENT TO NORTH the position equivalent to north in any diagram consisting of four points at 90-degree intervals ■ *adj.* **1.** IN THE NORTH situated in, facing, or coming from the north of a place, region, or country **2.** METEOROL FROM THE NORTH blowing from the north ○ *a north wind* ■ *adv.* TOWARDS THE NORTH in or towards the north [Old English *norþ,* of prehistoric Germanic origin]

North /nawrth/, **Frederick, 8th Baron North** (1732–92) British statesman. He was British prime minister from 1770 to 1782, and was widely held responsible for the US War of Independence despite his opposition to the war. Known as **Lord North**

North Africa northern part of the African continent, comprising Morocco, Algeria, Tunisia, Libya, and northern Egypt —**North African** *adj., n.*

Northallerton /náwrth állərtən/ market town in North Yorkshire, England. Population: 11,774 (1991).

Northam /náwrthəm/ town in Devon, southwestern England, situated 76 km/47 mi. north of Plymouth. Population: 8,715 (1981).

North America the third largest continent in the world, comprising Greenland, Canada, the United States, and Mexico —**North American** *adj., n.*

Northampton /náwr thámptən/ city and county town of Northamptonshire, central England. Population: 189,700 (1995).

Northamptonshire /náwr thámptənshər/ county in central England. It is predominantly rural, with industry near the county town of Northampton. Population: 599,300 (1995). Area: 2,370 sq. km/915 sq. mi.

Northants /náwr thants/ *abbr.* Northamptonshire

North Atlantic drift *n.* the relatively warm current, originating in the Gulf of Mexico, that flows across the surface of the North Atlantic Ocean from Newfoundland to northwestern Europe, influencing the latter's climate

North Atlantic Treaty Organization *n.* full form of NATO

North Borneo former name for **Sabah** (until 1963)

northbound /náwrth bownd/ *adj.* leading, going, or travelling towards the north

north by east *n.* the direction or compass point midway between north and north-northeast. —**north by east** *adj., adv.*

north by west *n.* the direction or compass point midway between north and north-northwest. —**north by west** *adj., adv.*

North Cape promontory in northern Norway, on Magerøya Island, on the Barents Sea

North Carolina

North Carolina /nawrth karə līnə/ state in the eastern United States, bordered by the Atlantic Ocean, South Carolina, Georgia, Tennessee, and Virginia. Capital: Raleigh. Population: 7,425,183 (1997). Area: 136,420 sq. km/52,672 sq. mi. —**North Carolinian** /nawrth karə līnee ən/ *adj., n.*

North Channel strait of the Atlantic Ocean between northeastern Ireland and southwestern Scotland. Width: 37 km/23 mi.

northcountryman /náwrth kúntrimən/ (*plural* **-men** /-mən/) *n.* a man who was born or brought up in the northern region of England

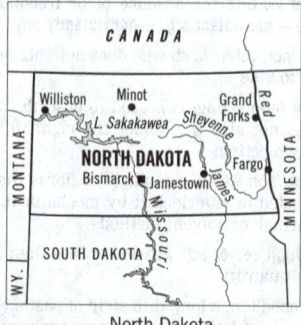

North Dakota

North Dakota state in the north-central United States, bordered by Minnesota, South Dakota, Montana, and Canada. Capital: Bismarck. Population: 640,883 (1997). Area: 183,123 sq. km/70,704 sq. mi. —**North Dakotan** *adj., n.*

North Downs /nawrth dównz/ range of chalk hills in

southern England, in Surrey and Kent. The highest peak is Leith Hill, 294 m/965 ft.

northeast /náwrth eest/; *nautical usage* /náwr eest/ *n.* **1.** COMPASS POINT BETWEEN N AND E the direction or compass point midway between north and east. **2. northeast, Northeast** AREA IN THE NORTHEAST the part of an area, region, or country that is situated in or towards the northeast ■ *adj.* **1. northeast, Northeast** situated in, facing, or lying towards the northeast of a region, place, or country **2.** METEOROL FROM NORTHEAST blowing from the northeast ○ *a northeast wind* ■ *adv.* TOWARDS THE NORTHEAST in or towards the northeast

Northeast *n.* **1.** NORTHEASTERN ENGLAND northeastern England, especially the area from the River Tees northwards including Tyneside, Northumberland, and Durham **2.** *US* NORTHEASTERN US REGION a region of the northeastern United States, usually thought of as consisting of the New England states, sometimes together with eastern New York, Pennsylvania, and New Jersey

northeast by east *n.* the direction or compass point midway between northeast and east-northeast. —**northeast by east** *adj., adv.*

northeast by north *n.* the direction or compass point midway between northeast and north-northeast. —**northeast by north** *adj., adv.*

northeaster /náwrth eester/; *nautical usage* /náwr eester/ *n.* a storm or wind that blows from the northeast

northeasterly /náwrth eesterli/; *nautical usage* /náwr eesterli/ *adj.* **1.** IN THE NORTHEAST situated in or towards the northeast **2.** METEOROL FROM THE NORTHEAST blowing from the northeast ○ *a northeasterly wind* ■ *n.* (*plural* **-lies**) METEOROL WIND FROM THE NORTHEAST a wind blowing from the northeast —**northeasterly** *adv.*

northeastern /náwrth eestern/; *nautical usage* /náwr eestern/ *adj.* **1.** IN THE NORTHEAST situated in the northeast of a region or country **2.** COMING FROM OR FACING NORTHEAST coming or blowing from, or facing towards the northeast **3. northeastern, Northeastern** OF THE NORTHEAST relating or native to the northeast of a region or country —**northeasterner** *n.* —**northeasternmost** *adj.*

Northeast Passage sea passage extending from the North Sea eastwards along the northern coast of Europe and Asia to the Pacific Ocean. It was first successfully navigated by Adolf Erik Nordenskøld in 1878–79.

northeastward /náwrth eestward/; *nautical usage* /náwr eestward/ *adj.* IN THE NORTHEAST towards or in the northeast ■ *n.* POINT IN THE NORTHEAST a direction towards or a point in the northeast ■ *adv.* EAST OF NORTH towards or from east of due north —**northeastwardly** *adj., adv.* —**northeastwards** *adv.*

northerly /náwrtherli/ *adj.* **1.** IN THE NORTH situated in or towards the north **2.** METEOROL FROM THE NORTH blowing from the north ○ *a northerly wind* ■ *n.* (*plural* **-lies**) METEOROL WIND FROM THE NORTH a wind blowing from the north [Mid-16thC. Ultimately from NORTH, on the model of *easterly*.] —**northerly** *adv.*

northern /náwrthern/ *adj.* **1.** IN THE NORTH situated in or towards the north of a region or country **2.** NORTH OF EQUATOR lying north of the equator or north of the celestial equator **3.** FACING NORTH situated on the north side of sth or facing north **4. northern, Northern** OF THE NORTH relating or native to the north of a region or country **5.** METEOROL FROM THE NORTH blowing from the north ○ *a northern wind*

Northern Cross *n.* a cross formed by six stars in the constellation Cygnus

Northern Crown *n.* ASTRON = **Corona Borealis**

northerner /náwrtherner/ *n.* sb who lives in or comes from the northern part of a country or region

northern harrier *n.* *US* = **hen harrier**

northern hemisphere *n.* **1.** GEOG HALF OF EARTH NORTH OF EQUATOR the half of the Earth that lies to the north of the equator **2.** ASTRON NORTHERN HALF OF CELESTIAL SPHERE the half of the celestial sphere north of the celestial equator

Northern Ireland province of the United Kingdom of Great Britain and Northern Ireland, situated in the northeastern portion of the island of Ireland.

Capital: Belfast. Population: 1,641,700 (1994). Area: 13,483 sq. km/5,206 sq. mi.

Northern Isles /náwrthern ílz/ ♦ **Orkney and Shetland islands**

Northernism /náwrthernizəm/ *n.* a pronunciation, word, or other linguistic construction typical of the northern region of a country

northern lights *npl.* ASTRON = **aurora borealis**

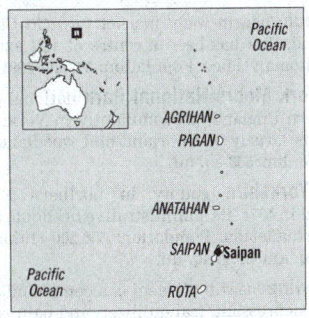
Northern Mariana Islands

Northern Mariana Islands /-marri ánnə-/ self-governing commonwealth of the United States, situated in the western Pacific Ocean and comprising all of the Mariana Islands except Guam. Area: 477 sq. km/184 sq. mi.

northernmost /náwrthern mōst/ *adj.* situated farthest north

northern oriole *n.* a North American oriole that has two subspecies, the Baltimore oriole and Bullock's oriole. The males have black and orange plumage. Latin name: *Icterus galbula*.

Northern Paiute (*plural* **Northern Paiute** or **Northern Paiutes**), **Northern Piute** (*plural* **Northern Piute** or **Northern Piutes**) *n.* ◊ **Southern Paiute 1.** PEOPLES MEMBER OF NATIVE N AMERICAN PEOPLE a member of a Native North American people of Oregon, Nevada, and northeastern California **2.** LANG NATIVE N AMERICAN LANGUAGE a Native North American language spoken in Oregon, Nevada, and northeastern California, belonging to the Uto-Aztecan branch of Aztec-Tanoan languages. Northern Paiute is spoken by about 6,000 people. —**Northern Paiute** *adj.*

northern pike *n.* ZOOL = **pike**[1] *n.* 1

Northern Piute PEOPLES, LANG = **Northern Paiute**

Northern Renaissance *n.* a northern European cultural and intellectual movement of the 15th century in France, England, Scotland, the Low Countries, and Germany that placed more emphasis on religion than the Italian Renaissance did

Northern Territory territory in north-central Australia. It became self-governing in 1978. Capital: Darwin. Population: 182,000 (1996). Area: 1,346,200 sq. km/519,771 sq. mi.

North Germanic *n.* a group of languages that includes Danish, Faroese, Icelandic, Norwegian, and Swedish and forms a subgroup of the Germanic branch of Indo-European languages. About 20 million people speak one of the North Germanic languages. —**North Germanic** *adj.*

northing /náwrthing, -thing/ *n.* **1.** MOVEMENT NORTH distance covered or movement made in a northerly direction, especially as measured by the difference in latitude between two points **2.** PROGRESS NORTH progress made in a northern direction **3.** MAPS LATITUDINAL GRID LINE ON MAP a grid line on a map that runs from east to west **4.** ◊ **easting** **5.** DISTANCE NORTHWARDS the distance northwards from a particular east-west grid line shown in the second half of a map reference

North Island island in New Zealand, in the southwestern Pacific Ocean. It is the smaller and more northern of the country's two main islands. Population: 2,749,980 (1996). Area: 115,777 sq. km/44,689 sq. mi.

North Korea ♦ **Korea**

North Lanarkshire /náwrth lánnərkshər/ council area in southern Scotland, established in 1996. Population: 326,799 (1997).

northland /náwrth land/ *n.* the northern part of a country

Northland[1] /náwrth land/ **1.** SCANDINAVIAN PENINSULA the Scandinavian peninsula containing Norway and Sweden **2.** *Can* FAR NORTHERN CANADA parts of Canada in the far north

Northland[2] administrative region in northern New Zealand, occupying most of the North Auckland Peninsula in the northwest of the North Island. Population: 141,865 (1996). Area: 30,105 sq. km/11,624 sq. mi.

north magnetic pole *n.* the point on the Earth's surface to which the north-seeking pole of a compass needle is attracted

Northman /náwrthmən/ (*plural* **-men** /-mən/) *n.* = **Norseman**

north-northeast *n.* COMPASS POINT BETWEEN N AND NE the direction or compass point midway between north and northeast. ■ *adj., adv.* IN NORTH-NORTHEAST in, from, facing, or towards the north-northeast —**north-northeast** *adj., adv.* —**north-northeasterly** *adj., adv.*

north-northwest *n.* COMPASS POINT BETWEEN N AND NW the direction or compass point midway between north and northwest. ■ *adj., adv.* IN NORTH-NORTHWEST in, from, facing, or towards the north-northwest —**north-northwest** *adj., adv.* —**north-northwesterly** *adj., adv.*

North Pennines /náwrth pénnīnz/ Area of Outstanding Natural Beauty in northern England, including part of the counties of Cumbria, Durham, and Northumberland, established in 1988. Area: 1,983 sq. km/773 sq. mi.

north pole *n.* **1. north pole, North Pole** NORTHERN END OF EARTH'S AXIS the northern end of the Earth's axis at a latitude of 90° N **2.** ASTRON NORTH END OF AXIS OF ROTATION the north end of the axis of rotation of a planet or other celestial body **3.** = **north magnetic pole 4.** POINT AT NORTHERN EXTENSION OF EARTH'S AXIS the point at infinity along the northern extension of one end of the Earth's axis of rotation

North Riding /náwrth ríding/ former division in Yorkshire, northern England. It became an administrative county, and now forms North Yorkshire County.

North Saskatchewan /nawrth sæss káchəwən/ river in Canada originating in the Canadian Rocky Mountains and flowing eastwards before joining the South Saskatchewan River. It empties into Lake Winnipeg. Length: 1,224 km/760 mi.

North Sea /nawrth see/ arm of the Atlantic Ocean between the eastern coast of Great Britain and the continent of Europe. Area: 575,000 sq. km/222,000 sq. mi.

North-South Divide *n.* term used to describe the political and economic difference between the north and the south of England

North Star *n.* ASTRON = **Polaris**

North Stradbroke Island /-strád brook-/ island of northeastern Australia, in Moreton Bay, off the coast of southeastern Queensland. Population: 2,290 (1994). Area: 319 sq. km/123 sq. mi.

North Uist /-yoo ist/ island in northwestern Scotland, in the Outer Hebrides, situated off the northwestern coast of the mainland. Population: 1,404 (1991).

Northumberland /nawr thúmbərlənd/ the northernmost county of England, and one of the largest and most sparsely populated. Population: 307,300 (1995). Area: 5,033 sq. km/1,944 sq. mi.

Northumberland National Park national park in northeastern England, in Northumberland, covering hilly country between Hadrian's Wall and the Scottish border. Area: 1,030 sq. km/398 sq. mi.

Northumbria /nawr thúmbri ə/ ancient region in northeastern England. It was one of the most powerful of the Anglo-Saxon kingdoms of England, from the 7th century AD to 954.

Northumbrian /nawr thúmbri ən/ *adj.* **1.** GEOG OF NORTHUMBERLAND relating to the English county of Northumberland, or its people or culture **2.** HIST OF NORTHUMBRIA relating to Northumbria, a region of Anglo-Saxon Britain, or its people or culture **3.** LANG OF DIALECT OF OLD AND MIDDLE ENGLISH relating to the dialect of Old and Middle English spoken in Northumbria ■ *n.* LANG **DIALECT OF OLD AND MIDDLE ENGLISH** a dialect of Old and Middle English spoken in Northumbria

North Vietnam /nawrth vi ət naám/ former republic in southeastern Asia, in the northern part of Vietnam. Capital: Hanoi. Area: 164,102 sq. km/63,360 sq. mi. Official name **Democratic Republic of Vietnam**

northwards /náwrthwərdz/; *nautical usage* **northward** /náwthərd/ *adv.* TOWARDS THE NORTH in a northerly direction ■ *n.* NORTHWARD POINT IN THE NORTH a direction towards or a point in the north —**northward** *adj.* —**northwardly** *adv.*

North Wessex Downs Area of Outstanding Natural Beauty, in southern England, including part of the counties of Hampshire, Oxfordshire, and Wiltshire, established in 1972. Area: 1,730 sq. km/675 sq. mi.

northwest /náwrth wést/; *nautical usage* /náwr wést/ *n.* **1.** COMPASS POINT BETWEEN N AND W the direction or compass point midway between north and west **2. northwest, Northwest** AREA IN THE NORTHWEST the part of an area, region, or country that is situated in or towards the northwest ■ *adj.* **1. northwest,** IN THE NORTHWEST situated in, facing, or lying towards the northwest of a region, place, or country **2.** METEOROL FROM NORTHWEST blowing from the northwest ○ *a northwest wind* ■ *adv.* TOWARDS THE NORTHWEST in or towards the northwest

Northwest /náwrth wést/ *n.* **1.** AREA OF ENGLAND the north-western region of England, especially Cumbria and Lancashire and including the Lake District **2.** *US* NORTHWESTERN UNITED STATES the northwestern area of the United States, including the states of Washington, Oregon, and Idaho **3.** *US* FORMER AREA OF THE UNITED STATES formerly, a region of the United States west of the Mississippi River and north of the Missouri River **4.** *Can* CANADIAN REGION the area of Canada north and west of the Great Lakes

northwest by north *n.* COMPASS POINT BETWEEN NW AND NNW the direction or compass point midway between northwest and north-northwest. ■ *adj., adv.* TOWARDS POINT BETWEEN NW AND NNW in, from, facing, or towards the point between northwest and north-north-west —**northwest by north** *adj., adv.*

northwest by west *n.* COMPASS POINT BETWEEN NW AND WNW the direction or compass point midway between northwest and west-northwest. See table at **compass** ■ *adj., adv.* TOWARDS POINT BETWEEN NW AND WNW in, from, facing, or towards the point between northwest and west-northwest —**northwest by west** *adj., adv.*

northwester /náwrth wéstər/; *nautical usage* /náwr wéstər/ *n.* a wind blowing from the northwest

northwesterly /náwrth wéstərli/; *nautical usage* /náwr wéstərli/ (*plural* **-lies**) *adj.* **1.** IN THE NORTHWEST situated in or towards the northwest **2.** METEOROL FROM THE NORTHWEST blowing from the northwest ○ *a north-westerly wind* —**northwesterly** *adv.*

northwestern /náwrth wéstərn/; *nautical usage* /náwr wéstərn/ *adj.* **1.** IN THE NORTHWEST situated in the north-west of a region or country **2.** FACING NORTHWEST coming or blowing from, or facing towards the northwest **3.** OF THE NORTHWEST typical of or native to the north-west of a region or country —**northwesterner** *n.* —**northwesternmost** *adj.*

Northwest Passage sea passage through the Arctic regions of North America, connecting the Pacific Ocean and the Atlantic Ocean

Northwest Territories region in northern Canada,

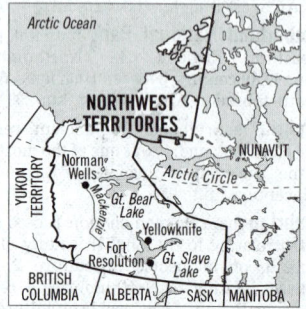

Northwest Territories

and its largest political subdivision, constituting a northern mainland region and numerous islands to the north. Capital: Yellowknife. Population: 64,402 (1996). Area: 3,426,320 sq. km/1,322,904 sq. mi.

northwestward /náwrth wéstwərd/; *nautical usage* /náwr wéstwərd/ *adj.* IN THE NORTHWEST towards or in the northwest ■ *n.* POINT IN THE NORTHWEST a direction towards or a point in the northwest —**northwestwardly** *adj., adv.* —**northwestwards** *adv.*

Northwich /náwrth wich/ market town in Cheshire, England, that has been a centre of salt extraction since Roman times. Population: 34,520 (1991).

North York Moors National Park national park in northern England, predominantly in Yorkshire. It consists largely of moorland and woodland. Area: 1,432 sq. km/553 sq. mi.

North Yorkshire county in northern England, created in 1974. Its administrative headquarters are in Northallerton. Population: 556,200 (1995). Area: 8,321 sq. km/3,213 sq. mi.

nortriptyline /nawr trípti leen/ *n.* a compound used as an antidepressant, tranquillizer, and pain reliever. Formula: $C_{19}H_{21}N$. [Mid-20thC. Coined from NOR- + TRI + ptyl (a shortening of *heptyl*) + -INE.]

Norw. *abbr.* **1.** Norway **2.** Norwegian

Norway

Norway /náwr way/ monarchy in northern Europe, occupying the western and northern portions of the Scandinavian Peninsula. Language: Norwegian. Currency: krone. Capital: Oslo. Population: 4,369,957 (1996). Area: 323,877 sq. km/125,016 sq. mi. Official name **Kingdom of Norway**

Norway maple *n.* a tall Eurasian maple with broad five-lobed green or reddish leaves, widely grown as a shade tree in the United States. Latin name: *Acer plantanoides.*

Norway rat *n.* = **brown rat**

Norway spruce *n.* a European spruce tree with dark green needles, drooping branches, and long cones, widely grown for its timber and as an ornamental. Latin name: *Picea abies.*

Norwegian /nawr wéej'n/ *n.* **1.** PEOPLES SB FROM NORWAY sb who was born or brought up in Norway, or who has Norwegian citizenship **2.** LANG OFFICIAL LANGUAGE OF NORWAY the official language of Norway, belonging to the North Germanic group of Indo-European languages. Norwegian is spoken by about five million people. ◊ **Landsmål** ■ *adj.* **1.** PEOPLES OF NORWAY relating to Norway, or its people or culture **2.** LANG OF NORWEGIAN relating to the Norwegian language [Early 17thC. Formed from medieval Latin *Norvegia* 'Norway', from Old Norse *Norvegr.*]

nor'wester /náwr wéstər/ *n.* **1.** METEOROL = **northwester 2.** BEVERAGES ALCOHOLIC DRINK a strong alcoholic drink (*slang*) **3.** *NZ* METEOROL HOT WIND IN NEW ZEALAND in New Zealand, a hot dry wind coming from the Southern Alps

Norwich /nórrich/ city and administrative centre of Norfolk, eastern England. Population: 120,895 (1991).

Norwich terrier *n.* a small short-legged dog with wiry fur and erect ears, belonging to a breed that originated in East Anglia

nos., Nos. *abbr.* numbers

n.o.s. *abbr.* not otherwise specified

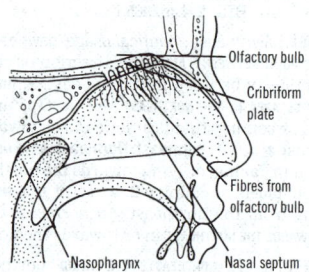

Nose: Cross-section of the human nose

nose /nōz/ *n.* **1.** ANAT ORGAN OF SMELL the part of the face or head through which a person or animal breathes and smells **2.** SENSE OF SMELL the sense of smell, especially the ability to recognize things by smell or to follow a scent **3.** TALENT FOR FINDING STH an intuitive ability to discover, detect, or recognize sth **4.** PART RESEMBLING NOSE a part that resembles the nose of a person or animal in appearance or function **5.** AUTOMOT, AIR PROJECTING FRONT PART OF VEHICLE the pointed or rounded front end of an aircraft, spacecraft, boat, car, or other vehicle **6.** DISTINCTIVE SMELL the characteristic aroma of sth, e.g. wine or tobacco ■ *v.* (**noses, nosing, nosed**) **1.** *vi.* PRY OR SNOOP to try to make discoveries by searching or asking questions in an inquisitive, impertinent, or intrusive manner (*informal*) **2.** *vti.* ADVANCE WITH CAUTION to move forwards slowly, carefully, or cautiously, or make sth move in this way **3.** *vt.* TOUCH STH WITH NOSE to touch, rub, or push sb or sth with the nose **4.** *vt.* SMELL STH to smell or sniff sth **5.** *vi.* SEARCH FOR BY SCENT to try to find sth by smelling or sniffing [Old English *nosu*. Ultimately from an Indo-European word that is also the ancestor of English *nasal, pince-nez,* and *nasturtium.*] —**noseless** *adj.* ◊ **keep your nose clean** to avoid getting into trouble (*informal*) ◊ **look down your nose at sb** *or* **sth** to regard sb or sth arrogantly or disdainfully as inferior or not worth your attention ◊ **nose to tail** so close together that the front of one vehicle almost touches the rear end of another ◊ **on the nose 1.** *US* absolutely on target, with total accuracy, or completely correctly (*informal*) ○ *at 10 o'clock on the nose* **2.** in betting on horseraces, for a horse to win only, not to be placed second or third (*slang*) **3.** *Aus* foul-smelling (*informal*) ◊ **put sb's nose out of joint** to make sb feel thwarted or offended because you do, obtain, or achieve sth that he or she was intending or hoping for ◊ **turn up your nose at sth** to refuse to accept sth because you feel it is inferior or unworthy of you (*informal*) ◊ **under sb's nose** in full view of or very close to sb

nose around, nose about *vti.* to look or search through a place in an inquisitive and often intrusive way (*informal*)

nose out *v.* **1.** *vt.* FIND STH OUT BY PRYING to discover sth by thorough and often cunning or intrusive searching or questioning **2.** *vt.* NARROWLY DEFEAT OPPONENT to defeat an opponent by a very narrow margin **3.** *vi.* DRIVE CAUTIOUSLY FORWARDS to move a vehicle very slowly and cautiously forwards out of a place **4.** *vt.* FIND STH BY SCENT to discover sth by smelling or sniffing, or as if by following a scent

nosebag /nōz bag/ *n.* a cylindrical or bucket-shaped bag containing a horse's food that can be hung around its head, over its nose. Also called **feedbag**

noseband /nōz band/ *n.* the part of a horse's bridle that goes over its nose

nosebleed /nōz bleed/ *n.* BLEEDING FROM NOSE a flow of blood from the nose. Technical name **epistaxis** ■ *adj. US* EXTREMELY HIGH extremely high or excessive, e.g. in price or profit level (*informal*)

nose candy *n. US* cocaine (*slang*)

nose cone *n.* the pointed front section of a missile, rocket, spacecraft, aircraft, or racing car, designed for aerodynamic efficiency

nose dive *n.* **1.** AIR STEEP PLUNGE THROUGH AIR an extremely steep sudden plunge by an aircraft towards the earth **2.** SHARP DECREASE a sudden very significant fall or decline in price, value, amount, or quality

nose-dive *vi.* **1.** AIR **PLUNGE VERY STEEPLY THROUGH AIR** to fall vertically or almost vertically with the front end pointing downwards (*refers to aircraft*) **2. DECREASE SHARPLY** to experience a sudden very significant fall or decline in price, value, amount, or quality —**nose-diver** *n.*

nose drops *npl.* liquid medication for the nose inserted in drops through the nostrils

nose flute *n.* a wind instrument of the South Pacific Islands, usually played by being breathed into through one nostril while the other one is plugged

nosegay /nṓz gay/ *n.* a small bouquet of flowers (*old*) [*Gay* from GAY in the obsolete sense 'ornament']

noseguard /nṓz gaard/ *n.* US in American football, a defensive lineman who plays opposite the centre in the offensive line

nose job *n.* a surgical operation to improve the shape or size of the nose (*informal*)

nose ornament *n.* a decorative ring or stud worn through the nostril or septum

nosepiece /nṓz peess/ *n.* **1. PART OF SPECTACLES** the part of a pair of spectacles that fits over the nose and connects the lenses **2. PART OF MICROSCOPE** the end piece of a microscope to which one or more objective lenses are attached **3. PROTECTION FOR NOSE** the part of a helmet or piece of armour that protects the nose **4.** = **noseband**

nose rag *n.* a handkerchief (*slang*)

nose ring *n.* **1. RING FIXED THROUGH ANIMAL'S NOSE** a ring put through an animal's nose to lead or control it **2. RING WORN IN NOSE AS ORNAMENT** a ring worn for adornment through a hole pierced in the nostril or septum

nose stud *n.* a small stud worn for adornment in a hole pierced in the nostril or septum

nose tackle *n.* US FOOTBALL = **noseguard**

nose wheel *n.* a landing-gear wheel at the front end of an aircraft

nosey *adj.* = **nosy**

nosh /nosh/ *n.* (*informal*) **1. MEAL** a meal **2. FOOD** prepared food ■ *vt.* (**noshes, noshing, noshed**) **EAT** to eat sth (*informal*) [Early 20thC. From Yiddish *nashen* 'to nibble', from Middle High German *naschen*.] —**nosher** *n.*

no-show *n.* sb who makes a reservation or appointment, or buys a ticket, but fails to arrive, without cancellation or explanation

nosh-up *n.* a large, satisfying, and enjoyable meal (*informal*)

no-side *n.* the end of a rugby match, as signalled by the referee's whistle

nosing /nṓzing/ *n.* **1. PROJECTING EDGE OF STAIR TREAD** the rounded edge of a stair tread that projects horizontally **2. PROTECTION FOR NOSING** a shield that protects a nosing on a staircase **3.** ARCHIT **PROJECTING EDGE OF MOULDING** the rounded projecting edge of a moulding

no-smoking *adj.* where smoking is not allowed, or that prohibits smoking

noso- *prefix.* disease ○ *nosophobia* [From Greek *nosos*, of unknown origin]

nosocomial /nóssō kṓmi əl/ *adj.* originating or occurring in a hospital [Mid-19thC. Formed from Greek *nosokomos* 'sb who tends the sick'.]

nosography /no sóggrəfi/ (*plural* **-phies**) *n.* a detailed classification and description of known diseases —**nosographer** *n.* —**nosographic** /nóssə gráffik/ *adj.* —**nosographically** /-gráffikli/ *adv.*

nosology /no sólləji/ (*plural* **-gies**) *n.* **1. CLASSIFYING OF DISEASES** the branch of medicine concerned with the classification and description of known diseases **2. CLASSIFIED LIST OF DISEASES** a completed classification of known diseases —**nosological** /nóssə lójjik'l/ *adj.* —**nosologically** /-lójjikli/ *adv.* —**nosologist** /no sólləjist/ *n.*

nosophobia /nóssō fṓbi ə/ *n.* an irrational fear of catching diseases

nostalgia /no stáljə, -ji ə/ *n.* **1. SENTIMENTAL RECOLLECTION** a mixed feeling of happiness, sadness, and longing when recalling a person, place, or event from the past, or the past in general **2. THINGS THAT AROUSE NOSTALGIA** sth, or things, intended to arouse a feeling of nostalgia or to evoke the past nostalgically **3. HOMESICKNESS** a longing for home or family when away from either (*dated*) [Late 18thC. From modern Latin, 'homesickness', from Greek *nostos* 'homecoming' + *algos* 'pain'.] —**nostalgic** *adj.* —**nostalgically** /no stáljikli/ *adv.*

nostoc /nóss tok/ *n.* a freshwater blue-green alga that lives in spherical colonies as coiled filaments and fixes atmospheric nitrogen. Genus: *Nostoc.* [Mid-17thC. From modern Latin; invented by Paracelsus (1493–1541), Swiss physician.]

nostology /no stólləji/ *n.* MED = **gerontology** [Mid-20thC. Coined from Greek *nostos* 'return home' (from the former idea that later life is like a return to early years) + -OLOGY.] —**nostologic** /nóstə lójjik/ *adj.* —**nostologically** *adv.* —**nostologist** /no stólləjist/ *n.*

Barnaby's

Nostradamus

Nostradamus /nóstrə daámass, -dáymass/ (1503–66) French astrologer and physician. His prophecies, composed in rhyming quatrains and first published as *Centuries* in 1555, were consulted for hundreds of years. Born **Michel de Notredame**

nostril /nóstrəl/ *n.* either of the two openings at the end of the nose of a person or animal [Old English *nosþyrl*, from *nosu*, an earlier form of NOSE + *þyrl* 'hole', from *þurh*, an earlier form of THROUGH]

nostrum /nóstrəm/ *n.* **1. INEFFECTIVE REMEDY** a remedy for a social, political, or economic problem, especially an idea or scheme that is often suggested but never proved to be successful **2. QUACK REMEDY** a medicine prepared or prescribed by an unqualified person whose claims for its effectiveness have no scientific basis [Early 17thC. From Latin *nostrum (remedium)* 'our (remedy)', a form of *noster* 'our'.]

nosy /nṓzi/ (**-ier, -iest**), **nosey** (**-ier, -iest**) *adj.* too curious about other people's affairs (*informal*) —**nosily** *adv.* —**nosiness** *n.*

nosy parker /-paàrkər/ *n.* sb who pries into other people's affairs, especially sb who asks impertinent or intrusive questions (*informal disapproving*) [Said to refer to Elizabeth I's Archbishop of Canterbury, Matthew Parker, who was noted for detailed inquiries concerning ecclesiastical affairs]

not /not/ *adv.* **1. FORMING NEGATIVES** a negative adverb used to form structures indicating that sth is to no degree or in no way the case or conveying the general notion 'no'. It is often used to express refusal, denial, or the negation of a statement just made. (*often contracted in spoken and informal written English to 'n't'*) ○ *Don't you think you've done enough?* ○ *Not every household has a dishwasher.* ○ *There's nothing in my account; not one penny.* ○ *Not only was the meal expensive, the service was bad too.* **2. SENTENCE SUBSTITUTE** used as a sentence substitute when indicating denial, refusal, or negation, in order to avoid repetition ○ *'Won't you come with us?'- 'Certainly not.'* ○ *I don't think I'll be late, at least I hope not.* [14thC. Contraction of NOUGHT.] ◇ **not at all** used as a polite way of acknowledging sb's thanks ◇ **not but what** = **not that** (*dated*) ◇ **not that** used to introduce a clause that explicitly denies sth that the listener might infer from a previous or subsequent statement ○ *I'm actually seeing her tonight. Not that it's any of your business!*

NOT /not/ *n.* a NOT circuit (*technical*)

nota plural of **notum**

nota bene /nṓtə bénni, -nay/ *interj.* used to draw sb's attention to sth particularly important, usually an addition to or qualification of a previous statement (*formal*) Full form of **n.b., N.B.** [From Latin, from *nota*, imperative form of *notare* 'to mark' + *bene* 'well']

notability /nṓtə bílləti/ (*plural* **-ties**) *n.* **1. SB IMPORTANT** a particularly important or distinguished person **2. SIGNIFICANCE** the importance of sb or sth, or the quality that makes sb or sth worth paying attention to

notable /nṓtəb'l/ *adj.* **1. WORTHY OF NOTE** significant or great enough to deserve attention or to be recorded ○ *a notable contribution to our understanding of this complex phenomenon* **2. INTERESTING** interesting, significant, and worth calling attention to ○ *more notable for what it leaves out than for what it includes* **3. DISTINGUISHED** particularly important, distinguished, or famous ■ *n.* **SB IMPORTANT** a particularly important or distinguished person [14thC. From Old French *notable*, from Latin *notare* 'to note'.] —**notableness** *n.*

notably /nṓtəbli/ *adv.* **1. ESPECIALLY** especially, or in the most significant case ○ *There has been much opposition, notably from the farming community.* **2. EXTREMELY** extremely or remarkably ○ *She seems notably unimpressed by all their arguments.*

notarial /nō táiri əl/ *adj.* relating to or done by a notary public —**notarially** *adv.*

notarize /nṓtə rīz/ (**-rizes, -rizing, -rized**), **notarise** (**-rises, -rising, -rised**) *vt.* to certify sth, e.g. a signature on a legal document, as authentic or legitimate by affixing a notary's stamp and signature —**notarization** /nṓtə rī záysh'n/ *n.*

notary /nṓtəri/ (*plural* **-ries**) *n.* **1.** LAW = **notary public 2. CLERK** a secretary or clerk (*archaic*) [14thC. Via Old French *notarie*, from Latin *notarius* 'shorthand writer, clerk'.]

notary public (*plural* **notaries public**) *n.* sb who is legally authorized to certify the authenticity of signatures and documents

notate /nō táyt/ (**-tates, -tating, -tated**) *vt.* to write sth down using notation, especially musical notation [Early 20thC. Back-formation from NOTATION.]

notation /nō táysh'n/ *n.* **1. SYMBOLIC REPRESENTATION** a set of written symbols used to represent sth, e.g. the length and pitch of musical notes **2. USE OF NOTATION** the process of using a system of notation **3. NOTING** the act of making a note or writing sth down **4. NOTE** a note or annotation [Late16thC. Via Old French or Latin from the Latin past participle stem *notat-*, from *notare* 'to note'.]

notch /noch/ *n.* **1. NICK OR INDENTATION** a small V-shaped cut in the edge or on the surface of sth **2. NICK USED AS TALLY** any of a series of cuts made to record a score, a debt, or the number of times sth has been done **3. DEGREE ON SCALE** a level or step on a scale, especially one measuring quality or achievement ○ *raise the tension on the wire another notch* ■ *vt.* (**notches, notching, notched**) **1. MAKE V-SHAPED CUT IN** to make a notch in or on sth **2. RECORD WITH NOTCHES** to record a score or debt by making a series of cuts in a surface **3. ACHIEVE OR SCORE** to achieve a victory or success, or score a point or goal (*informal*) ○ *notched up one more win* [Mid-16thC. Origin uncertain: perhaps from an Anglo-Norman word.] —**notchy** *adj.*

NOT circuit *n.* a logic circuit in a computer that produces a high-voltage output signal if the input signal is low, or a low-voltage output signal if the input signal is high

note /nōt/ *n.* **1. JOTTED RECORD OR SUMMARY** sth written down, often in abbreviated form, as a record or reminder **2. INFORMAL LETTER** a short written message or informal letter **3.** POL **OFFICIAL LETTER** a formal communication in writing, especially between governments **4. DOCUMENT** a short official document **5.** PRINTING, PUBL **ITEM OF SUPPLEMENTARY INFORMATION** a piece of additional information about sth in a printed text, usually given at the bottom of the relevant page or at the end of the book or article **6. WRITTEN COMMENT** a short written comment or item of information, e.g. written in the margin of a book or piece of work **7.** BANKING, FIN **BANKNOTE** a banknote. US term **bill**[1] *n.* 6 **8.** FIN = **promissory note 9.** MUSIC **MUSICAL OR VOCAL SOUND** a sound of a particular pitch, quality, or duration produced by a musical instrument or by the voice of a person or animal **10.** MUSIC **SYMBOL IN MUSIC** in written or printed music, a symbol representing a sound of a particular duration and pitch **11.** MUSIC **KEY ON KEYBOARD** a black or white key of a piano or other keyboard instrument **12.** LANG **INTONATION SHOWING EMOTION** a tone in the voice that indicates the speaker's feelings or adds to the meaning of what is said **13. CHARACTERISTIC FEATURE** a distinctive element, feeling, quality, or atmosphere **14. HINT** a hint or suggestion of sth **15. DISTINCTION** distinction or excellence ○ *a writer of note* **16.** MUSIC **TUNE** a tune (*archaic*) ■ **notes** *npl.* **SUMMARY FOR FUTURE REFERENCE** important facts written down by sb listening to sth, e.g. a student during a lesson ■ *vt.* **(notes, noting, noted) 1. OBSERVE STH** to notice or remember sth by paying particular attention to it **2. PERCEIVE STH** to notice or become aware of sth **3. MENTION STH** to mention sth important **4. WRITE STH DOWN** to write down sth important as a record or reminder [13thC. Via Old French *note* 'sign, characteristic, short letter', from Latin *nota* 'sign, mark'.] —**noteless** *adj.* —**noter** *n.*

notebook /nốt bŏŏk/ *n.* **1. SMALL WRITING BOOK** a small book in which to write, containing blank or lined pages **2.** COMPUT **SMALL PERSONAL COMPUTER** a small thin portable personal computer

note card *n.* US = **notelet**

notecase /nốt kayss/ *n.* a wallet (*dated*)

noted /nốtid/ *adj.* **1. WELL-KNOWN** well-known and especially distinguished by or admired for a particular thing or quality ○ *He is not noted for his generosity.* **2. MARKED OR SIGNIFICANT** significant or distinctive enough to be noticeable —**notedly** *adv.* —**notedness** *n.*

notelet /nốtlət/ *n.* a folded sheet of paper or thin card with a picture on the front, used for writing short informal letters. US term **note card**

note of hand *n.* FIN = **promissory note**

notepad /nốt pad/ *n.* a number of small sheets of blank or lined paper on which to write, fastened together in a way that makes it easy to detach a single page

notepaper /nốt paypər/ *n.* paper for writing letters or making notes on

note row *n.* MUSIC = **tone row**

noteworthy /nốt wurthi/ **(-thier, -thiest)** *adj.* deserving notice or attention, usually because of particular significance, excellence, uniqueness, or interest —**noteworthily** *adv.* —**noteworthiness** *n.*

NOT gate *n.* COMPUT = **NOT circuit**

nothing /núthing/ *pron.* **1. NOT ANYTHING** an indefinite pronoun indicating that there is not anything, not a single thing, or not a single part of a thing ○ *There is nothing more annoying than people who can't keep their personal lives private.* ○ *There's nothing else I can do for you.* ○ *There's nothing like a good soak in a hot bath to alleviate backache.* **2. STH OF NO IMPORTANCE** a thing or matter of no importance or significance ○ *It's nothing to me whether they win or lose.* **3. NOT HAVING A QUALITY** used to indicate the complete lack of the quality mentioned in sb or sth ○ *He wore an ordinary dark-blue jacket, with nothing special about it.* ○ *Nothing of any consequence was said.* **4. ZERO AMOUNT** a zero quantity or zero ○ *We won, three to nothing.* **5. STATE OF NONEXISTENCE** a state of nonexistence, or the absence of any perceptible qualities ○ *vanished into nothing* ■ *n.* **SB OR STH COMPLETELY UNIMPORTANT** sb who or sth that is totally unimportant ■ *adj.* **COMPLETELY UNDISTINGUISHED** completely lacking in distinguishing qualities, interest, or significance (*informal*) ○ *a nothing product, despite all the hype* [Old English *nāðinc*, from earlier forms of NO + THING] ◇ **all or nothing** used to indicate that only complete success or obtaining everything counts and anything less than that has no value ◇ **not for nothing** for a very good reason ◇ **nothing but** only ◇ **nothing doing** used to indicate a complete refusal to do sth or to cooperate (*informal*) ◇ **nothing for it** used to indicate that there is no other course of action open to sb ○ *There was nothing for it but for us to admit our error.* ◇ **nothing if not** definitely, undoubtedly, or at the very least ○ *He's nothing if not fair.* ◇ **nothing less than, nothing short of** used to emphasize forcefully that sth truly, definitely, or amazingly is as described ◇ **nothing like** having no resemblance to sb or sth else ◇ **nothing to it** used to indicate that sth is very easy

nothingness /núthingnəss/ *n.* **1. ABSENCE OF EVERYTHING** the absence of life, existence, and all discernible qualities **2. EMPTY SPACE** space with nothing in it **3. COMPLETE WORTHLESSNESS** complete worthlessness or insignificance **4. SB OR STH COMPLETELY WORTHLESS** sb or sth without any worth or significance **5.** PHILOSOPHY **LACK OF APPARENT MEANING** the condition of lacking any apparent meaning

WORD KEY: CULTURAL NOTE

Being and Nothingness, an extended essay by French philosopher Jean-Paul Sartre (1943). The fullest expression of Sartre's existential philosophy, it suggests that humans can be distinguished from the simple being or 'thing-ness' of objects and other creatures by their consciousness or 'no-thingness'. This awareness provides humans with their freedom, but it also leaves them searching for meaning in life.

notice /nốtiss/ *n.* **1. PUBLIC SIGN** a sign in a public place giving information, instructions, or a warning **2. WRITTEN ANNOUNCEMENT** a written or printed announcement or statement of information, often displayed on a board or wall or published in a newspaper or magazine **3. WARNING** advance warning or notification of sth ○ *gave us notice that the system would be changed* **4. PERIOD OF WARNING** the period of time between the giving of a warning or notification and its taking effect ○ *a day's notice of repairs to the water mains* **5.** LAW **WARNING OF END OF EMPLOYMENT** official notification of the exercise of a right, especially the right to terminate employment, or the amount of time in advance that such notification is given **6. ATTENTION** sb's attention, observation, or consideration ○ *How can such a glaring error possibly have escaped your notice?* **7. CRITICAL REVIEW** a written or published review of a book, play, or film ■ *v.* **(-tices, -ticing, -ticed) 1.** *vti.* **OBSERVE STH** to see or catch sight of sb or sth and register the fact in the mind ○ *Did you notice what he had in his hand?* **2.** *vti.* **PERCEIVE** to become aware of sth or sb and register the fact in the mind ○ *I noticed that he avoided mentioning her name.* **3.** *vt.* **MENTION STH** to mention or remark on sth **4.** *vt.* **RECOGNIZE** to recognize sb, or indicate that you recognize sb **5.** *vt.* **TREAT POLITELY** to treat sb with polite attention **6.** *vt.* **WRITE CRITICAL REVIEW OF** to write or publish a review of a book, play, or film **7.** *vt.* **GIVE OFFICIAL NOTICE TO** to give official notice to sb (*formal*) [15thC. Via Old French from Latin *notitia* 'being known, fame, knowledge', from *notus* 'known'.]

noticeable /nốtissəb'l/ *adj.* **1. EASILY SEEN** easy to see, hear, feel, or detect **2. NOTEWORTHY** important, distinctive, or worthy of comment —**noticeability** /nốtissə bílləti/ *n.* —**noticeableness** /nốtissəb'lnəss/ *n.* —**noticeably** *adv.*

noticeboard /nốtiss bawrd/ *n.* a board fixed to a wall on which notices, announcements, or advertisements can be fastened for temporary display. US term **bulletin board**

notifiable /nốti fī əb'l/ *adj.* used to describe an infectious disease of people or animals that must be reported to the appropriate authority when it occurs so that control or preventive measures can be taken

notification /nốtifi káysh'n/ *n.* **1. FORMAL ANNOUNCEMENT OR WARNING** official information about sth that has happened or will happen, or a document containing such information **2. ACT OF INFORMING OFFICIALLY** the act of informing sb officially about sth

notify /nốti fī/ **(-fies, -fying, -fied)** *vt.* **1. TELL OFFICIALLY** to inform or warn sb officially about sb or sth **2. MAKE STH KNOWN** to announce or report sth officially, or make sth officially known [14thC. Via Old French *notifier*, from Latin *notificare* 'to make known', from *notus* 'known'.] —**notifier** *n.*

no-tillage *n.* a method of farming in which crops are planted in narrow slit trenches, without any ploughing, and weeds are controlled with chemical weedkillers

notion /nốsh'n/ *n.* **1. IDEA** an idea, opinion, or concept **2. IMPRESSION** a vague understanding or impression **3. DESIRE** a sudden desire or whim [14thC. From the Latin stem *notion-* 'concept', from *not-*, past participle stem of *noscere* 'to know'.]

notional /nốsh'nəl/ *adj.* **1. IMAGINARY OR HYPOTHETICAL** existing only as an idea or in theory, not in reality **2. ABSTRACT OR SPECULATIVE** relating to or characteristic of ideas or concepts **3.** LING **USED WITH DEFINITE MEANING** used in a particular, concrete sense, like, e.g. 'did' in 'We did the work', as opposed to expressing a grammatical relationship, like 'did' in 'Why didn't she come?' ◊ **relational** —**notionally** *adv.*

notochord /nốtə kawrd/ *n.* a long flexible rod of cells that supports the body of chordates, e.g. the lamprey, and vertebrate embryos and is in effect a primitive backbone [Mid-19thC. From Greek *nōton* 'back' + CHORD, with the sense 'line'.] —**notochordal** /nốtə káwrd'l/ *adj.*

notorious /nō táwri əss/ *adj.* **1. FAMOUS FOR STH BAD** well-known for some undesirable feature, quality, or act **2. WELL-KNOWN** widely known (*archaic*) [Mid-16thC. Formed from medieval Latin *notorius*, from the past participle of *noscere* 'to know' (source of English *recognize*).] —**notoriety** /nṓtə rī́ əti/ *n.* —**notoriously** /nō táwri əssli/ *adv.* —**notoriousness** *n.*

notornis /nō táwrniss/ (*plural* **-nes** /-neez/) *n.* a rare flightless bird native to New Zealand, especially the takahe. Genus: *Notornis*. [Mid-19thC. From modern Latin, genus name, from Greek *notos* 'south' + *ornis* 'bird'.]

not proven *adj. Scotland* used as a verdict in Scottish courts as an alternative to guilty or not guilty, when there is a strong suspicion of guilt but not enough evidence to prove it

no trump, no trumps *n.* a bid or contract to play a hand of cards without a trump suit, especially in bridge —**no-trump** *adj.*

Nottingham /nóttingəm/ city in Nottinghamshire, England, of which it is the county town. Population: 284,000 (1996).

Nottinghamshire /nóttingəmshər/ county in central England. It is famous for Sherwood Forest and the legend of Robin Hood. Nottingham is the county town. Population: 1,031,900 (1995). Area: 2,165 sq. km/835 sq. mi.

Notts /nots/ *abbr.* Nottinghamshire

notum /nốtəm/ (*plural* **-ta** /-ə/) *n.* a hard protective covering on an insect's thorax [Late 19thC. From Greek *nōton* 'back'.]

notwithstanding /nót with stánding/ *prep.* **DESPITE** in spite of (*formal*) (*often used after a noun*) ○ *Its democratic structures, notwithstanding inevitable flaws, are among the most solid on the continent.* ○ *The lack of a decent catalogue notwithstanding, the exhibition contains much to marvel at.* ■ *adv.* **NEVERTHELESS** nevertheless, or in spite of this (*formal*) ○ *They, notwithstanding, persisted in their inquiries.* ■ *conj.* **ALTHOUGH** in spite of the fact that (*formal*) ○ *Notwithstanding they were provoked, they ought not to have reacted so violently.* [14thC. Modelled on Old French *non obstante* 'being of no hindrance'.]

notwork /nótwurk/ *n.* a computer network that is nonfunctional (*slang humorous*) [Late 20thC. Blend of NOT + NETWORK.]

nougat /nóo gaa/ *n.* a chewy sweet made with egg whites, honey, and usually chopped nuts or dried fruit that is wrapped in rice paper and cut into strips or pieces [Early 19thC. From Provençal *nogat*, from *noga* 'nut', from Latin *nux*.]

nought /nawt/ *n.* **1. ZERO** the number zero. US term **naught** *n.* **1 2. NOTHING** nothing (*archaic*) ◊ **naught** ■ *adv.* **NOT AT ALL** not in the least (*archaic*) ◊ **naught** ■ *adj.* **WORTH NOTHING** worthless in character or behaviour (*archaic*) ◊ **naught** [Old English *nōwiht*, from *ne* 'not' + *ōwiht* 'anything', a variant of AUGHT]

noughts and crosses *n.* a game in which two players alternately write '0' or 'X' on a grid of nine squares, until one player gets three of the same symbols in a line (*takes a singular verb*) US term **tick-tack-toe**

Nouméa /noo máyə/ capital city of New Caledonia, an overseas territory of France. It is situated on the southwestern coast of New Caledonia Island in the southwestern Pacific Ocean. Population: 65,110 (1989).

noumenon /nóomənən, -non, nów-/ (*plural* **-na** /-nə/) *n.* **1. OBJECT OF INTELLECT** sth beyond the tangible world that can only be known or identified by the intellect, not by the senses **2. INDEPENDENT OBJECT IN KANTIAN PHILOSOPHY** in Kantian philosophy, sth that exists independently of intellectual or sensory perception of it, e.g. the soul in some beliefs [Late 18thC. Via German from Greek, from the present participle of *noien* 'to apprehend, conceive'.] —**noumenal** *adj.* —**noumenally** *adv.*

noun /nown/ *n.* a word or group of words used as the name of a class of people, places, or things, or of a particular person, place, or thing. For example, the words *bottle*, *spider*, *charity*, and *Africa* are nouns. [14thC. Via Anglo Norman, 'name, noun', from Old French *nom*, from Latin *nomen* 'name' (source of English *nominal*).]

noun phrase *n.* a word or group of words that functions syntactically as a noun, e.g. as the subject, object, or topic, in a clause or sentence

nourish /núrrish/ (-ishes, -ishing, -ished) *vt.* **1. GIVE FOOD TO** to give people, animals, or plants the substances they require to live, grow, or remain fit and healthy **2. SUPPORT OR FOSTER** to encourage or strengthen a feeling or idea **3. HELP TO DEVELOP** to help sth to grow or develop [13thC. From the Old French stem *norriss-*, from *norir*, from Latin *nutrire* 'to suckle'.] —**nourisher** *n.*

nourishing /núrrishing/ *adj.* providing people, animals, or plants with a substantial quantity of the substances they require to live, grow, or remain fit and healthy —**nourishingly** *adv.*

nourishment /núrrishmənt/ *n.* **1. FOOD OR FOOD VALUE** food, or the valuable substances in food that a person, animal, or plant requires to live, grow, or remain fit and healthy **2. STH ENCOURAGING GROWTH** sth that provides a stimulating and healthy emotional and intellectual environment for people or animals

nous /nowss/ *n.* **1. COMMON SENSE** good sense or intelligence (*informal*) **2. INTELLECTUAL ABILITY** in ancient Greek philosophy, the capacity to reason and acquire knowledge, as distinguished from sensation **3. INTELLECT** the part of the human spirit that is capable of rational thought [Late 17thC. From Greek, 'intelligence'.]

nouveau /noóvō/ *adj.* having recently appeared or become fashionable (*humorous*) [Early 20thC. From French.]

nouveau riche /noóvō reésh/ (*plural* **nouveaux riches** /noóvō reésh/) *n.* sb who has recently become rich, especially a former member of the lower or middle classes who ostentatiously displays newly acquired wealth. ◊ **arriviste** [Early 19thC. From French, literally 'new rich'.] —**nouveau riche** *adj.*

nouveau roman /noó vō rō maaN/ (*plural* **nouveaux romans** /noóvō rō maaN/) *n.* LITERAT = **antinovel** [Mid-20thC. From French, literally 'new novel'.]

nouvelle cuisine /noó vel kwi zeén/ *n.* a style of French cooking consisting of tiny but beautifully presented dishes made from fresh lightly cooked ingredients in less rich sauces than in traditional French cookery [Late 20thC. From French, literally 'new cooking'.]

Nouvelle Vague /noó vel vaag/ *n.* CINEMA = **new wave** *n.* 3 [Mid-20thC. From French, literally 'new wave'.]

Nov., **Nov** *abbr.* November

nova /nṓvə/ (*plural* **-vas** *or* **-vae** /-vī/) *n.* a star that suddenly increases dramatically in brightness and then fades to its original luminosity over a short period of months or years [Late 19thC. From Latin, a form of *novus* 'new'.]

novaculite /nō vákyoō līt/ *n.* a hard dense fine-grained sedimentary rock containing quartz and feldspar and used as a whetstone [Late 18thC. Formed from Latin *novacula* 'razor'.]

Nova Scotia /nṓvə skóshə/ region of eastern Canada, and one of the three Maritime Provinces, consisting of a peninsula off New Brunswick and Cape Breton Island. Capital: Halifax. Population: 909,282 (1996). Area: 55,490 sq. km/21,425 sq. mi. —**Nova Scotian** *adj.*

novation /nō váysh'n/ *n.* the replacement of an old contract or obligation with a new one [Early 16thC. From the late Latin stem *novation-*, from, ultimately, *novare* 'to make new', from *novus* 'new'.]

novel[1] /nóvv'l/ *n.* **1. LONG STORY** a fictional prose work with a relatively long and often complex plot,

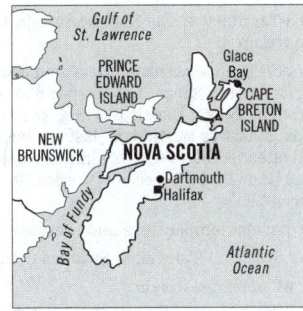

Nova Scotia

usually divided into chapters, in which the story traditionally develops through the thoughts and actions of its characters **2. LITERARY GENRE** novels considered collectively as a literary genre [15thC. Via Old French from Latin *novellus*, from *novus* 'new'. The meaning 'prose narrative' came from Italian *storia novella* 'short story' (literally 'new story').]

— **WORD KEY: SYNONYMS** —
See Synonyms at *new*.

novel[2] /nóvv'l/ *adj.* new, original, and different, and often particularly interesting or unusual as well [15thC. Via Old French from Latin *novellus*, literally 'slightly new', from *novus* 'new'.]

novel[3] /nóvv'l/ *n.* in Roman law, a new decree or sth that changes an existing statute [Early 17thC. From late Latin *novella* (*constitutio*), literally 'new (constitution)', a form of Latin *novellus* (see NOVEL).]

novelese /nóvvə leéz/ *n.* a type of language or style of writing that is typical of inferior novels (*disapproving*)

novelette /nóvvə lét/ *n.* **1. LITERAT SENTIMENTAL NOVEL** a light romantic novel, especially one that is considered trite or sentimental **2. LITERAT SHORT NOVEL** a long story or short novel **3. MUSIC SHORT LYRICAL MUSICAL COMPOSITION** a short piece of music written in a free lyrical style, usually for the piano —**novelettist** *n.*

novelettish /nóvvə léttish/ *adj.* having the qualities of an inferior piece of writing, especially triteness or sentimentality

novelise *vt.* = **novelize**

novelist /nóvvə list/ *n.* sb who writes novels

novelistic /nóvvə lístik/ *adj.* characteristic of a novel, especially in the treatment of real people or historical events —**novelistically** *adv.*

novelize /nóvvə līz/ (-izes, -izing, -ized), **novelise** (-ises, -ising, -ised) *vt.* **1. CONVERT FILM INTO NOVEL** to write the story of a film, play, or television series in the form of a novel **2. CONVERT FACT INTO FICTION** to retell a true story in the form of a novel, sometimes adding fictional details —**novelization** /nóvvə līz záysh'n/ *n.*

novella /nō vélla/ *n.* **1. SHORT NOVEL** a fictional prose work that is longer than a short story but shorter than a novel. ◊ **novelette 2. MORAL TALE** a moral or satirical tale (*archaic*) [Early 20thC. From Italian (*storia*) *novella* (see NOVEL[1]).]

novelty /nóvv'lti/ (*plural* **-ties**) *n.* **1. NEW THING OR EXPERIENCE** sth new, original, and different that is interesting or exciting, though often for only a short time **2. NEWNESS AND ORIGINALITY** the quality of being new, original, and different **3. SMALL TOY OR TRINKET** a small inexpensive toy, ornament, piece of jewellery, or trinket

November /nō vémbər/ *n.* **1. 11TH MONTH OF GREGORIAN CALENDAR** in the Gregorian calendar, the 11th month of the year, made up of 30 days **2. COMMUNICATION CODE WORD FOR LETTER 'N'** the NATO phonetic alphabet code word for the letter 'N', used in international radio communications [13thC. Via Old French *Novembre* from Latin *November*, the ninth month of the Roman calendar, from *novem* 'nine'.]

novena /nō veénə/ (*plural* **-nas** *or* **-nae** /-nee/) *n.* in the Roman Catholic Church, the recitation of prayers for nine consecutive days to achieve a particular purpose [Mid-19thC. From medieval Latin *novena*, a form of *novenus* 'ninefold', from *novem* 'nine'.]

novercal /nō vúrk'l/ *adj.* relating to or said to be typical of a stepmother (*literary*) [Early 17thC. From Latin *novercalis*, from *noverca* 'stepmother'.]

Novgorod /nóvgə rod/ city in western Russia, and the capital of Novgorod Oblast. Population: 235,000 (1992).

novice /nóvviss/ *n.* **1. BEGINNER** sb who has just started learning or doing sth new and has no previous experience in the skill or activity **2. RELIG RELIGIOUS PROBATIONER** sb who has joined a religious order but has not yet taken the final vows of a monk or nun [14thC. Via Old French from late Latin *novicius* 'newly enslaved person' or 'inexperienced person in a new situation', from *novus* 'new'.]

— **WORD KEY: SYNONYMS** —
See Synonyms at *beginner*.

novitiate /nō víshi ət/, **noviciate** *n.* **1. PROBATIONARY PERIOD** the period of time during which sb is a novice, especially in a religious order **2. NOVICES' LIVING QUARTERS** the part of a monastery or convent where novices live **3. = novice** *n.* 2 [Early 17thC. From French *noviciat*, or medieval Latin *noviciatus*, formed from late Latin *novicius* (see NOVICE).]

novocaine /nṓvō kayn/ *n.* = **procaine** [Early 20thC. Formed from Latin *novus* 'new' + *-caine* as in COCAINE.]

Novosibirsk /nóvvəsə beérsk/ city in southern Russia and capital of Novosibirsk Oblast, situated approximately 630 km/390 mi. east of Omsk. Population: 1,380,000 (1995).

now /now/ *adv.* **1. AT PRESENT TIME** at the present time, often as opposed to in the past or in the future ○ *I've never done this before, and I'm not starting now.* **2. IMMEDIATELY** at once or at this exact time ○ *We'll miss our train if we don't go now.* **3. GIVEN THE CURRENT SITUATION** under the present circumstances ○ *She asked me not to tell anyone, but now I don't suppose she'll mind.* **4. UP TO THE PRESENT TIME** used with statements of time to indicate that sth has been happening for a particular length of time up to the present ○ *For six months now, I've been telling you to clean this room.* **5. USED TO PREFACE OR CLARIFY REMARK** used to preface a remark, the second step in an argument, or a clarification of a statement, or to get sb's attention, or for emphasis ○ *Now, what would you like to drink?* **6. USED IN HESITATION** used in speech when hesitating, when thinking of what to say next (*informal*) **7. USED IN HESITATION** used in speech when hesitating and thinking of what to say next (*informal*) ■ *conj.* **SINCE** since, or in view of the fact that this is the present situation ○ *She can afford a decent car now that she's working.* ■ *n.* **PRESENT TIME** the present time or moment ○ *Now would be a good time to tell her.* ■ *adj.* **FASHIONABLE** in the latest fashion (*informal*) ○ *the now look in menswear* [Old English *nu*, ultimately from Indo-European] ◊ **(every) now and then**, **(every) now and again 1.** occasionally **2.** at the present moment **3.** a short time ago ◊ **for now** for the time being, as a temporary measure ◊ **now now 1.** used as a friendly way of trying to comfort sb **2.** used to warn or reprimand sb gently ◊ **now then** used to warn or reprimand sb gently

NOW /now/ *abbr.* National Organization for Women

nowadays /nów ə dayz/ *adv.* in the present, or in the times in which we are now living, usually in contrast to the past [14thC. Coined from NOW + *adayes* 'during the day', from DAY.]

noway /nṓ way/ *interj.* **noway, no way CERTAINLY NOT** used to express emphatic refusal or denial (*informal*) ■ *adv.* **NOT IN ANY WAY** in no way or not at all

nowhere /nṓ wair/; *occasional unstressed form* /nṓ wər/ *adv.* **NOT IN ANY PLACE** not in or to any place ○ *Nowhere does it mention any side-effects.* ■ *n.* **REMOTE PLACE** a remote or insignificant place ◊ **get nowhere**, **go nowhere** to fail to make any progress with sth you are trying to do ◊ **nowhere near** not at all, or a long way from being as specified (*informal*)

no-win *adj.* in which there is no chance of a successful outcome for a participant (*informal*)

nowise /nṓ wīz/ *adv.* in no manner or by no means at all

nowt /nowt, nōt/ *pron.* N England nothing [Old English. (See NOUGHT.)]

WORD KEY: REGIONAL NOTE

The poet John Dryden was among the first to tell users of English that 'two negatives make an affirmative'. This rule did not actually apply to English. Indeed, Shakespeare often doubles up his negatives (*You'll lie like dogs, and yet say nothing neither.* The Tempest, III.ii) and dialect speakers continue to use multiple negation for emphasis: *He said nowt to nobody didn't our kid.*

---

noxious /nókshəss/ *adj.* **1.** PHYSICALLY HARMFUL harmful to life or health, especially by being poisonous **2.** MORALLY HARMFUL likely to cause moral, spiritual, or social harm or corruption **3.** DISGUSTING very unpleasant ○ *a noxious smell* [15thC. Formed from Latin *noxius* 'hurtful, damaging'.] —**noxiously** *adv.* —**noxiousness** *n.*

Noyce /noyss/, **Phillip Roger** (*b.* 1950) Australian film director. He was director of *Newsfront* (1978) and *Dead Calm* (1988).

nozzle /nózz'l/ *n.* **1.** PROJECTING SPOUT a narrow or tapering part at the end of a tube or pipe, used to direct or control the flow of a liquid or gas **2.** SHORT TAPERED TUBE a short tapered tube that directs or accelerates the flow of a fluid, e.g. in a jet engine [Early 17thC. Literally 'noselike appliance', coined from NOSE + -*le*.]

np, n.p. *abbr.* PRINTING new paragraph

Np *symbol.* **1.** TELECOM neper **2.** CHEM neptunium

NP *abbr.* **1.** ANZ, S Africa National Party **2.** neuropsychiatry **3.** notary public **4.** noun phrase

NPA *abbr.* Newspaper Publishers' Association

NPD *abbr.* new product development

NPL *abbr.* National Physical Laboratory

NPN *abbr.* CHEM nonprotein nitrogen

NPV *abbr.* **1.** net present value **2.** no par value

NPWS *abbr.* Aus National Parks and Wildlife Service

nr *abbr.* near

NRA *abbr.* **1.** National Rivers Authority **2.** US National Rifle Association

NRDS *abbr.* neonatal respiratory distress syndrome

NREM *abbr.* nonrapid eye movement

NRMA *n.* the largest motoring organization in Australia, providing roadside assistance, travel information and other motor-related services to its members, as well as insurance and travel services to the general public. Full form **National Roads and Motorists Association**

NRV *abbr.* net realizable value

ns *abbr.* nanosecond

NS, N.S. *abbr.* **1.** New Style **2.** BANKING not sufficient (*funds*) **3.** US Nova Scotia **4.** nuclear ship

n.s. *abbr.* **1.** nearside **2.** new series **3.** not specified

n/s *abbr.* **1.** nonsmoking **2.** nonsmoker **3.** BANKING not sufficient (funds)

N/S *abbr.* nonsmoker

NSA *abbr.* US National Security Agency

NSAID *n.* a drug taken by mouth or applied externally and used to relieve pain and inflammation in a wide range of conditions, especially arthritic or muscular pain and menstrual period pain. Full form **nonsteroidal anti-inflammatory drug**

NSB *abbr.* National Savings Bank

NSC *abbr.* **1.** National Safety Council **2.** US National Security Council

nsec *abbr.* nanosecond

NSF, N.S.F., n.s.f., N/S/F *abbr.* BANKING not sufficient funds

NSG *abbr.* EDUC nonstatutory guidelines

N.S.P.C.A. *abbr.* US National Society for the Prevention of Cruelty to Animals

NSPCC *abbr.* National Society for the Prevention of Cruelty to Children

NSU *abbr.* nonspecific urethritis

NSW *abbr.* Aus New South Wales

NT *abbr.* **1.** National Trust **2.** New Testament **3.** Aus Northern Territory **4.** Can Northwest Territories **5.** CARDS no trump

nth /enth/ *adj.* **1.** MATH INDEFINITELY LARGE NUMERICALLY used to describe a very large, but unspecified, ordinal number, usually one that is the largest in a series of values **2.** LAST OR MOST RECENT last or latest in a long and often tedious series of similar occurrences (*informal*) [Mid-19thC. Formed from N 'indefinitely large or small amount'.]

NTP *abbr.* normal temperature and pressure

NTSC *abbr.* National Television Systems Committee

nt wt, nt. wt. *abbr.* net weight

nu /nyoo/ (*plural* **nus**) *n.* the 13th letter of the Greek alphabet, represented in the English alphabet as 'n'. See table at **alphabet** [Via Greek from a Semitic word]

NUAAW *abbr.* National Union of Agricultural and Allied Workers

nuance /nyoo aanss, noo oNss/ *n.* **1.** SUBTLE DIFFERENCE a very slight difference in meaning, feeling, tone, or colour **2.** USE OF NUANCES the use or awareness of subtle shades of meaning or feeling, especially in artistic expression or performance [Late 18thC. From French, 'slight difference of tone', from *nuer* 'to shade', ultimately from Latin *nubes* 'cloud'.] —**nuanced** *adj.*

nub /nub/ *n.* **1.** HEART OF STH the main point or core of sth **2.** SMALL LUMP a small lump or chunk **3.** SMALL PROJECTION a small protuberance **4.** TEXTILES FIBRE KNOT a knot of fibres in yarn [Late 16thC. From Middle Low German *knubbe*, variant of *knobbe* 'knob'. Originallly 'small lump or boil on the body'.] —**nubbiness** *n.* —**nubby** *adj.*

Nuba /nyóobə/ (*plural* **-ba** *or* **-bas**) *n.* **1.** PEOPLES MEMBER OF A SOUTHERN SUDANESE PEOPLE a member of any of various peoples inhabiting the mountains of central Sudan **2.** LANG = Nubian *n.* 2

nubbin /núbbin/ *n.* US a small undeveloped part of a fruit or vegetable, e.g. an ear of corn [Late 17thC. Literally 'small nub', formed from NUB.]

nubble /núbb'l/ *n.* a small lump or knob —**nubbliness** *n.* —**nubbly** *adj.*

nubecula /nyoo békyoolə/ (*plural* **-lae** /-lī/) *n.* a Magellanic Cloud (*technical*) [Late 17thC. From Latin, literally 'small cloud', from *nubes* 'cloud'.]

Nubia /nyóobi ə/ region in the River Nile valley in northeastern Africa between Aswan in Egypt and Khartoum in Sudan

Nubian /nyóobi ən/ *n.* **1.** PEOPLES INHABITANT OF NUBIA sb who lived in the ancient kingdom of Nubia **2.** LANG NILO-SAHARAN LANGUAGE a Nilo-Saharan language spoken in Sudan. Nubian is spoken by about one million people. [15thC. From medieval Latin *Nubianus*, from *Nubia*.] —**Nubian** *adj.*

nubile /nyóo bīl/ *adj.* **1.** READY FOR MARRIAGE used to describe a young woman who is physically mature enough to have sexual intercourse and therefore suitable for marriage (*dated*) **2.** YOUNG AND DESIRABLE young and sexually desirable (*informal*) [Mid-17thC. From Latin *nubilis*, from *nubere* 'to take a husband' (source of English *nuptial* and *connubial*).] —**nubility** /nyoo bílləti/ *n.*

nucellus /nyoo sélləss/ (*plural* **-li** /-lī/) *n.* the central part of a plant ovule in which the embryo develops [Late 19thC. From modern Latin, of uncertain origin: probably literally 'small kernel', formed from *nucleus* (see NUCLEUS).]

nucl- *prefix.* = nucleo- (used before vowels)

nuclear /nyóokli ər/ *adj.* **1.** NUCLEAR PHYS OF AN ATOM NUCLEUS relating to the nucleus of an atom **2.** ARMS, MIL OF NUCLEAR WEAPONS relating to or using weapons that produce a nuclear explosion **3.** NUCLEAR PHYS OF NUCLEAR ENERGY relating to, using, or producing nuclear energy through fission or fusion **4.** CELL BIOL, BIOL OF A CELL NUCLEUS relating to, involving, or contained in the nucleus of a cell **5.** BIOL FORMING A NUCLEUS forming or resembling a nucleus [Mid-19thC. Formed from Latin *nucleus*, from *nux* 'nut, kernel'. Ultimately from an Indo-European word meaning 'lump'.]

nuclear bomb *n.* a bomb in which the explosive potential is controlled by nuclear fission or fusion. ◊ **atom bomb, hydrogen bomb**

nuclear chemistry *n.* the branch of chemistry in which nuclear reactions are studied

nuclear deterrent *n.* the nuclear weapons possessed by a country or an alliance thought of as a means of discouraging enemy attack

nuclear disarmament *n.* the reduction or elimination of a nation's nuclear weapons or its capacity to manufacture them

nuclear emulsion *n.* a photographic emulsion used to identify and show the paths of subatomic particles after development

nuclear energy *n.* the energy released by nuclear fission or fusion

nuclear envelope *n.* CELL BIOL = nuclear membrane

nuclear family *n.* a social unit that consists of a mother, a father, and their children

nuclear fission *n.* = fission *n.* 2

nuclear-free zone *n.* an area, usually within a country, where all activities involving nuclear weapons or nuclear power are officially banned

nuclear fuel *n.* a substance such as an isotope of uranium that undergoes fission in a nuclear reactor and is used to provide power for electricity and submarines

nuclear fusion *n.* the process in which light atoms such as those of hydrogen and deuterium combine and form heavier atoms, releasing a great amount of energy, that primarily manifests itself in the form of heat

nuclearize /nyóokli ə rīz/ (**-izes, -izing, -ized**), **nuclearise** (**-ises, -ising, -ised**) *vt.* to provide or equip a military force with nuclear weapons —**nuclearization** /nyóokli ə rī záysh'n/ *n.*

nuclear magnetic resonance *n.* the energy pulse released by an atomic nucleus exposed to high-frequency radiation in a magnetic field, which is used to provide data about the atom that can be transformed into an image by computer techniques. This phenomenon is the basis of devices used in medicine, where it is called magnetic resonance imaging, to produce images of tissues, and in physics and chemistry to study molecular structure.

nuclear medicine *n.* the branch of medicine in which radioactive materials are used to diagnose and treat diseases

nuclear membrane *n.* a two-layered membrane surrounding the nucleus of a cell

nuclear physics *n.* the branch of physics in which the structure, forces, and behaviour of the atomic nucleus are studied —**nuclear physicist** *n.*

nuclear pore *n.* any of thousands of complex openings in a nuclear membrane

nuclear power *n.* the power, usually electrical or motive power, produced by nuclear fission or fusion —**nuclear-powered** *adj.*

nuclear power station, nuclear power plant *n.* a power station in which the heat for producing steam to drive electric turbogenerators is derived from a nuclear reactor

nuclear reaction *n.* a process in which energy is produced by either the splitting of heavy atoms (**nuclear fission**) or the combining of light atoms (**nuclear fusion**)

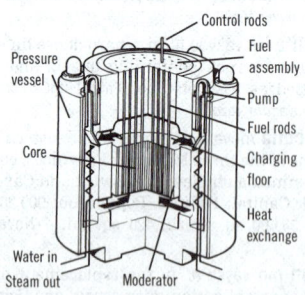

Nuclear reactor

nuclear reactor *n.* a device in which controlled nuclear fission takes place to produce heat energy

---

nuclear reprocessing plant *n.* a facility in which various useful isotopes are removed from used rods of nuclear reactors

nuclear sap *n.* the colourless liquid in the nucleus of a cell

nuclear submarine *n.* **1. SUBMARINE PROPELLED BY NUCLEAR ENERGY** a submarine in which a nuclear reactor produces steam to drive turbines for propulsion **2. SUBMARINE CARRYING NUCLEAR WEAPONS** a submarine that carries nuclear weapons

nuclear threshold *n.* the point in a war being fought with conventional weapons when one of the opposing forces decides to use nuclear weapons

nuclear warhead *n.* the forward part of a missile or other projectile whose explosive device derives its power from nuclear fission or fusion

nuclear waste *n.* unwanted, often radioactive, material that is produced by nuclear reactors and reprocessing plants

nuclear weapon *n.* a military weapon that derives its explosive power from nuclear fission or fusion

nuclear winter *n.* a period of continual cold and darkness believed to follow a nuclear war, caused by the blocking of the Sun's rays by high-altitude dust clouds, with disastrous environmental consequences

nuclease /nyóokli ayz/ *n.* an enzyme that breaks down nucleic acids [Early 20thC. Coined from a shortening of NUCLEIC + -ASE.]

nucleate /nyóokli ət, -ayt/, **nucleated** /nyóokli aytid/ *adj.* BIOL **WITH A NUCLEUS** having a nucleus or nuclei ■ *vti.* /nyóokli ayt/ (**-ates, -ating, -ated**) **FORM A NUCLEUS** to come together as a nucleus, or to bring things together to form a nucleus [Mid-19thC. Coined from a shortening of NUCLEAR + -ATE.] —**nucleator** /nyóokli aytər/ *n.*

nucleation /nyóokli áysh'n/ *n.* **1.** METEOROL **FORMATION PROCESS IN CLOUDS** the process by which ice crystals and rain drops form in clouds round a solid core **2.** GEOL **FORMATION OF CRYSTALS** the formation of crystals from a melt, often round a core of solid material

nuclei plural of **nucleus**

nucleic acid /nyoo kleé ik-, -kláy-/ *n.* any of various high-molecular-weight acids, e.g. DNA and RNA, consisting of nucleotide chains that convey genetic information and are found in all living cells and viruses

nuclein /nyóokli in/ *n.* BIOCHEM = **nucleoprotein**

nucleo- *prefix.* **1.** nucleus, nuclear ○ *nucleoplasm* **2.** nucleic acid ○ *nucleocapsid* [From NUCLEUS]

nucleocapsid /nyóokli ō kápsid/ *n.* the basic viral structure consisting of a core of nucleic acid surrounded by a protein coat

nucleolate /nyóokli ō layt/ *adj.* having a nucleolus or nucleoli

nucleolus /nyóokli óləss/ (*plural* **-li** /-lī/) *n.* a small round body inside a cell nucleus, composed of protein and RNA and associated with the formation of ribosomes and ribosomal RNA [Mid-19thC. From late Latin, 'little nucleus', from Latin *nucleus* (see NUCLEUS).] —**nucleolar** *adj.*

nucleon /nyóokli on/ *n.* a proton or neutron, especially when part of an atomic nucleus

nucleonics /nyóokli ónniks/ *n.* the branch of physics dealing with the properties of nucleons and the atomic nucleus (*takes a singular verb*)

nucleon number *n.* PHYS = **mass number**

nucleophile /nyóokli ō fīl/ *n.* a substance that becomes an electron donor in bonding during a chemical reaction —**nucleophilic** /nyóokli ō fíllik/ *adj.*

nucleoplasm /nyóokli ō plazəm/ *n.* the liquid matter (**protoplasm**) of a cell nucleus

nucleoprotein /nyóokli ō prō teen/ *n.* a protein in combination with a nucleic acid in cells that is the main constituent of genetic material in chromosomes

nucleoside /nyóokli ə sīd/ *n.* a type of organic compound, found especially in DNA and RNA in living organisms, consisting of a purine or pyrimidine base linked to a sugar, particularly ribose or deoxyribose [Early 20thC. Coined from NUCLEO- + GLYCOSIDE.]

nucleosome /nyóokli ə sōm/ *n.* a minute particle of DNA and protein that forms the basic packing unit of chromatin, the substance of chromosomes. Nucleosomes fit together rather like a tightly condensed string of beads.

nucleosynthesis /nyóokli ō sínthəssiss/ *n.* the synthesis of heavier elements from lighter elements by fusion reactions within stars

nucleotide /nyóokli ə tīd/ *n.* a type of chemical compound occurring most notably in nucleic acids such as RNA and DNA, consisting of a nucleoside linked to a phosphate group [Early 20thC. An alteration of NUCLEOSIDE.]

nucleus /nyóokli əss/ (*plural* **-i** /-li ī/ *or* **-uses**) *n.* **1. IMPORTANT ELEMENT** a central or most important item or part that has others grouped or built around it **2.** PHYS **CENTRAL REGION OF AN ATOM** the positively charged central region of an atom, consisting of protons and neutrons and containing most of the mass **3.** CHEM **STABLE ATOMS IN A MOLECULE** a stable group of atoms in a molecule, e.g. a benzene ring, that forms the base structure of many compounds and remains unchanged in chemical reactions **4.** BIOL **CENTRAL PART OF A LIVING CELL** the central body, usually spherical, within a eukaryotic cell, which is a membrane-encased mass of protoplasm containing the chromosomes and other genetic information necessary to control cell growth and reproduction **5.** BOT **STARCH GRANULE'S CENTRE** the central part of a starch granule **6.** BOT **INNER KERNEL OF A NUT** the central kernel of a nut seed **7.** ANAT **GROUP OF NERVE CELLS** a group of nerve cells in the central nervous system or a small mass of grey matter in the brain that has a specialized function **8.** ASTRON **CORE OF A COMET'S HEAD** the central core in the head of a comet, consisting of ice, frozen gases, and dust **9.** ASTRON **CENTRAL PORTION OF A NEBULA OR GALAXY** the central brighter portion of a nebula or galaxy **10.** PHON **MOST RESONANT PART OF A SYLLABLE** the most resonant part of a syllable, usually the vowel [Early 18thC. Via Latin *nuculeus* 'kernel of a nut', from *nuculus* 'little nut', from *nux* 'nut' (source of English *nougat*).]

nuclide /nyóo klīd/ *n.* one or more atomic nuclei identifiable as being of the same element by having the same number of protons and neutrons and the same energy content. Alternatively, the nuclide may be specified by its mass number, atomic number, and energy content. [Mid-20thC. Coined from NUCLEUS + -IDE.]

NUCPS *abbr.* National Union of Civil and Public Servants

nuddy /núddi/ *n.* nude (*informal*) [Mid-20thC. An alteration of NUDE.]

nude /nyood/ *adj.* (**nuder, nudest**) **1. UNCLOTHED** wearing no clothes ○ *the nude figure of a man* **2. FOR UNCLOTHED PEOPLE** intended for, or done by, people wearing no clothes **3. PLAIN** bare or plain, with no covering or decoration **4.** LAW **LACKING A LEGAL REQUISITE** lacking a legal requisite such as supporting evidence or a contract ■ *n.* **UNCLOTHED FIGURE** an unclothed person, especially an unclothed figure in a painting or other artistic work [Mid-16thC. From Latin *nudus*.] —**nudely** *adv.* —**nudeness** *n.* ◇ **in the nude** without clothes

WORD KEY: SYNONYMS

See Synonyms at ***naked***.

NUDETS *abbr.* nuclear detection system

nudge /nuj/ *v.* (**nudges, nudging, nudged**) **1.** *vt.* **PUSH SB OR STH GENTLY** to push or poke sb gently, usually with a motion of the elbow **2.** *vt.* **MOVE STH GENTLY** to move sth gently, especially by pushing it slowly and carefully **3.** *vt.* **APPROACH A LEVEL** to have very nearly reached a particular level or standard ○ *Their profits are nudging the 100 million mark.* **4.** *vi.* **MOVE SLOWLY** to move slowly or little by little **5.** *vt.* **GENTLY PERSUADE** to persuade sb into an action, gently and delicately ■ *n.* **1. GENTLE PUSH** a gentle push to get sb's attention **2. BIT OF PERSUASION** a gentle piece of persuasion [Late 17thC. Origin uncertain.] ◇ **nudge nudge** used to hint or suggest that sth is slightly lewd or sexually improper

nudism /nyóodizəm/ *n.* = **naturism** *n.* 1

nudist /nyóodist/ *n.* **SB PREFERRING NUDITY** sb who prefers to go about without clothes, especially sb who spends time in communes or designated areas with others who feel the same way ■ *adj.* **FOR NUDISTS** intended for people who prefer to go about without clothes

nudist colony *n.* a place, especially a holiday camp, where the wearing of clothes is not allowed, intended for people who believe nudity is a healthy natural state

nudity /nyóodəti/ *n.* **1. BEING UNCLOTHED** the state of having no clothes on **2. BARENESS** bareness or plainness, with no covering or decoration

Nuevo Laredo /nwáyvō lə ráydō/ city in northeastern Mexico, on the Rio Grande. Located opposite Laredo, Texas, it is the main drivers' entry point from the United States. Population: 217,912 (1990).

nuevo sol /nwáyvō sol/ (*plural* **nuevos soles** /nwáyvōs sólays/) *n.* MONEY = **sol**[4]

Nuffield /núf eeld/, **William Richard Morris, 1st Viscount** (1877–1963) British automobile manufacturer and philanthropist. He used his fortune for educational endowments and charitable causes.

nugatory /nyóogətəri/ *adj.* **1. TRIFLING** of no importance whatsoever **2.** LAW **NOT VALID** with no legal force [Early 17thC. Via Latin *nugatorius* from, ultimately, *nugae* 'trifling matters'.] —**nugatorily** *adv.*

nugget /núggit/ *n.* **1.** MINERALS **LUMP OF PRECIOUS METAL** a lump of gold or other precious metal in its natural state, dug up out of the ground **2. SMALL PRECIOUS THING** any small item or piece, especially of sth abstract such as knowledge or information, regarded as very precious **3.** FOOD **A SMALL ROUND PIECE OF FOOD** a small piece of food, usually coated with breadcrumbs and fried or baked in an oven [Mid-19thC. Origin uncertain: probably from an English dialect word meaning 'lump'.]

nuggety /núggiti/ *adj.* **1. OCCURRING AS NUGGETS** occurring as nuggets **2.** *ANZ* **BROAD AND STRONG-LOOKING** having a broad and strong-looking physique, and usually short in stature (*informal*)

nuisance /nyóoss'nss/ *n.* **1. SB OR STH IRRITATING** an annoying or irritating person or thing **2.** LAW **ILLEGAL THING** sth not allowed by law because it causes harm or offence, either to people in general (**public nuisance**) or to a private individual [15thC. Via Old French from, ultimately, Latin *nocere* 'to harm, injure' (source of English *innocent* and *innocuous*).]

nuisance call *n.* a usually anonymous telephone call made to annoy, harass, upset, or scare sb

nuisance value *n.* the relative usefulness of sth based on its potential to cause problems or difficulties for sb

NUJ *abbr.* National Union of Journalists

nuke /nyook/ *vt.* (**nukes, nuking, nuked**) **1.** MIL **ATTACK PEOPLE** to attack people or places with nuclear weapons (*slang*) **2.** FOOD **MICROWAVE STH** to cook sth in a microwave oven (*informal*) ■ *n.* **NUCLEAR WEAPON** a nuclear weapon (*slang*) [Mid-20thC. Shortening of NUCLEAR.]

null /nul/ *adj.* **1.** LAW **INVALID** having no legal validity **2. VALUELESS** having no value or importance **3. AMOUNTING TO NOTHING** amounting to nothing in terms of context or character **4. AT ZERO LEVEL** at the level of zero or nothing **5.** MATH **RELATING TO ZERO** equal to or relating to zero **6.** MATH **EMPTY** containing no elements ○ *the null set* **7.** MATH **ENDING IN ZERO** converging to zero ○ *a null sequence* **8.** PHYS **INDICATING A READING OF ZERO** indicating a reading of zero when a measured quantity is undetectable or equal to another in comparison ■ *n.* **ZERO** a zero (*literary*) [Mid-16thC. Via Old French *nul* from Latin *nullus* 'not any'.] ◇ **null and void** not legally valid

nullah /núllə/ *n.* a ditch or ravine in India and other parts of Asia [Late 18thC. From Hindi *nālā*.]

Nullarbor Plain /núllər bawr-/ dry plateau in southern South Australia. Area: 300,000 sq. km/116,000 sq. mi.

nullify /núlli fī/ (**-fies, -fying, -fied**) *vt.* **1.** LAW **MAKE STH INVALID** to make sth legally invalid or ineffective **2. CANCEL STH OUT** to have the effect of cancelling sth out —**nullifier** *n.*

WORD KEY: SYNONYMS

nullify, abrogate, annul, repeal, invalidate, negate

CORE MEANING: to put an end to the effective existence of sth

nullify a fairly formal word meaning to end the effectiveness of sth such as a contract, especially by doing sth that counteracts its terms; **abrogate** a formal word used mainly in official or legal contexts to indicate the bringing to an end of a formal agreement, treaty, or contract; **annul** to declare sth officially or legally invalid or ineffective in such a way as to indicate negation of its prior existence; **repeal** to end a law officially; **invalidate** to cause sth to be considered illegal, unsound, or ineffective, e.g. by failing to comply with certain terms and conditions; **negate** to render sth ineffective, for example by doing sth that counterbalances its force or effectiveness.

---

nullipara /nu líppərə/ (*plural* **-ras** *or* **-rae** /-ree/) *n.* a woman who has never given birth to a child [Late 19thC. Formed from Latin *nullus* 'none' + English *-para* 'woman who has given birth', from Latin *parere* 'to give birth'.]

nullity /núlləti/ *n.* **1.** LAW LEGAL INVALIDITY the state of being legally invalid **2.** NONEFFECTIVENESS lack of effectiveness or usefulness

NUM *abbr.* National Union of Mineworkers

num. *abbr.* **1.** number **2.** numeral

Num. *abbr.* BIBLE Numbers

numb /num/ *adj.* **1.** WITH NO FEELING unable to feel or have sensations, e.g. as a result of extreme cold or the application of a local anaesthetic **2.** EMOTIONLESS unable to feel emotions ■ *vt.* (**numbs, numbing, numbed**) **1.** TAKE SENSATION AWAY FROM STH to take away from a part of the body the power to feel or have sensations, or to take away the sensations themselves **2.** TAKE AWAY SB'S FEELINGS to make sb incapable of feeling emotion, or deaden sb's emotions or feelings [15thC. Originally a past participle of Old English *niman* 'to take'. Ultimately from a prehistoric Germanic word meaning 'to grasp', which is also the ancestor of English *nimble*.] —**numbly** *adv.* —**numbness** *n.*

number /númbər/ *n.* **1.** COUNTING, OR FIGURES USED TO COUNT the concept of calculating quantities of individual things, or any of the words, figures, or symbols used in doing this **2.** IDENTIFYING FIGURE any figure or group of figures identifying sb or sth, e.g. a set of figures identifying sb as a telephone subscriber, or a figure identifying a sports player or competitor ○ *What's your fax number?* **3.** QUANTITY a quantity of people or things, especially a large quantity ○ *We have received a number of complaints.* **4.** TOTAL a total or sum ○ *The number of people treated has risen to over 3 million.* **5.** SINGLE THING IN A SERIES a single one of a series of things produced in sequence, especially a single issue of a magazine **6.** MUSIC PIECE OF MUSIC a self-contained piece of popular music, especially one of several that feature in a performance **7.** CLOTHES GARMENT an item of clothing, especially women's clothing (*informal*) ○ *a little silk number* **8.** THING a thing of any kind, especially sth that gives pleasure or impresses (*informal*) **9.** PERSON sb regarded in sexual terms (*informal; sometimes considered offensive*) **10.** CANNABIS CIGARETTE a cannabis cigarette (*slang*) **11.** GRAM GRAMMATICAL QUANTITY quantity expressed, in some languages, by the form of a word ○ *The qualifying adjective agrees with the noun in gender and number.* ■ *v.* (**-bers, -bering, -bered**) **1.** *vt.* ASSIGN A NUMBER TO STH to give sth or sb an identifying number ○ *Don't forget to number the pages.* **2.** *vti.* MAKE AS TOTAL to reach a particular total amount ○ *Supporters numbered over 300, while there were only 15 dissenters.* **3.** *vt.* INCLUDE STH to include sb or sth as one of a group ○ *It is numbered among the world's most prestigious hotels.* [13thC. Via Anglo-Norman *numbre* from Latin *numerus* (source of English *numerous* and *enumerate*).] —**numberer** *n.* ◇ **do a number on sb** to treat sb unfairly or harshly, e.g. by criticizing or ridiculing him or her in a deliberate and systematic way (*slang*) ◇ **get** *or* **have sb's number** to understand sb's true motives or character and so be well placed to deal with him or her ◇ **sb's days are numbered** sb's life or career is about to come to an end

number-cruncher *n.* (*slang*) **1.** COMPUT COMPUTER a computer designed to perform large quantities of complex numerical calculations **2.** SB WHO DOES CALCULATIONS sb whose job consists of performing large quantities of arithmetical calculations —**number-crunching** *n.*

numbered account *n.* a bank account identified by a number only, allowing the account holder to keep his or her identity secret

numberless /númbərləss/ *adj.* **1.** COUNTLESS too numerous to be counted **2.** NOT NUMBERED not given a number or marked with a number

number one *n.* **1.** FIRST THING the first one in a series of things or people ○ *She's number one among the top candidates.* **2.** MUSIC BESTSELLING RECORD a recording in a particular category that has sold the most copies in a given week **3.** SELF yourself and your own interests (*informal*) **4.** IMPORTANT PERSON the leader or the most important person in a group or organization (*informal*) **5.** URINATION the act or an instance of urinating, or urine (*babytalk*) ◊ **number two** *n.* 2 ■ *adj.* **1.** MOST IMPORTANT first, best, or most important **2.** EXCELLENT of a very high standard or quality (*informal*)

Number One *n.* the first officer or first mate on a ship, next in rank after the captain (*informal*)

number plate *n.* a metal or plastic plate on the front and back of a motor vehicle, carrying the vehicle's registration number. US term **license plate**

Numbers *n.* the fourth book of the Bible

Number Ten *n.* 10 Downing Street, the official London home of the Prime Minister

number theory *n.* the branch of mathematics that deals with the properties of integers and relationships between integers

number two *n.* **1.** DEPUTY sb's deputy or second-in-command (*informal*) **2.** DEFECATION the act or an instance of defecating, or faeces (*babytalk*) ◊ **number one** *n.* 5

numbing /númming/ *adj.* **1.** CAUSING NUMBNESS causing numbness in part of the body **2.** DEADENING FEELINGS OR THOUGHTS temporarily taking away sb's ability to feel or think, e.g. as a result of shock

numbles /númb'lz/ *npl.* the edible inside organs of an animal, especially a deer, including the heart, liver, and lungs (*archaic*) [14thC. Via Old French from, ultimately, Latin *lumbulus*, from *lumbus* 'loin' (source of English *lumbar*, *loin*, and *sirloin*).]

numbskull *n.* = **numskull**

numdah /núm daa/ *n.* an embroidered rug made from felt, in a style from the Indian subcontinent and Middle East [Early 19thC. Via Urdu *namdā* from Persian *namad* 'felt, carpet'.]

numen /nyoo men/ (*plural* **-mina** /-minə/) *n.* **1.** SPIRIT INHABITING A PLACE a god or spirit believed to inhabit a place or living object such as a tree **2.** GUIDING FORCE any guiding force or influence [Early 17thC. From Latin, 'nod, command, divine power'.]

numerable /nyoómərəb'l/ *adj.* able to be counted

numeracy /nyoómərəssi/ *n.* competence in the mathematical skills needed to cope with everyday life and the understanding of information presented in mathematical terms like graphs, charts, or tables [Mid-20thC. Formed from NUMERATE, on the model of LITERACY.]

numeral /nyoómərəl/ *n.* SYMBOL REPRESENTING A NUMBER a symbol or set of symbols used to represent a number, e.g. the Arabic numeral 5, the equivalent Roman numeral V, and the equivalent binary numeral 101 ■ *adj.* OF NUMBERS relating to numbers or representing a number or numbers [14thC. Via late Latin *numeralis* from Latin *numerus* (see NUMBER).] —**numerally** *adv.*

numerary /nyoómərəri/ *adj.* relating to numbers [Early 18thC. Via medieval Latin *numerarius* from, ultimately, Latin *numerus* (see NUMBER).]

numerate *adj.* /nyoómərət/ **1.** MATHEMATICALLY COMPETENT able to do arithmetical calculations **2.** WITH SOME MATHS KNOWLEDGE having a basic understanding of mathematics ■ *vt.* /nyoómə rayt/ (**-ates, -ating, -ated**) ENUMERATE THINGS to name a number of things in turn

or in sequence (*archaic*) [Early 18thC. From Latin *numeratus*, the past participle stem of *numerare* 'to count', from *numerus* (see NUMBER).]

numeration /nyoo̅mə ráysh'n/ *n.* **1.** GIVING OR NAMING OF NUMBERS the naming of numbers, e.g. by schoolchildren, or the giving of numbers to items in a set or group **2.** COUNTING SYSTEM a system of symbols used for counting or numbering things

numerator /nyoo̅mə raytər/ *n.* the part of a common fraction appearing above the line, representing the number of parts of the whole that are being considered

numerical /nyoo mérrik'l/, **numeric** *adj.* **1.** CONSISTING OF NUMBERS using numbers or consisting of numbers **2.** OF NUMBERS OF THINGS in terms of the number of people or things [Early 17thC. Formed from Latin *numerus* (see NUMBER).]

numerical analysis *n.* a branch of mathematics dealing with the use of repeatedly used quantitative approximations to solve problems, and the measurement of the errors involved. Usually computers are used to execute the calculations. —**numerical analyst** *n.*

numerical control *n.* an often computerized technique for controlling machine tools where the position or action of a tool, e.g. the depth of a drill, is determined by a numerical value

numerically /nyoo mérrikli/ *adv.* in terms of the numbers of people or things involved ○ *His forces were numerically superior to those of the enemy.*

numerical order *n.* an ordering of people or things identified by number from the lowest to the highest

numerical taxonomy *n.* a procedure that involves comparing a large number of characteristics of one organism with the same characteristics of another

numeric control *n.* ENG = **numerical control**

numeric keypad *n.* a section of a computer keyboard, usually to the right of the main keypad, containing numbered keys in the same layout as the numbers on a calculator. The keys can be used in conjunction with other keys to perform special functions.

numerology /nyoómə rólləji/ *n.* the study of the occult use and supposed influence of numbers —**numerological** /nyoómərə lójik'l/ *adj.* —**numerologically** /-lójikli/ *adv.* —**numerologist** /nyoómə rólləjist/ *n.*

numero uno /noómərō oo̅nō/ *n.* (*informal humorous*) **1.** = **number one** *n.* 3 **2.** VIP the leader or most important person in a group or organization [Late 20thC. From Spanish or Italian, 'number one'.]

numerous /nyoómərəss/ *adj.* many in number [15thC. From Latin *numerosus*, from *numerus* (see NUMBER).] —**numerously** *adv.* —**numerousness** *n.*

numinous /nyoóminəss/ *adj.* **1.** MYSTERIOUSLY ASSOCIATED WITH A DEITY having a mysterious power that suggests the presence of a spirit or god (*formal*) **2.** HOLY filled with inextricable associations with God (*formal*) **3.** OF NUMINA relating to numina, the spirits or gods believed in some cultures to inhabit places or things [Mid-17thC. From the stem of Latin *numen* (see NUMEN).] —**numinously** *adv.* —**numinousness** *n.*

numismatic /nyoo̅miz máttik/ *adj.* relating to the study or collecting of coins and medals [Late 18thC. Via French *numismatique* from, ultimately, Greek *nomisma* 'coin, currency', from *nomizein* 'to have in use', from *nomos* 'custom'.] —**numismatically** *adv.*

numismatics /nyoo̅miz máttiks/ *n.* the study and collecting of coins and medals (*takes a singular verb*) —**numismatist** /nyoo mízmə tist/ *n.*

Num Lock /núm-/ *n.* a toggle feature of computer keyboards that cancels the scrolling and cursor-moving abilities of keys on the numeric keypad so that it can be used to input numbers

nummary /númməri/ *adj.* relating to coins, or to coins and banknotes [Early 17thC. From Latin *nummarius*, from *nummus* 'coin'.]

nummular /númmyoolər/ *adj.* shaped like a coin or disc (*formal*) [Mid-18thC. From Latin *nummulus* 'small coin', from *nummus* (see NUMMARY).]

nummulite /númmyoo lít/ *n.* a type of fossil commonly found in limestone dating from between 56.5 million and 5.2 million years ago. It is common in the

---

Mediterranean and is shaped like a flat disc. [Early 19thC. Formed from modern Latin *Nummulites*, former genus name, from Latin *nummulus* (see NUMMULAR), because of its shape.] —**nummulitic** /númmyŏŏ líttik/ *adj.*

numnah /núm naa/ *n.* a pad placed under a saddle [Mid-19thC. From Urdu *namadā* (see NUMDAH).]

numskull /núm skul/, **numbskull** *n.* an offensive term that deliberately insults sb's intelligence (*insult*) [Early 18thC. Formed from NUMB + SKULL.]

nun[1] /nun/ *n.* **1.** RELIG RELIGIOUS WOMAN a member of a religious community of women, e.g. any of various Christian orders of women who dedicate their lives to religious devotion and undertake not to marry **2.** BIRDS KIND OF PIGEON a variety of domestic pigeon with black-and-white feathers all over and a ring of white feathers round its neck and head that looks a little like a nun's headdress [Old English *nunne*. Via Old French *nonne* from ecclesiastical Latin *nonna*, from *nonnus* 'old man, monk'.]

nun[2] /noon/ *n.* the 14th letter of the Hebrew alphabet, represented in the English alphabet as 'n' [Early 19thC. From Hebrew *nûn*.]

nunatak /núnnə tak/ *n.* a mountain peak surrounded by glacial ice, originally in Norway and Greenland [Late 19thC. From Inuit (Eskimo) *nunataq*.]

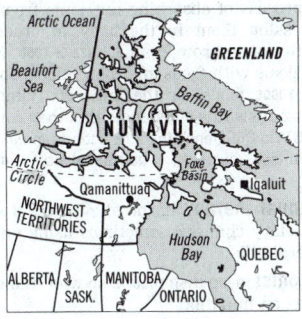
Nunavut

Nunavut /nóŏnnə vŏŏt/ territory created at the end of the 20th century in northern Canada, replacing the central and eastern part of the Northwest Territories. It is a homeland for the Inuit people. The name means 'our land' in Inuit. Capital: Iqaluit. Population: 22,000 (1997). Area: 2 million sq. km/770,000 sq. mi.

nun buoy *n.* a buoy with a rounded middle and tapering ends, used to mark the right-hand side of a channel that leads into a harbour [Early 18thC. From *nun* 'child's top'.]

Nunc Dimittis /núngk di míttiss, nŏŏngk-/ *n.* a hymn or canticle with a text from Luke 2:29–32, starting in Latin with 'Nunc dimittis servum tuum', in English meaning 'Lord, now you are dismissing your servant in peace'. The passage in the Bible describes Simeon being presented with the baby Jesus Christ.

nunchaku /nun cha'a koo/ *n.* a martial arts weapon consisting of two thick sticks joined at their ends by an untanned leather strip, a rope, or a chain [Late 20thC. From Japanese dialect.]

nuncheon /núnchən/ *n.* a drink or snack taken between meals, especially in the afternoon (*archaic*) [14thC. Formed from earlier *non* 'noon' (see NOON) + earlier *shench* 'drink', from Old English *scenc* (related to German *schenken* 'to give (to drink)'.]

nunciature /núnssi əchər/ *n.* the rank or position of a nuncio, or the period of time sb spends as a nuncio [Early 17thC. From Italian *nunciatura*, from *nuncio* (see NUNCIO).]

nuncio /núnssi ō, nŏŏn-, -shi ō/ (*plural* **-os**) *n.* **1.** CHR POPE'S REPRESENTATIVE sb appointed by the pope to represent him in a country, with the diplomatic status of an ambassador **2.** REPRESENTATIVE OR INTERMEDIARY sb sent by a person to act on his or her behalf, especially a person regarded as self-important or authoritarian (*formal humorous*) [Early 16thC. Via Italian from Latin *nuntius* 'messenger' (source of English *announce* and *enunciate*).]

nuncle /núngk'l/ *n.* an uncle (*archaic*) [Late 16thC. From *mine uncle* or *an uncle*.]

nuncupative /núngkyŏŏ paytiv, -pətiv/ *adj.* LAW given or declared orally by sb making a will, and written down later by sb else [Mid-16thC. Via late Latin *nuncupativus* to name, declare', from *nomen* 'name' + *capere* 'to take' (see CAPTIVE).]

Nuneaton /nun ée'tən/ industrial town in Warwickshire, England. Population: 66,715 (1991).

nunnery /núnnəri/ (*plural* **-ies**) *n.* a convent

Nupe /nŏŏ pay/ (*plural* **-pe** *or* **-pes**) *n.* **1.** PEOPLES MEMBER OF A NIGERIAN PEOPLE a member of a Nigerian people who live between the rivers Benue and Niger **2.** LANG LANGUAGE OF THE NUPE the language spoken by the Nupe, belonging to the Benue-Congo branch of the Niger-Congo family of languages. Nupe is spoken by about one million people. [Early 19thC. Named after a former kingdom at the junction of the Niger and Benue.]

NUPE /nyóōpi/ *abbr.* National Union of Public Employees

nuptial /núpsh'l, -chəl/ *adj.* **1.** OF MARRIAGE relating to marriage or weddings. ◊ **nuptials 2.** OF ANIMAL BREEDING relating to mating or breeding in animals [15thC. Via Old French from Latin *nuptiae* 'wedding', from *nubere* 'to take a husband' (source of English *nubile*).] —**nuptially** *adv.*

nuptial plumage *n.* the distinctive feathers that some birds grow during their mating season

nuptials /núpsh'lz, -chəlz/ *npl.* a wedding ceremony (*literary or humorous*)

Nuremberg /nyóŏrəm búrg/ city in Bavaria, southern Germany. After 1933 the German Nazi Party held annual rallies in a stadium in the city, and between 1945 and 1946 it was the scene of Allied trials of German war criminals. Population: 497,496 (1992).

Rudolf Nureyev

Nureyev /nyoòri ef, nyoo ráy-/, **Rudolf** (1938–93) Russian-born dancer and choreographer. He was connected from 1962 with Britain's Royal Ballet, where he often performed with Margot Fonteyn. Full name **Rudolf Hametovich Nureyev**

Nuristan /noòri staàn/ administrative province of eastern Afghanistan, south of the Hindu Kush. Area: 13,000 sq. km/5000 sq. mi.

Nurmi /núrmi/, **Paavo** (1897–1973) Finnish athlete. He won nine Olympic gold medals (1920, 1924, and 1928) in middle-distance and long-distance races. Known as **the Flying Finn**. Full name **Paavo Johannes Nurmi**

NURMTW *abbr.* National Union of Rail, Maritime, and Transport Workers

nurse /nurss/ *n.* **1.** MED SB CARING FOR PATIENTS sb trained to look after ill and injured people, especially sb who works in a hospital or clinic, administering the care and treatment that a doctor prescribes **2.** NANNY a nanny or nursemaid (*dated*) **3.** = **wet nurse 4.** NURSERY NURSE sb professionally qualified to look after young children in a nursery, nursery school, or crèche **5.** INSECTS INSECT LOOKING AFTER YOUNG an insect that looks after the young or the larvae in a colony of social insects such as ants or bees ■ *v.* (**nurses, nursing, nursed**) **1.** MED CARE FOR A SICK PERSON to take care of sb who is ill or injured **2.** *vi.* MED WORK AS A NURSE to do the work of a nurse, especially professionally in a hospital **3.** *vt.* TREAT A HEALTH PROBLEM to take care of yourself when ill or injured ○ *nursing a broken leg* **4.** *vt.* KEEP A FEELING to keep a feeling in the mind for a long time and perhaps indulge in it,

allowing it to grow or deepen ○ *nursing his resentment* **5.** *vt.* HOLD STH to hold sth precious with love or care **6.** *vt.* MANAGE SB OR STH CAREFULLY to manage, guide, or supervise sb or sth with care and devotion **7.** *vt.* CONSUME STH SLOWLY to consume sth, especially a drink, very slowly in order to make it last **8.** *vt.* HOLD SB IN YOUR ARMS to hold sb, especially a child, affectionately or protectively in your arms, or hold a part of sb's body in this way **9.** *vti.* BREASTFEED to breastfeed a baby, or suckle at a mother's breast [13thC. Via Old French *norrice* from, ultimately, Latin *nutricia* 'wet nurse', from Latin *nutrix*.] —**nurser** *n.*

nursemaid /núrss mayd/ *n.* a woman employed to look after sb's children when they are young (*dated*)

nurse practitioner *n.* a registered nurse trained in primary health care to assume certain responsibilities once assumed only by a doctor, such as the diagnosis and treatment of minor illnesses

nursery /núrssəri/ (*plural* **-ies**) *n.* **1.** EDUC = **nursery school 2.** CHILD'S ROOM a child's bedroom or playroom in a house **3.** GARDENING PLACE GROWING PLANTS COMMERCIALLY a place where plants are grown commercially, either for sale direct to the public or to other retailers **4.** PLACE FOSTERING STH a place where talents or abilities are allowed or encouraged to develop and flourish (*literary*) [14thC. Via Old French *norricerie* from *norrice* 'wet nurse' (see NURSE). Originally in English, 'attentive care'.]

nursery class *n.* a school class for children under five years of age, especially one in a school where the majority of children are older

nurserymaid /núrssəri mayd/ *n.* a woman employed to look after sb's children when they are young (*dated*)

nurseryman /núrssərimən/ (*plural* **-men** /-mən/) *n.* a man who works in or owns a nursery where plants are grown commercially

nursery rhyme *n.* a short song or poem for young children, especially one that has become traditional

nursery school *n.* a school for children between the ages of three and five, staffed wholly or partly by qualified teachers who encourage and supervise educational play rather than simply providing childcare

nursery slopes *npl.* SKIING the gentlest slopes in a ski resort or complex, designed for beginners to use. US term **bunny slopes**

nurse's aide *n.* US = **healthcare assistant**

nurse shark *n.* a warm-water shark that has a bristle (**barbel**) hanging from its jaw and a deep groove on either side of its mouth. Family: Orectolobidae. [So called because it tends its eggs until they hatch]

nursing /núrssing/ *n.* **1.** CARING FOR ILL PEOPLE the profession or task of looking after people who are ill or injured **2.** BREASTFEEDING breastfeeding, or the period of time that a mother spends breastfeeding her baby

nursing assistant *n.* = **healthcare assistant**

nursing auxiliary *n.* former name for **nursing assistant**

nursing bra *n.* a bra with removable or openable cups, worn by breastfeeding mothers

nursing home *n.* a long-term hospital or home that provides full-time care and medical treatment for people who are unable to take care of themselves

nursling /núrssling/ *n.* (*literary*) **1.** BREASTFED INFANT a baby that is being breastfed **2.** CHILD BEING CARED FOR a baby or child that sb is looking after or bringing up, especially sb else's child **3.** STH FOSTERED sth fostered or developed by a person, a place, or a set of circumstances

nurture /núrchər/ *vt.* (**-tures, -turing, -tured**) **1.** CARE FOR A YOUNG THING to give tender care and protection to a child, a young animal, or a plant, helping it to grow and develop **2.** ENCOURAGE TO FLOURISH to encourage sb or sth to grow, develop, thrive, and be successful ○ *an agent who nurtured several budding young playwrights* **3.** KEEP A FEELING to keep a feeling in the mind for a long time, allowing it to grow or deepen ■ *n.* **1.** CARE OR ENCOURAGEMENT care and protection given to a young child, animal, or plant, or support and encouragement given to sth to help it develop **2.** ENVIRONMENTAL INFLUENCE environmental influence on

Pecan   Walnut   Peanut   Brazil

Pistachio

Nut

an organism, especially when contrasted with what is determined genetically. ◊ **nature** [14thC. Via Old French from late Latin *nutritura*, from Latin *nutrire* 'to suckle' (see NOURISH).] —**nurturer** *n.*

NUS *abbr.* **1.** National Union of Seamen **2.** National Union of Students

Nusatenggara /noŏssə teng gaárə/ island group in Indonesia

nut /nut/ *n.* **1.** BOT **PLANT'S SHELL-COVERED FRUIT** the fruit of a plant, especially a tree, with a hard outer shell and a fairly hard kernel or inner part that is the plant's seed **2.** BOT, FOOD **EDIBLE KERNEL** the kernel of a plant's shell-covered fruit, especially when it is edible **3.** FOOD **PEANUT** a roasted peanut **4.** BOT **HARD FRUIT OF SOME PLANTS** the hard dry one-seeded fruit of various plants, which does not split open to scatter its seed when it is mature **5.** **FASTENING SCREWED ONTO A BOLT** a piece of metal, usually square or hexagonal, with a hole in the middle, screwed on the end of a bolt as a fastening for it **6.** MUSIC **PART OF A STRINGED INSTRUMENT** a ridge at the top end of the fingerboard of a violin, guitar, or other stringed instrument that the strings pass over just before they reach the tuning pegs **7.** MUSIC **PART OF AN INSTRUMENT'S BOW** a device like a screw at one end of a bow for a musical instrument that is turned to tighten the hairs of the bow **8.** **SMALL PIECE** a small piece of sth hard or solid ○ *a nut of coal* **9.** **HUMAN HEAD** a person's head (*informal*) **10.** **OFFENSIVE TERM** a highly offensive term for sb with a psychiatric disorder (*offensive*) **11.** **ENTHUSIAST** sb with a deep interest in sth (*informal*) ○ *a film nut* **12.** PRINTING = **en** ■ **nuts** *npl.* **TESTICLES** a man's testicles (*slang; sometimes considered offensive*) ■ *v.* (**nuts, nutting, nutted**) **1.** *vi.* **GATHER NUTS** to gather edible nuts from trees **2.** *vt.* **HIT SB WITH HEAD** to use the head to hit sb, usually in the face (*informal*) [Old English *hnutu*. Ultimately from an Indo-European base that is also the ancestor of Latin *nux* (source of English *nucleus* and *nougat*).]

NUT *abbr.* National Union of Teachers

nutation /nyoo táysh'n/ *n.* **1.** ASTRON **WOBBLY ROTATION** the wobbly rotation of a spinning object, especially a planet, caused by a temporary shift in the position of its axis **2.** BOT **PLANT'S IRREGULAR GROWTH** a spiral movement of a plant part caused by varying growth rates on each side **3.** **NODDING** the nodding of sb's head (*formal*) [Early 17thC. From Latin *nutation-*, from the past participle stem of *nutare* 'to nod'.] —**nutational** *adj.*

nut-brown *adj.* dark brown or reddish-brown in colour

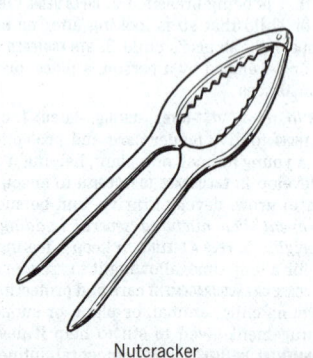

Nutcracker

nut butter *n.* nuts ground to a fine paste or spread, usually with oil and seasonings added and sometimes sugar

nutcase /nút kayss/ *n.* a highly offensive term for sb with a psychiatric disorder (*informal offensive*)

nutcracker /nút krakər/ *n.* **1.** **TOOL FOR CRACKING NUTS' SHELLS** a tool for cracking hard edible nutshells, usually consisting of two hinged metal arms between which the nut is squeezed **2.** BIRDS **BIRD THAT EATS PINE NUTS** a bird of the crow family that feeds mainly on nuts and the seeds of pines. Genus: *Nucifraga*.

─────── **WORD KEY: CULTURAL NOTE** ───────

The Nutcracker, a ballet by Russian composer Pyotr Illyich Tchaikovsky (1892). Based on Hoffmann's *The Nutcracker and the King of the Mice*, it depicts the dream of a young girl during which her nutcracker turns into a handsome prince who leads her to the magical realm of the Sugar Plum Fairy. Though the story is particularly popular with children, the music and choreography have universal and lasting appeal.

nut cutlet *n.* a vegetarian cake, patty, or burger made from chopped nuts and other vegetable ingredients mixed together and sometimes shaped into a meat chop or cutlet form. It is sometimes coated with breadcrumbs and is cooked by grilling, frying, or baking.

nutgall /nút gawl/ *n.* a hollow nut-shaped growth on the trunks of oak and other trees caused by the gall wasp, which uses the growth as a shelter for its larvae

nuthatch /nút hach/ *n.* a small bird with a blue-grey back that usually hangs upside down on a tree trunk and works its way down, eating insects, seeds, and nuts. Family: Sittidae. [14thC. From NUT + *hache* 'hatchet, axe', from Old French (see HATCHET), from its habit of hacking at nuts with its beak after wedging them into crevices.]

nuthouse /nút howss/ *n.* **1.** **OFFENSIVE TERM** a highly offensive term for psychiatric hospital (*slang offensive*) **2.** **CHAOTIC PLACE** a place full of noisy, boisterous, chaotic activity (*slang*)

nutlet /nútlət/ *n.* **1.** **SMALL NUT** a small nut, especially a small hard dry one-seeded fruit of various plants **2.** **FRUIT'S STONE** the stone of fruits such as the cherry and the plum

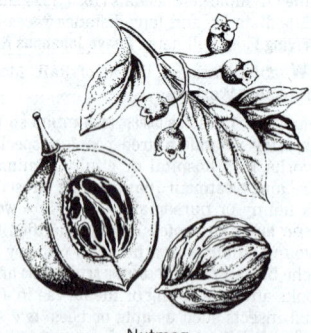

Nutmeg

nutmeg /nút meg/ *n.* **1.** COOK **SPICE** an aromatic spice made by grinding or grating the large hard seed of a nutmeg tree **2.** TREES **TROPICAL EVERGREEN TREE** an evergreen tree native to eastern India and widely grown in tropical regions for its seeds, which are

the source of nutmeg and mace. Latin name: *Myristica fragrans*. **3.** SOCCER **KICK OF BALL THROUGH OPPONENT'S LEGS** a kick of the ball through the open legs of an unsuspecting or off-guard opponent, made in order to regain possession of the ball behind the opponent (*informal*) ■ *adj.* COLOURS **LIGHT BROWN** of a light brown colour with a greyish tinge ■ *vt.* (**-megs, -megging, -megged**) SOCCER **KICK BALL THROUGH OPPONENT'S LEGS** to kick the ball through the open legs of an opponent (*informal*) [13thC. Origin uncertain: probably ultimately from medieval Latin *nux muscata*, literally 'nut smelling like musk', from *nux* 'nut' + late Latin *muscus* (see MUSK).]

nutria /nyoŏtri ə/ *n.* **1.** ZOOL = **coypu 2.** COYPU'S FUR the light brown fur of the coypu [Early 19thC. Via Spanish from, ultimately, Latin *lutra* 'otter'.]

nutrient /nyoŏtri ənt/ *n.* **NOURISHING SUBSTANCE** any substance that provides nourishment, e.g. the minerals that a plant takes from the soil or the constituents in food that keep a human body healthy and help it grow ■ *adj.* **NOURISHING** providing nourishment [Mid-17thC. From Latin *nutriens*, the present participle stem of *nutrire* (see NOURISH).]

nutriment /nyoŏtrimənt/ *n.* nourishment or nourishing substances [Mid-16thC. From Latin *nutrimentum*, from *nutrire* (see NOURISH).]

nutrition /nyoo trísh'n/ *n.* **1.** PHYSIOL **PROCESSING OF FOOD** the process of absorbing nutrients from food and processing them in the body in order to keep healthy or to grow **2.** SCI **SCIENCE OF FOOD** the science that deals with foods and their effects on health **3.** FOOD **FOODS** foods, or the minerals, vitamins, and other nourishing substances that they contain [Mid-16thC. Via Old French from the Latin stem *nutrition-*, from *nutrire* (see NOURISH).] —**nutritional** *adj.* —**nutritionally** *adv.*

nutritional therapy *n.* the alleviation of symptoms by dietary changes, sometimes using vitamin and mineral pills

nutritionist /nyoo trísh'nist/ *n.* sb who studies or is an expert on nutrition

nutritious /nyoo tríshəss/ *adj.* containing minerals, vitamins, and other substances that promote health —**nutritiously** *adv.* —**nutritiousness** *n.*

nutritive /nyoŏtrətiv/ *adj.* **1.** **NOURISHING** providing nutrients **2.** **OF NOURISHMENT** relating to or providing nutrition [15thC. Via Old French from medieval Latin *nutritivus*, from the past participle stem of *nutrire* (see NOURISH).] —**nutritively** *adv.*

nut roast *n.* a savoury vegetarian loaf made from chopped or ground-up nuts with onions, herbs, and seasonings, bound with breadcrumbs and baked

nuts /nuts/ *adj.* **1.** **OFFENSIVE TERM** a highly offensive term meaning having a psychiatric disorder (*slang offensive*) **2.** **ENTHUSIASTIC** wildly enthusiastic about sth, or extremely fond of sb (*slang*) ■ *interj.* **EXPRESSION OF ANNOYANCE** used to express annoyance, disbelief, or contempt (*slang*)

nuts and bolts *npl.* the most basic components, elements, or constituents of sth (*informal*)

nutshell /nút shel/ *n.* the hard outer shell of a nut that surrounds the edible inner nut or kernel ◊ **in a nutshell** in very few words, getting right to the main point

nutter /núttər/ *n.* an offensive term that deliberately insults sb's mental condition or way of behaving (*informal*)

nutty /nútti/ (**-tier, -tiest**) *adj.* **1.** **WITH NUTS** containing a large amount of nuts **2.** **LIKE NUTS** like nuts in taste, appearance, texture, or smell **3.** **OFFENSIVE TERM** an offensive term meaning having a psychiatric disorder (*slang offensive*) —**nuttily** *adv.* —**nuttiness** *n.*

Nuuk /nook/ capital and largest city of Greenland, situated on the southwestern coast. Population: 23,946 (1994).

nux vomica /núks vómmikə/ (*plural* **nux vomica**) *n.* **1.** TREES **ASIAN TREE** an Asian tree that has narrow leaves and orange-red berries containing seeds from which a former cardiac medication was made. Latin name: *Strychnos nux-vomica*. **2.** BOT **SEEDS OF NUX VOMICA TREE** the highly poisonous seeds of the nux vomica tree, which contain strychnine and other poisonous substances **3.** MED **MEDICINE** a medicine or homeopathic remedy made from the seeds of nux vomica [From medieval Latin, literally 'emetic nut']

nuzzle /núzz'l/ v. (-zles, -zling, -zled) 1. vti. **RUB STH WITH THE NOSE** to rub or push sth gently with the nose, especially as a way of showing affection 2. vi. **RUB STH WITH THE FACE** to make affectionate rubbing or stroking movements with the face ■ n. **RUBBING MOVEMENT** a rubbing or stroking movement with the nose or face [15thC. Origin uncertain: perhaps a back-formation from *noseling* 'on your nose', from NOSE.] — **nuzzler** n.

NV abbr. 1. MAIL Nevada 2. FIN non-voting

N/V abbr. BANKING no value

NVQ n. a UK qualification in a technical or vocational subject certifying the holder's proficiency in a range of work-related activities, awarded at a variety of levels. Full form **National Vocational Qualification**

NW abbr. 1. northwest 2. northwestern

NWbN abbr. northwest by north

NWbW abbr. northwest by west

Nwfld abbr. Newfoundland

NWT abbr. Can Northwest Territories

n.wt. abbr. net weight

NY, **N.Y.** abbr. New York

nyala /nyaále/ (plural **-la** or **-las**) n. 1. **CENTRAL AFRICAN ANTELOPE** an antelope found in central Africa, usually near water, that has vertical white stripes on its sides and, on the male, spiral horns. Latin name: *Tragelaphus angasi*. 2. **NE AFRICAN MOUNTAIN ANTELOPE** an antelope with spiral horns on the male found in mountainous regions in northeastern Africa, above 2,743/9,000 ft. Latin name: *Tragelaphus buxtoni*. [Late 19thC. From Zulu *i-nyala*.]

Nyanja /ni ánd jə/ (plural **-ja** or **-jas**), n. LANG = **Chewa** [Mid-19thC. From Bantu *nyanja* 'lake'.]

Nyasa, Lake /nī ássə-/ lake in southeastern Africa, between Malawi, Mozambique, and Tanzania. It is one of the world's largest lakes. Area: 22,490 sq. km/8,683 sq. mi.

nybble /níbb'l/ n. half of one byte, or four bits in size [Humorous play on the idea of a small bite]

NYC abbr. New York City

nyctalopia /níktə lópi ə/ n. the state of being unable to see well at night (technical) [Late 17thC. Via late Latin from Greek *nuktalōps* 'sightless at night', from the stem of *nux* 'night' + *alaos* 'sightless' + *ōps* 'eye' (source of English *myopia* and *triceratops*).] —**nyctalopic** /-lóppik/ adj.

nyctitropism /nik títtrəpizəm/ n. the movement of parts of a plant in response to light and temperature differences between night and day, such as the opening and closing of flowers and the folding together of leaves at night [Late 19thC. Formed from the stem of Greek *nux* 'night' (see NYCTALOPIA) + TROPISM.] —**nyctitropic** /níktə trópik, -tróppik/ adj.

nyctophobia /níktə fóbi ə/ n. an irrational fear of the night, or of darkness in general [Early 20thC. Formed from the stem of Greek *nux* 'night' (see NYCTALOPIA) + -PHOBIA.] —**nyctophobic** adj. —**nyctophobically** adv.

nyetwork n. = **notwork** (slang humorous) [Late 20thC. Blend of Russian *nyet* 'no' + NETWORK.]

nylon /ní lon/ n. TEXTILES **SYNTHETIC MATERIAL** a tough synthetic material widely used in different forms in manufactured articles, e.g. in food containers, in brush bristles, and in clothing ■ **nylons** npl. CLOTHES **WOMEN'S STOCKINGS** stockings made of a synthetic fibre such as nylon [Mid-20thC. Coined by its inventors, perhaps modeled on RAYON.]

NYMEX /ní meks/ abbr. New York Mercantile Exchange

nymph /nimf/ n. 1. MYTHOL **SPIRIT OF NATURE** a minor goddess or spirit of nature in mythology, inhabiting areas of natural beauty such as woods, mountains, and rivers and traditionally regarded as a beautiful young woman 2. **WOMAN** a beautiful young woman (literary) 3. INSECTS **INSECT LARVA** the larva of some insects, e.g. the mayfly, dragonfly, and grasshopper, that resembles the adult and develops into the adult insect directly, without passing through the intermediate pupa stage [14thC. Via Old French from, ultimately, Greek *nymphē* 'bride, nymph'.]

nympha /nímfə/ (plural **-phae** /-fee/) n. either of the small inner folds of skin (**labia minora**) that form the opening to the vagina [Late 17thC. Via Latin from Greek *nymphē* (see NYMPH).]

nymphalid /nímfəlid/ adj. belonging to a family of butterflies that has brightly coloured wings and includes the tortoiseshell butterfly and the red admiral. Family: Nymphalidae. [Late 19thC. Via modern Latin Nymphalidae, family name, from, ultimately, Latin *nympha* (see NYMPH).]

nymphet /nímfit, nim fét/, **nymphette** /nim fét/ n. a sexually aware and sexually desirable young woman, especially a woman in her early teens [Early 17thC. Originally, 'a small or young nymph'; the modern sense appeared in the mid-20thC.]

nympho /ním fō/ (plural **-phos**) n. a nymphomaniac (informal offensive) [Mid-20thC. Shortening.]

nymphomania /nímfə máyni ə/ n. a woman's compulsive desire to have sex with many different men, theorized to occur in some women (often considered offensive)

nymphomaniac /nímfə máyni ak/ n. 1. **WOMAN SUPPOSED TO HAVE SEXUAL COMPULSION** a woman supposed to have a compulsive desire to have sex with many different men 2. **OFFENSIVE TERM** an offensive term for a woman who is very active sexually, especially when she is regarded with distaste (informal offensive) —**nymphomaniacal** /nímfōmə ní ək'l/ adj.

Nynorsk /nee nawrsk/ n. LANG = **Landsmal** [Mid-20thC. From Norwegian, literally 'new Norwegian'.]

NYO abbr. National Youth Orchestra

NYP abbr. not yet published

NYSE abbr. New York Stock Exchange

nystagmus /ni stágməss/ n. an involuntary rhythmic movement of sb's eyes, usually from side to side, caused by some illnesses that affect the nerves and muscle behind the eyeball [Early 19thC. Via modern Latin from Greek *nustagmos* 'drowsiness', from *nustazein* 'to nod, be sleepy'.]

nystatin /nístətin/ n. an antibiotic drug used to treat fungal infections, especially thrush [Mid-20thC. Coined from N(ew) Y(ork) Stat(e), where it was developed.]

NZ abbr. New Zealand

NZBC abbr. New Zealand Broadcasting Commission

N Zeal. abbr. New Zealand

NZMA abbr. New Zealand Medical Association

NZRFU abbr. New Zealand Rugby Football Union

Oo

o /ō/ (*plural* **o's**), **O** (*plural* **O's** *or* **Os**) *n.* **1.** 15TH LETTER OF ENGLISH ALPHABET the 15th letter of the English alphabet **2.** SPEECH SOUND CORRESPONDING TO LETTER 'O' the speech sound that corresponds to the letter 'O' **3.** LETTER 'O' WRITTEN a written representation of the letter 'O'

o' /ō/ *contr.* of

O¹ /ō/ *interj.* **1.** USED TO ADDRESS SB used in addressing a person or topic or at the start of a plea or wish **2.** EXPRESSION OF WONDER used in expressing surprise or great wonderment (*literary*) [12thC. Representing a natural exclamation.]

O² *symbol.* CHEM oxygen

O³ *n.* MED a human blood type of the ABO group containing the O antigen. Somebody with type O blood can donate to all other types in the group but can receive only O blood.

o. *abbr.* **1.** **o., 0, O.** GEOG ocean **2.** **o., 0, O.** PRINTING octavo **3.** **o., 0.** old **4.** **o., 0.** MATH order **5.** **o., 0** BASEBALL out **6.** **o., 0, O** CRICKET over(s) **7.** PHARM pint [shortening of modern Latin *octarius*]

-o *suffix.* **1.** used to form abbreviated words ○ *aggro* ○ *demo* ○ *hypo* **2.** sb or sth associated with or having the characteristics of sth ○ *dumbo* [Origin uncertain: perhaps from OH]

OA *abbr.* MED osteoarthritis

o/a *abbr.* on or about

oaf /ōf/ *n.* (*insult*) **1.** SB UNINTELLIGENT an unintelligent person **2.** SB CLUMSY an awkward or clumsy person **3.** SB LOUTISH a rough loutish person [Early 17thC. From Old Norse *álfr* 'elf'.]

oafish /ōfish/ *adj.* resembling an oaf, e.g. in clumsiness, unintelligence, or loutishness (*insult*) — **oafishly** *adv.* —**oafishness** *n.*

Oahu /ō ä'a hoo/ island in Hawaii, the most populous and third largest of the Hawaiian Islands. Area: 1,575 sq. km/608 sq. mi.

Oak

oak /ōk/ *n.* **1.** TREES TREE BEARING ACORNS a deciduous or evergreen tree or shrub that has acorns as fruit, and leaves with several rounded or pointed projections. Genus: *Quercus.* **2.** PLANTS SHRUB WITH LOBED LEAVES a shrub such as the Jerusalem oak or poison oak with lobed leaves like those of oak trees **3.** INDUST HARD WOOD OF OAK TREE the hard wood of the oak tree, highly valued by furniture makers and formerly widely used in construction and shipbuilding **4.** OAK WREATH OR GARLAND a decoration made from the leaves of an oak tree, especially a wreath or garland ■ *adj.* COLOURS OF RICH BROWN COLOUR of a rich brown colour, similar to the colour of oak wood [Old English *āc*]

oak apple *n.* a rounded hollow growth on the trunk of an oak tree caused by infestation with gall wasps, which use the growths as shelters for their larvae

oaken /ōkən/ *adj.* made of oak wood (*literary*)

oak fern *n.* a light green woodland fern found in northern climates. Latin name: *Thelypteris dryopteris.*

oak gall *n.* = oak apple

Oakham /ōkəm/ market town in central England. It has a Norman castle. Population: 8,691 (1991).

Oakland /ōklənd/ city and county seat of Alameda County, western California, situated on the eastern side of San Francisco Bay. Population: 372,242 (1990).

oak leaf cluster *n.* a small decoration shaped like a bunch of oak leaves and acorns, added to another military decoration to show that it has been awarded to the wearer more than once

oakmoss /ōk moss/ *n.* any of various lichens that grow on oak trees and produce a resin used in the making of some perfumes. Latin name: *Evernia prunastri.*

oak pruner *n.* a long-horned beetle that as a larva bores oak twigs until they are cut off. Latin name: *Hypermallus villosus.*

oakum /ōkəm/ *n.* hemp or jute fibres, especially old ropes unravelled, soaked in tar, and used to seal the gaps between the planks forming a wooden ship's or boat's hull [Old English *ācumba* 'broken fibers', literally 'off-combing']

Oakville /ōkvil/ town in Halton Municipal Region, southeastern Ontario, Canada, situated 35 km/22 mi. southwest of Toronto. Population: 114,670 (1991).

oak wilt *n.* a disease of oak trees caused by a fungus that kills their leaves

OAM *abbr.* (Medal of the) Order of Australia

O & M *abbr.* organization and method

OAP *n.* sb who is old enough to draw a pension from the state

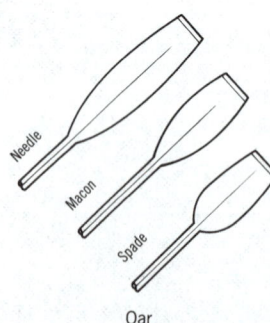

Oar

oar /awr/ *n.* ROWING **1.** POLE USED TO PROPEL BOAT a wooden pole with one broad flat end, used either singly or in pairs to propel a boat by dipping the broad end in the water **2.** SB ROWING sb who rows a boat, especially one of a team of rowers ■ *vti.* (**oars, oaring, oared**) TO ROW to row a boat [Old English *ār*]

oarfish /awr fish/ (*plural* **-fish** *or* **-fishes**) *n.* a long marine fish shaped like an eel that grows up to 7 m/23 ft and has a dazzling red head fin and a red dorsal fin running the length of its body. It is found in tropical seas and warmer parts of the Atlantic. Latin name: *Regalecus glesne.* [Mid-19thC. From the shape of its body.]

oarlock /awr lok/ *n.* US = rowlock [Old English *ārloc, ār* 'oar' + *loc* 'lock']

oarsman /awrzmən/ (*plural* **-men** /-mən/) *n.* a man who rows a boat, especially as part of a team of rowers — **oarsmanship** *n.*

oarswoman /awrz woŏmən/ (*plural* **-en** /-wimmən/) *n.* a woman who rows a boat, especially as part of a team of rowers

oar weed *n.* = tangle

oasis /ō áyssiss/ (*plural* **-ses** /-seez/) *n.* **1.** GEOG FERTILE LAND IN DESERT fertile ground in a desert where the level of underground water rises to or near ground level, where plants grow and travellers can replenish water supplies **2.** PLACE OR TIME OF RELIEF a place or period that gives relief from a troubling or chaotic situation [Early 17thC. Via late Latin from Greek. Probably ultimately of Egyptian origin.]

oast /ōst/ *n.* **1.** HOP-DRYING KILN a kiln used for drying hops, especially hops used to flavour beer **2.** = oasthouse [Old English *āst* 'kiln'. Ultimately from an Indo-European base meaning 'to be hot, burn' that is also the ancestor of English *estuary* and *edifice*.]

oasthouse /ōst howss/ (*plural* **-houses** /ōst howziz/) *n.* a building that contains, or formerly contained, hop-drying kilns and typically has conical or pyramid-shaped towers

Oat

oat /ōt/ *n.* BOT GRASS WITH EDIBLE SEED a grass that has edible seeds and is grown in numerous northern countries as a cereal crop. Latin name: *Avena sativa.* ■ **oats** *npl.* AGRIC EDIBLE SEEDS OF THE OAT the seeds of the oat grown as a cereal crop and used to make foods such as porridge and as a livestock feed [Old English *āte*]

oatcake /ōt kayk/ *n.* a hard unsweetened biscuit made from oatmeal, eaten with cheese and other savoury foods

oat-cell *adj.* relating to a highly malignant form of lung cancer characterized by the rapid growth of undifferentiated small round cells. Oat-cell carcinoma is usually related to smoking. [Because the cells look like grains of oats]

oaten /ōt'n/ *adj.* made from oats, oatmeal, or oat straw

Oates /ōts/, **Titus** (1649–1705) English conspirator. He fabricated the Popish Plot (1678). Initially rewarded, he was later found guilty of perjury and imprisoned.

oat grass *n.* a grass, especially in Africa and Asia, that looks like the oat. Genera: *Arrhenatherum* and *Danthonia.*

oath /ōth/ (*plural* **oaths** /ōthz/) *n.* **1.** SOLEMN PROMISE a formal or legally binding pledge to do sth such as tell the truth in a court of law, made formally and often naming God or a loved one as a witness **2.** WORDS OF PROMISE the words said when making a formal pledge, especially when reciting a conventional formula such as that used in a court of law **3.** SWEARWORD a swearword, especially one that uses the name of God or another sacred name in a disrespectful way [Old English *āþ*] ◇ **my oath** *ANZ* used to express strong confirmation or agreement (*slang*)

oatmeal /ót meel/ *n.* **1.** CRUSHED OATS oat grains ground or crushed into flakes or powder, used to make various foods such as porridge, flapjacks, and oatcakes ○ *oatmeal biscuits* **2.** FOOD = **porridge** ■ *adj.* COLOURS OF A LIGHT BROWN COLOUR of a light greyish-brown colour

OAU *abbr.* Organization of African Unity

Oaxaca /wə haákə/ historic city in southern Mexico, the capital of Oaxaca State. It was founded by the Aztecs. Population: 212,818 (1990).

OB *abbr.* **1. OB, ob.** MED obstetric **2. OB, ob.** MED obstetrics **3. OB, ob.** MED obstetrician **4.** BROADCAST outside broadcast

ob. *abbr.* **1.** MED obstetric **2.** MED obstetrics **3.** MED obstetrician **4.** MUSIC oboe **5.** he or she died [Shortening of Latin *obiit* (see OBIT)]

Ob. *abbr.* BIBLE Obadiah

ob- *prefix.* inverse, inversely ○ *obvolute* [From Latin *ob* 'in the way, against, towards']

oba /óbə/ *n.* a ruler among the Yoruba people of West Africa [Early 20thC. From Yoruba.]

Obad. *abbr.* BIBLE Obadiah

Obadiah /óbə dí ə/ *n.* **1.** BIBLICAL HEBREW PROPHET in the Bible, a minor Hebrew prophet of the 6th century BC **2.** BOOK OF THE BIBLE a book of the Bible containing the prophecies of Obadiah. Obadiah is the shortest book of the Bible. See table at **Bible**

Oban /óbən/ town, seaport and tourist centre in western Scotland. Population: 8,134 (1981).

obb. *abbr.* obbligato

obbligato /óbbli gaá tō/, **obligato** *adj.* NOT TO BE LEFT OUT not to be omitted from a musical piece, either as an instrumental part in the piece or as an instrument accompanying a singer (*used as a musical direction*) ■ *n.* (*plural* **-tos** *or* **-ti** /-tee/) ESSENTIAL PART a musical part or accompaniment that is not to be left out [Early 18thC. Via Italian, literally 'obliged', from Latin (see OBLIGATE).]

obcompressed /óbkəm prést/ *adj.* BOT flattened from back to front, like the fruits of penny grass

obconic /ob kónnik/, **obconical** /ob kónnik'l/ *adj.* cone-shaped and attached to a plant by the pointed end ○ *an obconic fruit*

obcordate /ob káwr dayt/ *adj.* heart-shaped and attached to a plant by the pointed end

obduracy /óbdyŏŏrəssi/ *n.* stubborn and total refusal to change an opinion or stance

obdurate /óbdyŏŏrət/ *adj.* **1.** STUBBORN not easily persuaded or influenced **2.** HARD-HEARTED not influenced by emotions, especially not inclined to feel sympathy or pity [15thC. From late Latin *obduratus*, the past participle of *obdurare* 'to be hard', from *durus* 'hard' (see ENDURE).] —**obdurately** *adv.* —**obdurateness** *n.*

OBE *abbr.* Officer of the (Order of the) British Empire

obeah /óbi ə/, **obi** *n.* **1.** WEST INDIAN RELIGION a religion that involves witchcraft, originally practised in Africa and surviving now in parts of the West Indies **2.** A CHARM an object believed to have magical powers, used in practising obeah [Mid-18thC. From Twi *ɔ̀bayifó.*]

obedience /ə beédi'nss/ *n.* **1.** ACT OF OBEYING the action or condition of obeying authority **2.** CHR CHURCH'S RULE the religious authority of a church or of a priest or other member of the clergy, or the people who are under this authority

obedient /ə beédi'nt/ *adj.* carrying out or willing to carry out what is demanded or ordered, particularly by sb in authority [13thC. Via Old French from Latin *oboediens*, the present participle stem of *oboedire* (see OBEY).]

obeisance /ō báyss'nss, ō beéss'nss/ *n.* **1.** RESPECTFUL GESTURE a gesture of respect or deference, e.g. a bow of the head (*formal*) **2.** RESPECTFUL BEHAVIOUR the attitude or behaviour of sb who pays respect or homage to sb or sth [14thC. From Old French, from *obeir* (see OBEY). Originally borrowed in its French meaning 'obedience'.]

obeli plural of **obelus**

obelia /ō beéli ə/ (*plural* **-lias**) *n.* a marine hydrozoan polyp that forms colonies that resemble moss on rocks, ships' hulls, and pilings. Genus: *Obelia.* [Late 19thC. Via modern Latin, genus name, from Greek *obelias* 'leaf baked on a spit', from *obelos* (see OBELUS).]

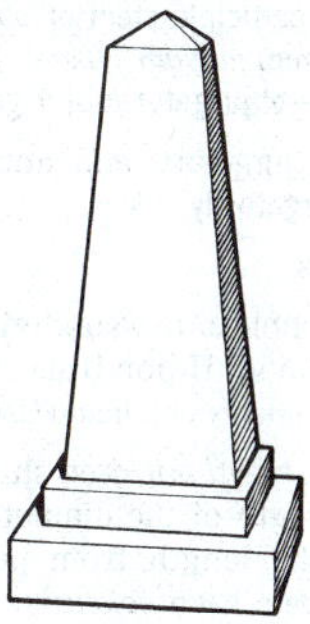

Obelisk

obelisk /óbbə lisk/ *n.* **1.** BUILDING STONE PILLAR a pillar of stone, especially one built as a monument, that has a square base and sides that taper like a pyramid towards a pointed top **2.** PRINTING = **dagger** [Mid-16thC. Via Latin *obeliscus* from Greek *obeliskos*, from *obelos* (see OBELUS).] —**obeliskoid** /óbbə lísk oyd/ *adj.*

obelize /óbbə līz/ (**-lizes, -lizing, -lized**), **obelise** (**-lises, -lising, -lised**) *vt.* to mark a written or printed word or passage with a dagger or obelus [Mid-17thC. From Greek *obelizein*, from *obelos* (see OBELUS).]

obelus /óbbələss/ (*plural* **-li** /-lī/) *n.* **1.** = **dagger 2.** MARK IN ANCIENT MANUSCRIPTS a printed mark (†) used in modern editions of ancient manuscripts to indicate that the passage marked is thought not to be genuine [14thC. Via late Latin from Greek *obelos* 'spit, obelisk'.]

obento /ō béntō/ (*plural* **-tos**), **bento** (*plural* **-tos**) *n.* a Japanese meal that is packaged in a partitioned lacquer box [Late 20thC. From Japanese.]

Oberammergau /óbər ámmər gow/ town in Bavaria, southeastern Germany, famous for producing a Passion Play every ten years. Population: 5,425 (1991).

Oberon /óbə ron/ *n.* the second-largest natural satellite of Uranus, discovered in 1787. It is 1,522 km in diameter and has a highly cratered surface.

obese /ō beéss/ *adj.* **1.** MED UNHEALTHILY OVERWEIGHT so overweight as to be at risk from several serious illnesses, including diabetes and heart disease, if action is not taken to control the weight **2.** OVERWEIGHT overweight (*informal*) [Mid-17thC. From Latin *obesus*, the past participle of assumed *obedere* 'to eat until overweight', from *edere* 'to eat' (see EDIBLE).] —**obesely** *adv.* —**obeseness** *n.*

obesity /ō beéssəti/ *n.* a condition in which sb's weight is more than 20% higher than is recommended for that person's height

obey /ə báy/ (**obeys, obeying, obeyed**) *vti.* **1.** DO AS TOLD to follow instructions or behave in accordance with a law, rule, or order **2.** BE CONTROLLED to be controlled by sb or sth [13thC. Via Old French *obeir* from Latin *oboedire* 'to listen to', from *audire* 'to hear' (source of English *audition*).] —**obeyer** *n.*

obfuscate /ób fuss kayt, óbfəss-/ (**-cates, -cating, -cated**) *v.* **1.** *vti.* MAKE STH OBSCURE to make sth obscure or unclear, especially by making it unnecessarily complicated **2.** *vt.* MAKE DARK to make sth dark or hard to see (*archaic*) **3.** *vt.* CONFUSE to make sb confused (*archaic*) [Mid-16thC. From late Latin *obfuscat-*, the past participle stem of *obfuscare* 'to darken', from *fuscus* 'dark'.] —**obfuscation** /ób fu skáysh'n, óbfə-/ *n.*

ob-gyn /ō bee jeé wī én/, **Ob-Gyn** *n. US* (*informal*) **1.** OBSTETRICS AND GYNAECOLOGY the branch of medicine that deals with obstetrics and gynaecology **2.** MEDICAL SPECIALIST IN BABIES AND WOMEN a specialist in obstetrics and gynaecology

obi[1] /óbi/ (*plural* **obis** *or* **obi**) *n.* a silk sash worn by a Japanese person in traditional dress to fasten the kimono [Late 19thC. From Japanese, literally 'belt, band, girdle'.]

obi[2] /óbi/ *n.* = **obeah**

Ob'-Irtysh river system in western Siberia, and the longest in Asia, incorporating the rivers Irtysh and Ob'. Length: 5,410 km/3,362 mi.

obit /óbit, ō bít/ *n.* an obituary (*informal*) [14thC. Via French from Latin *obitus* 'death', from (*mortem*) *obire* 'to die', literally 'to meet (death)', from *ire* 'to go'.]

obiter dictum /óbbitər díktəm, ṓbitər-/ (*plural* **obiter dicta** /-díktə, -/) *n.* **1.** JUDGE'S OBSERVATION an observation made by a judge that is incidental to the case being tried and, while being authoritative, is not binding on future courts under the doctrine of precedent **2.** PASSING COMMENT a comment made in passing [Early 19thC. From Latin, literally 'said by the way, said in passing'.]

obituary /ə bíchoo əri/ *n.* (*plural* **-ies**) ANNOUNCEMENT OF DEATH an announcement, especially in a newspaper, of sb's death, often with a short biography ■ *adj.* RECORDING A DEATH relating to or recording a death [Early 18thC. From medieval Latin *obituarius*, from Latin *obitus* 'death' (see OBIT).]

obj. *abbr.* **1.** GRAM object **2.** objection **3.** GRAM objective

object *n.* /óbb jikt/ **1.** STH VISIBLE OR TANGIBLE sth that can be seen or touched **2.** FOCUS a focus of sb's attention or emotion **3.** AIM an aim or purpose **4.** SB OR STH RIDICULOUS sb or sth ridiculous or pitiable (*informal*) **5.** GRAM NOUN AFFECTED BY VERB a noun, pronoun, or noun phrase denoting sb or sth that is acted on by a verb or affected by the action of a verb **6.** GRAM NOUN GOVERNED BY PREPOSITION a noun, pronoun, or noun phrase that is governed by a preposition **7.** PHILOS STH PERCEIVED AND NAMED AS SEPARATE sth that is perceived as an entity and referred to by a name ○ *mental objects* **8.** OPTICS SOURCE OF LIGHT RAYS the point or series of points that appear to be the source of light rays in an optical system. A point that is the source of the rays is called a real object, while a point that only appears to be the source is called a virtual object. **9.** COMPUT UNIT OF INFORMATION a block of information such as a text or graphics document or a part of a document that can be linked to and embedded in other documents. Changes subsequently made to the original information are reflected in the other documents in which it appears. **10.** COMPUT UNIT OF COMPUTER PROGRAMMING a collection of variables, data structures, and procedures stored as an entity and forming a basic building block of object-oriented programming ■ *v.* /əb jékt/ (**-jects, -jecting, -jected**) **1.** *vi.* BE OPPOSED to be opposed to sth, or express opposition to it **2.** *vt.* STATE AS OBJECTION to state sth as a reason for being opposed to sth [14thC. From medieval Latin *objectum* 'thing presented (to the sight)', ultimately from Latin *obicere* 'to present, throw against', from *jacere* 'to throw'.] ◇ **sth is no object** used in order to say that sth is not a concern or difficulty ○ *I want the best room you have – money's no object.*

WORD KEY: SYNONYMS

object, protest, demur, remonstrate, expostulate

CORE MEANING: to indicate opposition to sth

object a general word used to talk about being opposed or averse to sth, whether or not these feelings are expressed; **protest** to express strong feelings of objection in speech, writing, or actions; **demur** to raise objections in a hesitant or tentative way; **remonstrate** to indicate disagreement or objection by arguing with sb and trying to dissuade him or her from a course of action; **expostulate** a formal word used to indicate that a disagreement or objection is expressed very vehemently.

object ball *n.* in billiards, pool, or snooker, the ball that a player intends to hit with the cue ball in a particular shot

object code *n.* the binary version of a computer program that is used by the computer to run the program. ◊ **source code**

object complement *n.* a noun, pronoun, or adjective that is a complement of a verb and qualifies its direct object, e.g. *angry* in 'He makes me angry'. US term **objective complement**

object glass *n.* OPTICS = **objective** *n.* 5

objectify /əb jékti fī/ (**-fies, -fying, -fied**) *vt.* **1.** MAKE ACTUAL to think of or represent an idea or emotion as if it were sth that actually exists **2.** REDUCE TO OBJECT to reduce sb, or sth that is complex and multifaceted, to the status of a simple object

objection /əb jéksh'n/ *n.* **1.** EXPRESSION OF OPPOSITION a feeling or expression of opposition **2.** CAUSE OF OPPOSITION a reason for a feeling or expression of opposition

objectionable /əb jéksh'nəb'l/ *adj.* causing disapproval, offence, or opposition ○ *an objectionable habit* —**objectionableness** *n.* —**objectionability** /əb jéksh'nə bílləti/ *n.* —**objectionably** /əb jéksh'nə bli/ *adv.*

objective /əb jéktiv/ *adj.* **1.** FREE OF BIAS free of any bias or prejudice caused by personal feelings **2.** BASED ON FACTS based on facts rather than thoughts or opinions **3.** MED OBSERVABLE used to describe disease symptoms that can be observed by sb other than the person who is ill **4.** PHILOS EXISTING INDEPENDENTLY OF MIND existing independently of the individual mind or perception **5.** GRAM BEING OBJECT OF VERB in or constituting the grammatical case of a noun or pronoun that is the object of a verb ■ *n.* **1.** AIM an aim or goal **2.** MILITARY TARGET the target or goal of a military operation **3.** GRAM OBJECTIVE CASE the objective grammatical case **4.** GRAM NOUN IN OBJECTIVE CASE a noun or pronoun in the objective case **5.** OPTICS LENS NEAREST OBJECT the lens or combination of lenses in an optical instrument nearest to and facing the object being viewed —**objectiveness** *n.*

objective complement *n.* GRAM = **object complement**

objective correlative *n.* LITERAT sth in a written or performed work that is associated with a particular emotion and used to evoke it in the reader or audience

objective lens *n.* OPTICS = **objective** *n.* 5

objectively /əb jéktivli/ *adv.* **1.** WITHOUT BIAS without being influenced by personal feelings **2.** ACCURATELY on the basis of fact, experience, or some measurable quality ○ *objectively derived measures such as test scores*

objectivise *vt.* = **objectivize**

objectivism /əb jéktivizəm/ *n.* **1.** LITERAT EMPHASIS ON THE ACTUAL the emphasizing of external realities rather than beliefs or feelings in literature or art **2.** PHILOS BELIEF IN INDEPENDENT TRUTHS a philosophical belief that moral truths or external objects exist independently of the individual mind or perception —**objectivist** *n., adj.*

objectivity /òb jek tívvəti/ *n.* **1.** ABILITY TO VIEW THINGS OBJECTIVELY the ability to perceive or describe sth without being influenced by personal emotions or prejudices **2.** PHILOS ACTUAL EXISTENCE the actual existence of sth, without reference to people's impressions or ideas **3.** ACCURACY the quality of being accurate and independent of individual perceptions

objectivize /əb jékti vīz/ (**-vizes, -vizing, -vized**), **objectivise** (**-vises, -vising, -vised**) *vt.* = **objectify** *v.* 1

object language *n.* COMPUT **1.** LANGUAGE OF COMPUTER the language that a computer interprets in running programs **2.** = **target language** *n.* 3

object lens *n.* OPTICS = **objective** *n.* 5

object lesson *n.* an incident that provides an opportunity for learning sth, especially the best way to do sth ○ *an object lesson in tact*

object-oriented programming *n.* a form of computer programming based on objects arranged in a branching hierarchy

object permanence *n.* PSYCHOL the knowledge that objects have an existence in time and space, independent of whether or not they can be seen or touched

object relations *npl.* a psychoanalytic theory that sees an individual as motivated by a desire to form bonds with appropriate objects or people, rather than merely satisfying impulses in order to discharge tension

objet d'art /òb zhay daár/ (*plural* **objets d'art** /òb zhay daár/) *n.* an object that has artistic value, especially a small piece [Mid-19thC. From French, literally 'object of art'.]

objet trouvé /òb zhay tróo vay/ (*plural* **objets trouvés** /òb zhay tróo vay/) *n.* a natural or everyday object such as a pebble from a beach, treated as sth of artistic value or incorporated into a work of art [Mid-20thC. From French, literally 'found object'.]

objurgate /óbjur gayt/ (**-gates, -gating, -gated**) *vt.* to scold sb angrily (*literary*) [Early 17thC. From Latin *objurgat-*, the past participle stem of *objurgare*, literally 'to quarrel against', from *jurgium* 'quarrel'.] —**objurgation** /òb jur gáysh'n/ *n.* —**objurgator** /óbjur gaytər/ *n.*

objurgatory /ob júrgətəri/ *adj.* angry and scolding (*literary*) —**objurgatorily** *adv.*

obl. *abbr.* oblique

oblast /ób laast, óbblәst/ *n.* a subdivision of a republic of the former Soviet Union [Late 19thC. From Russian *óblast*, literally 'authority on', from *vlast* 'authority, power'.]

oblate[1] /ób layt, o bláyt/ *adj.* GEOM shaped like a sphere but with the length of the diameter at the equator greater than the length from pole to pole [Early 18thC. From modern Latin *oblatus* 'brought against or inversely', formed from Latin *latus* 'brought', past participle of *ferre* 'to bring', on the model of *prolatus* 'lengthened'.] —**oblately** *adv.* —**oblateness** *n.*

oblate[2] /ób layt/ *n.* CHR in the Roman Catholic Church, a lay person who is part of a religious community [Late 17thC. Via French from medieval Latin *oblatus*, literally 'brought to', from the past participle of Latin *offerre* (see OFFER).]

oblation /o bláysh'n/ *n.* **1.** RELIG OFFERING OF GIFT TO DEITY the offering of a gift or sacrifice to a deity **2.** CHR COMMUNION OFFERING the offering of bread and wine to God during the Christian service of Communion **3.** RELIGIOUS OR CHARITABLE GIFT sth offered in a religious rite or as a charitable gift [15thC. Directly or via Old French from the late Latin stem *oblation-*, from Latin *offerre* (see OFFER).] —**oblational** *adj.*

obligate /óbbli gayt/ *vt.* (**-gates, -gating, -gated**) COMPEL LEGALLY OR MORALLY to compel sb to do sth as a legal or moral duty ■ *adj.* BIOL ONLY EXISTING IN ONE ENVIRONMENT used to describe an organism that can exist only in a particular role or under particular environmental conditions. ◊ **facultative** [15thC. From Latin *obligatus*, past participle of *obligare* (see OBLIGE).] —**obligable** /óbbligəb'l/ *adj.* —**obligately** /-gaytli/ *adv.* —**obligator** /-gaytər/ *n.*

obligation /òbbli gáysh'n/ *n.* **1.** STATE OF OWING the state or condition of being obligated **2.** DUTY sth that must be done because of legal or moral duty **3.** STH OWED sth such as assistance or a debt that sb owes in return for sth given **4.** LAW BINDING LEGAL AGREEMENT a legal agreement by which sb is bound to do sth, especially pay money, or to refrain from doing sth **5.** LAW LEGAL CONTRACT a legal contract that contains a penalty for non-fulfilment of it —**obligational** *adj.*

obligatory /ə blíggətəri/ *adj.* **1.** LEGALLY, MORALLY, OR RELIGIOUSLY REQUIRED required by law or by a moral or religious rule **2.** COMPULSORY compulsory rather than optional —**obligatorily** *adv.*

oblige /ə blíj/ (**obliges, obliging, obliged**) *v.* **1.** *vt.* REQUIRE SB TO DO STH to bind sb morally or legally to do sth **2.** *vt.* FORCE SB TO DO STH to make it necessary for sb to do sth **3.** *vt.* CAUSE SB TO FEEL INDEBTED to cause sb to feel indebted by doing sth for that person **4.** *vt.* DO FAVOUR FOR SB to do a favour or service for sb ○ *Would you oblige me by closing the door?* **5.** *vi.* BE HELPFUL to do sth necessary or helpful ○ *was only too happy to oblige* [13thC. Via Old French *oblig(i)er* from Latin *obligare* 'to tie to', from *ligare* 'to tie, bind' (source of English *ligation*).] —**obliger** *n.*

obligee /òbbli jée/ *n.* LAW sb to whom another person is legally or morally bound, e.g. by a financial debt or obligation to do sth

obligement /ə blíjmənt/ *n.* *Scotland* a favour

obliging /ə blíjing/ *adj.* willing to be helpful or do favours —**obligingly** *adv.* —**obligingness** *n.*

obligor /òbbli gáwr/ *n.* LAW sb who makes a legally binding agreement to do or pay sth

oblique /ə bléek/ *adj.* **1.** SLOPING sloping or joining sth at an angle that is not a right angle **2.** INDIRECT not straightforward or direct ○ *an oblique reference to the lateness of the hour* **3.** GEOM NOT PARALLEL OR PERPENDICULAR neither perpendicular nor parallel to another line or plane **4.** GEOM NOT RIGHT-ANGLED not being or containing a right angle or a multiple of a right angle **5.** GRAM NOT BEING SUBJECT being a grammatical case other than the nominative or vocative **6.** BOT WITH SIDES OF DIFFERENT LENGTH used to describe leaves that have sides of different length **7.** ANAT NOT BEING ON ANATOMICAL PLANE slanting away from any of the anatomical planes of the body, e.g. the horizontal or perpendicular plane **8.** GEOG BEING AT TANGENT TO EARTH'S SURFACE used to describe a map projection based on a plane of projection that is at a tangent to the Earth's surface at a point between the poles and the equator ■ *adv.* MIL CHANGING DIRECTION AT 45° changing direction to or at an angle of 45° ■ *n.* **1.** STH SLANTING sth that is oblique, e.g. a slanting line **2.** PRINTING = **slash** *n.* 6 **3.** NAVIG COURSE CHANGE OF LESS THAN 90° a change of course of less than 90° ■ *vi.* (**obliques, obliquing, obliqued**) **1.** TAKE OBLIQUE DIRECTION to move or slant in an oblique direction **2.** MIL ADVANCE IN OBLIQUE DIRECTION to move forward at an angle in a military formation [15thC. From Latin *obliquus* 'slanting, sidelong', of unknown origin.] —**obliqueness** *n.*

obliquely /ə bléekli/ *adv.* **1.** INDIRECTLY in a way that is not direct or straightforward **2.** AT AN ANGLE at an angle that is not a right angle

oblique projection *n.* a map projection based on a plane of projection that is at a tangent to the Earth's surface at a point between the poles and the equator

oblique-slip fault *n.* GEOL a fracture in a layer of rock in which the movement is both horizontal and vertical

obliquity /ə blíkwəti/ (*plural* **-ties**) *n.* **1.** STATE OF BEING OBLIQUE the state or condition of being oblique **2.** DEVIATION FROM PLANE a deviation from the horizontal or perpendicular **3.** CHARACTER FLOW a departure from morality or reason **4.** LACK OF DIRECTNESS a lack of directness or straightforwardness in speech or conduct **5.** **obliquity, obliquity of the ecliptic** ASTRON ANGLE BETWEEN EARTH'S ORBIT AND EQUATOR the angle between the plane of the Earth's equator and the plane of the Earth's orbit around the sun, approximately 23.5°

obliquity of the ecliptic *n.* ASTRON = **obliquity** *n.* 5

obliterate /ə blíttə rayt/ (**-ates, -ating, -ated**) *vt.* **1.** DESTROY UTTERLY to destroy sth so utterly that nothing is left **2.** ERASE OR OBSCURE to erase or obscure sth completely, leaving no trace [Late 16thC. From Latin *oblitterat-*, the past participle stem of *oblitterare* 'to blot out, erase', from literally 'to remove letters', OB- and *littera* 'letter' (see LITERAL).] —**obliteration** /ə blíttə ráysh'n/ *n.* —**obliterative** /ə blíttərətiv/ *adj.* —**obliterator** /-raytər/ *n.*

oblivion /ə blívvi ən/ *n.* **1.** STATE OF BEING FORGOTTEN a state of being utterly forgotten **2.** STATE OF FORGETTING a state of forgetting everything or of being unaware of surroundings **3.** LAW OVERLOOKING OF PAST OFFENCES the deliberate overlooking of past offences [14thC. Via Old French from the Latin stem *oblivion-*, from *oblivisci* 'to forget', of uncertain origin: perhaps literally 'to smooth over', from *levis* 'smooth'.]

oblivious /ə blívvi əss/ *adj.* **1.** UNAWARE unaware of or paying no attention to sb or sth **2.** FORGETTING forgetting about sb or sth —**obliviously** *adv.* —**obliviousness** *n.*

oblong /óbb long/ *adj.* ELONGATED having a shape that is considerably longer than it is wide, especially a rectangular or roughly circular shape ■ *n.* ELONGATED SHAPE sth with a length greater than its width, especially a rectangle or distorted circle [15thC. From Latin *oblongus* 'rather long', from *longus* 'long'.]

obloquy /óbbləkwi/ *n.* (*formal or literary*) **1.** CENSURE statements that severely criticize or defame sb **2.** DISGRACE a state of disgrace brought about by being defamed [15thC. From late Latin *obloquium* 'contradiction', literally 'talking against', from *loqui* 'to talk'.]

obnoxious /əb nókshəss/ *adj.* very offensive and unpleasant ○ *obnoxious stench* [Late 16thC. Formed from Latin *obnoxius* 'vulnerable to harm' (its original English meaning), from *noxa* 'harm' (source of English *noxious*).] —**obnoxiously** *adv.* —**obnoxiousness** *n.*

o.b.o. *abbr.* or best offer (*used in advertisements*)

oboe /óbō/ *n.* **1.** WOODWIND INSTRUMENT a woodwind instrument that produces a penetrating high sound and consists of a long slim tube enclosing a double reed with a conical bore and keys operated by the fingers **2.** PLAYER OF OBOE sb who plays an oboe [Late 17thC. Via Italian from French *hautbois* (see HAUTBOY).] —**oboist** *n.*

oboe da caccia /óbō də káchə/ *n.* an early form of oboe from which the cor anglais was developed [Late 19thC. From Italian, literally 'hunting oboe'.]

oboe d'amore /-da máwray/ *n.* an oboe used mainly in baroque music that has a lower pitch than the standard instrument [Late 19thC. From Italian, literally 'oboe of love'.]

obol /óbbol/, **obolus** /óbbələss/ (*plural* **-li** /óbbə lī/) *n.* a coin or unit of weight used in ancient Greece, equal to one sixth of a drachma [Mid-17thC. Via Latin from Greek *obolos* 'obol' (unit of weight and of money), variant of *obelos* 'a spit'.]

Obon /ō bón/ *n.* a Buddhist festival celebrating All Souls, held in Japan from 13 to 31 July

Obote /o bṓt ay, o bṓti/, **Milton** (*b.* 1925) Ugandan statesman. Prime minister (1962–66) and president (1966–71 and 1980–85) of Uganda, he was overthrown in two military coups (1971 and 1985). Full name **Apollo Milton Obote**

obovate /ob ṓ vayt/ *adj.* BOT used to describe leaves that are oval with the narrow end at the base [Late 18thC. Coined from OB- + OVATE.]

obovoid /ob ṓ voyd/ *adj.* BOT used to describe fruits that are egg-shaped, with the narrow end at the base [Early 19thC. Coined from OB- + OVOID.]

obruk /ób ro͝ok/ *n.* work obligations owed by Russian peasants to either their aristocratic landlords or the state during the 18th century

obs. *abbr.* **1.** obscure **2.** observation **3.** **obs., Obs.** ASTRON observatory **4.** obsolete **5.** MED obstetrics

obscene /əb séen/ *adj.* **1.** INDECENT offensive to conventional standards of decency, especially by being sexually explicit **2.** LAW LIKELY TO DEPRAVE AND CORRUPT considered likely to deprave and corrupt people (*refers to publications*) **3.** DISGUSTING disgusting and morally offensive, especially because of showing total disregard for other people [Late 16thC. Via Old French from Latin *obscenus* 'ill-omened, offensive, hateful', of unknown origin.] —**obscenely** *adv.*

obscenity /əb sénnəti/ (*plural* **-ties**) *n.* **1.** INDECENCY offensiveness to conventional standards of decency, especially as a result of sexual explicitness **2.** OBSCENE EXPRESSION a word, phrase, or statement that is offensive, especially because of being sexually explicit **3.** STH OBSCENE sth that is disgusting and morally offensive

obscurant /əb skyóorənt/ *n.*, *adj.* = **obscurantist** ■ *adj.* CAUSING OBSCURITY concealing sth or making it obscure (*literary*) [Late 18thC. Via German from Latin *obscurant-*, present participle stem of *obscurare* 'to make dark', from *obscurus* (see OBSCURE).]

obscurantist /ób skyo͞o rántist/, **obscurant** *adj.* OPPOSED TO NEW IDEAS opposing or hindering the spread of new ideas and new social or political developments ■ *n.* OPPONENT OF NEW IDEAS sb who opposes or hinders the spread of new ideas and new social or political developments —**obscurantism** *n.*

obscure /əb skyóor/ *adj.* **1.** HARD TO UNDERSTAND difficult to understand because of not being fully or clearly expressed ○ *an obscure passage in the manuscript* **2.** INDISTINCT not able to be seen or heard distinctly **3.** UNIMPORTANT OR UNKNOWN not important or well-known ○ *an obscure portrait painter* **4.** KNOWN TO FEW PEOPLE unknown to most people, e.g. because of being hidden or remote **5.** DARK dark, shadowy, or clouded ○ *an obscure corner of the hall* **6.** LING UNSTRESSED used to describe a vowel that has a neutral, unstressed pronunciation (*technical*) ■ *vt.* (**-scures, -scuring, -scured**) **1.** MAKE UNCLEAR to make sth unclear, indistinct, or hidden **2.** DARKEN to make sth dark or cover sth with cloud [14thC. Via Old French from Latin *obscurus* 'dark, unknown', literally 'covered over', from the base *-scurus* 'covered'.] —**obscuration** /ób skyo͞o ráysh'n/ *n.* —**obscureness** /əb skyóornəss/ *n.*

WORD KEY: SYNONYMS

obscure, abstruse, recondite, arcane, cryptic, enigmatic

CORE MEANING: difficult to comprehend

obscure a general word for sth that is difficult to understand because it is expressed in a complicated way or because it involves areas of knowledge or study that are not known to most people; **abstruse** a formal word for sth that is difficult to understand, often because it involves specialist knowledge or is expressed in specialist language; **recondite** a formal word for sth that is difficult to understand without a high degree of scholarship or specialist knowledge; **arcane** a formal word for sth secret known only to very few people; **cryptic** puzzling, often because it is expressed in code or in terms that only some people would understand; **enigmatic** having a quality of mystery and ambiguity that makes it difficult to understand or interpret.

obscurely /əb skyóorli/ *adv.* **1.** UNCLEARLY in a way that is not clear, definite, or easy to understand **2.** DIMLY dimly or indistinctly **3.** AWAY FROM PEOPLE'S ATTENTION in a place or position that is remote, secluded, or not prominent or well-known

obscurity /əb skyóorəti/ (*plural* **-ties**) *n.* **1.** STATE OF BEING UNKNOWN a state of being unknown or inconspicuous ○ *plucked from obscurity to star in a Broadway musical* **2.** UNCLEARNESS difficulty in being understood or unclearness of meaning **3.** SB OR STH OBSCURE an obscure person or thing

obsecrate /óbssi krayt/ (**-crates, -crating, -crated**) *vt.* to beseech a god or important person to give or do sth (*archaic*) [Late 16thC. From Latin *obsecrat-*, the past participle stem of *obsecrare* 'to beseech (in the name of sth sacred)', ultimately from *sacer* (see SACRED).] —**obsecration** /óbssi kráysh'n/ *n.*

obsequent /óbssikwənt/ *adj.* GEOG used to describe a river, stream, or drainage system that flows into a subsidiary (**subsequent**) river in a direction contrary to that of the flow of the main (**consequent**) river [Late 19thC. From Latin *obsequent-*, present participle stem of *obsequi* 'to comply', literally 'to follow towards', from *sequi* 'to follow' (see SEQUENCE).]

obsequies /óbssi kwiz/ *npl.* rites or ceremonies carried out at a funeral [14thC. Via Anglo-Norman from late Latin *obsequiae*, alteration (influenced by *obsequium* 'compliance', see OBSEQUIOUS) of *exequiae*, literally 'those following out (to the grave)', from *exsequi* (see EXECUTE).]

obsequious /əb séekwi əss/ *adj.* excessively eager to please or to obey all instructions [15thC. From Latin *obsequiosus*, from *obsequium* 'compliance', from *obsequi* (see OBSEQUENT).] —**obsequiously** *adv.* —**obsequiousness** *n.*

observable /əb zúrvəb'l/ *adj.* **1.** NOTICEABLE able to be seen or detected **2.** WORTHY worthy of notice and attention (*archaic*) **3.** REQUIRING RESPECT needing to be followed or respected (*archaic*) ■ *n.* STH DIRECTLY MEASURABLE sth such as temperature that can be measured or observed directly —**observability** /əb zúrvə bílləti/ *n.*

observably /əb zúrvəbli/ *adv.* in a way or to an extent that can be seen or detected

observance /əb zúrvənss/ *n.* **1.** COMPLIANCE the execution of or compliance with laws, instructions, or customs **2.** RITUAL a custom, ritual, or ceremony, especially a religious one **3.** PERFORMANCE OF RELIGIOUS CEREMONIES the celebration of a religious occasion, or the practice of a religious rite, ceremony, or action **4.** RELIGIOUS RULE a rule of a religious order **5.** OBSERVATION careful watching or close attention

observant /əb zúrvənt/ *adj.* **1.** ATTENTIVE paying such careful attention that little or nothing is unnoticed **2.** OBEDIENT carrying out rituals or obeying laws, especially religious ones —**observantly** *adv.*

observation /óbzər váysh'n/ *n.* **1.** PAYING ATTENTION the attentive watching of sb or sth **2.** OBSERVING OF DEVELOPMENTS IN STH the careful observing and recording of sth that is happening, e.g. a natural phenomenon **3.** REMARK OR COMMENT a remark or comment on sth that has been noticed **4.** RECORD OF STH SEEN OR NOTED the result or record of observing sth such as a natural phenomenon and noting developments **5.** ACT OF OBSERVING OR OBEYING the act of observing a religious occasion or ritual or of obeying a law or rule **6.** NAVIG SIGHTING WITH NAVIGATIONAL INSTRUMENT a sighting with a navigational instrument to establish the observer's position in relation to a heavenly body such as the Sun **7.** NAVIG NAVIGATIONAL INSTRUMENT READING the reading taken from a navigational instrument that has been used to find the observer's position in relation to a heavenly body —**observational** *adj.* —**observationally** *adv.*

observation car *n.* a railway carriage fitted with extra or larger windows and often a partly transparent roof to allow passengers a better view of passing scenery

observation post *n.* a position from which soldiers can watch enemy movements and direct artillery fire

observatory /əb zúrvətəri/ (*plural* **-ries**) *n.* **1.** PLACE FOR SCIENTIFIC OBSERVATIONS a building, station, or artificial satellite used for scientific observation of natural phenomena such as astronomical objects, the weather, or earthquakes **2.** PLACE FOR LOOKING AT VIEW a place or building that commands an expansive view

observe /əb zúrv/ (**-serves, -serving, -served**) *v.* **1.** *vt.* NOTICE to see or notice sth, especially while watching carefully **2.** *vti.* WATCH ATTENTIVELY to watch sb or sth attentively, especially for scientific purposes **3.** *vti.* BE FORMAL WITNESS to be a formal witness to sth **4.** *vi.* BE SPECTATOR to watch sth without taking part **5.** *vt.* COMMENT to make a comment or remark on sth seen or noticed **6.** *vt.* COMPLY WITH to carry out or comply with sth such as a law or custom **7.** *vt.* CELEBRATE FESTIVAL to celebrate or keep a religious or traditional festival [14thC. Via Old French *observer* from Latin *observare*, literally 'to watch towards', from *servare* 'to watch, pay attention'.]

observer /əb zúrvər/ *n.* **1.** SB WHO SEES OR WATCHES STH sb who observes sth that is happening **2.** NONPARTICIPATING WITNESS sb who attends sth as a witness, often a formal one, without taking part **3.** SB OBSERVING CEREMONY OR OBEYING LAW sb who observes a religious ceremony or ritual, or obeys a rule or law **4.** AIRCRAFT IDENTIFIER sb trained in identifying aircraft **5.** WATCHER OF ENEMY MOVEMENTS a soldier who watches enemy movements or directs artillery fire

observingly /əb zúrvingli/ *adv.* in an attentive or considering manner

obsess /əb séss/ (**-sesses, -sessing, -sessed**) *v.* **1.** *vt.* PREOCCUPY to occupy sb's thoughts constantly and exclusively ○ *The desire for vengeance obsesses him.* **2.** *vi. US* BE PREOCCUPIED WITH to think or worry about sth constantly and compulsively [Early 16thC. From Latin *obsess-*, past participle stem of *obsidere* 'to besiege', literally 'to sit opposite to', from *sedere* 'to sit' (source of English *session*).]

obsession /əb sésh'n/ *n.* **1.** PREOCCUPATION an idea or feeling that completely occupies the mind **2.** STATE OF BEING OBSESSED the state of being obsessed by sb or sth ○ *Their devotion to each other borders on obsession.* **3.** PSYCHIAT UNCONTROLLABLE PERSISTENCE OF IDEA the uncontrollable persistence of an idea or emotion in the mind, sometimes associated with psychiatric disorder —**obsessional** *adj.* —**obsessionally** *adv.*

obsessive /əb séssiv/ *adj.* **1.** RESEMBLING OBSESSION amounting to an obsession or as strong as an obsession **2.** WORRYING UNCONTROLLABLY worrying compulsively about a particular thing, or things generally ■ *n.* PSYCHIAT SB WITH AN OBSESSION sb who has an obsession or a tendency to form obsessions —**obsessively** *adv.* —**obsessiveness** *n.*

obsessive-compulsive *adj.* PSYCHIAT WITH OBSESSIVE-COMPULSIVE DISORDER with or characteristic of obsessive-compulsive disorder such as hand-washing ■ *n.* OBSESSIVE-COMPULSIVE PERSON sb with obsessive-compulsive disorder

obsessive-compulsive disorder *n.* PSYCHOL a psychiatric disorder characterized by obsessive thoughts and compulsive behaviour, e.g. continual washing of the hands prompted by a feeling of uncleanliness

obsidian /ob síddi ən/ *n.* a jet-black volcanic glass, chemically similar to granite and formed by the rapid cooling of molten lava, that was used by early civilizations for manufacturing tools and ceremonial objects [14thC. From Latin *(lapis) Obsidianus*, a copyist's error for *Obsianus* '(stone) of Obsius', a Roman who according to Pliny the Elder discovered this or a similar stone in Ethiopia.]

obsolesce /óbssə léss/ (**-lesces, -lescing, -lesced**) *vi.* to become obsolete by being replaced by sth new [Late 19thC. From Latin *obsolescere* (see OBSOLESCENT).]

obsolescence /óbssə léss'nss/ *n.* the state of becoming obsolete by being replaced by sth new

obsolescent /óbssə léss'nt/ *adj.* becoming obsolete or disappearing from use or existence by being replaced by sth new [Mid-18thC. From Latin *obsolescent-*, present participle stem of *obsolescere* 'to wear out, decay', from *solere* 'to be accustomed'.] —**obsolescently** *adv.*

obsolete /óbssə leet, óbssə léet/ *adj.* **1.** NOT USED ANY MORE no longer in use because replaced by sth new **2.** OUT-OF-DATE superseded by sth newer, though possibly still in use **3.** BIOL UNDEVELOPED used to describe a part or an organ of an animal or plant that is undeveloped or no longer functional [Late 16thC. From Latin *obsoletus*, past participle of *obsolescere* (see OBSOLESCENT).] —**obsoletely** *adv.*

WORD KEY: SYNONYMS

See Synonyms at ***old-fashioned***.

obstacle /óbstək'l/ *n.* **1.** HINDRANCE sb or sth that hinders or prevents progress **2.** STH IN WAY sth that blocks or impedes a road, passage, or sb's way **3.** SPORTS HURDLE a fence or hedge set up for horses to jump over in showjumping [14thC. Via Old French from Latin *obstaculum*, from *obstare* 'to stand in the way, block', from *stare* 'to stand'.]

obstacle course *n.* **1.** *US* MIL = **assault course 2.** SPORTS SPORTS COURSE an area similar to a military assault course, used by competitors in an obstacle race

obstacle race *n.* a race in which competitors have to get past a range of obstacles

obstet. *abbr.* **1.** obstetric **2.** obstetrics

obstetric /ob stéttrik/ *adj.* relating to childbirth or obstetrics [Mid-18thC. From Latin *obstetricius* 'of a midwife', from the stem *obstetric-* 'midwife', literally 'woman who is present, stands before', from, ultimately, *stare* 'to stand'.]

obstetrician /óbstə trísh'n/ *n.* a doctor who specializes in pregnancy, delivering babies, and the care of women after childbirth

obstetrics /ob stéttriks/ *n.* the branch of medicine that deals with the care of women during pregnancy and childbirth, and for some six weeks following delivery (*takes a singular verb*)

obstinacy /óbstinəssi/ (*plural* **-cies**) *n.* **1.** STUBBORNNESS the quality of being obstinate **2.** OBSTINATE ACT an example of obstinate behaviour

obstinate /óbstinət/ *adj.* **1.** STUBBORN determined not to agree to other people's wishes or accept their suggestions **2.** REFUSING TO CHANGE unwilling to change or give up sth such as an idea or attitude **3.** DIFFICULT TO CONTROL difficult to control, get rid of, solve, or cure ○ *an obstinate blockage in the pipe* [14thC. From Latin *obstinatus*, past participle of *obstinare* 'to be resolved', literally 'to stand by', from *stare* 'to stand'.] —**obstinately** *adv.* —**obstinateness** *n.*

obstipation /óbsti páysh'n/ *n.* severe constipation, often caused by a blockage in the intestines [Late 16thC. From the late Latin stem *obstipation-*, literally 'pressing in the way of', from *stipare* 'to press'.]

obstreperous /əb stréppərəss/ *adj.* **1.** NOISY noisily and aggressively boisterous **2.** UNRULY strongly objecting to sth or noisily refusing to be controlled [Late 16thC. From Latin *obstreperus* 'clamorous', literally 'rattling against', from, ultimately, *strepere* 'to rattle, rustle'.] —**obstreperously** *adv.* —**obstreperousness** *n.*

WORD KEY: SYNONYMS

See Synonyms at ***unruly***.

obstruct /əb strúkt/ (**-structs, -structing, -structed**) *vt.* **1.** BLOCK to block a road, course, or passage **2.** HINDER to hinder or impede sb or sth **3.** IMPEDE VIEW to be in the way and prevent a clear view [Early 17thC. From Latin *obstructus*, past participle of *obstruere*, 'to build up against', from *struere* 'to heap up, pile'.] —**obstructor** *n.*

WORD KEY: SYNONYMS

See Synonyms at ***hinder***.

obstruction /əb strúksh'n/ *n.* **1.** BLOCK OR HINDRANCE sb or sth that causes or forms a blockage or hindrance **2.** ACT OF BLOCKING an act of blocking or hindering of sb or sth **3.** STATE OF BEING BLOCKED the state of being obstructed **4.** DELAYING OF STH the deliberate delaying of the business of sth such as a legislative body **5.** SPORTS UNFAIR IMPEDING OF OPPONENT in football and other sports, the unfair impeding of an opposing player or competitor

obstructionist /əb strúksh'nist/ *adj.* USING DELAYING TACTICS deliberately causing delay or impeding progress ■ *n.* SB WHO DELAYS STH sb who deliberately causes delay or impedes progress —**obstructionistic** /əb strúksh'n ístik/ *adj.* —**obstructionism** /əb strúksh'nizəm/ *n.*

obstruction of justice *n. US* the criminal offence of obstructing the administration and process of the law

obstructive /əb strúktiv/ *adj.* **1.** UNCOOPERATIVE hindering or preventing the progress of sth **2.** MED OF OR CAUSED BY OBSTRUCTION relating to or caused by the obstruction of a passage in the body —**obstructively** *adv.* —**obstructiveness** *n.*

obstructive sleep apnoea *n.* MED cessation or restriction of breathing during sleep that results in loud snoring

obstruent /óbb stroo ənt/ *adj.* **1.** MED OBSTRUCTING PASSAGE IN BODY obstructing or closing a passage in the body, e.g. the intestinal tract **2.** PHON PRODUCED BY CUTOFF OF AIR used to describe a speech sound produced by a stoppage of air from the lungs ■ *n.* **1.** MED OBSTRUCTION sth that obstructs or closes a passage in the body **2.** PHON SOUND PRODUCED BY CUTOFF OF AIR a speech sound produced by a stoppage of air from the lungs. ◊ **sonorant** [Mid-17thC. From Latin *obstruent-*, the present participle stem of *obstruere* (see OBSTRUCT).]

obtain /əb táyn/ (**-tains, -taining, -tained**) *v.* **1.** *vt.* GET to get possession of sth, especially by making an effort or having the necessary qualifications **2.** *vi.* BE ESTABLISHED to be established, valid, or current ○ *under the regulations that obtained at the time* **3.** *vi.* RESULT to follow as a result (*formal*) ○ *the unfortunate situation that obtains when such diverse elements are forced together* **4.** *vti.* ARRIVE AT to reach a place or goal (*archaic*) [15thC. Via Old French *obtenir* from Latin *obtinere* 'to take hold of', literally 'to hold to', from *tenere* 'to hold' (source of English *tenant*).] —**obtainer** *n.* —**obtainment** *n.*

WORD KEY: SYNONYMS

See Synonyms at ***get***.

obtainable /əb táynəb'l/ *adj.* able to be obtained or reached

obtrude /əb tróod, ob tróod/ (**-trudes, -truding, -truded**) *v.* **1.** *vti.* IMPOSE to impose sth such as opinions or yourself on other people **2.** *vt.* PUSH OUT to push sth out or forwards **3.** *vi.* APPEAR UNWELCOME to appear or be present in a way that is unwelcome but cannot be ignored ○ *'Not a leaf stirred; not a sound obtruded upon great Nature's meditation.'* (Mark Twain, *The Adventures of Tom Sawyer*; 1875) [Mid-16thC. From Latin *obtrudere* 'to thrust against', from *trudere* 'to thrust'.] —**obtruder** *n.* —**obtrusion** /əb tróozh'n/ *n.*

obtrusive /əb tróossiv/ *adj.* **1.** ANNOYING tending to force your presence or opinions on other people ○ *plagued by an obtrusive photographer* **2.** HIGHLY NOTICEABLE highly noticeable, often with a bad or unwelcome effect **3.** STICKING OUT projecting or sticking out [Mid-17thC. Formed from Latin *obtrusus*, past participle of *obtrudere* (see OBTRUDE).] —**obtrusively** *adv.* —**obtrusiveness** *n.*

obtund /ob-/ (**-tunds, -tunding, -tunded**) *vt.* to blunt, dull, or deaden sth (*formal*) [14thC. From Latin *obtundere* 'to strike against, blunt', from *tundere* 'to beat, strike'.] —**obtundent** *adj.*

obtuse /əb tyóoss/ *adj.* **1.** SLOW TO UNDERSTAND slow to understand or perceive sth **2.** MATH BETWEEN 90° AND 180° used to describe an angle greater than 90° and less than 180° **3.** MATH WITH INTERNAL ANGLE GREATER THAN 90° used to describe a triangle with one internal angle greater than 90° **4.** BLUNT not sharp or pointed **5.** BOT WITH ROUNDED OR BLUNT TIP used to describe a leaf that has a rounded or blunt tip [Early 16thC. From Latin *obtusus* 'blunted', past participle of *obtundere* (see OBTUND).] —**obtusely** *adv.* —**obtuseness** *n.*

obverse /ób vurss/ *n.* **1.** MAIN SIDE OF COIN OR MEDAL the side of a coin or medal that has the more important design on it, especially a head. ◊ **reverse 2.** COUNTERPART a counterpart, complement, or opposite **3.** LOGIC EQUIVALENT CATEGORICAL PROPOSITION a proposition derived from another proposition by denying it and then negating the predicate, e.g. 'Everything is possible' becomes 'Nothing is impossible' ■ *adj.* **1.** VISIBLE facing an observer **2.** BEING A COUNTERPART forming a counterpart to sth else **3.** BOT NARROWER AT BASE used to describe a leaf that is narrower at the base than the tip [Mid-17thC. From Latin *obversus*, past participle of *obvertere* (see OBVERT).]

obversion /ob vúrsh'n/ *n.* **1.** PROCESS OF SHOWING OTHER SIDE the process of turning sth so that the other side is seen **2.** LOGIC FORMING OF OBVERSE OF PROPOSITION the process of forming the obverse of a proposition

obvert /ob vúrt/ (**-verts, -verting, -verted**) *vt.* **1.** SHOW OTHER SIDE OF to turn sth such as a coin or medal so that the other side is seen **2.** LOGIC FORM OBVERSE OF to convert a proposition to its obverse [Early 17thC. From Latin *obvertere* 'to turn toward', from *vertere* 'to turn'.]

obviate /óbvi ayt/ (**-ates, -ating, -ated**) *vt.* **1.** MAKE UNNECESSARY to render sth unnecessary (*formal*) **2.** TO ANTICIPATE AND DISPOSE OF to avoid an anticipated difficulty by doing sth to prevent its arising [Late 16thC. From Latin *obviat-*, past participle stem of *obviare* 'to withstand', literally 'to stand in the way of', from *via* 'way'.] —**obviation** /óbvi áysh'n/ *n.*

WORD KEY: USAGE

obviate the need for Because one of the meanings of ***obviate*** is 'to make unnecessary', it is sometimes argued that *obviate the need* (or *necessity*) *for* is redundant. An older but still current meaning, however, is 'to anticipate and dispose of' obstacles, that is, 'to do away with' them. In a sentence like *Addressing these issues early can obviate any need for a joint resolution*, the need can be perceived as an obstacle — or early consideration can make the resolution unnecessary, in which case *any need for* is indeed redundant. There is little reason to prefer either interpretation to the other, except that the meaning 'to make unnecessary' allows much the same thought to be expressed with fewer words.

obvious /óbvi əss/ *adj.* **1.** EASY TO SEE easy to see or understand because not concealed, difficult, or ambiguous **2.** UNSUBTLE lacking subtlety or any attempt at concealment [Late 16thC. Formed from Latin *obvius* 'in the way', hence 'readily seen', from *via* 'way' (source of English *voyage*).] —**obviousness** *n.*

obviously /óbvi əssli/ *adv.* **1.** CLEARLY in a way or to an extent that is obvious **2.** UNDOUBTEDLY used to suggest that there can be no doubt or uncertainty about sth ○ *They want you to do it, obviously.*

obvolute /óbvə loot/ *adj.* BOT used to describe leaves or petals that are folded so as to overlap each other [Mid-18thC. From Latin *obvolutus*, past participle of *obvolvere* 'to wrap round', from *volvere* 'to roll'.] —**obvolution** /óbvə lóosh'n/ *n.* —**obvolutive** /óbvə lootiv/ *adj.*

OC *abbr.* **1.** MIL Officer Commanding **2.** STAMPS original cover

Oc., oc. *abbr.* GEOG Ocean

o.c. *abbr.* in the work cited [Shortening of Latin *opere citato*]

o/c *abbr.* overcharge

oca /ókə/ *n.* PLANTS a South American plant grown for its edible tubers. Genus: *Oxalis*. [Early 17thC. Via Spanish from Quechua *ócca*.]

OCAM *abbr.* African and Malagasy Common Organization

O Canada *n.* the title of the national anthem of Canada

ocarina /ókə reénə/ *n.* a simple wind instrument related to the flute that has an oval body, finger holes, and a protruding mouthpiece [Late 19thC. From Italian, literally 'little goose' (from its shape), from *oca* 'goose', from assumed Vulgar Latin *avica*, ultimately from Latin *avis* 'bird'.]

occ. *abbr.* **1.** GEOG occident **2.** occupation

Occam's razor /ókəmz-/ *n.* = **Ockham's razor**

occas. *abbr.* **1.** occasional **2.** occasionally

occasion /ə káyzh'n/ *n.* **1.** PARTICULAR TIME a particular time, especially a time when sth happens **2.** CAUSE OR REASON a cause of or reason for sth ○ *He has no occasion to criticize me.* **3.** CHANCE OR OPPORTUNITY a chance or opportunity to do sth ○ *You might never have another occasion to do it.* **4.** NEED the need for sth or to do sth ○ *has never had occasion to use it* **5.** IMPORTANT EVENT an important or special event ■ **occasions** *npl.* SB'S BUSINESS sb's business or needs (*archaic*) ■ *vt.* (**-sions, -sioning, -sioned**) CAUSE to cause or lead to sth [14thC. Via Old French from the Latin stem *occasion-* 'falling down, happening', ultimately from *cadere* 'to fall'.] ◇ **on occasion** from time to time

occasional /ə káyzh'nəl/ *adj.* **1.** INFREQUENT happening, seen, used, or doing sth from time to time but not regularly or frequently **2.** RELATING TO SPECIAL EVENT done for or connected with a special event ○ *occasional verse* **3.** FURNITURE DESIGNED FOR USE FROM TIME TO TIME intended for use as needed, but not essential or in constant use ○ *an occasional table* **4.** CAUSING serving as the cause of sth (*formal*)

——— **WORD KEY: SYNONYMS** ———
See Synonyms at *periodic*.

occasionally /ə káyzh'nəli/ *adv.* from time to time, but not regularly or frequently

occident /óksidənt/ *n.* the west (*literary or formal*) [14thC. Via Old French from Latin *occident-*, the present participle of *occidere* 'to fall down, set (of the sun)', ultimately from *cadere* 'to fall'.]

Occident *n.* the western hemisphere, especially the countries in Europe and America. ◇ **Orient**

occidental /óksi dént'l/ *adj.* western (*literary or formal*)

Occidental *adj.* PEOPLES OF OCCIDENT relating to or typical of any of the countries of the Occident, or their peoples or cultures. ◇ **Oriental** ■ *n.* WESTERNER sb who lives in or comes from the West. ◇ **Oriental**

occidentalize /óksi déntə līz/ (**-izes, -izing, -ized**), **Occidentalize, occidentalise** *vt.* to make sb or sth conform to the culture of the West

occipita plural of **occiput**

occipital /ok síppit'l/ *adj.* OF BACK OF HEAD relating to or located at the back of the head or skull ■ *n.* = **occipital bone** [Mid-16thC. From medieval Latin *occipitalis*, from Latin *occiput* (see OCCIPUT).]

occipital bone *n.* the saucer-shaped bone at the rear of the skull that connects with the spinal column and has an opening at its base through which the spinal cord passes

occipital lobe *n.* the pyramid-shaped area at the back of each hemisphere of the brain that deals with the interpretation of vision

occiput /óksi put, óksipət/ (*plural* **-ciputs** *or* **-cipita** /-síppitə/) *n.* ANAT the back part of the head or skull [14thC. From Latin, literally 'back of the head', from *caput* 'head'.]

occlude /ə kloód/ (**-cludes, -cluding, -cluded**) *v.* **1.** *vt.* STOP UP to block or stop up sth such as a passage **2.** *vt.* CUT OFF FLOW OF to cut off or prevent the flow or passage of sth such as light or liquid **3.** *vti.* DENT ALIGN TEETH PROPERLY to align the upper and lower teeth in the proper position for chewing or for being in normal contact when the mouth is closed **4.** *vt.* CHEM ABSORB OR ADSORB to absorb or adsorb a liquid or gas on the surface of or within a solid **5.** *vti.* METEOROL FORM OCCLUDED FRONT to form an occluded front, or to undercut a mass of warm air so that it is no longer in contact with the earth's surface [Late 16thC. From Latin *occludere* 'to close up', from *claudere* 'to close' (see CLOSE).]

occluded front *n.* METEOROL a composite front formed when a cold air mass meets and undercuts a warm air mass, and forces the warm air upwards and away from contact with the earth's surface

occlusal /ə kloóz'l/ *adj.* relating to the biting surface of a molar or pre-molar tooth

occlusion /ə kloózh'n/ *n.* **1.** ACT OF OCCLUDING an act of occluding or the state of being occluded **2.** OBSTRUCTION sth that obstructs or occludes **3.** METEOROL = **occluded front 4.** DENT MEETING OF UPPER AND LOWER TEETH the relation between the upper and lower teeth when the jaw is closed and their surfaces come in contact **5.** CLOSURE OF HOLLOW ORGAN the closure of a hollow organ such as the vocal tract in articulating a speech sound **6.** CHEM ABSORPTION OR ADSORPTION OF LIQUID the absorption or adsorption of a liquid or gas on or in a solid [Mid-17thC. Formed from Latin *occlus-*, past participle stem of *occludere* (see OCCLUDE).]

occlusive /ə kloóssiv/ *adj.* OF OCCLUSION relating to, involving, or producing an occlusion ■ *n.* CLOSED SPEECH SOUND a speech sound that involves a closure of the vocal tract

occult *adj.* /ókult, o kúlt/ **1.** SUPPOSEDLY SUPERNATURAL OR MAGIC relating to, involving, or typical of the supposed supernatural, magic, or witchcraft **2.** NOT UNDERSTANDABLE not capable of being understood by ordinary human beings **3.** SECRET secret or known only to the initiated **4.** MED HIDDEN used to describe a diseased condition that is hidden or difficult to detect **5.** MED DIFFICULT TO SEE not visible to the naked eye, and only detectable by microscope or chemical testing ■ *n.* /ókult, o kúlt/ THE SUPPOSED SUPERNATURAL the realm of the supposed supernatural, magic, or witchcraft ■ *vti.* /o kúlt/ (**-cults, -culting, -culted**) **1.** ASTRON TEMPORARILY HIDE CELESTIAL BODY to hide a celestial body temporarily by moving between it and an observer, or to be hidden in this way **2.** HIDE OR BE HIDDEN to hide sth from view or be hidden from view [Early 16thC. From Latin *occultus*, past participle of *occulere* 'to conceal', of uncertain origin: probably literally 'to conceal over', from *celare* 'to hide'.] —**occultly** /ó kúltli, o kúltli/ *adv.* —**occultness** /ókultnəss, o kúltnəss/ *n.*

occultation /ókul táysh'n, ók'l-/ *n.* **1.** TEMPORARY DISAPPEARANCE OF CELESTIAL BODY the temporary complete or partial disappearance of a celestial body when another moves between it and an observer **2.** ACT OF HIDING an act of hiding sth from view or the state of being hidden from view

occultism /ókultizəm, ók'ltizəm, o kúltizəm/ *n.* the belief in and study of the supposed supernatural, magic, or witchcraft

occupancy /ókyoŏpənssi/ (*plural* **-cies**) *n.* **1.** ACT OF OCCUPYING the act or state of occupying sth such as a building or an official position **2.** LEVEL OF OCCUPATION the level of occupation of a place ○ *a block of flats with high occupancy* **3.** TIME OF OCCUPYING the period of time during which sb occupies sth such as a building or an official position **4.** LAW USE WITHOUT OWNERSHIP the use and possession of property without claiming ownership of it **5.** LAW POSSESSION OF UNOWNED PROPERTY the act of taking possession of property, especially land, that has no owner, with the intention of becoming its owner

occupant /ókyoŏpənt/ *n.* **1.** HOLDER OR RESIDENT sb who lives or works in a place, or who holds a position of some sort **2.** LAW SB TAKING POSSESSION sb who takes possession of property, especially land, that has no owner, with the intention of becoming its owner

occupation /ókyoŏ páysh'n/ *n.* **1.** JOB the job by which sb earns a living **2.** ACTIVITY an activity on which time is spent **3.** ACT OF OCCUPYING an act of occupying or the state of being occupied **4.** MIL INVASION the invasion and control of a country or area by enemy forces **5.** TIME OF OCCUPYING the period of time during which sth is occupied

occupational /ókyoŏ pásh'nəl/ *adj.* relating to or caused by sb's job —**occupationally** *adv.*

occupational disease *n.* a disease that is directly caused by the conditions of sb's work

occupational hazard *n.* a risk associated with a particular type of work

occupational medicine *n.* the branch of medicine that deals with work-related diseases and injuries incurred at work

occupational pension *n.* a pension paid to an employee or former employee from a scheme set up by an employer, not the state

occupational therapy *n.* the use of regular periods of suitable productive activity as part of the treatment of illness or medical condition —**occupational therapist** *n.*

occupation groupings *npl.* SOC SCI the categories, e.g. C1 or C2, that people can be put into according to their occupation, often used in the advertising industry to define target markets

occupy /ókyoŏ pī/ (**-pies, -pying, -pied**) *vt.* **1.** LIVE IN PLACE to live in or be the established user of a place such as a home or office **2.** ENGAGE SB'S ATTENTION to take up sb's time or attention (*often passive*) **3.** FILL SPACE OR TIME to take up a space or an amount of time (*often passive*) **4.** MIL TAKE OVER PLACE to invade and take control of a country, area, or building **5.** HOLD POSITION to hold a post or rank [14thC. Via Old French from Latin *occupare* 'to take hold of', literally 'to take over', ultimately from *capere* 'to take' (source of English *captive*).] —**occupier** *n.*

occur /ə kúr/ (**-curs, -curring, -curred**) *vi.* **1.** HAPPEN to happen or come about **2.** EXIST to exist or be present **3.** ENTER MIND to come into sb's mind ○ *It didn't occur to him to lock the door.* [Early 16thC. From Latin *occurrere* 'to run to meet', literally 'to run against', from *currere* 'to run' (see COURSE).]

occurrence /ə kúrrənss/ *n.* **1.** HAPPENING sth that happens **2.** FACT OF OCCURRING the fact or act of sth happening —**occurrent** *adj.*

OCD *abbr.* obsessive-compulsive disorder

WORLD'S LARGEST OCEANS AND SEAS

1	Pacific Ocean	
Area	[64 million sq. mi. /165 million sq. km]	
2	Atlantic Ocean	
Area	[31.7 million sq. mi. / 82 million sq. km]	
3	Indian Ocean	
Area	[28.3 million sq. mi. / 73.4 million sq. km]	
4	Arctic Ocean	
Area	[5.4 million sq. mi. / 14 million sq. km]	
5	Mediterranean Sea	
Area	[0.97 million sq. mi. / 2.5 million sq. km]	
6	Bering Sea	
Area	[0.87 million sq. mi. /2.26 million sq. km]	
7	Caribbean Sea	
Area	[0.75 million sq. mi. /1.94 million sq. km]	
8	Sea of Okhotsk	
Area	[0.59 million sq. mi. /1.53 million sq. km]	
9	Sea of Japan	
Area	[0.39 million sq. mi. / 1 million sq. km]	
10	Hudson Bay	
Area	[0.28 million sq. mi. /0.73 million sq. km]	

ocean /ósh'n/ *n.* **1.** GEOG LARGE SEA a large expanse of salt water, especially any of the Earth's five largest seas, the Atlantic, Pacific, Indian, Arctic, and Antarctic Oceans. The oceans occupy huge regions of the Earth's surface, and their boundaries are usually established by continental land masses and ridges in the ocean floor. **2.** GEOG EARTH'S SEAS TOGETHER the whole body of salt water on the Earth **3.** SEA the sea (*literary*) **4.** LARGE AMOUNT a vast amount or expanse of sth [13thC. Via Old French from Latin *oceanus*, from Greek *ōkeanos*, the river surrounding the disc of the Earth, later applied to the Atlantic.]

oceanarium /ṓshə náiri əm/ (*plural* **-ums** *or* **-a**) *n.* a large saltwater aquarium for observing and exhibiting marine animals and plants [Mid-20thC. Blend of OCEAN and AQUARIUM.]

oceanaut /ṓshə nawt/ *n.* sb who swims underwater in an ocean using an aqualung [Mid-20thC. Blend of OCEAN and AQUANAUT.]

oceanfront /ṓsh'n frunt/ *n.* **1.** LAND BORDERING OCEAN land along the seashore (*often used before a noun*) ○ *ocean-front property* **2.** OCEANOG DIVISION BETWEEN WARM AND COLD OCEAN the point at which two oceanic water masses of different thermal characteristics meet

oceangoing /ṓsh'n gō ing/ *adj.* built, equipped, or used for travel on the ocean

ocean greyhound *n.* a fast ocean liner

Oceania /ṓssi áaniə, ṓshi-/ geographical region consisting of most of the smaller islands of the Pacific Ocean, sometimes including Australia and New Zealand —**Oceanian** *n.*, *adj.*

oceanic /ṓshi ánnik, ṓssi-/ *adj.* **1.** IN OR FROM AN OCEAN living, situated in, produced by, or taking place in an ocean, especially the depths of the open sea **2.** GEOL VOLCANIC resulting from volcanic activity in the ocean ○ *oceanic island* **3.** IMMENSE immense, vast, or overwhelming

Oceanic /ṓshi ánnik, ṓssi-/ *n.* LANGUAGE OF OCEANIA a group of languages spoken mainly on the Pacific islands lying to the north and east of Australia. It forms a branch of the Malayo-Polynesian family of languages. About two million people speak one of the Oceanic languages. ■ *adj.* OF OCEANIA relating to or typical of any of the countries of Oceania, or their peoples or cultures

oceanic ridge *n.* any section of a range of underwater mountains, found in all major oceans

oceanic trench *n.* a long narrow deep furrow in the earth's crust at the bottom of an ocean

oceanography /ṓshə nóggrəfi, ṓshi ə-/ *n.* the scientific study of oceans, including their chemistry, biology, and geology —**oceanographer** *n.* —**oceanographic** /ṓsh'nə gráffik, ṓshi ənə-/ *adj.* —**oceanographically** /-gráffikli/ *adv.*

oceanology /ṓshə nólləji, ṓshi ə-/ *n.* the branch of oceanography that studies how oceans may be used for economic or technological purposes —**oceanological** /ṓsh'nə lójjik'l, ṓ shi ənə-/ *adj.* —**oceanologically** /-lójjikli, -/ *adv.*

ocean perch *n.* = rosefish *n.* 1

ocean sunfish *n.* US = sunfish

ocean tramp *n.* = tramp steamer

Oceanus Procellarum /ṓssi áanəss prósse laáən/ *n.* a vast lunar lowland plain stretching between Mare Imbrium and Mare Humorum visible as a dark area in the west covering. Area: more than 2,000,000 sq. km/775,000 sq. mi.

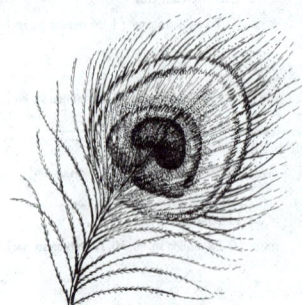

Ocellus: Peacock feather

ocellus /ō sélləss/ (*plural* **-li** /-lī/) *n.* **1.** INSECTS SIMPLE EYE IN INVERTEBRATES a simple eye in some insects and other invertebrates that is sensitive to light but unable to focus clearly **2.** BIRDS EYE-SHAPED SPOT ON FEATHERS an eye-shaped spot on the feathers of some birds such as the peacock **3.** BOT EYE-SHAPED SPOT ON LEAF an enlarged discoloured eye-shaped spot on a

leaf **4.** ZOOL EYE-SHAPED SPOT ON FISH an eye-shaped spot on a fish, usually dark-ringed with a lighter colour inside, believed to deceive predators [Early 19thC. From Latin, literally 'small eye', from *oculus* 'eye'.]

Ocelot

ocelot /óssə lot, -lot/ (*plural* **-lots** *or* **-lot**) *n.* a small wild cat with dark spots on a light brownish coat that is found in small numbers from the southern United States to South America. Latin name: *Felis pardalis.* [Late 18thC. Via French from Nahuatl *tlatlocelotl*, literally 'field jaguar'.]

och /okh/ *interj. Scotland, Ireland* an exclamation used to express disgust, disapproval, regret, weariness, or exasperation, depending on the intonation (*informal*) ○ *Och, it's too late now.* [Early 16thC. Natural exclamation.]

oche /óki/ *n.* the line behind which a darts player must stand when throwing [Mid-20thC. Origin uncertain: perhaps from Old French, 'groove'.]

ocher *n.*, *adj.* US = ochre

ochlocracy /ok lókrəssi/ (*plural* **-cies**) *n.* mobocracy [Late 16thC. Via French *ochlocratie* from Greek *okhlokratia* 'mob rule', from *okhlos* 'mob'.] —**ochlocrat** /óklə krat/ *n.* —**ochlocratic** /óklə kráttik/ *adj.* —**ochlocratically** /-kráttikli/ *adv.*

ochre /ṓkər/ *n.* COLOURS a brownish-yellow colour [14thC. Via French *ocre* from Latin *ochra* from, ultimately, Greek *ōkhros* 'pale, yellow'.] —**ocher** *adj.* —**ochreous** *adj.* —**ochry** /ṓkəri/ *adj.*

ochrea *n.* BOT = ocrea

-ock *suffix.* sth small or worthless ○ *hillock* ○ *mullock* [Old English *-oc, -uc*]

ocker /ókər/ *n. Aus* BOORISH CHAUVINISTIC AUSTRALIAN a boorish uncultivated chauvinistic Australian, especially an unreconstructed male with traditional views (*slang*) ■ *adj. Aus* BOORISH AND CHAUVINISTIC displaying the boorish, uncultivated, or chauvinistic attitudes thought by some to be typical of unreconstructed Australian men (*slang*) ○ *a raft of embarrassingly ocker uncles* [Late 20thC. Alteration of the male forename *Oscar*, as used for a character in a television series.]

Ockham /ókəm/, **William of** (1285?–1349) English philosopher. He revived nominalism, and enunciated the principle known as Ockham's razor.

Ockham's razor /ókəmz ráyzər/, **Occam's razor** *n.* the philosophical and scientific rule that simple explanations should be preferred to more complicated ones, and that the explanation of a new phenomenon should be based on what is already known [Mid-19thC. Named after William of OCKHAM.]

o'clock /ə klók/ *adv.* **1.** BEING A PARTICULAR HOUR IN TELLING THE TIME in telling the time, used to indicate an exact hour of the day or night, rather than some minutes past or before the hour ○ *woke up at six o'clock in the morning* **2.** INDICATING DIRECTION AS IF ON A CLOCKFACE used to describe a position or direction of sth by comparing it to the positions of numbers on a clockface, with the observer at the centre of the clock ○ *Look at the man sitting to your right, at three o'clock.* [15thC. Contraction of *of the clock*.]

O'Connell /ō kónn'l/, **Daniel** (1775–1847) Irish politician and a Roman Catholic, he succeeded in obtaining Catholic emancipation, becoming an MP at Westminster (1829). He agitated for repeal of the union of Ireland and Great Britain, and became Lord Mayor of Dublin (1841).

Daniel O'Connell

ocotillo /ókə teélyō, ókə teé ō/ (*plural* **-los** *or* **-lo**) *n.* TREES a spiny shrub with red flowers at the tip of each branch, found in dry parts of the southwestern United States and in Mexico. Latin name: *Fouqueria splendens.* [Mid-19thC. Via American Spanish, literally 'small ocote', from *ocote* 'Mexican pine tree', from Nahuatl *ocotl* 'torch'.]

OCR *abbr.* **1.** optical character reader **2.** optical character recognition

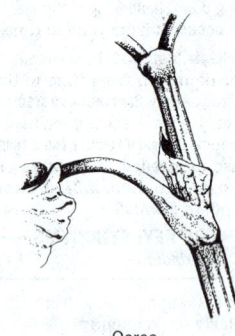

Ocrea

ocrea /ṓkri ə/ (*plural* **-ae** /-ri ee/), **ochrea** (*plural* **-ae**) *n.* BOT a cup-shaped sheath formed by appendages at the base of a leaf, as in rhubarb [Mid-19thC. From Latin, 'soldier's leg-armour'.]

OCS *abbr.* Officer Candidate School

oct. *abbr.* PRINTING octavo

Oct. *abbr.* October

oct- *prefix.* = octo- (*used before a vowel*)

octa- *prefix.* = octo-

octad /ók tad/ *n.* a group or series of eight [Mid-19thC. From Greek *oktad-*, the stem of *oktas*, from *oktō* (see OCTO-).] —**octadic** /ok táddik/ *adj.*

octagon /óktəgən/ *n.* a closed plane figure that has eight sides and eight angles

octagonal /ok tággənəl/ *adj.* having eight sides and eight angles

octahedral /óktə heédrəl/ *adj.* shaped like an octahedron —**octahedrally** *adv.*

octahedron /óktə heédrən/ (*plural* **-drons** *or* **-dra** /-drə/) *n.* a three-dimensional figure that has eight faces

octal /óktəl/ *adj.* MATH, COMPUT HAVING NUMBER SYSTEM BASED ON EIGHT using or having a number system based on eight instead of ten ■ *n.* COMPUT **1.** = octal notation **2.** OCTAL NUMBER a number with eight as its base

octal notation *n.* COMPUT a number system used in writing computer programs that is based on eight and uses numerals 0 to 7, one octal unit equalling three bits

octameter /ok támmitər/ *n.* a line of verse with eight metrical units or feet

octane /ók tayn/ *n.* **1.** PETROLEUM COMPONENT a liquid hydrocarbon found in petroleum that exists in 18 structurally different forms. Formula: C_8H_{18}. **2.** = octane number [Late 19thC. Coined from OCTO- + -ANE; from the number of carbon atoms in the hydrocarbon.]

octane number, **octane rating** *n.* a number that measures the ability of a liquid motor fuel such as petrol to prevent preignition or knocking. Fuels with higher numbers are less likely to cause knocking.

Octans /ók tanz/ *n.* a faint constellation of the southern hemisphere that contains the south celestial pole

octant /óktənt/ *n.* **1.** ASTRON **EIGHTH OF A CELESTIAL CIRCLE** the position of one body in the sky one-eighth of a circle (45°) from another **2. EIGHTH OF A CIRCLE** one-eighth of a circle, with or without the enclosed area **3.** MATH **REGION OF SPACE IN CARTESIAN SYSTEM** any one of the eight regions into which space is divided by the three planes of the Cartesian coordinate system [Late 17thC. From Latin *octant-*, the stem of *octans* 'half-quadrant' , from *octo* (see OCTO-).] —**octantal** /ok tánt'l/ *adj.*

octapeptide /óktə pép tīd/ *n.* a peptide consisting of eight amino acids

octavalent /óktə váylent/ *adj.* used to describe an element, atom, or group that has a valency of eight

octave /óktiv/ *n.* **1.** MUSIC **INTERVAL ON MUSICAL SCALE** an interval between two notes consisting of eight notes inclusive or seven steps on the diatonic scale **2.** MUSIC **NOTE AT EACH END OF OCTAVE** the note at each end of an octave, especially the higher one, considered in relation to the note at the other end **3.** MUSIC **NOTES AT END OF OCTAVE TOGETHER** the two notes at each end of an octave played together **4.** MUSIC **ALL NOTES INCLUDED WITHIN OCTAVE** the series of notes that fall within an octave, including the octave on each end, or the strings, keys, or other musical devices that produce these notes **5.** MUSIC **ORGAN STOP FOR PRODUCING HIGHER NOTES** an organ stop that causes tones to be produced an octave higher than the keys played alone **6.** POETRY **EIGHT LINES OF POETRY** a group of eight lines of verse, especially the first eight lines of a sonnet, or a poem that consists of eight lines **7.** CHR **CHRISTIAN FEAST DAY AND FOLLOWING WEEK** in Christianity, a feast day and the week following it **8.** CHR **EIGHTH DAY AFTER FEAST DAY** the eighth day after an octave feast day when the feast day is counted as one **9.** FENCING **EIGHTH DEFENSIVE POSITION IN FENCING** the eighth of eight basic defensive positions in fencing, known as a rotating perry **10. EIGHTH ITEM** the eighth in a series **11. SET OF EIGHT** a set or series of eight [14thC. Via French from Latin *octava*, the feminine of *octavus* 'eighth', from *octo* 'eight'.]

octave coupler *n.* MUSIC a mechanism on an organ or harpsichord that allows sb simultaneously to play one note and another one an octave higher or lower

Octavia /ok táyvi ə/ (69?–11 BC) Roman aristocrat. The sister of Augustus, she married Mark Antony in a vain attempt to effect a reconciliation between the two men.

octavo /ok táyvō, -taávō/ (*plural* **-vos**) *n.* a book size of about 16 by 23 cm/6 by 9 in, or a book of this size [Late 16thC. From Latin 'in an eighth (of a sheet)', from *octavus* (see OCTAVE) from the folding of a sheet eight times.]

octennial /ok ténni əl/ *adj.* **1. HAPPENING EVERY EIGHT YEARS** occurring at intervals of eight years **2. LASTING EIGHT YEARS** lasting for a period of eight years [Mid-17thC. Formed from late Latin *octennium* 'period of eight years', from Latin *octo* 'eight' + *annus* 'year'.] —**octennially** *adv.*

octet /ok tét/ *n.* **1. GROUP OF EIGHT, ESPECIALLY MUSICIANS** a group of eight, especially eight singers or instrumentalists **2.** MUSIC **MUSICAL COMPOSITION FOR GROUP OF EIGHT** a musical composition for a group of eight voices or instruments **3.** POETRY = **octave** *n.* 6 [Mid-19thC. Alteration of Italian *otteto* (from, ultimately, Latin *octo* 'eight'), influenced by OCTO-, on the model of words such as DUET.]

octo- *prefix.* eight ○ *octosyllable* [From Latin *octo* and Greek *oktō*. Ultimately from the Indo-European word for 'eight' that is also the ancestor of English *eight*.]

October /ok tṓbər/ *n.* in the Gregorian calendar, the tenth month of the year, made up of 31 days [Pre-12thC. From Latin, 'eighth month', from *octo* 'eight'. The early Romans calculated the beginning of their year from March, and so October was the eighth month.]

octocentenary /óktō sen teénəri/ (*plural* **-naries**) *n.* an 800th anniversary

octodecimo /óktō déssimō/ (*plural* **-mos**) *n.* a book size of about 10 by 16 cm/4 by $4\frac{1}{4}$ in, or a book of this size [Mid-19thC. From Latin, 'in an eighteenth (of a sheet)', from, ultimately, *octodecim*, literally 'eight and ten'; from the folding of a sheet 18 times.]

octogenarian /óktō jə náiri ən/ *n.* sb who is between 80 and 89 years old [Early 19thC. Formed from Latin *octogenarius*, from *octoginta* 'eighty', literally 'eight times ten'.]

octonary /óktənəri/ *adj.* **1. BASED ON EIGHT** based on the number eight **2. CONSISTING OF EIGHT** consisting of eight things ■ *n.* (*plural* **-ies**) **1. GROUP OF EIGHT** a group or set of eight things **2.** COMPUT = **octal** *n.* 2 [Mid-16thC. From Latin *octonarius* 'containing eight', from *octo* (see OCTO-).]

octoploid /óktə ployd/ *n.* GENETICS a cell nucleus or an organism, especially a plant, containing eight haploid sets of chromosomes. ◊ **haploid, diploid, triploid, tetraploid**

octopod /óktə pod/ *n.* a shell-less mollusc such as the octopus with a large head and eyes and eight tentacles. Order: Octopoda. [Early 20thC. From modern Latin *Octopoda*, order name, from Greek *oktōpod-*, the stem of *oktōpous* (see OCTOPUS).] —**octopodous** /ok tóppədəss/ *adj.*

octopus /óktəpəss/ (*plural* **-puses** *or* **-pi** /-pī/ *or* **-pus**) *n.* **1. SEA ANIMAL WITH EIGHT ARMS** a sea animal with a big head, a soft oval body, well-developed eyes, and eight arms containing rows of suckers. It usually lives on the ocean floor. Genus: *Octopus.* ◊ **squid 2. STH WITH FARFLUNG INFLUENCE** sth, especially an organization, that has many branches and forms of influence or control **3.** = **spider** *n.* 2 [Mid-18thC. From modern Latin, genus name, from Greek *oktōpous*, literally 'eight feet', from *oktō* 'eight' + *pous* 'foot'.]

octoroon /óktə ro͞on/ *n.* an offensive term for sb who has one Black grandparent and no other Black ancestors (*archaic offensive*) [Mid-19thC. Formed from OCTO- on the model of QUADROON.]

octosyllable /óktə siləb'l/ *n.* POETRY a language unit of eight syllables, usually a complete line of verse but occasionally just a word —**octosyllabic** /óktə si lábbik/ *adj.*

octroi /ók trwaa/ *n.* formerly, and especially in France and Italy, a local tax levied on goods entering a town or city [Late 16thC. Via French from, ultimately, medieval Latin *auctorizare* (see AUTHORIZE).]

octuple /óktyo͝op'l, ok tyo͞op'l/ *adj.* **1. EIGHT TIMES AS LARGE** eight times as large or effective **2. WITH EIGHT PARTS** consisting of eight parts ■ *vti.* **MULTIPLY BY EIGHT** to multiply sth by eight or to be multiplied by eight ■ *n.* **QUANTITY EIGHT TIMES GREATER** an amount that is eight times more than another amount

ocul- *prefix.* = **oculo-** (*used before vowels*)

ocular /ókyo͝olər/ *adj.* **RELATING TO EYES OR EYESIGHT** relating to, perceived by, or performed by the eye ■ *n.* **EYEPIECE** an eyepiece in an optical instrument [Late 16thC. Via French *oculaire* from late Latin *ocularis*, from Latin *oculus* 'eye'.]

WORD KEY: ORIGIN

The Indo-European ancestor of ***ocular*** is also the ultimate source of English *atrocious, eye, ferocious, inoculate*, and *optical*.

oculist /ókyo͝olist/ *n.* an optometrist or ophthalmologist (*dated*)

oculo- *prefix.* eye ○ *oculomotor* [From Latin *oculus* (see OCULAR)]

oculogyric /ókyo͝olō jírrik/ *adj.* relating to the movement of an eyeball in its socket

oculomotor /ókyo͝olō mṓtər/ *adj.* relating to or causing movement of the eyeball

oculomotor nerve *n.* either of the third pair of cranial nerves that carry nerve fibres from the brain to the eye muscles and eyelids

Od /od/ *interj.* used euphemistically as an oath to mean 'God' (*archaic*) [Late 16thC. Alteration of GOD.]

OD[1] *abbr.* **1.** overdraft **2.** overdrawn **3.** Officer of the Day **4.** Doctor of Optometry **5.** LANG Old Dutch **6.** MIL olive drab **7.** ordnance datum

OD[2] /ō deé/ *vi.* (**ODs, ODing, ODed**) **TAKE DEADLY AMOUNT OF DRUG** to take a dangerous amount of a drug, often causing hospitalization or death (*informal*) ■ *n.* **OVERDOSE** an overdose (*informal*) = **overdose** [Mid-20thC. Shortening of OVERDOSE.]

o.d. *abbr.* **1.** outside diameter **2.** on demand **3.** MIL olive drab **4.** MED right eye [Shortening of Latin *oculus dexter*]

O/D, o/d *abbr.* **1.** overdraft **2.** overdrawn

ODA *abbr.* Overseas Development Administration

odalisque /ódə lisk, óddə-/, **odalisk** *n.* **1. ENSLAVED WOMAN IN HAREM** an enslaved woman or concubine, especially, formerly, in a Turkish harem **2.** PAINTING, SCULPTURE **ARTISTIC REPRESENTATION OF ODALISQUE** a representation of an odalisque in art [Late 17thC. Via French from Turkish *ōdalik*, literally 'sb who works in a chamber', from *ōda* 'chamber'.]

Oda Nobunaga /ṓdə nóbbyoo naágə/ (1534–82) Japanese feudal lord. He began the 16th-century reunification of Japan.

odd /od/ *adj.* **1. UNUSUAL** peculiar, unusual, or out of the ordinary ○ *There's something very odd about the letter.* **2.** MATH **NOT DIVISIBLE EXACTLY BY 2** being a number such as 1, 3, 5, 7, 9, or 11 that, when divided by 2, leaves a remainder of 1. ◊ **even 3. LEFTOVER** leftover, and usually few in number ○ *a few odd coins* **4. SEPARATED FROM PAIR OR SET** left on its own without the other member or members of its pair, set, or series ○ *a number of odd socks in the drawer* **5. IRREGULAR** irregular or occasional ○ *We get the odd day off here and there.* **6. SLIGHTLY GREATER THAN STATED NUMBER** used after a number to mean a little more than the number stated ○ *I figured on paying 50-odd pounds for it.* **7. REMOTE** not usually visited or reached by many people ○ *We found the papers lying about in odd corners of the house.* **8.** MATH **HAVING CHANGING MATHEMATICAL SIGNS** used to refer to a function that changes sign but not value when the sign of each independent variable is changed at the same time ■ *n.* **STH ODD IN NUMBER** sth that is odd in number or numerical order [14thC. From Old Norse *oddi* 'third or odd number'. Ultimately from an Indo-European word meaning 'pointed upwards', the underlying idea being 'triangular', hence 'having one left over from two'.] —**oddish** *adj.* —**oddly** *adv.* —**oddness** *n.*

oddball /ód bawl/ *n.* sb who is unconventional, unusual, or not typical, usually in a harmless way (*informal insult; often used before a noun*)

odd bod *n.* = **oddball** (*informal*)

Oddfellow *n.* a member of the Independent Order of Oddfellows, a secret international social and charitable fraternity founded in England in the 18th century [From ODD 'remote, out-of-the-way', with reference to the Order's mystic practices]

oddity /óddəti/ (*plural* **-ties**) *n.* sb or sth unique, unusual, or unconventional

odd job *n.* any of a series of unrelated unspecialized jobs such as household repairs, usually done casually and for low pay (*often used in the plural*) ○ *does odd jobs for a living*

odd-job (**odd-jobs, odd-jobbing, odd-jobbed**) *vi.* to work at one or more odd jobs ○ *odd-jobbed around town* —**odd-jobber** *n.*

odd lot *n.* a quantity or number of shares that is smaller than the usual trading unit, e.g. fewer than 100 shares when traded on a stock exchange, or less than one whole share when liquidated

odd man out (*plural* **odd men out** *or* **odd ones out**) *n.* sb in a group who differs from the rest of the group in some way, or who is not treated as part of the group

oddment /ódmənt/ *n.* sth left over when most of sth has been used or disposed of (*usually used in the plural*) ○ *By the time she arrived there were only oddments left in the sale.* [Late 18thC. Formed from ODD on the model of FRAGMENT.]

odd-pinnate *adj.* used to describe a plant leaf such as that of the rose that is pinnate with a single leaflet at the top —**odd-pinnately** *adv.*

odds /odz/ *npl.* **1. CHANCES OF STH HAPPENING** the likelihood or probability that sth will occur, sometimes expressed as a ratio such as 10 to 1 ○ *The odds are that you'll never make it.* **2.** BETTING **PREDICTED CHANCES IN BETTING** a ratio of probability given to people placing a bet, usually the likelihood of a specific event happening, or of a competitor, team, or animal winning ○ *The horse was given odds of four to one.* **3.** SPORTS **HANDICAP OR ADVANTAGE USED IN COMPETITION**

an advantage or handicap given to a person, animal, or team in a sporting contest, to equalize the chances of winning **4.** **PERCEIVED ADVANTAGE OR DISADVANTAGE** a perceived advantage or disadvantage, especially one that one person is believed to have over another in a competition [Early 16thC. Plural of ODD.] ◇ **at odds with sb** *or* **sth** in disagreement with sb, or in conflict with sth ◇ **over the odds** more than is usual or necessary ◇ **what's the odds?** used to indicate that sth is of no importance

odds and ends *npl.* a group of miscellaneous items ○ *The top drawer is where I keep my odds and ends.*

odds and sods *npl.* miscellaneous people or items (*informal*)

oddsmaker /ódz maykər/ *n.* sb who officially calculates betting odds

odds-on *adj.* likeliest to win, succeed, or happen (*informal*) ○ *It was odds-on that he would succeed his father.*

ode /ōd/ *n.* **1.** POETRY **TYPE OF LYRIC POEM** a lyric poem, usually expressing exalted emotion in a complex scheme of rhyme and metre **2.** MUSIC, HIST **ANCIENT GREEK SONG** an ancient Greek song written either for a chorus or for a solo singer [Late 16thC. Via French from, ultimately, Greek *ōidē* 'song'. Ultimately from an Indo-European base meaning 'to speak', also the ancestor of English *melody* and *comedy*.]

-ode *suffix.* **1.** electrically conducting element ○ *electrode* **2.** electrode ○ *tetrode* [From Greek *hodos* 'way, road, journey' (source of English *exodus, method, odometer,* and *period*)]

Odense /ṓth'nssə/ city and port in south-central Denmark, on the island of Fyn. Population: 182,617 (1995).

Oder /ṓdər/ river in north-central Europe. Its northern course forms part of Poland's border with Germany. Length: 906 km/563 mi.

Odessa /ō déssə/, **Odesa** city and port in south-central Ukraine, on the Black Sea. Population: 1,060,000 (1995).

odeum /ṓdi-/ (*plural* **-a** /-ə/), **odeon** /ṓdi ən/ (*plural* **-a**) *n.* an ancient Greek or Roman building in which musical performances were held [Early 17thC. Directly or via French from Latin *odeum*, from Greek *ōideion*, from *ōidē* (see ODE).]

odious /ṓdi əss/ *adj.* inspiring hatred, contempt, or disgust [14thC. Via Old French from Latin *odiosus*, from *odium* (see ODIUM).] —**odiously** *adv.* —**odiousness** *n.*

odium /ṓdi əm/ *n.* **1.** **HATRED** intense dislike, repugnance, or contempt for sb or sth ○ *incurred scorn and odium for his actions* **2.** **STATE OF BEING ODIOUS** the state of being hateful, contemptuous, or disgusting [Early 17thC. From Latin (source also of English *annoy*).]

odometer /ō dómmitər, o-/ *n.* US = **mileometer** [Late 18thC. Via French *odomètre* or formed directly from Greek *hodos* 'way'.]

odonate /ṓdə nayt/ *n.* an insect belonging to the order of insects that includes the dragonfly and damselfly. Order: Odonata. [Early 20thC. From modern Latin *Odonata*, order name, from Greek *odōn*, a variant of *odous* 'tooth'.]

odont- *prefix.* = **odonto-** (*used before vowels*)

-odont *suffix.* having a particular kind of teeth ○ *acrodont* [From Greek *odont-*, the stem of *odous* (see ODONTO-)]

odontalgia /óddon tálji ə/ *n.* DENT toothache (*technical*)

-odontia *suffix.* condition or treatment of teeth ○ *anodontia* [Formed from Greek *odont-*, the stem of *odous* (see ODONTO-)]

odonto- *prefix.* tooth, teeth ○ *odontology* [From Greek *odont-*, the stem of *odous* 'tooth'. Ultimately from the Indo-European word for 'tooth', which is also the ancestor of English *tooth* and *dental*.]

odontoblast /o dóntə blast/ *n.* one of a layer of cells lining the pulp cavity of a tooth and taking part in the formation of dentine —**odontoblastic** /o dóntə blástik/ *adj.*

odontoglossum /o dóntə glóssəm/ *n.* a variety of orchid that grows on other plants in mountainous areas from Bolivia to Mexico and is widely cultivated for its clusters of brightly-coloured flowers. Genus: *Odontoglossum.* [Late 19thC. From modern Latin, genus name, literally 'tooth tongue', from Greek *odont-* 'tooth' + *glōssa* 'tongue'; from the toothlike projection on the end of the flower.]

odontoid /o dónt oyd/ *adj.* resembling a tooth, especially in shape

odontoid process *n.* a tooth-shaped peg that projects upwards from the second neck vertebra to engage with the first, acting as a pivot for side-to-side movements of the head

odontology /óddon tólləji/ *n.* the branch of science that studies the teeth and their anatomy, development, and diseases —**odontological** /o dóntə lójjik'l/ *adj.* —**odontologically** /-lójjikli/ *adv.* —**odontologist** /óddon tólləjist/ *n.*

odor *n.* US = **odour**

odorant /ṓdərənt/ *n.* sth that gives a characteristic smell to a product

odoriferous /ṓdə ríffərəss/ *adj.* having or diffusing a strong odour (*formal or technical*) —**odoriferously** *adv.* —**odoriferousness** *n.*

odorous *adj.* = **odoriferous** (*literary*) —**odorously** *adv.* —**odorousness** *n.*

odour /ṓdər/ *n.* **1.** **SMELL** smell or scent, whether pleasant or unpleasant ○ *the delicious odour of baking bread* **2.** **PERVASIVE QUALITY** a quality or attitude that suggests or resembles a particular thing ○ *They had an odour of propriety.* ○ *odour of sanctity* [13thC. Via Anglo-Norman and Old French *odor, odur* from Latin *odor* 'smell'.] ◇ **be in bad** *or* **good odour (with sb)** to be out of favour or in favour with sb

odourless /ṓdərləss/ *adj.* having no smell that is strong enough to be detected by the human nose —**odourlessness** *n.*

Odysseus /ō díssee əss/ *n.* in Greek mythology, the King of Ithaca and one of the senior Greeks in the Trojan War. He is the main character in Homer's epic poem the *Odyssey*. ◆ **Ulysses**

odyssey /óddissi/ (*plural* **-seys**) *n.* a long series of travels and adventures [Late 19thC. From the *Odyssey*, from, ultimately, Greek *Odusseia*, from ODYSSEUS.]

WORD KEY: CULTURAL NOTE

The Odyssey, an epic poem by the Greek writer Homer (?8th century BC). The oldest surviving source of Greek mythology along with the ***Iliad***, it describes Odysseus's ten-year journey home to Ithaca after the Trojan War. It provides both an insight into a long-lost civilization and a gripping narrative rich in evocative details, complex characters, and universal themes.

Oe *symbol.* oersted

OE *abbr.* LANG Old English ■ *n. NZ* **FIRST TRIP ABROAD** the first trip made overseas, especially to Europe. Abbr of **overseas experience**

OECD *abbr.* Organization for Economic Cooperation and Development

oedema /i deémə/ (*plural* **-mas** *or* **-mata** /-mətə/) *n.* **1.** MED **EXCESS FLUID** an abnormal buildup of serous fluid between tissue cells **2.** BOT **EXCESS FLUID IN PLANT** an abnormal swelling in a plant, chiefly caused by a buildup of excess water [15thC. From Greek *oidēma* 'swelling tumour', from *oidein* 'to swell'.] —**oedematous** /i démmətəss, i deémətəss/ *adj.*

Oedipal /eédip'l/ *adj.* referring or relating to Oedipus or the Oedipus complex [Mid-20thC. Formed from OEDIPUS.]

Oedipus /eédipəss/ *n.* in Greek mythology, a son of Jocasta and Laius, King of Thebes, who unwittingly killed his father and married his mother. He put out his own eyes when he discovered what he had done.

Oedipus complex /eédipəss-/ *n.* according to the controversial psychoanalytic theory of Sigmund Freud, feelings or desires originating when a child, especially a son, unconsciously seeks sexual fulfilment with the parent of the opposite sex. ◊ **Electra complex** [Early 20th C. Named after OEDIPUS.]

OEIC *abbr.* open-ended investment company

Ōe Kenzaburō /ō ay kénzə bóorō/ (*b.* 1935) Japanese writer. Perhaps the greatest Japanese novelist since World War II, he won the Nobel Prize in literature in 1994.

OEM *abbr.* original equipment manufacturer

oenology *n.* the scientific study of wine and the making of wine [Early 19thC. Coined from Greek *oinos* 'wine' + -LOGY.]

oenomel /eénə mel/ *n.* (*literary*) **1.** **HONEYED WINE** a drink of wine and honey made in ancient Greece **2.** **STRONG, SWEET LANGUAGE OR THOUGHT** words or ideas that combine strength and sweetness [Late 16thC. Via late Latin *oenomeli* from Greek *oinomeli*, literally 'honey wine', from *oinos* 'wine' + *meli* 'honey'.]

oenophile /eénə fīl/ *n.* sb who has a passionate interest in wine or is an expert on wines (*formal*) [Mid-20thC. From French, from *oeno-*, from Greek *oinos* 'wine'.]

o'er /ō ər, awr/ *prep., adv.* over (*literary*) ○ *The sun rose o'er the mountain.* [14thC. Contraction.]

oersted /-sted/ *n.* the unit measure of magnetic field strength in the centimetre-gram-second system. It is equal to the magnetic field strength experienced by a magnetic pole when undergoing a force of one dyne in a free space. Symbol **Oe** [Late19thC. Named after H.C. *Oersted* (1777–1851), Danish physicist who discovered the magnetic effect of an electric current.]

Oersted /úrstid, ŏrstid/, **Hans Christian** (1777–1851) Danish physicist and chemist. He pioneered the study of electromagnetism, and was the first to isolate aluminium (1825).

oesophagus (*plural* **-gi** /-gī/) *n.* the passage down which food moves between the throat and the stomach [14thC. Via medieval Latin *isophagus* from Greek *oisophagos*, of uncertain origin: perhaps literally 'carrier-eater', from *oisein* future infinitive of *pherein* 'to carry' + *phagein* 'to eat'.]

oestradiol /eéstrə dī ol, éstrə-/ *n.* an oestrogenic hormone produced in the ovaries and synthesized for use in treating oestrogen deficiency and breast cancer. Formula: $C_{18}H_{24}O_2$. [Mid-20thC. Coined from OESTRUS + DI- + -OL.]

oestral *adj.* = **oestrous**

oestriol /eéstri ol, és-/ *n.* an oestrogen hormone produced in the ovaries, secreted in the urine during pregnancy, and synthesized for use in treating oestrogen deficiency. Formula: $C_{18}H_{24}O_3$. [Early 20thC. Coined from OESTRUS + TRI- + -OL.]

oestrogen /eéstrəjən, éstrəjən/ *n.* any of several steroid hormones produced mainly in the ovaries that stimulate oestrus and the development of female secondary sexual characteristics [Early 20thC. Coined from OESTRUS + -O- + -GEN.] —**oestrogenic** /eéstrə jénnik, éstrə-/ *adj.*

oestrone /eéstrōn, és-/ *n.* an oestrogenic hormone produced in the ovaries and synthesized for use in treating oestrogen deficiency and breast cancer. Formula: $C_{18}H_{22}O_2$. [Early 20thC. Coined from OESTRUS + -ONE.]

oestrous /eéstrəss, és-/, **oestral** /eéstrəl, és-/ *adj.* ZOOL relating to or involving oestrus, or in oestrus

oestrous cycle *n.* a hormonally controlled reproductive cycle occurring in most female mammals, marked by a period of heat followed by ovulation and changes in the uterine lining

oestrus /eéstrəss, és-/ *n.* a regular period of sexual excitement in many female mammals during which the animal is receptive to mating [Late 19thC. Via Latin *oestrus* 'frenzy', from Greek *oistros* 'gad-fly', the underlying sense being 'sting', 'irritation' and hence 'stimulus to action'. Ultimately from an Indo-European word denoting 'passion' that is also the ancestor of English *irate*.]

oeuvre /úrvrə, urvr/ *n.* a work of art or literature, or such works considered as a unit, especially the complete work of a single artist (*formal*) [Late 19thC. Via French from Latin *opera*, the plural of *opus* 'work' (source of English *opus*).]

of (*stressed*) /ov/; (*unstressed*) /əv, ə/ CORE MEANING: used between two nouns, the second providing more information about the first ○ *Most software has complex sets of commands and options.* ○ *She let out a little squeal of delight.*
prep. **1.** **AFFECTED BY ACTION** used to indicate the person or thing affected by or performing an action ○ *the promotion of junior staff* ○ *the death of her father* **2.**

USED IN MEASURING QUANTITIES used after words or phrases expressing quantities to indicate the substance or thing being measured ○ *millions of dollars* ○ *a herd of cows* ○ *10 gallons of oil* **3.** CONNECTED WITH used to indicate the place that sb or sth belongs to or is connected with ○ *the president of France* **4.** CONTAINING containing the substance mentioned ○ *a mug of coffee* ○ *a busload of schoolchildren* **5.** PART OF STH used to indicate a part of sth that is normally considered as a whole ○ *a slice of cake* ○ *a square of fabric* **6.** MADE FROM made from or used as a material to form sth ○ *ruled with a rod of iron* ○ *a paste of flour and water* **7.** INDICATING RELATIONSHIP OR ASSOCIATION used to indicate a relationship, association, or cause ○ *I'll be thinking of you.* ○ *accused of negligence* **8.** RELATING TO used after words describing feelings and qualities to indicate the person or thing they relate to ○ *He's very sure of himself.* ○ *It's very kind of you to come.* **9.** INDICATING A PARTICULAR TYPE used to describe sb or sth in terms of a particular type or kind ○ *one heck of a gymnast* **10.** HAVING A PARTICULAR QUALITY used to indicate a quality that sb or sth has, or the person or thing having a particular quality ○ *announcements of a general nature* ○ *a musician of great talent* ○ *the gentleness of his manner* **11.** INDICATING AMOUNT used to indicate an amount, age, or value ○ *There is a limit of eight characters in a computer user name.* ○ *a young boy of 12* **12.** EVERY used to indicate a day or other period of time when an activity regularly occurs (*informal*) ○ *We usually go out for a meal of a Friday.* **13.** *US* BEFORE before the hour of ○ *It was a quarter of ten before she returned.* **14.** BY used to indicate the agent of an action (*archaic*) (*used in the passive*) ○ *admired of everyone* [Old English. Ultimately from a prehistoric Germanic word that is also the source of English *off* and German *ab* 'away'.]

OF *abbr.* LANG Old French

off /of/ CORE MEANING: a grammatical word used to indicate separation or distance between two points, especially movement away from the speaker ○ (adv) *He ran off before I could stop him.* ○ (prep) *The bottle rolled off the ledge and fell to the floor.*

1. *prep., adv.* SO AS TO LEAVE to come out of or leave a bus, train, or plane ○ *Check you have all your belongings before getting off the bus.* ○ *He got off at the next stop.* **2.** *prep., adv.* SO AS TO KEEP AWAY FROM so as to keep away from, avoid stepping on, or be at a distance from or to the side of ○ *The sign said 'Please keep off the grass'.* ○ *I stepped off the kerb.* **3.** *prep., adv.* AWAY FROM WORK away from work or usual duties owing to illness, holidays, or normal nonwork time ○ *trying to get time off work to visit her in hospital* ○ *I didn't see Jane – it must be her night off.* **4.** *prep., adv.* REDUCED BY so as to be reduced by the amount indicated ○ *10 percent off all swimwear this week* ○ *She knocked £10 off for the slight stain on the sleeve.* **5.** *prep., adv.* IN THE FUTURE a particular distance away in the future ○ *My fortieth birthday is only two years off!* **6.** *prep., adv.* SO AS TO REMOVE so as to eliminate or remove sth from view ○ *The dirt should wash off easily.* ○ *He was rubbing something off the board when I came in.* **7.** *adv.* TO A DISTANT PLACE so as to be away from the present location ○ *He hopped in the car, started it up, and took off.* **8.** *adv.* AWAY at a particular physical distance away ○ *The nearest stop's about two miles off.* **9.** *adv.* MEASURED so as to be divided or measured ○ *Measure the gap, mark it off with a pencil, and cut the wood to size.* **10.** *adv.* TO COMPLETION to the point of completion ○ *We're trying to get our bills paid off.* **11.** *adv.* INTO A PARTICULAR STATE into a particular state, especially an unconscious state ○ *The baby dozed off on the way over here.* **12.** *adv.* COMM REQUIRED NUMBER indicating the number of items required or produced (*preceded by a number*) **13.** *prep.* ABSTAINING FROM no longer participating in or using ○ *stay off caffeine for a week* **14.** *prep.* NOT LIKING no longer inclined towards ○ *I'm really off horror movies at the moment.* **15.** *prep.* ON A DIET OF using as a means of subsistence ○ *living off vegetables from our garden* **16.** *prep.* BRANCHING OUT FROM near or next to, and leading or branching away from ○ *He lives in an apartment block just off the high street.* **17.** *prep.* FROM used to show the object of an action (*nonstandard*) ○ *I got these sunglasses off my sister for my birthday.* **18.** *adv., adj.* NOT IN OPERATION not functioning or in use ○ *Shall I switch the engine off?* ○ *He was always constantly checking to make sure the lights were off.* **19.** *adv., adj.* CANCELLED so as to be no longer taking place ○ *The deal's off.* **20.** *adj.* NO LONGER FRESH smelling and tasting bad because of being no longer fresh ○ *We had to throw the fish away – it was going off.* **21.** *adj.* NOT ON THE MENU no longer on the menu in a restaurant, not being served at the moment ○ *I'm sorry sir, the steak is off.* **22.** *adj.* IN A PARTICULAR CONDITION in a particular condition with regard to sth ○ *How are you off for cash?* **23.** *adj.* NOT CORRECT in error or out of alignment **24.** *adj.* ON THE RIGHT OF situated on the right side of a vehicle, farthest away from the kerb **25.** *adj.* UNACCEPTABLE unacceptable or disappointing, not up to normal standards (informal) ○ *'She turned up two hours late.' 'Well I think that's a bit off.'* **26.** *n.* CRICKET PART OF CRICKET FIELD the side of the cricket field facing the batsman taking strike [Old English. Originally an emphatic variant of OF.] ◇ **off and on** occasionally

off. *abbr.* **1.** officer **2.** office **3.** official

Offa /óffə/, **King of Mercia** (730?–796). He ruled from 757, took control of much of southern England, and built Offa's Dyke.

off-air *adj.* spoken or occurring in broadcasting studios but not used during a broadcast —**off air** *adv.*

offal /óff'l/ *n.* **1.** EDIBLE INTERNAL ORGANS the edible, mainly internal organs of an animal, e.g. the heart, liver, brains, and tongue, sometimes regarded as unpalatable or even inedible **2.** STH THROWN AWAY sth discarded as refuse [14thC. Formed from OFF + FALL; probably modelled on Dutch *afval*.]

Offaly /óffəli/ county in the Republic of Ireland, in Leinster Province. The county town is Tullamore. Population: 59,080 (1996). Area: 1,997 sq. km/771 sq. mi.

Offa's Dyke /óffəz-/ series of earthworks along the border between England and Wales, constructed by King Offa of Mercia between 784 and 796. Length: 240 km/150 mi.

offbeat /óf beet/ *adj.* not conforming to convention or to expectations

off beat *n.* any unaccented beat in a bar of music

off-camera *adj.* out of sight of the camera —**off camera** *adv.*

off-centre *adj.* **1.** NOT AT THE CENTRE not at the centre and therefore sometimes causing a lack of symmetry, balance, or evenness of movement **2.** ECCENTRIC slightly unconventional or eccentric —**off centre** *adv.*

off chance, off-chance *n.* a slight or remote possibility ◇ **on the off chance (that)** just in case sth happens

off-colour *adj.* **1.** ILL ill or not very well ○ *I'm feeling a bit off-colour today.* **2.** RUDE lewd or indelicate (*informal disapproving*) **3.** NOT COLOURED NORMALLY not having the usual or desired colour

off-course *adj.* occurring somewhere other than a racecourse. US term **off-track**

offcut /óf kut/ *n.* a remnant left after the main pieces of sth such as fabric or paper have been cut

Offenbach /óff'n baak/ city in Hesse State, west-central Germany, on the River Main. Population: 116,700 (1994).

Offenbach, Jacques (1819–80) French composer. He wrote witty satirical operettas, one of which includes the famous 'Can-can', as well as the opera *The Tales of Hoffmann* (1880). Born **Jacob Eberst**

offence /ə fénss/ *n.* **1.** LEGAL OR MORAL CRIME an official crime, or a crime against moral, social, or other accepted standards ○ *He was convicted of a motoring offence* **2.** MIL, SPORTS ATTACK an attack or assault, usually in the military or in sports ○ *The army launched its great offence that spring.* **3.** SPORTS ATTACKING PLAYERS ON A TEAM the players making up the part of a team that attempts to score in a game, as distinct from the defence that tries to stop the other team from scoring ○ *We lacked a good offence last spring.* ◊ **defence** **4.** ANGER OR RESENTMENT anger, resentment, hurt, or displeasure ○ *'Please don't take offence'.* ○ *His remarks caused great offence.* **5.** CAUSE OF DISPLEASURE OR ANGER sth that causes displeasure, humiliation, anger, resentment, or hurt ○ *The request was an offence to their dignity.* [14thC. Via French from, ultimately, Latin *offens-*, the past participle stem of *offendere* (see OFFEND).]

offend /ə fénd/ (**-fends, -fending, -fended**) *v.* **1.** *vti.* CAUSE SB ANGER, RESENTMENT, OR HURT to hurt sb's feelings, or cause resentment, irritation, anger, or displeasure ○ *The book offended too many people.* **2.** *vi.* BREAK A LAW to violate a law or code of conduct ○ *he offended against the club's rules of proper dress* [14thC. Directly or via Old French *offendre* from Latin *offendere* 'to strike'. Ultimately from an Indo-European base that is also the ancestor of English *gun*.] —**offender** *n.* —**offending** *adj.*

offense *n.* US = **offence**

offensive /ə fénssiv/ *adj.* **1.** UPSETTING, INSULTING, OR IRRITATING causing anger, resentment, or moral outrage ○ *removed the offensive material from the play* **2.** UNPLEASANT TO THE SENSES causing physical repugnance ○ *an offensive smell* **3.** AGGRESSIVE demonstrating aggression ○ *warned that this would be seen as an offensive action* **4.** USED WHEN ATTACKING used, or designed to be used, when attacking ○ *an offensive weapon* ■ *n.* MIL ATTACK OR ASSAULT an attack, assault, or siege ○ *The platoon braced itself for the dawn offensive.*

offer /óffər/ *vt.* (**-fers, -fering, -fered**) **1.** PRESENT STH FOR ACCEPTANCE OR REJECTION to attempt to give sb sth that may be taken or refused, usually sth desirable ○ *They offered me the job.* **2.** HAVE STH FOR THE USE OF OTHERS to provide sth, or make sth available for those who want it ○ *The town offered many amenities.* **3.** VOLUNTEER TO DO STH to suggest doing sth yourself as a favour for sb else ○ *I offered to bring the salad.* **4.** COMM HAVE STH FOR SALE OR HIRE to present or have sth for sale or hire ○ *the first gym to offer professional trainers at a low cost* **5.** RELIG GIVE AS WORSHIP to present sth to God, often as part of worship ○ *We offer hymns of praise to God.* **6.** EXHIBIT A QUALITY to exhibit or demonstrate a particular quality ○ *The city offered little resistance against the army.* ○ *a plan that offers hope to millions* **7.** COMM MAKE A BID to make a bid or financial proposal for sth ○ *They offered 40 pence a share.* **8.** PRESENT PERFORMANCE to present an exhibition or performance ○ *They offered two films each night.* ■ *n.* **1.** PROPOSAL OF A SUGGESTED GIFT OR ACTION a suggestion from sb to give sth or do sth for sb else ○ *A home-cooked meal and a place to stay: that's the best offer I've had all day!* **2.** COMM FINANCIAL PROPOSAL OR BID a sum of money suggested as payment for sth such as a house ○ *They made an offer for the house but we refused it.* **3.** COMM REDUCED PRICE a reduced price for sth ○ *this week's special offer* **4.** LAW PROPOSAL LEADING TO A BINDING CONTRACT a proposal that, if accepted, creates a binding contract [Old English *offrian*. Via prehistoric Germanic from Latin *offerre*, literally 'to bring to', formed from *ferre* 'to bring'. Ultimately from an Indo-European word (ancestor also of English *bear* 'to carry').] —**offerer** *n.*

offer up *vt.* RELIG = **offer** *v.* 5

offering /óffəring/ *n.* **1.** CONTRIBUTION sth that is offered, or the act of offering ○ *The restaurant had some pretty awful offerings.* **2.** RELIG GIFT FOR GOD sth offered as a sacrifice to a deity **3.** CHR MONEY GIVEN DURING A CHURCH SERVICE a financial contribution to a church, often made during a church service [Old English *offrung*]

offer price *n.* the price at which sth, especially a share of a stock or mutual fund, is offered for sale

offertory /óffərtəri/ (*plural* **-ries**) *n.* **1.** OFFERING OF COMMUNION BREAD AND WINE the offering of the bread and wine during the Christian service of Holy Communion **2.** CHURCH COLLECTION the offering of money or gifts made by a church congregation **3.** PART OF A CHRISTIAN SERVICE a part of a church service during which prayers are said or sung while offerings are received [14thC. Via ecclesiastical Latin *offertorium* 'offering place', from, ultimately, Latin *offerre* (see OFFER).]

off-glide *n.* PHON a sound produced by the vocal organs prior to their making another sound or assuming a neutral position

off-guard *adj.* not paying attention or being prepared for possible attack (*not hyphenated after a verb*) ○ *caught the enemy off-guard*

offhand /of hánd/ *adv.* **1.** CASUALLY casually, thoughtlessly, or spontaneously **2.** WITHOUT PREPARATION

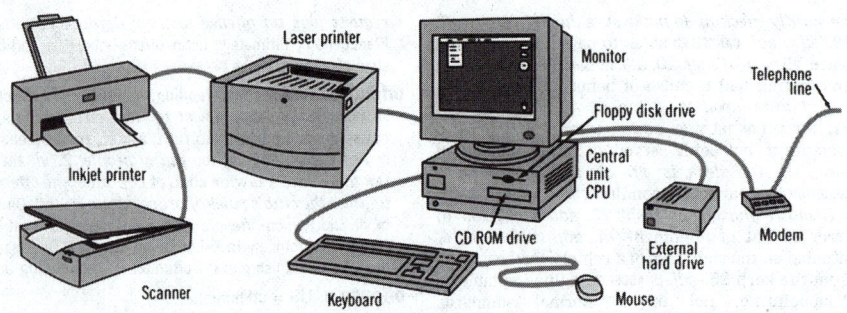

Office: Typical equipment used in an office

without preparation or research ○ *Offhand, I'd say there must be 50 people in there.* ■ *adj.* **offhand, offhanded 1. UNCONCERNED AND UNCARING** so casual, uninterested, or blunt as to appear impolite or uncaring (*disapproving*) ○ *She was pretty offhand about the whole affair.* **2. CASUALLY DONE** taken or made casually or without planning, usually on the spur of the moment ○ *Only through her offhand comment did I realize who she was.*

office /óffiss/ *n.* **1. ROOM USED FOR BUSINESS ACTIVITY** a room in which business or professional activities take place, often occupied by a single person or a single section of the business **2. PLACE OF BUSINESS** the quarters in which a commercial, professional, or government organization carries out its activities **3. OFFICIAL ORGANIZATION** a commercial or professional organization **4. STAFF IN AN OFFICE** the people who work in an office ○ *get-well cards from the office* **5. POL BRITISH GOVERNMENT DEPARTMENT** a department in the British Government ○ *He works for the Home Office.* **6. POL US GOVERNMENT AGENCY OR DEPARTMENT** a US government agency or subdivision, especially of the federal government **7. POSITION OF RESPONSIBILITY** an official post or position of duty, trust, or responsibility ○ *The mayor has been in office four years now.* **8. PLACE FOR TICKETS OR INFORMATION** a booth or other place where tickets or information may be obtained **9. CHR SET FORM OF A CHRISTIAN SERVICE** the prescribed order or form of a Christian church service, or of daily prayers **10. TASK OR ASSIGNMENT** a task, assignment, or chore (*formal*) (*usually used in the plural*) ■ **offices** *npl.* **1. STH DONE ON BEHALF OF ANOTHER** sth said or done by sb to or for another person (*formal*) ○ *I got the job through her kind offices.* **2. AREAS OR BUILDINGS WHERE SERVANTS WORK** the outbuildings or parts of a house in which servants work (*dated*) [13thC. Via French from Latin *officium*, literally 'doing work', from, ultimately, *opus* 'work' + *facere* 'to do'.]

office block *n.* a large building holding offices

office boy *n.* a boy or man who does errands around an office (*dated*)

office building *n.* = office block

office-free *adj.* US relating to or involving a workforce that is not required to work from or at an office

office hours *npl.* the regular times during which a business or profession, or business as a whole, is conducted

office junior *n.* a young office-worker entrusted only with minor clerical tasks

officer /óffissər/ *n.* **1. MIL** SB OF RANK IN THE ARMED FORCES sb in a military force who has rank or authority **2.** = **police officer 3. SHIPPING** SB IN AUTHORITY ON SHIP sb on a civilian ship who has a specialized or responsible post **4. ELECTED OR APPOINTED OFFICIAL** sb who is elected or appointed to an administrative position in a society, corporation, or government department ■ *vt.* (**-cers, -cering, -cered**) MIL, NAVY **SUPPLY STH WITH OFFICERS** to provide sth such as a military unit or a ship with officers

officer of arms *n.* HERALDRY a herald, especially one who devises, grants, or confirms coats of arms

official /ə físh'l/ *n.* **SB HOLDING OFFICE** sb who has a position of authority in an organization, corporation, or government department ■ *adj.* **1. OF A GOVERNMENTAL OR ORGANIZATIONAL OFFICE** relating to or concerned with a governmental or organizational office ○ *official*

rules and regulations **2. AUTHORIZED BY SOME AUTHORITY** approved, recognized, or issued by some authority ○ *No official statement has been issued.* **3. FORMAL** formal or ceremonial ○ *invited to attend the official opening* —**officially** *adv.*

official birthday *n.* in the United Kingdom, a date in June chosen as the occasion on which to celebrate the sovereign's birthday, with formal ceremonies taking place in London

officialdom /ə físh'ldəm/ *n.* bureaucracy and those who work within it, especially when viewed as inefficient or pompous (*informal*) ○ *caught up in the red tape of officialdom*

officialese /ə físhə leéz/ *n.* unclear, pedantic, and verbose language considered characteristic of official documents

officialism /ə físh'lizəm/ *n.* excessive respect or adherence to official routines and regulations, considered to be characteristic of officials (*informal*)

Official Receiver *n.* LAW an official appointed to manage a bankrupt's property prior to the appointment of a trustee

Official Referee *n.* LAW in England, a circuit judge with authority from the High Court to try cases involving examination of accounts or other documents

Official Solicitor *n.* LAW an officer of the Supreme Court of Judicature with special responsibilities for protecting the interests of people with disabilities

officiant /ə físhi ənt/ *n.* sb who conducts a religious ceremony

officiary /ə físhi əri/ *adj.* **DERIVED FROM HOLDING OF OFFICE** derived from the holding of an office, or having a title that is derived from an office held ○ *an officiary title* ■ *n.* (*plural* **-ies**) **OFFICIAL OR BODY OF OFFICIALS** an official or an organized group of officials [Early 17thC. Via medieval Latin *officiarius*, from Latin *officium* (see OFFICE).]

officiate /ə físhi ayt/ (**-ates, -ating, -ated**) *vi.* to preside in an official capacity, especially at a religious ceremony [Mid-17thC. Via medieval Latin *officiat-*, the past participle stem of *officiare* 'to conduct sacred service', from Latin *officium* (see OFFICE).]

officinal /o físsinəl, óffi sínəl/ *n.* PHARM **MEDICINE KEPT IN STOCK** a medicine kept in stock in a pharmacy rather than specially prepared according to a prescription (*archaic*) ■ *adj.* BOT **MEDICINAL** having medicinal properties, especially those recognized by a pharmacopoeia (*archaic*) [Late 17thC. Via medieval Latin *officinalis*, from *officina*, literally 'workshop' (later 'storeroom for medicines'), from Latin *officium* (see OFFICE).] —**officinally** *adv.*

officious /ə físhəss/ *adj.* **1. MEDDLESOME AND INTERFERING** characteristic of sb who is eager to give unwanted help or advice ○ *whisked away our unfinished meal in an officious manner* **2. UNOFFICIAL** unofficial or informal, especially in political or diplomatic dealings **3. HELPFUL** kind and helpful (*archaic*) [Late 15thC. Formed from Latin *officiosus*, from *officium* (see OFFICE). Originally in the sense 'performing a function eagerly'.] —**officiously** *adv.* —**officiousness** *n.*

offing /óffing/ *n.* NAUT the more distant part of the sea seen from the shore [Early 17thC. Origin uncertain: probably formed from OFF.] ◇ **in the offing** expected or likely in the future

offish /óffish/ *adj.* standoffish (*informal*)

off-key *adj.* (*not hyphenated after a verb*) **1. MUSIC OUT OF TUNE** not having the correct pitch **2. INAPPROPRIATE** not usual, conventional, or appropriate ■ *adv.* **OUT OF TUNE** above or below the correct pitch

off-label *adj.* US using or involving the use of a prescription drug to treat a condition for which the drug has not been approved by the US Food and Drug Administration

off-licence *n.* UK a shop or a pub where bottles or cans of alcoholic beverages may be bought for consumption elsewhere

off-limits *adj.* to which entry is forbidden or barred ○ *That part of town was off-limits to us.*

off-line *adj.* **1. COMPUT DISCONNECTED FROM A COMPUTER NETWORK** used to describe a computer terminal or peripheral device that is disconnected or is functioning separately from an associated computer or computer network ○ *The printer was taken off-line for repairs.* ◊ **online 2. COMMUNICATION RELATING TO PREPARING BROADCAST MATERIAL** involved in preparing but not transmitting material for broadcasting ○ *off-line editing* —**off line** *adv.* ◇ **take sth off-line** US to remove sth such as a discussion from a public forum to a more private one, e.g. from a chat room to personal e-mail

off-line newsreader *n.* COMPUT software that allows a user to read newsgroup articles when the computer is not connected to the Internet

offload /of lṓd, óf lōd/ (**-loads, -loading, -loaded**) *v.* **1.** *vti.* **UNLOAD GOODS** to unload goods or a cargo from a vehicle or container ○ *ships waiting to offload* **2.** *vt.* **GET RID OF** to get rid of sth unwanted by passing it on to sb else ○ *managed to offload some of the work onto colleagues* **3.** *vti.* **UNBURDEN YOURSELF** to relieve yourself of a stressful emotion such as anxiety or frustration by talking to someone (*informal*) **4.** *vti.* COMPUT **TRANSFER DATA** to transfer data from one computer to another in order to create spare capacity in the original computer

off-message *adj.* not following the official policy of a political party or other organization ○ *off-message MPs*

off-peak *adj.* relating to the periods outside that of maximum use, frequency, or demand —**off peak** *adv.*

off-piste *adj.* relating to or taking place on fresh trackless snow that is away from the regular skiing runs —**off piste** *adv.*

off-plan *adj.* based only on the plans of a building that has not yet been built —**off plan** *adv.*

offprint /óf print/ *n.* a separate printing of a single article from a periodical, often given in small quantities to each individual contributor

off-putting *adj.* arousing irritation, repugnance, or mild unease —**offputtingly** *adv.*

off-ramp *n.* US a one-way road serving as an exit from a main highway

off-rhyme *n.* POETRY a partial or near rhyme

off-road *adj.* designed, manufactured, or used for travel off public roads, especially over rough terrain

off-road vehicle *n.* any motorized vehicle designed or used for travel away from public roads or on rough terrain

off-sales *npl.* the sales within a pub of alcoholic beverages for consumption elsewhere ○ *Off-sales amounted to about 10% of gross takings.*

offscourings /óf skowringz/ *npl.* the leftover or discarded parts of sth

off-screen *adj.* **1. NOT VISIBLE ON A SCREEN** not visible on a television or cinema screen ○ *an off-screen commentator* **2. OCCURRING IN ORDINARY LIFE** occurring in ordinary life, not as fiction on television or in a film ○ *Her off-screen life was just as exciting.* ■ *adv.* **IN ORDINARY LIFE** aside from television or film performances ○ *Off-screen, he mostly played golf.*

off-season *n.* **TIME OF LESS ACTIVITY** a time of year when activity or business is at a low level (*often used before a noun*) ○ *Hotel rooms were cheaper in the off-season.* ■ *adv.* **IN THE OFF-SEASON** during the off-season ○ *He liked to travel off-season.*

offset *n.* /óf set/ **1.** STH COUNTERBALANCING STH ELSE sth that counterbalances or compensates, or an allowance made in order to counterbalance sth (*often used before a noun*) **2.** BEGINNING the beginning of sth (*dated*) **3.** STH SET APART anything set apart from sth else (*often used before a noun*) **4.** BOT OFFSHOOT CAPABLE OF PROPAGATION an offshoot or runner from the base of a plant that can propagate the plant **5.** PRINTING PRINTING PROCESS USING INK TRANSFER a method of printing in which inked impressions are transferred onto paper from another surface (*often used before a noun*) **6.** PRINTING UNINTENTIONAL MARKING FROM WET INK an accidental transfer of ink, usually from one piece of paper to another (*often used before a noun*) **7.** GEOL SPUR IN A MOUNTAIN RANGE a projecting spur or ridge in a mountain range (*often used before a noun*) **8.** GEOL HORIZONTAL DISPLACEMENT OF ROCK the horizontal displacement that occurs as a result of the movement of a rock mass along a fault **9.** ARCHIT = setback *n.* 2 **10.** SURVEYING LINE a short distance measured at right angles from a main survey line, used in finding the area of a piece of land **11.** CONSTR ABRUPT BEND IN A STRAIGHT LINE an abrupt bend put into an otherwise straight bar or pipe in order to avoid an obstruction **12.** GENETICS OFFSHOOT OR DESCENDANT sth that has developed from sth else, e.g. a collateral descendant or group of descendants of a family ■ *v.* /of sét, óf set/ (-sets, -setting, -set) **1.** *vt.* COUNTERACT STH to balance or make up for sth (*often passive*) ○ *These improved sales were offset by last month's losses.* **2.** *vti.* PRINTING PRINT STH BY TRANSFER to print sth by offset printing, or to accidentally transfer ink by an offset **3.** *vti.* CONSTR FORM OR BE AN OFFSET IN STH to make an offset in sth such as a wall or pipe, or to be formed into an offset —**offset** /óf sét/ *adv.*

offshoot /óf shoot/ *n.* **1.** PLANTS SHOOT FROM THE MAIN STEM OF PLANT a branch or shoot growing from the main stem of a plant **2.** STH THAT COMES FROM STH ELSE sth that springs or spreads from or that is a subsidiary of a main source or origin ○ *The company was an offshoot of their leisure empire.*

offshore *adv.* /of sháwr/ **1.** FROM WATER TO LAND on or over land that is near water, especially from a body of water ○ *An icy wind blew offshore.* **2.** IN WATER SOME WAY FROM SHORE in a body of water at some distance from the shore ○ *anchored offshore* ■ *adj.* when attributive /óf shawr/ **1.** BLOWING FROM WATER TO LAND blowing or moving from water to land ○ *offshore breezes* **2.** AT SEA SOME WAY FROM SHORE located at sea a considerable distance from shore **3.** FIN IN FOREIGN COUNTRY based in a foreign country, usually in order to avoid taxes

offside *adj.* when attributive /óf sīd/ **ILLEGALLY BEYOND THE BALL** illegally beyond or in advance of a ball or puck during play ■ *n.* /óf sīd/ AUTOMOT DRIVER'S SIDE OF VEHICLE the side of a motor vehicle away from the edge of the road, which when driving on the left of the road, as in the United Kingdom, is the right side of the vehicle. When driving is on the right of the road, as in North America and continental Europe, it is the left side of the vehicle. ○ *The offside wing mirror had been knocked off.* —**offside** /óf sīd/ *adv.*

offsider /óf sīdər/ *n.* Aus a male or female assistant ○ *Tony, my offsider, will meet you at the airport.*

offspring /óf spring/ (*plural* -spring *or* -springs) *n.* **1.** DESCENDANTS the descendants of people, animals, or sometimes plants **2.** RESULT OF STH the product, consequence, or effect of sth

offstage /óf stáyj/ *adv.* **1.** THEATRE OUTSIDE ACTING AREA away from the area of the stage used for a performance, usually out of the view of the audience **2.** IN PRIVATE LIFE in private life, especially as opposed to the character an actor plays or the personality a performer projects **3.** OUT OF PUBLIC VIEW unseen by the public and media ■ *adj.* **1.** THEATRE HAPPENING OFFSTAGE happening or situated outside the area of the stage visible to the audience **2.** PRIVATE occurring in or characteristic of sb's private life **3.** HAPPENING UNSEEN occurring out of the gaze of the public and the media

off-street *adj.* not in a street but in a car park, driveway, or another place

off-the-books *adj.* US **1.** NOT WRITTEN IN ACCOUNT BOOKS not recorded in the accounts of a company **2.** NOT

DECLARED FOR TAX not registered for the purposes of paying income tax

off-the-cuff *adj.* delivered spontaneously or without preparation or notes [From the custom of scribbling extempore remarks on a starched shirt cuff] —**off the cuff** *adv.*

off-the-peg *adj.* ready-made and sold in standard sizes, not tailored for the individual customer. US term **off-the-rack** —**off the peg** *adv.*

off-the-record *adj.* not intended for publication or to be attributed by name to the person who said it —**off the record** *adv.*

off-the-shelf *adj.* **1.** FROM EXISTING STOCK readily obtainable or taken from an existing stock of merchandise or supplies ○ *a mix of components that were both cheap and off the shelf* **2.** REGISTERED TO BE SOLD officially registered with the Registrar of Companies solely in order to be sold (*not hyphenated when used after a verb*) —**off the shelf** *adv.*

off-the-wall *adj.* unusual or unconventional in a way that is particularly bizarre (*informal*) [Late 20thC. Perhaps from the expression *bouncing off the walls*, ill, an allusion to the padded cells once used to contain people with psychiatric disorders.] —**off the wall** *adv.*

off-track *adj.* US = off-course

off-white *adj.* of a very pale colour, e.g. cream, that is a shade or two away from pure white —**off-white** *n.*

OFGAS /óff gass/, **Ofgas** *n.* a regulatory body set up to supervise the gas industry in the United Kingdom after privatization and deregulation. Full form **Office of Gas Supply**

O'Flaherty /ō fláhərti, ō flaá-/, **Liam** (1896–1984) Irish novelist. His works, notable for their realism and drama, include *The Informer* (1925).

OFM *abbr.* Order of Minor Friars (*a name used by the Franciscan friars*) [Latin, *Ordo Fratrum Minorum*]

OFris. *abbr.* Old Frisian

OFS *abbr.* Orange Free State

OFSTED /óff sted/, **Ofsted** *n.* the government department that monitors educational quality in schools and colleges in England and Wales. Full form **Office for Standards in Education**

oft /oft/ *adv.* often (*archaic or literary; often used in combination*) [Old English. Related to German *oft* and Swedish *ofta*.]

OFT *abbr.* Office of Fair Trading

OFTEL /óff tel/, **Oftel** *n.* a regulatory body set up to supervise the telecommunications industry in the United Kingdom after privatization and deregulation. Full form **Office of Telecommunications**

often /óff'n, óftən/ *adv.* at short intervals or repeatedly [13thC. An alteration of OFT, probably influenced by *selden* 'seldom'.] ◇ **every so often** regularly but with fairly long intervals between each occurrence ◇ **more often than not**, **as often as not** fairly frequently, or in a majority of instances

oftentimes /óff'n tīmz, óftən-/, **ofttimes** /óft tīmz/ *adv.* frequently (*archaic or literary*)

OFWAT /óff wot/, **Ofwat** *n.* a regulatory body set up to supervise water services in the United Kingdom after privatization and deregulation. Full form **Office of Water Services**

OG *abbr.* **1.** Officer of the Guard **2.** STAMPS original gum

o.g. *abbr.* SPORTS own goal

ogam *n.* = ogham

Ogbomosho /ógbə mósh ō/ *city in Oyo state, southwestern Nigeria, situated approximately 201 km/125 mi. northeast of Lagos. Population: 660,600 (1992).

Ogdon /ógdən/, **John** (1937–89) British pianist and composer. He was an ebullient champion of neglected virtuoso pieces and of 20th-century music. Full name **John Andrew Howard Ogdon**

ogee /ō jee/ *n.* **1.** S-SHAPED CURVE a decorative double curve like an elongated and flattened S **2.** S-SHAPED MOULDING a decorative moulding with an ogee-shaped profile **3.** = ogee arch [Late 17thC. An alteration of OGIVE.]

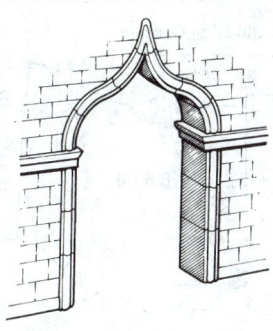

Ogee arch

ogee arch *n.* an arch whose sides curve gently inwards near the top and then curve upwards steeply to meet in a point

Ogen melon /ógen-/ *n.* a small variety of melon with a green skin and sweet pale green flesh [Named after *Ogen*, a kibbutz in Israel where it was developed]

ogham /óggəm/, **ogam** *n.* **1.** ANCIENT CELTIC WRITING SYSTEM an ancient British and Irish Celtic alphabet consisting of twenty characters formed by inscribing lines on either side of or across a long straight baseline **2.** CELTIC LETTER any of the characters used in the ogham alphabet **3.** CELTIC INSCRIPTION an inscription written in ogham, or a stone bearing such an inscription [Early 18thC. Via modern Irish from Old Irish *ogam*, named after *Ogma*, the Celtic god who supposedly invented it.]

ogive /ō jīv/ *n.* **1.** ARCHIT RIB IN GOTHIC VAULT a diagonal rib in a Gothic vault **2.** ARCHIT POINTED ARCH an arch that rises to a sharp point **3.** STATS CUMULATIVE FREQUENCY GRAPH a graph or curve that represents the cumulative frequencies of a set of values [Origin uncertain; perhaps via Old French *augive* from, ultimately, late Latin *obviare* 'to resist']

ogle /óg'l/ *vti.* (**ogles, ogling, ogled**) STARE AT SB LUSTFULLY to look at sb for sexual enjoyment or as a way of showing sexual interest ■ *n.* DESIROUS LOOK a prolonged flirtatious or lustful look at sb [Late 17thC. Origin uncertain: possibly from Low German *oegeln* 'to keep eyeing', from *oege* 'eye'. Related to Old English *ēage* 'eye'.] —**ogler** *n.*

─── **WORD KEY: SYNONYMS** ───
See Synonyms at **gaze**.

Ogooué /o gō way/ *river in Gabon, western-central Africa. Length: 970 km/683 mi.

O grade *n.* Scotland the lower-level examination for the Scottish Certificate of Education, now replaced by Standard grade. Full form **Ordinary grade**

ogre /ógər/ *n.* **1.** WICKED MONSTER a wicked giant or monster in fairy tales, especially one who eats people **2.** FRIGHTENING PERSON a person who is particularly unpleasant and frightening —**ogreish** *adj.*

ogress /ógriss/ *n.* **1.** WICKED FEMALE MONSTER a wicked female giant or monster in fairy tales, especially one who eats people **2.** OFFENSIVE TERM an offensive term that deliberately insults a woman's appearance and temperament [Early 18thC]

Ogun /ō gōon/ *state in southwestern Nigeria, north of Lagos State. Capital: Abeokuta. Population: 2,338,570 (1991). Area: 16,762 sq. km/6,472 sq. mi.

oh /ō/ *interj.* **1.** USED TO EXPRESS STRONG EMOTION used to express a strong emotional reaction to sth, e.g. surprise, shock, pain, or extreme pleasure ○ *Oh! That's wonderful news!* **2.** USED TO INTRODUCE STRONG REACTION used to introduce short phrases that express a strong emotion, e.g. anger, shock, delight, or triumph ○ *Oh what a fool I've been* **3.** USED TO INTRODUCE RESPONSE used to introduce a response to what sb has just said or asked ○ *Oh, I'm fine. How are you?* **4.** USED TO SHOW THOUGHT used to indicate thought or hesitation concerning what will be said next ○ *We've got, oh, fifteen minutes before the bus is due.* **5.** USED TO ATTRACT ATTENTION used to attract sb's attention or call attention to sth ○ *Oh, John, can you come over here a minute?* [Mid-16thC. An alteration of O.]

OH *abbr.* Ohio

OHG *abbr.* Old High German

Ohio

Ohio /ō hī´ō/ state of the United States bordered by Michigan, Lake Erie, Pennsylvania, West Virginia, Kentucky, and Indiana. Capital: Columbus. Population: 11,186,331 (1997). Area: 116,104 sq. km/44,828 sq. mi. —**Ohioan** *adj., n.*

ohm /ōm/ *n.* the SI unit of electrical resistance, equal to the resistance between two points on a conductor when a potential difference of 1 volt produces a current of 1 ampere. Symbol Ω [Mid-19thC. Named after Georg Simon Ohm, who studied the measurement of electrical resistance.]

Ohm /ōm/, **Georg Simon** (1787–1854) German physicist. His research on electric currents led to the formulation of Ohm's law. The ohm is named after him.

ohmage /ō´mij/ *n.* electrical resistance measured in ohms

ohmmeter /ōm´meetər/ *n.* an instrument that measures electrical resistance in ohms

OHMS *abbr.* On Her (or His) Majesty's Service

Ohm's law *n.* the law of physics that states that electric current is directly proportional to the voltage applied to a conductor and inversely proportional to that conductor's resistance [Named after Georg Simon Ohm, who formulated it]

oho /ō hō´/ *interj.* used to express surprise or exultation, e.g. at making a discovery [14thC. Formed from O + HO.]

OHP *abbr.* overhead projector

OHV *abbr.* **1.** off-highway vehicle **2. OHV, o.h.v.** MECH ENG overhead valve

-oid *suffix.* like, resembling, related to ○ *toxoid* ○ *cylindroid* [From Greek *-oeidēs*, from *eidos* 'form, shape' (see IDOL)]

oidium /ō idd´i əm/ *n.* (*plural* **-a** /ō idd´i ə/) *n.* a thin-walled egg-shaped fungal spore produced by the fragmentation of a hypha [Mid-19thC. Via modern Latin, genus name, from Greek *ōion* 'egg' (see OO-).]

oik /oyk/ *n.* sb, usually a man, who is considered to be ill-mannered, ignorant, and socially inferior (*informal insult*) [Early 20thC. Origin unknown.]

oil /oyl/ *n.* **1. THICK GREASY LIQUID** a liquid fat obtained from plant seeds, animal fats, mineral deposits, and other sources that is thicker than and does not dissolve in water and will burn. Oils are used for a wide variety of purposes, most commonly as lubricants and fuels and in cooking. **2. PETROLEUM** petroleum, the crude product that is distilled and refined to produce a wide variety of industrial oils and oil-based products (*often used before a noun*) ○ *oil prices* **3. PETROLEUM DERIVATIVE** any of various liquids extracted from petroleum, e.g. paraffin and motor oil, that are used as domestic fuels or as machinery and engine lubricants (*often used before a noun*) **4. PETROLEUM INDUSTRY** the worldwide industry that is based on petroleum extraction and refining (*often used before a noun*) ○ *oil companies* **5. THICK LIQUID CONTAINING OIL** a thick liquid containing oil or with the consistency of oil, especially a cosmetic **6.** = **oil paint** (*usually used in the plural*) **7. OIL PAINTING** a painting done in oil paints ■ *v.* (**oils, oiling, oiled**) **1.** *vt.* **APPLY OIL TO STH** to put oil into or onto sth in order to lubricate, polish, preserve, or soften it ○ *oiling the rusty gears* **2.** *vti.* **FUEL** to take on oil as a fuel, or supply a ship with oil **3.** *vti.* **TURN INTO OIL** to

become an oily liquid, or turn a solid fat, e.g. butter or lard, into an oily liquid [12thC. From Old French, via Latin *oleum* 'olive oil' from Greek *elaion*, from *elaia* 'olive' (source of English *oil*).] ◇ **burn the midnight oil** to work or study until very late at night

oil beetle *n.* a beetle that emits a foul-smelling oily substance from the joints of its legs to deter predators. Family: Meloidae.

oilbird /oyl´ burd/ *n.* a Central and South American bird whose young have fatty flesh that was once used as a source of oil for cooking and lighting. Latin name: *Steatornis caripensis.*

oil cake *n.* the solid residue remaining after extraction of the oil from some seeds, e.g. cottonseed and linseed. It is used as livestock feed.

oilcan /oyl´ kan/ *n.* a metal container with a long thin spout, used to squirt lubricating oil into machinery

oilcloth /oyl´ kloth/ *n.* cloth that has been treated with oil or a synthetic resin to make it waterproof, often used as a wipe-clean covering for tables (*often used before a noun*)

oil-cooled *adj.* with a cooling system that uses oil

oil drum *n.* a large metal cylinder designed for transporting and storing oil. Empty oil drums are often used as refuse containers, flotation devices, and braziers and to make instruments for steel bands.

oiled /oyld/ *adj.* treated with oil, usually for waterproofing or lubrication

oiler /oyl´ər/ *n.* **1. REFUELLING TANKER** an oil tanker, especially one that refuels ships at sea **2. OIL-FUELLED SHIP** a ship that uses oil as fuel **3. OIL WELL** an oil well (*informal*)

oil field /oyl´ feeld/, **oilfield** *n.* an area of land or sea under which there are substantial reserves of petroleum, especially one that is being exploited

oil-fired *adj.* burning oil as a fuel

oil gland *n.* a gland at the base of a bird's tail that secretes an oily substance that the bird uses to preen and waterproof its feathers

oilman /oyl´ man, óylmən/ (*plural* **-men** /-men, -mən/) *n.* **1. OIL EXECUTIVE** an executive in the petroleum industry **2. OIL FIELD WORKER** sb who works in an oil field

oil of cloves *n.* an essential oil extracted from clove flowers, used to relieve toothache and used by dentists, mixed with zinc oxide, to form a pain-killing cement for use in temporary fillings

oil of wintergreen *n.* an aromatic oil obtained from an evergreen North American shrub, used medicinally in liniments and also as a flavouring in food. It is the methyl ester of salicylic acid.

oil paint *n.* a paint that consists of pigment mixed with a drying oil

oil painting *n.* **1. PICTURE USING OIL PAINTS** a picture painted with oil paints **2. USE OF OIL PAINTS** the art of painting with oil paints ◇ **be no oil painting** to be physically unattractive, especially to have an unattractive face

oil palm *n.* an African palm tree whose fruit and seeds are the source of palm oil. Latin name: *Elaeis guineensis.*

oil pan *n. US* = sump

oil rig *n.* the equipment used for drilling for oil, including the platform that supports the drilling equipment

oil shale *n.* a black or dark brown type of shale from which petroleum can be extracted by distillation

oilskin /oyl´ skin/ *n.* **1. WATERPROOF FABRIC** cotton fabric that has been treated with oil to make it waterproof **2. WATERPROOF GARMENT** a garment, especially a coat, made of oilskin ■ **oilskins** *npl.* **WATERPROOF CLOTHING** waterproof overgarments consisting of a coat and trousers made of oilskin

oil slick *n.* a film of oil covering part of the surface of sth, especially a large expanse of oil floating on the sea following a spillage of oil from an oil tanker

oilstone /oyl´ stōn/ *n.* a fine-grained stone that is lubricated with oil and used to sharpen cutting tools

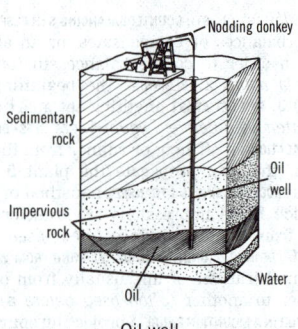

Oil well

oil well *n.* a shaft drilled into the earth or the bottom of the sea, through which petroleum is extracted

oily /óyli/ (**-ier, -iest**) *adj.* **1. DIRTY WITH OIL** covered, smeared, or dirtied with oil ○ *don't want to get my hands oily* **2. CONTAINING OIL** containing or producing a lot of oil **3. LIKE OIL** reminiscent of oil in texture, smell, or taste **4. INGRATIATING** unpleasantly eager to please or charm, or distressingly expert at doing this (*disapproving*) —**oiliness** *n.*

oink /oyngk/ *interj., n.* **PIG SOUND** a word used for the nasal grunting sound made by a pig ■ *vi.* (**oinks, oinking, oinked**) **MAKE PIG SOUND** to make the nasal grunting sound of a pig [Mid-20thC. An imitation of the sound.]

ointment /óyntmənt/ *n.* a smooth greasy substance used on the skin to soothe soreness or itchiness, help wounds heal, or make the skin softer [13thC. Via Old French *oignement* from, ultimately, Latin *unguentum* (source of English *unguent, unctuous,* and *anoint*).]

OIRO *abbr.* offers in the region of

Oise /waz/ river in western Europe, flowing from southern Belgium through France and into the Seine. Length: 299 km/186 mi.

Oita /óytə/ city and seaport in Japan. It is the capital of Oita prefecture, on northeastern Kyushu Island. Population: 417,051 (1992).

OJ, oj *abbr.* orange juice

Ojibwa /ō jíbbwə/ (*plural* **-was** or **-wa**), **Ojibway** /ō jíb way/ (*plural* **-ways** or **-way**) *n.* **1. NATIVE N AMERICAN PEOPLE** a Native North American people who once lived north of Lake Huron but who later moved into territories ranging from Saskatchewan across to Michigan **2. NATIVE N AMERICAN LANGUAGE** the Algonquian language spoken by the Ojibwa [Early 18thC. From Ojibwa *ojibwe.*] —**Ojibwa** *adj.*

OJT *abbr.* on-the-job training

OK[1] /ō káy/, **okay** *interj.* (*informal*) **1. INDICATING AGREEMENT** used to indicate agreement to or approval of what sb said or did ○ *'Can you help?' 'OK. What do you want me to do?'* **2. USED TO CHECK FOR APPROVAL** used at the end of a statement to inquire whether sb has understood and agrees with or approves of what was said ○ *It's your job to make the arrangements, OK?* **3. USED TO INDICATE FINISHING STH** used to indicate that sth is finished and that sth else will now be done or discussed ○ *OK, let's move to the next item on the agenda.* ■ *adj.* (*informal*) **1. PASSABLE** acceptable or tolerable but not exceptional ○ *It's OK for a first effort.* **2. RATHER GOOD OR PLEASANT** better than just satisfactory or acceptable ○ *Her parents are OK; we get on quite well.* **3. PHYSICALLY WELL** in good health or condition ○ *I'll be OK if I can just sit down for a minute.* **4. ALLOWABLE** acceptable to sb or permissible ○ *Is it OK for me to call home on the office phone?* ■ *adv.* **FAIRLY WELL** in an acceptable, tolerable, or satisfactory manner (*informal*) ○ *Everything's going OK, except that we're a little bit behind schedule.* ■ *vt.* (**OK's, OK'ing, OK'ed; okays, okaying, okayed**) (*informal*) **1. GIVE APPROVAL FOR STH** to approve of or consent to sth ○ *I just need you to OK the agenda.* **2. OBTAIN SB'S CONSENT** to obtain sb's approval of or consent to sth ○ *I'll need to OK that with my boss.* ■ *n.* (*plural* **OK's**) **APPROVAL** approval to do sth or consent to sth (*informal*) ○ *As soon as she gives the OK, we'll start work.* [Mid-19thC. Origin uncertain.]

Of the many competing theories about the origins of **OK**, the one now most widely accepted is that the letters stand for *oll* or *orl korrect*, a facetious early 19th-century American phonetic spelling of *all correct*, and that this was reinforced by the fact that they were also coincidentally the initial letters of *Old Kinderhook*, the nickname of US president Martin Van Buren (who was born in Kinderhook, New York State), which were used as a slogan in the presidential election of 1840 (a year after the first record of **OK** in print).

OK[2] *abbr.* Oklahoma

Okanagan /ókə náagən/ (*plural* -**gans** *or* -**gan**), **Okanogan** /ókə nógən/ (*plural* -**ans** *or* -**an**) *n.* **1.** NATIVE N AMERICAN PEOPLE a member of a Native North American people who live in and around the Okanagan river valley that runs from British Columbia down through Washington State **2.** LANG = **Okinagan** — **Okanagan** *adj.*

Okanagan, Lake /ókə náagən/ lake in southern British Columbia, Canada. Area: 352 sq. km/136 sq. mi.

Okapi

okapi /ō káapi/ (*plural* -**pis** *or* -**pi**) *n.* a plant-eating mammal of central Africa that looks rather like a small giraffe without the long neck. It is chestnut brown with white stripes on its hindquarters. Latin name: *Okapia johnstoni*. [Early 20thC. From an African language.]

Okavango /ókə váng gō/ river in south-central Africa, rising in Angola, where it is called Cubango, and flowing through Namibia and Botswana into the Okavango Swamp. Length: 1,600 km/1,000 mi.

Okavango Swamp marsh region in northwestern Botswana, southern Africa, occupying an inland drainage basin. Area: 16,800 sq. km/6,500 sq. mi.

okay *interj., adj., adv., vt., n.* = **OK**[1]

Okayama /ókə yáamə/ city and port in Japan, on western Honshu Island, on the Inland Sea. Population: 593,730 (1990).

Okeechobee, Lake /óki chóbi/ lake in Florida, north of the Everglades, forming part of the Cross-Florida Waterway. Area: 1,717 sq. km/663 sq. mi.

O'Keefe /ō keéf/, **Johnny** (1935–78) Australian singer. He is considered Australia's first rock-and-roll star. Full name **John Michael O'Keefe**

Georgia O'Keeffe

O'Keeffe /ō keéf/, **Georgia** (1887–1986) US artist. She is known for her stylized still lifes, notably of flowers and objects found in the desert.

Okefenokee Swamp /ókifi nóki-/ marsh region in southeastern Georgia and northeastern Florida, It is noted for its rich wildlife. Area: 1,709 sq. km/660 sq. mi.

okeydokey /óki dóki/, **okeydoke** /óki dók/ *interj.* OK (*informal humorous*) [Mid-20thC. An alteration of OK[1].]

Okhotsk, Sea of /ō kótsk, ō khótsk/ sea lying off the eastern coast of Siberia, part of the northwestern Pacific Ocean. Area: 1,530,000 sq. km/590,000 sq. mi.

Okie /óki/ *n. US* **1.** OFFENSIVE TERM an offensive term for a poor migrant farm labourer in the United States, especially one from Oklahoma or neighbouring Dust Bowl states during the 1930s (*slang insult*) **2.** OKLAHOMAN sb who was born or who lives in Oklahoma (*slang*)

Okinagan /óki náagən/ *n.* a Native North American language spoken by the Okanagan people. It belongs to the Salishan branch of Algonquian-Wakashan languages.

Okinawa /óki náawə/ **1.** city on south-central Okinawa Island, Japan. Population: 105,845 (1990). **2.** the largest of the Ryukyu Islands in southwestern Japan, between the East China Sea and the North Pacific Ocean. Area: 1,176 sq. km/454 sq. mi.

Okla. *abbr.* Oklahoma

Oklahoma

Oklahoma /óklə hómə/ state of the United States bordered by Colorado, Kansas, Missouri, Arkansas, Texas, and New Mexico. Capital: Oklahoma City. Population: 3,317,091 (1997). Area: 181,048 sq. km/69,903 sq. mi. —**Oklahoman** /óklə hómən/ *adj., n.*

Oklahoma City capital city of Oklahoma State, located in the central part of the state. Population: 463,201 (1994).

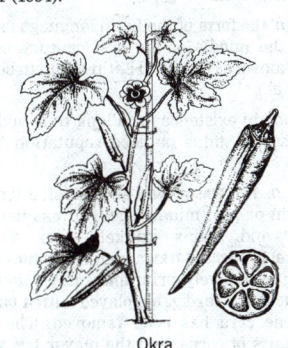
Okra

okra /ókrə, ókrə/ (*plural* **okra** *or* **okras**) *n.* **1.** PLANT WITH FINGER-SHAPED PODS a tall tropical Asian plant cultivated in warmer regions for its edible, usually green pods that are about as long as a finger. Latin name: *Abelmoschus esculentus*. **2.** POD USED AS VEGETABLE a pod from the okra plant, used as a vegetable and in soups and stews as a thickener [Early 18thC. Of West African origin, related to Igbo *okuro*.]

okta /óktə/ *n.* a unit of measure used to specify the amount of cloud cover, especially over an airfield, equivalent to enough cloud to cover one eighth of the sky [Mid-20thC. An alteration of OCTO-.]

-ol[1] *suffix.* compound containing hydroxyl, especially an alcohol or phenol ○ *glycerol* [From ALCOHOL]

-ol[2] *suffix.* = -ole

Olaf II /óləf/, **Olav II, St, King of Norway** (995–1030). During his reign (1015–28), he completed the conversion of Norway to Christianity. He was ousted by the Danes and killed in battle. Full name **Olaf Haraldsson**

Öland /ö land/ island of Sweden, located in the southwestern Baltic Sea. Population: 25,781 (1994). Area: 1,342 sq. km/518 sq. mi.

old /ōld/ *adj.* (**older, oldest**) **1.** HAVING LIVED LONG having lived for many years compared to others **2.** ORIGINATING YEARS AGO made, produced, or originating many years ago and still in existence **3.** ELDERLY showing physical or mental characteristics sometimes associated with long life **4.** WISE showing the understanding, wisdom, or behaviour that results from long experience of life ○ *She acts much older than she is.* **5.** EXISTING FOR SPECIFIED TIME having lived or existed for a specified amount of time (*usually used in combination*) ○ *The day was only a few hours old.* **6.** ANCIENT from the remote past ○ *the remains of an old civilization* **7.** FORMER from an earlier period of sth such as sb's life ○ *We drove past my old school.* **8.** FAMILIAR familiar from past experience ○ *She always makes the same old excuses.* **9.** EXISTING OR USED OVER TIME having existed or been used for a long time, especially if showing wear or age ○ *Change into old clothes before gardening.* **10.** EXPERIENCED skilled or knowledgeable as a result of much experience over time ○ *Take advice from someone who's an old hand at this work.* **11. old, Old** EARLIER existing before one or all of the other stages, forms, or instances of sth ○ *Old English words* **12.** USED FOR EMPHASIS used as an intensifier (*informal*) ○ *any old reason* **13.** EXPRESSING FAMILIARITY used to express affection or familiarity (*informal*) ○ *Good old Charlie!* **14.** US ANNOYINGLY FAMILIAR annoyingly familiar, especially as a result of repetition (*informal*) ○ *the kind of routine that gets old fast* **15.** GEOL, GEOG ERODED reduced through erosion and weathering. ◊ **young** **16.** GEOL, GEOG SLOWER-MOVING characterized by slower moving water and broad, flat floodplains. ◊ **young** ■ *n.* **1.** PERSON OF PARTICULAR AGE sb of a particular age (*used in combination*) ○ *childcare for three- and four-year-olds* **2.** OLD THINGS a thing or things that are old ○ *to balance the old with the new* **3.** *Aus* DARK BEER a dark beer brewed by top fermentation ■ *npl.* OFFENSIVE TERM an offensive term for people who have lived a long time (*offensive*) [Old English *eald* (source of *alderman*). Related to Dutch *oud* and German *alt*.]

Old is ultimately from an Indo-European word meaning 'to grow, nourish', which is also the ancestor of English *adult*, *alumnus*, and *alimony*. In Latin the meaning evolved into 'high', as seen in the English derivatives *altitude*, *exalt*, and *haughty*, whereas the Germanic languages preserved an old past participle meaning 'grown, old', which is also the ancestor of English *elder*, *eldest*, and *world*.

old age *n.* the latter years of sb's life lived out to its full term. ◊ **middle age**

Old Bill *n.* the police, or an individual police officer or a group of police (*slang*) ○ *Better watch it, lads, here come the Old Bill.* [Origin uncertain: probably from a moustached cartoon character created by Captain Bruce Bairnsfather (1887–1959), who was used in a recruitment campaign for the metropolitan police]

old boy *n.* **1.** FORMER STUDENT a former student at a boys' or men's school, especially a British public school or college **2.** MALE SENIOR CITIZEN a man who has reached an advanced age (*offensive*) **3.** FAMILIAR ADDRESS TO MAN a familiar way of addressing a man or boy (*dated informal*) ○ *See here, old boy, you can't enter this club uninvited.* [In school sense modelled on *new boy*]

old-boy network *n.* a system of informal contacts between men who belong to a particular group, especially former members of a school or university, and use their influence to help one another

Old Church Slavonic *n.* the earliest written Slavonic language, into which the Bible was translated in the ninth century. It is still used in religious services in some Eastern Orthodox Churches.

old country *n.* an immigrant's country of origin

Old Dart n. Aus the United Kingdom (informal ironic) [Dart from a dialect pronunciation of DIRT]

old dear n. a woman who has reached an advanced age (offensive)

olden /óldən/ adj. in or from the distant past (archaic or literary) [14thC. Formed from OLD + -EN.]

Old English n. 1. LANG EARLIEST FORM OF ENGLISH the earliest form of the English language, used up to around AD 1150. Its three main dialects were West Saxon, Kentish, and Anglian. It was first written using the runic alphabet. ◊ Middle English, Modern English 2. PRINTING TYPEFACE a form of black letter typeface used by English printers up to the 18th century —**Old English** adj.

Old English sheepdog

Old English sheepdog n. a large dog with a long shaggy coat and dark grey and white markings [Because they were originally bred in England]

olde-worlde /óldi wúrldi/ adj. quaintly historical in a way that may or may not be genuine [An alteration to resemble early English spellings]

old face n. a typeface that shows little difference between light and heavy strokes and has slanting serifs. It originated in the 18th century. US term **old style**

oldfangled /óld fáng g'ld/ adj. antiquated or out of date [Mid-19thC. Modelled on NEWFANGLED.]

old fart n. an offensive term referring to sb, usually a person in authority, who is regarded as being set in his or her ways and as lacking a sense of humour or fun (slang insult)

old-fashioned adj. 1. OUT OF DATE typical of or belonging to a time in the past and no longer considered fashionable or suitable for the present ◦ an old-fashioned car with a running board 2. MAINTAINING OLD-STYLE WAYS favouring or deliberately maintaining ideas, behaviour, or ways of doing things from an earlier time ■ n. BEVERAGES WHISKY COCKTAIL a cocktail made with whisky, bitters, sugar, and lemon peel and garnished with fruit

──── **WORD KEY: SYNONYMS** ────

old-fashioned, outdated, antiquated, archaic, obsolete, passe, antediluvian

CORE MEANING: no longer in current use or no longer considered fashionable

old-fashioned used to describe sth that is no longer in common use because of changes in taste or technology, although it may still be in existence. It is often used to suggest that sth is out of date, but can also be used nostalgically to recall how things used to be; **out-dated** used to describe sth that no longer seems relevant to modern life because it has been superseded by sth better, more fashionable, or more technologically advanced; **antiquated** used to describe sth such as a piece of machinery or a system that is old and outdated but still functioning or in use, although not very efficiently; **archaic** used to describe sth that is so old-fashioned that it seems to have no relevance to modern life. It can also be used to describe things such as words that are no longer in common use but that could be used to create a particular effect; **obsolete** used to describe sth that has passed totally out of use; **passe** a rather formal word used in a disapproving, sometimes even contemptuous, way to suggest sth that is no longer current or fashionable; **antediluvian** a formal or literary word often used in a deliberately humorous way to suggest that sth is extremely old-fashioned and outdated.

old-fashioned look n. a quizzical or reproving look directed at sb who has done or said sth amiss

Old French n. the earliest form of the French language, used until about AD 1400 or, in some analyses, AD 1600. ◊ Middle French —**Old French** adj.

old girl n. 1. FORMER STUDENT a former student at a girls' or women's school, especially a British public school or college 2. FEMALE SENIOR CITIZEN a woman who has reached an advanced age (offensive) 3. FAMILIAR ADDRESS TO WOMAN a familiar way of addressing a woman or girl (dated informal) ◦ Sorry, old girl, didn't mean to lose my temper like that.

old-girl network n. a system of informal contacts between women who belong to a particular group, especially former members of a school or university, and use their influence to help one another

Old Glory n. a nickname for the flag of the United States

old gold adj. of a dark dull yellow colour sometimes tinged with brown —**old gold** n.

old growth n. a long-established forest or woodland that contains some large old trees and has a relatively stable and diverse community of plants and animals (hyphenated when used before a noun)

old guard, **Old Guard** n. the members of a group or organization who have been in it longest, are the staunchest defenders of its traditions, and are the least amenable to change (takes a singular or plural verb)

Oldham /óldəm/ industrial town near Manchester, northwestern England. Population: 103,931 (1991).

old hand n. sb who has acquired skill and knowledge through long experience in a field of activity

old hat adj. boringly familiar or old-fashioned (informal)

Old High German n. the standard, literary form of German (High German) used in written documents up to around AD 1200 —**Old High German** adj.

oldie /óldi/ n. sth old, especially an old popular song (informal)

Old Kingdom n. the period of ancient Egyptian history that comprises the third to sixth dynasties, from around 2700 to 2150 BC, when the capital was at Memphis and the great pyramids were built

old lady n. (slang offensive) 1. OFFENSIVE TERM an offensive term for sb's mother 2. OFFENSIVE TERM an offensive term for a man's wife, or his girlfriend that he lives with

Old Latin n. the form of the Latin language used until around the middle of the first century BC, when what is known as Classical Latin began to be used —**Old Latin** n.

old-line adj. in existence for a long time and having a high social status or good reputation that has endured

old maid n. 1. OFFENSIVE TERM an offensive term for a woman in or past middle age who has never been married and seems unlikely ever to marry (offensive) 2. OFFENSIVE TERM a man or woman insulted as being excessively prim and fussy (offensive) 3. CARDS CARD GAME a card game played with a pack from which one card has been removed. The players collect pairs of cards, and the player left with the unpaired card loses. 4. CARDS LOSER IN OLD MAID the losing player in a game of old maid —**old-maidish** adj.

old man n. 1. OFFENSIVE TERM an offensive term for sb's father (slang offensive) 2. OFFENSIVE TERM an offensive term for a woman's husband, or the man that she lives with (slang offensive) 3. COMMANDING OFFICER a man in a position of authority, especially a commanding officer (slang) ◦ The old man is on the bridge, mad as can be. 4. FAMILIAR ADDRESS TO MAN a familiar way of addressing another man (informal dated) ◦ Look here, old man, I'm in a spot of bother and wonder if you could help me out.

old man's beard n. a popular name for several plants that have trailing or hanging whitish growths, especially traveller's joy, Spanish moss, and the fringe tree

old master n. 1. GREAT EUROPEAN PAINTER any of the great European painters of the period dating roughly from the late Middle Ages to the 18th century 2. PAINTING BY OLD MASTER a picture painted by an old master

Old Nick n. a nickname for the Devil (dated slang)

Old Norse n. the old Germanic language from which the modern Scandinavian languages are derived, in use in Scandinavia from around AD 700 to 1350 —**Old Norse** adj.

Old Red Sandstone n. a sedimentary rock, usually red in colour, formed during the Devonian period and found in Britain and northwestern Europe

old rose adj. of a deep pink colour tinged with grey —**old rose** n.

old salt n. a sailor who has years of experience at sea

Old Saxon n. = Saxon n. 2

old school n. a group of people who adhere to traditional or old-fashioned values and practices ◦ As a disciplinarian of the old school, he was horrified at the laxity of the new regime

old school tie n. 1. TIE a tie whose colours indicate which school, especially which British public school, the wearer attended 2. SCHOOL LOYALTY AND TRADITION the shared attitudes, traditions, and loyalties attributed to people who attended the same school, especially the same public school

old soldier n. 1. VETERAN SOLDIER an experienced and long-serving soldier, or a former soldier 2. VETERAN sb with a great deal of experience

oldsquaw /óld skwáw/, **old-squaw**, **old squaw** n. = long-tailed duck [Mid-19thC. Probably from its gabbling voice.]

old stager /-stáyjər/ n. sb with long experience in a particular activity

oldster /óldstər/ n. an offensive term for sb who has reached an advanced age (offensive) [Early 19thC. Modelled on YOUNGSTER. Originally it referred to a midshipman who had seen four years' service.]

old style n. 1. US = old face 2. OLD-LOOKING TYPEFACE a modern typeface that imitates the characteristics of old face

Old Style adj. used to indicate a date recorded according to the Julian calendar

old-style adj. typical of the past but now superseded by sth else

old sweat n. a veteran soldier (informal)

Old Testament n. the first part of the Christian Bible, corresponding to the Hebrew Bible, that recounts the creation of the world and the history of ancient Israel and contains the Psalms and the prophetic books

old-time adj. 1. OLD-FASHIONED typical of or dating from a time in the past ◦ the old-time music hall 2. LONG-ESTABLISHED in existence for a long time ◦ the old-time families of the town

old-timer n. 1. US SENIOR CITIZEN a senior citizen, especially a man (sometimes considered offensive) 2. EXPERIENCED PERSON sb who has lived in or worked at a particular place for a long time

Olduvai Gorge /óldə vī-/ ravine in northern Tanzania, where fossil remains of early humans and hominids have been found. It is the site of many important archaeological discoveries.

oldwife /óldwīf/ (plural -**wives** /-wīvz/ or -**wife**) n. ZOOL a popular name for several fishes, e.g. the alewife and the menhaden

old wives' tale n. a traditional belief or story, passed down by word of mouth, that is now considered untrue or superstitious ◦ Do what your doctor tells you and don't listen to old wives' tales. [From old wife, an old woman]

old woman n. (slang offensive) 1. OFFENSIVE TERM an offensive term for sb's mother 2. OFFENSIVE TERM an offensive term for a man's wife, or the woman that he lives with 3. OFFENSIVE TERM an offensive term that deliberately insults a man's courage and decisiveness —**old-womanish** adj.

Old World n. the part of the world that was known to Europeans before Columbus's first voyage to the

Americas, comprising Europe, Asia, and Africa. ◊ **New World**

old-world *adj.* considered to be typical of a former and more gracious age

Old World monkey *n.* any of a family of monkeys closely related to the great apes, with close-set nostrils and nongrasping tails. The family includes baboons and mandrills. Family: Cercopithecidae.

olé /ō láy/ *interj.* **EXPRESSION OF TRIUMPH** used to express triumph, excited approval, or encouragement in Spanish. It is a customary cry at bullfights and during flamenco dancing. ■ *n.* **CRY OF OLÉ** a cry or shout of olé [Early 20thC. From Spanish.]

OLE *abbr.* object linking and embedding

ole- *prefix.* = oleo- (*used before vowels*)

-ole *suffix.* **1.** a chemical compound containing a five-membered, usually heterocyclic ring ◊ *carbazole* **2.** a chemical compound, usually an ether, that does not contain hydroxyl ◊ *anisole* [Via French from Latin *oleum* (see OIL)]

olea plural of **oleum**

oleaginous /óli ájjənəss/ *adj.* **1.** **CONTAINING OIL** containing or producing oil **2.** **LIKE OIL** similar to oil in nature or consistency **3.** **INGRATIATING** unpleasantly eager to please, charm, or be of service to people ◊ *the oleaginous concierge* [Mid-17thC. Directly and via Old French *oleagineux* from Latin *oleaginus* 'of an olive tree, oily', from *olea* 'olive tree', an alteration of *oliva* (see OLIVE).] —**oleaginously** *adv.* —**oleaginousness** *n.*

oleander /óli ándər/ (*plural* **-ders** *or* **-der**) *n.* a poisonous evergreen shrub native to the Mediterranean region. It has leathery lance-shaped leaves, sweet-smelling white, pink, or purple flowers, and long seed pods. Latin name: *Nerium oleander.* [Mid-16thC. From medieval Latin.]

oleaster /óli ástər/ (*plural* **-ters** *or* **-ter**) *n.* **1.** **TREE WITH FRUITS LIKE OLIVES** a small tree that is similar to the olive tree. It has silvery leaves and branches, greenish yellow flowers, and fruits that resemble olives. Genus: *Elaeagnus.* **2.** **FRUIT OF OLEASTER** the fruit of the oleaster, which resembles an olive [14thC. Via Latin from *olea* 'olive tree', an alteration of *oliva* (see OLIVE).]

oleate /óli ayt/ *n.* a salt or ester of oleic acid

olecranon /ō lékrə non/ *n.* the upper end of the ulna bone that extends beyond the joint of the elbow to form the elbow's hard projecting point [Early 18thC. From Greek *ōlekranon*, from *ōlenē* 'elbow' + *kranion* 'head'.]

olefin /ólə fin/, **olefine** *n.* **1.** **olefin, olefin fibre SYNTHETIC FIBRE** any of a group of synthetic fibres that are long chains of polymers **2.** **CHEM** = **alkene** [Mid-19thC. From French (*gaz*) *oléfiant*, literally 'oil-forming (gas)', from Latin *oleum* 'oil' (see OIL).]

oleic /ō lee ik/ *adj.* **1.** **RELATING TO OIL** derived from or relating to oil **2.** **RELATING TO OLEIC ACID** derived from or relating to oleic acid

oleic acid *n.* a colourless oily liquid found in almost all animal and vegetable fats. An unsaturated fatty acid, it is used to make soap, ointments, cosmetics, and lubricating oils. Formula: $C_{18}H_{34}O_2$.

olein /óli in/, **oleine** *n.* a yellow oily liquid that occurs naturally in most fats and is mainly used as a textile lubricant

oleo /óli ō/ (*plural* **-os**) *n.* an oleograph (*informal*)

oleo- *prefix.* **1.** oil, oily ◊ *oleograph* **2.** oleic acid ◊ *oleate* [Via French *oléo-* from, ultimately, Latin *oleum* (see OIL)]

oleograph /óli ə graaf, -graf/ *n.* a coloured lithographic print made on canvas with oil colours in order to imitate an oil painting —**oleographic** /óli ə gráffik/ *adj.*

oleo oil *n.* a yellow fatty substance extracted from beef fat, used in the manufacture of margarine and soap

oleoresin /óli ō rézzin/ *n.* a mixture of a resin and an essential oil, either obtained naturally from plants or produced synthetically

oleum /óli əm/ (*plural* **-a** /óli ə/ *or* **-ums**) *n.* a solution of sulphur trioxide in sulphuric acid [Early 20thC. From Latin, 'oil' (see OIL).]

O level *n.* **1.** **FORMER UK SECONDARY SCHOOL EXAM** a former school examination primarily for fifth-year students at secondary schools in England and Wales, now replaced by the General Certificate of Secondary Education (**GCSE**). Full form **Ordinary level** **2.** **SUBJECT TAKEN AT O LEVEL** a subject studied, an examination taken, or a pass obtained at O level [Shortening of ORDINARY]

olfaction /ol fáksh'n/ *n.* **1.** **SMELLING SENSE** the sense of smell **2.** **ACT OF SMELLING** the smelling of sth [Mid-19thC. Formed from Latin *olfacere* 'to smell'.]

olfactometer /ól fak tómmitər/ *n.* an instrument for measuring the keenness of sb's sense of smell [Late 19thC. Coined from OLFACTION + -METER.]

olfactory /ol fáktəri/ *adj.* used in smelling or relating to the sense of smell [Mid-17thC. Via assumed Latin *olfactorius* 'used for smelling' from, ultimately, *olfacere* 'to smell', from *olere* (source of English *redolent*) + *facere* 'to do'.]

Olgas, The /ólgəz/ group of monolithic rocks in south-western Northern Territory, Australia, 26 km/16 mi. west of Ayers Rock. Their highest point is Mount Olga, 3,516ft/1,072m.

olibanum /o líbbənəm/ *n.* = **frankincense** [14thC. Via medieval Latin *olibanum* and Greek *libanos* from Arabic *al-lubān* 'storax'.]

oligarch /ólli gaark/ *n.* a ruler or leader in an oligarchy [Early 17thC. From Greek *oligarkhēs*, from *oligos* 'few' + *-arkhēs* '-ARCH'.]

oligarchy /ólli gaarki/ (*plural* **-chies**) *n.* **1.** **SMALL GOVERNING GROUP** a small group of people who together govern a nation or control an organization, often for their own purposes **2.** **ENTITY RULED BY OLIGARCHY** a nation governed or an organization controlled by an oligarchy **3.** **GOVERNMENT BY SMALL GROUP** government or control by a small group of people [Late 15thC. From Greek *oligarkhia*, from *oligos* 'few' + *-arkhia* '-archy' (see -ARCH).] —**oligarchic** /ólli gaárkik/ *adj.*

oligo- *prefix.* few ◊ *oligophagous* [From Greek *oligos* 'small, little, few']

Oligocene /ólligō seen/ *n.* the third geological period of the Tertiary Era, from 40 to 25 million years ago, when primates first appeared —**Oligocene** *adj.*

oligoclase /ólligō klayss/ *n.* a white, bluish, or reddish-yellow feldspar mineral of the plagioclase series, found especially in more acidic igneous and metamorphic rock [Mid-19thC. Formed from OLIGO- + Greek *klasis* 'breaking', from *klan* 'to break' (see CLASTIC), from its imperfect cleavage.]

oligomer /ólli gōmər/ *n.* a polymer consisting of less than five monomer units —**oligomeric** /ólligə mérrik/ *adj.* —**oligomerization** /ólli gōmə rī záysh'n/ *n.*

oligonucleotide /ólligō nyoókli ə tīd/ *n.* a polymeric chain containing ten nucleotides or fewer

oligophagous /ólli góffəgəss/ *adj.* feeding on a restricted range of foodstuffs, usually a small number of different plants

oligopoly /ólli góppəli/ (*plural* **-lies**) *n.* an economic condition in which there are so few suppliers of a particular product that one supplier's actions can have a significant impact on prices and on its competitors [Late 19thC. Coined from OLIGO- + MONOPOLY.] —**oligopolistic** /ólli góppə lístik/ *adj.*

oligopsony /ólli gópsəni/ (*plural* **-nies**) *n.* an economic condition in which there are so few buyers for a particular product that one buyer's actions can have a significant impact on prices and the market in general [Mid-20thC. Coined from OLIGO- + MONOPSONY.] —**oligopsonistic** /ólli gópsə nístik/ *adj.*

oligosaccharide /ólligō sákə rīd/ *n.* a carbohydrate made up of a relatively small number of linked monosaccharides. ◊ **polysaccharide**

oligotrophic /ólligō trôfik, -tróffik/ *adj.* containing relatively little plant life and nutrients in its waters but rich in dissolved oxygen

olingo /o líng gō/ (*plural* **-gos**) *n.* a small tree-dwelling nocturnal mammal that is native to the tropical forests of Central and South America and looks a little like a slim sleek raccoon. Latin name: *Bassaricyon gabbii.* [Early 20thC. From American Spanish.]

olio /óli ō/ (*plural* **-os**) *n.* **1.** **SPICED STEW** a highly spiced stew made from a variety of meats and vegetables **2.** **ASSORTMENT** a miscellaneous collection of things **3.** **ARTS MISCELLANY OR MEDLEY** sth made up of works of various kinds or works by different people, e.g. a literary miscellany or a musical medley [Mid-17thC. An alteration of Spanish *olla* 'pot, stew' (see OLLA).]

Oliphant /óllifənt/, **Sir Mark** (*b.* 1901) Australian physicist. He discovered tritium (1934) and designed the first proton synchrotron accelerator. Full name **Sir Marcus Laurence Elwin Oliphant**

Olive

olive /ólliv/ *n.* **1.** **FOOD GREEN OR BLACK FRUIT** a small oval bitter-tasting fruit with a stone, green when unripe and black when ripe. It is the source of olive oil. **2.** **TREES OLIVE TREE** an evergreen tree native to the Mediterranean that produces the olive. Latin name: *Olea europaea.* (*often used before a noun*) **3.** **INDUST OLIVE WOOD** the wood of the olive tree, used in decorative work **4.** **TREES TREE RESEMBLING OLIVE** a tree or shrub that resembles the olive tree ■ *n., adj.* **COLOURS** = **olive green** [12thC. Via Latin *oliva* from Greek *elaiwa*, a variant of *elaia* 'olive, olive oil' (source of English *oil*).]

olive branch *n.* **1.** **CONCILIATORY GESTURE** a gesture or offer intended to bring about a reconciliation **2.** **SYMBOL OF PEACE** a branch of an olive tree used as a symbol of peace [From Genesis 8:11]

olive drab *n.* **1.** **COLOURS GREYISH GREEN** a greyish-green colour **2.** **US TEXTILES GREEN CLOTH** cloth dyed in an olive drab colour, used especially for military uniforms **3.** **MIL GREEN MILITARY UNIFORM** a military uniform made of olive drab cloth, especially one worn in the United States army —**olive drab** *adj.*

olive green *adj.* of a deep yellowish green colour —**olive green** *n.*

olivenite /o lívvi nīt/ *n.* a rare mineral that is often olive green in colour. It is a hydrated arsenate of copper. Formula: $Cu_2(AsO_4)OH.$ [Early 19thC. From German *Olivenit*, from *Olive* 'olive', from its colour.]

olive oil *n.* monounsaturated oil with a distinctive flavour extracted from olives, extensively used in salad dressings and for cooking, and in the manufacture of soap and cosmetics. Extra virgin and virgin olive oil, pressed from olives without stones, are the best quality oils.

Oliver /óllivər/, **Isaac** (1560?–1617?) English painter of miniatures. He is noted for his naturalistic style, and painted portraits of the members of the court of James I.

Olives, Mount of /óllivz/ ridge in central Israel, east of Jerusalem, with many biblical associations. It is separated from Jerusalem by the Valley of Kidron. Height: 823 m/2,700 ft.

Olivier /ə lívvi ay/, **Laurence, 1st Baron Olivier of Brighton** (1907–89) British actor and director. An influential Shakespearean actor, he was a founding director of the National Theatre (1961–73). Full name **Laurence Kerr Olivier**

olivine /ólli veen/ *n.* an olive-green form of magnesium-iron silicate that occurs naturally in igneous rocks. It is used in refractories and as a gemstone. Formula: $(MgFe)_2SiO_4.$ —**olivinic** /ólli vínnik/ *adj.* —**olivinitic** /ólliviə níttik/ *adj.*

olla /óllə/ *n.* **1.** **HOUSEHOLD EARTHENWARE POT** a large, usually unglazed pot with a spherical body and a wide mouth, used in Latin America and the southwestern United States for storing water and for

Laurence Olivier

cooking **2.** FOOD = **olla podrida** [Early 17thC. Via Spanish from, ultimately, Latin *aulla* 'pot'. Ultimately from an Indo-European word meaning 'cooking pot' or 'oven', which is also the ancestor of English *oven*.]

olla podrida /-po dre̅édə/ (*plural* **olla podridas** *or* **ollas podridas**) *n.* **1.** TRADITIONAL SPANISH AND LATIN AMERICAN STEW a traditional Spanish and Latin American stew of meat and vegetables, usually containing sausage and chickpeas, and highly seasoned **2.** ASSORTMENT a miscellaneous mixture or assortment of things [From Spanish, literally 'rotten pot']

Olley /ólli/, **Margaret Hannah** (*b.* 1923) Australian painter. She is noted for her interiors and still life works.

Olmec /ól mek/ (*plural* **-mecs** *or* **-mec**) *n.* **1.** CENTRAL AMERICAN CIVILIZATION a Central American civilization that arose around AD 1200, before the Mayan civilization. It featured irrigated agriculture, urbanism, and the beginnings of calendar and writing systems. (*often used before a noun*) **2.** MEMBER OF OLMEC CIVILIZATION a member of any of the peoples who made up the Olmec civilization [Late 18thC. From Nahuatl *olmecatl*, literally 'sb who lives in the rubber country'.]

ology /óllə ji/ (*plural* **-gies**) *n.* any science or academic field, especially one whose name ends in '-ology' (*informal*) ○ *people studying ologies you've never heard of* [Early 19thC. From the suffix -OLOGY, as in 'biology', 'psychology', etc.]

oloroso /óllə ró̅sso̅/ (*plural* **-sos**) *n.* a golden-coloured full-bodied sherry, typically medium-sweet [Late 19thC. Via Spanish, literally 'fragrant', from Latin *olere* 'to smell'.]

Olsen /ólssən/, **John Henry** (*b.* 1928) Australian painter. Primarily a landscape artist, his works include the *Journey into the You Beaut Country* series (1961).

Olympia /ə límpi ə/ plain in southwestern Greece, in the western Peloponnese, near the Ionian Sea. It was an ancient religious site sacred to Zeus, and the first Olympic Games were held there in 776 BC.

Olympiad /ə límpi ad/ *n.* **1.** SINGLE OLYMPIC GAMES a holding of the modern Olympic Games **2.** FOUR-YEAR PERIOD a four-year interval between one holding of the Olympic Games and the next, used by the ancient Greeks as a way of calculating dates [14thC. Via Latin from, ultimately, Greek *Olumpia*, where the games were held.]

Olympian /ə límpi ən/ *adj.* **1.** MYTHOL RELATING TO MOUNT OLYMPUS relating to Mount Olympus, the home of the gods in Greek mythology **2.** ALOOF OR SUPERIOR so superior or grand as to be above everyday events and concerns ○ *his Olympian indifference to petty squabbles* **3.** ENORMOUS extraordinarily great or demanding **4.** GEOG OF OLYMPIA relating to ancient Olympia **5.** LIKE GREEK DEITY characteristic of a Greek god or goddess, or resembling one in power, majesty, or beauty (*literary*) ■ *n.* **1.** MYTHOL GREEK DEITY any one of the twelve major Greek gods or goddesses who had their home on Mount Olympus **2.** SPORTS OLYMPIC ATHLETE a competitor in the Olympic Games **3.** SUPERIOR PERSON sb who is so superior or grand as to be above everyday events and concerns **4.** PEOPLES SB FROM OLYMPIA an inhabitant of ancient Olympia [15thC. Formed from Greek *olumpios*.]

Olympic /ə límpik/ *adj.* relating to the Olympic Games

Olympic Games, **Olympic games** *npl.* **1.** INTERNATIONAL SPORTS CONTEST a large-scale international sports contest intended to promote international goodwill.

It has been held every four years since 1896 in different cities around the world. **2.** ANCIENT GREEK FESTIVAL an ancient Greek religious festival held every four years at Olympia in honour of Zeus, with athletic, literary, and musical contests involving participants from throughout Greece

Olympics /ə límpiks/ *npl.* the modern Olympic Games

Olympus, Mount /ə límpəss/ the highest mountain in Greece, located in the north of the country. In Greek mythology it was believed to be the home of the gods. Height: 2,917 m/9,570 ft.

Olympus Mons /ə límpəss mónz/ *n.* large volcano in the northern hemisphere of Mars. It is three times as high as Mount Everest. Height: 26,800 m/88,000 ft.

Om /óm/, **Aum** *n.* a sacred syllable that is chanted in Hindu and Buddhist prayers and mantras. It is symbolic of creation, destruction, and preservation or of the primary trinities of Hinduism or Buddhism.

OM *abbr.* Order of Merit

-oma *suffix.* tumour ○ *encephaloma* [Directly and via modern Latin from Greek *-ōma*]

Omagh /ómə, óm aa/ market town in central Northern Ireland. Population: 17,280 (1991).

Omaha[1] /ómə haa/ (*plural* **-has** *or* **-ha**) *n.* **1.** MEMBER OF NATIVE N AMERICAN PEOPLE a member of a Native North American people who have lived in northeastern Nebraska since the 17th century **2.** NATIVE N AMERICAN LANGUAGE the Siouan language spoken by the Omaha [Early 19thC. From Omaha *umonhon*, literally 'upstream people'.] —**Omaha** *adj.*

Omaha[2] /ómə haa/ city in eastern Nebraska, on the Missouri River. Population: 345,033 (1994).

Oman

Oman /ó ma̅an/ independent state in southwestern Asia, on the southeastern coast of the Arabian Peninsula. Language: Arabic. Currency: Omani rial. Capital: Muscat. Population: 2,251,000 (1996). Area: 212,457 sq. km/82,030 sq. mi. Official name **Sultanate of Oman** —**Omani** *adj.*, *n.*

Oman, Gulf of /ó ma̅an/ arm of the Arabian Sea, situated between northern Oman and the southeastern coast of Iran

Omar Khayyam /ó maar kī a̅am, -ám/ (1050?–1122) Persian poet, mathematician, and astronomer. His *Rubáiyát* is an extensive collection of four-line stanzas, some of which were translated into English by Edward Fitzgerald (1859). Full name **Abu ol-Fath Omar ebn Ebrahim ol-Khayyami**

omasum /ó máyssəm/ (*plural* **-sa** /-sə/) *n.* the third compartment of the stomach of a cow or other ruminant, situated between the abomasum and the reticulum. The inner surface has folds that break up food particles. [Early 18thC. From Latin, literally 'bullock's tripe'.]

ombre /ómbər/ *n.* a card game, popular in the 18th century, for three players using forty cards, with one player competing against the other two [Mid-17thC. From Spanish *hombre* 'man, ombre', from Latin *homo* 'man'.]

ombro- *prefix.* rainfall, precipitation ○ *ombrogenous* [From Greek *ombros*]

ombudsman /ómbʊdzmən/ (*plural* **-men** /-mən/) *n.* **1.** NONGOVERNMENTAL INVESTIGATOR sb responsible for investigating and resolving complaints from consumers or other members of the public against

a company, institution, or other organization **2.** GOVERNMENT OFFICIAL a government official responsible for impartially investigating citizens' complaints against a public authority or institution and trying to bring about a fair settlement [Mid-20thC. Via Swedish from Old Norse *umboðsmaðr* 'manager, deputy', which was formed from *umboð* 'commission' + *maðr* 'man' (related to English *man*).] —**ombudsmanship** *n.*

Omdurman /óm dur ma̅an/ city in east-central Sudan, on the west bank of the River Nile, opposite Khartoum. Population: 1,267,077 (1993).

-ome *suffix.* mass ○ *trichome* [Via modern Latin from Greek *-ōma*]

omega /ómigə/ *n.* **1.** LAST LETTER OF GREEK ALPHABET the 24th and final letter of the Greek alphabet, represented in the English alphabet as 'o'. See table at **alphabet** **2.** END the end, or the last thing in a series (*literary*) [Early 16thC. From Greek *ō mega* 'great (i.e, long) o', as opposed to 'small (short) o', 'o mikron'.]

omega hyperon *n.* a negatively charged elementary particle with a rest mass 3,272 times that of an electron

omega meson *n.* an extremely short-lived neutral meson with a rest mass 1,532 times that of an electron

omega minus *n.* = omega hyperon [From the symbol for the particle]

omelet *n.* US = omelette

omelette /ómlət/ *n.* a dish consisting of beaten eggs fried over high heat until set, often served folded in half over a savoury filling such as cheese or mushrooms [Early 17thC. Via French from, ultimately, Latin *lamella* 'small thin plate', from *lamina* 'thin plate' (source of English *laminate*).]

omen /ó men, ómən/ *n.* PROPHETIC SIGN a happening that is regarded as a sign of how sb or sth will fare in the future ■ *vti.* (**omens, omening, omened**) INDICATE STH'S FUTURE to indicate the future course of events relating to sth [Late 16thC. From Latin (source of English *abominable*).]

omentum /ó méntəm/ (*plural* **-ta** /-tə/) *n.* any of the folds of the peritoneum, especially the fold that covers the intestines (**greater omentum**) or the fold that connects to the liver (**lesser omentum**) [Mid-16thC. From Latin.]

Omer /ómər/ *n.* in Judaism, a seven-week period between the second day of Passover and the first day of Shavuoth, observed as a period of mourning, except on one day. Omer is named from the custom of offering an omer or sheaf of barley as a sacrifice in the Temple on the first day of this period.

omerta /ó mair taa/, **omertà** *n.* the code requirement alleged to apply to members of the Mafia, requiring that they remain silent about any crimes of which they have knowledge [Late 19thC. From Italian dialect, from Latin *humilitas* 'humility', from *humilis*, 'humble'. The underlying meaning is 'subjugation to the good of the society'.]

omicron /ó mí kron/ *n.* the fifteenth letter of the Greek alphabet, represented in the English alphabet as 'o'. See table at **alphabet** [Mid-17thC. From Greek *o mikron* 'small (i.e. short) o', as opposed to 'great (long) o', 'ō mega'.]

ominous /óminəss/ *adj.* suggesting or indicating that sth bad is going to happen or be revealed ○ *I think it's rather ominous that they haven't replied to your letter.* [Late 16thC. From Latin *ominosus* 'of an omen', from *omen* 'omen'.] —**ominously** *adv.* —**ominousness** *n.*

omissible /ó míssəb'l/ *adj.* able to be left out or left undone

omission /ó mísh'n/ *n.* **1.** STH LEFT OUT sth that has been deliberately or accidentally left out or not done ○ *errors and omissions excepted* **2.** ACT OF OMITTING the omitting of sth or the state of being omitted ○ *The omission of those three words changed the sense of the whole paragraph.* [14thC. Via Old French from the late Latin stem *omission-*, which was formed from *omittere* 'to OMIT'.]

omit /ó mít/ (**omits, omitting, omitted**) *vt.* **1.** LEAVE SB OR STH OUT to fail to include or mention sb or sth, either deliberately or accidentally **2.** FAIL TO DO STH to fail or forget to do sth, either deliberately or accidentally [15thC. From Latin *omittere*, which was formed from *ob-* 'away' + *mittere* 'to send' (source of English *mission*, *message*, and *promise*).]

WORD KEY: SYNONYMS

See Synonyms at ***neglect***.

omni- *prefix.* all ○ *omnicompetent* [From Latin *omnis*. Ultimately from an Indo-European word meaning 'abundance, to produce' that is also the ancestor of English *opulent*, *copy*, *optimum*, and *operate*.]

omnibus /ómnibəss/ *n.* **1.** BOOK COLLECTING SEPARATE WORKS a single book containing several works, usually by the same author, involving the same main character, or on the same subject, previously published separately **2. omnibus, omnibus edition** SINGLE BROADCAST OF PROGRAMMES a single continuous broadcast consisting of several radio or television programmes previously broadcast separately, e.g. instalments of a serial or soap opera **3.** BUS a bus (*archaic or formal*) ■ *adj.* WITH MANY DIFFERENT THINGS bringing many different things together as a single unit ○ *an omnibus education bill* [Early 19thC. Via French and directly from Latin 'for all', which was formed from *omnis* 'all' (see OMNI-).]

omnibus survey *n.* a survey in which data on a wide variety of subjects is collected during the same interview

omnicompetent /ómni kómpitənt/ *adj.* **1.** WIDELY COMPETENT able to deal successfully with any task or situation **2.** LAW WITH FULL JURISDICTION competent to judge or try any kind of case

omnidirectional /ómnidi réksh'nəl, -dī-/ *adj.* able to transmit or receive radio or sound waves in or from any direction

omnidirectional radio range *n.* = **omnirange**

omnificent /om nífiss'nt/, **omnific** /om nífik/ *adj.* with unlimited power to create (*literary*) [Late 17thC. Formed from Latin *omni-* (see OMNI-) + Latin *-ficus* '-fic' (see -FIC) + -ENT.] —**omnificence** *n.*

omnipotence /om níppətənss/ *n.* the possession of complete, unlimited, or universal power and authority [15thC]

omnipotent /om níppətənt/ *adj.* possessing complete, unlimited, or universal power and authority [13thC. Via Old French from the Latin stem *omnipotent-*, which was formed from *omnis* 'all' + *potens*, the present participle of *posse* 'to be able'.] —**omnipotently** *adv.*

Omnipotent *n.* a word sometimes used to refer to God (*literary*) [Early 17thC]

omnipresent /ómni prézz'nt/ *adj.* **1.** ALWAYS PRESENT EVERYWHERE continuously and simultaneously present throughout the whole of creation **2.** FOUND EVERYWHERE present or seemingly present all the time or everywhere [Early 17thC. From medieval Latin *omnipraesent-*, which was formed from *omni-* 'omni-' + *praesens* 'present'.] —**omnipresence** *n.*

omnirange /ómni raynj/ *n.* a very-high-frequency radio navigation network that enables aircraft pilots to choose and fly any bearing relative to a transmitter on the ground

omniscience /om níssi ənss/ *n.* knowledge of all things, whether real or apparent knowledge [Early 17thC. From medieval Latin *omniscientia*, literally 'knowledge of all', from *scientia* 'knowledge' (see SCIENCE).]

omniscient /om níssi ənt/ *adj.* knowing or seeming to know everything [Early 17thC. From medieval Latin *omniscient-*, which was formed from Latin *omni-* 'omni-' + *scire* 'to know' (see SCIENCE).]

omnium-gatherum /ómni əm gáthə rəm/ (*plural* **omnium-gatherums**) *n.* a collection of many different, often unsorted ideas or items (*humorous*) [From Latin *omnium* 'of all' + pseudo-Latin *gatherum*, an alteration of 'gathering']

omnivore /ómni vawr/ *n.* **1.** ANIMAL THAT EATS ANYTHING an animal that will feed on any kind or many different kinds of food, including both plants and animals **2.** SB WITH WIDE INTERESTS sb who has very wide interests and will read, study, or generally absorb anything that is available [Late 19thC. Via modern Latin *Omnivora* 'omnivores', from Latin *omnivorus* (see OMNIVOROUS).]

omnivorous /om nívvərəss/ *adj.* **1.** EATING MANY FOODS eating any kind or many different kinds of food, including both plants and animals **2.** INTERESTED IN RANGE OF THINGS wide-ranging and often undiscriminating in interests and tastes [Mid-17thC. Formed from Latin *omnivorus*, which in turn was formed from *omni-* (see OMNI-) + *-vorus* 'devouring'.] —**omnivorously** *adv.*

OMOV, **Omov** *abbr.* POL one member one vote

omphalos /ómfə loss/ *n.* **1.** ANCIENT GREEK SACRED STONE a conical stone with sacred significance in ancient Greek religion, especially the one at Delphi that was believed to mark the centre of the world **2.** FOCAL POINT the central or focal point, around which everything else revolves (*literary*) [Mid-19thC. From Greek, literally 'navel'.]

OMR *abbr.* optical mark reading

Omsk /omsk/ city and capital of Omsk Oblast, southwestern Russia, situated 772 km/480 mi. east of Chelyabinsk. Population: 1,160,000 (1995).

on /on/ *prep.* **1.** INDICATES POSITION used to describe sth in a position above and in contact with the surface of sth else ○ *sitting on the bed* **2.** ATTACHED TO STH used to indicate attachment to or suspension from a surface or object ○ *a wooden wheel mounted on the wall* **3.** SUPPORTING WEIGHT used to indicate what part of the body is supporting sb's weight ○ *They sat there leaning on their elbows.* **4.** CARRYING STH carrying sth that is therefore readily accessible ○ *I didn't have any cash on me at the time.* **5.** IN THE VICINITY OF located in a place or situated close to or alongside a place ○ *driving around on dirt roads* ○ *a small town on the coast of Trinidad* **6.** AT A TIME used to indicate when sth happens ○ *just before noon on Tuesday* **7.** RELATING TO STH concerned with or relating to a particular subject, thing, or activity **8.** WHERE STH IS AVAILABLE used to indicate that specific information is currently available from a machine or instrument ○ *a comedy show on the radio* **9.** AS MEANS OF FUNCTIONING used to indicate the means by which sb or sth subsists or functions ○ *animals that feed on the leaves of the trees* **10.** BY MEANS OF using sth as a means of transport ○ *They arrived on horseback.* **11.** DURING engaged in an activity ○ *My assistant is away on a course.* **12.** ACCORDING TO used to indicate that sth is grounds for a statement, way of thinking, or action ○ *allowing them to compete on an equal basis* **13.** IN CURRENT RANK OR POSITION used to indicate sb's current status or position in an organization or institution ○ *My sister is on the committee.* **14.** DIRECTED TOWARDS used to indicate that sth is directed towards sb or sth ○ *I shone my torch on the inscription.* **15.** CHARGED TO used to indicate that the cost of drinks or a meal is charged to a particular person ○ *The drinks are on me.* ■ *adv.* **1.** IN CONTACT WITH STH in contact with, attached to, or supported by sth ○ *an envelope with a stamp on* **2.** INTO STATE OF ATTACHMENT OR SUSPENSION into a condition of being attached to or suspended from sth ○ *sewing a button on* **3.** INTO OPERATION into the state of operating or functioning ○ *turned the television on* **4.** WITH CLOTHING wearing clothes or placing clothing over a part of the body ○ *I pulled my tee-shirt on.* **5.** PERSISTENTLY in a continuous or persistent way ○ *decided to stay on in Cambridge* **6.** IN PROGRESS in activity or performance at the present time or at some implied time ○ *putting a play on* **7.** BASEBALL INDICATING RUNNER'S POSITION in baseball, used to indicate whether an offensive player is on the bases ○ *left three runners on* **8.** BETTING WAGERED wagered as a bet ○ *put a bet on* ■ *adj.* **1.** TAKING PLACE happening or being performed at the present time ○ *There's nothing good on tonight.* ○ *I've got a lot on at the moment.* **2.** ARRANGED OR PLANNED indicating that an activity is arranged and will happen ○ *Are we still on for tomorrow?* **3.** FUNCTIONING indicating that a machine or device is functioning or in use ○ *Is the oven on?* **4.** CRICKET BOWLING indicating that a particular bowler is bowling **5.** CRICKET PART OF PITCH indicating or relating to the leg side of a cricket pitch **6.** CRICKET IN FIELDING POSITION indicating certain fielding positions on the leg side [Old English. Ultimately from an Indo-European word that is also the ancestor of English *aloft*.] ◇ **be on about** used to indicate what sb is talking about or what he or she means (*informal*) ◇ **be on it** *Aus* used to indicate that sb is drinking alcohol (*slang*) ◇ **be on to sb** *or* **sth** to have information on or be aware of the real nature of sb or sth (*informal*) ◇ **have sth on sb** to have unfavourable information about sb's activities ◇ **It's not on** used to indicate that sth is unacceptable ◇ **on and off** occasionally ◇ **on and on** in a continuous, persistent way ◇ **you're on** used to indicate that sb is agreeing to do sth proposed by sb else (*informal*)

ON *abbr.* **1.** Old Norse **2. ON, O.N.** Ontario

-on[1] *suffix.* **1.** subatomic particle ○ *fermion* **2.** fundamental hereditary unit ○ *muton* **3.** unit, quantum ○ *chronon* [From ION]

-on[2] *suffix.* = **-one** [Alteration of -ONE]

on-again, off-again *adj. US* happening or continuing intermittently, and thus difficult to predict (*informal*)

onager /ónnəjər/ (*plural* **-gers** *or* **-gri** /ónnə grī/) *n.* **1.** WILD ASIAN ASS a wild ass found in northern Iran and bordering areas that is dark yellow with a stripe along its back. Genus: *Equus hemionus.* **2.** ANCIENT WAR MACHINE in former times, a war machine used to throw stones [14thC. Via Latin from Greek *onagros*, from *onos* 'ass' + *agrios* 'wild'.]

onanism /ṓnənizəm/ *n.* **1.** MASTURBATION masturbation (*literary*) **2.** COITUS INTERRUPTUS coitus interruptus [Early 18thC. Named after Onan, a character in the Bible (Genesis 38:9), who spilled his semen onto the ground rather than impregnate his deceased brother's wife.] —**onanist** *n.* —**onanistic** /ṓnə nístik/ *adj.*

onboard /ón báwrd/ *adj.* carried or available on an aircraft, ship, or other vehicle or vessel [Mid-20thC. *Board* from BOARD 'side of a ship'.]

ONC /wunss/ *n.* (*plural* **ONCs**), *abbr.* Ordinary National Certificate

once *adv.* A TIME IN THE PAST used to indicate that sth happened or was the case at some time in the past ○ *The place must have been nice once.* ○ *a once comfortable lifestyle* ■ *conj.* AS SOON AS happening when or whenever sth else has happened ○ *Once he got started, it was clear we were dealing with an expert.* ■ *adv.* **1.** ARITH MULTIPLIED BY ONE indicating that a number is multiplied by one ○ *once three is three* **2.** BY ONE STEP distant by one place or degree ○ *a cousin once removed* ◇ **all at once 1.** happening suddenly, often unexpectedly ○ *I felt really sick all at once.* **2.** happening all at the same time ○ *She could not read the books all at once.* ◇ **at once 1.** immediately ○ *Tell him at once.* **2.** happening all at the same time ○ *It's a lot to take in at once.* ◇ **for once** happening on this particular occasion, if or but at no other time ○ *For once my strategy worked.* ◇ **once and away 1.** conclusively **2.** occasionally ◇ **once and for all** completely or finally ◇ **once in a while** occasionally ○ *You ought to sit back and relax every once in a while.* ◇ **once or twice** *or* **once and again** a few times, but not often ○ *pausing once and again to listen* ◇ **once upon a time** used at the beginning of fairy tales and children's stories to indicate that sth happened a long time ago or in an imaginary world

WORD KEY: CULTURAL NOTE

Once Upon a Time in the West, a spaghetti western directed by Sergio Leone (1968), is often considered the best of his films, and was reputedly Henry Fonda's favourite. He stars as a vicious gunman out to kill a feisty landowner, played by Claudia Cardinale, who is hoping to cash in on the Western expansion of the railway. Charles Bronson, in the role of a mysterious character known as 'Harmonica', is meanwhile hunting down Henry Fonda. Ennio Morricone, who wrote the music for many such films, composed the atmospheric score.

once-over *n.* a rapid inspection or examination of sb or sth (*informal*) ○ *I'll give the car a quick once-over.*

onchocerciasis /óngkōsur kī́ əssiss/ *n.* a disease caused by infestation with worms, especially a tropical disease of humans caused by a parasitic worm and transmitted by blackflies, causing skin nodules, lesions, and blindness [Early 20thC. Formed from modern Latin *Onchocerca*, a genus of worms, which was in turn formed from Greek *ogkos* 'barb' + *kerkos* 'tail', from their shape.]

onco- *prefix.* tumour ○ *oncolysis* [From Greek *onkos* 'mass']

oncogene /óngkō jeen/ *n.* a gene that can cause a cell to become malignant. Oncogenes are thought to be derived from normal cellular counterparts that have been taken up by certain viruses and altered so they malfunction when returned to the cell.

oncogenesis /óngkō jénnəssiss/ *n.* the development of a tumour or tumours

oncogenic /óngkō jénnik/, **oncogenous** /ong kójjənəss/ *adj.* relating to or causing the formation and growth of tumours —**oncogenicity** /óngkōjə níssəti/ *n.*

oncology /ong kólləji/ *n.* the branch of medicine that deals with the study and treatment of malignant tumours —**oncological** /óngkə lójjik'l/ *adj.* —**oncologist** *n.*

oncolysis /ong kóllǝssiss/ *n.* the destruction of tumour cells, either spontaneously or, more usually, in response to drug or radiographic treatment

oncoming /ón kuming/ *adj.* **APPROACHING** heading directly towards sb or sth ■ *n.* **ONSET** the approach of sth that is soon to occur

oncornavirus /ong káwrnə vírəss/ *n.* a virus containing single-stranded RNA and capable of causing cancer [Late 20thC. Coined from ONCO- + RNA + VIRUS.]

oncost /ón kost/ *n.* the general recurring expense of running a business, e.g. rent, maintenance, and utilities

OND *n.* (*plural* **ONDs**), *abbr.* Ordinary National Diploma

Michael Ondaatje

Ondaatje /on daátyə/, **Michael** (*b.* 1943) Sri Lankan-born Canadian writer. Among his many volumes of poetry and fiction is the Booker Prize-winning *The English Patient* (1992) that was made into a successful film.

Ondes Martenot /óNd maártǝnō/ *n.* an electronic musical instrument that can be played either on a keyboard or with a finger slider, producing a characteristic sliding sound. The instrument was favoured by the composer Olivier Messiaen. [From French *Ondes (musicales)* '(musical) waves', original name of the instrument, + *(Maurice) Martenot*, 1898–1980, French inventor]

on dit /oN deé/ (*plural* **on dits** /oN deé/) *n.* a piece of gossip [From French, 'they say']

one /wun/ CORE MEANING: a grammatical word indicating a single thing or unit, and not two or more ○ (*det*) *just one accident out of thousands* ○ (*det*) *a one-legged man* ○ (*pron*) *Central Newark, once home to several bank branches, now has one.* ○ (*pron+of*) *Bill got one of his boxing gloves off.*
1. *det., pron.* **UNIQUE** distinct from all others ○ *the one exception to this* **2.** *det., pron.* **USED TO DISTINGUISH STH** distinct from all others of its kind in a comparison ○ *from one thought to the next* **3.** *det.* A **NONSPECIFIC TIME** relating to an unspecified time in the past or future ○ *one August afternoon* **4.** *det.* **USED FOR EMPHASIS** used instead of 'a' and 'an' to emphasize a following adjective or expression (*informal*) ○ *She's written one great novel!* **5.** *det.* **PARTICULAR** introducing the name of sb who may not be known ○ *This plan, one Whitman concedes, is the most helpful.* **6.** *pron.* **TYPICAL INDIVIDUAL** used to refer to people in general (*formal*) ○ *One can eat well here.* **7.** *pron.* **SB OR STH UNSPECIFIED** used to indicate sb or sth not specifically identified (*dated*) ○ *the voice of one crying in the wilderness* **8.** *pron.* **PREVIOUSLY MENTIONED** used instead of a preceding noun to indicate sb or sth already mentioned ○ *nothing but an old vase, and a cracked*

one at that **9.** *pron.* **JOKE OR STORY** used to refer to a question, joke, or remark ○ *That's a good one!* **10.** *n.* ARITH **THE NUMBER 1** the number 1. It is the smallest whole number, designating a single unit, and the first cardinal number. **11.** *n.* STH **WITH VALUE OF 1** sth in a numbered series with a value of one ○ *to throw a one* **12.** *n.* US **DOLLAR BILL** used to refer to a one dollar bill (*informal*) **13.** *n.* TIME **MEASURE** used to indicate the time as one hour after twelve midday or midnight ○ *We'll stop for lunch at one.* **14.** *n.* MUSIC **MUSICAL NOTATION** the numeral 1 used as the bottom figure in a time signature to indicate that the beat is measured in semibreves [Old English *ān*. Ultimately from an Indo-European word that is also the ancestor of English *union.*] ◇ **as one** doing sth at the same time or in the same way ◇ **all one** not important enough to be of any consequence to sb ◇ **at one** in harmony with sb or sth ◇ **one and all** everyone in a group ◇ **one by one** happening individually in sequence ◇ **one or two** a few people or things ◇ **one and only 1.** unique and without comparison (*often used to introduce a performer on a show*) **2.** the person that sb loves

WORD KEY: USAGE

one of those people who is or *one of those people who are*? Sense determines whether the verb in a construction of this type should be singular or plural, and in any given case one choice is right and the other wrong. To decide which verb form to choose, start with the *of*. For example, *He is one of those people who is/are always trying to make a good impression* is not equivalent in meaning to *Of those people, he is one who is always trying to make a good impression*. Rather, the idea is *Of those people who are always trying to make a good impression, he is one.* Here the form of *to be* is not governed by *one* but by *people*, and therefore *one of those people who are* is right. In contrast, *He is the only one of those people who is/are worth talking to* surely does not mean *Of those people who are worth talking to, he is the only one.* Here the idea is *Of those people, he is the only one who is worth talking to*, so in this case *one of those people who is* is right.

-one *suffix.* ketone or related compound ○ *quinone* [Origin uncertain: possibly from Greek *-ōnē* 'daughter of']

one-acter *n.* a play that consists of only one act

one another *pron.* each of several members of a group to the others ○ *neighbours helping one another*

one-armed bandit *n.* a gambling machine that is operated by inserting a coin or token in a slot and pulling down a lever on one side (*informal*)

one-dimensional *adj.* **1.** IN ONE DIMENSION existing in or possessing only one dimension **2.** LACKING DEPTH presenting or perceiving only the most superficial aspects of sth

Onega, Lake /o náygə/ the largest lake in Europe, in northwestern Russia, east of Lake Ladoga, to which it is linked by the River Svir. Area: 9,700 sq. km/3,745 sq. mi.

one-horse *adj.* **1.** VERY SMALL AND BORING small, dull, and insignificant ○ *a one-horse town* **2.** HAVING ONE LIKELY WINNER fielding only one candidate or competitor who is likely to win ○ *a one-horse race* **3.** DRAWN BY SINGLE HORSE drawn by only one horse

Oneida[1] /ō nídə/ (*plural* **-das** or **-da**) *n.* **1.** MEMBER OF NATIVE N AMERICAN PEOPLE a member of a Native North American people who originally occupied lands in New York State and whose members now live mainly in Ontario, New York State, and Wisconsin. The Oneida were one of the five peoples who formed the Iroquois Confederacy, which later became known as the Six Nations. **2.** ONEIDA LANGUAGE the Iroquoian language of the Oneida people [Mid-17thC. From Oneida *onēr̨yote*, name of the main Oneida settlement.] —**Oneida** *adj.*

Oneida[2] /ō nídə/ city in Madison County, central New York State, situated 21 km/13 mi. southwest of Rome. Population: 10,850 (1990).

O'Neill /ō neél/, **Eugene** (1888–1953) US playwright. His realistic psychological dramas include *Mourning Becomes Electra* (1931), *The Iceman Cometh* (1946), and *Long Day's Journey into Night* (1956). He won the Nobel Prize in literature (1936). Full name **Eugene Gladstone O'Neill**

Eugene O'Neill

oneiric /ō ní érik/ *adj.* relating to, experienced in, or similar to a dream or dreams [Mid-19thC. Formed from Greek *oneiros* 'dream'.]

oneiromancy /ō ní ərō manssi/ *n.* the practice of divining the future through the interpretation of dreams [Mid-17thC. Coined from Greek *oneiros* 'dream' + -MANCY.] —**oneiromancer** *n.*

one-liner *n.* a short joke or funny remark in one sentence

one-man *adj.* consisting of, designed for, featuring, or performed by only one person ○ *a one-man tent*

one-man band *n.* **1.** STREET MUSICIAN WITH SEVERAL INSTRUMENTS a street performer who plays several musical instruments at once usually having them strapped to his or her body **2.** ORGANIZATION OF ONE PERSON a business or organization in which one person does all or most of the work

oneness /wúnn nəss/ *n.* **1.** SINGLENESS the quality of being one as opposed to many **2.** UNIQUENESS the quality of being unique **3.** AGREEMENT the state of being united or agreed **4.** SAMENESS the quality of being the same or monotonous [Old English]

one-night stand *n.* **1.** AFFAIR LASTING ONE NIGHT a sexual encounter that lasts for only one night (*informal*) **2.** ONE-NIGHT PERFORMANCE a single performance given at any one place for one night only

one-note *adj.* US limited in ability, scope, or range (*informal*) ○ *a one-note writer*

one-off *adj.* OCCURRING ONCE happening only once, not as part of a series ■ *n.* SINGLE UNREPEATED EVENT a unique and unrepeatable or unrepeated thing or event

one-on-one *adj.* US = one-to-one —**one-on-one** *adv.*

one-person *adj.* consisting of, designed for, featuring, or performed by only one person

one-piece *adj.* NOT SEPARATE consisting of a single, not two or more, components ■ *n.* ONE-PIECE SWIMSUIT a bathing suit consisting of a single piece

oner /wúnnər/ *n.* a unique or extraordinary person or thing (*informal*)

onerous /ónərəss, ónnərəss/ *adj.* **1.** DIFFICULT representing a great burden or much trouble **2.** LAW HAVING DISADVANTAGEOUS OBLIGATIONS involving obligations that are more disadvantageous than advantageous [14thC. Via Old French *onéreux*, from Latin *onerosus*, from *oner-*, stem of *onus* 'burden'.] —**onerously** *adv.* —**onerousness** *n.*

oneself /wun sélf/ *pron.* (*formal*) **1.** REFERRING TO THE SUBJECT used as a pronoun, the reflexive form of 'one', meaning a person's own self ○ *The aim is to improve oneself and one's ability.* **2.** WITHOUT HELP FROM OTHERS used to indicate that sth is done without help or interference from others ○ *One should always try and manage things oneself.* ■ NORMAL SELF your usual or normal self (*formal*) ○ *In such situations one never feels oneself.* [Mid-16thC. From *one's self*.]

one-shot *adj.* (*informal*) **1.** EFFECTIVE AT THE FIRST ATTEMPT taking effect after only one application or attempt ○ *a one-shot solution to financial problems* **2.** US HAPPENING ONLY ONE TIME happening or doing sth only once

one-sided *adj.* **1.** UNFAIRLY WEIGHTED dominated by or favouring one side more than the other in a competition **2.** BIASED presenting or considering one side of a matter whilst ignoring other aspects of it **3.** BIGGER ON ONE SIDE larger, more prominent, or more developed on one side than the other **4. BEING ON ONE SIDE** having or occurring on only one side —**one-sidedly** *adv.* —**one-sidedness** *n.*

one-step *n.* **1. DANCE BALLROOM DANCE** a ballroom dance similar to the foxtrot, in 2/4 time **2. MUSIC DANCE MUSIC** a piece of music written for the one-step ■ *vi.* (**one-steps, one-stepping, one-stepped**) **DANCE DANCE A ONE-STEP** to perform the one-step

one-stop *adj.* offering a wide variety of services or goods in one location so that a customer has to go to only one place ○ *a one-stop home design centre*

one-tailed *adj.* used to describe a statistical test in which all values of the critical region either fall below or exceed a given value, but not both

onetime *adj.* **1. FORMER** having been sth or played a particular role at a previous time ○ *the one-time world champion* **2. one-time HAPPENING ONLY ONCE** done or occurring only once and unlikely to happen again

one-to-one *adj., adv.* **INDIVIDUAL** involving contact or communication between only two people ○ *I find it much easier to teach one-to-one.* US form **one-on-one** ■ *adj.* **1. MATCHING** with one part that corresponds to or matches another **2. MATH WITH PAIRINGS THAT LEAVE NO REMAINDER** used to describe a mathematical set with members such that each member can be paired with one of another set leaving no remainder — **one-to-one** *adv.*

one-track *adj.* focused on, obsessed with, or restricted to only one issue or subject ○ *a one-track mind*

one-two *n.* **1. BOXING TWO SUCCESSIVE PUNCHES** a punch with one hand followed by a punch from the side (**cross**) with the other hand ○ *I gave him the one-two.* US term **one-two punch 2. QUICK SEQUENTIAL ACTIONS OR EVENTS** two actions or events producing an effect because delivered or happening quickly and in sequence ○ *The incumbent could not survive the one-two of a sex scandal and defections by supporters.* US term **one-two punch 3. SOCCER PASS TO ANOTHER PLAYER THEN BACK** a pass made to another player on the same team who then immediately passes to a new position taken up by the original passer

one-two punch *n.* US **1. BOXING** = **one-two** *n.* 1 **2.** = **one-two** *n.* 2 ○ *the one-two punch of a hurricane and then cholera*

one-up (**one-ups, one-upping, one-upped**) *vt.* US to gain an advantage over an opponent (*informal*) ○ *Looks like I've been one-upped again.*

one-upmanship /-úpmənship/ *n.* the practice of attempting to outdo or show yourself to be superior to a rival or opponent

one-way *adj.* **1. TRANSP GOING IN ONE DIRECTION** moving or allowing movement in one direction only ○ *a one-way street* **2. TRANSP NOT ALLOWING A RETURN** allowing sb to travel to a destination but not to return ○ *a one-way ticket* **3. INVOLVING ONLY ONE OF TWO PEOPLE** agreed on, felt, or involving a contribution from one person or party only ○ *a one-way agreement* **4. ALLOWING VIEWING FROM ONE SIDE** made in such a way that it can be looked through from one side but not from the other ○ *one-way glass* ■ *n.* **ONE-WAY ROAD SYSTEM** a one-way road system (*informal*)

one-way mirror *n.* US = **two-way mirror**

one-woman *adj.* consisting of, designed for, featuring, or performed by one woman ○ *a one-woman show*

ongoing /ónn gō ing, -gṓ-/ *adj.* having existed or been in progress for some time and continuing to do so

ONI *abbr.* Office of Naval Intelligence

onion /únnyən/ *n.* **1. EDIBLE BULB USED AS A VEGETABLE** a vegetable in the form of a rounded edible bulb with hard pungent flesh in concentric layers beneath a flaky brown skin **2. PLANT WITH PUNGENT BULBS** an Asian plant of the lily family with greenish-white flowers whose bulb is the onion. Latin name: *Allium cepa*. **3. PLANT RELATED TO THE ONION** any plant related to the onion, e.g. the Welsh onion [12thC. From Latin *unio* 'onion', of uncertain origin: perhaps directly or via *unio* 'pearl' (from the colour and shape), from *unus* 'one' (from the 'unity' formed by the layers).] —**oniony** *adj.*

Onion

onion dome *n.* a rounded dome resembling an onion in shape, typical of Russian and Byzantine church architecture

onionskin /únnyən skin/ *n.* a type of smooth thin translucent paper formerly used especially for making carbon copies

Onitsha /ō níchə/ city in Anambra State, southeastern Nigeria, situated about 362 km/225 mi. east of Lagos. Population: 336,600 (1992).

-onium *suffix.* a complex cation ○ *diazonium* [From AMMONIUM]

onium ion /óni əm-/ *n.* **CHEM** a positively charged ion (**cation**) that is analogous to the ammonium ion. Formula: NH_4^+. ◊ **cation**

on-label *adj.* US using or involving the use of a prescription drug to treat a condition for which the drug is approved by the US Food and Drug Administration

onlay *vt.* /on láy/ (**-lays, -laying, -laid**) **LAY STH ON A SURFACE** to lay sth on a surface, especially for decorative reasons, so that it stands in relief ■ *n.* /ónlay/ **1. MED SKIN GRAFT** a skin graft surgically transferred to the surface of an organ or other part of the body **2. DENT INLAY IN A TOOTH** an inlay fixed to the biting surface of a tooth [15thC. From ON + LAY (verb).]

online *pron., adj., adv.* **COMPUT CONNECTED VIA A COMPUTER** attached to or available through a central computer or computer network. ◊ **off-line** ■ *adj.* **1. CHEM ENG DIRECTLY CONNECTED TO A MEASURABLE PROCESS** used to describe an instrument or sensor that is connected directly to a process being measured, thus obviating the need to take samples for analysis in a laboratory or elsewhere **2. US ONGOING** currently going on or being done ■ *adv.* **WHILE CONNECTED TO A COMPUTER** while under the control of a computer or connected to a computer network

onliner /ón līnər/ *n.* a user or a supplier of online computer services

onload /on lṓd/ (**-loads, -loading, -loaded**) *vti.* to load freight onto a vehicle

onlooker /ón lŏŏkər/ *n.* sb who watches an event without participating in it —**onlooking** *adj.*

only /ónli/ **CORE MEANING:** an adverb used to indicate the one thing or person that solely or exclusively happens or is involved in a situation ○ *facilities for club members only* ○ *I will act only in the best interests of our country.* ○ *The regulations apply only to new firms.*
1. *adv.* **INDICATING A CONDITION** used to indicate the condition that exists for sth to happen or be true ○ *I'll go to the party, but only if you come with me.* **2.** *adv.* **MERELY** merely the situation, level, or amount stated ○ *I could only stand and look.* ○ *That's only part of the picture.* **3.** *adv.* **NO MORE AND NO LESS** just the particular amount specified ○ *There are only 3.3 people at work for every person retired.* **4.** *adv.* **AS RECENTLY AS** considered as happening very recently ○ *only last March* **5.** *adv.* **INDICATING AN EVENT HAPPENING IMMEDIATELY AFTER** used to introduce a surprising or unpleasant event that happens immediately after the one mentioned ○ *We rushed the cat to the vet, only to find there was nothing wrong with it.* **6.** *adv.* **Ireland EMPHASIZING** used to emphasize a statement ○ *It was only terrible.* **7.** *adj.* **THE SINGLE PERSON OR THING** used to indicate the single person or thing involved in a situation ○ *the only Democratic candidate* ○ *the only barrier between himself and the job* **8.** *adj.* **WITH**

NO SIBLINGS with no brothers or sisters ○ *an only child.* **9.** *conj.* **BUT** but or except ○ *It's the same product, only better.* [Old English *ānlic*, from *ān* 'one' (see ONE)] ◊ **only too** used to emphasize the extent to which sth is true ○ *Scenes like this are getting only too familiar.*

on-message *adj.* following the official policy of a political party or other organization ○ *The views expressed were most definitely not on-message.*

Yoko Ono and John Lennon

Ono, Yoko (b. 1933) Japanese-born US artist. She was known for her avant-garde performance art, which after her marriage to John Lennon in 1969 included protests against the Vietnam War.

o.n.o. *abbr.* or nearest offer (*used in advertisements*)

onomasiology /ónnō máyssi ólləjji/ *n.* **1. BRANCH OF SEMANTICS** the branch of linguistics that studies how meaning is expressed **2.** = **onomastics** *n.* 1 [Early 20thC. Coined from Greek *onomasia* 'name' + -LOGY.]

onomastic /ónnə mástik/ *adj.* relating to, connected with, or explaining names [Late 16thC. Via French, from Greek *onomastikos*, from, ultimately, *onoma* 'name' (source also of English *name*).]

onomastics /ónnə mástiks/ *n.* (*takes a singular verb*) **1. STUDY OF PROPER NAMES** the study of proper names, their origins, and their formation **2. SYSTEM OF NAMES IN A SPECIALIZED FIELD** the system underlying the creation and use of proper names in a specialized field

onomatopoeia /ónnō matə peé ə/ *n.* the formation or use of words that imitate the sound associated with the thing or action in question, e.g. 'hiss' and 'buzz' [Late 16thC. Via late Latin, from Greek *onomatopoiia* 'making of words', from, ultimately, *onoma* 'name' + *poiein* 'to make' (see POEM).] —**onomatopoeically** *adv.*

onomatopoeic /ónnə matə peé ik/ *adj.* imitative of the sound associated with the thing or action denoted by a particular word —**onomatopoeically** *adv.*

Onondaga /ónnən dáagə/ (*plural* **-gas** or **-ga**) *n.* **1. PEOPLES MEMBER OF A NATIVE AMERICAN PEOPLE** a member of a Native North American people that originally occupied lands in central New York State and whose members mainly continue to live there as well as in Ontario. The Onondaga were one of the five peoples who formed the Iroquois Confederacy, which later became known as the Six Nations. **2. LANG NATIVE AMERICAN LANGUAGE** an Iroquoian language spoken in central areas of New York State and in parts of Ontario, belonging to the Hokan-Siouan languages [Late 17thC. From Onondaga *onṓtà?ke*, the name of the main Onondaga settlement.] —**Onondaga** *adj.*

Onondaga, Lake /ónnən dáagə/ lake in Onondaga County, central New York State

onrush /ón rush/ *n.* a forward rush or push ○ *the onrush of enemy soldiers* ○ *the onrush of events* — **onrushing** *adj.*

on-screen *adj., adv.* appearing on the screen in a television programme or film and therefore visible to the audience ○ *Their private life was very different from their on-screen relationship.*

onset /ón set/ *n.* **1. START** the beginning of sth, especially of sth difficult or unpleasant ○ *the onset of winter* **2. MIL INITIAL MILITARY ATTACK** an initial attack or assault in battle [Early 16thC. Formed from SET (noun).]

onshore /ón sháwr/ *adj.* **ON LAND** on land as opposed to at sea ○ *onshore drilling* ■ *adj., adv.* **METEOROL IN THE DIRECTION OF LAND** towards land from the sea ○ *onshore breeze* —**onshore** *adv.*

onside /ón síd/ *adj., adv.* in a position that is allowed within the rules of the game, e.g. in soccer or hockey

on-site *adj., adv.* taking place or provided at the location where work or some other activity is being carried out

onslaught /ón slawt/ *n.* **1.** OVERWHELMING ASSAULT OR FORCE a powerful attack or force that overwhelms sb or sth **2.** VERY LARGE AMOUNT OF STH a very large quantity of people or things that is difficult to deal with or process ○ *faced with an onslaught of junk mail* [Early 17thC. Via Dutch *aanslag*, from Middle Dutch *aenslach*, literally 'blow on', from *slach* 'blow'. Influenced by obsolete English *slaught* 'slaughter'.]

onstage /ón stáyj/ *adj., adv.* performing, happening, or existing on the stage as opposed to in the wings, backstage, or somewhere not visible to the audience

on-stream *adj., adv.* in or into production or operation ○ *when the new system comes on-stream*

Ont., ON *abbr.* Ontario

ont- *prefix.* = onto- (*used before vowels*)

-ont *suffix.* cell, organism ○ *schizont* [From Greek *ont-*, literally 'being' (see ONTO-)]

Ontario

Ontario /on táiri ō/ Canadian province situated between the Great Lakes and Hudson Bay. Capital: Toronto. Population: 10,753,573 (1996). Area: 1,068,580 sq. km/412,579 sq. mi. —**Ontarian** *n., adj.*

Ontario, Lake lake in North America, the easternmost and smallest of the Great Lakes, straddling the US-Canadian border and bounded by New York State and Ontario Province. Its outflow is the St Lawrence River. Area: 19,011 sq. km/7,340 sq. mi.

on-the-job *adj.* provided or obtained while working at a job ○ *on-the-job training*

ontic /óntik/ *adj.* relating to real existence [Mid-20thC. Formed from the Greek stem *ont-* 'being' (see ONTO-).]

onto (*stressed*) /ón too/; (*unstressed*) /óntə, óntoō/ CORE MEANING: a preposition indicating that sb or sth is located on sth, or moves towards it so as to be on it ○ *I splashed water onto my face.* ○ *hop onto a bus* ○ *shine a flashlight onto the wall* ○ *loading the data onto a disk* ○ *come onto the market* *prep.* **1.** MAKING A DISCOVERY making or about to make a discovery, often about sth secret or illegal ○ *I'm really onto something big here.* ○ *The police were onto them.* **2.** IN CONTACT in contact with a person or organization ○ *Get onto the suppliers.* [Early 18thC. Formed from ON + TO.]

onto- *prefix.* **1.** being, existence ○ *ontology* **2.** organism ○ *ontogeny* [From Greek *ont-*, the present participle stem of *einai* 'to be'. Ultimately from an Indo-European base that is also the ancestor of English *am*, *is*, and *entity*.]

ontogeny /on tójjəni/, **ontogenesis** /óntə jénnəssiss/ *n.* the development of an individual from a fertilized ovum to maturity, as contrasted with the development of a group or species (**phylogeny**) — **ontogenic** /óntə jénnik/ *adj.* —**ontogenically** *adv.*

ontological argument /óntə lójjik'l-/ *n.* an argument made by St Anselm and others to prove the existence of God by pointing to God's essence as a perfect, necessary being

ontology /on tólləji/ (*plural* **-gies**) *n.* **1.** PHILOS STUDY OF EXISTENCE the most general branch of metaphysics, concerned with the nature of being **2.** THEORY OF EXISTENCE a particular theory of being [Early 18thC. From modern Latin, literally 'study of being', from the Greek

stem *ont-* 'being' (see ONT-).] —**ontological** /óntə lójjik'l/ *adj.* —**ontologically** *adv.* —**ontologist** /on tóllǝjist/ *n.*

onus /ónəss/ *n.* **1.** BURDEN a duty or responsibility ○ *The onus is on her to make the first move.* **2.** BLAME the blame for sth ○ *He'll always bear the onus of having caused the accident.* **3.** LAW BURDEN OF PROOF OR PROCEEDING the burden of proof or responsibility for acting in a legal proceeding [Mid-17thC. From Latin, 'burden, load' (source of English *onerous*).]

onward /ónwərd/ *adj.* MOVING FORWARD directed or moving forward in space, time, or development ○ *the great onward march of organization and life* ■ *adv.* **onward, onwards** AT OR TO A POINT AHEAD moving towards a point or position ahead in space, time, or development

onycholysis /ónni kólləssiss/ *n.* the separation of all or part of a fingernail or thumbnail from its bed, associated with psoriasis or a fungal skin condition [From modern Latin, from Greek *onukh-*, stem of *onux* 'nail, claw' (source of English *onyx*)]

onychophoran /ónni kóffərən/ *n.* a small invertebrate without jointed limbs, considered intermediate between annelid worms and arthropods. Order: Onychophora. [Late 19thC. Formed from modern Latin *Onychophora*, ultimately from the Greek stem *onukh-* 'claw' + *-phoros* 'bearing', from the curved claws.]

-onym *suffix.* name, word ○ *pseudonym* [From Greek *onuma* (see ONOMASTIC)]

onymous /ónnimǝss/ *adj.* having a name rather than being anonymous [Late 18thC. From ANONYMOUS.]

onyx /ónniks/ *n.* a fine-grained variety of the mineral chalcedony, used as a gemstone. It has alternating parallel layers of different colours, including white, brown, and black. Cameo brooches are sometimes carved from this stone with the white layer standing out in relief against a darker background. [13thC. Directly and via Old French and Latin from Greek *onux* 'fingernail, claw'. From the colour of some types of the stone.]

o.o., **o/o** *abbr.* on order

oo- *prefix.* ovum, egg ○ *oospore* [From Greek *ōion*. Ultimately from the Indo-European word for 'egg' that is also the ancestor of English *egg*, *oval*, *caviar*, and *cockney*.]

oocyst /ṓ əssist/ *n.* ZOOL the fertilized gamete of certain parasitic organisms (**sporozoans**) that is enclosed in a thick wall

oocyte /ṓ ə síīt/ *n.* BIOL a cell that develops into a female reproductive cell (**ovum**)

O.O.D. *abbr.* NAVY officer of the deck

O'Odham *n.* PEOPLES, LANG = Papago

oodles /ōōd'lz/ *npl.* a large amount or number of sth (*informal*) ○ *She has oodles of friends.* [Mid-19thC. Origin uncertain: perhaps from HUDDLE 'mass of things crowded together'.]

oogamete /ṓ óggə meet/ *n.* BIOL a female reproductive cell (**ovum**)

oogenesis /ṓ ə jénnəssiss/ *n.* BIOL the formation and development of an ovum —**oogenetic** /ṓ əjə néttik/ *adj.*

oogonium /ṓ ə gốni əm/ (*plural* **-a** /-i ə/ *or* **-ums**) *n.* **1.** CELL IN AN OVARY a cell in the ovary that develops into an oocyte **2.** ALGAL SEX ORGAN the female sex organ of some algae and fungi that contains oospheres [Mid-19thC. Formed from OO- + Greek *gonos* 'generation, seed'.] —**oogonial** *adj.*

ooh /ōō/ *interj.* USED TO EXPRESS SURPRISE used as an exclamation of surprise, excitement, pleasure, or pain (*informal*) ■ *vi.* (**oohs, oohing, oohed**) EXPRESS SURPRISE OR AWE to exclaim in surprise, excitement, pleasure, or pain, especially on first encountering sth ○ *When they went into the royal chambers, you could hear them oohing and aahing.* ■ *n.* EXCLAMATION OF SURPRISE an exclamation of surprise, excitement, pleasure, or pain [Early 20thC. Natural exclamation.] ◇ **ooh la la** used to show pleasant surprise or approval, or, humorously, to suggest that sth is scandalous

oolite /ṓ ə līt/ *n.* **1.** FORM OF SEDIMENTARY ROCK a sedimentary rock, often shale, clay, or sandstone, that is made up of small spherical grains consisting of concentric layers **2.** ROUND GRAIN OF ROCK any of the small spherical grains that make up oolite [Early

19thC. Via French *oölithe*, from modern Latin *oolites*, from Greek *ōion* 'egg' + *lithos* 'stone'.] —**oolitic** /ṓ ə líttik/ *adj.*

oolong /ōō long/ *n.* a type of dark Chinese tea that is partly fermented before being dried (*often used before a noun*) ○ *oolong tea* [Mid-19thC. From Chinese (Mandarin) *wulong*, from *wu* 'black' + *long* 'dragon'.]

oompah /ōō mpaa/, **oompah-pah** /ōō m paa paa/ *n.* a representation of the sound made by a bass brass instrument, considered typical of some kinds of band music (*often used before a noun*) ○ *an oompah band* [Late 19thC. An imitation of the sound.]

oomph /ōōmf/ *n.* **1.** ENERGY energy or enthusiasm ○ *Put some oomph into it!* **2.** US SEXUAL ATTRACTIVENESS strong or obvious sexual attractiveness (*slang*) [Mid-20thC. Origin uncertain: perhaps expressive of exertion.]

OOP *abbr.* COMPUT object-oriented programming

oophorectomy /ṓ əfə réktəmi/ (*plural* **-mies**) *n.* = ovariectomy [Late 19thC. Formed from modern Latin *oophoron* 'ovary', literally 'egg-bearer', ultimately from Greek *ōion* 'egg'.]

oophoritis /ṓ əfə ríītiss/ *n.* ovary inflammation [Late 19thC. Formed from modern Latin *oophoron* 'ovary' (see OOPHORECTOMY).]

oops /ōōps, oops/ *interj.* used as an exclamation when you drop sth, bump into sb, or do sth in a clumsy or awkward manner (*informal*) ○ *She dropped the entire tray? Oops!* [Mid-20thC. Natural exclamation.]

Oort cloud /áwrt-, oórt-/ *n.* a huge, roughly spherical, orbiting collection of comets thought to exist at the edge of the solar system [Late 20thC. Named after Jan Hendrix Oort (1900–92), the Dutch astronomer who postulated its existence.]

oose /ōōss/ *n. Scotland* fluff from textiles (*informal*)

oosphere /ṓ ə sfeer/ *n.* BIOL an unfertilized female reproductive cell in algae and fungi [Late 19thC. Coined from OO- + SPHERE.]

oospore /ṓ ə spawr/ *n.* BIOL a fertilized female reproductive cell in algae and fungi [Mid-19thC. Coined from OO- + SPORE.] —**oosporic** /ṓ ə spórrik/ *adj.* —**oosporous** /ṓ óspərəss/ *adj.*

ootid /ṓ ətid/ *n.* BIOL the stage in the development of an egg cell that becomes the mature ovum immediately prior to fertilization. It is a haploid cell formed by division of the secondary oocyte. [Early 20thC. Formed from OO-, modelled on SPERMATID.]

ooze[1] /ōōz/ *v.* (**oozes, oozing, oozed**) **1.** *vti.* FLOW OR LEAK SLOWLY to exude a liquid substance slowly and in small quantities, or to flow in this way ○ *Resin oozed from the trunk.* **2.** *vti.* OVERFLOW WITH SOME QUALITY OR EMOTION to possess a quality in abundance or express an emotion intensely, or to be expressed in an intense or overpowering way ○ *oozing charm and self-confidence* **3.** *vi.* MOVE SLOWLY BUT STEADILY to move slowly but steadily forward or outward ○ *The huge crowd oozed through the streets.* **4.** *vi.* EBB to disappear or decline slowly and gradually ■ *n.* **1.** VERY SLOW FLOW a slow and gradual leakage or flow **2.** TANNING SOLUTION an infusion used in tanning, made from oak bark and other plant materials [Old English *wōs* 'juice, sap']

ooze[2] /ōōz/ *n.* **1.** SLUDGE thick mud or slime that is found at the bottom of a river or lake **2.** BOG OR MARSH a soft or muddy area such as a bog or marsh **3.** MARINE BIOL SEDIMENT ON THE OCEAN FLOOR a layer of muddy sediment on the seafloor consisting mainly of the remains of microscopic organisms such as plankton [Old English *wāse*]

ooze leather *n.* a soft leather with a velvety finish [*Ooze* from OOZE[1] in the sense 'tanning solution']

oozy[1] /ōōzi/ (**-ier, -iest**) *adj.* leaking moisture [Old English; formed from OOZE[1]]

oozy[2] /ōōzi/ (**-ier, -iest**) *adj.* wet and muddy [Old English; formed from OOZE[2]]

op /op/ (*plural* **ops**) *n.* a surgical operation (*informal*)

OP *abbr.* **1.** order of preachers (*a title used by the Dominican order of friars*) **2.** observation post **3.** out of print

op. *abbr.* **1.** op., Op. opus **2.** operation **3.** opposite **4.** optical **5.** opera

opacify /ō pássi fī/ (**-fies, -fying, -fied**) *vti.* to become opaque or turn or make sth opaque [Early 20thC. Formed from OPACITY.] —**opacifier** *n.*

opacity /ō pássəti/ (*plural* **-ties**) *n.* **1.** BEING OPAQUE the quality, state, or degree of being opaque **2.** OBSCURITY the quality of being obscure in meaning **3.** PHOTOGRAPHY, PHYS ABILITY OF MATERIAL TO STOP LIGHT the capacity of a material such as photographic film to stop light, expressed as a comparison between light striking the material and light transmitted **4.** PHILOS PROPOSITIONS NOT ADHERING TO LEIBNITZ'S LAW propositions containing modal notions such as necessity or belief in which principles of logic such as Leibnitz's law do not obtain [Mid-16thC. Via French, from, ultimately, Latin *opacus* 'shaded, dark' (which also produced English *opaque*).]

opah /ṓpə/ *n.* a brightly coloured marine fish that can be up to 1.8 m/6 ft long. Latin name: *Lampris regius.* [Mid-18thC. From a West African language.]

opal /ṓp'l/ *n.* **1.** NON-CRYSTALLINE SILICA a non-crystalline variety of silica that can be of almost any colour and contains varying amounts of water **2.** GEMSTONE a piece of one of the non-crystalline varieties of opal, used as a gemstone [Late 16thC. From French *opale* or Latin *opalus*, of uncertain origin: probably ultimately from Sanskrit *upala* 'precious stone', from, ultimately, *upa* 'below' (source of English *Upanishad*.]

opalesce /ṓpə léss/ (**-esces, -escing, -esced**) *vi.* to display shimmering milky colours (*refers to opals*) [Early 19thC. Coined from OPAL + Latin *-esce* 'assuming a certain state'.]

opalescent /ṓpə léss'nt/ *adj.* showing or possessing shimmering milky colours —**opalescence** *n.*

opaleye /ṓp'l ī/ (*plural* **-eyes** or **-eye**) *n.* a common greenish omnivorous marine fish of the Californian and Mexican coast that has two white spots on its back. Latin name: *Girella nigricans.* [From the opalescent appearence of its eyes]

opaline /ṓpə līn, -leen/ *adj.* = opalescent ■ *n.* CRAFT OPAL GLASS a semi-translucent glass made by adding fluorides

opaque /ō páyk/ *adj.* **1.** NOT TRANSPARENT OR TRANSLUCENT impervious to light, so that images cannot be seen through it **2.** NOT SHINY dull and without lustre **3.** HARD TO UNDERSTAND obscure and unintelligible in meaning **4.** PHYS IMPENETRABLE BY RADIATION impenetrable by a specified form of radiation ■ *n.* MATERIAL THROUGH WHICH LIGHT CANNOT PASS sth opaque, especially a photographic pigment [15thC. Directly or via French, from Latin *opacus* 'shaded, dark'.] —**opaquely** *adv.* —**opaqueness** *n.*

opaque projector *n. US, Can* = episcope

op art *n.* a 20th-century school of abstract art that uses geometric patterns and colour to create the illusion of movement (*often used before a noun*) ○ *op art designs* [Shortening of OPTICAL ART, modelled on POP ART] —**op artist** *n.*

op. cit. *abbr.* in the text or texts quoted (*used in footnotes to refer to a source just mentioned*) [Shortening of Latin *opus citatum* or *opere citato*]

ope /ōp/ *adj.* OPEN open (*archaic or literary*) ■ *vti.* (**opes, oping, oped**) TO OPEN to open, or open sth (*archaic or literary*) [From OPEN]

OPEC /ṓ pek/ *n.* an organization of countries that share the same policies regarding the sale of petroleum. The members are Algeria, Gabon, Indonesia, Iran, Iraq, Kuwait, Libya, Nigeria, Qatar, Saudi Arabia, the United Arab Emirates, and Venezuela. Full form **Organization of Petroleum Exporting Countries**

open /ṓpən/ *adj.* **1.** NOT CLOSED OR LOCKED allowing people or things to pass through freely ○ *an open window* **2.** ALLOWING ACCESS TO THE INSIDE with the lid, cork, or other device removed or in a position that allows access to the inside ○ *an open box* **3.** NOT SEALED not sealed, fastened, or wrapped ○ *an open envelope* **4.** APART OR WIDE with a part of the body widened or apart ○ *The kitten's eyes were open.* **5.** UNFOLDED OR APART having been unfolded, extended, or left apart ○ *A newspaper lay open on the table.* **6.** FRANK AND HONEST not trying to hide anything or deceive anyone ○ *open hostility* **7.** PUBLIC conducted in a public manner ○ *open hearings* **8.** RECEPTIVE ready and willing to accept or listen to sth, e.g. new ideas or suggestions ○ *I'm always open to suggestions.* **9.** VULNERABLE in a position where blame, criticism, or attack are likely ○ *That remark left him open to criticism.* **10.** NOT ENCLOSED having no boundaries or enclosures ○ *open countryside* **11.** NOT COVERED having no cover or roof ○ *an open fire* **12.** AVAILABLE TO DO BUSINESS ready for business and available for use by customers or clients ○ *The garage is still open.* **13.** FREELY ACCESSIBLE accessible to all, with no restrictions on entry, membership, or acceptance ○ *an open meeting* **14.** ACCESSIBLE TO A PARTICULAR GROUP accessible to a particular group of interested people ○ *This competition is open to all students under the age of 18.* **15.** VACANT ready for or available to applicants ○ *The vacancy is no longer open.* **16.** *US* UTIL TURNED ON switched on and ready to use ○ *an open microphone* **17.** NOT PREDETERMINED OR DECIDED remaining undecided or unresolved ○ *I'm trying to keep my options open.* **18.** ALERT in a state of focused attention and alertness ○ *Keep your eyes and ears open.* **19.** WITH NO TIME RESTRICTION with no restrictions on the period of use ○ *an open ticket* **20.** *US* GENEROUS very free or generous, especially with money ○ *She gave to charity with an open hand.* **21.** *US* NOT HAVING LEGAL RESTRICTIONS not having restrictions that limit activities such as gambling or drinking ○ *an open town* **22.** SPORTS UNGUARDED unprotected by the assigned player ○ *He left the goal wide open.* **23.** UNPROTECTED BY SKIN unprotected and exposed, with the skin cut, torn, or missing ○ *an open wound* **24.** MED NOT BLOCKED free from blockage and therefore allowing unobstructed passage **25.** TEXTILES HAVING GAPS with small gaps or intervals between the stitches or threads ○ *an open weave* **26.** NAUT FREE FROM ICE OR OTHER HAZARDS not covered by ice or containing objects dangerous to shipping ○ *open water* **27.** MUSIC NOT CLOSED OR MUTED not closed off at the end, stopped by a finger, or covered with a mute ○ *an open organ pipe* **28.** METEOROL FROSTLESS mild and free of frost **29.** MIL KNOWN TO BE UNDEFENDED publicly declared not to be garrisoned or defended in wartime ○ *an open city* **30.** FIN AVAILABLE WITHOUT LIMITATIONS freely available without restrictions ○ *open credit* **31.** FIN CURRENTLY ACTIVE active and with transactions being made ○ *an open bank account* **32.** PRINTING HAVING UNUSUALLY WIDE SPACES with wide spacing between printed lines **33.** PHON ENDING IN A VOWEL used to describe a syllable that ends in a vowel **34.** GRAM HAVING SEPARATE ELEMENTS formed by two or more words that are spelled separately and without hyphenation ○ *an open compound* **35.** CHESS WITHOUT PAWNS not having pawns as part of a file **36.** SPORTS HAVING THE FRONT FOOT BACK having the front foot farther from the line along which the ball is to be hit than the back foot ○ *Adopting an open stance, he began hitting the ball to the opposite field.* **37.** MATH CONTAINING NO ENDPOINTS used to describe a mathematical interval that contains neither of a set's endpoints **38.** MATH REFERRING TO SET QUALITY used to describe a mathematical set that has at least one neighbourhood of every point within the set **39.** MATH SERVING AS A COMPLEMENT TO A CLOSED SET used to describe a mathematical set that is in a complementary relation to a closed set ■ *v.* (**opens, opening, opened**) **1.** *vti.* UNFASTEN FROM A LOCKED OR CLOSED POSITION to change position or move so as to allow access, or to change the position of or move sth such as a door or window in order to allow access **2.** *vt.* UNSEAL OR UNFASTEN STH to remove or unseal the lid, cork, or other device that keeps sth such as a container closed **3.** *vt.* UNWRAP STH to reveal the contents of sth, e.g. by removing its wrapping ○ *I opened the parcel.* **4.** *vti.* UNFOLD TO SHOW INSIDE to unfold sth or spread it apart so that the inner part is revealed ○ *Open your books at page 75.* **5.** *vti.* PART THE LIPS OR EYELIDS to move apart, or move the lips or eyelids apart **6.** *vti.* COMM START TRADING to start selling, trading, or doing business or to allow clients or customers access in order to buy, trade, or do business **7.** *vt.* GET UNDER WAY to start sth formally ○ *She opened the meeting with a speech about the environment.* **8.** *vt.* BANKING START AN ACCOUNT to start an active banking or investment account **9.** *vt.* DECLARE TO BE IN OPERATION OR SESSION to make an official and usually public declaration that sth is now ready for use or in session ○ *The sports centre was officially opened by the mayor.* **10.** *vti.* BEGIN SHOWING TO THE PUBLIC to start being shown to or performed for the general public for the first time ○ *The show opens on Friday.* **11.** *vt.* BECOME ACCESSIBLE TO THE PUBLIC to be visited by the public, or become accessible to the public ○ *The house opens to the public in August.* **12.** *vt.* REMOVE OBSTRUCTIONS to allow people free access when formerly this was denied or obstructed ○ *The country had finally opened its borders to the West.* **13.** *vt.* GIVE ACCESS TO A PLACE to provide access directly to another place (*refers to part of a building*) ○ *The bedroom opened onto a large living room.* **14.** *vti.* BE READY FOR NEW IDEAS to become or make sb ready to accept new ideas ○ *Try opening your mind a bit.* **15.** *vi.* BEGIN TO RAIN to produce a downpour ○ *The heavens opened.* **16.** *vi.* UNFOLD to open out fully (*refers to flowers or leaves*) ○ *The daffodils will open soon.* **17.** *vt.* MED EMPTY BOWELS to cause the bowels to evacuate **18.** *vi.* STOCK EXCH START TRADING AT A PARTICULAR VALUE to have a particular value at the start of a day's trading on a stock exchange ■ *n.* **1.** SPORTS COMPETITION ANYONE CAN ENTER a competition or championship in which anybody, amateur or professional, can compete **2.** OUTSIDE a large and unobstructed outdoor space ○ *in the open* **3.** UNCONCEALED STATE the state of being no longer hidden or held back ○ *It's good to get all the facts out in the open.* [Old English. Ultimately from an Indo-European word meaning 'up from under, over' that is also the ancestor of English *up*.] —**openness** *n.*

open up *v.* **1.** *vi.* UNFOLD to expand or unfold, e.g. before a viewer **2.** *vti.* MAKE STH ACCESSIBLE to make sth more accessible or available to a wider range of people **3.** *vt.* MAKE AN OPENING IN STH to make an opening in sth, especially in order to get access **4.** *vt.* REMOVE A COVER OR OBSTRUCTION FROM to remove the wrapping, restrictions, obstructions, or covering from sth **5.** *vti.* = open *v.* 6 ○ *A new video store is opening up next week* **6.** *vi.* SPEAK FREELY to speak honestly, especially about personal feelings or experiences ○ *She opens up when she gets to know you.* **7.** *vi.* TELL WHAT YOU KNOW to confess to a crime or give information about a crime under coercion (*informal*) **8.** *vi.* START SHOOTING A WEAPON to start firing or cause a gun or other weapon to start firing **9.** *vti.* OPEN BUSINESS FOR THE TRADING to unlock sth, especially a shop or business premises, so that trading can begin **10.** *vi.* MAKE A VEHICLE GO FASTER to cause a motor vehicle to accelerate, or to travel at an accelerated speed (*informal*) **11.** *vti.* SPORTS BECOME OR MAKE STH MORE EXCITING to become, or cause sth to become, more interesting or exciting ○ *After the first goal the match opened up.*

open-air *adj.* situated or happening outside a building

open-and-shut *adj.* simple and easily resolved ○ *an open-and-shut case*

open bar *n. US* a bar at a party, wedding, or other social function where the drinks are served free of charge

open book *n.* sb or sth that is very easy to understand or about which everything is known

open-cast *adj.* mined in such a way that minerals or other materials are excavated from the surface rather than deep underground ○ *open-cast mining*

open chain *adj.* an arrangement of atoms in a molecule in which the atoms are not joined at the ends to form a ring

open court *n.* a trial or court that is open to members of the public, and whose proceedings are recorded

open day *n.* a day on which an institution such as a school or university is open to the public for visitors to view aspects of its work and activities. US term **open house**

open door *n.* **1.** FREE TRADE POLICY a policy whereby a nation allows free and unrestricted trade with all other nations (*hyphenated before a noun*) **2.** UNRESTRICTED ACCESS free and unrestricted access at all times (*hyphenated when used before a noun*) ○ *open-door management*

open-end *adj. US* = open-ended

open-ended *adj.* **1.** WITH NO PREARRANGED END with no planned or defined end **2.** EASILY MODIFIED not definite and easily changed ○ *We'd left everything pretty open-ended about the holidays.* **3.** NEEDING MORE THAN A ONE WORD ANSWER requiring or allowing an answer that is fuller than a simple yes or no ○ *an open-ended question* **4.** HAVING NO LIMITS not having a fixed limit in either time or amount ○ *an open-ended contract.* US term **open-end** *adj.*

open-ended investment company (*plural* **open-ended investment companies**) *n.* a limited company managing investments for investors with holdings in the form of units representing a fraction of the value of the investments that are issued by and bought back by the managers

opener /ópənər/ *n.* **1.** OPENING DEVICE a device for opening containers such as tins, cans, or bottles **2.** INITIAL EVENT sb or sth that begins a discussion or event (*informal*) **3.** CARDS OPENING PLAYER sb who opens the bidding, betting, or play in a card game **4.** SPORTS FIRST GAME the first game in a series or season ■ **openers** *npl.* CARDS STARTING POINT a starting position or point, e.g. cards that allow sb to begin the betting in some card games ◇ **for openers** used to open a statement or discussion (*informal*)

open-eyed *adj.* **1.** WATCHFUL alert to all that is happening **2.** WITH EYES WIDE IN WONDER with the eyes wide open in wonder or surprise **3.** ASSESSING REALISTICALLY realistic in knowing and accepting all aspects of a situation

open-faced *adj.* with a face that suggests an honest, straightforward, and sincere character

open-faced sandwich *n.* US = **open sandwich**

openhanded /ópən hándid/ *adj.* generous with money or other material things —**openhandedly** *adv.* —**openhandedness** *n.*

openhearted /ópən haártid/ *adj.* sincere and generous in spirit towards other people —**openheartedly** *adv.* —**openheartedness** *n.*

open-hearth *adj.* used to describe a steel-making process that uses a furnace with a shallow hearth and a low roof (**reverberatory furnace**) to produce high-quality steel

open-heart surgery *n.* heart surgery during which the heart is exposed and blood is circulated outside the body by mechanical means

open house *n.* **1.** READY HOSPITALITY a situation or occasion when visitors are welcome at any time ○ *It's open house here – come over whenever you like!* **2.** US = **open day**

opening /ópəning/ *n.* **1.** GAP a gap or hole in sth, especially one through which you can see or through which people or animals can pass ○ *We found an opening in the fence.* **2.** FIRST PART the first part of sth ○ *The movie has a wonderful opening.* **3.** FIRST TIME STH IS USED OR DONE the often formal occasion when sth new such as a building or road is used for the first time, or when sth starts again after stopping for some time (*often used before a noun*) ○ *the opening ceremony* **4.** FIRST PERFORMANCE FOR THE GENERAL PUBLIC the first public performance or showing of a play, exhibition, or other production (*often used before a noun*) ○ *the opening night* **5.** OPPORTUNITY an opportunity to do sth ○ *It gave her an opening to say how delighted she was.* **6.** VACANCY a job that is available ○ *We have an opening for a young person with drive and enthusiasm.* **7.** ACT OF OPENING the act of opening sth **8.** US CLEARING IN WOODS an area in a wood or forest in which trees do not grow **9.** CHESS BEGINNING OF A GAME the first moves of a game, especially in chess and draughts **10.** LAW FIRST STATEMENT BY COUNSEL IN TRIAL the initial statement made by the prosecuting and defending barristers in a trial, before witnesses are called to give evidence

opening time *n.* the time at which pubs in the United Kingdom are legally allowed to start serving alcohol

open interval *n.* in mathematics, a set of real numbers consisting of all numbers between but excluding its endpoints, usually written (a,b) or]a,b[

open-jaw *adj.* AIR used to describe a flight or flight booking that goes to one destination and returns from another and is booked as a round-trip ticket

open learning *n.* a system of further education that allows people to learn on a flexible part-time basis (*often used before a noun*) ○ *open learning courses*

open letter *n.* a letter that is addressed to an individual or organization but is intended for every-

body to read and is published in a newspaper or magazine

openly *adv.* without making any attempt at concealment ○ *Many members were openly hostile to the proposed plan.*

open market *n.* a market with no commercial restrictions that allows free competition between buyers and sellers

open marriage *n.* a marriage in which each partner agrees to allow the other to engage in sexual relationships with other people

open-minded *adj.* free from prejudice and receptive to new ideas —**open-mindedly** *adv.* —**open-mindedness** *n.*

open-mouthed *adj.* **1.** WITH THE MOUTH OPEN with the mouth wide open in surprise or wonder **2.** VERY DEMANDING loudly and persistently demanding or complaining —**open-mouthedly** *adv.* —**open-mouthedness** *n.*

open-necked *adj.* with the top button unfastened ○ *an open-necked shirt*

open-plan *adj.* having a large space left open rather than divided up into smaller units, especially in a workplace

open-pollinated *adj.* pollinated naturally, without human intervention

open prison *n.* a prison with security measures that are appropriate to inmates who are not dangerous and are unlikely to try to escape

open punctuation *n.* minimal punctuation, especially minimal use of commas

open sandwich *n.* a sandwich consisting of a single slice of bread with filling on it but no second piece of bread on top, sometimes eaten with a knife and fork. US term **open-faced sandwich**

open season *n.* **1.** HUNT FREE HUNTING PERIOD a period during the year when certain restrictions concerning the hunting and killing of game or the catching of fish are lifted **2.** TIME OF UNRESTRAINED CRITICISM a period of unrestrained attack or criticism (*informal*) ○ *It seems to be open season on lawyers at the moment.*

open secret *n.* sth that is supposed to be secret but in actual fact is widely known

open sentence *n.* a formula containing a free variable, e.g. 'X is human', that cannot be said to be true or false because the referent of the variable is not determined

open sesame *n.* a sure means of gaining access to or obtaining sth [From the magical words used by Ali Baba, a character in the *Arabian Nights*, to open the door of the robbers' cave]

open set *n.* MATH a mathematical set that is included within a particular topology

open shop *n.* a workplace where being a member of a union, or of a specified union, is not a condition of being employed. ◇ **closed shop**, **union shop**

open side *n.* in rugby, the side of the field that lies between a scrum and the further touchline. ◇ **blind side** —**open-side** *adj.*

open-skies, **open-sky** *adj.* allowing aircraft belonging to any nation the freedom to fly over an area, and therefore placing no restrictions on aerial surveillance of military installations

open slather *n.* ANZ a situation in which there are no limits or constraints on behaviour (*informal*)

open society *n.* a society in which there is freedom of thought, ideas, speech, and communication

open system *n.* COMPUT a computer design system that has uniform industry standards and is compatible with any similar type of system or part

open-toe, **open-toed** *adj.* used to describe a shoe, especially a sandal, that is not closed at the front, allowing the toes to be seen

open-top, **open-topped** *adj.* used to describe cars and buses that have no roof or that have the roof removed

Open University *n.* a university, founded in 1969, offering degree courses primarily by correspondence to mature students studying part-time

and having many classes that are broadcast on TV and radio. Local tutoring sessions and summer schools are also provided. (*often used before a noun*) ◇ **distance learning**

open verdict *n.* in a coroner's court, the verdict given when the cause of death is not clear and no charge of murder or manslaughter can therefore be brought

openwork /ópən wurk/ *n.* **1.** DECORATIVE WORK USING PATTERNS OF HOLES decorative items that make use of patterns of holes, e.g. wrought-iron work, fretwork, or lace **2.** SEW EMBROIDERY WITH DECORATED HOLES an embroidery technique or the embroidery itself in which holes are formed in a fabric by either cutting or pulling threads and then embellishing with various stitches

opera[1] /óppərə/ *n.* **1.** MUSICAL DRAMA a dramatic work where music is a dominant part of the performance. It is usually highly stylized, with the actors often singing rather than reciting their lines, and typically has recurring themes intensified by musical repetitions developed as the piece progresses. **2.** OPERAS IN GENERAL operas thought of collectively or as an art form **3.** OPERATIC SCORE the musical score or libretto of an operatic work **4.** = **opera house** [Mid-17thC. Via Italian from Latin, 'works', from *opus* (see OPUS).]

opera[2] plural of **opus**

operable /óppərəb'l/ *adj.* **1.** MED SURGICALLY TREATABLE capable of being treated by surgery **2.** ABLE TO BE DONE capable of being done or put into practice —**operability** /óppərə bíllati/ *n.* —**operably** /óppərəbli/ *adv.*

opéra bouffe /óppərə boof/ (*plural* **opéras bouffes** /óppərə boof/) *n.* **1.** COMIC OPERA an opera with a comic or farcical theme **2.** OPÉRA BOUFFES AS A GROUP opéra bouffes thought of collectively or as an art form [From French, 'comic opera'; translation of Italian *opera buffa*]

opera buffa /óppərə boofə/ (*plural* **opera buffas** *or* **opere buffe** /óppə ray boo fay/) *n.* a comic opera of the kind that originated in Italy in the 18th century, using themes or characters from everyday life and usually having a happy ending. Mozart's *The Marriage of Figaro* is an example. [From Italian, 'comic opera']

opéra comique /óppərə ko meek/ (*plural* **opéras comiques**) *n.* an opera on a light-hearted theme with spoken dialogue. This style of opera was especially popular in 19th-century France. [From French, 'comic opera']

opera glasses *npl.* small decorative low-powered binoculars for use by people in the audience at theatrical, operatic, or ballet performances

operagoer /óppərə gō ər/ *n.* sb who attends opera performances regularly

opera hat *n.* a man's collapsible top hat that is spring-operated

opera house *n.* a theatre that is designed for putting on operas. It is usually much more ornate and sumptuous than a theatre designed for putting on plays.

operand /óppə rand/ *n.* **1.** MATH ENTITY WITH OPERATION PERFORMED ON IT a quantity, function, or other entity that is to have a mathematical operation performed on it **2.** COMPUT PART OF A COMPUTER INSTRUCTION the portion of a computer instruction that specifies the location in memory of the data to be manipulated [Late 19thC. From Latin *operandum*, literally 'thing to be worked on', from *operari* (see OPERATE).]

operant /óppərənt/ *n.* **1.** PERFORMER OF AN OPERATION sb or sth that operates or that carries out some kind of operation **2.** PSYCHOL VOLUNTARY ACTION in learning theory, an action or other unit of behaviour that does not appear to have a stimulus ■ *adj.* HAVING EFFECT producing a specified effect [Early 17thC. From Latin *operant-*, the present participle stem of *operari* (see OPERATE).] —**operantly** *adv.*

operant conditioning *n.* PSYCHOL a form of learning that takes place when an instance of spontaneous behaviour is either reinforced by a reward or discouraged by punishment. The principles involved have had a strong influence on behaviour modification as well as on other kinds of therapy.

opera seria /óppərə seéri ə/ (*plural* **opere serie** /óppəray seéri ay/) *n.* **1. TRAGIC OPERA WITH A MYTHOLOGICAL THEME** an opera that has a serious theme, often one taken from classical mythology, and usually a tragic ending. An example is Mozart's *The Clemency of Titus.* **2. OPERE SERIE AS A GROUP** opere serie thought of collectively or as an art form [From Italian, 'serious opera']

operate /óppə rayt/ (**-ates, -ating, -ated**) *v.* **1.** *vti.* **DO STH OR FUNCTION AS STH** to function or work, or make sth function or work **2.** *vti.* **BUSINESS MANAGE OR BE MANAGED** to exist as a working business or organization, or to oversee the running of a working business or organization **3.** *vi.* **MED PERFORM SURGERY** to perform surgery on a person or animal **4.** *vi.* **EXERT AN EFFECT** to have an effect or influence on sb or sth **5.** *vi.* **MIL PERFORM MILITARY MANOEUVRES** to carry out military manoeuvres **6.** *vi.* **FIN TRADE IN THE FINANCIAL MARKET** to trade or deal in securities or commodities on the stock exchange **7.** *vi.* **ENGAGE IN ILLEGAL ACTIVITIES** to be active in some illegal or underhand business [Early 17thC. From Latin *operat-*, the past participle of *operari* 'to work', from *oper-*, the stem of *opus* 'work'.]

operatic /óppə ráttik/ *adj.* **1. OF OPERA** belonging or relating to opera **2. FLAMBOYANT** overly or flamboyantly extravagant, especially in behaviour [Mid-18thC. Formed from OPERA[1], on the model of DRAMATIC.] —**operatically** *adv.*

operatics /óppə ráttiks/ *n.* flamboyantly exaggerated or extravagant behaviour (*takes a singular or plural verb*)

operating room *n. US* = operating theatre

operating system *n.* the essential program in a computer that maintains disk files, runs applications, and handles devices such as the keyboard, mouse, monitor, and printer

operating table *n.* a table on which sb undergoing a surgical operation lies

operating theatre *n.* a room in a hospital where surgical operations are performed. US term **operating room**

operation /óppə ráysh'n/ *n.* **1. CONTROLLING OF STH** the controlling of sth or the managing of the way it works **2. FUNCTIONING STATE** the state of functioning or of being in effect **3. STH DONE** sth that is carried out, especially sth difficult or complex ○ *the tricky operation of removing the sting* **4. MED SURGICAL INTERVENTION** any surgical procedure, e.g. one carried out to repair damage to a body part **5. ORGANIZED ACTION** an organized campaign, manoeuvre, or other form of action, especially one carried out by a rescue team, the police, or diplomatic personnel **6. operation, Operation MIL MILITARY ACTION** an action conducted by military forces or that can range in scope from a reconnaissance mission to an entire campaign (*often used before a noun*) ○ *Operation Desert Storm* **7. MATH MATHEMATICAL PROCESS** a mathematical process such as subtraction, multiplication, or differentiation in which certain entities are derived from others through the application of rules **8. COMPUT SINGLE PART OF A COMPUTER PROGRAM** a series of actions performed by a computer, defined by an instruction and forming part of a computer program **9. BUSINESS DEAL** a business deal or financial transaction **10. ILLEGAL BUSINESS** an illegal, dishonest, or underhand business

operational /óppə ráysh'nəl/ *adj.* **1. ABLE TO BE USED** in proper working order and able to be used ○ *The new transport link will be fully operational next month.* **2. OF THE OPERATION OF STH** relating to the operating of sth or to the way it operates **3. MIL COMBAT-READY** ready for combat or manoeuvres —**operationally** *adv.*

operational amplifier *n.* an amplifier with high gain and high stability that is controlled by way of externally connected negative-feedback circuits

operationalism /óppə ráysh'nəlizəm/, **operationism** /-sh'nizəm/ *n.* PHILOS the view that terms for scientific concepts should be defined in terms of the scientific operations, e.g. measuring or observing, performed to establish or disprove them —**operationalist** *n., adj.* —**operationalistic** /óppə ráysh'nə lístik/ *adj.*

operational research *n.* = operations research

operationism *n.* PHILOS = operationalism

operations /óppə ráysh'nz/ *npl.* the supervising, monitoring, and coordinating of the activities of a military or civilian organization (*often used before a noun*)

operations research *n.* analysis of the problems that exist in complex systems such as those used to run a business or a military campaign, designed to give a scientific basis for decision-making

operatise *vt.* = operatize

operative /óppərətiv/ *adj.* **1. IN EFFECT** in place and having an effect, especially the right or desired effect **2. SIGNIFICANT** carrying a special meaning or significance **3. MED OF SURGERY** relating to or resulting from a surgical procedure ■ *n.* **1. SKILLED WORKER** a skilled worker, especially in a manufacturing industry **2. WORKER** sb who performs a particular task or who works in a particular field (*formal or humorous*) ○ *a rodent operative* **3. POL POLITICAL WORKER** an employee of a political party who works in any behind-the-scenes capacity, e.g. political troubleshooting or manipulation of media stories **4. US DETECTIVE** a private detective **5. US SPY** a spy or secret agent —**operatively** *adv.* —**operativeness** *n.* —**operativity** /óppərə tívvəti/ *n.*

operatize /óppərə tīz/ (**-tizes, -tizing, -tized**), **operatise** (**-atises, -atising, -atised**) *vt.* to make an opera out of an existing novel, play, or other text [Mid-19thC. Formed from OPERA[1], on the model of DRAMATIZE.]

operator /óppə raytər/ *n.* **1. SB OPERATING STH** sb who operates machinery, an instrument, or other equipment **2. BUSINESS BUSINESS OWNER OR MANAGER** sb who owns or runs a business or other commercial enterprise **3. FIN STOCK-EXCHANGE DEALER** sb who deals on the stock exchange or in a money market, especially sb who makes aggressive or highly speculative moves **4. MANIPULATIVE PERSON** sb who behaves in a devious or manipulative way, especially in order to obtain some kind of self-advancement (*informal*) ○ *a smooth operator* **5. MATH DESCRIPTOR OR PERFORMER OF A MATHEMATICAL OPERATION** a mathematical symbol, term, or other entity that performs or describes an operation. Multiplication and subtraction signs are operators.

operculum /ō púrkyŏŏləm/ (*plural* **-la** /-lə/ *or* **-lums**) *n.* **1. ANAT MUCUS PLUG IN THE CERVIX** the plug of mucus that fills the opening of a woman's cervix while she is pregnant. It helps to prevent infection. **2. operculum ZOOL GILL-COVERING FLAP** the flexible bony flap covering the gills of bony fishes **3. BOT FLAP IN MOSSES AND FUNGI** a flap covering an aperture in the spore capsules of mosses and some fungi **4. ZOOL SEAL ON A MOLLUSC'S SHELL** a rounded plate that seals the mouth of the shell of some gastropod molluscs when the animal's body is inside [Early 18thC. From Latin, 'lid', formed from *operire* 'to cover'.] —**opercular** *adj.* —**operculardly** *adv.* —**operculate** /-lət/ *adj.* —**operculated** /-laytid/ *adj.*

opere buffe plural of opera buffa

opere serie plural of opera seria

operetta /óppə réttə/ *n.* a theatrical production, usually with a comic theme, similar to opera but with much spoken dialogue and usually some dancing. Gilbert and Sullivan wrote many operettas. [Late 18thC. From Italian, literally 'small opera', formed from *opera* (see OPERA[1]).] —**operettist** *n.*

operon /óppə ron/ *n.* GENETICS a segment of a chromosome containing the genes that specify the structure of a given protein, alongside the genes that regulate its manufacture. Operons are relatively simple units of genetic control, found only in bacteria. [Mid-20thC. From French *opéron*, from *opérer* 'to work', from Latin *operari* (see OPERATE).]

operose /óppə rōss/ *adj.* (*formal*) **1. TAXING** requiring a lot of effort **2. BUSY** busy, active, or hardworking [Late 17thC. From Latin *operosus*, from *oper-*, the stem of *opus* (see OPUS).] —**operosely** *adv.* —**operoseness** *n.*

Ophelia /ə feéli ə/ *n.* a very small inner natural satellite of Uranus, discovered in 1986 by the Voyager 2 planetary probe. Its gravitational influence seems to help stabilize the outer ring of Uranus.

ophicleide /óffi klīd/ *n.* an obsolete musical instrument similar to and superseded by the bass tuba [Mid-19thC. From French *ophicléide*, from Greek *ophis* 'snake' + the stem *kleid-* 'key'; from its resemblance to an earlier instrument called a 'serpent', but with keys.]

ophidian /ō fíddi ən/ *adj.* **1. OF SNAKES** belonging or relating to snakes **2. LIKE A SNAKE** resembling a snake in appearance, habits, or movement [Early 19thC. Formed from modern Latin *Ophidia*, suborder name, from the Greek stem *ophid-* 'snake'.] —**ophidian** *n.*

ophiolite /óffi ə līt/ *n.* any igneous and metamorphic rock that was formed from deep-sea sediment. Ophiolites are rich in iron and magnesium. [Mid-19thC. Coined from Greek *ophis* 'snake' + -LITE; from its snaky texture.]

ophiology /óffi ólləji/ *n.* the branch of zoology that is concerned with snakes [Early 19thC. Coined from Greek *ophis* 'snake' + -LOGY.] —**ophiological** /óffi ə lójjik'l/ *adj.* —**ophiologist** /óffi ólləjist/ *n.*

ophite /ō fīt/ *n.* any of several mottled green rocks, e.g. diabase or dolerite, that are made up of small long plagioclase crystals surrounded by larger pyroxene crystals [Mid-17thC. Via Latin from Greek *ophitēs* 'serpentine stone', from *ophis* 'snake'; from its markings, which are like a snake's.]

ophitic /ō fíttik/ *adj.* used to describe rocks consisting of small elongated plagioclase crystals completely enclosed by larger pyroxene crystals

Ophiuchus /o fyoōkəss/ *n.* a large constellation of the equatorial region located between Hercules and Scorpius

ophthal. *abbr.* **1.** ophthalmology **2.** ophthalmologist

ophthalm- *prefix.* = ophthalmo- (*used before vowels*)

ophthalmia /of thálmi ə/ *n.* inflammation of the eye, especially of the conjunctiva and surrounding area [14thC. Via late Latin from Greek, from *ophthalmos* 'eye' (see OPHTHALMO-).]

ophthalmic /of thálmik/ *adj.* relating to the eyes, or located in the region of the eye

ophthalmic optician *n.* = optician *n.* 2

ophthalmitis /óf thal mítiss/ *n.* inflammation of the eye

ophthalmo- *prefix.* eye, eyeball ○ *ophthalmoscope* [From Greek *ophthalmos*. Ultimately from an Indo-European word meaning 'to see', which is also the ancestor of English *eye*, *ogle*, and *optic*.]

ophthalmol. *abbr.* **1.** ophthalmology **2.** ophthalmologist

ophthalmologist /óf thal mólləjist/ *n.* a doctor qualified to diagnose and treat eye diseases and conditions with drugs, surgery, and corrective measures

ophthalmology /óf thal mólləji/ *n.* the branch of medicine that is concerned with the diagnosis and treatment of eye diseases and conditions —**ophthalmological** /óf thálmə lójjik'l/ *adj.* —**ophthalmologically** /óf thalmə lójjikli/ *adv.*

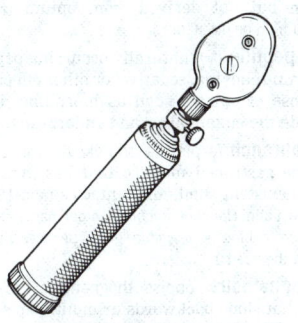

Ophthalmoscope

ophthalmoscope /of thálmə skōp/ *n.* a medical instrument used for examining the inside of the eye. A direct ophthalmoscope shines a fine beam of light into the eye and allows the examiner to see a magnified image of the spot where the beam falls. —**ophthalmoscopic** /of thálmə skóppik/ *adj.* —**ophthalmoscopically** /skóppikli/ *adv.*

ophthalmoscopy /óf thal móskəpi/ (*plural* **-pies**) *n.* a medical examination of the inside of the eye using an ophthalmoscope to detect changes to the retina, such as those associated with diabetes and hypertension

Ophuls /áwfəlz, áwfŭlz/, **Opüls, Max** (1902–57) German-born French film director. His romantic, opulent films include *La ronde* (1950) and *Madame de...* (1953). Real name **Maximilian Oppenheimer**

-opia *suffix.* condition or defect of vision ○ *hyperopia* ○ *protanopia* [From Greek, formed from *ops* 'eye, face'. Ultimately from an Indo-European word meaning 'to see', which is also the ancestor of English *eye, optic,* and *ocular.*]

opiate /ṓpi ət/ *n.* **1.** PHARM **OPIUM-CONTAINING DRUG** a drug such as morphine or heroin that contains opium or an opium derivative **2.** PHARM **SLEEP-INDUCING SUBSTANCE** a drug, hormone, or other substance that has sleep-inducing effects similar to those of opium or opium derivatives **3. STH WITH A SOOTHING OR DULLING EFFECT** sth that has a relaxing, pacifying, or dulling effect ■ *adj.* **1.** PHARM **CONTAINING OPIUM** containing opium or an opium derivative **2. BORING** mind-numbingly unexciting, especially because of being simplistic, cliché-ridden, or formulaic ■ *vt.* **(-ates, -ating, -ated) 1.** PHARM **TREAT WITH AN OPIATE** to treat sb, or sb's symptoms, with an opiate **2. DEADEN OR DULL** to dull or deaden pain, anguish, or some other unwanted condition [15thC. From medieval Latin *opiatus*, from, ultimately, Latin *opium* (see OPIUM).]

opine /ō pīn/ **(opines, opining, opined)** *vti.* to put forth an opinion (*formal*) [15thC. From Latin *opinari* 'to suppose, believe'.]

opinion /ə pínnyən/ *n.* **1. PERSONAL VIEW** the view sb takes about a certain issue, especially when it is based solely on personal judgement ○ *In my opinion it's all a waste of time.* **2. ESTIMATION** a view regarding the worth of sb or sth ○ *They had a pretty low opinion of me.* **3. EXPERT VIEW** an expert assessment of sth ○ *I told the doctor I wanted a second opinion.* **4. BODY OF GENERALLY HELD VIEWS** general assessment, judgement, or evaluation ○ *pundits and other opinion formers* **5.** LAW **CONCLUSION OF FACT** a conclusion drawn from observation of the facts [14thC. Via French from the Latin stem *opinion-* from *opinari* 'to suppose'.] ◇ **be a matter of opinion** to be open to dispute or debate ◇ **be of the opinion that** to think that sth is the case

opinionated /ə pínnyə naytid/ *adj.* always ready to express opinions and tending to hold to them stubbornly, unreasonably dismissing other people's views —**opinionatedly** *adv.* —**opinionatedness** *n.*

opinionative /ə pínnyənətiv/ *adj.* (*formal*) **1. OF OPINIONS** relating to opinions or to the stating of them **2.** = **opinionated** —**opinionatively** *adv.* —**opinionativeness** *n.*

opinion poll *n.* a survey that is carried out to discover what the general public think about sth. ◊ **poll**

opioid /ṓpi oyd/ *n.* **NATURALLY OCCURRING OPIUM-CONTAINING SUBSTANCE** any of various opium-containing substances that are produced naturally in the brain ■ *adj.* **SIMILAR TO OPIUM** similar in effect or properties to opium but not derived from opium [Mid-20thC. Coined from OPIUM + -OID.]

opioid peptide *n.* a naturally occurring peptide that has pain-relieving, sedative, or other effects similar to those of opiates such as morphine. Examples include the eukaphalins and endorphins.

opisthobranch /ə pís thə brangk/ *n.* MARINE BIOL any marine gastropod mollusc that has gills, a small or nonexistent shell, and tentacles [Mid-19thC. From modern Latin *Opisthobranchiata*, order name, from Greek *opisthen* 'behind' + *bragkhia* 'gills', because the gills are behind the heart.]

opisthognathous /óppiss thógnəthəss/ *adj.* having jaws that slope backwards or mouthparts that face backwards [Mid-19thC. Coined from Greek *opisthen* 'behind' + -GNATHOUS.] —**opisthognathism** *n.*

opisthosoma /o píss thə sṓmə/ *n.* the rear section of the body of a spider or other arachnid [Coined from Greek *opisthen* 'behind' + *sōma* 'body']

opium /ṓpi əm/ *n.* **1. ADDICTIVE DRUG** a brownish gummy extract from the unripe seed pods of the opium poppy that contains several highly addictive narcotic alkaloid substances, e.g. morphine and codeine. Crude opium is no longer used in medicine, but its extracts, especially morphine, are widely used. **2. STUPEFYING THING** sth that has a stupefying, numbing, or sleep-inducing effect ○ *soap operas dismissed as the opium of a bored populace* [14thC. Via Latin from Greek *opion* 'poppy juice', from *opos* 'vegetable juice'.]

WORD KEY: CULTURAL NOTE

Confessions of an English Opium-Eater, a memoir by Thomas de Quincey (1822). This autobiographical work focuses on the author's chronic addiction to opium, which he first took to relieve rheumatic pains. Its vivid descriptions of uncontrollable urges and withdrawal-induced nightmares make it one of the first works in English literature to openly examine the dark side of the human psyche.

opium den *n.* a place where opium is sold and smoked, especially one that has facilities where people using the drug can stay while under its influence

opium poppy *n.* a poppy of Europe and Asia with greyish-green leaves and attractive pink, red, or white flowers. It has long been grown as a source of opium. Latin name: *Papaver somniferum.*

Oporto /ō páwrt ō/ city and port in northwestern Portugal, situated about 274 km/170 mi. north of Lisbon. Population: 309,485 (1991).

Opossum

opossum /ə póssəm/ (*plural* **-sums** *or* **-sum**) *n.* **1. AMERICAN MARSUPIAL** a small nocturnal tree-dwelling marsupial found in the United States and Central and South America. It has dense fur, a long snout, and a hairless prehensile tail. Latin name: *Didelphis marsupialis.* **2. AUSTRALIAN MARSUPIAL** any one of several similar marsupials found in Australia and New Zealand. They are mostly nocturnal plant-eating tree-dwellers, and some have prehensile tails. Family: Phalangeridae. [Early 17thC. From Virginia Algonquian *opassom*, from *op* 'white' + *assom* 'dog, doglike creature'.]

opossum shrimp *n.* a crustacean that resembles a shrimp, the female of which carries the eggs and newly-hatched young in a brood pouch just below the thorax. Order: Mysidacae.

opp. *abbr.* opposite

Oppenheimer /óppən hīmər/, **J. Robert** (1904–67) US nuclear physicist. He was the director of the Los Alamos atom bomb project (1943–45) and the United States Atomic Energy Commission (1946–53). In 1953 he was suspended from nuclear work because of his past Communist associations. He won the Enrico Fermi Award in 1963.

Opperman /óppər man/, **Sir Hubert Ferdinand** (*b.* 1904) Australian cyclist. He was the first non-European to win the Paris-Brest-Paris marathon (1931). The following year he broke the world outdoor motor-paced speed record.

OPP film *n.* plastic film used for packaging

oppidan /óppidən/ *adj.* **OF TOWNS** belonging to, relating to, or found in a town, often the town in which a university is sited as distinct from the university itself (*formal*) ■ *n.* **TOWN DWELLER** sb who lives in a town (*formal*) [Mid-16thC. From Latin *oppidanus*, from *oppidum* 'fort, town'.]

oppilate /óppi layt/ **(-lates, -lating, -lated)** *vt.* MED to block up a body passage such as a duct or a body opening such as a pore [15thC. From Latin *oppilat-*, the past participle stem of *oppilare* 'to stop up', from *pilare*, literally 'to heap up', from *pila* 'heap of stones'.] —**oppilation** /óppi láysh'n/ *n.*

opponent /ə pṓnənt/ *n.* **1. RIVAL IN A CONTEST** a person or team faced in a competition, debate, battle, or other contest **2. SB OPPOSING STH** sb who is against a particular course of action or who does not support a particular cause or belief ○ *a fierce opponent of reform of the voting system* **3.** ANAT **OPPOSING MUSCLE** any muscle that counteracts the motion of another ■ *adj.* **1. CONTRARY** working or arguing against sth **2. CONTRADICTORY** serving to contradict sth [Late 16thC. From Latin *opponent-*, the present participle stem of *opponere*, literally 'to set against' (source of English *oppose*), from *ponere* 'to place'.] —**opponency** *n.*

opportune /óppər tyoon/ *adj.* suitable for a purpose or occurring at just the right time [15thC. Via French from Latin *opportunus* 'favourable' (used of the wind), from *ob portum veniens* 'coming towards port'.] —**opportunely** *adv.* —**opportuneness** *n.*

opportunist /óppər tyṓonist/ *n.* **UNPRINCIPLED RESOURCEFUL PERSON** sb who takes advantage of sth, especially sb who does so in a devious, unscrupulous, or unprincipled way ■ *adj.* = **opportunistic** —**opportunism** *n.*

opportunistic /óppərtyoo nístik/, **opportunist** *adj.* **1. TAKING ADVANTAGE OF OPPORTUNITIES** resourcefully taking advantage of all opportunities or situations, especially in a devious, unscrupulous, or unprincipled way **2.** MED **LIFE-THREATENING WHEN IMMUNITY IS LOW** used to describe a microorganism or relatively minor disease that is not normally serious but that can become pathogenic or life-threatening when the host has a low level of immunity ○ *opportunistic infections* —**opportunistically** *adv.*

opportunity /óppər tyṓonəti/ (*plural* **-ties**) *n.* **1. ADVANTAGEOUS CHANCE** a chance, especially one that offers some kind of advantage **2. FAVOURABLE CONDITIONS** a combination of favourable circumstances or situations

opportunity cost *n.* the cost of a commercial decision regarded as the value of the alternative that is forgone. For example, if the choice is between using a machine or scrapping it, the opportunity cost is the scrap value.

opportunity shop *n. ANZ* full form of **op shop**

opposable /ə pṓzəb'l/ *adj.* **1. RESISTIBLE** capable of being opposed or resisted **2. ABLE TO BE PLACED OPPOSITE STH** capable of being put in a position that is opposite sth else **3.** ANAT **TOUCHING THE END OF ANOTHER DIGIT** used to describe a thumb or big toe that can face and touch the end of one or more of the other digits of the same hand or foot —**opposability** /ə pṓzə bílləti/ *n.* —**opposably** /ə pṓzəbli/ *adv.*

oppose /ə pṓz/ **(-poses, -posing, -posed)** *v.* **1.** *vti.* **STAND IN OPPOSITION** to be against sth or to take an active stance against sth ○ *would not state openly that they oppose violence* **2.** *vt.* **SET IN CONTRAST TO** to set sth up as a contrast to sth else **3.** *vt.* **PUT OPPOSITE TO** to put one thing in a position directly facing another **4.** *vt.* **COMPETE WITH AS OPPONENTS** to be in competition, conflict, or battle with another person, team, or fighting force [14thC. From French *opposer*, an alteration (influenced by *poser* 'to place') of Latin *opponere* (see OPPONENT).] —**opposer** *n.* —**opposing** *adj.* ◇ **as opposed to** used to introduce sth that is in contrast or is distinct

opposed-cylinder engine *n.* an engine in which cylinders or banks of cylinders are mounted on opposite sides of the crankcase in the same plane, with their connecting rods mounted on a common crankshaft. Piston strokes on each side of the camshaft work in a direction opposite to one another.

opposite /óppəzit/ *adj.* **1. ON THE FACING SIDE** on the side that faces sth or at the furthest distance possible from sth **2. FACING AWAY** pointing, facing, or moving away from each other **3. TOTALLY DIFFERENT** of the same general class yet completely different **4.** BOT **LEVEL WITH ON THE OTHER SIDE** used to describe plant parts, especially pairs of leaves or flowers, that grow at the same level on a stem but on either side of it **5.** GEOM **FACING AN ANGLE** used to describe the side of a triangle facing a specified angle **6.** GEOM **FACING EACH OTHER GEOMETRICALLY** used to describe sides or angles in an even-sided polygon that face each other ■ *n.* **1. SB OR STH DIFFERENT FROM ANOTHER** sb or sth that is completely different from another or from what is expected **2. ANTONYM** a word that has an opposite meaning **3.** **OPPONENT** an opponent (*archaic or formal*) ■ *adv.* **IN THE OPPOSITE POSITION** in or into a position that is opposite ○ *They live directly opposite.* ■ *prep.* **1.** **ACROSS FROM** facing or across from sth or sb ○ *They moved to a house opposite the museum.* **2.** **IN A COMPLEMENTING ACTING ROLE TO** in an acting role that corresponds to or complements another, especially when the two roles are played by people of different genders ○ *excited to be playing opposite the great star* [14thC. Via French from Latin *oppositus*, the past participle of *opponere* (see OPPONENT).] —**oppositely** *adv.* —**oppositeness** *n.*

opposite number *n.* sb who does a similar job or who holds a similar post to another person, especially in another department or organization

opposite prompt *n.* in a theatre, the side of a stage that is to the actors' right when they face the audience. ◊ **stage right**

opposite sex *n.* women when thought of collectively as opposed to men, or men when thought of collectively as opposed to women

opposition /óppə zísh'n/ *n.* **1.** **ACTIVELY HOSTILE ATTITUDE** an actively hostile attitude towards sth, or a resistant stance against sth ○ *public opposition to the plan was growing* **2.** **SPORTS** **SPORTS OPPONENT** a person or team that plays against another (*takes a singular or plural verb*) **3.** **opposition, Opposition** **POL** **OUT-OF-POWER POLITICAL PARTY** a political party that is not in power (*often used before a noun; takes a singular or plural verb*) **4.** **LING** **LINGUISTIC CONTRAST** in linguistics, the contrast between two or more similar elements in a language **5.** **PHON** **PHONETIC CONTRAST BETWEEN SOUNDS** in phonetics, the contrast between two sounds that are articulated in a similar place in the mouth, e.g. between the voiced consonant /v/ and the voiceless consonant /f/ **6.** **CHESS** **THE ADVANTAGE OF NOT HAVING TO MOVE** a situation towards the end of a game of chess in which the two kings are in such a position that the opponent must make a king move and is therefore at a disadvantage **7.** **LOGIC** **RELATIONS BETWEEN LOGICAL PROPOSITIONS** the way in which logical propositions relate to each other **8.** **ASTRON** **MOON OR PLANET POSITION** the position of the Moon or one of the outer planets when it is on the opposite side of the Earth as seen from the Sun **9.** **ASTRON** **CELESTIAL BODY ALIGNMENT** the position of two celestial bodies when they are diametrically opposite on the celestial sphere **10.** **ASTROLOGICALLY OPPOSING PLANETARY POSITION** in astrology, a situation when two planets are 180 degrees from each other, believed to cause friction or symbolize confrontation —**oppositional** *adj.*

opposition research *n.* **US** research done in order to discover damaging or detrimental information about sb

oppress /ə préss/ (**-presses, -pressing, -pressed**) *vt.* **1.** **DOMINATE HARSHLY** to subject a person or a people to a harsh or cruel form of domination **2.** **INFLICT STRESS ON** to be a source of worry, stress, or trouble to sb **3.** **SUPPRESS** to hold sth in check or put an end to it (*archaic*) [14thC. From French *oppresser*, from Latin *oppress-*, the past participle stem of *opprimere*, literally 'to press against', from *premere* 'to press'.] —**oppression** *n.* —**oppressor** *n.*

oppressive /ə préssiv/ *adj.* **1.** **DOMINATING HARSHLY** imposing a harsh or cruel form of domination ○ *an oppressive regime* **2.** **HIGHLY STRESSFUL** exerting a worrying, troubling, or burdensome pressure on sb **3.** **STIFLING** so hot and humid as to make people feel tired, irritable, or sluggish —**oppressively** *adv.* —**oppressiveness** *n.*

opprobrious /ə próbri əss/ *adj.* **1.** **SCORNFUL** expressing scorn, contempt, or severe criticism **2.** **SHAMEFUL** bringing shame or disrepute [14thC. From late Latin *opprobriosus*, from Latin *opprobrium* (see OPPROBRIUM).] —**opprobriously** *adv.* —**opprobriousness** *n.*

opprobrium /ə próbri əm/ (*plural* **-a**) *n.* **1.** **SCORN** scorn, contempt, or severe criticism **2.** **DISGRACE** shame or disgrace that stems from disreputable behaviour **3.** **SOURCE OF SHAME** sth or sb that brings shame or disgrace (*archaic*) ○ *'would render him an object of scorn and an opprobrium of the religion with which he had diligently associated himself'* (George Eliot, *Middlemarch*; 1872) [Mid-17thC. From Latin, 'infamy,

reproach', from *opprobrare* 'to reproach', from *probrum* 'disgrace', literally 'sth brought before sb'.]

oppugn /ə pyoón/ (**-pugns, -pugning, -pugned**) *vt.* to question the validity or truthfulness of sth (*formal*) [15thC. From Latin *oppugnare*, literally 'to fight against', from *pugnare* 'to fight'.] —**oppugner** *n.*

oppugnant /ə púgnənt/ *adj.* wilfully hostile or opposed (*archaic or formal*) —**oppugnancy** *n.* —**oppugnantly** *adv.*

ops /ops/ *npl.* the controlling of organized military or civilian activities (*informal*) (*often used before a noun*) ○ *Who's in the ops room tonight?* [Early 20thC. Shortening of OPERATIONS.]

op shop *n.* **ANZ** a charity shop selling secondhand goods donated by members of the public (*informal*) Full form **opportunity shop**

opsin /ópsin/ *n.* a component of the visual pigment found in the retina of the eye. It is a glycoprotein, and in the vertebrate eye it combines with retinal to form rhodopsin. [Mid-20thC. Back-formation from RHODOPSIN.]

opsonic /op sónnik/ *adj.* **BIOL** relating to or involving opsonins

opsonic index *n.* **MED** a measure of the number of bacteria destroyed by certain blood cells, expressed as the ratio of opsonin in the infected patient's blood to the amount found in a healthy person's blood

opsonin /ópsənin/ *n.* **BIOL** a protein fragment in blood that binds to the surface of an invading antibody and promotes its destruction by white blood cells [Early 20thC. Coined from Latin *opsonare* 'to cater, buy provisions' (from Greek *opsōnein* 'condiment, delicacy', of unknown origin) + -IN.]

opsonize /ópsə nīz/ (**-nizes, -nizing, -nized**), **opsonise** (**-nises, -nising, -nised**), **opsonify** /op sónni fī/ (**-fies, -fying, -fied**) *vt.* **BIOL** to make foreign bodies such as bacteria susceptible to destruction by certain blood cells by coating them with opsonin —**opsonization** /ópsə nī záysh'n/ *n.*

-opsy *suffix.* examination ○ *biopsy* [From Greek *-opsia* 'sight, seeing', from *opsis* 'sight'. Ultimately from an Indo-European word meaning 'to see', which is also the ancestor of English *eye*, *optic*, and *ocular*.]

opt /opt/ (**opts, opting, opted**) *vi.* to choose sth or choose to do sth, usually in preference to other available alternatives [Late 19thC. Via French *opter* from Latin *optare* 'to choose, desire' (source of English *optative* and *adopt*).]

opt out *vi.* **1.** **CHOOSE NOT TO DO STH** to decide not to join in sth or not to go along with sth (*informal*) **2.** **CHOOSE SELF-ADMINISTRATION** to choose to manage financial and administrative affairs without any input or control from the relevant local authority (*refers to schools and hospitals*)

opt. *abbr.* **1.** **GRAM** optative **2.** optical **3.** optician **4.** optics **5.** optimum **6.** optional

optative /óptətiv/ *adj.* **1.** **OF CHOICE-MAKING** relating to the making of choices (*formal*) **2.** **GRAM** **CONTAINING A VERB EXPRESSING A WISH** containing a verb in the subjunctive mood that expresses a wish or desire, as does the independent clause 'God save the queen' ■ *n.* **GRAM** **1.** **OPTATIVE MOOD** the optative mood of a verb **2.** **VERB IN THE OPTATIVE MOOD** a verb in the optative mood [Mid-16thC. Via French from Latin *optativus*, from *optare* 'to choose, desire'.] —**optatively** *adv.*

optic[1] /óptik/ *adj.* **OF THE EYES** belonging or relating to the eyes, or situated in or near the eye ■ *n.* **1.** **INSTRUMENT'S LENS** any of the lenses or reflecting parts in an optical instrument **2.** **EYE** an eye (*archaic or humorous*) [14thC. Via French or medieval Latin from Greek *optikos*, from *optos* 'seen, visible'. Ultimately from an Indo-European word meaning 'to see', which is also the ancestor of English *eye* and *ocular*.]

optic[2] *tdmk.* a trademark for a device that fits over the neck of a bottle and dispenses a measure of spirits, used in pubs

optical /óptik'l/ *adj.* **1.** **OF VISIBLE LIGHT** relating to or producing light that can be seen **2.** **OF VISION** belonging or relating to the sense of sight **3.** **OPTICS** **OF CORRECTIVE LENSES** designed to correct or enhance faulty vision (*refers to a lens*) **4.** **LIGHT-SENSITIVE** sensitive to light (*refers to an instrument or device*) **5.** **PHYS** **OF OPTICS**

belonging or relating to the science of optics — **optically** *adv.*

optical activity *n.* **CHEM** the property of a crystal or a chemical solution to rotate the plane of polarized light that passes through it. In the case of solutions, the rotation is caused by asymmetrical molecules and the angle of rotation depends on the thickness of the substance.

optical art *n.* full form of **op art**

optical brightener *n.* any of several chemical substances used in the textile industry and in some washing powders to make the whiteness or colour of fabrics brighter

optical character reader *n.* a device for inputting material into a computer by digitizing the image of a printed page, identifying the characters, and storing them as machine code for further processing. Initially such devices could recognize only a specially designed typeface, but more modern readers can recognize a wide variety of typefaces and even handwriting.

optical character recognition *n.* the use of light-sensing methods to identify printed and hand-written material and encode it in machine-readable form for inputting into a computer

optical computer *n.* a proposed computer that uses optical switches, fibres, and laser light instead of wires, transistors, and printed circuits to achieve processing speeds far higher than those of conventional computers

optical disk, optical disc *n.* a rigid computer storage disk on which data is stored as tiny pits in the plastic coating and which is readable by laser beam, especially a recordable and erasable disk

optical double star *n.* a pair of stars that appear to lie close together as viewed from the Earth. They are actually a long way apart, though lying along the same line of sight.

optical fibre *n.* a fibre made of very pure glass or plastic that is used in modern communications systems to transmit information in the form of pulses of laser light. The core is usually of high refractive index and is enclosed in a sheath of lower refractive index, the light thus being transmitted by total internal reflection. ◊ **fibre optics**

optical glass *n.* any high-quality glass used in lenses for its superior refractive quality

optical illusion *n.* **1.** **FALSE VISUAL PERCEPTION** a visual experience in which there is some kind of false perception of what is actually there **2.** **SOURCE OF OPTICAL ILLUSION** sth that causes an optical illusion, especially sth drawn or designed deliberately to fool the eye

optical isomerism *n.* the property exhibited by a pair of molecules that differ only in being mirror images of each other and that rotate plane-polarized light in opposite directions when in solution — **optical isomer** *n.*

optical rotation *n.* the rotation of plane-polarized light as it passes through an optically active medium

optical scanner *n.* **COMPUT** = **scanner**

optical sound *n.* a form of sound reproduction in films that employs a photographed pattern of light on the film that is read by a lamp in the projector. It has now largely been superseded by digital sound.

optic axis *n.* a line passing through a lens, a curved mirror, or a crystal along which light can travel without undergoing double refraction

optic chiasma *n.* the X-shaped nerve tract beneath the brain where the optic nerves from each eye meet and that enables certain of their constituent nerve fibres to cross sides

optic cup *n.* a two-walled depression in a human embryo that develops into the retina

optic disc *n.* **ANAT** a small light-sensitive area of the retina marking the point where nerve fibres from the retinal cells converge to form the optic nerve

optician /op tísh'n/ *n.* **1.** **US** **MAKER AND SELLER OF LENSES** sb who is qualified to fit and supply spectacles and contact lenses, but not to examine eyes or prescribe corrective lenses 2. QUALIFIED EYE EXAMINER sb who is qualified to examine eyes and prescribe corrective lenses. US term **optometrist** 3. SHOP SELLING SPECTACLES a shop where eye examinations are carried out, corrective lenses are prescribed, and spectacles and contact lenses are supplied and fitted

optic nerve *n.* either of the paired second cranial nerves whose nerve fibres transmit visual light signals from the eye to the brain

optics /óptiks/ *n.* STUDY OF LIGHT the study of light or electromagnetic radiation in the visible, infrared, and ultraviolet regions (*takes a singular verb*) ■ *npl.* LENS-EQUIPPED INSTRUMENTS instruments used for detecting electromagnetic radiation and for attaining highly accurate long-range vision (*takes a plural verb*)

optic vesicle *n.* a fold of the embryonic forebrain that develops into the retina and optic nerve

optima plural of **optimum**

optimal /óptim'l/ *adj.* most desirable or favourable ○ *waited for optimal weather conditions* [Late 19thC. Formed from Latin *optimus* 'best', literally 'richest'. Ultimately from an Indo-European word meaning 'to produce', which is also the ancestor of English *opus* and *opulent*.] —**optimality** /ópti mállәti/ *n.* —**optimally** /óptim'li/ *adv.*

optimise *vt.* = **optimize**

optimism /óptimizәm/ *n.* 1. TENDENCY TO EXPECT THE BEST the tendency to believe, expect, or hope that things will turn out well 2. CONFIDENCE the attitude of sb who feels positive or confident 3. PHILOS DOCTRINE THAT OUR WORLD IS BEST a philosophical doctrine, first proposed by Leibnitz, that ours is the best of all possible worlds 4. PHILOS BELIEF IN THE ULTIMATE POWER OF GOOD the belief that things are continually getting better and that good will ultimately triumph over evil [Mid-18thC. From French *optimisme*, from, ultimately, Latin *optimum* (see OPTIMUM).]

optimist /óptimist/ *n.* 1. SB POSITIVE sb who tends to feel hopeful and positive about future outcomes 2. PHILOS FOLLOWER OF OPTIMISM sb who follows any philosophical doctrine of optimism

optimistic /ópti místik/ *adj.* tending to take a hopeful and positive view of future outcomes —**optimistically** *adv.*

optimize /ópti mīz/ (**-mizes, -mizing, -mized**), **optimise** (**-mises, -mising, -mised**) *v.* 1. *vt.* ENHANCE THE EFFECTIVENESS OF to make sth function at its best or most effective, or to use sth to its best advantage 2. *vt.* SOLVE IN THE BEST WAY POSSIBLE to find the best possible solution to a technical problem in which there are a number of competing or conflicting considerations 3. *vi.* SHOW OPTIMISM to feel and show optimism (*archaic or formal*) 4. *vt.* COMPUT WRITE CONCISELY to write computer programming instructions for a task in as few lines as possible to maximize the speed and efficiency of program execution. This will have the effect of, e.g. reducing the time it takes to store or retrieve data from a computer's memory. [Early 19thC. Formed from Latin *optimus* (see OPTIMAL).] —**optimization** /ópti mī záysh'n/ *n.*

optimum /óptimәm/ *n.* (*plural* **-ma** /-mә/ *or* **-mums**) BEST OF SEVERAL OUTCOMES the best out of a number of possible options or outcomes ■ *adj.* BEST most desirable or favourable ○ *optimum trading conditions* [Late 19thC. From Latin, 'best thing', from *optimus* (see OPTIMAL).]

option /ópsh'n/ *n.* 1. CHOICE a choice that is or can be taken ○ *Several options were ruled out right away.* 2. FREEDOM OF CHOICE the right, power, or freedom to make a choice ○ *I'd no option but to refuse.* 3. BUSINESS OPPORTUNITY AVAILABLE FOR A LIMITED TIME an opportunity, usually a commercial opportunity, that has been made available for a limited period only 4. FIN RIGHT TO BUY OR SELL the right to buy or sell sth, especially a stock-market commodity, at a specified price during a specified time period 5. POL = **local option** 6. PIECE OF NON-STANDARD EQUIPMENT an item of non-standard equipment that can be purchased separately, e.g. on a car ■ *vt.* (**-tions, -tioning, -tioned**) COMM HAVE OR GIVE A RIGHT TO to give or acquire an exclusive right to sth [Mid-16thC. Via French from the Latin stem *option-*, from *optare* (see OPT).] ◇ **keep** *or* **leave your options open** to put off making a decision or selection until a later time

optional /ópsh'nәl/ *adj.* left to individual choice ○ *It comes with optional air conditioning.* —**optionally** *adv.*

opto- *prefix.* 1. eye, vision ○ *optometry* 2. optical ○ *optoelectronics* [From Greek *optos* 'seen, visible' (see OPTIC)]

optoelectronics /óptō i lek trónniks, -ellek-/ *n.* the branch of electronics dealing with devices that generate, modulate, transmit, and sense electromagnetic radiation in the visible-light, infrared, and ultraviolet ranges (*takes a singular verb*) [Mid-20thC. Coined from Greek *optos* 'seen, visible' (see OPTIC) + ELECTRONICS.] —**optoelectronic** *adj.*

optometer /op tómmitәr/ *n.* an instrument used to examine the eye for defects in vision [Mid-18thC. Coined from Greek *optos* 'seen, visible' (see OPTIC) + -METER.]

optometrist /op tómmәtrist/ *n.* = **optician**

optometry /op tómmәtri/ *n.* the practice of examining eyes in order to determine levels of vision and then prescribing and supplying any necessary corrective lenses [Late 19thC. Coined from Greek *optos* 'seen, visible' (see OPTIC) + -METRY.] —**optometric** /óptә méttrik/ *adj.*

optophone /óptә fōn/ *n.* a device used especially by blind or visually impaired people that can convert written text into sounds [Early 20thC. Coined from Greek *optos* 'seen, visible' (see OPTIC) + -PHONE.]

opt-out *n.* a decision taken by the administration of a hospital or school to remove itself from local authority control and administer its own affairs (*often used before a noun*)

opulence /óppyŏŏlәnss/, **opulency** /-lәnssi/ *n.* 1. RICHES great wealth or affluence 2. LUXURY luxury, especially of an extravagant, showy, or vulgar nature

opulent /óppyŏŏlәnt/ *adj.* 1. LAVISH characterized by an obvious or lavish display of wealth or affluence 2. AMPLE in richly abundant supply [Mid-16thC. From Latin *opulentus*, literally 'producing much'. Ultimately from an Indo-European word meaning 'to produce', which is also the ancestor of English *opus, copious*, and *optimum*.] —**opulently** *adv.*

opuntia /ō púnshi ә/ *n.* a prickly pear cactus with attractive brightly coloured flowers and oval fruits. The fruits of some varieties are edible. Genus: *Opuntia.* [Early 17thC. From modern Latin, genus name, from *Opunt-*, the stem of *Opus*, a city in Greece. The word originally referred to a plant that grew there.]

opus /ṓpәss/ (*plural* **opuses** *or* **opera** /óppәrә/) *n.* 1. MUSIC ONE OF A SERIES OF MUSICAL WORKS a musical work, especially one of a numbered series by the same composer arranged to show the order in which they were written or catalogued 2. CREATIVE WORK a creative piece of work in any field of the arts. ◊ **magnum opus** [Early 18thC. From Latin, 'work'. Ultimately from an Indo-European word meaning 'to produce', which is also the ancestor of English *opulent* and *optimum*.]

opus anglicanum /-ang gli kaánәm/ *n.* a form of English embroidery that was popular in the Middle Ages, usually seen on ecclesiastical robes [Mid-19thC. From medieval Latin, literally 'English work'.]

opuscule /ō pús kyool/, **opusculum** /әpsskyŏŏlәm/ (*plural* **-la** /-lә/) *n.* a minor or insignificant creative work, especially a musical or literary work [Mid-17thC. Via French from Latin *opusculum*, literally 'little work', from *opus* (see OPUS).]

or[1] (*stressed*) /awr/; (*unstressed*) /әr/ CORE MEANING: a conjunction used to link two or more alternatives. In a series of alternatives, it is usually used only before the last alternative. ○ *Which do you prefer, butter or low fat spread?* ○ *factors that may trigger or exacerbate the illness*

1. *conj.* FOLLOWING 'EITHER' OR 'WHETHER' used to join two alternatives when the first is introduced by 'either' or 'whether' ○ *Either you typed the wrong name, or something is wrong with the equipment.* 2. *conj.* INDICATING APPROXIMATION used between two numbers to indicate an approximate quantity or to imply a few of sth ○ *Hit the return key every three or four seconds until you get a greeting message.* 3. *conj.* REPHRASING A STATEMENT used to introduce a rephrasing synonym or correction of a statement just made ○ *foetal oxygen deprivation, or hypoxia* 4. *conj.* OTHERWISE used to give an explanation of a statement just made ○ *You'd better leave or you'll be late.* 5. *conj.* WHETHER OR EITHER a poetic word for 'either' or 'whether', preceding the first of two alternatives, with 'or' also preceding the second alternative (*archaic or literary*) 6. *conj., prep.* BEFORE before (*archaic*)

or[2] /awr/ *adj.* HERALDRY used to describe an element of a coat of arms or other heraldic insignia that is coloured gold [15thC. Via French from Latin *aurum* 'gold' (see AURUM).]

OR[1] /awr/ *n.* a computer circuit that reproduces the logical element represented by the word 'or'. It is one of the basic interconnected circuits that perform a computer's logical functions.

OR[2] *abbr.* 1. INSUR owner's risk 2. operations research 3. Oregon 4. MIL other ranks

-or[1] *suffix.* sb or sth that does or performs ○ *conductor* [Via Old French *-eor, -eur* and Anglo-Norman *-(o)ur* from Latin *-or* and *-ator*]

-or[2] *suffix.* condition, state, activity ○ *horror* [Via Old French *-eur* from Latin *-or*]

ora plural of **os**

orache /órrәch/, **orach** *n.* a plant that has greyish-green edible leaves resembling spinach leaves and spikes of tiny green flowers. It grows wild throughout Europe. Genus: *Atriplex.* [13thC. Via Anglo-Norman *arasche* from, ultimately, Greek *atraphaxus*, of unknown origin.]

oracle /órrәk'l/ *n.* 1. SOURCE OF WISDOM sb or sth considered to be a source of knowledge, wisdom, or prophecy 2. WISE SAYING a wise or prophetic statement 3. SHRINE OF AN ANCIENT GOD in ancient Greece and Rome, a shrine dedicated to a particular god where people went to consult a priest or priestess in times of trouble or uncertainty. One of the most famous was the Delphic Oracle of Apollo, where Oedipus was given the prophetic warning that he would kill his father, Laius, and marry his mother, Jocasta. 4. GREEK OR ROMAN DEITY an ancient Greek or Roman deity that a priest or priestess would consult for advice on behalf of troubled or uncertain people 5. ADVICE FROM GREEK OR ROMAN DEITY a piece of advice, often in the form of a puzzle or an enigmatic statement, handed down by a Greek or Roman deity 6. GOD-GIVEN MESSAGE a message believed to come from God in response to a request, plea, or petition 7. BIBLE AREA OF A BIBLICAL TEMPLE the most sacred area in either of the biblical Temples, often referred to as the Holy of Holies [14thC. Via French from Latin *oraculum*, from *orare* 'to speak' (see ORATE).]

oracles /órrәk'lz/ *npl.* the books of the Bible

oracular /o rákyŏŏlәr/ *adj.* 1. OF OR AS AN ORACLE relating to oracles or in the form of an oracle 2. WISE knowing, wise, or prophetic 3. MYSTERIOUS puzzling, ambiguous, or enigmatic [Mid-17thC. Formed from Latin *oraculum* (see ORACLE).] —**oracularity** /o rákyŏŏ lárrәti/ *n.* —**oracularly** /o rákyŏŏlәrli/ *adv.*

oracy /áwrәssi/ *n.* the ability to speak fluently and articulately and to understand and respond to what other people say [Mid-20thC. Formed from ORAL, on the model of 'literacy'.]

ora et labora /áwrә et lә báwrә/ a Latin phrase meaning 'pray and work'

oral /áwrәl/ *adj.* 1. OF THE MOUTH relating to or belonging to the mouth ○ *oral hygiene* 2. FOR THE MOUTH designed for use in the mouth 3. SPOKEN existing in spoken form as distinct from written form 4. MED ADMINISTERED BY MOUTH used to describe medicines that are taken by mouth. ◊ **parenteral** 5. PHON WITH A RELEASE OF AIR THROUGH THE MOUTH used to describe a speech sound that is produced by means of an airstream that escapes through the mouth only, with the nasal cavity sealed off by the velum. ◊ **nasal** 6. PSYCHOANAL DERIVING PLEASURE VIA THE MOUTH used in Freudian analysis to describe a stage in child development when erotic pleasure is derived from mouth-associated sensations, especially through feeding, thumb-sucking, and putting objects into the mouth. ◊ **phallic** 7. PSYCHOANAL DEPENDENT AND AGGRESSIVE used in Freudian analysis to describe a dependent, selfish and aggressive personality type with a tendency to derive pleasure from mouth-related activities such as eating, drinking, or smoking 8. BIOL WHERE THE MOUTH IS SITED used to describe the surface of the body of an animal such as the underside of a starfish, on which the mouth is situated ∎ *n.* EDUC **TEST REQUIRING SPOKEN ANSWERS** an examination or test that involves candidates giving spoken answers to spoken questions, as distinct from one where the questions and answers are in written form. ◊ **viva** [Early 17thC. From late Latin *oralis*, from Latin *or-*, the stem of *os* 'mouth' (source also of English *orifice*, *oscillate*, and *usher*).] —**orally** *adv.*

—— **WORD KEY: SYNONYMS** ——
See Synonyms at **verbal**.

oral contraceptive *n.* a pill that is taken daily to prevent conception, especially one that combines an oestrogen and a progestogen

oral history *n.* **1.** HISTORY RECORDED BY PARTICIPANTS IN EVENTS the personal recollections of people who participated in historical events, recorded on audio or video tape or told to a younger generation **2.** STUDY OF HISTORY RECORDED ORALLY the branch of history that deals with personal accounts of historical events or periods recorded on audio or video tape —**oral historian** *n.*

oral hygiene *n.* = dental hygiene —**oral hygienist** *n.*

Oral Law, **Oral Torah** *n.* Jewish religious law that developed out of interpretations of the Torah and was originally passed on orally by rabbis and sages before being recorded in writing, principally in the Mishnah and Talmud

oral sex *n.* sexual activity that involves using the mouth and tongue to stimulate a partner's genitals

oral society *n.* a community in which people do not read or write

oral tradition *n.* a community's cultural and historical background preserved and passed on from one generation to the next in spoken stories and song, as distinct from being written down

Oran /ə rán/ city and port in Algeria, on the northwestern coast of the country. Population: 664,000 (1989).

orang *n.* = orang-utan [Late 18thC. Shortening.]

Orange

orange /órrinj/ *n.* **1.** TREES TREE YIELDING JUICY FRUIT a tree that is widely grown throughout warmer regions for its edible juicy citrus fruit. It has sweet-smelling blossoms and fine-grained wood. Genus: *Citrus*. **2.** FOOD CITRUS FRUIT a round or oval fruit of the orange tree, with a thick skin and juicy flesh divided into segments. As well as being eaten fresh, it is often squeezed for its juice. (*often used before a noun*) **3.** COLOURS COLOUR OF AN ORANGE the bright colour of the skin of an orange. It is a secondary colour that is a mixture of red and yellow. **4.** INDUST = orangewood **5.** TREES TREE WITH FRUITS SIMILAR TO THE ORANGE any tree or plant such as the mock orange and the Osage orange that produces fruits similar to the citrus orange **6.** ZOOL ORANGE-COLOURED BUTTERFLY a butterfly with predominantly orange colouration such as the sulphur butterfly. Family: Pieridae. **7.** ARTS PIGMENT MIXING YELLOW AND RED a pigment or dye that is a mixture of red and yellow **8.** TEXTILES, CLOTHES MATERIAL OF THE COLOUR ORANGE fabric or clothing that is orange in colour **9.** ORANGE-COLOURED OBJECT an object that is coloured orange ∎ *adj.* OF REDDISH-YELLOW COLOUR having the bright reddish-yellow colour of an orange [13thC. Via Old French *pomme d'orenge*, a translation (influenced by *Orange*, a town in France) of Italian *melarancia* 'orange

fruit', via Arabic *nāranj* and Persian *nārang* from Sanskrit *nāraṅgaḥ*.] —**orangey** *adj.*

Orange /órrinj/ *n.* DUTCH ROYAL HOUSE the royal house of the Netherlands from the accession of King William I in 1815. The family had earlier been Dutch princes and stadtholders, or magistrates. William of Orange became King William III of Great Britain and Ireland in 1689. ∎ *adj.* **1.** OF HOUSE OF ORANGE relating to or belonging to the house of Orange **2.** OF ORANGE ORDER relating to or belonging to the Orange Order

Orange[1] **1.** river in southern Africa. Its lower course forms the boundary between South Africa and Namibia. Length: 2,090 km/1,300 mi. **2.** town in central New South Wales, Australia. It is a centre for fruit and vegetable growing and light industry. Population: 34,980 (1996).

Orange[2] town in Vaucluse Department, Provence-Alpes-Côte d'Azur Region, southeastern France. Population: 26,964 (1996).

orangeade /órrinj áyd/ *n.* a still or fizzy nonalcoholic drink flavoured with orange or tasting like oranges [Early 18thC. Formed from ORANGE, on the model of 'lemonade'.]

orange badge *n.* an official sign displayed on vehicles of drivers with disabilities, entitling them to use reserved parking places

orange chromide *n.* a freshwater tropical fish native to Asia with distinctive orange spotty markings that make it a popular aquarium fish. Latin name: *Etropus maculatus.*

orange flower water *n.* a sweet aromatic liquid flavouring made from orange blossom. It is used in cakes, confectionery, and desserts.

orange hawkweed *n.* a perennial European variety of the hawkweed plant that has clusters of orange-red flower heads. Latin name: *Hieracium aurantiacum.*

Orange lodge *n.* a local branch of the Orange Order, or the building in which the branch has its headquarters

Orangeman /órrinjmən/ (*plural* -men /-mən/) *n.* **1.** ORANGE ORDER MEMBER a member of the Orange Order **2.** PROTESTANT IRISHMAN an Irishman of the Protestant faith [Late 18thC. From the name of the ORANGE ORDER.]

orange milkweed *n.* = butterfly weed

Orange Order *n.* a Protestant organization formed in 1795 with the aim of celebrating and defending Protestantism in Northern Ireland. In recent times it has been prominent in loyalist marches. [So called because it was originally formed out of loyalty to William of Orange (WILLIAM III)]

orange peel *n.* the thick dimpled skin of an orange

orange-peel *adj.* having a dimpled surface caused, e.g. by open pores or cellulite ○ *orange-peel skin*

orange-peel fungus *n.* a fungus that has an orange cup with a rough white underside resembling dry, curled-up orange peel. It grows singly or in groups, usually on decaying matter at the edge of woods, between September and January. Latin name: *Aleuria aurantia.*

orange pekoe *n.* a high-quality black tea grown in India and Sri Lanka and made using only the small, young, tender leaves growing at the tips of the stems

orangeroot /órrinj root/ *n.* BOT = goldenseal

orangery /órrinjəri/ (*plural* -ries) *n.* a building where orange trees are grown, especially a large greenhouse for use in cooler climates

orange squash *n.* a sweet nonalcoholic drink made from oranges or tasting of oranges. It comes in concentrated form, to be diluted with water.

orange stick *n.* a small stick used for manicuring the fingernails and cuticles that is usually wooden or plastic, with one pointed end and one rounded end [So called because it is usually made from orangewood]

orange-tip *n.* a common European butterfly with predominantly mottled white wings, and the front of the forewing tipped with orange in the males. Latin name: *Anthocaris cardamines.*

orangewood /órrinj wŏŏd/ *n.* the yellowish hard fine-grained wood of the orange tree, used for making furniture and carved objects

Orang-utan

orang-utan, **orang-utang** *n.* a large tailless ape with reddish-brown coarse shaggy hair and long powerful arms that is found only in the forests of Borneo and Sumatra. Latin name: *Pongo pygmaeus*. [Late 17thC. From Malay *orang hutan* 'forest person'.]

orate /aw ráyt/ (**orates, orating, orated**) *vi.* **1.** MAKE FORMAL PUBLIC SPEECH to make a speech, especially a public, formal, or ceremonial speech (*formal*) **2.** SPEAK POMPOUSLY to speak in a pompous or boring way, or for an inappropriately long time [Early 17thC. From Latin *orare* 'to speak, pray' (source of English *adore*, *oracle*, and *inexorable*).]

oration /aw ráysh'n/ *n.* **1.** FORMAL PUBLIC SPEECH a speech, lecture, or other instance of formal or ceremonial public speaking **2.** POMPOUS SPEECH a speech that is considered pompous, boring, or inappropriately long **3.** PUBLIC SPEECH SHOWING RHETORICAL SKILLS an academic speech that is designed to show the speaker's rhetorical skills, especially a speech given as an exercise in public speaking, often in a public speaking contest **4.** STYLE OF SPEECH DELIVERY the way in which a speech is delivered, or a way of speaking

orator /órrətər/ *n.* **1.** GIVER OF SPEECHES sb who gives speeches, especially sb practised and skilled in giving formal, ceremonial, or persuasive public addresses **2.** POMPOUS SPEAKER sb who has a tendency to speak in a pompous or boring way, or who speaks for an inappropriately long time **3.** LAW PETITIONER sb who files a petition or a complaint in a court of law (*archaic*)

oratorio /órrə táwri ō/ (*plural* -os) *n.* **1.** PIECE OF RELIGIOUS CLASSICAL MUSIC a musical composition for voices and instruments that has a religious theme, often telling a sacred story but not using costumes, scenery, or dramatic staging. Handel's *Messiah* is an example of this genre. **2.** ORATORIOS IN GENERAL oratorios as a musical genre [Mid-17thC. From Italian, named after the *Oratory* of Saint Philip Neri in Rome, where the form was used in musical services.]

oratory[1] /órrətəri/ *n.* **1.** ART OF PUBLIC SPEAKING the art of speaking in public with style, cogency, and grace **2.** RHETORICAL SKILL AND ELOQUENCE eloquence in public speaking, especially of the kind that shows the speaker's rhetorical skills **3.** POMPOSITY IN SPEECH pompous, boring, or inappropriately long speech [Early 16thC. From Latin (*ars*) *oratoria* '(art) of speaking', from *orator* (see ORATE).] —**oratorical** /órrə tórrik'l/ *adj.* —**oratorically** /-tórrikli/ *adv.*

oratory[2] /órrətəri/ (*plural* -ries) *n.* a place for private prayer or worship such as a small secluded chapel, usually set aside in a church [14thC. Via Anglo-Norman *oratorie* from, ultimately, Latin *orare* 'to speak, pray'.]

Oratory *n.* a religious society that has secular priests and is a branch of the Roman Catholic Church. It was founded in 1575 by Saint Philip Neri.

orb /awrb/ *n.* **1.** KING'S OR QUEEN'S JEWELLED SPHERE a small sphere usually made from a precious metal set with jewels and with a cross fixed to the top of it that forms part of a sovereign's ceremonial regalia. ◊ **sceptre 2.** SPHERE a sphere or spherical object **3.** EYE an eye (*literary*) **4.** AREA OF INTEREST a sphere of interest, influence, or activity (*literary*) **5.** ASTRON CELESTIAL BODY a planet or other celestial body, especially the Sun, the Moon, or the Earth (*archaic or literary*) **6.** CELESTIAL BODY'S PATH the orbiting path of a planet or other

Orb

celestial body (*archaic or literary*) **7. CIRCLE** a circle (*archaic or literary*) **8. ASTRON CONCENTRIC PLANET-HOLDING SPHERE** any one of the concentric spheres that were formerly believed by astronomers to hold the planets in their orbital paths ■ *v.* (**orbs, orbing, orbed**) **1.** *vt.* **ENCIRCLE** to encircle sth (*literary*) **2.** *vti.* **MAKE OR BECOME CIRCULAR** to become circular or make sth circular (*archaic*) [14thC. From Latin *orbis* 'wheel, circle', of unknown origin.]

orbicular /awr bíkyoōlər/, **orbiculate** /-lət/ *adj.* **1. ROUND** in the form of a circle or sphere (*formal*) **2. BOT FLAT AND ROUND** used to describe plant parts, especially leaves, that are flat and round or roundish [14thC. From late Latin *orbicularis*, from Latin *orbiculus*, literally 'small globe', from *orbis* 'globe'.] —**orbicularity** /awr bíkyoō lárrəti/ *n.* —**orbicularly** /awr bíkyoōlərli/ *adv.* — **orbiculately** /-lətli/ *adv.*

orbit /áwrbit/ *n.* **1. ASTRON, SPACE TECH PATH OF A PLANET, SATELLITE, OR MOON** the path that a celestial body such as a planet, moon, or satellite follows around a larger celestial body such as the Sun **2. ASTRON, SPACE TECH CELESTIAL BODY'S REVOLUTION** a single revolution of a celestial body around a larger body **3. AREA OF INTEREST** a sphere of interest, influence, or activity **4. ANAT, ZOOL EYE SOCKET** a round cavity in which an eye is located in the skull of a vertebrate **5. PHYS ELECTRON'S PATH AROUND AN ATOM'S NUCLEUS** the path that an electron takes as it moves around the nucleus of an atom ■ *v.* (**-bits, -biting, -bited**) **1.** *vti.* **ASTRON MOVE AROUND A CELESTIAL BODY** to move around a celestial body in a path dictated by the force of gravity exerted by that body **2.** *vt.* **SPACE TECH PUT INTO CELESTIAL ORBIT** to send sth, especially a spacecraft or an artificial satellite, into orbit **3.** *vi.* **FOLLOW A REGULAR PATH** to move regularly or repeatedly along the same path, especially a circular path [Mid-16thC. From Latin *orbita* 'wheel-track', of uncertain origin: probably formed from *orbis* 'wheel, circle'.]

orbital /áwrbit'l/ *adj.* **OF ORBITS** belonging to or relating to an orbit ■ *n.* **PHYS SPACE IN AN ATOM OCCUPIED BY AN ELECTRON** a subdivision of the available space within an atom for an electron to orbit the nucleus. An atom has many orbitals, each of which has a fixed size and shape and can hold up to two electrons. — **orbitally** *adv.*

orbital space vehicle *n. US* a vehicle that transports payloads to and from points in space having different orbits such as a space station, a satellite, and the Moon

orbital velocity *n.* the speed an object must maintain in order to remain in a given orbit. If the speed slows, the orbit will decay and the orbiting object will be drawn to the larger body.

orbiter /áwrbitər/ *n.* a spacecraft or satellite that is designed to orbit a celestial body but not to land on it

orb weaver *n.* a spider that weaves a broad intricate web of silk to entrap its prey

orca /áwrkə/ *n.* **MARINE BIOL** = **killer whale** [Mid-19thC. Via modern Latin, former genus name, from Latin *orca* 'large sea creature'.]

Orcadian /awr káydi ən/ *n.* sb who lives on or was born or brought up on Orkney, a group of islands lying to the north of Scotland [Mid-17thC. Formed from Latin *Orcades* 'Orkney Islands'.] —**Orcadian** *adj.*

orcein /áwrsi in/ *n.* a brown dye obtained from orcinol

and used as a biological stain [Mid-19thC. Formed from *orcin* 'orcinol', from modern Latin *orcina* 'orchil'.]

orch. *abbr.* **MUSIC 1.** orchestra **2.** orchestrated by

orchard /áwrchərd/ *n.* **1. AREA OF FRUIT OR NUT TREES** an area of land on which fruit or nut trees are grown, especially commercially **2. FRUIT OR NUT TREES COMMERCIALLY PLANTED** all the fruit or nut trees growing in a particular area, planted for commercial reasons [Old English *ortgeard*, from an uncertain first element + YARD]

—— **WORD KEY: CULTURAL NOTE** ——
The Cherry Orchard, a play by the Russian dramatist Anton Chekhov (1903–04). Chekhov described his last play as a comedy, but it is often played as tragedy. It depicts the decline of the Ranyevskayas, a family of upper-class landowners, who despite being faced with bankruptcy refuse to contemplate merchant Lopakhin's suggestion that they sell their beloved cherry orchard.

orchardist /áwrchərdist/ *n.* sb who owns or manages an orchard

orchestra /áwrkistrə/ *n.* **1. MUSIC LARGE GROUP OF CLASSICAL MUSICIANS** a large group of musicians playing classical music, consisting of sections of string, woodwind, brass, and percussion players, and directed by a conductor **2. MUSIC GROUP OF MUSICIANS** a group of musicians, especially a fairly large group usually but not always playing classical music **3.** *US* **THEATRE** = **orchestra pit 4. THEATRE PLACE FOR THE CHORUS** the semicircular area in front of the stage in ancient Greek theatres, reserved for the chorus [Early 17thC. Via Latin, 'space in front of the stage where the chorus danced', from Greek *orkhēstra*, from *orkheisthai* 'to dance'.]

orchestral /awr késtrəl/ *adj.* relating to orchestras or intended for an orchestra, especially a symphony orchestra —**orchestrally** *adv.*

orchestra pit *n.* the part of a theatre where the musicians sit, immediately in front of the stage or under the front part of the stage. US term **orchestra**

orchestra stalls *npl.* **THEATRE** the front seats on the lower floor of a theatre, situated just in front of the orchestra

orchestrate /áwrki strayt/ (**-trates, -trating, -trated**) *vt.* **1. MUSIC ARRANGE MUSIC FOR AN ORCHESTRA** to arrange or compose music to be played by an orchestra **2. ORGANIZE STH** to organize a situation or event unobtrusively so that a desired effect or outcome is achieved ○ *The press conference had clearly been carefully orchestrated.* —**orchestrator** *n.*

orchestration /áwrki stráysh'n/ *n.* **1. MUSIC MUSICAL ARRANGEMENT** the arrangement of a piece of music to be played by an orchestra **2. DISCREET ORGANIZING** the unobtrusive organizing of a situation or event to produce a desired effect or outcome

orchestrion /awr késtri ən/, **orchestrina** /áwrki strééna/ *n.* a mechanical musical instrument similar to a barrel organ, designed to imitate the sounds of an orchestra [Mid-19thC. Formed from ORCHESTRA on the model of *accordion*.]

Orchid

orchid /áwrkid/ *n.* **1. FLOWERING PLANT** any one of a large family of perennial plants prized for their beautiful and fragrant flowers and found mostly in tropical climates. Family: Orchidaceae. **2. ORCHID FLOWER** a flower from an orchid plant, typically a delicate fragrant flower with three petals [Mid-19thC. From the Latin stem *orchid-*, which was mistakenly formed from *orchis* (see ORCHIS).]

orchidaceous /áwrki dáyshəss/ *adj.* relating to, belonging to, or characteristic of the orchid family [Mid-19thC. Formed from modern Latin *Orchidaceae*, family name of the orchid.]

orchiectomy /áwrki éktəmi/ (*plural* **-mies**), **orchidectomy** /áwrki déktəmi/ (*plural* **-mies**) *n.* surgical removal of one or both testicles [Late 19thC. Coined from Greek *orkhis* (see ORCHIS) + -ECTOMY.]

orchil /áwrkil, -chil/ *n.* **1. LICHEN** a lichen that yields a reddish dye. Genera: *Roccella* and *Lecanora*. **2. RED DYE** a reddish dye derived from an orchil lichen, obtained by treating the lichen with aqueous ammonia [15thC. Via Spanish *orchilla* from Catalan *orxella* of, ultimately, Arabic origin.]

orchis /áwrkiss/ *n.* an orchid with a fleshy tuber and spikes of small flowers with spurred lips. Genus: *Orchis*. [Mid-16thC. Via Latin from Greek *orkhis*, literally 'testicle' (from the tuber's shape).]

orchitis /awr kítiss/ *n.* inflammation of one or both testicles, usually caused by infection. It can also develop in mumps, and if both testicles are affected it may result in sterility. [Late 18thC. Via modern Latin, which was coined from Greek *orkhis* 'testicle' + -ITIS.] —**orchitic** /awr kíttik/ *adj.*

OR circuit /áwr-/ *n.* a circuit with two or more inputs and one output, whose output is high if one input is high

Ord /awrd/ river in northern Western Australia. A dam for irrigation was built across it in 1972, forming Lake Argyle. Length: 320km/200 mi.

ord. *abbr.* **1. BIOL** order **2.** ordinal **3. BIOL** ordinance **4.** ordinary **5. MIL** ordnance

ordain /awr dáyn/ (**-dains, -daining, -dained**) *vt.* **1. COMMAND FORMALLY** to order or establish sth formally, especially by law or by another authority ○ *laws of commercial transactions that had long been ordained by the government* **2. RELIG MAKE A RELIGIOUS APPOINTMENT** to appoint sb officially as a priest, minister, or rabbi [13thC. Via Old French *ordener* from Latin *ordinare* 'to set in order', from *ordo* (see ORDER).] —**ordainer** *n.*

ordeal /awr deél, áwr deel/ *n.* **1. DIFFICULT EXPERIENCE** a very difficult or harrowing experience, especially one lasting a long time **2. ANCIENT TRIAL** a trial in the past that involved subjecting a defendant to life-threatening danger, e.g. from fire or water, with the outcome regarded as reflecting divine judgment [Old English *ordāl* 'trial, judgment'. Ultimately from a prehistoric Germanic base meaning 'to share out' that is also the ancestor of English *deal*.]

order /áwrdər/ *n.* **1. INSTRUCTION** an instruction to do sth **2. ARRANGEMENT OF ITEMS** the way in which several items are arranged, as an indication of their relative importance or size or when each will be dealt with ○ *I will announce the winners in reverse order.* **3. NEATNESS** an organized state, with elements arranged properly, neatly, or harmoniously ○ *We all need a little order in our lives.* **4. ABSENCE OF CRIME** a peaceful state in which laws are obeyed and misbehaviour or crime is not present or is prevented ○ *the establishment of law and order* **5. FUNCTIONING STATE** the state sth is in when it is functioning properly **6. INSTRUCTION TO PROVIDE STH** an instruction to bring or supply sth, e.g. a spoken instruction to a waiter or waitress, or a written instruction to a manufacturer or supplier of goods ○ *Can I take your order now?* **7. STH PROVIDED** sth provided in response to an instruction ○ *If you are not completely satisfied, you may return your order.* **8. SOCIAL GROUPING** the arrangement of society into groups or classes and the relationships between them ○ *a new world order* **9. SOCIAL GROUP** any one of the groups or classes into which a society is divided (*often used in the plural*) **10. BIOL SET OF RELATED FAMILIES** a taxonomic classification made up of related families of organisms ○ *the cat family, in the order Carnivora* **11. TYPE** a kind or type of sth, often one judged on importance or worth ○ *Exactly what order of stupidity are we dealing with?* **12. LAW COURT'S INSTRUCTION** an instruction issued by a judge or a court of law **13. FIN FINANCIAL INSTRUCTION** a written instruction to pay money **14. order, Order RELIG RELIGIOUS COMMUNITY** a religious community in which members live according to principles that are often based on the writings of a particular saint ○ *the Order of Saint*

Francis **15.** CHR **RELIGIOUS RANK** any one of the grades into which the ministry is divided in some Christian denominations, including deacons, priests, bishops, and archbishops **16.** CHR **RELIGIOUS SERVICE** a form of Christian religious service used on specific occasions **17. order, Order GROUP OF HONOURED PEOPLE** a prestigious group consisting of people who have been awarded an honour for services to their country, or the decoration indicating such an honour ○ *the Order of the Garter* **18.** ARCHIT **ARCHITECTURAL STYLE** any one of the five major styles of classical architecture, namely the Doric, Ionic, Corinthian, Tuscan, and Composite. They differ in the shapes and styles of columns and entablatures. **19.** MATH **NUMBER OF ROWS AND COLUMNS** the number of rows and columns in a matrix **20.** MATH **NUMBER OF DIFFERENTIATIONS** the number of times differentiation must be applied to a mathematical expression to obtain a specified derivative **21.** MATH **GROUP MEMBERS** the number of elements in a finite group **22.** SCI = **order of magnitude 23.** MATH **ORDER OF HIGHEST ORDER DIFFERENTIAL** in a differential equation, the order of the highest order differential **24.** CHEM **CLASSIFICATION OF CHEMICAL REACTIONS** a classification of chemical reactions based on the mathematical relationship between the rate of a given chemical reaction and the concentration of the reacting chemical compounds ■ **orders** *npl.* = **holy orders** ■ *v.* **(-ders, -dering, -dered) 1.** *vt.* **GIVE SB INSTRUCTIONS** to command sb to do sth ○ *The colonel ordered the troops to move out.* **2.** *vt.* **PRESCRIBE STH** to give an instruction for sth to be done **3.** *vti.* **REQUEST STH** to give an instruction for sth to be provided, e.g. food in a restaurant or goods from a manufacturer or supplier **4.** *vt.* **ARRANGE ITEMS** to arrange items in a particular way, especially in the sequence in which they are to be dealt with ○ *addresses ordered by postcode* **5.** *vt.* **ARRANGE THINGS NEATLY** to put things into a neat, well organized state or into the required state ○ *ordered her business affairs prior to leaving for the summer* ■ *interj.* **CALL FOR CALM** used to request calm or observance of correct procedure, e.g. by a person chairing a debate [13thC. Via French *ordre*, from, ultimately, Latin *ordin-*, the stem of *ordo* (source of English *ordinal*, *coordinate*, and *ordinary*). The underlying sense is 'conforming to order'.] —**orderer** *n.* ◇ **in order 1.** in a correct sequence or arrangement ○ *Put them in order alphabetically.* **2.** in a condition of being correct or appropriate ○ *The customs official was checking that the paperwork was in order.* ◇ **in order to** *or* **that** used to introduce the object or purpose of sth ◇ **on order** requested but not yet supplied or delivered ◇ **out of order 1.** not working properly or at all **2.** not in the correct sequence or place within a sequence **3.** not following accepted rules of procedure or conduct (*regional informal*) **4.** not done or behaving in a fair, appropriate, or tolerable way (*informal*) ◇ **a tall order** a request that is very difficult to fulfil (*informal*)

order about, order around *vt.* to subject sb to domineering or bullying treatment ○ *Don't think you can order me about.*

order arms *n.* **MILITARY DRILL MOVEMENT** an act of bringing a weapon, usually a rifle, from the shoulder to a resting position on the ground alongside the right leg, performed as part of a military drill ■ *interj.* **COMMAND TO ASSUME ORDER ARMS** used as a command in a military drill to assume the order arms position

orderly /áwrdərli/ *adj.* **1. WELL-BEHAVED** well-behaved or peaceful ○ *The meeting passed off in an orderly fashion* **2. NEATLY ARRANGED** arranged or organized in a neat, sensible, or proper way ○ *orderly bookshelves* ■ *n.* (*plural* **-lies**) **1.** MED **ASSISTANT WORKING IN A HOSPITAL** a hospital worker with no medical training who is employed to do various ancillary jobs such as transporting patients **2.** MIL **SOLDIER WITH MINOR DUTIES** a soldier acting as a senior officer's personal assistant who carries out a variety of minor duties such as carrying messages —**orderliness** *n.*

Order of Australia *n.* an order awarded in Australia to individuals who are seen to have made an outstanding contribution to society. There are general and military awards.

order of battle *n.* the way that military forces are organized in preparation for a battle

order of business *n.* the order in which a number of items are to be discussed or dealt with, e.g. at a meeting

order of magnitude *n.* MATH, SCI the difference in size, usually expressed in powers of 10, between two quantities. If a quantity were 10 times greater than another, it would be an order of magnitude greater; if 100 times greater, it would be two orders of magnitude greater. ○ *The mass of the Earth is an order of magnitude greater than that of Mars.*

Order of Merit *n.* a British honour awarded for eminence in any field

order of the day (*plural* **orders of the day**) *n.* **1. AGENDA** a programme of items to be discussed or dealt with on a particular day, e.g. by a legislative assembly **2. TYPICAL THING** sth that is regularly done, offered, chosen, or experienced during a particular period ○ *Heroism was the order of the day during the last big battle of the war.*

Order of the Garter *n.* the highest British order of knighthood

order paper *n.* a printed list given out daily to MPs showing the order and nature of business to be dealt with in Parliament

ordinal /áwrdin'l/ *adj.* **1.** MATH **SHOWING POSITION** showing the relative position in a sequence of numbers **2.** BIOL **RELATING TO BIOLOGICAL ORDERS** relating to a biological order in the classification of plants and animals ■ *n.* **1.** = **ordinal number** *n.* 1 **2.** CHR **CATHOLIC BOOKLET** in the Roman Catholic Church, an instruction booklet that lists the order of services in church worship **3.** CHR **CHRISTIAN BOOKLET** an instruction booklet that outlines rules and ceremony for the ordination of Christian ministers [Late 16thC. From late Latin *ordinalis* 'ordered', from the Latin stem *ordin-* (see ORDER).]

ordinal number *n.* **1. NUMBER SHOWING ORDER** a number used to show the relative position of sth or sb in a sequence. 'First' and 'second' are ordinal numbers. **2.** MATH, LOGIC **SIZE AND ORDER OF A SET** a measure of the size of an ordered set in addition to the order of its elements

ordinal scale *n.* STATS a list that shows only the relative positions of items on a scale, giving no measure of the difference between them

ordinance /áwrdinənss/ *n.* **1. LAW** a law or rule made by an authority, e.g. a local council **2. STH PRESCRIBED** sth regularly done because it is formally prescribed, especially a religious ceremony, such as Holy Communion (*formal*) [14thC. Via Old French from, ultimately, Latin *ordinare* (see ORDAIN).]

ordinand /áwrdi nand/ *n.* sb who is a candidate for ordination as a Christian minister [Mid-19thC. From Latin *ordinandus*, from *ordinare* (see ORDAIN).]

ordinarily /áwrd'nərəli/ *adv.* usually or normally

ordinary /áwrd'nəri/ *adj.* **1. COMMON** of a common everyday kind **2. UNREMARKABLE** not remarkable or special in any way, and therefore uninteresting and unimpressive ○ *He's just a pretty ordinary kind of guy.* **3. USUAL** usual or customary **4.** LAW **WITH IMMEDIATE JURISDICTION** with immediate jurisdiction, as opposed to jurisdiction by delegation or deputation **5.** MATH **WITH TWO VARIABLES** relating to a differential equation that has only two variables ■ *n.* (*plural* **-ies**) **1.** LAW **JUDGE** a judge who acts in his or her own right **2. ordinary, Ordinary** CHR **CLERIC WITH JUDGE'S POWERS** a member of the clergy, especially a bishop, whose position brings with it the power to act as a judge in some ecclesiastical matters **3. ordinary, Ordinary** CHR **UNCHANGING PARTS OF THE RELIGIOUS MASS** in the Roman Catholic Church, the parts of the daily Mass that do not change from day to day **4. ordinary, Ordinary** CHR **FORM FOR A RELIGIOUS SERVICE** in the Roman Catholic Church, the correct form that a religious service, especially Mass, should take, or a book that sets out the correct form **5.** HERALDRY **SIMPLE DESIGN** any one of the simpler shapes or designs used on coats of arms **6. EATING HOUSE** an eating establishment or a dining room in a tavern (*archaic*) [14thC. Via Old French from medieval Latin *ordinarius* 'following the usual course', from the Latin stem *ordin-* (see ORDER).] —**ordinariness** *n.* ◇ **out of the ordinary** unusual or extraordinary

Ordinary Grade *n. Scotland* EDUC full form of **O grade**

Ordinary level *n.* EDUC full form of **O level**

ordinary seaman *n.* the lowest rank of sailors in the navies of some countries, subordinate to the more experienced able seaman

ordinary share *n.* FIN a share that entitles the holder to a dividend in line with the company's profits, as distinct from a preference share that gives the holder priority when dividends are paid

ordinate /áwrd'nət/ *n.* MATH the vertical or y-coordinate of a point on a two-dimensional graph or diagram in which pairs of numbers denote distances along fixed horizontal and vertical axes. ◊ **abscissa** [Late 17thC. From Latin *ordinare* (see ORDAIN).]

ordination /áwrdi náysh'n/ *n.* an official investiture as a Christian priest or minister, or as a rabbi, or a ceremony during which sb is consecrated as a priest, minister, or rabbi [15thC. Directly or via French from the Latin stem *ordination-*, from *ordinare* (see ORDAIN).]

ordn. *abbr.* ordnance

ordnance /áwrdnənss/ *n.* **1. MILITARY WEAPONS SYSTEMS** military weapons systems, including supplies for their use and equipment for their maintenance **2. DEPARTMENT RESPONSIBLE FOR WEAPONS AND SUPPLIES** the army or government department that has responsibility for military weapons and supplies [14thC. Variant of ORDINANCE.]

ordnance datum *n.* the sea-level standard adopted by the Ordnance Survey for map-making purposes. It is established as sea-level as measured at Newlyn, in Cornwall.

Ordnance Survey *n.* the government body responsible for map-making in the United Kingdom

ordo /áwrdō/ (*plural* **-dos** *or* **-dines** /-di neez/) *n.* in the Roman Catholic Church, a calendar detailing the forms of Mass and other services to be followed for each day in the year [Mid-19thC. From Latin (see ORDER).]

ordonnance /áwrdənənss/ *n.* the general arrangement of elements in architecture and in works of art and literature (*formal*) [Mid-17thC. From French, an alteration of Old French *ordenance* 'ordinance'.]

Ordovician /áwrdō víshi ən/ *adj.* GEOL belonging to or dating from the second oldest period of the Palaeozoic era, approximately 500 to 440 million years ago. Primitive fish and other sea creatures appeared during this period. [Late 19thC. Formed from Latin *Ordovices*, the name of an ancient Celtic people of North Wales, where rocks from the period were first identified.]

ordure /áwr dyoor/ *n.* **1. EXCREMENT** excrement or dung (*formal*) **2. STH MORALLY CORRUPTING** obscene or otherwise morally corrupting material or behaviour, or an example of it (*literary*) [14thC. Via Old French from, ultimately, Latin *horridus* 'frightful', from *horrere* (see HORROR).]

ore /awr/ *n.* a naturally occurring mineral from which particular constituents, especially metals, can be profitably extracted [Old English *ōra*, *ār* 'brass, bronze' (later altered in form through confusion with Old English)]

öre /úrrə/ (*plural* **öre**) *n.* **1. SWEDISH CURRENCY UNIT** a subunit of currency in Sweden, worth one hundredth of a krona. See table at **currency 2. COIN WORTH ONE KRONA** a coin worth one krona [Early 18thC. From Swedish, from Old Norse *aurar*, of uncertain origin: probably from Latin *aureus* 'golden'.]

øre /úrə/ *n.* **1. DANISH OR NORWEGIAN CURRENCY UNIT** a subunit of currency in Denmark or Norway, worth one hundredth of a krone. See table at **currency 2. COIN WORTH ONE KRONE** a coin worth one krone [Early 18thC. From Danish or Norwegian, from Old Norse *aurar* (see ÖRE).]

Ore. *abbr.* Oregon

oread /áwri ad/ *n.* in Greek mythology, a mountain nymph [14thC. Via the Latin stem *Oread-* from, ultimately, Greek *Oreias*, from *oros* 'mountain'.]

Örebro /ōrə brōō/ city and county seat of Örebro Province, central Sweden, situated 160 km/100 mi. west of Stockholm. Population: 119,635 (1995).

ore dressing *n.* the separation of the mineral content of an ore from the unwanted rock or earth

Oreg. *abbr.* Oregon

oregano /órri gaáno/ *n.* **1.** AROMATIC PLANT a perennial plant of the mint family that is an aromatic Mediterranean variety of wild marjoram. Latin name: *Origanum vulgare.* **2.** OREGANO LEAVES the fresh or dried leaves of oregano, used to add flavour in cooking [Late 18thC. Via Spanish from, ultimately, Greek *origanon* 'wild marjoram', of uncertain origin: perhaps from *oros* 'mountain' + *ganos* 'brightness, joy'.]

Oregon

Oregon /órrigən/ state of the United States bordered by the Pacific Ocean, Washington, Idaho, Nevada, and California. Capital: Salem. Population: 3,243,487 (1997). Area: 251,470 sq. km/97,093 sq. mi. —**Oregonian** *n., adj.*

Oregon Trail *n.* a 19th-century route to the western United States extending from western Missouri to northern Oregon that was used by pioneers and settlers

Ore Mountains /áwr mówntinz/ range of mountains along the Czech-German border. Height: 1244 m/4080 ft.

Orenburg /órrən burg/ city in southwestern Siberian Russia, the capital of Orenburg Oblast. Population: 557,000 (1992).

Orense /aw rénss e/ city in northwestern Spain and capital of Orense Province, in the autonomous region of Galicia. Population: 110,796 (1995).

Öresund /ōrə sún, ōrə soónd/, **Øresend** channel in northern Europe, between the Kattigat Strait and the Baltic Sea. Length: about 105 km/65 mi.

Oreti /ō ráyti/ river in the south of the South Island, New Zealand. It rises in the Southern Alps and flows south to the Foveaux Strait. Length: 203 km/126 mi.

orf /awrf/ *n.* VET a pox caused by a virus, affecting sheep and goats, and also transmittable to humans, in which pus-filled blisters form on the animals' lips [Mid-19thC. Origin uncertain: probably from Old Norse *hrufa.*]

Orff /awrf/, **Carl** (1895–1982) German composer. He is noted for *Carmina Burana* (1937) and other highly rhythmic choral works.

orfray *n.* SEW = **orphrey**

org. *abbr.* **1.** organic **2.** organization **3.** organized

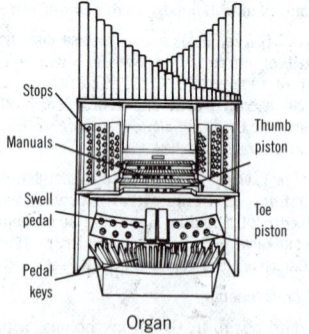

Organ

organ /áwrgən/ *n.* **1.** MUSIC MUSICAL KEYBOARD INSTRUMENT a large musical keyboard instrument that can produce a wide range of sounds at different volumes using compressed air passed through metal pipes **2.** MUSIC INSTRUMENT SIMILAR TO ORGAN any one of various musical instruments that make sounds similar to the organ without the use of pipes, e.g. electronically or using reeds **3.** BIOL BODY PART a complete and independent part of a plant or animal that has a specific function ○ *the organs of the digestive system* **4.** MEANS OF COMMUNICATION a newspaper or magazine regarded as a means of communication, especially one communicating the views of a particular group such as a political party (*formal*) ○ *the daily organ of left-of-centre politics* **5.** POL AGENCY an organization or body acting on behalf of a larger institution, especially a government (*formal*) ○ *There were no secrets about the institute's role as an organ of the business community* **6.** PENIS a penis (*used euphemistically*) [13thC. Via Old French *organe* and Latin *organum* from Greek *organon* 'tool, instrument'. Ultimately from an Indo-European word meaning 'to do', ancestor also of English *work* and *orgy*.]

organa plural of **organon, organum**

organdy /áwrgəndi, awr gándi/ (*plural* **-dies**), **organdie** *n.* a lightweight transparent stiff cotton fabric used especially in dressmaking [Early 19thC. From French *organdi*, of unknown origin.]

organelle /áwrgə nél/ *n.* CELL BIOL a specialized part of a cell, e.g. the nucleus or the mitochondrion, that has its own particular function [Early 20thC. From modern Latin *organella*, literally 'small organ', from medieval Latin *organum* (see ORGAN).]

organ grinder *n.* a street musician who plays a barrel organ, traditionally accompanied by a small monkey who circulates to collect money from bystanders [From the hand-cranked barrel organ]

organic /awr gánnik/ *adj.* **1.** OF LIVING THINGS relating to, derived from, or characteristic of living things **2.** DEVELOPING NATURALLY occurring or developing gradually and naturally, without being forced or contrived **3.** INTRINSIC forming a basic and inherent part of sth and largely responsible for its identity or makeup **4.** WITH ELEMENTS EFFICIENTLY COMBINED consisting of elements that exist together in a seemingly natural relationship that makes for organized efficiency **5.** AGRIC AVOIDING SYNTHETIC CHEMICALS relating to or employing agricultural practices that avoid the use of synthetic chemicals in favour of naturally occurring pesticides, fertilizers, and other growing aids **6.** FOOD PRODUCED WITHOUT SYNTHETIC CHEMICALS grown or reared without the use of synthetic chemicals ○ *a wide range of organic produce* **7.** MED OF BODY'S ORGANS relating to the organs of the body, specifically to basic changes in them brought about by physical disorders **8.** CHEM BASED ON CARBON belonging to a family of compounds characterized by chains or rings of carbon atoms that are linked to atoms of hydrogen and sometimes oxygen, nitrogen, and other elements ■ *n.* ORGANIC SUBSTANCE an organic substance, especially a fertilizer or pesticide —**organicity** /áwrgə níssəti/ *n.*

organically /awr gánnikli/ *adv.* **1.** NATURALLY in a natural or seemingly natural way ○ *paintings with elements organically arranged* **2.** WITHOUT CHEMICALS without the use of synthetic chemicals, especially fertilizers and pesticides ○ *organically raised chickens*

organic brain syndrome *n.* a psychiatric disorder caused by a permanent or temporary physical change in the brain

organic chemistry *n.* the scientific study of carbon-based compounds, originally limited to compounds that are the natural products of living things, now including the study of synthetic carbon compounds such as plastics. ◊ **inorganic chemistry**

organic disease *n.* MED a disorder associated with physical changes in one or more organs of the body

organicism /awr gánnissizəm/ *n.* **1.** BIOL = **holism 2.** MED THEORY CONCERNING DISEASE the theory that all diseases are due to structural changes in the body's organs **3.** SOC SCI THEORY CONCERNING SOCIETY the theory that society is analogous to, or shares characteristics with, living organisms —**organicist** *n.* —**organicistic** /awr gánni sístik/ *adj.*

organisation *n.* = **organization**

organise *vti.* = **organize**

organiser *n.* = **organizer**

organism /áwrgənizəm/ *n.* **1.** BIOL LIVING THING a living thing such as a plant, animal, virus, or bacterium **2.** SYSTEM OF INTERDEPENDENT PARTS a functioning system of interdependent parts that resembles a living creature ○ *Like any organism, public libraries and the people who run them must adapt and respond to change* (Laurence Arnold, *Pulse of the People*; 1997) —**organismal** /áwrgə nízm'l/ *adj.* —**organismic** /-nízmik/ *adj.* —**organismically** /-nízmikli/ *adv.*

organist /áwrgənist/ *n.* a musician who plays the organ

organization /áwrgə nī záysh'n/, **organisation** *n.* **1.** GROUP a group of people identified by shared interests or purpose, e.g. a business ○ *Each news organization sent its own photographer.* **2.** COORDINATION OF ELEMENTS the coordinating of separate elements into a unit or structure ○ *in charge of the organization of international conferences* **3.** RELATIONSHIP OF ELEMENTS the relationships that exist between separate elements arranged into a coherent whole ○ *changes to the organization of the party* **4.** EFFICIENCY IN ARRANGEMENT efficiency in the way separate elements are arranged into a coherent whole ○ *Your working method lacks organization.*

organizational /áwr gə nī záysh'nəl/, **organisational** *adj.* relating to the organizing of sth or to the way in which it is organized ○ *Events like these are an organizational nightmare.* —**organizationally** *adv.*

organizational psychology *n.* = **industrial psychology**

organization theory *n.* the branch of sociology that deals with the structure of organizations and the systems and processes that operate within them

organize /áwrgə nīz/ (**-izes, -izing, -ized**), **organise** (**-ises, -ising, -ised**) *v.* **1.** *vti.* FORM STH to form or establish sth such as a club, by coming together or bringing people together into a structured group (*often passive*) **2.** *vt.* COORDINATE to oversee the coordination of the various elements of sth **3.** *vt.* ARRANGE ELEMENTS to arrange the elements of sth in a way that creates a particular structure ○ *a society organized along democratic lines* ○ *candidates organized into groups of three* **4.** *vt.* MAKE MORE EFFECTIVE to apply or impose efficient working methods in order to work effectively, or make sb else work effectively ○ *Mature students are not necessarily better at organizing themselves.* **5.** *vti.* FORM TRADE UNION to recruit the workers in a place or industry into a trade union, or come together to form a trade union [15thC. Via French from medieval Latin *organizare*, literally 'to provide with bodily organs', from Latin *organum* (see ORGAN). The underlying meaning is 'having connecting parts like organisms'.]

organized /áwrgə nīzd/, **organised** *adj.* **1.** LARGE-SCALE existing on a large scale and involving the systematic coordination of many different elements ○ *organized religion* **2.** EFFICIENT working in a systematic and efficient way ○ *a motivated and organized self-starter*

organized crime *n.* a powerful ruthless large-scale network of professional criminals, or such networks in general

organizer /áwrgə nīzər/, **organiser** *n.* **1.** SB WHO ORGANIZES sb who is active in setting up or organizing projects and motivating others to take part **2.** DIARY a small portable calendar and diary used for planning, or a handheld computerized device with a simple database for managing appointments and other information **3.** CONTAINER WITH COMPARTMENTS a container with compartments for storing items in neat groups, e.g. a desktop container with compartments for pens, pencils, and other items of stationery **4.** EMBRYO EMBRYO PART a part of an embryo that controls the differentiation of cells, eventually leading to the formation of organs and all the other specialized parts that make up an individual organism

organo- *prefix.* **1.** organ ○ *organography* **2.** organic ○ *organophosphate* [From Greek *organon* (see ORGAN)]

organ of Corti /-káwrti/ *n.* ANAT a part of the cochlea of the inner ear that transforms sound energy into nerve impulses and sends those impulses to the brain [Late 19thC. Named after the Italian anatomist Alfonso *Corti* (1822–88).]

organogenesis /áwr gánnō jénnəssiss, áwrgən-/ *n.* the formation and development of animal or plant organs that takes place during the development of an embryo —**organogenetic** /awr gánnō jə néttik, áwrgənō-/ *adj.* —**organogenetically** /-jə néttikli/ *adv.*

organography /áwrgə nóggrəfi/ n. the scientific description of the organs and other main structures of plants and animals —**organographic** /áwrgənō gráffik/ adj. —**organographical** /-gráffik'l/ adj. —**organographically** /-gráffikli/ adv. —**organographist** /áwrgə nóggrəfist/ n.

organoleptic /awr gánnō léptik, áwrgənō-/ adj. BIOL affecting an organ, especially a sense organ [Mid-19thC. From French organoleptique, from Greek organon 'instrument' + lēptikos 'receptive'.] —**organoleptically** adv.

organology /áwrgə nóllə ji/ n. the study of plant and animal organs —**organological** /áwrgənō lójjik'l/ adj. —**organologist** /áwgə nólləjist/ n.

organometallic /awr gánnō me tállik, áwrgənō-/ adj. CHEM relating to an organic compound containing one or more metal atoms, e.g. the petrol additive tetraethyl lead

organon /áwrgə non/ (plural -na /-nə/ or -nons) n. a set of principles for use in philosophical or scientific investigation (formal) [Early 17thC. From Greek (see ORGAN).]

organophosphate /awr gánnō fóss fayt/ n. CHEM, AGRIC an organic compound containing phosphate groups. Organophosphates are widely used as pesticides and fertilizers, but there are medical concerns about their toxicity.

organotherapy /awr gánnō thérrəpi/ (plural -pies) n. MED treatment of diseases by administering substances derived from animal organs, e.g. bovine insulin, which is used to treat diabetes in humans —**organotherapeutic** /awr gánnō thérrə pyóotik/ adj.

organ-pipe cactus n. a tall branched cactus native to the southwestern United States and northern Mexico. Latin name: Lemaireocereus marginatus. [From its tall pipe-shaped stems]

organ screen n. an ornamental wooden or stone partition that separates the nave from the choir in a church or cathedral

organ stop n. 1. SET OF ORGAN PIPES a set of pipes on a musical organ, used to vary the tone and sometimes to imitate the sounds of other instruments 2. KNOB OPERATING PIPES a knob or handle that controls the flow of air to an organ stop

organum /áwrgənəm/ (plural -na /-nə/ or -nums) n. 1. MUSICAL STYLE a style of composition in western music of the late medieval period that combines plainsong melody with other melodies 2. MUSICAL PIECE a piece of music in the organum style [Early 17thC. From Latin (see ORGAN).]

organza /awr gánzə/ n. a stiff transparent fabric, usually silk, rayon, or nylon, used for dressmaking [Early 19thC. Origin uncertain: probably an alteration of the US trademark organza.]

organzine /áwrgən zeen, awrgán zeen/ n. yarn made from strands of silk twisted together, or fabric made from the yarn [Late 17thC. Via French organsin from Italian organzino, of uncertain origin: perhaps ultimately from Organzi, city in Uzbekistan (modern name Urgench).]

orgasm /áwr gazəm/ n. SEXUAL CLIMAX the climax of sexual excitement, consisting of intense muscle tightening around the genital area experienced as a pleasurable wave of tingling sensations through parts of the body ■ vi. (-gasms, -gasming, -gasmed) EXPERIENCE ORGASM to experience sexual orgasm [Late 17thC. Via French or modern Latin from Greek orgasmos, from organ 'to swell, be excited'.] —**orgasmic** /awr gázmik/ adj. —**orgastic** /-gástik/ adj. —**orgasmically** /-gázmikli/ adv. —**orgastically** /-gástikli/ adv.

OR gate n. ELECTRON ENG, COMPUT = OR circuit

orgeat /áwr zhaa/ n. a cooling drink made from almonds and orange-flower water. It was originally made from barley. [15thC. From French from, ultimately, Latin hordeum 'barley'.]

orgiastic /áwrji ástik/ adj. 1. MARKED BY WILD REVELRY full of a spirit of wild revelry ○ orgiastic gatherings 2. LACKING RESTRAINT showing extravagance or lack of restraint ○ orgiastic shopping sprees [Late 17thC. From Greek orgiastikos, from orgiazein 'to celebrate secret rites', from orgia (see ORGY).] —**orgiastically** adv.

orgone /áwrgōn/ n. a life force that is purported to exist in all living things. Some practitioners of alternative therapies claim it can be harnessed by patients sitting in specially designed booths. [Mid-20thC. Origin uncertain: probably formed from ORGANISM or ORGASM on the model of HORMONE.]

orgulous /áwrgyōōləss/ adj. proud (archaic) ○ 'The princes orgulous, their high blood chafed, Have to the port of Athens sent their ships'. (William Shakespeare, Troilus and Cressida; 1601) [13thC. Anglicization of French orgueilleux, from orgueil 'pride', of prehistoric Germanic origin.]

orgy /áwrji/ n. 1. GROUP SEX PARTY a gathering at which a group of people indulge in promiscuous sexual activity 2. DEBAUCHED PARTY a wild party or celebration characterized by excessive drinking and eating, with or without sexual promiscuity 3. PERIOD OF INDULGENCE a period of indulgence in a particular activity or emotion, especially sth that is disapproved of ○ an orgy of self-pity 4. HIST WORSHIP OF ANCIENT GODS in ancient Greece and Rome, a secret worshipping of the gods of pleasure, especially Bacchus or Dionysus, that involved much dancing, drinking, and singing (often used in the plural) [Mid-16thC. Via French from, ultimately, Greek orgia 'secret Dionysian rites'. Ultimately from an Indo-European word meaning 'to do' (ancestor also of English work and organ).]

oribi /órribi/ (plural -bis or -bi) n. a small fawn-coloured antelope with long legs and, in the male, short horns, native to the plains of southern and eastern Africa. Latin name: Ourebia ourebi. [Late 18thC. Via Afrikaans from Khoikho.]

Oriel

oriel /áwri əl/ n. 1. oriel, oriel window BAY WINDOW a bay window projecting from an outside wall and supported from beneath by a bracket 2. RECESS a recess or small room formed by an oriel [15thC. Via Old French oriol 'porch' from medieval Latin oriolum 'upper chamber', of unknown origin.]

orient /áwri ənt, órri-/ v. (-ents, -enting, -ented) 1. vt. POSITION to position sb or sth so that the person or thing faces in a particular direction ○ old stone buildings oriented north-south 2. vr. FIND YOUR POSITION to work out where you are and in which direction you need to travel ○ the seaman's skill of orienting himself by the stars 3. vt. DIRECT to direct sth in a particular way, e.g. towards a particular objective or audience ○ advertising oriented towards teenage girls 4. vt. MAKE FAMILIAR to accustom sb or yourself to a new situation or set of surroundings ○ It might take you a few weeks to orient yourself. 5. vt. POSITION TOWARDS EAST to position sth so that it faces east, especially to build a church so that its length lies east to west, with the main altar at the eastern end ■ n. 1. EASTERN SKY the eastern part of the sky, where the sun rises (archaic or literary) 2. DAWN the dawn (archaic or literary) 3. PEARL'S LUSTRE the lustre of a pearl, especially a pearl of high quality (archaic) 4. PEARL a pearl, especially one of high quality (archaic) ■ adj. (archaic) 1. EASTERN eastern 2. WITH GOOD LUSTRE having an exceptionally rich lustre (refers to pearls) ○ 'These pearls are orient, but they yield in whiteness to your teeth'. (Walter Scott, Ivanhoe; 1819) 3. GLOWING with a rich bright glow ○ 'her vanisht Night, Shot through with orient Beams' (John Milton, Paradise Lost; 1667) [14thC. Via Old French from Latin orient-, the present participle stem of oriri 'to rise' (source also of English origin and abort) because the sun rises in the east. The verb, borrowed from French orienter in the 18thC, originally meant 'to position towards the east'.]

Orient /áwri ənt, órri ənt/, **orient** n. the countries of eastern Asia, especially China, Japan, and their neighbours (dated) ◊ Occident

Oriental /áwri ént'l, órri-/, **oriental** adj. 1. RELATING TO EASTERN ASIA relating to the countries and peoples of eastern Asia, especially to China, Japan, and their neighbouring countries (dated) ◊ Occidental 2. HIGH IN QUALITY of high quality and value (refers to pearls and gems) ○ an oriental ruby ■ n. ASIAN PERSON a word used in the past to refer to sb from eastern Asia, now usually avoided because it generally causes offence (dated offensive)

Oriental fruit moth n. a small moth that in the larval stage is a damaging pest to fruit trees. Native to Asia, it has been introduced to other parts of the world. Latin name: Grapolitha molesta.

Orientalia /áwri en táyli ə, órri-/, **orientalia** n. artefacts from countries in eastern Asia [Early 20thC. From Latin, literally 'things from the Orient'.]

orientalism /áwri ént'lizəm, órri-/, **Orientalism** n. 1. ORIENTAL TRAIT a quality or characteristic typical of the countries, peoples, or cultures of eastern Asia 2. STUDY OF EASTERN ASIA the study of the civilizations of eastern Asia —**orientalist** n. —**orientalistic** /áwri entə lístik, órri-/ adj.

Oriental rug n. a brightly coloured and patterned carpet traditionally made by hand from high-quality wool in the Middle and Far East, now often factory-made from a variety of materials

orientate /áwri ən tayt/ (-tates, -tating, -tated) vt. to orient or be oriented [Mid-19thC. Back-formation from ORIENTATION.]

orientation /áwri ən táysh'n, órri-/ n. 1. POSITIONING the positioning of sth, or the position or direction in which sth lies ○ slopes with a southerly orientation 2. DIRECTION OF DEVELOPMENT the direction in which sth, e.g. a scheme, is developed or focused ○ the programme's clear orientation towards the white middle class 3. LEANING the direction in which sb's thoughts, interests, or tendencies lie ○ irrespective of sexual orientation 4. BECOMING ACCUSTOMED the process of becoming accustomed to a new situation or set of surroundings 5. BRIEFING MEETING a meeting at which introductory information or training is provided to people embarking on sth new, e.g. a course of study 6. CHEM MOLECULE ARRANGEMENT the arrangement of atoms, ions, radicals, or groups relative to each other in crystals or molecules 7. BIOL REACTION TO STIMULUS movement or direction of growth in response to a stimulus, e.g. the way a plant grows in response to light —**orientational** adj.

orientation week n. Aus the week before classes begin at a university or further-education college, during which first-year students participate in activities designed to introduce them to their new environment

oriented /áwri entid, órri-/ adj. openly supporting or favouring a particular point of view or set of beliefs (often used in combination) ○ a Marxist-oriented approach to economics

orienteer /áwri ən téer, órri-/ vi. (-teers, -teering, -teered) DO ORIENTEERING to take part in the sport of orienteering ■ n. PARTICIPANT IN ORIENTEERING sb who takes part in orienteering [Mid-20thC. Back-formation from ORIENTEERING.]

orienteering /áwri ən téering, órri-/ n. a sport that combines map-reading and cross-country running. Competitors make their way through unfamiliar terrain using a compass and a topographical map. [Mid-20thC. Anglicization of Swedish orientering, from orientera 'to orient', from French orienter (see ORIENT).]

orifice /órrə fiss/ n. an opening, especially the mouth, anus, vagina, or other opening into a cavity or passage in the body (literary) [Mid-16thC. Via Old French from Latin orificium, literally 'making a mouth', from the stem or- 'mouth' + -fic-, the stem of facere 'to make'.]

oriflamme /órri flam/ n. HIST a red banner or flag that was adopted as the national flag of France in the Middle Ages [15thC. From French oriflambe, of uncertain origin: perhaps from medieval Latin auriflamma, literally 'golden flame'.]

orig. abbr. 1. original 2. originally 3. origin

Origami: An origami paper pig

origami /órri gáami/ *n.* the Japanese art of paper folding [Mid-20thC. From Japanese, literally 'fold paper'.]

origin /órri jin/ *n.* **1. STARTING POINT** a starting point or first cause (*often used in the plural*) ○ *the origins of the universe* **2. SOURCE** the thing from which sth develops or the place where it comes from (*often used in the plural*) ○ *the uncertain origin of the expression* **3. ANCESTRY** the race, social class, or country that sb belongs to or that sb's family comes from (*often used in the plural*) ○ *a great family whose origins stretch back to the Middle Ages* **4.** ANAT **MUSCLE ATTACHMENT** the place where a muscle is attached **5.** ANAT **ANATOMICAL ROOT** the root of a nerve or blood vessel **6.** MATH **INTERSECTION OF AXES** the point of intersection of all axes in a coordinate system. In a plane it has the coordinates (0,0), while in a three-dimensional space it has the coordinates (0,0,0). [Mid-16thC. Directly or via French from the Latin stem *origin-*, from *oriri* 'to arise' (source of English *orient* and *abort*).]

WORD KEY: SYNONYMS

origin, source, derivation, provenance, root

CORE MEANING: the beginning of sth

origin used to talk about the beginning of sth in terms of the time, place, situation, or idea from which it arose. It can also be used to refer to sb's ancestry or social background; **source** used to describe the place, person, or thing through which sth has come into being or from which it has been obtained; **derivation** used to talk about the origin or source of sth, especially a word or phrase; **provenance** a formal word used to talk about the origin or history of sth, especially sth such as a work of art or archaeological artefact; **root** used to describe the cause or origin of sth, especially sth such as a feeling or a problem.

original /ə ríjj'nəl/ *adj.* **1. FIRST** existing first, from the beginning, or before other people or things ○ *The original plan was to turn the site into a shopping centre.* **2. NEW** completely new, and so not copied or derived from sth else ○ *She doesn't have a single original idea in her head.* **3. CREATIVE** possessing or demonstrating the ability to think creatively ○ *blessed with an original mind* **4. NOT TRADITIONAL** representing a departure from traditional or previous practice ○ *a refreshingly original interpretation of the classics* **5. SOURCE FOR COPIES** relating to or being sth from which a copy or alternative version has been made ○ *the original document* ■ *n.* **1. FIRST VERSION** the first or unique item from which copies or alternative versions are made ○ *The meaning of the original has been lost in translation.* **2. AUTHENTIC PIECE OF ART** a genuine work of art, and so not a copy or forgery ○ *verified as an original* **3. ECCENTRIC PERSON** an unusual or eccentric person **4. CREATIVE PERSON** a person of outstanding creativity or revolutionary thinking

WORD KEY: SYNONYMS

See Synonyms at ***new***.

originality /ə ríjjə nálləti/ *n.* **1. NEWNESS** the quality of newness that exists in sth not done before or not derived from anything else ○ *Improvised music lives on the tension between tradition and originality.* **2. CREATIVITY** the ability to think creatively and depart from traditional or previous forms **3.** (*plural* **-ties**) **ORIGINAL THING** sth original, e.g. a new idea or approach ○ *'That's always the case with my originalities – they are original to nobody but myself'.* (Thomas Hardy, *A Pair of Blue Eyes*; 1889)

originally /ə ríjj'nəli/ *adv.* **1. AT FIRST** at first or from the beginning ○ *Originally a ballet dancer, she trained to become a circus acrobat.* **2. INNOVATIVELY** in a creative or innovative way ○ *thoughtfully assembled and originally presented*

original sin *n.* the sinful state, deriving from the disobedience of Adam and Eve, that Christians believe all people are born into

originate /ə ríjjə nayt/ (**-nates, -nating, -nated**) *v.* **1.** *vi.* **HAVE ORIGIN** to begin or develop somewhere or from sth ○ *a custom that originated in the 19th century* **2.** *vt.* **INVENT** to invent sth or bring sth into being ○ *Einstein originated the theory of relativity.* **3.** *vt.* PRINTING, PUBL **CREATE FILM OF STH FOR REPRODUCTION** to reproduce an image on film from which printing plates will be made ○ *Colour plates originated by Smith and Jones, plc.* —**origination** /ə ríjjə náysh'n/ *n.* —**originator** /ə ríjjə naytər/ *n.*

originative /ə ríjjənətiv/ *adj.* with the ability to think of new ways of doing things —**originatively** *adv.*

orinasal /áwri náyz'l/ *adj.* **WITH ORAL AND NASAL PASSAGES** pronounced with both oral and nasal passages open, as the nasal vowels in French are ■ *n.* **ORAL-NASAL SPEECH SOUND** an orinasal speech sound [Mid-19thC. Coined from Latin *ori-*, from the stem *or-* 'mouth' + NASAL.] —**orinasally** *adv.*

O-ring /ó ring/ *n.* a plastic or rubber ring used in machinery as a seal against air, oil, or high pressure [Mid-20thC. From its shape.]

Orinoco /óri nṓkō/ large river in Venezuela. Its main channel discharges into the Atlantic Ocean, but one branch flows into the Amazon river system. Length: 2,560 km/1,590 mi.

oriole /áwri ōl/ *n.* **1. SONGBIRD OF EUROPE, ASIA, AND AFRICA** a forest-perching songbird, found throughout Europe, Asia, and Africa, with bold black and yellow markings and a loud melodious song. Family: Oriolidae. **2. N AMERICAN SONGBIRD** a brightly coloured North American songbird, especially an orange or yellow species called the Baltimore oriole. Family: Icteridae. [Late 18thC. Via medival Latin *oriolus* from Latin *aureolus* from, ultimately, *aurum* 'gold' (see AURIC).]

Orion /ə rí ən/ *n.* **1.** MYTHOL **MYTHOLOGICAL GIANT** in Greek mythology, a giant and hunter, the son of the sea god Poseidon, who was killed by the goddess Artemis and transformed into a constellation **2.** ASTRON **EQUATORIAL CONSTELLATION** an equatorial constellation near Gemini and Taurus, containing the Great Nebula and more than 200 stars visible to the naked eye

Orissa /o ríssə/ state in eastern India bordering Bihar, West Bengal, and the Bay of Bengal. Capital: Bhubaneswar. Population: 33,795,000 (1994). Area: 155,782 sq. km/60,148 sq. mi.

Oriya /o rée ə/ (*plural* **-ya**) *n.* **1.** PEOPLES **INDIAN PEOPLE** a member of a people who live mainly in Orissa and neighbouring Indian states **2.** LANG **LANGUAGE OF EASTERN INDIA** a language spoken in eastern parts of India, especially in Orissa and neighbouring states on the Bay of Bengal. Belonging to the Indo-Iranian branch of Indo-European languages, it is spoken by about 36 million people. [Early 19thC. Via *Oriya* from, ultimately, Sanskrit *Odra* 'Orissa', a state in eastern India.]

Orkney Islands /áwk nee-/ island group and council area of Scotland, 32 km/20 mi. northeast of the Scottish mainland. Kirkwall is the administrative centre. Population: 19,612 (1991). Area: 975 sq. km/375 sq. mi.

Orlando /awr lánd ō/ city and capital of Orange County, northern Florida, 126 km/78 mi. northeast of Tampa. Population: 164,693 (1990).

orle /awrl/ *n.* a border that runs inside and parallel to the edge of the shield of a coat-of-arms [Late 16thC. From French, from, ultimately, Latin *ora* 'border, edge'.]

Orleanist /awr lée ənist/ *n.* a supporter of the family of the Duke of Orléans and of their claim to the French throne, especially a supporter of King Louis-Philippe, who reigned 1830 to 1848 [Mid-19thC. From French *Orléaniste*, from *Orléans*, a city in France.]

Orléans /awr lée ənz/ city in north-central France, the capital of Loiret Department and Centre Region. Population: 107,965 (1990).

Orléans /awr lée ənz, awr lay aáN/, **Louis Philippe Joseph, Duc d'** (1747–93) French nobleman. He supported the French Revolution but was executed during the Reign of Terror. He was father of the future king, Louis Philippe. Known as **Philippe Egalité**

Orlon /áwr lon/ *tdmk.* a trademark for an acrylic fibre or yarn

Orly /áwrli/ southern suburb of Paris, location of an international airport

ormer /áwrmər/ *n.* MARINE BIOL an edible marine mollusc **(gastropod)** that has a large ear-shaped shell. Latin name: *Haliotis tuberculata.* [Mid-17thC. Via Channel Islands French, from, ultimately, Latin *auris maris*, literally 'sea ear', from its shape.]

ormolu /áwrmə loo/ *n.* a gold-coloured alloy of copper, zinc, and sometimes tin, used for decorating furniture and making jewellery and mouldings [Mid-18thC. From French *or moulu*, literally 'ground gold'.]

ornament *n.* /áwrnə mənt/ **1. DECORATIVE OBJECT** a small decorative object displayed for its beauty **2. DECORATION** decoration or decorative quality ○ *manuscript pages entirely without ornament* **3. STH THAT DECORATES** a thing that decorates or adds beauty to sth else **4.** MUSIC **EMBELLISHING NOTE** a note or set of notes added to embellish a melody or harmony **5. VALUED PERSON** sb whose presence is a source of pride or honour (*archaic or literary*) ■ *vt.* /áwrnə ment/ (**-ments, -menting, -mented**) **DECORATE** to make sth richer by adding decorative elements or items to it ○ *a stone facade ornamented with gargoyles* [14thC. Via Old French from Latin *ornamentum*, from *ornare* (see ORNATE).] —**ornamented** /áwrnə mentid/ *adj.*

ornamental /áwrnə mént'l/ *adj.* **1. DECORATIVE** serving as a decoration, as opposed to having any practical use ○ *The hitching post in the front yard was strictly ornamental.* **2. GROWN FOR SHOW** grown for beauty as distinct from food (*refers to plants*) ○ *an ornamental border* ■ *n.* **ORNAMENTAL PLANT** a plant that is grown for its beauty —**ornamentally** *adv.*

ornamentation /áwrnə men táysh'n/ *n.* **1. ADDITION OF DECORATIVE ELEMENTS** the addition of elements that enhance beauty or visual appeal, especially in the arts **2. DECORATIVE ELEMENT ADDED** one or more elements added to enhance beauty or visual appeal, especially in the arts **3.** MUSIC **ADDITION OF EMBELLISHING NOTES** the addition of a note or set of notes that embellishes a melody or harmony

ornate /awr náyt/ *adj.* **1. EXCESSIVELY DECORATIVE** with elaborate or excessive decoration **2. USING ELABORATE LANGUAGE** using or consisting of elaborate language, especially language that is designed to impress with its flair or literary quality ○ *expressions that are far too ornate for a TV soap opera* [Early 16thC. From Latin *ornatus*, the past participle of *ornare* 'to equip', hence 'to adorn'.] —**ornately** *adv.* —**ornateness** *n.*

ornery /áwrnəri/ *adj. US* **1. IRRITABLE** uncooperative and irritable (*informal*) **2. INSUFFICIENT** meagre, whether out of poverty or lack of generosity (*informal*) **3. COMMON** ordinary (*regional*) [Early 19thC. Dialectal variant of ORDINARY. The underlying meaning is 'common, mean'.] —**orneriness** *n.*

ornith. *abbr.* **1.** ornithology **2.** ornithological

ornith- *prefix.* = **ornitho-** (*used before vowels*)

ornithine /áwrni theen/ *n.* an amino acid formed in the liver as an intermediate in the manufacture of excretory urea. Formula: $C_5H_{12}O_2N_2$. [Late 19thC. Coined from ORNITH- +-INE; from its presence in birds' urine.]

ornithischian /áwrni thíski ən/ *adj.* **RELATING TO ORDER OF DINOSAURS** belonging or relating to an order of dinosaurs that had a backward-rotating pelvis similar to that of birds. The order includes the triceratops and stegosaurus. Order: Ornithischia. ■ *n.* **DINOSAUR** an ornithischian dinosaur, e.g. an ankylosaur [Early 20thC. From modern Latin *Ornithischia*, order name, which was coined from the Greek stem *ornith-* + Greek *iskhion* 'hip joint' (source of English *ischium*).]

ornitho- *prefix.* bird ○ *ornithophily* [From Greek *ornith-*, the stem of *ornis* 'bird']

ornithology /áwrni thólləji/ *n.* the branch of zoology that deals with the scientific study of birds —**ornithological** /áwrnithə lójjik'l/ *adj.* —**ornithologically** /-lójjikli/ *adv.* —**ornithologist** /áwrni thólləjist/ *n.*

ornithopod /awr níthə pod/ *n.* a plant-eating dinosaur, e.g. the hadrosaur and the iguanadon, that had hind feet similar to those of birds. Suborder: Ornithopoda. [Late 19thC. From modern Latin *ornithopoda*, suborder name, from the Greek stem *ornitho-* 'bird' + the stem *pod-* 'foot'.]

ornithopter /áwrni thoptər/ *n.* a flying machine that operates using flapping wings. Although the earliest aircraft designs imitated the flapping wings of birds and many prototypes have been flown in the past 100 years, no ornithopter has ever been commercially successful. [Early 20thC. From French *ornithoptère*, which was coined from the Greek stem *ornith-* 'bird' + *pteron* 'wing'.]

ornithosis /áwrni thóssiss/ *n.* the bacterial disease psittacosis, especially when contracted by humans from birds

oro- *prefix.* mountain ○ *orography* [From Greek *oros*, of unknown origin]

orogenesis /órrō jénnəssiss/ *n.* GEOL = **orogeny** —**orogenetic** /órrō jə néttik/ *adj.* —**orogenetically** /-néttikli/ *adv.*

orogenic belt /órrō jénnik-/ *n.* a large linear feature on the earth's surface that has undergone tectonic compression and uplift to form mountain ranges such as the Andes and the Alps

orogeny /o rójjəni/ *n.* GEOL the folding, faulting, and uplift of the earth's crust to form mountain ranges, often accompanied by volcanic and seismic activity —**orogenic** /órrə jénnik/ *adj.* —**orogenically** /-jénnikli/ *adv.*

orography /o róggrəfi/ *n.* GEOG the branch of physical geography involved with the study and mapping of variations in the earth's surface, including mountains and mountain ranges

oroide /áwrō īd/ *n.* an alloy of copper, zinc, tin, and iron that has a lustre similar to gold and is used in the manufacture of inexpensive jewellery [Late 19thC. From French, literally 'goldlike', from *or* 'gold' (see OR).]

orology /o rólləji/ *n.* GEOG = **orography** —**orological** /órrə lójjik'l/ *adj.* —**orologically** /-lójjikli/ *adv.* —**orologist** /o rólləjist/ *n.*

OROM /ó rom/ *abbr.* COMPUT optical read-only memory

Oromo /o rṓmō/ (*plural* **-mos** *or* **-mo**) *n.* **1.** PEOPLES **AFRICAN PEOPLE** a member of a people who originally occupied lands in Somalia, and whose members now live in parts of eastern Africa, especially in Ethiopia and Kenya **2.** LANG **LANGUAGE OF THE OROMO** the Cushitic language of this people. Over 7 million people speak Oromo. [Late 19thC. From *Oromo*.] —**Oromo** *adj.*

Orontes /ə rónt eez/ **1.** mountain in Iran, just southwest of Hamadan. Height: 3,548 m/11,640 ft. **2.** river in southwestern Asia, flowing through Lebanon, Syria, and Turkey, and into the Mediterranean Sea. Length: 571 km/355 mi.

oropharynx /órrō fárringks/ (*plural* **-pharynxes** *or* **-pharynges** /-fə rín jeez/) *n.* ANAT the part of the throat that is located below the soft palate and above the larynx [Late 19thC. Coined from the Latin stem *or-* 'mouth' (see ORAL) + PHARYNX.] —**oropharyngeal** /órrō fə rínji əl/ *adj.*

orotund /órrō tund/ *adj.* (*formal*) **1. STRONGLY CLEAR** loud, clear, and strong, as in tone or voice timbre **2. POMPOUS** pompous or bombastic in speech or prose [Late 18thC. From Latin *ore rotundo*, literally 'with a round mouth'.] —**orotundity** /órrō túndəti/ *n.*

orphan /áwrf'n/ *n.* **1. CHILD WITHOUT PARENTS** a child whose parents are both dead or who has been abandoned by his or her parents, especially a child not adopted by another family **2. ANIMAL WITHOUT MOTHER** a young animal whose mother is dead or has abandoned it **3.** PRINTING **STRANDED FIRST LINE** an opening line of a paragraph that is also the last line on a page, cut off from the rest of the paragraph by the page break. ◊ **widow** ■ *vt.* (**-phans, -phaning, -phaned**) **RENDER PARENTLESS** to make sb an orphan ○ *a young boy orphaned by the war* [14thC. Via late Latin from Greek *orphanos* 'orphaned'. Ultimately from an Indo-European word that is also the ancestor of English *robot*.] —**orphanhood** *n.*

orphanage /áwrfənij/ *n.* a home or other institutional setting for orphans, often operated by a local government or charitable organization

orphan site *n.* ENVIRON an area of contaminated land for which neither polluter nor owner will take responsibility. In such cases, the public sector normally assumes responsibility for decontaminating it.

orpharion /awr fárri ən/ *n.* a large lute, popular during the Renaissance, played by plucking or strumming the strings [Late 16thC. From the names of *Orpheus* and *Arion*, musicians in Greek mythology.]

Orphean /áwrfi ən/ *adj.* **1. RELATING TO ORPHEUS** relating to Orpheus **2. BEAUTIFUL** hauntingly beautiful or enchanting (*literary*)

Orpheus /áwrfyooss, áwrfi əss/ *n.* in Greek mythology, a poet and musician. He descended to the underworld to seek his wife, Eurydice, after her death but failed to bring her back.

Orphic /áwrfik/ *adj.* **1. RELATING TO POEMS OF ORPHEUS** relating to the poems and mystical writings associated with Orpheus **2. MYSTICAL** mystical or magical (*literary*)

Orphism /áwrfizəm/ *n.* ARTS an artistic movement within Cubism that flourished briefly at the beginning of the 20th century, concentrating on achievement of harmony of colour [Late 19thC. From ORPHEUS.] —**Orphist** *n.* —**Orphistic** /awr fístik/ *adj.*

orphrey /áwrfri/ (*plural* **-phreys**), **orfray** (*plural* **-frays**) *n.* SEW elaborate embroidery, often done in gold [13thC. Via Old French *orfreis* from, ultimately, medieval Latin *aurifrigium*, literally 'Phrygian gold'.]

orpiment /áwrpi mənt/ *n.* a crystalline bright yellow ore of arsenic, consisting of arsenic trisulphide, that is used in dyeing and tanning [14thC. Via French from Latin *auripigmentum*, literally 'gold pigment'.]

orpine /áwr pīn/, **orpin** /-pin/ *n.* a low-growing succulent plant with pink or purple flowers. Latin name: *Sedum telephium*. [14thC. From French *orpin*, from *orpiment* (see ORPIMENT).]

Orpington /áwrpingtən/ *n.* a breed of heavy deep-chested domestic fowl with a single comb, first bred in England [Late 19thC. Named after the town of *Orpington* in Kent, England.]

orrery /órrəri/ (*plural* **-ries**) *n.* ASTRON a mechanical model of the solar system that shows the orbits of the planets around the sun at the correct relative velocities [Early 18thC. Named after Charles Boyle, fourth Earl of *Orrery* 1676–1731, who had one made for him.]

orris /órriss/ (*plural* **-ris** *or* **-rises**) *n.* an iris with a fragrant root. Latin name: *Iris germanica*. [Mid-16thC. Origin uncertain: probably an alteration of IRIS.]

orrisroot /órriss root/ (*plural* **-roots** *or* **-root**), **orris root**, **orris** *n.* the fragrant rootstock of the orris, often used in perfumes and cosmetics

ortanique /áwrtə néek/ *n.* a hybrid fruit produced by crossing an orange with a tangerine [Mid-20thC. Contraction formed from ORANGE + TANGERINE + UNIQUE.]

orth. *abbr.* **1.** orthopaedic **2.** orthopaedics

ortho- *prefix.* **1.** correct; correction, straightening ○ *orthography* ○ *orthodontia* **2.** straight, upright, vertical ○ *orthotropous* **3.** perpendicular ○ *orthorhombic* **4.** fully hydrated or hydroxylated ○ *orthophosphate* [Via Old French and Latin from Greek *orthos* 'straight, right']

orthocentre /áwrthō sentər/ *n.* the point at which the three altitudes of a triangle intersect

orthochromatic /áwrthō krə máttik/ *adj.* sensitive to all the visible colours except red (*refers to film*)

orthoclase /áwrthō klayz, áwrthō klayss/ *n.* a type of feldspar of variable colour that has monoclinic crystalline structure and is commonly found in igneous rock

orthodontics /áwrthō dóntiks/, **orthodontia** /-dónti ə/ *n.* the area of dentistry concerned with the prevention and correction of irregularities of the teeth —**orthodontic** *adj.* —**orthodontist** *n.*

orthodox /áwrthə doks/ *adj.* **1. FOLLOWING TRADITIONAL DOCTRINE** following the established or traditional rules of social behaviour, a philosophy, or a faith **2. OBSERVING CHRISTIAN CREEDS** following the teachings of Jesus Christ and the Christian faith as set down in the ecumenical creeds [Late 16thC. Via French *orthodoxe* and late Latin from Greek *orthodoxos*, 'having the correct opinion', from *doxa* 'opinion'.] —**orthodoxly** *adv.*

Orthodox /áwrthə doks/ *adj.* **1. EASTERN ORTHODOX CHURCH** relating to the Eastern Orthodox Church **2. ORTHODOX JUDAISM** relating to Orthodox Judaism

Orthodox Church *n.* a Christian church that originated in the Byzantine Empire and recognizes the Patriarch of Constantinople as primate rather than the Pope. Orthodox Churches include the Eastern Orthodox Churches and the Coptic Church of Egypt.

Orthodox Judaism *n.* the branch of Judaism that accepts without reservation that the Torah was directly handed down from God to Moses

orthodoxy /áwrthə doksi/ *n.* the practice of observing established social customs and definitions of appropriateness

Orthodoxy /áwrthə doksi/ *n.* **Orthodoxy 1. PRACTICES OF EASTERN ORTHODOX CHURCH** the beliefs and practices of the Eastern Orthodox Church **2. ORTHODOX JUDAISM** the beliefs and practices of Orthodox Judaism

orthoepy /áwrthō epi/ *n.* **1. PRONUNCIATION** the study of the ways that words are pronounced **2. USUAL PRONUNCIATION** the usual pronunciation of words [Mid-17thC. Coined from ORTHO- + the Greek stem *epe-*, the stem of *épos* 'word, tale, story', the source of English *epic*.] —**orthoepic** /áwrthō éppik/ *adj.* —**orthoepically** /-éppikli/ *adv.* —**orthoepist** /áwr thō epist/ *n.*

orthogenesis /áwrthō jénnəssiss/ (*plural* **-ses** /-seez/) *n.* an obsolete theory that evolution can proceed in a specific direction determined by internal genetic factors rather than the external forces of natural selection —**orthogenetic** /áwrthō jə néttik/ *adj.* —**orthogenetically** /-néttikli/ *adv.*

orthogonal /awr thóggənəl/ *adj.* **1. RELATING TO RIGHT ANGLES** relating to or composed of right angles **2. DESCRIBING CRYSTAL STRUCTURE** all at right angles to each other in a crystal structure (*refers to a set of axes*) —**orthogonality** /awr thóggə nálləti/ *n.* —**orthogonally** /awr thóggənəli/ *adv.*

orthogonal matrix *n.* a matrix in which two rows or two columns are vectors whose scalar product is zero

orthogonal projection *n.* a way of providing a two-dimensional graphic view of an object in which the projecting lines are drawn at right angles to the plane of projection. In so doing this type of presentation appears to give the feeling of three dimensions.

orthograde /áwrthō grayd/ *adj.* carrying the body upright (*refers to primates*) [Early 20thC. Coined from ORTHO- + Latin *gradus* 'walking'.]

orthographic /áwrthə gráffik/, **orthographical** /-gráffik'l/ *adj.* **1. RELATING TO SPELLING** relating to the study of spelling **2. SPELLED CORRECTLY** correctly spelled **3.** MATH **MADE UP OF VERTICAL LINES** composed of vertical lines —**orthographically** *adv.*

orthographic projection *n.* = **orthogonal projection**

orthography /awr thóggrəfi/ (*plural* **-phies**) *n.* **1. STUDY OF CORRECT SPELLING** the study of correct spelling as it has come to be established by usage **2. STUDY OF HOW LETTERS ARE ARRANGED IN WORDS** the area of language study concerned with the letters of an alphabet and how those letters occur sequentially in words **3. RELATIONSHIP BETWEEN SOUNDS AND LETTERS** the way letters and diacritic symbols represent the sounds of a language in a spelling system

orthomorphic /áwrthō máwrfik/ *adj.* = **conformal**

orthopaedic /áwrthə péedik/, **orthopedic** *adj.* **1. RELATING TO ORTHOPAEDICS** relating to or used in orthopaedics **2. RELATING TO BONE DISORDERS** relating to or marked by disorders of the bones, joints, ligaments, or muscles [Mid-19thC. From French *orthopédique*, literally 'of correct child-rearing', from, ultimately, Greek *paideia* 'child-rearing', from the stem *paid-* 'child'; originally applied specifically to childhood bone disorders.] —**orthopaedically** *adv.* —**orthopaedist** *n.*

orthopaedics /áwrthə péediks/, **orthopedics** *n.* the branch of medicine concerned with the nature and correction of disorders of the bones, joints, ligaments, or muscles (*takes a singular verb*)

orthopedic *adj.* = **orthopaedic**

orthophosphate /áwrthō fóss fayt/ *n.* any salt or ester of phosphoric acid

orthophosphoric acid /áwrthō foss fórrik-/ *n.* = **phosphoric acid**

orthopsychiatry /áwrthō sī kī́ ətri/ *n.* a cross-disciplinary method of diagnosing, preventing, and treating childhood psychological problems that involves psychiatrists, child psychologists, paediatricians, and social workers —**orthopsychiatric** /áwrthō sī́ki áttrik/ *adj.* —**orthopsychiatrist** /áwrthō sī kī́ ətrist/ *n.*

orthopteran /awr thóptərən/, **orthopteron** *n.* PRIMITIVE INSECT any member of the order Orthoptera of primitive winged insects, including cockroaches, mantises, locusts, and crickets ■ *adj.* = **orthopterous** [Late 19thC. Formed from modern Latin *Orthoptera* (plural), order name, literally 'those with straight wings', ultimately from Greek *pteron* 'wing'.]

orthopterous /awr thóptərəss/ *adj.* relating to the order Orthoptera of primitive winged insects, including cockroaches, mantises, locusts, and crickets

orthoptics /awr thóptiks/ *n.* the study of eye disorders and their detection and correction, especially using nonsurgical treatments, e.g. eye exercises (*takes a singular verb*) —**orthoptic** *adj.* —**orthoptist** *n.*

orthorhombic /áwrthō rómbik/ *adj.* relating to a crystal system with three axes of different lengths that cross at right angles

orthoscopic /áwrthō skóppik/ *adj.* **1.** ABLE TO SEE NORMALLY able to see normally, without any visual distortion of images **2.** GIVING NORMAL VISION used to describe an optical instrument that gives normal vision

orthotics /awr thóttiks/ *n.* the branch of medical engineering concerned with the design and fitting of devices, e.g. braces, in the treatment of orthopaedic disorders (*takes a singular verb*) [Mid-20thC. Formed from *orthosis* 'artificial external device', from Greek *orthōsis* 'making straight', ultimately from *orthos* 'straight'.] —**orthotic** *adj.* —**orthotist** *n.*

orthotropic /áwrthə trópik, -tróppik/ *adj.* involving or characterized by vertical growth along a vertical axis —**orthotropically** *adv.* —**orthotropism** /awr thóttrəpizəm/ *n.*

orthotropous /awr thóttrəpəss/ *adj.* used to describe an ovule that grows straight

ortolan /áwrtələn/ (*plural* **-lan** *or* **-lans**) *n.* a small brownish bunting of Europe, Asia, and Africa that has a yellow throat and is known for its territorial display flight. It is sometimes eaten as a delicacy. Latin name: *Emberiza hortulana.* [Early 16thC. Via French from Provençal, literally 'gardener', from Latin *hortulanus*, from *hortus* 'garden', a source of English *horticulture*.]

ORV *abbr.* off-road vehicle

Orvieto /áwrvi áytō/ (*plural* **-tos**) *n.* a light white wine produced in the region of Orvieto, Italy

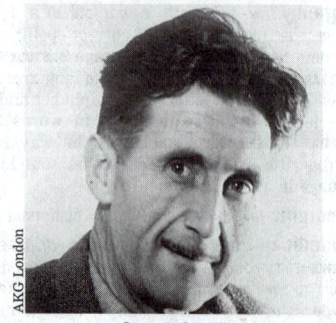
George Orwell

Orwell /áwr wel/, **George** (1903–50) British writer. A staunch critic of totalitarianism, he wrote political essays and fiction including the satirical political novels *Animal Farm* (1945) and *1984* (1949). Real name **Eric Arthur Blair** —**Orwellian** *adj.*

-ory *suffix.* **1.** of or relating to ○ *conclusory* **2.** place or thing connected with or used for ○ *crematory* [Via Anglo-Norman and Old French dialect *-orie* from Latin *-orius* and *-orium*]

oryx /órriks/ (*plural* **oryx** *or* **oryxes**) *n.* an antelope native to Africa and Arabia that has long horns, bold black and white markings on the face, and a hump above the shoulders. Genus: *Oryx.* [14thC. From Latin, from Greek *orux* 'spike, pickaxe, oryx'.]

orzo /áwrzō/ (*plural* **-zos**) *n.* pasta that is the size and shape of rice grains, often served with lamb in Greek cooking [Early 20thC. From Italian, literally 'barley', from Latin *hordeum*.]

os[1] /oss/ (*plural* **ora**) *n.* a mouth or mouth-like opening in an organism [Mid-18thC. From Latin, literally 'mouth, face, head' (stem *or*-) (source of English *oral*).]

os[2] /oss/ (*plural* **ossa**) *n.* a bone (*technical*) [Mid-16thC. From Latin, literally 'bone' (stem *oss*-) (source of English *ossify*).]

Os *symbol.* osmium

OS *abbr.* **1.** Ordnance Survey **2.** CLOTHES outsize **3.** ordinary seaman **4.** COMPUT operating system **5.** LAW old series **6.** Old Style **7.** Old Saxon **8.** COMM out of stock **9.** BANKING outstanding

o.s. *abbr.* **1.** oculus sinistrus **2.** LAW old series **3.** COMM out of stock **4.** BANKING outstanding

O/s *abbr.* **1.** COMM out of stock **2.** BANKING outstanding

OSA *abbr.* Order of Saint Augustine

Osage /ō sáyj, ṓ sayj/ (*plural* **Osage** *or* **Osages**) *n.* **1.** MEMBER OF NATIVE NORTH AMERICAN PEOPLE a member of a Native North American people that originally occupied lands in Ohio, before settling in parts of Missouri and Kansas, and whose members now live mainly in Oklahoma **2.** OSAGE LANGUAGE the language of the Osage people. It belongs to the Siouan branch of Hokan-Siouan languages. Osage is spoken by about 1,000 people. [Late 17thC. Alteration of Osage *Wazhazhe*, one of the three Osage bands.] —**Osage** *adj.*

Osaka /ō sáákə/ city and port in Japan, on southeastern Honshu Island. It is the capital of Osaka prefecture. Population: 2,481,000 (1994).

OSB *abbr.* Order of Saint Benedict

Oscan /óskən/ *n.* an extinct language spoken in southern parts of Italy during ancient times. It belongs to the Italic branch of Indo-European languages. [Late 16thC. Formed from Latin *Oscus* 'Oscan'.] —**Oscan** *adj.*

Oscar[1] /óskər/ *tdmk.* a trademark for the golden statuette awarded annually by the Academy of Motion Picture Arts and Sciences to people in the film industry for achievement in the making of films

—— WORD KEY: CULTURAL NOTE ——

Oscar and Lucinda, a novel by Australian writer Peter Carey (1988). Set in early nineteenth century Britain and Australia, the novel tells the story of a young English clergyman who shares a passion for gambling with a young, independent-minded Australian woman. It won the Booker Prize in 1989.

Oscar[2] *n.* the NATO phonetic alphabet code word for the letter 'O', used in international radio communications

Oscar II /óskər/, **King of Sweden and Norway** (1829–1907). He came to the thrones of Sweden and Norway in 1872, but relinquished the Norwegian throne in 1905 upon Norway's independence.

OSCE *n.*, *abbr.* Organization for Security and Co-operation in Europe

oscillate /óssi layt/ (**-lates, -lating, -lated**) *v.* **1.** *vi.* MOVE BACKWARDS AND FORWARDS to swing between two points with a rhythmic motion **2.** *vi.* BE INDECISIVE to keep changing your mind about which is better out of two positions, points of view, or courses of action **3.** *vti.* CAUSE TO CHANGE PREDICTABLY to cause or produce rhythmic, predictable variations between two extremes, usually within a set period of time [Early 18thC. From Latin *oscillat*-, the perfect participle stem of *oscillare* 'to swing', from *oscillum* 'swing, mask' (of Bacchus hung as a charm on a tree to swing), from os[1].] —**oscillator** *n.* —**oscillatory** *adj.*

oscillation /óssi láysh'n/ *n.* **1.** PREDICTABLE VARIATION an even, rhythmic change in value, position, or state around a mean value **2.** ONE CYCLE OF VARIATION a single cycle of variation between two values, positions, or states **3.** MOTION BETWEEN EXTREMES the act of moving backwards and forwards between two extreme points —**oscillational** *adj.*

oscillogram /o sílla gram/ *n.* the record produced by an oscillograph or oscilloscope [Early 20thC. Formed from a shortening of OSCILLOGRAPH + -GRAM.]

oscillograph /o sílla graaf, -graf/ *n.* a device that produces a visual record of variations between two points or states, e.g. of electric current [Late 19thC. From French *oscillographe*, literally 'that which swings while writing', formed from Latin *oscillare* 'to swing' (see OSCILLATE).] —**oscillographic** /o sílla gráffik/ *adj.* —**oscillographically** /-gráffikli/ *adv.* —**oscillography** /óssi lóggrəfi/ *n.*

oscilloscope /o sílla skōp/ *n.* a device that uses a cathode ray tube to produce a visual record of an electrical current on a fluorescent screen. Uses include testing electronic equipment and measuring the electrical impulses of the heart or the brain. [Early 20thC. Formed from a shortening of OSCILLATION + -SCOPE.] —**oscilloscopic** /o sílla skóppik/ *adj.*

oscine /óss īn, óssin/ *adj.* about, typical of, or belonging to the large suborder of passerine birds that includes most songbirds [Late 19thC. From modern Latin *Oscines*, suborder name, from Latin *oscen* 'songbird, bird whose cry is used in augury', literally 'singing towards', from *canere* 'to sing' (source of English *chant, charm,* and *enchant*).]

oscitancy /óssitənssi/ (*plural* **-cies**), **oscitance** /-tənss/ *n.* (*technical*) **1.** YAWN the act of yawning **2.** DROWSINESS a state of drowsiness or dullness [Early 17thC. From Latin *oscitant*-, the present participial stem of *oscitare* 'to yawn, gape', formed from os[1] + *citare* 'to put in motion, move'.] —**oscitant** *adj.*

Osco-Umbrian /óskō úmbri ən/ *n.* a group of extinct languages, including Oscan, Umbrian, and Faliscan, spoken in Italy during ancient times. It is a subgroup of the Italic branch of Indo-European languages. —**Osco-Umbrian** *adj.*

osculant /óskyŏŏlənt/ *adj.* BIOL having some of the characteristics of two related or similar taxonomic groups [Early 19thC. From Latin *osculant*-, the present participial stem of *osculari* (see OSCULUM).]

oscular /óskyŏŏlər/ *adj.* **1.** RELATING TO OSCULUM relating to or characteristic of an osculum **2.** RELATING TO THE MOUTH relating to the mouth or activities of the mouth, e.g. kissing (*technical*) [Early 19thC. Formed from Latin *osculum* (see OSCULUM).]

osculate /óskyŏŏ layt/ (**-lates, -lating, -lated**) *v.* **1.** *vt.* KISS to kiss (*formal or humorous*) **2.** *vt.* MATH TOUCH IN OSCULATION to touch at a point of common tangency to a line passing between two branches of a curve, each branch continuing in both directions of the line (*refers to arcs*) **3.** *vi.* MAKE CONTACT to make contact or come together (*technical*) [Mid-17thC. From Latin *osculatus*, the perfect participle of *osculari* (see OSCULUM).]

osculation /óskyŏŏ láysh'n/ *n.* **1.** KISSING a kiss or the act of kissing (*formal or humorous*) **2.** MATH POINT AT WHICH TWO SURFACES TOUCH the point at which two surfaces touch, particularly the point at which two curves have a common tangent —**osculatory** /óskyŏŏlətəri/ *adj.*

osculum /óskyŏŏləm/ (*plural* **-la** /-lə/) *n.* an opening like a mouth, through which a sponge expels water [Early 17thC. Via modern Latin from Latin, 'little mouth, kiss', from os 'mouth'.]

OSD *abbr.* Order of Saint Dominic

-ose[1] *suffix.* full of, having the qualities of, resembling ○ *frondose* [From Latin *-osus*]

-ose[2] *suffix.* **1.** carbohydrate, sugar ○ *maltose* **2.** product of primary hydrolysis ○ *proteose* [From GLUCOSE]

OSF *abbr.* **1.** Order of Saint Francis **2.** COMPUT Open Software Foundation

O'Shane /ō sháyn/, **Pat** (*b.* 1941) Australian lawyer. She was Australia's first Aboriginal barrister and magistrate. Full name **Patricia June O'Shane**

Oshawa /óshəwə/ city in southeastern Ontario, Canada, on Lake Ontario, northeast of Toronto. Population: 268,773 (1996).

Oshkosh /ósh kosh/ city and county seat of Winnebago County, eastern Wisconsin, situated on the western shore of Lake Winnebago. Population: 55,006 (1990).

Oshogbo /ə shóg bō/ capital city of Osun State, southwestern Nigeria, situated approximately 190 km/120 mi. northwest of Lagos. Population: 441,600 (1992).

OSI abbr. COMPUT open systems interconnection

osier /ózi ər/ n. **1.** WILLOW TREE a willow tree with long flexible twigs that are used to make baskets and furniture. Latin name: *Salix viminilis* and *Salix purpurea.* **2.** WILLOW BRANCH a branch or twig from a willow tree [14thC. From French, ultimately from medieval Latin *auseria*, of uncertain origin: perhaps from a Gaulish word meaning 'river-bed'.]

Osiris /ō sÍriss/ n. MYTHOL in Egyptian mythology, the god of the underworld and the dead, husband of Isis and father of Horus

-osis suffix. **1.** abnormal or diseased condition ○ *chlorosis* **2.** condition, action, or process ○ *osmosis* **3.** formation of or increase in ○ *thrombosis* [Via Latin from Greek]

Oslo /óz lō/ capital city of Norway, situated in the southeast of the country, at the head of Oslo Fjord. Population: 483,401 (1995).

Osmanli /oz mánli/ n. (plural **-lis** or **-li**) **1.** SUBJECT OF THE OTTOMAN EMPIRE a subject of the Ottoman Empire **2.** TURKISH LANGUAGE DURING THE OTTOMAN EMPIRE the Turkish language during the Ottoman Empire, especially when it was written in Arabic script ■ adj. RELATING TO THE OTTOMAN EMPIRE relating to or typical of the Ottoman Empire [Late 18thC. From Turkish *Osmānli*, from *Osman*.]

osmatic /oz máttik/ adj. having or characterized by a sensitive sense of smell [Late 19thC. From French *osmatique*, formed from Greek *osmē* 'smell, odour'.]

osmeterium /ózmi teÉri əm/ (plural **-a** /-ə/) n. a gland found on many caterpillars that secretes an unpleasant smelling substance as a defence against predators [Early 19thC. From modern Latin, ultimately from Greek *osmē* 'odour, smell'.]

osmic /ózmik/ adj. **1.** CONTAINING OSMIUM connected with or containing the element osmium, especially in a high valence state **2.** RELATING TO ODOURS OR SMELL relating to odours or the sense of smell (*technical*)

osmic acid n. = osmium tetroxide

osmiridium /ózmi ríddi əm/ n. a very hard white or grey naturally occurring alloy of osmium and iridium, which often contains platinum, rhodium, and other metals. Because it is resistant to corrosion, it is often used to make the nibs of pens. [Late 19thC. From German, a combination and shortening of OSMIUM + IRIDIUM.]

osmium /ózmi əm/ n. a hard white crystalline metallic chemical element, the densest known, occurring naturally in association with platinum. It is used as a catalyst and alloyed with iridium to form an extremely hard alloy from which pen nibs are made. Symbol **Os** [Early 19thC. From modern Latin, from Greek *osmē* 'smell, odour' + -IUM (from the pungent smell of osmium oxides).]

osmium tetroxide n. a colourless or yellow crystalline solid with an unpleasant smelling, poisonous vapour. It is used in solution as a stain for cell components in electron microscopy. Formula: OsO₄.

osmometer /oz mómmitər/ n. an instrument that measures osmotic pressure [Mid-19thC. A combination and shortening of OSMOSIS + -METER.] —**osmometric** /ózmə méttrik/ adj. —**osmometry** /oz mómmətri/ n.

osmoregulation /ózmō réggyōō láysh'n/ n. the control of the concentration of dissolved substances in the cells and body fluids of an animal [Mid-20thC. A combination and shortening of OSMOSIS + REGULATION.] —**osmoregulatory** /ózmō réggyōōlətəri/ adj.

osmose /oz mōz/ (**-moses, -mosing, -mosed**) vti. to cause or undergo diffusion by osmosis [Mid-19thC. Backformation from OSMOSIS.]

osmosis /oz móssiss/ n. **1.** SLOW CHANGE IN CONCENTRATION the flow of a solvent by diffusion through a semipermeable membrane from a more concentrated solution to a less concentrated one, until the concentrations are equalized. It is a major factor in

regulating the movement of water into and out of tissues in living organisms. **2.** GRADUAL ABSORPTION the gradual, often unconscious, absorption of knowledge or ideas through continual exposure rather than deliberate learning ○ *She seemed to have picked up a working knowledge of Greek by osmosis.* [Mid-19thC. Latinization of OSMOSE.] —**osmotic** /oz móttik/ adj.

osmotic pressure n. the pressure that must be applied to a solution to stop the inward diffusion of a solvent by osmosis through a semipermeable membrane

osmunda /oz múndə/ (plural **-das** or **-da**) n. any of several ferns with large spreading fronds, including the royal and cinnamon ferns. The fibrous roots are sometimes used as a potting medium for orchids. Genus: *Osmunda.* [13thC. From modern Latin *Osmunda*, genus name, from Old French *osmunde*, of unknown origin.]

osnaburg /óznə burg/ n. a heavy, coarse cotton cloth, used to make sacks for grain, upholstery, and draperies [Mid-16thC Named after *Osnaburg*, a variant of *Osnabrück*, a city in northwest Germany where the fabric was originally made]

Osprey

osprey /óss pray, óspri/ (plural **-preys** or **-prey**) n. a fisheating hawk that is distributed worldwide and has long wings and a white head with a dark strip around the eyes. Latin name: *Pandion haliaetus.* [15thC. Origin uncertain: probably from assumed Old French *ospreit*, ultimately from Latin *avis predae*, literally 'bird of prey'.]

Ossa, Mount /óssə/ mountain in northern Tasmania, Australia. It is the highest mountain in Tasmania. Height: 1,617 m/5,305 ft.

ossature /óssə tyoor, óssəchər/ n. the underlying structure or framework that supports a building or sculpture [Late 19thC. From French, formed from *os* 'bone' and modelled on MUSCULATURE.]

ossein /óssi in/ n. the organic component of bone, consisting mainly of collagen proteins [Mid-19thC. Formed from a contraction of OSSEOUS + -IN.]

osseous /óssi əss/ adj. made of or resembling bone [Late 17thC. From Latin *osseus* 'bony', from *os* 'bone'.]

Osset /óssit/, **Ossete** /ósseet/ n. a member of a people that lives in parts of southern European Russia and Georgia, especially Ossetia [Early 19thC. From Russian *osetin*, from Georgian *osetci* 'Ossetia'.]

Ossetic /o séttik/, **Ossetian** /o séesh'n/ n. LANGUAGE OF THE OSSETS the language spoken by the Ossets that belongs to the Iranian branch of Indo-European languages. Ossetic is spoken by about 300,000 people. ■ adj. RELATING TO OSSETIA OR OSSETS relating to or characteristic of Ossetia or the Ossets, their language, and culture

ossia /o séé ə, óssi ə/ conj. used to introduce an alternative version given by a composer of a piece of music, often in order to solve technical difficulties in the original version [Late 19thC. From Italian *o sia*, literally 'or let it be'.]

Ossian /óssi ən/ n. a legendary Gaelic hero and poet supposed to have lived in the 3rd century AD —**Ossianic** /óssi ánik/ adj.

ossicle /óssik'l/ n. a small bone, especially one of three bones of the middle ear in humans [Late 16thC. From Latin *ossiculum* 'little bone, ossicle', from *os* 'bone'.] —**ossicular** /o síkyōōlər/ adj. —**ossiculate** /-lət, o síkyōō layt/ adj.

ossification /óssifi káysh'n/ n. **1.** PROCESS OF BONE FORMATION the natural process of forming bone **2.** HARDENING OF SOFT TISSUE the hardening of soft tissue as a result of impregnation with calcium salts **3.** BONY MASS a mass or deposit of bony material in the human body **4.** PROCESS OF BECOMING INFLEXIBLE the process of becoming set and inflexible in behaviour, attitudes, and actions **5.** INFLEXIBLE CONFORMITY rigid, unthinking acceptance of social conventions

ossifrage /óssifrij, óssi frayj/ (plural **-frages** or **-frage**) n. (*archaic*) **1.** LAMMERGEIER a lammergeier **2.** OSPREY an osprey [Early 17thC. From Latin *(avis) ossifraga*, a bird of prey, literally 'bone-breaking (bird)', formed from *frangere* 'to break' (source of English *fragment* and *fraction*).]

ossify /óssi fī/ (**-fies, -fying, -fied**) vti. **1.** HARDEN INTO BONE to change or be changed from soft tissue, e.g. cartilage, into bone as a result of impregnation with calcium salts **2.** BECOME INFLEXIBLE to become or make sb become rigidly set in a conventional pattern of behaviour, beliefs, and attitudes [Early 18thC. From French *ossifier*, literally 'to turn into bone', from Latin *os* 'bone'.]

Ossining /óss'ning/ town in southeastern New York State, on the Hudson River, southeast of Peekskill. Population: 22,788 (1996).

osso buco /óssō bōōkō/ (plural **osso bucos** or **osso buchi** /óssō bōōkee/) n. an Italian casserole made with shin of veal cooked in white wine with tomatoes, traditionally served with risotto [From Italian, 'bone marrow']

ossuary /óssyoo əri/ (plural **-ies**) n. an urn or a vault used to hold the bones of the dead (*formal*) [Mid-17thC. From late Latin *ossuarium*, ultimately from Latin *os* 'bone'.]

ost- prefix. = osteo-

osteal /ósti əl/ adj. **1.** BONY made of, containing, or resembling bone **2.** RELATING TO BONES OR SKELETONS relating to bones or the skeletons of mammals [Late 19thC. Ultimately from Greek *osteon* 'bone'.]

osteitis /ósti Ítiss/ (plural **-tes** /-teez/) n. inflammation of a bone or bony tissue, caused by infection or injury

Ostend /o sténd/ town and seaport in West Flanders Province, western Belgium. Population: 68,635 (1996).

ostensible /o sténssəb'l/ adj. presented as being true or appearing to be true, but usually hiding a different motive or meaning [Mid-18thC. Via French from medieval Latin *ostensibilis*, from Latin *ostensus*, perfect participle of *ostendere* 'to show', literally 'to stretch before', from *tendere* 'stretch, spread' (source of English *tension*).]

ostensibly /o sténssəbli/ adv. apparently for a particular reason, but not really for that reason ○ *He left the room, ostensibly to go and use the phone.*

ostensive /o sténssiv/ adj. ostensible (*formal*) [Early 17thC. From Late Latin *ostensivus*, a derivative of Latin *ostensus*, perfect participle of *ostendere* (see OSTENSIBLE).] —**ostensively** adv.

ostensorium /óss ten sáwri əm/ (plural **-a** /-ə/), **ostensory** /o sténssəri/ (plural **-ries**) n. CHR = **monstrance** [Late 18thC. From medieval Latin, formed from the past participle stem of Latin *ostendere* (see OSTENSIBLE).]

ostentation /óss ten táysh'n/ n. a vulgar display of wealth and success designed to impress people (*disapproving*) [15thC. Via Old French from the Latin stem *ostentation-*, from *ostentare* 'to display, exhibit', from *ostendere* (see OSTENSIBLE).]

ostentatious /óss sten táysh əss/ adj. marked by a vulgar display of wealth and success designed to impress people (*disapproving*) [Mid-17thC. Formed from OSTENTATION.] —**ostentatiously** adv.

osteo- prefix. bone ○ *osteotomy* [From Greek *osteon*. Ultimately from an Indo-European word that is also the ancestor of English *ossify, ostracize,* and *oyster.*]

osteoarthritis /ósti ō aar thrÍtiss/ n. a form of arthritis characterized by gradual loss of cartilage of the joints, usually affecting people after middle age

osteoblast /ósti ō blast/ n. a cell from which bone develops —**osteoblastic** /ósti ō blástik/ adj.

osteoclasis /ósti ō klássiss/ (plural **-ses** /-seez/) n. **1.** osteoclasis, osteoclasia BONY TISSUE DISINTEGRATION the process of disintegration and assimilation of bony tissue that occurs during normal growth of bone, or as part of healing at a fracture site **2. SURGICAL BREAKING OF BONE** a surgical procedure in which a bone is broken in order to correct a natural deformity or a badly healed fracture [Early 20thC. Formed from OSTEO- + Greek *klasis* 'breaking', from *klan* 'to break'.]

osteoclast /ósti ō klast/ n. **1. BONE CELL** a large cell with many nuclei, found in growing bone. It assimilates bony tissue and is active in the formation of canals and cavities. **2. SURGICAL INSTRUMENT** an instrument used to break bones during surgery to correct a deformity [Late 19thC. Formed from OSTEO- + Greek *klastas* 'broken', from *klan* 'to break'.] —**osteoclastic** /ósti ō klástik/ adj.

osteogenesis /ósti ō jénnəssiss/ n. the formation of bone in the body

osteogenesis imperfecta /-ímpər féktə/ n. MED a rare hereditary disease in which abnormal connective tissue development causes fragile, brittle bones

osteogenic sarcoma n. = osteosarcoma

osteoid /ósti oyd/ adj. **LIKE BONE** resembling or having the characteristics of bone ■ n. **BONE TISSUE** the tissue from which bone develops (**bone matrix**), especially before it has hardened

osteology /ósti ólləji/ (plural -**gies**) n. **1. STUDY OF BONES** the branch of anatomy concerned with the study of the structure and functions of bones **2. SKELETON** the bone structure or skeleton of an animal — **osteological** /ósti ə lójjik'l/ adj. —**osteologically** /-lójjikli/ adv. —**osteologist** /ósti ólləjist/ n.

osteolysis /ósti ólləssiss/ n. the gradual disintegration of bone caused by disease

osteoma /ósti ṓmə/ (plural -**mata** /-mətə/ or -**mas**) n. a benign tumour made of bone, usually on the skull

osteomalacia /ósti ō mə láyshi ə/ n. a disease occurring mainly in women that results from a lack of vitamin D or calcium, causing softening of the bones and resulting pain and weakness

osteomyelitis /ósti ō mí ə lítiss/ n. inflammation of bone and bone marrow, caused by infection

osteopath /ósti ə path/ n. sb who practises osteopathy

osteopathy /ósti óppəthi/ n. a system of medicine based on the theory that many diseases are caused by misalignments of bones, ligaments, and muscles, and that correcting these through manipulation can cure the problems. It is often effective in treating joint and muscle disorders. —**osteopathic** /ósti ə páthik/ adj. —**osteopathically** adv.

osteophyte /ósti ə fīt/ n. a small abnormal outgrowth of bone that occurs within joints or at other sites where there is degeneration of cartilage, e.g. due to osteoarthritis —**osteophytic** /ósti ə fíttik/ adj.

osteoplastic /ósti ō plástik/ adj. **1. RELATING TO BONE SURGERY** relating to or typical of bone surgery **2. RELATING TO BONE DEVELOPMENT** relating to or important in the process of bone development

osteoplasty /ósti ə plásti/ n. the surgical repair or correction of distortions of bones

osteoporosis /ósti ō pə rṓssiss/ (plural -**ses**) n. a disease occurring among women after the menopause in which the bones become very porous, break easily, and heal slowly. It may lead to curvature of the spine after vertebrae collapse. [Mid-19thC. Formed from OSTEO- + Greek *poros* 'passage' (see PORE) + -OSIS.]

osteosarcoma /ósti ō saar kṓmə/ (plural -**mata** or -**mas**) n. a malignant bone tumour

osteosis /ósti ṓssiss/ n. the presence of bone-making nodules in the skin

osteotome /ósti ə tōm/ n. a surgical instrument used to cut or divide bone

osteotomy /ósti óttəmi/ (plural -**mies**) n. a surgical procedure in which bone is divided or sectioned — **osteotomist** n.

Ostia /ósti ə/ ancient Roman port in Italy, at the mouth of the River Tiber, southwest of Rome

ostiary /ósti əri/ (plural -**ies**) n. a doorkeeper in a Roman Catholic church [15thC. From Latin *ostiarius* 'doorkeeper', from *ostium* (see OSTIUM).]

ostinato /ósti naátō/ (plural -**tos**) n. a short musical phrase or melody that is repeated over and over, usually at the same pitch [Late 19thC. From Italian, literally 'stubborn, obstinate'.]

ostiole /ósti ōl/ n. a small pore or opening in some algae or fungi, through which reproductive spores pass [Mid-19thC. From Latin *ostiolum* 'little door', from *ostium* (see OSTIUM).]

ostium /ósti əm/ (plural -**a** /ósti ə/) n. **1. ANAT SMALL OPENING** a small pore or opening in a passage or organ of the body **2. ZOOL PORE IN SPONGE** a pore or small opening in a sponge through which water passes [Mid-17thC. From Latin, literally 'mouth of a river, opening'.]

ostler /ósslər/, **hostler** n. a person employed to look after horses at an inn (archaic) [14thC. Variant.]

ostmark /óst maark/ n. the unit of currency that was formerly used in the German Democratic Republic, divided into 100 pfennig [Mid-20thC. From German, literally 'east mark'.]

ostomate /óstə mayt/ n. sb who has had a stoma created, allowing the intestine to open at the body surface [Mid-20thC. Formed from OSTOMY.]

ostomy /óstəmi/ (plural -**mies**) n. a surgical procedure such as a colostomy or ileostomy, in which an artificial opening for excreting waste matter is created [Mid-20thC. Extracted as a general term from terms like COLOSTOMY, ILEOSTOMY.]

-ostosis suffix. formation of bone ◇ *hyperostosis* [Coined from Greek *osteon* 'bone' (see OSTEO- + -OSIS]

ostracize /óstrə sīz/ (-**cizes**, -**cizing**, -**cized**), **ostracise** (-**cises**, -**cising**, -**cised**) vt. **1. EXCLUDE FROM SOCIETY** to banish or exclude sb from society or from a particular group, either formally or informally ◇ *She was ostracized by all her former friends.* **2. BANISH** to banish sb by a popular vote because that person is regarded as dangerous to society, as was the practice in ancient Greece [Mid-19thC. From Greek *ostrakizein*, a derivative of *ostrakon* 'pottery fragment'.] — **ostracism** n.

— **WORD KEY: ORIGIN** —

Ostracize: In ancient Athens, when it was proposed that a particular person should be sent into exile for a period because he was becoming a danger to the state, a democratic vote was taken on the matter. The method of registering one's vote was to inscribe the name of the prospective banishee on a piece of broken pottery (*ostrakon*). The pieces were counted, and if enough votes were cast against him, he was sent away for ten years.

ostracod /óstrə kod/ (plural -**cod** or -**cods**) n. a tiny crustacean that lives inside a hard outer shell made of two hinged halves. Subclass: Ostracoda. [Mid-19thC. From modern Latin *Ostracoda*, subclass name, from Greek *ostrakōdēs* 'like a pottery fragment', from *ostrakon* 'shell'.]

Ostrava /óstrava/ city in the northeastern Czech Republic, situated about 16 km/10 mi. from the Polish border. Population: 325,827 (1994).

Ostrich

ostrich /óstrich/ (plural -**triches** or -**trich**) n. **1. FLIGHTLESS BIRD** a two-toed African bird that runs very fast but cannot fly. It is the largest living bird and has a long bare neck, small head, and fluffy drooping feathers. Latin name: *Struthio camelus*. **2. SB WHO IGNORES UNPLEASANT THINGS** sb who tries to avoid unpleasant situations by refusing to acknowledge that

they exist (informal) [13thC. Via Old French *ostrusce* from assumed Vulgar Latin *avistruthius*, ultimately from Latin *avis* 'bird' + Greek *strouthiōn*-, from *strouthos* 'sparrow'.]

Ostrogoth /óstrə goth/ n. a member of the eastern branch of Gothic peoples that invaded Italy, where they ruled from the end of the 5th to the middle of the 6th centuries. ◊ **Visigoth** [14thC. From late Latin *Ostrogothus* (plural) 'Ostrogoths', from a Germanic word that is also the ancestor of English *east* + Latin *Gothus* 'Goth'.] — **Ostrogothic** /óstrə góthik/ adj.

Ostyak /ósti ak/ (plural -**aks** or -**ak**), **Ostiak** (plural -**aks** or -**ak**) n. **1. PEOPLES MEMBER OF PEOPLE OF WESTERN SIBERIA** a member of a people that lives in parts of western Siberia **2. LANG OSTYAK LANGUAGE** the language of the Ostyak people. It belongs to the Finno-Ugric branch of Uralic languages. Ostyak is spoken by about 15,000 people. [Early 18thC. Via Russian from Tartar *ustyak* 'one of another tribe'.] —**Ostyak** adj.

OSU abbr. Order of Saint Ursula

Oswald /ózzwəld/, **St** (605?–641?) Anglo-Saxon monarch. He was king of Northumbria (634–41), where, with the help of St Aidan, he reestablished Christianity.

Oswald, Lee Harvey (1939–63) US alleged assassin. Accused of assassinating President John F. Kennedy (22 November, 1963), Oswald was fatally shot two days later while in police custody.

Oswestry /ózwəstri/ market town in Shropshire, west-central England. Population: 34,800 (1995).

OT abbr. **1.** overtime **2.** Old Testament **3.** occupational therapy

ot- prefix. = oto- (used before vowels)

Otago /ō taag ō/ administrative region of New Zealand, occupying the southeastern part of the South Island. Its principal city is Dunedin. Population: 193,132 (1996). Area: 38,638 sq. km/14,918 sq. mi.

Otago Peninsula /ōtaagō-/ peninsula on the southeastern coast of the South Island, New Zealand. It extends 25 km/16 mi. eastwards from Dunedin to Cape Saunders.

otalgia /ō tálji ə, -jə/ n. pain in the ear (technical) [Mid-17thC. From Greek *ōtalgia*, from *ōt-*, stem of *ous* 'ear'.]

OTC abbr. **1.** Officers' Training Corps **2.** over-the-counter

OTE abbr. on-target earnings (used in advertisements for jobs that pay commission)

other /úthər/ CORE MEANING: a grammatical word used to show that a thing, person, or situation is additional or different ◇ (adj) *He does much to help the homeless and other people in need.* ◇ (adj) *They met plenty of other children there.* ◇ (adj) *I went on ahead, and the other climbers struggled on behind.* ◇ (pron) *This is one problem, but there are many others.* ◇ (pron) *As much as I demand of others, I am much more demanding of myself.*

1. adj., pron. **FURTHER** refers to an additional or further person or thing of the type already mentioned ◇ (adj) *Let me make one other suggestion.* ◇ (pron) *A couple of students failed the exam, but many others passed.* **2.** adj., pron. **DIFFERENT** refers to a different thing or things from that or those already specified ◇ (adj) *Banks are unlike any other business.* ◇ (adj) *Are there any other items you'd like to take home?* ◇ (pron) *This problem, more than any other, has divided the critics.* **3.** adj., pron. **THE REMAINING** refers to the remaining people or things in a group, apart from the one specified ◇ (adj) *She left earlier, with the other kids.* ◇ (pron) *John and the others will be here soon.* **4.** adj., pron. **SECOND OF TWO THINGS** refers to the second of two things when the first is known or understood ◇ (adj) *He threw his other glove out of the window.* ◇ (pron) ◇ *She had a cup in one hand and a glass in the other.* ◇ (pron) *It goes in one ear and out the other.* [Old English *ōðer*] ◇ **every other** alternate ◇ *They give us meat every other day.* ◇ **or other** used to show that the preceding words you use are not exact or definite ◇ *For some reason or other, the house was crowded that night.* ◇ **other than** indicates an exception to a statement ◇ *Was anyone there other than the two of you?* ◇ **other things being equal** in a situation in which there is little difference between two or more people or things ○ *Other things being equal, I would choose the cheaper holiday.* ◇ **the other day** or **night** a few days or nights ago ○ *A funny thing happened the other day.*

other-directed *adj.* more concerned with what other people think than with your own values and standards —**other-directedness** *n.*

otherness /úthərnəss/ *n.* the condition of being perceived as strange or different

otherwise /úthər wīz/ *adv.* **1. OR ELSE** if things had been different ○ *'I overslept', said Joe, 'otherwise you would have heard from me earlier'.* **2. DIFFERENTLY** different from or opposite to sth stated ○ *You may take your hand luggage with you unless otherwise requested.* **3. IN OTHER WAYS** in any other ways ○ *An otherwise dull day was enlivened by her arrival.* [Old English (on) ōðre wīsan '(in) (an)other wise, manner']

otherworld /úthər wurld/ *n.* a world or life that is beyond the conventional perception of reality —**otherworldly** *adj.* —**otherworldliness** /úthər wúrldli nəss/ *n.*

otic /ṓtik, óttik/ *adj.* relating to or located near the ear [Mid-17thC. From Greek ōtikos, from ōt-, the stem of ous 'ear'.]

-otic *suffix.* **1.** relating to a particular condition, action, or process ○ *hypnotic* **2.** having a particular abnormal or diseased condition ○ *psychotic* [Via French and Latin from, ultimately, Greek -ōtikos]

otiose /ṓti ōss, -ōz/ *adj.* **1. NOT EFFECTIVE** with no useful result or practical purpose **2. WORTHLESS** with little or no value **3. LAZY** unwilling or uninterested in working or being active (*archaic*) [Late 18thC. From Latin *otiosus*, 'at leisure, idle', from *otium* 'leisure', of unknown origin.] —**otiosely** *adv.* —**otiosity** /ṓti óssəti/ *n.*

otitis /ō tī́tiss/ *n.* inflammation of the ear, caused by infection

otitis media *n.* a painful inflammation of the middle ear that can cause dizziness and temporary hearing loss

oto- *prefix.* ear ○ *otolith* [Via modern Latin from Greek ōt-, the stem of *ous* (see OTIC)]

otocyst /ṓtō sist/ *n.* **1. INNER EAR STRUCTURE** the structure from which the adult inner ear develops **2.** = statocyst

OTOH *abbr.* ONLINE on the other hand (*used in e-mail messages*)

otol. *abbr.* otology

otolaryngology /ṓtō lárring góllaji/ *n.* a branch of medicine concerned with the treatment and diagnosis of diseases of the ear, nose, and throat —**otolaryngological** /ṓtō lə ríng gə lójjik'l/ *adj.* —**otolaryngologist** /ṓtō lárring góllajist/ *n.*

otolith /ṓtō lith/ *n.* **1. ANAT GRANULE IN INNER EAR** a particle of calcium carbonate found in the inner ear of vertebrates and involved in sensory perception **2.** ZOOL = statolith

otology /ō tóllaji/ *n.* the branch of medicine concerned with the structure and function of the ear, its diseases, and their treatment —**otological** /ṓtə lójjik'l/ *adj.* —**otologist** /ō tóllajist/ *n.*

O'Toole /ō tool/, **Peter** (*b.* 1932) Irish-born British actor. He has starred in many films, notably *Lawrence of Arabia* (1964). Full name **Peter Seamus O'Toole**

otorhinolaryngology /ṓtō rī́nō lárring góllaji/ *n.* = otolaryngology —**otorhinolaryngological** /ṓtō rī́nō lə ríng gə lójjik'l/ *adj.* —**otorhinolaryngologist** /ṓtō rī́nō lárring góllajist/ *n.*

otosclerosis /ṓtō sklə rṓssiss/ *n.* a hereditary disease of the inner ear in which spongy bone growth leads to progressive hearing impairment

otoscope /ṓtō skōp/ *n.* an instrument incorporating a light and a magnifying lens, used to examine the external canal of the ear and the eardrum —**otoscopic** /ṓtō skóppik/ *adj.*

ototoxic /ṓtō tóksik/ *adj.* toxic to the ear and hence impairing hearing or balance —**ototoxicity** /ṓtō tok síssəti/ *n.*

Otranto, Strait of /ō tránt ō/ sea passage between the Adriatic and Ionian seas. It separates the 'heel' of Italy from Albania. Length: 69 km/43 mi.

OTS *abbr.* Officers' Training School

OTT *abbr.* over the top (*informal*)

ottava /ō taávə/ *adj.* sung or played at an octave higher or lower than the notes written on the staff, indicated by a sign placed above or below the staff [Early 19thC. From Italian, literally 'octave, eighth', from *otto* 'eight', from Latin *octo*.]

ottava rima /-reémə/ *n.* a verse form made up of eight lines in iambic pentameter with the rhyme scheme abababcc [Early 19thC. From Italian, literally 'eighth rhyme'.]

Ottawa /óttəwə/ **1.** river in Canada. It is the chief tributary of the St Lawrence River, forming part of the Ontario-Quebec border. Length: 1,271 km/789 mi. **2.** capital city of Canada, located in southeastern Ontario, on the Ontario-Quebec border. Population: 313,987 (1996).

Otter

otter /óttər/ (*plural* **-ter** or **-ters**) *n.* **1. WATER-LOVING ANIMAL** an aquatic fish-eating mammal with smooth dark brown fur and webbed feet. It is distributed worldwide except in Australia, and is related to the weasels and minks. Family: Mustelidae. **2. OTTER FUR** the fur of the otter [Old English ot(t)or. Ultimately from an Indo-European word meaning 'water', which is also the ancestor of English *water*, *hydrant*, and *whisky*.]

Otterburn /óttər burn/ village in Northumberland, northeastern England, site of the Scottish defeat of the English in the Battle of Otterburn in 1388

otter cat *n.* = jaguarundi

otter hound *n.* any of an English breed of large dogs, used to hunt otters

Otto cycle /óttō-/ *n.* a thermodynamic process for the conversion of heat into work, e.g. the sequential suction, compression, ignition, and expulsion in a four-stroke engine [Late 19thC. Named after Nikolaus August Otto (1832–91), German engineer and inventor.]

Ottoman

ottoman /óttəmən/ *n.* **1. LONG SEAT** an upholstered sofa that has no arms and is usually backless **2. STOOL FOR FEET** a low upholstered stool used for resting the feet or as a seat **3. HEAVY FABRIC** a heavy fabric made of silk or rayon that has a corded texture and is used to make coats and trimmings [Late 16thC. Via French or Italian from medieval Latin *ottomanus*, ultimately from Arabic ʻU̱tmān Osman.]

Ottoman /óttəmən/ *n.* a member of a Turkish people that conquered Asia Minor in the 13th century —**Ottoman** *adj.*

Ottoman Empire *n.* a Turkish empire established in the late 13th century in Asia Minor, eventually extending throughout the Middle East. It was responsible for the conquest of Constantinople and the end of the Byzantine Empire in 1453. It ended in 1922.

Otway Ranges /ót way ráynjiz/ range of hills in southern Victoria, Australia, which extends from Anglesea to Cape Otway

ou /ō/ *n.* S Africa a man (*slang*) [Mid-20thC. From Afrikaans, of uncertain origin: possibly from Dutch *ouwe* 'old man'.]

OU *abbr.* Open University

ouabain /waá bay in, -bayn/ *n.* a poisonous chemical compound that is sometimes used as a heart stimulant. It is extracted from an African tree. Latin name: *Strophanthus gratis*. [Late 19thC. Via French *oubaïo* from Somali *wabayo* 'arrow poison'.]

Ouagadougou /waágə dōog oo/ capital city of Burkina Faso, located in the centre of the country. Population: 690,000 (1993).

oubaas /ō baass/ *n.* S Africa a person who is above sb in age or rank [Mid-19thC. From Afrikaans, literally 'old boss', of uncertain origin: probably formed from Dutch *oud* 'old' + *baas* 'foreman'.]

oubliette /oóbli ét/ *n.* a dungeon made so that the only way in or out is through a trap door at the top [Early 19thC. From French, from *oublier* 'to forget', from assumed Vulgar Latin *oblitare*, from Latin *oblitus*, the perfect participle of *oblivisci*, the source of English *oblivion*.]

ouch /owch/ *interj.* an exclamation used to express sudden pain [Mid-19thC. Origin uncertain: possibly from German *autsch*, an exclamation of pain.]

oud /ood/ *n.* a stringed instrument of southwest Asia and northern Africa that resembles a lute or a mandolin [Mid-18thC. From Arabic *al-ʻūd* 'the wood' (see LUTE).]

ought[1] /awt/ CORE MEANING: a modal verb indicating what sb should do ○ *It seems to me that we ought to support their initiative.* ○ *You ought to tell her how you feel.*

v. **1. BE MORALLY RIGHT** indicates that sb has a duty or obligation to do sth or that it is morally right to do sth ○ *You ought to be ashamed of what you have done.* **2. BE IMPORTANT** indicates that sth is important or a good idea ○ *You ought to see a doctor as soon as possible.* **3. BE PROBABLE** indicates probability or expectation ○ *We ought to be there by now.* **4. BE WISHED FOR** indicates a desire or wish ○ *You ought to come to dinner sometime.* **5. BE THE CASE** indicates that sth should be the case but may not be ○ *That ought to be easy.* [Mid-18thC. From an erroneous division of 'a nought'.]

ought[2] *n.* MATH zero

ouguiya /oo gée yə/ *n.* the unit of currency of Mauritania [Late 20thC. Via French from Mauritanian Arabic *ūgiya*, ultimately from Greek *ougkia*, from Latin *uncia* (see OUNCE[1]).]

Ouija /weéjə/, **Ouija board** *tdmk.* a trademark for a board with letters and a pointer or planchette by which answers to questions are spelt out, supposedly by spiritual forces

ould /owld/ *adj.* Ireland old, especially when used as an intensifier (*nonstandard*) [Late 17thC. From the Irish pronunciation of OLD.]

Oulu /ṓ ōol oō/ city and port on the Gulf of Bothnia, west-central Finland. Population: 109,094 (1995).

ouma /ō maa/ *n.* S Africa **1. GRANDMOTHER** grandmother, often used as a title with the woman's last name **2.** any elderly woman (*slang*) [Early 20thC. From Afrikaans, 'grandmother', from *ou* 'old' + *ma* 'mother'.]

ounce[1] /ownss/ *n.* **1. UNIT OF WEIGHT** a unit of weight equal to one-sixteenth of a pound in the avoirdupois system **2. FLUID OUNCE** a unit for measuring liquid, equal to 0.0284 of a litre **3. SMALL AMOUNT** a small amount of sth ○ *Anyone with an ounce of common sense would take an umbrella on a day like this.* [14thC. Via Old French *unce* from Latin *uncia* 'twelfth part, inch, ounce', from *unus* 'one'.]

ounce[2] (*plural* **ounce** or **ounces**) *n.* = snow leopard [14thC. From Old French *once*, variant of *lonce* (the 'l' being mistaken for the definite article), from assumed Vulgar Latin *luncea*, from Latin *lync-* (see LYNX).]

oupa /ṓ paal/ *n. S Africa* **1.** GRANDFATHER grandfather, often used as a title with the man's last name **2.** any elderly man (*slang*) [Early 20thC. From Afrikaans, 'grandfather', formed from *ou* 'old' + *pa* 'father'.]

our /owr/ *det.* **1.** BELONGING TO US indicates that sth belongs to or is associated with the speaker or writer and at least one other person (*first person plural possessive determiner*) ○ *Where are all our bags?* ○ *Our house is just a few hundred yards from yours.* **2.** BELONGING TO EVERYONE indicates that sth belongs to or is associated with people in general ○ *the dreams that inspire us to do our best* **3.** REFERS TO MEMBER OF FAMILY refers to a member of the speaker's family (*informal*) ○ *Our John is an electrician now.* [Old English *ūre* 'of us', the genitive plural of WE]

Our Father *n.* = **Lord's Prayer**

Our Lady *n.* a title for the Virgin Mary

ours /owrz/ *pron.* refers to sth or sb that belongs to or is associated with the speaker and at least one other person (*first person plural possessive pronoun*) ○ *It's no surprise that their team is ahead of ours.* [13thC. Coined from OUR + *-'s* 'belonging to'.]

ourselves /owr sélvz, aar sélvz/ *pron.* **1.** BELONGING TO US refers to the speaker or writer and at least one other person, sometimes emphatically (*used as the object of a verb or preposition when the subject refers to the same people*) ○ *We ourselves can't work it out, so we don't expect others to be able to.* **2.** REFERS TO PEOPLE IN GENERAL refers to people in general ○ *Many of us have secrets that we find difficult to admit even to ourselves.* **3.** REFERS EMPHATICALLY TO US refers emphatically to the speaker or writer and at least one other person ○ *These papers are of no interest to anyone but ourselves.* **4.** OUR USUAL SELVES our usual selves ○ *At home with the family, we can really be ourselves.*

-ous *suffix.* **1.** full of, having the qualities of ○ *virtuous* ○ *traitorous* **2.** having a lower valence than a corresponding compound or ion the name of which ends in -ic ○ *chromous* [Via Old French from Latin *-osus* and *-us*]

Ouse /ooz/ **1.** river in eastern England that rises in Northamptonshire and empties into the Wash near King's Lynn, Norfolk. Length: 257 km/160 mi. **2.** river in northeastern England that rises in North Yorkshire and empties into the Humber Estuary. Length: 92 km/57 mi. **3.** river in southeastern England that rises in Sussex and empties into the English Channel. Length: 48 km/30 mi.

oust /owst/ *vt.* **1.** FORCE SB OUT to use force to remove sb from a place **2.** REMOVE SB FROM OFFICE to remove or force sb from an office or position [15thC. Via Old French *oster* from Latin *obstare* 'to stand in the way, hinder', from *stare* 'to stand', the source of English *obstetrics*.]

ouster /ówstər/ *n.* **1.** REMOVAL the act of removing or forcing sb out of a place or position **2.** WRONGFUL DISPOSSESSION the illegal removal or forceful dispossession of sb's property

out /owt/ CORE MEANING: a grammatical word indicating that sb or sth is away from a place or removed from somewhere ○ (adv) *The child ran out and got back onto the bike.* ○ (adv) *She took out her laptop.* ○ (adj) *She's been out late every night.*

1. *adv.* OUTSIDE outside a place rather than inside ○ *It's cold out.* **2.** *adv.* IN ANOTHER PLACE in another place, usually far away ○ *She's out in Australia, I think.* **3.** *adv.* INDICATES END POINT indicates a goal or objective achieved in the action specified by the verb ○ *Stick it out – never give up.* **4.** *adv.* IN EXISTENCE that there is in existence ○ *It's one of the best albums out.* **5.** *adj., adv.* AWAY FROM HOME away from home or your place of work ○ (adj) *He's not answering the doorbell – he must be out.* ○ (adv) *She's not answering the phone – she must have gone out.* **6.** *adj., adv.* FURTHER AWAY refers to the tide when the sea moves away from the shore ○ (adj) *We can cross to the island when the tide is out.* ○ (adv) *The tide goes out at around five o'clock.* **7.** *adj., adv.* NO LONGER BURNING of a light or a fire, no longer alight or no longer burning ○ (adj) *The fire is out.* ○ (adv) *The fire has gone out.* **8.** *adj., adv.* IN FLOWER in flower ○ (adj) *The daffodils are out at last.* ○ (adv) *All the wild flowers are coming out.* **9.** *adj., adv.* AVAILABLE of a book, record, etc., available for people to buy. ○ (adj) *Her new book is out in paperback at last.* ○ (adv) *Their new album came out last week.* **10.** *adj., adv.* ON STRIKE on strike ○ (adj) *The miners have been out for a month now.* ○ (adv) *500 workers came out in protest over the benefit cuts.* **11.** *adj.* NO LONGER IN A GAME unable to take part any longer in a game or sport **12.** *adj.* CONSIDERING A VERDICT of a jury, considering its verdict **13.** *adj.* INCORRECT inaccurate or incorrect ○ *Look – the figures are way out.* **14.** *adj.* UNACCEPTABLE unacceptable or not worth considering ○ *That possibility is out, I'm afraid.* **15.** *adj.* UNFASHIONABLE no longer in fashion **16.** *adj.* INTENT ON determined or intent on ○ *He's just out for what he can get.* **17.** *adj.* UNCONSCIOUS unconscious ○ *She was out cold.* **18.** *adj.* USED UP used up or exhausted ○ *All our rations are out.* **19.** *adj.* NOT IN GOVERNMENT not in power or office **20.** *adj.* FINISHED completed or concluded ○ *before the year is out* **21.** *adj.* NOT WORKING not working ○ *All the phones are out.* **22.** *interj.* AWAY FROM HERE! a command for sb to leave a place ○ *Out!* **23.** *vt.* TO EXPOSE SB to expose sb, especially a public figure or famous person, as a homosexual ○ *A gay action group outed a prominent celebrity.* **24.** *n. US* WAY OF AVOIDING BAD CONSEQUENCE a way of escaping from a predicament or avoiding the undesirable consequences of sth (*informal*) ○ *What's my out if things go wrong?* [Old English *ūt*] ◇ **out of 1.** indicates that sb leaves a place ○ *Three men came out of the store.* **2.** indicates that sb removes sth from a place ○ *In her enthusiasm, she pulled the drawer right out of the desk.* **3.** towards the outside ○ *She looked longingly out of the window.* **4.** no longer available or in sb's possession ○ *We're out of butter.* **5.** from ○ *Plastic products are made out of petroleum.* **6.** indicates proportion that sth is true of ○ *This applies to one out of five adults.* **7.** indicates that sb gains an advantage from sth ○ *I think I got a lot out of the course.* **8.** indicates that sb is sheltered from the weather ○ *Remember to keep out of the sun, or at least use sunblock.* **9.** beyond the range of a sound ○ *I called her, but she was out of earshot.* **10.** indicates the motivation behind an action ○ *He only did it out of spite.* **11.** indicates that sb is not or is no longer in a situation ○ *A police officer warned them to stay out of trouble.* ◇ **out of it** very drunk or under the influence of drugs (*informal*) ○ *You were totally out of it last night!* ◇ **out with it** a command to sb to let sth be known immediately ○ *Come on, what's going on? Out with it!*

outa *prep.* = **outta**

outage /ówtij/ *n.* **1.** AMOUNT MISSING an amount of sth that is missing after delivery or storage **2.** TEMPORARY LOSS OF POWER a temporary loss of function or interruption of a power source, especially a loss of electric power

out and away *adv.* without any question and by far

out-and-out *adj.* being a thorough, uncompromising, or unapologetic example of sth

out-and-outer *n.* a person who goes to extremes in some activity or endeavour

outback *n.* /owt bak/ REMOTE AREA, ESPECIALLY IN AUSTRALIA a sparsely inhabited or wilderness region of a country, especially of Australia ■ *adj.* RELATING TO AUSTRALIAN OUTBACK relating to a remote, sparsely inhabited region of a country, especially the Australian interior ○ *an outback community*

outbalance /owt bállənss/ (**-ances, -ancing, -anced**) *vt.* to go beyond sth in effect, influence, or importance

outbid /owt bíd/ (**-bids, -bidding, -bidded**) *vt.* to offer to pay more money for sth than sb else

outboard /ówt bawrd/ *adj.* **1.** ON THE OUTSIDE OF A BOAT located on the outside of the hull of a ship or boat **2.** LOCATED TOWARDS BOAT'S HULL positioned away from the centre of a ship or boat **3.** AWAY FROM THE FUSELAGE away from the main body of an aircraft and towards the wingtips ■ *adv.* TOWARDS OUTSIDE OF SHIP in a direction away from the centre of a ship or aircraft ■ *n.* BOAT WITH OUTBOARD MOTOR a boat with an engine mounted outside the stern

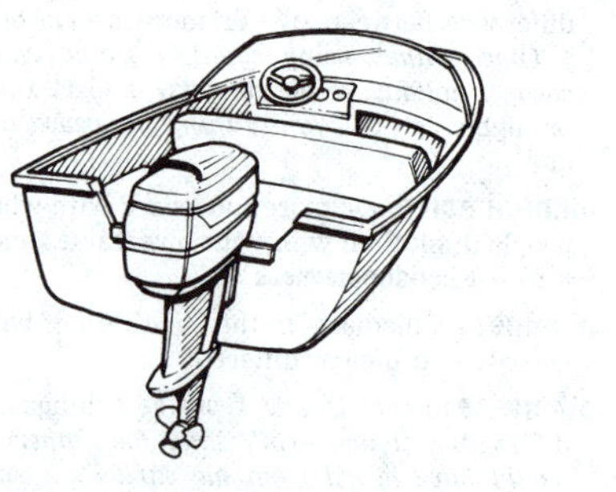

Outboard motor

outboard motor, outboard *n.* a small or medium-sized engine with a propeller that can be mounted outside the stern of a boat

outbound /ówt bownd/ *adj.* travelling away from rather than towards a particular place ○ *an outbound journey*

outbrave /owt bráyv/ *vt.* (*archaic*) **1.** FACE STH DEFIANTLY to face a threat with defiance **2.** BE MORE COURAGEOUS THAN SB to be braver than sb else

outbreak /ówt brayk/ *n.* a sudden occurrence, usually of sth unpleasant or dangerous such as illness or fighting ○ *the outbreak of war*

outbreed /owt bréed/ (**-breeds, -breeding, -bred** /-bréd/, **-bred**) *vti.* to bring together distantly related members of a species in order to breed genetically varied offspring, or to reproduce in this way [Early 20thC. Modelled on 'inbreed'.]

outbuilding /ówt bilding/ *n.* a barn, shed, or other structure that is situated away from the main building on a property

outburst /ówt burst/ *n.* **1.** SUDDEN DISPLAY OF EMOTION a sudden display of strong emotion ○ *an outburst of grief* **2.** INTENSE PERIOD OF ACTIVITY a sudden burst of energy or growth

outcall /ówt kawl/ *n.* a visit made by a doctor or other professional to the home of a client or patient

outcast /ówt kaast/ *n.* sb who has been rejected by a particular group or by society as a whole ○ *a social outcast* [Late 16thC. Formed from OUT + CAST.] —**outcast** *adj.*

outcaste /ówt kaast/ *n.* **1.** MEMBER EXPELLED FROM CASTE in India, sb who has been expelled from a Hindu caste for violating its rules or customs **2.** INDIAN WITHOUT CASTE sb in India who does not belong to a caste

outclass /owt klaass/ *vt.* to be so much better than others as to seem to be in a separate class altogether

outcome /ówt kum/ *n.* the way that sth turns out in the end

outcrop /ówt krop/ *n.* ROCK PROJECTING FROM SOIL the part of a rock formation that is exposed on the surface of the ground ■ *vi.* (**-crops, -cropping, -cropped**) PROJECT FROM GROUND to stick out of the ground as an outcrop [Mid-18thC. From *crop out*.]

outcross *vt.* /ówt kross/ (**-crosses, -crossing, -crossed**) BREED UNRELATED ANIMALS to mate two plants or animals not closely related but usually of the same breed in order to produce offspring ■ *n.* PRODUCT OF OUTCROSSING the process of outcrossing plants or animals, or the progeny produced as a result

outcry /ówt krī/ (*plural* **-cries**) *n.* **1.** STRONG REACTION a strong and widespread public reaction against sth **2.** CLAMOUR a loud cry from a crowd of people

outdated /owt dáytid/ *adj.* old-fashioned or out-of-date ○ *outdated notions about how to raise children*

WORD KEY: SYNONYMS

See Synonyms at ***old-fashioned.***

outdistance /owt dístənss/ (**-tances, -tancing, -tanced**) *vt.* **1.** GO FASTER THAN OTHER COMPETITORS to be faster than others in a race and leave other competitors behind **2.** BE BETTER THAN OTHERS to be considerably more successful than others

outdo /owt dóō/ (**-does, -doing, -did** /-díd/, **-done** /-dún/) *vt.* to do more or better than other people, or better than previously

outdoor /ówt dáwr/ *adj.* **1.** CONCERNED WITH THE OPEN AIR located in, belonging in, or suited to the open air ○ *outdoor activities* **2.** ENJOYING BEING OUTSIDE enjoying activities that take place in the open air

outdoors /owt dáwrz/ *adv.* OUTSIDE outside or in the open air ■ *n.* AREA NOT IN OR NEAR BUILDINGS the open air, especially when away from populated areas [Early 19thC. From the phrase 'out of doors'.]

outdoorsy /owt dáwrzi/ *adj.* suited to or fond of the open air (*informal*)

outdraw /owt dráw/ (**-draws, -drawing, -drew** /-dróo/, **-drawn** /-dráwn/) *vt.* **1.** DRAW WEAPON QUICKER THAN SB to draw a handgun faster than another person **2.** ATTRACT MORE PEOPLE to attract a larger audience than another performer or performance

outer /ówtər/ *adj.* **1.** ON THE OUTSIDE on or around the outside of sth ○ *the outer surface of the spacecraft* **2.** AWAY FROM THE CENTRE on the edge or away from the centre of sth ○ *the outer islands* **3.** ABOUT BODY RATHER THAN SPIRIT concerning or belonging to external or worldly things rather than the life of the mind or spirit [14thC. Formed from OUT, replacing earlier 'utter'.]

outer bar *n.* all the junior barristers practising at the bar

Outer Hebrides /ówtər hébrədeez/ island group in Scotland, comprising the westernmost islands of the Hebrides. ◆ **Hebrides**

outermost /ówtər mōst/ *adj.* farthest away from the centre [14thC. Formed from OUTER, on the model of 'innermost'.]

outer planet *n.* any of the five planets, Jupiter, Saturn, Uranus, Neptune, and Pluto, that have orbits lying beyond the asteroid belt

outer space *n.* all space in the universe beyond the earth and its atmosphere, especially interplanetary and interstellar space, but including the region where astronauts walk and satellites orbit the earth

outerwear /ówtər wair/ *n.* clothing that is designed to be worn outdoors over other clothing

outface /owt fáyss/ (**-faces, -facing, -faced**) *vt.* **1.** STARE SB DOWN to win a confrontation, especially by staring at sb or not looking away **2.** DEFY SB to confront sb boldly or confidently

outfall /ówt fawl/ *n.* the outlet of a sewer, drain, or stream, especially where it empties into a larger body of water

outfield /ówt feeld/ *n.* **1.** CRICKET OUTER PART OF CRICKET PITCH the part of a cricket pitch farthest from the bowler and the player who is batting **2.** BASEBALL AREA BEYOND THE INFIELD the part of a baseball or softball field beyond the diamond marked by the bases **3.** PLAYERS IN OUTFIELD the players in ball sports whose positions are in the outfield —**outfielder** *n.*

outfielder *n.* BASEBALL a player who defends in the outfield

outfit /ówt fit/ *n.* **1.** SET OF CLOTHES a set of clothes worn together **2.** EQUIPMENT a set of tools or equipment for a particular task or occupation ○ *a diving outfit* **3.** SMALL ORGANIZATION a team or group of people who work closely together, e.g. a military unit (*informal*) ■ *vt.* (**-fits, -fitting, -fitted**) **1.** EQUIP SB to provide sb with all the equipment that is needed to do a particular job **2.** DRESS SB to provide sb with a set of clothes

outfitter /ówt fittər/ *n.* a shop that sells men's clothes

outflank /owt flángk/ (**-flanks, -flanking, -flanked**) *vt.* **1.** ATTACK THE ENEMY INDIRECTLY to go around the main body of an enemy force and attack it from the side or from behind **2.** WIN BY MANOEUVRING to outwit or bypass an opponent or competitor

outflow /ówtflō/ *n.* the flow, movement, or transfer of sth such as gas, water, or money away from a place

outfox /owt fóks/ (**-foxes, -foxing, -foxed**) *vt.* to defeat sb by being more cunning

outgas /owt gáss/ (**-gases, -gassing, -gassed**) *vti.* to remove or release trapped or absorbed gas, or to be released as gas

outgo /owt gṓ/ *vt.* (**-goes, -going, -went** /-wént/, **-gone** /-gón/) OUTDO to go beyond or surpass sb or sth ■ *n.* **1.** EXPENDITURE sth that goes out, especially money that is paid out **2.** STH THAT FLOWS OUT sth that is flowing out

outgoing /ówt gō ing/ *adj.* **1.** LEAVING OR GOING OUT in the process of departing or going out of a building or place ○ *outgoing flights* **2.** LEAVING A JOB in the process of departing or being sent away after a period of office ○ *a dinner for the outgoing president* **3.** SOCIABLE confident and friendly in social situations ○ *a cheerful, outgoing child*

outgoings /ówt gō ingz/ *npl.* money paid out, especially on a regular basis

outgrew past tense of **outgrow**

out-group *n.* a group of people excluded from another group with higher status [Early 20thC. Modelled on 'in-group'.]

outgrow /owt grṓ/ (**-grows, -growing, -grew** /-gróo/, **-grown** /-grṓn/) *vt.* **1.** GET TOO LARGE to grow too large for sth **2.** MOVE BEYOND PREVIOUS INTERESTS to change so that old ideas, interests, or ways of behaving are lost in favour of new ones **3.** OUTSTRIP to grow larger or faster than other things or people

outgrowth /ówt grōth/ *n.* **1.** EXTENSION a natural development or result of sth else **2.** OFFSHOOT sth that is growing out from the main part

outguess /owt géss/ (**-guesses, -guessing, -guessed**) *vt.* to get an advantage over sb by anticipating what that person is thinking or planning to do

outgun /owt gún/ (**-guns, -gunning, -gunned**) *vt.* **1.** HAVE BETTER WEAPONS to have more guns or firepower than sb else **2.** OVERWHELM RIVAL to defeat a rival or competitor by being stronger or having better resources (*informal*)

outhaul /ówt hawl/ *n.* a rope used to pull a sail taut along a spar or boom

out-Herod (**out-Herods, out-Herodding, out-Herrodded, out-Herodded**) *vt.* to behave more excessively than sb else ○ *out-Herod Herod* [From Shakespeare's *Hamlet* III.2, referring to the traditionally overdramatic character of Herod in the medieval mystery plays.]

outhouse /ówt howss/ (*plural* **-houses** /-howziz/) *n.* **1.** OUTBUILDING a small building situated near the main building on a property **2.** *US* OUTDOOR TOILET an outdoor toilet consisting of a small building that encloses a seat with a hole in it built over a pit

outing /ówting/ *n.* **1.** EXCURSION a short pleasure trip usually lasting no more than a day **2.** TAKING PART IN EVENT an appearance at or participation in a public event, especially an athletic competition **3.** DECLARING SB TO BE HOMOSEXUAL the practice of making public the fact that sb is homosexual when that person wants the information kept private

outjockey /owt jóki/ (**-eys, -eying, -eyed**) *vt.* to get an advantage over sb by cleverness or trickery

outland /ówt land, -lənd/ *n.* **1.** HINTERLAND the remote or outlying areas of a country (*often used in the plural*) **2.** DIFFERENT COUNTRY a different country [Old English *ūtland*]

outlander /ówt landər/ *n.* sb from another country or from a different region, and thus a stranger [Late 16thC. Modeled on Dutch *uitlander* and German *Ausländer*.]

outlandish /owt lándish/ *adj.* **1.** VERY PECULIAR extremely unusual or bizarre **2.** ALIEN alien or foreign (*archaic*) [Old English *ūtlandisc*] —**outlandishly** *adv.* —**outlandishness** *n.*

outlast /owt láast/ (**-lasts, -lasting, -lasted**) *vt.* to last or exist longer than sb or sth else

outlaw /ówt law/ *n.* **1.** FUGITIVE a notorious criminal, especially one on the run **2.** SB WITHOUT LEGAL RIGHTS sb, often a criminal, who has been officially deprived of legal rights and so is not protected by the law **3.** REBEL sb who is rebellious or flouts the law **4.** VICIOUS ANIMAL a savage or uncontrollable animal ■ *vt.* (**-laws, -lawing, -lawed**) **1.** BAN STH to make sth illegal **2.** TAKE AWAY SB'S LEGAL RIGHTS to deprive sb officially of all their legal rights [12thC. Old English *ūtlaga*, from Old Norse *útlagi*, literally 'person outside the law', from *útlagr* 'outlawed, banished'.]

outlawry /ówt lawri/ *n.* **1.** DISREGARD FOR LAW refusal to obey the law **2.** STATE OF BEING LEGALLY OUTLAWED a state in which sb has been deprived of his or her legal rights and is no longer protected by the law, or the legal process by which this happens

outlay *n.* /ówt lay/ **1.** SPENDING the expending of resources or spending of money **2.** MONEY SPENT an amount of money spent ■ *vt.* /owt láy/ (**-lays, -laying, -laid** /-láyd/, **-laid**) SPEND MONEY to spend money on sth

outlet /ówt let, -lət/ *n.* **1.** VENT a passage or opening for letting sth out, e.g. water or steam **2.** RELEASE FOR EMOTIONS a way of releasing emotions or impulses **3.** STORE a place where sth is sold, often a shop that sells the products of a particular manufacturer **4.** MARKET FOR GOODS a market providing goods or services for purchasers **5.** HOLE ON ELECTRICAL DEVICE FOR PLUG a hole on a piece of electrical equipment into which a plug fits **6.** MOUTH OF RIVER the lower end of a river where it flows into a lake or the sea **7.** STREAM DRAINING LAKE a stream or channel flowing from a larger body of water

outlier /ówt lī ər/ *n.* **1.** GEOL ROCK FORMATION an outcrop of rock that is separated from a main formation **2.** OUTLYING PART OF STH a separate part of a system, organization, or body that is at some distance from the main part **3.** SB LIVING AT DISTANCE FROM WORK sb who lives a long way from his or her place of work

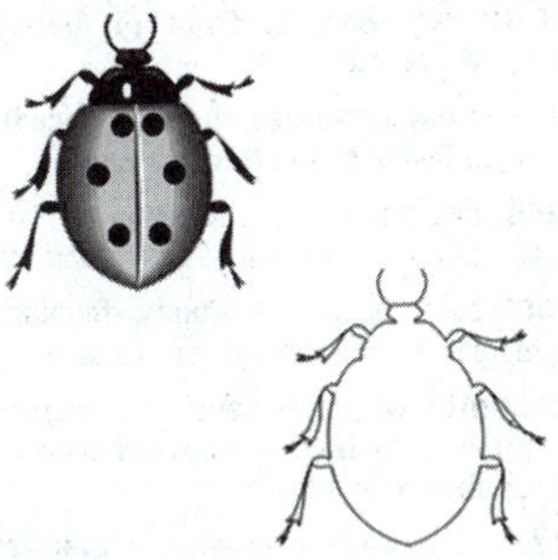

Outline

outline /ówt līn/ *n.* **1.** LINE THAT SHOWS SHAPE the edge or outer shape of sth **2.** LINE DRAWN ROUND STH a line drawn around the outside edge of sth **3.** DRAWING WITHOUT SHADING a style or example of drawing in which an object or figure is represented only by an outline **4.** ROUGH PLAN a list of the main points of a subject to be written about, or a rough idea of a proposed plan ■ *vt.* (**-lines, -lining, -lined**) **1.** DRAW MAIN FEATURES to draw a line showing or emphasizing the shape of sth **2.** GIVE ESSENTIAL ELEMENTS to give the main points of an argument or plan

outlive /owt lív/ (**-lives, -living, -lived**) *vt.* **1.** LIVE LONGER THAN to live longer than sb else **2.** OUTLAST to continue to exist beyond or last through sth ○ *The policy has outlived its usefulness.*

outlook /ówt lòok/ *n.* **1.** ATTITUDE an attitude or point of view **2.** LIKELY FUTURE expectations for the future, especially for the way a particular situation will develop **3.** VIEW a view seen from a particular place

out loud *adv.* aloud, rather than silently in sb's head

outlying /ówt lī ing/ *adj.* far from the central part of a particular place or region

outman /owt mán/ (**-mans, -manning, -manned**) *vt.* to have a larger force of people than an opponent has

outmanoeuvre /ówt mə nóovər/ (**-vres, -vring, -vred**) *vt.* to get the better of sb by using skill or cunning

outmatch /owt mách/ (**-matches, -matching, -matched**) *vt.* to prove stronger or better than sb else

outmoded /ówt mṓdid/ *adj.* **1.** OLD-FASHIONED no longer fashionable or widely used **2.** OBSOLETE having been superseded by sth newer or more efficient [Early 20thC. Translation of French *démodé*.] —**outmodedness** *n.*

outmost /ówt mōst/ *adj.* farthest away from the centre or main area [14thC. Alteration of UTMOST.]

outnumber /owt númbər/ (**-bers, -bering, -bered**) *vt.* to be more numerous than another group or set of things

out-of-body *adj.* undergoing an experience in which a person's consciousness appears to have an existence separate from the body, enabling the subject to see his or her own body from the outside

out of bounds *adj., adv.* in or indicating a place that is beyond the established or official boundaries

out-of-court *adj.* arranged without going to court or without completing a court case, usually in an effort to avoid a long court case or to minimize costs

out-of-date *adj.* old-fashioned or no longer current

out-of-doors *adj.* = **outdoors**

out of order *adj.* **1.** NOT FUNCTIONING used about a machine that is not working properly **2.** NOT OBEYING RULES OF SPEAKING used about sb who is not following the official procedures of a court or parliament, e.g. by speaking when told not to **3.** BEHAVING BADLY not acceptable, or behaving in an unacceptable way (*informal*) ○ *What he said was well out of order.*

out-of-pocket *adj.* **1.** HAVING LOST MONEY with less money than before, after spending some on sth that did not produce good results ○ *I was seriously out-of-pocket.* **2.** REQUIRING SB TO SPEND CASH relating to or being expenses paid for with cash ○ *out-of-pocket expenses* **3.** WITH NO MONEY with no money to spend

out-of-the-way *adj.* **1.** REMOTE far from a populated area or difficult to get to **2.** UNUSUAL uncommon or unconventional

out-of-town *adj.* coming from or happening in another town or city

outpace /owt pάyss/ (**-paces, -pacing, -paced**) *vt.* to do better or go faster than sth or sb else

outpatient /ówt paysh'nt/ *n.* a patient who receives treatment at a hospital without staying overnight

outperform /ówt pər fáwrm/ (**-forms, -forming, -formed**) *vt.* to perform better than sb or sth else

outplacement /ówt playssmənt/ *n.* a service offered by a company to help employees who are being dismissed find new jobs

outplay /owt pláy/ (**-plays, -playing, -played**) *vt.* to play better than an opponent

outpoint /owt póynt/ (**-points, -pointing, -pointed**) *vt.* **1.** SAIL CLOSER TO WIND to sail closer to the wind than another ship **2.** SCORE MORE POINTS to score more points than sb else

outport /ówt pawrt/ *n.* **1.** SECONDARY PORT a secondary port near another port but in deeper water, used for larger vessels **2.** *Can* NEWFOUNDLAND FISHING VILLAGE a small remote fishing village, especially one on the Newfoundland coast

outpost /ówt pōst/ *n.* **1.** TROOPS APART FROM MAIN FORCE a small group of troops stationed at a distance from the main body of an army and assigned to guard a particular place or area **2.** MILITARY BASE a small military base in a remote area or different country **3.** BASE a settlement in unfamiliar territory or on a frontier

outpour *vti.* /owt páwr/ (**-pours, -pouring, -poured**) FLOW OUT to flow out quickly or make sth flow out quickly ■ *n.* /ówt pawr/ STH FLOWING sth that flows out freely or the act of flowing out

outpouring /ówt pawring/ *n.* sth that pours or floods out, e.g. lava or a strong emotion

output /ówt pŏot/ *n.* **1.** PRODUCTION the act of producing **2.** YIELD an amount of sth produced or manufactured, especially during a fixed period of time **3.** CREATIVE OR ARTISTIC PRODUCTION creative or intellectual work produced by sb ○ *her literary output* **4.** ENERGY PRODUCED energy or power produced by a system **5.** ELEC ENG ELECTRICAL POWER the electrical energy, measured in watts, delivered by a generator or consumed by an electronic circuit **6.** COMPUT INFORMATION FROM COMPUTER information produced by a computer ■ *vt.* (**-puts, -putting, -put** *or* **-putted**) PRODUCE COMPUTER INFORMATION to display information from a computer on a monitor or direct it to a printer or other device

outrace /owt ráyss/ (**-races, -racing, -raced**) *vt.* to do sth better or faster than others

outrage /ówt rayj/ *n.* **1.** VIOLENT ACT an extremely violent or cruel act **2.** OFFENSIVE ACT a very offensive or insulting act **3.** FURY intense anger and indignation aroused by a violent or offensive act ■ *vt.* (**-rages, -raging, -raged**) **1.** ATTACK OR VIOLATE to commit a vicious crime against sb **2.** AROUSE ANGER IN SB to make sb feel intense anger or indignation **3.** RAPE to rape sb (*literary*) [13thC. Via French, 'excess, atrocity', from Old French *outrer* 'to exceed', ultimately from Latin *ultra* 'beyond' (see ULTRA-). The meaning was later influenced by RAGE.]

outrageous /owt ráyjəss/ *adj.* **1.** EXTRAORDINARY AND UNCONVENTIONAL extravagant or unconventional, and likely to shock people **2.** MORALLY SHOCKING violating accepted standards of decency or morality **3.** EXCESSIVE exceeding the bounds of what is reasonable or expected ○ *outrageous prices* **4.** VIOLENT OR CRUEL violent or unrestrained in mood or action —**outrageously** *adv.* —**outrageousness** *n.*

outrange /owt ráynj/ (**-ranges, -ranging, -ranged**) *vt.* to have a greater range than sth else of the same class, e.g. a firearm or missile

outrank /owt rángk/ (**-ranks, -ranking, -ranked**) *vt.* to have a higher rank or status than sb else

outré /ŏo tray/ *adj.* passing well beyond what is usual, normal, or generally acceptable [Early 18thC. Via French from Old French, the past participle of *outrer* 'to go too far' (see OUTRAGE).]

outreach *vt.* /owt réech/ (**-reaches, -reaching, -reached**) **1.** REACH FARTHER to reach or extend farther than sb or sth else **2.** EXCEED to exceed or go beyond a limit ■ *n.* /ówt reech/ **1.** PROVISION OF COMMUNITY SERVICES the provision of information or services to groups in society who might otherwise be neglected ○ *an outreach programme for people who cannot read* **2.** EXTENT OF REACH the length or extent of the reach of sb or sth ○ *the outreach of a communications network*

out relief *n.* money that was given by the state to poor people who were not living in a workhouse

outride /owt ríd/ (**-rides, -riding, -rode** /-rṓd/, **-ridden** /-rídd'n/) *vt.* **1.** RIDE BETTER OR FASTER to ride better, farther, or faster than sb else **2.** SHIPPING SURVIVE STORM to survive the violence of the wind and waves during a storm

outrider /ówt rīdər/ *n.* **1.** ESCORT sb who rides in front of or at the side of a carriage, motor vehicle, or race horse and acts as an escort **2.** FORERUNNER sb who goes ahead of a group and acts as a scout [Mid-16thC. The word originally denoted an officer of the sheriff's court who collected dues and issued summonses.]

outrigger /ówt riggər/ *n.* **1.** PART OF A BOAT a beam or framework sticking out from the side of a boat, used to extend a rope or sail or as a brace for an oarlock **2.** FRAMEWORK ON CANOE a long float attached to a framework that projects from the side of a seagoing canoe to prevent it from capsizing **3.** KIND OF BOAT OR CANOE a boat or canoe fitted with an outrigger **4.** AIR STRUCTURE ON AIRCRAFT a projection attached to an aircraft or other vehicle or machine to stabilize it or to support sth [Mid-18thC. Origin uncertain: perhaps an alteration (influenced by RIG) of obsolete *outligger*, a type of spar for extending a sail, from Dutch *uitligger*.]

outright *adv.* /owt rít/ **1.** WHOLLY wholly and completely ○ *He now owns the business outright.* **2.** INSTANTLY immediately or instantly ○ *They refused our offer outright.* **3.** CANDIDLY openly and without reservation ○ *I told him outright that he was making a big mistake.* ■ *adj.* /ówt rīt/ **1.** ABSOLUTE complete or total ○ *an outright lie* **2.** WITHOUT QUALIFICATIONS without restrictions or limitations ○ *The car was an outright gift from the corporation.*

outrun /owt rún/ (**-runs, -running, -ran** /-rán/, **-run**) *vt.* **1.** RUN FASTER to run faster or farther than sb else **2.** RUN AWAY to escape by or as if by running faster than a pursuer ○ *outrun the bill collectors* ○ *The hare outran the wolf.* **3.** EXCEED to develop faster or to exceed ○ *Demand for petrol began to outrun supply.*

outsell /owt sél/ (**-sells, -selling, -sold** /-sṓld/, **-sold**) *vt.* **1.** SELL MORE to be sold faster or in greater quantities than sth else **2.** BE BETTER AT SELLING to sell more than another salesperson

outset /ówt set/ *n.* the beginning or initial stage of an activity

outshine /owt shín/ (**-shines, -shining, -shone** /-shón/, **-shone**) *vt.* **1.** SHINE BRIGHTER to shine brighter than sth else **2.** SURPASS to surpass sb or sth else, especially in terms of excellence or quality

outshoot *vt.* /owt shŏot/ (**-shoots, -shooting, -shot** /-shót/, **-shot**) SHOOT BETTER to shoot better than sb else ■ *n.* /ówt shoot/ PROJECTION sth that projects or shoots out

outside /owt síd/ CORE MEANING: a grammatical word indicating the outer surface or appearance of sth ○ (noun) *Grill the chicken wings until the outsides are crisp.* ○ (adv) *The house still needs to be painted outside.*

1. *adv., prep., adj.* OUT OF DOORS in the open air rather than inside a building ○ (adv) *We should head outside soon if we're going to start the barbecue.* ○ (prep) *I'll meet you outside the post office.* ○ (adj) *an outside toilet* **2.** *adj., adv., prep.* BEYOND IMMEDIATE ENVIRONMENT happening, existing, or originating in places, people, or groups other than your own or what you are used to ○ (adj) *It was claimed that most of the substandard work had been done by outside contractors.* ○ (adv) *in the world outside* ○ (prep) *married outside her religion* **3.** *adj.* SLIGHT slight or remote ○ *There's an outside chance we may still be able to get tickets.* **4.** *adj.* MAXIMUM the most extreme possible or probable ○ *an outside estimate of three months to complete the job* **5.** *adj.* FARTHEST FROM SIDE OF ROAD farthest from the side of a road or centre of a race track ○ *coming up fast in the outside lane* **6.** *prep.* BEYOND THE SCOPE OF not included in the range or scope of sth ○ *Such behaviour is completely outside my comprehension.* **7.** *n.* EXISTENCE NOT IN AN INSTITUTION existence not in an institution such as prison or a psychiatric hospital ○ *We wondered what life was like on the outside.* **8.** *n.* AREA FARTHEST FROM SIDE OF ROAD the part farthest from the side of a road or centre of a race track ○ *Large crowds of shoppers forced her to walk on the outside of the pavement.* **9.** *n.* HEAVILY POPULATED AREA OF CANADA the most populous areas of Canada along the coasts ◇ **at the outside** at the maximum amount or time that can be expected ◇ **outside of** other than the person or thing mentioned

outside broadcast *n.* a radio or television programme not recorded or filmed in a studio. US term **remote**

outsider /owt sídər/ *n.* **1.** SB WHO DOES NOT BELONG sb who is not part of a particular group or organization **2.** COMPETITOR UNLIKELY TO WIN a competitor or candidate who is considered unlikely to win

WORD KEY: CULTURAL NOTE

The Outsider, a novel by French writer Albert Camus (1942). This classic existentialist work is also known as *The Stranger*. It is set in Algiers and recounts how a young man's extreme sense of alienation leads him to commit murder. During his trial, however, the absurdities of the judicial process compel him to acknowledge the value of human life.

outsight /ówt sīt/ *n.* the ability to take note of or judge external things [Early 17thC. Modelled on 'insight'.]

outsize /ówt síz, ówt sīz/ *n.* EXTRA LARGE SIZE a size that is larger than usual ■ *adj.* **outsize, outsized** EXTRA LARGE much larger, heavier, or more extensive than is usual or expected ○ *an outsize ego*

outskirts /ówt skurts/ *npl.* the areas at the edge of a town or city, farthest from the centre

outsmart /owt smaárt/ (**-smarts, -smarting, -smarted**) *vt.* to use cunning or cleverness to get an advantage over sb

outsold past participle, past tense of **outsell**

outsole /ówt sōl/ *n.* the outer sole of a boot or shoe [Late 19thC. Modelled on 'insole'.]

outsource /ówt sawrss/ (**-sources, -sourcing, -sourced**) *vt.* to buy labour or parts from a source outside a company or business, usually as a means of cutting costs or to employ expertise not available within the company

outspan *n.* /ówt span/ *S Africa* PLACE FOR PEOPLE TO STOP a place kept available on a farm for people travelling to stop to rest their animals ■ *vti.* /owt spán/ (**-spans, -spanning, -spanned**) *S Africa* UNHARNESS ANIMAL to remove a yoke or harness from an animal [Early 19thC. Via Afrikaans *uitspan* 'to unyoke, unharness' from Middle Dutch *uitspannen*.]

outspend /owt spénd/ (**-spends, -spending, -spent** /-spént/, **-spent**) *vt.* **1.** SPEND MORE THAN to spend more than sb else **2.** EXCEED SPENDING LIMITS OF to exceed fixed limits for sth in spending ○ *outspent our budget*

a at; aa father; aw all; ay day; air hair; ə about, edible, item, common, circus; e egg; ee eel; hw when; i it, happy; ī ice; 'l apple; 'm rhythm; 'n fashion; o odd; ō open; ŏo good; oo pool; ow owl; oy oil; th thin; t͟h this; u up; ur urge;

outspoken /owt spṓkən/ adj. expressing opinions directly, frankly, and fearlessly —**outspokenly** adv. —**outspokenness** n.

outspread adj. /owt spred/ STRETCHED OUT extended or spread out flat ■ vt. /owt spréd/ (-spreads, -spreading, -spread) EXTEND to stretch out or extend sth ■ n. ACT OF SPREADING OUT the act or an example of extending outwards

outstand /owt stánd/ (-stands, -standing, -stood /-stŏod/, -stood) vi. to stand out or be prominent

outstanding /owt stánding/ adj. 1. UNUSUALLY EXCELLENT excellent, and superior to others in the same group or category ○ outstanding work 2. NOT YET RESOLVED not yet paid, resolved, or dealt with ○ outstanding debts 3. JUTTING OUT jutting outwards or upwards 4. STOCK EXCH PUBLICLY SOLD publicly issued and sold as securities —**outstandingly** adv.

outstare /owt staír/ (-stares, -staring, -stared) vt. to make sb look away or submit by staring hard

outstation /owt staysh'n/ n. a post or station in a remote unsettled spot

outstay /owt stáy/ (-stays, -staying, -stayed) vt. 1. STAY LONGER THAN to stay longer than other people, or longer than is appropriate ○ outstayed their welcome 2. SHOW GREATER ENDURANCE THAN to show greater endurance than sb ○ outstayed their rivals

outstood past participle, past tense of **outstand**

outstretch /owt stréch/ (-stretches, -stretching, -stretched) vt. to hold out or extend sth

outstrip /owt stríp/ (-strips, -stripping, -stripped) vt. 1. DO BETTER THAN to achieve more or go faster than sb, especially a competitor 2. EXCEED to be greater than sth ○ Demand for their products has already outstripped supply.

outswing /owt swing/ n. the movement of a bowled cricket ball from the leg side to the off side

outta, **outa** prep. used as a written representation of 'out of', reflecting popular pronunciation (informal) ○ I'm outta here. [From a pronunciation of out of]

outtake /owt tayk/ n. 1. EXCLUDED SECTION OF FILM a recorded scene or sequence that is not included in the final version of a film or television programme, usually because it contains mistakes ○ The outtakes were funnier than the movie itself. 2. REJECTED RECORDING a recording not used in the final version of an album

outthrust /owt thrúst/ adj. extending out beyond sth ○ the dog's outthrust paw

outturn /owt turn/ n. the amount produced during a specific period [Late 18thC. From turn out.]

outvote /owt vṓt/ (-votes, -voting, -voted) vt. to defeat other candidates or a proposal by a majority of votes

outward /ówtwərd/ CORE MEANING: a grammatical word indicating that sth is outside or on or towards the exterior of sth, or relates to the exterior of sth ○ the rustic balustrading that bounded the arbour on the outward side
1. adj. VISIBLE clearly observable ○ She gave no outward indication that she was upset. 2. adj. RELATING TO THE PHYSICAL BODY relating to the physical body rather than the mind or spirit ○ his outward appearance reflected his inner turmoil 3. adj. APPARENT apparent or superficial ○ can't judge by outward appearances 4. adj. OUTBOUND heading away from a place 5. adv. = outwards 6. n. MATERIAL WORLD the reality of the external world (literary) [Old English ūtanweard, ūteweard] —**outwardness** n.

outward-bound adj. making an outgoing journey or passage

outwardly /ówtwərdli/ adv. in appearance rather than in reality

outwards /ówtwərdz/, **outward** adv. towards the outside and away from the inside or middle

outwash /owt wosh/ n. sand and gravel deposited by streams that are flowing away from a glacier

outwear /owt waír/ (-wears, -wearing, -wore /-wáwr/, -worn /-wáwrn/) vt. to last longer or wear better than sth else

outweigh /owt wáy/ (-weighs, -weighing, -weighed) vt. 1. BE MORE CRUCIAL THAN to be more important or valu-

able than sth else 2. WEIGH MORE THAN to weigh more than sb or sth else

outwit /owt wít/ (-wits, -witting, -witted) vt. 1. GAIN ADVANTAGE OVER SB THROUGH CUNNING to use cunning or trickery to get an advantage over sb 2. BE SMARTER THAN SB to be more intelligent than sb (archaic)

outwith /owt wíth/ prep. Scotland outside or beyond ○ working outwith normal hours [Pre-12thC]

outwore past tense of **outwear**

outwork vt. /owt wúrk/ (-works, -working, -worked) WORK HARDER THAN to work harder or faster than sb ■ n. /owt wurk/ 1. MILITARY OUTPOST a trench or fortification built beyond the main line of defence 2. WORK DONE AT HOME work done for a company outside the company's premises

outworker /owt wurkər/ n. sb who works for a company from home rather than on the company's premises

outworn /owt wáwrn/ adj. outdated or no longer useful. Past participle of **outwear**

ouzel /ṓoz'l/ n. a small European bird of the thrush family that has dark plumage with a white band across its throat. Latin name: Turdus torquatus. [Old English ōsle 'blackbird'. Ultimately from an Indo-European word that is also the ancestor of English merle and merlon.]

ouzo /ṓozṓ/ (plural -zos) n. a colourless Greek alcoholic spirit flavoured with aniseed [Late 19thC. From modern Greek, of uncertain origin.]

ova npl. plural of **ovum**

oval /ṓv'l/ adj. EGG-SHAPED shaped like an egg ■ n. EGG SHAPE sth shaped like an egg [Late 16thC. From medieval Latin ovalis, from Latin ovum 'egg' (see OVUM).] —**ovally** adv. —**ovalness** n.

ovalbumin /ōv álbyŏomin, ōv al byŏomin/ n. the main crystalline protein or albumin found in egg whites [Mid-19thC. From Latin ovi albumen, literally 'white of egg', from ovum 'egg' + albumen (see ALBUMEN).]

Oval Office n. 1. US PRESIDENT'S OFFICE an oval-shaped room in the White House that is the private office used by the president of the United States 2. US PRESIDENCY the power and authority of the president of the United States

oval window n. a membranous opening between the middle ear and the inner ear that transmits sound vibrations [From its shape]

Ovambo /ō vámbō/ (plural -bo or -bos) n. 1. MEMBER OF AFRICAN PEOPLE a member of a Black people that lives in parts of southern Africa, especially in Angola and Namibia 2. OVAMBO LANGUAGE the Bantu language of the Ovambo people. It belongs to the Benue-Congo branch of Niger-Congo languages. Ovambo is spoken by about 700,000 people. [Mid-19thC. Of Bantu origin, literally 'people of leisure'.] —**Ovambo** adj.

ovariectomy /ō vári éktəmi/ (plural -mies) n. the surgical removal of one or both ovaries

ovariotomy /ō vári óttəmi/ (plural -mies) n. 1. INCISION INTO OVARY a surgical incision into an ovary 2. = ovariectomy

ovaritis /ōvə rítiss/ n. = oophoritis

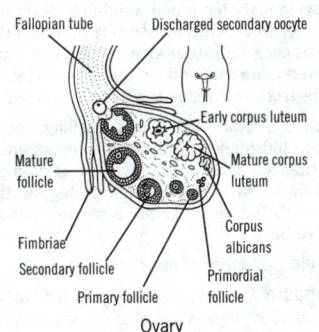

Ovary

ovary /ṓvəri/ (plural -ries) n. 1. FEMALE REPRODUCTIVE ORGAN either of the two female reproductive organs that produce eggs and, in vertebrates, also produce the sex hormones oestrogen and progesterone 2. PART OF A FLOWER the lower part of a pistil that bears ovules and ripens into a fruit [Mid-17thC. From modern Latin

ovarium, from Latin ovum (see OVUM).] —**ovarian** /ō vári ən/ adj.

ovate /ṓ vayt/ adj. 1. EGG-SHAPED shaped like an egg 2. BOT SHAPED LIKE A POINTED OVAL used to describe a leaf or petal that is broad and rounded at the base and tapers towards the tip [Mid-18thC. From Latin ovatus 'egg-shaped', from ovum (see OVUM).] —**ovately** adv.

ovation /ō váysh'n/ n. 1. LOUD AND LONG APPLAUSE enthusiastic applause or cheering, especially from a crowd or large group of people 2. HIST ROMAN VICTORY CELEBRATION an ancient Roman victory ceremony for a returning military hero [Mid-16thC. Via the Latin stem ovation- from ovare 'to rejoice', ultimately from an imitation of the sound of exulting.] —**ovational** adj.

oven /úvv'n/ n. a compartment warmed by a heat source and used for baking, roasting, or drying [Old English ofen. Ultimately from an Indo-European word meaning 'cooker' that is also the ancestor of English olla.]

ovenable /úvv'nəb'l/ adj. heat-resistant, or in heat-resistant packaging and ready to be cooked without further preparation ○ The frozen dinner came in an ovenable paperboard tray.

ovenbird /úvv'n burd/ n. 1. NORTH AMERICAN BIRD a North American warbler that has a shrill call and builds a dome-shaped nest on the ground. Latin name: Seiurus aurocapillus. 2. SOUTH AMERICAN BIRD small brown South American bird that builds a dome-shaped nest from clay and dried leaves. Genus: Furnarius. [Early 19thC. From the oven-like shape of the birds' nests.]

oven glove n. a padded hand covering used as protection when putting hot dishes into and taking them out of an oven

ovenproof /úvv'n proof/ adj. capable of being used in an oven without being damaged by the heat

oven-ready adj. already prepared and ready to be cooked or heated before eating

ovenware /úvv'n wair/ n. heat-resistant dishes that can be used for baking or roasting as well as for serving

over /ṓvər/ (overs, overing, overed) CORE MEANING: a grammatical word used to indicate a position directly above sth, either resting on the top of sth, or above the upper surface of sth with a space in between ○ (prep) a framed portrait over the fireplace ○ (prep) He wore a red flannel shirt over a T-shirt. ○ (prep) Julia was bent over the sink washing glasses. ○ (adv) flocks of geese flying over ○ (adv) Heat the milk and pour it over.
1. prep., adv. ON OR TO OTHER SIDE OF positioned on or moving to the other side of sth such as a barrier, obstacle, or area of land ○ (prep) To see the cathedral you need to cross over the river. ○ (adv) He climbed over into the next field. 2. prep., adv. THROUGHOUT throughout the whole extent of sth ○ (prep) travelling over Europe ○ (prep) In the past few years, fifties diners have sprung up all over town. ○ (adv) People are the same the world over. 3. prep., adv. MORE THAN more than a particular amount, measurement, or age ○ (prep) go over your quota ○ (adv) people 30 and over 4. adv. ACROSS INTERVENING SPACE positioned in or moving to a point across intervening space ○ She reached over and turned off the TV. ○ Jim sent a couple of guys over to help out. 5. adv. SO AS TO FALL so as to change position, especially from being upright ○ knocked over a pile of books ○ He rolled over and turned out the light. 6. adv. REMAINING remaining or surplus after what was needed has been used ○ There was plenty of food left over from the party. 7. adv. US AGAIN doing sth again, or again from the beginning ○ If you make a mistake you'll just have to start over. 8. prep. BY MEANS OF by means of a device for communication such as a radio or telephone ○ talk over the phone 9. prep. ABOUT on the subject of or related to ○ grieving over the loss of her husband 10. prep. AFFECTING as an effect or influence upon sb or sth ○ exercise more control over file access. 11. prep. DURING happening during or throughout a period of time or an occasion ○ We can discuss this over lunch. 12. prep. RECOVERED FROM having recovered from the bad effects of sth such as an illness ○ get over a virus. 13. prep. IN PREFERENCE TO in preference to sth else ○ I'd choose steak over fish every time. 14. adj. FINISHED finished or no longer in progress ○ When

all this is over I'm going on holiday. **15.** *adv.* **VERY** to a great extent or degree ○ *He's not over happy at the moment* **16.** *interj.* RADIO **WORD SHOWING SB'S TURN TO SPEAK** used when communicating via radio to indicate that sb has finished talking and it is the other person's turn to speak **17.** *n.* *US* GAMBLING **SCORE ABOVE PARTICULAR NUMBER IN A WAGER** in a wager, the score above a particular number of points or an amount above a particular total ○ *bet the over in the Super Bowl* **18.** *n.* CRICKET **BOWLING OF SIX BALLS** a series of six correctly bowled balls in cricket, or the play during this [Old English *ofer.* Ultimately from an Indo-European word that is also the ancestor of English *super-* and *hyper-*.] ◇ **over again** once more ◇ **over against 1.** opposite to **2.** in contrast with or in opposition to ◇ **over and above** in addition to or in excess of sth ○ *benefits over and above the basic salary* ◇ **over and over** repeatedly or a great deal

overabundance /ṓvər ə bʊ́ndənss/ *n.* an amount greater than what is needed or appropriate —**overabundant** *adj.*

overachieve /ṓvər ə chéev/ **(-achieves, -achieving, -achieved)** *vi.* to perform better or be more successful than expected —**overachiever** *n.* —**overachievement** *n.*

overact /ṓvər ákt/ **(-acts, -acting, -acted)** *vti.* to exaggerate movements or emotions, especially when acting in a performance

overactive /ṓvər áktiv/ *adj.* excessively or abnormally active

overage[1] /ṓvər áyj/ *adj.* **1. TOO OLD FOR STH** older than the age fixed as a standard or considered appropriate for a particular activity **2. NO LONGER USEFUL** too old to be useful (*offensive if used of people*)

overage[2] /ṓvərij/ *n.* money, goods, or sth else in excess of what is proper or shown in the records [Mid-20thC. Formed from OVER.]

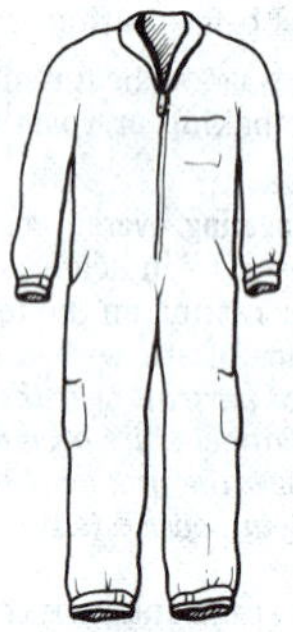

Overalls

overall *adj.* /ṓvər awl/, *adv.* /ṓvəráwl/ **1. END TO END** from one extremity to the other **2. TOTAL** including everything ■ *adj.* /ṓvər awl/ **GENERAL** considered as a whole ○ *an overall impression* ■ *adv.* /ṓvəráwl/ **ON THE WHOLE** in general or as a whole ○ *Overall, we were disappointed with the results.* ■ *n.* /ṓvər awl/ CLOTHES **PROTECTIVE GARMENT** a loose-fitting lightweight piece of clothing like a coat, worn over ordinary clothes to protect them ■ **overalls** *npl.* **1. ONE-PIECE PROTECTIVE GARMENT** a one-piece garment with long sleeves and trousers worn to protect a worker's clothes from dirt or wear **2. WORK TROUSERS WITH BIB** loose-fitting trousers that have a bib and shoulder straps, originally worn over ordinary clothing as a protection from dirt and wear

overall majority *n.* a majority of votes in an election when measured against the total combined votes of all other competing political parties

overarch /ṓvər áarch/ **(-arches, -arching, -arched)** *vt.* to form an arch over sth or somewhere

overarching /ṓvər áarching/ *adj.* embracing or overshadowing everything

overarm /ṓvər aarm/ *adj.* **1. WITH ARM ABOVE SHOULDER** thrown or done with the arm raised above the shoulder and rotating forward **2. WITH ARM RAISED** beginning a stroke in swimming with the arm raised above the shoulder and rotating forward ■ *adv.* SPORTS **WITH HAND ABOVE SHOULDER** with the hand coming forward in a semicircular motion from behind and above the shoulder. US term **overhand**

overate past tense of **overeat**

overawe /ṓvər áw/ **(-awes, -awing, -awed)** *vt.* to make sb feel subdued or inhibited by inspiring respect and some fear

overbalance /ṓvər bállənss/ *v.* **(-ances, -ancing, -anced) 1.** *vti.* **LOSE BALANCE** to lose balance, or make sb or sth lose balance **2.** *vt.* **BE MORE IMPORTANT THAN** to have greater weight or importance than sth else ■ *n.* **PREPONDERANCE** an excess of an amount, quantity, or weight

overbear /ṓvər báir/ **(-bears, -bearing, -bore** /-báwr/, **-borne** /-báwrn/) *v.* **1.** *vt.* **OVERPOWER SB** to defeat sb by having superior weight or strength **2.** *vt.* **OUTWEIGH** to be more important than other considerations **3.** *vi.* **PRODUCE TOO MUCH** to produce too much fruit or too many offspring

overbearing /ṓvər báiring/ *adj.* arrogant and tending to order people around —**overbearingly** *adv.* —**overbearingness** *n.*

overbid *v.* /ṓvər bíd/ **(-bids, -bidding, -bid, -bidden** *or* **-bid) 1.** *vti.* **BID MORE THAN WORTH OF STH** to bid more than sth is worth **2.** *vi.* BRIDGE **BID FOR TOO MANY TRICKS** to bid for more tricks than can be won ■ *n.* /ṓvərbid/ **HIGHER BID** a bid that is higher than sb else's bid —**overbidder** /ṓvər bíddər/ *n.*

overbite /ṓvər bīt/ *n.* a faulty alignment of the teeth in which the upper front teeth project too far over the lower teeth when the mouth is closed

overblouse /ṓvər blowz/ *n.* a blouse designed to be worn outside the waistband of a skirt or trousers

overblow /ṓvər blṓ/ **(-blows, -blowing, -blew** /-blóo/, **-blown** /-blṓn/) *vti.* to blow a wind instrument with extra force so as to produce an overtone

overblown /ṓvər blṓn/ *adj.* **1. EXAGGERATED** done to excess and seeming exaggerated ○ *overblown stories that are barely credible* **2. PRETENTIOUS** showing pomposity or pretentiousness ○ *His style of writing is overblown and excessively wordy.* **3. PAST BEST** past full bloom and beginning to die ○ *an overblown rose*

overboard /ṓvər bawrd, ṓvər báwrd/ *adv.* over the side of a ship and into the water [Old English *ofer bord,* literally 'over the side']

overbook /ṓvər bóok/ **(-books, -booking, -booked)** *vti.* to take more reservations than there are seats or places available in a place

overbore past tense of **overbear**

overborne, overborn past participle of **overbear**

overbought /ṓvər báwt/ *adj.* characterized by high prices on the stock exchange as the result of recent heavy trading, and so not likely to rise further in the near future

overbuild /ṓvər bíld/ **(-builds, -building, -built** /-bílt/, **-built) *v.* 1.** *vti.* **BUILD TOO MUCH** to construct more buildings than are necessary or desirable in an area **2.** *vti.* **BUILD OVERAMBITIOUSLY** to construct sth that is too large or elaborate **3.** *vt.* **BUILD ON STH ELSE** to build sth on top of a particular place or thing

overburden *vt.* /ṓvər búrd'n/ **(-dens, -dening, -dened) OVERLOAD** to place too much weight or worry on sb or sth ○ *overburdened with debt* ■ *n.* /ṓvər burd'n/ **1. EXCESSIVE BURDEN** an excessive or onerous burden **2. SOIL LAYERED OVER ROCK** soil or other material layered over bedrock or over any geological deposit

overcall *vti.* /ṓvər káwl/ **(-calls, -calling, -called) BID HIGHER** to bid higher than a bridge opponent before a partner has made a positive bid ■ *n.* /ṓvər kawl/ **HIGHER BID** a bid in bridge that is higher than an opponent's bid, made before a partner has made a positive bid

overcame past tense of **overcome**

overcapacity /ṓvər kə pássəti/ *n.* an ability to produce goods or provide services that exceed demand

overcapitalize /ṓvər káppit'l īz/ **(-izes, -izing, -ized), overcapitalise (-ises, -ising, -ised)** *vt.* **1. SUPPLY TOO MUCH CAPITAL TO** to provide a business with more capital than is justified by its condition or its ability to make profits **2. OVERVALUE** to give a corporation a nominal value that is higher than its fair market value

overcast *adj.* /ṓvər kaast/ **1.** METEOROL **CLOUDY** very cloudy, with no sun showing **2.** SEW **SEWN WITH LONG STITCHES** sewn along the edge with long loose stitches that prevent a piece of fabric from unravelling ■ *n.* /ṓvər kaast/ **1.** METEOROL **HEAVY CLOUD COVER** a heavy covering of clouds in the sky **2.** MINING **MINE ARCH** an arch in a mine supporting a passage above it ■ *v.* /ṓvər káast/ **(-casts, -casting, -casted) 1.** *vi.* METEOROL **BECOME CLOUDY** to become cloudy or dull **2.** *vt.* SEW **SECURE WITH LOOSE STITCHES** to sew the edge of a piece of fabric with an overcast stitch

overcasting /ṓvər kaasting/ *n.* long slanting stitches sewn loosely across the edge of a piece of fabric to prevent it from unravelling

overcharge *v.* /ṓvər cháarj/ **(-charges, -charging, -charged) 1.** *vti.* **CHARGE TOO MUCH** to charge sb too much money for sth **2.** *vt.* **PUT EXCESSIVE POWER INTO** to charge a battery or circuit with more electricity than it can safely hold **3.** *vt.* **OVERFILL OR OVERLOAD STH** to fill or load sth with more than it can hold or bear **4.** *vt.* **EXAGGERATE STH** to make sth seem greater or more important than it actually is (*literary*) ■ *n.* /ṓvər chaarj/ **1. EXCESSIVE CHARGE** an excessively high charge for sth **2. ACT OF CHARGING TOO MUCH** an act of charging too much for sth

overcloud /ṓvər klówd/ **(-clouds, -clouding, -clouded)** *vti.* **1. CLOUD OVER** to cover sth, or become covered, with clouds **2. MAKE OR BECOME DIM** to become, or to make sth become, dim and gloomy (*formal*)

overcoat /ṓvər kōt/ *n.* **1. THICK OUTER COAT** a heavy coat worn over other outer clothes **2. overcoat, overcoating TOP LAYER OF PAINT** an additional protective layer of sth such as paint or varnish on top of a treated surface

overcome /ṓvər kúm/ **(-comes, -coming, -came** /ṓvər káym/, **-come)** *v.* **1.** *vt.* **MAKE SB HELPLESS** to make sb incapacited or helpless, or to break down sb's normal self-control (*usually passive*) ○ *completely overcome with emotion* **2.** *vt.* **SURMOUNT DIFFICULTY** to struggle successfully against a difficulty or disadvantage **3.** *vti.* **DEFEAT SB** to defeat sb or sth, especially in a conflict or competition (*formal*) **4.** *vi.* **WIN DESPITE OBSTACLES** to win or be successful, especially in spite of obstacles [Old English; from OVER + COME]

WORD KEY: SYNONYMS

See Synonyms at ***defeat.***

overcommit /ṓvər kə mít/ **(-mits, -mitting, -mitted)** *vti.* to undertake, or to make sb or yourself undertake, more than can be accomplished (*often passive*)

overcompensate /ṓvər kómpən sayt/ **(-sates, -sating, -sated)** *vti.* **1. TRY TOO HARD TO OVERCOME** to try too hard to make up for a disadvantage or shortcoming and fall into a fault of another kind **2. REWARD TOO MUCH** to pay sb too much in recompense or compensation for sth done —**overcompensation** /-kómpən sáysh'n/ *n.* —**overcompensatory** *adj.*

overconfident /ṓvər kónfidənt/ *adj.* excessively confident or self-assured —**overconfidently** *adv.*

overcook /ṓvər kóok/ **(-cooks, -cooking, -cooked)** *vt.* to cook sth so long that it loses its flavour and texture

overcorrect /ṓvər kə rékt/ *vti.* **(-rects, -recting, -rected) CORRECT STH MORE THAN IS NECESSARY** to do too much when trying to correct a mistake or fault, usually so that a further mistake is made ■ *adj.* **TOO CORRECT** excessively exact or proper

overcorrection /ṓvər kə réksh'n/ *n.* **1.** LING = **hypercorrection 2. UNNECESSARY CORRECTING OF STH** the fact of overcorrecting a mistake or fault

overcritical /ṓvər kríttik'l/ *adj.* judging or criticizing sb or sth too harshly or too fastidiously —**overcriticalness** *n.*

overcrop /ṓvər króp/ **(-crops, -cropping, -cropped)** *vt.* to make soil infertile by removing its nutrients through continuous cultivation

overcrowd /ṓvər krówd/ **(-crowds, -crowding, -crowded)** *vt.* to put more people or things into an area than it is comfortably able to hold (*often passive*) —**overcrowded** *adj.* —**overcrowding** *n.*

overdevelop /ṓvər di véllәp/ **(-ops, -oping, -oped)** *vt.* **1. DEVELOP STH EXCESSIVELY** to develop sth to excess **2. DEVELOP FILM TOO MUCH** to exceed the amount of time, temperature, or strength of solution required to develop a photographic film, thereby producing too much contrast —**overdevelopment** *n.*

overdo /ṓvər dóo/ (**-does, -doing, -did** /-díd/, **-done** /-dún/) *vt.* **1.** OVERCOOK STH to cook food for too long **2.** SPOIL EFFECT BY EXAGGERATION to spoil the effect of sth by exaggerating it ○ *You rather overdid the sympathetic friend act on that occasion.* **3.** DO STH TO EXCESS to do sth too much, often with a harmful effect [Old English] —**overdoer** *n.* ◇ **overdo it** *or* **things 1.** to work too hard and tire yourself **2.** to do sth to excess

overdone past participle of **overdo**

overdose *n.* /ṓvər dōss/ DANGEROUS AMOUNT OF DRUG dangerously large dose of a drug, especially a narcotic, causing hospitalization or death ■ *vti.* /ṓvər dṓss/ (**-doses, -dosing, -dosed**) TAKE OR GIVE OVERDOSE to take or give sb an overdose

overdraft /ṓvər draaft/ *n.* **1.** AMOUNT OWED TO BANK the amount that an account holder owes a bank because the balance in the account does not cover the amount that he or she has withdrawn from or debited to it **2.** BORROWING LIMIT a limit up to which an account holder may borrow from a bank when there are no funds in his or her current account **3.** *US* = **overdraught**

overdramatize /ṓvər drámmə tīz/ (**-tizes, -tizing, -tized**), **overdramatise** (**-tises, -tising, -tised**) *vti.* to behave, or to treat sth, in an excessively dramatic way, e.g. by exaggerating the strength of your feelings or the gravity of a situation

overdraught /ṓvər draaft/ *n.* a current of air passed over a fire, e.g. in a furnace or kiln. US term **overdraft**

overdraw /ṓvər dráw/ (**-draws, -drawing, -drew** /-dróo/, **-drawn** /-dráwn/) *v.* **1.** *vti.* FIN LACK ENOUGH FUNDS IN BANK ACCOUNT to withdraw or have debited more money from a bank account than it has credited to it, so that money is owed to the bank **2.** *vt.* EXAGGERATE STH to exaggerate in describing or telling about sth **3.** *vti.* ARCHERY PULL BOW TOO TIGHT to pull a bow too tight

overdrawn /ṓvər dráwn/ *adj.* **1.** HAVING WITHDRAWN MORE THAN ACCOUNT CONTAINS owing money to a bank because an account has had more money withdrawn or debited from it than credited to it **2.** EXAGGERATED showing exaggeration in the description of sth

overdress *vti.* /ṓvər dréss/ (**-dresses, -dressing, -dressed**) DRESS TOO ELABORATELY to dress, or to dress sb, more formally or elaborately or in more clothes than the situation requires (*often passive*) ■ *n.* /ṓvər dress/ DRESS WORN OVER OUTER CLOTHING a dress that is intended to be worn over other outer clothing

overdrew *v.* past tense of **overdraw**

overdrive *n.* /ṓvər drīv/ **1.** HIGHEST ENGINE GEAR the highest gear in the engine of a motor vehicle that is used at high speeds for fuel economy and to save engine wear **2.** EXTRA HARD LEVEL OF ACTIVITY a particularly intense and productive mode of activity, usually possible only for short periods (*informal*) ○ *Production has gone into overdrive.* ■ *vt.* /ṓvər drīv/ (**-drives, -driving, -drove** /-drṓv/, **-driven** /-drívv'n/) DRIVE TOO HARD to drive sb, sth, or yourself too hard

overdub /ṓvər dub/ *vti.* (**-dubs, -dubbing, -dubbed**) RECORD EXTRA SOUND OR MUSIC FOR to add supplementary sound or music to a recording ■ *n.* EXTRA LAYER OF RECORDED SOUND a supplementary layer of sound or music added onto a recording

overdue /ṓvər dyóo/ *adj.* late or after the scheduled time, especially in arriving, occurring, or being paid ○ *The library said the books were overdue.*

overdye /ṓvər dī/ (**-dyes, -dying, -dyed**) *vt.* **1.** DYE STH TOO MUCH to use too much dye on sth **2.** DYE WITH ANOTHER COLOUR to dye a fabric with another colour over the original one

overeat /ṓvər éet/ (**-eats, -eating, -ate** /-áyt, -ét/, **-eaten** /-éet'n/) *vi.* to eat too much food, especially habitually —**overeater** *n.* —**overeating** *n.*

overelaborate *adj.* /ṓvər i lábbərət/ TOO ELABORATE excessively elaborate, fussy, or detailed ■ *vti.* /ṓvər i lábbə rayt/ (**-rates, -rating, -rated**) MAKE STH TOO ELABORATE to add or give too much elaboration or detail to sth

overemphasize /ṓvər émfə sīz/ (**-sizes, -sizing, -sized**), **overemphasise** (**-sises, -sising, -sised**) *vt.* to give sth too much importance, attention, or force

overestimate *vt.* /ṓvər ésti mayt/ (**-mates, -mating, -mated**) **1.** CALCULATE STH TOO HIGHLY to calculate the amount, value, or quantity of sth at too high a level **2.** GIVE EXCESSIVE MERIT OR IMPORTANCE TO to judge sb or sth to be better, greater, or more important than he, she, or it actually is ■ *n.* /ṓvər éstimət, -ésti mayt/ EXCESSIVELY HIGH ESTIMATE an estimate that is too high —**overestimation** /ṓvər ésti máysh'n/ *n.*

overexpose /ṓvər ik spṓz/ (**-poses, -posing, -posed**) *vt.* **1.** EXPOSE FILM TO TOO MUCH LIGHT to expose a photographic medium such as film to too much light or for too long a time, so that the colours or tones in the resulting photograph are too light **2.** ALLOW SB TOO MUCH OF STH to allow sb, or expose sb to, too much of sth, especially to allow sb to appear in public or in the media too often

overextend /ṓvər ik sténd/ (**-tends, -tending, -tended**) *v.* **1.** *vt.* STRETCH LIMITS OF RESOURCES to force sb, sth, or yourself beyond a safe or reasonable limit **2.** *vt.* PROLONG STH BEYOND EXPECTED DURATION to prolong sth beyond its normal or expected duration **3.** *vr.* RISK FINANCIAL RUIN to risk financial ruin by borrowing excessively, spending too much, or overcommitting resources

overfamiliar /ṓvər fə mílli ər/ *adj.* **1.** TOO FRIENDLY more friendly, informal, or intimate than is appropriate **2.** TOO WELL KNOWN used so much or so well known as to be boring or ineffective —**overfamiliarity** /ṓvər fə mílli árrəti/ *n.*

overfill /ṓvər fíl/ (**-fills, -filling, -filled**) *vti.* to become, or to make sb or sth become, too full

overfish /ṓvər físh/ (**-fishes, -fishing, -fished**) *vti.* to take too many fish from a body of water and so deplete its population

overflew past tense of **overfly**

overflight /ṓvər flīt/ *n.* the flight of an aircraft over an area

overflow *v.* /ṓvər flṓ/ (**-flows, -flowing, -flowed**) **1.** *vti.* FLOW OR POUR OVER to pour out over the limits or edge of a container because the container is too full of liquid **2.** *vt.* FLOOD STH to flood, cover, or flow over the surface of sth **3.** *vt.* SPREAD BEYOND LIMITS OF STH to spread beyond the area intended to contain it ○ *The crowd overflowed the hall into the street outside.* **4.** *vi.* BE OVERWHELMED BY EMOTION to be so full of an emotion as to feel the need to express it ■ *n.* /ṓvər flō/ **1.** EXCESS LIQUID CONTENTS excess liquid that flows or pours over the edge of sth **2.** EXCESS PEOPLE OR THINGS people or things that cannot be contained in the space originally set aside for them **3.** OUTLET THAT PREVENTS FLOODING an outlet that allows sth, usually a liquid, to escape before it runs over the top of its container, e.g. water in a cistern **4.** AMOUNT IN EXCESS OF LIMIT the amount by which a limit is exceeded **5.** COMPUTER'S INABILITY TO HANDLE LARGE DATA the inability of a location in computer memory to handle data of an excessively large magnitude, or an instance of this ○ *an overflow error.* ◊ **underflow**

overfly /ṓvər flī/ (**-flies, -flying, -flew** /-flóo/, **-flown** /-flṓn/) *vti.* **1.** FLY ABOVE AREA to fly over an area **2.** OVERSHOOT to fly past a specific point ○ *The plane has overflown the runway.*

overfold /ṓvər fōld/ *n.* a geological fold that has turned over on itself so that both sides dip in the same direction, causing the middle strata to be upside down

overfunding /ṓvər fúnding/ *n.* the policy of selling more securities than are needed to finance government spending

overgarment /ṓvər gaarmənt/ *n.* an article of clothing such as an outer garment or protective wear worn on top of other clothes

overglaze *n.* /ṓvər glayz/ **1.** EXTRA GLAZE ON POTTERY an additional coat of glaze applied to pottery or porcelain **2.** TOP LAYER OF DECORATION ON POTTERY a decoration applied to pottery or porcelain on top of the glaze ■ *vt.* /ṓvər gláyz/ (**-glazes, -glazing, -glazed**) APPLY GLAZE OR OVERGLAZE TO POTTERY to apply a glaze or overglaze to pottery or porcelain ■ *adj.* /ṓvər glayz/ APPLIED ON TOP OF GLAZE applied on top of a ceramic glaze ○ *overglaze colours*

overgraze /ṓvər gráyz/ (**-grazes, -grazing, -grazed**) *vt.* to graze land to the point that vegetation is harmed and as a consequence can no longer support stock (*often passive*)

overgrow /ṓvər grṓ/ (**-grows, -growing, -grew** /-gróo/, **-grown** /-grṓn/) *vti.* to grow so large, dense, or extensive as to cover the area of ground or container it is planted in and hinder the growth of other plants —**overgrowth** /ṓvər grōth/ *n.*

overgrown /ṓvər grṓn/ *adj.* **1.** COVERED WITH VEGETATION GROWING WITHOUT CHECK covered with plants or weeds that have been allowed to grow without check **2.** GROWN TOO MUCH FOR ALLOTTED SPACE grown too dense, large, or extensive for the area of ground or container in which it is planted **3.** IMMATURE grown to a large or adult size, but remaining immature ○ *behaving like an overgrown schoolboy*

overhand /ṓvər hand/ *adj.* **1.** SPORTS MADE WITH HAND RAISED OVER SHOULDER made with the hand coming forward in a semicircular motion from behind and above the shoulder **2.** SEWN ON TOP OF SEAM sewn with small vertical stitches passing over the two edges that are being joined together to make a seam ■ *adv.* *US* SPORTS = **overarm**

overhand knot *n.* a knot formed by passing one end of a cord or rope through a loop formed on another part of it, often used to prevent an end from fraying

overhang *v.* /ṓvər háng/ (**-hangs, -hanging, -hung** /-húng/) **1.** *vti.* PROJECT OVER to project or extend over sth leaving a sheltered space beneath **2.** *vt.* LOOM OVER SB to threaten or loom over sb or sth ■ *n.* /ṓvər hang/ **1.** PROJECTION sth, e.g. part of a rock face or the edge of a roof, that projects out over the space beneath **2.** EXTENT OF PROJECTION the degree or amount by which sth projects or extends over sth **3.** HALF DIFFERENCE IN WINGSPAN half the difference in the span of the two wings of a biplane **4.** DISTANCE TO WING END ON MONOPLANE the distance from the last outer strut to the end of a monoplane's wing

overhaul *vt.* /ṓvər háwl/ (**-hauls, -hauling, -hauled**) **1.** LOOK FOR MECHANICAL DEFECTS to examine a piece of machinery thoroughly to identify defects **2.** REPAIR MACHINE EXTENSIVELY to carry out comprehensive repairs and adjustments to a piece of machinery **3.** REVISE STH THOROUGHLY to examine and revise sth thoroughly **4.** GRADUALLY OVERTAKE SB to catch up with and overtake sb or sth **5.** SAILING SLACKEN OR RELEASE STH to slacken or release sth such as a rope or the blocks of a tackle ■ *n.* /ṓvər hawl/ COMPREHENSIVE REPAIR a comprehensive examination and repair of sth —**overhauler** /ṓvər hawlər, -háwlər/ *n.*

overhead *adv.* /ṓvər héd/ DIRECTLY ABOVE directly above sb or sth, especially up in the air ■ *adj.* /ṓvər hed/ **1.** POSITIONED DIRECTLY ABOVE positioned directly above sb or sth **2.** HIT WITH RACQUET ABOVE HEAD played hard and downwards, with the racquet held high above the head **3.** RELATING TO ONGOING COSTS relating to the general recurring costs of running a business, e.g. rent, maintenance, and utilities ■ *n.* /ṓvər hed/ **1.** SHOT IN RACQUET GAMES a shot played hard and downwards, with the racquet held above head height **2.** STH LOCATED ABOVE sth such as a light that is mounted or located in an overhead position ■ **overheads** *npl.* ONGOING BUSINESS COSTS the general recurring costs of running a business, excluding the costs of labour and materials, e.g. rent, maintenance, and utilities ■ *n.* /ṓvər hed/ = **overhead projection**

overhead camshaft, **overhead cam** *n.* a camshaft in an internal-combustion engine that is mounted above the cylinder heads and controls the operation, opening, and closing of the cylinder's valves

overhead compartment *n.* a luggage compartment above the passenger seats for holding luggage in an aeroplane

overhead projection *n.* **1.** TRANSPARENCY FOR OVERHEAD PROJECTOR a transparent sheet placed on an overhead projector so that its enlarged image can be projected on a screen or other surface **2.** USE OR RESULT OF OVERHEAD PROJECTOR the use or the image produced by the use of an overhead projector

overhead projector *n.* a projector with a flat, transparent top on which a sheetlike transparency is placed, the enlarged image being projected on a screen or other surface

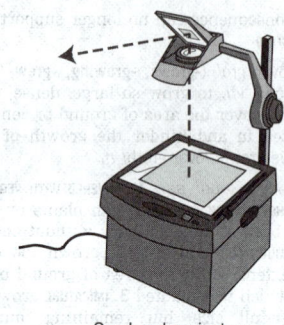

Overhead projector

overhead-valve engine *n.* an internal-combustion engine with the inlet and exhaust valves located in the cylinder head above the pistons. US term **valve-in-head engine**

overhear /óvər heér/ (-hears, -hearing, -heard /óvər húrd/, -heard) *vti.* to hear what sb is saying, either deliberately or accidentally, without the speaker's knowledge [Old English]

overheat /óvər heét/ (-heats, -heating, -heated) *vti.* **1.** BECOME OR MAKE TOO HOT to become, or to make sb or sth become, too hot **2.** ECON GROW TOO QUICKLY to experience too rapid growth in demand with a resultant increase in inflation, or to cause too rapid growth in an economy **3.** MAKE OR BECOME TOO EXCITED to become, or to make sb become, too excited, agitated, or angry (*usually passive*)

overhit /óvər hít/ (-hits, -hitting, -hit) *vti.* to hit a ball too hard or put too much force into a stroke

overhung past tense, past participle of **overhang**

overhype /óvər híp/ (-hypes, -hyping, -hyped) *vt.* to praise and publicize sb or sth excessively or misleadingly (*informal*)

overindulge /óvər in dúlj/ (-dulges, -dulging, -dulged) *v.* **1.** *vti.* PERMIT TOO MUCH to give in to a desire for sth too lavishly or too often, especially to eat or drink too much **2.** *vt.* BE TOO INDULGENT WITH SB to allow sb to do or have what he or she wants too much —**overindulgence** *n.* —**overindulgent** *adj.* —**overindulgently** /óvər in dúljəntli/ *adv.*

overjoyed /óvər jóyd/ *adj.* extremely delighted

overkill /óvər kil/ *n.* **1.** EXCESS action that far exceeds what is needed in order to achieve a result **2.** GREATER DESTRUCTIVE CAPACITY THAN NEEDED the capacity of weaponry, especially nuclear weapons, to cause greater damage or destruction than is necessary to accomplish a mission ■ *vti.* (-kills, -killing, -killed) DESTROY WITH EXCESS OF WEAPONS to use excessive force, especially far more nuclear weapons than necessary, to destroy an enemy or place

overladen /óvər láyd'n/ *adj.* carrying too heavy a physical or emotional load

overland /óvər land/ *adv.* BY LAND by or across land ■ *adj.* TAKING PLACE ON LAND made by land or used for moving across land ■ *vti.* (-lands, -landing, -landed) *Aus* DRIVE LIVESTOCK OVERLAND to drive cattle or sheep long distances across land (*archaic*) —**overlander** *n.*

overlap *v.* /óvər láp/ (-laps, -lapping, -lapped) **1.** *vti.* PLACE OR BE OVER to position things in such a way that the edge of one thing is on top of and extending past the edge of another, or to be positioned in this way ○ *The roofers overlapped the slates.* **2.** *vt.* EXTEND BEYOND STH to cover sth such as a boundary or edge, and extend beyond it ○ *The tablecloth overlapped the table by several inches.* **3.** *vti.* COINCIDE to coincide or correspond in part with sth in time, function, or purpose, or to make sth coincide or correspond with sth else ○ *Her area of responsibility in some extent overlaps mine.* ■ *n.* /óvər lap/ **1.** PARTIAL OVERLAY an edge that partly covers or is covered by sth else **2.** EXTENT OF OVERLAP the amount by which sth overlaps sth else ○ *It needs an overlap of six centimetres.* **3.** PARTIAL COINCIDENCE OR CORRESPONDENCE a partial coincidence or correspondence of two things in time, function, or purpose **4.** GEOL YOUNGER SEDIMENTARY ROCK OVER OLDER LAYER a younger layer of sedimentary rock that extends over an older layer and conceals it completely [Early 18thC. Formed from LAP.]

overlay[1] /óvər láy/ (-lays, -laying, -laid /-láyd/, -laid) **1.** PLACE STH AS COVERING to place a covering or covering layer of sth on top of sth else **2.** COVER STH to cover the surface of sth with sth else **3.** APPLY DECORATION TO SURFACE to apply a decorative material to a surface (*often passive*) **4.** PRINTING EQUALIZE PRESSURE OVER to affix a piece of paper to the surface of a press to help make a uniform impression on a forme or plate ■ *n.* /óvər lay/ **1.** COVERING a covering or covering layer laid on top of sth else **2.** EXTRA DECORATIVE LAYER an layer of decorative material applied to a surface **3.** ADDITIONAL TRANSPARENCY LAID ON TOP a transparent sheet containing additional details, e.g. a chart or map, that is placed on top of another transparency in an overhead projector during a presentation or lecture **4.** PRINTING PAPER TO EQUALIZE PRINTING PRESSURE a piece of paper used to equalize the pressure on a forme or printing plate before printing

overlay[2] past tense of **overlie**

overleaf /óvər leéf/ *adv.* on the other side of the page

overlie /óvər lí/ (-lies, -lying, -lay /-láy/, -lain /-láyn/) *vt.* **1.** LIE ON TOP OF to lie on top of sb or sth **2.** SMOTHER OFFSPRING to kill a newborn baby or animal by accidentally lying on and smothering it

overload *vt.* /óvər lód/ (-loads, -loading, -loaded) **1.** PUT EXCESSIVE LOAD ON STH to put too large or heavy a load on sb or sth or in sth **2.** ELEC FUSE ELECTRICAL SYSTEM to use more current than an electrical system can handle, e.g. by using too many electrical appliances simultaneously **3.** OVERBURDEN SB to give sb too much work, stress, or other difficulty ■ *n.* /óvər lód/ **1.** ELEC EXCESSIVE ELECTRICAL LOAD a greater amount of electrical current than an electrical system can handle **2.** EXCESSIVE PHYSICAL WEIGHT sth that is physically too heavy or too much to carry **3.** EXCESSIVE MENTAL OR EMOTIONAL BURDEN sth that is mentally or emotionally too difficult to cope with **4.** *US* MENTAL OR EMOTIONAL EXHAUSTION OR CONFUSION the condition of having an excessive mental or emotional burden (*informal*) ○ *I'm in overload right now.*

overlock /óvər lok/ *n.* a sewing technique using an invisible hem stitch made by a sewing machine or a special device

overlong /óvər lóng/ *adj.* too long in extent or duration ■ *adv.* FOR TOO LONG for too long a time

overlook /óvər loók/ (-looks, -looking, -looked) *vt.* **1.** MISS STH to miss or fail to notice sth **2.** IGNORE to choose to disregard or ignore a shortcoming or fault **3.** LOOK DOWN AT STH to look at sth from above **4.** PROVIDE VIEW OF STH to provide a view of sth, especially from above **5.** BE ABOVE STH to be located high above sth **6.** EXAMINE STH to look at sth with care

━━━━━━ WORD KEY: SYNONYMS ━━━━━━
See Synonyms at **neglect**.

overlord /óvər lawrd/ *n.* **1.** PRINCIPAL RULER a ruler with overall power, usually over several subservient rulers, and especially sb who ruled over other lords in a feudal system **2.** SB POWERFUL sb of great power or influence —**overlordship** *n.*

overly /óvərli/ *adv.* to an extreme or excessive degree [Old English]

overman *vt.* /óvər mán/ (-mans, -manning, -manned) = **overstaff** ■ *n.* /óvər man/ (*plural* -men /-men/) **1.** SUPERVISOR a man who supervises other workers (*archaic*) **2.** SUPERMAN IN NIETZSCHEAN THOUGHT in the thought of Friedrich Nietzsche, a man whose superior powers of creativity and insight enable him to live beyond standards of good and evil —**overmanning** *n.*

overmantel /óvər mant'l/ *n.* an ornamental shelf above a mantelpiece

overmaster /óvər maastər/ (-ters, -tering, -tered) *vt.* to conquer sb's resistance or break down sb's self-control and take control of him or her (*literary*) ○ *an overmastering urge to tell her precisely what I thought of her*

overmatch *vt.* /óvər mách/ (-matches, -matching, -matched) *US* **1.** DEFEAT to be superior enough to defeat or overpower sb or sth **2.** PROVIDE WITH SUPERIOR OPPONENT to provide sb with an opponent who is likely to defeat him or her easily ■ *n.* /óvər mach/

US UNEQUAL CONTEST a contest in which one competitor is far superior to another

overmatter /óvər matər/ *n.* copy typeset in excess of the space available for it

overmedicate /óvər méddi kayt/ (-cates, -cating, -cated) *vt.* to give sb or yourself too much medication —**overmedication** /óvər méddi káysh'n/ *n.*

overmuch /óvər múch/ *adv.* EXCESSIVELY to an excessive degree ■ *adj.* EXCESSIVE too much ■ *n.* EXCESSIVE QUANTITY an excessive quantity or amount

overnight /óvər nít/ *adv.* **1.** THROUGHOUT THE NIGHT for the duration of the entire night **2.** DURING NIGHT at some point in the course of the night **3.** VERY QUICKLY within a very short time ○ *It became a bestseller overnight.* ■ *adj.* **1.** LASTING ONE NIGHT lasting throughout a night **2.** SPENDING NIGHT resident for the night **3.** OCCURRING AT NIGHT taking place during the night **4.** USED WHEN SPENDING A NIGHT used when staying overnight somewhere **5.** EXTREMELY SUDDEN happening in a very short time ○ *an overnight success* **6.** *US* INTENDED FOR NEXT-DAY DELIVERY guaranteed to get to the intended destination by the next day ■ *vi.* (-nights, -nighting, -nighted) SPEND NIGHT to stay somewhere for the night

overnight bag, **overnight case** *n.* a small piece of luggage used to carry necessities for a stay lasting one night

overnighter /óvər nítər/ *n.* **1.** OVERNIGHT STAY an stay lasting one night (*informal*) **2.** SB ON AN OVERNIGHT STAY sb who takes an overnight trip or stays somewhere overnight

overoptimistic /óvər opti místik/ *adj.* unrealistically hopeful about the future —**overoptimism** /óvər óptimizəm/ *n.* —**overoptimistically** /óvər opti místikli/ *adv.*

overpass *n.* /óvər paass/ *US, Can, ANZ* a road, bridge, or passage that crosses over another route

overpay /óvər páy/ (-pays, -paying, -paid /-páyd/, -paid) *vti.* **1.** PAY MORE THAN JOB WARRANTS to pay sb at a rate that is too high for the job **2.** PAY TOO MUCH BY MISTAKE to pay sb too much for sth as a result of an error

overpersuade /óvər pər swáyd/ (-suades, -suading, -suaded) *vt.* to persuade sb to act contrary to his or her inclination or judgment

overpitch /óvər pích/ (-pitches, -pitching, -pitched) *vti.* to bowl a ball in cricket so that it lands too close to the batsman

overplay /óvər pláy/ (-plays, -playing, -played) *v.* **1.** *vti.* OVERDO to play a part or role in an exaggeratedly dramatic or theatrical way **2.** *vt.* OVERSTATE STH to exaggerate the importance or strength of sth **3.** *vt.* SPORTS HIT STH TOO HARD OR FAR to hit or kick a ball too hard or too far ◇ **overplay your hand** to make overconfident or heavy-handed use of an advantage or strong position and fail as a result

overplus /óvər pluss/ *n.* a larger amount than is needed or appropriate [14thC. Translation of French *surplus.*]

overpopulate /óvər póppyoō layt/ (-lates, -lating, -lated) *v.* **1.** *vt.* INCREASE POPULATION OF PLACE TOO MUCH to increase the population of a place so much that the amount of space, food, water, or other resources available to support it is insufficient (*often passive*) **2.** *vi.* REPRODUCE TO EXCESS to increase to unsustainable or undesirable numbers by excessive reproduction —**overpopulation** /óvər póppyoō láysh'n/ *n.*

overpotted /óvər póttid/ *adj.* growing in a pot too large for healthy development

overpower /óvər pów ər/ (-ers, -ering, -ered) *vt.* **1.** SUBDUE SB PHYSICALLY to use superior strength or force to defeat sb, especially to make sb physically helpless and unable to fight **2.** OVERWHELM SB MENTALLY to have so strong an effect on sb that he or she is unable to resist or control it **3.** GIVE STH EXCESSIVE POWER to supply sth, especially a car, with more power than necessary, especially mechanical or electrical power

overpowering /óvər pów əring/ *adj.* **1.** IRRESISTIBLE impossible to resist or control ○ *an overpowering urge to laugh* **2.** PHYSICALLY OVERWHELMING with overwhelmingly superior physical strength —**overpoweringly** *adv.*

overprescribe /ṓvər pri skrī́b/ (**-scribes, -scribing, -scribed**) *vti.* to prescribe too much medication for sb ○ *The doctor was prone to overprescribe for his patients.* —**overprescription** /-pri skrípsh'n/ *n.*

overpressure /ṓvər preshər/ *n.* the amount by which atmospheric pressure exceeds normal levels, e.g. in a shock wave from an explosion or an accelerating aircraft

overprice /ṓvər prī́ss/ (**-prices, -pricing, -priced**) *vt.* to charge too high a price for sth (*often passive*)

overprint *vti.* /ṓvər prínt/ (**-prints, -printing, -printed**) ADD PRINTING TO STH to print sth additional on an already printed surface, especially in order to add text, numbers, or another colour ■ *n.* /ṓvər print/ **1.** ADDITIONAL PRINTING an additional printing on a surface, especially text, numbers, or another colour **2.** OVERPRINTED POSTAGE STAMP a postage stamp with additional information printed on its surface

overprivileged /ṓvər prívvilijd/ *adj.* having too many advantages in life

overprize /ṓvər prī́z/ (**-prizes, -prizing, -prized**) *vt.* to regard sth as more valuable and important than it really is

overproof /ṓvər pro͞of/ *adj.* higher in alcohol content than proof spirit. ◊ **proof**

overproportion /ṓvər prə páwrsh'n/ (**-tions, -tioning, -tioned**) *vt.* to make sth larger than is usual or needed and out of proportion to other things —**overproportionately** *adv.*

overprotect /ṓvər prə tékt/ (**-tects, -tecting, -tected**) *vt.* to protect sb or sth more than is necessary or wise, especially to shield a child too much from the realities of life —**overprotection** *n.* —**overprotective** *adj.*

overqualified /ṓvər kwólli fīd/ *adj.* with more academic or vocational qualifications or experience than is necessary or desirable for a job

overrate /ṓvər ráyt/ (**-rates, -rating, -rated**) *vt.* to regard sb as better or more capable, or sth as greater, than is in fact the case —**overrated** *adj.*

overreach /ṓvər re͞ech/ (**-reaches, -reaching, -reached**) *v.* **1.** *vr.* FAIL THROUGH OVERAMBITION to fail through trying to do things that are beyond your abilities **2.** *vti.* EXTEND TOO FAR OR BEYOND STH to reach or extend too far or beyond sth **3.** *vti.* DEFEAT BY TRICKERY to get the better of sb by trickery or deception **4.** *vt.* OVERTAKE SB to catch up with and pass sb or sth **5.** *vi.* HURT ONE FOOT WITH ANOTHER to strike and injure the forefoot with the hindfoot while walking or running (*refers to a horse*) **6.** *vi.* SAIL ON TACK LONGER THAN NECESSARY to sail on a tack longer than is wanted or needed

overreact /ṓvər ri ákt/ (**-acts, -acting, -acted**) *vi.* to react to sth with disproportionate action or excessive emotion —**overreaction** *n.* —**overreactive** *adj.*

overrefine /ṓvər ri fī́n/ (**-fines, -fining, -fined**) *vti.* to make sth more refined, subtle, or fastidious than is desirable or appropriate, especially to make too many subtle points or distinctions in presenting an argument —**overrefinement** *n.*

overregulate /ṓvər réggyo͝o layt/ (**-lates, -lating, -lated**) *vt.* to impose too many regulations on sb or sth, especially an industry

overrepresented /ṓvər réppri zéntid/ *adj.* having too many representatives or represented by too many examples in proportion to the total ○ *His earlier work is rather overrepresented in this collection.* —**overrepresentation** /ṓvər réppri zen táysh'n/ *n.*

override *vt.* /ṓvər rī́d/ (**-rides, -riding, -rode** /-rṓd/, **-ridden** /-rídd'n/) **1.** CANCEL STH to cancel or change an action or decision taken by sb else **2.** OUTWEIGH STH to be more important than and take priority over sth else **3.** TAKE MANUAL CONTROL OF to take manual control of an automatic control system **4.** RIDE HORSE OVER to ride a horse over or across an area **5.** RIDE HORSE TOO HARD to tire a horse by riding it too hard **6.** OVERLAP STH to extend over sth, especially by overlapping it ■ *n.* /ṓvər rīd/ **1.** ASSUMPTION OF MANUAL CONTROL the condition, process, or action of temporarily taking manual control of an automatic system **2.** SWITCH FOR MANUAL CONTROL a switch or some other manual control that temporarily cancels or reverses the effect of an automatic system [Old English from OVER + RIDE]

overrider /ṓvər rīdər/ *n.* either of a pair of projections on the bumper of a motor vehicle, designed to prevent damage in a collision with the bumper of another vehicle

overriding /ṓvər rī́ding/ *adj.* highest in priority —**overridingly** *adv.*

overripe /ṓvər rī́p/ *adj.* too ripe, and past its best flavour and texture —**overripeness** *n.*

overrode past tense of **override**

overruff /ṓvər rúf/ (**-ruffs, -ruffing, -ruffed**) *vti.* = **overtrump**

overrule /ṓvər ro͞ol/ (**-rules, -ruling, -ruled**) *vt.* **1.** RULE AGAINST SB'S ARGUMENT to rule authoritatively that sb's argument is unsound, especially in the case of a judge disallowing a barrister's arguments ○ *Objection overruled!* **2.** DECIDE AGAINST SB to decide against sb or to overturn a decision taken by sb with lesser authority **3.** EXERCISE CONTROL OVER SB to exercise dominion or control over sb or sth (*literary*)

overrun *v.* /ṓvər rún/ (**-runs, -running, -ran** /-rán/, **-run**) **1.** *vt.* SPREAD RAPIDLY AND INFEST STH to arrive in such large numbers or spread so rapidly in a place that it becomes infested or overcrowded (*often passive*) ○ *The cathedral square was overrun with tourists.* **2.** *vt.* CONQUER ENEMY AND TERRITORY to attack an enemy force, defeat it conclusively, and take over the territory occupied by it ○ *The rebels overran the government forces.* **3.** *vti.* EXCEED LIMIT to continue beyond a predetermined limit, especially a time limit or fixed budget **4.** *vt.* OVERSHOOT STH to go on beyond an intended stopping point such as a boundary line or the end of an airport runway **5.** *vti.* OVERFLOW to overflow or spill over sth **6.** *vt.* PRINTING PRINT MORE THAN PLANNED to print extra copies of a publication **7.** *vt.* PRINTING MOVE TYPESET MATERIAL to transfer set type or illustrated material from one column, page, or line to another **8.** *vi.* RUN WITH THROTTLE CLOSED to run at higher revolutions than the throttle setting dictates. A vehicle engine most commonly overruns when the vehicle is running downhill with the throttle closed and the engine speed is dictated by the speed of the wheels. ■ *n.* /ṓvər run/ **1.** ACT OF OVERRUNNING an instance of sb or sth overrunning, especially of going on beyond the intended stopping point **2.** AMOUNT EXCEEDING ESTIMATE the amount by which sth exceeds a preset limit, an estimated cost, or a budget **3.** EXTRA QUANTITY PRODUCED an extra quantity of sth produced, e.g. manufactured items or copies of printed matter **4.** EXTRA AREA AT END OF RUNWAY a cleared level area at the end of a runway, available in case a plane overshoots

overrun brake *n.* a brake on a vehicle being towed, to prevent it from running into the back of the vehicle towing it

oversaw past tense of **oversee**

overscore /ṓvər skáwr/ (**-scores, -scoring, -scored**) *vt.* to draw a line over or through written text, usually so as to cancel or revise it

oversea /ṓvər se͞e/ *adj., adv.* = **overseas**

overseas /ṓvər se͞ez/ *adv.* ACROSS THE SEA across or beyond a sea, especially in another country ○ *They live overseas.* ■ *adj.* **overseas, oversea 1.** RELATING TO PLACE ACROSS SEA relating to, located in, or coming from, a foreign country or place beyond a sea ○ *overseas visitors* **2.** TRAVELLING ACROSS SEA involving travel across a sea ○ *an overseas assignment* ■ *n.* SOMEWHERE BEYOND SEA a foreign country, or foreign countries and places beyond the sea collectively (*takes a singular verb*) ○ *come from overseas*

oversee /ṓvər se͞e/ (**-sees, -seeing, -saw** /-sáw/, **-seen** /-se͞en/) *vt.* **1.** SUPERVISE STH to watch over, manage, and direct sb or a task done by sb **2.** OBSERVE STH to observe sth covertly or secretly while it is happening [Old English; from OVER + SEE]

overseer /ṓvər seer/ *n.* sb who supervises workers, especially those engaged in manual labour

oversell /ṓvər sél/ (**-sells, -selling, -sold** /-sṓld/) *v.* **1.** *vt.* PRAISE STH TOO HIGHLY to exaggerate the value or worth of sb, sth, or yourself to an implausible extent **2.** *vti.* SELL TOO AGGRESSIVELY to use excessively aggressive sales techniques when selling a product **3.** *vti.* SELL TOO MUCH OF to sell too much of a product, especially more than can be produced or supplied

overset (**-sets, -setting, -set**) *v.* /ṓvər sét/ **1.** *vti.* PRINTING TYPESET TOO MUCH COPY to set too much type or copy for the available space **2.** *vt.* TIP STH OVER to tip or turn sth over (*archaic*) **3.** *vt.* DISTURB SB to disturb or upset sb (*archaic*)

oversew /ṓvər sṓ/ (**-sews, -sewing, -sewed, -sewn** /-sṓn/) *vt.* to sew two edges together, with small stitches overlapping both edges

oversexed /ṓvər sékst/ *adj.* having an excessive preoccupation with or need for sex

overshadow /ṓvər sháddō/ (**-ows, -owing, -owed**) *vt.* **1.** TAKE ATTENTION AWAY FROM SB to take attention away from sb or sth by appearing more important or interesting **2.** CAST SHADOW OVER STH to cast a physical shadow over sth, or make sth become gloomy [Old English]

overshirt /ṓvər shurt/ *n.* a loose shirt that is worn on top of another garment such as a sweater or another shirt

overshoe /ṓvər shoo/ *n.* a shoe, usually made of rubber or plastic, that is worn over an ordinary shoe to protect it from dampness or dirt

overshoot *v.* /ṓvər sho͞ot/ (**-shoots, -shooting, -shot** /-shót/) **1.** *vti.* SEND OR GO FARTHER THAN INTENDED to shoot a projectile beyond the target that was being aimed at or be shot in this way **2.** *vti.* MISS TARGET to miss a target by missing or being shot too far **3.** *vti.* AIR RUN OFF END OF RUNWAY to fail to complete a take-off or landing before reaching the end of the runway and run off the end of it **4.** *vti.* EXCEED LIMIT to exceed a fixed or prearranged limit **5.** *vt.* MOVE QUICKLY OVER STH to move at a high speed over sth ■ *n.* /ṓvər shoot/ **1.** ACT OF OVERSHOOTING an instance of sb or sth overshooting an intended stopping point, especially the end of an airport runway **2.** AMOUNT BY WHICH STH EXCEEDS an instance of sth exceeding a prearranged limit or the amount or extent by which it exceeds it

overshot /ṓvər shot/ *adj.* **1.** WITH UPPER PART EXTENDING PAST LOWER used to describe a jaw with an upper part that is longer than and sticks out over the lower part **2.** DRIVEN BY WATER ON UPPER SURFACE used to describe a waterwheel driven by water flowing onto it from above

oversight /ṓvər sīt/ *n.* **1.** FAILURE BY OMISSION a mistake, especially as a result of a failure to do or notice sth **2.** SUPERVISION the responsibility of supervising sth (*formal*)

oversimplify /ṓvər símpli fī/ (**-fies, -fying, -fied**) *vt.* to reduce sth to such a level of simplicity that it becomes distorted or falsified —**oversimplification** /ṓvər sim plif i káy shən/ *n.*

oversize *adj.* /ṓvər sī́z/ **oversize, oversized** UNUSUALLY LARGE larger than is usual or necessary ■ *n.* /ṓvər sīz/ **1.** UNUSUALLY LARGE SIZE a size that is larger than usual **2.** EXTRA-LARGE ARTICLE an article that comes in a larger size than usual

overskirt /ṓvər skurt/ *n.* a skirt that is worn on top of another garment, often revealing part of the lower one

oversleep /ṓvər sle͞ep/ (**-sleeps, -sleeping, -slept** /-slépt/, **-slept**) *vi.* to continue sleeping for longer than desired or intended

oversold /ṓvər sṓld/ past participle, past tense of **oversell** ■ *adj.* STOCK EXCH UNREASONABLY LOW IN PRICE available at or characterized by prices that are excessively low as a result of previous heavy selling on the stock market. ◊ **overbought**

overspend *v.* /ṓvər spénd/ (**-spends, -spending, -spent, -spent** /-spént/) **1.** *vti.* SPEND TOO MUCH to spend more money than can be afforded **2.** *vt.* EXHAUST STH to tire sb or sth out completely ■ *n.* /ṓvər spend/ **1.** EXTRAVAGANCE an act or instance of spending more money than can be afforded **2.** AMOUNT OVERSPENT an amount by which sb overspends

overspill *n.* /ṓvər spil/ **1.** STH SPILLED sth that spills or has spilled over from sth **2.** PEOPLE MOVING FROM CITY TO OUTSKIRTS the part of a crowded city's population that leave to live in new housing areas outside it ■ *vti.* /ṓvər spíl/ (**-spills, -spilling, -spilled** *or* **-spilt** /-spílt/, **-spilled** *or* **-spilt**) SPILL OVER to spill over, or to make sth spill over

overspread /ṓvər spréd/ (**-spreads, -spreading, -spread**) *vt.* to spread widely over or cover the surface of sth [Old English]

overstaff /ṓvər staáf/ (**-staffs, -staffing, -staffed**) *vt.* to supply a workplace with too large a staff (*usually passive*)

overstate /ṓvər stáyt/ (**-states, -stating, -stated**) *vt.* to exaggerate sth in talking or writing about it —**overstatement** *n.*

overstay /ṓvər stáy/ (**-stays, -staying, -stayed**) *vti.* to remain beyond the expected, planned, or desired time

oversteer *vi.* /ṓvər stéer/ (**-steers, -steering, -steered**) MAKE SHARPER TURN THAN EXPECTED to turn more sharply than expected, especially in a motor vehicle ○ *We oversteered and landed in a ditch.* ■ *n.* /ṓvər steer/ TENDENCY TO TURN TOO SHARPLY the tendency of a motor vehicle to turn more sharply than expected

overstep /ṓvər stép/ (**-steps, -stepping, -stepped**) *vt.* to go beyond the limit of sth [Old English]

overstock *v.* /ṓvər stók/ (**-stocks, -stocking, -stocked**) **1.** *vti.* STOCK IN EXCESS to stock more of sth than is necessary or desirable **2.** *vt.* KEEP TOO MANY ANIMALS ON to graze an area with more livestock than it can support ■ *n.* /ṓvər stok/ *US* EXCESS an excessively large supply of sth

overstrain /ṓvər stráyn/ (**-strains, -straining, -strained**) *vti.* to try to force sb, sth, or yourself to perform beyond capacity, especially so that damage, injury, or breakdown results

overstress *vt.* /ṓvər stréss/ (**-stresses, -stressing, -stressed**) **1.** PUT EXCESSIVE EMPHASIS ON STH to put too much emphasis on sth **2.** PUT SB UNDER TOO MUCH STRESS to subject sb to too much mental or emotional pressure **3.** DEFORM AS RESULT OF EXCESSIVE FORCE to deform material permanently by exerting too much force on it ■ *n.* /ṓvər stress/ EXCESSIVE EMPHASIZING OF STH the putting of too much emphasis on sth

overstretch /ṓvər stréch/ (**-stretches, -stretching, -stretched**) *v.* **1.** *vti.* STRETCH STH TOO FAR to stretch sth such as a muscle too much, so as to cause injury or damage **2.** *vt.* STRETCH RESOURCES TOO FAR to try to do too much with the resources available, with consequent strain on those resources and, usually, poor performance (*often passive*) ○ *Absenteeism is often a sign that employees are overstretched.* **3.** *vt.* STRETCH OVER STH to extend or stretch over sth

overstrung /ṓvər strúng/ *adj.* **1.** TOO NERVOUS excessively nervous and tense **2.** MUSIC WITH DOUBLE SET OF STRINGS used to describe a piano fitted with two sets of strings, one crossing the other at an angle **3.** ARCHERY STRUNG TOO TIGHTLY having the bowstring fixed too tightly

overstuff /ṓvər stúf/ (**-stuffs, -stuffing, -stuffed**) *vt.* **1.** PUT TOO MUCH MATERIAL INTO STH to stuff a cavity or object with too much material **2.** UPHOLSTER COMPLETELY to upholster a piece of furniture using a large amount of padding to make it soft, deep, and comfortable

oversubscribe /ṓvər səb skrīb/ (**-scribes, -scribing, -scribed**) *vt.* to apply to participate in sth in numbers in excess of the available number of places (*usually passive*) ○ *The course on modern poetry was heavily oversubscribed.* —**oversubscription** /ṓvər səb skrípsh'n/ *n.*

oversupply *n.* /ṓvər sə plī/ (*plural* **-plies**) EXCESSIVE SUPPLY an excessive supply of sth ■ *vti.* /ṓvər sə plī/ (**-plies, -plying, -plied**) SUPPLY TOO MUCH OF to provide sb or sth with an excessive supply of sth

overt /ō vúrt/ *adj.* **1.** UNCONCEALED done openly and without any attempt at concealment **2.** LAW OPEN AND INTENTIONAL done openly and intentionally, and therefore able to be taken as a sign of criminal intent [14thC. From Old French, the past participle of *ovrir* 'to open', from Latin *aperire* (see APERTURE).] —**overtly** *adv.* —**overtness** *n.*

overtake /ṓvər táyk/ (**-takes, -taking, -took** /-tŏŏk/, **-taken** /-táyk'n/) *v.* **1.** *vti.* GO PAST to draw level with and pass a person or vehicle travelling in the same direction **2.** *vt.* DO BETTER THAN SB to reach and then surpass a level achieved by sb or sth **3.** *vt.* COME OVER SB SUDDENLY to come over sb suddenly or catch sb by surprise ○ *Sleep overtook them.* **4.** *vt.* CATCH UP WITH SB to go after and catch up with sb

overtax /ṓvər táks/ (**-taxes, -taxing, -taxed**) *vt.* **1.** EXHAUST SB to impose too great a strain on sb, sth, or yourself **2.** LEVY EXCESSIVE TAX ON to levy more tax on sb or sth than is justified or considered fair

over-the-air *adj.* transmitted by radio or television —**over the air** *adv.*

over the counter *adv.* directly to a customer, without requiring a doctor's prescription

over-the-counter *adj.* **1.** BUYABLE WITHOUT PRESCRIPTION sold directly to the public without a doctor's prescription **2.** BOUGHT AND SOLD ELECTRONICALLY not quoted as a security on an exchange, but bought and sold electronically **3.** DEALING IN OVER-THE-COUNTER SECURITIES relating to or dealing in over-the-counter securities [From the idea that anybody can buy such items directly from the seller, as in a shop]

over-the-hill *adj.* **1.** PAST PRIME past the point at which talent, energy, or physical performance is at its peak **2.** OLD no longer young (*sometimes considered offensive*) [From the idea of being past your peak]

over-the-shoulder shot *n.* CINEMA a shot taken from over the shoulder of a character whose back can be seen at side of frame. It is frequently used for filming conversations.

over-the-top *adj.* so exaggerated as to appear ridiculous or outrageous (*informal*)

overthrow *vt.* /ṓvər thrṓ/ (**-throws, -throwing, -threw** /-thrṓō/, **-thrown** /-thrṓn/) **1.** REMOVE SB FROM POWER BY FORCE to remove a person or group of people from a position of power by force **2.** SPORTS THROW BALL TOO FAR OR HARD to throw a ball too far so that it goes beyond the player or target it was intended to reach ■ *n.* /ṓvər thrō/ **1.** REMOVAL FROM POWER BY FORCE the removal of a person or group of people from a position of power by force **2.** SPORTS THROW THAT GOES TOO FAR a throw of a ball that goes beyond the player or target, e.g. the stumps in cricket, it was intended to reach **3.** CRICKET ADDITIONAL RUN FROM OVERTHROW an additional run scored as a result of an overthrow by a fielder [14thC. The underlying meaning is 'to overturn, knock down'.]

overthrust fault /ṓvər thrust fáwlt, -folt/, **overthrust** *n.* a rock fault produced by thrust action that causes older rocks to move long distances and eventually settle on top of younger rocks **(horizontal displacement)**

overtime /ṓvər tīm/ *n.* **1.** ADDITIONAL TIME WORKED extra time worked beyond the normal hours of employment **2.** PAY FOR ADDITIONAL TIME WORKED payment, usually at a higher rate, for time worked beyond the normal hours of employment **3.** *US, Can* SPORTS = **extra time** ■ *adv.* **1.** BEYOND NORMAL LENGTH OF TIME beyond the normal or contracted length of time **2.** VERY HARD using a great deal of energy and effort (*informal*) ○ *been working overtime to try and make them see sense*

overtone /ṓvər tōn/ *n.* **1.** SUPPLEMENTARY MEANING a subtle additional meaning, nuance, or quality **2.** MUSIC HIGHER MUSICAL TONE a higher tone produced at the same time as the lowest tone that helps to determine the overall quality of the sound

overtook past tense of **overtake**

overtop /ṓvər tóp/ (**-tops, -topping, -topped**) *vt.* **1.** RISE ABOVE STH to rise above sb or sth **2.** SURPASS SB to surpass sb or sth **3.** OVERRIDE to be more important than sb or sth

overtrade /ṓvər tráyd/ (**-trades, -trading, -traded**) *vi.* to trade beyond the level that can be supported by the trader's financial means or the market involved

overtrain /ṓvər tráyn/ (**-trains, -training, -trained**) *vti.* to train or exercise, or make sb train or exercise, excessively, especially before a competition, with a resulting decrease in effectiveness

overtrick /ṓvər trik/ *n.* a trick taken in bridge in addition to the number needed to make a contract

overtrump /ṓvər trúmp/ (**-trumps, -trumping, -trumped**) *vti.* to play a higher trump card than one already played by another player in a trick

overture /ṓvər tyoor, -chər/ *n.* **1.** MUSIC MUSICAL INTRODUCTION a single orchestral movement that introduces an opera, play, ballet, or longer musical work, often including the work's themes **2.** = **concert overture 3.** INTRODUCTORY PROPOSAL OR INITIATIVE an introductory proposal or initiative made to mark the beginning of a discussion, agreement, or relationship ○ *make overtures to someone* **4.** INTRODUCTION TO A POEM an introduction to a written work such as a poem or play [15thC. Via Old French, 'opening', from, ultimately, Latin *apertura* (see APERTURE).]

overturn (**-turns, -turning, -turned**) *v.* /ṓvər túrn/ **1.** *vti.* TIP OVER to turn sb or sth upside down **2.** *vt.* OVERTHROW SB to remove a person or a group of people from a position of power **3.** *vt.* REVERSE PREVIOUS DECISION to reverse a previous decision, ruling, or law by using legal or legislative procedures —**overturn** /ṓvər turn/ *n.*

overuse *n.* /ṓvər yōōss/ EXCESSIVE USE the excessive use of sth ■ *vt.* /ṓvər yōōz/ (**-uses, -using, -used**) USE STH TOO MUCH to use sth excessively, often wearing it out or making it ineffective

overvalue /ṓvər vállyoo/ (**-ues, -uing, -ued**) *vt.* to set too high a value or price on sth —**overvaluation** /ṓvər vállyoo áysh'n/ *n.*

overview /ṓvər vyoo/ *n.* **1.** BROAD SURVEY a general or comprehensive outline of sth **2.** SUMMARY a brief summary of sth

overvoltage /ṓvər vōltij/ *n.* a voltage that is in excess of the normal voltage for which an electrical circuit or system was designed and may sometimes cause damage to components

overweening /ṓvər wéening/ *adj.* **1.** ARROGANT intolerably arrogant or conceited **2.** EXCESSIVE excessive, especially in an arrogant and conceited way [14thC. Formed from WEEN 'to think, believe'.] —**overweeningly** *adv.*

overweigh /ṓvər wáy/ (**-weighs, -weighing, -weighed**) *vt.* **1.** = **outweigh** *v.* 2 **2.** WEIGH ON SB to oppress or burden sb heavily

overweight *adj.* /ṓvər wáyt/ **1.** TOO HEAVY FOR GOOD HEALTH with more weight than is considered healthy for sb of a specific height, build, or age **2.** ABOVE WEIGHT LIMIT heavier than the allowed weight limit ○ *an overweight letter* ■ *vt.* /ṓvər wáyt/ (**-weights, -weighting, -weighted**) **1.** OVEREMPHASIZE STH to give too much emphasis or consideration to sth **2.** OVERLOAD STH to weigh sth down with an excessive load ■ *npl.* OVERWEIGHT PEOPLE people who weigh too much for their height, build, or age (*sometimes considered offensive*)

overwhelm /ṓvər wélm/ (**-whelms, -whelming, -whelmed**) *vt.* (*often passive*) **1.** OVERPOWER SB EMOTIONALLY to affect sb's emotions in a complete or irresistible way **2.** MIL OVERCOME SB PHYSICALLY to use superior strength, force, or numbers to defeat sb, especially an enemy, completely **3.** SURGE OVER AND COVER to flow over the top of and submerge or cover sb or sth **4.** PROVIDE WITH HUGE AMOUNT OF STH to supply sb with a very large or excessive amount of sth [14thC. Formed from OVER + WHELM.]

overwhelming /ṓvər wélming/ *adj.* **1.** EMOTIONALLY OVERPOWERING having such a great effect as to be emotionally overpowering **2.** PHYSICALLY OVERPOWERING overpowering in strength, force, or numbers **3.** EXTREMELY LARGE extremely large in amount or proportion —**overwhelmingly** *adv.*

overwind /ṓvər wīnd/ (**-winds, -winding, -wound** /-wównd/, **-wound**) *vt.* to wind up the spring of a clockwork device, especially a watch or clock, too tightly, so that it will not operate or the spring breaks

overwinter /ṓvər wíntər/ (**-ters, -tering, -tered**) *v.* **1.** *vti.* KEEP OR STAY ALIVE THROUGHOUT WINTER to keep livestock or plants alive through the winter by sheltering them, or to be kept alive in this way **2.** *vi.* STAY FOR WINTER to spend the winter by taking up residence in a particular place

overwore past tense of **overwear**

overwork *v.* /ṓvər wúrk/ (**-works, -working, -worked**) **1.** *vti.* DO TOO MUCH WORK to work, or to make sb, yourself, or an animal work, excessively **2.** *vt.* OVERUSE STH to use sth too often, especially a word or expression **3.** *vt.* DECORATE SURFACE OF to apply decoration to the surface of sth **4.** *vt.* WORK TOO MUCH ON STH to expend too much effort on sth, especially so as to reduce its quality or effectiveness ■ *n.* /ṓvər wurk/ EXCESSIVE WORK too much work [Old English]

overworn past participle of **overwear**

overwound past participle, past tense of **overwind**

overwrite /óvər rít/ (-writes, -writing, -wrote /-rót/, -written /-rítt'n/) v. 1. vti. REPLACE COMPUTER FILE to replace data or a program in memory or on a disk with a new file of the same name 2. vti. WRITE STH TOO ELABORATELY to make a piece of writing too elaborate, polished, or decorative 3. vt. COVER WRITING WITH MORE WRITING to cover a piece of writing by writing on top of it

overwrought /óvər ráwt/ adj. 1. VERY UPSET extremely upset, emotional, or agitated 2. TOO ELABORATE fashioned or decorated too elaborately 3. ORNAMENTED ON SURFACE ornamented on the surface with sth

overzealous /óvər zélləss/ adj. too enthusiastic or eager, especially in carrying out a duty, and usually causing trouble or annoyance as a result

ovi- prefix. egg, ovum ○ *oviform* [Formed from Latin *ovum* (see OVUM)]

Ovid /óvvid/ (43 BC–AD 17) Roman poet. His works include *Amores* and *Metamorphoses*, a collection of mythical and historical tales. —**Ovidian** /o víddi ən/ adj.

oviduct /óvi dukt/ n. either of a pair of tubes in the body that transport eggs from the ovary to the uterus. ◊ **fallopian tube**

Oviedo /óvvi áyd ō/ city and capital of Oviedo Province, Asturias autonomous region, northern Spain. Population: 202,421 (1995).

oviform /óvi fawrm/ adj. shaped like an egg

ovine /ó vīn/ adj. relating to or like a sheep [Early 19thC. Via late Latin *ovinus* from Latin *ovis* 'sheep'. Ultimately from the Indo-European word for 'sheep' that is also the ancestor of English *ewe*.]

oviparous /ō víppərəss/ adj. 1. PRODUCING EGGS THAT HATCH OUTSIDE BODY used to describe birds, fish, reptiles, and insects that reproduce by means of eggs that develop and hatch outside the mother's body. ◊ **viviparous** 2. RELATING TO EGG PRODUCTION OUTSIDE BODY relating to the production of eggs that develop and hatch outside the mother's body —**oviparously** adv.

oviposit /óvi pózzit/ (-its, -iting, -ited) vi. to lay eggs (refers usually to insects) [Early 19thC. Coined from OVI- + Latin *posit-*, the past participle stem of *ponere* 'to place' (see POSITION).]

ovipositor /óvi pózzitər/ n. a tubular organ at the end of the abdomen of some female fish or animals, especially insects, that is used to deposit eggs

ovisac /óvi sak/ n. a sac or capsule in the ovary of a mammal that contains a mature ovum. When the ovisac is ruptured the ovum is released. ◊ **Graafian follicle**

ovo- prefix. = **ovi-**

ovoid /ó voyd/ adj. 1. WITH FORM OF EGG with the solid form of an egg 2. BOT SHAPED LIKE AN EGG used to describe a fruit or similar plant part that is shaped like an egg ■ n. STH EGG-SHAPED sth with the shape or form of an egg [Early 19thC. Via French from, ultimately, Latin *ovum* 'egg' (see OVUM).]

ovolactovegetarian /óvō láktō vejjə táiri ən/ n. a vegetarian who eats eggs and dairy products, but no products that involve the killing of animals. ◊ **vegan**

ovolo /óvəlō/ (plural -li /-lī/) n. a convex moulding that resembles a quarter-circle or ellipse when viewed in cross section [Mid-17thC. From Italian, literally 'little egg', ultimately from Latin *ovum* 'egg' (see OVUM).]

ovonic /ō vónnik/ adj. relating to, consisting of, or using glassy materials that can rapidly and reversibly become electrical conductors after a minimum voltage is applied [Mid-20thC. Coined from OVSHINSKY EFFECT + ELECTRONIC.]

ovonics /ō vónniks/, **Ovonics** n. the study or use of glassy materials that can rapidly and reversibly become electrical conductors after a minimum voltage is applied (takes a singular verb)

ovotestis /óvō téstiss/ (plural -tes /-teez/) n. the sexual organ of a hermaphroditic animal such as the garden snail that produces both sperm and eggs

ovoviviparous /óvō vi víppərəss/ adj. used to describe insects, fish, and reptiles that reproduce by means of eggs that develop within the female, deriving some nutrition from her but remaining encased within an egg membrane —**ovoviviparously** adv.

Ovshinsky effect /ov shínski-/ n. an effect that occurs in thin films of glass containing selenium and tellurium in which the resistance of the material drops rapidly when a particular voltage is applied across it. Switches made from these materials will stay on after the voltage has been removed. [Mid-20thC. Named after the US physicist Stanford R. *Ovshinsky* (b. 1922).]

ovulate /óvvyoō layt/ (-lates, -lating, -lated) vi. to ripen and release an egg or eggs from the ovary for possible fertilization [Late 19thC. Formed from OVULE.] —**ovulatory** adj.

ovulation /óvvyoō láysh'n/ n. the ripening and discharge of an egg or eggs from the ovary for possible fertilization

ovule /óvvyool/ n. 1. BOT SMALL PLANT PART DEVELOPING INTO SEED a small structure in a seed plant that contains the embryo sac and develops into a seed after fertilization 2. BIOL IMMATURE EGG a small or immature egg [Early 19thC. Via French from modern Latin *ovulum*, literally 'little egg', from Latin *ovum* 'egg' (see OVUM).] —**ovular** /óvyoōlər/ adj.

ovum /óvəm/ (plural **ova** /óvə/) n. a female reproductive cell [Early 18thC. From Latin, 'egg' (source of English *oval* and *ovary*). Ultimately from an Indo-European word that is also the ancestor of English *egg*, *cockney*, and *caviar*.]

ow /ow/ interj. used to represent an involuntary expression of pain [Early 20thC. Natural exclamation.]

owe /ō/ (owes, owing, owed) v. 1. vt. BE OBLIGATED TO PAY SB MONEY to be under an obligation to pay or repay sb an amount of money ○ *She owed the bank a lot of money.* 2. vti. BE FINANCIALLY IN DEBT to be financially in debt to sb or for sth ○ *She claims she doesn't owe anyone.* 3. vt. BE INDEBTED FOR STH to have sth, usually some desirable thing, only because of sth or sb else ○ *I owe my success to my father.* 4. vt. FEEL THAT RESPONSE IS DESERVED to feel that sth should be given to or done for sb in recompense for sth ○ *She owes you an explanation.* ○ *I owe myself a night out.* 5. vt. BEAR GRUDGE TOWARDS SB to feel a particular emotion, especially a grudge, towards sb ○ *owe sb a grudge* [Old English *āgan* (source of English *ought*). Ultimately from an Indo-European word meaning 'to own' that is also the ancestor of English *own*.]

Owen /ó in/, **Robert** (1771–1858) British social reformer. A pioneer of socialist industrial communities, he wrote *Revolution in Mind and Practice* (1849).

Owen, Wilfred (1893–1918) British poet. Famous for his war poetry, he was killed in World War I a week before the armistice.

Jesse Owens: Photographed in the long jump competition at the Berlin Olympics (1936)

Owens /ó inz/, **Jesse** (1913–80) US athlete. One of the greatest sprinters of all time, he won four gold medals at the 1936 Olympics, setting multiple Olympic and world records. Real name **James Cleveland Owens**

Owerri /ə wérri/ capital city of Imo State, southern Nigeria. Population: 35,010 (1983).

owing /ó ing/ adj. due to be given, especially in payment or repayment of a debt ○ *amounts still owing* ◊ **owing to** as a result or consequence of sth

Owl

owl /owl/ n. 1. HOOTING BIRD OF PREY a predatory, usually nocturnal bird with a large head, large front-facing eyes, hooked and feathered talons, a small beak, short neck, and a distinctive hooting call. The owl is traditionally described as wise, perhaps because of its fixed gaze, as if it were considering sth carefully. Order: Strigiformes. 2. FANCY PIGEON a domestic pigeon belonging to a breed resembling the owl 3. SB RESEMBLING OWL sb who has habits or characteristics attributed to owls, e.g. wisdom, contemplativeness, solemnity, or staying up all night [Old English *ūle*, from a prehistoric Germanic word of uncertain origin: probably an imitation of an owl's call]

owl butterfly n. a South American butterfly that has a spot like an owl's eye on the underside of each hind wing. Genus: *Caligo*.

owlet /ówl ət/ n. a young or baby owl

owlet frogmouth n. = **owlet nightjar**

owlet moth n. = **noctuid** ['Owlet' from the fact that its eyes shine in the dark when light strikes them]

owlet nightjar n. a bird native to Australia and Papua New Guinea that is related to the nightjar but resembles a small owl and swoops down on insects from a perch. Family: Aegothelidae.

owlish /ówlish/ adj. physically resembling an owl or displaying a characteristic attributed to owls, e.g. wisdom, contemplativeness, solemnity, or staying up all night —**owlishly** adv. —**owlishness** n.

owl parrot n. = **kakapo**

owl's clover n. a plant of the figwort family found in western North and South America that has dense spikes of variously-coloured flowers. Genus: *Orthocarpus*. [*Owl's* from the fact that its flowers look like owls' faces]

own /ōn/ adj. EMPHASIZES POSSESSIVE a grammatical word emphasizing that sb or sth belongs to a particular person or thing and not to sb or sth else ○ (adj) *I always wanted to have my own business.* ○ *Her own mother wouldn't have recognized her.* ○ (pron) ○ *At last he had a house of his own.* ■ adj., pron. INDICATES THAT SB DOES STH UNAIDED used to indicate that sb does sth without help or interference ○ (adj) *She made her own dress.* ○ *I can make my own decisions.* ○ (pron) *I'd rather make my own than buy them readymade.* ■ v. (owns, owning, owned) 1. vt. HAVE STH AS PROPERTY to have sth as your property ○ *He owns a chain of hotels.* 2. vti. ACKNOWLEDGE to acknowledge or admit sth (archaic or formal) ○ *He owned that the struggle had been hard.* [Old English *āgnian*, from *āgen* 'one's own', past participle of *āgan*, an earlier form of OWE] ◊ **come into your own** to start to be really effective, useful, or successful ◊ **hold your own 1.** put up effective resistance in an argument or contest **2.** remain in a stable condition after an illness or injury, often when it might not be expected ◊ **on your own 1.** alone **2.** without help or interference **own up** vi. to admit to having done sth

own brand n. an item for sale that has the trademark or label of the retailer, usually a large supermarket chain, instead of that of the manufacturer (hyphenated when used before a noun) US term **store brand**

owner /ónər/ n. sb who owns sth

owner-occupied adj. used as a residence by the person who owns it

owner-occupier *n.* sb who owns or is in the process of buying the house or apartment he or she is living in

ownership /ṓnər ship/ *n.* **1.** RIGHT OF POSSESSION the legal right of possessing sth **2.** FACT OR STATE OF OWNING STH the fact or condition of being an owner of sth

own goal *n.* **1.** GOAL SCORED ACCIDENTALLY FOR OPPONENTS a goal scored by mistake for the opposing team, usually by being miskicked or mishit by, or deflected off, a defender **2.** ACTION THAT BACKFIRES ON DOER an action, especially one intended to damage sb, that ends up harming its initiator (*informal*)

own label *n.* = **own brand** (*hyphenated when used before a noun*)

Ox

ox /oks/ (*plural* **oxen** /óks'n/) *n.* **1.** BOVINE DRAUGHT ANIMAL an adult castrated bull, sometimes used for pulling heavy loads and ploughs. Genus: *Bos*. **2.** COW OR BULL a male or female bovine mammal, especially one belonging to a domestic breed **3.** SB UNINTELLIGENT AND CLUMSY sb who is unintelligent and clumsy, especially sb with a large build (*insult*) [Old English *oxa*, from a prehistoric Germanic word that is also the ancestor of English *aurochs*]

ox- *prefix*. oxygen ○ *oxime* [From OXYGEN]

oxacillin /óksə síllin/ *n.* an antibiotic used to treat bacterial infections that are resistant to penicillin [Mid-20thC. Coined from *isoxazole* + PENICILLIN.]

oxalate /óksə layt/ *n.* a salt or ester of oxalic acid

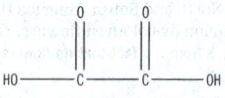

Oxalic acid

oxalic acid /ok sállik-/ *n.* a colourless poisonous acid found in plants as an oxalate and synthetically made for use in bleaching, dyeing, and cleaning. Formula: $H_2C_2O_4$. ['Oxalic' formed from Latin *oxalis* 'wood sorrel' (see OXALIS), because it occurs naturally in the plant's leaves]

oxalis /ok sálliss, óksəliss/ *n.* a plant such as wood

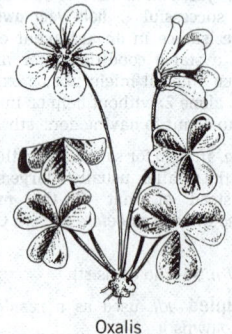

Oxalis

sorrel with leaves similar to those of clover. Genus: *Oxalis*. [Early 17thC. Via Latin from Greek, 'wood sorrel', from *oxus* 'sour' (see OXYGEN), because of the taste of its leaves.]

oxazepam /ok sázzə pam/ *n.* a tranquillizer used to manage anxiety, insomnia, and alcohol withdrawal. Formula: $C_{15}H_{11}ClN_2O_2$. [Mid-20thC. Coined from HYDROXY- + BENZODIAZEPINE + AMINE.]

oxblood /óks blud/, **oxblood red** *adj.* of a dark brownish-red colour —**oxblood** *n.*

oxbow /óks bō/ *n.* **1.** U-SHAPED COLLAR FOR OX a collar for an ox used as a draught animal, consisting of a U-shaped piece of wood attached to a yoke **2.** BEND IN RIVER a bend in a river shaped like an oxbow, or the land found in the bend of a river **3.** = **oxbow lake**

oxbow lake *n.* a small curved lake developed on a river floodplain by a river abandoning its original meandering course and cutting a new channel

Oxbridge /óksbrij/ *n.* the universities of Oxford and Cambridge, seen as forming an institution distinct from all the other more recently established universities in England [Mid-19thC. Blend of *Oxford* and *Cambridge*.]

oxcart /óks kaart/ *n.* a cart drawn by oxen, for transporting heavy goods

oxen plural of **ox**

oxeye /óks ī/ *n.* **1.** PLANT WITH FLOWER HEADS LIKE A DAISY'S a composite plant of Europe, Asia, and North America that has flower heads resembling a daisy's. Genus: *Buphthalum* and *Heliopsis*. **2.** = **daisy** *n.* 2

ox-eyed *adj.* with big round eyes like those of an ox

oxeye daisy, **oxeye** *n.* = **daisy** *n.* 2

Oxfam /óks fam/ *n.* an international charity dedicated to providing poverty and disaster relief overseas. It was founded in Oxford in 1942.

oxford /óksfərd/, **Oxford** *n.* a sturdy leather shoe that laces over the instep [Late 19thC. Named after OXFORD.]

Oxford /óksfərd/ city in south-central England, and administrative centre of Oxfordshire. Its university is the oldest in England. Population: 118,795 (1991).

Oxford accent *n.* a way of speaking using the pronunciation associated with Oxford English

Oxford bags *npl.* trousers with extremely loose baggy legs, popular during the 1920s [Named after Oxford University, where they were once fashionable]

Oxford blue *adj.* DARK BLUE of a dark blue colour. ○ **Cambridge blue** ■ *n.* **1.** DARK BLUE COLOUR a dark blue colour. ○ **Cambridge blue 2.** OXFORD UNIVERSITY SPORTSPERSON sb who has represented Oxford University in a sporting competition. ○ **blue, Cambridge blue**

Oxford English *n.* a variety of English, associated with Oxford University, that uses a form of Received Pronunciation, the educated standard speech of southern England

Oxford Movement *n.* CHR a movement in the Church of England that began in Oxford in the 1830s and advocated a renewal of Roman Catholic doctrine and practices. Its most influential leaders were John Henry Newman (later to become a Roman Catholic cardinal), John Keble, and Edward Pusey.

Oxfordshire /óksfərdshər, óksfərd sheer/ inland county in south-central England. Oxford is the county town. Population: 593,700 (1995). Area: 2,610 sq. km/1,010 sq. mi.

oxidant /óksidənt/ *n.* **1.** OXIDIZING AGENT a substance that oxidizes other substances **2.** SUBSTANCE IN FUEL a substance in a bipropellant rocket fuel that contains oxygen to support the combustion of another substance, usually liquid oxygen, hydrogen peroxide, or nitric acid [Late 19thC. Via French from, ultimately, *oxide* (see OXIDE).]

oxidase /óksi dayz, -dayss/ *n.* an enzyme that catalyses biological oxidation, especially in living organisms [Late 19thC. Formed from OXIDATION.]

oxidation /óksi dáysh'n/ *n.* ○ **reduction 1.** ADDITION OF OXYGEN a chemical reaction in which oxygen is added

to an element or compound **2.** LOSS OF ELECTRONS the process of losing electrons from a chemical element or compound [Late 18thC. Via French from, ultimately, *oxide* (see OXIDE).] —**oxidative** /óksi daytiv, óksidətiv/ *adj.*

oxidation-reduction *n.* a chemical reaction in which one component loses electrons or is oxidized and another gains electrons or is reduced

oxidative phosphorylation *n.* a process that takes place in all living cells in the presence of oxygen, in which they convert food to the energy that is required to maintain life. This process produces ATP, the body's high-energy fuel, through the phosphorylation of ADP driven by the oxidation of NADH and other donors of electrons.

oxidative stress *n.* the impaired performance of cells, caused by the presence of too many oxygen molecules in them

oxide /óks īd/ *n.* any compound containing oxygen, especially in combination with a metal [Late 18thC. From French, formed from *oxygène* 'oxygen', on the model of *acide* 'acid'.]

oxidize /óksi dīz/ (-**dizes**, -**dizing**, -**dized**), **oxidise** (-**dises**, -**dising**, -**dised**) *vti.* **1.** REACT OR MAKE REACT WITH OXYGEN to react or cause a chemical to react with oxygen, e.g. in forming an oxide. ○ **reduce** *v.* 12 **2.** LOSE OR MAKE LOSE ELECTRONS to lose electrons, or to cause a chemical element or compound to lose electrons. ○ **reduce** *v.* 13 **3.** COVER WITH OXIDE COATING to form an oxide coating or to cover sth with an oxide coating — **oxidization** /óksi dī záysh'n/ *n.* —**oxydizable** /óksi dízəb'l/ *adj.*

oxidizer /óksi dīzər/, **oxidiser** *n.* = **oxidant** *n.* 1

oxidizing agent *n.* a substance that oxidizes other substances and undergoes reduction in the process

oxidoreductase /óksidō ri dúk tayss, -tayz/ *n.* an enzyme that catalyses a reaction involving oxidation and reduction

oxime /óks eem, -īm/ *n.* an organic compound containing a hydroxile group bonded to a nitrogen atom [Late 19thC. Coined from OXY- + IMIDE.]

oximeter /ok símmitər/ *n.* an instrument that measures the amount of oxygen in sth, especially in blood [Mid-19thC. Coined from OXY- + -METER.] —**oximetric** /óksi méttrik/ *adj.* —**oximetrically** /-rikli/ *adv.* —**oximetry** /ok símmətri/ *n.*

oxlip /ókslip/ *n.* a woodland plant of Europe and Asia that has clusters of small yellow flowers. Latin name: *Primula elatior*. [Old English *oxanslyppe*, literally 'ox dung', from *oxa* 'ox' + *slyppe* 'slime' (see SLIP)]

Oxo /óksō/ *tdmk.* a trademark for an extract of beef stock condensed and sold in small cubes for use in cooking or, mixed with hot water, as a beverage

Oxon. *abbr.* Oxfordshire ■ *adj.* RELATING TO OXFORD relating to the University of Oxford (*used after titles of academic awards*) Abbr of **Oxoniensis**. ○ **Cantab.**

Oxonian /ok sṓni ən/ *adj.* **1.** RELATING TO OXFORD UNIVERSITY relating to or typical of Oxford University, or its students and staff **2.** RELATING TO OXFORD relating to or typical of the city of Oxford or its inhabitants [Mid-16thC. Formed from *Oxonia*, Latinized form of Old English *Ox(e)naford* 'Oxford'.] —**Oxonian** *n.*

oxpecker /óks pekər/ *n.* an African starling that climbs on the back of wild and domestic mammals and eats parasites from their skin. Genus: *Buphagus*. [Mid-19thC]

oxtail /óks tayl/ *n.* the tail of a beef animal, skinned and chopped into short lengths and simmered for a long time to make rich soups or stews

oxter /ókstər/ *n.* the armpit (*regional*) [Old English *ōxta*. Ultimately from an Indo-European word meaning 'axis' that is also the ancestor of English *axle*, *axis*, and *alar*.]

——————— **WORD KEY: REGIONAL NOTE** ———————
Old English speakers used *ohsta*, *oxta* for 'armpit', and dialect speakers in Ireland, Scotland, and the North of England have preserved the usage: *He had it hid under his oxter*. They have also created the verb *oxtercog*, meaning 'to go arm in arm', as in *They may be arguing now but they'll be oxtercogging tomorrow!*

oxtongue /óks tung/ *n.* a plant of Europe and Asia that has bristly leaves and flowers like the dandelion. Genus: *Picris*. [14thC. From the shape of its leaves.]

oxy- *prefix.* oxygen ○ *oxyacid* [Shortening of OXYGEN]

oxyacetylene /óksi ə séttə leen, -lin/ *n.* a mixture of oxygen and acetylene that is used to produce an extremely hot flame for cutting and welding metal

oxyacid /óksi assid/ *n.* an acid that contains oxygen

oxycephaly /óksi séffəli/ *n.* a condition in which the skull becomes slightly pointed as a result of the premature closure of some connective bones (sutures) [Late 19thC. Formed from Greek *oxukephalos*, literally 'pointed-headed', from *oxus* 'sharp' (see OXYGEN) + *kephalē* 'head'.]

oxygen /óksijən/ *n.* a colourless odourless gas that is the most abundant chemical element and forms compounds with most others. It is necessary in most cases for combustion and essential for plant and animal respiration. Symbol **O** [Late 18thC. From French, literally 'acid-former' (because it was thought to be a basic component of acids), formed from Greek *oxus* 'sharp, sour'.] —**oxygenic** /óksi jénnik/ *adj.*

oxygenase /óksijə nayz, -nayss/ *n.* an enzyme that promotes a reaction in which oxygen is incorporated into the molecules of the substrate

oxygenate /óksijə nayt, ok síjjə nayt/ *vti.* (**-ates, -ating, -ated**) **COMBINE WITH OXYGEN** to combine sth, or to be combined, with oxygen ■ *n.* **OXYGEN SUBSTANCE ADDED TO FUELS** a substance added to fuels, especially petrol, to make them burn more efficiently

oxygen debt *n.* the amount of oxygen needed to replenish the stores the body uses for its normal physiological processes after these have been depleted during strenuous physical exercise

oxygen demand *n.* = **biochemical oxygen demand**

oxygen mask *n.* a device fitting closely over the nose and mouth through which oxygen is supplied to assist breathing, e.g. at high altitudes

oxygen tent *n.* a structure enclosing a patient in bed and resembling a transparent plastic tent, into which oxygen can be pumped to assist breathing

oxyhaemoglobin /óksi heémə glóbin/ *n.* the bright red form of haemoglobin when it is combined with oxygen molecules, which it transports from the lungs to the tissues

oxyhydrogen /óksi hí drə gən/ *adj.* using a mixture of oxygen and hydrogen gases, thus allowing hydrogen to burn in an oxygen atmosphere and giving a flame temperature of 2,400°C ○ *oxyhydrogen welding*

oxymetazoline /óksi méttə zṓlin/ *n.* a nasal decongestant, usually administered as a spray

oxymoron /óksi máwron, óksi máwrən/ (*plural* **-ra**) *n.* a phrase in which two words of contradictory meaning are used together for special effect, e.g. 'wise fool' or 'legal murder' [Mid-17thC. From Greek *oxumōron*, a substantival use of the neuter singular of *oxumōros* 'pointedly foolish', from *oxus* 'sharp' (source of English *oxygen*) + *mōros* 'foolish' (source of English *moron*).]

oxyntic /ok síntik/ *adj.* producing or secreting acid ○ *oxyntic cells*

oxysulphide *n.* any compound in which a chemical element is combined with sulphur and oxygen

oxytetracycline /óksi téttrə sí kleen/ *n.* a yellow crystalline antibiotic obtained from a soil bacterium *Streptomyces rimosus* and used to treat a wide variety of bacterial infections

oxytocic /óksi tóssik/ *adj.* **SPEEDING UP CONTRACTIONS IN CHILDBIRTH** inducing or speeding up childbirth by stimulating the muscles of the womb and causing contractions ■ *n.* **DRUG ACCELERATING CHILDBIRTH** a drug that induces or speeds up childbirth [Mid-19thC. Formed from Greek *oxutokia* 'sudden delivery' (literally 'sharp birth'), which in turn was formed from Greek *tokos* 'birth' (related to English *thane*).]

oxytocin /óksi tóssin/ *n.* a hormone released by the pituitary gland that stimulates contractions of the womb during childbirth and triggers the secretion of milk from the breast during nursing. It may be given to women during childbirth to assist labour.

oxytone /óksi tōn/ *adj.* **1. WITH ACUTE ACCENT ON LAST SYLLABLE** in classical Greek, having an acute accent on the final syllable **2. WITH STRESS ON FINAL SYLLABLE** with the stress on the final syllable ■ *n.* an oxytone word or syllable [Mid-18thC. From Greek *oxutonos*, literally 'sharp pitch', which was formed from *tonos* 'pitch, force' (see TONE).]

oxyuriasis /óksi yŏŏ ríˈəssəss/ *n.* infestation with pinworms [Early 20thC. From modern Latin, from *Oxyuris* 'name of a genus of worms'.]

oyer and terminer /óyər ənd túrminə/ *n.* **1. BRITISH COMMISSION TO JUDGE ON ASSIZE** a commission from the British Crown empowering a judge to try cases in English courts of assize, abolished along with the assize system in 1972 **2. US CRIMINAL COURT** a high court with general criminal jurisdiction in some states of the US [Partial translation of Anglo-Norman *oyer et terminer*, literally 'to hear and determine' (*terminer* from Latin *terminare*, source of English *terminate*)]

oyez /ō yéz, -yéss, -yáy/, **oyes** *interj.* **CALL FOR SILENCE** used, usually three times in succession, to call for silence and indicate that an official announcement is about to be made, e.g. in court or by a town-crier ■ *n.* a cry of 'oyez' [From Anglo-Norman, the imperative plural ('hear ye!') of *oyer* 'to hear', from Latin *audire* 'to hear']

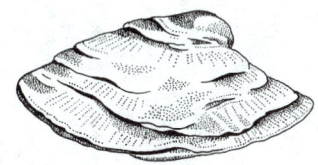

Oyster

oyster /óystər/ *n.* **1. EDIBLE SHELLFISH** an edible shellfish with a rough irregularly shaped shell that lives mainly on the sea bed in coastal waters. Oysters are generally eaten raw and considered a delicacy. Genera: *Ostrea* and *Crassostrea*. **2. SHELLFISH SIMILAR TO OYSTER** any shellfish similar to an edible oyster, e.g. a pearl oyster **3. SLIGHTLY GREYISH OFF-WHITE** a pale beige or pink colour with a greyish tinge **4. PIECE OF DARK MEAT IN FOWL** a small piece of dark meat found in a hollow on either side of the pelvic bone of a fowl such as a chicken or turkey **5. UNCOMMUNICATIVE PERSON** a person who does not say much or is secretive (*archaic informal*) ■ *vi.* (**-ters, -tering, -tered**) **GATHER OYSTERS** to grow or gather oysters [Via Old French *oistre* from Latin *ostrea, ostreum*, from Greek *ostreon*, etymologically an allusion to its shell, being related to *ostrakon* 'shell' (source of English *ostracize*) and *osteon* 'bone' (source of English *osteo-*)] ◇ **the world is your oyster** the world provides unlimited opportunities for you to be successful and prosper

Oystercatcher

oyster bed *n.* an area of seabed where oysters grow or are grown

oystercatcher /óystər katshər/ *n.* a common large shore bird, found worldwide, that has a long flat almost chisel-shaped red bill and black or black-and-white plumage, and lives on shellfish and worms. Genus: *Haematopus*.

oyster crab *n.* a small soft-bodied crab that lives harmlessly inside the shell of a live oyster or other mollusc. Latin name: *Pinnotheres ostreum*.

oysterman /óystər mən/ (*plural* **-men**) *n.* **1. SB WHO GROWS OR GATHERS OYSTERS** sb who grows, collects, or sells oysters **2.** a boat used in gathering oysters

oyster mushroom *n.* an edible mushroom that grows on dead wood and has a soft flavourful grey cap. Latin name: *Pleurotus ostreatus*.

oyster plant *n.* **1.** = **salsify** *n.* **1 2.** = **lungwort**

oyster sauce *n.* a salty bottled sauce flavoured with oysters, used as a seasoning or flavouring in Chinese cooking

oyster shell scale *n.* an insect pest of shade trees and shrubs that in its wingless and eyeless adult form lives under an impenetrable white shell and sucks the sap of its host. Latin name: *Lepidosaphes ulmi*.

oz *abbr.* ounce [From Italian *ōz*, abbreviation of *onza* 'ounce', from Latin *uncia* 'twelfth part' (see OUNCE)]

Oz /oz/ *n.* Australia (*informal*)

oz ap *abbr.* apothecaries' ounce

Ozark Plateau /ṓz aark-/ mountainous region in the southern United States, predominantly in Arkansas, Missouri, and Oklahoma. Area: 130,000 sq. km/50,000 sq. mi.

oz av *abbr.* avoirdupois ounce

Seiji Ozawa

Ozawa /ō záˈawə/, **Seiji** (*b.* 1935) Japanese conductor. He has conducted the Boston Symphony Orchestra since 1973.

ozocerite /ṓzō sírrit/, **ozokerite** /ṓzō kírrit/ *n.* a waxy hydrocarbon substance occurring naturally in irregular veins in sandstone rock, ranging in colour from brown to jet black, and used in making candles, wax paper, and polishes [Mid-19thC. From German *Ozokerit*, from Greek *ozein* 'to smell' (source of English *ozone*) + *kēros* 'beeswax'.]

ozone /ṓ zōn, ṓ zṓn/ *n.* **1. FORM OF OXYGEN** a gaseous form of oxygen with three oxygen atoms per molecule, formed by electrical discharge in oxygen. It acts as a strong oxidizing agent and is used in water purification. Although considered a pollutant in the lower atmosphere where it is present in very small quantities, it forms a protective ozone layer in the upper atmosphere. Formula: O_3. **2. FRESH AIR** fresh pure air, especially sea air (*informal*) [Mid-19thC. Via German *Ozon* from Greek *ozon*, the neuter present participle of *ozein* 'to smell'; so called from its pungent smell.]

ozone-friendly *adj.* causing no harm to the ozone layer

ozone hole *n.* an area of the upper atmosphere where the ozone layer is absent or has become unusually thin

ozone layer *n.* the layer of the upper atmosphere, from 15 to 50 km/10 to 30 miles above the Earth's surface, where most atmospheric ozone collects, absorbing harmful ultraviolet radiation from the Sun. In the 1980s it was realized that industrial pollutants such as CFCs were damaging the ozone layer and that holes had appeared in it, especially over the Antarctic.

ozonide /ṓ zōnīd/ *n.* an explosive organic compound

formed by the addition of ozone to any organic compound with a double or triple carbon bond

ozonize /ṓ zōnīz/ (-nizes, -nizing, -nized), **ozonise** (-nises, -nising, -nised) *vt.* **1.** CONVERT OXYGEN TO OZONE to convert oxygen into ozone **2.** TREAT WITH OZONE to treat sth with ozone, or add ozone to an organic compound with a double or triple carbon bond

ozonizer /ṓzən īzzər/ *n.* a device that produces ozone from oxygen gas

ozonosphere /ṓ zṓnə sfeer, ō zónnə sfeer/ *n.* = **ozone layer**

oz t *abbr.* troy ounce

p[1] /pee/ (*plural* **p's**), **P** (*plural* **P's**) *n.* **1.** 16TH LETTER OF THE ALPHABET the 16th letter of the modern English alphabet **2.** SPEECH SOUND CORRESPONDING TO LETTER 'P' the sound made when speaking that corresponds to the letter 'P' **3.** LETTER 'P' WRITTEN a written representation of the letter 'P' ◇ **mind your p's and q's** to be careful to be polite, tactful, and well-behaved

p[2] *symbol.* **1.** penny *or* pence **2.** MUSIC piano (*used as a direction*)

P[1] *symbol.* **1.** CHEM ELEM phosphorus **2.** peso **3.** pataca **4.** pula

P[2] *abbr.* **1.** PHYS parity **2.** park (*used on gear sticks*) **3.** CHESS pawn **4.** played (*used in sports tables*) **5.** after noon **6.** PHYS power **7.** PHYS pressure **8.** peseta

p. *abbr.* **1.** page **2.** part **3.** GRAM participle **4.** GRAM past **5.** per **6.** pint **7.** pipe **8.** population **9.** KNITTING purl

P. *abbr.* **1.** Pastor **2.** President **3.** Priest **4.** Prince

pa[1] /paa/ (*plural* **pa's** *or* **pas**) *n.* father (*informal*) [Early 19thC. Shortening of PAPA.]

pa[2] /paa/ (*plural* **pa**), **pah** (*plural* **pah**) *n.* **1.** NZ MAORI VILLAGE a Maori village **2.** MAORI HILLTOP FORT AND SETTLEMENT a fortified Maori settlement on a hilltop [Mid-18thC. From Maori *pà*, from *pā* 'to block up'.]

Pa *symbol.* **1.** PHYS pascal **2.** CHEM ELEM protactinium

PA[1] *abbr.* **1.** INSUR particular average **2.** MAIL Pennsylvania **3.** BANKING personal account **4.** personal appearance **5.** personal assistant **6.** MIL Post Adjutant **7.** LAW power of attorney **8.** press agent **9.** Press Association

PA[2] *n.* an electronic amplification system used to increase the sound level of speech or music in a large or open space such as a stadium or auditorium. Full form **public-address system**

Pa. *abbr.* Pennsylvania

p.a. *abbr.* yearly

P/A *abbr.* LAW power of attorney

pa'anga /páang gə, paa áang-/ *n.* **1.** TONGAN UNIT OF CURRENCY the main unit of currency of Tonga, worth 100 seniti. See table at **currency 2.** NOTE WORTH A PA'ANGA a note worth one pa'anga

PABA /pábbə, páabə/ *n.* a colourless form of aminobenzoic acid used in sunscreens to absorb ultraviolet light and in dyes and pharmaceuticals. It is part of the vitamin B complex and is found in yeast and liver. Full form **para-aminobenzoic**

Pabst /paapst/, **G. W.** (1885–1967) Austrian film director. His expressionist anti-establishment films include *Pandora's Box* (1928), *Westfront* (1930), and *The Threepenny Opera* (1931). Full name **Georg Wilhelm Pabst**

pabulum /pábbyoōləm/ *n.* **1.** PLANT OR ANIMAL FOOD a source of nourishment in an easily absorbable liquid, especially the nutrient intake of plants and lower animals **2.** UNSATISFYING INTELLECTUAL MATERIAL material whose intellectual content is thin, trite, bland, or generally unsatisfying (*literary*) [Mid-17thC. From Latin, where it was formed from the stem of *pascere* 'to feed' (source of English *pasture*).]

PABX *abbr.* private automatic branch exchange

Pac. *abbr.* Pacific

Paca

paca /paákə, pákə/ *n.* a large burrowing plant-eating rodent with a large head and brown fur with white spots, found in the rainforests of South and Central America. Genus: *Cuniculus*. [Mid-17thC. Via Spanish and Portuguese from Tupi.]

pace[1] /payss/ *n.* **1.** SPEED OF MOVEMENT the particular speed at which sb or sth moves, especially when walking or running ○ *She quickened her pace.* **2.** SPEED OF EVENTS the rate or speed at which things happen or develop ○ *the pace of modern life* **3.** SPEED IN PERFORMANCE the degree of urgency, sharpness, or speed in the writing, composition, or performance of a dramatic or musical work **4.** STEP a step taken when walking or running **5.** DISTANCE COVERED IN A STEP the distance covered in a single step or stride **6.** UNIT OF LENGTH any of several units of distance ranging from .76 to 1.52 m/30 to 60 in, based on the length of one or two human strides **7.** WAY OF WALKING a particular manner or style of walking **8.** EQU GAIT OF HORSE a distinctive way in which a four-legged animal walks or runs at different speeds, e.g. a walk, trot, or canter, especially as executed by a trained horse **9.** 2-BEAT GAIT a two-beat gait of a four-legged animal where both legs on one side of the body move and are put down together. It is natural in camels but the product of training in horses. ■ *v.* (**paces, pacing, paced**) **1.** *vti.* WALK TO AND FRO to walk to and fro within a restricted area, especially in a state of nervous anxiety or deep thought ○ *paced up and down all night worrying* **2.** *vti.* WALK ALONG STH to walk along or through sth with regular strides **3.** *vti.* MEASURE BY COUNTING STEPS to measure a distance by counting the paces taken to cover it ○ *I paced out the width of the room.* **4.** *vt.* SET THE SPEED OF STH to set the speed at which sb runs, moves, or does sth ○ *I helped her train for the marathon by pacing her on a bicycle.* **5.** *vt.* DO STH AT CONTROLLED RATE to run or work at an even controlled speed so as not to waste energy ○ *Learn to pace yourself.* **6.** *vi.* MOVE AT A PACE to move at a pace (*refers to horses*) [13thC. Directly or via French *pas* 'step' from Latin *passus*, literally 'stretch (of the leg)', ultimately from *pandere* 'to stretch, extend' (source of English *expand*).] ◇ **at sb's own pace** at the rate that is natural or comfortable for sb ◇ **force the pace** to do sth to force sb to go faster or to make sth happen more quickly ◇ **off the pace** SPORTS behind the leader or the score of the leading competitor ◇ **put sth through its paces** to make sth demonstrate its capabilities, as a test or in order to impress other people ◇ **set the pace** to go at a speed or establish a standard that others have to keep up with ◇ **stand or stay the pace** to be able to keep up with other people, especially when the pace is fast, the standard high, or the competition fierce

pace[2] /páyssi, páa chay/ *prep.* used in front of a name or title as a gesture of real or ironic respect to sb who is mistaken and about to be corrected ○ *Pace the critic of this newspaper, the character's name is Prospero, not Prosperus.* [Late 18thC. From Latin, literally 'with peace, with permission', a form of *pax* 'peace' (source of English *peace*).]

PACE /payss/ *abbr.* Police and Criminal Evidence Act

pace bowler *n.* a fast bowler in cricket

pace car *n.* a car that leads the competitors in a motor race through a pace lap before the start of a race but does not participate in the race itself

pace lap *n.* a lap of the course driven by all the competitors in a motor race before the race begins, to warm up the engines

pacemaker /páyss maykər/ *n.* **1.** SPORTS COMPETITOR WHO SETS THE PACE a competitor in a race who sets the speed at which the whole or part of the race is run **2.** = **pacesetter** *n.* 1 **3.** MED DEVICE THAT REGULATES THE HEARTBEAT a battery-operated electrical device inserted into the body to deliver small regular shocks that stimulate the heart to beat in a normal rhythm **4.** ANAT NATURAL HEARTBEAT REGULATOR a small area of specialized heart-muscle tissue in the wall of the upper right chamber of the heart that sends out rhythmic electrical impulses to regulate the heartbeat

pacer /páyssər/ *n.* **1.** SPORTS = **pacemaker** *n.* 1 **2.** EQU HORSE TRAINED TO PACE a horse trained to move at a pace in races

pacesetter /páyss setər/ *n.* **1.** LEADER IN A FIELD OF ACTIVITY a person or group regarded as being a leader in any field and one whom others may emulate **2.** SPORTS = **pacemaker** *n.* 1

pacey /páyssi/ (**pacier, paciest**), **pacy** (**pacier, paciest**) *adj.* with fast-moving action or a fast-moving, exciting plot ○ *a pacey story*

pacha *n.* = **pasha**

pachisi /pə cheézi, paa-/ *n.* an ancient Indian four-handed game similar to backgammon played on a cross-shaped board with six cowrie shells used as dice [Early 19thC. From Hindi *pac(c)īsī*, literally '(throw of) 25' (this being the highest in the game).]

pachouli *n.* = **patchouli**

pachyderm /páki durm/ *n.* a large mammal with a thick skin, especially the elephant, rhinoceros, or hippopotamus [Mid-19thC. From French *pachyderme*, from Greek *pachydermos* 'thick-skinned', from *pachys* 'thick' + *derma* 'skin'.] —**pachydermal** /páki dúrm'l/ *adj.*

pachydermatous /páki dúrmətəss/ *adj.* **1.** RESEMBLING A PACHYDERM having the thick skin or some other physical characteristic typical of a pachyderm **2.** EMOTIONALLY THICK-SKINNED insensitive to other people and unworried by criticism or attack (*literary or humorous*) [Early 19thC. Ultimately from Greek *pakhus* 'thick' + *dermat-*, stem of *derma* 'skin'.]

pachysandra /páki sándrə/ (*plural* **-dras** *or* **-dra**) *n.* a low-growing shrubby evergreen plant of the box family with toothed leaves and tiny white flowers, often used as ground cover. Genus: *Pachysandra*. [Early 19thC. From modern Latin (genus name), from Greek *pakhus* 'thick' + *andr-* 'man, male' (see ANDRO-); from the thick stamens.]

pachytene /páki teen/ *n.* BIOL the third stage of cell division, during which the paired chromosomes become shorter and thicker and divide into four chromatids [Early 20thC. From French *pachytène*, from Greek *pakhus* 'thick' + French *-tène* 'ribbon' (from, ultimately, Greek *tainia*).]

Pacif. *abbr.* Pacific

pacific /pə síffik/ *adj.* **1.** BRINGING PEACE leading to or promoting peace and an end to conflict **2.** HAVING A PEACEFUL TEMPERAMENT calm and peaceful by nature **3.** UNAGGRESSIVE avoiding the use of force [Mid-16thC. Directly or via French *pacifique* from Latin *pacificus*, from *pac-*, stem of *pax* 'peace' (see PEACE).]

Pacific /pə síffik/ *n.* PACIFIC OCEAN the Pacific Ocean ■ *adj.* RELATING TO THE PACIFIC OCEAN relating to the Pacific Ocean, or to the territories that surround it or are surrounded by it

pacification /pássi fi káysh'n/ *n.* **1.** PROCESS OF PACIFYING the process of bringing about peace by calming sb or putting an end to conflict **2.** MIL ESTABLISHMENT OF AN ENFORCED PEACE the use of military force or other measures to eradicate rebellion and restore an area to peace and government control

Pacific Northwest *n.* a region of the northwestern United States on the Pacific coast that includes the states of Washington and Oregon and sometimes southwestern British Columbia, in Canada

Pacific Ocean the largest ocean in the world, stretching from the Arctic Ocean in the north to Antarctica in the south, and from North and South America in the east to eastern Asia, the Malay Archipelago, and Australia in the west. Its deepest point is the Mariana Trench, 10,924 m/35,840 ft. Area: 165,000,000 sq. km/64,000,000 sq. mi.

Pacific Rim *n.* the countries that border the Pacific, especially the countries of East Asia, considered as a political or economic unit

Pacific Standard Time, **Pacific Time** *n.* the standard time for the western coastal regions of North America, one hour behind Mountain Time and eight hours behind Greenwich Mean Time

pacifier /pássi fī ər/ *n.* **1.** SB OR STH THAT PACIFIES sb or sth that calms a person or situation **2.** *US* BABYWARE = **dummy**

pacifism /pássi fizzəm/ *n.* **1.** BELIEF IN THE PEACEFUL RESOLUTION OF CONFLICTS a belief that violence, war, and the taking of lives are unacceptable ways of resolving disputes **2.** REFUSAL TO PARTICIPATE IN WAR the refusal to take up arms or participate in war because of moral or religious beliefs **3.** POL BELIEF IN DIPLOMACY OVER WAR a belief that international conflicts should be settled by negotiation rather than war

pacifist /pássi fist/ *n.* **1.** BELIEVER IN PACIFISM sb who believes in, advocates, or practises pacifism **2.** CONSCIENTIOUS OBJECTOR sb who refuses to perform military service or take part in a war ■ *adj.* SUPPORTING PACIFISM believing in, advocating, or practising pacifism —**pacifistic** /pássi fístik/ *adj.* —**pacifistically** /-fístikli/ *adv.*

pacify /pássi fī, pássə-/ (**-fies, -fying, -fied**) *vt.* **1.** CALM to calm sb who is angry or agitated, or soothe violent or angry feelings **2.** MIL BRING PEACE TO to bring peace to an area, people, or situation, often by using military force to end conflict or unrest [15thC. Directly or via French *pacifier* from Latin *pacificare*, literally 'to make peace', from *pac-*, stem of *pax* 'peace' (see PEACE).] —**pacifiable** *adj.*

Pacinian corpuscle /pə sínni ən-/ *n.* a pressure-sensitive nerve ending resembling a tiny white onion that is connected to the end of nerve fibres in the skin, especially of the hands and feet, and in connective tissue [Mid-19thC. Named after Filippo *Pacini* (1812–83) an Italian anatomist.]

Pacino /pə chéenō/, **Al** (*b.* 1940) US actor. He starred in *The Godfather* films and won an Academy Award for *Scent of a Woman* (1992). Full name **Alfredo Pacino**

pack[1] /pak/ *v.* (**packs, packing, packed**) **1.** *vti.* PUT BELONGINGS INTO A CONTAINER to put personal belongings into a bag or other container for transporting **2.** *vti.* PUT PRODUCTS IN CONTAINERS to put sth into a container or fill a container with sth for sale, transport, or storage **3.** *vt.* MAKE STH INTO A PARCEL OR BUNDLE to make up a parcel or bundle, or to wrap or roll sth up in one **4.** *vt.* FILL STH WITH A LARGE QUANTITY to fill sth, especially a limited space, tightly (*often passive*) ○ *a book packed with useful information* **5.** *vti.* CROWD INTO OR FILL A PLACE to crowd into a place so that it is full or overfull, or to fill a place with people **6.** *vt.* FIT STH INTO A LIMITED TIME to fit many different activities or events into a limited period of time ○ *packed a lot of sightseeing into one weekend* **7.** *vt.* COMPUT = **compress** *v.* 3 **8.** *vti.* COMPACT STH OR BECOME COMPACTED to compact a substance such as snow or soil into a dense mass, or to become densely compacted **9.** *vt.* PRESS STH ROUND AN OBJECT to wrap or press sth in around an object to hold it firmly or protect it **10.** *vt.* MED USE A PACK ON A WOUND to apply a medical pack to a wound or insert one into a body cavity **11.** *vt.* MED APPLY A COMPRESS TO A BODY PART to apply cold compresses to part of a patient's body in order to control body temperature **12.** *vt.* MECH ENG SEAL STH TO PREVENT LEAKAGE to seal a mechanical joint by inserting a layer of compressible material between the moving parts to prevent leakage of fluid **13.** *vt.* MECH ENG FILL A CAVITY WITH GREASE to fill a cavity containing bearings with grease **14.** *vti. US* CARRY A GUN to carry a weapon, especially a gun (*informal*) **15.** *vt.* POSSESS STH AS A FORCEFUL CAPABILITY to be capable of delivering sth that has a powerful or devastating effect (*informal*) **16.** *vt.* LOAD BAGGAGE ONTO AN ANIMAL to put goods or belongings onto a horse, donkey, or other animal in order to transport them **17.** *vti.* CARRY A LOAD to carry a load **18.** *vi.* RUGBY FORM SCRUM OR MAUL to get into a compact group for a scrum or maul ■ *n.* **1.** COMMERCIAL CONTAINER a container or piece of packaging holding several products or items of the same kind, or such a container and its contents **2.** COLLECTION OF THINGS IN A PACKAGE a set of documents or other materials relating to a subject that are packaged together ○ *a free information pack* **3.** AMOUNT CONTAINED IN A PACK the contents of a pack, or the amount of sth that can be contained in a pack **4.** LARGE AMOUNT a large amount of sth ○ *a pack of lies* **5.** BAG CARRIED ON THE BACK a bag or bundle, especially one designed to be carried on a person's or animal's back **6.** SOLDIER'S BAG FOR EQUIPMENT a soldier's canvas or nylon bag with shoulder straps used to carry personal clothing and equipment in the field **7.** PARACHUTE IN A CONTAINER a parachute, rigged, folded, and in its container ready for use **8.** SET OF CARDS a set of 52 playing cards, including the four suits plus jokers ○ *a pack of cards* **9.** GROUP OF ANIMALS a group of animals that live and hunt together, especially wolves or dogs ○ *a pack of wolves* **10.** LARGE GROUP OF PEOPLE ACTING TOGETHER a group of people who behave in the same way, especially a group whose behaviour appears to be threatening, predatory, or criminal ○ *always followed by a pack of photographers* **11.** GROUP OF BROWNIES OR CUBS a local organized unit of Brownie Guides or Cub Scouts **12.** RUGBY RUGBY TEAM'S FORWARDS the forwards playing for a particular rugby team, or the forwards from both sides during a match, especially when involved in a scrum or maul **13.** SPORTS MAIN BODY OF COMPETITORS the main body of competitors in a race or competition **14.** MIL GROUP OF SUBMARINES OR AIRCRAFT a number of submarines, aircraft, or other military units who hunt and fight the enemy as a group **15.** MED COMPRESS USED IN SURGERY a wad of soft absorbent material applied to a wound or temporarily inserted into a body cavity to control bleeding or keep tissues dry during surgery **16.** MED MEDICINAL COMPRESS a compress placed on the body for medicinal purposes **17.** COSMETIC PASTE a quantity of moist material applied to part of the body, especially the face, for cosmetic purposes ○ *a mud pack* **18.** = **pack ice** **19.** AMOUNT OF FOOD PRESERVED an amount of food canned or preserved in a particular year or season [12thC. From Dutch or Low German *pakken* (noun of uncertain origin: probably from Flemish, Dutch, or Low German *pak*).] —**packable** *adj.* ◇ **send sb packing** to dismiss or send sb away brusquely and unceremoniously (*informal*)

pack away *vt.* **1.** STORE AWAY to put things into storage containers after use or for reuse at a later time **2.** EAT IN LARGE QUANTITIES to eat food in large quantities (*informal*)

pack in *v.* **1.** *vt.* ATTRACT IN LARGE NUMBERS to attract very large audiences ○ *The show has been running three years and is still packing them in night after night.* **2.** *vti.* STOP DOING STH to stop or give up doing sth (*informal*) ○ *She's packed in her job.* **3.** *vt.* END RELATIONSHIP WITH to end a sexual or romantic relationship with sb (*informal*) ◇ **pack it in** to stop doing sth (*informal*) (*often used as a command*)

pack off *v.* **1.** *vt.* SEND UNCEREMONIOUSLY to send sb away unceremoniously to another place (*informal*) ○ *They were packed off to boarding school at the age of seven.* **2.** *vi.* GO SOMEWHERE UNCEREMONIOUSLY to leave or to go somewhere hastily or unceremoniously ○ *They packed off home as soon as the work was done.*

pack up *v.* **1.** *vti.* STOP DOING STH to stop doing sth **2.** *vi.* STOP WORKING to stop working properly (*informal*) ○ *The washing machine has packed up.* **3.** *vi.* FINISH WORK to finish work for the day (*informal*) ○ *I'm packing up and going home.*

pack[2] /pak/ (**packs, packing, packed**) *vt.* to ensure that a group such as a jury or committee is made up wholly or mainly of supporters of a particular side [Early 16thC. Origin uncertain: probably an alteration of PACT with the idea of private or secret dealings.]

package /pákij/ *n.* **1.** PARCEL an object or set of objects, wrapped, boxed, or tied in a bundle for transportation or mailing **2.** DIFFERENT THINGS CONSTITUTING A SINGLE ITEM a number of different components intended to constitute a single item **3.** COMPUT PIECE OF GENERAL ADAPTABLE COMPUTER SOFTWARE a piece of computer software that can be used for a range of related purposes, such as word processing or financial analysis **4.** = **package holiday** ■ *vt.* (**-ages, -aging, -aged**) **1.** PUT STH INTO PACKAGE to put things into or wrap them up as a package **2.** PRODUCE ATTRACTIVE PACKAGING FOR STH to create suitable or attractive packaging in which a product is to be sold **3.** PROMOTE OR PRESENT STH to present sb or sth to others in a way intended to ensure appeal and acceptance ○ *It wasn't so much the policy that was wrong as the way it was packaged.* **4.** GROUP STH AS A PACKAGE to group or offer several different items together in a package **5.** PUBL, BROADCAST PRODUCE STH FOR OTHERS TO MARKET to produce a book or television programme or series in finished form ready to be published or broadcast by another company

package deal *n.* a proposal or agreement comprising a number of different items that must all be accepted together

package holiday *n.* a holiday or tour organized in advance by a travel company to whom the holidaymaker pays a single fee covering transport, accommodation, board, and often entertainment. US term **package tour**

packager /pákijər/ *n.* **1.** SB OR STH THAT PACKS GOODS a person or machine that packs or wraps goods for sale, storage, or transport **2.** PUBL, BROADCAST SUBCONTRACTED PRODUCER OF BOOKS OR PROGRAMMES a company that produces books or television programmes in finished form for another company to publish or broadcast

package tour *n. US* = **package holiday**

packaging /pákijing/ *n.* **1.** WRAPPING OR CONTAINER the wrapping or container in which an item is presented for sale, or the materials used to make it **2.** DESIGN OR STYLE OF WRAPPING the design or style of the wrapping or container in which sth is offered for sale, especially from the point of view of its appeal to buyers **3.** PRESENTATION the manner in which sth or sb is presented to the public in order to create a favourable image or impression **4.** WORK OF PACKAGER the work done by a packager

pack animal *n.* an animal that is used to carry goods or equipment, e.g. a horse, donkey, or mule

pack drill *n.* a military punishment in which the offender has to march carrying a full load of equipment

packed /pakt/ *adj.* **1.** FULL OF PEOPLE full of people and extremely crowded ○ *played to a packed house every night* **2.** CONTAINING A LOT OF STH containing or offering sth in excitingly large quantities (*often used in combination*) ○ *a fun-packed adventure* **3.** COMPRESSED pressed together to form a compact mass ○ *packed snow*

packed lunch *n.* a lunch that has been prepared and put into a container to be eaten later, usually on a picnic or excursion. US term **box lunch**

packer /pákər/ *n.* **1.** SB OR STH THAT PACKS GOODS a person or machine that packs goods in containers or in packaging **2.** WHOLESALE PROCESSOR OF MEAT a person or company involved in the processing and packing of goods, especially meat or fresh produce, for the wholesale market

Packer /pákər/, **Sir Frank** (1906–74) Australian journalist and newspaper proprietor. He was chairman of Australian Consolidated Press (1957–74), one of the country's largest media groups. Full name **Sir Douglas Frank Hewson Packer**

Packer, Kerry (*b.* 1937) Australian media proprietor. His television coverage of cricket revolutionized the way the game is presented. Full name **Kerry Francis Bullimore Packer**

packet /pákit/ *n.* **1.** SMALL CONTAINER FOR GOODS a small box, envelope, or bag in which goods are sold or stored **2.** CONTENTS OR QUANTITY IN PACKET the contents of a packet, or the quantity of goods contained in a packet ○ *still have half a packet of crisps* **3.** SMALL PARCEL a small parcel or package **4.** COMPUT MESSAGE FRAGMENT IN A COMPUTER NETWORK a small piece of a message for transmission through a computer network **5. packet, packet boat** BOAT ON A REGULAR SHORT RUN a small ship that provides a regular service carrying passengers, freight, and mail over a fixed short route ■ *vt.* **(-ets, -eting, -eted)** PUT STH IN A PACKET to put sth into a packet or wrap it up as a parcel [15thC. Origin uncertain: probably literally 'small pack', formed from PACK[1] (perhaps on the model of Anglo-Norman *pacquet*).] ◇ **catch** *or* **cop** *or* **get a packet** to be seriously injured (*slang*) ◇ **cost a packet** to cost a great deal of money

packet switching *n.* the process of transmitting and routing data in the form of packet segments sent rapidly and sequentially over a channel that is occupied only during the actual transmission of data

packframe /pák fraym/ *n.* a lightweight frame with shoulder straps to which equipment or unwieldy loads can be strapped to be carried on a person's back

packhorse /pák hawrss/ *n.* a horse used for carrying goods or equipment

pack ice *n.* floating ice, especially in polar regions, that has formed itself into a solid mass covering a wide area

packing /páking/ *n.* **1.** ACT OF PUTTING THINGS INTO CONTAINERS the task of putting things into containers, usually for storage or transport **2.** MATERIAL FOR PROTECTING A PACKED OBJECT material used to surround and protect sth packed inside a container **3.** WATERTIGHT OR AIRTIGHT MATERIAL material used to fill or surround sth such as a joint in a pipe in order to make it watertight or airtight **4.** FOOD TECH PROCESSING AND PACKAGING OF FOOD the processing and packaging of food such as meat or produce for sale **5.** MED ABSORBENT MATERIAL FOR MEDICAL PACKS absorbent material such as gauze for insertion in body cavities or wounds **6.** MECH ENG SPACERS BETWEEN CLAMPED SURFACES shims, washers, or other pieces of metal used to adjust the distance between component surfaces before they are secured

packing case *n.* a large wooden box or crate in which objects are packed for transportation or storage

packing fraction *n.* a measure of the stability of an atomic nucleus, arrived at by dividing the difference between its mass in atomic mass units and its mass number by that mass number

pack rat *n.* a North American rat that lives in woodlands and collects and carries away objects to its nest. The best-known species has a long bushy tail and cheek pouches. Latin name: *Neotoma cinerea.*

packsaddle /pák sad'l/ *n.* a saddle for carrying loads on a pack animal

packthread /pák thred/ *n.* strong twine used for sewing up packages wrapped in sacking or other fabric

pack train *n.* a line of pack animals carrying loads

pact /pakt/ *n.* an agreement made between two or more groups or individuals, either formally or informally, to do sth together or for each other [15thC. Via French *pacte* from Latin *pactum*, a form of *pactus*, past participle of *pacisci* 'to agree'.]

pacy *adj.* = **pacey**

pad[1] /pad/ *n.* **1.** PIECE OF SOFT MATERIAL a piece of soft material used to protect sth or give it shape, to clean or polish articles, or to absorb moisture **2.** SPORTS PROTECTIVE MATERIAL WORN BY SPORTS PLAYERS a specially shaped covering of impact-absorbing material used to protect part of the body, especially when playing a sport **3.** BLOCK OF PAPER SHEETS a number of sheets of paper of the same size fastened together along one edge **4.** INK-FILLED MATERIAL a thick firm piece of material saturated with ink onto which a rubber stamp is pressed so that ink is transferred onto it **5.** AIR AREA FOR TAKING OFF AND LANDING a place where a helicopter can land and take off or from which a rocket is launched **6.** SANITARY TOWEL a strip of absorbent material used externally during menstruation **7.** BACKING MATERIAL a firm backing or support for sth that is laid on a surface **8.** ZOOL FLESHY CUSHION OF AN ANIMAL'S PAW a small rounded fleshy cushion on the underside of an animal's paw **9.** ANAT FLESHY TIP OF A FINGER OR TOE the rounded fleshy part at the end of a human finger or toe **10.** LIVING QUARTERS sb's flat or house (*slang dated*) **11.** BOT WATER LILY LEAF the broad leaf of an aquatic plant such as a water lily that floats on the surface of the water **12.** ELEC ENG SET OF RESISTORS a fixed configuration of resistors designed to reduce the strength of an electrical signal without distorting the signal itself ■ *vt.* **(pads, padding, padded) 1.** LINE OR COVER STH WITH SOFT MATERIAL to use soft material to give sth shape, to make it more comfortable, or to protect it **2.** ADD UNNECESSARY MATERIAL TO STH to add unnecessary material to sth, especially a piece of writing or a speech, in order to lengthen it ○ *padded out the speech with anecdotes* **3.** INFLATE STH BY ADDING BOGUS EXPENSES to add extra charges to a bill or expense account to make it higher than it should be [Mid-16thC. Origin uncertain: perhaps from a Low Dutch word. Originally 'bundle of straw'.]

pad[2] /pad/ *vti.* **(pads, padding, padded) 1.** WALK QUIETLY to walk, or to walk along or through somewhere, with soft or silent steps ○ *She padded along in her slippers.* **2.** WALK SLOWLY to walk along a route very slowly ■ *n.* **1.** SOUND OF FOOTSTEPS the sound of soft steady footsteps **2.** FOOTPAD a footpad (*archaic*) **3.** EQU SLOW HORSE a horse that goes at a slow ambling gait (*archaic or regional*) [Mid-16thC. Origin uncertain: perhaps from Low German *padden* 'to tread' (noun from Low German or Dutch *pad* 'path').]

padded cell *n.* formerly, a room in a psychiatric hospital with its walls and floor covered with padding to prevent a patient from doing himself or herself physical harm

padding /pádding/ *n.* **1.** THICK SOFT MATERIAL thick soft material used as a protective lining or covering or to fill and give shape to things **2.** UNNECESSARY ADDITIONS TO SPEECH OR WRITING unnecessary or irrelevant material added to a piece of writing or speech to make it longer **3.** BOGUS ADDITIONS TO BILL extra charges added to a bill or expense account to make it higher than it should be

paddle[1] /pádd'l/ *n.* **1.** NAUT SHORT FLAT-BLADED OAR a short oar with a flat blade at one or both ends used to propel a canoe or small boat **2.** NAUT BLADE OF A PADDLE WHEEL a blade of a paddle wheel **3.** *US* RACKET GAMES TABLE TENNIS BAT a round wooden bat with a short handle used in table tennis **4.** *US* PIECE OF WOOD FOR SPANKING a usually short piece of wood with a flattened end used for physical punishment **5.** ZOOL = **flipper** *n.* 1 **6.** FLAT-BLADED STIRRING TOOL a tool with a flat blade used for shaping, stirring, or beating **7.** VIDEO EARLY INPUT DEVICE FOR VIDEO GAMES an input device for early video games with a dial that allowed the user to move an on-screen object either up and down or from side to side ■ *v.* **(-dles, -dling, -dled) 1.** *vti.* NAUT PROPEL A CANOE WITH A PADDLE to propel a canoe or small boat through water using a paddle **2.** *vt.* NAUT CARRY IN A CANOE to carry sb or sth somewhere in a canoe or paddleboat **3.** *vt. US* SPANK to spank sb with a paddle or with the hand **4.** *vt.* STIR WITH PADDLE to stir, beat, or shape sth using a paddle **5.** *vti.* ROW AT AN EASY PACE to row a boat at an easy pace [15thC. Origin uncertain: perhaps via medieval Latin *padela* from Latin *patella* 'small dish', from *patina* 'shallow dish' (source of English *patina*).] —**paddler** *n.*

paddle[2] /pádd'l/ *v.* **(-dles, -dling, -dled) 1.** *vi.* WALK ABOUT IN SHALLOW WATER to walk or play, usually with bare feet, in shallow water **2.** *vti.* DABBLE IN WATER to move the hands or feet about gently in shallow water **3.** *vi.* WADDLE to walk along unsteadily like a very small child ■ *n.* ACT OF PLAYING IN WATER an act or period of walking or playing in shallow water ○ *go for a paddle* [Mid-16thC. Origin uncertain: perhaps from a Low Dutch word.] —**paddler** *n.*

paddleball /pádd'l bawl/ *n.* a game for two to four players played by hitting a ball against a wall with small paddles, or the ball used in this game

paddleboard /pádd'l bawrd/ *n.* a long narrow surfboard used especially in rescuing swimmers

paddleboat /pádd'l bōt/ *n.* a boat propelled by one or more paddle wheels

paddlefish /pádd'l fish/ (*plural* **-fishes** *or* **-fish**) *n.* a large freshwater fish with a long flat snout and a cartilage skeleton, found in the Mississippi River and its tributaries and in the Yangtze River. Family: Polyodontidae.

paddle steamer *n.* a steamship propelled by paddle wheels on each side of the hull or by a single paddle wheel at the stern. US term **paddle wheeler**

Paddle wheeler

paddle wheel *n.* a wheel with flat blades fixed all round its edge, attached to the hull of a ship and usually turned by an engine to propel the ship through water

paddle wheeler *n. US* = **paddle steamer**

paddock /páddək/ *n.* **1.** EQU ENCLOSED FIELD FOR HORSES a small field near a house or stable with grazing for horses **2.** EQU AREA FOR MOUNTING RACEHORSES an area on a racecourse where the racehorses are paraded before a race and the jockeys mount **3.** MOTOR SPORTS AREA FOR CARS BEFORE A RACE an area near the pits on a motor-racing track where cars are worked on before a race **4.** *ANZ* FENCED AREA OF LAND a field or other fenced-off area of land **5.** *ANZ* PLAYING AREA the playing area for a sport, e.g. a football pitch ■ *vt.* **(-docks, -docking, -docked)** EQU KEEP HORSES IN PADDOCK to keep animals, especially horses, in a paddock [Early 17thC. Alteration of *parro(c)k*, from Old English *pearroc* 'fence, enclosed land', from a prehistoric Germanic word perhaps from assumed Vulgar Latin *parricus* (source of English *park*).]

paddy[1] /páddi/ (*plural* **-dies**) *n.* **1. paddy, paddy field** RICE FIELD a field, usually kept covered with shallow water, in which rice is grown **2.** RICE rice as a crop in the field or when harvested but not yet processed [Early 17thC. From Malay *padi*.]

paddy[2] /páddi/ (*plural* **-dies**) *n.* a fit of rage or bad temper (*informal*) [Late 19thC. From PADDY.]

Paddy /páddi/ (*plural* **-dies**) *n.* an offensive term for an Irish person (*slang insult*) [Late 18thC. From the pet form of Irish *Pádraig* 'Patrick'.]

paddy field *n.* = **paddy**[1] *n.* 1

paddymelon *n.* = **pademelon**

paddy wagon *n. US, ANZ* a patrol wagon (*informal*) [Late 19thC. *Paddy* is said to have originally referred to Irish policemen in New York and New England.]

paddywhack /páddi wak/ *n.* (*dated informal*) **1.** TEMPER a bad temper **2.** SPANKING a spank or spanking [Early 19thC. [Paddy] from PADDY.]

pademelon /páddi melən/ (*plural* **-melons** *or* **-melon**), **paddymelon** (*plural* **-ons** *or* **-on**) *n.* a small wallaby that lives at the edges of forests in Australia. Genus: *Thylogale.* [Early 19thC. Alteration of an Aboriginal name.]

Padishah /páddi shaa/ *n.* a title used by or to refer to the former Shahs of Iran and Sultans of

Turkey [Early 17thC. From Persian *pād(i)šāh*, literally 'lord-shah', from *pati* 'lord, master' + *šāh* 'shah' (source of English *shah*).]

padlock /pád lok/ *n.* **SMALL DETACHABLE LOCK** a detachable lock with a movable semicircular bar at the top, the free end of which is usually passed through a hasp and then locked shut ■ *vt.* (**-locks, -locking, -locked**) **LOCK STH WITH A PADLOCK** to secure sth using a padlock [15thC. *Pad-* is of unknown origin.]

padre /paádri, -dray/ *n.* **1.** MIL **CHRISTIAN CHAPLAIN IN THE ARMED FORCES** a Christian clergyman who ministers to the armed forces **2. USED TO ADDRESS A PRIEST** used to address or refer to a Roman Catholic priest in a country where Spanish, Italian, or Portuguese is spoken [Late 16thC. Via Italian, Spanish, or Portuguese from Latin *pater* 'father' (source of English *patron*).]

padrone /pə drṓni/ (*plural* **-nes** *or* **-ni** /-nee/) *n.* the owner or manager of an Italian business, especially a restaurant or café [Late 17thC. Via Italian from Latin *patronus* 'protector, patron', from *pater* (see PADRE).] —**padronism** *n.*

padsaw /pádd saw/ *n.* a small narrow saw with a handle at one end only, used for cutting curves. US term **keyhole saw** [Late 19thC. *Pad* from PAD[1] in the sense 'handle into which different tools can be fitted'.]

Padua /páddyoo ə/ city in northeastern Italy, and the capital of Padua Province, Veneto Region. Population: 213,656 (1992).

paduasoy /páddyoo ə soy/ *n.* a rich heavy silk fabric [Late 16thC. Alteration (influenced by *Padua say* 'cloth from *Padua*', Italian city known for textile manufacturing) of French *pou-de-soie* 'pou of silk' (from Old French *pout*, of unknown origin).]

paean /peé ən/ *n.* a written, spoken, or musical expression of enthusiastic praise or rapturous joy [Late 16thC. Via Latin, 'religious hymn (originally in honour of Apollo)', from Greek *paian*, from *Paian* 'name for Apollo'.]

paed- *prefix.* = **ped-** (*used before vowels*)

paediatrician /peédi ə trísh'n/, **pediatrician** *n.* a doctor who specializes in the care and development of children and in the prevention and treatment of children's diseases. US term **pediatrician**

paediatrics /peédi áttriks/, **pediatrics** *n.* the branch of medicine concerned with the care and development of children and with the prevention and treatment of children's diseases (*takes a singular verb*) US term **pediatrics** —**paediatric** *adj.*

paedo- *prefix.* = **pedo-** [From Greek *paid-*, stem of *pais* 'child, boy' (source of English *encyclopedia*). Ultimately from an Indo-European word meaning 'little', which is also the ancestor of English *poor*.]

paedodontics /peédə dóntiks/, **pedodontics** *n.* the branch of dentistry concerned with dental care and treatment for children (*takes a singular verb*) US term **pedodontics**

paedology /pi dólləji/, **pedology** *n.* the scientific study of the physical and mental development of children. US term **pedology** —**paedologic** /peédəlójjik/ *adj.* —**paedological** /-lójjik'l/ *adj.* —**paedologically** /-lójjikli/ *adv.* —**paedologist** /pi dólləjist/ *n.*

paedomorphosis /péddə máwrfəssiss, peédə-/ *n.* = **pedomorphosis**

paedomorphosis /peédə máwrfəsiss, péddə máwrfəsiss/ *n.* = **neoteny**

paedophile /peédə fīl/, **pedophile** *n.* an adult who has sexual desire for children or who has committed the crime of sex with a child. US term **pedophile** —**paedophilic** /peédə fíllik/ *adj.*

paedophilia /peédə fílli ə/, **pedophilia** *n.* sexual desire felt by an adult for children, or the crime of sex with a child. US term **pedophilia** —**paedophiliac** /-fílli ak/ *n., adj.*

paella /pī éllə/ *n.* **1. SPANISH RICE DISH** a Spanish dish made of saffron-flavoured rice with chicken, shellfish, and other ingredients that vary from region to region **2. PAN FOR PAELLA** a large shallow frying pan, with a handle on each side, that allows rice to cook in a shallow depth of liquid that evaporates quickly and evenly [Late 19thC. Via Catalan from, ultimately, Latin *patella* 'small dish', from *patina* 'shallow dish'.]

paeon /peé ən/ *n.* a metrical foot consisting of one long and three short syllables arranged in any order [Early 17thC. Via Latin from Greek *paiōn*, variant of *paian* (see PAEAN).]

Paestum /péstəm/ ancient city in southern Italy, noted for its Greek ruins

pagan /páygən/ *n.* **1. FOLLOWER OF A LESS POPULAR RELIGION** sb who does not follow one of the world's main religions, especially sb who is not a Christian, Muslim, or Jew, and whose religion is regarded as questionable (*sometimes considered offensive*) **2. POLYTHEIST OR PANTHEIST** a follower of an ancient polytheistic or pantheistic religion **3. HEATHEN** sb who has no religion (*disapproving*) ■ *adj.* **1. OF A LESS POPULAR RELIGION** believing in or relating to a religion that is not one of the world's main religions and is regarded as questionable **2. FOLLOWING POLYTHEISTIC OR PANTHEISTIC RELIGION** believing in or relating to an ancient polytheistic or pantheistic religion **3. NONRELIGIOUS** having no religion (*sometimes considered offensive*) [14thC. Via late Latin *paganus* from Latin, 'villager, civilian', from *pagus* 'rural district' (source of English *peasant*).] —**paganism** *n.* —**paganistic** /páygə nístik/ *adj.*

WORD KEY: ORIGIN

The Latin word *pagus*, from which ***pagan*** is derived, originally meant 'sth stuck in the ground as a landmark'. It was extended metaphorically to 'rural district, village', and the noun *paganus* was derived from it, denoting 'country dweller, villager'. This shifted in meaning, first to 'civilian', and then (based on the early Christian notion that all members of the Church were 'soldiers' of Christ) to 'heathen'.

Paganini /pággə neéni/, **Niccolò** (1782–1840) Italian composer and violinist. Renowned as a virtuoso, his compositions include violin sonatas, caprices for solo violin, and concertos.

page[1] /payj/ *n.* **1. ONE SIDE OF SHEET OF PAPER** one side of a single sheet of paper, especially one bound into a book, newspaper, or magazine, or forming part of a piece of written work **2. SINGLE SHEET IN A BOOK** a single sheet of paper, especially one bound into a book, newspaper, or magazine ○ *a book with some pages missing* **3. AMOUNT OF WRITING ON A PAGE** the amount of writing or printed matter that can be contained on a page **4.** COMPUT **COMPUTER DATA PRINTING OUT AS A PAGE** the amount of text or graphics in a computer document that will print out as a single page **5.** COMPUT **SCREENFUL OF COMPUTER DISPLAY** the portion of text or graphics that can be seen on a computer screen at one time **6. NOTEWORTHY PERIOD OR EVENT** a period or event, especially a noteworthy one, in the history of sth or sb's life ○ *Antibiotics wrote an important page in the history of medical research.* ■ *v.* (**pages, paging, paged**) **1.** *vi.* **LOOK THROUGH PAGES** to turn and look over the pages of sth **2.** *vt.* = **paginate** [Late 16thC. From French, shortening of *pagene*, from Latin *pagina*, literally '(strips of papyrus) fastened together'.]

page[2] /payj/ *n.* **1. BOY ATTENDANT** a youth acting as an attendant to sb on a ceremonial occasion, e.g. to a bride at her wedding **2. BOY WHO RUNS ERRANDS** a youth employed to run errands or carry messages for guests in a hotel or club **3.** HIST **BOY SERVANT IN MEDIEVAL TIMES** a youth who acted as a personal or household servant to sb, especially a royal or noble person, in medieval times **4.** HIST **BOY APPRENTICED TO KNIGHT** a youth who acted as the personal servant to a knight in medieval times as the first stage of his training to become a knight **5.** POL **ERRAND RUNNER IN US CONGRESS** sb who is employed to run errands, carry messages, act as a guide, and perform other duties in the US Congress ■ *vt.* (**pages, paging, paged**) **1. SUMMON SB BY NAME** to summon sb by calling out his or her name, e.g. over a loudspeaker system **2. CONTACT SB ON A PAGER** to try to contact sb on his or her pager **3.** HIST **SERVE SB AS PAGE** to serve sb in the capacity of page [13thC. From French, of uncertain origin: perhaps ultimately from Greek *paidion* 'little child, slave-boy', from *paid-* (see PAEDO-).]

Page /payj/, **Sir Earle** (1880–1961) Australian statesman. He was founder and leader of the Country Party (1920–39), held various ministerial posts, and was briefly prime minister in 1939.

pageant /pájjənt/ *n.* **1. LARGE-SCALE PLAY REPRESENTING A HISTORICAL EVENT** a large-scale stage production representing historical or legendary events, especially local ones, in scenes or tableaux in which dramatic interest is less important than spectacle **2. ELABORATE AND COLOURFUL PROCESSION** an elaborate and colourful procession, display, or ceremonial occasion [14thC. Alteration of earlier *pagyn* 'scene, stage', from Anglo-Latin *pagina*, of uncertain origin: perhaps from Latin, 'page, leaf' (see PAGE[1]).]

pageantry /pájjəntri/ *n.* **1. MAGNIFICENT CEREMONIAL DISPLAY** highly colourful, splendid, and stately display or ceremonies, usually with a historical or traditional flavour **2. PAGEANTS** pageants considered collectively (*archaic*)

pageboy /páyj boy/ *n.* **1.** = **page**[2] *n.* 1 **2.** HAIR **HAIRSTYLE WITH FRINGE** a hairstyle in which the hair is cut to one length, usually jaw-length, and curls under slightly at the ends, with a fringe at the front

page break *n.* a code or symbol on a computer screen that shows where a printer will start a new page, e.g. in a word processing document

pager /páyjər/ *n.* a small electronic message-receiving device, often with a small screen, that beeps, flashes, or vibrates to let the user know that sb is trying to contact him or her

page three *n.* the page on which some tabloid newspapers habitually print a large photograph of a naked or bare-breasted woman (*hyphenated when used before a noun*) ○ *a page-three girl*

Paget's disease /pájjəts-/ *n.* **1. BONE DISEASE** a chronic disease in which the bones become enlarged and weakened and subject to fracture **2. Paget's disease, Paget's cancer CANCEROUS CONDITION OF THE BREAST** a cancerous inflammatory condition of the nipple and areola, associated with breast cancer [Late 19thC. Named after Sir James *Paget* (1814–99), English surgeon and pathologist who described these diseases.]

page-turner *n.* a book with a very gripping plot

paginal /pájjin'l/ *adj.* **1.** PUBL **DUPLICATING PAGE FOR PAGE** exactly duplicating a previous edition or version, so that the same text appears on the same page in both **2. RELATING TO PAGES** consisting of, relating to, or like a page or pages [Mid-17thC. From late Latin *paginalis*, from Latin *pagina* (see PAGE[1]).]

paginate /pájji nayt/ (**-nates, -nating, -nated**) *vt.* to number the pages of a book or document [Late 19thC. Origin uncertain: probably a back-formation from PAGINATION.]

pagination /pájji náysh'n/ *n.* **1. PAGE NUMBERS** the sequential numbers given to pages in a book or document **2. ACT OF NUMBERING PAGES** the process or work of numbering pages [Mid-19thC. From French, from Latin *pagina* (see PAGE[1]).]

paging[1] /páy jing/ *n.* the movement of a fixed-size block of data between faster main and slower auxiliary memories to optimize performance without the user being aware that the transfer has taken place

paging[2] /páy jing/ *n.* a facility that enables sb to be contacted via a pager (*often used before a noun*) ○ *a paging service*

Paglia /páyli ə/, **Camille** (*b.* 1947) US writer. Her books, which mainly examine art and culture, take a controversial anti-feminist position. Full name **Camille Anna Paglia**

Pagnol /pán yol/, **Marcel** (1895–1974) French playwright and film director. Many of his films, including *Manon des Sources* (1952), are set in southern France.

pagoda /pə gṓdə/ *n.* **1.** EASTERN RELIG **BUDDHIST TEMPLE WITH PROJECTING ROOFS** a Buddhist temple building, especially one in the form of a tower with several storeys, each with an upward curving roof that tapers slightly towards the top **2.** ARCHIT **BUILDING DESIGNED LIKE A BUDDHIST PAGODA** a building that is shaped like a Buddhist pagoda but has a decorative rather than a religious purpose [Late 16thC. From Portuguese *pagode*, of uncertain origin: perhaps ultimately from Persian *butkada*, literally 'idol dwelling', but altered by association with Prakrit *bhagodī* 'holy'.]

Pagoda

Library of Congress

Thomas Paine

pagoda tree *n.* a Chinese tree that grows into a shape similar to a pagoda, has dark green leaves, and bears clusters of creamy-white flowers. Latin name: *Sophora japonica*.

pah /paa/ *interj.* used to show disgust, contempt, or annoyance [Late 16thC. Natural exclamation.]

Pahlavi /páylǝvi/, **Pehlevi** *n.* a literary form of classical Persian used especially in Zoroastrian and Mani-chaean texts [Late 18thC. From Persian *pahlawī*, from *pahlav*, from *parthava* 'Parthia (country of ancient Asia)'.]

paid /payd/ past participle, past tense of **pay** ■ *adj.* **GIVEN MONEY OR EARNING MONEY** given money in return for work, or done for the purpose of earning money ◇ **put paid to** to destroy or put an end to sb or sth

paid-up *adj.* (*not hyphenated after a verb*) **1. NOT OWING ANYTHING** having paid all the money owed to an organization or individual **2. COMMITTED** enthusiastic and committed **3. FULLY PAID FOR** for which the full price or all instalments have been paid ○ *paid-up shares* **4. RECEIVED FROM SHAREHOLDERS** constituting the amount of a company's capital that has actually been received from its shareholders ○ *paid-up capital*

paigle /páyg'l/ *n.* = **oxlip** [Mid-16thC. Origin unknown.]

pail /payl/ *n.* a bucket [14thC. From Old French *paielle* 'warming pan, liquid measure', of uncertain origin: perhaps from Latin *patella* 'small dish' (see PAELLA).]

paillasse *n.* = **palliasse**

paillette /pal yét/, pálli ét/ *n.* a sequin or spangle sewn onto a piece of clothing [Mid-19thC. From French, literally 'small straw', from *paille* 'straw, chaff', from Latin *palea* (see PALLIASSE).]

pain /payn/ *n.* **1. UNPLEASANT PHYSICAL SENSATION** the acutely unpleasant physical discomfort experienced by sb who is violently struck, injured, or ill in certain ways ○ *cried out in pain* **2. FEELING OF DISCOMFORT** a sensation of pain in a particular part of the body (*often used in the plural*) ○ *was complaining of pains in the lower abdomen* **3. EMOTIONAL DISTRESS** severe emotional or mental distress ○ *the pain of rejection* **4. SB OR STH TROUBLESOME** sb or sth that is extremely annoying or causes many problems (*informal*) ■ **pains** *npl.* **1. TROUBLE TAKEN TO DO STH** conscientious effort or trouble taken, usually in tackling a piece of work **2. LABOUR PAINS** the painful spasms experienced by a woman during childbirth, caused by the contraction of the womb ■ *v.* (**pains, paining, pained**) **1.** *vt.* **SADDEN SB** to make sb feel saddened or distressed ○ *It pains me to hear you speak like that.* **2.** *vti.* **CAUSE OR FEEL PAIN** to cause physical pain to sb, or experience pain [13thC. Via French *peine* from Latin *poena* 'penalty, punishment', from Greek *poinē* 'penalty' (source of English *punish* and *subpoena*).] ◇ **a pain in the arse** or **backside** sb or sth that is extremely annoying or troublesome or causes a great many problems (*slang*) ◇ **a pain in the neck** sb or sth that is extremely annoying or troublesome or causes a great many problems (*informal*) ◇ **on** or **under pain of sth** risking or threatened with sth, e.g. death or instant dismissal, as punishment

Paine /payn/, **Thomas** (1737–1809) British writer and political philosopher. His pamphlet *Common Sense* (1776) influenced the move towards American independence.

pained /paynd/ *adj.* expressing wounded feelings or a sense of being disappointed or offended by sth that sb has done ○ *a pained expression*

painful /páynf'l/ *adj.* **1. CAUSING PAIN** causing acute physical discomfort ○ *a painful cut* **2. HURTING** hurting as a result of an injury or disease ○ *My arm's still quite painful.* **3. CAUSING DISTRESS** causing emotional or mental distress ○ *painful memories* **4. DIFFICULT** accomplished with laborious effort ○ *making painful progress with the work* **5. VERY BAD** embarrassingly bad ○ *Her performance was painful to watch.* —**painfully** *adv.* —**painfulness** *n.*

painkiller /páyn kilǝr/ *n.* sth, especially a drug, that reduces pain —**painkilling** *adj.*

painless /páynlǝss/ *adj.* **1. CAUSING NO PAIN** not causing any pain **2. TROUBLE-FREE** involving little or no difficulty or effort ○ *a painless solution to our problem* —**painlessly** *adv.* —**painlessness** *n.*

painstaking /páynz tayking/ *adj.* involving or showing great care and attention to detail [Late 17thC. From *pains taking*.]

────── **WORD KEY: SYNONYMS** ──────
See Synonyms at *careful*.

paint /paynt/ *n.* **1. COLOURED LIQUID APPLIED TO A SURFACE** a coloured liquid applied to a surface in order to decorate or protect it, or in order to create a painting **2. DRIED PAINT ON A SURFACE** a film of dried paint on a surface (*often used before a noun*) ○ *paint remover* **3. SOLID PIGMENT** a solid block of pigment that forms liquid paint when moistened or dissolved **4. FACIAL MAKEUP** makeup for the face (*informal*) **5.** THEATRE = **greasepaint** ■ *v.* (**paints, painting, painted**) **1.** *vti.* **COVER STH WITH PAINT** to cover the surface of sth with paint in order to decorate or protect it **2.** *vti.* **CREATE A PICTURE USING PAINT** to create a picture, or create a picture of sth, by applying paint in different colours to paper, canvas, or some other surface **3.** *vt.* **ADD STH TO A SURFACE USING PAINT** to mark designs or words on a surface using paint ○ *The words 'No Parking' were painted on the wall.* **4.** *vt.* **APPLY LIQUID WITH A BRUSH** to apply a liquid to a surface using a brush, e.g. to brush a medicated liquid onto the skin ○ *My father used to paint iodine onto our grazed knees.* **5.** *vt.* **APPLY COSMETICS TO THE FACE OR NAILS** to apply makeup to the face or lips, or varnish to the nails **6.** *vi.* **USE COSMETICS** to use cosmetics, especially to cover blemishes or to lend a false attractiveness (*archaic*) **7.** *vt.* **DESCRIBE IN WORDS** to describe sth in words, especially to give a vivid description of sth ○ *In his autobiography, he paints his uncle's home as a palace* [12thC. From French *peint*, past participle of *peindre*, from Latin *pingere* 'to paint' (source of English *depict* and *picture*).]

paintball /páynt bawl/ *n.* a team game in which each player has a gun that fires gelatin capsules filled with water-soluble marking dye, the object being to shoot members of the opposing team —**paintballing** *n.*

paintbrush /páynt brush/ *n.* a brush for putting paint onto surfaces or painting pictures

Painted Desert /páyntid-/ plateau region in Arizona noted for its vividly coloured rocks. Parts of it lie within Native American reservations. Area: 19,425 sq. km/7,500 sq. mi.

painted lady *n.* a widely distributed migratory butterfly with reddish-brown, black, and orange wings. Latin name: *Vanessa cardui*.

painter[1] /páyntǝr/ *n.* **1. SB WHO PAINTS PICTURES** an artist who paints pictures ○ *a portrait painter* **2. SB WHO PAINTS HOUSES** sb whose job is to cover surfaces with paint, especially to paint and decorate the interiors of buildings

painter[2] /páyntǝr/ *n.* NAUT a rope attached to the front of a boat that is used to tie it to sth such as a mooring [14thC. Origin uncertain: probably from Old French *penteur* 'rope running from masthead, cord for hanging', from *pendre* 'to hang', from, ultimately, Latin *pendere* (source of English *suspend*).]

painterly /páyntǝrli/ *adj.* **1. USING COLOUR RATHER THAN LINE** characterized by the use of colour rather than line to represent shapes or to structure a composition **2. LIKE A PAINTER'S WORK** typical of a good painter and his or her work

painting /páynting/ *n.* **1. PAINTED PICTURE** a picture made using paint **2. ACTIVITY OF APPLYING PAINT** the art or work of applying paint to surfaces

paintwork /páynt wurk/ *n.* the painted surfaces of sth, e.g. a vehicle's bodywork or the interior of a building

pair /pair/ *n.* **1. 2 SIMILAR THINGS USED TOGETHER** two matching objects that are designed to be used together ○ *a pair of socks* **2. THING WITH TWO JOINED PARTS** a garment or article consisting of two matching or identical parts joined together ○ *a pair of binoculars* **3. 2 PEOPLE TOGETHER** two people who are doing sth together, or who are considered together because there is some connection between them **4. COUPLE** two people in a relationship such as a marriage **5.** ZOOL **2 MATING ANIMALS** a male and female animal of the same species who are together for mating **6. ONE OF TWO MATCHED ARTICLES** one of two matched articles such as shoes or gloves ○ *lost the pair to his cufflink* **7.** EQU **2 HORSES HARNESSED TOGETHER** two horses harnessed together to pull a carriage ○ *a coach and pair* **8.** CARDS **2 PLAYING CARDS** two playing cards that have the same value ○ *a pair of aces* **9.** POL **2 OPPOSING MEMBERS MAKING A VOTING AGREEMENT** two members from opposing sides in a legislative body who each agree not to vote on issues if the other is not present and able to vote. The arrangement covers occasions when members cannot vote because of illness or other commitments, the effect being to maintain the usual balance of numbers between the two opposing sides. **10.** POL **AGREEMENT TO FORM A PAIR** an arrangement between two members on opposing sides in a legislative body to form a pair **11.** ROWING = **pair-oar 12.** MATH, LOGIC **SET OF 2 ELEMENTS IN ORDER** a set consisting of two elements in order **13.** CHEM **ELECTRON BOND** two electrons forming a bond between atoms **14.** CRICKET **ZERO IN BOTH INNINGS** a score of zero in both innings of a match ■ **pairs** *npl.* = **pelmanism** ■ *v.* (**pairs, pairing, paired**) **1.** *vti.* **PUT INTO GROUP OF 2** to form a pair with sb, or to partner sb with sb else, for some shared activity or for romance or friendship **2.** *vt.* **MATCH 2 THINGS TOGETHER** to put two matching articles together **3.** *vt.* POL **FORM A LEGISLATIVE PAIR** to arrange a pair between two members of a voting assembly or to form a pair with another member **4.** *vi.* ZOOL **FORM A MATING PAIR** to form a mating pair [13thC. Directly or via French *paire* from Latin *paria* 'equals', a plural form of *par* 'equal, a pair' (source of English *compare* and *umpire*).]

pair bond *n.* ZOOL a relationship between a male and female animal, formed either during courtship and breeding or for life, that excludes others of the same species —**pair bonding** *n.*

pair-oar *n.* a racing shell in which two rowers with one oar each sit one behind the other

pair production *n.* the creation of a negative particle (**electron**) and a positive particle (**positron**) when a fast particle (**photon**) passes through a strong electric field such as that surrounding an atomic nucleus

pair royal (*plural* **pairs royal**) *n.* in some card games, a set of three cards of the same value

paisa /pí saa/ (*plural* **-se** or **-sa**) *n.* **1. S ASIAN SUBUNIT OF CURRENCY** a subunit of currency in India, Pakistan, Bangladesh, and Nepal. See table at **currency 2. COIN WORTH A PAISA** a coin worth one paisa [Late 19thC. From Hindi *paisā*.]

paisley /páyzli/ (*plural* **-leys**) *n.* **1. PATTERN WITH CURVING SHAPES** a distinctive bold design consisting of multi-coloured curving shapes, stylized cones, and feathers **2. GARMENT WITH A PAISLEY DESIGN** a fabric or piece of clothing with a paisley design, especially a type

Paisley

of woollen shawl popular in the 19th century [Early 19thC. Named after *Paisley*, town in south-western Scotland where material with this pattern was first made.] —**paisley** *adj.*

Paisley /páyzli/ town and administrative centre of Renfrewshire, Scotland. Population: 75,526 (1991).

Paiute /pí óot/ (*plural* **-utes** *or* **-ute**), **Piute** /pí óot, pí yóot, pí oot/ (*plural* **-utes** *or* **-ute**) *n.* a Native North American language spoken in various parts of the United States, especially in California. It belongs to the Uto-Aztecan branch of Aztec-Tanoan languages and is spoken by about 12,000 people. [Early 19thC. From Spanish *payuchi*, of unknown origin.] —**Paiute** *adj.*

pajamas *npl.* US = **pyjamas**

pak choi /pák chóy/ *n.* a type of Chinese vegetable with tender wide white stems and bright green leaves, similar to Swiss chard in appearance [From Chinese (Cantonese) *paǎk ts'oi*, literally 'white vegetable']

Paki /páki, paaki/ (*plural* **-is**) *n.* **1.** OFFENSIVE TERM a highly offensive term for sb from Pakistan or with ancestors from Pakistan (*slang insult*) **2.** OFFENSIVE TERM FOR INDIAN a highly offensive term for any person from the Indian subcontinent (*slang offensive*) [Mid-20thC. Shortening.]

Paki-bashing *n.* an offensive term for aggressive and violent attacks on immigrants from Pakistan or the Indian subcontinent or their descendants in the UK (*slang offensive*)

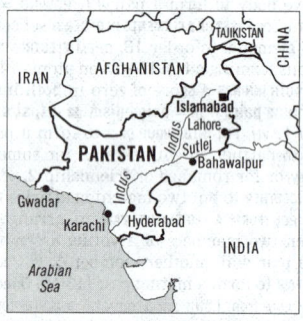

Pakistan

Pakistan /paáki staán/ republic on the Arabian Sea in southern Asia. It occupies the northwestern corner of the Indian subcontinent. Language: Urdu. Currency: Pakistani rupee. Capital: Islamabad. Population: 132,185,388 (1997). Area: 796,095 sq. km/307,293 sq. mi. Official name **Islamic Republic of Pakistan** —**Pakistani** *n., adj.*

pakora /pə káwrə/ *n.* an Indian deep-fried fritter made by dipping pieces of vegetable, meat, or shellfish in a chickpea-flour batter and generally eaten as a snack [Mid-20thC. From Hindi *pakorā*, literally 'dish of vegetables in gram-flour'.]

pal /pal/ *n.* AGGRESSIVE FORM OF ADDRESS used to address sb, often in an unfriendly or aggressive way (*informal*) ○ *Listen, pal, you'd better watch out!* ■ *vi.* (**pals, palling, palled**) BECOME FRIENDS WITH SB to become friends with sb and spend time with sb [Late 17thC. Via English Romany, 'pal, brother', from, ultimately, Sanskrit *bhrātṛ* 'brother'.]

pal around *vi.* to become friends with and spend time with sb (*informal*)

pal up *vi.* to form a friendship or friendly partnership

PAL *n.* the system used for broadcasting television programmes in the UK and many other European countries. Abbr of **phase alternation line**

Pal. *abbr.* Palestine

palace /pálləss/ *n.* **1.** OFFICIAL RESIDENCE OF A SOVEREIGN a grand and imposing building that is the official residence of a king or queen, a head of state such as a president, or a high-ranking aristocrat or church dignitary **2.** LARGE BUILDING FOR ENTERTAINMENT a large public or private building with an imposing ornate style, used for entertainment or exhibitions ○ *an old movie palace fallen into disrepair* [13thC. Via Old French *palais* from Latin *palatium*, named after *Palatium* 'Palatine Hill' where the emperor Augustus built a house.]

palace revolution *n.* the overthrow of a ruler by those who are already in the ruling group, often carried out with little violence

paladia plural of **palladium**[2]

paladin /pállədin/ *n.* **1.** MEDIEVAL CHAMPION a champion or hero, especially in medieval legend or history **2.** CHAMPION OF A CAUSE sb known for championing a cause **3.** ONE OF CHARLEMAGNE'S COMPANIONS any one of the 12 legendary companions of Charlemagne [Late 16thC. Via French from, ultimately, Latin *palatinus* (see PALATINE).]

Palaearctic /páyli aártik, -aártik, pálli-/, **Palearctic** *adj.* relating to the biogeographic region of the Arctic and immediately adjacent temperate regions of Europe, Asia, and Africa, or to a species within that range such as the Eurasian sparrowhawk. US term **Palearctic**

palaeo- *prefix.* **1.** ancient, prehistoric ○ *palaeozoology* **2.** primitive, early ○ *palaeoethnology* [From Greek *palaios*, which was formed from *palai* 'long ago'. Ultimately related to *tēle* 'far off', the source of English *tele-*.]

palaeoanthropic /páyli ō an thróppik, pálli-/, **palaeoanthropic** *adj.* relating to prehistoric human beings. US term **paleoanthropic**

palaeoanthropology /páyli ō ánthrə pólləji, pálli-/, **paleoanthropology** *n.* the study of early human beings and related species through fossil evidence. US term **paleoanthropology** —**palaeoanthropological** /páyli ō ánthrəpə lójjik'l, pálli-/ *adj.* —**palaeoanthropologist** *n.*

palaeobiochemistry /páyli ō bío kémmistri, pálli-/, **paleobiochemistry** *n.* US term **paleobiochemistry 1.** STUDY OF THE EVOLUTION OF BIOCHEMISTRY the study of the development and change in biochemical processes as indicated in fossils and other geological evidence **2.** FOSSIL CHEMICALS the biological chemicals found in fossils of ancient organisms

palaeobiogeography /páyli ō bío ji óggrəfi, pálli-/, **paleobiogeography** *n.* the study of the locations of prehistoric species on the basis of fossil evidence. US term **paleobiogeography**

palaeobotany /páyli ō bóttəni, pálli-/, **paleobotany** *n.* the study of prehistoric plants on the basis of fossil evidence. US term **paleobotany** —**palaeobotanical** /páyli ō bə tánnik'l, pálli-/ *adj.* —**palaeobotanist** *n.*

Palaeocene /páyli ə seen, pálli-/, **Paleocene** *n.* the epoch of geological time when placental mammals first appeared, 65 to 55 million years ago. US term **Paleocene** [Late 19thC. Coined from PALAEO- + Greek *kainos* 'new'.] —**Palaeocene** /páyli ə seen, pálli-/ *adj.*

palaeoclimatology /páyli ō klímə tólləji, pálli-/, **paleoclimatology** *n.* the study of prehistoric climates on a global or regional scale from evidence preserved in glacial deposits, sedimentary structures, and fossils. US term **paleoclimatology** —**palaeoclimatologist** *n.*

palaeocurrent /páyli ō kúrrənt, pálli-/, **paleocurrent** *n.* a prehistoric current of water or wind, revealed by the study of the sedimentary structures and textures that it deposited. US term **paleocurrent**

palaeoecology /páyli ō i kólləji, pálli-/, **paleoecology** *n.* the study of the interaction of prehistoric life forms and their environments. US term **paleoecology** —**palaeoecological** /páyli ō eèkə lójjik'l, pálli-, -ékə-/ *adj.* —**palaeoecologist** *n.*

palaeoethnobotany /páyli ō éthnō bóttəni, pálli-/, **paleoethnobotany** *n.* the study of fossilized seeds and grain in order to gain information about prehistoric patterns of cereal growth. US term **paleoethnobotany**

Palaeogene /páyli ə jeen, pálli-/, **Paleogene** *n.* the early part of the Tertiary period of geological time, comprising the Palaeocene, Eocene, and Oligocene epochs. US term **Paleogene** —**Palaeogene** *adj.*

palaeogeography /páyli ō ji óggrəfi, pálli-/, **paleogeography** *n.* the study of the geographical features of past epochs. US term **paleogeography** —**palaeogeographer** *n.* —**palaeogeographic** /páyli ō jeè ə gráffik, pálli-/ *adj.* —**palaeogeographical** *adj.* —**palaeogeographically** *adv.*

palaeography /páyli óggrəfi, pálli-/, **paleography** *n.* US term **paleography 1.** STUDY OF ANCIENT WRITINGS the study of ancient handwriting and manuscripts **2.** OLD MANUSCRIPT an ancient manuscript or piece of handwriting —**palaeographic** /páyli ə gráffik, pálli-/ *adj.* —**palaeographical** *adj.* —**palaeographer** /páyli óggrəfər/ *n.*

Palaeo-Indian, **Paleo-Indian** *adj.* relating to the earliest inhabitants of the Americas, who arrived from Asia by the Bering land bridge that connected Alaska and Siberia. By 12,000 to 10,000 years ago they were hunting game and living in small groups throughout North America. US term **Paleo-Indian** —**Palaeo-Indian** *n.*

palaeolith /páyli ə lith, pálli-/, **paleolith** *n.* a stone tool from the Palaeolithic age. US term **paleolith**

Palaeolithic /páyli ə líthik, pálli-/ *n.* the early part of the Stone Age, when early human beings made chipped-stone tools, from 750,000 to 15,000 years ago —**Palaeolithic** *adj.*

Palaeolithic man, **Paleolithic** *n.* a member of any of the various peoples who lived in the Palaeolithic period, such as Neanderthal, Cro-Magnon, or Java man. US term **Paleolithic**

palaeomagnetism /páyli ō mágnitizəm, pálli-/, **paleomagnetism** *n.* **1.** MAGNETISM IN ANCIENT ROCK the polarity and intensity of residual magnetism in ancient rock. US term **paleomagnetism 2.** STUDY OF THE EARTH'S PREHISTORIC MAGNETIC FIELD the study of changes in the intensity and direction of the Earth's magnetic field throughout geological time. The recurring reversals of the Earth's magnetic field and the changing configurations of the continents have been established through such studies. —**palaeomagnetic** /páyli ō mag néttik, pálli-/ *adj.*

palaeontography /páyli on tóggrəfi, pálli-/, **paleontography** *n.* the branch of palaeontology concerned with describing fossils. US term **paleontography** —**palaeontographic** /páyli óntə gráffik, pálli-/ *adj.* —**palaeontographical** *adj.*

palaeontol. *abbr.* palaeontology

palaeontology /páyli on tólləji, pálli-/, **paleontology** *n.* the study of life in prehistoric times by using fossil evidence. US term **paleontology** —**palaeontological** /páyli óntə lójjik'l, pálli-/ *adj.* —**palaeontologically** *adv.* —**palaeontologist** *n.*

palaeopathology /páyli ō pə thólləji, pálli-/, **paleopathology** *n.* the study of the evidence of disease processes in early human and animal remains, e.g. by using DNA analysis. US term **paleopathology**

Palaeozoic /páyli ə zō ik, pálli-/, **Paleozoic** *n.* the era of geological time when fish, insects, amphibians, reptiles, and land plants first appeared, about 600 million to 230 million years ago. US term **Paleozoic** —**Palaeozoic** *adj.*

palaeozoology /páyli ō zoo ólləji, pálli-/, **paleozoology** *n.* the study of ancient animals and animal life using fossils and other palaeontological evidence —**palaeozoological** /páyli ō zoò ə lójjik'l, pálli-/ *adj.*

palaestra (*plural* **-tras** *or* **-trae** /-tree/), **palestra** *n.* a public sports ground or gymnasium in ancient Greece. US term **palestra** [14thC. Via Latin from Greek *palaistra*, from *palaiein* 'to wrestle'.]

palanquin /pállən keèn/ *n.* a covered seat carried on poles held parallel to the ground on the shoulders of two or four people. It was formerly used to transport an important person, especially in East Asia. [Late 16thC. Via Portuguese *palanquim* from, ultimately, Sanskrit *palyanka* 'bed, litter'.]

palatable /pállətəb'l/ *adj.* **1.** PLEASANT-TASTING having a good enough taste to be eaten or drunk **2.** ACCEPTABLE acceptable to sb's sensibilities [Mid-17thC. Formed from PALATE.]

palatal /pállət'l/ *adj.* **1.** ANAT FACING OR RELATING TO THE PALATE occurring at, facing, or relating to the palate **2.** PHON PRONOUNCED WITH THE TONGUE AT THE PALATE used to describe a consonant sound that is produced by raising the tongue to or near the hard palate ○ *The 'sh' sound is a palatal fricative.* **3.** PHON PRONOUNCED WITH THE TONGUE FORWARD used to describe a vowel sound that is produced with the tongue moved forward in the mouth ○ *The vowel in 'meet' is palatal.* ■ *n.* PHON PALATAL SPEECH SOUND a speech sound pronounced with the tongue at or near the hard palate or with the tongue pushed forward, especially a palatal consonant — **palatally** *adv.*

palatalise *vt.* = palatalize

palatalization /pállətə līz áysh'n/, **palatalisation** *n.* the pronunciation of a speech sound by raising the tongue to or towards the hard palate

palatalize /pállətə līz/ (**-izes, -izing, -ized**), **palatalise** (**-ises, -ising, -ised**) *vt.* **1.** PRODUCE AT THE HARD PALATE to make a speech sound by raising the tongue to or towards the hard palate **2.** MAKE MORE PALATAL to alter a speech sound in pronunciation by placing the tongue closer to the hard palate, rather than to the teeth, alveolar ridge, or velum

palate /pállət/ *n.* **1.** ANAT ROOF OF THE MOUTH the roof of the mouth that separates it from the nasal cavity. It consists of a bony hard palate at the front and a muscular soft palate at the rear. **2.** SENSE OF TASTE a personal sense of taste and flavour **3.** AESTHETIC TASTE intellectual or aesthetic tastes or sensibilities [14thC. From Latin *palatum*.]

palatial /pə láysh'l/ *adj.* **1.** LUXURIOUS grand or luxurious ○ *palatial mansions* **2.** SUITABLE FOR A PALACE appropriate for a palace [Mid-18thC. From Latin *palatium* (see PALACE).] —**palatialness** *n.*

palatinate /pə látti nayt, -nət/ *n.* the territory, office, or responsibilities of a feudal palatine

palatine¹ /pállə tīn/ *n.* **1.** POWERFUL FEUDAL LORD a feudal lord in central Europe with sovereign powers within his territory **2.** IMPERIAL COURT OFFICIAL a court official in the late Roman and Byzantine empires ■ *adj.* **1.** SUITABLE FOR A PALACE relating to or suitable for a palace **2.** HAVING POWER OVER TERRITORY used to describe an official or feudal lord who had sovereign power over a territory **3.** RULED BY LORD used to describe a territory that is ruled by a sovereign feudal lord [15thC. Via French *palatine* from Latin *palatinus* 'of the palace, palace official', from *palatium* (see PALACE).]

palatine² /pállə tīn/ *adj.* ANAT OF THE PALATE relating to the palate ■ *n.* ANAT HARD PALATE BONE either of the two bones that form the hard palate

Palatine¹ /pállə tīn/ *adj.* relating to the German Palatinate, or its people or culture

Palatine² /pállə tīn/ *n.* the central hill of the seven on which Rome was built, considered the oldest and the site of many of the imperial palaces

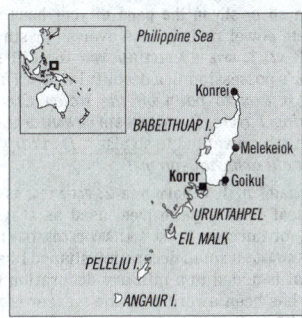

Palau

Palau /pä lów/ republic in the western Pacific Ocean comprising a group of islands that are part of the Caroline Islands. Language: English, Palauan. Currency: US dollar. Capital: Koror. Population: 17,000 (1996). Area: 495 sq. km/191 sq. mi. Official name **Republic of Palau**

palaver /pə láavər/ *n.* **1.** INCONVENIENT BOTHER irritating and time-consuming activity and bother **2.** EMPTY TALK idle, flattering, or time-wasting talk **3.** CONFERENCE BETWEEN DIFFERENT CULTURES a conference between European explorers or colonialists and local African officials, usually requiring the use of a pidgin language (*archaic*) **4.** CONFERENCE BETWEEN DIFFERENT PARTIES a conference or meeting between different parties (*humorous*) ■ *vi.* (**-ers, -ering, -ered**) **1.** TALK IDLY to talk idly, emptily, or with the intention of flattering (*archaic*) **2.** CONFER to confer or hold a conference (*humorous*) [Mid-18thC. Via Portuguese *palavra* 'speech' from Latin *parabola* (see PARABLE). The word was adopted from Portuguese by British sailors visiting West Africa, where it was used to denote negotiations between Europeans and Africans.]

palazzo /pə látsō/ (*plural* **-zos** or **-zi** /-tsee/) *n.* a large ornate building such as a museum or official residence, especially in Italy [Mid-17thC. Via Italian from Latin *palatium* (see PALACE).]

palazzo pants *npl.* women's loose-fitting lightweight trousers with flared legs

pale¹ /payl/ *adj.* (**paler, palest**) **1.** LACKING COLOUR lacking in colour or intensity ○ *pale blue* **2.** PALLID FROM ILLNESS unusually light in skin complexion because of illness, shock, or worry **3.** PRODUCING LITTLE LIGHT producing or reflecting little light **4.** INADEQUATE inadequate or faint ○ *a pale version of his former flamboyant self* ■ *v.* (**pales, paling, paled**) **1.** *vi.* BECOME WHITER to become whiter or lose brilliance **2.** *vi.* BECOME LESS IMPORTANT to be or become less important, remarkable, or intense, especially in comparison to sth more important or serious **3.** *vt.* CAUSE TO LOSE COLOUR to cause sb or sth to lose colour or brilliance [14thC. Via Old French from Latin *pallidus* (see PALLID).]

pale² /payl/ *n.* **1.** FENCE STAKE a pointed slat of wood for a fence **2.** FENCE a fence marking a boundary **3.** FENCED-IN AREA an area fenced in or its boundary **4.** HERALDRY VERTICAL STRIPE ON A SHIELD a wide vertical band down the centre of a shield ■ *vt.* (**pales, paling, paled**) FENCE IN to fence in an area [12thC. Via Old French *pal* from Latin *palus* 'stake'.] ◇ **beyond the pale** outside the limits of what is considered to be acceptable

Pale *n.* **1.** AREA OF JEWISH SETTLEMENT formerly, a restricted area in Imperial Russia where Jews were allowed to settle **2.** PART OF IRELAND UNDER ENGLISH RULE the area of Ireland, based around Dublin, that was controlled by England from the 12th century until the final conquest of the entire country in the 16th century

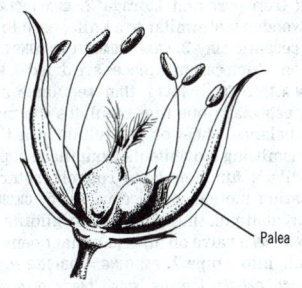

Palea

palea /páyli ə/ (*plural* **-ae** /-li ee/) *n.* **1.** LEAF ON FLOWERING GRASS a dry membranous leaf with a single flower (**bract**) on a flowering grass **2.** FLOWER SCALE a dry membranous scale on the head of a composite flower such as a sunflower [Mid-18thC. From Latin 'chaff'.]

paleface /páyl fayss/ *n.* an offensive term for a Caucasian person, allegedly used by Native North Americans (*offensive*)

paleo- US = palaeo- [From Greek *palaios*]

paleoanthropic *adj.* US = palaeoanthropic

paleoanthropology *n.* US = palaeoanthropology

paleobiochemistry *n.* US = palaeobiochemistry

paleobiogeography *n.* US = palaeobiogeography

paleobotany *n.* US = palaeobotany

Paleocene *adj., n.* US = Palaeocene

paleoclimatology *n.* US = palaeoclimatology

paleocurrent *n.* US = palaeocurrent

paleoecology *n.* US = palaeoecology

paleoethnobotany *n.* US = palaeoethnobotany

Paleogene *adj., n.* US = Palaeogene

paleogeography *n.* US = palaeogeography

paleography *n.* US = palaeography

Paleo-Indian *n., adj.* US = Palaeo-Indian

paleolith *n.* US = palaeolith

Paleolithic *adj., n.* US = Palaeolithic

paleomagnetism *n.* US = palaeomagnetism

paleontography *n.* US = palaeontography

paleontol. US = palaeontol.

paleontology *n.* US = palaeontology

paleopathology *n.* US = palaeopathology

Paleozoic *adj., n.* US = Palaeozoic

paleozoology *n.* US = palaeozoology

Palermo /pə láirm ō/ city and port in Sicily, Italy. It is the largest city on the island, and is situated on the northwestern coast. Population: 694,749 (1993).

Palestine /pállə stīn/ area in southwestern Asia between the River Jordan and the eastern coast of the Mediterranean Sea. During biblical times it was the Jewish homeland, comprising the kingdoms of Israel and Judah. The country was then successively occupied by the Romans, the Arabs, and the Ottoman Turks. In 1947 Palestine was partitioned between the new state of Israel and Jordan, which assumed control of the West Bank territories. Wars fought in 1948, 1967, and 1972 between Israel and the surrounding Arab states saw an increase in the land held by Israel. In 1993 an agreement was signed under which the Palestinian Arabs gained limited self-rule in territories in the Gaza Strip and on the West Bank of the River Jordan. —**Palestinian** *n., adj.*

palestra *n.* US = palaestra

paletot /páltō/ *n.* a fitted coat worn by women in the 19th century, usually over a bustle or crinoline [Mid-19thC. From French, of unknown origin.]

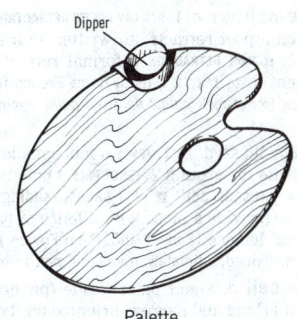

Palette

palette /pállət/ *n.* **1.** PAINTING BOARD FOR ARTIST'S PAINTS a board or tray on which an artist arranges and mixes paints. A traditional style of palette is an oval board that curves in near a thumbhole, so that the artist can hold the board steadily from underneath. **2.** PAINTING RANGE OF COLOURS USED BY AN ARTIST the assortment of colours on a palette, in a painting, or typical of an artist's work **3.** COMPUT COLOUR RANGE OF A COMPUTER DISPLAY the range of colours that can be reproduced on a computer display **4.** ARTS QUALITIES IN NONGRAPHIC ART a range of qualities or elements in a nongraphic art such as music or literature [Late 18thC. Via French (see PALLET¹).]

palette knife *n.* **1.** BLUNT FLEXIBLE KNIFE a kitchen implement with a long flexible blunt-edged blade for lifting and turning food or for spreading, particularly when filling or icing cakes **2.** SPATULA FOR MIXING PAINTS a spatula-shaped implement with a slender flexible metal blade and a handle, used by an artist to mix and apply thick paints

palfrey /páwlfri, pól-/ (*plural* **-freys**) *n.* a horse for everyday riding, especially one for a woman to ride (*archaic*) [12thC. Via Old French *palefrei* from, ultimately, late Latin *paraveredus*, literally 'extra horse', from *veredus* 'light horse used by couriers', ultimately of Gaulish origin.]

Pali /paáli/ *n.* an ancient Indo-European language derived from Sanskrit and formerly spoken in various parts of India. It survives in the language of Hinayana Buddhist scriptures. [Late 18thC. From Pali *pāli*, denoting the canonical text, as opposed to the commentary, shortened from Sanskrit *pāli-bhāsā*, literally 'language of the line'.] —**Pali** *adj.*

palimony /pállimәni/ (*plural* **-nies**) *n. US* a maintenance allowance for an ex-lover or member of an unmarried couple, when required by a court of law [Late 20thC. A blend of PAL and ALIMONY.]

palimpsest /pállimp sest/ *n.* **OVERWRITTEN MANUSCRIPT** a manuscript written over a partly erased older manuscript in such a way that the old words can be read beneath the new ■ *adj.* **OVERWRITTEN** used to describe a document that has been overwritten [Mid-17thC. Via Latin *palimpsestus* from Greek *palimpsestos*, literally 'sth rubbed smooth again'.]

palindrome /pállin drōm/ *n.* **1. TEXT READING THE SAME BACKWARDS AS FORWARDS** a word, phrase, passage, or number that reads the same forwards and backwards, e.g. 'Anna', 'Draw, o coward', or '23832' **2.** GENETICS **MIRROR-IMAGE DNA SEQUENCE** a segment of DNA in which the nucleotide sequence in one strand read from one end is the same as the sequence in the complementary strand read from the opposite end. For example the sequence GGTACC is a palindrome when the complementary strand is CCATGG. [Early 17thC. From Greek *palindromos*, literally 'running back again'.] —**palindromic** /pállin drómmik/ *adj.*

paling /páyling/ *n.* **1. FENCE OF STAKES** a fence formed by a line of pointed stakes planted in the ground **2.** = **pale**[2] *n.* 1 [14thC. Originally in the meaning 'making of a fence with pales', hence, the fence itself.]

palingenesis /pállin jénnәssiss/ *n.* **1.** BIOL = **recapitulation** *n.* 2 **2.** CHR **SPIRITUAL REGENERATION** spiritual rebirth by means of baptism **3. MIGRATION OF THE SOUL TO ANOTHER BODY** the supposed transmigration of the soul of sb who has died into the body of another person or animal [Early 19thC. Coined from Greek *palin* 'again' + *genesis* 'birth'.] —**palingenetic** /pállin jә néttik/ *adj.* —**palingenetically** *adv.*

palinode /pálli nōd/ *n.* **1.** POETRY **POETIC RETRACTION** a poem in which a poet retracts sth written in a previous poem **2. FORMAL RETRACTION** a formal retraction of a statement [Late 16thC. Directly or via French from Latin *palinodia*, from Greek *palinōdia*, from *palin* 'again, back' + *ōdē* 'ODE'.]

palisade /pálli sayd/ *n.* **1. FENCE** a fence made of pales driven into the ground **2. FENCE PALE** a pale in a fence **3.** BOT = **palisade cell** ■ *vt.* (**-sades, -sading, -saded**) **FENCE IN** to provide a place with a fence of pales as a means of defence [Early 17thC. From French *palissade*, which was formed, ultimately, from Latin *palus* (see PALE[2]).]

palisade cell *n.* a soft plant tissue (**parenchyma**) cell that is long and narrow, oriented on its vertical axis, and adjacent to the upper epidermis in a leaf

palisade layer, palisade mesophyll, palisade parenchyma *n.* a layer of long cells under the upper epidermis of a leaf that are full of specialized chlorophyll-containing cell parts (**chloroplasts**)

Palk Strait /páwk-, páwlk-/ inlet of the Bay of Bengal, separating southeastern India from northwestern Sri Lanka. Length: 137 km/85 mi.

pall[1] /pawl/ *n.* **1. DARK COVERING** a covering that makes a place dark and gloomy ○ *a pall of thick black smoke* **2. GLOOMY ATMOSPHERE** a prevailing gloomy mood or oppressive atmosphere ○ *Her departure cast a pall over the weekend.* **3. COFFIN COVERING** a cloth covering for a coffin, bier, hearse, or tomb **4. COFFIN** a coffin, especially when being carried in a funeral **5.** CHR **CHALICE COVER** a square cover for a communion chalice, especially a linen-covered board **6.** CHR **PALLIUM** a pallium (*archaic*) **7.** HERALDRY **HERALDIC BEARING** a heraldic bearing representing an archbishop's pallium in the form of three bands in a Y-shape, charged with crosses ■ *vt.* (**palls, palling, palled**) **COVER WITH A PALL** to cover sb or sth with a pall or with sth that resembles a pall [Pre-12thC. From Latin *pallium* 'covering'.]

pall[2] /pawl/ (**palls, palling, palled**) *vi.* to be or become uninteresting, unsatisfying, or insipid ○ *The music soon began to pall on us.* [14thC. Alteration of APPAL.]

Palladian[1] /pә láydi әn/ *adj.* ARCHIT typical of or similar to the classical architectural style developed by Andrea Palladio in the 16th century

Palladian[2] /pә láydi әn/ *adj.* **1.** MYTHOL **OF ATHENA** relating to the goddess Pallas Athena **2. RELATING TO WISDOM** relating to wisdom or knowledge [Mid-16thC. From Latin *palladium* (see PALLADIUM[2]).]

Palladio /pә laádi ō, -laádee-/, **Andrea** (1508–80) Italian architect. Working in the classical tradition of ancient Rome, he produced villa designs and wrote his *Four Books on Architecture* (1570), which influenced several generations of architects. Born **Andrea di Pietro della Gondola**

palladium[1] /pә láydi әm/ *n.* a malleable silvery-white metallic chemical element that resembles platinum and is used as a chemical catalyst and in electrical contacts, jewellery, dental alloys, and medical instruments. Symbol **Pd** [Early 19thC. From *Pallas* (see PALLADIUM[2]), the name given to an asteroid discovered shortly before the metal.] —**palladic** /pә láddik, -láy-/ *adj.* —**palladous** /pә láydәss, pállәdәss/ *adj.*

palladium[2] /pә láydi әm/ (*plural* **-ums** *or* **-a** /pә láydi ә/) *n.* **1. SAFEGUARD** a protection or safeguard, especially one protecting social and civic institutions **2. palladium, Palladium PROTECTIVE CHARM** an object believed to have the power to protect a city or nation, especially the statue of Pallas Athena that was believed to protect Troy [14thC. Via Latin from Greek *palladion*, from *Pallas*, epithet of Athena, goddess of wisdom.]

Pallas /pállәss/ *n.* **1.** ASTRON **SECOND LARGEST ASTEROID** the second largest asteroid, discovered in 1802. It has an average diameter of approximately 530 km. **2. Pallas, Pallas Athena** MYTHOL = **Athena**

Pallas's cat /pállәssiz-/ *n.* a small wild cat of mountainous Tibet and Siberia, with small ears and luxurious grey fur with dark stripes. Latin name: *Felis manul.* [Named after the German naturalist Peter *Pallas* (1741–1811)]

pallbearer /páwl bairәr/ *n.* sb who helps to carry or escort a coffin at a funeral or burial

pallet[1] /pállәt/ *n.* **1. PLATFORM FOR LOADS** a standardized platform or open-ended box, usually made of wood, that allows mechanical handling of bulk goods during transport and storage **2.** CRAFT **CLAY-WORKING TOOL** a wooden tool similar to a knife, used to mix and shape ceramic clay **3.** CRAFT **BOARD FOR DRYING CERAMICS** a board on which ceramic pieces are dried **4. REGULATING LEVER IN A TIMEPIECE** a lever that regulates a ratchet wheel, especially one that regulates the movement of the balance wheel or pendulum in a timepiece by transmitting movements from the escape wheel. The pallet's function is to convert rotary to reciprocating motion, or vice versa. **5. GILDING TOOL** a tool for manipulating gold leaf in gilding **6.** MUSIC **VALVE ON ORGAN** a valve on an organ that opens in order to let air into a pipe **7.** PAINTING = **palette** *n.* 1 [15thC. Via French *palette*, literally 'small blade or spade', from Latin *pala* 'spade, shovel'.]

pallet[2] /pállәt/ *n.* **1. STRAW MATTRESS** a straw-filled mattress **2. MAKESHIFT BED** a temporary and usually uncomfortable bed, made from materials at hand [14thC. From Anglo-Norman *paillete*, from *paille* 'straw', from Latin *palea*.]

palletize /pállә tīz/ (**-tizes, -tizing, -tized**), **palletise** (**-tises, -tising, -tised**) *vt.* to put, transport, or store a load of sth on a standardized platform

pallia plural of **pallium**

palliasse /pálli ass, -áss/ *n.* a straw-filled mattress

palliate /pálli ayt/ (**-ates, -ating, -ated**) *vt.* **1.** MED **ALLEVIATE** to alleviate a symptom without curing the underlying medical condition **2. MITIGATE** to reduce the intensity or severity of sth **3. PARTIALLY EXCUSE** to make an offence seem less serious by providing excuses or mitigating evidence [15thC. From the past participle stem of *palliare* 'to cover or hide', from *pallium* 'a covering' (source of English *pallium*).] —**palliation** /pálli áysh'n/ *n.* —**palliator** /pálli aytәr/ *n.*

palliative /pálli әtiv/ *adj.* **1. TREATING SYMPTOMS ONLY** alleviating pain and symptoms without eliminating the cause **2. SOOTHING** soothing anxieties or other intense emotions ■ *n.* MED **SYMPTOM-TREATING MEDICINE** sth that palliates, especially a medicine that treats symptoms only —**palliatively** *adv.*

palliative care *n.* the treatment and relief of mental and physical pain without curing the causes, especially in patients suffering from a terminal illness

pallid /pállid/ *adj.* **1. PALE** having an unhealthily pale complexion **2. LACKLUSTRE** lacking colour, spirit, or intensity [Late 16thC. From Latin *pallidus*, from *pallere* 'to be pale'.] —**pallidity** /pә líddәti/ *n.* —**pallidly** /pállidli/ *adv.*

Palliser /pállissәr/ the southernmost point of the North Island, New Zealand, situated at the eastern end of the Cook Strait

pallium /pálli әm/ (*plural* **-a** /-ә/ *or* **-ums**) *n.* **1.** CHR **VESTMENT WORN BY A POPE OR ARCHBISHOP** a white vestment that rests on the shoulders with pendants hanging at its front and back, worn by a pope, all Roman Catholic archbishops, and some bishops **2.** ZOOL = **mantle** *n.* 5 **3.** BIRDS = **mantle** *n.* 6 **4.** ANAT = **cerebral cortex 5.** ANAT **PART OF THE BRAIN** the layer of grey matter forming the surface of the cerebral cortex **6.** HIST **ANCIENT CLOAK** a man's rectangular cloak worn in ancient Rome [Late 16thC. From Latin, literally 'covering'.] —**pallial** *adj.*

pall-mall /pál mál/ *n.* **1. OLD MALLET-AND-BALL GAME** a 17th-century game in which players used a mallet to hit a wooden ball through an iron hoop suspended at the end of a long alley **2. ALLEY FOR PLAYING PALL-MALL** an alley in which pall-mall is played [Mid-16thC. Via obsolete French *palle maille* from Italian *pallamaglio*, which was formed, ultimately, from *balla* 'ball' + *maglio* 'mallet'.]

pallor /pállәr/ *n.* an unhealthy-looking paleness of complexion [14thC. From Latin, from *pallere* 'to be pale'.]

pally /pálli/ (**-lier, -liest**) *adj.* having a friendly relationship (*informal*) [Late 19thC. From PAL.]

palm[1] /paam/ *n.* **1.** ANAT **INNER SURFACE OF THE HAND** the inner surface of the hand, extending from the base of the fingers to the wrist **2.** ZOOL **UNDERSIDE OF A MAMMAL'S FOREFOOT** the part of a mammal's forefoot that is most often in contact with the ground **3.** MEASURE **HAND-SIZED MEASURE** a unit of length, based on the length or width of a hand **4. COVERING FOR THE PALM OF THE HAND** sth that covers the palm of the hand, e.g. the inner hand surface of a glove **5. FLAT PART OF A BRANCHED STRUCTURE** the broad flat lobe of a branched structure such as the antler of a moose or deer, or of a cactus stalk **6.** ROWING **OAR BLADE** the blade of an oar **7.** NAUT **INNER FACE OF AN ANCHOR POINT** the inner face of an anchor's point ■ *vt.* (**palms, palming, palmed**) **1. HIDE IN THE HAND** to hide sth in the hand, especially as part of a trick **2. TAKE STEALTHILY** to take sth secretly by hiding it in the hand **3. TOUCH WITH THE PALM** to touch sth with the palm **4.** BASKETBALL **HOLD INSTEAD OF DRIBBLING** to let a basketball come to rest in the hands during a dribble, thereby committing a foul [Old English. Via a prehistoric Germanic word from Latin *palma* 'palm of the hand, PALM[2]'.] ◇ **grease sb's palm** to bribe sb (*slang*) ◇ **have sb or sth in the palm of your hand** to have complete power or influence over sb or sth

palm off *vt.* **1. GIVE IN A DECEITFUL WAY** to shift sth into another's possession in a deceitful way ○ *The crooks needed a way to palm off the stolen CDs on unsuspecting buyers.* **2. PASS ON STH UNWANTED** to give or pass on sth unwanted to sb else ○ *Don't try to palm off that old armchair on me!*

palm[2] /paam/ *n.* **1.** = **palm tree 2. PALM LEAF AS A VICTORY SIGN** a leaf from a palm tree, used as a symbol of victory or success **3.** MIL **MILITARY DECORATION INDICATING MULTIPLE AWARDS** a small decoration shaped like a palm leaf that is added to a military decoration to show that it has been awarded to the wearer more than once [12thC. Via French *paume* from Latin *palma* 'palm of the hand, palm tree' (because a cluster of palm leaves was thought to look like a hand and fingers).]

Palma /pálmә/ port on Majorca. It is the capital city of the Spanish Balearic Islands. Population: 323,138 (1995).

palmar /pálmәr/ *adj.* relating to the palm of the hand or to the underside of an animal's forefoot

palmate /pál mayt, -mәt/ *adj.* **1. palmate, palmated** /pál maytәd/ BOT, ZOOL **HAVING SEVERAL LOBES** forming a branching pattern that spreads like fingers from a hand **2.** BIRDS **HAVING WEBBED TOES** having three toes that are connected by webbing [Mid-18thC. From Latin *palmatus*, which was formed from *palma* (see PALM[1].) — **palmately** *adv.*

palmation /pal máysh'n/ *n.* **1.** BOT LOBE OF A PALMATE STRUCTURE any of the lobes of a palmate formation **2.** BEING PALMATE the state of having a palmate shape

Palm Beach /paam béech/ town in southeastern Florida on the Atlantic Ocean. It is a fashionable winter resort. Population: 9,814 (1990).

palm chat *n.* a gregarious bird of open woodlands and cultivated fields of the West Indies. It is olive-brown above and yellow with dark streaks below. Latin name: *Dulus dominicus.*

palm civet *n.* a tree-dwelling mammal of Africa and Asia, with short legs and sharp claws. Family: Viverridae.

palmcorder /paam kawrdər/ *n.* a small portable video camera and recorder that fits in the palm of the hand [Late 20thC. Blend of PALM + RECORDER.]

AKG London

Olof Palme

Palme /pálmə/, **Olof** (1927–86) Swedish statesman. He was Social Democratic prime minister of Sweden (1969–76, 1982–86) and was noted for his efforts to secure world peace. Full name **Sven Olof Joachim Palme**

palmer /paamər/ *n.* **1.** MEDIEVAL PILGRIM a pilgrim, especially a medieval Christian pilgrim who carried or wore palm leaves as proof of a visit to the Holy Land **2.** ZOOL = **palmer worm** [14thC. Via Anglo-Norman *palmer* from medieval Latin *palmarius*, from *palma* (see PALM[2]).]

Express Newspapers

Arnold Palmer

Palmer /paamər/, **Arnold** (*b.* 1929) US golfer. He won the US Masters (1958, 1960, 1962, and 1964), the US Open (1960), and the British Open (1960, 1961) tournaments.

Palmer, Sir Geoffrey (*b.* 1942) New Zealand statesman. He was Labour prime minister of New Zealand (1989–90). Full name **Sir Geoffrey Winston Russell Palmer**

Palmerston /paamərstən/, **Lord, Viscount** (1784–1865) British statesman. Changing from Tory to Whig (1830), he became prime minister (1855–58; 1859–65). His robust manner led to the nickname "Firebrand Palmerston".

Palmerston North city in the south of the North Island, New Zealand, situated 140 km/87 mi. north of Wellington. Population: 73,862 (1996).

palmer worm *n.* a destructive, swarming moth caterpillar

palmette /pal mét/ *n.* a stylized palm leaf used as an ornament or in a decoration [Mid-19thC. From French,

literally 'small palm', from, ultimately, Latin *palma* (see PALM[2]).]

palmetto /pal méttō/ (*plural* **-tos** *or* **-toes**) *n.* **1.** LOW PALM PLANT a low growing palm plant with fan-shaped leaves, especially the cabbage palmetto **2.** BLADE USED FOR WEAVING the blade of a palmetto leaf, used for weaving [Mid-16thC. From Spanish *palmito*, literally 'small palm', from, ultimately, Latin *palma* (see PALM[2]). The ending was changed by association with Italian words ending in *-etto*.]

palmist /paamist/ *n.* sb who practises palmistry

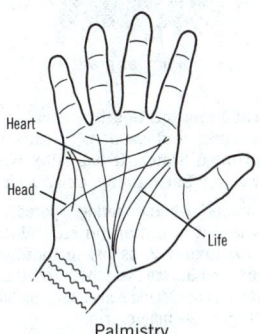

Palmistry

palmistry /paamistri/ *n.* the practice of examining the features of sb's palms in order to predict that person's destiny

palmitate /pálmi tayt/ *n.* a salt or ester of palmitic acid

palmitic acid /pal míttik-/ *n.* a waxy acid found in plant and animal fats and oils and used in making soap, candles, and food additives. Formula: $C_{16}H_{32}O_2$. [*Palmitic* from French *palmitique*, from *palme* (see PALMITIN)]

palmitin /pálmitin/ *n.* an ester of palmitic acid and glycerol, found in animal fats and palm oil and used in soap-making [Mid-19thC. From French *palmitine*, from *palme* 'palm tree', from Old French *paume* (see PALM[2]).]

palm oil *n.* a yellowish oil extracted from the fruit of oil palms and used as a lubricant and in soaps, foods, and cosmetics. Palm oil is high in saturated fats.

Palm Springs /paam springz/ city in southern California, a resort and residential centre. Population: 40,181 (1990).

palm sugar *n.* sugar made from palm tree sap

Palm Sunday *n.* the Sunday before the Christian festival of Easter that commemorates Jesus Christ's triumphal entry into Jerusalem through a crowd waving palm branches, as narrated in the Bible. Palm fronds are distributed at some church services on this day.

Palmtop

palmtop /paam top/ *n.* a computer with a miniature keyboard and screen that fits into the palm of the hand

palm tree *n.* a tree, shrub, or plant typically with a branchless trunk and a crown of pinnate or palmate leaves on top, found in tropical and subtropical regions. Family: Palmae.

palm vaulting *n.* ARCHIT = **fan vaulting**

palm wine *n.* an alcoholic drink made from fermented palm sap, common in parts of Africa

Palm tree

palmy /paami/ (**-ier, -iest**) *adj.* **1.** OF PALM TREES relating to, consisting of, or abundant in palm trees **2.** FLOURISHING prosperous or flourishing (*literary*) ○ *in her palmy days*

palmyra /pal mírə/ (*plural* **-ras** *or* **-ra**) *n.* a tall Asian fan-leafed palm tree whose fronds, wood, and sap are harvested for various uses. Latin name: *Borassus flabellifer*. [Late 17thC. Alteration (influenced by *Palmyra*, the name of an ancient city in Syria) of Portuguese *palmeira* 'palm tree', from Latin *palma* (see PALM[2]).]

Palomar, Mount /pállə maar/ mountain in southern California, northeast of San Diego. It is the site of an astronomical observatory. Height: 1,871 m/6,138 ft.

palomino /pállə meenō/ (*plural* **-nos**) *n.* a golden-coloured horse with a pale mane and tail, originally bred in the southwestern United States [Early 20thC. Via American Spanish from, ultimately, Latin *palumbinus* 'like a dove'.]

palooka /pə lookə/ *n.* US **1.** OAF sb considered to be very clumsy and unintelligent (*slang insult*) **2.** POOR BOXER an easily beaten athlete, especially a boxer (*slang*) [Early 20thC. Origin unknown.]

Palouse /pə looss/ (*plural* **-louse** *or* **-louses**) *n.* a member of a Native North American people who originally occupied lands in southern Washington and northern Idaho, and who now live mainly in northern Washington

paloverde /pállō vúrdi/ (*plural* **-des** *or* **-de**) *n.* BOT = **Jerusalem thorn** [Early 19thC. From American Spanish, literally 'green tree'.]

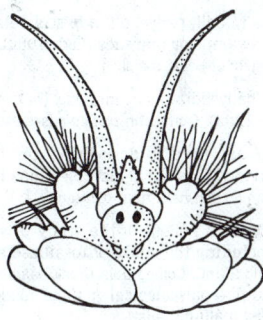

Palp

palp /palp/ *n.* a sensory appendage situated near the mouth of many invertebrate animals, used to assess or manipulate food before it is eaten [Mid-19thC. Via French *palpe* from Latin *palpus*, from *palpare* 'to touch gently, palpate'.]

palpable /pálpəb'l/ *adj.* **1.** INTENSE so intense as to be almost able to be felt physically ○ *the palpable tension in the room* **2.** OBVIOUS obvious or easily observed ○ *a palpable need for change* **3.** MED FEELABLE able to be felt by the hands, especially in a medical examination ○ *a palpable lump in the abdomen* [14thC. From late Latin *palpabilis*, from Latin *palpare* 'to touch gently, palpate'.] —**palpability** /pálpə bílləti/ *n.* —**palpableness** /pálppəb'lnəss/ *n.* —**palpably** *adv.*

palpate[1] /pal páyt/ (**-pates, -pating, -pated**) *vt.* to examine a part of the body by feeling with the hands and fingers, especially to distinguish between swellings that are solid and those that are filled with fluid [15thC. From Latin *palpatus*, from *palpare* 'to touch gently'.]

palpate[2] /pál payt/ *adj.* used to describe an invertebrate animal that is equipped with one or more palps [Mid-19thC. Coined from PALP + -ATE.]

palpebral /pálpəbrəl/ *adj.* relating to the eyelids [Mid-19thC. From Latin *palpebra* 'eyelid'.]

palpi plural of **palpus**

palpitate /pálpi tayt/ (**-tates, -tating, -tated**) *vi.* to beat in an irregular or abnormally rapid way, either because of a medical condition or because of exertion, fear, or anxiety (*refers to the heart*) [15thC. From Latin *palpitatus*, past participle stem of *palpitare*, from *palpare* 'to touch gently, palpate'.] —**palpitant** *adj.*

palpitation /pálpi táysh'n/ *n.* an irregular or unusually rapid beating of the heart, either because of a medical condition or because of exertion, fear, or anxiety (*usually used in the plural*)

palpus /pálpəss/ (*plural* **-pi** /-pee/) *n.* = palp [Early 19thC. From Latin (see PALP).]

palsgrave /páwlz grayv/ *n.* a count palatine, especially in Germany [Mid-16thC. From early Dutch *paltsgrave*, from *palts* 'palatinate' + *grave* 'count'.]

palstave /páwl stayv/ *n.* a metal axe that fits into a split handle, especially one of a distinctive bronze type found in ancient Europe [Mid-19thC. From Danish *paalstav*.]

palsy /páwlzi/ *n.* muscular inability to move part or all of the body (*archaic*) ◊ **Bell's palsy, cerebral palsy** [13thC. Via Old French *paralisie* from, ultimately, Latin *paralysis* (see PARALYSIS).]

palsy-walsy /pálzi wálzi/, **palsy** *adj.* very friendly, often in an insincere or unpleasant way (*slang*) [Mid-20thC. Humorous formation based on PAL.]

palter /páwltər/ (**-ters, -tering, -tered**) *vi.* (*archaic*) **1. ACT OR TALK INSINCERELY** to act or talk insincerely or deceitfully **2. HAGGLE** to haggle in bargaining [Mid-16thC. Origin unknown.] —**palterer** *n.*

paltry /páwltri, pól-/ (**-trier, -triest**) *adj.* **1. INSIGNIFICANT** insignificant or unimportant ○ *a paltry sum of money* **2. DESPICABLE** low and contemptible [Mid-16thC. Origin uncertain: probably from Scots and northern English dialect *pelt* 'coarse cloth, rubbish', of uncertain origin.] —**paltrily** *adv.* —**paltriness** *n.*

paludal /pə lyoōd'l, pállyoōd'l/ *adj.* ECOL relating to or living in swamps or marshes [Early 19thC. From Latin *paludem*, stem of *palus* 'marsh'.]

paludism /pállyoōdizəm/ *n.* malaria (*not in technical use*) [Late 19thC. From Latin *paludem* (see PALUDAL).]

paly /páyli/ *adj.* used to describe a heraldic shield that is divided into equal-sized sections by vertical lines [From French *palé*, from *pal* (see PALE[2])]

palynology /pálli nólləji/ *n.* the study of spores and pollen, including the study of fossilized spores and pollen [Mid-20thC. Coined from Greek *palunein* 'to sprinkle' + -LOGY.] —**palynological** /pállinə lójjik'l/ *adj.* —**palynologist** /pálli nólləjist/ *n.*

pam /pam/ *n.* the jack of clubs in some card games such as loo, where it is the highest trump card [Late 17thC. Shortening of French *pamphile*, from the Greek name *Pamphilos*, literally 'loved by all'.]

pam. *abbr.* pamphlet

Pama-Nyungan /páʹamə nyoōngən/ *n.* a family of about 175 Native Australian languages, many of which are now extinct, spoken across most of the continent apart from some northwestern parts and Tasmania. About 100,000 people speak a Pama-Nyungan language.

Pamirs /pə meerz/ high plateau region in Central Asia, located mainly in Tajikistan. The highest point is Communism Peak, 7,495 m/24,590 ft.

pampas /pámpəss, -pəz/ *n.* treeless grassy plains in temperate South America, especially Argentina (*takes a singular or plural verb*) [Early 18thC. Via Spanish *pampa* from Quechua, literally 'plain'.] —**pampean** /pámpi ən, pam pee ən/ *adj.*

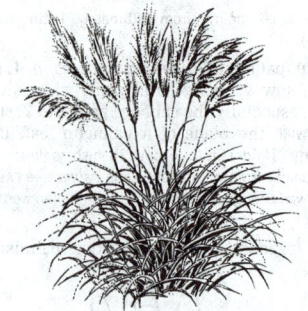
Pampas grass

pampas grass *n.* a tall South American grass often grown in parks and gardens, naturalized in the southern United States. It has silky white plumes when flowering. Latin name: *Cortaderia selloana*.

pamper /pámpər/ (**-pers, -pering, -pered**) *vt.* **1. TREAT LAVISHLY** to lavish attention on sb, indulging his or her taste for luxury **2. GRATIFY** to indulge or gratify a desire or need **3. FEED EXCESSIVELY** to fill sb with rich food (*archaic*) [14thC. Origin uncertain: probably from Low German or Dutch.] —**pamperer** *n.*

pampero /pam páirō/ (*plural* **-ros**) *n.* a strong, cold, dry wind that blows southwest from the Andes to the Atlantic, across the South American pampas [Late 18thC. From Spanish, formed from *pampa*, literally 'plain'.]

Pampers /pámpərz/ *tdmk.* a trademark for a brand of disposable nappies

pamph. *abbr.* pamphlet

pamphlet /pámflət/ *n.* a small leaflet or paper booklet, usually unbound and coverless, that gives information or supports a position [14thC. From *Pamphilet* or *Pamflet*, popular names of *Pamphilus, seu de Amore*, a short anonymous 12thC Latin love poem, later used for any short text.]

pamphleteer /pámflə teer/ *n.* **PAMPHLET WRITER** sb who writes pamphlets that contain opinionated essays, usually on a political topic ■ *vi.* (**-eers, -eering, -eered**) **WRITE PAMPHLETS** to write material for pamphlets, especially political ones

pamphrey /pámfri/ (*plural* **-phreys**) *n.* Ireland a cabbage, especially a variety of dark green, open-leaved spring cabbage [Origin unknown]

Pamplona /pam plōnə/ city in northeastern Spain. It is the capital of the autonomous region of Navarre. Population: 181,776 (1995).

pamprodactylous /pámprō dáktiləss/ *adj.* BIRDS used to describe a bird such as the swift that has all four toes facing forwards [Late 19thC. Coined from PAN- + PRO- + DACTYL + -OUS.]

pan[1] /pan/ *n.* **1. COOK COOKING POT** a cooking pot, usually metal and with a handle, for use on the hob of a cooker **2. COOK** = baking tin **3. HOUSEHOLD CONTAINER FOR WASTE** shallow container that household waste is put into for easy disposal **4. SHALLOW, OPEN CONTAINER** any shallow open container used to store, catch, or heat liquids or other substances **5. MINING DISH FOR SORTING MINERALS** a flat metal dish, shaped like a pie plate, used to separate precious minerals, especially gold, from loose soil, gravel, or sediment **6. SCALE DISH** either of the dishes suspended in a balance scale **7. GEOL CONCAVITY IN EARTH** a natural shallow sink or basin in the ground, usually filled with rainwater or mud **8. SHALLOW AREA FOR EVAPORATING BRINE** a natural or artificial concavity in the earth, in which brine is evaporated, leaving behind salt **9. TRANSP** = hardpan **10. THIN ICE FLOE** a small, flat, thin ice floe of the type that forms near a shore or in a bay **11. ARMS PRIMING CONTAINER IN GUN** the hollow part of a flintlock gun, into which the gunpowder is loaded ■ *v.* (**pans, panning, panned**) **1.** *vt.* **CRITICIZE SEVERELY** to criticize sb or sth severely, especially in a review (*informal*) **2.** *vi.* **MINING SORT THROUGH DIRT FOR MINERALS** to use a shallow dish to separate valuable minerals from loose soil, gravel, or sediment by washing or shaking **3.** *vi.* **YIELD PRECIOUS METALS** to yield valuable metals when separating minerals and leavings by means of washing or shaking using a shallow dish [Old English

panne. From a prehistoric Germanic word that may derive, ultimately, from Latin *patina* (see PATEN).]

pan out *vi.* (*informal*) **1. CONCLUDE** to turn out or result ○ *After all our careful planning, it's a shame that things didn't pan out as we had hoped.* **2. BE SUCCESSFUL** to turn out well or successfully ○ *Her new career in moviemaking never panned out.* [From the practice by prospectors of washing gravel in a pan in order to separate the gold]

pan[2] /pan/ *vti.* (**pans, panning, panned**) **MOVE A CAMERA HORIZONTALLY FROM A FIXED POINT** to move a camera horizontally from a stationary point in order to capture a broad view of a scene or to film or photograph a moving object ■ *n.* **HORIZONTAL CAMERA MOVEMENT FROM A FIXED POINT** a horizontal movement of a camera from a fixed point, or the resulting filmed shot [Early 20thC. Shortening of PANORAMA or PANORAMIC.]

pan[3] /paan/ *n.* **1. BOT BETEL LEAF** a leaf of the betel plant **2. ROLLED BETEL LEAF WITH SPICES** a leaf of the betel plant rolled and filled with spices and lime, chewed for its flavour and as a stimulant in southwestern Asia [Early 17thC. From Hindi *pān*.]

Pan[1] /pan/ *n.* in Greek mythology, the god of nature, pastures, flocks, and forests, believed to have a human torso and head, and the hind legs, ears, and horns of a goat. Roman equivalent **Faunus**

Pan[2] /pan/ *n.* the innermost known natural satellite of Saturn, discovered in 1990. It is approximately 20 km in diameter.

Pan. *abbr.* Panama

pan- *prefix.* all, any, everyone ○ *panchromatic* ○ *Pan-Slavism* [From Greek, a form of *pas* 'all' (source also of English *pancreas*)]

panacea /pánnə seé ə/ *n.* a supposed cure for all diseases or problems [Mid-16thC. Via Latin from Greek *panakeia*, from *panakēs* 'all-healing', from *akos* 'remedy'.] —**panacean** *adj.*

panache /pə násh/ *n.* **1. DASHING STYLE** a sense or display of spirited style and self-confidence **2. CLOTHES HELMET PLUME** a plume or tuft of feathers, especially on a hat or helmet [Mid-16thC. Via French from Italian *pennacchio* 'plume of feathers', from, ultimately, Latin *pinna* 'feather' (source of English *pin, pinnacle*, and *pinion*).]

panada /pə náadə/ *n.* a very thick paste of flour or some other starchy ingredient and a liquid such as milk or stock that is used as a base for sauces or as binding for stuffing [Late 16thC. Via Spanish or Portuguese from, ultimately, Latin *panis* 'bread'.]

pan-African *adj.* relating to the nations of Africa, collectively or in cooperation with one another, or advocating freedom and independence for African people —**Pan-Africanism** *n.*

panama /pánnə maa, -máa/, **Panama** *n.* = Panama hat

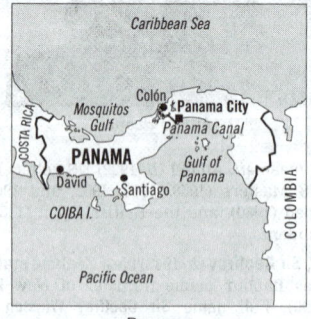
Panama

Panama /pánnə maa, -máa/ republic in Central America. It has the Caribbean Sea to its north and the Pacific Ocean to its south, connected by the Panama Canal, and is situated between Costa Rica and Colombia. Language: Spanish. Currency: balboa. Capital: Panama City. Population: 2,674,490 (1996). Area: 75,517 sq. km/29,157 sq. mi. Official name **Republic of Panama** —**Panamanian** /pánnə máyni ən/ *n., adj.*

Panama, Isthmus of /pánnə maa, -máa/ narrow neck of land occupied by Panama, separating the Pacific Ocean and the Caribbean Sea

Panama Canal /pánnə maa kə nál/ canal across the Isthmus of Panama, completed in 1914. Length: 82 km/50 mi.

Panama City /pánnə maa sítti/ capital city of Panama, located in the centre of the country, on the Pacific Ocean. Population: 485,490 (1996).

Panama hat, **panama hat**, **panama**, **Panama** *n.* a brimmed men's hat made from the plaited leaves of the jipijapa, or an imitation of such a hat

Pan-American *adj.* relating to the nations of North, South, and Central America, collectively or in co-operation with one another —**Pan-Americanism** *n.*

Pan-Arabism *n.* a movement for greater cooperation among and self-reliance within Arab or Islamic nations —**Pan-Arab** *n., adj.* —**Pan-Arabic** *adj.* —**Pan-Arabist** *n., adj.*

panatella /pánnə téllə/, **panatela** *n.* a long thin cigar that does not bulge in the middle [Mid-19thC. Via American Spanish, denoting a long thin biscuit, from Italian *panatello* 'small loaf', from, ultimately, Latin *panis* 'bread' (source of English *pannier*).]

Panathenaea /pan áthə née ə/ *n.* a summer festival held annually in ancient Athens but with extra ceremony every fourth year. It involved games, sacrifices, and music and poetry contests. [Early 17thC. From Greek *panathēnaia hiera*, literally 'festival of all Athenians'.]

pancake /pán kayk/ *n.* **1.** THIN FRIED CAKE a thin flat cake made by pouring batter onto a hot greased flat pan, and cooking it on both sides **2.** *Scotland* DROP SCONE a drop scone **3.** AIR = **pancake landing** ■ *v.* (**-cakes**, **-caking**, **-caked**) **1.** *vti.* AIR MAKE PANCAKE LANDING to make a pancake landing or cause an aircraft to make such a landing **2.** *vt.* US FLATTEN to turn sth parallel to the ground, especially a tennis racquet in the course of a stroke

Pan-Cake *tdmk.* a trademark for a semi-solid theatrical makeup, typically applied with a damp sponge

Pancake Day *n.* = **Shrove Tuesday** [So called because it is celebrated by eating pancakes, which were traditionally made to use up eggs and fat before the fast of Lent]

pancake ice *n.* a small flat thin piece of sea ice that drifts out into deeper water from near the shore or the bay in which it was formed

pancake landing *n.* an aeroplane landing in which the aircraft drops abruptly straight to the ground from a low altitude, usually due to engine failure

pancake tortoise *n.* a Tanzanian turtle with a flattened flexible shell. It can slip between rocks and narrow crevices and then slightly inflate to resist being pulled out. Latin name: *Malachersus tornieri*.

Pancake Tuesday *n.* = **Shrove Tuesday**

pancetta /pan chéttə/ *n.* a salt-cured and spiced form of unsmoked belly of pork, used in Italian dishes [Mid-20thC. From Italian, literally 'little belly', from, ultimately, Latin *pantix* 'bowel, intestine' (source of English *paunch*).]

panchax /pán chaks/ *n.* a small tropical freshwater Southeast Asian fish that is olive, red, and yellow and is often kept as an aquarium fish. Latin name: *Aplocheilus panchax*. [Mid-20thC. From modern Latin, the former genus name.]

panchayat /pun chī ət/ *n.* S Asia a village council in India [Early 19thC. Via Hindi *pañcāyat* from Sanskrit *pañcāyatta*, literally 'depending on five' (the original number of members).]

Panchen Lama /púnchən-/ *n.* the second highest ranking Lama in Tibetan Buddhism [From Tibetan, contraction of *pandi-tachen-po* 'great learned one']

panchromatic /pán krō máttik/ *adj.* used to describe photographic film that is sensitive to all visible colours and some ultraviolet light

pancratium /pan kráyshi əm/ (*plural* **-a** /-shi ə/) *n.* an athletic event in ancient Greece, involving boxing and wrestling contests [Early 17thC. From Greek *pagkration*, from *kratos* 'strength'.] —**pancratic** /pan kráttik/ *adj.*

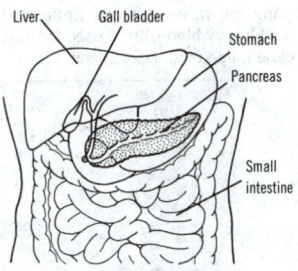

Pancreas

pancreas /pángkri əss/ *n.* a large elongated glandular organ lying near the stomach. It secretes juices into the small intestine and the hormones insulin, glucagon, and somatostatin into the bloodstream. [Late 16thC. Via modern Latin from Greek *pagkreas*, from *kreas* 'flesh'.]

pancreat- *prefix.* pancreas ○ *pancreatitis* [From Greek *pankreat-*, the stem of *pankreas* (see PANCREAS)]

pancreatectomy /pángkri ə téktəmi/ (*plural* **-mies**) *n.* whole or partial removal of the pancreas by surgery

pancreatic duct /pángkriáttik/ *n.* a duct that carries pancreatic juice and, in human beings, runs from the pancreas to join the common bile duct, which empties into the small intestine

pancreatic juice *n.* a watery alkaline fluid secreted by the pancreas. It contains enzymes that break down partially digested food in the small intestine.

pancreatin /pángkri ətin, pan krée ətin/ *n.* **1.** DIGESTIVE AID FROM PANCREATIC ENZYMES a digestive aid made from a mixture of pancreatic enzymes extracted from domestic animals **2.** MIXTURE OF PANCREATIC ENZYMES the mixture of digestive enzymes produced by the pancreas, including amylase, lipase, and trypsin

pancreatitis /pángkri ə títiss/ *n.* inflammation of the pancreas

pancreozymin /pángkri ō zímin/ *n.* = **cholecystokinin** [Mid-20thC. From PANCREAS + *zymin*.]

Panda

panda /pándə/ *n.* **1.** LARGE BLACK-AND-WHITE CHINESE MAMMAL a large bamboo-eating mammal of central China, with bold black-and-white markings, including black patches over the eyes. Latin name: *Ailuropodia melanoleuca*. **2.** = **red panda** [Mid-19thC. Via French from the Nepalese name of the red panda.]

panda car *n.* a police patrol car (*informal*) [So called because its colour scheme, black or blue with a broad white stripe, was thought to resemble the markings of the giant panda]

pandanus /pan dáynəss/ (*plural* **-nuses** *or* **-nus**) *n.* a tropical plant resembling a palm, with prop roots and a crown of narrow leaves that are often used to make mats. Genus: *Pandanus*. [Mid-19thC. Via modern Latin from Malay *pandan*.]

Pandean /pan dée ən/ *adj.* relating to the mythological Greek god Pan

Pandean pipes *npl.* = **panpipes**

pandect /pán dekt/ *n.* **1.** BODY OF LAWS a set of documents containing all the laws of a country or society **2.** COMPREHENSIVE TREATISE a comprehensive treatise on a subject [Mid-16thC. Directly or via French from Latin *pandecta*, from Greek *pandektēs* 'all-receiving', from *dekhesthai* 'to receive'.]

Pandects /pán dekts/ *n.* = **Digest** *n.*

pandemic /pan démmik/ *adj.* HAVING WIDESPREAD EFFECT existing in the form of a widespread epidemic that affects people in many different countries. AIDS is currently considered to be pandemic ■ *n.* VERY WIDESPREAD DISEASE a disease or condition that is found in a large part of a population [Mid-17thC. From Greek *pandēmos* 'public', literally 'of all the people', from *dēmos* 'people' (source of English *democracy*).]

pandemonium /pándə móni əm/ *n.* **1.** CHAOS wild uproar and chaos **2.** NOISY CONFUSED PLACE a place or situation that is noisy and chaotic [Mid-17thC. From modern Latin *Pandaemonium*, from Greek *daimōn* (see DEMON).] —**pandemoniac** *adj.* —**pandemonic** /-mónnik/ *adj.*

Pandemonium /pándə móni əm/ *n.* Hell, or any place of chaos or torment (*literary*) [From the name of the capital of Hell in Milton's *Paradise Lost*]

pander /pándər/ *vi.* (**-ders**, **-dering**, **-dered**) **1.** INDULGE WEAKNESSES to indulge sb's weaknesses or questionable wishes and tastes ○ *tired of pandering to their children's demands* **2.** PROCURE SEXUAL FAVOURS to procure sexual favours for sb (*disapproving*) ■ *n.* **1.** **pander**, **panderer** SB WHO INDULGES ANOTHER'S WEAKNESSES sb who indulges another's weaknesses or questionable wishes and tastes (*disapproving*) **2.** **pander**, **panderer** ROMANTIC GO-BETWEEN a go-between in an illicit or secret romantic or sexual relationship (*disapproving*) **3.** PIMP a pimp (*archaic*) [14thC. From *pandarus*.]

pandit /pándit/ *n.* a wise or learned man in India, especially a Brahman who is an expert in Hindu culture, law, and philosophy

P & L *abbr.* profit and loss

Pandora[1] /pan dáwrə/ *n.* in Greek mythology, the first woman, who was sent by the gods with a jar full of evils in order to avenge Prometheus's theft of fire. She opened the jar out of curiosity, thus releasing the evils into the world.

Pandora[2] /pan dáwrə/ *n.* a small inner natural satellite of Saturn, discovered in 1980 by Voyager 2. It is irregular in shape with a maximum dimension of 110 km.

Pandora's box *n.* **1.** OBJECT IN GREEK MYTHOLOGY in Greek mythology, the jar, later referred to as a box, from which Pandora allowed all the world's evils to escape **2.** SET OF ILLS the source of a great collection of ills that need not be faced unless an unwise action is taken ○ *If you criticize her work, you'll be opening a real Pandora's box.*

pandore /pán dawr/ *n.* = **bandore**

pandour /pán door/ *n.* HIST, MIL **1.** 18C CROATIAN SOLDIER a soldier in a notorious Croatian regiment in the 18th-century Austrian army **2.** KHOIKHOI SOLDIER a Khoikhoi soldier belonging to the Dutch East India Company's force in South Africa at the beginning of the 19th century [Mid-18thC. Via French *pandur* or German *Pandur* from Serbo-Croat *pandur* 'constable, bailiff', of uncertain origin: probably from medieval Latin *banderius* 'guard of vineyards or fields'.]

pandowdy /pan dówdi/ (*plural* **-dies**) *n.* US a dish made of sliced apples and spices covered with a biscuit crust and baked in a deep pan [Mid-19thC. Origin uncertain: probably ultimately from PAN[1] + a variant of DOUGH.]

p & p *abbr.* postage and packing

pandurate /pándyōōrət, -dŏŏrayt/, **panduriform** /pan dyŏŏri fawrm, -dŏŏri-/ *adj.* used to describe a leaf that is shaped like a violin, with rounded ends and a tapering middle [Late 18thC. From Latin *pandura*, from Greek *pandoura* (see BANDORE).]

pandy /pándi/ (**-dies**, **-dying**, **-died**) *vt.* Ireland, Scotland to hit sb on the palm as punishment, especially with a ruler or strap (*archaic*) [Mid-18thC. From Latin *pande manum* 'hold out your hand', from *pandere* 'to stretch out'.]

pane /payn/ *n.* **1.** GLAZED SECTION OF A WINDOW a glazed section of a window or door **2.** PIECE OF GLASS IN A WINDOW a piece of plate glass in a window or door **3.** SECTION OF SURFACE a distinct section of a surface such as a door or wall **4.** SURFACE OF A FACETED OBJECT a surface on a faceted object, e.g. a metal nut or cut jewel **5.** SECTION OF A SHEET OF STAMPS rectangular section into which a sheet of postage stamps is divided before being sold [13thC. Via French *pan* from Latin *pannus* 'piece of cloth'. Current senses evolved from 'piece of cloth' via 'distinct part or panel of a garment'.]

panegyric /pánnə jírrik/ *n.* extravagant praise delivered in formal speech or writing (*formal*) [Early 17thC. Via French *panégyrique* from Latin *panegyricus* 'public eulogy' from, ultimately, Greek *panēguris* 'public assembly', from *aguris* 'assembly, marketplace'.] —**panegyrical** *adj.* —**panegyrically** *adv.* —**panegyrist** *n.*

panegyrize /pánnəjə rīz/ (**-rizes, -rizing, -rized**), **panegyrise** (**-rises, -rising, -rised**) *vti.* to praise sb or sth, especially extravagantly in formal speech or writing (*formal*)

panel /pánn'l/ *n.* **1.** BUILDING FLAT RECTANGULAR PART a flat rectangular piece of hard material that serves as a part of sth such as a door or wall, often raised above or sunk in the surface **2.** BUILDING FENCE SECTION a section between two posts in a fence or gate **3.** SEW STRIP OF FABRIC IN GARMENT a vertical section of fabric sewn onto other such sections in a flowing garment or drapery **4.** PAINTING WOODEN SURFACE FOR PAINTING a thin piece of wood used as a surface for oil painting, or the painting on it **5.** DRAWING COMIC STRIP FRAME a section depicting a single scene in a comic strip **6.** AEROSP PART OF AN AIRCRAFT WING a section or surface of an aeroplane wing **7.** ENG CLUSTER OF PERFORMANCE-MEASURING INSTRUMENTS a surface on which performance-measuring instruments such as gauges, dials, lights, and digital displays are clustered **8.** COMPUT CONTROL AREA OF A COMPUTER the collection of lights, digital displays, and switches used to monitor and control the operation of a computer **9.** COMPUT DISPLAY ON A COMPUTER SCREEN a display of related information on a computer screen, often a list of options **10.** ARTS GROUP OF JUDGES OR SPEAKERS a group of people who publicly discuss or judge sth, usually in a situation where they sit in a row to face an audience or a competition arena **11.** LAW LIST OF PEOPLE FOR JURY DUTY a list of people summoned as potential jurors, or the people themselves **12.** LAW JURY a jury in a court proceeding **13.** *Scotland* LAW ACCUSED PERSON an accused person or group of accused people brought into court to face charges ■ *vt.* (**-els, -elling, -elled**) **1.** BUILDING SUPPLY WITH PANELS to furnish, cover, or decorate sth with panels, especially wooden panelling for walls **2.** LAW EMPANEL to make a list of potential jurors or select a jury from such a list **3.** *Scotland* LAW INDICT to indict sb for a crime [14thC. Via Old French from *pan* 'piece of cloth' (see PANE). The underlying sense is of a distinct part.]

panel beater *n.* a person or business that repairs car bodies, especially by beating out dents

panel heating *n.* a domestic heating system in which heating elements are housed in panels attached to walls or floors

paneling *n.* US = panelling

panelist *n.* US = panellist

panelling /pánn'ling/ *n.* **1.** WOODEN WALL COVERING thin boards or sheets of wood for covering walls, especially as decoration **2.** PANEL-COVERED WALL a panel-covered wall or other surface

panellist /pánn'list/ *n.* sb who is a member of a panel

panel van *n.* ANZ a small van with rear doors used for carrying goods and tools

panettone /pánnə tóni/ (*plural* **-ettones** or **-ettoni**) *n.* a tall Italian yeast cake flavoured with vanilla and dried and candied fruits, traditionally eaten at Christmas [Early 20thC. From Italian, from *pane* 'bread', from Latin *panis*.]

Pan-European *adj.* relating to all the nations of Europe, collectively or in cooperation with one another

pan-fry (**pan-fries, pan-frying, pan-fried**) *vt.* to fry food, usually fish or meat, in a frying pan with a little fat

pang /pang/ *n.* **1.** SHARP PAIN a short sharp pain **2.** INTENSE EMOTION a sudden, intense, and distressing feeling [15thC. Origin uncertain: perhaps an alteration of PRONG.]

panga /páng gə/ *n.* an African knife with a long, broad, and heavy blade, often used for cutting down sugar cane [Mid-20thC. From Swahili.]

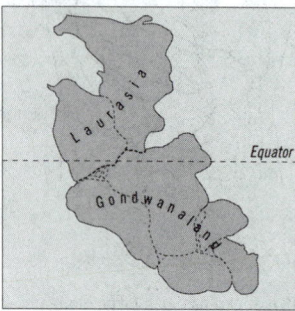
Pangaea

Pangaea /pan jée ə/ *n.* ancient supercontinent incorporating all the Earth's major landmasses. It is thought to have begun splitting up about 200 million years ago. [Early 20thC. Coined from PAN- 'all' + Greek *gaia* 'earth'.]

pangenesis /pan jénnəssiss/ *n.* a disproved hypothesis of heredity according to which somatic cells influenced by the environment send information concerning that influence to reproductive cells, where it is passed to the next generation —**pangenetic** /pánjə néttik/ *adj.* —**pangenetically** /-néttikli/ *adv.*

Panglossian /pan glóssi ən/ *adj.* excessively and inappropriately optimistic (*literary*) [Mid-19thC. From Dr *Pangloss*, a philosopher in Voltaire's *Candide* (1759), who always asserts that 'all is for the best in the best of all possible worlds'.]

Pangolin

pangolin /páng gəlin, pang gṓlin/ *n.* an African and Asian mammal with horny scales, a long tapering snout and tail, and a long sticky tongue for catching ants and termites. Order: Pholidota. [Late 18thC. From Malay *peng-guling*, literally 'roller', because it rolls itself up when frightened.]

panhandle[1] /pán hand'l/ *n.* **1.** HANDLE OF A PAN the handle of a cooking pan **2.** **panhandle, Panhandle** US GEOG STRIP OF LAND EXTENDING FROM US STATE a narrow section of land shaped like the handle of a cooking pan that extends away from the body of the US state or territory it belongs to ◇ *the Texas Panhandle*

panhandle[2] /pán hand'l/ (**-dles, -dling, -dled**) *v.* US **1.** *vi.* BEG MONEY FROM STRANGERS to beg for money on the street by approaching and talking to passers-by **2.** *vt.* GET BY BEGGING to get money from a stranger by approaching him or her in the street and begging **3.** *vt.* BEG MONEY FROM to approach and beg for money from sb [Late 19thC. Probably so called from the beggar's outstretched arm, thought to resemble the handle of a pan.] —**panhandler** *n.*

Panhellenic /pán he lénnik/ *adj.* relating to all Greek peoples or all of Greece

Panhellenism /pan héllənizəm/ *n.* a philosophy or movement advocating a single political system for all Greek people

panic[1] /pánnik/ *n.* OVERPOWERING FEAR OR ANXIETY a sudden feeling of fear or anxiety, especially among many people, that comes on suddenly, is overwhelming, appears to be uncontrollable, and may seem to be unfounded ■ *adj.* INVOLVING OR RESULTING FROM PANIC relating to, responding to, or resulting from panic or possible panic ◇ *panic selling on the stock market* ■ *vti.* (**-ics, -icking, -icked**) BE OR MAKE SB EXTREMELY AFRAID to feel panic, or make a person or animal feel panic [Early 17thC. Via French *panique* and modern Latin *panicus* 'terrified', from, ultimately, Greek *Pan*, the Greek god of nature whose appearance was believed to induce irrational fear.] —**panicky** /pánniki/ *adj.*

panic[2] *n.* = panic grass

Panic *adj.* relating to Pan, a god in Greek mythology

panic attack *n.* a sudden overpowering feeling of fear or anxiety that prevents sb from functioning, often triggered by a past or present source of anxiety

panic bolt *n.* a bolt released by a waist-high bar that is fitted on emergency exit doors in buildings used by large numbers of people

panic button *n.* an alarm to call security staff or summon help in an emergency ◇ **hit** *or* **press** *or* **push the panic button** to react to a perceived emergency or crisis by panicking and responding too hastily (*informal*)

panic buying *n.* the buying of a particular product or products in quantity by a large number of people who fear a possible shortage

panic disorder *n.* a condition in which sb has recurrent panic attacks

panic grass, **panic, pannick** *n.* a grass, e.g. millet, used for grain fodder and as a cereal. Genus: *Panicum.* [*Panic* from Latin *panicum* 'foxtail millet', used as genus name]

panicle /pánnik'l/ *n.* **1.** FLOWER CLUSTER ALONG STEM a cluster of flowers on a plant consisting of a number of individual stalks (**racemes**) each of which has a series of single flowers along its length **2.** PYRAMID-SHAPED FLOWER CLUSTER a loose branching pyramid-shaped cluster of flowers [Late 16thC. From Latin *panicula*, literally 'little ear of millet', from *panus* 'swelling, ear of millet'.]

panicled *adj.* = paniculate

panicmonger /pánnik mung gər/ *n.* sb who creates a sense of panic in others through his or her own agitation, or who deliberately fosters a sense of panic in others

panic stations *n.* a state of panic, confusion, and commotion immediately following an unexpected event that requires immediate action (*informal; takes a singular verb*)

panic-stricken, **panic-struck** *adj.* suddenly affected by or characterized by panic

paniculate /pə níkyoōlət/, **paniculated** /-laytid/, **panicled** /pánnik'ld/ *adj.* growing in, forming, or resembling a panicle

Panislamism /pán iz laámizəm, pan ízləmizəm/ *n.* a movement that aims to unify Muslim countries and spread the Islamic religion [Late 19thC. Coined from PAN- + ISLAMISM.] —**Panislamic** /pániz lámmik/ *adj.* —**Panislamist** /pán iz laámist, pan ízləmist/ *n., adj.*

Panjabi *n., adj.* = Punjabi

panjandrum /pan jándrəm/ (*plural* **-drums** or **panjandra** /-drə/) *n.* sb, especially an official, who is pompous or pretentious [Mid-18thC. Nonsense word.]

——— **WORD KEY: ORIGIN** ———
Panjandrum was coined in 1755 by the English actor and playwright Samuel Foote (1720–77) to test the memory of the actor Charles Macklin, who claimed to be able to memorize and repeat anything said to him (it was one of several inventions in the same vein that Foote put to him): 'And there were present the Picninnies, and the Joblillies, and the Garyulies, and the Grand Panjandrum himself, with the little round button at top'. It did not spread into general use until the 19th century.

Pankhurst /pángk hurst/, **Emmeline** (1858–1928) British suffragette. She founded the Women's Social and Political Union (1903) in Manchester. She was frequently imprisoned for destroying property, but during World War I abandoned her campaign and encouraged women to do industrial war work.

panleucopenia /pán lookō peéni ə/, **panleukopenia** *n.*

Emmeline Pankhurst

feline distemper (*technical*) [Mid-20thC. Coined from PAN- + LEUCOPENIA.]

pan loaf *n*. COOK **LOAF BAKED IN TIN** a baker's loaf of white bread with a thin soft crust all the way round it that is baked individually in a tin (*regional*) ■ *adj., adv. Scotland* **AFFECTED** with an affected way of speaking (*informal humorous*) [*Pan* because it is baked in a pan. The sense 'affected(ly)' arose from the fact that a pan loaf was once more expensive than a plain loaf.]

panmixia /pan míksi ə/, **panmixis** /-míksiss/ *n*. random breeding and free interchange of genes within a population [Late 19thC. Via modern Latin from German *Panmixie*, literally 'all mixing', from, ultimately, Greek *mixis* 'mixing, mingling'.] —**panmictic** *adj*.

panne /pan/ *n*. a lightweight silk or rayon fabric resembling velvet [Late 18thC. From French, of unknown origin.]

pannick *n*. = panic grass

pannier /pánni ər/ *n*. **1.** **BASKET ON BACK OF ANIMAL** a large basket, often one of a pair, that is placed on the back of a horse, donkey, or other pack animal **2.** **BAG ON BACK OF BICYCLE** one of a pair of bags carried on either side of the back or front wheel of a bicycle or motorcycle **3.** CLOTHES, HIST **FRAMEWORK TO WIDEN SKIRT** a framework of cane worn by women in the 18th century at each side of the hips to widen a skirt **4.** CLOTHES, HIST **OVERSKIRT LOOPED UP AT HIPS** an overskirt looped up at the hips to show the underskirt and give the impression of fullness, worn in the second half of the 19th century [13thC. Via Old French *pannier* from Latin *panarium* 'breadbasket', from *panis* 'bread', earlier 'food' (source also of English *pantry*).]

pannikin /pánnikin/ *n*. a small metal drinking cup [Early 19thC. Formed from PAN¹, on the model of CANNIKIN 'cup'.]

panoply /pánnəpli/ (*plural* **-plies**) *n*. **1.** **FULL ARRAY** an impressive and magnificent display or array of sth **2.** CLOTHES **FULL CEREMONIAL DRESS** ceremonial dress with all the necessary accessories **3.** MIL **FULL ARMOUR** a full suit of armour and equipment for a warrior **4.** **PROTECTIVE COVERING** a covering that protects sth [Late 16thC. Via French from Greek *panoplia*, literally 'all weapons', from *hopla* 'weapons'.] —**panoplied** *adj*.

panoptic /pan óptik/, **panoptical** /-óptik'l/ *adj*. taking in or showing everything in a single view [Early 19thC. Formed from Greek *panoptos*, literally 'seen by all', and *panoptēs*, literally 'all-seeing', both formed in turn from *optos* 'visible'.] —**panoptically** *adv*.

panorama /pánnə raámə/ *n*. **1.** **ALL-ROUND VIEW** an unobstructed view extending in all directions, especially of a landscape **2.** **COMPREHENSIVE SURVEY** an all-encompassing survey of a particular topic or issue **3.** ARTS, PHOTOGRAPHY **PICTURE WITH A WIDE VIEW** a picture or photograph that has a wide view, especially one that is unrolled gradually in front of the spectator **4.** ARTS = cyclorama [Late 18thC. Coined from PAN- + Greek *horama* 'view', from *horan* 'to see'.] —**panoramic** /-rámmik/ *adj*. —**panoramically** *adv*.

───────── **WORD KEY: ORIGIN** ─────────

Panorama was coined in the late 1780s by an Irish artist called Robert Barker for a method he had invented for painting a scene on the inside of a cylinder in such a way that its perspective would seem correct to someone viewing it from inside the cylinder. He put his invention into practice in 1793 when he opened his 'Panorama', a large building in Leicester Square, London, where the public could come and gaze at such all-encompassing

scenes. The modern abstract meaning was in use by the early 19th century.

panoramic sight *n*. a sight on a military weapon that gives the user a wide-angled view of the target area

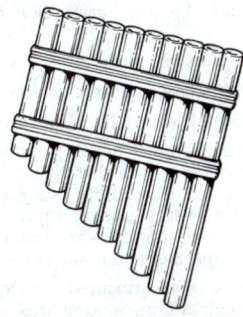

Panpipes

panpipes /pán pīps/ *npl*. a set of reeds of different lengths that are bound together in a row and played by blowing across the top of each pipe. Panpipes have been in use since ancient times and are today often associated with Peruvian music. [Early 19thC. *Pan* from the name of the mythological Greek god supposed to have invented them.]

pansexual /pán sékshoo əl/ *adj*. relating to a sexuality that expresses itself in many different forms [Early 20thC. Coined from PAN- + SEXUAL.] —**pansexuality** /pán sekshoo álləti/ *n*.

Pan-Slavism *n*. a 19th-century political and cultural movement aiming at the union of all Slav people —**Pan-Slavic** *adj*. —**Pan-Slavist** *n., adj*.

panspermia /pan spúrmi ə/ *n*. a theory of biogenetics that states that the universe is full of spores that germinate when they find a favourable environment [Mid-19thC. From Greek, 'doctrine that the elements are made of all the seeds of things', from, ultimately, *sperma* 'seed' (source also of English *sperm*).]

pansy /pánzi/ *n*. (*plural* **-sies**) **1.** PLANTS **FLOWER WITH BRIGHT VELVETY PETALS** a European plant with brightly coloured velvety flowers that usually have black or dark centres. Genus: *Viola* and *Achimenes*. **2.** OFFENSIVE TERM a highly offensive term for a gay man or boy (*dated offensive*) **3.** OFFENSIVE TERM a highly offensive term for an effeminate man or boy (*dated offensive*) **4.** COLOURS **DEEP VIOLET** a deep violet colour ■ *adj*. COLOURS **DEEP VIOLET IN COLOUR** of a deep violet colour [15thC. From French *pensée*, literally 'thought' (from its lowered head), feminine past participle of *penser* 'to think' (source also of English *pensive*).]

pant¹ /pant/ *v*. (**pants, panting, panted**) **1.** *vi*. **TAKE SHORT FAST SHALLOW BREATHS** to take short fast shallow breaths, especially when excited, hot, or after physical exertion **2.** *vt*. **SAY STH BREATHLESSLY** to say sth while trying to catch your breath **3.** *vi*. **YEARN** to have a strong desire and yearning for sb or sth **4.** *vi*. **PULSATE QUICKLY** to throb at a fast rhythm ■ *n*. **SHALLOW BREATH** a short fast shallow breath [15thC. From assumed Anglo-Norman, 'to gasp', ultimately from Vulgar Latin *phantasiare* 'to gasp in horror', from Latin *phantasia* 'apparition' (source also of English *fancy* and *fantasy*).]

pant² /pant/ *n*. US a pair of trousers (*formal*) ◊ **pants** [Late 19thC. Back-formation.]

pant- *prefix*. = panto- (*used before vowels*)

pantalets /pántə léts/, **pantalettes** *npl*. HIST **1.** **WOMEN'S LONG UNDERPANTS** long underpants extending below the skirt, usually with a frill round the bottom of each leg, worn by women in the first half of the 19th century **2.** **FRILLS ON PANTALETS** a pair of frills, one at the bottom of each leg, on a pair of pantalets [Mid-19thC. Formed from PANTALOON with the literal sense 'little pantaloons'.]

pantaloon /pántə loon/ *n*. a character in pantomime who is the victim of the clown's jokes and tricks [Late 16thC. Via French *pantalon* from Italian *Pantalone* (see PANTALOON).]

Pantaloon /pántə loon/ *n*. a character in Italian commedia dell'arte, a very thin man of advanced years who is easily tricked and who wears pantaloons

and slippers [Late 16thC. Origin uncertain: probably named after *San Pantaleone* 'Saint Pantaleon', patron saint of Venice.]

pantaloons /pántə loonz/ *npl*. **1.** **WIDE TROUSERS GATHERED AT ANKLE** loose-fitting trousers that are gathered at the ankle **2.** **BAGGY TROUSERS** trousers that fit very loosely (*informal humorous*) **3.** HIST **TIGHT-FITTING MEN'S TROUSERS** tight-fitting men's trousers fastened with buttons or ribbons at the ankle and sometimes held with a strap under the instep, worn in the early 19th century **4.** HIST **17C ENGLISH TROUSERS** men's wide ankle-length breeches, worn especially in England during the reign of Charles II [Mid-17thC. See PANTALOON.]

pantechnicon /pan téknikən/ *n*. a large furniture-removal van [Mid-19thC. Coined from PAN- + Greek *tekhnikos* 'artistic', because it originally denoted a building in London used as a bazaar (and, later, as a furniture warehouse).]

───────── **WORD KEY: ORIGIN** ─────────

The original *Pantechnicon* was a huge complex of warehouses, wine vaults, and other storage facilities in Motcomb Street, in London's Belgravia. Built in 1830 and supposed to be fireproof, it was almost totally destroyed by fire in 1874. It seems originally to have been intended to be a bazaar. Hence its name, literally 'everything artistic', denoting that all sorts of manufactured wares were to be bought there. But it was its role as a furniture repository that brought it into the general language. Removal vans taking furniture there came to be known as 'pantechnicon vans', and by the 1890s *pantechnicon* was a generic term for 'removal van'.

pantheism /pánthi izəm/ *n*. **1.** **BELIEF THAT GOD IS EVERYTHING** the belief that God and the material world are one and the same thing and that God is present in everything **2.** **BELIEF IN ALL DEITIES** the belief in and worship of all or many deities [Mid-18thC. Coined from PAN- + Greek *theos* 'god' + -ISM.] —**pantheist** *n*. —**pantheistic** /pánthi ístik/ *adj*. —**pantheistically** /-ístikli/ *adv*.

pantheon /pánthi ən, pan thée-/ *n*. **1.** RELIG **TEMPLE** a temple dedicated to all deities **2.** RELIG **ALL DEITIES OF SPECIFIC RELIGION** all the deities of a particular religion considered collectively **3.** ARCHIT **MEMORIAL TO DEAD HEROES** a monument or public building commemorating the dead heroes of a nation **4.** **GROUP OF IMPORTANT PEOPLE** a group of people who are the most famous or respected in a particular field [15thC. Via Latin from Greek *pantheion*, literally 'of all the gods', from, ultimately, *theos* 'god'.]

Pantheon /pánthi ən, pan thée ən/ *n*. a circular temple in Rome that was completed in 27 BC and dedicated to all the deities but which has been used as a Christian church since AD 609

panther /pánthər/ (*plural* **-thers** *or* **panther**) *n*. **1.** **BLACK LEOPARD** a leopard, especially in its black unspotted phase **2.** US = puma [13thC. Via Old French *pantere* from, ultimately, Greek *panthēr*.]

pantie girdle /pánti-/, **panty girdle** *n*. a woman's undergarment with a sewn-in crotch like underpants, but made of elasticated material in order to give the abdomen a flatter appearance

panties /pántiz/ *npl*. short light fitted underpants for women or girls (*informal*) [Mid-19thC. Formed from PANTS.]

pantihose *npl*. = pantyhose

pantile /pán tīl/ *n*. a roof tile made in an S shape so that the downcurving tail of the S overlaps the upcurving head of the S of the tile next to it [Mid-17thC. From PAN¹ + TILE, probably modelled on Dutch *dakpan* 'roof pan'.]

pantisocracy /pánti sókrəssi/ (*plural* **-cies**) *n*. a planned Utopian community in which everyone shares power and is equal [Late 18thC. Coined from PANTO- + Greek *isokratia* 'equality of power'.]

panto /pántō/ (*plural* **-tos**) *n*. pantomime (*informal*) [Mid-19thC. Shortening.]

panto- *prefix*. all ◊ *pantograph* [From Greek *pant-*, the stem of *pas* (source also of English *pan* and *pancreas*)]

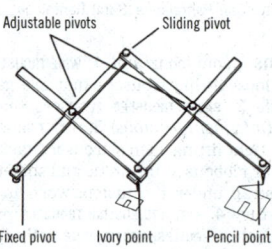

Pantograph

pantograph /pántə graaf, -graf/ *n.* 1. DRAWING COPYING INSTRUMENT an instrument that consists of a set of adjustable interconnected bars forming a parallelogram and is used to copy line drawings or maps to any scale 2. TECH FRAME OR BRACKET a device shaped like a pantograph and used as a frame or bracket 3. RAIL CURRENT-SUPPLY DEVICE FOR ELECTRIC TRAIN a device on the roof of electric trains and locomotives for picking up electric current from overhead wires [Early 18thC. Coined from PANTO- + -GRAPH.] —**pantographer** /pan tóggrəfər/ *n.* —**pantographic** /pántə gráffik/ *adj.* —**pantographically** /-gráffikli/ *adv.*

pantomime /pántə mīm/ *n.* 1. THEATRE HUMOROUS THEATRICAL ENTERTAINMENT a style of theatre, or a play in this style, traditionally performed at Christmas, in which a folktale or children's story is told with jokes, songs, and dancing. Pantomime stories include *Cinderella*, *Dick Whittington*, and *Aladdin*. 2. LUDICROUS SITUATION a ridiculous and farcical situation that results from confusion and misunderstanding (*informal*) 3. THEATRE MIME ARTIST a person who acts without speaking, using gesture and expression 4. HIST, THEATRE ROMAN THEATRICAL PERFORMANCE a theatrical performance in ancient Rome by one masked actor who played all the characters, using only dance, gesture, and expression, and no words, while a chorus narrated the story 5. HIST, THEATRE ROMAN ACTOR an actor in a Roman pantomime [Late 16thC. Via Latin *pantomimus* 'mime artist', from Greek *pantomōmos*, literally 'complete imitator', from *mōmos* 'imitator' (source of English *mime*).] —**pantomimic** /pántə mímmik/ *adj.* —**pantomimist** /-mīmist/ *n.*

pantomime horse *n.* a comic character in a pantomime played by two actors in a horse costume, with one forming the front half of the horse and the other the back half

pantothenate /pántə thénnayt, pan tóthə nayt/ *n.* a salt or an ester of pantothenic acid [Mid-20thC. Coined from PANTOTHENIC ACID.]

pantothenic acid /pántə thénnik-/ *n.* a thick oily acid that belongs to the vitamin B complex, is found in living tissue, and is essential for the growth of some animals. Formula: $C_9H_{17}NO_5$. [Formed from Greek *pantothen* 'from every side', because it is widely found]

pantoum /pan tóom/ *n.* a form of verse in which the second and fourth lines of each four-line verse are repeated as the first and third lines of the following verse [Late 18thC. Via French from Malay *pantun*.]

pantropic /pan trópik, -tróppik/, **pantropical** /-trópik'l, -tróppik'l/ *adj.* found throughout the tropics [Mid-20thC. Coined from PAN- + TROPIC.]

pantry /pántri/ *n.* (*plural* **pantries**) 1. PLACE FOR STORING FOOD a small closed space connected to a kitchen, often with a door, in which food and utensils for food preparation can be stored 2. SMALL ROOM FOR STORING FOOD a highly ventilated cold small room or walk-in cupboard with shelves and a marble surface used for storing food [13thC. Via Old French *paneterie* 'cupboard for bread', from, ultimately, late Latin *panarius* 'breadseller', from Latin *panis* 'bread' (source also of English *company*).]

pants /pants/ *npl.* 1. ITEM OF UNDERWEAR an item of clothing worn next to the skin that covers the buttocks and genital area 2. *US, Can, Aus* MEN'S OR WOMEN'S TROUSERS an item of clothing that covers the part of the body from the waist to the ankles or, sometimes, the knees, each leg having a separate tubular piece [Mid-19thC. Shortening of PANTALOONS.] ◇ **beat the**

pants off sb to defeat sb decisively (*informal*) ◇ **bore or scare** or **charm the pants off sb** to bore, scare, or charm sb very much (*informal*) ◇ **caught with your pants down** to be caught in an unprepared or embarrassing position ◇ **wear the pants** *US, Can, ANZ* to be the boss

pantsuit /pánt soot, -syoot/, **pants suit** *n. US* = trouser suit

panty girdle *n.* = pantie girdle

pantyhose /pánti hōz/, **pantihose** *npl. US* = tights

pantyliner /pánti līnər/ *n.* a light, thin sanitary towel

pantywaist /pánti wayst/ *n. US* 1. OFFENSIVE TERM an offensive term for a man that deliberately insults his courage and masculinity (*slang offensive*) 2. CLOTHES ITEM OF CHILDREN'S CLOTHING a piece of clothing for children, consisting of a shirt and trousers that are buttoned together at the waist (*dated*)

panzer /pánzər/ *n.* an armoured vehicle such as a tank, especially a German armoured vehicle used in World War II [Mid-20thC. Shortening of German *Panzerdivision* 'armoured unit', ultimately from Old French *pancier* 'armour for the belly', from *pance* 'belly' (see PAUNCH).]

Paolozzi /pow lótsi/, **Sir Eduardo** (b. 1924) Scottish sculptor. He was an important exponent of pop art during the 1950s, after which he turned to abstract sculpture incorporating mechanistic forms.

pap[1] /pap/ *n.* 1. FOOD SEMI-LIQUID FOOD soft semiliquid food, usually mashed or pulped, especially for babies or sick people 2. TRIVIAL OR WORTHLESS MATERIAL sth, especially a book, film, television programme, or idea, that is so lacking in depth and substance that it is considered worthless [14thC. Via Old French *papa* (and probably also via medieval Latin), from Latin *pappa*, a children's word meaning 'food'.]

pap[2] /pap/ *n.* 1. NIPPLE a nipple or teat (*archaic*) 2. **pap, Pap** GEOG ROUNDED HILL a round, conical hill (*often used in placenames*) [12thC. Origin uncertain: perhaps from Latin *papilla* (see PAPILLA), or perhaps an imitation of the sound of sucking.]

papa[1] /pə paá/ *n.* 1. FATHER a father (*informal dated*) 2. COMMUNICATION CODE WORD FOR LETTER 'P' the NATO phonetic alphabet code word for the letter 'P', used in international radio communications [Late 17thC. Via French from Latin, from Greek *pappas* 'father'.]

papa[2] /paápə/ *n.* a soft blue-grey clay of marine origin [Late 19thC. From Maori.]

papacy /páypəssi/ *n.* (*plural* **-cies**) 1. PAPAL POWER OR STATUS the power or position of the pope 2. POPE'S PERIOD IN POWER the period of office of a pope 3. PAPAL GOVERNMENT the system of government in the Roman Catholic Church with the pope as the head [14thC. From medieval Latin *papatia*, from late Latin *papa* 'pope'.]

papad /páppad/ *n. S Asia* a fried or roasted plate-sized wafer, eaten as an appetizer or accompaniment

Papago /páppə gō/ *n.* (*plural* **-go** or **Papagos**) 1. PEOPLES MEMBER OF A NATIVE N AMERICAN PEOPLE a member of a Native North American people that originally occupied lands in central Arizona, and whose members now live mainly in parts of northern Mexico and southern Arizona 2. LANG NATIVE N AMERICAN LANGUAGE a Native North American language, spoken in parts of Arizona and northern Mexico, that belongs to the Uto-Aztecan branch of Aztec-Tanoan languages and is closely related to Pima. Papago is spoken by about 9,000 people. [Mid-19thC. Via Spanish *pápago* from, ultimately, a Pima-Papago word.] —**Papago** *adj.*

papain /pə páy in, -pī-/ *n.* an enzyme found in the juice of papaya and used as a meat tenderizer and in medicine to promote digestion and healing of wounds [Late 19thC. Formed from PAPAYA.]

papal /páyp'l/ *adj.* relating to the pope or the papacy [14thC. Via Old French from medieval Latin *papalis*, from late Latin *papa* 'pope' (see POPE).] —**papally** *adv.*

papal cross *n.* a cross consisting of a long upright and three crossbars of successively decreasing length, with the shortest at the top

Papal States /páyp'l-/ former territories in Italy over which the pope had sovereignty between 754 and 1870

Papandreou /páppən dráy oo/, **Andreas** (1919–96) Greek statesman. He was the founder of the Pan-Hellenistic Socialist Movement (1974), and prime minister of Greece (1981–89 and 1993–96).

Papanicolaou test /páppə níkə loo-/, **Papanicolaou smear** *n. US* a smear test [Mid-20thC. Named after G. N. *Papanicolaou*, 1883–1962, a Greek-born US anatomist.]

paparazzo /páppə ráts ō/ (*plural* **-zi** /páppə rátsi/) *n.* a freelance photographer who follows famous people hoping to catch a newsworthy story, especially sth shocking or scandalous (*often used in the plural*) [Mid-20thC. From Italian, with reference to the surname of a freelance photographer in the film *La Dolce Vita*, 1959, by Federico Fellini.]

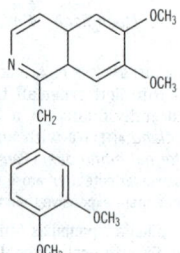

Papaverine

papaverine /pə pávvə reen, -páyvə-/ *n.* a toxic white crystalline alkaloid, found in opium or derived synthetically, that is nonaddictive and is used as an antispasmodic to treat asthma and colic. Formula: $C_{20}H_{21}O_4N$. [Mid-19thC. Formed from Latin *papaver* 'poppy' (see POPPY).]

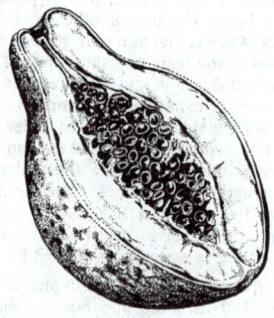

Papaya

papaya /pə pī ə/ *n.* 1. TREES TROPICAL TREE WITH OBLONG FRUIT a tropical evergreen tree that has a crown of broad leaves and large elongated or round yellow edible fruit. Latin name: *Carica papaya*. 2. FOOD PAPAYA FRUIT the edible fruit of the papaya tree [Late 16thC. From Spanish *papaya*, from Carib or Arawak.]

paper /páypər/ *n.* 1. INDUST THIN FLAT MATERIAL FROM WOOD PULP a thin material consisting of flat sheets, made from pulped wood, cloth, or fibre, used for various purposes, e.g. for writing and printing on, or for wrapping things in, or for covering walls 2. SHEET OR SHEETS OF PAPER one or more pieces or sheets of paper, especially for writing or drawing on 3. PRESS = newspaper 4. EDUC EXAMINATION a set of examination questions prepared on paper 5. EDUC SET OF EXAM ANSWERS a written set of answers by a student to a set of examination questions 6. EDUC ACADEMIC ARTICLE OR TALK an essay or article, particularly an academic one, read at a conference or to a society, or submitted for publication 7. EDUC STUDENT'S ESSAY an essay written by a student for a class 8. = wallpaper 9. WRAPPER a piece of paper, especially one used to wrap a sweet or a cigarette (*often used in the plural*) 10. POL GOVERNMENT DOCUMENT a white paper, green paper, or command paper 11. FIN COMMERCIAL NEGOTIABLE DOCUMENT a negotiable instrument, e.g. a bill of exchange or promissory note 12. THEATRE FREE THEATRE TICKET a free ticket that is given out in order to fill up a theatre (*slang*) 13. THEATRE THEATREGOERS WITH FREE TICKETS members of the audience who have been given free tickets in order to fill up a theatre (*slang*) ■ **papers** *npl.* 1. POL PERSONAL IDENTITY DOCUMENTS a document or documents, e.g. a passport, showing sb's identity or status **2. ASSORTMENT OF DOCUMENTS** a collection of documents relating to a particular issue or subject ○ *official papers in the archives* **3. SB'S PERSONAL WRITINGS** sb's diaries, letters, and other personal writings **4. SHIPPING** = *ship's papers* ■ *adj.* **1. MADE OF PAPER** consisting of or made of paper **2. RESEMBLING PAPER** similar to paper, e.g. in flimsiness **3. EXISTING IN DOCUMENTARY FORM** written in a document but not necessarily effective or useful in reality **4. IN WRITING** conducted in writing ■ *vt.* (**-pers, -pering, -pered**) **1. WALLPAPER STH** to cover a wall or room with wallpaper **2. COVER STH WITH PAPER** to cover sth with paper **3. THEATRE FILL UP THEATRE** to fill up a theatre by giving out free tickets (*slang*) [14thC. Via Old French *papier* and Anglo-Norman *papir* from Latin *papyrus* (see PAPYRUS).] —**paperer** *n.* ◇ **on paper 1.** in theory, but not in fact **2.** in writing

paper over *vt.* **1. COVER STH WITH PAPER** to cover sth up with paper, especially to cover a wall's imperfections or old paint with wallpaper **2. CONCEAL STH** to conceal sth without resolving it, especially mistakes, disagreements, or faults

paperback /páypər bak/ *n.* **SOFTCOVER BOOK** a book that has a thin flexible cover instead of a hard cover ■ *adj.* **WITH FLEXIBLE COVER** with a thin flexible cover, instead of a hard cover ■ *vt.* (**-backs, -backing, -backed**) **PUBLISH AS PAPERBACK** to publish a book in paperback form —**paperbacker** *n.*

paperbark /páypər baark/ *n.* an Australian species of tree with pale thin papery bark that peels off in large sheets. Genus: *Melaleuca.* [From the colour and texture of the bark]

paper birch (*plural* **paper birches** *or* **paper birch**) *n.* a North American birch tree that has toothed oval leaves, valuable wood, and white peeling bark that is used to make baskets and other articles. Latin name: *Betula papyrifera.* [From the white colour of the bark]

paperboard /páypər bawrd/ *n.* a type of thick cardboard

paperbound /páypər bownd/ *adj.* = **paperback**

paperboy /páypər boy/ *n.* a boy who delivers newspapers to people's homes, or who sells newspapers

paper chase *n.* **1. SEARCH OF DOCUMENTS** an intense searching and collation of files, books, or documents **2. RACE FOLLOWING PAPER TRAIL** a cross-country race in which runners follow a trail of shredded paper that has been left by an earlier runner or runners

paperclip /páypər klip/ *n.* a clip designed to be slipped over two or more sheets of paper to hold them together, especially a piece of wire that is bent into a long flat oval spiral

paper-cutter *n.* **1. MACHINE FOR CUTTING PAPER** a machine or device for cutting paper, especially a flat platform with a long arm containing a blade that can be raised and lowered in order to cut straight edges **2.** *US* = **paperknife**

paper filigree *n.* = **rolled paperwork**

papergirl /páypər gurl/ *n.* a girl who delivers newspapers to people's homes, or who sells newspapers

paperhanger /páypər hangər/ *n.* **1. SB WHO HANGS WALLPAPER** sb who puts up wallpaper, especially sb who does this professionally **2.** *US* **CRIMINOL PASSER OF BAD CHEQUES** sb who regularly passes bad cheques in order to obtain money (*slang*) —**paperhanging** *n.*

paper jam *n.* a situation in which paper becomes jammed in a printer or photocopier, causing the device to stop working

paperknife /páypər nīf/ (*plural* **paperknives** /páypər nīvz/) *n.* a blunt knife for slitting open envelopes, or for slitting folded paper, especially leaves of books

paperless /páypərləss/ *adj.* using records or means of communication that are electronic rather than on paper ○ *the age of the paperless office*

paper money *n.* currency in the form of banknotes, as opposed to coins

paper mulberry (*plural* **paper mulberries**) *n.* a small Asian tree with an inner bark that was once used in Japan for making paper, now commonly grown as a shade tree. Latin name: *Broussonetia papyrifera.*

paper nautilus (*plural* **paper nautiluses** *or* **paper nautili**) *n.* a cephalopod mollusc, the female of which has a thin delicate shell. Genus: *Argonauta.* ◊ **pearly nautilus** [From the delicacy and whiteness of its shell]

paper profit *n.* a profit that is not generated from the normal trading of a business and may or may not be realized (*often used in the plural*)

paper-pusher *n.* sb with a routine clerical job involving much paperwork (*informal*)

paper round *n.* US term **paper route 1. NEWSPAPER DELIVERY JOB** the job of delivering newspapers to people's homes **2. COURSE OF PAPER ROUND** the course followed from house to house by sb delivering newspapers

paper route *n.* *US* = **paper round**

paper-thin *adj.* **THIN** extremely thin, like paper ■ *adv.* **THINLY** extremely thinly

paper tiger *n.* a person or thing, especially an organization or a nation, that appears to be very strong and powerful but is in fact weak and ineffectual

paper trail *n.* a sequence of documents that reflects the stages in the actions of a person or organization, especially as the object of an investigation (*informal*)

paper wasp *n.* a large slender wasp known for its elaborate nest that is made up of individual cells built of papery material. Genus: *Polistes.*

paperweight /páypər wayt/ *n.* a small heavy, usually ornamental object that is used to hold down papers and keep them in place

paperwork /páypər wurk/ *n.* routine work that involves tasks such as filling in forms, keeping files up to date, or writing reports and letters

papery /páypəri/ *adj.* similar to paper in texture or thickness —**paperiness** *n.*

papeterie /pápitri/ *n.* a box that holds paper and writing instruments [Mid-19thC. From French 'paper manufacture, writing-case', from, ultimately, *papier* (see PAPER).]

Paphian /páyfi ən/ *adj.* **1. GEOG RELATING TO PAPHOS** relating to the village of Paphos **2. MYTHOL RELATING TO APHRODITE** relating to the deity Aphrodite, who, in Greek mythology, rose fully formed from the sea at Paphos **3. CONCERNING SEXUAL ACTIVITY** relating to sexual love (*literary*) ■ *n.* **1. PEOPLES, GEOG SB FROM PAPHOS** sb who lives or was born in Paphos **2. Paphian, paphian PROSTITUTE** a prostitute (*literary*)

Paphos[1] /páy foss/ *n.* a village in Cyprus that is the site of an ancient city near which, according to Greek mythology, Aphrodite was born, rising fully formed from the sea

Paphos[2] /páy foss/, **Paphus** /páyfəss/ *n.* in Greek mythology, a king of Cyprus who was the son of Pygmalion and Galatea

Papiamento /páppi ə méntō/ *n.* a Spanish-based creole spoken in the Netherlands Antilles, derived from a Portuguese pidgin and including many Dutch words. Papiamento is spoken by about 200,000 people. [Mid-20thC. From Spanish, from Papiamento *papya* 'talk' + *-mentu* '-ment'.] —**Papiamento** *adj.*

papier collé /páppi ay kóllay/ *n.* scraps of paper and other objects that are glued onto a sheet as an abstract artistic composition [From French, literally 'glued paper']

papier-mâché /páppi ay máshay, páypər-/ *n.* sheets of paper pulp and glue stuck together in layers, usually onto a frame or mould, used to make various objects such as boxes, bowls, and masks [From French, literally 'mashed paper'] —**papier-mâché** *adj.*

papilla /pə píllə/ (*plural* **papillae** /-lee/) *n.* **1. ANAT NIPPLE** a nipple or teat (*technical*) **2. ANAT, BIOL SMALL LUMP OF TISSUE** a small nipple-shaped protuberance, e.g. on the tongue enclosing the taste buds, or at the root of a hair or feather **3. BOT SMALL PROJECTION ON PETAL OR LEAF** a small elevated pad on the surface of a stigma, petal, or leaf **4. SMALL PROJECTION RESEMBLING NIPPLE** a very small projection like a nipple on the surface of sth [Late 17thC. From Latin, literally 'a little swelling', from PAPULE 'a swelling' (see PAPULE).] —**papillary** *adj.* —

papillate *adj.* —**papilliferous** /páppi lífférəss/ *adj.* —**papilliform** /pə pílli fawrm/ *adj.*

papilloma /páppi lómə/ (*plural* **-mata** /-mətə/ *or* **-mas**) *n.* a benign tumour of the skin or mucous membrane projecting from a surface, e.g. a wart —**papillomatous** *adj.*

papillon /páppi lon/ *n.* a small spaniel with a silky coat and heavily fringed tail and ears [Early 20thC. From French, literally 'butterfly', because its pointed ears resemble the shape of a butterfly's wings.]

papist /páypist/ *n.* an offensive term for a member of the Roman Catholic Church (*insult*) [Mid-16thC. Directly or via French from modern Latin *papista*, from ecclesiastical Latin *papa* 'pope'.] —**papism** *n.* —**papistic** /pə pístik/ *adj.* —**papistry** /páypistri/ *n.*

papoose /pə póoss/, **pappoose** *n.* **1. OFFENSIVE TERM** a Native North American baby or young child (*offensive*) **2. BAG FOR CARRYING BABY** a bag that fits over the shoulders, used for carrying a baby, especially in front of the body [Mid-17thC. From Algonquian, literally 'very young'.]

papovavirus /pə póvə vīrəss/ *n.* any of a group of DNA-containing viruses, many of which can cause cancers in animals, including the papillomaviruses that are responsible for warts [Mid-20thC. Coined from PAPILLOMA + POLYOMA + VACUOLATION + VIRUS.]

pappus /páppəss/ (*plural* **-pi** /-pī/) *n.* a covering of scales, bristles, and feathery hairs that surrounds the fruit of plants such as dandelions and thistles and helps to disperse the fruits [Early 18thC. Via Latin, from Greek *pappos*, literally 'grandfather', hence 'the down on seeds', from the idea of a grey-bearded man.] —**pappose** /páppōss/

pappy[1] /páppi/ (**-pier, -piest**) *adj.* with a mushy consistency [Late 17thC. Formed from PAP[1].]

pappy[2] /páppi/ (*plural* **-pies**) *n.* *US* a father (*regional dated*) [Mid-18thC. Formed from PAPA.]

paprika /pápprikə, pə préekə/ *n.* **1. COOK MILD RED SPICE FROM SWEET PEPPER** a mild red spice made from various sweet red peppers and used especially in Hungarian cooking **2. PLANTS, FOOD SWEET RED PEPPER** a sweet red pepper or the plant on which it grows. Genus: *Capsicum.* **3. COLOURS REDDISH-ORANGE COLOUR** a bright reddish-orange colour, like that of paprika seasoning [Late 19thC. Via Hungarian from Serbian *pàpar* 'pepper', from Latin *piper* (see PEPPER).]

Pap smear /páp-/, **Pap test** *n.* *US* = **cervical smear** [Pap a shortening of *Papanicolaou* (see PAPANICOLAOU TEST)]

Papuan /páppōō ən/ *n.* **1. PEOPLES SB FROM PAPUA NEW GUINEA** sb who was born in or is a citizen of Papua New Guinea **2. GROUP OF LANGUAGES OF NEW GUINEA** a group of languages spoken in much of New Guinea and nearby islands. They are not related to the Malayo-Polynesian languages, but exact classification has not yet proved possible. The Papuan languages are spoken by about two million people. —**Papuan** *adj.*

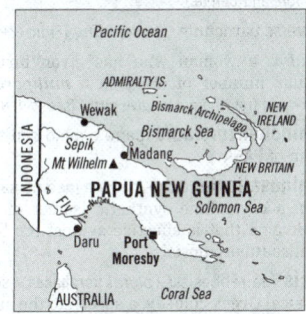
Papua New Guinea

Papua New Guinea /páppōō ə nyōō gínni/ independent nation in Oceania, situated northeast of Australia, in the southwestern Pacific Ocean, consisting of the eastern half of the island of New Guinea together with many other islands. Language: English. Currency: kina. Capital: Port Moresby. Population: 4,394,537 (1996). Area: 462,840 sq. km/178,704 sq. mi. Official name **Independent State of Papua New Guinea** —**Papua New Guinean** *n., adj.*

papule /páppyool/ *n.* a small hard round protuberance on the skin [Early 18thC. From Latin *papula*.] —**papular** /páppyoolər/ *adj.* —**papuliferous** /páppyoo líffərəss/ *adj.*

papyraceous /páppi ráyshəss/ *adj.* made of or resembling paper [Mid-18thC. Formed from Latin *papyrus* (see PAPYRUS).]

papyrology /páppə rólləji/ *n.* the study of ancient papyrus manuscripts —**papyrological** /páppərə lójjik'l/ *adj.* —**papyrologist** /páppə rólləjist/ *n.*

papyrus /pə pírəss/ (*plural* **-ri** /-rī/ *or* **papyruses**) *n.* 1. PLANTS **TALL MARSH PLANT** a tall aquatic plant of the sedge family, native to southern Europe and the Nile valley, that has small flowers resembling umbrellas. Latin name: *Cyperus papyrus*. 2. INDUST **MATERIAL RESEMBLING PAPER MADE FROM PAPYRUS** writing material made from the pith of the stem of the papyrus plant that was used by the ancient Egyptians, Greeks, and Romans 3. PAPYRUS **DOCUMENT** an ancient manuscript written on material made from the papyrus plant [14thC. Via Latin from Greek *papuros* 'papyrus plant'.]

par /paar/ *n.* 1. AVERAGE **LEVEL** a level or standard considered to be average or normal 2. FIN **ACCEPTED VALUE OF CURRENCY** the accepted value of one country's currency in terms of the currency of another country that uses the same metal standard 3. COMM = **par value** 4. GOLF **ALLOCATED STANDARD SCORE** the standard score assigned to each hole on a golf course, or to the sum total of these holes ■ *adj.* AVERAGE average or normal ■ *vt.* (**pars, parring, parred**) GOLF **SCORE PAR ON** to score the equivalent of the par on a hole or course [Late 16thC. From Latin, 'equal' (source of English *pair* and *umpire*.] ◇ **be feeling below par** to feel slightly unwell or out of sorts (*informal*) ◇ **be on (a) par (with sb** *or* **sth)** to be on the same level or status, or generally have the same status or value ◇ **be par for the course** to be usual or to be expected under the circumstances (*informal*)

par. *abbr.* 1. paragraph 2. parallel 3. parenthesis 4. parish

Par. *abbr.* Paraguay

par- *prefix.* = **para-**¹

para¹ /párrə/ *n.* a paratrooper (*informal; usually used in the plural*) [Mid-20thC. Shortening.]

para² /paárə/ (*plural* **-ras** *or* **-ra**) *n.* 1. A SUBUNIT OF YUGOSLAV **CURRENCY** a subunit of currency in Yugoslavia, 100 of which are worth one new dinar. See table at **currency** 2. COIN **WORTH ONE PARA** a coin worth one para [Late 17thC. Via Turkish, from Persian *pāra* 'piece, para'.]

para-¹ *prefix.* 1. beside, near, along with ○ *parataxis* 2. beyond ○ *paranormal* 3. isomeric or related compound ○ *paraldehyde* 4. resembling ○ *paramyxovirus* 5. faulty, undesirable ○ *paraphasia* 6. assistant, auxiliary ○ *paralegal* 7. occupying the para position in the benzene ring ○ *paradichlorobenzene* [From Greek *para* 'beside'. Ultimately from an Indo-European word meaning 'next to, in front of' that is also the ancestor of English *fore* and *before*.]

para-² *prefix.* parachute ○ *paraskiing* [From PARACHUTE]

-para *suffix.* a woman who has given birth to a particular number of children ○ *nullipara* [From Latin, formed from *parere* 'to give birth' (see PARENT).]

para-aminobenzoic acid /párrə ə mīnō ben zóik-/ *n.* full form of PABA

para-aminosalicylic acid /párrə ə meé nō sállisilik-, -mí-/ *n.* a crystalline synthetic isomer of aminosalicylic acid that is effective against the bacteria that cause tuberculosis

parabasis /pə rábbəsiss/ (*plural* **parabases** /-seez/) *n.* in classical Greek comedy, a speech to the audience that is made by the chorus [Early 19thC. From Greek, where it was formed from *parabainein* 'to go aside', from *bainein* 'to step'.]

parabiosis /párrə bī óssiss/ (*plural* **-ses** /-seez/) *n.* 1. BIOL **ANATOMICAL UNION OF TWO INDIVIDUALS** the state in which two individuals are joined together and share the same circulation of blood. This is the case for conjoined twins, and it can also be induced experimentally or to establish a blood supply for some grafts. 2. MED **TEMPORARY CESSATION OF NERVE ACTIVITY** the temporary suppression of nerve conduction [Early

20thC. Coined from PARA-¹ + Greek *biosis* 'way of life', from *bios* 'life'.] —**parabiotic** /párrə bī óttik/ *adj.*

parablast /párrə blast/ *n.* the yolk of a fertilized egg [Mid-19thC. Coined from PARA-¹ + Greek *blastos* 'a bud, shoot'.] —**parablastic** /párrə blástik/ *adj.*

parable /párrəb'l/ *n.* 1. LITERAT **MORAL OR RELIGIOUS STORY** a short simple story intended to illustrate a moral or religious lesson 2. BIBLE **STORY ASCRIBED TO JESUS CHRIST** a parable that appears in the Bible as told by Jesus Christ [14thC. Via Old French *parabole* and Latin *parabola* from, ultimately, Greek *paraballein*, literally 'to put beside' (formed from *ballein* 'to throw', hence 'to compare'.]

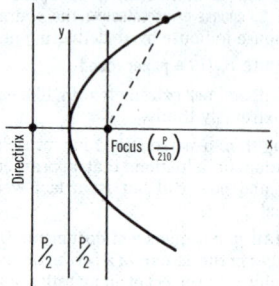

Parabola

parabola /pə rábbələ/ *n.* a curve formed by the intersection of a cone with a plane parallel to its side [Late 16thC. Via modern Latin, from Greek *parabolē* 'application, comparison', from the relationship between the section of a cone that forms the parabola and part of the cone's surface.]

parabolic¹ /párrə bóllik/ *adj.* 1. RELATING TO PARABOLA relating to, resembling, or having the form of a parabola 2. WITH PARABOLOID **SHAPE** with the form of a paraboloid

parabolic² /párrə bóllik/, **parabolical** /párrə bóllik'l/ *adj.* relating to or resembling a parable [15thC. Via late Latin *parabolicus* from late Greek *parabolikos* 'figurative', from *parabolē* (see PARABLE).] —**parabolically** *adv.*

parabolic aerial *n.* = **dish aerial**

parabolize /pə rábbə līz/ (**-lizes, -lizing, -lized**), **parabolise** (**-lises, -lising, -lised**) *vt.* to explain sth or tell a story by means of a parable [Early 17thC. From medieval Latin *parabolizare* 'to speak in parables', from Latin *parabola* (see PARABLE).]

paraboloid /pə rábbə loyd/ *n.* a mathematical surface in which intersections with planes produce parabolas, ellipses, or hyperbolas [Mid-17thC. Coined from PARABOLA + -OID.] —**paraboloidal** /pə rábbə lóyd'l/ *adj.*

para boots /párrə-/ *npl.* high-lacing boots worn by paratroopers that are popular in various street fashions

parabrake /párrə brayk/ *n.* = **brake parachute**

parabuntal /párrə búnt'l/ *n.* fine straw used in hat-making

Paracelsus /párrə sélssəss/, **Philippus Aureolus** (1493?–1541) German physician and alchemist. His belief that disease is caused by outside agents and could be treated by chemical remedies defied the medical tenets of his time. Pseudonym of **Theophrastus Bombastus von Hohenheim**

paracentesis /párrə sen teéssiss/ *n.* = **thoracentesis** [Late 16thC. Via Latin 'the removing of a cataract', from, ultimately, Greek *parakentein*, literally 'to pierce at the side', from *kentein* 'to prick, stab'.]

paracetamol /párrə seétə mol, -séttə-/ *n.* 1. PAIN **RELIEVER** a drug sold in tablet form that is used to relieve pain and reduce fever. US term **acetaminophen** 2. PARACETAMOL **TABLET** a tablet or capsule containing paracetamol [Mid-20thC. From 'par(a)acet(yl)am(inophen)ol'.]

parachronism /pə rákrənizəm/ *n.* an error in assigning a date to sth, especially when the date given is later than it should be [Mid-17thC. Origin uncertain: either coined from PARA-¹ + Greek *khronos* 'time' + -ISM, or an alteration of ANACHRONISM.]

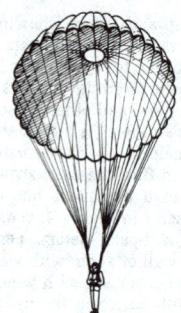

Parachute

parachute /párrə shoot/ *n.* 1. CANOPY FOR SLOWING FALL FROM **AIRCRAFT** a device consisting of a canopy fitted to a harness that is used to slow the speed at which a person or object drops from an aircraft 2. ZOOL = **patagium** *n.* 1 ■ *vti.* (**-chutes, -chuting, -chuted**) DROP BY **PARACHUTE** to drop, or allow sb or sth to drop, from an aircraft by parachute [Late 18thC. From French, literally 'protection against a fall', from *chute* 'a fall'.] —**parachutist** *n.*

parachute spinnaker *n.* a very large light triangular sail used on a racing yacht

Paraclete /párrə kleet/ *n.* CHR in Christianity, the Holy Spirit [13thC. Via French *paraclet*, literally 'someone called to assist', from, ultimately, Greek *parakalein*, literally 'to call to your side', from *kalein* 'to call'.]

parade /pə ráyd/ *n.* 1. CELEBRATORY PROCESSION OF PEOPLE an organized procession of people celebrating a special occasion and often including decorated vehicles or floats, a marching band, people twirling batons, and people on horseback 2. DISPLAY **OF PEOPLE OR THINGS** a long moving line of people or things intended to be publicly displayed 3. SUCCESSION **OF PEOPLE OR THINGS** a large number of people or things in succession ○ *a parade of visitors to the palace* 4. MIL **PROCESSION OF TROOPS** a march by troops along the streets or in a large area such as a square, usually as a celebration of an important event 5. MIL **GATHERING OF TROOPS IN FORMATION** a formal gathering of a troop of soldiers in a regimented formation for a ceremonial march, inspection, or training 6. MIL **PARADE GROUND** a parade ground 7. PEOPLE **IN PARADE** people marching in a parade 8. FLAMBOYANT **OR FLAUNTING EXHIBITION OF STH** a showy or ostentatious exhibition or display of sth 9. **parade, Parade** STREET a street with a row of shops (*often used in placenames*) 10. FENCING **PARRY** a type of parry in fencing ■ *v.* (**-rades, -rading, -raded**) 1. *vti.* GO ON FESTIVE **PROCESSION** to march in a festive public parade 2. *vti.* USE IN FESTIVE **PROCESSION** to use sth or be used in a festive public parade 3. *vti.* MIL **ASSEMBLE FOR MILITARY PARADE** to gather for and march in a military parade 4. *vti.* SHOW SB **OR STH OFF** to display or show sb or sth, especially proudly and ostentatiously 5. *vi.* WALK **ABOUT TO BE SEEN** to walk or stroll about in public, especially in order to be seen or admired 6. *vti.* CLAIM **TO BE STH ELSE** to claim to be other than you really are, or claim that one person or thing is another person or thing ○ *parading old ideas as new reforms* [Mid-17thC. Via French from Spanish *parada* 'display', literally 'stopping' (from the act of stopping a horse), ultimately from Latin *parare* 'to prepare' (see PREPARE).] ◇ **rain on sb's parade** US to spoil things for sb (*informal*)

parade ground *n.* a place where troops regularly gather in formation for inspection or training

paradichlorobenzene /párrə dī kláw rō bén zeen/ *n.* a white crystalline compound used as a moth repellent. Formula: $C_6H_4Cl_2$. [Late 19thC. Coined from PARA-¹ + DI- + CHLORO- + BENZENE.]

paradiddle /párrə did'l/ *n.* a drum roll in which left and right drumsticks alternate [Early 20thC. An imitation of the sound.]

paradigm /párrə dīm/ *n.* 1. TYPICAL **EXAMPLE** a typical example of sth 2. MODEL **THAT FORMS BASIS OF STH** an example that serves as a pattern or model for sth, especially one that forms the basis of a methodology or theory 3. GRAM **SET OF ALL FORMS OF WORD** a set of word forms giving all of the possible inflections of a word 4. SCI, PHILOS **RELATIONSHIP OF IDEAS TO ONE ANOTHER** in the philosophy of science, a generally accepted model of how ideas relate to one another, forming a conceptual framework within which scientific research is carried out [15thC. Via late Latin from Greek *paradeigma* 'example', from *paradeiknunai*, literally 'to show beside', from *deiknunai* 'to show'.] —**paradigmatic** /párrədig máttik/ *adj.* —**paradigmatically** /-máttikli/ *adv.*

paradise /párrə dīss/ *n.* **1.** PLACE OR STATE OF PERFECT HAPPINESS a place, situation, or condition in which sb finds perfect happiness **2.** PLACE IDEALLY SUITED TO SB a place where there is everything that a particular person needs for his or her interest (*informal*) ○ *a surfer's paradise* **3.** paradise, Paradise JUD-CHR HEAVEN in religions such as Christianity, Islam, and Judaism, the place where good people are believed to go or the state they are believed to attain after death **4.** paradise, Paradise BIBLE GARDEN OF EDEN according to the Bible, the perfect garden where Adam and Eve were placed at the Creation [12thC. Via Old French and late Latin *paradisus* from Greek *paradeisos* 'enclosed place, park', from Avestan *pairidaeza*, literally 'to form around', from *diz* 'to form'.] —**paradisaic** /párrədi sáy ik, -záy ik/ *adj.* —**paradisiacally** *adv.*

──────── WORD KEY: CULTURAL NOTE ────────

Paradise Lost, an epic poem by John Milton (1667). This monumental work describes Satan's rebellion against God, his corruption of Adam and Eve, and their subsequent expulsion from the Garden of Eden. The sustained brilliance of its language, structure, characterization, and imagery make it arguably the greatest epic poem in English literature. A sequel, *Paradise Regained*, was published in 1671.

───

paradise duck *n.* a large New Zealand duck. The male is dark-coloured with a black head, while the female is chestnut-coloured with a white head and wing patches. Latin name: *Tadorna variegata*. [*Paradise* from its bright colours]

paradise flycatcher *n.* a brightly coloured Asian and African flycatcher. The males have very long slender forked tails. Genus: *Terpsiphone*.

parador /párrə dawr/ *n.* **1.** SPANISH TOURIST HOTEL a tourist hotel in Spain, operated by the national government and located in a castle, monastery, convent, or other historic site **2.** LATIN AMERICAN HOTEL a privately owned and operated hotel or resort in Latin America [Mid-19thC. From Spanish, from *parar* 'to stop, stay', from Latin *parare* 'to prepare' (see PREPARE).]

parados /párrə doss/ *n.* a bank built up behind a trench or other fortification that gives protection from attack from the rear [Mid-19thC. From French, literally 'defend the back', from *dos* 'back'.]

paradox /párrə doks/ *n.* **1.** STH ABSURD OR CONTRADICTORY a statement, proposition, or situation that seems to be absurd or contradictory, but in fact is or may be true **2.** SELF-CONTRADICTORY STATEMENT a statement or proposition that contradicts itself **3.** PERSON OF OPPOSITES sb who has qualities that seem to contradict each other **4.** STH CONTRARY TO POPULAR BELIEFS sth that is contrary to or conflicts with conventional or common opinion (*archaic*) [Mid-16thC. Via Latin *paradoxum* from, ultimately, Greek *paradoxos*, literally 'contrary to opinion', from *doxa* 'opinion', from *dokein* 'to think'.] —**paradoxical** /párrə dóksik'l/ *adj.* —**paradoxically** /-dóksikli/ *adv.* —**paradoxicalness** /-dóksik'lnəss/ *n.*

paradoxical frog *n.* a frog of the Amazon forest and the island of Trinidad. The adult frog is less than a third of the size of the tadpole. Latin name: *Pseudis paradoxa*.

paradoxical sleep *n.* = REM sleep [*Paradoxical* from the fact that the electrical brain patterns of this deep sleep more closely resemble those of the waking state]

paradrop /párrə drop/ *n.* DELIVERY BY PARACHUTE the delivery of personnel, materials, provisions, or other supplies to a place by attaching them to a parachute and dropping them from an aircraft ■ *vt.* (-drops, -dropping, -dropped) PARACHUTE SB OR STH to deliver sb or sth to a place by paradrop

paraesthesia /párress theezi ə/ *n.* an abnormal or unexplained tingling, pricking, or burning sensation on the skin [Late 19thC. Coined from PARA-¹ + Greek *aesthēsis* 'feeling'.]

paraffin /párrəfin/ *n.* **1.** INDUST, DOMESTIC FUEL OIL a mixture of liquid hydrocarbons obtained from pet-

roleum and used as a domestic heating fuel and as fuel for aircraft. ◊ **kerosene 2.** CHEM = alkane **3.** = **paraffin wax** ■ *vt.* (-fins, -fining, -fined) INDUST TREAT WITH PARAFFIN to treat sth by saturating, impregnating, or coating it with paraffin or paraffin wax [Mid-19thC. Coined from Latin *parum* 'little' + *affinis* 'related' (source of English *affinity*), because it is not closely related to any other substance.] —**paraffinic** /párrə fínnik/ *adj.*

paraffin oil *n.* = paraffin *n.* 1

paraffin wax *n.* a white waxy solid mixture of hydrocarbons obtained from petroleum and used in making candles, pharmaceuticals, and cosmetics, and as a sealing agent

paraformaldehyde /párrə fawr máldi hīd/, **paraform** /párrə fawrm/ *n.* a white combustible polymer of formaldehyde used as a disinfectant and a fungicide, and as a component of contraceptive creams. Formula: (HCHO)ₙ, where *n* is greater than or equal to 6. [Late 19thC. Coined from PARA-¹ + FORMALDEHYDE.]

paragenesis /párrə jénnəsiss/, **paragenesia** /párrəjə neézi ə/, **paraform** *n.* the order in which the mineral constituents of a rock are formed [Mid-19thC. Coined from PARA-¹ + -GENESIS.] —**paragenetic** /párrəjə néttik/ *adj.* —**paragenetically** /-néttikli/ *adv.*

Paragliding

paragliding /párrə glīding/ *n.* a sport in which an individual jumps from an aircraft or an elevation wearing a rectangular parachute that allows control of direction in the descent to the ground [Coined from PARA-² + *gliding*] —**paraglider** *n.*

paragnathous /párrəg náythəss/ *adj.* with upper and lower jaws of the same length [Late 19thC. Coined from PARA-¹ + -GNATHOUS.]

paragoge /párrə gog/, **paragogue** *n.* the addition of a letter, sound, or syllable at the end of a word as a word develops, e.g. the 's' in 'towards' [Mid-16thC. Via late Latin from Greek *paragōgē*, literally 'carrying beyond', from *agōgē* 'carrying'.] —**paragogic** /párrə gójjik/ *adj.* —**paragogically** /-gójjikli/ *adv.*

paragon /párrəgən/ *n.* **1.** EXAMPLE OF EXCELLENCE sb or sth that is the very best example of sth **2.** MINERALS LARGE UNFLAWED DIAMOND a perfect diamond that weighs at least 100 carats [Mid-16thC. Via archaic French from Italian *paragone*, originally 'touchstone to test gold', ultimately from medieval Greek *parakonan*, literally 'to sharpen against', hence 'to compare'.]

paragraph /párrə graaf, -graf/ *n.* **1.** SECTION OF WRITING a piece of writing that consists of one or more sentences, begins on a new and often indented line, and contains a distinct idea or the words of one speaker **2.** PRESS SHORT NEWS STORY a short item of news or editorial comment in a newspaper ■ *vt.* (-graphs, -graphing, -graphed) **1.** SET OUT IN PARAGRAPHS to arrange sth in a series of paragraphs **2.** PRESS WRITE NEWS IN A PARAGRAPH to report news or a story in a short paragraph [15thC. Via Old French from, ultimately, Greek *paragraphos* 'stroke marking a line in which there is a break in sense', literally 'writing beside', ultimately from *graphein* 'to write'.] —**paragrapher** *n.*

paragraphia /párrə gráffi ə, -gráafi-/ *n.* the writing of words or letters different from the ones intended, as a result of a stroke or disease [Late 19thC. Coined from PARA-¹ + Greek *-graphia* 'writing'.]

Paraguay¹ /párrə gwī/ *republic in South America, bordered by Bolivia, Brazil, and Argentina. Language: Spanish. Currency: kina. Capital: Asunción. Population: 5,504,146 (1996). Area: 406,752 sq.

Paraguay

km/157,048 sq. mi. Official name **Republic of Paraguay** —**Paraguayan** *n., adj.*

Paraguay² *river of central South America, a tributary of the River Paraná. Length: 2,550 km/1,580 mi.*

Paraguay tea *n.* = maté *n.* 2 [Late 18thC. Named after the country in which the tree proliferates.]

parahydrogen /párrə hídrəjən/ *n.* a form of molecular hydrogen in which the two atomic nuclei spin in opposite directions. Parahydrogen makes up about 25 per cent of hydrogen molecules. [Early 20thC. Coined from PARA-¹ + HYDROGEN.]

para-influenza virus *n.* any of a group of four viruses, similar to the influenza virus, that cause respiratory illnesses, especially in children, with symptoms of severe sore throat, croup, and pneumonia

parakeet /párrə keet/ *n.* a small tropical parrot that has a long tail and is usually very brightly coloured [Mid-16thC. Anglicization of Old French *paraquet*, of uncertain origin: perhaps ultimately a form of *Pierre* 'Peter', in the sense of 'little Peter'.]

paralanguage /párrə lang gwij/ *n.* nonverbal vocal elements in communication that may add a nuance of meaning to language as it is used in context, e.g. tone of voice or whispering

paraldehyde /pə ráldi hīd/ *n.* a colourless liquid polymer of acetaldehyde used as a sedative and as a solvent. Formula: $C_6H_{12}O_3$. [Mid-19thC. Coined from PARA-¹ + ALDEHYDE.]

paralegal /párrə leeg'l/ *n.* LAWYER'S ASSISTANT sb with specialist legal training who assists a fully qualified lawyer ■ *adj.* OF A PARALEGAL relating to a paralegal or the work of a paralegal [Late 20thC. Coined from PARA-¹ + LEGAL.]

paraleipsis *n.* = paralipsis

paralinguistics /párrə ling gwístiks/ *n.* the study of paralanguage (*takes a singular verb*) —**paralinguistic** *adj.*

paralipomena /párrə lī pómmənə/ *npl.* material added to a literary work as a supplement [Late 17thC. Via late Latin (plural) from Greek *paraleipomena* '(things) left out', ultimately from *leipein* 'to leave'.]

Paralipomena /párrə lī pómmənə/ *npl.* the title used for the Book of Chronicles in the Vulgate (*sometimes used in the singular*) [14thC. Via ecclesiastical Latin from, ultimately, Greek *paraleipein*, literally 'to leave to one side' (because it contains material omitted from the Books of Kings).]

Paralipomenon singular of **paralipomena**

paralipsis /párrə lípsiss/ (*plural* **paralipses** /-seez/), **paraleipsis** /-lī́psiss/ (*plural* **paraleipses** /-seez/) *n.* a rhetorical technique of emphasizing a topic by saying in some way that you will not talk about it, e.g. by using the phrase 'not to mention' [Mid-16thC. Via late Latin from Greek *paraleipsis* 'omission', from *paraleipein*, literally 'to leave on one side', from *leipein* 'to leave'.]

parallax /párrə laks/ *n.* **1.** PHYS APPARENT CHANGE OF POSITION an apparent change in the position of an object when the person looking at the object changes position **2.** ASTRON ANGLE MEASURING A STAR'S DISTANCE FROM THE EARTH the angle between two imaginary lines from two different observation points meeting at a star or celestial body that is used to measure its distance from the Earth [Late 16thC. Via French from Greek *parallaxis* 'alternation, angle between two lines', from *parallassein* 'to alter', ultimately from *allos* 'other'.] —**pa-**

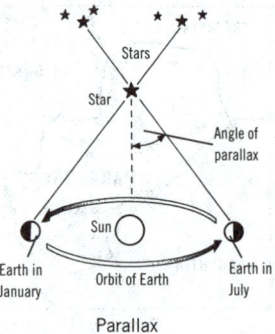

Parallax

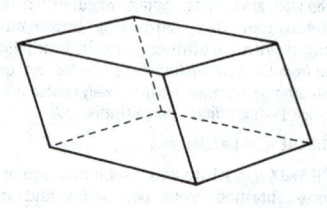

Parallelepiped

rallactic /párrə láktik/ *adj.* —**parallactically** /-láktikli/ *adv.*

parallel /párrə lel/ *adj.* **1.** GEOM ALWAYS SAME DISTANCE APART relating to or being lines, planes, or curved surfaces that are always the same distance apart and therefore never meet **2.** RESEMBLING EACH OTHER relating to two things that are comparable because they are similar and share many characteristics **3.** GRAM OF IDENTICAL SYNTACTIC CONSTRUCTIONS used to describe two or more phrases or clauses in a single sentence that have identical syntactic constructions **4.** COMPUT USING SEVERAL ITEMS OF INFORMATION SIMULTANEOUSLY relating to a computer that processes several items of information at the same time. ◊ **serial 5.** MUSIC KEEPING SAME MUSICAL INTERVAL THROUGHOUT used to describe the movement of two voices or melodies that match each other exactly in pitch, while preserving the same interval between them ■ *n.* **1.** GEOM PARALLEL LINE OR PLANE any of a set of parallel geometric forms, especially lines or planes **2.** SB OR STH EQUIVALENT sb or sth that is very similar to another, sharing many characteristics **3.** COMPARISON a comparison between two things that reveals their similarity ○ *It's easy to draw a parallel between their two careers* **4.** GEOG LINE PARALLEL TO THE EQUATOR an imaginary line round the Earth that lies parallel to the equator and represents a particular degree of latitude from the equator **5.** GEOG LINE ON MAP a line on a map representing a parallel of latitude **6.** ELEC ENG CONFIGURATION OF ELECTRICAL COMPONENTS the way in which electrical components or circuits are connected so that the same voltage is applied across each component or circuit ○ *connected in parallel* ■ *vt.* (-**lels**, -**leling**, -**leled**) **1.** BE PARALLEL to be or run parallel to sth **2.** MAKE STH PARALLEL TO STH to make sth be or run parallel to sth else **3.** CORRESPOND TO STH to be similar to sth else, especially in following a similar course of events **4.** COMPARE STH TO STH ELSE to compare sth with, or show sth to be similar to, sth else **5.** MATCH SB OR STH to be equal to or as good as sb or sth else ■ *adv.* ALONGSIDE in a parallel manner so as to keep the same distance away from sth and never meet it [Mid-16thC. Via French and Latin from Greek *parallēlos*, literally 'beside each other', from *allēlōn* 'each other', ultimately from *allos* 'other'.] ◇ **in parallel (with sb** *or* **sth)** in conjunction with and at the same time as sb or sth else

parallel bars *npl.* GYMNASTICS BARS FOR GYMNASTIC EXERCISES a piece of gymnastic equipment consisting of two horizontal bars parallel to each other and supported on vertical posts. The bars may be at either the same or different heights. ■ *n.* GYMNASTICS SPORTS EVENT USING PARALLEL BARS an event in a gymnastics competition that uses the parallel bars (*takes a singular verb*)

parallel cousin *n.* a cousin who is the child of your mother's sister or your father's brother. ◊ **cross-cousin**

parallelepiped /párrə lellə pí ped, -le léppi-/ *n.* a polyhedron consisting of six faces that are parallelograms [Late 16thC. From Greek *parallēlepipedon*, literally 'parallel surface', from *epipedon* 'surface', from, ultimately, *pedon* 'ground'.]

paralleling /párrə leling/ *n.* the exploitation of differences in commercial markets by buying an expensive product in a place where prices are relatively low and selling it on in a place where prices are higher

parallelism /párrə lelizəm/ *n.* **1.** SIMILARITY the condition of being parallel **2.** LITERAT REPETITION FOR EFFECT in writing, the deliberate repetition of particular words or sentence structures for effect **3.** PHILOSOPHY THEORY OF MIND-BODY RELATIONSHIP the philosophical theory that mind and body do not interact but follow separate parallel tracks, without any relationship of cause and effect existing between the two —**parallelist** *n.*

parallel of latitude *n.* = parallel *n.* 4

parallelogram /párrə léllə gram/ *n.* a four-sided plane figure in which both pairs of opposite sides are parallel and of equal length, and the opposite angles are equal [Late 16thC. Via late Latin from Greek *parallēlogrammon*, from *parallēlos* 'parallel'.]

parallel play *n.* play in which two or more children who are in close proximity and possibly involved in similar activities, do not interact with each other socially

parallel port *n.* a connection point through which a computer sends and receives data simultaneously by means of a number of separate wires, commonly used for connecting a printer or external storage device. Computers transmit data through the parallel port at higher speeds and with fewer errors than through the serial port. [Because it transfers data over more than one channel at the same time]

parallel processing *n.* the use of two or more computer processors to run parts of the same program together and merge the results, with significantly faster program execution as a result. Parallel processing is used when many complex calculations are required, e.g. in weather modelling and digital special effects. [Because instructions are sent to multiple processors at the same time]

parallel ruler *n.* a ruler designed for drawing parallel lines, constructed with two linked straight edges that remain parallel although the distance between them may be varied

parallel turn *n.* SKIING a turn executed by shifting the bodyweight and keeping the skis parallel, rather than by adjusting the line of the skis

paralogism /pə rálləjizəm/ *n.* in logic, an invalid argument that is unintentional or that has gone unnoticed [Mid-16thC. Via late Latin *paralogismus* from, ultimately, Greek *paralogos* 'contrary to reason', from *logos* 'reason' (see LOGIC).] —**paralogist** *n.* —**paralogistic** /pə rállə jístik/ *adj.*

Paralympic Games

Paralympic Games /párrə límpik-/, **Paralympics** /párrə límpiks/ *npl.* an international sports competition for disabled athletes —**Paralympian** *n.*

paralyse /párrə līz/ (-**lyses**, -**lysing**, -**lysed**) *vt.* **1.** MED DEPRIVE OF VOLUNTARY MOVEMENT to cause sb to lose the ability to move a part of the body, either by damaging nerve or muscle function, or through the use of a paralysing drug **2.** MAKE TEMPORARILY UNABLE TO MOVE to make sb temporarily unable to move, e.g. with fear **3.** BRING SYSTEM TO STANDSTILL to bring a system or network to a stop or prevent it from functioning effectively [Late 18thC. Via French *paralyser* from, ultimately, Latin *paralysis* (see PARALYSIS).]

paralysis /pə rálləssiss/ *n.* **1.** MED LOSS OF MOVEMENT loss of voluntary movement as a result of damage to nerve or muscle function **2.** INACTIVITY failure to take action or make progress [Pre-12thC. Via Latin from Greek *paralusis*, from *paraluesthai* 'to be disabled', from *para-* 'on one side' + *luein* 'to release'.]

paralysis agitans /-ájji tanz/ *n.* = **Parkinson's disease** [*Agitans* from Latin, the present participle of *agitare* 'to shake']

paralytic /párrə líttik/ *adj.* **1.** DRUNK extremely drunk (*informal*) **2.** OF PARALYSIS relating to paralysis ■ *n.* OFFENSIVE TERM an offensive term for sb affected by paralysis (*offensive*) [14thC. Via Old French and Latin from Greek *paralutikos*, from *paralusis* (see PARALYSIS).] —**paralytically** *adv.*

paralyze *vt.* US = paralyse

paramagnetic /párrə mag néttik/ *adj.* used to describe a substance that is weakly magnetized so that it will lie parallel to a magnetic field. The phenomenon results from the presence of unpaired electrons in the atoms of the substance, which cause the atoms to act as tiny magnets when a magnetic field is applied. ◊ **diamagnetic, ferromagnetic** —**paramagnetism** /párrə mágnətizəm/ *n.*

Paramaribo /párrə márribō/ port and capital city of Suriname, located in the north of the country near the Atlantic Ocean. Population: 180,000 (1994).

paramatta /párrə máttə/, **parramatta** *n.* a lightweight fabric made from wool blended with silk or cotton [Early 19thC. Named after the settlement of *Parramatta* in New South Wales, Australia, where a similar fabric was produced.]

paramecium /párrə meéssi əm/ (*plural* **paramecia** /-si ə/ *or* -**ums**) *n.* a single-celled microscopic aquatic organism (**protozoan**) with hair-like appendages (**cilia**) around its body that it uses to move around and to capture bacteria. Genus: *Paramecium*. [Mid-18thC. From modern Latin, genus name, from Greek *paramēkēs* 'oval', from its shape.]

paramedic /párrə méddik/ *n.* **1.** EMERGENCY MEDICAL WORKER sb trained to perform emergency medical procedures in the absence of a doctor, especially a member of an ambulance crew **2.** MEDICAL WORKER SUPPORTING DOCTORS a medical worker whose work supports the work of doctors and nurses, e.g. a radiologist or a laboratory technician —**paramedical** *adj.*

parament /párrəmənt/ *n.* an object made of richly decorated fabric, especially a ceremonial robe, tapestry, or wall hanging (*archaic*) [14thC. From Old French, 'ornament', from *parer* 'to prepare, trim' (see PARE).]

parameter /pə rámmitər/ *n.* **1.** LIMITING FACTOR a fact or circumstance that restricts how sth is done or what can be done **2.** SCI VARIABLE QUANTITY DETERMINING OUTCOME a measurable quantity, e.g. temperature, that determines the result of a scientific experiment and can be altered to vary the result **3.** MATH VARIABLE MATHEMATICAL VALUE in a mathematical expression, a variable value that, when it changes, gives another different but related mathematical expression from a limited series of such expressions **4.** STATS OVERALL QUANTITY a general quantity that relates to an entire population, as distinct from an individual statistic that relates to a sample [Mid-17thC. From modern Latin *parametrum*, from PARA-[1] + Greek *metron* 'measure'.] —**parametric** /párrə méttrik/ *adj.*

parametric equalizer *n.* a device used with audio equipment to cut or boost selected frequencies of an output signal by continuously widening or narrowing the filtered frequencies of the signal. It is a more sophisticated version of the standard bass and treble controls on a stereo system. ◊ **graphic equalizer**

parametric equations *npl.* a set of mathematical equations in which coordinates of points are explicitly expressed in terms of independent parameters

paramilitary /párrə míllitəri/ *adj.* **1. USING MILITARY TECHNIQUES** using military weapons and tactics to fight within a country against the official ruling power **2. MILITARY IN STYLE** similar to or modelled on the military but not belonging to it **3. ASSISTING OFFICIAL MILITARY FORCES** organized and staffed by civilians to provide support to the regular military services ○ *a paramilitary unit* ■ *n.* (*plural* **-ies**) **UNOFFICIAL SOLDIER** a member of a paramilitary organization, especially one fighting against the official ruling power

paramnesia /párram neézi ə/ *n.* **1. FALSE MEMORY** false memories of events that did not really take place **2. INABILITY TO RECALL MEANINGS OF WORDS** an inability to recall the meanings of common words

paramorph /párrə mawrf/ *n.* a mineral that changes its crystalline structure without any change in its chemical composition. Aragonite changes to calcite in this way. —**paramorphism** /párrə máwrfizəm/ *n.*

paramorphine /párrə máwr feen/ *n.* = **thebaine**

paramount /párrə mownt/ *adj.* greatest in importance or significance [Mid-16thC. From Anglo-Norman *paramont*, from *par* 'by' + *amont* 'above'.] —**paramountcy** *n.* —**paramountly** *adv.*

paramour /párrə moor/ *n.* a lover, especially one in a relationship with a married person (*literary*) ○ *'found thee out even in the arms of thy paramour'* (Sir Walter Scott, *Ivanhoe*; 1819) [14thC. From *par amur* 'passionately', from Anglo-Norman *par amour* 'by way of love'.]

paramyxovirus /párrə míksō vīrəss/ *n.* a virus belonging to the group that includes the mumps and measles viruses and the parainfluenza virus

Paraná /párrə naá/ **1.** river in eastern South America, formed by the confluence of two other rivers and flowing through Brazil, along the border of Paraguay, and through Argentina, reaching the Atlantic Ocean at the Río de la Plata. Length: 2,800 km/1,740 mi. **2.** city in northeastern Argentina, on the River Paraná. Population: 206,848 (1991).

parang /paá rang/ *n.* a large knife with a short straight-edged blade, used in Malaysia and Indonesia as a weapon and as a tool [Mid-19thC. From Malay.]

paranoia /párrə nóy ə/ *n.* **1. DISTRUST** extreme and unreasonable suspicion of other people and their motives **2.** PSYCHIAT **PSYCHIATRIC DISORDER** a psychiatric disorder involving systematized delusion, usually of persecution [Early 19thC. From Greek, 'unreason', literally 'out of one's mind', from *nous* 'mind'.]

paranoiac /párrə nóy ak/ *adj.* **RELATING TO PARANOIA** characteristic of or resembling paranoia ■ *n.* **SB WITH PARANOIA** sb who has paranoia

paranoid /párrə noyd/ *adj.* **1. DISTRUSTFUL** obsessively anxious about sth, or unreasonably suspicious of other people and their thoughts or motives **2.** PSYCHIAT **SHOWING CHARACTERISTICS OF PARANOIA** relating to or showing the characteristics of paranoia ■ *n.* **PARANOID PERSON** sb who is paranoid (*dated*)

paranormal /párrə náwrm'l/ *adj.* **IMPOSSIBLE TO EXPLAIN SCIENTIFICALLY** unable to be explained or understood in terms of scientific knowledge ■ *n.* **PARANORMAL THINGS** paranormal events or phenomena

paraparesis /párrəpə reéssiss/ *n.* a medical condition in which both legs, and often the bladder, have little voluntary control —**paraparetic** /-réttik/ *adj.*

parapet /párrəpət, -pet/ *n.* **1. LOW WALL** a low protective wall built where there is a sudden dangerous drop, e.g. along the edge of a balcony, roof, or bridge. Some parapets are battlemented, especially on castles, and many are built as ornamental features. **2.** MIL **PROTECTIVE WALL OF EARTH** a bank of earth, rubble, or sandbags piled up along the edge of a military trench for protection from enemy fire [Late 16thC. Via French from Italian *parapetto*, from *parare* 'to shield' (see PARASOL) + *petto* 'chest', from Latin *pectus* (see PECTORAL).]

paraph /párrəf, pə ráff/ *n.* a decorative flourish written under a signature to finish it off, or formerly to protect against forgery [Late 16thC. Via French from, ultimately, medieval Latin *paragraphus* 'paragraph'.]

paraphasia /párrə fáyzi ə/ *n.* a speech defect of neurological origin in which the speaker's words are jumbled unintelligibly. ◊ **aphasia**

paraphernalia /párrəfər náyli ə/ *n.* **1. ASSORTED OBJECTS** assorted objects or items of equipment, often things that seem amusing, strange, or irritating **2.** LAW **WEDDING GIFTS TO WIFE** in former times, items of property given to a wife on her wedding by her new husband and regarded by law as belonging to her [Mid-17thC. Via medieval Latin from, ultimately, Greek *parapherna*, 'married woman's own property', literally 'beside the dowry', from *phernē* 'dowry'.]

paraphilia /párrə fílli ə/ *n.* the need for an abnormal stimulus, e.g. a sadistic or masochistic practice, in order to achieve sexual arousal or orgasm —**paraphiliac** *n.*

paraphrase /párrə frayz/ *vt.* (**-phrases, -phrasing, -phrased**) **REPHRASE AND SIMPLIFY** to restate sth using other words, especially in order to make it simpler or shorter ■ *n.* **REPHRASED VERSION** sth that is rephrased and simplified through being made shorter [Mid-16thC. Via French from, ultimately, Greek *paraphrazein*, literally 'to explain alongside', from *phrazein* 'to explain'.] —**paraphrastic** /párrə frástik/ *adj.*

paraphysis /pə ráffississ/ (*plural* **-ses** /-seez/) *n.* an erect sterile filament that grows among the reproductive organs of fungi, algae, and mosses [Mid-19thC. From modern Latin, literally 'growth beside', from Greek *phusis* 'growth'.] —**paraphysate** /pə ráffisət, -sayt/ *adj.*

paraplegia /párrə pleéjə/ *n.* total inability to move both legs and usually the lower part of the trunk, often as a result of disease or injury of the spine [Mid-17thC. Via modern Latin from Greek *paraplēgiē* 'stroke on one side', from *paraplēssein* 'to strike on one side', from *plessein* 'to strike'.] —**paraplegic** *adj.*, *n.*

parapodium /párrə pṓdi əm/ (*plural* **parapodia** /-di ə/) *n.* an appendage on the body of some marine worms, occurring in pairs on each segment of the worm's body, used for swimming, crawling, or holding onto things

parapsychology /párrə sī kólləji/ *n.* the study of supposed mental phenomena that cannot be explained by known psychological or scientific principles, e.g. extrasensory perception and telepathy —**parapsychological** /párrə sīkə lójjik'l/ *adj.* —**parapsychologist** /párrə sī kóllәjist/ *n.*

Paraquat /párrə kwot/ *tdmk.* a trademark for a weedkiller

Pará rubber /pə raá-/ *n.* rubber made from the latex of the Pará rubber tree [Mid-19thC. Named after the state of *Pará* in Brazil.]

parasailing /párrə sayling/ *n.* a sport in which a waterskier wearing a parachute or holding onto a type of hang-glider is towed along behind a motorboat and rises up into the air [Mid-20thC. Coined from PARA[2] + SAIL.]

parasang /párrə sang/ *n.* an old unit of measure for distance used in Persia, equal to about 5.6 km/31/2 mi [Late 16thC. Via Latin from Greek *parasaggēs*, of Persian origin.]

parascending /párrə sending/ *n.* a sport in which sb wearing an open parachute is towed along by a speedboat or land vehicle, rises into the air, and descends independently using the parachute [Late 20thC. Coined from PARA[2] + ASCEND.]

parascience /párrə sī ənss/ *n.* the study of phenomena that cannot be explained or tested by conventional scientific methods

paraselene /párrəsi leéni/ (*plural* **-nae** /-nee/) *n.* an image of the Moon seen within a lunar halo [Mid-17thC. Coined from PARA-[1] + Greek *selēnē* 'moon'.] —**paraselenic** /-lénnik/ *adj.*

parasensory /párrə sénssəri/ *adj.* extrasensory (*technical*)

parasexual /párrə sékshoo əl/ *adj.* used to describe a type of reproduction, seen in certain fungi, in which the recombination of parental chromosomes takes place without the usual formation of sex cells by cell division (**meiosis**) —**parasexuality** /párrə sékshoo álləti/ *n.*

Parashah /párrə shaa/ (*plural* **Parashoth** /-shōt/) *n.* in Judaism, a passage from the Torah read during traditional weekly worship at the synagogue [Early 17thC. From Hebrew *pārāšāh* 'division'.]

parasite /párrə sīt/ *n.* **1.** BIOL **ORGANISM LIVING ON ANOTHER** a plant or animal that lives on or in another, usually larger, host organism in a way that harms or is of no advantage to the host **2. SCROUNGER** sb who lives off the generosity of others and does nothing in return [Mid-16thC. Via Latin from Greek *parasitos* 'one who eats from another's table', from *sitos* 'grain, food'.]

parasitic /párrə síttik/ *adj.* **1.** BIOL **LIVING IN OR ON ANOTHER ORGANISM** living in or on another host organism, usually causing it harm **2. LIVING OFF OTHER PEOPLE** living off the generosity of others without doing anything in return —**parasitically** *adv.*

parasiticide /párrə sítti sīd/ *adj.* **KILLING PARASITES** used or designed to destroy parasites ■ *n.* **PARASITE-KILLING SUBSTANCE** a substance that is used to destroy parasites —**parasiticidal** /párrə sítti sīd'l/ *adj.*

parasitise *vt.* = **parasitize**

parasitism /párrə sītizəm/ *n.* **1.** BIOL **PARASITIC BEHAVIOUR** a type of symbiosis in which one organism lives as a parasite in or on another organism **2.** VET = **parasitosis**

parasitize /párrəssi tīz, -sī tīz/ (**-izes, -izing, -ized**), **parasitise** (**-ises, -ising, -ised**) *vt.* to infest an animal or plant with a parasite, or to live on it as a parasite

parasitoid /párrəssi toyd, -sī toyd/ *adj.* **LAYING EGGS INSIDE HOST** used to describe an insect that lays its eggs inside the living body of another animal or insect. The hatched newborns feed off the body, eventually killing the host. ■ *n.* **PARASITOID INSECT** an insect that lays its eggs within a host, eventually causing the death of the host

parasitology /párrə sī tólləji/ *n.* the scientific study of plants and animals that live as parasites —**parasitological** /párrə sītə lójjik'l/ *adj.*

parasitosis /párrə sī tṓssiss/ (*plural* **parasitoses** /-seez/) *n.* VET a disease that develops as a result of infestation by parasites

paraskiing /párrə skee ing/ *n.* the sport of skiing off high mountains and descending using a light, steerable parachute composed of inflatable tubes of fabric [Mid-20thC. Coined from PARA[2] + SKI.]

parasol /párrə sol/ *n.* an umbrella made to provide shade from the sun [Early 17thC. Via French from Italian *parasole*, from *parare* 'to protect' + *sole* 'sun'.]

parasuicide /párrə sṓo i sīd/ *n.* **1. ACT BORDERING ON SUICIDE** a suicide attempt or act of self-injury that is motivated by a desire to draw attention to other personal problems rather than by a genuine wish to die **2. SB CARRYING OUT PARASUICIDE** sb who carries out a parasuicide

parasympathetic /párrə simpə théttik/ *adj.* relating or belonging to the parasympathetic nervous system [Early 20thC. Because some of the nerves run beside sympathetic nerves.]

parasympathetic nervous system *n.* one of the two divisions in the part of the nervous system that controls involuntary and unconscious bodily functions (**autonomic nervous system**). Its actions include slowing the heart, constricting the pupils, and relaxing the bowels. ◊ **sympathetic nervous system**

parasynthesis /párrə sínthississ/ (*plural* **-ses** /-seez/) *n.* the formation of words by a combination of smaller words and additional elements. For example, 'heavy-handed' combines the adjective 'heavy' with 'handed', which in turn is 'hand' with '-ed' added. —**parasynthetic** /párrəsin théttik/ *adj.*

parasyntheton /párrə sínthi ton/ (*plural* **-ta** /-tə/) *n.* a word formed by the combination of smaller words and additional elements

parataxis /párrə táksiss/ *n.* the combination of clauses or phrases without the use of conjunctions such as 'and' or 'so', e.g. in 'He saved my life – he deserves a medal'. ◊ **asyndeton** [Mid-19thC. From Greek, from *parataessein* 'to place side by side', from *tassein* 'to arrange'.] —**paratactic** /párrə táktik/ *adj.* —**paratactically** /-táktikli/ *adv.*

paratha /pə raátə/ *n.* a flat unleavened bread of Indian origin, made from flour, water, and clarified butter. It is smaller and thinner than a nan. [Mid-20thC. From Hindi *parāṭhā*.]

parathion /párrə thī on/ *n.* a colourless highly toxic oil that is used as an insecticide. Formula: $C_{10}H_{14}NO_5PS$. [Mid-20thC. Coined from PARA-[1] + *thiophosphate* + -ON.]

parathyroid /párrə thī royd/ *adj.* **1.** **OF PARATHYROID GLANDS** relating to or produced by the parathyroid glands **2.** **NEAR THYROID GLAND** in the area around the thyroid gland ■ *n.* = **parathyroid gland**

parathyroidectomy /párrə thī royd éktəmi/ (*plural* **-mies**) *n.* the surgical removal of one or more of the parathyroid glands

parathyroid gland *n.* any of four small glands that lie in or near the walls of the thyroid gland. They secrete a hormone that controls the depositing of calcium and phosphorus in bones.

parathyroid hormone *n.* a hormone secreted by the parathyroid glands that controls the depositing of calcium and phosphorus in bones

paratrooper /párrə troopər/ *n.* a soldier trained to go into battle by parachute, especially one who is also a member of an airborne unit

paratroops /párrə troops/ *npl.* soldiers trained to parachute directly into action, or into enemy territory ○ *a paratroop regiment* —**paratroop** *adj.*

paratyphoid fever /párrə tī foyd-/ *n.* an infectious bacterial disease similar to typhoid but with much less severe symptoms, usually limited to a pink rash, diarrhoea, and some abdominal pain

paravane /párrə vayn/ *n.* a torpedo-shaped device with sharp fins at the front, towed by a ship to cut the moorings of submerged mines [Early 20thC. Coined from PARA- 'protector' (modelled on PARASOL) + VANE.]

par avion /-ávvi on/ *adv.* by air mail [From French, literally 'by aeroplane']

parazoan /párrə zṓ ən/ (*plural* **-a** /-ə/) *n.* a member of the subkingdom of invertebrate animals that includes sponges. Subkingdom: *Parazoa*. [Early 20thC. From modern Latin, subkingdom name, from PARA-[1] on the model of PROTOZOAN and METAZOAN.]

parboil /paár boyl/ (**-boils, -boiling, -boiled**) *vt.* to boil sth, especially a vegetable, until it is partly cooked, usually before frying or roasting it [15thC. Via Old French *parboillir* 'to boil thoroughly' from, ultimately, Latin *bullire* 'to boil'. Originally 'boil thoroughly', later 'boil partially' (influenced by PART).]

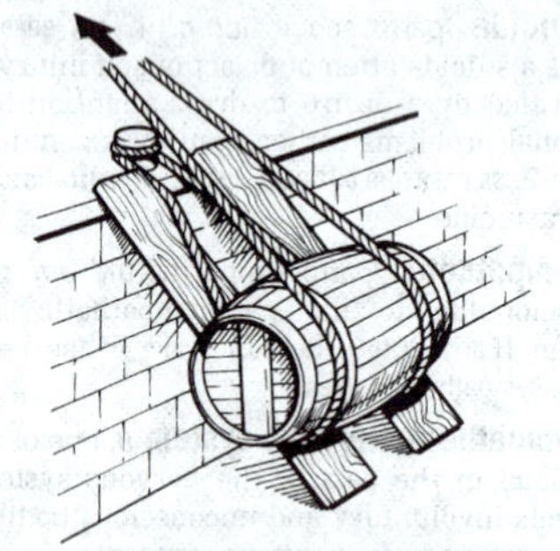

Parbuckle

parbuckle /paár buk'l/ *n.* a rope sling for lifting or lowering barrels, logs, or similar objects [Early 17thC. Alteration (influenced by BUCKLE) of earlier *parbunkle*, of unknown origin.]

Parcae /paár see/ *npl.* in Roman mythology, the Fates. Greek equivalent **Moirai** [Late 16thC. From Latin.]

parcel /paárss'l/ *n.* **1.** **STH WRAPPED UP** one or more things wrapped up together in paper or other packaging **2.** **PORTION** any of the portions into which sth is divided, especially a piece of land that was originally part of a larger area **3.** COMM **BATCH OF COMMERCIAL GOODS** a specific quantity of wholesale merchandise, or a sales transaction involving such a batch **4.** **BUNCH** a collection of people or things (*archaic or literary*) ○ *'a parcel of rascals'* (Thomas Paine, *The Age of Reason*; 1794) ■ *vt.* (**-cels, -celling, -celled**) **1.** **MAKE PARCEL OF STH** to wrap sth or a group of things into a parcel **2.** NAUT **PROTECT ROPE** to bind canvas tightly round rope or cable to protect it [14thC. Via Old French from, ultimately, Latin *particula*, literally 'small part'. Originally 'part, detail'.]

parcel out *vt.* to divide and distribute sth between a number of people

parcel-gilt *adj.* partly gilded, often on the inside but not on the outside

parcel post *n.* a postal service that collects, processes, and delivers parcels

parcenary /paárssinəri/ *n.* LAW = **coparcenary** [15thC. From Anglo-Norman, from *parcen* 'portion'.]

parch /paarch/ (**parches, parching, parched**) *vt.* to make sb or sth extremely dry through water deprivation or exposure to heat [14thC. Origin unknown.]

parched /paarcht/ *adj.* **1.** **THIRSTY** very thirsty (*informal*) **2.** **DRY** completely lacking in moisture because of hot conditions or lack of rainfall

WORD KEY: SYNONYMS

See Synonyms at ***dry***.

Parcheesi /paar cheézi/ *tdmk.* a trademark for a board game based on pachisi, an ancient game [Late 19thC]

parchment /paárchmənt/ *n.* **1.** **FORMER WRITING MATERIAL** a creamy or yellowish material made from dried and treated sheepskin, goatskin, or other animal hide, used in former times for books and documents **2.** **DOCUMENT** a manuscript or other work written, drawn, or painted on a sheet of parchment **3.** PRINTING, PAPER **HIGH-QUALITY PAPER** strong, smooth or textured, usually off-white paper that is used for special documents, letters, or artwork [13thC. From Old French *parchemin*, via Latin *pergamena* from, ultimately, Greek *Pergamon*, the city of Pergamum in Asia Minor.]

parclose /paár klōz/ *n.* CHR a screen or railing that separates or encloses a side chapel, private tomb, or other special area within a large church [15thC. From Old French, the past participle of *parclore* 'to close off, enclose', from Latin *claudere* 'to close'.]

parcourse /paár kawrss/ *n.* *US* a training circuit in a park or other open space, where people can walk or run between stations fitted with equipment and instructions for specific fitness exercises [Partial translation of French *parcours* 'course', a loan translation of medieval Latin *percursus*, literally 'running through', from *percurrere*, literally 'to run through']

pard[1] /paard/ *n.* a large cat, especially a leopard or a panther (*archaic*) [13thC. Via Old French from, ultimately, Greek *pardos*, of Iranian origin.]

pard[2] /paard/ *n.* *US* = **pardner** (*slang*) [Mid-19thC. Shortening.]

pardner /paárdnər/ *n.* *US* used to address a friend, in imitation of the cowboy's supposed pronunciation of the word 'partner' (*slang*)

pardon /paárd'n/ *vt.* (**-dons, -doning, -doned**) **1.** **FORGIVE SB FOR WRONGDOING** to pronounce the official release of sb who has committed a crime or other wrongdoing from punishment, or the official forgiving of a crime or wrongdoing **2.** **EXCUSE SB FOR STH IMPOLITE** to excuse sb for doing sth impolite, or to excuse sth impolite, e.g. interrupting or contradicting sb ■ *n.* **1.** **RELEASE FROM PUNISHMENT** the act of officially releasing sb guilty of a crime or wrongdoing from facing punishment **2.** **PAPER AUTHORIZING FREEDOM FROM PUNISHMENT** an official document stating that sb may be released without receiving any or any further punishment **3.** **ACT OF EXCUSING SB** the excusing of an impolite act or the forgiving of the person committing it **4.** CHR **INDULGENCE** an indulgence (*dated informal*) ■ *interj.* **1.** **WHAT DID YOU SAY?** used as a request to sb to repeat sth that has just been said **2.** used as an apology for doing sth impolite or wrong [13thC. Via Old French *pardun* (noun) and *pardoner* (verb), literally 'to grant thoroughly', from, ultimately, Latin *donare* 'to give, grant'.] —**pardonable** *adj.* —**pardonably** *adv.* ◇ **pardon me 1.** used as an apology for doing sth impolite or wrong **2.** *US* used as a request to sb to repeat sth that has just been said

pardoner /paárd'nər/ *n.* **1.** **SB WHO PARDONS** sb who gives a pardon **2.** CHR, HIST **SELLER OF RELIGIOUS PARDONS** sb who, in medieval times, made a living by selling papal indulgences that were believed to free people from their sins

pare /pair/ (**pares, paring, pared**) *vt.* **1.** **TRIM NAILS** to trim sth such as fingernails or toenails **2.** **REMOVE OUTER LAYER** to remove the skin or outer layer of sth such as a vegetable or fruit thinly and neatly [13thC. Via Old French *parer* 'to prepare, trim', from Latin *parare* (source of English *prepare, repair, rampart*, and *parade*).]

pare down *vt.* to reduce a total amount or number, usually an amount of money or a number of workers, slowly and steadily

paregoric /párrə górrik/ *n.* **OPIUM-BASED PAINKILLER** a former painkilling medicine in the form of camphorated tincture of opium. Originally freely available without prescription, it was a major source of opium addiction. ■ *adj.* **SOOTHING** soothing or painkilling [Late 17thC. Via late Latin from Greek *parēgorikos* 'soothing', from *para* 'beside' + *agoreuein* 'to speak'.]

paren. *abbr.* parenthesis

parenchyma /pə réngkimə/ *n.* **1.** BOT **PLANT TISSUE** soft plant tissue made up of thin-walled cells that forms the greater part of leaves, stem pith, roots, and fruit pulp **2.** ANAT **SPECIALIZED ORGAN TISSUE** the tissue that makes up the specialized parts of particular organs, rather than the blood vessels and connective or supporting tissue **3.** ZOOL **WORM TISSUE** the loose meshwork of cells that surrounds internal organs and fills spaces inside the body of animals such as flatworms [Mid-17thC. Via modern Latin from Greek *parегkhuma* 'soft tissue', from *paregkhein* 'to pour in beside', from *khein* 'to pour'.] —**parenchymatous** /párren kímmətəss/ *adj.*

parent /páirənt/ *n.* **1.** **MOTHER OR FATHER** sb's mother, father, or legal guardian **2.** **ORIGIN OF STH ELSE** sth from which one or more similar and separate things have developed, or to which they are attached (*often used before a noun*) ○ *money transferred from the parent fund* **3.** SCI **EARLIER ATOMIC FORM** an atom, molecule, or ion that undergoes change to become a new product. The starting components in a chemical reaction are the parent molecules. (*often used before a noun*) **4.** NUCLEAR PHYS **PARTICLE'S EARLIER FORM** a radioactive particle that disintegrates to give a new particle (**nuclide**) as a subsequent member of a radioactive decay series (*often used before a noun*) ■ *vt.* (**-ents, -enting, -ented**) **ACT AS PARENT TO** to be or act as a parent to sb or sth [15thC. Via Old French from Latin *parent-*, the present participle stem of *parere* 'to give birth' (source of English *parturition, viper*, and *repertory*).]

parentage /páirəntij/ *n.* **1.** **SB'S PARENTS** the parents or ancestors of a particular person, especially when regarded in terms of social characteristics **2.** **DERIVATION** the particular origins or sources that sth has developed from **3.** = **parenthood**

parental /pə rént'l/ *adj.* **1.** **OF PARENTS** relating to, belonging to, or provided by parents **2.** GENETICS **ORIGINAL** used to describe the original generation of individuals from which all subsequent generations have been bred —**parentally** *adv.*

parenteral /pa réntərəl/ *adj.* **1.** **INJECTED, INFUSED, OR IMPLANTED** used to describe drug administration other than by the mouth or the rectum, e.g. by injection, infusion, or implantation **2.** **INJECTABLE, INFUSABLE, OR IMPLANTABLE** used to describe drugs that are administered by injection, infusion, or implantation [Early 20thC. Formed from PARA-[1] + Greek *enteron* 'intestine' (source of English *dysentery*).] —**parenterally** *adv.*

parenthesis /pə rénthississ/ (*plural* **-ses** /-seez/) *n.* **1.** = **bracket** *n.* 1 **2.** **BRACKETED MATTER** a word or phrase that comments on or qualifies part of the sentence in which it is found and is isolated from it by brackets or dashes **3.** **DEPARTURE FROM TOPIC** a piece of speech or writing that wanders off from the main topic **4.** **INTERVAL** sth that acts as a pause or break in sth (*formal*) [Mid-16thC. Via late Latin from Greek, formed from *parentithenai* 'to insert', from *tithenai* 'to place'.] ◇ **in parenthesis** as an additional qualifying, explanatory, or otherwise separate comment

parenthesize /pə rénthə sīz/ (**-sizes, -sizing, -sized**), **parenthesise** (**-sises, -sising, -sised**) *v.* **1.** *vt.* **PUT STH IN BRACKETS** to enclose part of a written or printed passage in brackets **2.** *vt.* **ADD STH AS EXTRA COMMENT** to add a word, phrase, or opinion as an extra comment that is not wholly related to what is being said **3.**

vti. INSERT EXTRA COMMENTS to break up speech or writing with extra comments added throughout

parenthetical /párrən théttik'l/, **parenthetic** /-théttik/ *adj.* **1.** ADDITIONAL added as an extra comment or parenthesis **2.** CONTAINING PARENTHESES used to describe writing that uses or contains additional comments or notes added as parentheses [Early 17thC] —**parenthetically** *adv.*

parenthood /páirənt hòod/ *n.* the role or experience of being a parent, or the way of life that being a parent imposes

parenting /páirənting/ *n.* the experiences, skills, qualities, and responsibilities involved in being a parent and in teaching and caring for a child (*often used before a noun*) ○ *parenting skills*

parent metal *n.* in welding, the metal of any of the components that are to be welded together

parents' evening *n.* an evening meeting at which teachers make themselves available in school for parents to discuss their children's progress

Parent-Teacher Association *n.* a school body run by teachers and parents to organize fundraising and social events and encourage cooperation and understanding

Parer /páirər/, **Damien Peter** (1912–44) Australian photographer and film director. His World War II documentary *Kokoda Front Line* (1942) was the first Australian film to win an Academy Award.

parergon /pə ráir gon, pə rúr-/ (*plural* **-ga** /-gə/) *n.* sth that exists as an addition or as an additional detail to sth else, especially an employment or activity that is subsidiary to a person's main occupation (*archaic or literary*) [Early 17thC. From Greek, formed from *para* 'beside' + *ergon* 'work'.]

paresis /pə réessiss, párrississ/ *n.* muscular weakness or partial inability to move caused by diseases of the nervous system [Late 17thC. From Greek, literally 'letting go', formed from *para* 'aside' + *hienai* 'to throw' (see CATHETER).]

paresthesia *n.* US = **paraesthesia**

pareu /paa ráy oo/ *n.* a length of fabric worn wrapped round the hips by both men and women in Polynesian countries [Mid-19thC. From Tahitian.]

parev /páarvə/, **pareve** /páarəvə/, **parveh** /páarvə/, **parve** *adj.* used to classify a food that, under Jewish law, is neither a dairy nor a meat product and can therefore be eaten with either as part of the same meal. ◊ **fleishig, milchig** [Mid-20thC. From Yiddish.]

par excellence /paar éksə loNss, -éksə lóNss, -éksələnss/ *adj.* of the very best kind or highest quality [From French, literally 'by virtue of preeminence']

parfait /paar fáy/ (*plural* **-faits** *or* **-fait**) *n.* a rich dessert consisting of frozen whipped cream or rich ice cream flavoured with fruit. It is sometimes lightened with egg whites to give it a texture similar to that of mousse. [Late 19thC. Via French, literally 'perfect', from Latin *perfectus* 'perfect'.]

parfleche /páar flesh/ *n. US, Can* **1.** DRIED ANIMAL SKIN the hide of an animal, soaked and scraped to remove the hair, then stretched and dried, but not tanned **2.** ANIMAL-SKIN ARTICLE a shield, bag, or other item made of parfleche [Early 19thC. From Canadian French, formed from French *parer* 'to defend' + *flèche* 'arrow'.]

parget /páarjit/ *n.* **1.** PLASTER FOR WALLS OR CHIMNEYS plaster, whitewash, roughcast, or any similar material used to coat walls or line chimneys **2.** PLASTERWORK ornamental plasterwork on a wall ■ *vt.* (**-gets, -geting, -geted**) COAT STH WITH PARGET to cover walls, line chimneys, or decorate sth with parget [14thC. Alteration (influenced by Old French *parjeter* 'to throw about') of Old French *porgeter* 'to plaster a wall', from *jeter* 'to throw'.] —**pargeting** *n.*

parhelia plural of **parhelion**

parhelic circle /paar héelik-, -héllik-/ *n.* a luminous horizontal band in the sky that passes through the Sun and is caused by the Sun's rays reflecting off ice crystals in the atmosphere

parhelion /paar héeli ən/ (*plural* **-a** /-li ə/) *n.* a bright coloured spot on a parhelic circle, often seen in pairs and caused by ice crystals in the atmosphere diffracting light. ◊ **anthelion** [Mid-17thC. Via Latin from Greek *parēlion*, from *para* 'beside' + *hēlios* 'sun' (see HELIO-).] —**parheliacal** /páarhə lí ək'l/ *adj.* —**parhelic** /paar héelik, -héllik/ *adj.*

pari- *prefix.* equal ○ *parisyllabic* [From Latin, formed from *par* (see PAR)]

pariah /pə rí ə, párri ə/ *n.* **1.** OUTCAST sb who is despised and avoided by other people **2.** SB OF LOW CASTE in India and Myanmar, a member of a caste that is lower than the four main Hindu castes. A pariah usually does domestic or agricultural work. [Early 17thC. From Tamil *paraiyan*, literally 'drummer', from *parai* 'festival drum', because hereditary drummers belonged to this caste.]

pariah dog *n.* = **pye-dog** [Because it is seen as belonging to the fringes of society, like the pariah caste]

Parian /páiri ən/ *adj.* **1.** INDUST OF MARBLE FROM PAROS used to describe a fine white marble that was mined on the Greek island of Paros in ancient times **2.** CERAMICS OF PORCELAIN FROM PAROS used to describe a variety of fine porcelain used mainly to make figures and originally from the Greek island of Paros **3.** OF PAROS relating to or from the Greek island of Paros ■ *n.* PEOPLES SB FROM PAROS sb who was born in or is an inhabitant of the Greek island of Paros [Mid-16thC. Formed from Latin *Parius*.]

parietal /pə rí ət'l/ *adj.* **1.** BIOL OF WALLS OF HOLLOW PART relating to the walls of any hollow part of a plant or animal such as a plant's ovary or an animal's skull **2.** *US* EDUC OF IN-COLLEGE RESIDENCE relating to residence within a college ■ *n.* BIOL PARIETAL PART a parietal part of a plant or animal [Early 16thC. Directly or via French from late Latin *parietalis*, from *paries* 'wall'.]

parietal bone *n.* either of two bones, one on each side of the skull, that form a part of the sides and roof of the skull

parietal cell *n.* any of the cells that make up the peptic glands of the stomach and secrete hydrochloric acid

parietal lobe *n.* the middle region of each of the two hemispheres of the brain, lying beneath the crown of the skull

pari-mutuel /párri myóotyoo əl/ (*plural* **pari-mutuels** *or* **paris-mutuels**) *n. US* = **tote** [From French, literally 'mutual wager']

paring /páiring/ *n.* sth such as a thin slice of fruit or vegetable peel that has been pared or cut off sth larger

paring knife *n.* a short tapered knife with a sharp blade designed for removing the outer skin of vegetables or fruit

pari passu /párri pássoo, páari-/ *adv.* **1.** LAW FAIRLY at an equal rate or in an otherwise fair way, with no one person or group taking precedence over another **2.** AT SAME RATE together, step for step (*literary*) [From Latin, literally 'with equal step']

paripinnate /párri pínnayt, -nət/ *adj.* = **even-pinnate**

Paris[1] /párriss/ *n.* in Greek mythology, a Trojan prince whose abduction of Helen, the wife of Menelaus started the Trojan War [Via Latin from Greek]

Paris[2] *English* /párriss/; *French* /pa rée/ capital city of France, situated in the north-central part of the country. Population: 2,152,423 (1990).

Paris green *n.* a bright blue-green toxic powder used to add colour to paint. It is also used as an insecticide and a wood preserver. It is a double salt of copper acetate and copper arsenate. Formula: $(CuO)_3As_2O_3.Cu(Cu_2H_3O_2)_2$. [Mid-19thC. Named after the city of PARIS, France.]

parish /párrish/ *n.* **1.** CHR DISTRICT WITH OWN CHURCH in the Anglican, Roman Catholic, and some other churches, a division of a diocese that has its own church and clergy member (*often used before a noun*) ○ *the parish priest* **2.** CHR PEOPLE OF PARISH the people who live in a particular parish **3.** SMALL LOCAL GOVERNMENT UNIT the smallest defined area of local government in rural areas of England, containing a village with its own elected council [13thC. Via Old French *parroche* and ecclesiastical Latin *parochia* from, ultimately, Greek *paroikos* 'neighbour', literally 'dwelling nearby', from *oikos* 'dwelling'.]

parish council *n.* in England, a local government body that meets regularly to make decisions concerning a civil parish

parishioner /pə rísh'nər/ *n.* sb who lives in a particular religious or civil parish [15thC. Formed from earlier *parishon*, from Old French *parochien*, from *parroche* (see PARISH).]

parish pump *adj.* of interest only to a small group in a particular area [*Parish* because use of the pump is limited to members of the local parish]

parish register *n.* a book in which the births, baptisms, marriages, and burials in a parish are recorded

Parisian /pə rízzi ən/ *n.* RESIDENT OF PARIS sb who was born in or who lives in the French city of Paris ■ *adj.* OF PARIS relating to Paris, its people, or its culture

parisyllabic /párri si lábbik/ *adj.* used to describe a noun or verb that contains the same number of syllables in all of its inflections

parity[1] /párriti/ *n.* **1.** EQUALITY equality of status or position, especially in terms of pay or rank **2.** SIMILARITY BETWEEN THINGS the quality of being similar or identical **3.** MATH RELATIONSHIP BETWEEN NUMBERS a relationship of oddness or evenness between two numbers (**integers**). If two numbers are both odd or both even, they are said to have the same parity. If one is odd and one is even, they have different parity. **4.** FIN EQUALITY OF EXCHANGE RATE equivalence in the rate of exchange between several currencies **5.** COMPUT INTEGRITY OF TRANSMITTED DATA equivalence between the data transmitted, e.g. by fax or e-mail, and the data received. Errors are checked by comparing the quantity of 1s in the message sent with the quantity in the message received. [Late 16thC. Directly or via Old French *parite* from late Latin *paritas*, from *par* 'equal' (see PAR).]

parity[2] /párriti/ *n.* **1.** CONDITION OF HAVING GIVEN BIRTH the condition or fact of having given birth **2.** NUMBER OF CHILDREN the number of children that a particular woman has given birth to [Late 19thC. Coined from PAROUS + -ITY.]

park /paark/ *n.* **1.** LEISURE AREA FOR PUBLIC RECREATION a publicly owned area of land, usually with grass, trees, paths, sports fields, playgrounds, picnic areas, and other features for recreation and relaxation **2.** ENVIRON PROTECTED AREA OF COUNTRYSIDE an area of land reserved and managed so that it remains unspoilt, undeveloped, and as natural as possible **3.** PRIVATE AREA OF LAND a large privately owned area of land that forms a private estate **4.** LEISURE PRIVATELY OWNED RECREATION FACILITY an area of privately owned land, developed to offer recreation or amusements to paying customers **5.** BUSINESS BUSINESS SITE an area of land developed for a group of related commercial enterprises ○ *a science park* **6.** *US, Can* SPORTS STADIUM OR SPORTS FIELD a sports stadium or sports field ○ *a ball park* **7.** TRANSP ROAD OR DISTRICT a street or district, especially in a suburban area (*often used in placenames*) **8.** SOCCER FOOTBALL PITCH a football pitch (*informal*) **9.** CARS POSITION ON AUTOMATIC GEARBOX a position on the gear selector of an automatic gearbox that acts as a parking brake for a motor vehicle **10.** MIL AREA HOUSING MILITARY VEHICLES a designated area where military vehicles are kept, within a military base ■ *v.* (**parks, parking, parked**) **1.** *vti.* CARS STOP AND LEAVE VEHICLE to stop a motor vehicle beside or off the road and leave it there for some time **2.** *vti.* CARS MANOEUVRE MOTOR VEHICLE INTO SPACE to manoeuvre a motor vehicle into a space in order to park it **3.** *vt.* SETTLE SOMEWHERE to sit down somewhere, usually with the intention of staying there for some time (*informal*) ○ *Just park yourself over there.* **4.** *vt.* LEAVE STH SOMEWHERE to place or leave sth somewhere temporarily, especially sth heavy, bulky, or unwanted (*informal*) **5.** *vi. US* KISS IN PARKED CAR to kiss and cuddle in a parked car in a quiet and secluded location (*slang*) **6.** *vt.* SPACE TECH PLACE SPACECRAFT IN ORBIT to place a spacecraft or satellite in orbit, usually temporarily [13thC. Via Old French *parc* from medieval Latin *parricus*, ultimately from a prehistoric Germanic word meaning 'enclosure' that is also the ancestor of English *paddock*.]

Mansfield Park, a novel by Jane Austen (1814). It tells the story of young Fanny Price, who is sent to live with her wealthy relatives, the Bertrams. Fanny's warmth and moral strength, which are contrasted with her uncle's stern traditionalism and the irresponsible flirtations of her neighbours Mary and Henry Crawford, eventually win her the respect of the family and the hand of her cousin Edmund.

Park /paark/, **Sir Keith** (1892–1975) New Zealand air marshal. He was an RAF commander during the evacuation from Dunkirk and the Battle of Britain.

Park, Mungo (1771–1806) Scottish explorer. He explored the River Niger and wrote *Travels in the Interior Districts of Africa* (1799). In a subsequent expedition his party was attacked, and he was drowned.

Park, Ruth (b. 1923) New Zealand-born Australian novelist. Her works include *The Harp in the South* (1948), an account of life in a Sydney slum.

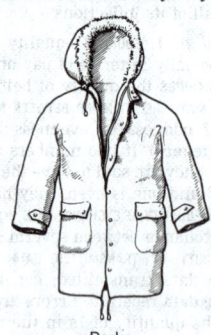
Parka

parka /paarkə/ *n.* **1. LONG, HOODED JACKET** a warm, knee- or thigh-length jacket with a hood that is often lined with fur or imitation fur **2. COAT OF ANIMAL SKIN** a thick, fur-lined, hooded outer garment for Arctic conditions, pulled on over the head. Traditionally, parkas are made of animal hide and worn by the Inuit and Aleut people. [Late 18thC. From Russian, 'pelt, skin jacket', of Nenets origin.]

park-and-ride *n.* a transport scheme designed to reduce car use in city centres in which motorists drive to out-of-town car parks from where buses or trains run regularly into the city

Dorothy Parker

Parker /paarkər/, **Dorothy** (1893–1967) US writer and critic. She is known for her sardonic stories, poetry, and reviews for the *New Yorker* magazine. Full name **Dorothy Rothschild Parker**

Parkes /paarks/ town in central New South Wales, Australia. It is the site of the Parkes Observatory. Population: 10,094 (1996).

Parkes, Sir Henry (1815–96) Australian statesman. He was premier of New South Wales five times between 1872 and 1891, and the architect of Australian federation.

parkie /paarki/ *n.* a park keeper (*informal*)

parkin /paarkin/ (*plural* **-kins** or **-kin**) *n.* N England, Scotland, NZ a heavy moist dark ginger cake made with oatmeal and treacle [Early 19thC. Origin uncertain: possibly from the surname *Parkin*.]

parking /paarking/ *n.* **1. SPACE TO LEAVE VEHICLES** spaces in which vehicles may be parked **2. STOPPING AND LEAVING VEHICLE** the action of driving a road vehicle into a position beside or off the road and leaving it there **3.** *US* **KISSING IN PARKED CAR** kissing and cuddling in a parked car in a quiet and secluded location (*slang*)

parking light *n. US* = **sidelight**

parking lot *n. US, Can* = **car park**

parking meter *n.* a coin-operated roadside meter that displays the length of time for which a vehicle may remain legally parked in a parking space

parking orbit *n.* a temporary orbit of a spacecraft while preparations are made for the next step in its programme

parking station *n. ANZ* a multistorey car park

Parkinsonism /paarkins'nizəm/ *n.* any of a group of incurable nervous disorders that includes Parkinson's disease, marked by the symptoms of trembling limbs and muscular rigidity. These disorders may be caused by the frequent use of certain drugs or by exposure to chemicals.

Parkinson's disease /paarkins'nz-/ *n.* an incurable nervous disorder marked by the symptoms of trembling hands, lifeless face, monotone voice, and a slow, shuffling walk. It is generally caused by the degeneration of dopamine-producing brain cells, and is the commonest form of Parkinsonism. [Late 19thC. Named after the English physician James *Parkinson* (1755–1824), who described it.]

Parkinson's law *n.* the observation that work always expands to fill the time set aside for it [Mid-20thC. Named after the English historian C. Northcote *Parkinson* (1909–93), who formulated it.]

Parkinson's syndrome *n.* = **Parkinsonism**

park keeper *n.* a public official who patrols, supervises, and maintains a public park

parkland /paark land/ *n.* the land contained within a park, especially when the grassland contains shrubs and trees

Rosa Parks

Parks /paarks/, **Rosa** (b. 1913) US civil rights leader. Her arrest in Alabama for not relinquishing her bus seat to a white passenger (1955) led to Martin Luther King's boycott campaign of the bus company and gave impetus to the campaign for civil rights. Full name **Rosa Louise Parks**

parkway /paark way/ *n. US, Aus* a wide stretch of public highway with grassy areas on both sides, often divided by a grassy central reservation

parky /paarki/ (**-ier, -iest**) *adj.* cold or chilly (*informal*) ○ *It does get a bit parky at night.* [Late 19thC. Origin unknown.]

Parl. *abbr.* **1.** Parliament **2. Parl., parl.** parliamentary

parlance /paarlənss/ *n.* **1. PARTICULAR WAY OF TALKING** the style of speech or writing used by people in a particular context or profession **2. SPEECH** speech, especially in a conversation [Late 16thC. Via Old French from *parler* 'to speak'.]

parlando /paar lándō/ *adv.* sung in a style that suggests speech, usually without pitch or with less clear pitch (*used as a musical direction*) [Late 19thC. From Italian, literally 'speaking'.] —**parlando** *adj.*

parlay /paarli, -lay/ *vt.* (**-lays, -laying, -layed**) *US, Can* **1. BET WINNINGS ON** to stake an original bet and its winnings on a subsequent bet **2. USE ADVANTAGE** to make good use of an asset or advantage to obtain success ■ *n. US, Can* **INSTANCE OF BETTING WINNINGS** a bet in which winnings from a previous bet are gambled [Late 19thC. Alteration of obsolete *paroli*, via French and Italian from, ultimately, Italian *parare* 'to place a bet', from Latin (see PREPARE).]

parley /paarli/ *vi.* (**-leys, -leying, -leyed**) **CONFER** to talk or negotiate, especially with an enemy ■ *n.* (*plural* **-leys**) **DISCUSSION** a talk or negotiation, especially between opposing military forces (*dated*) [Late 16thC. From Old French *parlee*, via *parler* 'to speak' from late Latin *parabolare*, from *parabola* 'talk'.]

parliament /paarləmənt/ *n.* **1. LEGISLATIVE BODY** a nation's legislative body, made up of elected and sometimes nonelected representatives **2. ASSEMBLY OR CONFERENCE** an assembly or conference held to make laws or discuss sth **3. ASSEMBLY OF PARLIAMENT** an assembly of a parliament, created following a general election and dissolved before the next general election [13thC. From Old French *parlement*, from *parler* 'to speak'. The underlying meaning is 'discussion, consultation'.]

Parliament *n.* the supreme legislative body in various countries. In the United Kingdom, Parliament consists of the House of Commons and the House of Lords.

parliamentarian /paarlə men táiri ən/ *n.* **1. SB IN PARLIAMENT** a member of a parliament **2. EXPERT IN HOW PARLIAMENTS WORK** an expert in parliamentary procedures and parliamentary history [Early 17thC]

Parliamentarian *n.* during the English Civil War, a supporter or member of Oliver Cromwell's parliamentary army against King Charles I

parliamentarianism /paarlə men táiri ənizəm/ *n.* government of a country by a parliament, or support for this kind of government

parliamentary /paarlə méntəri/ *adj.* **1. OF PARLIAMENTS** relating to parliaments, or in the form of a parliament ○ *parliamentary government* **2. FITTING FOR PARLIAMENT** used to describe language and behaviour considered to conform to the standards that apply to a parliament

Parliamentary Commissioner, **Parliamentary Commissioner for Administration** *n.* = **ombudsman** *n.* 2

parliamentary private secretary (*plural* **parliamentary private secretaries**) *n.* a backbench MP who acts as an assistant to a government minister in parliamentary dealings, especially dealings with other backbench MPs

parliamentary secretary (*plural* **parliamentary secretaries**) *n.* a Member of Parliament, especially one appointed as a junior minister, who assists a Minister of the Crown in the running of a government department

parlor *n. US* = **parlour**

parlor car *n.* in the United States and Canada, a railway carriage containing individual reserved seats

parlor grand *n. US* = **boudoir grand**

parlour /paarlər/ *n.* **1. WORK PREMISES** a room or set of rooms equipped and used for a specific line of business (*often used in combination*) ○ *a beauty parlour* **2. LIVING ROOM FOR ENTERTAINING GUESTS** a living room that is set aside for entertaining guests **3. SMALL QUIET ROOM** a room in a hotel or pub that offers more privacy and comfort than the main or public bar areas (*dated*) [13thC. From Old French, formed from *parler* 'to talk'. The underlying meaning is 'room for polite conversation'.]

parlour game *n.* a game that can be played indoors (*dated or formal*)

parlous /paarləss/ *adj.* **1. DANGEROUS** very unsafe, uncertain, or difficult (*archaic or humorous*) ○ *'Thou art in a parlous state, shepherd'*. (William Shakespeare, *As You Like It*; 1599) **2. CRAFTY** mischievous, devious, or cunning (*archaic*) ■ *adv.* **VERY** used to emphasize the extreme or excessive nature of sth (*archaic*) [14thC. Shortening and alteration of PERILOUS.] —**parlously** *adv.* —**parlousness** *n.*

Parma /paarmə/ city in northern Italy. It is the capital of Parma Province, in Emilia-Romagna Region. Population: 170,555 (1992).

Parmenides /paar ménni deez/ (fl. 500 BC) Greek philosopher. He was a leader of the Eleatic school and author of *On Nature*, which anticipates the idealism of Plato.

Parmesan /páarmi zan, -zən, -zán/ (*plural* **-sans** *or* **-san**) *n.* a pale yellow hard strong Italian cheese made with unpasteurized skimmed milk, often served grated as a garnish on pasta dishes. Parmesan is aged for at least two years before use. [Mid-16thC. Via French from Italian *parmigiano*, 'from the city of Parma', where it is traditionally made.]

parmigiana /paármi jaánə/ *adj.* used to describe a dish that has been prepared using Parmesan cheese ○ *veal parmigiana* [Late 19thC. From Italian, feminine of *parmigiano* 'Parmesan' (see PARMESAN).]

Parnassian /par nássi ən/ *adj.* POETIC found in poetry or associated with poetic works (*literary*) ■ *n.* FRENCH 19C POET one of a late 19th-century French poetic school that advocated emotional detachment and purity of metrical form [Mid-17thC. Formed from Latin *Parnassius*, from Greek *Parnasos* 'Parnassus'. *Poet* from *Le Parnasse contemporain* (1866), a poetry anthology.]

Parnassus /paar nássəss/ mountain in central Greece, directly north of Delphi. In ancient times it was sacred to Apollo and thought to be the home of the Muses. Height: 2,457 m/8,061 ft.

Parnell /paar nél/, **Charles Stewart** (1846–91) Irish politician. In 1880 he became leader of the Home Rule Party. He lost support after being cited in the divorce case of Katherine O'Shea, whom he later married.

parochial /pə róki əl/ *adj.* 1. NARROW-MINDED concerned only with narrow local concerns without any regard for more general or wider issues 2. CHR OF A PARISH relating to or belonging to a parish, or to parishes [14thC. Via Old French from ecclesiastical Latin *parochia* 'parish'.] —**parochialism** *n.* —**parochialist** *n.* —**parochially** *adv.*

parochial school *n.* US a private school affiliated with a church that provides children with a general education as well as religious instruction

parody /párrədi/ *n.* (*plural* **-dies**) 1. AMUSING IMITATION a piece of writing or music that deliberately copies another work in a comic or satirical way 2. PARODIES IN GENERAL parodies as a literary or musical style or type 3. POOR IMITATION an attempt or imitation that is so poor that it seems ridiculous ■ *vt.* (**-dies, -dying, -died**) IMITATE COMICALLY to write or perform a parody of sb or sth [Late 16thC. Via late Latin from Greek *parōidia*, from *para* 'secondary, indirect' + *ōidē* 'song'.] —**parodic** /pə róddik/ *adj.* —**parodical** *adj.* —**parodist** /párrədist/ *n.*

parol /pə ról, párrəl/ *adj.* SPOKEN used to describe a legal contract or lease that is made, done, or given by word of mouth only, rather than in writing ■ *n.* ORAL CONTRACT a legal contract or lease that is made, done, or given orally only [15thC. Via Anglo-Norman from, ultimately, Latin *parabola* 'speech, talk' (see PARABLE).]

parole /pə ról/ *n.* 1. CONDITIONAL RELEASE OF PRISONER the early release of a prisoner, with conditions such as good behaviour and regular reporting to the authorities applying for a stated period of time ○ *on parole* 2. PRISONER'S PROMISE the promise to fulfil set conditions, given by a prisoner released on parole 3. CONDITIONAL PERIOD the period after a prisoner's release on parole during which the conditions of release continue to apply 4. US PRISONER OF WAR'S PROMISE a promise given by a prisoner of war, either not to escape, or not to take up arms again as a condition of release 5. LING REAL-WORLD LANGUAGE language considered as the utterances of real people, as distinct from the system of language (**langue**) that governs how those utterances are constructed. ◊ **competence, performance** ■ *vt.* (**-roles, -roling, -roled**) GIVE PRISONER PAROLE to release a prisoner on parole [15thC. Via French from, ultimately, Latin *parabola* 'speech, talk' (see PARABLE).] —**parolable** *adj.*

paronomasia /párrənō máyzi ə/ *n.* a play on words, especially a pun [Late 16thC. Via Latin from, ultimately, Greek *paronomazein*, literally 'to name differently', from *onomazein* 'to name'.] —**paronomastic** /-mástik/ *adj.* —**paronomastically** *adv.*

paronym /párrənim/ *n.* a word that is derived from the same root as another word, e.g. 'wise' and 'wisdom' [Mid-19thC. From Greek *parōnumon*, from *para-* 'beside' + *onuma* 'name'.] —**paronymic** /párrə nímmik/ *adj.* —**paronymous** /pə rónniməss/ *adj.* —**paronomously** *adv.*

parotic /pə róttik/ *adj.* situated close to or beside the ear [Mid-19thC. Formed from the Greek stem *ŏt-* 'ear' (see OTO-).]

parotid /pə róttid/ *adj.* 1. NEAR EAR situated close to or beside the ear 2. RELATING TO PAROTID GLAND relating to the parotid gland ■ *n.* = **parotid gland** [Late 17thC. Via French from, ultimately, the Greek stem *parōtid-*, literally 'beside the ear', from the stem *ŏt-* 'ear' (see OTO-).]

parotidectomy /pə rótti déktəmi/ (*plural* **-mies**) *n.* the surgical removal of a parotid gland

parotid gland, **parotid** *n.* a salivary gland located below the ear in humans

parotitis /párrə títiss/, **parotiditis** /pə rótti dítis/ *n.* inflammation of a parotid gland or the parotid glands —**parotitic** /-títtik/ *adj.*

parous /párrəss/ *adj.* having given birth on at least one occasion [Late 19thC. From -PAROUS.]

-parous *suffix.* giving birth to, producing ○ *uniparous* [Formed from Latin *-parus*, from *parere* 'to give birth' (see PARENT)]

Parousia /pə roóssi ə/ *n.* = **Second Coming** [Late 19thC. From Greek, literally 'presence', from the present participle of *pareinai*, from *einai* 'to be' (see ONTO-).]

paroxysm /párrək sizəm/ *n.* 1. SUDDEN OUTBURST OF EMOTION a sudden and uncontrollable expression of emotion 2. OUTBURST OF SYMPTOM a sudden onset or intensification of a pathological symptom or symptoms, especially when this is recurrent [Late 16thC. Via medieval Latin from, ultimately, Greek *paroxunein* 'to irritate', literally 'to sharpen beyond', from, ultimately, *oxus* 'sharp' (see OXYGEN).] —**paroxysmal** /párrək sízm'l/ *adj.* —**paroxysmally** *adv.* —**paroxysmic** *adj.*

paroxytone /pə róksi tōn/ *n.* 1. WORD WITH PENULTIMATE STRESS a word in which the main stress is on the second-last syllable 2. GREEK WORD CATEGORY in ancient Greek, a word with an acute accent on the second-last syllable ■ *adj.* WITH STRESSED PENULTIMATE SYLLABLE with the main stress on the second-last syllable [Mid-18thC. From Greek *paroxutonos*, from *para-* 'beside' + *oxutonos* 'oxytone'.] —**paroxytonic** /pə róksi tónnik/ *adj.*

parpen /paárpən/, **parpend** /-pənd/ *n.* a stone or brick built into a wall to go from one side of the wall to the other and act as a binder. US term **perpend** [15thC. Via Old French from medieval Latin *parpannus*, of unknown origin.]

parquet /paár kay, paárki/ *n.* DECORATIVE WOODEN FLOORING flooring consisting of blocks of wood laid in a decorative pattern ■ *vt.* (**-quets, -queting, -queted**) COVER FLOOR WITH PARQUET to cover a floor in parquet [Early 19thC. From French, literally 'small enclosed space', from *parc* 'enclosure' (see PARK).]

Parquetry: Parquetry floor in an anonymous painting (1860?)

parquetry /paárkitri/ *n.* flooring or a decorative inlay for furniture made with blocks of wood

parr /paar/ (*plural* **parrs** *or* **parr**) *n.* 1. YOUNG SALMON a young salmon up to two years old that has dark transverse bands (**parr marks**) and lives in freshwater 2. YOUNG FISH the young of some fishes other than the salmon [Early 18thC. Origin unknown.]

Parr /paar/, **Catherine, Queen of England** (1512–48) English queen She married Henry VIII in 1543, becoming his sixth queen. After his death in 1547 she married Thomas Seymour.

Parramatta /párrə máttə/ city in New South Wales, Australia, a western suburb of Sydney. Population: 142,993 (1996).

parrel /párrəl/, **parral** *n.* a ring, loop, or band that secures a boom to a mast while allowing it to move up and down [15thC. Shortening and alteration of APPAREL, in the earlier sense of 'rigging'.]

parricide /párri síd/ *n.* 1. MURDER OF RELATIVE the murder of a parent or close relative 2. MURDERER OF RELATIVE sb who murders a parent or close relative [Mid-16thC. From Latin *parricidium* 'kin-slaying' and *parricida* 'kin-slayer', which were both formed from assumed *parri-* 'relative', of unknown origin.] —**parricidal** /párri síd'l/ *adj.* —**parricidally** /-síd'li/ *adv.*

parritch /párrich, paá-/ *n. Scotland* porridge (*dated*) [Variant of PORRIDGE]

Parrot

parrot /párrət/ *n.* 1. BRIGHTLY COLOURED TROPICAL BIRD a tropical or subtropical bird with a stout hooked bill and variously coloured, often brilliant plumage. Some species have the ability to mimic speech. Order: Psittaciformes. 2. SB WHO COPIES OTHERS sb who simply repeats things that sb else has said, without thought or understanding ■ *vt.* (**-rots, -roting, -roted**) COPY OTHER PEOPLE to repeat what sb else says or writes without having thought about it or understood it [Early 16thC. Origin uncertain: probably from French dialect *Perrot* 'little Pierre'.] —**parroter** *n.*

parrot-fashion *adv.* a way of repeating sth mindlessly, like a parrot (*informal*)

parrot fever *n.* = **psittacosis** [From the fact that humans can contract it from pet birds such as parrots]

parrotfish /párrət fish/ (*plural* **-fish** *or* **-fishes**) *n.* a brightly coloured tropical marine fish with jaws shaped like a parrot's beak that it uses for scraping coral. Family: Scaridae. [Early 18thC. From its beak-shaped jaw and brilliant red, green, and blue colouring.]

parry /párri/ *v.* (**-ries, -rying, -ried**) 1. TURN BLOW ASIDE to block or deflect the damaging effect of a blow or weapon 2. *vt.* AVOID ANSWERING to evade a question by cleverly saying sth that does not answer it ■ *n.* (*plural* **-ries**) ACT OF EVADING an act of evading a blow, criticism, or question [Late 17thC. Origin uncertain: probably via French *parez* 'defend (yourself)'! from, ultimately, Latin *parare* 'to prepare' (see PARE).]

Parry, Cape /párri/ promontory in Canada, in the Northwest Territories, jutting into Amundsen Gulf between Franklin and Darnley bays

Parry, Sir William Edward (1790–1855) British explorer. He mapped many areas in the Arctic but failed in his attempt to find the North West Passage or reach the North Pole.

parse /paarz/ (**parses, parsing, parsed**) *vti.* 1. DESCRIBE GRAMMATICAL ROLE OF WORD to describe the grammatical role of a word in a sentence, or to be subject to this process 2. ANALYSE GRAMMATICAL STRUCTURE OF SENTENCE to analyse and describe the grammatical structure of a sentence, or to be subject to this process of analysis and description [Mid-16thC. Origin uncertain; probably from earlier *pars* 'part of speech', from Latin, *part* (see PART).] —**parsable** *adj.*

parsec /paár sek/ *n.* an astronomical unit of distance equal to 3.262 light years. A parsec is the distance from which the Earth's distance from the Sun would subtend one second of arc. [Early 20thC. Coined from PARALLAX + SECOND.]

Parsee /paár see, paar seé/, **Parsi** n. a member of a Zoroastrian group living mainly in western India, descended from Persian refugees of the 7th and 8th centuries [Early 17thC. From Persian *Pārsī*, from *Pārs* 'Persia'.] —**Parsee** adj. —**Parseeism** n.

parser /paárzər/ n. **1.** COMPUT SOFTWARE FOR ANALYSING LANGUAGE a computer program that breaks natural language or programming language statements or instructions into smaller more easily interpreted units understandable to the computer. The parser determines how a sentence can be constructed from the grammar of the language, producing a parse tree about the statement as the output. **2.** ANALYSER sb or sth that analyses sth into its component parts [Mid-19thC. Originally in the general sense 'one who parses'.]

Parsi n., adj. = Parsee

parsimonious /paárssi móni əss/ adj. very frugal or ungenerous —**parsimoniously** adv. —**parsimoniousness** n.

parsimony /paárssiməni/ n. **1.** FRUGALITY great frugality or unwillingness to spend money **2.** PHILOS PRINCIPLE OF ECONOMY economy in the use of means to achieve sth, especially the principle of endorsing the simplest explanation that covers a case [15thC. From Latin *parsimonia*, from *pars-*, past participle stem of *parcere* 'to spare'.]

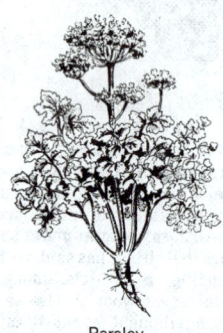
Parsley

parsley /paárssli/ n. a widely cultivated plant of the carrot family with small compound leaves that are used in cooking and as a garnish. Latin name: *Petroselinum crispum*. [Pre-12thC. From late Latin *petrosilium*, ultimately from Greek *petroselinon*, from *petra* 'rock' + *selinon* 'parsley'.]

parsley fern n. a bright green European fern with leaves that look like parsley leaves. Latin name: *Cryptogramma crispa*.

parsley piert /-peért/ n. a small plant of the rose family with three-lobed leaves and tiny green flowers. Latin name: *Aphanes arvensis*. [Late 16thC. Alteration of French *perce-pierre*, literally 'stone-piercer'.]

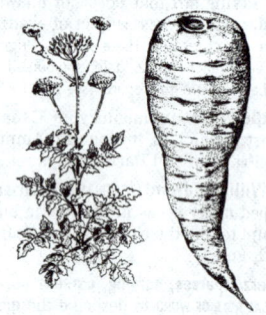
Parsnip

parsnip /paárssnip/ n. **1.** PLANT OF CARROT FAMILY an aromatic plant of the carrot family cultivated for its edible root. Latin name: *Pastinaca sativa*. **2.** ROOT VEGETABLE the long cone-shaped cream-coloured root of the parsnip plant, cooked and eaten as a vegetable [14thC. Alteration (influenced by English *neep* 'turnip') of Old French *pasnaie*, from Latin *pastinum* 'two-pronged gardening fork', probably because of its shape.]

parson /paárs'n/ n. **1.** ANGLICAN PARISH PRIEST an Anglican parish priest **2.** CLERIC a member of the clergy, especially of the Protestant Church [13thC. From Old French *persone* 'person' (see PERSON). The underlying meaning may be 'important personage', or perhaps the 'person' legally responsible for parish property.] —**parsonic** /paar sónnik/ adj. —**parsonical** /-sónnik'l/ adj.

parsonage /paárss'nij/ n. the house, usually provided by the parish, where a parson lives

parson bird n. NZ = **tui** [From resemblance of its markings to the dark suit and white preaching bands of a parson in church]

Parsons /paárss'nz/, **Sir Charles Algernon** (1854–1931) British engineer. He invented the first successful steam turbine engine, and built the first turbine-driven steamship (1897).

Parsons, Geoffrey Penwill (b. 1930) Australian pianist. As an accompanist he has performed with many of the world's leading singers.

parson's nose n. the fatty piece of flesh at the rear end of a cooked chicken, turkey, or other bird, to which the tail feathers were attached. US term **pope's nose** [Variant of *Pope's nose*, an insulting term that originated during a period of anti-Catholicism during the reign of James II (1685–88)]

part /paart/ n. **1.** PORTION OR DIVISION a portion or section of sth ○ *the early part of the century* **2.** EQUAL PORTION any of several equal portions that make up sth such as a mixture ○ *pastry that is one part fat to three parts flour* **3.** COMPONENT a separable piece or component of sth such as a machine, system, or device ○ *a motor with only three moving parts* **4.** IMPORTANT ELEMENT OF STH an integral and essential feature or component of sth ○ *She wants to be part of the community.* **5.** THEATRE ACTOR'S ROLE a role in a dramatic performance ○ *played the part of Hamlet in the school play* **6.** INVOLVEMENT IN AN EVENT sb's participation in or influence on sth ○ *What part did he have to play in all this?* **7.** SIDE sb's side or viewpoint ○ *You're always taking her part.* **8.** ORGANIC CONSTITUENT an organ, system, or other discrete element of an organism ○ *the part of the plant that carries out photosynthesis* **9.** MUSIC SEPARATE MUSICAL ROLE the score for a single voice or instrument in a symphonic, orchestral, or choral work **10.** LOGICAL DIVISION a logical division of sth such as a report, book, or presentation ○ *Part three of the paper deals with environmental issues.* **11.** US HAIR = **parting** ■ **parts** npl. **1.** AREA a geographical region or local area (*informal*) ○ *That's unheard of in these parts.* **2.** ABILITIES intellectual abilities or talents (*literary*) ○ *a man of parts* ■ v. (**parts, parting, parted**) **1.** vti. SEPARATE to move or to move sth in different directions so that there is a space between them ○ *They had to part the children to keep them from fighting.* ○ *The curtains parted.* **2.** vti. DIVIDE INTO PARTS to divide sth into parts, or to undergo division into parts **3.** vti. HAIR DIVIDE HAIR to make a line in the hair by combing in opposite directions from it, or to separate naturally in this way **4.** vi. END RELATIONSHIP to finish a relationship with sb ○ *We parted on bad terms.* **5.** vi. GO AWAY to go away from sb ○ *They parted at the corner of the street.* ■ adj. PARTIAL partial or less than the whole ○ *part owner of a beach house* ■ adv. PARTIALLY to some extent but not completely ○ *She's part Irish, part French.* [13thC. The noun came from Old French; the verb via French *partir* from Latin *partire*; both from Latin *part-*, stem of *pars* 'part' (source of English *parcel*).] ◇ **for the most part** in general, or mostly ○ *She does OK at school, for the most part.* ◇ **in good part** without taking offence or becoming angry ◇ **in part** to an extent but not completely ◇ **on the part of** as far as sb is concerned, or with regard to sb ◇ **part and parcel** an essential, indivisible element of sth

part with vt. to give sth up or to give sth away, especially unwillingly

part. abbr. **1.** particle **2.** participle **3.** particular

partake /paar táyk/ (**-takes, -taking, -took** /-toók/, **-taken** /-táykən/) vi. **1.** EAT OR DRINK STH to have sth to eat or drink (*formal*) **2.** HAVE OR SEEM TO HAVE to have or appear to have a certain amount of some quality or char-

acteristic (*formal*) **3.** PARTICIPATE to share in or take part in sth ○ *How many students partake in sports activities?* [Mid-16thC. Back-formation from *partaker* 'participator', from *part-taker*, a translation of Latin *particeps* (see PARTICIPATE).] —**partaker** n.

partan /paárt'n/ n. Scotland an edible crab [15thC. Origin uncertain: probably from Scottish Gaelic *partan* 'red'.]

parted /paártid/ adj. **1.** IN PARTS divided into parts **2.** SEPARATED separated or kept separate **3.** DIVIDED BY A PARTING having a parting ○ *a hairstyle parted on the left* **4.** BOT DIVIDED TO BASE used to describe a leaf or plant part that is separated or cleft nearly to the base

parterre /paar táir/ n. GARDENING an ornamental garden laid out in a formal pattern that is usually marked out with low evergreen hedges and filled in with annual bedding plants [Early 17thC. From French, 'ornamental garden', from *par terre* 'on the ground'.]

part exchange n. the practice of paying part of the price of sth by giving the seller sth that the buyer owns

part-exchange vt. to accept or give goods as part payment for sth being bought

parthenocarpy /paar theénō kaarpi/ n. the production of fruits without fertilization or seeds [Early 20thC. From German *Parthenocarpie*, from Greek *parthenos* 'virgin' + *karpos* 'fruit'.] —**parthenocarpic** /paar theénō kaárpik/ adj. —**parthenocarpous** /paar theénō kaárpəss/ adj.

parthenogenesis /paáthənō jénnəssiss/ n. a form of reproduction, especially in plants, insects, and arthropods, in which a female gamete develops into a new individual without fertilization by a male gamete [Mid-19thC. Coined from Greek *parthenos* 'virgin' + GENESIS.] —**parthenogenetic** /-jə néttik/ adj. —**parthenogenetically** /-néttikli/ adv.

Parthenon, Athens, Greece

Parthenon n. a large temple to the goddess Athena on the Acropolis in Athens. Built in the 5th century BC, it is considered the greatest example of Doric architecture.

Parthian /paárthi ən/ n. sb from Parthia, an ancient country in Asia that ruled an empire until the 3rd century —**Parthian** adj.

Parthian shot n. a final hostile remark or gesture made while leaving [From the Parthians' legendary tactic of firing arrows over their shoulders while retreating]

partial /paársh'l/ adj. **1.** INCOMPLETE not complete or total **2.** AFFECTING PARTS affecting a part or parts but not the whole **3.** LIKING STH having a particular liking for sth ○ *partial to chocolate cake* **4.** BIASED showing an unfair preference for one person or another ■ n. **1.** MATH = **partial derivative 2.** MUSIC = **overtone** n. 2 [15thC. Via Old French *parcial* from late Latin *partialis*, from the stem *part-* (see PART).] —**partialness** n.

partial derivative, **partial** n. the derivative of a function of two or more variables calculated with respect to one of the variables and on the assumption that the others are fixed

partial differential equation n. a differential equation that involves partial derivatives of more than one variable

partial eclipse n. an eclipse in which only part of sth such as the Sun or Moon is covered or darkened

partial fraction n. any of a set of simpler fractions, the sum of which comprises a more complex fraction

partiality /paárshi állәti/ (*plural* **-ties**) *n.* **1.** FONDNESS a liking for sth **2.** BIASED ATTITUDE OR BEHAVIOUR an unfair preference for one person or thing over another

partially /paársh'li/ *adv.* **1.** NOT COMPLETELY to a degree but not completely **2.** IN A BIASED WAY in a way that shows an unfair preference for one person or thing over another

partially sighted *adj.* having a visual impairment that cannot be completely corrected by the use of glasses or contact lenses

partial pressure *n.* the pressure that one gas in a mixture of gases would exert if it were the only gas present

partial product *n.* the result when a quantity is multiplied by one digit of a number with two or more digits

partible /paártәb'l/ *adj.* able to be divided [Mid-16thC. Via late Latin *partibilis* from Latin *partire* 'to part' (see PART).]

participant /paar tíssipәnt/ *n.* SB TAKING PART sb who takes part in sth ■ *adj.* PARTICIPATING taking part in sth [Mid-16thC. From French, present participle of *participer*, from Latin *participare* (see PARTICIPATE).]

participate /paar tíssi payt/ (**-pates, -pating, -pated**) *v.* **1.** *vi.* TAKE PART to take part in an event or activity **2.** HAVE A QUALITY to have a particular quality (*archaic*) [15thC. From, ultimately, Latin *participare*, from *particeps* 'sharing', literally 'taking part', from the stem *part-* 'part' (see PART).] —**participative** *adj.* —**participatory** *adj.* —**participator** *n.*

participating insurance *n.* a type of insurance in which people who hold a policy are entitled to a dividend from the insurance company's profits

participation /paar tíssi páysh'n, paár ti-/ *n.* the act of taking part in an activity ○ *We would welcome your participation in any of the events.*

participial /paárti síppi әl/ *adj.* with the form or function of a verb that can be used as both adjective or verb [Late 16thC. From Latin *participialis*, from *participium* (see PARTICIPLE).] —**participially** *adv.*

participle /paárti sip'l, paar tíssip'l/ *n.* a form of a verb that is used to form complex tenses, such as 'was loving' and 'has loved' in English, and may also be used as an adjective [14thC. Via Old French from Latin *participium*, from *particeps* 'sharing' (see PARTICIPATE), because it shares qualities of both adjectives and verbs.]

particle /paártik'l/ *n.* **1.** TINY PIECE a very small piece of sth ○ *airborne particles* **2.** TINY AMOUNT a very small amount of sth ○ *There wasn't a particle of truth in anything he said.* **3.** PHYS BODY WITH FINITE MASS a minute body that is considered to have finite mass but negligible size **4.** PHYS BASIC UNIT OF MATTER any of the basic units of matter, e.g. a molecule, atom, or electron **5.** PHYS SUBATOMIC UNIT a unit of matter smaller than the atom or its main components **6.** GRAM PART OF MULTI-WORD VERB an adverb or preposition that occurs as part of a multi-word verb, such as 'up' in 'blow up' **7.** CHR PIECE OF CONSECRATED BREAD OR WAFER in the Roman Catholic Mass, a small piece of consecrated bread or wafer [14thC. From Latin *particula* 'small part', from the stem *part-* (see PART).]

particle accelerator *n.* NUCLEAR PHYS = **accelerator** *n.* 2

particle beam *n.* a very narrow concentrated stream of charged particles such as electrons or protons that is produced by a particle accelerator or a particle-beam weapon. Lenses are used to focus the beam and magnets change its direction.

particle physics *n.* the branch of physics that deals with the study of subatomic particles, particularly the many unstable particles produced in particle accelerators and high-energy collisions (*takes a singular verb*)

parti-coloured /paárti-/, **party-coloured** *adj.* with different parts in different colours [*Parti* from PARTY, in the sense 'multi-coloured']

particular /pәr tíkyoolәr/ *adj.* **1.** ONE OUT OF SEVERAL relating to one person or thing out of several ○ *Which particular dress do you prefer?* **2.** PERSONAL belonging to one person and different from other people's **3.** EXCEPTIONAL great or more than usual **4.** SPECIAL special and worth mentioning **5.** FUSSY having or demanding high standards ○ *She's very particular about standards of hygiene.* **6.** CHOOSY taking great care when making a choice **7.** DETAILED going into great detail about sth (*formal*) **8.** LOGIC NOT DEALING WITH ALL relating to or being a proposition that deals with some but not all members of a class ■ *n.* **1.** ITEM an individual fact, item, or detail (*often used in the plural*) **2.** SINGLE INSTANCE an individual case or instance, as opposed to a more general theory **3.** PHILOS REAL THING an entity with definite spatial and temporal properties [14thC. Via Old French from Latin *particularis* 'concerned with small parts or details', from *particula* 'small part' (see PARTICLE).] ◇ **in particular** specifically or especially

particularise *vti.* = **particularize**

particularism /pәr tíkyoolәrizәm/ *n.* **1.** COMMITMENT TO ONE GROUP undivided commitment to one particular group with exclusive concern for its interests, especially if this is detrimental to the interests or well-being of a larger group **2.** POL SELF-RULE PRINCIPLE a policy of allowing political divisions within a state or federation to be self-governing, without regard to what effect this may have on the larger body **3.** CHR BELIEF THAT GOD BESTOWS GRACE INDIVIDUALLY the belief that God chooses to bestow grace and salvation on particular individuals —**particularist** *n.* —**particularistic** /pәr tíkyoolә rístik/ *adj.*

particularity /pәr tíkyoo lárrәti/ (*plural* **-ties**) *n.* (*formal*) **1.** EXACTITUDE attention to detail and concern for accuracy **2.** FASTIDIOUSNESS the practice of taking great care when making a choice **3.** USE OF DETAIL the use of great detail in describing sth **4.** = **particular 5.** STH CHARACTERISTIC a peculiarity or characteristic **6.** INDIVIDUALITY the condition of being peculiar to an individual rather than a group

particularize /pәr tíkyoolә rīz/ (**-izes, -izing, -ized**), **particularise** (**-ises, -ising, -ised**) *v.* **1.** *vt.* FOCUS ON INDIVIDUAL to make sth become particular, e.g. by focusing on a particular person or thing **2.** *vt.* PROVIDE WITH SPECIFIC EXAMPLES to provide sth with specific examples **3.** *vti.* GO INTO DETAIL to go into detail about sth —**particularization** /pәr tíkyoolә rī záysh'n/ *n.* —**particularizer** /pәr tíkyoolә rīzәr/ *n.*

particularly /pәr tíkyoolәrli/ *adv.* **1.** VERY MUCH to a great degree **2.** MORE THAN USUAL more than usual or more than in other cases **3.** SPECIFICALLY as a specific example **4.** IN DETAIL with great attention to detail

particulate /paar tíkyoolәt, -layt/ *adj.* OF PARTICLES relating to or consisting of separate particles ■ *n.* SUBSTANCE CONSISTING OF PARTICLES a substance that consists of separate particles, especially airborne pollution [Late 19thC. Formed from Latin *particula* (see PARTICLE).]

particulate inheritance *n.* a theory advanced by Gregor Mendel that parental genes do not blend in offspring but rather retain their characteristics from generation to generation

parting /paárting/ *n.* **1.** LEAVING the act of leaving sb or sth, especially if the separation is sad or upsetting **2.** SEPARATION the process or action of separating or dividing **3.** HAIR DIVIDING LINE IN HAIR the line in a hairstyle from which the hair is combed or brushed in different directions. US term **part 4.** CRYSTALS, MINERALS BREAKING OF CRYSTAL ALONG PLANE the tendency of some crystals to break along a plane of weakness through deformation ■ *adj.* **1.** DONE WHILE LEAVING done, made, or given when leaving ○ *a parting remark* **2.** DEPARTING leaving or coming to an end (*literary*) ○ *'The curfew tolls the knell of parting day...'* (Thomas Gray, *Elegy Written in a Country Churchyard*; 1751) **3.** DIVIDING used to divide or separate sth

parting shot *n.* a final, often hostile, remark or gesture made by sb who is leaving [Origin uncertain: possibly an alteration of PARTHIAN SHOT]

parting strip *n.* a thin strip of a material such as wood or metal used to keep two adjacent parts separate

parti pris /paárti preé/ (*plural* **partis pris**) *n.* a preconceived opinion or bias [From French, literally 'side taken']

partisan[1] /paárti zán/, **partizan** *n.* **1.** BIASED SUPPORTER a strong supporter of a person, group, or cause, especially one who does not listen to other people's opinions **2.** RESISTANCE FIGHTER a member of a group that has taken up armed resistance against occupying enemy forces ■ *adj.* SHOWING UNREASONING SUPPORT showing strong and usually biased support for a cause, especially a political one [Mid-16thC. Via French and Italian dialect *partisano* from Italian *parte* 'part, side', from the Latin stem *part-* (see PART).] —**partisanship** *n.*

partisan[2], **partizan** *n.* ARMS, HIST a weapon with a long shaft and a blade, used in the 16th and 17th centuries [Mid-16thC. Via obsolete French from obsolete Italian *partesana*, variant of *partigiana (arma)*, literally 'partisan (weapon)', feminine of *partigiano* (see PARTISAN[1]).]

partita /paar teétә/ (*plural* **-te** /-teé tay/ *or* **-tas**) *n.* a suite or set of musical variations, especially in Baroque music [Late 19thC. Via Italian, literally 'composition divided into parts', from, ultimately, Latin *partire* 'to divide' (see PART).]

partite /paár tīt/ *adj.* **1.** BOT DEEPLY SPLIT used to describe a plant part such as a leaf that is split almost to its base **2.** IN PARTS divided into or consisting of two or more parts (*usually used in combination*) [Late 16thC. From Latin *partitus*, the past participle of *partire* 'to divide' (see PART).]

partition /paar tísh'n/ *n.* **1.** STH THAT DIVIDES SPACE sth that divides a space, e.g. a wall built to make two rooms out of one **2.** DIVIDED PART a section or part of sth divided **3.** DIVISION OF COUNTRY the division of a country into two or more separate states or countries ○ *the partition of India* **4.** DIVIDING UP the division of sth into parts, or the state of being divided into parts (*formal*) ■ *v.* (**-tions, -tioning, -tioned**) **1.** *vt.* DIVIDE WITH A PARTITION to divide or separate sth by means of a partition **2.** *vti.* SPLIT A COUNTRY to divide a country into two or more separate states **3.** *vt.* DIVIDE to divide sth into separate parts [15thC. Via Old French from, ultimately, Latin *partire* 'to divide' (see PART).] —**partitioner** *n.* —**partitionist** *n.* —**partitionment** *n.*

partitive /paártәtiv/ *adj.* **1.** SEPARATING separating or dividing sth (*formal*) **2.** GRAM EXPRESSING PART OF STH used to describe a grammatical construction expressing a part of sth, such as 'of' in 'a lump of coal' or the possessive form in 'the dog's tail' ■ *n.* GRAM PARTITIVE CONSTRUCTION a partitive construction [14thC. Via Old French from, ultimately, Latin *partit-*, the past participle stem of *partire* 'to divide' (see PART).] —**partitively** *adv.*

partly /paártli/ *adv.* to some extent, but not completely ○ *The road was partly blocked by a heavy snowfall.*

partner /paártnәr/ *n.* **1.** SB WHO SHARES ACTIVITY sb who takes part in an activity or undertaking with sb else **2.** MEMBER OF RELATIONSHIP either member of an established couple in a relationship **3.** FELLOW PARTICIPANT IN SEXUAL ACTIVITY either of two people who have or have had sex together **4.** ASSOCIATE IN DANCE OR GAME sb who dances with another person or who plays on the same side as another person in a game **5.** COMM BUSINESS ASSOCIATE sb who owns part of a company, usually a company he or she works in, and who shares both the financial risks and the profits of the business **6.** STH RELATED sth that is related in some way to sth else **7.** NAUT SUPPORTING TIMBER ON SHIP one of the timbers on a ship underneath the deck that is used to support the mast (*often used in the plural*) ■ *vt.* (**-ners, -nering, -nered**) BE SB'S PARTNER to be sb's partner, e.g. in a game or dance [14thC. Alteration (influenced by PART) of *parcener*, via Anglo-Norman, literally 'one who shares', from, ultimately, the Latin stem *partition-* 'sharing' (see PARTITION).]

partnership /paártnәr ship/ *n.* **1.** RELATIONSHIP BETWEEN PARTNERS the relationship between two or more people or organizations that are involved in or share the same activity **2.** COOPERATION cooperation between people or groups working together **3.** GROUP OF PEOPLE WORKING TOGETHER an organization formed by two or more people or groups to work together for some purpose **4.** COMM, LAW COMPANY OWNED BY PARTNERS a company set up by two or more people who put money into the business and who share the financial risks and profits **5.** PARTNERS IN BUSINESS the people who make up a partnership, collectively

part of speech *n.* a grammatical category or word group in a language to which words may be assigned on the basis of how they are used in sentences. The traditional main parts of speech in English are noun, verb, adjective, adverb, pronoun, preposition, conjunction, and interjection. Others sometimes used are article and determiner. [Translation of Latin *pars orationis*]

parton /paár ton/ *n.* a postulated elementary particle, proposed as a constituent of neutrons and protons [Mid-20thC. Formed from PARTICLE.]

partook past tense of **partake**

Partridge

partridge /paártrij/ *n.* **1.** MEDIUM-SIZED GAME BIRD a medium-sized ground-nesting bird with variegated plumage, native to Europe and Asia and related to the pheasants and grouse. Genera: *Alectoris* and *Perdix.* **2.** PARTRIDGE FLESH the flesh of the partridge served as food [13thC. Via Old French *perdriz* from, ultimately, Greek *perdix*, of uncertain origin: perhaps literally 'farter'.]

partridgeberry /paártrij beri/ (*plural* **-ries**) *n.* **1.** N AMERICAN EVERGREEN PLANT a trailing evergreen plant of eastern North America that has rounded leaves, small white fragrant flowers, and scarlet berries. Latin name: *Mitchella repens.* **2.** BERRY OF PARTRIDGEBERRY PLANT the scarlet, relatively tasteless berry of the partridgeberry plant [Early 18thC. From the fact that partridges use it for food.]

part song, **part-song** *n.* a vocal musical composition with parts for different voices, usually performed without accompaniment

part-time *adj., adv.* for less than the usual amount of time associated with a particular activity ○ *a part-time job* —**part-timer** *n.*

parturient /paar tyóori ənt/ *adj.* **1.** GIVING BIRTH about to give birth (*technical*) **2.** RELATING TO CHILDBIRTH relating to the process or time of childbirth **3.** ABOUT TO PRODUCE on the verge of producing sth or coming forth (*literary*) [Late 16thC. From Latin *parturient-*, present participle stem of *parturire* (see PARTURITION).] —**parturiency** *n.*

parturifacient /paar tyóori fáysh'nt/ *adj.* INDUCING BIRTH inducing birth or making it easier to give birth ■ *n.* BIRTH-INDUCING DRUG a drug that induces birth or makes it easier to give birth [Late 19thC. Coined from Latin *parturire* 'to be in labour' (see PARTURITION) + -FACIENT.]

parturition /paártyōo rísh'n/ *n.* the act of giving birth to offspring (*formal*) [Mid-17thC. Via the late Latin stem *parturition-* from, ultimately, Latin *parturire* 'to be in labour', from *parere* 'to give birth' (see PARENT).]

partway /paárt way/, **part way** *adv.* some but not all of the way through a process or distance

partwork /paárt wurk/, **part work** *n.* a series of magazines on a particular topic or area of interest, published in weekly, fortnightly, or monthly instalments and intended to be collected to form a complete volume

party /paárti/ *n.* (*plural* **-ties**) **1.** SOCIAL GATHERING FOR FUN a social gathering to which people are invited in order to enjoy themselves and often to celebrate sth ○ *Are you coming to my birthday party?* **2.** GROUP ACTING TOGETHER a group of people who are doing sth together ○ *a search party* **3.** POL POLITICAL ORGANIZATION an organization of people who share the same broad political views and aims, usually attempting to have members elected to government **4.** MIL GROUP OF SOLDIERS a detachment of soldiers given a particular task **5.** LAW ONE SIDE IN AGREEMENT OR DISPUTE a person or a group of people acting together and forming one side in an agreement, contract, dispute, or lawsuit **6.** PERSON an individual ■ *vi.* (**-ties**, **-tying**, **-tied**) BE AT PARTY to socialize and have fun at a party or in a situation resembling a party (*informal*) ■ *adj.* HER-

ALDRY OF TWO COLOURS divided into parts of two different colours [13thC. Via French *partie* 'part, side', and Old French *parti* 'political faction' from, ultimately, Latin *partitus*, the past participle of *partire* 'to divide' (see PART).] ◇ **be (a) party to sth** to participate or be involved in a particular activity

party animal *n.* sb who is a regular and enthusiastic participant at informal social occasions, especially parties (*informal*)

partygoer /paárti gō ər/ *n.* sb who goes to a party or who goes to a lot of parties

party line *n.* **1.** POL POLITICAL POLICY the official policy of a political party or other organization **2.** TELECOM MULTI-USER TELEPHONE LINE a telephone line shared by more than one subscriber —**partyliner** *n.*

party man *n.* a man who is a loyal member or supporter of a political party

party piece *n.* sth such as a song or an impression regularly performed at parties to entertain people

party political broadcast *n.* a short television or radio programme in which a political party is allowed to comment on political issues or to campaign, especially during an election

party politics *n.* political activity as carried on by political parties, especially if carried on by them more in their own interests than for the benefit of the people (*takes a singular or plural verb*) —**party-political** *adj.*

party pooper /-poopər/ *n.* sb who spoils other people's fun or fails to join in the general enthusiasm for sth (*informal*)

party wall *n.* a wall separating adjoining homes, buildings, or pieces of land

parulis /pə roóliss/ (*plural* **-lides** /-deez/) *n.* a gumboil (*technical*) [From modern Latin, literally 'beside the gums', from Greek *oulon* 'gums']

parure /pə roór/ *n.* a matching set of jewellery that includes earrings, a brooch, ring, necklace, and bracelet, and sometimes other items such as buckles [Early 19thC. From French, formed from *parer* 'to adorn' (see PARE).]

par value *n.* the value printed on a security such as a share certificate or bond at the time of issue. It is used to calculate interest or dividend payments. ◊ **market value**

Parvati *n.* a Hindu mother and fertility goddess, the wife of Shiva. She is thought of as the model Hindu wife and is often depicted with a conch, mirror, and lotus.

parvenu /paárvə nyoo/ (*plural* **-nus**) *n.* sb who has recently become wealthy or risen to a higher position in society but who is still considered as inferior by established wealthy and powerful people [Early 19thC. Via French, literally 'one who has arrived', from, ultimately, Latin *pervenire* 'to arrive', from *venire* 'to come' (see VENUE).]

parvis /paárviss/, **parvise** *n.* an enclosed area or portico at the front of a building, especially a church [14thC. Via Old French from, ultimately, late Latin *paradisus* 'garden' (see PARADISE).]

parvo /paárvō/ *n.* = **parvovirus** *n.* 2 [Shortening]

parvovirus /paárvō vírəss/ *n.* **1.** SINGLE-STRANDED DNA VIRUS any of a group of viruses that have a single strand of DNA, especially those causing disease in mammals **2.** VIRAL DISEASE OF DOGS a contagious disease of dogs caused by a parvovirus and marked by fever, loss of appetite, and diarrhoea [Mid-20thC. Coined from Latin *parvus* 'small' + VIRUS.]

pas /paa/ (*plural* **pas**) *n.* a step in dancing, especially in classical ballet [Early 18thC. Via French from Latin *passus* 'step' (see PACE).]

Pasadena /pássə deénə/ **1.** city in southwestern California, the home of the California Institute of Technology. Population: 134,170 (1994). **2.** city in southeastern Texas, a centre of the oil industry. Population: 129,292 (1994).

pascal /pásk'l, pa skál/ *n.* a unit of pressure or stress equal to one newton per square metre. Symbol **Pa** [Mid-20thC. Named after Blaise PASCAL.]

Pascal /pa skál, pásk'l/ *n.* a high-level general-purpose computer language designed to encourage structured programming [Mid-20thC. Acronym for *programme appliqué à la sélection et la compilation automatique de la littérature*; also named after Blaise PASCAL.]

Pascal /pa skaál/, **Blaise** (1623–62) French philosopher and mathematician. He is considered one of the great minds in Western intellectual history. Among his achievements are the invention of the first mechanical adding machine and the development of the modern theory of probability.

Pascal's triangle *n.* a triangular arrangement of numbers with a 1 at the top and at the beginning and end of each row, with each of the other numbers being the sum of the two numbers above it [Named after Blaise PASCAL, who devised it]

Pasch /paask, pask/ *n.* (*archaic*) **1.** PASSOVER the religious holiday of Passover **2.** EASTER the religious holiday of Easter [Pre-12thC. From Old French *pasches* (plural), from, ultimately, Greek *paskha*, via Aramaic from Hebrew *pesaḥ*.]

paschal /pásk'l/ *adj.* **1.** RELATING TO EASTER relating to Easter **2.** RELATING TO PASSOVER relating to Passover (*archaic*) [15thC. Via Old French *pascal* from, ultimately, ecclesiastical Latin *pascha*, from Greek *paskha* (see PASCH).]

paschal flower *n.* = **pasqueflower**

pas de deux /paá də dö́/ (*plural* **pas de deux**) *n.* BALLET a dance or dance sequence for two dancers [From French, 'step for two']

paseo /paa sáy ō/ (*plural* **-os**) *n.* the procession of the matadors and other bullfighters into the arena before the bullfight begins [Mid-19thC. Via Spanish from, ultimately, assumed Vulgar Latin *passare* 'to pass' (see PASS).]

pash /pash/ *n.* a brief infatuation for sb (*dated informal*) [Early 20thC. Shortening of PASSION.]

pasha /paáshə, páshə/, **pacha** *n.* in the past in Turkey and other Middle Eastern countries, an official of high rank [Mid-17thC. From Turkish *paşa*.]

pashm /páshəm/ *n.* the fine wool that grows beneath the outer wool of some goats, especially the soft, downy fibre from the undercoat of the Kashmir goat, used for cashmere shawls and other articles [Late 19thC. From Persian *pašm* 'wool'.]

pashmina /push meénə/ *n.* a fine woollen fabric made from the hair of the belly of goats raised in northern India, used especially for making shawls [Late 19thC. From Persian *pašm*'wool'.]

Pashto /púsh tō/ (*plural* **-to** *or* **-tos**), **Pushto** /púsh too/ (*plural* **-to** *or* **-tos**), **Pushtu** (*plural* **-tu** *or* **-tus**) *n.* **1.** LANG LANGUAGE OF AFGHANISTAN one of the official languages of Afghanistan, also spoken in parts of northwestern Pakistan. It belongs to the Indo-Iranian branch of the Indo-European languages and is spoken by about 21 million people. **2.** PEOPLES PASHTO SPEAKER sb who speaks the Pashto language [Late 18thC. From Pashto *pəštō*.] —**Pashto** *adj.*

Pasiphaë /pə síffi ee/ *n.* **1.** MYTHOL MOTHER OF MINOTAUR in Greek mythology, the wife of Minos, King of Crete, who fell in love with a bull and gave birth to the Minotaur **2.** ASTRON MOON OF JUPITER the eighth moon of Jupiter [Via Latin from Greek, literally 'all-shining']

paso doble /pássō dố blay/ (*plural* **pao dobles** /páyo dốblayz/ *or* **pasos dobles** /pássō dốblayz/) *n.* **1.** LATIN AMERICAN BALLROOM DANCE a quick ballroom dance inspired by a Latin American style of marching. The movements of the man are intended to symbolize those of a bullfighter with the woman as his cape. **2.** MUSIC MUSIC FOR PASO DOBLE a piece of music for dancing the paso doble [Early 20thC. From Spanish, literally 'double step'.]

Pasolini /pázzō leéni/, **Pier Paolo** (1922–75) Italian film director. His films include *The Gospel According to St Matthew* (1964) and *The Decameron* (1971).

pasqueflower /pásk flowər, paásk-/ *n.* a small perennial plant of the buttercup family with hairy compound leaves and large blue, purple, or white flowers that bloom in the spring. Genus: *Anemone.* [Late 16thC. Anglicization and alteration (influenced by French *pasque* 'Easter', because it blooms in the spring) of French *passefleur*.]

pasquinade /pásskwi náyd/ *n.* SATIRE an often anonymous lampoon or satire that traditionally was left displayed in a public place (*archaic*) ■ *vt.* **(-nades, -nading, -naded)** LAMPOON SB OR STH to ridicule sb or sth with a pasquinade (*archaic*) [Late 16thC. Via French from Italian *pasquinata*, from *Pasquino*, the name of a statue in Rome where lampoons were posted.] —**pasquinader** *n.*

pass /paass/ *v.* **(passes, passing, passed) 1.** *vti.* MOVE PAST to move past or through a place, or past a person ○ *dark clouds passing overhead* **2.** *vti.* OVERTAKE to overtake and leave behind sb or sth **3.** *vti.* SPORTS THROW OR KICK BALL TO PLAYER to throw, kick, or hit a ball or other object to another player during a game **4.** *vt.* HAND OVER to hand sth to sb ○ *Could you pass me the salt, please?* **5.** *vti.* TRANSFER OR BE TRANSFERRED to transfer sth such as property, authority, or responsibility to sb, or to be transferred in this way ○ *The house will pass to his daughter when he dies.* **6.** *vti.* MOVE INTO DIFFERENT PLACE OR CONDITION to make sb or sth move, or to move from one place or condition to another **7.** *vti.* MOVE IN A PARTICULAR WAY to move sth or move in a particular way in relation to sth else ○ *He passed his hand along the banister.* **8.** *vt.* GUIDE to guide sth into a particular position ○ *Pass the wire over that hook.* **9.** *vi.* EXTEND PAST to extend through, in front of, or along sth such as a road or area ○ *The road passes by the cemetery.* **10.** *vi.* CHANGE to go from one condition, stage, or state to another ○ *It sheds its skin before it passes to the pupal stage.* **11.** *vt.* SPEND TIME to use up time doing sth ○ *We passed the time playing cards.* **12.** *vi.* ELAPSE to elapse or go by ○ *Time passes quickly.* **13.** *vi.* END to come to an end ○ *The storm finally passed.* **14.** *vti.* BE SUCCESSFUL IN AN EXAM to be successful in a test or examination, or officially decide that sb has been successful in a test or examination **15.** *vti.* SUCCEED IN SUBJECT to meet the requirements of a course of study **16.** *vi.* BE ACCEPTABLE to be of an acceptable standard ○ *It's not the best but it will pass.* **17.** *vti.* APPROVE MEASURE OR BE APPROVED to approve sth such as a law, measure, or proposal, or to get official approval **18.** *vti.* DIE to stop living (*formal*) ○ *She passed from this life in 1967.* **19.** *vi.* GO UNREMARKED to allow to happen, without comment or intervention ○ *She could not let such rude behaviour pass.* **20.** *vi.* HAPPEN BETWEEN PEOPLE OR THINGS to happen or be exchanged between two or more people or things ○ *A look passed between them.* **21.** *vi.* NOT DO STH to decide not to do sth that is suggested or accept sth that is offered **22.** *vi.* CARDS NOT RAISE BID to stop raising a bid in a card game **23.** *vt.* EXCRETE to process and excrete sth from the body **24.** *vt.* GIVE JUDGMENT to give a judgment or opinion ○ *pass judgment* **25.** *vt.* STATE to say sth or give an opinion ○ *She didn't pass any comment at all.* **26.** *vt.* CIRCULATE FAKE MONEY to use fake money to pay for sth ○ *passing counterfeit bills* ■ *n.* **1.** DOCUMENT GIVING PRIVILEGES a document such as a ticket that entitles the holder to do sth such as enter a place ○ *a press pass* **2.** SPORTS ACT OF THROWING TO PLAYER an act of throwing, kicking, or hitting a ball or other object to another player in a sport **3.** SUCCESSFUL GRADE a successful outcome in a test, examination, or course of study **4.** GEOG WAY THROUGH MOUNTAINS a way through or over mountains (*often used in placenames*) **5.** ATTEMPT TO KISS OR TOUCH SB an uninvited attempt to kiss or touch sb in a sexual way **6.** ACT OF GOING BY an instance of sth going past, through, over, or round a place **7.** MOVEMENT a particular movement of sth such as the hand **8.** OPERATION a single cycle or complete operation of sth such as machinery **9.** DOCUMENT EXCUSING SB FROM STH a document that excuses the holder from normal activities **10.** ACT OF NOT DOING STH an instance of not doing sth that is suggested or not accepting sth that is offered **11.** CARDS FAILURE TO BID an instance of not bidding or raising the bid in a card game **12.** STATE OF AFFAIRS a particular and usually undesirable state of affairs ○ *How did we let things get to such a pass?* **13.** FENCING SWORD THRUST a thrust with a sword ■ *interj.* I DON'T KNOW used by sb in answer to a question to say that he or she does not know the answer or does not want to give an answer (*informal*) ○ *'Guess who I've just seen'. – 'Pass!'* ○ *'How would you rate him as a manager?' – 'Pass!'* [13thC. Via Old French *passer* from assumed Vulgar Latin *passare*, from Latin *passus* 'step' (source of English *passage* and *passenger*; see PACE).]

pass as *vt.* = **pass for**

pass away *vi.* **1.** DIE to stop living (*often used as a euphemism for 'die'*) **2.** COME TO END to come to an end or no longer exist

pass by *vt.* to leave sb or sth unaffected or uninvolved ○ *The usual troubles of adolescence seemed to pass her by.*

pass for, pass as *vt.* to be so like sb or sth as to be easily mistaken for the real person or thing

pass off *v.* **1.** *vt.* MAKE ACCEPTED UNDER FALSE IDENTITY to cause sb or sth to be accepted under a different, false identity **2.** *vi.* HAPPEN to have a particular outcome (*refers to a planned event*) **3.** *vi.* DIMINISH to end or disappear gradually

pass on *v.* **1.** *vi.* DIE to stop living (*often used as a euphemism for 'die'*) **2.** *vt.* CONVEY STH to convey or transmit sth that has been received to sb else

pass out *v.* **1.** *vi.* FAINT to lose consciousness **2.** *vt.* DISTRIBUTE to distribute things among a number of people **3.** *vi.* COMPLETE TRAINING to complete a course of training, especially as a military officer

pass over *vt.* **1.** IGNORE to ignore sb's right to be considered for sth, especially a job or a promotion **2.** DISREGARD to fail to consider or include sb or sth **3.** DIE to stop living (*dated*)

pass up *vt.* to decide not to take advantage of an opportunity

pass. *abbr.* 1. passage 2. passenger 3. GRAM passive

passable /paassəb'l/ *adj.* **1.** ACCEPTABLE adequate or good enough **2.** ABLE TO BE CROSSED capable of being crossed or travelled on **3.** POL ABLE TO BE ENACTED able to be passed or made law **4.** FIN SUITABLE FOR CIRCULATION suitable for circulation as legal and valid —**passably** *adv.*

passacaglia /pássə kaályə/ *n.* a baroque musical composition in slow triple time composed on a repeated bass line [Mid-17thC. Via Italian from Spanish *pasacalle*, from *pasar* 'to pass' + *calle* 'street', because it was often played in the streets.]

passade /pa sáyd/ *n.* a movement in dressage in which a horse is made to move forwards and back again on the same spot [Mid-17thC. Via French from Italian *passata*, ultimately from assumed Vulgar Latin *passare* (see PASS).]

passado /pə saádō/ (*plural* **-dos** *or* **-does**) *n.* in fencing, a thrust made while stepping forwards [Late 16thC. Alteration of Spanish *pasada* or French *passade*, ultimately from assumed Vulgar Latin *passare* (see PASS).]

passage[1] /pássij/ *n.* **1.** CORRIDOR OR PATHWAY a corridor in an enclosed area or an outdoor path enclosed on both sides **2.** WAY THROUGH a path made for sb through an obstruction such as a crowd of people **3.** ARTS PIECE OF WRITING OR MUSIC a section of a piece of writing, speech, or music **4.** CHANGE OF PLACE OR CONDITION the act of going from one place to another or changing from one condition to another (*formal*) **5.** PROCESS OF TIME PASSING the process of time going by ○ *the passage of time* **6.** TRANSP JOURNEY a journey, especially one made by sea or air **7.** RIGHT TO TRAVEL the right to come and go, travel, or pass through somewhere ○ *The guides ensured our safe passage.* **8.** POL APPROVAL OF NEW LAW official approval of a new law or other proposal **9.** ANAT TUBE IN THE BODY a tube or channel in the body **10.** GEOG SEA CHANNEL a sea channel or strait (*often used in placenames*) **11.** MED BOWEL MOVEMENT the act or process of expelling sth from the body, e.g. emptying the bowels or the bladder **12.** INTERCHANGE an exchange of words, blows, or information between people or parties (*formal*) [13thC. Via Old French from, ultimately, assumed Vulgar Latin *passare* 'to pass' (see PASS).]

WORD KEY: CULTURAL NOTE

A Passage to India, a novel by the E.M. Forster (1924). In Forster's last and most highly regarded novel, an Englishwoman travelling in colonial India accuses a local doctor of assaulting her during a visit to the mysterious Marabar Caves. The conflicting responses of English expatriates and local Indians to the subsequent trial highlight the limitations of their belief systems and the problems of human understanding.

passage[2] /pássij, pə saázh/ *n.* MOVEMENT IN DRESSAGE either of two movements in dressage, one being a sideways walk and the other a slow deliberate trot ■ *vti.* **(-sages, -saging, -saged)** PERFORM A PASSAGE to perform a passage or make a horse do this [Late 18thC. Via French *passager* from, ultimately, Latin *passus* 'step' (see PACE).]

passage hawk /pássijər-/, **passager hawk** *n.* a hawk or falcon captured while in its first plumage

passageway /pássij way/ *n.* = **passage**[1] *n.* 1

passagework /pássij wurk/ *n.* **1.** NONTHEMATIC PASSAGES parts of a musical work that are thematically unrelated to the whole but enable a performer to display virtuosity **2.** PERFORMANCE OF PASSAGEWORK the performance or execution of passagework

passant /páss'nt/ *adj.* HERALDRY used in heraldry to describe an animal shown walking to the left or right [15thC. From French, the present participle of *passer* (see PASS).]

passback /paàss bak/ *n.* SPORTS the act of passing the ball or puck to another player who is closer to the home goal

pass band *n.* RADIO the range of frequencies that an electronic filter will allow to pass without attenuation. A voice band filter in a telephone exchange will pass a frequency band of approximately 3,000 cycles.

passbook /paàss bòok/ *n.* **1.** BANKING RECORD OF BANK TRANSACTIONS a book in which a record is kept of the money put into and taken out of a bank account or a building society account **2.** COMM BOOK RECORDING CREDIT PURCHASES a book in which a trader records the items a customer has bought on credit **3.** POL IDENTITY DOCUMENT a mandatory identification document issued to Black people in South Africa during apartheid that gave details of their ancestry and spelled out restrictions on their movement [Early 19thC. *Pass* of uncertain origin: possibly from the fact that it is handed back and forth between the bank and the customer.]

Passchendale /pásh'n dayl/ village in western Belgium. It was the scene of heavy fighting in October and November 1917, during World War I.

passé /pássay, paà-/ *adj.* **1.** OUT-OF-DATE out-of-date or no longer fashionable **2.** PAST PRIME no longer in prime condition [Late 18thC. From French, the past participle of *passer* 'to pass' (see PASS).]

WORD KEY: SYNONYMS

See Synonyms at ***old-fashioned***.

passed pawn *n.* CHESS a pawn with no opposing pawn in front of it on its own or on either adjacent file that could become a queen

passementerie /pass méntri/ *n.* **1.** DECORATIVE TRIMMING FOR CLOTHES a decorative trimming for clothing made, e.g. of beads, braid, or lace **2.** MAKING OF CLOTH DECORATIONS the craft of making fringes, tassels, and cords to embellish soft furnishings and upholstery [Early 17thC. From French, formed from *passement* 'decorative lace or braid', literally 'passing (over one another)', from *passer* (see PASS).]

passenger /pássinjər/ *n.* **1.** SB TRAVELLING IN VEHICLE sb who travels in a motor vehicle, train, aircraft, or ship, but is not a driver or crew member **2.** SB NOT DOING SHARE OF WORK sb in a team who does not do his or her fair share of the work [14thC. Alteration of Old French *passageor* 'one who makes a passage', from *passage* (see PASSAGE).]

passenger pigeon *n.* an extinct migratory North American pigeon that was abundant until it was hunted to extinction in the 19th century. Latin name: *Ectopistes migratorius.* [*Passenger* in the earlier sense 'migrating bird', because of its long migrations in huge flocks]

passe-partout /páss paar tòo/ (*plural* **passe-partouts** /-tòo/) *n.* **1.** MASTER KEY sth such as a master key that gives unrestricted access to a building or area **2.** PICTURE FRAME a decorated mat round a framed picture **3.** ADHESIVE TAPE OR GUMMED PAPER adhesive tape or gummed paper used to fix pictures to mats before framing [From French, literally 'pass everywhere']

passepied /paàss pyáy/ *n.* a French court dance in triple time similar to the minuet, often part of instrumental dance suites [From French, literally 'foot-pass']

passer-by /paàssər-/ (*plural* **passers-by**) *n.* sb who happens to be going past a place, especially on foot

passerine /pássə rīn, -reen/ *adj.* RELATING TO PERCHING SONGBIRDS relating or belonging to an order of mainly perching songbirds. It is the largest order of birds and comprises more than half of all species. Order: Passeriformes. ■ *n.* PASSERINE BIRD any bird that belongs to the passerine order [Late 18thC. From late Latin *passerinus* 'of sparrows', from *passer* 'sparrow', of unknown origin.]

pas seul /paá sŏl/ (*plural* **pas seuls**) *n.* a dance or passage performed by a single dancer [From French, literally 'solo step']

passible /pássəb'l/ *adj.* sensitive to feeling emotions, especially when this causes pain (*formal*) [14thC. Via Old French from Latin *passibilis*, from *pass-*, the past participle stem of *pati* 'to feel, suffer' (see PATIENT).] —**passibility** /paássə bíllәti/ *n.* —**passibly** /paássəbli/ *adv.*

passim /pássim/ *adv.* used especially in footnotes to indicate that what is being referred to occurs in various places in a book or other text (*formal*) [Early 19thC. From Latin, literally 'scatteredly', from *passus*, past participle of *pandere* 'to spread out'.]

passing /paássing/ *adj.* **1.** GOING PAST moving past ○ *a passing car* **2.** TRANSITORY lasting only a short time **3.** BRIEF AND WITHOUT MUCH ATTENTION done briefly and without much attention being paid ○ *a passing interest* **4.** EXTREMELY very or extremely (*archaic*) ○ *She was passing fair.* ■ *n.* **1.** CEASING TO EXIST the fact or process of sth becoming obsolete or ceasing to exist **2.** PLACE WHERE IT IS POSSIBLE TO PASS a place where it is possible to pass or cross sth **3.** PROCESS OF TIME GOING BY the elapsing of time **4.** DEATH death ■ *adv.* EXCEEDINGLY very (*archaic*)

passing bell *n.* a bell rung to mark a death or a funeral

passing lane *n.* a lane designated for passing slower traffic

passing note *n.* MUSIC a note played between two chords or pitches to provide a melodic transition from one to the other

passing out *n.* the successful completion of a course of training, especially as a military officer (*hyphenated when used before a noun*)

passing shot *n.* TENNIS in racket games such as tennis, a winning shot that passes beyond the reach of a player at the net

passion /pásh'n/ *n.* **1.** INTENSE EMOTION intense or overpowering emotion such as love, joy, hatred, or anger ○ *Try and play it with a little more passion.* **2.** STRONG SEXUAL DESIRE strong sexual desire and excitement **3.** OUTBURST OF EMOTION a sudden outburst of an emotion such as rage, hatred, or jealousy ○ *He flew into a passion.* **4.** INTENSE ENTHUSIASM FOR STH a keen interest in a particular subject or activity ○ *a passion for music* **5.** OBJECT OF ENTHUSIASM the object of sb's intense interest or enthusiasm ○ *Orchids are my passion.* ■ **passions** *npl.* EMOTIONS strong emotions, especially as distinct from reason or intellect ○ *a meeting at which passions were running high* [12thC. Via French from the ecclesiastical Latin stem *passion-* 'suffering, affection', from, ultimately, *pati* 'to suffer' (source of English *patient, passive,* and *compatible*).]

WORD KEY: SYNONYMS

See Synonyms at ***love***.

Passion *n.* **1.** CHR SUFFERINGS OF JESUS CHRIST the sufferings of Jesus Christ from the Last Supper until his crucifixion **2.** BIBLE STORY OF JESUS CHRIST'S SUFFERING any of the accounts of the Passion in the Gospel, or a musical work based on one of these

passional /pásh'nəl/ *adj.* OF PASSION relating to passion or arising from passion (*literary*) ■ *n.* CHR BOOK RECOUNTING MARTYRS' STORIES a book that tells of the sufferings of Christian saints and martyrs [15thC. From Latin *passionalis*, from *passion-* (see PASSION).]

passionate /pásh'nət/ *adj.* **1.** SHOWING SEXUAL DESIRE expressing or showing strong sexual desire ○ *a passionate kiss* **2.** SHOWING INTENSE EMOTION expressing intense or overpowering emotion ○ *a passionate speech on human rights* **3.** ENTHUSIASTIC having a keen enthusiasm or intense desire for sth ○ *a passionate golfer* **4.** HAVING STRONG EMOTIONS tending to have strong feelings, especially of love, desire, or enthusiasm ○ *a fiery, passionate personality* **5.** QUICK-TEMPERED easily made angry —**passionately** *adv.*

Passionflower

passionflower /pásh'n flow ər/ *n.* a chiefly tropical American climbing vine with large flowers. Some varieties have edible fruit. Genus: *Passiflora.* [Mid-17thC. Because parts of the flower are taken as symbols of Jesus Christ's Passion.]

passion fruit *n.* the edible fruit of a passionflower, especially a granadilla

Passionist /pásh'nist/ *n.* CHR a member of a Roman Catholic mendicant order devoted to commemorating the Passion of Jesus Christ by missionary work. The order was founded in Italy in 1720 by St Paul of the Cross.

passionless /pásh'nləss/ *adj.* **1.** LACKING LOVE empty of romantic or sexual love ○ *a passionless film* **2.** EMOTIONALLY DETACHED feeling or expressing no emotion —**passionlessness** *n.*

Passion play *n.* a play that tells the story of the sufferings and crucifixion of Jesus Christ

Passion Sunday *n.* CHR **1.** 5TH SUNDAY IN LENT the fifth Sunday in Lent, or the second Sunday before Easter, when Passiontide begins **2.** = **Palm Sunday**

Passiontide /pásh'n tīd/ *n.* CHR the last two weeks of Lent, from Passion Sunday to Easter

Passion Week *n.* CHR **1.** WEEK FOLLOWING PASSION SUNDAY the second week before Easter, from Passion Sunday to Palm Sunday (*archaic*) **2.** WEEK BEFORE EASTER Holy Week

passivate /pássi vayt/ (**-vates, -vating, -vated**) *vt.* to coat the surface of a metal with a substance that protects it against corrosion

passive /pássiv/ *adj.* **1.** NOT ACTIVELY TAKING PART tending not to participate actively, and usually letting others make decisions **2.** OBEYING READILY tending to submit or obey without arguing or resisting **3.** NOT OPERATIONAL not working or operating **4.** INFLUENCED BY STH EXTERNAL influenced, affected, or produced by sth external **5.** GRAM EXPRESSING ACTION DONE TO THE SUBJECT indicating that the apparent subject of a verb is the person or thing undergoing, not performing, the action of the verb, as in 'We were given work to do' **6.** CHEM UNREACTIVE chemically inactive or resistant to corrosion **7.** ELECTRON ENG LACKING A POWER SOURCE used to describe an electronic circuit or device that does not contain a source of energy **8.** FIN NOT PRODUCING INTEREST used to describe a form of investment that does not produce interest ■ *n.* GRAM PASSIVE VOICE the passive voice, or a verb in the passive voice [14thC. Directly or via French from Latin *passivus*, from, ultimately, *pati* (see PASSION).] —**passively** *adv.* —**passiveness** *n.*

passive-aggressive *adj.* used to describe, or relating to, a personality type or way of behaving that seeks to manipulate others indirectly and resist their demands rather than confronting or opposing directly —**passive aggression** *n.*

passive immunity *n.* immunity from disease acquired by the transfer of antibodies from one person to another, e.g. through injections or between a mother and a fetus through the placenta

passive resistance *n.* resistance to authority using only nonviolent methods such as peaceful demonstration or noncooperation —**passive resister** *n.*

passive smoking *n.* the involuntary breathing in of other people's tobacco smoke

passivism /pássivizəm/ *n.* **1.** = **passive resistance** **2.** PASSIVE CONDUCT passive behaviour or attitudes —**passivist** *n.*

passivity /pa sívvəti/ *n.* the quality of being passive, or passive behaviour

passkey /paáss kee/ (*plural* **-keys**) *n.* **1.** PRIVATE KEY TO RESTRICTED ENTRANCE a key that gives the holder access via a restricted entrance **2.** = **skeleton key**

pass law *n.* a law operating in South Africa before the abolition of apartheid restricting the movement of Black people within the country

Passmore /paáss mawr/, **John** (1904–84) Australian painter. He was a pioneer of abstract art in Australia.

Passmore, John Arthur (*b.* 1914) Australian philosopher and historian. His works include *A Hundred Years of Philosophy* (1957).

Passover /paáss ōvər/ *n.* a Jewish festival beginning on the 14th day of Nisan and continuing for seven or eight days in commemoration of the exodus of the Hebrews from captivity in Egypt [Mid-16thC.Translation of Hebrew *pesaḥ*, 'to pass without affecting', alluding to the Bible (Exodus 12:11–27) where God passes over the Israelites, while the firstborn of other families are killed.]

passport /paáss pawrt/ *n.* **1.** OFFICIAL IDENTIFICATION DOCUMENT an official document issued by the government of a country to a citizen that identifies the bearer and gives permission to travel to and from that country **2.** ANY AUTHORIZATION TO TRAVEL any authorization or official permission to travel in or through a country **3.** MEANS OF ACCESS sth that grants sb access to sth ○ *Education is the passport to a more fulfilling life.* [15thC. From French *passeport*, literally 'to pass the seaport'.]

password /paáss wurd/ *n.* **1.** WORD SECURING ACCESS a secret word or phrase that must be used by sb who wants to be allowed in somewhere **2.** COMPUT KEYED CHARACTERS GIVING COMPUTER ACCESS a sequence of characters that you have to key in to gain access to part of a computer system ○ *Don't let anyone know your password.*

past[1] /paast/ CORE MEANING: movement that involves passing or going beyond sb or sth ○ (prep) *Walk past the library and you'll arrive at the park.* ○ (adv) *She walked right past without saying a word to us.*

1. *prep., adv.* LATER later than a particular time ○ *It's twenty past seven.* ○ *It's past your bedtime.* ○ *It's half past.* **2.** *prep.* ON THE FARTHER SIDE OF STH on the farther side of or beyond sth ○ *We prefer the bakery that's just past the school.* **3.** *prep.* BEYOND A NUMBER, AMOUNT, OR POINT beyond a particular number, amount, or point, especially a point at which sth can be done ○ *Do what you like; I'm past caring.* **4.** *adv.* AGO before the present time (*archaic*) ○ *He left home six months past.* **5.** *adv.* *Scotland* AWAY away, for the sake of tidiness or for future use (*informal*) ○ *Be a good wee soul and put your toys past.* [13thC. Originally the past participle of PASS.] ◇ **past it** not as effective or vigorous as in former times, usually owing to old age (*humorous or informal*) ◇ **not put sth past sb, not put it past sb** to believe that sb is quite capable of doing sth, usually sth disreputable or outrageous (*informal*)

past[2] /paast/ *adj.* **1.** ELAPSED gone by ○ *the past few days* **2.** RELATING TO AN EARLIER TIME having existed or occurred in a previous time ○ *in a past job* **3.** ONE-TIME having formerly occupied a particular position ○ *a gathering of past presidents* **4.** GRAM EXPRESSING ACTION THAT TOOK PLACE PREVIOUSLY used to describe or relating to the verb tense that is used for an action that took place previously ■ *n.* **1.** TIME BEFORE THE PRESENT the time before the present and the events that happened then **2.** GRAM PAST TENSE the past tense of a language, or a verb form in the past tense **3.** SB'S PREVIOUS HISTORY everything that has happened previously to sb or sth ○ *She has a mysterious past.* **4.** SHAMEFUL HISTORY a shameful or scandalous earlier period in sb's life [13thC. Originally the past participle of PASS.] —**pastness** *n.*

pasta /pástə/ *n.* **1.** FOOD MADE FROM FLOUR a fresh or dried food that is usually made from flour, eggs, and water formed into a variety of shapes, e.g. macaroni or spaghetti **2.** PASTA DISH a dish made with cooked pasta [Late 19thC. Via Italian, from late Latin (see PASTE).]

paste[1] /payst/ *n.* **1.** ADHESIVE MIXTURE a soft mixture of flour and water or starch and water used as an adhesive, especially for sticking paper to sth **2.** FOOD SEMI-SOLID MIXTURE a soft mass or mixture with a consistency between a liquid and a solid **3.** COOK PASTRY DOUGH pastry dough usually made with shortening and used especially to make pie crusts **4.** FOOD FOOD SPREAD a soft food product that can be spread on sth such as bread ○ *anchovy paste* **5.** GLASS FOR IMITATION GEMS a hard, brilliant glass used to make imitation jewels **6.** PORCELAIN CLAY the clay mixture used to make porcelain ■ *vt.* **(pastes, pasting, pasted) 1.** GLUE STH TO STH ELSE to stick things together using paste **2.** COVER A SURFACE WITH PASTE to cover a surface by sticking things to it with paste **3.** SPREAD STH THICKLY to spread a soft substance onto a surface in a thick layer **4.** COMPUT PLACE TEXT IN DOCUMENT ELECTRONICALLY to place text, data, or an image into a document electronically as an addition or alteration from another location [13thC. Via Old French from late Latin *pasta* from, ultimately, Greek *passein* 'to sprinkle' (source of English *pastel*). Originally used for 'dough', the underlying sense is 'moist mixture'.] —**paster** *n.*

paste up *vt.* PRINTING to take printed pages or proofs and stick them onto separate sheets of paper so that they can be read and amended

paste[2] /payst/ **(pastes, pasting, pasted)** *vt.* to give sb a severe beating or defeat sb heavily (*informal*)

pasteboard /páyst bawrd/ *n.* THICK STIFF PAPER a stiff board made either of sheets of paper pasted together or of layers of paper pulp pressed together ■ *adj.* **1.** FLIMSY not of good quality, or not very substantial ○ *pasteboard houses* **2.** FAKE intended to pass for the genuine article

pastel /pást'l, pa stél/ *adj.* PALE IN COLOUR having a pale soft colour ■ *n.* **1.** PALE COLOUR a pale soft colour **2.** PASTE USED FOR MAKING CRAYONS a paste of powdered pigment and gum, used for making crayons **3.** CRAYON a crayon for doing pastel drawings **4.** DRAWING sth drawn using pastel crayons **5.** ART USING PASTELS the technique or process of drawing with pastels [Late 16thC. Directly or via French from Italian *pastello*, literally 'small amount of paste', from *pasta* 'paste', from late Latin (see PASTE).] —**pastellist** *n.*

pastern /pástərn/ *n.* **1.** PART OF A HORSE'S FOOT the part of a horse's foot between the fetlock and the top of the hoof **2.** BONE IN A HORSE'S FOOT either of two bones in a horse's foot that connect the hoof with the fetlock [13thC. Via Old French *pasturon*, from *pasture* 'hobble for pastured animal' (the original sense in English), from, ultimately, Latin *pascere* 'to feed' (source of English *pasture*).]

paste-up *n.* **1.** SHEETS WITH PAGES FOR CHECKING a number of sheets of paper onto which printed pages or proofs have been pasted for checking **2.** PREPARATION FOR PRINTING PLATES cards on which pieces of typesetting or artwork have been pasted to be photographed for making printing plates **3.** TECHNIQUE OF MAKING PASTE-UPS the technique or process of making paste-ups (*often used before a noun*) ○ *a paste-up artist*

Pasteur /pas túr/, **Louis** (1822–95) French scientist. He developed the process of pasteurization and invented vaccinations to induce immunity against certain viral diseases. He founded, and was the first director of, the Pasteur Institute in Paris.

pasteurization /paáschə rī záysh'n, páschə-/, **pasteurisation** *n.* treatment of a liquid such as milk by heating it in order to destroy harmful bacteria

pasteurize /paáschə rīz, páschə-/ **(-izes, -izing, -ized), pasteurise (-ises, -ising, -ised)** *vt.* to treat a liquid such as milk by heating it in order to destroy harmful bacteria [Late 19thC. Named after Louis PASTEUR, who developed it.] —**pasteurizer** *n.*

Pasteur treatment /pass tốr-/ *n.* a treatment for sb infected with rabies in which increasingly strong injections of a less infective form of the virus are given to produce antibodies against it [Late 19thC. Named after Louis PASTEUR, who devised the technique.]

pasticcio /pa stíchō/ (*plural* **-ci** /-chi/ *or* **pasticcios**) *n.* a pastiche [Mid-18thC. Via Italian, literally 'pie, pasty', from, ultimately, late Latin *pasta* (see PASTE).]

pastiche /pa stéesh/ *n.* **1.** IMITATIVE WORK a piece of creative work, e.g. in literature, drama, or art, that imitates and often satirizes another work or style **2.** MIXTURE a piece of creative work, e.g. in literature, drama, or art, that is a mixture of things borrowed from other works **3.** USE OF PASTICHE the creation or use of a pastiche [Late 19thC. Via French from Italian *pasticcio* (see PASTICCIO). The underlying sense is 'mixture' or 'medley'.]

pastille /pást'l/ *n.* **1.** SWEET a small flavoured or medicated sweet **2.** FUMIGATING SUBSTANCE a substance, usually in tablet or paste form, that is burnt to scent or fumigate a room [Mid-17thC. Via French from Latin *pastillus*, literally 'little loaf' (from the shape), from *panis* 'loaf'.]

pastime /paáss tīm/ *n.* an interest or activity that sb pursues in his or her spare time [15thC. From PASS + TIME.]

pasting /páysting/ *n.* a severe beating or a complete defeat (*informal*)

pastis /pa stéess/ *n.* a yellowish French liqueur flavoured with aniseed, often drunk as an aperitif [Early 20thC. Via French, literally 'muddle, mixture', from, ultimately, late Latin *pasta* (see PASTE).]

pastitsio /pa stítsi ō/ (*plural* **-os**) *n.* a Greek dish of minced meat mixed with cooked macaroni and topped with bechamel sauce, baked in a dish

past master *n.* **1.** EXPERT sb who has great experience and skill in doing sth **2.** FORMER MASTER sb who has held a position as master at one time, e.g. in the Freemasons

pastor /paástər/ *n.* **1.** MINISTER a Christian minister or priest in charge of a congregation **2.** SPIRITUAL ADVISER sb who is not a minister or priest but who gives spiritual advice to a group of people **3.** SHEPHERD a shepherd (*archaic*) **4.** ASIAN STARLING an Asian starling with a black head and wings and a pink body that often feeds on the parasites that live on sheep. Latin name: *Sturnus roseus.* [14thC. Via Old French *pastre* from Latin *pastor* 'herdsman, shepherd', from *past-*, the past participle stem of *pascere* 'to feed or graze'.] —**pastorship** *n.*

pastoral /paástərəl/ *adj.* **1.** RURAL relating to the countryside or to rural life ○ *pastoral living* **2.** ARTS IDEALIZING RURAL LIFE presenting an idealized image of rural life and nature ○ *pastoral poetry* **3.** CHR OF CLERGY relating to religious ministers or priests or their duties **4.** AGRIC USED FOR PASTURE used to describe land that is used as pasture **5.** GIVING ADVICE TO STUDENTS relating to the duties of a teacher who gives personal advice and support to students rather than just teaching them **6.** AGRIC OF SHEEP OR CATTLE relating to or keeping sheep or cattle ■ *n.* **1.** ARTS DESCRIPTION OF RURAL LIFE a literary work or painting that portrays rural life in an idealized way **2.** MUSIC = **pastorale 3.** CHR LETTER FROM A RELIGIOUS MINISTER a letter written by a religious minister to his or her congregation **4.** CHR BISHOP'S STAFF a staff carried by a bishop as a symbol of office [15thC. From Latin *pastoralis*, literally 'to do with herdsmen or shepherds', from *pastor* (see PASTOR).] —**pastorally** *adv.*

WORD KEY: CULTURAL NOTE

Pastoral Symphony, a composition by German composer Ludwig van Beethoven (1808). Also known as Symphony No. 6 in F major, op. 68, this widely performed work was described by Beethoven as a 'recollection of country life'. It describes a day's outing to the Viennese countryside and features peasant dances, bird song, and a storm.

pastorale /pástə raál, pástə raáli/ (*plural* **-rales** *or* **-rali**), **pastoral** /paástrəl, paástə raál/ *n.* **1.** RUSTIC OPERA an opera with a rural story and setting, popular in the 16th and 17th centuries **2.** MUSIC WITH A PASTORAL THEME a piece of music with a pastoral theme [Early 18thC. Via Italian, literally 'pastoral', from, ultimately, Latin *pastor* (see PASTOR).]

Pastoral Epistles *n.* in the Bible, the three epistles, two to Timothy and one to Titus, traditionally attributed to St Paul

pastoralism /paástrəlizəm/ *n.* **1.** LIVESTOCK RAISING the raising of livestock, especially by traditional methods, as the main economic activity of a society **2.** ARTS ARTISTIC TREATMENT OF RURAL LIFE the style in literary work or painting that portrays rural life, especially that of shepherds, in an idealized way **3.** WAY OF LIFE DEPENDENT ON LIVESTOCK a way of life that depends on raising livestock and living on its milk and meat

pastoralist /paástrəlist/ *n.* **1.** SB LIVING A PASTORAL LIFE sb who has a pastoral way of life **2.** *Aus* AUSTRALIAN LIVESTOCK FARMER a cattle or sheep farmer, especially the owner of a large area of land in the Australian outback

pastorate /paástərət/ *n.* **1.** OFFICE OF PASTOR the office, term of office, or jurisdiction of a pastor **2.** PASTORS COLLECTIVELY pastors considered as a group

past participle *n.* a participle that expresses past time or a completed action. It is used with auxiliaries to form perfect tenses in the active voice and all tenses in the passive voice. In the sentence 'I waited until he had rung the bell', the past participle is 'rung'.

past perfect *n.* VERB TENSE WITH 'HAD' a verb tense that is formed with 'had' and expresses an action that was completed at a time in the past ■ *adj.* BEING IN PAST PERFECT TENSE being in or relating to the past perfect tense

pastrami /pə straámi/ *n.* smoked and strongly seasoned beef, usually prepared from a shoulder cut, that is served cold in thin slices [Mid-20thC. Via Yiddish from Romanian *pastramă*.]

pastry /páystri/ (*plural* **-tries**) *n.* **1.** DOUGH FOR PIES a dough made with flour, water, and shortening, used to make crusts for pies **2.** FOODS MADE FROM PASTRY sweet baked food made from pastry **3.** STH MADE WITH PASTRY a pie or small cake made with pastry [15thC. Formed from PASTE on the model of Old French *pastaierie*.]

past tense *n.* a verb tense that expresses sth that happened or was done in the past. In the sentence 'I felt very proud of them', the verb 'felt' is in the past tense.

pasturage /paáschərij/ *n.* **1.** = **pasture** *n.* 1 **2.** GRAZING OF LIVESTOCK the grazing of livestock, or the right to graze livestock on a particular area of land

pasture /paáschər/ *n.* **1.** LAND FOR GRAZING grass-covered land used for grazing livestock **2.** PLANTS FOR GRAZING grass and other growing plants that are suitable food for livestock ■ *vti.* **(-tures, -turing, -tured)** GRAZE to graze, or to put livestock somewhere to graze [13thC. Via Old French from late Latin *pastura*, from *past-*, the past participle stem of Latin *pascere* 'to feed'.] ◇ **pastures new** somewhere different to work or live (*informal*) ◇ **put sb out to pasture 1.** to put a grazing animal into a field to graze **2.** to impose retirement on sb, usually on grounds of age (*informal or humorous*)

pasty[1] /pásti/ (*plural* **-ties**) *n.* a pie made from a folded round of pastry with a savoury or sweet filling in the middle [Via Old French *pasté(e)* from, ultimately, late Latin *pasta* (see PASTE)]

pasty[2] /páysti/ *adj.* **(-ier, -iest) 1.** UNHEALTHILY PALE having a pale unhealthy appearance **2.** RESEMBLING PASTE resembling paste in consistency, colour, or texture ■ *n.* (*plural* **-ies**) NIPPLE COVERING either of a pair of small adhesive coverings for a woman's nipples, worn usually by erotic dancers [Early 17thC. Formed from PASTE.] —**pastily** *adv.* —**pastiness** *n.*

PA system *abbr.* public-address system. = **PA**

pat[1] /pat/ *vt.* **(pats, patting, patted) 1.** STRIKE LIGHTLY to strike sth lightly with the palm of the hand or sth flat **2.** LAY THE HAND ON STH REPEATEDLY to touch sb or sth repeatedly with the palm of your hand, e.g. to show affection or to congratulate sb ○ *I patted the child's curly head.* **3.** SHAPE STH WITH THE HANDS to shape or smooth sth with the hands or with a flat object ■ *n.* **1.** LIGHT BLOW a light blow with the palm of the hand or with a flat object **2.** LIGHT TOUCH a light, usually repeated, touch with the hand to show affection or to congratulate sb **3.** SOFT SOUND the sound made by a light blow with the hand or with a flat object, or by a light footstep **4.** SMALL PIECE a small piece of sth soft, especially butter [14thC. Imitative of the sound of patting.] ◇ **a pat on the back** an expression of praise or congratulation (*informal*) ○ *You deserve a pat on the back for getting the work done so quickly.*

pat² /pat/ *adv.* **1.** EXACTLY in an exact, accurate, or fluent way ○ *He has his lines off pat.* **2.** OPPORTUNELY at the most appropriate time or place ■ *adj.* **1.** GLIB so easily and readily produced as to suggest lack of proper thought ○ *pat answers* **2.** CARDS NOT TO BE IMPROVED used to describe a poker hand that is not likely to be improved by drawing additional cards [Late 16thC. Origin uncertain: probably from PAT¹, the underlying sense being 'hitting the mark'.]

Pat *n.* an offensive term for an Irishman (*offensive*) [Early 19thC. Pet-form of the name *Patrick*, common in Ireland.]

pat. *abbr.* **1.** patent **2.** patented

pataca /pə taákə/ *n.* **1.** UNIT OF CURRENCY the basic unit of currency of Macau, worth 100 avos **2.** COIN WORTH A PATACA a coin worth one pataca [Mid-19thC. Via Portuguese from Arabic *abū ṭāqah*, a kind of coin.]

patagium /pə táyji əm/ (*plural* **-a** /-ə/) *n.* **1.** FOLD OF MAMMAL SKIN a loose fold of skin between the fore and hind limbs in some mammals, used as an aid to flying or gliding by, e.g. bats and flying lemurs **2.** FOLD OF BIRD SKIN a thin fold of skin between a bird's wing and its shoulder [Early 19thC. From Latin, literally 'gold edging on a tunic'.]

Patagonia /páttə g-ni ə/ *n.* region of southern Argentina, between the Andes Mountains and the South Atlantic Ocean. Area: 777,000 sq. km/300,000 sq. mi. —**Patagonian** *n.*, *adj.*

pataphysics /páttə fízziks/ *n.* an imaginary science invented by the French absurdist dramatist Alfred Jarry, supposedly investigating and explaining what is beyond metaphysics (*takes a singular verb*) [Mid-20thC. Via French *pataphysique*, an alteration of Greek *ta epi ta metaphusika*, 'that which comes after the metaphysics'.]

patch /pach/ *n.* **1.** STH THAT COVERS OR MENDS a piece of material used to cover, strengthen, or mend a hole in sth ○ *an elbow patch* **2.** SMALL AREA a small area of sth within a larger one ○ *a patch of ice* **3.** SMALL GROWING AREA a small area of land used for growing a particular crop ○ *a cabbage patch* **4.** PERIOD a period of time in which a particular situation exists ○ *a relationship going through a rough patch* **5.** AREA OF CONTROL an area under sb's control or jurisdiction ○ *They warned him to stay off their patch.* **6.** EYE SHIELD a pad worn over an injured or missing eye ○ *an eye patch* **7.** MED COVER FOR WOUND a piece of material used to cover a wound **8.** SEWN-ON BADGE a cloth badge sewn onto clothing as identification, a sign of rank, or to commemorate sth **9.** COMPUT SOFTWARE BUG CORRECTOR OR UPDATE a fragment of program code made available to fix a bug in a software application or to add a new feature before an updated version of the application is released ○ *a patch available on the Internet* **10.** MED, PHARM DRUG-IMPREGNATED MATERIAL a piece of material impregnated with a drug and worn on the skin to allow the gradual absorption of the drug ○ *a nicotine patch* **11.** FASHION ARTIFICIAL BEAUTY SPOT a small piece of black silk or velvet, often in a distinct shape, worn on the face by men and women as an adornment in the 17th and 18th centuries ■ *vt.* (**patches, patching, patched**) **1.** REPAIR STH WITH MATERIAL to cover or mend a hole in sth or to strengthen a weak place using cloth or other substance **2.** MAKE STH FROM CLOTH PIECES to make sth by sewing together pieces of fabric **3.** COMPUT AMEND A PROGRAM USING A PATCH to fix or update software using a patch **4.** TELECOM CONNECT A CALL to connect one telephone or radio caller with another or transfer a call to somewhere else ○ *Patch me through to headquarters.* [14thC. Origin uncertain: perhaps ultimately from a dialect variant of Old French *piece* (see PIECE).] ◇ **not a patch on sb** *or* **sth** not nearly as good as sb or sth (*informal*) ◇ **hit a bad patch**, **strike a bad patch** go through a period of misfortune or difficulty

patch up *vt.* **1.** MEND STH HURRIEDLY to mend or assemble sth hurriedly or as a temporary measure **2.** MAKE FRIENDS AGAIN to become friends with sb again after an argument **3.** GIVE TREATMENT TO SB to give sb medical treatment for an injury (*informal*)

patch board, **patch panel** *n.* an electrical panel with numerous sockets into which electrical cords (**patch cords**) can be plugged to form temporary circuits. Telephone exchanges used to use patch boards before the advent of electronic switchboards.

patchouli /páchooli, pə choóli/, **pachouli** *n.* **1.** TROPICAL ASIAN SHRUB a tropical Asian shrub of the mint family whose leaves produce a fragrant oil. Latin name: *Pogostemon cablin.* **2.** AROMATIC OIL the aromatic oil obtained from the patchouli shrub, used in perfumes and in aromatherapy [Mid-19thC. From Tamil *pacculi*.]

patch pocket *n.* a pocket made by sewing a patch of fabric on the outside of a garment

patch test *n.* a test for allergies in which small pads impregnated with allergens are applied to sb's skin to check whether there is any negative reaction

patchwork /pách wurk/ *n.* **1.** PATCHES SEWN TOGETHER needlework in which patches or scraps of fabric are sewn together to make a decorative cover ○ *a patchwork quilt* **2.** MIXTURE sth made up of many different parts

patchy /páchi/ (**-ier, -iest**) *adj.* **1.** OCCURRING IN PATCHES occurring only in patches, rather than throughout an area, or consisting only of patches, rather than a large expanse ○ *patchy fog* **2.** OF VARYING QUALITY good only at times or in places —**patchily** *adv.* —**patchiness** *n.*

patd *abbr.* patented

pate /payt/ *n.* the head, especially the top of the head (*archaic or humorous*) [14thC. Origin unknown.]

pâté /páttay, pátti/ *n.* a paste made from meat, fish, or vegetables, often served as an appetizer [Mid-19thC. Via French from Old French *paste* (see PASTE).]

pâté de foie gras /páttay də fwaà graà, pátti-/ (*plural* **pâtés de foie gras** /páttay də fwaà graà, pátti-/) *n.* a rich pâté made from the livers of geese that are fattened specifically for this purpose [From French, literally 'pâté of fatty liver']

patella /pə téllə/ (*plural* **-lae** /-lee/ *or* **-las**) *n.* a kneecap (*technical*) [15thC. From Latin, literally 'small shallow dish' (from the shape), from *patina* (see PATEN).] —**patellar** *adj.*

patellate /pə téllət/, **patelliform** /pə télli fawrm/ *adj.* BIOL shaped like a saucer or a shallow cup

paten /pátt'n/, **patin**, **patine** *n.* a shallow metal plate, often made of gold or silver, used to carry the bread at the celebration of the Christian ceremony of Communion [13thC. Directly or via French *patène* from Latin *patena*, *patina* 'shallow dish or pan', from Greek *patanē* 'plate'.]

patency /páyt'nssi/ *n.* **1.** OBVIOUSNESS the obvious nature of sth **2.** MED UNBLOCKED CONDITION the naturally open and unblocked state of an artery, duct, or other tube in the body

patent /páyt'nt, pátt'nt/ *n.* **1.** EXCLUSIVE RIGHT TO MARKET AN INVENTION an exclusive right officially granted by a government to an inventor to make or sell an invention **2.** DOCUMENT GRANTING A PATENT an official document setting out the terms of a patent **3.** INVENTION PROTECTED BY PATENT an invention for which a patent has been granted **4.** DOCUMENT GRANTING A RIGHT any official document that grants a right to sb ■ *adj.* **1.** CLEAR OR OBVIOUS very obvious and not needing any further explanation or not being open to doubt ○ *his patent discomfiture* **2.** LAW OPEN FOR INSPECTION used to describe a legal document that is accessible to anyone for inspection **3.** OF PATENTS relating to or dealing in patents ○ *a patent lawyer* **4.** PROTECTED BY PATENT protected by a patent from being copied or sold by sb else **5.** MED UNBLOCKED used to describe an artery, duct, or other tube in the body that is naturally open and unblocked **6.** BOT SPREADING used to describe plant parts that spread out widely from a centre ■ *vt.* (**-ents, -enting, -ented**) PROTECT RIGHTS TO STH BY PATENT to obtain a patent on or for sth, especially an invention [14thC. Directly or via French from Latin *patent-*, the present participle stem of *patere* 'to lie open'.]

patentee /páyt'n tee, pátt'n-/ *n.* a person or group to whom a patent has been granted

patent leather *n.* leather that has been treated with lacquer to give it a hard, glossy surface [From the idea of protection]

patent log *n.* NAUT an instrument used to measure a ship's speed or the distance it has travelled by means of fins that rotate as the instrument is dragged through the water behind the vessel [Because it was patented]

patently /páyt'ntli, pátt-/ *adv.* in a way that can easily be seen or understood ○ *He was patently ill at ease.*

Patent Office *n.* a government office that evaluates patent claims and grants patents

patentor /páyt'n táwr, pátt'n-/ *n.* a person or office that grants a patent

patent right *n.* the exclusive right to make or sell sth that is granted to sb by a patent

Patent Rolls *npl.* the register of patents granted in the United Kingdom

patent still *n.* an alcohol still that uses steam heat and runs continuously [Because it was patented]

pater /páytər/ *n.* sb's father (*dated slang or humorous*) [14thC. From Latin, 'father'.]

---- WORD KEY: ORIGIN ----

The Latin word *pater*, from which **pater** is derived, is also the source of English *paternal*, *patrician*, *patrimony*, *patron*, and *pattern*. Its ultimate Indo-European ancestor also produced English *father* and *patriot*.

----

paterfamilias /páytərfə mílli ass, páttər-/ (*plural* **patresfamilias** /paà trayz-/) *n.* a man in the role of father and head of a household [15thC. From Latin, literally 'father of a family'.]

paternal /pə túrn'l/ *adj.* **1.** OF FATHERS OR FATHERHOOD relating to fathers or typical of a father **2.** RELATED THROUGH A FATHER being on a father's side of a family ○ *her paternal grandfather* **3.** INHERITED FROM A FATHER inherited or deriving from a father [15thC. Via late Latin *paternalis*, from, ultimately, Latin *pater* 'father'.] —**paternally** *adv.*

paternalism /pə túrn'lizəm/ *n.* a style of government or management, or an approach to personal relationships, in which the desire to help, advise, and protect may neglect individual choice and personal responsibility —**paternalist** *n.* —**paternalistic** /pə túrnə lístik/ *adj.* —**paternalistically** /-lístikli/ *adv.*

paternity /pə túrnəti/ *n.* **1.** FATHERHOOD a man's role or status as a father **2.** ANCESTRY descent from a father **3.** ORIGIN the origin or authorship of sth (*literary*) [15thC. Directly or via French *paternité* from late Latin *paternitas* from, ultimately, Latin *pater* 'father'.]

paternity leave *n.* time off work that an employer grants to a man whose partner has just had, or is about to have, a baby

paternity suit *n.* a lawsuit brought by a woman against a man whom she claims is the father of her child and therefore liable for contributing to the child's financial support

paternity test *n.* a medical test using DNA fingerprinting or other genetic information to determine whether or not a man is the father of a particular child

paternoster /páttər nóstər, -nostər/ *n.* **1.** paternoster, **Paternoster** CHR LORD'S PRAYER in the Roman Catholic Church, the Lord's Prayer, or a recitation of it **2.** CHR LARGE BEAD IN A ROSARY in Roman Catholicism, a large bead in a rosary, used to indicate when the Lord's Prayer is to be recited **3.** WORDS IN PRAYER OR ATTEMPTED MAGIC a set form of words used in prayer or in attempting magic **4.** NONSTOP LIFT a doorless lift in which compartments move continuously and people step on and off as they wish [Pre-12thC. From Latin *pater noster* 'our father', the first two words of the Lord's Prayer.]

Paterson /páttərssən/, **Banjo** (1864–1941) Australian poet. His works include *The Man from Snowy River and Other Verses* (1895) and the lyrics to the song 'Waltzing Matilda'. Real name **Andrew Barton Paterson**.

path /paath/ *n.* **1.** TRODDEN TRACK a track that has been made by people using it continuously **2.** SURFACED TRACK a surfaced track made for walking or cycling **3.** COURSE a route along which sth moves ○ *the path of the Earth's orbit round the Sun* **4.** COURSE OF ACTION a course of action or a way of living **5.** COMPUT ROUTE TO A COMPUTER FILE the route that a computer operating system follows through the directories on a disk to locate a file, or the sequence of keyed characters that identifies this route [Old English *pæth*. Ultimately from an Indo-European word meaning 'to tread', which is also the ancestor of English *find, pontiff,* and *sputnik.*] ◇ **lead sb up the garden path** to deceive or mislead sb (*informal*) ◇ **the primrose path** an enjoyable, easy way of life considered to be the route to ruin or degeneration

path. *abbr.* pathology

-path *suffix.* **1.** sb with a particular disorder ○ *neuropath* **2.** sb who practices a particular type of treatment ○ *osteopath* **3.** sb who possesses a particular ability ○ *telepath* [Back-formation from -PATHY]

Pathan /pə taán/ (*plural* **-than** *or* **-thans**) *n.* a member of a people that lives in Afghanistan, where Pathans are the largest ethnic group, and in parts of Pakistan [Mid-17thC. From Hindi *Paṭhān.*]

pathetic /pə théttik/ *adj.* **1. PITIFUL** provoking or expressing feelings of pity **2. CONTEMPTIBLY INADEQUATE** so inadequate as to be laughable or contemptible (*informal*) [Late 16thC. Via French *pathétique* from, ultimately, Greek *pathētikos* 'sensitive', which was formed, ultimately, from *pathos* 'feeling' (source of English *pathos*). The underlying sense is 'moving, arousing emotion'.] — **pathetically** *adv.*

WORD KEY: SYNONYMS

See Synonyms at ***moving***.

pathetic fallacy *n.* the attribution of human characteristics to nature or to inanimate objects, as in the phrase 'the angry waves'

pathfinder /paáth fīndər/ *n.* sb who discovers a route, especially through unexplored territories or uncharted areas of knowledge —**pathfinding** *n.*

patho- *prefix.* disease ○ *pathogen* [From Greek *pathos* (see PATHOS)]

pathogen /páthəjən, -jen/ *n.* sth that can cause disease, such as a bacterium or a virus

pathogenesis /páthə jénnəssiss/, **pathogeny** /pə thójjəni/ *n.* the cause, development, and effects of a disease —**pathogenetic** /páthəjə néttik/ *adj.*

pathogenic /páthə jénnik/ *adj.* **1. CAUSING DISEASE** causing disease, or able to cause disease **2. OF THE CAUSES OF DISEASE** relating to the causes and development of diseases

pathognomonic /páthəgnə mónnik/ *adj.* MED used to describe a symptom or sign that indicates almost beyond doubt the correct diagnosis of a disease [Early 17thC. From Greek *pathognōmonikos*, literally 'that is a judge of disease', from *pathos* 'disease' + *gnōmōn* 'judge'.]

pathol. *abbr.* **1.** pathological **2.** pathology

pathological /páthə lójjik'l/ *adj.* **1.** MED **OF PATHOLOGY** relating to pathology or used in pathology **2.** MED **DISEASE** relating to disease or arising from disease **3. EXTREME** uncontrolled or unreasonable ○ *a pathological fear of heights* [Late 17thC. From Greek *pathologikos*, from *pathos* 'disease'.] —**pathologically** *adv.*

pathologist /pə thóllәjist/ *n.* a scientist who is skilled in identifying the nature, origin, progress, and cause of disease, especially one who determines the cause of sb's death by a post-mortem

pathology /pə thólləji/ (*plural* **-gies**) *n.* **1. STUDY OF DISEASE** the scientific study of the nature, origin, progress, and cause of disease **2. PROCESSES OF A PARTICULAR DISEASE** the processes of a particular disease, observable either with the naked eye or by microscopy, or, at a molecular level, as inferred from biochemical tests **3. CONDITION THAT IS NOT NORMAL** any condition that is a deviation from the normal [Late 16thC. Directly or via French *pathologie* from medieval Latin *pathologia*, from Greek *pathos* 'disease'.]

pathophysiology /páthō fízzi ólləji/ *n.* the disturbance of function that a disease causes in an organ, as distinct from any changes in structure that might be caused

pathos /páy thoss/ *n.* **1. QUALITY THAT AROUSES PITY** the quality in sth that makes people feel pity or sadness **2. EXPRESSION OF PITY** feelings of pity, especially when they are expressed in some way [Late 16thC. From Greek, 'feeling, disease' (source also of English *pathetic*).]

pathway /paáth way/ *n.* **1. PATH** a path or route **2.** MED **SEQUENCE OF REACTIONS** a sequence of biochemical reactions involved in a metabolic process

-pathy *suffix.* **1.** disorder, disease ○ *retinopathy* **2.** system of treating medical disorders ○ *hydropathy* **3.** feeling, perception ○ *telepathy* [From Greek *-patheia*, from *pathos* (see PATHOS)] —**-pathic** *suffix.*

patience /páysh'nss/ *n.* **1. CAPACITY FOR WAITING** the ability to endure waiting or delay without becoming annoyed or upset, or to persevere calmly when faced with difficulties ○ *This job needs time and patience.* **2. ABILITY TO TOLERATE TRYING CIRCUMSTANCES** the ability to tolerate being hurt, provoked, or annoyed without complaint or loss of temper **3.** CARDS **CARD GAME FOR ONE** a card game for one player. US term **solitaire** [12thC. Via French from Latin *patientia*, from *patient-* (see PATIENT).]

patient /páysh'nt/ *adj.* **1. CAPABLE OF WAITING** able to endure waiting or delay without becoming annoyed or upset or to persevere calmly when faced with difficulties **2. ABLE TO TOLERATE DIFFICULT CIRCUMSTANCES** able to tolerate being hurt, provoked, or annoyed without complaint or loss of temper ■ *n.* **SB GIVEN MEDICAL TREATMENT** sb who is being given medical treatment [14thC. Via French from Latin *patient-*, the present participle stem of *pati* 'to suffer' (source of English *passion*).] —**patiently** *adv.*

patin *n.* = **paten**

patina /páttinə/ *n.* **1. THIN GREEN LAYER ON COPPER** a thin layer formed by corrosion on the surface of some metals and minerals, especially the green layer that covers copper and bronze and is valued for its colour **2. SURFACE SHEEN** a pleasing surface sheen on sth that develops with age or frequent handling **3. SUPERFICIAL LAYER** any thin or superficial layer on sth [Mid-18thC. Via Italian from Latin (see PATEN).] — **patinated** /pátti naytid/ *adj.*

patine *n.* = **paten**

patio /pátti ō/ (*plural* **-os**) *n.* **1. PAVED AREA OUTSIDE A HOUSE** a paved area adjoining a house, used for outdoor dining, growing plants in containers, and recreation **2. ROOFLESS COURTYARD** a roofless inner courtyard typical of a Spanish-style house [Early 19thC. From Spanish, literally 'courtyard of a house', of unknown origin.]

patio doors *npl.* a pair of glazed doors in an outside wall of a house that open onto a patio

patisserie /pə téssəri, -tíssəri/ *n.* **1. CAKE SHOP** a bakery that specializes in pastries and cakes **2. CAKES** sweet pastries or cakes collectively [Late 16thC. From French *pâtisserie*, from *patissier* 'pastry chef', from, ultimately, late Latin *pasta* (see PASTE).]

Pátmos /pát moss/ island in the Aegean Sea, one of the Greek Dodecanese island group. It is thought to be the place where John the Evangelist wrote the biblical book of Revelation. Population: 2,650 (1995). Area: 34 sq. km/13 sq. mi.

Patna /pátnə/ capital city of Bihar State, northern India. Population: 916,980 (1991).

Patna rice /pátnə-/ *n.* a variety of long-grained rice; used in savoury dishes [Mid-19thC. Named after PATNA, where it is grown.]

Pat. Off. *abbr.* Patent Office

patois /pát waa/ (*plural* **patois** /pát waaz/) *n.* **1. REGIONAL DIALECT** a regional form of a language, used informally and usually containing elements regarded as nonstandard **2. JARGON** the jargon used by a particular group [Mid-17thC. From French 'native speech', of uncertain origin: probably from *patoier*, literally 'to paw roughly', from *patte* 'paw' (probable source of English *patrol*).]

pat. pend. *abbr.* patent pending

patr- *prefix.* = **patri-** (*used before vowels*)

Patras /pə tráss, pátrəss/ city in Greece, on the northwestern Peloponnesian Coast, facing the Ionian Sea. It is the country's main port. Population: 152,570 (1991).

patresfamilias plural of **paterfamilias**

patri- *prefix.* father, paternal ○ *patrilineal* [From Latin *patr-*, the stem of *pater*, and Greek *patr-*, the stem of *patēr* (see PATER)]

patrial /páytri əl, páttri əl/ *n.* formerly, sb entitled to enter and stay in the United Kingdom without being regarded as an immigrant, e.g. sb from a Commonwealth country [Early 17thC. Via French or medieval Latin *patrialis* 'of one's country' (the original sense in English), from, ultimately, Latin *pater* 'father'.]

patriarch /páytri aark, páttri-/ (*plural* **-archs**) *n.* **1. HEAD OF A FAMILY** a man who is the head of a family or group **2. RESPECTED ELDERLY MAN** a respected and experienced elderly man within a group or family **3.** BIBLE **BIBLICAL ANCESTOR** a figure mentioned in the Bible considered as the ancestor of the whole human race, e.g. Adam or Noah **4.** BIBLE **HEBREW LEADER** any of the ancestors and religious leaders of the Hebrew people in Hebrew Scriptures, especially in the book of Genesis, e.g. Abraham, Isaac, or Jacob **5. OLDEST MEMBER** the oldest male member of sth, such as a community of people or a herd of livestock **6. FOUNDER** a man who is a founder of sth **7.** CHR **EASTERN ORTHODOX BISHOP** in the Eastern Orthodox Church, a bishop of the sees of Constantinople, Alexandria, Antioch, or Jerusalem, and also of Russia, Romania, or Serbia **8.** CHR **SENIOR ROMAN CATHOLIC BISHOP** in the Roman Catholic Church, a leading bishop in a Uniat church **9.** CHR **DIGNITARY OF THE LATTER-DAY SAINTS** a high dignitary of the Latter-Day Saints with the power to invoke blessings, especially one of the Melchizedek order of priests [12thC. Directly and via French from ecclesiastical Latin, from Greek *patriarkhēs*, literally 'head of a family', from *patria* 'family'.]

patriarchal /páytri aárk'l, pátri-/ *adj.* **1. RELATING TO A PATRIARCH** relating to or held to be typical of a patriarch **2. TYPICAL OF A CULTURE RULED BY MEN** relating to or typical of a culture in which men are the most powerful members **3.** CHR **RULED BY A BISHOP** in Roman Catholicism, governed by a bishop —**patriarchally** *adv.*

patriarchal cross *n.* a Christian cross with a second and shorter horizontal bar above the main bar

patriarchalism /páytri aárkəlizəm, páttri-/ *n.* institutionalized domination by men, with women being regarded as socially or constitutionally inferior

patriarchate /páytri aarkət, páttri-/ *n.* **1.** CHR **OFFICE OF A CHRISTIAN PATRIARCH** the office, term of office, area of jurisdiction, or residence of a patriarch of a Christian church **2.** = **patriarchy** [Early 17thC. Via medieval Latin *patriarchatus*, from, ultimately, ecclesiastical Latin *patriarcha* (see PATRIARCH).]

patriarchy /páytri aarki, páttri-/ (*plural* **-chies**) *n.* **1. SOCIAL SYSTEM IN WHICH MEN DOMINATE** a social system in which men are regarded as the authority within the family and society, and in which power and possessions are passed on from father to son **2. PATRIARCHAL SOCIETY** a form of society based on a system of patriarchy [Mid-16thC. Via medieval Latin *patriarchia* from, ultimately, Greek *patriarkhēs* (see PATRIARCH).]

patrician /pə trísh'n/ *n.* **1. ARISTOCRATIC ROMAN** a member of an aristocratic family of ancient Rome whose privileges included the exclusive right to hold certain offices **2. NONHEREDITARY BYZANTINE TITLE** a nonhereditary honorary title bestowed by Byzantine emperors on people who had been of great service to the empire **3. ARISTOCRAT** a member of the aristocracy in any country **4. SB TYPICAL OF THE UPPER CLASS** sb who has the qualities and manners typical of those of the upper class ■ *adj.* **1. OF PATRICIANS** relating to patricians, or belonging to a class of patricians **2. ARISTOCRATIC** typical of aristocrats or the upper class **3.** POL **OPPOSED TO DEMOCRACY** against the idea that people in all social classes should have voting rights [15thC. Via French *patricien* from Latin *patricius* 'of a noble father', from *pater* 'father'.]

patriciate /pə tríshi ət/ *n.* **1. RANK OF PATRICIAN** the position or rank of a patrician **2. PATRICIANS AS A GROUP** the social class to which patricians belong [Mid-17thC. From Latin *patriciatus*, from *patricius* (see PATRICIAN).]

patricide /páttri sīd, páytri-/ *n.* **1. MURDER OF OWN FATHER** the murder of a father by his own child or children **2. MURDERER OF OWN FATHER** sb who murders his or her own father [Late 16thC. From Late Latin *patricidium*, from Latin *pater* 'father'.] —**patricidal** /páttri sīd'l, páytri-/ *adj.*

Patrick /páttrik/, **St** (389?–461?) British-born Irish churchman. He spread Christianity throughout Ireland, and reorganized the church there. He is the patron saint of Ireland. Known as **the Apostle of Ireland**

patriclinous /pə trɪ́klinəss/, **patroclinous** *adj.* descended or inherited from the men's line [Early 20thC. Coined from PATRI- + Greek *klinein* 'to lean'.]

patrilineage /páttrə lɪnni ij/ *n.* **1. DESCENT ON THE FATHER'S SIDE** descent traced through the male line **2. ANCESTRAL GROUP ON THE FATHER'S SIDE** a group of people who are related to each other on the father's side of a family

patrilineal /páttrə lɪnni əl/, **patrilinear** /-ər/ *adj.* used to describe family relationships traced through the male line, or societies in which only such relationships are recognized —**patrilineally** *adv.*

patrilocal /páttri lṓk'l/ *adj.* used to describe a custom in which the wife goes to live with the husband's family or people after marriage, or a society in which this custom prevails —**patrilocally** /páttri lṓk'li/ *adv.*

patrimony /páttrimǝni/ (*plural* **-nies**) *n.* **1. INHERITANCE FROM A FATHER** an inheritance from a father or man ancestor **2. HERITAGE** the things that one generation has inherited from its ancestors **3.** CHR **ESTATE BELONGING TO A CHURCH** an estate or endowment that belongs to a church [14thC. Via French from Latin *patrimonium*, from *pater* 'father'.] —**patrimonial** /páttri mṓni əl/ *adj.* —**patrimonially** /-mṓni əli/ *adv.*

patriot /páttri ət, páy-/ *n.* sb who proudly supports or defends his or her country and its way of life [Late 16thC. Via French from late Latin *patriota* 'fellow countryman', from, ultimately, Greek *patris* 'fatherland'.] —**patriotic** /páttri óttik, páytri-/ *adj.* —**patriotically** /-óttikli/ *adv.*

patriotism /páttri ə tizəm, páy-/ *n.* pride in or devotion to the country sb was born in or is a citizen of

patristic /pə trɪ́stik/, **patristical** /pə trɪ́stik'l/ *adj.* CHR relating to the early Christian writers such as St Augustine or St Ambrose whose works have helped to shape the Christian church [Mid-19thC. From German *Patristik*, from Latin *pater* 'father'.] —**patristically** *adv.*

patristics /pə trɪ́stiks/ *n.* the study of the writings and lives of the early Christian theologians (*takes a singular verb*) [Mid-19thC. Via German *Patristik* from Latin *pater.*]

patro- *prefix.* = **patri-**

patroclinous *adj.* = **patriclinous**

Patroclus /pə trókləss/ *n.* in Greek mythology, a friend of Achilles and a warrior in the Trojan War. When Hector killed Patroclus, Achilles avenged his death by killing Hector.

patrol /pə trṓl/ *n.* **1. REGULAR TOUR MADE BY A GUARD** a regular tour made of a place in order to guard it or to maintain order **2. SB CARRYING OUT A PATROL** a person or group that carries out a patrol **3.** MIL **MILITARY UNIT ON A MISSION** a military unit sent on a particular mission, e.g. to carry out an attack or reconnaissance **4.** SCOUTING **SUBDIVISION OF A SCOUT TROOP** a subdivision of a troop of Scouts or Guides ■ *vti.* (**-trols, -trolling, -trolled**) **GO ON PATROL** to guard or protect a place ○ *the troops patrolling the border* [Mid-17thC. Directly or via German *Patrolle* from French *patrouiller*, originally 'to walk through mud in a military camp', from, ultimately, Old French *patte* 'paw' (source of English *patois*).]

patrol car *n.* = **squad car**

patrolman /pə trṓlmən/ (*plural* **patrolmen** /-mən/) *n.* **1. MECHANIC PROVIDING BREAKDOWN SERVICE** an employee of a motoring organization who patrols an area and responds to calls from members **2.** *US* **PATROLLING POLICE OFFICER** a police officer who patrols a beat

patrology /pə trólləji/ *n.* CHR the study of the writings of the Fathers of the Christian church [Early 17thC. From Greek *patēr* 'father'.] —**patrological** /páttrə lójjik'l/ *adj.* —**patrologist** /pə trólləjist/ *n.*

patrol wagon *n. US, ANZ* an enclosed police vehicle for transporting prisoners

patron /páytrən/ *n.* **1. SPONSOR** sb who gives money or other support to sb or sth, especially in the arts **2. REGULAR CUSTOMER** a customer, especially a regular one, of a shop or business **3.** RELIG = **patron saint 4.** HIST **ROMAN SLAVE MASTER** a slave master in ancient Rome who freed a slave but retained some rights over him or her **5.** CHR **SB ABLE TO MAKE CHURCH APPOINTMENTS** sb who holds the right to appoint a member of the clergy to an ecclesiastical benefice in the Church of England [14thC. Via French from Latin *patronus*, literally 'one who protects, as a father does', from *pater* 'father'.] —**patronal** /pə trṓn'l/ *adj.* —**patronly** /páytrənli/ *adj.*

WORD KEY: SYNONYMS

See Synonyms at ***backer***.

patronage /páttrənij/ *n.* **1. SUPPORT OF A PATRON** the encouragement, monetary support, or influence of a patron **2. BUSINESS PROVIDED BY CUSTOMER** the trade that a regular customer brings to a shop or business (*formal*) **3. CONDESCENDING KINDNESS** support or kindness offered in a condescending way **4. POWER TO MAKE APPOINTMENTS** the political power to grant privileges or appoint people to positions **5. APPOINTMENTS ASSIGNED BY A POLITICIAN** the appointments or privileges that a politician can give to loyal supporters **6.** CHR **RIGHT OF ECCLESIASTICAL APPOINTMENT** the right to appoint a member of the clergy to an ecclesiastical benefice in the Church of England [14thC. From French, from *patron* (see PATRON).]

patronize /páttrə nīz/ (**-izes, -izing, -ized**), **patronise** (**-ises, -ising, -ised**) *v.* **1.** *vti.* **BE CONDESCENDING TO** to treat sb as if he or she were less intelligent or knowledgeable than yourself **2.** *vt.* **BE A REGULAR CUSTOMER OF** to be a regular customer of a particular shop or business (*formal*) **3.** *vt.* **SUPPORT SB** to give money or other material support to sb or sth, especially in the arts —**patronizer** *n.*

patronizing /páttrə nīzing/, **patronising** *adj.* treating sb as if he or she is less intelligent or knowledgeable than yourself —**patronizingly** *adv.*

patron saint *n.* a saint who is believed to be the special guardian of sb or sth, especially a country, trade, or group of people

patronymic /páttrə nímmik/ *adj.* **DERIVED FROM A MAN ANCESTOR'S NAME** used to describe a name derived from a man ancestor's name, especially one that adds a prefix, e.g. 'Mac-', or a suffix, e.g. '-son', to the earlier name ■ *n.* **PATRONYMIC NAME** a patronymic name [Early 17thC. Via late Latin *patronymicus* from Greek *patrōnumikos*, from *patrōnumos* 'father's name'.]

patsy /pátsi/ (*plural* **-sies**) *n.* sb who is easily victimized, cheated, or manipulated (*insult*) [Late 19thC. Origin uncertain: perhaps from Italian *pazzo* 'fool'.]

pattée /páttay, pátti/ *adj.* used to describe a cross with triangular arms that widen towards the ends [15thC. From French, from *patte* 'paw'.]

patten /pátt'n/ *n.* a clog, sandal, or overshoe with a raised wooden sole to raise the wearer's feet above mud [14thC. From French *patin*, from *patte* 'paw' (source of English *patrol*).]

patter[1] /páttər/ *vi.* (**-ters, -tering, -tered**) **1. MAKE A QUICK TAPPING SOUND** to make a quick light tapping sound on sth ○ *The rain pattered against the window.* **2. STEP LIGHTLY** to move or run with short quick light steps ○ *She pattered across the floor in her pyjamas.* ■ *n.* **TAPPING NOISE** a quick light tapping sound [Early 17thC. Formed from PAT 'to hit', with the literal sense 'to keep on hitting', thought to suggest the action.]

patter[2] /páttər/ *n.* **1. GLIB AND RAPID TALK** the fast well-prepared talk of someone such as a comedian or salesperson **2. JARGON** the language that belongs to a specific group or class of people **3. SMALL TALK** meaningless empty chatter ■ *v.* (**-ters, -tering, -tered**) **1.** *vi.* **TALK QUICKLY** to speak rapidly and glibly **2.** *vt.* **REPEAT STH RAPIDLY** to repeat sth quickly in a mechanical way [14thC. Shortening of PATERNOSTER. The modern meaning 'fast speech' evolved from 'to mumble prayers quickly' (the way the paternoster was said in church) via 'to speak quickly and glibly'.]

pattern /pátt'n/ *n.* **1. DESIGN** a repeated decorative design, e.g. on fabric ○ *a zigzag pattern* **2. REGULAR FORM** a regular or repetitive form, order, or arrangement ○ *a predictable pattern of behaviour* **3. PROTOTYPE** an original design or model from which exact copies can be made **4. PLAN FOR MAKING STH** a plan or model used as a guide for making sth ○ *a knitting pattern* **5. GOOD EXAMPLE** a model that is considered to be worthy of imitation **6. REGULAR WAY OF DOING STH** a regular or standard way of moving or behaving ○ *the flight patterns of birds* **7. SAMPLE** a specimen of a piece of fabric, wallpaper, or other material **8.** METALL **MODEL USED FOR MAKING A MOULD** a wood, plaster, or metal shape used to make a mould for casting in a foundry. The original model is often slightly oversize to allow for the contraction on cooling. **9.** ARMS **GUNSHOTS ON TARGET** marks made by shots from a gun on a target **10.** ARMS **SPREAD OF SPENT PROJECTILES** the dispersal of projectiles such as artillery shells and shrapnel on the ground around a target ■ *vt.* (**-terns, -terning, -terned**) **1. MIMIC** to imitate the design of sth **2. PUT A PATTERN ON** to make sth into, or decorate sth with, a repeated decorative design [14thC. Via Old French *patron* 'pattern', also 'patron', from Latin *patronus* 'patron'. The underlying meaning is of a patron commissioning work and providing a model or example to be copied.]

patterning /pátt'ning/ *n.* a design or configuration that is in accordance with a pattern

patter song *n.* a comic song, especially in the works of Gilbert and Sullivan, that consists of words that are sung together in rapid succession

USMA Archives, West Point

George S. Patton

Patton /pátt'n/, **George S.** (1885–1945) US general. In World War II he commanded the Third Army in France, successfully defeating the Germans.

patty /pátti/ (*plural* **-ties**) *n.* **1. FLAT PORTION OF FOOD** a small flat individual cake made from minced meat, vegetables, or other food **2. SMALL PIE** a small pie or pasty [Mid-17thC. Anglicization of French *pâté*, influenced by PASTY.]

pattypan squash *n.* a variety of wheel-shaped summer squash with a ribbed edge. Latin name: *Cucurbita pepo*. [*Pattypan* from PATTY + PAN]

patulous /páttyŏŏləss/ *adj.* BOT used to describe branches that spread or expand from a central point [Early 17thC. Formed from Latin *patulus*, 'standing open', from *patere* 'to be open'.] —**patulously** *adv.* —**patulousness** *n.*

patzer /pátsər, paátsər/ *n. US* sb who plays chess badly (*insult*) [Mid-20thC. Origin uncertain: perhaps from German *patzen* 'to bungle'.]

Pau /pō/ city in southwestern France. It is the capital of the Pyrénées-Atlantiques Department, in Aquitaine Region. Population: 83,928 (1990).

PAU *abbr.* Pan American Union

paua /pów ə/ (*plural* **pauas** *or* **paua**) *n. ANZ* an edible abalone native to New Zealand with an iridescent shell used in ornaments and jewellery. Latin name: *Haliotis iris*. [Mid-19thC. From Maori.]

paucity /páwssəti/ *n.* **1. DEARTH** an inadequacy or lack of sth **2. FEWNESS** a small number of sth [14thC. Via Old French *paucité* from Latin *paucitas*, from *paucus* 'few, little'.]

Paul /pawl/, **St** (AD 3?–62?) Early Christian missionary. He became a Christian after having a vision of Jesus Christ on the road from Jerusalem to Damascus. A major missionary of Christianity, he was also its first theologian. His life and teachings are described in the Epistles and the Acts of the Apostles in the Bible. Known as **Saul of Tarsus, Paul the Apostle** —**Pauline** /páwl īn/ *adj.*

Paul VI, Pope (1897–1978). He became pope in 1963, and presided over the Second Vatican Council. He travelled widely to extend the Vatican's influence. Real name **Giovanni Batista Montini**

Pauli exclusion principle /pówli-/ *n.* the law of quantum physics stating that no two identical particles of a particular type (**fermions**) may occupy the same quantum state at the same time [Early 20thC. Named after Wolfgang *Pauli*, the Austrian-born US physicist who enunciated it.]

Paul Jones (*plural* **Paul Joneses**) *n.* a dance in which partners are exchanged following a fixed pattern [Early 20thC. Named after John *Paul Jones* (1747–92), a Scottish naval officer known for his victories in the American War of Independence.]

paulownia /paw lṓni ə/ (*plural* **-as** *or* **-a**) *n.* a deciduous Chinese tree of the snapdragon family, especially one that has large heart-shaped leaves and pyramid-shaped clusters of purple or white flowers. Latin name: *Paulownia tomentosa*. [Mid-19thC. From modern Latin, named after Anna *Paulowna* (1795–1865), wife of William II of the Netherlands and daughter of Tsar Paul I of Russia.]

paunch /pawnch/ *n.* **1.** BIG STOMACH a large round stomach on sb **2.** ZOOL = **rumen 3.** SAILING ROPE MAT a thick rope mat that protects against chafing [14thC. Via Old French *pance*, *panche*, from Latin *panticem* 'belly, bowels'.]

paunchy /páwnchi/ (**-ier**, **-iest**) *adj.* having a large round stomach —**paunchiness** *n.*

pauper /páwpər/ *n.* **1.** VERY POOR PERSON sb who is in extreme poverty **2.** RECIPIENT OF PUBLIC AID formerly, a needy person who was eligible to receive aid from public funds (*archaic*) [15thC. From Latin, literally 'getting little', from *paucus* 'little' + *parare* 'to get'.] —**pauperism** *n.*

pauperize /páwpə rīz/ (**-izes**, **-izing**, **-ized**), **pauperise** (**pauperises**, **pauperising**, **pauperised**) *vt.* to make sb become extremely poor

paupiette /pṓ pyét/ *n.* a piece of meat or fish that is cut or rolled out very thin, topped with a stuffing, then rolled up into a neat shape and cooked [Early 18thC. Via French, and Italian *polpetta* from Latin *pulpa*, 'pulp' (source also of English *pulp*).]

pauropod /páwrə pod/ *n.* a small eyeless invertebrate with eleven segments and nine pairs of legs. Class: Pauropoda. [Late 19thC. From modern Latin *pauropoda*, literally 'small-footed', from Greek *pauros* 'small' + *podos* '-footed', from its tiny feet.]

pause /pawz/ *v.* (**pauses**, **pausing**, **paused**) **1.** *vi.* STOP BRIEFLY to stop doing sth before carrying on ○ *He paused for a moment and then continued eating.* **2.** *vi.* STAY BRIEFLY to stop somewhere for a short time ○ *I paused to glance into a shop window.* **3.** *vi.* HESITATE to hesitate before doing or saying sth **4.** *vt.* CAUSE STH TO PAUSE to cause sth such as a machine to stop temporarily, e.g. by pressing a pause button ○ *Can you pause the video for a moment?* ■ *n.* **1.** BRIEF STOP a temporary break in an activity **2.** SHORT SILENCE a brief moment of silence between words, sounds, or musical notes **3.** HESITATION a brief moment of hesitation or uncertainty before sth happens or is done **4.** MUSIC MUSICAL SYMBOL FOR TIME EXTENSION a musical symbol indicating that a note, chord, or pause is to be held longer than the indicated time value. It is represented by a full stop with an upside-down 'u' above it. **5.** POETRY = **caesura** *n.* **6.** **pause**, **pause button** a control on an electronic or mechanical device such as a video machine that brings it temporarily to a halt [15thC. Via Middle French, and Latin *pausa* 'stopping, cessation', from, ultimately, Greek *pauein* 'to stop, cease'.] —**pausal** *adj.* —**pauser** *n.* —**pausing** *n.* ◇ **to give sb pause** to make sb hesitate or reconsider

— WORD KEY: SYNONYMS —
See Synonyms at *hesitate*.

pav /pav/ *n.*, *abbr. ANZ* pavlova (*informal*)

pavane /pə ván, -vaan/ *n.* **1.** DANCE STATELY DANCE a slow stately court dance performed in the 16th and 17th centuries **2.** MUSIC MUSIC FOR A PAVANE a piece of music written for a pavane, usually in slow duple metre [Mid-16thC. Via French from Italian *pavana* 'Paduan', from *Pavo*, a dialect name for the city of Padua.]

Pavarotti /pávvə rótti/, **Luciano** (*b.* 1935) Italian tenor. Known for his great vocal power and range, he is associated with 19th-century Italian opera.

pave /payv/ (**paves**, **paving**, **paved**) *vt.* **1.** PROVIDE WITH A SURFACE FOR WALKING ON to cover with stone, brick, concrete, or other hard materials in order to make it a suitable surface for walking or travelling on **2.**

Luciano Pavarotti

BE A SURFACE FOR WALKING ON to serve as the material that is used to cover the surface of sth in order to make it suitable for walking or travelling on ○ *Large stone slabs paved the path.* **3.** COVER to cover a surface with a flat, uniform material, e.g. leaves or flowers [14thC. Via Old French *paver* from Latin *pavire* 'to beat, tread down'.] —**paver** *n.* ◇ **pave the way** to prepare for and facilitate the progress of sb or sth

pavé /pávvay/ *n.* a jewel setting in which small stones are set very close together so as to cover the surface of the piece and obscure the metal base [Late 19thC. From French, 'paved'.]

pavement /páyvmənt/ *n.* **1.** PATH FOR PEDESTRIANS a paved path for pedestrians alongside a street. US term **sidewalk 2.** *US* TRANSP ASPHALT SURFACE an asphalt surface, especially of a road **3.** GEOL LEVEL AREA OF ROCK a level area of bare rock that resembles a pavement **4.** INDUST MATERIAL FOR PAVEMENTS material such as concrete or stone that is used to make a pavement **5.** CIV ENG LAYERED SURFACE OF A PATH the layered structure that forms the surface of a path, road, carriageway, or aircraft runway [13thC. Via Old French from Latin *pavimentum* 'beaten floor', from *pavire* 'to beat, tread down'.]

pavid /pávvid/ *adj.* timid and fearful (*literary*) [Mid-17thC. From Latin *pavidus*, from *pavere* 'to quake with fear'.]

pavilion /pə vílli ən/ *n.* **1.** BUILDING OUTDOOR STRUCTURE a summer house or other ornamental building in a garden **2.** SPORTS SPORTS CLUBHOUSE a building at a cricket or other sports ground with players' changing rooms and where refreshments are served **3.** EXHIBITION TENT a large tent or other temporary structure used for displaying or exhibiting things **4.** BIG TENT a large and often extremely ornate tent **5.** BUILDING ANNEX a detached building that forms part of a complex for a hospital or other large public building **6.** MINERALS FACET OF A GEM a facet of a brilliant-cut gem that comes below the girdle ■ *vt.* (**-ions**, **-ioning**, **-ioned**) **1.** SET IN A PAVILION to enclose or house sth inside a pavilion **2.** ENCLOSE STH to enclose or completely surround sth (*literary*) ○ '*Pavilioned in splendour, And girded with praise*' (Sir Robert Grant, *O Worship the King*; 1833) **3.** CONSTRUCT A PAVILION FOR to construct a pavilion for sth [Pre-12thC. Via Old French *pavilloun*, *paveillon*, *pavilun* from Latin *papilio* 'butterfly, tent', because a tent was thought to resemble a butterfly's wings.]

paving /páyving/ *n.* **1.** SURFACE FOR PATH, ROAD, ETC. a surface of paved stone, brick, concrete, or other material **2.** MATERIAL FOR MAKING A HARD SURFACE material such as concrete or stones used for making a firm surface, e.g. for a path or road **3.** CONSTRUCTION OF PAVED SURFACE the act of making a paved surface

paving stone *n.* a large flat rectangular slab usually made from concrete or stone that is used in making a paved surface

pavior *n.* US = **paviour**

paviour /páyvyər/ *n.* a person who lays paving [15thC. From Old French *paveur*, from *paver* 'to pave' (see PAVE).]

pavis /pávviss/ *n.* a large heavy medieval shield used to protect the whole body [14thC. Via French and Italian *pavese* from medieval Latin *pavense* 'from Pavia', a city in northern Italy where these shields were originally made.]

Pavlov /páv lof/, **Ivan Petrovich** (1849–1936) Russian physiologist. He became famous for his studies on

conditioned reflexes with dogs. He won a Nobel Prize in 1904.

pavlova /pav lṓvə, pávvləvə/ *n.* a dessert consisting of a large meringue shell filled with cream and fruit [Early 20thC. Named after Anna PAVLOVA, in whose honour the dish was created.]

Anna Pavlova

Pavlova /pav lṓvə, pávvləvə/, **Anna** (1882–1931) Russian ballet dancer. Admired for the poetic quality of her movement, she performed many classic roles. The solo dance 'The Dying Swan' was created for her.

Pavlovian /pav lṓvi ən/ *adj.* **1.** AUTOMATIC produced involuntarily in response to a stimulus **2.** RELATING TO PAVLOV relating to Ivan Pavlov and his work [Mid-20thC. Named after Ivan Petrovich PAVLOV.]

Pavlovian conditioning *n.* = **classical conditioning**

Pavo /páavō/ *n.* a constellation of the southern hemisphere lying near the South Pole between Indus and Ara. It contains the bright star Peacock.

pavonine /pávvə nīn/ *adj.* resembling a peacock, especially the colours and design of its tail (*literary*) [Mid-17thC. From Latin *pavoninus* 'peacock'.]

paw /paw/ *n.* **1.** ZOOL ANIMAL'S FOOT the foot of a four-legged mammal, usually having claws or nails **2.** HUMAN HAND a human hand, especially one that is large or clumsy (*informal*) ■ *vti.* (**paws**, **pawing**, **pawed**) **1.** STRIKE REPEATEDLY WITH THE HOOF to scrape or strike sth repeatedly with a paw or hoof **2.** TOUCH CLUMSILY to touch or caress sb roughly or rudely with the hands [13thC. Via Old French *powe*, *poue*, *poe* from, ultimately, the prehistoric Germanic language.]

pawky /páwki/ (**-ier**, **-iest**) *adj.* witty or shrewd in a dry or sly manner (*regional*) [Mid-17thC. Formed from earlier *pawk* 'trick, artifice, cunning plan'.] —**pawkily** *adv.* —**pawkiness** *n.*

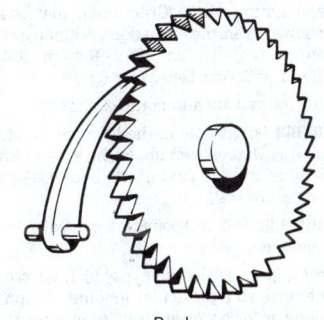
Pawl

pawl /pawl/ *n.* a hinged or pivoted catch, often spring-controlled, that is designed to catch in the teeth of a ratchet wheel to prevent reverse motion [Early 17thC. Origin uncertain: perhaps via French or Dutch *pal* 'stake', from Latin *palus*.]

pawn[1] /pawn/ *n.* **1.** CHESS CHESS PIECE a chess piece of the lowest value that can move one square forward at a time, with an optional first move of two squares. It can take other pieces by moving diagonally and can be exchanged for any other captured piece on reaching the farthest rank of the board. **2.** MANIPULATED PERSON OR THING sb or sth that is being used for the advantage of another person or thing [14thC. Via Anglo-Norman *poun* and Old French *peon* from medieval Latin *pedon-* 'footsoldier', from Latin *ped-* 'foot'.]

pawn[2] /pawn/ *vt.* **(pawns, pawning, pawned) 1.** DEPOSIT WITH A PAWNBROKER to leave sth with a pawnbroker as security against money borrowed **2.** TO STAKE to stake or pledge your honour, life, or word on sth ■ *n.* **1.** OBJECT DEPOSITED AS SECURITY an object that is left as security with a pawnbroker in exchange for a loan of money **2.** HOSTAGE sb who is held as security, usually as a hostage **3.** ACT OF PAWNING the act of pawning sth [15thC. Via Old French *pan, pand, pant,* 'pledge, security, plunder', from a Germanic word.] — **pawnage** *n.* —**pawner** *n.* ◇ **in pawn** left or held as security with a pawnbroker in exchange for a loan of money

pawnbroker /páwn brōkər/ *n.* sb who lends money at a fixed rate of interest in exchange for articles of personal property that are left as security

Pawnee /paw neé/ (*plural* **-nee** *or* **-nees**) *n.* **1.** PEOPLES MEMBER OF A NATIVE N AMERICAN PEOPLE a member of a confederation of Native North American peoples who originally occupied lands in Nebraska and Kansas and who, apart from a small community in Oklahoma, are now mainly dispersed **2.** LANG PAWNEE LANGUAGE the Caddoan language of the Pawnee people. Pawnee is spoken by about 3,000 people. [Late 18thC. Via Canadian French *Pani* from a Native North American language.]

pawnshop /páwn shop/ *n.* a shop where articles or personal property may be left as security in exchange for a loan of money

pawn ticket *n.* a ticket that serves as a receipt for sth that has been pawned

pawpaw /páwpaw/ *n.* BOT = **papaw, papaya**

pawpaw /páw paw/, **papaw** /páw paw, pə páw/ *n.* **1.** TREES N AMERICAN TREE WITH EDIBLE FRUIT a small North American deciduous tree or shrub of the custard apple family that has large oblong leaves, purple flowers, and small fleshy edible fruit. Latin name: *Asimina triloba.* **2.** FOOD PAWPAW FRUIT the edible fruit of the pawpaw tree **3.** TREES, FOOD = **papaya** *n.* **2** [Early 17thC. Alteration of PAPAYA.]

Pawtucket /paw túkit/ city in northeastern Rhode Island, at the confluence of the Blackstone and Seekonk rivers. Population: 72,644 (1990).

pax /paks/ *interj.* SCHOOLCHILDREN'S TRUCE a call for a truce or a break in a game used by children and usually signalled by holding up crossed fingers (*informal*) ■ *n.* **1. pax, Pax** POL STABLE PERIOD UNDER A POWERFUL EMPIRE a period of peace and stability under the influence of a powerful country or empire **2.** CHR KISS OF PEACE IN CHURCH a kiss or other greeting given as a sign of peace during the Christian ceremony of Communion, especially in the Roman Catholic Mass **3.** CHR TABLET KISSED AT CHRISTIAN COMMUNION a tablet bearing a representation of the Crucifixion that is kissed by participants in the Christian ceremony of Communion, especially in the Roman Catholic Mass [Pre-12thC. From Latin, 'peace'.]

PAX *abbr.* UTIL private automatic exchange

Pax Romana /-rō maánə/ *n.* the long period of peace and stability that existed under the Roman Empire, especially in the 2nd century AD [From Latin, literally 'peace of the Romans']

pax vobiscum /-vō bískoōm/ *interj.* peace be with you [From Latin]

pay[1] /pay/ *v.* **(pays, paying, paid** /payd/**) 1.** *vti.* GIVE MONEY FOR STH to give sb a particular amount of money for work done or for goods or services provided ○ *They were paid a small fortune for it.* **2.** *vti.* SETTLE A DEBT to settle a debt or other obligation **3.** *vti.* BRING IN MONEY to bring in a certain amount of money ○ *How much will the job pay?* **4.** *vti.* BE PUNISHED to be punished or suffer the bad consequences of sth you have done ○ *He's paid the price for what he did.* **5.** *vt.* FIN YIELD INTEREST to yield a specific amount as a return on a sum of money invested ○ *The account pays 12% interest.* **6.** *vi.* GIVE A POSITIVE RESULT to be profitable or beneficial ○ *Crime doesn't pay.* **7.** *vt.* BESTOW to give sth, e.g. attention or a compliment, to sb or sth ○ *pay a compliment* **8.** *vt.* VISIT to make a visit or call to see sb **9.** *vt.* = **pay out 10.** *vt.* SAILING LET GO LEEWARD to allow a vessel to make leeway **11.** *vt. Aus* ACKNOWLEDGE STH IS TRUE to acknowledge the truth of a statement or that you were wrong (*informal*) ○ *OK, I'll pay that.* ■ *n.* **1.** MONEY GIVEN IN RETURN FOR WORK money that is given in return for work or services provided, especially in the form of a salary or wages **2.** REWARD reward, recompense, or recognition granted to sb **3.** MINING = **pay dirt** ■ *adj.* **1.** NEEDING THE INSERTION OF A COIN TO FUNCTION requiring the insertion of coins or a card in order to function ○ *pay TV* **2.** MINING RICH IN METALS yielding metal or minerals valuable enough to make mining them profitable [12thC. Via Old French *payer* 'to satisfy, pacify' (the original sense in English, hence 'to satisfy by handing over money'), from Latin *pacare,* from *pax* 'peace'.] ◇ **in the pay of sb** employed by sb, especially for a dishonest or criminal purpose ◇ **pay your way** to pay your share of expenses ◇ **put paid to** to put an end to or ruin sth (*informal*)

WORD KEY: SYNONYMS

See Synonyms at ***wage.***

pay back *vt.* **1.** REPAY to repay money that has been lent ○ *I'll pay you back on Friday.* **2.** TAKE REVENGE ON to revenge yourself on sb

pay for *vt.* to undergo the bad consequences of sth you have done

pay in *vt.* to deposit money in a bank or other account

pay off *v.* **1.** *vt.* REPAY IN FULL to repay the full amount of a bill, debt, or other financial obligation, especially one that has been paid in instalments **2.** *vt.* BRIBE SB to give sb money as a bribe, usually to prevent that person from causing trouble (*informal*) **3.** *vt.* PAY AND LAY OFF WORKERS to give employees or workers the money owing to them for work performed before dismissing them **4.** *vi.* BE SUCCESSFUL to be successful or profitable ○ *All that preparation paid off in the end.* **5.** *vt.* TAKE REVENGE ON to take revenge on sb for sth he or she has done to you **6.** *vi.* SAILING MAKE LEEWAY to make leeway

pay out *v.* **1.** *vti.* PAY MONEY to spend or pay money **2.** *vt.* UNWIND to release a rope or cable gradually by hand **3.** *vt.* TAKE REVENGE to take revenge on sb **4.** *vti. Aus* CRITICIZE to criticize or abuse sb (*informal*)

pay over *vi.* to transfer money to sb officially

pay up *vi.* to pay money that is due

pay[2] /pay/ **(pays, paying, payed)** *vt.* to make a ship's hull waterproof with pitch or tar [Early 17thC. Via Old French *peier* from Latin *picare,* from *pix* 'pitch'.]

payable /páy əb'l/ *adj.* **1.** REQUIRING PAYMENT due or needing to be paid **2.** BANKING GRANTING PAYMENT TO SB requesting payment to be made to a particular person ○ *Shall I make the cheque payable to you or to Jean?*

pay and display *n.* a parking system in which motorists buy a ticket from a machine to cover the amount of time that they intend to leave their vehicle in the car park. The ticket is then displayed in the windscreen or one of the windows of the vehicle. [Late 20thC]

pay-as-you-earn *n.* full form of **PAYE**

payback /páy bak/ *n.* **1.** FIN RETURN ON INVESTMENT a financial return on an investment equalling the initial capital invested **2.** FIN TIME REQUIRED TO RECOVER OUTLAY the period of time required to recover the return on an initial investment **3.** REVENGE revenge or retaliation (*informal*)

pay bed *n.* = **amenity bed**

paycheque /páy chek/ *n.* **1.** SALARY CHEQUE a cheque issued to an employee as payment for salary or wages **2.** SALARY wages or salary

payday /páy day/ *n.* the day on which employees are paid their wages or salary

pay dirt *n.* **1.** *US* POTENTIALLY PROFITABLE DISCOVERY a discovery or idea that is likely to be useful or profitable **2.** MINING DEPOSIT WORTH MINING gravel, sand, earth, or ore that is worth mining

paydown /páy down/ *n. US* the reduction of a debt by paying back some of the money borrowed

PAYE *n.* a system in which income tax is deducted as wages are earned. Full form **pay-as-you-earn**

payee /pay eé/ *n.* a person to whom money is being paid or is due, especially in a transaction such as the payment of a cheque or money order

pay envelope *n. US* = **pay packet**

payer /páyər/ *n.* **1.** SB WHO PAYS a person who pays sb or sth **2.** SB RESPONSIBLE FOR PAYMENT the person named as responsible for the payment of a cheque, money order, or other financial paper when it is redeemed

paying guest *n.* sb who pays to stay in another person's home for a temporary period, e.g. as a holiday

payload /páy lōd/ *n.* **1.** FREIGHT QUANTITY OF CARGO the quantity of cargo or load that a plane, train, or other vehicle can carry, often expressed as weight or volume **2.** AIR PLANE PASSENGERS AND EQUIPMENT the passengers and instruments carried by an aircraft or spacecraft **3.** ARMS EXPLOSIVE CHARGE the explosive charge of a rocket or missile or the total explosive charge of the bomb load carried by an aircraft

paymaster /páy maastər/ *n.* the person who is responsible for paying wages or salaries in a business or government organization

Paymaster-General (*plural* **Paymasters-General**) *n.* the government minister who heads the office that acts as paying agent for government departments

payment /páymənt/ *n.* **1.** FIN MONEY PAID an amount of money that is paid or is due to be paid **2.** REWARD a reward or punishment given in return for sth **3.** FIN ACT OF PAYING the act of paying money, or fact of being paid ○ *Payment will be made at the end of the month.* [14thC. From Old French *paiement,* from *payer* (see PAY).]

payment by results *n.* a system of payment in which the salary paid depends on how well sb does the job

paynim /páynim/ *n.* (*archaic*) **1.** PAGAN a pagan **2.** SB NOT A CHRISTIAN sb who is not a Christian, especially a Muslim [13thC. Via Old French *pai(e)nime* from ecclesiastical Latin *paganismus* 'paganism', from *paganus* 'pagan'. Originally meaning 'all non-Christian countries'.]

payoff /páy of/ *n.* **1.** FIN FULL PAYMENT full payment of a salary, wages, or a debt **2.** FIN TIME FOR FULL PAYMENT the time when full and final payment of a debt, salary, or wage is due **3.** SETTLEMENT a final settlement, reward, or reckoning **4.** CLIMAX OF NARRATIVE the final climax of a narrative or sequence of events **5.** REVENGE final retribution or revenge **6.** FIN BRIBE a payment made to someone as a bribe (*informal*) **7.** PSYCHOL HIDDEN BENEFIT OF NEGATIVE BEHAVIOUR an often unconscious or hidden benefit of a negative thought pattern or action

payola /pay ólə/ (*plural* **-las** *informal*) *n. US* a payment given in exchange for promoting a commercial product, or the system of making such payments, especially to disc jockeys [Mid-20thC. Coined from PAY + -OLA.]

payout /páy owt/ *n.* the act of paying out money or the sum of money paid

pay packet *n.* US term **pay envelope 1.** WAGE CONTAINER an envelope containing an employee's wages **2.** WAGES wages received for a job or service

pay-per-view *n.* a cable or satellite television system in which individual programmes can be watched for a fee

payphone /páy fōn/ *n.* a public telephone that operates only when coins or a card are used to pay for calls

payroll /páy rōl/ *n.* **1.** LIST OF PAID EMPLOYEES a list of employees and their salaries or wages **2.** TOTAL PAID TO EMPLOYEES the total sum of money to be paid to employees at a given time

payroller /páy rōlər/ *n.* an employee, often in a government department, who does little or no work, having acquired the job through connections or as reward for political favours

payslip /páy slip/ *n.* a printed statement of the amount an employee is paid, showing deductions for tax, pensions, and National Insurance. US term **paystub**

paystub /páy stub/ *n. US* = **payslip**

payt *abbr.* payment

pay television *n.* a system in which television programmes are transmitted in a scrambled form that can be decoded by viewers who have paid for the appropriate equipment

paytrain /páy trayn/ *n.* a train on which passengers pay fares to the guard or conductor because there are no ticket offices open on the stations

pay TV *n.* = **pay television**

payware /páy wair/ *n.* commercial software as opposed to freeware or shareware

Octavio Paz

Paz /pass/, **Octavio** (1914–98) Mexican writer. Known for his poetry and essays, he won a Nobel Prize in literature in 1990.

Pb *symbol.* lead

PB *abbr.* **1.** SPORTS personal best **2.** PHARM Pharmacopoeia Britannica **3.** AUTOMOT power brakes **4.** CHR prayer book

PBB *abbr.* polybrominated biphenyl

PBX *abbr.* UTIL private branch exchange

pc *abbr.* **1.** per cent **2.** postcard **3.** PHARM after meals (*used in prescriptions*) [From Latin *post cibum* 'after food']

PC *abbr.* **1.** COMPUT personal computer **2.** politically correct **3.** Police Constable **4.** POL Privy Councillor **5.** *Can* POL Progressive Conservative **6.** Prince Consort **7.** POL Privy Council **8.** MIL Past Commander **9.** MIL Post Commander **10.** POL Parish Council **11.** POL Parish Councillor **12.** ELECTRON ENG printed circuit

pc. *abbr.* **1.** piece **2.** price

p.c., **p/c** *abbr.* **1.** petty cash **2.** price current

PCB *n.* a compound derived from biphenyl and containing chlorine that is used in electrical insulators, flame retardants, and plasticizers. PCB is a hazardous pollutant that is difficult to dispose of safely and has been banned in several countries. Full form **polychlorinated biphenyl**

PCI *n.* a specification for extending the internal circuitry (**bus**) that transmits data from one part of a computer to another. It allows the expansion of a computer by inserting printed circuit boards, or expansion boards, into sockets (**slots**) inside the PCI bus. Full form **peripheral component interconnect local bus**

pcm *abbr.* **1.** per calendar month **2.** UTIL pulse code modulation

PCMCIA *n.* a specification for extending the internal circuitry (**bus**) that transmits data from one part of a computer to another. Originally designed for adding memory to portable computers, the PCMCIA bus is used to connect credit-card-sized peripheral devices as well. Full form **Personal Computer Memory Card Interface Adapter**

PCP *abbr.* **1.** CHEM phencyclidine **2.** MED pneumocystis carinii pneumonia **3.** *Can* POL Progressive Conservative Party

PCR *abbr.* polymerase chain reaction

PCV *abbr.* passenger carrying vehicle

pd *abbr.* paid

Pd *symbol.* palladium

PD *abbr.* **1.** police department **2.** MAIL postal district

p.d., **P.D.** *abbr.* **1.** PHYS potential difference **2.** per diem

PDA *abbr.* Personal Digital Assistant

PDL *abbr.* page description language

pdq *adv.* at once or immediately (*informal*) Full form **pretty damn quick**

PDR *abbr.* STOCK EXCH price-dividend ratio

P-D ratio *abbr.* STOCK EXCH price-dividend ratio

PDSA *abbr.* People's Dispensary for Sick Animals

PDT *abbr.* Pacific Daylight Time

pe /pay/ *n.* the 17th letter of the Hebrew alphabet, represented in the English alphabet as 'p' or 'f'. See table at **alphabet**

PE *abbr.* **1.** Peru (*international vehicle registration*) **2.** EDUC physical education **3.** PHYS potential energy **4.** STATS probable error **5.** CHR Protestant Episcopal

p.e. *abbr.* printer's error

P/E *abbr.* price-earnings

Pea

pea /pee/ *n.* **1.** FOOD SEED AS A VEGETABLE a round green seed that grows in a pod, eaten as a vegetable **2.** PLANTS LEGUMINOUS PLANT WITH EDIBLE SEEDS an annual vine of Europe and Asia of the legume family with compound leaves and small white flowers that is widely grown for its peas, contained in pods. Latin name: *Pisum sativum.* **3.** PLANTS PLANT RELATED TO THE PEA any of various plants related to or similar to the pea, such as the chickpea, sweet pea, or cowpea **4.** STH RESEMBLING A PEA sth resembling a pea in form or size [Mid-17thC. Back-formation from *pease* (originally the singular form, wrongly thought to be a plural), which came from Latin *pisa*.]

peace /peess/ *n.* **1.** FREEDOM FROM WAR freedom from war, or the time when a war or conflict ends **2.** MENTAL CALM a state of mental calm and serenity, with no anxiety **3.** PEACE TREATY a treaty agreeing to an end of hostilities between two warring parties **4.** LAW AND ORDER the absence of violence or other disturbances within a state ○ *Peace reigned throughout the land.* **5.** STATE OF HARMONY freedom from conflict or disagreement among people or groups of people ■ *interj.* BE CALM OR SILENT used to tell sb to be calm or silent or as a greeting or farewell (*archaic*) [12thC. Via Anglo-Norman *pes* from Latin *pax* 'peace, peace treaty', which is also the source of English *appease*, *pacific*, and *pay*.] ◊ **at peace 1.** in a state of friendship and freedom from conflict **2.** dead (*used euphemistically*) **3.** in a state of calm and serenity ◊ **hold your peace** to refrain from speaking (*dated*) ◊ **keep the peace** to refrain from or prevent conflict or violence ◊ **make peace** to bring a disagreement or war to an end ◊ **make your peace with sb** to become friends with sb again after an argument

peaceable /peéssəb'l/ *adj.* **1.** DISPOSED TOWARDS PEACE inclined towards peace and avoiding contentious situations **2.** TRANQUIL tranquil and free from strife and disorder [14thC. Formed from PEACE, or via French *peisible* and *plaisible* from late Latin *placibilis* 'pleasing', from *placere* 'to please'.] —**peaceableness** *n.* —**peaceably** *adv.*

peace camp *n.* a camp set up by antiwar demonstrators, usually in the vicinity of a military establishment

Peace Corps *n.* a United States government organization that trains volunteers to work in developing countries on educational and agricultural projects. ◊ **VSO**

peaceful /peéssf'l/ *adj.* **1.** QUIET AND CALM quiet, calm, and tranquil ○ *a peaceful atmosphere* **2.** MENTALLY CALM serene and untroubled in the mind **3.** APPROPRIATE FOR PEACETIME appropriate for a time of peace rather than war —**peacefully** *adv.*

— **WORD KEY: SYNONYMS** —
See Synonyms at *calm.*

peacekeeping /peéss keeping/ *n.* the preservation of peace, especially as a military mission in which troops attempt to keep formerly warring armed forces from starting to fight again —**peacekeeper** *n.*

peacemaker /peéss maykər/ *n.* sb who brings about peace and reconciliation between others —**peacemaking** *n.*

peace offering *n.* sth done for or given to an enemy or sb you have quarrelled with in the hope of bringing about a reconciliation

peace pipe *n.* a long-stemmed ceremonial pipe used by some Native North American peoples

peace sign *n.* a sign used to indicate peaceful intentions, made by holding the palm upright and outwards and forming a V with the middle and index fingers

peacetime /peéss tīm/ *n.* a time when there is no war

Peach

peach[1] /peech/ *n.* **1.** FOOD SWEET ROUND FRUIT WITH STONE sweet round juicy fruit with yellow flesh, a single stone, and a soft downy orange-yellow skin **2.** TREES SMALL TREE WITH EDIBLE FRUIT a small tree that originated in China and has pink flowers, is widely grown in temperate regions, and bears peaches as fruit. Latin name: *Prunus persica.* **3.** SB OR STH EXCELLENT sb or sth that is particularly good or pleasing (*informal*) ○ *That was a peach of a throw!* **4.** COLOURS CREAMY ORANGE-YELLOW COLOUR a creamy orange colour tinged with yellow, like a ripe peach ■ *adj.* CREAMY ORANGE of a creamy orange colour tinged with yellow [13thC. Via Old French from medieval Latin *persica*, an alteration of earlier *persicum*, from *mālum Persicum*, literally 'Persian apple', because it first became known in Europe through that country.]

peach[2] /peech/ (**peaches, peaching, peached**) *vi.* to inform against sb, especially an accomplice (*dated informal*) [15thC. Shortening of earlier *appeach*, via Anglo-Norman from late Latin *impedicare* (see IMPEACH).] —**peacher** *n.*

peach melba *n.* a dessert made with fresh or canned peaches, vanilla ice cream, and a raspberry sauce

peach palm *n.* a dense spiny Amazonian palm with an edible heart. Latin name: *Bactris gasipaes.*

peachy /peéchi/ (**-ier, -iest**) *adj.* **1.** RESEMBLING A PEACH resembling a peach in colour, taste, or texture **2.** EXCELLENT excellent or wonderful (*informal*) [Late 16thC. Formed from PEACH[1].] —**peachily** *adv.* —**peachiness** *n.*

peacoat /peé kōt/ *n.* = **pea jacket**

Peacock

peacock /peé kok/ *n.* **1.** MALE PEAFOWL a male peafowl with a crested head and a large fan-shaped tail with brilliantly coloured blue and green spots **2. PEAFOWL** a peafowl, either male or female **3. VAIN PERSON** sb who is very vain, and who shows this especially in the way he or she behaves and dresses ■ *vi.* (**-cocks, -cocking, -cocked**) **SHOW OFF** to strut about in a vain and self-important way (*archaic*) [14thC. *Pea* originally an Old English word meaning 'peacock', from Latin *pavo*.] — **peacockish** *adj.*

peacock blue *adj.* of a brilliant greenish-blue colour, like the plumage on a peacock's breast and neck — **peacock blue** *n.*

peacock butterfly *n.* a European butterfly with bold iridescent colours that makes communal nests. Latin name: *Nymphalis io.*

peacock ore *n.* a copper ore such as bornite or chalcopyrite that becomes iridescent as it tarnishes

peafowl /peé fowl/ (*plural* **-fowls** *or* **-fowl**) *n.* either of two large pheasants native to India and Southeast Asia. The male holds up its brilliant iridescent tail like a fan in courtship displays. Latin name: *Pavo cristatus* and *Pavo muticus.* [Early 19thC. From 'pea' (see PEACOCK).]

peag /peeg/ *n.* = **wampum** *n.* [Early 17thC. Shortening of WAMPUMPEAG.]

pea green *adj.* of a medium yellowish-green colour — **pea green** *n.*

peahen /peé hen/ *n.* a female peafowl with much plainer plumage than the peacock [14thC. From 'pea' (see PEACOCK).]

pea jacket *n.* a heavy double-breasted jacket or short coat, made of mohair or thick wool and originally worn by sailors [By folk etymology from Dutch *pijjakker, pijjekker,* literally 'coarse cloth jacket', from *pij* 'coarse cloth' (by association with PEA) + *jekker* 'jacket']

peak[1] /peek/ *n.* **1. MOUNTAIN TOP** the pointed summit of a mountain **2. MOUNTAIN** a mountain with a pointed summit **3. POINTED PART** a sharp projecting pointed part of sth, e.g. the brim of a cap **4. HIGHEST POINT** the point of greatest success, development, or strength of a process or activity ○ *She's at the peak of her career.* **5. TOP OF CURVE** the highest point in a curve, especially the curve of a wave **6. HAIR = widow's peak** ■ *n., n.* PHYS **MAXIMUM VALUE OF QUANTITY** a point at which a variable physical quantity such as temperature or voltage changes from rapidly increasing to rapidly decreasing, or the value of the quantity at such a point ■ *n.* **1.** NAUT **EXTREME END OF HULL** narrow part at the front or back end of a boat's hull **2.** SAILING **CORNER OF FORE-AND-AFT SAIL** the top rear corner of a fore-and-aft sail **3.** SAILING **GAFF END** the outermost end of a gaff sail ■ *v.* (**peaks, peaking, peaked**) **1.** *vi.* **REACH HIGHEST POINT** to reach the point of greatest success, development, intensity, or strength ○ *Sales peaked in July.* **2.** *vi.* **FORM PEAK** to form a peak or peaks ○ *The waves peaked as the storm grew.* **3.** *vt.* **CAUSE PEAK IN** to cause sth to come to a high point or peak ■ *adj.* **1. HIGHEST** being at a maximum or highest point ○ *peak efficiency* **2. OF GREATEST USE** relating to the maximum use of sth or the maximum demand on sth ○ *peak viewing time* [Mid-16thC. Back-formation from PEAKED, a variant of PICKED 'pointed'.]

peak[2] /peek/ *v.* (**peaks, peaking, peaked**) *vi.* to become thin, pale, and sickly in appearance (*archaic*) [Early 16thC. Origin unknown.] —**peakish** *adj.*

Peak District region in northern England forming the southern part of the Pennine Hills

Peak District National Park national park in northern England, mainly in Derbyshire, within the Peak District. It was founded in 1951. Area: 1,404 sq. km/542 sq. mi.

peaked[1] /peekt/ *adj.* having a peak or point —**peakedness** *n.*

peaked[2] /peekt/ *adj.* US = **peaky**

peak hour *n.* ANZ the rush hour, when the greatest number of people are travelling to or from work

peak load *n.* the maximum instantaneous rate of power consumption in a load circuit

peak programme meter *n.* a device attached across an electrical transmission circuit to measure changes in volume of the sound reproduction

peaky /peéki/ (**-ier, -iest**) *adj.* thin, pale, and sickly in appearance. US term **peaked** [Early 19thC. Formed from PEAK 'to be sickly'.]

peal[1] /peel/ *n.* **1.** MUSIC **RINGING OF BELLS** a ringing of bells, especially a change or series of changes rung on bells **2.** MUSIC **GROUP OF BELLS** a set of tuned bells **3.** NOISY **OUTBURST** a loud repetitive sound, especially of thunder or laughter ■ *v.* (**peals, pealing, pealed**) **1.** *vti.* MUSIC **RING** to ring a bell loudly and sonorously, or to be rung in this way **2.** *vt.* **SAY LOUDLY** to say sth loudly and sonorously [14thC. Variant of APPEAL 'call, request'.]

peal[2] /peel/ (*plural* **peals** *or* **peal**) *n.* a grilse (*regional*) [Mid-16thC. Origin unknown.]

peamouse /peé mowss/ (*plural* **-mice** /-mīss/) *n.* N England a shrew mouse (*informal*)

pean /peen/ *n.* sable fur spotted with a gold or yellow colour [Mid-16thC. Origin unknown.]

Peanut

peanut /peé nut/ *n.* **1.** FOOD **OILY EDIBLE SEED** an oily edible seed with a thin shell that grows underground and is a source of vegetable oil **2.** PLANTS **PLANT PRODUCING PEANUTS** a low-growing annual plant of the legume family whose seeds are contained in pods that are forced underground as they grow. Latin name: *Arachis hypogaea.* ■ **peanuts** *npl.* **SMALL AMOUNT OF MONEY** a very small amount of money, especially when smaller than would be expected (*informal*) ○ *They're paid peanuts!* [Early 19thC. From PEA (from the similarity of peanuts to peas, because peanuts also grow in a pod) + NUT.]

peanut butter *n.* an oily paste made from ground roasted peanuts and usually spread on bread or used in cooking

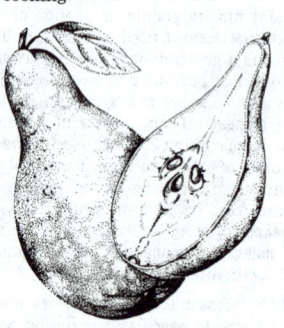

Pear

pear /pair/ *n.* **1.** FOOD **GREEN-SKINNED FRUIT** a sweet juicy fruit with firm white flesh, a usually green skin, and an approximately oval shape, larger and rounded at the base and tapering towards the stem **2.** TREES **TREE BEARING PEARS** a tree of the rose family that has shiny leaves and bears pears as fruit. Latin name: *Pyrus communis.* [Pre-12thC. Via assumed Vulgar Latin *pira* from, ultimately, Latin *pirum.*]

pearl[1] /purl/ *n.* **1.** GEM **FORMED IN MOLLUSC** a small lustrous sphere of calcium carbonate that forms round a grain of sand in a mollusc such as an oyster, and is valued as a gem **2.** = **mother-of-pearl 3.** SB **OR STH MUCH VALUED** sb or sth highly esteemed or valued **4.** COLOURS **PALE GREYISH-WHITE COLOUR** a pale greyish-white colour tinged with blue ■ *adj.* COLOURS **PALE GREYISH-WHITE** of a pale greyish-white colour tinged with blue ■ *v.* (**pearls, pearling, pearled**) **1.** *vi.* **HARVEST PEARLS** to fish or dive for pearls **2.** *vi.* **MAKE BEADS** to form a pearl or pearl-shaped drops **3.** *vt.* **DECORATE WITH PEARLS**

to decorate sth with pearls or with things that resemble pearls **4.** *vt.* **MAKE STH INTO SHAPE OF PEARLS** to make sth into the shape or colour of pearls [14thC. Via Old French from assumed Vulgar Latin *pernula,* literally 'little mollusc whose feet resemble hams in shape', from Latin *perna,* 'leg, ham, ham-shaped mollusc'.]

pearl[2] /purl/ (**pearls, pearling, pearled**) *n.* = **purl**[1] *n.* **2**, **purl**[1] *n.* **3**

pearl ash *n.* the commercial form of potassium carbonate

pearl barley *n.* grains of barley that have been polished and are used in soups and stews

pearler /púrlər/ *n.* **1. PEARL DIVER OR TRADER** sb who dives for pearls or trades in them **2. BOAT USED FOR PEARL-DIVING** a boat used for pearl-diving or for trading pearls

pearl essence *n.* a silvery translucent substance extracted from the scales of fish such as herring, used to make artificial pearls, lacquers, and other products

pearl grey *adj.* of a pale blue-grey colour —**pearl grey** *n.*

Pearl Harbor /purl-/ inlet in Hawaii, on Oahu Island. The Japanese attack on it in 1941 prompted the United States' entry into World War II.

pearlite /púrl īt/ *n.* a microstructure of steel or cast iron made up of bands (**lamellae**) of pure iron (**ferrite**) and iron carbide (**cementite**) [Late 19thC. Coined from PEARL + -ITE.] —**pearlitic** /pur líttik/ *adj.*

pearlized /púrl īzd/, **pearlised** *adj.* having a pearly iridescent lustre

pearl millet *n.* a tall cereal grass widely grown for its whitish seeds. Latin name: *Pennisetum americanum.*

pearl onion *n.* a very small white onion that is often pickled

pearl oyster *n.* a tropical marine mollusc that is a source of pearls. Genus: *Pinctada.*

pearly /púrli/ *adj.* (**-ier, -iest**) **1. RESEMBLING PEARL** resembling pearls or mother-of-pearl, particularly in having an iridescent lustre **2. DECORATED WITH PEARLS** adorned or decorated with pearls or mother-of-pearl **3.** COLOURS **PALE GREYISH-WHITE** of a pale greyish-white colour tinged with blue ■ *n.* (*plural* **-ies**) COCKNEY **WEARING PEARL-DECORATED COSTUME** a member of a Cockney family who, on ceremonial occasions, traditionally wears a special costume covered with pearl buttons arranged in ornamental patterns. ◊ **pearly king, pearly queen** —**pearliness** *n.*

Pearly Gates *npl.* in Christianity, the gates of heaven (*informal*)

pearly king *n.* a man from one of the Cockney families traditionally entitled to wear a pearl-covered costume, who is chosen as the one with the finest costume

pearly nautilus *n.* a mollusc that has a spiral pearl-coloured shell divided internally by cross walls into a series of chambers. Genus: *Nautilus.* ◊ **paper nautilus** [From the colour of its shell]

pearly queen *n.* a woman from one of the Cockney families traditionally entitled to wear a pearl-covered costume, who is chosen as the one with the finest costume

pearmain /páir mayn/ (*plural* **-mains** *or* **-main**) *n.* a variety of red-skinned apple [13thC. Via Old French *parmaine, permaine* from Latin *Parmensis,* 'from Parma' (in Italy), because this fruit originally came from there.]

Pears /peerz/, **Sir Peter** (1910–86) British tenor. He is noted for his interpretation of music for tenor by Benjamin Britten, much of which Britten wrote for him. Full name **Sir Peter Neville Luard Pears**

Pearse /peerss/, **Patrick Henry** (1879–1916) Irish nationalist leader. He led the Irish Republican Brotherhood in the Easter Rising (1916), after which he was executed.

Pearse, Richard William (1877–1953) New Zealand inventor. He is said to have achieved a brief powered flight on 31 March 1903, eight months before the flight of the Wright brothers.

pear-shaped *adj.* having a shape similar to that of a pear with a rounded bottom part and narrower top part ◇ **go pear-shaped** to get out of control or go wrong (*informal*)

peart /peert/ *adj.* lively and brisk (*regional*) [15thC. Variant of PERT.]

Peary /peeri/, **Robert** (1856–1920) US explorer. He is generally credited with leading the first expedition to reach the North Pole (1909). Full name **Robert Edwin Peary**

peasant /pézz'nt/ *n.* **1.** AGRICULTURAL LABOURER OR SMALL FARMER a member of a class of people living in rural areas who are engaged in agricultural labouring or are small farmers **2.** RURAL PERSON a country-dweller or rustic **3.** UNEDUCATED PERSON sb considered to be ill-mannered or uneducated (*informal offensive*) [15thC. Via Anglo-Norman *paisant* and Old French *païsant, païsenc* 'inhabitant of rural district', from, ultimately, Latin *pagus* 'rural district'.]

peasantry /pézz'ntri/ *n.* **1.** PEASANTS peasants as a class in society **2.** RANK OR CHARACTERISTICS OF PEASANTS the status or characteristic behaviour of a peasant

pease-brose /peez bróz/ *n. Scotland* a thick porridge made from dried peas [From 'pease', an earlier form of PEA, + 'brose', originally a Scottish dialect word]

peasecod /peez kod/ *n.* a pea pod (*archaic*) [14thC. From 'pease', an earlier form of PEA + COD 'pod, husk'.]

pease pudding *n.* a thick puree made from dried peas and served usually with ham, pork, or bacon [*Pease* an earlier form of PEA]

peashooter /pee shooter/ *n.* a toy in the form of a pipe through which dried peas or similar small pellets can be blown

pea soup *n.* **1.** SOUP WITH PEAS soup made with fresh or dried peas **2.** *US* = **peasouper** (*informal*)

peasouper /pee sóopər/ *n.* **1.** THICK FOG an extremely thick fog (*informal*) US term **pea soup 2.** CAN OFFENSIVE TERM an offensive term for a French Canadian (*slang offensive*) [Late 19thC. Because the thick yellow fog resembles pea soup.]

peat /peet/ *n.* **1.** DEPOSIT OF ORGANIC DEBRIS a compacted deposit of partially decomposed organic debris, usually saturated with water **2.** PIECE OF PEAT USED FOR FUEL a cut and dried piece of peat used as fuel [14thC. Via Anglo-Latin from a Celtic word meaning 'bit, part, piece'.] —**peaty** *adj.*

peat bog *n.* an area of land composed primarily of peat

peat moss *n.* a moss that grows in wet places, and whose partially decomposed remains form peat. Genus: *Sphagnum*.

peat reek *n.* **1.** SMOKE FROM PEAT FIRE the smoke from a peat fire that is said to impart a distinctive flavour to whisky **2.** WHISKY DISTILLED OVER PEAT FIRE whisky that is distilled over a peat fire, thereby gaining a distinctive smoky flavour

peau de soie /pó də swaá/ *n.* a silk or artificial fabric such as rayon with a smooth texture and a fine grainy or ribbed surface [From French, literally 'silk skin']

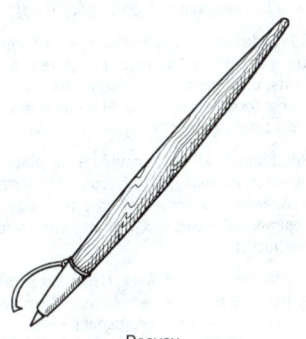
Peavey

peavey /peevi/ (*plural* **-veys**), **peavy** (*plural* **-vies**) *n.* a pointed lever with a hinged hook, used for handling logs [Late 19thC. Named after Joseph *Peavey*, its US inventor.]

pebble /pébb'l/ *n.* **1.** SMALL ROUND STONE a small rounded stone that has been worn smooth by erosion **2.** GEOL ROCK FRAGMENT a rock fragment with a diameter between 4 mm/0.16 in and 64 mm/2.51 in **3.** GEOL ROCK CRYSTAL USED FOR LENSES a colourless form of quartz (**rock crystal**) used for making lenses **4.** OPTICS CRYSTAL LENS a lens made from colourless rock crystal **5.** IRREGULAR SURFACE a rough grainy surface, especially of leather ■ *adj.* THICK AND DISTORTING being or containing lenses that make the eyes of the wearer seem very large and distorted (*informal*) ○ *wearing thick pebble glasses* ■ *vt.* (**-bles, -bling, -bled**) **1.** COVER WITH PEBBLES to cover or pave sth with pebbles **2.** GIVE IRREGULAR SURFACE TO to give a rough grainy surface to sth [Old English *papolstān, popelstān*. Ultimate origin unknown.]

pebbledash /pébb'l dash/ *n.* a finish for exterior walls, consisting of small stones set in plaster

pec /pek/ *n.* a pectoral muscle (*informal*) (*often used in the plural*) ○ *exercises to strengthen the pecs* [Mid-20thC. Shortening.]

pecan /peekən, pi kán/ *n.* **1.** FOOD EDIBLE NUT an edible nut resembling a long walnut with a thin dark red shell **2.** TREES TREE WITH EDIBLE NUT a large hickory tree with deeply furrowed bark and hard brittle wood, grown in the United States and Mexico for its nuts. Latin name: *Carya illinoensis.* [Late 18thC. Via French *pacane* from Algonquian *pakani.*]

peccable /pékəb'l/ *adj.* open or prone to sin or temptation (*formal*) [Early 17thC. Via French from medieval Latin *peccabilis*, from Latin *peccare* 'to sin'.] —**peccability** /pékə bílləti/ *n.*

peccadillo /pékə díllō/ (*plural* **-loes** *or* **-los**) *n.* a petty or unimportant offence or fault [Late 16thC. Via Spanish 'little fault or sin', from *peccado* 'sin', from, ultimately, Latin *peccare* 'to sin'.]

peccant /pékənt/ *adj.* (*formal*) **1.** SINFUL guilty of a sin **2.** WILFUL violating a rule or practice [Late 16thC. From Latin *peccant-*, the present participle stem of *peccare* 'to sin'.] —**peccancy** *n.* —**peccantly** *adv.*

peccary /pékəri/ (*plural* **-ries**) *n.* a wild pig of Mexico and South America with a rudimentary tail and small tusks on the upper jaw that grow downwards. Genus: *Tayassu.* [Early 17thC. From Carib *pakira.*]

peccavi /pe kaá vee/ (*plural* **-vis**) *n.* an admission of sin or guilt (*literary*) [Early 16thC. From Latin, literally 'I have sinned'.]

pech /pekh/ *n. Scotland* PANTING BREATH a short, fast, and forceful breath ■ *vi.* (**peches, peching, peched**) *Scotland* PANT FOR BREATH to pant or struggle for breath from exertion [15thC. An imitation of the sound of breathing heavily.]

Pechora /pi cháwrə/ river in northwestern European Russia, flowing northwards to the Barents Sea. Length: 1,809 km/1,124 mi.

peck[1] /pek/ *v.* (**pecks, pecking, pecked**) **1.** *vt.* PICK UP WITH BEAK to take small bits of food using a beak **2.** *vti.* STRIKE WITH BEAK to strike sb or sth with a beak **3.** *vt.* MAKE HOLE IN to make a hole in sth by repeatedly striking it with a beak **4.** *vi.* NIBBLE to eat small quantities of food with little interest ○ *She just pecked at her food.* **5.** *vt.* KISS LIGHTLY to kiss sb lightly and briefly ■ *n.* **1.** SWIFT BITE WITH BEAK a quick light stroke, blow, or bite with a beak **2.** HOLE MADE BY BEAK a mark or hole made by a beak or pointed object **3.** LIGHT KISS a quick light kiss (*informal*) [14thC. Origin uncertain: probably originally a variant of PICK 'to poke, pierce', perhaps influenced by Middle Low German *pekken* 'to peck'.]

peck[2] /pek/ *n.* **1.** UNIT OF DRY MEASURE a unit of dry measure equal to 9.09 litres/8 quarts **2.** CONTAINER FOR PECK a container that holds a peck of material **3.** LARGE QUANTITY a large amount or number of sth (*informal*) [13thC. Origin unknown.]

pecker /pékər/ *n.* **1.** STH THAT PECKS sth that pecks, especially a woodpecker **2.** *US* PENIS a penis (*slang*) (*sometimes considered offensive*) ◇ **keep your pecker up** used to tell sb to keep his or her spirits up (*informal*)

pecking order *n.* **1.** SOC SCI SOCIAL HIERARCHY a social hierarchy in which some members of a group are established as superior to others **2.** BIRDS SOCIAL HIERARCHY AMONG FOWL a social hierarchy among domestic fowl in which each member maintains its place by dominance over the lower members ['Pecking' formed from PECK 'to strike with beak']

peckish /pékish/ *adj.* slightly hungry (*informal*)

Pecksniffian /pek sníffi ən/ *adj.* hypocritical and making a show of having high moral principles [Mid-19thC. Named after *Pecksniff*, a highly hypocritical character in *Martin Chuzzlewit* (1844) by Charles Dickens.]

pecorino /pékə reénō/ (*plural* **-nos**) *n.* a hard pungent Italian cheese made from ewe's milk [Mid-20thC. From Italian *pecora* 'sheep'.]

Pécs /paych/ town and capital of Baranya County, southwestern Hungary, situated about 170 km/105 mi. southwest of Budapest. Population: 172,177 (1994).

pectate /pék tayt/ *n.* a salt or ester of pectic acid [Mid-19thC. Formed from PECTIC ACID.]

pectic acid /péktik-/ *n.* a gelatinous acid that does not dissolve in water and is formed from certain esters of pectin. Formula: $C_{17}H_{24}O_{16}$. [*Pectic* from Greek *pēktikos*, from *pēktos* 'curdled, congealed', which was formed in turn from *pēgnunai* 'to make solid']

pectin /péktin/ *n.* a soluble chemical substance found mainly in the rinds of citrus fruits that binds cells together and is used to gel foods and various commercial products [Mid-19thC. Via French from Greek *pektos* (see PECTIC ACID).] —**pectic** *adj.* —**pectinous** *adj.* —**pectinaceous** /-náyshəss/ *adj.*

pectinate /pékti nayt/, **pectinated** /pékti naytid/ *adj.* ZOOL having projections that resemble the teeth of a comb —**pectination** /pékti náysh'n/ *n.*

pectinesterase /pékti néstə rayz, -rayss/ *n.* an enzyme that catalyses the hydrolytic breakdown of pectin into pectic acid and methanol [Mid-20thC. Coined from PECTIN + -ESTERASE.]

pectize /pék tīz/ (**-tizes, -tizing, -tized**), **pectise** (**-tises, -tising, -tised**) *vt.* to change sth into a gel —**pectizable** *adj.* —**pectization** /pék tī záysh'n/ *n.*

pectoral /péktərəl/ *adj.* **1.** ANAT OF THE CHEST relating to or located in or on the chest **2.** WORN ON CHEST worn on the chest ○ *a pectoral medal* ■ *n.* **1.** ANAT CHEST MUSCLE a chest muscle or organ ○ *an exercise for the pectorals* **2.** ZOOL = **pectoral fin 3.** BREASTPLATE sth that is worn on the chest as a decoration or ornament **4.** MED CHEST MEDICINE a medicine for chest or respiratory disorders (*dated*) [15thC. Via French *pectorale* 'sth worn on the chest', from Latin *pectorale* 'breastplate' and *pectoralis* 'of the chest', which were formed from *pectus* 'chest'.] —**pectorally** *adv.*

pectoral arch *n.* ZOOL = **pectoral girdle**

pectoral fin *n.* either of a pair of fins of a fish located either directly behind the gill openings or below them

pectoral girdle *n.* the part of the skeleton of a vertebrate animal that consists of bone or cartilage and provides attachment and support for the forelimbs

pectoral muscle *n.* any of four flat muscles, two on each side of the front of the chest, that help to move the upper arm and shoulder. The large fan-shaped pectoralis major pulls the arm forwards across the chest, while the pectoralis minor beneath it depresses the shoulder.

pectoral sandpiper *n.* a rare North American shorebird with mottled brown markings that breeds only in the Arctic and migrates to Central and South America for the winter. Latin name: *Calidris melanotos.* [Because the male inflates its breast during courtship]

peculate /pékyŏo layt/ (**-lates, -lating, -lated**) *vt.* to appropriate money or property by embezzlement or theft (*formal*) [Mid-18thC. From Latin *peculari*, from *peculium* (see PECULIAR).] —**peculator** *n.* —**peculation** /pékyŏo láysh'n/ *n.*

peculiar /pi kyŏoli ər/ *adj.* **1.** UNUSUAL unusual, strange, or unconventional ○ *The situation was very peculiar.* **2.** UNIQUE belonging exclusively to or identified distinctly with sb or sth ■ *n.* **1.** SB'S PROPERTY OR RIGHT a privilege or property that belongs uniquely to sb (*archaic*) **2.** CHR CHURCH EXEMPT FROM DIOCESAN JURISDICTION a church or parish that is exempt from the jurisdiction of the diocese in which it is situated [15thC.

From Latin *peculiaris* 'of private property' (later 'individual', hence 'strange'), from *peculium* 'private property', from *pecus* 'cattle', hence 'wealth'.] —**peculiarly** *adv.*

peculiarity /pi kyoŏli árrəti/ (*plural* **-ties**) *n.* **1.** INDIVIDUAL CHARACTERISTIC a characteristic or trait that belongs distinctively to a particular person, place, or thing **2.** ODDNESS the quality or state of being unusual or strange

peculium /pi kyoŏli əm/ *n.* LAW, HIST in Roman law, property that a father allowed his child, or a master his slave, to own independently [Late 17thC. From Latin (see PECULIAR).]

pecuniary /pi kyoŏni əri/ *adj.* **1.** OF MONEY relating to or involving money **2.** LAW INVOLVING FINANCIAL PENALTY involving a financial penalty such as a fine ○ *a pecuniary offence* [Early 16thC. From Latin *pecuniarius*, from *pecunia* 'money, wealth in cattle', from *pecus* 'cattle'.] —**pecuniarily** *adv.*

pecuniary advantage *n.* in law, a financial benefit gained by fraud or deception

ped. *abbr.* pedal

ped- *prefix.* = **pedo-** (*used before vowels*)

pedagogics /péddə gójjiks/ *n.* = **pedagogy** (*formal*) (*takes a singular verb*)

pedagogue /péddə gog/ *n.* **1.** TEACHER an educator or schoolteacher **2.** PEDANTIC TEACHER a teacher who teaches in a particularly pedantic or dogmatic manner [14thC. Via Latin *paedagogus* from Greek *paidagōgos* 'slave who leads a child to school', from *pais* 'child' + *agōgos* 'leader'.]

pedagogy /péddə goji/ *n.* the science or profession of teaching [Mid-16thC. Via French *pédagogie* from Greek *paidagōgia* 'duties of a pedagogue'.] —**pedagogic** *adj.* —**pedagogical** *adj.* —**pedagogically** *adv.*

pedal[1] /péddˈl/ *n.* **1.** FOOT-OPERATED LEVER FOR MACHINE a lever operated by the foot that powers a mechanism such as a bicycle, sewing machine, or the foot controls of a car **2.** MUSIC FOOT-OPERATED LEVER FOR MUSICAL INSTRUMENT a foot-operated lever used in playing the piano, organ, and other musical instruments **3.** MUSIC = **pedal point** ■ *vti.* (**-als, -alling, -alled**) **1.** TRANSP MAKE BICYCLE MOVE to use the pedals to make a bicycle or other vehicle move forward **2.** OPERATE OR PLAY INSTRUMENT USING FOOT MECHANISM to operate the pedals of sth such as a piano, organ, or machine in order to make it work [Early 17thC. Via French, ultimately, Latin *pedalis* 'of the foot', from *ped-, pes* 'foot' (source also of English *impede* and *pedigree*).] —**pedaller** *n.*

pedal[2] /peédˈl, péddˈl/ *adj.* relating to the foot or feet [Early 17thC. From Latin *pedalis* 'of the foot'.]

pedalo /péddəlō/ (*plural* **-alos** *or* **-aloes**) *n.* a small pleasure boat that is powered by paddles and operated by pedals [Mid-20thC. Formed from PEDAL.]

pedal point *n.* a note, usually in the bass, that is sustained while other musical parts and harmonies continue

pedal pushers *npl.* calf-length trousers for women, originally designed for cycling

pedal steel, **pedal steel guitar** *n.* an electrically amplified floor-mounted guitar that is fretted with a steel bar and usually has ten strings, whose pitch can be varied by the use of pedals

pedant /péddˈnt/ *n.* **1.** SB TOO CONCERNED WITH RULES AND DETAILS sb who pays excessive attention to formal scholarship and to unimportant rules and details **2.** SB WHO SHOWS OFF KNOWLEDGE sb who makes an ostentatious display of learning **3.** TEACHER a schoolteacher (*archaic*) [Late 16thC. Via French *pédant* from Italian *pedante*, of uncertain origin: perhaps from, ultimately, Latin *paedagogus* (see PEDAGOGUE).]

pedantic /pi dántik/ *adj.* too concerned with what are thought to be correct rules and details, e.g. in language —**pedantically** *adv.*

pedantry /péddˈntri/ (*plural* **-ries**) *n.* a pedantic attitude or an example of pedantic behaviour

pedate /péddayt/ *adj.* possessing, used as, or resembling a foot or feet [Late 18thC. From Latin *pedatus* 'having feet', from *pes* 'foot'.] —**pedately** *adv.*

peddle /péddˈl/ (**-dles, -dling, -dled**) *v.* **1.** *vti.* SELL GOODS to sell goods, especially while travelling from place to place **2.** *vt.* DRUGS SELL DRUGS to sell sth illegal,

especially drugs (*dated*) **3.** *vt.* PROMOTE IDEA to promote an idea or belief insistently [Mid-16thC. Back-formation from PEDDLER.]

peddler /péddlər/ *n.* **1.** DRUGS DRUG SELLER sb who sells sth, especially illegal drugs **2.** *US* = **pedlar** [14thC. Alteration of earlier *pedder*, of uncertain origin: perhaps from an obsolete word meaning 'basket'.]

pederast /péddə rast/, **paederast** *n.* a man who has sex with a boy (*formal*) [Mid-17thC. From Greek *paiderastēs*, literally 'lover of boys'.]

pederasty /péddə rasti/, **paederasty** *n.* sexual relations between a man and a boy (*formal*) —**pederastic** /péddə rástik/ *adj.*

pedes plural of **pes**

pedestal /péddistˈl/ *n.* **1.** ARCHIT BASE OF COLUMN a base or support for a column or statue **2.** FURNITURE SUPPORTING BASE the column-shaped base of a piece of furniture such as a table or washbasin **3.** POSITION OF BEING EXALTED OR ADMIRED a position in which sb admires another person so much that he or she thinks that person is perfect ○ *I don't want to be put on a pedestal – I just want to be treated as a normal person!* ■ *vt.* (**-tals, -talling, -talled**) PUT STH ON PEDESTAL to provide sb or sth with a pedestal [Mid-16thC. Via French *piédestal* from Italian *piedestallo*, literally 'foot of a stall'.]

pedestrian /pə déstri ən/ *n.* SB WALKING sb who is travelling on foot, especially in an area also used by cars ■ *adj.* DULL ordinary, unimaginative, or uninspired [Early 18thC. Directly or via French *pédestre* from Latin *pedester* 'going on foot', from *pes* 'foot'.] —**pedestrianism** *n.*

pedestrian crossing *n.* a place marked on a road as a place for people to cross. ◊ *pelican crossing*, *zebra crossing*. US term **crosswalk**

pedestrianize /pə déstri ə nīz/, **pedestrianise** (**-izes, -izing, -ized**) *vt.* to change a street into an area for pedestrians only by banning motor vehicles —**pedestrianization** /pə déstri ə nī záysh'n/ *n.*

Pedi /péddi/ (*plural* **-dis** *or* **-di**) *n.* **1.** PEOPLES SOUTH AFRICAN PEOPLE a member of a people that lives in parts of South Africa, mainly in Transvaal **2.** LANG LANGUAGE OF THE PEDI the Bantu language of the Pedi people, belonging to the Benue-Congo branch of Niger-Congo languages. Pedi is spoken by about three million people. —**Pedi** *adj.*

pedi- *prefix.* foot, feet ○ *pedipalp* [From Latin *ped-*, the stem of *pes* (see PEDAL).]

pediatrician *n.* US = **paediatrician**

pediatrics *n.* US = **paediatrics**

pediatrist *n.* US = **paediatrist**

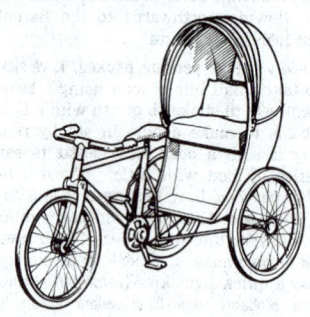
Pedicab

pedicab /péddi kab/ *n.* a pedal-operated tricycle with a seat in front for the driver and a passenger seat behind covered by a hood, available for hire in some Southeast Asian countries

pedicel /péddi sel, -s'l/, **pedicle** /péddik'l/ *n.* **1.** BOT STALK OF INDIVIDUAL FLOWER a stalk bearing a single flower or spore-producing body within a cluster **2.** ANAT STALK-SHAPED BODY PART an anatomical part that resembles a stem or stalk **3.** INSECTS NARROW SEGMENT a narrow anatomical part such as the waist between the thorax and abdomen of wasps and related insects [Late 17thC. From modern Latin *pedicellus*, from Latin *pediculus* 'footstalk', from *pes* 'foot'.] —**pedicellar** /péddi séllər/ *adj.* —**pedicellate** /-séllit, -layt/ *adj.*

pediculate /pi díkyoŏlit, -layt/ *adj.* relating to the anglerfishes, which are characterized by a modified dorsal spine with an attachment for luring prey [Mid-19thC. From modern Latin *Pediculati*, order name, from Latin *pediculus* (see PEDICEL).] —**pediculate** *n.*

pediculicide /pi díddi kyoŏli sīd/ *n.* a chemical substance that kills lice, used to treat infestations of humans and animals [Early 20thC. Coined from Latin *pediculus* 'louse' + -CIDE.]

pediculosis /pi díkyoŏ lóssiss/ *n.* infestation with lice, specifically the head and body louse *Pediculus humanus*. It can cause insomnia, irritability, and depression. [Early 19thC. Formed from Latin *pediculus* 'louse'.] —**pediculous** /pi díkyoŏləss/ *adj.*

pedicure /péddi kyoor/ *n.* **1.** MED MEDICAL CARE OF FEET medical treatment of the feet, e.g. the removal of corns **2.** COSMETICS COSMETIC TREATMENT OF FEET cosmetic treatment of the feet, e.g. the application of nail varnish **3.** COSMETICS, MED SESSION OF TREATMENT FOR FEET a session of cosmetic or medical treatment of the feet ■ *vt.* (**-cures, -curing, -cured**) TREAT FEET OF SB to give a pedicure to sb [Mid-19thC. From French *pédicure*, from the Latin stem *ped-* 'foot' + *cura* 'care'.] —**pedicurist** *n.*

pediform /péddi fawrm/ *adj.* in the shape of a foot (*technical*)

pedigree /péddi gree/ *n.* **1.** LINE OF ANCESTORS the line of ancestors of an individual animal or person, especially a pure-bred animal **2.** LIST OF ANIMAL'S ANCESTORS a document recording the line of ancestors of an animal, especially a pure-bred animal **3.** FAMILY TREE a table showing the line of ancestors of a person, especially an aristocratic or upper class person **4.** BACKGROUND the background, history, or origin of sth, especially a group ■ *adj.* PURE-BRED descended from a line of animals whose purity of breed has been recorded over several generations [15thC. From Anglo-Norman *pe de gru*, literally 'crane's foot'. From the resemblance of a family tree's branching lines to a bird's foot.] —**pedigreed** *adj.*

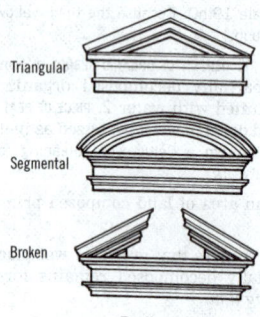

Triangular

Segmental

Broken

Pediment

pediment /péddimənt/ *n.* **1.** ARCHIT GABLE ON COLONNADE a broad triangular or segmental gable surmounting a colonnade as the major part of a facade **2.** GEOG BROAD ROCK AREA a broad flat rock surface of low relief adjacent to a steeper slope in an arid region, e.g. that of a mountain range, often covered with rock debris [Late 16thC. Origin uncertain: perhaps an alteration of PYRAMID.] —**pedimental** /péddi mént'l/ *adj.*

pedipalp /péddi palp/ *n.* either of a pair of appendages that are part of the mouths of spiders and other arachnids, used for various functions including manipulating food [Early 19thC. From modern Latin *pedipalpi*, from Latin *pes* 'foot' and *palpus* 'palp'.]

pedlar /péddlər/ *n.* sb who travels from place to place or from door to door selling goods. US term **peddler** [14thC. Alteration of *pedder*, of uncertain origin: perhaps from medieval Latin *pedarius* 'one who goes on foot', from Latin *pes* 'foot'.]

pedo- *prefix.* soil ○ *pedology* [From Greek *pedon*. Ultimately from the Indo-European word for 'foot' that is also the ancestor of English *foot* and *pedal*.]

pedodontics *n.* US = **paedodontics**

pedogenesis /peédə jénnisiss/ *n.* the natural process of soil formation, including erosion and leaching —**pedogenetic** /peédəjə néttik/ *adj.* —**pedogenic** /-jénnik/ *adj.*

pedology[1] *n.* US = paedology

pedology[2] /pi dólləji/ *n.* the scientific study of soil properties and the classification of soil types —**pedologic** /peèdəlójjik/ *adj.* —**pedological** /-lójjik'l/ *adj.* —**pedologically** /-lójjikli/ *adv.* —**pedologist** /pi dóllǝjist/ *n.*

pedometer /pi dómmitər/ *n.* an instrument that measures the distance covered by a walker by recording the number of steps taken [Early 18thC. From French *pédomètre*, from the Latin stem *ped-* 'foot' + French *-mètre* '-meter'.]

pedophile *n.* US = paedophile

pedophilia *n.* US = paedophilia

peduncle /pi dúngk'l/ *n.* **1.** BOT STALK the stalk of a plant **2.** ZOOL PART RESEMBLING STALK a part resembling a stalk in shape or function, e.g. the base of a fish's tail or a structure attaching an invertebrate animal to the place where it lives [Mid-18thC. From modern Latin *pedunculus*, literally 'a small foot', from Latin *pes* 'foot'.] —**peduncled** *adj.* —**peduncular** /pi dúngkyoōlər/ *adj.*

pedunculate /pi dúngkyoōlət, -layt/, **pedunculated** /-laytid/ *adj.* having or resembling a stalk, or a structure with the shape or function of a stalk

pee /pee/ *vi.* (**pees, peeing, peed**) URINATE to pass urine (*informal*) ■ *n.* (*informal*) **1.** URINE urine **2.** URINATION an act of urinating [Late 18thC. From the first letter of PISS.]

Peebles /peéb'lz/ town in southern Scotland, on the River Tweed. Population: 7,065 (1991).

peek /peek/ *vi.* (**peeks, peeking, peeked**) LOOK QUICKLY to take a quick look at sth, especially in a secretive way or at sth you should not be looking at ○ *I peeked at the name at the foot of the letter.* ■ *n.* QUICK LOOK a quick or secret look at sth [14thC. Origin uncertain: perhaps from earlier Dutch *kieken* 'to look'.]

peekaboo /peékə bóo, peékə boo/ *n.* CHILDREN'S GAME a game played to amuse small children, in which the face is hidden in the hands and then suddenly uncovered as 'peekaboo!' is shouted ■ *interj.* WORD SAID IN GAME OF PEEKABOO the word used when playing a game of peekaboo ■ *adj.* CLOTHES HAVING HOLES having holes or gaps intended to reveal parts of the body [Late 16thC. Coined from PEEK + BOO.]

Peekskill /peék skil/ city in southeastern New York State, on the Hudson River, southeast of Newburgh. Population: 20,805 (1996).

peel[1] /peel/ *v.* (**peels, peeling, peeled**) **1.** *vt.* REMOVE OUTER LAYER OF STH to cut away or pull off the skin or outer layer of sth, especially a fruit or vegetable **2.** *vi.* HAVE REMOVABLE SKIN to have a skin that can be removed **3.** *vt.* PULL STH OFF to pull or strip off sth, especially sth that is stuck to a surface **4.** *vi.* LOSE OUTER LAYER to lose or shed an outer layer or covering, e.g. of paint or sunburnt skin ○ *The skin on her nose was peeling.* **5.** *vi.* COME OFF IN THIN PIECES to come off in flakes, small pieces, or thin strips **6.** *vt.* SPORTS PUT BALL THROUGH CROQUET HOOP to make another player's ball go through a hoop in croquet ■ *n.* FOOD FRUIT OR VEGETABLE SKIN the rind or skin of a fruit or vegetable ○ *apple peel* [13thC. From Latin *pilare*, literally 'to deprive of hair', from *pilus* 'hair'. Originally in the meaning 'to plunder'.]

peel[2] /peel/ *n.* COOK a shovel with a long handle, used by bakers to move bread in and out of an oven [14thC. Via Old French *pele* from Latin *pala* 'spade'.]

peel[3] /peel/ *n.* ARCHIT a fortified tower of the type built in the border counties of Scotland and England in the 16th century to withstand raids [13thC. Via Anglo-Norman *pel* from, ultimately, Latin *palus* 'stake'.]

Peel /peel/, **Sir Robert** (1788–1850) British statesman. As home secretary (1822–27 and 1828–30) he organized the London police force, later known as "Bobbies" or "Peelers". He also served as Conservative prime minister (1834–35 and 1841–46).

peelable /peélǝb'l/ *adj.* **1.** WITH A SKIN THAT PEELS with a skin that can be peeled off **2.** REMOVABLE AND REUSABLE used to describe an adhesive label that can be removed and reused

peeler /peélǝr/ *n.* **1.** DEVICE FOR REMOVING SKIN FROM VEGETABLES a device for removing the skin from fruit or vegetables, usually a hand-held utensil with a blade **2.** US STRIPPER a striptease dancer (*slang*)

peeling /peéling/ *n.* a piece of sth, especially fruit or vegetable skin, that has been peeled off (*often used in the plural.*) ○ *potato peelings*

peely-wally /peéli wólli/, **peelie-wallie** *adj.* Scotland pale, sickly, or feeling ill (*informal*) [Mid-19thC. Origin uncertain: perhaps an imitation of a whining sound, or perhaps a playful alteration of PALE.]

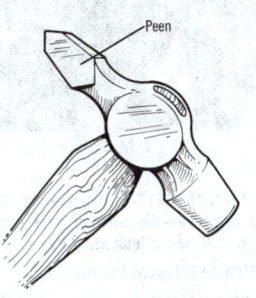

Peen

peen /peen/ *n.* END OF HAMMER HEAD OPPOSITE FACE the end of a hammer head opposite the flat face, often rounded or wedge-shaped, and used for bending and shaping ■ *vt.* (**peens, peening, peened**) SHAPE STH USING PEEN to bend or shape sth by striking it with the peen of a hammer [Late 17thC. Origin uncertain: perhaps from a Scandinavian word.]

peep[1] /peep/ *v.* (**peeps, peeping, peeped**) **1.** *vi.* LOOK QUICKLY OR SECRETLY to look quickly or secretly, e.g. through a small opening or from a hiding place **2.** *vti.* EMERGE OR MAKE STH EMERGE to become or make sth become partly visible or visible only for a short time ■ *n.* **1.** QUICK LOOK a quick or secret look at sth **2.** THE FIRST SIGHT OF STH the first appearance or sight of sth [15thC. Origin uncertain: perhaps an alteration of PEEK.]

peep[2] /peep/ *vi.* (**peeps, peeping, peeped**) **1.** MAKE A SHORT, HIGH-PITCHED NOISE to make a high-pitched little noise like a baby bird or a mouse **2.** SPEAK IN HIGH OR QUIET VOICE to speak in a quiet, weak, or high-pitched voice **3.** MAKE QUIET NOISE to make the quietest possible noise or remark ■ *n.* **1.** SHORT HIGH-PITCHED SOUND a high-pitched sound like that of a baby bird or a mouse **2.** SMALLEST SOUND a very quiet utterance ○ *I don't want to hear another peep out of any of you!* [15thC. An imitation of the sound.]

peeper[1] /peépər/ *n.* **1.** SB WHO PEEPS sb who looks secretly at sb or sth **2.** EYE sb's eye (*dated slang*) (*often used in the plural*)

peeper[2] /peépər/ *n.* AMPHIB = spring peeper

peephole /peép hōl/ *n.* **1.** SMALL OPENING a small crack or hole that sb can look through **2.** SPYHOLE IN DOOR a small hole in a door that allows sb to see people on the other side without being observed

Peeping Tom, **peeping Tom** *n.* a man who gets sexual pleasure from secretly watching sb undressing or sexual activity between other people [Early 19thC. Named after a tailor in English legend who was the only person to look at Lady Godiva riding naked.]

peepshow /peép shō/, **peep show** *n.* **1.** EROTIC SHOW an erotic or pornographic film or show viewed from individual booths **2.** BOX FOR VIEWING a sequence of pictures viewed through a hole or lens in a box, viewed as a form of entertainment in former times

peep sight *n.* a metal tab at the rear of a rifle barrel, containing a small circular opening through which the user looks to align the front sight with the target

peepul *n.* = bo tree

peer[1] /peer/ *vi.* (**peers, peering, peered**) **1.** LOOK CLOSELY to look very carefully or hard, especially at sb or sth that is difficult to see, often with narrowed eyes **2.** BE PARTIALLY OR BRIEFLY VISIBLE to be partially visible or appear briefly [Late 16thC. Origin uncertain: perhaps from Low German *pīren* 'to look'.]

peer[2] /peer/ *n.* **1.** PERSON OF EQUAL STANDING WITH ANOTHER sb who is equal to another person or to other people in some respect such as age or social class **2.** MEMBER OF BRITISH OR N IRISH NOBILITY member of the nobility in Great Britain and Northern Ireland **3.** FRIEND a companion, fellow, or mate (*archaic*) [13thC. Via Old French from Latin *par* 'equal' (source of English *pair* and *par*).]

peerage /peérij/ *n.* **1.** NOBLES AS A GROUP peers considered as a class or group **2.** NOBLE RANK the rank, status, or title of a peer **3.** PUBL LIST OF NOBLES a book listing the members of the nobility and giving information about their families

peeress /peer éss/ *n.* **1.** WOMAN PEER a woman who is a peer **2.** WIFE OF PEER the wife or widow of a peer

peer group *n.* a social group consisting of people who are equal in such respects as age, education, or social class ○ *Teenagers usually prefer to spend time with their own peer group.*

peerie /peéri/ *adj.* Scotland small [Early 19thC. Origin unknown.]

peerless /peérləss/ *adj.* incomparable, matchless, or without equal —**peerlessly** *adv.* —**peerlessness** *n.*

peer of the realm (*plural* **peers of the realm**) *n.* in Great Britain and Northern Ireland, a member of the nobility who has the right to sit in the House of Lords

peer pressure *n.* social pressure on sb to adopt a particular type of behaviour, dress, or attitude in order to be accepted as part of a group

peer review *n.* assessment of an article, piece of work, or research by people who are experts on the subject

peer-review (**peer-reviews, peer-reviewing, peer-reviewed**) *vt.* to assess an article, piece of work, or research as an expert on the subject —**peer-reviewed** *adj.*

peeve /peev/ *vt.* (**peeves, peeving, peeved**) ANNOY SB to make sb feel annoyed, irritated, or resentful (*informal*) ■ *n.* (*informal*) **1.** STH THAT ANNOYS sth that annoys or irritates sb **2.** BAD MOOD an irritated or resentful mood [Early 20thC. Back-formation from PEEVISH.]

peevish /peévish/ *adj.* bad-tempered, irritable, or tending to complain [14thC. Origin unknown.] —**peevishly** *adv.* —**peevishness** *n.*

peewee[1] /peé wee/ *n.* VERY SMALL PERSON OR THING sb or sth that is extremely or exceptionally small, especially a small child ■ *adj.* TINY very small [Late 19thC. Reduplication of WEE.]

peewee[2] /peé wee/ *n.* BIRDS = pewee [Late 19thC. An imitation of the sound made by the bird.]

peewit /peé wit/ *n.* = lapwing [Early 16thC. An imitation of the sound made by the bird.]

peezle /peéz'l/ *n.* the penis of an animal, especially a bull or horse (*regional informal*) [Variant of PIZZLE.]

peg /peg/ *n.* **1.** PIN FOR FASTENING OR MARKING STH a small piece of metal, plastic, or wood used to secure or mark sth or to join two parts together **2.** HOOK FOR HANGING THINGS a hook or projecting piece of wood or metal that is attached to a surface such as a door or wall and used to hang things on, especially clothes **3.** FASTENER FOR CLOTHES ON WASHING LINE a hinged piece of wood or plastic used to fasten washing to a clothes line **4.** MUSIC PART FOR TUNING STRING a screw or pin around which a string is wound in the head (**pegbox**) of a stringed instrument. The string can be tightened or loosened to raise or lower its pitch by turning the peg. **5.** REASON FOR DOING STH sth used as an excuse or reason for doing sth, or as a support for an argument **6.** DEGREE OR STEP a degree, notch, or step, especially in sb's opinion of a person or thing **7.** SMALL DRINK OF SPIRITS a small drink of spirits such as brandy or whisky (*dated informal*) **8.** BASEBALL FAST THROW in baseball, a fast, low throw of the ball that puts a base runner out **9.** SPORTS CROQUET PIN in croquet, a post that must be hit with a ball in order for a player to win the game ■ *vt.* (**pegs, pegging, pegged**) **1.** SECURE STH WITH PEGS to fasten sth with one or more pegs **2.** PUT A PEG IN STH to insert a peg into sth **3.** MARK STH WITH PEG to mark sth, such as the score in a game, with a peg or pegs **4.** COMM FIX STH AT CERTAIN LEVEL to fix the cost or value of sth at a certain level **5.** US CATEGORIZE SB to classify sb or sth, especially as having a particular character **6.** THROW A BASEBALL to throw sth, especially a low and fast baseball (*informal*) [15thC. Origin uncertain: probably from obsolete Dutch *pegge*.] ◇ **bring** *or* **take sb down a peg (or two)** to make sb more humble ◇ **off the peg** ready to wear, not tailor-made ◇ **a square peg in a round hole** sb who is completely unsuited to the situation he or she is in

peg away *vi.* to persist or continue working at sth

peg down *vt.* to fasten sth down with pegs

peg out *v.* **1.** *vi.* COLLAPSE FROM EXHAUSTION to collapse from exhaustion or to be too exhausted to continue (*informal*) **2.** *vt.* FASTEN CLOTHES TO WASHING LINE to attach wet clothes to a washing line with pegs **3.** *vt.* SECURE STH WITH PEGS to fasten sth, such as a tent, with pegs **4.** *vi.* DIE to die (*informal*) **5.** *vt.* MARK OUT LAND WITH PEGS to mark out a piece of land with pegs **6.** *vi.* WIN CROQUET GAME in croquet, to hit the peg, thereby winning the game **7.** *vt.* EXCLUDE OPPONENT'S BALL IN CROQUET to make an opponent's croquet ball hit the peg, thereby causing it to be out of the game **8.** *vi.* SCORE WINNING POINT IN CRIBBAGE to score the winning point in cribbage

Pegasus /péggəssəss/ *n.* **1.** MYTHOL HORSE WITH WINGS in Greek mythology, a horse with wings, born of the shed blood of Medusa **2.** ASTRON LARGE NORTHERN CONSTELLATION NEAR ANDROMEDA a large constellation of the northern hemisphere between Andromeda and Aquarius

Pegasus Bay /péggəssəss-/ bay on the eastern coast of the South Island, New Zealand, situated between the Banks Peninsula to the south and Motunau Beach to the north

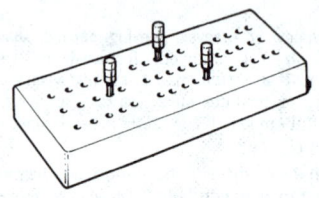

Pegboard

pegboard /pég bawrd/ *n.* **1.** BOARD WITH HOLES FOR PLAYING GAMES a board with a pattern of holes into which pegs are placed in games such as solitaire **2.** BOARD WITH HOLES FOR KEEPING SCORE a board with a pattern of holes into which pegs are placed to keep the score in some games, especially card games such as cribbage

Peg-Board *tdmk.* a trademark for a thin board with evenly spaced holes into which pegs or hooks can be placed for displaying, hanging, or storing things

pegbox /pég boks/ *n.* the portion of a stringed instrument that holds the tuning pegs

peg leg *n.* **1.** WOODEN LEG a prosthetic leg, especially a simple wooden one fitted at the knee (*informal*) (*often considered offensive*) **2.** OFFENSIVE TERM an offensive term for sb who has a prosthetic leg

pegmatite /pégmə tīt/ *n.* a coarse-grained igneous rock, usually granite, that is characterized by large well-formed crystals and often contains rare elements [Mid-19thC. Formed from the Greek stem *pēgmat*- 'sth joined together'.] —**pegmatitic** /pégmə títtik/ *adj.*

peg top *n.* SPINNING TOP a spinning top that is thrown from the hand and is caused to spin as a string quickly unwinds from around a central metal peg ■ **peg tops** *npl.* TROUSERS THAT NARROW TOWARDS ANKLES trousers that are full and gathered at the hips and narrow at the ankle (*dated*)

peg-top *adj.* used to describe a garment, especially a skirt or pair of trousers, that is wide at the hips and narrow at the hem (*dated*)

Pegu /pe góo/ city in Myanmar, formerly Burma. Between 1531 and 1635 it was the country's capital. Population: 150,447 (1983).

Pehlevi *n., adj.* = **Pahlavi**

I. M. Pei

Pei /pay/, **I. M.** (*b.* 1917) Chinese-born US architect. His work combines elegance of form with functional efficiency. Full name **Ieoh Ming Pei**

PEI *abbr.* Prince Edward Island

peignoir /páyn waar/ *n.* a woman's loose-fitting dressing gown, bathrobe, or negligée [Mid-19thC. From French, from *peigner* 'to comb', from, ultimately, Latin *pecten* 'comb'.]

pejoration /péejə ráysh'n/ *n.* **1.** WORSENING STATE a worsening, deterioration, or decline in quality, status, or value (*formal*) **2.** LING CHANGE TO NEGATIVE MEANING OF WORD a change over time in the meaning of a word so that it becomes less favourable or more negative. An example is the English word 'cunning', formerly used to mean 'learned' but now used to mean 'cleverly deceitful'. [Mid-17thC. From the medieval Latin stem *peioration*-, from late Latin *peiorare* 'to worsen', from Latin *peior* 'worse' (source of English *impair*).]

pejorative /pi jórrətiv/ *adj.* EXPRESSING DISAPPROVAL expressing criticism or disapproval (*formal*) ■ *n.* DISAPPROVING WORD a word, expression, or affix that expresses criticism or disapproval [Late 19thC. Via French *péjoratif* from, ultimately, late Latin *peiorare* (see PEJORATION).] —**pejoratively** *adv.*

peke /peek/, **Peke** *n.* a Pekingese dog (*informal*) [Early 20thC. Shortening.]

pekin /péekin/ *n.* **1.** TEXTILES SILK FABRIC WITH STRIPES silk fabric with broad stripes in various colours or patterns **2.** pekin, Pekin BIRDS LARGE WHITE DUCK a large white duck of a breed that originated in China [Late 18thC. From French. Named after *Pékin* 'Beijing'.]

Pekinese *n., adj.* = **Pekingese**

Peking /pee kíng/ former name for **Beijing**

Peking duck *n.* **1.** CHINESE DISH OF CRISPY DUCK Chinese dish in which small portions of duck meat, strips of crisp duck skin, cucumber, and spring onions are rolled in pancakes **2.** *Hong Kong* OVER-LOADED STUDENT a student who is expected to cope with a lot of school work and learn by rote

Pekingese

Pekingese /péeki néez/, **Pekinese** *n.* (*plural* -**ese**) **1.** ZOOL SMALL CHINESE DOG a small pet dog of a Chinese breed with a short flat nose, a long straight silky coat, and a tail that curls over its back **2.** MANDARIN CHINESE Mandarin Chinese (*dated*) **3.** PEOPLES SB FROM BEIJING sb who was born or lives in Beijing ■ *adj.* OF BEIJING relating to Beijing, or its people or culture

Peking man *n.* the fossilized remains of an extinct human species that lived 400,000 to 500,000 years ago, originally classified as Pithecanthropus and now regarded as a subspecies of Homo erectus [Early

20thC. Named after PEKING because its remains were discovered in China.]

pekoe /péekō/ *n.* a high-quality black tea [Early 18thC. From Chinese *pekho*, literally 'white down'. From the downy young leaves used.]

pel /pel/ *n., abbr.* pixel

pelage /péllij/ *n.* a mammal's coat of fur, hair, or wool (*technical*) [Early 19thC. Via French from, ultimately, Latin *pilus* 'hair'.]

Pelagian /pi láyji ən/ *adj.* CHR OF PELAGIUS OR PELAGIANISM relating to Pelagius or his teachings ■ *n.* CHR BELIEVER IN PELAGIANISM a believer in the teachings of the Christian heretic Pelagius

Pelagianism /pi láyji ənizəm/ *n.* CHR the belief of the heretical Christian Pelagius that people can earn salvation through their own efforts, without relying on the grace of God, and the rejection of the concept of original sin [Late 16thC. Named after PELAGIUS.]

pelagic /pə lájjik/ *adj.* **1.** FOUND IN OPEN SEA living, occurring, or deposited in the deep waters of the ocean or the open sea as opposed to near the shore **2.** FOUND IN SURFACE WATERS living, occurring, or found in the surface waters of the ocean or the open sea **3.** DEPOSITED ON OCEAN BED used to describe sediments deposited beneath deep ocean waters that are rich in the remains of microscopic organisms [Mid-17thC. Via Latin from Greek *pelagikos*, from *pelagos* 'sea'.]

Pelagius /pi láyji əss/ (360?–420?) Romano-British monk. His doctrine, known as Pelagianism, denies the existence of original sin and was condemned as heretical.

pelargonic acid /pélaar gonnik-/ *n.* = **nonanoic acid**

pelargonium /péllə góni əm/ (*plural* -**ums** *or* -**um**) *n.* a plant of South African origin with rounded or lobed leaves and clusters of red, pink, or white flowers. Many geraniums are cultivated forms of pelargoniums. Genus: *Pelargonium.* [Early 19thC. From modern Latin, genus name, from Greek *pelargos* 'stork'. From the resemblance of its capsules to a stork's bill.]

Pelasgian /pi lázji ən, -lázgi ən/ *n.* ANCIENT INHABITANT OF GREECE a member of any of the ancient peoples that lived in Greece and the Aegean Islands before the arrival of the Bronze Age Hellenic peoples ■ *adj.* **Pelasgian, Pelasgic** OF PELASGIANS OR THEIR CULTURES relating to the Pelasgian peoples or their cultures [15thC. Formed from Latin *Pelasgus*, from Greek *Pelasgos*, name of the Pelasgians' mythical founder.]

Pele

Pele /pél ay/ (*b.* 1940) Brazilian football player. He is considered one of the greatest players of all time. His Brazilian team won the World Cup in 1958, 1962, and 1970. He played for the New York Cosmos (1975–77) and then retired, having scored 1,281 goals during his career. Real name **Edson Arantes do Nascimento**

pelecypod /pi léssipod/ *n.* = **bivalve** [Late 19thC. From modern Latin *Pelecypoda*, class name, from Greek *pelekus* 'axe' + -*podos* 'footed'.]

pelerine /péllə reen, -rin/ *n.* a woman's short narrow cape with long pointed ends that meet at the front [Mid-18thC. Via French *pèlerine*, the feminine form of *pèlerin* 'pilgrim' from late Latin *pelegrinus* (source of English *pilgrim*).]

Pele's hair /péllayz-/ *n.* fine threads of volcanic glass formed by the action of the wind on jets of lava erupting into the air [Mid-19thC. Translation of Hawaiian *lauoho o Pele.* Named after *Pele*, the goddess of volcanoes in Hawaiian mythology.]

Peleus /péeli əss, péel yoos/ *n.* in Greek mythology, the king of the Myrmidons in Thessaly. He and the sea nymph Thetis were the parents of Achilles.

pelf /pelf/ *n.* money, wealth, or riches, especially if obtained dishonestly (*dated*) [14thC. Via Anglo-Norman from Old French *pelfre* 'booty', of unknown origin.]

pelham /péllam/ *n.* a bit for a horse's bridle that is midway between the simple snaffle bit and the harsher curb bit [Mid-19thC. From the surname *Pelham*.]

Pelican

pelican /péllikən/ *n.* a large web-footed bird found on warm-water coasts worldwide that has a large flat bill with a hanging pouch that can be expanded to catch and store fish. Family: Pelecanidae. [Pre-12thC. Via late Latin *pelicanus* from Greek *pelekan*, of uncertain origin: perhaps formed from *pelekus* 'axe', in allusion to the shape of its bill.]

pelican crossing *n.* a pedestrian crossing where people wishing to cross the road can stop the traffic by pressing a button that controls traffic lights at the side of the road [Acronym formed from *pedestrian light controlled*]

pelisse /pə léess/ *n.* **1. MILITARY GARMENT WITH FUR** a cloak, coat, or jacket lined or trimmed with fur, often worn as part of a military uniform, e.g. by members of the Hussar regiments **2. WOMAN'S COAT** a woman's long fitted coat or dress that opens at the front and is often trimmed with fur [Early 18thC. Via French and late Latin *pellicia* from, ultimately, Latin *pellis* 'skin'.]

pelite /pée līt/, **pelyte** *n.* aluminium-rich metamorphic rock formed by the action of temperature and pressure on clay-rich sedimentary rocks [Late 19thC. Formed from Greek *pēlos* 'clay'.] —**pelitic** /pi líttik/ *adj.*

pellagra /pə lággrə, pə láygrə/ *n.* a disease caused by a dietary deficiency of niacin and marked by dermatitis, diarrhoea, and disorder of the central nervous system [Early 19thC. From Italian, from *pelle* 'skin' + *agra* 'rough' or *-agra* 'seizure'.] —**pellagrous** *adj.*

pellagrin /pə lággrin, pə láygrin/ *n.* sb who has the dietary deficiency disease pellagra

pellet /péllət/ *n.* **1. SMALL BALL OF COMPRESSED MATERIAL** a small ball, or piece of material that has been pressed tightly together e.g. for animal feed or a medicine **2. ARMS SMALL BULLET** a small bullet or ball of metal fired from a gun **3. IMITATION BULLET** an imitation bullet for use in a toy gun **4. ARMS, HIST STONE MISSILE FOR CANNON OR CATAPULT** a ball, usually made of stone, formerly used as a cannonball or as a missile fired from a catapult **5. BIRDS UNDIGESTED MATTER REGURGITATED BY PREDATORY BIRDS** an undigested mass of food, mostly bone and hair, that is regurgitated by owls and other birds of prey **6. ANIMAL FAECES** a small round piece of the faeces of some animals such as sheep or rabbits ■ *vt.* (**-lets, -leting, -leted**) **1. STRIKE STH WITH PELLETS** to bombard or hit sb or sth with pellets **2. MAKE PELLETS OF STH** to make or form sth into pellets [14thC. Via French *pelote* from assumed Vulgar Latin *pilotta*, literally 'a small ball', from Latin *pila* 'ball' (source of English *pill*).] —**pelletization** /péllə tī záysh'n/ *n.* —**pelletize** /péllə tīz/ *vt.* —**pelletizer** /péllə tīzər/ *n.*

pellicle /péllik'l/ *n.* **1. THIN FILM OR MEMBRANE** a thin film, membrane, or skin **2. MICROBIOL FLEXIBLE SHEATH BENEATH PROTOZOAN CELL MEMBRANE** a multilayered flexible sheath that lies immediately beneath the cell membrane of many protozoans [Mid-16thC. Via French *pellicule* from

Latin *pellicula*, literally 'a small skin', from *pellis* 'skin'.] —**pellicular** /pə líkyoŏlər/ *adj.*

pellitory /péllitəri/ (*plural* **-ries**) *n.* a Mediterranean plant whose oil was formerly used for the relief of toothache. Latin name: *Anacyclus pyrethrum*. [Mid-16thC. Via Old French *peletre* from Latin *pyrethrum* (see PYRETHRUM).]

pell-mell /pél mél/ *adv.* **1. IN A DISORDERLY RUSH** in a disorderly frantic rush **2. UNTIDILY** in a confused, jumbled, or untidy manner ■ *adj.* **1. DISORDERLY** confused, frantic, or disorderly **2. CONFUSION OR DISORDER** a confused or disorderly condition or situation [Late 16thC. Via French *pêle-mêle* from Old French *pesle mesle*, a playful development of *mesler* 'to mix'.]

pellucid /pə loŏssid/ *adj.* **1. TRANSPARENT** allowing all or most light to pass through (*literary*) **2. CLEAR IN MEANING** easy to understand or clear in meaning (*formal*) [Early 17thC. From Latin *pellucidus*, from *pel-lucere* 'to shine through', from *lucere* 'to shine'.] —**pellucidity** /péllyoŏ síddəti/ *n.* —**pellucidly** /pə loŏssidli/ *adv.* —**pellucidness** /-sidnəss/ *n.*

Pelly /pélli/ river in Canada. It is a tributary of the Yukon River in southeastern Yukon Territory and originates in the Mackenzie Mountains. Length: 530 km/330 mi.

pelmanism /pélmənizəm/, **Pelmanism** *n.* a game in which a pack of cards is laid face down on a table and players try to select matching pairs by remembering their positions from previous attempts [Early 20thC. Named after Christopher Louis *Pelman*, English psychologist and specialist in memory techniques.]

pelmet /pélmət/ *n.* a narrow piece of fabric or board fitted above a window for decoration and to hide the curtain rail

pelobatid /péllō báttid, peélō-/ *n.* a frog with the backbone development of more primitive frogs and the leg-muscle structure of more advanced ones. The European spadefoot toad is a pelobatid. Family: Pelobatidae. [Mid-20thC. Coined from Greek *pelos* 'mud' + *bates* 'walker' + -ID.]

Peloponnese /péllapə neess/ peninsula in southern Greece, linked to the rest of mainland Greece by the Isthmus of Corinth. Area: 21,439 sq. km/8,278 sq. mi. —**Peloponnesian** /péllapə neézh'n, -neésh'n/ *n., adj.*

Pelops /peé lops/ *n.* in Greek mythology, the son of Tantalus, killed by his father and served up as a meal to the gods. The gods punished Tantalus and restored Pelops to life.

peloria /pə láwri ə/ *n.* unusual regularity of form in a flower that is commonly irregular [Mid-19thC. Via modern Latin from, ultimately, Greek *pelōr* 'monster'.] —**peloric** /pə láwrik, -lórrik/ *adj.*

pelorus /pi láwrəss/ *n.* a device used to measure bearings relative to the direction in which a boat is travelling [Mid-19thC. Origin uncertain: perhaps named after *Pelorus*, Hannibal's alleged guide from Italy.]

pelota /pə lóttə, -lōtə/ *n.* **1. FAST COURT GAME OF BASQUE ORIGIN** a fast court game of Basque origin, in which two players use long wickerwork baskets strapped to their wrists to hurl a ball against a marked wall and catch it. ◊ **jai alai 2. BALL FOR PELOTA** the ball used in pelota [Early 19thC. Via Spanish, literally 'ball', from, ultimately, Latin *pila* (see PELLET).]

pelt[1] /pelt/ *n.* **INDUST 1. ANIMAL SKIN WITH FUR** the skin of an animal with the fur, hair, or wool still attached **2. ANIMAL SKIN READY FOR TANNING** the skin of an animal with the fur, hair, or wool removed so that it is ready for tanning into leather ■ *vt.* (**pelts, pelting, pelted**) **REMOVE ANIMAL'S SKIN** to remove the skin of an animal [15thC. Origin uncertain: perhaps from Old French *pelete*, literally 'a small skin', from *pel* 'skin', from Latin *pellis*.]

pelt[2] /pelt/ *v.* (**pelts, pelting, pelted**) **1.** *vt.* **THROW THINGS AT SB OR STH** to bombard sb or sth with many blows or missiles **2.** *vt.* **BEAT AGAINST STH** to beat against sth continuously **3.** *vi.* **RAIN HEAVILY** to fall fast and hard as hail or rain **4.** *vi.* **TO MOVE QUICKLY** to hurry or move quickly ■ *n.* **A BLOW** a strong blow [15thC. Origin uncertain: perhaps a contraction of PELLET, or perhaps from Latin *pultare* 'to hit'.] —**pelter** *n.* ◊ **at full pelt** extremely fast

peltast /pél tast/ *n.* a foot soldier of ancient Greece armed with a light shield and a javelin [Early 17thC. Via Latin *peltasta* from, ultimately, Greek *peltē* 'a small light shield'.]

peltate /pél tayt/ *adj.* BOT used to describe a leaf that has its stalk attached to the lower surface in the centre rather than at the edge [Mid-18thC. Via Latin, literally 'armed with a light shield', from, ultimately, Greek *peltē* (see PELTAST).] —**peltately** *adv.* —**peltation** /pel táysh'n/ *n.*

Peltier effect /pélti ay-/ *n.* the production or absorption of heat at the junction of two metals when an electric current is passed from one metal to another. Heat is produced or absorbed depending on the direction and amount of current flow. [Mid-19thC. Named after its discoverer, the French scientist J. C. A. *Peltier* (1785–1845).]

Pelton wheel /pélt'n-/ *n.* an impulse turbine in which cup-shaped buckets on the edge of a rotor are hit with a high-pressure jet of water, causing the rotor to turn [Late 19thC. Named after its inventor, the US engineer L. A. *Pelton* (1829–1908).]

peltry /péltri/ *n.* the skins of animals collectively, especially when the fur is still attached [15thC. Via Anglo-Norman *pelterie* from, ultimately, Old French *pel* (see PELT[1]).]

pelves *n.* plural of **pelvis**

pelvic /pélvik/ *adj.* relating to, involving, or located in or near the pelvis

pelvic fin *n.* either of a pair of fins on the lower surface of a fish that have skeletal support and are analogous to the hind limbs of land animals

pelvic inflammatory disease *n.* an inflammation of a woman's reproductive organs in the pelvic area which can cause infertility

pelvimetry /pel vímmətri/ *n.* measurement of the inlet and outlet diameters of the pelvis, usually to assess whether there will be any difficulty during childbirth

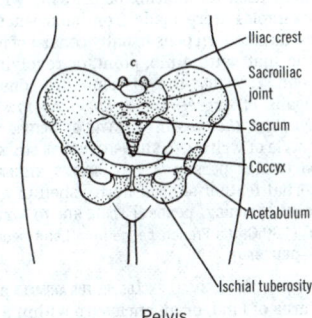

Pelvis

pelvis /pélviss/ (*plural* **-vises** *or* **-ves** /-veez/) *n.* **1. BASIN-SHAPED SKELETAL STRUCTURE IN VERTEBRATES** the strong basin-shaped ring of bone near the bottom of the spine formed by the hip bones on the front and sides, and the triangular sacrum on the back **2. BASIN-SHAPED CAVITY OR BODY PART** any basin- or cup-shaped anatomical cavity such as the region of the kidney into which urine is discharged before its passage into the ureter [Early 17thC. From Latin, literally 'basin'.]

pelycosaur /péllikə sawr/ *n.* a large extinct reptile that was common in Europe and North America during the Permian period, 290 to 245 million years ago. Order: Pelycosauria. [Mid-20thC. Coined from the Greek stem *peluk-* 'bowl' + -SAUR.]

Pemba /pémbə/ island in northeastern Tanzania, in the Indian Ocean. Its main towns are Wete and Chake Chake. Population: 265,039 (1988). Area: 984 sq. km/380 sq. mi.

Pembroke /pém broŏk, pémbrək/ town in southwestern Wales, in Pembrokeshire. Population: 15,820 (1991).

Pembrokeshire /pém broŏkshər, -brəkshər, -broŏk sheer, -brək sheer/ county in southwestern Wales. It is the site of many prehistoric and Roman remains. Haverfordwest is its administrative centre. Population: 113,500 (1995). Area: 1,591 sq. km/614 sq. mi.

Pembroke table /pémbroŏk-/, **pembroke table** *n.* a small four-legged table with a top that folds down on two sides and one or two drawers [Late 18thC. Origin uncertain: perhaps named after PEMBROKE.]

pemmican /pémmikən/, **pemican** *n.* **1.** NATIVE NORTH AMERICAN FOOD OF DRIED MEAT a traditional Native North American food made with strips of lean dried meat pounded into paste, mixed with melted fat and dried berries or fruits, and pressed into small cakes **2.** FOOD USED AS EMERGENCY RATIONS a nutritious food adapted from traditional Native North American pemmican and used as emergency rations, e.g. by explorers [Late 18thC. From Cree *pimihkan*, from *pimiy* 'fat'.]

pemoline /pémmə leen/ *n.* a synthetic stimulant of the central nervous system, used to treat depression and given to children who have attention deficit disorder. Formula: $C_9H_8N_2O_2$. [Mid-20thC. Coined from parts of *phenyliminooxooxazolidine*, its chemical name.]

pemphigus /pémfigəss/ *n.* a disease characterized by large blisters on the skin and mucous membranes, often accompanied by itching or burning sensations [Late 18thC. Via modern Latin from the Greek stem *pemphig-* 'pustule'.]

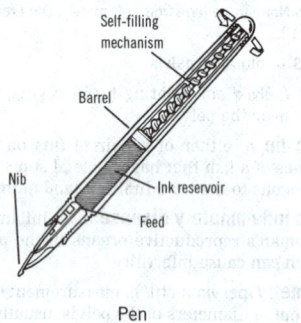

Self-filling mechanism

Barrel

Nib

Ink reservoir

Feed

Pen

pen¹ /pen/ *n.* **1.** INSTRUMENT FOR WRITING IN INK a long thin instrument used for writing or drawing with ink. Early examples were made from sharpened quill feathers, but modern pens usually consist of a metal or plastic shaft with a nib, point, or revolving ball at one end. **2.** WRITING the written word considered as a means of expression ○ *They say the pen is mightier than the sword.* **3.** STYLE OF WRITING a particular style of writing **4.** STH WRITTEN BY SB sth written by a particular person **5.** ZOOL SQUID'S INTERNAL SHELL the internal feather-shaped horny shell of a squid ■ *vt.* (**pens, penning, penned**) WRITE STH to write sth (*formal*) [13thC. Via French *penne* from Latin *penna* 'feather'.] —**penner** *n.*

pen² /pen/ *n.* **1.** AGRIC SMALL ENCLOSURE FOR ANIMALS a small fenced area of land, or an enclosure within a building, used to keep farm animals in **2.** AGRIC ANIMALS KEPT IN PEN the farm animals kept in a pen **3.** AREA THAT CONFINES SB OR STH an enclosed area where sb or sth is confined or controlled **4.** NAVY FORTIFIED DOCK FOR REPAIRING SUBMARINES a heavily fortified dock for repairing or servicing submarines ■ *vt.* (**pens, penning, penned**) CONFINE SB OR STH to keep or shut sb or sth in a pen or other enclosed area [Old English *penn*. Origin unknown.]

pen³ /pen/ *n.* BIRDS a female swan [Mid-16thC. Origin unknown.]

pen⁴ /pen/ *n.* US, Can CRIMINOL a state, provincial, or federal prison (*slang*) [Late 19thC. Shortening of *penitentiary*.]

PEN /pen/ *abbr.* International Association of Poets, Playwrights, Editors, Essayists, and Novelists

Pen. *abbr.* Peninsula (*used in place names*)

penal /peén'l/ *adj.* **1.** OF PUNISHMENT relating to, forming, or prescribing punishment, especially by law ○ *the penal system* **2.** PUNISHABLE BY LAW subject to punishment under the law **3.** USED AS PLACE OF PUNISHMENT used as a place of imprisonment and punishment ○ *a penal institution* **4.** PAYABLE AS PENALTY required to be paid as a penalty [15thC. Via French *pénal* from, ultimately, Latin *poenalis*, from *poena* 'penalty'.]

penal code *n.* a body or system of laws concerned with the punishment of crime

penal colony *n.* a place of imprisonment and punishment at a remote location

penalize /peénə līz/ (**-izes, -izing, -ized**), **penalise** (**-ises, -ising, -ised**) *vt.* **1.** SUBJECT SB OR STH TO PENALTY to impose a penalty on sb or sth for breaking a law or rule **2.** PUT SB OR STH AT DISADVANTAGE to put sb or sth at a disadvantage or treat him or her unfairly **3.** SPORTS PUNISH PLAYER FOR BREAKING RULE to punish a team or player for breaking a rule by giving an advantage to the opposing team or player **4.** MAKE ACT PUNISHABLE to make sth punishable by a law or rule —**penalization** /peénə līt záysh'n/ *n.*

penal servitude *n.* confinement in a penal colony as a result of conviction of a crime

penalty /pénn'lti/ (*plural* **-ties**) *n.* **1.** LEGAL PUNISHMENT FOR COMMITTING CRIME a legal or official punishment such as a fine or imprisonment for committing a crime or other offence **2.** LAW LEGAL PUNISHMENT FOR BREAKING CONTRACT a punishment such as a fine for failing to fulfil the terms of a legal agreement **3.** UNPLEASANT CONSEQUENCE sth unpleasant suffered as the result of an unwise action **4.** SPORTS DISADVANTAGE FOR BREAKING RULE a disadvantage imposed on a player or team for breaking a rule in a sport or game, e.g. a free shot at the goal awarded to the opposing side **5.** SOCCER = **penalty kick 6.** SOCCER GOAL FROM PENALTY a goal scored from a penalty in football

penalty area *n.* a rectangular area in front of a football goal within which the goalkeeper is allowed to handle the ball. A foul by the defending team within this area may result in a free shot at the goal being awarded to the opposing side.

penalty box *n.* **1.** SOCCER = **penalty area 2.** ICE HOCKEY AREA WHERE PENALIZED PLAYERS MUST WAIT an area with a bench beside an ice-hockey rink where penalized players must stay during the period they have to serve as a time penalty

penalty kick *n.* **1.** SOCCER FREE KICK AT GOAL in football, a free kick from the penalty spot at the opposing team's goal, which is defended only by its goalkeeper. It is awarded for certain types of foul within the penalty area. **2.** RUGBY KICK AWARDED AFTER FOUL a kick worth three points that can be aimed at the goal after a serious foul by a member of the opposing side

penalty rates *npl.* ANZ rates of pay that are higher than normal rates and that are paid for work performed outside normal working hours

penalty shoot-out *n.* a way of deciding a tied football game in which players from opposing sides take alternate free kicks at the goal from the penalty spot

penalty spot *n.* **1.** SOCCER SPOT FOR PENALTY KICK a designated spot on a football field, 11 m/12 yd from the goal line, from which penalty kicks are taken **2.** HOCKEY CIRCLE ON HOCKEY PITCH in hockey, a designated spot 7 m/23 ft from the goal line from which the shot is taken

penance /pénnənss/ *n.* **1.** SELF-PUNISHMENT FOR COMMITTING SIN self-punishment or an act of religious devotion performed to show sorrow for having committed a sin **2.** CHRISTIAN SACRAMENT OF RECONCILIATION a sacrament in some Christian churches in which a person confesses sins to a priest and is forgiven after performing a religious devotion or duty such as praying or fasting **3.** DUTY IMPOSED BY PRIEST a duty or religious devotion imposed by a priest during the sacrament of confession in some Christian churches ■ *vt.* (**-ances, -ancing, -anced**) IMPOSE PENANCE ON SB to make sb do penance for a sin [13thC. Via Old French from Latin *paenitentia* 'regret', from *paenitere* 'to regret'.]

Penang /pə náng/, **Pinang** state in northwestern Malaysia, comprising Penang Island and a small mainland area on the Malay Peninsula. Capital: George Town. Population: 1,065,075 (1990). Area: 1,031 sq. km/398 sq. mi.

penannular /pen ánnyoŏlər/ *adj.* in the shape of an almost complete circle [Mid-19thC. Coined from *pene-*, from Latin *paene* 'almost' + ANNULAR.]

penates /pə naá teez, -náy-/, **Penates** *npl.* in ancient Roman religious belief, the gods of a household or state [Early 16thC. From Latin, from *penus* 'provisions'.]

pence plural of **penny**

pencel /péns'l/, **pensil** *n.* a small narrow flag (**pennon**) or streamer, especially one carried at the end of a lance [13thC. Via Anglo-Norman from Old French *penoncel*, literally 'a small pennon'.]

penchant /póN shoN/ *n.* a strong liking, taste, or tendency for sth [Late 17thC. From French, the present participle of *pencher* 'to incline', from, ultimately, Latin *pendere* (see PENDANT).]

pencil /péns'l/ *n.* **1.** INSTRUMENT FOR DRAWING AND WRITING a thin cylindrical instrument used for drawing, or writing. It consists of a rod of graphite or some other erasable marking material inside a wooden or metal shaft. **2.** STH RESEMBLING PENCIL sth that has a similar shape, structure, or function to a pencil, e.g. a stick for applying cosmetics ○ *an eyebrow pencil* **3.** OPTICS NARROW CYLINDER OF LIGHT a long narrow cylinder or cone of light with a small angle of convergence **4.** GEOM SET OF LINES THROUGH A POINT the set of all lines passing through a fixed point or of all lines parallel to a given line **5.** PAINTING ARTIST'S FINE BRUSH a fine brush used by an artist (*archaic*) **6.** DRAWING ARTIST'S INDIVIDUAL STYLE the individual drawing style or technique of an artist ■ *vt.* (**-cils, -cilling, -cilled**) DRAW OR WRITE STH WITH PENCIL to draw, mark, write, or colour sth with a pencil [14thC. Via Old French *pincel* from, ultimately, Latin *peniculus* 'brush', literally 'a small tail', from *penis* 'tail'.]

pencil in *vt.* to note or enter sth provisionally, e.g. the time of a proposed engagement in an appointments book or on a calendar

pencil moustache *n.* a very thin moustache

pencil pusher *n.* US = pen pusher (*slang*)

pencil skirt *n.* a narrow, straight skirt

pen computer *n.* a computer that uses pattern-recognition circuitry or software to enable it to accept sb's handwriting as a form of data input

pend¹ /pend/ (**pends, pending, pended**) *vi.* **1.** AWAIT JUDGMENT to remain unsettled or wait to be judged **2.** HANG to hang **3.** DEPEND to depend (*archaic*) [15thC. Origin uncertain: probably from French *pendre* (see PENDANT).]

pend² /pend/ *n.* Scotland a vaulted or arched passageway, especially from the street to the back of a group of houses [15thC. Directly or via French *pendre* from Latin *pendere* (see PENDANT).]

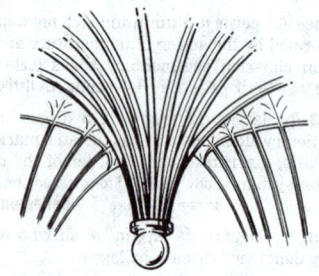

Pendant

pendant /péndənt/, **pendent** *n.* **1.** HANGING ORNAMENT OR JEWELLERY an ornament or a piece of jewellery that hangs from a necklace, bracelet, or earring **2.** NECKLACE WITH HANGING ORNAMENT a necklace with a hanging ornament attached to it **3.** HANGING LIGHT a lamp, chandelier, or other lighting fixture that hangs from the ceiling **4.** ARCHIT ORNAMENT HANGING FROM CEILING an architectural ornament hanging from a vaulted ceiling or roof **5.** ONE OF MATCHING PAIR a piece of art that matches or goes with another piece **6.** NAUT LENGTH OF WIRE OR ROPE a length of wire or rope attached at the upper end to a spar or similar part and at the lower end to a block and tackle ■ *adj.* = **pendent** [14thC. From French, the present participle of *pendre* 'to hang', from Latin *pendere*.]

pendent /péndənt/, **pendant** *adj.* **1.** HANGING OR SUSPENDED dangling, hanging, or suspended (*formal or literary*) **2.** OVERHANGING jutting, overhanging, or sticking out (*formal or literary*) **3.** GRAM GRAMMATICALLY INCOMPLETE used to describe an incomplete grammatical structure **4.** PENDING not yet dealt with, decided, or settled (*formal or literary*) ■ *n.* = **pendant** [13thC. Variant of PENDANT, influenced by Latin *pendent-*, the present participle stem of *pendere* 'to hang'.] —**pendency** *n.* —**pendently** *adv.*

WORD KEY: ORIGIN

The Latin word *pendere*, from which **pendent** is derived, is also the source of English *append*, *appendix*, *compendium*, *depend*, *impend*, *penchant*, *pendulum*, *penthouse*, *perpendicular*, and *suspend*.

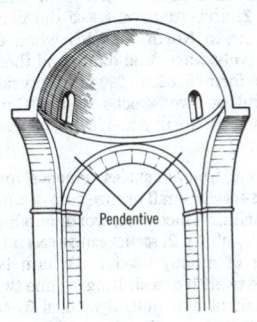

Pendentive

pendentive /pen déntiv/ *n.* a sloping triangular piece of vaulting between the arches that support a dome and its rim [Early 18thC. Via French *pendentif* from, ultimately, Latin *pendere* 'to hang'.]

Penderecki /péndə rétski/, **Krzysztof** (*b.* 1933) Polish composer. He is noted for his eerie, often aleatoric music. His works include *Threnody for the Victims of Hiroshima* (1961).

pending /pénding/ *adj.* **1.** NOT YET TAKEN CARE OF not yet dealt with, decided, or settled **2.** ABOUT TO HAPPEN about to happen or come into effect ■ *prep.* **1.** UNTIL until or while waiting for ○ *pending further enquiries* **2.** DURING during sth [Mid-17thC. Anglicization of French *pendant* (see PENDANT).]

pendragon /pen drággən/, **Pendragon** *n.* a supreme leader of the ancient Britons [15thC. From Welsh, from *pen* 'head' + *dragon* 'military standard' (from Latin *draco*).] —**pendragonship** *n.*

pendular /péndyōōlər/ *adj.* swinging to and fro with the motion of a pendulum

pendulous /péndyōōləss/ *adj.* **1.** HANGING LOOSELY hanging loosely or swinging freely **2.** UNDECIDED undecided or wavering in making a decision [Early 17thC. Formed from Latin *pendulus* (see PENDULUM).] —**pendulously** *adv.* —**pendulousness** *n.*

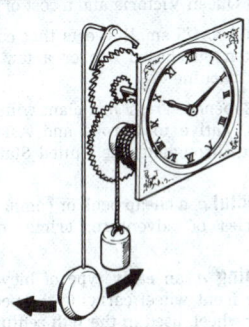

Pendulum

pendulum /péndyōōləm/ *n.* **1.** WEIGHT SWINGING FREELY FROM A FIXED POINT a weight hung from a fixed point so that it can swing freely to and fro under the influence of gravity **2.** SWINGING ROD CONTROLLING A CLOCK MECHANISM a rod with a weight at its base that swings from side to side and controls the mechanism of a clock **3.** STH THAT CHANGES REGULARLY sth that changes its direction or position regularly, often alternating between two extremes ○ *The pendulum has swung back to more traditional teaching methods.* [Mid-17thC. Via modern Latin from, ultimately, Latin *pendulus* 'hanging', from *pendere* (see PENDANT).]

Penelope /pə nélləpi/ *n.* in Greek mythology, the wife of Odysseus, who waited for his return from the Trojan War and was the mother of his son, Telemachus

peneplain /péeni playn/, **peneplane** *n.* an area of nearly flat featureless land that is the result of a prolonged period of erosion —**peneplanation** /péeniplə náysh'n/ *n.*

penes plural of **penis**

penetrable /pénnitrəb'l/ *adj.* capable of being penetrated —**penetrability** /pénnitrə bílləti/ *n.* —**penetrably** /pénnitrəbli/ *adv.*

penetralia /pénni tráyli ə/ *npl.* the innermost parts of a place, especially a sanctuary within a temple (*formal*) [Mid-17thC. From Latin, from *penetralis* 'innermost', from *penetrare* (see PENETRATE).] —**penetralian** *adj.*

penetrameter *n.* = penetrometer

penetrance /pénnitrənss/ *n.* the frequency with which a particular hereditary characteristic, e.g. a genetic disease, occurs among individuals carrying the gene or genes for that characteristic [Mid-20thC. From German *Penetranz*.]

penetrant /pénnitrənt/ *n.* **1.** CHEM SUBSTANCE THAT HELPS A LIQUID TO PENETRATE a substance that encourages a liquid to penetrate a porous material by lowering the surface tension of the liquid **2.** STH THAT PENETRATES sb or sth that penetrates

penetrate /pénni trayt/ (-trates, -trating, -trated) *v.* **1.** *vti.* ENTER OR PASS THROUGH STH to enter or pass through sth, e.g. by piercing it or forcing a way in ○ *The aim of the mission was to penetrate deep into enemy territory.* **2.** *vt.* SPREAD THROUGH STH to enter and spread through sth ○ *The fumes had penetrated the entire building.* **3.** *vt.* COMM GET A SHARE OF A MARKET to succeed in getting a share of a particular market **4.** *vt.* INFILTRATE A GROUP to enter sth such as an organization or country, usually secretly, in order to influence or gather information from within **5.** *vt.* SEE INTO STH to see into or through sth that is dark or obscuring **6.** *vt.* DECIPHER A MEANING to understand or discover the meaning of sth ○ *an enigma few were able to penetrate* **7.** *vi.* BE UNDERSTOOD to be understood or taken in by the mind ○ *It took a few seconds for the news to penetrate.* **8.** *vt.* INSERT THE PENIS to insert the penis into a vagina or anus [Mid-16thC. From Latin *penetrat-*, the past participle stem of *penetrare* 'to penetrate'.] —**penetrator** *n.*

penetrating /pénni trayting/ *adj.* **1.** ABLE OR TENDING TO PENETRATE strong enough to enter or spread through sth ○ *a penetrating odour* **2.** PIERCING OR PROBING apparently able to see or understand things that are hidden ○ *a penetrating glance* **3.** LOUD AND PIERCING loud, piercing, shrill, or unpleasant to the ears **4.** SHARP OR PERCEPTIVE able to understand or accurately identify sth ○ *a penetrating observation*

penetration /pénni tráysh'n/ *n.* **1.** ENTERING OR PASSING THROUGH the action of penetrating, entering, or passing through sth ○ *Penetration of the foundations by torrential rain resulted in structural damage.* **2.** ABILITY TO PENETRATE the ability or power to penetrate, enter, or pass through sth **3.** UNDERSTANDING the ability to understand or perceive sth **4.** MIL ATTACK THAT ENTERS ENEMY TERRITORY an attack that succeeds in penetrating an enemy's territory or defences **5.** ARMS DEPTH PROJECTILE GOES INTO A TARGET a measure of the depth a projectile reaches beneath the surface of its target **6.** COMM DEGREE OF SUCCESS IN A MARKET the extent to which a commercial product or service is recognized or bought in a particular market ○ *The launch of the new product should improve the company's market penetration.* **7.** INSERTION OF PENIS the insertion of the penis into a vagina or anus

penetrative /pénnitrətiv, -traytiv/ *adj.* **1.** PENETRATING piercing sth or able to get through sth **2.** KEEN mentally perceptive or insightful **3.** INVOLVING INSERTION OF PENIS used to describe sexual activity that involves putting the penis into a vagina or anus

penetrometer /pénni trómmitər/, **penetrameter** /-trám-/ *n.* **1.** INSTRUMENT FOR MEASURING RADIATION an instrument for measuring the penetrating power of forms of electromagnetic radiation such as X-rays by comparing the transmission through standard absorbers **2.** DEVICE FOR MEASURING FIRMNESS an instrument for measuring the penetrability of a solid material by measuring the depth to which it may be pierced with a standard needle [Early 20thC. Coined from PENETRATION + -METER.]

pen friend *n.* a person, especially one living in another country, with whom you establish a friendship through an exchange of letters and who you may never meet in person. US term **pen pal**

Penguin

penguin /péng gwin/ *n.* **1.** SEABIRD THAT CANNOT FLY an upright web-footed seabird with contrasting black-and-white plumage, native to cold regions of the southern hemisphere. Penguins cannot fly but use their flipper-shaped wings for swimming. Family: Spheniscidae. **2.** GREAT AUK the great auk (*archaic*) [Late 16thC. Origin uncertain: perhaps from Welsh *pen gwyn* 'white head', in allusion to the great auk or to the snow-covered headland of Newfoundland.]

penholder /pén hōldər/ *n.* **1.** HANDLE FOR HOLDING A PEN NIB a handle for a pen point or nib, consisting of a metal, plastic, or wooden rod **2.** HOLDER FOR A PEN OR PENS a holder for a pen or pens in the form of, e.g. a beaker, rack, or stand

-penia *suffix.* deficiency ○ *thrombocytopenia* [Via modern Latin from Greek *penia* 'poverty, want']

penicillamine /pénni sílla meen/ *n.* a drug formed by the breakdown of penicillin, used in the treatment of rheumatoid arthritis and for the removal of toxic metals from the body. Formula: $C_5H_{11}NO_2S$. [Mid-20thC. A blend of PENICILLIN and AMINE.]

penicillate /pénni síllət/ *adj.* having or resembling a tuft of hair [Early 19thC. Formed from Latin *penicillus* (see PENICILLIUM).] —**penicillately** *adv.* —**penicillation** /pénnissi láysh'n/ *n.*

R = an organic group (e.g. C_6H_5)

Penicillin

penicillin /pénni síllin/ *n.* an antibiotic originally derived from mould but now also produced synthetically. It is used to treat a wide range of bacterial infections. Genus: *Penicillium*. [Early 20thC. Formed from PENICILLIUM.]

penicillinase /pénni sílli nayz, -nayss/ *n.* an enzyme found in some bacteria that makes penicillin inactive and is therefore used to stop adverse reactions to the antibiotic. Production of this enzyme plays a role in the development of penicillin-resistant strains of bacteria.

penicillium /pénni sílli əm/ *n.* a bluish-green fungus that grows on stale or ripening food. Some forms of penicillium are used to make cheese and others are a source of the antibiotic penicillin. Genus: *Penicillium*. [Mid-19thC. From modern Latin, from Latin *penicillus* 'paintbrush', from *peniculus* (see PENCIL). From its brushlike spore-bearing structures.]

penile /pée nīl/ *adj.* relating to, affecting, or resembling the penis

penillion /pe nílli ən/, **pennillion** *npl.* Welsh songs, often improvised, sung to a fixed harp accompaniment [Late 18thC. From Welsh, literally 'verses', from *pen* 'head'.]

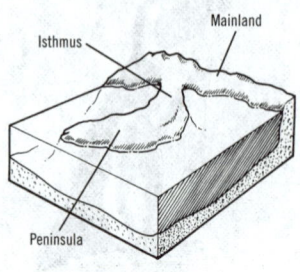

Peninsula

peninsula /pə nínsyŏŏlə/ *n.* a narrow piece of land that juts out from the mainland into a sea or lake [Mid-16thC. From Latin *paeninsula*, from *paene* 'almost' + *insula* 'island'.] —**peninsular** *adj.*

penis /peéniss/ (*plural* **-nises** *or* **-nes** /-neez/) *n.* the external male organ of copulation, used to transfer semen to the female. In most mammals, it is also used to expel urine from the body. [Late 17thC. From Latin, 'tail, penis'.]

penis envy *n.* in Freudian psychoanalysis, the theory that some girls' and women's psychological problems stem from a sense of deprivation about not having a penis. Very few psychologists now accept this concept.

penitence /pénnitənss/ *n.* regret or sorrow for having committed sins or misdeeds [12thC. Via French *pénitence* from Latin *paenitentia* (see PENANCE).]

penitent /pénnitənt/ *adj.* FEELING REGRET FOR SINS expressing or feeling regret or sorrow for having committed sins or misdeeds ■ *n.* **1.** SB REGRETTING HIS OR HER OWN SINS sb who feels regret or sorrow for his or her sins or misdeeds **2.** SB DOING PENANCE AFTER CONFESSION sb who does a penance under the direction of a priest or minister after confessing his or her sins [14thC. Via French *pénitent* from, ultimately, Latin *paenitere* (see PENANCE).] —**penitently** *adv.*

penitential /pénni ténsh'l/ *adj.* constituting or expressing penance or penitence —**penitentially** *adv.*

penitentiary /pénni ténshəri/ *n.* (*plural* **-ries**) **1.** *US, Can* CRIMINOL PRISON a prison, especially for people who have been convicted of serious crimes **2.** CHR ROMAN CATHOLIC OFFICIAL GRANTING ABSOLUTION a high official in the Roman Catholic Church who can grant absolution in extraordinary cases **3.** CHR ROMAN CATHOLIC TRIBUNAL a tribunal of the Roman Catholic Church dealing with penance ■ *adj.* **1.** OF PENANCE relating to penance **2.** CRIMINOL CONCERNING PUNISHMENT OR REFORM OF OFFENDERS involving or used for the punishment or reform of offenders **3.** *US* CRIMINAL LAW PUNISHABLE BY IMPRISONMENT IN A PENITENTIARY punishable by a term of imprisonment in a penitentiary [15thC. Via medieval Latin *paenitentiaria* from, ultimately, Latin *paenitentia* (see PENANCE).]

penknife /pén nīf/ (*plural* **-knives** /-nīvz/) *n.* a small knife with one or more blades that can be folded back into the handle. US term **pocketknife** [15thC. From its original use for making quill pens.]

penlight /pén līt/ *n.* a small electric torch that is similar in size and shape to a fountain pen

penman /pénmən/ (*plural* **-men** /-mən/) *n.* **1.** SB SKILLED AT WRITING sb who is skilled at handwriting, especially with a pen **2.** SB SKILLED AT HANDWRITING sb who writes or uses a pen with a particular level of skill **3.** AUTHOR an author or writer **4.** HIST SCRIBE sb who wrote or copied documents as a profession

penmanship /pénmən ship/ *n.* **1.** TECHNIQUE OF WRITING BY HAND the art, skill, or technique of writing by hand **2.** TYPE OF HANDWRITING the manner, quality, or style of sb's handwriting

Penn /penn/, **William** (1644–1718) English Quaker reformer and colonialist. After religious persecution in England he travelled to North America, where he founded Pennsylvania (1681).

Penn. *abbr.* Pennsylvania

penna /pénnə/ (*plural* **-nae** /-nee/) *n.* a feather that helps to form the outer contour of a bird's plumage, as opposed to a down feather [From Latin, 'feather'] —**pennaceous** /pe náyshəss/ *adj.*

pennae plural of **penna**

pen name *n.* a name used by a writer instead of his or her real name

pennant /pénnənt/ *n.* **1.** NAUT TRIANGULAR FLAG DISPLAYED ON A SHIP a small narrow triangular flag displayed on boats and ships for identification and signalling **2.** FLAG RESEMBLING A SHIP'S PENNANT a flag that has a shape similar to a ship's pennant **3.** NAUT = **pendant 4.** *US, Can, Aus* SPORTS FLAG SYMBOLIZING A SPORTS CHAMPIONSHIP a flag that symbolizes a championship in some sports, especially baseball **5.** *US, Can, Aus* SPORTS CHAMPIONSHIP SYMBOLIZED BY A PENNANT a championship that is symbolized by a pennant [Early 17thC. A blend of PENNON and PENDANT.]

pennate /pénnayt/, **pennated** /pénnaytid/ *adj.* **1.** ZOOL WITH FEATHERS having feathers or wings **2.** MARINE BIOL BILATERALLY SYMMETRICAL used to describe diatoms in the class Pennales, which are bilaterally symmetrical **3.** BOT = **pinnate**

penne /pénnay/ *n.* short tube-shaped pasta cut diagonally at the ends [Late 20thC. From Italian, the plural of *penna* 'feather, quill pen'.]

Penney /pénni/, **William George, Baron** (1909–91) British physicist. He developed the British atom and hydrogen bombs.

penni /pénni/ (*plural* **-nia** /pénni ə/ *or* **-nis**) *n.* **1.** a monetary unit of Finland, 100 of which are worth one markka. See table at **currency 2.** COIN WORTH A PENNI a coin worth one penni [Late 19thC. From Finnish.]

penniless /pénniləss/ *adj.* very poor or without any money —**pennilessly** *adv.* —**pennilessness** *n.*

pennillion *npl.* = **penillion**

Pennine Hills /pén īn-/ range of hills in northern England, forming the 'spine' of England

penninite /pénni nīt/, **pennine** /pénīn/ *n.* a green-blue hydrated crystalline silicate of magnesium, aluminium, and iron, a member of the chlorite group of minerals, occurring in low-grade metamorphic rocks [Mid-19thC. Named after the *Pennine* Alps, on the Swiss-Italian border.]

pennon /pénnən/ *n.* **1.** LONG NARROW FLAG CARRIED ON A LANCE a long narrow flag, usually triangular, tapering, or divided at the end, originally carried on a lance by a medieval knight **2.** NAUT = **pennant** *n.* 1 **3.** BIRDS WING OR PINION a bird's wing or the pinion of a wing (*literary*) [14thC. Via French *penon*, literally 'a large feather', from, ultimately, Latin *penna* 'feather'.]

Pennsylvania

Pennsylvania /pénss'l váyni ə/ state in the eastern United States bordered by New York State, New Jersey, Delaware, Maryland, West Virginia, and Ohio. Capital: Harrisburg. Population: 12,019,661 (1997). Area: 118,515 sq. km/45,789 sq. mi.

Pennsylvania Dutch *npl.* GERMAN AND SWISS IMMIGRANTS IN PENNSYLVANIA a group of people who emigrated from Germany and Switzerland to eastern Pennsylvania in the 17th and 18th centuries, or their descendants ■ *n.* **1.** **Pennsylvania Dutch, Pennsylvania German** LANG GERMAN DIALECT SPOKEN IN PENNSYLVANIA a dialect of German mixed with some English that is spoken in eastern parts of Pennsylvania by the Pennsylvania Dutch. Pennsylvania Dutch is spoken by about 70,000

people. **2.** FOLK ART THAT USES STYLIZED FIGURES a type of folk art developed by the Pennsylvania Dutch that uses stylized figures of people, plants, and animals, primarily in the decoration of household objects and in needlework [Mid-18thC. Alteration of German *Deutsch* 'German'.]

Pennsylvanian /péns'l váyni ən/ *n.* **1.** PEOPLES SB FROM PENNSYLVANIA sb who was born in or lives in Pennsylvania **2.** GEOL GEOLOGICAL PERIOD the period of geological time in North America when the climate was relatively warm and damp and the major coal beds were formed, 320 to 290 million years ago. It is the second of two epochs of the Carboniferous Period used by North American geologists. —**Pennsylvanian** *adj.*

penny /pénni/ (*plural* **pennies** *or* **pence** /penss/) *n.* **1.** SMALL BRITISH COIN a small bronze coin or unit of money used in Britain since 1971, worth one hundredth of a pound. Symbol **p 2.** FORMER BRITISH COIN a bronze coin or a unit of money used in Britain before 1971, worth one twelfth of a shilling, or one two-hundred-and-fortieth of a pound. Symbol **d 3.** COIN IN UNITED STATES AND CANADA a small coin worth one cent used in the United States and Canada **4.** COIN WITH LOW VALUE a coin or monetary unit with a low value or equal to one hundredth of a pound or one hundredth of a dollar in some countries **5.** VERY SMALL AMOUNT OF MONEY a very small amount of money ○ *It won't cost you a penny.* [Old English *penig.* Ultimately, from a prehistoric Germanic word that also produced German *Pfennig* 'penny'.] ◇ **a penny for your thoughts** used to ask sb what he or she is thinking about ◇ **cost a pretty penny** to cost a great deal of money ◇ **the penny dropped** used to say that you suddenly understood or realized sth ◇ **in for a penny, in for a pound** if you decide to do sth, you should do it wholeheartedly and boldly, and accept any resulting problems or difficulties ◇ **penny wise and pound foolish** economical with regard to small items of expenditure but extravagant with regard to large items ◇ **spend a penny** to urinate (*used euphemistically*) ◇ **turn up like a bad penny** to keep making unwelcome appearances

penny ante *n.* **1.** CARDS TYPE OF POKER a game of poker in which the bets are limited to small sums of money **2.** *US* COMM BUSINESS TRANSACTION INVOLVING VERY LITTLE MONEY any business arrangement that involves very little money or is inconsequential (*informal*) ○ *We're talking penny ante here.* —**penny-ante** *adj.*

penny arcade *n.* = **amusement arcade**

penny black, Penny Black *n.* the first adhesive postage stamp, issued by Britain in 1840, with a portrait of Queen Victoria and a cost of one penny

penny candy *n. US* small sweets that cost about a penny, often purchased one or a few at a time through a machine

pennycress /pénnee kress/ *n.* a plant with round flat seed pods, native to Europe and Asia but now naturalized throughout the United States. Genus: *Thlaspi.*

penny dreadful *n.* a cheap book or comic containing lurid stories of adventure, crime, or passion (*informal*)

penny-farthing *n.* an early type of bicycle with a very large front wheel carrying the pedals and a small rear wheel, used in the 19th century

penny pincher *n.* sb who is extremely mean or excessively careful with his or her money (*informal*)

pennyroyal /pénnee róyəl/ *n.* **1.** MINT PLANT OF EUROPE AND ASIA a plant of the mint family with clusters of small purple flowers that is native to Europe and Asia and is used in medicines and as an insect repellent. Latin name: *Mentha pulegium.* **2.** N AMERICAN MINT PLANT an aromatic plant of the mint family that grows in eastern North America, especially a variety with bluish flowers. Latin name: *Hedeoma pulegioides.* [Mid-16thC. Alteration of Anglo-Norman *puliol real*, literally 'royal thyme'.]

penny shares *npl.* securities that sell on a stock exchange at less than 20p a share

pennyweight /pénnee wayt/ *n.* a unit of weight in the troy system, equal to 1.555 g/1/20 oz [Old English *penega gewiht*, the weight of a silver penny]

penny whistle *n.* a small high-pitched flute with six finger holes, similar to a recorder but made of metal and very inexpensive to buy

penny-wise *adj.* extremely careful about spending even small amounts of money

pennywort /pénnee wurt/ *n.* **1. ROCK PLANT** a plant that grows on rocks in Europe and Asia and has whitish-green tubular flowers and rounded leaves. Latin name: *Umbilicus rupestris.* **2. MARSH PLANT** a plant that grows in marshy areas in Europe and North Africa and has greenish-pink flowers and rounded leaves. Latin name: *Hydrocotyle vulgaris.* **3. PLANT WITH ROUNDED LEAVES** a North American plant of the gentian family with small white or purplish flowers and rounded leaves. Latin name: *Obolaria virginica.*

pennyworth /pénnee wurth, pénnərth/ *n.* **1.** (*plural* **-worths** *or* **-worth**) **AMOUNT COSTING A PENNY** the amount of sth that can be bought for a penny (*dated*) **2. SMALL AMOUNT** a small amount or the slightest amount (*dated*) **3. COMMENT OR OPINION** sb's comment or opinion, especially an unwelcome one (*informal*) [Old English *penig weorð*]

penology /pee nólləji/ *n.* the theory, scientific study of, and practice of how crime is punished, how prisons are managed, and how rehabilitation is handled [Mid-19thC. Formed from Latin *poena* (see PENAL).] —**penological** /peeenə lójjik'l/ *adj.* —**penologically** *adv.* —**penologist** /-óllənjist/ *n.*

pen pal *n.* either of two people usually in different countries, who become friends through an exchange of letters but who may never meet (*informal*) = **pen friend**

penpusher /pén pooshər/ *n.* sb who has a boring administrative job (*informal*) US term **pencil pusher** —**penpushing** *adj.*, *n.*

Penrith /pén rith, pen ríth/ market town in England, in Cumbria. Population: 12,049 (1991).

Penrose /pénnröz/, **Sir Roger** (*b.* 1931) British mathematician. He worked with Stephen Hawking on black holes, and has also made important contributions to pure mathematics.

pensile /pén sīl/ *adj.* **1. HANGING** hanging or suspended ○ *a pensile nest* **2. BUILDING A HANGING NEST** used to describe a bird such as the Baltimore Oriole that builds a hanging nest [Early 17thC. Via Latin *pensilis*, from *pens-*, the past participle stem of *pendere* (see PENDANT).] —**pensileness** *n.* —**pensility** /pen sílləti/ *n.*

pension[1] /pénsh'n/ *n.* **1. RETIREMENT PAY** a fixed amount of money paid regularly to sb during retirement by the government, a former employer, or insurance company **2. REGULAR SUM PAID** a sum of money paid regularly as compensation, e.g. for an injury sustained on a job, or as a reward for service, e.g. to an ex-soldier ■ *vt.* (**-sions, -sioning, -sioned**) **PAY A PENSION** to pay a pension to sb [14thC. Via French from Latin *pension-* 'payment', from *pens-*, the past participle stem of *pendere* (see PENDANT).]
pension off *vt.* **1. FORCE SB TO RETIRE** to force sb into retirement with a pension, e.g. as a cost-cutting measure or because of age **2. GET RID OF** to get rid of sth because it is useless or no longer needed (*informal*)

pension[2] /paànsyáwn/ *n.* **1. SMALL HOTEL** a boarding house or small inexpensive hotel in continental Europe, especially in France **2.** = **full board**

pensionable /pénsh'nəb'l/ *adj.* entitled to or relating to entitlement to receive a pension —**pensionability** /pénsh'nə bílləti/ *n.*

pensionary /pénsh'n-ri/ *adj.* **OF A PENSION** relating to a pension or the paying of a pension ■ *n.* (*plural* **-ies**) = **pensioner 2** (*archaic or literary*)

pensioner /pénsh'nər/ *n.* **1. SB RECEIVING PENSION** sb who is paid a pension, especially sb who has retired from work on the grounds of age **2. PENSIONS HIRED PERSON** sb whose services are bought, especially sb paid to do menial or unpleasant work (*archaic or literary*) **3. EDUC STUDENT WITHOUT SCHOLARSHIP** a student at Cambridge University who does not have a scholarship

pensive /pénssiv/ *adj.* thinking deeply about sth, especially in a sad or serious manner [14thC. Via French, from *penser* 'to think', from Latin *pensare*, literally

'to keep on weighing', from *pendere* 'to weigh', from English *poise*).] —**pensively** *adv.* —**pensiveness** *n.*

penstemon /pénstimən, pen steémən/, **pentstemon** *n.* a North American plant belonging to the figwort family that has large brightly coloured flowers with five stamens, one of which is sterile. Genus: *Penstemon* and *Pentstemon.* [Mid-18thC. From modern Latin, the genus name, literally 'five stamens', from Greek *penta-* 'five' + *stēmōn* 'stamen'.]

penstock /pén stòk/ *n.* a sluice, channel, or pipe used to control water flow or supply water to sth such as a hydroelectric plant [Early 17thC. From PEN 'enclosure'.]

pent /pent/ *adj.* (*archaic*) **1. SHUT IN** shut in or confined **2. REPRESSED** stifled or repressed ■ past tense, past participle of **pen** (*archaic*) [Late 16thC. Originally, the past participle of PEN 'to enclose'.]

pent- *prefix.* = **penta-** (*used before vowels*)

penta- *prefix.* five ○ *pentaploid* [From Greek *pente* 'five' (source of English *pentagon*). Ultimately from the Indo-European word for 'five', which is also the ancestor of English *five*, *finger*, and *fist*, as well as Latin *quinque*.]

pentachlorophenol /péntə klawrə feé nol/ *n.* a white chemical compound that is used in fungicides, disinfectants, and wood preservatives. Formula: C_6Cl_5OH.

pentacle /péntək'l/ *n.* MATH = **pentagram** [Late 16thC. From medieval Latin *pentaculum*, literally 'little five', from Greek *penta-* (see PENTA-).]

pentad /pén tàd/ *n.* **1.** MATH **GROUP OF FIVE** any group or series of five **2.** CHEM **ATOM WITH VALENCY OF FIVE** an atom or chemical group with a valency of five **3.** METEOROL **5 DAYS** a period of five days [Mid-17thC. From Greek, from *pente* (see PENTA-).]

pentadactyl /péntə dákt'l/ *adj.* ZOOL having five fingers on each hand or five toes on each foot —**pentadactylism** *n.*

pentagon /péntəgən/ *n.* MATH a geometrical figure that has five sides and five angles [Late 16thC. Via late Latin *pentagonum* from, ultimately, Greek *pentagōnon*, literally 'five-angled', from *penta-* (see PENTA-).] —**pentagonal** /pentágənəl/ *adj.* —**pentagonally** *adv.*

Pentagon /péntəgən/ *n.* the US Department of Defense, or the five-sided main building that houses it

Pentagram

pentagram /péntə gràm/ *n.* MATH a star-shaped geometrical figure with five points, especially one used as a magical or occult symbol [Mid-19thC. From Greek *pentagrammon*, a form of *pentagrammos* 'of five lines'.]

pentahedron /péntə heédrən/ (*plural* **-drons** *or* **-dra** /-heédrə/) *n.* MATH a solid geometrical figure that has five faces —**pentahedral** *adj.*

pentamerous /pen támmərəss/ *adj.* **1. WITH 5 SIMILAR PARTS** divided into or having five similar parts **2. BOT WITH 5 SIMILAR FLOWER PARTS** used to describe flowers that have petals or other parts such as sepals or stamens arranged in groups of five —**pentamerism** *n.*

pentameter /pen támmitər/ *n.* a line of poetry that is made up of five units of rhythm, e.g. five pairs of stressed and unstressed syllables [Early 16thC. Via Latin from Greek *pentametros*, literally 'having five measures', from *penta-* (see PENTA-) + *metron* (see METER).]

pentamidine /pén támmi deen, -din/ *n.* a drug used in treating protozoan infections, such as the African

forms of sleeping sickness and the form of pneumonia often caught by AIDS patients. Formula: $C_{19}H_{24}N_4O_2$. [Mid-20thC. From PENTANE + amidine.]

pentane /pén tàyn/ *n.* an organic chemical belonging to the group containing only hydrogen and carbon (**hydrocarbons**). It has three isomers, one of which produces a colourless flammable liquid used as a solvent. Formula: C_5H_{12}. [Late 19thC. Formed from PENTA-.]

pentangle /pént àng g'l/ *n.* MATH = **pentagram**

pentangular /pen táng gjŏŏlər/ *adj.* MATH having five angles and five sides

pentanoic acid /péntə nō ik-/ *n.* = **valeric acid**

pentapeptide /péntə pép tīd/ *n.* a peptide with five amino acids in its molecules

pentaprism /péntəprizəm/ *n.* OPTICS a prism with five faces that deviates light at a 90-degree angle, making it useful in correctly presenting an image in the viewfinder of a single-lens reflex camera

pentaquine /péntə kweən, -kwin/, **pentaquin** /-kwin/ *n.* a synthetic drug used together with quinine in treating or preventing malaria. Formula: $C_{18}H_{27}N_3O$. [Coined from PENTA- + QUINOLINE]

pentarchy /pén taàrki/ (*plural* **-chies**) *n.* **1. GOVERNMENT BY 5 RULERS** a system of government by five rulers **2. 5 POLITICAL UNITS** a federation of five political units **3. 5 RULERS** the group of five rulers who rule a pentarchy [Late 16thC. From Greek *pentarkhia* 'rule of five', from *penta-* (see PENTA-) + *-arkhia* (see -ARCHY).] —**pentarchical** /pen taàrkik'l/ *adj.*

pentastich /péntəstik/ *n.* a poem or section of a poem consisting of five lines [Mid-17thC. Via modern Latin from Greek *pentastikhos*, literally 'having five rows', from *penta-* (see PENTA-) + *stikhos* 'row'.]

pentastome /péntəstöm/ *n.* ZOOL = **tongue worm**

Pentateuch /péntə tyoòk/ *n.* the first five books of the Bible, traditionally regarded as having been written by Moses [15thC. Via ecclesiastical Latin from Greek *pentateukhos*, literally 'having five books', from *penta-* (see PENTA-) + *teukhos* 'book'.] —**Pentateuchal** *adj.*

pentathlete /pen táthleet/ *n.* an athlete who takes part in a pentathlon

pentathlon /pen táthlən/ *n.* **1.** = **modern pentathlon 2. OLYMPIC TRACK AND FIELD CONTEST** the Olympic competition consisting of five track and field events, usually sprinting, hurdling, long jumping, and discus and javelin throwing [Early 17thC. From Greek, literally 'contest of five', from *penta-* (see PENTA-) + *athlon* 'contest'.]

pentatomic /péntə tómmik/ *adj.* having five atoms in a molecule

pentatonic scale /péntə tonnik-/ *n.* any musical scale that has five notes to an octave, especially a major scale in which the fourth and seventh tones are omitted [*Pentatonic* from PENTA- + TONIC]

pentavalent /péntə váylənt/ *adj.* used to describe chemical elements that have a valency of five

pentazocine /pen tázzō seen/ *n.* a synthetic narcotic drug used as a painkiller. Formula: $C_{19}H_{27}NO$. [Mid-20thC. Coined from PENTA- + AZO- + OCTA- + -INE.]

Pentecost /péntə kàwst, -kòst/ *n.* **1.** CHR = **Whit Sunday 2.** JUDAISM = **Shavuoth** [Pre-12thC. Via late Latin from, ultimately, Greek *pentēkonta* 'fifty' (because it falls fifty days after the second day of the Passover), from *pentē* 'five'.]

Pentecostal /pénti kóst'l/ *adj.* **1. EMPHASIZING THE HOLY SPIRIT** belonging or relating to any Christian denomination that emphasizes the workings of the Holy Spirit, interprets the Bible literally, and adopts an informal demonstrative approach to religious worship **2. OF PENTECOST** relating to the Christian festival of Pentecost ■ *n.* **MEMBER OF A PENTECOSTAL DENOMINATION** a member of a Pentecostal denomination —**Pentecostalism** *n.* —**Pentecostalist** *n.*, *adj.*

pentene /pén teen/ *n.* a colourless flammable liquid with several isomers that is used in making organic compounds. Formula: C_5H_{10}.

penthouse /pént howss/ (*plural* **-houses** /-howziz/) *n.* **1. ROOFTOP DWELLING** an expensive and comfortable flat on the top floor of a building or built on the roof (*often used before a noun*) ○ *a penthouse apartment* **2. HOUSING FOR SERVICE EQUIPMENT** a structure on the roof of a building to house lift machinery, a water tank, or other service equipment **3. ADJOINING ROOF OR SHED** a sloping roof, or a shed with a sloping roof, built against the outer wall of a building **4. SPORTS ROOFED CORRIDOR** in real tennis, a roofed corridor that runs along three sides of a court [14thC. Alteration (influenced by HOUSE) of Anglo-Norman *pentiz* 'lean-to', via Old French *apentis* from, ultimately, Latin *appendere*, literally 'to hang onto', from *pendere* 'to hang'.]

pentimento /pént i méntō/ (*plural* **-ti** /-ti/) *n.* **1. TECHNIQUE FOR RESTORING PAINTINGS** the technique of removing a top layer of paint to reveal a painting or part of a painting that has been painted over **2. REVEALED PAINTING** a painting or part of a painting that is revealed by pentimento [Early 20thC. Via Italian, 'correction', literally 'repentance', from Latin *paenitere* 'to repent' (source also of English *penitent*).]

Pentland Firth /péntlənd-/ sea passage in Scotland separating the Orkney Islands from the mainland, and linking the North Sea to the Atlantic Ocean. Length: 32 km/20 mi.

pentlandite /péntlən dīt/ *n.* a brownish-yellow mineral that is the principal ore and main source of nickel [Mid-19thC. Named after the Irish scientist Joseph B. *Pentland* (1797–1873), who discovered it.]

pentobarbital sodium /péntō báarbit'l-/ *n. US* = **pentobarbitone sodium** [*Pentobarbital* formed from *pentobarbitone* (see PENTOBARBITONE)]

pentobarbitone sodium /péntō báarbitōn-/ *n.* a barbiturate used as a hypnotic and a sedative. Formula: $C_{11}H_{17}N_2O_3Na$. US term **pentobarbital sodium** [*Pentobarbitone* coined from PENTANE + BARBITONE]

pentode /pén tōd/ *n.* **ELECTRONIC DEVICE WITH 5 ELECTRODES** an electronic valve that has five electrodes. They are a cathode, an anode, and three grids. ■ *adj.* **WITH 3 ELECTRODES** used to describe a transistor that has three electrodes at the base or gate [Early 20thC. Formed from PENTA-.]

pentosan /péntə san/ *n.* an organic compound found mainly in plants, whose polysaccharide carbohydrates break down to form pentoses

pentose /péntōss, -tōz/ *n.* a carbohydrate found in plants and nucleic acids that is a monosaccharide whose molecules each contain five carbon atoms

pentose phosphate pathway *n.* BIOCHEM a cyclic sequence of chemical reactions in the cytoplasm of animal and plant cells in which glucose molecules are converted into biochemically useful smaller molecules. These smaller molecules include ribose molecules needed for nucleic acid synthesis.

Pentothal /péntə thal/ *tdmk.* a trademark for thiopental sodium, also known as sodium pentothal, a barbiturate drug used in medicine

pentoxide /pen tók sīd/ *n.* a chemical element whose oxides contain five atoms of oxygen in each molecule

pentstemon *n.* = penstemon

pent-up *adj.* repressed or stifled rather than being released or freely expressed ○ *pent-up emotions*

pentyl /pén tīl, péntil/ *adj.* relating to a chemical group containing carbon and hydrogen, deriving from pentane. Formula: C_5H_{11}. [Late 19thC. Formed from PENTA-.]

pentyl acetate *n.* a colourless combustible liquid used as a solvent for paints, in extracting penicillin, in photographic film, and as a flavouring. Formula: $CH_3COOC_5H_{11}$.

pentylenetetrazol /pénta leen téttra zol/ *n.* a white crystalline powder used to stimulate the central nervous system. Formula: $C_6H_{10}N_4$. [Mid-20thC. Coined from PENTA- + METHYLENE + *tetrazole*.]

penult /pe núlt, pénnult/ *n.* the second to last item in a series of things, especially the second to last syllable of a word [15thC. Shortening of Latin *penultima*, the feminine of *paenultimus* (see PENULTIMATE).]

penultimate /pe núltimət/ *adj.* **1. SECOND TO LAST** second to last in a series or sequence ○ *the penultimate chapter* **2. LING OF A PENULT** relating to a penult [Late 17thC. From Latin *paene* 'almost' + *ultimus* 'last' (see ULTIMATE).] —**penultimately** *adv.*

penumbra /pə númbrə/ (*plural* **-brae** /-bree/ *or* **-bras**) *n.* **1. ASTRON PARTIAL SHADOW** a partial outer shadow that is lighter than the darker inner shadow (**umbra**), e.g. the area between complete darkness and complete light in an eclipse **2. ASTRON EDGE OF A SUNSPOT** a greyish area surrounding the dark centre of a sunspot **3. INDETERMINATE AREA** an indistinct area, especially a state in which sth is unclear or uncertain [Mid-17thC. From modern Latin, literally 'almost shadow', from Latin *paene* 'almost' + *umbra* 'shadow'.] —**penumbral** *adj.* —**penumbrous** *adj.*

penurious /pə nyoori əss/ *adj.* (*literary*) **1. POOR** having very little money **2. NOT GENEROUS** not generous with money **3. BARREN** barren or yielding little —**penuriously** *adv.* —**penuriousness** *n.*

penury /pényŏori/ *n.* extreme poverty [15thC. From Latin *penuria*, of uncertain origin.]

WORD KEY: SYNONYMS
See Synonyms at **poverty**.

Penzance /pen zánss/ town in England, in western Cornwall, on Mounts Bay. It is a port and seaside resort. Population: 17,500 (1994).

peon /pée ən/ *n.* **1. LABOURER** in Latin America and the southern United States, a farm labourer, especially in former times, who was forced to work for a creditor until a debt was paid off **2. LOW-PAID WORKER** formerly, in India and Sri Lanka, a low-paid office worker, soldier, or public servant **3. DRUDGE** sb who does boring menial work [Early 17thC. Via Spanish *peón* and Portuguese *peão* 'foot soldier', from the medieval Latin stem *pedon-*, from Latin *pes* 'foot'.]

peonage /pée ənij/ *n.* **1. DEBT-REPAYMENT SYSTEM** a former system used in Latin America and the southern United States under which a debtor was forced to work for a creditor until a debt was paid **2. STATUS OF PEON** the status or condition of being a peon

peony /pée əni/ (*plural* **-nies**), **paeony** (*plural* **-nies**) *n.* **1. SHOWY FLOWERING PLANT** a shrub belonging to the buttercup family that has large globe-shaped red, white, or pink flowers and is native to Europe, Asia, and North America. Genus: *Paeonia*. **2. PEONY FLOWER** the flower of a peony [Old English *peonie*. Via medieval Latin from, ultimately, Greek *paiōnia*, from *Paiōn* 'Paian', the physician of the deities.]

people /pée p'l/ *n.* (*plural* **-ples**) **NATION** a nation, community, ethnic group or nationality ○ *a proud people* ■ *npl.* **1. HUMAN BEINGS COLLECTIVELY** human beings considered collectively or in general ○ *People tend not to mind if you ask them for help.* **2. SUBORDINATES** persons such as employees, subjects, or followers who are under the authority or leadership of sb or sth ○ *I'll get one of my people to phone them.* **3. FAMILY MEMBERS** the members of sb's family, especially sb's wider family (*informal*) ○ *My people were farmers.* **4. ORDINARY MEN AND WOMEN** the general population, as distinct from the government or higher social classes ○ *the will of the people* **5. POLITICAL UNIT** a group of persons comprising a political unit, electorate, or group ■ *vt.* (**-ples, -pling, -pled**) **POPULATE AREA** to populate an area (*usually passive*) ○ *mountain regions that are sparsely peopled* [13thC. Via Anglo-Norman from Latin *populus* (source of English *popular* and *public*), of Etruscan origin.]

people carrier *n.* a versatile passenger vehicle for large families, van-like in shape and with three rows of seats

peoplehood /pée p'l hŏod/ *n.* identity as a member of a particular people, especially a nation or ethnic group

people mover *n.* any automated means of transporting large numbers of people over short distances

people person (*plural* **people persons**) *n.* sb who enjoys the company of other people and is particularly good at communicating with them

people skills *npl.* the ability to deal with people and get along with them, e.g. because of being sensitive or diplomatic

people's republic *n.* a Socialist or Communist republic

pep /pep/ *n.* liveliness or vigour (*informal*) [Early 20thC. Shortening of PEPPER.]

pep up (**peps, pepping, pepped**) *vt.* to make sb or sth more lively, energetic, or interesting (*informal*)

PEP /pep/ *n.* a tax-free investment plan that allows small investors to own shares in British companies. Full form **Personal Equity Plan**

peperomia /péppə rṓmi ə/ *n.* a tropical or subtropical plant belonging to the pepper family that is often cultivated as a house plant for its attractive heavily veined foliage. Genus: *Peperomia*. [Late 19thC. From modern Latin *Peperomia*, the genus name, from Greek *peperi* (see PEPPER).]

pepino /pə péenō/ (*plural* **-nos**) *n.* **1. PLANTS SPINY PLANT** a Peruvian plant belonging to the nightshade family that has spiny foliage, bright blue flowers, and edible purple-streaked fruit. Latin name: *Solanum muricatum*. **2. PLANTS FRUIT OF PEPINO PLANT** the aubergine-shaped fruit of the pepino plant that has a flavour like that of a melon **3. GEOG CONE-SHAPED HILL** a steep conical hill, especially in Puerto Rico [Mid-19thC. Via American Spanish from, ultimately, Latin *pepo* (see PUMPKIN).]

pepla plural of **peplum**

peplos /pépplɒss/, **peplus** *n.* a loose-fitting garment worn by women in ancient Greece, draped in folds around the shoulders and reaching the waist [Late 18thC. From Greek.]

peplum /péppləm/ (*plural* **-lums** *or* **-la** /-plə/) *n.* a short flared ruffle attached to the waist of a jacket or blouse [Late 17thC. From Latin, from Greek *peplos* (see PEPLOS).]

pepo /pée pō/ (*plural* **-pos**) *n.* a fruit of the gourd family such as a melon, squash, pumpkin, or cucumber that typically has a firm or hard rind, a large number of flat seeds, and soft watery flesh [Mid-19thC. From Latin (see PUMPKIN).]

Pepper

pepper /péppər/ *n.* **1. FOOD SEASONING** a hot condiment or seasoning made from the ground dried berries of a tropical climbing plant. Black pepper is made from berries that are dried before they ripen, and white pepper from berries that ripen before being dried. **2. PLANTS PLANT WITH BERRIES** a tropical climbing plant such as betel, cubeb, or kava whose berries are dried for use as pepper. Genus: *Piper*. **3. FOOD HOLLOW VEGETABLE** a green, red, or yellow vegetable that is hollow with firm walls containing seeds and has mild or pungent flesh that can be eaten either raw or cooked **4. PLANTS PLANT WITH EDIBLE PODS** a tropical plant of the nightshade family that bears mild or pungent peppers as fruit. Genus: *Capsicum*. **5. FOOD PUNGENT CONDIMENTS** condiments such as chilli or cayenne pepper made from the more strongly pungent peppers ■ *v.* (**-pers, -pering, -pered**) **1.** *vt.* **SPRINKLE WITH PEPPER** to add or sprinkle pepper as a seasoning onto sth **2.** *vt.* **ASSAIL SB OR STH** to bombard sb or sth with sth **3. SPRINKLE STH AROUND** to scatter things liberally on to or among sth (*often passive*) ○ *manuscripts peppered with typing errors* **4.** *vt.* **MAKE STH LIVELY** to liven up sth such as a speech with wit [Old English *piper*. Via the prehistoric West Germanic language from Latin *piper* (source of English *pimpernel*), from, ultimately, Sanskrit *pippalī* 'berry, peppercorn'.]

pepper-and-salt *adj.* flecked with dark and light colours ○ *pepper-and-salt hair*

pepperbox /péppər boks/ *n.* **1. ARCHIT CYLINDRICAL TURRET** a cylindrical turret or cupola **2. ARMS SMALL PISTOL** a small 18th-century pistol with several short revolving barrels

peppercorn /péppər kawrn/ n. a small dried tropical berry that is ground to make pepper. Black peppercorns are dried before they ripen, giving them a sweeter deeper flavour than white peppercorns. [Old English *piporcorn*]

peppered moth n. a moth that is grey and speckled when found in rural areas and black in smoke-darkened industrial regions. Latin name: *Biston betularia*.

peppergrass /péppər graass/ n. US = **pepperwort**

pepperidge /péppərij/ n. TREES = **sour gum** [Mid-16thC. Origin unknown.]

pepper mill n. a kitchen utensil for storing and grinding peppercorns

Peppermint

peppermint /péppər mint/ n. **1.** PLANTS PUNGENT HERB a plant of the mint family whose dark green downy leaves yield a pungent oil. Latin name: *Mentha piperita*. **2.** FOOD FLAVOURING a flavouring prepared from the peppermint plant's aromatic oil, used in the food and pharmaceutical industries (*often used before a noun*) **3.** FOOD PEPPERMINT SWEETS a sweet flavoured with peppermint

pepperoni /péppə róni/ n. a hard dry Italian sausage spiced with pepper, or a slice of this, often used on pizzas [Mid-20thC. Via Italian *peperone* 'red pepper', from, ultimately, Latin *piper* (see PEPPER).]

pepper pot n. **1.** PEPPER CONTAINER a small cylindrical container for ready-ground pepper with a perforated top for sprinkling. US term **peppershaker 2.** FOOD STEW a Guyanese or West Indian stew made with meat, rice, and vegetables and seasoned with cassava syrup

peppershaker /péppər shaykər/ n. US = **pepper pot**

peppershrike /péppər shrīk/ n. a small stocky North American bird of the vireo family with a thick hook-tipped bill. Genus: *Cyclarhis*.

pepper tree n. a subtropical South American tree belonging to the cashew family that is cultivated as an ornamental tree for its bright red fruits. Genus: *Schinus*.

pepperwort /péppər wurt/ n. **1.** MARSH FERN a freshwater fern with floating leaves and slender tangled stems that grows in marshes and ponds. Genus: *Marsilea*. **2.** PUNGENT PLANT a plant of the mustard family whose pungent lower leaves are used in salads and to season dishes. Genus: *Lepidium*. US term **peppergrass**

peppery /péppəri/ adj. **1.** FOOD CONTAINING PEPPER strongly flavoured with pepper or tasting of pepper **2.** ANGRY angry and critical **3.** EASILY ANNOYED easily annoyed

pep pill n. any pill that contains a stimulant drug, especially an amphetamine (*dated informal*)

peppy /péppi/ (-**pier**, -**piest**) adj. lively and vigorous (*informal*) —**peppily** adv. —**peppiness** n.

pepsin /pépsin/ n. an enzyme produced in the stomach that breaks down proteins into simpler compounds. It can be extracted from the stomachs of calves and hogs for use as a digestive aid and in the production of cheese. [Mid-19thC. Coined from Greek *pepsis* 'digestion', from *peptein* (see PEPTIC).]

pepsinogen /pep sínnəjən/ n. a substance produced by stomach glands that is converted into pepsin after contact with hydrochloric acid during digestion

pep talk n. a short speech designed to give advice and generate enthusiasm, e.g. in a sports team or among a company's employees (*informal*)

peptic /péptik/ adj. **1.** HELPING DIGESTION relating to or helping digestion **2.** INVOLVING PEPSIN relating to, caused by, or producing pepsin **3.** OF THE STOMACH relating to or involving the stomach, especially any digestive actions or their results [Mid-17thC. Via Latin from Greek *peptikos* 'capable of digesting', from *peptein* 'to digest'.]

peptic ulcer n. erosion of the mucous membrane that lines the upper digestive tract, caused by excess secretion of acid in the stomach

peptidase /pépti dayz, -dayss/ n. an enzyme that breaks down peptides into amino acids

peptide /pép tīd/ n. **1.** COMPOUND WITH AMINO BONDS a chemical compound whose amino acids have chemical bonds between carboxyl and amino groups **2.** LINEAR MOLECULE OF AMINO ACIDS a linear molecule made up of two or more amino acids linked by peptide bonds [Early 20thC. From German *Peptid*, a back-formation from *Polypeptid* (see POLYPEPTIDE).] —**peptidic** /pep tíddik/ adj.

peptide bond n. a chemical bond formed when the amino group of one amino acid condenses with the carboxyl group of another

peptidoglycan /pep tídə glī kan/ n. a large molecule found in the cell walls of bacteria, giving the walls their strength and the cell its shape

peptize /pép tīz/ (-**tizes**, -**tizing**, -**tized**), **peptise** (-**tises**, -**tising**, -**tised**) vt. to disperse fine particles of one substance evenly throughout another substance to create a state intermediate between a suspension and a solution (**colloid**) [Mid-19thC. Formed from PEPTONE.] —**peptizable** adj. —**peptization** /pép tī záysh'n/ n. —**peptizer** /pép tīzər/ n.

peptone /péptōn/ n. a compound formed during the hydrolysis of proteins that does not dissolve in water and is used as a food source for microorganisms grown in laboratories [Mid-19thC. Via German from Greek *peptos* 'digested', from *peptein* (see PEPTIC).]

peptonize /péptə nīz/ (-**nizes**, -**nizing**, -**nized**), **peptonise** (-**tonises**, -**tonising**, -**tonised**) vt. to digest food using an enzyme that breaks down protein —**peptonization** /péptə nī záysh'n/ n. —**peptonizer** /péptə nīzər/ n.

Pepys /peeps/, **Samuel** (1633–1703) English diarist. His *Diary* (1660–69) includes detailed descriptions of the Plague and the Fire of London.

Pequot /pée kwot/ (*plural* -**quot** or -**quots**) n. **1.** PEOPLES MEMBER OF A NATIVE N AMERICAN PEOPLE a member of a Native North American people who originally lived, and whose descendants still live, in eastern Connecticut **2.** LANG PEQUOT LANGUAGE an Algonquian language spoken in parts of New England, especially Connecticut. It is one of the Algonquian-Wakashan languages and is spoken by about seven thousand people. [Mid-17thC. From Narragansett *Pequtôog* 'Pequot people'.] —**Pequot** adj.

per /pər/ prep. **1.** FOR EACH for each or for every thing mentioned ○ *50 miles per hour* **2.** ACCORDING TO STH by, through, or according to sth ○ *per instructions* [14thC. From Latin. Ultimately, from an Indo-European base meaning 'through, forward', which is also the ancestor of English *for*, *pro*, and *pre-*.]

per. abbr. **1.** period **2.** person

per- prefix **1.** through ○ *peroral* **2.** containing a large proportion of an element ○ *peroxide* **3.** containing an element in its highest oxidation state ○ *perchlorate* **4.** containing a peroxide group ○ *peracid* [From Latin *per* (see PER)]

peracid /pər ássid/ n. an acid such as perchloric acid or permanganic acid in which one element is in its highest possible state of oxidation —**peracidity** /pérrə síddəti/ n.

peradventure /púrəd vénchər/ adv. PERHAPS possibly or perhaps (*archaic*) ■ n. CHANCE chance, doubt, or uncertainty (*literary*) [13thC. From Old French *per aventure* 'by chance'.]

perambulate /pə rámbyoo layt/ (-**lates**, -**lating**, -**lated**) vti. to walk about a place (*archaic or literary*) [Mid-16thC. From Latin *perambulare*, from *ambulare* 'to walk'

(source of English *amble*).] —**perambulatory** adj. —**perambulation** /pə rámbyoŏ láysh'n/ n.

perambulator /pə rámbyoŏ laytər/ n. **1.** PRAM a baby's pram (*archaic or formal*) **2.** TECH MEASURING DEVICE a device consisting of a wheel on a long handle, used to measure distance while walking [Early 17thC. Originally in the sense 'sb who walks'.]

per annum /pər ánnəm/ adv. in or for every year, or by the year [From modern Latin, literally 'by the year']

per ardua ad astra /pər aárdyoo ə ad ástrə/ used as the motto of the Royal Air Force with the meaning 'by endeavour to the stars'

p/e ratio abbr. price-earnings ratio

perborate /pər báw rayt/ n. a salt compound of borate used as a bleaching agent in washing powder

percale /pər káyl/ n. a smooth-textured closely woven cotton or polyester fabric used for bedsheets and clothing. It sometimes has a glazed finish. [Early 17thC. From French, of uncertain origin: possibly from Persian *pargālah* 'rag'.]

percaline /púrkə leen, -lin/ n. a glossy lightweight cotton fabric used for linings and book bindings [Mid-19thC. From French, from *percale* (see PERCALE).]

per capita /pər káppitə/ adv., adj. by or for each person ○ *earnings per capita* [From modern Latin, literally 'per head']

perceive /pər séev/ (-**ceives**, -**ceiving**, -**ceived**) vt. **1.** NOTICE USING THE SENSES to notice sth, especially sth that escapes the notice of others **2.** UNDERSTAND OR COMPREHEND to understand sth in a particular way [13thC. Via Anglo-Norman and Old French variants of *perçoivre*, from Latin *percipere*, literally 'to seize completely', from *capere* 'to seize', (source of English *capture*).] —**perceivable** adj. —**perceivably** adv. —**perceiver** n.

per cent, **percent** adv. AS EXPRESSED IN HUNDREDTHS used to express a proportion of an amount in hundredths, represented by the symbol % ○ *a 10 per cent rise* ■ n. (*plural* **per cent**; *plural* -**cent**) **1.** ONE HUNDREDTH one hundredth part of sth **2.** PERCENTAGE a part or percentage [From Latin *per centum*, literally 'by a hundred']

percentage /pər séntij/ n. **1.** PROPORTION IN ONE-HUNDREDTHS a proportion stated in terms of one-hundredths that is achieved by multiplying an amount by a per cent **2.** PROPORTION a proportion of a larger group or set ○ *A larger percentage of pupils are choosing to go on to college.* **3.** FIN COMMISSION OR CUT an amount charged that is based on the total amount involved, e.g. a commission charged on a sale, especially the commission that an agent charges a client (*informal*) **4.** ADVANTAGE advantage or benefit (*informal*) ○ *There's no percentage in accepting the proposal.*

percentile /pər sén tīl/ n. a value on a scale of one hundred that indicates whether a distribution is above or below it

percept /púr sept/ n. sth that is perceived by the senses (*formal*) [Mid-19thC. From Latin *perceptum* 'sth perceived', the past participle of *percipere* (see PERCEIVE).]

perceptible /pər séptəb'l/ adj. large enough, great enough, or distinct enough to be noticed ○ *a perceptible difference* —**perceptibility** /pər séptə bílləti/ n. —**perceptibly** adv.

perception /pər sépsh'n/ n. **1.** PERCEIVING the process of using the senses to acquire information about the surrounding environment or situation ○ *the range of human perception* **2.** RESULT OF PERCEIVING the observation or result of the process of perception ○ *After watching the experiment closely, he noted his perceptions in his lab notebook.* **3.** IMPRESSION an attitude or understanding based on what is observed or thought ○ *a news report that altered the public's perception of the issue* **4.** POWERS OF OBSERVATION the ability to notice or discern things that escape the notice of most people **5.** PSYCHOL NEUROLOGICAL PROCESS OF OBSERVATION AND INTERPRETATION any of the neurological processes of acquiring and mentally interpreting information from the senses [14thC. Via Old French from the Latin stem *perception-*, from *percipere* (see PERCEIVE).] —**perceptional** adj.

perceptive /pər séptiv/ adj. **1.** QUICK TO UNDERSTAND quick to understand or discern things or showing understanding of a person or situation **2.** PERCEPTUAL relating to perception or capable of perceiving — **perceptively** *adv.* —**perceptiveness** *n.* —**perceptivity** /púr sep tívvəti/ *n.*

perceptual /pər sépchoo əl/ *adj.* relating to perception with the senses —**perceptually** *adv.*

perceptual defence *n.* the process by which the mind may ignore or distort unwanted or threatening perceptions

Perceval /púrssəv'l/, **John de Burgh** (b. 1923) Australian painter and ceramicist. His early works were influenced by surrealism, and his later paintings are noted for their spontaneity and bright colours.

Perceval, Spencer (1762–1812) British statesman. He was Tory prime minister (1809–12).

perch[1] /purch/ *n.* **1.** PLACE FOR BIRD TO SIT a place for a bird to land or rest on, e.g. a branch or a pole in a cage **2.** RESTING PLACE any temporary resting place for a person or thing **3.** MEASURE SOLID MEASURE FOR STONE a unit of measure for the volume of stone, equal to about 0.7 cu m/24 cu ft **4.** MEASURE UNIT OF LENGTH a unit of length equal to 5.03 m/5½ yd **5.** MEASURE UNIT OF AREA a unit of area equal to 25.3 m²/30¼ sq. yd **6.** TEXTILES INSPECTION FRAME a frame that woven fabric is laid on to be inspected after weaving **7.** TRANSP = pole ■ *v.* (**perches**, **perching**, **perched**) **1.** *vt.* SIT PRECARIOUSLY to sit or stand somewhere awkwardly and precariously ○ *He was perched on a high stool.* **2.** *vt.* PUT IN A HIGH PLACE to situate sth in a place high up ○ *the ruins of a castle perched on the clifftops* **3.** *vi.* BIRDS BE ON A PERCH to land or rest on a perch ○ *A pair of doves perched on the apple tree.* **4.** *vti.* TEXTILES LAY AN ITEM ON A PERCH to place sth such as woven fabric on a perch to inspect after weaving [13thC. Via Old French from Latin *pertica* 'pole, stick'.] —**percher** *n.* ◇ **fall off your perch** to die (*informal*) ◇ **knock sb off his** *or* **her perch** to make sb feel less proud or superior

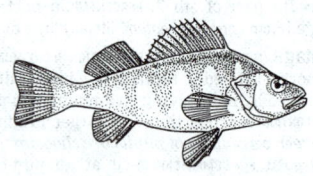

Perch

perch[2] /purch/ (*plural* **perches** *or* **perch**) *n.* an edible bony freshwater fish native to North America and Europe that has rough scales and two dorsal fins, one spiny and one soft. Genus: *Perca*. [14thC. Via Old French from, ultimately, Greek *perkē*.]

perchance /pər cháanss/ *adv.* (*archaic or literary*) **1.** PERHAPS possibly or perhaps **2.** BY CHANCE by chance [14thC. From Anglo-Norman *par chance*, literally 'by chance'.]

Percheron /púrshə ron/ *n.* a large black or grey draught horse of a breed that originated in France [Late 19thC. From French, 'of the Percheron breed', named after *le Perche*, a region of France where it was first bred.]

perching bird *n.* a bird such as a lark, finch, or crow with feet adapted for clinging to horizontal branches

perchlorate /pər kláw rayt/ *n.* a salt or ester of perchloric acid

perchloric acid /pər kláwrik-/ *n.* a colourless acid of chlorine that is explosive under some conditions and that is used as a powerful oxidizing agent in laboratory work. Formula: $HClO_4$.

perchloride /pər kláw rīd/ *n.* a chloride of an element that contains more chlorine than all other chlorides of the same element

perchloroethylene /pər kláwrō éthə leen/ *n.* a colourless toxic organic solvent used in dry-cleaning fluid. Formula: C_4C_{14}.

perciatelli /púrchə télli/ *n.* pasta in the form of long thin tubes, thicker than spaghetti [From Italian dialect, literally 'little pierced thing', from *perciato* 'pierced', the past participle of *perciare* 'to pierce', from Old French *percer* (see PIERCE)]

percipient /pər síppi ənt/ *adj.* INSIGHTFUL perceptive, observant, or discerning ■ *n.* SB OR STH THAT PERCEIVES sb or sth capable of perceiving [Mid-17thC. From Latin *percipere* (see PERCEIVE).] —**percipiently** *adv.*

percoid /púr koyd/ *adj.* BONY AND SPINY-FINNED belonging or relating to a large suborder of bony spiny-finned fishes that includes the perch, sea bass, sunfishes, and red mullet. Suborder: Percoidea. ■ *n.* PERCOID FISH a fish belonging to the percoid suborder [Mid-19thC. From modern Latin *Percoidea*, the suborder name, from Latin *perca* (see PERCH).]

percolate /púrkə layt/ (**-lates**, **-lating**, **-lated**) *v.* **1.** *vti.* PASS THROUGH A FILTER to make a liquid or gas pass through a filter or porous substance, or filter through in this way **2.** *vi.* PASS THROUGH SLOWLY to pass slowly through sth or spread throughout a place ○ *I let the idea percolate through my mind.* **3.** *vti.* BEVERAGES MAKE COFFEE to prepare coffee in a percolator, or undergo preparation in a percolator [Early 17thC. From Latin *percolare* 'to sieve through', from *colare* 'to sieve', from *colum* 'sieve' (source of English *colander*).] — **percolable** /púrkələb'l/ *adj.* —**percolation** /púrkə láysh'n/ *n.* —**percolative** /púrkələtiv/ *adj.*

percolator /púrkə laytər/ *n.* a coffeepot in which boiling water rises repeatedly through a narrow stem, spills over into a sieve-like basket containing coffee grounds, mixes with them, and returns to the water below

per contra /pər kóntrə/ *adv.* on the other hand, or by way of contrast [From Italian, literally 'by the opposite side']

per curiam decision /pər kyoóri am-/ *n.* a court judgement given without the need to retire to consider a verdict [From Latin *per curiam*, literally 'by the court']

percurrent /pər kúrrənt/ *adj.* used to describe a leaf's main vein when it runs the entire length of the leaf [Late 16thC. From Latin *percurrere* 'to run through', from *currere* 'to run' (source of English *current*).]

percuss /pər kúss/ (**-cusses**, **-cussing**, **-cussed**) *vt.* MED to gently tap a part of a patient's body in order to diagnose an illness or condition [Mid-16thC. From Latin *percuss-*, the past participle stem of *percutere* 'to strike hard', from *quatere* 'to strike' (source of English *concuss*).] —**percussor** *n.*

percussion /pər kúsh'n/ *n.* **1.** MUSIC INSTRUMENTS THAT ARE HIT the group of instruments that produce sound by being struck, including drums and cymbals, or the section of the orchestra playing such instruments **2.** MED TAPPING OF THE BODY examination of part of a patient's body by tapping with the fingers to assess the presence of fluid, the enlargement of organs, or the solidification of normally hollow parts **3.** IMPACT the impact of one object striking another, or the noise or shock created when two objects hit each other (*formal*) **4.** ACT OF DETONATING A PERCUSSION CAP the striking or detonating of a percussion cap in a firearm [Mid-16thC. From the Latin stem *percussion-*, from *percussus*, the past participle of *percutere* (see PERCUSS).]

percussion cap *n.* a detonator consisting of a thin metal cap or strip of paper containing explosive powder, formerly used to fire some pistols

percussion instrument *n.* a musical instrument such as a drum, cymbal, or triangle that is hit to produce sound

percussionist /pər kúsh'nist/ *n.* a musician who plays a percussion instrument

percussion lock *n.* a mechanism on a gun that fires by striking a percussion cap

percussion tool *n.* any power tool that delivers repeated heavy blows e.g. a pneumatic drill

percussive /pər kússiv/ *adj.* having the effect of an impact or a blow —**percussively** *adv.* —**percussiveness** *n.*

percutaneous /púrkyoo táyni əss/ *adj.* MED administered or absorbed through the skin, as an injection or, e.g. ointment —**percutaneously** *adv.*

Percussion

Percy /púrssi/, **Sir Henry** (1366–1403) English military leader. The son of the Earl of Northumberland, he rebelled against Henry IV, and was killed at the Battle of Shrewsbury. Known as **Harry Hotspur**

per diem /pər dée em, -dī em/ *adv., adj.* BY THE DAY by the day or every day ■ *n.* DAILY PAYMENT a daily payment or allowance [From Latin, literally 'by the day']

perdition /pər dísh'n/ *n.* **1.** CHR PUNISHMENT IN HELL in some religions, the state of everlasting punishment in Hell that sinners endure after death **2.** CHR HELL Hell itself as a location **3.** COMPLETE DESTRUCTION complete destruction or ruin (*archaic*) [14thC. Via Old French from, ultimately, Latin *perdere*, literally 'to put to destruction', from *dare* 'to put' (source of English *render*).]

perdu /púr dyoo/, **perdue** *adj.* hidden or out of sight (*archaic or literary*) [Late 16thC. Via French, the past participle of *perdre* 'to lose', from Latin *perdere* (see PERDITION).]

perdurable /pər dyoórəb'l/ *adj.* extremely durable or imperishable (*archaic*) [13thC. Via Old French from, ultimately, Latin *perdurare* (see PERDURE).] —**perdurably** *adv.* —**perdurability** /pər dyŏŏrə bílləti/ *n.*

perdure /pər dyŏŏr/ (**-dures, -during, -dured**) *vi.* to last for a long time (*archaic*) [15thC. Via Old French from Latin *perdurare*, literally 'to last through', from *durare* 'to last' (source of English *duration, during*, and *endure*).]

père /pair/ *n.* **1. FRENCH PRIEST** the title given to Roman Catholic priests in France and French-speaking countries **2. SENIOR** in France and French-speaking countries, used after a man's surname to distinguish him from his son ○ *M. Doucet père.* ◊ **fils** [Early 17thC. Via French from, ultimately, Latin *pater* (see PATERNAL).]

Père David's deer *n.* a large reddish-grey deer that survives in captivity after having become extinct in China, its native habitat. Latin name: *Elaphurus davidianus.* [Late 19thC. Named after the French missionary and naturalist *Père* Armand *David* (1826–1900).]

peregrinate /pérrəgri nayt/ (**-nates, -nating, -nated**) *vti.* to travel around a place or from place to place (*literary*) [Late 16thC. From Latin *peregrinari*, from *peregrinus* (see PEREGRINE).] —**peregrinator** *n.*

peregrination /pérrəgri náysh'n/ *n.* a journey or voyage (*literary*) [15thC. Directly or via French from Latin, from, ultimately, *peregrinari* 'to travel', from *peregrinus* (see PEREGRINE).]

peregrine /pérrəgrin/ *n.* BIRDS = **peregrine falcon** ■ *adj.* (*archaic*) **1. FROM A FARAWAY PLACE** coming from another region or country **2. WANDERING** wandering or travelling [14thC. Via French from Latin *peregrinus* 'travelling', from *pereger*, literally 'through fields', from *ager* 'field' (source of English *agrarian*).]

peremptory /pə rémptəri/ *adj.* **1. DICTATORIAL** expecting to be obeyed and unwilling to tolerate disobedience, **2.** LAW **CLOSED TO FURTHER CONSIDERATION OR ACTION** ending, or not open to, discussion, debate, or further action **3. EXPRESSING URGENCY** communicating urgency, command, or instruction [13thC. Via Anglo-Norman from, ultimately, Latin *perimere* 'to take away completely', from *emere* 'to buy, to take'. The underlying meaning is 'taking away possibility of debate'.] —**peremptorily** *adv.* —**peremptoriness** *n.*

Perendale /pérrən dayl/ *n. NZ* a sheep that is a cross between a Romney and a Cheviot

perennate /pérrə nayt, pə rénnayt/ (**-nates, -nating, -nated**) *vi.* BOT to survive from one growing season to the next with reduced or arrested growth between seasons [Early 17thC. From Latin *perennare* 'to last for years', from *perennis* (see PERENNIAL).] —**perennation** /pérrə náysh'n/ *n.*

perennial /pə rénni əl/ *adj.* **1.** BOT **LASTING OVER 2 YEARS** used to describe a plant that lasts for more than two growing seasons, either dying back after each season, as some herbaceous plants do, or growing continuously, as some shrubs do **2. RECURRING OR ENDURING** constantly recurring, or lasting for an indefinite time ○ *perennial problem of litter* ■ *n.* BOT **PERENNIAL PLANT** a plant that lasts for more than two growing seasons [Mid-17thC. Formed from Latin *perennis*, literally 'through the year', from *annus* 'year' (source of English *annual*).] —**perennially** *adv.*

perentie /pə rénti/, **perenty** (*plural* **-ties**) *n.* a large burrowing lizard that has brown skin with yellow patches and is found in the semiarid and desert regions of central and northern Australia. It can grow to 2.5 m/8 ft in length and is the largest Australian lizard, and the second-largest in the world. Latin name: *Varanus giganteus.* [Early 20thC. Of Aboriginal origin, probably from Diyari *pirindi.*]

perestroika /pérrə stróykə/ *n.* the political and economic restructuring in the former Soviet Union initiated by Mikhail Gorbachev from about 1986. The stated aims included decentralized control of industry and agriculture and some private ownership. [Late 20thC. From Russian, literally 'rebuilding, reconstruction'.]

perf. *abbr.* **1.** STAMPS perforated **2.** GRAM perfect **3.** performance

perfect *adj.* /púrfikt/ **1. WITHOUT FAULTS** without errors, flaws, or faults ○ *in perfect condition* **2. COMPLETE AND WHOLE** complete and lacking nothing essential ○ *We had a perfect day together.* **3. EXCELLENT OR IDEAL** excellent or ideal in every way ○ *That's the perfect word to describe him.* **4. ESPECIALLY SUITABLE** having all the necessary or typical characteristics required for a given situation ○ *the perfect candidate for the job* **5. FLAWLESS** without any flaw or blemish ○ *perfect teeth* **6. UTTER, ABSOLUTE, COMPLETE** used to emphasize the extent or degree of sth ○ *a perfect nuisance* **7. EXACTLY REPRODUCING STH** exactly reproducing an original ○ *a perfect likeness* **8.** BOT **WITH STAMENS AND PISTILS TOGETHER** used to describe a flower that has functional stamens and pistils in the same flower **9.** MATH **EXACTLY DIVISIBLE** exactly divisible into equal roots **10.** GRAM **WITH THE VERB ACTION FINISHED** used to describe a verb or verb tense for an action that is brought to a close **11.** MUSIC **OF MUSICAL INTERVALS** used collectively to describe the differences in pitch between the fourth, the fifth, and the octave, common to both major and minor scales **12.** FUNGI **WITH SEXUAL AND ASEXUAL REPRODUCTION** used to describe a fungus that reproduces both sexually and asexually during its life cycle **13.** INSECTS **SEXUALLY MATURE** sexually mature and completely differentiated ■ *vt.* /pər fékt/ (**-fects, -fecting, -fected**) **1. COMPLETE STH** to make sth as good as possible, or to bring sth to completion ○ *They perfected the process last year.* **2.** PRINTING **PRINT THE REVERSE SIDE** to complete a printed page by printing its reverse side ■ *n.* /púr fikt/ GRAM **1. PERFECT TENSE OF VERB** the perfect tense of a verb. ◊ **future perfect 2. VERB IN THE PERFECT TENSE** a verb that is in the perfect tense [13thC. Directly and via Old French *parfit* from, ultimately, Latin *perficere* 'to make completely, finish', from *facere* 'to make' (source of English *fact*).] —**perfectness** *n.*

perfect binding *n.* a book binding in which the leaves of a book are cut into pages whose edges are bound with glue to the spine, as opposed to being stitched uncut —**perfect bound** *adj.*

perfect competition *n.* a market condition in which a product is traded freely by buyers and sellers in large numbers without any individual transaction affecting the price

perfect game *n.* BOWLING a game of bowling in which 12 consecutive strikes occur

perfect gas *n.* PHYS, CHEM = **ideal gas**

perfectible /pər féktəb'l/ *adj.* capable of being improved or made perfect —**perfectibility** /pər féktə bílləti/ *n.*

perfection /pər féksh'n/ *n.* **1. PERFECT NATURE** the quality of sth that is as good or suitable as it can possibly be ○ *to strive for perfection as a goal* **2. PROCESS OF PERFECTING** the process of becoming or making sth perfect ○ *The perfection of the technique will require another two years research.* **3. EXAMPLE OR INSTANCE OF BEING PERFECT** sb or sth that reaches the highest attainable standard, or an instance of this ○ *His cooking that evening was sheer perfection* ◇ **to perfection** perfectly ○ *The piece showed off her talent as a pianist to perfection.*

perfectionism /pər féksh'nizəm/ *n.* **1.** PHILOSOPHY **BELIEF IN EXISTENCE OF PERFECTION** the doctrine that perfection is possible in human beings **2. DEMAND FOR PERFECTION** rigorous rejection of anything less than perfect

perfectionist /pər féksh'nist/ *n.* **1. DEMANDING PERSON** sb who demands perfection in all things, especially his or her own work **2.** PHILOSOPHY **BELIEVER IN PERFECTIONISM** sb who believes in the doctrine of perfectionism

perfective /pə féktiv/ *adj.* **1. TOWARDS PERFECTION** tending towards perfection **2.** GRAM **DESCRIBING COMPLETED ACTION** used to describe a verb that reports a completed action ■ *n.* GRAM **PERFECTIVE VERB OR ASPECT** a verb in the perfective aspect, or the aspect itself —**perfectively** *adv.* —**perfectiveness** *n.* —**perfectivity** *n.*

perfective aspect *n.* the aspect that a verb is said to be in when it is in a perfect tense, reporting a completed action rather than an incomplete or continuing one

perfectly /púrfiktli/ *adv.* **1. IN A PERFECT WAY** in exactly the way desired or required ○ *That will suit her perfectly.* **2. USED FOR EMPHASIS** used to emphasize the degree or extent of sth ○ *They're perfectly capable of managing on their own.*

perfect number *n.* a positive whole number that is equal to the sum of the numbers that can be multiplied to give it as a result, excluding itself

perfecto /pər féktō/ (*plural* **-tos**) *n.* a medium-sized cigar with tapered ends and a thick centre [Late 19thC. From Spanish, 'perfect'.]

perfector /pər féktər/, **perfecter** *n.* **1.** PRINTING **PRINTING MACHINE** a printing press that prints on both sides of a page simultaneously **2. SB MAKING STH PERFECT** sb who makes sth perfect

perfect participle *n.* GRAM = **past participle**

perfect pitch *n.* MUSIC = **absolute pitch**

perfect rhyme *n.* **1. RHYME OF DIFFERENTLY SPELT WORDS** a rhyme of two words that are pronounced the same but spelt differently and have different meanings, e.g. 'flew' and 'flue' **2. RHYME WITH LAST PARTS THE SAME** a rhyme in which the stressed vowel and consonants following it are the same, e.g. 'alive' and 'contrive'

perfect square *n.* a rational number equal to the square of another rational number

perfervid /pur fúrvid/ *adj.* extremely passionate or enthusiastic (*literary*) [Mid-19thC. From modern Latin *perfervidus*, literally 'extremely vehement', from Latin *fervidus* (see FERVID).] —**perfervidly** *adv.* —**perfervidness** *n.*

perfidious /pər fíddi əss/ *adj.* guilty of treachery or deceit (*literary*) —**perfidiously** *adv.* —**perfidiousness** *n.*

perfidy /púrfidi/ *n.* treachery or deceit (*literary*) [Late 16thC. From Latin *perfidia*, from *perfidus*, literally 'through faith' (found in *per fidem decipere* 'to deceive through trustingness'), formed in turn from *fides* (see FAITH).]

perfin /púrfin/ *n.* a postage stamp with initials perforated in it by a business or other organization to prevent misuse [Mid-20thC. Blend of PERFORATED + INITIAL.]

perfoliate /pər fóli ət/ *adj.* BOT used to describe a leaf that encloses a stem so that the stem seems to pass through it [Late 17thC. From modern Latin *perfoliatus*, literally 'through a leaf', from Latin *folium* 'leaf' (source of English *foliage*).] —**perfoliation** /pər fóli áysh'n/ *n.*

perforate *v.* /púrfə rayt/ (**-rates, -rating, -rated**) **1.** *vt.* **PUNCTURE STH** to make a hole or holes in sth **2.** *vt.* **MAKE HOLES FOR TEARING** to make a line of small holes in paper to make tearing it easier **3.** *vi.* **PENETRATE STH** penetrate or pass through sth ■ *adj.* /púrfərət/ **1.** BIOL **WITH SMALL HOLES** dotted with small holes **2.** BIOL **WITH TRANSPARENT SPOTS** dotted with transparent spots **3.** STAMPS = **perforated** [Mid-16thC. From Latin *perforare* 'to bore through', from *forare* 'to bore'.] —**perforable** /púrfərəb'l/ *adj.* —**perforative** /-rətiv/ *adj.* —**perforator** /-raytər/ *n.* —**perforatory** /-rətəri/ *adj.*

perforated /púrfə raytid/ *adj.* **1. WITH HOLES** pierced with a hole or holes, especially with a line of small holes designed to make tearing easy **2.** MED **WITH A HOLE** in which a hole has developed ○ *a perforated eardrum*

perforation /púrfə ráysh'n/ *n.* **1. HOLE** a hole made in sth **2. MAKING HOLES OR HAVING THEM** the act of making a hole or holes in sth or the state of being perforated **3. HOLES FOR TEARING** a small hole or series of holes punched into a piece of paper to make tearing easy **4.** MED **FORMATION OF A HOLE** the formation of a hole in an organ, tissue, or tube, usually as a consequence of disease

perforation gauge *n.* STAMPS a small ruler used to measure the number of perforations along the borders of a postage stamp

perforce /pər fáwrss/ *adv.* unavoidably or as forced by circumstances (*archaic or literary*) [14thC. From Old French *par force* 'by force'.]

perform /pər fáwrm/ (**-forms, -forming, -formed**) *v.* **1.** *vt.* **ACCOMPLISH** to carry out an action or accomplish a task ○ *the surgeon who performed the operation* **2.** *vt.* **FULFIL** to do what is stated or required **3.** *vti.* ARTS **PRESENT AN ARTISTIC WORK** to present or enact an artistic work such as a piece of music or a play to an audience **4.** *vi.* **FUNCTION OR BEHAVE** to function, operate, or behave in a particular way or to a particular standard ○ *athletes who perform best under pressure* [14thC. From Anglo-Norman *parformer*, an alteration of Old French *parfornir*, literally 'to accomplish completely', from *fournir* 'to accomplish' (source of English *furnish*).] —**performable** *adj.* —**performer** *n.*

WORD KEY: SYNONYMS

perform, do, carry out, fulfil, discharge, execute

CORE MEANING: to complete a task or duty

perform a fairly formal word meaning to complete a task

or duty, especially when this requires skill or care or when it forms part of a set procedure; **do** a general word meaning to complete a task or duty; **carry out** a general expression meaning to perform a task or procedure; **fulfil** to achieve the successful accomplishment or realization of sth planned, promised, or anticipated, or the complete performance of a duty or obligation; **discharge** a fairly formal word meaning to fulfil duties or responsibilities successfully; **execute** a formal word meaning to complete an action or procedure that requires skill and expertise. It can also be used to refer to the accomplishment of a plan.

performance /pər fáwrmənss/ *n.* **1.** ARTS **ARTISTIC PRESENTATION** a presentation of an artistic work to an audience e.g. a play or piece of music **2. MANNER OF FUNCTIONING** the manner in which sth or sb functions, operates, or behaves **3. WORKING EFFECTIVENESS** the effectiveness of the way sb does his or her job (*often used before a noun*) **4. DISPLAY OF BEHAVIOUR** a public display of behaviour that others find distasteful, e.g. an angry outburst that causes embarrassment (*informal*) **5. IRRITATING PROCEDURE** an irritating or troublesome procedure (*informal*) **6. THING ACCOMPLISHED** sth that is carried out or accomplished **7. THE PERFORMING OF** the performing of sth, e.g. a task or action **8.** LING **LANGUAGE PRODUCED** the language that a speaker or writer actually produces, as distinct from his or her understanding of the language. ◊ **competence, parole**

performance art *n.* art that combines two or more artistic media, a traditionally static medium, e.g. sculpture or photography, and a dramatic medium,e.g. recitation or improvisation —**performance artist** *n.*

performance enhancer *n.* any one of various dietary supplements used by athletes to enhance bursts of high performance

performative /pər fáwrmətiv/ *adj.* **PERFORMING SPEECH ACT** used to describe speech that constitutes an act of some kind, e.g. the phrase 'I promise I'll do my best', that constitutes a promise in itself ■ *n.* **SPEECH THAT CONSTITUTES AN ACT** a performative utterance [Mid-20thC. Formed from PERFORM, on the model of *declarative*.] —**performatively** *adv.*

performing arts *npl.* the forms of art that involve theatrical performance, especially drama, dance, and music

perfume /púr fyoom/ *n.* **1. FRAGRANT LIQUID** a fragrant liquid that is sprayed or rubbed on the skin or clothes to give a pleasant smell **2. PLEASANT SCENT** a pleasant smell ■ *vt.* (**-fumes, -fuming, -fumed**) **GIVE STH PLEASANT SCENT** to give sth a pleasant smell [Mid-16thC. Via French *parfum* from, ultimately, obsolete Italian *parfumare*, literally 'to smoke through', from *fumare* 'to smoke'.] —**perfumed** /púr fyoomd, pər fyoómd/ *adj.* —**perfumey** /púrf yoomi/ *adj.*

WORD KEY: SYNONYMS

See Synonyms at ***smell***.

perfumer /pər fyoómər/ *n.* sb who manufactures or sells perfumes

perfumery /pər fyoóməri/ (*plural* **-ies**) *n.* **1. PERFUMES IN GENERAL** perfumes generally **2. PLACE MAKING OR SELLING PERFUMES** a place of business where perfumes are manufactured or sold **3. MAKING OF PERFUMES** the manufacture of perfumes, or the art of making perfumes

perfunctory /pər fúngktəri/ *adj.* **1. DONE ROUTINELY** done as a matter of duty or custom, without thought, attention, or genuine feeling ○ *a perfunctory kiss* **2. HASTY** done hastily or superficially ○ *a perfunctory search* [Late 16thC. Via late Latin *perfunctorius* from, ultimately, *perfungi*, literally 'to work through', from *fungi* (source of English *function*).] —**perfunctorily** *adv.* —**perfunctoriness** *n.*

perfuse /pər fyoóz/ (**-fuses, -fusing, -fused**) *vt.* **1. PERMEATE STH** to spread throughout sth, or spread a substance or quality, e.g. liquid, light, or colour, throughout sth **2.** MED **INJECT LIQUID INTO BODY** to introduce a liquid into tissue or an organ by circulating it through blood vessels or other channels within the body [Early 16thC. From Latin *perfus-*, the past participle stem of *perfundere*, literally 'to pour over', from *fundere* 'to pour' (source of English *found*).] —**perfused** *adj.* —**perfusion** *n.* —**perfusive** /pər fyoósiv/ *adj.*

Pergamum /púrgəməm/ ancient city in northwestern Asia Minor, in present-day Turkey. It was a major cultural centre in the 3rd and 2nd centuries BC.

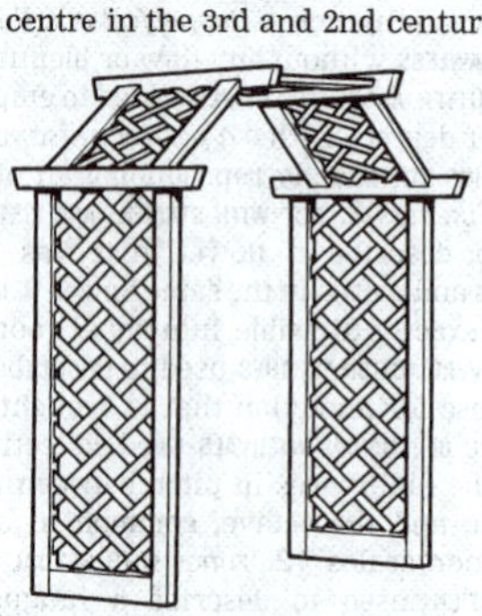

Pergola

pergola /púrgələ/ *n.* a frame structure consisting of colonnades or posts with a latticework roof, designed to support climbing plants [Late 17thC. Via Italian from Latin *pergula*.]

perhaps /pər háps/; *informal* /praps/ CORE MEANING: an adverb expressing uncertainty, or indicating that sth is possibly true or may possibly happen, often used to make remarks appear less definite ○ *Perhaps it will be warmer later.* ○ *He wondered if perhaps he had been mistaken.* ○ *Perhaps his best-known ceramic work is his public mural 'Voyage'.*

adv. **1. APPROXIMATELY** used to show approximation ○ *The house is perhaps five miles from here.* **2. USED FOR POLITENESS** used in requests and suggestions in order to sound more polite ○ *Perhaps we should help Dad in the kitchen.* [15thC. From PER 'by' + an earlier form of HAP 'chance'.]

peri /péeri/ *n.* **1. MYTHOLOGICAL FIGURE** in Persian mythology, a beautiful supernatural being descended from the fallen angels **2. BEAUTIFUL WOMAN** a graceful and beautiful girl or woman (*literary*) [Late 18thC. From Persian *perī*.]

peri- *prefix.* **1.** around, surrounding ○ *pericarp* **2.** near ○ *perilune* ○ *perinatal* [From Greek *peri* 'around, about'. Ultimately from an Indo-European word which is also the ancestor of English *far*, *per-*, and *paradise*.]

perianth /pérri anth/ *n.* the outer structure of a flower, made up of the corolla, the calyx, or both [Early 19thC. Via French from modern Latin *perianthium*, literally 'around a flower', from Greek *peri* 'around' + *anthos* 'flower'.]

periapt /pérri apt/ *n.* a charm worn to protect the wearer from harm [Late 16thC. Via French from Greek *periapton*, literally 'sth fastened around', from *peri* 'around' + *haptein* 'to fasten'.]

periastron /pérri ás tron/ *n.* the points in space and time in the orbits of two stars in a binary system at which they are closest together [Mid-19thC. Coined from PERI- + Greek *astron* 'star', on the model of *perihelion*.]

pericarditis /pérri kaar dítiss/ *n.* inflammation of the pericardium —**pericarditic** /-díttik/ *adj.*

pericardium /pérri kaárdi əm/ (*plural* **-a** /-di ə/) *n.* a fibrous membrane that forms a sac surrounding the heart and attached portions of the main blood vessels [Late 16thC. Via medieval Latin from Greek *perikardion*, literally 'around the heart', from *peri* 'around' + *kardia* 'heart'.] —**pericardial** *adj.* —**pericardiac** *adj.*

pericarp /pérri kaarp/ *n.* the part of a fruit that surrounds the seed or seeds, including the skin, flesh, and, e.g. in apples, the core —**pericarpial** /pérri kaárpi əl/ *adj.* —**pericarpic** /-kaárpik/ *adj.*

perichondrium /pérri kóndri əm/ (*plural* **-a** /-dri ə/) *n.* the fibrous membrane that covers the surface of cartilage except at joints [Mid-18thC. Via modern Latin, literally 'around the cartilage', from Greek *peri* 'around' + *khondros* 'cartilage'.] —**perichondrial** *adj.*

periclase /pérri klayss/ *n.* a colourless, grey, green, or yellow mineral consisting of magnesium oxide, often found in limestones [Mid-19thC. Directly or via German *Periklas* from modern Latin *periclasia*, literally 'breaking around', from Greek *peri* 'around' + *klasis* 'breaking', from its perfect cleavage.] —**periclastic** /pérri klástik/ *adj.*

Pericles /pérri kleez/ (495?–429? BC) Athenian statesman. He dominated Athens during its golden age by means of his oratory skills and honesty. He ordered the construction of the Parthenon and established Athens as a great centre of art and literature. —**Periclean** /pérri kleé ən/ *adj.*

periclinal /pérri klín'l/ *adj.* **1.** GEOL **DOME-SHAPED** used to describe a fold in sedimentary rocks that appears as a regular dome on the surface of the earth **2.** BOT **PARALLEL TO OUTSIDE WALL** used to describe cell walls that are parallel to the outer surface of a plant part [Late 19thC. Formed from Greek *periklinēs*, literally 'sloping all around', from *peri* 'all around' + *klinein* 'to slope'.]

pericline /pérri klīn/ *n.* **1.** GEOL **FOLD IN ROCK** a dome-shaped fold in sedimentary rock **2.** MINERALS **MINERAL WITH LONG WHITE CRYSTALS** a variety of the mineral albite, usually found in the form of long white crystals [Mid-19thC. From Greek *periklinēs*.]

pericope /pə ríkəpi/ *n.* an extract from a book, especially a passage from the Bible selected for reading during a Roman Catholic Mass [Mid-17thC. Via late Latin from Greek *perikopē*, literally 'cutting around', from *peri* 'around' + *koptein* 'to cut'.] —**pericopic** /pérri kóppik/ *adj.*

pericranium /pérri kráyni əm/ (*plural* **-a** /-ni ə/) *n.* the membrane of connective tissue that surrounds the skull [Early 16thC. Via modern Latin from Greek *perikranion*, literally 'round the skull', from *peri* 'round' + *kranion* 'skull'.] —**pericranial** *adj.*

pericycle /pérri sīk'l/ *n.* the outer layer of plant tissue surrounding the inner tissues in the roots and stems of plants (**stele**) that conducts moisture and nutrients around the plant [Late 19thC. Via French from Greek *perikuklos*, literally 'circling around', from *peri* 'around' + *kuklos* 'circle'.] —**pericyclic** /pérri síklik/ *adj.*

pericynthion /pérri sínthi ən/ (*plural* **-thia** /-thi ə/) *n.* ASTRON = **perilune** [Mid-20thC. Coined from PERI- + Greek *Kunthios* 'of' Mount Cynthus (the supposed birthplace of ARTEMIS or DIANA, hence 'the moon').]

periderm /pérri durm/ *n.* the outer layer of plant tissue in woody roots and stems —**peridermal** /pérri dúrm'l/ *adj.* —**peridermic** /-dúrmik/ *adj.*

peridium /pə ríddi əm/ (*plural* **-a** /-di ə/) *n.* the covering of the spore-bearing organ in many kinds of fungi [Early 19thC. Via modern Latin from Greek *pēridion*, literally 'small leather wallet', from *pēra* 'wallet'.]

peridot /pérri dot/ *n.* a pale green or yellowish green transparent form of the mineral olivine, used as a gemstone [Early 18thC. From French, of unknown origin.]

peridotite /pérri dṓ tīt/ *n.* a coarse-grained igneous rock rich in iron and magnesium. It is found in meteorites and also on Earth, where it is thought to form much of the Earth's core. —**peridotitic** /pérri dō títtik/ *adj.*

perigee /pérri jee/ *n.* the point in the orbit of a satellite, moon, or planet at which it comes nearest to the object it is orbiting [Late 16thC. Via French from, ultimately, late Greek *perigeios* 'close round the earth', from *peri* 'close round' + *gaia* 'earth'.] —**perigeal** /pérri jeé əl/ *adj.* —**perigean** /-jeé ən/ *adj.*

periglacial /pérri gláysh'l/ *adj.* relating to or found in a region that borders on a glacier

Périgueux /pérri gṓ/ town in southwestern France, in Dordogne Department, Aquitaine Region. Population: 32,848 (1990).

perigynous /pə ríjjinəss/ *adj.* used to describe a flower that has petals, stamens, and sepals arranged around a cup-shaped receptacle that contains the ovary, e.g. the flowers of cherries and roses —**perigyny** *n.*

perihelion /pérri heéli ən/ (*plural* **-a** /-li ə/) *n.* the point in the orbit of a planet or other astronomical body at which it comes closest to the Sun [Mid-17thC. Via modern Latin *perihelium*, literally 'close round the sun', from Greek *peri* 'close round' + *helios* 'sun', on the model of *perigee*.] —**perihelial** *adj.*

perikaryon /pérri kárri ən/ (*plural* **-a** /-ri ə/) *n.* the part of a nerve cell that contains cytoplasm [Late 19thC. Coined from PERI- + KARYO- + -ON.] —**perikaryal** *adj.*

peril /pérrəl/ *n.* **1. EXPOSURE TO RISK** exposure to risk of harm **2. DANGER** a source of possible harm ■ *vt.* (**-illing, -illed**) **IMPERIL SB OR STH** to expose sb or sth to the risk of harm (*archaic*) [13thC. Via French from Latin *periculum* 'experiment, risk'. Ultimately from an Indo-European base meaning 'to try', which is also the ancestor of English *fear*, *experiment*, *expert*, and *empiric*.]

perilous /pérrələss/ *adj.* involving exposure to very great danger —**perilously** *adv.* —**perilousness** *n.*

perilune /pérri loon/ *n.* the point at which a planet or other body orbiting the Moon comes closest to the Moon's surface [Mid-20thC. Coined from PERI- + Latin *luna* 'moon', on the model of *apolune*.]

perilymph /pérri limf/ *n.* the fluid that fills the space between the membranous labyrinth and the bony labyrinth in the inner ear [Mid-19thC. Coined from PERI- + LYMPH.]

perimeter /pə rímmitər/ *n.* **1.** BOUNDARY ENCLOSING AN AREA a boundary that encloses an area **2.** GEOM CURVE ENCLOSING AREA a curve enclosing an area on a plane, or the length of such a curve **3.** OUTER EDGE OF TERRITORY the outer edge of an area of defended territory [Late 16thC. Via Latin from Greek *perimetros*, literally 'measuring around', from *peri* 'around' + *metron* 'measure'.] —**perimetric** /pérri méttrik/ *adj.* —**perimetrical** /-méttrik'l/ *adj.* —**perimetrically** /-métrikli/ *adv.*

perimorph /pérri mawrf/ *n.* a mineral that crystallizes around a grain of a different kind of mineral —**perimorphic** /pérri máwrfik/ *adj.* —**perimorphous** /-máwrfəss/ *adj.* —**perimorphism** /-máwrfizəm/ *n.*

perimysium /pérri mízzi əm/ *n.* the sheath of connective tissue that surrounds bundles of muscle fibres [Mid-19thC. Coined from PERI- + Greek *mus* 'muscle'.]

perinatal /pérri náyt'l/ *adj.* relating to or occurring during the period around childbirth, specifically from around week 28 of pregnancy to around one month after the birth —**perinatally** *adv.*

perinatology /pérri nay tólləji/ *n.* a medical speciality concerned with the care and treatment of mother and infant immediately prior to, during, and following childbirth —**perinatologist** *n.*

perinephrium /pérri néffri əm/ (*plural* **-a** /-fri ə/) *n.* the fatty tissue that surrounds the kidney [Late 19thC. Coined from PERI- + Greek *nephros* 'kidney'.] —**perinephric** *adj.*

perineum /pérri neé əm/ (*plural* **-a** /-neé ə/) *n.* the region of the abdomen surrounding the urogenital and anal openings [Mid-17thC. Via late Latin from Greek *perinaion*, literally 'near to where excretion takes place', from *peri* 'near to' + *inan* 'to excrete'.] —**perineal** *adj.*

perineuritis /pérrinyoō rítiss/ *n.* inflammation of a perineurium —**perineuritic** /-nyoō ríttik/ *adj.*

perineurium /pérri nyoōri əm/ (*plural* **-a** /-ri ə/) *n.* the sheath of connective tissue that surrounds a bundle of nerve fibres [Mid-19thC. Coined from PERI- + NEURO-.] —**perineurial** *adj.*

period /peéri əd/ *n.* **1.** INTERVAL OF TIME an interval of time **2.** IDENTIFIABLE TIME an interval of time that is identified by what happens or exists during it **3.** TIMETABLE SECTION a division of a schedule or timetable, e.g. a portion of the school day **4.** MENSTRUATION TIME an occurrence of menstruation (*often used before a noun*) **5.** GEOL UNIT OF GEOLOGICAL TIME a division of geological time shorter than an era and longer than an epoch **6.** = **full stop 7.** DIVISION OF GAME a division of playing time in some sports **8.** PHYS TIME FOR SINGLE CYCLE the time required for one complete cycle of a repetitive system, e.g. the rotation of a star or the movement of an electromagnetic wave. Symbol *T* **9.** MATH INTERVAL BETWEEN EQUAL VALUES the interval between the points at which the values of a periodic function are equal **10.** CHEM ROW IN PERIODIC TABLE any of the horizontal rows of elements in the periodic table **11.** POETRY UNIT OF POETIC RHYTHM one of the longer units in the classical system of analysing the rhythms of poetry **12.** MUSIC MUSICAL PASSAGE a long passage of music consisting of two or more contrasting musical phrases ■ *interj.* SHOWING FINALITY a word added to the end of a statement to emphasize that the speaker will not discuss it further (*informal*) ■ *adj.* RELATING TO PARTICULAR HISTORICAL TIME belonging to or intended to suggest a particular historical time ○ *actors in period costume* [14thC. Via French from, ultimately, Greek *periodos*, literally 'way around', from *hodos*

'way' (source of English *exodus* and *episode*), the underlying meaning being 'circuit, cycle'.]

periodic /peéri óddik/ *adj.* **1.** OCCASIONAL recurring or reappearing from time to time **2.** REGULAR occurring or appearing at regular intervals or in regular cycles **3.** INVOLVING PERIODS associated with or occurring in periods [Mid-17thC. Via French and Latin from Greek *periodikos*, from *periodos* (see PERIOD).] —**periodically** *adv.*

───── WORD KEY: SYNONYMS ─────
periodic, intermittent, occasional, sporadic
CORE MEANING: recurring over a period of time
periodic used to indicate that sth occurs at intervals, suggesting a degree of regularity; **intermittent** used to indicate that sth occurs at irregular intervals and emphasizing the absence of continuity or regularity; **occasional** used to indicate that sth occurs infrequently and irregularly, often used to describe sth fairly minor or unimportant; **sporadic** used to indicate that sth occurs irregularly and unpredictably, often implying scattered instances.

periodic acid *n.* any strongly oxidizing acid of iodine [Coined from PER- + IODIC]

periodical /peéri óddik'l/ *n.* MAGAZINE a magazine or journal published at regular intervals such as weekly, monthly, or quarterly ■ *adj.* **1.** PUBLISHED REGULARLY published at regular intervals **2.** OCCASIONAL recurring or reappearing from time to time

periodical cicada *n.* = **seventeen-year locust**

periodic function *n.* a mathematical function whose value is the same at regular intervals

periodicity /peéri ə díssəti/ *n.* **1.** REGULAR RECURRENCE recurrence at regular intervals **2.** CHEM CHEMICAL SIMILARITY similarity between the properties of chemical elements that are close to each other in the periodic table

periodic law *n.* the law stating that chemical elements fall into groups sharing similar properties when they are arranged according to atomic number

periodic sentence *n.* in rhetoric, a complex sentence in which the main clause is left unfinished until the end in order to create the effect of anticipation or suspense

periodic system *n.* the system of arranging chemical elements in a table according to the periodic law

periodic table *n.* a table of the chemical elements arranged according to their atomic numbers

periodization /peéri ə dī záysh'n/, **periodisation** *n.* the dividing of history into distinct and identifiable periods

periodontal /pérri ō dónt'l/ *adj.* relating to or affecting the tissues that surround the neck and root of a tooth [Mid-19thC. Coined from PERI- + Greek *odont* 'tooth'.] —**periodontally** *adv.*

periodontics /pérri ō dóntiks/, **periodontology** /pérri ō don tólləji/ *n.* the branch of dentistry concerned with the treatment of diseases of the gums and other periodontal tissues —**periodontic** *adj.* —**periodontical** *adj.* —**periodontically** *adv.* —**periodontist** *n.*

period piece *n.* sth, especially a curio or a work of art, that dates from or evokes a particular historical period, often sth with no other value

perionychium /pérri ō níki əm/ (*plural* **-a** /-ki ə/) *n.* the areas of skin that surround a fingernail or toenail [Early 20thC. From modern Latin, literally 'round the nail', from Greek *onux* 'nail'.]

periosteum /pérri ósti əm/ (*plural* **-a** /-ti ə/) *n.* the sheath of connective tissue that surrounds all bones except those at joints [Late 16thC. Via modern Latin from, Greek *periosteon*, literally 'around the bone', from *osteon* 'bone'.] —**periosteal** *adj.*

periostitis /pérri ō stítiss/ *n.* inflammation of the periosteum —**periostitic** /-stíttik/ *adj.*

periostracum /pérri óstrəkəm/ (*plural* **-ca** /-kə/) *n.* the hard outer layer of the shell of some molluscs, especially freshwater molluscs [Mid-19thC. From modern Latin, literally 'shell around', from Greek *ostrakon* 'shell'.]

periotic /pérri ótik/ *adj.* involving the area around the ear, especially the bones around the inner ear

peripatetic /pérripə téttik/ *adj.* GOING FROM PLACE TO PLACE travelling from place to place, especially working in several establishments and travelling between them ■ *n.* PERIPATETIC WORKER a peripatetic worker, especially a teacher who travels between schools [Early 17thC. Via French or Latin from Greek *peripatētikos*, from *peripatein* 'to walk around', which in turn was formed form *patein* 'to walk'.] —**peripatetically** *adv.*

Peripatetic /pérripə téttik/ *adj.* RELATING TO ARISTOTLE'S PHILOSOPHY belonging or relating to the school of philosophy founded by Aristotle, who gave lectures while walking about the Lyceum in Athens ■ *n.* ARISTOTELIAN PHILOSOPHER a member of the Aristotelian school of philosophy

peripatus /pə ríppətəss/ *n.* = **onychophoran** [Mid-19thC. Via modern Latin, the genus name, from Greek *peripatos*, literally 'way around', from *peripatos* 'way'.]

peripeteia /pérripə teé ə, pérripə tí ə/, **peripetia** *n.* an abrupt change in events or circumstances, especially in drama (*formal*) [Late 16thC. From Greek, literally 'falling down around', from *pet-*, the stem of *piptein* 'to fall'.] —**peripeteian** *adj.*

peripheral /pə ríffərəl/ *adj.* **1.** AT THE EDGE at or relating to the edge of sth, as opposed to its centre **2.** NOT SIGNIFICANT minor or incidental in importance or relevance **3.** ANAT NEAR THE SURFACE near the surface of an organ or the body ■ *n.* COMPUT PERIPHERAL PIECE OF HARDWARE a piece of computer hardware such as a printer or a disk drive that is external to but connected with and controlled by a computer's central processing unit —**peripherally** *adv.*

peripheral nervous system *n.* the part of the nervous system that lies outside the brain and spinal cord

periphery /pə ríffəri/ (*plural* **-ies**) *n.* **1.** BOUNDARY the area around the edge of a place **2.** SURFACE the surface of an object **3.** POSITION OF LITTLE INVOLVEMENT the position or state of having only a minor involvement in sth [Late 16thC. Via late Latin from, ultimately, Greek *peripherēs*, literally 'carrying around', from *pherein* 'to carry'.]

periphrasis /pə ríffrəssiss/ (*plural* **-ses** /-seez/) *n.* **1.** INDIRECT SPEECH the use of excessively long or indirect speech in order to say sth **2.** INDIRECT STATEMENT an expression that states sth indirectly [Mid-16thC. Via Latin from, ultimately, Greek *periphrazein*, literally 'to explain around', from *phrazein* 'to explain'.]

periphrastic /pérri frástik/ *adj.* **1.** USING PERIPHRASIS concerning or using periphrasis **2.** GRAM NOT FORMED WITH INFLECTIONS formed using two or more words rather than an inflected form, especially used to describe a verb tense formed using an auxiliary verb rather than by inflecting the main verb [Early 19thC. From Greek *periphrastikos*, from *periphrazein* (see PERIPHRASIS).] —**periphrastically** *adv.*

periphyton /pə ríffi ton/ *n.* aquatic plants and animals that live attached to rocks and other submerged objects [Mid-20thC. Origin uncertain: probably coined from PERI- + Greek *phuton* 'plant', on the model of *plankton*.]

periplasm /pérri plazəm/ *n.* the area of a cell that lies immediately inside the cell wall but outside the plasma membrane

periplast /pérri plast/ *n.* a cell wall or cell membrane

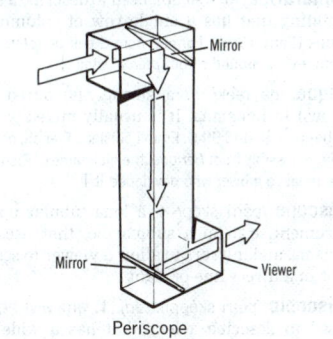

Periscope

PERIODIC TABLE

Chemical elements are indicated by their symbols. The numbers above the elements are the atomic numbers, and those below are the atomic weights (those in parentheses are for the longest-lived isotopes, while those for Np, Pa, and Tc are for the most technologically important isotopes). The lanthanides and actinides do not fit easily into any group and are thus shown separate from the main table. Elements 113–118 are not known but are included in the table to show their expected positions.

Period \ Group	1	2	3	4	5	6	7	8	9	10	11	12	13	14	15	16	17	18
1	1 H 1.01																	2 He 4.00
2	3 Li 6.94	4 Be 9.01											5 B 10.81	6 C 12.01	7 N 14.01	8 O 16.00	9 F 19.00	10 Ne 20.18
3	11 Na 22.99	12 Mg 24.31											13 Al 26.98	14 Si 28.09	15 P 30.97	16 S 32.06	17 Cl 35.45	18 Ar 39.95
4	19 K 39.10	20 Ca 40.08	21 Sc 44.96	22 Ti 47.90	23 V 50.94	24 Cr 52.00	25 Mn 54.94	26 Fe 55.85	27 Co 58.93	28 Ni 58.71	29 Cu 63.55	30 Zn 65.38	31 Ga 69.72	32 Ge 72.59	33 As 74.92	34 Se 78.96	35 Br 79.90	36 Kr 83.80
5	37 Rb 85.47	38 Sr 87.62	39 Y 88.91	40 Zr 91.22	41 Nb 92.91	42 Mo 95.94	43 Tc 98.91	44 Ru 101.07	45 Rh 102.91	46 Pd 106.40	47 Ag 107.87	48 Cd 112.40	49 In 114.82	50 Sn 118.69	51 Sb 121.75	52 Te 127.60	53 I 126.90	54 Xe 131.30
6	55 Cs 132.91	56 Ba 137.34	* 71 Lu 174.97	72 Hf 178.49	73 Ta 180.95	74 W 183.85	75 Re 186.2	76 Os 190.2	77 Ir 192.22	78 Pt 195.09	79 Au 196.97	80 Hg 200.59	81 Tl 204.37	82 Pb 207.20	83 Bi 208.98	84 Po 209	85 At (210)	86 Rn (222)
7	87 Fr (223)	88 Ra (226)	** 103 Lr (256)	104 Rf (261)	105 Db (262)	106 Sg (266)	107 Bh (264)	108 Hs (269)	109 Mt (268)	110 Uun (269)	111 Uuu (272)	112 Uub (277)	113 Uut	114 Uuq	115 Uup	116 Uuh	117 Uus	118 Uuo

Lanthanides *	57 La 138.91	58 Ce 140.12	59 Pr 140.91	60 Nd 144.24	61 Pm (145)	62 Sm 150.40	63 Eu 151.96	64 Gd 157.25	65 Tb 158.93	66 Dy 162.50	67 Ho 164.93	68 Er 167.26	69 Tm 168.93	70 Yb 173.04
Actinides **	89 Ac (226)	90 Th 232.04	91 Pa 231.04	92 U 283.04	93 Np 237.05	94 Pu (244)	95 Am (243)	96 Cm (247)	97 Bk (247)	98 Cf (251)	99 Es (254)	100 Fm (257)	101 Md (258)	102 No (255)

periproct /pérri prokt/ *n.* the area surrounding the anus of some invertebrate animals such as sea urchins [Late 19thC. Coined from PERI- + Greek *prōktos* 'anus'.]

peripteral /pə ríptərəl/ *adj.* used to describe a classical building that has a single row of columns on all sides [Early 19thC. Formed from Greek *peripteros*, literally 'with a wing around', from *pteron* 'wing'.]

perique /pə reèk/ *n.* a strongly-flavoured tobacco grown in Lousiana. It is usually mixed with other tobaccos. [Late 19thC. From Louisiana French, of uncertain origin: possibly from *Périque*, the nickname of Pierre Chenet, the tobacco grower who developed it.]

periscope /pérri skōp/ *n.* a long tubular optical instrument, e.g. on a submarine, that uses lenses, prisms, and mirrors to allow a viewer to see objects not in a direct line of sight

periscopic /pérri skóppik/ *adj.* **1. WITH WIDE FIELD OF VIEW** used to describe a lens that has a wide field of view **2. RELATING TO PERISCOPES** relating to or using a periscope —**periscopically** *adv.*

perish /pérrish/ (-ishes, -ishing, -ished) *v.* **1.** *vi.* **DIE** to die, e.g. because of harsh conditions or accident (*literary*) **2.** *vi.* **DISAPPEAR** to come to an end or cease to exist (*formal*) **3.** *vti.* **DECAY** to deteriorate or decay, or to make a material, e.g. rubber, deteriorate or decay [13thC. Via French *périss-*, the stem of *périr*, from Latin *perire*, literally 'to go completely', from *ire* 'to go' (source of English *exit*).]

perishable /pérrishəb'l/ *adj.* **SPOILING EASILY** liable to decay, rot, or spoil ▪ *n.* **PERISHABLE ITEM** sth that is perishable, especially an item of food —**perishability** /pérrishə bílləti/ *n.* —**perishableness** /pérrishəb'lnəss/ *n.* —**perishably** /pérrishəbli/ *adv.*

perished /pérrisht/ *adj.* feeling extremely cold (*informal*)

perisher /pérrishər/ *n.* an annoying person, especially a naughty child (*dated informal*)

perishing /pérrishing/ *adj.* **1. COLD** extremely cold **2. USED FOR EMPHASIS** used to emphasize how annoying sth or sb is (*dated informal*) —**perishingly** *adv.*

perisperm /pérri spurm/ *n.* nutritive tissue from a plant nucleus that surrounds the seed embryo —**perispermal** /pérri spúrm'l/ *adj.*

perissodactyl /pə rísso dáktil/ *n.* a large mammal that belongs to the order of mammals with hooves and an odd number of toes, which includes horses, rhinoceroses, and tapirs. Order: Perissodactyla. [Mid-19thC. From modern Latin *Perissodactyla*, the order name, literally 'uneven finger or toe', from Greek *perissos* 'uneven' + *daktulos* 'finger, toe'.] —**perissodactyl** *adj.* —**perissodactylous** *adj.*

peristalsis /pérri stálssiss/ (*plural* -ses /-seez/) *n.* the waves of involuntary muscle contractions that transport food, waste matter, or other contents through a tube-shaped organ such as the intestine [Mid-19thC. Via modern Latin from Greek *peristaltikos* 'clasping, compressing', from *peristellein*, literally 'to place around', from *stellein* 'to place'.] —**peristaltic** *adj.* —**peristaltically** *adv.*

peristome /pérri stōm/ *n.* the mouthparts of an invertebrate such as an earthworm or echinoderm —**peristomal** /pérri stṓm'l/ *adj.* —**peristomial** /-stṓmi əl/ *adj.*

peristyle /pérri stīl/ *n.* **1.** ENCIRCLING COLUMNS a line of columns (**colonnade**) that encircles a building or a courtyard **2.** BUILDING WITH PERISTYLE a building or courtyard that has a peristyle [Early 17thC. Via French from, ultimately, Greek *peristulos* 'having columns around', from *stulos* 'column'.] —**peristylar** /pérri stílər/ *adj.*

perithecium /pérri théessi əm/ (*plural* **-a** /-si ə/) *n.* in some kinds of fungus, a flask-shaped fruiting body that contains spores [Mid-19thC. From modern Latin, literally 'case around', from Greek *peri* 'around' + *thēkē* 'case'.]

peritoneum /pérritō née əm/ (*plural* **-a** /-née ə/ *or* **-ums**) *n.* a smooth transparent membrane that lines the abdomen and doubles back over the surfaces of the internal organs to form a continuous sac [Mid-16thC. Via late Latin from, ultimately, Greek *peritonos* 'stretched around', from *teinein* 'to stretch'.] —**peritoneal** *adj.* —**peritoneally** *adv.*

peritonitis /pérritō nítiss/ *n.* inflammation of the membrane that lines the abdomen (**peritoneum**). Symptoms can include swelling of the abdomen, severe pain, and weight loss. —**peritonitic** /-níttik/ *adj.*

peritrack /pérri trak/ *n.* = **taxiway** [Late 20thC. Coined from PERIMETER + TRACK.]

peritrich /pérri trik/ (*plural* **-tricha** /pə ríttrikə/) *n.* a simple microscopic invertebrate (**protozoan**) covered in tiny filaments (**cilia**) that it uses to move around [Early 20thC. Shortening of modern Latin *peritricha*, literally 'hair around', from Greek *peri* 'around' + *trikh-*, the stem of *thrix* 'hair'.] —**peritrichous** /pə ríttrikəss/ *adj.*

periwig /pérri wig/ *n.* a wig, especially of the kind that men wore in the 17th and 18th centuries [Early 16thC. Alteration of an earlier form of PERUKE.]

periwinkle[1] /pérri wingk'l/ *n.* MARINE BIOL = **winkle** [Mid-16thC. Origin uncertain: perhaps an alteration of Old English *pinewincle* 'mussel shell'.]

Periwinkle

periwinkle[2] /pérri wingk'l/ *n.* PLANTS **TRAILING PLANT** a European or Asian trailing evergreen plant with blue or white flowers and dark-green glossy leaves. Genus: *Vinca.* ■ *adj.* PALE BLUISH-PURPLE of a pale bluish-purple colour [Pre-12thC. From late Latin *pervinca*, which evolved from Latin *vincapervinca*, of uncertain origin: perhaps formed from *pervincire*, literally 'to wind around'.]

perjink /pər jíngk/ *adj.* *Scotland* caring too much about neatness or unimportant details (*humorous*) [Early 19thC. Origin unknown.]

perjure /púrjər/ (**-jures, -juring, -jured**) *vr.* to tell a lie in a court of law and therefore be guilty of perjury [15thC. Via French from Latin *perjurare* 'to swear falsely', from *jurare* (see JURY).] —**perjurer** *n.*

perjured /púrjərd/ *adj.* **1.** GUILTY OF PERJURY guilty of telling a lie in a court of law and therefore of committing perjury **2.** CONTAINING PERJURY containing lies and therefore breaking an oath to tell the truth in a court of law

perjury /púrjəri/ (*plural* **-ries**) *n.* **1.** TELLING LIES UNDER OATH the telling of a lie after having taken an oath to tell the truth, usually in a court of law **2.** LIE UNDER OATH a lie told in a court of law by sb who has taken an oath to tell the truth [14thC. Via Anglo-Norman from Latin *perjurium*, from *perjurare* (see PERJURE).] —**perjurious** /pər jóori əss/ *adj.* —**perjuriously** /-əssli/ *adv.* —**perjuriousness** /-əssnəss/ *n.*

perk[1] /purk/ *n.* **1.** ADDITIONAL BENEFIT a benefit given to an employee in addition to a salary, e.g. the use of a car or membership of a club **2.** INCIDENTAL GAIN anything that sb gains incidentally or as a consequence of sth else ○ *Taking time off whenever you want is one of the perks of being self-employed.* [Early 19thC. Shortening of PERQUISITE.]

perk up *vti.* **1.** MAKE OR BECOME LIVELY to become or make sb more cheerful, positive, or active **2.** STICK UP to stick up or make sth stick up, especially quickly ○ *saw the dog's ears perk up* [*Perk* is of uncertain origin: perhaps from an obsolete word meaning 'to perch', via medieval Latin *perca* 'perch' from Latin *pertica* (see PERCH)]

perk[2] /purk/ (**perks, perking, perked**) *vti.* to percolate, or to percolate coffee (*informal*) [Mid-20thC. Shortening.]

Perkins /púrkinz/, **Charles Nelson** (*b.* 1936) Australian Aboriginal activist. He led antidiscrimination protests in the 1960s, and subsequently became head of the federal Department of Aboriginal Affairs (1984–89).

perky /púrki/ (**-ier, -iest**) *adj.* **1.** LIVELY AND CHEERFUL lively, cheerful, and energetic **2.** TOO CONFIDENT irritatingly self-confident —**perkily** *adv.* —**perkiness** *n.*

perlite /púr līt/ *n.* a greyish volcanic glass in the form of grains that resemble pearls. It is often added to potting compost as a soil conditioner and is also used as a heat insulator. —**perlitic** /pur líttik/ *adj.*

perlocution /púr lō kyóosh'n/ *n.* the effect that a speaker's words have on sb. Their effect might be, e.g. to reassure or frighten. [Mid-20thC. Coined from PER + LOCUTION.] —**perlocutionary** *adj.*

perm[1] /purm/ *n.* HAIR TREATMENT a hair treatment that uses chemicals to give hair long-lasting curliness or waviness ■ *vt.* (**perms, perming, permed**) GIVE HAIR A PERM to treat hair chemically to give it long-lasting curliness or waviness [Early 20thC. Shortening of PERMANENT.]

perm[2] /purm/ *n.* SELECTION OF WINNERS the selection of possible winners made by sb making a bet, especially, in football pools, a selection of matches that are thought likely to end in a score draw (*informal*) ■ *vt.* (**perms, perming, permed**) SELECT WINNERS to select a number of possible winners to bet on from a larger field, especially, in football pools, a number of matches thought likely to end in a score draw (*informal*) [Mid-20thC. Shortening of PERMUTATION.]

Perm /purm/, **Perm'** city in eastern European Russia. Population: 1,098,600 (1992).

permaculture /púrmə kulchər/ *n.* a system of agriculture that uses a mix of trees, shrubs, other perennial plants, and livestock to create a self-sustaining ecosystem that yields crops and other products [Late 20thC. Blend of PERMANENT and AGRICULTURE.]

permafrost /púrmə frost/ *n.* underlying soil or rock that remains permanently frozen, found mainly in the polar regions [Mid-20thC. Coined from PERMANENT + FROST.]

permalloy /pur mállоy/ *tdmk.* a trademark for various nickel-iron alloys that are highly valued in the electronics industry because they allow magnetic fields to pass through them

permanence /púrmənənss/, **permanency** /púrmənənssi/ *n.* existence in the same form forever or for a very long time [15thC. Directly or via French or medieval Latin *permanentia*, from the Latin stem *permanent-* (see PERMANENT).]

permanent /púrmənənt/ *adj.* **1.** EVERLASTING lasting for ever or for a very long time, especially without undergoing significant change **2.** UNCHANGING never changing or not expected to change ■ *n.* *US* HAIR **PERM** a perm (*formal*) [15thC. Directly or via French from Latin *permanere*, literally 'to remain through', from *manere* 'to remain' (source of English *remain*).] —**permanently** *adv.* —**permanentness** *n.*

permanent magnet *n.* a magnet that retains its properties after the magnetizing force has been removed from it. Permanent magnets are used in loudspeakers and small motors. —**permanent magnetism** *n.*

permanent press *n.* any chemical process, e.g. the use of resin, used to give fabric shape and make it resistant to wrinkling (*hyphenated when used before a noun*)

permanent tooth *n.* any of the second and final set of teeth that grow to replace the milk teeth. A human adult has 32 permanent teeth.

permanent wave *n.* HAIR a perm (*formal*)

permanent way *n.* a railway track intended for long-term public use, laid with sleepers on a prepared bed of ground and supported by stones, as opposed to a lightweight or temporary track

permanganate /pər máng gə nayt/ *n.* a chemical compound that is a salt of permanganic acid [Mid-19thC. Formed from MANGANESE.]

permanganic acid /púr man gánnik-/ *n.* an unstable acid that exists only in dilute solution. Formula: $HMnO_4$. [*Permanganic* formed from PERMANGANATE]

permeability /púrmi ə bílləti/ (*plural* **-ties**) *n.* **1.** PERMEABLE NATURE the property of being permeable **2.** RATE SUBSTANCE PASSES THROUGH POROUS MEDIUM the rate at which sth such as a liquid or a magnetic field passes through a membrane or other medium **3.** MAGNETIC PROPERTY the property of a material to alter a magnetic field in which it is placed, or a measure of this property. Symbol μ

permeable /púrmi əb'l/ *adj.* allowing liquids, gases, or magnetic fields to pass through —**permeably** *adv.*

permeance /púrmi ənss/ *n.* **1.** ACT OF PERMEATING the act of passing through a porous substance or membrane **2.** ABILITY TO BE MAGNETIZED the ability of a magnetic component or assembly to be magnetized, measured in henries and calculated by dividing the magnetic flux by the magnetomotive force —**permeant** *adj.*, *n.*

permease /púrmi ayz, -ayss/ *n.* an enzyme that brings about a chemical reaction to carry a substance across a cell membrane [Mid-20thC. Formed from PERMEATE.]

permeate /púrmi ayt/ (**-ates, -ating, -ated**) *vti.* **1.** SPREAD THROUGH to enter sth and spread throughout it, so that every part or aspect of it is affected **2.** SCI PASS THROUGH to pass through the minute openings in a porous substance or membrane, or make sth such as a liquid pass through [Mid-17thC. From Latin *permeare* 'to pass through', from *meare* 'to pass'.] —**permeation** /púrmi áysh'n/ *n.* —**permeative** /púrmi ətiv/ *adj.*

per mensem /pər ménssəm/ *adv.* monthly or by the month (*formal*) [From modern Latin, literally 'by the month']

Permian /púrmi ən/ *n.* the period of geological time when reptiles flourished, 290 million to 245 million years ago [Late 16thC. Named after the province of *Perm* in eastern Russia, where strata from the period are easily visible.] —**Permian** *adj.*

per mill /pər míl/, **per mil** *adv.* in every thousand or by the thousand ['Mill' from Latin *mille* 'thousand']

permissible /pər míssəb'l/ *adj.* allowable or permitted [15thC. Via French from, ultimately, Latin *permiss-*, the past participle stem of *permittere* (see PERMIT).] —**permissibility** /pər míssə bílləti/ *n.* —**permissibly** /pər míssəbli/ *adv.*

permission /pər mísh'n/ *n.* agreement to allow sth to happen or be done [15thC. Via French from, ultimately, Latin *permiss-*, the past participle stem of *permittere* (see PERMIT).]

permissive /pər míssiv/ *adj.* **1.** ALLOWING FREEDOM OF BEHAVIOUR allowing or enjoying the freedom to behave in ways others might consider unacceptable, particularly in sexual matters **2.** GIVING PERMISSION granting permission **3.** OPTIONAL not required (*archaic*) [15thC. Via French from, ultimately, Latin *per.*] —**permissively** *adv.* —**permissiveness** *n.*

permit *v.* /pər mít/ (**-mits, -mitting, -mitted**) **1.** *vti.* ALLOW STH to allow sth or give permission for it **2.** *vti.* MAKE STH POSSIBLE to allow sb the possibility of doing sth **3.** *vr.* ALLOW YOURSELF STH to allow yourself to have or do sth, especially as a luxury or for a special occasion ■ *n.* /púrmit/ **1.** DOCUMENT GIVING PERMISSION an official document or certificate giving permission for sth **2. PERMISSION** permission granted, especially in written form (*formal*) [15thC. From Latin *permittere*, literally 'to let go through', from *mittere* 'to let go' (source of English *mission*).] —**permittee** /púrmi teé/ *n.* —**permitter** /pər míttər/ *n.*

permittivity /púrmi tívvəti/ (*plural* **-ties**) *n.* the measure of the ability of a nonconducting material to retain electric energy when placed in an electric field. Symbol *v* [Late 19thC. Formed from PERMIT, on the model of *conductivity*.]

permutate /púrmyŏo tayt/ (**-tates**, **-tating**, **-tated**) *vt.* to change the order of items in a group, especially to rearrange them in every possible way [Late 16thC. From Latin *permutare* (see PERMUTE).]

permutation /púrmyŏo táysh'n/ *n.* **1. ARRANGEMENT** an arrangement of items created by moving or re-ordering them **2. REARRANGING** the reordering or re-arranging of items in a group **3. TRANSFORMATION** a change or transformation **4. MATH ORDER OF MATHEMATICAL ELEMENTS** an ordered arrangement of elements from a set **5.** BETTING **PERM** a perm (*formal*) —**permutational** *adj.*

permute /pər myŏot/ (**-mutes**, **-muting**, **-muted**) *vt.* **1. REARRANGE THINGS** to change the order of items in a group, especially to rearrange them in every possible way **2.** MATH **REARRANGE MATHEMATICAL ELEMENTS** to reorder the elements in a mathematical set [Late 19thC. From Latin *permutare*, literally 'to change completely', from *mutare* 'to change' (source of English *mutate*).] —**permutability** /pər myŏotə bílləti/ *n.* —**permutable** /pər myŏotəb'l/ *adj.* —**permutably** /-əbli/ *adv.*

pernicious /pər níshəss/ *adj.* **1. MALICIOUS** wicked or meaning to cause harm **2. CAUSING SERIOUS HARM** causing great harm, destruction, or death [Early 16thC. Via Old French from, ultimately, Latin *pernicies*, literally 'complete destruction', from *nec-*, the stem of *nex* 'destruction'.] —**perniciously** *adv.* —**perniciousness** *n.*

pernicious anaemia *n.* a severe form of anaemia, found mostly in older adults, that results from the body's inability to absorb vitamin B₁₂. Symptoms include weakness, breathing difficulties, and weight loss.

pernickety /pər níkəti/ *adj.* (*informal*) US term **persnickety 1. FINICKY** excessively concerned about unimportant details **2. REQUIRING PRECISION** requiring precise attention to detail [Early 19thC. Origin unknown: perhaps thought to suggest small pieces.] —**pernicketiness** *n.*

Pernod /púrnō/ *tdmk.* a trademark for an alcoholic spirit with the flavour of aniseed

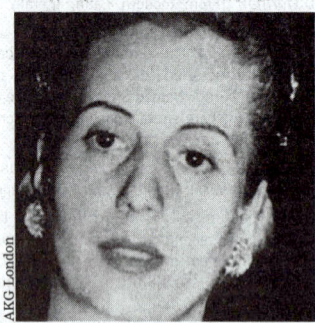

Eva de Perón

Perón /pə rón/, **Eva de** (1919–52) Argentinian political figure. Married to President Juan Perón, she was adored by the Argentinian people for her charitable work. Born **María Eva Duarte**. Known as **Evita**

Perón, Isabel de (*b.* 1931) Argentinian politician. She was the third wife of Juan Perón, and after his death succeeded him as president (1974–76). Born **María Estela Martínez Cartas**

Perón, Juan (1895–1974) Argentinian statesman. He rose to power by a military coup (1943) and as president (1946–55 and 1973–74) enacted populist economic reforms. His wife Eva Perón was idolized by the poor, and, losing popularity after her death in 1952, he spent 18 years in exile. Full name **Juan Domingo Perón** —**Peronist** /pə rónnist/ *n.*, *adj.*

peroneal /pérrə neé əl/ *adj.* relating to the narrower of the two bones in the lower leg (**fibula**) [Mid-19thC. Formed from Greek *peronē* 'pin of a brooch, fibula'.]

peroral /pər áwrəl/ *adj.* occurring by way of the mouth —**perorally** *adv.*

perorate /pérrə rayt/ (**-rates**, **-rating**, **-rated**) *vi.* (*formal*) **1. END SPEECH** to finish a speech by summarizing its main points **2. GIVE SPEECH** to speak at length, especially in a formal or pompous way [Early 17thC. From Latin *perorare*, literally 'to speak all the way through', from *orare* 'to speak' (source of English *oration*).]

peroration /pérrə ráysh'n/ *n.* **1. SPEECH'S CONCLUSION** a conclusion to a speech in which the main points of the speech are summarized (*formal*) **2. LONG-WINDED SPEECH** a long speech making much use of rhetorical devices —**perorational** *adj.*

perovskite /pe róv skīt/ *n.* a black, yellow, or brown mineral consisting of calcium titanate, with applications in superconductivity [Mid-19thC. Named after the Russian mineralogist L. A. Perovski, 1792–1856.]

peroxidase /pə róksi dayz, -dayss/ *n.* an enzyme found in plants that speeds up oxidation reactions involving hydrogen peroxide or other peroxides

peroxide /pə rók sīd/ *n.* **1.** CHEM **CHEMICAL COMPOUND** a chemical compound such as hydrogen peroxide that contains oxygen atoms in the group -O₂- **2. HAIR COLOURING SUBSTANCE** a solution of hydrogen peroxide used as a hair lightener. It gives hair an unnaturally light blond tint that is almost white. (*often used before a noun*) ○ *a peroxide blonde* ■ *vt.* (**-ides**, **-iding**, **-ided**) **1. BLEACH HAIR WITH PEROXIDE** to bleach hair using peroxide **2.** CHEM **TREAT STH WITH PEROXIDE** to treat sth with peroxide or hydrogen peroxide

peroxisome /pə róksi sōm/ *n.* a tiny part within a cell containing enzymes that oxidize toxic substances such as alcohol and prevent them from doing any harm. There are many peroxisomes in the cells of the liver and kidney. [Mid-20thC. Coined from PEROXIDE + -SOME.]

perp /purp/ *n.* US sb responsible for a crime (*slang*) [Late 20thC. Shortening of PERPETRATOR.]

perpend¹ /púr pend/ *n.* US BUILDING = **parpen** [15thC. Variant of PARPEN.]

perpend² /pər pénd/ (**-pends**, **-pending**, **-pended**) *vti.* to ponder sth (*archaic*) [Early 16thC. From Latin *perpendere*, literally 'to weigh thoroughly', from *pendere* 'to weigh' (source of English *pensive*).]

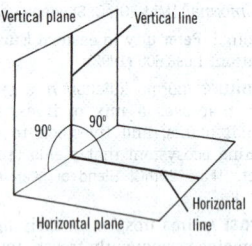

Perpendicular

perpendicular /púrpən díkyŏolər/ *adj.* **1. VERTICAL** perfectly vertical **2. STEEP** very steep **3. AT RIGHT ANGLES** at right angles to a line or plane **4. perpendicular, Perpendicular** ARCHIT **IN LATE GOTHIC STYLE** relating to or typical of a style of Gothic architecture whose characteristic elements are tall narrow facades, windows, and doors, and vaulted ceilings. It was popular in England in the 14th and 15th centuries. ■ *n.* **1. PERPENDICULAR LINE** a perpendicular line or plane **2. DEVICE FINDING THE VERTICAL** any device used to establish a vertical line such as a spirit level or a plumb line **3. perpendicular, Perpendicular** ARCHIT **ARCHITECTURAL STYLE** the perpendicular style of architecture **4.** MOUNTAINEERING **SHEER ROCK** a sheer rock face [14thC. Via Old French from, ultimately, Latin *perpendiculum* 'plumb line', literally 'sth weighed thoroughly', formed from *perpendere*, literally 'to weigh thoroughly', formed in turn from *pendere* 'to weigh'.] —**perpendicularity** /púrpən díkyŏo lárrəti/ *n.* —**perpendicularly** /púrpən díkyŏolərli/ *adv.*

perpetrate /púrpi trayt/ (**-trates**, **-trating**, **-trated**) *vt.* to commit or be responsible for sth, usually sth criminal or morally wrong [Mid-16thC. From Latin *perpetrare*, literally 'to completely bring about', from *patrare* 'to bring about', literally 'to father', from *pater* 'father'.] —**perpetration** /púrpi tráysh'n/ *n.* —**perpetrator** /púrpə traytər/ *n.*

perpetual /pər péchoo əl/ *adj.* **1. LASTING FOR EVER** lasting for all time **2. LASTING INDEFINITELY** lasting for an indefinitely long time **3. OCCURRING REPEATEDLY** occurring over and over **4.** BOT **BLOOMING THROUGHOUT SEASON** used to describe flowers or flowering plants that bloom throughout the season [14thC. Via French from, ultimately, Latin *perpes* 'continuous', literally 'going towards throughout', from *petere* 'to go towards' (source of English *petition*).]

perpetual calendar *n.* a calendar set out in such a way that it can be used for several years or for any year

perpetual check *n.* a situation in chess in which one player's king is placed in check with every move the other player makes, resulting in a draw

perpetually /pər péchoo əli/ *adv.* **1. FOR EVER** for ever or for a very long time **2. REPEATEDLY** repeatedly at very short intervals, and so appearing to be continuous

perpetual motion *n.* **1. HYPOTHETICAL MOTION** the hypothetical continuous operation of a mechanism without the introduction of energy from an external source, known as perpetual motion of the first kind. A device demonstrating this would violate the first law of thermodynamics, which states that energy can neither be created nor destroyed. **2. HYPOTHETICAL CONVERSION OF HEAT** the hypothetical operation of a mechanism that would convert heat directly into work, known as perpetual motion of the second kind. A device demonstrating this would violate the second law of thermodynamics, which states that heat cannot be converted into work without producing some other effect.

perpetuate /pər péchoo ayt/ (**-ates**, **-ating**, **-ated**) *vt.* **1. MAKE STH LAST** to make sth continue, usually for a very long time **2. MAKE STH BE REMEMBERED** to make sth or sb be remembered [Early 16thC. From Latin *perpetuare*, from *perpetuus* (see PERPETUAL).] —**perpetuation** /pər péchooáysh'n/ *n.* —**perpetuator** /pər péchoo aytər/ *n.*

perpetuity /púrpi tyŏo əti/ (*plural* **-ties**) *n.* **1. PERPETUAL CONDITION** the state of continuing for a long time or indefinitely **2. ETERNITY** eternity or the rest of time ○ *a sacrifice honoured in perpetuity* **3.** LAW **TRANSFER OF PROPERTY FOR EVER** the transfer of property for an unlimited period of time, restricted in law by the rule against perpetuity. The maximum legal period of transferred ownership is based on the length of a life in existence at the time plus 21 years plus a nine month period of gestation. **4.** FIN **INVESTMENT** an investment designed to pay an annual return indefinitely, having no maturity date [15thC. Via French from, ultimately, Latin *perpetuus* (see PERPETUAL).]

perphenazine /pər fénnə zeen, -zin/ *n.* a drug used to relieve anxiety, tension, and nausea. Formula: C₂₁H₂₆ClN₃OS. [Mid-20thC. Coined from PIPERIDINE + PHENYL + AZINE.]

Perpignan /púrp een yaaN/ city in southern France, near the Mediterranean Sea and the border with Spain. Population: 108,049 (1990).

perplex /pər pléks/ (**-plexes**, **-plexing**, **-plexed**) *vt.* **1. PUZZLE SB** to puzzle or confuse sb, especially causing doubt **2. COMPLICATE STH** to make sth excessively complicated or intricate [Late 16thC. Back-formation from PERPLEXED.]

perplexed /pər plékst/ *adj.* **1. PUZZLED** puzzled, and usually troubled by doubt **2. TOO COMPLICATED OR INTRICATE** very complicated or intricate, especially in a way that causes difficulties [15thC. Via French from Latin *perplexus*, literally 'completely woven together', from *plexus*, the past participle of *plectere* 'to weave together' (source of English *plexus*).] —**perplexedly** /pər pléksidli/ *adv.*

perplexing /pər pléksing/ *adj.* disconcertingly difficult to understand or come to terms with —**perplexingly** *adv.*

perplexity /pər pléksəti/ (*plural* **-ties**) *n.* **1. BEING PERPLEXED** the state of being perplexed **2. PERPLEXING THING** sth that is difficult to understand, especially because it is complex or part of a complicated whole (*often used in the plural*) **3. COMPLEX NATURE** the nature of sth that is disconcertingly complex

per pro /per pró/ *prep.* a fuller form of the abbreviation 'pp' that is written in formal correspondence by sb who is signing on behalf of another person [Shortening of Latin *per procurationem*, literally 'by proxy']

perquisite /púrkwizit/ *n.* **1. PERK** a perk (*formal*) **2. CUSTOMARY TIP** a tip that is customary on some occasions **3. A RIGHT** sth considered to be an exclusive right [Early 18thC. From medieval Latin *perquisitum*, literally 'sth searched for', from *perquirere* 'to seek for', from *quaerere* 'to seek'.]

Perrault /pérrō/, **Charles** (1628–1703) French writer. In *Tales of Mother Goose* (1697) he set down from oral tradition such fairy tales as *Cinderella* and *Sleeping Beauty.*

Perrier /pérri ay/ *tdmk.* a trademark for a sparkling mineral water from France

perron /pérrən/ *n.* **1. PLATFORM** a raised platform at an entrance that is not at ground level **2. STAIRWAY** an external stairway leading up to a perron [14thC. Via French from the assumed Vulgar Latin stem *petron-*, literally 'large stone', from Latin *petra* 'stone'.]

perry /pérri/ (*plural* **-ries**) *n.* a drink made from fermented pear juice, similar to cider or wine [14thC. Via Old French *pere* from, ultimately, Latin *pirum* (see PEAR).]

Perry /pérri/, **Fred** (1909–95) British tennis player. He was winner of the US Open (1933, 1934, 1936), Wimbledon (1934, 1935, 1936), Australian Open (1934), and French Open (1935) singles titles. Full name **Frederick John Perry**

pers. *abbr.* **1.** personal **2.** person

perse /purss/ *adj.* COLOURS of a dark bluish-grey or purplish-black colour [14thC. Via French from medieval Latin *persus.*] —**perse** *n.*

per se /per sáy/ *adv.* in itself, by itself, or intrinsically (*formal*) [From Latin, literally 'by itself']

Perse /purss/, **Saint-John** (1887–1975) French poet and diplomat. His poetry deals chiefly with the themes of solitude and exile. He won the Nobel Prize for literature (1960). Pseudonym of **Alexis Saint-Léger Léger**

persecute /púrssi kyoot/ (**-cutes, -cuting, -cuted**) *vt.* **1. OPPRESS PEOPLE** to systematically subject a race or group of people to cruel or unfair treatment, e.g. because of their ethnic origin or religious beliefs **2. PESTER SB** to make sb the victim of continual pestering or harassment [15thC. Via French from, ultimately, Latin *persecut-*, the past participle stem of *persequi*, literally 'to keep following', from *sequi* 'to follow' (source of English *sequence*).] —**persecutee** /púrssi kyoo teé/ *n.* —**persecutive** /púrssi kyootiv/ *adj.* —**persecutor** /-kyootər/ *n.* —**persecutory** /-kyootəri/ *adj.*

persecution /púrssi kyoósh'n/ *n.* **1. THE PERSECUTING OF SB** the subjecting of a group of people to cruel or unfair treatment, e.g. because of their ethnic origin or religious beliefs **2. SUFFERING OF PERSECUTED PEOPLE** the suffering felt by persecuted people

Perseid /púrsi id/ *n.* any meteor forming part of a meteor shower that appears around 12 August and seems to originate from the vicinity of the constellation Perseus

Persephone /pər séffəni/ *n.* in Greek mythology, the daughter of Demeter and Zeus who was abducted by Hades, king of the underworld. She spent half the year in the underworld and half the year on earth with her mother. Her return to earth symbolized the arrival of spring. Roman equivalent **Proserpina**

Persepolis /pər séppəliss/ ruined city situated northeast of Shiraz in modern-day Iran. It was founded by Darius I in the 6th century BC as the Persian capital and destroyed by Alexander the Great.

Perseus[1] /púrssi əss, púr syooss/ *n.* a constellation in the northern hemisphere between Auriga and Andromeda

Perseus[2] /púrs yooss, púrsi əss/ *n.* in Greek mythology, the son of Zeus and Danae. He killed the Gorgon Medusa and also rescued the princess Andromeda as she was about to be sacrificed to a sea monster.

perseverance /púrssi veérənss/ *n.* **1. DETERMINED CONTINUATION WITH STH** steady and continued action or belief, usually over a long period and especially despite difficulties or setbacks **2. CHR CALVINIST CONCEPT OF DIVINE GRACE** in Calvinism, the belief that God's grace brings selected people, the elect, to salvation **3. CHR ROMAN CATHOLIC BELIEF IN GOD'S GRACE** in the Roman Catholic Church, the belief that God's grace lasts to the end of sb's life if that person has maintained his or her good works and faith —**perseverant** *adj.*

perseveration /pə sévvə ráysh'n/ *n.* a tendency to repeat the response to an experience in later situations where it is not appropriate [Early 20thC. Formed from Latin *perseverare* (see PERSEVERE).]

persevere /púrssi veér/ (**-veres, -vering, -vered**) *vi.* to persist steadily in an action or belief, usually over a long period and especially despite problems or difficulties [14thC. Via French *persévérer* from Latin *perseverare* 'to follow strictly', from *perseverus* 'very strict', from *severus* (see SEVERE).] —**persevering** *adj.* —**perseveringly** *adv.*

Pershing /púrshing/ *n.* a two-stage US Army ballistic missile capable of delivering a nuclear warhead [Mid-20thC. Named in honour of General J. J. PERSHING.]

Pershing /púrshing/, **John J.** (1860–1948) US general. He led the American Expeditionary Force in Europe during World War I. Full name **John Joseph Pershing**

Persia /púrshə, púrzhə/ **1. IRAN** Iran (*archaic*) **2.** ancient empire in southwestern Asia that, at its height under Darius the Great in the 6th century BC, stretched from the shores of the eastern Mediterranean to the Indus River in modern-day Tibet. It was conquered by Alexander the Great in 330 BC.

Persian /púrsh'n, púrzhn/ *n.* **1. PEOPLES RESIDENT OR NATIVE OF IRAN** sb who was born in or is a citizen of Iran **2. LANG** = Farsi **3. HIST PEOPLE OF ANCIENT PERSIA** a member of a people who lived in ancient Persia and who founded an empire around 500 BC **4. LANG LANGUAGE OF ANCIENT PERSIANS** the language spoken by the ancient Persians ■ *adj.* **PEOPLES 1. ABOUT ANCIENT PERSIA** relating to or typical of ancient Persia, or its people or culture **2. ABOUT MODERN IRAN** relating to modern Iran, or its people or culture

Persian blinds *npl.* = **persiennes** [From their use and manufacture in that country]

Persian carpet, **Persian rug** *n.* a carpet consisting of a woven backing to which wool or silk threads have been hand-knotted, made in the Middle East and typically having rich colours and strong designs

Persian cat

Persian cat *n.* a domestic cat with long silky hair belonging to a breed originally from the Middle East

Persian Gulf gulf of the Arabian Sea, with Iran to its northeast and the Arabian peninsula to its southwest. Area: 233,000 sq. km/90,000 sq. mi.

Persian lamb *n.* **1. SOFT CURLED FUR FROM KARAKUL LAMB** the soft curled usually black fur from the karakul lamb **2. KARAKUL LAMB** a lamb of the karakul sheep

Persian melon *n.* a melon that has musky orange flesh and a rind with a netted pattern. Latin name: *Cucumis melo.*

Persian wool *n.* a loosely twisted three-strand wool yarn used in needlepoint, each strand being two-ply

persiennes /púrssi énz/ *npl.* outside louvred shutters for blocking sunlight while allowing ventilation. US term **Persian blinds** [Mid-19thC. From French, formed from *persian* 'Persian'.]

persiflage /púrssi flaazh/ *n.* **1. LIGHT TEASING CHAT** light or teasing good-natured talk **2. LIGHT-HEARTED STYLE** light-heartedness or frivolity in the treatment of sth [Mid-18thC. From French, formed from *persifler* 'to banter', from *siffler* 'to whistle', via Old French from, ultimately, Latin *sibilare* (see SIBILANT).]

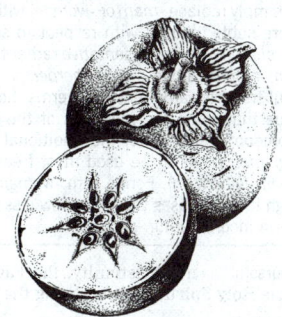

Persimmon

persimmon /pər símmən/ *n.* **1. FOOD TROPICAL FRUIT** a sweet juicy orange-red fruit with a slightly tough outer skin that is edible only when fully ripe **2. TREES TREE BEARING PERSIMMONS** a tropical tree that has hard wood and bears persimmons as fruit. Genus: *Diospyros.* [Early 17thC. Alteration of Virginia Algonquian *pessemins.*]

persist /pər síst/ (**-sists, -sisting, -sisted**) *vi.* **1. KEEP CARRYING ON** to continue steadily or obstinately despite problems, difficulties, or obstacles **2. CONTINUE TO BE BELIEVED WRONGLY** to continue being widely believed or accepted despite evidence or proof to the contrary ○ *a view that persists to this day* **3. CONTINUE** to continue happening [Mid-16thC. From Latin *persistere*, literally 'to stand through', from *sistere* 'to make stand', from *stare* (see STATION).] —**persister** *n.*

persistence /pər sístənss/, **persistency** /-tənssi/ *n.* **1. THE QUALITY OF PERSISTING** the quality of continuing steadily despite problems or obstacles **2. ACT OF PERSISTING** the action of sb who persists with sth **3. LONG CONTINUANCE OF STH** continuance of an effect after its cause has ceased or been removed **4. ZOOL RESILIENCE OF ORGANISM** the ability of a living organism to resist being disturbed or altered

persistent /pər sístənt/ *adj.* **1. CONTINUING DESPITE PROBLEMS** tenaciously or obstinately continuing despite problems or difficulties **2. INCESSANT OR UNRELENTING** existing or continuing for a long time **3. BOT PERSISTING BEYOND MATURATION** used to describe a plant part such as a scale on a pine cone that lasts beyond maturity without falling off **4. ZOOL SUSTAINING CONTINUAL GROWTH** used to describe a body part such as a tooth that grows throughout life **5. ECOL ABLE TO REMAIN IN THE ENVIRONMENT** used to describe a chemical that remains in the environment or a living organism for months or years, usually because of resistance to attack by oxygen, light, and micro-organisms —**persistently** *adv.*

persistent vegetative state *n.* a medical condition in which a patient has severe brain damage and as a result is unable to stay alive without the aid of a life-support system, showing no response to stimuli

person /púrs'n/ (*plural* **people** /peép'l/ *or* **persons** *formal*) *n.* **1. HUMAN BEING** an individual human being **2. HUMAN'S BODY** a human being's body, often including the clothing ○ *objects found on her person* **3. HUMAN'S APPEARANCE** an individual human being's general appearance (*formal*) **4. A CHARACTER OR ROLE** a character or role, e.g. in a play (*archaic*) **5. GRAM FORM OF VERB AND PRONOUN** any one of three forms of verbs and pronouns used to denote the speaker, the person addressed, or sb else being referred to **6. ETHICS OBJECT WITH SPECIAL MORAL VALUE** an object with special moral value because of some spiritual status, or autonomous nature, or importance for other people **7. LAW INDIVIDUAL OR BODY OF INDIVIDUALS** a living human being or a group, either or both having legal rights and responsibilities [12thC. Via Old French from Latin *persona* 'mask worn by an actor, character', of uncertain origin: probably from Etruscan *phersu* 'mask'.] ◇ **in person** personally rather than being represented by sb or sth else

WORD KEY: USAGE

In combining forms: terms that are not gender-specific have increasingly grown in prominence, and ones incorporating the combining form ***-person*** are now common (*chairperson, spokesperson*). The terms that have taken hold most strongly, however, tend to be those that do not simply replace *-man* (or *-woman*) with ***-person*** but are more subtly neutral with respect to sex: *chair* rather than *chairperson*, *representative* rather than *congressperson*, *angler* rather than *fisherperson*. Despite the powerful trend towards inclusive terms, however, it remains true that when the members of the group at issue are predominantly male, the traditional term incorporating *-man* tends to be used most frequently of all (*chairman, fisherman*). Forms with *-woman* are also seen, though in most cases these are now less common than the form incorporating ***-person.***

Person /púrss'n/ *n.* in Christianity, the Father, the Son, or the Holy Spirit, together being the Trinity

persona /pər sṓnə/ (*plural* **-nae** /-nee/ *or* **-nas**) *n.* **1.** LITERAT **CHARACTER IN LITERATURE** a character in a literary work, especially a play (*often used in the plural*) **2. ASSUMED IDENTITY OR ROLE** an identity or role that sb assumes **3.** PSYCHOL **PERSONAL FACADE** the image of character and personality that sb wants to show the outside world. This concept originated in *Jungian* psychology. [Early 20thC. From Latin (see PERSON).]

personable /púrss'nəb'l/ *adj.* having a pleasant personality and appearance —**personableness** *n.* —**personably** *adv.*

personage /púrss'nij/ (*plural* **-ages**) *n.* (*formal*) **1. IMPORTANT PERSON** sb who is distinguished, important, or famous **2.** LITERAT, HIST **HISTORICAL FIGURE OR FICTIONAL CHARACTER** a historical figure or a character in a work of literature [15thC. From Old French, formed from *persone* (see PERSON).]

persona grata /pər sṓnə graáatə/ (*plural* **personae gratae** /-neé graá tee/) *n.* sb who is acceptable, especially as a diplomat, to the authorities of a country to which he or she is sent. ◊ **persona non grata** [From late Latin, 'acceptable person'] —**persona grata** *adj.*

personal /púrss'nəl/ *adj.* **1. RELATING TO SB'S PRIVATE LIFE** relating to the parts of sb's life that are private **2. RELATING TO ONE PERSON** relating to a particular individual **3. BELIEVED BY INDIVIDUAL PERSON** believed by or originating from an individual person ○ *personal opinion* **4. DONE BY ONE INDIVIDUAL ONLY** done by a particular individual rather than by that person's delegate ○ *that personal touch* **5. INTENDED FOR PARTICULAR INDIVIDUAL** intended for or owned by a particular individual rather than anyone else **6. REFERRING OFFENSIVELY TO PARTICULAR PERSON** referring, especially in an offensive way, to sb's beliefs, actions, or physical characteristics ○ *That personal remark was definitely uncalled for.* **7. UNFAIRLY REMARKING OR QUESTIONING ABOUT OTHERS** making unacceptable remarks or being too probing about other people ○ *There's no need to get personal.* **8. OF THE BODY** relating to sb's body **9.** RELIG **CONSCIOUS AND INDIVIDUAL** having the character or nature of a conscious and individual entity **10.** LAW **OF MOVABLE PROPERTY** relating to or constituting an individual's movable property ■ *n. US* PRESS = **personal ad** (*often used in the plural*)

personal ad *n.* a usually classified newspaper or magazine advertisement in which sb expresses interest in meeting others or sends a message of a personal nature to sb else. US term **personal**

personal allowance *n.* an amount of money sb is entitled to earn before paying tax

personal assistant *n.* sb employed to perform secretarial and administrative tasks for sb such as an executive who has many responsibilities

personal column *n.* a section of a newspaper or magazine in which personal ads are printed

personal computer *n.* a computer with its own operating system and wide selection of software intended to be used by one person

Personal Digital Assistant *n.* a small handheld computer with a built-in notebook, diary, and fax capability, usually operated using a stylus rather than a keyboard

personal effects *npl.* possessions that sb carries or wears either regularly or at a particular time

Personal Equity Plan *n.* full form of **PEP**

personal foul *n.* a foul, especially one committed in football or basketball, involving illegal physical contact with an opponent during a game and also sometimes involving unnecessary roughness

Personal Information Manager *n.* software that organizes random notes, contacts, and appointments for fast access

personal injury *n. US* an actionable injury to an individual person, whether involving physical contact or not and whether fatal or not, but causing pain, discomfort, or injury

personalism /púrss'nəlizəm/ *n.* a quirky or highly individualistic mode of expression or behaviour —**personalist** *n., adj.* —**personalistic** /púrss'nə lístik/ *adj.*

personality /púrssə nálləti/ (*plural* **-ties**) *n.* **1. SB'S SET OF CHARACTERISTICS** the totality of sb's attitudes, interests, behavioural patterns, emotional responses, social roles, and other individual traits that endure over long periods of time **2. CHARACTERISTICS MAKING SB APPEALING** the distinctive or very noticeable characteristics that make sb socially appealing ○ *a partner with real personality* **3. SB REGARDED AS EPITOMIZING TRAITS** an individual regarded as epitomizing particular character traits **4. FAMOUS PERSON** sb who is famous, especially an entertainer or a sportsperson **5. UNUSUAL PERSON** sb who is very unusual and distinctive **6. QUALITY OF BEING A PERSON** the quality of existing as a person ○ *Do you think that computers will ever achieve personality?* **7. DISTINGUISHING CHARACTERISTICS** the distinguishing characteristics of a place or situation

personality disorder *n.* a psychiatric disorder in attitude or behaviour that makes it difficult for sb to get along with other people or to succeed at work or in social situations but that does not involve loss of touch with reality

personality test *n.* a standardized psychological test in which the subject is given questions about various aspects of personality, the answers supplying a character-trait profile unique to that individual

personality type *n.* a set of categories based on attitudes or behavioural tendencies into which people are grouped, e.g. introvert and extrovert

personalize /púrss'nə līz/ (**-izes, -izing, -ized**), **personalise** (**-ises, -ising, -ised**) *vt.* **1. PUT INITIALS OR NAME ON STH** to mark sth such as a wallet, pen, or item of clothing with sb's initials or name **2. CHANGE STH TO REFLECT OWNER'S PERSONALITY** to change or modify sth showing that it obviously originated from or belonged to a particular person **3. TAKE REMARK PERSONALLY** to take a remark in a personal way **4.** = **personify** *v.* 3 —**personalization** /púrss'nə lī záysh'n/ *n.*

personally /púrss'nəli/ *adv.* **1. AS OWN OPINION** in one's own experience or showing one's own opinion ○ *Personally, I would have given it back.* **2. AS AN INDIVIDUAL** as a particular individual **3. WITHOUT OTHERS** without intervention or assistance from others ○ *I'll handle it personally.* **4. AS PERSON IN SOCIAL CONTEXT** as a person, considered in a social context ○ *personally likable but professionally inept* **5. OF SB ONE HAS MET** relating to sb known by personal contact rather than by reputation ○ *I never knew your brother personally.*

personal organizer *n.* **1. DIARY WITH CHANGEABLE PAGES** a diary that also contains personal information and has replaceable pages so that it can be kept up to date **2. HAND-HELD MULTIFUNCTIONING COMPUTER** a hand-held computer with a small keyboard and display that can function as a diary, an address book, a scheduler, and a calculator

personal pronoun *n.* a pronoun such as 'I', 'you', or 'she' that refers to a speaker, sb being addressed, or another person

personal property *n.* in law, the tangible, movable property of an individual, exclusive of land and including items such as automotive vehicles, boats, and money

personal stereo *n.* a small audio cassette or CD player used with earphones, designed to be carried in a pocket or worn attached to a belt

personalty /púrss'nəlti/ (*plural* **-ties**) *n.* = **personal property** [Mid-16thC. Via Anglo-Norman from, ultimately, late Latin *personalitas* (see PERSONALITY).]

personal unconscious *n.* in Jungian and related forms of psychotherapy, a section of an individual's unconscious mind that contains impulses, fears, and memories that have been repressed

personal watercraft *n. US* a jet-propelled vehicle for one or two people used for travelling on water. It is similar in appearance to a motorcycle.

persona non grata /pər sṓnə non graáatə/ (*plural* **personae non gratae** /-nee non graá tee/) *n.* **1. UNWELCOME OR UNACCEPTABLE PERSON** sb who is unwelcome or unacceptable. ◊ **persona grata 2. SB UNACCEPTABLE AS DIPLOMAT** sb who is unacceptable as a diplomat to the authorities of a country to which he or she is sent [From late Latin, 'unacceptable person'] —**persona non grata** *adj.*

personate[1] /púrssə nayt/ (**-ates, -ating, -ated**) *vt.* **1.** THEATRE **PLAY ROLE IN PLAY** to play a dramatic role, especially in a play **2.** CRIMINAL LAW **IMPERSONATE SB AS DECEPTION** to impersonate sb in order to deceive or defraud [Late 16thC. From late Latin *personare*, from Latin *persona* (see PERSON).] —**personation** /púrssə náysh'n/ *n.* —**personative** /púrss'nətiv/ *adj.* —**personator** /púrssə naytər/ *n.*

personate[2] /púrsə nayt/ *adj.* used to describe a flower such as a snapdragon that has two lips with one lip curling over the other to close the opening between them [Late 16thC. From Latin *personatus* 'masked', from *persona* (see PERSON).]

personhood /púrss'n hood/ *n.* the state of being human

person-hour *n.* a unit that measures the amount of work that can be done by one person in one hour and the cost of that hour's work

personification /pər sónnifi káysh'n/ *n.* **1. SB WHO EMBODIES STH** sb who is an embodiment or perfect example of sth **2. REPRESENTATION OF AN ABSTRACT QUALITY AS HUMAN** a representation of an abstract quality or notion as a human being, especially in art or literature **3. ATTRIBUTION OF HUMAN QUALITIES TO ABSTRACTS** the attribution of human qualities to objects or abstract notions

personify /pər sónni fī/ (**-fies, -fying, -fied**) *vt.* **1. BE PERFECT EXAMPLE OF STH** to be an embodiment or perfect example of sth **2. REPRESENT STH ABSTRACT AS HUMAN** to represent an abstract quality as a human being, especially in art or literature **3. ASCRIBE HUMAN QUALITIES TO NONHUMAN** to ascribe human qualities to an object or abstract notion —**personifiable** *adj.* —**personifier** *n.*

personnel /púrssə nél/ *n.* **DEPARTMENT OF ORGANIZATION DEALING WITH EMPLOYEES** the department of an organization or business that deals with employing staff and staffing issues generally ■ *npl.* **PEOPLE EMPLOYED IN ORGANIZATION** the people employed in an organization, business, or armed force [Early 19thC. From French, formed from *personne* 'person', on the model of 'matériel'.]

person-to-person *adj. US* relating to or being a telephone call chargeable only when a particular person is reached

perspective /pər spéktiv/ *n.* **1. PARTICULAR EVALUATION OF STH** a particular evaluation of a situation or facts, especially from one person's point of view **2. MEASURED ASSESSMENT OF SITUATION** a measured or objective assessment of a situation, giving all elements their comparative importance ○ *He's having trouble keeping things in perspective right now.* **3. APPEARANCE OF DISTANT OBJECTS TO OBSERVER** the appearance of objects to an observer allowing for the effect of their distance from the observer **4.** DRAWING, PAINTING **ALLOWANCE FOR ARTISTIC PERSPECTIVE WHEN DRAWING** the theory or practice of allowing for artistic perspective when drawing or painting **5. VISTA** a vista or view [14thC. Via Old French from, ultimately, late Latin *perspectivus*

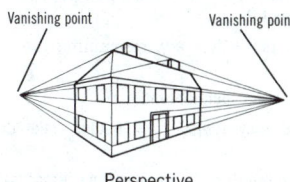

Perspective

'optical', from Latin *perspicere* 'to look closely', from *specere* (see SPECTACLE).] —**perspectively** *adv.*

Perspex /púr speks/ *tdmk.* a trademark for a tough transparent acrylic plastic that can be used in place of glass

perspicacious /púrspi káyshəss/ *adj.* penetratingly discerning, perceptive, or astute [Early 17thC. Formed from Latin *perspicac-*, the stem of *perspicax*, from *perspicere* (see PERSPECTIVE).] —**perspicaciously** *adv.* —**perspicaciousness** *n.*

perspicacity /púrspi kássəti/ *n.* acuteness of discernment or perception

perspicuity /púrspi kyoo əti/ *n.* **1.** = perspicacity **2.** BEING PERSPICUOUS the quality of being perspicuous

perspicuous /pər spíkyoo əss/ *adj.* clearly expressed and therefore easily understood [Late 16thC. Formed from Latin *perspicuus*, from *perspicere* (see PERSPECTIVE).] —**perspicuously** *adv.* —**perspicuousness** *n.*

perspiration /púrspə ráysh'n/ *n.* **1.** FLUID EXCRETED BY SWEAT GLANDS fluid lost from the body both in the form of sweat secreted by the sweat glands and as water that diffuses through the skin **2.** PROCESS OR ACT OF EXCRETING PERSPIRATION the process or act of excreting sweat secreted by the sweat glands or fluid that diffuses through the skin

perspiratory /pər spírətəri/ *adj.* relating to or causing perspiration

perspire /pər spír/ (**-spires, -spiring, -spired**) *vti.* to secrete fluid from the sweat glands through the pores of the skin [Mid-17thC. Via obsolete French *perspirer*, from Latin *perspirare*, literally 'to breathe through', from *spirare* 'to breathe' (see SPIRIT).] —**perspiringly** *adv.*

persuade /pə swáyd/ (**-suades, -suading, -suaded**) *vt.* **1.** GET SB TO DO STH to successfully urge sb to perform a particular action, especially by reasoning, pleading, or coaxing **2.** CONVINCE SB OF STH to make sb believe sth, especially by giving good reasons for doing so [Early 16thC. From Latin *persuadere*, literally 'to urge strongly', from *suadere* 'to urge'.] —**persuadable** *adj.* —**persuadability** /pər swáydə bílləti/ *n.* —**persuader** /pər swáydər/ *n.*

——— **WORD KEY: USAGE** ———
See Usage note at *convince*.

persuasion /pər swáyzh'n/ *n.* **1.** ACT OF PERSUADING the act of persuading sb to do sth **2.** ABILITY TO PERSUADE the ability to persuade sb **3.** SET OF BELIEFS a set of beliefs, e.g. a set of religious or political beliefs **4.** GROUP WITH PARTICULAR BELIEFS a group whose members share a particular set of beliefs or views or a particular lifestyle [14thC. Via Old French from, ultimately, Latin *persuas-*, the past participle stem of *persuadere* (see PERSUADE).]

persuasive /pər swáyssiv/ *adj.* having the ability to persuade people or the effect of persuading them [Late 16thC. Via French or medieval Latin from Latin *persuas-*, the past participle stem of *persuadere* (see PERSUADE).] —**persuasively** *adv.* —**persuasiveness** *n.*

pert /purt/ *adj.* **1.** AMUSINGLY CHEEKY cheeky and lively in a pleasant or amusing way **2.** JAUNTY jaunty and stylish in design ○ *a pert hat* **3.** SMALL AND WELL-SHAPED small, well-shaped, and pretty ○ *a pert nose* [13thC. Via Old French *apert* 'open, frank' from Latin *apertus* 'open' (see APERTURE), influenced by Old French *espert* 'clever' (from Latin *expertus*; see EXPERT).] —**pertly** *adv.* —**pertness** *n.*

PERT /purt/ *n.* a method of charting and scheduling a complex set of interrelated activities that identifies the most time-critical events in the process. Full form **programme evaluation and review technique**

pert. *abbr.* pertaining

pertain /pər táyn/ (**-tains, -taining, -tained**) *vi.* **1.** RELATE OR HAVE RELEVANCE to relate to sth or have relevance, reference, or a connection to it **2.** BE APPROPRIATE to be appropriate, fitting, or suitable **3.** BE PART OR BELONG to be part of sth or belong to sth, especially as an attribute or accessory [14thC. Via Old French *partenir* from Latin *pertinere*, literally 'to hold to', from *tenere* (see TENANT).]

Perth /purth/ **1.** town on the River Tay in Perth and Kinross Council Area, central Scotland. Population: 41,453 (1991). **2.** capital city of Western Australia, located on the River Swan. Population: 1,096,829 (1996).

Perth and Kinross council area in north-central Scotland. Perth is its administrative centre. Population: 133,000 (1996).

pertinacious /púrti náyshəss/ *adj.* **1.** RESOLUTE determinedly resolute in purpose, belief, or action **2.** PERSISTENT highly persistent [Early 17thC. From Latin *pertinac-*, the stem of *pertinax*, literally 'very tenacious', from *tenax* (see TENACIOUS).] —**pertinaciously** *adv.* —**pertinaciousness** *n.* —**pertinacity** /-nássəti/ *n.*

pertinent /púrtinənt/ *adj.* relevant to the matter being considered [14thC. Via Old French from, ultimately, Latin *pertinere* (see PERTAIN).] —**pertinence** *n.* —**pertinently** *adv.*

perturb /pər túrb/ (**-turbs, -turbing, -turbed**) *vt.* **1.** DISTURB SB to disturb and trouble or worry sb **2.** PHYS CAUSE STH TO UNDERGO A PERTURBATION to cause a small deviation in the behaviour of a physical system, e.g. in the orbit of an electron or a planet [14thC. Via Old French from Latin *perturbare*, literally 'to disturb thoroughly', from *turbare* 'to disturb', from *turba* 'turmoil' (see TURBID).] —**perturbable** *adj.* —**perturbably** *adv.* —**perturbing** *adj.* —**perturbingly** *adv.*

perturbation /púrtə báysh'n/ *n.* **1.** BEING PERTURBED the act of being disturbed and troubled, or a disturbed and troubled state **2.** CAUSE OF TROUBLE sth causing disruption, trouble, or disorder **3.** PHYS SECONDARY INFLUENCE ON A SYSTEM a slight disturbance of a system by a secondary influence within it **4.** ASTRON DEVIATION IN ORBIT CAUSED BY GRAVITY a deviation in an astronomical body's orbit or path caused by the gravitational attraction of another astronomical body —**perturbational** *adj.*

pertussis /pər tússiss/ *n.* whooping cough (*technical*) [Late 18thC. From modern Latin, from *per-* 'extreme' + *tussis* 'cough' (see TUSSIS).] —**pertussal** *adj.*

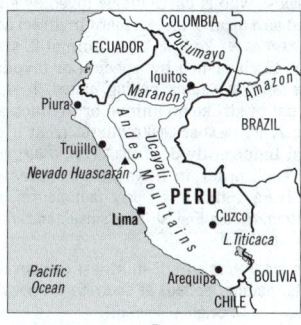

Peru

Peru /pə roo/ country in western South America, on the Pacific Ocean, bounded by Ecuador, Colombia, Brazil, Bolivia, and Chile. It is the third largest country in South America. Language: Spanish. Currency: nuevo sol. Capital: Lima. Population: 24,523,408 (1996). Area: 1,285,216 sq. km/496,225 sq. mi. Official name **Republic of Peru**

Perugia /pə roojə/ city in central Italy. It is the capital of Perugia Province and Umbria Region. Population: 146,160 (1992).

Peruke: Samuel Pepys wearing a peruke

peruke /pə rook/ *n.* a periwig (*archaic*) [Mid-16thC. Via French *perruque* (source of English *periwig*) from Italian *perrucca* 'head of hair', of unknown origin.]

peruse /pə rooz/ (**-ruses, -rusing, -rused**) *vt.* to read or examine sth in a leisurely or careful way [Mid-16thC. From PER- + USE; the word originally meant 'to use thoroughly, use up'.] —**perusable** *adj.* —**perusal** *n.* —**peruser** *n.*

Perutz /pə roots/, **Max Ferdinand** (*b.* 1914) Austrian-born British biochemist. He shared the Nobel Prize for chemistry for his work on haemoglobin, using X-ray crystallography.

Peruvian /pə roovi ən/ *adj.* OF PERU relating to or typical of Peru, or its people or culture ■ *n.* SB FROM PERU sb who was born or brought up in Peru, or who has Peruvian citizenship

Peruvian balsam *n.* = balsam of Peru

Peruvian bark *n.* the bark of the cinchona tree, formerly used to make quinine and other alkaloid drugs [So called because the trees originally grew in Peru]

perv /purv/, **perve** *n.* **1.** PERVERT a pervert (*slang insult*) **2.** ANZ LUSTFUL LOOK a voyeuristic glance or look (*slang*) ■ *vi.* (**pervs, perving, perved**) ANZ LEER to give sb a lustful look (*slang*) [Mid-20thC. Shortening of PERVERT.] —**pervy** *adj.*

pervade /pər váyd/ (**-vades, -vading, -vaded**) *vt.* to spread through or be present throughout sth [Mid-17thC. From Latin *pervadere*, literally 'to go throughout', from *vadere* 'to go' (see EVADE).] —**pervader** *n.* —**pervasion** /pər váyzh'n/ *n.*

pervasive /pər váyssiv/ *adj.* spreading widely [Mid-18thC. Formed from Latin *pervas-*, the past participle stem of *pervadere* (see PERVADE).] —**pervasively** *adv.* —**pervasiveness** *n.*

perve *n., vi.* ANZ = perv (*informal*)

perverse /pər vúrss/ *adj.* **1.** PURPOSELY BEING UNREASONABLE purposely deviating from what is accepted as good, proper, or reasonable **2.** UNREASONABLY STUBBORN unreasonably stubborn, contrary, or awkward **3.** WILFULLY DOING WRONG wilfully persisting in what is wrong **4.** PERVERTED perverted (*archaic*) [14thC. Via Old French from Latin *perversus*, the past participle of *pervertere* (see PERVERT).] —**perversely** *adv.* —**perverseness** *n.*

perversion /pər vúrsh'n/ *n.* (*disapproving*) **1.** UNUSUAL SEXUAL PRACTICE a sexual practice regarded as abnormal **2.** TURNING OF GOOD INTO BAD the changing of sth good, true, or correct into sth bad or wrong or a situation in which the change has occurred ○ *perversion of justice*

perversity /pər vúrssəti/ (*plural* **-ties**) *n.* **1.** STUBBORN UNREASONABLE BEHAVIOUR being unreasonable or wilfully persisting in doing wrong **2.** PERVERSE ACTION sth such as an action or activity that is perverse

perversive /pər vúrssiv/ *adj.* tending or able to pervert sth

pervert /pər vúrt/ *vt.* (**-verts, -verting, -verted**) **1.** LEAD AWAY SB FROM GOOD to lead sb or sth away from what is considered good, normal, moral, or proper **2.** MISINTERPRET OR DISTORT STH to misinterpret or distort sth such as a piece of text **3.** USE STH IMPROPERLY to use sth incorrectly or improperly **4.** DEBASE STH to bring sth into a state regarded as morally inferior or reprehensible ■ *n.* SB WITH UNUSUAL SEXUAL BEHAVIOUR sb whose sexual activities are considered abnormal (*disapproving*) [14thC. Via Old French *pervertir* from Latin *pervertere*, literally 'to turn wrong', from *vertere* (see VERSE).] —**perverter** /pər vúrtə/ *n.* —**pervertible** *adj.*

perverted /pər vúrtid/ *adj.* **1.** DEVIATING FROM WHAT IS PROPER deviating greatly from what is accepted as right, normal, or proper **2.** RELATING TO UNUSUAL SEXUAL ACTIVITIES relating to or practising sexual activities considered abnormal (*disapproving*) **3.** DISTORTED misinterpreted or distorted —**pervertedly** *adv.* —**pervertedness** *n.*

pervious /púrvi əss/ *adj.* **1.** ABLE TO BE PERMEATED able to be penetrated or permeated **2.** OPEN TO NEW THINGS open to ideas, suggestions, and change [Early 17thC. Formed from Latin *pervius*, from *per-* 'through' + *via* 'way' (see VIA).] —**perviously** *adv.* —**perviousness** *n.*

pes /pays, peez/ (*plural* **pedes** /pée deez/) *n.* **1.** FOOT OR SIMILAR APPENDAGE the foot or a part resembling a foot **2.** FOUR-FOOTED ANIMAL'S HIND FOOT a hind foot of a four-footed vertebrate [Mid-19thC. From Latin, 'foot' (source of English *pedal*). Ultimately from the Indo-European word for 'foot', which is also the ancestor of *foot*, *fetter*, *impede*, and *podium*.]

Pesach /páy saakh/ *n.* JUDAISM the Passover festival [Early 17thC. From Hebrew *pesaḥ*, from *pāsaḥ* 'to pass over'.]

pesante /pay sáanti/ *adv.* in a heavy or ponderous manner (*used as a musical direction*) [From Italian]

peseta /pə sáytə/ *n.* **1.** UNIT OF SPANISH CURRENCY the unit of currency in Spain. See table at **currency 2.** COIN WORTH A PESETA a coin worth a peseta [Early 19thC. From Spanish, literally 'small peso', formed from *peso* (see PESO).]

pesewa /pay sáy waa/ *n.* **1.** MINOR UNIT OF GHANAIAN CURRENCY a minor unit of currency in Ghana, 100 of which are worth a new cedi **2.** COIN WORTH A PESEWA a coin worth a pesewa, 100 of which are worth a new cedi [Mid-20thC. From Fante and Twi, 'penny'.]

Peshawar /pə shaáwər/ city near the Khyber Pass in the North-West Frontier District, Pakistan. Population: 1,676,000 (1995).

Peshitta /pə sheétə/, **Peshitto** *n.* the Syriac version of the Bible, written around the 4th century [Late 18thC. From Syriac *pšīṭṭā*, 'the simple one'.]

pesky /péski/ (**-kier, -kiest**) *adj.* US, Can troublesome or irritating (*informal*) [Late 18thC. Origin uncertain: probably from an alteration of PEST.] —**peskily** *adv.* —**peskiness** *n.*

peso /páyssō/ (*plural* **-sos**) *n.* See table at **currency 1.** UNIT OF MEXICAN CURRENCY the unit of currency in Mexico **2.** NOTE WORTH A PESO a note worth a peso [Mid-16thC. Via Spanish from Latin *pensum* 'weight', from the past participle of *pendere* 'to weigh' (see PENSIVE).]

pessary /péssəri/ (*plural* **-ries**) *n.* **1.** UTERINE SUPPORT a plastic device such as a ring placed in the vagina to keep the womb in position following a prolapse due to weakened ligaments **2.** VAGINAL SUPPOSITORY a suppository containing medication for insertion into the vagina [14thC. Via late Latin *pessarium* from, ultimately, Greek *pessos*, originally an oval stone used in board games.]

pessimism /péssəmizəm/ *n.* **1.** TENDENCY TO EXPECT WORST a tendency to see only the negative or worst aspects of all things and to expect only bad or unpleasant things to happen **2.** PHILOS DOCTRINE ABOUT EVIL a doctrine that all things become evil or that evil outweighs good in life [Late 18thC. From French *pessimisme*, from Latin *pessimus* 'worst', on the model of 'optimisme'.]

pessimist /péssə mist/ *n.* sb who always expects the worst to happen in every situation —**pessimistic** /pessə místik/ *adj.* —**pessimistically** /pessə místikli/ *adv.*

pest /pest/ *n.* **1.** BIOL DAMAGING ORGANISM an organism that is damaging to livestock, crops, humans, or land fertility **2.** ANNOYING PERSON OR THING sb or sth that is a nuisance (*informal*) **3.** OUTBREAK OF DISEASE an epidemic of infectious or contagious disease (*archaic*) [Mid-16thC. Via French, 'pestilence' from Latin *pestis*, of unknown origin.]

Pestalozzi /péstə lótsi/, **Johann Heinrich** (1746–1827) Swiss educator. He developed teaching methods adapted to children's natural development, the basis of modern primary education.

pester /péstər/ (**-ters, -tering, -tered**) *vt.* to be a constant source of annoyance to sb, e.g. by harassing him or

her with demands [Mid-16thC. Via French *empestrer* 'to embarrass' (influenced by PEST), of uncertain origin: perhaps via assumed Vulgar Latin *impastoriare* 'to hobble' from, ultimately, Latin *pastor* 'herdsman' (see PASTOR).] —**pesterer** *n.* —**pesteringly** *adv.*

pesthole /pést hōl/ *n.* a place where epidemic diseases are rife and from where they might spread (*dated*) [Early 20thC. Formed from PEST in the obsolete meaning 'contagious disease'.]

pesthouse /pést howss/ (*plural* **-houses** /-howziz/) *n.* a hospital where patients suffering from infectious disease were once treated [Early 17thC. Formed from PEST in the obsolete meaning 'contagious disease'.]

pesticide /pésti sīd/ *n.* a chemical substance used to kill pests, especially insects [Mid-20thC. Coined from PEST + -CIDE.] —**pesticidal** /pésti sīd'l/ *adj.*

pestiferous /pə stíffərəss/ *adj.* **1.** ANNOYING troublesome or annoying **2.** MED CAUSING INFECTIOUS DISEASE breeding or spreading a virulently infectious disease **3.** CORRUPTING wicked and corrupting (*formal*) [15thC. Formed from Latin *pestifer* 'plague-carrying', from *pestis* 'plague'.] —**pestiferously** *adv.* —**pestiferousness** *n.*

pestilence /péstilənss/ *n.* (*archaic*) **1.** MED EPIDEMIC OF DISEASE an epidemic of a highly contagious or infectious disease such as bubonic plague **2.** MED DISEASE a serious infectious disease **3.** STH EVIL a malevolent belief, influence, or presence

pestilent /péstilənt/ *adj.* **1.** CAUSING OR INFECTED WITH CONTAGIOUS DISEASE likely to cause a contagious disease or to be infected with one **2.** DEADLY causing or tending to cause death **3.** HARMFUL very harmful morally, socially, or physically (*archaic*) **4.** ANNOYING annoying or infuriating (*dated*) [14thC. Via Old French from the Latin stem *pestilent-*, from *pestis* 'plague'.] —**pestilential** /pésti lénsh'l/ *adj.* —**pestilentially** /-lénsh'li/ *adv.* —**pestilently** /péstiləntli/ *adv.*

pestle /péss'l/ *n.* (*plural* **-tles**) OBJECT FOR CRUSHING OR GRINDING a rod-shaped object made from hard material with a rounded end that is used for crushing or grinding substances in a mortar ■ *vti.* (**-tles, -tling, -tled**) CRUSH OR POUND SUBSTANCE USING PESTLE to crush, grind, or pound a substance or object using a pestle [14thC. Via Old French from Latin *pistillum* (source also of English *pistil*).]

pesto /péstō/ *n.* **1.** BASIL SAUCE a sauce or paste made by crushing together basil leaves, pine nuts, oil, Parmesan cheese, and garlic. It is traditionally served hot or cold with pasta or on meat. **2.** FLAVOURFUL PASTE a pureed or finely minced paste of herbs and vegetables, tomatoes, or olives, used as pasta sauce [Mid-20thC. From Italian, from the past participle of *pestare* 'to pound, crush', via late Latin *pistare* from Latin *pinsere* 'to beat'.]

pet[1] /pet/ *n.* **1.** ANIMAL KEPT AT HOME an animal kept for companionship, interest, or amusement **2.** FAVOURITE PERSON sb who is indulged, especially a favourite **3.** LOVED PERSON sb who is particularly loved by another, often used as a term of endearment in direct address ■ *adj.* **1.** KEPT AS PET kept as a pet animal **2.** SPECIAL OR FAVOURITE TO SB cherished by, special, or favourite to sb ○ *a pet topic* ■ *v.* (**pets, petting, petted**) **1.** *vt.* STROKE ANIMAL to pat or stroke an animal or to touch a child similarly **2.** *vt.* TREAT SB INDULGENTLY to treat a person or animal indulgently **3.** *vi.* TOUCH FOR SEXUAL PLEASURE to touch each other in a way that causes sexual pleasure [Early 16thC. Origin uncertain: perhaps a back-formation from Middle English *pety* 'small', an earlier form of PETTY.] —**petter** *n.*

pet[2] /pet/ *n.* SULKY MOOD a fit of sulkiness or peevishness ■ *vi.* (**pets, petting, petted**) BE SULKY to be peevish or sulky [Mid-16thC. Origin unknown.]

PET /pet/ *abbr.* **1.** positron emission tomography **2.** polyethylene terephthalate

Pet. *abbr.* BIBLE Peter

peta- *prefix.* one thousand million million (10^{15}). Symbol **P** [Formed from PENTA-, on the model of 'tera-' (as if from 'tetra-'); so called because it represents 1,000 to the fifth power]

petal /pétt'l/ *n.* one of the showy coloured parts that form the outer part of a flower that together are the corolla [Early 18thC. Via modern Latin *petalum* from Greek *petalon* 'leaf'. Ultimately from an Indo-European base meaning 'to spread', which is also the ancestor of English

fathom and *patent*.] —**petaline** /péttə līn/ *adj.* —**petalled** /pétt'ld/ *adj.*

-petal *suffix.* moving toward ○ *centripetal* [Formed from modern Latin *-petus*, from Latin *petere* 'to seek' (see PETITION).]

petaliferous /pétt'l íffərəss/, **petalous** /pétt'ləss/ *adj.* having petals

petaloid /pétt'l oyd/ *adj.* resembling the petal of a flower

petalous *adj.* = petaliferous

pétanque /pay tóngk/ *n.* = **boules** [Mid-20thC. From French.]

petard /pe taárd/ *n.* **1.** ARMS EXPLOSIVE CHARGE FOR BREACHING FORTIFICATION a small explosive charge or grenade used to blow a hole in a door, wall, or fortification **2.** FIRECRACKER a powerful firecracker [Mid-16thC. Via French from, ultimately, Latin *pedere* 'to break wind'. Ultimately from an Indo-European word that is also the ancestor of English *fizzle* and *feisty*.] ◇ **be hoist with your own petard** to be the victim of your own attempt to harm sb else

petaurist /pə táwrəst/ *n.* ZOOL = flying phalanger [Mid-17thC. From Greek *petauristēs* 'acrobat', from *petauron* 'springboard'.]

Petavius /pə táyvi əss/ *n.* a walled enclosure on the Moon with a prominent crack (**rill**) across the floor and a complex central peak, located south of Mare Fecundatis, 177 km/110 mi. in diameter

petcock /pét kok/ *n.* a small manually operated valve or tap used to drain off waste material or excess fluid from the cylinder of an internal combustion engine [Mid-19thC. From *pet* (of uncertain origin: perhaps from PET[1] or obsolete *pet* 'fart', via French from, ultimately, Latin *peditus*) + COCK[1] in the meaning of 'spout'.]

petechia /pi teéki ə/ (*plural* **-ae** /-teéki ee/) *n.* a tiny purplish red spot on the skin caused by the release into the skin of a very small quantity of blood from a capillary [Late 18thC. Via modern Latin from Italian *petecchie* 'spots on the skin', ultimately from Latin *impetigo* (see IMPETIGO).] —**petechial** *adj.*

peter[1] /peétər/ (**-ters, -tering, -tered**) *vi.* to become less [12thC. From the name *Peter*.]

peter out *vi.* to dwindle and finally stop or disappear [Early 19thC. Origin unknown.]

peter[2] /peétər/ *n.* (*slang*) **1.** CASH BOX a safe or cash box **2.** LAW WITNESS BOX IN COURT the witness box in a court **3.** US PENIS a penis (*considered offensive by some people*)

peter[3] /peétər/ (**-ters, -tering, -tered**) *vi.* in bridge and whist, to play a high card first, followed by a low card [Late 19thC. Shortening of an obsolete sense of BLUE PETER, a higher card than necessary, played as a signal to one's partner.]

Peter, **St** (*d.* AD64?). One of the 12 disciples of Jesus Christ, he was a leader and missionary in the early church, and traditionally the first bishop of Rome. Born **Simon**

Peterborough /peétərbərə/ **1.** city in Cambridgeshire, England. Population: 160,000 (1996). **2.** city in southeastern Ontario, Canada, approximately 40 km/25 mi. north of Lake Ontario. Population: 100,193 (1996).

Peterborough, Soke of former administrative county of England, from 1884 to 1965

Peterhead /peétər héd/ town and fishing port in Aberdeenshire, and the most easterly town in Scotland. Population: 19,000 (1991).

Peterlee /peétər leé/ town in northern England, in County Durham. It was built as a new town in 1948. Population: 31,139 (1991).

peterman /peétərmən/ (*plural* **-men** /-mən/) *n.* a burglar who specializes in breaking safes (*slang*) [Early 19thC. From PETER[1].]

Peter Pan *n.* a man who looks very young or behaves in a boyish way (*informal*) [Early 20thC. From the name of the hero of J. M. Barrie's play *Peter Pan, or The Boy Who Wouldn't Grow Up* (1904).]

Peter Pan collar *n.* a flat collar attached to a round neck with rounded ends visible at the front

Peter Principle *n.* the theory that all members of an organization will eventually be promoted to a level at which they are no longer competent to do their job [Mid-20thC. Named after the US author Laurence Johnston *Peter* 1919–90, who propounded it.]

Peters /peétərz/, **Winston Raymond** (*b.* 1945) New Zealand politician. He founded the New Zealand First Party in 1993, and served as deputy prime minister and treasurer (1996–98).

petersham /peétərshəm/ *n.* TEXTILES a strong ribbed ribbon used to reinforce parts of garments such as waistbands [Early 19thC. Named after the English army officer Viscount *Petersham* (1790–1851), who wore such an overcoat.]

Peter's pence *n.* **1.** ROMAN CATHOLIC DONATION a voluntary financial contribution made by some Roman Catholic dioceses to the Papal See **2.** HIST MEDIEVAL TAX TO PAPAL SEE a tax of one penny per household paid to the Papal See in medieval times until it was abolished by Henry VIII [From the tradition that the papacy was founded by Saint PETER]

Peters' projection *n.* a form of map projection that represents the relative size of land masses more accurately than Mercator's projection [Late 20thC. Named after Arno *Peters*, who created it.]

Peter the Great /peétər thə gráyt/, **Tsar** (1672–1725) Russian emperor. His victory over Sweden established Russia as a major European power.

pethidine /péthi deen/ *n.* a white crystalline compound used as a painkiller and sedative. Formula: $C_{15}H_{21}NO_2$. US term **meperidine** [Mid-20thC. A blend of P(IPER)IDINE and ETH(YL).]

pétillant /pétti oN, péttilənt/ *adj.* used to describe wine that is slightly sparkling [Late 19thC. From French, 'effervescent', literally 'passing gas'.]

petiolar /pétti ōlər/ *adj.* relating to the growth of petioles

petiolate /pétti ə layt/ *adj.* having a petiole

petiole /pétti ōl/ *n.* a leafstalk (*technical*) [Mid-18thC. From modern Latin *petiolus*, a variant of Latin *peciolus*, literally 'little foot' (see PEDICEL).]

petiolule /pétti ə lyool/ *n.* the stalk of a leaflet in a compound leaf [Mid-19thC. From modern Latin *petiolulus*, literally 'little petiole', from *petiolus* (see PETIOLE).]

petit bourgeois /pétti boórzhwaa/ (*plural* **petits bourgeois** /pétti boórzhwaa/) *n.* a member of the lower middle class [From French, literally 'little citizen']

petite /pə teét/ *adj.* **1.** SMALL AND DELICATELY BUILT having a small and delicate build ○ *a petite woman* **2.** CLOTHES FOR SMALLER WOMEN designed to fit smaller women or girls [Mid-16thC. From French, feminine of *petit* 'little'.]

petite bourgeoisie /pə teét boor zhwaa zeé/ (*plural* **petites bourgeoisies**) *n.* people in the lower middle class, a group traditionally including small business operators and tradespeople

petit four /pétti fáwr/ (*plural* **petits fours** /pétti fáwr, -fáwrz/) *n.* any one of a mixture of bite-size sweet biscuits or cakes served at the end of a meal with coffee [From French, literally 'little oven']

petition /pə tísh'n/ *n.* **1.** DEMAND FOR ACTION WITH SIGNATURES a written request signed by many people demanding a particular action from an authority or government **2.** APPEAL OR REQUEST TO HIGHER AUTHORITY an appeal or request to a higher authority or being **3.** STH REQUESTED sth requested or appealed for **4.** ACT OF PETITIONING the act of making a petition **5.** LAW DOCUMENT INITIATING LEGAL ACTION a written application for a legal action to be taken, particularly at the start of divorce proceedings ■ *v.* (**-tions, -tioning, -tioned**) **1.** *vti.* GIVE PETITION TO SB to give or address a petition to sb, especially sb in authority or a representative of an organization **2.** *vi.* MAKE DEMAND USING PETITION to urge for or against a course of action by presenting a petition **3.** *vi.* LAW MAKE FORMAL REQUEST to request formally, using a petition [14thC. Via Old French from, ultimately, Latin *petere* 'to seek, go toward'. Ultimately from an Indo-European base meaning 'to fly', which is also the ancestor of English *feather* and *symptom*.] —**petitionary** *adj.*

──────── **WORD KEY: ORIGIN** ────────
The Latin word *petere*, from which **petition** is derived, is

also the source of English *appetite, compete, impetus, perpetual, petulant,* and *repeat.*

petitioner /pə tísh'nər/ *n.* **1.** SB PETITIONING FOR STH sb who requests or demands sth using a petition **2.** LAW SB PETITIONING FOR DIVORCE sb who is beginning divorce proceedings

petitio principii /pə tíshi ō prin kíppi ī, -síppi ī/ *n.* logically fallacious reasoning in which what has to be proved is already assumed [From Latin, literally 'assuming the first thing']

petit larceny /pétti-/, **petty larceny** *n.* the theft of sth whose value lies below a particular standard in a particular jurisdiction

petit mal /pétti mál/ *n.* a form of epilepsy marked by episodes of brief loss of consciousness without convulsions or falling. It is found most frequently in children and adolescents. ◊ **grand mal** [From French, literally 'small illness']

petit point /pétti póynt/ (*plural* **petits points**) *n.* **1.** SMALL STITCH IN NEEDLEPOINT FOR DETAILS a small stitch used in needlepoint when creating details **2.** EMBROIDERY WITH SMALL STITCHES work embroidered using small stitches [From French, 'small stitch']

petits pois /pétti pwaá/ *npl.* small sweet green peas [From French, 'small peas']

pet name *n.* a name showing endearment used for a family member or special friend

petnapping /pét naping/ *n.* the stealing or kidnapping of a pet animal [Late 20thC. Modelled on 'kidnapping'.] —**petnapper** *n.*

Petra /péttrə/ ancient ruined city in southwestern Jordan, famous for its buildings and tombs that are carved out of solid rock

Petrarch /pét raark/ (1304–74) Italian lyric poet and scholar. He is best remembered for his series of love poems addressed to Laura, the *Canzoniere* (1327). Born **Francesco Petrarca**

Petrarchan sonnet /pə traákən-/ *n.* a form of poetry that has an eight line stanza with the rhyme scheme abbaabba followed by six lines with various rhyme schemes, usually cdcdcd or cdecde [Early 19thC. Named after the Italian poet Francesco PETRARCH 1304–74, who developed the form.]

petrel /péttrəl/ *n.* a bird that lives on the sea such as the storm-petrel, the diving petrel, or the fulmar. Petrels are widespread in ocean environments and move awkwardly on land. Family: Hydrobatidae and Pelecanoididae and Procellariidae. [Early 17thC. Origin uncertain: perhaps formed from Saint *Peter*, who walked on water (Matthew 14:29), because the bird flies close to the surface.]

petri- *prefix.* = **petro-**

Petri dish

Petri dish /péttri-, peétri-/ *n.* a shallow flat-bottomed dish with a loose cover used especially to grow bacterial cultures in the laboratory [Named after Julius *Petri* (1852–92), the German bacteriologist who invented it]

Petrie /péttri/, **Sir Flinders** (1853–1942) British archaeologist. He is noted for his work in Egypt and Palestine. He devised a method of relative dating based on pottery types. Full name **Sir William Matthews Flinders Petrie**

petrifaction /péttri fáksh'n/, **petrification** /péttrifi káysh'n/ *n.* **1.** CONVERSION OF SUBSTANCE TO STONE the process in which the porous structure of organic

material such as bones, shell, and wood is infiltrated by salt-bearing groundwater, which preserves the structure when it solidifies. The Petrified Forest in Arizona contains whole tree trunks that have been turned into stone. **2.** CONDITION OF BEING PETRIFIED the condition of being turned into stone

petrify /péttri fī/ (**-fies, -fying, -fied**) *v.* **1.** *vt.* IMMOBILIZE SB WITH FEAR to cause a person or animal to become immobile with terror **2.** *vti.* GEOL CAUSE PETRIFICATION to cause or bring about the process by which sth organic is turned into stone **3.** *vti.* MAKE OR BECOME DEADENED OR STIFF to become or cause sth to become dull, stiff, or deadened [15thC. From French *pétrifier* or medieval Latin *petrificare*, both formed from Latin *petra* 'stone', from Greek *petra* (see PETRO-).] —**petrifier** *n.*

Petrine /peé trīn/ *adj.* **1.** OF THE APOSTLE PETER relating to or associated with St. Peter, the Apostle. **2.** OF CATHOLIC DISSOLUTION OF MARRIAGE in the Roman Catholic Church, associated with or used to describe a dissolved marriage between sb who has been baptized and sb who has not [Mid-19thC. Formed from ecclesiastical Latin *Petrus* 'Peter'.]

petro- *prefix.* **1.** rock, stone ○ *petrography* **2.** petroleum ○ *petrodollar* [From Greek *petros* 'a stone' and *petra* 'rock' (source also of English *petrify, parsley* and *saltpeter*)]

petrochemical /péttrō kémmik'l/ *n.* DERIVATIVE OF PETROL OR NATURAL GAS a substance derived from petroleum or natural gas, such as petrol or paraffin wax ■ *adj.* RELATING TO PETROCHEMICALS relating to or derived from petrochemicals —**petrochemically** *adv.*

petrochemistry /péttrō kémmistri/ *n.* **1.** CHEMISTRY OF PETROLEUM the branch of chemistry that is concerned with petroleum and derivatives of petroleum **2.** GEOCHEMISTRY OF ROCKS the chemistry of rocks, especially with reference to their composition

petrodollar /péttrō dolər/ *n.* a unit of foreign currency earned by an oil-exporting country

petrog. *abbr.* petrography

petrogenesis /péttrō jénnəssiss/ *n.* the origin, formation, and history of rocks

petroglyph /péttrōglif/ *n.* a prehistoric drawing done on rock [Late 19thC. From French, from Greek *petros* 'stone' + *glyphē* 'carving'.]

petrography /pə tróggrəfi/ *n.* the systematic description of the texture of rocks and the minerals they contain, often using microscopy of thin slices of the rock to determine the mineral content —**petrographer** *n.* —**petrographic** /péttrə gráffik/ *adj.* —**petrographically** /-gráffikli/ *adv.*

petrol /pétrəl/ *n.* a volatile flammable liquid made from petroleum, used as fuel in internal-combustion engines. US term **gasoline** [Mid-16thC. Via French *pétrole* from medieval Latin *petroleum* (see PETROLEUM).]

petrol. *abbr.* petrology

petrol blue *adj.* of a greyish-blue colour tinged with green

petrol bomb *n.* BOTTLE OF PETROL USED AS BOMB a crude bomb usually made of a bottle filled with a flammable liquid such as petrol with a rag for a wick that is lighted just before it is thrown. US term **Molotov cocktail** ■ *vt.* ATTACK TARGET WITH PETROL BOMB to use a petrol bomb on a target —**petrol bomber** *n.*

petrol cap *n.* a sealing device for the pipe that leads to the petrol tank of a motor vehicle

petroleum /pə tróli əm/ *n.* crude oil that occurs naturally in sedimentary rocks and consists mainly of hydrocarbons. A wide variety of commercially important petrochemicals, such as petrol and paraffin are derived from it. [Early 16thC. From medieval Latin, from Latin *petra* 'rock' + *oleum* (see OIL).]

petroleum jelly *n.* a greasy substance derived from petroleum and used as an ointment base, lubricant, and a protective covering

petrolhead /pétrəl hed/ *n.* ANZ sb whose principal interest is fast cars or motor-racing (*slang*)

petrolic /pə tróllik/ *adj.* obtained from or containing petroleum

petrology /pə tróllǝji/ *n.* the study of sedimentary, igneous, and metamorphic rocks with respect to their occurrence, structure, origin, history, and mineral content —**petrological** /péttrə lójjik'l/ adj. —**petrologically** /-lójjikli/ adv. —**petrologist** /pe tróllǝjist/ n.

petrol pump n. a device usually located at a petrol station for delivering fuel to a vehicle. US term **gas pump**

petrol station n. a place at which drivers can buy fuel, oil, and other motoring supplies. US term **gas station**

petronel /pétrǝ nel/ n. a short firearm with a curved butt whose length was between that of a long pistol and a short carbine, used mostly by cavalry in the 16th and 17th centuries [Late 16thC. Via French petrinal from, ultimately, Latin pectus 'chest' (see PECTORAL), so called because the butt-end rested against the chest when the gun was fired.]

petrosal /pǝ tróss'l/ adj. affecting or belonging to the hard (**petrous**) portion of the temporal bone surrounding the inner ear [Mid-18thC. Formed from Latin petrosus (see PETROUS).]

petrous /péttrǝss/ adj. 1. GEOL OF ROCK relating to or resembling rock or stone 2. ANAT OF HARD PART OF TEMPORAL LOBE used to describe the hard portion of the temporal bone surrounding the inner ear [Mid-16thC. Formed from Latin petrosus 'rocky', from petra 'rock' (see PETRIFY).]

PET scan /pét-/ n. an image of a bodily cross-section, usually of the brain, that reveals metabolic processes and that is obtained by means of positron emission tomography —**PET scanner** n. —**PET scanning** n.

petticoat /pétti kōt/ n. 1. CLOTHES WOMAN'S UNDERGARMENT a woman's undergarment that is sometimes decorated and consists of an underskirt with or without a bodice 2. CLOTHES FORMERLY, ANY SKIRT until the 20th century, any skirt whether worn on its own with a jacket or bodice, or underneath a gown 3. CLOTHES SKIRT UNDER SARI a long skirt worn under a sari 4. OFFENSIVE TERM an offensive term for a woman or girl (dated offensive) [15thC. From PETTY 'small' + COAT. The modern meaning evolved from 'padded coat worn under armour' via 'short coat worn by men'.]

pettifogger /pétti fogǝr/ n. sb who argues or fusses over trivia and details [Mid-16thC. Origin uncertain: probably from PETTY + fogger, of unknown origin.]—**pettifog** vi. —**pettifoggery** n.

pettifogging /pétti foging/ adj. 1. TRIVIAL petty or trivial ○ pettifogging details 2. QUIBBLING quibbling or fussing over trivial matters (insult)

petting /pétting/ n. touching between people that causes sexual pleasure but does not include sexual intercourse (dated informal)

pettish /péttish/ adj. peevish, irritable, or sulky [Late 16thC. Formed from PET².]—**pettishly** adv. —**pettishness** n.

pettitoes /pétti tōz/ npl. pig's feet when used as food [Mid-16thC. Origin uncertain: perhaps by folk-etymology from French petite oie 'giblets of a goose', by association with PETTY and TOE.]

petty /pétti/ (-**tier**, -**tiest**) adj. 1. INSIGNIFICANT of little importance 2. NARROW-MINDED narrow-minded in nature 3. MEAN spiteful in character 4. OF RELATIVELY LITTLE IMPORTANCE subordinate in rank or importance [14thC. From Old French peti, a variant of petit 'small', of unknown origin.]—**pettily** adv. —**pettiness** n.

Petty /pétti/, **Bruce Leslie** (b. 1929) Australian cartoonist and filmmaker. He won an Academy Award for his short animated film Leisure '77 (1977).

petty cash n. a small amount of money kept, e.g. in an office, and used to cover minor everyday expenses

petty larceny n. = petit larceny

petty officer n. a noncommissioned naval officer ranking above enlisted sailors and below commissioned officers

petty sessions n. a court of summary jurisdiction, no longer used formally

petulant /péttyŏŏlǝnt/ adj. ill-tempered or sulky in a peevish manner [Late 16thC. Via French from Latin petulans 'insolent', from petere 'to seek, assail' (see PETITION).]—**petulance** n. —**petulantly** adv.

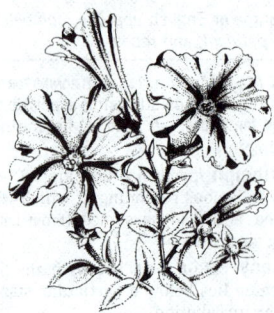
Petunia

petunia /pǝ tyóoni ǝ/ n. PLANTS TROPICAL PLANT WITH BRIGHT FLOWERS a flowering plant native to tropical America that has sticky stems and brightly coloured funnel-shaped flowers. Genus: Petunia. ■ adj. COLOURS OF DARK PURPLE COLOUR of a dark purple or violet colour [Early 19thC. Via modern Latin, genus name, from, ultimately, Portuguese petum 'tobacco', from Tupi or Guarani; so called because it is related to tobacco.]

petuntse, **petunze** n. a variety of feldspar that can be melted and is used in the manufacture of Chinese porcelain [Early 18thC. From Chinese (Mandarin) bái-dūnzi, literally 'white stone block'.]

pew /pyoo/ n. 1. CHURCH OR SYNAGOGUE BENCH a usually wooden bench with a straight back and often a kneeling bench attached to the one in front of it, used by worshippers in a church or synagogue 2. SEAT a seat (informal humorous) ○ take a pew [14thC. Via Old French puie 'balcony' from, ultimately, Latin podium (see PODIUM). The word originally denoted a raised seating area in a church.]

pewee /pée wee/, **peewee** n. a drab medium-sized flycatcher with a plaintive song. Genus: Contopus. [Late 18thC. An imitation of its call.]

pewit /pée wit/ n. BIRDS = lapwing [Early 16thC. An imitation of its call.]

pewter /pyóotǝr/ n. 1. METAL TIN AND LEAD ALLOY a silver-grey alloy of tin and lead sometimes containing antimony and copper 2. HOUSEHOLD PEWTER OBJECTS COLLECTIVELY articles made from pewter 3. COLOURS DARK GREYISH COLOUR a dark, dull grey colour tinged with blue or purple ■ adj. COLOURS OF DARK DULL GREY COLOUR of a dark dull grey colour, with a tinge of blue or purple [14thC. Via Old French peutre from assumed Vulgar Latin peltrum, of unknown origin.]

pewterer /pyóotǝrǝr/ n. a craftsperson who makes or repairs pewter articles

peyote /pay ṓti/ n. 1. US PLANTS GLOBESHAPED CACTUS a spineless globeshaped cactus native to Mexico and the southwestern United States that has small rounded nodules containing mescaline. Genus: Lophophora williamsii. 2. peyote, peyote button DRUGS CACTUS USED AS DRUG any one of the buttonshaped nodules on the stem of the peyote cactus that contains mescaline and is used as a hallucinogenic drug [Mid-19thC. Via American Spanish from Nahuatl peyotl.]

pF symbol. picofarad

pf. abbr. 1. perfect 2. pfennig

PFD abbr. personal flotation device

pfennig /fénnig/ (plural -**nigs** or **pfennige**) n. 1. MINOR UNIT OF GERMAN CURRENCY a minor unit of currency in Germany, 100 of which are worth a mark. See table at currency 2. COIN WORTH A PFENNIG a coin worth a pfennig [Mid-16thC. From German, ultimately related to English penny.]

PG¹ adj. CINEMA used to describe a film that would be inappropriate for children, unless accompanied by a parent. Full form **parental guidance** [Abbreviation of parental guidance]

PG² abbr. postgraduate

pg. abbr. page

Pg. abbr. Portuguese

P.G. abbr. paying guest

PGA abbr. Professional Golfers' Association

PGCE abbr. Postgraduate Certificate of Education

PGP n. a program to encrypt data for security purposes when the data is transmitted over public networks like the Internet. PGP uses public key encryption, a system that provides for privacy and authentication of both the sender and the receiver of the message. Abbr of **Pretty Good Privacy**

PGR adj. ANZ used to describe a film that would be inappropriate for children, unless accompanied by a parent. Full form **parental guidance recommended**

pH n. a measure of the acidity or alkalinity of a solution, such as vinegar, or a damp substance, such as soil. The pH of pure water is 7 with lower numbers indicating acidity and higher numbers indicating alkalinity. Full form **potential of hydrogen**

Ph symbol. phenyl group

PH, **P.H.** abbr. public health

ph. abbr. phase

phacoemulsification /fákō i múlssifi káysh'n/ n. an ultrasonic technique using microsurgical instruments that allows a cataract-affected lens to be liquefied and removed by suction using a very small incision near the edge of the cornea. A foldable plastic lens is then inserted through the incision and unfolded. [Late 20thC. Coined from Greek phakos 'lentil' (because of the shape of the lens) + emulsification.]

phaeton /fáytǝn/ n. a small light four-wheeled carriage, usually with two seats and usually drawn by two horses [Late 16thC. Via French from, ultimately, Greek Phaethōn, the son of Helios, who was killed by Zeus while trying to drive his father's chariot across the sky.]

phage /fayj/ (plural **phages**) n. = bacteriophage [Early 20thC. Shortening.]

-phage suffix. sth that eats ○ xylophage [From Greek -phagos '-eating', which was formed from phagein 'to eat' (see PHAGO-)]

phagedaena /fájjǝ deénǝ/, **phagedena** n. an ulcer that spreads rapidly [Late 16thC. Via Latin from Greek phagedaina.]

-phagia suffix. eating ○ aerophagia ○ hyperphagia [From Greek, formed from phagein 'to eat' (see PHAGO-)]

phago- prefix. eating, consuming ○ phagocyte [From Greek phagein 'to eat'. Ultimately from an Indo-European word meaning 'to share out, distribute', which is also the ancestor of English pagoda and nebbish.]

phagocyte /fággǝ sīt/ n. a cell in the body's bloodstream and tissues such as a white blood cell that engulfs and ingests foreign particles, cell waste material, and bacteria —**phagocytic** /fággǝ síttik/ adj.

phagocytosis /fággǝ sī tṓsiss/ n. BIOL the engulfing and ingesting of foreign particles or waste matter by phagocytes —**phagocytotic** /fággǝ sī tóttik/ adj.

-phagous suffix. eating ○ polyphagous [Formed from Latin -phagus, via Greek -phagos from phagein 'to eat' (see PHAGO-)]

-phagy suffix. = -phagia

Phalange /fǝ lánj/ n. a Lebanese Christian paramilitary group [Mid-20thC. Variant of Falange, from Spanish, literally 'phalanx'.]—**Phalangist** n., adj.

phalangeal /fe lánji ǝl/ adj. relating to a phalanx or the phalanges

phalanger /fǝ lánjǝr/ n. a small tree-dwelling marsupial with dense woolly fur and a long tail, found in Australia and nearby islands. Family: Phalangeridae. [Late 18thC. Via modern Latin from the Greek stem phalang- 'toe bone', because of the webbed or fused toes on its hind feet.]

phalanx /fállanks/ (plural -**lanxes** or -**langes** /fǝ lán jeez/) n. 1. TIGHT GROUP a group of people, animals, or objects that are moving or standing closely together 2. ARMY, HIST BODY OF TROOPS especially in ancient Greece, a group of soldiers that attacks in close formation, protected by their overlapping shields and projecting spears 3. (plural -**langes**) ANAT FINGER AND TOE BONE a finger or toe bone of a human being or vertebrate animal [Mid-16thC. Via Latin (stem phalang-) from Greek phalanx (stem phalagx 'line of battle, finger, or toe bone'.]

phalarope /fállǝ rōp/ n. a small wading bird that is related to the sandpiper but has lobed toes adapted for swimming. Genus: *Phalaropus*. [Late 18thC. Via French from modern Latin *Phalaropus*, genus name, from Greek *phalaris* 'coot' + *pous* 'foot'.]

Phalguna /fúl go͝onə/ *n.* in the Hindu calendar, the 12th month of the year, made up of 29 or 30 days and occurring about the same time as February or March

phalli plural of **phallus**

phallic /fállik/ *adj.* **1.** OF A PHALLUS relating to or resembling a phallus **2.** PSYCHOANAL RELATING TO THEORETICAL STAGE OF DEVELOPMENT in psychoanalytic theory, relating to a stage of psychosexual development during which a young child's sexual feelings are concentrated on the genitals **3.** RELIG OF PHALLICISM relating to phallicism [Late 18thC. From Greek *phallikos*, from *phallos* (see PHALLUS).]

phallicism /fállisizəm/ *n.* the worshipping of the reproductive forces of life as symbolized by the penis —**phallicist** *n.*

phallocentric /fállō séntrik/ *adj.* centred on men, or showing a preference for traditionally masculine qualities rather than traditionally feminine ones [Early 20thC. Coined from PHALLUS + -CENTRIC.]

phallus /fálləss/ (*plural* **-luses** *or* **-li** /-lī/) *n.* **1.** STYLIZED PENIS a picture, sculpture, or other representation of a penis, especially one regarded as a symbol of the reproductive force of life **2.** PENIS the human penis, especially when erect [Early 17thC. Via late Latin from Greek *phallos*. Ultimately, from an Indo-European base denoting 'to swell', which is also the ancestor of English *bowl*, *bull*, and *bold*.]

-phan *suffix.* = -phane

-phane *suffix.* a substance having the appearance or qualities of ○ *cymophane* [From Greek *-phanēs*, which was formed from *phainesthai* 'to appear' (see PHENOMENON)]

phanerogam /fánnərō gam/ *n.* a plant that produces seeds [Mid-19thC. Via French from modern Latin *phanerogamus*, from Greek *phaneros* 'visible', which was formed from *phainein* (see PHENOMENON) + *gamos* 'sexual union' (see -GAMOUS).] —**phanerogamic** /fánnərō gámmik/ *adj.*

phantasm /fán tazəm/ *n.* **1.** SUPPOSED GHOST OR SPIRIT a supposed being such as a ghost or a disembodied spirit that can be seen but does not have physical substance **2.** PHILOS DELUSION OR ILLUSION an understanding or perception that is not based on reality [13thC. Via Old French *fantasme* from, ultimately, Greek *phantasma*, from *phantazesthai* 'to appear' (see FANTASTIC).] —**phantasmal** /fan tázm'l/ *adj.* —**phantasmally** /-m'li/ *adv.* —**phantasmic** /-tázmik/ *adj.* —**phantasmically** /-tázmikli/ *adv.*

phantasmagoria /fán tazmə gáwri ə/, **phantasmagory** /fan tázmə gawri/ (*plural* **-ries**) *n.* **1.** BIZARRE IMAGES a series or group of strange or bizarre images seen as if in a dream **2.** EVER-CHANGING SCENE a scene or view that encompasses many things and changes constantly [Early 19thC. From French *fantasmagorie* 'art of making optical illusions', from *fantasme* (see PHANTASM), possibly on the model of *allégorie* 'allegory'.] —**phantasmagoric** /fán tazmə górrik/ *adj.* —**phantasmagorical** /-górrik'l/ *adj.* —**phantasmagorically** /-górrikli/ *adv.*

phantasy /fántəssi/ (*plural* **-sies**) *n.* = **fantasy** (*archaic*)

phantom /fántəm/ *n.* **1.** UNREAL BEING OR SENSATION sth that can be seen or heard or whose presence can be felt, but that is not physically present **2.** ILLUSION sb or sth that does not exist, or whose existence is difficult to prove **3.** APPARENT POWER sb or sth that appears to have power over sb but has no reality ○ *The phantom of disaster seemed to threaten their success.* ■ *adj.* NOT REAL appearing to be real but not actually existing ○ *The local branch of the organization turned out to have a lot of phantom members.* [13thC. Via Old French *fantosme* from, ultimately, Greek *phantasma* (see PHANTASM).]

■ WORD KEY: CULTURAL NOTE

The Phantom of the Opera, a novel by French writer Gaston Leroux (1910). This romantic melodrama about a disfigured musical genius who dwells in the passageways of a Paris opera house was not widely known until the appearance of Rupert Julian's film adaptation of 1925. This in turn inspired other film adaptations as well as Andrew Lloyd Webber's 1986 musical, one of the most successful musicals of all time.

---

phantom limb *n.* the powerful illusion that an amputated limb is still attached. This illusion may persist for weeks or months after the limb has been lost.

phantom limb pain *n.* pain that appears to come from an amputated limb

phantom pregnancy *n.* a condition in which a woman has the delusional belief that she is pregnant and suffers symptoms and displays signs of pregnancy. US term **false pregnancy**. Technical name **pseudocyesis**

-phany *suffix.* a manifestation of sth ○ *epiphany* [Formed from Greek *phan-*, the stem of *phainesthai* 'to appear' (see PHENOMENON)]

Phar., **phar.** *abbr.* **1.** pharmacist **2.** pharmacopoeia **3.** pharmaceutical **4.** pharmacy

Pharaoh /fáirō/, **pharaoh** *n.* **1.** ANCIENT EGYPTIAN RULER the ancient Egyptian title for a ruler of Egypt **2.** POWERFUL PERSON sb in a position of authority, especially sb who is harsh, gives unreasonable orders, and expects unquestioning obedience [Pre-12thC. Via ecclesiastical Latin and Greek *Pharaō* and Hebrew *par'ōh* from Egyptian *pr-' o*, literally 'great house'.] —**Pharaonic** /fair rónnik/ *adj.*

Pharaoh ant, **Pharaoh's ant** *n.* a small yellowish-red ant that is a household pest in many tropical countries. Latin name: *Monomorium pharaonis*. [*Pharaoh* because it is common in warm parts of the world such as Egypt]

Pharaoh's cat *n.* = **English mongoose**

Pharisaic /fárri sáy ik/, **Pharisaical** /fárri sáy ik'l/ *adj.* **1.** ASSOCIATED WITH THE PHARISEES relating to or characteristic of the Pharisees **2.** Pharisaic, pharisaic, Pharisaical, pharisaical SELF-RIGHTEOUSLY OBSESSED WITH RULES acting with hypocrisy, self-righteousness, or obsessiveness with regard to the strict adherence to rules and formalities (*disapproving*) [Early 17thC. Via ecclesiastical Latin *pharisaïcus* from, ultimately, Greek *pharisaios* (see PHARISEE).] —**Pharisaically** *adv.* —**Pharisaicalness** *n.*

Pharisaism /fárri say izəm/, **Phariseeism** /fárri see izəm/ *n.* **1.** PRACTICES OF PHARISEES the beliefs and practices of the Pharisees, especially the great attention they paid to the detailed rules of everyday life **2.** Pharisaism, Phariseeism, pharisaism, phariseeism SELF-RIGHTEOUSNESS ABOUT ADHERING TO RULES hypocritical, self-righteous, or obsessive behaviour or attitudes towards the observing of rules and formalities (*disapproving*) [Late 16thC. Via French from, ultimately, Greek *pharisaios* (see PHARISEE).]

Pharisee /fárri see/ *n.* **1.** JUDAISM MEMBER OF ANCIENT JEWISH RELIGIOUS GROUP a member of an ancient Jewish religious group who followed the Oral Law in addition to the Torah and attempted to live in a constant state of purity **2.** Pharisee, pharisee SELF-RIGHTEOUS OR HYPOCRITICAL PERSON sb who is self-righteous or hypocritical, especially with regard to adherence to rules and formalities (*disapproving*) [Pre-12thC. Via ecclesiastical Latin from Greek *pharisaios*, ultimately, from Aramaic *prīšayyā*, literally 'those who are separate'.]

Pharm., **pharm.** *abbr.* **1.** pharmacist **2.** pharmacopoeia **3.** pharmaceutical **4.** pharmacy

pharmac- *prefix.* = pharmaco- (*used before vowels*)

pharmaceutical /fáarmə syóotik'l/ *adj.* involved in or associated with the manufacturing, preparation, dispensing, or sale of the drugs used in medicine [Mid-17thC. Formed from late Latin *pharmaceuticus* from, ultimately, Greek *pharmakeutēs* 'one who prepares drugs', from *pharmakon* 'drug'.] —**pharmaceutically** *adv.*

pharmaceutics /fáarmə syóotiks/ *n.* SCIENCE OF DRUGS the science of the preparation and dispensing of the drugs prescribed by doctors (*takes a singular verb*) ■ *npl.* MEDICINAL DRUGS drugs prescribed as medicines

pharmacist /fáarməsist/ *n.* sb trained and licensed to dispense medicinal drugs and to advise on their use [Mid-19thC. Formed from PHARMACY.]

pharmaco- *prefix.* drugs, medicine ○ *pharmacodynamics* [From Greek *pharmakon* 'drug, poison']

pharmacodynamics /fáarməkō dī námmiks/ *n.* the study of the effects of drugs on living organisms (*takes a singular verb*) —**pharmacodynamic** *adj.*

pharmacognosy /fáarmə kógnəssi/ *n.* a branch of pharmacology dealing with active substances found in plants [Mid-19thC. Coined from PHARMACO- + Greek *gnōsis* 'knowledge' (see GNOSIS).] —**pharmacognosist** *n.* —**pharmacognostic** /fáarmə kog nóstik/ *adj.*

pharmacokinetics /fáarmōkō ki néttiks, -kī-/ *npl.* BODY'S REACTION TO DRUGS the body's reaction to drugs, including their absorption, metabolism, and elimination (*takes a plural verb*) ■ *n.* STUDY OF REACTION TO DRUGS the study of the body's reaction to drugs (*takes a singular verb*)

pharmacol. *abbr.* pharmacology

pharmacology /fáarmə kólləji/ (*plural* **-gies**) *n.* **1.** SCI STUDY OF DRUGS the science or study of drugs, including their sources, chemistry, production, use in treating diseases, and side effects **2.** MED, PHARM DRUG'S EFFECTS the effects that a drug has when taken by sb, especially as a medical treatment —**pharmacological** /fáarməkə lójjik'l/ *adj.* —**pharmacologically** /-lójjikli/ *adv.* —**pharmacologist** /fáarmə kólləjist/ *n.*

pharmacopoeia /fáarməkə pee ə/, **pharmacopeia** *n.* **1.** BOOK DESCRIBING DRUGS AND THEIR USES a book or database listing drugs used in medical practice and describing their composition, preparation, use, dosages, effects, and side effects, especially one published as an official guide for pharmacists **2.** COLLECTION OF DRUGS a stock or collection of drugs [Early 17thC. Via modern Latin from Greek *pharmakopoiia* 'preparing of drugs', from *pharmakon* 'drug'.] —**pharmacopoeial** *adj.* —**pharmacopoeic** *adj.* —**pharmacopoeist** *n.*

pharmacotherapy /fáarməkō thérrəpi/ (*plural* **-pies**) *n.* the use of drugs to treat conditions, especially psychiatric disorders

pharmacy /fáarməssi/ (*plural* **-cies**) *n.* **1.** DRUG DISPENSING the science or profession of dispensing drugs used as medical treatments **2.** SHOP SELLING OR DISPENSING MEDICINE a place where the drugs used for treating diseases are dispensed or sold [14thC. Via Old French *farmacie* from, ultimately, Greek *pharmakeia* 'use of drugs', from *pharmakon* 'drug'.]

pharyng- *prefix.* = pharyngo- (*used before vowels*)

pharyngeal /fə rínji əl, fárrin jeé əl/ *adj.* found in, affecting, or relating to the throat [Early 19thC. Formed from modern Latin *pharyngeus*, from the stem *pharyng-* (see PHARYNX).]

pharyngitis /fárrin jítiss/ *n.* MED inflammation of the pharynx, commonly known as a sore throat

pharyngo- *prefix.* pharynx ○ *pharyngoscope* [Via modern Latin from Greek, the stem of *pharugx* 'throat' (see PHARYNX)]

pharyngology /fárring gólləji/ *n.* the branch of medicine concerned with the throat, its diseases, and their treatment —**pharyngological** /fárring gə lójjik'l/ *adj.* —**pharyngologist** /-gólləjist/ *n.*

pharyngoscope /fə ríng gə skōp/ *n.* a medical instrument for examining the throat —**pharyngoscopic** /fə ríng gə skóppik/ *adj.* —**pharyngoscopy** /fárring góskəpi/ *n.*

pharynx /fárringks/ (*plural* **pharynges** /fə rín jeez/ *or* **pharynxes**) *n.* **1.** ANAT THROAT the throat, the region of the alimentary canal in humans and in vertebrate animals that lies between the mouth and oesophagus **2.** ZOOL PART SIMILAR TO THROAT a region between the mouth and the digestive system in sea anemones, worms, insects, and other invertebrate animals [Late 17thC. Via modern Latin (stem *pharyng-*) from Greek *pharugx* 'throat'. Ultimately, from an Indo-European word meaning 'to pierce', which is also the ancestor of English *perforate*.]

phase /fayz/ *n.* **1.** STAGE OF DEVELOPMENT a clearly distinguishable period or stage in a process, in the development of sth, or in a sequence of events **2.** PATTERN OF BEHAVIOUR any period of time when a situation or particular pattern of behaviour persists and is often annoying or worrying **3.** PART OR ASPECT one of the many parts or aspects of sth ○ *We needed to restructure all phases of our business.* **4.** ASTRON RECURRING SHAPE OF MOON any of the recurring forms seen in the sky of the Moon or a planet. The four principal phases of the Moon are the first quarter, full moon, last quarter, and new moon. **5.** PHYS PART OF REPEATING CYCLE any part of a repeated uniform pattern of occurrence of a phenomenon or process, relative to a fixed starting point or time **6.** PHYS STATE OF MATTER any of the states in which matter can exist, depending on temperature and pressure, e.g. the solid, liquid, gaseous, and plasmic states **7.** ZOOL VARIATION IN ANIMAL FORM an alternative stage, appearance, or colouring that distinguishes a group of animals from most of their kind, or that a particular animal adopts under specific conditions **8.** BIOL STAGE IN ORGANISM'S LIFE CYCLE a stage in the life cycle of an organism ■ *vt.* (**phases, phasing, phased**) **1.** DO STH IN STAGES to plan or arrange sth so that it is carried out in stages (*often passive*) ○ *a takeover that is being phased to minimize disruption* **2.** SYNCHRONIZE THINGS to cause two or more things to happen or operate simultaneously or in a coordinated way ○ *to phase the departure of one train with the arrival of another* [Early 19thC. Partly via French, partly a back-formation from modern Latin *phases* 'moon phases', both, ultimately, from Greek *phasis* 'appearance', from *phainein* 'to show'.] —**phaseal** /fáyzi əl/ *adj.* —**phasic** *adj.* ◇ **in phase** in the same phase at the same time, or operating in a synchronized or coordinated way ◇ **out of phase** not in the same phase, or not synchronized or coordinated with each other

phase in *vt.* to introduce sth in stages over a period of time

phase out *vt.* to bring sth to an end or remove it in stages over a period of time

phase-contrast microscope *n.* a microscope sensitive to small differences in the phase of light reflected by or passing through different parts of an object. By enhancing the differences, it provides a clearly contrasted image. Phase-contrast microscopes are particularly useful for examining colourless or transparent objects.

phase modulation *n.* a method of transmitting a voice or other signal in which the phase of a radio carrier wave is varied in accordance with the signal

phase music *n.* a type of musical composition, associated with minimalism, in which the different parts use the same material at the same time, but only sometimes in phase with each other

-phasia *suffix.* speech disorder ○ *aphasia* [Formed from Greek *phasis* 'utterance', from *phanai* 'to say'. Ultimately from an Indo-European word meaning 'to speak', which is also the ancestor of English *fable*, *fame*, and *boon*.]

phasmid /fázmid/ *n.* TROPICAL PLANT-EATING INSECT a tropical plant-eating insect that has a body that looks like a twig with long legs and antennae. Stick insects and leaf insects are phasmids. Family: Phasmidae. ■ *adj.* RELATING TO PHASMIDS belonging or relating to the phasmids [Late 19thC. Via modern Latin *Phasmida*, order name, from, ultimately, Greek *phasma* 'apparition', from *phainein* 'to show' (see PHASE).]

phat /fat/ *adj.* of a very high quality or standard (*slang*) ○ '*music...set to the phat beats of hip-hop*' (*The New York Times*; November 1998) [Late 20thC. Origin unknown.]

phatic /fáttik/ *adj.* spoken in order to share feelings, create goodwill, or set a pleasant social mood, rather than to convey information. 'Have a nice day!' is a phatic phrase. [Early 20thC. Formed from Greek *phatos* 'spoken', from *phanai* 'to say' (see -PHASIA).]

PhB *abbr.* Bachelor of Philosophy [Latin, *Philosophiae Baccalaureus*]

PHC *abbr.* Pharmaceutical Chemist

PhD *abbr.* Doctor of Philosophy [Latin, *Philosophiae Doctor*]

pheasant /fézz'nt/ (*plural* -**ants** *or* -**ant**) *n.* **1.** BIRDS LARGE LONG-TAILED BIRD a large bird related to and resembling domestic poultry. Male pheasants have long curved tails, and are often brightly coloured. Pheasants are frequently bred for shooting. Family: Phasianidae. **2.** FOOD PHEASANT MEAT the meat obtained from a pheasant [13thC. Via Old French *fesan* from, ultimately, Greek *phasianos (ornis)*, '(bird) from the river Phasis' in western Georgia, where it was supposed to have originated.]

pheasant's eye (*plural* **pheasant's eyes** *or* **pheasant's eye**) *n.* **1.** PLANT WITH DEEP RED FLOWER a plant of the buttercup family with very narrow twiggy leaves and a deep red flower with a dark centre or a yellow cup-shaped flower. Genus: *Adonis*. **2.** VARIETY OF NARCISSUS a variety of narcissus with white petals sur-

Pheasant

rounding a red-rimmed cup. Latin name: *Narcissus poeticus*.

phellem /féllem/ *n.* = **cork** *n.* 4 [Late 19thC. Formed from Greek *phellos* 'cork', on the model of PHLOEM and XYLEM.]

phelloderm /féllə durm/ *n.* a layer of plant cells produced by the inner surface of the cork cambium in woody plants, from which cork tissue develops [Late 19thC. Coined from Greek *phellos* 'cork' + -DERM.] —**phellodermal** /féllō dúrm'l/ *adj.*

phellogen /félləjen/ *n.* = **cork cambium** [Late 19thC. Coined from Greek *phellos* 'cork' + -GEN.] —**phellogenetic** /félləjə néttik/ *adj.* —**phellogenic** /-jénnik/ *adj.*

phen- *prefix.* CHEM = **pheno-**

phenacaine /fénnə kayn/ *n.* a white crystalline compound used as a local anaesthetic in ophthalmology. Formula: $C_{18}H_{22}N_2O_2$. [Early 20thC. Coined from *phen-*, variant of PHENO-, + -CAINE.]

phenacetin /fə nássetin/ *n.* **1.** DRUG USED TO TREAT PAIN a white crystalline compound used in drugs to reduce fever or relieve pain. Formula: $C_{10}H_{13}NO_2$. **2.** **phenacetin** (*plural* -**tin** *or* -**tins**) PILL a tablet containing phenacetin [Late 19thC. Alteration of acetophenetidin, its chemical name.]

phenacite /fénnə kīt, fénnə sīt/, **phenakite** /fénnə kīt/ *n.* a colourless glassy mineral consisting of beryllium silicate that is sometimes used as a gemstone [Mid-19thC. Formed from Greek *phenak-*, stem of *phenax* 'impostor', because it was mistaken for quartz.]

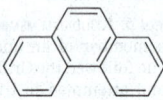

Phenanthrene

phenanthrene /fə nánth reen/ *n.* a colourless crystalline aromatic hydrocarbon used in the manufacture of dyes, drugs, and explosives. Formula: $C_{14}H_{10}$. [Late 19thC. Contraction of PHENO- + ANTHRACENE.]

phencyclidine /fen síkli deen, -síkli-/ *n.* a drug used as an anaesthetic in veterinary medicine and illegally as a hallucinogen. Formula: $C_{17}H_{25}N$. [Mid-20thC. Coined from *phen-* (variant of PHENO-) + CYCLO- + PIPERIDINE.]

phenetics /fi néttiks/ *n.* a system of biological classification based on overall similarities between organisms rather than on their genetic or developmental relationships (*takes a singular verb*) [Mid-20thC. Formed from Greek *phainesthai* 'to appear' (see PHENOMENON + -ETIC).] —**phenetic** /fi néttik/ *adj.* —**phenetically** *adv.* —**pheneticist** *n.*

pheno- *prefix.* **1.** containing phenyl ○ *phenobarbitone* **2.** related to or derived from benzene ○ *phenol* **3.** appearing ○ *phenocryst* [From Greek *phainein* 'to show' (see PHASE)]

phenobarbital /feenō baárbit'l/ *n.* US = **phenobarbitone**

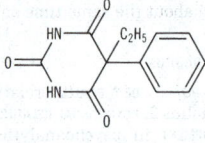

Phenobarbitone

phenobarbitone /feenō baárbitōn/ *n.* a crystalline barbiturate used as a sedative, hypnotic, and anticonvulsant. Formula: $C_{12}H_{12}N_2O_3$. US term **phenobarbital**

phenocopy /feenō koppi/ (*plural* -**ies**) *n.* a non-inheritable change in an organism induced by its response to its environment but resembling a genetic mutation [Mid-20thC. Blend of PHENOTYPE and COPY.]

phenocryst /feenə krist, fénnə-/ *n.* any of the large embedded crystals in a porphyritic rock [Late 19thC. From French *phénocryste*, from *phéno-* 'pheno-' (see PHENO-) + Greek *krustallos* 'crystal' (see CRYSTAL).] —**phenocrystic** /feenə krístik, fénnə-/ *adj.*

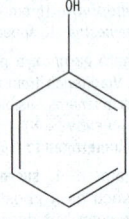

Phenol

phenol /feenol/ *n.* **1.** POISONOUS CAUSTIC COMPOUND a poisonous caustic crystalline compound obtained from coal, wood tar, or benzene, used in the manufacture of resins, dyes, and pharmaceuticals and as an antiseptic and disinfectant. Formula: C_6H_5OH. **2.** COMPOUND BASED ON BENZENE RING a chemical compound that has one or more hydroxyl groups attached to a benzene ring [Mid-19thC. Coined from *phen-*, variant of PHENO-, + -OL.]

phenolic /fi nóllik/ *n.* phenolic, phenolic resin RESIN USED IN PAINTS AND ADHESIVES a type of thermosetting resin derived from phenol and used in plastics, paints, and adhesives ■ *adj.* CHEM RELATING TO PHENOL derived from or containing phenol

phenology /fi nólləji/ (*plural* -**gies**) *n.* **1.** STUDYING HOW CLIMATE AFFECTS BIOLOGICAL CYCLES the study of regularly recurring biological phenomena such as animal migrations or plant budding, especially as influenced by climatic conditions **2.** RELATIONSHIP BETWEEN RECURRING PHENOMENON AND CLIMATE the relationship between a regularly recurring biological phenomenon and climatic or environmental factors that may influence it [Late 19thC. Coined from PHENOMENON + -LOGY.] —**phenological** /feenə lójjik'l/ *adj.* —**phenologist** /fi nólləjist/ *n.*

phenolphthalein /feé nol tháleen, -tháy-/ *n.* a colourless or yellowish compound used as a chemical indicator and as a laxative. Alkalis turn a solution of phenolphthalein red. Formula: $C_{20}H_{14}O_4$.

phenol red *n.* a red dye used as an acid-base indicator and, in medicine, to test kidney function

phenom /fə nóm/ *n.* an outstanding or unusual person or thing (*slang*) [Late 19thC. Shortening of PHENOMENON.]

phenomena plural of **phenomenon**

Phenolphthalein

Phenylalanine

phenomenal /fə nómminəl/ adj. **1.** REMARKABLE remarkable, especially if remarkably and impressively good or great ○ a phenomenal talent **2.** GREAT very great in extent or degree (informal) ○ a phenomenal success **3.** PHILOS PERCEIVED BY SENSES perceived by or perceptible to the senses, rather than the mind, and thus having at least an apparent external existence **4.** OF A PHENOMENON constituting or relating to a phenomenon —**phenomenally** adv.

phenomenalism /fə nómminəlizəm/ n. a philosophical theory stating that knowledge of the external world is limited to appearances so that we know what our senses tell us about things (**sense-data**), not what they are in themselves —**phenomenalist** n., adj. —**phenomenalistically** /fə nómminə lístikli/ adv.

phenomenology /fə nómmi nólləji/ n. **1.** STUDY OF PHENOMENA in philosophy, the science or study of phenomena, things as they are perceived, as opposed to the study of being, the nature of things as they are **2.** PHILOSOPHICAL INVESTIGATION OF EXPERIENCE the philosophical investigation and description of conscious experience in all its varieties without reference to the question of whether what is experienced is objectively real —**phenomenological** /fə nómminə lójjik'l/ adj. —**phenomenologically** /-lójjikli/ adv. —**phenomenologist** /-óllejist/ n.

phenomenon /fə nómminən/ (plural **-na** /-nə/) n. **1.** STH EXPERIENCED a fact or occurrence that can be observed **2.** STH NOTABLE sth that is out of the ordinary and excites people's interest and curiosity ○ a strange phenomenon **3.** EXTRAORDINARY PERSON OR THING sb or sth that is, or that is considered to be, truly extraordinary and marvellous **4.** PHILOS OBJECT OF PERCEPTION sth perceived or experienced, especially an object as it is apprehended by the human senses as opposed to an object as it intrinsically is in itself [Late 16thC. Via late Latin from Greek phainomenon 'that which appears', from the past participle of phainein 'to bring to light' (source of English fantasy), ultimately 'to shine'.]

phenothiazine /feeno thí ə zeen, fénno-/ n. **1.** VET COMPOUND KILLING INTESTINAL WORMS AND INSECTS a yellowish crystalline compound used in veterinary medicine to destroy intestinal worms and as an insecticide. Formula: $C_{12}H_9NS$. **2.** MED DRUG USED TO TREAT SCHIZOPHRENIA a derivative of phenothiazine used as a tranquillizer and in the treatment of schizophrenia

phenotype /feeno tīp/ n. the visible characteristics of an organism resulting from the interaction between its genetic makeup and the environment [Early 20thC. From German Phänotypus, literally 'type that shows', from Greek phainein (see PHENOMENON).] —**phenotypic** /feeno típpik/ adj. —**phenotypical** /-típpik'l/ adj. —**phenotypically** /-típpikli/ adv.

phenoxide /fi nók sīd/ n. any chemical compound that is a salt of phenol

phenyl /feé nīl, fénn'l/ n. a chemical group derived from benzene by removing a hydrogen atom, thus having a valency of one. Formula: C_6H_5. [Mid-19thC. From French phényle, from Greek phainein 'to show' (see PHENOMENON), because it was first used to name compounds formed from lighting gas.]

phenylalanine /feé nīl állə neen, fénn'l-/ n. an essential amino acid found in many proteins and converted to a nonessential amino acid (**tyrosine**) by the body. Formula: $C_9H_{11}O_2N$.

phenylbutazone /feé nīl bjóōtəzōn, fénn'l-/ n. an anti-inflammatory drug used to treat arthritis, bursitis, and gout. Formula: $C_{19}H_{20}N_2O_2$.

phenylketonuria /feé nīl keétə nyoóri ə, fénn'l-/ n. a condition, resulting from a genetic mutation, in which the body lacks the enzyme to metabolize phenylalanine which, if untreated, results in developmental deficiency, seizures, and tumours

phenylpropanolamine /feé nīl própə nóllə meen, fénn'l-/ n. a drug that constricts blood vessels and is used as a nasal and bronchial decongestant, and an appetite suppressant. Formula: $C_9H_{13}NO$.

phenylthiocarbamide /feé nīl thī ō kaárbə mīd, fénn'l-/, **phenylthiourea** /feé nīl thī ō yoóri ə, fénn'l-/ n. a crystalline compound that tastes extremely bitter to people who possess a particular dominant gene, and is thus used to test for the presence of that gene

phenytoin /fénni tō in/ n. an anticonvulsant drug used to treat epilepsy. Formula: $C_{15}H_{12}N_2O_2$. [Mid-20thC. Coined form DI- + PHENYL + HYDANTOIN.]

pheromone /férrəmōn/ n. a chemical compound produced and secreted by an animal that influences the behaviour and development of other members of the same species [Mid-20thC. Coined from Greek pherein 'to carry' (see -PHORE) + HORMONE.] —**pheromonal** /férrə mōn'l/ adj.

phew /fyoo/ interj. **1.** EXPRESSING TIREDNESS, RELIEF, OR DISGUST used to express tiredness, relief, surprise, or disgust **2.** EXPRESSING REPULSION used to express disgust at an unpleasant smell [Early 17thC. An imitation of the sound made by blowing through partly closed lips.]

phi /fī/ (plural **phis**) n. the 21st letter of the Greek alphabet, represented in the English alphabet as 'ph'. See table at alphabet [Mid-20thC. Via late Greek from Greek phei.]

PHI /fī/ abbr. permanent health insurance

phial /fí əl/ n. = **vial** [14thC. Via Old French fiole from, ultimately Greek phialē 'broad flat vessel'.]

Phi Beta Kappa n. **1.** ACADEMIC HONORARY SOCIETY an honorary society of American college and university students showing high academic achievement. It was founded in 1776. **2.** HONOUR SOCIETY MEMBER a member of Phi Beta Kappa

phi effect n. = phi phenomenon

PHIGS /figz/ abbr. programmers' hierarchical interactive graphics standard

phil. /fil/ abbr. **1.** philosophy **2.** philosopher **3.** philosophical **4.** philology **5.** philological

Phil. abbr. **1.** Philippines **2.** BIBLE Philippians **3.** MUSIC Philharmonic

phil- prefix. = **philo-** (used before vowels or l)

-phil suffix. = **-phile**

Phila. abbr. Philadelphia

Philadelphia /fíllə délfi ə/ the largest city in Pennsylvania, situated on the Delaware River in the southeastern part of the state. It is known as the Birthplace of the Nation because both the US Declaration of Independence and the Constitution of the United States were drawn up there. Population: 1,478,000 (1996).

philadelphus /fíllə délfəss/ n. PLANTS = **mock orange** n.
1 [Late 18thC. Via modern Latin from Greek philadelphos

'loving one's brother', from philos 'loving' + adelphos 'brother'.]

Philae /fí ee/ submerged island in southern Egypt, in the River Nile, south of Aswan. It was the site of ancient temples that were moved when the island was flooded after the building of the Aswan High Dam.

philander /fi lándər/ (**-ders, -dering, -dered**) vi. to flirt with and have casual sexual affairs with women, especially when married to another woman (dated disapproving) [Late 17thC. From Greek philandros 'loving men', from the stem andr- 'man' (source of English andro-). Originally 'lover'.] —**philanderer** n.

philanthropic /fíllən thróppik/, **philanthropical** /-pik'l/ adj. **1.** CHARITABLE AND GENEROUS showing kindness, charitable concern, and generosity towards other people **2.** DEVOTED TO HELPING OTHER PEOPLE devoted to helping other people, especially through giving charitable aid —**philanthropically** adv.

philanthropy /fi lánthrəpi/ n. **1.** DESIRE TO BENEFIT HUMANITY a desire to improve the material, social, and spiritual welfare of humanity, especially through charitable activities **2.** LOVE FOR ALL HUMANITY general love for, or benevolence towards, the whole of humankind (formal) [Early 17thC. Via late Latin from, ultimately, Greek philanthrōpos 'humane', from philos 'loving' + anthrōpos 'human being'.] —**philanthropist** n.

philately /fi láttəli/ n. the collection and study of postage stamps and related items [Mid-19thC. From French philatélie, from Greek philos 'loving' + ateleia 'exemption from tax', ultimately from telos 'tax'; from the freedom from charges that a stamped letter provides.] —**philatelic** /fíllə téllik/ adj. —**philatelically** /-téllikli/ adv. —**philatelist** /fi láttəlist/ n.

Philby /fílbi/, **Kim** (1912–88) British intelligence agent and Soviet spy. During the 1940s and 1950s he penetrated the upper levels of British intelligence and passed vital information to the Union of Soviet Socialist Republics. Real name **Harold Adrian Russell Philby**

-phile suffix. **1.** one that loves or has an affinity for ○ nucleophile ○ Europhile **2.** loving or having an affinity for ○ homophile [Via Latin -philus from, ultimately, Greek philos 'loving'] —**philic** suffix. —**philous** suffix. —**phily** suffix.

Philemon /fi leé mən/ n. BIBLE a book in the Bible, written by St Paul, appealing to Philemon to take pity on his slave who had escaped and converted to Christianity. See table at Bible

philharmonic /fíl haar mónnik, fíllər-/, **Philharmonic** adj. PERFORMING OR PROMOTING MUSIC used to describe an orchestra or choir that performs music or a society that promotes the study, performance, and appreciation of music ■ n. PHILHARMONIC ORCHESTRA, CHOIR, OR SOCIETY a symphony orchestra, choir, or musical society that has the word 'philharmonic' in its title [Mid-18thC. Via French philharmonique from, ultimately, Greek philos 'loving' + harmonia 'harmony' (see HARMONY).]

philhellene /fíl he leen, fil hélleen/, **philhellenist** /fil héllənist/ n. sb who greatly admires ancient or modern Greece, the Greeks, and their culture [Early 19thC. From Greek philellēn, from philos 'loving' + Hellēn 'a Greek' (source of English Hellene).] —**philhellenic** /fíl he leénik, -lénnik/ adj. —**philhellenism** /fil héllənizəm/ n. —**philhellenistic** /fil héllə nístik/ adj.

Phil. I. abbr. Philippine Islands

-philia suffix. **1.** intense or abnormal attraction to ○ neophilia ○ zoophilia **2.** tendency towards ○ basophilia [Via modern Latin from Greek philia 'fondness', from philos 'loving'] —**philiac** suffix.

philibeg /fílli beg/ *n.* = **filibeg**

Philip /fíllip/, **St** (*fl.* 1st century AD) New Testament apostle. One of the original 12 disciples of Jesus Christ, he was born in Bethsaida and was present at the feeding of the 5,000.

Philip I /fíllip thə fúrst/, **Duke of Burgundy and King of Castile** (1478–1506). Father of Charles V and Ferdinand I, he founded the Hapsburg dynasty in Spain through his marriage to Joanna the Mad of Castile. Known as **Philip the Handsome**

Philip II /fíllip thə sékənd/, **King of Macedonia** (382–336 BC). After becoming king (359) he extended Macedonian power over the whole of Greece. He was the father of Alexander the Great.

Philip IV /fíllip thə fáwrth/, **King of France** (1268–1314). He succeeded to the throne in 1285. His conflict with Pope Boniface VII led to the residence of the popes in Avignon (1309–77). Known as **Philip the Fair**

Philip V /fíllip thə fífth/, **King of Spain** (1683–1746). The grandson of Louis XIV of France, he was the first of the Spanish Bourbons. His accession to the throne (1700) led to the War of the Spanish Succession.

Philip, Prince, Duke of Edinburgh (*b.* 1921). The son of Prince Andrew of Greece and the great-great-grandson of Queen Victoria, he married Princess Elizabeth, later Queen Elizabeth II, in 1947.

Philippi /fi líp ī, fílli pī/ town in northern Greece, situated northwest of the town of Kavála. It was the site of a battle in 42 BC in which forces led by Mark Antony and Octavian defeated Marcus Brutus and Gaius Cassius Longinus. Population: 728 (1981).

Philippians /fi líppi ənz/ *n.* a book of the Bible consisting of a letter (**Epistle**) from St. Paul to the Christian church at Philippi. (*takes a singular verb*)

philippic /fi líppik/ *n.* a verbal attack on sb or sth delivered in the most savage, bitter, and insulting terms, usually as a speech [Late 16thC. Via Latin *philippicus* from Greek *philippikos*, the speech of the fourth-century BC Greek orator *Demosthenes* urging the citizens of Athens to rise up against Philip of Macedon (see PHILIP II).]

Philippine *adj.* **1.** OF PHILIPPINES relating to or typical of the Philippines, or its people or culture **2.** = **Filipino** *adj.*

Philippine English *n.* a variety of English spoken in the Philippines

WORD KEY: WORLD ENGLISH

Philippine English, also Filipino English, is the English language as used in the Philippines. It has some co-official status with Filipino. English is the second Western colonial language, after Spanish; the United States took the territory in 1898 from Spain, whose colony it had been since 1521. The nation is diverse, with a Malay majority, a Chinese minority, and many people of mixed Malay, Chinese, Spanish, and US backgrounds. Because English is used in varying degrees by over half the population of about 60 million, the Philippines rightly claims to be a major English-speaking country. Like US English, Philippine English is 'rhotic' (that is, 'r' is pronounced in words such as *art, door,* and *worker*). Also, *h* is pronounced as a retroflex 'r' (that is, it is pronounced with the tip of the tongue curled back and raised). Vowels tend to be full in all syllables (e.g. seven being pronounced "seh-ven", not 'sevn'). An 's' or 'sh' sound may serve instead of a 'z' or 'zh', as in 'carss' (cars), 'pleshure' (pleasure). In grammar, the present continuous is commonly used for habitual behaviour, rather than the simple present ('We are doing this work all the time' for 'We do this work all the time'), the present perfect may be used rather than the simple past ('We have done it yesterday' for 'We did it yesterday') and the past perfect rather than the present perfect ('They had already been there' for 'They have already been there'). Distinctive vocabulary includes: (1) Hispanicisms, unchanged or adapted, e.g. *asalto* (surprise party), *querida* (mistress), *aggrupation* (from *agrupación* meaning 'group'); (2) words from Tagalog, e.g. *boondock* (mountain) – whence 'the boondocks', *kundiman* (love song), *tao* (man) – as in 'the common tao'; (3) local coinages, e.g. *carnap* (to steal a car), the formation by analogy with *kidnap* and *jeepney* (blending *Jeep* and *jitney*, 'small bus', a Jeep adapted for passengers).

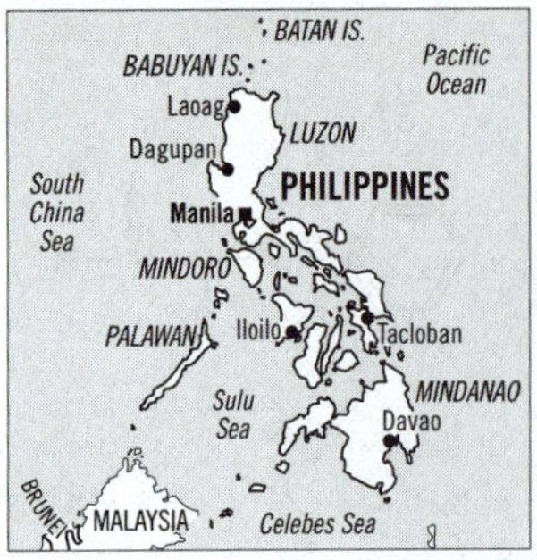

Philippines

Philippines /fílləpeenz/ republic in Asia, in the western Pacific Ocean, in the Malay Archipelago. It comprises over 7,000 islands. Language: Filipino. Currency: Philippine peso. Capital: Manila. Population: 68,614,612 (1995). Area: 300,000 sq. km/115,830 sq. mi. Official name **Republic of the Philippines**

Philistine /fíllistīn/ *n.* **1.** PEOPLES SB FROM ANCIENT PHILISTIA a member of the Aegean people who settled in ancient Philistia around the 12th century BC **2. philistine, Philistine** SB WHO DOES NOT APPRECIATE ART a materialistic person who is indifferent to artistic and intellectual achievements and values (*disapproving*) ■ *adj.* **1.** PEOPLES RELATING TO PHILISTINES relating to or typical of the ancient Philistines or their culture **2. philistine, Philistine** UNCULTURED ignorant, uncultured, and indifferent or hostile to artistic and intellectual achievement [14thC. Via late Latin and Greek from Hebrew *Pəlištī* 'people of Philistia' in Palestine. Derogatory sense from, ultimately, the hostility of the Philistines towards the ancient Israelites.] —**philistinism** /fíllistinizəm/ *n.*

Phillip /fíllip/, **Arthur** (1738–1814) British naval officer. He transported the first convicts to Australia in 1788, and was first governor of New South Wales (1788–92).

Phillips screw /fíllips-/ *tdmk.* a trademark for a screw with a cross-shaped slot on its head

Phillips screwdriver *tdmk.* a trademark for a screwdriver that has a cross-shaped tip so that it can be used to turn a Phillips screw

phillumenist /fi lóomənist/ *n.* sb who collects matchboxes and matchbooks as a hobby [Mid-20thC. Coined from PHILO- + Latin *lumen* 'light' (see LUMEN).] —**phillumeny** *n.*

philo- *prefix.* loving, having an attraction to or affinity for ○ *philoprogenitive* [From Greek *philos* 'loving']

Philoctetes /fíllək tée teez, fi lók ti teez/ *n.* in Greek mythology, a friend of Achilles and the slayer of the Trojan prince Paris

philodendron /fíllə déndrən/ (*plural* **-drons** *or* **-dra** /-drə/) *n.* a tropical American climbing plant of the arum family, grown as a house plant for its evergreen leaves. Genus: *Philodendron.* [Late 19thC. Via modern Latin from, ultimately, Greek *philodendros* 'loving trees' (because it climbs trees in its native habitat), from *dendron* 'tree' (see DENDRON).]

philogyny /fi lójjəni/ *n.* a positive and admiring attitude towards women in general (*literary*) —**philogynist** *n.* —**philogynous** *adj.*

philol. *abbr.* **1.** philology **2.** philological

philology /fi lólləji/ *n.* **1.** LING STUDY OF LANGUAGE IN TEXTS the scientific study of the relationship of languages to one another, and their history, especially based on the analysis of texts **2.** HIST STUDY OF ANCIENT TEXTS the study and analysis of ancient texts, especially as an approach to the cultural history of a period or people **3.** LITERAT STUDY OF LITERATURE the study of literature in general (*archaic*) [14thC. Via Latin *philologia* from, ultimately, Greek *philologos* 'fond of words', from *philos* 'loving' + *logos* 'word'.] —**philological** /fíllə lójjik'l/ *adj.* —**philologically** /-lójjikli/ *adv.* —**philologist** /fi lólləjist/ *n.*

philoprogenitive /fíllō prō jénnitiv/ *adj.* **1.** PRODUCING OFFSPRING producing a large number of offspring (*formal*) **2.** LOVING CHILDREN loving children, especially your own offspring (*literary*)

philos. *abbr.* **1.** philosophical **2.** philosopher **3.** philosophy

philosophe /fíllə sóf, -zóf/ *n.* any of the leading writers and thinkers of the Enlightenment in 18th-century France, who advocated a rational approach to philosophy and government and criticized the French social and political system [Pre-12thC. From Latin *philosophus* 'philosopher' (see PHILOSOPHER).]

philosopher /fi lóssəfər/ *n.* **1.** PHILOSOPHY SB WHO STUDIES LIFE AND REALITY sb who seeks to understand and explain the nature of life and reality, especially a scholar of philosophy or related fields **2.** THINKING PERSON sb who is given to thinking deeply and seriously about human affairs and life in general **3.** CALM AND RATIONAL PERSON sb who responds calmly and rationally to events, especially adversity [14thC. Formed from Old French *philosophe* via Latin from Greek *philosophos*, literally 'lover of knowledge', from *sophia* 'learning, wisdom'.]

philosopher's stone, philosophers' stone *n.* a substance that medieval alchemists believed could be used to convert other metals into gold

philosophical /fíllə sóffik'l, -zóffik'l/, **philosophic** /-sóffik, -zóffik/ *adj.* **1.** PHILOSOPHY RELATING TO STUDYING NATURE OF REALITY concerned with the study of the nature of life and reality, or of related areas such as ethics, logic, or metaphysics **2.** CONCERNED WITH DEEP QUESTIONS OF LIFE concerned with or given to thinking about the larger issues and deeper meanings in life and events **3.** SHOWING CALMNESS AND RESIGNATION showing calmness, restraint, or resignation, especially reacting to adversity in a restrained or resigned way —**philosophically** *adv.*

philosophize /fi lóssə fīz/ (**-phizes, -phizing, -phized**), **philosophise** (**-phises, -phising, -phised**) *v.* **1.** *vi.* DISCUSS NATURE OF REALITY to comment on or attempt to explain the nature of life and reality, or some part of it such as logic, ethics, knowledge, or existence **2.** *vi.* EXPLAIN OR MORALIZE IN SUPERFICIAL WAY to express opinions of a supposedly philosophical nature in a superficial, tedious, or moralistic way **3.** *vt.* PHILOSOPHY DEAL WITH STH FROM PHILOSOPHICAL STANDPOINT to consider, explain, or deal with sth from a philosophical standpoint —**philosophization** /fi lóssə fī záysh'n/ *n.* —**philosophizer** /fi lóssə fīzər/ *n.*

philosophy /fi lóssəfi/ (*plural* **-phies**) *n.* **1.** PHILOSOPHY EXAMINATION OF BASIC CONCEPTS the branch of knowledge or academic study devoted to the systematic examination of basic concepts such as truth, existence, reality, causality, and freedom **2.** PHILOSOPHY SYSTEM OF THOUGHT a particular system of thought or doctrine **3.** PHILOSOPHY GUIDING OR UNDERLYING PRINCIPLES a set of basic principles or concepts underlying a particular sphere of knowledge **4.** SET OF BELIEFS OR AIMS a precept, or set of precepts, beliefs, principles, or aims, underlying sb's practice or conduct **5.** CALM RESIGNATION restraint, resignation, or calmness and rationality in a person's behaviour or response to events **6.** EDUC THE LIBERAL ARTS the branch of learning that includes the liberal arts and sciences and excludes medicine, law, and theology (*archaic*) [14thC. Via Old French *filosofie* from, ultimately, Greek *philosophia*, from *philosophos* 'philosopher' (see PHILOSOPHER).]

philter *n.* US = **philtre**

philtre *n.* a magical potion or charm, especially one that causes sb to fall in love (*literary*) [Late 16thC. Via French from, ultimately, Greek *philtron*, from *philein* 'to love', from *philos* 'loving'.]

phimosis /fī mósiss/ *n.* an abnormal narrowing of the opening in the foreskin to the extent that it cannot be drawn back over the penis. This precludes washing and often leads to irritation and infection. [Late 17thC. Via modern Latin from Greek *phimōsis* 'muzzling'.]

phi phenomenon, phi effect *n.* an optical illusion in which the rapid appearance and disappearance of two stationary objects, e.g. flashing lights, is perceived as the movement back and forth of a single object

phiz /fiz/, **phizog** /fízzog, fi zóg/ *n.* a person's face (*slang*) [Late 17thC. Shortening of PHYSIOGNOMY.]

phleb- *prefix.* = **phlebo-** (*used before vowels*)

phlebitis /fli bítiss/ n. inflammation of the wall of a vein

phlebo- prefix. vein ○ phlebotomy [From Greek phleb-, the stem of phleps 'blood vessel']

phlebography /fli bóggrəfi/ n. = **venography**

phlebotomize /fli bóttə mīz/ (-mizes, -mizing, -mized), **phlebotomise** (-mises, -mising, -mised) vt. to make an incision into sb's vein, formerly often done to release blood from a vein as a therapeutic treatment

phlebotomy /fli bóttəmi/ (plural -mies) n. a surgical incision made in a vein, or a puncture made by a needle to draw blood for testing —**phlebotomist** n.

phlegm /flem/ n. 1. MED THICK MUCUS the thick mucus secreted by the walls of the respiratory passages, especially during a cold 2. UNFLAPPABILITY calmness or composure that is not easily disturbed 3. MED BODILY FLUID DETERMINING HEALTH AND EMOTIONS in medieval medicine, one of the four basic bodily fluids (**humours**). Phlegm was believed to be cold and moist in nature and to cause sluggishness and apathy. 4. INDIFFERENCE sluggishness, apathy, or indifference (archaic) [14thC. Via Old French fleume from, ultimately, Greek phlegma, literally 'heat', from phlegein 'to burn'. Ultimately, from an Indo-European word meaning 'to shine'.] —**phlegmy** adj.

phlegmatic /fleg máttik/, **phegmatical** /-máttik'l/ adj. characterized by a lack of emotion or emotional display, and not easily worried, excited, or annoyed [14thC. Via Old French fleumatique and Latin phlegmaticus from Greek phlegmatikos, from phlegma (see PHLEGM).] —**phlegmatically** adv.

─── **WORD KEY: SYNONYMS** ───
See Synonyms at impassive.

phloem /fló em/ n. one of the two main types of tissue in the more highly developed plants. Phloem conducts synthesized foodstuffs to all parts of the plant. [Late 19thC. From German, where it was formed from Greek phloos 'bark'.]

phlogiston /flə jístən, -gístən/ n. HIST a hypothetical element that some early scientists, before the discovery of oxygen, believed to be present in all combustible substances to make them burn [Mid-18thC. From Greek, literally 'inflammable thing', from phlogizein 'to set on fire', from phlox 'flame' (see PHLOX).] —**phlogistic** /flə jístik, -gístik/ adj.

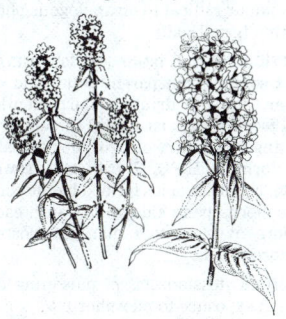
Phlox

phlox /floks/ (plural **phlox** or **phloxes**) n. a common garden plant, originally native to North America, that has slim stems with oval narrow leaves and clusters of scented white, red, or purple flowers. Genus: Phlox. [Early 18thC. Via modern Latin, genus name, from Greek, 'flame', from its brightly coloured flowers. Ultimately from an Indo-European word that is also the ancestor of English black.]

Phnom Penh /nóm pén/ capital city of Cambodia, situated at the confluence of the Mekong and Tonle Sap rivers in the southern part of the country. Population: 900,000 (1991).

-phobe suffix. sb who fears or dislikes sth ○ computerphobe [Via French from, ultimately, Greek phobos 'fear']

phobia /fóbi ə/ n. an irrational or very powerful fear and dislike of sth, e.g. spiders or confined spaces [Late 18thC. From -PHOBIA.]

-phobia suffix. an exaggerated or irrational fear

○ claustrophobia [Via Latin from, ultimately, Greek phobos 'fear']

phobic /fóbik/ adj. 1. INTENSELY FEARFUL OF STH having or showing an intense fear and dislike of sth 2. PSYCHIAT RELATING TO PHOBIAS affected with or arising out of a phobia ■ n. PSYCHIAT SB WITH A PHOBIA sb who has a strong or irrational fear and dislike of sth

-phobic suffix. with a strong or irrational fear or dislike of sb or sth ○ claustrophobic

Phobos /fó boss/ n. the innermost of the two natural satellites of Mars, both of which are small. It was discovered in 1877 and is ellipsoidal in shape.

phocine /fó sīn/ adj. relating to or resembling seals [Mid-19thC. From modern Latin Phocinae, subfamily name, from, ultimately, Greek phōkē 'seal'.]

phocomelia /fókō meéli ə/ n. a condition, present at birth, characterized by an absent or under-developed upper section of a limb, with a normal-sized hand or foot attached to the trunk by a short, broad, flat limb [Late 19thC. Formed from Greek phōkē 'seal' + melos 'limb'; from the short limbs of seals.]

Phoebe[1] /feébi/ n. 1. MYTHOL TITAN GODDESS in Greek mythology, a Titan goddess who later became identified with the goddess of the moon, Artemis 2. MOON a personification of the moon (literary) [14thC. Via Latin from Greek Phoibē, feminine of phoibos 'bright, shining'.]

Phoebe[2] /feébi/ n. the outermost known natural satellite of Saturn, discovered in 1898. It is irregular in shape and has a maximum dimension of approximately 230 km.

Phoebus /feébəss/ n. 1. = **Apollo** 2. SUN a personification of the sun (literary) [14thC. Via Latin from, ultimately, Greek phoibos 'bright, shining'.]

Phoenician /fə nísh'n, fə neésh'n/ n. 1. PEOPLES SB FROM ANCIENT PHOENICIA a member of an ancient people that occupied Phoenicia, coastal lands in present-day Syria, where they established thriving trading ports. During pre-Christian times, their influence spread throughout the eastern Mediterranean. 2. LANG LANGUAGE OF ANCIENT PHOENICIA an extinct language formerly spoken in ancient Phoenicia. It belongs to the Canaanitic group of the Semitic branch of Afro-Asiatic languages. —**Phoenician** adj.

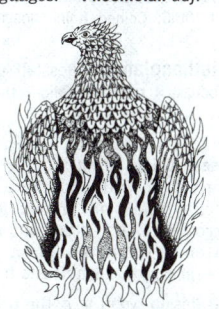
Phoenix

phoenix /feéniks/ n. 1. MYTHOL MYTHOLOGICAL BIRD in ancient mythology, a bird resembling an eagle that lived for 500 years and then burned itself to death on a pyre from whose ashes another phoenix arose. It commonly appears in literature as a symbol of death and resurrection. 2. SB OR STH BEAUTIFUL OR UNIQUE a supremely beautiful, rare, or unique person or thing (literary) ○ a phoenix of princes [Pre-12thC. Via Old French from, ultimately, Greek phoinix.]

Phoenix[1] /feéniks/ n. a constellation of the southern hemisphere situated between Sculptor and Eridanus

Phoenix[2] /feéniks/ capital of Arizona and its largest city, located in the southern part of the state. Population: 1,159,014 (1996).

phon /fon/ n. a unit of subjective measure of loudness level. The level in phons is equal in number to the sound intensity of a 1,000-hertz reference sound, measured in decibels, judged to be the same loudness as the measured sound.

phon. abbr. 1. phonology 2. phonetics

phon- prefix. = **phono-** (used before vowels)

phonate /fó nayt, fō náyt/ (-nates, -nating, -nated) v. 1. vti. VOICE A SOUND to make a voiced sound or make a sound voiced by vibrating the vocal cords 2. vi. PRODUCE SOUNDS WITH THE VOICE to produce sounds, especially speech sounds, with the voice —**phonation** /fō náysh'n/ n. —**phonatory** /-təri/ adj.

phone[1] /fōn/ n. TELEPHONE a telephone ■ **phones** npl. EARPHONES a set of earphones (informal) ■ v. (**phones**, **phoning**, **phoned**) 1. vti. CALL SB BY TELEPHONE to call sb on the telephone 2. vt. REPORT STH BY TELEPHONE to report or communicate sth using a telephone [Late 19thC. Shortening.]

phone[2] /fōn/ n. a single basic speech sound [Mid-19thC. See -PHONE.]

-phone suffix. 1. device that emits or receives sounds, musical instrument ○ diaphone ○ hydrophone ○ sousaphone 2. telephone ○ speakerphone 3. sound, speech sound ○ isophone 4. speaker of a particular language ○ Francophone [From Greek phōnē (see PHONO-)] —**phonic** suffix. —**phony** suffix.

phone book n. a telephone directory

phone box n. a telephone box

phonecard /fón kaard/ n. a rectangular plastic card that can be used instead of money when making calls from some public telephones

phone-in n. BROADCAST a radio or television programme in which audience members call in to discuss topics with the host and guest. US term **call-in**

phoneme /fó neem/ n. a speech sound that distinguishes one word from another, e.g. the sounds 'd' and 't' in the words 'bid' and 'bit'. A phoneme is the smallest phonetic unit. [Late 19thC. Via French from Greek phōnēma 'sound produced', from phōnein 'to produce a sound', from phōnē 'sound, voice'.]

phonemic /fə neémik, fō-/ adj. 1. OF PHONEMES relating to a phoneme 2. OF DIFFERENT PHONEMES relating to speech sounds that belong to different phonemes rather than being different ways of pronouncing the same phoneme 3. OF PHONEMICS relating to the branch of linguistics that studies phonemes [Mid-20thC] —**phonemically** adv.

phonemics /fə neémiks, fō-/ n. the branch of linguistics involved in the classification and analysis of the phonemes of a language (takes a singular verb) [Mid-20thC] —**phonemicist** /fə neémissist, fō-/ n.

phone phreak n. COMPUT sb who breaks into telephone systems and other secure networks, often for the purpose of making free long-distance telephone calls (slang)

phone sex n. the act of talking in an erotic and explicit way to sb on the telephone for sexual pleasure

phonet. abbr. phonetics

phonetic /fə néttik, fō-/ adj. 1. OF SPEECH SOUNDS belonging to or associated with the sounds of human speech 2. SHOWING PRONUNCIATION representing the sounds of human speech in writing, often with special symbols or unconventional spelling 3. OF PHONETICS relating to the science of phonetics [Early 19thC. Via modern Latin from Greek phōnētikos 'spoken', ultimately from phōnein (see PHONEME).] —**phonetically** adv.

phonetic alphabet n. 1. PHON SYMBOLS SHOWING PRONUNCIATION a set of letters and symbols used to represent the sounds of human speech in writing 2. TELECOM = **NATO Phonetic Alphabet**

phonetician /fónə tísh'n, fónnə-/ n. sb who specializes in the branch of linguistics involved in the study of speech sounds [Mid-19thC]

phonetics /fə néttiks, fō-/ n. (takes a singular verb) 1. STUDY OF SPEECH SOUNDS the scientific study of speech sounds and how they are produced 2. SOUND SYSTEM OF A LANGUAGE the system or pattern of speech sounds used in a particular language [Mid-19thC]

phoney /fóni/, **phony** adj. (-nier, -niest) 1. NOT GENUINE not genuine and used to deceive 2. GIVING A FALSE IMPRESSION putting on a false show of sth such as sincerity or expertise ■ n. (plural **-neys** or **-nies**) SB OR STH PHONEY a phoney person or thing [Late 19thC.

Origin uncertain: possibly an alteration of slang *fawney* 'gilt brass ring used by swindlers', from Irish Gaelic *fáinne* 'ring'.] —**phonily** *adv.* —**phoniness** *n.*

phoney war *n.* a period when enemies are officially at war but not actively engaged in armed conflict, e.g. the period of relative calm at the beginning of World War II

phonic /fónnik/ *adj.* **1. USING PHONICS** using or involving phonics as a method of teaching people to read **2. OF SOUND** associated with sound or the scientific study of sound **3. OF SPEECH SOUNDS** relating to the sounds used in speech [Early 19thC. Formed from Greek *phōnē* 'sound, voice'.] —**phonically** *adv.*

phonics /fónniks/ *n.* (*takes a singular verb*) **1. READING METHOD INVOLVING LETTER RECOGNITION** a method of teaching reading in which people learn to associate letters with the speech sounds they represent, rather than learning to recognize the whole word as a unit **2. ACOUSTICS** acoustics (*archaic*) [Late 17thC. Formed from Greek *phōnē* 'sound, voice'.]

phono- *prefix.* **1.** sound, speech, voice ○ *phonogram* **2.** telephone ○ *phonecard* [From Greek *phōnē* 'sound'. Ultimately from an Indo-European base meaning 'to speak', which is also the ancestor of English *fame, fable, fate,* and *ban.*]

phonocardiogram /fónō kaárdi ə gram/ *n.* a visual record of heart sounds and murmurs made by a phonocardiograph

phonocardiograph /fónō kaárdi ə graaf, -graf/ *n.* an instrument that amplifies heart sounds and converts them into a visual display —**phonocardiographic** /fónō kaárdi ə gráffik/ *adj.* —**phonocardiography** /-óggrəfi/ *n.*

phonochemistry /fónō kémmistri/ *n.* a branch of science and technology dealing with the effect of sound and ultrasonic waves on chemical reactions

phonogram /fónə gram/ *n.* **1. CHARACTER REPRESENTING A WORD OR SOUND** a symbol that represents a word, part of a word, or an individual speech sound **2. LETTER GROUP WITH A PARTICULAR SOUND** a sequence of letters that have the same pronunciation in several different words, e.g. 'ear' in 'earth', 'heard', and 'learn' [Mid-19thC] —**phonogramic** /fónə grámmik/ *adj.* —**phonogramically** /-grámmikli/ *adv.*

phonograph /fónə graaf, fónə graf/ *n. US* a record player [Late 19thC]

phonography /fə nóggrəfi/ *n.* **1. USE OF SYMBOLS FOR SOUNDS** the use of symbols to represent speech sounds in writing **2. SHORTHAND WITH SYMBOLS FOR SOUNDS** a method of writing in shorthand that uses symbols to represent speech sounds —**phonographer** *n.* —**phonographic** /fónə gráffik/ *adj.* —**phonographically** /-gráffikli/ *adv.* —**phonographist** /fə nóggrəfist/ *n.*

phonol. *abbr.* phonology

phonolite /fónə līt/ *n.* a fine-grained light-coloured volcanic rock characterized by the presence of alkali feldspar and nepheline [Early 19thC. Coined from PHONO- + -LITE; from the resonance of the rock when hit with a hammer.] —**phonolitic** /fónə líttik/ *adj.*

phonology /fə nólləji, fō-/ (*plural* **-gies**) *n.* **1. STUDY OF SPEECH SOUNDS** the scientific study of the system or pattern of speech sounds used in a particular language or in language in general **2. SOUND SYSTEM OF A LANGUAGE** the system or pattern of speech sounds used in a particular language —**phonological** /fónə lójjik'l, fónnə-/ *adj.* —**phonologically** /fónə lójjikli/ *adv.* —**phonologist** /fə nólləjist, fō-/ *n.*

phonon /fó non/ *n.* PHYS a quantum of vibrational or acoustic energy in a crystal lattice [Mid-20thC]

phonoreception /fónō ri sépsh'n/ *n.* the perception of or response to high-frequency vibration, especially sound waves

phonoscope /fónə skōp/ *n.* a device that produces a visual representation of the vibrations of sound waves, used especially with musical instruments [Mid-19thC. Originally the name of a device for testing the quality of musical strings.]

phonotactics /fónō táktiks, fónə-/ *n.* the study of the sounds it is possible to put together to form words and parts of words in a language (*takes a singular verb*)

phonotypy /fónə tīpi, fónō-/ *n.* the representing of speech sounds with phonetic symbols in writing or print —**phonotyper** *n.* —**phonotypist** *n.*

phooey /fóo i/ *interj.* used to express contempt, disbelief, disgust, or disappointment (*informal*) [Early 20thC. Partly an alteration of *pfui*. Suggestive of the sound associated with spitting.]

-phore *suffix.* sth that carries ○ *sporophore* [From Greek *-phoros* 'bearing', from *pherein* 'to carry'. Ultimately from an Indo-European word that is also the ancestor of English *bear* and *transfer*.] —**-phorous** *suffix.*

-phoresis *suffix.* transmission ○ *diaphoresis* [From Greek *phorēsis*, which was formed from *phorein*, literally 'to keep carrying', from *pherein* (see -PHORE)]

phosgene /fóss jeen, fóz-/ *n.* a highly toxic colourless gas used as a chemical weapon in World War I and in the manufacture of pesticides, plastics, and dyes. Formula: $COCl_2$. [Early 19thC]

phosgenite /fóssji nīt, fózji-/ *n.* a rare greyish fluorescent crystalline mineral consisting of a carbonate and chloride of lead. Formula: $Pb_2(Cl_2CO_3)$. [Mid-19thC. Formed from PHOSGENE, because the minerals are formed from the same substances as phosgene gas.]

phosph- *prefix.* = **phospho-** (*used before vowels*)

phosphatase /fóssfə tayz, -tayss/ *n.* an enzyme that catalyses the breakdown and synthesis of phosphoric acid esters and the transfer of phosphate groups from these acids to other compounds [Early 20thC. Coined from PHOSPHATE + -ASE.]

phosphate /fóss fayt/ *n.* any salt or ester formed by the reaction of a metal, alcohol, or other radical with phosphoric acid. A tribasic acid, phosphoric acid forms three series of phosphates by replacement of one, two, or all three of its hydrogen ions. [Late 18thC. From French *phosphate*, from *phosphore* 'phosphorus'.] —**phosphatic** /foss fáttik/ *adj.*

phosphate rock *n.* any of several sedimentary rocks that have a naturally high phosphate concentration and are used as fertilizers and in the manufacture of phosphorus compounds

phosphatide /fóssfə tīd/ *n.* BIOCHEM = **phospholipid** —**phosphatidic** /fóssfə tíddik/ *adj.*

phosphatidylcholine /fóssfəti dīl kó leen/ *n.* BIOCHEM = **lecithin** [Mid-20thC. Coined from PHOSPHATIDE + -YL + CHOLINE.]

phosphatidylethanolamine /fóssfəti dīl éthə nóllə meen/ *n.* BIOCHEM = **cephalin** [Mid-20thC. Coined from PHOSPHATIDE + -YL + ETHANOLAMINE.]

phosphatize /fóssfə tīz/ (**-tizes, -tizing, -tized**), **phosphatise** (**-tises, -tising, -tised**) *v.* **1.** *vt.* **TREAT STH WITH PHOSPHATE** to treat sth with phosphoric acid or with a phosphate, typically to protect ferrous metal against corrosion **2.** *vti.* **CHANGE INTO A PHOSPHATE** to convert sth or be converted into a phosphate or phosphates —**phosphatization** /fóssfə tī záysh'n/ *n.*

phosphaturia /fóssfə tyóori ə/ *n.* the presence in the urine of a high concentration of phosphate salts, giving it a cloudy appearance. It is associated with the formation of kidney stones. [Late 19thC. Coined from PHOSPHATE + -URIA.] —**phosphaturic** *adj.*

phosphene /fóss feen/ *n.* a sensation of seeing light caused by pressure or electrical stimulation of the eye [Late 19thC. From modern French *phosphène*, from Greek *phōs* 'light' + *phainein* 'to show'.]

phosphide /fóss fīd/ *n.* any compound of phosphorus with a more electropositive element, e.g. a metal [Mid-19thC]

phosphine /fóss feen/ *n.* a colourless inflammable gas with a fishy smell, used as a pesticide. Formula: PH_3. [Late 19thC]

phosphite /fóss fīt/ *n.* any salt or ester of phosphorous acid [Late 18thC]

phospho- *prefix.* **1.** phosphorus ○ *phosphate* **2.** phosphate ○ *phosphocreatine* [From PHOSPHORUS]

phosphocreatine /fóssfō kreé ə teen/, **phosphocreatin** /-tin/ *n.* an organic acid derived from creatine that is present in muscles and other tissue and is capable of storing and providing energy for muscle contraction. Formula: $C_4H_{10}N_3O_5P$.

phosphofructokinase /fóssfō frúktō kíe nayz, -kí nayz, -kee nayss/ *n.* an enzyme found in cytoplasm that catalyses the transfer of a phosphate group to a fructose compound during the metabolism of glucose

phosphoglucomutase /fóssfō glóokō myóo tayz, -tayss/ *n.* a reversible enzyme found in all living cells that catalyses both the breakdown and the synthesis of glycogen, thus serving a cell's immediate need for energy storage or use

phospholipase /fóssfō lí payz, fóssfó lí payss/ *n.* an enzyme often found in the membrane of a cell that catalyses the hydrolysis of phospholipids

phospholipid /fóssfō líppid/ *n.* a phosphorus-containing lipid that is soluble in organic solvents and is found in the cells of all living tissue, especially in the two-layered cellular membranes

phosphonic acid /foss fónnik-/ *n.* CHEM = **phosphorous acid**

phosphonium /foss fóni əm/ *n.* a univalent radical derived from phosphene. Formula: PH_4. [Late 19thC. Coined from PHOSPHO- + ending of AMMONIUM.]

phosphor /fóssfər/ *n.* a substance that can emit light when irradiated with particles of electromagnetic radiation [Early 17thC. From Latin *phosphorus* (see PHOSPHORUS).]

phosphorate /fóssfə rayt/ (**-ates, -ating, -ated**) *vt.* to treat, combine, or impregnate sth with phosphorus

phosphor bronze *n.* any one of several alloys containing copper, tin, and phosphorus that are resistant to wear and corrosion and are used in bearings, gears, and components exposed to sea water

phosphoresce /fóssfə réss/ (**-resces, -rescing, -resced**) *vi.* to continue to emit light without accompanying heat after exposure to and removal of a source of stimulating radiation

phosphorescence /fóssfə réss'nss/ *n.* the continued emission of light without heat after exposure to and removal of a source of electromagnetic radiation

phosphorescent /fóssfə réss'nt/ *adj.* continuing to emit light after the source of stimulating radiation has been removed —**phosphorescently** *adv.*

phosphoric /foss fórrik/ *adj.* containing phosphorus with a valence state higher than that of the phosphorus ion or radical in an analogous phosphorous compound [Late 18thC]

phosphoric acid *n.* **1. TRANSPARENT SOLID USED AS FERTILIZER** a water-soluble transparent solid acid used as a fertilizer, in soft drinks, pharmaceuticals, and animal feeds, and to rust-proof metals. It is formed by boiling a solution of phosphorus pentoxide in water. Formula: H_3PO_4. **2. ACID FORMED FROM PHOSPHORUS PENTOXIDE** any of the acids formed by the combination of phosphorus pentoxide with water, each having one more oxygen atom than the corresponding phosphorous acid

phosphorism /fóssfərizəm/ *n.* poisoning caused by long-term exposure to phosphorus

phosphorite /fóssfə rīt/ *n.* **1. MINERAL DEPOSIT OF PHOSPHATES** a mineral deposit consisting of apatite and other phosphates **2.** = **phosphate rock** —**phosphoritic** /fóssfə ríttik/ *adj.*

phosphorolysis /fóssfə róllississ/ *n.* a reversible reaction in which the covalent bonds of a molecule are broken by the addition of atoms of phosphoric acid, e.g. during the breakdown of glycogen [Mid-20thC. A blend of PHOSPHORUS or *phosphorylation* + HYDROLYSIS.]

phosphorous /fóssfərəss/ *adj.* relating to phosphorus with a valence state lower than that of the phosphorus ion or radical in an analogous phosphoric compound [Late 18thC. Coined from PHOSPHORUS + -OUS.]

phosphorous acid *n.* **1. WHITE OR YELLOWISH CYSTALLINE SOLID** a white or yellowish cystalline solid that absorbs water from the atmosphere. It is used as a reducing agent and to produce phosphite salts, and is formed by reacting cold water with phosphorus pentoxide. Formula: H_3PO_3. **2. DIBASIC ACID FORMED FROM PHOSPHORUS PENTOXIDE** any of the acids formed by the combination of phosphorus pentoxide with water, each having one less oxygen atom than the corresponding phosphoric acid

phosphorus /fóssfərəss/ *n.* a phosphorescent substance or object [Early 17thC. Via modern Latin from Greek *phōsphoros* 'morning star', literally 'light-bringing', from *phōs* 'light'.]

phosphorus pentoxide, **phosphorus oxide** *n.* a flammable hygroscopic white solid formed by burning phosphorus in air and used primarily to manufacture orthophosphoric acid by reacting it with water. Formula: P_2O_5.

phosphoryl /fóssfəril/ *n.* a chemical group, usually with a valence of three, consisting of one phosphorus atom and one oxygen atom

phosphorylase /foss fórri layz, -layss/ *n.* an enzyme usually found in the cytoplasm of a cell that catalyses the phosphorolysis of a molecule such as glycogen and the production of organic phosphates

phosphorylate /foss fórri layt/ (-ates, -ating, -ated) *vt.* to add a phosphate group to an organic molecule to produce an organic phosphate —**phosphorylation** /fóss forri láysh'n/ *n.* —**phosphorylative** /foss fórrilətiv/ *adj.*

phot /fōt, fot/ *n.* a unit of illumination in the centimetre-gram-second system equal to one lumen per square centimetre [Late 19thC. Via French from Greek *phōt*-, stem of *phōs* 'light' (See PHOS-).]

phot. *abbr.* 1. photograph 2. photographer 3. photographic 4. photography

phot- *prefix.* = photo- (used before vowels)

photic /fótik/ *adj.* 1. OF LIGHT relating to light, especially when produced by living organisms 2. ECOL OF THE OCEAN DEPTH WHERE PHOTOSYNTHESIS OCCURS relating to or used to describe the area of the ocean where light penetrates and photosynthesis occurs [Mid-19thC. Formed from PHOT.]

photo /fótō/ *n.* (*plural* -tos) = photograph ■ *vt.* (-tos, -toing, -toed) PHOTOGRAPH SB OR STH to take a photograph or photographs of sb or sth [Mid-19thC. Shortening.]

photo- *prefix.* 1. light, radiant energy ○ *photochemistry* 2. photographic ○ *photodrama* 3. photoelectric ○ *photocurrent* [From Greek *phōt*-, the stem of *phōs* 'light'. Ultimately from an Indo-European base meaning 'to shine', which is also the ancestor of English *beacon*, *banner*, and *phenomenon*.]

photoactinic /fótō ak tínnik/ *adj.* emitting radiation similar to visible and ultraviolet light in its chemical effects on such substances as photographic emulsions

photoactive /fótō áktiv/ *adj.* exhibiting a reaction to electromagnetic radiation, especially visible light, either by chemical reaction or photoelectrically

photoautotroph /fótō áwtō trof/ *n.* an organism that derives its energy exclusively from light and uses it to synthesize food —**photoautotrophic** /fótō áwtō tróffik/ *adj.* —**photoautotrophically** /-tróffikli/ *adv.*

photobiology /fótō bī ólləji/ *n.* a branch of biology concerned with the interaction of living organisms with light —**photobiological** /fótō bī ə lójjik'l/ *adj.* —**photobiologist** /fótō bī ólləjist/ *n.*

photobiotic /fótō bī óttik/ *adj.* used to describe organisms that need light in order to live and grow

photo call *n.* an occasion when celebrities pose for the press and other photographers, usually for publicity purposes

photocatalysis /fótō kə tállississ/ *n.* the acceleration or deceleration of the speed at which a chemical reaction occurs, caused by electromagnetic radiation and especially visible light

photocathode /fótō káthōd/ *n.* an electrode that emits electrons when exposed to electromagnetic radiation such as light. Photocathodes are used in television and digital cameras and photoelectric cells.

photo CD *n.* COMPUT a compact disc that stores images from photographs that can be displayed on a computer or television screen

photocell /fótō sel/ *n.* = photoelectric cell

photochemical smog /fótō kémmik'l-/ *n.* air pollution caused by the effect of strong sunlight on nitrogen

dioxide and hydrocarbons emitted by motor vehicles, creating a harmful haze of minute droplets in the air

photochemistry /fótō kémmistri/ *n.* a branch of chemistry that studies the effect of radiation, especially of visible and ultraviolet light, on chemical reactions and of the emission of radiation by chemical reactions —**photochemical** *adj.* —**photochemically** /-kémmikli/ *adv.* —**photochemist** *n.*

photochromic /fótō krómik/ *adj.* changing colour or becoming darker or lighter in colour as light increases or decreases in intensity

photocoagulation /fótō kō ággyoō láysh'n/ *n.* the use of a high-energy light source such as a laser to harden tissue for surgical repair, especially in eye injuries

photocomposition /fótō kómpə zísh'n/ *n.* = filmsetting —**photocompose** /fótō kəm pōz/ *vt.* —**photocomposer** /-pōzər/ *n.*

photoconduction /fótō kən dúksh'n/ *n.* the conduction of electricity resulting from the absorption of electromagnetic radiation, especially visible light

photoconductivity /fótō kón duk tívvəti/ *n.* an increase in the electrical conductivity of a substance on exposure to electromagnetic radiation, especially visible light —**photoconductive** /fótō kən dúktiv/ *adj.* —**photoconductor** /-dúktər/ *n.*

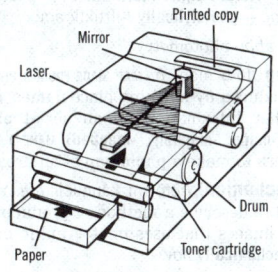

Photocopier

photocopier /fótə kopi ər/ *n.* a machine that uses a photographic process to produce an almost instant copy of sth printed, written, or drawn

photocopy /fótə kopi/ *n.* (*plural* -ies) PHOTOGRAPHIC REPRODUCTION OF A TEXT OR PICTURE a copy of sth printed, written, or drawn that is produced almost instantly by a photographic process in a machine designed for this purpose ■ *vti.* (-ies, -ying, -ied) MAKE PHOTOCOPY to make a photocopy of sth, or be photocopied

photocurrent /fótō kurrənt/ *n.* an electric current that is produced by and varies with the intensity of illumination. The current is a result of photoconductivity or of the photoelectric or photovoltaic effect.

photodecomposition /fótō dee kómpə zísh'n/ *n.* the breakdown of a chemical compound into simpler substances by means of incident electromagnetic energy, especially visible light

photodegradable /fótō di gráydəb'l/ *adj.* able to be decomposed into simpler substances through prolonged exposure to incident electromagnetic energy, especially ultraviolet light

photodiode /fótō dí ōd/ *n.* a semiconductor device in which the flow of current is controlled by the intensity of light and which can therefore be used to detect light

photodisintegration /fótō diss ínti gráysh'n/ *n.* the ejection of a proton, neutron, or other elementary particle from an atomic nucleus as a result of its absorption of a photon, usually in the form of gamma radiation —**photodisintegrate** /fótō diss íntigrayt/ *vti.*

photoduplicate /fótō dyoópli kayt/ *vt.* (-cates, -cating, -cated) MAKE A PHOTOCOPY OF STH to make a photocopy of sth ■ *n.* PHOTOCOPY a copy of sth made using a photocopier —**photoduplication** /fótō dyoópli káysh'n/ *n.*

photodynamic /fótō dī námmik/ *adj.* 1. BIOL OF PHOTODYNAMICS relating to photodynamics or to the energy of light 2. BIOL INVOLVING AN ADVERSE REACTION TO LIGHT bringing about or enhancing the toxic effects of some wavelengths of light, especially ultraviolet, on living tissue 3. MED OF A LASER CANCER TREATMENT relating to or used to describe a cancer treatment in which the drug used is activated by a laser beam —**photodynamically** *adv.*

photodynamics /fótō dī námmiks/ *n.* a branch of biology dealing with the effects of light on living organisms (*takes a singular verb*)

photoelectric /fótō i léktrik/, **photoelectrical** /-trik'l/ *adj.* relating to any electrical effects that are due to the action of electromagnetic radiation, especially visible light —**photoelectrically** *adv.* —**photoelectricity** /fótō ilek tríssiti, -éllek-/ *n.*

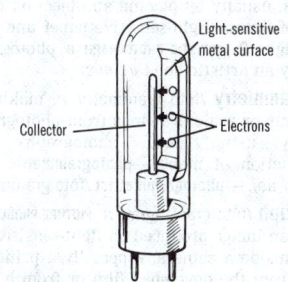

Photoelectric cell

photoelectric cell *n.* a solid-state device sensitive to varying levels of light that is used to generate or control an electric current, e.g. in burglar alarms, smoke detectors, and exposure meters

photoelectric effect *n.* the emission of electrons from a substance exposed to electromagnetic radiation

photoelectron /fótō i lék tron/ *n.* an electron released from the surface of a substance that has been struck by a photon of electromagnetic radiation

photoemission /fótō i mísh'n/ *n.* the release of electrons from a substance by incident electromagnetic radiation —**photoemissive** /fótō i míssiv/ *adj.*

photoengrave /fótō in gráyv/ (-graves, -graving, -graved) *vt.* to make a copy of sth using photoengraving —**photoengraver** *n.*

photoengraving /fótō ingráyving/ *n.* 1. PROCESS OF ETCHING A PRINTING PLATE the process of making a printing plate by photographing an image onto a metal plate and then etching the image 2. PRINTING PLATE MADE BY PHOTOENGRAVING a printing plate made by photographing an image onto a metal 3. PRINT MADE BY PHOTOENGRAVING a print made using a photoengraved printing plate

photoessay /fótō éssay/, **photo essay** *n.* = photo story

photo finish *n.* 1. RACE RESULT DETERMINED FROM A PHOTOGRAPH the end of a race in which two or more contestants are so close that the result must be determined from a photograph taken as they cross the finish line 2. VERY CLOSE CONTEST a race or competition won by a very small margin

Photofit /fótō fit/ *tdmk.* a trademark for a way of constructing a photograph of sb using photographs of individual facial features arranged to fit a description closely. This method is often used to try to identify criminals.

photoflash /fótō flash/ *n.* = flashbulb

photoflood /fótō flud/ *n.* a very bright incandescent lamp used in photography and filming

photofluorogram /fótō floorə gram/ *n.* a photograph of an image produced using X-rays

photofluorography /fótō floor róggrəfi/ *n.* a technique that photographs an X-ray image onto a fluorescent screen for diagnostic purposes [Mid-20thC] —**photofluorographic** *adj.*

photog /fə tóg/ *n.* a photographer (*informal*)

photog. *abbr.* 1. photograph 2. photographic 3. photography

photogelatin process /fṓtō jéllətin-/ *n.* = **collotype**

photogene /fṓtō jeen/ *n.* = **afterimage** [Mid-19thC]

photogenic /fṓtə jénnik/ *adj.* **1.** LOOKING ATTRACTIVE IN PHOTOGRAPHS tending to look good in photographs **2.** BIOL PRODUCING LIGHT used to describe an organism that produces its own light, especially by phosphorescence **3.** CAUSED BY LIGHT caused or aggravated by light, e.g. an epileptic episode brought about by blinking lights [Mid-19thC. Coined from PHOTO- + -GENIC.] —**photogenically** *adv.*

photogeology /fṓtō ji óllәji/ *n.* the study and identification of landforms and other geologic features by means of aerial and satellite photographs —**photogeologic** /fṓtō jee ə lójjik/ *adj.* —**photogeologist** /fṓtōji óllәjist/ *n.*

photogram /fṓtə gram/ *n.* **1.** PHOTOGRAPHIC IMAGE LIKE A SHADOW a photographic image produced without a camera, usually by placing an object on or near a piece of film or light-sensitive paper and exposing it to light **2.** ARTISTIC PHOTOGRAPH a photograph, especially an artistic one (*archaic*)

photogrammetry /fṓtō grámmətri/ *n.* making measurements or scale drawings from photographs, especially using aerial photography in the construction of maps —**photogrammetric** /fṓtō grə méttrik/ *adj.* —**photogrammetrist** /fṓtō grámmətrist/ *n.*

photograph /fṓtə graaf, -graf/ *n.* PICTURE PRODUCED WITH A CAMERA an image produced on light-sensitive film or array inside a camera, especially a print or slide made from the developed film or from a digitized array image, or a reproduction in a newspaper, magazine, or book ■ *v.* (**-graphs, -graphing, -graphed**) **1.** *vti.* TAKE A PHOTOGRAPH OF SB OR STH to produce an image of sth by pointing a camera at it and allowing light briefly to fall on the film inside **2.** *vi.* BE PHOTOGRAPHED WITH A PARTICULAR RESULT to be able to be photographed, or to have a particular quality or appearance in a photograph ○ *Scenes like this photograph best in bright sunlight.* [Mid-19thC]

photographer /fə tóggrəfər/ *n.* sb who takes photographs as a profession, hobby, or art form

photographic /fṓtə gráffik/ *adj.* **1.** OF PHOTOGRAPHY relating to, used in, or produced by photography **2.** LIKE A PHOTOGRAPH as accurate and detailed as a photograph —**photographically** *adv.*

photographic magnitude *n.* the magnitude of a star determined by measuring its size on a photographic plate. Depending on the colour of the star, photographic magnitude and visual magnitude can differ because the eye and standard photographic plates have different colour sensitivities.

photographic memory *n.* the ability to recall information, especially visual images, with great accuracy and clarity

photography /fə tóggrəfi/ *n.* **1.** PRODUCING PICTURES WITH A CAMERA the art, hobby, or profession of taking photographs, and developing and printing the film or processing the digitized array image **2.** USING LIGHT TO MAKE PICTURES the process of recording images by exposing light-sensitive film or array to light or other forms of radiation

photogravure /fṓtō grə vyóor/ *n.* the process of using photography to make a printing plate with an image engraved into it [Late 19thC. From French, formed from *photo* + *gravure* 'engraving', from *graver* 'to engrave'.]

photoheliograph /fṓtō heéli ə graaf, -graf/ *n.* = **heliograph** *n.* 2

photoinduced /fṓtō in dyóost/ *adj.* initiated through exposure to light —**photoinduction** /fṓtō in dúksh'n/ *n.* —**photoinductive** /-dúktiv/ *adj.*

photointerpretation /fṓtō in túr pri táysh'n/ *n.* the science of identifying objects in photographs, especially in order to determine their potential military or topographic importance —**photointerpreter** /fṓtō in túrpritər/ *n.*

photoionization /fṓtō ī ə nī záysh'n/ *n.* the removal of one or more electrons from an atom or molecule by absorption of a photon of electromagnetic radiation, especially visible or ultraviolet light. The free electrons in the ionosphere are believed to be a product of molecular absorption of ultraviolet radiation from the Sun. —**photoionize** /fṓtō ī ə nīz/ *vti.*

photojournalism /fṓtō júrnəlizəm/ *n.* form of journalism in which photographs play a more important role than the accompanying text —**photojournalist** *n.* —**photojournalistic** /-lístik/ *adj.*

photokinesis /fṓtō ki neéssiss, -kī-/ *n.* movement of an organism when stimulated by light [Early 20thC] —**photokinetic** /-ki néttik, -kī-/ *adj.* —**photokinetically** /-néttikli/ *adv.*

photolithograph /fṓtō líthə graaf, fṓtō líthə graf/ *n.* a picture made by using photolithography

photolithography /fṓtō li thóggrəfi/ *n.* **1.** LITHOGRAPHY USING PHOTOGRAPHY the process of creating lithographs using photographic methods **2.** PHOTOGRAPHIC TRANSFER OF PATTERNS FOR ETCHING a process of producing integrated circuits and printed circuit boards by photographing the circuit pattern on a photosensitive substrate and then chemically etching away the background —**photolithographer** *n.* —**photolithographic** /fṓtō líthə gráffik/ *adj.* —**photolithographically** /-gráffikli/ *adv.*

photoluminescence /fṓtō lóomi néss'nss/ *n.* the emission of light from a substance as a result of the absorption of electromagnetic radiation. The frequency of the light emitted is lower than that absorbed. [Late 19thC] —**photoluminescent** /fṓtō lóomi néss'nt/ *adj.*

photolysis /fō tólləsiss/ *n.* the irreversible decomposition of a chemical compound as a result of the absorption of electromagnetic radiation, especially visible light [Late 20thC] —**photolytic** /fṓtō líttik/ *adj.* —**photolytically** /-líttikli/ *adv.*

photom. *abbr.* photometry

photomap /fṓtō map/ *n.* MAP MADE FROM A PHOTOGRAPH a map produced by marking place names, grid lines, and other information on an aerial photograph ■ *vti.* (**-maps, -mapping, -mapped**) MAKE A MAP FROM A PHOTOGRAPH to make a photomap of an area

photomechanical /fṓtō mi kánnik'l/ *adj.* relating to or used to describe a method of producing printed text or images that uses photographic methods —**photomechanically** *adv.*

photometer /fō tómmitər/ *n.* an instrument for measuring the luminous intensity of light sources by comparison with a standard source [Late 18thC]

photometry /fō tómmətri/ *n.* **1.** MEASUREMENT OF LIGHT the measurement of the luminous intensities of visible light sources. This is sometimes expanded to include near-infrared and near-ultraviolet light. **2.** BRANCH OF PHYSICS the branch of physics concerned with the measurement of the intensity of light [Early 19thC] —**photometric** /fṓtə méttrik/ *adj.* —**photometrically** /-méttrikli/ *adv.* —**photometrist** /fō tómmətrist/ *n.*

photomicrograph /fṓtō míkrə graaf, -graf/ *n.* a photograph made of sth seen through a microscope —**photomicrographic** /fṓtō míkrə gráffik/ *adj.* —**photomicrography** /fṓtō mī króggrəfi/ *n.*

photomontage /fṓtō mon taázh/ *n.* **1.** MAKING PICTURES FROM PARTS OF PHOTOGRAPHS the technique of combining a number of photographs or parts of photographs to form a composite picture, used especially in art and advertising **2.** PICTURE COMBINING PARTS OF PHOTOGRAPHS a composite picture made up of many photographs or parts of photographs, used especially in art and advertising

photomosaic /fṓtō mō záy ik/ *n.* a large picture made up of many photographs, e.g. one combining aerial photographs to produce a detailed picture of an area

photomultiplier /fṓtō múlti plī ər/, **photomultiplier tube** *n.* an evacuated electronic device used to convert low-intensity electromagnetic radiation, especially visible light, into an electrical current, and to amplify this current significantly

photomural /fṓtō myóorəl/ *n.* a large picture decorating a wall, made up of one or more photographs or parts of photographs applied directly to the surface of the wall

photon /fṓ ton/ *n.* a quantum of visible light or other form of electromagnetic radiation demonstrating both particle and wave properties. A photon has neither mass nor electric charge but possesses energy and momentum. [Early 20thC] —**photonic** /fō tónnik/ *adj.*

photonegative /fṓtō néggətiv/ *adj.* **1.** PHYS SHOWING DECREASING CONDUCTIVITY AS LIGHT INCREASES used to describe a conductive material whose electrical conductivity decreases in response to increasing illumination **2.** BIOL MOVING AWAY FROM LIGHT used to describe organisms that move away from a source of light

photonuclear /fṓtō nyóokli ər/ *adj.* relating to a nuclear reaction caused by the absorption of a photon, usually in the form of gamma radiation, by an atomic nucleus

photo opportunity, **photo op** *n.* an opportunity for the media to photograph a politician or other public figure doing sth newsworthy, especially when this is deliberately staged to produce favourable publicity

photoperiod /fṓtō peéri əd/ *n.* the daily cycle of light and darkness that affects the behaviour and physiological functions of organisms —**photoperiodic** /fṓtō péeri óddik/ *adj.* —**photoperiodically** /-óddikli/ *adv.*

photoperiodism /fṓtō peéri ədizəm/ *n.* the influence of the daily cycle of light and darkness on the physiology and behaviour of an organism [Early 20thC]

photophilous /fō tóffələss/ *adj.* used to describe an organism such as a plant that grows well in strong light [Early 20thC]

photophobia /fṓtō fṓbi ə/ *n.* **1.** OPHTHALMOL SENSITIVITY TO LIGHT very low tolerance of the eye for light, sometimes a symptom of disease or migraine **2.** PSYCHIAT FEAR OF LIGHT an irrational fear and avoidance of light or lighted spaces

photophobic /fṓtō fṓbik/ *adj.* **1.** OPHTHALMOL AFFECTED BY PHOTOPHOBIA relating to or having a condition in which the eye has very low tolerance to light **2.** PSYCHIAT HAVING A FEAR OF LIGHT being abnormally afraid of light **3.** BIOL GROWING WELL IN REDUCED LIGHT used to describe an organism such as a plant that grows well in reduced light

photophore /fṓtə fawr/ *n.* a luminous light organ on many deep-sea and some nocturnal fish, squids, and shrimps [Late 19thC]

photophosphorylation /fṓtō fóss fórri láysh'n/ *n.* the process in photosynthesis that converts light energy to stored energy in plants and bacteria

photopia /fō tṓpi ə/ *n.* normal vision during daylight, when the activity of the cones in the retina enables the eye to perceive colour [Early 20thC] —**photopic** /fō tóppik, fō tṓpik/ *adj.*

photopolymer /fṓtō póllimər/ *n.* a light-sensitive plastic whose physical properties change on exposure to visible or ultraviolet light

photopositive /fṓtō pózzətiv/ *adj.* **1.** PHYS SHOWING INCREASING CONDUCTIVITY AS LIGHT INCREASES used to describe a conductive material whose electrical conductivity increases in response to increasing illumination **2.** BIOL MOVING TOWARDS LIGHT used to describe organisms that move towards a light source

photorealism /fṓtō reé əlizəm/ *n.* an artistic style, e.g. in painting or sculpture, that produces an accurate and detailed representation of the subject without attempting to conceal any unattractive aspects —**photorealist** *adj.*, *n.* —**photorealistic** /-lístik/ *adj.*

photoreception /fṓtō ri sépsh'n/ *n.* BIOL the perception, absorption, and use of light, e.g. for vision in animals or photosynthesis in plants —**photoreceptive** *adj.*

photoreceptor /fṓtō rə séptər/ *n.* a cell or organ that responds to light. Simple ones may sense only changes in light intensity while more complex ones such as the eye may also form images of objects in the visual field.

photoreconnaissance /fṓtō ri kónniss'nss/ *n.* reconnaissance undertaken using cameras, usually from an aircraft or drone

photoresist /fṓtō ri zist, -zíst/ *n.* a photosensitive material that is applied to a surface, exposed to visible or ultraviolet light, and developed prior to chemical etching during the photolithographic process

photorespiration /fótō respi ráysh'n/ *n.* the oxidation of carbohydrates in plants with the release of carbon dioxide during photosynthesis

photosensitive /fótō sénssətiv/ *adj.* reacting to incident electromagnetic radiation, especially visible, infrared, and ultraviolet light —**photosensitivity** /fótō sénssə tívvəti/ *n.*

photosensitize /fótō sénssə tīz/ (**-tizes, -tizing, -tized**), **photosensitise** (**-tises, -tising, -tised**) *vt.* to increase the sensitivity of an organism or substance to electromagnetic radiation, especially visible light —**photosensitization** /fótō sénssətī záysh'n/ *n.* —**photosensitizer** /fótō sénssə tīzər/ *n.*

photosphere /fótə sfeer/ *n.* the intensely bright gaseous outer layer of a star, especially the Sun. Sunspots and faculae are both features of the photosphere. [Mid-17thC. The word originally meant 'orb of light' and acquired its more technical meaning in the mid-19thC.] —**photospheric** /fótə sférrik/ *adj.*

Photostat /fótō stat/ *tdmk.* a trademark for a kind of photocopier [Early 20thC]

photo story *n.* a collection of photographs in a magazine or book, often accompanied by a short commentary, that tells a story

photosynthesis /fótō sínthəssiss/ *n.* a process by which green plants and other organisms produce simple carbohydrates from carbon dioxide and hydrogen, using energy that chlorophyll or other organic cellular pigments absorb from radiant sources [Late 19thC] —**photosynthetic** /fótō sin théttik/ *adj.* —**photosynthetically** /-théttikli/ *adv.*

photosynthesize /fótō sínthə sīz/ (**-sizes, -sizing, -sized**), **photosynthesise** (**-sises, -sising, -sised**) *vti.* to produce carbohydrates and oxygen by photosynthesis [Early 20thC. Formed from PHOTOSYNTHESIS.]

phototaxis /fótō táksiss/, **phototaxy** /fótō táksi/ *n.* movement of an organism either towards or away from a source of light [Late 19thC] —**phototactic** /-táktik/ *adj.* —**phototactically** /-táktikli/ *adv.*

phototherapy /fótō thérrəpi/, **phototherapeutics** /fótō thérrə pyóotiks/ *n.* the use of light of particular wavelengths, especially ultraviolet light, in the treatment of disease —**phototherapeutic** /fótō thérrə pyóotik/ *adj.*

phototoxic /fótō tóksik/ *adj.* making the skin unusually sensitive to and subject to damage by light, e.g. by sunburn —**phototoxicity** /fótō tok síssəti/ *n.*

phototransistor /fótō tran zístər/ *n.* a light-sensitive junction transistor that amplifies the base current as the illumination increases

phototrophic /fótō trófik, -tróffik/ *adj.* used to describe organisms that can utilize light as a source of energy —**phototroph** /fótō trof/ *n.*

phototropism /fótō trópizəm/ *n.* the tendency of an organism to grow towards or away from a source of light [Late 19thC. Coined from Greek *tropikos* 'relating to turning', from *tropē* 'turn'.]

phototropy /fótō trópi/ *n.* a property of some solids whereby they change colour in relation to the wavelength of the incident electromagnetic radiation, especially visible light [Early 20thC]

phototube /fótō tyoob/ *n.* an electron tube that uses a cathode to convert visible light into electrical current at a rate proportional to the intensity of the illumination

phototypography /fótō tī póggrəfi/ *n.* a printing process that uses photography —**phototypographical** /fótō tīpə gráffik'l/ *adj.* —**phototypographically** /-gráffikli/ *adv.*

photovoltaic /fótō vol táy ik/ *adj.* able to generate a current or voltage when exposed to visible light or other electromagnetic radiation

photovoltaic cell *n.* a type of photoelectric cell that detects and measures light intensity using the potential difference that arises between dissimilar materials when they are exposed to electromagnetic radiation

photovoltaic effect *n.* the production of a potential difference across the junction of dissimilar materials or in a nonhomogeneous semiconductor material by the absorption of visible light or other electromagnetic radiation

phr. *abbr.* phrase

phrasal /fráyz'l/ *adj.* consisting of or belonging to a phrase [Late 19thC] —**phrasally** *adv.*

phrasal verb *n.* a verb followed by an adverb, a preposition, or both, used with an idiomatic meaning that is often quite different from the literal meaning of the individual words. Examples include 'put up with' meaning 'tolerate' and 'stand for' meaning 'represent'.

phrase /frayz/ *n.* **1.** GRAM GRAMMATICAL UNIT a string of words that form a grammatical unit, usually within a clause or sentence **2.** LANG FIXED EXPRESSION a string of words that are used together with an idiomatic meaning **3.** SHORT UTTERANCE a short expression **4.** LITERAT, POETRY WORDS SPOKEN AS GROUP a group of words that form a unit of meaning or rhythm in prose or poetry, often separated by a punctuation in writing and by pauses in speech **5.** MUSIC MELODIC DIVISION a sequence of notes that form a unit of melody within a piece of music **6.** DANCE PART OF A CHOREOGRAPHIC PATTERN a short sequence of dance steps or movements ■ *v.* (**phrases, phrasing, phrased**) **1.** *vt.* EXPRESS IN PARTICULAR WAY to express sth with a particular pattern of words in speech or writing **2.** *vt.* SEPARATE TEXT INTO PHRASES to show clearly which groups of words belong together when reading sth aloud or making a speech, usually by pausing in appropriate places or by stress and intonation **3.** *vti.* MUSIC SEPARATE MUSIC INTO PHRASES to show clearly which sequences of notes belong together in a piece of music, especially when performing it [Mid-16thC. Via Latin from Greek *phrasis* 'speech, way of speaking', from *phrazein* 'to show, explain' (source of English *paraphrase* and *phraseology*).]

phrase book *n.* a book of useful words and phrases in a foreign language with translations for visitors to a country or region where that language is spoken

phrasemaker /fráyz maykər/ *n.* sb who produces impressive phrases in speech or writing —**phrasemaking** *n.*

phrase marker *n.* a representation of the structure of a sentence, usually in the form of a tree diagram

phraseogram /fráyzi ə gram/ *n.* a symbol used to represent a particular phrase in shorthand

phraseograph /fráyzi ə graaf, -graf/ *n.* a phrase that is or can be represented by a symbol, usually in shorthand

phraseology /fráyzi óllǝji/ *n.* **1.** SET OF PHRASES the phrases used in a particular sphere of activity **2.** USE OF LANGUAGE the way words and phrases are chosen or used [Mid-17thC. From modern Latin *phraseologia* from, ultimately, Greek *phrasis* 'speech' (see PHRASE).] —**phraseological** /fráyzi ə lójjik'l/ *adj.* —**phraseologist** /fráyzi óllǝjist/ *n.*

phrase-structure grammar *n.* a grammar that describes the structure and linear sequence of a sentence in terms of the phrases of which it is made up

phrasing /fráyzing/ *n.* **1.** COMBINATION OF WORDS the way words are chosen and put together for a particular purpose, or the words themselves **2.** MUSIC GROUPING OF NOTES the way sequences of notes are grouped together to form units of melody in a piece of music, especially when it is played or sung

phratry /fráytri/ (*plural* **-tries**) *n.* **1.** RELATED GROUP OF CLANS a group of clans claiming descent from a common ancestor **2.** KINSHIP GROUP a kinship group in ancient Greece [Mid-19thC. From Greek *phratria*, from *phratēr* 'clansman, brother'. Ultimately from an Indo-European word that is also the ancestor of English *brother*, *fraternal*, and *friar*.] —**phratric** *adj.*

phreak /freek/ (**phreaks, phreaking, phreaked**) *vi.* to use computer and telecommunications skills to illegally break into a telephone system in order to make free long-distance calls [Late 20thC. Alteration of FREAK on the model of PHONE.]

phreaking /fréeking/ *n.* using computer and telecommunications skills to break into the telephone system to make free long-distance calls (*slang*) [Late 20thC. From PHONE PHREAK. Variation of FREAK, on the model of PHONE.]

phreatic /fri áttik/ *adj.* **1.** OF SOIL BELOW WATER LEVEL relating to or used to describe the soil or rock below the water level, where all the pores and intergranular spaces are full of water **2.** CAUSED BY HEATED GROUNDWATER relating to an explosion caused by groundwater coming into contact with ascending magma, e.g. in a volcano [Late 19thC. Formed from Greek *phreat-*, stem of *phrear* 'well, cistern'. Ultimately from an Indo-European word meaning 'to boil, bubble', which is also the source of English *brew* and *fervour*.]

phren. *abbr.* phrenology

phrenic /frénnik/ *adj.* **1.** ANAT OF THE DIAPHRAGM belonging to or supplying the diaphragm **2.** OF THE MIND belonging to or associated with the mind [Early 18thC. From French *phrénique*, from Greek *phrēn* (see -PHRENIA).]

phrenol. *abbr.* phrenology

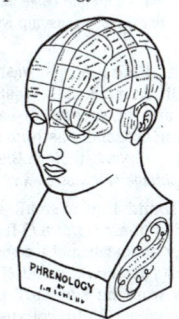

Phrenology

phrenology /frə nóllǝji/ *n.* the study of the bumps on the outside of the skull, based on the now discredited theory that these bumps reflect sb's character [Early 19thC] —**phrenological** /frénnə lójjik'l/ *adj.* —**phrenologist** /frə nóllǝjist/ *n.*

Phrygia /fríjji ə/ ancient country in Asia Minor, in present-day west-central Turkey. It reached the height of its importance in the 8th century BC, and was conquered by Croesus, king of Lydia, in the 6th century BC.

Phrygian /fríjji ən/ *n.* **1.** PEOPLES SB FROM ANCIENT PHRYGIA sb who was born in or was a citizen of ancient Phrygia **2.** LANG EXTINCT LANGUAGE OF ANCIENT PHRYGIA an extinct language spoken in ancient Phrygia, usually classified as belonging to the Anatolian branch of Indo-European languages —**Phrygian** *adj.*

Phrygian cap *n.* = liberty cap [*Phrygian* from the fact that the cap was worn by the ancient Phrygians]

PHS *abbr.* Public Health Service

phthalein /tháy leen, tháy li in, thálleen, tháli in/ *n.* an organic dye obtained by reacting phthalic anhydride with a phenol [Late 19thC. Formed from PHTHALIC ACID.]

phthalic acid /thállik-/ *n.* one of three isomers obtained by the oxidation of benzene derivatives and used in the manufacture of dyes, perfumes, pharmaceuticals, and synthetic fibres. Formula: $C_6H_4(CO_2H)_2$. [*Phthalic*, formed from a shortening of NAPHTHALENE]

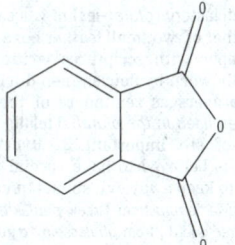

Phthalic anhydride

phthalic anhydride *n.* a white crystalline organic compound derived from naphthalene and used in the manufacture of dyes, insecticides, and plastics. Formula: $C_6H_4(CO)_2O$.

phthalocyanine /thállō sí ə neen, tháy lō-/ *n.* **1.** BRIGHT GREENISH-BLUE PIGMENT a bright greenish-blue crystalline compound derived from phthalic anhydride and used as a pigment, coating for CD-ROMs, and as an anti-cancer agent. Formula: $(C_6H_4C_2N)_4N_4H_2$. **2.** BLUE OR GREEN PIGMENTS a blue or green pigment developed as a metal-substituted form of phthalocyanine and used in enamels, plastics, printing inks, wallpaper, and linoleum

phthiriasis /thi rí əssiss/ *n.* an infestation of the pubic hair of human beings with lice whose bite can irritate the skin [Late 16thC. Via Latin from Greek *phtheiriasis*, from *phtheirian* 'to be infested with lice', from *phtheir* 'louse'.]

phthisic /thí sik, tí sik/ *n.* = phthisis ■ *adj.* **phthisic, phthisical** RELATING TO PHTHISIS relating to or having phthisis [14thC. Via Old French *tisike*, later *ptisique* from, ultimately, Greek *phthisikos* 'consumptive', from *phthisis* (see PHTHISIS).]

phthisis /thíssiss, tíssiss/ *n.* **1.** WASTING DISEASE any disease or condition marked by wasting of the body **2.** LUNG DISEASE any of several diseases of the respiratory system, especially asthma or tuberculosis (*archaic*) [Mid-16thC. Via Latin from Greek *phthisis* 'consumption', from *phthinein* 'to waste away'.]

phut /fut/ *n.* a sound like a small explosion or a sudden expulsion of air (*informal*) [Late 19thC. Origin uncertain: perhaps an imitation of the sound of a burst of air, or from Hindi *phat* 'crack, sound of a slap'.] ◇ **go phut 1.** to stop working suddenly or break down completely (*informal*) **2.** to collapse or come to nothing (*informal*)

phyco- *prefix.* relating to seaweed or algae [From Greek *phukos* 'seaweed']

phycocyanin /fíkō sí ənin/ *n.* a protein pigment in blue-green algae

phycoerythrin /fíkō érrithrin/ *n.* a red protein pigment in red algae

phycology /fī kólləji/ *n.* = algology —**phycological** /fíkə lójjik'l/ *adj.* —**phycologist** /fī kólləjist/ *n.*

phycomycete /fíkō mí seet, fíkō mī seét/ *n.* a mould resembling algae. Class: Phycomycetes. [Mid-20thC. Ultimately from Greek *phukos* 'seaweed' + *mukētes*, plural of *mukēs* 'fungus', from its supposed resemblance to algae.] —**phycomycetous** /fíkō mī seétəss/ *adj.*

phyl- *prefix.* = phylo- (used before vowels)

phyla plural of **phylum**

Phylactery

phylactery /fi láktəri/ (*plural* -ies) *n.* **1.** JUDAISM JEWISH AID TO PRAYER either of two small leather boxes containing slips of paper with scriptures written on them, traditionally worn by Jewish men during morning weekday prayers as reminders of their religious duties (*often used in the plural*) ◊ tefillin **2.** REMINDER a reminder of sth important **3.** AMULET sth worn because it is believed to have special powers, e.g. the power to keep away evil spirits (*archaic*) [14thC. Via Latin *phylacterium* from Greek *phulaktērion* 'amulet', from *phulaktēr* 'guard', from *phulassein* 'to guard'.]

phyle /fí li/ (*plural* -lae /fí lī/) *n.* any of a number of tribes or clans into which some peoples of ancient Greece were divided. The phylae formed political and administrative units within the large city-states. [Mid-19thC. From Greek *phulē* 'tribe'.] —**phylic** *adj.*

phyletic /fī léttik/ *adj.* relating to the hereditary descent of a species or its evolutionary de-

velopment [Late 19thC. From Greek *phuletikos*, from *phulē* 'tribe'.] —**phyletically** *adv.*

phyll- *prefix.* = phyllo- (used before vowels)

-phyll *suffix.* leaf ○ *microphyll* [From Greek *phyllon* (see PHYLLO-)] —**phyllous** *suffix.*

phyllid /fíllid/ *n.* a moss or liverwort leaf

phyllite /fíllīt/ *n.* a fine-grained metamorphic rock with a distinctive shiny surface, containing large quantities of mica and resembling slate or schist [Early 19thC. Coined from Greek *phullon* 'leaf' (see PHYLLO-) + -ITE.] —**phyllitic** /fi líttik/ *adj.*

phyllo /feélō/, **phyllo pastry** *n.* US = filo [Mid-20thC. Via modern Greek, 'leaf, sheet', from Greek *phullon* 'leaf' (see PHYLLO-).]

phyllo- *prefix.* leaf ○ *phyllotaxis* [From Greek *phullon*. Ultimately from an Indo-European word that is also the ancestor of English *foliage*.]

phylloclade /fíllō klayd/, **phylloclad** /-klad/ *n.* = cladophyll [Mid-20thC. From modern Latin, from Greek *phullon* 'leaf' (see PHYLLO-) + *klados* 'shoot'.] —**phyllocladous** /fíllóklədəss/ *adj.*

phyllode /fíllōd/, **phyllodium** /filōdi əm/ (*plural* -a /-ə/) *n.* a flat leaf stalk that functions as a leaf in certain plants, such as the acacia [Mid-19thC. From modern Latin *phyllodium*, from Greek *phullōdēs* 'leaflike', from *phullon* (see PHYLLO-).] —**phyllodial** *adj.*

phylloid /fílloyd/ *adj.* like a leaf in shape or function [Mid-19thC. From modern Latin *phylloides*, from Greek *phullon* (see -PHYLL).]

phyllophagous /fi lóffəgəss/ *adj.* used to describe an animal that eats leaves

phylloquinone /fíllō kwi nōn/ *n.* = vitamin K_1 [Mid-20thC. Coined from PHYLLO- + QUINONE, on the model of German *Phyllochinon*.]

phyllotaxis /fíllō táksis/ (*plural* -es), **phyllotaxy** /-táksi/ (*plural* -ies) *n.* **1.** POSITIONS OF PLANT'S LEAVES the way the leaves on a particular plant are arranged in relation to one another **2.** STUDY OF LEAF POSITIONING the study of the factors that determine the growth patterns and arrangement of plant leaves —**phyllotactic** /fíllō táktik/ *adj.*

phylloxera /fi lóksərə/ (*plural* -ra *or* -ras *or* -rae /-rī/) *n.* an aphid that is a major pest in wine-producing areas. Latin name: *Viteus vitifolii*. [Mid-19thC. From modern Latin, genus name, from PHYLLO- + Greek *xeros* 'dry'; from the insect's effect on leaves.]

phylo- *prefix.* race, kind, tribe, phylum ○ *phylogeny* [From Greek *phulon* (see PHYLUM)]

phylogeny /fī lójjəni/ (*plural* -nies), **phylogenesis** /fíllō jénnəssiss/ (*plural* -ses /-seez/) *n.* the evolutionary history of a species, genus, or group, as contrasted with the development of an individual (**ontogeny**) —**phylogenetic** /fíllō jénnik/ *adj.* —**phylogenetically** /fíllō jə néttikli/ *adv.* —**phylogenetics** /-jə néttiks/ *n.* —**phylogenic** /fíllō jénnik/ *adj.* —**phylogenically** *adv.*

phylum /fíləm/ (*plural* -la /-lə/) *n.* **1.** ZOOL MAJOR TAXONOMIC GROUP IN BIOLOGICAL CLASSIFICATION a major taxonomic group into which animals are divided, made up of several classes. The corresponding taxonomic group for plants and fungi is the division. **2.** LANG GROUP OF LANGUAGES a large group of languages or language stocks thought to be historically related, e.g. Afro-Asiatic or Indo-European [Late 19thC. Via modern Latin from Greek *phulon* 'race'.]

phys. *abbr.* **1.** physiological **2.** physiology **3.** physical **4.** physicist **5.** physics

physalis /fī sáyliss/ (*plural* -ises *or* -es /-leez/) *n.* a tropical plant of the nightshade family that is native to the Americas and bears edible yellow berries. Latin name: *Physalis peruviana*. US term **Cape gooseberry** [Early 19thC. Via modern Latin, genus name, from Greek *phusallis* 'bladder', with reference to the inflated calyx.]

phys. ed. *abbr.* physical education

physi- *prefix.* = physio- (used before vowels)

physiatrics /fízzi áttriks/ *n.* US MED = physical medicine (*takes a singular verb*) [Mid-20thC. Coined from Greek *phusis* 'nature' (see PHYSICS) + *iatrikos* 'medical'.]

physic /fízzik/ *n.* (*archaic*) **1.** MED PROFESSION OF MEDICINE medicine or healing as an art or profession **2.** MED A MEDICINE a medicine, especially one that purges the bowels **3.** PHYS PHYSICS physics ■ *vt.* (**-ics, -icking, -icked**) (*archaic*) **1.** PURGE STH to purge sth such as the bowels **2.** TREAT SB OR STH to treat sb or sth with a medicine or cure [13thC. Directly or via Old French *fisique* from Latin *physica* (see PHYSICS). The original meaning was 'knowledge of the natural world', which survives in PHYSICS.]

physical /fízzik'l/ *adj.* **1.** OF THE BODY relating to the body, rather than with the mind, the soul, or the feelings **2.** REAL AND TOUCHABLE existing in the real material world, rather than as an idea or notion, and able to be touched and seen **3.** NEEDING BODILY STRENGTH involving or needing a lot of bodily strength or energy **4.** WITH BODILY CONTACT involving a lot of bodily contact or aggression ○ *Some of the players were a little too physical.* **5.** INVOLVING TOUCHING tending to touch people or involving touching, especially in an affectionate or sexual way (*informal*) **6.** SCI NOT SOCIAL OR BIOLOGICAL used to describe sciences such as physics and chemistry that deal with nonliving things such as energy and matter ○ *the physical sciences* ■ *n.* MED PHYSICAL EXAMINATION a physical examination (*informal*) ■ **physicals** *npl.* COMM TANGIBLE GOODS articles of trade or commerce that can be bought and used, as distinct from articles bought and sold in a futures market —**physicality** /fízzi kálləti/ *n.* —**physicalness** /fízzik'lnəss/ *n.*

physical anthropology *n.* the branch of anthropology that studies the evolutionary development of human physical characteristics and the differences in appearance among the peoples of the world, as distinct from cultural differences

physical challenge *n.* **1.** RESTRICTED CAPABILITY TO PERFORM PARTICULAR ACTIVITIES an inability to perform some or all of the tasks of daily life **2.** MEDICAL CONDITION RESTRICTING ACTIVITIES a medically diagnosed condition that makes it difficult to engage in the activities of daily life

physical chemistry *n.* the branch of chemistry that studies the physical and thermodynamic properties of substances in relation to their structures and chemical reactions

physical education *n.* gymnastics, athletics, team sports, and other forms of physical exercise taught to children at school

physical examination, **physical** *n.* a doctor's general examination to determine sb's state of physical health and fitness, sometimes as a requirement for a specific job or activity

physical geography *n.* the branch of geography that studies the natural features of the Earth's surface as well as their formation

physicalism /fízzik'lizəm/ *n.* in philosophy, a form of materialism that explains the phenomena of reality, including perceptual and intellectual processes, in terms of the physical —**physicalist** *n.*, *adj.* —**physicalistic** /fízzikə lístik/ *adj.*

physical jerks *npl.* physical exercises of the kind done regularly to keep fit, such as press-ups (*dated informal*) ['Jerks' is the plural of JERK]

physically /fízzikli/ *adv.* **1.** IN THE REAL WORLD in terms of what is real or what exists in the material world, as opposed to what is theoretical or exists only in the mind ○ *physically impossible* **2.** OF THE BODY relating to sb's body or appearance ○ *physically unattractive*

physically challenged *adj.* UNABLE TO PERFORM PARTICULAR ACTIVITIES used to describe sb with a condition that makes it difficult to perform some or all the basic tasks of daily life ■ *npl.* PHYSICALLY CHALLENGED PEOPLE people who are physically challenged

physical medicine *n.* the branch of medicine concerned with the diagnosis of injuries or physical disabilities and their treatment by external means, including heat, massage, or exercise, rather than by medication or surgery

physical science *n.* any of the sciences such as physics and chemistry that study nonliving things

physical therapy *n.* US = physiotherapy —**physical therapist** *n.*

physician /fi zísh'n/ *n.* a doctor who diagnoses and treats diseases and injuries using methods other than surgery [13thC. From Old French *fisicien*, from *fisique* (see PHYSIC).]

physicist /fízzisist/ *n.* a student of physics or a scientist who specializes in physics [Mid-19thC. Coined from PHYSICS + -IST.]

physicochemical /fízzikō kémmik'l/ *adj.* **1.** OF PHYSICS AND CHEMISTRY relating to both physical and chemical characteristics **2.** OF PHYSICAL CHEMISTRY relating to physical chemistry [Mid-17thC. Coined from Greek *physikos* (see PHYSICS) + CHEMICAL.] —**physicochemically** *adv.*

physics /fízziks/ *n.* PHYS STUDY OF PHYSICAL FORCES AND QUALITIES the scientific study of matter, energy, force, and motion, and the way they relate to each other. Physics traditionally incorporates mechanics, electromagnetism, optics, and thermodynamics and now includes modern disciplines such as quantum mechanics, relativity, and nuclear physics. (*takes a singular verb*) ■ *npl.* PHYSICAL ASPECTS the physical processes, interactions, qualities, properties or behaviour of sth [15thC. Formed from PHYSIC; translation of Latin *physica* (plural), from Greek *phusika*, plural of *phusikos* 'of nature', from *phusis* 'nature', from *phuein* 'to make grow'.]

physio /fízzi ō/ (*plural* -os) *n.* (*informal*) **1.** PHYSIOTHERAPIST a physiotherapist **2.** = physiotherapy [Mid-20thC. Shortening of PHYSIOTHERAPY.]

physio- *prefix.* physical ○ *physiotherapy* [From Greek *phusis* 'nature'; related to *phuein* 'to make grow' (see PHYTO-)]

physiognomy /fízzi ónnəmi/ (*plural* -mies) *n.* **1.** FACIAL FEATURES the features of sb's face, especially when they are used as indicators of that person's character or temperament **2.** JUDGMENT OF CHARACTER FROM FACIAL FEATURES the use of facial features to judge sb's character or temperament **3.** CHARACTER OR APPEARANCE OF STH the character or outward appearance of sth, e.g. the physical features of a landscape [13thC. Via Old French from, ultimately, Greek *phusiognōmonia* 'judging of sb's character by their features', from *phusis* 'nature, character' (see PHYSICS) + *gnomon* 'judge' (see GNOMON).] —**physiognomic** /fízzi ə nómmik/ *adj.* —**physiognomically** *adv.* —**physiognomist** /fízzi ónnəmist/ *n.*

physiography /fízzi óggrəfi/ *n.* physical geography (*dated*) —**physiographer** *n.* —**physiographic** /fízzi ə gráffik/ *adj.* —**physiographically** /fízzee ə gráffikli/ *adv.*

physiol. *abbr.* **1.** physiological **2.** physiology

physiological /fízzi ə lójik'l/, **physiologic** /fízzi ə lójjik/ *adj.* **1.** OF ORGANISM'S FUNCTION relating to the way that living things function, rather than to their shape or structure **2.** OF PHYSIOLOGY relating to physiology —**physiologically** *adv.*

physiological psychology *n.* a branch of psychology that studies the interactions between physical or chemical processes in the body and mental states or behaviour

physiological saline *n.* an aqueous salt solution used to keep cells alive and to administer medication intravenously. The solution is prepared so that it exerts the same osmotic pressure as that of fluids inside the cells.

physiology /fízzi ólləji/ *n.* **1.** STUDY OF THE FUNCTIONING OF LIVING THINGS the branch of biology that deals with the internal workings of living things, including such functions as metabolism, respiration, and reproduction, rather than with their shape or structure **2.** BODY'S INTERNAL PROCESSES the way a particular body or organism works [Mid-16thC. Via French *physiologie* or Latin *physiologia* from Greek *phusiologia* *phusis* 'nature' (see PHYSICS) + *-logia* '-logy'.] —**physiologist** *n.*

physiopathology /fízzi ōpə thólləji/ *n.* the branch of medicine that studies how disease disrupts normal body functions —**physiopathologic** /fi zzi ōpathə lójjik/ *adj.* —**physiopathologist** /fízzi ō pə thólləjist/ *n.*

physiotherapy /fízzi ō thérrəpi/, **physical therapy** *n.* the treatment of injuries and physical disabilities by a trained person under the supervision of a specialist in physical medicine. US term **physical therapy** —**physiotherapeutic** /fízzi ō therə pyootik/ *adj.* —**physiotherapeutically** *adv.* —**physiotherapist** /-thérrəpist/ *n.*

physique /fi zéek/ *n.* the shape and size of sb's body [Early 19thC. From French, from *physique* 'physical', from, ultimately, Greek *phusikos* (see PHYSICS).]

physostigmine /físsō stíg meen/, **physostigmin** /físs ō stígmin/ *n.* a drug derived from the dried leaves of the poisonous Calabar bean and used to treat glaucoma and counteract adverse effects of anticholinergic drugs on the central nervous system. Formula: $C_{15}H_{21}N_3O_2$. [Mid-19thC. Coined from modern Latin *Physostigma*, genus name (from Greek *phusa* 'bladder' + STIGMA, from its distended form) + -INE.]

phyt- *prefix.* = phyto- (used before vowels)

-phyte *suffix.* **1.** plant ○ *saprophyte* **2.** pathological growth ○ *osteophyte* [From Greek *phuton* (see PHYTO-)]

phyto- *prefix.* plant ○ *phytohormone* [Via modern Latin from, ultimately, Greek *phuton*, from *phuein* 'to make grow'. Ultimately from an Indo-European base meaning 'to be' that is also the ancestor of English *be*, *build*, *physical*, and *future*.]

phytoalexin /fítō ə léksin/ *n.* a chemical produced by a plant to protect it from infection by a pathogen or exposure to some agents of stress

phytochemistry /fítō kémmistri/ *n.* the chemistry of plants and their metabolic processes —**phytochemical** *adj.* —**phytochemically** *adv.* —**phytochemist** *n.*

phytochrome /fítōkrōm/ *n.* the pigment in green plants that absorbs light and controls dormancy, flowering, and the germination of seeds [Late 19thC. Coined from PHYTO- + Greek *khrōma* 'colour'.]

phytogenesis /fítō jénnəssiss/, **phytogeny** /fī tójjəni/ *n.* the evolutionary development of plants —**phytogenetic** /fítō jə néttik/ *adj.* —**phytogenetically** /-néttik'li/ *adv.*

phytogenic /fítō jénnik/, **phytogenous** /fītójənəss/ *adj.* used to describe substances, such as coal, that are formed from plants

phytogeny *n.* = phytogenesis

phytogeography /fítōji óggrəfi/ *n.* the study of the geographical distribution of plants —**phytogeographer** *n.* —**phytogeographic** /-jee ə gráffik/ *adj.* —**phytogeographically** /-gráffik'li/ *adv.*

phytography /fī tóggrəfi/ *n.* the branch of botany concerned with the accurate description of plants —**phytographic** /fítō gráffik/ *adj.*

phytohormone /fítō háwrmōn/ *n.* = plant hormone

phytol /fí tol/ *n.* a liquid alcohol found in plants and used to synthesize vitamins E and K. Formula: $C_{20}H_{40}O$.

phytology /fī tólləji/ *n.* botany (*archaic*)

phyton /fí ton/ *n.* the smallest part of a plant, usually a leaf and its stem, that can grow when it has been cut from the parent plant [Mid-19thC. From French, formed from Greek *phuton* (see -PHYTE) + *-on* '-on'.]

phytopathogen /fítō páthəjən/ *n.* sth that causes disease in plants

phytopathology /fítō pə thólləji/ *n.* the branch of botany that studies plant diseases —**phytopathological** /fítō pathə lójjik'l/ *adj.* —**phytopathologically** /-lójjikli/ *adv.* —**phytopathologist** /fítō pə thólləjist/ *n.*

phytophagous /fī tóffəgəss/ *adj.* used to describe animals, especially insects, that feed on plants —**phytophagy** /fī tóffəji/ *n.*

phytoplankton /fítō plángktən/ *n.* very small free-floating aquatic plants such as one-celled algae, found in plankton. ◊ **zooplankton** —**phytoplanktonic** /fítō plangk tónnik/ *adj.*

phytoremediation /fítō ri méedi áysh'n/ *n.* the process of decontaminating soil by using plants to absorb heavy metals or other pollutants

phytosociology /fítō sōssi ólləji, -sōshi ólləji/ *n.* the branch of ecology concerned with the identification, analysis, and classification of plant communities or plant associations —**phytosociological** /fítō sōssi ə lójjik'l/ *adj.* —**phytosociologically** /-lójjikli/ *adv.* —**phytosociologist** /fítō sōssi ólləjist, -sōshi-/ *n.*

phytotoxic /fítō tóksik/ *adj.* poisonous to plants [Mid-20thC] —**phytotoxicity** /fítō tok síssəti/ *n.*

phytotoxin /fítō tóksin/ *n.* **1.** POISON MADE BY PLANTS a poisonous substance obtained from plants such as the drug digitalis **2.** STH POISONOUS TO PLANTS sth that is poisonous to plants

phytotron /fítō tron/ *n.* a place in which plants can be grown under controlled conditions, such as a glasshouse or a more complex facility

pi[1] /pī/ *n.* **1.** 16TH LETTER OF THE GREEK ALPHABET the 16th letter of the Greek alphabet, represented in the English alphabet as 'p'. ♦ **alphabet 2.** MATH MATHEMATICAL CONSTANT a number approximately equal to 3.14159 that is the ratio of the circumference of a circle divided by its diameter and is represented by the symbol π [Early 19thC. From Greek. In the sense 'number', representing the first letter of Greek *peripheria* 'circumference' or of its English equivalent *periphery*.]

pi[2] /pī/, **pie** *n.* **1.** PRINTING JUMBLE OF PRINTER'S TYPE a pile of printer's type that has been mixed up together **2.** DISORDERED MIXTURE a disorganized combination of things ■ *v.* (**pies, piing, pied; pies, pieing, pied**) **1.** *vt.* PRINTING JUMBLE TYPE to mix printer's type up together **2.** *vti.* MAKE OR BECOME JUMBLED to mix things up in a confusing way or to become mixed up or confused [Mid-17thC. Origin uncertain: perhaps a translation of French *pâté* 'pie, patty', with reference to the jumbled contents of a pie.]

pi[3] /pī/ *adj.* pretending to be very religious or virtuous (*archaic informal*) [Mid-19thC. Shortening of PIOUS.]

PI *abbr.* **1.** Philippines (*international vehicle registration*) **2.** US private investigator

pia *n.* ANAT = pia mater —**pial** *adj.*

PIA *abbr.* **1.** FIN Personal Investment Authority **2.** COMPUT peripheral interface adaptor

Piacenza /pya chéntsa/ capital city of Piacenza Province, Emilia-Romagna Region, northern Italy. Population: 102,161 (1992).

piacular /pī ákyoōlər/ *adj.* RELIG **1.** ATONING FOR SIN done or offered in order to make up for a sin or sacrilegious action **2.** SINFUL wicked or sinful and requiring the offender or sinner to atone [Early 17thC. From Latin *piacularis*, from *piaculum* 'atonement', from *piare* 'to appease'.]

AKG London

Edith Piaf

Piaf /pee af/, **Édith** (1915–63) French singer. Her expressive performance of songs such as 'Je ne regrette rien' and 'La Vie en rose' led to international fame. Real name **Edith Giovanna Gassion**

piaffe /pi áf/ *n.* **piaffe, piaffer** TROTTING IN PLACE a dressage movement performed by a horse in which it trots in one place and raises its legs very high ■ *vi.* (**piaffes, piaffing, piaffed**) PERFORM A PIAFFE to perform a dressage movement that involves trotting on the spot with the legs raised high [Mid-18thC. From French, formed from *piaffer* 'to strut'.]

Piaget /pi azh ay/, **Jean** (1896–1980) Swiss psychologist. His pioneering study of the intellectual development in children has had a major impact in psychology and education.

pia mater /pīə máytər/ *n.* the innermost and most delicate of the three membranes (**meninges**) that surround the brain and the spinal cord [14thC. From Latin, literally 'tender mother', translated from Arabic *al-'umm ar-rakika*.]

pianism /pee ənizəm/ *n.* piano-playing skill or technique —**pianistic** /pee ə nístik/ *adj.*

pianissimo /peé ə níssimō/ *adv.* VERY SOFTLY very softly and quietly (*used as a musical direction*) ■ *n.* (*plural* **-mos** *or* **-mi**) SOFTLY PLAYED MUSICAL PART a part of a musical composition that is played very softly [Early 18thC. From Italian, 'very quiet', from *piano* (see PIANO²).] —**pianissimo** *adj.*

pianist /peé ənist/ *n.* sb who plays the piano

piano¹ /pi ánnō/ *n.* (*plural* **-os**) MUSICAL INSTRUMENT WITH KEYBOARD a large musical instrument consisting of a wooden case with wires stretched inside it and a row of white and black keys. It is played by pressing the keys, each of which is attached to a small hammer that strikes one of the strings and makes a sound. ◊ **grand piano, upright piano** ■ *adj.* **1.** OF OR FOR PIANO relating to or played on a piano ○ *a piano sonata* **2.** OF OR FOR ENSEMBLE CONTAINING PIANIST used to describe a small musical ensemble that contains a pianist, and usually a violinist and cellist, or a piece of music written for such an ensemble ○ *a piano trio* [Early 19thC. From Italian, shortening of PIANOFORTE.]

WORD KEY: CULTURAL NOTE

The Piano, a film by New Zealand director Jane Campion (1993). Set in the mid-nineteenth century, it is the story of the mute Scots wife of a New Zealand landowner who falls in love with a settler who has acquired her beloved piano. Holly Hunter won an Academy Award for her performance in the lead role.

piano² /pyáanō/ *adv.* SOFTLY softly and quietly (*used as a musical direction*) ■ *n.* (*plural* **-nos** *or* **-ni** /-ee/) SOFTLY PLAYED MUSICAL PART a part of a musical composition that is played softly [Late 17thC. Via Italian from Latin *planus* 'soft, flat'.] —**piano** *adj.*

piano accordion *n.* an accordion with a keyboard on one side to play the notes of the melody on —**piano accordionist** *n.*

piano bar *n.* a bar, or a lounge in a hotel, where a pianist plays to entertain customers or provide background music

pianoforte /pi ánnō fáwti/ (*plural* **-tes**) *n.* a piano (*formal*) [Mid-18thC. From Italian, from *gravecembalo col piano e forte* 'harpsichord with soft and loud', referring to the instrument's variation in tone compared with a standard harpsichord.]

piano hinge *n.* a long narrow hinge that has a pin running the length of its joint

Pianola /peé ə nṓlə/ *tdmk.* a trademark for a type of player piano

piano nobile /pyáanō nṓbili/ *n.* the first floor of a large residence or public building (*formal*) [From Italian, literally 'noble floor', because it is high above the ground and provides a view]

piano player *n.* **1.** SB WHO PLAYS PIANO sb who plays the piano, especially sb who plays popular or jazz music **2.** MECHANICAL DEVICE a mechanical device that plays a piano automatically

piano roll *n.* a roll of paper with patterns of perforations whose positions determine the sequence of notes played on a player piano

piano stool *n.* an adjustable stool for a pianist to sit on and often having a hollow compartment under the seat for storing sheet music

piassava /peé ə saávə/, **piassaba** /peéə saábə/ *n.* **1.** TREES FIBRE-PRODUCING PALM TREE a Brazilian palm tree that produces a coarse fibre. Latin name: *Attalea funifera* and *Leopoldinia piassaba.* **2.** INDUST COARSE FIBRE the coarse fibre obtained from the piassava tree, used to make rope, brooms, and brushes [Mid-19thC. Via Portuguese from Tupi *piaçába.*]

piastre /pi ástə/ *n.* **1.** SUBUNIT OF MIDDLE EASTERN CURRENCY a subunit of currency in Egypt, Lebanon, Sudan, and Syria, 100 of which are worth one pound **2.** COIN WORTH ONE PIASTRE a coin worth one piastre [Late 16thC. Via French from Italian *piastra (d'argento)* '(silver) plate', from Latin *emplastrum* (see PLASTER).]

Piave /pyaáv e/ river in northeastern Italy. Length: 220 km/137 mi.

piazza /pi átsə/ (*plural* **-zas**) *n.* **1.** (*plural* **-ze**) ITALIAN PUBLIC SQUARE a large open square, especially one in an Italian town **2.** OPEN-SIDED PASSAGEWAY a covered passageway that has arches on one or both sides and is usually attached to a building, e.g. along the inner walls of a courtyard or quadrangle **3.** *US* PORCH a veranda or porch, especially one attached to a house (*regional dated*) [Late 16thC. Via Italian from Latin *platea* 'open space' (see PLACE).]

pibroch /peéb rokh/ *n.* a piece of music written for the Scottish Highland bagpipes, consisting of a theme and variations, often with a mournful tone [Early 18thC. From Gaelic *piobaireachd* 'the art of piping', from, ultimately, English *pipe.*]

pic /pik/ (*plural* **pics** *or* **pix** /piks/) *n.* a picture, especially a photograph, illustration, or cinema film (*informal*) [Late 19thC. Shortening of PICTURE.]

pica¹ /píkə/ *n.* **1.** MEASURE OF TYPE SIZE a unit of measurement for printing type, equal to 12 points or 0.422 cm/0.166 in **2.** TYPOGRAPHIC MEASURE a linear measure used in typography, equal to about 0.422 cm/0.166 in [15thC. From Anglo-Latin, 'church almanac'; from the resemblance to the handwriting in such books.]

pica² /píkə/ *n.* indiscriminate craving for and eating of substances such as paint chips, clay, plaster, or dirt. It is found mostly among children and pregnant women and may result from mineral deficiencies. [Mid-16thC. From Latin, 'magpie', as a literal translation of Greek *kissa, kitta* 'magpie, false appetite'; from the magpie's indiscriminate feeding habits.]

picador /píkə dawr/ *n.* a bullfighter on horseback, who attacks the bull with a spear early in the fight, making it easier for the main bullfighter (**matador**) to kill with his sword [Late 18thC. From Spanish, formed from *picar* 'to prick, pierce'.]

pica em *n.* = **pica¹** *n.* 1

picara /píkərə/ *n.* (*archaic literary*) **1.** DISHONEST WOMAN a woman who is a cheat or swindler **2.** WOMAN PIRATE a woman pirate [Mid-20thC. From Spanish, feminine form of *picaro* (see PICARO).]

Picardy third /píkərdi-/ *n.* a major third that appears in the final chord of some Baroque works that are predominantly in a minor key [Translation of *tierce de Picardy*; from its use in the church music of *Picardy*, France]

picaresque /píkə résk/ *adj.* **1.** TYPICAL OF ROGUES relating to or typical of rogues or scoundrels **2.** LITERAT HAVING ROGUE AS HERO belonging to or characteristic of a type of prose fiction that features the adventures of a roguish hero and usually has a simple plot divided into separate episodes ■ *n.* LITERAT PICARESQUE FICTION a type of prose fiction featuring the adventures of a roguish hero [Early 19thC. Via French from Spanish *picaresco*, from *picaro* 'rogue', from, ultimately, assumed Vulgar Latin *piccare* 'to prick, pierce', possible source of English *pick.*]

picaro /píkərō/ (*plural* **-ros**) *n.* (*archaic literary*) **1.** ROGUE a cheat, swindler, or rogue **2.** PIRATE a pirate or adventurer [Early 17thC. From Spanish (see PICARESQUE).]

picaroon /píkə ro͞on/, **pickaroon** *n.* (*archaic literary*) **1.** ROGUE a rogue **2.** PIRATE a pirate **3.** PIRATE SHIP a pirate ship ■ *vi.* (**-roons, -rooning, -rooned**) LIVE ADVENTUROUS LIFE to live the adventurous life of a pirate, thief, swindler, or scoundrel (*archaic literary*) [Early 17thC. From Spanish *picaron*, literally 'great rogue', from *picaro* (see PICARESQUE).]

Pablo Picasso: Photographed in 1933 by Man Ray

Picasso /pikássō/, **Pablo** (1881–1973) Spanish painter and sculptor. An exceptionally versatile and prolific artist, he was the leading figure in the development of modern abstract art. Among his major works are the cubist masterpiece *Les Demoiselles d'Avignon* (1906–07) and *Guernica* (1937), which expresses his horror of war.

picayune /píkə yo͞on/ *adj.* *US, Can* (*informal*) **1.** TRIFLING of very little importance **2.** SMALL-MINDED tending to fuss about unimportant things and to be childishly spiteful ■ *n.* **1.** *US, Can* TRIFLING THING sth unimportant or of little value (*informal*) **2.** MONEY SPANISH-AMERICAN COIN a small silver coin formerly used in Spanish America, worth half of a real **3.** *US* MONEY SMALL COIN a low-value coin, especially a five-cent piece (*archaic informal*) [Early 19thC. Via French *picaillon*, a Piedmontese coin, from Provençal *picaioun*, of unknown origin.]

piccalilli /píkə lílli/ *n.* pickle consisting of mixed vegetables, especially cauliflower, small whole onions, and cucumber, in a sauce containing mustard and vinegar [Mid-18thC. Origin uncertain: probably from PICKLE + CHILLI.]

piccaninny /píkə nínni/ (*plural* **-nies**) *n.* **1.** highly offensive term for a small Black child (*offensive*) **2.** *Aus* OFFENSIVE TERM FOR AN ABORIGINAL CHILD an offensive term for an Aboriginal child (*informal offensive*) [See PICCANINNY]

Piccard /pík aar/, **Auguste** (1884–1962) Swiss physicist. He is noted for his exploration of the deep sea, and of the stratosphere, to which he made the first balloon ascent.

piccata /pi kaátə/ *adj.* used to describe meats sautéed in slices and served in a spicy lemon and butter sauce ○ *veal piccata* [Via Italian from French *piqué*, past participle of *piquer* 'to attach ingredients, to lard', literally 'to prick']

piccolo /píkəlō/ (*plural* **-los**) *n.* a musical instrument that is the smallest member of the flute family, with a range one octave higher than the standard flute [Mid-19thC. From Italian, 'small'.]

pice /pīss/ (*plural* **pice**) *n.* MONEY a subunit of currency formerly used in the Indian subcontinent, 4 of which were worth an anna [Early 17thC. From Hindi *paisā* 'paisa' (see PAISA).]

piceous /píssi əss/ *adj.* thick and sticky or brownish-black in colour, like pitch (*formal*) [Mid-17thC. Formed from Latin *piceus* 'pitchy', from the stem *pic-* 'pitch' (source of English *pitch*).]

pichiciego /píchissi áygō/ (*plural* **-go** *or* **-gos**), **pichiciago** (*plural* **-go** *or* **-gos**) *n.* **1.** SMALL ARMADILLO a very small silky-haired armadillo with pink armour found in Argentina. Latin name: *Chlamyphorus truncatus.* **2.** LARGE ARMADILLO a large armadillo found in South America that has yellowish-brown armour and coarse whitish hair. Latin name: *Burmeisteria retusa.* [Early 19thC. From Spanish *pichiego*, probably from Guarani *pichey*, name of a type of armadillo, literally 'small' + Spanish *ciego* 'sightless', from Latin *caecus.*]

pick¹ /pik/ *v.* (**picks, picking, picked**) **1.** *vt.* REMOVE STH FROM PLANT to remove sth, especially in quantity and by hand, from a plant on which it has grown ○ *picking strawberries* **2.** *vt.* STRIP STH OF FRUIT OR FLOWERS to strip a plant or all the plants in a particular place of fruit or flowers ○ *The bushes nearest the path had already been picked.* **3.** *vt.* CHOOSE to take or decide to take one or more things or people from a larger number ○ *Pick three people for your team.* **4.** *vt.* REMOVE STH IN SMALL PIECES to remove sth bit by bit from the surface or middle of sth using a sharp or pointed object such as a fingernail or a beak **5.** *vt.* SCRAPE BODY PART WITH FINGERNAIL to use a fingernail to loosen and remove sth, or to loosen and remove sth attached to the surface of a part of the body ○ *pick a scab* **6.** *vt.* OPEN STH WITHOUT PROPER KEY to use a special device or pointed instrument to open a lock, usually illegally ○ *pick a lock* **7.** *vt.* UNDO to loosen, unfasten, or separate sth into disconnected parts, especially sth that was sewn together ○ *pick a seam apart* **8.** *vi.* FIND FAULT to be petty or fault-finding **9.** *vt.* START FIGHT OR QUARREL to begin a fight or quarrel with sb, usually deliberately **10.** *vt.* MUSIC PLUCK OR PLAY BY PLUCKING to pluck the strings of a stringed instrument or to play a tune on such an instrument in this way ■ *n.* **1.** CHOICE the act or right of choosing sb or sth ○ *I was first so I got to take my pick.* **2.** BEST the very best of a wide selection of people or things ○ *the pick of the bunch* **3.** CROP PORTION the amount of a crop gathered by hand at one time [13thC. Origin uncertain: probably from assumed Old English *pīcian* 'to prick' and Old

Icelandic *pikka* 'to prick, peck'; later reinforced by French *piquer* 'to prick, pick'.] —**pickable** *adj.* ◇ **pick and choose** to take a lot of time or trouble when selecting sth ◇ **pick holes in** *vt.* to look for and find mistakes or problems in sth, especially sb's argument ◇ **pick sb's pocket** to steal sth from sb's pocket without the person feeling or noticing ◇ **pick your way** to step very carefully through a dirty, untidy, or dangerous area of ground

pick at *vt.* 1. EAT LITTLE FOOD to eat very little of a meal ○ *He only picked at his breakfast.* 2. SCRAPE STH WITH FINGERNAILS to scrape away surface pieces of sth with the fingernails 3. NAG SB to nag or criticize sb in a petty way (*informal*)

pick off *vt.* to shoot a number of targets one by one, usually from a distance

pick on *vt.* 1. PERSISTENTLY TREAT SB UNFAIRLY to blame, criticize, or bully sb repeatedly in a way that is considered unfair or unkind 2. SELECT SB OR STH to choose sb or sth from among others

pick out *vt.* 1. CHOOSE STH to choose or select sth from among others ○ *She picked out her favourite chocolate.* 2. IDENTIFY SB FROM CROWD OR BACKGROUND to recognize or distinguish sb or sth from among others or against a background that makes this difficult ○ *I couldn't pick him out in the crowd.* 3. MAKE STH STAND OUT to make sth stand out against its background, especially by giving it a strikingly different colour ○ *The design was picked out in green.* 4. MUSIC PLAY STH NOTE BY NOTE to play a tune slowly, note by note

pick over *vt.* to go through sth, selecting the best items or discarding unwanted items

pick up *v.* 1. LIFT STH to take hold of and raise or remove sth or sb 2. *vti.* GATHER DROPPED THINGS to collect things that have been dropped or have fallen to the ground 3. *vr.* REGAIN UPRIGHT OR STRONGER POSITION to stand up after falling down, or recover strength, courage, or sense of purpose after a setback ○ *She picked herself up.* 4. *vti.* TAKE ON PASSENGERS to stop a vehicle and let a passenger or passengers in ○ *picked up a hitchhiker* 5. *vt.* CLAIM STH to collect sth such as items left for repair or goods ordered from a shop ○ *pick up a library book* 6. *vt.* PAY FOR STH to take on the responsibility for providing payment for sth such as a bill 7. *vt.* BUY STH ON IMPULSE to buy sth in a casual or unplanned way 8. *vt.* ACQUIRE STH CHEAPLY OR EASILY to get or buy sth easily or cheaply 9. *vt.* ACQUIRE STH CASUALLY to acquire sth casually, without meaning to and without knowing it ○ *has picked up some bad habits* 10. *vt.* MED CATCH A DISEASE to become infected with a disease 11. *vt.* NOTICE STH to notice sth or become aware of it 12. *vt.* FIND STH to find and follow sth, such as a scent or trail ○ *pick up the scent* 13. *vt.* UNDERSTAND STH to understand sth that is communicated indirectly 14. *vt.* LEARN STH to learn sth in a casual or unsystematic way, e.g. by frequently hearing it, seeing it done, or trying to do it 15. *vi.* BECOME BETTER to improve after being ill, injured, bad, or unsuccessful (*informal*) ○ *He picked up quickly* 16. *vti.* ACCELERATE to increase in strength, speed, or intensity, or to cause sth to increase ○ *Her speed picked up.* 17. *vti.* RETURN TO STH AGAIN to continue sth at a later time, usually after an interruption or break, or to be continued in this way ○ *She wanted to pick up her career.* 18. *vt.* FIND SEXUAL PARTNER to make the acquaintance of a stranger, often in a public place, usually for sexual purposes (*informal*) ○ *picked him up in a pub* 19. *vt.* ARREST to arrest sb (*informal*) ○ *He was picked up on a burglary charge.* 20. *vt.* RECEIVE SIGNAL to receive sth such as a radio or television signal or a radar image on a piece of equipment

pick up on *vt.* (*informal*) 1. NOTICE STH to notice sth, and perhaps mention or question it 2. CRITICIZE SB to criticize sb for an action or behaviour, often in a condescending way

pick[2] /pík/ *n.* 1. TOOL FOR BREAKING UP HARD SURFACES a tool used for breaking up hard surfaces, consisting of a long handle and a curved metal head that is pointed at one or both ends 2. SMALL TOOL FOR BREAKING INTO PIECES a small tool used to break up sth into smaller pieces (*often used in combination*) 3. SHARP TOOL FOR PICKING a sharp tool for cleaning sth such as the teeth or for getting into small places, such as a lock (*often used in combination*) 4. MUSIC = **plectrum** ■ *vi.* (**picks,**

picking, picked) WORK WITH PICK to use a pick or do labouring work with a pick [14thC. Variant of PIKE.]

pickaback *n., adj., adv.* a piggyback (*dated*)

pickaninny *n.* US = **piccaninny** (*taboo insult*)

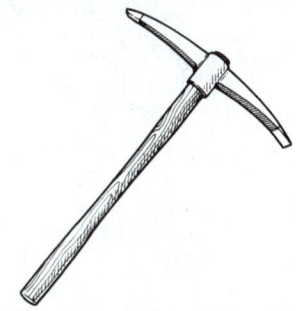

Pickaxe

pickaxe /pík aks/ *n.* a tool consisting of a long handle and a metal head that usually has one pointed end and one flattened end, used for breaking up sth hard or cutting sth [13thC. Middle English *pikois* from Old French *picois* (ultimately from Latin *picus* 'woodpecker'), altered in the 15thC by association with AXE.]

picker /píkər/ *n.* a person or a machine that picks sth, especially fruit or other crops (*often used in combination*)

pickerel /píkərəl/ (*plural* **-el** *or* **-els**) *n.* 1. N AMERICAN FISH OF PIKE FAMILY a North American river fish of the pike family that is a fierce predator and is popular with anglers. Latin name: *Esox niger.* 2. PIKE a young pike [14thC. Literally 'small pike'; partly modelled on Anglo-Latin *picerellus.*]

pickerelweed /píkərəl weed/ *n.* a North American plant with heart-shaped leaves and purple flowers that grows in shallow water in rivers and lakes. Latin name: *Pontederia cordata.*

picket /píkit/ *n.* 1. POINTED POST STUCK IN THE GROUND a post or plank with a pointed end that is hammered into the ground, e.g. as a marker, as a support for a fence, or to tether an animal 2. **picket, picquet, piquet** MIL SOLDIER OR SOLDIERS ON GUARD a soldier or small body of troops used to occupy ground of tactical importance 3. PROTESTER OR PROTESTERS OUTSIDE BUILDING a person or group of people demonstrating or protesting outside a building, e.g. a striking worker who tries to persuade other people not to enter during a strike ■ *v.* (**-ets, -eting, -eted**) 1. *vt.* ENCLOSE OR MARK STH WITH STAKES to enclose or mark sth with wooden stakes driven into the ground, or enclose it with a picket fence 2. *vt.* MIL POST GUARDS to post troops as guards 3. *vt.* MIL GUARD to patrol or guard a place, especially a military site or position 4. *vti.* HOLD PROTEST OUTSIDE PLACE to hold a demonstration or protest outside a place, e.g. as part of a strike in order to persuade others not to enter a place of business 5. *vt.* TETHER ANIMAL to tether a horse or other animal [Late 17thC. From French *piquet* 'pointed stake', from *piquer* 'to prick, pierce' (see PICK[1]). The meaning 'guard' comes from the practice of soldiers tethering their horses to stakes.] —**picketer** *n.*

picket fence *n.* a fence made of pointed stakes or posts driven into the ground and connected by one or more horizontal bars

picket line *n.* a line of people who are protesting outside a building, e.g. striking workers outside their workplace, who attempt to persuade other people not to enter

Pickford /píkfərd/, **Mary** (1893–1979) Canadian-born US actor and producer. She starred in films such as *Poor Little Rich Girl* (1917), and cofounded United Artists Studio (1919). Real name **Gladys Marie Smith.** Known as **America's Sweetheart**

pickings /píkingz/ *npl.* things available to be earned or taken in a particular place ○ *easy pickings*

pickle /pík'l/ *n.* 1. FOOD SAVOURY PRESERVE a lumpy mixture of chopped vegetables, typically cauliflower, onions, cucumbers, and gherkins, preserved in vinegar or brine to give it a sharp or spicy flavour and eaten with other foods. US term **relish** 2. FOOD VEGETABLE PRESERVED IN VINEGAR a small vegetable,

AKG London

Mary Pickford

such as an onion or gherkin, that has acquired a sharp taste by being preserved in vinegar or brine, usually with added spices (*usually used in the plural*) 3. FOOD LIQUID FOR PRESERVING FOOD liquid, usually brine or a vinegar solution, used to preserve cold foods such as vegetables or fish 4. INDUST CLEANING OR PROCESSING SOLUTION an industrial or commercial solution used to clean or process sth 5. AWKWARD SITUATION a difficult or problematic situation (*informal*) 6. TROUBLESOME PERSON a mildly troublesome person, especially a naughty child (*informal*) 7. **pickle, puckle** *Scotland* SMALL AMOUNT a small amount (*informal*) ■ *vt.* (**-les, -ling, -led**) 1. FOOD PRESERVE FOOD to preserve food, especially vegetables or fish, in vinegar, brine, or another solution 2. DIP OR SOAK STH IN LIQUID to clean or process sth by dipping or soaking it in a liquid [14thC. From Middle Low German *pekel*, of unknown origin.] —**pickler** *n.*

pickled /pík'ld/ *adj.* 1. PRESERVED preserved in vinegar, brine, or another liquid 2. INEBRIATED inebriated (*informal*)

picklock /pík lok/ *n.* 1. LOCK-OPENING TOOL a tool used to open locks without using the key 2. SB WHO OPENS LOCKS UNLAWFULLY sb who opens locks without using a key, especially a burglar

pick-me-up *n.* sth that lifts the spirits and energizes sb, especially a stimulating drink (*informal*)

pick 'n' mix /píkən míks/ *n.* a wide range of items, especially sweets, cheeses, or salads, from which you choose whatever combination you want (*hyphenated when used before a noun*)

pickoff /pík of/ *n.* an electronic device that senses movement used, e.g. in the guidance system of an aircraft or as part of a surveillance system

pickpocket /pík pokit/ *n.* sb who steals from people's pockets and bags in public places, usually secretly and unnoticed

pick-up *n.* 1. LIFTING OR COLLECTING OF STH the raising, gathering, collection, or removal of sth to be taken somewhere else 2. SB OR STH TAKEN SOMEWHERE sb or sth that is moved from one place to another 3. HITCHHIKER a hitchhiker (*informal*) 4. = **pick-up truck** 5. IMPROVEMENT OR INCREASE an improvement or increase (*informal*) 6. = **pick-me-up** 7. PROSPECTIVE SEXUAL PARTNER sb met casually with the aim of developing a sexual relationship (*informal*) 8. ARREST the taking of sb into custody by a police officer (*informal*) 9. US POWER TO ACCELERATE the ability of a vehicle to accelerate quickly (*informal*) 10. RECORDING TONE ARM the tone arm of a record player 11. **pick-up, pick-up arm** RECORDING PART OF TONE ARM a device inside the tone arm of a record player that converts the needle's vibrations into electrical signals that are converted into sound 12. MUSIC CONVERTER OF VIBRATIONS ON MUSICAL INSTRUMENT an electromagnetic device that converts the vibrations from the strings of an electric guitar or other amplified instrument into electrical signals that are amplified into sound 13. PHYS RECEIVING OF LIGHT OR SOUND WAVES the receiving and gathering of light or sound waves that are to be converted into electrical impulses 14. TECH RECEIVER FOR LIGHT OR SOUND WAVES a device used to receive light or sound waves ■ *adj.* US INFORMAL AND IMPROMPTU informally organized on the spot and made up of or involving people available at the time

pick-up truck, pick-up *n.* a light truck with a low-sided open back and a tailgate that drops down for easy loading and unloading

Pickwickian /pik wíki ən/ adj. **1.** GENEROUS OR NAIVE generous, naive, or benevolent **2.** UNUSUAL not literal or typical in usage or meaning [Mid-19thC. From the character of Mr Pickwick in Charles Dickens' novel *The Pickwick Papers* (1837).]

picky /píki/ (**-ier, -iest**) adj. having specific and inflexible likes and dislikes and, therefore, hard to please or satisfy [Mid-19thC. Formed from PICK[1].] —**pickily** adv. —**pickiness** n.

pick-your-own adj. used to describe crops that can be picked by customers from the plants, or such a service offered to customers

picloram /píklə ram/ n. CHEM a herbicide permitted for use on plants other than crops, such as the grass of playing fields. Formula: $C_6H_3Cl_3N_2O_2$. [Mid-20thC. Coined from PICOLINE + CHLOR- + AMINE.]

picnic /píknik/ n. **1.** FOOD MEAL TAKEN AND EATEN OUTDOORS an informal meal prepared for eating in the open air or the food that makes up such a meal **2.** EASY OR PLEASANT THING sth easy to do or pleasant to experience (*informal*) ○ *It was no picnic.* ■ vi. (**-nics, -nicking, -nicked**) HAVE A PICNIC to eat an informal meal outdoors [Mid-18thC. From French *pique-nique*, of unknown origin.] —**picnicker** n.

— WORD KEY: CULTURAL NOTE —

Picnic at Hanging Rock, a novel by Australian author Joan Lindsay (1967). Set in turn-of-the-century Australia, it tells the story of the disappearance of three school girls during a St Valentine's Day picnic at Hanging Rock in Victoria. Although one girl reappears, the mystery is never explained. It was made into a film by Peter Weir in 1976.

picnic day n. Aus an extra day off work granted by many employers, sometimes used for a picnic for company employees

picnic races npl. Aus horse races for amateur riders, usually local farmers or farmhands, that are major social events in rural areas of Australia

pico- prefix. **1.** ONE MILLION MILLIONTH one million millionth (10^{-12}) ○ *picofarad*. Symbol **p 2.** very small ○ *picornavirus* [Via Spanish *pico* 'beak, small amount' from Latin *beccus*; ultimately of Celtic origin]

Pico della Mirandola /peèkō délla mi rándōlə/, **Giovanni, Conte** (1463–94) Italian humanist philosopher. His 900 propositions about all subjects attracted accusations of heresy.

picofarad /peèkō farəd, -farad/ n. one million millionth of a farad. Symbol **pF**

picogram /peèkō gram/ n. one million millionth of a gram

picoline /píkə leen/ n. a liquid found in coal tar and bone oil, used as a solvent and in organic synthesis. Formula: C_6H_7N. [Mid-19thC. Coined from the Latin stem *pic-* 'pitch' (source of English *pitch*) + *oleum* 'oil' (source of English *oil*) + -INE.] —**picolinic** /píkə línnik/ adj.

picomole /peèkōmōl/ n. one million millionth of a mole

picornavirus /pi káwrnə vírəss/ n. a small infectious virus, such as the virus that causes polio or the common cold. Family: Picornaviridae. [Mid-20thC. Coined from PICO- + RNA + VIRUS.]

picosecond /peèkō sekənd/ n. a million millionth of a second

picot /peèkō/ n. DECORATIVE LOOP a loop that forms a pattern with others, e.g. in lace ■ vt. (**-cots, -coting, -coted**) DECORATE WITH PICOTS to embroider small loops on fabric [Early 17thC. From French, literally 'small point', formed from *pic* 'peak, point', from *piquer* 'to prick' (see PICK[1]).]

picotee /píkə teé/ n. a flower, especially a carnation or tulip, that has petals edged with a different, usually darker colour [Early 18thC. From French *picotée*, feminine past participle of *picoter* 'to prick', from *picot* (see PICOT).]

picowave /peèkō wayv/ vt. (**-waves, -waving, -waved**) to expose food to radiation in order to kill insects, worms, or bacteria

picquet n. = picket

picr- prefix. = picro- (*used before vowels*)

picrate /pík rayt/ n. a salt or ester of picric acid [Mid-19thC. Coined from Greek *pikros* 'bitter' + -ATE.]

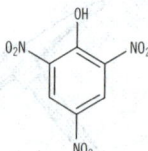

Picric acid

picric acid /píkrik-/ n. a strong toxic yellow crystalline acid used in dyes, antiseptics, and high explosives. Formula: $C_6H_3N_3O_7$. [From Greek *pikros* 'bitter' + -IC]

picrite /pík rīt/ n. a dark-coloured igneous rock made up primarily of coarse grains of olivine and other ferromagnesian minerals [Early 19thC. Coined from Greek *pikros* 'bitter' + -ITE.]

picro- prefix. **1.** bitter ○ *picrotoxin* **2.** picric acid ○ *picrate* [From Greek *pikros* 'sharp, bitter'. Ultimately from an Indo-European base meaning 'to cut, scratch' that is also the ancestor of English *paint* and *file*.]

picrotoxin /píkrə tóksin/ n. a bitter crystalline compound derived from the seeds of an Indian vine and used as an antidote to barbiturate poisoning. Formula: $C_{30}H_{34}O_{13}$.

Pict /pikt/ n. a member of any of the ancient peoples that occupied lands north of the Forth and Clyde Rivers in Scotland from the 1st to the 4th centuries AD. The Picts prevented the Romans from spreading into central and northern Scotland and later joined with the Scots to form the unified kingdom of Scotland. [Pre-12thC. From late Latin *Picti* (plural), of uncertain origin: perhaps from Latin *pictus* 'painted' (see PICTURE), from the Picts' painted or tattooed skin.]

Pictish /píktish/ adj. OF PICTS relating to the Picts, their culture, or their language ■ n. LANGUAGE FORMERLY USED IN SCOTLAND an extinct language spoken in an area that is now part of Scotland to the north of the Forth and Clyde Rivers. Its relationship with other languages remains unclear. Pictish had died out by about the 10th century AD, but it survives in some Scottish placenames. [Late 16thC]

pictograph /píktō graaf, -graf/, **pictogram** /-gram/ n. **1.** LANG PICTURE REPRESENTING WORD a graphic symbol or picture representing a word or idea in some writing systems, as opposed to a symbol such as a letter of the alphabet representing an individual sound **2.** CHART WITH PICTURES OR SYMBOLS a chart or diagram that uses symbols or pictures to represent values [Mid-19thC. Coined from Latin *pictus* (see PICTURE) + -GRAPH.] —**pictographer** /pik tóggrəfər/ n. —**pictographic** /píktə gráffik/ adj. —**pictographically** /-gráffik'li/ adv. —**pictography** /pik tóggrəfi/ n.

Picton /píktən/ town on the northeastern coast of the South Island, New Zealand. It is a ferry port and tourist centre. Population: 3,061 (1996).

Pictor /píktər/ n. an inconspicuous constellation of the southern hemisphere between Dorado and Columba

pictorial /pik táwri əl/ adj. **1.** OF PICTURES relating to, composed of, or shown by pictures **2.** ILLUSTRATED containing illustrations or photographs, as opposed to writing or text **3.** DESCRIPTIVE used to describe language that conjures up vivid images ■ n. HIGHLY ILLUSTRATED PERIODICAL a newspaper or magazine that has many pictures in it, especially one with far more pictures than text [Mid-17thC. Formed from late Latin *pictorius*, from Latin *pictor* 'painter', from *pictus* (see PICTURE).] —**pictoriality** /pik táwri álləti/ n. —**pictorially** /pik táwri əli/ adv. —**pictorialness** n.

pictorialize /pik táwri ə līz/ (**-izes, -izing, -ized**), **pictorialise** (**-ises, -ising, -ised**) vt. to represent sth in drawings, paintings, or photographs, or illustrate sth with them —**pictorialization** /pik táwri ə līzáysh'n/ n.

picture /píkchər/ n. **1.** STH DRAWN OR PAINTED a shape or set of shapes and lines drawn, painted, or printed on paper, canvas, or some other flat surface, especially shapes that represent a recognizable form or object **2.** PHOTOGRAPHY PHOTO a photograph **3.** TV TV IMAGE the image on a television screen **4.** CINEMA FILM a cinema film or motion picture **5.** MENTAL IMAGE a vivid image or impression in the mind of how sb or sth looks **6.** ARTISTIC DESCRIPTION OR REPRESENTATION a description or representation of sth in writing, in a film, in music, or some other art form **7.** OBSERVED SITUATION a situation regarded as a scene being observed **8.** EMBODIMENT OR EPITOME a typical or perfect example of the way sth looks, or sb or sth that embodies a quality or state perfectly ○ *They're the picture of the happily married couple.* **9.** SB WHO CLOSELY RESEMBLES ANOTHER sb who looks very much like sb else ○ *The daughter was the absolute picture of the grandmother.* **10.** BEAUTIFUL THING sth that is beautiful to look at ■ **pictures** npl. CINEMA CINEMA the cinema as entertainment, rather than an industry (*informal dated*) ■ vt. (**-tures, -turing, -tured**) **1.** IMAGINE STH to imagine or have an image of sb or sth in mind **2.** DESCRIBE STH to describe sb or sth in a particular way **3.** FEATURE PICTURE OF SB to feature a picture, especially a photograph, of sb or sth in a newspaper, magazine, or book (*often passive*) [15thC. From Latin *pictura*, from *pictus*, the past participle of *pingere* 'to paint' (source also of English *depict*, *paint*, and *pigment*).]

— WORD KEY: CULTURAL NOTE —

The Picture of Dorian Gray, a novel by the Oscar Wilde (1890). In Wilde's update of the Faust legend, the decadent young gentleman Dorian Gray trades his soul for eternal youth and beauty, but is subsequently tormented by a portrait of himself that constantly changes to reflect the ravages of time and of his debauched lifestyle. It was made into a film by Albert Lewin in 1945.

picture book n. a highly illustrated book, especially one for children, written in a simple style

picture card n. = court card. US term face card

picturegoer /píkchər gō ər/ n. sb who goes to the cinema (*dated*)

picture hat n. a woman's elaborately decorated hat with a very broad brim, of the kind often featured in informal portraits of women painted in the 18th century

picture hook n. a hook that is nailed to a wall or suspended from a rail fixed to the wall and used to hang a picture

picture house (plural **picture houses**) n. a cinema (*dated*)

picture library n. a place where photographs and other images are stored, from which they may be borrowed for use in books, magazines, and newspapers

picture moulding n. **1.** US = picture rail **2.** WOOD FOR PICTURE FRAMES carved or moulded wood used to make picture frames

picture palace n. a cinema (*dated*)

picture-perfect adj. very clean, tidy, ordered, and pleasing, as the subjects of paintings and photographs often are

picture postcard n. a postcard with a picture, often a photograph of a landmark or landscape, on one side (*dated*)

picture-postcard adj. very attractive, like the scenes typically photographed for picture postcards

picture rail n. a strip of wood or plaster, usually a cornice-like moulding, fixed high up around the walls of a room, from which you can hang pictures. US term picture molding

picture researcher n. sb whose job is finding the photographs, drawings, and other illustrative material for a book or magazine, using picture libraries and other sources

picturesque /píkchə résk/ adj. **1.** VERY ATTRACTIVE visually pleasing enough to be the subject of a painting or photograph **2.** VIVID so accurate or detailed as to evoke a clear mental image of what has been described **3.** OBSCENE containing a lot of swearwords (*used euphemistically*) **4.** DISTINCTIVE having a pleasingly distinctive or unusual atmosphere ○ *We ate* *lunch in a picturesque fishing village.* ■ *n.* PLEASING OR DISTINCTIVE THINGS things that are unusually pleasing or distinctive, spoken of collectively [Early 18thC. Anglicization (modelled on PICTURE) of French *pittoresque*, from Italian *pittoresco*, from *pittore* 'painter', from Latin *pictor* (see PICTORIAL).] —**picturesquely** *adv.* —**picturesqueness** *n.*

picture tube *n.* = tube *n.* 7

picture window *n.* a large window, usually with a single pane of glass, especially one that has a pleasant view

picture writing *n.* 1. WRITING WITH SYMBOLS FOR WHOLE WORDS a writing system such as that of Chinese that uses symbols or pictures to represent whole words or ideas rather than individual sounds 2. PICTURES RECOUNTING OR REPORTING STH the reporting of an event or telling of a story using pictures instead of words, e.g. in ancient cave paintings

picul /pík'l/ *n.* any of various units of weight used in Southeast Asia, especially the Chinese unit, which is equal to 60 kg/133 lb [Late 16thC. From Malay and Javanese *pikul* 'load'.]

piculet /píkyŏŏlət/ (*plural* -let *or* -lets) *n.* a very small tropical woodpecker. Genus: *Picumnus.* [Mid-19thC. Literally 'small small woodpecker', formed from Latin *picus* 'woodpecker'.]

PID *n.*, *abbr.* 1. MED pelvic inflammatory disease 2. COMPUT personal identification device

piddle /pídd'l/ *v.* (-dles, -dling, -dled) 1. *vi.* URINATE to urinate (*informal; usually used by or to children*) 2. *vti.* DO THINGS HAPHAZARDLY to do sth in a casual, unhurried, or disorganized way, often spending time on unimportant things ■ *n.* (*plural* -dles) URINATION an act of urinating (*informal; usually used by or to children*) [Late 18thC. Origin uncertain: perhaps a blend of PISS and PUDDLE.] —**piddler** *n.*

piddling /pídtling/ *adj.* very small, insignificant, or trivial (*informal*) [Mid-16thC. Formed from PIDDLE.] —**piddlingly** *adv.*

piddock /pídtdak/ *n.* MARINE BIOL a saltwater mollusc that has a hinged shell, like the mussel or clam, but with serrated edges that it uses to bore into rock and wood. Family: Pholadidae. [Mid-19thC. Origin unknown.]

pidgin /píjjin/ *n.* a simplified language made up of elements of two or more languages, used as a communication tool between speakers whose native languages are different [Early 19thC. From Chinese, alteration of BUSINESS.] —**pidginization** /píjji nī záysh'n/ *n.* —**pidginize** /píjji nīz/ *vt.*

pidgin English *n.* a pidgin containing elements of English vocabulary, grammar, and pronunciation, especially one formerly used between Chinese people and Europeans, or one currently spoken in West Africa and some Pacific islands

pi-dog *n.* = pye-dog

PIDS *abbr.* primary immune deficiency syndrome

pie[1] /pī/ *n.* 1. BAKED FOOD WITH PASTRY a baked dish consisting of a filling such as chopped meat or fruit enclosed in or covered with pastry and usually cooked in a container 2. DIVISIBLE WHOLE sth regarded as a resource to be shared or divided up ○ *Our competitors are always claiming for a larger piece of the overseas pie.* [14thC. Origin uncertain: perhaps from PIE[4], since the assorted contents of a pie resemble items collected by a magpie.] ◇ **pie in the sky** sth described very attractively that is not likely to happen or materialize

pie[2] /pī/ *n.* a very small coin formerly used in India, worth one third of a pice [Mid-19thC. Via Hindi *paī* from Sanskrit *pādikā*, from *pāda* 'quarter'.]

pie[3] *n.* PRINTING = pi[1] *n.* 2

pie[4] /pī/ (*plural* pie *or* pies) *n.* a magpie (*archaic*) [14thC. Via French from Latin *pica* 'magpie'.]

piebald /pī bawld/ *adj.* used to describe a horse whose coat has patches of two or more contrasting colours, especially black and white ■ *n.* a piebald horse [Late 16thC. From pie[4] (from the resemblance to a magpie's plumage) + bald]

piece /peess/ *n.* 1. PART DETACHED FROM LARGER WHOLE a part that has been broken, torn, or cut from a larger

whole 2. PORTION OR SERVING a portion or serving from a larger block or whole 3. INDIVIDUAL ITEM OR ARTICLE an item or article of a particular kind or class ○ *an expensive piece of equipment* 4. INTERCONNECTING PART any of a set of parts that fit together to form a whole or unit 5. EXAMPLE OF STH an instance or example of sth, often sth abstract such as luck 6. DECLARATION OF OPINION a statement of opinion on a particular subject, event, or situation ○ *At least I said my piece.* 7. ARTS ARTISTIC WORK a single artistic work, such as a musical composition, play, or painting 8. PRESS PUBLISHED ARTICLE an article in a newspaper or magazine 9. MONEY COIN a coin of a specified value ○ *a fifty-pence piece* 10. BOARD GAMES OBJECT MOVED IN BOARD GAME any of a set of objects that players on board games move on the board 11. FIREARM a gun, especially a handgun (*slang*) 12. OFFENSIVE TERM an offensive term for a woman (*slang offensive*) 13. US OFFENSIVE TERM an offensive term for sexual intercourse (*slang offensive*) 14. US, Can ESTIMATE OF DISTANCE an unspecified distance (*informal*) ○ *You go down the road a piece and then you come to the bridge.* 15. Scotland, UK SLICE OF BREAD OR SNACK a slice of bread, a sandwich, or a snack taken to be eaten somewhere, especially school or work (*regional*) 16. ANZ FLEECE a fragment of fleece (*often used in the plural*) ■ *vt.* (**pieces**, **piecing**, **pieced**) 1. WORK STH OUT to put sth together gradually, bit by bit ○ *We finally managed to piece together the events of that night.* 2. MEND STH to mend sth by patching it [12thC. From Old French *piece*, probably of Gaulish origin.]

piece out *vt.* to share or dispense sth, such as food, in a makeshift, piecemeal way

pièce de résistance /pi éss de re zís toNss/ (*plural* **pièces de résistance** /pi éss de re zís toNss/) *n.* 1. MOST IMPRESSIVE THING the most impressive thing or sth that brings the greatest pride or satisfaction 2. MOST IMPORTANT DISH the most important dish served at a meal (*formal*) [Late 18thC. From French, literally 'piece of resistance', originally applied to the most substantial dish in a meal.]

piece-dyed *adj.* dyed after being woven

piece goods *npl.* fabrics made and sold in standard lengths

piecemeal /peéss meel/ *adv.* 1. GRADUALLY little by little 2. IN PARTS in separate parts or fragments ■ *adj.* DONE BIT BY BIT done in a disorganized or fragmentary way ○ *His novel is a ragtag, piecemeal work.* [13thC. From PIECE + obsolete -*meal* 'measure', from Old English *mæl* 'measure, meal' (see MEAL).]

piece of cake *n.* sth that is very easy to do (*informal*) [From the easiness of eating cake, a soft food]

piece of eight *n.* an old Spanish gold coin worth eight reals

piece of piss *n.* sth that is very easy to do (*slang*)

piece of work *n.* sb or sth remarkable or outstanding

piecework /peéss wurk/ *n.* work that is paid by the amount rather than by the time spent doing it

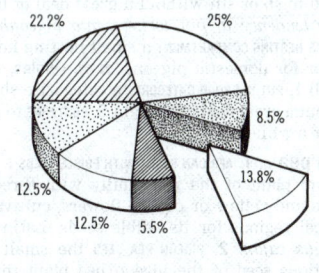

Piechart

piechart /pī chaart/ *n.* a diagrammatic representation of a group shown as a circle divided into sections by straight lines from its centre with areas proportional to the relative size of the quantity represented

piecing /peéssing/ *n.* the sewing together of various pieces of cloth or leather to make a larger decorative fabric

pied-à-terre /pi áyd aa taír, peé edaa táir/ (*plural* **pieds-à-terre**) *n.* a small flat or house used as a second home for holidays or business purposes [From French, literally 'foot to earth']

piedmont /peéd mont/ *n.* AREA AT FOOT OF MOUNTAINS a region at the base of a mountain range ■ *adj.* AT FOOT OF MOUNTAINS lying or formed at the base of a mountain range [Mid-19thC. From *Piedmont*, hilly region of the eastern United States, named after *Piemonte*, a region of northwest Italy, literally in Italian 'foot of the mountain'.]

Piedmont Plateau /peéd mont-/ region of the eastern United States between the Appalachian Mountains and the Atlantic Coastal Plain

Pied Piper /pīd pípər/ *n.* 1. LEGENDARY PLAYER OF ENCHANTING MUSIC a visiting piper in German folklore whose entrancing music rid the town of Hamelin of its rats. He later lured away its children after town officials refused to pay him for his services. 2. **Pied Piper**, **pied piper** SB OTHERS FOLLOW sb who attracts supporters and followers, especially by making unrealistic promises

──────── **WORD KEY: CULTURAL NOTE** ────────
The Pied Piper of Hamelin, a poem by Robert Browning (1842). Based on a medieval legend, it tells the story of a piper who successfully rids a town of rats by luring the animals into a river with his music. When the citizens refuse to pay him for his services, he uses the same technique to abduct their children. The term *pied piper*, a charismatic leader who makes attractive but false promises, is taken from the title and main character of this poem.

pied wagtail *n.* 1. SMALL EUROPEAN BIRD a small European bird with black-and-white plumage and a long black tail. Latin name: *Motacilla alba yarrellii*. 2. LONG-TAILED AFRICAN BIRD a long-tailed black-and-white bird found throughout Africa. Latin name: *Motacilla aguimp*.

pie-eyed *adj.* very drunk (*informal*) [Because vision is affected by the alcohol]

pier /peer/ *n.* 1. SEASIDE STRUCTURE a platform built on stilts jutting out into a body of water, used as a boat jetty, a place from which to fish, or as an entertainment centre 2. VERTICAL STRUCTURAL SUPPORT a pillar, especially a rectangular one supporting the end of an arch, lintel, or vault 3. BRIDGE SUPPORT a vertical structural support between two spans of a bridge 4. WALL BETWEEN ADJACENT DOORS an area of wall between two adjacent doors, windows, or other openings 5. COLUMN PROJECTING FROM WALL a column of masonry projecting from a wall 6. WALL REINFORCEMENT a vertical structure, usually of masonry, built against a wall to support it 7. BREAKWATER a barrier built out to sea to protect a harbour from heavy waves [12thC. From Anglo-Latin *pera*.]

──────── **WORD KEY: CULTURAL NOTE** ────────
The Road to Wigan Pier, a book by George Orwell (1937). It combines a first-hand account of the appalling living conditions endured by workers in northern England with a penetrating analysis of class interests and prejudices. Its graphic and moving descriptions, compelling arguments, and restrained anger make it a classic of literary journalism.

pierce /peerss/ (**pierces**, **piercing**, **pierced**) *v.* 1. *vti.* BORE INTO STH to penetrate through or into sth with a sharp pointed object 2. *vt.* PUT HOLE IN to make a hole through sth ○ *She had her ears pierced.* 3. *vti.* PENETRATE A BARRIER to break through a barrier of some kind, e.g. a defensive line or security system 4. *vti.* GAIN SIGHT OR KNOWLEDGE to perceive sth with the eyes or the mind 5. *vti.* PENETRATE STH WITH SOUND OR LIGHT to sound or shine suddenly and sharply through sth, such as silence or darkness ○ *A dreadful scream pierced the silence.* 6. *vt.* AFFECT DEEPLY to have a sudden intense, often painful effect on sb ○ *A stab of fear pierced his heart.* [13thC. Via French *percer* from, ultimately, Latin *pertundere* 'to bore through', from *tundere* 'to bore'.] —**piercer** *n.*

Pierce /peerss/, **Franklin** (1804–69) US statesman and 14th President of the United States (1853–57). A Democrat, he sided with the South on the slavery issue, yet was committed to the Union.

──
zh vision   In foreign words: kh German Bach; aN French vin; aaN French blanc; ö German schön, French feu; oN French bon; öN French un; ü French rue   Stress marks: ´ as in **secret** \seék rət\; **academic** \àkə démmik\

Franklin Pierce

piercing /péerssing/ adj. **1.** PENETRATING with an unpleasantly intense quality ○ a piercing cry **2.** PERCEPTIVE capable of perceiving acutely ○ her piercing gaze **3.** INTENSELY COLD with a sharp deeply chilling cold ○ a piercing wind ■ n. **1.** MAKING HOLES FOR RINGS IN BODY the practice of piercing holes in parts of the body so that rings or studs can be inserted ○ body piercing **2.** HOLE FOR RING IN BODY a hole pierced in a part of the body to take a ring or stud ○ She had piercings on her eyebrow and nose. —**piercingly** adv.

Pieria /pī éeri ə/ region of ancient Macedonia where, according to Greek mythology, the Pierian Spring was located

Pierian /pī éeri ən/ adj. **1.** OF ANCIENT PIERIA relating to the region of Pieria in ancient Macedonia, to its spring, or to the Muses who lived there **2.** INSPIRING providing poetic inspiration (literary)

Pierian Spring n. in Greek mythology, the spring at Pieria in ancient Macedonia that was sacred to the Muses, who lived there, and gave poetic inspiration to anyone who drank from it

Piero della Francesca /pyáirō déllə fran chéskə/ (1420?–92) Italian painter. One of the leading figures of the early Renaissance, he is noted particularly for his frescoes for the church of San Francesco, Arezzo.

Pierrot /péerō/ n. **1.** FRENCH PANTOMIME CHARACTER a character in traditional French pantomime. He is a white-faced clown with a white costume and pointed hat, and is often represented as sad or crying. **2.** **pierrot, Pierrot** CLOWN any clown with a white face and a baggy white costume [Mid-18thC. From French, literally 'little Peter', from Pierre 'Peter'.]

Pietà /pée e taá/, **pietà** n. a painting or sculpture of the Virgin Mary mourning over Jesus Christ's dead body [Mid-17thC. Via Italian from Latin pietas (see PIETY).]

Pietermaritzburg /péetər márrits burg/ capital city of Kwazulu-Natal Province, South Africa, situated 72 km/45 mi. northwest of Durban. Population: 156,473 (1991).

pietism /pī ətizəm/ n. **1.** PIOUSNESS devotion to a deity or deities and observance of religious principles in everyday life **2.** SANCTIMONIOUSNESS excessive or insincere religious devotion [Early 19thC. From PIETISM.] —**pietist** /pī ətist/ n. —**pietistic** /pī ə tístik/ adj. —**pietistically** /-tístik'li/ adv.

Pietism /pī ətizəm/ n. a German Protestant movement in the 17th and 18th centuries that changed the focus of Lutheranism from ritual and church government to personal piety. It was founded by Philipp Jakob Spener. [Late 17thC. Via German Pietismus from Latin pietas (see PIETY).]

piety /pī ə ti/ (plural **-ties**) n. **1.** RELIGIOUS DEVOTION strong respectful belief in a deity or deities and strict observance of religious principles in everyday life **2.** DEVOUT ACT an action inspired by devout religious principles **3.** INSINCERE ATTITUDE a conventional or hypocritical statement or observance of a belief **4.** FAMILY LOYALTY loyalty to parents and family (archaic) [14thC. Via Old French piete from Latin pietas, from pius 'devout', source of English pious.]

piezo- prefix. pressure ○ piezoelectric crystal [From Greek piezein 'to press'. Ultimately from an Indo-European base meaning 'to sit' that is also the ancestor of English sit and Sanskrit upaniṣad (see UPANISHAD).]

piezoelectricity /péezō i lék tríssəti, -éllek-/ n. PHYS the electric current produced by some crystals and ceramic materials when they are subjected to mechanical pressure —**piezoelectric** /péezō i léktrik/ adj.

piezometer /pee zómmitər/ n. an instrument for measuring the compressibility of a material or fluid under pressure —**piezometric** /péezō méttrik/ adj. —**piezometrically** /-méttrik'li/ adv.

piffle /píff'l/ n. NONSENSE silly talk or ideas (informal) ○ Don't talk piffle! ■ vi. (**-fles, -fling, -fled**) BEHAVE THOUGHTLESSLY to behave in a silly or ineffective way (dated informal) [Mid-19thC. Origin uncertain: perhaps suggesting the sound of silly talk.]

piffling /píff'ling/ adj. of little use, value, or importance (informal)

pig /pig/ n. **1.** FARM ANIMAL WITH BROAD SNOUT a sturdy short-legged mammal with a broad snout, especially a domesticated pig, commonly kept as a farm animal and traditionally represented as fat and pink with a curly tail. Latin name: Sus scrofa. **2.** PORK the meat of a pig **3.** GREEDY PERSON sb who is slovenly, greedy, or gluttonous (informal) **4.** COARSE PERSON sb who behaves in a coarse, discourteous, or brutal manner (informal) **5.** STH UNPLEASANT a thing or situation that is difficult or unpleasant (informal) ○ a pig of a job **6.** METALL BLOCK OF METAL a casting of metal in a basic shape suitable for storage or transportation **7.** METALL METAL MOULD a basic mould for casting metal, especially iron **8.** OFFENSIVE TERM an offensive term for a member of the police force (slang offensive) ■ v. (**pigs, pigging, pigged**) **1.** vi. GIVE BIRTH TO PIGS to give birth to a litter of pigs **2.** vt. EAT GREEDILY to eat gluttonously or excessively (informal) ○ Who's pigged all the chocolate biscuits? [Assumed Old English picga. Originally in the sense 'young pig'.] ◇ **a pig in a poke** sth that is bought or obtained without being inspected to see if it is worth having ◇ **make a pig's ear of sth** to do sth very badly (informal)

pig out vi. to eat greedily or gluttonously (informal)

pigeon[1] /píjjən/ n. **1.** BIRD COMMON IN CITIES a medium-sized bird with a stocky body and short legs, especially a domesticated variety of the rock dove, commonly seen in cities and throughout most of the world, or trained for racing and carrying messages. Latin name: Columba livia. **2.** GULLIBLE PERSON sb who is easily swindled or deceived (informal) [14thC. Via Old French pijon 'young bird' from a Vulgar Latin alteration of late Latin pipio, from an assumed base imitative of the sound of cheeping.]

pigeon[2] /píjjən/ n. a matter of concern or responsibility to sb in particular ○ Matters of this kind are not my pigeon. [Early 19thC. Alteration of PIDGIN, in allusion to pigeon-fancying.]

pigeon breast, **pigeon chest** n. a condition in which the sides of the chest are flattened and the centre protrudes like the keel of a boat —**pigeon-breasted** adj.

pigeonhole /píjjən hōl/ n. **1.** PLACE TO PUT MESSAGES any of a series of small compartments in a desk or wall unit into which papers or messages can be sorted or placed **2.** BROAD CATEGORY a category or label assigned to sb or sth without a great deal of thought ○ the tendency to put writers into pigeonholes **3.** PIGEON'S NESTING COMPARTMENT a small nesting hole in a shelter for domestic pigeons ■ vt. (**-holes, -holing, -holed**) **1.** PUT IN BROAD CATEGORY to categorize sb or sth without a great deal of thought **2.** POSTPONE to put sth off for a while

pigeon pea n. **1.** AFRICAN PLANT WITH EDIBLE SEEDS a woody African plant of the pea family with three-lobed leaves and yellow or orange flowers, cultivated in tropical regions for its edible seeds. Latin name: Cajanus cajan. **2.** PIGEON PEA SEED the small edible nutritious seed of the pigeon pea plant that is a popular ingredient in West Indian cookery [From the use of its seeds as pigeon-feed]

pigeon-toed adj. tending to walk or stand with the toes turned inwards

pigfish /píg fish/ n. a food fish of the grunt family found on the Atlantic coast of North America. Latin name: Orthopristis chrysoptera.

piggery /píggəri/ (plural **-ies**) n. **1.** PLACE FOR RAISING PIGS a farm or a building on a farm where pigs are

bred and raised **2.** COARSE BEHAVIOUR coarse, greedy, or otherwise distasteful behaviour

piggish /píggish/ adj. **1.** GLUTTONOUS eating too much too fast **2.** OBSTINATE behaving in a stubborn, uncooperative, or obstructive way —**piggishly** adv. —**piggishness** n.

piggy /píggi/ n. (plural **-gies**) (informal babytalk) **1.** PIG a pig or piglet **2.** TOE a toe, especially a small child's toe ■ adj. (**-gier, -giest**) = **piggish**

piggyback /píggi bak/, **pickaback** /píkə bak/ n. **1.** RIDE ON SB'S BACK a ride on sb's back or shoulders **2.** TRANSP HAULING OF ONE VEHICLE BY ANOTHER the transporting of one vehicle by another, e.g. cars by lorry or lorry trailers by railway wagon ■ adj., adv. **1.** ON SB'S BACK carried on the back or shoulders of another person **2.** TRANSP ON OTHER VEHICLE transported on another vehicle **3.** AS AN ADDITION linked with or added onto sth larger or more important ■ v. (**-backs, -backing, -backed**) **1.** vt. CARRY ON BACK to carry sb on the back or shoulders **2.** vt. TRANSP TRANSPORT to transport one vehicle on another **3.** vti. ATTACH ONE THING TO ANOTHER to link or add sth to a larger or more important item, or to become linked or added to sth else [Mid-16thC. Origin uncertain: perhaps originally a dialect form of earlier English pick back, literally 'to throw back' or 'to throw a pack', which by folk etymology was associated with PIG.]

piggy bank n. a child's money box, especially but not necessarily one in the shape of a pig

piggy in the middle n. **1.** CHILDREN'S GAME a game played by children, in which two people throw a ball to each other and a third person stands in the middle and tries to intercept it. US term **monkey in the middle** **2.** SB CAUGHT UP IN ARGUMENT sb who is uncomfortably caught up in a disagreement between two people or groups

pigheaded /píg héddid/ adj. stubbornly adhering to a belief, decision, or course of action —**pigheadedly** adv. —**pigheadedness** n.

pig iron n. a crude form of iron made in a blast furnace and shaped into rough blocks for storage or transportation. Pig iron is processed further to make steel, wrought iron, and other alloys. [From PIG]

pig Latin n. any joke dialect coined and used by children, especially one in which first consonants are moved to the end of the words and extra syllables added [From the perception of pigs as vulgar]

piglet /píglət/ n. a newborn or immature pig

pigment n. /pígmənt/ **1.** COLOURING SUBSTANCE a substance that is added to give sth, such as paint or ink its colour. Pigments are often available in the form of dry powders to be added to liquids. **2.** NATURAL PLANT COLOURING a natural substance in plant or animal tissue that gives it its colour ■ vt. /píg mént/ (**-ments, -menting, -mented**) GIVE COLOUR TO to impart colour to sth [Pre-12thC. From Latin pigmentum, from pingere 'to paint' (source of English picture). Ultimately from an Indo-European base meaning 'to cut' (ancestor also of English file).] —**pigmentary** /pígməntəri/ adj.

pigmentation /pígmen táysh'n/ n. **1.** NATURAL COLOUR the natural colour of plants and animals **2.** DISCOLOURATION abnormal colouring in plant or animal tissue that occurs as a result of disease

Pigmy /pígmi/ n. = **Pygmy**

pigmy hippopotamus n. = **pygmy hippopotamus**

pignut /píg nut/ n. **1.** PLANT WITH EDIBLE TUBERS a plant found in woods and the shaded sides of fields with edible underground tubers. Latin name: Conopodium majus. **2.** EDIBLE TUBER OF PIGNUT the roundish edible tuber of the pignut

pigpen /píg pen/ n. **1.** US = **pigsty** **2.** ENCLOSURE FOR PIGS an indoor enclosure in which pigs are kept on a modern pig farm, as distinct from the traditional outdoor pigsty **3.** US = **pigsty**

Pigs, Bay of /pigz/ ◆ **Bay of Pigs**

pigskin /píg skin/ n. LEATHER FROM PIG the skin of a pig, especially when made into leather ■ adj. MADE OF LEATHER FROM PIG made of leather prepared from the skin of a pig

pigsty /píg stī/ (plural **-sties**) n. US term **pigpen 1.** PLACE FOR PIGS a building or enclosure where pigs are kept, especially a traditional outdoor enclosure **2. UNTIDY PLACE** a dirty or disorderly place

pigswill /píg swil/ *n.* waste food and kitchen scraps that are fed to pigs

pigtail /píg tayl/ *n.* **1. HAIR PLAIT** a plait or bunch, often in pairs, into which the hair is either plaited or gathered **2. HAIR** = **queue** *n.* 4 **3. TOBACCO STRAND** a thin twisted piece of tobacco **4. ELEC BRAIDED WIRE** a short length of flexible electrical cable or wire, usually braided, connecting two terminals —**pigtailed** *adj.*

pigweed /píg weed/ *n.* **1. WEED WITH HAIRY LEAVES** a North American weed of the amaranth family with hairy leaves and green flowers growing in spikes. Latin name: *Amaranthus retroflexus.* **2.** = **fat hen**

pika /píːkə/ (*plural* -**kas** *or* -**ka**) *n.* a small short-eared burrowing mammal that is related to the rabbit and lives in rocky mountainous regions of western North America and Asia. Family: Ochotonidae. [Early 19thC. From Tungus *piika*.]

Pike

pike[1] /píːk/ (*plural* **pikes** *or* **pike**) *n.* **1. LARGE SHARP-TOOTHED FRESHWATER FISH** a large predatory freshwater fish of northern waters with a long body, long broad snout, and sharp teeth. It is a popular food and game fish. Latin name: *Esox lucius.* **2. FISH RESEMBLING PIKE** a fish that resembles the pike or belongs to the same family, especially the muskellunge and the pickerel [14thC. From PIKE[3]; from its long pointed jaws.]

pike[2] /píːk/ *n.* **SPIKE ON POLE** a weapon, used in the past by foot soldiers, consisting of a very long pole with a pointed metal head ■ *vt.* (**pikes, piking, piked**) **ATTACK WITH PIKE** to stab or kill sb with a pike [Early 16thC. From French *pique*, from *piquer* (see PIQUE).]

pike[3] /píːk/ *n.* a sharp pointed object of any kind [Old English *pic*]

pike[4] /píːk/ *n.* **N England** a pointed rugged summit of a steep hill or mountain [13thC. Origin uncertain: either from PIKE[3], or of Scandinavian origin.]

pike[5] /píːk/ *n.* a road on which a toll is paid [Early 19thC. Shortening of TURNPIKE.]

pike[6] /píːk/ *n.* a diving or gymnastic position in which the body is bent at the hips with the head tucked under and the hands touching the toes or behind the knees [Early 20thC. Origin unknown.] —**piked** *adj.*

pike[7] /píːk/ (**pikes, piking, piked**) *vi.* **Aus** to let sb down by breaking an arrangement or commitment (*slang*) ○ *We're playing this evening, but no doubt John will pike on us.* [Late 19thC. From earlier pike 'to leave quickly', of uncertain origin.]

pikelet /píːklət/ *n.* **1. THIN CRUMPET** a soft flat yeast cake, traditionally made in northern England. It is similar to a crumpet but thinner and is usually eaten buttered. **2. ANZ SMALL PANCAKE** a small thick pancake made of batter [Late 18thC. From Welsh *pyglyd* 'pitchy', in the phrase *bara pyglyd* 'pitchy bread', perhaps because of its dark colour.]

pikeman /píːkmən/ (*plural* -**men** /-mən/) *n.* a foot soldier armed with a pike

pikeperch /píːk purch/ (*plural* -**perches** *or* -**perch**) *n.* = **walleye** *n.* 4

piker /píːkər/ *n.* **1. US CAUTIOUS GAMBLER** sb who gambles cautiously with little money (*informal*) **2. US STINGY PERSON** sb who is stingy with money (*informal*) **3. US PETTY PERSON** sb who does things in a small-minded or petty way (*informal*) **4. Aus UNRELIABLE PERSON** sb who lets people down, especially repeatedly, by

withdrawing from agreements or commitments (*slang*)

pikestaff /píːk staaf/ *n.* **1. SHAFT OF PIKE** the wooden shaft of a pike, which forms the handle **2. POINTED WALKING STICK** a walking stick with a pointed metal end

pilaf *n.* = **pilau**

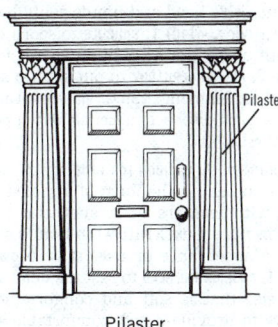

Pilaster

Pilaster

pilaster /pi lástər/ *n.* a vertical structural part of a building that projects partway from a wall and is made to resemble an ornamental column by adding a base and capital [Late 16thC. Via French *pilastre* from Italian *pilastro* or medieval Latin *pilastrum*, from Latin *pila* 'pillar'.] —**pilastered** *adj.*

Pilate /píːlət/, **Pontius** (*fl.* 1st century AD) Roman administrator. As procurator of Judaea (AD 26–36) he condemned Jesus Christ to death, albeit reluctantly, according to the Bible.

pilau /peé low/, **pilaf** /peé laf/ *n.* a dish of spiced rice, often with chopped vegetables, fish, or meat added [Early 17thC. From Turkish *pilâv* 'cooked rice'.]

Pilbara /púbrə/ region in northwestern Western Australia, located between the De Grey and Ashburton rivers

pilchard /píːlchərd/ (*plural* -**chards** *or* -**chard**) *n.* a small edible marine fish of the herring family that lives in European waters and has a rounded body and large scales. It is often sold in tins. Latin name: *Sardinia pilchardus.* [Mid-16thC. Origin unknown.]

pile[1] /píːl/ *n.* **1. MOUND OF THINGS** a number of things heaped or stacked one on top of another **2. LARGE QUANTITY** a very large amount of sth (*informal*) (*often used in the plural*) ○ *I've got piles of work to do.* **3. FORTUNE** a very large amount of money, especially one large enough to retire on (*informal*) ○ *He'd already made his pile by the age of 30.* **4. BUILDING** a large impressive building **5. PYRE** a funeral pyre (*archaic*) **6. ELEC** = **voltaic pile 7. NUCLEAR PHYS NUCLEAR REACTOR** a nuclear reactor (*dated*) ■ *v.* (**piles, piling, piled**) **1.** *vt.* **MAKE INTO A MOUND** to heap or stack things one on top of another **2.** *vt.* **PLACE LARGE AMOUNTS ON STH** to heap a large amount of sth somewhere ○ *plates piled high with mussels* **3.** *vi.* **GO AS A CROWD** to move hurriedly in a large disorganized group ○ *We all piled into the car and headed for the seaside.* [15thC. Via French, from Latin *pila* 'pillar' (source also of English *pillar*).] ◇ **pile it on (thick)** to exaggerate sth, especially its intensity or severity (*informal*)

pile on *vt.* to continually add more and more of sth ○ *Arsenal piled on the pressure in the second half.*

pile up *vti.* **1. AMASS** to accumulate, or accumulate sth, rapidly, forming a large amount **2. CRASH** to crash a vehicle, or to collide with other vehicles, forming a chain of collisions

pile[2] /píːl/ *n.* **CONSTR SUNKEN SUPPORT FOR BUILDING** a vertical wood, metal, or concrete support for a building or other structure that is driven into the ground **2. HERALDRY HERALDIC SYMBOL** a heraldic figure in the shape of an arrowhead, usually displayed with the point downwards **3. ARMS ARROWHEAD** the pointed head of an arrow (*technical*) **4. ARMS ANCIENT ROMAN JAVELIN** a javelin used by foot soldiers in ancient Rome ■ *vt.* (**piles, piling, piled**) **CONSTR SUPPORT A STRUCTURE WITH PILES** to use piles as a support for a building or other structure [Pre-12thC. From Latin *pilum* 'javelin'.]

pile[3] /píːl/ *n.* **1. LOOPED FABRIC SURFACE** the surface of a carpet or of a fabric such as velvet that is formed of short, sometimes cut, loops of fibre **2. FUR** the fine soft fur or hair of an animal [Mid-16thC. Origin

uncertain: probably via Anglo-Norman *peile* from, ultimately, Latin *pilus* 'hair' (source of English *depilatory*, *pluck* and, perhaps, *pillage*).]

pilea plural of **pileum**

pileate /píːli ət/, **pileated** /píːli əytid/ *adj.* **1. BIRDS CRESTED** used to describe a bird that has a crest of feathers on its head **2. FUNGI WITH CAP-SHAPED PART** used to describe a fungus that has a cap-shaped upper part (**pileus**) [Early 18thC. From Latin *pileatus*, literally 'wearing a felt cap', from *pileus* 'felt cap'.]

pile-driver *n.* **1. MACHINE THAT HAMMERS PILES** a large mechanical hammering device that uses steam, compressed air, or gravity to drive construction piles into the ground **2. STRONG BLOW** a very strong blow or kick (*informal*)

pile-driving *adj.* very powerful or strong (*informal*) ○ *a rock number with a pile-driving beat*

pilei plural of **pileus**

pileous /píːli əss/ *adj.* **BIOL** covered with hair [Mid-18thC. From Latin *pileus*, literally 'felt cap'.]

piles /píːlz/ *npl.* haemorrhoids (*informal*) [15thC. Origin uncertain: probably from Latin *pila* 'ball', from their shape.]

pileum /píːli əm/ (*plural* -**a** /píːli ə/) *n.* the top of a bird's head from the base of the bill to the nape of the neck [Late 19thC. Via modern Latin from Latin *pileus* 'felt cap'.]

pile-up *n.* **1. LARGE-SCALE COLLISION** a collision involving several vehicles (*informal*) **2. ACCUMULATION OF THINGS** an accumulated number or amount of things such as tasks

pileus /píːli əss/ (*plural* -**i** /píːli ī/) *n.* **1. BOT CAP OF MUSHROOM** the top cap-shaped part of a mushroom or other fungus **2. MARINE BIOL JELLYFISH'S BODY** the part of the body of a jellyfish that resembles an opened umbrella **3. CLOTHES ROMAN SKULLCAP** a close-fitting brimless cap worn by ancient Romans [Mid-18thC. From Latin *pileus* 'felt cap'.]

pilewort /píːl wurt/ (*plural* -**worts** *or* -**wort**) *n.* a flowering plant of the buttercup family such as the lesser celandine, sometimes used as a remedy for haemorrhoids [15thC. PILE the singular of PILES.]

pilfer /pílfər/ (-**fers**, -**fering**, -**fered**) *vti.* to steal small items of little value, especially habitually [14thC. From Anglo-Norman *pelfrer* 'to rob', of uncertain origin.] —**pilferage** *n.* —**pilferer** *n.* —**pilfering** *n.*

— **WORD KEY: SYNONYMS** —
See Synonyms at **steal.**

pilgrim /pílgrim/ *n.* **1. RELIGIOUS TRAVELLER** sb who goes on a journey to a holy place for religious reasons **2. TRAVELLER** sb who is making a journey of any kind (*literary*) [12thC. Via Provençal *pelegrin* from Latin *peregrinus* (see PEREGRINE).]

— **WORD KEY: CULTURAL NOTE** —
The Pilgrim's Progress, a story by John Bunyan (1678, 1684). An allegorical account of religious conversion, it describes the journey of a man called Christian from the City of Destruction (the contemporary, corrupt world) to the Celestial City (a state of religious grace). Much of its immense and lasting popularity can be attributed to the author's skill in rendering complex abstract issues immediate, entertaining, and accessible. It is the source of three well-known expressions in use today – *muck-raker* (an investigative journalist seeking sensational stories), *slough of despond* (a state of profoundly deep depression), and *vanity fair* (a place or situation of ostentatious, empty pride).

Pilgrim /píll grim/ *n.* one of the English Puritans who founded Plymouth Colony in Massachusetts in 1620

pilgrimage /pílgrimij/ *n.* **1. RELIGIOUS JOURNEY** a journey to a holy place, undertaken for religious reasons **2. TRIP TO SPECIAL PLACE** a journey to a place with special significance ○ *Thousands of fans make the pilgrimage to Elvis's birthplace every year.* [13thC. From Provençal *pelegrinatge*, from Latin *peregrinus* (see PEREGRINE).]

Pilgrim's Way /pílgrimz-/ track in southern England. Dating from prehistoric times, it runs from Winchester, in Hampshire, to Canterbury, in Kent.

pili **BIOL** plural of **pilus**

piliferous /pī líffərəss/ *adj.* used to describe plant parts that are covered in fine hairs or have hairs growing at the tip [Mid-19thC. Coined from PILUS + -I- + -FEROUS.]

piliform /pílli fawrm/ *adj.* used to describe a plant part that takes the form of a hair [Early 19thC. Coined from PILUS + -FORM.]

Pilipino /pílli pe'enō/ *n., adj.* LANG = **Filipino**

pill /pil/ *n.* **1.** **ROUND TABLET OF MEDICINE** a round solid tablet of medicine to be taken orally **2. pill, Pill ORAL CONTRACEPTIVE** a contraceptive that is taken orally in pill form **3. STH ROUND** sth round such as a ball, bullet, or bomb (*informal*) **4. TIRESOME PERSON** sb who is unpleasant or boring (*dated slang*) ■ **pills** *npl.* **TESTICLES** a man's testicles (*slang*) ■ *v.* **(pills, pilling, pilled) 1.** *vi.* **FORM LITTLE BALLS WHEN RUBBED** to become covered in small balls of matted fibre as a result of friction (*refers to fabrics*) **2.** *vt.* **EXCLUDE** to reject sb either by vote or consensus (*dated slang*) [15thC. From Middle Low German or Middle Dutch *pille*, of uncertain origin: probably from Latin *pilula*, literally 'little ball', from *pila* 'ball'.] ◇ **a bitter pill (to swallow)** sth that it difficult or painful to accept ◇ **sugar** *or* **sweeten the pill** to make sth unpalatable easier to accept or deal with

pillage /píllij/ *vti.* **(-lages, -laging, -laged) 1. PLUNDER A PLACE** to rob a place using force, especially during a war **2. STEAL PEOPLE'S POSSESSIONS** to steal goods using force, especially during a war ■ *n.* **1. STEALING OF SB'S POSSESSIONS** theft of goods from a place using force, especially during a war **2. STOLEN POSSESSIONS** goods that are stolen using force, especially during war [14thC. From French, from *piller* 'to plunder', of uncertain origin: perhaps from Latin *pilare* 'to remove hair', or from assumed Vulgar Latin *piliare*, from Latin *pilum* 'javelin'.] —**pillager** *n.*

pillar /píllər/ *n.* **1. COLUMN USED FOR SUPPORT OR DECORATION** a vertical column that is part of a building or other structure and can be either a support or decoration **2. STH TALL AND NARROW** sth that is tall and slender like a pillar **3. CENTRAL FIGURE** sb who is a mainstay of an organization or society ○ *She was a pillar of the community.* ■ *vt.* **(-lars, -laring, -lared) SUPPORT WITH PILLARS** to support or strengthen sth with pillars [13thC. Via Anglo-Norman *piler* from, ultimately, Latin *pila* 'pillar' (source of English *compile* and *pile* 'heap').] ◇ **from pillar to post** from one place to another

pillar box *n.* a tall round red postbox where letters can be posted for collection

pillar-box red *adj.* of a bright red colour, like a British letter box

pillarization /píllə rī záysh'n/, **pillarisation** *n.* the division of society into autonomous groups whose members share a common language or set of beliefs. Each group retains its own identity, while crossing lines of class and status. In Dutch society pillarization is based upon Calvinist, Roman Catholic, and Humanist social groupings. [Translation of Dutch *verzuiling*]

Pillars of Hercules two promontories, the Rock of Gibraltar and Jebel Musa, on either side of the Strait of Gibraltar at the far western end of the Mediterranean. According to legend, the two rocks were separated by Hercules.

Pillars of Islam, Five Pillars of Islam *npl.* the basic tenets of Islam, which are a belief in Allah and in Muhammad as his prophet, in prayer, in charity, in fasting, and in making a pilgrimage to Mecca

pillbox /píl bokss/ *n.* **1. PILL-CONTAINER** a small container for pills **2. pillbox, pillbox hat WOMAN'S BRIMLESS HAT** a woman's shallow brimless hat with a flat top **3. GUN SHELTER** a small fortified shelter with a flat roof

pillion /pílli ən/ *n.* **PASSENGER SEAT** a seat for a passenger behind the driver of a motorbike or the rider of a horse ■ *adv.* **BEHIND THE RIDER** seated behind the driver of a motorbike or the rider of a horse [15thC. From Gaelic *pillean* and Irish *pillin*, literally 'little couch', from *pell* 'couch', from Latin *pellis* 'skin' (source of English *pelt* 'skin').]

pilliwinks /pílli wingks/ *npl.* an instrument of torture used on the fingers and thumbs in medieval times (*takes a singular or plural verb*) [15thC. Origin unknown.]

pillock /píllək/ *n.* sb who behaves in a thoughtless or unintelligent way (*informal insult*) [Mid-16thC. Contraction of earlier *pillicock* 'penis', from an uncertain, possibly Scandinavian word + COCK[1].]

pillory /píllәri/ *n.* (*plural* **-ries**) **OLD PUNISHMENT DEVICE** a device used in the past as a means of public punishment, in the form of a wooden frame with holes into which sb's head and hands could be locked ■ *vt.* **(-ries, -rying, -ried) 1. RIDICULE** to scorn or ridicule sb or sth openly, or expose sb or sth to scorn or ridicule **2. PUNISH IN PILLORY** to put sb into a pillory as a public punishment [13thC. Via Anglo-Latin *pillorium* from Old French *pillorie*, of uncertain origin: perhaps from Provençal *espilori*.]

pillow /píllō/ *n.* **1. CUSHION FOR HEAD** a soft support for the head in bed, in the form of a sealed fabric bag stuffed with feathers or a synthetic filling **2.** = **cushion** *n.* 7 **3. STH LIKE A PILLOW** sth that is similar to a pillow in appearance or use ■ *vt.* **(-lows, -lowing, -lowed) 1. CUSHION THE HEAD** to rest the head on a pillow or sth else that is soft and comfortable **2. ACT AS PILLOW FOR** to provide a soft comfortable surface on which to rest sth [Pre-12thC. Via a prehistoric West Germanic word (source also of German *pfühl* and Dutch *peluw*), from Latin *pulvinus*.]

pillow block *n.* an enclosure and support for a shaft or axle of a machine

pillowcase /píllō kayss/ *n.* a fabric cover for a pillow

pillow lace *n.* lace made using bobbins and a firm pad, or pillow as a base, as distinct from lace made with a needle and a paper pattern

pillow lava *n.* lava that has solidified into pillow-shaped masses, formed from underwater lava flows or from lava flowing into water from land. Each pillow can be up to 2 m/6 ft across and is surrounded by a fine-grained skin.

pillowslip /píllō slip/ *n.* = **pillowcase**

pillow talk *n.* the discussion of intimate or private matters in bed with a sexual partner

pilocarpine /pīlō kaar pīn, -pin/ *n.* a poisonous colourless or yellow alkaloid obtained from the leaves of the jaborandi tree, used in the past to promote sweating and to treat glaucoma. Formula: $C_{11}H_{16}N_2O_2$. [Late 19thC. Coined from modern Latin *Pilocarpus*, genus name of the tree.]

pilose /pīlōss/, **pilous** /pīləs/ *adj.* used to describe plant parts that are covered with soft hair [Late 18thC. From Latin *pilosus* 'hairy', from *pilus* 'hair'.] —**pilosity** /pī lóssəti/ *n.*

pilot /pīlət/ *n.* **1.** AIR **SB WHO FLIES PLANE** sb who is qualified to fly an aircraft or spacecraft **2.** NAVIG **SB STEERING SHIPS THROUGH DIFFICULT AREA** sb with local knowledge whose job is to navigate ships in and out of a harbour or through a particular stretch of water **3.** SHIPPING **STEERER OF SHIP** sb who steers a ship or boat **4. LEADER** sb who acts as a leader or guide **5.** BROADCAST **TELEVISION PROGRAMME** a television or radio programme made as a prototype for a projected series **6. TRIAL RUN** a test of sth, e.g. a proposed manufacturing process, to discover and solve problems before full implementation **7.** = **pilot light** *n.* 1 **8.** ENG **MACHINE GUIDE** a guiding part of a tool or machine ■ *vt.* **(-lots, -loting, -loted) 1.** AIR **FLY AN AIRCRAFT** to fly an aircraft or spacecraft **2. NAVIGATE** to navigate a ship **3. BE IN CHARGE OF STH** to direct the course of sth, e.g. a project or a programme of research **4. RUN A TRIAL** to test sth, such as a proposed manufacturing process, to discover and solve problems before full implementation [Early 16thC. Via French *pilote*, from medieval Latin *pilotus*, an alteration of *pedota*, from, ultimately, Greek *pēdon* 'oar'.]

pilotage /pīlətij/ *n.* **1.** NAVIG **PILOTING OF CRAFT** the controlling of a ship, aircraft, or spacecraft **2.** FIN **HARBOUR OR RIVER PILOT'S FEE** the fee paid to a harbour or river pilot for steering a ship along a short difficult stretch **3.** NAVIG **MANUAL NAVIGATION** the navigation of an aircraft using landmarks and maps, rather than an aircraft's own navigation systems

pilot balloon *n.* a small balloon launched to study the speed and direction of winds at high altitudes. The balloon is visually tracked by a theodolite.

pilot fish *n.* a small striped marine fish, often found swimming with sharks, mantas, and other large fishes, where it finds stray scraps of food. Latin name: *Naucrates ductor*.

pilot house *n.* an enclosed control room on or near the bridge of a ship, containing the steering wheel and navigational and communication equipment

pilot lamp *n.* a small light in an electric circuit to show if the power is on or if an electrical device is operating

pilot light *n.* **1. pilot light, pilot FLAME USED FOR IGNITION** a small gas flame that remains lit in order to ignite a burner when it is turned on **2.** = **pilot lamp**

pilot officer *n.* a junior commissioned officer in the Royal Air Force or in the air forces of some other countries, ranking above acting pilot officer

pilot whale *n.* a large black toothed whale with a bulbous head, found in warm seas. Genus: *Globicephala*.

pilous *adj.* = **pilose**

Pils /pilz/ (*plural* **Pils**) *n.* any kind of lager beer similar to Pilsner [Mid-20thC. Shortening of PILSNER.]

Pilsener *n.* = **Pilsner**

Pilsner /pílznər/, **Pilsener** *n.* lager beer with a strong hops flavour, originally and especially made in Pilsen in the Czech Republic [Late 19thC. From German, literally 'of Pilsen', from *Pilsen* (Czech *Plzeň*), the name of a province in the Czech Republic.]

Piłsudski /pil sóotski/, **Józef Klemens** (1867–1935) Polish statesman. He fought to free Poland from Russian rule. He was Poland's head of state (1918–22) and later its virtual dictator (1926–35).

Piltdown man /pílt down-/ *n.* a supposed primitive form of human being represented by remains of bones found in Sussex in 1912, shown in 1953 to be a hoax [Early 20thC. Named after the village in Sussex where the remains were found.]

pilule /píllyool/ *n.* a small pill [15thC. Via French from Latin *pilula*, literally 'little ball', from *pila* 'ball' (source of English *pill*.]

pilus /pīləss/ (*plural* **-li** /pī lī/) *n.* any part of a plant or animal organism that looks like a hair [Mid-20thC. From Latin, 'hair'.]

PIM /pim/ *n., abbr.* COMPUT Personal Information Manager

Pima /pe'emə/ *n.* **1.** PEOPLES **NATIVE N AMERICAN PEOPLE** a member of a Native North American people that originally occupied lands in southern and central Arizona, and whose members now live mainly in central Arizona **2.** LANG **NATIVE N AMERICAN LANGUAGE** a Native American language spoken in parts of Arizona. It belongs to the Uto-Aztecan branch of Aztec-Tanoan languages and is closely related to Papago. Pima is spoken by about 15,000 people. [Early 19thC. From Spanish, a shortening of *Pimahito*, from Pima *pimahaitu* 'nothing', perhaps because of a misunderstanding by missionaries.] —**Pima** *adj.*

pimento /pi méntō/ *n.* **1.** FOOD = **pimiento 2.** = **allspice** [Late 17thC. Via Spanish *pimiento*, from Latin *pigmentum* (see PIGMENT).]

pi meson /pī me'ezon/ *n.* = **pion**

pimiento /pim yén tō, pi méntō/ (*plural* **-tos**), **pimento** (*plural* **-tos**) *n.* **1.** FOOD **MILD RED PEPPER** a large sweet red pepper that is used especially to stuff olives, as a garnish, and to make paprika **2.** PLANTS **EUROPEAN PEPPER PLANT** a European plant that produces pimiento peppers. Latin name: *Capsicum annuum*. [Mid-17thC. From Spanish (see PIMENTO).]

pimp /pimp/ *n.* **MAN SOLICITING FOR PROSTITUTES** a man who finds customers for a prostitute in return for a portion of the prostitute's earnings ■ *vi.* **(pimps, pimping, pimped) BE A PIMP** to work as a pimp, finding customers for prostitutes [Late 16thC. Origin uncertain.]

pimpernel /pímpər nel/ (*plural* **-nels** *or* **-nel**) *n.* a small plant with long trailing stems and small red, white, or purple flowers. Pimpernels belong to the primrose family. Genus: *Anagallis*. [15thC. Via Old French *pimpernelle* 'burnet' (the plant), the original sense in English, from earlier *piprenelle*, from, ultimately, Latin *piper* 'pepper', because its fruit resembles peppercorns.]

pimple /pímp'l/ n. a small inflamed or pus-filled spot on the skin [14thC. From an alteration of the base that produced Old English *piplian* 'to break out in spots'.] —**pimpled** adj. —**pimply** adj.

pin /pin/ n. **1.** THIN POINTED METAL STICK a small thin metal stick with a sharp point and a rounded head, used for holding pieces of fabric together **2.** POINTED METAL FASTENER any fastener that has a sharp metal point designed to pierce the things it is fastening **3.** = safety pin n. 1, safety pin n. 2 **4.** STH DECORATIVE ATTACHED TO CLOTHING a badge, piece of jewellery, or other decorative item that attaches to clothing by means of a sharp metal point or a clasp **5.** = hairpin n. 1 **6.** = cotter pin **7.** LEAST BIT the smallest amount (*dated informal*) ○ *not worth a pin* **8.** ELEC PART OF ELECTRICAL CONNECTOR a thin metal terminal extending from an electrical or electronic device such as a plug or a valve, used to connect the device by socket to other circuitry ○ *a three-pin plug* **9.** SURG ROD TO JOIN BROKEN BONE a thin metal rod used to hold the ends of a fractured bone together **10.** DENT PEG USED IN DENTISTRY a peg used to attach a crown to the root of a tooth **11.** TECH KEY PART ENTERING LOCK the part of a key that inserts into a lock **12.** MUSIC PEG HOLDING INSTRUMENT STRING any of the pegs on a stringed instrument such as a piano that hold the strings and can be turned to tighten or loosen them to tune the instrument **13.** ARMS SAFETY CLIP ON GRENADE the safety clip on a hand grenade that must be removed before the grenade can be detonated **14.** SPORTS SKITTLE any of the club-shaped targets used in various games of bowling **15.** GOLF HOLE MARKER IN GOLF a pole with a flag on it, used to mark each hole on a golf course **16.** WRESTLING WRESTLING FALL a fall in wrestling in which an opponent's shoulders are made to touch the mat **17.** BEVERAGES BEER CASK a small beer barrel holding 4.5 gallons **18.** COMPUT GUIDE ON COMPUTER PRINTER any of the rounded pegs that guide the paper through a computer printer **19.** COMPUT PART OF PRINTHEAD THAT FORMS LETTERS any of the tiny wires on the printhead of a dot matrix printer that form one dot of a letter or symbol ■ **pins** npl. LEGS sb's legs (*informal*) ○ *He's a bit unsteady on his pins.* ■ vt. (**pins, pinning, pinned**) **1.** FASTEN STH WITH PINS to fasten, attach, or secure sth with a pin **2.** KEEP SB OR STH FROM MOVING to hold sb or sth immobile, e.g. on the ground ○ *The beam fell across his back, pinning him to the ground.* **3.** CHESS RESTRICT OPPONENT'S CHESS PIECE to make it impossible for a chess opponent to move a piece without exposing the king to check or a valuable piece to capture **4.** WRESTLING HOLD WRESTLING OPPONENT DOWN to hold a wrestling opponent's shoulders to the mat [12thC. From Latin *pinna* 'feather, pointed peak'. Ultimately from an Indo-European base meaning 'to fly, rush' which is also the ancestor of English *feather*.] —**pinner** n. **pin down** vt. **1.** IDENTIFY PRECISELY to determine sth with certainty ○ *Can you pin down the time of death?* **2.** FORCE TO DECIDE to force sb to keep a commitment or come to a decision ○ *I haven't managed to pin him down to a date for our meeting yet.* **3.** PREVENT SB FROM MOVING to prevent sb from going anywhere ○ *The platoon was pinned down by enemy fire.*

PIN /pin/ (*plural* **PINs**), **PIN number** n. a multidigit number unique to an individual that is used, with a card, to get money from a cashpoint machine or to gain access to a computer or telephone system. Abbr of **personal identification number**

piña cloth /peeenyə-/ n. a fine transparent fabric made of fibre from pineapple leaves [Piña via Spanish, 'pineapple, pine cone', from Latin *pinea* 'pine cone', from *pinus* (see PINE¹)]

piña colada /peeenə kō laádə, peeenyə-/ n. a cocktail made from pineapple juice, rum, and coconut [From Spanish, literally 'strained pineapple']

pinafore /pínnə fawr/ n. **1.** DRESS WORN OVER STH ELSE a sleeveless dress, usually worn over a blouse or sweater. US term **jumper 2.** APRON an apron, usually one with a bib (*dated*) **3.** GIRL'S OVERGARMENT a sleeveless collarless garment worn by girls in the past over a dress and fastened at the top and back [Late 18thC. From PIN + AFORE, because it was originally used for a garment pinned to the front of a dress.]

pinafore dress n. = pinafore

Pinang = Penang

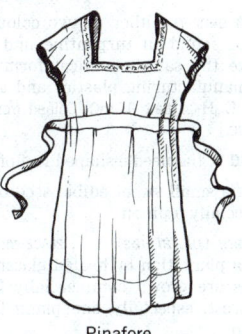

Pinafore

pinaster /pī nástər/ n. a pyramid-shaped Mediterranean pine tree with needles in pairs and clusters of long prickly cones. Latin name: *Pinus pinaster*. [Mid-16thC. From Latin, from *pinus* (see PINE).]

pinball /pínn bawl/ n. a game played on an electronic table fitted with obstacles, targets, and pivoted flippers. The player controls the flippers to keep a ball in play, hitting targets to score points. (*often used before a noun*)

Pince-nez

pince-nez /pánss náy/ (*plural* **pince-nez** /pánss náyz/) n. a pair of spectacles without side arms, held in place by a clip that fits over the nose [From French, literally 'to pinch the nose']

pincer movement /pínssər-/ n. a military manoeuvre that attempts to surround an enemy by simultaneous attack from the front and two side columns that curve around the enemy and back towards each other

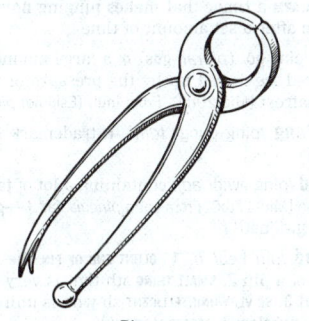

Pincers

pincers /pínssərz/ npl. **1.** LARGE CLAWS OF LOBSTER the front claws of some crustaceans and arachnids, e.g. the lobster and scorpion, used for grasping things **2.** TOOL FOR GRIPPING THINGS a tool, resembling a pair of pliers or scissors, with curved pivoted jaws that are used to grip sth, e.g. a nail, when they are closed [14thC. From Anglo-Norman, a variation of Old French *pincier* (see PINCH).]

pinch /pinch/ v. (**pinches, pinching, pinched**) **1.** vti. GRIP STH BETWEEN FINGER AND THUMB to grip or squeeze sth tightly between finger and thumb or between two hard objects or edges **2.** vti. BE TOO TIGHT AND PAINFUL to painfully constrict or squeeze a part of the body ○ *These shoes are pinching my feet.* **3.** vt. GARDENING REMOVE SHOOTS TO ENCOURAGE BUSHY GROWTH to remove new shoots and buds from a plant to make it become more bushy **4.** vt. WITHER STH to make sb or sth become

shrunken or withered, especially through harsh conditions like cold or hunger ○ *a face pinched with grief and pain* **5.** vti. STEAL STH to steal sth or take sth without permission (*informal*) ○ *Who's pinched my pen?* **6.** vt. ARREST SB to arrest sb (*informal*) **7.** vt. IMPOSE HARDSHIP ON to put sb in financial difficulty ○ *Unexpected expenses have really pinched me this month.* **8.** vt. SAILING SAIL A VESSEL INTO THE WIND to sail a sailing vessel too close to the wind, so that it loses wind from its sails **9.** vi. MINING NARROW AND DISAPPEAR to become gradually narrower, eventually disappearing entirely (*refers to a vein of ore*) ■ n. **1.** PAINFUL SQUEEZE a painful squeeze or nip, especially with the thumb and finger ○ *a pinch on the arm* **2.** VERY LITTLE a very small amount of a substance, especially the amount held between the thumb and first finger ○ *add a pinch of salt* **3.** ROBBERY a robbery (*informal*) **4.** AN ARREST an arrest made by the police (*informal*) **5.** CRITICAL TIME an emergency or critical situation ○ *If it comes to the pinch, we'll have to sell the house.* [13thC. Via assumed Anglo-Norman *pincher*, a variant of Old French *pincier*, from assumed Vulgar Latin *pinctiare* 'to prick'.] ◇ **at a pinch** if absolutely necessary, although preferably not ◇ **feel the pinch** to have financial problems

—————— **WORD KEY: SYNONYMS** ——————
See Synonyms at *steal*.

pinch bar n. a crowbar with a pointed end and a projection that provides a fulcrum, used as a lever, often having a notch, or claw, at the other end

pinchbeck /pínch bek/ n. **1.** GOLD-COLOURED METAL ALLOY an alloy of copper and zinc used as imitation gold in inexpensive jewellery **2.** CHEAP COPY an inferior imitation ■ adj. **1.** MADE OF PINCHBECK made from pinchbeck alloy **2.** IMITATION made in imitation of sth and usually of inferior quality [Mid-18thC. Named after Christopher *Pinchbeck*, died 1732, English watchmaker and inventor of the alloy.]

pinchbuck /pínch buk/ n. a long-bodied beetle, native to Europe, with long curving antennae. Latin name: *Harpium sycophanta*.

pinchcock /pínch kok/ n. a clamp used to control the flow of fluid through a flexible tube

pinch effect n. PHYS the narrowing of a beam of charged particles caused by the interaction of each particle with the magnetic field generated by the movement of the beam

pinchpenny /pínch peni/ adj. UNGENEROUS unwilling to spend or give money ■ n. (*plural* -nies) MISER sb who is unwilling to spend or give money

pin curl n. a flat curl in hair, made by winding strands of hair into a circle and securing it with a clip or hairpin

pincushion /pín kŏosh'n/ n. a small stuffed pad used for sticking dressmaking pins into when they are not being used

Pindar /píndər/ (*fl.* 522? BC–443 BC) Greek poet. He was the chief lyric poet of Greece, his *Triumphal Odes* surviving intact.

Pindaric /pin dárrik/ adj. **1.** RELATING TO PINDAR relating to the poet Pindar **2.** IN STYLE OF PINDAR'S POETRY relating to Pindaric odes or in the form of a Pindaric ode

Pindaric, **Pindaric ode** n. a form of ode with three-stanza sections, the first and second stanzas having one metrical form and the third having a different form

pine¹ /pīn/ n. **1.** TREES EVERGREEN TREE an evergreen co-

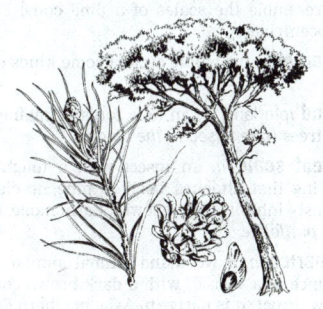

Pine

niferous tree with needle-shaped leaves and woody cones. The sticky sap of some species is used to make turpentine, and many species are planted as ornamentals. Genus: *Pinus*. (*often used before a noun*) **2.** INDUST **WOOD FROM PINE** the wood of any pine tree, varying from soft to hard. It is widely used for furniture and as a structural and finishing building material. **3.** TREES **TREE RESEMBLING THE PINE** a coniferous tree or shrub similar to the pine but unrelated, e.g. the Norfolk Island pine or ground pine [Pre-12thC. From Latin *pinus*, of uncertain origin: perhaps from, ultimately, an Indo-European base meaning 'to swell' (ancestor also of English *fat*), the tree being 'swollen' with resin.] — **piney** *adj.*

pine² /pīn/ (**pines, pining, pined**) *vi.* **1.** YEARN to long for sb or sth, especially sb or sth unattainable **2.** WASTE AWAY to become weak and lose vitality as a result of grief or longing [Pre-12thC. Origin uncertain: probably from, ultimately, Latin *poena* 'penalty' (source of English *pain* and *penal*), from Greek *poinē*. Originally in the sense 'torture'.]

pineal /pīnni əl, pī neé əl/ *adj.* **1.** BIOL **RELATING TO PINEAL GLAND** relating to or secreted by the pineal gland **2.** BOT **CONE-SHAPED** shaped like a pine cone [Late 17thC. Via French *pinéal* from Latin *pinea* 'pine cone', from its pine-cone-like shape, from *pinus* (see PINE¹).]

pineal gland, **pineal body** *n.* a small cone-shaped organ of the brain that secretes the hormone melatonin into the bloodstream. It is one of the endocrine glands and is situated beneath the back part of the corpus callosum.

Pineapple

pineapple /pī nap'l/ *n.* **1.** FOOD **JUICY YELLOW FRUIT** a large fruit with juicy yellow flesh, a thick lumpy yellowish brown skin, and a tuft of tough pointed leaves at the top **2.** (*plural* **-ples** *or* **-ple**) PLANTS **PLANT ON WHICH PINEAPPLES GROW** a tropical American plant that produces pineapples. It has a tall thick stem, tough sword-shaped leaves, and dense clusters of small flowers. Latin name: *Ananas comosus*. **3.** ARMS **GRENADE WITH PATTERNED SURFACE** a hand grenade with a surface of raised geometric shapes (*slang*) [14thC. Originally used for 'pine cone'; the modern sense evolved because the fruit was thought to resemble a pine cone.]

pineapple weed *n.* a plant with greenish-yellow flower heads that smell like pineapple when crushed. It is native to Asia, but is naturalized in North America and Europe. Latin name: *Matricaria matri.*

pine cone *n.* a pine tree's seed case, usually woody, oval, and scaly [See PINEAPPLE]

pinecone fish /pínkōn-/ *n.* either of two marine fishes of the Indian and Pacific Oceans with heavy scales that resemble the scales of a pine cone. Family: Monocentridae.

pine kernel *n.* the edible seed of some kinds of pine tree

pineland /pín land/ *n.* an area forested mainly with pine trees (*often used in the plural*)

pine leaf scale *n.* an insect with a tough outer covering that attaches itself to pine needles and seriously inhibits their growth. Latin name: *Chionaspis pinifoliae.*

pine marten *n.* a woodland animal similar in appearance to a weasel, with a dark brown coat and yellow throat. It is native to Asia, northern Europe, and northern North America. Genus: *Martes.*

pinene /pín een/ *n.* either of two colourless liquid compounds found in turpentine and eucalyptus. They have the same chemical formula and are used in manufacturing plastics and as a solvent. Formula: $C_{10}H_{16}$. [Late 19thC. Coined from Latin *pinus* 'pine' + -ENE.]

pine needle *n.* the needle-shaped leaf of a pine tree

pine nut *n.* a small sweet edible seed of some pine trees, especially a piñon

pinery /pínəri/ (*plural* **-ies**) *n.* **1.** PLACE WHERE PINEAPPLES ARE GROWN a plantation or heated glasshouse where pineapples are grown commercially **2.** PINE FOREST a pine forest, especially one planted for timber production

pine tar *n.* a thick sticky brown to black substance obtained by the destructive distillation of pine wood and used in making roofing materials, paints, medicines, and shampoos

pinewood /pín woŏd/ *n.* **1.** WOOD FROM PINE the wood of a pine tree (*often used before a noun*) **2.** BOT FOREST OF PINES a small forest of pine trees (*often used in the plural*)

pinfeather /pínn fethər/ *n.* a feather only recently emerged from a bird's skin and still surrounded by a horny sheath

pinfish /pínn fish/ (*plural* **-fishes** *or* **-fish**) *n.* a small marine fish of the porgy family with a thin dark green body and sharp dorsal spines, found along the southern Atlantic coast of the United States. Latin name: *Lagodon rhomboides.*

pinfold /pínn fōld/ *n.* **1.** PLACE FOR STRAY ANIMALS an enclosure for stray animals, especially farm animals **2.** CONFINING PLACE any place or situation that confines [Pre-12thC. From an alteration of earlier *pund-* 'enclosure' (source also of *pound*) + FOLD.]

ping /ping/ *n.* **1.** SOUND a single short ringing sound **2.** *US* AUTOMOT = **knock** **3.** ACOUSTICS SONAR PULSE a brief sonic or ultrasonic pulse emitted by a sonar, the reflection or echo of which is used in detecting submarines or shoals of fish ■ *v.* (**pings, pinging, pinged**) ACOUSTICS **1.** *vti.* RING to make a single short ringing sound, or to make sth such as a bell produce a ringing sound **2.** *vi.* DETECT UNDERWATER OBJECTS to detect submarines or shoals of fish by emitting and receiving the echo of a brief sonic or ultrasonic pulse [Mid-18thC. An imitation of the sound.]

pinger /píngər/ *n.* (*informal*) **1.** DEVICE THAT PINGS a device that produces pinging noises, especially one used as part of underwater detection equipment **2.** TIMER WITH ALARM a timer that makes pinging noises as an alarm after a set amount of time

pingo /píng gō/ (*plural* **-gos**) *n.* a large mound of soil-covered ice forced up by the pressure of water in permafrost [Mid-20thC. From Inuit (Eskimo) *pinguq.*]

Ping-Pong /píng pong/ *tdmk.* a trademark for table tennis

pinguid /píng gwid/ *adj.* containing a lot of fat, oil, or grease [Mid-17thC. From Latin *pinguis* 'fat'.] —**pinguidity** /ping gwíddəti/ *n.*

pinhead /pín hed/ *n.* **1.** BLUNT END OF PIN the rounded head of a pin **2.** SMALL THING sth that is very small or trivial **3.** SB VERY UNINTELLIGENT sb who is unintelligent or thoughtless (*informal insult*)

pinheaded /pín hedid/ *adj.* unintelligent or very thoughtless (*informal*)

pinhole /pín hōl/ *n.* a tiny hole or puncture of the size made by a pin

pinhole camera *n.* a basic form of camera with a tiny hole for the aperture, and no lens. Light passes through the hole to form an inverted image on the film emulsion.

pinion¹ /pínnyən/ *n.* ZOOL **BIRD'S WING** a bird's wing, especially the tip of the wing where the stiff flight feathers are found, containing the carpus, metacarpus, and phalanx bones ■ *vt.* (**-ions, -ioning, -ioned**) **1.** RESTRAIN to restrain or immobilize sb, especially by tying his or her arms **2.** KEEP FROM FLYING to prevent a bird from flying by removing or binding its wing feathers [15thC. Via French *pignon* from, ultimately, Latin *pinna* (see PIN).]

pinion² /pínnyən/ *n.* a small gear wheel that engages with a larger gear or with a rack, e.g. in a vehicle steering system [Mid-17thC. Via French *pignon*, an alteration of earlier *pignol*, from, ultimately, Latin *pinea* 'pine cone', from *pinus* (see PINE 1).]

pinite /pínnīt, pī nīt/ *n.* a grey-green mineral that is a mixture of mica and chlorite, formed by the alteration of the mineral cordierite [Early 19thC. From German *Pinit*, named after *Pini*, a mine in Saxony.]

pink¹ /pingk/ *n.* **1.** COLOURS **PALE REDDISH COLOUR** a pale reddish colour that, as a pigment, is formed by mixing red and white **2.** PLANTS **PLANT WITH FRAGRANT FLOWERS** a plant with narrow greyish-green leaves and fragrant flowers in various colours, especially pink, white, or red. The carnation and sweet william are types of pink. Genus: *Dianthus*. **3.** PLANTS **FRAGRANT FLOWER** the fragrant pink, white, or red flower of a pink plant **4.** PLANTS **PLANT SIMILAR TO TRUE PINK** a plant that is similar but not related to the pink such as the wild pink or moss pink **5.** HIGHEST FORM the highest degree or perfect example of sth ○ *the pink of perfection* **6.** CLOTHES **RED HUNTING JACKET** the scarlet riding coat traditionally worn by fox hunters **7.** = **pinko** (*slang disapproving*) ■ *adj.* **1.** COLOURS **COLOURED PINK** of the colour pink **2.** POL **SLIGHTLY LEFT-WING** relating to or holding political views that tend towards the left (*informal disapproving*) **3.** RELATING TO HOMOSEXUALS relating to homosexuals (*informal*) ■ *vi.* AUTOMOT = **knock** [Late 16thC. Origin uncertain: probably from earlier Dutch *pinck* 'small', from the phrase *pinck oogen*, literally 'small eyes', translated in English as 'pink eyes'. Originally used for the plant.] ◇ **in the pink** in excellent physical health (*dated*)

— **WORD KEY: ORIGIN** —

The Dutch phrase *pinck oogen* meant literally 'small eyes'. It was adopted into English in the partially translated form *pink eyes*, and it is thought that this may have been used as the name of a plant of the genus *Dianthus*. The abbreviated form *pink* emerged as a plant name in the 16th century. Many of these plants have pale red flowers, and by the 18th century *pink* was being used as a colour term.

pink² /pingk/ (**pinks, pinking, pinked**) *vt.* **1.** CUT WITH PINKING SHEARS to cut fabric with pinking shears to make a zigzag edge that will not easily fray **2.** STAB to prick sb's skin with a sword or other pointed weapon **3.** DECORATE WITH LITTLE HOLES to make a pattern on leather or other material by punching little holes in the surface [14thC. Origin uncertain: perhaps from Low German.]

pink³ /pingk/ *n.* a sailing ship with a narrow overhanging stern [Late 15thC. From Middle Dutch *pincke.*]

pink⁴ /pingk/ (**pinks, pinking, pinked**) *vi.* AUTOMOT = **knock** [Early 20thC. Imitation of the sound.]

pink-collar *adj.* *US* relating to jobs, especially clerical jobs, traditionally associated with women. ◊ **blue-collar, white-collar**

pink dollar *n.* *US* = **pink pound**

pink elephants *npl.* hallucinations in any form that are sometimes experienced by sb who has overindulged in alcohol or drugs (*informal humorous*)

pinkeye /pingk ī/ *n.* **1.** INFLAMMATION OF THE EYE a contagious form of acute conjunctivitis in human beings and some domestic animals marked by inflammation of the eyelid and eyeball **2.** CATTLE ILLNESS an eye infection of cattle, caused by any of several different viruses or bacteria. It is characterized by redness of the eye, production of tears that attract flies, and sometimes blindness.

pink gin *n.* gin that has Angostura™ bitters added to it, giving it a pale pinkish colour and an aromatic spicy flavour

pinkie /píngki/, **pinky** (*plural* **-ies**) *n.* *US, Can, Scotland* the little finger (*informal*) [Late 16thC. Origin uncertain: probably from Dutch *pinkje*, from *pink* 'little finger'.]

pinking shears, **pinking scissors** *npl.* scissors for cutting cloth that have one blade or both blades serrated, so that whatever they cut has a zigzag edge, either for decoration or to prevent fraying [From PINK]

pink lady *n.* a cocktail that is made by mixing gin,

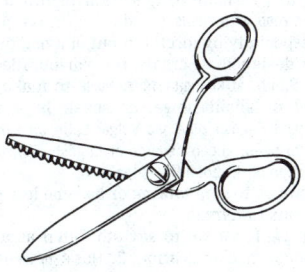

Pinking shears

brandy, lemon or lime juice, egg white, and grenadine

pinko /píngkō/ (*plural* **-os** *or* **-oes**) *n.* sb who leans towards the political left (*slang disapproving*) [Early 20thC. Formed from PINK, alluding to RED in the sense 'communist'.]

pink pound *n.* the collective spending power of the gay and lesbian community, especially when targeted as consumers. US term **pink dollar**

pinkroot /píngk root/ (*plural* **-roots** *or* **-root**) *n.* **1.** PLANTS PLANT WITH RED AND YELLOW FLOWERS a tropical or subtropical perennial plant with pinkish roots that grows in the southeastern United States and has red flowers tinged with yellow on the inside. Genus: *Spigelia*. **2.** MED POWDERED ROOT OF PINKROOT PLANT the powdered root of the pinkroot plant, formerly used to treat intestinal worms **3.** BOT PLANT DISEASE a fungal plant disease that affects bulbous plants, especially onions, causing the roots to become pink and shrivelled, and stunting root growth

pink salmon *n.* **1.** ZOOL SMALL PACIFIC SALMON a small salmon of northern Pacific waters, the male of which has a pinkish body and a distinctive hump on the back at breeding times. Latin name: *Oncorhynchus gorbuscha*. **2.** FOOD FLESH OF PINK SALMON the edible pink flesh of the pink salmon, often tinned

pink slip *n.* US a termination of employment notice that an employer gives to an employee in the United States (*informal*) [From the traditional colour of such notices]

pinky *n.* = PINKIE

pin money *n.* **1.** MONEY FOR BUYING PERSONAL THINGS money that is earned, put aside, or used for buying personal, often nonessential, things **2.** NOT MUCH MONEY a small amount of money **3.** MONEY THAT MAN GIVES TO WIFE money that a man gives to his wife, woman partner, or daughter for personal use (*dated*)

pinna /pínnə/ (*plural* **-nae** /-nee/ *or* **-nas**) *n.* **1.** ZOOL FEATHER, WING, OR FIN a feather, wing, fin, or other similarly shaped body part or appendage **2.** BOT LEAFLET any one of the several leaflets that make up a pinnate compound leaf **3.** ANAT = AURICLE n. 1 [Late 18thC. From Latin *penna* 'feather' (source of English *pen*¹). Ultimately from an Indo-European base meaning 'to fly', which is also the ancestor of English *feather*.] —**pinnal** *adj.*

pinnace /pínnəss/ *n.* a small boat such as a sailing boat carried by a larger vessel and used as a gig or a tender [Mid-16thC. Via French from, ultimately, Latin *pinus* 'pine' (see PINE).]

pinnacle /pínnək'l/ *n.* **1.** HIGHEST POINT the highest or

topmost point or level of sth ○ *at the pinnacle of a career* **2.** GEOG MOUNTAIN PEAK a natural peak, especially a distinctively pointed one on a mountain or in a mountain range **3.** ARCHIT POINTED ORNAMENT a pointed ornament on top of a buttress or parapet ■ *vt.* (**-cles, -cling, -cled**) **1.** ARCHIT ADD PINNACLE TO STH to provide sth with a pinnacle **2.** PUT STH ON PINNACLE to put or set sth on a pinnacle or on sth resembling a top or peak [13thC. Via Old French from late Latin *pinnaculum* literally 'little feather', from Latin *pinna* 'feather' (see PINNA).]

pinnae plural of PINNA

pinnate /pínnayt/, **pinnated** /pínnaytid/ *adj.* resembling a feather in appearance or structure, especially in having a central axis or stem with parts branching off it [Early 18thC. From Latin *pinnatus*, from *pinna* (see PINNA).] —**pinnately** *adv.* —**pinnation** /pi náysh'n/ *n.*

pinnati- *prefix.* like a feather ○ *pinnatiped* [From Latin *pinnatus* (see PINNATE)]

pinnatifid /pi náttifid/ *adj.* used to describe leaves that have a central axis with parts branching off it [Mid-18thC. Formed from PINNATI- + -FID.] —**pinnatifidly** *adv.*

pinniped /pínni ped/, **pinnipedian** /pínni péedi ən/ *n.* any sea-dwelling mammal such as a walrus, sea lion, or seal that has a streamlined body and four flippers and eats fish and other meat. Suborder: Pinnipedia. [Mid-19thC. From modern Latin *Pinnipedia*, order name, from Latin *pinna* 'wing, fin' + *pes* 'foot'.] —**pinniped** *adj.*

pinnule /pín yool/, **pinnula** /pínnyōōlə/ (*plural* **-lae** /pínnyōōlee/) *n.* **1.** ZOOL FIN-SHAPED PART a small fin or fin-shaped part of an organ or organism **2.** BOT LOBES OF A LEAFLET any of the small divisions or lobes of a leaf that has a central axis with parts branching off it [Late 16thC. From Latin *pinnula* 'little feather' from PINNA.] —**pinnular** *adj.*

PIN number *n.* = PIN

pinny /pínni/ (*plural* **-nies**) *n.* an apron (*informal; often used by or to children*) [Mid-19thC. Shortening of PINAFORE.]

Pinochet /peénō shay/, **Augusto** (*b.* 1915) Chilean military dictator. Under his right-wing regime (1973–90) dissidence was brutally suppressed. Full name **Augusto Pinochet Ugarte**

pinochle /peé nuk'l/, **pinocle, penuchle, penuckle** *n.* **1.** CARD GAME WITH INCOMPLETE PACKS a card game for two or four players using two packs of cards that do not include two to eight. Certain combinations of cards score points, as do tricks taken. **2.** WINNING COMBINATION OF CARDS a combination of the queen of spades and the jack of diamonds in the game of pinochle [Mid-19thC. Origin uncertain.]

pinocytosis /peénō sī tóssiss/ *n.* the ingestion of fluid into a cell by turning a portion of the cell membrane inwards to form a sheath that is then pinched off to form an internal vesicle [Late 19thC. Formed from Greek *pinein* 'to drink', on the model of 'phagocytosis'.] —**pinocytotic** /-sī tóttik/ *adj.* —**pinocytotically** /-sī tóttikli/ *adv.*

piñon /pi nyón, pínnyən/ (*plural* **-ñons** *or* **-ñones** /pi nyō neez/), **pinyon** *n.* **1.** TREES US PINE TREE any of several low-growing pines of the southwestern United States that bear edible seeds. Latin name: *Pinus edulis* and *Pinus monophylla*. **2.** piñon, piñon nut FOOD EDIBLE SEED OF PIÑON the small sweet edible nut of the piñon [Mid-19thC. Via Spanish *piñón* from, ultimately, Latin *pineus* 'of pines', from *pinus* (see PINE).]

Pinot Grigio /peénō gríjjō/ (*plural* **Pinot Grigios**) *n.* **1.** ITALIAN WINE GRAPE a white grape grown in Italy, used for making wine **2.** ITALIAN WHITE WINE a crisp dry white wine made from the Pinot Grigio grape [From Italian, literally 'grey Pinot', a grape variety (from French; see PINOT NOIR)]

Pinot Noir /peénō nwaár/ *n.* **1.** RED WINE GRAPE a black grape grown in the Burgundy area of France and also in Australia, the United States, and elsewhere, used for making wine **2.** RED WINE red wine made from the Pinot Noir grape [From French, literally 'black Pinot' (a grape variety), from, ultimately, *pin* 'pine-cone', from the resemblance of the grape bunch to a pine-cone]

pinpoint /pín poynt/ *vt.* (**-points, -pointing, -pointed**) IDENTIFY STH CORRECTLY to identify or locate sth accurately ■ *n.* **1.** STH SMALL OR TRIVIAL sth small or trivial and

with no value or consequence **2.** PIN'S POINT the sharp end of a pin or sth that resembles it ■ *adj.* PRECISELY EXACT reflecting exact meticulous precision

pinprick /pín prik/ *n.* **1.** SMALL HOLE MADE BY PIN a small puncture, especially to the skin, made by a pin or sth with a similarly sharp end **2.** SLIGHT WOUND a very minor wound **3.** MINOR IRRITANT a minor annoyance, nuisance, or distraction **4.** SMALL MARK a very small dot or mark of sth ■ *vt.* (**-pricks, -pricking, -pricked**) PUNCTURE STH WITH PIN to puncture sth, especially the skin, with a pin or sth with a similarly sharp end

pins and needles *n.* a tingling sensation, especially in the feet or hands, sometimes experienced when a temporarily restricted blood flow to the affected body parts returns to normal (*takes a singular or plural verb*)

pinscher /pínshər/ *n.* short-haired German dog belonging to breeds that traditionally had their ears clipped and tails docked. ◊ **Doberman pinscher** [Early 20thC. From German, of uncertain origin: probably from English *pinch*, because of the practice of clipping the dog's ears.]

pinsetter /pín setər/ *n.* a person or machine in a bowling alley that sets up and resets the pins

Pinsk /pinsk/ city in southwestern Belarus. Population: 130,000 (1996).

pinstripe /pín strīp/ *n.* **1.** NARROW LINE IN FABRIC any one of many very narrow lines in a fabric **2.** MATERIAL WITH VERY NARROW LINES material that has very narrow lines in it, especially the kind of fabric used for making business suits (*often used before a noun*) **3.** PINSTRIPE SUIT a suit made of pinstripe fabric (*often used in the plural*) —**pinstriped** *adj.*

pint /pīnt/ *n.* **1.** MEASURE UNIT OF LIQUID MEASURE a unit of liquid measure equal to one eighth of a gallon, which is equal to 0.568 litre in the United Kingdom and 0.473 litre in the United States **2.** MEASURE UNIT OF DRY MEASURE a unit of dry measure equal to one eighth of a gallon, which is equal to 0.568 litre in the United Kingdom and 0.551 litre in the United States **3.** CONTAINER a container or measure that has the capacity of a pint **4.** PINT OF LIQUID a pint of a liquid, especially of beer or milk (*informal*) **5.** UK BEVERAGES DRINK SERVED IN PUB a drink of beer or some similar alcoholic drink in a pub or bar perhaps, but not necessarily, a single or exact pint (*informal*) [14thC. From French *pinte*, of uncertain origin: possibly via assumed Vulgar Latin *pincta* 'painted (mark on a container)' from, ultimately, Latin *pingere* 'to paint'.]

pinta /píntə/ *n.* an infectious bacterial skin disease of tropical America that is marked by the formation and eruption of papules, loss of pigmentation, and thickening of the skin [Early 19thC. Via Spanish, literally 'painted spot', from assumed Vulgar Latin *pincta* (see PINT).]

pintail /pín tayl/ (*plural* **-tails** *or* **-tail**) *n.* a slender duck of the northern hemisphere that has a long pointed tail and brown and white plumage. Latin name: *Anas acuta*. [From the pointed tip of the male bird's tail]

pintle /pínt'l/ *n.* a pin or bolt, especially one used as a vertical pivot or hinge, e.g. on a rudder [Old English *pintle* 'peg, penis', of prehistoric Germanic origin]

pinto /píntō/ *n.* (*plural* **-tos**), *adj.* US, Can = PIEBALD [Mid-19thC. Via Spanish, literally 'painted', from, ultimately, Latin *pingere* 'to paint'.]

pinto bean *n.* **1.** PLANTS BEAN PLANT a variety of the kidney bean grown in the southwestern United States for food and fodder **2.** FOOD EDIBLE SEED a mottled brown and pink kidney-shaped bean of the pinto bean plant [*Pinto* from Spanish, 'painted, mottled']

pint-size, **pint-sized** *adj.* very small, especially smaller than usual or than expected (*informal*)

pin tuck *n.* a narrow vertical fold stitched in place and used for decoration, especially on the front of clothes —**pin-tucked** *adj.*

Pintupi /píntəpi/ (*plural* **-pi** *or* **-pis**), **Pintubi** /píntəbi/ (*plural* **-bi** *or* **-bis**) *n.* PEOPLES a member of a Native Australian people that lives in the border regions between Western Australia and Northern Territories [Mid-20thC. Of Australian Aboriginal origin.] —**Pintupi** *adj.*

pin-up *n.* **1.** PICTURE OF SEXUALLY ATTRACTIVE PERSON a photograph or poster of an attractive person, especially

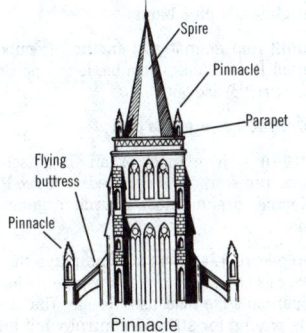

Pinnacle

Labels: Spire, Pinnacle, Parapet, Flying buttress, Pinnacle

one in which the person is posing in a seductive way and scantily clothed or naked **2.** **SEXUALLY ATTRACTIVE PERSON** sb considered attractive enough to appear in a pin-up picture

pinwheel /pín weel/ *n.* *US, Can* **1.** = **windmill** **2.** = **Catherine wheel**

pinwork /pín wurk/ *n.* the delicate stitches that are raised above the main design in the embroidery of needlepoint lace

pinworm /pín wurm/ *n.* **1.** ZOOL **PARASITIC NEMATODE WORM** a threadlike nematode worm that occurs as a parasite in the intestines of vertebrate animals, including human beings. Family: Oxyuridae. **2.** MED **PINWORM INFESTATION** an infestation of pinworms

pin wrench *n.* a specialized wrench containing a pin fitted for insertion into the head of a bolt so as to be able to drive the bolt

piny /pīni/ **(-ier, -iest), piney (pinier, piniest)** *adj.* relating to or resembling pine trees, e.g. in smell

Pinyin /pín yín/ *n.* a system for transliterating written Chinese characters into the Roman alphabet for diplomatic, official, and media uses, introduced in 1959 and adopted by the People's Republic of China in 1979 [Mid-20thC. From Mandarin Chinese *pīnyīn*, literally 'spell sound'.]

piolet /pée ə lay/ *n.* a double-headed ice axe used by mountaineers [Mid-19thC. From French dialect, formed from *piola* 'small axe'; ultimately of Germanic origin.]

pion /pí on/ *n.* any of the group of three mesons that have either single positive, negative, or zero charge, a mass approximately 270 times that of the electron, and spin zero [Mid-20thC. Formed from *pi meson*.]

pioneer /pí ə néer/ *n.* **1.** **INVENTOR OR INNOVATOR** a person or group that is the first to do sth or that is a forerunner in creating or developing sth new **2.** **FIRST PERSON TO EXPLORE TERRITORY** sb who goes into previously uncharted or unclaimed territory with the aim of exploring it and possibly colonizing it or settling there **3.** ARMY **SOLDIER WHO BUILDS THINGS** a foot soldier whose duties include going ahead of the main company to pave the way for them by building roads, ditches, bridges, and other constructions **4.** ECOL **FIRST SPECIES TO GROW SOMEWHERE** the first species of plant or animal life to begin living in a previously unoccupied site, e.g. a moss beginning to grow on otherwise bare rock ■ *v.* **(-neers, -neering, -neered)** **1.** *vt.* **INVENT OR DEVELOP NEW THING** to experiment with or develop sth new **2.** *vt.* **GO INTO UNEXPLORED TERRITORY** to go into previously uncharted or unclaimed territory with the aim of exploring it and possibly colonizing it or settling there **3.** *vi.* **ACT AS PIONEER** to act as a pioneer in a specified field [Early 16thC. Via French *pionnier* from, ultimately, the medieval Latin stem *pedon-* 'foot soldier', from Latin *ped-*, the stem of *pes* 'foot'.]

pious /pí əss/ *adj.* **1.** RELIG **RELIGIOUS** devoutly religious **2.** RELIG **RELIGIOUSLY REVERENT** characterized by religious reverence **3.** **ACTING IN FALSELY MORALIZING WAY** talking or acting in a falsely, hypocritically, or affectedly moralizing way **4.** RELIG **HOLY OR SACRED** holy or sacred, especially as distinct from worldly **5.** **PRAISEWORTHY** deserving to be praised **6.** **SHOWING DUE RESPECT** showing appropriate respect, especially towards parents (*archaic*) [15thC. Formed from Latin *pius* 'dutiful' (source of English *pity* and *expiate*).] —**piously** *adv.* —**piousness** *n.*

pip[1] /pip/ *n.* **1.** **SEED OF FRUIT** a small hard seed of an edible fruit such as an apple, pear, or orange **2.** **SECTION OF PINEAPPLE SKIN** any one of the many irregular diamond-shaped sections on the outer skin of a pineapple **3.** **ROOTSTOCK OR FLOWER** a rootstock or flower of certain plants, especially the lily of the valley [Late 18thC. A shortening of PIPPIN.]

pip[2] /pip/ *n.* **1.** **SPOT ON DIE OR DOMINO** a single spot on a die or domino **2.** CARDS **MARK ON PLAYING CARD** a single symbol of a club, diamond, heart, or spade on a playing card. The type of symbol designates the suit and the number of them indicates the value of the card. **3.** **SHORT HIGH-PITCHED SOUND** a short, usually high-pitched sound, especially of the kind used in broadcasting as a time signal **4.** MIL **STH INDICATING RANK** sth such as a diamond-shaped insignia on the shoulder of a British Army officer's uniform that indicates rank (*informal*) **5.** **SPECK** a very small mark or piece of sth ■ *v.* **(pips, pipping, pipped)** **1.** *vi.* BIRDS **CHEEP** to make a cheeping sound, especially when newly hatched (*refers to birds*) **2.** *vti.* BIRDS **USE BEAK TO BREAK SHELL** to use the beak to break through the shell during hatching (*refers to birds*) **3.** *vi.* **MAKE SHRILL NOISE** to make or emit a short shrill noise [Late 16thC. Origin unknown.]

pip[3] /pip/ *n.* **1.** VET **CONTAGIOUS POULTRY DISEASE** a contagious disease of birds, especially domestic ones, characterized by the presence of a thick crust in the mouth and throat, caused by an abnormal secretion of mucus **2.** MED **MINOR AILMENT** a slight ailment in humans (*informal dated*) ■ *vt.* **(pips, pipping, pipped)** **IRRITATE SB** to make sb annoyed or upset (*informal dated*) [14thC. Via Middle Dutch *pippe* from, ultimately, Latin *pituita* 'phlegm'.] ◇ **give sb the pip** to annoy or irritate sb (*dated*)

pip[4] /pip/ **(pips, pipping, pipped)** *vt.* (*informal*) **1.** **BEAT SB IN COMPETITION** to beat sb in competition, especially when it looked as though the other person was going to stay ahead **2.** **WOUND OR KILL SB WITH GUN** to wound or kill a person or animal with a bullet from a gun [Late 19thC. Origin uncertain: perhaps from PIP[1] or PIP[2].]

pipa[1] /péepə/ *n.* a completely aquatic American toad that has a flattened body, large webbed feet, and no eyelids or tongue. Genus: *Pipa*. [Early 18thC. Probably from Galibi.]

pipa[2] /pée paá/ *n.* a plucked four-string Chinese instrument with a fretted fingerboard like a guitar's [Mid-19thC. From Chinese *píba*, literally 'loquat'; so called from the instrument's shape.]

pipage /pípij/ *n.* **1.** **PIPES COLLECTIVELY** a number of pipes thought of collectively or as a functioning system **2.** **TRANSPORTATION USING PIPES** the transportation or delivery of sth by means of pipes **3.** **COST OF TRANSPORTING STH BY PIPE** the cost of transporting or delivering sth by means of pipes

pipal /péep'l/ *n.* = **bo tree**

pipe[1] /pīp/ *n.* **1.** **TUBE FOR TRANSPORTING LIQUID OR GAS** a long cylindrical tube that water, oil, gas, or other such material passes through **2.** **TUBE OF ANY KIND** an object in tubular form **3.** **DEVICE FOR SMOKING TOBACCO** a small bowl with a hollow stem coming from it, used for smoking tobacco or other substances. Pipes are usually made of wood or clay. The tobacco is burnt in the bowl and the smoke drawn into the mouth through the stem. **4.** **AMOUNT IN SMOKER'S PIPE** the amount of tobacco or other substance that the bowl of a smoker's pipe holds **5.** BIOL **HOLLOW BODY PART** a tubular part or organ in a plant or animal, especially one in an animal's respiratory system **6.** MUSIC **TUBULAR MUSICAL INSTRUMENT PLAYED BY BLOWING** any of several tubular musical instruments that are played by blowing air into them **7.** MUSIC **TUBULAR PART OF MUSICAL ORGAN** any of the upright tubular parts of a musical organ that produce sound when air is blown into them **8.** MUSIC, HIST **WIND INSTRUMENT OF MIDDLE AGES** a three-holed wind instrument, popular during the Middle Ages, played with one hand while the other hand beats on a small drum called a tabor **9.** NAUT **SAILOR'S WHISTLE** a small whistle used for signalling orders to a crew, usually by a boatswain **10.** GEOL **CYLINDER-SHAPED GEOLOGICAL FORMATION** a vertical cylinder-shaped geological formation such as a vein of ore **11.** GEOL **PASSAGE THROUGH WHICH LAVA FLOWS** a vertical passage through which molten lava flows **12.** METALL **HOLE IN CAST METAL** a conical cavity in the middle of a piece of metal, produced by gas escaping as the metal cools **13.** **HIGH-PITCHED NOISE** a high-pitched or shrill noise such as a birdcall ■ **pipes** *npl.* **1.** MUSIC **BAGPIPES** the bagpipes **2.** **HUMAN RESPIRATORY SYSTEM** the human respiratory system or vocal cords (*slang*) ■ *v.* **(pipes, piping, piped)** **1.** *vt.* **CARRY STH BY PIPE** to carry sth, especially water, gas, or a semisolid, by means of a pipe, pipeline, or system of pipes ○ *The company pipes crude oil to the refinery.* **2.** *vti.* **INSTALL AND CONNECT PIPES** to equip sth with pipes or install pipes and their connections in sth **3.** *vt.* MUSIC **PLAY TUNE ON PIPE** to play a tune on a musical pipe **4.** *vt.* MUSIC **SEND PIPED MUSIC THROUGH PLACE** to send piped music through a public place or workplace **5.** *vt.* MUSIC **SIGNAL STH USING PIPE** to signal the arrival or departure of sb or sth using a pipe **6.** *vt.* NAUT **ORDER CREW USING BOATSWAIN'S PIPE** to give orders to a crew using a boatswain's pipe **7.** *vt.* SEW **DECORATE GARMENT WITH PIPING** to add decorative piping to a garment or to soft furnishing **8.** *vt.* FOOD **DECORATE FOOD WITH PIPING** to add decorative piping to food, especially by forcing it out of a bag that has a nozzle designed to create the various decorative forms **9.** *vti.* **MAKE HIGH-PITCHED NOISE** to make a high-pitched or shrill noise, or speak in a squeaky voice [Old English *pīpe*, via Vulgar Latin *pipa* from Latin *pipare* 'to peep, cheep' (source of English *fife*), ultimately an imitation of the sound] —**pipeful** *n.*

pipe down *vi.* to stop talking or become less noisy or boisterous (*informal*)

pipe up *vi.* **1.** **SAY STH** to say sth, often as an interruption or a clarification **2.** MUSIC **BEGIN TO SING OR PLAY INSTRUMENT** to begin to sing or play a musical instrument

pipe[2] /pīp/ *n.* **1.** **LARGE CONTAINER FOR LIQUID** a large container for wine, oil, or some other liquid **2.** MEASURE **UNIT OF LIQUID CAPACITY** a unit of liquid measure for wine, equal to four barrels, two hogsheads, or 105 gallons **3.** MEASURE **CASK** a cask that has the capacity of four barrels, two hogsheads, or 105 gallons [14thC. Via Anglo-Norman from Vulgar Latin *pipa* (see PIPE[1]).]

pipe band *n.* a marching or military band with bagpipes, drums, and often a drum major, typically playing traditional Scottish music

pipe bomb *n.* a bomb made of a length of pipe that is filled with explosives and is capped at its ends

pipeclay /píp klay/ *n.* **FINE WHITE CLAY** a very fine white pure clay used in the manufacture of pottery and smokers' pipes, and for whitening leather and other materials ■ *vt.* **(-clays, -claying, -clayed)** **USE PIPECLAY FOR WHITENING LEATHER** to use pipeclay for whitening leather or some other, usually natural, material

pipe cleaner *n.* a flexible wire covered with fluffy material that is used for cleaning the stems of smokers' pipes and other things that are difficult to access

piped music *n.* pre-recorded, usually easy-listening music played through speakers in public places and some workplaces to create a soothing atmosphere

pipe dream *n.* an aim, hope, idea, or plan so fanciful that it is very unlikely to be realized [From the dreams caused by smoking opium]

pipefitting /píp fiting/ *n.* **1.** **BRANCH OF PLUMBING INVOLVING PIPES** the branch of plumbing that involves measuring, cutting, bending, and joining lengths of pipe, either in installation or repairs **2.** **ACT OR PROCESS OF PIPE INSTALLATION** an act or process of installing or connecting pipes **3.** **STH USED IN CONNECTING PIPES** sth that is used in the connection or joining of pipes —**pipefitter** *n.*

pipeline /píp līn/ *n.* **1.** **LONG PIPE SYSTEM FOR TRANSPORTING STH** a pipe or system of pipes designed to carry sth such as oil, natural gas, or other petroleum-based products over long distances, often underground **2.** **CHANNEL OF COMMUNICATIONS** a channel of communications, especially a private one among several people within a single organization **3.** **SYSTEM FOR SUPPLYING STH** a system for the supply or transfer of sth, especially goods or information ■ *vt.* **(-lines, -lining, -lined)** **1.** **SEND STH BY PIPE SYSTEM** to send, connect, or carry sth by way of a long system of pipes **2.** TECH **FIT STH WITH LONG PIPE SYSTEM** to fit or supply sth with a long system of pipes ◇ **in the pipeline** in preparation but not yet ready

pipe major *n.* a noncommissioned officer in charge of a regiment's pipe band

pip-emma /píp émmə/ *adv.* in the afternoon (*dated informal*) [Early 20thC. From the former phonetic names for the letters 'p' and 'm'.]

pipe of peace *n.* = **peace pipe**

pipe organ *n.* a musical organ that uses pipes to produce the sound, as opposed to a reed organ or an electric organ. Most church organs are pipe organs.

piper /pípər/ *n.* **1.** **BAGPIPER** sb who plays the bagpipes **2.** **PLAYER ON PIPE** sb who plays a pipe ◇ **he who pays the piper calls the tune** used to say that the person who is paying for sth will control what happens

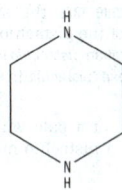

Piperazine

piperazine /pi pérrə zeen/ *n.* a colourless crystalline compound used to kill or expel parasitic worms and as an insecticide. Formula: $C_4H_{10}N_2$. [Late 19thC. Blend of PIPERIDINE and AZINE.]

Piperidine

piperidine /pi pérri deen/ *n.* a colourless liquid compound that has a peppery odour resembling ammonia and is used in making rubber and epoxy resins. Formula: $C_5H_{11}N$. [Mid-19thC. Coined from PIPERINE + -IDINE.]

piperine /píppə reen/ *n.* a white crystalline alkaloid compound that is the chief active component of pepper. Formula: $C_{17}H_{19}NO_3$. [Early 19thC. Formed from Latin *piper* (see PEPPER).]

pipe roll *n.* a collection of accounts dating from the 12th to the 19th century that were submitted annually by sheriffs and other crown ministers and are kept at the British Exchequer [So called perhaps because they were rolled up into a tubular shape]

piperonal /píppərō nal/ *n.* a white crystalline compound that has an odour resembling heliotrope and is used in perfumes and flavourings. Formula: $C_{19}H_{63}$. [Mid-19thC. From German, formed from *Piperin* 'piperine'.]

pipe snake *n.* a snake found mostly in tropical areas that has a fused inflexible skull, vestiges of hind limbs, and two unequally-sized lungs. Family: Anillidae.

pipes of Pan *npl.* = panpipes

pipestone /píp stōn/ *n.* a reddish or pinkish stone resembling clay in consistency that some Native North Americans harden and use for decorative objects and long, often ornate pipes

pipette /pi pét/ *n.* SMALL TUBE FOR SUCKING UP LIQUID a small glass tube that liquid is drawn into so that it can be measured, often before delivering it to another container, e.g. in experiments or in medication doses ■ *vt.* (-pettes, -petting, -petted) MEASURE OR TRANSFER LIQUID USING PIPETTE to measure or deliver an accurate amount of liquid using a pipette [Mid-19thC. From French, literally 'little pipe', from *pipe* 'pipe', from Vulgar Latin *pipa* (see PIPE[1]).]

pipi /píppee/ (*plural* -pi *or* -pis) *n.* ANZ a name given to various edible shellfish [Mid-19thC. From Maori.]

piping /píping/ *n.* 1. CONSTR PIPES COLLECTIVELY pipes thought of collectively, especially when they form a connected plumbing system in a house or other building 2. SEW DECORATIVE TWISTED CORD a twisted cord covered with a folded strip of bias-cut fabric inserted into a seam as a decoration, e.g. on clothes and soft furnishings 3. FOOD DECORATIVE EFFECT ON FOOD a decorative effect used on food, especially strands or swirls of icing in a contrasting colour 4. MUSIC SKILL OF PLAYING MUSICAL PIPE the art, technique, or skill of playing the bagpipes or another kind of musical pipe 5. MUSIC SOUND OF MUSICAL PIPE the sound of bagpipes or some other musical pipe 6. SHRILL NOISE a shrill, high-pitched, or whistling noise ■ *adj.* SHRILLY PITCHED shrill and very high in pitch, as some voices are

pipistrelle /píppi strél/, **pipistrel** *n.* a small brown insect-eating bat found throughout the world. Genus: *Pipistrellus.* [Late 18thC. Via French and Italian from, ultimately, Latin *vespertilio* 'bat', from *vesper* 'evening'.]

pipit /píppit/ *n.* a small songbird in the wagtail family, resembling the lark, with brown speckled plumage and a long tail. Family: Motacillidae. [Mid-18thC. An imitation of the bird's call.]

pipkin /pípkin/ *n.* a small cooking pot, usually made of metal or earthenware and with a handle going across the top [Mid-16thC. Origin uncertain: possibly formed from PIPE[2].]

pippin /píppin/ *n.* 1. FOOD VARIETY OF APPLE any of several varieties of cultivated eating or cooking apples 2. BOT PIP OR SEED a pip or seed, especially an apple pip 3. DESIRABLE OR ADMIRABLE PERSON OR THING sb or sth that is particularly desirable or admirable (*dated informal*) [14thC. From French *pepin*.]

pipsissewa /pip síssəwə/ (*plural* -was *or* -wa) *n.* an evergreen herb of the wintergreen family that has white or pinkish flowers and jagged astringent leaves that are used medicinally as a diuretic. Genus: *Chimaphila.* [Late 18thC. From Abnaki *kpi-pskwàhsawe* 'flower of the woods'.]

pipsqueak /píp skweek/ *n.* sb or sth that is small or insignificant, but nevertheless often annoying or troublesome (*informal*) [Early 20thC. Thought to suggest smallness and insignificance.]

piquant /peékənt, -kaant/ *adj.* 1. SPICY OR SAVOURY having a flavour, taste, or smell that is spicy or savoury, often with a slightly tart or bitter edge to it 2. SHARPLY STIMULATING OR PROVOCATIVE refreshingly interesting, stimulating, or provocative 3. SHARPLY CRITICAL AND BITING excessively severe or hurtful, e.g. in tone or content [Early 16thC. From French, the present participle of *piquer* 'to prick, sting' (see PIQUE[1].)] —**piquancy** *n.* —**piquantly** *adv.* —**piquantness** *n.*

pique[1] /peek/ *n.* BAD MOOD a bad mood or feeling of resentment, especially when brought on by an insult, hurt pride, or loss of face ■ *v.* (**piques, piquing, piqued**) 1. *vt.* PUT SB IN BAD MOOD to cause sb to be in a bad mood or to feel resentful 2. *vt.* AROUSE SB'S INTEREST to cause a feeling of interest, curiosity, or excitement in sb 3. *vr.* TAKE PRIDE IN STH to take pride in sth, especially a personal attribute or ability [Mid-16thC. Via French *piquer* 'to prick, irritate' from assumed Vulgar Latin *piccare* (source of English *pick*[1] and *picket*).]

pique[2] /peek/ *n.* WINNING SCORE IN PIQUET in the game of piquet, a score of 30 points to an opponent's 0 from the hand as dealt ■ *vti.* (**piques, piquing, piqued**) SCORE A PIQUE AGAINST SB in the game of piquet, to score a pique against an opponent [Mid-17thC. From French *pic*, of uncertain origin.]

piqué /peé kay/ *n.* a closely woven ribbed fabric produced from natural fibres, especially cotton or silk, and used mainly in making clothes [Mid-19thC. From French, the past participle of *piquer* 'to prick, stitch' (see PIQUE[1].)]

piquet /pi két, -káy/, **picquet** *n.* a card game for two players who use only 32 cards instead of the usual 52, all the twos, threes, fours, fives, and sixes having been left out. Scoring is by declaring and winning tricks. [Mid-17thC. From French, of uncertain origin: probably from Old French *pic* (see PIQUE[2].)]

piracy /pírəssi/ *n.* 1. SHIPPING ROBBERY ON HIGH SEAS robbery on the high seas, especially the stealing of a ship's cargo 2. TRANSP ROBBERY ON ANY FORM OF TRANSPORT robbery committed on board any form of transport, especially an aircraft 3. TRANSP HIJACKING the hijacking of an aircraft or another form of transport 4. USE OF COPYRIGHT MATERIAL WITHOUT PERMISSION the taking and using of copyright or patented material without authorization or without the legal right to do so 5. BROADCAST ILLEGAL BROADCASTING the unauthorized or illegal broadcasting of TV or radio programmes [Mid-16thC. From medieval Latin *piratia*, from Latin *pirata* (see PIRATE).]

Piraeus /pī reé əss/ industrial city and seaport serving Athens, in Greece. Population: 182,671 (1991).

piragua /pi raágwə, pi rággwə/ *n.* = pirogue [Early 17thC. Via American Spanish from Carib, 'dugout'.]

piraña *n.* = piranha

Pirandello /pírrən délló/, **Luigi** (1867–1936) Italian playwright. His works, such as *Six Characters in Search of an Author* (1921), explore the human condition with grim humour. He won a Nobel Prize in literature (1934).

Piranesi /pírrə náyssi/, **Giovanni Battista** (1720–78) Italian graphic artist. He is noted for his *Imaginary Prisons* (1745), and other engravings and etchings of real or imaginary buildings.

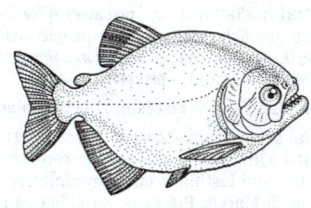

Piranha

piranha /pi raánə/ (*plural* -nhas *or* -nha), **piraña** (*plural* -ñas *or* -ña) *n.* a small South American freshwater fish that has sharp teeth, strong jaws, and is a dangerous predator when attacking in large numbers. Genus: *Serrasalmo.* [Mid-18thC. Via Portuguese from Tupi *piráya*.]

pirate /pírət/ *n.* 1. SHIPPING ROBBER AT SEA sb who commits robbery on the high seas, especially regularly 2. SHIPPING SHIP USED BY SEA ROBBERS a ship used by people who rob or otherwise attack shipping on the high seas 3. SB USING COPYRIGHT MATERIAL WITHOUT PERMISSION sb who duplicates or uses copyright or patented material without authorization or without the legal right to do so 4. BROADCAST SB INVOLVED IN ILLEGAL BROADCASTING sb who takes part in or manages the unauthorized or illegal broadcasting of TV or radio programmes ■ *v.* (**-rates, -rating, -rated**) 1. *vti.* ROB STH ON HIGH SEAS to rob a vessel or commit robbery on the high seas 2. *vt.* USE COPYRIGHT MATERIAL WITHOUT PERMISSION to duplicate or use copyright or patented material without authorization or without the legal right to do so [13thC. Via Latin *pirata* from Greek *peiratēs*, from *peiran* 'to attempt, attack'. Ultimately from an Indo-European word that is also the ancestor of English *peril* and *empiric*.] —**piratic** /pī ráttik/ *adj.* —**piratically** /-ráttikli/ *adv.*

pirog /pi rốg/ (*plural* -rogi /-rốgi/ *or* -roghi) *n.* a large rectangular pie that has a pastry crust top and bottom, filled with chopped meat or cabbage, onions, and hard-boiled eggs [Mid-19thC. From Russian.]

pirogue /pi rốg/ *n.* a canoe made from a hollowed-out tree trunk [Early 17thC. Via French from Carib *piragua* (source of English *piragua*).]

pirouette /pírroo ét/ *n.* BODY SPIN WHEN DANCING a fast complete spin of the body, especially one performed on the tip of the toe or the ball of one foot in ballet ■ *vi.* (**-ettes, -etting, -etted**) PERFORM A PIROUETTE to perform a fast body spin on one foot, especially in ballet [Mid-17thC. Via French from Old French, 'spinning top', of unknown origin.]

pirozhki /pi róshki/, **piroshki** *npl.* very small fried or baked pastries, filled with finely chopped meat or cabbage and onions, sometimes also with chopped hard-boiled eggs, or with potato or some similar filling (*takes a singular or plural verb*) [Early 20thC. From Russian, literally 'little pirog', from PIROG.]

Pisa /peézə/ capital of Pisa Province, Tuscany Region, central Italy. It is known for its leaning bell tower. Population: 97,872 (1993). ◊ **Leaning Tower of Pisa**

pis aller /peéz állay/ (plural **pis allers** /peéz állay/) n. sth that is done as a last resort or when no other option is available [From French, from pis 'worse' + aller 'to go']

Pisano /pi saáno͞/, **Giovanni** (1250?–1314?) Italian sculptor. The son of Nicola Pisano, he incorporated Gothic elements into his sculptures for Siena Cathedral and pulpits for the cathedrals of Pistoia and Pisa.

Pisano, Nicola (1220?–84?) Italian sculptor. The father of Giovanni Pisano, his fame rests chiefly on his relief sculptures for the Pisa Baptistry, based on Roman models.

piscary /pískəri/ (plural **-ries**) n. **1.** PLACE WHERE PEOPLE FISH a place where people fish or are allowed to fish **2.** LAW LEGAL RIGHT TO FISH the legal right to fish in a particular place even if it belongs to another person [15thC. Via medieval Latin piscaria from, ultimately, Latin piscis 'fish' (see PISCI-).]

piscatorial /pískə táwri əl/, **piscatory** /pískətəri/ adj. relating to fish, fishing, or people who fish (formal) [Early 19thC. Via Latin piscatorius from, ultimately, piscis 'fish' (see PISCI-).] —**piscatorially** adv.

Piscean /píssi ən/ n. = Pisces n. 2 —Piscean adj.

Pisces /pí seez/ (plural **-sces**) n. **1.** ZODIAC 12TH SIGN OF ZODIAC the 12th sign of the zodiac, represented by two fishes and lasting from approximately 19 February to 20 March. Pisces is classified as a water sign and its ruling planets are Jupiter and Neptune. **2.** ZODIAC SB BORN UNDER PISCES sb whose birthday falls between 19 February and 20 March **3.** ASTRON ZODIACAL CONSTELLATION BETWEEN AQUARIUS AND PISCES a large faint zodiacal constellation between Aquarius and Pisces [Pre-12thC. From Latin, plural of piscis 'fish' (source of English porpoise).] —**Pisces** adj.

pisci- prefix. fish ○ pisciform [From Latin piscis. Ultimately from the Indo-European word for 'fish' that is also the ancestor of English fish and porpoise.]

pisciculture /píssi kulchər/ n. the controlled breeding, hatching, and rearing of fish, especially for scientific or commercial purposes [Mid-19thC. Formed from Latin piscis 'fish' (see PISCI-), on the model of 'agriculture'.] —**piscicultural** /píssi kúlchərəl/ adj. —**pisciculturally** /-kúlchərəli/ adv. —**pisciculturist** /-kúlchərəlist/ n.

pisciform /píssi fawrm/ adj. shaped like or otherwise resembling a fish (formal)

piscina /pi seénə/ (plural **-nas** or **-nae** /-nee/) n. **1.** SACRED CONTAINER FOR HOLY WATER in some Christian churches, a sacred container or basin that holds holy water, used to carry it away after ablutions have been completed **2.** PLACE WHERE PRIEST WASHES SACRED CONTAINERS the place where a priest can wash his hands and the sacred containers used in Mass, located in the sacristy, especially in a Roman Catholic church [Late 16thC. Via medieval Latin, literally 'fish pond', from piscis 'fish' (see PISCI-).] —**piscinal** /píssin'l/ adj.

piscine /píssīn/ adj. relating to, characteristic of, or resembling fish (formal) [Late 18thC. Via medieval Latin piscinus from Latin piscis 'fish' (see PISCI-).]

Piscis Austrinus /píssiss o stríʳnəs, píssiss-/ n. a small constellation of the southern hemisphere between Grus and Aquarius

piscivorous /pi sívvərəss/ adj. feeding habitually or mainly on fish

pisé /peé zay/, **pisé de terre** /-de táir/ n. compressed earth or clay used for making floors or walls [Late 18thC. From French pisé de terre, literally 'beaten earth'.]

pish /pish/ interj. used to express contempt, annoyance, or impatience (dated) [Late 16thC. Natural exclamation.]

pishogue /pi shóg/, **pishoge** n. Ireland **1.** OLD-FASHIONED NONSENSE superstition or old-fashioned nonsense **2.** SUPERSTITIOUS BELIEF a superstitious belief or practice [Early 19thC. From Irish piseog.]

pisiform /píssi fawrm/ adj. LIKE A PEA resembling a pea in shape or size ■ n. = pisiform bone [Mid-18thC. Formed from Latin pisum 'pea'.]

pisiform bone n. the small knobbly bone at the place where the inner bone of the forearm (**ulna**) joins the wrist (**carpus**)

pismire /píss mīr/ n. an ant (regional archaic or informal) [14thC. From PISS (from the smell of formic acid) + obsolete mire 'ant'.]

pisolite /pissō līt/ n. an inorganic limestone consisting of individual spherical concretions (**pisoliths**) [Early 18thC. Formed from Greek pisos 'pea' + -LITE.] —**pisolitic** /pissō líttik/ adj.

pisolith /pissəlith/ n. a spherical concretion with concentric laminations that with others makes up an inorganic limestone. Pisoliths can be up to 10 cm/4 in in diameter. [Late 18thC. Formed from Greek pisos 'pea' + -LITH.]

piss /piss/ v. (**pisses, pissing, pissed**) (slang offensive) **1.** vi. OFFENSIVE TERM an offensive term meaning to urinate **2.** vt. OFFENSIVE TERM an offensive term meaning to discharge sth, e.g. blood, when urinating **3.** vt. OFFENSIVE TERM an offensive term meaning to urinate on or into sth ■ n. (slang offensive) **1.** OFFENSIVE TERM an offensive term for urine **2.** OFFENSIVE TERM an offensive term for an act or instance of urinating **3.** ANZ BEVERAGES BEER beer [13thC. Via French pisser from assumed Vulgar Latin pissiare, ultimately an imitation of the sound.] ◊ **on the piss** taking part in a heavy alcohol-drinking session (slang offensive) ◊ **piss and vinegar** US an offensive term for feisty strength of character and physical vigour (slang offensive) ◊ **piss yourself (laughing)** to laugh uncontrollably (slang offensive) ◊ **take the piss** to ridicule or mock sb or sth (slang offensive)

piss about, piss around v. (slang offensive) **1.** vt. ANNOY SB to annoy sb or waste sb's time, especially deliberately **2.** vi. BEHAVE IN SILLY OR CHILDISH WAY to behave in a silly or childish way, especially by wasting time

piss away vt. an offensive term meaning to waste or squander sth, e.g. money or time (slang offensive)

piss down vi. to rain heavily (slang offensive)

piss off v. (slang offensive) **1.** vt. OFFENSIVE TERM an offensive term meaning to annoy, irritate, or upset sb **2.** vi. OFFENSIVE TERM an offensive term meaning to go away and stop being annoying (often used as a command)

Pissarro /pi saáro͞/, **Camille** (1830–1903) French painter. He was a major exponent of the impressionist style, and is known for his landscapes, river scenes, and street scenes. Full name **Camille Jacob Pissarro**

piss artist n. **1.** HABITUAL HEAVY DRINKER sb who regularly drinks a lot of alcohol or who regularly gets drunk (slang) **2.** SB INCOMPETENT sb who is completely incompetent or who exaggerates his or her competence (slang insult)

pissed /pist/ adj. (slang offensive) **1.** OFFENSIVE TERM an offensive term meaning extremely drunk **2.** US = **pissed off**

pissed off adj. very annoyed or angry (slang offensive) US term **pissed**

pisser /píssər/ n. (slang offensive) **1.** OFFENSIVE TERM an offensive term for a situation that is extremely annoying or disappointing **2.** Australian PUB a public house

pisshead /píss hed/ n. sb who frequently or habitually gets very drunk (slang disapproving)

pissoir /píss waar/ n. a public urinal, especially one on the streets of some European cities, with a circular screen round it [Early 20thC. From French, formed from pisser (see PISS).]

pisspot /píss pot/ n. (slang offensive) **1.** US OFFENSIVE TERM an offensive term for sb regarded as ill-tempered and generally mean **2.** ANZ DRUNKARD a habitual drunkard [Originally in the literal meaning 'chamber pot']

piss-take n. a parody, especially one that involves mockery or ridicule (slang offensive) —**piss-taker** n. —**piss-taking** n.

piss-up n. (slang offensive) **1.** DRINKING BOUT a heavy alcohol-drinking session **2.** MESSED-UP SITUATION a deplorable mess or mix-up

pistachio /pi staáshi ō, pi stásh-/ n. (plural **-os** or **-o**) **1.** TREES SMALL ASIAN TREE a small Mediterranean or Asian tree of the cashew family that yields hard-shelled

nuts, the kernels of which are edible. Latin name: Pistachia vera. **2.** pistachio (plural **-os**), pistachio nut NUT KERNEL OF PISTACHIO TREE the small edible green kernel of the nut of the pistachio tree [15thC. Via Old French pistace and Italian pistacchio from, ultimately, Greek pistakion, from pistakē 'pistachio tree', possibly of Iranian origin.]

pistachio green n. of a pale whitish-green colour, like the kernel of a pistachio nut —**pistachio green** n.

piste /peest/ n. **1.** SKIING SNOW-COVERED SLOPE FOR SKIING a downhill track or area of densely packed snow that provides good skiing conditions **2.** SPORTS AREA FOR SPORTS CONTEST a rectangular area, sometimes cordoned off, where a contest, especially a fencing bout, takes place [Early 18thC. Via French, 'track', from, ultimately, Latin pinsere 'to beat'; the underlying meaning is 'beaten track'.]

pistil /pístil/ n. a carpel or group of fused carpels forming the female reproductive part of a flower and including the ovary, style, and stigma [Early 18thC. Directly or via French pistile from Latin pistillum 'pestle', because of its shape.]

pistillate /písti layt/ adj. having one or more pistils but usually without stamens

pistol /píst'l/ n. SMALL GUN a small short-barrelled gun designed to be held in one hand ■ vt. (**-tols, -tolling, -tolled**) SHOOT SB OR STH WITH PISTOL to shoot sb or sth using a pistol [Mid-16thC. Via French pistole from, ultimately, Czech pišt'ala, literally 'pipe', from pištěti 'to whistle', ultimately an imitation of the sound.]

pistole /pis tṓl/ n. a gold coin used in some European countries during the 17th and 18th centuries [Late 16thC. From French, a shortening of pistolet, of unknown origin.]

pistoleer /pístə leér/ n. sb, especially a soldier, who carries or uses a pistol (archaic)

pistol grip n. a handle that resembles the butt of a pistol, especially in being shaped to fit the hand

pistol-whip vt. to hit or beat sb or sth with the butt or barrel of a pistol

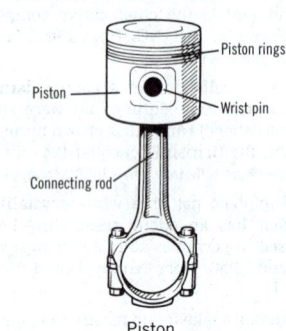

Piston

piston /píst'n/ n. **1.** ENG METAL CYLINDER SLIDING WITHIN TUBE a metal cylinder that slides up and down inside a tubular housing, receiving pressure from or exerting pressure on a fluid, used e.g. in an internal-combustion engine **2.** MUSIC VALVE IN BRASS INSTRUMENT the valve mechanism in a brass musical instrument that is used to alter its pitch [Early 18thC. Via French from Italian pestone 'large pestle', from pestare 'to crush'.]

piston ring n. a metal ring or series of rings fitted round a piston to ensure a tight seal with the cylinder wall and prevent gaseous leakage

piston rod n. a rod connected to a piston that transmits the motion of the piston to a pump or an engine

pistou /peé too/ n. a sauce from Provence made of basil, garlic, and olive oil, similar to Italian pesto [Mid-20thC. Via French from Provençal, the past participle of pestar 'to crush', from late Latin pistare (see PESTO).]

pit[1] /pit/ n. **1.** BIG HOLE IN GROUND a large hole in the ground **2.** MINING HOLE IN GROUND FOR MINING a deep hole in the ground that gives access to a mining resource, especially coal **3.** MINING MINESHAFT a shaft that gives access to a mine **4.** MED SMALL INDENTATION LEFT BY ILLNESS a small indentation in the skin, usually permanent, left by a disease such as chickenpox or by a skin disorder such as acne **5.** MOTOR SPORTS **SERVICING AREA FOR RACING CARS** an area, or section of an area, off the side of a motor-racing track where vehicles can get fuel, fresh tyres, and repairs (*often used in the plural*) **6.** AUTOMOT **SUNKEN AREA FOR EXAMINING CARS** a sunken area, especially in a garage, where the undersides of cars and other motor vehicles can be inspected and repaired **7.** ATHLETICS **SANDY AREA WHERE JUMPERS LAND** a soft sandy area where a long-jumper, triple-jumper, or pole-vaulter can land safely **8.** ANAT **NATURAL HOLLOW** a natural hollow, especially on the surface of a body part **9.** BOT **CONCAVE SPOT ON PLANT WALL** a tiny concavity or thin-walled area in the wall of a plant serving to help transport water and nutrients **10. LOWEST PART** the very bottom of sth **11. AREA CONTAINING PARTICULAR SUBSTANCE** an area filled with a particular material or substance ○ *a tar pit* **12.** THEATRE = **orchestra pit 13.** = **pitfall** *n.* 2 **14.** GAMBLING **AREA IN CASINO** the area in a casino where the gambling takes place **15.** *US* STOCK EXCH **AREA ON FLOOR OF EXCHANGE** the area of the floor of an exchange where commodities trading takes place **16.** SPORTS **ARENA FOR FIGHTING** an arena that is cordoned off for bouts of fighting, especially illegal fighting between cocks or dogs. ◊ **cockpit 17. BED** a bed (*slang*) **18.** CHR **HELL** Hell (*archaic*) ■ *vt.* **(pits, pitting, pitted) 1. SET UP IN OPPOSITION** to set sb or sth up in opposition to sb or sth else **2. MARK SURFACE WITH SMALL HOLES** to cause small holes or indentations to form in a surface **3. PUT SB OR STH INTO DEEP HOLE** to put or bury sb or sth in a deep hole ■ **pits** *npl.* **WORST POSSIBLE THING, PERSON, OR PLACE** the worst or most unpleasant thing, person, or place it is possible to find (*informal*) [Old English *pytt*, ultimately from a prehistoric Germanic word that was borrowed from Latin *puteus* 'pit, well']

pit[2] /pit/ *n.* *US* BOT **FRUIT KERNEL** the kernel or stone of a fruit ■ *vt.* **(pits, pitting, pitted)** *US* **REMOVE KERNEL FROM FRUIT** to remove the kernel or stone from a fruit [Mid-19thC. Origin uncertain: probably from Dutch, from a prehistoric Germanic word that was also the ancestor of English *pith*.]

pita[1] /píttə, peétə/ *n.* a plant such as the agave that yields a strong fibre used to make paper and cordage [Late 17thC. Via American Spanish from Taino.]

pita[2] *n.* = **pitta**

pitapat /píttə pát/ *adv.* **WITH TAPPING SOUND** with quick light tapping noises ■ *n.* **SERIES OF TAPPING NOISES** a series of quick light tapping noises, especially those made by light, running feet ■ *vi.* **(-pats, -patting, -patted) MAKE SERIES OF TAPPING NOISES** to make a series of quick light tapping noises [Early 16thC. An imitation of the sound.]

pit bull *n.* = **pit bull terrier**

pit bull terrier, pit bull *n.* a large bull terrier similar to the Staffordshire bull terrier but more muscular and powerful. The breed was first developed in the United States in dog-fighting circles and remains unrecognized by the Kennel Clubs.

Pitcairn Island /pít kairn-/ island in the central South Pacific Ocean. It is the main island of a group forming a dependency of the United Kingdom. It was first inhabited by mutineers from the HMS *Bounty* in 1790. Population: 61 (1991). Area: 5 sq. km/2 sq. mi.

pitch[1] /pich/ *v.* **(pitches, pitching, pitched) 1.** *vti.* **THROW STH** to throw or hurl sth **2.** *vt.* **SET UP TEMPORARY STRUCTURE** to set up a camp, tent, marquee, or other temporary structure **3.** *vt.* **SECURE STH IN GROUND** to secure, embed, or implant sth in the ground **4.** *vti.* **FALL OR MAKE FALL DOWN** to fall or stumble, or cause sb or sth to fall or stumble, especially headfirst **5.** *vi.* **SLANT IN PARTICULAR WAY** to slant or slope in a particular way or to a particular level **6.** *vi.* **WOBBLE UP AND DOWN** to move with the front and rear being alternately uppermost, e.g. in rough water or turbulent air currents (*refers especially to ships and aircraft*) **7.** *vt.* **SET STH AT PARTICULAR INTELLECTUAL LEVEL** to put, set, or have sth at a particular intellectual level **8.** *vt.* CRICKET **BOWL BALL TO BATSMAN** to bowl a ball so that it hits the ground at a particular spot or distance from the batsman **9.** *vti.* BASEBALL **THROW BALL TO BATTER** to throw a baseball from the mound to the batter **10.** *vti.* GOLF **HIT GOLF BALL HIGH** to hit a high ball, usually onto the green and often with some backspin so that it does not roll too much on landing **11.** *vt.* **TRY TO SELL OR PROMOTE STH** to try to sell or promote sth such as a product, personal viewpoint, or potential business venture, often in an aggressive way **12.** *vt.* MUSIC **SET INSTRUMENT TO PARTICULAR KEY** to set a musical instrument to a particular key **13.** *vt.* CARDS **LEAD CARD TO ESTABLISH TRUMPS** to lead a card of a particular suit in order to establish that suit as trumps for the trick **14.** *vi.* *US, Can* **GIVE ENTHUSIASTIC SUPPORT** to provide enthusiastic support for sb or sth ■ *n.* **1. PARTICULAR DEGREE OF STH** a particular degree or level of sth ○ *What drove him to such a pitch of anxiety?* **2. DEGREE OF SLOPE OF STH** the degree, angle, or extent of the slope of sth, especially a hill, road, or other feature **3.** SPORTS **FIELD FOR GAME** a playing area for a team ball game **4.** CRICKET **AREA BETWEEN CRICKET STUMPS** the area between the two sets of stumps. The regulation size is 22 yards long and 10 feet wide. **5.** CRICKET **PLACE WHERE BALL BOUNCES** the point where a cricket ball lands when it is bowled **6.** BASEBALL **THROW OF BALL** the act or an instance of pitching the ball in baseball **7. WAY OF THROWING STH** a particular way or manner of throwing sth, especially a ball **8.** ARCHIT **HIGHEST OR LOWEST POINT ON FEATURE** the highest or lowest point on a feature such as an arch **9.** BUILDING **DEGREE OF ELEVATION OF ROOF** the degree of elevation of a roof, usually expressed in terms of the ratio between its height and its span **10.** TECH **DISTANCE BETWEEN SIMILAR FORMS** the spacing between adjacent forms on an object that has repeated elements, e.g. the distance between threads on a screw thread **11.** MUSIC **PARTICULAR FREQUENCY OF SINGLE NOTE** the level of a sound in the scale, defined by its frequency **12.** AIR **ANGLE TO WHICH PROPELLER SET** the angle between the plane passing through a propeller blade and the plane of rotation of the propeller **13. TOSSING MOTION** an act or instance of pitching up and down, e.g. in rough water or air turbulence **14. PLACE WHERE STALL IS ERECTED** a place where a stall is erected, especially in a street market **15. AGGRESSIVE SPEECH AIMING TO PERSUADE SB** an aggressive speech given, often more than once, in order to try to persuade sb to accept or buy sth (*informal*) **16.** GEOL **TILT OF GEOLOGICAL FORMATION** the inclination from the horizontal of a geological formation or structure, e.g. a vein or stratum **17.** MOUNTAINEERING **DISTANCE SEPARATING CLIMBERS** the distance between climbers making an ascent or descent using the same ropes, equal to one rope length or less **18.** GOLF **HIGH GOLF SHOT** a golf shot, especially one from fairway to green, in which the ball lofts high in the air, often with some backspin, so that it does not roll too far on landing [12thC. Origin uncertain.] ◇ **queer sb's pitch** to spoil sb's plans or prevent sb from doing sth (*informal*)

pitch in *vi.* **1. HELP WILLINGLY** to help or cooperate, especially in a very willing way **2. BEGIN TO DO STH** to begin to do or participate in sth, especially with great enthusiasm

pitch into *vt.* to begin to attack sb, either verbally or physically (*informal*)

pitch up *vi.* to arrive at a place (*informal*)

pitch[2] /pich/ *n.* **1. SUBSTANCE OBTAINED FROM TAR** a dark sticky substance obtained from tar and used in the building trade, especially for waterproofing roofs **2. NATURAL TARRY SUBSTANCE** a sticky dark substance such as asphalt, found naturally **3. RESIN** resin that is obtained from the sap of certain pine trees ■ *vt.* **(pitches, pitching, pitched) SPREAD PITCH ON SURFACE** to coat a surface with pitch [Partly Old English *pic*, and partly from Anglo-Norman *piche*, both ultimately from Latin *pix* (source also of English *pay*)]

pitch-and-putt *n.* **1. SHORTENED VERSION OF GOLF** a game similar to regulation golf, but played on a much shorter course, in which players use only two clubs, an iron and a putter. The distance to each hole is around one third of the length of the average golf hole. **2. PITCH-AND-PUTT COURSE** a course for pitch-and-putt, with holes shorter than those for regulation golf

pitch-and-toss *n.* a game of skill and luck that involves each player throwing a coin towards a designated spot. The person whose coin lands closest to the mark then takes up all the coins and drops them, and any coins that land heads up are won by that player.

pitchbend /pích bend/ *n.* an instrumental and vocal technique by which the pitch of a note is modified by raising or lowering it slightly

pitch-black *adj.* extremely dark, especially when dark enough to make seeing difficult or impossible

pitchblende /pích blend/ *n.* a dark-coloured naturally occurring form of the mineral uraninite that is the principal source of uranium and radium [Late 18thC. From German *Pechblende*, from *Pech* 'pitch' + *Blende* (see BLENDE).]

pitch-dark *adj.* = **pitch-black**

pitched battle *n.* **1. FIERCE BATTLE AT PREARRANGED LOCATION** a fierce battle, usually involving a large number of people and fought between two sides who take up prearranged positions in close proximity to each other **2. FIERCE CONFLICT OR ARGUMENT** a large-scale, usually bitter conflict or confrontation, often including people who have no direct involvement with the matter

pitcher[1] /píchər/ *n.* **1. LARGE SINGLE-HANDLED JUG** a large single-handled water jug, usually wide around the middle, gradually narrowing towards the neck, and flaring out at the lip or spout **2.** BOT **URN-SHAPED LEAF** any of the modified urn-shaped leaves of the pitcher plant [13thC. Via Old French *pichier* from, ultimately, medieval Latin *bicarium*, from an assumed Vulgar Latin word that is also the ancestor of English *beaker*.]

pitcher[2] /píchər/ *n.* **1.** BASEBALL **PLAYER WHO THROWS BALL TO BATTER** the player on the fielding side who stands on the mound and throws the ball in the direction of the batter, attempting to cause the batter to make an out **2.** BUILDING **PAVING STONE** a paving stone, especially one made of granite [Early 18thC. Formed from PITCH[1].]

pitcher plant *n.* a plant with leaves that are pitcher-shaped to attract, trap, and digest insects. Family: Sarraceniaceae.

pitchfork /pích fawrk/ *n.* **PRONGED FARMING TOOL** a farming implement, usually with a long handle and two or three widely spaced, slightly curved prongs, that is used for stacking, turning, and moving hay ■ *vt.* **(-forks, -forking, -forked) 1. USE PITCHFORK TO MOVE HAY** to use a pitchfork to lift, turn, or move hay **2. THRUST SB INTO DIFFICULT SITUATION** to cause sb to become involved in a situation that is extremely difficult and unwanted [13thC. Alteration of earlier *pickfork* (influenced by PITCH[1]), of uncertain origin: perhaps 'fork with pikes', from PICK[2]; or 'fork for pitching (sheaves, etc.)', from, ultimately, PITCH[1].]

pitch pine *n.* **1.** TREES **PINE TREE YIELDING PITCH** an eastern North American pine tree that yields pitch or turpentine. Latin name: *Pinus rigida.* **2. PITCH PINE WOOD** the wood of the pitch pine tree

pitchstone /pích stōn/ *n.* a dark hydrated volcanic glass similar to obsidian

pitchy /píchi/ **(-ier, -iest)** *adj.* **1. STICKY WITH PITCH** covered with or full of pitch **2. LIKE PITCH** resembling pitch, especially in colour, smell, or consistency —**pitchiness** *n.*

piteous /pítti əss/ *adj.* **1. DESERVING PITY** deserving pity or bringing out feelings of pity **2. FULL OF PITY** full of or expressing pity or compassion (*archaic*) [13thC. Via Old French *piteus*, literally 'full of pity', from, ultimately, Latin *pietas* 'compassion'.] —**piteously** *adv.* —**piteousness** *n.*

pitfall /pít fawl/ *n.* **1. POTENTIAL DISASTER** a potential disaster or difficulty, often one that is unexpected or cannot be anticipated **2. DISGUISED HOLE ACTING AS TRAP** a deep hole in the ground disguised in some way, often with a canopy of foliage covering its top opening and sides so steep that escape is impossible

pith /pith/ *n.* **1. TISSUE UNDER RIND OF CITRUS FRUITS** the soft whitish fibrous tissue that lies under the outer rind of citrus fruits **2. TISSUE INSIDE STEM OF PLANT** the central spongy tissue of the stem of a vascular plant **3. CENTRAL PART OF STH** the central or most important or significant part of sth such as an argument or discussion **4. SPONGY INTERIOR OF BODY PART** the soft spongy inner material of a part of the body such as a hair shaft or bone **5. VIGOUR** vigour, stamina, weight, or substance ■ *vt.* **(piths, pithing, pithed) 1. CUT LABORATORY ANIMAL'S SPINAL CORD** to cut or destroy the spinal cord of a vertebrate as part of a laboratory experiment **2. KILL ANIMALS BY CUTTING SPINAL CORD** to kill animals, especially cattle, by cutting through the spinal cord **3. REMOVE PITH FROM PLANT STEM** to remove the pith from the centre of a plant stem [Old English *piþa*, from a prehistoric Germanic word that is also the ancestor of PITH[2]]

pithead /pít hed/ *n.* the top part of a mineshaft, including the machinery, equipment, and buildings

Pithecanthropus /píthi kánthrəpəss/ (*plural* **-pi** /-pī/) *n.* the original genus name of Java Man, now classified as Homo erectus (*dated*) [Late 19thC. From modern Latin, former genus name, from Greek *pithēkos* 'ape' + *anthrōpos* 'human being'.] —**pithecanthropic** /píthi kan thróppik/ *adj.* —**pithecanthropine** /píthi kánthrə pīn/ *adj.* —**pithecanthropoid** /-kánthrə poyd/ *adj.*

Pith helmet

pith helmet *n.* a lightweight hat made from dried pith or some other material, worn in hot climates to protect the head, face, and the back of the neck from strong sunlight

pithos /píth oss, pī́-/ (*plural* **-oi** /-thoy/) *n.* a large jar, usually made of pottery, used in ancient Greece for storing oil or grain [Late 19thC. From Greek.]

pithy /píthi/ (**-ier**, **-iest**) *adj.* **1.** BRIEF AND TO THE POINT brief yet forceful and to the point, often with an element of wit **2.** OF PITH relating to, full of, or resembling pith —**pithily** *adv.* —**pithiness** *n.*

pitiable /pítti əb'l/ *adj.* **1.** EVOKING COMPASSION arousing or deserving pity or compassion **2.** EVOKING CONTEMPT arousing or deserving contempt or derision —**pitiableness** *n.* —**pitiably** *adv.*

pitiful /píttif'l/ *adj.* **1.** AROUSING PITY arousing or deserving pity or compassion **2.** AROUSING CONTEMPT arousing or deserving contempt or derision —**pitifully** *adv.* —**pitifulness** *n.*

pitiless /píttiləss/ *adj.* **1.** WITHOUT MERCY lacking in pity, mercy, or sympathy **2.** SEVERE severe to the highest degree possible ○ *the blazing, pitiless sun* —**pitilessly** *adv.* —**pitilessness** *n.*

Pitjantjatjara /píchənchə chárrə/ (*plural* **-ra** *or* **-ras**), **Pitjantjara** /píchən járrə/ (*plural* **-ra** *or* **-ras**) *n.* **1.** PEOPLES MEMBER OF ABORIGINAL PEOPLE a member of an Australian Aboriginal people who live in the desert regions in the south of the continent **2.** LANG PITJANTJATJARA LANGUAGE the language of the Pitjantjatjara people, which belongs to the Pama-Nyungan family. About 2,000 people speak Pitjantjatjara. [From Pitjantjatjara]

Pitlochry /pit lókhri/ town in Scotland, in Perth and Kinross council area, on the River Tummel. Population: 2,541 (1991).

pitman /pítmən/ (*plural* **-men** /-mən/) *n.* sb who is employed in a mine, especially sb who works at a coalface

piton /pée ton/ *n.* a metal spike for driving into ice or a rock crevice, with an eye at the other end so that a rope can be passed through it and then secured [Late 19thC. From French, 'eye-bolt'.]

Pitot-static tube /pée̅to̅ staáttik-/ *n.* a device consisting of a Pitot tube and a static tube, used to measure fluid velocity and especially as an air speed indicator in aircraft [Early 20thC. See PITOT TUBE.]

Pitot tube /pée̅to̅-/ *n.* **1.** DEVICE FOR MEASURING FLUID VELOCITY an instrument placed in a moving fluid and used along with a manometer to measure fluid velocity **2.** = **Pitot-static tube** [Late 19thC. Named after the French physicist Henri *Pitot* 1695–1771, who invented it.]

pit stop *n.* **1.** MOTOR SPORTS REFUELLING STOP FOR CAR DURING RACE a stop in the pits to allow a racing car to be refuelled and serviced during a race **2.** BRIEF STOP DURING ROAD JOURNEY a brief stop during a journey by road to rest, refuel, use a toilet, or buy refreshments (*informal*) **3.** PLACE TO MAKE PIT STOP a place to make a pit stop during a road journey (*informal*)

Pitt /pít/, **William, 1st Earl of Chatham** (1708–78) British statesman. As secretary of state (1756–61), he was the most powerful politician in Britain and effectively prime minister. He headed a new government from 1766 to 1768. Known as **Pitt the Elder**

William Pitt (the Younger)

Pitt, William (1759–1806) British statesman. He was Great Britain's youngest prime minister, at the age of 24 (1783–1801). He resigned following George III's refusal to accept Roman Catholic emancipation, but returned to office (1804–06) for a second administration. Known as **Pitt the Younger**

pitta, **pita, pitta bread, pita bread** *n.* a flat round Middle Eastern unleavened bread that can be opened to insert a filling [Mid-20thC. From modern Greek *pētta*, *pit(t)a* 'bread, pie'.]

pittance /pítt'nss/ *n.* a very small amount of sth, especially a very small sum of money, wage, or allowance [13thC. Via Old French *pietance* from medieval Latin *pietantia* 'pious or charitable gift', from Latin *pietas* 'piety'.]

pitter-patter /píttər patər/ *n.* LIGHT CONTINUOUS TAPPING SOUND a light, rapid, and continuous tapping sound, similar to the sound of raindrops falling on sth ■ *vi.* (**pitter-patters**, **pitter-pattering**, **pitter-pattered**) MAKE LIGHT CONTINUOUS TAPPING SOUND to make or move with a light, rapid, and continuous tapping sound ■ *adv.* WITH LIGHT CONTINUOUS TAPPING SOUND with a light, rapid, and continuous tapping sound [15thC. An imitation of the sound.]

Pitt Street Farmer *n. Aus* = **Collins Street Farmer** (*informal*)

pituitary /pi tyo̅o̅ itəri/ *n.* (*plural* **-ies**) **1.** PHYSIOL = **pituitary gland 2.** PHARM = **pituitary extract** ■ *adj.* PHYSIOL OF PITUITARY GLAND relating to or produced by the pituitary gland [Early 17thC. From Latin *pituitarius* 'of slime or mucus', from *pituita* 'slime'. From the fact that the pituitary gland was originally thought to secrete nasal mucus.]

pituitary extract *n.* a pharmaceutical preparation made from substances obtained from the pituitary gland that is rich in beneficial hormones

pituitary gland, **pituitary body** (*plural* **pituitary bodies**) *n.* a small oval gland at the base of the brain in vertebrates, producing hormones that control other glands and influence growth of the bone structure, sexual maturing, and general metabolism

pit viper *n.* a venomous American snake that has heat-sensitive pits below its eyes used to detect prey. Rattlesnakes and copperheads are pit vipers. Family: Crotalidae.

pity /pítti/ *n.* **1.** FEELING OF SYMPATHY a feeling of sadness because sb else is in trouble or pain, or the capacity to feel this **2.** REGRETTABLE THING a sad or regrettable thing ○ *It's a pity you couldn't make it.* **3.** MERCY a willingness to help or to forgive sb who is in pain or who has done wrong ■ *vt.* (**-ies**, **-ying**, **-ied**) FEEL PITY FOR SB OR STH to feel pity for sb or for sb's pain or trouble ■ *interj.* EXPRESSION OF SYMPATHY OR REGRET used to express sympathy or regret about sth (*informal*) [13thC. Via Old French *pité* from Latin *pietas* 'piety, dutifulness, compassion' (see PIETY).] —**pitying** *adj.* —**pityingly** *adv.* ◇ **have** *or* **take pity on sb** to feel pity for sb or for sb's pain or trouble, or show mercy to sb ◇ **(the) more's the pity** used to express regret, disappointment, or annoyance that sth is the case (*informal*)

pityriasis /pítti rī́ əssiss/ *n.* a skin disease affecting humans and animals in which the skin comes off in dry flakes [Late 17thC. Via modern Latin from Greek *pituriasis*, from *pituron* 'corn husks'.]

più /pyoo/ *adv.* more or increasingly (*used as a musical direction*) [Early 18thC. Via Italian from Latin *plus* (see PLUS).]

piupiu /pée oo pee oo/ *n.* a skirt worn by Maori men and women for traditional ceremonies and dances, made from the leaves of the New Zealand flax [Late 19thC. From Maori.]

Pius IX /pī́ əss/, **Pope** (1792–1878). His pontificate (1846–78) was marked by the loss of the Papal States, the declaration of papal infallibility, and condemnation of all forms of liberalism. Real name **Giovanni Maria Mastai-Ferretti**

Pius XI, Pope (1857–1939). As pope (1922–34) he presided over the signing of the Lateran Treaty (1929), and spoke out against fascism, Nazism, and communism. Real name **Ambrogio Damiano Achille Ratti**

Pius XII, Pope (1876–1958). As pope (1939–58) he condemned modernism and communism. He sought to prevent World War II, although his role in the war is the subject of controversy. Real name **Eugenio Pacelli**

Pius X, St, Pope (1835–1914). During his pontificate (1903–14) he opposed modernism in the Roman Catholic Church, initiated changes to canon law, and introduced a new breviary. Real name **Giuseppe Melchiorre Sarto**

Piute *n., adj.* = **Paiute**

pivot /pívvət/ *n.* **1.** TECH OBJECT ON WHICH LARGER OBJECT TURNS a small object such as a bar or pin that supports a larger object and lets it turn or swing **2.** CRUCIAL PERSON OR THING the one person or thing that is essential to the success or effectiveness of sth **3.** TURNING MOVEMENT a turning movement carried out by pivoting on sth **4.** MIL CENTRE POINT OF WHEELING MOVEMENT a person, a group of people, or point that acts as the centre around which a military formation carries out a wheeling movement **5.** BASKETBALL BASKETBALL POSITION OR PLAYER an offensive position in basketball in which a player faces away from the opposing basket, relays passes, and screens other members of the team, or a player in this position ■ *v.* (**-ots**, **-oting**, **-oted**) **1.** *vi.* TURN ON PIVOT to turn or swing supported by a pivot **2.** *vi.* DEPEND ON STH to depend on sb or sth, usually a single person, thing, or factor **3.** *vt.* PROVIDE WITH PIVOT to provide sth with a pivot on which it can turn or swing [From French, of unknown origin]

pivotal /pívvət'l/ *adj.* **1.** VITALLY IMPORTANT vitally important, especially in determining the outcome, progress, or success of sth **2.** TECH ACTING AS PIVOT relating to or functioning as a pivot

pivot bridge *n.* = **swing bridge**

pivot man *n.* **1.** SB ACTING AS PIVOT sb who acts as the pivot for a military formation or who has a pivotal role in any organization or formation **2.** = **pivot** *n.* 5

pix[1] plural of **pic**

pix[2] *n.* = **pyx**

pixel /píks'l/ *n.* an individual tiny dot of light that is the basic unit from which the images on a computer or television screen are made [Mid-20thC. Coined from PIX[1] + ELEMENT.]

pixie /píksi/, **pixy** (*plural* **-ies**) *n.* a type of fairy or elf often depicted as having pointed ears, wearing a long pointed hat, and being cheerful and rather mischievous [Mid-17thC. Origin unknown.]

pixilated[1] /píksi laytid/, **pixillated** *adj.* **1.** BEWILDERED feeling bewildered because unable to understand what is happening **2.** DRUNK drunk (*slang*) [Mid-19thC. Coined humorously from PIXIE + *-lated* (as in English words such as 'elated' and 'titillated').] —**pixilation** *n.*

pixilated[2] /píksi laytid/ *adj.* used to describe an image on a computer or television screen that is made up of pixels, especially one that is unclear or distorted [Mid-20thC. Coined from PIXEL + *-ated*.]

pixy *n.* = pixie

pizz. *abbr.* pizzicato

pizza /péetsə/ *n.* a flat round piece of bread dough topped with a tomato sauce and cheese, and often with other toppings such as sliced ham, sausage, or vegetables, then baked [Late 19thC. From Italian, 'pie', of uncertain origin.]

pizzazz /pə záz/, **pizazz, pizzaz, pzazz** *n.* an attractive and exciting vitality, especially when combined with style and glamour (*informal*) [Mid-20thC. The origin of this word is uncertain, but it may have been an invention of Diana Vreeland who was fashion editor for the publication *Harper's Bazaar* during the 1930s.]

pizzeria /péetsə rée ə/ (*plural* **-as**) *n.* a restaurant that specializes in making and serving pizzas [Mid-20thC. From Italian *pizzeria*, from PIZZA.]

pizzicato /pítsi kaátō/ *adv.* BY PLUCKING STRINGS by using the fingers to pluck the strings of an instrument that is normally played with a bow, especially a violin (*used as a musical direction*) ■ *n.* (*plural* **-tos** *or* **-ti** /-ti/) PIZZICATO PIECE OF MUSIC a piece of music, or a section of a piece, played pizzicato [Mid-19thC. From Italian, from *pizzicare* 'to pluck', from *pizzare* 'to prick, sting', from *pizza* 'point'.] —**pizzicato** *adj.*

pizzle /pízz'l/ *n.* the penis of an animal, especially a bull (*archaic; sometimes considered offensive*) [Late 15thC. From Low German *pēsel*, literally 'little penis', from Middle Low German *pēse* 'penis'.]

pk *abbr.* **1.** pack **2.** park **3.** peak **4.** MEASURE peck

PK *abbr.* **1.** PARANORMAL psychokinesis **2.** CARS Pakistan (*international vehicle registration*)

pkg. *abbr.* package

pkt *abbr.* packet

PKU *abbr.* phenylketonuria

pkwy, pky *abbr.* parkway

pl *abbr.* GRAM plural

PL *abbr.* **1. PL, pl** GRAM plural **2.** LAW public law

Pl. *abbr.* Place (*used in addresses*)

PL/1 *n., abbr.* programming language 1

PLA *abbr.* Port of London Authority

placable /plákəb'l/ *adj.* easily placated (*literary*) [14thC. Directly or via Old French from Latin *placabilis*, from *placare* 'to calm' (see PLACATE).] —**placability** /plákə bíləti/ *n.* —**placably** /plákəbli/ *adv.*

placard /plákaard/ *n.* **1.** NOTICE DISPLAYED IN PUBLIC a large piece of card or board with sth written or printed on it, displayed to be read by the public or carried by sb such as a demonstrator **2.** SMALL CARD OR METAL PLAQUE a small card or metal plaque such as a door-plate, with a name or some other piece of writing on it ■ *vt.* (**-ards, -arding, -arded**) **1.** PUT PLACARDS ON STH to put up placards on or in sth **2.** ADVERTISE OR ANNOUNCE WITH PLACARDS to display sth on or advertise sth with placards, or in a very conspicuous way [Late 15thC. From French, formed from Old French *plaquier* 'to flatten, plaster', from Middle Dutch *placken* 'to flatten, patch' (source also of English *plaque*).]

placate /plə káyt/ (**-cates, -cating, -cated**) *vt.* to make sb less angry, upset, or hostile, usually by doing or saying things to please him or her [Late 17thC. From Latin *placat-*, the past participle stem of *placare* 'to calm'. Ultimately from an Indo-European base that is also the ancestor of English *please, flake,* and *plank*.] —**placation** *n.* —**placatory** *adj.*

place /playss/ *n.* **1.** AREA OR PORTION OF SPACE an area, position, or portion of space that sb or sth can be in ○ *This is a good place to plant the sapling.* **2.** LOCALITY a particular geographical locality such as a town, country, or region ○ *People come here to work from lots of different places.* **3.** AREA IN TOWN a relatively open area in a town, e.g. a public square or a short street **4.** DWELLING the house or other type of accommodation where sb lives ○ *a place of our own* **5.** AREA WHERE STH HAPPENS a building or area where sth in particular happens or is located ○ *the firm's place of business* **6.** PARTICULAR POINT IN STH a particular point in sth, e.g. a book, film, or story ○ *I lost my place when you interrupted me.* **7.** PROPER POSITION the position or location where sb or sth belongs ○ *A place for everything, and everything in its place.* **8.** OPPORTUNITY TO STUDY an opportunity to study at school or university ○ *hoping for a place at Oxford.* **9.** STATUS sb's social position or rank in an organization ○ *know your place* **10.** RESPONSIBILITY sb's responsibility or right, especially one arising from who the person is or the status he or she has ○ *It's not your place to tell me what to do.* **11.** JOB a job or position ○ *offered a place on the board* **12.** SOMEWHERE TO SIT somewhere for sb to sit, e.g. at a table during a meal or in the audience of a theatre ○ *I'll keep a place for you next to me.* **13.** POSITION IN RANK the position of sb or sth in a rank, sequence, or series ○ *She finished in second place.* **14.** HORSERACING WINNING, SECOND, OR THIRD POSITION the winning, second, or third position in a race, especially a horse race **15.** *US* HORSERACING SECOND POSITION second position in a race, especially a horse race **16.** MATH POSITION OF DIGIT IN NUMBER the relative position of a particular digit in a number ■ *vt.* (**places, placing, placed**) **1.** PUT SOMEWHERE to put sth or sb in a particular location or position ○ *placed the box on the table* **2.** PUT IN PARTICULAR STATE to cause sb or sth to be in a particular state or condition ○ *Your actions placed all of us in danger.* **3.** SEE SB IN PARTICULAR WAY to see or treat sb or sth as having a particular value or character ○ *He placed his family above everything else in his life.* **4.** REMEMBER SB OR STH to be able to recognize or remember sb or sth ○ *I know the face but I can't place the name.* **5.** ASSIGN SB to assign sb to a job, position, home, or the care of sb else ○ *I'll see if I can place you with the sales team.* **6.** AIM STH CAREFULLY to aim or calculate sth carefully so that it lands in a particular spot or has a desired effect ○ *The champion's experience showed in the way he placed his punches.* **7.** HAVE STH ACCEPTED to have sth accepted and dealt with by sb else ○ *placed an order for a new car* **8.** HORSERACING WIN OR BE SECOND OR THIRD to finish or cause to finish in the winning, second, or third position in a contest, especially a horse race (*usually passive*) ○ *This horse has been placed in its last three outings.* [Pre-12thC. Via French from, ultimately, Latin *platea* 'broad way', from the Greek phrase *plateia hodos*. *Plateia* 'broad' came from an Indo-European base meaning 'to spread' that is also the ancestor of English *flat* and *plant*. The Latin word is the ultimate source also of English *plaza* and *piazza*.] ◇ **all over the place 1.** everywhere (*informal*) **2.** in a state of disorder or confusion (*informal*) ◇ **a place in the sun** a position of success, happiness, or prosperity ◇ **give place (to)** to make room for sb or sth or allow sb or sth to take precedence ◇ **go places** to be successful (*informal*) ◇ **in place 1.** where sb or sth belongs or ought to be **2.** in position or ready for use ◇ **in place of** instead of or as a replacement for sb or sth ◇ **out of place 1.** not where sth or sb should be **2.** inappropriate or incongruous ◇ **put sb in his or her place** to humble sb who is behaving in an arrogant, presumptuous, or insolent way (*informal*) ◇ **take place** to happen ◇ **take the place of** to be a substitute for or replace sth or sb

placebo /plə séebō/ (*plural* **-bos** *or* **-boes**) *n.* **1.** MED DRUG WITH NO REAL EFFECT a drug containing no active ingredients given to a patient participating in a clinical trial in order to assess the performance of a new drug. It may also may be given to patients because it may benefit them psychologically to believe they are receiving treatment. **2.** STH DONE TO PLACATE SB sth done or said simply to placate or reassure sb that has no actual effect on whatever is causing his or her problems or anxiety **3.** CHR VESPERS OF OFFICE FOR DEAD in the Roman Catholic Church, the vespers of the office for the dead [13thC. From Latin, 'I shall please' (first word in the Vulgate text of Psalm 114:9, used in the Roman Catholic service for the dead), from *placere* 'to please' (see PLEASE).]

placebo effect *n.* a sense of benefit felt by a patient that arises solely from the knowledge that treatment has been given

place card *n.* a small card with sb's name on it, put on a table to show where that person is to sit, especially for a formal meal

placeholder /pláyss hōldər/ *n.* a symbol in a mathematical or logical expression used to show a pattern, e.g. by representing a term in an equation or a statement in an argument

place kick *n.* a kick to resume play after a stoppage, especially in American football or rugby, for which the ball is propped or held up on the ground

place-kick (**place-kicks, place-kicking, place-kicked**) *vt.* to kick the ball or to score a goal or points by kicking the ball while it is propped up on the ground —**place-kicker** *n.*

placeman /pláyssmən/ (*plural* **-men** /-mən/) *n.* sb appointed to public office simply as a reward for services to a political party or who uses public office simply to satisfy personal greed or ambition

place mat *n.* a protective mat set out for the plate of someone eating at a table

placement /pláyssmənt/ *n.* **1.** PLACING OR BEING PLACED the act of placing or arranging sth in a particular place or position, or the fact of being placed or arranged in this way **2.** MATCHING SB TO PARTICULAR SITUATION the task of finding sth such as jobs or accommodation for people, or of assigning people to particular jobs, classes, or accommodation, or an instance of doing so **3.** WORK EXPERIENCE AS PART OF STUDY a period of work for practical experience as part of an academic course. US term **practicum 4.** SPORTS SKILFUL PLAYING OF BALL a player's skill in accurately playing the ball in a sport such as tennis or rugby

placename /pláyss naym/ *n.* the name of a geographical area or feature such as a town, settlement, hill, or body of water

placenta /plə séntə/ (*plural* **-tas** *or* **-tae** /-tee/) *n.* **1.** BIOL ORGAN IN UTERUS OF PREGNANT MAMMAL a vascular organ that develops inside the uterus of most pregnant mammals to supply food and oxygen to the foetus through the umbilical cord. It is expelled after birth. **2.** BOT PART OF OVARY OF PLANT the part of the ovary in a flowering plant that bears ovules **3.** BOT SPORE-BEARING MASS OF TISSUE the tissue in a nonflowering plant where the sporangia or spores develop [Late 17thC. Via Latin, 'cake', from, ultimately, Greek *plakous* 'flat cake', from the stem *plak-* 'flat surface'. Ultimately from an Indo-European base meaning 'to be flat'.] —**placentary** *adj.*

placental /plə sént'l/ *adj.* WITH PLACENTA having a placenta ■ *n.* ANIMAL WITH PLACENTA an animal that has a placenta, in contrast to marsupials or those that lay eggs

placentation /plássen táysh'n/ *n.* **1.** BIOL FORMATION OR ATTACHMENT OF PLACENTA the process of forming a placenta during pregnancy, or the way in which the placenta is attached to the wall of the uterus **2.** BOT WAY OVULES ARE ATTACHED the way in which ovules are attached to the ovary of a plant **3.** BIOL PLACENTA TYPE the form, structure, or type of a placenta

place of safety order *n.* a court order enabling sb to remove a child or young person temporarily to a place of safety from actual or likely abuse or neglect

placer /pláyssər/ *n.* a deposit of sand or gravel found, e.g. in the bed of a stream, containing particles of gold or some other valuable mineral [Early 19thC. From American Spanish, 'shoal'.]

placer mining *n.* the process of obtaining valuable minerals from placers by washing or dredging

place setting *n.* the set of items such as cutlery, plates, and glasses arranged on a table to be used by one person at a meal, or the cutlery or plates alone

place value *n.* MATH the value of the place that a digit occupies in a numeral

placid /plássid/ *adj.* calm and tending not to become excited, upset, or disturbed, or appearing so [Early 17thC. Directly or via French *placide* from Latin *placidus* 'gentle', from *placere* 'to please' (see PLEASE).] —**placidity** /plə síddəti/ *n.* —**placidly** /plássidli/ *adv.*

WORD KEY: SYNONYMS

See Synonyms at ***calm***.

placing /pláyssing/ *n.* the issuing of securities to the public through a stockbroker or another intermediary

placket /plákit/ *n.* **1.** OPENING IN WOMAN'S GARMENT an opening in a woman's garment such as a skirt or blouse, either where it fastens or at a pocket **2.** PIECE OF CLOTH BEHIND OPENING a piece of cloth sewn in behind an opening in a woman's garment [Early 17thC. Alteration of PLACARD.]

placoderm /plákə durm/ *n.* an extinct creature resembling a fish that was covered with bony plates and lived in the Palaeozoic era. Class: Placodermi. [Mid-19thC. Coined from the Greek stem *plak-* 'flat stone' (see PLACENTA) + -DERM.]

placoid /plák oyd/ *adj.* used to describe fish scales that have a flat base and a sharp projecting spine tipped with enamel. The subclass of fish that includes sharks, rays, and skates have placoid scales. [Mid-19thC. Coined from the Greek stem *plak-* 'flat stone' (see PLACENTA) + -OID.]

pladdy /pláddi/ (*plural* **-dies**) *n. Ireland* one of the low flat islands in Strangford Lough

plafond /plə fón, pla fóN/ *n.* a ceiling, especially one that is highly ornamented [Mid-17thC. From French, literally 'flat bottom'.]

plagal /pláyg'l/ *adj.* MUSIC **1. FROM SUBDOMINANT TO TONIC** used to describe a musical cadence or harmonic progression in which the subdominant chord is immediately followed by the tonic chord **2. RELATING TO MUSICAL MODE** relating to or being a musical mode beginning on the note a fourth below the keynote of its equivalent authentic mode but ending on the same final note [Late 16thC. From medieval Latin *plagalis*, from, ultimately, medieval Greek *plagios hēkhos* 'plagal mode'. *Plagios* 'oblique' was formed from *plagos* 'side'.]

plage /plaazh/ *n.* a mark on the Sun's surface often associated with sunspots [Via Old French, 'region', from, ultimately, Greek *plagos* 'side' (see PLAGAL)]

plagiarise *vti.* = **plagiarize**

plagiarism /pláyjərizəm/ *n.* **1. STEALING SB'S WORK OR IDEA** copying what sb else has written or taking sb's else's idea and trying to pass it off as original **2. STH PLAGIARIZED** sth copied from sb else's work, or sb else's idea that sb presents as his or her own —**plagiarist** *n.* —**plagiaristic** /pláyjə rístik/ *adj.*

plagiarize /pláyjə rīz/ (**-rizes, -rizing, -rized**), **plagiarise** (**-rises, -rising, -rised**) *vti.* to take sth that sb else has written or thought and try to pass it off as original —**plagiarizer** *n.*

plagio- *prefix.* **1.** oblique, offset ○ *plagiotropism* **2.** disturbance ○ *plagioclimax* [From Greek *plagios*, literally 'sideways', from *plagos* 'side'. Ultimately from an Indo-European base meaning 'to be flat', which is also the ancestor of English *flake*, *flag*, *plank*, and *placate*.]

plagioclase /pláyji ə klayz/ *n.* a feldspar consisting of sodium and calcium aluminium silicates and belonging to a common series whose cleavages are not at right angles [Mid-19thC. Coined from PLAGIO- + Greek *klasis* 'breaking'.] —**plagioclastic** /pláyji ə klástik/ *adj.*

plagioclimax /pláyji ō klī maks/ *n.* a stable plant community that has arisen due to human intervention in the natural succession of communities [Mid-20thC. Coined from PLAGIO- + CLIMAX.]

plagiotropism /pláyji ō trópizəm/ *n.* BOT the tendency of a plant's roots, stems, or branches to grow at an angle away from the vertical in response to a stimulus —**plagiotropic** /pláyji ō trópik, pláyji ə-/ *adj.* —**plagiotropically** /pláyji ə trópik'li, -tróppik'li/ *adv.*

plague /playg/ *n.* **1.** MED **EPIDEMIC DISEASE** a disease that spreads very rapidly, infecting very large numbers of people and killing a great many of them, or an outbreak of such a disease **2.** MED **BUBONIC PLAGUE** the bubonic plague **3. APPEARANCE OF STH IN LARGE NUMBERS** the appearance of sth harmful or annoying such as vermin in abnormally large numbers, or with abnormal frequency **4. SB OR STH TROUBLESOME** an affliction or extremely troublesome or annoying person or thing ■ *vt.* (**plagues, plaguing, plagued**) **1. AFFLICT SB OR STH** to occur or recur frequently, causing a great deal of trouble, difficulty, or pain to sb or sth (*often passive*) **2. ANNOY SB CONSTANTLY** to harass or annoy sb constantly, usually by asking questions or making requests or demands [14thC. Via Latin *plaga* 'blow, stroke, wound' from, possibly, Greek. Ultimately from an Indo-European word meaning 'to strike' which is also the ancestor of English *complain* and *plankton*.]

plaguy /pláygi/, **plaguey** *adj.* (**-guier, -guiest**) **TROUBLESOME** causing trouble or irritation (*archaic informal*) ■ *adv.* **ANNOYINGLY** in a troublesome or annoying way or to a troublesome or annoying degree (*archaic informal*) —**plaguily** *adv.*

plaice /playss/ (*plural* **plaice**) *n.* **1. LARGE FLAT EDIBLE SEAFISH** a large edible flat-bodied fish that lives in European seas and has brown skin with red or orange spots. Latin name: *Pleuronectes platessa.* **2. FLATFISH OF NORTH AMERICAN ATLANTIC WATERS** a fish similar and related to the European plaice, found in North American Atlantic waters. Latin name: *Hippoglossoides platessoides.* [13thC. Via Old French *plaïs* from late Latin *platessa* 'flatfish', from Greek *platus* 'broad'.]

plaid /plad/ *n.* **1.** CLOTHES **TARTAN CLOTH WORN OVER SHOULDER** a long rectangular piece of tartan material worn draped over the shoulder as part of traditional Scottish Highland dress **2.** TEXTILES **TARTAN FABRIC** a fabric usually made of wool and woven in a tartan or chequered pattern **3.** TEXTILES **TARTAN PATTERN** a tartan or checked pattern [Early 16thC. Via Gaelic from Middle Irish, of unknown origin.]

Plaid Cymru /plīd kúmri/ *n.* the Welsh Nationalist Party [Mid-20thC. From Welsh, literally 'party of Wales'.]

plain /playn/ *adj.* **1. SIMPLE AND ORDINARY** simple and ordinary in nature or appearance and without additions or decorations ○ *plain, homely food* ○ *a plain brown envelope* **2. CLEARLY VISIBLE** not blocked or obscured by anything, so as to be clearly visible ○ *in plain view* **3. CLEAR IN MEANING** quite clear in meaning and easy to recognize or understand ○ *The plain fact is that they lied to us.* **4. FRANK** stating the truth clearly without concealing anything or sparing sb's feelings ○ *The time has come for plain speaking.* **5. PURE** not combined with any other substances ○ *plain water* **6. LACKING PATTERN OR COLORATION** uncoloured or unpatterned ○ *plain fabric* **7. NOT PRETTY** not pretty or striking in looks ○ *plain looks* **8.** KNITTING **IN SIMPLEST KNITTING STYLE OR STITCH** done in the simplest knitting style or stitch ■ *adv.* **1. ABSOLUTELY** used to emphasize an adjective or adverb ○ *just plain wrong* **2. CLEARLY** in a clear or distinct way ○ *I'll tell you plain, I've had enough of this.* ■ *n.* **1.** GEOG **FLAT EXPANSE OF LAND** a large expanse of fairly flat dry land, usually with few trees **2.** KNITTING **KNITTING STYLE OR STITCH** the simplest knitting style or stitch. The right needle goes into a loop of wool on the left needle and the wool is then passed around the right needle. ■ **plains** *npl.* GEOG **TREELESS LEVEL EXPANSES** large expanses of level, almost treeless country in some central states of the United States [13thC. Via Old French from Latin *planus* 'flat' (also the source of English *plane* and *piano*).] —**plainly** *adv.* —**plainness** *n.*

plain bread *n. Scotland* bread cut from a loaf of white bread that has flat sides and a dark crust on the top and bottom

plainchant /pláyn chaant/ *n.* = **plainsong**

plain chocolate *n.* **1. CHOCOLATE WITHOUT ADDED MILK** chocolate with no added milk that is darker and less sweet than milk chocolate **2. CHOCOLATE SWEET** a sweet coated with plain chocolate

plain clothes *npl.* ordinary civilian clothes when worn by a police officer on duty —**plain-clothes** *adj.*

plain dealing *n.* open and honest behaviour or business

plain flour *n.* flour that has had no baking powder added to it

plain Jane /-jáyn/ *n.* a woman who is not pretty or striking in looks (*informal; often considered offensive*)

plain loaf (*plural* **plain loaves**) *n. Scotland* a white loaf baked in a batch, so the sides are flat and there is a dark crust on its top and bottom only

plain sailing *n.* sth that is straightforward and easy to do [Origin uncertain: perhaps an alteration of PLANE SAILING, from the comparative simplicity of this sort of navigation]

Plains Indian /pláynz-/ *n.* a member of any of the Native American peoples that in the past lived on the Great Plains of North America

plainsman /pláynzmən/ (*plural* **-men** /pláynzmən/) *n.* a man who lives on a plain, especially sb who settled or lives on the Great Plains of North America

plainsong /pláyn song/ *n.* **1. TYPE OF CHURCH MUSIC** a type of church music intended to be sung in unison and unaccompanied by instruments that is particularly associated with services held in monasteries **2.** = **Gregorian chant** [15thC. Translation of Latin *cantus planus*.]

plain-spoken *adj.* saying or tending to say precisely what is thought without concealing anything or sparing other people's feelings —**plain-spokenness** *n.*

plainswoman /pláynz wŏŏmən/ (*plural* **-en** /-wimin/) *n.* a woman who lives on a plain, especially one who settled or lives on the Great Plains of North America

plaint /playnt/ *n.* **1.** LAW **STATEMENT OF GROUNDS FOR COURT ACTION** a statement in writing to a court of law showing the grounds on which a complainant is bringing an action and asking for the grievance to be redressed **2. EXPRESSION OF GRIEF** an expression of grief or sadness (*archaic literary*) [12thC. Via French from Latin *planctus* 'a beating of the breast', from *plangere* 'to beat' (see PLANGENT).]

plain text *n.* a form of a message that is in ordinary readable language rather than in code

plaintiff /pláyntif/ *n.* sb who begins a lawsuit against another person (**defendant**) in a civil court [14thC. From French (see PLAINTIVE).]

plaintive /pláyntiv/ *adj.* expressing sadness or sounding sad [14thC. From French *plaintive*, *plaintif*, from *plaint* (see PLAINT).] —**plaintively** *adv.* —**plaintiveness** *n.*

plain weave *n.* a type of weave in which the weft passes alternately under and over the warp so that the threads form a simple criss-cross pattern

plain-woven *adj.* woven in plain weave

plait /plat/ *n.* **1. WOVEN STRANDS** sth made by weaving strands together, especially a length of hair with strands woven together like rope or a loaf made by weaving strands of dough together **2.** SEW **PLEAT** a pleat ■ *vt.* (**plaits, plaiting, plaited**) **1. WEAVE STRANDS TOGETHER** to weave three or more strands of sth over and under each other, usually to form them either into sth that looks like a rope or into a flat band **2. MAKE STH BY PLAITING** to make sth by plaiting **3.** SEW **PLEAT STH** to pleat sth [15thC. Via Old French *pleit* from, ultimately, Latin *plicit-*, the past participle stem of *plicare* 'to fold' (source of English *pleat* and *plight*).]

plan /plan/ *n.* **1. SCHEME FOR ACHIEVING OBJECTIVE** a method of doing sth that is worked out usually in some detail before it is begun and that may be written down in some form or simply retained in memory **2. INTENTION** sth that sb intends or has arranged to do (*often used in the plural*) **3. DIAGRAM OF LAYOUT** a drawing or diagram showing the layout, arrangement, or structure of sth **4. LIST OR OUTLINE** a list, summary, or diagram that shows how the items that make up sth such as a piece of writing or an organized meeting are to be arranged **5.** ARCHIT **HORIZONTAL SECTION OF BUILDING** a scale diagram showing a horizontal view of the arrangement of rooms and fixtures in a building on a particular level ■ *v.* (**plans, planning, planned**) **1.** *vti.* **WORK OUT HOW TO DO STH** to work out in advance and in some detail how sth is to be done or organized **2.** *vt.* **INTEND TO DO STH** to intend or to make arrangements to do sth **3.** *vt.* ARCHIT **MAKE A SCALE DRAWING** to make a scale drawing of sth, especially a building [Late 17thC. From French, 'ground plan', an alteration (influenced by *plan* 'flat') of *plant*, from, ultimately, Latin *plantare* 'to push in with the sole of the foot' (see PLANT).]

plan ahead *vi.* to make preparations or arrangements for the future

plan for *vt.* to make preparations and arrangements for sth based on what is expected to happen

plan on *vt.* to intend to do sth (*informal*)

plan out *vt.* to make a detailed plan for sth to be done or organized

plan- *prefix.* = **plano-**

planar /pláynər/ *adj.* flat or lying in a single geometric plane —**planarity** /play nárrəti/ *n.*

planarian /plə náiri ən/ *n.* a small flatworm that mainly lives in fresh water, is not a parasite, and has a three-branched intestine. Order: Tricladida. [Mid-19thC. Via modern Latin *Planaria*, the name of the genus, from Latin *planarius* 'on level ground', from *planus* 'flat' (see PLAIN).]

planation /play náysh'n/ n. the levelling out of natural surfaces on land or under water by erosion or the depositing of new material [Late 19thC. Formed from PLANE².]

planchet /plaánchit/ n. **1.** BLANK DISC OF METAL FOR STAMPING a flat disc of metal ready to be stamped as a coin or medal **2.** US CHEM SMALL METAL CUP a small metal container used to measure a radioactive substance [Early 17thC. Literally 'little plank', formed from obsolete English planch 'wooden plank, metal plate', from French planche (see PLANK).]

planchette /plaán shét/ n. a small heart-shaped or triangular wooden board on two castors and with a pencil attached that spells out messages supposed to be from the spirit world when people touch it lightly [Mid-19thC. From French, literally 'little plank', formed from planche 'plank' (see PLANK).]

Planck /plangk/, **Max** (1858–1947) German physicist. The originator and developer of quantum theory, he won a Nobel Prize in physics (1918). Full name **Max Karl Ernst Ludwig Planck**

Planck's constant /plángks-/, **Planck constant** n. a basic physical constant that is equal to the energy of a photon divided by its frequency, with an approximate value of 6.6261 x 10^{-34} joule-seconds. Symbol h [Early 20thC. Named after Max PLANCK.]

Planck's law n. a basic law of quantum theory stating that the energy of electromagnetic radiation is absorbed or emitted in discrete amounts that are directly proportional to the radiation's frequency

plane[1] /playn/ n. **1.** AIR AIRCRAFT an aeroplane **2.** FLAT SURFACE a flat or level material surface **3.** LEVEL OF REALITY a level or category of existence, mental activity, or achievement **4.** MATH TWO-DIMENSIONAL SURFACE OR SPACE a two-dimensional surface in which a straight line between any two points will lie wholly on that surface **5.** AIR WING OR HYDROFOIL a flat surface such as a wing of a hydrofoil that provides lift for an aircraft or hydroplane ■ adj. **1.** FLAT completely flat and level **2.** MATH TWO-DIMENSIONAL lying within a particular plane ■ vi. (**planes, planing, planed**) AIR TRAVEL BY PLANE to travel by aeroplane [Early 17thC. From Latin planus 'flat' (see PLAIN).] —**planeness** n.

plane[2] /playn/ (**planes, planing, planed**) vi. **1.** SKIM OVER WATER'S SURFACE to rise partly out of water and skim along the surface, in the way that a hydroplane does **2.** AIR SOAR to glide through the air without propulsion, in the way that a bird does without flapping its wings or an aeroplane does with its engine off

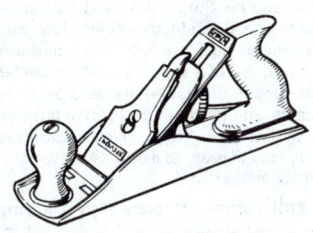

Plane

plane[3] /playn/ n. **1.** WOODWORK TOOL FOR SMOOTHING WOOD a hand tool for smoothing or shaping wood consisting of a wooden or metal body with a flat base in which an adjustable metal blade is held at an angle **2.** CERAMICS SMOOTHING TROWEL a hand tool with a flat metal blade used for smoothing the surface of clay or of plaster in a mould ■ vt. (**planes, planing, planed**) WOODWORK SMOOTH WOOD to use a plane to smooth or shape the surface of wood, to reduce it to the required size, or to remove material from it [14thC. Via French from late Latin plana, from Latin planare 'to make level', from planus 'flat' (see PLANE¹).]

plane[4] /playn/ n. = plane tree

plane geometry n. a branch of geometry dealing with the study of curves and figures

planeload /pláyn lōd/ n. the number of passengers or the quantity of goods that can be carried in an aircraft

planer /pláynər/ n. **1.** WOODWORK PLANING MACHINE a person or machine that planes, especially a machine used to plane wood or to cut flat surfaces into metal **2.** PRINTING WOODEN BLOCK TO KEEP TYPE LEVEL a flat block of wood used to hold type level in a chase [15thC. Formed from PLANE².]

plane sailing n. sailing using a form of navigation that treats the earth's surface as if it were flat for the purposes of calculating a ship's position and course

plane surveying n. surveying in the field, using a plane table, to produce a map of a relatively small area

planet /plánnit/ n. **1.** ASTRON ASTRONOMICAL BODY ORBITING STAR an astronomical body that orbits a star and does not shine with its own light, especially one of the nine such bodies orbiting the Sun in the solar system **2.** ZODIAC ASTROLOGICAL INFLUENCE in astrology, any of the planets of the solar system, the Sun, the Moon, but not the Earth, that are considered to influence events on Earth and the fate or character of individuals **3.** EARTH the Earth ◊ save the planet [12thC. Via French planète from Latin planeta 'planet, wandering star', from Greek planētēs 'wanderer'.]

— **WORD KEY: CULTURAL NOTE** —
The Planets, an orchestral work by English composer Gustav Holst (1914–16). This suite for orchestra, organ, and chorus is divided into seven movements, each of which represents the astrological character of a planet with appropriate music. Thus, the section called 'Mars, Bringer of War' consists of a brooding, sinister theme, while 'Venus, Bringer of Peace' is calm and serene.

plane table n. a surveying instrument for use in the field, consisting of a drawing board mounted on adjustable legs with a sighting telescope and ruler

planetarium /plánnə táiri əm/ n. (plural **-ums** or **-a** /-ri ə/) n. **1.** BUILDING WITH IMAGE OF NIGHT SKY a building with a domed ceiling onto which movable images of the stars, planets, and other objects seen in the night sky are projected for an audience **2.** PROJECTOR USED IN PLANETARIUM the special projector used to project images of the night sky for an audience in a planetarium **3.** SOLAR SYSTEM MODEL a model of the solar system, often a working model showing how the planets revolve around the Sun (archaic) [Mid-18thC. Via modern Latin from late Latin planetarius 'astrologer', from planeta 'planet' (see PLANET).]

planetary /plánnitəri/ adj. **1.** ASTRON INVOLVING PLANETS relating to, belonging to, involving, or typical of planets **2.** INVOLVING ALL OF EARTH involving or relating to the whole Earth, all the people or countries of the world, or a large proportion of them ■ n. (plural **-taries**) ENG = planetary gear

planetary gear, **planetary** (plural **-ies**) n. a gearwheel especially in an epicyclic train that travels around another usually central gearwheel

planetary nebula n. a glowing ring-shaped nebula of expanding gases surrounding a small very hot white star

planetesimal /plánni téssim'l/ n. a small rocky celestial object thought to have orbited the Sun in the early stages of the solar system before coalescing with others to form the planets [Early 20thC. Coined from PLANET + -esimal (as in 'infinitesimal').]

planetoid /plánni toyd/ n. = **asteroid** —**planetoidal** /plánni tóyd'l/ adj.

planetology /plánni tólləji/ n. a branch of astronomy that studies the origin and composition of the planets and other solid bodies in the solar system such as comets and meteors —**planetological** /plánnitə lójjik'l/ adj. —**planetologist** /plánni tólləjist/ n.

plane tree, **plane** n. a tall deciduous tree that has leaves with pointed lobes, ball-shaped clusters of flowers and fruit, and bark that peels off in patches. Genus: *Platanus*. [14thC. 'Plane' via French from, ultimately, Greek *platanos*, from *platus* 'broad', from the shape of its leaf.]

planet wheel n. a wheel in an epicyclic gear system that rotates around the wheel with which it meshes

plangent /plánjənt/ adj. **1.** EXPRESSING OR SUGGESTING SADNESS expressing or suggesting grief or sadness, or resonating with a mournful sound (literary) **2.** RESONANT making a loud and resonant sound [Early 19thC. From Latin plangent-, the present participle stem of plangere 'to beat' (source also of English complain and plaint).] —**plangency** n. —**plangently** adv.

plani- prefix. = **plano-**

planimeter /pla nímmitər/ n. a mechanical instrument that measures the area of a plane figure as a pointer is moved around the figure's edge [Mid-19thC. From French planimètre.] —**planimetric** /plánni méttrik/ adj. —**planimetrically** /-méttrikli/ adv.

planish /plánnish/ (-ishes, -ishing, -ished) vt. to toughen and smooth the surface of a metal by hammering or rolling it [Late 16thC. From Old French planiss-, the stem form of planir 'to smooth', from plain 'flat' (see PLAIN).] —**planisher** n.

planisphere /plánni sfeer/ n. a representation on a flat surface of all or part of a sphere, especially a map of the night sky as seen at a particular time and place [From medieval Latin planisphaerium, from Latin planus 'flat, plane' (see PLAIN) + sphaera 'sphere', from Greek sphaira] —**planispheric** /-sférrik/ adj.

plank /plangk/ n. **1.** WOODWORK, BUILDING LONG FLAT PIECE OF WOOD a piece of wood that has been sawn into a long flat fairly narrow rectangular shape, for use especially in building floors, shelves, and boats **2.** POL POLICY OF POLITICAL PARTY a policy that is part of a political party's platform ■ vt. (**planks, planking, planked**) BUILDING COVER STH WITH PLANKS to cover sth with planks [13thC. Via Old Northern French planke, a variation of Old French planche (source of English planchette), from late Latin planca 'slab', from the feminine of Latin plancus 'flat'.]

planking /plángking/ n. **1.** WOODWORK, BUILDING PLANKS a number of planks especially when they are used as building material or as part of a boat **2.** BUILDING COVERING STH WITH PLANKS the work of covering sth with planks or fixing planks to sth

plank spanker n. a guitarist (slang)

plankter /plángktər/ n. one of the tiny organisms that make up plankton [Mid-20thC. Via German from Greek plagktēr 'wanderer', from plazein 'to wander' (see PLANKTON).]

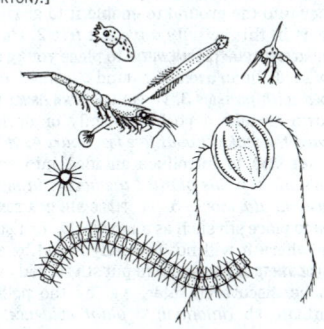

Plankton

plankton /plángktən/ n. a mass of tiny animals and plants floating in the sea or in lakes usually near the surface and eaten by fish and other aquatic animals [Late 19thC. Via German from Greek, 'wandering thing', from plazein 'to wander, lead astray'.] —**planktonic** /plangk tónnik/ adj.

planned obsolescence n. a policy of designing and making products so that they will quickly become outdated or wear out, so that people will have to buy a replacement

planner /plánnər/ n. **1.** SB WHO PLANS STH sb who plans sth, especially sb whose job is to plan the development of an area **2.** PLANNING AID a chart or notebook in which future events can be indicated or noted

planning permission n. the authorization that people must apply for to a local authority before they can build a new building or structure or alter an existing one

plano- prefix. flat ◊ planosol ◊ plano-concave [From Latin planus (see PLANE¹)]

plano-concave /pláynō kón kayv/ *adj.* flat on one side and concave on the other

plano-convex /pláynō kón veks/ *adj.* flat on one side and convex on the other

planogamete /plánnəgə meet, plánnō gámmeet/ *n.* a gamete such as a spermatozoon that is capable of moving

planography /plə nóggrəfi/ *n.* a printing process such as lithography in which the printing is done from a flat surface —**planographic** /pláynə gráffik/ *adj.* —**planographically** /-gráffikli/ *adv.*

planometer /plə nómmitər/ *n.* a flat metal plate used to test the flatness of other surfaces in metalwork —**planometric** /pláynə méttrik/ *adj.* —**planometrically** /-méttrikli/ *adv.* —**planometry** /plə nómmətri/ *n.*

planosol /pláynə sol/ *n.* a type of soil formation found on flat uplands that have high to moderate rainfall, in which a strongly leached upper layer overlies a layer of compacted clay or silt

plant /plaant/ *n.* **1.** PLANTS **VEGETABLE ORGANISM** a photosynthetic organism that has cellulose cell walls, cannot move of its own accord, grows on the earth or in water, and usually has green leaves. Kingdom: *Plantae.* **2.** PLANTS **SMALLER VEGETABLE ORGANISM** a vegetable organism that does not have a permanent woody stem, e.g. a flower or herb rather than a bush or tree **3.** GARDENING **SEEDLING** a cutting or seedling that is ready to be planted out **4.** INDUST **FACTORY** a factory, power station, or other large industrial complex where sth is manufactured or produced **5.** INDUST **INDUSTRIAL EQUIPMENT** equipment together with the buildings and land necessary for carrying on an industrial process or running a business **6.** LITERAT, THEATRE **ACTION OR REMARK THAT BECOMES SIGNIFICANT** an action or remark seemingly casually introduced into a narrative or play that turns out later to have great significance (*informal*) **7.** **STH DISHONESTLY HIDDEN TO INCRIMINATE** sth secretly and dishonestly put somewhere it can be discovered later, e.g. by the police, in order to incriminate sb (*informal*) **8.** **SB SECRETLY INTRODUCED INTO GROUP** sb who is secretly introduced into an organization in order to spy on it or to influence the behaviour of its members (*informal*) ■ *v.* **(plants, planting, planted) 1.** *vti.* BOT, AGRIC **PUT STH INTO THE GROUND TO GROW** to put sth such as a seed, plant, or tuber into the ground to enable it to grow, or to take part in this activity ○ *plant a tree* **2.** *vti.* AGRIC, GARDENING **PLACE PLANTS SOMEWHERE** to place young plants or sow seeds in an area of ground ○ *wanted to plant that bed with pansies* **3.** *vt.* **PUT STH DOWN FIRMLY** to put sth down or take a position firmly or decisively ○ *planted the stakes about five feet apart* **4.** *vt.* **PUT AN IDEA IN SB'S MIND** to introduce an idea into another person's mind ○ *She planted the notion in my head that we should move.* **5.** *vt.* **PLACE STH IN A CONCEALED POSITION** to place sth such as an explosive or listening device where it will not be easily found by others **6.** *vt.* **HIDE STH TO INCRIMINATE SB** to put sth secretly where it can be discovered later, e.g. by the police, to incriminate sb (*informal*) ○ *plant evidence* **7.** *vt.* **INTRODUCE A SPY INTO GROUP** to introduce sb into an organization in order to spy on it or to influence the behaviour of its members (*informal*) ○ *planted an informer in the group* **8.** *vt.* **STRIKE SB** to land a blow on sb (*informal*) **9.** *vt.* AGRIC **STOCK WITH FISH** to place spawn, young fish, or shellfish into an area of water so that they will develop there ○ *plant oysters* **10.** *vt.* **ESTABLISH A COLONY** to establish a colony or settlement in a place, or send people to a place as colonists or settlers [Pre-12thC. From late Latin *plantare* 'to plant'. Latin *plantare* meant 'to push in with the sole of the foot' and was formed from *planta* 'sole of the foot'.] —**plantable** *adj.* —**plantlike** *adj.*

WORD KEY: ORIGIN

There did exist a Latin noun *planta* which meant 'shoot, cutting', of uncertain origin, but the meaning of the English noun ***plant*** is not found. It is likely that this sense developed after the classical Latin period and is linked with the action of pressing on a shovel, or some other tool, with the 'sole of the foot' in order to work the soil for planting. Latin *planta* 'sole of the foot' is ultimately from an Indo-European base meaning 'to spread' which is also the ancestor of English *flat* and *place.*

plant out *vt.* to transplant a seedling that has been grown in a pot or in a sheltered place to open ground

Plantagenet /plan tájjənət/ *adj.* **OF ENGLISH ROYAL FAMILY OR REIGN** belonging or relating to the English royal family that ruled between 1154 and 1485, or to this period of English history. The period is spanned by the reigns of Kings Henry II, Richard I, John, Henry III, Edward I, Edward II, Edward III, Richard II, Henry IV, Henry V, Henry VI, Edward IV, Edward V and Richard III. ■ *n.* **MEMBER OF PLANTAGENET ROYAL FAMILY** a member of the Plantagenet royal family [From Latin *planta* 'sprig' + Latin *genista* 'broom', after the sprig of broom worn by Geoffrey IV, father of Henry II, in his cap]

plantain[1] /plántin, -tayn/ *n.* a small plant mostly growing wild in northern temperate regions with leaves that grow mainly from the plant's base and spikes of tiny greenish flowers. Family: Plantaginaceae. [14thC. Via French from Latin *plantago*, from *planta* 'sole of the foot' (see PLANT).]

plantain[2] /plántin, -tayn/ *n.* **1.** FOOD **FRUIT LIKE BANANA** a green fruit resembling a banana, eaten cooked as a staple food in many tropical countries **2.** PLANTS **TROPICAL PLANT LIKE BANANA TREE** a large tropical plant of the banana family that produces clusters of green fruit that resemble bananas. Latin name: *Musa paradisiaca.* [16thC. Via Spanish *plátano* 'plane tree' from Latin *platanus* (see PLANE TREE).]

plantain lily (*plural* **plantain lilies**) *n.* = **hosta**

plantar /plántər/ *adj.* relating to, affecting, or occurring on the sole of the foot [Early 18thC. From Latin *plantaris*, from *planta* 'sole of the foot' (see PLANT).]

plantar wart *n.* = **verruca**

plantation /plaan táysh'n, plan-/ *n.* **1.** AGRIC **LARGE ESTATE OR FARM** a large estate or farm especially in a hot country where crops such as cotton, coffee, tea, or rubber trees are grown, usually worked by resident labourers **2.** AGRIC **AREA OF PLANTED LAND** an area of land on which trees or crops are planted **3.** AGRIC **GROUP OF CULTIVATED PLANTS** a large group of plants, especially trees, that are being cultivated **4.** *US* AGRIC **ESTATE IN SOUTHERN UNITED STATES** a large landed estate in the southern United States **5.** HIST **COLONY** a colony or settlement **6.** HIST **COLONIZATION** the act of colonizing a place (*archaic*)

plantcutter /plaánt kutər/ *n.* a South American bird that has a short conical bill with a serrated edge. It eats fruit, leaves, and buds, often destroying crops. Family: Phytotomidae.

planter /plaántər/ *n.* **1.** AGRIC **HEAD OF PLANTATION** sb who owns or manages a plantation **2.** GARDENING **LARGE CONTAINER** a large decorative container for houseplants or small trees **3.** AGRIC **PLANTING MACHINE** a machine for planting seeds, tubers, or other plant parts **4.** HIST **SETTLER** a colonist (*archaic*) **5.** HIST **SCOTS OR ENGLISH SETTLER IN ULSTER** one of the Scots or English settlers who arrived in Ulster in the 17th century under official patronage

planter's punch *n.* a drink made with rum, lime or lemon juice, sugar, water, or soda, and sometimes bitters

plant hormone *n.* a hormone produced naturally by plants that activates or regulates their growth, or a synthetic equivalent used to promote growth in cultivated plants

plantigrade /plánti grayd/ *adj.* **WALKING ON SOLES OF FEET** used to describe an animal such as a bear or a human being that walks on the soles of its feet with the heel touching the ground ■ *n.* **PLANTIGRADE ANIMAL** an animal that walks on the soles of its feet [Mid-19thC. Via French from modern Latin *plantigradus*, from Latin *planta* 'sole of the foot' (see PLANT) + *-gradus* 'stepping' (see GRADE).]

plantlet /plaántlət/ *n.* a young or very small plant

plant louse *n.* = **aphid**

plantocracy /plaan tókrəssi/ (*plural* **-racies**) *n.* a ruling class made up of the owners and managers of large plantations, or a society they rule

plantsman /plaántsmən/ (*plural* **-men** /-mən/) *n.* a man who has expert knowledge of garden plants and gardening

plantswoman /plaánts wòomən/ (*plural* **-men** /-wimin/) *n.* a woman who has expert knowledge of garden plants and gardening

planula /plánnyòolə/ (*plural* **-lae** /-lī/) *n.* a free-swimming larva of a coelenterate such as a hydra that has cilia and usually a flattened oval body [Late 19thC. From modern Latin, literally 'little flat one', formed from Latin *planus* 'flat' (see PLAIN).] —**planular** *adj.*

plaque /plak, plaak/ *n.* **1.** **INSCRIBED METAL OR STONE** a small flat piece of metal, stone, or other hard material with an inscription or decoration on it that is fixed onto a surface, often to commemorate sb or sth **2.** DENT **DEPOSIT ON SURFACE OF TEETH** a film of saliva, mucus, bacteria, and food residues that builds up on the surface of teeth and can cause gum disease **3.** MED **SMALL PATCH** a small flattened patch or deposit, e.g. on the skin in psoriasis or on the inner wall of an artery in arteriosclerosis **4.** BIOL **CLEAR PATCH IN CULTURE** a clear patch in a bacterial or cell culture caused by a virus destroying the cells **5.** **SMALL BADGE OR BROOCH** a small badge or brooch worn to show membership of or rank in an organization [Mid-19thC. Via French from Dutch *plak* 'tablet', from *plakken*, from Middle Dutch *placken* 'to flatten, patch' (source also of English *placard*).]

plash[1] /plash/ *n.* **LIGHT SPLASH** a light splash or splashing sound (*literary*) ■ *v.* **(plashes, plashing, plashed)** (*literary*) **1.** *vi.* **SPLASH IN OR THROUGH LIQUID** to move in or through sth liquid, scattering drops of it and making a light splashing sound **2.** *vt.* **SPLASH STH** to splash or spatter sth liquid [Early 16thC. An imitation of the sound.]

plash[2] *vt.* = **pleach**

plashy /pláshi/ (**-ier, -iest**) *adj.* (*literary*) **1.** **SPLASHY** liable to splash or be splashed **2.** **WET** wet and marshy

-plasia *suffix.* growth, formation ○ *hyperplasia* [Via modern Latin from, ultimately, Greek *plassein* 'to form, mould' (source of English *plaster*)]

plasm /plázzəm/ *n.* **1.** = **plasma 2.** **PROTOPLASM** protoplasm of a specified type [Early 17thC. From late Latin *plasma* 'image, creation' (see PLASMA).]

plasm- *prefix.* = **plasmo-** (*used before vowels*)

-plasm *suffix.* material that forms or is formed ○ *protoplasm* ○ *neoplasm* [Shortening of PROTOPLASM]

plasma /plázmə/, **plasm** /plázəm/ *n.* **1.** MED **FLUID COMPONENT OF BLOOD** the clear yellowish fluid component of blood, lymph, or milk, excluding the suspended corpuscles and cells **2.** MED **BLOOD SUBSTITUTE** a blood substitute prepared by removing the cells and corpuscles from donated sterile blood and freezing the resulting fluid until it is needed **3.** PHYS **IONIZED GAS** a hot ionized gas made up of ions and electrons that is found in the Sun, stars, and fusion reactors. Plasma is a good conductor of electricity and reacts to a magnetic field but otherwise has properties similar to those of a gas. **4.** MINERALS **GREEN CHALCEDONY** a green variety of chalcedony used as a gemstone, in mosaics, and for other decorative purposes [Early 18thC. Via late Latin, 'image, creation', from Greek, 'sth moulded', from *plassein* 'to mould' (see PLASTIC).] —**plasmatic** /plaz máttik/ *adj.*

plasma cell /plázmə sĕl/, **plasmacyte** *n.* a lymphocyte that produces antibodies and is derived from a B cell

plasma engine *n.* an engine used in space travel that generates thrust by using magnetic fields to emit a jet of plasma

plasmagel /plázmə jel/ *n.* a form of cytoplasm, often forming an outer layer in cells, that resembles jelly

plasmagene /plázmə jeen/ *n.* a particle in the cytoplasm of organisms that can replicate itself and is thought to be able to pass on hereditary characteristics in the same way as a chromosomal gene —**plasmagenic** /plázmə jénnik/ *adj.*

plasmalemma /plázmə lémmə/ *n.* = **cell membrane**

plasma membrane *n.* = **cell membrane**

plasmapheresis /plázmə férrəssiss/ *n.* a process in which blood taken from a patient is treated to extract the cells and corpuscles, which are then added to another fluid and returned to the patient's body. It is performed, e.g. to remove harmful antibodies or immune complexes from the blood, especially in autoimmune diseases such as myasthenia gravis.

plasmasol /plázmə sol/ *n.* a form of cytoplasm that is more fluid than plasmagel, often forming an inner layer in cells

plasma torch *n.* a metal-cutting device in which a cutting flame is produced by the conversion of a gas into plasma

plasmid /plázmid/ *n.* a small circle of DNA that replicates itself independently of chromosomal DNA, especially in the cells of bacteria. Plasmids often contain genes for drug resistance and are used in genetic engineering, since they can be transmitted between bacteria of the same and different species.

plasmin /plázmin/ *n.* an enzyme found in plasma that catalyses the breakdown of blood-clotting agents such as fibrin [Mid-19thC. From French, coined from *plasma* 'plasma'.]

plasminogen /plaz mínnəjən/ *n.* a substance found in body fluids and blood plasma that when activated becomes plasmin

plasmo-[1], **plasm-** *prefix.* involving or like plasma [From late Latin *plasma* 'image' (see PLASMA)]

plasmo-[2] *prefix.* plasma ○ *plasmogamy* [From PLASMA]

plasmodesma /plázmō dézmə/ (*plural* **-mata** /-mətə/) *n.* a very fine thread of cytoplasm that in some plants passes through openings in the walls of adjacent cells and forms a living bridge between them [Early 20thC. From German, coined from *Plasma* 'plasma' + Greek *desma* 'bond'.]

plasmodium /plaz mṓdi əm/ (*plural* **-a** /plazmṓdi ə/) *n.* **1.** MASS OF PROTOPLASM a mass of protoplasm containing many nuclei that is a stage in the life cycle of some organisms, especially slime moulds **2.** PARASITIC PROTOZOAN CAUSING MALARIA a parasitic protozoan, especially one that causes malaria. Genus: *Plasmodium.* [Late 19thC. Coined from PLASMA + modern Latin *-odium* 'resembling', from Greek *-ōdēs* (see -OID).] —**plasmodial** *adj.*

plasmogamy /plaz móggəmi/ *n.* a type of fusion between cells in certain fungi in which the cytoplasm merges but the nuclei remain distinct

plasmolyse *vti.* = **plasmolyze**

plasmolysis /plaz mólləssiss/ *n.* the shrinking of the protoplasm in a plant or bacterial cell away from the cell wall, caused by loss of water through osmosis —**plasmolytic** /plázmə líttik/ *adj.* —**plasmolytically** /-líttikli/ *adv.*

plasmolyze /plázmə līz/ (**-lyzes, -lyzing, -lyzed**), **plasmolyse** (**-lyses, -lysing, -lysed**) *vti.* to undergo plasmolysis, or make this happen in a cell

plasmon /pláz mon/ *n.* GENETICS the sum total of the genetic material in the cytoplasm, as opposed to the nucleus or nuclei, of a cell or an organism

-plast *suffix.* living cell, small body ○ *spheroplast* [From Greek *plastos*, a past participle of *plassein* (see -PLASIA)]

plaster /plaástər/ *n.* **1.** LIME MIXTURE FOR WALLS a mixture of lime, sand, and water that is applied as a liquid paste to the ceilings and internal walls of a building and dries to a smooth hard surface **2.** STICKY BANDAGE a strip of adhesive material, usually with a dressing attached, for sticking over a cut or wound **3.** PIECE OF IMPREGNATED MUSLIN a piece of muslin spread with a curative preparation formerly used for placing over a wound or sore. ◊ **mustard plaster 4.** = **plaster of Paris** ○ *had his leg in plaster* ■ *vt.* (**-ters, -tering, -tered**) **1.** COVER WALLS WITH PLASTER to apply plaster to the interior walls and ceilings of a building **2.** APPLY STH THICKLY to apply a thick layer of sth to a surface (*informal*) **3.** STICK A MASS OF THINGS OVER A SURFACE to stick or spread objects in great profusion over a surface **4.** MAKE STH APPEAR IN MANY LOCATIONS to cause a name, story, or image to appear in many conspicuous places ○ *woke up to find her name plastered over every front page* **5.** BOMBARD to hit sb or sth repeatedly and effectively with blows or weapons (*informal*) **6.** APPLY MEDICINAL PLASTER to apply a medicinal plaster to a wound or sore [Old English *plaster* 'medical dressing' and Old French *plastre* 'wall plaster', both via medieval Latin *plastrum* from, ultimately, Greek *emplastron*, from *emplassein* 'to plaster up', from *plassein* (see -PLASIA)] —**plasterer** *n.* —**plastery** *adj.*

plasterboard /plaástər bawrd/ *n.* reinforced gypsum plaster sandwiched between two layers of strong paper in large sheets, used chiefly for interior walls

plaster cast *n.* **1.** RIGID COVERING FOR BROKEN LIMB a rigid covering of plaster of Paris moulded round a broken limb to immobilize the fracture site during healing **2.** PLASTER COPY OF STH a copy or mould of an object, such as a statue or footprint in plaster of Paris

plastered /plaástərd/ *adj.* very drunk (*informal*) [Early 20thC. From PLASTER in the sense 'to hit hard'.]

plastering /plaástəring/ *n.* **1.** APPLICATION OF PLASTER TO WALLS the application of a layer of plaster to walls **2.** PLASTER COVERING SURFACE the plaster that covers a surface **3.** SEVERE DEFEAT a severe beating or defeat (*informal*)

plaster of Paris *n.* a white powder, calcium sulphate, mixed with water to form a quick-hardening paste, used in the arts for sculpting and making casts and used in medicine for moulding casts round broken limbs [Named after PARIS, where it originated]

plasterwork /plaástər wurk/ *n.* objects in plaster, especially the layer of plaster applied to interior wall surfaces or decorative plaster mouldings on ceilings or walls

plastic /plástik/ *n.* **1.** SYNTHETIC MATERIAL an extremely versatile synthetic material made from the polymerization of organic compounds. It can be moulded into shapes or fabricated in many different forms for use in commerce and industry. **2.** CREDIT CARDS debit or credit cards as a form of payment as distinct from cash or a cheque (*informal*) ■ *adj.* **1.** MADE OF PLASTIC made of or consisting of plastic **2.** ABLE TO BE MOULDED able to be shaped, moulded, or modelled **3.** OF MOULDING, MODELLING, OR SCULPTING relating to or involving moulding, modelling, or sculpting **4.** PHYS ABLE TO HAVE SHAPE PERMANENTLY CHANGED able to be bent, stretched, squeezed, or pulled out so that the resulting change of shape is permanent **5.** BIOL ADAPTING TO CONDITIONS capable of adapting to conditions during growth or development **6.** ARTIFICIAL seeming artificial and unnatural ○ *a plastic smile* **7.** ADAPTING EASILY adapting easily and readily to change **8.** OF PLASTIC SURGERY relating to or involving plastic surgery [16thC. Via French *plastique* and Latin *plasticus* from Greek *plastikos* 'mouldable', from *plastos*, the past participle of *plassein* 'to form, mould' (see -PLASIA).] —**plastically** *adv.*

plastic art *n.* **1.** THREE-DIMENSIONAL ART a three-dimensional art such as sculpture, modelling or bas-relief work, pottery, or ceramics **2.** VISUAL ART an art that represents subjects for visual appreciation, such as painting, sculpture, or architecture

plastic bomb *n.* a bomb that employs a plastic explosive for its destructive force

plastic bullet *n.* a large bullet made of PVC, sometimes used by the police for riot control in place of metal bullets

plastic explosive *n.* an explosive with the consistency of putty that allows it to be easily moulded

Plasticine /plásti seen/ *tdmk.* a trademark for a soft coloured modelling material used especially by children

plasticise *vti.* = **plasticize**

plasticity /pla stíssəti/ *n.* **1.** ABILITY TO BE MOULDED the condition of being soft and capable of being moulded **2.** ABILITY TO KEEP SHAPE AFTER CHANGE the quality that will allow a substance to retain its change in shape after being bent, stretched, or squeezed **3.** THREE-DIMENSIONAL QUALITY the three-dimensional quality of an image

plasticize /plásti sīz/ (**-cizes, -cizing, -cized**), **plasticise** (**-cises, -cising, -cised**) *v.* **1.** *vti.* MAKE OR BECOME PLASTIC to give plastic or mouldable qualities to sth, or become plastic or mouldable **2.** *vt.* TREAT WITH PLASTIC to impregnate or coat sth with plastic, usually to make it waterproof —**plasticization** /plásti sī záysh'n/ *n.*

plasticizer /plásti sīzər/, **plasticiser** *n.* an industrial compound that affects the physical properties of a substance to which it is added

plastic money *n.* debit and credit cards as distinct from cash or cheques

plastic surgeon *n.* a physician who performs or specializes in plastic surgery

plastic surgery *n.* the branch of surgery that is concerned with repairing damage, relieving impairments, or improving appearance. Cosmetic surgery is a branch of plastic surgery.

plastic wrap *n.* *US* a clear plastic film that sticks to itself and to surfaces, used to wrap food for storage

plastid /plástid/ *n.* a specialized organ or part (**organelle**) in a photosynthetic plant cell that contains pigment, ribosomes, and DNA, and serves particular physiological purposes such as food synthesis and storage [Late 19thC. Via the Greek stem *plastid-* from, ultimately, *plastos* 'moulded' (see PLASTIC).]

plastique /pla steék/ *n.* **1.** PLASTIC EXPLOSIVE plastic explosive **2.** GRACEFUL DANCE POSES graceful sustained movement or held poses in dance [Late 19thC. From French (see PLASTIC).]

plastisol /plásti sol/ *n.* a suspension of synthetic resin particles convertible by heat into solid plastic [Mid-20thC. Coined from PLASTIC + SOL.]

plastometer /pla stómmitər/, **plastimeter** /pla stímmitər/ *n.* an instrument for measuring the plasticity of materials [Early 20thC. Coined from PLASTICITY + -METER.] —**plastometric** /plástō méttrik/ *adj.* —**plastometry** /pla stómmətri/ *n.*

plastron /plástrən/ *n.* **1.** UNDER PART OF TORTOISE SHELL the under portion of the shell of a turtle or tortoise that is made up of several, often hinged bony plates joined to the carapace by bridges located between the animal's legs **2.** WATER-REPELLENT GILL IN AQUATIC INSECTS a tuft of water-repellent hairs on the bodies of some aquatic insects that traps air bubbles and acts as an external gill **3.** STEEL BREASTPLATE a steel breastplate worn as part of medieval armour beneath a chain-mail tunic (**hauberk**) **4.** CHEST PAD FOR FENCERS a leather-covered pad for protecting the chest, worn by professional fencers [Early 16thC. Via French from Italian *piastrone*, literally 'large breastplate', from *piastra* 'metal plate'.] —**plastral** *adj.*

-plasty *suffix.* surgical repair, plastic surgery ○ *angioplasty* ○ *rhinoplasty* [Via modern Latin from, ultimately, Greek *plastos* (see PLASTIC)]

plat[1] /plat/ *n.* **1.** *US* PLAN OR MAP a plan or map showing property boundaries and geographical features **2.** PLOT OF LAND a small plot or area of land (*archaic*) ■ *vt.* (**plats, platting, platted**) *US* MAP AREA OF LAND to map an area of land to show boundaries and features [Early 16thC. Origin uncertain: probably an alteration of PLOT.]

plat[2] /plat/ *n.* PLAIT a plait (*archaic*) ■ *vt.* (**plats, platting, platted**) PLAIT STH to plait sth (*archaic*) [14thC. Alteration of PLAIT.]

plat. *abbr.* **1.** plateau **2.** platoon

Plata, Río de la /plaátə/ large inlet on the eastern coast of South America, an estuary of the Paraná and Uruguay rivers, lying between Uruguay and Argentina. Length: 300 km/190 mi.

platan /plátt'n/, **platane** *n.* = **plane tree** [14thC. Via modern Latin *Platanus*, genus name, from Greek *platanos* (see PLANE TREE).]

plat du jour /plaà doo zhóor/ (*plural* **plats du jour** /plaà doo zhóor/) *n.* the featured dish on the menu of a restaurant for a particular day [Early 20thC. From French, 'dish of the day'.]

plate /playt/ *n.* **1.** HOUSEHOLD DISH FROM WHICH FOOD IS EATEN a flat or shallow dish, usually round and made of earthenware, china, glass, or sometimes plastic or metal, from which food is eaten **2.** FOOD CONTENTS OF PLATE a portion of food consisting of the amount served on a plate **3.** *US* FOOD SERVED FOOD a specified variety of prepared and served food ○ *a low-calorie plate* **4.** CHR COLLECTION DISH FOR MONEY a shallow metal or wooden container passed round a church for members of the congregation to put money in **5.** SCI DISH FOR GROWING CULTURES a small flat glass or plastic dish with a vertical rim, used in laboratories for growing cultures of microorganisms **6.** THIN SHEET a thin flat rigid sheet or slice of some material, usually of uniform thickness and with a smooth surface **7.** ANAT FLAT ANATOMICAL STRUCTURE a thin flat bony or horny anatomical part or formation **8.** METALL THINLY BEATEN METAL metal produced in thin sheets of uniform thickness by beating, rolling, or casting **9.** ARMS SHEET OF ARMOUR PLATING a sheet of metal used as part of the cladding of a warship or tank

10. HIST SECTION OF SUIT OF ARMOUR a thin piece of steel or iron used to make up a suit of armour (*often used in combination*) **11.** METALL COATING OF METAL a thin coating of metal, typically silver or gold, applied by electrolysis to copper or another base metal **12.** HORSERACING PRIZE OF GOLD OR SILVER CUP a prize, especially in horseracing, consisting of a silver or gold cup **13.** HORSERACING RACE WITH CUP AS PRIZE a race, especially a horserace, in which the prize is a silver or gold cup **14.** ENGRAVED PLAQUE a metal plaque that bears an engraved or printed legend, name, number, or other inscription (*often used in combination*) **15.** AUTOMOT NUMBER PLATE a vehicle's number plate **16.** GEOL SECTION OF EARTH'S CRUST any of the segments of the earth's crust that move in relation to one another as defined by the theory of plate tectonics **17.** ENG FLAT CONSTITUENT PART OR FITTING a flat slab of metal or other material that constitutes part of a machine or mechanism **18.** DENT ARTIFICIAL PALATE FITTED WITH FALSE TEETH a piece of plastic moulded to fit the mouth and holding false teeth or an orthodontic device such as a brace **19.** PHOTOGRAPHY SENSITIZED SHEET OF GLASS a sheet of glass or other material coated with a light-sensitive film to receive a photographic image **20.** PRINTING SURFACE FROM WHICH TO PRINT a template for printing, either an engraved metal sheet or a phototypeset page **21.** PRINTING PRINT TAKEN FROM ENGRAVED SURFACE a print made from a printing plate, especially one inserted into a book on paper different from that on which the text is printed **22.** PRINTING ILLUSTRATION IN BOOK a full-page illustration or photograph in a book, especially on glossy or coated paper **23.** ELEC ELECTRODE a thin flat piece of metal acting as an electrode in a re-chargeable battery **24.** BASEBALL = **home plate 25.** HORSERACING SHOE WORN BY RACEHORSE a light shoe with which racehorses are shod in preparation for racing **26.** BUILDING HORIZONTAL SUPPORTING TIMBER a horizontal timber laid along the top of a wall of a building to support the ends of timbers laid at right angles to the wall **27.** *US* FOOD CUT OF BEEF a thin cut of beef from the breast or ribs ■ *vt.* (**plates, plating, plated**) **1.** METALL COVER STH WITH GOLD OR SILVER to cover sth with a thin coating or film of metal, especially to overlay sth made of a baser metal with gold or silver **2.** ARMS COVER STH WITH METAL SHEETS to cover sth, especially a ship or tank, with sheets of metal for protection and strength **3.** PRINTING SET UP TYPE IN PAGE FORM to set up movable type into page form ready for printing **4.** SURG STRENGTHEN BROKEN BONE WITH PLATE to hold a fractured bone in position once it has been set by screwing it, on either side of the fracture, to a metal plate [13thC. Via Old French from, ultimately, Greek *platus* 'flat'. Ultimately from an Indo-European base meaning 'to spread flat' that is also the ancestor of English *flat*, *plan*, and *flounder²*.] ◇ **have sth handed to you on a plate** to obtain sth without having to put any effort into obtaining it (*informal*) ◇ **have sth on your plate** to have sth that requires your attention

plate armour *n.* body armour made up of metal plates, as distinct from the chain mail that it superseded

plateau /pláttō/ *n.* (*plural* **-teaus** *or* **-teaux** /pláttōz/) **1.** RAISED AREA WITH LEVEL TOP a hill or mountain with a level top **2.** STABLE PHASE a period or phase in sth when there is little increase or decrease **3.** PHASE OF STAGNATION a phase in mental or physical development during which little headway is made ■ *vi.* (**-teaus, -teauing, -teaued**) LEVEL OUT to reach a stable phase after a period of movement or development [Late 18thC. Via French from Old French *platel*, literally 'small flat thing', from *plate* (see PLATE).]

plate boundary *n.* an area on the margins of tectonic plates where seismic, volcanic, and tectonic activity takes place as a consequence of the relative motion of the plates

plated /pláytid/ *adj.* **1.** OVERLAID WITH GOLD OR SILVER covered with a thin layer of gold or silver **2.** ENG COVERED WITH PLATES protected and strengthened by a covering of plates **3.** KNITTING KNITTED WITH TWO YARNS knitted with two kinds of yarn, one appearing on the front and one on the back of the fabric

plateful /pláytfŏŏl/ *n.* the amount of food that a plate will hold

plate glass *n.* strong thick glass in large sheets used for windows and as a construction material for larger buildings (*hyphenated when used before a noun*)

platelayer /pláyt layər/ *n.* sb whose job is to lay and maintain railway lines. US term **trackman** ['Plate' from PLATE RAIL]

platelet /pláytlət/ *n.* a tiny colourless disc-shaped particle found in large quantities in the blood that plays an important part in the clotting process

platemaker /pláyt maykər/ *n.* a person or machine that prepares plates for printing

platemark /pláyt maark/ *n.* METALL = **hallmark** *n.* 3

platen /plátt'n/ *n.* **1.** METAL PLATE IN PRINTING PRESS a flat metal plate in a printing press that holds the paper against the inked type **2.** TYPEWRITER ROLLER the cylindrical roller against which the paper is held in a typewriter, and against which the type strikes **3.** WORKTABLE the movable worktable of a machine tool [Mid-16thC. From Old French *platine* 'metal plate', from *plat* 'flat', via assumed Vulgar Latin *plattus* from Greek *platus* (see PLATE).]

plater /pláytər/ *n.* **1.** SB OR STH THAT PLATES a person or machine that plates things **2.** RACEHORSE IN MINOR RACES a racehorse of average quality that is entered for minor races **3.** BLACKSMITH a blacksmith who specializes in shoeing racehorses

plate rail *n.* an early type of rail with a flange along the outer edge to keep the unflanged wheels on the track

plateresque /pláttə résk/ *adj.* relating to a heavily decorated architectural style fashionable in 16th-century Spain, reminiscent of elaborate silverware [Late 19thC. From Spanish *plateresco*, from *platero* 'silversmith', from *plata* 'silver' (see PLATINA).]

plate tectonics *n.* a theory that ascribes continental drift, volcanic and seismic activity, and the formation of mountain belts to moving plates of the earth's crust supported on less rigid mantle rocks (*takes a singular verb*)

platform /plát fawrm/ *n.* **1.** STAGE FOR PERFORMERS OR SPEAKERS a raised level area of flooring for speakers, performers, or participants in a ceremony, making them easily visible to the audience **2.** FLAT RAISED STRUCTURE a simple structure, especially one composed of wooden planks, serving as base for keeping things clear of the ground **3.** RAIL RAISED AREA PROVIDING ACCESS TO TRAINS a raised structure beside the line at a railway station that makes it easier to get on or off and load or unload a train **4.** TRANSP REAR STEP ON BUS OR TRAM an open step at the rear of a bus or tram for passengers to stand on as they get into or out of the vehicle **5.** POL STATED POLICY OF PARTY SEEKING ELECTION the publicly announced policies and promises of a party seeking election, understood as the basis of its actions should it come to power **6.** OPPORTUNITY FOR DOING STH a position of authority or prominence that provides a good opportunity for doing sth **7.** INDUST OFFSHORE DRILLING STRUCTURE an anchored offshore structure with living and working accommodation above water level, from which oil or gas wells can be drilled or maintained **8.** GEOG RAISED AREA OF GROUND a flat raised area of ground **9.** THICKENED SOLE OF SHOE a thick layer of leather or other material between the sole and upper of a shoe **10.** ACCESSORIES SHOE WITH PLATFORM SOLE a shoe or boot with a platform sole **11.** COMPUT COMPUTER OPERATING SYSTEM a computer operating system, often along with the associated equipment [Mid-16thC. From French *plateforme* 'diagram', from *plat* 'flat' + *forme* 'form'.]

platform balance *n.* = **platform scale**

platform rocker *n.* *US* a rocking chair with the rocker set into a stable base that lies flat on the floor

platform scale *n.* a scale with a flat surface that supports the object to be weighed

platform ticket *n.* a ticket allowing access to a station platform, formerly purchased by non-travellers so that they could meet or see off passengers

CORBIS/Bettmann

Sylvia Plath

Plath /plath/, **Sylvia** (1932–63) US poet. Her work is best known for its savage imagery and themes of self-destruction, anticipating her own suicide. She was married to Ted Hughes.

platin- *prefix.* platinum ○ *platinic* [From PLATINUM]

platina /plátinə, plə téenə/ *n.* a naturally occurring platinum alloy [Mid-18thC. From Spanish, formed from *plata* 'silver' (because of its silvery colour), from assumed Vulgar Latin *plattus*.]

plating /pláyting/ *n.* **1.** THIN COVERING CONSISTING OF VALUABLE METAL a thin covering of a valuable metal applied to a surface of base metal ○ *gold plating* **2.** COVERING OF METAL PLATES a covering or armour of metal plates applied to the surface of sth, especially a ship or tank **3.** APPLICATION OF A COVERING OF METAL the process of applying a covering of metal or metal plates to the surface of sth

platinic /plə tínnik/ *adj.* relating to, containing, or consisting of platinum, especially in a valency state of four

platiniferous /plátti níffərəss/ *adj.* containing or yielding platinum

platinize /plátti nīz/ (**-nizes, -nizing, -nized**), **platinise** (**-nises, -nising, -nised**) *vt.* to coat, combine, or treat sth with platinum or a platinum compound —**platinization** /plátti nī záysh'n/ *n.*

platinoid /plátti noyd/ *adj.* RESEMBLING PLATINUM resembling or containing platinum ■ *n.* **1.** METAL CHEMICALLY SIMILAR TO PLATINUM a metal that is chemically similar to platinum, specifically iridium, osmium, palladium, rhodium, or ruthenium **2.** ALLOY SIMILAR TO PLATINUM an alloy of copper, zinc, nickel, and tungsten that resembles platinum in not tarnishing readily and in having a strong resistance to the passage of an electric current

platinous /pláttinəss/ *adj.* relating to, containing, or consisting of platinum, especially in a valency state of two

platinum /pláttinəm/ *n.* CHEM ELEM PRECIOUS METALLIC ELEMENT a precious silvery-white metallic element, highly malleable and ductile and highly resistant to chemicals and heat, used in jewellery and chemically as a catalyst and in electroplating. Symbol **Pt** ■ *adj.* MUSIC TOP-SELLING having sold 300,000 copies of a single or an album [Early 19thC. Formed from PLATINA, on the model of the names of other metals ending in *-um*.]

platinum black *n.* platinum in the form of a fine black powder, used as a catalyst in organic synthesis

platinum blonde, **platinum blond** *adj.* SILVERY-BLONDE pale silvery-blonde in colour (*hyphenated before a noun*) ■ *n.* SB WITH PLATINUM-BLONDE HAIR sb who has platinum-blonde hair

platinum metal *n.* platinum or any of the metals in its group, specifically iridium, osmium, palladium, rhodium, or ruthenium

platitude /plátti tyood/ *n.* **1.** BANAL STATEMENT a pointless, unoriginal, or empty comment or statement made as though it was significant or helpful **2.** USE OF PLATITUDES the making of platitudes [Early 19thC. From French, literally 'flatness', from *plat* 'flat' (see PLATE).]

platitudinarian /plátti tyoodi náiri ən/ *n.* SB WHO TALKS IN PLATITUDES sb whose speech or writing is full of platitudes ■ *adj.* FULL OF PLATITUDES using, containing, or resembling platitudes

platitudinize /plátti tyoōdi nīz/ (**-nizes, -nizing, -nized**), **platitudinise** (**-nises, -nising, -nised**) *vi.* to produce or talk in platitudes —**platitudinizer** /plátti tyoōdi nīzər/ *n.*

platitudinous /plátti tyoōdinəss/, **platitudinal** /-dinəl/ *adj.* using, containing, or resembling platitudes

Plato /pláytō/ *n.* a distinctive dark-floored large crater on the Moon just north of Mare Imbrium, approximately 100 km/60 mi. in diameter

Plato (428?–347 BC) Greek philosopher. A disciple of Socrates and teacher of Aristotle, he founded the Athenian Academy. His works, written in dialogue form, include *Phaedo*, *Symposium*, and *Republic*.

platonic /plə tónnik/ *adj.* **1. NOT INVOLVING SEXUAL RELATIONS** involving friendship, affection, or love without sexual relations between people who might be expected to be sexually attracted to each other **2. PERFECT BUT UNREAL** perfect in form or conception but not found in reality [Mid-16thC. Via Latin from Greek *Platōnikos*, from *Platōn* (see PLATO).] —**platonically** *adv.*

Platonic *adj.* relating to Plato or his philosophy

Platonism /pláytənizəm/ *n.* the philosophy or teachings of Plato, especially the theory that both physical objects and instances of qualities are recognizable because of their common relationship to an abstract form or idea [Late 16thC. From modern Latin *Platonismus*, from Greek *Platōn* (see PLATO).] —**Platonist** *n.*

platoon /plə toōn/ *n.* **1. MILITARY SUBDIVISION** a subdivision of a company of soldiers, usually led by a lieutenant and consisting of two to three sections or squads of ten to twelve people **2. PEOPLE OR THINGS WORKING TOGETHER** a body of people or things with a common purpose or goal [Mid-17thC. From French *peloton*, literally 'small ball', from *pelote* 'ball' (see PELLET).]

platoon sergeant *n.* a non-commissioned officer in the US army who assists a lieutenant in leading a platoon

Plattdeutsch /plát doych/ *n., adj.* LANG = **Low German** [Mid-19thC. Via German from Dutch *Platduitsch*, literally 'low German', from the flat landscape of the North German lowlands where it is spoken.]

platteland /plát land/ *n.* remote rural areas in South Africa [Mid-20thC. Via Afrikaans from Middle Dutch, literally 'flat country'.]

platter /pláttər/ *n.* **1.** HOUSEHOLD **LARGE FLAT DISH** a large flat dish for serving food **2.** FOOD **SERVED FOOD** a particular variety of prepared and served food (*often used in combination*) ○ *seafood platter* **3.** MUSIC **RECORD** a gramophone record (*dated informal*) **4.** COMP SCI **RECORDING SURFACE OF A HARD DISK** the recording surface of a hard disk [14thC. Via Anglo-Norman *plater* from Old French *plat* (see PLATE).]

platy[1] /pláyti/ (**-ier, -iest**) *adj.* used to describe minerals that crystallize in thin sheets and tend to flake along cleavage planes

platy[2] /plátti/ (*plural* **-ys** *or* **-ies** *or* **-y**) *n.* a brightly coloured Central American fish that bears live young, not eggs, and is popular as an aquarium fish. Genus: *Xiphophorus*. [Early 20thC. Shortening of modern Latin *Platypoecilus*, former genus name, from Greek *platus* 'flat' + *poikilos* 'spotted'.]

platyhelminth /plátti hélminth/ *n.* a flatworm (*technical*) [Late 19thC. From modern Latin *Platyhelminthes*, phylum name, from Greek *platus* 'flat' + *helminth-* 'worm'.] —**platyhelminthic** /plátti hel mínthik/ *adj.*

platypus /pláttipəss/ (*plural* **-puses** *or* **-pi** /-pī/) *n.* = **duckbilled-platypus** [Late 18thC. Via modern Latin *Platypus*, genus name, from Greek *platupous* 'flat-footed', from *platus* 'flat' + *pous* 'foot'.]

platyrrhine /plátti rīn/ *adj.* **HAVING WIDELY SPACED NOSTRILS** used to describe animals, especially New World monkeys, whose nostrils are well separated and point to either side ■ *n.* **PLATYRRHINE MONKEY** a platyrrhine animal, especially a monkey [Mid-19thC. Via modern Latin *Platyrrhini*, division name, from Greek *platurrhis* 'broad-nosed'.]

plaudit /pláwdit/ *n.* an expression of praise or approval ○ *won plaudits for her skilful handling of the crisis* [Early 17thC. From Latin *plaudite* 'applaud!', from *plaudere*; from the customary appeal made by Roman actors at the end of a play.]

WORD KEY: ORIGIN

The Latin word *plaudere* from which **plaudit** is derived is also the source of English *applaud* and *explode*.

plausible /pláwzəb'l/ *adj.* **1. BELIEVABLE** believable and appearing likely to be true, usually in the absence of proof **2. PERSUASIVE** having a persuasive manner in speech or writing, often combined with an intention to deceive [Mid-16thC. From Latin *plausibilis*, literally 'deserving applause', from *plaus-*, the past participle stem of *plaudere*.] —**plausibility** /pláwzə bílləti/ *n.* —**plausibleness** /pláwzəb'lnəss/ *n.* —**plausibly** /-əbli/ *adv.*

plausive /pláwziv/ *adj.* (*archaic*) **1. EXPRESSING PRAISE** characterized by or expressing praise or approval **2. PLAUSIBLE** plausible [Early 17thC. Formed from Latin *plaus-*, the past participle stem of *plaudere* (source of English *applaud* and *explode*).]

Plautus /pláwtəss/, **Titus Maccius** (254?–184 BC) Roman comic dramatist. His 21 surviving plays, modelled on Greek New Comedy, influenced both Shakespeare and Molière.

play /play/ *v.* (**plays, playing, played**) **1.** *vi.* LEISURE **ENGAGE IN ENJOYABLE ACTIVITY** to take part in enjoyable activity for the sake of amusement **2.** *vi.* **ACT IN JEST** to do sth for fun, not in earnest **3.** *vti.* GAME, SPORT **TAKE PART IN A GAME OR SPORT** to take part in a game or a sporting activity ○ *likes to play football* **4.** *vt.* GAME, SPORT **COMPETE AGAINST** to compete against sb in a game or sporting event ○ *They play their biggest rival tomorrow.* **5.** *vti.* SPORTS **ASSIGN OR HAVE A POSITION ON FIELD** to assign a player to a particular position on the field, or be assigned such a position **6.** *vt.* SPORTS **HIT BALL** to hit or kick a ball, puck, or shuttlecock in a particular direction, especially as a way of beating an opponent ○ *playing the ball straight down the line* **7.** *vt.* SPORTS **HIT A SHOT** to make a particular shot or stroke in a sporting event **8.** *vt.* GAMES **USE A PIECE OR CARD IN A GAME** to use a card from a hand in a card game or a piece in a board game **9.** *vti.* **ACT IN A PARTICULAR MANNER** to deal with a situation in a particular way to achieve a desired result ○ *Whether you get what you want depends on how you play it.* **10.** *vti.* GAMBLING **GAMBLE** to gamble on a game of chance such as roulette or on horse races **11.** *vt.* FIN **SPECULATE IN A MARKET** to speculate with securities or commodities in a market **12.** *vti.* ARTS **ACT A PART IN A PLAY** to portray a character in a theatrical or film production ○ *'He that plays the king shall be welcome'.* (Shakespeare, *Hamlet*; 1602) **13.** *vti.* ARTS **PERFORM OR BE PERFORMED SOMEWHERE** to perform a play or show a film at a particular theatre or cinema, or be performed or shown there ○ *What's playing at the Luxor?* **14.** *vt.* THEATRE **PERFORM A DRAMATIC WORK BY** to perform the work of a particular dramatist **15.** *vt.* THEATRE **PERFORM IN PARTICULAR PLACES** to perform in particular places or types of places ○ *playing the northern industrial towns* **16.** *vt.* **PRETEND TO BE** to pretend to be a particular type of person ○ *Don't play the innocent with me.* **17.** *vti.* MUSIC **PERFORM ON A MUSICAL INSTRUMENT** to use a musical instrument to produce music ○ *plays the trombone* **18.** *vt.* MUSIC **PERFORM MUSIC** to use an instrument or the voice to perform a piece of music ○ *play a sonata* **19.** *vt.* MUSIC **PERFORM A COMPOSER** to perform the music of a particular composer ○ *Chopin is notoriously difficult to play well.* **20.** *vti.* MUSIC **REPRODUCE RECORDED MUSIC** to reproduce recorded music for listening, or be reproduced in this way ○ *played my favourite CD* **21.** *vti.* **DIRECT LIGHT OR WATER** to direct light or water over a surface or in a particular way, or be directed in this manner **22.** *vti.* **MOVE IRREGULARLY OVER A SURFACE** to move or cause sth to move unsteadily or irregularly over a surface, usually in a pleasing way ○ *sunlight playing on her brown hair* **23.** *vt.* **LET A FISH PULL ON A LINE** to tire an already hooked fish by letting it pull on the line as it tries to escape **24.** *vi.* **MAKE A PARTICULAR IMPRESSION ON SB** to be received in a particular way by sb or to make a particular impression on that person ○ *a policy that is likely to play well with middle-class voters* ■ *n.* **1.** THEATRE **DRAMATIC COMPOSITION OR PRODUCTION** a dramatic work written to be performed by actors on the stage, on television, or on the radio **2. PLOY** a ploy or deceptive act intended to achieve a particular end ○ *The defendant's tears were just a play for your sympathy.* **3.** LEISURE **ENJOYABLE ACTIVITIES** activities bringing amusement or enjoyment, especially the spontaneous activity of young children or young animals ○ *young cubs at play* **4.** LANGUAGE **PUN** a pun on a word **5.** SPORTS **ACTION DURING A GAME** the action during a game or series of games ○ *Bad light eventually stopped play.* ○ *The play was skilled during the first half but then the team began to tire.* **6.** *US* SPORTS **ACTION OR MOVE IN A GAME** a particular action or move in a game ○ *drilled the team in several new offensive plays* **7.** GAME, SPORT **TURN IN A GAME** sb's turn to move in a game **8.** GAME, SPORT **HANDLING OF A SHOT OR MOVE** a player's handling of a shot or move or use of a piece or card **9.** GAMBLING **GAMBLING** participation in betting or gambling **10. FLICKERING MOVEMENT** flickering or shimmering movement, especially of light through or on sth **11. LOOSENESS** the amount of looseness in sth, such as a rope or between moving parts [Old English *pleg(i)an*. Ultimately from a prehistoric Germanic word meaning 'to risk, exercise' that is also the ancestor of English *plight* and *pledge*.] —**playability** /pláyə bílləti/ *n.* —**playable** /pláyəb'l/ *adj.* ◇ **make a play for sb** *or* **sth** to try openly to gain sth ◇ **play away from home** to be sexually unfaithful to a spouse or partner (*informal*) ◇ **play fair** to act in an honest and reasonable way ◇ **play fast and loose** to act irresponsibly or recklessly without regard to facts or others' feelings ◇ **play for time** to delay action or a decision in the hope that conditions will be more favourable later on ◇ **play hard to get** to avoid agreeing to a suggestion, invitation, or proposal, with the intention of appearing to be desirable or in demand ◇ **play safe** to exercise caution and take few risks

play about *vi.* = **play around** *v.* 2

play along *vi.* to pretend to agree with sb or sth in order to gain an advantage or avoid conflict

play around *vi.* **1. SLEEP AROUND** to engage in sexual activity with sb other than a spouse or long-term partner **2. WASTE TIME** to behave in an irresponsible or childish way

play at *v.* **1.** *vt.* **PRETEND** to pretend to do or be sth, usually without conviction or commitment ○ *I was tired of playing at being an entrepreneur.* **2.** *vi.* **ENGAGE IN A ROLE-PLAY GAME** to engage in a game that involves role-playing (*refers typically to children*) ○ *playing at doctors and nurses*

play back *vti.* to reproduce recorded sound or video material

play down *vt.* to represent sth as being less important or significant than it is ○ *While some patients exaggerate their symptoms, others play them down.* ○ *The spin doctors are playing down the significance of the charge.*

play off *v.* **1. TAKE PART IN DECIDING GAME** to take part in a deciding game to find the winner of a tied contest **2.** *vt.* **BRING INTO CONFLICT** to set one person or group against another in order to gain an advantage ○ *children playing their parents off against each other*

play on, play upon *v.* **1.** *vt.* **TAKE ADVANTAGE OF** to use sb's hope, fear, or insecurity as a way of manipulating that person **2.** *vt.* **MAKE A PUN** to make a pun on a word **3.** *vi.* **HIT BALL INTO OWN WICKET** in cricket, to hit the ball into your own wicket, putting yourself out of the game

play out *v.* **1.** *vt.* **ACT OUT STH** to act out a scene or situation that has been rehearsed or envisaged previously **2.** *vt.* **FINISH PLAYING STH** to continue to play sth to the finish or end ○ *We'll play out this hand, then go home.* **3.** *vt.* **LET STH OUT GRADUALLY** to release sth such as a rope bit by bit **4.** *vti.* *US* **END** to bring sth to an end, or come to an end ○ *The calamity has yet to play out.*

play up *v.* **1.** *vt.* **EMPHASIZE** to emphasize or exaggerate sth ○ *She played up her commercial know-how for all she was worth.* **2.** *vi.* **BEHAVE BADLY** to be uncooperative or disruptive ○ *The children are playing up again.* **3.** *vi.* **MALFUNCTION** to fail to function properly ○ *My printer's playing up.* **4.** *vti.* **HURT** to cause pain to sb (*refers to parts of the body*)

play up to *v.* **1.** *vt.* **TRY TO PLEASE** to attempt to please sb by flattery and obsequiousness **2.** *vi.* **SUPPORT ACTOR** to support another actor in a play

play with *vt.* **1. THINK ABOUT** to consider a plan or idea without doing very much to make it happen **2. TREAT CARELESSLY** to treat sb or sb's feelings carelessly or irresponsibly **3. DEAL WITH STH HALF-HEARTEDLY** to deal with sth unenthusiastically or haphazardly, e.g.

by pushing food around a plate without eating **4.** MASTURBATE to masturbate

playa /plī ə/ *n.* the lower part of an inland desert drainage basin that is periodically filled with alkaline and briny salts washed down by rainwater from surrounding highlands [Mid-19thC. Via Spanish, 'beach', from late Latin *plagia* 'plain, shore', of uncertain origin: perhaps ultimately from Greek *plagos* 'side'.]

play-act (**play-acts, play-acting, play-acted**) *v.* **1.** *vi.* BEHAVE INSINCERELY to behave in an insincere and excessively dramatic fashion, usually in order to get attention (*informal*) **2.** *vti.* PRETEND TO BE ACTING to pretend to be acting a part, usually for fun **3.** *vi.* ACT IN A PLAY to take part in drama, especially as an amateur —**play-acting** *n.* —**play-actor** *n.*

playback /pláy bak/ *n.* **1.** REPLAY OF A RECORDING the replay of a sound or video recording after it has been made, often as a check for quality or accuracy **2.** DEVICE FOR REPLAYING RECORDINGS the device or facility in a recording apparatus for replaying recordings

playbill /pláy bil/ *n.* **1.** POSTER ADVERTISING A PLAY a poster advertising a play or other theatrical perfomance (*dated*) **2.** *US* THEATRE PROGRAMME the printed programme accompanying a theatrical performance or concert, sold to theatregoers before the performance ○ *We had barely two minutes to study the playbill before the lights went down.*

playboy /pláy boy/ *n.* a rich man who does not work and devotes himself to a life of pleasure without commitments or responsibilities

play-by-play *adj. US* LIVE AND DETAILED consisting of a description of each event as it happens, especially in a sports contest ■ *n. US* = **commentary**

Play-Doh /pláy dō/ *tdmk.* a trademark for a soft coloured modelling material used especially by children

played out *adj.* **1.** EXHAUSTED drained of energy or inspiration as a result of excessive or prolonged effort or of being too long in the public eye **2.** NO LONGER POPULAR OR FASHIONABLE having lost all usefulness or relevance through overuse or overexposure (*hyphenated before a noun*) [Originally describing a fish that has fought until it is exhausted]

player /pláyər/ *n.* **1.** SB TAKING PART IN GAME sb taking part in a sport or game, e.g. a member of a team (*often used in combination*) ○ *a hockey player* **2.** MUSICIAN sb who plays a musical instrument (*usually used in combination*) ○ *a trumpet player* **3.** PARTICIPANT IN AN ACTIVITY a person, group, or business that has an influential role in a particular political or commercial activity ○ *a major player in the direct banking sector* **4.** STAGE ACTOR an actor, especially a member of a theatrical company **5.** DEVICE FOR PLAYING RECORDED SOUND a device for playing recorded sound (*usually used in combination*) ○ *a CD player*

player piano *n.* a piano with a mechanism for playing music automatically, usually by means of a perforated metal disc or roll of paper

playfellow /pláy felō/ *n.* a friend with whom a child plays (*dated*)

playful /pláyf'l/ *adj.* **1.** ENJOYING FUN AND GAMES fond of having fun and playing games with others **2.** SAID OR DONE IN FUN said or done in a teasing way or in fun ○ *a playful poke in the ribs* —**playfully** *adv.* —**playfulness** *n.*

playgirl /pláy gurl/ *n.* a rich woman who does not work and devotes herself to a life of pleasure without commitments or responsibilities

playgoer /pláygō ər/ *n.* sb who frequents the theatre as a spectator —**playgoing** *adj., n.*

playground /pláy grownd/ *n.* **1.** ENCLOSED PLAY AREA an outdoor recreation area for children, usually equipped with swings, slides, seesaws, and other play equipment **2.** SCHOOL YARD the yard attached to a school, for children to play in during break times. US term **schoolyard 3.** RESORT a resort or other place used for a recreation by a particular group of people ○ *The coast has become a playground for millionaires.*

playgroup /pláy groop/ *n.* an organized meeting for preschool children to play together under supervision

playhouse /pláy howss/ (*plural* **-houses** /-howziz/) *n.* **1.** THEATRE a theatre, especially the main theatre in a town or city (*often used in placenames*) ○ *appearing at the Nottingham Playhouse* **2.** = **Wendy house**

playing card *n.* any of a set of cards printed with an identical design on the back and symbols on the face representing the numbers in different suits, used for playing various games. Playing cards were introduced to the West from Asia and were probably first used in China in the 10th century. The pack was standardized at 52 in the 15th century.

playing field *n.* an area of level ground used for organized sporting activities ◇ **a level playing field** a situation in which all those involved have an equal chance of being successful

playlet /pláylət/ *n.* a short play, often one with a rather slight plot

playlist /pláy list/ *n.* a list of musical recording that are to be played on a radio programme or by a radio station —**playlist** *vt.*

play lunch *n. ANZ* a snack to eat at school during the mid-morning break

playmaker /pláy maykər/ *n.* in team games, a player who initiates moves that create scoring opportunities

playmate /pláy mayt/ *n.* sb, especially a child, who plays with another

play-off *n.* **1.** TIEBREAKER an additional match, game, or round to decide the winner in the case of a tie **2.** *US, Can* ONE OF A SERIES OF MATCHES one of a series of matches that decides a championship competition ○ *One more win should guarantee a spot in the playoffs.*

play on words *n.* a pun

playpen /pláy pen/ *n.* a portable structure that forms a small enclosure for a baby to play in safely

playroom /pláy room, -rŏom/ *n.* a room reserved, designed, or equipped for children to play in

playschool /pláy skool/ *n.* a place where pre-school children can be taken for supervised play and learning, usually for half-day sessions

playsuit /pláy soot, -syoot/ *n.* an outfit for a child or woman to wear when relaxing, either consisting of shorts and a top or made in one piece

plaything /pláy thing/ *n.* **1.** TOY a toy or other object with which to play **2.** SB OR STH TREATED AS A TOY sb or sth used for amusement rather than being treated with respect or taken seriously

playtime /pláy tīm/ *n.* a time set aside for play, especially as a break for children at school

playwright /pláy rīt/ *n.* sb who writes plays

plaza /plaázə/ *n.* **1.** SPANISH SQUARE an open square or marketplace in a Spanish-speaking country or somewhere influenced by Hispanic culture **2.** *US* = **shopping centre** [Late 17thC. Via Spanish from Latin *platea* 'broad street' (see PLACE).]

PLC *abbr.* **PLC, plc** public limited company ■ *n., abbr.* product life cycle

plea /plee/ *n.* **1.** URGENT REQUEST an urgent, often emotional, request ○ *a plea for understanding* **2.** LAW DEFENDANT'S ANSWER TO CHARGE the defendant's answer to a charge in a court of law, especially one stating that he or she is guilty or not guilty **3.** LAW STATEMENT SUPPORTING DEFENDANT'S OR CLAIMANT'S CASE a statement or argument made in a court of law in support of a defendant's or claimant's case **4.** COURT CASE in Scotland, a legal case conducted through the courts **5.** EXCUSE an excuse or pretext [13thC. Via Anglo-Norman *plai* 'lawsuit, agreement' from, ultimately, Latin *placitum* 'decree', from the past participle of *placere* (see PLEASE).]

plea bargaining *n.* the practice of arranging with the prosecution, and sometimes a judge, for a defendant to plead guilty to a less serious charge rather than be tried for a more serious one —**plea bargain** *n.* —**plea-bargain** *vi.*

pleach /pleech/ (**pleaches, pleaching, pleached**), **plash** /plash/ (**plashes, plashing, plashed**) *vt.* to form or reinforce a hedge or arch by intertwining shoots or branches [14thC. From Old French dialect *plechier*, a variant of Old French *plassier* (source of English *plash*) from, ultimately, Latin *plectere* 'to plait' (see PLEXUS).]

plead /pleed/ (**pleads, pleading, pleaded** *or* **pled** *US, Can, Scotland* /pled/, **pleaded** *or* **pled** *US, Can, Scotland*) *v.* **1.** *vi.* BEG EARNESTLY to make an earnest or urgent entreaty, often in emotional terms ○ *I pleaded with her to stay.* **2.** *vt.* OFFER STH AS AN EXCUSE to use a particular reason or circumstance to excuse or justify behaviour ○ *It's no good pleading ignorance.* **3.** *vt.* DECLARE GUILT OR INNOCENCE to answer 'guilty' or 'not guilty' in response to a charge in a court of law **4.** *vti.* OFFER AN ARGUMENT IN SUPPORT to argue a case in support of sb or sth, especially in a court of law [13thC. Via Anglo-Norman *pleder* from, ultimately, medieval Latin *placitare* 'to appeal', from *placitum* 'decree' (see PLEA).] —**pleadable** *adj.* —**pleader** *n.*

pleadings /pleédingz/ *npl.* the formal written statements made by the plaintiff and the defendant in a lawsuit

pleasance /plézz'nss/ *n.* **1.** SECLUDED AREA OF A GARDEN a quiet tree-planted area laid out with walks and often statues and fountains **2.** PLEASURE pleasure or delight (*archaic*) [14thC. From French *plaisance*, from *plaisant* (see PLEASANT).]

pleasant /plézz'nt/ *adj.* **1.** ENJOYABLE bringing feelings of pleasure, enjoyment, or satisfaction ○ *We spent a very pleasant evening together.* **2.** GOOD-NATURED friendly, kind, or good-natured **3.** FULL OF JOKES inclined to make jokes and be facetious (*archaic*) [14thC. From Old French *plaisant*, the present participle of Old French *plaisir* (see PLEASE).] —**pleasantly** *adv.* —**pleasantness** *n.*

pleasantry /plézz'ntri/ (*plural* **-ries**) *n.* **1.** POLITE REMARK a conventionally polite remark or enquiry **2.** WITTY REMARK a humorous or witty remark **3.** AGREEABLE CONVERSATION pleasing light conversation

please /pleez/ *adv., interj.* USED IN REQUESTS used to add politeness or urgency to requests, commands, and published rules and regulations ○ *Please be quiet.* ■ *interj.* USED TO EXPRESS INDIGNATION used to express astonishment or indignation, often facetiously ○ *Please! Do you expect me to believe that?* ■ *v.* (**pleases, pleasing, pleased**) **1.** *vti.* GIVE PLEASURE to give pleasure or satisfaction to sb **2.** *vt.* BE WHAT SB WANTS to be the wish or will of sb (*formal or literary*) **3.** *vi.* LIKE to like or wish to do sth ○ *You can do as you please.* [14thC. Via Old French *plaisir* from Latin *placere* (source of English *placid* and *complacent*).] —**pleaser** *n.* ◇ **if you please 1.** used to make a polite request or command (*dated formal*) **2.** used to indicate mild annoyance, indignation, or amazement (*dated*)

pleased /pleezd/ *adj.* **1.** HAPPY OR SATISFIED feeling or expressing satisfaction or pleasure ○ *I'm really pleased with their progress.* ○ *Pleased to meet you.* **2.** WILLING willing to do sth ○ *We would be pleased to answer any further requests you have.*

pleasing /pleézing/ *adj.* **1.** PLEASANT pleasant or gratifying ○ *a pleasing contrast* **2.** SATISFYING welcome or satisfying —**pleasingly** *adv.* —**pleasingness** *n.*

pleasurable /plé<u>zh</u>ərəb'l/ *adj.* giving pleasure or enjoyment —**pleasurability** /plé<u>zh</u>ərə bílləti/ *n.* —**pleasurably** /plé<u>zh</u>ərəbli/ *adv.*

pleasure /plé<u>zh</u>ər/ *n.* **1.** HAPPINESS OR SATISFACTION a feeling of happiness, delight, or satisfaction ○ *I took great pleasure in pointing out his mistake to him.* **2.** SENSUAL GRATIFICATION gratification of the senses, especially sexual gratification **3.** RECREATION recreation, relaxation, or amusement, especially as distinct from work or everyday routine ○ *travelling for pleasure* **4.** STH SATISFYING a source of happiness, joy, or satisfaction **5.** SB'S DESIRE sb's desire, wish, or preference (*formal or literary*) ■ *v.* (**-ures, -uring, -ured**) **1.** *vt.* GIVE SB PLEASURE to give sb pleasure, especially through sensual or sexual stimulation or gratification **2.** *vi.* ENJOY to derive satisfaction or happiness from sth (*archaic*) [14thC. From Old French *plaisir* 'to please', used as a noun (see PLEASE).] —**pleasureful** *adj.* —**pleasureless** *adj.*

pleasure principle *n.* in Freudian psychology, the principle that guides instinctive behaviour, directing the subject towards gratifying immediate needs and avoiding pain

pleat /pleet/ *n.* PRESSED FOLD a vertical fold in cloth or other material, usually one of a number, sewn into position or pressed flat ■ *vt.* (**pleats, pleating, pleated**) PUT PLEATS IN STH to put pleats into cloth or a piece of clothing [14thC. From an early variant of PLAIT.] — **pleater** *n.*

pleb /pleb/ *n.* **1. SB REGARDED AS ILL-EDUCATED** sb who is regarded ill-educated and unrefined and behaves in a coarse or crude manner, especially sb from a lower social class (*insult*) **2.** HIST = **plebeian** *n.* 1 **3.** *US* MIL = **plebe** [Mid-17thC. Originally a back-formation from PLEBS, misunderstood as a plural, later also a shortening of PLEBEIAN.]

plebby /plébbi/ (**-bier, -biest**) *adj.* ill-educated and coarse, vulgar, or tasteless (*insult*)

plebe /pleeb/ *n. US* a first-year student at the US Military Academy or the US Naval Academy [Mid-19thC. Origin uncertain: probably a shortening of PLEBEIAN.]

plebeian /plə beé ən/ *n.* **1. MEMBER OF THE ROMAN PLEBS** one of the ordinary citizens of ancient Rome as distinct from the patricians **2. SB REGARDED AS ILL-EDUCATED** sb who behaves in a coarse or crude manner, and has common or vulgar tastes, especially sb from a lower social class (*insult*) ■ *adj.* **1. OF THE ROMAN PLEBS** relating or belonging to the ordinary people in a society, especially the plebs of ancient Rome **2. COMMON OR VULGAR** coarse, vulgar, or tasteless (*insult*) [Mid-16thC. Formed from Latin *plebeius*, from *plebs* (see PLEBS).] — **plebeianism** *n.*

plebiscite /plébbi sīt/ *n.* **1. VOTE OF ALL CITIZENS** a vote by a whole electorate to decide a question of importance. ◊ **referendum 2. EXPRESSION OF PUBLIC WILL** a public expression of the will or opinion of a whole community **3.** HIST **COMMON PEOPLE'S LAW** a law enacted by the plebs or ordinary citizens of ancient Rome gathered in assembly [Mid-16thC. Via French from Latin *plebiscitum*, literally 'decree of the common people'.] — **plebiscitary** /plə bíssitəri/ *adj.*

plebs /plebz/ *npl.* HIST the ordinary citizens of ancient Rome, as distinct from the patricians [Mid-19thC. From Latin.]

plecopteran /plə kóptərən/ *n.* = **stonefly** ■ *adj.* **OF STONEFLIES** relating or belonging to the stoneflies. Order: Plecoptera. [Late 19thC. Formed from modern Latin *Plecoptera*, order name, from Greek *plekos* 'wickerwork' + *pteron* 'wing'; so called because of its netted wings.]

plectognath /plék tog nath/ *n.* a bony strong-toothed marine fish with a small mouth and small gill openings, e.g. the triggerfish or the puffer. Order: Plectognathi. [Late 19thC. From modern Latin *Plectognathi*, order name, from Greek *plektos* 'twisted' + *gnathos* 'jaw'.]

plectrum /pléktrəm/ (*plural* **-tra** /-trə/ *or* **-trums**) *n.* a small flat pointed piece of plastic or other material, used for plucking or strumming the strings of a guitar or similar instrument [Early 17thC. Via Latin from Greek.]

pled /pled/ *US, Can, Scotland* past participle, past tense of **plead**

pledge /plej/ *n.* **1. SOLEMN UNDERTAKING** a solemn promise or vow ○ *stood by her election pledges* **2. STH GIVEN AS SECURITY** sth delivered as security for the keeping of a promise or the payment of a debt or as a guarantee of good faith **3.** a promise to donate money, e.g. to a charity or a political cause ○ *They have raised over $10,000 in donations and pledges.* **4. BEING HELD AS SECURITY** the state of being held as security ○ *goods in pledge* **5. TOKEN OF STH** sth given or received as a token of sth such as love or friendship **6. TOAST** a toast drunk to sb or sth as a gesture of goodwill or support **7.** *US* UNIV **RECRUIT TO A UNIVERSITY SOCIETY** a student who has been invited, and has promised, to join a fraternity or sorority in a university in the United States ■ *v.* (**pledges, pledging, pledged**) **1.** *vt.* **PROMISE STH** to promise sth solemnly, or promise solemnly to do sth **2.** *vt.* **BIND** to submit sb to a binding pledge **3.** *vt.* **GIVE STH AS SECURITY** to hand over sth as security for the payment of a debt, repayment of a loan, or the carrying out of some obligation (*dated*) **4.** *vti.* **DRINK TO SB** to drink a toast to sb (*archaic*) ○ *'Drink to me, only with thine eyes, And I will pledge with mine'* (Ben Jonson *'To Celia'*; 1616) **5.** *vti. US* UNIV **PROMISE TO JOIN A UNIVERSITY SOCIETY** to promise to join a society, fraternity, or sorority in a university in the United States [14thC. Via Old French *plege* from late Latin *plebium*, from *plebire* 'to pledge', of Germanic origin.] —**pledgable** *adj.* ◇ **sign** *or* **take the pledge** to undertake solemnly to abstain forever from alcoholic drink (*dated*)

pledgee /ple jeé/ *n.* sb with whom a pledge or pawned object is deposited

Pledge of Allegiance *n.* a formula recited by citizens of the United States when saluting the US flag as a promise of loyalty to the country

pledger /pléjjər/, **pledgor, pledgeor** *n.* **1. SB WHO DEPOSITS A PLEDGE** sb who deposits a pledge or puts sth in pawn **2. SB WHO MAKES A PLEDGE** sb who takes a pledge or vow

pledget /pléjjit/ *n.* a small tuft of cotton wool or other material used on forceps to cleanse or apply medication to a confined space such as the ear passage [Mid-16thC. Origin unknown.]

pledgor *n.* = **pledger**

-plegia *suffix.* inability to move ○ *quadriplegia* [Formed from *plēgē* 'a blow, stroke', from *plēg-*, the stem of *plēssein* 'to strike' (see PLECTRUM)]

Pleiad /plí əd/, **pleiad** *n.* a brilliant group of seven people or things, specifically the group of poets of the French Renaissance, La Pléiade, which included Ronsard and Du Bellay, or seven Alexandrian Greek poets of the 3rd century BC [Early 17thC. Back-formation from PLEIADES.]

Pleiades /plí ə deez/ *npl.* **1.** MYTHOL **7 DAUGHTERS OF ATLAS** in Greek mythology, the seven daughters of Atlas and Pleione who were pursued by Orion and were turned into a constellation to escape him **2.** ASTRON **CLUSTER OF STARS** an open cluster of more than 300 stars in the constellation Taurus, six or seven of which are blue-white giants clearly visible to the naked eye [14thC. Via Latin from Greek (singular *Pleias*), related to *plein* 'to sail'.]

plein-air /pláyn áir/ *adj.* relating to or in the style of the French impressionist painters who sought to capture effects of light and atmosphere by completing their work out of doors [Late 19thC. From French *(en) plein air* '(in) the open air'.] —**plein-airist** *n.*

pleio- *prefix.* = **pleo-**

Pleiocene *adj., n.* GEOL = **Pliocene**

pleiotaxy /plí ō taksi/ *n.* BOT the development of more petals or sepals than normal

pleiotropism /plī óttrəpizəm/, **pleiotropy** /plī óttrəpi/ (*plural* **-pies**) *n.* the phenomenon in which a single gene determines two or more apparently unrelated characteristics of the same organism, or an instance of this —**pleiotropic** /plī ə tróppik/ *adj.* —**pleiotropically** /-tróppikli/ *adv.*

Pleistocene /plístō seen/ *adj.* **GEOLOGICAL PERIOD** relating to or used to describe the earlier epoch of the Quaternary Period in the Cenozoic Era, characterized by the disappearance of continental ice sheets and the appearance of humans ■ *n.* **PLEISTOCENE EPOCH** the Pleistocene epoch [Mid-19thC. Coined from Greek *pleistos* 'most' + *kainos* 'recent'.]

plenary /pleénəri/ *adj.* **1. FULL OR UNLIMITED** full and complete and not limited in any respect (*formal*) **2. ATTENDED BY EVERYONE** attended or meant to be attended by every member or delegate ○ *a plenary session* ■ *n.* (*plural* **-ries**) **1. PLENARY MEETING** a plenary meeting, session, or lecture, e.g. at a conference **2.** CHR **BOOK OF GOSPELS OR EPISTLES** a book containing all the gospels or all the epistles and accompanying homilies or sermons [Early 16thC. From late Latin *plenarius*, from Latin *plenus* 'full' (see PLENTY).] —**plenarily** *adv.*

plenary indulgence *n.* in the Roman Catholic Church, a complete remission of temporal punishment

plenipotent /plə níppətənt/ *adj.* having complete authority [Mid-17thC. From late Latin (see PLENIPOTENTIARY).]

plenipotentiary /plénnipə ténshəri/ *adj.* **1. HAVING FULL POWER** invested with complete authority to act independently **2. CONFERRING FULL POWER** giving the holder complete authority to act independently ■ *n.* (*plural* **-ies**) **OFFICIAL WITH FULL POWERS** an ambassador, envoy, or delegate invested with full authority to act or negotiate independently on behalf of a government or sovereign [Mid-17thC. Via medieval Latin *plenipotentiarius* from the late Latin stem *plenipotent-*, literally 'having full power', from *plenus* 'full' + *potens* 'powerful'.]

plenitude /plénni tyood/ *n.* (*literary*) **1. ABUNDANCE** an abundance or plentiful supply of sth **2. COMPLETENESS OR FULLNESS** the state of being full or complete [15thC. Via Old French from late Latin *plenitudo*, from *plenus* 'full' (see PLENTY).]

plenteous /plénti əss/ *adj.* (*literary*) **1. ABUNDANT** being in plentiful supply **2. PRODUCTIVE** giving an abundant yield [13thC. Via Old French from *plentivous* from, ultimately, *plentet* (see PLENTY).] —**plenteously** *adv.* —**plenteousness** *n.*

plentiful /pléntif'l/ *adj.* **1. ABUNDANT** present or existing in good supply ○ *Water is plentiful on the island.* **2. PRODUCTIVE** supplying a large amount or number — **plentifully** *adv.* —**plentifulness** *n.*

plenty /plénti/ *n.* **1. LOTS** an adequate or more than adequate amount or quantity ○ *There's plenty for the kids to do there.* ○ *Get plenty of rest.* **2. PROSPERITY** a situation in which there is a more than adequate supply of food, money, and other necessities ○ *had grown up in a time of plenty* ■ *adj.* **AMPLY SUFFICIENT** ample or more than sufficient (*informal*) ■ *adv. US* **SUFFICIENTLY** used to emphasize the degree to which sth is the case (*informal*) ○ *It should be plenty big enough.* [13thC. Via Old French *plentet* from Latin *plenitas*, from *plenus* 'full'. Ultimately, from an Indo-European word that is also the ancestor of English *full* and *folk*.]

plenum /pleénəm/ (*plural* **-nums** *or* **-na** /pleénə/) *n.* **1.** PHYS **ENCLOSURE CONTAINING GAS AT A HIGHER PRESSURE** an enclosure or chamber containing gas that is at a higher pressure than the surrounding atmosphere. Plenum systems may be used in air conditioning. **2. GENERAL ATTENDANCE AT A MEETING** a full or general assembly, e.g. of all the branches of a legislature **3.** PHILOS **MATTER-FILLED SPACE** space entirely filled with matter [Late 17thC. From Latin *plenum spatium*, literally 'full space'.]

pleo- *prefix.* more ○ *pleomorphism* [From Greek *pleīon*. Ultimately from an Indo-European base meaning 'full, to fill', which is also the ancestor of English *complete*, *supply*, and *plethora*.]

pleochroism /plee ókrō izəm/ *n.* the property in some crystals of transmitting different colours when viewed along different axes [Mid-19thC. Coined from PLEO- + Greek *khrōs* 'skin, colour'.] —**pleochroic** /pleé ə krṓ ik/ *adj.*

pleomorphism /pleé ə máwrfizəm/, **pleomorphy** /pleé ə mawrfi/ *n.* BIOL the characteristic in some organisms of taking on at least two different forms during the life cycle, or the ability to do this under certain conditions —**pleomorphic** /pleé ə máwrfik/ *adj.*

pleonasm /pleé ə nazəm/ *n.* **1. USE OF SUPERFLUOUS WORDS** the use of more words than are necessary to express a meaning **2. EXAMPLE OF USING SUPERFLUOUS WORDS** an example of using more words than are necessary to express a meaning, such as 'free gift' or 'sufficient enough' [Mid-16thC. Via late Latin from Greek *pleonasmos*, from *pleonazein* 'to be in excess', from *pleōn* 'more' (see PLEO-).] —**pleonastic** /pleé ə nástik/ *adj.* —**pleonastically** /-nástik'li/ *adv.*

pleopod /pleé ə pod/ *n.* ZOOL = **swimmeret**

pleotropic /pleé ə tróppik/ *adj.* used to describe a gene that affects more than one characteristic of the phenotype

plesiosaur /pleéssi ə sawr/ *n.* an extinct marine reptile of the Mesozoic era with limbs like paddles, a large flattened body, and a short tail. Suborder: Sauropterygia. [Mid-19thC. From modern Latin *Plesiosaurus*, genus name, from Greek *plēsios* 'near' + *sauros* 'lizard', because it was similar to the saurians.]

plethora /pléthərə/ *n.* **1. LARGE OR EXCESSIVE AMOUNT OR NUMBER** a very large amount or number of sth, especially an excessive amount ○ *a plethora of new TV channels* **2. EXCESS OF BLOOD** an excess of blood in part of the body, especially in the facial veins, causing a ruddy complexion (*archaic*) [Mid-16thC. Via late Latin from Greek *plēthōrē*, from *plēthein* 'to be full'.] — **plethoric** /ple thórrik/ *adj.* —**plethorically** /-thórrikli/ *adv.*

pleur- *prefix.* = **pleuro-** (*used before vowels*)

pleura /plóorə/ *n.* (*plural* **-rae** /plóoree/ *or* **-ras**) ANAT **MEMBRANE AROUND THE LUNGS** the thin transparent membrane that lines the chest wall and doubles back to cover the lungs, thereby forming a continuous sac enclosing the narrow pleural cavity. The inner faces of the cavity are lubricated by fluid to ease breathing movements. ■ ZOOL plural of **pleuron** [15thC. Via medieval Latin from Greek, 'side, rib' (source of English *pleurisy*).] —**pleural** *adj.*

pleural cavity *n.* the cavity formed between the pleural layer surrounding the lungs and the other layer lining the chest wall

pleurisy /plóorəssi/ *n.* inflammation of the membrane (**pleura**) surrounding the lungs, usually involving painful breathing, coughing, and the buildup of fluid in the pleural cavity [14thC. Via Old French from, ultimately, Greek *pleuritis*, from *pleura* 'side, rib'.] —**pleuritic** /plóoríttik/ *adj.*

pleuro- *prefix.* **1.** side, lateral ○ *pleurodont* **2.** pleura, pleural ○ *pleuropneumonia* [From Greek *pleura* 'side, rib']

pleurodont /plóorə dont/ *adj.* **1.** FUSED RATHER THAN ROOTED used to describe teeth, e.g. those found in some reptiles, that are not rooted in the jawbone but fused to its inner side **2.** HAVING TEETH NOT ROOTED IN THE JAWBONE used to describe reptiles that have teeth not rooted in the jawbone but fused to its inner side

pleurodynia /plóorə dínni ə/ *n.* **1.** PLEURITIC PAIN pain in the pleura, or between the ribs or in the chest wall area **2.** VIRAL ILLNESS WITH CHEST PAIN a Coxsackie viral illness resulting in pain in the muscles between the ribs or in other structures of the chest wall (*not used technically*) [Early 19thC. Coined from PLEURO- + Greek *odunē* 'pain' (source of English *anodyne*).]

pleuron /plóor on/ (*plural* -**ra** /plóorə/) *n.* a membrane that encases the lung. ♦ **pleura** [Early 18thC. Via modern Latin from Greek, 'rib, side'.]

pleuropneumonia /plóorō nyoo mṓni ə/ *n.* inflammation of the membrane (**pleura**) surrounding the lungs and of the lungs themselves at the same time

pleurotomy /plóo róttəmi/ (*plural* -**mies**) *n.* a surgical incision of the membrane (**pleura**) surrounding the lungs to permit drainage of fluid, especially in pleurisy

pleuston /plóostən/ *n.* small animals and plants such as algae that float on the surface of a pool of fresh water [Mid-20thC. Coined from Greek *pleusis* 'sailing', on the model of PLANKTON. Ultimately, from an Indo-European base meaning 'to flow', which is also the ancestor of English *float*.] —**pleustonic** /ploo stónnik/ *adj.*

Pleven /plév en/ capital city of Pleven Province, northern Bulgaria, situated about 129 km/80 mi. northeast of Sofia. Population: 125,000 (1996).

plexiform /pléksi fawrm/ *adj.* resembling or in the form of a plexus or network [Early 19thC. Coined from PLEXUS + -FORM.]

Plexiglas /pléksi glaass/ *tdmk.* US a trademark for a tough transparent acrylic plastic that can be used in place of glass

plexor /pléksər/ *n.* MED a small rubber-headed hammer formerly used to tap the body in a medical examination by percussion and in testing reflexes, e.g. by tapping the knee [Mid-19thC. Formed from Greek *plēxis* 'percussion', from *plēssein* 'to strike'.]

plexus /pléksəss/ (*plural* -**uses** *or* -**us**) *n.* **1.** ANAT NETWORK IN THE BODY a network of nerves, blood vessels, or other vessels in the body **2.** COMPLEX NETWORK any complex network or interwoven structure [Late 17thC. From Latin, past participle of *plectere* 'to plait' (source of English *complex*). Ultimately, from an Indo-European word that is also the ancestor of English *flax*.]

plf, plff *abbr.* plaintiff

pliable /plī əb'l/ *adj.* **1.** FLEXIBLE flexible and easily bent **2.** EASILY INFLUENCED easily persuaded or influenced **3.** ADAPTABLE adaptable to change [15thC. From Old French, where it was formed from *plier* 'to bend' (see PLY².)] —**pliability** /plī ə bílləti/ *n.* —**pliableness** /plī əb'lnəss/ *n.* —**pliably** /plī əbli/ *adv.*

— **WORD KEY: SYNONYMS** —
pliable, ductile, malleable, elastic, pliant
CORE MEANING: ready to be bent or moulded
pliable used to refer to a substance or material that can be easily bent or moulded; **ductile** a technical word used to describe metals that can be easily drawn out into a long continuous wire; **malleable** used to describe metals

that can be worked and hammered or pressed into various shapes without breaking or cracking; **elastic** used to describe substances or materials that can be stretched without breaking and that return to their original shape after this; **pliant** used to describe sth that is supple and springy and therefore easily bent or stretched

pliant /plī ənt/ *adj.* **1.** SUPPLE supple and bending easily ○ *a pliant tree branch* **2.** ADAPTABLE easily adapted or modified **3.** EASILY INFLUENCED easily persuaded or influenced [14thC. From Old French, present participle of *plier* 'to fold, bend' (see PLY².)] —**pliancy** *n.* —**pliantly** *adv.* —**pliantness** *n.*

— **WORD KEY: SYNONYMS** —
See Synonyms at *pliable.*

plica /plīkə/ (*plural* -**cae** /-see/) *n.* ANAT a fold or folded part, e.g. of skin [Early 18thC. Via medieval Latin, 'fold', from Latin *plicare* 'to fold' (see PLY².)] —**plical** *adj.*

plicate /plī kayt/, **plicated** /plī kaytid/ *adj.* **1.** BOT FOLDED LIKE A FAN arranged in folds like a fan **2.** GEOL WITH A PLEATED TEXTURE used to describe rock with a folded wrinkled texture [Late 17thC. From Latin *plicat-*, past participle stem of *plicare* 'to fold' (see PLY².)] —**plicately** *adv.* —**plicateness** *n.*

plication /plī káysh'n/, **plicature** /plíkəchər/ *n.* **1.** SURG STITCHING THE SIDES OF A BODY ORGAN the pleating and stitching of the walls of a body organ in order to reduce its size **2.** FOLDING the action of folding or the condition of being folded **3.** A FOLD a fold in sth

plié /plee ay/ *n.* a ballet movement in which the knees are bent and the back is kept straight [Late 19thC. From French, the past participle of *plier* 'to bend' (see PLY².)]

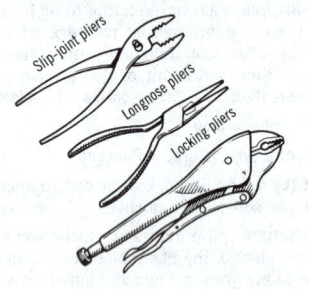

Pliers

pliers /plī ərz/ *npl.* a hand tool with two hinged arms ending in jaws that are closed by hand pressure to grip sth [Mid-16thC. Formed from PLY¹.]

plight¹ /plīt/ *n.* a difficult or dangerous situation, especially a sad or desperate predicament [14thC. Via Anglo-Norman *plit* 'wrinkle, situation' (influenced by PLIGHT²) from Latin *plicitum*, from the past participle of *plicare* 'to fold' (see PLY².)]

plight² /plīt/ *vt.* (**plights, plighting, plighted, plighted** *or* **plight**) MAKE A VOW to make a formal pledge, especially when promising to marry ■ *n.* PLEDGE a formal promise or pledge (*archaic*) [Old English *plihtan* 'to endanger', from *pliht* 'risk, danger', from a prehistoric Germanic word meaning 'to risk, pledge yourself', which is also the ancestor of English *pledge*] —**plighter** *n.*

plimsoll /plíms'l/, **plimsole** *n.* UK a light canvas shoe with a rubber sole [Late 19thC. Origin uncertain; probably from PLIMSOLL LINE, because the line around the shoe resembles it.]

Plimsoll line, **Plimsoll mark** *n.* any of several marks on the side of a merchant ship indicating the limit to which it can legally be submerged when loaded [Named after the British politician and reformer Samuel *Plimsoll* (1824–98) who introduced the Merchant Shipping Act of 1876, which advocated its use]

plink /plingk/ *n.* HIGH-PITCHED SOUND a short high-pitched metallic sound such as the sound made when the string of a musical instrument is plucked or a pebble is dropped into an empty glass bottle ■ *vti.* (**plinks, plinking, plinked**) **1.** MAKE HIGH-PITCHED SOUND to produce or make sth produce a short high-pitched metallic sound **2.** SHOOT AT A TARGET to shoot at or hit targets for fun, especially targets that make a short

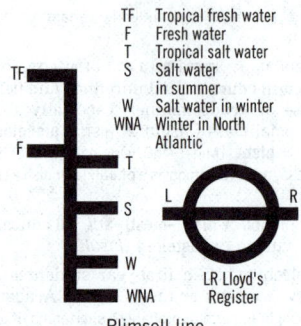

TF	Tropical fresh water
F	Fresh water
T	Tropical salt water
S	Salt water in summer
W	Salt water in winter
WNA	Winter in North Atlantic

LR Lloyd's Register

Plimsoll line

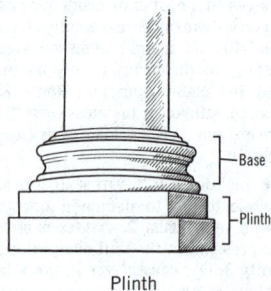

Plinth

high-pitched metallic sound when hit [Mid-20thC. An imitation of the sound.] —**plinker** *n.*

plinth /plinth/ *n.* **1.** SUPPORTING BLOCK a square block beneath a column, pedestal, or statue **2.** ARCHIT SUPPORTING PART OF A WALL the part of the wall of a building immediately above the ground, usually a course of stones or bricks **3.** ARCHIT PART OF A DOORFRAME the square block at the base on each side of a doorframe **4.** FLAT BASE any flat block used as a base for sth, e.g. underneath a heavy machine [Late 16thC. Via French from, ultimately, Greek *plinthos* 'tile, squared building stone'.]

Pliny (the Elder) /plínni/ (23–79) Roman scholar. His *Natural History* (77 AD) was a major source of knowledge until the 17th century.

Pliny (the Younger) (62–113) Roman politician and writer. He was the nephew of Pliny the Elder and author of nine books of Letters (100–109).

plio- *prefix.* = pleo-

Pliocene /plī ō seen/, **Pleiocene** *adj.* BELONGING TO THE TERTIARY PERIOD belonging to or typical of the last epoch of the Tertiary period, 5.4 to 1.6 million years ago, during which time a hominid species (**Homo erectus**) first appeared ■ *n.* PLIOCENE EPOCH OR ROCKS the Pliocene epoch, or rocks formed during that period [Mid-19thC. Coined from Greek *pleiōn* 'more' (see PLEO-) + *kainos* 'recent' (see -CENE), because it is later than the Miocene.]

Pliofilm /plī ō film/ *tdmk.* a trademark for a type of plastic made of rubber hydrochloride that forms a clear flexible sheeting, used for packaging and raincoats

plissé /plee say/, **plisse** *n.* **1.** WRINKLED FINISH a permanently wrinkled finish given to a fabric by treating it chemically **2.** FABRIC WITH A WRINKLED FINISH fabric with a plissé finish [Late 19thC. From French, past participle of *plisser* 'to pleat', from *pli* 'fold', from *plier* (see PLY².)]

PLO *abbr.* Palestine Liberation Organization

plod /plod/ *vi.* (**plods, plodding, plodded**) **1.** WALK HEAVILY to walk with a slow heavy tread **2.** WORK SLOWLY BUT STEADILY to work slowly but steadily, especially on sth uninteresting or laborious ■ *n.* **1.** SLOW HEAVY STEPS a walk with slow heavy steps **2.** SOUND OF SB PLODDING the sound of slow, heavy steps **3.** LABORIOUS TASK a task involving long and laborious work **4.** POLICE OFFICER a police officer, especially one of lower rank (*slang insult*) [Mid-16thC. Origin uncertain; thought to suggest the motion.] —**plodder** *n.* —**ploddingly** *adv.* —**ploddingness** *n.*

plodge /plodj/ (**plodges, plodging, plodged**) *vi.* to wade in water or through mud (*regional*) [Early 19thC. Origin uncertain.]

-ploid *suffix.* having a chromosome number in a particular relationship to the basic number of chromosomes in a group ○ *tetraploid* [From DIPLOID and HAPLOID]

ploidy /plóydi/ *n.* the multiple of the number of chromosome sets in a cell [Mid-20thC. Formed from -PLOID.]

Ploieşti /plaw yéshtyə/ city in southeastern Romania. It is the capital of Prahova County and centre of the national oil industry. Population: 254,408 (1994).

plonk[1] *v.* (**plonks, plonking, plonked**) **1.** *vti.* DROP HEAVILY OR SUDDENLY to drop, be dropped, or sit down heavily or suddenly (*informal*) **2.** *vt.* ABRUPTLY LAY STH DOWN to drop or lay sth down heavily or suddenly, often with deliberate emphasis ○ *She plonked the book down in front of me.* **3.** *vi.* PLAY MUSIC INEXPRESSIVELY to play a musical instrument heavily, and without much expression or skill ■ *n.* ACTION OR SOUND OF SUDDEN FALL the thudding action or sound of a sudden heavy fall (*informal*) ■ *adv.* WITH PLONKING SOUND with a plonking sound or action (*informal*) ○ *It landed plonk in my lap.* [Late 19thC. An imitation of the sound.]

plonk[2] /plongk/ *n.* cheap inferior wine (*informal*) [Mid-20thC. Shortening of *plink-plonk*, of uncertain origin: possibly an alteration of French *vin blanc* 'white wine'.]

plonker /plóngkər/ *n.* **1.** STUPID PERSON sb who is stupid or foolish (*slang insult*) **2.** UNINTELLIGENT PERSON sb who is unintelligent or thoughtless (*slang*) [Mid-19thC. Formed from PLONK[1].]

plook /plook/ *n. Scotland* = **plouk**

plop /plop/ *n.* **1.** SOUND OF STH DROPPING INTO WATER the sound made by sth dropping into water without making a large splash **2.** DEFECATION OF FAECES a human stool or animal dropping (*informal*) (*usually used by or to children*) ■ *v.* (**plops, plopping, plopped**) **1.** *vti.* FALL WITH A PLOP to fall or drop sth into water without making a large splash **2.** *vi.* DROP DOWN QUICKLY AND HEAVILY to drop or sit down quickly and heavily ■ *adv.* WITH A PLOP with a plopping sound or action ■ *interj.* IMITATION OF THE SOUND OF DROPPING INTO WATER used to imitate the sound of sth dropping into water without splashing [Early 19thC. An imitation of the sound.]

plosion /plṓzh'n/ *n.* PHON the sound made by a sudden release of breath in pronouncing certain sounds, especially a stop consonant [Early 20thC. Back-formation from EXPLOSION.]

plosive /plṓssiv/ *adj.* PRONOUNCED WITH A SUDDENLY RELEASED BREATH used to describe a consonant such as the 'p' in 'pear' that is pronounced by completely closing the breath passage and then releasing air ■ *n.* CONSONANT PRONOUNCED WITH PLOSION a consonant pronounced with a sudden release of breath [Late 19thC. Back-formation from EXPLOSIVE.]

plot /plot/ *n.* **1.** SECRET HOSTILE PLAN a plan decided on in secret, especially to bring about an illegal or subversive act **2.** ARTS STORYLINE the story or sequence of events in a narrated or presented work such as a novel, play, or film **3.** PIECE OF GROUND a small piece of ground **4.** *US* BUILDING PLAN OF A BUILDING OR ESTATE an architectural plan of a building or estate **5.** *US* A CHART a graph, chart, or diagram ■ *v.* (**plots, plotting, plotted**) **1.** *vti.* MAKE SECRET PLANS to make secret plans, especially to do sth illegal or subversive with others **2.** *vt.* MARK STH ON A CHART to mark sth on a chart, especially the course of a ship or aircraft **3.** *vt. US* BUILDING MAKE A PLAN to make a plan or map of sth, e.g. a building or estate **4.** *vti.* MARK ON A GRAPH to mark points on a graph or diagram using coordinates, or to be located on a graph by coordinates **5.** *vt.* DRAW ON A GRAPH to draw a line or curve through points marked on a graph or diagram **6.** *vt.* ARTS PLAN EPISODES OF A STORY to devise the sequence of events in a story or script [From Old English, 'area of ground', and Old French *complot* 'secret scheme', both of unknown origin]

plotline /plót līn/, **plot line** *n.* the plot or storyline in a book or dramatic presentation, or the dialogue needed to develop the plot

plotter /plóttər/ *n.* **1.** SB WHO SECRETLY PLANS sb who makes secret plans, especially to do sth illegal or subversive **2.** COMPUT COMPUTER DEVICE FOR DRAWING GRAPHS a computer output device that draws graphs and other pictorial images on paper, sometimes using attached pens. Large plotters are used in computer-aided design applications to produce more rapidly the engineering drawings and architectural plans once prepared by skilled draughtspeople.

plough /plow/ *n.* **1.** AGRIC FARM IMPLEMENT a heavy farming tool with a sharp blade or series of blades for breaking up soil and making furrows, usually pulled by a tractor or draught animal **2.** HEAVY TOOL any of various heavy tools or machines used like a plough to cut a cleared route or channel, e.g. a snowplough **3.** WOODWORK NARROW-BLADED PLANE THAT CUTS GROOVES a plane with a narrow blade used to cut grooves in wood **4.** AGRIC PLOUGHED LAND land that has been ploughed ■ *v.* (**ploughs, ploughing, ploughed**) **1.** *vti.* AGRIC MAKE FURROWS IN THE EARTH to break up earth and turn it over into furrows ○ *ploughing a field* **2.** *vti.* CUT THROUGH STH to cut or force a way through sth ○ *I ploughed my way through the crowd.* **3.** *vt.* MAKE A CLEARING IN STH to make a channel or cleared route in sth **4.** *vt.* AGRIC PUT UNDER SOIL to put sth such as fertilizer or a crop under the surface of the soil, using a plough **5.** *vti.* FAIL to fail at an examination (*informal*) **6.** *vti.* WORK METHODICALLY AT STH to work at sth and progress slowly and steadily ○ *We ploughed through the backlog of applications.* ○ *ploughing my way through pages of job ads* **7.** *vti.* to sail through a stretch of water (*literary*) ○ *a ship in full sail, ploughing an azure sea* **8.** *vt. US* HAVE SEX to have sexual intercourse with sb (*slang*) [Old English *ploh*, via prehistoric Germanic from a northern Italic word] —**plougher** *n.*

plough back *vt.* to invest profits from a business back into the business

plough in *vt.* to contribute or devote sth, especially money, to a project or place

plough into *v.* **1.** *vt.* CRASH INTO to crash into or hit with a great deal of force ○ *We lost control and ploughed into the car in front.* **2.** *vi.* TO EAGERLY START STH to start a job or undertaking, especially with energy and determination

plough under *vt.* **1.** BURY to bury sth so that it disappears ○ *Large tracts of forest had been ploughed under by the bulldozers.* **2.** OVERWHELM STH OR SB to overwhelm sb with too many responsibilities or jobs, or to overwhelm sth with too heavy a burden ○ *I was ploughed under for the whole weekend trying to fix the mess in the computer files.*

ploughboy /plów boy/ *n.* **1.** BOY LEADING PLOUGH ANIMALS a boy who leads one or more animals while they pull a plough **2.** COUNTRY BOY any boy who lives in the country and may not be very sophisticated (*archaic*)

ploughman /plów mən/ (*plural* **-men** /-mən/) *n.* sb who operates a plough, especially a plough drawn by animals —**ploughmanship** *n.*

ploughman's lunch *n.* a cold lunch, typically served in a pub, consisting of a plate of bread, cheese, pickle or chutney, and a pickled onion [Origin uncertain: probably from the belief that bread and cheese were the staple lunch of the ploughman in former times]

ploughman's spikenard *n.* a European plant with yellow flowers and purple bracts. Latin name: *Inula conyza*. [*Ploughman* in the meaning of 'farm labourer, country person'; from the idea that spikenard, which had a reputation for curative powers, could heal wounds incurred in working]

ploughshare /plów shair/ *n.* the part of a plough that cuts the soil for the furrow

plouk /plook/, **plook** *n. Scotland* a pimple [15thC. Origin unknown.] —**plouky** *adj.*

Plovdiv /plóv dif/ city in southern Bulgaria, the administrative centre of Plovdiv Region. Population: 344,000 (1996).

plover /plúvvər/ *n.* **1.** WADING BIRD a wading bird that lives on the shoreline and has a short bill and tail and long pointed wings. Family: Charadriidae. **2.** BIRD SIMILAR TO THE PLOVER a bird that resembles the plover but is in a different taxonomic family, e.g. the Egyptian plover or upland plover [14thC. Via Anglo-Norman from assumed Vulgar Latin *pluviarius*, from Latin *pluvia* 'rain' (see PLUVIAL); from the fact that it lives near water.]

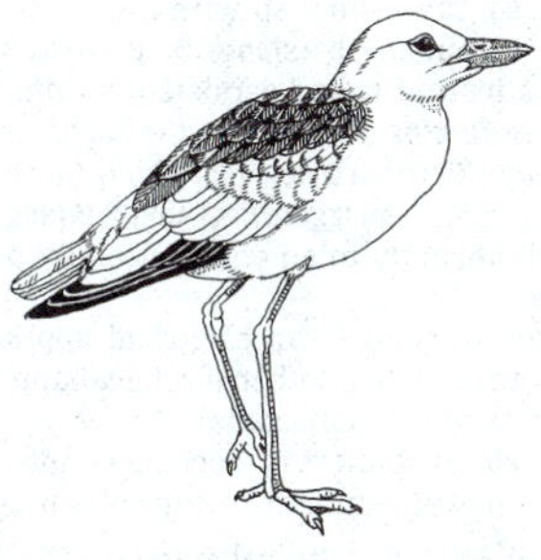

Plover

plow /plow/ *n., vti.* US = **plough**

plowter /plówtər/ (**-ters, -tering, -tered**), **plouter** (**-ters, -tering, -tered**) *vi. Scotland* **1.** SPLASH THROUGH WATER to splash through or play in water or mud **2.** DO STH IDLY to do sth in an idle or careless way [Early 19thC. Origin uncertain: perhaps literally 'to plout repeatedly', formed from *plout* 'to splash in water', an imitation of the sound.]

ploy /ploy/ *n.* **1.** DECEPTIVE TACTIC a tactic or manoeuvre, especially one calculated to deceive or frustrate an opponent **2.** ACTIVITY sth sb does as a job, amusement, or pastime **3.** *Scotland* PIECE OF FUN a lighthearted or carefree piece of fun [Late 17thC. Origin uncertain: possibly from EMPLOY.]

PLP *abbr.* Parliamentary Labour Party

PLR *abbr.* LIBRARIES Public Lending Right

PLSS *abbr.* MED portable life-support system

plu. *abbr.* plural

pluck /pluk/ *v.* (**plucks, plucking, plucked**) **1.** *vt.* TAKE STH AWAY QUICKLY to take sth away swiftly, often by means of skill or strength **2.** *vt.* QUICKLY REMOVE STH ROOTED to pull out by the roots some or all of the feathers or hair from sth **3.** *vt.* PULL OFF STH to pull sth off or out of sth else, e.g. fruit from a tree **4.** *vt.* TAKE STH CASUALLY to select sth randomly or with no obvious reason **5.** *vti.* TUG AT STH to tug quickly at sth ○ *felt someone plucking at my sleeve* **6.** *vt.* MUSIC PULL AND RELEASE STRINGS to play a stringed musical instrument by quickly pulling and releasing strings with a finger or plectrum ■ *n.* **1.** BRAVERY courage and determination in meeting danger or difficulty **2.** ACT OF PLUCKING one act or instance of plucking sth **3.** FOOD ANIMAL'S HEART, LIVER, AND LUNGS the heart, liver, and lungs of an animal used as meat [Old English *pluccian*, from prehistoric Germanic, of uncertain origin: perhaps from assumed Vulgar Latin *piluccare*, literally 'to pluck hair', from, ultimately, Latin *pilus* 'hair'] —**plucker** *n.*

WORD KEY: SYNONYMS

See Synonyms at ***courage***.

pluck up *vt.* to muster courage or audacity

plucky /plúki/ (**-ier, -iest**) *adj.* showing courage and determination, especially in the face of difficulties or superior odds —**pluckily** *adv.* —**pluckiness** *n.*

plug /plug/ *n.* **1.** FILLER FOR A HOLE sth used to fill and tightly close up a hole **2.** STOPPER FOR A SINK a rubber or plastic stopper for the drainage hole in a sink or bath **3.** ELEC ELECTRICAL CONNECTION the connection at the end of the wire leading from an electrical device, with prongs or pins that allow it to fit into the socket of a power supply **4.** ELEC SOCKET an electrical socket, e.g. on a wall (*informal*) **5.** BROADCAST PUBLICIZING MENTION a favourable mention of sth to publicize it, e.g. during a broadcast about sth else (*informal*) **6.** WEDGE FOR A SCREW a hollow piece of plastic pushed inside a hole to act as a holder for a screw that, when inserted, makes the plug expand and completely fill the hole **7.** AUTOMOT SPARK PLUG a spark plug **8.** CAKE OF CHEWING TOBACCO a cake of compressed or twisted tobacco or a piece of it used for chewing **9.** SEISMOL = **volcanic plug 10.** OLD HORSE an old and worn-out horse (*slang*) **11.** ANGLING WEIGHTED LURE an artificial weighted lure that has hooks attached to it **12.** SMALL PIECE CUT FROM STH a small wedge cut away from sth, especially as a test sample ■ *v.* (**plugs, plugging, plugged**) **1.** *vt.* CLOSE UP STH to close up a hole or gap **2.** *vt.* GIVE STH A FAVOURABLE MENTION to make a favourable mention of sth to publicize it, e.g. during a broadcast about sth else (*informal*) ○ *a chance to plug her latest novel* **3.**

vt. US **SHOOT SB** to shoot sb with a gun (*slang*) **4.** *vt.* **PUNCH SB** to punch sb (*slang*) **5.** *vi.* **WORK STEADILY** to work at sth steadily and persistently (*informal*) ○ *He is still plugging away in the insurance business.* [Early 17thC. Via Dutch from Middle Dutch *plugge*, of unknown origin.] —**plugger** *n.* ◇ **pull the plug on sth** to bring sth abruptly to an end, especially by cutting off funds

plug in *vti.* to connect an electrical appliance to a power source or to another electrical appliance, or to function when connected in this way

plug into *vti.* to connect or become connected to an electrical power source by means of a plug

plug and play *n.* a technical standard that allows a peripheral device such as a printer or DVD drive to be connected to a computer and to function immediately without the need for the user to alter the system's configuration files

plug gauge *n.* a tool for checking the diameter of a hole, consisting of a plug of a known size that is put into the hole

plughole /plúg hōl/ *n.* an opening in sth, such as a basin or bath, where liquid can drain away when a plug is removed

plug-ugly *adj.* **VERY UGLY** extremely unattractive (*insult*) ■ *n.* (*plural* **plug-uglies**) US **TOUGH RUTHLESS PERSON** a tough and intimidating person, especially a gangster (*slang*) [From the *Plug Uglies*, a gang of hoodlums in several US cities in the 1850s]

plum /plum/ *n.* **1.** TREES **SMALL FRUIT TREE** a small tree of the rose family that produces a round or oval smooth-skinned fruit. Genus: *Prunus.* **2.** FOOD **FRUIT OF THE PLUM TREE** the round or oval smooth-skinned edible fruit of a plum tree, containing a flattened stone **3.** FOOD **DRIED FRUIT** a raisin or other dried fruit used in a cake, pie, or pudding (*archaic*) **4.** COLOURS **DARK REDDISH-PURPLE** a dark reddish-purple colour **5.** **STH CHOICE** sth that is highly desirable or enviable, especially a job or contract (*informal*) ■ *adj.* **1.** **DESIRABLE** highly desirable or profitable (*informal*) ○ *a plum job* **2.** COLOURS **DARK REDDISH-PURPLE** of a dark reddish-purple colour [12thC. Alteration of Middle Low German and Middle Dutch *prūme* and Old High German *pfrūma*, ultimately, from Latin *prunum* (see PRUNE).]

plumage /plóomij/ *n.* the feathers that cover a bird's body, considered collectively [14thC. Via Old French from, ultimately, Latin *pluma* 'feather, plume' (see PLUME).]

plumate /plóo mayt/ *adj.* resembling, having, or producing feathers [Early 19thC. From Latin *plumatus* 'feathered', from *pluma* 'feather' (see PLUME).]

plumb /plum/ *n.* **1.** **WEIGHT ATTACHED TO A LINE** a weight, usually made of lead, attached to a line and used to find the depth of water or to verify a true vertical alignment **2.** **TRUE VERTICAL POSITION** a true vertical position or alignment ■ *adv.* **1.** **IN TRUE VERTICAL OR PERPENDICULAR POSITION** in perfect alignment or a true vertical position **2.** **EXACTLY** precisely or exactly (*informal*) ○ *plumb in the middle* **3.** US **COMPLETELY** utterly or totally (*informal*) ○ *plumb lazy* ■ *vt.* (**plumbs, plumbing, plumbed**) **1.** **FULLY COMPREHEND** to succeed in fully understanding sth, especially sth mysterious **2.** to experience sth, especially sth unpleasant, to an extreme degree ○ *had plumbed the depths of despair* **3.** **FIND THE DEPTH OR VERTICAL ALIGNMENT OF** to find the depth of water or a vertical alignment with a plumb **4.** **MAKE VERTICAL** to make sth properly vertical **5.** **TO INSTALL PLUMBING** to equip with plumbing [13thC. Via Old French *plomb* 'lead weight' from Latin *plumbum* 'lead' (source of English *plumber* and *aplomb*).]

plumb in *vt.* to attach a device such as a washing machine to a system of inlet and drainage pipes

plumbago /plum báygō/ (*plural* **-gos**) *n.* **1.** PLANTS **FLOWERING PLANT** an evergreen Mediterranean or tropical plant of the leadwort family that has clusters of blue, white, or red flowers. Genus: *Plumbago.* **2.** MINERALS = **graphite** [Early 17thC. From Latin, 'lead ore, plumbago', from *plumbum* 'lead', translation of Greek *molubdaina* 'lead ore', hence 'flowering plant', from the flower's colour.]

plumb bob *n.* the weight, usually a conical metal one, at the end of a plumb line

plumbeous /plúmbi əss/ *adj.* made of, concerning, or like lead [Late 16thC. Formed from Latin *plumbeus* 'of lead', from *plumbum* 'lead' (see PLUMB).]

plumber /plúmmər/ *n.* sb who installs and repairs pipes and fixtures, especially for water, drainage, or heating systems in a building [14thC. Via Old French *plommier* 'lead worker' from, ultimately, Latin *plumbum* 'lead' (see PLUMB). The modern meaning developed because water pipes were originally made of lead.]

plumber's snake *n.* = **snake** *n.* 3

plumbic /plúmbik/ *adj.* CHEM containing or relating to lead, especially in a valence state of four [Late 18thC. Formed from Latin *plumbum* 'lead' (see PLUMB).]

plumbiferous /plum bíffərəss/ *adj.* containing or yielding lead [Late 18thC. Coined from Latin *plumbum* 'lead' (see PLUMB) + -FEROUS.]

plumbing /plúmming/ *n.* **1.** CONSTR **PLUMBER'S WORK** the work that a plumber does **2.** CONSTR **PIPES AND FIXTURES** the pipes and fixtures that carry or use water or gas in a building **3.** **USE OF A PLUMB LINE** the use of a plumb line to test depth or show a vertical alignment

plumbism /plúmbizəm/ *n.* long-term lead poisoning (*technical*) [Late 19thC. Formed from Latin *plumbum* 'lead' (see PLUMB).]

plumb line *n.* a line with a weight attached, used to find the depth of water or to verify a true vertical alignment

plumbous /plúmbəss/ *adj.* CHEM containing or relating to lead, especially in a valence state of two [Mid-19thC. Formed from Latin *plumbum* 'lead' (see PLUMB).]

plumb rule *n.* a plumb line attached to a board, used to check whether sth is truly vertical

plume /ploom/ *n.* **1.** **FEATHER** a feather, especially a large or ornamental one **2.** **FEATHERS USED AS A CREST** a feather or bunch of feathers used as a decoration, especially on a hat or helmet **3.** **COLUMN OF STH** a rising column of sth, e.g. smoke, dust, or water **4.** BIOL **PART RESEMBLING A FEATHER** any plant part or formation that looks like a feather, e.g. the part of some seeds that allows them to be blown about by the wind **5.** **TOKEN OF HONOUR** a prize, awarded decoration, or token of honour ■ *v.* (**plumes, pluming, plumed**) **1.** *vt.* BIRDS **PREEN FEATHERS** to preen, smooth, or clean the feathers **2.** *vr.* **BE PROUD OF STH** to take pride in or congratulate yourself on sth **3.** *vt.* **DECORATE WITH FEATHERS** to decorate sth with feathers [14thC. Via Old French from Latin *pluma* 'down, feather'. Ultimately from an Indo-European base denoting 'fleece, feather', which is also the ancestor of English *fleece*.] —**plumed** *adj.*

plumelet /plóomlət/ *n.* a little plume or tuft

plummet /plúmmit/ *vi.* (**-mets, -meting, -meted**) **1.** **DROP DOWNWARDS** to drop steeply and suddenly downwards ○ *temperatures have plummeted* **2.** FIN **SUDDENLY FALL IN VALUE** to take a sudden unexpected drop in value or price **3.** **SUDDENLY BECOME PESSIMISTIC** to decline or drop suddenly, particularly from a state of optimism to one of pessimism ■ *n.* **1.** **SUDDEN DECLINE** a sudden sharp fall in value or amount **2.** CONSTR = **plumb bob** [14thC. Via Old French *plomet* 'small lead ball' from, ultimately, Latin *plumbum* 'lead' (see PLUMB).]

plummy /plúmmi/ (**-mier, -miest**) *adj.* **1.** **LIKE PLUMS** resembling, full of, or tasting like plums **2.** **RICH AND RESONANT** with a voice or tone that is rich, resonant, and mellow, and is thought to be typical of the British upper classes **3.** **DESIRABLE** highly desirable or of superior quality (*informal*)

plumose /plóomōss/ *adj.* = **plumate** [Mid-18thC. From Latin *plumosus*, from *pluma* 'feather' (see PLUME).] —**plumosely** *adv.* —**plumosity** /ploo móssəti/ *n.*

plump[1] /plump/ *adj.* **1.** **SLIGHTLY OVERWEIGHT** rounded and somewhat overweight (*sometimes considered offensive*) **2.** **WELL-FLESHED** having a pleasing amount of flesh ○ *a plump chicken* **3.** **FILLED WITH STH** rounded and filled with sth ○ *a plump cushion* ■ *vti.* (**plumps, plumping, plumped**) **FATTEN OR ROUND** to become or make sth fatter, rounder, or softer ○ *plump up the cushions* [15thC. From Middle Dutch or Middle Low German *plomp* 'blunt, thick'.] —**plumply** *adv.* —**plumpness** *n.*

plump[2] /plump/ *vti.* (**plumps, plumping, plumped**) **DROP ABRUPTLY OR HEAVILY** to fall or come down heavily or suddenly, or to cause sb or sth to do so ○ *plumped down into an armchair* ■ *n.* **1.** **ABRUPT FALL OR ITS SOUND** a heavy or abrupt fall, or its sound **2.** *Scotland* a sudden rainstorm (*nonstandard*) ○ *a thunder plump* ■ *adv.* **1.** **HEAVILY** in a sudden or heavy way **2.** **DIRECTLY** directly or in a direct line **3.** **BLUNTLY** in a blunt and direct way ■ *adj.* **DIRECT** blunt, direct, and forceful [13thC. Origin uncertain: probably from Dutch *plompen* or Low German *plumpen* 'to fall into water', an imitation of the sound.]

plumper /plúmpər/ *n.* a pad worn by an actor between the teeth and the inside of the cheeks to make the face seem fatter

plum pudding *n.* a rich steamed pudding made from flour, suet, dried fruit, and spices that is often flavoured with brandy or rum [*Plum* from the use of PLUM to mean 'raisin']

plum tomato *n.* an elongated firm-textured tomato that is often used in cooking and is the usual variety used for tinned tomatoes [*Plum* from its shape]

plumule /plóo myool/ *n.* **1.** BOT **RUDIMENTARY SHOOT** the rudimentary primary shoot of a plant embryo **2.** BIRDS **YOUNG BIRD'S DOWN FEATHER** one of a young bird's soft down feathers [Early 18thC. From Latin *plumula* 'small feather', from *pluma* 'feather' (see PLUME).]

plumy /plóomi/ (**-ier, -iest**) *adj.* **1.** **LIKE FEATHERS** like a feather or plume **2.** **COVERED WITH PLUMES** made of, covered with, or decorated with feathers or plumes

plunder /plúndər/ *v.* (**-ders, -dering, -dered**) **1.** *vti.* **ROB A PLACE OR STEAL GOODS** to rob a place or the people living there or steal goods using violence and often causing damage, especially in wartime or during civil unrest ○ *gangs of looters plundering the electrical stores* **2.** *vt.* **ROB OR STEAL BY FRAUD** to rob a place or steal goods or money by fraudulent means ○ *a military government that had steadily plundered the country's wealth* **3.** *vt.* **GET BY SUPERIOR STRENGTH** to gain or acquire by superior strength or skill ○ *They plundered five goals in a one-sided game.* ■ *n.* **1.** **STOLEN GOODS** sth stolen by force, especially during wartime or civil unrest **2.** **ROBBERY** the theft of goods by force or fraud [Mid-17thC. Via German *plündern* or Low German *plünderen* from, ultimately, Middle Low German *plunder* 'household goods', of unknown origin.] —**plunderable** *adj.* —**plunderer** *n.* —**plunderous** *adj.*

plunderage /plúndərij/ *n.* **1.** **EMBEZZLEMENT ABOARD SHIP** the embezzlement of goods aboard a ship **2.** **STOLEN GOODS ABOARD SHIP** goods embezzled aboard a ship

plunge /plunj/ *v.* (**plunges, plunging, plunged**) **1.** *vti.* **MOVE OR BE THROWN SUDDENLY** to move, rush, dive, or be thrown suddenly downwards or forwards ○ *plunged into the undergrowth and disappeared* **2.** *vt.* **PUT SUDDENLY IN AN UNPLEASANT CONDITION** to bring or force sb or sth suddenly into an unpleasant or undesirable situation **3.** *vt.* **THRUST QUICKLY OR FIRMLY** to put or push sth firmly into sth such as a liquid or container ○ *Drain the beans and plunge them into cold water.* **4.** *vi.* **BECOME INVOLVED ENTHUSIASTICALLY** to become involved in sth with great enthusiasm ○ *She plunged into student life.* **5.** **EMBARK ON RECKLESSLY** to begin a course of action suddenly and in a reckless or impetuous way ○ *warned against plunging into full monetary union* **6.** *vi.* **GO DOWN SUDDENLY** to go or drop downwards suddenly or steeply **7.** *vi.* **DROP SUDDENLY IN VALUE** to drop suddenly and unexpectedly in value or price ○ *Prices plunged.* **8.** *vi.* GAMBLING **GAMBLE RECKLESSLY** to gamble, speculate, or take risks in a reckless way (*informal*) ■ *n.* **1.** **LEAP INTO WATER** a dive or leap into water ○ *a headlong plunge into the sea* **2.** **SUDDEN SHARP FALL** a sudden sharp fall in value or amount ○ *a 38% plunge in PC sales* **3.** **SUDDEN RUSH** a sudden or violent rush ○ *The dog made a plunge for the open door.* **4.** **GAMBLE** a reckless gamble or speculation (*informal*) [14thC. Via Old French *plongier* from assumed Vulgar Latin *plumbicare* 'to heave a sounding lead', from Latin *plumbum* 'lead' (see PLUMB).] ◇ **take the plunge 1.** to commit suddenly to doing sth new, difficult, or irrevocable **2.** to get married or decide to get married (*informal humorous*)

plunge bath (*plural* **plunge baths**) *n.* a bath large enough for the whole body to be immersed

plunge pool *n.* a small deep swimming pool used for cooling the body

plunger /plúnjər/ *n.* **1.** CONSTR **TOOL FOR CLEARING DRAINS** a tool for clearing clogged drains consisting of a rubber suction cup attached to a long handle **2.** MECH ENG **THRUSTING MACHINE PART** a part of a machine that thrusts or drops downwards, e.g. a piston **3.** US **GAMBLER** sb who gambles a lot (*informal*) [Early

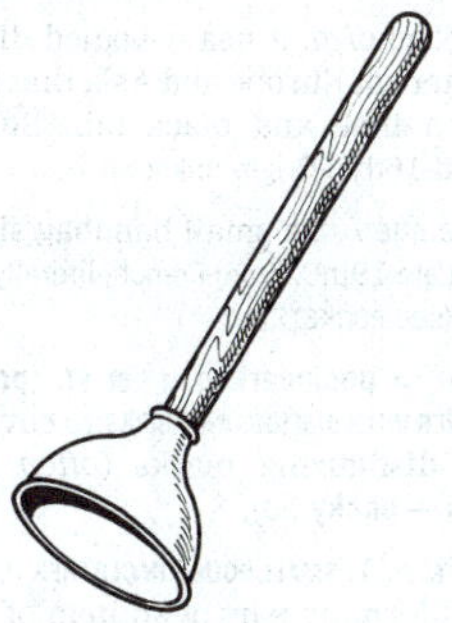

Plunger

17thC. The earliest meaning was 'sb who dives into water'.]

plunging /plúnjing/ *adj.* in a direction or at an angle that plunges downwards

plunk /plungk/ *vti.* **(plunks, plunking, plunked) 1.** MUSIC **TWANG STRINGS** to twang the strings of a stringed instrument, especially in an inexpert or unexpressive way **2. DROP DOWN** to fall or cause sth to drop heavily or suddenly ■ *n.* **1. TWANGING SOUND** a twanging sound, e.g. of a string on a stringed instrument being plucked **2.** *US* **SUDDEN HEAVY FALL** the action or sound of a sudden heavy fall ○ *A stone hit the tin roof with a plunk.* **3. HARD BLOW** a hard blow (*informal*) ■ *adv.* **1.** *US* **WITH A PLUNK** with a plunking sound or action **2. EXACTLY** precisely or exactly (*informal*) ○ *plunk in the middle* [Early 19thC. An imitation of the sound.]

pluperfect /ploo púrfikt/ *adj., n.* GRAM = **past perfect** [15thC. From Latin *plus quam perfectum* 'more than perfect'.]

plural /plóorəl/ *adj.* **1.** GRAM **REFERRING TO MORE THAN ONE** having a grammatical form that refers to more than one person or thing **2. CONCERNING MORE THAN ONE** concerning, involving, or made up of more than one, or more than one kind of, person or thing ■ *n.* GRAM **1. PLURAL CATEGORY** the plural number category **2. PLURAL FORM OF A WORD** the plural form of a word ○ *What's the plural of mouse in the computer sense?* [14thC. Via Old French from Latin *pluralis*, from *plus* 'more'.] —**plurally** *adv.*

pluralism /plóorəlizəm/ *n.* **1. SOCIETY WITH DIFFERENT INTERNAL GROUPS** the existence of groups with different ethnic, religious, or political backgrounds within one society **2.** SOCIOL **SOCIAL POLICY AND THEORY** a policy or theory that minority groups within a society should maintain cultural differences but share overall political and economic power **3.** CHR **HOLDING OF MULTIPLE OFFICES** the holding of more than one office or position by an individual, especially in a church **4.** PHILOS **THEORY OF VARIED BEING OR SUBSTANCE** the philosophical theory that reality is made up of many kinds of being or substance **5. STATE OF BEING PLURAL** state or condition of being plural —**pluralist** *n.* —**pluralistic** /plóorə lístik/ *adj.* —**pluralistically** /-lístikli/ *adv.*

plurality /ploor rálləti/ (*plural* **-ties**) *n.* **1.** GRAM **CONDITION OF BEING PLURAL** the condition of being plural or numerous **2. GREAT NUMBER OR PART OF STH** a great number or part of sth, particularly when this represents more than half of the whole **3.** *US, Can* POL **MARGIN GAINED BY AN ELECTION CANDIDATE** the number of votes an election winner gets, or the number exceeding the nearest rival, when no one has more than fifty percent of the total votes cast **4.** CHR = **pluralism** *n.* 3

pluralize /plóorə līz/ (**-izes, -izing, -ized**), **pluralise** (**-ises, -ising, -ised**) *v.* **1.** *vti.* **MAKE PLURAL** to make sth plural or to become plural **2.** *vi.* CHR **HOLD MULTIPLE OFFICES** to hold more than one office, especially ecclesiastical ones, at the same time —**pluralization** /plóorə lī záysh'n/ *n.* —**pluralizer** /plóorə līzər/ *n.*

plural marriage *n.* = **polygamy** *n.* 1

plural voting *n.* a system of voting that formerly permitted certain voters to vote more than once in an election, or to vote in different constituencies

plus /pluss/ *prep.* **1. USED FOR ADDING** used to show that one number or amount is added to another ○ *The flight cost £180, plus £20 airport tax.* **2. AND ALSO** together with (*informal*) ○ *Exports have been affected by transport problems plus the effect of a strong pound.* ■ *adj.* **1.** ARITH **INVOLVING ADDITION** showing or involving addition **2.** MATH **ON POSITIVE SIDE** with a figure or value on the positive side of a scale or axis (*often written as '+'*) **3.** ELEC ENG **ON THE ELECTRICAL POSITIVE SIDE** on or involving the positive side of an electrical circuit **4. ADVANTAGEOUS** favourable, desirable, or advantageous ○ *On the plus side, there's a big garden.* ○ *one of its plus points* **5. SOMEWHAT MORE THAN STATED GRADE** somewhat higher than a stated grade for academic work (*often written as '+'*) **6.** FUNGI **REPRODUCING ONLY WITH OPPOSITE STRAIN** reproducing as an alga or fungus only with an opposite strain ■ *n.* (*plural* **pluses** *or* **plusses**) **1.** MATH = **plus sign 2. POSITIVE QUANTITY** a positive quantity **3. ADVANTAGEOUS FACTOR** sth beneficial or advantageous (*informal*) ○ *Having her in the team is a real plus.* **4. SURPLUS** a surplus ■ *conj.* **AND ALSO** and also or furthermore (*informal*) ○ *I'm too busy to come, plus I'm short of cash.* [Mid-16thC. From Latin *plus* 'more'.]

plus fours *npl.* baggy trousers gathered and fastened just below the knee, worn mainly for sports or hunting ○ *golfers in their plus fours* [Because they were four inches longer in the leg than standard knickerbockers]

plush /plush/ *n.* TEXTILES **SOFT FABRIC** a rich smooth fabric with a long soft nap ■ *adj.* **plush, plushy LUXURIOUS** luxurious, expensive, or lavish (*informal*) [Late 16thC. Via French *pluche* from, ultimately, assumed Vulgar Latin *piluccare* 'to pluck' (see PLUCK); because loops of the woven fabric must be cut ('plucked') in making plush.]

plus sign *n.* the symbol '+', used to show addition or a positive quantity

plus-size *adj.* larger than average ○ *our new range of plus-size fashions*

Plutarch /ploo taark/ (46–120) Greek historian, biographer, and philosopher. His *Parallel Lives* (1st century) was used by Shakespeare as a source for his history plays.

Pluto /plóotō/ *n.* **1. ROMAN GOD OF THE UNDERWORLD** in Roman mythology, the god of the underworld and husband of Proserpine. He was the god of the dead and also of riches, since precious metals and crops were believed to come from his underground realm. Greek equivalent **Hades 2.** ASTRON **SMALLEST, MOST DISTANT PLANET** the planet in the solar system that is the smallest in diameter and is, on average, the furthest away from the Sun. It was discovered in 1930, has one moon (**Charon**), and an equatorial radius 0.18 times that of the Earth. [Via Latin from Greek *Ploutōn*, from *ploutos* 'wealth'] —**Plutonian** /ploo tṓni ən/ *adj.*

plutocracy /ploo tókrəssi/ (*plural* **-cies**) *n.* **1. RULE BY THE WEALTHY** the rule of a society by its wealthiest people **2. SOCIETY RULED BY THE WEALTHY** a society that is ruled by its wealthiest members **3. WEALTHY RULING CLASS** any wealthy social class that controls or greatly influences the government of a society [Mid-17thC. From Greek *ploutokratia*, from *ploutos* 'wealth'.] —**plutocrat** /plóotə krat/ *adv.* —**plutocratic** /-kráttik/ *adj.* —**plutocratically** *adv.*

pluton /plóo ton/ *n.* a mass of intrusive igneous rock that solidified underground by the crystallization of magma [Mid-20thC. From German, back-formation from *plutonisch* 'plutonic', from Latin *Pluto* (see PLUTO).] —**plutonic** /ploo tónnik/ *adj.*

plutonium /ploo tṓni əm/ *n.* a highly toxic silvery radioactive metallic chemical element, found in small amounts in uranium ores. The isotope plutonium-239 is used to produce atomic energy and in nuclear weapons. Symbol **Pu** [Mid-20thC. Named after the planet PLUTO, because it follows uranium and neptunium in the periodic table.]

pluvial /plóovi əl/ *adj.* **1. RELATING TO RAIN** concerning, involving, or caused by rain **2. RAINY** involving a lot of rain ■ *n.* **WET PERIOD** a period of increased rainfall [Mid-17thC. From Latin *pluvialis*, from *pluvia* 'rain', from *pluere* 'to rain' (source of English *plover*).]

pluviometer /plóovi ómmitər/ *n.* = **rain gauge** [Late 18thC. Coined from Latin *pluvia* 'rain' (see PLUVIAL) + -METER.] —**pluviometric** /plóovi ō méttrik/ *adj.* —**pluviometrically** /-méttrikli/ *adv.* —**pluviometry** /plóovi ómmətri/ *n.*

Pluviôse /plóovi ōss/ *n.* the fifth month of the year in the French revolutionary calendar, corresponding to 21 January to 19 February in the Gregorian calendar. This was typically a rainy period in France. [Late 18thC. From French, literally 'rainy'.]

pluvious /plóovi əss/, **pluviose** /plóovi ōss/ *adj.* concerning, involving, or typical of rain, especially heavy rainfall [15thC. Via Old French from Latin *pluviosus*, from *pluvia* 'rain' (see PLUVIAL).]

ply[1] /plī/ (**plies, plying, plied**) *v.* **1.** *vti.* **WORK HARD AT STH** to work at a trade or occupation, especially with diligence **2.** *vt.* **USE STH DILIGENTLY** to use sth such as a tool or weapon in a diligent or skilful way ○ *the dexterity with which she plied her needle* **3.** *vt.* COMM **OFFER STH FOR SALE** to offer goods or services for sale, especially regularly or as an occupation **4.** *vt.* **SUPPLY SB WITH STH** to keep supplying sb with sth, especially in an insistent way ○ *kept plying us with offers of food* **5.** *vt.* **SUBJECT TO URGENTLY AND INSISTENTLY** to keep subjecting sb to sth in an urgent and insistent way ○ *we were plied with questions* **6.** *vti.* **TRAVEL A ROUTE REGULARLY** to travel a route regularly, especially on water **7.** *vi.* SAILING **SAIL AGAINST THE WIND** to sail a boat on a zigzag course against the wind [14thC. Shortening of APPLY.]

ply[2] /plī/ *n.* (*plural* **plies**) (*often used in combination*) **1. TWISTED STRAND** a twisted single strand, especially in a yarn or rope **2. THIN LAYER OF STH** a layer, sheet, or thickness of sth such as wood or a tyre ■ *vti.* (**plies, plying, plied**) **TWIST TOGETHER** to twist or fold things together [14thC. From Old French *pli*, from *plier* 'to fold', from Latin *plicare*. Ultimately, from an Indo-European word that is also the ancestor of English *plait*.]

Plymouth /plímməth/ **1.** town and seaport in southwestern England, in Devon. Population: 260,000 (1996). **2.** town in southeastern Massachusetts, on Plymouth Bay, south of Duxbury. It was settled by the Pilgrims in 1620. Population: 48,329 (1996).

Plymouth Brethren *n.* a Protestant group founded in the United Kingdom in the late 1820s that has no organized ministry or formal creed, and accepts the Bible as its sole guide [Named after the town of PLYMOUTH, where it was founded]

Plymouth Rock *n.* a US breed of domestic hen with white or grey barred plumage, raised for its eggs and meat

plywood /plī wŏŏd/ *n.* a type of board made by gluing and compressing thin layers of wood together with the grain of each layer at right angles to the layer next to it [Early 20thC. *Ply* from PLY[2].]

Plzeň /pəl zénya/ capital city of the Západoceky Region in the western part of the Czech Republic. Population: 171,908 (1994).

pm, **PM, P.M.** *abbr.* **1.** between twelve noon and midnight. Abbr of **post meridiem 2.** phase modulation **3.** premium **4.** postmortem

Pm *symbol.* promethium

PM *abbr.* **1.** Prime Minister **2.** Postmaster **3.** Provost Marshal **4.** Past Master (*of a fraternity*) **5. PM, p.m., P.M.** postmortem

PMG *abbr.* **1.** Postmaster General **2.** Provost Marshal General **3.** Paymaster General

PMS *abbr.* premenstrual syndrome

PMT *abbr.* premenstrual tension

PN, **P/N, pn** *abbr.* promissory note

PNdB *abbr.* perceived noise decibel

pneum- *prefix.* = **pneumo-** (*used before vowels*)

pneuma /nyóomə/ *n.* in Stoicism, the vital spirit or soul [Late 19thC. From Greek, literally 'breath, spirit', from *pnein* 'to breathe'. Ultimately, from an Indo-European word that is also the ancestor of English *sneeze* and *snort*.]

pneumatic /nyoo máttik/ *adj.* **1. USING COMPRESSED AIR** operated by compressed air in a tool or machine **2. FILLED WITH AIR** filled with air, especially compressed air **3.** PHYS **INVOLVING COMPRESSED GASES** relating to, involving, operated by, or typical of the pressure of compressed gases, especially air pressure or compressed air **4. OF GASES OR WIND** concerning, involving, or typical of air, gases, or wind **5.** RELIG **OF THE SOUL** concerning or involving the soul or spirit **6.** BIRDS **WITH AIR-FILLED CAVITIES IN THE BONES** used to describe birds that have air-filled cavities in the bones **7. FULL-BREASTED** having large breasts (*informal; offensive in some contexts*) [Mid-17thC. Via French and Latin from

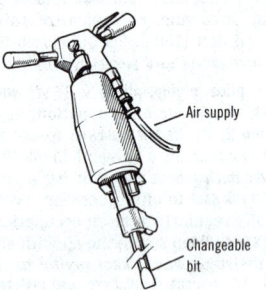

Pneumatic drill

Greek *pneumatikos*, from *pneuma* (see PNEUMA).] —**pneumatically** *adv.*

pneumatic drill *n.* a heavy powerful drill operated by compressed air and used especially for breaking up the surface of roads or pavements. ◊ **jackhammer**

pneumatics /nyoo máttiks/ *n.* PHYS the branch of physics dealing with the mechanical properties of air and other gases (*takes a singular verb*)

pneumatic tube *n.* a tube through which letters and packets are propelled by compressed air

pneumato- *prefix.* **1.** air, gas, vapour ○ *pneumatolysis* **2.** respiration, breathing ○ *pneumatometer* **3.** spirits, spiritual ○ *pneumatology* [Formed from Greek *pneumat-*, the stem of *pneuma* (see PNEUMA)]

pneumatology /nyoomə tólləji/ *n.* **1.** THEOLOGY OF THE HOLY SPIRIT the branch of Christian theology that deals with the Holy Spirit **2.** STUDY OF SPIRITS the study of spirits or spiritual beings —**pneumatological** /nyoomətə lójjik'l/ *adj.* —**pneumatologist** /nyoomə tólləjist/ *n.*

pneumatolysis /nyoomə tólləssiss/ *n.* the alteration caused in rocks by hot gases escaping from solidifying magma —**pneumatolytic** /nyoo máttō líttik/ *adj.*

pneumatophore /nyoo máttō fawr, nyoóməttə fawr/ *n.* **1.** BOT SPECIALIZED PLANT BRANCH a type of branch in swamp plants such as the mangrove or bald cypress that grows upwards from roots and carries out respiration **2.** BIOL SAC ACTING AS A FLOAT a gas-filled sac that acts as a float in coelenterates such as the Portuguese man-of-war

pneumo- *prefix.* **1.** air, gas ○ *pneumoencephalogram* **2.** lung, pulmonary ○ *pneumocystis* **3.** pneumonia ○ *pneumobacillus* **4.** respiration ○ *pneumograph* [Formed from Greek *pneuma* 'air, breath' (see PNEUMA)]

pneumobacillus /nyoomōbə silləss/ (*plural* **-li** /-sīllee/) *n.* BIOL a gram-negative bacterium that occurs in the respiratory tract and is one cause of pneumonia. Latin name: *Klebsiella pneumoniae.*

pneumococcus /nyoomō kókəss/ (*plural* **-ci** /-kók sī/) *n.* BIOL a gram-positive bacterium that occurs in the respiratory tract and is one cause of pneumonia. Latin name: *Streptococcus pneumoniae.* —**pneumococcal** *adj.*

pneumoconiosis /nyoomō kōni óssiss/, **pneumonoconiosis** /nyoomənō kōni óssiss/ *n.* a disease of the lungs, such as silicosis, caused by inhaling mineral or metallic dust over a long period [Late 19thC. Formed from PNEUMO- + Greek *konis* 'dust'.]

pneumocystis /nyoomō sístiss/ *n.* a form of pneumonia that mainly affects people with weakened immune systems. It is caused by the microorganism *Pneumocystis carinii.*

pneumonectomy /nyoomə néktəmi/ (*plural* **-mies**) *n.* the surgical removal of a lung [Late 19thC. Coined from Greek *pneumōn* 'lung' (see PNEUMONIA) +-ECTOMY.]

pneumonia /nyoo mōni ə/ *n.* an inflammation of one or both lungs, usually caused by infection from a bacterium or virus or, less commonly, by a chemical or physical irritant [Early 17thC. Via modern Latin from, ultimately, Greek *pneumōn* 'lung', alteration (influenced by *pneuma* 'breath') of *pleumōn*.]

pneumonic /nyoo mónnik/ *adj.* **1.** OF THE LUNGS relating to or affecting the lungs **2.** OF PNEUMONIA relating to, involving, or affected by pneumonia [Late 17thC.

Via French from, ultimately, Greek *pneumōn* 'lung' (see PNEUMONIA).]

pneumonitis /nyoomə nítiss/ *n.* any inflammation of the air sacs in the lungs, usually caused by a virus [Early 19thC. Via modern Latin from Greek *pneumōn* 'lung' (see PNEUMONIA).]

pneumonoconiosis *n.* = pneumoconiosis [Mid-19thC. Formed from Greek *pneumōn* 'lung' + *konis* 'dust'.]

pneumothorax /nyoomō tháwr aks/ *n.* the presence of air or gas in a pleural cavity surrounding the lungs, causing pain and difficulty in breathing. Pneumothorax can occur spontaneously because of accidental rupture or perforation of the pleura, and in the past it was also a deliberate medical procedure in the treatment of tuberculosis.

PNG *abbr.* Papua New Guinea

po /pō/ (*plural* **pos**) *n.* a chamber pot (*informal*) [Late 19thC. Shortening of French *pot de chambre* 'chamber pot'.]

Po[1] *symbol.* polonium

Po[2] /pō/ the longest river in Italy. It rises in the Alps near Italy's northwestern border and flows into the Adriatic Sea. Length: 670 km/417 mi.

PO *abbr.* **1.** Post Office **2.** PO, p.o. postal order **3.** Pilot Officer **4.** Petty Officer

p.o. *abbr.* per os (*used on prescriptions*)

POA *abbr.* Prison Officers' Association

poach[1] /pōch/ (**poaches, poaching, poached**) *v.* **1.** *vti.* CATCH GAME ILLEGALLY to catch wild animals or fish illegally on public land or while trespassing on private land **2.** *vti.* ENCROACH ON STH to encroach on other people's rights, territory, or sphere of operation in order to appropriate or remove sb or sth ○ *A rival company was poaching our customers.* **3.** *vti.* RACKET GAMES PLAY SB ELSE'S SHOT to play a shot that properly should be handled by a partner in badminton, tennis, squash, or handball **4.** *vti.* SOCCER SCORE SNEAK GOAL to score a goal at close range by lingering inside the opposing penalty area while unobserved by defenders ○ *Their striker is an expert at poaching.* **5.** *vti.* MAKE GROUND MUDDY to become muddy or make ground muddy by trampling it **6.** *vi.* SINK INTO MUD to sink into soft earth or mud while walking across it [Early 17thC. From Old French *pocher* 'to trample, trespass', origin uncertain: probably of Germanic origin.] —**poachable** *adj.*

poach[2] /pōch/ (**poaches, poaching, poached**) *vt.* to cook sth by simmering it in or over water or another liquid [15thC. From Old French *pochier*, originally 'to enclose in a bag', from *poche* 'bag' (see POCKET).]

poacher[1] /pōchər/ *n.* **1.** ILLEGAL HUNTER sb who hunts or fishes illegally, usually while trespassing on other people's property **2.** SOCCER OPPORTUNISTIC PLAYER a player in football who scores a goal while lingering around the opposition's penalty area, unobserved by defenders

poacher[2] /pōchər/ *n.* a pan for poaching eggs that has a tightly fitting lid and small metal cups

POB *abbr.* Post Office Box

PO Box *abbr.* post office box

AKG London

Pocahontas: Posthumous portrait (1666)

Pocahontas /pókə hóntəss/ (1595?–1617?) Native American princess. According to legend she saved the life of colonist John Smith (1608). Born **Matoaka**

pochard /póchərd/ *n.* a heavy-bodied diving duck of coastal waters of Europe and Asia that has a reddish head and a blue and black bill. Subfamily: Aythyini. [Mid-16thC. Origin unknown.]

pochette /po shét/ *n.* a small handbag shaped like an envelope [Late 19thC. From French, literally 'small pouch', from *poche* (see POCKET).]

pock /pok/ *n.* **1** ■ *vt.* (**pocks, pocking, pocked**) COVER WITH DISFIGURING MARKS to cover with pockmarks or disfiguring marks (*often passive*) [Old English *poc*] —**pocky** *adj.*

pocket /pókit/ *n.* **1.** SMALL POUCH IN CLOTHES a shaped piece of material forming part of an item of clothing and used to hold small items, e.g. inside trousers or on the outside of a shirt **2.** SMALL FITTED POUCH a small fitted pouch, e.g. a pouch-shaped compartment on the inside of a bag ○ *The suitcase has several inside pockets.* **3.** SMALL POUCH any small pouch, bag, or purse **4.** PERSONAL MONEY sb's personal financial resources ○ *a holiday paid for out of his own pocket* **5.** SMALL DIFFERENTIATED AREA a small area differentiated from neighbouring areas by some feature ○ *pockets of wealth* **6.** CAVITY any type of cavity or opening **7.** GEOL ORE IN A CAVITY the quantity of petroleum, natural gas, or mineral found in an underground cavity, or the cavity that contains this substance **8.** SPORTS POSITION IN A RACE a position in a race in which a competitor is blocked by others **9.** CUE GAMES POUCH ON A PLAYING TABLE any of the pouches or nets at the corners and sides of a billiard, snooker, or pool table ○ *He sank the red in the side pocket.* **10.** ZOOL SAC ON AN ANIMAL any pouch-shaped sac on an animal's body **11.** *Aus* FOOTBALL PLAYER IN SIDE POSITION in Australian Rules football, a player in one of two side positions at the ends of the ground **12.** AIR AIR POCKET an air pocket ■ *vt.* (**-ets, -eting, -eted**) **1.** PUT IN A POCKET to put sth into a pocket ○ *She pocketed the change.* **2.** TAKE STH DISHONESTLY to appropriate sth, often dishonestly ○ *They buy tickets cheaply, sell them for high prices, and pocket the difference.* **3.** CUE GAMES HIT A BALL INTO A POCKET to hit a ball into one of the pockets on a billiard, snooker, or pool table ○ *pocket the black* **4.** PUT UP WITH STH to tolerate sth unpleasant, especially an insult, without protesting or retaliating **5.** SUPPRESS FEELINGS to hide or suppress feelings **6.** ENCLOSE OR SURROUND to enclose or hem in sb or sth **7.** *US* POL RETAIN A PIECE OF LEGISLATION to retain a legislative bill without signing it, especially as a US president, in order to stop it becoming approved by Congress ■ *adj.* **1.** SMALL ENOUGH TO CARRY IN THE POCKET designed for carrying in a pocket ○ *a pocket torch* **2.** SMALL small, especially smaller than sth larger of the same type ○ *a pocket trumpet* **3.** CONTAINED isolated and contained in small areas [15thC. From Anglo-Norman *pokete*, literally 'small bag', from *poke* 'bag'.] —**pocketability** /pókitə billəti/ *n.* —**pocketable** /pókitəb'l/ *adj.* ◊ **have deep pockets** to have large financial resources ○ *a price-cutting war which will be won by whoever has the deepest pockets* ◊ **in pocket** making a profit from sth ◊ **in sb's pocket 1.** fully under sb's control **2.** almost certain to be won by sb ○ *We thought she had the race in her pocket.* ◊ **line your pocket(s)** to profit at the expense of others ◊ **out of pocket** having lost money on sth

pocket battleship *n.* a small but powerful and heavily armed battleship, especially one built by Germany in the 1930s to conform to limitations that were placed by treaty on size and armament

pocketbook /pókit bŏok/ *n.* **1.** *US, Can* SMALL CASE CARRIED IN THE POCKET a small case or folder for money and documents, suitable for carrying in a pocket **2.** *US, Can* HANDBAG a purse or handbag **3.** *US, Can* MONEY sb's financial resources **4.** SMALL BOOK a book or notebook small enough to be carried in a pocket

pocket borough *n.* POL a political constituency in Britain before the Reform Act of 1832, whose representative in Parliament was determined by one landowner or landowning family [*Pocket* from the idea that the landowner had the borough 'in his pocket']

pocket calculator *n.* a calculator small enough to be carried in a pocket

pocketful /pókitfŏol/ *n.* **1.** AMOUNT IN A POCKET the amount of sth that would fit in a pocket **2.** A LARGE AMOUNT a large amount of sth, especially money (*informal*)

pocket gopher *n.* = gopher

pocketknife /pókit nīf/ (*plural* **-knives** /-nīvz/) *n.* = penknife

pocket money *n.* **1. MONEY GIVEN TO CHILD BY PARENTS** a small sum of money paid regularly by parents to a child so that the child can make his or her own purchases. US term **allowance 2. SMALL AMOUNT OF MONEY** a small amount of personal money, sufficient only for making minor purchases or to cover incidental expenses

pocket mouse *n.* a small nocturnal rodent of the deserts of the western United States and Mexico, with long hind legs, a long tail, and fur-lined cheek pouches for carrying food. Genus: *Perognathus*.

pocket-sized, **pocket-size** *adj.* **1. SMALL ENOUGH FOR THE POCKET** small enough or almost small enough to be carried in a pocket **2. SMALL** very small compared to things of the same type

pocket veto *n.* *US* in the United States, a US presidential failure to return a bill passed by Congress during its last days in session, to prevent its being enacted [From the notion of the executive's holding the bill in a coat pocket]

pockmark /pók maark/ *n.* (*often used in the plural*) **1. MED SCAR ON THE SKIN** a scar on the skin, especially one left by smallpox, chickenpox, or acne **2. SMALL HOLLOW MARK** a small hollow mark disfiguring a surface ■ *vt.* (**-marks**, **-marking**, **-marked**) **1. MED COVER THE SKIN WITH POCKMARKS** to disfigure the skin with pockmarks **2. MAKE POCKMARKS IN STH** to make many small indentations or marks in the surface of sth

poco /pókō/ *adv.* a little or slightly (*used in musical directions*) [Early 18thC. From Italian, 'little'.]

poco a poco *adv.* little by little (*used in musical directions*) [From Italian, 'little by little']

pococurante /pókō kyoo ránti/ *adj.* **APATHETIC** uninterested, indifferent, or nonchalantly detached (*literary*) ■ *n.* **APATHETIC PERSON** sb who does not care about sth or remains unworried and indifferent (*literary*) [Mid-18thC. From Italian, from *poco* 'little' + *curare* 'to care'.] —**pococurateism** /-ránti izəm/ *n.* —**pococurantism** /-rántizəm/ *n.*

Pocono Mountains /pókə no mówntinz/ range of forested mountains in northeastern Pennsylvania, reaching about 640 m/2,100 ft

pod[1] /pod/ *n.* **1. BOT SEED CASE** the long narrow outer case holding the seeds of a plant such as the pea, bean, or vanilla **2. SPACE TECH DETACHABLE COMPARTMENT OF A SPACECRAFT** a specialized detachable compartment on a spacecraft, usually for carrying personnel or instruments **3. AEROSP, NAVY STREAMLINED HOUSING FOR EQUIPMENT** a streamlined housing attached to the wing or fuselage of an aircraft, or to the hull of a submarine, to carry fuel, an engine, weaponry, or other equipment **4. ZOOL PROTECTIVE EGG CASE** a protective case surrounding the eggs of some fishes and insects, e.g. the grasshopper ■ *v.* (**pods**, **podding**, **podded**) **1.** *vt.* **TAKE PEAS FROM POD** to strip peas out of their pod so that they can be eaten or cooked **2.** *vi.* **PRODUCE PODS** to produce fruit in the form of pods [Late 17thC. Origin unknown.]

pod[2] /pod/ *n.* **ZOOL** a small group of marine animals, especially seals, whales, or dolphins [Mid-19thC. Origin unknown.]

pod[3] /pod/ *n.* **1. SOCKET FOR A BORING-TOOL BIT** a socket holding the bit in a boring tool **2. CHANNEL IN THE BARREL OF A BORING TOOL** a lengthwise channel in the barrel of a boring tool [Late 16thC. Origin unknown.]

PO'd /pee ṓd/, **p.o.'d** *adj.* quite annoyed (*slang*) [Shortening of pissed off]

POD *abbr.* pay on delivery

-pod *suffix.* foot, part like a foot ○ *stomatopod* [From Greek *-pod*, the stem of *pous*. Ultimately from the Indo-European word for 'foot', which is also the ancestor of English *foot*, *podium*, and *pedestrian*.] —**-podous** *suffix.*

podagra /po dágrə/ *n.* gout in the foot or the big toe [13thC. Via Latin from Greek, literally 'foot-trap', from *pod-* (the stem of *pous* 'foot') + *agra* 'trap'.] —**podagral** *adj.* —**podagric** *adj.* —**podagrical** *adj.* —**podagrous** *adj.*

Steve Podborski

Edgar Allan Poe

Podborski /pod báwrski/, **Steve** (*b.* 1957) Canadian skier. He won seven World Cup events in downhill skiing between 1979 and 1982.

-pode *suffix.* = -pod

podesta /pō déstə/ *n.* HIST formerly, a chief magistrate or governor of an Italian town, especially during the Middle Ages and Renaissance [Mid-16thC. Via Italian from Latin *potestas* 'power', from *potis* 'powerful'. Ultimately from an Indo-European word that is also the ancestor of English *potent* and *despot*.]

podge /poj/, **pudge** /puj/ *n.* **1. EXCESS FAT** excess fat on a person (*sometimes considered offensive*) **2. SHORT TUBBY PERSON** a short and rather tubby person [Mid-19thC. Origin uncertain: probably a back-formation from PODGY.]

Podgorica /pód go reetsə/ capital city of Montenegro, Federal Republic of Yugoslavia, situated about 19 km/12 mi. north of Lake Shkoder. Population: 118,059 (1991).

podgy /pójji/ (**-gier**, **-giest**) *adj.* short and chubby (*sometimes considered offensive*) [Mid-19thC. Variant of PUDGY.] —**podgily** *adv.* —**podginess** *n.*

podia *plural of* **podium**

podiatry /po dī ətri/ *n.* *US* = chiropody [Early 20thC. Coined from Greek *pod-*, the stem of *pous* 'foot' + -IATRY.] —**podiatric** /pódi áttrik/ *adj.* —**podiatrist** /po dī ətrist/ *n.*

podium /pṓdi əm/ (*plural* **-ums** *or* **-a** /pódi ə/) *n.* **1. SMALL RAISED PLATFORM** a small raised platform that the conductor of an orchestra, a lecturer, or sb giving a speech can stand on **2.** *US* = lectern **3.** ARCHIT **FOUNDATION WALL** a low wall forming a foundation or base, e.g. for a colonnade **4.** ARCHIT **WALL AROUND AN AMPHITHEATRE'S ARENA** a low wall encircling the arena of an ancient amphitheatre [Mid-18thC. Via Latin from Greek *podion*, literally 'small foot', from *pous* 'foot'.]

-podium *suffix.* foot, part like a foot ○ *pseudopodium* [Via modern Latin from Greek *podion* (see PODIUM)]

podophyllin /póddə fíllin/, **podophyllin resin** *n.* a greenish or brownish bitter resin obtained from the root of the May apple, used medicinally to remove warts [Mid-19thC. Formed from modern Latin *Podophyllum*, genus name of the May apple, from the Greek stem *pod-* 'foot' + *phullon* 'leaf', so called because of the shape of its leaves.]

podsol *n.* = podzol

podsolization *n.* = podzolization

podzol /pód zol/, **podsol** /pód sol/ *n.* a basically infertile type of soil that forms in cool moist climates, usually under coniferous or mixed forests. The topsoil consists of leached clay under a layer of organic material. [Early 20thC. From Russian, from *pod-* 'under' + *zol* 'ash'.] —**podzolic** /pod zóllik/ *adj.*

podzolization /pód zo lī záysh'n/, **podzolisation, podsolization, podsolisation** *n.* the process whereby minerals are leached from the upper into the lower layers of a soil, leaving the topsoil acidic and infertile and forming a podzol —**podzolize** /pódzə līz/ *vti.*

Poe /pō/, **Edgar Allan** (1809–49) US writer and critic. His poems and short stories, including *The Pit and the Pendulum* (1842), deal with the mysterious and the macabre.

POE *abbr.* **1. MIL** port of embarkation **2.** port of entry

poem /pṓ im/ *n.* **1. POETRY PIECE WRITTEN IN VERSE** a complete and self-contained piece of writing in verse that is

set out in lines of a particular length and uses rhythm, imagery, and often rhyme to achieve its effect **2. WRITING WITH POETIC EFFECT** a piece of writing that is not in verse but that has the imaginative, rhythmic, or metaphorical qualities and the intensity usually associated with a poem **3. BEAUTIFUL OR DELIGHTFUL THING** sth particularly lovely, beautiful, or delightful [15thC. Via French *poème* from, ultimately, Greek *poiēma*, literally 'making', from *poiein* 'to make'.]

poenology /pee nólləji/ *n.* = penology

poesy /pṓ əzi/ *n.* poetry or poetic compositions in general, or a particular piece of poetry (*archaic or literary*) [14thC. Via French *poésie*, from, ultimately, Greek *poiēsis*, literally 'making' (see -POIESIS).]

poet /pṓ it/ *n.* **1. POETRY SB WHO WRITES POEMS** sb who writes poems, especially a regular and recognized writer of poems **2. SB IMAGINATIVE OR CREATIVE** sb who is very imaginative and creative or who possesses great skill and artistry and is able to produce beautiful things [13thC. Via French *poète* and Latin *poeta* from Greek *poiētēs* 'maker, author', from *poiein* 'to make'.]

poet. *abbr.* **1.** poetic **2.** poetical **3.** poetry

poetaster /pṓ i tástər/ *n.* sb who writes bad poetry [Late 16thC. From modern Latin, formed from Latin *poeta* (see POET).]

poetic /pō éttik/, **poetical** /-ik'l/ *adj.* **1. POETRY RELATING TO POETRY** relating to, typical of, or in the form of poetry **2. RESEMBLING POETRY** having qualities usually associated with poetry, especially in being gracefully expressive, romantically beautiful, or elevated and uplifting **3. SENSITIVE OR INSIGHTFUL** characteristic of a poet, especially in possessing unusual sensitivity or insight or in being able to express things in a beautiful or romantic way —**poetically** *adv.*

poetical /pō éttik'l/ *adj.* **1.** = poetic **2. EXCESSIVELY POETIC** inappropriately, exaggeratedly, or sentimentally poetic —**poeticality** /pō étti kálləti/ *n.* —**poetically** /-étti kli/ *adv.* —**poeticalness** /-étti'lnəss/ *n.*

poeticize /pō étti sīz/ (**-cizes, -cizing, -cized**), **poeticise** (**-cises, -cising, -cised**), **poetize** /pṓ i tīz/ (**-izes, -izing, -ized**), **poetise** (**-ises, -ising, -ised**) *vti.* to express or describe sth in a poetic style or in poetry

poetic justice *n.* a situation in which sb meets a fate that seems a fitting punishment or, less often, a fitting reward for their past actions

poetic licence *n.* liberties with the normal rules of fact, style, or grammar taken by a writer or speaker in order to achieve a particular effect

poetics /pō éttiks/ *n.* **1. BASIC PRINCIPLES OF POETRY** the literary or philosophical study of the basic principles, forms, and techniques of poetry or of imaginative writing in general (*takes a singular verb*) **2. TREATISE ON POETRY** a treatise on the nature or principles of poetry **3. WAY OF COMPOSING A POEM** the art or technique of writing poetry (*takes a plural verb*)

poetize, **poetise** *vti.* = poeticize

poet laureate (*plural* **poets laureate**) *n.* **1. BRITISH COURT POET** a poet who is appointed a member of the royal household for life by a British monarch and, especially formerly, is expected to write poems celebrating great national or royal events **2. EMINENT POET** any poet who is specially honoured for his or her work, or who is considered to be the most eminent poet in a particular country, state, or group

poetry /pṓ itri/ *n.* **1. LITERAT LITERATURE IN VERSE** literary work written in verse, in particular verse writing of high quality, great beauty, emotional sincerity or intensity, or profound insight **2.** LITERAT **POEMS COLLECTIVELY** all the poems written by a particular poet, in a particular language or form, or on a particular subject ○ *a collection of love poetry* **3.** LITERAT **WRITING OF POEMS** the art or skill of writing poems **4.** LITERAT **PROSE LIKE POETRY** writing in prose that has a poetic quality **5. BEAUTY OR GRACE** sth that resembles poetry in its beauty, rhythmic grace, or imaginative, elevated, or decorative style **6. POETIC QUALITY** a poetic or particularly beautiful or graceful quality in sth [14thC. Via Old French from, ultimately, Latin *poeta* (see POET).]

POEU *abbr.* Post Office Engineers Union

po-faced *adj.* **1. HUMOURLESS AND DISAPPROVING** inappropriately solemn or disapproving **2. EXPRESSIONLESS** remaining expressionless or wearing a stern expression, especially when others are laughing or responding in some way [Origin uncertain: possibly from PO]

pogo /pṓgō/ (**-gos, -going, -goed**) *vi.* to dance in a punk style of the 1970s by jumping up and down on the spot [Late 20thC. From POGO STICK.] —**pogo** *n.* —**pogoer** *n.*

pogo stick *n.* a strong metal pole with a spring at the bottom and two footrests to stand on, used to jump up and down or hop along on for play or exercise [Early 20thC. Formerly a trademark; of unknown origin.]

pogrom /póggrəm/ *n.* a planned campaign of persecution or extermination sanctioned by a government and directed against an ethnic group, especially against the Jewish people in tsarist Russia [Early 20thC. From Russian, 'devastation', formed from *gromit* 'to wreak havoc', from *grom* 'thunder'.]

poi[1] /poy/ *n.* a dish made from the root of the taro, cooked, pounded to a paste, and fermented. It is eaten as a staple in Hawaii and other Pacific islands. [Early 19thC. From Hawaiian.]

poi[2] /poy/ *n.* a light ball on a string, swung as a rhythmic accompaniment to Maori dance and song

poi dance *n.* a Maori dance in which women performers swing pois in unison [From Maori]

-poiesis *suffix.* creation, formation, production ○ *erythropoiesis* [From Greek *poiēsis*, which was formed from *poiein* 'to make' (source also of English *poem* and *onomatopoeia*)]

poignant /póynyənt/ *adj.* **1. CAUSING SADNESS OR PITY** causing a sharp sense of sadness, pity, or regret **2. SHARPLY PERCEPTIVE** particularly penetrating and effective or relevant (*literary*) **3. SHARPLY PAINFUL** causing acute physical pain (*literary*) **4. STRONG SMELLING OR TASTING** having an often pleasurably strong sharp smell or taste (*archaic*) [14thC. From French, the present participle of *poindre* 'to prick', from Latin *pungere* 'to prick, sting'.] —**poignance** *n.* —**poignantly** *adv.*

poikilocyte /póykilō sīt/ *n.* an abnormally shaped red blood cell [Late 19thC. Coined from Greek *poikilos* 'spotted, irregular' + -CYTE.]

poikilotherm /póykilō thurm/ *n.* an organism such as a reptile, amphibian, insect, or fish that has a body temperature that varies according to the temperature of the local atmosphere. ◊ **ectotherm**

poikilothermic /póykilō thúrmik/, **poikilothermal** /póykilō thúrm'l/, **poikilothermous** /póykilō thúrməss/ *adj.* having a body temperature that varies according to the temperature of the local atmosphere. Reptiles, amphibians, insects, and fish are all poikilothermic. [Late 19thC. Coined from Greek *poikilos* 'spotted, varied' + -THERMIC.] —**poikilothermism** *n.* —**poikilothermy** *n.*

poilu /pwaáloo/ *n.* a soldier in the French infantry, especially during World War I [Early 20thC. Via French, literally 'hairy', from, ultimately, Latin *pilus* 'hair' (see PILE[3]).]

poinciana /póynssi áanə/ (*plural* **-as** *or* **-a**) *n.* a tropical tree grown for its large reddish-orange flowers. Genera: *Caesalpinia* and *Delonix.* [Mid-18thC. From modern Latin, former genus name, named in honour of M. de *Poinci*, a 17thC governor of the Antilles.]

poind /poynd/ (**poinds, poinding, poinded**) *vt. Scotland* **1. SEIZE DEBTOR'S GOODS** to seize the goods of a debtor so that they can be sold to meet an unpaid debt **2. IMPOUND** to impound stray animals [Old English *gepyndan* 'to impound', formed from *pund* 'enclosure' (see POUND[3])]

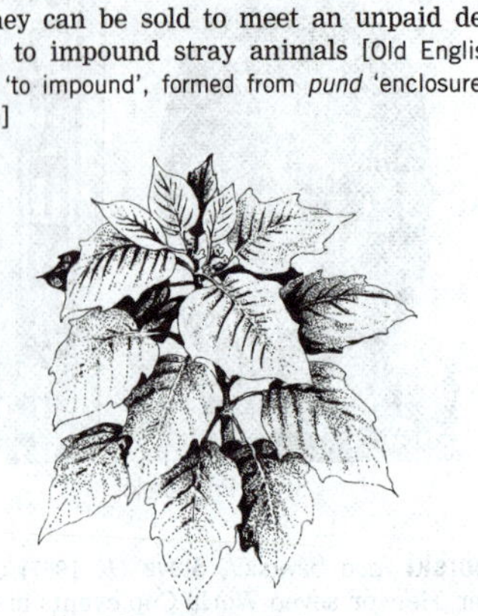

Poinsettia

poinsettia /poyn sétti ə/ (*plural* **-as** *or* **-a**) *n.* a Central American shrub of the spurge family that has distinctive bright red bracts resembling petals surrounding a cluster of tiny yellow flowers. It is popular as a house plant at Christmas. Latin name: *Euphorbia pulcherrima.* [Mid-19thC. Named after Joel R. *Poinsett* (1775–1851), US botanist and ambassador to Mexico, who introduced the plant to the United States.]

point /poynt/ *n.* **1. OPINION, IDEA, OR FACT** a particular opinion, idea, or fact put forward in the course of, or forming one of the main elements of, a discussion or argument ○ *She made several valid points in her report.* **2. UNDERLYING ESSENTIAL IDEA** the essential idea conveyed or intended in sth that is said or written ○ *He seems to have missed the point entirely.* **3. PURPOSE** the purpose or usefulness of sth ○ *Is there really any point in continuing?* **4. ITEM IN A LIST OR PLAN** one of several individual items or details in sth such as a plan, a contract, or a list ○ *a four-point plan to revive the coal industry* ○ *a point-by-point examination of the contract* **5. CONVINCING ARGUMENT OR VIEWPOINT** a cogent or persuasive argument or observation ○ *You have to admit that she has a point there.* **6. QUALITY OR FEATURE** a distinguishing quality, feature, or item in the makeup of sb or sth ○ *Generosity is one of his strong points.* **7.** ZOOL **PHYSICAL FEATURE OF A LIVESTOCK ANIMAL** an external feature such as the face or fetlock that is assessed when judging the overall shape of a livestock animal **8. LOCATION** a particular place or position ○ *a point six miles east of here* **9. MOMENT** a particular moment in time ○ *At that point, the door opened and the teacher walked in.* **10. PARTICULAR STAGE IN A PROCESS** a particular moment or stage in a process, especially one at which a significant change or development occurs or a particular condition is reached ○ *We have reached the point at which a decision will have to be made.* **11. LEVEL OR DEGREE** a particular level or degree of a quality ○ *He was confident to the point of almost being arrogant* **12. TIME JUST BEFORE STH HAPPENS** the moment or period of time just before sth happens ○ *at the point of death* **13. SHARP END OF STH** the sharp narrowed end of sth such as a needle, pencil, or weapon **14. END OR TIP** the end or tip of sth such as a finger or the projecting angle of sth such as the elbow or chin **15. SMALL PROJECTION** a small sharp or perceptible projection such as that in a piece of writing in Braille **16. OBJECT WITH A SHARP END** an object that has a sharp narrowed end or tip, e.g. a needle, pin, or sword (*archaic*) **17.** MUSIC **TIP OF A BOW** the tip of the bow of a string instrument. ◊ **heel 18.** ZOOL **ANTLER PRONG** one of the prongs on a deer's antlers **19.** GEOG **HEADLAND** a prominent headland on the coast that juts out into the sea, often the projecting tip of a peninsula (*often used in placenames*) **20. ACT OF POINTING** the act of pointing, e.g. with a finger **21. DOT** a small dot or source of sth such as colour or light **22.** MATH **DECIMAL POINT** the dot separating the whole number and fraction in a decimal number. The term 'point' is used particularly when such numbers are spoken aloud. ○ *five point nine* **23.** GEOM **DIMENSIONLESS GEOMETRIC ELEMENT** a dimensionless geometric element whose location in space is defined solely by its coordinates. Geometric figures such as circles, planes, or spheres can be treated as if they are sets of points. **24.** GRAM, PRINTING **PUNCTUATION MARK** in printing or writing, a punctuation mark, especially a full stop **25.** PHON = **vowel point 26.** SPORTS, LEISURE **UNIT USED IN SCORING** a unit used in scoring a sport, game, or competition, or as a means of making a quantitative evaluation of sth ○ *Using a points system, each employee was rated on a scale from one to five.* **27. UNIT ON A SCALE** a single unit on a scale of measurement ○ *The earthquake measured 6 points on the Richter scale.* ○ *opened up a 10-point lead over her rivals in the polls* **28.** STOCK EXCH **INVESTMENT PRICE UNIT** a unit used to measure change in the value of an investment, e.g. on the Stock Exchange ○ *The FTSE index is up 5 points.* **29.** *US* FIN **PERCENTAGE OF A LOAN** an amount equivalent to one percent of the value of a loan, used to calculate the sum the borrower pays up front to the lender as a service charge **30.** LAW **MOTORISTS' PENALTY UNIT** a penalty unit given for a driving offence recorded on a sb's driving licence. Receiving a certain number of points leads automatically to a penalty. **31.** *US* EDUC **STUDENT'S UNIT OF CREDIT** a unit of academic credit for a student that is equivalent to one hour of class work per week over a period of one term **32.** BRIDGE **UNIT OF WINNING POTENTIAL** a unit used in assessing the strength of a hand in bridge **33.** PRINTING, MEASURE **PRINTING UNIT OF MEASUREMENT** a unit of measurement in printing equal to one twelfth of a pica, or approximately 0.03515 cm/ 0.01384 in **34.** MEASURE **DIAMOND WEIGHT UNIT** a unit of weight for a diamond equivalent to one-hundredth of a metric carat **35.** COMPASS **MARK ON A COMPASS** any of the 32 individual bearings or directions marked on a compass, e.g. west, west by north, west-northwest, or northwest **36.** COMPASS **ANGLE BETWEEN ADJACENT BEARINGS** the angle between any two adjacent bearings marked on a compass, measuring 11° 15′ **37.** MIL **UNIT AHEAD OF A FORMATION** an individual or unit that moves ahead of a larger formation, acting as a scout and advance guard **38.** MIL **ADVANCE MILITARY POSITION** the position ahead of a larger formation taken by an individual or unit acting as point **39.** BASKETBALL **OFFENSIVE BASKETBALL POSITION** in basketball, the position in front court taken by the guard who directs the offensive **40.** CRICKET **OFF-SIDE FIELDING POSITION** a fielding position on the off side, level with the batsman's wicket and at a distance from it that varies between three or four yards (*silly point*) and about thirty yards (*deep point*) **41.** CRICKET **FIELDER FIELDING AT POINT** a fielder fielding at point **42.** HERALDRY **DIVISION OF A HERALDIC SHIELD** any of the positions on or divisions of a heraldic shield in which a charge can be placed ■ **points** *npl.* **1.** RAIL **JUNCTION OF TWO CONVERGING RAILWAY TRACKS** the mechanical arrangement by which one railway track diverges or converges with another, allowing trains to change to another line or route **2.** AUTOMOT **ELECTRICAL CONTACTS IN A DISTRIBUTOR** the two electrical contacts that act as circuit breakers in the distributor of an internal-combustion engine as current is passed in turn to the cylinders **3. BALLERINA'S TIPTOES** the ends of the toes on which a ballerina wearing special shoes raises herself up for certain moves and positions while performing **4.** ZOOL **EXTREMITIES OF A DOMESTIC ANIMAL** the ears, feet, and tail of a domestic animal ■ *v.* (**points, pointing, pointed**) **1.** *vi.* **INDICATE WITH AN EXTENDED FINGER** to extend the finger or a long and thin object in the direction of sth in order to draw attention to it ○ *I pointed at one of the shrubs and asked its cost.* **2.** *vt.* **AIM AT STH** to hold an object so that its end is aimed at sb or sth ○ *pointed the hose towards the flowers* **3.** *vi.* **BE TURNED TOWARDS** to be turned towards or aimed in a particular direction ○ *The arrow on the signpost was pointing to the right.* **4.** *vt.* **DIRECT SB TOWARDS** to indicate the direction in which sb should go ○ *If you can just point me in the right direction I expect I'll find it.* **5.** *vti.* COMPUT **AIM A MOUSE OR JOYSTICK** to move a mouse, joystick, or other device so that the cursor on a computer screen is positioned over or touching sth ○ *Point at the icon, then double click on it.* **6.** *vi.* **SUGGEST STH IS THE CASE** to be strong evidence of sth or lead the mind to believe or conclude sth ○ *It all points to one conclusion.* **7.** *vi.* **CALL ATTENTION TO STH** to call attention to a particular fact or situation as being important **8.** *vt.* **GIVE FORCE TO A REMARK** to give additional force, emphasis, or incisiveness to sth said or written **9.** *vt.* CONSTR **REPAIR WITH MORTAR** to repair or finish a wall, chimney, or other structural component by putting mortar or cement between the bricks or stones **10.** *vt.* **SHARPEN STH** to sharpen sth so that it has a point at the end **11.** *vt.* **STRETCH THE FOOT DOWNWARDS** to stretch out the foot or toes so that leg and foot make one comparatively straight line, especially in ballet **12.** *vti.* SAILING **SAIL CLOSE TO THE WIND** to sail a boat close to the wind **13.** *vti.* HUNT **POINT THE MUZZLE AT GAME** to stand still with muzzle and tail outstretched indicating the whereabouts of game (*refers to a gun dog*) **14.** *vt.* MUSIC **MARK A PSALM FOR CHANTING** to mark a psalm to indicate how it is to be chanted **15.** *vt.* PHON **ADD MARKS OVER LETTERS** to place diacritics or vowel points over the relevant letters in a text **16.** *vt.* GRAM **PUNCTUATE** to put punctuation marks into a text **17.** *vi.* MED **COME TO A HEAD** to reach the stage of spontaneous rupture or surgical opening, allowing pus to drain (*refers to boils and abscesses*) [13thC. Via French from, ultimately, Latin *punctum* 'prick-mark, dot, particle' (source of English *punctual* and *punctuation*), from the past participle of Latin *pungere* 'to prick, pierce' (see PUNGENT).] ◇ **a sore point** a cause of annoyance ◇ **be on the point of doing sth** to be just about to do sth ○ *I was just on the point of leaving.* ◇ **beside the point** irrelevant or unimportant ◇ **in point of fact** ◆ **fact** ◇ **make a point of doing sth** to be careful to do sth and, often, to be seen by others to do it ◇ **not to put too fine a point on it** used to indicate that sb is being or is about to be frank or blunt ◇ **stretch a point 1.** to allow sth as an exception to the rule **2.** to exaggerate ◇ **stretch the point** to exaggerate ◇ **to the point** relevant or worth paying attention to ◇ **up to a point, to a point** to a certain extent, but not completely

point out *vt.* **1. SHOW SB STH** to point at or otherwise indicate sth so that sb will look at it ○ *Our guide pointed out the most interesting architectural features of the building.* **2. TELL SB STH** to tell sb about or draw sb's attention to sth ○ *She did point out some of the difficulties we might expect to face.*

point up *vt.* to emphasize sth or an aspect of sth

point-and-shoot *adj.* used to describe cameras that require no adjustment by the user before taking a photograph because the focus and exposure are adjusted automatically or are fixed

point-blank *adv.* **1.** ARMS **AT CLOSE RANGE** at or from very close range **2. OUTRIGHT** directly or bluntly and without further explanation ○ *told them point-blank what I thought of them* ■ *adj.* **1.** ARMS **FIRED AT CLOSE RANGE** fired straight and from so close to the target that no adjustment to the aim is necessary for the drop in the bullet's trajectory ○ *point-blank shot* **2.** ARMS **CLOSE TO THE TARGET** very close to the target when shooting ○ *at point-blank range* **3. OUTRIGHT** direct and blunt ○ *a point-blank refusal* [Origin uncertain: possibly from French *point (de tir)* 'firing point' + *blanc* 'target']

point defect *n.* an imperfection in the lattice structure of a crystal

point duty *n.* the task, usually undertaken by a police officer or traffic warden, of standing at a road junction in order to direct traffic

Barnaby's

Pointe

pointe /pwaNt/ *n.* the ends of the toes, a position on which a ballerina wearing special shoes raises herself up for certain moves and positions while performing [Mid-19thC. From French, 'point'.]

pointed /póyntid/ *adj.* **1. ENDING IN A POINT** ending in a point or sharp angle **2. MADE WITH EMPHASIS** made with emphasis and carrying an unmistakable message, often a criticism **3. CONSPICUOUS** made studiedly obvious or noticeable —**pointedness** *n.*

pointed arch *n.* ARCHIT = **lancet arch**

pointedly /póyntidli/ *adv.* in a deliberate or emphatic way and with no attempt at tact or subtlety ○ *They pointedly ignored me.*

Pointe-Noire /pwaàNt nwaàr/ city in the Republic of Congo, and the country's main port. Population: 576,206 (1992).

pointer /póyntər/ *n.* **1. CANE USED FOR POINTING** a stick or cane used, especially by a teacher or lecturer, to point sth out, e.g. on a chart or large map **2. INDICATOR ON A MEASURING DEVICE** a needle that moves round on a measuring instrument to point to part of a dial **3. HELPFUL ADVICE OR INFORMATION** a piece of advice or information given to help sb achieve sth or do sth the right way ○ *My coach gave me a few pointers on how to hold the racket.* **4. SIGN INDICATING A SITUATION** a sign of what is happening or what might happen in the future **5.** HUNT **GUN DOG THAT INDICATES THE POSITION OF GAME** a gun dog, usually with a shorthaired white coat with coloured patches, belonging to a breed trained to indicate the whereabouts of shot game by standing still with the muzzle and tail outstretched **6.** COMPUT **ARROW ON A COMPUTER SCREEN** an arrow or other symbol on a computer screen that shows the current position of the mouse or other pointing device. The symbol may change shape depending on the task being performed. **7.** COMPUT **COMPUTER MEMORY ADDRESS** an address, stored as data in a computer's memory, that is the location at which the desired data is stored ■ **pointers, Pointers** *npl.* ASTRON **GUIDE STARS IN THE PLOUGH CONSTELLATION** the two bright stars in the Plough constellation forming the side of the quadrilateral farthest from the handle, and used as a guide to find the Pole Star

pointillism /póyntilizəm/ *n.* **1.** PAINTING **STYLE OF 19C PAINTING** a late 19th-century style of painting in which a picture is constructed from dots of pure colour that blend, at a distance, into recognizable shapes and various colour tones. Pointillism developed out of impressionism and its best-known exponent is the French painter Georges Seurat. **2.** MUSIC **MUSICAL COMPOSITION TECHNIQUE** a technique of musical composition using sparse isolated notes in widely varying registers rather than traditional closely connected melodies [Early 20thC. From French *pointillisme*, via *pointiller* 'to mark with dots' from, ultimately, Latin *punctum* 'dot'.] —**pointillist** *n.*, *adj.* —**pointillistic** /póynti lístik/ *adj.*

pointing /póynting/ *n.* **1. ACTIVITY OF POINTING** the act or activity of, or an instance of, pointing **2. MORTAR BETWEEN BRICKS** the cement or mortar between the bricks of a wall

pointing device *n.* an input device such as a mouse, trackball, or joystick used to manipulate a pointer on a computer display

point lace *n.* lace made with a needle instead of bobbins [From POINT in the sense 'to prick, stitch']

pointless /póyntləss/ *adj.* **1. WITHOUT PURPOSE OR BENEFIT** having no purpose, use, or sense, or any positive or beneficial effect ○ *It's pointless even attempting to make sense of it.* **2.** SPORTS **SCORING NO POINTS** in sports, having or scoring no points —**pointlessly** *adv.* —**pointlessness** *n.*

point man *n.* **1.** MIL **LEAD SOLDIER IN A MILITARY FORMATION** the lead soldier in a military formation or patrol **2.** *US* **SB IN THE FOREFRONT** sb who is in the forefront of an activity or endeavour and playing a crucial and possibly hazardous role in it

point mutation *n.* a mutation that involves a change in a single base or base pair of the nucleotides in a gene, occurring as a result of addition, deletion, or substitution

point of departure *n.* a starting point

point of honour *n.* sth that a sense of honour, self-respect, or pride obliges sb to do

point of no return *n.* **1. CRITICAL STAGE IN A PROCESS** the time or stage in a process beyond which it becomes impossible to stop or discontinue it **2.** AIR **POINT ON A JOURNEY** the point in an aircraft's flight after which there will be insufficient fuel left to enable it to return to its starting point

point of order *n.* a question raised by one of the participants in a formal debate or meeting that relates to the rules of procedure governing it, in particular as to whether those rules are being breached

point of presence *n.* **1.** COMPUT full form of **POP 2. PLACE TO CONNECT TO A NETWORK** a location where a user can connect to a network, e.g. a place where subscribers can dial in to an Internet service provider

point of reference *n.* sth to which sb can refer in order to check direction or progress, as a guide to action or conduct, or as an aid to understanding or communication

point-of-sale *adj.* located, used, or occurring at the place where a product is sold —**point of sale** *n.*

point of view *n.* **1. PERSPECTIVE SB BRINGS** sb's particular way of thinking about or approaching a subject, as shaped by his or her own character, experience, mindset, and history **2. OPINION** sb's personal opinion on a subject **3. PARTICULAR ASPECT ON A SUBJECT** any of the various aspects from which a subject may be considered or judged **4.** LITERAT **ANGLE OF THE NARRATOR** the perspective on events of the narrator or a particular character in a story **5. POSITION OF AN OBSERVER** the position or angle from which sb observes an event or a scene

point-of-view shot *n.* a film or television shot that shows an event or scene as a particular character sees it

point source *n.* PHYS, ENVIRON a source of sth such as radiant energy or pollution that is or appears to be very small

point-to-point *n.* **CROSS-COUNTRY STEEPLECHASE FOR AMATEURS** a type of horse race for amateurs in which horses regularly used in hunting are raced over a marked cross-country course that includes various jumps and obstacles ■ *adj.* **FROM PLACE TO PLACE** from one particular place to another —**point-to-pointer** *n.* —**point-to-pointing** *n.*

Point-to-Point Protocol *n.* a protocol for dial-up access to the Internet using a modem

point woman *n.* *US* a woman who is in the forefront of any activity or endeavour, playing a crucial and possibly hazardous role in it

pointy /póynti/ (**-ier, -iest**) *adj.* ending in a point (*informal*)

pointy-headed *adj.* *US* intelligent or intellectual in an arrogant or impractical way (*slang*)

poise[1] /poyz/ *n.* **1. COMPOSURE** calm self-assured dignity, especially in dealing with social situations **2. CONTROLLED GRACE IN MOVEMENT** a graceful controlled way of standing, moving, or performing an action **3. EQUILIBRIUM** a stable state of balance **4. SUSPENDED STATE** a state of hovering or being in suspension (*literary*) ■ *v.* (**poises, poising, poised**) **1.** *vti.* **BALANCE OR SUSPEND** to be balanced or suspended, or to place or hold sth in balance or suspension **2.** *vt.* **WEIGH** to weigh things, especially by holding them in the hands, or to weigh sth up, especially alternatives (*archaic*) [14thC. The noun is via Old French *pois* 'weight, balance'; the verb via *peser* 'to weigh', both ultimately from Latin *pensare* (see PENSIVE).]

poise[2] /poyz/ *n.* the centimetre-gram-second unit of viscosity equal to one dyne-second per square centimetre [Early 20thC. Shortening of *Poiseuille*, named after the French physiologist J. L. M. *Poiseuille* (1799–1868).]

poised /poyzd/ *adj.* **1. READY TO ACT** fully prepared or in position and about to do sth ○ *We are now poised to take over the company.* **2. READY TO MOVE** motionless and balanced, or motionless and suspended in the air, often just before or in the midst of an action ○ *a bird poised on a branch* **3. WITH COMPOSURE** calm, self-assured, and dignified **4. IN DANGER OF STH** teetering on the edge of a sudden change ○ *stock prices seemingly poised to rise*

poison /póyz'n/ *n.* **1. TOXIC SUBSTANCE** a substance that causes illness, injury, or death if taken into the body or produced within the body **2. STH EXERCISING AN INSIDIOUS INFLUENCE** sth that exercises a powerful destructive or corrupting force, especially in an insidious way **3.** CHEM **REACTION-INHIBITING SUBSTANCE** a substance that inhibits a chemical reaction or diminishes the activity of a catalyst **4.** NUCLEAR PHYS **SUBSTANCE SLOWING A NUCLEAR REACTION** any substance in a nuclear reactor that can absorb neutrons without undergoing fission and that therefore slows down the reaction ■ vt. (-sons, -soning, -soned) **1. GIVE POISON TO SB** to administer poison to a person or animal, especially with malicious intention **2. HARM WITH A TOXIC SUBSTANCE** to cause illness, injury, or death to sb with a poison or other harmful chemical substance **3. ADD POISON TO STH** to put poison into or onto sth so as to harm or kill sb ○ *poisoned bait used to kill rats* **4. POLLUTE THE ENVIRONMENT** to pollute water, land, or air severely with harmful substances **5. CORRUPT OR UNDERMINE STH** to have an evil or corrupting influence on sb or sth, especially by planting hostility or suspicion in sb's mind against another person **6. SPOIL A SITUATION** to have a harmful spoiling effect on sth that should be pleasant, enjoyable, or friendly **7. CHEM INHIBIT A CHEMICAL REACTION** to inhibit a chemical reaction or activity **8. NUCLEAR PHYS SLOW DOWN A NUCLEAR REACTION** to slow down or stop a nuclear reaction by the addition of a substance that can absorb neutrons without undergoing fission [13thC. Via Old French from the Latin stem *potion-* from, ultimately, *potare* 'to drink'.] —**poisoner** n. ◇ **what's your poison?, name your poison** used to ask what sb would like to drink (*informal*)

poisoned chalice n. a task or decision that will almost inevitably bring harm or unpopularity upon the person who is forced to undertake it

poison gas n. a lethal or incapacitating gas used as a weapon in warfare

poison hemlock n. *US* = hemlock

Poison ivy

poison ivy n. **1. VINE CAUSING AN ITCHING RASH** a North American climbing vine of the cashew family that has three-part leaves, small green flowers, and white berries. Contact with the plant produces an itching rash. Genus: *Rhus*. **2. RELATED PLANT** any plant related to poison ivy, such as poison oak **3. MED RASH** the rash produced by poison ivy

poison oak n. a plant similar or related to poison ivy that produces a skin rash as a result of being touched. Genus: *Rhus*.

poisonous /póyz'nəss/ adj. **1. CONTAINING OR PRODUCING POISON** containing, producing, or acting as a poison **2. MALICIOUS** filled with or creating malice, distrust, or hostility —**poisonously** adv. —**poisonousness** n.

poison-pen letter n. a letter sent anonymously to sb that contains unpleasant or abusive comments

poison pill n. a strategic move adopted by a company designed to make an unwelcome takeover by another firm less attractive to that firm

poison sumac, poison sumach n. a shrub native to swampy areas of the southeastern United States that has compound leaves, greenish flowers, and greenish-white berries. Contact with the plant produces an irritating rash. Poison sumac is in the same family as poison ivy and poison oak. Latin name: *Toxicodendron vernix*.

Poisson /pwáass on, pwáss-/, **Siméon-Denis** (1781–1840) French mathematician and physicist. He is noted for his work on electricity, magnetism, elasticity, and for the Poisson distribution in statistics.

Poisson distribution /pwáass on-/ n. a probability distribution that represents the number of random events occurring over a fixed period of time [Early 20thC. Named after Siméon Poisson, who first described it.]

Poisson's ratio n. PHYS the ratio of the decrease in width to the increase in length of a material when it is stretched [Early 20thC. Named after Siméon Poisson.]

Poitiers /pwaati ay/ city in west-central France. It is the capital of Vienne Department in Poitou-Charente Region. Population: 78,894 (1990).

poke[1] /pōk/ v. (pokes, poking, poked) **1.** vti. **PROD WITH STH** to push the point of sth such as an outstretched finger, elbow, or stick against sb or sth else **2.** vt. **MAKE A HOLE IN STH** to make a hole or opening in sth by pushing at it with a finger or a sharp object **3.** vt. **PUSH INTO A HOLE** to push a finger or a long thin object into a hole, space, or opening **4.** vti. **PROTRUDE FROM STH** to stick, or stick sth, out of or through an opening, surface, or covering in such a way that part of the object is visible ○ *One foot was poking out from under the covers.* **5.** vi. **SEARCH HAPHAZARDLY** to search or investigate in a haphazard or aimless manner ○ *poking around in a second-hand bookshop* **6.** vi. **MEDDLE** to pry or intrude into sth, or meddle with sth ○ *Stop poking around in my affairs.* **7.** vt. **STIR A FIRE** to stir a fire with a poker or similar object to make it burn better **8.** vt. **OFFENSIVE TERM** an offensive term meaning to have penetrative sex (*taboo offensive*) **9.** vt. **PUNCH SB** to hit sb with one of the fists (*informal*) **10.** vi. **GO SLOWLY** to move around or do things in a slow unhurried way ■ n. **1. PROD** a push or prod with a finger, elbow, stick, or similar pointed object **2. LOOK OR SEARCH** the activity of haphazard or casual browsing or investigating **3. PROD** a short prod with the fist (*informal*) **4. OFFENSIVE TERM** an offensive term for a penetrative sex act (*taboo offensive*) [13thC. Origin uncertain.]

poke[2] /pōk/ n. **1. BAG** a small bag or sack (*regional*) **2.** *Scotland* **PAPER BAG** a paper bag especially to hold groceries (*informal*) [13thC. From Old French dialect, a variant of *poche* (see POUCH).]

poke[3] n. = pokeweed [Mid-17thC. From Virginia Algonquian *poughkone* (source of English *puccoon*).]

pokeberry /pók̄bəri/ n. **1.** (*plural* -ries) **POKEWEED BERRY** the berry that grows on a pokeweed plant **2.** (*plural* -ry *or* -ries) = pokeweed

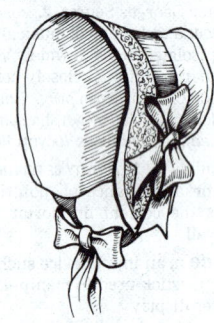

Poke bonnet

poke bonnet n. a woman's bonnet with a deep projecting rim, fashionable in the first half of the 19th century [From POKE[2]]

poker[1] /pók̄ər/ n. CARDS a card game in which players attempt to acquire a winning combination of cards that involves betting at every deal [Mid-19thC. Origin uncertain: possibly from German *Pochspiel*, literally 'bragging game', from *pochen* 'to brag'.]

poker[2] /pók̄ər/ n. **1. METAL ROD FOR STIRRING A FIRE** a metal rod for stirring a fire to make it burn better **2. SB OR STH THAT POKES** sb or sth that pokes, or sth used for poking [Mid-16thC. Formed from POKE[1].]

poker face n. a face showing no expression and revealing nothing about what sb is thinking or feeling [From POKER[1]] —**poker-faced** adj.

poker machine n. ANZ a gambling machine in which a player inserts coins in a slot and pulls a lever that spins symbols in matching combinations that determine winnings

pokerwork /pók̄ər wurk/ n. decorative designs burned into white wood with the heated end of a metal rod

pokeweed /pók̄ weed/ n. (*plural* -weed *or* -weeds) n. a tall North American plant that has white flowers, juicy blackish berries in elongated clusters, edible shoots, and a poisonous root. Latin name: *Phytolacca americana*. [Mid-18thC. From POKE[3].]

pokey adj. = poky (*informal*)

pokie /pók̄i/, **pokey** (*plural* -eys) n. ANZ a slot machine (*informal*) [Late 20thC. Shortening of POKER MACHINE.]

poky /pók̄i/ (-ier, -iest), **pokey** (-ier, -iest) adj. (*informal*) **1. CRAMPED** uncomfortably small and cramped **2. *US* SLOW** annoyingly slow **3.** *US* **FRUMPY** shabby and old-fashioned [Mid-19thC. From POKE[1]. The word originally meant 'petty, pottering', and came from the idea of poking aimlessly at sth.] —**pokily** adv. —**pokiness** n.

POL abbr. MIL petroleum, oil, and lubricants

pol. abbr. **1.** political **2.** politics

Pol. abbr. **1.** Poland **2.** Polish

Polack /pól ak/ n. *US* an offensive term referring to a Polish person (*slang offensive*) [Late 16thC. Directly or via French *Polaque* from Polish *Polak* (source of English *polka*).]

Poland

Poland /pólənd/ republic in eastern Europe. Language: Polish. Currency: zloty. Capital: Warsaw. Population: 38,612,000 (1996). Area: 312,677 sq. km/120,725 sq. mi. Official name **Republic of Poland**

polar /pólər/ adj. **1. GEOG OF OR NEAR THE EARTH'S POLES** relating to, located at, or found in the regions surrounding the North or South Pole **2. SCI OF A POLE OR POLES** relating to a pole or poles of a rotating body, a magnet, or an electrically charged object **3. ASTRON, SPACE TECH PASSING OVER A PLANET'S POLES** passing over, or travelling in an orbit that passes over, a planet's poles ○ *polar orbit* **4. UTTERLY OPPOSITE** completely opposite to each other, or at the other extreme from sth else **5. PIVOTAL** of pivotal or central importance **6. GUIDING** serving as a guide or giving direction (*literary*) **7. CHEM HAVING A DIPOLE** having a permanent dipole, or having molecules with permanent dipoles ○ *polar molecule* **8. CRYSTALS HAVING AN IONIC BOND** having an ionic bond, or having crystals with ionic bonds ○ *polar crystal* **9. MATH IN A POLAR COORDINATE SYSTEM** relating to or measured with reference to a system of polar coordinates

polar axis n. MATH the fixed horizontal line in a system of polar coordinates from which the angle made by the radius vector is measured

Polar bear

polar bear n. a large white mainly meat-eating bear that lives in the Arctic on coasts and ice floes. It has wide front feet for swimming. Latin name: *Ursus maritimus*.

polar body n. a cell with a nucleus but little cytoplasm that is produced along with an oocyte, and later discarded, in the process of cell division that leads to an ovum

polar cap *n.* **1.** GEOG **ICY AREA AROUND THE POLES** the area around either the North or South Pole that is permanently covered in ice **2.** ASTRON **POLAR ICECAP ON MARS** either of the two polar regions on Mars that are permanently covered with frozen carbon dioxide and water

polar circle *n.* the lines of latitude that define the Arctic and Antarctic regions, 66°33' N and 66°33' S

polar coordinates *npl.* MATH the two coordinates that locate a point in a plane by specifying the length of a radius vector and the angle it makes with a horizontal line (**polar axis**)

polar front *n.* a weather front separating cold polar air and warmer air

polarimeter /pṓlə rímmitər/ *n.* OPTICS an instrument used to measure the rotation of the plane of polarization of light as it passes through a substance, especially a liquid or solution. It is an important tool in the analysis of sugar solutions. [Mid-19thC. Coined from POLARIZATION + -METER.] —**polarimetric** /pṓləri méttrik/ *adj.* —**polarimetry** /pṓlə rímmətri/ *n.*

Polaris /pō laáriss/ *n.* **1.** ASTRON **BRIGHT STAR NEAR THE NORTH POLE** the brightest star in the constellation Ursa Minor, located very near the celestial North Pole. Because it always indicates due north from an observer anywhere on the Earth, Polaris is important for navigation. **2.** ARMS **MISSILE WITH A NUCLEAR WARHEAD** a US intermediate-range ballistic missile that usually carries a nuclear warhead and is launched from a submarine

polariscope /pō lárriskōp/ *n.* an instrument used to study either a substance exposed to polarized light or the effects of a substance on polarized light [Early 19thC. Coined from POLARIZATION + SCOPE.]

polarise *vti.* = **polarize**

polarity /pō lárrəti/ (*plural* **-ties**) *n.* **1.** **EXTREME DIFFERENCE** a situation in which two individuals or groups have qualities, ideas, or principles that are diametrically opposed to each other **2.** PHYS **OPPOSITE PHYSICAL CHARACTERISTICS IN A SYSTEM** the condition, in a system, of having opposite characteristics at different points, especially with respect to electric charge or magnetic properties

polarization /pṓlə rī záysh'n/, **polarisation** *n.* **1.** **DIVISION INTO OPPOSITE VIEWS** a process in which the differences between groups or ideas become ever more clear-cut and extreme and the opposition between them hardens **2.** PHYS **HAVING OR CAUSING POLARITY** the state of being polarized or the process of polarizing sth **3.** OPTICS **PROCESS LIMITING LIGHT VIBRATIONS** the process or property by which radiation, especially light, is restricted to vibrate in particular directions **4.** PHYS **POLARIZING OF CHARGES** the process in which the positive and negative charges in an atomic, molecular, or chemical system develop polarity

polarize /pṓlə rīz/ (**-izes, -izing, -ized**), **polarise** (**-ises, -ising, -ised**) *vti.* **1.** **CAUSE A DIVISION OF OPINION** to make the differences between groups or ideas ever more clear-cut and extreme and harden the opposition between them, or to become ever more sharply divided and opposed **2.** PHYS **ACQUIRE POLARITY** to acquire, or cause sth to acquire, polarity **3.** PHYS **RESTRICT LIGHT VIBRATION** to cause light to vibrate within certain planes, or to be restricted to vibration within certain planes —**polarizable** *adj.* —**polarizer** *n.*

polarizing microscope *n.* a microscope in which polarized light is used to examine specimens

polar nucleus *n.* either of the two nuclei in the centre of the sac of a seed plant embryo that eventually fuse into the endosperm

polarography /pṓlə róggrəfi/ *n.* an analytic technique used to study ions in a solution that compares the strength of electric currents passing through the solution during electrolysis and the voltages needed to produce them [Mid-20thC. Coined from POLARIZATION + -GRAPHY.] —**polarographic** /pṓlərə gráffik/ *adj.*

Polaroid /pṓlə royd/ *tdmk.* **1.** a trademark for a camera that produces pictures that develop within seconds of being taken, or the film used in such a camera **2.** a trademark for a specially treated transparent plastic that allows polarized light through and is used to reduce glare in sunglasses

polar star *n.* ASTRON = **Polaris**

polder /pṓldər/ *n.* an area of land reclaimed from the sea and protected by dykes, especially in the Netherlands [Early 17thC. From Dutch.]

pole[1] /pōl/ *n.* **1.** GEOG **NORTH OR SOUTH POLE** either of the two points on the Earth, the North and South Poles, that are the endpoints of its axis of rotation, are furthest from the equator, and are surrounded by icecaps **2.** ASTRON, GEOM **AXIS ENDPOINTS OF A SPHERE** either of the two endpoints of the axis of rotation of a sphere or a planet or other celestial body **3.** ASTRON = **celestial pole** **4.** **EITHER OF TWO OPPOSITES** one of two completely opposed or contrasted positions, states, or views ○ *They're at opposite poles as far as their taste in music is concerned.* **5.** PHYS **END OF A MAGNET** either of the two ends of a magnet or magnetized body where the lines of force are most concentrated **6.** ELEC **ELECTRIC TERMINAL** either of two terminals in sth such as a battery, generator, or motor that have opposite electric charges **7.** BIOL **DISTINCT REGION IN A CELL** either of two opposite regions that are physiologically or functionally distinct in an organism, cell, or structure, e.g. the opposite ends of the spindle structure formed in the nucleus of a cell during cell division **8.** MATH **ORIGIN OF POLAR COORDINATES** the origin in a polar coordinate system **9.** **REFERENCE POINT** a fixed point of reference (*literary*) [14thC. Via Latin from Greek *polos* 'axis' (source of English *pulley*). Ultimately from an Indo-European word meaning 'to turn around', which is also the ancestor of *wheel* and *cycle*.] ◇ **be poles apart** to be as different or as opposed as it is possible to be

pole[2] /pōl/ *n.* **1.** **LONG STRAIGHT OBJECT** a long, straight, strong piece of wood, metal, or other material, usually with a round cross-section and thin enough to hold in the hands or arms **2.** SPORTS **POLE-VAULTER'S POLE** the long flexible shaft made of wood, metal, or fibreglass used by competitors in the pole vault **3.** MOTOR SPORTS = **pole position** **4.** TRANSP **SHAFT ON A HORSE-DRAWN VEHICLE** a single shaft projecting forward from the front of a vehicle between the animals that draw it and to which those animals are hitched **5.** MEASURE = **perch**[1] *n.* 4 **6.** MEASURE = **perch**[1] *n.* 5 ■ *v.* (**poles, poling, poled**) **1.** *vti.* NAUT **PROPEL A BOAT WITH A POLE** to move a boat along by pushing with a pole against a firm surface **2.** *vt.* GARDENING **SUPPORT A PLANT WITH A POLE** to use a pole to provide support for a plant **3.** *vti.* SKIING **USE SKI POLES** to make forward progress on skis by pushing with ski poles [Old English *pāl*. From a prehistoric Germanic ancestor that was borrowed from Latin *palus* 'stake'.] ◇ **not touch sb** *or* **sth with a bargepole** to avoid any contact or involvement with sb or sth

Pole *n.* **1.** **SB FROM POLAND** sb who was born or brought up in Poland or who has Polish citizenship **2.** **SB WITH A POLISH ANCESTOR** sb who is of Polish descent [Late 16thC. Via German from, ultimately, Old Polish *Polanie*, literally 'field-dwellers', from *pole* 'field', from Slavic.]

poleax *vt., n.* US = **poleaxe**

poleaxe /pṓl aks/ *n.* **1.** **BUTCHER'S AXE** a specialized axe with a hammer face opposite the blade, used, especially formerly, for slaughtering animals **2.** ARMS **BATTLE-AXE** a battle-axe with a long or short handle, especially one with a hammer or spike opposite the axe blade **3.** NAVY **AXE FOR CUTTING RIGGING** a short-handled axe used to cut rigging or ropes on sailing ships, especially during combat ■ *vt.* (**-axes, -axed**) **1.** **AMAZE AND STUPEFY SB** to leave sb stupefied and speechless with astonishment **2.** **HIT SB VERY HARD** to hit sb hard enough to cause unconsciousness **3.** **HIT WITH A POLEAXE** to hit sb or sth with a poleaxe [14thC. Alteration of *pollax*, literally 'head-axe', from POLL, perhaps because it was for splitting heads or because it had a special kind of head.]

polecat /pṓl kat/ *n.* an animal related to but larger than the weasel that lives in woodlands in Europe, Asia, and North Africa, has brown fur, and emits a foul smell when disturbed. Genus: *Mustela* and *Vormela.* ◊ **ferret** [14thC. Origin uncertain: perhaps from French *poule* 'hen' (because it was known to take hens from farmyards) + CAT.]

pole horse *n.* a horse harnessed to the pole of a carriage or wagon

poleis plural of **polis**

Polecat

polemic /pə lémmik/ *n.* **1.** **PASSIONATE ARGUMENT** a passionate, strongly worded, and often controversial argument against or, less often, in favour of sth or sb **2.** **PASSIONATE CRITIC** sb who engages in a dispute or argues strongly or passionately against sth or sb (*literary*) ■ *adj.* **polemic, polemical** **CONTAINING PASSIONATE ARGUMENT** containing or expressing passionate and strongly worded argument against or in favour of sth or sb [Mid-17thC. Via medieval Latin from Greek *polemikos*, from *polemos* 'war', of unknown origin.] —**polemically** *adv.*

polemicist /pə lémmissist/, **polemist** /pə lémmist/ *n.* sb who writes or delivers a polemic or is skilled in polemical argument

polemics /pə lémmiks/ *n.* the art or practice of arguing powerfully and effectively for or against sth and engaging in controversy (*takes a singular verb*)

polemist *n.* = **polemicist**

polenta /pō léntə/ *n.* in Italian cooking, fine yellow maize meal cooked to a mush with water or stock and served with meat, fish, or vegetables, or cooled, set, sliced, and baked or fried [Mid-16thC. Via Italian from Latin, 'barley meal'.]

pole piece *n.* a shaped piece of ferromagnetic material, usually soft iron, that concentrates and directs the magnetic field of a magnet to maximize the efficiency of devices such as loudspeakers and generators

pole position *n.* **1.** MOTOR SPORTS **BEST STARTING POSITION IN A MOTOR RACE** the best position on the starting grid of a motor race, usually on the inside of the front row and taken by the driver with the fastest pre-race practice time **2.** **GOOD BEGINNING** a very good or advantageous position at the beginning of sth

poler /pṓlər/ *n.* **1.** = **pole horse** **2.** NAUT **SB POLING A BOAT** sb who uses a pole to move a boat along [Late 17thC. From POLE[2].]

pole star *n.* sth considered as a guiding light and giver of direction (*literary*)

Pole Star *n.* ASTRON = **Polaris**

pole vault *n.* **1.** **HIGH JUMP WITH A POLE** a field event in which the competitors use a long flexible pole to swing themselves up and over a very high crossbar **2.** **JUMP IN THE POLE VAULT** a jump in the pole vault, or any jump made with the help of a pole —**pole-vault** *vti.* —**pole-vaulter** *n.*

poley /pṓli/ *adj. Aus* AGRIC having no horns [Mid-19thC. Formed from POLL.]

police /pə leéss/ *n.* **1.** **ORGANIZATION FOR MAINTAINING LAW AND ORDER** a civil organization whose members are given special legal powers by the government and whose task is to maintain public order and to solve and prevent crimes **2.** **POLICE OFFICERS** police officers considered as a group (*takes a plural verb*) **3.** **SPECIALIZED FORCE** an organized group of people whose job is maintaining order, ensuring that regulations are obeyed, and preventing crime within a particular area or sphere of activity **4.** **ENFORCEMENT OF LAW** the enforcement of law and the prevention of crime in a community (*archaic*) ■ *vt.* (**-lices, -licing, -liced**) **1.** **ENSURE LAW AND ORDER** to ensure that law and order is maintained in a particular area or at a particular event, using the police or a military force **2.** **ENSURE RULES ARE FOLLOWED** to ensure that rules and procedures are followed correctly in sth or that sth is implemented as agreed [15thC. Via French from, ultimately,

Greek *politeia* 'civil organization, the state', from *politēs* 'citizen'(see POLITIC).]

police action *n.* a relatively small-scale military action undertaken without a declaration of war, e.g. to prevent violation of an international agreement. Soldiers used in police actions are usually deployed aiding the civil police.

police constable *n.* = constable

police dog *n.* a dog trained to work with the police in tracking or searching for people or in detecting illegal substances by smell

police force *n.* an organized body of police with jurisdiction within a particular geographical area or over a particular group of people

policeman /pə lēessmən/ (*plural* **-men** /-mən/) *n.* a man who is a police officer

Police Motu = Hiri Motu

police officer *n.* sb who belongs to a police force

police procedural *n.* a crime novel or drama in which the crime is investigated by police officers

police state *n.* a country in which the government uses police, especially secret police, to exercise strict or repressive control over the population and deny them full civil liberties

police station *n.* the local headquarters of a police force

policewoman /pə lēess wŏŏmən/ (*plural* **-en** /-wimin/) *n.* a woman who is a police officer, especially a constable

policy[1] /pólləssi/ *n.* (*plural* **-cies**) **1.** COURSE OF ACTION a programme of actions adopted by an individual, group, or government, or the set of principles on which they are based **2.** PRUDENCE shrewdness or prudence, especially in the pursuit of a particular course of action ■ *npl.* *Scotland* ESTATE GROUNDS the grounds attached to a large country house [14thC. From Old French *policie* 'government, civil organization' (see POLICE). The underlying meaning is 'an established system of government'.]

policy[2] /pólləssi/ (*plural* **-cies**) *n.* a contract that exists between an insurance company and an individual or organization buying insurance services, or the document that lists the contract terms [Mid-16thC. From French *police*, of uncertain origin; probably via Latin *apodixis* from, ultimately, Greek *apodeiknunai* 'to demonstrate, prove'.]

policyholder /pólləssi hōldər/ *n.* a named person or organization responsible for an insurance policy

policymaking /pólləssi mayking/ *n.* DRAWING UP OF POLICY the drawing up of policies, especially the formulating of political policies by members of a government ■ *adj.* MAKING POLICIES having the task of formulating policies, especially in a government — **policymaker** *n.*

policy science *n.* the study of how policies are made and executed in governments and bureaucracies

polio /póli ō/ *n.* = poliomyelitis [Mid-20thC. Shortening.]

poliomyelitis /póli ō mí ə lítiss/ *n.* a severe infectious viral disease, usually affecting children or young adults, that inflames the brainstem and spinal cord, sometimes leading to paralysis and muscular wasting [Late 19thC. From modern Latin, from Greek *polios* 'grey' (because the motor neurons it affects are known as 'grey matter') + MYELITIS.] — **poliomyelitic** /-mí ə lítik/ *adj.*

poliovirus /póli ō vírəss/ *n.* any of three forms of an enterovirus that causes poliomyelitis

polis[1] /pólliss/ (*plural* **-leis** /pó līss/) *n.* **1.** ANCIENT GREEK CITY-STATE a city-state in ancient Greece, typical of Greek political organization from 800 to 400 BC **2.** GOVERNMENT USING CITY-STATES the city-state form of government [Late 19thC. From Greek, 'city' (source of English *metropolis*, *police*, and *politics*).]

polis[2] /pólliss/ (*plural* **-lis**) *n.* *Scotland* the police as a force, or an individual police officer (*nonstandard*) [Late 19thC. Alteration of POLICE.]

polish /póllish/ *v.* (**-ishes**, **-ishing**, **-ished**) **1.** *vti.* MAKE SMOOTH OR GLOSSY to make sth smooth or shiny, or become smooth or shiny, by rubbing with sth **2.** *vt.* REMOVE THE OUTER LAYER OF to remove the outer layers of

brown rice to make white rice by rotating the grain in a drum **3.** *vti.* IMPROVE to make sth more refined, elegant, or complete, or to become so ■ *n.* **1.** SUBSTANCE USED FOR POLISHING a substance used to make sth smooth or shiny ○ *furniture polish* **2.** SMOOTHNESS the smoothness or glossiness of sth that has been polished ○ *car paintwork with a high polish* **3.** RUB GIVEN TO STH a rubbing of sth designed to make it smooth or glossy **4.** REFINEMENT refinement, especially of style, that is the mark of expertise or experience [13thC. Via the Old French stem *poliss-* from Latin *polire* (source also of English *polite*). Ultimately from an Indo-European base meaning 'to push', which also produced English *push*.] — **polisher** *n.*

polish off *vt.* **1.** FINISH QUICKLY AND COMPLETELY to finish sth, especially food or a task, quickly and completely **2.** KILL to kill or eliminate sb (*informal*) [From the idea of putting the finishing touches to sth]

polish up *vt.* **1.** MAKE SHINY to make sth smooth or shiny by rubbing it **2.** IMPROVE to improve or refine sth, e.g. a prepared speech or knowledge of a foreign language

polish up on *vt.* to improve knowledge or skill in a particular area

Polish /pólish/ *npl.* PEOPLES PEOPLE OF POLAND the people of Poland ■ *n.* LANG OFFICIAL LANGUAGE OF POLAND the official language of Poland, also spoken in parts of the United States and Europe, especially Germany. It belongs to the Balto-Slavic branch of Indo-European languages and is spoken by about 44 million people. ■ *adj.* **1.** OF POLAND relating to Poland, its people, or culture **2.** OF POLISH relating to the Polish language

Polish notation *n.* a notation for symbolic logic where the logical operators are placed as prefixes in front of formulas instead of between them, allowing parentheses to be dispensed with. For example, 'p or (q and r)' becomes 'or p and q r'. [From the fact that it was developed by mathematicians in Poland]

polit. *abbr.* **1.** politics **2.** political

Politburo /póllit byoorō, pə lít-/ *n.* the executive and policymaking committee of a governing Communist Party, especially the committee consisting of twenty members in the former Soviet Union [Early 20thC. From Russian *politbyuro*, literally 'political bureau'.]

polite /pə līt/ (**-liter**, **-litest**) *adj.* **1.** WELL-MANNERED showing or possessing good manners or common courtesy **2.** ELEGANT socially superior to ordinary people and considered refined or cultivated [15thC. From Latin *politus*, the past participle of *polire* 'to polish' (see POLISH).] — **politely** *adv.* — **politeness** *n.*

politesse /pólli téss/ *n.* politeness of a very formal or genteel kind [Early 18thC. From French, literally 'politeness'.]

politic /póllətik/ *adj.* possessing or displaying tact, shrewdness, or cunning [15thC. Via Old French from, ultimately, Greek *politēs* 'citizen', from *polis* 'city' (see POLIS).] — **politicly** *adv.*

political /pə líttik'l/ *adj.* **1.** CONCERNED WITH PARTY POLITICS relating to politics, especially party politics **2.** CONCERNED WITH GOVERNMENT relating to civil administration or government **3.** RESULTING FROM UNACCEPTABLE BELIEFS arising from sb's voiced opposition to a government or from voiced support for policies and principles regarded by authorities as unacceptable **4.** PRAGMATIC carried out for reasons that best serve a desired outcome rather than for reasons that are, e.g. morally justifiable ○ *denies that this was a political decision* — **politically** *adv.*

political economy *n.* the study of ways in which economics and government policies interact (*dated*) — **political economist** *n.*

politically correct *adj.* marked by language or conduct that deliberately avoids giving offence, e.g. on the basis of ethnic origin or sexual orientation — **political correctness** *n.*

political party *n.* an organization that collectively represents a political ideology, especially in a constitutional government or opposition

political prisoner *n.* sb who is imprisoned because his or her political actions or beliefs are regarded as unacceptable or subversive

political science *n.* the study of political organizations and institutions, especially governments — **political scientist** *n.*

political terrorism *n.* the use of intimidating violence for political ends, or a specific instance of this — **political terrorist** *n.*

political theatre *n.* dramatic performances designed to advance or promote a political cause

politician /póllə tísh'n/ *n.* **1.** SB ACTIVE IN POLITICS sb who is actively or professionally engaged in politics **2.** GOVERNMENT MEMBER a member of a branch of government **3.** *US* SB SEEKING PERSONAL POWER sb whose main political motive is self-advancement (*disapproving*) **4.** SCHEMER sb who deviously manipulates interrelationships, especially in a workplace [Late 16thC. Formed from POLITIC.]

politicize /pə lítti stz/ (**-cizes**, **-cizing**, **-cized**), **politicise** (**-cises**, **-cising**, **-cised**) *v.* **1.** INTRODUCE INTO THE POLITICAL ARENA to bring sth such as an issue of public interest into the political arena **2.** *vt.* GIVE A POLITICAL AWARENESS OR FLAVOUR TO to make sb politically aware or active, or introduce a political element to sth — **politicization** /pə lítti st záysh'n/ *n.*

politicking /póllə tiking/ *n.* political activity, especially campaigning or speech-making, often when disapproved of as insincere or self-serving

politico /pə líttikō/ (*plural* **-cos**) *n.* a politician, especially one whose words are dismissed as trite or whose motives are disapproved of as self-serving (*informal*) [Mid-17thC. From Italian or Spanish, 'politician'.]

politics /póllətiks/ *n.* **1.** THEORY AND PRACTICE OF GOVERNMENT the theory and practice of forming and running organizations connected with government (*takes a singular verb*) **2.** POLICYMAKING ACTIVITY activity within a political party or organization that is concerned with debate and the creation and carrying out of distinctive policies rather than merely the administration of the state (*takes a singular or plural verb*) **3.** INTERRELATIONSHIPS IN A SPECIFIC FIELD the totality of interrelationships in a particular area of life involving power, authority, or influence, and capable of manipulation (*takes a singular or plural verb*) ○ *the politics of education* **4.** CALCULATED ADVANCEMENT the use of tactics and strategy to gain power in a group or organization (*takes a singular or plural verb*) **5.** POLITICAL LIFE political life as a profession (*takes a singular verb*) ■ *npl.* **1.** POLITICAL ACTIVITY political activity at any level **2.** POLITICAL BELIEFS political persuasions or beliefs

polity /pólləti/ (*plural* **-ties**) *n.* **1.** PARTICULAR FORM OF GOVERNMENT a particular form of government that exists within a state or an institution **2.** POLITICS AND GOVERNMENT WITHIN SOCIETY that aspect of society that is oriented to politics and government **3.** POLITICAL ENTITY a state, society, or institution regarded as a political entity [Mid-16thC. Via Latin from Greek *politeia* (see POLICE).]

polje /pólyə/ *n.* GEOG a large steep-walled plain in a limestone region, containing a marsh or small lake [Late 19thC. From Serbo-Croat, 'field'. Ultimately from an Indo-European base denoting 'flat, to spread', which is also the ancestor of English *field*, *plain*, and *polka*.]

James Knox Polk

Polk /pōk/, **James Knox** (1795–1849) US statesman and 11th president of the United States. Under his Democratic administration (1845–49), the United States expanded westwards to the Pacific Ocean.

polka /pólkə, pṓl-/ *n.* **1.** LIVELY DANCE a lively dance for couples consisting of three quick steps and a hop and originating in Central Europe **2.** MUSIC FOR THE POLKA a piece of music for the polka, in fast two-four time ■ *vi.* **(-kas, -kaing, -kaed)** DANCE THE POLKA to dance the polka [Mid-19thC. Origin uncertain: probably via Czech from Polish, the feminine form of *Polak* 'Pole', which developed from a prehistoric Slavic word meaning 'field' (source also of English *polje*).]

polka dot *n.* a dot or round spot repeated to form a regular pattern in a contrasting colour, especially on fabric

poll /pōl/ *n.* **1.** POL ELECTION a political election in its entirety, including the casting, recording, and counting of votes **2.** SURVEY OF THE PUBLIC a questioning of the population or of a representative sample to tally opinions or gather other information. ◊ **opinion poll 3.** POL NUMBER OF VOTES the total number of votes cast in an election **4.** HEAD the head, or the back part of the head (*archaic*) **5.** TECH STRIKING SURFACE OF A HAMMER the broad, hitting part of a hammer ■ **polls** *npl.* POL = **polling station** ■ *v.* **(polls, polling, polled) 1.** *vt.* SAMPLE OPINION METHODICALLY to sample the opinions or attitudes of a group of people systematically **2.** *vt.* POL RECEIVE A CERTAIN NUMBER OF VOTES to receive a particular number of votes in an election **3.** *vti.* CAST A VOTE IN AN ELECTION to cast a vote in an election **4.** *vt.* COMPUT CHECK THE AVAILABILITY OF COMPUTER COMMUNICATION LINES to check communication lines in a computer or computer network to determine if they can receive or transmit data **5.** *vt.* AGRIC SHEAR AN ANIMAL to clip or shear an animal **6.** *vt.* AGRIC REMOVE AN ANIMAL'S HORNS to cut an animal's horns short or cut them off [13thC. Origin uncertain: probably from Middle Dutch or Middle Low German. The original meaning underlying all its senses is 'head'; the 'voting' meaning comes from the idea of counting heads.]

pollack /póllək/ (*plural* **-lacks** *or* **-lack**), **pollock** (*plural* **-locks** *or* **-lock**) *n.* a marine fish with a protruding lower jaw, found in North Atlantic waters. It belongs to the cod family and is an important food fish. Genus: *Pollachius*. [Early 16thC. Alteration of Scots *podlok*, of unknown origin.]

pollard /póllərd, -aard/ *n.* **1.** BOT TREE WITH BRANCHES CUT a tree whose branches are cut back extensively to encourage denser growth **2.** ZOOL ANIMAL WITH HORNS REMOVED OR SHED an animal that has shed its horns or antlers, or has had its horns removed ■ *vt.* **(-lards, -larding, -larded)** CUT BRANCHES OR HORNS to cut back the branches of a tree, or remove the horns of an animal [Mid-17thC. Formed from POLL. The underlying meaning is 'having its head cut'.]

poll card *n.* = **polling card**

pollen /póllən/ *n.* a powdery substance produced by flowering plants that contains male reproductive cells. It is carried by wind and insects to other plants, which it fertilizes. [Mid-18thC. From Latin, 'fine flour, dust'.]

Pollen /póllən/, **Daniel** (1813–96) New Zealand statesman. He was premier of New Zealand (1875–76).

pollen analysis *n.* = **palynology**

pollen basket *n.* the hollow part of a bee's hind leg, used to transport pollen

pollen count *n.* a scientific measure of the amount of pollen in a specific volume of air during a 24-hour period

pollen mother cell *n.* a cell in a flowering plant that produces four pollen grains after cell division

pollen sac *n.* a cavity in the anther of a flower, where pollen is produced

pollen tube *n.* a hollow tube that develops from a pollen grain and conveys male reproductive cells to the egg cell

poll evil *n.* inflammation around the ligaments and tendons under the skin between a horse's ears, usually due to bacterial infection

pollex /pólleks/ (*plural* **-lices** /-seez/) *n.* the first digit of the forelimb in birds and animals, or the thumb in humans (*technical*) [Mid-19thC. From Latin, of uncertain origin.]

pollie /pólli/, **polly** (*plural* **pollies**) *n. Aus* a politician (*informal*)

pollinate /póllə nayt/ **(-nates, -nating, -nated)** *vt.* to transfer pollen from the anthers to the stigma, usually from one plant to another, and fertilize it [Late 19thC. Formed from Latin *pollin-*, the stem of *pollen* (see POLLEN).] —**pollination** /póllə náysh'n/ *n.* —**pollinator** /-naytər/ *n.*

polling booth *n.* a booth in which an individual voter marks a ballot paper during an election

polling card, **poll card** *n.* a postcard giving details of time and place of voting, sent to all who are on the electoral register

polling station *n.* a building officially designated for casting votes during an election

pollinia plural of **pollinium**

polliniferous /póllə nífərəss/ *adj.* producing or carrying pollen [Mid-19thC. Coined from the Latin stem *pollin-* (see POLLINATE) + -FEROUS.]

pollinium /pə línni əm/ (*plural* **-ia** /-ə/) *n.* a cohering mass of pollen grains transported as a whole during pollination, typical of orchids and milkweeds [Mid-19thC. From modern Latin, formed from the Latin stem *pollin-* (see POLLINATE).]

pollinosis /pólli nṓssiss/ *n.* hay fever (*technical*) [Early 20thC. Formed from the Latin stem *pollin-* (see POLLINATE).]

polliwog /pólliwog/, **pollywog** *n. UK, US, Can* a tadpole (*regional*) [15thC. Alteration of earlier *polwygle*, from *poll* 'head' (see POLL) + WIGGLE.]

pollock *n.* = **pollack**

Pollock /póllək/, **Jackson** (1912–56) US artist. A leading abstract expressionist, he used action-painting techniques to create intricate interlaced webs of paint. Full name **Paul Jackson Pollock**

pollster /pṓlstər/ *n.* sb who conducts public opinion polls

poll tax *n.* **1.** TAX LEVIED EQUALLY ON ALL any flat-rate tax levied on all the individuals in a population, often as a prerequisite to voting **2.** COMMUNITY CHARGE a community charge (*informal*)

pollucite /póllyoo sīt, pə lóoss īt/ *n.* a colourless rare mineral that occurs in coarse granite and is a source of caesium [Mid-19thC. Alteration of its earlier name *pollux*, from the fact that it is associated with the mineral CASTOR[2] (in allusion to Castor and Pollux, sons of Zeus in Greek mythology).]

pollutant /pə lóot'nt/ *n.* sth that pollutes, e.g. chemicals or waste products that contaminate the air, soil, or water

pollute /pə lóot/ **(-lutes, -luting, -luted)** *vt.* **1.** CONTAMINATE to cause harm to an area of the natural environment, e.g. the air, soil, or water, usually by introducing damaging substances such as chemicals or waste products **2.** CORRUPT OR DEFILE to make sb morally or spiritually impure **3.** DESECRATE to violate the sacred nature of a holy place [14thC. From Latin *pollut-*, the past participle stem of *polluere*. Ultimately from an Indo-European base meaning 'dirt, to make dirty'.] —**polluter** *n.*

pollution /pə lóoshən/ *n.* **1.** ACT OF POLLUTING the act of polluting sth, especially the natural environment **2.** POLLUTED STATE the state or condition of being polluted, or the presence of pollutants ○ *Pollution will destroy fish in the rivers.*

Pollux *n.* ◆ **Castor and Pollux**

polly *n.* = **pollie**

Pollyanna /pólli ánnə/ *n.* sb who is invariably and unrealistically optimistic [Early 20thC. Named after the heroine of children's stories written by the US author Eleanor Hodgman Porter (1868–1920).]

pollywog *n.* = **polliwog**

polo /pṓlō/ *n.* **1.** SPORTS TEAM GAME PLAYED ON HORSEBACK a game played by teams on horseback, with players using long-handled mallets to drive a wooden ball into a goal **2.** SPORTS TEAM GAME PLAYED WITH BALL any of several team games whose object is to drive a ball into a goal, e.g. water polo (*usually used in combination*) **3.** (*plural* **-los**) CLOTHES POLO SHIRT a polo shirt (*informal*) **4.** POLO NECK a polo neck (*informal*) [Late 19thC. From Tibetan *pholo*, literally 'ball game'.]

Polo /pṓlō/, **Marco** (1254–1324) Venetian merchant and traveller. His accounts of his travels to China offered Europeans a firsthand view of Asian lands and stimulated interest in Asian trade.

polo coat *n.* a double-breasted overcoat, usually made of camelhair

polonaise /póllə náyz/ *n.* **1.** DANCE SLOW FORMAL DANCE FOR COUPLES a slow and stately dance of Polish origin, for couples **2.** MUSIC MUSIC FOR A POLONAISE a piece of music for the polonaise, in $\frac{3}{4}$ time **3.** CLOTHES CUTAWAY DRESS WITH UNDERSKIRT a dress with a tight bodice, cut away at the waist to reveal an inner skirt [Mid-18thC. From French, 'Polish'.]

polo neck *n.* US term **turtleneck 1.** HIGH ROLLOVER COLLAR high rollover collar that fits closely to the neck **2.** SWEATER WITH HIGH ROLLOVER COLLAR a sweater with a high rollover collar that fits closely to the neck —**polo-necked** *adj.*

polonium /pə lṓni əm/ *n.* a very rare naturally radioactive metallic element found in uranium ores, used to remove static electricity. Symbol **Po** [Late 19thC. Formed from medieval Latin *Polonia* 'Poland', the home of Marie CURIE, one of the element's discoverers.]

polony /pə lṓni/ *n.* a large smoked sausage made with a variety of finely ground seasoned meats, usually including beef and pork [Mid-18thC. Probably an alteration of BOLOGNA.]

polo pony *n.* a horse ridden in the game of polo

polo shirt *n.* **1.** CASUAL COTTON SHIRT a lightweight casual shirt, usually made of knitted cotton, with a small square collar and a buttoned opening at the neck **2.** POLO-NECKED SHIRT a shirt with a polo neck [From the fact that it is traditionally worn by polo players]

Pol Pot /pól pót/ (1928–98) Cambodian political leader. He led the communist Khmer Rouge to victory, and approximately 1.7 million people died under his rule (1975–79). Real name **Saloth Sar**

poltergeist /póltərgīst/ *n.* a supposed supernatural spirit that reveals its presence by creating disturbances, e.g. by knocking over objects [Mid-19thC. From German, literally 'noisy ghost'.]

poltroon /pol tróon/ *n.* an offensive term for a contemptible coward (*archaic*) [Early 16thC. Via French from Italian *poltrone* 'coward, lazy person', of uncertain origin.]

poly[1] /pólli/ (*plural* **-ys**) *n.* (*informal*) **1.** MED POLYMORPHONUCLEAR LEUCOCYTE a polymorphonuclear leucocyte **2.** CHEM POLYETHYLENE polyethylene **3.** EDUC POLYTECHNIC a polytechnic [Late 20thC. Shortening.]

poly[2] /pólli/ (*plural* **-lies**) *n.* an aromatic plant of the mint family, found in southern Europe. Latin name: *Teucrium polium*. [Early 16thC. Via Latin *polium* from Greek *polion*.]

poly- *prefix.* **1.** more than one ○ *polyandry* **2.** more than normal ○ *polyphagia* **3.** polymer ○ *polyethylene* [From Greek *polus* 'much' (source of English *hoi polloi*). Ultimately from an Indo-European base meaning 'to fill', which is also the ancestor of *full, plenty, plus*, and *plural*.]

polyA /póli áy/ *n.* = **polyadenylic acid**

polyacrylamide /pólli ə krílla mīd/ *n.* a white solid polymer of acrylamide, used as a thickening, clouding, and absorbent agent

polyadelphous /pólli ə délfəss/ *adj.* used to describe flowers with stamens whose filaments are arranged in bundles [Early 19thC. Coined from POLY- + Greek *adelphos* 'brother', because the stamens are the male part of the flower.]

polyadenylic acid /pólli áddə níllik-/ *n.* a segment of RNA made up of multiple units of adenylic acid, found in messenger RNA molecules. It stabilizes RNA during protein synthesis.

polyalcohol /pólli álkə hol/ *n.* = **polyol**

polyamide /pólli ámmīd, -mid/ *n.* any synthetic polymer that has recurring amide groups. Nylon is a polyamide.

polyamine /pólli ámm een, -ə méen/ *n.* any organic compound containing more than one amino group

polyandry /pólli ándri/ *n.* **1.** ANTHROP HAVING MULTIPLE HUSBANDS the custom of having more than one husband **2.** ZOOL HAVING MULTIPLE MATES animal mating in which a female mates with more than one male during any single breeding season **3.** BOT **HAVING MANY STAMENS** possession by a plant of a large number of stamens [Late 17thC. From Greek *poluandria*, literally 'many husbands', from the stem *andr-* 'man, husband'.] —**polyandrous** /pólli ándrəss/ *adj.*

polyanthus /pólli ánthəss/ *n.* **1.** **HYBRID PRIMROSE** a hybrid primrose with bright flowers in a variety of colours. Latin name: *Primula polyantha*. **2.** = **polyanthus narcissus** [Early 18thC. Via modern Latin from Greek *poluanthos*, literally 'having many flowers'.]

polyanthus narcissus *n.* a narcissus with small white or yellow flowers, native to Europe and Asia. Latin name: *Narcissus tazetta*.

polyatomic /pólli ə tómmik/ *adj.* used to describe a molecule that has more than two atoms

polybasic /pólli báyssik/ *adj.* used to describe a molecule or compound that has two or more atoms of replaceable hydrogen

polybasite /pólli báy sīt/ *n.* a rare grey to black crystalline mineral containing silver, found near silver ores [Mid-19thC. From German *Polybasit*, from Greek *polus* 'much' + German *Basis* 'base', from its chemical composition.]

polycarbonate /pólli ka árbə nayt, -bənət/ *n.* a strong synthetic resin used in moulded products, unbreakable windows, and optical components such as spectacle lenses

polycarboxylic acid /pólli kaar bok síllik-/ *n.* carboxylic acid that contains more than one carboxyl group

polycarpic /pólli ka árpik/, **polycarpous** /-ka árpəss/ *adj.* used to describe a plant that is capable of producing flowers and fruit several times in succession —**polycarpy** /pólli kaarpi/ *n.*

polycentrism /pólli séntrizəm/ *n.* the belief, formerly held, that national spheres of power not modelled on the Soviet Union were possible within Communism —**polycentric** *adj.* —**polycentrist** *n., adj.*

polychaete /pólli keet/, **polychete** *n.* a marine worm with a segmented body and bristled fleshy appendages used in swimming. Class: Polychaeta. [Late 19thC. From modern Latin *Polychaeta*, class name, from Greek *polukhaitēs* 'having much hair', from *khaitē* 'long hair'.] —**polychaetous** /pólli ke étəss/ *adj.*

polychete /pólli keet/ *n.* US = MARINE BIOL **polychaete**

polychlorinated biphenyl /pólli kláwrə naytid bī féen'l/ *n.* full form of **PCB**

polychromatic /pólli krō máttik/ *adj.* **1.** **WITH MANY COLOURS** having, showing, or consisting of many colours, either at the same time or in sequence **2.** **WITH MANY WAVELENGTHS** used to describe electromagnetic radiation that has multiple wavelengths

polychrome /póllikrōm/ *adj.* **1.** **WITH MULTI-COLOURED DECORATION** decorated with many or varied colours **2.** PHYS = **polychromatic** *adj.* 1 ■ *n.* ARTS **MULTICOLOURED OBJECT** a polychrome object or artefact

polyclinic /pólli klínnik/ *n.* a clinic, often independent of a hospital, in which medical care is provided by a range of specialists

polyclone /pólliklōn/ *n.* a clone derived from groups of cells of different ancestry or genetic constitution —**polyclonal** /pólli klōn'l/ *adj.* —**polyclonally** /-klōn'li/ *adv.*

polyconic projection /pólli kónnik-/ *n.* a conic map projection in which all meridians, except the central, are curved and the parallels are non-concentric arcs

polycotton /pólli kot'n/ *n.* a fabric that is made from a mixture of polyester fibre and cotton [Late 20thC. Blend of POLYESTER and COTTON.]

polycotyledon /pólli kótti leéd'n/ *n.* a plant with more than two cotyledons —**polycotyledonous** *adj.*

polycrystal /pólli kríst'l/ *n.* a crystalline structure whose crystals were formed rapidly and randomly

polycyclic /pólli síklik/ *adj.* **1.** BIOL **WITH SEVERAL WHORLS** used to describe a shell that has two or more whorls **2.** CHEM **WITH SEVERAL RINGS OF ATOMS** used to describe a compound that has two or more closed rings of atoms —**polycyclic** *n.*

polycystic /pólli sístik/ *adj.* used to describe an organ, e.g. a kidney or ovary, that has developed multiple cysts

polycythaemia /póllisī theémi ə/ *n.* an abnormal increase in red blood cells, occurring on its own or in conjunction with other diseases, especially of the respiratory or circulatory systems [Mid-19thC. Coined from POLY- + -CYTE + HAEMO- + -IA, literally 'many-blood-cell disease'.]

polycythemia *n.* US = **polycythaemia**

polydactyl /pólli dáktil/ *adj.* used to describe vertebrates, including human beings, that have more than the normal number of fingers or toes —**polydactyl** *n.*

polydipsia /pólli dípsi ə/ *n.* abnormally excessive thirst [Mid-17thC. Coined from POLY- + Greek *dipsa* 'thirst' + -IA.] —**polydipsic** *adj.*

polyelectrolyte /pólli i léktrə līt/ *n.* an electrolyte that has a high molecular weight, e.g. a protein

polyembryony /pólli émbri əni/ *n.* the production of more than one embryo from a single egg —**polyembryonic** /pólli émbri ónnik/ *adj.*

polyene /pólli een/ *n.* a hydrocarbon that has many alternating single and double carbon-carbon bonds

polyester /pólli éstər/ *n.* **1.** **SYNTHETIC POLYMER** a synthetic polymer used in making resins, plastics, and textile fibres. The monomer units of polyesters are linked together by the chemical group -COO-. **2.** **SYNTHETIC FABRIC** a strong hard-wearing synthetic fabric with low moisture absorbency, made from a polyester

polyethylene /pólli éthə leen/ *n.* US = **polythene**

polyethylene glycol *n.* any of several polymers of ethylene compounds that are used as emulsifiers and lubricants in ointments and cosmetics

Polyfilla /póllifillə/ *tdmk.* a trademark for a multipurpose filling plaster

polygamy /pə líggəmi/ *n.* **1.** ANTHROP **HAVING MULTIPLE SPOUSES** the custom of having more than one spouse at the same time **2.** ZOOL **HAVING MULTIPLE MATES** animal mating in which an individual mates with more than one animal during any single breeding season [Late 16thC. Via French from, ultimately, ecclesiastical Greek *polugamos* 'often married', from Greek *gamos* 'marriage'.] —**polygamist** *n.* —**polygamous** *adj.* —**polygamously** *adv.*

polygene /pólli jeen/ *n.* any in a group of genes where the number of those genes present collectively determines the extent of a characteristic, e.g. height —**polygenic** /pólli jénnik/ *adj.* —**polygenically** /-jénnikli/ *adv.*

polygenesis /pólli jénnəssiss/ *n.* origin from more than one species, line of ancestors, or source —**polygenetic** /póllijə néttik/ *adj.* —**polygenetically** /-néttikli/ *adv.*

polyglot /pólli glot/ *adj.* **1.** **COMPETENT IN MANY LANGUAGES** capable of reading, writing, or speaking many languages **2.** **IN MANY LANGUAGES** written or communicated in many languages ■ *n.* **1.** **MULTILINGUAL PERSON** sb who has a command of many languages **2.** **BOOK CONTAINING TEXT IN MANY LANGUAGES** a book, especially a Bible, that gives the text in several languages **3.** **MIX OF LANGUAGES** a confused mixture of languages [Mid-17thC. Via French from Greek *poluglōttos*, from *glōtta* 'tongue, language' (source of English *glottis* and *glossary*).] —**polyglotism** /pólli glotizəm/ *n.*

polygon /pólligən, -gon/ *n.* a geometrical plane figure with three or more straight sides [Late 16thC. Via late Latin from Greek *polugōnos* 'many-angled', from -*gōnos* '-angled'.] —**polygonal** /pə líggən'l/ *adj.* —**polygonally** *adv.*

polygonum /pə líggənəm/ *n.* a plant with bulbous stem joints and spikes of small flowers. Genus: *Polygonum*. [Early 18thC. Via modern Latin, genus name, from Greek *polugonon* 'knotgrass', literally 'many-jointed', from *gonu* 'knee, joint'.]

polygraph /pólli graaf, -graf/ *n.* **1.** **DEVICE RECORDING INVOLUNTARY RESPONSES** an electrical device that registers several involuntary physical activities, including pulse rate and perspiration. It is often used as a lie detector. **2.** **TEST USING POLYGRAPH** a test using a polygraph, or a result of this test ■ *vt.* (-**graphs**, -**graphing**, -**graphed**) **TEST SB USING POLYGRAPH** to test sb,

usually sb suspected of committing a crime, using a polygraph [Mid-20thC. From the fact that it measures a number of physiological indicators at the same time.] —**polygraphic** /pólli gráffik/ *adj.* —**polygraphically** *adv.*

polygyny /pə líjjəni/ *n.* **1.** ANTHROP **HAVING MULTIPLE WIVES** the custom of being married to more than one wife at the same time. ◊ **polygamy 2.** ZOOL **HAVING MULTIPLE MATES** animal mating in which a male mates with more than one female during any single breeding season **3.** BOT **HAVING MANY PISTILS OR STYLES** the possession by a plant of many pistils or styles [Late 18thC. Formed from Greek *gunē* 'woman' (source of English *gynaeco-*).] —**polygynist** *n.* —**polygynous** *adj.*

polyhedra *n.* plural of **polyhedron**

polyhedral /pólli heédrəl/ *adj.* relating to or in the form of a polyhedron

polyhedral angle *n.* a geometrical angle formed by the intersection of three or more planes meeting at a point, e.g. the peak of a pyramid

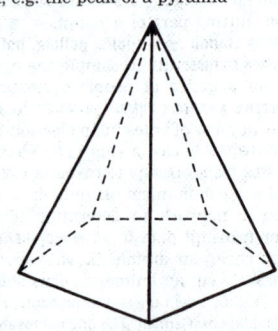

Polyhedron

polyhedron /pólli heédrən/ (*plural* -**drons** *or* -**dra** /-drə/) *n.* a solid geometrical figure that has many faces. A regular polyhedron has its faces formed from identical regular polygons that make equal angles with each other. [Late 16thC. From Greek *poluedron* 'many-based figure', from *hedra* 'base'.]

polyhydroxy /pólli hī dróksi/, **polyhydric** /-hídrik/ *adj.* used to describe a compound that has two or more hydroxyl groups in each molecule

Polyhymnia /pólli hímni ə/ *n.* in Greek mythology, the Muse responsible for songs and dances dedicated to the deities

polyimide /pólli ímmīd/ *n.* any tough durable polymer that contains an imido group, chiefly used in heat-resistant coatings

polyisoprene /pólli ísə preen/ *n.* a polymeric form of isoprene found in natural or synthetic rubber

polymath /pólli math/ *n.* sb who is knowledgeable in a variety of subjects [Early 17thC. From Greek *polumathēs*, literally 'sb with much learning', from *manthanein* 'to learn' (source of English *mathematics*).] —**polymathic** /pólli máthik/ *adj.* —**polymathy** /pə límməthi/ *n.*

polymer /póllimər/ *n.* a natural or synthetic compound that consists of large molecules made of many chemically bonded smaller identical molecules. Starch and nylon are polymers. [Mid-19thC. From Greek *polumerēs* 'having many parts', from *meros* 'part'.] —**polymeric** /pólli mérrik/ *adj.*

polymerase /póllimə rayz, pə límmə-/ *n.* any enzyme that catalyses a polymer, especially in DNA or RNA

polymerase chain reaction *n.* a technique used to replicate a fragment of DNA in order to replicate the DNA sequence

polymerization /pə límmə rī záysh'n, póllimə rī-/, **polymerisation** *n.* the chemical reaction in which a compound is made into a polymer by the addition or condensation of smaller molecules —**polymerize** /póllimə rīz, pə límmə rīz/ *vti.*

polymerous /pə límmərəss/ *adj.* **1.** BIOL **WITH MANY PARTS** used to describe an organism that consists of many parts or segments **2.** BOT **WITH PETALS IN MANY WHORLS** used to describe a flower that has its petals or sepals arranged in many whorls

polymorph /pólli mawrf/ *n.* **1.** BIOL **ANIMAL OR PLANT WITH MANY FORMS** an animal or plant that has several different adult forms **2.** CHEM **CHEMICAL COMPOUND WITH DIF-**

FERENT FORMS a chemical compound that has several crystalline forms **3.** BIOL WHITE BLOOD CELL WITH SEGMENTED NUCLEUS a white blood cell whose nucleus is segmented into lobes —**polymorphic** /pólli máwrfik/ adj. —**polymorphism** /-máwrfizəm/ n.

polymorphonuclear leucocyte /pólli máwrfō nyoōkli ər-/ n. = **polymorph** n. 3

polymyxin /pólli míksin/ n. a peptide antibiotic that is derived from a soil bacterium [Mid-20thC. Formed from modern Latin *Polymyxa*, species name, from POLY- + Greek *muxa* 'slime'.]

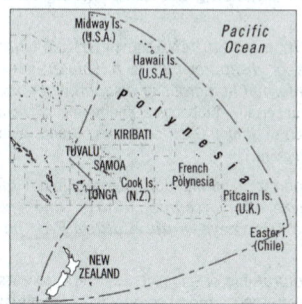

Polynesia

Polynesia /pólla neézi ə/ one of three major divisions of the Pacific Islands, encompassing a number of island groups in the central and southern Pacific Ocean, including Hawaii, Samoa, and the Cook Islands

Polynesian /pólli neézi ən/ n. **1.** PEOPLES SB FROM POLYNESIA sb who was born or brought up on any of the many islands of the central and southern Pacific **2.** LANG LANGUAGE GROUP OF POLYNESIA a group of languages, including Fijian, Hawaiian, and Maori, spoken on islands of the central and southern Pacific. They form a branch of the Austronesian family of languages. About 800,000 people speak a Polynesian language. ■ adj. **1.** OF POLYNESIA relating to any of the countries or islands of Polynesia, their people, or their cultures **2.** LANG OF POLYNESIAN relating to the group of languages called Polynesian

polyneuritis /pólli nyoor rítiss/ n. simultaneous inflammation of several nerves at once

Polynices /pólli ní seez/ n. in Greek mythology, one of the sons of Oedipus and Jocasta. He and his brother Eteocles killed each other in a struggle over the throne of Thebes.

polynomial /pólli nṓmi əl/ adj. SCI WITH MORE THAN TWO TERMS used to describe a mathematical expression that has more than two terms, or a system of taxonomic nomenclature that uses more than two names ■ n. **1.** MATH MATHEMATICAL EXPRESSION a mathematical expression consisting of the sum of a number of terms, each of which contains a constant and variables raised to a positive integral power **2.** BIOL MULTI-TERM TAXONOMIC NAME a taxonomic name of a plant or animal that has more than two terms, e.g. one giving a genus, species, and subspecies [Late 17thC. Modelled on BINOMIAL.]

polynucleotide /pólli nyoōkli ə tīd/ n. a chemical compound made up of many nucleotides linked to one another, forming a chain

polyol /pólli ol/ n. any alcohol that contains more than two hydroxyl groups. Glycerol is a polyol.

polyoma /pólli ṓmə/, **polyoma virus** n. a virus in rodents that can produce tumours

polyp /póllip/ n. **1.** MARINE BIOL SEDENTARY STAGE OF MARINE INVERTEBRATE a single-cavity marine invertebrate (**coelenterate**) in its sedentary stage. It attaches to rock at one end of its cylindrical body and has a tentacled mouth at the other end. This stage usually alternates with a free-swimming form. **2.** MED BENIGN GROWTH ON BODY a small stalk-shaped growth sticking out from the skin or from a mucous membrane. Polyps are mostly benign, but some become malignant. [14thC. Via French *polipe* and Latin *polypus* from Greek *polupous* 'octopus', literally 'many-footed', from *pous* 'foot' (source of English *podium*).] —**polypoid** /pólli poyd/ adj. —**polypous** adj.

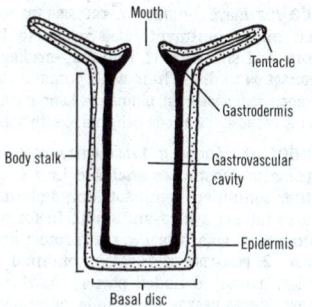

Polyp: Cross-section of a polyp

polypeptide /pólli pép tīd/ n. a natural or synthetic compound consisting of linked amino acids. Proteins are polypeptides.

polypetalous /pólli péttələss/ adj. used to describe flowers with many separate petals, e.g. roses and carnations

polyphagia /pólli fáyjə/ n. **1.** MED ABNORMALLY HUGE APPETITE an abnormally insatiable appetite for food **2.** BIOL DIET OF MANY FOODS the habit on the part of certain animals of feeding on many different types of food —**polyphagous** /pə líffəgəss/ adj.

polyphase /pólli fayz/ adj. producing two or more phases of alternating current, or two or more alternating voltages of the same frequency

Polyphemus /pólli feéməss/ n. in Greek mythology, a cyclops who imprisoned Odysseus, who put out Polyphemus's one eye

polyphemus moth n. a large North American moth with a large transparent blue eyespot on each hind wing. Latin name: *Antheraea polyphemus*.

polyphone /pólli fōn/ n. a letter or character that has more than one way of being pronounced

polyphonic /pólli fónnik/ adj. **1.** MUSIC WITH SEVERAL MELODIES consisting of two or more largely independent melodic lines, parts, or voices that sound simultaneously **2.** LING WITH SEVERAL POSSIBLE PRONUNCIATIONS used to describe a letter or character that may be pronounced in several different ways —**polyphonically** adv.

polyphonic prose n. highly rhythmic prose that makes use of poetic devices such as alliteration and assonance

polyphony /pə líffəni/ n. **1.** MUSIC MUSIC WITH SEVERAL MELODIES musical composition that uses simultaneous, largely independent, melodic parts, lines, or voices **2.** LING USE OF LETTER FOR DIFFERENT SOUNDS the representation of different sounds by the same letter in a writing system [Early 19thC. From Greek *poluphōnia* 'multiplicity of sounds', from, ultimately, *phōnē* 'voice, sound' (see -PHONE).] —**polyphonous** adj. —**polyphonously** adv.

polyphyletic /pólli fī léttik/ adj. derived or descended from several groups of ancestors —**polyphyletically** adv.

polyphyodont /pólli fī ō dont/ adj. used to describe a fish or other vertebrate that grows several sets of teeth in succession [Late 19thC. Modelled on DIPHYODONT.]

polyploid /pólli employ/ adj. having more than twice the basic number of chromosomes —**polyploid** n. —**polyploidy** n.

polypod /pólli pod/ adj. used to describe an insect larva with a large number of legs and feet, or this larval stage in the development of some insects [Mid-18thC. Via French from the Greek stem *polupod-* 'many-footed', from *pous* 'foot' (source of English *podium*).] —**polypod** n.

polypody /póllipōdi/ n. (plural **-dies**) n. a fern with evergreen pinnate leaves and a creeping rootstock. Genus: *Polypodium*. [15thC. Via Latin *polypodium* from Greek *polupodion*, literally 'many-footed one'.]

polyposis /pólli pṓssiss/ n. a condition in which numerous polyps develop in a hollow organ, e.g. the bowel

polypropylene /pólli prṓpə leen/, **polypropene** /pólli prṓpeen/ n. a thermoplastic substance that is a synthetic polymer of propylene, used in making pipes, industrial fibres, and moulded objects

polyprotodont /pólli prṓtə dont/ n. any marsupial that has two or more incisors in the lower jaw. Opossums and bandicoots are polyprotodonts. Order: Polyprotodontia. [Late 19thC. Coined from POLY- + PROTO- + -ODONT, literally 'many front teeth'.]

polyptych /pólliptik/ n. an arrangement of three or more panels with a painting or carving on each, usually hinged together and used as an altarpiece in a church [Mid-19thC. Modelled on DIPTYCH.]

polypus /póllipəss/ (plural **-pi** /-pī/) n. MED = **polyp** n. 2 [14thC. From Latin (see POLYP).]

polyrhythm /pólliritħ'm/ n. musical composition that employs several simultaneous, contrasting rhythms —**polyrhythmic** /pólli ríthmik/ adj. —**polyrhythmically** /-ríthmikli/ adv.

polyribosome /pólli ríbəsōm/ n. a cluster of ribosomes linked by a strand of messenger RNA and functioning as a site of protein synthesis

polysaccharide /pólli sákə rīd/, **polysaccharose** /pólli sákərōss/ n. a complex carbohydrate, e.g. starch or cellulose, made up of sugar molecules linked into a branched or chain structure

polysemy /pólli líssimi, pólli seemi, pólli seémi/ n. the existence of several meanings for a single word or phrase [Early 20thC. Via modern Latin *polysemia* from, ultimately, Greek *polusēmos* 'having many meanings', from *sēma* 'sign' (see SEMANTIC).] —**polysemous** /pə líssiməss, pólli seémass/ adj.

polysepalous /pólli séppələss/ adj. used to describe flowers that have distinctly separate sepals

polysome /póllisōm/ n. = **polyribosome** [Mid-20thC. Contraction.]

polysomic /pólli sṓmik/ adj. used to describe a diploid cell or organism in which some of the chromosomes occur more than twice

polysorbate /pólli sáwr bayt/ n. an emulsifier used in preparing some foods and drugs [Mid-20thC. Coined from POLY- + SORBITOL + -ATE.]

polyspermy /pólli spurmi/ n. the fertilization of an egg by several spermatozoa

polystichous /pə lístikəss, pólli stíkəss/ adj. used to describe parts of a plant that are arranged in two or more series of rows [Late 19thC. Modelled on DISTICHOUS.]

polystyrene /pólli stí reen/ n. a synthetic polymer of styrene that is stable in various physical forms. As a white rigid foam (**expanded polystyrene**) it is used for packing and insulation.

polysulphide /pólli súlfīd/ n. a sulphide whose molecules have two or more atoms of sulphur

polysyllabic /pólli si lábbik/ adj. **1.** WITH SEVERAL SYLLABLES having more than one or two syllables **2.** WITH MANY LONG WORDS using or containing very long words, often where shorter words would be adequate or better —**polysyllabically** adv.

polysyllable /pólli siləb'l, pólli sílləb'l/ n. a word that has more than one or two syllables

polysyllogism /pólli síllǝjizəm/ n. a chain of syllogisms in which each conclusion forms the premise for the next

polysynaptic /pólli si náptik/ adj. used to describe a reflex in the central nervous system that uses two or more synapses

polysyndeton /pólli síndətən/ n. the use of multiple conjunctions or coordinate clauses in close succession, as, in 'The bad news caused him to weep and cry and wail' [Late 16thC. Modelled on ASYNDETON.]

polysynthetic /pólli sin théttik/ adj. used to describe a language in which the syntax is conveyed by means of multiple affixes to single words —**polysynthesis** /pólli sínthəssiss/ n. —**polysynthetically** /pólli sin théttikli/ adv.

polytechnic /pólli téknik/ n. a college offering a range of courses, some of them vocational or technical, at or below the bachelor's degree level. In 1992 all polytechnics in England and Wales became universities. [Early 19thC. Via French from Greek *polutekhnos* 'multi-skilled', from *tekhnē* 'skill' (source of English *technical*).]

polytene /pólli teen/ *adj.* with multi-stranded chromosomes in contact with corresponding chromosomes —**polytenic** /pólli teénik/ *adj.* —**polyteny** /-teeni/ *n.*

polytetrafluoroethylene /pólli téttrə floorō éthə leen/ *n.* a durable, chemically resistant, nonflammable thermoplastic substance widely used to coat metal surfaces, especially the surfaces of cooking pots to make them nonstick

polytheism /pólli thi izəm, pólli theé izəm/ *n.* worshipping of or believing in more than one deity, especially several deities [Early 17thC. Via French from Greek *poluthaos* 'of many deities', from *theos* 'deity' (see THEO-).] —**polytheist** *n.* —**polytheistic** /pólli thi ístik/ *adj.* —**polytheistically** /-ístikli/ *adv.*

polythene /pólli theen/ *n.* a malleable thermoplastic used to make containers, packaging, and electrical insulation materials. It is a polymer of ethylene. US term **polyethylene** [Mid-20thC. Contraction of POLY-ETHYLENE.]

polytonality /pólli tō nálləti/ *n.* music composed in such a way that several keys are used at once — **polytonal** /pólli tốn'l/ *adj.* —**polytonally** /-tốn'li/ *adv.*

polytrophic /pólli trốfik, -tróffik/ *adj.* used to describe bacteria that derive food from several different sources

polytypic /pólli típpik/, **polytypical** /-típpik'l/ *adj.* used to describe a taxonomic subset, especially a species, that has many subdivisions

polyunsaturated /pólli un sáchə raytid/ *adj.* belonging to a class of fats, especially plant oils, that are less likely to be converted into cholesterol in the body. Their molecules have long carbon chains with many double bonds unsaturated by hydrogen atoms.

polyurethane /pólli yoorə thayn/ *n.* any of a group of thermoplastic polymers that are used in resins, coatings, insulation, adhesives, foams, and fibres. They contain the NHCOO chemical group.

polyuria /pólli yoóri ə/ *n.* the passing of abnormally large amounts of urine, e.g. in untreated diabetes

polyvalent /pólli váylənt, pə lívvələnt/ *adj.* **1.** CHEM WITH MORE THAN ONE VALENCY used to describe a chemical element that has more than one valency or a valency of more than two **2.** BIOL EFFECTIVE AGAINST MULTIPLE AGENTS used to describe a vaccine that is effective against more than one strain of microorganism, toxin, antigen, or antibody —**polyvalency** /pólli váylənssi/ *n.*

polyvinyl /pólli vín'l/ *adj.* used to describe plastics and resins produced by the polymerization of vinyls

polyvinyl acetate *n.* full form of **PVA**

polyvinyl chloride *n.* full form of **PVC**

Polyxena /pə líksənə/ *n.* in Greek mythology, one of the daughters of King Priam and Queen Hecuba of Troy, sacrificed at the command of the ghost of Achilles

polyzoan /pólli zố ən/ *n.* BIOL = **bryozoan** [Mid-19thC. Formed from modern Latin *Polyzoa*, former phylum name, from POLY- + -ZOON.]

pom /pom/ *n.* ANZ a British person (*informal humorous or disapproving*) [Early 20thC. Shortening of POMMY.]

pomace /púmmiss, pómmiss/ *n.* **1.** REMAINS OF CRUSHED FRUIT the pulpy mass that remains after apples or other fruits have been crushed and pressed to extract the juice, e.g. to make cider **2.** FOOD REMAINS AFTER OIL EXTRACTION the pulpy mass that remains after nuts, fish, or other foods have been crushed and pressed to extract oil or another liquid [Mid-16thC. Via medieval Latin *pomacium* 'cider' from, ultimately, Latin *pomum* 'apple, fruit'.]

pomace fly *n.* a tiny fly that lives on decaying fruit, commonly found where cider or wine is being made. Family: Drosophilidae.

pomaceous /po máyshəss/ *adj.* used to describe a fruit in the form of a large fleshy receptacle with a central seed-bearing core (**pome**), e.g. the apple and the pear [Early 18thC. Formed from Latin *pomum* 'apple'.]

pomade /pə máyd, -maád/ *n.* DRESSING FOR HAIR a perfumed oil or ointment used to make hair look smooth and shiny ■ *vt.* (**-mades, -mading, -maded**) PUT POMADE ON to dress hair with pomade [Mid-16thC. Via French *pommade* from, ultimately, Latin *pomum* 'apple', probably because it was originally made with apples.]

pomander /pə mándər/ *n.* **1.** AROMATIC MIXTURE a mixture of aromatic substances enclosed in a sachet, ball, or other container, kept near stored clothes or in a room to impart a pleasant smell. In former times, a pomander was worn as a protection against disease. **2.** POMANDER CONTAINER a container for a pomander, usually a lidded pottery bowl with holes **3.** CLOVE-STUDDED ORANGE an orange or apple studded with cloves and used to scent clothes or a room [15thC. From Old French *pome d'embre*, literally 'apple of amber'.]

Pomare /po maári/, **Sir Maui Wiremu Pita Naera** (1876–1930) New Zealand Maori leader and politician. He was minister of health and minister of internal affairs during the Massey government.

pome /pōm/ *n.* BOT a fleshy fruit that has a central core typically containing five seeds, e.g. an apple or pear [14thC. Via Old French from, ultimately, Latin *pomum* 'apple'.]

Pomegranate

pomegranate /pómmi granit/ *n.* **1.** FOOD ROUND RED FRUIT a round reddish orange-sized fruit with a tough rind enclosing several chambers that are filled with numerous seeds surrounded by tart juicy red pulp **2.** TREES ASIAN TREE the tropical tree, native to Asia, that bears the pomegranate. Latin name: *Punica granatum*. [14thC. From Old French *pome grenate*, literally 'seedy apple'.]

pomelo /pómmələ/ (*plural* **-los**) *n.* **1.** FOOD CITRUS FRUIT a yellowy-orange citrus fruit similar to a large grapefruit **2.** (*plural* **-los** *or* **-lo**) TREES CITRUS TREE the citrus tree, native to Southeast Asia, that bears the pomelo. Latin name: *Citrus maxima*. [Mid-19thC. Origin uncertain: possibly an alteration of *pompelmous*, from Dutch *pompelmoes*.]

Pomeranian /pómmə ráyni ən/ *n.* **1.** ZOOL SMALL DOG a breed of small dog with a long silky coat, pointed ears, a pointed muzzle, and a long curling tail **2.** PEOPLES SB FROM POMERANIA sb who was born in or is an inhabitant of the central European region of Pomerania, which lies mostly in modern Poland ■ *adj.* OF POMERANIA relating to the central European region of Pomerania, its people, or their culture [Mid-18thC. Formed from *Pomerania* in central Europe.]

pomfret[1] /póm frit/, **pomfret-cake** *n.* a small flat round liquorice sweet [Mid-19thC. Named after the town of *Pomfret* (now 'Pontefract') in West Yorkshire, where they were originally made.]

pomfret[2] /póm frit/ (*plural* **-frets** *or* **-fret**) *n.* a tropical sea fish whose white flesh is used especially in Southeast Asian, Chinese, and Indian cooking. Latin name: *Stromateoides argenteus*. [Early 18thC. Origin uncertain: probably literally 'little pampo', formed from Portuguese *pampo*.]

pomiculture /pómmi kulchər/ *n.* the cultivation of fruit [Late 19thC. Coined from Latin *pomum* 'apple, fruit' + CULTURE.]

pomiferous /po mífferəss/ *adj.* used to describe fruit plants that bear apples, pears, or any related fleshy fruit with five seeds (**pome**) [Mid-17thC. Formed from Latin *pomum* 'apple, fruit'.]

pommel /pómm'l, púmm'l/ *n.* **1.** EQU FRONT OF SADDLE the front part of a saddle that curves upwards **2.** ARMS PART OF SWORD HANDLE the knob at the hilt of a sword **3.** GYMNASTICS HANDLE ON POMMEL HORSE either of the two curved handles on the top of a pommel horse ■ *vt.* = **pummel** [14thC. Via Old French *pomel*, literally 'little fruit', from, ultimately, Latin *pomum* 'fruit'.]

pommel horse *n.* **1.** GYMNASTICS APPARATUS a padded oblong piece of gymnastics apparatus that is raised off the floor and has two curved handles on the top **2.** GYMNASTICS EVENT the men's gymnastics event that involves balancing and manoeuvring on a pommel horse

pommy /pómmi/ *adj.* ANZ BRITISH British (*informal humorous or disapproving*) ■ *n.* (*plural* **-mies**) ANZ = **pom** (*informal humorous or disapproving*) [Early 20thC. Origin uncertain: probably a shortening of *pomegranate*, alteration of *Jimmy Grant* or *Pummy Grant*, rhyming slang for *immigrant*.]

pomo /pốmō/, **po-mo** *adj.* postmodern (*informal*) ○ '*beat-generation, counterculture, and pomo literature*' (Hawkeye, *FutureCulture FAQ part 1 & 2*; 1992)

Pomo (*plural* **-mo** *or* **-mos**) *n.* **1.** PEOPLES MEMBER OF NATIVE N AMERICAN PEOPLE a member of a group of Native North American peoples living in northern California **2.** LANG NATIVE AMERICAN LANGUAGE any of several closely related Native American languages spoken in parts of northern California. They belong to the Hokan branch of Hokan-Siouan languages. [Late 19thC. From northern Pomo *P ó mo* 'at the red earth hole'.] —**Pomo** *adj.*

pomology /po mólləji/ *n.* the study or practice of cultivating fruit [Early 19thC. Coined from Latin *pomum* 'fruit' + -LOGY.] —**pomological** /pómmə lójjik'l/ *adj.* —**pomologically** /-lójjikli/ *adv.* —**pomologist** /po móllə jist/ *n.*

Pomona /pə mốnə/ *n.* the Roman goddess of fruit [Mid-17thC. From Latin, from *pomum* 'fruit'.]

pomp /pomp/ *n.* **1.** CEREMONIAL SPLENDOUR a display of great splendour and magnificence **2.** SELF-IMPORTANCE an ostentatious and vain display of importance [14thC. Via Old French from, ultimately, Greek *pompē* 'solemn procession, send-off, escort', from *pempein* 'to send', of unknown origin.]

━━━━ **WORD KEY: CULTURAL NOTE** ━━━━

Pomp and Circumstance, an orchestral work by British composer Edward Elgar (parts 1 to 4: 1901–07; part 5: 1930). The title of this series of five military marches (op. 39) derives from the reference in Shakespeare's *Othello* (III iii) to the 'pride, pomp, and circumstance of glorious war'. The first march includes a melody later used for the finale of Elgar's *Coronation Ode*, 'Land of Hope and Glory'.

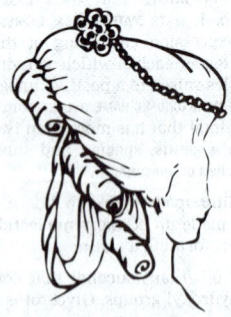

Pompadour

pompadour /pómpə door/ *n.* a woman's hairstyle, popular in the 18th century, in which the hair is swept back high off the face over a pad [Mid-18thC. Named after Jeanne-Antoinette Poisson, Marquise de *Pompadour* (1721–64), who popularized the style.]

pompano /pómpənố/ (*plural* **-nos** *or* **-no**) *n.* **1.** ATLANTIC FISH a marine food fish with a deep flat body and forked tail, found off the southern Atlantic and Gulf coasts of North America. Latin name: *Trachinotus carolinus*. **2.** = **butterfish** [Late 18thC. From Spanish *pámpano*, of uncertain origin: possibly from *pámpana* 'vine leaf' (from its shape) or Latin *pampinus* 'tendril' (from its markings).]

Pompeian red /pom páy ən-/ *adj.* of a red colour that is tinged with orange, resembling the colour of the walls of houses found in Pompeii —**Pompeian red** *n.*

Pompeii: View of the Forum, with Vesuvius in the background

Pompeii /pom páy i/ ancient Roman city in southern Italy. It was buried by volcanic ash during the eruption of Mount Vesuvius in AD 79, and has since been partly excavated.

Pompey /pómpi/ (106–48 BC) Roman general and statesman. He formed the First Triumvirate with Caesar and Crassus. After quarrelling with Caesar, he was defeated by him at Pharsalus (48 BC) and escaped to Egypt, where he was assassinated. Full name **Gnaeus Pompeius Magnus**. Known as **Pompey the Great**

Pompidou /pómpi doo/, **Georges** (1911–74) French statesman. He was four times prime minister, and followed de Gaulle as president (1969–74).

pompilid /pómpilid/ *n.* = **spider hunting wasp** [Early 20thC. From modern Latin *Pompilidae*, family name, ultimately from Greek *pompilos* 'pilot-fish'.]

pompom /póm pom/ *n.* **1.** CLOTHES SMALL TUFTED WOOL BALL a small tufted ball made from wool, silk, or other material, attached as a decoration to hats, shoes, and other articles of clothing **2.** CHEERLEADER'S ACCESSORY a cheerleader's accessory in the form of a large white or brightly coloured ball-shaped mass of thin paper or plastic strips connected to a handle **3.** BOT = **pompon** *n.* 2 [Mid-18thC. From French, of unknown origin.]

pom-pom /póm pom/ *n.* a rapid-firing automatic weapon, especially a cannon used in the Boer War or a double-barrelled anti-aircraft gun used in World War II (*slang*) [An imitation of the sound]

pompon /póm pon/ *n.* **1.** CLOTHES = **pompom** *n.* 1 **2.** BOT SMALL ROUND FLOWER a small round flower of some chrysanthemum or dahlia varieties, or a variety that has this kind of flower [Mid-18thC. From French, of unknown origin.]

pomposity /pom póssəti/ (*plural* -**ties**) *n.* **1.** SELF-IMPORTANCE an excessive sense of self-importance, usually displayed through exaggerated seriousness or stateliness in speech and manner **2.** POMPOUS ACT an act, remark, or gesture that is exaggerated in its seriousness or stateliness and conveys an excessive sense of self-importance

pompous /pómpəss/ *adj.* **1.** SELF-IMPORTANT having an excessive sense of self-importance, usually displayed through exaggerated seriousness or stateliness in speech or manner **2.** REVEALING SELF-IMPORTANCE displaying exaggerated seriousness or stateliness ○ *a pompous gesture* **3.** CEREMONIALLY GRAND full of splendour and magnificence [14thC. Via Old French *pompeux* from, ultimately, Greek *pompē* (see POMP).] —**pompously** *adv.* —**pompousness** *n.*

'pon /pon/ *prep.* upon (*archaic or literary*) [Mid-16thC. Shortening.]

Ponca /póngkə/ (*plural* -**ca** or -**cas**) *n.* **1.** PEOPLES MEMBER OF NATIVE N AMERICAN PEOPLE a member of a Native North American people who formerly occupied lands around the Niobrara River in Nebraska and now live mainly in parts of Oklahoma and Nebraska **2.** LANG NATIVE AMERICAN LANGUAGE a Native American language spoken in parts of Oklahoma and Nebraska. It belongs to the Siouan branch of the Hokan-Siouan languages and is closely related to Omaha. [Late 18thC. From Ponka *ppákka*.] —**Ponca** *adj.*

ponce /ponss/ *n.* **1.** OFFENSIVE TERM an offensive term that deliberately insults a man's sexuality and appearance (*slang insult*) **2.** PIMP a pimp (*slang*) [Late 19thC. Origin unknown.] —**poncy** *adj.*

ponce about, ponce around *vi.* (*slang*) **1.** BEHAVE EFFEMINATELY to act in an effeminate manner **2.** WASTE TIME to spend time doing or achieving nothing at all

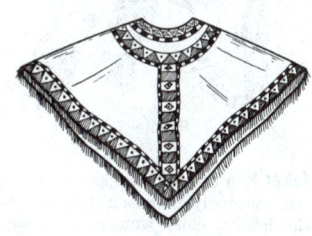

Poncho

poncho /pónchō/ (*plural* -**chos**) *n.* a simple outer garment for the upper body in the form of a single piece of heavy cloth, often wool, with a slit in it for the head. Ponchos were originally worn in South America. [Early 18thC. From American Spanish, of uncertain origin: perhaps from Spanish, variant of *pocho* 'faded'.]

pond /pond/ *n.* POOL a small still body of water formed naturally or created artificially, e.g. as a feature in a garden ■ *vi.* (**ponds, ponding, ponded**) FORM POOLS to collect into shallow pools (*refers to water*) [13thC. Alteration of POUND, in the sense 'enclosure for fish'.]

ponder /póndər/ (-**ders**, -**dering**, -**dered**) *vti.* to think over sth carefully over a period of time [14thC. Via Old French *ponderer* from Latin *ponderare* 'to weigh, consider', from *pondus* 'weight' (see PONDEROUS).]

ponderable /póndərəb'l/ *adj.* **1.** APPRECIABLE significant enough in size or extent to have an effect or be worth taking into consideration **2.** MEASURABLE able to be measured, calculated, or predicted ■ *n.* PONDERABLE THING sth that is ponderable —**ponderability** /póndərə bílləti/ *n.* —**ponderably** /póndərəbli/ *adv.*

ponderous /póndərəss/ *adj.* **1.** MOVING HEAVILY lumbering and laborious in movement **2.** DULL without liveliness or wit **3.** HEAVY-LOOKING disproportionately thick and heavy [14thC. Via Old French *pondereux* from Latin *ponderosus*, from *ponder-*, stem of *pondus* 'weight'.] —**ponderously** *adv.* —**ponderousness** *n.*

pond lily *n.* = **water lily**

pondokkie /pon dóki/ *n.* S Africa a roughly made house, especially one improvised from available materials (*informal*) [Early 19thC. From Afrikaans, of uncertain origin: probably via Malay from, ultimately, Arabic *fundug* 'hotel'.]

pond scum *n.* green freshwater algae that form a layer on the surface of stagnant water

pond-skater *n.* any of several types of long-legged insects that have slender hairy bodies and travel about on the surface of water. Family: Gerridae. US term **water strider**

pondweed /pónd weed/ (*plural* -**weed** or -**weeds**) *n.* **1.** AQUATIC PLANT an aquatic plant that has jointed stems, floating or submerged leaves, and greenish flowers. It grows in ponds and slow streams. Genus: *Potamogeton*. **2.** PLANT LIKE TRUE PONDWEED any of several aquatic plants such as mare's-tail unrelated to but resembling pondweed proper

pone[1] /pōn/ *n.* = **corn pone** [Early 17thC. From Virginia Algonquian *poan*.]

pone[2] /pōn, póni/ *n.* in card games, the person who does not deal in two-handed games, or the person sitting to the right of the dealer [Early 19thC. From Latin *pone* 'put', imperative of *ponere* 'to place' (see POSITION).]

pong /pong/ *n.* STINK an unpleasant smell (*informal*) ■ *vi.* (**pongs, ponging, ponged**) TO STINK to give off an unpleasant smell (*informal*) [Early 20thC. Origin unknown.] —**pongy** *adj.*

ponga /póngə/ (*plural* **pongas** or **ponga**) *n.* a tall evergreen tree fern found in New Zealand. Latin name: *Cyathea dealbata*. [Mid-19thC. From Maori.]

pongee /pon jee, pón jee/ *n.* **1.** SILK a type of soft, usually unbleached, silk fabric from China or India **2.** IMITATION SILK an imitation of silk pongee, usually made of cotton or rayon [Early 18thC. Origin uncertain, probably from Chinese *běnjī*, literally 'own loom', or *běnzhī*, literally 'home-woven'.]

pongid /pónjid, póng gid/ *n.* any ape of the family that includes the gibbon and the great apes. Family: Pongidae. [Mid-20thC. Via modern Latin *Pongidae*, family name, from, ultimately, Congolese *mpongo* 'ape'.]

pongo /póng gō/ (*plural* -**gos**) *n.* **1.** ORANG-UTAN an orang-utan **2.** SOLDIER a naval term for a soldier (*slang*) [Early 17thC. From Congolese *mpongo* 'ape'. Originally in the meaning of 'chimpanzee, gorilla'.]

poniard /pónnyərd, -yaard/ *n.* DAGGER a small dagger with a slim blade that is triangular or square in its cross section (*literary*) ■ *vt.* (-**iards**, -**iarding**, -**iarded**) STAB WITH PONIARD to stab sb with a poniard (*literary*) [Mid-16thC. Via French *poignard* from, ultimately, Latin *pugnus* 'fist' (see PUGNACIOUS). The underlying meaning is 'weapon held in a clenched fist'.]

pons /ponz/ (*plural* **pontes** /pón teez/) *n.* a whitish band of nerve fibres on the surface of the brainstem between the medulla oblongata and midbrain [Late 17thC. From Latin, 'bridge' (source of English *pontoon* and *pontiff*). Ultimately from an Indo-European word meaning 'to pass over', which is also the ancestor of English *path*.]

pons asinorum /pónz ássi náwrəm/ *n.* a proposition or problem that is especially difficult for an inexperienced person to understand [From Latin, literally 'bridge of asses', originally applied to the proposition of Euclid that the base angles of an isosceles triangle are equal]

pons Varolii /pónz və róli i/ *n.* ANAT = **pons** [Late 17thC. From Latin, literally 'bridge of Varolius', named after C. *Varoli* (1543–75), Italian anatomist.]

pont /pont/ *n.* S Africa a flat-bottomed ferryboat [Mid-17thC. Via Dutch from Middle Dutch *ponte* 'ferryboat'.]

Ponta Delgada /póntə del gaːdə/ city in Portugal, on São Miguel Island. It is the capital of the autonomous region of the Azores. Population: 21,091 (1991).

Pontefract cake /pónti frakt-/ *n.* = **pomfret**[1] [See POMFRET]

pontes plural of **pons**

pontifex /pónti feks/ (*plural* -**tifices** /pon tíffi seez/) *n.* a member of the highest council of priests in ancient Rome [Late 16thC. From Latin, literally 'way-maker', formed from *pont-*, stem of *pons* 'bridge, way' (see PONS).]

Pontifex Maximus /pónti feks máksiməss/ (*plural* **Pontifices Maximi** /pon tíffi seez máksi mīʹ/) *n.* the chief priest who presided over the highest council of priests in ancient Rome

pontiff /póntif/ *n.* **1.** ROMAN CATHOLIC POPE the head of the Roman Catholic Church and bishop of Rome **2.** ROMAN CATHOLIC BISHOP a bishop in the Roman Catholic Church (*archaic*) **3.** HIST = **pontifex** [Late 16thC. Via Old French from Latin *pontifex* (see PONTIFEX).]

pontifical /pon tíffik'l/ *adj.* **1.** OF A PONTIFF belonging to, befitting, or involving the Pope, a bishop, or a pontifex **2.** POMPOUS displaying an exaggerated sense of self-importance ■ *n.* BISHOP'S BOOK a book containing the rites that may be performed only by a bishop ■ **pontificals** *npl.* PONTIFF'S VESTMENTS the vestments and insignia of a pope or bishop [15thC. From Latin *pontificalis*, from *pontifex* (see PONTIFEX).] —**pontifically** *adv.*

Pontifical Mass *n.* a High Mass that is celebrated by a bishop, especially in the Roman Catholic Church

pontificate *vi.* /pon tíffi kayt/ (-**cates**, -**cating**, -**cated**) **1.** SPEAK POMPOUSLY to speak about sth in a knowing and self-important way, especially when not qualified to do so **2.** SERVE AS A BISHOP to officiate as a bishop, especially in celebrating Mass ■ *n.* /pon tíffikət, -kayt/ TERM OF OFFICE the office or term of office of a pope or bishop [Early 19thC. From medieval Latin *pontificat-*, the past participle stem of *pontificare*, from Latin *pontifex* (see PONTIFEX).] —**pontification** /pon tíffi káysh'n/ *n.* —**pontificator** /-kaytər/ *n.*

pontil /póntil/ n. = **punty** [Mid-19thC. From French, of uncertain origin: probably from Italian *puntello*, literally 'small point', from *punto* 'point'.]

pontine /pón tīn/ adj. relating to or situated in the whitish band of nerve fibres (**pons**) on the surface of the brainstem between the medulla oblongata and midbrain [Late 19thC. Formed from Latin *pont-*, stem of *pons* 'bridge, way' (see PONS).]

pontoon[1] /pon tóon/ n. **1.** CIV ENG **FLOATING SUPPORT FOR BRIDGE** a floating structure used as a support for a bridge across a river, especially one put in place temporarily **2.** AIR **FLOAT ON AN AIRCRAFT** a float on an aircraft providing buoyancy or stability when on water **3.** SHIPPING **FLOATING DOCK** a floating structure used as a dock [Late 17thC. Via French *ponton* from the Latin stem *ponton-* 'floating bridge', from *pont-*, stem of *pons* 'bridge' (see PONS). Originally 'flat-bottomed boat'.]

pontoon[2] /pon tóon/ n. **1.** CARDS **CARD GAME** a gambling card game in which the aim is to accumulate cards that add up to an exact value of 21. US term **blackjack** n. **1 2.** **HAND WITH 21 POINTS** a hand that contains exactly 21 points in the first deal in pontoon. US term **blackjack** [Early 20thC. Origin uncertain: probably an alteration of French *vingt-et-un* 'twenty-one'.]

pontoon bridge n. a temporary bridge built across a river, supported by floating structures

Pontypool /póntə póol/ town in Monmouthshire, Wales. Population: 35,564 (1991).

Pontypridd /póntə preeth/ town near Cardiff, Wales. Population: 28,487 (1991).

pony /póni/ n. (*plural* **-nies**) n. **1.** **SMALL HORSE** any of several small horse breeds **2.** **ANY HORSE** a horse of any kind, especially a racehorse (*informal*) **3.** **POLO HORSE** a horse used in polo **4.** **SMALL GLASS** a small drinking glass, especially one used for liqueurs **5.** **£25** the sum of £25 (*slang*) [Mid-17thC. Origin uncertain: possibly via French *poulenet*, literally 'little foal', from, ultimately, Latin *pullus* 'young animal' (see PULLET).]

pony up vti. US to pay sb the money that is owed to him or her (*dated informal*)

pony express n. a system of carrying mail using relays of horses and riders that operated in the American West from St Joseph, Missouri, to Sacramento, California, from 1860 to 1861

Ponytail

ponytail /póni tayl/ n. a hairstyle in which long hair is pulled back and tied behind the head so that it hangs down the back like a pony's tail —**ponytailed** adj.

pony-trekking n. a leisure activity that involves riding across open countryside on a pony, usually in organized groups

poo /poo/ n. **EXCREMENT** excrement, or an act of defecating (*informal; usually used by or to children*) ■ vti. (**poos, pooing, pooed**) **DEFECATE** to excrete faeces (*informal; usually used by or to children*) [Variant of POOH]

pooch /pooch/ n. a dog (*informal*) [Early 20thC. Origin unknown.]

poodle /póod'l/ n. a dog with a thick curly coat usually clipped short, belonging either to a small breed (**toy poodle**), or a large breed (**standard poodle**) originally developed in Europe for hunting [Early 19thC. From German *Pudel*, shortening of *Pudelhund*, from Low German *pudeln* 'to splash in water' + German *Hund* 'dog'.]

Poodle

poodle-faker n. a man who seeks out the company of women, especially a nauseatingly genteel young man who flatters older women, often for selfish reasons (*dated informal disapproving*) [From the idea that the man resembles a fawning lap dog]

poof[1] /poof, poof/, **pouf** n. an offensive term that deliberately insults a man for being homosexual or behaving in a way considered more characteristic of or suitable for a woman (*slang insult*) [Mid-19thC. Origin uncertain: probably an alteration (influenced by French *pouf* 'women's hairstyle') of PUFF 'powder-puff'.]

poof[2] /poof, poof/ interj. (*informal*) **1.** **INDICATING SUDDENNESS** used to indicate that sth happens suddenly **2.** **EXPRESSING DISDAIN** used to express disdain for or dismissal of sth

poofter /póoftər, poofter/ n. = **poof**[1] (*slang insult*) [Early 20thC. Alteration of POOF.]

poofy /póoffi, póoffi/ (**-ier, -iest**) adj. used disparagingly and often offensively to describe effeminate or homosexual men, or features of appearance or behaviour regarded as typical of effeminate or homosexual men (*slang disapproving*) [Mid-20thC. Formed from POOF[1].]

pooh /poo/ interj. (*informal*) **1.** **INDICATING STINK** used to indicate that there is an unpleasant smell. US term **phew 2.** **EXPRESSING DISDAIN** used to express disdain or dismissal [Late 16thC. An imitation of the sound made by blowing sth away with the lips.]

Pooh-Bah /póo baa/, **pooh-bah** n. **1.** **POMPOUS BUT USELESS OFFICIAL** a pompous self-important official, especially one who holds more than one office but is ineffectual in all of them **2.** **IMPORTANT PERSON** a leader, high official, or important person [Late 19thC. Named after a character in *The Mikado*, an operetta by W. S. Gilbert and Arthur Sullivan.]

pooh-pooh (**pooh-poohs, pooh-poohing, pooh-poohed**) vt. to dismiss or express disdain for sth [Late 18thC. Doubled form of POOH.]

pooka /póokə/ n. *Ireland* a mischievous spirit in Irish folklore, especially one who takes on the form of an animal [Early 19thC. Via Irish *púca* from Old English *pūca* 'puck' (see PUCK).]

pool[1] /pool/ n. **1.** **WATER** a small body of still water, usually one that occurs naturally **2.** **PUDDLE** a small amount of any liquid lying on a surface **3.** **LEISURE SWIMMING POOL** a swimming pool or paddling pool **4.** **DEEP PART OF WATER** a deep place in a river or stream where the water runs more slowly **5.** CIV ENG **WATER BEHIND DAM** a body of water collected behind a dam **6.** **PATTERN RESEMBLING A POOL** a pattern or arrangement of sth, e.g. light, that resembles a pool of liquid **7.** **UNDERGROUND OIL OR GAS** an accumulation of oil or gas in a region of porous sedimentary rock ■ vi. (**pools, pooling, pooled**) **1.** **FORM A POOL** to collect in or form a pool **2.** PHYSIOL **ACCUMULATE IN A BODY PART** to collect in a body part or organ (*refers to blood*) [Old English *pōl*, from prehistoric Germanic]

pool[2] /pool/ n. **1.** CUE GAMES **FORM OF BILLIARDS** a form of billiards played with a cue ball and 15 balls on a felt-covered table with six pockets **2.** GAMBLING **FORM OF GAMBLING** a form of gambling in which the participants contribute an amount to a common fund that is divided among the winners **3.** GAMBLING **TOTAL AMOUNT STAKED** the collective amount that the players in a gambling game have staked **4.** **COLLECTIVE RESOURCE** a joint supply of vehicles, commodities, or workers that is shared and used by members of a group **5.**

PRESS **GROUP OF REPORTERS** a selected group of reporters who cover an event and make their reports available to all participating news organizations **6.** FIN **INVESTMENT FUND** a collection of investments, e.g. properties in an investment trust, that are managed as a group for a common purpose or group of owners **7.** COMM **BUSINESS TRUST** an agreement between competing businesses to control production and sales in order to guarantee profits ■ vt. (**pools, pooling, pooled**) **SHARE RESOURCES** to combine sth to form a supply that can be shared by a group of people or companies [Late 17thC. Via French *poule* 'hen, gambling stakes' (hens were used as game prizes) from, ultimately, Latin *pullus* 'young animal' (see PULLET). 'Collective resource' arose via 'players' collected bets'.]

Poole /pool/ city and port in southern England. It is a resort and sailing centre. Population: 140,000 (1995).

pools /poolz/ n. an organized form of gambling, mainly by post, that involves predicting the outcome of football matches

poolside /póol sīd/ n. the area around the sides of a swimming pool (*often used before a noun*)

pool table n. a felt-covered table used for playing pool. It is rectangular and has six pockets, one at each corner and one in the middle of each of the longer sides.

poon /poon/ (*plural* **poons** *or* **poon**) n. a southern Asian tree that has shiny leathery leaves and strong light wood that is used for masts and spars. Genus: *Calophyllum*. [Late 17thC. Via Sinhalese *pūna* from Malayalam *punna* or Tamil *punnai*.]

poop[1] /poop/ n. **1.** **RAISED AREA AT SHIP'S REAR** the raised cabins at the stern of an old sailing ship, or the raised area at the stern of a modern ship, lying above the level of the main deck **2.** = **poop deck** ■ v. (**poops, pooping, pooped**) **1.** vt. **BREAK OVER STERN** to break over a ship at the stern **2.** vi. **HAVE WAVES BREAKING OVER STERN** to have waves break over its stern, especially repeatedly (*refers to ships*) [15thC. Via Old French *pupe* from, ultimately, Latin *puppis*, of unknown origin.]

poop out vi. (*slang*) **1.** **STOP DOING STH** to stop doing sth, usually because of exhaustion or fear **2.** **STOP WORKING** to stop operating, e.g. because of mechanical failure

poop[2] /poop/ (**poops, pooping, pooped**) vt. to make sb feel exhausted (*informal*) (*usually passive*) ○ *pooped by the long hike* [Mid-20thC. Origin unknown.]

poop[3] /poop/ n. US facts or information about sth (*slang*) = **dirt** [Mid-20thC. Origin unknown.]

poop[4] /poop/ n. **EXCREMENT** excrement, or a stool (*informal*) (*often used by or to children*) ■ vi. (**poops, pooping, pooped**) **DEFECATE** to defecate (*informal*) (*often used by or to children*) [Mid-16thC. Originally in the meaning of 'to make a short blast of sound'.]

poop[5] /poop/ n. an offensive term that deliberately insults sb's intelligence or consideration for others (*slang*) [Early 20thC. Origin uncertain: perhaps a shortening of NINCOMPOOP.]

poop deck n. a raised open deck at the stern of a ship, with cabins below it

pooped /poopt/ adj. extremely tired (*informal*)

pooper-scooper /póopər skoopər/ n. a small shovel used to clean up dog excrement, used especially by a dog owner whose dog defecates in a public place (*informal*)

poo-poo n. **EXCREMENT** excrement, or the act of defecating (*babytalk*) ■ vi. (**poo-poos, poo-pooing, poo-pooed**) **DEFECATE** to defecate (*babytalk*) [Doubled form of POO]

poor /pawr, poor/ adj. **1.** **NOT RICH** lacking money or material possessions **2.** **AFFECTED BY POVERTY** where there is a lot of poverty, or where poverty is evident **3.** **INFERIOR** less than adequate, or below average in quality or condition **4.** **LACKING SKILL** below average in skill or ability **5.** **LOW OR INADEQUATE** lower than expected or needed in quantity, number, or amount **6.** **WEAK** lacking strength, power, stamina, or resilience **7.** **DEFICIENT** lacking or deficient in sth (*often used in combination*) **8.** **LACKING PRODUCTIVE POTENTIAL** lacking fertility or nutrients **9.** **LOW IN VALUATION** low in a scale of value ○ *has a poor opinion of himself* **10.** **DESERVING PITY** deserving pity or compassion, especially because of sth that has just happened ■ *npl.* **PEOPLE WHO ARE POOR** people who lack money or material possessions (*takes a plural verb*) ○ *The poor are always with us.* [12thC. Via Old French *povre* from Latin *pauper* (see PAUPER).] —**poorness** *n.* ◇ **a poor man's sth** a cheaper or inferior version of sth, especially one that is more widely available than the original

poor box *n.* a box, especially one kept in a church, that is used to collect money for the poor

poorhouse /páwr howss, poor-/ (*plural* -**houses** /-howziz/) *n.* a publicly funded institution that existed in the past to house people who were too poor to provide for themselves

poori /poori/ *n.* a thin flat unleavened Indian wheat bread, shaped into a small round and deep-fried, making it puff up and become crisp [Mid-20thC. From Hindi *pūrī*.]

Poor Knights Islands /páwr nīts-/ group of uninhabited islands in the southwestern Pacific Ocean, 24 km/15 mi. off the northeastern coast of the North Island, New Zealand. Area: 2.7 sq. km/1 sq. mi.

poor law *n.* a law or system of laws relating to the provision of support for poor people

poorly /páwrli, poorli/ *adv.* **1.** **INADEQUATE** in an inferior or inadequate way **2.** **UNFAVOURABLY** with an unfavourable opinion or attitude ■ *adj.* **1.** **PHYSICALLY UNWELL** feeling physically unwell, or in poor physical health (*informal*) **2.** **VERY ILL** very ill (*regional informal*) ○ *The victim is in a poorly condition.*

poor mouth *n.* *US, Ireland* complaints about being poor, regarded as made to win sympathy, sometimes when the complainer is not truly poor (*disapproving*)

poor-mouth (**poor-mouths, poor-mouthing, poor-mouthed**) *vi.* to complain of a lack of money, especially when feigning or exaggerating poverty, often in order to win sympathy (*informal disapproving*)

poor rate *n.* HIST a tax levied from parishes in the past to raise money for housing and feeding poor people

poor relation *n.* sb who or sth that is inferior compared to another

poor white *n.* *US* an offensive term for a poor and uneducated lower-class white person (*informal offensive*)

Pooterish /pootərish/ *adj.* self-importantly genteel or middle-class, especially amusingly so [Mid-20thC. Named after Charles *Pooter*, a character in *Diary of a Nobody* (1892), by George and Weedon Grossmith.]

poove /poov/ *n.* = **poof**¹ (*slang insult*) [Variant]

pop¹ /pop/ *n.* **1.** **SUDDEN BURSTING SOUND** a sudden explosive sound, like the sound produced when a balloon bursts or a cork comes out of a bottle **2.** **FIZZY DRINK** a carbonated drink, usually sweet and flavoured with fruit (*informal*) **3.** **GUNSHOT** a shot with a firearm **4.** **ATTEMPT** a try at doing sth (*informal*) ■ *v.* (**pops, popping, popped**) **1.** *vti.* **MAKE A BURSTING SOUND** to make, or cause sth to make, a sudden explosive sound, like the sound of a cork out of a bottle or a balloon bursting **2.** *vti.* **BURST** to burst, or make sth burst, with a sudden explosive sound **3.** *vi.* **BULGE** to become wide open and seem to bulge out of the sockets (*refers to somebody's eyes*) **4.** *vi.* **GO BRIEFLY TO** go, come, or visit for a brief time (*informal*) **5.** *vt.* **OPEN OR CLOSE STH** to move sth quickly and suddenly into an open or closed position (*informal*) **6.** *vt.* **PUT QUICKLY** to put or place sth somewhere with a sudden rapid movement (*informal*) **7.** *vt.* **TAKE BY SWALLOWING** take a drug orally (*informal*) **8.** *vt.* **PAWN** to pawn sth (*informal*) ■ *adv.* **1.** **WITH BURSTING NOISE** with a sudden bursting sound **2.** **UNEXPECTEDLY** suddenly or abruptly ■ *interj.* **INDICATING BURSTING NOISE** used to indicate a sudden bursting noise [14thC. An imitation of the sound.] ◇ **a pop** for each one (*slang*) ○ *It'll cost you £10 a pop.*

pop off *vi.* to die suddenly (*informal*)

pop² /pop/ *n.* **1.** **FATHER** a word used to refer to or address your father (*informal*) **2.** **OLDER MAN** a word used to address a much older man (*dated slang*) [Mid-19thC. Shortening of POPPA.]

pop³ /pop/ *n.* **1.** MUSIC = **pop music** (*often used before a noun*) **2.** ARTS = **pop art** ■ *adj.* **POPULAR** intended for or appreciated by a wide public, and often regarded as oversimplified for the sake of greater accessibility (*informal*) ○ *magazines full of pop psychology* [Late 19thC. Shortening of POPULAR.]

POP *abbr.* **1.** Post Office Preferred (*used to describe the size of envelopes and packages*) **2.** COMM proof of purchase

pop. *abbr.* **1.** popular **2.** population

pop art *n.* an art movement of the 1960s and 1970s that incorporated elements of modern popular culture and the mass media. It included such artists as Andy Warhol and Roy Lichtenstein.

popcorn /póp kawrn/ *n.* **1.** HEATED MAIZE KERNELS the kernels of a variety of maize, heated until they become puffy, usually flavoured with butter, caramelized sugar, or cheese and eaten as a snack **2.** MAIZE a variety of maize with hard kernels that pop open to form white puffs when heated. Latin name: *Zea mays praecox.*

pope¹ /pōp/ *n.* **1.** pope, Pope ROMAN CATHOLIC CHURCH HEAD the head of the Roman Catholic Church and bishop of Rome **2.** pope, Pope COPTIC CHURCH HEAD the head of the Coptic Church **3.** pope, Pope ORTHODOX PRIEST a priest in the Eastern Orthodox Church **4.** POWERFUL PERSON sb who has authority or status similar to that of a pope [Pre-12thC. Via Latin from, ultimately, Greek *pappas* 'father'.]

pope² /pōp/ (*plural* **popes** *or* **pope**) *n.* = **ruffe** [Mid-17thC. From POPE¹.]

Pope /pōp/, **Alexander** (1688–1744) English poet. He wrote the mock-heroic poem *The Rape of the Lock* (1712) and *An Essay on Man* (1733–34).

popedom /pópdəm/ *n.* the office, tenure, or dominion of a pope

popery /pópəri/ *n.* an offensive term for the Roman Catholic Church, its doctrines, or its practices (*offensive*)

pope's nose *n.* = **parson's nose** (*offensive in some contexts*)

popeyed /póp īd/ *adj.* **1.** WITH BULGING EYES with the eyes bulging out **2.** WIDE-EYED with eyes wide open in surprise or disbelief

popgun /póp gun/ *n.* **1.** TOY GUN a toy gun that uses compressed air to shoot pellets, balls, or a cork tied to a string. It makes a popping sound. **2.** USELESS GUN a useless or unimpressive firearm (*informal*)

popinjay /póppin jay/ *n.* a vain and conceited person (*dated*) [13thC. Via Old French *papegay* 'parrot' from, ultimately, Arabic *babbağā.* 'Arrogant person' from the parrot's gaudy colours and meaningless chattering.]

popish /pópish/ *adj.* an offensive term used to describe things associated with the Roman Catholic Church, its doctrines, or its practices (*offensive*) —**popishly** *adv.*

poplar /póplər/ *n.* **1.** TREES SLENDER QUICK-GROWING TREE a slender quick-growing tree of the willow family with triangular leaves, flowers in catkins, and light-coloured soft wood. It is native to northern temperate regions. Genus: *Populus.* **2.** TREES = **tulip tree 3.** INDUST POPLAR'S WOOD the light-coloured wood of a poplar (*often used before a noun*) [14thC. Via Anglo-Norman *popler* from, ultimately, Latin *populus.*]

poplin /pópplin/ *n.* a plain strong fabric with fine ribbing, usually made of cotton. It is used for making clothes and upholstery. (*often used before a noun*) [Early 18thC. Via obsolete French *papeline* from, ultimately, medieval Latin *papalis* 'papal' (because it was made at the papal town of Avignon), from Latin *papa* (see POPE).]

popliteal /póppli tee əl, po plítti əl/ *adj.* relating to or located in the part of the leg behind the knee joint [Late 18thC. Formed from modern Latin *popliteus,* from Latin *poples* 'ham, back of the knee'.]

popmobility /póp mō bílləti/ *n.* a form of exercise that combines aerobics with elements of modern dance and is performed to music, usually by large groups of people

pop music *n.* modern commercial music, usually tuneful, uptempo and repetitive, that is aimed at the

general public and the youth market in particular

Popocatepetl /póppə kátta pet'l, -pett'l/ *n.* volcano in southern-central Mexico. Height: 5,452 m/17,887 ft.

popover /póp ōvər/ *n.* **1.** *US* HOLLOW MUFFIN a light hollow muffin-shaped quick bread made from eggs, flour, and milk **2.** SIMPLE DRESS OR TOP a simple garment for women or girls that can be slipped over the head

poppa /póppə/ *n.* *US* = **papa** (*informal*) [Late 19thC. Alteration.]

poppadom /póppədəm, -dom/, **poppadum** *n.* a thin crisp circular Indian bread made from gram flour or flour from pulses and flavoured with spices. Poppadoms are dried and fried in hot fat. [Early 19thC. From Tamil *pappaṭam,* of uncertain origin: perhaps from *paruppa aṭam* 'lentil cake'.]

popper /póppər/ *n.* **1.** = **press stud 2.** DRUGS AMYL NITRATE a small capsule of amyl nitrate or butyl nitrate, prepared as an illicit drug (*slang*)

poppet /póppit/ *n.* **1.** USED AS TERM OF ENDEARMENT used to address a sweet and dear person, especially a child (*informal*) **2.** ENG = **poppet valve 3.** NAUT SUPPORT FOR SHIP a steel beam or timber that is used to support the front and back ends of a ship when it is launched [14thC. Origin uncertain: perhaps from French *poupette,* literally 'small doll', from assumed *poupe* 'doll', from Latin *pupa* 'girl, doll'.]

poppet head *n.* MINING the framework at the top of a mineshaft that supports the pulleys for the winding mechanism

poppet valve *n.* a valve that is raised and lowered by a vertical guide, e.g. the intake and exhaust valves of the cylinders in an internal-combustion engine also called poppet

popping crease /pópping-/ *n.* the line at which a cricket batsman stands when facing the bowler. It runs parallel to the wicket and lies four feet in front of it. [Probably because it originally marked the line that the ball had to cross before it could be struck]

popple¹ /pópp'l/ (**-ples, -pling, -pled**) *vi.* to move in an irregular tumbling or bubbling manner, like water does when it boils [14thC. Origin uncertain: probably from Middle Dutch *popelen* 'to babble, murmur', originally an imitation of the sound.]

popple² /pópp'l/ *n.* a poplar tree (*informal*) [14thC. From Latin *populus.*]

Poppy

poppy /póppi/ (*plural* -**pies**) *n.* **1.** PLANTS PLANT WITH RED FLOWERS an annual or perennial plant that has large red, orange, or white flowers, cup-shaped seed pods, and milky sap. Genus: *Papaver.* **2.** PHARM, DRUGS PLANT EXTRACT an extract from the poppy that is used in drugs such as opium and medicine **3.** PLANTS PLANT LIKE A TRUE POPPY any of several flowering plants that are similar or related to the poppy, e.g. the California poppy and Welsh poppy **4.** COLOURS ORANGE-RED COLOUR a bright red colour tinged with orange [Pre-12thC. Via assumed Vulgar Latin *papavum* from Latin *papaver.*]

poppycock /póppi kok/ *n.* absurd speech or writing (*dated informal*) [Mid-19thC. From Dutch dialect *pappekak,* from *pap* 'soft, pap' + *kak* 'dung'.]

Poppy Day *n.* = Remembrance Sunday

poppyhead /póppi hed/ *n.* an ornamental carved top on the end of a pew in a Gothic church

poppy seed *n.* the small black seed of the poppy, used in cooking and in baking

pops /pops/ *n.* = **pop²** (*dated slang*) [Early 20thC. Extended form.]

pop shop *n.* a pawn shop (*informal*) ['Pop' from POP¹ in the sense 'to pawn']

Popsicle /pópsik'l/ *tdmk. US* a trademark for a coloured fruit-flavoured ice on one or two sticks

popsock /póp sok/ *n.* a woman's short stocking, reaching up to the knee. Popsocks are usually sheer and are often worn under trousers. (*usually used in the plural*)

pop-top *n.* **1.** *US, Can* = **ring pull** **2.** VAN ROOF a van roof that can be raised to create extra headroom while the van is stationary **3.** VAN a van with a pop-top

populace /póppyŏŏləss/ *n.* **1.** INHABITANTS the inhabitants of a town, region, or other area **2.** GENERAL PUBLIC ordinary people, as distinct from the political elite or the aristocracy [Late 16thC. Via French from Italian *popolaccio* 'rabble', from *popolo* 'people', from Latin *populus* (see POPULAR).]

popular /póppyŏŏlər/ *adj.* **1.** APPEALING TO THE GENERAL PUBLIC appealing to or appreciated by a wide range of people ○ *the most popular name for babies this year* **2.** WELL-LIKED liked by a particular person or group of people ○ *popular with young audiences* **3.** OF THE GENERAL PUBLIC relating to the general public ○ *popular appeal* **4.** AIMED AT NON-SPECIALISTS designed to appeal to or be comprehensible to the non-specialist ○ *a popular gardening magazine* **5.** BELIEVED BY PEOPLE IN GENERAL believed, embraced, or perpetuated by ordinary people ○ *popular myths* **6.** INEXPENSIVE designed to be affordable to people on average incomes ○ *a new popular car* [15thC. Via Anglo-Norman *populer* from Latin *popularis* 'of the people', from *populus* 'people' (source of English *people* and *public*), of uncertain origin: probably from Etruscan.]

popular etymology *n.* = **folk etymology**

popular front *n.* a broad-based coalition of left-wing political parties, formed to oppose fascism or institute social reforms, especially in Europe in the mid-1930s

popularise *vt.* = **popularize**

popularity /póppyŏŏ lárrəti/ *n.* **1.** FACT OF BEING WELL LIKED admiration, approval, or acceptance of sb or sth by people in general or by a particular group of people **2.** DEMAND FOR STH desire or demand for sth, e.g. a manufactured product

popularize /póppyŏŏlə rīz/ (**-izes, -izing, -ized**), **popularise** (**-ises, -ising, -ised**) *vt.* **1.** MAKE POPULAR to make sth widely liked or appreciated **2.** MAKE UNDERSTANDABLE to make sth accessible and comprehensible to a wide audience —**popularization** /póppyŏŏlə rī záysh'n/ *n.* —**popularizer** *n.*

popularly /póppyŏŏlərli/ *adv.* **1.** GENERALLY by most people or in most situations **2.** BY NON-SPECIALISTS by the general public, as distinct from specialists

popular music *n.* = **pop music**

popular sovereignty *n.* **1.** GOVERNMENT'S SUBJECTION TO PEOPLE the doctrine in the United States that the people are sovereign and a government is subject to the will of the people **2.** HIST DOCTRINE PERMITTING CHOICE ON SLAVERY a pre-Civil War political doctrine in the United States that held that individual states should decide whether to permit slavery or not. It was espoused mainly by opponents of the abolition of slavery.

populate /póppyŏŏ layt/ (**-lates, -lating, -lated**) *vt.* **1.** INHABIT A PLACE to live in an area, region, or country (*often passive*) **2.** PEOPLE A PLACE to supply an area with inhabitants [Late 16thC. From medieval Latin *populat-*, the past participle stem of *populare*, from Latin *populus* 'people' (see POPULAR).] —**populated** *adj.*

population /póppyŏŏ láysh'n/ *n.* **1.** PEOPLE IN PLACE all of the people who inhabit an area, region, or country **2.** ALL PEOPLE OF GROUP all of the people of a particular nationality, ethnic group, religion, or class who live in an area **3.** NUMBER OF PEOPLE the total number of people who inhabit an area, region, or country, or the number of people in a particular group who inhabit an area **4.** SUPPLYING WITH INHABITANTS the populating of an area with inhabitants **5.** STATS GROUP STATISTICALLY SAMPLED the entire group of individuals or items from which a sample may be selected for

statistical measurement **6.** ECOL INDIVIDUALS OF SAME SPECIES all the plants or animals of a particular species present in a place

population control *n.* the limiting of numbers of individuals living in an area. In humans it may be achieved through contraception while in animals it may occur through killing or the introduction of predators.

population explosion *n.* a sudden and rapid increase in the number of individuals living in an area. In humans, this may be as a result of an increased birth rate or a decline in mortality, while in the case of animals it may be because of a lack of predators or altered environmental conditions.

population genetics *n.* the study of genetic variation in populations, particularly how and why the frequencies of different genes change over time or in different localities (*takes a singular verb*)

population revolution *n.* the huge growth in population in western Europe that began about 1730. It was a prelude to the Industrial Revolution.

populism /póppyŏŏlizəm/ *n.* **1.** ANTI-ELITE POLITICS politics or political ideology based on the perceived interests of ordinary people, as opposed to those of a privileged elite **2.** FOCUS ON ORDINARY PEOPLE focus or emphasis on the lives of ordinary people, e.g. in the arts and in politics [Late 19thC. Formed from Latin *populus* 'people' (see POPULAR).]

Populism *n.* the political philosophy and programme of the Populist Party of the United States

populist /póppyŏŏlist/ *n.* SUPPORTER OF ORDINARY PEOPLE an advocate of the rights and interests of ordinary people, e.g. in politics or the arts ■ *adj.* OF ORDINARY PEOPLE emphasizing or promoting ordinary people, their lives, or their interests [Late 19thC. Formed from Latin *populus* 'people' (see POPULAR).]

Populist *n.* POPULIST PARTY SUPPORTER a political supporter of the Populist Party of the United States ■ *adj.* OF THE POPULIST PARTY belonging or relating to the Populist Party of the United States

populous /póppyŏŏləss/ *adj.* with a large number of inhabitants [15thC. From late Latin *populosus*, from Latin *populus* 'people' (see POPULAR).] —**populously** *adv.* —**populousness** *n.*

pop-up *adj.* **1.** UPWARD-LIFTING with a mechanism that makes it, or sth in it move quickly upwards ○ *pop-up headlights* **2.** COMP PRESENTED ON SCREEN TEMPORARILY appearing quickly and temporarily on a computer screen when a special key is pressed or a button is clicked with a mouse ○ *a pop-up menu* **3.** PUBL WITH RISING CUT-OUT FIGURES containing cut-out figures that rise up as a page is opened ○ *a pop-up book* ■ *n.* PUBL ITEM WITH POP-UP FIGURES a book or card that contains pop-up figures, or a pop-up figure

porbeagle /páwr beeg'l/ (*plural* **-gles** *or* **-gle**) *n.* a large and voracious shark with a crescent-shaped tail, found in North Atlantic waters. Latin name: *Lamna nasus*. [Mid-18thC. From Cornish *porbugel*.]

porcelain /páwrssəlin, -layn/ *n.* **1.** CERAMIC MATERIAL a hard translucent ceramic material used for making plates, cups, and other items (*often used before a noun*) **2.** ITEMS MADE OF PORCELAIN objects made of porcelain, e.g. expensive crockery or decorative figurines **3.** DECORATIVE OBJECT a single object made from porcelain, especially a decorative object [Mid-16thC. Via French from Italian *porcellana* 'cowrie shell, porcelain' (from its texture), literally 'like a young sow' (from its shape), via *porca* 'sow' from, ultimately, Latin *porcus* 'pig'.]

porcelain clay *n.* = **kaolin**

porcelain enamel *n.* a glass coating that is fused to a metal by firing

porcellaneous /páwrssə láyni əss/ *adj.* made of porcelain, or resembling porcelain in its translucence or whiteness [Late 18thC. Coined from Italian *porcellana* 'porcelain' (see PORCELAIN) + -EOUS.]

porch /pawrch/ *n.* **1.** COVERED ENTRANCE a covered shelter at the entrance to a building **2.** US, Can ROOFED EXTERIOR ROOM a raised platform with a roof that runs along the side of a house, partly enclosed with low walls or fully enclosed with screens or windows [13thC. Via Old French from Latin *porticus*

'covered entry' (source of English *portico*), from *porta* 'gate' (see PORT²).]

porcine /páwr sīn/ *adj.* relating to or resembling pigs [Mid-17thC. Via French from Latin *porcinus*, from *porcus* 'pig' (see PORK).]

porcino /pawr seénō/ (*plural* **-ni** /-seéni/), **porcini mushroom** *n.* = **cep** [Late 20thC. From Italian, shortening of *fungo porcino*, literally 'porcine mushroom'.]

Porcupine

porcupine /páwrkyŏŏ pīn/ *n.* a large rodent whose body is covered with long protective quills that it can erect in defence against predators. Families: Hystricidae and Erethizontidae. [14thC. From Old French *porc espin*, literally 'spiny pig'.]

— **WORD KEY: ORIGIN** —
When French *porc espin* was adopted by English for **porcupine** it underwent a range of odd transformations, including *portpen*, *porpoynt*, *porpentine* (the form used by Shakespeare: the ghost of Hamlet's father speaks of the 'quills upon the fretful porpentine'), *porkenpick*, and *porpin* before finally settling down in the 17th century to **porcupine**. Around 1700 the fanciful variant *porcupig* was coined.

Porcupine /páwrkyŏŏ pīn/ river in North America that originates in northern Yukon Territory, Canada, joining the Yukon River in northeastern Alaska. Length: 721 km/448 mi.

porcupine fish *n.* a tropical marine fish that has strong sharp spines covering its body. It inflates the spines when attacked. Family: Diodontidae.

porcupine grass *n.* = **spinifex** *n.* 1

porcupine provisions *npl.* measures taken by a business company to discourage an unwanted takeover

pore¹ /pawr/ *n.* **1.** ANAT TINY OPENING IN SKIN a tiny opening in human skin, or in the skin or other outer covering of an animal, through which substances can pass. Perspiration is released through the pores. **2.** BOT TINY OPENING IN PLANT a tiny opening in a leaf or stem of a plant used to absorb or release substances, e.g. in photosynthesis or respiration **3.** GEOL SMALL SPACE IN ROCK a small space that is surrounded by rock or soil. It may be filled with water, crude oil, or natural gas. [14thC. Via Old French and Latin from Greek *poros* 'passage' (source of English *emporium*). Ultimately from an Indo-European word that is also the ancestor of English *fare* and *ford*.]

— **WORD KEY: USAGE** —
See Usage note at *pour*.

pore² /pawr/ (**pores, poring, pored**) *vi.* **1.** LOOK CONCENTRATEDLY to study sth carefully and thoughtfully ○ *poring over a book* **2.** REFLECT to meditate on or think carefully about sth [13thC. Origin uncertain: possibly related to PEER.]

pore fungus *n.* any fungus that has spores in tiny tubules that lead to outside pores. Families: Boletaceae and Polyporaceae.

porgy /páwrgi/ (*plural* **-gy** *or* **-gies**) *n.* **1.** MARINE FOOD FISH a marine food fish that has a deep flat body with large scales, found in the Mediterranean Sea and Atlantic Ocean. Latin name: *Pagrus pagrus*. **2.** FISH RELATED TO PORGY any marine food fish related to the porgy, with a similarly deep flat body. Family: Sparidae. **3.** UNRELATED FISH LIKE PORGY any of various fishes that are similar to the porgy but unrelated, e.g. the menhaden [Mid-17thC. Via Spanish or Portuguese *pargo* from, ultimately, Greek *phagros* 'sea bream'.]

poriferan /paw ríffərən/ *n.* = **sponge** *n.* 1 (*technical*) ■ *adj.* RELATING TO SPONGES belonging or relating to the sponges [Mid-19thC. Formed from modern Latin *Porifera*, phylum name, literally 'passage-bearing', ultimately from Latin *porus* (see PORE[1]).]

pork /pawrk/ *n.* **1.** FOOD PIG MEAT the flesh of a pig eaten as food, usually cooked fresh. Cured pig flesh is usually referred to as bacon or ham. (*often used before a noun*) **2.** *US* POL POLITICAL HANDOUTS government money and jobs awarded by politicians to their supporters or constituents to win their favour, especially when awarded wastefully (*informal*) [13thC. Via Old French from Latin *porcus* 'pig' (source of English *porcupine* and *porcelain*). Ultimately from an Indo-European word meaning 'pig', which is also the ancestor of English *farrow*.]

pork barrel *n. US* government-funded projects that bring jobs and other benefits to an area and give its political representative the opportunity to award favours and reap the ensuing prestige (*informal*) (*hyphenated when used before a noun*)

pork belly *n.* a side of fresh pork, commonly traded on the commodities markets, or a cut of meat from this

porker /páwrkər/ *n.* **1.** AGRIC FAT YOUNG PIG a young fattened pig, especially one raised for its meat. ◊ **baconer 2.** OVERWEIGHT PERSON an overweight person or animal (*informal insult*)

pork pie *n.* **1.** PIE CONTAINING MINCED PORK a round raised pie filled with minced pork and usually eaten cold **2.** = **porky** (*slang*)

porkpie hat /páwrk pī-/, **porkpie** *n.* **1.** MAN'S HAT a man's hat with a flat crown and small brim that can be turned up, first popular in the 1850s **2.** WOMAN'S HAT a woman's round hat without a brim, first popular in the 1860s [*Porkpie* from its shape]

pork rinds *npl. US* = **pork scratchings**

pork scratchings *npl.* small pieces of fried pork rind and fat that are eaten as a snack. US term **pork rinds**

porky /páwrki/ *adj.* (**porkier, porkiest**) **1.** RELATING TO PORK relating to or resembling pork **2.** OVERWEIGHT overweight (*informal insult*) ■ *n.* (*plural* **porkies**) LIE a lie (*slang*) (*often used in the plural*)

porn /pawrn/, **porno** /páwrnō/ *n.* pornography (*informal*) (*often used before a noun*) [Mid-20thC. Shortening.]

pornographic /páwrnə gráffik/ *adj.* **1.** PORTRAYING SEX EXPLICITLY sexually explicit and intended to cause sexual arousal **2.** SELLING PORNOGRAPHY producing or selling sexually explicit magazines, films, or other materials —**pornographically** *adv.*

pornography /pawr nóggrəfi/ *n.* **1.** SEXUALLY EXPLICIT MATERIAL films, magazines, writings, photographs, or other materials that are sexually explicit and intended to cause sexual arousal **2.** SEXUAL IMAGES INDUSTRY the production or sale of sexually explicit films, magazines, or other materials [Mid-19thC. Via French from, ultimately, Greek *pornographos* 'writing about prostitutes', from *pornē* 'prostitute'. Ultimately from an Indo-European word denoting 'to sell'.] —**pornographer** *n.*

porosity /paw róssəti/ (*plural* **-ties**) *n.* **1.** POROUS QUALITY the porous nature of sth, or the extent to which sth is porous **2.** GEOL, ENG PERCENTAGE OF PORE SPACE the ratio of the space taken up by the pores in a soil, rock, or other material to its total volume. It is expressed as a percentage. **3.** GEOL, ENG PORE a pore in soil, rock, or other material (*technical*) [14thC. Via French from, ultimately, medieval Latin *porosus* (see POROUS).]

porous /páwrəss/ *adj.* **1.** WITH PORES with a surface that contains pores or a body that contains cavities **2.** PERMEABLE permitting the movement of fluids or gases through it by way of pores or other passages **3.** BREACHABLE easy to cross, infiltrate, or penetrate [14thC. Via Old French *poreux* from medieval Latin *porosus*, from Latin *porus* 'passage' (see PORE[1]).] —**porously** *adv.* —**porousness** *n.*

porphyria /pawr fírri ə/ *n.* a medical condition caused by the body's failure to metabolize porphyrins. Symptoms of the hereditary form include abdominal pain, sensitivity to sunlight, confusion, and excretion of porphyrins in the urine. [Early 20thC. Formed from PORPHYRIN.]

porphyrin /páwrfərin/ *n.* any of various organic compounds that are common in animal and plant tissue, e.g. as components of haemoglobin, chlorophyll, and some enzymes. They consist of four pyrrole rings linked by methylene groups. [Early 20thC. Formed from Greek *porphura* 'purple' (source of English *purple*), from their colour.]

porphyritic /páwrfə ríttik/ *adj.* **1.** RELATING TO PORPHYRY relating to or containing porphyry **2.** WITH LARGE CRYSTALS containing isolated large and distinct crystals in a mainly fine-grained rock

porphyry /páwrfəri/ (*plural* **-ries**) *n.* **1.** REDDISH-PURPLE ROCK a reddish-purple rock containing large distinct feldspar crystals embedded in a fine-grained groundmass **2.** ROCK WITH LARGE CRYSTALS any predominantly fine-grained igneous rock that contains isolated large crystals [14thC. Via Old French *porfire* from, ultimately, Greek *porphuritēs*, from *porphura* 'purple' (see PURPLE), from its colour.]

porpoise /páwrpəss/ (*plural* **-poise** *or* **-poises**) *n.* **1.** MARINE MAMMAL a toothed marine mammal, related to the whales and dolphins, that has a blunt snout and a triangular dorsal fin. Family: Phocaenidae. **2.** DOLPHIN a popular but technically inaccurate term for a dolphin [14thC. From Old French *porpeis*, literally 'pig-fish', ultimately from Latin *porcus* 'pig' (see PORK) + *piscis* 'fish'; perhaps from its snout or its curved back.]

porrect /pə rékt/ *adj.* used to describe animal parts that extend forwards [Early 19thC. From Latin *porrectus*, the past participle of *porrigere* 'to stretch forward', from *regere* 'to direct'.]

porridge /pórrij/ *n.* **1.** FOOD HOT BREAKFAST CEREAL a dish made from oatmeal or another cereal cooked with milk or water to form a thick liquid, often eaten at breakfast. US term **oatmeal** *n.* 2 **2.** IMPRISONMENT a term of imprisonment (*slang*) [Mid-16thC. Alteration of POTTAGE. In the meaning of 'imprisonment', from the idea that porridge is a common prison food, with a punning allusion to *stir* 'prison'.]

porringer /pórrinjər/ *n.* a small bowl, usually with a handle, used for soup, stew, or porridge [Early 16thC. Alteration of *potinger*, via Old French *potager* from *potage* 'pottage' (see POTTAGE).]

port[1] /pawrt/ *n.* **1.** HARBOUR a place by the sea, or by a river or other waterway, where ships and boats can dock, load, and unload **2.** TOWN WITH A HARBOUR a town or city built around a port **3.** WATERFRONT the waterfront area of a port **4.** COVE a sheltered place along a coast, where boats are protected from storms and rough seas **5.** = **port of entry** [Pre-12thC. From Latin *portus* (source of English *opportune*). Ultimately from an Indo-European word meaning 'to go across', which is also the ancestor of English *pore*[1].]

port[2] /pawrt/ *n.* **1.** NAUT OPENING IN BOAT a watertight opening in the side of a boat, used for loading and unloading and as a means of general access to the holds **2.** NAUT = **porthole** *n.* 1 **3.** MIL GUN HOLE a small opening in an armoured vehicle, military aircraft, naval vessel, or fortification through which a gun can be fired **4.** ENG VALVE-OPERATED OPENING an opening controlled by a valve, e.g. any of the openings in the cylinder of an internal combustion engine **5.** COMPUT EXTERNAL COMPUTER CONNECTION an external socket on a computer's main unit (**CPU**) where a peripheral device such as a printer, keyboard, or network cable is plugged in **6.** *Scotland* CITY GATE a city gate, or the original site of a gate that is no longer there (*often used in placenames*) [13thC. Via Old French, 'gate', from Latin *porta* (source of English *porch* and *portal*).]

port[3] /pawrt/ *n.* LEFT SIDE ON SHIP OR PLANE the left-hand side of a boat or aeroplane when facing forwards ■ *adj., adv.* ON LEFT on or to the left-hand side of boat or aeroplane when facing forwards ■ *vti.* (**ports** /pawrt/, **porting, ported**) TURN TO PORT to make a turn towards the port side, or make a ship do this [Mid-16thC. Shortening of *port side*, from PORT[1], because it was the side that faced the pier and over which cargo was loaded.]

port[4] /pawrt/ *n.* a strong sweet fortified wine usually drunk after dinner. It is usually a deep red colour, but some kinds are brownish (**tawny port**) and some white. Originally from Portugal, port is now made in other countries. [Late 17thC. Named after the city of *Oporto* in Portugal, from where it was shipped.]

port[5] /pawrt/ *vt.* (**ports, porting, ported**) CARRY ACROSS THE BODY to carry a weapon positioned diagonally across the body with the muzzle or blade in front of the left shoulder ■ *n.* DIAGONAL POSITION the position of a rifle or sword when ported [Mid-16thC. Via French *porter* 'to carry' from Latin *portare* (source of English *portable, transport, important*, and *portfolio*); see PORT[1].]

port[6] /pawrt/ (**ports, porting, ported**) *vt.* to convert software to run on different computer operating systems [Mid-20thC. From PORT[2].]

port[7] /pawrt/ *n. Aus* a suitcase or other travelling bag (*dated*) [Early 20thC. Shortening of PORTMANTEAU.]

Port. *abbr.* **1.** Portugal **2.** Portuguese

porta /páwrtə/ (*plural* **-tas** *or* **-tae**) *n.* an opening into an organ or other bodily part, especially the opening in the liver through which most of the blood vessels enter [14thC. Via modern Latin from Latin, 'gate'.]

portable /páwrtəb'l/ *adj.* **1.** EASILY MOVED ABOUT designed to be light or compact enough to carry or move easily from place to place **2.** COMPUT EASY TO CONVERT easily converted to run on different computer operating systems ■ *n.* EASILY TRANSPORTED OBJECT a device or an appliance that is designed to be easily carried or moved from place to place [14thC. Via Old French from late Latin *portabilis*, from *portare* 'to carry'.] —**portability** /páwrtə bílləti/ *n.* —**portably** /páwrtəbli/ *adv.*

Portadown /páwrtə dówn/ town in the Craigavon District of County Armagh, in southern Northern Ireland. Population: 21,299 (1991).

portae plural of **porta**

portage /páwrtij, pawr taázh/ *n.* **1.** ACT OF CARRYING the carrying or transporting of sth **2.** CHARGE FOR CARRYING a charge made for carrying or transporting sth **3.** CARRYING OF BOATS OVERLAND the carrying of boats or cargo across land from one waterway to another or around an unnavigable section of a waterway **4.** OVERLAND ROUTE TO WATERWAY an overland route used when transporting a boat or its cargo from one waterway to another ■ *vti.* (**-ages, -aging, -aged**) CARRY STH OVERLAND TO WATERWAY to carry boats or cargo across land from one waterway to another or around an unnavigable portion of a waterway [13thC. Via Old French from, ultimately, Latin *portare* 'to carry'.]

Portakabin /páwrtə kabin/ *tdmk.* a trademark for a portable building that can be assembled quickly and used for a variety of purposes, e.g. as an office or a schoolroom

portal /páwrt'l/ *n.* **1.** LARGE GATE a large or elaborate gate or entrance (*literary*) **2.** ENTRANCE TO STH any entrance to a place, or any means of access to sth (*literary*) **3.** **portal, portal site** COMPUT HOME SITE FOR WEB BROWSER on the Internet, a website that provides links to information and other websites ■ *adj.* ANAT OF PORTAL VEIN OR SYSTEM relating to the portal vein, portal system, or the opening in the liver (**porta**) through which the portal vein passes [14thC. Via Old French from, ultimately, Latin *porta* 'gate' (see PORT[1]).]

portal system *n.* a network of blood vessels that begin in the capillaries of one organ and end in the capillaries of another, especially the portal veins connecting the liver and intestines

portal vein *n.* a vein that carries blood from the digestive organs, gall bladder, and spleen to the liver, especially the vein from the intestines carrying nutrient-rich blood

portamento /páwrtə méntō/ (*plural* **-ti** /-ti/) *n.* a smooth glide from one note to another when singing or playing a stringed instrument [Late 18thC. From Italian, literally 'carrying', because the player slides the same finger from one note to the next.]

Port Arthur /páwrt aárthər/ **1.** town in Australia, in southern Tasmania. It was the site of a major penal settlement between 1830 and 1837. Population: 190 (1994). **2.** city in southeastern Texas, the largest petrol-refining centre in the United States. Population: 58,724 (1990). **3.** former name for **Lüshun**

portative /páwrtətiv/ *adj.* (*formal*) **1.** portable **2.** RELATING TO OR FOR CARRYING relating to the carrying of things, or used for carrying things [14thC. Via Old French from, ultimately, Latin *portare* 'to carry'.]

portative organ *n.* a small portable organ operated by bellows, used in medieval and Renaissance music

Port Augusta /pawrt aw gústə/ city in South Australia, at the head of the Spencer Gulf. The city is a railway junction and industrial centre. Population: 13,914 (1996).

Port-au-Prince /páwrt ō prínss/ capital city and chief port of Haiti, on Gonâve Gulf. Population: 743,000 (1994).

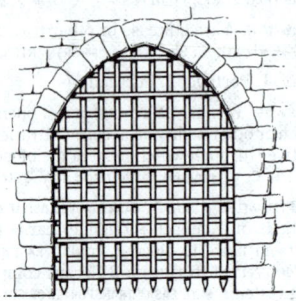

Portcullis

portcullis /pawrt kúlliss/ *n.* a heavy iron or wooden grating that is set in vertical grooves and suspended by chains. It is lowered to block the gateway to a castle or fortification. [14thC. From Old French *porte coleïce*, from *porte* 'door', from Latin *porta* 'gate', + *col(e)ïce*, a form of *couleïs* 'sliding', ultimately from Latin *colare* 'to filter'.]

port de bras /páwr də braá/ *n.* the proper movement of the arms in ballet, or exercises for developing this [From French, literally 'carriage of the arms']

Port du Salut *n.* = **Port-Salut** *n.*

Porte /pawrt/ *n.* the court or government of the Ottoman Empire. It was situated in Constantinople. [Early 17thC. From French *(la Sublime) Porte* '(the exalted) Gate', translation of the Turkish title of the central office; from the palace gate where justice was administered.]

porte-cochere *n.* **1.** COVERED ENTRANCE a large covered entrance for vehicles in a wall or building leading to a courtyard **2.** EXTENDED ROOF a large roof or awning extending from the entrance of a building to the driveway [Late 17thC. From French *porte cochère*, literally 'door for coaches'.]

Port Elizabeth /páwrt ilízzəbəth/ city in Eastern Cape Province, southeastern South Africa, situated on Algoa Bay, on the Indian Ocean. Population: 853,205 (1991).

portend /pawr ténd/ (**-tends**, **-tending**, **-tended**) *vt.* **1.** BE AN OMEN to be an indication that sth, especially sth unpleasant, is going to happen (*formal*) **2.** INDICATE to indicate or signify sth [15thC. From Latin *portendere*, literally 'to stretch forward', from *tendere* (see TENDER[2]).]

portent /páwr tent/ *n.* **1.** OMEN an indication that sth, often sth unpleasant, is going to happen **2.** SIGNIFICANCE ominous or prophetic significance **3.** MARVEL a wonderful or marvellous thing (*formal*) [Late 16thC. From Latin *portentum*, from *portendere* (see PORTEND).]

portentous /pawr téntəss/ *adj.* **1.** SIGNIFICANT very serious and significant, especially in terms of future events **2.** POMPOUS excessively serious or pompous (*disapproving*) **3.** AMAZING inspiring wonder and amazement —**portentously** *adv.* —**portentousness** *n.*

porter[1] /páwrtər/ *n.* **1.** LUGGAGE CARRIER sb who is employed to carry people's luggage, e.g. at an airport, railway station, or in a hotel **2.** MED HOSPITAL EMPLOYEE sb who moves patients between departments or wards in a hospital **3.** US, Can TRANSP TRAIN ATTENDANT an attendant in a train [14thC. Via French *porteur* from medieval Latin *portator*, literally 'carrier', from *portare* (see PORT[1]).]

porter[2] /páwrtər/ *n.* **1.** GATEKEEPER sb who is in charge of the door or gate of a building or institution **2.** EDUC COLLEGE RECEPTION PERSON sb who is in charge of the main gate in a university or college and who answers enquiries and performs other administrative tasks **3.** CARETAKER the caretaker of a

building, especially a block of flats, who is responsible for the general maintenance of the building. US term **superintendent** *n.* **3** [13thC. Via French *portier* from late Latin *portarius*, from *porta* 'gate' (see PORT[1]).]

porter[3] /páwrtər/ *n.* a dark sweet beer, similar to light stout, made from malt that has been browned or charred [Early 18thC. Shortening of *porter's ale*, from PORTER[1]; probably because the beer was drunk mainly by porters.]

Porter, Cole (1891–1964) US composer and lyricist. He is known for his witty sophisticated songs, and for musicals such as *Kiss Me Kate* (1949). Full name **Cole Albert Porter**

Porter, Peter (*b.* 1929) Australian-born British poet and critic. His many collections of formally elegant verse include *The Automatic Oracle* (1987). Full name **Peter Neville Frederick Porter**

Porter, Rodney Robert (1917–85) British biochemist. He is noted for his work on the chemical structure of antibodies, for which he shared a Nobel Prize in physiology or medicine (1972).

porterage /páwrtərij/ *n.* **1.** CARRYING WORK the work of carrying that is performed by porters **2.** FEE FOR CARRYING a fee charged by porters for carrying things

porterhouse /páwrtər howss/ (*plural* **-houses** /-howziz/) *n.* an establishment that in the past sold porter and sometimes also served meals (*archaic*)

porterhouse steak *n.* a beef steak from the thick end of the sirloin

portfire /páwrt fīr/ *n.* a slow fuse that was used in the past for explosives in mining as well as for rockets and fireworks [Mid-17thC. Anglicization of French *porte-feu*, literally 'fire-carrier'.]

portfolio /pawrt fóli ō/ (*plural* **-os**) *n.* **1.** FLAT CASE a large flat case for carrying documents, e.g. maps, photographs, or drawings **2.** PORTFOLIO CONTENTS the contents of a portfolio, especially as representing sb's creative work **3.** POL MINISTERIAL RESPONSIBILITIES the post or responsibilities of a cabinet minister, or minister of state **4.** FIN GROUP OF INVESTMENTS all the investments held by an individual or organization **5.** RANGE OF PRODUCTS the complete range of products or designs offered by a company (*formal*) [Early 18thC. From Italian *portafoglio*, from *portare* 'to carry' + *foglio* 'sheet, page'.]

Port-Gentil /pawr zhaaN teé/ city and seaport in western Gabon. It is the capital of Ogooué-Maritime Province. Population: 97,900 (1993).

Port Harcourt /-haárkərt/ major port and capital city of Rivers State, southern Nigeria. Population: 400,000 (1995).

Porthcawl /pawrth káwl/ town near Bridgend in southern Wales. Population: 15,922 (1991).

Port Hedland /-hédlənd/ town in northwestern Western Australia. It is a mining centre and port. Population: 12,846 (1996).

porthole /páwrt hōl/ *n.* **1.** NAUT ROUND WINDOW a small round window with a metal frame in the side of a ship **2.** MIL OPENING FOR WEAPON a small opening in a fortified wall through which weapons can be fired

Portia /páwrshə/ *n.* a small inner natural satellite of Uranus, discovered in 1986 by the Voyager 2 planetary probe. It is approximately 110 km/68 mi. in diameter.

portico /páwrtikō/ (*plural* **-coes** *or* **-cos**) *n.* **1.** PORCH a

Portico

covered entrance to a large building **2.** COVERED WALKWAY a covered walkway, often leading to the main entrance of a building, that consists of a roof supported by pillars [Early 17thC. Via Italian from Latin *porticus*, from *porta* 'gate' (see PORT[2]).]

portière /páwrti áir/ *n.* a heavy curtain hung across a doorway (*formal*) [Mid-19thC. From French, formed from *porte* 'door', ultimately from Latin *porta* (see PORT[2]).]

portion /páwrsh'n/ *n.* **1.** FRACTION a part or section of a larger whole **2.** FOOD HELPING OF FOOD an amount of food for one person **3.** LAW INHERITANCE a part of an estate that has been bequeathed to an heir **4.** LAW = **dowry** *n.* **1 5.** FATE an unavoidable event or part of sb's life (*literary*) ■ *vt.* (**-tions**, **-tioning**, **-tioned**) **1.** DIVIDE to divide sth into parts for use **2.** LAW ENDOW to give a dowry to a woman (*archaic*) [14thC. Via French from the Latin stem *portion-*, of uncertain origin: possibly sth related to *pars* 'share' (source of English *part*).] —**portionable** *adj.* —**portioner** *n.*

Port Jackson /-jáksən/ coastal inlet in eastern New South Wales, Australia. It is the site of the city of Sydney. Area: 54 sq. km/20 sq. mi.

Portland /páwrtlənd/ **1.** city in southwestern Maine, on the southern shore of Casco Bay, northeast of Saco. Population: 63,123 (1996). **2.** city in Oregon, situated in the northwestern part of the state on the Willamette River. It is the state's largest city, and its economic and cultural centre. Population: 437,319 (1990).

Portland, Isle of peninsula on the coast of Dorset, southern England, connected to the mainland by the Chesil Bank, a shingle ridge. Population: 12,000 (1995). Area: 11.5 sq. km/4.5 sq. mi.

Portland cement /páwrtlənd-/ *n.* a cement that hardens under water, made by burning limestone and clay [So called because its colour resembles that of Portland stone, a limestone named after the Isle of PORTLAND, where it was quarried]

Port Laoise /-leéshə/ county town of Laois, central Ireland. Population: 3,773 (1986).

Port Lincoln town on Boston Bay in South Australia. It is a fishing port and tourist resort. Population: 11,678 (1996).

Port Louis /-loó iss, -loó i/ capital city and chief port of Mauritius, on the northeastern coast of the island. Population: 142,850 (1992).

portly /páwrtli/ (**-lier**, **-liest**) *adj.* **1.** SLIGHTLY OVERWEIGHT slightly overweight but dignified **2.** STATELY having an air of grandeur (*archaic*) [15thC. Formed from PORT[5] in the sense 'bearing, manner'.] —**portliness** *n.*

Port Macquarie /-mə kwórri/ coastal town in southeastern New South Wales, Australia. It is a residential and tourist centre. Population: 33,709 (1996).

portmanteau /páwrt mántō/ *n.* (*plural* **-teaus** *or* **-teaux** /páwrt mán tōz/) LARGE SUITCASE an old type of large leather suitcase, especially one that opened out into two compartments ■ *adj.* MULTIPLE combining several uses or qualities [Mid-16thC. From French *portemanteau*, from *porter* 'to carry' + *manteau* 'cloak'.]

portmanteau word *n.* a word that combines the sound and meaning of two words, e.g. 'smog', a combination of 'smoke' and 'fog' [From Humpty Dumpty's description (in Lewis Carroll's *Through the Looking Glass*) of the word 'slithy' as a *portmanteau* because 'there are two meanings packed up into one word']

Port Moresby /-máwrzbi/ capital city of Papua New Guinea, situated on the southern coast of the island of New Guinea. Population: 193,242 (1990).

Porto Alegre /páwrtoo ə légri/ capital city of Rio Grande do Sul State, southeastern Brazil, and the country's leading river port. It lies at the junction of five rivers. Population: 1,286,251 (1996).

port of call *n.* **1.** NAUT PORT AWAY FROM HOME any port, other than the home port, that a vessel visits on a journey **2.** VISITED PLACE a place visited during a holiday, trip, or excursion (*informal*)

port of entry *n.* a place, e.g. a port or an airport, where passengers and goods may enter a country under the supervision of customs officials

Port-of-Spain /páwrt əv spáyn/, **Port of Spain** capital city and main port of Trinidad and Tobago. It is situated in the northwestern part of the island of Trinidad. Population: 59,200 (1988).

Porto-Novo /páwrt o nóv ō/ capital city of Benin, and its main seaport, situated on a lagoon that extends along the Gulf of Guinea. Population: 179,000 (1994).

Port Phillip Bay /páwrt fíllip-/ bay in southern Victoria, Australia. The city of Melbourne lies on its southern shore. Area: 2,000 sq. km/800 sq. mi.

Port Pirie /-pírri/ city in South Australia, on the Spencer Gulf. It is a port and industrial centre. Population: 13,633 (1996).

portrait /páwrtrit, páwr trayt/ n. **1.** ARTS **PICTURE OF A PERSON** a painting, photograph, or drawing of sb, sb's face, or a related group **2.** DESCRIPTION a description of sth, e.g. a person, place, or period ■ adj. PRINTING **TALLER THAN WIDE** used to describe a piece of paper, illustration, book, or page that is taller than it is wide. ◊ **landscape** [Mid-16thC. From French, from past participle of Old French *portraire* (see PORTRAY).]

WORD KEY: CULTURAL NOTE
Portrait of a Lady, a novel by US writer Henry James (1881). Through the story of Isabel Archer, a young American woman who travels to Europe and is duped into marrying an urbane but materialistic fellow expatriate, the author explores the contrasting characteristics of the Old World (sophisticated but corrupt) and the New (idealistic but naive). It was made into a film by Jane Campion in 1997.

portraitist /páwrtrətist, páwrtritist/ n. sb such as a photographer or painter who specializes in portraits

portraiture /páwrtrichər/ n. **1.** MAKING OF PORTRAITS the art or practice of making portraits **2.** PORTRAITS portraits considered collectively **3.** PORTRAIT a portrait painting, drawing, or photography (*formal*)

portray /pawr tráy/ (**-trays, -traying, -trayed**) vt. **1.** ARTS **DEPICT VISUALLY** to depict sth, e.g. a person or a scene, in a painting, photograph, drawing, or sculpture **2.** DEPICT VERBALLY to represent sb or sth in words **3.** PLAY A ROLE IN DRAMA to play a character in drama [13thC. From Old French *portraire*, literally 'to draw forth', from *traire* 'to draw', from Latin *trahere* (see TRACTION.] —**portrayable** adj. —**portrayer** n.

portrayal /pawr tráy əl/ n. **1.** ACTING REPRESENTATION the way an actor conveys the character of the role being played **2.** ARTISTIC DEPICTION an artist's depiction or representation of a subject **3.** REPRESENTATION a representation of sb or sth in words or images

portress /páwrtrəss/ n. a woman who is a doorkeeper or caretaker, especially in a convent [15thC. Formed from PORTER[2].]

Port Said /-síd/ city and port in northeastern Egypt, at the Mediterranean end of the Suez Canal. Population: 460,000 (1992).

Port-Salut /páwr sa loó/, **Port du Salut** /páwr doo sa loó/ n. a flat round mild French cheese with an orange rind, made from whole milk [Late 19thC. Named after Notre Dame de *Port-du-Salut*, a Trappist monastery in northwestern France where the cheese was first produced.]

Portsmouth /páwrtsməth/ n. **1.** city and naval base in southern England, in Hampshire. Population: 192,000 (1996). **2.** city in southeastern Virginia. It is a major seaport. Population: 103,907 (1990).

Port Stanley /-stánli/ capital town of the Falkland Islands, a British dependency in the southern Atlantic Ocean. Population: 1,232 (1986).

Port Sudan /-soodán/ city in northeastern Sudan, the country's only seaport, situated on the Red Sea 322 km/200 mi. northeast of Khartoum. Population: 305,385 (1993).

Port Sunlight /-sún līt/ village in Merseyside, northwestern England. It was created in 1888 to provide accommodation for the workers of the Sunlight soap factory.

Port Talbot /-táwlbət, pawr táwlbət/ town in southern Wales. It is the administrative centre of Neath and Port Talbot unitary authority, and was a major steel-making centre. Population: 37,647 (1991).

Portugal

Portugal /páwrchoõg'l/ republic in southwestern Europe, in the southwestern part of the Iberian peninsula. Language: Portuguese. Currency: escudo. Capital: Lisbon. Population: 9,865,114 (1996). Area: 92,082 sq. km/35,553 sq. mi. Official name **Portuguese Republic**

Portuguese /páwrchoõ geéz/ n. **1.** LANG **LANGUAGE OF PORTUGAL AND BRAZIL** the official language of Portugal and Brazil, also an official language in some African countries, belonging to the Italic branch of Indo-European languages. Portuguese is spoken by about 150 million people, with a further approximately 30 million using it as a second language. **2.** PEOPLES **SB FROM PORTUGAL** sb who was born in or brought up in Portugal, or who has Portuguese citizenship ■ adj. **1.** OF PORTUGAL relating to Portugal, or its people or culture **2.** LANG **RELATING TO PORTUGUESE** relating to the Portuguese language [Late 16thC. Via Portuguese *português* from, ultimately, medieval Latin *Portus Cale*, the port of Gaya (Oporto).]

Portuguese India territories in India formerly ruled by Portugal, considered as a group. They included Goa, Daman, Diu, Dadra, and Nagar Haveli. They were taken over by India between 1954 and 1961.

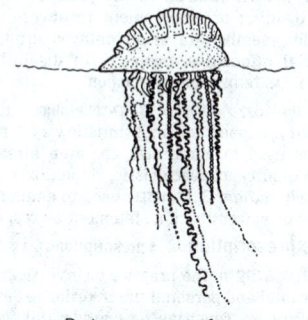
Portuguese man-of-war

Portuguese man-of-war n. a sea organism (**hydrozoan**) resembling a jellyfish, that lives in warm waters, has a transparent gas-filled float, and long stinging often poisonous tentacles. Genus: *Physalia*. [From its crest, resembling a sail]

portulaca /páwrtyoõ láke/ n. a plant with fleshy leaves and brightly coloured flowers, native to tropical and subtropical America but widely cultivated. Genus: *Portulaca*. [Mid-16thC. Via Latin, 'purslane', from *portula*, literally 'little gate', from *porta* (see PORT[2]); from the covering of the seed capsule, that resembles a gate.]

port-wine stain n. a conspicuous purplish birthmark, especially on the face or neck

POS abbr. point of sale

pos. abbr. **1.** position **2.** positive

posada /pō saáde/ n. a hotel, pension, or hostel in a Spanish-speaking country [Mid-18thC. From Spanish, formed from *posar* 'to stay, lodge', via late Latin *pausare* from Latin *pausa* 'rest' (see PAUSE).]

pose[1] /pōz/ v. (**poses, posing, posed**) **1.** vti. **ADOPT A POSTURE** to adopt a particular physical posture for a photograph or painting, or position sb or sth for this purpose **2.** vi. **IMPERSONATE** to pretend to be sb or sth else ○ *got past the security guards by posing as a journalist* **3.** vt. **PRESENT** to be the cause of sth, e.g. a problem, threat, danger, or challenge ○ *a breakdown of negotiations that poses a threat to*

peace **4.** vt. **ASK** to ask a question, often one that requires some consideration **5.** vi. **BE PRETENTIOUS** to behave, dress, or assume a mental attitude intended to impress others (*disapproving*) ■ n. **1.** **POSTURE** a particular physical posture, e.g. one adopted for a painting or photograph **2.** **PRETENCE** a way of behaving or dressing calculated to impress others (*disapproving*) ○ *His sudden interest in opera is just a pose.* [14thC. Via Old French *poser* from, ultimately, late Latin *pausare* 'to rest, cease', from *pausa* (see PAUSE).]

pose[2] /pōz/ (**poses, posing, posed**) vt. to confuse or baffle sb (*dated*) [Early 16thC. Partly a shortening of *appose* (variant of OPPOSE), and partly from Old French *poser* 'to assume'.]

Poseidon /pə síd'n/ n. a US ballistic missile capable of being launched from a submarine and carrying a nuclear warhead

poser[1] /pózər/ n. **1.** **SB WHO POSES** sb who adopts a particular posture for a photograph or painting **2.** **POSEUR** a poseur (*informal disapproving*) [Late 19thC. Formed from POSE[1].]

poser[2] /pózər/ n. a difficult question or problem [Late 16thC. Formed from POSE[2].]

poseur /pō zúr/ n. sb who behaves or dresses to impress others [Late 19thC. From French, formed from *poser* 'to pose' (see POSE[1]).]

posey /pózi/ (**-ier, -iest** *informal*) adj. frequented by affected people and posers (*disapproving informal*)

posh /posh/ adj. (*informal*) **1.** **FOR THE WELL-OFF** elegant, fashionable, and expensive **2.** **UPPER-CLASS** from, imitative of, or characteristic of the upper classes ■ adv. **LIKE AN UPPER CLASS PERSON** like sb from the upper classes (*informal*) ○ *She talks posh on the phone to try to impress people.* [Early 20thC. Origin uncertain.] —**poshly** adv. —**poshness** n.

WORD KEY: ORIGIN
The legend has become widely circulated that *posh* is an acronym formed from the initial letters of *port out, starboard home*, an allusion to the fact that wealthy passengers could afford the more expensive cabins on the port side of the ships going out to India, and on the starboard side returning to Britain, which kept them out of the heat of the sun. Pleasant as this story is, it has never been substantiated. Another possibility is that *posh* may be the same word as the now obsolete *posh* 'dandy, swell', a slang term current around the end of the 19th century. This too is of unknown origin, but it has been linked with the still earlier 19th-century slang term *posh* 'halfpenny', hence broadly 'money', which may have come ultimately from Romany *posh* 'half'.

posit /pózzit/ vt. (**-its, -iting, -ited**) (*formal*) **1.** **PUT STH FORWARD** to put sth forward for consideration, e.g. a suggestion, assumption, or fact **2.** **POSITION STH** to place sth firmly in position ■ n. **STH PUT FORWARD** a fact, assumption, or suggestion for consideration (*formal*) [Mid-17thC. From Latin *posit-*, the past participle stem of *ponere* 'to place' (see POSITION).]

positif /póssitif/ n. a manual that controls the softer stops on a church organ [Via Old French, 'positive organ', from Latin *positivus* (see POSITIVE).]

position /pə zísh'n/ n. **1.** **LOCATION** the place where sb or sth is, especially in relation to other things ○ *confirm their position and direction by radio* **2.** **POSTURE** the posture that sb's body is in ○ *The accident victim had been placed in the recovery position.* **3.** **ARRANGEMENT** the way or direction in which an object is placed or arranged ○ *the position of the hour hand* **4.** **SITUATION** a particular set of circumstances ○ *I wouldn't sell just yet if I were in your position.* **5.** **RANK** sb's standing or level of importance in society or an organization ○ *In her position she should set an example for others.* **6.** **POST** a job or post in a company or organization ○ *the position of marketing manager* **7.** **VIEW** a policy, view, or opinion, especially an official one ○ *What's your position on the euro?* **8.** **CORRECT PLACE** the correct or usual place or arrangement of an object or person ○ *Once the dignitaries are in position, the ceremony can start.* **9.** MIL **STRATEGIC PLACE** a strategic area or point that is occupied by military personnel or where weapons are placed ○ *The enemy took up positions on a hill overlooking the fort.* **10.** **PLACE IN ORDER** the place a person, team, or organization occupies in a race, contest, or list ○ *The liberals were squeezed into third position by the two main parties.* **11.** SPORTS **ROLE IN A TEAM** the part of a playing area where a player is based and usually plays ○ *The substitute took up a midfield position.* **12.** GAME **ARRANGEMENT OF PIECES** the arrangement of the pieces or counters in a board game, e.g. chess or backgammon, at a given time **13. SEXUAL POSTURE** the posture used by a couple in sexual intercourse **14.** FIN **DEALER'S RESPONSIBILITY** a dealer's commitment to buy or sell a particular number of securities or commodities **15.** FIN **INVESTOR'S VULNERABILITY** an investor's status based on holdings with regard to market trends **16.** MUSIC **HAND PLACEMENT** the placement of the fingers on a keyboard or string instrument **17.** MUSIC **DEGREE OF EXTENSION OF TROMBONE SLIDE** the extent to which a trombone slide is pushed out **18.** MUSIC **ARRANGEMENT OF NOTES IN A CHORD** the arrangement of individual notes within a chord. Root position is the most fundamental position. **19.** POETRY **VOWEL TYPE IN CLASSICAL POETRY** a short vowel counting as a long vowel in classical poetry because it comes before two or more consonants ■ *vt.* **(-tions, -tioning, -tioned) 1. PUT STH IN PLACE** to put sth in a particular or suitable place ○ *Position the two pieces so that they are at right angles.* **2. PLACE SB** to place sb or yourself in a particular or suitable area, place, or situation ○ *This strategy will position us advantageously in the market.* **3. LOCATE STH** to determine the site or location of sth ○ *Air traffic controllers have positioned the unknown aircraft at 50 miles north of the airport.* [14thC. Via French from, ultimately, Latin *posit-*, the past participle stem of *ponere* 'to place'. Ultimately from an Indo-European word meaning 'to drop off'.] —**positional** *adj.* —**positionally** *adv.* —**positioner** *n.*

WORD KEY: ORIGIN

The Latin word *ponere*, from which ***position*** is derived, is also the source of English *compose, compost, compound, deposit, dispose, expose, impose, oppose, positive, post, postpone, posture, repose, suppose,* and *transpose.*

positional notation *n.* the method of denoting numbers by using digits in such a way that the value contributed by the digit depends on its position as well as its independent value. In the decimal system the value of the digits '37' is $(3 \times 10^1) + (7 \times 10^0)$, while in the octal system it is $(3 \times 8^1) + (7 \times 8^0)$, or 31 decimal.

position audit *n.* an assessment of a company's or organization's commercial standing carried out to help future planning

position effect *n.* a change in a gene's expression depending on its location on the chromosome relative to other genes

position paper *n.* an in-depth report on a particular matter that gives the official view and recommendations of a government or organization

positive /pózzətiv/ *adj.* **1. OPTIMISTIC** confident, optimistic, and focusing on the good things rather than bad ○ *a positive attitude about work* **2. SURE** certain and not in doubt ○ *'Are you sure that's what you want to do?' 'Yes, I'm positive'.* **3.** LAW **IRREFUTABLE** conclusive and beyond doubt or question ○ *positive identification of the suspect* **4. BENEFICIAL** producing good results because of having an innately beneficial character ○ *It was a positive experience.* **5. AFFIRMATIVE** indicating agreement or affirmation ○ *got some positive feedback from the survey* **6. QUANTIFIABLE** capable of being measured, detected, or perceived ○ *a positive correlation between investment in telecommunications and economic development* **7.** MED **INDICATING PRESENCE OF STH IN TEST** indicating the presence or existence of a particular organism, illness, or condition in the results of a test or examination ○ *a positive test for diabetes* **8.** MED = **Rh positive 9. ENCOURAGING GOOD BEHAVIOUR** encouraging behaviour, especially in the young, that is considered morally good ○ *a positive role model* **10. ADDING EMPHASIS** used to emphasize the degree to which sth is true, striking, or impressive (*informal*) ○ *Hiring her is a positive triumph for the department.* **11.** MATH **MORE THAN ZERO** with a value higher than zero. Symbol **+ 12.** MATH **NOT NEGATIVE** measured in a direction or designated as a quantity equal in magnitude but opposite to that regarded as negative **13.** PHILOS **EMPIRICAL** relating to the theory that knowledge can be acquired only through direct observation and experimentation rather than metaphysics and theology **14.** BIOL **SHOWING RESPONSE** indicating growth, response, or movement towards a stimulus, e.g. light **15.** PHYS **WITH ELECTRICAL CHARGE LIKE A PROTON** with an electrical charge of an opposite polarity to an electron's and the same polarity as a proton's **16.** PHYS **WITH POSITIVE CHARGE** with an overall positive electrical charge, sometimes caused by the loss of one or more electrons **17.** PHYS **WITH HIGHER ELECTRICAL POTENTIAL** with a higher electrical potential than the earth or the defined neutral point ○ *a positive electrode* **18.** ELEC = **electropositive** *adj.* 1 **19.** PHOTOGRAPHY **LIKE THE SUBJECT** used to describe photographic images that have colours or values of dark and light corresponding to the subject **20.** OPTICS **MAKING LIGHT CONVERGE** making a parallel beam of light converge **21.** GRAM **NOT COMPARATIVE OR SUPERLATIVE** relating to the basic form of an adjective or adverb, rather than its comparative or superlative forms **22.** ENG **MECHANICAL ACTION WITH NO SLACK** used to describe a mechanical action or device having little or no play **23.** ZODIAC **OF CERTAIN ZODIAC SIGNS** relating to the air and fire signs of the zodiac ■ *n.* **1. POSITIVE THING** sth that shows agreement, support, or affirmation (*informal*) ○ *Not a bad situation when we weigh up all the positives.* **2.** MATH **STH GREATER THAN ZERO** a value or number higher than zero **3.** PHOTOGRAPHY **IMAGE LIKE THE SUBJECT** a photographic image in which the light and dark tones and colours correspond to those of the original subject **4.** PHYS **STH WITH POSITIVE CHARGE** sth that carries a positive electrical charge **5.** PHYS **CELL PLATE OR TERMINAL** a positively charged plate or terminal in a cell **6.** GRAM **BASIC FORM OF MODIFIER** an adjective or adverb in its basic form rather than the comparative or superlative **7.** MUSIC **MEDIEVAL ORGAN** a small medieval organ with just one manual and no pedals **8.** MUSIC = **positif** [14thC. Via French from Latin *positivus*, from *posit-*, the past participle stem of *ponere* (see POSITION); the underlying meaning is 'firmly set down'.] —**positiveness** *n.* —**positivity** *n.*

positive discrimination *n.* the practice of setting aside training or employment resources or positions for members of disadvantaged groups such as racial minorities, people with disabilities, or women. US term **affirmative action**

positively /pózzətivli/ *adv.* **1. ENCOURAGINGLY** in an encouraging, supportive, or optimistic way **2. FOR ADDING EMPHASIS** used to emphasize an often already emphatic quality, characteristic, or action ○ *looking positively radiant* **3. DEFINITELY** used to emphasize the finality or extremity of a statement or response

positive prescription *n.* = **prescription** *n.* 7

positive vetting *n.* the practice of investigating sb's background and personal life in order to determine suitability for sensitive or confidential work, especially work involving matters of national security

positivism /pózzətivizəm/ *n.* **1.** PHILOS **THEORY OF KNOWLEDGE** the theory that knowledge can be acquired only through direct observation and experimentation rather than through metaphysics and theology **2. POSITIVE STATE** the state or quality of being positive —**positivist** *n., adj.* —**positivistic** /pózzəti vístik/ *adj.* —**positivistically** /-vístikli/ *adv.*

positron /pózzi tron/ *n.* an elementary particle of antimatter that has the same mass as an electron but the opposite electrical charge [Mid-20thC. Coined from POSITIVE + ELECTRON.]

positron emission tomography *n.* a method of medical imaging capable of displaying the metabolic activity of organs in the body, and useful in diagnosing cancer, locating brain tumours, and investigating other brain disorders

positronium /pózzi trṓni əm/ *n.* a combination of a positron and an electron that rapidly decays to produce two or three photons

posology /pə sólləji/ *n.* the study of the dosage of medicines [Early 19thC. From French *posologie*, from Greek *posos* 'how much'.] —**posological** /póssə lójjik'l/ *adj.*

poss. *abbr.* **1.** possession **2.** GRAMMAR possessive **3.** possible **4.** possibly

posse /póssi/ *n.* **1.** *US* **SHERIFF'S HELPERS** a group of able-bodied citizens that a sheriff can call upon to assist in maintaining law and order. They are associated mainly with the 19th-century American South and West. **2. ASSEMBLED GROUP** a group of people assembled for a common purpose (*informal*) **3. STREET GANG** a group of youths who hang around together and have a leader (*slang*) [Mid-17thC. Shortening of POSSE COMITATUS.]

posse comitatus /póssi kommi táatəss/ *n. US* a posse (*formal*) [From medieval Latin, literally 'force of the county']

possess /pə zéss/ **(-sesses, -sessing, -sessed)** *vt.* **1. OWN** to have or own sth **2. HAVE AS AN ABILITY** to have a particular ability, quality, or characteristic **3. HAVE KNOWLEDGE OF STH** to have or acquire skill or knowledge of sth **4. TAKE CONTROL** to take control of or influence sb, affecting the person's behaviour or thinking ○ *possessed by fear and unable to speak* **5. INFLUENCE** to cause sb to be influenced or controlled by sth, especially an emotion ○ *The news possessed us with foreboding.* **6. CONTROL FEELING** to control yourself or a feeling in a particular situation (*formal*) **7. HAVE SEX** to have sex with sb (*dated; sometimes considered offensive*) **8. SEIZE STH** to gain or seize sth (*archaic*) [14thC. Via Old French *possesser* from Latin *possess-*, the past participle stem of *possidere*, literally 'to sit on as head of', from *sedere*.] —**possessor** *n.*

possessed /pə zést/ *adj.* **1. OWNING** being the owner of sth ○ *an only child possessed of a great fortune* **2. HAVING QUALITY** having as a quality, characteristic, or belief (*literary*) **3. CONTROLLED** controlled or strongly influenced, especially by a supposed evil supernatural force or a strong emotion ○ *screaming and shouting like a man possessed* **4.** = **self-possessed**

possession /pə zésh'n/ *n.* **1. OWNERSHIP** the act or state of owning or holding sth **2. STH OWNED** sth owned or held **3.** POL **COLONY** a country or region controlled or governed by another country (*often used in the plural*) **4. STATE OF BEING CONTROLLED** the condition of being controlled by or appearing to be controlled by a supernatural force or strong emotion **5.** LAW **OCCUPANCY** the physical occupancy of sth, e.g. a house, whether or not accompanied by ownership **6.** CRIMINOL **HAVING STH ILLEGAL** the crime of having or owning sth illegal, e.g. a weapon, contraband, stolen property, or illegal drugs **7.** SPORTS **CONTROL OF A BALL** control of the ball or puck in various sports ■ **possessions** *npl.* **PERSONAL PROPERTY** personal property and wealth —**possessional** *adj.*

possession order *n.* a court order authorizing sb to take possession of or recover property

possessive /pə zéssiv/ *adj.* **1. EAGER TO DOMINATE** wishing to control sb exclusively or to be the sole object of sb's love (*disapproving*) **2. SELFISH** tending not to share possessions with others **3. OF OWNERSHIP** relating to ownership ○ *possessive pride* **4.** GRAM **SHOWING OWNERSHIP IN GRAMMATICAL TERMS** indicating grammatical ownership, e.g. in pronouns such as 'his' or 'her' ■ *n.* GRAM **1. WORD SHOWING OWNERSHIP** a noun, pronoun, determiner or form of a word that indicates ownership or association **2. POSSESSIVE CASE** the possessive or genitive case —**possessively** *adv.* —**possessiveness** *n.*

possessory /pə zéssəri/ *adj.* **1. RELATING TO POSSESSION** relating to possession or a possessor (*formal*) **2.** LAW **DEPENDING ON POSSESSION** arising from or depending on possession

posset /póssit/ *n.* **SPICY HOT MILK DRINK** a drink made from hot milk curdled with beer or wine and flavoured with spices, drunk in the past as a remedy for colds ■ *vi.* **(-sets, -seting, -seted) REGURGITATE MILK** to regurgitate milk (*refers to babies*) [15thC. Origin uncertain: perhaps via Old French from Latin *posca* 'drink of water and vinegar', from *potare* 'to drink' + *esca* 'food'.]

possibility /póssə bílləti/ *n.* (*plural* **-ties**) **1. STH POSSIBLE** sth that is possible **2. STATE OF BEING POSSIBLE** the condition or quality of being possible **3. CONTENDER** sb who is considered a possible winner, choice, or candidate ■ **possibilities** *npl.* **POTENTIAL** the potential for successful future development ○ *The house needs a lot of work, but it's got possibilities*

possible /póssəb'l/ *adj.* **1. LIKELY TO HAPPEN** capable of happening or likely to happen in the future **2. MAYBE REAL OR TRUE** capable of being real, present, or true **3. CAPABLE OF HAPPENING BUT UNLIKELY** theoretically capable of being done, of happening, or of existing, although

a at; aa father; aw all; ay day; air hair; ə about, edible, item, common, circus; e egg; ee eel; hw when; i it, happy; ī ice; 'l apple; 'm rhythm; 'n fashion; o odd; ō open; ŏŏ good; oo pool; ow owl; oy oil; th thin; th this; u up; ur urge;

difficult or unlikely in practice **4. POTENTIAL** having potential as a particular thing or for a particular purpose **5. PROPER** in keeping with convention, decorum, or tradition ■ *n.* **POSSIBILITY** sb who or sth that is a possibility [14thC. Via French from Latin *possibilis*, from *posse* 'to be able' (see POTENT).]

possible world *n.* a philosophical idea postulating an alternative world or situation in which a proposition's truth can be evaluated. A proposition is true if there is such a world in which it would be true and it is necessary if it is true in every such world.

possibly /póssəbli/ *adv.* **1. PERHAPS** likely, or maybe so, but not known for certain **2. AS A POSSIBILITY** as sth that is possible or may be realized **3. ADDING EMPHASIS** used to express shock, disbelief, or amazement ○ *How could you possibly have believed that?* **4. SUGGESTING EFFORT** used to indicate the magnitude of effort or difficulty **5. SUGGESTING IMPOSSIBILITY** used in negative sentences and phrases to emphasize that sth cannot be done or cannot happen **6. USED AS REQUEST MODIFIER** used with requests to suggest the speaker's awareness of an imposition ○ *Could you possibly post this letter for me on your way to the station?*

possie /pózzi/, **pozzie** (*plural* **-zies**) *n.* ANZ a position or location (*informal*) [Early 20thC. Shortening.]

possum /póssəm/ *n.* **1.** = **opossum** (*informal*) **2.** ANZ = **phalanger** [Early 17thC. Shortening.] ◇ **play possum** to feign death, illness, or sleep, or pretend to be uninvolved in sth, in order to protect yourself

post¹ /pṓst/ *n.* **1. UPRIGHT POLE** a pole of wood or metal fixed in the ground in an upright position, serving as a support, marker, or place for attaching things **2. BUILDING UPRIGHT FRAME PART** a vertical piece in a building frame that supports a beam **3. HORSERACING RACECOURSE INDICATOR** either of two upright poles marking the starting point and finishing line on a racecourse **4. SPORTS GOALPOST** a goalpost (*informal*) **5. FURNITURE FURNITURE SUPPORT** any of the upright supports of a piece of furniture such as a chair or a four-poster bed **6. ACCESSORIES EARRING PART** a metal stem on a pierced earring that passes through the ear, and fits into a cap at the back **7. COMPUT** = **posting¹** *n.* 1 ■ *vt.* (**posts, posting, posted**) **1. DISPLAY STH** to display sth, e.g. an announcement, name, or result, in a public place **2. ONLINE PUBLISH ELECTRONICALLY** to make text appear online or at an Internet location **3. GIVE NOTICE OF MARRIAGE** to announce a forthcoming marriage in a church ○ *post the banns* **4. NAUT NAME A SHIP** to publish the name of a ship presumed lost or sunk [Pre-12thC. From Latin *postis*, literally 'sth that stands in front', ultimately from an Indo-European base meaning 'to stand', which is also the ancestor of English *stud*, *stem*, and *station*.]

post² /pṓst/ *n.* **1. MAIL POSTAL SERVICE** the official system for collecting, delivering, and sending letters and parcels from one place to another ○ *I'll send the contract to you by post.* **2. MAIL LETTERS AND PARCELS** letters and parcels that have been sent or are to be sent through the postal system ○ *Is there any post for me today?* **3. MAIL LETTER COLLECTION TIME** the time when letters and parcels are collected from a post box or delivered ○ *If you rush you'll catch the last post.* **4. HIST STATION ON A ROUTE** any of a series of stations along a route where, in the past, mounted messengers or couriers rested and changed horses **5. HIST MAIL DELIVERER** a rider who, in the past, covered the distance from one post to the next in a delivery system ■ *v.* (**posts, posting, posted**) **1.** *vi.* **EQU KEEP RHYTHM WITH HORSE** to bob up and down in the saddle in time with a horse's trot **2.** *vt.* **COMPUT UPDATE DATABASE** to update a database record by entering or transferring information **3.** *vti.* **COMPUT SEND MESSAGE ELECTRONICALLY** to place or send a message on the Internet or on some other electronic network **4.** *vi.* **HIST TRAVEL BY POST** to travel using relays of horses **5.** *vi.* **TRAVEL FAST** to travel in haste (*archaic*) **6.** *vt.* **MAIL SEND A LETTER** to send a letter or parcel through the postal system. ◇ **mail 7.** *vt.* **ACCT WRITE IN LEDGER** to enter a transaction in a ledger ■ *adv.* (*archaic*) **1. QUICKLY** quickly **2. BY POST HORSE** by mounted messengers or couriers riding between posts [Early 16thC. Via French, 'relay station', from, ultimately, Latin *posita*, the feminine past participle of *ponere* (see POSITION).] ◇ **keep sb posted** to keep sb

informed by supplying new information regularly ◇ **pip sb at the post** to beat sb in the very final stages of sth

post³ /pṓst/ *n.* **1. EMPLOYMENT SITUATION** a position of employment **2. WORKPLACE OR STATION** a place where sb has particular responsibilities **3. MIL MILITARY BASE** a place where a military operation is carried out **4. MIL BUGLE CALL** in the British army, either of two evening bugle calls given as a signal for army personnel to retire to their quarters **5. COMM** = **trading post** ■ *vt.* (**posts, posting, posted**) **1. SEND SB TO WORK** to assign sb to a particular position for a period of duty ○ *post a security guard at the exit* **2. SEND SB AWAY TO WORK** to send sb somewhere, often abroad, to do a particular job for a specific period of time ○ *After she qualified, she was posted to South America for two years.* **3. MIL TRANSFER SOLDIER** to send sb to a new military assignment or unit **4. US LAW PAY TO SET FREE** to pay sb's bond or bail [Mid-16thC. Via French *poste* from, ultimately, Latin *positum*, from the past participle of *ponere* 'to place' (see POSITION).]

post⁴ *n.* a postmortem examination of a corpse (*informal*)

POST /pṓst/ *abbr.* **1. COMM** point-of-sale terminal **2. COMPUT** Power On Self-Test

post- *prefix.* **1.** after, later ○ *postwar* **2.** behind ○ *postorbital* [From Latin *post*. Ultimately from an Indo-European word meaning 'off, away', which is also the ancestor of English *off*, *after*, and *ebb*.]

postage /pṓstij/ *n.* the amount of money paid for the delivery of a piece of mail

postage due stamp *n.* a stamp on a letter indicating that the postage charge has not been fully paid

postage stamp *n.* **1. GUMMED POSTAGE MARKER** an illustrated paper stamp affixed to letters and parcels to show payment of postage **2. PRINTED MARK** a printed mark or impression on an envelope indicating that the postage charge has been paid ■ *adj.* **TINY** unusually small (*hyphenated when used before a noun*)

postal /pṓst'l/ *adj.* relating to a post office or the delivery of post —**postally** *adv.*

postal code *n. Can* = postcode. ◇ **zip code**

postal order *n.* a voucher for a sum of money that can be bought at the Post Office and that is payable to a particular person or organization. US term **money order**

postal vote *n.* a vote that is posted instead of made in person, usually because the voter cannot get to the polling station. US term **absentee ballot**

post-and-rail fence *n.* a fence of horizontal timbers threaded between upright posts

postbag /pṓst bag/ *n.* US term **mailbag 1. BAG FOR MAIL** a bag or satchel used to carry mail by the person who delivers it **2. RECEIVED MAIL** the mail received by an MP, a famous person, or television or radio programme on a particular subject

post-bellum /pṓst belləm/, **postbellum** *adj.* relating to or during the period after a war, especially the American Civil War [From Latin *post bellum* 'after the war']

post-boost phase *n.* the last phase of a multistage missile's flight, when it releases its payload

postbox /pṓst boks/ *n. UK* a box in a public place where letters can be posted for collection. US term **mailbox**

postboy /pṓst boy/ *n.* **1. MAIL OFFICE MAIL DISTRIBUTOR** a boy or man who delivers mail in an office (*dated*) **2. TRANSP** = **postilion**

postbus /pṓst buss/ *n.* a bus in rural districts that carries mail as well as passengers

post captain *n.* in the past, a naval officer with a commission as captain [From POST³]

postcard /pṓst kaard/, **post card** *n.* a card used to carry a message, usually with a picture or a photograph on one side, that can be sent through the postal system without an envelope. ◇ **picture postcard**

post chaise *n.* a closed horse-drawn carriage with four wheels that was used in the 18th and 19th centuries as a fast means of transporting mail and passengers [From POST²]

postcode /pṓst kōd/ *n.* a group of letters and numbers added at the end of an address that helps to speed delivery. US term **zip code**

postdate /pṓst dáyt/ (**-dates, -dating, -dated**) *vt.* **1. FIN DATE A CHEQUE LATER** to put a date on a cheque later than the current day's date in order to delay payment **2. HAPPEN LATER** to happen or be at a later date than sth **3. ASSIGN LATER DATE** to assign a date to sth, e.g. an event in history, that is later than the one previously assigned

postdiluvian /pṓst dī looʹvi ən/, **postdiluvial** *adj.* **AFTER THE FLOOD** existing or occurring after the flood described in the book of Genesis in the Bible ■ *n.* **FLOOD SURVIVOR** sb or sth existing or surviving after the flood described in the book of Genesis [Late 17thC. Modelled on ANTEDILUVIAN.]

postdoc /pṓst dok/ *n.* **POSTDOCTORAL STUDENT OR AWARD** a postdoctoral grant, fellowship, or scholar (*slang*) ■ *adj.* **POSTDOCTORAL** relating to postdoctoral work or students (*slang*) [Late 20thC. Shortening.]

postdoctoral /pṓst dóktərəl/ *adj.* relating to academic work or research done after a doctorate has been awarded

poster /pṓstər/ *n.* **1. PRINTED PICTURE** a printed picture, often a reproduction of a photograph or artwork, used for decoration **2. ADVERTISEMENT** a bill or placard in a public place advertising sth **3. COMPUT SENDER** sb who posts a message to an online or Internet location, e.g. a newsgroup

poste restante /pṓst ri stánt/ *n.* **1. POST OFFICE DEPARTMENT** a department of a post office where mail is held for people until they collect it. US term **general delivery 2. SPECIAL ADDRESS** an address on an item of mail indicating that it should be held at a post office until collection by the addressee [From French, 'mail remaining' (at the post office)]

posterior /po stéeri ər/ *adj.* **1. BEHIND** situated at the rear or behind sth **2. ZOOL, ANAT NEAR THE BACK** situated near or towards the back of a human being's or animal's body **3. BOT NEAREST THE STEM** nearest the main stem or axis of a plant ○ *the posterior flower* **4. COMING AFTER** coming after sth in an order or series (*formal*) **5. SUBSEQUENT** following sth in time (*formal*) ■ *n.* **BUTTOCKS** the buttocks (*humorous*) [Early 16thC. From Latin, 'coming farther after', from *posterus* 'coming after', from *post* (see POST-).] —**posteriorly** *adv.*

posterity /po stérrəti/ *n.* (*formal*) **1. PEOPLE IN FUTURE** all future generations **2. ALL DESCENDANTS** all of sb's descendants [14thC. Via French *postérité* from Latin *posteritas*, from *posterus* (see POSTERIOR).]

postern /pṓstərn/ *n.* **REAR GATE** a small gate or entrance at the back of a building, especially a castle or a fort ■ *adj.* **AT THE BACK** situated at the rear or at the side (*archaic*) [13thC. Via Old French *posterne* from, ultimately, late Latin *posterula* 'small back door', from Latin *posterus* (see POSTERIOR).]

poster paint *n.* a type of paint made from pigment mixed with water-soluble gum that is often used for painting posters and by children. US term **poster color**

post exchange *n. US* a shop on a US military camp selling food, clothes, and other things

postexilian /pṓst ek síʹli ən, pṓst ig zíʹli ən/, **postexilic** /-ek síllik, -ig zíllik/ *adj.* occurring or in existence after the period of Babylonian captivity of the Jewish people, 587–539 BC

postfeminist /pṓst fémminist/ *adj.* **1. REFLECTING FEMINISM** developing out of or including the principles of feminism **2. GOING BEYOND FEMINISM** differing from or showing a re-evaluation of the principles of feminism **3. AFTER FEMINISM** occurring or having developed after the feminist movement of the 1970s (*offensive in some contexts*) ■ *n.* **SUPPORTER OF POSTFEMINIST IDEAS** a supporter of or believer in postfeminist ideas — **postfeminism** *n.*

postfix *vt.* /pṓst fíks/ (**-fixes, -fixing, -fixed**) **ADD SUFFIX** to add a letter or group of letters to the end of a word (*formal*) ■ *n.* /pṓst fiks/ **SUFFIX** a suffix [Late 20thC. Modelled on PREFIX.] —**postfixal** /pṓst fíks'l/ *adj.*

post-free *adj.* = postpaid

postglacial /pṓst gláyssi əl/ *adj.* occurring after a

glacial period, especially one during the Quaternary Period

postgraduate /póst gráddyoŏ ət/, **postgrad** informal adj. **RELATING TO GRADUATES** relating to academic study after graduation from a university or college or to students who have graduated. US term **graduate** n. 2 ■ n. **STUDENT WITH FIRST DEGREE** sb who has graduated from a university or college with a first degree, especially one who is doing further study

posthaste /póst háyst/ adv. **FAST** as quickly as possible ■ n. **SPEED** great speed (archaic) [Mid-16thC. From haste, post, haste, an instruction on letters.]

post hoc /póst hók/ n. the fallacy of arguing that since one event happened before a second, the first caused the second [Mid-19thC. From Latin, 'after this', referring to the fallacy post hoc, ergo propter hoc 'after this, therefore because of this'.]

post horn n. a simple, usually valveless horn, used in the past to announce the arrival of a mail-coach [From POST²]

post horse n. a horse that used to be kept at inns or post houses for use by postriders or for hire by travellers

post house n. an inn where post horses were kept in the past

posthumous /póstyoŏoməss/ adj. **1.** **AFTER SB'S DEATH** occurring after sb's death **2.** **PUBL** **PUBLISHED AFTER DEATH** published or printed after the author's death **3.** **BORN AFTER FATHER'S DEATH** born after the death of the father ○ a posthumous heir [Early 17thC. Formed from late Latin posthumus, an alteration of Latin postumus 'last' (from posterus; see POSTERIOR), under the influence of humare 'to bury'.] —**posthumously** adv. —**posthumousness** n.

posthypnotic suggestion /póst hip nóttik-/ n. a suggestion made to sb under hypnosis that is to be acted upon at a later time after the period of hypnosis is over

postiche /po stéesh/ adj. **FAKE** fake or artificial (formal) ■ n. (formal) **1.** **FAKE COPY** an artificial or fake version or copy of sth **2.** **HAIR** **HAIRPIECE** a small hairpiece or toupee [Early 18thC. Via French from Italian posticcio, of uncertain origin: perhaps ultimately from Latin positus 'placed, added on', from ponere (see POSITION).]

posticous /po stéekəss/ adj. situated behind another part of the same plant [Mid-19thC. Formed from Latin posticus 'behind', from post (see POST-).]

postie /pósti/ n. a postman or postwoman (informal) [Late 19thC. Formed from POST².]

postil /póstil/ n. **MARGINAL COMMENTARY** A note or commentary on a text in the margin (formal) ■ vti. (-tils, -tilling, -tilled) **ANNOTATE BIBLICAL TEXT** to annotate a text, especially a Biblical text (archaic) [14thC. Via Old French postille from medieval Latin postilla, of uncertain origin: possibly from Latin post illa (verba) 'after those (words)'.]

postilion /po stílli ən/, **postillion** n. sb riding the near front horse in a team of horses drawing a carriage [Early 17thC. Via French postillon 'postrider' from Italian postiglione, from posta, from Latin posita (see POST².]

postimpressionism /póst im présh'nizəm/ n. a school of painting in late 19th century France that rejected the naturalism of impressionism but adapted its use of colour and form to a more subjective style — **postimpressionist** n., adj. —**postimpressionistic** /póst im présha nístik/ adj.

postindustrial /póst in dústri əl/ adj. relating to or characteristic of the decline of heavy industry in the western nations as an economic base and the rise of service industries, information technology, and research

posting¹ /pósting/ n. **1.** **COMPUT** **MESSAGE** a message posted online, e.g. to an Internet newsgroup or forum **2.** **ACCT** **BOOKKEEPING ACTIVITY** the activity of making entries in a ledger **3.** **ACCT** **LEDGER ENTRY** an entry made in a ledger

posting² /pósting/ n. an appointment to a job, position, or unit, usually overseas

posting³ /pósting/ adj. relating to sending and collecting post [Late 16thC. From POST².]

Post-it /póstit/ tdmk. a trademark for self-sticking slips of paper sold in pad form

postlude /póst lood/ n. **1.** **MUSIC** **ORGAN VOLUNTARY** a piece of organ music played at the end of a church service **2.** **FINAL PART** a final or concluding phase, chapter, or development (literary) [Mid-19thC. Modelled on PRELUDE.]

postman /póstmən/ (plural -men /-mən/) n. a man whose job it is to collect and deliver letters and parcels that have been sent by post. US term **mailman**

postman's knock n. a children's game in which one player gives another a pretend letter and is given a kiss in return [From the knocks of the player in the role of the postman]

postmark /póst maark/ n. **OFFICIAL STAMP** an official mark, usually covering a postage stamp, that indicates when and where a piece of mail was posted ■ vt. (-marks, -marking, -marked) **USE A POSTMARK** to stamp a postmark on an item of mail

postmaster /póst maastər/ n. the person in charge of a post office or postal district

postmaster general (plural **postmasters general**) n. the executive head of the postal service in some countries, e.g. the United Kingdom

postmenopausal /póst mennə páwz'l/ adj. relating to or occurring in the time following the menopause

postmeridian /póst mə ríddi ən/ adj. relating to or occurring in the afternoon (formal) [Early 17thC. From Latin postmeridianus, from post 'after' + meridiem 'midday'.]

post meridiem /póst mə ríddi əm/ adv. full form of **pm** [From Latin, 'after midday']

post mill n. a windmill with its machinery assembled around an upright spindle and with a blade at the back that makes the sails turn to face the direction of the wind

postmillennial /póst mi lénni əl/ adj. occurring or existing after the millennium

postmillennialism /póst mi lénni əlizəm/, **postmillennarianism** /póst milli náiri ənizəm/ n. the belief that Jesus Christ will return to earth after, and not at, the millennium —**postmillennialist** n. —**postmillennian** n., adj.

postmistress /póst mistrəss/ n. a woman who has charge of a post office (dated)

postmodern /póst módd'n/ adj. relating to art, architecture, literature, or thinking developed after and usually in reaction to modernism, returning to more classical or traditional elements and techniques —**postmodernism** n. —**postmodernist** n.

postmodernity /póst mo dúrnəti/ n. an intellectual movement against modernity and the certainty of universal rational scientific explanation

postmortem /póst máwrtəm/ n. **1.** **MEDICAL EXAMINATION OF CORPSE** a detailed medical examination of a corpse in order to determine the cause of death. Full form **postmortem examination**. US term **autopsy** **2.** **RETROSPECTIVE ANALYSIS** an analysis carried out shortly after the conclusion of an event, especially an unsuccessful one ○ the usual media postmortems the day after the election ■ adj. **AFTER DEATH** occurring after death [Mid-18thC. From Latin post mortem 'after death'.]

postnasal drip /póst náyz'l-/ n. a continual dripping of mucus from the rear of the nose into the throat, often caused by allergy or a cold

postnatal /póst náyt'l/ adj. occurring immediately or soon after childbirth —**postnatally** adv.

postnatal depression n. a state of severe, even suicidal depression that can affect a woman soon after giving birth to a baby. US term **postpartum depression**

postnuptial /póst núpsh'l/ adj. occurring in the period after a marriage —**postnuptially** adv.

post-obit n. **BOND PAYABLE AFTER SB'S DEATH** a bond that pays after the death of a particular person (dated) ■ adj. **AFTER DEATH** coming into effect after sb's death (formal) ○ post-obit payments [Mid-18thC. From Latin post obitum 'after death'.]

post office n. **1.** **PLACE FOR MAILING AND STAMPS** an office or building where the public has access to services of the postal system **2.** **NATIONAL MAIL SYSTEM** the national organization or government department that is responsible for a country's postal service

post office box n. a private numbered box in a post office where letters are held until collected by the addressee

postop /póst óp/, **post-op** adj. postoperative (informal) [Late 20thC. Shortening.]

postoperative /póst ópprətiv/ adj. occurring after a surgical operation —**postoperatively** adv.

postorbital /póst áwrbit'l/ adj. situated behind the eye or the eye socket

postpaid /póst páyd/ adj. with the postage paid in advance

postpartum /póst paártəm/ adj. occurring in or relating to the period immediately after childbirth [Mid-19thC. From Latin post partum 'after childbirth'.]

postpartum depression n. US = postnatal depression

postpone /póst pón/ (-pones, -poning, -poned) vt. **1.** **DELAY** to put sth off until a later time or date **2.** **DEFER** to treat sth with less importance (formal) [15thC. From Latin postponere, literally 'to place later', from ponere (see POSITION).] —**postponable** adj. —**postponement** n. —**postponer** n.

postpose /póst póz/ (-poses, -posing, -posed) vti. **GRAM** to place a word or phrase after another or at the end of a sentence or construction [Late 19thC. Back-formation from POSTPOSITION.]

postposition /póstpə zísh'n/ n. **GRAM** **1.** **PLACEMENT AFTER HEAD OF PHRASE** the placing of a word or phrase after the word or phrase it qualifies, e.g. the placing of 'bold and free' in the phrase 'poets bold and free' **2.** = **postpositive** n. [Mid-17thC. Modelled on 'preposition'.] —**postpositional** adj. —**postpositionally** adv.

postpositive /póst pózzətiv/ adj. **GRAM** **PLACED AFTER HEAD OF PHRASE** used to describe an adjective or modifier that is placed after the word or phrase it qualifies ■ n. **GRAM** **WORD PLACED AFTER** an adjective or modifier that is placed after the word it qualifies [Late 18thC. Via late Latin postpositivus from, ultimately, Latin postponere (see POSTPONE).] —**postpositively** adv.

postprandial /póst prándi əl/ adj. occurring after a meal, especially an evening meal (formal or humorous) —**postprandially** adv.

post-print adj. belonging to the era of electronic communication rather than printing ○ the post-print revolution

postproduction /póst prə dúksh'n/ n. the final stage of making a recording, film, or television programme that includes editing, sound dubbing, and adding special effects

postrider /póst rídər/ n. sb who delivered or relayed post on horseback in the past

post road n. a road or route used regularly by the postal delivery service in the past

postscript /póst skript/ n. **1.** **SHORT MESSAGE** a short message added on to the end of a letter, after the signature **2.** **ADDED-ON PART** an addition to the end of sth such as a book, story, or document [Mid-16thC. From Latin postscriptum, from the past participle of postscribere 'to write after', from scribere (see SCRIBE).]

PostScript /póst skript/ tdmk. a trademark for a page description language used in design, typesetting, and printing, usable on a variety of platforms

post-structuralism n. an intellectual movement derived from structuralism but questioning the basis upon which the structures of society, language, and mores have been conceptualized

postsynaptic /póst si náptik/ adj. used to describe a nerve cell, muscle cell, or a region of cell membrane that receives signals transmitted across a synapse from another nerve cell

postsynch /póst síngk/ (-synchs, -synching, -synched) vt. to add sound or music to a film at a later time

post town n. a town with a main post office (archaic)

posttranscriptional /póst tran skrípsh'nəl/ adj. used to describe processes or components involved in carrying out the genetic instructions of a living cell that participate only after the stage of transcription of a gene or genes

posttransfusion /pōst trans fyóozh'n/ *adj.* occurring after or because of a blood transfusion

posttranslational /pōst trans láysh'nəl/ *adj.* used to describe processes or components involved in carrying out the genetic instructions of living cells that participate only after translation of RNA to protein

post-traumatic stress disorder *n.* a psychological condition that may affect people who have suffered severe emotional trauma, e.g. combat, crime, or natural disaster, and may cause sleep disturbances, flashbacks, anxiety, tiredness, and depression

postulant /póstyōōlənt/ *n.* **1.** RELIG **RELIGIOUS ORDER APPLICANT** sb who applies to join a religious order (*formal*) **2. PETITIONER** sb who submits a request for sth (*archaic or formal*) [Mid-18thC. Directly or via French from Latin *postulant-*, the present participle stem of *postulare* (see POSTULATE).] —**postulancy** *n.*

postulate *vt.* /póst yōō layt/ (**-lates, -lating, -lated**) **1. ASSUME** to assume or suggest that sth is true or exists, especially as the basis of an argument **2. CLAIM STH** to demand or claim sth **3. NOMINATE** to put forward a candidate for a post or office pending approval from a higher authority (*formal*) ■ *n.* /póstyōōlət/ **1. STH ASSUMED TRUE** sth that is assumed or believed to be true and that is used as the basis of an argument or theory **2. PRINCIPLE** a basic principle **3. PRECONDITION** an essential precondition or requirement **4.** MATH, LOGIC **STATEMENT UNDERPINNING A THEORY** a statement that is assumed to be true but has not been proved and that is taken as the basis for a theory, line of reasoning, or hypothesis [Mid-16thC. From medieval Latin *postulare* 'to nominate', originally 'to demand'. Ultimately from an Indo-European base meaning 'to ask', which is also the ancestor of English *pray* and *precarious*.] —**postulation** /póstyōō láysh'n/ *n.* —**postulational** /-láysh'nəl/ *adj.*

postulator /póstyōō laytər/ *n.* **1.** CHR **ADVOCATE FOR SAINTHOOD** in the Roman Catholic Church, an official, usually a priest, who presents a request for a deceased person to be beatified or canonized **2. SB WHO POSTULATES** sb who postulates sth

posture /póschər/ *n.* **1. BODY POSITION** a position the body can assume, e.g. standing, sitting, kneeling, or lying down **2. CARRIAGE** the way in which sb carries his or her body, especially when standing ○ *had poor posture as a child* **3. POSE CONVEYING ATTITUDE** a physical pose that conveys a mental or emotional attitude ○ *a posture of defiance* **4. DECEPTIVE STANCE** a position, attitude, or stance that is intended to deceive **5. CULTIVATED POSITION** a practised or cultivated arrangement of the body, e.g. a position used in yoga **6. ATTITUDE** a frame of mind or attitude towards a particular subject ○ *a conciliatory posture* **7. ARRANGEMENT OF PARTS** the way that components of an object or situation are arranged in relation to one another ■ *v.* (**-tures, -turing, -tured**) **1.** *vi.* **ASSUME STANCE** to assume an affected or exaggerated pose or attitude **2.** *vti.* **MAKE A POSTURE** to arrange sb in, or adopt, a particular posture [Late 16thC. Via French from, ultimately, Latin *positura*, from *posit-*, the past participle stem of *ponere* (see POSITION).] —**postural** *adj.* —**posturer** *n.*

posturize /pósch ərīz/ (**-izes, -izing, -ized**), **posturise** (**-ises, -ising, -ised**) *vi.* = **posture** *v.* 1

postviral syndrome /póst vírəl-/ *n.* = **ME**

postvocalic /pōst vō kállik/ *adj.* PHON coming after a vowel

postwar /pōst wáwr/ *adj.* occurring or existing after a war, especially World War II

postwoman /pōst wōōmən/ (*plural* **-en** /-wimən/) *n.* a woman whose job it is to collect and deliver letters and parcels that have been sent by post

posy /pōzi/ (*plural* **-sies**) *n.* **1. FLOWERS** a small bunch of flowers **2. INSCRIPTION** a short verse or inscription, especially on a trinket or ring (*archaic*) [Mid-16thC. Alteration of POESY.]

pot[1] /pot/ *n.* **1. WATERTIGHT CONTAINER FOR COOKING OR STORAGE** a container made of metal, pottery, or glass that is usually cylindrical and watertight with an open top and sometimes a lid, used especially for cooking or storage **2. STH RESEMBLING POT IN SHAPE** sth similar to a pot in shape or function e.g. a flowerpot, teapot, or chamber pot **3. CONTENTS OF POT** the contents of a pot, or the amount that it will hold ○ *made a pot of coffee* **4.** CERAMICS **OBJECT MADE FROM CLAY** a dish or container that is made from clay, especially one of artistic or historical interest **5.** = **potty**[2] (*informal*) **6. LARGE AMOUNT OF MONEY** a large amount of money (*informal*) **7.** CARDS **MONEY BET IN CARD GAME** all the money that is bet in a game of cards, especially poker, and that is taken by the winning player **8. DRINKING VESSEL** a large drinking vessel, usually glass or pewter, for beer **9.** *US* **COMMON FUND** a common fund of money that is contributed to by the members of a group, usually for a particular purpose, e.g. a party or trip (*informal*) **10.** CUE GAMES **HIT OF BALL INTO POCKET** in billiards or snooker, a hit of a ball that sends it into any of the pockets at the edge of the table **11.** SPORTS **CUP WON IN COMPETITION** a vessel, especially a silver cup, that is won in a competition, especially a sports contest (*informal*) **12.** AGRIC **FISH OR LOBSTER TRAP** a basket or cage used for catching lobsters, eels, or fish **13. POTBELLY** a round bulging stomach or abdomen (*informal*) **14.** = **potshot** *n.* 1 (*informal*) **15.** *Aus* **BEER GLASS** in Victoria and Queensland, a 10-oz beer glass ■ *v.* (**pots, potting, potted**) **1.** *vt.* GARDENING **PUT PLANT IN POT** to put a plant into a pot with soil or compost **2.** *vti.* **SHOOT ANIMAL FOR FOOD** to shoot or shoot at a bird or animal, especially for food **3.** *vti.* **SHOOT AT STH WITHIN EASY REACH** to shoot or shoot at an easy target, especially casually **4.** *vt.* COOK **PRESERVE FOOD IN POT** to preserve food in a pot **5.** *vti.* CUE GAMES **HIT BALL INTO POCKET** in billiards or snooker, to hit a ball into any of the pockets at the edge of the table **6.** *vti.* CERAMICS **SHAPE STH WITH CLAY** to shape a pot or other item from clay **7.** *vt.* ELECTRON ENG to encapsulate electronic components in an insulating resin to protect them and hold them in place. The technique is used in high technology industries such as avionics as well as in automotive, medical, and consumer electronics. **8.** *vt.* **PUT CHILD ON POTTY** to put a young child on a potty [Pre-12thC. From assumed Vulgar Latin *pottus* of unknown origin. Later also probably from French *pot*, of the same origin.] ◇ **go to pot** to get much worse or become useless, worthless, or extremely unsatisfactory (*informal*)

pot on *vt.* to transfer a growing plant from a smaller to a larger pot

pot up *vt.* to plant a seedling or cutting in a pot, separating it from others with which it originally grew

pot[2] *n.* the plant or drug cannabis (*slang*) [Mid-20thC. Origin uncertain: probably a shortening of Mexican Spanish *potiguaya* 'marijuana leaves'.]

pot[3] /pot/ *n.* a potentiometer (*informal*) [Mid-20thC. Shortening.]

pot. *abbr.* potential

potable /pṓtəb'l/ *adj.* **SUITABLE FOR DRINKING** suitable for drinking because it contains no harmful elements ■ *n.* **STH TO DRINK** a liquid that is suitable for drinking, especially an alcoholic drink [15thC. Directly or via French from late Latin *potabilis*, from Latin *potare* 'to drink', from *potus* 'drink' (source of English *potion*).] —**potability** /pṓtə bílləti/ *n.* —**potableness** /pṓtəb'lnəss/ *n.*

potage /po táazh, pó taazh/ *n.* a thick soup [Mid-16thC. From French (see POTTAGE).]

potamic /pə támmik/ *adj.* relating to rivers or river navigation (*technical*) [Late 19thC. Formed from Greek *potamos* 'river'.]

potash /pót ash/ *n.* **1. POTASSIUM COMPOUND USED IN FERTILIZER** a potassium compound, especially potassium chloride, sulphate, or oxide, primarily used in fertilizers. The concentration of potassium in the fertilizer is usually expressed as a percentage. **2.** = **potassium carbonate 3.** = **potassium hydroxide** [Early 17thC. From obsolete Dutch *potasschen*, plural of *potasch*, literally 'pot ash' (originally obtained by soaking wood ash in water and evaporating the resulting solution in iron pots).]

potash alum *n.* = **alum**

potassium /pə tássi əm/ *n.* a soft silvery-white very reactive element of the alkali metal group, commonly found combined in minerals. The metal has few uses other than being alloyed with sodium as a coolant in nuclear reactors, although its compounds are widely used, especially in fertilizers. Symbol K [Early 19thC. From modern Latin, from *potassa* 'potash', from POTASH; from potassium being the basis of potash.]

potassium-argon dating *n.* a technique for estimating the age of rocks older than 250,000 years, based on the time taken for the radioactive decay of the potassium-40 isotope into a stable argon isotope. The half-life of potassium-40 is about 1.28 x 10^9 years, and the ratio of potassium to argon in the specimen gives an indication of its age.

potassium bitartrate /-bī táar trayt/ *n.* a white powder or crystalline compound used in baking powder, in medicine, and in food preparation. Formula: $KHC_4H_4O_6$.

potassium bromide *n.* a white crystalline compound used in lithography, medicine, photography, and soaps. Formula: KBr.

potassium carbonate *n.* a white salt used in brewing, ceramics, explosives, fertilizers, glass, and soap. Formula: K_2CO_3.

potassium chlorate *n.* a white salt that detonates with heat and is used in the manufacture of fireworks, matches, and explosives, in textile printing and paper manufacture, and as a bleach and disinfectant. It is also known to chemistry students for its use in the laboratory preparation of oxygen. Formula: $KClO_3$.

potassium chloride *n.* a colourless crystalline salt used as a fertilizer and in photography and medicine. Formula: KCl.

potassium cyanide *n.* a very poisonous white crystalline chemical salt used in the extraction of gold and silver from their ores, electroplating, photography, and as an insecticide. Formula: KCN.

potassium dichromate *n.* a yellow-red poisonous crystalline compound used in the manufacture of explosives, safety matches, and dyes. Formula: $K_2Cr_2O_7$.

potassium ferricyanide *n.* a bright red poisonous crystalline compound that decomposes when heated. It is used in textile printing, wool dyeing, blueprint paper, and as a fertilizer. Formula: $K_3Fe(CN)_6$.

potassium ferrocyanide *n.* a yellow crystalline compound used in medicine and explosives. Formula: $K_4Fe(CN)_6$.

potassium hydrogen carbonate *n.* a white powder or granular compound, used in baking powder and in medicine as an antacid. Formula: $KHCO_3$.

potassium hydrogen tartrate *n.* = **potassium bitartrate**

potassium hydroxide *n.* a caustic toxic white solid used to make soap, detergents, liquid shampoos, and matches. Formula: KOH.

potassium iodide *n.* a white crystalline compound with a salty taste, used in medicine and photography and added to table salt to provide a source of iodine. Formula: KI.

potassium nitrate *n.* a white crystalline salt used in fireworks, explosives, and matches, as a fertilizer, and as a preservative for meats. Formula: KNO_3.

potassium permanganate *n.* a dark purple toxic odourless crystalline compound used as a bleach, disinfectant, and antiseptic, and in deodorizers and dyes. Formula: $KMnO_4$.

potassium sodium tartrate *n.* Rochelle salt (*technical*)

potassium sulphate *n.* a colourless crystalline compound used in aluminium, glass, and cement manufacture, in fertilizers, and in medicine. Formula: K_2SO_4.

potation /pō táysh'n/ *n.* (*literary*) **1. DRINKING** the act or an instance of drinking **2. ALCOHOLIC DRINK** a drink, especially an alcoholic drink [15thC. Directly or via Old French from the Latin stem *potation-*, from, ultimately, *potare* 'to drink' (see POTABLE).]

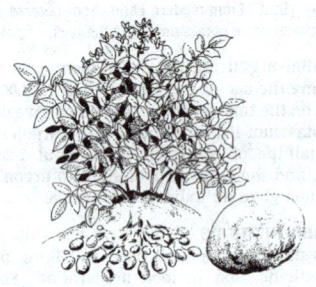

Potato

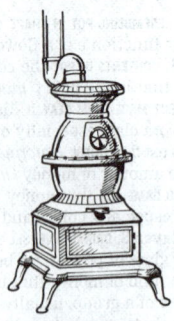

Potbelly stove

potato /pə táytō/ (*plural* **-toes**) *n.* **1.** FOOD ROOT VEGETABLE a rounded white tuber with a thin skin, cooked as a vegetable. It is an important source of starch, especially in Europe and North America. Potatoes can be boiled, baked, roasted, or fried, have many different varieties, and are used in many dishes. **2.** PLANTS POTATO PLANT a perennial plant, originally from South America and belonging to the nightshade family, that is widely cultivated for its fleshy underground tuber. Latin name: *Solanum tuberosum.* **3.** = **sweet potato** [Mid-16thC. From Spanish *patata*, an alteration of Taino *batata* 'sweet potato'.]

potato beetle *n.* = **Colorado beetle**

potato blight *n.* a highly destructive disease of the potato caused by the fungus *Phytophthora infestans.* It was the cause of the loss of the potato crop in Ireland in the 19th century.

potato cake *n.* a flat round mass of seasoned potato, either cooked and mashed or raw and grated, that has been fried or sautéed

potato chip *n.* US, ANZ a very thin slice of potato that has usually been deep-fried in oil, salted, sometimes flavoured, and packaged and sold to be eaten cold as a snack

potato crisp *n.* = **crisp** *n.* 1

potato pancake *n.* a pancake made from a mixture of coarsely grated potato with egg, flour, and seasonings

potato scone *n.* a griddle cake of dough containing mashed potato and flour, served hot

potato skin *n.* a piece of skin from a hollowed-out baked potato that is then baked further, or a piece of deep-fried skin of a raw potato, served as an appetizer (*often used in the plural*)

pot-au-feu /pót ō fő/ (*plural* **pot-au-feu** /pót ō fő/) *n.* **1.** FOOD DISH OF MEAT AND VEGETABLES a French stew of slowly boiled meat and vegetables, the meat usually being eaten separately from the vegetables and stock, which are served first as a soup **2.** HOUSEHOLD LARGE COOKING POT a large earthenware pot in which pot-au-feu is traditionally cooked [From French, literally 'pot on the fire']

Potawatomi /póttə wóttəmi/ (*plural* **-mi** or **-mis**) *n.* **1.** PEOPLES MEMBER OF NATIVE N AMERICAN PEOPLE a member of a Native North American people who originally occupied lands in various northern central states, and whose members now live mainly in Kansas, Oklahoma, Michigan, and Ontario **2.** LANG POTAWATOMI LANGUAGE the Algonquian language of the Potawatomi people —**Potawatomi** *adj.*

potbelly /pót beli/ (*plural* **-lies**) *n.* **1.** BULGING STOMACH a round bulging stomach or abdomen **2.** SB WITH POTBELLY sb who has a potbelly —**potbellied** *adj.*

potbelly stove, potbellied stove *n.* US a wood- or coal-burning stove that has a rounded bulbous body

potboiler /pót boylər/ *n.* a book, film, or other work that is produced quickly to make money and has little literary or artistic quality (*informal*) [From its exclusive purpose of 'boiling the pot', that is, providing a livelihood so that sb can eat]

pot-bound /pót bownd/ *adj.* used to describe a pot plant whose roots have grown very dense and have filled its pot so that its growth is restricted. Some plants grow well in this condition.

potboy /pót boy/ *n.* a boy or man employed in a public house, especially to collect empty glasses (*archaic*)

poteen /po teén, po cheén/ *n.* in Ireland, a spirit that has been distilled illegally, especially from potatoes [Early 19thC. From Irish *(fuisce) poitín*, literally 'small pot (whiskey)', from *pota* 'pot', from POT[1].]

potency /pót'nssi/ (*plural* **-cies**) *n.* **1.** STRENGTH OF MEDICINE the strength of sth such as a drug, medicine, or alcoholic drink **2.** STATE OF BEING POTENT the state or quality of being potent **3.** ABILITY TO DEVELOP a capacity to grow or develop in the future

potent[1] /pót'nt/ *adj.* **1.** STRONG AND EFFECTIVE very strong, effective, or powerful **2.** PERSUASIVE exerting persuasion, influence, or force **3.** WITH STRONG CHEMICAL EFFECT with a strong or concentrated chemical or medicinal effect **4.** HAVING POWER having or using power, control, or authority **5.** CAPABLE OF SEXUAL INTERCOURSE capable of having an erection, sexual intercourse, or an ejaculation [15thC. From Latin *potent-*, present participle stem of *posse* 'to be powerful' (source of English *posse*), contraction of *potis esse*, from *potis* 'able' + *esse* 'to be'.] —**potently** *adv.* —**potentness** *n.*

potent[2] /pót'nt/ *adj.* HERALDRY used to describe a heraldic cross that has four arms with a bar across the end of each arm [14thC. Alteration of obsolete English *potence* 'crutch' or its Old French source, from Latin *potentia* 'power', from the stem *potent-* (see POTENT[1]).]

potentate /pót'n tayt/ *n.* sb who has power, authority, and influence, especially a monarch or other leader who has the power to rule over others

potential /pə ténsh'l/ *adj.* **1.** POSSIBLE BUT NOT YET REALIZED with a possibility or likelihood of occurring, or of doing or becoming sth in the future **2.** GRAM EXPRESSING POSSIBILITY used to describe a verb or verb form that expresses possibility, e.g. 'may' or 'might' in English ■ *n.* **1.** CAPACITY TO DEVELOP the capacity or ability for future development or achievement **2.** GRAM POTENTIAL VERB FORM a verb or verb form that expresses possibility, e.g. 'may' or 'might' in English **3.** PHYS = **electric potential** [14thC. Directly or via Old French *potenciel* from late Latin *potentialis*, ultimately from the Latin stem *potent-* (see POTENT[1]).] —**potentially** *adv.*

potential difference *n.* the work done in moving a unit electric charge between two points in an electric field. Symbol ΔV, ΔU

potential divider *n.* = **voltage divider**

potential energy *n.* the energy that a body or system has stored because of its position in an electric, magnetic, or gravitational field, or because of its configuration. Symbol V, E_p

potentiality /pə ténshi álləti/ (*plural* **-ties**) *n.* **1.** CAPACITY FOR DEVELOPMENT the capacity or ability for future development or for a future achievement or action **2.** SB OR STH WITH POTENTIAL sb who or sth that has potentiality

potential well *n.* a region in an electric, magnetic, or gravitational field in which an object has a lower potential energy than it would have in all adjacent regions

potentiate /pə ténshi ayt/ (**-ates**, **-ating**, **-ated**) *vt.* MED to improve the effectiveness of a drug or treatment, especially by adding another drug or agent —**potentiator** *n.*

potentilla /pót'n tíllə/ (*plural* **-las** or **-la**) *n.* a flowering plant or small shrub cultivated for its small yellow,

white, or red flowers that have five petals and many pistils. Genus: *Potentilla.* [Mid-16thC. From medieval Latin, literally 'powerful little (plant)' (from its use in medicine), from the Latin stem *potent-* (see POTENT[1]).]

potentiometer /pə ténshi ómmitər/ *n.* **1.** INSTRUMENT FOR MEASURING ELECTROMOTIVE FORCE a device for measuring an unknown potential difference or electromotive force by balancing part of it against a known standard **2.** VOLUME OR BRIGHTNESS CONTROL a three-terminal component, typically used as a volume or brightness control, that gives a variable electric potential by rotating a shaft or moving a slider [Late 19thC. Coined from POTENTIAL + -METER.] —**potentiometry** *n.*

potentiometric /pə ténshi ə méttrik/ *adj.* indicating the completion of a chemical reaction by a change in potential at an electrode immersed in the solution where the reaction is taking place [Early 20thC. Coined from POTENTIAL + -METRIC.]

potful /pót fool/ *n.* the amount that a pot will hold

pothead /pót hed/ *n.* sb who regularly smokes cannabis, especially in large amounts (*slang disapproving*)

pothecary /póthəkəri/ (*plural* **-ies**) *n.* an apothecary (*archaic*) [14thC. Shortening.]

pother /póthər/ *n.* **1.** NERVOUS STATE a state of emotional agitation, especially over sth trivial **2.** COMMOTION a great deal of frenzied activity or conversation, especially over sth trivial **3.** CHOKING CLOUD a cloud of smoke or dust that chokes ■ *vti.* (**-ers, -ering, -ered**) CONFUSE SB OR BE CONFUSED to confuse or worry sb or to become confused or worried [Late 16thC. Origin uncertain.]

potherb /pót hurb/ *n.* a herb or vegetable used to add flavour in cooking

potholder /pót hōldər/ *n.* a pad of fabric used to protect the hands from hot pots and cooking utensils

pothole /pót hōl/ *n.* **1.** TRANSP HOLE IN ROAD SURFACE a hole that has formed in the surface of a road and that can be hazardous to motorists **2.** GEOL, GEOG VERTICAL HOLE IN LIMESTONE AREA a vertical deep hole or shaft formed naturally in limestone regions by the erosive action of running water **3.** GEOL, GEOG HOLE IN RIVER BED a bowl-shaped hole in the bed of a river or stream, formed by the abrasive action of stone, gravel, or ice being churned in an eddy

potholing /pót hōling/ *n.* the activity of exploring potholes and underground caves connected by them, especially as a hobby or sport —**potholer** *n.*

pothook /pót hŏŏk/ *n.* **1.** DOMESTIC HOOK OVER FIRE an S-shaped hook fixed above an open fire, from which a pot or kettle is hung **2.** CURVED SHAPE MADE IN HANDWRITING a handwriting mark beginning or ending in a curve

pothouse /pót howss/ (*plural* **-houses** /-howziz/) *n.* a public house (*archaic*)

pothunter /pót huntər/ *n.* **1.** HUNT HUNTER OF GAME FOR PROFIT sb who hunts game for food or as a source of income, often indiscriminately and disregarding rules **2.** SPORTS, LEISURE PRIZE-SEEKER sb who takes part in competitions and races with more interest in the prizes than the sport (*informal disapproving*) **3.** ARCHAEOL AMATEUR ARCHAEOLOGIST sb who digs in search of ancient pots and other objects but is not a professional archaeologist —**pothunting** *n.*

potion /pósh'n/ *n.* a liquid to be drunk that is medicinal, supposedly magical, or poisonous [13thC. Via Old French from the Latin stem *potion-*, from, ultimately, *potare* 'to drink'.]

Potiphar /póttifər/ *n.* in the Bible, the Egyptian who bought Joseph as a slave and later imprisoned him when falsely accused of attempting to sleep with his wife. (Genesis 37).

potlatch /pót lach/ *n.* among Native American peoples of the northwest coast of North America, a ceremony of feasting in which the host gains prestige by giving gifts or, sometimes, destroying wealth [Mid-19thC. From Chinook Jargon.]

potluck /pot lúk/ *n.* **1.** WHATEVER IS AVAILABLE whatever happens to be available to satisfy a need **2.** FOOD FOOD AVAILABLE TO UNEXPECTED GUEST whatever food happens to be available to give to an unexpected guest **3.** US

FOOD **MEAL TO WHICH EVERYONE BRINGS STH** a meal to which each participant brings one dish that is shared with everyone else [Late 16thC. From POT[1] + LUCK.]

potman /pótmən/ (*plural* **-men** /-mən/) *n.* a man employed in a public house, especially to collect empty glasses (*archaic*)

pot marigold *n.* a European garden plant of the daisy family with large bright yellow or orange flowers. Latin name: *Calendula officinalis.* US term **calendula** ['Pot' from its being grown for decoration]

Potomac /pə tóm ak/ river of the eastern United States, formed by the confluence of its own north and south branches near Cumberland, Maryland, and emptying into Chesapeake Bay. It flows through Washington, D.C. Length: 460 km/285 mi.

potometer /pə tómmitər/ *n.* an instrument used to determine the rate of a plant's transpiration by measuring water uptake [Late 19thC. Coined from Greek *poton* 'drink' + -METER.]

potoroo /póttə roó/ (*plural* **-roos**) *n.* a rabbit-sized member of the kangaroo family that looks like a rat and has powerful hind legs that it uses for jumping. Latin name: *Potorous tridactylus.* [Late 18thC. From Aboriginal.]

pot plant *n.* a plant that is growing in a flowerpot and is kept in a house or office for display and decoration. US term **potted plant**

potpourri /pō poóri, pồpə rée/ (*plural* **-ris**) *n.* **1.** DOMESTIC **COLLECTION OF FRAGRANT DRIED FLOWERS** a collection of dried flower petals, leaves, herbs, and spices, sometimes coloured and scented, that are used to scent the air **2.** MISCELLANEOUS MIXTURE a miscellaneous mixture of things [Early 17thC. From French, literally 'rotten pot' (translation of Spanish *olla podrida*); *pourri,* past participle of *pourrir* 'to rot', from, ultimately, Latin *putris* 'rotten'.]

pot roast *n.* a dish consisting of a piece of beef cooked slowly in the oven in a closed pot in its own juices, often on a bed of vegetables —**pot-roast** *vti.*

Potsdam /póts dam/ city in northeastern Germany, in Brandenburg State, approximately 29 km/18 mi. southwest of Berlin. It was the site of the Potsdam Conference (July-August 1945), at which US, British, and Soviet leaders discussed the postwar administration of Germany. Population: 139,000 (1994).

potsherd /pót shurd/, **potshard** /-shard/ *n.* a fragment of pottery, especially one found at an archaeological site [14thC. From POT + SHERD.]

potshot /pót shot/ *n.* **1.** EASY SHOT a shot taken quickly, carelessly, or on a chance opportunity at sth such as game, especially when within easy reach **2.** HASTY **CRITICISM** a criticism made without careful consideration and aimed at an easy target ○ *journalists taking potshots at the government* [Mid-19thC. From the purpose of the shot originally being to get food for the cooking 'pot' (not in accordance with the strict codes of shooting as a sport).]

pot still *n.* an apparatus for distilling whisky that applies heat directly to the container holding the wash

potstone /pót stōn/ *n.* an impure variety of talc, used in the past to make cooking vessels

pottage /póttij/ *n.* a thick vegetable, or meat and vegetable, soup [12thC. Originally *potage,* from Old French, literally 'what is put in a pot', from *pot* (see POT).]

potted /póttid/ *adj.* **1.** GROWING IN POT planted in a pot **2.** PRESERVED IN POT cooked or preserved in a vessel such as a pot or jar **3.** SUPERFICIALLY SUMMARIZED reproduced in a brief and often superficial form (*informal*)

potted plant *n.* US = pot plant

potter[1] /póttər/ *n.* sb who makes pottery [Pre-12thC.]

potter[2] /póttər/ (**-ters, -tering, -tered**) *vi.* **1.** ENGAGE IN **ACTIVITY IN UNHURRIED MANNER** to do relatively unimportant things in a relaxed and unhurried way ○ *pottering about in the greenhouse.* US term **putter 2.** PROCEED AIMLESSLY to proceed slowly and without any particular goal [Mid-16thC. Formed from obsolete *pote* 'to push', from Old English *potian,* of uncertain origin.] —**potterer** *n.*

Beatrix Potter

Potter /póttər/, **Beatrix** (1866–1943) British children's writer and illustrator. Her illustrated animal stories, including *The Tale of Peter Rabbit* (1900) and *The Tailor of Gloucester* (1902), became children's classics. Full name **Helen Beatrix Potter**

Potteries /póteriz/ region in Staffordshire, west-central England, famous for its ceramics factories

potter's clay *n.* clay that does not contain any iron and is suitable for making pottery

potter's field *n.* in the Bible, an area of land near Jerusalem bought as a burial ground for strangers with the money that was given to Judas for betraying Jesus Christ

potter's wheel *n.* a device for moulding clay into pottery by hand, consisting of a horizontal disc that holds the clay and is rotated manually or by electricity. A technological advance in pottery-making, it was invented around 6000 BC and made faster and higher-quality ceramic pottery production possible.

potter wasp *n.* a small solitary wasp that constructs elaborate clay pots in which it lays its eggs and puts caterpillars to serve as food for the young. Genus: *Eumenes.*

pottery /póttəri/ (*plural* **-ies**) *n.* **1.** OBJECTS MADE OF BAKED **CLAY** objects such as vases, pots, plates, or sculptured articles that are made by moulding or shaping moist clay and hardening it by heating it in a kiln **2.** MAKING **OF POTTERY** the art, craft, or occupation of making pottery **3.** PLACE WHERE POTTERY IS MADE a workshop, factory, or other place where pottery is made

potting compost *n.* any mixture, e.g. based on soil or peat, with a balance of nutrients used for growing plants in pots

potting shed *n.* a small shed in a garden for storing flowerpots, compost, and gardening materials

pottle /póttʼl/ *n.* (*archaic*) **1.** HALF A GALLON a measure for liquids that is equal to 1.9 litres/half a gallon **2.** CONTAINER HOLDING POTTLE a container, especially a drinking vessel, that can hold a pottle [14thC. From Old French *potel,* literally 'small pot', from *pot* (see POT).]

potto /póttō/ (*plural* **-tos**) *n.* a small primate of West and Central African rain forests that has small ears, large eyes, and a short bushy tail and lives in the lower branches of trees. Latin name: *Perodicticus potto.* [Early 18thC. Origin uncertain: probably from a West African source.]

Pott's disease /póts-/ *n.* a tubercular disease of the spine, marked by the destruction of the bone and discs and curvature of the spine [Mid-19thC. Named after Sir Percivall Pott (1713–88), the English surgeon who described the disease.]

potty[1] /pótti/ (**-tier, -tiest**) *adj.* (*informal*) **1.** IRRATIONAL slightly irrational **2.** KEEN OR ENTHUSIASTIC very enthusiastic about or obsessed by sb or sth **3.** TRIVIAL trivial and unimportant [Mid-19thC. Origin uncertain: perhaps formed from POT[1] in the sense of 'container'.] —**pottiness** *n.*

potty[2] /pótti/ (*plural* **-ties**) *n.* a bowl, used especially by young children who cannot yet use a toilet, to eliminate body waste (*informal*) [Mid-20thC. Formed from POT[1].]

potty-chair *n.* a small chair with a pot in the seat, used by young children who are being trained to use a toilet

potty-train (**potty-trains, potty-training, potty-trained**) *vti.* to train a young child to use a potty instead of a nappy (*informal*)

pot-walloper *n.* in some English boroughs before 1832, a man entitled to vote because he had his own fireplace as a homeowner, tenant, or lodger [Early 18thC. Alteration (modelled on WALLOP) of *potwaller,* literally 'pot-boiler', from POT[1] + obsolete *wall* 'to boil' (from Old English *weallan,* from prehistoric Germanic).]

pouch /powch/ *n.* **1.** SMALL SOFT BAG a small bag or container made of a soft material such as fabric or leather **2.** STH RESEMBLING POUCH sth that looks like a pouch, especially a small baggy fold of skin **3.** ZOOL POCKET OF SKIN IN ANIMAL a structure in an animal resembling a pouch, especially one on the abdomen of a marsupial for carrying young, or in the cheek of a rodent for carrying food **4.** ANAT BODY CAVITY **RESEMBLING POCKET** a pocket-shaped space or structure in the body **5.** BOT PLANT CAVITY a cavity in a plant shaped like a pocket **6.** Scotland POCKET a pocket **7.** MAIL BAG FOR MAIL a lockable bag or sack for carrying mail, especially diplomatic correspondence ■ *v.* (**pouches, pouching, pouched**) **1.** *vt.* PUT IN POUCH to put sth into a pouch **2.** *vt.* POCKET STH to take sth by putting it into your pocket **3.** *vti.* FORM POUCH to make sth, or be made, into a shape resembling a pouch [13thC. Via Anglo-Norman *puche,* Old Northern French *pouche,* and Old French *poche,* from a prehistoric Germanic word meaning 'bag' that is also the ancestor of English *pocket.*] —**pouchy** *adj.*

pouf[1] /poof/, **pouffe** *n.* **1.** FURNITURE PADDED STOOL a round or square piece of padded furniture with an upholstered cover, used as a seat or footrest. US term **hassock 2.** HAIR PUFFED-OUT HAIRSTYLE a puffed-out hairstyle, similar to a bouffant, fashionable especially in the 18th century **3.** HAIR PAD IN HAIR a pad worn in the hair to help shape a pouf **4.** CLOTHES BUNCHED-UP **PART OF DRESS** a part of a dress or skirt gathered up to form a soft projecting shape [Early 19thC. Via French from, ultimately, an imitation of the sound of a puff.]

pouf[2] /poof, poof/, **pouffe** *n.* = poof[1] (*slang offensive*)

Pouilly-Fuissé /poo yee fwee say/ *n.* a dry white wine produced from the Chardonnay grape in the area around Pouilly and Fuissé in the Burgundy region of France

Pouilly-Fumé /poo yee fyoo may/ *n.* a dry white wine produced from the Sauvignon Blanc grape in the area around Pouilly-sur-Loire in the Loire valley of France [Mid-20thC. From French; *fumé* is the past participle of *fumer* 'to smoke', from, ultimately, Latin *fumus* 'smoke'.]

Poujadism /poo zhaadizəm/ *n.* a very right-wing political movement in France in the 1950s, with mainly middle-class support [Mid-20thC. From French *Poujadisme,* which was named after the French publisher and politician Pierre Poujade born 1920.] —**Poujadist** *n., adj.*

poulard /poo laard/, **poularde** *n.* a young domestic hen (**pullet**) that has been spayed to encourage fattening. Spaying of hens is rarely done in modern poultry production. [Mid-18thC. From French *poularde,* from *poule* 'hen', from, ultimately, Latin *pulla,* feminine of *pullus* 'chicken' (source of English *pony* and *poultry*).]

Poulenc /pool angk, pool aNk/, **Francis** (1899–1963) French composer and pianist. He was one of Les Six. His music, tuneful and satirical, includes ballets, operas, chamber music, and songs.

poult /pōlt/ *n.* a young fowl, especially a turkey or pheasant [15thC. Contraction of PULLET.]

poulterer /pôltərər/ *n.* sb who buys, prepares, and sells poultry [Late 16thC. Alteration of archaic *poulter,* from Old French *pouletier,* from *poulet* 'young fowl'.]

poultice /póltiss/ *n.* a warm moist preparation placed on an aching or inflamed part of the body to ease pain, improve circulation, or hasten the expression of pus. Poultices may be made from bread, clay, mustard, medicinal herbs, or other materials, but are now considered to have little medical benefit. [14thC. Originally *pultes,* from Latin, plural of *puls* 'pottage, thick gruel' (source of English *pulse* 'lentils').]

poultry /pôltri/ *n.* **1.** DOMESTIC FOWL domestic fowl in general, e.g. chickens, turkeys, ducks, or geese, raised for meat or eggs **2.** MEAT FROM POULTRY the meat of domestic fowl such as chickens and ducks [14thC. From Old French *pouletrie*, from *pouletier* 'poulterer', from *poulet* 'young fowl'.]

pounamu /pŏonə moo/ *n.* = **greenstone** *n.* 2 [Mid-19thC. From Maori.]

pounce[1] /pownss/ *v.* (**pounces, pouncing, pounced**) **1.** *vi.* JUMP SUDDENLY ON to jump or swoop suddenly towards or onto sb or sth, especially onto prey **2.** *vi.* ATTACK OR TAKE QUICKLY to move very quickly and suddenly in attacking sb or obtaining sth ○ *He pounced on the book and carried it off to his room.* **3.** *vt.* REACT SWIFTLY TO to be quick to notice and make use of sth ○ *She immediately pounced on his admission that he'd known all about it.* ■ *n.* ACT OF SUDDENLY JUMPING ON an act of suddenly jumping or swooping towards or onto sb or sth, especially onto prey [14thC. Origin uncertain: either a shortening of PUNCHEON, or from Old French *poinson* 'pointed tool', via the assumed Vulgar Latin stem *punction-* from, ultimately, the Latin stem *punct-* (see PUNCTURE).] —**pouncer** *n.*

pounce[2] /pownss/ *n.* **1.** POWDER TO STOP INK RUNNING a very fine powder used in the past to stop ink from spreading on unglazed paper **2.** POWDER USED FOR PRODUCING IMAGE powdered charcoal or other fine powder sprinkled over a stencil to reproduce the main lines of a pattern or design on the surface beneath the stencil ■ *vt.* (**pounces, pouncing, pounced**) **1.** SPRINKLE PAPER WITH POUNCE to sprinkle paper with pounce **2.** REPRODUCE STH WITH POUNCE to reproduce a pattern or design on sth by sprinkling pounce over a stencil [Late 16thC. Via Old French *ponce* (noun) and *poncer* (verb) from, ultimately, Latin *pumic-*, stem of *pumex* 'pumice' (source of English *pumice*).]

pouncet box /pównssət-/ *n.* a small box with a perforated lid, used in the past to hold a perfumed substance [Late 16thC. 'Pouncet' of uncertain origin: perhaps a misprint for *pounced* 'perforated', from *pounce* 'to ornament with perforation', ultimately from Old French *poinson* 'pointed tool' (see POUNCE[1]).]

pound[1] /pownd/ *n.* **1.** MONEY COMMON UNIT OF CURRENCY a unit of currency used in the United Kingdom, Cyprus and several Middle Eastern countries. See table at **currency 2.** MONEY COIN OR NOTE WORTH A POUND a coin or note worth a pound **3.** = **pound scots 4.** MEASURE AVOIRDUPOIS UNIT OF WEIGHT a unit of weight in the avoirdupois system, divided into 16 ounces and equivalent to 0.45 kg **5.** MEASURE TROY UNIT OF WEIGHT a unit of weight in the troy system that is divided into 12 ounces and is equivalent to 0.37 kg **6.** MEASURE UNIT OF FORCE a unit of force, equal to the gravitational force experienced by a pound mass accelerating at 9.80665 m/32.174 ft per second per second [Old English *pund* via prehistoric Germanic from Latin *pondo* 'weight of a pound', from *(libra) pondo* '(pound) by weight', a form of assumed *pondos* 'weight'] ◇ **get** *or* **have your pound of flesh** to get what is due to you, even if it causes difficulties or hardship to others

pound[2] /pownd/ *v.* (**pounds, pounding, pounded**) **1.** *vti.* STRIKE HARD AND REPEATEDLY to strike sb or sth repeatedly and heavily **2.** *vt.* BEAT STH TO PULP OR POWDER to beat sth into very fine pieces or to a mass, with repeated heavy blows **3.** *vi.* THROB to beat or throb heavily ○ *My heart was pounding.* **4.** *vt.* ATTACK CONTINUOUSLY to attack a place continuously with bombs or large guns ○ *pounding the city for a few weeks* **5.** *vi.* RUN HEAVILY to run with heavy steps **6.** *vt.* TEACH BY REPETITION to ensure that sb learns or understands sth by using constant repetition and drilling ■ *n.* ACT OF POUNDING the act or sound of pounding [15thC. Alteration of *pounen*, from Old English *pūnian*, from a prehistoric Germanic base that is also the ancestor of Dutch *puin* 'rubbish, rubble'.] —**pounder** *n.*

pound out *vt.* **1.** PRODUCE STH WITH HARD WORK to produce sth by working in a diligent continuous way ○ *pound out an essay* **2.** PRODUCE STH WITH HEAVY BLOWS to produce sth with heavy blows or loud thumping noises ○ *pound out a tune on the piano*

pound[3] /pownd/ *n.* **1.** ENCLOSURE FOR STRAY ANIMALS a fenced-off area where stray animals, especially dogs, are kept **2.** CRIMINOL ENCLOSURE FOR VEHICLES OR OTHER GOODS a fenced-off area where vehicles or other goods that have been taken by the police or another authority are kept until a debt or fine has been paid **3.** HUNT, AGRIC PLACE FOR ANIMALS OR FISH an area in which animals or fish are trapped or kept **4.** PRISON AREA a place where people are held prisoner ■ *vt.* (**pounds, pounding, pounded**) PUT STH IN POUND to confine sb or sth in a pound [From the Old English stem *pund-*]

US Office of War Information

Ezra Pound

Pound /pownd/, **Ezra** (1885–1972) US writer. He was an influential poet, critic, translator, and mentor of other poets, and a founder of imagism. His major work is *Cantos* (1925–70). Full name **Ezra Loomis Pound**

poundage[1] /pówndij/ *n.* **1.** COMM PAYMENT PER POUND OF WEIGHT a tax, charge, commission, or other payment for sth calculated per pound of weight **2.** FIN PAYMENT PER POUND STERLING a tax, charge, commission, or other payment for sth calculated per pound sterling **3.** MEASURE WEIGHT IN POUNDS the weight of sb or sth expressed in pounds

poundage[2] /pówndij/ *n.* **1.** CONFINEMENT IN ENCLOSURE the confinement of animals in an enclosed area or pound **2.** FEE FOR RETURN OF STH the fee that must be paid for the return of an impounded vehicle, animal, or other goods

poundal /pównd'l/ *n.* a British unit of force, equal to the force that will impart an acceleration of one foot per second per second to a mass of one pound [Late 19thC. Formed from POUND[1], perhaps on the model of QUINTAL.]

pound cake *n.* *US* a rich dense yellow cake that is traditionally made with a pound each of butter, sugar, flour, and eggs, or with equal weights of each of these ingredients

pound cost averaging *n.* the periodic purchase of the same amount in pounds sterling of the same security at regular time intervals regardless of the price of the security

pound-foolish *adj.* unwise when dealing with large sums of money [From the phrase *penny-wise and pound-foolish*]

pound scots (*plural* **pounds scots**) *n.* an obsolete unit of currency in Scotland worth one shilling and eight pence (1s 8d.) in 1707 at the time of the Union of the Parliaments of Scotland and England

pound sign *n.* **1.** MONEY SYMBOL FOR MONEY the symbol (£) which indicates pound sterling **2.** *US* UTIL, COMPUT = **hash**

pound sterling (*plural* **pounds sterling**) *n.* the official name for the unit of currency used in the United Kingdom

pour /pawr/ (**pours, pouring, poured**) *v.* **1.** *vt.* MAKE STH FLOW to make a substance flow in a stream ○ *poured the sugar into the bowl* **2.** *vti.* SERVE DRINK to serve a drink from a container such as a pot or jug into a cup, mug, or glass ○ *Let me pour you some tea.* **3.** *vi.* FUNCTION AS CONTAINER FOR POURING to function as a container from which liquid is poured ○ *This teapot doesn't pour very well.* **4.** *vi.* FLOW IN LARGE QUANTITIES to flow down or out, especially in large quantities ○ *Smoke poured from the burning building.* **5.** *vi.* RAIN HEAVILY to rain very heavily ○ *It poured for hours.* **6.** *vi.* COME IN LARGE QUANTITIES to come or go quickly and in large quantities ○ *Letters of complaint came pouring in.* **7.** *vt.* EXPRESS FEELING to express a feeling at length and without restraint **8.** *vt.* GIVE LARGE AMOUNT OF to give a large amount of sth such as effort or support to sth ○ *poured a lot of blood, sweat, and tears into that project* [13thC. Origin uncertain: probably via Old French dialect *purer* 'to sift, pour out' from Latin *purare* 'to purify', from *purus* 'pure' (source of English *pure*).]

WORD KEY: USAGE

pour or **pore**? 'To gaze at or study intently' (***pore***) might seem to have more in common with 'to drench' (***pour***) than with 'a small opening in skin or a rock' (***pore***). Perhaps it has, but all three words have been derived separately, despite the fact that one of the verbs has the same spelling as the noun. You ***pour*** from the pot into a teacup, ***pore*** over a text, and have ***pores*** in your skin.

pourboire /pŏor bwaar/ *n.* a sum of money given for services rendered or anticipated [Early 19thC. From French, literally 'for drinking'.]

pourparler /poor paar lay/ *n.* an informal discussion or round of talks, often diplomatic, that precedes a larger and more important conference with official negotiations (*formal*) [Early 18thC. From French, literally 'for talking'.]

pour point *n.* the lowest temperature at which a liquid will continue to flow

pousse-café /póoss ka fáy/ *n.* **1.** LAYERED DRINK a drink consisting of different-coloured liqueurs poured in one glass and forming layers because each liqueur has a different density **2.** AFTER-DINNER DRINK a liqueur served after dinner, with or after coffee [From French, literally 'push coffee']

poussette /poo sét/ *n.* MOVEMENT IN COUNTRY DANCING a movement in country dancing in which one or more couples hold hands and move up or down the row of other dancers in order to change their position ■ *vi.* (**-settes, -setting, -setted**) DANCE POUSSETTE to perform a poussette in a dance [Early 19thC. From French, literally 'small push', ultimately from *pousser* 'to push', from Latin *pulsare*, literally 'to push frequently', from *pellere* 'to push'.]

poussin /pŏo saN/ *n.* a chicken reared to be eaten when very young and tender [Mid-20thC. Via French from late Latin *pullicenus*, literally 'small young fowl', from Latin *pullus* 'young fowl' (source of English *pony*).]

Poussin /pŏo saN/, **Nicolas** (1594–1665) French-born Italian painter. He was a master of French classicism, and was influenced by Raphael.

pout[1] /powt/ *v.* (**pouts, pouting, pouted**) **1.** *vti.* PUSH LIPS OUTWARDS to move the lower lip or both lips outwards to form an expression of bad temper or sulkiness, or in order to look sexually provoking **2.** *vi.* SULK to show disappointment, anger, or resentment, usually in silence ○ *still pouting because he missed the game* **3.** *vt.* SAY STH SULKILY to say sth with a pout ○ *pouted that the whole thing wasn't fair* ■ *n.* **1.** EXPRESSION WITH LIPS PUSHED OUT an expression of the face with the lower lip or both lips pushed out **2.** SULKY MOOD a period or fit of sulking [14thC. Origin uncertain: perhaps from a Scandinavian source.] —**pouty** *adj.* —**poutingly** *adv.*

pout[2] /powt/ (*plural* **pout** *or* **pouts**) *n.* **1.** = **bib** *n.* 3 **2.** = **hornpout** [Old English stem *-pūte*, of uncertain origin: perhaps from the same Scandinavian source as POUT[1]]

pouter /pówtər/ *n.* **1.** POUTING PERSON sb who pouts **2.** **pouter, pouter pigeon** BIRDS DOMESTIC PIGEON WITH AN INFLATABLE CROP a domesticated pigeon belonging to a breed with a crop that can be greatly inflated [Early 18thC. Formed from POUT[1].]

poutine /poo téen/ *n.* a dish originating in Quebec that consists of chips and curd cheese, covered with tomato sauce or gravy

poverty /póvvərti/ *n.* **1.** STATE OF BEING POOR the state of not having enough money to take care of basic needs such as food, clothing, and housing **2.** LACK a deficiency or lack of sth ○ *poverty of emotion* **3.** INFERTILITY OF SOIL lack of soil fertility or nutrients [12thC. Via Old French *poverte* from Latin *paupertas*, from *pauper* 'poor' (source of English *pauper* and *poor*).]

WORD KEY: SYNONYMS

poverty, destitution, indigence, deprivation, penury, social exclusion, want

CORE MEANING: insufficiency of resources on which to live

poverty a general word for the state of being without enough money or resources to live at a standard considered normal or basic by society. It can be used to describe varying states of need, from lack of material comfort to near-starvation; **destitution** poverty that is so extreme as to be life-threatening; **indigence** a formal word used to describe a state of very severe poverty; **deprivation** a state of severe poverty, emphasizing the fact that those affected have been denied the material benefits that others enjoy; **penury** a fairly severe state of economic need; **social exclusion** used in political or sociological contexts to suggest a lack of money or resources sufficient to sustain a basic standard of living, causing those affected to be disadvantaged; **want** a formal or literary word used to describe a situation where people do not have the money, food, or resources they need to have a basic standard of living.

Poverty Bay /póvvərti-/ bay on the east coast of the North Island, New Zealand. The city of Gisborne lies on its northern shore.

poverty line, **poverty level** n. a level of income below which sb is considered to be living in poverty. It is based on the price of basic necessities and is usually determined by a government.

poverty-stricken adj. extremely poor and with intense problems as a result

poverty trap n. a situation in which an unemployed person will lose money by working because more will be lost in state benefits than is gained in income

pow /pow/ interj. used to imitate the sound of an explosion or gun, or of a sudden impact, e.g. when sb is hit (informal) [Late 19thC. An imitation of the sound.]

POW abbr. prisoner of war

powder /pówdər/ n. **1. TINY LOOSE PARTICLES** a substance in the form of a loose grouping of many tiny dry grains **2. POWDER FOR PARTICULAR PURPOSE** a substance in the form of powder that is produced for a particular purpose by crushing or drying a solid, or by mixing various powders ○ face powder **3. ARMS GUNPOWDER** gunpowder **4. DRY SNOW** light dry snow ■ v. (**-ders, -dering, -dered**) **1.** vt. **PUT POWDER ON** to cover sth with powder, or to sprinkle powder on sth **2.** vti. **TURN INTO POWDER** to turn a solid into powder or to become a powder [13thC. Via French poudrer (verb) and poudre (noun, alteration of poldre), from, ultimately, Latin pulver-, stem of pulvis 'dust' (source of English pulverize).] — **powderer** n. —**powdery** adj.

powder blue adj. of a very pale blue colour with a slight tinge of purple (hyphenated when used before a noun) —**powder blue** n.

powder burn n. a minor skin burn caused by being very close to a brief intense explosion, especially gunfire, sometimes used as evidence in a court of law

powder compact n. = compact¹ n. 1

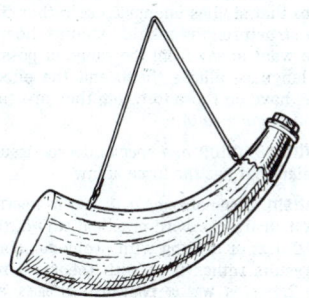

Powder horn

powder horn n. a small container to hold gunpowder

powder keg n. **1. ARMS KEG FOR GUNPOWDER** a small barrel used to hold gunpowder or blasting powder **2. TENSE SITUATION** a tense situation that may easily erupt into violence

powder metallurgy n. the technology of working powdered metals or some carbides by compressing or heating without melting, or by compressing and heating without melting, to produce solid objects such as self-lubricating bearings

powder monkey n. (informal) **1. NAVY BOY CARRYING GUNPOWDER ON SHIP** a boy employed on a warship in the past to carry gunpowder from the store to the guns **2. SB WHO WORKS WITH EXPLOSIVES** sb who delivers, works

with, or is in charge of explosives in fields such as mining or construction

powder puff n. a soft or fluffy pad used for putting powder on the face or skin

powder room n. a toilet for women

powdery mildew n. a fungal disease that produces a white powdery covering on plant leaves caused by various fungi

Powell /pów əl/, **Cecil Frank** (1903–69) British physicist. He was a pioneer in the photography of nuclear processes, and discovered the pi-meson. He won a Nobel Prize in physics (1950).

Colin Powell

Powell, Colin (b. 1937) US military leader. He was chairman of the Joint Chiefs of Staff during the Gulf War (1991). Full name **Colin Luther Powell Jr.**

Powell, Michael (1905–90) British film director. In partnership with Emeric Pressburger, he made a number of films noted for their imagery and technical virtuosity, including The Red Shoes (1998).

power /pówər/ n. **1. ABILITY OR CAPACITY TO DO STH** the ability, skill, or capacity to do sth **2. CONTROL AND INFLUENCE** control and influence over other people and their actions **3. AUTHORITY TO ACT** the authority to act or do sth according to a law or rule **4. POLITICAL CONTROL** the political control of a country, exercised by its government or leader **5. SB WITH POWER** sb who has political or financial power **6. IMPORTANT COUNTRY** a country that has military or economic resources and is considered to have political influence over other countries **7. STRENGTH** physical force or strength **8. PERSUASIVENESS** the ability to influence people's judgment or emotions **9. SKILL** a faculty, skill, or ability ○ musical powers **10. ENERGY ENERGY TO DRIVE MACHINERY** energy or force used to drive machinery or produce electricity **11. ELECTRICITY** electricity made available for use **12. ENG, PHYS MEASURE OF RATE OF DOING WORK** a measure of the rate of doing work or transferring energy, usually expressed in terms of wattage or horsepower. Symbol P **13. MATH NUMBER OF MULTIPLICATIONS** the number of times a quantity is to be successively multiplied by itself, usually written as a small number to the right of and above the quantity **14. OPTICS MAGNIFYING ABILITY** a measure of the ability of a lens, mirror, or prism to magnify an image **15. STATS PROBABILITY OF REJECTING NULL HYPOTHESIS** the probability of rejecting the null hypothesis as false when a particular alternative hypothesis is true ■ adj. **1. RUN BY ELECTRICITY OR FUEL** receiving power from a motor using electrical energy or fuel such as petrol, instead of relying on manual labour ○ power tools **2. INTENDED FOR BUSINESS SUCCESS** designed or believed to improve sb's status, influence, or effectiveness in business ○ power dressing ■ v. (**-ers, -ering, -ered**) **1.** vt. **PROVIDE ENERGY TO OPERATE STH** to supply sth such as a machine or tool with energy **2.** vi. **MOVE ENERGETICALLY** to move fast and with great power and energy (informal) [13thC. Via Anglo-Norman poer and Old French poeir from assumed Vulgar Latin potere 'to be powerful', from potis 'powerful' (source of English potent¹).] ◇ **do sb** or **sth a** or **the power of good** to benefit sb or sth greatly (informal) ◇ **the powers that be** the people in authority

power down vti. to switch a computer off in the correct way, bringing an orderly end to system operation

power up vti. to switch on a computer, printer, or other peripheral device

power base n. a position, area, or group of voters providing the foundation of sb's political power or support

powerboat /pówər bŏt/ n. a small motorboat with a powerful outboard or inboard motor, used especially for racing —**powerboating** n.

power broker n. a person or country that has great influence, especially in politics or commerce, and is able to use this influence to affect the policies and decisions of others

power centre n. Can a shopping centre containing several large superstores or discount stores

power cut n. a temporary loss of electricity supply to a building or to an area of a town. US term **power outage**

power dive n. a steep dive made by an aircraft with its engines at high power to increase the speed —**power-dive** vti.

powerful /pówərf'l/ adj. **1. INFLUENTIAL** able to exert a lot of influence and control over people and events ○ a powerful nation **2. STRONG** with great physical or mental strength or force **3. EFFECTIVE** with the strength or qualities to be effective in producing a result ○ a powerful antibiotic **4. PERSUASIVE** able to produce a strong effect on people's ideas or emotions ○ a powerful film ■ adv. **VERY** extremely (regional) ○ He was powerful thirsty. —**powerfully** adv. —**powerfulness** n.

powerhouse /pówər howss/ (plural **-houses** /pówər howziz/) n. sb or sth that is full of energy and very productive, especially of new ideas (informal)

powerless /pówərləss/ adj. lacking power, strength, or effectiveness —**powerlessly** adv. —**powerlessness** n.

power line n. a cable that carries electricity from a power station to the users of the electricity or between electric utilities in a network

power nap n. a short sleep taken by a businessperson in the office in order to feel revitalized

power of appointment n. the authority given to sb to select beneficiaries and to allocate money and other property from a person's estate to those beneficiaries

power of attorney n. the legal authority to act for another person in legal and business matters

power outage n. US = power cut

power pack n. a device for converting electrical supply to direct or alternating current at the correct voltage for a piece of electrical or electronic equipment

power plant n. **1. ENERGY** = power station **2. TRANSP UNIT POWERING SELF-PROPELLED OBJECT** a unit that supplies the power to move a self-propelled object, e.g. a diesel-electric engine in a locomotive or an internal-combustion engine in an automobile

power play n. **1. BID FOR ADVANTAGE** an attempt to gain an advantage by a display of strength or superiority, e.g. in a negotiation or relationship **2. TACTIC OF CONCENTRATING RESOURCES** a tactic in business, commerce, or politics of concentrating resources and effort on one particular area **3. SPORTS TACTIC OF CONCENTRATING PLAYERS** a tactic used in sport consisting of concentrating players in a particular area **4. ICE HOCKEY NUMERICAL ADVANTAGE IN ICE HOCKEY** a situation or period of time in ice hockey during which one team has a numerical advantage because the other team has one or more players in the penalty box

power point n. = socket n. 2

power politics n. political relations and actions based on an implied threat of use of political, economic, or military power by a participant (takes a singular verb)

power series n. an infinite series in which the terms contain regularly increasing integral powers of a variable. A typical series would be $Sn = 1 + 2x + 3x^2 + 4x^3 + \ldots + nx^{n-1}$.

power shovel n. a mobile machine for excavating and removing debris, with a movable lever arm ending in a hinged digging bucket

---

power station *n.* an industrial complex where power, especially electricity, is generated from another source of energy such as burning coal, nuclear reactions, or flowing water. US term **power plant**

power steering *n.* a system of steering for a motor vehicle in which turning the steering wheel is made easier by supplementary power from the vehicle's engine

power takeoff *n.* 1. POWER DIVERSION FROM ENGINE the transfer of power from a vehicle's engine to another piece of machinery such as a winch or hydraulic pump 2. DEVICE FOR DIVERTING POWER FROM ENGINE a device for transferring power from a vehicle's engine to another piece of machinery

power train *n.* the portion of a vehicle's drive mechanism that transmits power from the engine to the wheels, tracks, or propellers. A car's power train includes the clutch, transmission, driveshaft, and differential.

power trip *n.* (*informal*) 1. ASSERTION OF CONTROL OVER OTHERS an action designed to gain or keep control over other people in order to increase and enjoy a feeling of power 2. SITUATION GIVING CONTROL OVER OTHERS a situation that increases sb's feeling of being powerful or in control of others

power user *n.* a computer user who is expert in one or more software applications (*informal*)

power walking *n.* a form of exercise involving energetic walking in which the arms are swung backwards and forwards, sometimes using weights, in order to increase the heart rate —**power walker** *n.*

powwow /pów wow/ *n.* 1. MEETING a meeting or gathering to discuss sth (*informal*) 2. NATIVE AMERICAN CEREMONY a traditional Native American ceremony featuring dance, feasting, and a blessing by a shaman for an event such as a marriage, a major hunt, or a gathering of nations ■ *vi.* (**-wows, -wowing, -wowed**) HAVE POWWOW to hold a powwow (*informal*) [Early 19thC. From Narragansett *powah*, *powwaw*, literally 'shaman'.]

Powys /pów iss/ county in central Wales. Llandrindod Wells is its administrative centre. Population: 122,300 (1995). Area: 5,205 sq. km/2,009 sq. mi.

pox /poks/ *n.* MED 1. VENEREAL DISEASE a venereal disease, especially syphilis (*informal*) 2. DISEASE CAUSING SPOTS ON SKIN a viral disease such as smallpox or chickenpox that causes pus-filled blisters (**pustules**) to form on the skin, and often leaves scars (**pockmarks**) [Alteration of the plural of POCK] ◇ **a pox on sb** *or* **sth** used to express a wish that misfortune will come to sb or sth (*archaic*)

poxvirus /póks vīrəss/ *n.* an oval-shaped DNA-containing virus responsible for diseases that cause pus-filled blisters (**pustules**) to form on the skin

poxy /póksi/ *adj.* so contemptible or unpleasant that it is worthless (*informal*) [Early 20thC. The literal sense is 'infected with pox'.]

Poynting theorem /póynting-/ *n.* PHYS the theorem stating that the rate of flow of electromagnetic energy per unit area equals the cross product of the electric and magnetic vectors [Late 19thC. Named after J. H. *Poynting* (1852–1914), an English physicist.]

Poznán /pŏz nan/ city in western Poland. It is the capital of Poznán Province. Population: 581,800 (1995).

pozzuolana /pótswə láanə/, **pozzolana** /pótsə-/ *n.* a porous volcanic ash that when mixed with cement hardens either in air or under water [Early 18thC. From Italian *pozz(u)olana (terra)* '(earth) of Pozzuoli (the name of a town near Naples in Italy)'.]

Pozzuoli /pot swáwli/ town in Campania Region, southern Italy. Population: 75,706 (1991).

pp *abbr.* 1. privately printed 2. pianissimo 3. past participle 4. by proxy (*used when signing documents on behalf of somebody else*)

PP *abbr.* 1. past president 2. parish priest 3. postpaid 4. prepaid 5. after a meal (*used in prescriptions*) 6. parcel post 7. prepositional phrase

pr. *abbr.* GRAM pronoun

Pr. *abbr.* 1. Priest 2. Prince 3. preferred (stock)

practicable /práktikəb'l/ *adj.* 1. CAPABLE OF BEING DONE capable of being carried out or put into effect 2. USABLE capable of being used [Mid-17thC. Via medieval Latin *practicabilis* from, ultimately, Greek *praktikē*, the feminine of *praktikos* 'practical' (see PRACTISE).]

practical /práktik'l/ *adj.* 1. CONCERNED WITH MATTERS OF FACT concerned with actual facts and experience, not theory ○ *the practical applications of this research* 2. USEFUL sensible or useful, and likely to be effective ○ *practical advice* 3. GOOD AT SOLVING PROBLEMS good at managing matters and dealing with problems and difficulties 4. SUITABLE FOR EVERYDAY USE plain, functional, and suitable for everyday use 5. VIRTUAL resembling a particular thing in almost every way (*informal*) ○ *The campaign was a practical disaster.* ■ *n.* EDUC LESSON WITH HANDS-ON ACTIVITIES a lesson or examination that requires actually doing sth such as an experiment or a medical procedure ○ *a physics practical* [Via medieval Latin *practicalis* from, ultimately, Greek *praktikos* (see PRACTICE)] —**practicality** /prákti kálәti/ *n.*

practical joke *n.* a trick that is carried out on sb to make him or her look silly and to amuse others —**practical joker** *n.*

practically /práktikli/ *adv.* 1. ALMOST very nearly but not quite 2. IN PRACTICAL WAY in a way that is useful, sensible, or practical

practice /práktiss/ *n.* 1. REPETITION IN ORDER TO IMPROVE the process of repeating sth such as an exercise many times in order to improve performance 2. PERFORMANCE OF RELIGION, PROFESSION, OR CUSTOMS the performance of a religion, profession, set of customs, or established habit 3. PROCESS OF CARRYING OUT AN IDEA the process of carrying out an idea, plan, or theory 4. WORK OF PROFESSIONAL PERSON the business of a lawyer, doctor, dentist, or other professional 5. HABIT a habit, custom, or usual way of doing sth ○ *good business practices* ■ *vti.* *US* = **practise** [15thC. From PRACTISE.]

WORD KEY: SYNONYMS

See Synonyms at ***habit***.

practiced *adj.* *US* = **practised**

practicing *adj.* *US* = **practising**

practicum /práktikəm/ *n.* *US* = **placement** [Early 20thC. From late Latin, the neuter of *practicus* 'active, practical', from Greek *praktikos* (see PRACTISE).]

practise /práktiss/ (**-tises, -tising, -tised**) *v.* 1. *vti.* REPEAT IN ORDER TO IMPROVE to do sth, especially exercises, repeatedly in order to improve performance 2. *vt.* DO STH AS CUSTOM to do sth as an established custom or habit 3. *vti.* WORK IN LAW OR MEDICINE to work in a particular job or profession, especially law or medicine 4. *vt.* FOLLOW RELIGION to act according to the beliefs and customs of a religion 5. *vt.* PERPETRATE to perpetrate sth morally bad, e.g. deceit or cruelty 6. *vi.* TAKE ADVANTAGE OF SB to take advantage of sb, especially sb who is gullible [14thC. Directly or via obsolete French *practiser* from medieval Latin *practizare*, an alteration of *practicare*, from, ultimately, Greek *praktikos* 'practical', from *prattein* 'to do'.]

practised /práktisst/ *adj.* expert in doing sth because of long experience

practising /práktissing/ *adj.* actively involved in a particular activity, e.g. a profession, religion, or way of life

practitioner /prak tísh'nər/ *n.* 1. SB WHO PRACTISES A PROFESSION sb who practises a particular profession, especially medicine 2. CHR CHRISTIAN SCIENCE HEALER in Christian Science, sb who carries out ministry and spiritual healing [Mid-16thC. Formed from obsolete *practician*, from Old French *practicien*, from *practiser* 'to practise' (see PRACTISE).]

Prado /práadō/ *n.* a museum in Madrid that contains the Spanish national collection of paintings, sculptures, and drawings. It was founded by Fernando VII in 1810.

praedial /préedi əl/, **predial** *adj.* relating to land or farming [From medieval Latin *praedialis*, from Latin *praedium* 'farm, estate'] —**praediality** /préedi állәti/ *n.*

praemunire /prée myoo nīri, -neeri/ *n.* the offence under English law of accepting the authority of some other power over that of the English crown, or an accusation to that effect [From medieval Latin *praemunire facias* 'that you warn' (these words being part of the writ), the first word of which meant 'to warn' (by association with Latin *praemonere* 'to forewarn', source of English *premonition*) and came from Latin, 'to fortify in front', from *munire* 'to fortify, defend' (see MUNITION)]

praenomen /pree nōmən/ (*plural* **-nomens** *or* **-nomina** /-nómminə/) *n.* in ancient Rome, sb's first name [Early 17thC. From Latin, 'forename', from *nomen* 'name' (source of English *nominal, noun,* and *renown*).] —**praenominal** /pree nómmin'l/ *adj.* —**praenominally** /pree nómmin'li/ *adv.*

praesidium *n.* = **presidium**

praetor /préetər, -tawr/, **pretor** *n.* in ancient Rome, any of several magistrates ranking immediately below the consuls and acting as the chief law officers of the state. At first there was only one praetor, but there were later as many as eight who were also responsible for organizing the public games. [15thC. From Latin, of uncertain origin: possibly formed from *praeire*, literally 'to go in front'.] —**praetorial** /pree táwri əl/ *adj.* —**praetorship** /préetərship/ *n.*

praetorian /pree táwri ən/, **pretorian** *adj.* 1. RELATING TO PRAETORS relating to praetors or to the office of praetor 2. CORRUPT corrupt and venal (*formal*) ■ *n.* ANCIENT ROMAN OF PRAETOR RANK in ancient Rome, a holder or former holder of the office of praetor, e.g. an ex-praetor who became governor of a province

Praetorian, **Pretorian** *adj.* OF THE PRAETORIAN GUARD belonging or relating to the Praetorian Guard ■ *n.* MEMBER OF PRAETORIAN GUARD a member of the Praetorian Guard

Praetorian Guard *n.* 1. ANCIENT ROMAN EMPEROR'S BODYGUARD the emperor's bodyguard in ancient Rome. The members of the Guard were reputed to be corrupt and often interfered with the selection of the emperor in later periods of the Roman Empire. 2. MEMBER OF PRAETORIAN GUARD a soldier of the emperor's bodyguard in ancient Rome

pragmatic /prag máttik/ *adj.* 1. CONCERNED WITH PRACTICAL RESULTS more concerned with practical results than with theories and principles 2. PHILOS RELATING TO PHILOSOPHICAL PRAGMATISM relating to or characteristic of philosophical pragmatism 3. POL POLITICAL relating to the political affairs of a country (*formal*) 4. LEARNING LESSONS FROM HISTORY dealing with or looking at the facts of history with particular regard to the lessons that can be learned from them 5. LING RELATING TO PRAGMATICS relating or belonging to pragmatics [Late 16thC. Via late Latin *pragmaticus* from, ultimately, Greek *pragma* 'deed, action'.] —**pragmaticality** /prag mátti kállәti/ *n.* —**pragmatically** /prag máttikli/ *adv.*

pragmatics /prag máttiks/ *n.* LING the branch of linguistics that studies language use rather than language structure. Pragmatics studies how people choose what to say from the range of possibilities their language allows them, and the effect their choices have on those to whom they are speaking. (*takes a singular verb*)

pragmatic sanction *n.* a special decree issued by a sovereign that has the force of law

pragmatism /prágmətizəm/ *n.* 1. WAY OF THINKING ABOUT RESULTS a straightforward practical way of thinking about things or dealing with problems, concerned with results rather than with theories and principles 2. PHILOS WAY OF EVALUATING THEORIES a philosophical view that a theory or concept should be evaluated in terms of how it works and its consequences as the standard for action and thought. ◊ **instrumentalism** —**pragmatist** *n.* —**pragmatistic** /prágmə tístik/ *adj.*

Prague /praag/ capital city of the Czech Republic, located in the west of the country. Population: 1,213,000 (1995).

prahu *n.* = **proa**

Praia /prí ə/ capital city of the Republic of Cape Verde, in southeastern São Tiago Island. Population: 69,000 (1992).

Prairial /práiri ál/ *n.* the ninth month of the year in the French Revolutionary calendar, corresponding to 21 May to 19 June in the Gregorian calendar [Late 18thC. From French *Prairial*, from *prairie* 'meadow'.]

prairie /práiri/ *n.* **N AMERICAN GRASSLAND** a treeless grass-covered plain in the United States and Canada, especially in the Midwest and the West ■ **prairies** *npl. Can* **PRAIRIE PROVINCES** the Prairie Provinces of Manitoba, Alberta, and Saskatchewan in Canada [Late 18thC. Via French from assumed Vulgar Latin *prataria*, from Latin *pratum* 'meadow', of unknown origin.]

prairie chicken *n.* a game bird belonging to the grouse family with mottled brownish plumage, native to grasslands of the United States. The male has inflatable air sacs on its throat, used in courtship. Latin name: *Tympanuchus cupido* and *Tympanuchus pallidicinctus.*

prairie dog *n.* a burrowing rodent of the squirrel family that lives in large underground colonies on the grasslands of North America. It has light-brown fur and a sharp barking or whistling warning call. Genus: *Cynomys.*

prairie falcon *n.* a large falcon, native to the western United States, that has a squarish head, dark-brown back feathers with pale edges, and pale spotted underparts. Latin name: *Falco mexicanus.*

prairie oyster *n.* **1. RAW EGG DRINK** a drink consisting of a raw egg, Worcestershire sauce, salt, and pepper, taken as a cure for a hangover or hiccups **2.** *US* **COOKED CALF OR PIG TESTICLE** the fried testicle of a calf or pig, eaten as a delicacy in the Midwestern United States (*usually used in the plural*)

prairie schooner *n.* a large covered wagon, pulled by horses or oxen that was used by pioneers crossing the North American prairies in the 19th century [From the imagined resemblance of their canvas tops, seen from a distance, to a ship's sails]

prairie soil *n.* a type of soil that typically forms under the grasses of the North American prairie. It is rich in plant nutrients and is nearly black in colour.

prairie wolf *n.* = **coyote**

praise /prayz/ *n.* **1. EXPRESSION OF ADMIRATION** words that express great approval or admiration, e.g. for sb's ability or achievements or for sth's good qualities **2. WORSHIP** worship and thanks to God or a deity (*often used in the plural*) ■ *vt.* (**praises, praising, praised**) **1. EXPRESS ADMIRATION FOR SB OR STH** to express great approval or admiration, e.g. for sb's ability or achievements or for sth's good qualities **2. WORSHIP GOD** to give worship and thanks to God or a deity [13thC. Via Old French *preisier* from late Latin *pretiare* 'to prize', from *pretium* 'price'.] —**praiser** *n.*

praiseworthy /práyz wurthi/ *adj.* deserving praise —**praiseworthily** *adv.* —**praiseworthiness** *n.*

prajna /prújnə, prúzhnə/ *n.* in Buddhist teaching, direct awareness and understanding of truth not achieved by intellectual or rational means [Early 19thC. From Sanskrit *prajñā*, literally 'to know directly'.]

Prakrit /praákrit/ *n.* a language belonging to a group spoken in northern India from approximately 400 BC to AD 1000. Prakrits are Indic languages that developed form Sanskrit, the most well-known being Pali. [Mid-18thC. From Sanskrit *prākṛta* 'natural, vernacular', from *pra-* 'forward' + *kṛta-*, past participle stem of *karoti* 'it makes' (see SANSKRIT).] —**Prakrit** *adj.*

praline /praá leen/ *n.* **1. NUTS BOILED IN SUGAR** a nut caramelized in boiling sugar syrup that hardens when cold, or a substance made from crushed caramelized nuts and used as a dessert topping or chocolate filling **2. CHOCOLATE** a chocolate with a soft filling made from crushed caramelized nuts, usually almonds [Early 18thC. Named after the French officer Marshal de Plessis-*Praslin* (1598–1675), whose cook invented it.]

pralltriller /praál trilər/ *n.* a musical embellishment made by the quick alternation of a particular note with the note immediately above it [Mid-19thC. From German, literally 'bouncing trill'.]

pram[1] /pram/ *n.* a cot on four wheels with a handle at one end and a hood at the other, in which a baby can be transported out of doors. US term **baby carriage** [Late 19thC. Contraction of PERAMBULATOR.]

pram[2] /praam/, **praam** *n.* **1. FLAT-BOTTOMED FISHING BOAT** a small fishing boat boat with a flat bottom and a square front **2. FLAT-BOTTOMED BARGE** a flat-bottomed barge used in Baltic ports [Mid-16thC. Via Dutch *praam* from, ultimately, Czech *prám* 'raft'.]

prana /praánə/ *n.* **1. BREATH CONTROL IN YOGA** in yoga, the use of inhalation, holding the breath, and exhalation, according to particular patterns and time periods. It is designed to aid self-awareness, focus, and meditation. **2. BREATH OR BREATHING** in Hinduism, breath or breathing [Mid-19thC. From Sanskrit *prāṇa*, literally 'breathing out'.]

prance /praanss/ *v.* (**prances, prancing, pranced**) **1.** *vi.* **MOVE IN LIVELY WAY** to move about in a lively and carefree, but often silly or annoying, way **2.** *vi.* **SWAGGER** to walk in a way that displays excessive pride, arrogance, or a desire to be noticed and admired (*disapproving*) **3.** *vti.* EQU **JUMP FORWARD ON BACK LEGS** to raise the front legs and jump forward on the back legs, or to make a horse perform this step **4.** *vti.* EQU **WALK WITH LIVELY STEPS** to walk with lively springing steps, or to make a horse walk this way ■ *n.* **PRANCING MOVEMENT** a lively, springing, or carefree movement [14thC. Origin unknown.] —**prancer** *n.* —**prancing** *adj.* —**prancingly** *adv.*

prandial /prándi əl/ *adj.* relating to a meal, especially lunch or dinner (*formal or humorous*) [Early 19thC. Formed from Latin *prandium* 'late breakfast'.] —**prandially** *adv.*

prang /prang/ *vt.* (**prangs, pranging, pranged**) **1. CRASH STH** to crash or damage a vehicle or aircraft (*informal*) **2. BOMB STH** to bomb a target (*dated slang*) ■ *n.* **1. CRASH** a crash in a vehicle or aircraft (*informal*) **2. BOMBING RAID** a bombing raid (*dated slang*) [Mid-20thC. Origin unknown.]

prank[1] /prangk/ *n.* a mischievous trick or silly stunt done for amusement [Late 16thC. Origin unknown.] —**prankish** *adj.*

prank[2] /prangk/ *vti.* (**pranks, pranking, pranked**) to embellish or display sth in an ostentatious manner (*formal*) ○ *Don't prank yourself up, it's only a family dinner.* [Mid-16thC. Origin uncertain: probably from Middle Dutch *pronken* or Middle Low German *prunken* 'to show off'.]

prankster /prángkstər/ *n.* sb who enjoys playing mischievous tricks on people

Prasad /prə saád/, **Rajendra** (1884–1963) Indian statesman. A member of Indian National Congress, he presided over the Constituent Assembly (1946–49) and was the first president of India (1950–62).

prase /práyz/ *n.* a green form of quartz [Late 18thC. Via French from, ultimately, Greek *prasios* 'leek-coloured', from *prason* 'leek'.]

praseodymium /práyzi ō dímmi əm/ *n.* a soft ductile silvery metallic chemical element belonging to the rare-earth group. It is characterized by a green tarnish and is used in alloys and to colour glass. Symbol **Pr** [Late 19thC. Coined from Greek *prasios* 'leek-coloured' (see PRASE) + DIDYMIUM.]

prat /prat/ *n.* **1. prat, pratt FOOL** an unintelligent person (*slang insult*) **2. BUTTOCKS** the buttocks (*slang*) ■ *vi.* **BEHAVE THOUGHTLESSLY OR EXASPERATINGLY** to behave in an unintelligent way, especially when this causes exasperation or leads to time-wasting (*insult*) [Mid-16thC. Origin unknown.]

prate /prayt/ *vi.* (**prates, prating, prated**) **CHATTER** to talk in a silly way and at length about nothing important ■ *n.* **PRATTLE** silly or idle talk [15thC. From Middle Dutch *praten*.] —**prater** *n.* —**pratingly** *adv.*

pratfall /prát fawl/ *n. US* (*slang*) **1. COMIC FALL** a backward fall onto the buttocks, especially one executed deliberately for comic effect **2. EMBARRASSING MISTAKE** an embarrassing or humiliating mistake or failure

praties /prátiz/ *npl. Ireland* potatoes (*informal*) [Late 18thC. Plural of *pratie* 'potato', from Irish *prátai*, plural of *práta*.]

pratincole /prátting kōl/ *n.* a brown or grey bird that is native to Europe and has long pointed wings, a forked tail, and a short bill. It lives on stony or grassy land, usually near water. Family: Glareolidae. [Late 18thC. From modern Latin *pratincola*, from Latin *pratum* 'meadow' (source of English *prairie*) + *incola* 'dweller'.]

pratique /pra teék/ *n.* permission granted to a ship or boat to use a port on satisfying the local quarantine regulations or on producing a clean bill of health [Early 17thC. From French, literally 'practice'.]

pratt *n.* = **prat** (*slang insult*)

prattle /prátt'l/ *vi.* (**-tles, -tling, -tled**) **TALK IDLY OR CHILDISHLY** to talk in a silly, idle, or childish way ■ *n.* **IDLE OR CHILDISH TALK** silly, idle, or childish talk [Mid-16thC. Origin uncertain: possibly formed from PRATE, or from Middle Low German *pratelen*.] —**prattler** *n.* —**prattlingly** *adv.*

prau *n.* = **proa**

pravastatin /právvə státtin/ *n.* a drug used to reduce abnormally high levels of blood cholesterol

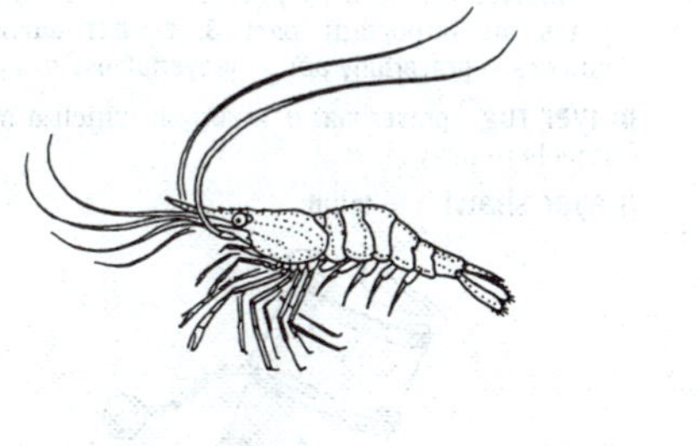

Prawn

prawn /prawn/ *n.* **EDIBLE CRUSTACEAN** an edible marine animal resembling a shrimp, with a slender body, a long tail, five pairs of legs, and two pairs of pincers. Genera: *Palaemon.* Latin name: *Penaeus.* ■ *vi.* (**prawns, prawning, prawned**) **FISH FOR PRAWNS** to fish for prawns [15thC. Origin unknown.] —**prawner** *n.* ◇ **come the raw prawn** *Aus* to try to deceive or mislead someone, usually by acting or pleading innocent (*informal*)

prawn cocktail *n.* cooked and shelled prawns in a seafood dressing, usually served in a small bowl or glass with salad garnish and eaten cold as a starter

prawn cracker *n.* a light and puffy prawn-flavoured snack food resembling a crisp, made from rice flour and often served with a Chinese meal as an appetizer

praxeology /práksi ólləji/, **praxiology** *n.* the study of human behaviour [Early 20thC. Formed from Greek *praxis* 'custom, behaviour' (see PRAXIS).] —**praxeological** /práksi ə lójjik'l/ *adj.*

praxis /práksiss/ *n.* (*formal*) **1. PERFORMANCE OR APPLICATION OF SKILL** the practical side and application of sth such as a professional skill, as opposed to its theory **2. ESTABLISHED PRACTICE** an established custom or habitual practice [Late 16thC. Via medieval Latin from Greek, where it was formed from *prattein* 'to do'.]

Praxiteles /prak síttə leez/ (390?–330? BC) Greek sculptor. Apart from *Hermes with the Infant Dionysus*, his work is known only in the form of Roman copies.

pray /pray/ *v.* (**prays, praying, prayed**) **1.** *vti.* **SPEAK TO GOD OR OTHER BEING** to speak to God, a deity, or a saint, e.g. in order to give thanks, express regret, or ask for help **2.** *vti.* **HOPE STRONGLY** to hope strongly for sth ○ *I'm just praying that it won't rain on Saturday.* **3.** *vti.* **MAKE AN EARNEST REQUEST** to ask sb for sth, especially earnestly or with passion ○ *He prayed to be allowed to go back home to his family.* **4.** *vt.* to attempt to achieve sth by prayer ○ *The villagers tried to pray the drought away.* ■ *interj.* **EMPHASIZING A QUESTION OR COMMAND** used to emphasize a question or a command, either politely or sarcastically ○ *And what, pray, do you think you're doing?* [13thC. Via Old French *preier* from Latin *precari* 'to entreat', from *prec-*, stem of prex 'prayer' (source of English *deprecate* and *precarious*).]

prayer /prair/ *n.* **1. COMMUNICATION WITH GOD OR OTHER BEING** a spoken or unspoken communication with God, a deity, or a saint. It may express praise, thanksgiving, confession or a request for sth such as help or sb's wellbeing. **2. COMMUNICATING WITH GOD OR OTHER BEING** the act or practice of making spoken or unspoken communication with God, a deity, or a saint **3. RELIGIOUS SERVICE WITH PRAYERS** a religious service at which prayers are said (*often used in the plural*) **4. EARNEST REQUEST** an earnest request for sth **5. STH WISHED**

FOR sth that is wanted or hoped for very much ○ *My only prayer is to see grandchildren before I die.* **6.** LAW **REQUEST IN PETITION** a request contained in a petition **7.** **SLIGHT CHANCE** a slight chance or hope ○ *I don't have a prayer of getting the manager's job.* [13thC. Via Old French *preiere* from, ultimately, Latin *precarius* 'obtained by entreaty', from *precari* 'to entreat' (see PRAY).]

prayer beads *npl.* a string of beads such as a rosary used to keep count of prayers being recited

prayer book *n.* a book containing the prayers regularly used in religious services

prayerful /práirf'l/ *adj.* **1.** **PRAYING FREQUENTLY** liking to pray or praying frequently **2.** **INFLUENCED BY PRAYER** strongly influenced by prayer, or in which prayer plays an important part **3.** **EARNEST** earnest or sincere —**prayerfully** *adv.* —**prayerfulness** *n.*

prayer rug, **prayer mat** *n.* a rug on which a Muslim kneels to pray

prayer shawl *n.* = **tallith**

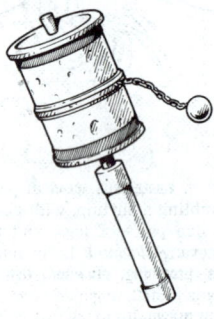

Prayer wheel

prayer wheel *n.* in Tibetan Buddhism and some other religions, a hollow cylinder that contains prayers written on a scroll. It must be turned by hand or machinery to make the prayers effective.

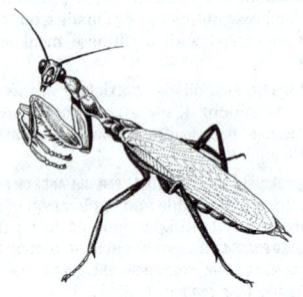

Praying mantis

praying mantis *n.* a large greenish brown predatory insect originating in Europe, with long forelegs that are raised and folded at rest, as if in prayer. Latin name: *Mantis religiosis.*

PRB *abbr.* Pre-Raphaelite Brotherhood (*used after the name of a painter*)

PRC *abbr.* People's Republic of China

pre- *prefix.* **1.** before, earlier ○ *preschool* **2.** in advance, preparatory ○ *presell* ○ *prerelease* **3.** in front of ○ *premolar* [From Latin *prae* 'in front, before'. Ultimately from an Indo-European word which is also the ancestor of English *prior, prime,* and *private.*]

preach /preech/ (**preaches, preaching, preached**) *v.* **1.** *vti.* **GIVE SERMON** to give a talk on a religious or moral subject, especially in church **2.** *vi.* **GIVE ADVICE IN IRRITATING WAY** to give people advice on their morals or behaviour in an irritatingly tedious or overbearing way **3.** *vt.* **URGE PEOPLE TO ACCEPT STH** to make an opinion or attitude known to others and urge others to share it [13thC. Via Old French *prechier* from, ultimately, Latin *praedicare* (see PREDICATE).] —**preachable** *adj.*

preacher /preecher/ *n.* (*informal*) **1.** **MINISTER** sb whose occupation is to give sermons, preach the gospel, or conduct religious services, especially a minister of a Protestant church **2.** **SB WHO PREACHES** sb who gives advice in an irritatingly tedious or over-

bearing way, or who urges others to share a belief or support a cause

preachify /preechi fī/ *vi.* to preach or give advice on morals or behaviour in an irritatingly tedious or overbearing way (*informal*) —**preachifying** *n.*

preachment /preechmənt/ *n.* (*informal*) **1.** **SERMON** a sermon or talk on a moral or religious subject **2.** **OVERBEARING ADVICE** tedious or overbearing advice on morals or behaviour

preachy /preechi/ *adj.* giving, or in the habit of giving, advice on morals or behaviour in an irritatingly tedious or overbearing way (*informal*) —**preachiness** *n.*

preadamite /pree áddə mīt/, **pre-Adamite** *n.* **1.** **BELIEVER IN PEOPLE BEFORE ADAM** sb who believes that there were people living on earth before Adam **2.** **SB LIVING BEFORE ADAM** any of the people believed to have been living on earth before Adam ■ *adj.* **RELATING TO PREADAMITES** relating to the belief or those who believe that people existed on earth before Adam

preadaptation /pree áddəp táysh'n/ *n.* anatomical or behavioural feature of an organism that is highly suited to an adjacent habitat, thus allowing for migration and increased survival rate in response to environmental change. The lungs that have developed in some fish were probably originally buoyancy aids, but were preadapted for breathing air. —**preadapt** /pree ə dápt/ *vti.* —**preadapted** /-dáptid/ *adj.* —**preadaptive** /-dáptiv/ *adj.*

preadolescence /pree áddə léssənss/ *n.* the period of two or three years before adolescence —**preadolescent** *n., adj.*

preagricultural /pree ággri kúlchərəl/ *adj.* having not yet developed agriculture as a means of providing food. ◊ **hunter-gatherer**

preamble /pree ámb'l/ *n.* **1.** **INTRODUCTORY EXPLANATION** a section at the beginning of a speech, report, or formal document that explains the purpose of what follows **2.** **STH THAT PRECEDES** sth that precedes, introduces, or leads up to sth else [14thC. Via French *préambule* from, ultimately, Latin *praeambulus*, literally 'going in front', from *ambulare* 'to walk'.]

preamplifier /pree ámpli fīər/ *n.* an amplifying circuit, e.g. in a radio or television, that is designed to strengthen very weak signals and then transmit them to a more powerful amplifier

prearrange /pree ə ráynj/ (**-ranges, -ranging, -ranged**) *vt.* to arrange, plan, or agree on sth beforehand —**prearrangement** *n.*

preatomic /pree ə tómmik/ *adj.* relating or belonging to the time before atomic energy was developed or atomic weapons existed

prebend /prébbənd/ *n.* **1.** **PAYMENT TO CATHEDRAL CLERGY** an allowance paid by a cathedral or collegiate church to a member of its clergy, or the property or tithe that is the source of this allowance **2.** = **prebendary** **3.** **POSITION OF PREBENDARY** the position of prebendary in the Church of England [15thC. Via French from late Latin *praebenda*, literally 'things to be supplied' (source of English *provender*), from Latin *praebere* 'to offer', literally 'to hold in front'.] —**prebendal** *adj.*

prebendary /prébbəndəri/ *n.* a member of the clergy of a cathedral or collegiate church, either one who receives an allowance from it or an honorary member who receives no payment —**prebendaryship** *n.*

prebiological /pree bī ə lójjik'l/ *adj.* relating or belonging to a time in geological history before the appearance of living organisms

prec. *abbr.* preceding

Precambrian /pree kámbri ən/ *n.* the period of geological time when the Earth's crust consolidated and primitive life first appeared, 4,650 to 700 million years ago —**Precambrian** *adj.*

precancel /pree kánss'l/ *vt.* (**-cels, -celling, -celled**) **CANCEL STAMP BEFORE POSTING** to cancel the postage stamp on an envelope, e.g. before posting it ■ *n.* **PRE-CANCELLED STAMP** a stamp that has been cancelled before posting, or an item bearing such a stamp —**precancellation** /pree kánssə láysh'n/ *n.*

precancerous /pree kánssərəss/ *adj.* used to describe conditions or tissue abnormalities that are capable of becoming cancerous if left untreated

precarious /pri káiri əss/ *adj.* **1.** **UNSAFE** dangerously unstable, unsteady, uncertain, or insecure **2.** **NOT WELL FOUNDED** based on uncertain premises or unwarranted assumptions (*formal*) [Mid-17thC. Formed from Latin *precarius* 'depending on entreaty, uncertain'.] —**precariously** *adv.* —**precariousness** *n.*

precast /pree kaast/ *adj.* poured into a cast of the required shape and allowed to harden before being taken out and put into position ○ *buildings made entirely of precast concrete* —**precast** *vt.*

precatory /prékətəri/ *adj.* expressing a wish, a request, an entreaty, or a recommendation (*formal*) [Mid-17thC. From late Latin *precatorius*, from *precari* 'to entreat' (see PRAY).]

precaution /pri káwsh'n/ *n.* **1.** **PROTECTION AGAINST POSSIBLE UNDESIRABLE EVENT** an action taken to protect against possible harm or trouble, or to limit the damage if sth goes wrong ○ *wearing a hat as a precaution against sunstroke* **2.** **CAUTION TO FORESTALL FUTURE TROUBLE** the foresight to protect against possible harm or trouble [Late 16thC. Via French from, ultimately, Latin *precaut-*, past participle stem of *praecavere*, literally 'to take care before', from *cavere* 'to take heed' (see CAUTION).] —**precautional** *adj.* —**precautionary** *adj.* —**precautious** *adj.*

precede /pri-/ (**-cedes, -ceding, -ceded**) *vt.* **1.** **COME OR GO BEFORE STH** to come, go, be, or happen before sb or sth else in time, position, or importance **2.** **INTRODUCE STH WITH STH** to say or do sth before sth else [14thC. Via French from Latin *praecedere*, literally 'to go in front', from *cedere* 'to give way'.]

precedence /préssidənss/, **precedency** /préssidənssi/ *n.* **1.** **PRIORITY** the right or need to be dealt with before sb or sth else or to be treated as more important than sb or sth else **2.** **RELATIVE IMPORTANCE** relative importance in rank and status that determines sth, e.g. the order in which participants are placed in a formal situation **3.** **GREATER IMPORTANCE** the fact of being more important than others (*formal*)

precedent *n.* /préssidənt/ **1.** **EXAMPLE FOR LATER ACTION OR DECISION** an action or decision that can be subsequently used as an example for a similar decision or to justify a similar action **2.** **ESTABLISHED PRACTICE** an established custom or practice **3.** LAW **REQUIREMENT TO FOLLOW EARLIER COURT DECISIONS** the doctrine that requires a court to follow decisions of superior or previous courts ■ *adj.* /préssidənt, pri seed'nt/ **PRECEDING** coming, going, existing, or happening before sb or sth else (*formal*) —**precedently** *adv.*

precedential /préssi dénsh'l/ *adj.* (*formal*) **1.** **RELATING TO OR BEING PRECEDENT** relating to or serving as a precedent **2.** **MORE IMPORTANT** taking precedence over sth or sb else —**precedentially** *adv.*

preceding /pri seeding/ *adj.* coming, going, existing, or happening immediately before sb or sth else

precensor /pree sénssər/ (**-sors, -soring, -sored**) *vt.* to lay down rules in advance stating what will or will not be allowed in a publication, broadcast, or other item for public performance or release —**precensorship** *n.*

precentor /pri séntər/ *n.* **1.** **LEADER OF CHURCH SINGING** sb who leads the singing of the congregation or choir in a church **2.** **SB IN CHARGE OF CATHEDRAL MUSIC** a member of the clergy of a cathedral who is nominally in charge of the music in the cathedral **3.** *Scotland* **OFFICIAL SINGER IN SOME PRESBYTERIAN CHURCHES** in small Presbyterian denominations that disapprove of instrumental music in church, an official appointed by the Kirk Session to lead the singing by singing lines for the congregation to repeat [Early 17thC. From Latin *praecentor*, from *praecinere*, literally 'to sing before', from *canere* 'to sing'.] —**precentorship** *n.*

precept /pree sept/ *n.* **1.** **PRINCIPLE** a rule, instruction, or principle that guides sb's actions, especially one that guides moral behaviour (*formal*) **2.** LAW **WARRANT OR WRIT** a warrant or writ that is issued by a legal authority **3.** LAW **ORDER FOR PAYMENT** an order for the payment of money [14thC. From Latin *praeceptum*, literally 'sth taught', the past participle of *praecipere*, literally 'to take before', from *capere* 'to take'.]

preceptive /pri séptiv/ *adj.* giving instructions or orders, or setting out principles (*formal*) —**preceptively** *adv.*

preceptor /pri séptər/ *n.* **1. TEACHER** a teacher or instructor (*formal*) **2. SPECIALIZED TUTOR** a specialist in a profession, especially medicine, who gives practical training to a student **3. HEAD OF PRECEPTORY** the head of a community of Knights Templars —**preceptoral** *adj.* —**preceptorate** *n.* —**preceptorship** /pri séptər ship/ *n.*

preceptory /pri séptəri/ (*plural* **-ries**) *n.* a community of Knights Templars

precess /pri séss/ (**-cesses, -cessing, -cessed**) *vti.* to spin or make sth spin with a motion in which the axis of rotation sweeps out a cone [Late 19thC. Back-formation from PRECESSION.]

precession /pri sésh'n/ *n.* the regular motion of a spinning body such as a spinning top or a planet, in which the axis of rotation sweeps out a cone [Late 16thC. From the late Latin stem *praecession-*, from *praecess-*, the past participle stem of *praecedere* 'to go before' (see PRECEDE).] —**precessional** *adj.*

precession of the equinoxes *n.* the slow westward movement of the equinoxes, resulting from the Earth's precessional motion, making them occur slightly earlier each year

pre-Christian *adj.* existing or occurring before Jesus Christ or Christianity

precinct /pree singkt/ *n.* **1. SPECIAL PART OF TOWN** a part of a town designated for a particular use, especially an area accessible only to pedestrians or a purpose-built area containing many shops ○ *a shopping precinct* **2.** *US* **CITY AREA PATROLLED BY POLICE UNIT** a district of a city or town under a particular unit of the police force **3.** *US* **POLICE UNIT OR STATION** the police unit or police station of a city or town district **4.** *US* **ELECTORAL DISTRICT** a small electoral district of a city or town, part of a ward **5. BOUNDARY** a boundary marking out an area ■ **precincts** *npl.* **AREA AROUND STH** the area surrounding a building or institution such as a cathedral or college [15thC. From medieval Latin *praecinctum*, literally 'sth encircled', the past participle of Latin *praecingere*, literally 'to gird about', from *cingere* 'to gird'.]

preciosity /préshi óssəti/ (*plural* **-ties**) *n.* ridiculous overrefinement in language and manners, or an example of this ○ *It might be quite a good poem if all the preciosities were removed.* [14thC. Via French from, ultimately, Latin *pretiosus* 'precious' (see PRECIOUS).]

precious /préshəss/ *adj.* **1. VALUABLE** worth a great deal of money **2. VALUED** highly valued, much loved, or considered to be of great importance ○ *Your friendship is very precious to me.* **3. NOT TO BE WASTED** rare or unique and therefore to be used wisely or sparingly or treated with care **4. USED FOR EMPHASIS** used for emphasis to express irritation, dislike, contempt, bemusement, or some other strong emotion (*informal*) ○ *I'm tempted to tell them what they can do with their precious training course!* **5. FASTIDIOUS OR AFFECTED** too carefully refined in language, dress, and manners ■ *adv.* **VERY** very ○ *And precious little thanks I got!* ■ *n.* **TERM OF ENDEARMENT** used as term of affection in talking to sb ○ *Good morning, my precious.* [13thC. Via Old French *precios* from Latin *pretiosus*, from *pretium* 'price'.] —**preciously** *adv.* —**preciousness** *n.*

precious coral *n.* = **red coral**

precious metal *n.* the metals gold, silver, or platinum, usually when found in the native state

precious stone *n.* any relatively rare and valuable mineral used in jewellery such as a diamond or ruby

precipice /préssəpiss/ *n.* **1. HIGH CLIFF OR CRAG** a high, vertical, or very steep rock face **2. DANGEROUS STATE** a very dangerous situation [Late 16thC. Directly or via French from Latin *praecipitium*, from the stem *praecipit-* 'headlong' (see PRECIPITATE).] —**precipiced** *adj.*

precipitancy /pri síppitənssi/ (*plural* **-cies**), **precipitance** /-tənss/ *n.* **1. RECKLESS HASTE** reckless haste or suddenness **2. HASTY ACTION** a reckless, hasty, or impulsive action

precipitant /pri síppitənt/ *adj.* **1. TOO HASTY** done too quickly and impulsively, often resulting in mistakes **2. SUDDEN OR UNEXPECTED** happening suddenly or unexpectedly **3. RUSHING** acting too quickly ■ *n.* CHEM **STH CAUSING PRECIPITATION** a substance that causes precipitation [Early 17thC. From French *précipitant*, present participle of *précipiter* (see PRECIPITATE).] —**precipitantly** *adv.*

precipitate *adj.* /pri síppi tayt, -síppitət/ **1. DONE OR ACTING RASHLY** done or acting too quickly and without enough thought ○ *I may have been precipitate in accepting their offer.* **2. HURRIED** very hurried **3. SUDDEN** sudden and unexpected ■ *v.* /pri síppi tayt/ (**-tates, -tating, -tated**) **1.** *vt.* **MAKE STH HAPPEN QUICKLY** to make sth happen suddenly and quickly **2.** *vt.* **SEND SB OR STH RAPIDLY** to send sb or sth suddenly and rapidly into some state or condition ○ *A minor border skirmish precipitated the two countries into war.* **3.** *vti.* **THROW OR FALL FROM ABOVE** to throw sb or sth or fall from a great height (*formal*) **4.** *vti.* METEOROL **MAKE RAIN OR SNOW FALL** to cause liquid or solid forms of water, condensed in the atmosphere, to fall to the ground as rain, snow, or hail, or to fall in such a form **5.** *vti.* CHEM **SEPARATE SOLID OUT OF SOLUTION** to cause a solid to separate out from a solution as a result of a chemical reaction, or to separate out in this way ■ *n.* CHEM **SUSPENSION OF SMALL PARTICLES** a suspension of small solid particles that are formed in a solution as a result of a chemical reaction and usually settle out of the solution [Early 16thC. From Latin *praecipitat-*, past participle stem of *praecipitare* 'to throw down', from *praeceps* 'headlong', from *caput* 'head'.] —**precipitability** /pri síppitə bílləti/ *n.* —**precipitable** /-síppitəb'l/ *adj.* —**precipitately** /-tətli/ *adv.* —**precipitateness** *n.* —**precipitative** /-taytiv/ *adj.* —**precipitator** *n.*

precipitation /pri síppi táysh'n/ *n.* **1. RAIN OR SNOW OR HAIL** rain, snow, or hail, all of which are formed by condensation of moisture in the atmosphere and fall to the ground **2. FORMATION OF RAIN OR SNOW OR HAIL** the formation of rain, snow, or hail from moisture in the air **3. FORMATION OF SUSPENSION IN SOLUTION** the formation of a suspension of an insoluble compound by mixing two solutions **4. HASTE** great or excessive haste (*formal*) ○ *He deeply regretted the precipitation of his elopement.* **5. A QUICKENING OF STH** a bringing about of sth earlier or more suddenly than expected (*formal*) ○ *circumstances that led to the precipitation of my divorce* **6. PROPULSION** the propelling or throwing of sb or sth (*formal*)

precipitin /pri síppitin/ *n.* an antibody that, when combined with its antigen, forms a substance that separates out of solution and can be detected visually [Early 20thC. Coined from PRECIPITATE + -IN.]

precipitinogen /pri síppi tinnəjən/ *n.* an antigen that causes the formation of a specific precipitin. This reaction can be used to identify an unknown antigen. [Early 20thC. Coined from PRECIPITIN + -GEN.]

precipitous /pri síppitəss/ *adj.* **1. DONE RASHLY** done or acting too quickly and without enough thought **2. LIKE A PRECIPICE** very high and steep **3. WITH A PRECIPICE** having several precipices [Mid-17thC. Via French *précipiteux* from, ultimately, Latin *praecipitium* (see PRECIPICE).] —**precipitously** *adv.* —**precipitousness** *n.*

précis /práy see/ *n.* (*plural* **-cis**) **SHORTENED VERSION** a shortened version of a speech or written text, containing the main points and omitting minor details ■ *vt.* (**-cis, -cising, -cised**) **MAKE SHORTENED VERSION OF STH** to make a précis of sth [Mid-18thC. From French, literally 'abridged'.]

precise /pri síss/ *adj.* **1. EXACT OR DETAILED** exact and accurate, or detailed and specific ○ *The train leaves an hour from now, or 57 minutes, to be precise.* **2. HANDLING SMALL DETAILS** able to assimilate details or wanting to be given details **3. INDICATING STH SPECIFIC** indicating that sth is the exact one that is being referred to ○ *At that precise moment, in he came.* **4. CAREFUL ABOUT DETAILS** very careful about small details, especially of correct behaviour **5. CLEAR** distinct and correct [Early 16thC. Via French from Latin *praecisus*, the past participle of *praecidere*, literally 'to cut off in front', from *caedere* 'to cut'.] —**preciseness** *n.*

precisely /pri síssli/ *adv.* **1. EXACTLY** exactly ○ *That is precisely what I mean.* **2. IN DETAIL** in complete and accurate detail ○ *Tell me precisely what happened.* **3. ACCURATELY** with absolute accuracy ○ *instruments that must be adjusted precisely before use* **4. CLEARLY** clearly and distinctly ○ *She speaks very precisely.* **5. USED FOR EMPHASIS** used to add emphasis when specifying sth ○ *It was precisely because you didn't ask that she thought you didn't need her help.* **6. EXPRESSING AGREEMENT** used to indicate complete agreement with what has been said ○ *'But I don't think they can be relied on.' 'Precisely.'*

precisian /pri sízh'n/ *n.* sb who is very concerned about the observance of rules and correct behaviour, especially in matters of morality and religion —**precisianism** *n.*

precision /pri sízh'n/ *n.* **1. EXACTNESS** exactness or accuracy **2.** MATH **MATHEMATICAL ACCURACY** the accuracy to which a calculation is performed, specifying the number of significant digits with which the result is expressed ■ *adj.* **RELATING TO EXACTNESS OR ACCURACY** allowing for, made with, or requiring great exactness or accuracy [Late 16thC. Via French from, ultimately, Latin *praecis-*, the past participle stem of *praecidere* (see PRECISE).]

precisionist /pri sízh'nist/ *n.* sb who insists on or strives for absolute precision —**precisionism** *n.*

preclinical /pree klínnik'l/ *adj.* relating to or characteristic of a disease before the symptoms become evident —**preclinically** *adv.*

preclude /pri klóod/ (**-cludes, -cluding, -cluded**) *vt.* **1. PREVENT STH** to prevent sth or make it impossible, or to prevent sb from doing sth (*formal*) ○ *That shouldn't preclude a satisfactory outcome.* **2. DEBAR SB** to exclude sb or sth, especially in advance ○ *Having a relative in the company precludes me from entering the contest.* [Early 17thC. From Latin *praecludere*, literally 'to close off ahead', from *claudere* 'to close'.] —**preclusion** /pri klóozh'n/ *n.* —**preclusive** /-klóossiv/ *adj.* —**preclusively** *adv.*

precocial /pri kósh'l/ *adj.* used to describe some animals that display independent activity at birth, especially young birds that are hatched covered with down and with open eyes [Late 19thC. Formed from modern Latin *Praecoces* 'the precocial birds', the plural of Latin *praecox* 'precocious' (see PRECOCIOUS).]

precocious /pri kóshəss/ *adj.* **1. MENTALLY ADVANCED FOR AGE** more developed, especially mentally, than is usual or expected at a particular age, or showing such advanced development (*sometimes used disapprovingly*) **2.** BOT **BLOSSOMING OR RIPENING EARLY** used to describe a plant or tree that blossoms before its leaves appear, e.g. the magnolia, or one whose fruits ripen early [Mid-17thC. Formed from Latin *praecox* 'ripening early', literally 'cooked ahead', ultimately from *coquere* 'to cook'.] —**precociously** *adv.* —**precociousness** /pri kóshəssnəss/ *n.* —**precocity** /pri kóssəti/ *n.*

precognition /pree kog nísh'n/ *n.* **1. ABILITY TO FORESEE THE FUTURE** the ability to know what is going to happen in the future, especially if based on extrasensory perception **2. PRETRIAL INVESTIGATION IN SCOTLAND** in Scotland, an official investigation of the facts of a case by interrogating witnesses in preparation for a trial, to make it possible to prepare a relevant charge in defence. This is done by the procurator fiscal. —**precognitive** /pree kógnitiv/ *adj.*

pre-Columbian *adj.* relating to North, Central, or South America before the arrival of Christopher Columbus in 1492

preconceive /pree kən seév/ (**-ceives, -ceiving, -ceived**) *vt.* to form an opinion or idea about sb or sth before enough information or experience is available to make an educated or fair judgment

preconceived /pree kən seévd/ *adj.* formed in the mind in advance, especially if based on little or no information or experience and reflecting personal prejudices

preconception /pree kən sépsh'n/ *n.* an idea or opinion formed in advance, especially if it is based on little or no information or experience and reflects personal prejudices

preconcert /pree kónssərt/ (**-certs, -certing, -certed**) *vt.* to agree, arrange, or organize sth beforehand (*formal*)

precondition /pree kən dísh'n/ *n.* **STH THAT MUST BE DONE FIRST** sth that must be done or agreed before sth else will happen ○ *They made a total ceasefire a precondition of the talks.* ■ *vt.* (**-tions, -tioning, -tioned**) **PREPARE SB OR STH** to prepare sb or sth for a process or put sb into a desired mental state

preconize /preēkə nīz/ (**-izes, -izing, -ized**), **preconise** (**-ises, -ising, -ised**) *vt.* **1. PROCLAIM STH** to proclaim or announce sth (*formal*) **2. SUMMON SB** to summon sb publicly (*formal*) **3.** CHR **GIVE PAPAL APPROVAL TO BISHOP** in the Roman Catholic Church, to make a public announcement of papal approval of the appointment of a bishop [15thC. From medieval Latin *praeconizare*, from Latin *praecon-*, stem of *praeco* 'public crier'.] —**preconization** /preēkə nī záysh'n/ *n.*

preconscious /pree kónshəss/ *n.* **RECALLABLE THOUGHTS AND FEELINGS** in Freudian theory, the part of the mind lying between the conscious and the unconscious. It contains information, thoughts, and feelings that are not present in conscious awareness but can readily be brought into the conscious mind. ■ *adj.* **RELATING TO RECALLABLE PART OF MIND** relating to or contained in the preconscious —**preconsciously** *adv.* —**preconsciousness** *n.*

precontract /pree kón trakt/ *n.* **CONTRACT MADE IN ADVANCE** a contract made in advance to prevent a subsequent contract, especially a betrothal ■ *vti.* (**-tracts, -tracting, -tracted**) **1. MAKE AGREEMENT IN ADVANCE** to make a contract or enter into an agreement in advance **2. MAKE CONTRACT FOR ARRANGED MARRIAGE** to pledge sb to marriage by an earlier agreement or to become pledged in this way

precook /pree kóok/ (**-cooks, -cooking, -cooked**) *vt.* to cook food completely or partially in advance, especially before it is sold, so that only minimal cooking or merely reheating is required —**precooked** *adj.*

precritical /pree kríttik'l/ *adj.* relating to the time or state before a crisis or before sth such as a disease reaches a critical condition

precursive *adj.* = **precursory**

precursor /pri kúrssər/ *n.* **1. SB OR STH THAT COMES EARLIER** sb or sth that comes before, and is often considered to lead to the development of, another person or thing **2. PREVIOUS HOLDER OF JOB** sb who has held a particular position before sb else **3.** CHEM **CHEMICAL COMPOUND PRECEDING ANOTHER** a chemical compound that leads to another, usually more stable, product in a series of connected reactions [Early 16thC. From Latin *praecursor*, from *praecurs-*, the stem of *praecurrere*, literally 'to run before', from *currere* 'to run'.]

precursory /pree kúrssri, pri-/, **precursive** /-kúrssiv/ *adj.* **1. AT INITIAL STAGE** at an initial or preparatory stage **2. INDICATING STH TO COME** serving as an indication of sth to come (*formal*)

pred. *abbr.* LOGIC, GRAM predicate

predacious /pri dáyshəss/, **predaceous** *adj.* **1. PREDATORY** used to describe animals that hunt, kill, and eat other animals **2. ATTACKING OTHERS** attacking and stealing from other people (*formal*) [Early 18thC. Formed from Latin *praedari* 'to seize as plunder' (see PREDATORY).] —**predaciousness** *n.* —**predacity** /pri dássəti/ *n.*

predate /preē dáyt/ (**-dates, -dating, -dated**) *vt.* **1. EXIST EARLIER THAN STH OR SB** to come before sth or sb in time **2. PUT EARLY DATE ON STH** to put a date on sth that is earlier than the actual date, or to say that sth occurred at an earlier date than it actually did

predation /pri dáysh'n/ *n.* **1. PREYING OF ONE SPECIES ON ANOTHER** the relationship between two groups of animals in which one species hunts, kills, and eats the other **2. PLUNDERING** the act of plundering, stealing, or destroying [15thC. From the Latin stem *praedation-*, from *praedari* 'to seize as plunder' (see PREDATORY).]

predator /préddətər/ *n.* **1. CARNIVOROUS ANIMAL OR DESTRUCTIVE ORGANISM** a carnivorous animal that hunts, kills, and eats other animals in order to survive, or any other organism that behaves in a similar manner **2. SB WHO PLUNDERS OR DESTROYS** a person, group, company, or state that steals from others or destroys others for gain **3. RUTHLESSLY AGGRESSIVE PERSON** sb who is extremely aggressive, determined, or persistent (*disapproving*) [Early 20thC. From Latin *praedator*, from *praedari* 'to seize as plunder' (see PREDATORY).]

predatory /préddətəri/ *adj.* **1. RELATING TO PREDATORS** relating to or characteristic of animals that survive by preying on others **2. GREEDILY DESTRUCTIVE** greedily eager to steal from or destroy others for gain **3. RUTHLESSLY AGGRESSIVE** extremely aggressive, determined, or persistent (*disapproving*) [Late 16thC. From Latin *praedatorius*, from *praedari* 'to seize as plunder', from *praeda* 'booty' (source of English *prey, spree,* and *osprey*).] —**predatorily** *adv.* —**predatoriness** *n.*

predatory pricing *n.* the act of setting prices at very low levels in order to force other companies out of the market

predecease /preēdi seēss/ (**-ceases, -ceasing, -ceased**) *vt.* to die before sb else (*formal*) ○ *His eldest son predeceased him.* —**predecease** *n.*

predecessor /preēdi sessər/ *n.* **1. PREVIOUS HOLDER OF JOB** sb who held a particular position or job before sb else **2. STH REPLACED BY STH ELSE** sth previously in use or existence that has been replaced or succeeded by sth else ○ *I hope my new car will be more reliable than its predecessor.* **3. ANCESTOR** an ancestor [14thC. Via French from late Latin *praedecessor*, literally 'one who has departed before', from *decedere* 'to depart'.]

predelinquent /preē di língkwənt/ *adj.* *US* showing signs of becoming a delinquent ○ *a program for predelinquent youths* [Late 20thC. From PRE- + DELINQUENT.]

predella /pri déllə/ *n.* **1. ALTAR PLATFORM** the platform for an altar, or the step on which an altar rests **2. DECORATED BASE OF ALTARPIECE** the decorative base of an altarpiece, embellished with small paintings or sculptures [Mid-19thC. From Italian, 'stool'.]

predestinarian /preē desti náiri ən/ *n.* **BELIEVER IN PREDESTINATION** sb who believes in predestination ■ *adj.* **RELATING TO PREDESTINATION** relating to predestination or to people who believe in it —**predestinarianism** *n.*

predestinate /pree désti nayt/ *vt.* (**-nates, -nating, -nated**) **PREDESTINE** to predestine sth or sb ■ *adj.* **1. FOREORDAINED** decided in advance **2. FOREORDAINED BY GOD OR A DEITY** decided and decreed by in advance by God, a deity, or fate [14thC. From ecclesiastical Latin *praedestinatus*, the past participle of *praedestinare* (see PREDESTINE).]

predestination /pree désti náysh'n/ *n.* **1. ADVANCE DECISION BY GOD ABOUT EVENTS** the doctrine holding that God, a deity, or fate has established in advance everything that is going to happen and that nothing can change this course of events **2. GOD'S DECISION WHO GOES TO HEAVEN** the doctrine that God decided at the beginning of time who would go to Heaven after death and who would not **3. FOREORDAINING** the divine or human act of deciding the fate of people or things beforehand

predestine /pree déstin/ (**-tines, -tining, -tined**) *vt.* **1. FOREORDAIN EVENTS** to decide in advance what is going to happen **2. PRESELECT WHO WILL GO TO HEAVEN** to select in advance who will go to Heaven after death and who will not [14thC. Directly or via French from ecclesiastical Latin *praedestinare*, literally 'to foreordain', from Latin *destinare* 'to decree'.] —**predestinable** *adj.*

predeterminate /preē di túrminət/ *adj.* decided in advance (*formal*) —**predeterminately** *adv.*

predetermine /preē di túrmin/ (**-mines, -mining, -mined**) *vt.* **1. ARRANGE IN ADVANCE** to decide, agree, or arrange sth in advance **2. INCLINE SB TOWARDS OPINION OR ACTION** to make sb inclined in advance towards a particular opinion or course of action —**predetermination** /preē di túrmi náysh'n/ *n.* —**predeterminative** /preē di túrminətiv/ *adj.*

predeterminer /preē di túrminər/ *n.* a word that precedes and qualifies another determiner, as 'both' does in 'both my hands'

predial *adj.* = **praedial**

predicable /préddikəb'l/ *adj.* **ABLE TO BE ASSERTED** able to be stated, or able to be said about sb or sth (*formal*) ■ *n.* **QUALITY THAT DESCRIBES STH** a quality or attribute by which sb or sth can be described (*formal*) [Mid-16thC. From medieval Latin *praedicabilis*, from Latin *praedicare* (see PREDICATE).] —**predicability** /préddikə bílləti/ *n.* —**predicableness** *n.*

predicament /pri díkəmənt/ *n.* **1. DIFFICULT SITUATION** a difficult, unpleasant, or embarrassing situation from which there is no clear or easy way out **2.** LOGIC **CATEGORY** any category or class that can be assigned to sth [14thC. From late Latin *praedicamentum* 'class, category' (translation of Greek *katēgoria*), from Latin *praedicare* 'to proclaim' (see PREDICATE).]

predicant /préddikənt/ *adj.* **RELATING TO PREACHING** relating to or involved in preaching (*formal*) ■ *n.* **1. PREACHING FRIAR** a member of a religious order, especially the Dominicans, that has a particular commitment to preaching **2.** = **predikant** [Late 16thC. From Latin *praedicant-*, present participle stem of *praedicare* 'to preach' (see PREDICATE).]

predicate *n.* /préddikət/ **1.** GRAM **PART OF SENTENCE EXCLUDING SUBJECT** a word or combination of words, including the verb, objects, or phrases governed by the verb that make up one of the two main parts of a sentence **2.** LOGIC **EVERYTHING IN SENTENCE EXCLUDING NAMES** everything in a simple sentence other than names, e.g. 'runs' in 'Fred runs' and 'is taller than' in 'Fred is taller than Ginger' **3.** LOGIC **STH AFFIRMED OR DENIED** that which is affirmed or denied about sth ■ *vt.* /préddi kayt/ (**-cates, -cating, -cated**) **1. BASE STH ON STH** to base an opinion, an action, or a result on sth (*formal*) ○ *predicated on reason* **2. STATE STH** to state or assert sth (*formal*) **3. IMPLY STH** to imply sth (*formal*) **4.** LOGIC **ASSERT STH ABOUT SUBJECT OF STATEMENT** to assert or affirm sth about the subject of a statement **5.** LOGIC **MAKE EXPRESSION PREDICATE OF STATEMENT** to make an expression or term the predicate of a statement [Mid-16thC. From late Latin *praedicatum*, from the past participle of Latin *praedicare* 'to declare publicly', literally 'to declare before', from *dicare* 'to state'.] —**predication** /préddi káysh'n/ *n.* —**predicative** /pri díkətiv/ *adj.*

predicate calculus *n.* the branch of symbolic logic that uses symbols to explore relationships between and within propositions

predicate nominative *n.* a noun or pronoun that completes the meaning of a sentence containing a linking verb, such as 'you' in the sentence 'Is that you?'

predicatory /préddikətəri/ *adj.* relating to or characteristic of a preacher or preaching (*formal*) [Early 17thC. From late Latin *praedicatorius*, from Latin *praedicare* 'to proclaim, teach' (see PREDICATE).]

predict /pri díkt/ (**-dicts, -dicting, -dicted**) *vti.* to say what is going to happen in the future, often on the basis of present indications or past experience [Mid-16thC. From Latin *praedict-*, the past participle stem of *praedicere*, literally 'to say in advance', from *dicere* 'to say'.] —**predictor** *n.*

predictable /pri díktəb'l/ *adj.* **1. HAPPENING AS EXPECTED** happening or turning out in the way that might have been expected or predicted **2. SELDOM UNEXPECTED** rarely or never being or doing anything unusual or unexpected —**predictability** /pri díktə bílləti/ *n.* —**predictableness** /-díktəb'lnəss/ *n.* —**predictably** /-díktəbli/ *adv.*

prediction /pri díksh'n/ *n.* **1. STATEMENT ABOUT FUTURE** a statement of what someone thinks will happen in the future **2. ACT OF PREDICTING** the making of a statement or forming of an opinion about what will happen in the future —**predictive** *adj.* —**predictively** *adv.* —**predictiveness** *n.*

predigest /preē dī jést, pree di jést/ (**-gests, -gesting, -gested**) *vt.* **1. MAKE FOOD MORE DIGESTIBLE** to treat food with chemicals or enzymes so that it is more easily digested, especially for people with digestion problems **2. SIMPLIFY STH** to produce information in a simplified form so that it is easy to understand —**predigestion** /-jésch'n/ *n.*

predikant /préddikənt/, **predicant** *n.* a minister of the Dutch Reformed Church in South Africa [Early 19thC. From Dutch, 'predicant'.]

predilection /preēdi léksh'n/ *n.* a particular liking or preference for sth (*formal*) [Mid-18thC. Via French from, ultimately, medieval Latin *praediligere*, literally 'to love first', from Latin *diligere* 'to love'.]

predispose /preēdi spṓz/ (**-poses, -posing, -posed**) *vt.* **1. MAKE SB FAVOURABLE** to make sb feel favourably about sb or sth in advance (*formal*) **2. MAKE SB LIABLE TO STH** to make sb liable or inclined to do sth, e.g. catch an illness or behave in a particular way (*formal*) ○ *Her fair skin predisposes her to sunburn.* **3.** LAW **DISPOSE OF STH AHEAD OF TIME** to dispose of sth, e.g. property, in advance (*archaic*) —**predisposal** *n.*

predisposition /preē dispə zísh'n/ *n.* **1. FAVOURABLE ATTITUDE OR INCLINATION** a favourable attitude towards sb or sth or an inclination to do sth **2. LIABILITY TO STH** a liability or tendency to do sth, e.g. behave in a particular way **3.** MED **TENDENCY TO DEVELOP DISEASE** a susceptibility to a disease, arising from a hereditary or another factor

prednisolone /pred níssə lōn/ *n.* a synthetic steroid hormone, similar to cortisone, used to treat allergies and suppress inflammatory diseases such as rheumatoid arthritis [Mid-20thC. Blend of PREDNISONE and -OL.]

prednisone /préddni sōn/ *n.* a synthetic steroid hormone produced from cortisone and used to treat allergies and autoimmune diseases [Mid-20thC. Coined from *pregnane* + DIENE + CORTISONE.]

predoctoral /pree dóktərəl/ *adj.* relating to or involving research or studies that will lead to a doctoral degree

predominance /pri dómminənss/, **predominancy** /-ənssi/ *n.* **1.** **MAJORITY** the state of being the commonest or greatest in number or amount **2.** **SUPERIORITY** greater or greatest importance, power, or influence

predominant /pri dómminənt/ *adj.* **1.** **MOST COMMON** commonest or greatest in number or amount **2.** **MOST IMPORTANT** most important, powerful, or influential

predominantly /pri dómminəntli/ *adv.* in the greatest number or amount

predominate *v.* /pri dómmi nayt/ (**-nates, -nating, -nated**) **1.** *vi.* **BE IN MAJORITY** to be the most common or greatest in number or amount **2.** *vi.* **BE MORE IMPORTANT** to have greater importance, power, or influence than others **3.** *vt.* **DOMINATE SB OR STH** to dominate or control sb or sth [Late 16thC. From medieval Latin *predominat-*, the past participle stem of *predominari*, literally 'to rule over', from Latin *dominari* 'to rule'.] —**predominately** /pri dóminətli/ *adv.* —**predomination** /pri dómmi náysh'n/ *n.* —**predominator** /pri dómmi naytər/ *n.*

pre-eclampsia /preé i klámpsi ə/ *n.* a potentially dangerous condition that may develop in late pregnancy and may lead to convulsions if not treated. Symptoms are high blood pressure, fluid retention, abnormal weight gain, and the presence of protein in the urine. [Early 20thC. Coined from PRE- + ECLAMPSIA.]

pre-embryo /pree émbri ō/ *n.* a fertilized ovum before implantation in the womb and before differentiation of embryonic tissue —**pre-embryonic** /preé embri ónnik/ *adj.*

preemie /preémi/, **premie** *n. US, Can* a premature baby born before it is fully developed, usually before 35 weeks of gestation [Early 20thC. From shortening of PREMATURE.]

pre-eminent /pri émminənt/ *adj.* standing out among all others because of superiority in a particular field or activity [From Latin *praeeminent-*, the present participle stem of *praeeminere*, literally 'to stand out in front', from *eminere* 'to stand out'] —**pre-eminence** *n.* —**pre-eminently** *adv.*

pre-empt /pri émpt/ (**-empts, -empting, -empted**) *v.* **1.** *vt.* **ACT TO PREVENT STH** to do sth that makes it pointless or impossible for sb else to do what he or she intended **2.** *vt. US* **OCCUPY STH** to occupy land in order to have the right to buy it later **3.** *vt.* **REPLACE STH** to take the place of sth, especially of sth less important **4.** *vi.* BRIDGE **MAKE BRIDGE BID THAT BLOCKS OTHERS** to make a bid intended to prevent further bidding [Back-formation from PREEMPTION] —**pre-emptor** *n.* —**pre-emptory** *adj.*

pre-emption /pri émpsh'n/ *n.* **1.** **ACTION PREVENTING STH** action that makes it pointless or impossible for sb else to do what he or she intended **2.** *US* **OCCUPATION OF PUBLIC LAND** the occupation of public land in order to have the right to buy it later, or the right to buy that is gained in this way **3.** **OPTION TO BUY PROPERTY** an option to purchase property if and when it is put up for sale **4.** **STRATEGY OF FIRST ATTACK** the strategy of attacking an enemy in order to prevent that enemy from attacking first [From the medieval Latin stem *praeemption-*, ultimately from *praeemere*, literally 'to buy first', from Latin *emere* 'to buy']

pre-emptive /pri émptiv/ *adj.* **1.** **DONE BEFORE OTHERS CAN ACT** done before sb else has had an opportunity to act so making his or her planned action pointless or impossible **2.** MIL **INTENDED TO PREVENT ATTACK** intended to eliminate or lessen an enemy's capacity to attack ○ *a preemptive strike* **3.** BRIDGE **PREVENTING FURTHER BIDDING** intended to prevent further bidding —**pre-emptively** *adv.*

pre-emptive right *n.* a right to be offered first refusal in selling or buying an asset

preen[1] /preen/ (**preens, preening, preened**) *vti.* **1.** **GROOM FEATHERS WITH BEAK** to clean, smooth, or arrange the feathers with the beak ○ *swans preening their feathers* **2.** **GROOM FUR WITH TONGUE** to clean and smooth the fur by licking it ○ *The cat was quietly preening on the windowsill.* **3.** **CARE FOR PERSONAL APPEARANCE** to spend a long or excessive time attending to personal appearance, especially making small finishing touches to the hair, the face, or clothes ○ *busy preening in front of the mirror* **4.** **SHOW SELF-SATISFACTION** to feel excessively self-satisfied and display that feeling by gloating (*disapproving*) ○ *He preens himself on his ability to deflect criticism.* [15thC. Origin uncertain: probably from Old French *proignier* 'to prune'.] —**preener** *n.*

preen[2] /preen/ *n.* **1.** *Scotland* **PIN** a pin **2.** **BROOCH** a decorative pin or brooch [Old English *prēon*, from a prehistoric Germanic word]

pre-engineered /preé enji neérd/ *adj.* constructed using prefabricated parts

pre-establish /preé i stáblish/ (**-lishes, -lishing, -lished**) *vt.* to set up, decide, or arrange sth in advance

pre-exilian /preé ig zílli ən/ *adj.* relating to the Jewish people before their exile to Babylon in the sixth century BC

pre-exist /preé ig zíst/ (**-ists, -isting, -isted**) *vti.* to exist before another person, group, thing, or event

pre-existence /preé ig zístənss/ *n.* the existence of sth at an earlier time and often in a different state —**pre-existent** *adj.*

pref. *abbr.* **1.** preface **2.** prefatory **3.** preference **4.** preferred **5.** prefix

prefab /preé fab/ *adj.* **MANUFACTURED IN SECTIONS** relating to or constructed from prefabricated parts (*informal*) ■ *n.* **STH PREFABRICATED** a prefabricated house or building (*informal*) [Mid-20thC. Shortening.]

prefabricate /pree fábbri kayt/ (**-cates, -cating, -cated**) *vt.* **1.** **PRODUCE IN SECTIONS** to manufacture sections of sth, especially a building, that can be transported to a site and easily assembled there **2.** **PRODUCE IN STANDARDIZED FORM** to produce sth in an unoriginal or standardized way —**prefabrication** /pree fábbri káysh'n/ *n.* —**prefabricator** /-kaytər/ *n.*

preface /préffəss/ *n.* **1.** **INTRODUCTORY PART OF TEXT** an introductory section at the beginning of a book or speech that comments on aspects of the text such as the writer's intentions ○ *in the preface to the second edition* **2.** **PRELIMINARY ACTION** an action or thing that precedes sth more important **3.** **preface, Preface** CHR **PRAYER TO GOD** a prayer said by a priest during Mass, especially the prayer that begins 'Lift up your hearts' **4.** **preface, Preface** CHR **PRAYER FOR PARTICULAR PURPOSE** in the Roman Catholic Church, any one of a number of prayers used for particular purposes ■ *vt.* (**-aces, -acing, -aced**) **1.** **INTRODUCE WITH PREFACE** to introduce an action, speech, or piece of writing with sth ○ *He prefaced his remarks with an apology.* **2.** **SERVE AS INTRODUCTION TO** to act as a preface to an action, speech, or piece of writing [14thC. Via French from, ultimately, Latin *praefatus*, the past participle of *praefari* 'to say before', from *fari* 'to speak'.] —**prefacer** *n.*

prefaded /preé fáydid/ *adj.* given an artificially faded, worn, or old appearance ○ *prefaded denim*

prefatory /préffətəri/ *adj.* serving to introduce sth else such as a main body of text or a speech ○ *prefatory remarks introducing the Prime Minister* [Late 17thC. Formed from Latin *praefatus*, the past participle of *praefari* (see PREFACE).] —**prefatorily** *adv.*

prefect /preé fekt/ *n.* **1.** EDUC **PUPIL ASSISTING WITH DISCIPLINE** a senior pupil who is given some authority over other pupils in matters of discipline **2.** PUBLIC ADMIN **HIGH-RANKING ADMINISTRATIVE OFFICIAL** the highest official in an administrative district (**department**) or former territorial possession of France, or in an administrative region of Italy **3.** **FRENCH CHIEF OF POLICE** the head of a French police force, especially in Paris **4.** HIST **ROMAN MAGISTRATE OR COMMANDER** a senior administrative or military official in ancient Rome **5.** CHR **SENIOR MASTER AT JESUIT SCHOOL** a senior master or administrator with special responsibilities at a Jesuit school or college [14thC. Via Old French from Latin *praefectus* 'overseer', the past participle of *praeficere* 'to set over', from *facere* 'to make'.] —**prefectorial** /preé fek táwri əl/ *adj.*

prefecture /preé fekchər/ *n.* **1.** **PREFECT'S JURISDICTION** the district over which a prefect has jurisdiction **2.** **OFFICE OF PREFECT** the office or authority of a prefect **3.** **PREFECT'S RESIDENCE** the official residence of a prefect in countries such as France or Italy —**prefectural** /pree fékchərəl/ *adj.*

prefer /pri fúr/ (**-fers, -ferring, -ferred**) *vt.* **1.** **LIKE BETTER THAN STH ELSE** to like or want one thing more than another ○ *I prefer tea to coffee.* **2.** LAW **LAY BEFORE COURT** to make a charge against sb by submitting details of the alleged offence to a court, magistrate, or judge for examination, or prosecute such a charge ○ *prefer charges* **3.** LAW **GIVE PRIORITY TO** to give priority to one person, especially a creditor, over others **4.** **PROMOTE** to promote sb to a higher position or rank (*archaic*) [14thC. Via French *préferer* from Latin *praeferre*, from *prae-* 'before, in front' (see PRE-) + *ferre* 'to carry, bear'.] —**preferrer** *n.*

preferable /préffərəb'l/ *adj.* more likely to be enjoyable, useful, or desired than sth else —**preferability** /préffərə bílləti/ *n.* —**preferableness** /préffərəb'lnəss/ *n.*

preferably /préffərəb'li/ *adv.* used to specify more exactly what is required or desired ○ *Plan to arrive early, preferably before the rush hour.*

preference /préffərənss/ *n.* **1.** **SELECTION OF SB OR STH** the view that a particular person, object, or course of action is more desirable than another, or a choice based on such a view ○ *The judges showed a marked preference for representational art* **2.** **SB OR STH PREFERRED** a person, object, or course of action that is more desirable than another, or the state of being that desirable choice ○ *State your preferences clearly.* **3.** **RIGHT TO EXPRESS CHOICE** the right or opportunity to choose a person, object, or course of action that is considered more desirable than another ○ *We exercised our preference.* **4.** LAW **PRIORITY OF ONE CREDITOR OVER OTHERS** priority given to a particular creditor, e.g. when a debtor goes bankrupt, or the right of a particular creditor to receive payment before others **5.** COMM **FAVOURITISM IN INTERNATIONAL TRADE** priority given to a particular country or group of countries in international trade ■ **preferences** *npl.* POL **VOTES UNDER PREFERENTIAL VOTING SYSTEM** votes assigned to second or third choice candidates, and so on, under the preferential voting system, e.g. in Australia

preference shares *npl.* shares whose holders are the first to receive dividends from available profit. Preference shares are redeemed before ordinary shares when a company is liquidated. US term **preferred stock**

preferential /préffə rénsh'l/ *adj.* **1.** **SHOWING FAVOURITISM** giving advantage or priority to a particular person or group ○ *preferential treatment* **2.** COMM **SHOWING FAVOURITISM IN INTERNATIONAL TRADE** giving advantage or priority to a particular country or group of countries in international trade —**preferentialism** *n.* —**preferentialist** *adj.* —**preferentiality** /préffə rénshi álləti/ *n.* —**preferentially** /préffə rénsh'li/ *adv.*

preferential voting *n.* an electoral system used in some countries, e.g. Australia, in which voters indicate their chosen candidates in order of preference

preferment /pri fúrmənt/ *n.* (*formal*) **1.** **PROMOTION** appointment to a higher position or rank, especially in the church **2.** **HIGH-RANKING POSITION** an office, appointment, or position of high rank or honour, especially one that brings social advancement or financial reward

preferred stock *n. US* = **preference shares**

prefiguration /preé figə ráysh'n/ *n.* **1.** **INDICATION OF FUTURE PERSON OR THING** a representation, often in form or likeness, of a person, thing, or event that is to come **2.** **STH REPRESENTING FUTURE PERSON OR THING** sb or sth that represents, often in form or likeness, a person, thing, or event that is to come

prefigure /pree fíggər/ (**-ures, -uring, -ured**) *vt.* **1.** **INDICATE FUTURE EXISTENCE OF** to represent or suggest, often in form or likeness, a person, thing, or event that will come later ○ *designs that prefigured modern architecture* **2.** **THINK ABOUT BEFOREHAND** to think about or imagine a person, thing, or event in advance [15thC. From ecclesiastical Latin *praefigurare*, literally 'to depict beforehand', from Latin *figura* 'figure'.] —**prefigurative** /preefíggərətiv/ *adj.* —**prefiguratively** *adv.* —**prefigurativeness** *n.* —**prefigurement** /pree fíggərmənt/ *n.*

prefix /préefiks/ *n.* **1.** GRAM **WORD ELEMENT BEGINNING VARIOUS WORDS** a linguistic element that is not an independent word but is attached to the beginning of words to modify their meaning. For example, 'un-' is a prefix meaning 'not'. **2.** **TITLE** a title before sb's name ○ *the prefix 'The Honourable' before an MP's full name* **3.** **STH PRECEDING STH ELSE** sth that comes before sth else, e.g. a fixed group of digits at the beginning of a telephone number ■ *vt.* (**-fixes, -fixing, -fixed**) **1.** **PUT BEFORE STH** to place sth in front of sth else ○ *You must prefix the number with the area code.* **2.** **INTRODUCE WITH STH** to say or do sth by way of introduction ○ *His requests for money were usually prefixed by an apology.* **3.** GRAM **ADD PREFIX TO** to attach a prefix at the beginning of a word to alter its meaning **4.** **ARRANGE IN ADVANCE** to decide on sth such as a price, date, or meeting place beforehand ○ *They duly arrived at the prefixed hour.* [15thC. Via French from Latin *praefixus*, *praefixum*, the past participle of Latin *praefigere* 'to fix in front', from *figere* 'to fasten'.] —**prefixal** /pree fíks'l, pree fíks'l/ *adj.* —**prefixally** *adv.* —**prefixation** /pree fik sáysh'n/ *n.* —**prefixion** /pree fíksh'n/ *n.*

preflight /pree flīt/ *adj.* **CARRIED OUT BEFORE TAKEOFF** occurring before an aircraft takes off ○ *The fault was discovered during a preflight check.* ■ *vt.* (**-flights, -flighting, -flighted**) **CHECK TO DETERMINE AIRWORTHINESS** to carry out a technical inspection of an aircraft before it takes off to ensure that it is airworthy ■ *n.* **PREFLIGHT CHECK** the set of procedures and checks that pilots and ground crew are required to carry out before an aircraft's takeoff ○ *During the preflight, the pilot discovered a problem in the landing gear.*

preform /pree fáwm/ (**-forms, -forming, -formed**) *vt.* **1.** **FORM BEFOREHAND** to shape or form sth beforehand **2.** **GIVE INITIAL SHAPE** to give sth a preliminary shape [Early 17thC. From Latin *praeformare*.]

preformation /pree fawr máysh'n/ *n.* the preliminary shaping or forming of sth beforehand

preformation theory *n.* the obsolete theory that sperm and egg cells (**gametes**) contain miniature adults that grow during development

prefrontal /pree frúnt'l/ *adj.* **1.** **AT VERY FRONT OF BRAIN** relating to or situated in the foremost part of the brain **2.** **ANTERIOR TO FRONTAL BONE** located in front of the frontal bone

prefrontal lobe *n.* the area of the brain at the very front of each of the two cerebral hemispheres. The prefrontal lobes are concerned with the functions of learning, behaviour, and the emotions.

prefrontal lobotomy *n.* a surgical operation in which the nerves connecting the front part of the brain (**prefrontal lobe**) to the thalamus are severed. Prefrontal lobotomy was a method of reducing severe emotional disturbances, but the operation had serious side effects.

preganglionic /pree gang gli ónnik/ *adj.* used to describe fibres in a nerve pathway that end in a cluster of nerve cell bodies (**ganglion**), continuing on to muscles or organs

preggers /préggərz/ *adj.* pregnant (*informal*) [Mid-20thC. Alteration of PREGNANT.]

preglacial /pree gláysh'l/ *adj.* formed or occurring before a glacial period, especially the period that began about a million years ago (**Pleistocene epoch**), when the surface of the Earth was covered with ice

pregnable /prégnəb'l/ *adj.* able to be captured or attacked [15thC. Via Old French from, ultimately, Latin *prehendere* (see PREHENSION).] —**pregnability** /prégnə bílləti/ *n.*

pregnancy /prégnənssi/ (*plural* **-cies**) *n.* **1.** **CONDITION OF BEING PREGNANT** the physical condition of a woman or female animal carrying unborn offspring inside her body, from fertilization to birth. Technical name **cyesis** **2.** **INSTANCE OF BEING PREGNANT** an individual occurrence or experience of being pregnant. Technical name **cyesis** **3.** **TIME OF CARRYING UNBORN OFFSPRING** the period during which a woman or female animal carries an unborn offspring inside her body, from fertilization to birth. Technical name **cyesis** **4.** **SIGNIFICANCE** importance or fullness of meaning ○ *the pregnancy of his words*

pregnant /prégnənt/ *adj.* **1.** BIOL **CARRYING OFFSPRING WITHIN THE BODY** carrying unborn offspring inside the body **2.** **SIGNIFICANT** full of meaning or importance ○ *After a pregnant pause, the general began briefing the media on the surprise attack.* **3.** **FULL OF STH** pervaded by sth, usually sth intangible **4.** **CREATIVE** full of creative power ○ *the child's pregnant imagination* **5.** **PRODUCTIVE** producing a lot of useful results ○ *It was a pregnant endeavour, yielding much experience, information, and help.* [15thC. Via Old French *preigne* from, ultimately, Latin *praegnas* 'before birth', from *prae-* 'before' + *gnatus* 'born' (source of English *native*).] —**pregnantly** *adv.*

preheat /pree héet/ (**-heats, -heating, -heated**) *vt.* to heat an oven, dish, or other item before using it ○ *Preheat the oven to gas mark 7.*

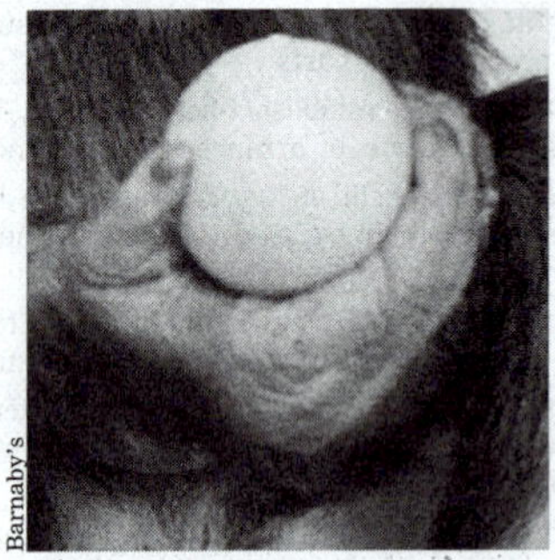

Barnaby's

Prehensile: Chimpanzee grasping a ball

prehensile /pri hén sīl/ *adj.* **1.** ZOOL **ABLE TO GRASP STH** able to take hold of things, especially by wrapping around them ○ *The monkey has a prehensile tail.* **2.** **QUICK TO UNDERSTAND** skilled at grasping ideas and concepts **3.** **AGGRESSIVELY EAGER** excessively eager for gain or profit [Late 18thC. Via French from, ultimately, Latin *prehendere* (see PREHENSION).] —**prehensility** /pree hen sílləti/ *n.*

WORD KEY: ORIGIN

The Latin word *prehendere*, from which ***prehensile*** is derived, is also the source of English *apprehend, apprentice, comprehend, comprise, depredation, impregnable, predator, prey, prison, reprehensible, reprieve*, and *surprise*.

prehension /pri hénsh'n/ *n.* (*formal*) **1.** **ACT OF FIRMLY GRASPING** the act of firmly taking hold of sth **2.** **PERCEIVING OF STH THROUGH SENSES** the perception by the senses of a sight, sound, smell, taste, or texture **3.** **COMPREHENSION** the process of understanding [Mid-16thC. From Latin *prehensionem*, from *prehendere* 'to seize'.]

prehistorian /pree hi stáwri ən/ *n.* sb who studies or specializes in the period before recorded history [Late 19thC. Formed from PREHISTORY on the model of HISTORIAN.]

prehistoric /pree hi stórrik/, **prehistorical** /-stórrik'l/ *adj.* **1.** **BEFORE RECORDED HISTORY** relating to the period before history was first recorded in writing **2.** **RELATING TO LANGUAGE BEFORE WRITING** relating or belonging to a language before it was recorded in writing **3.** **VERY OLD OR OLD-FASHIONED** relating to or being an object, idea, or attitude that is very old or out of date ○ *prehistoric views about nutrition* —**prehistorically** *adv.*

prehistory /pree hístəri/ *n.* **1.** **HISTORY BEFORE WRITTEN WORD** the period before history was first recorded in writing **2.** **STUDY OF PREHISTORIC PERIOD** the study of the prehistoric period using archaeological evidence **3.** **EVENTS LEADING UP TO STH** the events and circumstances preceding a current event or situation (*informal*)

prehominid /pree hómmənid/ *n.* any one of various animals believed to be early ancestors of the modern human race —**prehominid** *adj.*

preignition /pree ig nísh'n/ *n.* ignition of fuel in an internal-combustion engine before the spark has been generated, causing inefficient operation. Preignition may be caused by a hot spot in the cylinder. —**preignite** *vti.*

preindustrial /pree in dústri əl/ *adj.* relating to a society, country, or economic system in which industry has not yet developed on an extensive scale

prejudge /pree júj/ (**-judges, -judging, -judged**) *vt.* to judge a person, issue, or case before sufficient evidence is available [Late 16thC. Via French *préjuger* from Latin *praejudicare*.] —**prejudger** *n.* —**prejudgment** *n.*

prejudice /préjjədiss/ *n.* **1.** **OPINION FORMED BEFOREHAND** a preformed opinion, usually an unfavourable one, based on insufficient knowledge, irrational feelings, or inaccurate stereotypes **2.** **THE HOLDING OF ILL-INFORMED OPINIONS** the holding of opinions that are formed beforehand on the basis of insufficient knowledge **3.** **IRRATIONAL DISLIKE OF SB** an unfounded hatred, fear, or mistrust of a person or group, especially one of a particular religion, ethnicity, nationality, or social status **4.** LAW **DISADVANTAGE OR HARM** disadvantage or harm caused to sb or sth ■ *vt.* (**-dices, -dicing, -diced**) **1.** **CAUSE TO PREJUDGE SB OR STH** to make sb form an opinion about sb or sth in advance, especially an irrational one, based on insufficient knowledge **2.** **AFFECT ADVERSELY** to cause harm or disadvantage to sb or sth [13thC. Via French from Latin *praejudicium* 'judgment in advance', from *judicium* 'judgment'.] ◇ **without prejudice** LAW without doing any harm to sb's legal rights or any claim that sb has (*formal*)

prejudiced /préjjədist/ *adj.* holding opinions, especially unfavourable ones, that are based on insufficient knowledge, irrational feelings, or inaccurate stereotypes

prejudicial /préjjoo dísh'l/ *adj.* **1.** **RESULTING IN HARM** causing disadvantage or harm to sb or sth **2.** **ENCOURAGING PREJUDICE** leading to the formation of prejudiced ideas or opinions —**prejudicially** *adv.*

prelacy /préləssi/ (*plural* **-cies**) *n.* **1.** **POSITION OF PRELATE** the office or position of a prelate **2.** **PRELATES COLLECTIVELY** prelates considered as a group **3.** = **prelatism** [14thC. Via Anglo-Norman from medieval Latin *prelatia*, from *praelatus* (see PRELATE).]

prelapsarian /pree lap sáiri ən/ *adj.* relating or belonging to the biblical time before Adam and Eve lost their innocence in the Garden of Eden [Late 19thC. Coined from PRE- + Latin *lapsus* 'sin, fall'.]

prelate /préllət/ *n.* a high-ranking member of the clergy, e.g. an abbot, bishop, or cardinal [13thC. Via Old French from medieval Latin *praelatus*, the past participle of Latin *praeferre* 'to prefer'.] —**prelatic** /pri láttik/ *adj.*

prelatism /préllətizəm/ *n.* government of a church by high-ranking members of the clergy (*disapproving*) —**prelatist** *n.*

prelature /préllachər/ *n.* = **prelacy** *n.* 1, **prelacy** *n.* 2

prelect /pri lékt/ (**-lects, -lecting, -lected**) *vi.* to give a lecture or speech in public (*formal*) [Late 18thC. From Latin *praelect-*, the past participle stem of *praelegere* 'to read in front of', from *legere* 'to read'.] —**prelection** /-léksh'n/ *n.* —**prelector** *n.*

prelibation /pree lī báysh'n/ *n.* a sample or taste of sth in advance (*formal*) [Early 16thC. From Latin *praelibationem*, from *praelibare* 'to taste beforehand', from *libare* 'to pour out'.]

prelim /préelim/ *n.* **1.** SPORTS **PRELIMINARY CONTEST** a preliminary contest or event (*informal*) **2.** *Scotland* EDUC **SCOTTISH SCHOOL EXAMINATION** in Scotland, a school examination taken to prepare students for a public examination (*informal*) **3.** EDUC **UNIVERSITY EXAM** the first public examination in some universities ■ **prelims** *npl.* PUBL **BOOK FRONT MATTER** the initial pages of a book, including the title page and table of contents, that precede the main text (*informal*) [Late 19thC. Contraction of PRELIMINARY.]

prelim. *abbr.* preliminary

preliminary /pri límminəri/ *adj.* **COMING BEFORE STH** occurring before and leading up to sth, especially an event of greater size and importance ■ *n.* (*plural* **-ies**) **1.** **INTRODUCTORY OR PREPARATORY ACTIVITY** sth said or done before sth else, often by way of introduction to or preparation for sth of greater size and importance (*often used in the plural*) **2.** SPORTS **INTRO-**

DUCTORY CONTEST a sporting contest held before the main event, especially in boxing and wrestling **3.** SPORTS **ELIMINATORY CONTEST** an eliminatory contest to select the finalists in a sporting competition **4.** EDUC **PREPARATORY EXAMINATION** a test that prepares students for a subsequent examination of greater difficulty and importance [Mid-17thC. Directly or via French from modern Latin *praeliminaris*, from Latin *prae-* 'before' + *limen* 'threshold'.] —**preliminarily** /pri límminərəli/ *adv.*

preliterate /pree líttərət/ *adj.* **WITHOUT WRITTEN LANGUAGE** used to describe a society that has no written language ■ *n.* **MEMBER OF A PRELITERATE SOCIETY** a member of a society with no written language —**preliteracy** /preè líttərəssi/ *n.*

preloved /pree lúvd/ *adj.* *ANZ* used euphemistically to describe an article for sale second-hand (*informal*)

prelude /prélyood/ *n.* **1.** MUSIC **INTRODUCTORY PIECE OF MUSIC** a piece of music that introduces or precedes another one **2.** MUSIC **FREE-STANDING PIECE OF MUSIC** a short musical composition, often one for piano, and often forming part of a set of such works **3. INTRODUCTORY EVENT OR OCCURRENCE** an event or action that introduces or precedes sth else, especially sth longer and more important ■ *v.* (**-udes, -uding, -uded**) **1.** *vti.* **ACT AS PRELUDE TO STH** to act as an introduction to sth else, especially sth that is longer and more important **2.** *vt.* **INTRODUCE WITH PRELUDE** to precede sth, especially a piece of music, with a prelude [Mid-16thC. Via French from, ultimately, Latin *praeludere* 'to play before', from *ludere* 'to play'.] —**prelusive** /pri lóossiv/ *adj.* —**prelusively** /-lóossivli/ *adv.* —**prelusorily** /-lóossərəli/ *adv.* —**prelusory** /-lóossəri/ *adj.*

WORD KEY: CULTURAL NOTE

The Prelude, a poem by William Wordsworth (1798–1850). Planned as a preface to a never-completed philosophical poem called *The Recluse*, this autobiographical account of the poet's intellectual and spiritual development was written over a period of more than 40 years and published posthumously. Rejecting contemporary rationalist philosophies, it proclaims Wordsworth's faith in the redeeming power of poetry and the imagination.

prelusion /pri lóozh'n/ *n.* = **prelude** *n.* 3

prem /prem/ *n.* a premature baby (*informal*) [Mid-20thC. Shortening of PREMATURE.]

prem. *abbr.* premium

premalignant /preèmə lígnənt/ *adj.* = **precancerous**

premarital /pree márrit'l/ *adj.* occurring or existing before marriage

premature /prémməchər/ *adj.* **1. HAPPENING TOO SOON** occurring, existing, or developing earlier than is expected, normal, or advisable ○ *It would be premature to suggest that there is a link between these events.* **2.** MED **BORN TOO EARLY** born before completing the normal gestation period, or, for a human infant, weighing less than 2.5 kg/5 lb 8 oz at birth [Early 16thC. From Latin *praematurus* 'ripening too early', from *maturus* 'ripe'.] —**prematurely** *adv.* —**prematureness** *n.* —**prematurity** /prémmə chóorəti/ *n.*

premaxilla /preè mak síllə/ (*plural* **-lae**) *n.* either of two bones that form the front part of the upper jaw in vertebrates and that bear the incisors. In humans, it merges with the rest of the maxilla during embryonic life. —**premaxillary** *adj.*

premed /pree méd/ *n.* (*informal*) **1. PREMEDICATION** drugs administered to a patient before a general anaesthetic, e.g. to relieve anxiety before a surgical operation **2.** *US* **PREMEDICAL STUDENT** a student in a premedical programme ○ *The premeds will be taking their exams soon.* **3.** *US* **PREMEDICAL COURSEWORK** a premedical course of study ○ *majoring in premed* ■ *adj.* **PREMEDICAL** premedical (*informal*) [Mid-20thC. Shortening.]

premedical /pree méddik'l/ *adj.* relating to or engaged in the course of studies that sb must complete before entering medical school —**premedically** *adv.*

premedication /preè medi káysh'n/ *n.* the practice of giving drugs to a patient before a general anaesthetic, or the drugs given, to relieve anxiety, diminish body reactions to pain, or improve post-operative comfort

premeditate /pri méddi tayt/ (**-tates, -tating, -tated**) *v.* **1.** *vt.* **PLAN BEFOREHAND** to plan or devise sth, especially a crime, in advance **2.** *vti.* **PONDER STH IN ADVANCE** to consider or think carefully about sth beforehand [Mid-16thC. From Latin *praemeditatus*, the past participle of *praemeditari* 'to think about beforehand', from *meditare* (see MEDITATE).] —**premeditative** /-tətiv/ *adj.* —**premeditator** /-taytər/ *n.*

premeditated /pri méddi taytid/ *adj.* not committed in a moment of passion or mindlessness, e.g. intense rage or drunkenness, but thought out and decided on beforehand ○ *was charged with premeditated murder* —**premeditatedly** *adv.*

premeditation /pri méddi táysh'n/ *n.* **1.** LAW **CONTEMPLATION OF INTENDED CRIME** thinking about and planning a crime beforehand, rather than acting on impulse in a moment of passion or mindlessness **2. REFLECTION BEFORE ACTION** thinking about sth before doing it [15thC. Directly or via French from Latin *praemeditationem*, from *praemeditari* (see PREMEDITATE).]

premenopausal /preè menō páwz'l/ *adj.* used to describe the stage in a woman's life just before the onset of the menopause, or a woman at this stage. Such a woman is still menstruating, but may show some signs of the menopause, e.g. irregular menstrual periods.

premenstrual /pree ménstruəl/ *adj.* relating to or occurring in the days immediately before the start of a woman's menstrual period

premenstrual syndrome *n.* a group of symptoms, e.g. nervous tension, irritability, tenderness of the breasts, and headache, experienced by some women in the days preceding menstruation and caused by hormonal changes

premie *n.* = **preemie**

premier /prémmi ər/ *adj.* **1. BEST OR MOST IMPORTANT** first in importance, size, or quality **2. COMING FIRST** happening or existing first ■ *n.* **1. PRIME MINISTER** a prime minister or head of government **2. LEADER OF AUSTRALIAN STATE GOVERNMENT** the head of government of an Australian state or territory **3. LEADER OF CANADIAN PROVINCE** the governmental head of a Canadian province ■ **premiers** *npl.* *Aus* SPORTS **WINNERS OF SPORTING CHAMPIONSHIP** the winners of the premiership in Australian Rules football, rugby league, and some other sports [15thC. Via French from Latin *primarius* 'foremost'.]

premier danseur /prémm yay daaN súr/ (*plural* **premiers danseurs** /prémm yay daaN súr/) *n.* the principal man dancer in a ballet company [Early 19thC. From French, literally 'first dancer'.]

premiere /prémmi air/ *n.* **1. FIRST PUBLIC PERFORMANCE** the first public performance or showing of sth such as a play or film **2. LEADING WOMAN ACTOR** the principal woman performer in a theatre company ■ *v.* (**-mieres, -miering, -miered**) **1.** *vti.* **PRESENT OR BE PRESENTED AS PREMIERE** to be publicly performed, shown, or broadcast for the first time, or present the first performance of sth such as a play or film ○ *The film premiered in Britain.* **2.** *vi.* **GIVE FIRST PUBLIC PERFORMANCE** to appear on stage or screen for the first time, especially in a leading role ○ *Not many young performers get to premiere on Broadway.* ■ *adj.* **BEST OR MOST IMPORTANT** first in importance, quality, or size [Mid-20thC. From French, the feminine form of *premier* 'first' (see PREMIER).]

première danseuse /prémm yair daaN sőz/ (*plural* **premières danseuses** /prémm yair daaN sőz/) *n.* the principal female dancer in a ballet company [Early 19thC. From French, literally 'first (female) dancer'.]

premiership /prémmi ərship/ *n.* **1.** POL **POSITION OF PREMIER** the office or position of premier **2.** SPORTS **CHAMPIONSHIP** a championship in some sports, e.g. football and rugby, or the competition to decide this

premillenarian /preè milə náiri ən/ *adj.* **RELATING TO PREMILLENNIALISM** relating or belonging to premillennialism ■ *n.* **BELIEVER IN PREMILLENNIALISM** sb who believes in premillennialism —**premillenarianism** *n.*

premillennial /preè mi lénni əl/ *adj.* relating to or occurring in the period immediately before a millennium —**premillennially** *adv.*

premillennialism /preè mi lénni əlizəm/ *n.* the belief that Jesus Christ will return to earth for the Last Judgment just before the one-thousand-year reign of peace (**millennium**) mentioned in the Bible —**premillennialist** *n.*

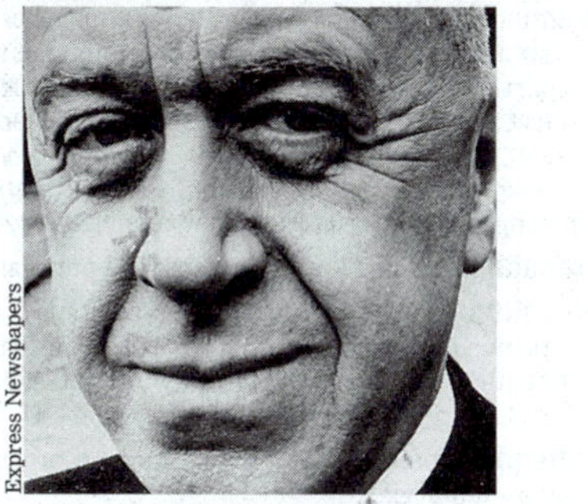
Express Newspapers

Otto Preminger

Preminger /prémminjər/, **Otto** (1906–86) Austrian-born US film director, producer, and actor. His films include *Laura* (1944), *Carmen Jones* (1954), and *Exodus* (1960). Full name **Otto Ludwig Preminger**

premise /prémmiss/ *n.* **1. EVIDENCE FOR CONCLUSION** a statement given as the evidence for a conclusion **2. BASIS OF ARGUMENT** a proposition that forms the basis of an argument or from which a conclusion is drawn ○ *I question the premise on which your whole theory is based.* ■ *v.* (**-ises, -ising, -ised**) **1.** *vt.* **SAY BY WAY OF INTRODUCTION** to state sth in advance to introduce or explain what follows (*formal*) **2.** *vti.* **PROPOSE AS PREMISE** to put forward a proposition as a premise in an argument [14thC. Via French from medieval Latin *praemissa (propositio)* '(the proposition) set before', from the past participle of *praemittere* 'to set in front', from *mittere* 'to send'.]

premises /prémmissiz/ *npl.* **1. LAND AND BUILDINGS** a piece of land and the buildings on it **2. PART OR ALL OF BUILDING** a building or part of a building, especially when used for commercial purposes **3.** LAW **MATTERS PREVIOUSLY MENTIONED** matters previously stated or referred to in a legal document such as a deed **4.** LAW **PRELIMINARY EXPLANATORY SECTION** the introductory part of a legal document, e.g. the part giving the names and other details of those concerned [15thC. From medieval Latin *praemissa* 'things stated at the beginning' (see PREMISE).]

premiss /prémmiss/ *n.* = **premise** *n.* 1, **premise** *n.* 2

premium /preèmi əm/ *n.* **1. COST OF INSURANCE** the sum of money paid, usually at regular intervals, for an insurance policy ○ *My insurance premium went up as a result of the accident.* **2. ADDITIONAL SUM** a sum of money paid in addition to a normal wage, rate, price, or other amount **3. PRIZE** an award or prize given, e.g. to the winner of a competition **4. INDUCEMENT TO BUY** a gift or reduced price offered as an incentive to purchase another product or service ○ *The manufacturer offered premiums, in the form of free merchandise and trips, for every purchase of a new car.* **5. AMOUNT ABOVE PAR VALUE** the amount above its nominal value at which sth such as a security sells **6.** *US* **EXTRA CHARGE FOR BORROWING MONEY** an amount charged in addition to interest on a loan **7. COST OF SECURITIES OPTION** the sum or cost at which a securities option is bought or sold **8. FEE FOR INSTRUCTION** a fee paid for training or apprenticeship in a profession or trade ■ *adj.* **1. HIGH-QUALITY** of very high quality **2. UNUSUALLY HIGH** higher than normal, especially in price ○ *premium petrol prices* [Early 17thC. From Latin *praemium* 'reward', from *prae-* 'pre-' + *emere* 'to take, buy' (source of English *example, exempt*, and *redeem*).] ◇ **at a premium 1.** much in demand and therefore difficult to obtain **2.** selling for a high price, or for a higher price than usual, because of scarcity ◇ **put a premium on** to place a high value on sb or sth

Premium Bond, **Premium Savings Bond** *n.* a savings bond issued by the Treasury and purchased by the public, on which no interest is paid. Instead, there are monthly draws for cash prizes.

premix *n.* /preè miks/ **PREPARED MIXTURE** a product consisting of previously mixed ingredients or elements ■ *vt.* /pree míks/ (**-mixes, -mixing, -mixed**) **COMBINE AHEAD OF TIME** to mix sth beforehand

premolar /pree mṓlər/ *n.* either of two teeth on each side of both jaws that lie immediately behind the canines and in front of the molars and are used for grinding and chewing —**premolar** *adj.*

premonition /prémmə nísh'n/ *n.* 1. INTUITION OF FUTURE EVENT a strong feeling, without a rational basis, that a particular thing is going to happen 2. WARNING ABOUT FUTURE an advance warning about a future event [Mid-16thC. Via French from, ultimately, Latin *praemonere* 'to forewarn', from *monere* 'to warn'.] —**premonitorily** /pri mónnitərəli/ *adv.* —**premonitory** /-mónnitəri/ *adj.*

prenatal /pree náyt'l/ *adj.* = **antenatal** —**prenatally** *adv.*

prenotion /prée nōsh'n/ *n.* 1. PRECONCEPTION a preconceived idea about sb or sth 2. PREMONITION a feeling that sth is about to occur or may occur [Early 17thC. From Latin *praenotionem*.]

prenuptial /pree núpsh'l/ *adj.* occurring or existing before a marriage

prenuptial agreement *n.* an agreement made between a couple before marriage relating to the arrangement of financial matters and division of property in the event of their divorce

preoccupancy /pree ókyoŏpənssi/ *n.* 1. PRIOR HABITATION occupancy of a place in advance or before sb else 2. PREOCCUPATION the state of being interested in sth, especially to the exclusion of other things

preoccupation /pri ókyoŏ páysh'n/, **preoccupancy** (*plural* **-cies**) *n.* 1. CONSTANT THOUGHT ABOUT STH constant thought about or persistent interest in sth ○ *a preoccupation with fame and fortune* 2. FOCUS OF SB'S ATTENTION a particular subject or activity that constantly occupies sb's thoughts ○ *His children are his main preoccupation at the moment.* 3. = **preoccupancy** *n.* 1 [Early 17thC. Via Latin *praeoccupationem* 'action', from *praeoccupare*.]

preoccupied /pri ókyoŏ pīd/ *adj.* 1. HAVING ATTENTION TAKEN UP WITH STH completely absorbed in doing or thinking about sth else, sometimes excessively ○ *She was too preoccupied to notice what was going on.* 2. OCCUPIED already occupied by sb or sth else ○ *a preoccupied airline seat* 3. BIOL ALREADY IN USE used to describe a scientific name that has already been used to designate a species, genus, or other taxonomic group and therefore cannot be used again

preoccupy /pri ókyoŏ pī/ (**-pies, -pying, -pied**) *vt.* 1. ABSORB SB'S THOUGHTS to fill sb's thoughts completely, sometimes excessively 2. OCCUPY BEFOREHAND to occupy sth in advance or before sb else

preop /pree óp/ *adj.* preoperative (*informal*) [Mid-20thC. Shortening.]

preoperative /pree óppərətiv/ *adj.* occurring or done before a surgical operation

preordain /prée awr dáyn/ (**-dains, -daining, -dained**) *vt.* 1. PREDESTINE to decide in advance that sth will happen, or determine sb's future, usually by fate or divine decree 2. ARRANGE IN ADVANCE to decide, determine, or arrange sth beforehand —**preordainment** *n.* —**preordination** /prée awrdi náysh'n/ *n.*

preovulatory /prée ovyoŏ laytəri/ *adj.* relating to the stage of the menstrual cycle between menstruation and ovulation, lasting from 6 to 13 days

preowned /pree ṓnd/ *adj.* US, ANZ previously owned and now for sale

prep /prep/ *n.* (*informal*) 1. HOMEWORK at a boarding school or private school, work to be done by pupils outside normal school hours 2. STUDY TIME at a boarding school, the time during which pupils do homework or prepare for lessons ○ *No talking was allowed during prep.* 3. PREPARATION preparation for activity 4. US PRIVATE SECONDARY SCHOOL a preparatory school in the United States, preparing students for college 5. US = **preppy** *n.* 2 ■ *v.* (**preps, prepping, prepped**) 1. *vi.* US PREPARE FOR STH to study or train for a particular examination, sporting event, or other activity (*informal*) 2. *vt.* SURG PREPARE SB FOR SURGERY to make a patient ready for an operation or other hospital procedure (*informal*) 3. *vt.* PAINTING PREPARE STH FOR PAINTING to prime a surface for painting ■ *adj.* PREPARATORY serving as preparation (*informal*) [Mid-19thC. Shortening of PREPARATION.]

prep. *abbr.* 1. preparation 2. preparatory 3. GRAM preposition

prepackage /pree pákij/ (**-ages, -aging, -aged**) *vt.* 1. PACKAGE BEFORE SALE to package goods before selling them 2. ARRANGE COMPLETELY BEFOREHAND to arrange all the elements of sth in advance, allowing no individual variation ○ *a prepackaged holiday*

preparation /préppə ráysh'n/ *n.* 1. PREPARING STH OR SB the work or planning involved in making sth or sb ready or in putting sth together in advance (*often used before a noun*) ○ *a preparation time of about 45 minutes* 2. READINESS a state of readiness ○ *Twenty place settings lay carefully arranged in preparation for the guests.* 3. PREPARATORY MEASURE sth done in advance in order to be ready for a future event (*often plural*) ○ *Preparations for the next Olympic Games are already under way.* 4. MIXTURE a substance, e.g. a medicine, that is made for a specific purpose by combining various ingredients ○ *a cough preparation* 5. EDUC HOMEWORK at a boarding school or private school, work to be done by pupils outside normal school hours 6. EDUC STUDY TIME at a boarding school, the time during which pupils do homework or prepare for lessons 7. MUSIC SOFTENING APPROACH TO DISSONANCE in traditional composition, a lessening of the effect of a dissonant chord by using the discordant note harmonically in a preceding chord [14thC. Via French from Latin *praeparationem*, from *praeparare* 'to prepare'.]

preparative /pri párrətiv/ *adj.* having the purpose of making sth ready or of introducing sth (*formal*) ○ *a series of preparative lectures* [15thC. Via French *préparatif* from medieval Latin *praeparativus*, from *praeparare* 'to prepare'.] —**preparatively** *adv.*

preparatory /pri párrətəri/ *adj.* 1. MAKING STH READY serving to make sth ready ○ *preparatory design work* 2. INTRODUCTORY acting as an introduction to sth [15thC. From medieval Latin *praeparatorius*, from *praeparator* 'preparer' (see PREPARE).] —**preparatorily** *adv.* ◇ **preparatory to** before or in preparation for

preparatory school *n.* 1. PRIVATE JUNIOR SCHOOL in the United Kingdom, a private, usually single-sex school that prepares students between the ages of 6 and 13 for entrance into a private boarding school 2. US PRIVATE SECONDARY SCHOOL in the United States, a private secondary school that prepares students for college, often with academic requirements for entry

prepare /pri páir/ (**-pares, -paring, -pared**) *v.* 1. *vti.* MAKE READY to make sth ready for use or action, or for a particular event or purpose ○ *preparing the aircraft for takeoff* 2. *vti.* MAKE SB READY to get ready or make sb ready for sth ○ *They prepared to go.* ○ *Prepare yourselves for a shock.* 3. *vt.* MAKE BY PUTTING THINGS TOGETHER to make sth by combining various elements or ingredients ○ *meals that can be prepared in less than half an hour* 4. *vt.* PREPLAN to plan sth in advance 5. *vt.* EQUIP to provide a person or group with necessary equipment, e.g. for a ship or an expedition 6. *vt.* MUSIC LESSEN EFFECT OF DISSONANCE to lessen the effect of a dissonant chord by using the discordant note harmonically in a preceding chord [15thC. Directly or via French from Latin *praeparare* 'to make ready beforehand', from *parare* 'to make ready'.] —**preparer** *n.*

prepared /pri páird/ *adj.* 1. ABLE AND WILLING willing and able to do sth ○ *Are you prepared to testify in court?* 2. READY AND ABLE TO DEAL WITH STH ready and able to cope with sth, often sth hard or bad ○ *The students were prepared for the last exam.* 3. MADE, OR MADE READY, BEFOREHAND made ready or put together in advance ○ *a specially prepared surface* ○ *a prepared statement* —**preparedly** /pri páiridli/ *adv.*

preparedness /pri páiridnəss/ *n.* readiness for action, especially military action

prepared piano *n.* a piano that has been modified to produce special effects, usually by placing objects on or between its strings

prepay /pree páy/ (**-pays, -paying, -paid** /-páyd/) *vt.* to pay in advance for sth, e.g. the postage on a letter or parcel —**prepayable** *adj.*

prepayment /pree páymənt/ *n.* 1. ADVANCE PAYMENT a payment made in advance, usually for a service (*often used in the plural*) 2. PAYING IN ADVANCE the act of paying for sth in advance

prepense /pri pénss/ *adj.* LAW planned or contemplated in advance (*formal*) ○ *acted with malice prepense* [Early 18thC. Alteration of *purpensed* 'premeditated', via Anglo-Norman *purpenser* 'to premeditate' from, ultimately, Latin *pensare* 'to think'.]

preponderance /pri póndərənss/, **preponderancy** /-rənssi/ *n.* (*formal*) 1. MAJORITY a large number or the majority (*takes a singular or plural verb*) ○ *A preponderance of the settlers in this area were French.* 2. DOMINANCE OR SUPERIORITY dominance or superiority in force, importance, or influence ○ *The preponderance of the evidence is in support of this theory.*

preponderant /pri póndərənt/ *adj.* greater in number, power, or importance than sth else of the same nature or class [Mid-17thC. Via Latin *praeponderantem* from *praeponderare* 'to outweigh'.] —**preponderantly** *adv.*

preponderate /pri póndə rayt/ (**-ates, -ating, -ated**) *vi.* to be greater in weight, strength, number, or importance than sth else [Early 17thC. From Latin *praeponderat-*, the past participle stem of *praeponderare* 'to weigh more', from *ponderare* 'to weigh'.] —**preponderately** /-póndərətli/ *adv.* —**preponderation** /-póndə ráysh'n/ *n.*

preposition /préppə zísh'n/ *n.* a member of a set of words used in close connection with, and usually before, nouns and pronouns to show their relation to some other part of a clause. An example is 'off' in 'He fell off his bike' and 'What did he fall off?' [14thC. From the Latin stem *praepositiōn-* 'putting before', from *praeponere* 'to put before', from *ponere* 'to put' (see POSITION).]

prepositional /préppə zísh'nəl/ *adj.* used as or belonging to a preposition —**prepositionally** *adv.*

prepositional phrase *n.* a phrase made up of a preposition followed by a noun or pronoun, e.g. 'over the hill'. Prepositional phrases can be used adverbially or adjectivally.

prepositive /pree pózzətiv/ *adj.* GRAM PLACED BEFORE WORD used to describe a word that is placed before the word it modifies ■ *n.* GRAM PREPOSITIVE TERM a prepositive word or element [Late 16thC. Formed from Latin *praepositivus*, the past participle of *praeponere* (see PREPOSITION).] —**prepositively** *adv.*

prepossess /prée pə zéss/ (**-sesses, -sessing, -sessed**) *vt.* 1. IMPRESS FAVOURABLY IN ADVANCE to make a good impression on sb before a more important moment 2. INFLUENCE BEFOREHAND to cause sb to form an opinion about sb or sth before it is necessary or appropriate to do so 3. OCCUPY SB'S MIND to occupy the thoughts of sb to an excessive degree

prepossessing /prée pə zéssing/ *adj.* creating a pleasing impression (*formal*) —**prepossessingly** *adv.* —**prepossessingness** *n.*

prepossession /prée pə zésh'n/ *n.* 1. PREJUDICE prejudice or bias towards or against a particular person or thing 2. ABSORPTION OF MIND the occupation of the mind by thoughts on a particular subject

preposterous /pri póstərəss/ *adj.* going very much against what is thought to be sensible or reasonable [Mid-16thC. From Latin *praeposterus* 'inverted', literally 'having the first thing last'. The underlying meaning is 'unnatural, perverse'.] —**preposterously** *adv.* —**preposterousness** *n.*

prepotency /pri pṓt'nssi/ (*plural* **-cies**) *n.* 1. GENETICS ABILITY TO TRANSMIT MORE GENETIC TRAITS the ability of one parent to confer more genetic traits on the offspring than the other parent 2. BOT GREATER ABILITY TO FERTILIZE PLANT the dominance of pollen from one strain over pollen from others in its ability to fertilize a plant 3. SUPERIORITY OF STRENGTH a superiority in power, force, authority, or influence

prepotent /pri pṓt'nt/ *adj.* 1. MORE POWERFUL AND INFLUENTIAL greater in power, force, or influence 2. BOT, GENETICS EXHIBITING PREPOTENCY having or exhibiting prepotency in conferring genetic traits or in fertilization [15thC. Via Latin *praepotentem* from *praeposse* 'to be more powerful', from *posse* 'to be able'.] —**prepotently** *adv.*

preppy /préppi/, **preppie** *adj.* US RELATING TO YOUNG WELL-EDUCATED AFFLUENT PEOPLE relating to or characteristic of well-educated, fairly affluent young people who are known for their neat, traditional, often expensive clothing style (*informal*) ■ *n.* (*plural* **-pies**) US (*informal*) 1. WELL-EDUCATED AFFLUENT YOUNG PERSON a young person who dresses with preppy style or behaves in a preppy manner 2. PREPARATORY SCHOOL STUDENT a young person who is studying or has studied at a preparatory school —**preppily** *adv.* —**preppiness** *n.*

preprandial /pree prándi əl/ *adj.* taking place before a meal, especially an evening meal (*formal or humorous*)

preprocess /pree prṓssess/ (**-esses, -essing, -essed**) *vt.* to analyse computer data, e.g. control statements embedded in a program, and take appropriate action before processing the data

preproduction /pree prə dúksh'n/ *n.* PRELIMINARY WORK the plans and activities, e.g. those relating to finance, equipment, and personnel, that precede the production phase of a project, especially in the entertainment and manufacturing industries ■ *adj.* **1.** HAPPENING BEFORE PRODUCTION preceding a production phase **2.** PROTOTYPIC produced as a trial or prototype

prep school *n.* a preparatory school (*informal*)

prepuberty /pree pyoobəti/ *n.* the phase of physical and emotional development that immediately precedes puberty —**prepubertal** /pree pyoobətəl/ *adj.*

prepubescent /preepyoo béss'nt/ *adj.* RELATING TO PERIOD BEFORE PUBERTY at or characteristic of the stage of life just before puberty ■ *n.* PREPUBESCENT CHILD a child at the stage of development just before puberty

prepuce /preé pyooss/ *n.* (*technical*) **1.** FORESKIN the foreskin **2.** SKIN COVERING CLITORIS the loose fold of skin that covers the tip of the clitoris [14thC. Via French from Latin *praeputium*.] —**preputial** /pri pyoosh'l/ *adj.*

prequel /preékwəl/ *n.* a film or novel set at a time preceding the action of an existing work, especially one that has achieved commercial success [Late 20thC. Blend of PRE- and SEQUEL.]

Pre-Raphaelite /preé ráffə līt, -ráffi ə-/ *n.* MEMBER OF 19C GROUP OF PAINTERS a member of a group of painters and writers **(the Pre-Raphaelite Brotherhood)** founded in 1848 with the aim of reviving the realistic style of Italian painting before Raphael. The group included Rossetti and Millais. ■ *adj.* RELATING TO PRE-RAPHAELITES relating or belonging to the Pre-Raphaelites, or characteristic of their style of painting or writing —**Pre-Raphaelitism** *n.*

prerecord /preé ri káwrd/ (**-cords, -cording, -corded**) *vt.* to record sth such as a message or television or radio programme for later use or broadcasting

prerecorded /preé ri káwrdid/ *adj.* **1.** RECORDED IN ADVANCE recorded in advance for later use or broadcasting **2.** WITH MUSIC OR FILM ALREADY RECORDED with sound or pictures already recorded on it, e.g. an audio cassette or CD

prerelease /peé ri leéss/ *n.* STH RELEASED EARLY a publication, recording, or product that is released before the appointed or official time ○ *The single is a prerelease from their forthcoming album.* ■ *adj.* BEFORE AUTHORIZED RELEASE relating to or occurring during the period before the appointed or official time of release ○ *prerelease publicity*

prerequisite /pre rékwəzit/ *n.* STH NEEDED AS PRIOR CONDITION an object, quality, or condition that is required in order for sth else to happen ○ *A degree is a prerequisite for entry into this profession.* ■ *adj.* NEEDED AS PRIOR CONDITION required in order for sth else to happen ○ *A good command of Spanish is prerequisite for the Spanish literature course.*

preretirement /preé ri tīrmənt/ *n.* the period of sb's life just before retirement (*often used before a noun*) ○ *preretirement planning*

prerogative /pri róggətiv/ *n.* **1.** PRIVILEGE RESTRICTED TO PEOPLE OF RANK an exclusive privilege or right enjoyed by a person or group occupying a particular rank or position ○ *Being the leader, it was her prerogative to choose a successor.* **2.** INDIVIDUAL RIGHT OR PRIVILEGE a privilege or right that allows a particular person or group to give orders or make decisions or judgments ○ *It's not his prerogative to say who can come.* **3.** PRIVILEGE RESULTING FROM NATURAL ADVANTAGE the right conferred by a natural advantage that places sb in a position of superiority ○ *the prerogatives conferred by age* **4.** SOVEREIGN POWER, PRIVILEGE, OR IMMUNITY the power or right of a monarch or government to do sth or be exempt from sth **5.** SUPERIORITY superiority in rank or nature [14thC. Via Old French from, ultimately, Latin *praerogare* 'to ask first', from *rogare* 'to ask'.]

pres. *abbr.* **1.** GRAM present **2.** presidential

Pres. *abbr.* President

presage /préssij/ *n.* **1.** PORTENT OR OMEN a sign or warning of a future event **2.** SENSE OF STH TO COME a feeling that a particular thing, often sth unpleasant, is about to happen **3.** FUTURE IMPORT significance with regard to future events ○ *a moment of great presage* **4.** PREDICTION a prediction of a future event (*archaic*) ■ *v.* (**presages, presaging, presaged**) **1.** *vt.* FORETELL to be or give a sign or warning of a future event ○ *Clear skies that night presaged fine weather for the picnic.* **2.** *vt.* HAVE PRESENTIMENT OF STH to know intuitively that a particular thing is going to happen **3.** *vti.* PREDICT to predict a future event [14thC. Directly or via French from, ultimately, Latin *praesagire* 'to forebode', from *sagire* 'to perceive'.] —**presager** *n.*

presale /pree sáyl/ *n.* a private sale of products, objects, or works of art that takes place before a public sale

Presb., **Presby.** *abbr.* Presbyterian

presbyopia /prézbi ṓpi ə/ *n.* progressive reduction in the eye's ability to focus, with consequent difficulty in reading at the normal distance, associated with ageing. It typically starts at middle age, and is due to age-related loss of elasticity of the lens. [Late 18thC. Coined from Greek *presbus* 'old man' (see PRESBYTER) + -OPIA.] —**presbyope** /prézbi ōp/ *n.* —**presbyopic** /prézbi óppik/ *adj.*

presbyter /prézbitər/ *n.* **1.** MEMBER OF EARLY CHURCH ADMINISTRATION in early Christianity, an administrative official of a local church **2.** MEMBER OF CLERGY an ordained member of the clergy in many Christian churches **3.** LAY OFFICIAL IN PRESBYTERIAN CHURCH any of the lay people chosen by the congregation to govern a Presbyterian or other Reformed church [Late 16thC. Via ecclesiastical Latin from Greek *presbuteros* 'elder' (source of English *priest*), from *presbus* 'old man'.]

presbyterate /prez bíttərət/ *n.* **1.** PRESBYTER'S POSITION the office or position of a presbyter **2.** GROUP OF PRESBYTERS an order or group of presbyters

presbyterial /prézbi teéri əl/ *adj.* relating to a presbyter or presbytery

presbyterian /prézbi teéri ən/ *adj.* RELATING TO ADMINISTRATION BY PRESBYTERS characterized by or relating to the government of a church by democratically elected lay officials ■ *n.* SUPPORTER OF ADMINISTRATION BY PRESBYTERS sb who supports and advocates church government by democratically elected lay officials

Presbyterian /prézbi teériən/ *adj.* RELATING TO ONE OF REFORMED CHURCHES relating or belonging to one of the Reformed churches or any of the presbyterian churches ■ *n.* PRESBYTERIAN CHURCH-MEMBER a member of a presbyterian church —**Presbyterianism** *n.*

presbytery /prézbitəri/ (*plural* **-ies**) *n.* **1.** GROUP OF PRESBYTERS a group of presbyters in the early Christian church or in a modern Presbyterian church **2.** COURT OF PRESBYTERIAN CHURCH a court composed of ministers and lay officials in a Presbyterian Church, or the churches under the jurisdiction of such a court **3.** GOVERNMENT BY PRESBYTERS the government of a church by democratically elected lay officials **4.** PART OF CHURCH FOR CLERGY part of a church or cathedral, or a separate building, for the use of clergy only **5.** HOME OF ROMAN CATHOLIC PARISH PRIEST the home of a Roman Catholic parish priest

preschool /preé skool/ *adj.* **1.** UNDER SCHOOL AGE below the age at which compulsory schooling begins **2.** FOR PRESCHOOL CHILDREN relating to or provided for children below the age at which compulsory schooling begins —**preschooling** *n.*

prescience /préssi ənss/ *n.* knowledge of actions or events before they happen [14thC. Via French from late Latin *praescientia* 'foreknowledge' (see PRESCIENT).]

prescient /préssi ənt/ *adj.* having or showing knowledge of actions or events before they take place [Early 17thC. Via Latin *praescientem* from *praescire* 'to know beforehand', from *scire* 'to know'.] —**presciently** *adv.*

prescientific /preé sī ən tíffik/ *adj.* relating to or happening during the time before the development of modern science and the application of modern scientific methods

prescind /pri sínd/ (**-scinds, -scinding, -scinded**) *vi.* to detach the mind from sth, typically a concept, notion, or fixed idea (*formal*) ○ *if we can, for a moment, prescind from a focus on motive per se and consider instead opportunity and means* [Mid-17thC. From Latin *praescindere* 'to cut off in front', from *scindere* 'to cut off'.]

prescribe /pri skríb/ (**-scribes, -scribing, -scribed**) *v.* **1.** *vti.* MED ORDER USE OF MEDICATION to direct a patient to follow a particular course of treatment, specifically to use a particular drug at set times and in specified dosages ○ *arguments that nurses should be allowed to prescribe as well as doctors* **2.** *vt.* RECOMMEND STH AS REMEDY to recommend a particular course of action or treatment as a remedy for sth ○ *I prescribe lots of tender loving care* **3.** *vt.* LAY STH DOWN AS RULE to say with authority that a certain course of action should be taken ○ *the penalties prescribed by law* **4.** *vi.* SET DOWN REGULATIONS to lay down rules or laws **5.** *vti.* LAW CLAIM PROPERTY AS RIGHT to claim a right to sth on the grounds of possession over a long period of time [15thC. From Latin *praescribere* 'to write before', from *scribere* 'to write'.] —**prescribable** *adj.* —**prescriber** *n.*

prescribed illness *n.* an illness arising from chemical hazards in the workplace, e.g. mercury poisoning, or from dangerous circumstances, e.g. decompression sickness

prescript /preéskript/ *n.* STH PRESCRIBED a rule or regulation that has been laid down (*formal*) ■ *adj.* PRESCRIBED laid down as a rule or regulation (*formal*) [Mid-16thC. From Latin *praescriptum* 'sth prescribed', the past participle of *praescribere* 'to prescribe'.]

prescription /pri skrípsh'n/ *n.* **1.** WRITTEN ORDER FOR MEDICINE a written order issued by a doctor or other qualified practitioner that authorizes a chemist to supply a particular medication for a particular patient, with instructions on its use (*often used before a noun*) **2.** PRESCRIBED MEDICINE a drug or other medication prescribed by a doctor or other qualified practitioner ○ *I've got to pick up my son's prescription.* **3.** ORDER FOR LENS TO CORRECT EYESIGHT a written order from an optometrist or ophthalmologist for glasses or contact lenses of a particular type and strength to correct the eyesight of a particular person (*often used before a noun*) ○ *prescription sunglasses* **4.** PROVEN FORMULA FOR STH a proven formula for causing sth else to happen ○ *Caring about others' feelings is a prescription for a fulfilling life.* **5.** ESTABLISHING OF REGULATIONS laying down of laws, rules, and regulations **6.** STH PRESCRIBED AS RULE a practice or course of action laid down as a regulation **7.** **prescription, positive prescription** LAW PRESUMPTION OF RIGHT OF POSSESSION a presumption of the right of possession of property, based on long-term exercise of property rights [14thC. Via French from the Latin stem *praescription-*, from *praescribere* (see PRESCRIBE).]

prescription drug *n.* a drug that can be dispensed only upon presentation of a legally valid prescription

prescriptive /pri skríptiv/ *adj.* **1.** MAKING OR ADHERING TO REGULATIONS establishing or adhering to rules and regulations ○ *prescriptive grammarians* **2.** LAW GROUNDED IN LEGAL PRESCRIPTION based on legal prescription **3.** CUSTOMARY based on or authorized by long-standing custom (*dated*) —**prescriptively** *adv.* —**prescriptiveness** *n.*

preseason /pree seéz'n/ *n.* the period just before the start of a new sporting season, during which players train intensively and play matches that are not part of a competition (*often used before a noun*) ○ *a preseason game*

preselect /preési lékt/ (**-lects, -lecting, -lected**) *vt.* to select a person, object, place, or course of action in advance, usually on the basis of specific requirements

presell /pree sél/ (**-sells, -selling, -sold, -sold**) *vt.* **1.** MARKETING POPULARIZE STH BEFOREHAND to promote a product or entertainment before it is generally available to the public, by means of advertising and publicity **2.** PUBL SELL BOOK EARLY to sell a book before its official publication date **3.** COMM ARRANGE SALE OF STH BEFOREHAND to agree to sell a house, car, or other item before it is actually available

presence /prézz'ns/ *n.* **1.** BEING PRESENT the physical existence of sb or sth in a particular place ○ *Our presence is requested at the board meeting.* **2.** AREA WITHIN SIGHT OR EARSHOT the immediate vicinity of sb or sth ○ *How dare you use that kind of language in my presence!* **3.** PERSONAL DIGNITY dignified appearance and bearing ○ *has a certain presence about her that garners respect* **4.** IMPRESSIVE PERSON sb who inspires awe and respect **5.** INVISIBLE SUPPOSED SUPERNATURAL BEING a supernatural spirit that is felt to be nearby ○ *a malevolent presence filled the room* **6.** PERSON PRESENT sb who is present in a particular place ○ *the venerable scholar, a dignified presence in the academic procession* **7.** ARTS ABILITY TO CAPTIVATE AUDIENCE a quality of certain performers that enables them to achieve a rapport with and hold the attention of their audiences **8.** STATIONING OF PERSONNEL the existence of official personnel in a place, especially police, military, or diplomatic personnel ○ *maintained a heavy military, diplomatic, and intelligence presence in the capital* [14thC. Via French from Latin *praesentia*, from *praesent-* (see PRESENT[2]).]

presence chamber *n.* the room in which a ruler or other important person receives guests and holds assemblies

presence of mind *n.* the ability to remain calm and act decisively and effectively in a crisis ○ *At least she had the presence of mind to call the fire brigade.*

present[1] *v.* /pri zént/ (**-sents, -senting, -sented**) **1.** *vt.* GIVE SB STH to give sth to sb, often in a formal manner ○ *Then she presented me with the bill!* **2.** *vt.* MAKE AWARD TO SB to make a gift or award of sth to sb **3.** *vt.* OFFER STH FORMALLY to offer formally sth such as compliments or apologies to sb (*formal*) ○ *May I present my warmest congratulations?* **4.** *vt.* MAKE STH VISIBLE IN PARTICULAR WAY to show or display sth in a particular way ○ *taking care to present his best side to the camera* **5.** *vt.* HAND STH OVER OFFICIALLY to put sth forward for inspection or consideration, typically in a formal or official manner or capacity ○ *proposals to be presented at the next meeting* **6.** *vt.* POSE STH AS PROBLEM to pose a problem or difficulty to sb ○ *presenting a direct threat to national security* **7.** *vt.* LAW PUT STH BEFORE COURT to submit a criminal charge to a court for consideration and judgment **8.** *vt.* LAW BRING CHARGE to put a charge before a court of law so that it can be considered or tried **9.** *vt.* INTRODUCE WOMAN INTO SOCIETY to introduce a young woman formally into fashionable society ○ *Her family planned to present her at the Christmas debutante ball in New York.* **10.** *vt.* INTRODUCE SB FORMALLY to introduce sb formally, especially to sb of higher rank ○ *They were presented to the Queen.* **11.** *vt.* BE HOST OF PROGRAMME to introduce, or act as the host of, a television or radio programme or an infomercial ○ *He used to present a game show on ITV.* **12.** *vt.* OFFER STH AS PUBLIC ENTERTAINMENT to bring a film, play, or other form of entertainment to the public **13.** *vt.* PORTRAY STH ARTISTICALLY to represent sth or sb in a particular way in the arts ○ *In the film, Romeo and Juliet are presented as modern teenagers.* **14.** *vr.* BE IN APPOINTED PLACE to appear, especially at an appointed time and place ○ *Present yourselves at the gate at eight o'clock.* **15.** *vr.* ARISE to come into being or happen ○ *when an opportunity presents itself* **16.** *vi.* MED HAVE PARTICULAR SYMPTOMS to exhibit the specified symptom or symptoms on examination ○ *Monday, July 5th: The patient presents with arrhythmia and complains of arthralgia.* **17.** *vi.* MED EXIT BIRTH CANAL IN POSITION to appear during the process of being born (*refers to a foetus*) ○ *In most births, the first part to present is the back of the head.* **18.** *vi.* PRODUCE SPECIFIED IMPRESSION to produce a particular impression, especially a favourable one (*formal*) ○ *She presents as a pleasant young woman.* ■ *n.* /prézz'nt/ GIFT sth that is given to sb out of kindness or to celebrate an occasion such as a birthday [13thC. Via French from Latin *praesentare* 'to make present', from *praesent-* (see PRESENT[2]).]

WORD KEY: SYNONYMS

See Synonyms at ***give***.

present[2] /prézz'nt/ *adj.* **1.** CURRENTLY HAPPENING taking place or existing now ○ *in our present circumstances* **2.** IN A PLACE in a particular place ○ *There were over a hundred people present at the reception* **3.** NOW UNDER DISCUSSION being considered or talked about at this time **4.** GRAM RELATING TO CURRENT TIME used to describe a verb form or tense that expresses the current time **5.** AT HAND readily available (*archaic*) **6.** ON HAND TO ACT ready to take action (*archaic*) ■ *n.* **1.** THE HERE AND NOW the current time or moment ○ *The story takes place in the present.* **2.** GRAM CURRENT-TIME VERB TENSE the verb tense that expresses current time **3.** GRAM CURRENT-TIME VERB a verb in the present tense, indicating that the action is happening now [13thC. Via French from Latin *praesent-*, the present participle stem of *praeesse* 'to be in front of', from *esse* 'to be'.] ◇ **at present** just now ◇ **for the present** as far as the present time is concerned

presentable /pri zéntəb'l/ *adj.* **1.** FIT TO APPEAR IN PUBLIC looking or being good enough to be introduced to other people ○ *Make sure you look presentable.* **2.** FIT TO BE DISPLAYED OR GIVEN good enough to be offered, shown, or given to other people ○ *still a presentable gift* —**presentability** /pri zéntə bílləti/ *n.* —**presentableness** /-zéntəb'lnəss/ *n.* —**presentably** /-zéntəbli/ *adv.*

present arms *n.* a drill movement in which a salute is given by bringing a rifle vertically in front of the body, or the command to give such a salute — **present arms** *vi.*

presentation /prézz'n táysh'n/ *n.* **1.** ACT OF PRESENTING STH an act of presenting sth or the state of being presented **2.** WAY STH APPEARS WHEN OFFERED the manner in which sth is shown, expressed, or laid out for other people to see ○ *Presentation is an important part of the chef's job.* **3.** PREPARED REPORT READ BEFORE AUDIENCE a formal talk made to a group of people, e.g. on sb's recent work or some aspect of business, often with handouts, diagrams, or other visual aids ○ *He gave a presentation on modern irrigation methods.* **4.** PREPARED PERFORMANCE FOR AUDIENCE a performance, exhibition, or demonstration put on before an audience **5.** FORMAL HANDING-OVER OF GIFT the action of presenting sb with an award or a token of appreciation in front of other people, or an occasion when this is done ○ *the presentation of the trophy* **6.** MED PART OF BABY APPEARING FIRST the part of a baby that appears first at birth, normally the crown of the head ○ *a breech presentation* **7.** SB'S INTRODUCTION INTO SPECIAL SOCIAL GROUP an occasion when sb is first presented at court or into society, or the official or recognized process of first presenting sb in this way **8.** CHR ACT OF NOMINATING CLERGY MEMBER the act or power of nominating a member of the clergy to a particular paid office in a church **9.** OBJECT OF PERCEPTION sth that is perceived, remembered, or acquired as knowledge **10.** = **presentment** *n.* 3 —**presentational** *adj.*

presentationism /prézz'n táysh'nizzəm/ *n.* the theory that things in the external world are identical with people's perceptions of them —**presentationist** *n.*

Presentation of the Virgin Mary *n.* the Roman Catholic festival that commemorates the Virgin Mary's presentation at the temple, held on 21 November

presentative /pri zéntətiv/ *adj.* able to be known directly without any reflective or cognitive process being necessary —**presentativeness** *n.*

present-day *adj.* found or existing in modern times ○ *out of touch with present-day society and the TV culture*

presentee /prézz'n tee/ *n.* (*formal*) **1.** SB WHO IS PRESENTED TO OTHERS sb who is introduced in a formal or official way **2.** SB WHO IS GIVEN STH sb who is presented with sth formally, e.g. an award or prize, or a gift from a large body of other people

presenter /pri zéntər/ *n.* **1.** TV OR RADIO ANNOUNCER sb who introduces a particular programme on television or radio and provides comments linking individual items or contributors during the programme ○ *a local radio presenter* **2.** SB WHO PRESENTS STH sb who presents sth, e.g. an award or a gift (*formal*) **3.** INFOMERCIAL SALESPERSON sb who presents and discusses a particular product during a television infomercial

presentient /pri sénshənt, pree sénshənt/ *adj.* having a definite and usually uneasy sense that sth is going to happen, or being aware of sth before it occurs (*formal*) [Early 19thC. From, ultimately, Latin *praesentire* 'to perceive beforehand', which was formed from *sentire* 'to feel'.]

presentiment /pri zéntimənt/ *n.* an awareness of some event, especially an unpleasant event, before it takes place and before there is any reason to suspect it or know about it ○ *She had a presentiment that something terrible would happen.* [Early 18thC. Via obsolete French *présentiment* from, ultimately, Latin *praesentire* (see PRESENTIENT).] —**presentimental** /pri zénti mént'l/ *adj.*

presently /prézz'ntli/ *adv.* **1.** SOON not at this exact moment but in a short while ○ *I'll be there presently.* **2.** AT THE PRESENT TIME now, or during the current period (*some people object to this usage*) ○ *Yes, he's presently engaged in a research job for the company.* **3.** STRAIGHT AWAY immediately and without delay (*archaic*)

presentment /pri zéntmənt/ *n.* **1.** PRESENTATION the act of presenting sth or the way in which sth is presented **2.** STATEMENT BY JURY in the past, a formal statement made on oath by a jury to a court concerning facts and matters within their own knowledge **3.** PRESENTING OF NEGOTIABLE INSTRUMENT the presenting of a negotiable instrument for payment

present participle *n.* the form of a verb that suggests a continuous or active sense and that ends in '-ing' in English, e.g. 'flying'

present perfect *n.* the form of a verb that suggests sth completed, in English by preceding the verb with 'have' or 'has' and usually putting '-ed' after it, e.g. 'have departed' —**present perfect** *adj.*

presents /prézz'nts/ *npl.* the words that are used in a legal or formal document (*formal*)

present tense *n.* the tense of a verb that suggests actions or the situation at the time of speaking or writing

present value *n.* the value now of a sum of money expected to be received in the future, calculated by subtracting the interest and other value that will accrue in the intervening period

preservable /pri zúrvəb'l/ *adj.* able to be kept safe, unchanged, or unspoilt ○ *The east wing is preservable but the rest of the building will have to be demolished.* —**preservability** /pri zúrvə bílləti/ *n.* — **preservably** /pri z/ *adv.*

preservation /préssər váysh'n/ *n.* **1.** PROTECTION FROM HARM the guarding of sth from danger, harm, or injury **2.** KEEPING OF STH UNCHANGED maintenance of sth, especially sth of historic value, in an unchanged condition **3.** UPHOLDING OF STH the keeping of sth intangible intact ○ *preservation of freedom of speech*

preservationist /prézzər váysh'nist/ *n.* sb who tries to prevent things from being damaged, destroyed, or altered from their current condition, particularly things of natural or historical interest —**preservationism** *n.*

preservative /pri zúrvətiv/ *adj.* ABLE TO KEEP FROM DECAY having the ability to protect sth from decay or spoilage ■ *n.* STH THAT PREVENTS SPOILAGE sth that provides protection from decay or spoilage, e.g. a food additive

preserve /pri zúrv/ *vt.* (**-serves, -serving, -served**) **1.** MAKE SURE STH LASTS to keep sth protected from anything that would cause its current quality or condition to change or deteriorate or fall out of use ○ *They are anxious to preserve the area's rural character.* ○ *We need to preserve professional standards of conduct.* **2.** MAINTAIN STH TO keep up or maintain sth ○ *She preserved a cool and composed manner throughout the interrogation.* **3.** STOP FOOD GOING BAD to treat or store food in such a way as to protect it from decay, e.g. by pickling, drying, salting, freezing, or canning **4.** MAKE JAM to make jam or marmalade **5.** PROTECT SB OR STH to protect sb or sth from danger, especially the danger of being killed or damaged (*formal or literary*) ○ *'The Lord shall preserve thee from all evil'* (*Psalm 121*) **6.** KEEP ANIMALS IN SECURE AREA to rear wild animals, especially fish and birds, in a protected area of water or land, so that they can be fished or shot for sport in the hunting season ■ *n.* **1.** EXCLUSIVE AREA OF ACTIVITY a type of work, sport, or interest that one particular person or group retains exclusive use of, or a place kept for one person or group to enjoy exclusively ○ *The children considered the treehouse their own preserve and resented adults intruding.* **2.** FOOD FRUIT JAM a sweet thick substance eaten on bread or in desserts and cakes, made by boiling fruit in sugar and water. Preserves can be kept for several years in airtight jars, bottles, or cans. (*often used in the plural*) **3.** *US* = **reserve** *n.* 2 **4.** **AREA FOR PRIVATE HUNTING** an area where game is kept for private hunting [14thC. Via French *préserver* from medieval Latin *praeservare* 'to guard beforehand', from Latin *servare* 'to keep'. Ultimately from an Indo-European word meaning 'to protect'.]

preserver /pri zúrvər/ *n.* sth used to keep sb or sth safe, undamaged, or unchanged

preset /pree sét/ *vt.* (**-sets, -setting, -set**) **SET MACHINE TO COME ON LATER** to arrange the settings of a timing device controlling or built into an electrical appliance so that the appliance is automatically switched on at a specified time ○ *The central heating is preset to come on in the morning and evening.* ■ *n.* **GADGET THAT TURNS MACHINE ON LATER** an electronic timing device or system that is used to make an appliance operate at a later time

preshrunk /preé shrúngk/ *adj.* with the fabric already shrunk before being sold, so that it will not shrink when the consumer washes it

preside /pri zíd/ (**-sides, -siding, -sided**) *vi.* **1.** **BE OFFICIALLY IN CHARGE** to be the chairperson or hold a similar position of authority at a formal gathering of people **2.** **HAVE CONTROL** to be the most powerful person or the one everyone else obeys, usually in a specified place or situation ○ *the question of who will preside over the business once their mother retires* **3.** **MUSIC PERFORM AS INSTRUMENTALIST** to be the featured instrumentalist in a performance ○ *preside at the organ* [Early 17thC. Via French *présider* from Latin *praesidere*, literally 'to sit in front of', from *sedere* 'to sit'.] —**presider** *n.*

presidency /prézzidənssi/ (*plural* **-cies**) *n.* **1.** **POSITION OF PRESIDENT OF NATION** the job or function of president of a republic, or a president's term of office **2.** **JOB OF PRESIDENT** the status, post, or function of being president of a company, society, institution, or similar body ○ *The presidency of the club turned out to be a thankless task.* **3.** **LATTER-DAY SAINTS COUNCIL** a three-person executive council in the Church of Jesus Christ of Latter-day Saints **4.** **LATTER-DAY SAINTS GOVERNING COUNCIL** the governing body of the Church of Jesus Christ of Latter-day Saints

president /prézzidənt/ *n.* **1.** **HEAD OF STATE OF A REPUBLIC** the chief politician of a republic, e.g. the United States of America ○ *President Kennedy was shot in 1963.* **2.** **HIGHEST-RANKING MEMBER OF AN ASSOCIATION** sb who holds the top official position in an organization, club, or society ○ *president of the Lawn Tennis Association* **3.** *US* **HEAD OF A COMPANY** the highest-ranking executive officer of a business or corporation **4.** **HEAD OF EDUCATIONAL ESTABLISHMENT** the highest-ranking executive officer of certain universities and colleges **5.** **SB IN CHARGE OF A MEETING** sb who has been appointed or elected to take charge at a formal gathering of people **6.** **LATTER-DAY SAINTS LEADER** in the Church of Jesus Christ of Latter-day Saints, a man who is a member of the church's governing board. He, together with counsellors and the Council of the Twelve Apostles, makes major church policy and decisions. [14thC. Via French *président* from, ultimately, Latin *praesidere* (see PRESIDE).] —**presidentship** *n.*

president-elect (*plural* **presidents-elect**) *n.* sb who has been elected or appointed as president but who has not yet been officially installed into the job

presidential /prézzi dénsh'l/ *adj.* **1.** **RELATING TO PRESIDENT** concerning the post of president, or used or owned by a president ○ *The presidential elections dominated the news.* **2.** **LED BY A PRESIDENT** presided over by a president, or presiding like one —**presidentially** *adv.*

presidio /pri síddi ō, pri zíddi ō/ (*plural* **-os**) *n.* a fortified settlement, especially of the type established by Spanish colonizers in the southwestern part of what is now the United States [Mid-18thC. Via Spanish from Latin *praesidium* 'garrison, fortification', from *praesidere* (see PRESIDE).]

presidium /pri síddi əm, -zíddi-/ (*plural* **-ums** *or* **-a** /-di ə/), **praesidium** (*plural* **-ums** *or* **-a**) *n.* a permanent executive committee that acted for a larger legislature in the former Soviet Union and other Communist countries [Early 20thC. Via Russian from Latin *praesidium* (see PRESIDIO).]

PRESIDENTS OF THE UNITED STATES

Term of office	President	Political party
1789–1797	George Washington	
1797–1801	John Adams	*Federalist*
1801–1809	Thomas Jefferson	*Democratic-Republican*
1809–1817	James Madison	*Democratic-Republican*
1817–1825	James Monroe	*Democratic-Republican*
1825–1829	John Quincy Adams	*Democratic-Republican*
1829–1837	Andrew Jackson	*Democrat*
1837–1841	Martin Van Buren	*Democrat*
1841	William Henry Harrison	*Whig*
1841–1845	John Tyler	*Whig*
1845–1849	James Polk	*Democrat*
1849–1850	Zachary Taylor	*Whig*
1850–1853	Millard Fillmore	*Whig*
1853–1857	Franklin Pierce	*Democrat*
1857–1861	James Buchanan	*Democrat*
1861–1865	Abraham Lincoln	*Republican*
1865–1869	Andrew Johnson	*Democrat*
1869–1877	Ulysses S. Grant	*Republican*
1877–1881	Rutherford B. Hayes	*Republican*
1881	James Garfield	*Republican*
1881–1885	Chester A. Arthur	*Republican*
1885–1889	Grover Cleveland	*Democrat*
1889–1893	Benjamin Harrison	*Republican*
1893–1897	Grover Cleveland	*Democrat*
1897–1901	William McKinley	*Republican*
1901–1909	Theodore Roosevelt	*Republican*
1909–1913	William Howard Taft	*Republican*
1913–1921	Woodrow Wilson	*Democrat*
1921–1923	Warren G. Harding	*Republican*
1923–1929	Calvin Coolidge	*Republican*
1929–1933	Herbert Hoover	*Republican*
1933–1945	Franklin Delano Roosevelt	*Democrat*
1945–1953	Harry S. Truman	*Democrat*
1953–1961	Dwight D. Eisenhower	*Republican*
1961–1963	John F. Kennedy	*Democrat*
1963–1969	Lyndon Johnson	*Democrat*
1969–1974	Richard Nixon	*Republican*
1974–1977	Gerald Ford	*Republican*
1977–1981	Jimmy Carter	*Democrat*
1981–1989	Ronald Reagan	*Republican*
1989–1993	George Bush	*Republican*
1993–	Bill Clinton	*Democrat*

presignify /pree sígni fī/ (**-fies, -fying, -fied**) *vt.* to indicate in advance sth that is going to result or take place (*formal*)

Elvis Presley

Presley /prézzli/, **Elvis** (1935–77) US singer and actor. Renowned as a pioneer of rock-and-roll, he also acted in several Hollywood films. Full name **Elvis Aron Presley**. Known as **The King**

press[1] /press/ *v.* (**presses, pressing, pressed**) **1.** *vti.* **PUSH AGAINST STH** to use a steady and significant force to put weight on sth, sometimes to make it move or start working ○ *I got into the lift and pressed the down button but nothing happened.* **2.** *vt.* **SQUEEZE JUICE OUT OF STH** to squeeze the juice or oil out of sth using force or weight to compress it ○ *pressing grapes* **3.** *vt.* **SMOOTH STH OUT** to push a flat object, especially a hot iron, onto a garment or piece of cloth so as to smooth out unwanted creases or make a crease where desired ○ *pressed a shirt and put it on* **4.** *vt.* **CHANGE STH'S SHAPE BY SQUEEZING** to change the shape of sth by squeezing it or putting a steady weight on it, especially in order to make it more compact ○ *pressed the clay into a ball* **5.** *vt.* **HOLD SB OR STH TIGHTLY** to grip or clasp sb or sth firmly but not roughly with the hands or arms, especially to show affection or moral support ○ *She pressed his hand in sym-*

pathy. **6.** *vt.* **FORCE SB TO DO STH** to force sb into doing sth he or she did not want or intend to do ○ *They pressed her into standing for the election.* **7.** *vt.* **TRY TO OBTAIN STH FROM SB** to ask sb persistently or forcefully to supply, accept, or do a specific thing ○ *They pressed him for an immediate response.* **8.** *vt.* **EMPHASIZE STH** to make sure that sth is fully recognized and understood, or stress its importance ○ *It is vital that you press the main items of the manifesto in your speech.* **9.** *vt.* **DEMAND STH** to plead or demand sth insistently **10.** *vti.* **PESTER SB** to pester or worry sb continually (*dated or literary*) ○ *They pressed her every day until she agreed to go with them.* **11.** *vi.* **MOVE AS CROWD** to crowd around or together (*literary*) ○ *The crowd pressed forward as the gates opened.* **12.** *vi.* **REQUIRE ATTENTION** to need to be dealt with urgently (*dated or formal*) ○ *I'd like to help now, but business presses.* **13.** *vt.* **DRY STH OUT AND PRESERVE IT** to flatten and dry a natural object such as a flower so that it does not decompose and can be kept or used decoratively ○ *pressed flowers as a hobby* **14.** *vt.* **MAKE STH WITH A MOULD** to form sth in a mould, especially to make gramophone records ○ *went down to the studio to press a record* **15.** *vti.* **BASKETBALL HARASS BASKETBALL OPPONENT** to use a harassing and aggressive defence against an opponent in basketball ■ *n.* **ACT OF PRESSING 1.** an act of pressing sth ○ *I gave the doorbell a few presses but nobody answered.* **2.** **CROWD** a tightly-packed crowd of people **3.** **POWERFUL MOVEMENT** the crowding and pressing together of a lot of people or things at the same time (*literary*) ○ *He could not move because of the press of people.* **4.** **DEVICE FOR SQUEEZING STH** a piece of equipment designed to crush sth to release the juices or create a pulp ○ *a garlic press* **5.** **DEVICE FOR FLATTENING STH** a piece of equipment used to keep or make sth smooth and uncreased **6.** **HOUSEHOLD LINEN CUPBOARD** a shelved cupboard, usually of a large size, for storing bed or table linens or clothes **7.** **MECH ENG MACHINE THAT APPLIES MECHANICAL PRESSURE** a machine that, by applying pressure to a piece of metal or other material, can shape, form, cut, stamp, or otherwise cause a physical change to occur **8.** **PRESS NEWSPAPERS OR NEWS REPORTERS** the newsgathering business generally or all the people involved in gathering and reporting on the news, but in particular journalists working on newspapers ○ *She agreed to appear on television but refused to talk to the press.* **9.** PRESS **COMMENTS BY JOURNALISTS** the opinions expressed in articles or reviews in the newspapers or magazines ○ *His new musical had a lot of good press.* **10.** PRINTING = **printing press 11.** PUBL **PUBLISHING COMPANY** a company that publishes books (*used especially in names*) **12.** PRINTING **BUSINESS OR SKILL OF PRINTING** the technical or physical process used by a printer and the skills a printer requires **13.** RACKET GAMES **CLAMP FOR RACKETS** a clamp for holding a tennis or other racket to prevent it from warping when it is not in use **14.** SPORTS **DEFENCE IN SPORT** an aggressive defence, especially in basketball **15.** **LIFTING OF WEIGHT ABOVE HEAD** in weightlifting, a lift in which the weight is raised to shoulder height and then to above the head without moving the legs [14thC. Via French *presser* from Latin *pressare* 'to keep on pressing', from *press-*, the past participle stem of *premere* 'to press'.] —**presser** *n.* ◇ **be pressed for sth** to be short of sth, usually time

WORD KEY: ORIGIN

The Latin word *pressare*, from which **press** is derived, is also the source of English *compress, depress, express, impress, oppress, repress,* and *suppress*.

press for *vt.* to seek or demand sth with great urgency ○ *They pressed for an immediate review of the situation.*

press on *vi.* to continue in an urgent or persistent manner ○ *Night was falling but they pressed on despite their weariness.*

press[2] /press/ *vt.* (**presses, pressing, pressed**) **1.** **FORCE SB INTO MILITARY SERVICE** to forcibly recruit sb into military service **2.** **USE STH FOR NEW PURPOSE** to take sth out of its intended place or function and make use of it in a different way (*literary*) ■ *n.* **FORCING OF SB INTO MILITARY SERVICE** the act of recruiting people into military service by force [Late 16thC. Alteration (influenced by PRESS[1]) of obsolete *prest* 'to enlist by paying in advance', via Old French *prester* from Latin *praestare*, literally 'to stand before', from *stare* 'to stand'.]

press agency *n.* = **news agency**

press agent *n.* sb who is responsible for promoting clients by contacting and liaising with the press, and supplying the press with information, advertising material, photographs, and stories about them

Press Association *n.* the national news agency for the United Kingdom and Ireland

press box *n.* a section in a sports stadium or similar venue kept exclusively for journalists to work in

Pressburger /préss burgər/, **Emeric** (1902–88) Hungarian-born British film director. In partnership with Michael Powell, he made a number of films exploring complex moral themes, including *Black Narcissus* (1946). Real name **Imre Pressburger**

press conference *n.* an invited meeting for members of the press to enable them to hear a prepared statement by sb in the news, and usually to ask questions about that statement

pressed /prest/ *adj.* **1.** **PROCESSED AND PACKED INTO TIGHT SHAPE** made compact and firm by being forced mechanically into cans or containers ○ *pressed meat* **2.** **BUSY AND UNDER STRAIN** having urgent or worrying things to deal with ○ *She is particularly pressed today, so I won't ask her to help if I can avoid it.*

press gallery *n.* a raised gallery with seating at the back of a courtroom or legislative assembly room, where newspaper reporters and other members of the press can sit

press gang *n.* in former times, a group of military personnel whose job was to find people to force into military service

press-gang *vti.* to force people into military service or into doing anything that they are reluctant to do ○ *I never wanted to go to camp – my parents press-ganged me into it.*

pressie *n.* = **prezzie**

pressing /préssing/ *adj.* **1.** **URGENT** needing to be attended to without delay ○ *He had a pressing engagement and had to leave immediately.* **2.** **VERY PERSISTENT** persistent and demanding, and therefore difficult to ignore or refuse ○ *Her invitations were so pressing that we eventually had to accept.* ■ *n.* **GRAMOPHONE RECORDS MADE AT ONE TIME** all the gramophone records produced at one time from a master mould —**pressingly** *adv.* —**pressingness** *n.*

press kit *n.* a package of background and promotional material relating to a product, distributed to the media by a press agent or publicity department

pressman /préss man, -mən/ (*plural* **-men** /-men, -mən/) *n.* **1.** **JOURNALIST** a man working as a newspaper reporter (*dated*) **2.** **OPERATOR OF PRINTING PRESS** sb who operates a printing press

pressmark /préss maark/ *n.* a mark on a book denoting where it should be placed in a library

press of sail *n.* the largest amount of sail that a ship can safely carry

pressor /préssər/ *adj.* relating to or bringing about an increase in blood pressure

press release *n.* an official statement or account of a news story that is specially prepared and issued to newspapers and other news media for them to make known to the public

pressroom /préss room, préssrōōm/ *n.* an enclosed area in a newspaper plant or printing works where the presses are located

pressrun /préss run/ *n.* **1.** **CONTINUOUS RUNNING OF PRINTING PRESS** the continuous running of a printing press until a specified number of copies is printed **2.** **NUMBER OF COPIES RUN** the number of copies run off in a continuous printing operation

press secretary *n.* an employee responsible for managing the news media on behalf of an organization or a prominent individual

press stud *n.* a manufactured device with two halves that push tightly into each other, generally used instead of a button to keep a piece of clothing fastened. US term **snap**

press-up *n. UK, NZ* any one of a series of identical exercise movements performed with the body straight and facing the floor. The arms are used to raise the body and then lower it again. ◊ **pushup**

pressure /préshər/ *n.* **1.** **PROCESS OF PRESSING STEADILY** the applying of a firm regular weight or force against sth or sb ○ *The pressure of her hand on his was comforting.* **2.** **CONSTANT STATE OF WORRY AND URGENCY** powerful and stressful demands on sb's time, attention, and energy, or one of many demands of this sort **3.** **FORCE THAT PUSHES OR URGES** sth that affects thoughts and behaviour in a powerful way, usually in the form of several outside influences working together persuasively **4.** PHYS **FORCE PER UNIT AREA** the force acting on a surface divided by the area over which it acts. Symbol *p* **5.** = **compression 6.** **ATMOSPHERIC PRESSURE** atmospheric pressure ■ *vt.* (**-sures, -suring, -sured**) **MAKE SB DO STH** to apply great persuasion or a strong influence on sb to force him or her to do sth [14thC. From Latin *pressura*, which was formed from the stem *press-* (see PRESS).] —**pressureless** *adj.*

pressure cabin *n.* an airtight cabin in an aircraft or spacecraft in which air pressure is maintained at a greater level than that of the outside atmospheric pressure for the comfort and safety of the occupants

pressure-cook *vt.* to cook sth in a pressure cooker

pressure cooker *n.* a specially-designed pan used to steam food at high pressure, at a higher temperature and in a shorter time than by boiling

pressure gauge *n.* a device or instrument used to measure the pressure of a gas or liquid, e.g. a gauge that measures the air pressure in the tyres of a car

pressure group *n.* a number of people who work together to make their particular concerns known to those in government, and to influence the passage of legislation

pressure point *n.* any point at which an artery can be compressed against a bone using a finger, so stemming blood flow to the part of the body that the artery supplies. Compression of such a point can, at certain sites, reduce bleeding from a wound.

pressure sore *n.* = **bedsore**

pressure suit *n.* an inflatable airtight suit, similar to that worn by deep sea divers, used to protect against the effects of low pressure at very high altitude or in space

pressure vessel *n.* a cylindrical or spherically shaped container designed to withstand bursting pressures

pressurize /préshə rīz/ (**-izes, -izing, -ized**), **pressurise** (**-ises, -ising, -ised**) *vt.* **1.** **INCREASE AIR PRESSURE IN ENCLOSED SPACE** to increase the air pressure in an enclosed space, e.g. inside an aircraft, to maintain air at close to normal atmospheric pressure when the external pressure falls **2.** **INCREASE AIR PRESSURE IN CONTAINER** to increase the air pressure in a container beyond normal levels **3.** **MAKE SB DO STH** to apply great persuasion or a strong influence on people to force them, or try to force them, to do sth they would not otherwise have done ○ *colleagues who had pressurized me to apply for membership* **4.** **PUT FLUID UNDER PRESSURE** to apply increased pressure to a fluid —**pressurization** /préshə rī záysh'n/ *n.* —**pressurizer** /préshə rīzər/ *n.*

presswoman /préss wōōmən/ *n.* a woman working as a newspaper reporter (*dated*)

presswork /préss wurk/ *n.* the operation, management, or work done by a printing press

Prestel /préss tel/ *tdmk.* a trademark for a British Telecom service that provides information to subscribers on a television screen

Prester John *n.* a Christian priest-king who was believed to rule over a vast kingdom of great wealth in Asia or Africa during the Middle Ages [From Old French *prestre Jehan* and medieval Latin *presbyter Johannes* 'John the priest']

prestidigitation /présti dĭjji táysh'n/ *n.* sleight of hand used in performing magic tricks (*formal*) [Mid-19thC. From French, from *prestidigitateur* 'person practising sleight of hand', from *preste* 'nimble' + Latin *digitus* 'finger' (source of English *digit*).] —**prestidigitator** /présti dĭjji taytər/ *n.*

prestige /pre stéezh, -stéej/ *n.* **1.** **RESPECT ASSOCIATED WITH HIGH QUALITY** the kind of honour, awe, or high opinion that is inspired by a high-ranking, influential, or successful person or product **2.** **GLAMOUR** the kind of attractiveness and importance that is very obvious or enviable, associated with wealthy and successful people ○ *It's a prestige car and its price reflects that.* [Mid-17thC. Via French from Latin *praestigiae* 'illusions, juggler's tricks', of uncertain origin: probably ultimately from *praestringere* 'to make dull, confuse', from *stringere* 'to bind tight'.]

prestigious /pre stĭjjəss/ *adj.* having a distinguished reputation or bringing prestige to the person who has it —**prestigiously** *adv.* —**prestigiousness** *n.*

prestissimo /pre stíssi mō/ *adv.* **EXTREMELY FAST** played or to be played as fast as possible (*used especially as a musical direction*) ■ *n.* (*plural* **-mos**) **EXTREMELY FAST MUSICAL PIECE** a musical composition or passage that is meant to be played as fast as possible [Early 18thC. From Italian, the superlative of *presto* 'presto'.] —**prestissimo** *adj.*

presto /préstō/ *adv.* MUSIC **VERY FAST** played or to be played very fast (*used as a musical direction*) ■ *n.* (*plural* **-tos**) **VERY FAST MUSICAL PIECE** a musical composition or passage that is meant to be played very fast ■ *adv.* **SUDDENLY** instantly, as if magically (*informal*) [Late 16thC. Via Italian 'quick', from, ultimately, Latin *praesto* 'at hand'.] —**presto** *adj.*

Preston /préstən/ town and seaport in northwestern England, in Lancashire. It is the county's administrative centre. Population: 134,300 (1995).

Preston, Margaret Rose (1875–1963) Australian artist. Sometimes influenced by Aboriginal art, her paintings, engravings, and woodcuts are executed in a bold, decorative style.

prestress /pree stréss/ (**-stresses, -stressing, -stressed**) *vt.* to apply stress to sth such as a cable or beam so that it will bear a load better when in use

prestressed concrete /préé strest-/ *n.* concrete that is cast over cables that are under tension, so as to increase its strength

Prestwich /préstwich/ industrial town 8 km/5 mi. northwest of Manchester, England. Population: 31,801 (1991).

Prestwick /préstwik/ town near Ayr, Scotland, on the Firth of Clyde. It is home to an international airport. Population: 13,705 (1991).

presumable /pri zyóoməb'l/ *adj.* probable, or capable of being assumed to be true

presumably /pri zyóoməbli/ *adv.* used to show that you expect that a specified thing is the case or will happen or has happened ○ *Presumably that man is her father.*

presume /pri zyóom/ (**-sumes, -suming, -sumed**) *v.* **1.** *vti.* **BELIEVE STH TO BE TRUE** to accept that sth is virtually certain to be correct even though there is no proof of it, on the grounds that it is extremely likely ○ *After several days of searching, they presumed that there were no survivors.* **2.** *vi.* **BEHAVE ARROGANTLY OR OVERCONFIDENTLY** to behave so inconsiderately, disrespectfully, or overconfidently as to do sth without being entitled or qualified to do it (*usually used negatively*) ○ *I would never presume to tell you how to run your business.* **3.** *vt.* **REGARD STH AS TRUE WITHOUT PROOF** to assume that sth is true in the absence of proof that will confirm or contradict it **4.** *vt.* **SEEM TO PROVE STH** to indicate the existence or truth of sth (*formal*) ○ *Your line of reasoning presumes his being at home the whole evening.* **5.** *vi.* **TAKE ADVANTAGE** to exploit or take advantage of sb unscrupulously ○ *would not want to presume on the generosity of a stranger* [14thC. Via French *présumer* from Latin *praesumere* 'to take before, anticipate', which was formed from *sumere* 'to take'.] —**presumer** *n.* —**presuming** *adj.* —**presumingly** *adv.*

presumption /pri zúmpsh'n/ *n.* **1. STH BELIEVED WITHOUT ACTUAL EVIDENCE** a belief based on the fact that sth is considered to be extremely reasonable or likely ○ *I acted on the presumption that their IDs were genuine.* **2. RUDENESS OR ARROGANCE** behaviour that is inconsiderate, disrespectful, or overconfident **3.** LAW **LEGAL INFERENCE** an inference that sth is the case, in the absence of evidence rebutting that assumption and on the basis of other known facts ○ *a presumption of innocence* **4. BELIEF IN STH THAT SEEMS REASONABLE** the acceptance that sth is correct, without having proof of it, on the grounds that it is extremely likely (*formal*) ○ *a decision based on presumption rather than on the facts* **5. STH THAT COULD BE PROOF** an indication that sth exists or is true (*formal*) [12thC. Via Old French *presumpcion* from, ultimately, Latin *praesumere* (see PRESUME).]

presumptive /pri zúmptiv/ *adj.* **1. PROBABLE** based on what is thought most likely or reasonable (*formal*) **2. CAUSING PEOPLE TO PRESUME STH** forming a reasonable basis for the acceptance that sth exists or is true (*formal*) **3. EXPECTED TO BECOME** expected or thought likely to become (*archaic or formal*) ○ *heir-presumptive* **4.** BIOL **POTENTIALLY ABLE TO DIFFERENTIATE** used to describe cells or tissue of an early embryo that, in the normal course of development, will differentiate to form a particular organ or tissue in the mature embryo [Mid-16thC. Via French *présomptif* from, ultimately, Latin *praesumere* (see PRESUME).] —**presumptively** *adv.* —**presumptiveness** *n.*

presumptuous /pri zúmptyoo əss, -zúmpshəss/ *adj.* inconsiderate, disrespectful, or overconfident, especially in doing sth when not entitled or qualified to do it [14thC. Via Old French *presumptueux* from, ultimately, Latin *praesumere* (see PRESUME).] —**presumptuously** *adv.* —**presumptuousness** *n.*

presuppose /pree səpṓz/ (**-poses, -posing, -posed**) *vt.* **1. ASSUME STH IN ADVANCE** to believe that a particular thing is true before there is any proof of it ○ *the tendency to presuppose that everybody will understand English* **2.** LOGIC **REQUIRE STH AS PRIOR CONDITION** to make sth necessary if a particular thing is to be shown to be true or false. The sentence 'Fred loves his daughter' presupposes that Fred has a daughter. —**presupposition** /prée supə zísh'n/ *n.*

presystolic /prée sis tóllik/ *adj.* used to describe the interval immediately before systole in the heart

pret. *abbr.* preterite

prêt-à-porter /prét aa páwr tay/ *adj.* manufactured in standard sizes ready to be bought off the peg in shops [Mid-20thC. From French, literally 'ready to wear'.]

pretax /prée táks/ *adj.* before tax is or was deducted ○ *the firm's pretax profits*

preteen /prée téen/, **preteenager** /-téen ayjər/ *n.* a girl or boy in the few years before becoming a teenager

pretence /pri ténss/ *n.* **1. INSINCERE OR FEIGNED BEHAVIOUR** sth done or a way of behaving that is not genuine but is meant to deceive other people ○ *His display of affection was certainly a pretence.* **2. UNWARRANTED CLAIM** a claim, especially one with few facts to support it (*often used in the negative*) ○ *He makes no pretence to being an expert.* **3. MAKE-BELIEVE** make-believe or things imagined **4.** = **pretext 5.** = **pretension** *n.* 2 [14thC. Via Anglo-Norman from medieval Latin *pretensus* 'alleged', from the past participle of Latin *praetendere* (see PRETEND).]

pretend /pri ténd/ *v.* (**-tends, -tending, -tended**) **1.** *vti.* **ACT AS IF STH WERE TRUE** to make believe, e.g. by using the imagination or acting skills ○ *The little girl liked to pretend that she was an astronaut.* **2.** *vt.* **MAKE INSINCERE CLAIM ABOUT STH** to claim untruthfully or exaggeratedly to be or to have a particular thing, or to imply sth in this way ○ *I won't pretend to be an expert on the subject, but I can't believe those figures are correct.* **3.** *vt.* **MAKE STH SEEM TO BE TRUE** to act in a way intended to make people believe sth untrue or misleading about sb or sth ○ *She pretended to be an orphan just to get our sympathy.* **4.** *vi.* **CLAIM TO OWN STH** to make an untruthful or dubious claim of ownership or the right to sth, especially sth valuable, admirable, or prestigious (*formal*) ○ *pretends to the throne* ■ *adj.* **IMAGINARY** existing only in the imagination, not real (*informal; usually used by or to children*) ○ *I made a pretend house where my pretend horse lives.* [14thC. Directly or via French *prétendre* from Latin *praetendere*, literally 'to extend in front', from *tendere* 'to stretch'.]

pretended /pri téndid/ *adj.* appearing or claiming to be real, but in fact false or insincere ○ *I find her pretended caring and concern quite offensive.*

pretender /pri téndər/ *n.* **1. SB CLAIMING THE RIGHT TO STH** sb who either sincerely or dishonestly claims the right to a special rank, title, or privilege, especially a royal title, although many people question or doubt the claim. The son and grandson of James II of England both claimed the throne and were known as the Old Pretender and the Young Pretender. **2. SB GIVING FALSE IMPRESSION** sb who acts or speaks in a way that is designed to make people believe sth that is untrue

pretension /pri ténsh'n/ *n.* **1. QUESTIONABLE CLAIM TO STH** an untruthful or dubious assertion of a right to sth, especially sth valuable, admirable, or prestigious (*often used in the plural and with negatives*) ○ *His pretensions to aristocratic birth were unconvincing.* **2. AFFECTED BEHAVIOUR** behaviour that is artificial, especially that which is given to display and grandeur **3. MAKING OF CLAIM TO STH** the formal act of putting forward a claim (*formal*) [15thC. From the medieval Latin stem *praetension-*, which was formed from the past participle stem of Latin *praetendere* (see PRETEND).]

pretentious /pri ténshəss/ *adj.* **1. SELF-IMPORTANT AND AFFECTED** acting as though more important, valuable, or special than is warranted, or appearing to have an unrealistically high self-image **2. MADE TO LOOK OR SOUND IMPORTANT** presenting itself unjustifiably as having a special quality or significance, and often seeming forced or too clever ○ *dismissed it as yet another pretentious film* **3. OSTENTATIOUS** extravagantly and consciously showy or glamourous [Mid-19thC. Via French *prétentieux* from, ultimately, the medieval Latin stem *praetension-* (see PRETENSION).] —**pretentiously** *adv.* —**pretentiousness** *n.*

preter- *prefix.* beyond ○ *preterhuman* [From Latin *praeter*, from *prae* 'before' (see PRE-)]

preterhuman /préetər hyóomən/ *adj.* more than human or beyond what is usually thought of as human (*literary*)

preterite /préttərit/ *n.* the past tense [14thC. Via Old French from Latin *(tempus) praeteritum* 'past (tense)', from the past participle of *praeterire* (see PRETERITION)] —**preterite** *adj.*

preterition /préttə rísh'n/ *n.* **1. OMITTING OF STH** the act of passing over sth or leaving sth out (*formal*) **2.** CHR **PASSING OVER OF THE NONELECT** the Calvinist doctrine that those people who were not predestined to be saved were passed over by God [Late 16thC. From the late Latin stem *praeterition-* 'a passing by', from Latin *praeterire* 'to go by', from *ire* 'to go'.]

preteritive /pri térritiv/ *adj.* used to describe a verb that is in the past tense

preterm /prée túrm/ *adj.* **PREMATURE** born before completion of a pregnancy of normal length ■ *adv.* **PREMATURELY** before completion of a pregnancy of normal length

preterminal /pree túrmin'l/ *adj.* occurring at a time just before death

pretermit /préetər mít/ (**-mits, -mitting, -mitted**) *vt.* (*formal*) **1. OVERLOOK STH** to overlook or ignore sth deliberately **2. LEAVE STH OUT** to leave sth out or undone [15thC. From Latin *praetermittere* 'to let go by', which was formed from *mittere* 'to let go'.] —**pretermission** /préetər mísh'n/ *n.* —**pretermitter** /-míttər/ *n.*

preternatural /préetər nácherəl/ *adj.* **1. GOING BEYOND NATURE** exceeding what is normal in nature (*formal or literary*) **2. SUPERNATURAL** supernatural or uncanny (*literary*) [Late 16thC. From medieval Latin *praeternaturalis*, from the Latin phrase *praeter naturam* 'beyond nature'.] —**preternaturalism** *n.* —**preternaturality** /préetər náchə rálləti/ *n.* —**preternaturally** /-rəli/ *adv.* —**preternaturalness** /-rəlnəss/ *n.*

pretext /prée tekst/ *n.* a misleading or untrue reason given for doing sth in an attempt to conceal the real reason [Early 16thC. From Latin *praetextus* 'show, display', from *praetext*, the past participle stem of *praetexere* 'to weave before, adorn', from *texere* 'to weave'.]

pretor *n.* = **praetor**

Pretoria /pri táwri ə/ city in northeastern South Africa, and the country's administrative capital. It is situated in Gauteng Province, about 48 km/30 mi. north of Johannesburg. Population: 1,080,187 (1991).

pretorian /pri táwri ən/ *adj., n.* = **praetorian**

Pretorius /pri táwri əss/, **Andries** (1798–1853) South African soldier and statesman. The father of Marthinus Pretorius, he was a leader of the Great Trek, and fought the Zulus and the British. Pretoria is named after him. Full name **Andries Wilhemus Jacobus Pretorius**

Pretorius, Marthinus Wessels (1819–1901) South African statesman. The son of Andries Pretorius, he was president of the South African Republic, which then comprised only the Transvaal (1857–71), and of the Orange Free State (1859–63).

prettify /prítti fī/ (**-fies, -fying, -fied**) *vt.* to give a person, place, or thing some added decoration, especially of a rather superficial or fussy kind —**prettification** /príttifi káysh'n/ *n.* —**prettifier** /prítti fī ər/ *n.*

pretty /prítti/ *adj.* (**-tier, -tiest**) **1. HAVING A PLEASANT FACE** with an attractive, pleasant face that is graceful and appealing rather than outstandingly beautiful **2. NICE TO LOOK AT** pleasing or charming in appearance in a delicate, gentle, or decorative way ○ *The garden looks so pretty at this time of year.* **3. NICE TO LISTEN TO** with a pleasant, gentle, or delicate sound quality ○ *operas with pretty music* **4. LARGE** large in size, extent or value (*dated informal*) ○ *a pretty sum* **5. GRACEFUL AND EFFEMINATE** having, as a boy or man, the pleasing looks and graceful manner often associated with a woman (*offensive in some contexts*) **6. UNSATISFACTORY** very bad or unsatisfactory (*dated informal*) ○ *That's a pretty mess you've got yourself into.* **7. WEAK AND SUPERFICIAL** appealing or charming to hear or look at, but without any deep meaning or sincerity ○ *He knows how to paint pretty pictures but he's not an artist.* ■ *adv.* **FAIRLY** to quite a large, noticeable, or reasonable extent (*informal*) ○ *I'm pretty sure I left my keys on the kitchen table.* ■ *n.* (*plural* **-ties**) **SB WHO IS PRETTY** a pretty person, thing, or animal (*archaic informal*) [Old English, *prættig*. Ultimately from a prehistoric Germanic base meaning 'trick', of unknown origin. In Old English, 'pretty' meant 'clever' in a bad sense – 'crafty, cunning'. Not until the 15thC had it passed via 'clever', 'skilfully made', and 'fine' to 'beautiful'.] ◇ **sitting pretty** in a good or favourable position (*informal*) ◇ **a pretty penny** a large amount of money (*informal*) ◇ **pretty well** nearly completely (*informal*)

WORD KEY: SYNONYMS

See Synonyms at ***goodlooking***.

Pretty Good Privacy full form of **PGP**

pretty-pretty *adj.* so pretty that it looks unnatural or silly (*informal*) ○ *a pretty-pretty hat covered in flowers and ribbons*

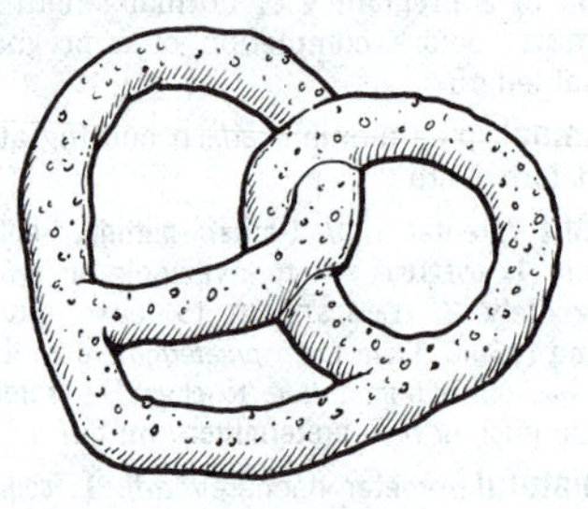

Pretzel

pretzel /préts'l/ *n.* a usually small crisp knot-shaped or stick-shaped biscuit with a golden-brown glaze (*used especially in the plural*) [Mid-19thC. From German, of uncertain origin: perhaps ultimately from Latin *brachiatus* 'branched, wearing bracelets', which was formed from *brachium* 'arm' (see BRACHIUM). According to tradition, the shape of the pretzel was devised by a Christian monk to represent arms and hands folded in prayer.]

prevail /pri váyl/ (**-vails, -vailing, -vailed**) *v.* **1.** *vi.* BE UNBEATEN AND IN CONTROL to prove to be stronger and in the position of greater influence and power ○ *He prevailed over his enemies.* **2.** WIN THROUGH to prove to be effective ○ *Justice will prevail.* **3.** *vi.* BE THE NORMAL THING to predominate or be the most common or frequent ○ *Middle-class families prevail in this street.* **4.** *vi.* BE CURRENT to remain in general use or effect (*formal*) ○ *Witchcraft still prevails in some parts of the country.* [14thC. From Latin *praevalere* 'to be stronger', from *valere* 'to be strong'.] —**prevailer** *n.*

prevail on, prevail upon *vt.* to persuade sb to do sth ○ *They prevailed on her to take part.*

prevailing /pri váyling/ *adj.* **1.** USUAL found most commonly or having the most power or effect in a particular area ○ *prevailing winds* **2.** found, existing, or in force currently ○ *the prevailing view among modern scientists* —**prevailingly** *adv.*

prevalence /prévvələnss/ *n.* **1.** STATE OF BEING COMMON the state of being frequent or widespread **2.** MED NUMBER OF CASES OF DISEASE the number of cases of an illness or condition that exists at a particular time in a defined population ○ *The prevalence of asthma in the country is increasing steadily.*

prevalent /prévvələnt/ *adj.* occurring, or accepted and practised, commonly or widely ○ *Roman Catholicism is the prevalent religion in most of southern Europe.* [Late 16thC. From Latin *praevalere* (see PREVAIL).] —**prevalently** *adv.*

WORD KEY: SYNONYMS

See Synonyms at ***widespread***.

prevaricate /pri várri kayt/ (**-cates, -cating, -cated**) *vi.* to avoid giving a direct and honest answer or opinion, or a clear and truthful account of a situation, especially by quibbling or being deliberately ambiguous or misleading [Mid-16thC. From Latin *praevaricari* 'to walk crookedly', from, ultimately, *varus* 'crooked, knock-kneed'.] —**prevaricator** *n.*

prevarication /pri várri káysh'n/ *n.* the attempt to avoid giving a direct and honest answer or opinion, or a clear and truthful account of a situation

prevenient /pri veéni ənt/ *adj.* (*formal*) **1.** PRECEDING STH coming or occurring in advance of another thing **2.** CREATING ANTICIPATION producing a sense of anticipation [Early 17thC. From Latin *praevenient-*, the present participle stem of *praevenire* 'to come before' (see PREVENT).]

prevent /pri vént/ (**-vents, -venting, -vented**) *v.* **1.** *vt.* STOP STH FROM TAKING PLACE to cause sth not to happen or not to be done ○ *Rain prevented them from playing the match.* **2.** *vt.* STOP SB FROM DOING STH to be the reason why sb does not or cannot do a particular thing ○ *a sense of duty that prevented him from abandoning the project* **3.** *vi.* STAND IN THE WAY to be the reason that sth is impossible or very difficult ○ *Modesty prevents that I reveal the true reason.* [15thC. From Latin *prevent-*, the past participle stem of *praevenire* 'to come before, prevent', which was formed from *venire* 'to come'. Ultimately from an Indo-European word meaning 'to go, come' that is also the ancestor of English *come* and *basis*. The meaning 'hinder' developed in Latin via 'act in advance of, anticipate'.] —**preventability** /pri véntə bílləti/ *n.* —**preventable** *adj.* —**preventably** /-təbli/ *adv.* —**preventer** /-tər/ *n.*

preventative /pri véntətiv/ *adj., n.* = **preventive**

prevention /pri vénsh'n/ *n.* **1.** ACTION THAT STOPS STH FROM HAPPENING an action or actions taken to stop sb from doing sth or to prevent sth from taking place ○ *the prevention of crime* **2.** STH THAT ACTS TO PREVENT STH an action or measure that makes it impossible or very difficult for sb to do a certain thing, or for sth to happen

preventive /pri véntiv/ *adj.* WITH THE PURPOSE OF PREVENTING STH used or devised to stop sth from happening, or to stop people from doing a particular thing ○ *preventive dentistry* ■ *n.* STH THAT PREVENTS sth that stops sth unwanted from happening, especially sth that protects against illness ○ *The best preventive against heart disease is a healthy lifestyle.* —**preventively** *adv.* —**preventiveness** *n.*

preventive detention *n.* **1.** LONG TERM OF IMPRISONMENT imprisonment for a term of up to 14 years for criminals over the age of 30 **2.** PRETRIAL IMPRISONMENT the pretrial jailing without bail of sb accused of a crime who is thought likely to attempt to flee, commit additional crimes, or intimidate witnesses or prosecutors, or an instance of such jailing

preverbal /preé v/ *adj.* **1.** NOT YET ABLE TO TALK at the stage of development when a child is not yet able to use speech **2.** GRAM PRECEDING VERB coming before a verb

preview /preé vyoo/ *n.* **1.** OPPORTUNITY TO SEE STH IN ADVANCE a showing of sth, especially a film, play, exhibition, or work of art, to a select audience before the general public sees it **2.** DESCRIPTION OF A FORTHCOMING SHOW a piece printed in a paper or magazine or broadcast on radio or TV describing and commenting on sth that is soon to be broadcast or presented to the public **3.** PROMOTIONAL FILM a short film shown on TV or at the cinema promoting an upcoming film or programme ■ *vt.* (**-views, -viewing, -viewed**) **1.** SHOW STH IN ADVANCE to put on a performance or showing of sth for a select audience before the general public has the opportunity to see it **2.** DESCRIBE A SHOW IN ADVANCE to write, print, or broadcast a short piece that describes and comments on sth that is soon to be broadcast or presented to the public

previous /preévi əss/ *adj.* **1.** COMING BEFORE STH occurring before sth or sb of the same kind ○ *his previous girlfriend* ○ *the previous edition* **2.** ALREADY ARRANGED existing, made, or settled before the one being referred to now ○ *She was unable to come because of a previous engagement.* **3.** ACTING TOO HASTILY saying or doing sth earlier than is appropriate (*informal*) [Early 17thC. From Latin *praevius* 'going before', from *prae* 'before'.] —**previousness** *n.* ◇ **previous to sth** before a particular thing took place

previously /preévi əsli/ *adv.* at an earlier time or on an earlier occasion

previous question *n.* **1.** MOTION TO STOP QUESTION in the House of Commons, a motion to stop a question being debated, so that a vote cannot be held on it **2.** MOTION TO PUT QUESTION in the House of Lords and US legislative bodies, a motion to put a question that will end a debate so that a vote on a bill can be taken without delay

previse /pri víz/ (**-vises, -vising, -vised**) *vt.* (*formal or literary*) **1.** PREDICT STH to predict or foresee sth **2.** WARN SB to warn sb about sth [15thC. From Latin *praevis-*, the past participle stem of *praevidere* 'to foresee', which was formed from *videre* 'to see'.]

prevision /pri vízh'n/ (**-sions, -sioning, -sioned**) *n.* (*formal or literary*) **1.** ABILITY TO PREDICT the ability to predict or foresee things **2.** PREDICTION a prediction or premonition

prevocalic /preé vō kállik/ *adj.* used to describe a consonant that comes immediately before a vowel —**prevocalically** *adv.*

prewar /preé wáwr/ *adj.* BEFORE THE WAR dating from or belonging to the period before a particular war, especially World War II or World War I ○ *prewar fashions* ■ *adv.* AT A TIME BEFORE THE WAR during the period before a particular war took place, especially World War II or World War I

prewashed /preé wósht/, **pre-washed** *adj.* washed before being packaged and sold in the shops

prey /pray/ (*plural* **prey** *or* **preys**) *n.* **1.** ANIMALS HUNTED BY OTHER ANIMALS an animal or animals that are caught, killed, and eaten by another animal as food ○ *The common shrew's prey consists largely of earthworms and woodlice.* **2.** SB TREATED UNKINDLY BY OTHERS sb who is attacked or receives cruel or unfair treatment from sb else ○ *a young heiress who became prey to fortune hunters* **3.** LIKELY PERSON TO SUFFER FROM STH sb who is prone to some particular ailment, worry, or upsetting condition, or who seems vulnerable in this way ○ *She was tense, nervous, and prey to headaches.* **4.** KILLING OF OTHER ANIMALS AS FOOD the natural practice or habit of predatory animals to hunt, kill, and eat other animals ○ *a bird of prey* **5.** PLUNDER items stolen or plundered (*archaic or literary*) [13thC. Via Old French *preie* from Latin *praeda* 'booty' (related to Latin *praehendere* 'to seize', which is the source of English *apprehend* and *prison*). Ultimately from an Indo-European word meaning 'to take' that is also the ancestor of English *get*.] —**preyer** *n.* ◇ **be prey to sth** to experience sth unpleasant regularly or be at risk of sth

prey on, prey upon *vt.* **1.** HUNT AND KILL OTHER ANIMALS to hunt and kill other animals for food ○ *Owls prey on mice and rabbits.* **2.** VICTIMIZE SB to victimize or exploit sb **3.** WORRY SB to cause sb constant anxiety or distress ○ *an ever-increasing debt that preyed on his mind*

prezzie /prézzi/ (*plural* **-zies**), **pressie** (*plural* **-sies**) *n.* a gift or present (*informal*) ○ *Did you get lots of prezzies on your birthday?* [Mid-20thC. Shortening and alteration of PRESENT¹.]

Priam /prí əm/ *n.* in Greek mythology, the king of Troy, husband of Hecuba, and father of Hector, Paris, and Cassandra. He was killed during the Trojan War.

priapic /prī áppik/ *adj.* **1.** RELATING TO PHALLUS relating to or resembling a phallus (*dated or literary*) **2.** MED WITH PENIS PERMANENTLY ERECT having a permanently erect penis **3.** FASCINATED BY MALE SEXUAL ACTIVITY showing a preoccupation with male sexual activity [Late 18thC. Formed from Latin *Priapus*, the god of procreation, symbolized by the erect phallus, from Greek *Priapos*.]

priapism /prí əpizəm/ *n.* a medical disorder in which there is persistent, often painful erection of the penis in the absence of sexual interest [Early 17thC. Formed from Latin *Priapus* (see PRIAPIC).]

Priapus /prī áypəss/ *n.* in Greek mythology, the god of fertility. He was the son of Aphrodite and Dionysus.

Pribilof Islands /príbbi lof-/ group of islands off southwestern Alaska, in the southeastern Bering Sea, approximately 290 km/180 mi. north of Unalaska Island. Population: 901 (1990). Area: 161 sq. km/62 sq. mi.

price /prīss/ *n.* **1.** COST OF STH BOUGHT OR SOLD the particular amount, usually of money, that is offered or asked for when sth is bought or sold ○ *The price of food continued to soar.* **2.** STH SACRIFICED TO GET STH ELSE sth lost or given in order to achieve a particular position or condition ○ *Unwanted media attention is the price of fame.* **3.** SUFFICIENT BRIBE the sum of money or other payment for which sb is willing to do sth or to refrain from doing sth ○ *The price of her cooperation was an invitation to the gala dinner.* **4.** REWARD MONEY a sum of money offered as a reward for the capture or killing of a particular criminal or outlaw (*dated or literary*) ○ *an outlaw with a price on his head* **5.** MEASURE OF STH'S VALUE an estimate of what sb or sth is worth, e.g. how important, useful, or irreplaceable it is (*dated or literary*) **6.** BETTING BETTING ODDS betting or gambling odds ■ *vt.* (**prices, pricing, priced**) **1.** DECIDE HOW MUCH STH COSTS to state or fix the exact price that a customer or consumer must pay for sth ○ *He* *priced the antique clock at £500.* **2. MARK STH WITH ITS PRICE** to show how much sth costs, especially by writing on the article itself or by attaching a label or price tag ○ *spent the morning pricing merchandise* **3. FIND OUT WHAT STH COSTS** to check the price that has been set for a certain product, or compare the different prices charged at a variety of shops or from different companies ○ *priced a few computers before deciding which one to buy* [13thC. Via Old French *pris* from Latin *pretium* 'price, money' (source of English *prize* and *praise*). Ultimately from an Indo-European base meaning 'to sell' that is also the ancestor of English *pornography*.] —**pricer** *n.* ◇ **at any price** no matter how much it costs (*often used with a negative*) ◇ **at a price** for a lot of money ◇ **be beyond price** to be priceless ◇ **what price sth?** used to suggest that sth such as an ideal or a promise has no value ○ *'What Price Glory?'* (Maxwell Anderson, *What Price Glory?*; 1924)

US Information Agency

Leontyne Price

Price /prīss/, **Leontyne** (*b.* 1927) US soprano. During a long career as a major international opera star (1952–85), she was especially associated with Italian opera. Full name **Mary Violet Leontyne Price**

price control *n.* government control over prices of goods and services, usually introduced as an emergency measure

price-cutting *n.* the reduction of prices below their usual level in order to sell more than competitors

price discrimination *n.* the charging of different prices for the same product or service in different markets

price-dividend ratio *n.* on the stock exchange, the ratio of a share's price to the dividends paid in the previous year

price-earnings ratio *n.* on the stock exchange, the ratio of a share's price to its earnings, providing an indication of its value

price fixing *n.* the setting of prices by government or following an agreement between producers, rather than by free market operation

price index *n.* a mathematical quantity that is used to measure movements in price levels over different periods of time

price leadership *n.* the setting of a price by the market leader at a level that competitors can match in order to avoid price-cutting

priceless /prīssləss/ *adj.* **1. IMPOSSIBLE TO PUT A VALUE ON** worth more than can be calculated in terms of money ○ *the priceless treasures of the pharaohs' tombs* **2. HILARIOUS** extremely comic and amusing (*informal*) ○ *You should have seen his face when I walked in – it was priceless!* —**pricelessness** *n.*

price ring *n.* a group of traders who cooperate, usually illegally, to maintain the price of the goods they sell, thus preventing competition

price support *n.* government maintenance of prices levels by means such as subsidy

price tag *n.* **1. LABEL SAYING WHAT STH COSTS** a small label attached to an article that is for sale, with the price written or printed on it **2. PRICE THAT MUST BE PAID** the amount sth costs, whether in money or in sth else, e.g. emotional outlay or loss of life or health (*informal*) ○ *The price tag for involvement in the war was more than the country could stand.*

price war *n.* extreme competition within a market, characterized by price-cutting

pricey /prīssi/ (**-ier, -iest**), **pricy** (**-ier, -iest**) *adj.* charging high prices or costing a great deal (*informal*) ○ *a pricey restaurant* —**priceyness** *n.*

Prichard /prícherd/, **Katherine Susannah** (1883–1969) Australian writer. Her fiction including *Working Bullocks* (1926) and *Coonardoo* (1930) interprets Australian life in terms of class struggle.

prick /prik/ *v.* (**pricks, pricking, pricked**) **1.** *vt.* **MAKE SMALL HOLE THROUGH SURFACE** to puncture the surface of sth, especially the skin, by piercing it lightly with sth sharp and finely pointed ○ *pricked her finger on a cactus needle* **2.** *vti.* **HURT IN A STINGING WAY** to feel a sharp, stinging pain that makes you want to rub it, or to cause sth such as the eyes or the skin to hurt in this way ○ *The shampoo got into his eyes and pricked them.* **3.** *vt.* **SUDDENLY DISTURB SB EMOTIONALLY OR MENTALLY** to make sb feel a sudden strong emotional twinge, e.g. of guilt or shame ○ *His conscience began to prick him.* **4.** *vt.* **MARK OUT SHAPE USING TINY HOLES** to make a number of small indentations in or through the surface of sth such as a board or a piece of card or fabric so as to form the outline of sth **5.** *vti.* **RAISE THE EARS** to stick up straight or cause an animal's ears to stick up straight ○ *The dog pricked its ears at the sound of its master's voice.* **6.** *vt.* **MAKE AN ANIMAL MOVE FASTER** to urge an animal, especially a horse, to gallop or move more quickly by digging the spurs or heels into its flank (*archaic or literary*) **7.** *vt.* **PUSH SB INTO ACTIVITY** to force or encourage sb to speed up with some task or project or to get started on some definite course of action ○ *If only we could prick him into action on this.* ■ *n.* **1. QUICK, SHARP PAIN** a sudden twinge of pain caused by a fine point being pushed into the skin **2. SMALL PUNCTURE** a small puncture hole or indented mark or an act of piercing that causes such a puncture **3. OFFENSIVE TERM** an offensive term for a penis (*taboo offensive*) **4. OFFENSIVE TERM** a highly offensive term for a man regarded as pathetically inadequate or unpleasant (*taboo insult*) **5. STH THAT ENTERS THE MIND PAINFULLY** a sudden, unpleasant thought or feeling, often one related to some past action or event **6. POINTED IMPLEMENT** any pointed implement or weapon such as a goad (*archaic*) **7. HARE'S FOOTPRINT** the footprint of a hare [Old English *prica*, of unknown origin. *Prick* is a word of the Low German area, which English shares with Dutch (*prik*). The earliest record of its use for 'penis' is from the late 16thC, and in the 16th and 17th centuries women used it as a term of endearment.] ◇ **kick against the pricks** to show opposition to authority, rules, or circumstances that you have no power to influence ◇ **prick up your ears** to begin to listen very carefully

prick out *vt.* to make a series of small holes in an area of earth and put young seedlings into these holes to grow

pricker /príker/ *n.* a tool used to prick or pierce small holes in sth

pricket /príkit/ *n.* **1. YOUNG MALE DEER** a male deer in its second year, typically one with unbranched antlers **2. CANDLEHOLDER** a metal spike for sticking a candle on [14thC. Literally 'small prick'.]

prickle /prík'l/ *n.* **1. BOT PROJECTION ON PLANT** a sharp pointed projection on the outer surface of a leaf or plant **2. TINGLING FEELING** a tingling or stinging sensation ■ *vti.* (**-les, -ling, -led**) **HURT IN A STINGING WAY** to feel a sharp, stinging pain or to cause sth such as the eyes or the skin to hurt in this way [Old English *pricel*, literally 'small prick', formed from the same prehistoric Germanic base that produced English *prick*]

prickly /príkli/ (**-led, -lier, -liest**) *adj.* **1. WITH SMALL SHARP SPIKES** having a surface or skin with prickles on it **2. UNCOMFORTABLE** irritating to the skin, especially because of fibres or prickles that are rough to the touch **3. OVERSENSITIVE** easily angered, offended, or upset (*informal*) ○ *He's very prickly on that subject.* **4. TRICKY TO HANDLE OR SOLVE** especially difficult and likely to upset people (*informal*) ○ *They tried to keep off prickly subjects like politics and religion.* —**prickliness** *n.*

prickly ash *n.* **1. AROMATIC SHRUB OF EASTERN AMERICA** an aromatic shrub or small tree, native to eastern North America, that has prickly branches and bears clusters of small greenish flowers. Latin name: *Zanthoxylum americanum*. ◇ **toothache tree 2. PRICKLY SHRUB OF SOUTHERN UNITED STATES** a spiny shrub or tree of

the southern United States with pinnately compound leaves. Latin name: *Zanthoxylum clavaherculis*. ◇ **Hercules' club** *n.* 1

prickly heat *n.* a rash of tiny raised spots, accompanied by redness and itching, appearing in hot or humid conditions. It is due to obstruction of the sweat-gland ducts. Technical name **miliaria**

prickly pear *n.* any of various tropical cacti that have flattened jointed spiny stems, large yellow or orange flowers, and pear-shaped fruits that are edible in some species. Native to North and South America, prickly pears have been introduced elsewhere, often becoming troublesome weeds. Genus: *Opuntia*.

prickly poppy *n.* any of various plants of the poppy family that have bristly stems and leaves and bear yellow, lavender, or white flowers. Some are cultivated as ornamentals. They were traditionally used by herbalists as a source of medicines. Genus: *Argemone*.

prick-teaser, **prick-tease** *n.* = **cock-teaser** (*taboo offensive*)

pride /prīd/ *n.* **1. FEELING OF SUPERIORITY** a haughty attitude shown by people who consider, often unjustifiably, that they are better than others ○ *Her pride prevented her from mixing with those she considered her social inferiors.* **2. PROPER SENSE OF OWN VALUE** the correct level of respect for the importance and value of your personal character, life, efforts, or achievements ○ *He had lost all his confidence and pride.* **3. SATISFACTION WITH SELF** the happy, satisfied feeling sb experiences when having or achieving sth special that other people admire ○ *She felt a sense of pride when she looked at her finished work.* **4. SOURCE OF PERSONAL SATISFACTION** sth that sb feels especially pleased and satisfied to own or to have achieved ○ *His grandchildren were his pride and joy.* **5. THE BEST TIME** the best condition or period of sth (*literary*) **6. GROUP OF LIONS** a group of lions, typically consisting of comprises up to a dozen related adult females, their cubs and juveniles, plus from one to six adult males ■ *vr.* (**prides, priding, prided**) **BE PROUD OF STH** to obtain personal satisfaction and pleasure from a particular source, especially sth accomplished or a quality possessed ○ *He prides himself on his meticulous timekeeping.* [Old English *prȳde*, a variant of *prȳte*, which was formed from *prūd* 'proud'. There is an isolated example of the use of the word for a 'group of lions' from the 15thC, but the modern usage seems to be a 20th-century revival.] —**prideful** *adj.* —**pridefully** *adv.* ◇ **take pride in sth** to have a sense of personal satisfaction because of a particular achievement or effort that you or sb connected with you has made ◇ **pride of place** the most important or prominent position

─── **WORD KEY: CULTURAL NOTE** ───
Pride and Prejudice, a novel by Jane Austen (1813). Through the story of the relationship between Elizabeth Bennet, the fiercely independent daughter of minor gentry, and Mr Darcy, a wealthy and haughty nobleman, Austen reveals how both pride and prejudices create barriers to mutual understanding. One of Austen's lighter social comedies, it was made into a film by Robert Leonard in 1940.

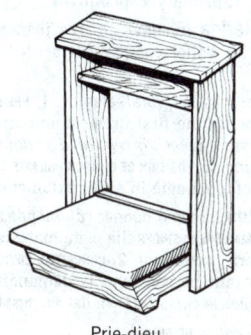

Prie-dieu

prie-dieu /pree dyŏ/ (*plural* **prie-dieux**) *n.* a shelved wooden desk for use when praying, usually with a low surface for kneeling on and a higher surface for resting the elbows or a book on [Mid-18thC. From French, literally 'pray God'.]

prier /prī ər/, **pryer** *n.* sb who pries

priest /preest/ *n.* **1. ORDAINED PERSON** an ordained minister, especially in the Roman Catholic, Anglican, and Eastern Orthodox churches, responsible for administering the sacraments, preaching, and ministering to the needs of the congregation **2. MINISTER OF NON-CHRISTIAN RELIGION** a spiritual leader or teacher of a non-Christian religion **3. DESCENDANT OF FAMILY OF AARON** sb descended from the family of Aaron of the tribe of Levi, appointed as priests in the Hebrew Scriptures ■ *vt.* **(priests, priesting, priested) ORDAIN SB** to perform the necessary ceremonies to make sb into a priest (*archaic*) [Old English *prēost* via prehistoric Germanic from ecclesiastical Latin *presbyter* (see PRESBYTER)]

priestess /pree stéss, preést ess, preéstiss/ *n.* a woman who is a spiritual leader in a non-Christian religion

priest-hole /preésts-/, **priest's hole** *n.* a small hidden room or space in an English house, created as a hiding-place for Roman Catholic priests and others trying to escape persecution after the English Reformation

priesthood /preést hòòd/ *n.* **1. PRIEST'S POSITION** the official role, position, or office of a priest **2. PRIESTS AS A GROUP** all Roman Catholic priests considered together, or all the priests of another religion [Old English *prēosthād*]

Priestley /preéstli/, **Joseph** (1733–1804) British chemist, Unitarian minister, and political radical. He isolated and described the properties of oxygen and other gases, and is considered one of the founders of modern chemistry.

priestly /preéstli/ *adj.* used, worn, or performed exclusively by priests, or in some way typical of or suitable for a priest (*formal or literary*) ○ *priestly garments* [Old English *prēostlic*] —**priestliness** *n.*

priest-ridden *adj.* influenced or controlled by priests or religious dogma to what the speaker or writer regards as an unacceptable degree (*dated or literary*)

prig /prig/ *n.* sb who takes pride in behaving in a very correct and proper way, and who feels morally superior to people with more relaxed standards (*insult*) [Late 17thC. Origin uncertain: perhaps the same word as obsolete slang *prig* 'tinker', of unknown origin. Its original meaning was 'dandy'.] —**priggery** *n.* —**priggish** *adj.* —**priggishly** *adv.* —**priggishness** *n.* —**priggism** *n.*

prill /pril/ *vt.* **(prills, prilling, prilled) MAKE SOLID INTO GRANULES** to make a solid into granules or pellets that flow freely and do not clump together ■ *n.* **PRILLED GRANULE** a granule or pellet made by prilling [Late 18thC. Origin unknown.]

prim /prim/ *adj.* **(primmer, primmest) 1. PRUDISH** easily shocked by vulgar or obscene language or behaviour **2. FORMAL AND PROPER** excessively formal and proper in manner or appearance ■ *v.* **(prims, primming, primmed) 1.** *vti.* **ASSUME PROPER EXPRESSION** to take on an affectedly proper expression **2.** *vt.* **MAKE SB LOOK VERY PROPER** to make sb look excessively proper [Early 18thC. Origin uncertain: perhaps via Old French *prin* 'excellent, delicate' from Latin *primus* (see PRIME).] —**primly** *adv.* —**primness** *n.*

prim. *abbr.* **1.** primary **2.** primitive

prima ballerina /preémə-/ *n.* the principal woman dancer in a ballet company [From Italian, 'first ballerina']

primacy /prímassi/ (*plural* **-cies**) *n.* **1. PRE-EMINENCE** the state of being the first or most important part or aspect of sth ○ *Speech is regarded as having primacy over writing.* **2. POSITION OF CHURCH PRIMATE** the position or office of a primate in a Christian church

prima donna /preémə dònnə/ (*plural* **prima donnas**) *n.* **1. LEAD WOMAN OPERA SINGER** the principal woman soloist in an opera production **2. CONCEITED, DIFFICULT PERSON** a self-important person who is demanding and difficult to please (*insult*) [From Italian, 'first lady']

primaeval *adj.* = **primeval**

prima facie /prímə fáyshi/ *adv.* **AT FIRST GLANCE** on initial examination or consideration ○ *Prima facie, this lawsuit seems spurious.* ■ *adj.* **1. APPARENT** clear from a first impression ○ *a prima facie counterexample to your hypothesis* **2. LEGALLY SUFFICIENT** sufficient in law to establish a case or fact, unless disproved [From Latin, literally 'at first appearance']

primage /prímij/ *n.* *NZ* a tax payable in addition to customs duty [15thC. From Anglo-Latin *primagium*, of uncertain origin: probably formed from Latin *primus* (see PRIME).]

primal /prím'l/ *adj.* **1. ORIGINAL** first or earliest, and often basic ○ *the primal instinct for survival* **2. BASIC** most significant and primary ○ *our primal need for a new fuel source* [Mid-16thC. From medieval Latin *primalis*, from Latin *primus* (see PRIME).] —**primality** /prī málləti/ *n.*

primal scream *n.* a cry of extreme anger that a client undergoing primal therapy is encouraged to use

primal therapy *n.* a style of psychotherapy in which clients relive past traumas and unleash repressed anger and frustration through screams, tantrums, or beating inanimate objects

primaquine /prímə kween/, **primaquine phosphate** *n.* a synthetic drug used to treat malaria. Formula: $C_{15}H_{21}N_3O$. [Mid-20thC. Origin uncertain: possibly from Latin *primus* 'first' + an alteration of QUINOLINE.]

primarily /prímərəli, prī márrəli/ *adv.* **1. CHIEFLY** mainly or mostly ○ *Baldness is primarily found among adult men.* **2. ORIGINALLY** originally or at first

primary /príməri/ *adj.* **1. FIRST IN SEQUENCE** first or earliest in a sequence ○ *the primary stage of development* **2. MOST IMPORTANT** ranked as most important **3. BASIC** essential or basic to sth **4. ORIGINAL** being the first form of sth ○ *Unlike musical chords, notes are primary.* **5. RELATING TO EARLY EDUCATION** relating to the early years of formal education, usually for children between the ages of 5 and 12 **6. RELATING TO NATURAL RESOURCE INDUSTRY** relating to or produced by an industry such as forestry, mining, or agriculture, that collects and processes a natural resource **7.** ELEC **PRODUCING ELECTRICITY** used to describe a cell that uses an irreversible chemical reaction to generate electricity and, as a result, cannot be recharged **8.** ELEC **RELATING TO CURRENT-INDUCING COMPONENT** used to describe a circuit component such as a coil that induces a current in a neighbouring circuit **9.** CHEM **SUBSTITUTING ATOMS** relating to or resulting from the replacement of one or more atoms in a molecule **10.** CHEM **RELATING TO ATTACHED CARBON ATOM** having or used to describe a carbon atom in a molecule that is bonded to one other carbon atom only **11.** BIOCHEM **RELATING TO AMINO ACID SEQUENCE** relating to or used to describe the basic type, number, or sequence of component units in a polypeptide, especially a protein **12.** BIRDS **RELATING TO MAIN WING FEATHERS** relating to or used to describe any of the main flight feathers on the outer edge of a bird's wing **13.** BOT **GROWN FROM EMBRYONIC TISSUE** relating to or used to describe growth from embryonic tissue in the tip of a root or shoot ■ *n.* (*plural* **-ies**) **1. FIRST THING** sth that is first in time or order **2. MOST IMPORTANT THING** a part or aspect of sth that is the most important **3. BASIC PART OR ASPECT** sth that is essential or basic to sth **4. ORIGINAL FORM** sth that is the earliest form of sth **5.** POL **ELECTION OF CANDIDATES FOR GOVERNMENTAL POSITION** in the United States, an election in which members of a party choose candidates for a governmental position **6.** POL **ELECTION OF DELEGATES TO CHOOSE CANDIDATES** in the United States, an election to choose delegates who will choose the party's candidates at a political convention **7.** EDUC = **primary school** (*used in school names*) **8.** COLOURS = **primary colour** **9.** ELEC = **primary coil** **10.** ASTRON **BRIGHTER STAR OF DOUBLE STAR** the brighter or larger of two stars in a double star **11.** ASTRON = **primary planet** **12.** BIRDS = **primary feather** [15thC. From Latin *primarius*, from *primus* (see PRIME).]

primary accent *n.* LING = **primary stress**

primary care *n.* the level of health care at which a patient is assessed and treated by a general practitioner or nurse, or, if necessary, is referred to a specialist

primary cell *n.* an electrical cell that uses an irreversible chemical reaction to generate electricity and, as a result, cannot be recharged

primary coil *n.* a coil that forms part of a machine or circuit in which the current flow sets up the magnetic flux necessary for the operation of the machine or circuit

primary colour *n.* **1. RED, GREEN, OR BLUE** any one of the three basic colours of the spectrum, red, green, or blue, from which all other colours can be blended **2. CYAN, MAGENTA, OR YELLOW** any one of the three basic colours cyan, magenta, or yellow, which when subtracted from white can produce all other colours

primary consumer *n.* an animal that eats plants, in terms of its position in a food chain

primary election *n.* = **primary** *n.* **5**, **primary** *n.* **6**

primary feather *n.* any one of the main flight feathers on the outer edge of a bird's wing

primary group *n.* the group of people that sb regularly interacts with face-to-face

primary growth *n.* a growth from the tips of roots and shoots of a plant that develops into the main part of the mature plant

primary meristem *n.* a plant tissue derived from the tip of a root or shoot

primary planet *n.* a planet in direct orbit around a sun

primary process *n.* in Freudian terminology, a basic process that is involved in the functioning of the id and is ruled by the pleasure principle

primary production *n.* the total chemical energy produced by photosynthesis

primary qualities *npl.* properties, e.g. spatial location, that are independent of the mind and are inseparable from the objects studied by sciences such as physics

primary root *n.* the first root to grow from a seed

primary school *n.* **1. UK SCHOOL FOR YOUNGER CHILDREN** in the United Kingdom, a school in which children usually aged between 5 and 11 or 12 are taught **2. US SCHOOL FOR YOUNGER STUDENTS** in the United States, a school in which the first three, or sometimes four, grades are taught, often including kindergarten as well

primary storage *n.* the main memory in a computer, including the random-access memory, or RAM, and the read-only memory, or ROM, directly accessible by the processor

primary stress *n.* the strongest force used in pronouncing one of the syllables of a multisyllabic word or the mark, usually ', used to indicate this. For example, in the word 'secondary', the primary stress falls on the first syllable. US term **primary accent**

primary syphilis *n.* the first of the three stages of syphilis, in which a painless growth (**chancre**) grows at the site of infection and the infecting bacterium (**spirochaete**) spreads throughout the body

primary tooth *n.* = **milk tooth**

primary wave *n.* a seismic wave that creates vibrations parallel to its direction

primary winding *n.* ELECTRON ENG = **primary coil**

primate /prí mayt/ *n.* **1. MEMBER OF MAMMAL ORDER** a member of an order of mammals with a large brain and complex hands and feet, including humans, apes, and monkeys. Order: Primates. **2. primate, Primate ARCHBISHOP** an archbishop or high-ranking bishop **3. SB OF HIGHEST RANK** sb holding the highest rank (*archaic*) [12thC. From Latin *primat-*, the stem of *primas* 'of the first rank', from *primus* (see PRIME).] —**primatial** /prī máysh'l/ *adj.*

primatology /prímə tólləji/ *n.* the scientific study of primates, especially nonhuman primates —**primatological** /prímə tə lójjik'l/ *adj.* —**primatologist** /prímə tólləjist/ *n.*

primavera /preémə váirə/ *adj.* made with an assortment of fresh spring vegetables, especially sliced as an accompaniment to pasta, meat, or seafood [Late 20thC. From Italian *(alla) primavera* '(in the) spring (style)', from late Latin *prima vera* 'early spring', from Latin *primum ver*, literally 'first spring'.]

prime /prīm/ *adj.* **1. BEST** of the highest quality ○ *prime grade beef* **2. FIRST IN IMPORTANCE** of the greatest importance or the highest rank **3. EARLIEST** earliest in time or sequence **4.** MATH **NOT DIVISIBLE WITHOUT REMAINDER** used to describe a number that can be divided without a remainder only by one and itself **5.** MATH **BEING WITHOUT COMMON FACTORS** used to describe a number that has no common factors with another number ○ *15 is prime to 8.* ■ *n.* **1. BEST STAGE OF STH** the best state or stage of sth, especially the most active and enjoyable period in adult life ○ *In his prime, he was one of the country's best tennis players.* **2. EARLIEST PERIOD OF STH** the earliest part of sth, e.g. the early hours of daylight or the first season of the year **3. DISTINGUISHING MARK** a mark (′) added to a number, character, or expression in order to distinguish it from another, or as the symbol for measurement in feet **4.** FENCING **FIRST PARRYING POSITION** the first of the eight parrying positions in fencing **5.** MUSIC **FIRST NOTE IN MUSICAL SCALE** the first note of a musical scale **6.** MUSIC = **unison 7.** CHR **SECOND CANONICAL HOUR** the second of the seven canonical hours assigned to morning prayer at the first hour of the day **8.** MATH = **prime number 9.** FIN = **prime rate** ■ *v.* **(primes, priming, primed) 1.** *vti.* **MAKE OR BECOME READY** to make sth ready for use or become ready for use **2.** *vt.* **PREPARE SURFACE FOR PAINTING** to prepare a surface for painting or a similar process by treating it with a sealant or an undercoat of paint **3.** *vt.* **PUT CHARGE IN GUN** to make a firearm ready for use by putting a charge in it **4.** *vt.* **PROVIDE EXPLOSIVE WITH FUSE** to make an explosive ready for use by inserting a fuse **5.** *vt.* **PREPARE PUMP** to put liquid in a pump in order to get it started **6.** *vt.* **PUT FUEL INTO CARBURETTOR** to put fuel into a carburettor in order to start an internal-combustion engine **7.** *vt.* **BRIEF SB** to give sb, especially a witness in a court case, information or instructions on how to behave or answer questions **8.** *vt.* **PLY SB WITH DRINK** to provide sb with large quantities of alcohol in order to prepare him or her for doing sth [Pre-12thC. Via Old French from, ultimately, Latin *primus* 'first'. Ultimately from an Indo-European word that is also the ancestor of English *principal* and *pristine.*] —**primely** *adv.* —**primeness** *n.*

WORD KEY: CULTURAL NOTE

The Prime of Miss Jean Brodie, a novel by the British writer Muriel Spark (1961). The best-known of Spark's novels, it is set in an Edinburgh girls' school and describes the powerful and lasting influence of an unconventional schoolteacher, Miss Jean Brodie, on a group of promising but impressionable pupils. It was adapted for the theatre in 1966 and made into a film by Ronald Neame in 1968.

prime cost *n.* the cost of the material and labour necessary to make a product

prime interest rate *n.* = **prime rate**

prime meridian *n.* the 0° longitude meridian, from which other longitudes are calculated. It passes through Greenwich.

prime minister *n.* **1. HEAD OF CABINET** in a parliamentary system, the head of the cabinet and, usually, chief executive **2. RULER'S CHIEF MINISTER** the chief minister appointed by the ruler of a country —**prime ministerial** *adj.* —**prime ministership** *n.*

prime mover *n.* **1. MOST IMPORTANT CAUSE OF STH** sb or sth that initiates a process or activity and is usually the most important factor in its continuation **2.** GOD God, considered to be the first cause or origin of everything **3.** PHILOS **SOURCE OF ALL MOTION** in Aristotelian philosophy, the initial source of all movement **4. NATURAL OR PHYSICAL ENERGY SOURCE** a natural or physical source of energy such as wind or electricity that can be harnessed to power a machine **5. ENERGY CONVERTER** a machine that converts energy from a natural or physical source in order to power equipment such as a windmill or turbine

prime number *n.* a whole number that can only be divided without a remainder by itself and one

primer[1] /prímər/ *n.* **1. BASIC READING TEXTBOOK** a book used to teach young children to read, typically containing simple stories **2. INTRODUCTORY TEXT** a book that provides an introduction to a topic [14thC. Via Anglo-Norman from, ultimately, Latin *primarius* (see PRIMARY).]

primer[2] /prímər/ *n.* **1. PRIMING AGENT** sb or sth that primes sth **2. UNDERCOAT** a paint or sealant used to prepare a surface for painting or a similar process, or a coat of this material **3. EXPLOSIVE IGNITER** a small container or wafer of explosive material such as gunpowder, used to ignite the main explosive charge of a firearm or explosive **4.** BIOCHEM **GENETIC MATERIAL** a molecular substrate such as a DNA molecule needed in the polymerization reaction that produces another molecule structurally similar to the substrate [15thC. Formed from PRIME.]

prime rate, **prime interest rate** *n.* the lowest rate of interest on loans that is available from a bank at a given time

primero /pri máirō/ *n.* a card game played for money in the 16th and 17th centuries [Mid-16thC. Alteration of Spanish *primera*, literally 'first', from Latin *primarius* (see PRIMARY).]

primers /prímərz/ *n.* *NZ* the earliest classes of primary school (*informal*) (*takes a singular verb*) [Early 20thC. Shortening of PRIMARY.]

prime time *n.* the hours when television audiences are usually largest, typically from 7:00 pm to 11:00 pm. Advertising rates are most expensive during these hours. —**primetime** *adj.*

primeval /prī mēev'l/, **primaeval** *adj.* at or from the ancient, original stages in the development of sth [Mid-17thC. Formed from Latin *primaevus*, from *primus* 'first' + *aevum* 'age'.] —**primevally** *adv.*

prime vertical *n.* the imaginary circle around the Earth that goes through the highest point of the celestial sphere directly above an observer and meets the horizon at east and west

primigravida /prími grávvidə/ (*plural* **-das** *or* **-dae** /-dee/) *n.* a woman during her first pregnancy [Late 19thC. From modern Latin, formed from *gravida* 'pregnant', on the model of PRIMIPARA.]

priming /príming/ *n.* a small container or wafer of explosive material such as gunpowder, used to ignite the main explosive charge of a firearm or explosive

primipara /prī míppərə/ (*plural* **-ras** *or* **-rae** /prī míppəree/) *n.* a woman who has given birth only once, whether it was a single or a multiple birth, and whether the baby was alive or stillborn [Mid-19thC. From modern Latin, from Latin *primus* 'first' + *-para* 'bearing', feminine form of *-parus* (see -PAROUS).] —**primiparity** /prími párrəti/ *n.* —**primiparous** /prī míppərəss/ *adj.*

primitive /prímmətiv/ *adj.* **1. FIRST** at or relating to the first stages or form of sth **2.** BIOL **DEVELOPMENTALLY EARLY** relating to or appearing in an earlier stage of biological development, particularly of an embryo or species **3. VERY SIMPLE IN DESIGN** crudely simple in design or construction (*offensive in some contexts*) **4. ORIGINAL** not derived from other things **5. WITH SIMPLE TECHNOLOGICAL DEVELOPMENT** not using or relying on complex modern technologies (*sometimes considered offensive*) **6.** MATH **BEING BASIS** acting as a basis from which sth else is derived **7. NATURAL** arising from some inherent characteristic **8.** ARTS **ARTISTICALLY UNTRAINED** created by an artist with no formal training, especially using a simple style **9.** ARTS **EARLY MEDIEVAL** created by an early medieval European artist or a folk artist **10.** LING **FROM WHICH OTHER FORM DERIVES** used to describe a word form from which another word is derived ○ *The primitive root in 'children' is 'child'.* **11.** LING **EARLIER IN LINGUISTIC DEVELOPMENT** being or belonging to an earlier form of a language ■ *n.* **1. SB OR STH FROM ORIGINAL STAGE** sb or sth from the first stage or form of sth **2. SB FROM A CULTURE WITH SIMPLE TECHNOLOGIES** a member of a people who do not use or rely on complex modern technologies (*often considered offensive*) **3.** ARTS **UNTRAINED ARTIST** an artist without formal training, especially one using a simple style **4.** ARTS **EARLY MEDIEVAL ARTIST** an artist or folk artist, especially a painter, whose work was typical of the style of early medieval Europe **5.** ARTS **EARLY MEDIEVAL WORK OF ART** a painting or other work by an early medieval artist or a folk artist **6. DERIVATION** sth such as a concept, feature, or formula from which sth else is derived **7.** MATH **BASIC GEOMETRIC FORM OR FUNCTION** a geometric form or function from which another is derived **8.** LING **WORD ROOT** a word root (*dated technical*) **9.** COMPUT **BASIC ELEMENT OF COMPUTER PROGRAM** a simple element of a computer program or graphic design from which larger programs or images can be constructed [14thC. Via French from, ultimately, Latin *primitus* 'in the first place', from *primus* (see PRIME).] —**primitively** *adv.* —**primitiveness** *n.*

primitivism /prímmətivizəm/ *n.* **1. STATE OF BEING PRIMITIVE** the state of being primitive or the qualities associated with being primitive **2.** ARTS **SIMPLICITY OF STYLE** simplicity or naivety of artistic style **3. ANTI-MODERNISM** the belief that less technologically dependent cultures and ways of living are inherently better than more technologically dependent ones —**primitivist** *n.*, *adj.* —**primitivistic** /prímmәti vístik/ *adj.*

primo /prēemō/ *n.* (*plural* **-mos** *or* **-mi** /-mi/) **LEAD MUSICAL PART** the lead musical part in a duet, trio, or ensemble composition ■ *adj.* **FIRST** first in a sequence or series (*formal*) [Mid-18thC. Via Italian and Spanish, 'first, prime', both from Latin *primus* (see PRIME).]

primogenitor /prímō jénnitər, prēemō-/ *n.* **1. ORIGINAL ANCESTOR** the first ancestor of a people or other group **2. ANCESTOR** sb who lived earlier in sb's line of descent [Mid-17thC. Variant of PROGENITOR, on the model of *primogeniture.*]

primogeniture /prímō jénnichər, prēemō-/ *n.* **1. FIRST-BORN STATUS** the state of being the first-born child of a set of parents **2. FIRST-BORN'S RIGHT OF INHERITANCE** the right of the first-born child, usually the eldest son, to inherit the parents' entire estate [Early 17thC. From medieval Latin *primogenitura*, from Latin *primus* 'first' + *genitura* 'birth'.] —**primogenitary** /-jénnitəri/ *adj.*

primordial /prī máwrdi əl/ *adj.* **1. EXISTING FIRST** existing at the beginning of time or the development of sth **2. BASIC** essential or basic to sth **3.** BIOL **OF EARLIEST STAGE OF DEVELOPMENT** relating to cells, tissues, organs, or individuals at the earliest stage of development [14thC. From late Latin *primordialis*, from Latin *primordium* 'origin', from *primus* 'first' + *ordiri* 'to begin'.] —**primordiality** /prī máwrdi álləti/ *n.* —**primordially** /-əli/ *adv.*

primordium /prī máwrdi əm/ (*plural* **-a** /-di ə/) *n.* a tissue or organ in the earliest stage of embryonic development, found when the dividing cells in the fertilized ovum first differentiate [Late 16thC. From Latin (see PRIMORDIAL).]

primp /primp/ **(primps, primping, primped)** *vti.* to groom yourself, sb, or sth in a fussy way ○ *spending all day primping in front of the mirror* [Late 16thC. Origin uncertain.]

primrose /prím rōz/ *n.* **1. SPRING PLANT WITH PALE YELLOW FLOWERS** a small European perennial plant with pale yellow flowers that appear in early spring. Latin name: *Primula vulgaris.* **2.** = **primula 3. PRIMROSE FLOWER** a flower of the primrose plant [14thC. Via Old French *primerose* from medieval Latin *prima rosa* 'first rose', so called because of its early flowering.]

primrose path *n.* an easy or pleasurable way of life, especially one that leads to disaster (*literary*) [From the phrase 'the primrose path of dalliance' in Shakespeare's *Hamlet*]

primula /prímmyŏŏlə/ (*plural* **-las** *or* **-la**) *n.* a small perennial plant with colourful flowers. Genus: *Primula.* [Mid-18thC. Via modern Latin, genus name, from medieval Latin *primula (veris)*, literally 'first fruit (of spring)', from Latin *primulus*, literally 'small first', from *primus* (see PRIME).] —**primulaceous** /prímmyŏŏ láyshəss/ *adj.*

primum mobile /prīməm mṓbili/ *n.* **1.** ASTRON **OUTERMOST SPHERE OF UNIVERSE** in Ptolemaic astronomy, the outermost sphere of the universe, thought to revolve every 24 hours, moving the inner spheres with it **2.** PHILOS = **prime mover** *n.* 3 [15thC. From medieval Latin, literally 'first moving thing'. Translation of Arabic *al-muḥarrik al-awwal.*]

primus /príməss/, **Primus** *n.* *Scotland* the highest ranking bishop in the Scottish Episcopal Church [Late 16thC. From Latin, 'first' (see PRIME).]

primus inter pares /príməss intər paá reez, prēe-/ *n.* the representative or leader of a group of equals [From Latin, 'first among equals']

Primus stove /príməss-/ *tdmk.* a trademark for a brand of portable paraffin cooking stove, used by campers

prin. *abbr.* **1.** principal **2.** principle

prince /prinss/ *n.* **1. SON OF MONARCH** a man or boy in a royal family, especially the son of a reigning king

PRIME MINISTERS OF AUSTRALIA, CANADA, NEW ZEALAND, AND THE UNITED KINGDOM AFTER 1900

Prime Ministers of Australia

Term of Office	Prime Minister
1903–1904	John Christian Watson
1904–1905	George Houston Reid
1905–1908	Alfred Deakin
1908–1909	Andrew Fisher
1909–1910	Alfred Deakin
1910–1913	Andrew Fisher
1913–1914	Joseph Cook
1915–1923	Andrew Fisher
1914–1915	William Morris Hughes
1923–1929	Stanley Shelbourne Bruce
1929–1932	James Henry Scullin
1932–1939	Joseph Aloysius Lyons
1939	Earle Page
1939–1941	Robert Menzies
1941	Arthur William Fadden
1941–1945	John Curtin
1945	Francis Michael Forde
1945–1949	Joseph Benedict Chifley
1949–1966	Robert Menzies
1966–1967	Harold Holt
1967–1968	John McEwen
1968–1971	John Gorton
1971–1972	William McMahon
1972–1975	Gough Whitlam
1975–1983	Malcolm Fraser
1983–1991	Bob Hawke
1991–1996	Paul Keating
1996–	John Howard

Prime Ministers of Canada

Term of Office	Prime Minister
1896–1911	Wilfred Laurier
1911–1920	Robert Laird Borden
1920–1921	Arthur Meighen
1921–1926	W.L. Mackenzie King
1926	Arthur Meighen
1926–1930	W.L. Mackenzie King
1930–1935	Richard Bedford Bennett
1935–1948	W.L. Mackenzie King
1948–1957	Louis St. Laurent
1957–1963	John G. Diefenbaker
1963–1968	Lester B. Pearson
1968–1979	Pierre Trudeau
1979–1980	Joseph Clark
1980–1984	Pierre Trudeau
1984	John M. Turner
1984–1993	Brian Mulroney
1993	Kim Campbell
1993–	Jean Chrétien

Prime Ministers of New Zealand

Term of Office	Prime Minister
1893–1906	Richard John Seddon
1906	William Hall-Jones
1906–1912	Joseph George Ward
1912	Thomas Mackenzie
1912–1925	William Ferguson Masey
1925	Francis Henry Dillon Bell
1925–1928	Joseph Gordon Coates
1928–1930	Joseph George Ward
1930–1935	George William Forbes
1935–1940	Michael Joseph Savage
1940–1949	Peter Fraser
1949–1957	Sydney George Holland
1957	Keith Jacka Holyoake
1957–1960	Walter Nash
1960–1972	Keith Jacka Holyoake
1972	John Ross Marshall
1972–1974	Norman Eric Kirk
1974–1975	Wallace Edward Rowling
1975–1984	Robert David Muldoon
1984–1989	David Russell Lange
1989–1990	Geoffrey Palmer
1990	Michael Moore
1990–1997	James Bolger
1997–	Jenny Shipley

Prime Ministers of the United Kingdom

Term of Office	Prime Minister
1902–1905	Arthur James Balfour
1905–1908	Henry Campbell-Bannerman
1908–1916	Herbert Henry Asquith
1916–1922	David Lloyd George
1922–1923	Andrew Bonar Law
1923–1924	Stanley Baldwin
1924	Ramsay MacDonald
1924–1929	Stanley Baldwin
1929–1935	Ramsay MacDonald
1935–1937	Stanley Baldwin
1937–1940	Neville Chamberlain
1940–1945	Winston Churchill
1945–1951	Clement Attlee
1951–1955	Winston Churchill
1955–1957	Anthony Eden
1957–1963	Harold Macmillan
1963–1964	Alec Douglas-Home
1964–1970	Harold Wilson
1970–1974	Edward Heath
1974–1976	Harold Wilson
1976–1979	James Callaghan
1979–1990	Margaret Thatcher
1990–1997	John Major
1997–	Tony Blair

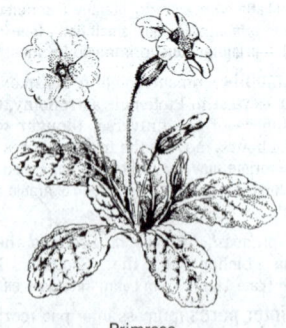
Primrose

or queen **2. MAN RULER** a man who rules a principality **3. EUROPEAN NOBLEMAN** a nobleman in some European countries, usually ranked below a duke **4. HIGHLY REGARDED MAN** a man or boy who is ranked highly in his field ○ *Robin Hood was the prince of thieves.* **5. US GENEROUS, KIND MAN** a man who is extremely nice, especially in a generous or chivalrous way (*in-*

formal) [12thC. Via French from Latin *princeps*, literally 'one who takes first place' (source of English *principal*).]

──── **WORD KEY: CULTURAL NOTE** ────
The Prince, a political treatise by Italian writer Niccolò Machiavelli (1513). Machiavelli based this guide to gaining and maintaining political power on his study of history and his experience of politics. The first work of its kind to present a political philosophy derived from a study of human behaviour rather than traditional ethics, it gained lasting notoriety by justifying the judicious use of ruthlessness and deceit.

Prince Albert (*plural* **Prince Alberts**) *n.* in body piercing, a ring put through the tip of the penis [Late 19thC. Named after Prince ALBERT.]

Prince Charles Island /prinss chaárlz-/ the largest island in Foxe Basin, west of Baffin Island, in Nunavut, Canada. Area: 9,521 sq. km/3,676 sq. mi.

prince charming, **Prince Charming** *n.* **1. ROMANTICALLY IDEAL MAN** a man who fulfils the romantic ideal of the perfect lover (*informal*) **2. CHARMER** a man who actively seeks to charm people, especially women,

and gain their liking [Mid-19thC. From the name of the hero of the fairy tale *Cinderella*.]

prince consort *n.* a prince who is married to a reigning queen

princedom /prínssdəm/ *n.* **PRINCE'S POSITION OR TERRITORY** the position, territory, jurisdiction, or estate of a prince ■ **princedoms** *npl.* = principalities

Prince Edward Island /prinss edwóod-/ the smallest province in Canada, in the east of the country, in the Gulf of St Lawrence, opposite New Brunswick and Nova Scotia. Capital: Charlottetown. Population: 134,557 (1996). Area: 5,660 sq. km/2,185 sq. mi. —**Prince Edward Islander** *n.*

Prince Edward Island National Park national park in eastern Canada, on the northern shore of Prince Edward Island. Area: 22 sq. km/9 sq. mi.

princeling /prínssling/, **princelet** /prínsslət/ *n.* a prince of low rank, age, or importance

princely /prínssli/ (**-lier**, **-liest**) *adj.* **1. RELATING TO PRINCE** relating to, belonging to, or suitable for a prince **2. VERY EXPENSIVE OR GENEROUS** generous as an amount of money or requiring the expenditure of large sums

a at; aa father; aw all; ay day; air hair; ə about, edible, item, common, circus; e egg; ee eel; hw when; i it, happy; ī ice; 'l apple; 'm rhythm; 'n fashion; o odd; ō open; oō good; oo pool; ow owl; oy oil; th thin; th this; u up; ur urge;

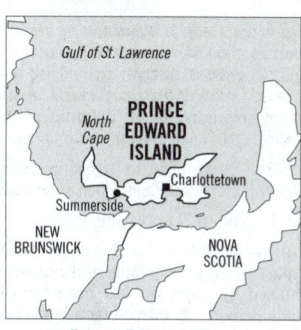

Prince Edward Island

of money ○ *a princely manor in the country* — **princeliness** *n.*

Prince of Darkness *n.* Satan (*literary*) [Modelled on PRINCE OF PEACE]

Prince of Peace *n.* Jesus Christ (*literary*) [From the Christian interpretation of 'and his name shall be called ... Prince of Peace' in the Bible, *Isaiah* 9:6]

Prince of Wales Island /prinss əv wáyəlz-/ **1.** island in southeastern Alaska. It is the largest island in the Alexander Archipelago. Population: 6,278 (1990). Area: 5,778 sq. km/2,231 sq. mi. **2.** island in northern Canada, in Nunavut, between Victoria and Somerset islands. Area: 33,338 sq. km/12,872 sq. mi. **3.** island in northern Australia, in Queensland. Area: 180 sq. km/70 sq. mi.

prince regent (*plural* **prince regents** *or* **princes regent**) *n.* a prince who rules in the monarch's place, e.g. when the monarch is abroad, ill, or still a child

prince royal (*plural* **princes royal**) *n.* the eldest son of a reigning monarch

prince's-feather (*plural* **prince's-feathers** *or* **prince's-feather**) *n.* a tall annual plant with reddish leaves and spikes of red flowers. Family: Amaranthus.

princess /prin séss, prínsess/ *n.* (*plural* **-cesses**) **1.** MONARCH'S DAUGHTER a woman member of a royal family, other than the queen, especially a daughter of the reigning monarch **2.** PRINCE'S WIFE the wife of a prince **3.** DAUGHTER OF MONARCH'S SON a daughter of a son of the sovereign **4.** WOMAN RULER a woman who rules a principality **5.** EUROPEAN NOBLEWOMAN a noblewoman in some European countries, usually ranked below a duchess **6.** HIGHLY REGARDED WOMAN a woman who is ranked highly in her field, or who has other qualities suitable for a princess (*dated*) **7.** SPOILED WOMAN a rich, spoiled young woman (*informal*) ■ *adj.* **princess, princesse** FITTED AT TOP WITH FLARED SKIRT made with long triangular pieces of fabric that reach from neck to hem, fitted at the bodice with a flared skirt

princesse /prin séss/ *adj.* = **princess** *adj.* [Mid-19thC. From French, 'princess'.]

princess royal (*plural* **princesses royal**) *n.* the eldest daughter of a reigning monarch, especially of a British monarch, who confers the title on her as a special honour

Princeton /prínstən/ town in west-central New Jersey. It is the site of Princeton University, founded in 1746. Population: 13,198 (1990).

principal /prínsip'l/ *adj.* **1.** PRIMARY first or among the first in importance or rank **2.** FIN INITIALLY INVESTED relating to the initial amount of money that was invested or borrowed ■ *n.* **1.** MOST IMPORTANT PERSON sb who is in charge or most highly ranked **2.** SIGNIFICANT PARTICIPANT any one of the most significant participants in an event or a situation ○ *the principals in the debate* **3.** EDUC HEAD OF SCHOOL the head administrator of a school, college, or university **4.** **principal, principal teacher** HEAD OF SCHOOL DEPARTMENT the head of a department in a Scottish school ○ *She was promoted to principal of English.* **5.** SENIOR CIVIL SERVANT a civil servant ranked immediately below a Secretary **6.** ARTS LEAD PERFORMER a lead actor, singer, or dancer in a theatrical or musical performance **7.** MUSIC LEAD MUSICIAN the lead musician in a section of an orchestra, or the part played by that musician **8.** FIN ORIGINAL AMOUNT INVESTED the initial sum of money invested or borrowed, before interest or other

revenue is added, or the remainder of that sum after payments have been made **9.** LAW REPRESENTED PERSON sb for whom a representative or proxy acts in a legal matter **10.** LAW RESPONSIBLE PARTY sb who has ultimate responsibility for sth, rather than an accomplice or representative **11.** LAW CRIMINAL the perpetrator of a crime **12.** ARCHIT MAIN SUPPORT BEAM the main support beam, girder, or truss in a roof, bridge, or other construction [13thC. Via French from Latin *principalis*, from *princip-*, the stem of *princeps* (see PRINCE).] —**principally** *adv.* —**principalship** *n.*

principal axis *n.* OPTICS the line that passes through the centre of curvature of a lens

principal boy *n.* a woman who plays the lead male part in a pantomime

principal diagonal *n.* in a square matrix, the diagonal line that extends from the upper left corner to the lower right corner

principal focus *n.* OPTICS = focal point *n.* 1

principality /prínssə pálləti/ *n.* (*plural* **-ties**) **1.** PRINCE'S OR PRINCESS'S COUNTRY a territory ruled by a prince or princess **2.** POSITION OF PRINCE the position or jurisdiction of a prince ■ **principalities** *npl.* ORDER OF ANGELS one of the nine orders of angels in the traditional Christian hierarchy

principal parts *npl.* **1.** VERB FORMS OF INFLECTED LANGUAGE the basic forms of a verb, from which other forms are derived, in an inflected language such as Latin **2.** ENGLISH VERB FORMS the infinitive, past tense, and participial forms of an English verb

principate /prínssi payt, -pət/ *n.* **1.** LAND RULED BY PRINCE a territory ruled by a prince **2.** **principate, Principate** PERIOD OF EARLY ROMAN EMPIRE a period of the early Roman empire in which some traditions and institutions of the Republic were preserved **3.** **principate, Principate** ROMAN POLITICAL SYSTEM the political system of the Roman principate [14thC. Directly or via French from Latin *principatus*, from *princeps* (see PRINCE).]

Príncipe /prínssi pay/ the second largest island in São Tomé and Príncipe. Population: 5,900 (1995). Area: 109 sq. km/42 sq. mi.

principium /prin síppi əm, pring kípp-/ (*plural* **-a** /-pi ə/) *n.* an essential or basic principle (*formal*) (*often used in the plural*) [Late 16thC. From Latin, formed from *princip-*, the stem of *princeps* (see PRINCE).]

principle /prínssip'l/ *n.* **1.** BASIC ASSUMPTION an important underlying law or assumption required in a system of thought **2.** ETHICAL STANDARD a standard of moral or ethical decision-making ○ *I buy recyclable products as a matter of principle.* **3.** WAY OF WORKING the basic way in which sth works **4.** SOURCE the primary source of sth **5.** CHEM CHARACTERISTIC INGREDIENT an ingredient of a substance that gives the substance a particular quality [14thC. Alteration of French *principe*, from Latin *principium*, from *princip-*, the stem of *princeps* (see PRINCE).] ◇ **in principle** in theory or in the essentials ◇ **on principle** because of a particular ethical standard that sb believes in

Principle /prínssip'l/ *n.* a term used in Christian Science for God

principled /prínssip'ld/ *adj.* based on or possessing moral principles, especially ones held in high regard

prink /pringk/ (**prinks, prinking, prinked**) *vti.* to dress or groom sb or yourself in a fancy or fussy way [Late 16thC. Origin uncertain.] —**prinker** *n.*

print /print/ *n.* **1.** MARK PRESSED INTO STH a mark made by pressing sth onto a surface **2.** WRITING ON A SURFACE words, figures, or symbols on a surface, especially when produced by a machine ○ *books available in large print* **3.** PUBL PUBLISHED TEXT the state of being in a printed form or being published ○ *We don't want these typographical errors to make it into print.* **4.** ARTS ARTWORK MADE BY PRESSING DESIGN a work of art made by inking a surface with a raised design and pressing it onto paper or another surface **5.** ARTS FABRIC WITH INKED DESIGN a fabric with an ink or paint design on its surface, or the design itself (*often used before a noun*) ○ *She was wearing a new print dress.* **6.** PHOTOGRAPHY PHOTOGRAPH a photograph, usually made from a negative **7.** CINEMA FILM COPY a copy of a film **8.** STAMP OR DIE a stamp or die used to make marks on a surface **9.** CRIMINOL FINGERPRINT a

fingerprint (*informal*) ■ *v.* (**prints, printing, printed**) **1.** *vti.* PRINTING MAKE STH WITH PRINTING MACHINE to make a copy, document, or publication using a printing press or a computer printer ○ *These books were printed in Canada.* **2.** *vti.* PUBL PUBLISH STH to publish information or a publication ○ *The company prints several news magazines in addition to books.* **3.** *vti.* MARK STH USING PRESSURE to produce a mark, design, or lettering on a surface by pressing sth on it ○ *A machine prints the corporate logo onto pencils.* **4.** *vti.* PRESS DESIGNS ONTO STH to press a mark, design, or lettering onto sth ○ *We printed enough T-shirts for the whole team.* **5.** *vti.* WRITE SEPARATED LETTERS to write sth by hand, using separated letters rather than script ○ *Print your name under your signature.* **6.** *vti.* PHOTOGRAPHY, CINEMA MAKE A COPY FROM A NEGATIVE to make a positive image or copy of a photograph or film from a negative **7.** *vi.* PRINTING WORK AS PRINTER to do the work of a printer ■ *adj.* **1.** PUBL RELATING TO PUBLISHED MEDIA produced by or relating to the published media [13thC. From Old French *preinte*, the feminine past participle of *preindre* 'to press', from Latin *premere* (see PRESS).] ◇ **in print 1.** currently available from a publisher **2.** printed in a book, newspaper, or magazine ◇ **out of print** not currently available from a publisher

print out *vt.* COMPUT to produce a printed copy of data from a computer

printable /príntəb'l/ *adj.* **1.** ABLE TO BE PUBLISHED sufficiently inoffensive, correct, or well-written as to be fit to be printed in a publication ○ *Some of the player's comments weren't printable.* **2.** ABLE TO BE PRINTED capable of being printed or printed on ○ *This paper's too glossy to be printable.* —**printability** /príntə bílləti/ *n.*

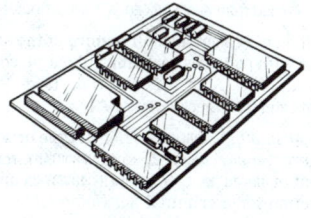

Printed circuit

printed circuit *n.* an electronic circuit in which some components and the connections between them are formed by etching a metallic coating on one or both sides of an insulating board

printed matter *n.* published material such as books, newspapers, magazines, or catalogues

printer /príntər/ *n.* **1.** PRINTING PERSON OR COMPANY IN PRINTING TRADE a person or company that prints books, newspapers, or magazines **2.** PRINTING, PUBL MACHINE FOR PRINTING BOOKS OR NEWSPAPERS a machine that prints books, newspapers, or magazines **3.** COMPUT MACHINE FOR PRINTING COMPUTER DATA a peripheral output device designed to produce computer-generated text or graphics on paper, transparencies, or similar media **4.** PHOTOGRAPHY MACHINE FOR MAKING COPIES OF FILM a machine that makes duplicates of film, normally a positive from a negative

printer's devil *n.* an apprentice or young assistant to a printer (*dated*) [From DEVIL in the sense 'apprentice']

printhead /print hed/ *n.* COMPUT a part of a computer printer that prints out the characters on paper

printing /prínting/ *n.* **1.** PRODUCTION OF COPIES the process or business of producing copies of documents, publications, or images **2.** PRINTED CHARACTERS typographical characters as they appear on paper or another surface ○ *The printing has washed off this bottle.* **3.** LETTERS WRITTEN SEPARATELY letters written separately or the act of writing letters separately, in contrast to script characters ○ *Her printing is easier to read than her handwriting.* **4.** PRINT RUN the process or output of one print run of a publication ○ *This book is in its eighth printing.*

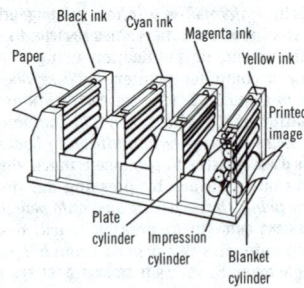

Printing press

printing press *n.* a machine that presses inked set type or etched plates onto paper or textiles that are fed through the machine

printmaker /prínt maykər/ *n.* an artist who designs and makes prints —**printmaking** *n.*

printout /prínt owt/ *n.* a paper copy of data from a computer

print run *n.* the process or output of one printing of a publication, document, or artwork ○ *an initial print run of 30,000 copies*

print shop *n.* a small building, room, or business where documents, publications, or artworks are printed

prion[1] /prí ən/ *n.* BIOL an infectious particle of protein that, unlike a virus, contains no nucleic acid, does not trigger an immune response, and is not destroyed by extreme heat or cold. These particles are considered responsible for such diseases as scrapie, BSE, kuru, and Creutzfeldt-Jakob disease. [Late 20thC. Coined from PROTEINACEOUS + INFECTIOUS + -ON.]

prion[2] /prí ən/ *n.* BIRDS a small seabird of the southern oceans with soft grey markings like a pigeon and a serrated bill. Genus: *Pachyptila.* [Mid-19thC. Via modern Latin from Greek *priōn* 'saw'.]

prior[1] /prí ər/ *adj.* **1.** EARLIER earlier in time or sequence ○ *a prior engagement* **2.** MORE IMPORTANT more important or basic ■ *n.* US EARLIER CONVICTION an earlier conviction for a criminal act (*informal*) ○ *Check to see whether the suspect has any priors.* [Early 18thC. From Latin, 'former, elder, superior', literally 'more before'.]

prior[2] /prí ər/ *n.* **1.** ABBOT'S DEPUTY an officer in a monastery who is ranked below an abbot **2.** MAN RELIGIOUS SUPERIOR a man superior in some religious communities **3.** SENIOR MEDIEVAL MAGISTRATE a senior magistrate in some medieval Italian republics, especially Florence [Pre-12thC. Via medieval Latin from Latin, 'elder, superior' (see PRIOR[1]).]

priorate /prí ərət/ *n.* the position or term of office of a prior or prioress

prioress /prí ə réss/ *n.* **1.** ABBESS'S DEPUTY an officer in a convent who ranks below an abbess **2.** WOMAN RELIGIOUS SUPERIOR a woman superior in some religious communities

prioritize /prī órri tīz/ (**-tizes, -tizing, -tized**), **prioritise** (**-tises, -tising, -tised**) *vti.* **1.** RANK THINGS ACCORDING TO IMPORTANCE to order things according to their importance or urgency ○ *I must prioritize my list of things to do.* **2.** RANK STH AS MOST IMPORTANT to regard sth as most important or urgent ○ *I have to prioritize finding a job.*

priority /prī órriti/ (*plural* **-ties**) *n.* **1.** GREATEST IMPORTANCE the state of having most importance or urgency ○ *Give this case priority treatment.* **2.** SB OR STH IMPORTANT sb or sth that is ranked highly in terms of importance or urgency ○ *You've got to get your priorities right.* **3.** EARLINESS the state of having preceded sth else **4.** RIGHT OF PRECEDENCE the right to be ranked above others

priory /prí əri/ (*plural* **-ies**) *n.* a religious community or home such as a monastery or convent, headed by a prior or prioress

Pripet Marshes /preepyət maárshiz/, **Pripyat' Marshes** swamp region in southern Belarus and northwestern Ukraine, along the River Pripet

prise /prīz/ (**prises, prising, prised**) *vt.* **1.** LEVER STH to open or part sth by levering ○ *I used a screwdriver to prise the lid off the paint.* **2.** EXTRACT INFORMATION to get sth, especially information, from sb or sth with difficulty [14thC. Origin uncertain: probably from French *prise* 'seizing, capture' (see PRIZE[2]).]

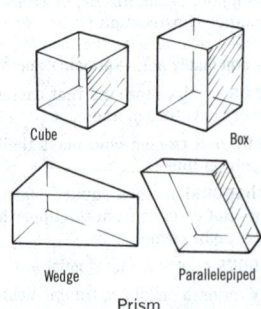

Prism

prism /prízzəm/ *n.* **1.** OPTICS POLYGONAL SOLID FOR DISPERSING LIGHT a transparent polygonal solid object with flat faces and a usually triangular cross-section, used for separating white light into a spectrum of colours **2.** STH MADE OF CUT GLASS a cut-glass object, especially one that can separate white light into a spectrum **3.** CRYSTALS CRYSTAL TYPE a crystal form with faces that are parallel to a single axis **4.** GEOM PARALLELOGRAM-SIDED SOLID a solid figure with ends that are identical polygons and with sides that are parallelograms [Late 16thC. Via late Latin from Greek *prisma*, literally 'sth sawn' (because of its shape), from *prizein* 'to saw', of unknown origin.]

prismatic /priz máttik/ *adj.* **1.** RELATING TO PRISM resembling or relating to a prism **2.** SEPARATED BY PRISM used to describe light that shows the colours of the spectrum, as refracted by a prism **3.** COLOURFUL brightly coloured, like a rainbow [Early 18thC. Via French *prismatique* from Greek *prismat-*, the stem of *prisma* (see PRISM).] —**prismatically** *adv.*

prismatoid /prízmə toyd/ *n.* a polyhedron with all its vertices in one of two parallel planes [Mid-19thC. Formed from Greek *prismat-*, the stem of *prisma* (see PRISM).] —**prismatoidal** /prízmə tóyd'l/ *adj.*

prismoid /príz moyd/ *n.* a prismatoid with sides that are parallelograms or trapezoids and equal-sided polygons as bases [Early 18thC. Formed from PRISM, on the model of *rhomboid.*] —**prismoidal** /priz móyd'l/ *adj.*

prison /prízz'n/ *n.* **1.** PLACE WHERE CRIMINALS ARE CONFINED a secure place where sb is confined as punishment for a crime or while waiting to stand trial **2.** CONFINEMENT a place or condition of captivity or unwanted restraint ○ *His fears are a prison that he cannot escape.* ■ *vt.* (**-ons, -oning, -oned**) IMPRISON to put sb in prison (*archaic or literary*) [12thC. Via Old French from, ultimately, the Latin stem *prension-* 'seizing', from *prehendere* 'to seize'.]

prison camp *n.* a camp where prisoners of war are confined

prisoner /prízz'nər/ *n.* **1.** SB HELD IN PRISON sb confined in a prison as a punishment for a crime or while waiting to stand trial **2.** SB HELD AGAINST WILL sb who has been captured and is held in confinement in a place **3.** SB WHO IS OR FEELS TRAPPED sb who is unable to escape a situation or condition

prisoner of conscience *n.* sb held in a prison by a state, especially an oppressive regime, because of his or her political or religious beliefs

prisoner of war *n.* sb who has been captured and held captive by the enemy during a war

prisoner's base *n.* a children's game in which two teams try to tag each other's members, thereby adding them to their team at their base [Alteration of earlier *prison-bars*]

prissy /príssi/ (**-sier, -siest**) *adj.* behaving in a very prudish and proper way [Late 19thC. Origin uncertain: probably a blend of PRIM and SISSY.] —**prissily** *adv.* —**prissiness** *n.*

Priština /préeshtina/ the largest city in the region of Kosovo in the Federal Republic of Yugoslavia. Population: 108,083 (1991).

pristine /prís teen/ *adj.* **1.** IMMACULATE so clean and neat as to look as good as new ○ *The house is in pristine condition.* **2.** UNSPOILT not yet ruined by human encroachment ○ *acres of pristine forest* **3.** IN OR OF ORIGINAL STATE in or belonging to an original state or condition [Mid-16thC. From Latin *pristinus* 'former'.]

prithee /príthi/ *interj.* used to introduce a request to sb (*archaic*) [Late 16thC. Contraction of (*I*) *pray thee.*]

priv. *abbr.* **1.** private **2.** privative

privacy /prívvəssi, prívəssi/ *n.* **1.** SECLUSION the state of being apart from other people and not seen, heard, or disturbed by them ○ *Shut the door so we can have some privacy.* **2.** FREEDOM FROM ATTENTION OF OTHERS freedom from the observation, intrusion, or attention of others ○ *If you seek celebrity, you must sacrifice privacy.* **3.** HIDDEN CONDITION the state of being kept secret

private /prívət/ *adj.* **1.** NOT FOR OTHERS concerning matters that are not for other people to see or know about **2.** SECLUDED sufficiently secluded for it to be possible to be alone and not watched, heard, or disturbed by others ○ *Let's find a private corner where we can talk.* **3.** PERSONAL belonging to, restricted to, or intended for an individual **4.** NOT PUBLIC not open to the public **5.** ACTING IN PERSONAL CAPACITY not holding an official position in government, or not relating to the official role of a government person ○ *a private citizen* **6.** NONGOVERNMENTAL not supported by government funding **7.** RESERVED AND SECRETIVE preferring not to disclose personal information or to discuss personal feelings with others ○ *She's a very private person.* **8.** NOT UNDERSTANDABLE BY EVERYONE excluding people who do not share the knowledge required to understand **9.** MIL LOWEST-RANKING belonging to the lowest rank of soldier ■ *n.* MIL LOWEST-RANKING SOLDIER a soldier of the lowest rank ■ **privates** *npl.* GENITALS the genitals (*informal*) [14thC. From Latin *privatus* 'isolated, not in public life', the past participle of *privare* (see PRIVATION).] —**privately** *adv.* —**privateness** *n.*

private bill *n.* a legislative bill presented in Parliament that affects only an individual or corporation

private company *n.* a company that is not listed on the stock market and does not issue its shares to the public

private detective *n.* a detective who is not a member of the police, but who is hired by individuals or companies

private enterprise *n.* **1.** BUSINESS NOT REGULATED BY GOVERNMENT business activities that are not regulated or owned by the government **2.** PRIVATELY OWNED COMPANY a company that is owned by a private individual or individuals and not by the government

privateer /prívə teér/ *n.* **1.** PRIVATE SHIP USED IN WAR a ship that belongs to and is run by a person or company but is authorized by the government to engage in battle during war **2.** SB SAILING ON PRIVATEER the commander or a crew member of a privateer [Mid-17thC. Modelled on *volunteer.*]

private eye *n.* a private detective (*informal*) [*Eye*, spelling of *I.*, a shortening of *investigator.*]

private hotel *n.* a privately run hotel that has the right to refuse potential guests

private income *n.* income from sources other than employment, e.g. from investments or allowances

private investigator *n.* = private detective

private language *n.* an exclusive language devised and spoken by a restricted group of people, especially twins

private law *n.* the branch of law concerned with the rights and responsibilities of individuals. ◊ **public law**

private life *n.* the part of sb's life that relates to his or her personal activities and relationships and not to his or her job or public duties

private means *npl.* = private income

private member *n.* a member of the House of Commons who does not hold a ministerial position

private member's bill *n.* a bill introduced in the House of Commons by a private member

private parts *npl.* the genitals

private patient *n.* a patient who chooses to pay for medical treatment outside the National Health Service, usually to obtain advantages such as the avoidance of a long wait for surgery

private pay bed *n.* MED a hospital bed reserved for a paying patient, rather than a National Health Service patient

private practice *n.* **1.** **BUSINESS RUN BY AN INDIVIDUAL PROFESSIONAL** a professional business owned and managed by an individual professional such as a lawyer, rather than by an organization **2.** MED **PRACTICE OUTSIDE NHS** a doctor's practice that is not part of the National Health Service. Few doctors engage in full-time private practice, but many NHS consultants pursue part-time private practice.

private property *n.* **1.** **STH OWNED BY INDIVIDUAL** sth, especially land or buildings, owned by an individual or a nongovernmental corporation **2.** **IDEA OF LAND OWNERSHIP** the idea that land can be divided up, bought or claimed, and owned by an individual, company, or government

private secretary *n.* a secretary employed to manage sb's personal or confidential affairs, especially those of a business executive or public figure

private sector *n.* the part of a free market economy that is made up of companies and organizations that are not owned or controlled by the government

private treaty *n.* sale of property according to terms negotiated by buyer and vendor

private view, **private viewing** *n.* a preview of a film or an exhibition that is open only to invited guests

privation /prī vāysh'n/ *n.* **1.** **LACK OF LIFE'S NECESSITIES** lack of the basic necessities of life such as food, housing, and heating **2.** **ACT OF DEPRIVING SB** the act of depriving sb of sth [14thC. From Latin *privare* 'to deprive, isolate', from *privus* 'single, isolated', literally 'standing in front'.]

privatise *vt.* = **privatize**

privative /prívvətiv/ *adj.* **1.** **RELATING TO LACK OR NEGATION** indicating the absence or negation of some quality ○ *a privative term* **2.** **CAUSING DEPRIVATION** causing or experiencing deprivation ■ *n.* **AFFIX DENOTING LACK OR NEGATION** an affix, word, or expression that denotes the absence or negation of some quality, e.g. English 'non-' or Greek 'a-' [Late 16thC. Directly or via French from, ultimately, Latin *privare* (see PRIVATION).] —**privatively** *adv.*

privatization /prívə tī záysh'n/, **privatisation** *n.* the practice of transferring to private ownership an economic enterprise or public utility that has been under state ownership

privatize /prívə tīz/ (**-tizes, -tizing, -tized**), **privatise** (**-tises, -tising, -tised**) *vt.* to transfer to private ownership an economic enterprise or public utility that has been under state ownership

privet /prívvit/ *n.* an evergreen shrub with small white flower clusters and black berries that is commonly used for hedges. Latin name: *Ligustrum vulgare* and *Ligustrum ovalifolium.* [Mid-16thC. Origin uncertain.]

privilege /prívvəlij/ *n.* **1.** **RESTRICTED RIGHT OR BENEFIT** an advantage, right, or benefit that is not available to everyone **2.** **RIGHTS AND ADVANTAGES ENJOYED BY ELITE** the rights and advantages enjoyed by a relatively small group of people, usually as a result of wealth or social status ○ *a system founded on privilege* **3.** **SPECIAL HONOUR** a special treat or honour ○ *It was a privilege to work with you.* **4.** **LAWMAKER'S RIGHT TO SPECIAL TREATMENT** the right to, or granting of, special treatment or benefits to members of a lawmaking body, e.g. freedom from prosecution ■ *vt.* (**-leges, -leging, -leged**) **1.** **GIVE SB OR STH SPECIAL RIGHTS** to grant special rights or benefits to sb or sth **2.** **GRANT SB OR STH EXEMPTION** to exempt or release sb or sth from sth [12thC. Via Old French from Latin *privilegium* 'private law', from *privus* (see PRIVATION) + the stem *leg-* 'law'.]

privileged /prívvəlijd/ *adj.* **1.** **ENJOYING SPECIAL ADVANTAGES** enjoying privileges, especially the resources and advantages associated with the upper classes or the rich **2.** **HONOURED OR FORTUNATE** fortunate in having a special advantage or opportunity to do sth ○ *I feel privileged to be here today.* ■ *npl.* **PEOPLE ENJOYING SPECIAL ADVANTAGES** a class of people, especially the rich or the upper classes, that benefits from special rights or resources (*takes a plural verb*)

privileged communication *n.* LAW **1.** **CONFIDENTIAL COMMUNICATION** a confidential conversation or correspondence that does not have to be disclosed in a court of law **2.** **COMMUNICATION EXEMPT FROM LIBEL OR SLANDER** speech or writing that is not subject to libel or slander laws

privily /prívvili/ *adv.* in a secret or private way (*archaic*)

privity /prívvəti/ (*plural* **-ties**) *n.* **1.** **SHARED KNOWLEDGE OF SECRET** the state of sharing knowledge of, or colluding in, sth secret **2.** LAW **LEGALLY RECOGNIZED RELATIONSHIP** a legally recognized relationship between two parties, e.g. between members of a family, between an employer and employees, or between others who have entered into a contract together **3.** LAW **RELATIONSHIP TO PROPERTY** a successive or mutual relationship to some property [12thC. Via Old French from medieval Latin *privitas*, from Latin *privus* (see PRIVATION).]

privy /prívvi/ *adj.* **1.** **SHARING SECRET KNOWLEDGE** sharing knowledge of sth secret or private ○ *I was privy to their plans to elope.* **2.** **RELATING TO SB IN PRIVATE CAPACITY** relating to sb, especially a British monarch, as a private individual, not as an official personage **3.** **SECRET** done or spoken secretly or privately (*archaic*) ■ *n.* (*plural* **-ies**) **1.** **OUTSIDE TOILET** an outside toilet or latrine **2.** LAW **SB INVOLVED IN STH** an individual who has an interest or agency in sth that involves another party [12thC. Via French *privé* from Latin *privatus* (see PRIVATE).]

privy chamber *n.* an apartment reserved for private use in a royal residence

privy council *n.* a committee that advises a ruler — **privy counsellor** *n.*

Privy Council *n.* the committee that advises a British king or queen —**Privy Counsellor** *n.*

Privy Purse *n.* **1.** **BRITISH MONARCH'S PERSONAL ALLOWANCE** the allowance from public funds given to the British monarch to cover personal expenses **2.** **MONARCH'S FINANCIAL OFFICIAL** the official who manages the personal finances of the British monarch. Full form **Keeper of the Privy Purse**

Privy Seal *n.* **1.** **BRITISH MONARCH'S SEAL OF AUTHORITY** a seal that used to be attached to documents authorized by the British king or queen **2.** = **Lord Privy Seal**

prix fixe /prée féeks/ (*plural* **prix fixes**) *n.* **1.** **RESTAURANT MEAL SERVED AT FIXED PRICE** a meal with several courses that is offered by a restaurant at a set price **2.** **SET PRICE FOR MEAL** a set price for a restaurant meal with several courses [From French, 'fixed price']

prize[1] /prīz/ *n.* **1.** **AWARD FOR WINNER** sth that is given to the winner of a contest or competition **2.** **STH HIGHLY VALUED** sth that sb values highly, especially because it takes great skill, effort, or luck to get ■ *vt.* (**prizes, prizing, prized**) **TREASURE STH** to value sth highly ○ *This award is something I'll always prize.* ■ *adj.* **COMPLETE** perfect as an example of sth, especially sth undesirable (*dated informal*) ○ *I made a prize fool of myself.* [Late 16thC. From earlier *prise* 'value, reward'.]

prize[2] /prīz/ *n.* sth captured and kept, especially a ship or its contents taken by another ship in wartime [13thC. From Old French *prise*, literally 'sth seized', the feminine past participle of *prendre* 'to take, seize', from Latin *prehendere* (see PREHENSION).]

prize[3] *vt., n.* US = **prise**

prizefight /príz fīt/ *n.* a boxing match in which the winner receives a cash prize —**prizefighter** *n.* — **prizefighting** *n.*

prize ring *n.* **1.** **BOXING RING** a boxing ring where prizefights are held **2.** **PROFESSIONAL BOXING** the sport or business of professional boxing

prizewinner /príz winər/ *n.* sb or sth that wins a prize in a competition, or that habitually wins prizes — **prizewinning** *adj.*

prn *abbr.* as required (*used on medical prescriptions*) [From Latin *pro re nata*]

pro[1] /prō/ *n.* (*plural* **pros**) **1.** **ARGUMENT FOR STH** an argument in favour of a proposal or position **2.** **SIDE ARGUING FOR STH** a person or side in a debate, argument, or campaign that is in favour of a proposal or proposition ■ *prep.* **FOR** in favour of ■ *adv.* **IN SUPPORT OF STH** on the side that favours one side of an issue [14thC. From Latin, 'for' (see PRO-).]

pro[2] /prō/ *n.* (*plural* **pros**) **1.** **PROFESSIONAL PERSON** a professional, especially in sports (*informal*) **2.** **SKILLED PERSON** sb who is very skilled at what he or she does **3.** **PROSTITUTE** a prostitute (*slang*) ■ *adj.* **PROFESSIONAL** relating to or typical of an activity, especially a sport, from which sb earns a living ■ *adv.* **PROFESSIONALLY** as a professional [Mid-20thC. Shortening.]

PRO *n., abbr.* **1.** Public Record Office **2.** public relations officer

pro-[1] *prefix.* **1.** substituting for, acting in place of ○ *proconsul* **2.** in favour of ○ *pronuclear* [Via Old French from, ultimately, Latin *pro* 'for'. Ultimately from an Indo-European word meaning 'forward, before' that is also the ancestor of English *fro, from,* and *pro*[2].]

pro-[2] *prefix.* **1.** rudimentary, precursor ○ *promycelium* **2.** before, earlier than ○ *procambium* **3.** in front of ○ *procephalic* [Via Old French from, ultimately, Greek *pro* 'in front, before'. Ultimately from an Indo-European word meaning 'forward, before' that is also the ancestor of English *fro, from,* and *pro*[1].]

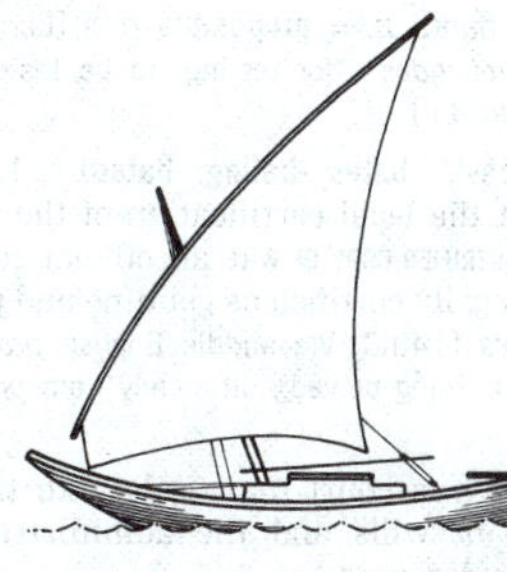

Proa

proa /prṓ ə/ (*plural* **-as**), **prau** /prow/ (*plural* **praus**), **prahu** /praá oo/ (*plural* **-us**) *n.* a Malayan boat with a triangular sail and a single outrigger [Late 16thC. From Malay *pārāhū* 'boat'.]

proactive /prō áktiv/ *adj.* taking the initiative by acting rather than reacting to events [Mid-20thC. Modelled on *retroactive.*] —**proactively** *adv.*

WORD KEY: USAGE

Jargon? When people name words they despise as jargon, ***proactive*** is often on the list. However, ***proactive*** does meet a need, serving as the opposite of *reactive* more naturally than, for example, *anticipatory* or *assertive* is able to. Nonetheless, it should be used sparingly.

pro-am /prō ám/ *adj.* **COMBINING PROFESSIONALS AND AMATEURS** involving or composed of professional and amateur sports players ■ *n.* **PRO-AM COMPETITION** a competition in which professional players compete against amateurs, or in which professionals and amateurs compete together [Mid-20thC. Contraction.]

prob. *abbr.* **1.** probable **2.** probably **3.** problem

probabilism /próbbəbəlizzəm/ *n.* **1.** PHILOSOPHY **RELIANCE ON PROBABILITIES** the belief that certainty is impossible, and that therefore decisions must be based on probabilities **2.** PHILOSOPHY, CHR **THE CHOOSING OF FAVOURABLE PROBABILITY** the principle whereby, in moral questions in which nothing is certain, sb may follow the probability favourable to him or her rather than a more probable, but less favourable view —**probabilist** *n., adj.* —**probabilistic** /próbbəbə lístik/ *adj.* — **probabilistically** /-lístik'li/ *adv.*

probability /próbbə bílləti/ (*plural* **-ties**) *n.* **1.** **STATE OF BEING PROBABLE** the state of being probable or the extent to which sth is probable ○ *We must take into account the probability of another earthquake.* **2.** **STH LIKELY TO HAPPEN** sth that is likely to happen or exist ○ *We must prepare for all probabilities.* **3.** STATS **MATHEMATICAL LIKELIHOOD OF EVENT** the likelihood that an event will occur expressed as the ratio of the number of favourable outcomes in the set of outcomes divided by the total number of possible outcomes ◇ **in all probability** used to suggest that sth is highly probable

probability density function *n.* **1.** = **probability function 2.** STATS **FUNCTION OF CONTINUOUS VARIABLE** a function of a continuous variable such that the integral of the function over a specific region yields the probability that its value will fall within the region

probability function *n.* a function of a discrete random variable that yields the probability of occurrence of distinct outcomes

probability theory *n.* the branch of mathematics that deals with quantities having random distributions, with the aim of predicting how defined systems will behave

probable /próbbəb'l/ *adj.* LIKELY likely to exist, occur, or be true, although evidence is insufficient to prove or predict it ■ *n.* LIKELY CHOICE sb or sth that is likely to be chosen for sth or likely to do sth ○ *a probable for the team* [14thC. Directly or via French from Latin *probabilis* 'provable, plausible', from *probare* (see PROVE).]

probable cause *n.* sufficient reason to believe that an arrest or search of a suspect is warranted

probable error *n.* the amount by which a statistic may vary from fact, based on chance factors

probably /próbbəbli/ *adv.* as is likely or to be expected ○ *I'll probably come tonight.*

proband /prṓ band/ *n.* = **propositus** *n.* 3 [Early 20thC. From Latin *probandus-*, 'for testing, to be tested', from *probare* (see PROVE).]

probate /prṓ bayt/ (**-bates, -bating, -bated**) *n.* **1.** PROOF OF VALIDITY OF WILL the legal certification of the validity of a will **2.** VERIFIED COPY OF WILL an official copy of a will that is legally certified as genuine and given to the executors [14thC. Via Middle English *probat* from Latin *probatum* 'thing proved', ultimately from *probare* 'to test'.]

probate court *n.* a court that deals with the legal certification of wills and the administration of estates of the deceased

probation /prə báysh'n/ *n.* **1.** SUPERVISION BY PROBATION OFFICER the supervision of the behaviour of a young or first-time criminal offender by a probation officer. During the period of supervision, the offender must regularly report to the probation officer and must not commit any further offences. **2.** PERIOD OF TESTING SB'S SUITABILITY a period during which sb's suitability for a job or other role is being tested **3.** TESTING OF STH the testing or proving of sth (*formal*) —**probational** *adj.* —**probationally** *adv.* —**probationary** *adj.*

probationary assistant *n.* *NZ* in New Zealand, a teacher undergoing a probation period

probationer /prə báysh'nər/ *n.* **1.** SB ON PROBATION sb who is on probation, especially a newly qualified nurse or teacher, or a criminal offender who is under the supervision of a probation officer **2.** STUDENT PRESBYTERIAN MINISTER a student Scottish Presbyterian minister who has received a licence but has not yet been ordained

probation officer *n.* sb who supervises the behaviour of criminal offenders on probation

probation service *n.* the branch of the criminal justice system that deals with the supervision of criminal offenders after their release from prison or as an alternative to prison

probative /prṓbətiv/, **probatory** /prṓbətəri/ *adj.* **1.** PROVIDING PROOF supplying proof or evidence **2.** TESTING designed to test or prove sb or sth [15thC. Via Old French *probatif* from, ultimately, Latin *probare* (see PROVE).]

probe /prōb/ *n.* **1.** INVESTIGATION a thorough investigation, often into illegal or suspicious activities **2.** ELEC ENG CIRCUIT-TESTING DEVICE a device with a metal tip used to test or the behaviour of electrical circuits **3.** SURG, DENT SURGICAL INSTRUMENT FOR EXPLORING a long thin instrument used by doctors and dentists for exploring or examining **4.** SPACE TECH = **space probe** ■ *vti.* (**probes, probing, probed**) **1.** INVESTIGATE COMPLETELY to conduct a thorough investigation into sth **2.** CHECK USING PROBE to examine sth with a probe **3.** EXAMINE AREA to search or explore a place [Mid-16thC. Via medieval latin *proba* 'examination', from, ultimately, Latin *probare* 'to test'.] —**probeable** *adj.* —**prober** *n.*

probenecid /prō bénnəssid/ *n.* a drug that promotes the excretion of uric acid and is used to treat gout [Mid-20thC. From PROPYL + BENZENE + ACID.]

probity /prṓbəti/ *n.* absolute moral correctness (*formal*) [Early 16thC. Via Old French *probité* from, ultimately Latin *probus-*, 'good, honest, upright'.]

problem /próbbləm/ *n.* **1.** DIFFICULTY a difficult situation, matter, or person **2.** PUZZLE TO BE SOLVED a question or puzzle that needs to be solved **3.** MATH STATEMENT REQUIRING MATHEMATICAL SOLUTION a statement or proposition requiring an algebraic, geometric, or other mathematical solution ■ *adj.* HARD TO DEAL WITH difficult to discipline or deal with [14thC. Via Old French from, ultimately, Greek *problēmat-*, 'projection, obstacle', literally 'thing thrown in front', from *ballein*, 'to throw'.] ◇ **no problem** used to indicate that sth will not cause any difficulty or inconvenience (*informal*)

WORD KEY: SYNONYMS

problem, mystery, puzzle, riddle, conundrum, enigma

CORE MEANING: sth difficult to solve or understand

problem a general word for a question or difficult situation in need of a solution; **mystery** sth that has never been fully explained or understood and may never be so; **puzzle** a problem whose solution requires ingenuity as well as facts and skills and often involves the use of clues; **riddle** a problem or puzzling question deliberately devised to require a degree of skill and ingenuity in its solution. It can also be used to refer to sth that has not yet been fully explained or understood; **conundrum** a problem that is so complicated or strange that it seems impossible to solve; **enigma** sb or sth that is mysterious and hard to understand.

problematic /próbblə máttik/, **problematical** /-máttik'l/ *adj.* involving difficulties or problems —**problematically** *adv.*

problem play *n.* a dramatic work that deals with moral or social problems

pro bono /prō bṓnō/ *adj.*, *adv.* done or undertaken for the public good without any payment or compensation [Shortening of Latin *pro bono publico* 'for the public good']

proboscidean /próbbə síddi ən/, **proboscidian** *n.* a very large mammal that has a trunk and tusks, e.g. the elephant or extinct mammoth or mastodon. Order: Proboscidea. [Mid-19thC. Formed from modern Latin *Proboscidea*, order name, from Latin *proboscid-*, the stem of *proboscis*.] —**proboscidean** *adj.*

proboscis /prō bóssis/ (*plural* **-cises** *or* **-cides** /-bóssi deez/) *n.* **1.** ELEPHANT'S TRUNK the trunk of an elephant or related extinct mammal **2.** LONG FLEXIBLE SNOUT the long flexible snout of some mammals such as the tapir, the elephant seal, and the proboscis monkey **3.** LONG MOUTHPARTS OF INVERTEBRATE the long or tubular mouthparts of certain insects, worms, and spiders, used for feeding, sucking, and other purposes **4.** LARGE NOSE a human nose, especially a large one (*humorous*) [Late 16thC. Via Latin from Greek *proboskis*, 'elephant's trunk', from *boskein*, 'to feed'.]

proboscis monkey *n.* a large monkey found in Borneo that has reddish fur and a protruding bulbous nose that in older males becomes pendulous. Latin name: *Nasalis larvatus*.

proc. *abbr.* **1.** procedure **2.** proceedings **3.** process

procaine /prṓ kayn, -káyn/, **procain** *n.* a white or colourless crystalline ester formerly used as a local anaesthetic in medicine and dentistry in the form of its hydrochloride. Formula: $C_{13}H_{20}N_2O_2$.

procambium /prō kámbi əm/ *n.* BOT undifferentiated plant tissue that develops into cambium and vascular tissue [Late 19thC. From PRO[2] + CAMBIUM.] —**procambial** *adj.*

procarp /prṓ kaarp/ *n.* BIOL the female sex organ of red algae

procaryote *n.* = **prokaryote**

procathedral /prṓkə theédrəl/ *n.* a local or parish church that is temporarily being used as a cathedral

procedural /prə seéjərəl/ *adj.* involving a procedure, especially a legal procedure —**procedurally** *adv.*

procedural language *n.* a high-level programming language that requires the programmer to specify the sequence of operations that the computer must follow to accomplish a specific task. Pascal, BASIC, and COBOL are procedural languages.

procedure /prə seéjər/ *n.* **1.** ESTABLISHED METHOD an established or correct method of doing sth **2.** ANY METHOD any means of doing or accomplishing sth ○ *an extremely unorthodox procedure* **3.** COMPUT = **routine** *n.* 5 **4.** COMPUT = **subroutine** [Early 17thC. From French *procédure*, from *procéder* from Old French (see PROCEED).]

proceed /prə seéd/ (**-ceeds, -ceeding, -ceeded**) *vi.* **1.** BEGIN ACTION to go on to do sth **2.** CONTINUE WITH ACTION to continue with a course of action **3.** PROGRESS to progress in a steady or particular manner **4.** GO IN SOME DIRECTION to go in a particular direction, especially forward **5.** LAW SUE to bring legal action against sb **6.** DEVELOP to come from or arise from sth [14thC. Via Old French *proceder* from Latin *procedere*, 'to go forward', from *cedere*, 'to go'.] —**proceeder** *n.*

proceeding /prə seéding/ *n.* PROCEDURE an action or course of action ■ **proceedings** *npl.* **1.** LAW LEGAL ACTION legal action brought against sb **2.** SERIES OF EVENTS a series of related events occurring at one time or in one place **3.** PUBLISHED RECORDS published records of a meeting or conference

proceeds /prṓ seedz/ *npl.* the money derived from a sale or other commercial transaction

process[1] /prṓ sess/ *n.* **1.** SERIES OF ACTIONS a series of actions directed towards a particular aim **2.** SERIES OF NATURAL OCCURRENCES a series of natural occurrences that produce change or development **3.** LAW SUMMONS TO APPEAR IN COURT a summons or writ ordering sb to appear in court **4.** LAW LEGAL PROCEEDINGS the entire proceedings in a lawsuit **5.** BIOL NATURAL OUTGROWTH a part that naturally grows on or sticks out on an organism ■ *v.* (**-esses, -essing, -essed**) **1.** *vt.* PREPARE STH USING A PROCESS to treat or prepare sth in a series of steps or actions, e.g. using chemicals or industrial machinery **2.** *vt.* PHOTOGRAPHY TREAT STH WITH PHOTOGRAPHIC CHEMICALS to treat light-sensitive film or paper with chemicals in order to make a latent image visible **3.** *vt.* USE PROCEDURES TO DO STH to deal with sb or sth according to an established procedure **4.** *vti.* COOK PREPARE FOOD IN FOOD PROCESSOR to chop, mix, or otherwise prepare food in food processor or blender **5.** *vt.* COMPUT USE PROGRAM ON DATA to use a computer program to work on data in some way, e.g. to sort a database or recalculate a spreadsheet **6.** *vt.* LAW SERVE SUMMONS ON SB to serve a summons or writ on sb **7.** *vt.* LAW BRING LEGAL ACTION to bring a legal action against sb **8.** *vt.* *US* STRAIGHTEN HAIR USING LYE to straighten curly hair using lye [14thC. Directly and via Old French *proces* from Latin *processus*, the past participle of *procedere* (see PROCEED).]

process[2] /prə séss/ (**-esses, -essing, -essed**) *vi.* to move forwards in a procession

processed cheese *n.* a blend of several types of cheese with emulsifiers added, sometimes sold in individually wrapped thin slices

process engineering *n.* the branch of engineering that determines the sequence of operations and the selection of tools required to manufacture a product

process industry *n.* an industry in which raw materials are treated or prepared in a series of stages, e.g. using chemical processes. Process industries include oil refining, petrochemicals, water and sewage treatment, food manufacture, and pharmaceuticals.

procession /prə sésh'n/ *n.* **1.** GROUP OF PEOPLE MOVING FORWARDS a group of people or vehicles moving forwards in a line as part of a celebration, commemoration, or demonstration **2.** FORWARD MOVEMENT the movement forwards of a group of people or vehicles as part of a celebration, commemoration, or demonstration **3.** SUCCESSION a series of people or things coming one after the other [12thC. Via Old French from ultimately Latin *process*, the past participle stem of *procedere* (see PROCEED).]

processional /prə sésh'nəl/ *adj.* **1.** FOR PROCESSION used for or in a procession **2.** FORMING PROCESSION taking the form of a procession ■ *n.* **1.** MUSIC MUSIC FOR PROCESSION a piece of music suitable for accompanying a procession **2.** MUSIC, CHR MUSIC FOR ENTRY OF CLERGY a hymn or other piece of music that accompanies the entry of the clergy into a church **3.** CHR BOOK OF HYMNS AND PRAYERS a book of hymns and prayers for use during a religious procession —**processionally** *adv.*

processor /prṓ sessər/, **processer** *n.* **1.** STH THAT PROCESSES sb or sth that processes things **2.** CENTRAL PROCESSING UNIT OF COMPUTER the central processing unit of a computer **3.** COMPUT = **microprocessor 4.** HOUSEHOLD = **food processor**

process printing *n.* a method of full-colour printing using multiple images from plates printed in yellow, magenta, blue, and cyan

process-server *n.* sb who serves a writ or summons ordering sb to appear in court

procès-verbal /próssay vur baál/ (*plural* **procès-verbaux** /próssay vur bṓ/) *n.* a written account of official proceedings [Mid-17thC. From French, literally 'oral proceedings', originally with reference to the oral reports of evidence from police officers who could not write.]

pro-choice *adj.* advocating open legal access to voluntary abortion

proclaim /prə kláym/ (**-claims, -claiming, -claimed**) *vt.* **1.** DECLARE STH PUBLICLY to announce sth publicly or formally **2.** DECLARE SB TO BE STH to declare publicly that sb is sth **3.** SHOW WHAT STH IS to show or reveal clearly what sth is **4.** MAKE STH CLEAR to state sth emphatically or openly [14thC. Via Old French *proclamer* from Latin *proclamare*, literally 'to cry forth', from *clamare* 'to cry'.] —**proclaimer** *n.* —**proclamatory** /prə klámmətəri/ *adj.*

proclamation /próklə máysh'n/ *n.* **1.** PUBLIC ANNOUNCEMENT a public or formal announcement **2.** MAKING OF PUBLIC ANNOUNCEMENT the act of announcing sth publicly or formally [14thC. Via Old French from, ultimately, Latin *proclamare* (see PROCLAIM).]

proclitic /prō klíttik/ *adj.* used to describe a reduced form of a word that is closely attached in pronunciation to the word following it and has no accent of its own, e.g. 'd' in 'd'you' [Mid-19thC. From modern Latin *procliticus*-, from PRO[2] on the model of ENCLITIC.] —**proclitic** *n.*

proclivity /prə klívvəti/ (*plural* **-ties**) *n.* a natural tendency to behave in a particular way [Late 16thC. From Latin *proclivitas*, from *proclivis* 'inclined', literally 'leaning forward', from *clivus*, 'slope'.]

Procne /prókni/ *n.* in Greek mythology, an Athenian princess whose husband, Tereus, raped her sister, Philomela. She avenged this act by killing their own son and feeding him to Tereus.

proconsul /prō kónss'l/ *n.* **1.** HIST GOVERNOR OF ANCIENT ROMAN PROVINCE a governor of an ancient Roman province, usually a former consul **2.** GOVERNOR OF COLONY a governor or administrator of a colony or other dependency [14thC. From Latin '(person acting) for the consul', from *consul* (see CONSUL).] —**proconsular** /prō kónssjŏolər/ *adj.* —**proconsulate** /-kónssjŏolət/ *n.* —**proconsulship** /-ship/ *n.*

Procopius /prō kṓpi əss/ (500?–565?) Byzantine historian. He wrote *The Books About the Wars* and other texts that document the reign of Justinian I and the Byzantine court.

procrastinate /prō krásti nayt/ (**-nates, -nating, -nated**) *vti.* to postpone doing sth, especially as a regular practice [Late 16thC. From Latin *procrastinare*, 'to put off until tomorrow', from *crastinus* 'of tomorrow', from *cras*, 'tomorrow'.] —**procrastination** /prō krásti náysh'n/ *n.* —**procrastinator** /-naytər/ *n.*

procreate /prṓkri ayt, -áyt/ (**-ates, -ating, -ated**) *v.* **1.** *vti.* HAVE OFFSPRING to produce offspring by reproduction **2.** *vt.* CREATE STH to create or produce sth [Mid-16thC. From *procreare*, 'to bring forth', from *creare* (see CREATE).] —**procreant** /prṓkri ənt/ *adj.* —**procreation** /-áysh'n/ *n.* —**procreative** /-aytiv/ *adj.* —**procreator** /prṓkri aytər, -áytər/ *n.*

Procrustean /prō krústi ən/ *adj.* trying to establish conformity by using any and all means, including violence [Mid-19thC. Formed from PROCRUSTES.]

Procrustes /prō krús teez/ *n.* in Greek mythology, a robber who abducted strangers and forced them to fit perfectly into a bed by either cutting off or stretching their limbs

procryptic /prō kríptik/ *adj.* used to describe an animal that has a coloration or pattern of shading that provides concealment [Late 19thC. Origin uncertain: probably from PROTECTIVE + CRYPTIC.] —**procryptically** *adv.*

proct- *prefix.* = **procto-** (*used before vowels*)

proctitis /prok tī́tiss/ *n.* inflammation of the rectum [Early 19thC. Formed from Greek *prōktos* 'anus'.]

procto- *prefix.* anus, anal, rectum, rectal ○ *proctoscope* [From Greek *prōktos*]

proctodaeum /proktə dée əm/ (*plural* **-a** /-dée ə/ *or* **-ums**) *n.* the exterior section of an embryo that develops into part of the anal canal [Late 19thC. From modern Latin, from PROCTO- + Greek *hodaios*, 'on the way', from *hodos* 'way'.]

proctology /prok tólləji/ *n.* the branch of medicine concerned with disorders of the colon, rectum, and anus —**proctological** /proktə lójjik'l/ *adj.* —**proctologist** /prok tóllәjist/ *n.*

proctor /próktər/ *n.* **1.** UNIVERSITY OFFICER IN CHARGE OF DISCIPLINE either of two officers at certain universities elected annually and assigned to supervise undergraduate discipline **2.** *US* = **invigilator 3.** REPRESENTATIVE sb who conducts another person's case in court (*dated*) **4.** CLERGY REPRESENTATIVE any one of the representatives of the clergy in the Church of England convocation ■ *vt.* (**-tors, -toring, -tored**) *US* = **invigilate** [14thC. Contraction of PROCURATOR.] —**proctorial** /prok táwri əl/ *adj.* —**proctorship** /próktər ship/ *n.*

proctoscope /próktə skōp/ *n.* a tubular medical instrument with an integral light source, used for examining the anal canal and rectum —**proctoscopic** /próktə skóppik/ *adj.* —**proctoscopy** /prok tóskəpi/ *n.*

procumbent /prō kúmbənt/ *adj.* **1.** LYING FACE DOWN lying down with the face to the ground **2.** BOT GROWING ALONG GROUND used to describe a plant stem that grows along the ground without taking root [Mid-17thC. From Latin *procumbent-*, the present participle of *procumbere*, 'to fall forward', from *-cumbere* 'to lie down'.]

procuration /prókyŏo ráysh'n/ *n.* **1.** ACQUIRING OF STH the obtaining of sth, especially by effort (*formal*) **2.** CRIMINAL LAW PROVIDING OF PROSTITUTE the crime of providing sb for prostitution **3.** LAW ENGAGING OF PROCURATOR the engaging of an agent to manage sb's affairs **4.** LAW AUTHORIZING OF PROCURATOR the authorization given to sb who acts as an agent to manage sb else's affairs

procurator /prókyŏo raytər/ *n.* **1.** LAW AGENT MANAGING SB'S AFFAIRS an agent engaged to manage sb else's affairs **2.** HIST ANCIENT ROMAN OFFICIAL in ancient Rome, an administrative official with legal or fiscal powers —**procuratorial** /prókyŏorə táwri əl/ *adj.* —**procuratorship** /prókyŏo raytər ship/ *n.*

procurator fiscal (*plural* **procurators fiscal** *or* **procurator fiscals**) *n.* a public prosecutor and coroner in Scotland

procure /prə kyóor/ (**-cures, -curing, -cured**) *v.* **1.** *vt.* ACQUIRE STH to obtain sth, especially by effort **2.** *vti.* CRIMINAL LAW PROVIDE PROSTITUTES to provide sb for prostitution [13thC. Via Old French from Latin *procurare*, 'to take care of, manage', from *curare* 'to care for'.] —**procurable** *adj.* —**procural** *n.* —**procurance** *n.*

WORD KEY: SYNONYMS

See Synonyms at ***get***.

procurement /prə kyóormənt/ *n.* **1.** OBTAINING OF STH the obtaining of sth, especially by effort **2.** PURCHASING OF STH the purchasing of sth, especially for a company, government, or other organization

procurer /prə kyóorər/ *n.* **1.** SB GETTING STH sb who obtains sth **2.** CRIMINAL LAW SB SUPPLYING PROSTITUTES sb who provides people for prostitution

procuress /prə kyóor ess/ (*plural* **-esses**) *n.* a woman who provides people for prostitution

prod /prod/ *vti.* (**prods, prodding, prodded**) **1.** POKE SB OR STH to poke sb or sth with a finger, elbow, or pointed object **2.** INCITE SB TO ACTION to incite or encourage sb to take action ■ *n.* **1.** A POKE a poke with a finger, elbow, or pointed object **2.** INCITEMENT TO ACTION an incitement or encouragement to do sth **3.** POKING INSTRUMENT an instrument used for poking a person or animal [Mid-16thC. Origin uncertain: perhaps a variant of obsolete *brod* 'goad', of uncertain origin: probably from Old Norse *broddr*.] —**prodder** *n.*

Prod /próddi/, **Proddie** *n. Scotland, Ireland* an offensive term referring to a Protestant (*slang insult*)

prod. *abbr.* **1.** produce **2.** produced **3.** product **4.** production

prodigal /próddig'l/ *adj.* **1.** WASTEFUL tending to spend money wastefully **2.** PRODUCING GENEROUS AMOUNTS giving or producing sth in large amounts ■ *n.* **1.** SPENDTHRIFT sb who spends money wastefully **2.** REPENTANT WASTREL sb who leaves home and spends parental money wastefully or behaves in a depraved manner but returns repentant to a warm welcome (*literary*) [Early 16thC. Via French from, ultimately, Latin *prodigus*, 'wasteful', from *prodigere*, 'to drive away, squander', from *agere*, 'to drive'.] —**prodigality** /próddi gálləti/ *n.* —**prodigally** /próddig'li/ *adv.*

prodigious /prə díjjəss/ *adj.* **1.** SIZABLE great in amount, size, or extent **2.** MARVELLOUS very impressive or amazing [Mid-16thC. From Latin *prodigiosus* 'marvellous', from *prodigium* (see PRODIGY).] —**prodigiously** *adv.* —**prodigiousness** *n.*

prodigy /próddiji/ (*plural* **-gies**) *n.* **1.** SB WITH EXCEPTIONAL TALENT sb who shows an exceptional natural talent for sth from an early age **2.** STH MARVELLOUS sth very impressive or amazing [15thC. From Latin *prodigium* 'prophetic sign, portent', of uncertain origin: perhaps literally 'sth foretold', formed from *-igium*, from *aio* 'I say'.]

prodrome /prṓdrōm/ *n.* a symptom indicating the start of a disease. ◊ **syndrome** [Mid-17thC. Via French from, ultimately, Greek *prodromos*, literally 'a running before', from *dromos* 'running' (see -DROME).] —**prodromal** /prō drṓm'l/ *adj.* —**prodromic** /-drómmik/ *adj.*

produce *v.* /prə dyóoss/ (**-duces, -ducing, -duced**) **1.** *vti.* MAKE STH to make or create sth **2.** *vti.* MANUFACTURE STH to manufacture goods for sale **3.** *vt.* CAUSE STH to cause sth to happen or arise **4.** *vti.* YIELD STH to bring forth or bear sth **5.** *vt.* OFFER STH to present or show sth **6.** *vt.* ARTS ORGANIZE THE MAKING OF STH to organize and supervise the making of sth **7.** *vt.* GEOM EXTEND STH IN SPACE to extend the length of a line ■ *n.* /próddyooss/ FARM OR GARDEN PRODUCTS products of farms or gardens, especially fruits and vegetables [15thC. From Latin *producere* 'to lead or bring forth', from *ducere* 'to lead'.] —**producibility** /prə dyóossə bílləti/ *n.* —**producible** /prə dyóossəb'l/ *adj.*

WORD KEY: SYNONYMS

See Synonyms at ***make***.

producer /prə dyóossər/ *n.* **1.** STH THAT PRODUCES sb or sth that produces sth **2.** STH GENERATING ITEMS FOR SALE a person, company, or country that produces goods or services for sale **3.** ARTS ORGANIZER OF FILM, RECORDING, ETC sb who organizes and supervises the making of a film, play, broadcast, or recording **4.** INDUST APPARATUS FOR PRODUCER GAS a furnace used for making producer gas **5.** ECOL ORGANISM THAT MAKES ITS FOOD an organism such as a green plant, that manufactures its own food from simple inorganic substances. Producers are ultimately the sole source of food for all animals and other consumer organisms.

producer gas *n.* a fuel consisting of carbon monoxide, nitrogen, and hydrogen, made by passing air and steam over hot coke in a furnace

producer goods, **producer's goods** *npl.* raw materials, equipment, and other goods that are used to manufacture consumer goods

product /pródukt/ *n.* **1.** COMMODITY PRODUCED FOR SALE a commodity that is produced by manufacture or by a natural process and is offered for sale **2.** COMPANY'S GOODS OR SERVICES the goods or services produced by a company **3.** RESULT sth that arises as a consequence of sth else **4.** MATH RESULT OF MULTIPLYING the result of the multiplication of two or more quantities **5.** CHEM CHEMICAL SUBSTANCE a substance produced in a chemical reaction [15thC. From Latin *productus*, the past participle of *producere* (see PRODUCE).]

production /prə dúksh'n/ *n.* **1.** MAKING OF STH the making or creation of sth **2.** STH PRODUCED sth that has been made or created **3.** ECON PRODUCING OF GOODS the process of manufacturing a product for sale **4.** ECON COMPANY'S PRODUCT the goods or services produced by a company **5.** ARTS SUPERVISION OF FILM, RECORDING, ETC the organization and supervision of the making of a film, play, broadcast, or recording **6.** ARTS FILM, RECORDING, ETC a film, play, broadcast, or recording that has been produced for the public **7.** SHOWING OF STH the showing or presenting of sth such as evidence —**productional** *adj.*

production assistant *n.* an assistant to a film producer who performs a variety of errands and tasks

production company *n.* an organization that makes films

production designer *n.* sb who is responsible for the look of the physical world on screen in a film, including sets and costumes

production line *n.* a sequence of machines or processes in a factory through which the products pass until they are fully assembled

production manager *n.* sb who is in charge of arranging the shooting of a film or the producing of a play, e.g. by planning schedules, ordering equipment, and hiring extras

production number *n.* a piece of music in a musical that is sung and danced by featured actors supported by the chorus

productive /prə dúktiv/ *adj.* **1.** PRODUCING STH producing or able to produce sth **2.** PRODUCING MUCH producing sth abundantly and efficiently **3.** WORTHWHILE producing satisfactory or useful results **4.** ECON PRODUCING GOODS producing goods and services of exchangeable value **5.** MED PRODUCING MUCUS used to describe a cough that produces mucus **6.** GRAM USED TO FORM WORDS used to describe a prefix or suffix that is used in forming new words —**productively** *adv.* —**productiveness** *n.*

productivity /pródduk tívvəti/ *n.* **1.** ABILITY TO PRODUCE the ability to be productive **2.** ECON RATE OF PRODUCTION the rate at which a company produces goods or services, in relation to the amount of materials and number of employees needed

productivity bargaining *n.* the process of bargaining between unions and management by which a pay rise is offered in exchange for improved productivity

product liability *n.* the liability of manufacturers and traders for damage or injury caused to purchasers or bystanders by their products

product line *n.* **1.** COMPANY'S WHOLE RANGE OF PRODUCTS the whole range of products marketed by a company **2.** COMPANY'S GROUP OF RELATED PRODUCTS a group of related products marketed by the same company that differ only in size or style

proem /prō em/ *n.* an introduction to a literary work or a speech [14thC. Via Old French *pro(h)eme* from, ultimately, Greek *prooimion*, literally 'song before', from *oimē* 'song'.] —**proemial** /prō émmi əl/ *adj.*

proenzyme /prō én zīm/ *n.* the inactive precursor of an enzyme, especially one secreted by living cells and activated by an acid, another enzyme, or other catalytic means

proestrus *n.* US = **pro-oestrus**

prof /prof/ *n.* a college or university professor (*informal*) [Mid-19thC. Shortening.]

Prof. *abbr.* professor

profane /prə fáyn/ *adj.* **1.** IRREVERENT showing disrespect for God, any deity, or religion **2.** SECULAR not connected with or used for religious matters **3.** UNINITIATED not initiated into sacred or secret rites ■ *vt.* (**-fanes, -faning, -faned**) TREAT STH IRREVERENTLY to treat sth sacred with disrespect [14thC. Via Old French *prophane* from Latin *profanus*, literally 'outside the temple', hence 'not sacred', from *fanum* 'temple' (source of English *fanatic*).] —**profanation** /próffə náysh'n/ *n.* —**profanatory** /prə fánnətəri/ *adj.* —**profanely** /-fáynli/ *adv.* —**profaneness** /-fáyn nəss/ *n.* —**profaner** /-fáynər/ *n.*

profanity /prə fánnəti/ (*plural* **-ties**) *n.* **1.** PROFANE LANGUAGE OR BEHAVIOUR language or behaviour that shows disrespect for God, any deity, or religion **2.** PROFANE WORD OR PHRASE a word or phrase that shows disrespect for God, any deity, or religion

profess /prə féss/ (**-fesses, -fessing, -fessed**) *v.* **1.** *vti.* DECLARE STH OPENLY to acknowledge sth publicly **2.** *vt.* DECLARE STH FALSELY to make a false claim about sth **3.** *vt.* RELIG BELIEVE A RELIGION to follow a particular religion **4.** *vti.* RELIG BECOME PRIEST, NUN, ETC to admit sb, or be admitted, into a religious order [15thC. From Old French *profes*, 'having taken religious vows', ultimately from Latin *profess-*, the past participle of *profiteri* 'to declare publicly', from *fateri* 'to acknowledge'.] —**professed** *adj.* —**professedly** /prə féssidli/ *adv.*

profession /prə fésh'n/ *n.* **1.** OCCUPATION REQUIRING EXTENSIVE EDUCATION an occupation that requires extensive education or specialized training **2.** PEOPLE IN PROFESSION the members of a particular profession **3.** DECLARATION a public acknowledgment or declaration of sth **4.** RELIG DECLARATION OF RELIGIOUS BELIEF a declaration of belief in a religion or faith

professional /prə fésh'nəl/ *adj.* **1.** OF A PROFESSION relating to or belonging to a profession **2.** FOLLOWING OCCUPATION AS PAID JOB engaged in an occupation as a paid job rather than as a hobby **3.** VERY COMPETENT showing a high degree of skill or competence **4.** DOING STH HABITUALLY habitually, and usually annoyingly, indulging in a particular activity ○ *a professional complainer* ■ *n.* **1.** MEMBER OF PROFESSION sb whose occupation requires extensive education or specialized training **2.** SB DOING STH AS PAID JOB sb who is engaged in an occupation as a paid job rather than as a hobby **3.** SB VERY COMPETENT sb who shows a high degree of skill or competence **4.** TEACHER AT SPORTS CLUB an expert player of a sport who is paid to teach other players in a club —**professionally** *adv.*

professional association *n.* a society of members of a profession that regulates entry to, and sets and maintains standards for, the profession

professional foul *n.* a deliberate foul in football, usually committed in order to prevent the opposing team gaining a potentially crucial advantage in field position or goal-scoring opportunity

professionalise *vt.* = **professionalize**

professionalism /prə fésh'nəlizəm/ *n.* **1.** PROFESSIONAL STANDARDS the skill, competence, or character expected of a member of a highly trained profession **2.** FOLLOWING ACTIVITY FOR GAIN the following of an activity for financial gain rather than as an amateur

professionalize /prə fésh'nə līz/ (**-izes, -izing, -ized**), **professionalise** (**-ises, -ising, -ised**) *vt.* to make an occupation professional, especially by paying the people who engage in it or improving the conditions or standards of their work

professor /prə féssər/ *n.* **1.** MOST SENIOR LECTURER the most senior lecturer in a university department **2.** *US* EDUC UNIVERSITY TEACHER a teacher in a university or college **3.** TEACHER OF A SKILL a senior teacher of a nonacademic discipline in an institution other than a university such as a music or drama school **4.** RELIG SB PROFESSING BELIEF sb who professes a religion or other belief (*formal*) —**professorial** /próffə sáwri əl/ *adj.* —**professorially** /-sáwri əli/ *adv.* —**professorship** /-ship/ *n.*

professoriate /próffə sáwri ət/, **professorate** /prə féssərət/ *n.* **1.** PROFESSORS professors as a group **2.** PROFESSOR'S POSITION the status or position of professor

proffer /próffər/ (**-fers, -fering, -fered**) *vt.* **1.** HOLD STH OUT to hold sth out to sb so that he or she can take or grasp it **2.** PROPOSE STH to offer sth for consideration to sb [13thC. From Old French *proffrir*, literally 'to offer forth', from *offrir* 'to offer'.] —**profferer** *n.*

proficiency /prə físh'nssi/ *n.* competence in sth, or knowledge of it

proficient /prə físh'nt/ *adj.* VERY SKILLED having a high degree of skill in sth ■ *n.* SB VERY SKILLED sb with a high degree of skill in sth (*archaic*) [Late 16thC. Via Old French from Latin *proficient-*, the present participle of *proficere* 'to make progress', literally 'to make forward', which was formed from *facere* 'to make'.] —**proficiently** *adv.*

profile /prō fīl/ *n.* **1.** SIDE VIEW OF FACE the outline of sb's face as seen from the side **2.** ARTS ARTWORK OF SB'S PROFILE a visual representation of the outline of sb's face as seen from the side **3.** COMMUNICATION SHORT BIOGRAPHY a short biographical account of sb **4.** STATS DATA DESCRIBING STH a set of data, usually in graph or table form, that indicates the extent to which sth matches tested or standard characteristics **5.** VISIBILITY a level or degree of noticeability ○ *Though he had become famous, he still tried to keep a low profile.* **6.** GEOG VERTICAL SECTION OF PHYSICAL FEATURE a vertical section through a physical feature, e.g. through soil, showing its development from bedrock, or through a river, showing its height above sea level along its course **7.** PUPIL ASSESSMENT an assessment of the range of qualities, attitudes, and behaviour of a pupil, providing a fuller picture of the pupil than that given by traditional school reports ■ *vt.* (**-files, -filing, -filed**) **1.** COMMUNICATION DO SHORT BIOGRAPHY OF SB to write or present a short biographical account of sb **2.** ARTS DRAW PROFILE OF SB to draw or paint the outline of sb's face as seen from the side [Mid-17thC. From Italian *profilo*, from *profilare* 'to draw in outline', literally 'to draw or spin forth', ultimately from *filo* 'thread', from Latin *filum*.] —**profiler** *n.*

profit /próffit/ *n.* **1.** BUSINESS EXCESS OF INCOME OVER EXPENDITURE the excess of income over expenditure during a particular period of time **2.** FIN INCOME FROM STH income from an investment or transaction **3.** BUSINESS MONEY FROM BUSINESS ACTIVITY money made or to be made from business activity **4.** ADVANTAGE an advantage or benefit derived from an activity ■ *v.* (**-its, -iting, -ited**) **1.** *vi.* FIN MAKE MONEY ON STH to gain financial profit from sth **2.** *vti.* BENEFIT FROM STH to gain an advantage or benefit from sth, or to provide an advantage or benefit (*formal*) [13thC. Via Old French from Latin *profectus* 'advance', the past participle of *proficere* (see PROFICIENT).] —**profiter** *n.* —**profitless** *adj.* —**profitlessly** *adv.*

profitable /próffitəb'l/ *adj.* **1.** FIN LUCRATIVE yielding a financial profit **2.** USEFUL of some use, benefit, or advantage to sb —**profitability** /próffitə bílləti/ *n.* —**profitableness** /-b'lnəss/ *n.* —**profitably** *adv.*

profit and loss *n.* an account showing income and expenditure over a given period and indicating net profit or loss

profit centre *n.* a section or activity of a company that is independently profitable

profiteer /próffi teer/ *vi.* (**-eers, -eering, -eered**) MAKE EXCESSIVE PROFITS to make excessive profits by charging high prices for scarce, necessary, or rationed goods ■ *n.* SB MAKING EXCESSIVE PROFITS sb who makes excessive profits by charging high prices for scarce, necessary, or rationed goods —**profiteering** *n.*

profiterole /prə fíttərōl/ *n.* a small ball of choux pastry filled with cream and usually served with chocolate sauce [Early 16thC. From French, literally 'small gain', from *profit* (see PROFIT).]

profit margin *n.* the amount by which income exceeds related expenditure

profit sharing *n.* a system by which the employees of a company receive a prearranged share of the company's profits (*hyphenated when used before a noun*)

profit taking *n.* the selling of commodities, securities, or shares at a time when their current market value is greater than the price at which they were purchased

profligate /próffligət/ *adj.* **1.** WASTEFUL extremely extravagant or wasteful **2.** WITH LOW MORALS having or showing extremely low moral standards ■ *n.* **1.** SB WASTEFUL sb who is extremely extravagant or wasteful **2.** SB WITH LOW MORALS sb with extremely low moral standards [Mid-16thC. From Latin *profligatus*, the past participle of *profligare* 'to strike down, ruin', from *fligere* 'to strike' (source of English *conflict*).] —**profligacy** *n.* —**profligately** *adv.*

profluent /prófloo ənt/ *adj.* flowing smoothly or freely [15thC. From Latin *profluere* 'to flow forth', from *fluere* 'to flow'.]

pro forma /prō fáwrmə/ *adj.* **1.** FORMAL OR CONVENTIONAL done or existing only as a formality **2.** PROVIDED IN ADVANCE provided in advance in order to supply descriptions of sth or to serve as a model, e.g. of a later version of a document ■ *adv.* FOR CONVENTION'S SAKE for the sake of or in accordance with convention [From Latin, literally 'for form's sake']

profound /prə fównd/ *adj.* **1.** GREAT very great, strong, or intense **2.** SHOWING GREAT UNDERSTANDING showing great perception, understanding, or knowledge **3.** REQUIRING GREAT UNDERSTANDING requiring great perception, understanding, or knowledge **4.** VERY DEEP extending to or situated at a great depth [13thC. Via Old French *profond* from Latin *profundus*, literally 'bottom forward or downward', from *fundus* 'bottom'.] —**profoundly** *adv.* —**profoundness** *n.*

profundity /prə fúndəti/ (*plural* **-ties**) *n.* **1.** GREAT UNDERSTANDING great perceptiveness, understanding, or knowledge **2.** STH REQUIRING GREAT UNDERSTANDING sth requiring great understanding, perceptiveness, or knowledge **3.** INTELLECTUAL COMPLEXITY the intellectual complexity or abstruseness of sth **4.** GREATNESS the greatness, strength, or intensity of sth **5.** GREAT DEPTH extension to, or location at, a great depth [15thC. Via Old French *profundite* from late Latin *profunditas*, from *profundus* (see PROFOUND).]

profuse /prə fyōoss/ *adj.* **1.** GENEROUSLY PROVIDED given freely and extravagantly ○ *profuse apologies* **2.** GENEROUS IN GIVING giving sth freely and extravagantly **3.** COPIOUS being or appearing in large amounts [15thC. From Latin *profusus*, the past participle of *profundere* 'to pour forth', from *fundere* 'to pour'.] —**profusely** *adv.* —**profuseness** *n.*

profusion /prə fyōozh'n/ *n.* **1.** A GREAT DEAL a large quantity of sth **2.** PROFUSE QUALITY the quality of being profuse

prog /prog/ *n.* a television or radio programme (*informal*) [Late 20thC. Shortening.]

prog. *abbr.* **1.** program **2.** programme **3.** progress **4.** progressive

Prog. *abbr.* Progressive

progenitor /prō jénnitər/ *n.* **1.** ANCESTOR a direct ancestor of sb or sth **2.** ORIGINATOR the originator of, or original model for, sth [14thC. From Latin, literally 'begetter', from *progenit-*, the past participle stem of *progignere* 'to beget', literally 'to create forth', from *gignere* (see GENITAL).]

progeny /prójjəni/ (*plural* **-nies**) *n.* **1.** OFFSPRING OF ORGANISM the offspring of a person, animal, or plant **2.** RESULTING THINGS things that develop or result from sth [13thC. Via Old French *progenie* from Latin *progenies* 'offspring', from *progignere* (see PROGENITOR).]

progeria /prō jeéri ə/ *n.* a rare condition of premature ageing that begins in childhood or early adult life and leads to death within a few years [Early 20thC. Via modern Latin from Greek *progērōs*, literally 'aged forward', from *gēras* 'old age'.]

progestational /prō je stáysh'nəl/ *adj.* **1.** PHYSIOL RELATING TO MENSTRUAL CYCLE PHASE relating to the stage of the menstrual cycle following ovulation during which progesterone is produced and the womb is prepared for pregnancy **2.** BIOCHEM, PHARM OF OR LIKE PROGESTERONE relating to or resembling progesterone or its effects

Progesterone

progesterone /prō jéstərōn/ *n.* a sex hormone produced in women, first by the corpus luteum of the ovary to prepare the womb for the fertilized ovum, and later by the placenta to maintain pregnancy. Formula: $C_{21}H_{30}O_2$. [Mid-20thC. Formed from PRO- + GESTATION + STEROL + -ONE.]

progestin /prə jéstin/ *n.* any progestogen, usually progesterone [Early 20thC. Formed from PRO- + GESTATION + -IN.]

progestogen /prə jéstəjən/ *n.* a steroid hormone or agent having effects similar to those of progesterone [Mid-20thC. Formed from PRO- + GESTATION + -IN.]

proglottid /prō glóttid/, **proglottis** /-glóttiss/ (*plural* **-tides**) *n.* a segment of a tapeworm's body. Each segment contains a complete reproductive system. —**proglottic** *adj.*

prognathous /prógnəthəss, prog náythəss/, **prognathic** /prog náthik/ *adj.* used to describe an animal with a jaw that sticks out markedly [Mid-19thC. Coined from PRO- + Greek *gnathos* 'jaw'.] —**prognathism** /prógnəthizəm/ *n.*

prognosis /prog nóssiss/ (*plural* **-ses** /-seez/) *n.* **1.** MED OPINION ON COURSE OF DISEASE a medical opinion as to the likely course and outcome of a disease **2.** PREDICTION a prediction about how a given situation will develop [Mid-17thC. Via late Latin from Greek *prognōsis*, literally 'knowledge beforehand', ultimately from *gignōskein* 'to know'.]

prognostic /prog nóstik/ *adj.* **1.** MED OF DISEASE PROGNOSIS relating to or acting as a prognosis of a disease **2.** OF PREDICTION relating to or acting as a prediction ■ *n.* **1.** MED INDICATION OF COURSE OF DISEASE an indicator used in making a prognosis concerning a disease **2.** PREDICTION a prediction as to how a given situation will develop [15thC. Via Old French from, ultimately, Greek *prognōstikos* 'of knowledge beforehand', from *prognōsis* (see PROGNOSIS).]

prognosticate /prog nósti kayt/ (**-cates**, **-cating**, **-cated**) *v.* **1.** *vti.* PREDICT THE FUTURE to predict or foretell future events **2.** *vt.* BE INDICATION OF STH to be an indication of the likely future course of sth —**prognostication** /prog nósti káysh'n/ *n.* —**prognosticative** /-kətiv/ *adj.* —**prognosticator** /-kaytər/ *n.*

prograde /prō grayd/ *adj.* moving in the same orbital or rotational direction as another astronomical body

program /prō gram/ *n.* **1.** US = programme **2.** INSTRUCTIONS OBEYED BY COMPUTER a list of instructions in a programming language that tells a computer to perform a certain task **3.** TECH OPERATING INSTRUCTIONS FOR MACHINE a set of coded operating instructions that is used to run a machine automatically ■ *v.* (**-grams, -gramming** *or* **-graming, -grammed** *or* **-gramed**) **1.** *vt.* US = programme **2.** *vti.* WRITE COMPUTER PROGRAM to write or load a program for a computer **3.** *vt.* TECH INSERT OPERATING INSTRUCTIONS INTO MACHINE to insert coded operating instructions into a machine [Mid-17thC. Via French from, ultimately, Greek *programma* 'public notice', literally 'sth written publicly', ultimately from *graphein* 'to write'.]

program director *n.* US = head of programming

programer *n.* US = programmer

program evaluation and review technique *n.* full form of PERT

programing *n.* US = programming

programmatic /prōgrə máttik/ *adj.* **1.** RELATING TO PROGRAMME relating to or consisting of a programme **2.** SYSTEMATIC following a plan or programme **3.** MUSIC OF PROGRAMME MUSIC relating to or composed as programme music —**programmatically** *adv.*

programme /prō gram/ *n.* US term **program** **1.** PLAN A plan of action **2.** BROADCAST a television or radio broadcast **3.** BOOKLET GIVING DETAILS OF A PERFORMANCE a booklet or leaflet giving details of a theatrical or musical performance **4.** SERIES OF CLASSES a series of classes or lectures ■ *vt.* (**-grammes, -gramming, -grammed**) US term **program** **1.** SCHEDULE STH to schedule sth as part of a programme **2.** TRAIN SB TO DO STH AUTOMATICALLY to train a person or an animal to do a particular thing automatically [Mid-17thC. Via French from, ultimately, Greek *programma* 'written public notice', literally 'written publicly', ultimately from *graphein* 'to write'.] —**programmability** /prō gramə bílləti/ —**programmable** /prō grámməb'l, prō graməb'l/ *adj.*

programmed learning, **programmed instruction** *n.* a learning method based on self-instructional materials that are designed to allow pupils to progress at their own pace, step by step, through structured sequences

programme music *n.* music that depicts or is inspired by a specific story, object, or scene

programme of study *n.* the subjects and skills taught to pupils of different abilities and maturities during each key stage of the National Curriculum in England and Wales

programmer /prō gramər/ *n.* sb who writes computer programs

programming /prō graming/ *n.* **1.** CREATING OF COMPUTER PROGRAMS the designing or writing of computer programs **2.** BROADCAST BROADCASTING OF PROGRAMMES the selection and scheduling of television or radio programmes, or the programmes themselves

programming language *n.* a unique vocabulary and set of rules for writing computer programs. This term is usually applied to high-level languages, e.g. C, C++, Java, Pascal, and BASIC.

program trading *n.* the automatic buying and selling of large quantities of shares using computer programs that monitor price changes —**program trade** *n.* —**program trader** *n.*

progress /prə gréss, prō gress/ *n.* **1.** IMPROVEMENT gradual development or improvement of sth **2.** MOTION TOWARDS STH movement forwards or onwards **3.** (*plural* **-gresses**) ROYAL TOUR an official royal tour (*archaic*) ■ *v.* (**-gresses, -gressing, -gressed**) **1.** *vi.* IMPROVE to develop or advance continuously **2.** *vi.* MOVE ALONG to move forwards or onwards **3.** *vt.* HELP COMPLETE STH to bring sth towards completion [15thC. From Latin *progressus*, the past participle of *progredi* 'to go forward', from *gradi* 'to walk'.]

progress chaser *n.* sb employed to check the progress of a piece of manufacturing work and ensure its prompt delivery

progression /prə grésh'n/ *n.* **1.** GRADUAL ADVANCEMENT a gradual change or advancement from one state to another **2.** FORWARD MOVEMENT movement forwards or onwards **3.** SERIES OF RELATED THINGS a series or succession of related things **4.** MATH SEQUENCE OF RELATED NUMBERS a sequence of numbers or terms in which each can be derived from its predecessor using a constant formula **5.** MUSIC SERIES OF NOTES OR CHORDS a movement from one note or chord to another —**progressional** *adj.* —**progressionally** *adv.*

progressive /prə gréssiv/ *adj.* **1.** PROGRESSING GRADUALLY progressing gradually over a period of time **2.** POL FAVOURING REFORM advocating social, economic, or political reform **3.** EDUC INFORMAL AND LESS STRUCTURED EDUCATIONALLY relating to or using a more informal, less structured approach to the education of children **4.** FIN WITH HIGHER RATES FOR HIGHER INCOMES used to describe a form of taxation in which the tax rate increases in proportion to the taxable income **5.** CARDS, DANCING HAVING CHANGES OF PARTNER characterized by changes of partner at stages of a card game or dance **6.** GRAM EXPRESSING CONTINUOUS ACTION used to express continuous action ■ *n.* **1.** POL ADVOCATE OF REFORM sb who advocates social, political, or economic reform **2.** GRAM PROGRESSIVE FORM OF VERB the progressive aspect of a verb, or a verb in the progressive aspect —**progressively** *adv.* —**progressiveness** *n.*

Progressive *adj.* **1.** POL OF PROGRESSIVE POLITICAL PARTY belonging to or associated with a Progressive Party **2.** JUDAISM OF NONORTHODOX JEWISH RELIGIOUS MOVEMENT relating to a Jewish religious movement whose members do not believe that the Torah was given literally and directly by God to Moses ■ *n.* POL MEMBER OF PROGRESSIVE PARTY sb who is a member of a Progressive Party

Progressive Conservative *n.* MEMBER OF CANADIAN PROGRESSIVE CONSERVATIVE PARTY in Canada, a member or supporter of the Progressive Conservative Party ■ *adj.* OF CANADIAN PROGRESSIVE CONSERVATIVE PARTY in Canada, belonging to or supporting the Progressive Conservative Party

Progressive Conservative Party *n.* a Canadian federal and provincial political party founded in the 1850s as the Liberal-Conservative Party, becoming the Conservative Party after the 1870s and taking its present name in 1942

progressive education *n.* a 20th-century theory of education that stresses children's self-expression, an informal classroom atmosphere, and individual attention

Progressive Federal Party *n.* a South African political party formed in 1977 by a merger between the Progressive Party and members of the United Party

progressive jazz *n.* a form of experimental, free-flowing, and improvisational jazz that uses dissonance and complex rhythms

Progressive Party *n.* **1.** US POLITICAL PARTY in the United States, any of three related political parties that favoured social reform and were active in the presidential elections of 1912, 1924, and 1948 **2.** CANADIAN POLITICAL PARTY a Canadian national political party formed in 1920 from members of farmers' movements and dissident Liberals that was dissolved in 1942

Progressive Rock *n.* a type of rock music originating in the early 1970s and characterized by technically elaborate and sometimes experimental arrangements

progressivism /prə gréssivizəm/ *n.* **1.** BELIEFS OF PROGRESSIVES the beliefs and practices of progressives **2.** EDUC **BELIEFS AND PRACTICES OF PROGRESSIVE EDUCATION** the theories and practices of progressive education — **progessivist** *n.*

progress payment *n.* a part of a larger payment made to a contractor when a stage of a job is completed

prohibit /prə híbbit/ (**-its, -iting, -ited**) *vt.* **1. FORBID SB** to forbid sb to do sth by a law or rule **2. PREVENT SB** to prevent sb from doing sth [15thC. Formed from Latin *prohibit-*, the past participle stem of *prohibere*, literally 'to hold back', from *hibere* 'to hold'.] —**prohibiter** *n.*

prohibition /prṓ i bísh'n/ *n.* **1. FORBIDDING OF STH** the act or process of forbidding sth **2. ORDER THAT FORBIDS** an act or order that forbids sth **3.** LAW **COURT ORDER** an order from a superior court that forbids an inferior court to decide on a matter beyond its jurisdiction **4. OUTLAWING OF TRADE IN ALCOHOLIC BEVERAGES** a policy that forbids by law the manufacture, sale, and transport of alcoholic beverages [14thC. Via French from, ultimately, Latin *prohibere* (see PROHIBIT).] —**prohibitionary** *adj.*

Prohibition Party *n.* a political party in the United States founded in 1869 that advocated the banning of alcoholic beverages

prohibitive /prə híbbitiv/ *adj.* **1. TOO EXPENSIVE FOR MOST PEOPLE** too expensive or costly for most people to buy **2. FORBIDDING STH** prohibiting or forbidding sth — **prohibitively** *adv.* —**prohibitiveness** *n.*

prohibitory /prə híbbitəri/ *adj.* (*formal*) **1. LIKELY TO FORBID STH** likely to prevent or forbid sth **2. FORBIDDING STH** preventing or forbidding sth

proinsulin /prō ínssyŏŏlin/ *n.* the inactive precursor of insulin that is converted to the active substance by the action of enzymes in the pancreas

project *n.* /prójjekt/ **1. TASK OR SCHEME** a task or scheme that requires a large amount of time, effort, and planning to complete **2. UNIT OF WORK** an organized unit of work ○ *a school project* **3. PUBLIC WORK** an extensive organized public undertaking ○ *a construction project* **4.** US PUBLIC ADMIN = **housing project** (*often used in the plural*) ■ *v.* /prə jékt/ (**projects, projecting, projected**) **1.** *vt.* **ESTIMATE** to estimate sth by extrapolating data ○ *They projected 3% annual growth.* **2.** *vti.* **STICK OUT** to jut out beyond or farther than sth ○ *The balcony projected several metres.* **3.** *vt.* **COMMUNICATE STH** to communicate sth effectively ○ *He projects himself as a confident man.* **4.** *vt.* PSYCHOL **BELIEVE OTHERS SHARE A MENTAL LIFE** to make a thought or feeling seem to have an external and objective reality, especially to ascribe sth personal to others ○ *He had projected his fear of heights onto her.* **5.** *vt.* **THROW STH** to throw or cast sth (*formal*) (*usually passive*) ○ *The ball was projected several metres upwards.* **6.** *vt.* **PROPOSE A PLAN** to propose a plan of action (*often passive*) ○ *The tour was projected for the following summer.* **7.** *vt.* **DIRECT AN IMAGE ONTO SURFACE** to make an image appear on a surface ○ *projected the photograph onto the screen* **8.** *vt.* **IMAGINE STH** to use the imagination to see or remember sth ○ *She projected herself back into the past.* **9.** *vti.* **MAKE THE VOICE AUDIBLE** to make the voice heard clearly and at a distance, or be effective in making the voice heard ○ *She projected her voice to the back of the auditorium.* **10.** *vt.* GEOM **DRAW A PROJECTION OF A FIGURE** to transform a geometric figure into another by drawing straight lines through every point of the figure to another plane. In this way, a circle may be projected as an ellipse and a square as a rectangle. [14thC. From Latin *projectum* 'sth thrown forwards', from, ultimately, *proicere* 'to throw forwards', from *jacere* 'to throw'.]

projectile /prō jék tīl/ *n.* **MISSILE OR SHELL** an object that can be fired or launched, e.g. an artillery shell or a rocket ■ *adj.* **1.** ZOOL **CAPABLE OF BEING THRUST FORWARDS** used to describe a part of an animal's body that can be thrust forwards such as the jaws in some types of fish **2. IMPELLED FORWARDS** hurled or impelled forwards

projection /prə jéksh'n/ *n.* **1. ESTIMATE** an estimate of the rate or amount of sth **2. STH THAT STICKS OUT** sth that juts out or overhangs **3. PROTRUSION** the act or process of protruding **4. CASTING OF STH ON SURFACE** the projecting of an image or picture on a surface **5. STH CAST ON SURFACE** an image or picture projected on a surface **6.** PSYCHOL **UNCONSCIOUS TRANSFER OF INNER MENTAL LIFE** the unconscious ascription of a personal thought, feeling, or impulse to sb else, especially a thought or feeling considered undesirable **7.** MAPS **REPRESENTATION ON SURFACE** a means of representing lines, figures, or solids on a flat surface such as a map that conforms to the viewing direction or follows particular rules **8.** GEOM **DRAWN REPRESENTATION** the representation of a line, figure, or solid on a flat surface **9.** HIST **MIXING BY ALCHEMISTS** in alchemy, the mixing of powdered philosopher's stone with base metals in order to supposedly transmute them into gold or silver —**projectional** *adj.*

projection booth *n.* US = **projection room**

projectionist /prə jéksh'nist/ *n.* sb whose job is to operate the projector and screen the film in a cinema and take responsibility for the quality of the image and sound

projection room *n.* an enclosed compartment in a theatre from where films, slides, or lights are projected onto a screen or a stage. US term **projection booth**

projection television, **projection TV** *n.* a television picture display system in which an enlarged picture is projected onto a screen

projective /prə jéktiv/ *adj.* **1. MADE BY PROJECTION** relating to or made by projection **2.** PSYCHOL **OF A TYPE OF PSYCHOLOGICAL TEST** relating to or involving a psychological test in which sth mentally hidden is revealed by a personal response to an image or group of images —**projectively** *adv.*

projective geometry *n.* the study of those properties of plane geometric figures that do not vary when they are projected onto another plane and of the transformations of size and perspective that accompany this

projective test *n.* a psychological test that uses images in order to evoke responses from a subject and reveal hidden elements of the subject's mental life

projector /prə jéktər/ *n.* equipment for projecting the image from film onto a screen and for playing back recorded sound from tracks on the film

projet /prózhay/ *n.* a plan or outline, especially of a draft law or treaty [Early 19thC. Via French from Latin *projectum* (see PROJECT).]

prokaryon /prō kárri on/ *n.* the nucleus of a cell or organism with no membrane separating the area containing DNA from the rest of it [Mid-20thC. Formed from Greek *pro-* 'before' + *karuon* 'nut'.]

prokaryote /prō kárri ot/, **procaryote** *n.* an organism whose DNA is not contained within a nucleus. Bacteria are prokaryotes. [Mid-20thC. Via French, literally 'having nuts before', from Greek *karuōtos* 'having nuts', from *karuon* 'nut'.] —**prokaryotic** /prō kárri óttik/ *adj.*

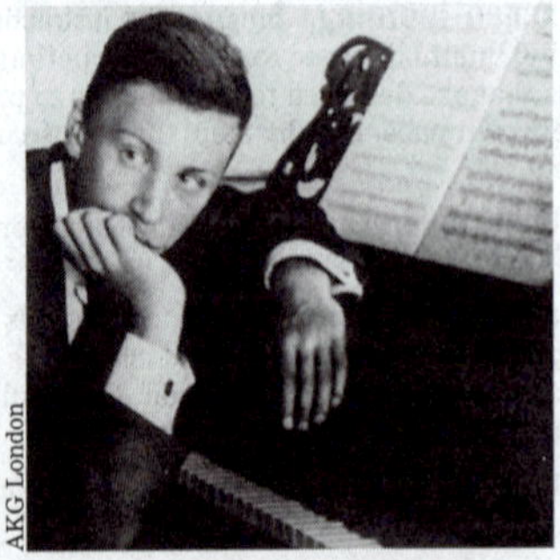

Sergey Sergeyevich Prokofiev

Prokofiev /prə kóffi ef/, **Sergey Sergeyevich** (1891–1953) Russian composer. His symphonies, concertos, ballets, and operas include *The Love of Three Oranges* (1921), *Peter and the Wolf* (1934), and *Romeo and Juliet* (1936).

prolactin /prō láktin/ *n.* a hormone produced by the pituitary gland that stimulates lactation and the secretion of progesterone in mammals, as well as secretion by the crop gland in some birds [Mid-20thC. Coined from PRO- + LACTO- + -IN.]

prolamine /prṓlə meen, -min/ *n.* a plant protein soluble in diluted alcohol that is found in rye, wheat, and other grains [Early 20thC. Coined from PROLINE + AMMONIA + -INE.]

prolapse /prṓ laps, prō láps/, **prolapsus** /prō lápsəss/ *n.* (*plural* **-suses**) **SLIPPAGE OF BODY PART** a slippage or sinking of a body organ or part such as a valve of the heart from its usual position ■ *vi.* (**-lapses, -lapsing, -lapsed**) **BE DISPLACED IN BODY** to slip or fall out of its proper place in the body [Late 16thC. Formed from Latin *prolaps-*, the past participle stem of *prolabi* 'to fall forwards', from *labi* 'to fall'. Originally in English, 'gliding forwards'.] —**prolapsed** *adj.*

prolate /prṓ layt/ *adj.* used to describe rock fragments that are elongated in the direction of the polar diameter [Late 17thC. From Latin *prolatus*, the past participle of *proferre*, literally 'to carry forwards', from *ferre* 'to carry'.] —**prolately** *adv.* —**prolateness** *n.*

prole /prōl/ *n.* **PROLETARIAN** a proletarian (*informal*) ■ *adj.* **PROLETARIAN** proletarian (*informal*) [Late 19thC. Shortening.]

proleg /prṓ leg/ *n.* a leg on the abdomen of a caterpillar or other insect larva

prolegomenon /prṓ le gómminən/ (*plural* **-na** /-gómminə/) *n.* a preliminary discussion or introductory essay, especially to a book or treatise (*formal*) [Mid-17thC. From Greek, from, ultimately, *prolegein*, literally 'to say before', from *legein* 'to say'.] — **prolegomenal** *adj.*

prolepsis /prō lépsiss, -leépsiss/ (*plural* **-ses** /-seez/) *n.* **1.** LOGIC **INTRODUCTORY ANTICIPATION OF OBJECTION** a preface intended to anticipate and answer an objection to an argument **2.** GRAM **ANTICIPATORY ADJECTIVE** the use after a verb of an adjective that anticipates the result of the verb's action, e.g. 'to iron a shirt smooth' [Late 16thC. Via Latin from, ultimately, Greek *prolambanein*, literally 'to take before', from *lambanein* 'to take'.] —**proleptic** /prō léptik/ *adj.*

proletarian /prṓlə táiri ən/ *adj.* SOC SCI **OF WORKING CLASS** relating to the working class ■ *n.* **1.** SOC SCI **WORKER** a member pf the working class **2.** SOC SCI **INDUSTRIAL WAGE-EARNER** in Marxist theory, a member of the industrial working class whose only asset is labour sold to an employer **3.** HIST **IMPOVERISHED ANCIENT ROMAN** a member of an impoverished social class of ancient Rome that had the lowest status and possessed no property [Mid-17thC. Formed from Latin *proletarius* 'low-status Roman who serves the state only by producing offspring', from *proles* 'offspring'.] —**proletarianism** *n.*

proletariat /prṓlə táiri ət/ *n.* **1. WORKING CLASS** the class of wage-earning workers in society (*takes a singular or plural verb*) **2. CLASS OF INDUSTRIAL WAGE-EARNERS** in Marxist theory, the class of industrial workers whose only asset is the labour they sell to an employer **3.** HIST **ANCIENT ROMAN SOCIAL CLASS** social class of ancient Rome that had the lowest status and possessed no property [Mid-19thC. Via French *prolétariat* from, ultimately, Latin *proles* (see PROLETARIAN).]

pro-life *adj.* in favour of bringing the human foetus to full term, especially by campaigning against abortion and experimentation on embryos —**pro-lifer** *n.*

proliferate /prə líffə rayt/ (**-ates, -ating, -ated**) *v.* **1.** *vi.* **INCREASE GREATLY** to increase greatly in number **2.** *vti.* BIOL **REPRODUCE RAPIDLY** to multiply or be multiplied in the process of reproducing new cells, offspring, or parts, as in the budding of plants [Late 19thC. Back-formation from PROLIFERATION.] —**proliferative** /-ərətiv/ *adj.*

proliferation /prə líffə ráysh'n/ *n.* **1. RAPID INCREASE** the rapid spread or increase of sth **2.** BIOL **ORGANIC MULTIPLICATION** the multiplication of parts in an organism

proliferous /prə líffərəss/ *adj.* producing or growing many cells, buds, or shoots [Mid-17thC. Formed from medieval Latin *prolifer*, literally 'bearing offspring', from *proles* 'offspring'.]

prolific /prə líffik/ *adj.* **1.** PRODUCTIVE highly productive **2.** FRUITFUL abounding or fruitful (*formal*) **3.** BIOL PRODUCING FRUIT OR OFFSPRING producing a lot of fruit or many offspring [Mid-17thC. From medieval Latin *prolificus*, from *proles* 'offspring'.] —**prolificacy** *n.* —**prolifically** *adv.*

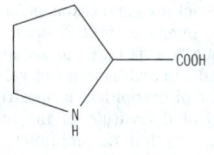

Proline

proline /prố leen/ *n.* an amino acid found in many proteins, particularly in collagen. Formula: $C_5H_9NO_2$. [Early 20thC. Contraction of *pyrrolidine*.]

prolix /prốliks, prō líks/ *adj.* tiresomely wordy [15thC. Directly or via French from Latin *prolixus*, literally 'that has flowed out', from the past participle of *liquere* 'to flow' (source of English *liquid*).] —**prolixity** /prō líksəti/ *n.* —**prolixly** /prō líksli/ *adv.*

───── **WORD KEY: SYNONYMS** ─────
See Synonyms at *wordy*.

prolocutor /prō lókyōōtər/ *n.* CHR sb who chairs an ecclesiastical convocation in the Anglican Church [15thC. Via Latin, 'pleader, advocate', from, ultimately, *proloqui* 'to speak out', from *loqui* 'to speak' (source of English *locution*).] —**prolocutorship** *n.*

prolog *n.* US = prologue

Prolog /prố log/, **PROLOG** *n.* a high-level programming language based on logical rather than mathematical relationships

prologue /prố log/ *n.* **1.** INTRODUCTORY STATEMENT an introductory passage or speech before the main action of a novel, play, or long poem **2.** THEATRE ACTOR INTRODUCING ACTION OF PLAY an actor who speaks introductory lines to a dramatic performance before the main action begins **3.** PRELIMINARY EVENT an event or act that leads to sth more important ■ *vt.* (**-logues, -loguing, -logued**) PREFACE WITH PROLOGUE to preface sth such as a novel or play with a prologue [14thC. Via French and Latin from Greek *prologos*, literally 'speech before', from *logos* 'speech'.]

prolong /prə lóng/ *vt.* (**-longs, -longing, -longed**) to make sth go on longer [15thC. Directly or via French *prolonger* from late Latin *prolongare*, literally 'to lengthen out', from Latin *longus* 'long'.] —**prolongation** /prố long gáysh'n/ *n.* —**prolonger** /prə lóngər/ *n.* —**prolongment** /prə lóngmənt/ *n.*

prolonge /prə lónj/ *n.* a rope with a hook and a toggle used to tow sth heavy, especially a gun carriage [Mid-19thC. From French *prolonger* (see PROLONG).]

prolusion /prə lōōzh'n/ *n.* a tentative, preliminary, or introductory essay (*formal*) [Early 17thC. Formed from Latin *prolusion-*, the stem of *prolusio* from, ultimately, *proludere*, literally 'to play before', from *ludere* 'to play'.] —**prolusory** /-lōōzəri/ *adj.*

prom /prom/ *n.* **1.** = promenade *n.* 1 (*informal*) **2.** MUSIC = promenade concert (*informal*) **3.** US STUDENT DANCE a formal high-school or college dance for students, usually held at the end of the school year [Late 19thC. Shortening.]

PROM /prom/ *abbr.* programmable read-only memory

prom. *abbr.* promontory

promenade /prómmə na'ad/ *n.* **1.** SEAFRONT PATH a paved path or terrace along a seafront **2.** WALK FOR PLEASURE a leisurely walk or stroll, usually in a public place, that is taken for pleasure or to be seen (*formal*) **3.** DANCE MARCHING DANCE MOVEMENT a marching step or sequence in square or country dancing ■ *v.* (**-nades, -nading, -naded**) **1.** *vti.* TAKE A STROLL IN A PUBLIC PLACE to walk in a slow and leisurely way, especially up and

down a street or in a public place **2.** *vi.* DANCE MARCH DURING A DANCE to perform a marching step or sequence in square or country dancing [Mid-16thC. Via French, *se promener* 'to go for a walk' from, ultimately, late Latin *prominare* 'to drive forwards', formed from *minare* 'to drive'.]

promenade concert *n.* a concert, usually of classical music, at which part of the audience stand in an area without seating

promenade deck *n.* a covered upper deck on a passenger ship on which passengers can walk

promethazine /prō méthə zeen/ *n.* an antihistamine drug used to treat allergies and motion sickness. Formula: $C_{17}H_{20}N_2S$. [Mid-20thC. Coined from PROPYL + METHYL + AZINE.]

Promethean /prə méethi ən/ *adj.* **1.** MYTHOL OF PROMETHEUS relating to Prometheus **2.** BOLDLY CREATIVE creative and imaginatively original

Prometheus[1] /prə méethi əss/ *n.* in Greek mythology, a Titan who became a hero to humankind because he stole fire from the gods and gave it to them. His eternal punishment was to be chained to a rock and have an eagle eat his liver, which would grow in the night only to be eaten again. [Late 16thC. Via Latin from Greek.]

Prometheus[2] /prə méethi əss/ *n.* a small inner natural satellite of Saturn, discovered in 1980 by Voyager 2. It is irregular in shape having a maximum dimension of 150 km.

promethium /prə méethi əm/ *n.* a radioactive metallic element produced by the fission of uranium, thorium, or plutonium. It is used in phosphorescent paints and as an X-ray source. Symbol **Pm** [Mid-20thC. Named after PROMETHEUS[1] because it is the result of mankind's ability to utilize the energy of nuclear fission.]

prominence /prómminənss/, **prominency** /-nənssi/ (*plural* **-cies**) *n.* **1.** CONSPICUOUS IMPORTANCE the condition or quality of being significantly important or well-known **2.** STH THAT STICKS OUT sth that projects or protrudes, especially a geographical feature or a body part **3.** ASTRON GAS STREAM FROM SUN a visible stream of glowing gas that shoots out from the Sun, seen in the upper chromosphere and lower corona. Prominences are best seen during an eclipse when they are visible at the rim of the Sun.

prominent /prómminənt/ *adj.* **1.** STICKING OUT large and projecting **2.** NOTICEABLE noticeable or conspicuous **3.** WELL-KNOWN distinguished, eminent, or well-known [15thC. From Latin *prominere*, literally 'to project forwards', from *-minere* 'to project' (source of English *imminent*).] —**prominently** *adv.* —**prominentness** *n.*

promiscuity /prómmi skyōō əti/ *n.* **1.** UNDISCRIMINATING SEXUAL BEHAVIOUR behaviour characterized by casual and indiscriminate sexual intercourse, often with many people (*disapproving*) **2.** CONFUSED MIXING a confused or indiscriminate mixing of elements (*formal*)

promiscuous /prə mískyoo əss/ *adj.* **1.** SEXUALLY INDISCRIMINATE having many indiscriminate or casual sexual relationships (*disapproving*) **2.** CONFUSEDLY MIXED mixed in an indiscriminate or disorderly way (*formal*) **3.** CHOOSING WITHOUT DISCRIMINATING choosing carelessly or without discrimination (*disapproving*) **4.** CASUAL casual and unplanned [Early 17thC. Formed from Latin *promiscuus*, literally 'mixed forwards', from *miscere* 'to mix' (source of English *mixed* and *miscellaneous*).] —**promiscuously** *adv.* —**promiscuousness** *n.*

promise /prómmiss/ *v.* (**-ises, -ising, -ised**) **1.** *vti.* MAKE A VOW TO SB to assure sb that sth will certainly happen or be done ○ *Promise that you'll be home on time.* **2.** *vt.* PLEDGE STH to pledge to sb to provide or do sth ○ *He promised the children a kitten.* **3.** *vti.* MAKE SB EXPECT STH to cause sb to expect sth ○ *The overcast sky promised rain.* **4.** *vt.* ASSURE OR WARN to assure or warn sb that sth is true or inevitable ○ *Things will be fine, I promise you.* **5.** *vt.* AFFIANCE to engage sb to be married (*dated*) ○ *She told him that she was promised to someone else.* ■ *n.* **1.** ASSURANCE OR UNDERTAKING an assurance that sth will be done or not done ○ *He never keeps his promises.* **2.** GOOD INDICATION an indication that sb or sth will turn out well or successfully ○ *She showed great promise as an athlete.* [14thC. Directly or via French *promesse* from, ultimately, Latin *promittere*, literally 'to send forward', from

mittere 'to send' (source of English *mission, missile,* and *transmit*).] —**promiser** *n.*

promisee /prómmi seé/ *n.* sb to whom a promise is made (*formal*)

promising /prómmissing/ *adj.* likely to be successful or to turn out well —**promisingly** *adv.*

promisor /prómmi sáwr/ *n.* sb who undertakes to do sth (*formal*)

promissory /prómmissəri/ *adj.* **1.** CONTAINING A PROMISE concerning, containing, or implying a promise **2.** INSUR SHOWING INSURANCE CONTRACT PROVISIONS stating how the terms of an insurance contract will be fulfilled [15thC. Via medieval Latin *promissorius* from, ultimately, Latin *promittere* (see PROMISE).]

promissory note *n.* a signed agreement promising payment of a sum of money on demand or at a particular time

promo /prốmō/ *n.* (*plural* **-mos**) STH TO PROMOTE PRODUCT sth that promotes or advertises a product, e.g. a recorded announcement, commercial, or video (*informal*) ■ *adj.* CONNECTED WITH PROMOTION OF STH involved or engaged in the promotion or advertising of sth [Mid-20thC. Shortening of PROMOTION or PROMOTIONAL.]

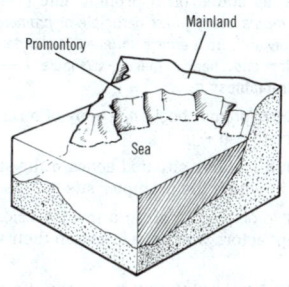

Promontory

promontory /prómməntəri/ (*plural* **-ries**) *n.* **1.** GEOG PROJECTING POINT OF LAND a point of land that juts out into the sea **2.** ANAT PROJECTING PART OF BODY a prominent or protruding part of the body [Mid-16thC. From medieval Latin *promontorium*, an alteration of Latin *promunturium*, of uncertain origin: perhaps formed from *mons* 'mountain' (source of English *mountain*).]

promote /prə mốt/ *vt.* (**-motes, -moting, -moted**) **1.** HR ADVANCE IN POSITION to raise sb to a more senior job or a higher position or rank **2.** SUPPORT OR ENCOURAGE to encourage the growth and development of sth **3.** BUSINESS ADVERTISE STH to publicize a product so that people will buy or hire it **4.** ADVANCE STH to further sth by helping to arrange or introduce it **5.** CHESS EXCHANGE PAWN FOR MORE POWERFUL PIECE in chess, to exchange a pawn for a more powerful piece, especially a queen, when it reaches an opponent's end of the board [14thC. Formed from Latin *promot-*, the past participle stem of *promovere* 'to move forwards', from *movere* 'to move' (source of English *move, motor,* and *moment*).] —**promotable** *adj.*

promoter /prə mốtər/ *n.* **1.** SB OR STH ARRANGING PUBLIC EVENT a person or organization that stages entertainment, a sporting contest, or other public event **2.** FIN ACQUIRER OF CAPITAL FOR VENTURE sb who secures capital for a financial or commercial undertaking such as a public company **3.** GENETICS BINDING SITE IN A DNA CHAIN in a DNA chain, a sequence to which the enzyme RNA polymerase binds so as to start transcription **4.** CHEM SUBSTANCE ADDED TO CATALYST a chemical additive that increases the efficiency of a catalyst **5.** MED STH THAT ENCOURAGES TUMOUR CELLS a substance that when given after a carcinogen encourages tumour cells to form or grow

promotion /prə mốsh'n/ *n.* **1.** HR ADVANCEMENT IN POSITION an advancement to a more senior job or a higher rank, grade, or position **2.** BUSINESS STH THAT PROMOTES sth that is designed to promote or advertise a product, cause, or organization **3.** ENCOURAGEMENT FOR ACTIVITY encouragement for the growth or development of sth **4.** SPORTS ADVANCE INTO HIGHER DIVISION advance by a sports team into a higher division of a league **5.** CHESS EXCHANGE OF PAWN FOR SUPERIOR PIECE in chess, the act of exchanging a pawn for a more powerful piece, usually a queen, when it reaches an opponent's end of the board

promotional *adj.* relating to the promotion of a product or organization so that people become more aware of it

promotive /prə mṓtiv/ *adj.* tending to further or encourage sth —**promotiveness** *n.*

prompt /prompt/ *adj.* **1.** DONE IMMEDIATELY done at once and without delay **2.** QUICK TO ACT ready, punctual, or quick to act ■ *adv.* PUNCTUALLY in a punctual way (*informal*) ■ *v.* (**prompts, prompting, prompted**) **1.** *vt.* URGE INTO ACTION to incite or urge sb to do sth **2.** *vt.* BRING ABOUT STH to give rise to sth **3.** *vti.* THEATRE PROVIDE ACTOR WITH LINES to provide actors or performers with the words or lines they have forgotten **4.** *vt.* REMIND OR SUGGEST to suggest sth or give a reminder to a speaker ■ *n.* **1.** THEATRE REMINDER OF WORDS TO PERFORMER words or lines supplied to a performer who has forgotten them **2.** THEATRE OCCURRENCE OF PROMPT the act or occasion of words being supplied to a performer who has forgotten them **3.** COMPUT STH CUEING RESPONSE a symbol or message displayed on a computer monitor or an audio signal informing a computer user that some input is required **4.** COMM TIME LIMIT FOR PAYMENT the time limit of payment for goods or services, as stated on a prompt note [14thC. From Latin *promptus* 'ready', past participle of *promere*, literally 'to take forward', from *emere* 'to take'. The underlying idea is 'bringing out', hence 'making available'.] —**promptly** *adv.* —**promptness** *n.*

promptbook /prómpt bo͝ok/ *n.* a copy of a script for a prompter to use

prompt box *n.* a box situated beneath the stage in a theatre in which the prompter sits

prompter /prómptər/ *n.* sb in a theatre whose job is to prompt actors who have forgotten their words or lines

promptitude /prómpti tyood/ *n.* punctuality or quickness to act (*formal*)

prompt note *n.* a written reminder sent to the purchaser of sth, stating when payment is due

prompt side *n.* the side of the stage in a theatre where the prompter sits. In Britain the prompt side is usually on the actor's left, and in the United States usually on the actor's right.

promulgate /prómm'l gayt/ (**-gates, -gating, -gated**) *vt.* (*formal*) **1.** DECLARE STH OFFICIALLY to proclaim or declare sth officially, especially to publicize formally that a law or decree is in effect **2.** MAKE KNOWN to make sth widely known [Mid-16thC. From Latin *promulgare*, literally 'to milk forward', from *mulgere* 'to milk'. The underlying idea is of 'bringing out into the light of day'.] —**promulgation** /-gáysh'n/ *n.* —**promulgator** /-gaytər/ *n.*

pron. *abbr.* **1.** pronominal **2.** pronoun **3.** pronounced **4.** pronunciation

pronate /pró nayt/ (**-nates, -nating, -nated**) *v.* **1.** *vt.* TURN HAND PALM DOWN to turn the hand or forearm so that the palm faces downwards **2.** *vti.* ROTATE FOOT INWARDS to rotate the bones of the foot so that the weight is borne mainly on the inside of the foot [Mid-19thC. Back-formation from PRONATE, from PRONE or Latin *pronus* (see PRONE).] —**pronation** /prō náysh'n/ *n.*

pronator /pró naytər/ *n.* a muscle that turns a part of the body so that it faces downwards, e.g. one of the muscles in the forearm that rotates the hand into the palm-down position [Early 18thC. From modern Latin, from Latin *pronus* (see PRONE), on the model of SUPINATOR.]

prone /prōn/ *adj.* **1.** DISPOSED TO STH inclined to do or be affected by sth **2.** FACE DOWN lying face down **3.** IN DOWNWARD DIRECTION sloping, leaning, or moving downwards [15thC. From Latin *pronus* 'bent forwards', from *pro* 'forwards'.] —**pronely** *adv.* —**proneness** *n.*

pronephros /prō néf ross/ (*plural* **-roi** /-roy/ *or* **-ra** /-rə/) *n.* the first of three segments of the kidney, functional in some vertebrate embryos but not in adults [Late 19thC. Formed from PRO² + Greek *nephros* 'kidney'.] —**pronephric** *adj.*

prong /prong/ *n.* SHARP POINT a thin sharp point at the end of sth ■ *vt.* (**prongs, pronging, pronged**) PIERCE WITH STH SHARP to prick or stab sth with a sharp pointed end [15thC. From Anglo-Latin *pronga* of uncertain origin: perhaps from, ultimately, a prehistoric Germanic word meaning 'pinching'.]

pronged /prongd/ *adj.* with a thin sharp point at the end (*often used in combination*)

pronghorn /próng hawrn/, **pronghorn antelope** *n.* an animal similar to an antelope found in Mexico and the western United States that is the fastest North American mammal. The male has two horns, shed annually, each with a curved prong. Latin name: *Antilocapra americana.*

pronograde /prṓnō grayd/ *adj.* used to describe quadrupeds that walk with the body parallel to the ground [Early 20thC. Formed from Latin *pronus* 'leaning forwards' + *-gradus* 'walking'.]

pronominal /prō nómmin'l/ *adj.* ACTING AS PRONOUN like or functioning as a pronoun ■ *n.* WORD ACTING LIKE PRONOUN a word that functions like a pronoun [Late 17thC. From late Latin *pronominalis* 'belonging to a pronoun', from Latin *pronomen* (see PRONOUN).] —**pronominally** *adv.*

pronominalize /prō nómminə līz/ (**-izes, -izing, -ized**), **pronominalise** (**-ises, -ising, -ised**) *vt.* in transformational grammars, to replace a noun or noun phrase in a sentence with a pronoun —**pronominalization** *n.*

pronoun /prṓ nown/ *n.* a word that substitutes for a noun or a noun phrase, such as 'I', 'you', 'them', 'it', 'ours', 'who', 'which', 'myself', and 'anybody'. Pronouns are sometimes distinguished from nouns by having objective form, e.g. 'her' for 'she' and 'me' for 'I'. [15thC. Formed from NOUN on the model of French *pronom* and its source Latin *pronomen*, literally 'in place of a name', from *nomen* 'name'.]

pronounce /prə nówns/ (**-nounces, -nouncing, -nounced**) *v.* **1.** *vti.* UTTER SOUNDS OR WORDS to articulate sounds or words, especially in a way acceptable to the person to whom they are spoken or by most speakers of a language **2.** *vti.* FORMALLY DECLARE to declare sth officially to be the case **3.** *vt.* GIVE JUDGMENT to render an opinion or judgment **4.** *vt.* PHON SYMBOLIZE SOUND OF WORD to indicate with symbols how a word should be spoken [14thC. Via Old French *pronuncier* from Latin *pronuntiare*, literally 'to announce before', from *nuntiare* 'to announce'.] —**pronounceable** *adj.* —**pronouncer** *n.*

pronounced /prə nównst/ *adj.* **1.** NOTICEABLE noticeable or obvious **2.** VOICED voiced or spoken —**pronouncedly** /prə nównssidli/ *adv.*

pronouncement /prə nównssmənt/ *n.* **1.** OFFICIAL STATEMENT an official or formal statement **2.** AUTHORITATIVE STATEMENT a formal or authoritative statement

pronto /próntō/ *adv.* in a prompt or rapid way (*informal*) [Mid-19thC. Via Spanish from Latin *promptus* (see PROMPT).]

pronuclear /prō nyo͝okli ər/ *adj.* **1.** FAVOURING NUCLEAR POWER in favour of using nuclear power in weapons or as a source of energy **2.** BIOL OF PRONUCLEUS relating to a pronucleus —**pronuclearist** *n., adj.*

pronucleus /prō nyo͝okli əss/ (*plural* **-i** /-ī/ *or* **-uses**) *n.* the nucleus of a fully matured ovum or spermatozoan before the nuclei are fused during fertilization

pronunciamento /prə núnssi ə méntō/ (*plural* **-tos**) *n.* an announcement, proclamation, or manifesto, especially one issued by a revolutionary group [Mid-19thC. Via Spanish from, ultimately, Latin *pronuntiare* (see PRONOUNCE).]

pronunciation /prə núnssi áysh'n/ *n.* **1.** MAKING SOUNDS OF SPEECH the way in which a sound, word, or language is articulated, especially in conforming to an accepted standard **2.** ACT OF SPEECH the act of articulating a sound or word **3.** PHON TRANSCRIPTION OF SOUNDS a phonetic transcription of sounds

pro-oestrus /prō éestrəss/ *n.* the period in the oestrus cycle immediately preceding oestrus

proof /proof/ *n.* **1.** CONCLUSIVE EVIDENCE evidence or an argument that serves to establish a fact or the truth of sth **2.** TEST OF STH a test or trial of sth to establish whether it is true **3.** STATE OF HAVING BEEN PROVED the quality or condition of having been proved **4.** LAW TRIAL EVIDENCE the evidence in a trial that helps to determine the court's decision **5.** LAW SCOTTISH LEGAL PROCESS OR TRIAL in Scottish law, a process by which evidence in a civil case is heard prior to a trial, or a civil trial before a judge and without a jury to determine the issues on which the trial will take place **6.** BEVERAGES STRENGTH OF ALCOHOLIC CONTENT the relative strength of an alcoholic beverage measured against a standard and expressed by a number that is twice the percentage of the alcohol present in the liquid **7.** PRINTING PRINTING IMPRESSION an impression used for checking corrections before the final printing of an image or text **8.** MATH, LOGIC SEQUENCE OF STEPS TO VALIDATE A SOLUTION the sequence of steps or stages used in establishing the validity of a mathematical or philosophical proposition. These steps are a logical derivation of the proposition from axioms, or explicit assumptions, and previously proved propositions. **9.** ARTS ARTIST'S IMPRESSION an impression taken from an engraved plate before it is printed **10.** PHOTOGRAPHY PRINT FROM A NEGATIVE a photographic print made from a negative and checked for quality prior to further reproduction **11.** COINS COIN IMPRESSION a preliminary impression of a coin, intended as a specimen for display ■ *adj.* **1.** IMPERVIOUS TO STH capable of resisting sth that may have a harmful or unwanted effect **2.** BEVERAGES HAVING RELATIVE ALCOHOLIC STRENGTH having a specific alcoholic strength that is expressed by a number that is twice the percentage of alcohol present in the liquid (*often used in combination*) **3.** RESISTANT capable of resisting or withstanding sth ■ *vt.* (**proofs, proofing, proofed**) **1.** MAKE RESISTANT to make sth capable of resisting harm, injury, or damage **2.** PRINTING, ARTS MAKE A PROOF OF STH to make a trial impression of sth printed or engraved **3.** PRINTING INSPECT FOR ERRORS to proofread a text, or inspect a printed impression for errors **4.** *US* COOK ACTIVATE YEAST to cause yeast to become active by adding water and often sugar [13thC. Alteration of earlier *pref* (influenced by PROVE) via Old French *preve* from Latin *proba*, from *probare* 'to prove, test' (source also of English *prove*).]

proof of purchase *n.* evidence such as a receipt that shows that sth has been paid for

proofread /pro͞of reed/ (**-reads, -reading, -read** /-red/) *vti.* to read the proofs of a text in order to correct them [Early 20thC. Back-formation from PROOFREADER.]

proofreader /pro͞of reedər/ *n.* sb whose job is to read printer's proofs of a text and correct them

proof sheet *n.* a sheet of paper that has a printer's proof on it, usually with wide margins so that corrections can be marked up easily

proof spirit *n.* an alcoholic beverage or a mixture of alcohol and water formerly used as a standard for measuring alcoholic strength. In the United Kingdom and Canada proof spirit is 57.1 per cent alcohol by volume at 10.6°C/51°F, in the United States, 50 per cent alcohol at 15.6°C/60°F.

proof theory *n.* the part of the theory of logic concerned with the exact nature of deriving propositions and conclusions

prop¹ /prop/ *n.* **1.** RIGID SUPPORT a rigid object such as a beam, stake, or pole that supports sth or holds it in place **2.** COMFORTING PERSON OR THING sb or sth that provides comfort or assistance **3.** RUGBY RUGBY FORWARD in rugby, a forward at either end of the front row of a scrum **4.** *Aus* SUDDEN STOP a sudden or unexpected stop, especially of a horse ■ *v.* (**props, propping, propped**) **1.** *vt.* SUPPORT WITH PROP to use a rigid object to support sth or hold it in place **2.** *vi. Aus* STOP ABRUPTLY to come to a sudden and unexpected stop (*refers to a horse*) [15thC. From Middle Dutch *proppe* 'vine prop, support'.]

prop up *vt.* to give support or help to sb or sth

prop² /prop/ *n.* ARTS = **property** *n.* 4 [Mid-19thC. Shortening.]

prop³ /prop/ *n.* an aircraft propeller (*informal*) [Early 20thC. Shortening.]

prop. *abbr.* **1.** proper **2.** properly **3.** property **4.** PHILOS, MATH proposition **5.** proprietor

propaedeutic /pró pee dyo͞otik/ *adj.* GIVING PRELIMINARY TEACHING providing preparatory instruction (*formal*) ■ *n.* INTRODUCTORY STUDY a preliminary course of study that introduces more advanced instruction (*often used in plural*) [Late 18thC. Formed from PRO² + *pae-*

PROOFREADERS' MARKS

General

Mark in margin	Instruction	Textual mark	Corrected type
✔	Delete	the new dictionary	the dictionary
✔	Delete and close up space	the dicti on ary	the dictionary
new/	Insert indicated material	the/dictionary	the new dictionary
✔ or (stet)	Leave unchanged/ as before	the new dictionary	the new dictionary
(?)	Query	the newt dictionary	
(sp)	Spell out	③ dictionaries	three dictionaries

Paragraphing

Mark in margin	Instruction	Textual mark	Corrected type
⌐	New paragraph	It was a gift. The new dictionary was excellent.	It was a gift. The new dictionary was excellent.
⌐	Flush paragraph	It was a gift. The new dictionary was excellent.	It was a gift. The new dictionary was excellent.
⌒	Run on	It was a gift. The new dictionary was excellent.	It was a gift. The new dictionary was excellent.

Position and Spacing

Mark in margin	Instruction	Textual mark	Corrected type
∼	Transpose	the dictionary new	the new dictionary
←	Move left	←the dictionary	the dictionary
→	Move right	the dictionary→	the dictionary
⌐	Move down	the dictionary	the dictionary
⌐	Move up	dictionary the	the dictionary
‖	Align	the dictionary the dictionary	the dictionary the dictionary
—	Straighten line	the dictionary	the dictionary
Y	Insert space	thedictionary	the dictionary
Y	Equalize space	the | new | dictionary	the new dictionary
⌣	Close up	the diction ary	the dictionary
1 2 3 |||	Set characters/ words in order	the dict ion ary	the dictionary

Punctuation

Mark in margin	Instruction	Textual mark	Corrected type
⊙	Full stop/ Decimal point	The new dictionary is excellent	The new dictionary is excellent.
,	Comma	scribble scribble scribble	scribble, scribble, scribble
⊢⊣	Hyphen	20th century dictionary	20th-century dictionary
:	Colon	The dictionary definition	The dictionary definition:
;	Semicolon	Look it up find it.	Look it up; find it.
✓	Apostrophe	the worlds dictionary	the world's dictionary
⁶⁶/⁹⁹	Double quotation marks	the world dictionary	the "world" dictionary
⁶/⁹	Single quotation marks	the world dictionary	the 'world' dictionary
[ ]	Brackets	the world dictionary	the [world] dictionary
|en|	En dash/rule	1900 2000	1900–2000
|em|	Em dash/rule	the dictionary the world	the dictionary—the world
✳	Asterisk	the dictionary	the dictionary*
§	Section symbol	World Dictionary	World Dictionary
/	Virgule/ Oblique/ slash	dictionary world English	dictionary/world/English
⋯	Ellipsis	world dictionary a gift	world dictionary ... a gift

Style of Type

Mark in margin	Instruction	Textual mark	Corrected type
≡	Upper case/ capital letters	the dictionary	The Dictionary
≢	Lower case	The Dictionary	the dictionary
=	Small capitals	the dictionary	THE DICTIONARY
///	Italic	the world dictionary	the *world* dictionary
⌐	Roman	the *world* dictionary	the world *dictionary*
∼	Bold face	the world dictionary	the **world** dictionary
∼	Light face	**the world dictionary**	**the** world **dictionary**
Ƴ	Superior/ superscript	85°F	85°F
⅄	Inferior/ subscript	H2O	H_2O

deutics 'teaching' on the model of Greek *propaideuein* 'to teach beforehand'.]

propagable /próppəgəb'l/ *adj.* **1.** BIOL, BOT CAPABLE OF BEING PROPAGATED capable of being grown or bred from a parent stock **2.** PHYS CAPABLE OF BEING IMPELLED FORWARDS capable of being transmitted or impelled forwards, especially in the form of light or sound waves — **propagability** /próppəgə bílləti/ *n.*

propaganda /próppə gándə/ *n.* **1.** PUBLICITY TO PROMOTE STH information or publicity put out by an organization or government to spread and promote a policy, idea, doctrine, or cause **2.** MISLEADING PUBLICITY deceptive or distorted information that is systematically spread [Early 18thC. From modern Latin *Propaganda Fide*, literally 'propagating the faith' (see PROPAGANDA).] —**propagandism** *n.* —**propagandist** *n.*, *adj.*

Propaganda *n.* a committee of Roman Catholic cardinals, the Congregation for the Propagation of the Faith, in charge of supervising foreign missions and educating priests to serve in them

propagandize /próppə gán dīz/ (-**dizes**, -**dizing**, -**dized**), **propagandise** (-**dises**, -**dising**, -**dised**) *vti.* to organize or spread propaganda

propagate /próppə gayt/ (-**gates**, -**gating**, -**gated**) *v.* **1.** *vti.* BIOL REPRODUCE ORGANISM to reproduce a plant or animal or, cause one to reproduce **2.** *vti.* GARDENING CREATE NEW PLANTS to multiply plants by the use of seeds or cuttings **3.** *vt.* SPREAD STH WIDELY to spread ideas or customs to many people **4.** *vti.* PHYS IMPEL STH FORWARDS to move or transmit sth forwards in space, especially as a light or sound wave [Late 16thC. From Latin *propagare* 'to breed plants in layers (of vines)', from, ultimately, *propago* 'layer', literally 'planting out', from an assumed base meaning 'to plant'.] —**propagation** /próppə gáysh'n/ *n.* —**propagational** *adj.* —**propagative** /próppəgaytiv/ *adj.*

propagator /próppə gaytər/ *n.* **1.** SPREADER OF IDEAS sb who spreads ideas or beliefs widely **2.** GARDENING BOX FOR SEEDS OR CUTTINGS a shallow box with a transparent cover used for germinating seeds or allowing cuttings to take root, especially one that can be heated

propagule /próppə gyool/, **propagulum** /pró pággyŏoləm/ *n.* a part of a plant or fungus such as a bud or a spore that becomes detached from the rest and forms a new organism [Mid-19thC. From modern Latin *propagulum*, literally 'little shoot', from *propago* (see PROPAGATE).]

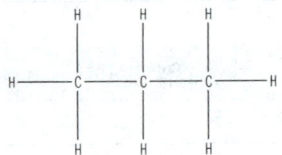

Propane

propane /pró payn/ *n.* a flammable colourless hydrocarbon gas that is used as a fuel, propellant, and refrigerant. Formula: C_3H_8. [Mid-19thC. Formed from PROPIONIC.]

propanoic acid /própə nó ik-/ *n.* = **propionic acid** [*Propanoic* was coined from PROPANE + -IC]

propanone /própə nōn/ *n.* acetone (*technical*)

proparoxytone /própə róksitōn/ *n.* ACCENTED WORD IN CLASSICAL GREEK in classical Greek grammar, a word that has an acute accent on the third syllable from the end, or a heavy stress on this syllable ■ *adj.* WITH PROPAROXYTONE with or using a proparoxytone [Mid-18thC. From Greek *proparoxutonos*, literally 'having an accent before the last syllable', from, ultimately, *oxutonos* 'having an accute accent'.]

pro patria /prō páttri ə/ *adv.* for sb's own country (*formal*) [From Latin, literally 'for the fatherland']

propel /prə pél/ (-**pels**, -**pelling**, -**pelled**) *vt.* **1.** PUSH FORWARDS to move or push sth or sb forwards **2.** CAUSE ACTION to impel or cause a course of action [15thC. From Latin *propellere* 'to drive forwards', from *pellere* 'to drive' (source of English *pulse* and *repel*).]

propellant /prə péllənt/, **propellent** *n.* **1.** SPACE TECH EXPLOSIVE SUBSTANCE a substance that is burned to give upward thrust to a rocket **2.** ARMS EXPLOSIVE CHARGE FOR GUN an explosive charge that projects a bullet from a gun **3.** GAS IN AEROSOLS a compressed inert gas used to dispense the contents of an aerosol container when pressure is applied and released

propellent /prə péllənt/ *adj.* tending to drive or move sth forwards

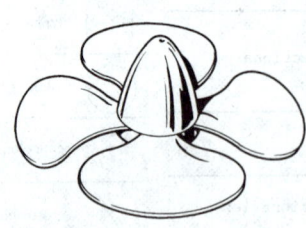

Propeller

propeller /prə péllər/ *n.* a revolving shaft with spiral blades that causes a ship or an aircraft to move by the backward thrust of water or air

propeller shaft *n.* **1.** SHAFT TRANSMITTING POWER the shaft in a ship or aircraft that transmits power from the engine to the propeller **2.** = **drive shaft** *n.* 1

propelling pencil *n.* a pencil with a replaceable lead that can be extended as it gets worn down. US term **mechanical pencil**

propend /prō pénd/ (-**pends**, -**pending**, -**pended**) *vi.* to incline to or towards sth (*archaic*) [Mid-16thC. From Latin *propendere* 'to hang forwards', from *pendere* 'to hang' (source of English *pendant*).]

propene /pró peen/ *n.* = **propylene** [Mid-19thC. Coined from PROPYL + -ENE.]

propenoic acid /própə nó ik-/ *n.* = **acrylic acid**

propensity /prə pénssəti/ (*plural* -**ties**) *n.* a tendency to demonstrate particular behaviour (*formal*) [Late 16thC. Formed from obsolete English *propense* 'inclined, prone', from, ultimately, Latin *propendere* (see PROPEND).]

proper /próppər/ *adj.* **1.** CORRECT appropriate or correct ○ *proper winter clothing* **2.** NEEDED AND APPROPRIATE fulfilling all expectations or criteria ○ *proper equipment for the task* **3.** WITH CORRECT MANNERS behaving in a respectable or socially acceptable way **4.** BELONGING EXCLUSIVELY TO SB characteristic of or belonging exclusively to sb or sth **5.** NARROWLY IDENTIFIED strictly identified and distinguished from sth else **6.** UK, Can COMPLETE thorough and complete **7.** HERALDRY SHOWING NATURAL COLOURS showing the natural colours in the design or device of a heraldic object **8.** CHR USED ON HOLY OCCASION reserved as a prayer, lesson, or rite for a holy day or festival **9.** GOODLOOKING physically handsome and admirable (*archaic*) **10.** MATH NON-IDENTICAL SET WITHIN SECOND SET included as a mathematical set in a second set but not being the same ■ *adv.* **1.** TOTALLY exceedingly or completely (*regional*) **2.** PROPERLY in a correct or proper way (*nonstandard*) ■ *n.* **proper, Proper** CHR SERVICE FOR HOLY OCCASION a Christian church service that is used for a holy day or festival [13thC. Directly or via Old French *propre* from Latin *proprius* 'one's own, particular, special', of uncertain origin: perhaps from *pro privo*, literally 'for the individual'.] —**properness** *n.*

proper adjective *n.* an adjective that is formed from a proper noun, as 'Canadian' is from 'Canada'

proper fraction *n.* a fraction in which the value of the numerator is less than the value of the denominator, e.g. $\frac{5}{8}$

properly /próppərli/ *adv.* **1.** APPROPRIATELY in a suitable or appropriate way ○ *properly dressed for the occasion* **2.** CORRECTLY in a correct or well-mannered

way ○ *If you can't behave properly, we'll have to go home.* **3.** IN REALITY in a correct and appropriate situation ○ *The chair properly belongs in the corner.* **4.** TOTALLY to the fullest degree or extent ○ *By the end of the day she was properly tired.*

proper noun, **proper name** *n.* the name of sth particular, normally beginning with a capital letter and not used with the indefinite article or a modifier, e.g. 'York', 'Sally', or 'Henderson'

propertied /próppərtid/ *adj.* owning property, especially land

property /próppərti/ (*plural* -**ties**) *n.* **1.** STH OWNED sth of value such as land or a patent that is owned **2.** OWNED LAND OR REAL ESTATE a piece of land or real estate that is owned by sb **3.** LAW RIGHT TO OWN STH the right to own, possess, or use sth **4.** TRAIT OR ATTRIBUTE a characteristic quality or distinctive feature of sth (*often used in the plural*) **5.** ARTS PROP a prop (*formal*) **6.** STH AT SB'S DISPOSAL sth at the disposal of a person, a group, or the public ○ *community property* **7.** PHILOS DISTINCTIVE BUT NOT ESSENTIAL QUALITY in the thought of Aristotle, an attribute or quality that is peculiar to a whole class or species but not essential to it **8.** Aus LAND IN COUNTRY a piece of rural land, usually a farm, ranch, or estate [13thC. Via Anglo-Norman *proprete* and French *propriété* (source also of English *propriety*) from Latin *proprietas* 'ownership', from *proprius* (see PROPER).]

property centre *n.* a place where property is advertised for sale or purchase and where conveyancing is offered by a group of solicitors

property man *n.* = **propman** (*dated*)

property mistress *n.* a woman who looks after stage properties (*dated*)

property tax *n.* a tax that is based on the value of a house or other property

prop forward *n.* RUGBY = **prop**[1] *n.* 3

prophage /pró fayj/ *n.* a stable form of virus that infects bacteria, with genetic material that is integrated into and replicated with that of its host without harming the host [Mid-20thC. Formed from PRO[2].]

prophase /pró fayz/ *n.* the first phase in cell division, when chromosomes condense and can be seen as two chromatids. ◊ **anaphase, metaphase, telophase** [Late 19thC. Formed from PRO[2].]

prophecy /próffəssi/ (*plural* -**cies**) *n.* **1.** RELIG DIVINE PREDICTION a prediction of a future event that reveals the will of a deity **2.** PREDICTION a prediction that sth will occur in the future **3.** RELIG ABILITY TO PREDICT THE FUTURE the ability to predict the future when inspired by a deity

prophesy /próffə sī/ *v.* **1.** *vti.* PREDICT to predict what is going to happen **2.** *vi.* RELIG PREDICT WITH DIVINE AUTHORITY to reveal the will of a deity in predicting a future event —**prophesiable** *adj.* —**prophesier** *n.*

prophet /próffit/ *n.* **1.** RELIG SB WHO INTERPRETS DIVINE WILL sb who interprets or passes on the will of a deity **2.** SB PREDICTING THE FUTURE sb who foretells the future **3.** ADVOCATE OF STH sb who advocates a cause or idea **4.** SB WHO IS INSPIRED sb considered to be an inspired leader or teacher [12thC. Via French *prophète* and Latin *propheta* from Greek *prophētēs*, literally 'someone who speaks beforehand', from *phētēs* 'speaker'.]

Prophet /próffit/ *n.* **1.** MUHAMMAD Muhammad, the founder of Islam **2.** FOUNDER OF LATTER DAY SAINTS Joseph Smith, the founder of the Church of Jesus Christ of Latter-Day Saints. ■ **Prophets** *npl.* PROPHETIC BOOKS OF BIBLE the prophetic books of the Bible, comprising the second half of the Christian Old Testament, and the second of the three divisions of the Hebrew Bible. See table at **Bible**

prophetess /próffi téss/ *n.* a woman prophet

prophetic /prə féttik/ *adj.* **1.** CORRECTLY PREDICTING predicting or foreshadowing sth that does eventually happen **2.** OF PROPHET relating to a prophet —**prophetical** *adj.* —**prophetically** *adv.*

Prophet's Birthday *n.* = **Mawlid al-Nabi**

prophylactic /próffi láktik/ *adj.* MED GUARDING AGAINST DISEASE guarding against infection or disease ■ *n.* **1.** PHARM DRUG THAT GUARDS AGAINST DISEASE a drug or agent such as anti-malarial pills that prevents the development of a disease **2.** *US* **CONDOM** a condom (*regional formal*) [Late 16thC. Via French *prophylactique* from, ultimately, Greek *prophulassein* 'to keep guard in front of', from *phulassein* 'to guard'.] —**prophylactically** *adv.*

prophylaxis /próffi láksiss/ (*plural* **-es** /-lák seez/) *n.* **1.** MED **TREATMENT TO PREVENT DISEASE** treatment such as vaccination that prevents disease or stops it spreading **2.** DENT **REMOVAL OF PLAQUE AND TARTAR** a dental treatment to remove plaque and tartar from the teeth [Mid-19thC. From modern Latin, literally 'guarding in front of', from Greek *pro* 'in front of' + *phulaxis* 'guarding', modelled on English *prophylactic*.]

propinquity /prə píngkwəti/ *n.* nearness in space, time, or relationship (*formal*) [14thC. Directly or via Old French *propinquité* from Latin *propinquitas*, from, ultimately, *prope* 'near' (source of English *approach*).]

propionate /própi ə nayt/ *n.* a chemical compound that is a salt or ester of propionic acid [Late 19thC. Formed from PROPIONIC.]

propionic /própi ónnik/ *adj.* derived from propionic acid [Mid-19thC. Formed from Greek *pro* 'in front' + *piōn* 'fat', because it is first in order of the fatty acids.]

propionic acid *n.* a colourless liquid fatty acid that is used in making artificial flavours, perfumes, and preservatives. Formula: $C_3H_6O_2$.

propitiate /prə píshi ayt/ (**-ates, -ating, -ated**) *vt.* to appease or conciliate sb or sth (*formal*) [Late 16thC. From Latin *propitiare* 'to make favourable', from *propitius* 'favourable'.] —**propitiable** *adj.* —**propitiation** /prə píshi áysh'n/ *n.* —**propitiative** /prə píshi ətiv/ *adj.* —**propitiator** /-aytər/ *n.*

propitiatory /prə píshi ətəri/ *adj.* designed to appease or win favour (*formal*) —**propitiatorily** *adv.*

propitious /prə píshəss/ *adj.* **1. FAVOURABLE** favourable and likely to lead to success **2. KINDLY** kindly disposed or gracious (*formal*) [15thC. Directly or via Old French *propicieus* from Latin *propitius* (see PROPITIATE).] —**propitiously** *adv.* —**propitiousness** *n.*

propjet /próp jet/ *n.* = **turboprop** *n.* **1**, **turboprop** *n.* **2** [Mid-20thC. Coined from PROPELLER + JET.]

propman /próp man/ (*plural* **-men** /-men/) *n.* a man who looks after stage properties

propolis /próppəliss/ *n.* a waxy resinous substance that comes from buds, used by bees as a cement and caulking in making their hives [Early 17thC. Via Latin from Greek, literally 'before a city', from *polis* 'city', because it originally referred to a structure around the opening of the hive.]

proponent /prə pṓnənt/ *n.* **1. ADVOCATE** sb who advocates sth **2.** LAW **PRESENTER OF WILL** sb who presents a will for probate **3. PROPOSER** sb who proposes sth [Late 16thC. From Latin *proponent-*, present participle stem of *proponere* 'to put forth', from *ponere* 'to place'.]

proportion /prə páwrsh'n/ *n.* **1. PART OF WHOLE** a quantity of sth that is part of the whole amount or number ○ *What proportion of their time is spent on administration?* **2. RELATIONSHIP BETWEEN QUANTITIES** the relationship between two or more amounts or numbers, or between the parts of a whole ○ *The proportion of lorries to cars on the road has remained the same.* **3. RELATIVE SIZE OF THINGS** the correct or desirable relationship of size, quantity, or degree between two or more things or parts of sth ○ *An understanding of proportion is essential for an architect.* **4. RELATIVE IMPORTANCE** the importance of different aspects of a situation when compared with each other ○ *The media blew the incident all out of proportion.* **5.** MATH **RATIO** a relationship or ratio between two variables that remains fixed **6.** MATH **EQUALITY OF TWO RATIOS** a relationship of equality between two ratios, in which the first term divided by the second equals the third divided by the fourth, as in 1/2 = 3/6 ■ **proportions** *npl.* **1. SIZE OF STH** the size or shape of sth **2. IMPORTANCE OF STH** the importance or seriousness of sth ■ *vt.* (**-tions, -tioning, -tioned**) **1. KEEP THINGS IN SAME RELATIONSHIP** to create or maintain a relationship of size, quantity, or degree between two or more things **2. MAKE STH BALANCED IN APPEARANCE** to give sth a pleasing shape, appropriate dimensions, or a harmonious arrangement of parts (*usually passive*) ○ *a beautifully proportioned design* [14thC. Directly or via Old French from the Latin stem *proportion-*, from the phrase *pro portione* 'according to (each) part', from the stem *portion-* (see PORTION).] —**proportionability** /prə páwsh'nə bílləti/ *n.* —**proportionable** *adj.* —**proportionably** *adv.* —**proportionment** *n.*

proportional /prə páwrsh'nəl/ *adj.* **1. IN PROPORTION** in the correct relationship of size, quantity, or degree to sth else, or remaining in the same relationship when things change ○ *The rate of pay is proportional to the complexity of the task.* **2.** MATH **RELATED BY A RATIO** related by or possessing a constant ratio ■ *n.* MATH **TERM IN PAIR OF EQUIVALENT RATIOS** any one of the four terms in a relationship of proportion between two ratios, where the first term divided by the second equals the third divided by the fourth —**proportionality** /prə páwrsh'n álləti/ *n.* —**proportionally** /-páwrsh'nəli/ *adv.*

proportional representation *n.* an electoral system in which each party's share of the seats in government is the same as its share of all the votes cast

proportional tax *n.* a tax in which the proportion of income paid in tax is constant when income rises

proportionate *adj.* /prə páwrsh'nət/ **IN PROPORTION** having the correct relationship of size, quantity, or degree to sth else, or remaining in the same relationship when things change ○ *The fall in price led to a proportionate rise in sales.* ■ *vt.* /prə páwshə nayt/ (**-ates, -ating, -ated**) **MAKE THINGS PROPORTIONAL** to give two or more things the correct relationship of size, quantity, or degree —**proportionately** /prə páwsh'nətli/ *adv.* —**proportionateness** *n.*

proposal /prə pṓz'l/ *n.* **1. IDEA OR PLAN** a suggestion or intention, especially one put forward formally or officially **2. ACT OF PROPOSING** the act of making a suggestion or stating an intention **3. REQUEST TO MARRY SB** a request for sb to enter into marriage **4.** POL, LAW **DRAFT LAW FROM EC** a draft law proposed by the European Commission to the Council of Ministers

propose /prə pṓz/ (**-poses, -posing, -posed**) *v.* **1.** *vt.* **MAKE SUGGESTION** to put sth forward, often formally or officially, e.g. an idea or suggested course of action ○ *Harsher penalties have been proposed.* **2.** *vt.* **STATE AN INTENTION** to announce a plan or intended course of action ○ *What do you propose to do about it?* **3.** *vt.* **NOMINATE SB** to put forward sb's name for an elected position or a promotion ○ *propose her for the new position* **4.** *vti.* **REQUEST MARRIAGE** to ask sb to marry ○ *He proposed while we were on holiday.* **5.** *vt.* **SUGGEST TOAST OR VOTE OF THANKS** to ask others to join in sth such as a toast or a vote of thanks ○ *I propose a toast to Chris and Sarah.* [14thC. From Old French *proposer*, literally 'to put forward', from *poser* (see POSE), modelled on Latin *proponere* 'to put forward'.] —**proposable** *adj.* —**proposer** *n.*

proposita /prō pózzitə/ (*plural* **-tae** /-tee/) *n.* a woman who is involved in legal proceedings [From Latin, feminine of *propositus* (see PROPOSITUS)]

propositi plural of **propositus**

proposition /próppə zísh'n/ *n.* **1. PROPOSAL** an idea, offer, or plan put forward for consideration or discussion **2. STATEMENT** a statement of opinion or judgment **3. SUGGESTION OF SEXUAL INTERCOURSE** an invitation to have sexual intercourse **4. PRIVATE AGREEMENT** a private deal or agreement **5. STH TO BE FACED** sth or sb to be dealt with (*informal*) ○ *The news that he would be there certainly made the party a more attractive proposition.* **6.** MATH **THEOREM** a statement or theorem to be demonstrated **7.** PHILOSOPHY **MEANING OF DECLARATIVE SENTENCE** the meaning of a declarative sentence and what is said to be true or false ■ *vt.* (**-tions, -tioning, -tioned**) **1. SUGGEST SEX** to invite sb to have sexual intercourse **2. OFFER SB A DEAL** to offer to make a private deal or agreement with sb [14thC. Directly or via French from the Latin stem *proposition-*, from *proposit-*, past participle stem of *proponere*, literally 'to put forth', from *ponere* 'to place'.] —**propositional** *adj.* —**propositionally** *adv.*

propositional attitude *n.* in philosophy, an attitude taken by sb towards a proposition, e.g. in believing it, knowing it, or desiring it

propositional calculus *n.* the branch of deductive logic that deals with the relationships formed between propositions by connectives, e.g. 'and', 'but', 'if', or 'or'

propositional function *n.* = **open sentence**

propositus /prō pózzitəss/ (*plural* **-ti** /-tī/) *n.* **1.** LAW **ORIGINAL ANCESTOR** sb who is the original ancestor of a line of descent **2. MAN LITIGANT** a man who is involved in legal proceedings **3.** MED **FIRST PERSON INVESTIGATED IN FAMILY STUDY** the first person to be investigated in the genetic study of a family [Mid-18thC. From Latin, past participle of *proponere* (see PROPONE).]

propound /prə pównd/ (**-pounds, -pounding, -pounded**) *vt.* **1. SUGGEST IDEA OR EXPLANATION** to put forward a suggestion or theory for others to consider **2. PRODUCE DOCUMENT FOR AUTHENTICATION** to present a document to a court or other authority in order that its validity can be established [Mid-16thC. Alteration of PROPONE.] —**propounder** *n.*

propr *abbr.* proprietor

propraetor /prō préetər/, **propretor** *n.* an ancient Roman citizen sent to govern a province, usually after serving as a senior magistrate (**praetor**) in Rome [Late 16thC. From Latin, from earlier phrase *pro praetore* '(one acting) for the praetor'.]

propranolol /prō pránnə lol/ *n.* PHARM a drug used to treat angina pectoris, abnormal heart rhythms, migraine, and high blood pressure. Formula: $C_{16}H_{21}NO_2$. [Mid-20thC. Coined from PROPYL + PROPANOL with repetition of *-ol*.]

proprietary /prə prī ətəri/ *adj.* **1. USED WITH EXCLUSIVE LEGAL RIGHT** used, manufactured, or sold by a person or company with an exclusive property right, e.g. a patent or trademark ○ *a proprietary drug* **2. EXHIBITING CHARACTERISTICS OF OWNERSHIP** exhibiting characteristics that imply or assume ownership of sb or sth ○ *The child kept a proprietary hold on the toy.* **3. RELATING TO OWNERS OR OWNERSHIP** relating to, involving, or associated with an owner, ownership, or sth owned **4. PRIVATELY OWNED** privately owned and run ■ *n.* (*plural* **-ies**) **1.** PHARM **PROPRIETARY AGENT** a drug or other substance made and sold under the legal protection of a trademark or patent **2. OWNER** an owner or a group of owners **3. OWNERSHIP** the right of ownership, or sth exclusively owned [15thC. Directly or via French from medieval Latin *proprietarius*, both from late Latin, 'of a property holder', from Latin *proprietas* (see PROPERTY).] —**proprietarily** *adv.*

proprietary colony (*plural* **proprietary colonies**) *n.* a North American colony granted to an individual or group by the Crown with full ownership rights

proprietary name *n.* a product name that is registered as a trademark

proprietor /prə prī ətər/ *n.* **1. OWNER OF A BUSINESS** the owner of a commercial enterprise or business establishment such as a shop, hotel, or restaurant **2. LEGAL OWNER** the legal owner of sth **3. FREEHOLDER OF PROPERTY** sb identified on the Land Registry as the freeholder of a property [15thC. Coined from PROPRIETARY + -OR.] —**proprietorial** /prə prī ə táwri əl/ *adj.* —**proprietorially** /-táwri əli/ *adv.* —**proprietorship** /prə prīətər ship/ *n.*

propriety /prə prī əti/ *n.* (*plural* **-ties**) **1. SOCIALLY CORRECT OR APPROPRIATE BEHAVIOUR** conformity to the standards of politeness, respect, decency, or morality conventionally accepted by a society **2. QUALITY OF BEING SOCIALLY APPROPRIATE** quality of displaying behaviour thought to be correct or appropriate ■ **proprieties** *npl.* **RULES OF ETIQUETTE** the accepted standards of correct or appropriate social behaviour [15thC. Via Old French from Latin *proprietas* 'appropriateness, ownership', from *proprius* (see PROPER).]

proprioceptor /própri ə séptər/ *n.* a sensory nerve ending in muscles, tendons, and joints that provides a sense of the body's position by responding to stimuli from within the body [Early 20thC. Coined from Latin *proprius* 'your own' + RECEPTOR.] —**proprioception** /própri ə sépsh'n/ *n.* —**proprioceptive** *adj.*

prop root *n.* a root that grows from the stem of a plant above the ground and helps to support it. The mangrove and maize are examples of plants with prop roots.

props master *n.* sb who looks after stage props

proptosis /prop tṓssiss/ *n.* the forward displacement or protrusion of an organ of the body, especially an eyeball [Late 17thC. Via late Latin from Greek *proptōsis* 'a falling forward', from *propiptein* 'to fall forward'.]

propulsion /prə púlsh'n/ *n.* **1. ACT OF DRIVING STH FORWARDS** the process by which an object such as a motor vehicle, ship, aircraft, or missile is moved forwards **2. DRIVING FORCE** the force by which sth such as a motor vehicle, rocket, or ship is moved forwards [Early 17thC. Ultimately from Latin *propuls-*, past participle stem of *propellere* (see PROPEL).] —**propulsive** /prə púlssiv/ *adj.* —**propulsory** *adj.*

propyl /prṓp il/ *n.* either of two isomeric chemical groups or radicals derived from propane. Formula: C_3H_7. [Mid-19thC. Coined from PROPIONIC + -YL.]

propylaeum /próppi leé əm/ (*plural* **-a** /próppi leé ə/) *n.* a colonnaded gate or entrance to a building, especially a temple, or to a group of buildings [Early 18thC. Via Latin from, ultimately, Greek *propulaios* 'before the gate', from *pulē* 'gate'.]

propyl alcohol *n.* a colourless alcohol used as a solvent and antiseptic. Formula: C_3H_8O.

propylene /prṓpi leen/ *n.* a flammable gaseous hydrocarbon derived from petroleum and used in organic synthesis. Formula: C_3H_6.

propylene glycol *n.* a colourless thick sweet-tasting liquid derived from propylene and used as an antifreeze in brake fluid, and as a solvent and lubricant. Formula: $C_3H_8O_2$.

propylon /prṓpi lon/ *n.* = **propylaeum** [Mid-19thC. Via Latin from Greek *propulon*, literally 'before the gate', from *pulē* 'gate'.]

pro rata /prō raátə/ *adv., adj.* in accordance with a fixed proportion [From Latin, 'according to the rate']

prorate /prō ráyt/ (**-rates, -rating, -rated**) *vti. US, Can* to calculate, divide, or distribute sth on a pro rata basis [Mid-19thC. Anglicization of PRO RATA.] —**proratable** *adj.* —**proration** /-ráysh'n/ *n.*

prorogue /prō rṓg/ (**-rogues, -roguing, -rogued**) *v.* **1.** *vti.* **SUSPEND PARLIAMENTARY SESSION** to discontinue the meetings of a parliament or other body without formally ending the session **2.** *vt.* **POSTPONE STH** to defer sth to a later date or to a subsequent meeting [15thC. Via French *proroguer* from Latin *prorogare* 'to prolong', literally 'to ask the people (whether a term of office should be extended)', from *rogare* 'to ask'.] —**prorogation** /prṓ rō gáysh'n/ *n.*

pros. *abbr.* prosody

prosaic /prō záy ik/ *adj.* **1. LACKING IMAGINATION** not having any features that are interesting or imaginative **2. RESEMBLING PROSE** characteristic of, resembling, or consisting of prose [Late 16thC. Directly and via French from late Latin *prosaicus*, from Latin *prosa* (see PROSE).] —**prosaically** *adv.* —**prosaicness** *n.*

prosaism /prō záy izzəm/, **prosaicism** /prō záy i sizzəm/ *n.* **1. BORING WORD OR QUALITY** a dull or unimaginative expression or style of writing **2. STH CHARACTERISTIC OF PROSE** a word, phrase, or style of writing used in prose —**prosaist** *n.*

pros and cons *npl.* the arguments for and against sth

Pros. Atty *abbr. US* prosecuting attorney

proscenium /prə seéni əm/ (*plural* **-a** /-ə/ *or* **-ums**) *n.* **1. FRONT OF STAGE** the part of a theatre stage that is in front of the curtain **2. STAGE IN ANCIENT GREECE OR ROME** the stage of a theatre in ancient Greece or Rome [Early 17thC. Via Latin from Greek *proskēnion* 'fore-estage', from *skēnē* (see SCENE).]

prosciutto /prō shóotō/ *n.* a type of cured ham from Italy, usually served cold and uncooked in thin slices [Mid-20thC. Via Italian from, ultimately, Latin *exsuctus* 'lacking juice', past participle of *exsugere* 'to suck out', from *sugere* 'to suck'.]

proscribe /prō skríb/ (**-scribes, -scribing, -scribed**) *vt.* **1. CONDEMN OR BAN STH** to prohibit sth that is considered undesirable by those in authority **2. CONDEMN STH** to denounce or condemn sth **3. BANISH SB** to banish or exile sb **4. OUTLAW SB PUBLICLY** to state publicly that sb is no longer protected by the law, especially in ancient Rome (*archaic*) [15thC. From Latin *proscribere* 'to publish in writing, to publish sb's name as outlawed', from *pro-* 'in front of' + *scribere* (see SCRIBE).] —**proscriber** *n.*

proscription /prō skrípsh'n/ *n.* (*formal*) **1. CONDEMNATION OF STH** an act of condemning or forbidding sth **2. CONDITION OF BEING BANNED** the condition of having been denounced or exiled **3. BANISHING OR BEING BANISHED** the act of banishment or exile, or the state of being banished or exiled —**proscriptive** /-skríptiv/ *adj.* —**proscriptively** /-skríptivli/ *adv.* —**proscriptiveness** *n.*

prose /prōz/ *n.* **1. LANGUAGE THAT IS NOT POETRY** writing or speech in its normal continuous form, without the rhythmic or visual line structure of poetry **2. ORDINARY STYLE OF EXPRESSION** writing or speech that is ordinary or matter-of-fact, without embellishment **3. PASSAGE FOR TRANSLATION** a piece of text to be translated into another language as an exercise for students **4.** CHR = **sequence** *n.* 6 ■ *v.* (**proses, prosing, prosed**) **1.** *vti.* **WRITE IN PROSE** to write sth in prose, as opposed to poetry **2.** *vt.* **REWRITE AS PROSE** to turn poetry into prose **3.** *vi.* **SPEAK OR WRITE PROSAICALLY** to speak or write in an ordinary, matter-of-fact, or unimaginative style [13thC. Via Old French from Latin *prosa (oratio)* 'straightforward (discourse)' from, ultimately, *provertere* 'to turn forward', from *vertere* (see VERSE).]

prosector /prō séktər/ *n.* sb who prepares or dissects cadavers for anatomic demonstrations [Mid-19thC. Directly or via French from late Latin, literally 'in place of the cutter', from Latin *sector* (see SECTOR).]

prosecute /próssi kyoot/ (**-cutes, -cuting, -cuted**) *v.* **1.** *vti.* **TAKE LEGAL ACTION AGAINST SB** to have sb tried in a court of law for a civil or criminal offence ○ *Trespassers will be prosecuted.* **2.** *vti.* **TRY TO PROVE SB IS GUILTY** to represent the person or people who are taking legal action against sb in a court of law **3.** *vt.* **PERFORM ACTIVITY OR OCCUPATION** to engage in or carry on some activity or occupation (*formal*) ○ *prosecute a trade* **4.** *vt.* **CONTINUE TO COMPLETION** to carry on doing sth, usually until it is finished or accomplished (*formal*) ○ *prosecute an investigation* [15thC. From Latin *prosecut-*, the past participle stem of *prosequi* (see PURSUE).] —**prosecutable** *adj.*

prosecuting attorney *n. US* a lawyer representing the state or the people in a criminal trial

prosecution /próssi kyóosh'n/ *n.* **1. PURSUIT OF LEGAL ACTION** the trial of sb in a court of law for a criminal offence **2. LAWYERS TRYING TO PROVE SB'S GUILT** the lawyers representing the person or people who are taking legal action against sb in a court of law, especially the Crown or the people in a criminal trial ○ *a witness for the prosecution* **3. PERFORMANCE OF ACTIVITY OR OCCUPATION** the carrying on of an activity or occupation (*formal*) ○ *the prosecution of your duty* **4. CONTINUATION TO COMPLETION** the continuation of or perseverance in some task or pursuit, usually until it is finished or accomplished (*formal*)

prosecutor /próssi kyootər/ *n.* **1.** *US* = **prosecuting attorney 2. INITIATOR OF LEGAL PROCEEDINGS** sb who initiates a court prosecution

proselyte /próssə līt/ (**-lytes, -lyting, -lyted**) *n.* a new convert to a religious faith or political doctrine [14thC. Via late Latin *proselytus* from Greek *prosēluthos* 'person who comes to a place', from *proserkhesthai* 'to come to'.] —**proselytic** /prόssə líttik/ *adj.* —**proselytism** /-lə tizəm/ *n.*

proselytize /próssələ tīz/ (**-tizes, -tizing, -tized**), **proselytise** (**-tises, -tising, -tised**) *vti.* to try to convert sb to a religious faith or political doctrine —**proselytization** /-tī záysh'n/ *n.* —**proselytizer** /-tīzər/ *n.*

prose poem *n.* a piece of creative writing that has the structure of prose but the style and language of poetry

Proserpina /prə súrpinə/, **Proserpine** /próssər pīn/ *n.* the Roman goddess of the earth

prosimian /prō símmi ən/ *n.* a nocturnal lower primate with large eyes and ears, e.g. a lemur, tarsier, or bush baby. Suborder: Prosimii.

prosit /prṓzit/ *interj.* used as a drinking toast, to wish sb good health or good fortune [Mid-19thC. Via German from Latin, 'may it benefit', 3rd person present subjunctive singular of *prodesse* (see PROUD).]

prosody /próssədi/ (*plural* **-dies**) *n.* **1. STUDY OF POETIC STRUCTURE** the study of the structure of poetry and the conventions or techniques involved in writing it, including rhyme, metre, and the patterns of verse forms **2. SYSTEM OR THEORY OF WRITING VERSE** a particular system or theory of writing poetry **3. RHYTHM OF SPEECH** the rhythm of spoken language, including stress and intonation, or the study of these patterns [15thC. Via Latin *prosodia* from Greek *prosōidiā* 'song with an instrumental accompaniment', from *pros* 'in addition to' + *ōidē* 'song' (source of English *ode*).] —**prosodic** /prə sóddik/ *adj.* —**prosodically** /-sóddikli/ *adv.* —**prosodist** /próssədist/ *n.*

prosoma /prō sṓmə/ (*plural* **-mas** *or* **-mata** /-sṓmətə/) *n.* the region near the head of spiders and some related arthropods, consisting of fused segments of head and thorax [Late 19thC. Coined from PRO- 'in front of' + Greek *sōma* 'body'.]

prosopography /próssə póggrəfi/ (*plural* **-phies**) *n.* a collection of biographical sketches used by social and political historians to convey larger patterns in a historical period [Mid-16thC. From modern Latin *prosopographia*, literally 'writing about sb', from Greek *prosōpon* 'face, person'.] —**prosopographer** *n.* —**prosopographical** /próssə pə gráffik'l/ *adj.*

prosopopoeia /próssəpə peé ə/, **prosopopeia** *n.* **1. RHETORICAL FIGURE OF SPEECH** a figure of speech in which an imaginary, dead, or absent person speaks **2.** = **personification** [Mid-16thC. Via Latin from Greek *prosōpopoiia* 'representation in human form', from *prosōpon* 'face, person' + *poiein* 'to make'.] —**prosopopoeial** *adj.*

prospect *n.* /prós pekt/ **1. POSSIBILITY OF STH HAPPENING SOON** a chance or the likelihood that sth will happen in the near future, especially sth desirable **2. VISION OF FUTURE** sth that is expected or certain to happen in the future, or a mental picture of this ○ *I don't relish the prospect of spending five months at sea.* **3. EXTENSIVE OUTLOOK OR SCENE** a view, especially one from a high position over a large expanse of land or water ○ *a pleasant prospect* **4. DIRECTION FACED** the direction in which sth faces ○ *a northerly prospect* **5.** COMM **LIKELY CUSTOMER** sb who is likely to be interested in buying a product or service **6. SB OR STH WITH POTENTIAL** sb or sth that is likely to succeed ○ *She's our brightest prospect.* **7. SURVEY** an act of making a survey, examination, or observation **8.** MINING **MINERAL LOCATION** location of a mineral deposit, or an area believed to have mineral deposits **9.** MINING **MINERAL DEPOSIT** a probable mineral deposit or one that definitely exists **10.** MINING **MINERAL SAMPLE TO BE ANALYZED** a sample of a mineral to be analyzed for its components **11.** MINING **MINERAL YIELD** the yield that can be obtained by mining a mineral ■ **prospects** *npl.* **EXPECTATIONS OF SUCCESS** the likelihood of being successful or prosperous in the future, especially in a job or career ○ *Young people who leave school early certainly limit their prospects.* ■ *v.* /prə spékt, prós pekt/ (**-pects, -pecting, -pected**) **1.** *vti.* MINING **SEARCH FOR MINERAL DEPOSITS** to explore an area in search of oil or valuable minerals, especially gold **2.** *vt.* MINING **WORK A MINE** to work a mine to see how profitable it is **3.** *vi.* **LOOK FOR STH** to search or watch for sth ○ *prospect for business* [15thC. From Latin *prospectus* 'view', from the past participle of *prospicere* 'to look forward', from *specere* (see SPECTACLE).] —**prospectless** /prós pektləss/ *adj.*

prospective /prə spéktiv/ *adj.* **1. LIKELY TO BE STH** expected or hoping to do or become sth ○ *his prospective mother-in-law* **2. LIKELY TO HAPPEN** likely or expected to happen ○ *prospective changes* —**prospectively** *adv.*

prospector /prə spéktər, prós pektər/ *n.* sb who explores an area in search of oil, gold, or other mineral deposits

prospectus /prə spéktəss/ *n.* **1. INFORMATION ABOUT INSTITUTION OR ORGANIZATION** a brochure or pamphlet that advertises or describes the activities, staff, and facilities of an organization or an institution such as a school, college, or university. US term **catalog 2. OFFICIAL ADVANCE INFORMATION ABOUT STH** an official document giving details about sth that is going to happen, e.g. an issue of shares, a forthcoming publication, a new business, or a proposed project [Mid-18thC. From Latin (see PROSPECT).]

prosper /próspər/ (**-pers, -pering, -pered**) *v.* **1.** *vi.* **SUCCEED FINANCIALLY** to be successful, especially in financial or economic terms, through effort or good fortune **2.** *vt.* **MAKE STH THRIVE** to make sth or sb successful or profitable (*archaic*) [14thC. Directly or via Old French from Latin *prosperare*, from *prosperus* 'doing well'.]

prosperity /pro spérrəti/ *n.* the condition of enjoying great wealth, success, or good fortune

prosperous /próspərəss/ *adj.* **1.** FINANCIALLY SUCCESSFUL successful and flourishing, especially earning or producing great wealth **2.** WEALTHY having great wealth, or associated with wealthy people **3.** FULL OF GOOD FORTUNE characterized by success or good fortune ○ *wishing you a prosperous New Year* **4.** PROMISING likely to be successful or bring a good result —**prosperously** *adv.* —**prosperousness** *n.*

pross /pross/, **prossie** /próssi/ *n.* a prostitute (*slang*) [Early 20thC. Shortening.]

Alain Prost

Prost /prost/, **Alain** (*b.* 1955) French racing driver and team owner. He was Formula One world champion (1985, 1986, 1989, and 1993) and four times runner-up.

prostacyclin /próstə sīklin/ *n.* a type of unsaturated fatty acid (**prostaglandin**) that dilates blood vessels and inhibits the formation of blood clots [Late 20thC. Coined from PROSTATE + CYCLIC + -IN.]

prostaglandin /próstə glándin/ *n.* an unsaturated fatty acid found in all mammals that resembles hormones in its activity, e.g. controlling smooth muscle contraction, blood pressure, inflammation, and body temperature [Mid-20thC. Coined from PROSTATE + GLAND + -IN.]

prostate /pró stayt/ *n.* ANAT = **prostate gland** [Mid-17thC. Ultimately via modern Latin *prostata* from Greek *prostatēs* 'guardian' (of the bladder), from *proïstanai* 'to set before', from *histanai* 'to cause to stand'.] —**prostatic** /pro státtik/ *adj.*

prostatectomy /próstə téktəmi/ (*plural* **-mies**) *n.* surgical removal of the whole or part of the prostate gland

prostate gland *n.* an O-shaped gland in males that surrounds the urethra below the bladder, secreting a fluid into the semen that acts to improve the movement and viability of sperm

prostatism /próstə tizəm/ *n.* a disorder of the prostate gland, especially enlargement that blocks or inhibits urine flow

prostatitis /próstə tītiss/ *n.* inflammation of the prostate gland

prosthesis /pross théessiss/ (*plural* **-ses** /-seez/) *n.* **1.** MED ARTIFICIAL BODY PART an artificial body part, e.g. an artificial limb or eye **2.** SURG REPLACEMENT OF BODY PART the branch of surgery concerned with replacing missing body parts with artificial devices **3.** LING = **prothesis** *n.* 1 [Mid-16thC. Via late Latin from Greek, 'addition', from *prostithenai* 'to add to', from *tithenai* 'to place' (source of English *thesis*).] —**prosthetic** /pross théttik/ *adj.* —**prosthetically** /-théttikli/ *adv.*

prosthetic group *n.* the part of a conjugated protein that is not an amino acid, e.g. the lipid group in lipoprotein

prosthetics /pross théttiks/ *n.* a branch of medicine dealing with the design, production, and use of artificial body parts (*takes a singular verb*) —**prosthetist** /prósthətist/ *n.*

prosthodontics /prósstha dóntiks/ *n.* a branch of dentistry dealing with the replacement of teeth and parts of the jaw (*takes a singular verb*) [Mid-20thC. Coined from PROSTHESIS + -ODONTIA modelled on ORTHODONTICS.] —**prosthodontic** *adj.* —**prosthodontist** *n.*

prostitute /prósti tyoot/ *n.* **1.** SB PAID FOR SEXUAL INTERCOURSE sb who receives money in return for sexual intercourse or other sex acts **2.** SB WHO DEGRADES TALENT FOR MONEY sb who uses a skill or ability in a way that is considered unworthy, usually for financial gain ■ *vt.* (**-tutes, -tuting, -tuted**) **1.** MISUSE STH FOR GAIN to use a skill or ability in a way that is considered unworthy, usually for financial gain ○ *He has been accused of prostituting his talent by appearing in TV commercials.* **2.** WORK OR OFFER SB AS PROSTITUTE to work as a prostitute or offer sb else for sexual intercourse or other sex acts in exchange for money [Mid-16thC. From the past participle of Latin *prostituere* 'to expose publicly, offer for sale', from *statuere* 'to set, place' (source also of English *statute*).] —**prostitutor** *n.*

prostitution /prósti tyóosh'n/ *n.* **1.** WORK OF A PROSTITUTE the act of engaging in sexual intercourse or performing other sex acts in exchange for money, or of offering another person for such purposes **2.** MISUSE OF TALENT FOR GAIN the use of a skill or ability in a way that is considered unworthy, usually for financial gain

prostomium /prō stōmi əm/ (*plural* **-a** /-ə/) *n.* the part of the head of certain worms, including the earthworm, that is in front of the mouth [Late 19thC. Via modern Latin, from Greek *prostomion*, literally 'sth in front of the mouth', from *stoma* 'mouth' (source also of English *stomach*).] —**prostomial** *adj.*

prostrate *v.* /pro stráyt/ (**-trates, -trating, -trated**) **1.** *vr.* LIE FACE DOWNWARDS to lie flat on the face or bow very low, e.g. in worship or humility ○ *He prostrated himself before the soprano.* **2.** *vt.* LAY SB OR STH ON GROUND to lay or throw sb or sth flat on the ground ○ *prostrated by a blow on the head* **3.** *vt.* INCAPACITATE SB to make sb physically or emotionally weak or helpless ○ *prostrated by illness* ■ *adj.* /pró strayt/ **1.** LYING FLAT ON FACE lying prone or stretched out with the face downwards, e.g. in worship or submission **2.** LYING DOWN stretched out in a horizontal position, often because of illness or injury **3.** DRAINED OF ENERGY drained of physical strength or incapacitated by overexertion or powerful emotion ○ *prostrate with grief* **4.** BOT GROWING ALONG THE GROUND used to describe a plant that grows or trails along the ground ○ *a prostrate shrub* [14thC. From Latin *prostratus*, the past participle of *prosternere* 'to throw in front of', from *sternere* 'to spread out, lay down' (source also of English *strata*).] —**prostration** /pro stráysh'n/ *n.*

prostyle /prō stīl/ *adj.* used to describe a building, e.g. a Greek temple, with a row of columns at the front [Late 17thC. From Latin *prostylos* 'having pillars in front', from *stilus* 'pointed writing instrument, stake' (source of English *style*).]

prosy /prōzi/ (**-ier, -iest**) *adj.* dull and commonplace, with no interesting, imaginative, or eloquent features —**prosily** *adv.* —**prosiness** *n.*

Prot. *abbr.* **1.** Protestant **2.** HIST Protectorate

prot- *prefix.* = **proto-** (*used before vowels*)

protactinium /prō tak tínni əm/ *n.* a toxic radioactive metallic chemical element found in uranium ores. Symbol **Pa** [Early 20thC. Coined from PROTO- + ACTINIUM, because the commonest isotope decays to give actinium.]

protagonist /prō tággənist/ *n.* **1.** LITERAT MAIN CHARACTER the most important character in a novel, play, story, or other literary work **2.** HIST MAIN CHARACTER IN ANCIENT GREEK DRAMA the first actor who interacted with the chorus in ancient Greek drama **3.** LEADING FIGURE a main participant in an event, e.g. a contest or dispute ○ *two protagonists in a long-running dispute* **4.** SUPPORTER an important or influential supporter or advocate of sth such as a political or social issue ○ *an early protagonist of educational reform* [Late 17thC. From Greek *protagōnistēs* 'actor who plays the chief part', from *agōnistes* 'actor, competitor', from *agōn* 'contest' (see AGONY).] —**protagonism** *n.*

protamine /prōtə meen/ *n.* a water-soluble, strongly basic protein that has a low molecular weight, does not coagulate when heated, hydrolyzes to yield amino acids, in particular arginine, and is found in fish sperm. It is used therapeutically to control haemorrhage and diabetes.

protanopia /prōtə nōpi ə/ *n.* a form of colour blindness in which the retina fails to distinguish between red and green. ◊ **Daltonism** [Early 20thC. Coined from PROTO- (red being regarded as the first of the primary colours) + AN- + -OPIA.] —**protanopic** /-nóppik/ *adj.*

protasis /próttəssiss/ (*plural* **-ses** /-seez/) *n.* GRAM the part of a conditional sentence that contains the condition, e.g. 'if he asks' in 'if he asks, I'll tell him' [Mid-16thC. Via Latin from Greek from *proteinein* 'to put forward, propose', from *teinein* 'to stretch'.] —**protatic** /pro táttik/ *adj.*

prote- *prefix.* = **proteo-**

protea /prōti ə/ (*plural* **-as** *or* **-a**) *n.* an evergreen shrub or tree of southern Africa, grown for its colourful bracts and dense flower heads. Genus: *Protea.* [Mid-18thC. From modern Latin, named after PROTEUS, from the variety of form in the genus.]

protean /prō tée ən, prōti ən/ *adj.* **1.** ABLE TO CHANGE FORM variable or continually changing in nature, appearance, or behaviour **2.** VERSATILE showing great variety, diversity, or versatility

protease /prōti ayz, -ayss/ *n.* an enzyme found in plant and animal cells that breaks down proteins or peptides by catalysing the hydrolysis of peptide bonds

protease inhibitor *n.* a compound, naturally occurring in plants, that breaks down the enzyme protease, inhibiting the replication and development of certain cells such as cancers and viruses, including the Aids virus

protect /prə tékt/ (**-tects, -tecting, -tected**) *vt.* **1.** KEEP STH OR SB SAFE to prevent sb or sth from being harmed or damaged **2.** ECON HELP HOME INDUSTRIES BY TAXING IMPORTS to help the industries in a country by imposing customs duties on imports from other countries **3.** FIN GUARANTEE PAYMENT OF DRAFT to put up money in advance to guarantee that a draft or note is paid [15thC. From Latin *protect-*, past participle stem of *protegere*, literally 'to cover in front', from *tegere* 'to cover' (source of English *integument*).]

WORD KEY: SYNONYMS

See Synonyms at ***safeguard***.

protectant /prə téktənt/ *n.* a substance that prevents sth from being damaged, e.g. a coating used to stop metal going rusty

protected /prə téktid/ *adj.* **1.** ECOL ENDANGERED legally classified as a species in danger of extinction **2.** SHELTERED sheltered from the elements **3.** COMPUT LOCKED AGAINST UNAUTHORIZED CHANGES locked against changes by unauthorized users of a computer program

protection /prə téksh'n/ *n.* **1.** SAFEGUARDING OF SB OR STH the act of preventing sb or sth from being harmed or damaged, or the state of being kept safe **2.** STH THAT PROTECTS SB OR STH sth that prevents sb or sth from being harmed or damaged **3.** INSUR INSURANCE COVER an insurance company's agreement to pay compensation or costs if some specified undesirable event occurs **4.** CRIMINOL PROMISE OF SAFETY FROM CRIMINAL ATTACK a promise made by a gangster that sb or sth will not be harmed if money is paid, or the payment extorted in return for such a promise (*informal*) **5.** *US* CONDOM a form of contraception, usually a condom, used during sexual intercourse to prevent sperm or disease-causing organisms from entering the body **6.** GUARANTEE OF FREEDOM AND SAFETY a document that enables sb to travel around in freedom and safety, especially in another country or in enemy territory **7.** ECON = **protectionism** **8.** MOUNTAINEERING MOUNTAIN CLIMBERS' SAFETY EQUIPMENT the safety equipment used by mountain climbers to keep them from falling, e.g. pitons, harnesses and ropes

protectionism /prə téksh'nizəm/ *n.* the system of imposing duties on imports into a country in order to protect domestic industries —**protectionist** *n., adj.*

protection money *n.* money paid to a gangster or other person who threatens to damage sth or harm sb unless the money is paid

protective /prə téktiv/ *adj.* **1.** GIVING PROTECTION preventing sth or sb from being harmed or damaged, or designed or intended for this purpose **2.** TAKING GREAT CARE OF SB very anxious to protect or defend sb or sth, often excessively so ○ *She had always felt protective towards her younger brother.* **3.** ECON INTENDED TO HELP DOMESTIC INDUSTRIES intended to give an advantage to a country's domestic industries ○ *a protective tariff* ■ *n.* **1.** STH THAT PROTECTS sth that prevents sb or sth from being harmed or damaged

2. CONDOM a condom (*formal*) —**protectively** *adv.* —**protectiveness** *n.*

protective coloration, protective colouring *n.* the combination of surface colours and patterns of an animal that helps it blend into its surroundings and so evade predators

protective custody *n.* detention in a particular place by the police in order to give protection from harm by other people

protector /prə téktər/ *n.* **1. STH THAT PROTECTS** sth that prevents sb or sth from being harmed or damaged **2. SB WHO PROTECTS** sb who protects or defends sb or sth **3. protector, Protector SB RULING IN PLACE OF MONARCH** sb in charge of a country while the monarch is absent or too young or unfit to rule —**protectoral** *adj.* —**protectorship** *n.*

Protector *n.* the title given to the head of the Commonwealth of England, Scotland, and Ireland during the period without a monarch that lasted from 1653 to 1659. The title was held by Oliver Cromwell (1653–58) and Richard Cromwell (1658–59).

protectorate /prə téktərət/ *n.* **1. STATE DEPENDENT ON ANOTHER** a country or region that is defended and controlled by a more powerful state, or the relationship between the two **2. PLACE THAT IS DEPENDENT ON ANOTHER** an area or country that is dependent on another more powerful nation **3. OFFICE OF PROTECTOR** the position or term of office of a protector

protégé /prótti zhay, prṓti-/ *n.* a young person who receives help, guidance, training, and support from sb who is older and has more experience or influence [Late 18thC. From French, from the past participle of *protéger* 'to protect', from Latin *protegere* (see PROTECT).]

protégée /próti zhay, prṓti-/ *n.* a young woman who receives help, guidance, training, and support from sb who is older and has more experience or influence [Late 18thC. From French, feminine of *protégé* (see PROTÉGÉ).]

protei plural of **proteus**

proteid /prṓti id/ *n.* a salamander such as an olm or a mudpuppy that retains its larval form. Family: Proteidae. [Late 19thC. Formed from modern Latin *Proteus*, genus name, named after PROTEUS.]

protein /prṓ teen/ *n.* **1.** BIOCHEM **COMPLEX NATURAL COMPOUND** a complex natural substance that has a high molecular weight and a globular or fibrous structure composed of amino acids linked by peptide bonds. Proteins are essential to the structure and function of all living cells and viruses. **2.** FOOD **FOOD RICH IN PROTEIN** a food source that is rich in protein molecules ○ *a protein-rich diet* [Mid-19thC. Via French from Greek *prōteios* 'primary', from *prōtos* 'first'; from its importance to the proper functioning of the body.] —**proteinaceous** /prṓti náyshəss/ *adj.* —**proteinic** /prō teénik/ *adj.* —**proteinous** /prō teénəss/ *adj.*

proteinase /prṓti nayz, -nayss/ *n.* an enzyme (**protease**) that catalyses the hydrolysis of proteins into their component amino acids or simpler peptides

proteinuria /prṓti nyoóri ə/ *n.* the presence of protein in the urine, usually indicating disease

pro tem /prō tém/ *adv., adj.* at the present time but not permanently [Shortening of PRO TEMPORE]

proteolysis /prṓti ólləssiss/ *n.* the breakdown of proteins or peptides into simpler molecules, e.g. in digestion —**proteolytic** /prṓti ə líttik/ *adj.* —**proteolytically** /-líttikli/ *adv.*

proteose /prṓti ōz/ *n.* a water-soluble protein derivative formed during hydrolytic processes such as digestion that does not coagulate when heated and precipitates if mixed with certain sulphur-containing compounds

Proterozoic /prṓtərō zṓ ik/ *n.* the latter half of the Precambrian era, during which sea plants and animals first appeared [Early 20thC. Coined from PROTERO- + Greek *zōē* 'life' + -IC.] —**Proterozoic** *adj.*

protest *v.* /prə tést/ (**-tests, -testing, -tested**) **1.** *vti.* **COMPLAIN OR OBJECT STRONGLY** to express strong disapproval of or disagreement with sth, or to refuse to obey or accept sth, often by making a formal statement or taking action in public **2.** *vti.* **SAY FIRMLY THAT STH IS TRUE** to state or affirm sth in strong or formal terms ○ *He continued to protest his innocence.* **3.** *vt.* FIN **DECLARE FINANCIAL NOTE DISHONOURED** to state formally that a note or bill has been dishonoured **4.** *vt.* **ANNOUNCE STH** to declare or proclaim sth (*archaic*) ■ *n.* /prṓ test/ **1. STRONG COMPLAINT OR OBJECTION** an expression or display of strong disapproval of or disagreement with sth, or a refusal to obey or accept sth, often in the form of a public statement **2. DEMONSTRATION OF PUBLIC OPPOSITION OR DISAPPROVAL** an expression of strong opposition to or disapproval of sth in the form of a public demonstration or other action ○ *student protests* **3.** LAW **CREDITOR'S FORMAL STATEMENT** a formal statement drawn up by a notary on behalf of a creditor, declaring that sb has refused to honour a bill **4. CAPTAIN'S STATEMENT ABOUT DAMAGE TO SHIP** a statement made by the master of a damaged vessel, declaring when and how a ship was damaged [14thC. Via French from, ultimately, Latin *protestari* 'to declare publicly', from *testari* 'to declare' (source of English *testament*).] —**protestant** /próttistənt/ *n., adj.* —**protester** /prə téstər/ *n.* —**protestingly** *adv.*

WORD KEY: SYNONYMS

See Synonyms at ***complain***. See Synonyms at ***object***.

Protestant /próttistənt/ *n.* a member or adherent of any denomination of the Western Christian church that rejects papal authority and some fundamental Roman Catholic doctrines, and believes in justification by faith. The formulation of Protestants' beliefs began with the Reformation in the 16th century. —**Protestant** *adj.*

Protestant ethic *n.* = **Protestant work ethic**

Protestantism /próttistəntizəm/ *n.* **1. BELIEF IN PROTESTANT DOCTRINES** adherence to Protestant beliefs **2. RELIGIOUS MOVEMENT OPPOSING ROMAN CATHOLICISM** a Christian religious movement originating in the 16th century from Martin Luther's attack on Roman Catholic doctrine. It grew to encompass many churches and denominations denying papal authority and believing in justification by faith. **3. ALL PROTESTANT CHURCHES** the Protestant churches as a group

Protestant work ethic *n.* a belief in the moral value of work, thrift, and the responsibility of the individual for his or her actions

protestation /prótti stáysh'n/ *n.* **1. FORMAL AFFIRMATION** a strong or firm declaration that sth is true or false (*often used in the plural*) ○ *protestations of loyalty* **2. ACT OF COMPLAINING OR OBJECTING** the expression of strong disapproval of or disagreement with sth **3. COMPLAINT OR OBJECTION** an individual expression of strong disapproval of or disagreement with sth

proteus /prṓti əss/ (*plural* **-i** /-ī/) *n.* a rod-shaped bacterium associated with enteritis and urinary tract infections. Genus: *Proteus.* [Early 19thC. From modern Latin, named after PROTEUS.]

Proteus /prṓti əss/ *n.* **1. GREEK SEA GOD** in Greek mythology, a prophetic sea god who could change his shape at will **2. SECOND-LARGEST MOON OF NEPTUNE** the second-largest natural satellite of Neptune, discovered in 1989 by Voyager 2. It is irregular in shape, having a maximum dimension of approximately 440 km.

prothalamion /prṓthə láymi ən/ (*plural* **-a** /-ə/), **prothalamium** /-mi əm/ (*plural* **-a** /-ə/) *n.* a song or poem written or performed in celebration of a marriage (*formal*) [Late 16thC. From *'Prothalamion'*, a poem by Spenser (1597), modelled on *epithalamion*, a variant of EPITHALAMIUM.]

prothallus /prō thálləss/ (*plural* **-li** /-lī/), **prothallium** /prō thálli əm/ (*plural* **-a** /-ə/) *n.* a flat green organ bearing the reproductive organs (**gametophytes**) of ferns and related plants [Mid-19thC. From modern Latin, from *pro-* 'before' + Greek *thallos* 'green shoot'.] —**prothallial** /prō thálli əl/ *adj.* —**prothallic** *adj.*

prothesis /próthəssiss/ (*plural* **-ses** /próthə seez/) *n.* **1.** LING **ADDITION OF SYLLABLE TO HELP PRONUNCIATION** the addition of a sound or sounds at the beginning of a word to make the word easier to pronounce **2.** CHR **PREPARATIONS FOR OFFERING EUCHARIST** the preparations for the offering of the Eucharist in the Eastern Orthodox Church [Late 16thC. From Greek, 'a placing before or in public', from *thesis* 'placing' (source of English *thesis*).] —**prothetic** /prō théttik/ *adj.* —**prothetically** /-théttikli/ *adv.*

prothonotary /prótthə nṓtəri, prō thónnətəri/ (*plural* **-ies**), **protonotary** /prṓtə nṓtəri, prō tónnətəri/ (*plural* **-ies**) *n.* **1.** LAW **CHIEF CLERK IN COURT** the chief clerk in some courts of law **2. prothonotary, prothonotary apostolic** (*plural* **prothonotaries apostolic**) **ROMAN CATHOLIC CHURCH OFFICIAL** in the Roman Catholic Church, any one of twelve officials who can act as a notary to authenticate papal proceedings, documents, and acts [15thC. Via medieval Latin from Greek *prōto* + Latin *notarios* 'first notary', from *notarios* (see NOTARY).] —**prothonotarial** /prō thónnə táiri əl/ *adj.*

prothoraces plural of **prothorax**

prothoracic /prṓ thaw rássik/ *adj.* relating to the front segment (**prothorax**) of the thorax of an insect

prothoracic gland *n.* a gland in insects that secretes the steroid hormone ecdysone, responsible for controlling moulting and metamorphosis

prothorax /prō tháw raks/ (*plural* **-raxes** *or* **-races** /-seez/) *n.* the front segment of the thorax of an insect, where the first pair of legs is located [Early 19thC. From modern Latin, literally 'thorax in front', from *thorax* 'thorax'.]

prothrombin /prō thrómbin/ *n.* a plasma protein produced in the liver and converted to thrombin during the clotting of blood

protist /prṓtist/ *n.* an organism belonging, in an older classification system, to the kingdom that includes protozoans, bacteria, and single-celled algae and fungi. Kingdom: *Protista.* ◊ **protoctist** [Late 19thC. Formed from modern Latin *Protista*, former kingdom name, ultimately from Greek *prōtistos* 'very first', from *prōtos* 'first'.] —**protistan** /prō tístən/ *adj.* —**protistology** /prṓtis tólləji/ *n.*

protium /prṓti əm/ *n.* the most common and lightest isotope of hydrogen, with atomic mass 1 [Mid-20thC. Coined from Greek *prōtos* 'first' + -IUM.]

proto- *prefix.* **1.** first in time, earliest ○ *protolithic* ○ *protomartyr* **2.** original, ancestral ○ *protostar* ○ *Proto-Norse* **3.** first in a series, having the least amount of a particular element or radical ○ *protactinium* [From Greek *prōtos*; ultimately related to *pro* (see PRO[2])]

protocol /prṓtə kol/ *n.* **1. ETIQUETTE OF STATE OCCASIONS** the rules or conventions of correct behaviour on official or ceremonial occasions **2. CODE OF CONDUCT** the rules of correct or appropriate behaviour for a particular group of people or in a particular situation **3.** INTERNAT REL **INTERNATIONAL AGREEMENT** a formal agreement between states or nations **4. AMENDMENT** sth that amends a treaty or other formal document **5.** INTERNAT REL **STH ADDED TO TREATY** sth added to a treaty that deals with minor details or that makes it easier to understand **6. RECORD OR DRAFT OF AGREEMENT** a written record or preliminary draft of a treaty or other agreement **7.** COMPUT **RULES FOR EXCHANGING INFORMATION BETWEEN COMPUTERS** a set of technical rules about how information should be transmitted and received using computers **8.** PHILOSOPHY = **protocol statement 9.** *US* MED, SCI **RESEARCH PLAN** the detailed plan of a scientific experiment, medical trial, or other piece of research [15thC. Directly and via Old French from medieval Latin from Greek *prōtokollon* 'first leaf of a book'. The modern meaning evolved via 'draft of a diplomatic document'.]

protocol statement *n.* a statement that can be immediately verified by experience

protoderm /prṓtə durm/ *n.* BOT = **dermatogen** —**protodermal** *adj.*

protogalaxy /prṓtō gálləksi/ (*plural* **-ies**) *n.* a hypothetical cloud of gas believed to have been formed about 14 billion years ago from dark matter, neutral hydrogen, and helium, from which all the galaxies and stars evolved

Proto-Germanic /prṓtō-/ *n.* the reconstructed hypothetical language that is believed to be the ancestor of the Germanic branch of the Indo-European family of languages —**Proto-Germanic** *adj.*

protohistory /prṓtō hístəri/ *n.* the archaeological period of human development, before recorded history (*dated*) —**protohistoric** /prṓtō hi stórrik/ *adj.*

protohuman /prṓtō hyō'əmən/ *n.* an extinct hominid or primate that has some of the characteristics of modern people —**protohuman** *adj.*

Proto-Indo-European *n.* the reconstructed hypothetical language that is believed to be the ancestor of all the Indo-European languages —**Proto-Indo-European** *adj.*

protoindustrialization /prṓtō in dústri ə līt záysh'n/, **protoindustrialisation** *n.* the preliminary shift from an agricultural to an industrial economy, marked by the rapid spread of home-based manufacturing

protolanguage /prṓtō lang gwij/ *n.* a recorded or reconstructed language that is the ancestor of another language or family of languages

protolithic /prṓtō líthik/ *adj.* relating to the earliest part of the Stone Age [Late 19thC. Coined from PROTO- + -LITHIC on the model of NEOLITHIC.]

protomartyr /prṓtō maártər/ *n.* **1.** FIRST CHRISTIAN MARTYR St Stephen, the first Christian martyr **2.** FIRST MARTYR FOR CAUSE the first person to die for a particular cause

protomorphic /prṓtō máwrfik/ *adj.* having a primitive structure

proton /prṓ ton/ *n.* a stable elementary particle of the baryon family that is a component of all atomic nuclei and carries a positive charge equal to that of the electron's negative charge. Symbol **p** [Late 19thC. From Greek *prōton*, a form of *prōtos* 'first, elementary'.] —**protonic** /prṓ tónnik/ *adj.*

protonema /prṓtə neémə/ (*plural* **-mata** /-mətə/) *n.* the primary thread-shaped structure of mosses and certain liverworts that results from the germination of a spore and gives rise to a new plant [Mid-19thC. Coined from PROTO- + Greek *nēma* 'thread'.] —**protonemal** *adj.*

proton number *n.* PHYS = atomic number

Proto-Norse *n.* the form of the North Germanic language used in parts of Scandinavia, especially Norway and Iceland, until about the 8th century AD —**Proto-Norse** *adj.*

protonotary *n.* = prothonotary

proton synchrotron *n.* a circular very high-energy particle accelerator that accelerates protons through the action of magnetic fields and a high-frequency electric field

protoplasm /prṓtō plazzəm/ *n.* the colourless liquid or colloidal contents of a living cell, composed of proteins, fats, and other organic substances in water, and including the nucleus and cytoplasm [Mid-19thC. From German *Protoplasma*, literally 'first created thing', from Greek *plasma* (see PLASMA).] —**protoplasmic** /prṓtō plázmik/ *adj.*

protoplast /prṓtō plast/ *n.* the living substance of a plant or bacterial cell, excluding the cell wall [Mid-16thC. Directly or via French from late Latin *protoplastus* 'first created being', from Greek *prōtoplastos*, from *plastos* 'formed', from *plassein* 'to form'.] —**protoplastic** /prṓt ō plástik/ *adj.*

protoporphyrin /prṓtō páwrfirin/ *n.* a purple porphyrin acid that combines with iron to form the deep red of iron-containing proteins, e.g. haemoglobin and cytochrome. Formula: $C_{34}H_{34}N_4O_4$.

Protosemitic /prṓtō si míttik/ *n.* the hypothetical reconstructed language that is believed to be the ancestor of the Semitic branch of the Afro-Asiatic family of languages —**Protosemitic** *adj.*

protostar /prṓtō staar/ *n.* an interstellar cloud of gas and dust thought to develop into a star when it has collapsed sufficiently for nuclear reactions to begin

protostele /prṓtə steel, -steeli/ *n.* the conducting tissue (**stele**) of stems and roots, consisting of a core of xylem surrounded by phloem —**protostelic** /prṓtə steélik/ *adj.*

protostome /prṓtə stōm/ *n.* an invertebrate animal such as a mollusc or arthropod in which the mouth forms directly from the blastopore

protostherian /prṓtō theéri ən/ *n.* an echidna, platypus, or any of the many extinct related mammals. Subclass: Prototheria. [Late 19thC. Formed from PROTO- + Greek *therion* 'wild animal'.]

prototroph /prṓtə trōf/ *n.* an organism such as a bacterium or fungus that can grow without having to find nutrients in its surrounding environment. ◊ **auxotroph**

prototrophic /prṓtə trṓfik, -trṓffik/ *adj.* having the same nutritional needs and metabolic characteristics as the wild parent strain

prototype /prṓtə tīp/ *n.* **1.** ORIGINAL USED AS MODEL sth having the essential features of a subsequent type, and on which later forms are modelled **2.** STANDARD EXAMPLE a standard example of a particular kind, class, or group **3.** FULL-SIZE FUNCTIONAL MODEL a first full-size functional model to be manufactured, e.g. of a car or a machine ○ *A prototype of the new convertible will be on display at the Motor Show.* **4.** BIOL PRIMITIVE FORM a primitive form believed to be the original type of a species or group, exhibiting the essential features of the later type ■ *vti.* (-**types**, -**typing**, -**typed**) CREATE A PROTOTYPE to create a prototype of sth [Early 17thC. Via French from late Latin *prototypus* 'original, primitive' and Greek *prototypon* 'primitive form', from *proto* 'first' + *typos* 'impression'.] —**prototypal** /prṓtə típ'l/ *adj.* —**prototypic** /-típpik/ *adj.* —**prototypical** /-típpik'l/ *adj.*

protoxide /prō tók sīd/ *n.* an oxide of an element that has the lowest proportion of oxygen of all the oxides of that element

protoxylem /prṓtə zílləm/ *n.* the part of the water-carrying tissue (**xylem**) of a plant that develops first and has narrow thin-walled cells

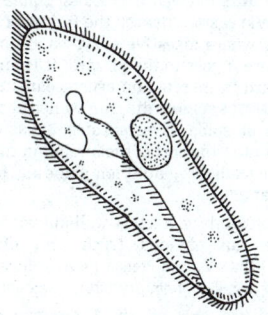

Protozoan

protozoan /prṓtə zṓ ən/ (*plural* **-ans** *or* **-a** /-ə/), **protozoon** /-on/ (*plural* **-ons** *or* **-a** /-ə/) *n.* a single-celled organism such as an amoeba that can move and feeds on organic compounds of nitrogen and carbon. Kingdom: *Protoctista*. [Mid-19thC. Formed from modern Latin *Protozoa*, literally 'first animals', from Greek *zōia*, plural of *zōion* 'animal'.] —**protozoan** *adj.* —**protozoic** *adj.*

protozoology /prṓtō zō ólləji, -zoo-/ *n.* the branch of zoology that studies protozoans [Early 20thC. Formed from modern Latin *Protozoa* (see PROTOZOAN).] —**protozoological** /prṓtō zō ə lójjik'l, -zoo-/ *adj.* —**protozoologist** /prṓtō zō ólləjist, -zoo-/ *n.*

protract /prə trákt/ (-**tracts**, -**tracting**, -**tracted**) *vt.* **1.** MAKE STH LAST to make sth last longer **2.** ANAT EXTEND A BODY PART to extend or lengthen a body part **3.** MATH PLOT AND DRAW LINES to plot lines and draw them using a scale and protractor [Mid-16thC. Back-formation from PROTRACTION.] —**protractive** *adj.*

protracted /prə tráktid/ *adj.* lasting or drawn out for a long time —**protractedly** *adv.* —**protractedness** *n.*

protractile /prə trák tīl/ *adj.* **1.** THAT CAN BE PROTRUDED capable of being thrust out **2.** ZOOL = protrusile

protraction /prə tráksh'n/ *n.* **1.** PROTRACTING OF STH the act of protracting sth **2.** SCALE DRAWING OF BUILDING OR LAND the act of drawing sth such as a building or an area of land to scale, or a drawing of this kind

protractor /prə tráktər/ *n.* **1.** GEOM INSTRUMENT FOR MEASURING ANGLES an instrument shaped like a semicircle marked with the degrees of a circle, used to measure or mark out angles **2.** LENGTHENER sb or sth that extends or lengthens sth else **3.** ANAT MUSCLE THAT EXTENDS BODY PART a muscle with the function of extending a body part

protrude /prə trōod/ (-**trudes**, -**truding**, -**truded**) *vti.* to stick out from the surroundings, or make sth stick out [Early 17thC. From Latin *protrudere* 'to thrust forward', from *trudere* 'to thrust'. Ultimately from an Indo-European

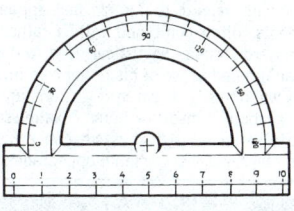

Protractor

word that is also the ancestor of English *thrust*.] —**protrudable** *adj.* —**protrudent** *adj.*

protrusile /prə trōo sīl/, **protrusible** /prə trōozəb'l/ *adj.* used to describe an organ or appendage that can be quickly extended, as can the mouth of many fishes or the proboscis of nemertine worms [Mid-19thC. Formed from the Latin stem *protrus-* (see PROTRUSION).]

protrusion /prə trōozh'n/ *n.* **1.** ACT OF PROTRUDING the act of protruding, or the state of being protruded **2.** STH THAT PROTRUDES sth that sticks out from its surroundings [Mid-17thC. From the medieval Latin stem *protrusion-*, from Latin *protrus-*, past participle stem of *protrudere* (see PROTRUDE).]

protrusive /prə trōossiv/ *adj.* **1.** JUTTING OUT jutting or sticking out **2.** FORWARD IN MANNER having a brash forward manner [Late 17thC. Formed from the Latin stem *protrus-* (see PROTRUSION).] —**protrusively** *adv.* —**protrusiveness** *n.*

protuberance /prə tyōobərənss/, **protuberancy** /-ssi/ (*plural* -**cies**) *n.* **1.** STH THAT STICKS OUT sth, or a part of sth, that sticks out from its surroundings ○ *the small fleshy protuberance that dangles down from the soft palate* **2.** FACT OF STICKING OUT the fact or condition of sticking out or being swollen or bulging [Mid-17thC. Formed from *protuberant* 'bulging out', from, ultimately, late Latin *protuberare*, literally 'to swell in front', from *tuber* 'lump'.]

protuberant /prə tyōobərənt/ *adj.* projecting out from the surroundings in a bulging, rounded manner [Mid-17thC. Formed from late Latin *protuberant-*, present participle stem of *protuberare*, literally 'to swell forward', from *tuber* 'lump'.] —**protuberantly** *adv.*

protuberate /prə tyōobə rayt/ (-**ates**, -**ating**, -**ated**) *vi.* to swell out from surroundings [Late 16thC. From Latin *protuberat-*, past participle stem of *protuberare* (see PROTUBERANT).]

protyle /prṓ tīl/ *n.* an imaginary substance from which the chemical elements were supposed to have been formed [Late 19thC. Formed from PROTO- + Greek *hulē* 'matter, hyle'.]

proud /prowd/ *adj.* **1.** PLEASED AND SATISFIED feeling pleased and satisfied, e.g. about having done sth or about owning sth ○ *I am very proud to be here today to give you this award.* **2.** HAVING SELF-RESPECT having a proper amount of self-respect **3.** FOSTERING FEELINGS OF PRIDE characterized by feelings of pride ○ *the proudest moment in your life* **4.** ARROGANT having an exaggerated opinion of personal worth or abilities **5.** IMPRESSIVE looking magnificent and impressive, or behaving in an impressive way ○ *the proud spires of Oxford* **6.** HIGH-SPIRITED high-spirited and strong ○ *a proud horse* **7.** PROJECTING projecting slightly from a surrounding surface [12thC. Via Old French *prud*, from Latin *prodesse* 'to be beneficial', literally 'to be for', from *esse* 'to be' (source of English *essence*).] —**proudly** *adv.* —**proudness** *n.* ◊ **do sb proud 1.** to treat sb well and generously **2.** to bring honour or distinction to sb

— **WORD KEY: SYNONYMS** —
proud, arrogant, conceited, egotistical, vain
CORE MEANING: describing sb who is pleased with himself or herself

proud can be used to describe sb who is rightly self-satisfied. It can also be used disapprovingly to describe sb who shows a lack of humility or who has an inordinately high opinion of himself or herself; **arrogant** used disapprovingly to describe sb who seems inordinately self-confident or pleased with his or her achievements and who lacks humility; **conceited** used to describe sb who displays excessive satisfaction and smugness with regard to his or her appearance or achievements, often combined with a rather superior attitude towards others; **egotistical** used to describe sb who has an inflated sense of his or her own importance, especially when this is shown through constantly talking or thinking about himself or herself; **vain** used to describe sb who shows an excessive concern with and admiration for his or her personal appearance.

Marcel Proust

Proust /proost/, **Marcel** (1871–1922) French novelist. He is author of a 13-volume series of partly autobiographical novels, *À la recherche du temps perdu* (1913–27). —**Proustian** /próosti ən/ *adj.*

proustite /próost īt/ *n.* a deep red mineral consisting of silver arsenic sulphide. It occurs in crystals or masses and is an ore of silver. Formula: Ag_3AsS_3. [Mid-19thC. Named after the French chemist Joseph L. *Proust* (1754–1826).]

prov. *abbr.* **1.** province **2.** provincial **3.** provisional

Prov. *abbr.* **1.** Provost **2.** BIBLE Proverbs **3.** Provençal

prove /proov/ (**proves, proving, proved, proved** *or* **proven** /prṓv'n, próov'n/) *v.* **1.** *vt.* ESTABLISH TRUTH OF STH to establish the truth or existence of sth by providing evidence or argument **2.** *vt.* CHEM, MINERALS TEST STH TO DETERMINE CHARACTERISTICS to subject sth to scientific analysis to determine its worth or characteristics **3.** *vr.* DEMONSTRATE COMPETENCE to show yourself to be competent and worthy **4.** *vt.* MATH CHECK A MATHEMATICAL RESULT to verify that a mathematical result is correct **5.** *vt.* MATH DEMONSTRATE THE TRUTH OF A HYPOTHESIS to demonstrate that a hypothesis or proposition is true **6.** *vt.* LAW DEMONSTRATE THAT A WILL IS GENUINE to establish that a will is genuine or valid **7.** *vt.* PRINTING, ARTS MAKE AN IMPRESSION OF STH to make a test impression of a negative, etching, or type **8.** *vi.* FOOD RISE IN WARM PLACE to rise in a warm place before being baked (*refers to dough*) **9.** *vti.* TURN OUT TO BE to turn out to be a particular thing or a thing of a particular character after time or testing [12thC. Via Old French *prover* from Latin *probare*, literally 'to prove to be good', from *probus* 'good'.] —**provability** /próovə bílləti/ *n.* —**provable** /próovəb'l/ *adj.* —**provably** /próovəbli/ *adv.*

WORD KEY: USAGE

Form of the past participle: The past participles ***proved*** and ***proven*** are both often used as verbs, with auxiliaries, and also as predicate adjectives: whether to say, for example, *We have proved our case* or *We have proven our case*, and *The case is proved* or *The case is proven* is a matter of choice. ***Proved*** is not, however, ordinarily employed as an adjective preceding a noun: *proven case* is the standard form.

WORD KEY: ORIGIN

The Latin word *probus*, from which ***prove*** is derived, is also the source of English *approve, probable, probe, probity, proof, reprobate,* and *reprove.*

proven /prṓv'n, próov'n/ *adj.* **1.** TRIED AND TESTED done or used before and known to work or be satisfactory **2.** LAW PROVED TRUE having been demonstrated beyond a doubt to be true —**provenly** *adv.*

provenance /próvvənəss/ *n.* **1.** ORIGIN the place of origin of sth **2.** SOURCE AND OWNERSHIP HISTORY the source and ownership history of a work of art or literature, or of an archaeological find [Late 18thC. Via French from Latin *provenire* 'to arise', literally 'to come forth', from *venire* 'to come'.]

WORD KEY: SYNONYMS

See Synonyms at ***origin.***

Provençal /próvvon saál/ *adj.* OF PROVENCE relating to Provence, or its people or culture ■ *n.* **1.** LANGUAGE OF SE FRANCE a Romance language spoken in southeastern parts of France. It is closely related to French, Italian, and Catalan. Provençal is spoken by about four million people. **2.** SB FROM PROVENCE sb who was born, brought up or who lives in, Provence [Late 16thC. Via French from Latin *provincialis* 'provincial', from *provincia* 'province', a colloquial name for southern Gaul during Roman rule.]

Provençale /próvvon saál/ *adj.* prepared with olive oil, garlic, herbs, and tomatoes [Mid-19thC. From French *à la provençale* 'in the Provençal manner'.]

Provence /pro vóNss/ region in southeastern France, bordering the Mediterranean Sea. It was an ancient Roman province.

provender /próvvindər/ *n.* **1.** FOOD FOR LIVESTOCK food for livestock, especially hay or other dry fodder (*archaic*) **2.** FOOD food (*literary or humorous*) [14thC. From Old French *provendre*, variant of *provende*, alteration (influenced by Latin *providere* 'to supply') of *praebenda* 'things to be given'.]

provenience /prō véeni ənss/ *n.* *US* = **provenance** [Late 19thC. Formed from Latin *provenient-*, present participle stem of *provenire* (see PROVENANCE).]

proventriculus /prṓ ven tríkyŏŏləss/ (*plural* **-li** /-lī/) *n.* **1.** BIRDS PART OF BIRD'S STOMACH the first part of a bird's stomach, where digestive enzymes are mixed with food before it goes to the gizzard. It is analogous to the gizzard in insects and crustaceans. **2.** ZOOL PART OF INVERTEBRATE'S STOMACH the thin-walled section of the stomach of some invertebrates **3.** INSECTS PART OF INSECT'S STOMACH the part of the foregut in some insects that has teeth or plates for grinding food —**proventricular** *adj.*

proverb /próvvurb/ *n.* a short well-known saying that expresses an obvious truth and often offers advice [14thC. Via Old French *proverbe* from Latin *proverbium* 'saying, saw', from *pro* 'forth' + *verbum* 'word'.]

proverbial /prə vúrbi əl/ *adj.* **1.** EXPRESSED AS A PROVERB expressed as a proverb, or resembling a proverb either in form or because of being widely known or referred to **2.** USED IN A PROVERB often referred to metaphorically or as another descriptive device ○ *She was behaving like the proverbial cat on hot bricks.* —**proverbially** *adv.*

Proverbs /próvvurbz/ *n.* a book of the Bible made up of the proverbs of wise men, including Solomon

provide /prə víd/ (**-vides, -viding, -vided**) *v.* **1.** *vt.* SUPPLY SB WITH STH to supply sb with or be a source of sth needed or wanted **2.** *vt.* MAKE STH AVAILABLE to make sth available to sb **3.** *vt.* LAW REQUIRE STH AS A CONDITION to require sth in advance as a condition or as part of a contract **4.** *vi.* TAKE PRECAUTIONS to take precautions to prevent harm or bring about good **5.** *vi.* SUPPLY MEANS OF SUPPORT to supply the material means of support for sb ○ *provides for his children* **6.** *vt.* PREPARE STH IN ADVANCE to get sth ready in advance (*archaic*) [15thC. From Latin *providere* 'to prepare in advance, supply', literally 'to see ahead', from *videre* 'to see'.]

providence /próvvid'nss/ *n.* **1. providence, Providence** GOD'S GUIDANCE the wisdom, care, and guidance believed to be provided by God **2. providence, Providence** GOD God perceived as a caring force guiding humankind **3.** GOOD JUDGMENT AND MANAGEMENT good judgment and foresight in the management of affairs or resources [14thC. Directly and via Old French from Latin *providentia* 'foresight', from *provident-*, the present participle stem of *providere* 'to provide'.]

Providence /próvvidənss/ capital of Rhode Island and its largest city, located in the northeastern part of the state. Population: 152,558 (1996).

provident /próvvid'nt/ *adj.* **1.** PREPARING FOR THE FUTURE carefully preparing for future needs **2.** FRUGAL economical in the use of resources [15thC. From Latin *provident-*, the present participle stem of *providere* 'to prepare in advance, supply'.]

providential /próvvi dénsh'l/ *adj.* **1.** OF PROVIDENCE relating to or believed to be determined by providence **2.** VERY LUCKY so lucky that it seems determined by providence

WORD KEY: SYNONYMS

See Synonyms at ***lucky.***

provident society *n.* = **friendly society**

provider /prə vídər/ *n.* **1.** SUPPLIER OF SUPPORT sb who provides the material means of support for sb, especially a family **2.** SUPPLIER OF SERVICE an organisation or company that provides access to a service or system, e.g. a cellular phone, cable, or computer network ○ *an Internet provider* ○ *a health care provider*

province /próvvinss/ *n.* **1.** POL ADMINISTRATIVE DIVISION OF NATION an administrative region or division of a country **2.** AREA OF KNOWLEDGE a sphere of knowledge or activity **3.** CHR ECCLESIASTICAL TERRITORY an ecclesiastical territory of more than two dioceses, under the jurisdiction of an archbishop or metropolitan **4.** HIST REGION OF ROMAN EMPIRE a country or region controlled by the ancient Roman Empire through an appointed governor **5.** ECOL CATEGORY FOR RANKING VEGETATION a category superior to a subregion and subordinate to a subkingdom, used in certain biogeographical systems for ranking global vegetation types ■ **provinces** *npl.* NONMETROPOLITAN PARTS OF NATION the parts of a country exclusive of the capital and larger cities [14thC. Directly and via Old French from Latin *provincia* 'Roman territory', from *pro* 'before' + *vincere* 'to conquer'.]

Provincetown /próvvins town/ town in eastern Massachusetts, at the tip of Cape Cod, north of Dennis. It is an artists' colony, and the site of the Pilgrims' first landing in 1620. Population: 3,681 (1996).

provincial /prə vínsh'l/ *adj.* **1.** OF A PROVINCE belonging to or coming from a province **2.** UNSOPHISTICATED AND NARROW-MINDED unsophisticated and unwilling to accept new ideas or ways of thinking (*disapproving*) **3.** ARCHIT, FURNITURE SIMPLE AND PLAIN in a simple and plain decorative style ■ *n.* **1.** SB FROM PROVINCES sb from the provinces, as opposed to sb from a city or the capital **2.** UNSOPHISTICATED PERSON an unsophisticated or narrow-minded person (*disapproving*) **3.** CHR HEAD OF A PROVINCE the head of an ecclesiastical province or of a religious order in a province [14thC. Directly and via Old French from Latin *provincialis*, from *provincia* (see PROVINCE).] —**provinciality** /prə vínshi állәti/ *n.* —**provincially** /prə vínsh'li/ *adv.*

Provincial Council *n.* a council that formerly administered a New Zealand province

provincial court *n.* a Canadian court that deals with less serious offences and whose judges are appointed and paid by the province

provincialism /prə vínshəlizəm/ *n.* **1.** NARROW-MINDED AND UNSOPHISTICATED ATTITUDE narrowness in outlook and lack of sophistication (*disapproving*) **2.** STH FROM A PROVINCE sth such as a word, phrase, trait, or custom that originates in a province

provincial police *n.* a Canadian police force that has jurisdiction within a province but not in urban areas that have their own municipal police

proving ground *n.* a place or situation in which sb or sth new is tried out or tested

provirus /prṓ vīrəss/ *n.* a form of a virus that is integrated into the genetic material of the host and passed on from one cell generation to the next

provision /prə vízh'n/ *n.* **1.** SUPPLYING OF STH the act of providing or supplying sth ○ *the provision of after-school clubs* **2.** ACTION TAKEN TO PREPARE a preparatory step taken to meet a possible or expected need ○ *No provision has been made for people with disabilities.* **3.** LAW LEGAL CLAUSE STATING CONDITION a clause in a law or contract stating that a particular condition must be met **4.** STH PROVIDED sth provided or supplied **5.** ACCT ESTIMATE OF LIABILITY an estimate of a known liability, e.g. depreciation, the value of which cannot be explicitly determined ■ **provisions** *npl.* FOOD AND OTHER SUPPLIES supplies of food and other things required, especially for a journey ■ *vt.* (**-sions, -sioning, -sioned**) PROVIDE SB WITH SUPPLIES to provide sb with supplies, especially for a journey [14thC. Via French from the Latin stem *provision-* 'foresight, preparation', from *provis-*, past participle stem of *providere* (see PROVIDE).] —**provisioner** *n.*

provisional /prə vízh'nəl/ *adj.* **TEMPORARY OR CONDITIONAL** temporary or conditional, pending confirmation or validation ○ *a provisional government* ■ *n.* **1.** *US* HR **SB HIRED TEMPORARILY** sb hired temporarily for a job, especially before being qualified to do it permanently **2.** STAMPS **TEMPORARY POSTAGE STAMP** a postage stamp used temporarily until an official permanent stamp is issued —**provisionally** *adv.*

Provisional *n.* **MEMBER OF IRA FACTION** a member of the faction of the Irish Republican Army that strives to achieve its goals through using force ■ *adj.* **RELATING TO IRA FACTION** relating to the faction of the Irish Republican Army that strives to achieve its goals through using force

provisional licence *n.* a driving licence for people who have not yet passed a driving test and are subject to various restrictions. US term **learner's permit**

provisional tax *n.* in Australia, tax that is paid in advance on sb's estimated earnings in the next financial year

proviso /prə vízō/ (*plural* **-sos** *or* **-soes**) *n.* **1. CONDITION WITHIN AGREEMENT** a condition asked as part of an agreement **2.** LAW **CLAUSE ADDED TO CONTRACT** a clause introducing a condition in a contract [15thC. From medieval Latin *proviso quod* 'provided that', from Latin *proviso*, a form of *provisus*, past participle of *providere* 'to prepare in advance, supply'.]

provisory /prə vízəri/ *adj.* **1. LAW CONDITIONAL** stating a condition **2.** = **provisional** *adj.* [Early 17thC. From medieval Latin *provisorius* 'of papal provision', from *provisus* (see PROVISO).] —**provisorily** *adv.*

provitamin /prō víttəmin/ *n.* a substance that is converted into an active vitamin as a result of the body's normal biochemical processes

Provo /prṓvō/ (*plural* **-vos**) *n.* a provisional member of the faction of the Irish Republican Army that advocates the use of force (*informal*) [Late 20thC. Shortening.]

provocation /próvvə káysh'n/ *n.* **1. ACT OF PROVOKING** the act of provoking sb or sth **2. CAUSE OF ANGER** sth that makes sb angry or indignant **3.** LAW **REASON FOR ATTACKING SB** sth that incites sb to attack sb else [14thC. Directly or via French from the Latin stem *provocation-*, ultimately from *provocare* (see PROVOKE).]

provocative /prə vókətiv/ *adj.* **1. MAKING PEOPLE ANGRY OR EXCITED** deliberately aimed at exciting or annoying people ○ *a provocative remark* **2. SEXUALLY AROUSING** intended to arouse other people sexually [15thC. Directly and via Old French *provocatif* from late Latin *provocativus*, from *provocare* (see PROVOKE).] —**provocatively** *adv.* —**provocativeness** *n.*

provoke /prə vṓk/ (**-vokes, -voking, -voked**) *vt.* **1. MAKE SB FEEL ANGRY** to make sb feel angry or exasperated **2. ELICIT A RESPONSE** to be the cause or occasion of an emotion or response ○ *Her bravery provoked a lot of sympathy.* **3. STIR SB TO EMOTION** to stir sb to an emotion or response **4. INCITE STH** to act in a way intended to bring sth about **5. BE THE CAUSE OF AN ACTIVITY** to serve as the stimulating factor for an activity [14thC. Directly or via Old French *provoker* from Latin *provocare* 'to summon', from *vocare* 'to call', from *vox* 'voice'.]

provost /próvvəst/ *n.* **1. HEAD OF EDUCATIONAL ESTABLISHMENT** the head of some educational establishments, especially Oxford or Cambridge colleges **2.** CHR **SENIOR DIGNITARY OF CATHEDRAL** the senior dignitary of a cathedral or collegiate church **3. HEAD OF SCOTTISH CITY GOVERNMENT** until 1975, the person elected to be head of government in a city, town, or borough in Scotland. Provost is still used as a courtesy title by some Scottish local authorities. ◊ **Lord Provost 4. PRISON WARDEN** the keeper of a prison (*archaic*) [Pre-12thC. From medieval Latin *propositus*, alteration of Latin *praepositus*, literally 'sb placed in front', ultimately from *ponere* 'to place' (source of English *preposition*).]

provost court /prə vṓ-/ *n.* a military court set up in an occupied hostile territory for the trial of minor offences

provost guard /prə vṓ-/ *n. US* a detail of soldiers having police duties under the authority of the provost marshal

provost marshal /prə vṓ-/ *n.* the army officer in charge of a unit of military police

prow /prow/ *n.* **1. FRONT OF SHIP** the forward part of a ship **2. PROJECTING FRONT PART** the projecting front part of sth other than a ship [Mid-16thC. Via French *proue* from Latin *prora*, from Greek *prōra* 'front of a ship', from *pro* 'forward'.]

prowess /prów ess/ *n.* **1. SUPERIOR SKILL** exceptional ability or skill **2. VALOUR IN COMBAT** extraordinary valour and ability in combat [13thC. From Old French *proesce* 'bravery', from *prou* 'brave', variant of *prud* (see PROUD).]

prowl /prowl/ *vti.* (**prowls, prowling, prowled**) **ROAM AN AREA STEALTHILY FOR PREY** to roam around an area stealthily in search of prey, food, or opportunity ■ *n.* **ACT OF ROAMING** the act of roaming stealthily for prey [14thC. Origin unknown.] ◇ **on the prowl** moving around stealthily looking for sth or sb

prowl car *n. US* a police patrol car (*dated*)

prowler /prówlər/ *n.* **1. SB PROWLING WITH UNLAWFUL INTENT** sb who roams or looks around somewhere stealthily waiting for the opportunity to commit criminal acts **2. SB OR STH THAT PROWLS** an animal that or person who prowls

prox. *abbr.* proximo

proxemics /prok séemiks/ *n.* the study of the distance individuals maintain between each other in social interaction and how this separation is significant [Mid-20thC. Formed from PROXIMITY on the model of PHONEMICS.]

proximal /próksim'l/ *adj.* **1.** ANAT **NEARER CENTRE OF BODY** nearer to the point of reference or to the centre of the body. For example, the elbow is proximal to the hand. ◊ **distal 2.** DENT **NEAREST ANOTHER TOOTH** used to describe the surface of a tooth nearest to either the one behind it or the one in front of it **3.** = **proximate** [Early 18thC. Formed from Latin *proximus* (see PROXIMITY).] —**proximally** *adv.*

proximate /próksimət/ *adj.* **1. NEAREST** nearest in order, time, or place **2. VERY CLOSE** very close in space or time **3. ABOUT TO HAPPEN** soon to appear or take place **4. APPROXIMATE** almost accurate [Late 16thC. From Latin *proximat-*, past participle stem of *proximare* 'to come near', from *proximus* (see PROXIMITY).] —**proximately** *adv.* —**proximateness** *n.* —**proximation** /próksi máysh'n/ *n.*

proxime accessit /próksimi ak séssit, próksi may ək-/ *n.* the person who comes immediately after the winner in a competitive examination (*formal*) [From Latin, literally 'he or she came very close']

proximity /prok símməti/ *n.* closeness in space or time [15thC. From Latin *proximitas* 'nearness', from *proximus* 'nearest', the superlative form of *prope* 'near' (source of English *approach*).]

proximity card *n.* a plastic card carrying electronically coded information accessed by holding the card near a reading device. Proximity cards are often used to open doors as part of a security system.

proximity fuse *n.* a fuse, typically part of a warhead, that will activate and cause detonation when the warhead is at a specified distance from the target

proximo /próksimō/ *adv.* occurring during the next month (*formal*) ○ *propose a meeting for the fifth proximo* [Mid-19thC. From Latin *proximo (mense)* 'in the next (month)'.]

proxy /próksi/ (*plural* **-ies**) *n.* **1. FUNCTION OR POWER OF SUBSTITUTE** the function, power, or capacity to act of a deputy authorized to substitute for another **2. SB ACTING AS SUBSTITUTE** sb authorized to substitute for sb else **3. AUTHORIZATION DOCUMENT FOR STAND-IN** a document authorizing sb to act for another person **4.** LAW, STOCK EXCH **DOCUMENT AUTHORIZING VOTE ON ANOTHER'S STOCK** a document authorizing sb to vote on matters of corporate stock on behalf of sb else [15thC. From medieval Latin *procuratia*, alteration of Latin *procuratio* 'care, management', from *procurare* 'to take care of'.]

Prozac /prṓ zak/ *tdmk.* a trademark for an antidepressant drug that slows down the uptake of serotonin by the central nervous system

PRP *abbr.* **1.** profit-related pay **2.** performance-related pay

prs *abbr.* pairs

prude /prood/ *n.* sb who is easily shocked by sex or nudity and who pays a great deal of attention to proper social behaviour (*disapproving*) [Early 18thC. From French, back-formation from Old French *prudefemme* (misunderstood as 'virtuous woman'), feminine of *prud'homme*, from assumed *pro de ome*, literally 'fine (thing) of a man'.] —**prudery** *n.* —**prudish** *adj.* —**prudishly** *adv.* —**prudishness** *n.*

prudence /pro͞od'nss/ *n.* **1. PRACTICALITY** good sense in managing practical matters **2. TENDENCY TO AVOID RISK** a tendency to evaluate situations carefully so as to avoid risk **3. FRUGALITY** careful management of resources [14thC. Directly or via French from Latin *prudentia*, contraction of *providentia* (see PROVIDENCE).]

prudent /pro͞od'nt/ *adj.* **1. HAVING GOOD SENSE** having good sense in dealing with practical matters **2. CAREFULLY CONSIDERING CONSEQUENCES** using good judgment to consider consequences and to act accordingly **3. CAREFUL IN MANAGING RESOURCES** careful in managing resources so as to provide for the future [14thC. Directly or via French from Latin *prudent-*, contraction of the stem *provident-* (see PROVIDENT).] —**prudently** *adv.*

WORD KEY: SYNONYMS

See Synonyms at ***cautious***.

prudential /proo dénsh'l/ *adj.* **1. RESULTING FROM PRUDENCE** resulting from, depending on, or marked by prudence **2. USING PRUDENCE** using prudence, especially in business matters —**prudentially** *adv.*

pruinose /pro͞o i nōss, -nōz/ *adj.* having a white powdery coating, e.g. on a fruit or leaf [Early 19thC. From Latin *pruinosus*, from *pruina* 'hoarfrost'.]

prune[1] /proon/ (**prunes, pruning, pruned**) *v.* **1.** *vti.* **CUT BRANCHES** to cut branches away from a plant to encourage fuller growth **2.** *vt.* **REDUCE STH BY REMOVING UNWANTED MATERIAL** to reduce sth by removing whatever is unnecessary or unwanted **3.** *vt.* **REMOVE STH UNNECESSARY** to remove sth considered unnecessary or unwanted [14thC. From Old French *proignier* 'to cut in a rounded shape in front', from Latin *rotundus* 'round' (source of English *rotund*).] —**prunable** *adj.* —**pruner** *n.*

prune[2] /proon/ *n.* **1. DRIED PLUM** a plum that has been preserved by drying **2.** *US* **PLUM TO BE DRIED** a plum suitable for drying (*informal*) **3. OFFENSIVE TERM** an offensive term that deliberately insults sb's intelligence, competence or ability to interest others (*informal insult*) [14thC. From French, ultimately from Latin *prunum*, from Greek *prounon*, variant of *proumnon* 'plum'.]

prunella[1] /proo néllə/ *n.* a wool fabric with a twill weave, used for academic gowns, clerical robes, and shoe uppers [Mid-17thC. From French *prunelle* 'sloe', a diminutive of *prune* 'plum'. Probably from its colour.]

prunella[2] /proo néllə/ (*plural* **-las** *or* **-la**) *n.* PLANTS = **selfheal** [Late 16thC. From modern Latin *Prunella*, genus name, from prunella, in medieval Latin *brunella*, a disease with a brown coating of the tongue, which selfheal was thought to cure.]

pruning hook *n.* a tool with a hooked blade and sometimes a long handle, used to prune trees and bushes

prurient /pro͝ori ənt/ *adj.* having or intended to arouse an unwholesome interest in sexual matters (*disapproving*) [Mid-17thC. From Latin *prurient-*, the present participle stem of *prurire* 'to itch, long for', of uncertain origin: perhaps formed from *pruna* 'burning coal'.] —**prurience** *n.* —**pruriently** *adv.*

prurigo /proor rígō/ *n.* a chronic inflammatory skin disease causing small itchy swellings [Mid-17thC. From Latin, 'itching', from *prurire* (see PRURIENT).] —**pruriginous** /proor ríjjinəss/ *adj.*

pruritus /proor rítəss/ *n.* an intense feeling of itchiness [Mid-17thC. From Latin, past participle of *prurire* (see PRURIENT).]

prusik /prússik/ *n.* **1. prusik, Prusik, prusik knot KNOT ATTACHING SLING TO ROPE** a knot used to tie a small sling to a climbing rope, forming a loop that holds fast when weighted but can be slid along the rope when unweighted **2. prusik, Prusik SLING ATTACHED TO ROPE** a small sling attached to a climbing rope using a prusik knot ■ *vi.* (**-siks, -siking, -siked**) **ASCEND OR DESCEND ROPE** to ascend or descend a climbing rope using a prusik sling [Mid-20thC. Named after the Austrian mountaineer, Karl *Prusik*.]

Prussia /prúsha/ former state and kingdom in Germany. Its capital was Berlin. —**Prussian** *adj.*, *n.*

Prussian blue *n.* **1.** Prussian blue, prussian blue BLUE IRON PIGMENT a water-insoluble blue iron pigment **2.** DARK GREENISH-BLUE a rich dark blue colour with a tinge of green ■ *adj.* OF DEEP GREENISH-BLUE of a rich dark blue colour with a tinge of green [*Prussian* because its discoverer, Diesbach, was Prussian]

prussiate /prúshi ət/ *n.* **1.** FERROCYANIDE OR FERRICYANIDE a chemical compound that is ferrocyanide or ferricyanide **2.** SALT OF HYDROCYANIC ACID a chemical compound that is a salt of hydrocyanic acid [Late 18thC. Formed from *prussic* (see PRUSSIC ACID).]

prussic acid /prússik-/ *n.* = **hydrocyanic acid** [*Prussic* formed from *Prussian*, because it was first obtained from Prussian blue]

pry[1] /prī/ *vi.* (**pries**, **prying**, **pried**) INQUIRE NOSILY to look inquisitively or inquire nosily about sb's private affairs ■ *n.* (*plural* **pries**) **1.** ACT OF PRYING the act of prying into sb's private affairs **2.** SB WHO PRIES sb who engages in prying into other people's private affairs [14thC. Origin unknown.]

pry[2] /prī/ (**pries**, **prying**, **pried**) *vt.* US to open or part sth by using leverage [Early 19thC. Back-formation from PRISE, misunderstood as 3rd person present singular.]

pryer *n.* = **prier**

prytaneum /prítta neé əm/ (*plural* **-a** /-ttə neé ə/) *n.* a public building in ancient Greece used as a meeting place [Early 17thC. Via Latin from Greek *prutaneion*, from *prutanis* 'prince, ruler'.]

Przewalski's horse /prézhi válskiz-, shi-/ *n.* a wild Asian horse with a stocky body, a chestnut coat, and an erect dark mane. It is the only surviving wild horse, with just a tiny population found in the Gobi Desert on the border of China and Mongolia. Latin name: *Equus caballus przewalskii*. [Late 19thC. Translation of Latin *equus przewalskii*, named after the Russian explorer N. M. Przhevalskiĭ (1839–88), who was the first European to report seeing it.]

PS *abbr.* **1.** GRAM phrase structure **2.** Police Sergeant **3.** PS, ps postscript **4.** Permanent Secretary **5.** private secretary **6.** THEATRE prompt side **7.** Passenger Steamer

Ps. *abbr.* (Book of) Psalms

PSA *abbr.* Public Service Association

Psa. *abbr.* (Book of) Psalms

psalm /saam/, **Psalm** *n.* a sacred song or poem of praise, especially one in the Book of Psalms in the Bible [12thC. Via late Latin *psalmus* from Greek *psalmos* 'harpsong', from *psallein* 'to pluck'.] —**psalmic** *adj.*

psalmist /saámist/ *n.* the author of a psalm

psalmody /saámədi, sálm-/ (*plural* **-dies**) *n.* **1.** RELIG PSALM SINGING the singing of psalms in divine worship **2.** MUSIC MUSICAL ARRANGEMENTS FOR PSALMS the prescribed arrangements for singing individual psalms from the Book of Psalms **3.** SET OF PSALMS a collection of psalms [14thC. Via late Latin *psalmodia* from Greek *psalmōidia*, ultimately from *psalmos* (see PSALM) + *ōidē* 'song'.] —**psalmodic** /saa móddik, sal-/ *adj.* —**psalmodist** /saámədist, sálm-/ *n.*

Psalms /saamz/ *n.* a book of the Bible made up of 150 poems and hymns to God, traditionally believed to have been written by King David

Psalter /sáwltər, sóltər/, **psalter** *n.* a book containing psalms, or the Book of Psalms, used in worship [Pre-12thC. From Latin *psalterium* 'book of psalms' in ecclesiastical Latin (see PSALTERY); reinforced by Old French *sautier*.]

psalterium /sawl teéri əm, sol-/ (*plural* **-a** /-ə/) *n.* ZOOL = **omasum** [Mid-19thC. Formed from Latin, 'stringed instrument' (see PSALTERY).]

psaltery /sáwltəri, sóltəri/ (*plural* **-ies**) *n.* an ancient musical instrument with numerous strings that can be plucked with the fingers or with a plectrum [13thC. Via Old French *sauterie*, from Latin *psalterium* 'stringed instrument', from Greek *psaltērion* 'stringed instrument played by plucking', from *psallein* 'to pluck'.]

psammite /sámmīt/ *n.* **1.** SANDSTONE rock formed principally of sand **2.** METAMORPHOSED SANDSTONE a metamorphosed sandstone containing large amounts of quartz [Mid-19thC. Formed from Greek *psammos* 'sand'.] —**psammitic** /sa míttik/ *adj.*

p's and q's /peéz ən kyooź/ *npl.* the polite manners and behaviour that sb adopts, e.g., when eager to make a good impression ○ *We'd better mind our p's and q's.* [From *mind one's p's and q's*, of uncertain origin: perhaps a warning to children to distinguish the two letters when learning to write, or to printers' apprentices in handling type]

PSBR *abbr.* public sector borrowing requirement

PSE *n.* the study of social, especially health-related, issues as a school subject. Full form **Personal and Social Education**

psephology /si fólləji/ *n.* the statistical study of elections [Mid-20thC. Formed from Greek *psephos* 'pebble, vote'; from the Greek practice of using pebbles to vote.] —**psephological** /séfə lójjik'l/ *adj.* —**psephologically** /-lójjikli/ *adv.* —**psephologist** /si fólləjist/ *n.*

pseud /syood/ *n.* sb who pretends to know a lot about art, literature, or music [Mid-20thC. Shortening of PSEUDO.]

pseud. *abbr.* pseudonym

pseud- *prefix.* = **pseudo-** (*sometimes used before vowels*)

pseudaxis /syoo dáksiss/ (*plural* **-es** /-seez/) *n.* BOT = **sympodium**

pseudepigrapha /syoódi piggrəfə/ *npl.* certain anonymous or pseudonymous writings professing to be biblical but not included in any biblical canon [Late 17thC. From Greek, a form of *pseudepigraphos* 'with false title', from PSEUDO- + *epigraphein* 'to write on' (see EPIGRAPH).] —**pseudepigraphic** /syoód eppi gráffik/ *adj.* —**pseudepigraphical** /-gráffik'l/ *adj.* —**pseudepigraphous** /syoódi piggrəfəss/ *adj.*

pseudo /syoódō/ *adj.* not authentic or sincere, in spite of appearances [14thC. From Greek *pseudo-*, from *pseudēs* (see PSEUDO-).]

pseudo- *prefix.* **1.** similar ○ *pseudobulb* **2.** false, spurious ○ *pseudoscience* [From Greek *pseudēs*, from *pseudein* 'to lie', of unknown origin]

pseudobulb /syoódō bulb/ *n.* a thickened part of a stem that lies above the ground, e.g. in many orchids

pseudocarp /syoódō kaarp/ *n.* a fruit formed by combining the ripened ovary with another structure, often the receptacle, e.g. in strawberries [Mid-19thC. Formed from PSEUDO- + Greek *karpos* 'fruit'.] —**pseudocarpous** /syoódō kaárpəss/ *adj.*

pseudoclassicism /syoódō klássissizəm/ *n.* the use in art and literature of ancient Greek and Roman styles —**pseudoclassical** *adj.*

pseudocoel /syoódō seel/, **pseudocoelom** /-seéləm/ *n.* a body cavity of some primitive invertebrates that has no mesodermal lining

pseudocyesis /syoódō sī eéssiss/ (*plural* **-ses** /-seez/) *n.* a phantom pregnancy (*technical*) [Mid-19thC. Formed from Greek *kuesis* 'conception'.]

pseudogene /syoódō jeen/ *n.* a nonfunctional DNA sequence that is very similar to the sequence of a functional gene

pseudohermaphroditism /syoódō hur máffrə dītizəm/ *n.* a condition in which sb has either ovaries (**female pseudohermaphroditism**) or testes (**male pseudohermaphroditism**) but has external genitalia of ambiguous appearance

pseudomonad /syoódō mố nad/ *n.* a rod-shaped bacterium that lives in soil or decomposing organic material, some of which are pathogenic to plants and animals. Genus: *Pseudomonas*. [Early 20thC. From modern Latin *Pseudomonad-*, stem of *Pseudomonas*, literally 'false monad', from the stem *monad-* 'monad'.]

pseudomorph /syoódō mawrf/ *n.* **1.** MINERAL WITH UNUSUAL CRYSTALLINE SHAPE a mineral that does not have its usual crystalline form as a result of having replaced another mineral in a rock and taken its shape **2.** IRREGULAR FORM an irregular or deceptive form —**pseudomorphic** /syoódō máwrfik/ *adj.* —**pseudomorphism** /-fizəm/ *n.* —**pseudomorphous** /-fəss/ *adj.*

pseudonym /syoódənim/ *n.* a name that is not sb's correct name, especially one used by an author in publications [Mid-19thC. Via French *pseudonyme* from Greek *pseudōnumon*, literally 'false name', ultimately from *onuma*, variant of *onoma* 'name' (source of English *anonymous*).] —**pseudonymity** /syoódə nímməti/ *n.*

pseudonymous /syoo dónniməss/ *adj.* bearing or written under a name that is not the correct name of the person concerned —**pseudonymously** *adv.* —**pseudonymousness** *n.*

pseudopodium /syoódō pốdi əm/ (*plural* **-a** /-ə/), **pseudopod** /syoódō pod/ *n.* a temporary cytoplasmic protrusion in amoeba and other protozoa used for locomotion and to take up food

pseudopregnancy /syoódō prégnənssi/ (*plural* **-cies**) *n.* = **phantom pregnancy**

pseudorandom /syoódō rándəm/ *adj.* relating to random numbers generated by a computational process

pseudoscience /syoódō sī ənss/ *n.* a theory or method doubtfully or mistakenly held to be scientific

pseudosophistication /syoódō sə físti káysh'n/ *n.* false or pretended sophistication

pseudotuberculosis /syoódō tyoō búrkyoō lốssiss/ *n.* a disease marked by the formation of nodules of inflamed tissue similar to those in tuberculosis but not caused by the tubercle bacillus

psf, p.s.f. *abbr.* pounds per square foot

pshaw /pshaw/ *interj.* used to express disbelief, impatience, or contempt [Late 17thC. An imitation of the sound made.]

PSHE *abbr.* Personal, Social, and Health Education

psi[1] /psī/ *n.* the 23rd letter of the Greek alphabet, represented in the English alphabet as 'ps'. See table at alphabet [15thC. From Greek *psei*.]

psi[2], **p.s.i.** *abbr.* pounds per square inch

psia, p.s.i.a. *abbr.* pounds per square inch, absolute

psid, p.s.i.d. *abbr.* pounds per square inch, differential

psig, p.s.i.g. *abbr.* pounds per square inch, gauge

psilocin /sílləssin, síll-/ *n.* a hallucinogenic compound produced in the body after eating a particular mushroom. Formula: $C_{12}H_{16}N_2O$. [Mid-20thC. Formed from Greek *psilos* 'smooth'.]

psilocybin /sílə síbin, síllə-/ *n.* a crystalline hallucinogen obtained from a particular mushroom. Formula: $C_{13}HN_2O_3P_2$. [Mid-20thC. Formed from Greek *psilos* 'smooth' + *kubē* 'head'.]

psilomelane /si lómmi layn/ *n.* a mixed hydrated manganese oxide ore, occurring in dark-coloured rounded masses [Mid-19thC. Formed from Greek *psilos* 'smooth' + *melas* 'black'.]

psi particle *n.* = **J/psi particle**

psittacine /sítta sīn, -ssin/ *adj.* OF PARROTS belonging to the parrot family, or affecting, resembling, or relating to parrots or related birds ■ *n.* MEMBER OF PARROT FAMILY a bird that belongs to the parrot family [Late 19thC. Via Latin *psittacinus* from *psittacus*, from Greek *psittakos* 'parrot'.]

psittacosis /sítta kốssiss/ *n.* a contagious disease of parrots and related birds that can be transmitted to humans, sometimes causing serious lung infection. It is caused by the bacterium *Chlamydia psittaci*. [Late 19thC. Via Latin *psittacus* from Greek *psittakos* 'parrot'.]

PSL *abbr.* private sector liquidity

psoas /só əss/ (*plural* **-ai** /-ī/ *or* **-ae** /-ee/) *n.* either of two pairs of muscles that are located in the groin and help to flex the hip joint. The psoas in oxen is the fillet muscle. [Late 17thC. From Greek, a plural form of *psoa* 'muscle of the loins'.]

psoralen /sáwrələn/ *n.* a toxic substance present in certain plants and used to treat severe acne and psoriasis [Mid-20thC. Via modern Latin *Psoralea*, genus name, from Greek *psoraleos* 'itchy', from *psora* 'itch, mange'.]

psoriasis /sə rí əssiss/ *n.* a skin disease marked by red scaly patches [Late 17thC. Via Latin, 'scurvy, mange', from Greek *psōriasis* 'being itchy', ultimately from *psōra* 'itch, mange'.] —**psoriatic** /sáwri áttik/ *adj.*

PSS, **pss** *abbr.* postscripts

psst /pst/ *interj.* used to get the attention of one person without alerting others [Early 20thC. An imitation of the sound.]

PST *abbr.* **1.** Pacific Standard Time **2.** *Can* provincial sales tax

PSTN *abbr.* Public Switched Telephone Network

PSU *abbr.* COMPUT power supply unit

PSV *n.* (*plural* **PSVs**), *abbr.* public service vehicle

psych /sīk/ (**psychs, psyching, psyched**) *v. US* **1.** *vt.* **MAKE UNEASY** to make sb fearful, uneasy, or intimidated **2.** *vr.* **PREPARE TO PERFORM WELL** to prepare sb psychologically to perform at peak levels [Early 20thC. Origin uncertain: perhaps partly a shortening of PSYCHOANALYSE and partly from PSYCH-.]

psych out *v.* (*informal*) **1.** *vt.* **INTIMIDATE SB** to intimidate or undermine the confidence of sb. US term **psych 2.** *vt.* **PUZZLE STH OUT** to analyse, solve, or understand sth such as a problem **3.** *vt.* **GUESS SB'S THOUGHT PROCESSES** to guess or anticipate correctly the intentions or thoughts of another person **4.** *vi.* **COLLAPSE EMOTIONALLY** to break down psychologically ○ *The prisoner psyched out completely.*

psych up *vr.* to prepare yourself mentally for a task or action (*informal*) ○ *She's been psyching herself up for this interview all week.* US term **psych** *v.* 2

psych. *abbr.* **1.** psychological **2.** psychology

psych- *prefix.* = **psycho-** (*used before vowels*)

psyche /sīki/ *n.* **1.** RELIG **HUMAN SPIRIT** the human spirit or soul **2.** PSYCHOL **HUMAN MIND** the human mind as the centre of thought and behaviour [Mid-17thC. Via Latin from Greek *psukhē* 'breath, soul, mind', from *psukhein* 'to breathe'.]

Psyche /sīki/ *n.* in Roman mythology, a beautiful young woman loved by Cupid. He visited her secretly at night, forbidding her ever to look at him. When she did, he abandoned her. They were eventually reunited and Jupiter made her immortal.

psychedelia /sīkə déeli ə/ *n.* the subculture of artefacts, phenomena, writings, or art associated with psychedelic drugs [Mid-20thC. Back-formation from PSYCHEDELIC.]

psychedelic /sīkə déllik/ *adj.* **1.** **RELATING TO HALLUCINOGENIC DRUGS** used to describe, or relating to or caused by, drugs that generate hallucinations, abnormal psychic states, or states that resemble psychiatric disorders **2.** **OVERLOADING THE SENSES** weird, distorted, wildly colourful, or otherwise resembling images or sounds experienced by sb under the influence of a psychedelic drug ■ *n.* **DRUG** a psychedelic drug [Mid-20thC. From Greek *psukhē* 'mind' + *dēloun* 'to reveal, make visible', from *dēlos* 'clear'.] —**psychedelically** *adv.*

psychiatric /sīki áttrik/ *adj.* relating to psychiatry or its patients

psychiatric hospital *n.* a hospital dedicated to the treatment, care, and protection of people with serious psychiatric disorders who are judged to be unfit or unsafe to be at large

psychiatric social worker *n.* a social worker specializing in psychiatric cases

psychiatrist /sī kī ətrist/ *n.* a doctor trained in the treatment of people with mental illnesses

psychiatry /sī kī ətri/ *n.* a medical specialization concerned with the diagnosis and treatment of disorders that have primarily mental or behavioural symptoms and with the care of people having such disorders [Mid-19thC. From French *psychiatrie*, from Greek *psukhē* (see PSYCHE) + *iatreia* 'cure'.]

psychic /sīkik/ *adj.* **1.** **OF THE MIND** relating to the human mind **2.** **OUTSIDE SCIENTIFIC KNOWLEDGE** outside the sphere of scientific knowledge **3.** **SUPPOSEDLY SENSITIVE TO SUPERNATURAL FORCES** claiming or believed to have extraordinary perception and sensitivity to nonphysical or supernatural forces ■ *n.* **SB SUPPOSEDLY SENSITIVE TO SUPERNATURAL** sb who claims or is believed to be sensitive to nonphysical or supernatural forces [Late 18thC. From Greek *psukhikos* 'pertaining to the soul or spirit', from *psukhē* (see PSYCHE).] —**psychical** *adj.* —**psychically** *adv.*

psycho /sīkō/ *n.* (*plural* **-chos**) **OFFENSIVE TERM** a highly offensive term for sb who has a psychiatric or personality disorder (*slang*) ■ *adj.* **OFFENSIVE TERM** an offensive term used for sb who behaves in an uncontrolled and unpredictable way (*slang offensive*) [Mid-20thC. Shortening of PSYCHOPATHIC.]

WORD KEY: CULTURAL NOTE

Psycho, a film by English director Alfred Hitchcock (1960). A disturbing horror film with a rich vein of black comedy, it tells the story of a woman who flees her home after stealing money from her boss. Stopping at a motel run by the sinister Norman Bates and his apparently domineering mother, she is brutally murdered while taking a shower. Members of her family subsequently investigate the death. As a result of the impact of the film, the term *Bates Motel* came to mean any rundown rooming house, motel, or structure redolent of oppressive fear and underlying horror.

psycho- *prefix.* **1.** mind, mental ○ *psychoactive* **2.** psychology, psychological ○ *psychobabble* [From Greek *psukhē* (see PSYCHE)]

psychoacoustics /sīkō ə kóostiks/ *n.* the scientific study of the psychological and physiological principles of sound perception (*takes a singular verb*)

psychoactive /sīkō áktiv/ *adj.* used to describe drugs or medication having a significant effect on mood or behaviour

psychoanal. *abbr.* psychoanalysis

psychoanalyse /sīkō ánnə līz/ (**-lyses, -lysing, -lysed**) *vt.* to apply the methods of psychoanalysis in a psychotherapeutic setting —**psychoanalyser** *n.*

psychoanalysis /sīkō ə nálləssiss/ *n.* **1.** **METHOD OF UNDERSTANDING MENTAL LIFE** a psychological theory and therapeutic method developed by Sigmund Freud, based on the ideas that mental life functions on both conscious and unconscious levels and that childhood events have a powerful psychological influence throughout life **2.** **TREATMENT BY PSYCHOANALYSIS** treatment by psychoanalysis, interpreting material presented by a patient in order to bring the processes of the unconscious into conscious awareness —**psychoanalyst** /sīkō ánnəlist/ *n.* —**psychoanalytic** /sīkō ánnə líttik/ *adj.* —**psychoanalytical** /-ánnə líttik'l/ *adj.* —**psychoanalytically** /-ánnə líttikli/ *adv.*

psychoanalyze *vt.* US = **psychoanalyse**

psychobabble /sīkō babb'l/ *n.* psychological jargon used inaccurately to talk about personal problems

psychobiography /sīkō bī óggrəfi/ (*plural* **-phies**) *n.* a biography that focuses on the psychological profile of the subject

psychobiology /sīkō bī ólləji/ *n.* the study of the biological bases of behaviour. ◊ **sociobiology** —**psychobiological** /sīkō bī ə lójjik'l/ *adj.* —**psychobiologically** /-lójjikli/ *adv.* —**psychobiologist** /sīkō bī ólləjist/ *n.*

psychochemical /sīkō kémmik'l/ *n.* **PSYCHOACTIVE DRUG** a drug that affects mood or behaviour ■ *adj.* **OF PSYCHOACTIVE DRUGS** relating to or acting like a psychoactive drug

psychodrama /sīkō draamə/ *n.* a form of psychotherapy pioneered by Jacob Moreno in which patients are required to perform roles in dramas illustrating their own particular problems before an audience of other patients —**psychodramatic** /sīkō drə máttik/ *adj.*

psychodynamics /sīkō dī námmiks/ *n.* **1.** **INTERACTION OF EMOTIONAL FORCES** the interaction of the emotional and motivational forces that affect behaviour and mental states, especially on a subconscious level (*takes a singular or plural verb*) **2.** **INNER FORCES AFFECTING BEHAVIOUR** the study of the emotional and motivational forces that affect behaviour and mental states (*takes a singular verb*) —**psychodynamic** *adj.* —**psychodynamically** *adv.*

psychogenesis /sīkō jénnəssiss/ *n.* the psychological rather than physical cause of a psychological disorder —**psychogenetic** /-jə néttik/ *adj.* —**psychogenetically** *adv.*

psychogenic /sīkō jénnik/ *adj.* originating in mental or emotional rather than in physiological processes —**psychogenically** *adv.*

psychogeriatric /sīkō jérri áttrik/ *adj.* MED relating or referring to mental disorders in senior citizens, or to senior citizens with such disorders

psychogeriatrics /sīkō jérri áttriks/ *n.* psychology and psychiatric disorders of senior citizens (*takes a singular verb*)

psychohistory /sīkō hístəri/ (*plural* **-ries**) *n.* psychological analysis of sb's life or of historical events —**psychohistorian** /-hi stáwri ən/ *n.* —**psychohistorical** /-stórrik'l/ *adj.*

psychokinesis /sīkō ki néessiss, -kī néessiss/ *n.* the supposed ability to use mental powers to make objects move or to otherwise affect them —**psychokinetic** /-ki néttik/ *adj.*

psychol. *abbr.* **1.** psychological **2.** psychologist **3.** psychology

psycholinguistics /sīkō ling gwístiks/ *n.* the study of language acquisition and use in relation to the psychological factors controlling its use and recognition (*takes a singular verb*) —**psycholinguist** /sīkō líng gwist/ *n.* —**psycholinguistic** /-gwístik/ *adj.*

psychological /sīkə lójjik'l/ *adj.* **1.** **OF PSYCHOLOGY** relating to psychology **2.** **OF THE MIND** relating to the mind or mental processes **3.** **AFFECTING THE MIND** affecting or intended to affect the mind or mental processes **4.** **EXISTING ONLY IN THE MIND** existing only in the mind, without having a physical basis ○ *His health problem is psychological.* —**psychologically** *adv.*

psychological dependence *n.* strong desire for sth without being physically addicted to it

psychological moment *n.* the time at which the mental state of a person or group of people is most receptive or appropriate

psychological warfare *n.* **1.** MIL **WARFARE BY PROPAGANDA** tactics that use propaganda to try to demoralize an enemy in war, usually including the civilian population **2.** **NONMILITARY PSYCHOLOGICAL UNDERMINING** the use of psychological tactics to disconcert and disadvantage an opponent in an everyday or a business context, e.g. causing fear or anxiety

psychologise *vti.* = **psychologize**

psychologism /sī kólləjizəm/ *n.* a belief in or emphasis on the importance of psychology in other fields, e.g. history or philosophy —**psychologistic** /sī kóllə jístik/ *adj.*

psychologist /sī kólləjist/ *n.* **1.** **PROFESSIONAL IN PSYCHOLOGY** a professional who studies behaviour and experience, usually either licensed to provide therapeutic services to the public or working in an academic setting **2.** **STUDENT OF PSYCHOLOGY** sb who is studying or has studied psychology, especially as a main subject at university or college

psychologize /sī kóllə jīz/ (**-gizes, -gizing, -gized**), **psychologise** (**-gises, -gising, -gised**) *v.* **1.** *vt.* **INTERPRET BEHAVIOUR PSYCHOLOGICALLY** to interpret behaviour in psychological terms or concepts **2.** *vi.* **ANALYSE PSYCHOLOGICALLY** to think, analyse, or reason psychologically

psychology /sī kólləji/ (*plural* **-gies**) *n.* **1.** **STUDY OF MIND** the scientific study of the human mind and mental states, and of human and animal behaviour **2.** **CHARACTERISTIC MENTAL MAKEUP** the characteristic temperament and associated behaviour of an individual or group, or that exhibited by those engaged in a particular activity **3.** **SUBTLE MANIPULATIVE BEHAVIOUR** subtle clever actions and words used to influence a person or group

psychomachia /sīkō máki ə/, **psychomachy** /sīkómmaki/ *n.* conflict of the soul between the spirit and the flesh (*literary*) [Early 17thC. From late Latin, from Greek *psukhē* 'soul' + *makhē* 'battle'.]

psychometrics /sīkō méttriks/ *n.* a branch of psychology dealing with the measurement of mental traits, capacities, and processes (*takes a singular verb*)

psychometry /sī kómmətri/ *n.* **1.** PSYCHOL = **psychometrics 2.** PARAPSYCHOL **DIVINATION BY TOUCHING OBJECT** the alleged ability to obtain information about a person or event by touching an object related to that person or event —**psychometric** /-méttrik/ *adj.* —**psychometrical** /-méttrik'l/ *adj.* —**psychometrically**

/-méttrikli/ *adv.* —**psychometrician** /sīkō mə trísh'n/ *n.* —**psychometrist** /sī kómmətrist/ *n.*

psychomotor /sīkō mótər/ *adj.* relating to bodily movement triggered by mental activity, especially voluntary muscle action

psychoneuroimmunology /sīkō nyoórō ímmyoo nólləji/ *n.* a branch of medicine concerned with how emotions affect the immune system

psychoneurosis /sīkō nyoō rṓssiss/ (*plural* -**roses** /-seez/) *n.* = neurosis —**psychoneurotic** /-róttik/ *adj.*

psychopath /sīkō path/ *n.* an offensive term for sb with a personality disorder marked by antisocial thought and behaviour —**psychopathic** /sīkō páthik/ *adj.* —**psychopathically** *adv.*

psychopathology /sīkō pə thólləji/ *n.* the study of the causes and development of psychiatric disorders —**psychopathological** /sīkō páthə lójjik'l/ *adj.* —**psychopathologist** /sīkō pə thólləjist/ *n.*

psychopathy /sī kóppəthi/ (*plural* -**thies**) *n.* **1. PERSONALITY DISORDER** a severe personality disorder marked by antisocial thought and behaviour (*informal*) **2. PSYCHIATRIC DISORDER** any psychiatric illness (*dated*)

psychopharmacology /sīkō fa'ármə kólləji/ *n.* the scientific study of the effects of drugs on thought and behaviour —**psychopharmacological** /-kə lójjik'l/ *adj.* —**psychopharmacologist** /-kólləjist/ *n.*

psychophysics /sīkō fízziks/ *n.* a branch of psychology dealing with the effects of physical stimuli on sensory perceptions and mental states (*takes a singular verb*) —**psychophysical** *adj.*

psychophysiology /sīkō fízzi ólləji/ *n.* = physiological psychology

psychosexual /sīkō sékshoo əl/ *adj.* relating to the mental and emotional aspects of sexuality and sexual development —**psychosexuality** /-sékshoo álləti/ *n.* —**psychosexually** /-sékshoo əli/ *adv.*

psychosis /sī kṓssiss/ (*plural* -**ses** /-seez/) *n.* a psychiatric disorder such as schizophrenia or mania that is marked by delusions, hallucinations, incoherency, and distorted perceptions of reality —**psychotic** /sī kóttik/ *adj.* —**psychotically** *adv.*

psychosocial /sīkō sṓsh'l/ *adj.* relating to both the psychological and the social aspects of sth, or relating to sth that has both of these aspects

psychosomatic /sīkō sə máttik/ *adj.* **1. MED MENTALLY INDUCED** used to describe a physical illness that is caused by mental factors such as stress, or the effects related to such illnesses **2. RELATING TO MIND AND BODY** involving both the mind and body [Mid-19thC. Coined from PSYCHO- + SOMATIC.] —**psychosomatically** *adv.*

psychosynthesis /sīkō sínthəssiss/ *n.* **1. PSYCHOTHERAPEUTIC MOVEMENT** a psychotherapeutic movement, opposed to psychoanalysis, that attempts to restore useful inhibitions and control **2. HOLISTIC FORM OF PSYCHOTHERAPY** a holistic form of psychotherapy involving clients in an exploration of the emotional, intellectual, physical, and spiritual elements of the self

psychotherapy /sīkō thérrəpi/ *n.* the treatment of mental disorders by psychological methods —**psychotherapeutic** /sīkō thérrə pyoótik/ *adj.* —**psychotherapeutically** /-pyoótikli/ *adv.* —**psychotherapist** /-thérrəpist/ *n.*

psychotomimetic /sī kóttō mi méttik/ *adj.* **PRODUCING A REACTION LIKE PSYCHOSIS** used to describe a drug or other factor that produces a condition resembling psychosis ■ *n.* **PSYCHOTOMIMETIC DRUG** a drug or other factor that produces a condition resembling psychosis [Mid-20thC. Coined from PSYCHOSIS + MIMETIC on the model of *psychotic.*]

psychotropic /sīkō trópik, -tróppik/ *adj.* **CAPABLE OF AFFECTING THE MIND** used to describe drugs that are capable of affecting the mind, e.g. those used to treat psychiatric disorders ■ *n.* **PSYCHOTROPIC DRUG** a drug capable of affecting the mind, e.g. one used to treat psychiatric disorders

psychro- *prefix.* cold ○ *psychrophilic* [From Greek *psukhros,* of unknown origin]

psychrometer /sī krómmitər/ *n.* an instrument consisting of two thermometers, used to measure at-

mospheric humidity. The bulb of one thermometer is kept moist and the effect of evaporative cooling on it is compared to the other, which is kept dry.

psychrophilic /sīkrō fíllik/ *adj.* thriving at low temperatures ○ *psychrophilic bacteria* [Mid-20thC]

psyllium /sílli əm/ *n.* an annual plant of the plantain family that is native to Europe and Asia and has dense spikes of small flowers. Latin name: *Plantago psyllium.* [Mid-16thC. Via Latin from Greek *psullion,* literally 'little flea', from *psulla* 'flea'; because the seeds resemble fleas.]

pt *abbr.* **1.** part **2.** patient **3.** FIN payment **4.** pint **5.** point **6.** port

Pt[1] *abbr.* (*used in place names*) **1.** Point **2.** Port

Pt[2] *symbol.* CHEM ELEM platinum

PT[1] *n.* gymnastics, athletics, team sports, and other forms of physical exercise taught to children at school. Full form **physical training**

PT[2] *abbr.* postal telegraph

pt. *abbr.* preterite

p.t. *abbr.* **1.** past tense **2.** part-time **3.** pro tem

pta *symbol.* MONEY peseta

PTA *abbr.* **1.** Parent Teacher Association **2.** Passenger Transport Authority

Ptarmigan

ptarmigan /ta'ármigən/ (*plural* -**gan** *or* -**gans**) *n.* a wild grouse of cold or mountainous regions that has feet covered with feathers and white plumage in the winter. Genus: *Lagopus.* [Late 16thC. Alteration (influenced by Greek *pt-* as in *pteron* 'wing') of Gaelic *tarmachan,* literally 'little ptarmigan', from *tarmach* 'ptarmigan'.]

PT boat *n.* US = motor torpedo boat

PTC *abbr.* phenylthiocarbamide

Pte *abbr.* Private

PTE *abbr.* Passenger Transport Executive

-pteran *prefix.* = -pterous

pteranodon /tə ránnə don/ *n.* an extinct toothless flying reptile with a bony crest. Genus: *Pteranodon.*

pteridology /térri dólləji/ *n.* a branch of botany dealing with ferns [Mid-19thC. Coined from Greek *pterid-,* the stem of *pteris* 'fern' + -LOGY.] —**pteridological** /térridə lójjik'l/ *adj.* —**pteridologist** /térri dólləjist/ *n.*

pteridophyte /térridə fīt/ *n.* a plant that has no flowers or seeds and reproduces by means of spores. Ferns and some mosses are pteridophytes. Division: *Pteridophyta.* [Late 19thC. Coined from Greek *pterid-* (see PTERIDOLOGY) + -PHYTE.] —**pteridophytic** /térridə fíttik/ *adj.* —**pteridophytous** /térri dóffitəss/ *adj.*

pteridosperm /térridə spurm/ *n.* an extinct plant resembling a fern that bore seeds [Early 20thC. Coined from Greek *pterid-* (see PTERIDOLOGY) + SPERM.]

pterodactyl /térrə dáktil/ *n.* an extinct flying reptile (**pterosaur**) of the Jurassic and Cretaceous Periods with membranous wings and a rudimentary tail and beak. Genus: *Pterodactylus.* [Early 19thC. From modern Latin *Pterodactylus,* the genus name, literally 'wing finger', from Greek *pteron* 'wing' + *daktulos* 'finger'.]

pteropod /térrə pod/ *n.* a marine gastropod mollusc that has a foot with wing-shaped lobes that are used as swimming organs. Group: *Pteropoda.* [Mid-19thC. Formed from modern Latin *Pteropoda,* the class name, which was coined from Greek *pteron* 'wing' + modern Latin *-poda* '-pod'.]

pterosaur /térrə sawr/ *n.* an extinct flying reptile of the Triassic, Jurassic, and Cretaceous Periods that had membranous featherless wings supported by an elongated fourth digit. Order: Pterosauria. [Mid-19thC. From modern Latin *Pterosauria,* the order name, literally 'lizard with wings', from Greek *pteron* 'wing' + *sauros* 'lizard'.]

-pterous *suffix.* having wings of a particular kind or number ○ *orthopterous* ○ *dipterous* [Formed from Greek *pteron* 'wing, feather'. Ultimately from an Indo-European base meaning 'to fly, fall', which is also the ancestor of English *feather* and *pen.*]

pteroylglutamic acid /térrō īl gloo támmik-/ *n.* folic acid (*technical*) [*Pteroylglutamic* coined from PTEROIC + -YL + GLUTAMIC]

pterygium /tə ríjji əm/ (*plural* -**ums** *or* -**a** /-ə/) *n.* a triangular patch of tissue that obstructs vision by growing over usually the inner side of the eye. It results from degeneration of the cornea and is associated with prolonged exposure to sun and wind. [Mid-17thC. Via modern Latin from Greek *pterugion,* literally 'little wing', from *pterux* 'wing'.]

pterygoid process /térri goyd-/ *n.* either of two bony plates extending downwards from the sphenoid bone of the skull [*Pterygoid* via modern Latin *pterygoides* 'like a wing', from Greek *pterux* 'wing']

pteryla /térrilə/ (*plural* -**lae** /-lī/) *n.* a defined area on the skin of a bird from which feathers grow [Mid-19thC. From modern Latin, literally 'feather forest', from Greek *pteron* 'feather' + *hulē* 'forest'.]

PTFE *abbr.* polytetrafluoroethylene

ptg *abbr.* printing

PTH *abbr.* parathyroid hormone

PTN *abbr.* public telephone network

PTO, **pto** *abbr.* please turn over

Ptolemaeus /tóllə máyess/ *n.* a large walled plain on the Moon that is noticeably hexagonal in shape and has a highly cratered floor. Located northeast of Mare Imbrium, it is approximately 140 km/85 mi. across.

Ptolemaic /tóllə máy ik/ *adj.* **1.** ASTRON OF THE ASTRONOMER PTOLEMY relating to the geographer and astronomer Ptolemy or to his system of planetary motion **2.** HIST OF THE EGYPTIAN PTOLEMIES relating to the Ptolemies, Pharaohs of ancient Egypt, or to Egypt during their rule

Ptolemaic system *n.* a theory of planetary motion developed by Ptolemy that held that the Earth was at the centre of the universe with the Sun, Moon, and planets revolving around it. The most influential of the geocentric theories, it dominated thinking for 14 centuries until the Copernican system was accepted

Ptolemaist /tóllə máy ist/ *n.* a believer in the Ptolemaic system of planetary motion

Ptolemy /tólləmi/ (AD. 100?–170) Greek astronomer, mathematician, and geographer. His Earth-centred model of the universe prevailed until the 16th century. His writings are collected in the *Almagest.* Full name **Claudius Ptolemaeus**

Ptolemy I /tólləmi/ (367?–283? BC) Macedonian king of Egypt. A general in Alexander the Great's army, he became king of Egypt in 305 BC, thereby founding the Ptolemaic dynasty. Known as **Ptolemy Soter**

ptomaine /tṓ mayn/ *n.* any one of a group of foul-smelling organic bases containing nitrogen, produced by bacteria during the decay of proteins [Late 19thC. Via French from Italian *ptomaina,* from Greek *ptōma,* 'fallen body, corpse', from *piptein* 'to fall' (source of English *symptom*).]

ptomaine poisoning *n.* food poisoning caused by bacteria, but formerly believed to be caused by ptomaines

ptosis /tṓssiss/ (*plural* -**ses** /-seez/) *n.* MED a drooping of the upper eyelid, resulting from muscle weakness or inability to move muscles [Mid-18thC. From Greek *ptōsis* 'a falling', from *piptein* (see PTOMAINE).]

pts *abbr.* **1.** parts **2.** payments **3.** pints **4.** points **5.** ports

PTSD *abbr.* post-traumatic stress disorder

PTV *abbr.* pay television

Pty *abbr.* proprietary (*used in 'Pty Ltd' to indicate a private limited company*)

ptyalin /tí əlin/ *n.* an enzyme in saliva that catalyses the conversion of starch into sugars [Mid-19thC. Coined from Greek *ptualon* 'saliva' + -IN.]

ptyalism /tí əlizəm/ *n.* excessive production of saliva [Late 17thC. From Greek *ptualismos* 'salivation', from *ptualon* 'spittle', from, ultimately, *ptuein* 'to spit'.]

Pu *symbol.* plutonium

pub /pub/ *n.* **1. PLACE FOR DRINKING** a building where drinks, especially alcoholic ones, can be bought and consumed. Food, and sometimes accommodation, may also be available. **2. HOTEL** hotel (*informal*) [Mid-19thC. Shortening of PUBLIC HOUSE.]

pub. *abbr.* **1.** public **2.** publication **3.** published **4.** publisher **5.** publishing

pubbing /púbbing/ *n.* the social activity of going to a pub or pubs (*informal*) ○ *Monday morning can look grim after a weekend's pubbing.*

pub-crawl *n.* **ROVING DRINKING SESSION** a session of drinking at several pubs or bars in succession (*informal*) ■ *vi.* (**pub-crawls, pub-crawling, pub-crawled**) **GO ON PUB-CRAWL** to go drinking at several pubs or bars in succession (*informal*)

puberty /pyóobərti/ *n.* the stage of becoming physiologically capable of sexual reproduction, marked by genital maturation, development of secondary sex characteristics, and the first occurrence of menstruation [14thC. Directly or via French *puberté* from Latin *pubertas*, from, ultimately, *pubes* 'adult'.] —**pubertal** *adj.*

puberulent /pyoo bérr yóolənt/ *adj.* BOT, ZOOL covered with fine down or hairs [Mid-19thC. Formed from *puber-*, the stem of *pubes* 'adult'.]

pubes[1] *n.* /pyóo beez/ (*plural* -**bes** /pyóo beez/) **AREA ABOVE THE EXTERNAL GENITALIA** the part of the abdomen immediately above the external genitalia that is covered with hair from puberty onwards ■ *npl.* /pyoobz/ **PUBIC HAIR** the hair growing on the lower abdomen from puberty onwards (*informal*) (*takes a plural verb*) [Late 16thC. From Latin *pubes* 'adult males, genitals'.]

pubes[2] *plural of* **pubis**

pubescent /pyoo béss'nt/ *adj.* **1. AT PUBERTY** reaching or having attained puberty **2.** BOT, ZOOL **HAIRY** covered with down or fine hair [Mid-17thC. Directly or via French from Latin *pubescent-*, the present participle stem of *pubescere* 'to reach puberty', from *pubes* 'adult'.] —**pubescence** *n.*

pub grub *n.* food, usually of a relatively simple and inexpensive type, served in a pub (*informal*)

pubic /pyóobik/ *adj.* relating to or located near or on the pubes or pubis ○ *pubic hair*

pubic bone *n.* = **pubis**

pubic louse *n.* = **crab**[1] *n.* 4

pubis /pyóobiss/ (*plural* -**bes** /-beez/) *n.* the joined pair of bones comprising the lower front of the hipbone in humans. Although a separate bone at birth, it later fuses with the ilium and the ischium. [Late 16thC. From the Latin phrase *os pubis*, literally 'bone of the genital region'.]

publ. *abbr.* **1.** publication **2.** published **3.** publisher

public /públik/ *adj.* **1. CONCERNING ALL MEMBERS OF THE COMMUNITY** relating to or concerning people as a whole or all members of a community ○ *public health* **2. FOR COMMUNITY USE** provided for the use of a community **3. OPEN TO ALL** open to everyone, and typically frequented by large numbers of people **4. OF THE STATE** relating to or involving government and governmental agencies rather than private corporations or industry ○ *working in the public sector* ○ *a public servant* **5. WELL KNOWN** known to large numbers of the community because of being involved in activities such as politics or entertainment ○ *a public figure* **6. DONE OPENLY** made, done, or happening openly, for all to see ○ *a public debate* **7. KNOWN BY ALL MEMBERS OF COMMUNITY** known or potentially known by all members of a community ○ *make the information public* **8.** POL **BELONGING TO THE COMMUNITY** belonging to the community as a whole

and administered through its representatives in government ○ *public land* **9.** FIN **HAVING OPENLY PURCHASABLE SHARES** used to describe companies whose shares are available, or are made available, for anyone to buy ■ *n.* **1. EVERYONE** the community as a whole **2. PARTICULAR PART OF COMMUNITY** a part of a community sharing a particular interest ○ *the reading public* **3. FANS OR FOLLOWERS** the fans or followers of a performer or author **4.** = **public bar** [15thC. Directly or via French from Latin *publicus*, an alteration of *poplicus* (apparently under the influence of *pubes* 'adult'), from *populus* 'people'.] —**publicness** *n.*

public access *n.* in US law, the availability of cable broadcasting facilities for the transmission of programmes produced by members of the public (*hyphenated before a noun*)

public-address system *n.* full form of **PA**

publican /públikən/ *n.* **1. PUB OWNER** the owner or manager of a pub **2.** HIST **TAX COLLECTOR IN ANCIENT ROME** a collector of taxes in ancient Rome [12thC. Via French *publicain* from, ultimately, Latin *publicus* (see PUBLIC). The modern meaning presumably arose from an association with PUBLIC HOUSE.]

publication /públi káysh'n/ *n.* **1. PUBLISHING OF STH** the publishing of sth, especially printed material for sale **2. PUBLISHED ITEM** an item that has been published, especially in printed form **3. PUBLIC COMMUNICATION OF STH** the communication of information to the public [14thC. Via French from, ultimately, *publicare* (see PUBLISH).]

public bar *n.* a bar in a pub that is furnished basically and in which drinks are sold more cheaply than in a lounge bar

public bill *n.* a bill presented in Parliament by a government, dealing with public policy

public company *n.* a limited company whose shares can be bought and sold on the stock market. US term **public corporation**

public convenience *n.* a toilet in a public place, e.g. a town centre, for use by members of the public

public corporation *n.* **1. ORGANIZATION RUNNING STATE-OWNED ENTERPRISE** in the United States, an organization set up by the government that runs a state-owned enterprise. Its chairman and governors are appointed by a government minister. **2.** *US* = **public company**

public defender *n.* in the United States, an attorney who represents defendants who cannot afford their own lawyer

public domain *n.* **1. NOT IN COPYRIGHT** in US law, the condition of not being protected by patent or copyright and so freely available for use ○ *public domain software* **2. REVEALED CONDITION** the condition of being openly known or revealed as opposed to being kept a secret ○ *The information is now in the public domain.* **3.** *US* **GOVERNMENT LAND** land that is owned and administered by a government

public enemy *n.* sb who is thought to be a threat to the public, especially a violent criminal

public enterprise *n.* economic activity by government departments and quangos

public expenditure *n.* spending by the state or state-owned bodies

public eye ◇ **in the public eye** regularly receiving attention from the media

public figure *n.* sb who is well known to people generally

public health *n.* the general health of a community and the practice and study of ways to preserve and improve this. It includes health education, sanitation, control of diseases, and regulation of pollution.

public house *n.* a pub (*formal*)

public interest *n.* **1. COMMON BENEFIT** the general benefit of the public ○ *a law that would be contrary to the public interest* **2. GENERAL INTEREST IN ISSUE** the general level of interest shown by people towards an issue or event

publicise *vt.* = **publicize**

publicist /púbblissist/ *n.* **1. SB WHO GETS PUBLICITY FOR A CLIENT** sb who is responsible for obtaining media publicity for a client **2. JOURNALIST** a journalist

(*dated*) [Late 18thC. Via French *publiciste* (modelled on *canoniste* 'canon lawyer'), from, ultimately, Latin *publicus* (see PUBLIC).]

publicity /pu blíssəti/ *n.* **1. STH STIMULATING PUBLIC INTEREST** sth such as advertising designed to increase public interest or awareness in sth or sb (*often used before a noun*) ○ *The event was dismissed as a mere publicity stunt.* **2. INTEREST CREATED BY PUBLICITY** public interest or awareness created by publicity **3. ATTENTION-GETTING INFORMATION** information used to attract public attention, or the business of disseminating this ○ *She works in publicity.* ○ *the company's publicity campaign for their new product* **4. CONDITION OF BEING PUBLIC** the condition of being known or available to the public [Late 18thC. From French *publicité*, from *public* (see PUBLIC).]

publicize /púbbli sīz/ (-**cizes**, -**cizing**, -**cized**), **publicise** (-**cises**, -**cising**, -**cised**) *vt.* to make sth generally known or known to members of a particular group, typically by advertising

public key encryption *n.* in computing, a message encryption technique in which encoding is done using a generally available public key but decoding is done using a private key available only to the receiver

public law *n.* **1. BRANCH OF LAW** the branch of law that deals with a state and its relationships with its citizens. ◇ **private law 2. LAW APPLYING TO THE PUBLIC** a law that applies to the public

Public Lending Right *n.* the right for authors to receive a small fee every time their books are borrowed from UK public libraries

public-liability insurance *n.* insurance that compensates individuals if they experience injury or damage resulting from lack of reasonable care by an insured business or organization

public life *n.* **1. LIFESTYLE ATTRACTING PUBLICITY** a lifestyle that attracts a lot of publicity and public scrutiny, especially that of a politician **2. PUBLIC SERVICE** public service, especially by a politician

public limited company *n.* a company whose shares can be bought and sold on the stock market and whose shareholders are subject to restricted liability for any debts or losses. Full form of **PLC**

publicly /públikli/ *adv.* **1. OPENLY** in a public or open manner **2. BY THE PUBLIC** by or in the name of the public

public nuisance *n.* **1.** LAW **ILLEGAL ACTION HARMING THE COMMUNITY** an illegal action that harms the members of a community in general **2. UNACCEPTABLE PERSON** sb who is generally thought to be irritating or offensive (*insult*)

public opinion *n.* the general attitude or feeling of the public concerning an issue, especially when this has an effect on political decision-making

public ownership *n.* ownership by the state of sth regarded as a national asset, e.g. coal, water, or the telecommunications industry

public prosecutor *n.* a government law official prosecuting criminal offences on behalf of the community or the state

Public Record Office *n.* a British institution in which official documents, historical and modern, are stored after they are released under the thirty-year rule. They may be consulted by the public.

public relations *n.* **1. PROMOTION OF A FAVOURABLE IMAGE** the practice or profession of establishing, maintaining, or improving a favourable relationship between an institution, or person, and the public (*takes a singular verb*) **2. PUBLIC IMAGE** how well or badly sth such as an institution or person is regarded by the public (*takes a singular or plural verb*) ○ *Such projects provide good public relations for the government.* **3. DEPARTMENT MANAGING PUBLIC RELATIONS** the department in an organization that is responsible for public relations (*takes a singular verb*)

public room *n. Scotland* a term used by solicitors and estate agents to describe any of the rooms in a private house into which strangers may traditionally be invited, e.g. a sitting room, dining room, or study

public school *n.* **1.** INDEPENDENT FEE-PAYING SECONDARY SCHOOL in England and Wales, an independent fee-paying secondary school, typically a single-sex boarding school **2.** STATE-FUNDED SCHOOL in the United States, a state-funded elementary or secondary school providing education free for all local children and young people

public sector *n.* the part of the economy that is controlled by government spending and employment (*hyphenated when used before a noun*)

public-sector borrowing requirement *n.* the amount that the UK government needs to borrow in any fiscal year in order to be able to meet its budgeted costs

public servant *n.* **1.** HOLDER OF A GOVERNMENT POSITION an appointed or elected holder of a government position or office **2.** ANZ CIVIL SERVANT a civil servant

public service *n.* **1.** GOVERNMENT EMPLOYMENT government employment, especially within the civil service **2.** PROVISION OF ESSENTIAL SERVICES the business or activity of providing the public with essential goods or services such as electric power **3.** ANZ POL DEPARTMENTS IMPLEMENTING GOVERNMENT POLICY the range of departments and organizations responsible for implementing government policy **4.** SERVICE BENEFITING THE GENERAL PUBLIC a service that is run for the benefit of the general public, e.g. the utilities, the emergency services, transport, and broadcasting (*hyphenated when used before a noun*)

public-service broadcasting *n.* noncommercial broadcasting, specifically programmes broadcast by the BBC

public speaking *n.* the skill, practice, or process of making speeches to large groups of people —**public speaker** *n.*

public spending *n.* spending by government and government bodies (*hyphenated when used before a noun*)

public-spirited *adj.* motivated by or showing genuine concern for others in the community

public transport *n.* a network of passenger vehicles for use by the public running on set routes, usually at set times and charging set fares (*hyphenated when used before a noun*)

public trustee *n.* Can in Canada, an official who manages the estates of those who are deemed not mentally competent in law or those who die without wills but have minor heirs

public utility *n.* a government-regulated company that provides an essential public service such as water, gas, or electricity (*hyphenated before a noun*)

public works *npl.* civil-engineering projects that are government owned or financed, and undertaken specifically for the benefit of the public

publish /púbblish/ (-lishes, -lishing, -lished) *v.* **1.** *vti.* PREPARE AND PRODUCE TEXT OR SOFTWARE to prepare and produce material in printed or electronic form for distribution and, usually, sale **2.** *vt.* PUBLISH THE WORK OF AN AUTHOR to publish the work of a particular author **3.** *vt.* MAKE STH PUBLIC KNOWLEDGE to announce sth publicly [14thC. Via Old French *publiss-*, the stem of *publier*, from, ultimately, Latin *publicus* 'public' (source of English *public*).] —**publishable** *adj.*

publisher /púbblishər/ *n.* **1.** PUBLISHING COMPANY OR PERSON a company or person that publishes products such as books, journals, or software **2.** OWNER OF A PUBLISHING BUSINESS the owner or representative of the owner of a newspaper, periodical, or publishing house

publishing /púbblishing/ *n.* the trade, profession, or activity of preparing and producing material in printed or electronic form for distribution to the public

publishing house *n.* an established publishing company that prepares and produces material in printed or electronic form for distribution and, usually, sale

PUC *n.* S Asia EDUC a preuniversity junior college

Puccini /poo cheeni/, **Giacomo** (1858–1924) Italian composer. His lyrical, theatrical operas include *La Bohème* (1896), *Tosca* (1900), *Madame Butterfly* (1904), and *Turandot* (1926).

puccoon /pə koón/ (*plural* -coons *or* -coon) *n.* **1.** PLANTS PLANT YIELDING A RED DYE an American plant of the borage or poppy family such as gromwell or bloodroot whose roots yield a reddish dye. Latin name: *Lithospermum canescens* and *Sanguinaria canadensis.* **2.** INDUST DYE FROM PUCCOON a dye made from puccoon [Early 17thC. From Algonquian *poughkone.*]

puce /pyooss/ *adj.* of a brilliant purplish-red colour [Late 18thC. Via French, 'flea' (in the phrase *couleur puce* 'flea-coloured'), from Latin *pulex*. Ultimately from an Indo-European word meaning 'flea', which is also the ancestor of English *flea*.] —**puce** *n.*

puck /puk/ *n.* **1.** ICE HOCKEY DISC IN HOCKEY a small disc of hard rubber that the players hit in hockey **2.** SPORTS STROKE AT THE BALL a player's stroke at the ball in the Irish sport of hurling ■ *vt.* (pucks, pucking, pucked) **1.** SPORTS STRIKE A BALL to strike the ball in the Irish sport of hurling **2.** *Ireland* HIT STH HARD to hit sth with great force (*slang*) [Late 19thC. Origin uncertain: perhaps originally in dialect, 'to strike'.]

Puck[1], **puck** *n.* a mischievous or malevolent spirit in English folklore [Old English *pūca*]

Puck[2] *n.* a small natural satellite of Uranus, discovered in 1985 by the Voyager 2 planetary probe. It is approximately 154 km in diameter.

pucka *adj.* = pukka

pucker /púkər/ *vti.* (-ers, -ering, -ered) GATHER INTO WRINKLES to gather sth such as cloth or the skin around the lips in such a way that wrinkles or small creases are formed, or to become gathered in this way ■ *n.* SMALL WRINKLE a small wrinkle, fold, or crease [Late 16thC. Origin uncertain: probably from the stem of POCKET, in which case the underlying idea is of forming into pockets or small bag-shaped wrinkles.]

puckeroo /púkə roo/ *adj.* NZ broken, destroyed or not working (*informal*) [Late 19thC. From Maori *pakaru* 'broken'.]

puckish /púkish/ *adj.* mischievous or naughty in a playful way [Late 19thC. Formed from PUCK[1].] —**puckishly** *adv.* —**puckishness** *n.*

pud /pood/ *n.* pudding (*informal*)

pudding /poóding/ *n.* **1.** SWEET COOKED DESSERT a sweet cooked dessert containing flour or a cereal product and other ingredients such as sugar, fruit, or eggs (*often used in combination*) **2.** DESSERT the dessert course of a meal ○ *What's for pudding?* **3.** COOKED SAVOURY DISH a substantial savoury cooked dish usually covered with, or encased in, suet pastry or sometimes breadcrumbs (*often used in combination*) **4.** TYPE OF SAUSAGE a kind of sausage made with ingredients such as minced meat, seasonings, and oatmeal packed into a skin or bag and usually boiled (*usually used in combination*) ○ *black pudding* [13thC. Via French *boudin* 'black pudding', from, ultimately, Latin *botellus* 'sausage', the original sense in English. The modern meaning evolved via 'any food cooked in a bag or cloth'.] —**pudding** *adj.* ◇ **in the pudding club** pregnant (*slang; often considered offensive*)

pudding basin *n.* a deep bowl used for making puddings, especially steamed puddings (*hyphenated when used before a noun*)

pudding-basin haircut *n.* a haircut with the hair cut in a continuous straight line all the way round the head, generally regarded as unflattering

pudding stone *n.* a conglomerate rock in which the pebbles have a different colour and texture from the material binding them together (**matrix**)

puddle /púdd'l/ *n.* **1.** SHALLOW POOL OF WATER a shallow pool of water, e.g. one formed by rainwater in a hollow on a road **2.** POOL OF LIQUID a small pool of liquid **3.** CIV ENG WATERPROOF LINING MATERIAL nonporous material made from thoroughly mixed wet clay and sand and used as a waterproof lining, e.g. in constructing a canal **4.** ROWING EDDY FROM OAR STROKE the swirling surface of the water after the blade of an oar has completed a stroke ■ *v.* (-dles, -dling, -dled) **1.** *vi.* MESS ABOUT to potter or mess about **2.** *vi.* SPLASH IN SHALLOW WATER to wade, dabble, or splash in shallow water or puddles **3.** *vt.* CIV ENG WATERPROOF STH WITH PUDDLE to make a canal or pool waterproof by lining it with puddle **4.** *vt.* CIV ENG MIX CLAY AND SAND to work clay and sand to make puddle **5.** *vt.* METALL PROCESS PIG IRON to convert pig iron to wrought iron by

heating it in a furnace in the presence of an oxidizing agent such as ferric oxide to remove carbon [14thC. Formed from Old English *pudd* 'ditch', with the literal sense 'small ditch'.] —**puddler** *n.* —**puddly** *adj.*

puddock /púddək/ *n. Scotland* a frog or toad

pudendum /pyoo déndəm/ (*plural* -da /-déndə/) *n.* human external genital organs [Mid-17thC. From Latin, from, ultimately, *pudere* 'to make or feel ashamed' (source of English *impudent*).] —**pudendal** *adj.*

pudge /puj/ *n.* excess weight on a person (*regional*)

pudgy /pújji/ (-ier, -iest) *adj.* short and carrying more bodyweight than is desirable or advisable (*informal; sometimes considered offensive*) —**pudginess** *n.*

Pudsey /púdsi/ town in Yorkshire, England, 10 km/6 mi. west of Leeds. Population: 31,636 (1991).

pudu /poó doo/ (*plural* -dus *or* -du) *n.* a very small deer with tiny straight antlers, found in the forests of Central and South America. Genus: *Pudu*. [Late 19thC. From Araucanian.]

Puebla /pwéblə/ city in central Mexico, and the capital of Puebla State. It has one of the oldest cathedrals in Latin America. Population: 1,057,454 (1990).

pueblo /pwébblō/ (*plural* -los) *n.* **1.** NATIVE N OR CENTRAL AMERICAN VILLAGE a village built by Native North or Central Americans in the southwestern United States and Central America, containing at least one, but typically a cluster of multi-storey stone or adobe houses **2.** VILLAGE IN SPANISH-SPEAKING COUNTRIES a town or village in a Spanish-speaking country [Early 19thC. Via Spanish from Latin *populus* (see PUBLIC).]

Pueblo /pwébblō/ (*plural* -lo *or* -los) *n.* PEOPLES a member of any Native North or Central American people who live or lived in pueblos. The Hopi, Taos, and Zuñi are all Pueblo peoples. —**Pueblo** *adj.*

puerile /pyóor īl/ *adj.* **1.** SILLY silly or immature, especially in a childish way **2.** RELATING TO CHILDHOOD relating to or characteristic of childhood [Late 16thC. Directly or via French *puéril* from Latin *puerilis*, from *puer* 'child, boy'. Ultimately from an Indo-European base meaning 'little' (ancestor also of English *few*).] —**puerilely** *adv.* —**puerility** /pyoor rílləti/ *n.*

puerilism /pyóorilizəm/ *n.* childish or immature behaviour by an adult

puerperal /pyoo úrpərəl/ *adj.* relating to childbirth or the time immediately following childbirth [Mid-18thC. From Latin *puerperus* 'bringing forth children', from *puer* 'child' + *-parus* 'bringing forth'.]

puerperal fever *n.* = puerperal sepsis

puerperal psychosis *n.* a psychiatric disorder that may affect women in the first two weeks after giving birth. It may be depressive or schizophrenic and may involve false ideas concerning the baby.

puerperal sepsis *n.* blood poisoning following childbirth, caused by infection of the placental site

puerperium /pyóor peeri əm/ *n.* the period immediately after childbirth when the womb is returning to its normal size, lasting approximately six weeks [Early 17thC. From Latin, from Latin *puerperus* (see PUERPERAL).]

Puerto Rico

Puerto Rico /púərtə reékō/ commonwealth of the United States, occupying one large island and several small ones in the northern Caribbean, east of the Dominican Republic. Language: Spanish, English. Currency: US dollar. Capital: San Juan.

Population: 3,522,037 (1990). Area: 8,876 sq. km/3,427 sq. mi. —**Puerto Rican** *n., adj.*

puff /puf/ *n.* **1. SHORT SUDDEN RUSH OF AIR** a short sudden rush of air, wind, gas, or smoke **2. SOUND OF PUFF** the short sound made by a puff **3. AMOUNT IN A PUFF** the amount of substance contained in a puff **4. SHORT EXHALATION** a short blowing out of breath **5. INHALING FOLLOWED BY EXHALING** an inhalation followed by an exhalation, especially when smoking **6. LIGHT PASTRY SNACK** a snack or cake consisting of puff pastry with a sweet or sometimes a savoury filling (*often used in combination*) ○ *a cream puff* **7. EXAGGERATED PRAISE OR PUBLICITY** an exaggerated or flattering expression of praise, especially in publicizing sth or sb **8.** COSMETICS = **powder puff 9. SWELLING** a rounded swelling or projection on sth **10.** CLOTHES **GATHERED SECTION OF FABRIC** a piece of fabric gathered around the edges and bulging in the middle **11.** *US* **QUILTED BEDSPREAD** a quilted and padded covering for a bed (*dated*) **12.** HAIR **VOLUMINOUS HAIRSTYLE** hair arranged in an enlarged mass by combing, rolling, or padding it **13.** GENETICS **ENLARGED REGION ON A CHROMOSOME** an enlarged region on a chromosome resulting from active RNA synthesis ■ *v.* (**puffs, puffing, puffed**) **1.** *vt.* **MAKE SB BREATHLESS** to make sb breathless, e.g. after heavy exercise (*informal*) ○ *Phew! I'm puffed!* **2.** *vi.* **BREATHE QUICKLY** to breathe quickly in short blasts **3.** *vti.* **EMIT GAS IN SHORT BLASTS** to emit or blow steam, gas, or smoke in short blasts **4.** *vti.* **INHALE AND EXHALE SMOKE** to inhale and exhale smoke from a cigarette, cigar, or pipe **5.** *vi.* **MOVE EMITTING SMOKE PUFFS** to move in a particular direction or way emitting puffs of smoke or steam **6.** *vi.* **MOVE WHILE PANTING** to move in a particular direction or way while panting ○ *He puffed up the hill.* **7.** *vti.* **SWELL** to swell or make sth swell, e.g. with air or pride **8.** *vt.* **SPEAK HIGHLY OF SB OR STH** to praise sb or sth extravagantly, especially in publicity material [12thC. Origin uncertain: perhaps from Old English *pyf*, in which case an imitation of the sound.] ◇ **out of puff** out of breath (*informal*) ◇ **puffed out** out of breath because of exertion (*informal*)

puff adder *n.* **1. AFRICAN INFLATING VIPER** an African viper that inflates its body and hisses when alarmed. Genus: *Bitis.* **2.** = **hognose snake**

puffball /púf bawl/ *n.* a round fungus that produces a cloud of dark spores when disturbed. Many species are edible when immature. Genus: *Lycoperdon* and *Calvatia.*

puffbird /púf burd/ *n.* a medium-sized bird with rounded wings and a large head, found in the forests of Central and South America. Family: Bucconidae. [Early 19thC. Because it puffs out its feathers.]

puffed-up *adj.* self-important or pompous

puffer /púffər/ *n.* **1. PUFFING PERSON OR THING** sth or sb that puffs, especially a steam-driven train or cargo vessel **2.** ZOOL **INFLATING MARINE FISH** a marine fish of tropical waters that can inflate its body with water to appear larger to predators. Although poisonous, some varieties can be eaten as food after special preparation. Family: Tetraodontidae.

puffery /púffəri/ *n.* exaggerated or excessively flattering praise, especially in publicity (*informal*)

Puffin

puffin /púffin/ (*plural* **-fins** *or* **-fin**) *n.* a black-and-white diving bird of the auk family with a short neck and a triangular brightly coloured bill. Genus: *Fratercula.* [14thC. Origin uncertain: perhaps by folk etymology from a Celtic word by association with PUFF because of its plump appearance.]

puff pastry *n.* a light flaky multi-layered pastry made by repeated rolling and folding of extremely rich buttery pastry dough, which then rises during baking

puffy /púffi/ (**-ier, -iest**) *adj.* **1. SWOLLEN** swollen, especially because of tiredness, injury, crying, or poor health **2. SHORT OF BREATH** with a tendency to puff and pant **3. POMPOUS** pompous or self-important —**puffily** *adv.* —**puffiness** *n.*

Pug

pug[1] /pug/ *n.* a short compact dog with a wrinkled face, short coat, and curled tail, belonging to a breed of Asian origin [Mid-18thC. Origin uncertain: perhaps from Dutch.]

pug[2] /pug/ *vt.* (**pugs, pugging, pugged**) **1.** BUILDING, CERAMICS **KNEAD CLAY WITH WATER** to mix clay with water to make it pliable enough to form bricks or pottery **2.** BUILDING **FILL A GAP WITH CLAY** to fill in a gap with clay or mortar ■ *n.* BUILDING, CERAMICS **CLAY SUITABLE FOR MOULDING** clay mixed with water until it is pliable enough to form bricks or pottery [Early 19thC. Origin unknown.] —**puggy** *adj.*

pug[3] /pug/ *n.* a boxer (*slang*) [Mid-19thC. Shortening of PUGILISM.]

Puget Sound /pyŏŏjit-/ deep inlet of the Pacific Ocean, in northwestern Washington State. Area: 1,453 sq. km/561 sq. mi.

puggled /púgg'ld/, **puggled out** *adj. Scotland* in a state of extreme tiredness, usually from working hard at sth (*informal*) [Early 20thC. Formed from earlier *puggle* 'crazy', from Hindi *pāgal*, *paglā* 'idiot'.]

puggree /púggri/, **pugree, pugaree** /púggəri/ *n. S Asia* a turban [Mid-17thC. From Hindi *pagṛī*.]

pugilism /pyŏŏjilizəm/ *n.* the practice, sport, or profession of boxing [Late 18thC. Formed from Latin *pugil* 'boxer'. Ultimately from an Indo-European base meaning 'to prick', which is also the ancestor of English *poignant*.] —**pugilist** *n.* —**pugilistic** /pyŏŏji lístik/ *adj.* —**pugilistically** /-lístikli/ *adv.*

pugil-stick *n.* a long stick with padded ends used in game shows involving mock combats [*Pugil* probably a shortening of PUGILISM]

Pugin /pyŏŏjin/, **Augustus Welby Northmore** (1812–52) British architect and designer. A leader of the Gothic revival, his most influential work was the interior and exterior decoration of the Houses of Parliament.

pug mill *n.* a machine in which materials are ground and mixed, e.g. clay with water for building or pottery-making, or cement for building [From PUG[2]]

pugnacious /pug náyshəss/ *adj.* inclined to fight or be aggressive [Mid-17thC. Formed from Latin *pugnax*, from, ultimately, *pugnus* 'fist'.] —**pugnaciously** *adv.* —**pugnaciousness** *n.* —**pugnacity** /pug nássəti/ *n.*

pug nose *n.* a short stubby nose with a turned-up or flattened end [From PUG[1]] —**pug-nosed** *adj.*

puh-leeze /pə léez/, **puh-lease** *interj.* used facetiously to express astonishment, disbelief, or indignation (*informal*) [Late 20thC. Alteration of PLEASE.]

puisne /pyŏŏni/ *adj.* used to describe a justice of the High Court of England [Late 16thC. From Old French, literally 'born after', from *puis* 'after' + *né* 'born'. Originally used in the sense 'younger'.]

puissance /pwée soNs, pyŏŏ iss'nss/ *n.* **1.** SHOWJUMPING **SPECIAL SHOWJUMPING COMPETITION** a competition in showjumping in which horses attempt to clear an obstacle that is raised higher for each round, until all but the winner are eliminated **2. STRENGTH** power or might (*literary*) [15thC. Via French from, ultimately, Latin *potis* (see PUISSANT).]

puissant /pyŏŏ iss'nt/ *adj.* powerful or mighty (*literary*) [15thC. Via French from, ultimately, Latin *potis* 'able'. Ultimately from an Indo-European base meaning 'powerful', which is also the ancestor of English *despot*.] —**puissantly** *adv.*

puja /pŏŏjə/ *n.* daily devotion in Hinduism, consisting of a ritual offering of food, drink, and ritual actions and prayers, most commonly to an image of a deity [Late 17thC. From Sanskrit *pūjā* 'worship'.]

puke /pyook/ *vti.* (**pukes, puking, puked**) **BE SICK** to vomit, or vomit sth up (*slang*) ■ *n.* (*slang*) **1. STH VOMITED** vomited food or other matter **2. VOMITING** the vomiting up of sth **3. DESPICABLE PERSON** a contemptible or annoying person [Late 16thC. Origin uncertain: probably an imitation of the sound of vomiting.]

pukeko /pŏŏkəkō/ (*plural* **-kos** *or* **-ko**) *n. ANZ* a wading bird native to New Zealand with glossy black-and-blue plumage and a bright red bill and beak. Latin name: *Porphyrio porphyrio.* [Mid-19thC. From Maori.]

pukka /púkə/, **pucka** *adj.* **1.** *S Asia* **WELL DONE OR MADE** properly done or made, or of superior quality **2. GENUINE** genuine or authentic (*informal*) **3. RESPECTABLE** of high social status (*informal*) **4. EXCELLENT** of the highest quality or standard [Late 17thC. From Hindi *pakkā* 'cooked, ripe'.]

pul /pool/ (*plural* **puls** *or* **puli** /pŏŏli/) *n.* an Afghan monetary unit worth one hundredth of an afghani [Mid-19thC. From Pashto.]

pulchritude /púlkri tyood/ *n.* physical beauty (*literary or humorous*) [14thC. From Latin *pulchritudo*, from *pulcher* 'beautiful'.] —**pulchritudinous** /púlkri tyŏŏdinəss/ *adj.*

pule /pyool/ (**pules, puling, puled**) *vi.* to whine, whimper, or cry plaintively (*archaic*) [Early 16thC. Origin uncertain: probably an imitation of the sound of whimpering.] —**puler** *n.* —**pulingly** *adv.*

puli /pyŏŏli/ (*plural* **-lik** /pyŏŏlik/ *or* **-lis**) *n.* a medium-sized Hungarian sheepdog with long hair that can be combed out or left corded [Mid-20thC. From Hungarian.]

Pulitzer prize /pŏŏlitsər-/ *n.* any of several prizes awarded annually for excellence in U.S. journalism, literature, and music [Early 20thC. Named after Joseph PULITZER.]

pull /pŏŏl/ *v.* (**pulls, pulling, pulled**) **1.** *vti.* **DRAW A PHYSICAL OBJECT NEARER** to apply force to a physical object so as to draw or tend to draw it towards the force's origin **2.** *vt.* **REMOVE STH FORCIBLY** to remove or extract sth by exerting force **3.** *vt.* **DRAW A LOAD** to draw a load, e.g. a trailer or plough **4.** *vti.* **TUG** to tug at or jerk sth or sb **5.** *vt.* MED **STRAIN AND DAMAGE A MUSCLE** to strain and damage a muscle, ligament, or tendon **6.** *vt.* **ATTRACT CROWD** to draw a large number of people (*informal*) **7.** *vt.* **TAKE OUT A WEAPON** to take out a weapon in readiness to attack sb (*informal*) **8.** *vt.* **APPLY FORCE TO A TRIGGER** to apply force to a trigger, lever, or switch so as to operate a weapon or machine **9.** *vt.* **OPEN OR CLOSE CURTAINS** to open or close curtains or window coverings **10.** *vti.* **TEAR** to tear or rip sth **11.** *vt.* **STRETCH STH** to stretch sth elastic **12.** *vt.* **DO STH UNDERHAND** to do sth undesirable or despicable in an underhand way (*informal*) ○ *I just know they're trying to pull something, but I don't know what.* **13.** *vti.* CARS **MANOEUVRE A VEHICLE** to manoeuvre a vehicle in a particular direction **14.** *vi.* CARS **DRIFT TO ONE SIDE BECAUSE FAULTY** to drift to one side or the other, usually because of a fault (*refers to motor vehicles or their steering*) ○ *My car pulls to the left.* **15.** *vi.* CARS **PRODUCE SUFFICIENT DRIVING POWER** to produce sufficient driving power to move a vehicle **16.** *vi.* **INTAKE DEEPLY** to inhale deeply when smoking, or take a deep gulp at a drink **17.** *vt.* BEVERAGES **POUR DRINK FROM CASK** to extract beer or a similar drink from a cask by operating a handle attached to a pump **18.** *vt.* COMM, PUBL **REMOVE STH FROM CIRCULATION** to remove sth from circulation, or prevent it from ever getting into circulation (*informal*) **19.** *vti.* **ATTRACT SEXUAL PARTNER** to meet and succeed in attracting sb, often so as to have a casual and usually brief sexual relationship (*slang*) ○ *Did you pull at the party?* **20.** *vt.* PRINTING **MAKE A PRINTING PROOF** to make a proof from type **21.** *vt.* HORSERACING **REIN A**

HORSE BACK to rein in a horse, especially so as to prevent it from winning a race **22.** vt. **SPORTS HIT A BALL TOO FAR TO THE SIDE** to hit a ball farther left for a right-handed player or right for a left-handed player than intended ■ n. **1. PULLING OR BEING PULLED** the pulling of sb or sth, or an instance of being pulled **2. PULLING FORCE** the physical force involved in the action of pulling **3. SUSTAINED EFFORT** a sustained effort, especially under difficult circumstances **4. INFLUENCE** special influence, typically because of personal position within an organization or society, or personal connection with an individual (informal) **5. POWER TO ATTRACT** the ability or power to attract an audience or supporters (informal) **6. STH USED FOR PULLING** sth such as a knob, handle, or tab used for pulling (often used in combination) **7. DEEP INHALING OR GULP** the inhaling or drinking of sth deeply **8.** PRINTING **PRINTING PROOF** a proof made from type **9.** HORSERACING **RESTRAINT OF A HORSE** the restraining of a horse by its rider, especially to keep it from winning **10. SPORTS PULLING OF A BALL** the pulling of a ball, or a ball that is pulled **11.** ARMS **RESISTANCE IN A FIRING MECHANISM** the amount of resistance in a firing mechanism such as a trigger or bowstring [Old English pullian, originally 'to pluck'] — **puller** n.

─── **WORD KEY: SYNONYMS** ───
pull, drag, draw, haul, tow, tug, yank
CORE MEANING: move sth towards you or in the same direction as you
pull a general word meaning to move sth towards you or in the same direction as you; **drag** to pull sth with laborious effort, caused by the weight of the object or the type of surface it is being moved across; **draw** to pull sth with a smooth movement; **haul** to pull sth with a steady strong movement, often involving strenuous effort; **tow** to pull sth along behind by means of a rope; **tug** to pull sth with brief, energetic, or violent movements performed intermittently, without necessarily producing much movement in the object; **yank** an informal word meaning to pull sth with a single strong movement.

pull about vt. to treat sb or sth roughly or brutally
pull ahead vi. to move in front of or gain a lead over sb or sth moving in the same direction
pull away vi. **1. MOVE AWAY** to move away from sb or sth **2. DRAW BACK** to draw back from sb or sth, either physically or emotionally
pull back vti. to withdraw, or make people, especially troops, withdraw
pull down vt. **1. DEMOLISH STH** to destroy or demolish sth, especially a building **2. REDUCE STH TO A LOWER LEVEL** to reduce sth such as a price to a lower level or value **3. DECREASE SB'S WELL-BEING** to have a detrimental effect on sb's health or mental well-being **4.** US **EARN AN AMOUNT** to earn a particular amount of money (slang) **5.** COMPUT **MAKE A MENU APPEAR** to make a menu appear on a computer screen by clicking on its heading
pull for vt. US to hope that sb or sth will succeed in an endeavour
pull in v. **1.** vi. TRANSP **ARRIVE** to arrive and stop, usually at a station **2.** vti. = **pull over** v. **3.** vi. **EARN AMOUNT** to earn a particular amount of money (informal) **4.** vt. **ARREST SB** to arrest sb, or take sb in to the police station for questioning (slang)
pull off vt. to accomplish or arrange sth despite difficulties (informal)

─── **WORD KEY: SYNONYMS** ───
See Synonyms at **accomplish**.

pull on vt. to put on clothing or an item of clothing, especially in haste
pull out v. **1.** vti. TRANSP **MANOEUVRE INTO THE TRAFFIC FLOW** to drive a vehicle away from the side of a road, e.g. to join a flow of traffic **2.** vi. TRANSP **MANOEUVRE A VEHICLE BEFORE OVERTAKING** to drive a vehicle out from behind another vehicle so as to overtake **3.** vi. TRANSP **DEPART** to depart from a station or stopping place **4.** vti. **RETREAT** to retreat or cause sb to retreat ○ the army is pulling out **5.** vi. **WITHDRAW** to withdraw from an obligation or commitment ○ they are threatening to pull out of the deal **6.** vti. AIR **LEVEL OUT AN AIRCRAFT** to level out or make an aircraft level out from a dive
pull over vti. to drive a vehicle to the side of a road and stop, or force the driver of a vehicle to do this
pull through vti. to recover or help sb recover from a period of illness or difficulties

pull together v. **1.** vi. **WORK TOGETHER** to cooperate, collaborate, or otherwise work together **2.** vr. **RECOVER COMPOSURE** to recover your composure or self-control (informal)
pull up v. **1.** vi. TRANSP **STOP SOMEWHERE** to arrive and stop at a place **2.** vt. **TELL SB OFF** to scold or reprimand sb sharply **3.** vi. **CATCH UP IN A RACE** to move into a closer or level position with sb, e.g. in a race
pullback /pŏŏl bak/ n. **1. ACT OF PULLING BACK** an act or the process of pulling back, especially a withdrawal of troops **2. DEVICE FOR PULLING BACK** a device for holding, restraining, or drawing sth back
pull-down adj. **MADE TO APPEAR ON A COMPUTER SCREEN** used to describe a menu or other screen item that can be made to appear on a computer screen by clicking on its heading ■ n. **PULL-DOWN ITEM** a pull-down feature on a computer screen
pulled threadwork n. an embroidery technique in which tight stitches are used to draw some threads together and separate others, thereby forming lacy patterns
pullet /pŏŏl it/ n. a young female chicken, especially one that has not started to lay eggs [14thC. Via French poulet, literally 'little hen', from poule 'hen', from, ultimately, Latin pullus 'young animal' (source of English pony).]

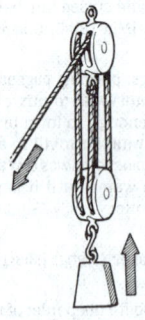
Pulley

pulley /pŏŏl i/ (plural -leys) n. **1. WHEEL WITH A GROOVED RIM** a mounted rotating wheel with a grooved rim over which a belt or chain can move to change the direction of a pulling force **2. SYSTEM OF PULLEYS** a system of pulleys along with a mounting block and tackle, used to improve leverage in lifting heavy weights **3.** Scotland **CLOTHES AIRER ON PULLEYS** in Scotland, a clothes airer that is raised to the ceiling by means of pulleys [14thC. Via Old French polie from, ultimately, Greek polos 'pole' (source of English pole). Ultimately from an Indo-European base meaning 'to revolve' (ancestor also of English wheel).]
pull-in n. a café catering for drivers, situated beside a road (dated)
Pullman /pŏŏlmən/ n. a comfortable train-carriage for sitting or sleeping in [Mid-19thC. Named after George M. PULLMAN.]
Pullman /pŏŏlmən/, **George Mortimer** (1831–97) US inventor and manufacturer. He designed the first modern railroad sleeping car (1863).
pullorum disease /pŏŏ láwrəm-/ n. a highly infectious disease of young poultry caused by the bacterium Salmonella pullorum, and marked by diarrhoea. It is often fatal to chicks. [Pullorum from modern Latin, 'of chickens']
pullout /pŏŏl owt/ n. **1.** PUBL **OBJECT FOR PULLING OUT** an object intended to be pulled out of a publication, e.g. a removable section of a magazine or a part of a book that folds out **2. WITHDRAWAL** a withdrawal from an obligation or other demanding situation **3. RETREAT** a retreat from a place or military involvement **4.** AIR **LEVELLING-OUT MANOEUVRE OF AIRCRAFT** an aircraft manoeuvre in which a dive changes to level flight
pullover /pŏŏl ōvər/ n. a garment, especially a jumper, put on by being pulled over the head
pull-tab n. US = **ring-pull**
pull-through n. a weighted cord with a cleaning rag at one end, dragged through the barrel of a rifle to clean it

pullulate /púllyŏŏ layt/ (-lates, -lating, -lated) vi. **1.** BOT **GERMINATE** to germinate or sprout (technical) **2.** ZOOL **BREED** to breed freely or rapidly (technical) **3.** TEEM to teem or swarm with sth (literary) [Early 17thC. From Latin pullulare, from, ultimately, pullus (see PULLET).] — **pullulation** /púllyŏŏ láysh'n/ n.
pull-up n. **1. PHYSICAL EXERCISE** a physical exercise in which the hands are placed on an overhead horizontal bar, and the body is lifted by pulling upwards with the arms **2.** = **pull-in** (dated)
pulmonary /púlmənəri, pŏŏl-/ adj. **1.** MED **RELATING TO LUNGS** concerning, affecting, or associated with the lungs **2.** ZOOL = **pulmonate** adj. **1** [Early 18thC. From Latin pulmonarius, from Latin pulmo 'lung'. Ultimately from an Indo-European base meaning 'to flow', which is also the ancestor of English flow and pneumonia.]
pulmonary artery n. either of the two arteries that carry blood in need of oxygen from the right side of the heart to the lungs
pulmonary vein n. any of the four veins that carry oxygen-rich blood from the lungs to the left side of the heart
pulmonate /púlmənət, pŏŏl-/ adj. ZOOL **1. WITH LUNGS** with lungs or organs that function as lungs **2. WITH SAC LIKE LUNG** used to describe a mollusc that has a sac functioning as a lung ■ n. ZOOL **MOLLUSC WITH LUNG SAC** a mollusc with a sac functioning as a lung. Examples include land snails, slugs, and many freshwater snails. Subclass: Pulmonata. [Mid-19thC. From modern Latin pulmonatus, from Latin pulmo (see PULMONARY).]
pulmonic /pul mónnik, pŏŏl-/ adj. = **pulmonary** adj. 1 [Mid-17thC. Directly or via French from modern Latin pulmonicus, from Latin pulmo (see PULMONARY).]
pulp /pulp/ n. **1.** BOT **SOFT FLESHY PLANT TISSUE** soft or fleshy plant tissue such as the inner part of a fruit or vegetable **2.** BOT **STEM PITH** the pith inside a plant stem **3. SOFT MATERIAL** a soft or soggy mass **4.** PAPER **CRUSHED WOOD FOR PAPER** crushed wood or other materials that are used to make paper **5.** PUBL **CHEAP BOOKS AND MAGAZINES** thrilling novels and magazines produced on cheap paper, especially crime, horror, or science fiction stories (often used before a noun) ○ a prize collection of classic pulp fiction **6.** DENT **INSIDE OF TOOTH** the sensitive tissue at the centre of a tooth, consisting of nerves and blood vessels **7.** MINING **PULVERIZED ORE** ore that has been mined and pulverized, especially when mixed with water ■ v. (pulps, pulping, pulped) **1.** vti. COOK, INDUST **CRUSH STH** to crush sth, or to be crushed, into pulp **2.** vt. COOK **REMOVE PULP FROM FRUIT** to remove the soft fleshy tissue from fruit or vegetables [14thC. From Latin pulpa, of unknown origin.]

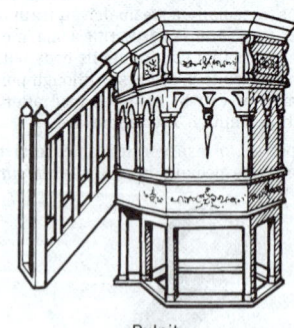
Pulpit

pulpit /pŏŏlpit/ n. **1. PLATFORM IN CHURCH** a raised platform or stand in a church that is used by the priest or minister for preaching or leading a service **2. CLERGY** the clergy considered as a group [14thC. Via late Latin from Latin pulpitum 'platform, scaffold', of unknown origin.]
pulpwood /púlp wŏŏd/ n. a soft wood such as aspen, pine, or spruce that is used to make paper
pulpy /púlpi/ (-ier, -iest) adj. soft, moist, and smooth in consistency —**pulpiness** n.
pulque /pŏŏlki, pŏŏl kay/ n. a thick alcoholic drink made in Mexico from the sap of the agave plant [Late 17thC. Via Mexican Spanish from Nahuatl puliúhki, literally 'decomposed'.]

pulsar /púl saar/ *n.* a small dense star that emits brief, intense bursts of visible radiation, radio waves, and X-rays, and is generally believed to be a rapidly rotating neutron star [Mid-20thC. Contraction of *pulsating star*, on the model of 'quasar'.]

pulsate /pul sáyt/ (**-sates, -sating, -sated**) *vi.* **1.** THROB to expand and contract with a strong regular beat **2.** VIBRATE to vibrate or quiver **3.** BE FULL OF ENERGY to be full of energy, bustling activity, and excitement ○ *The whole city is pulsating with excitement at this time of year.* **4.** PHYS VARY REPEATEDLY IN INTENSITY OR MAGNITUDE to vary in intensity or magnitude, especially in a repeated way [Late 18thC. From Latin *pulsare*, literally 'to beat repeatedly', from *pellere* (see PULSE[1]).]

pulsatile /púlssə tīl/, **pulsative** /-tiv/ *adj.* pulsating or vibrating rhythmically —**pulsatility** /púlssə tílləti/ *n.*

pulsation /pul sáysh'n/ *n.* **1.** PULSATING the action of pulsating **2.** PHYSIOL BEATING OF HEART the rhythmic change in volume that takes place in the heart or an artery **3.** ONE BEAT a single beat or pulse

pulsator /pul sáytər/ *n.* **1.** MACHINE THAT PULSATES a device or machine that pulsates **2.** MED, PHYS VIBRATING DEVICE a device that stimulates or maintains a rhythmic motion

pulsatory /púlssətəri, pul sáytəri/ *adj.* **1.** VIBRATING RHYTHMICALLY contracting and expanding or vibrating rhythmically **2.** OF PULSATION relating to or involving pulsation

pulse[1] /pulss/ *n.* **1.** PHYSIOL REGULAR BEAT OF BLOOD FLOW the regular expansion and contraction of an artery, caused by the heart pumping blood through the body. It can be felt through an artery that is near the surface, e.g. the one in the wrist on the same side as the thumb. **2.** PHYSIOL SINGLE BEAT OF BLOOD FLOW a single expansion and contraction of an artery, caused by a beat of the heart **3.** RHYTHMICAL BEAT a beat or throb, e.g. of a drum, or a series of rhythmical beats or throbs **4.** PHYS CHANGE OR REPEATING CHANGE IN MAGNITUDE a brief temporary change in a normally constant quantity, e.g. in a voltage, or a series of intermittent disturbances that are regular in form and frequency of occurrence **5.** CURRENT ATTITUDES the sentiments, opinions, or attitudes current among the public or a particular group ○ *a journalist who really has a finger on the pulse of society* **6.** VITALITY energy and excitement ○ *I love the pulse of city life.* ■ *vi.* (**pulses, pulsing, pulsed**) **1.** BEAT RHYTHMICALLY to move or throb with a strong regular rhythm **2.** PHYS UNDERGO BRIEF SUDDEN CHANGES to undergo a series of brief sudden changes in quantity, e.g. in voltage **3.** BE ENERGETIC to be full of energy and excitement ○ *an area pulsing with creative energy* [14thC. Via Old French from Latin *puls-*, past participle stem of *pellere* 'to beat' (source of English *push*). Ultimately from an Indo-European base that also produced English *anvil*.]

pulse[2] /pulss/ *n.* **1.** FOOD EDIBLE SEED an edible seed from a pod, e.g. a pea or bean, eaten fresh or dried **2.** PLANTS SEED-POD PLANT a plant such as the pea, the bean, alfalfa, or clover that has pods as fruits and roots that bear nodules containing nitrogen-fixing bacteria [13thC. Via Old French from Latin *puls* 'porridge' (source of English *poultice*), of uncertain origin: perhaps via Etruscan from Greek *poltos*.]

pulse code modulation *n.* a technique for electronic transmission of voice signals by sampling the amplitude of the signal and converting it to a coded digital form for transmission

pulsejet /púlss jet/ *n.* a ramjet engine in which air, admitted through moveable vanes, mixes with fuel in the combustion chamber. The resulting explosion forces the vanes shut, causing a pulsating thrust.

pulse modulation *n.* a way of transmitting information using a series of electrical pulses, with the duration, amplitude, or frequency of the pulses modified to carry the information

pulsometer /pul sómmitər/ *n.* a lightweight pistonless pump that works using the partial vacuum created by pulses of condensing steam being forced between two chambers [Mid-19thC. Coined from PULSE[1] + -METER.]

pulverable /púlvərəb'l/ *adj.* capable of being pulverized [Early 17thC. Formed from Latin *pulverare* 'to reduce to dust', from *pulvis* (see PULVERIZE).]

pulverize /púlvə rīz/ (**-izes, -izing, -ized**), **pulverise** (**-ises, -ising, -ised**) *v.* **1.** *vti.* CRUSH STH TO POWDER to crush or grind sth, or become crushed or ground, into a powder or dust **2.** *vt.* DEFEAT SB to subject an opponent to a crushing defeat (*informal*) ○ *We completely pulverized the opposition.* [15thC. From late Latin *pulverizare*, from Latin *pulver-*, the stem of *pulvis* 'powder, dust' (source of English *powder*).] —**pulverizable** *adj.* —**pulverization** /púlvər ī záysh'n/ *n.* —**pulverizer** /púlvə rīzər/ *n.*

pulvillus /pul vílləss/ (*plural* **-li** /pul vílī/) *n.* a small cushion or pad between the claws at the tip of an insect's foot, used to cling to a surface [Early 18thC. From Latin, literally 'small pad', from *pulvinus* 'cushion', of unknown origin.]

pulvinate /púlvi nayt/ *adj.* **1.** CUSHION-SHAPED shaped like a cushion **2.** SWELLING AT BASE with a swelling at the base

pulvinus /pul vínəss/ (*plural* **-ni** /-nī/) *n.* a swelling at the base of a leafstalk. Changes in its rigidity cause changes in the position of the leaf. [Mid-19thC. From Latin, 'cushion, pillow', of unknown origin.]

puma /pyoomə/ (*plural* **-mas** or **-ma**) *n.* a large tawny wild cat that is found from the mountains of Canada to the forests of South America. Latin name: *Felis concolor*. US term **mountain lion** [Late 18thC. Via Spanish from Quechua *púma*.]

pumice /púmmiss/ *n.* a very light porous rock formed from solidified lava, used in solid form as an abrasive and in powdered form as a polish [15thC. Via Old French from, ultimately, Latin *pumic-*, the stem of *pumex* 'foam', because of the stone's spongy appearance.] —**pumiceous** /pyoo míshəss/ *adj.*

pummel /púmm'l/ (**-mels, -melling, -melled**), **pommel** (**-mels, -melling, -melled**) *vt.* to hit sb or sth with repeated blows, especially using the fists [Mid-16thC. Alteration of POMMEL.]

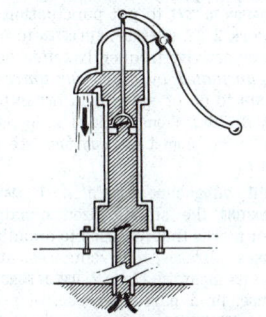

Pump: Cross-section of a water pump

pump[1] /pump/ *v.* (**pumps, pumping, pumped**) **1.** *vti.* SHIFT LIQUID OR GAS to force a liquid or gas to flow in a particular direction **2.** *vt.* MAKE STH MOVE UP AND DOWN to work a handle, lever, or other device energetically **3.** *vt.* ASK SB QUESTIONS to try to get information from sb by asking questions repeatedly and forcefully **4.** *vt.* MED FLUSH OUT SB'S STOMACH to flush out the contents of sb's stomach, usually to remove poison, drugs, or alcohol. A tube and a funnel are used to pour in water and allow the diluted stomach contents to run out. ■ *n.* **1.** MECH ENG DEVICE FOR SHIFTING LIQUID OR GAS a device that is used to raise, compress, or transfer liquids or gases and is operated by a piston or similar mechanism **2.** PHYSIOL WAY OF MOVING IONS OR MOLECULES a mechanism for the active movement of ions or molecules across a cell membrane [15thC]
pump out *vt.* **1.** PRODUCE A GREAT DEAL OF STH to produce sth continually and in large quantities ○ *a new radio station pumping out dance music 24 hours a day* **2.** REMOVE FLUID FROM STH to remove fluid from sth using a pump ○ *We had to pump out the boat again because it was leaking so badly.*
pump up *vt.* **1.** INFLATE STH to inflate sth such as a tyre or ball using a pump **2.** TURN STH UP to turn up the sound, especially of music, produced by amplifiers or speakers (*informal*) **3.** US GYM BUILD BODY MUSCLE to increase the mass of a muscle by bodybuilding techniques (*informal*)

pump[2] *n.* **1.** CANVAS SHOE WITH RUBBER SOLE a low flat canvas shoe with a rubber sole, worn especially by children for gym **2.** US = **court shoe 3.** US MAN'S

FORMAL SHOE a man's patent leather slip-on shoe worn with formal attire **4.** SOFT SHOE FOR DANCING a light, soft shoe for dancing [Mid-16thC. Origin uncertain.]

pumped storage *n.* in hydroelectric systems, a way of generating power during peak periods that involves pumping water up to a reservoir during periods of low demand and releasing it during peak periods

pumpernickel /púmpər nik'l, póom-/ *n.* a dark, dense, slightly sour bread that originated in Germany and is made from coarse rye flour [Mid-18thC. From German dialect, earlier 'lout', from *pumpern* 'to break wind' + *Nickel* 'goblin'.]

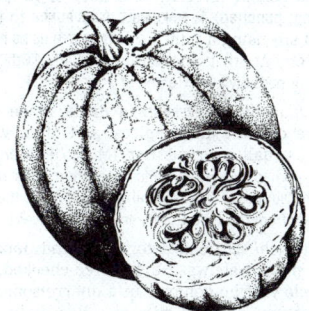

Pumpkin

pumpkin /púmpkin/ *n.* **1.** FOOD LARGE ORANGE FRUIT a round large fruit with a thick orange-skinned rind, pulpy flesh, and many seeds **2.** PLANTS PLANT THAT PUMPKINS GROW ON a trailing or climbing plant with yellow flowers and large round orange edible fruit. Genus: *Cucurbita*. [Late 17thC. Alteration of earlier *pumpion*, via obsolete French *pompon* from, ultimately, Latin *pepo* (see PEPO).]

pumpkinseed /púmpkin seed/ *n.* a common North American freshwater sunfish that has an olive-coloured upper body shading to yellow or orange on its belly, with one red spot on each gill cover. Latin name: *Lepomis gibbosus*. [Early 19thC. From its shape and its orange colour.]

pump priming *n.* **1.** ECON INVESTMENT TO STIMULATE REGIONAL GROWTH the use of investment to stimulate the economy in depressed regions and bring about self-sustaining growth **2.** PROCESS TO GET PUMP WORKING the process or act of making a pump work more effectively by pouring fluid into it as it starts up

pump room *n.* a building or room at a spa where mineral water can be drunk

pun /pun/ *n.* PLAY ON WORDS a humorous use of words that involves a word or phrase that has more than one possible meaning ■ *vi.* (**puns, punning, punned**) USE PLAY ON WORDS to make a pun or use puns [Mid-17thC. Origin uncertain: perhaps a shortening of obsolete *pundigrion*, from Italian *puntiglio* (see PUNCTILIOUS).] —**punner** *n.*

puna /poonə/ *n.* **1.** MED = **altitude sickness 2.** GEOG PLATEAU IN ANDES a cold dry flat treeless area at a high altitude in the Andes [Early 17thC. Via American Spanish from Quechua.]

Puncak Jaya /poon chaak jaá yaa/ the highest mountain in Indonesia, on the western half of the island of New Guinea, in the Surdiman Range. Height: 5,030 m/16,503 ft.

punch[1] /punch/ *vt.* (**punches, punching, punched**) **1.** HIT SB WITH FIST to hit sb or sth with the fist **2.** PRESS BUTTON to press a key or button on a computer keyboard or some other device with a quick thrusting movement of the finger ○ *Punch the return key.* **3.** US POKE STH to poke or prod sth ○ *He punched the pile of debris with a stick to see what was under it.* **4.** US, Can AGRIC HERD CATTLE to herd cattle on horseback **5.** Aus PASS BALL in Australian Rules football, to pass the ball by punching it to another player ■ *n.* **1.** BLOW WITH FIST a blow with the fist **2.** VIGOUR drive, energy, or power that livens or invigorates sth ○ *performance lacked that punch* **3.** Aus FOOTBALL PASS in Australian Rules football, a pass made by punching the ball to another player [14thC. From Old French *poinsonner* 'to prick', from *poinson, poinchon* (see PUNCHEON[2]).] ◇ **pack a punch** to be very powerful or strong (*informal*) ◇ **not pull your punches, pull no punches, not pull any punches** to use as much force and energy as necessary or possible to attain a goal or convey a message ◇ **roll with the punches** to adapt easily to a difficult situation (*informal*)

punch in *vt.* COMPUT to enter information into a computer using the keyboard

punch[2] /punch/ *n.* **1. TOOL FOR MAKING HOLES** a tool used to make holes in sth **2. STAMPING TOOL** a tool that is hit to stamp a design on sth or to cut sth to a particular shape **3. STAMPING OR CUTTING PART OF PUNCH** the die or solid part of a punch, containing the stamping or cutting tool **4. TOOL FOR DRIVING BOLTS OUT** a tool used to knock a bolt or rivet out of a hole ■ *vt.* **(punches, punching, punched) 1. MAKE HOLE USING PUNCH** to make a hole in sth using a punch **2. STAMP STH USING PUNCH** to stamp or cut sth using a punch [Early 16thC. Origin uncertain: possibly a shortening of PUNCHEON[1].]

punch[3] /punch/ *n.* BEVERAGES a drink made with a mixture of fruit juice, spices, and often wine or spirits, usually served hot [Mid-17thC. Origin uncertain: perhaps via Hindi *pañc-* 'five' from Sanskrit *pañca* (from the supposed five original ingredients of the drink); ultimately from the Indo-European word for 'five'.]

Punch /punch/ *n.* a character from traditional children's puppet shows. He is a red-cheeked, hook-nosed clown who behaves in a quarrelsome or aggressive manner. His wife is called Judy. ◊ **Punchinello** [Late 17thC. Shortening of PUNCHINELLO.] ◇ **pleased as Punch** extremely pleased (*informal*)

Punch and Judy /púnch ən jóodi/, **Punch-and-Judy, Punch-and-Judy show** *n.* a comic children's puppet show featuring Punch and Judy, a quarrelsome couple, together with a number of other standard characters. The show is often used as a belittling image of confrontation, e.g. when referring to politics.

punchbag /púnch bag/ *n.* a large heavy bag, usually suspended from a rope, used by boxers to improve their punching skills. US term **punching bag**

punchball /púnch bawl/ *n.* a large heavy ball on a stand, used for training or exercise, especially by boxers

punchboard /púnch bawrd/ *n.* a board with small holes, each containing a slip of paper. Players buy a chance to punch out a slip to see if they have won a prize.

punchbowl /púnch bōl/ *n.* **1. BOWL FOR SERVING PUNCH** a large bowl for serving punch, often with a matching ladle and cups **2.** GEOG **HOLLOW IN GROUND** a bowl-shaped hollow found on hills or mountains

punch card, punched card *n.* a card with patterns of holes punched in it, used to store information in early computers and telex machines

punch-drunk *adj.* **1. DAZED BY EVENTS** dazed or confused by sth such as a bad experience (*informal*) **2.** BOXING **DISORIENTATED BY PUNCHES** showing signs of confusion and disorientation as a result of brain damage caused by blows to the head

punched card *n.* = **punch card**

punched tape *n.* a strip of paper tape with patterns of holes punched in it, used to store information in early computers and telex machines

puncheon[1] /púnchən, púnshən/ *n.* **1. LARGE CASK** a large cask containing between 70 and 100 gallons **2.** MEASURE **UNIT OF CAPACITY** a unit of capacity, equal to between 70 and 100 gallons [15thC. From Old French *poinçon, poinchon*, of uncertain origin: possibly the same word as PUNCHEON[2].]

puncheon[2] /púnchən, púnshən/ *n.* CONSTR a short upright piece of wood used for structural framing [15thC. Via Old French *poinchon* from, ultimately, Latin *punct-*, the past participle stem of *pungere* (see PUNGENT).]

Punchinello /púnchi néllō/ (*plural* **-los**) *n.* **1.** THEATRE **ITALIAN PUPPET CHARACTER** a short character who appears in Italian puppet and clown shows and is probably the source of Punch **2. LUDICROUS PERSON** sb who is considered a buffoon [Mid-17thC. From Italian dialect *Pollecinella*, of uncertain origin: perhaps via *pollecena* 'turkey pullet', from, ultimately, Latin *pullus* (see PULLET); from the resemblance of his nose to a turkey's beak.]

punching bag *n.* *US* = **punchbag**

punch line *n.* the last part of a joke or funny story that delivers the meaning and the bulk of the humour [From PUNCH[1]]

punch-up *n.* a fist-fight or brawl (*informal*)

punchy /púnchi/ (**-ier, -iest**) *adj.* (*informal*) **1. EFFECTIVE** forceful and concise ○ *What we need is a good punchy slogan.* **2. PUNCH-DRUNK** punch-drunk [Early 20thC. Formed from PUNCH[1].] —**punchily** *adv.* —**punchiness** *n.*

punctate /púngk tayt/ *adj.* with tiny spots, holes, or dents ○ *a punctate leaf* [Mid-17thC. Formed from Latin *punctum* (see POINT).] —**punctation** /pungk táysh'n/ *n.*

punctilio /pungk tílli ō/ (*plural* **-os**) *n.* (*formal*) **1. OBSERVANCE OF ETIQUETTE** strict adherence to even the finest points of etiquette **2. POINT OF ETIQUETTE** a very fine point of etiquette [Late 16thC. Via obsolete Italian *puntiglio* and Spanish *puntillo*, literally 'small point', from, ultimately, Latin *punctum* (see POINT).]

punctilious /pungk tílli əss/ *adj.* **1. CAREFUL ABOUT CORRECT BEHAVIOUR** very careful about the conventions of correct behaviour and etiquette ○ *a courteous, punctilious manner* **2. FASTIDIOUS** showing great care in small details ○ *a punctilious execution of a complex design* [Mid-17thC. From French *pointilleux*, from *pointille* 'small point', from *pointe*.] —**punctiliously** *adv.* —**punctiliousness** *n.*

WORD KEY: SYNONYMS

See Synonyms at *careful*.

punctual /púngkchoo əl/ *adj.* **1. KEEPING TO ARRANGED TIME** arriving or taking place at the arranged time ○ *a punctual start to a meeting* **2.** MATH **OF POINT IN SPACE** relating to or with the properties of a point in space [14thC. From medieval Latin *punctualis*, from Latin *punctum* (see POINT).] —**punctuality** /púngkchoo állәti/ *n.* —**punctually** /púngkchoo əli/ *adv.*

punctuate /púngktyoo ayt/ (**-ates, -ating, -ated**) *v.* **1.** *vti.* **ADD PUNCTUATION TO TEXT** to put punctuation marks in written work **2.** *vt.* **INTERRUPT STH OFTEN** to interrupt a situation or activity frequently (*often passive*) ○ *a meeting punctuated by humorous anecdotes* **3.** *vt.* **EMPHASIZE STH** to do or say sth in order to add emphasis [Mid-17thC. From medieval Latin *punctuare* 'to mark with points', from Latin *punctum* (see POINT).] —**punctuator** *n.*

punctuation /púngkchoo áysh'n/ *n.* **1. MARKS USED TO ORGANIZE WRITING** the standardized nonalphabetical symbols or marks that are used to organize writing into clauses, phrases, and sentences, and in this way make its meaning clear **2. USE OF PUNCTUATION** the general use, or a particular use, of punctuation marks **3. ACT OF PUNCTUATING WRITING** the act of punctuating writing, or an occasion during which writing is punctuated

punctuation mark *n.* a symbol, e.g. a comma, full stop, or question mark, that is used to organize writing

puncture /púngkchər/ *n.* **SMALL HOLE** a small hole or wound made by a sharp object ■ *v.* **(-tures, -turing, -tured) 1.** *vti.* **MAKE OR GET HOLE** to sustain or cause a small hole or wound in sth such as a tyre or the skin **2.** *vt.* **RUIN SB'S CONFIDENCE** to rapidly reduce or destroy sb's confidence, arrogance, or conviction ○ *The interview punctured his self-esteem.* [14thC. From Latin *punctura*, from *punct-*, the past participle stem of *pungere* 'to prick' (see PUNGENT).] —**puncturable** *adj.* —**puncturer** *n.*

pundit /púndit/ *n.* **1. SB WHO EXPRESSES OPINION** sb who acts as a critic or authority on a particular subject, especially in the media ○ *The election results threw the political pundits into confusion.* **2.** = **pandit 3. SB WISE** sb with knowledge and wisdom [Late 17thC. Via Hindi *paṇḍit* from Sanskrit *paṇḍita-* 'learned', of uncertain origin.]

Pune /póonə/ city in western India, in Maharashtra State. It is the administrative headquarters of Pune district. Population: 1,567,000 (1991).

pung /pung/ *n. Can, New England* a low one-horse sleigh shaped like a box [Early 19thC. Shortening of *tom pung*, from an Algonquian word.]

pungent /púnjənt/ *adj.* **1. STRONG-SMELLING OR STRONG-TASTING** with a strong smell or powerfully sharp or bitter taste **2. CAUSTIC AND POINTED** expressed in or showing a witty and biting manner ○ *pungent observations about government corruption* **3.** BIOL **SHARP AND POINTED** used to describe a plant or animal part that ends in a sharp point ○ *a plant with elongated pungent leaves* [Late 16thC. From Latin *pungent-*, the present participle stem of *pungere* 'to prick, sting' (source of English *point, puncture,* and *poignant*).] —**pungency** *n.* —**pungently** *adv.*

Punic /pyóonik/ *adj.* **CARTHAGINIAN** relating to the ancient Carthaginians, Carthage, or the Carthaginian language. Carthage was eventually destroyed by the Roman Empire following the three Punic Wars, fought in 264–261 BC, 218–201 BC, and 149–146 BC. ■ *n.* **CARTHAGINIAN LANGUAGE** the Semitic language of ancient Carthage, which was related to Phoenician [15thC. Via Latin *Punicus* from, ultimately, Greek *Phoinix* 'Phoenician'.]

punish /púnnish/ (**-ishes, -ishing, -ished**) *v.* **1.** *vti.* **MAKE SB UNDERGO A PENALTY** to subject sb to a penalty for doing sth wrong **2.** *vt.* **IMPOSE CRIMINAL PENALTY** to respond to a crime or other wrong act by imposing a penalty (*often passive*) ○ *Any infringement of the rules will be punished by a fine.* **3.** *vt.* **TREAT SB OR STH HARSHLY** to treat sb or sth harshly, causing damage or pain ○ *Lopez punished the champ with some powerful blows to the body.* **4.** *vt.* **TREAT SB UNFAIRLY** to treat sb unfairly or discriminate against sb **5.** *vt.* **EAT OR DRINK STH** to eat or drink sth quickly and enthusiastically (*informal*) ○ *The guests were really punishing the red wine.* [14thC. Via Old French *puniss-*, the stem of *punir*, from Latin *punire*, from *poena* (see PENAL).] —**punisher** *n.*

punishable /púnnishəb'l/ *adj.* leading to or liable to punishment ○ *a punishable offence* —**punishability** /púnnishə bílləti/ *n.*

punishing /púnnishing/ *adj.* very demanding, either physically or mentally. ◊ **punitive** —**punishingly** *adv.*

punishment /púnnishmənt/ *n.* **1. ACT OF PUNISHING** the act or an instance of punishing **2. PENALTY FOR DOING STH WRONG** a penalty that is imposed on sb for wrongdoing **3. ROUGH USE** rough treatment or heavy use ○ *a sturdy car that can take a lot of punishment*

punitive /pyóonətiv/, **punitory** /pyóonitəri/ *adj.* **1. OF OR AS PUNISHMENT** relating to, done as, or imposed as a punishment ○ *punitive air strikes* **2. CREATING BURDEN** causing great difficulty or hardship [Early 17thC. From medieval Latin *punitivus*, from Latin *punit-*, the past participle stem of *punire* (see PUNISH).] —**punitively** *adv.* —**punitiveness** *n.*

punitive damages *npl.* damages that are awarded by a court to punish the defendant rather than to compensate the victim

punitory *adj.* = **punitive**

Punjab /pun jaáb/ **1.** state in northern India, bordering Pakistan on the west. Capital: Chandigarh. Population: 21,695,000 (1994). Area: 50,362 sq. km/19,445 sq. mi. **2.** province of eastern Pakistan. Capital: Lahore. Population: 50,460,000 (1983). Area: 206,014 sq. km/79,542 sq. mi.

Punjabi /pun jaábi/, **Panjabi** *adj.* PEOPLES, LANG **OF PUNJAB** relating to or typical of Punjab, or its people or culture ■ *n.* **1.** PEOPLES **SB FROM PUNJAB** sb who was born or lives in the Punjab **2.** LANG **LANGUAGE OF PUNJAB** the official language of Punjab. Punjabi is an Indo-European language belonging to the Indo-Iranian family. It is spoken by about 70 million people, and is the language in which the Sikh scriptures are written. [Early 19thC. From Urdu *Panjābī*, from *Panjāb* 'Punjab', from Sanskrit *pañca āpas* 'five rivers'.]

punk /pungk/ *n.* **1. YOUTH MOVEMENT** a youth movement of the late 1970s, characterized by loud aggressive rock music, confrontational attitudes, body piercing, and unconventional hairstyles, makeup, and clothing **2. SB BELONGING TO PUNK MOVEMENT** a member of the punk movement **3.** = **punk rock 4.** *US* **OFFENSIVE TERM** an offensive term referring to a young man regarded as worthless, lazy, or arrogant (*insult*) **5. PROSTITUTE** a prostitute (*archaic*) **6. DRIED WOOD** dried or decayed wood used as tinder (*archaic*) ■ *adj.* **NO GOOD** inferior in quality or condition (*informal*) [Late 17thC. Originally 'rotten wood used as tinder', of uncertain origin: perhaps from Algonquian (Delaware) *ponk*, literally 'living ashes'.]

punka /púngkə/, **punkah** n. a large fan used in India, consisting of palm leaves or a large cloth-covered frame suspended from the ceiling and operated by a servant [Early 17thC. Via Hindi *paṅkhā* from Sanskrit *pakṣakaḥ*, from *pakṣaḥ* 'wing'.]

punkie /púngki/, **punky** (*plural* **-ies**) n. US = **biting midge** [Mid-18thC. Via assumed New York Dutch *punkje* from Delaware *pónkwas* 'dust, ashes'.]

punk rock n. fast loud rock music often with confrontational lyrics that characterized the punk movement —**punk rocker** n.

punnet /púnnit/ n. a small, light, rectangular basket or tray in which fruits such as strawberries or raspberries are often sold [Early 19thC. Origin uncertain: perhaps literally 'small pound', formed from a dialectal variant of POUND[1].]

punster /púnstər/ n. sb who frequently makes puns

Punt

punt[1] /punt/ n. FLAT-BOTTOMED BOAT a narrow, open boat with square ends that has a flat bottom and is propelled using a long pole ■ v. (**punts, punting, punted**) **1.** vi. GO IN PUNT to travel in a punt **2.** vti. BOATS POLE PUNT to propel a punt using a long pole [Pre-12thC. From Latin *ponto* (see PONTOON).] —**punter** n.

punt[2] /punt/ vti. SPORTS KICK BALL to drop a ball and then kick it before it hits the ground ■ n. SPORTS KICK a kick in which sb drops a ball and kicks it before it hits the ground [Mid-19thC. Origin uncertain: perhaps originally a variant of BUNT[1].] —**punter** n.

punt[3] /punt/ n. BET PLACED WITH A BOOKMAKER a bet or gamble, especially one placed with a bookmaker (*informal*) ■ vti. (**punts, punting, punted**) GAMBLE to bet or gamble, especially with a bookmaker [Early 18thC. From French *ponter*, of uncertain origin.]

punt[4] /punt/ n. MONEY **1.** IRISH UNIT OF CURRENCY unit of currency in the Republic of Ireland. See table at **currency 2.** COIN WORTH A PUNT a coin worth a punt [Late 20thC. From Irish *púnt*.]

punt[5] /punt/ n. WINE the indentation in the bottom of a champagne or wine bottle [Mid-19thC. Origin uncertain: perhaps from PUNTY, or from French *pontil* (see PONTIL).]

Punta Arenas /póonta ə ráynəss/ city on the Strait of Magellan in southern Chile. It is one of the southernmost cities in the world. Population: 109,110 (1992).

punter /púntər/ n. (*informal*) **1.** CUSTOMER an ordinary member of the public, especially a customer or a member of an audience ○ *Give the punters what they want, that's my motto.* **2.** GAMBLER sb who bets money on sth **3.** PROSTITUTE'S CLIENT a prostitute's client [Early 18thC. Formed from PUNT[3]; the word's meaning developed from 'gambler' to 'victim of a swindle'.]

punty /púnti/ n. (*plural* **-ties**) n. a long metal rod on which molten glass is turned and worked during the glass blowing process [Mid-17thC. From French *pontil* (see PONTIL).]

puny /pyóoni/ (**-nier, -niest**) adj. **1.** SMALL AND WEAK very small or thin and weak **2.** INADEQUATE less than is required to be effective ○ *a puny attempt at an apology* [Late 16thC. Anglicization of puisne.] —**punily** adv. —**puniness** n.

pup /pup/ n. **1.** ZOOL YOUNG DOG a dog under a year old **2.** ZOOL YOUNG ANIMAL a young animal of various species including mice, rats, and seals **3.** CONCEITED YOUTH an inexperienced or arrogant young person, especially a boy or young man ■ vi. (**pups, pupping, pupped**)

BEAR PUPS to give birth to pups [Late 16thC. Shortening of PUPPY.] ◇ **be sold a pup** to buy sth worthless or useless (*informal*)

pupa /pyóopə/ (*plural* **-pae** /-pee/ *or* **-pas**) n. an insect at the stage between a larva and an adult in complete metamorphosis, during which the insect is in a cocoon or case, stops feeding, and undergoes internal changes [Late 18thC. From Latin, 'girl, doll', feminine of *pupus* 'boy' (source of English *pupil*[1]).] —**pupal** adj.

puparium /pyoo páiri əm/ (*plural* **-a** /-ri ə/) n. the hard case that encloses the pupa of the housefly and various other insects while they develop into adults [Early 19thC. From modern Latin, formed from Latin *pupa* (see PUPA).]

pupate /pyoo páyt/ (**-pates, -pating, -pated**) vi. to develop from a larva into a pupa —**pupation** /pyoo páysh'n/ n.

pupil[1] /pyóop'l/ n. **1.** EDUC STUDENT a young student, taught at school or by a private teacher **2.** FOLLOWER OR STUDENT OF SB sb who is taught by or is influenced by the teachings of a particular person, usually an expert in a field ○ *a pupil of Jung* **3.** LAW TRAINEE BARRISTER sb who is training to become a barrister **4.** LAW CHILD IN CARE OF LEGAL GUARDIAN in Scottish law, a girl under 12 or a boy under 14 who is in the care of a legal guardian [14thC. From Latin *pupillus*, literally 'little boy', from *pupus* 'boy'.]

pupil[2] /pyóop'l/ n. ANAT the dark circular opening at the centre of the iris in the eye, where light enters the eye. The iris closes the pupil in bright light and opens it in dim light. [14thC. Via French *pupille* from Latin *pupilla*, literally 'little doll', from *pupa* (see PUPA); so called from the tiny image that you see when looking into another person's eye.]

pupillage /pyóopəlij/ n. **1.** BEING A STUDENT the state of being a pupil, or the period during which sb is a pupil (*formal*) **2.** LAW PERIOD TRAINEE BARRISTER SPENDS IN CHAMBERS in English law, the period of time that a trainee barrister spends working in the chambers of a member of the bar immediately before qualifying

pupillary[1] /pyóopələri/ adj. LAW relating to a pupil or a legal ward of a guardian

pupillary[2] adj. ANAT relating to or affecting the pupil of the eye

puppet /púppit/ n. **1.** ARTS MOVABLE DOLL a doll or figure representing a person or animal that is moved using the hands inside the figure or by moving rods, strings, or wires attached to it **2.** SB WHO CAN BE MANIPULATED a person, government, or organization whose actions are controlled by others [Mid-16thC. Variant of earlier *poppet*, of uncertain origin: possibly via Anglo-Norman *poppe* 'doll' from, ultimately, Latin *pupa* (source of English *pupa*).]

puppeteer /púppi teér/ n. sb who operates puppets or who gives puppet shows

puppetry /púppitri/ n. the art of making or operating puppets

Puppis /púppiss/ n. a constellation of the southern hemisphere lying partly in the Milky Way, located between Vela and Canis Major

puppy /púppi/ (*plural* **-pies**) n. **1.** YOUNG DOG a dog under a year old **2.** CONCEITED YOUTH an inexperienced or arrogant young person, especially a boy or young man (*informal*) [15thC. Origin uncertain: possibly via Old French *popée* 'doll, toy' from, ultimately, Latin *pupa*.] —**puppyhood** n. —**puppyish** adj.

puppy dog n. a dog under a year old, especially one kept as a pet

puppy fat n. the plumpness that some children develop when they are young but that disappears as they mature

puppy love n. the love or infatuation felt by adolescents

pup tent n. = shelter tent

Purana /poo ráanə/ (*plural* **-nas**) n. one of a group of sacred Hindu texts written in Sanskrit that recount the lives of deities and the creation, destruction, and recreation of the universe [Late 17thC. From Sanskrit *purāṇah*, from *purāṇa-* 'belonging to former times', from *purā* 'formerly'.] —**Puranic** /poo ráanik/ adj.

Purbach /púr bak/ n. a walled plain on the Moon having a noticeably hexagonal shape and ridges

on the floor. Located east of Mare Nubium, it is approximately 120 km/75 mi. across.

purblind /púr blīnd/ adj. **1.** OFFENSIVE TERM an offensive term meaning partly or completely unable to see (*offensive*) **2.** LACKING UNDERSTANDING slow or unwilling to understand (*formal*) [13thC. From PURE + BLIND.]

Purcell /pər séll/, **Henry** (1659–95) English composer. He wrote numerous instrumental and vocal pieces ranging from sacred to theatrical music. His works include the opera *Dido and Aeneas* (1689) and incidental music for *The Tempest* (1695).

purchasable /púrchəssəb'l/ adj. **1.** FOR SALE available to be bought **2.** CAPABLE OF BEING BRIBED willing to accept a bribe —**purchasability** /púrchəssə bílləti/ adj.

purchase /púrchəss/ v. (**-chases, -chasing, -chased**) **1.** vti. GET STH BY PAYING MONEY to buy sth using money or its equivalent **2.** vt. OBTAIN STH THROUGH EFFORT to obtain sth by hard work or sacrifice ○ *a victory purchased with great effort* **3.** vt. MOVE STH USING A LEVER to move, lift, or hold on to sth using a device such as a lever ■ n. **1.** ACT OF BUYING the act of buying sth **2.** STH BOUGHT sth that sb has bought **3.** HOLD a firm grip or hold on sth ○ *hands too slippery to get a purchase on the rock* **4.** ADVANTAGE influence, power, or another advantage that can be exercised ○ *an attempt to gain some purchase over his rivals* **5.** POWER GIVEN BY A LEVER a measure of the mechanical advantage given by a pulley or lever [13thC. From Anglo-Norman *purchacer* 'to pursue', literally 'to chase eagerly', from Old French *chacier* (see CHASE).] —**purchaser** n.

purchase ledger n. a record kept by a business of its accounts with other businesses from which it buys goods on credit

purchase tax n. UK a tax on nonessential consumer goods. It was replaced in the UK by value-added tax or VAT.

purchasing power n. **1.** ABILITY TO SPEND the ability to make purchases based on income and savings **2.** VALUE OF CURRENCY the value of a particular currency, measured in terms of the goods and services it can buy ○ *the purchasing power of the yen*

purdah /púrdə/ n. **1.** KEEPING WOMEN FROM PUBLIC VIEW the Hindu and Islamic custom of keeping women fully covered with clothing and apart from the rest of society **2.** SCREEN a screen or curtain used in Hindu communities to keep women out of view **3.** VEIL a veil worn by Hindu and Muslim women as part of purdah [Early 19thC. Via Urdu *pardah* 'veil' from Middle Persian *pardak*.]

pure /pyoor, pyawr/ (**purer, purest**) adj. **1.** WITHOUT ANOTHER SUBSTANCE not mixed with any other substance ○ *This jacket is pure wool.* **2.** FREE FROM CONTAMINATION clean and free from impurities ○ *The water from the spring is completely pure.* **3.** COMPLETE sheer or complete ○ *a look of pure terror* **4.** CHASTE virtuous and chaste (*literary*) **5.** CLEAR pleasingly clear and vivid (*refers to colour, sound, or light*) **6.** RELATING TO THEORY relating to theory rather than practical applications ○ *Opportunities for pure research are increasingly rare nowadays.* ◊ applied **7.** OF UNMIXED ANCESTRY with unmixed parentage or ancestry **8.** BIOL PRODUCED BY CONSTANT INBREEDING produced by continual inbreeding or self-fertilization and breeding true **9.** MUSIC, PHYS COMPOSED OF SINGLE FREQUENCY consisting of a single frequency without any overtones (*refers to sound*) ○ *a pure middle C* **10.** MUSIC WITHOUT DISCORD free of discord and in tune (*refers to a musical tone*) **11.** PHON PRONOUNCED WITH ONE UNCHANGING SOUND used to describe a vowel that is pronounced with a single unchanging sound **12.** PHON PRONOUNCED WITHOUT ANOTHER CONSONANT used to describe a consonant that is pronounced unaccompanied by any other consonant [13thC. Via French from Latin *purus* (source of English *purée*, *pour*, and *puritanical*).] —**pureness** n.

pureblood /pyóor blud, pyáwr-/, **pureblooded** /pyóor bludid, pyáwr-/ adj. with an ancestry that is exclusively of a particular type —**pureblood** n.

purebred /pyóor bred, pyáwr-/ adj. WITH ANCESTORS OF SAME BREED having ancestors that belong to the same breed or variety as a result of controlled breeding ○ *a purebred Arabian stallion* ■ n. STH PUREBRED a purebred plant or animal

pure democracy *n.* a form of democracy in which the people exercise direct power rather than electing representatives to govern on their behalf

purée /pyoόr ay, pyáwr ay/, **puree** *n.* **FOOD IN FORM OF PASTE** food that has been made into a thick moist paste by rubbing it through a sieve, mashing it, or blending it ■ *vti.* (**-rées, -réeing, -réed; -rees, -reeing, -reed**) **MAKE FOOD INTO PURÉE** to become a purée, or sieve, mash, or blend food into a purée ○ *Purée the vegetables and add them to the stock.* [Early 18thC. From French *purée*, from the feminine past participle of *purer* 'to squeeze out', literally 'to make pure', from Latin *purare*, from *purus* 'pure'.]

Pure Land Buddhism *n.* groups of Mahayana Buddhism that venerate the Buddha Amitabha, or Amida, as a compassionate saviour and promise rebirth in paradise, known as the Pure Land, as a reward for faith. These groups are commonest in East Asia, especially Japan and Korea. [*Pure Land* is a translation of Chinese *Qingtu*]

purely /pyoόrli, pyáwrli/ *adv.* **1. ENTIRELY** in a complete, entire, or total way ○ *It was a purely financial decision.* **2. MERELY** for the sole reason of ○ *surgery for purely cosmetic purposes* **3. WITH NOTHING ADDED** in a way that is free of any added substances or elements or of contaminants ○ *sheep that have been purely bred from the original stock* **4. INNOCENTLY** in a way that is innocent, pure, or chaste

purfle /púrf'l/ *n.* **ORNAMENTAL BORDER** an ornamental border on clothes or furniture, consisting of a ruffled or curved band ■ *vt.* (**-fles, -fling, -fled**) **DECORATE STH WITH PURFLE** to decorate clothes or furniture with a purfle [14thC. Via Old French *porfil* from, ultimately, assumed Vulgar Latin *profilare*, literally 'to spin forward', from Latin *filum* 'thread' (see **FILUM**).]

purgation /pur gáysh'n/ *n.* the act of purging or being purged, especially when freeing sb or being freed from guilt or sin (*literary*)

purgative /púrgətiv/ *n.* **SUBSTANCE FOR PURGING THE BOWELS** a drug or other substance that causes evacuation of the bowels (*dated or literary*) ■ *adj.* **EMPTYING THE BOWELS** acting as a purgative (*dated or literary*) —**purgatively** *adv.*

purgatorial /púrgə táwri əl/ *adj.* (*literary*) **1. LIKE PURGATORY** relating to or similar to purgatory **2. PURGING SB OF SIN** serving to rid sb of sin —**purgatorially** *adv.*

purgatory /púrgətəri/ *n.* **1. purgatory, Purgatory PLACE OF SUFFERING** in Roman Catholic doctrine, the place in which the souls remain until they have expiated their sins before they go to heaven **2. MISERABLE SITUATION** an extremely uncomfortable, painful, or unpleasant situation or experience ○ *the purgatory of lost love* [12thC. Via Old French *purgatoire* from, ultimately, Latin *purgare* 'to purify' (see **PURGE**).]

purge /purj/ *v.* (**purges, purging, purged**) **1.** *vt.* **GET RID OF OPPONENTS** to remove opponents or people considered undesirable from a state or organization **2.** *vt.* **REMOVE STH UNDESIRABLE** to get rid of sth undesirable, impure, or imperfect **3.** *vt.* **RELIG FREE SB FROM GUILT OR SIN** to make sb or sth pure and free from guilt, sin, or defilement (*formal*) ○ *purge a soul of its sins* **4.** *vi.* **PSYCHOL, MED VOMIT OR USE LAXATIVES** to rid the body of food by using laxatives or inducing vomiting **5.** *vt.* **COMPUT DELETE DATA** to delete unwanted or unneeded data from disk storage in a systematic fashion so as to remove all references to the data **6.** *vti.* **MED EMPTY THE BOWELS** to empty the bowels or cause sb to empty the bowels (*archaic*) ■ *n.* **1. GETTING RID OF OPPONENTS** the removal of opponents or people considered undesirable from a state or organization **2. GETTING RID OF STH UNDESIRABLE** the removal of sth unwanted, unneeded, imperfect, or impure **3. MED LAXATIVE SUBSTANCE** sth that acts as a laxative (*archaic*) [13thC. Via Old French *purgier* from Latin *purgare* 'to purify'.] —**purger** *n.*

puri /poόri/ (*plural* **-ri** or **-ris**), **poori** (*plural* **-ri** or **-ris**) *n.* a small piece of light, flat, unleavened Indian bread that is fried and served hot [Mid-20thC. Via Hindi *pūrī* from Sanskrit *pūrikā*.]

purification /pyoόrifi káysh'n, pyáwr-/ *n.* **1. PROCESS OF PURIFYING STH** the process of ridding sth of anything harmful, inferior, or unwanted **2. RELIG RITUAL CLEANS-ING** an act of purifying sb as part of a religious ceremony or ritual to remove guilt, sin, or un-

cleanness ○ *a ritual of purification carried out by the priests*

purificator /pyoόrifi kaytər, pyáwr-/ *n.* a linen cloth used in some Christian churches to wipe the chalice after the celebration of Communion —**purificatory** /pyoόrifi kaytəri, pyáwr-/ *adj.*

purify /pyoόri fī, pyáwr-/ (**-fies, -fying, -fied**) *v.* **1.** *vti.* **MAKE STH PURE** to rid sth or become rid of sth harmful, inferior, or unwanted ○ *We use special filters to purify the water.* **2.** *vt.* **RELIG MAKE SB SPIRITUALLY PURE** to free sb of sin, guilt, or uncleanness, e.g. in a ceremony or a ritual cleansing —**purifier** *n.*

Purim /poόrim, pyoόrim, poo reém/ *n.* a Jewish festival celebrated on the 14th day of Adar that commemorates the Jewish people's deliverance from Haman's plot to massacre them, as told in the Book of Esther. A lot was drawn, in Haman's presence, to decide the day and month of the massacre. [14thC. From Hebrew *pū'rīm*, literally 'lots', from *pūr* 'lot'.]

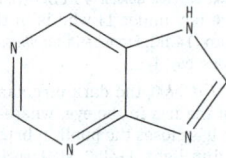

Purine

purine /pyoόr een, pyáwr-/ *n.* **1. CRYSTALLINE SOLID** a colourless crystalline solid that can be prepared from uric acid and is the parent compound of several biologically important substances. Formula: $C_5H_4N_4$. **2. DERIVATIVE FOUND IN RNA AND DNA** a biologically significant derivative of purine, especially either of the bases adenine and guanine, which are found in RNA and DNA [Late 19thC. From German *Purin*, formed from a blend of Latin *purus* 'pure' and modern Latin *uricum* 'uric acid'.]

purism /pyoόrizəm, pyáwr-/ *n.* insistence on the maintenance or observance of traditional standards in a field, especially in the use of language

purist /pyoόrist, pyáwr-/ *n.* sb who insists on maintaining sth in its traditional form —**puristic** /pyoor ístik, pyáw-/ *adj.* —**puristically** /-ístikli/ *adv.*

puritan /pyoόrit'n, pyáwrit'n/ *n.* **SB WITH STRICT MORAL CODE** sb who lives according to strict moral or religious principles, especially sb who regards pleasure as suspect ■ *adj.* = **puritanical** —**puritanism** *n.*

Puritan /pyoόrit'n, pyáwr-/ *n.* **PROTESTANT** a member of a group of Protestants in 16th- and 17th-century England and 17th-century America who believed in strict religious discipline and called for the simplification of acts of worship. The movement was an attempt to remove Roman Catholic influences from the Church of England. ■ *adj.* **OF PURITANS** relating to Puritans, their beliefs, or movement ○ *a Puritan form of worship* [Late 16thC. Formed from Latin *puritas* 'purity', from *purus* 'pure'.] —**Puritanism** *n.*

puritanical /pyoόri tánnik'l, pyáwr-/, **puritan** /-it'n/, **puritanic** /-itánnik/ *adj.* adhering to strict moral or religious principles —**puritanically** *adv.* —**puritanicalness** *n.*

purity /pyoόrəti, pyáwrəti/ (*plural* **-ties**) *n.* **1. FREEDOM FROM ADDED ELEMENTS** the absence, or degree of absence, of anything harmful, inferior, unwanted, or of a different type ○ *tests to establish the purity of the water in the river* **2. INNOCENCE** virtue and innocence ○ *the purity of young children* **3. LING CORRECTNESS** the observance of traditional standards of correctness in speech and writing **4. COLOUR SATURATION** the degree of saturation or lack of white in a colour **5. CLARITY** clarity of tone or sound

Purkinje cell /pur kínjee-/ *n.* one of the many densely-branching neurons found in the middle layer of the brain's cerebellar cortex [Late 19thC. Named after J.

E. *Purkinje* (1787–1869), the Bohemian physiologist who originally described the structure.]

purl¹ /purl/ *n.* **1. KNITTING STITCH IN KNITTING** a reverse plain knitting stitch, often combined with a plain stitch to create a ribbed effect. ◊ **knit 2. purl, pearl SEW GOLD OR SILVER THREAD** sewing thread that is made from gold or silver wire **3. purl, pearl SEW BORDER ON LACE OR BRAID** a decorative looped border sewn on lace or braid ■ *vti.* (**purls, purling, purled**) **KNITTING KNIT WITH PURL** to knit sth using a purl stitch. ◊ **knit** [14thC. Origin unknown.]

purl² /purl/ *vi.* (**purls, purling, purled**) **FLOW GENTLY** to flow with a soft murmuring sound, producing gentle ripples (*literary*) (*refers to rivers and streams*) ■ *n.* **GENTLE FLOW** the soft sound and gentle movement of a river or stream (*literary*) [15thC. Origin uncertain: probably from a Scandinavian source.]

purler /púrlər/ *n.* a headlong fall (*informal*) [Mid-20thC. Origin uncertain.]

purlieu /púr lyoo/ *n.* **1. OUTLYING DISTRICT** a district on the outskirts of a city or town **2. SHABBY AREA** an area or district, especially one that is old and poor (*formal*) ○ *the lowest slums and purlieus of our great towns* **3. FREQUENTED PLACE** a place that sb often visits (*formal*) **4. LAND ON EDGE OF ROYAL FOREST** land that once lay within the boundary of a royal forest and was later separated from it, but remained subject to royal laws on hunting ■ **purlieus** *npl.* **ENVIRONS** the outer regions or boundaries of a place (*formal*) ○ *the purlieus of the city* [15thC. Origin uncertain: probably an alteration (influenced by **LIEU**) of Anglo-Norman *puralee* 'king's trip around the borders', from *pur-* 'forth' + *aller* 'to go'.]

purlin /púrlin/ *n.* a horizontal roof beam that supports the rafters [15thC. Origin uncertain.]

purloin /pur lóyn/ (**-loins, -loining, -loined**) *vt.* to steal sth (*formal*) ○ *He purloined my watch when I visited him.* [14thC. From Anglo-Norman *purloigner*, literally 'to move far away', from Old French *loing* 'far', from Latin *longus* 'long' (see **LONGITUDE**).] —**purloiner** *n.*

—— **WORD KEY: SYNONYMS** ——
See Synonyms at *steal.*

purple /púrp'l/ *n.* **1. COLOURS COLOUR COMBINING RED AND BLUE** a dark colour that reflects very little light and that is formed as a pigment by combining red and blue **2. PURPLE OBJECT** an object, substance, or fabric that is purple in colour **3. CLOTHES ROBE IN COLOUR PURPLE** a cloth or robe in the colour purple that was formerly worn as a symbol of imperial, royal, or other high rank **4. IMPERIAL RANK** imperial power or high rank **5. CHR RANK OF CARDINAL OR BISHOP** the rank or office of a cardinal or a bishop **6. CHR BISHOPS** bishops regarded as a group ■ *adj.* **1. COLOURS OF A DARK RED-BLUE** of a dark colour that reflects very little light and that is formed as a pigment by combining red and blue **2. LITERAT ELABORATE OR EXAGGERATED** elaborate in style and containing too many literary effects ○ *purple prose* ■ *vti.* (**-ples, -pling, -pled**) **TURN STH PURPLE** to become or make sth become purple ○ *His eyes narrowed and his cheeks purpled.* [Pre-12thC. Alteration of Latin *purpura*, from Greek *porphura* 'shellfish yielding purple dye' (source of English *porphyry*).] —**purpleness** *n.* —**purplish** *adj.* —**purply** *adj.*

purple gallinule /-gálli nyool/ *n.* a water-loving bird with dark bluish-purple plumage and red legs. One species lives in the Mediterranean region, the other in North and South America. Genus: *Porphyrio*.

purpleheart /púrp'l haart/, **purple heart** *n.* **1. TREES TROPICAL S AMERICAN TREE** a tropical tree of South America with hard brownish wood that turns purple when it is exposed to air. Genus: *Peltogyne*. **2. INDUST, WOODWORK PURPLE WOOD** the hard decorative purplish wood of the purpleheart

purple heart *n.* a purple, heart-shaped amphetamine tablet (*slang dated*)

Purple Heart *n.* a decoration awarded to members of the US armed forces who have been wounded in action [From the silver heart and the purple ribbon from which it is suspended]

purple loosestrife *n.* a marsh plant with lance-shaped leaves and spikes of purple flowers. Latin name: *Lystrum salicaria.*

purple patch *n.* **1.** TIME OF GOOD LUCK a period of good luck or success (*informal*) **2. purple patch, purple passage** ELABORATE WRITING a section in a piece of writing that is very elaborate or contains too much imagery [Translation of Latin *purpureus pannus* in Horace; from the qualities of brilliance and ornateness ascribed to the colour purple]

purport *vti.* /pur páwrt/ (**-ports, -porting, -ported**) **1.** CLAIM TO BE STH to claim, seem, or profess to be sth specified ○ *The letter is purported to be by Napoleon.* **2.** INTEND STH to intend to do sth (*formal*) ○ *While this new measure provided money for research, it also purported to cut spending overall.* ■ *n.* /pər páwrt, púr pawrt/ (*formal*) **1.** SENSE the meaning or significance of sth ○ *The purport of the remarks was difficult to discern.* **2.** INTENT intention or purpose of sth ○ *The principal purport of his letter was to inform them that he would soon be leaving the country.* [15thC. Via Anglo-Norman *purporter*, literally 'to carry forward', from Latin *portare* 'to carry' (see PORT[1]).]

purported /pur páwrtid/ *adj.* supposed or claimed to be, but without any evidence or proof of it (*formal*) —**purportedly** *adv.*

purpose /púrpəss/ *n.* **1.** REASON FOR EXISTENCE the reason for which sth exists or for which it has been done or made ○ *the purpose of life* **2.** DESIRED EFFECT the goal or intended outcome of sth ○ *The purpose of the law is to control pollution.* **3.** DETERMINATION the desire or the resolve necessary to accomplish a goal ○ *You need to act with purpose.* ■ *vt.* (**-poses, -posing, -posed**) SET STH AS GOAL to intend or determine to do sth [13thC. From Old French *purpos*, from *purposer* 'to intend', literally 'to put forth', an alteration (influenced by *poser* 'to put') of Latin *proponere* (see PROPOSE).] ◇ **at cross purposes 1.** to be talking about different things and so be involved in a misunderstanding **2.** to have intentions that conflict with sb else's, when you should both be working together ◇ **on purpose** deliberately ◇ **to good purpose** successfully, or with good results (*formal*) ◇ **to no purpose** without success or achieving useful results (*formal*) ◇ **to the purpose** relevant

purpose-built *adj.* designed for a particular use or to meet specific needs ○ *a purpose-built swimming pool*

purposeful /púrpəssf'l/ *adj.* **1.** DETERMINED showing a clear determination ○ *She set off with a purposeful stride.* **2.** HAVING A GOAL having a definite purpose or aim ○ *purposeful activity* —**purposefully** *adv.* —**purposefulness** *n.*

purposeless /púrpəssləss/ *adj.* **1.** WITHOUT REASON lacking a reason ○ *animal behaviour that to human eyes seems entirely purposeless* **2.** WITHOUT PURPOSE lacking an aim or purpose ○ *walking about in a purposeless kind of way*

purposely /púrpəssli/ *adv.* deliberately or with an express purpose in mind ○ *They purposely humiliated me at the meeting.*

purposive /púrpəssiv/ *adj.* **1.** USEFUL having a use or purpose ○ *Most human activity is purposive.* **2.** DETERMINED showing determination ○ *She had a purposive air about her that morning.* —**purposively** *adv.* —**purposiveness** *n.*

purpura /púrpyŏŏrə/ *n.* a condition in which bleeding under the skin causes purplish blotches to appear on the skin [Mid-18thC. From Latin, 'purple' (see PURPLE).] —**purpuric** /pur pyŏŏrrik/ *adj.*

purpure /púrpyoor/ *n.* in heraldry, the colour purple [Pre-12thC. From Latin *purpura* 'purple', strengthened by Old French *purpre* (see PURPLE).]

purpurin /púrpyŏŏrin/ *n.* a reddish-orange crystalline compound used in the manufacture of dyes, as a stain for biological specimens, and as a reagent for the detection of boron. Formula: $C_{14}H_8O_5$.

purr /pur/ *n.* **1.** CAT'S LOW MURMURING NOISE the characteristic soft low murmuring noise that a cat makes when it seems to be contented **2.** PURRING SOUND a sound similar to the purr of a cat ○ *the purr of the engine* ■ *v.* (**purrs, purring, purred**) **1.** *vi.* EMIT PURR to emit a purr **2.** *vti.* SPEAK IN SOFT THROATY VOICE to speak, or say sth, in a soft throaty voice that suggests pleasure, contentment, or sensuality **3.** *vi.* MAKE LOW REGULAR MECHANICAL SOUND to make the soft low vibrating noise that a machine, especially an engine, makes when it is perfectly tuned and is running well [Early 17thC. An imitation of the sound of a cat.] —**purringly** *adv.*

purse /purss/ *n.* **1.** SMALL BAG FOR CARRYING PERSONAL MONEY a small bag holding personal money, often with separate compartments for coins and notes, carried in the pocket or kept inside a handbag or other bag **2.** *US* = **handbag 3.** PRIZE MONEY a sum of money offered as a prize, especially the total sum of money offered in prizes ○ *with a purse of over £20,000* **4.** AVAILABLE FUNDS an amount of money available to spend ○ *The legislators overestimated the size of the public purse.* ■ *vt.* (**purses, pursing, pursed**) DRAW LIPS TOGETHER AT SIDES to draw the lips together at the sides so that they wrinkle and form a circle, usually when deep in thought or to express disapproval [13thC. Alteration of late Latin *bursa*, variant of *byrsa*, from Greek *byrsa* 'hide' (see BURSA).] ◇ **you can't make a silk purse out of a sow's ear** used to emphasize the impossibility of making sth of superior quality from inferior materials or beginnings

purser /púrssər/ *n.* the officer on a merchant ship or commercial aircraft who is responsible for managing the money and who, on a passenger ship, is responsible for the well-being of the passengers

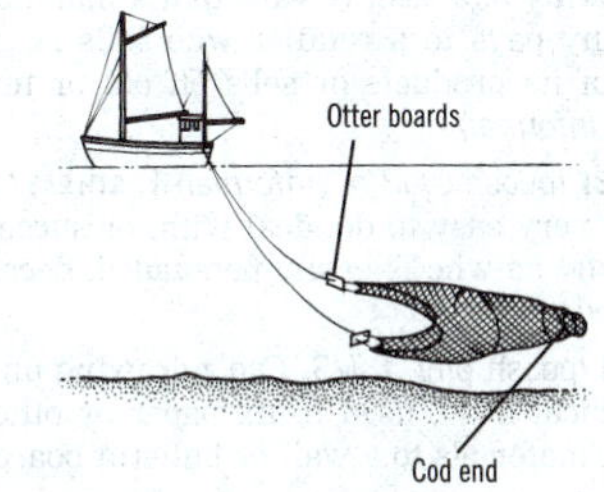

Purse seine

purse seine *n.* a large commercial fishing net pulled by two boats, with ends that are pulled together round a shoal of fish so that the net forms a pouch

purse strings *npl.* control over the money that is available to spend

purslane /púrsslən/ (*plural* **-lanes** *or* **-lane**) *n.* a trailing weed sometimes used in salad or cooked and served as a vegetable. Genus: *Portulaca.* [14thC. From Old French *porcelaine*, which was formed (by confusion with *porcelaine*; see PORCELAIN) from Latin *porcilaca*, from *portulaca*.]

pursuance /pər syŏŏ ənss/ *n.* the process of doing sth or carrying it out in the way that is expected or required (*formal*) ○ *in pursuance of our agreement*

pursuant /pər syŏŏ ənt/ *adj.* following in order to catch [Mid-16thC. From Old French *poursuiant*, present participle of *poursuir* (see PURSUE).] —**pursuantly** *adv.* ◇ **pursuant to** in accordance with (*formal*)

pursue /pər syŏŏ/ (**-sues, -suing, -sued**) *v.* **1.** *vti.* CHASE SB to follow or chase sb in order to catch, overtake, or attack him or her **2.** *vt.* BE EVER-PRESENT PROBLEM FOR SB to be an ongoing, persistent problem for a person or organization ○ *Poor investment decisions pursued the company.* **3.** *vt.* STRIVE FOR STH to try hard to achieve or obtain sth over a period of time **4.** *vt.* CONTINUE WITH STH to continue with sth or follow it up ○ *pursuing a number of lines of inquiry* **5.** *vt.* CARRY STH OUT to work at sth or carry it out ○ *pursuing his studies* **6.** *vt.* SEEK SB PERSISTENTLY FOR SEXUAL PARTNER to make persistent attempts to start a sexual relationship with sb **7.** *vt.* FOLLOW ROUTE to go along a specified route or direction [14thC. Via Anglo-Norse *pursuer* and Old French *poursuir* from *pursivre*, ultimately from Latin *prosequi*, literally 'to follow forward' (see PROSECUTE).] —**pursuable** *adj.* —**pursuer** *n.*

WORD KEY: SYNONYMS

See Synonyms at ***follow.***

pursuit /pər syŏŏt/ *n.* **1.** ACT OF CHASING AFTER STH the act of chasing after sb or sth in order to catch, attack, or overtake that person or thing **2.** ACT OF STRIVING FOR STH the effort made to try to achieve or obtain sth over a period of time ○ *the pursuit of happiness* **3.** HOBBY a pastime, hobby, or leisure activity **4.** CYCLE RACE WITH OBJECT OF OVERTAKING a cycle race in which the riders start from points on opposite sides of a ring-shaped track and race to overtake each other rather than reach a set finish line first [14thC. From Anglo-Norse *purseute* and Old French *poursuite*, formed from *poursuir* (see PURSUE).]

pursuit plane *n.* a fighter plane before World War II

pursuivant /púrssivənt/ *n.* **1.** JUNIOR OFFICER IN COLLEGE OF ARMS an officer who ranks below a herald in a college of arms **2.** ROYAL OR STATE MESSENGER a messenger employed by the British government or the monarch to deliver warrants **3.** FOLLOWER a follower or attendant (*archaic*) [14thC. From Old French *pursivant*, present participle of *pursivre* 'to pursue', ultimately from Latin *prosequi* (see PURSUE).]

pursy /púrssi/ (**-sier, -siest**) *adj.* (*archaic*) **1.** SHORT-WINDED getting out of breath easily **2.** OVERWEIGHT weighing more than is healthy [15thC. From Anglo-Norman *porsif*, variant of Old French *polsif*, from *polser* 'to pant', from Latin *pulsare* 'to agitate, drive' (see PUSH).] —**pursiness** *n.*

purulent /pyŏŏrŏŏlənt/ *adj.* relating to, containing, or consisting of pus [15thC. From French or Latin *purulentus* 'full of pus', from the stem *pur-* 'pus'. Ultimately from an Indo-European word that is also the ancestor of English *foul*.] —**purulence** *n.* —**purulently** *adv.*

purvey /pər váy/ *vt.* (**-veys, -veying, -veyed**) **1.** SUPPLY GOODS to be a commercial supplier of goods, especially foods (*formal*) **2.** CIRCULATE GOSSIP to publish or pass on news or information, especially gossip, scandal, or other kinds of information that people generally feel should not be circulated ■ *n. Scotland* FOOD LAID ON the food and drink that is provided at a party or other gathering (*dated*) [12thC. Via Anglo-Norman *purveier* from Latin *providere* 'to provide' (see PROVIDE).]

purveyance /pər váyənss/ *n.* **1.** PROVISION OF FOOD the supplying of sth, especially food **2.** PROVIDING OF SUPPLIES FOR MONARCH the task of providing, collecting, or requisitioning supplies for a king or queen (*archaic*)

purveyor /pər váyər/ *n.* **1.** COMMERCIAL SUPPLIER OF GOODS a person or company supplying goods, especially foods (*formal*) **2.** SB CIRCULATING STH sb who supplies, deals in, or circulates anything, especially sth that is disapproved of or ridiculed **3.** OFFICER PROVIDING MONARCH'S SUPPLIES an officer employed to buy or commandeer supplies for a king or queen (*archaic*)

purview /púr vyoo/ *n.* **1.** SCOPE OR RANGE the scope or range of sth, e.g. a court's jurisdiction or sb's knowledge **2.** LAW MAIN ENACTING PART OF WRITTEN LEGISLATION the main body of a written piece of legislation that follows the introductory section or preamble and contains the clauses that state what the law requires [15thC. From Anglo-Norman *purveü* and Old French *porveü*, past participle of *porve(i)er* (see PURVEY).]

pus /puss/ *n.* the yellowish or greenish fluid that forms at sites of infection, consisting of dead white blood cells, dead tissue, bacteria, and blood serum [14thC. From Latin (stem *pur-*) 'pus' (see PURULENT).]

Pusan /poo sán/ city and port on Korea Strait in southeastern South Korea. It is the second largest city in the country. Population: 3,813,814 (1995).

Pusey /pyŏŏzi/, **Edward** (1800–82) British clergyman and theologian. He became a leader of the Oxford movement in 1841 after John Henry Newman converted to Roman Catholicism. Full name **Edward Bouverie Pusey**

Puseyism /pyŏŏzi izəm/ *n.* the teachings of Edward Bouverie Pusey, leader of the Oxford Movement, who advocated a renewal of Catholic practices in the Church of England [Mid-19thC. Named after the Oxford don, Edward PUSEY, who advocated the observance of Catholic doctrine in the Church of England.]

push /pŏŏsh/ *v.* (**pushes, pushing, pushed**) **1.** *vti.* PRESS AGAINST TO MOVE to press against sb or sth in order to move that person or object **2.** *vti.* ADVANCE BY USING PRESSURE OR FORCE to advance or make sb or sth advance by using pressure or force ○ *She pushed to the front.* **3.** *vt.* ENCOURAGE SB STRONGLY to urge sb strongly to take some action or direction ○ *pushed their children to succeed* **4.** *vt.* DEPEND ON OR EXPLOIT STH to depend on or exploit sth to the limits of what is wise or acceptable ○ *Don't push your luck, friend.* **5.** *vt.* **USE ENERGY TO ACCOMPLISH STH** to use effort or energy to promote or accomplish sth ○ *push a bill through the legislative process* **6.** *vti.* **EXTEND BEYOND LIMITS** to extend sth beyond the usual limits ○ *pushing the boundaries of knowledge in this field* **7.** *vt.* **FORCE STH TO CHANGE** to force sth, especially a financial system, to change in a particular way ○ *a fear that increased competition will push prices down* **8.** *vt.* **SELL DRUGS** to engage in the sale of illegal drugs (*slang*) **9.** *vi.* MIL **ADVANCE AGAINST ENEMY** to make a sustained military advance **10.** *vt.* COMPUT **ADD DATA TO PUSHDOWN LIST** to add an item at the top of a pushdown list ■ *n.* **1. APPLICATION OF PRESSURE** the act of applying pressure to sb or sth in order to move that person or object **2. ACT OF ADVANCING** an act of advancing by using pressure or force **3. ENERGETIC EFFORT** an energetic effort used to promote or accomplish sth ○ *make a push to reform the tax code* **4. DETERMINATION** vigorous energy or will to succeed ○ *dynamic graduates with plenty of push* **5. MILITARY ADVANCE** a sustained military advance ○ *a push into enemy territory* **6. STIMULUS** a stimulus or encouragement that helps the process of starting, finishing, or changing sth **7.** HOCKEY **CONTINUOUS NUDGING SHOT WITH STICK** in hockey, a shot in which the ball is moved forwards along the ground to another player by the application of continuous pressure with the stick, instead of being hit **8.** COMPUT **NETWORK SERVICE TRANSMITTING DATA** a network service in which the source of the data initiates the transmission. ◊ **pull** [14thC. Via French *pousser* from Latin *pulsare*, literally 'to drive repeatedly', from *pellere* 'to drive, thrust' (source of English *pulse* 'beat').] ◇ **at a push** if really necessary (*informal*) ◇ **be pushing 40** to be approaching the age of 40 (*informal; can be applied to other ages*) ◇ **give sb the push** to dismiss sb (*informal*) ◇ **when push comes to shove** at the point when sth must be done or a decision must be made

push about, push around *vt.* to treat sb in a domineering way, especially by making unfair demands or giving repeated orders, and generally showing no respect (*informal*)

push along *vi.* to leave or go away (*informal*) ○ *It's time I was pushing along.*

push in *vi.* to force yourself unfairly into a queue of people, ahead of others who arrived before you

push off *v.* **1.** *vti.* **MOVE BOAT AWAY FROM MOORING** to move a boat out into open water, away from the place where it has been tied up **2.** *vi.* **GO AWAY** to leave or go away (*informal*)

push on *vi.* to continue on a journey, or carry on with an activity with renewed determination or effort

push through *vt.* to get sth accepted or agreed quickly, especially by using persuasion or force

pushback /po͝osh bak/ *n.* **1. MECHANISM THAT FORCES STH BACKWARDS** a mechanism that forces sth backwards, e.g. a device fitted to a door that forces it back into its closed position after sb has opened it **2. METHOD OF STARTING HOCKEY GAME** a stick stroke used in hockey to start a game or to restart it after a goal has been scored

push-bike *n.* a bicycle that is propelled by being pedalled (*dated informal*)

push broom *n.* a very wide brush designed to sweep large areas of flooring by pushing

push button *n.* a button that, when pushed, mechanically opens or closes an electrical circuit, e.g. a doorbell ○ *a row of levers and push buttons*

push-button *adj.* **1. OPERATED BY PUSHING BUTTON** operated by pushing a button or buttons to open or close an electrical circuit **2. EQUIPPED WITH AUTOMATIC DEVICES** equipped with modern devices that perform tasks more or less automatically ○ *the push-button kitchen* **3. INSTANTLY PROVIDED** obtained, provided, or produced easily and instantly

pushcart /po͝osh kaart/ *n. US* a cart or barrow light enough to be pushed by hand, e.g. one from which goods are sold

pushchair /po͝osh chair/ *n.* a lightweight wheeled chair for pushing a baby or young child around in, especially one that can be folded or collapsed for easy storage. ◊ **stroller**

pushdown /po͝osh down/ *n.* a technique for organizing a list or storage of data in which the item most recently added to the list or storage becomes the next item to be retrieved. This is also called a last in, first out (or LIFO) algorithm. ○ *a pushdown stack*

pushed /po͝osht/ *adj.* (*informal*) **1. SHORT OF STH** lacking in sth, usually time or money ○ *We're pushed for time now.* **2. ALMOST UNABLE TO DO STH** able to do sth only with difficulty or effort

pusher /po͝oshər/ *n.* **1. SELLER OF ILLEGAL DRUGS** sb who sells illegal drugs, especially addictive drugs (*slang*) **2. SB FIERCELY COMPETITIVE OR AMBITIOUS** sb ambitious who is always trying aggressively to outdo others (*informal*)

push fit *n.* a join that enables two pieces to be pushed together rather than fixed in some other way

pushing /po͝oshing/ *adj.* **1. AMBITIOUS** showing energy, initiative, and ambition **2. ASSERTIVE** aggressively self-confident or assertive —**pushingly** *adv.* —**pushingness** *n.*

Pushkin /po͝oshkin/, **Aleksandr Sergeyevich** (1799–1837) Russian writer. He was an author of plays, novels, and short stories, and his best-known works include the verse novel *Eugene Onegin* (1831) and the tragic play *Boris Godunov* (1825).

push money *n.* a cash reward that a manufacturing company pays to a retailer who sells large quantities of its products or sells off old or unwanted stock (*informal*)

pushover /po͝osh ōvər/ *n.* (*informal*) **1. STH EASY TO DO** sth that is very easy to do, deal with, or succeed at **2. EASY VICTIM** sb who is easily persuaded, deceived, or defeated

pushpin /po͝osh pin/ *n. US, Can* a drawing pin with a cylindrical head, used to fix paper or other lightweight materials to a wall or bulletin board

push-pull *adj.* used to describe an electronic circuit in which two components are arranged so that an alternating input makes them transmit a current alternately. This type of circuit is commonly used in audio amplifiers to reduce harmonic distortion.

push rod *n.* a metal rod operated by a cam to open and close a valve in an internal combustion engine

push-start *vt.* (**push-starts, push-starting, push-started**) **START VEHICLE BY PUSHING IT** to start a motor vehicle's engine by pushing the vehicle with the gear engaged and the clutch pressed down until it picks up speed, then releasing the clutch ■ *n.* **ACT OF PUSH-STARTING ENGINE** an act of push-starting a vehicle's engine

push-up *n.* **1.** *Aus, Can, US* **EXERCISE OF RAISING BODY FROM FLOOR** a physical exercise in which, from a position of lying flat on the front with the hands under the shoulders, the body is pushed off the floor until the arms are straight **2.** *US* COMPUT **COMPUTER STORAGE TECHNIQUE** a set of stored data in which the first item to be retrieved is the one stored earliest

pushy /po͝oshi/ (**-ier, -iest**) *adj.* excessively aggressive or forceful in competing or dealing with others (*informal*) ○ *pushy sales techniques* —**pushily** *adv.* —**pushiness** *n.*

pusillanimous /pyo͞ossi lánniməss/ *adj.* showing a lack of courage or determination (*formal*) [15thC. Formed from late Latin *pusillanimis*, from *pusillis* 'very small' + *animus* 'mind'.] —**pusillanimity** /pyo͞ossilə nímməti/ *n.* —**pusillanimously** /pyo͞ossi lánniməssli/ *adv.*

WORD KEY: SYNONYMS

See Synonyms at ***cowardly***.

puss[1] /po͝oss/ *n.* an affectionate word used for or to address a cat (*informal; often used by or to children*) [Early 16thC. Origin uncertain: probably from Middle Low German *pūs*, of unknown origin.]

puss[2] /po͝oss/ *n.* sb's face or mouth (*slang*) ○ *a familiar puss* [Late 19thC. From Irish *pus* 'lip, mouth'.]

pussy[1] /po͝ossi/ (*plural* **-ies**) *n.* **1. CAT** an affectionate word used for or to address a cat (*informal; often used by or to children*) **2. CATKIN** a furry hanging flower (**catkin**) that some trees produce, especially the catkin of the pussy willow tree [Late 16thC. Coined from PUSS[1] + -Y. Originally a term of endearment for a girl or woman.]

pussy[2] /po͝ossi/ (*plural* **-ies**) *n.* **1. OFFENSIVE TERM** an offensive term for the vulva (*taboo offensive*) **2. OFFENSIVE TERM** an offensive term for sexual intercourse with a woman (*slang offensive*) **3. OFFENSIVE TERM** a highly offensive term for women regarded as a source of sexual pleasure (*slang offensive*) [See PUSSY[1]]

pussy[3] /pússi/ (**-sier, -siest**) *adj.* resembling or full of pus [Late 19thC. Formed from PUS.]

pussycat /po͝ossi kat/ *n.* **1. CAT** an affectionate word for a cat (*often used by or to children*) **2. SB GENTLE AND AMIABLE** sb who is gentle and easy-going (*informal*)

pussyfoot /po͝ossi fo͝ot/ (**-foots, -footing, -footed**) *vi.* (*informal*) **1. BEHAVE HESITANTLY OR SPEAK VAGUELY** to behave hesitantly or indecisively, or avoid speaking frankly or openly **2. MOVE STEALTHILY** to move quietly and usually secretively

pussytoes /po͝ossi tōz/ (*plural* **-toes**) *n.* a low-growing perennial herb of the composite family with woolly leaves and clusters of small whitish flower heads resembling a cat's paws. Genus: *Antennaria.* [Late 19thC. So-called because the plant resembles a cat's paw.]

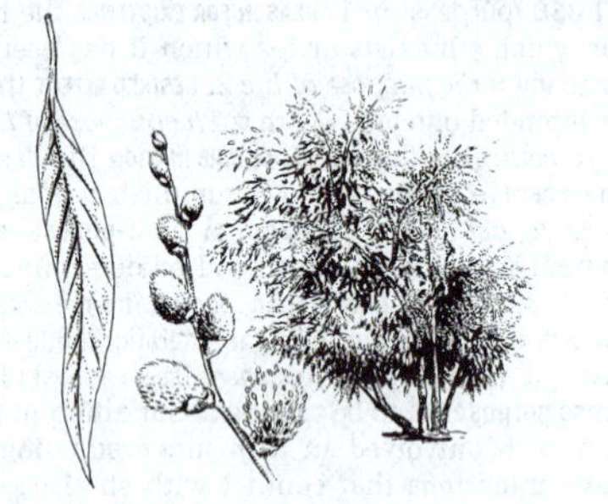

Pussy willow

pussy willow *n.* **1. N AMERICAN WILLOW TREE** a North American willow shrub or small tree that has fluffy grey flowers (**catkins**) along its branches. Latin name: *Salix discolor.* **2. WILLOW TREE** a willow tree. Genus: *Salix.*

pustulant /pústyo͝olənt/ *adj.* **CAUSING PUSTULES** causing pustules to form on the skin ■ *n.* **SUBSTANCE CAUSING PUSTULES** a substance that causes pustules to form on the skin

pustulate *vti.* /pústyo͞o layt/ (**-lates, -lating, -lated**) **CAUSE OR FORM PUSTULES** to become covered with pustules, or cause pustules to form on the skin ■ *adj.* /pústyo͞olət/ **HAVING PUSTULES** covered with pustules —**pustulation** /pústyo͞o láysh'n/ *n.*

pustule /pús tyool/ *n.* **1.** ANAT **PIMPLE** a small round raised area of inflamed skin filled with pus **2.** BIOL **RAISED DISCOLOURED SPOT** a small raised discoloured area, especially on a plant [14thC. From Latin *pustula.*] —**pustular** /pústyo͞olər/ *adj.*

put /po͝ot/ *v.* (**puts, putting, put**) **1.** *vt.* **PLACE STH** to move sth into a particular place or position ○ *I put my arms around her.* ○ *They put the child's money into a trust fund.* **2.** *vt.* **CAUSE SB TO GO** to cause sb to go to a place and stay there for a period of time **3.** *vt.* **PLACE SB IN SITUATION** to place sb or sth in a particular state or situation **4.** *vt.* **MAKE SB DO STH** to make sb do sth ○ *She was put to work in the garden.* **5.** *vt.* **MAKE SB HAVE STH** to make sb or sth have or be affected by sth ○ *They put pressure on him to accept the offer.* **6.** *vt.* **EXPRESS JUDGMENT OF STH** to express or experience a feeling about sb or sth ○ *Most people put a high value on educational qualifications.* **7.** *vt.* **USE STH** to use or apply sth for a particular purpose ○ *Put your mind to it.* **8.** *vt.* **INVEST STH** to invest money, time, or effort in sth ○ *We offered to put some money into the scheme.* **9.** *vt.* **EXPRESS STH** to express or state sth in a particular way ○ *How can I put this without offending you?* **10.** *vt.* **CREATE SPECIFIED DISTANCE** to create a distance of time or space between the self and sth or sb else **11.** *vt.* **BRING STH UP FOR SB** to bring sth up as a question, vote, or proposal for sb **12.** *vt.* **SET WORDS TO MUSIC** to provide words with a musical form ○ *put the words to music* **13.** *vt.* **ESTIMATE STH** to make an estimate of sth, e.g. the time ○ *I put the time at about 11 o'clock.* **14.** *vt.* **SET RESTRICTION** to set a limit or a restriction ○ *We must put a stop to this at* *once!* **15.** *vt.* WRITE OR PRINT STH to change or translate information from one kind of language to another **16.** *vt.* PLACE BET to bet an amount of money on a race or contest **17.** *vt.* THROW HEAVY METAL BALL to throw the heavy metal ball in the shot put **18.** *vi.* NAUT SET COURSE to take a particular course ○ *lifted anchor and put to sea* ■ *n.* **1.** THROW OF HEAVY METAL BALL in the shot put, a throw of the heavy metal ball **2. put, put option** STOCK EXCH OPTION TO SELL a type of option giving the owner of an underlying asset the right to sell a set quantity at a set price during a specific time period [Assumed Old English *putian* 'to urge'] ◇ **not know where to put yourself** to feel embarrassed (*informal*) ◇ **stay put** remain in the same place

put about *v.* **1.** *vt.* CIRCULATE INFORMATION to circulate sth such as news or gossip **2.** *vr.* MAKE YOURSELF KNOWN TO MANY PEOPLE to make yourself known to many different people, e.g. in order to start friendships or establish business contacts (*informal*) **3.** *vti.* NAUT CHANGE COURSE to make a ship change course, or to change course

put across *vt.* to make sth understood or accepted by expressing it clearly ◇ **put one across (on) sb** to deceive or trick sb (*informal*)

put aside *vt.* **1.** SEPARATE STH FOR DISCARDING OR SAVING to separate sth from sth else and discard it or save it for later use **2.** IGNORE STH to disregard sth ○ *They agreed to put aside their differences.* **3.** SET STH DOWN to stop holding, looking at, or concentrating on sth and set it to one side

put away *vt.* **1.** PUT STH IN USUAL STORAGE PLACE to put sth in the place where it is normally stored or kept ready for use **2.** SAVE STH FOR THE FUTURE to save sth, especially money, for future use **3.** EAT FOOD QUICKLY to eat food, especially quickly, greedily, or in large quantities (*informal*) **4.** CONFINE SB to put sb in prison or another form of confinement (*informal*) **5.** = **put down** *v.* 7

put back *vt.* **1.** RETURN STH TO WHERE IT BELONGS to return sth to the place it was taken from or to the place where it is normally kept **2.** PAY STH BACK to give sth back to a person or group in exchange for help or benefits received **3.** RESTORE STH TO OPERATION to restore machine to operation **4.** RESTORE PIECES TO WHOLE to restore pieces or fragments to a unified whole **5.** DELAY OR POSTPONE STH to delay sb or sth, or postpone sth **6.** MAKE CLOCK SHOW EARLIER TIME to change the time on a clock so that it shows an earlier time **7.** DRINK ALCOHOL QUICKLY to drink alcoholic drinks, especially quickly

put by *vt.* to save sth, especially money, for future use

put down *v.* **1.** *vt.* WRITE STH to write sth on paper **2.** *vt.* SUPPRESS REBELLION to use force to bring a rebellion to an end **3.** *vt.* DISPARAGE OR BELITTLE SB to make sb or sth appear ridiculous or unimportant by being critical or scornful (*informal*) **4.** *vt.* SUBMIT FOR FORMAL DISCUSSION to submit sth formally so that it can be discussed or debated **5.** *vt.* PAY DEPOSIT ON STH to pay part of the cost of a purchase as a deposit **6.** *vt.* ATTRIBUTE STH TO STH to give sth as or understand sth to be a cause or reason for sth else ○ *I put his unfriendliness down to shyness.* **7.** *vt.* KILL ANIMAL HUMANELY to kill an animal in a humane way, usually because it is old, injured, or terminally ill **8.** *vt.* DEPOSIT PASSENGER to let a passenger get off or get out **9.** *vti.* LAND AEROPLANE to land an aircraft somewhere **10.** *vt.* PUT CHILD TO BED to put a baby or small child to bed

WORD KEY: SYNONYMS

See Synonyms at ***kill***.

put forth *vt.* (*formal*) **1.** MAKE STH KNOWN to make sth known, e.g. by stating it, publishing it, or formally submitting it for discussion **2.** GROW LEAVES OR OTHER PARTS to send out new leaves or new growth **3.** EXERT EFFORT to exert strength or make an effort in an attempt to accomplish sth **4.** START JOURNEY to begin a journey or voyage

put forward *vt.* **1.** MAKE STH KNOWN to make sth known, e.g. by stating it, publishing it, or formally submitting it for discussion **2.** OFFER SB AS CANDIDATE to suggest sb as a candidate for sth **3.** MAKE CLOCK SHOW LATER TIME to change the time on a clock so that it shows a later time

put in *v.* **1.** *vt.* GIVE TIME OR ENERGY to devote time or effort **2.** *vt.* INSTALL STH to install sth, especially equipment or fittings in a house **3.** *vt.* MAKE CLAIM to make a claim or application for sth **4.** *vt.* SAY STH to make a remark, especially to add sth to a conversation **5.** *vi.* BRING SHIP INTO PORT to bring a ship into a port, especially for a short stay **6.** *vt.* MAKE OPPOSING CRICKET TEAM BAT in cricket, to decide that the opposing team should bat first

put off *v.* **1.** *vt.* POSTPONE STH to delay or postpone sth **2.** *vt.* DELAY OR HINDER SB to delay sb or stop sb from acting or proceeding **3.** *vt.* MAKE SB DISGUSTED to disgust or repel sb **4.** *vt.* DISCOURAGE SB to make sb lose interest in or enthusiasm for sth **5.** *vt.* DISTRACT SB to disturb sb's concentration or divert sb's attention **6.** *vi.* START BOAT JOURNEY to start a journey in a boat or ship **7.** *vt.* TAKE CLOTHING OFF to remove clothes or an article of clothing (*archaic*) ○ *Put off that wet cloak.* ◇ **put sb off his** *or* **her stride** *or* **stroke** to distract sb from what he or she is doing and make that person do it less well

put on *vt.* **1.** START STH OPERATING to make sth electrical or mechanical start operating, e.g. by turning a knob or pressing a switch **2.** COVER WITH CLOTHING to cover the body or a part of the body with clothing, headgear, footwear, or other accessories **3.** APPLY STH TO SKIN to apply sth, e.g. make-up or lotion, to the skin **4.** ORGANIZE STH to organize and present an event, e.g. a theatrical entertainment **5.** GAIN OR ADD STH to gain sth that is additional or extra ○ *He's been putting on weight.* **6.** PRESCRIBE STH FOR SB to prescribe sth for sb, e.g. medication or a special diet **7.** ADD STH to add sth to a cost or value **8.** ADOPT FALSE BEHAVIOUR to adopt an attitude or way of behaving that is false or insincere **9.** PROVIDE STH to provide sth as a service or facility **10.** MAKE STH SUBJECT TO IMPOSITION to impose sth such as a tax or a restriction **11.** PLACE BET to make a bet, or offer money as a stake for a bet **12.** HAND TELEPHONE TO SB to hand a telephone to sb so that he or she can speak to sb on the other end **13.** TEASE SB to make fun of sb, especially by pretending sth (*informal*) ○ *You're putting me on.*

put on to *vt.* **1.** INFORM SB ABOUT STH to tell a person about sb or sth previously unknown to him or her **2.** ALLOW PEOPLE TO SPEAK BY TELEPHONE to allow sb to speak to sb else by telephone, e.g. by handing over the telephone or making a connection via a switchboard **3.** REVEAL TRUTH ABOUT SB to make sb suspect, or realize the truth about, sb else (*informal*)

put out *v.* **1.** *vt.* EXTINGUISH LIGHT OR FIRE to switch off a light or extinguish a fire **2.** *vt.* ANNOY SB to annoy, upset, or offend sb ○ *He was very put out with me.* **3.** *vt.* MAKE STH KNOWN to make sth widely known, e.g. by announcing or broadcasting it **4.** *vt.* CAUSE INCONVENIENCE to cause sb inconvenience **5.** *vt.* TO CAUSE INJURY TO STH to cause injury to a part of the body ○ *I put my back out* **6.** *vt.* PRODUCE STH to manufacture or produce sth **7.** *vi.* *US* AGREE TO SEX of a woman, to agree to have sex (*slang; often considered offensive*) **8.** *vt.* ELIMINATE PLAYER to eliminate a player from a game or competition **9.** *vi.* SET OFF IN BOAT to start sailing in a boat after a period spent at rest in harbour or on shore ◇ **put sb out to pasture** *or* **grass** to make sb retire

put over *vt.* to make sth understood by expressing it clearly ◇ **put one over (on sb)** to make sb believe or accept sth by using deceit (*informal*)

put through *vt.* **1.** MAKE SB UNDERGO STH to make sb experience sth difficult or unpleasant **2.** MAKE TELEPHONE CALL to make a telephone call to sb **3.** CONNECT BY TELEPHONE to connect sb by telephone to sb else **4.** CARRY STH OUT to process sth or take it to a successful conclusion

put to *vi.* **1.** BRING BOAT TO SHORE to tie up a boat in a sheltered spot or harbour **2.** PUT HORSE BETWEEN SHAFTS to hitch a horse to a cart or other vehicle (*archaic*)

put up *v.* **1.** *vt.* INCREASE STH to raise or increase sth **2.** *vt.* BUILD STH to build or erect sth **3.** *vt.* FASTEN STH TO WALL to fasten sth to a wall, fence, or other upright surface **4.** *vti.* GIVE OR FIND SHELTER AND FOOD to give sb accommodation, or find accommodation somewhere ○ *put us up for the night* **5.** *vt.* ENGAGE IN STH to engage in or carry on sth ○ *put up a fight* **6.** *vt.* PROVIDE MONEY to offer or provide sth, especially money **7.** *vt.* OFFER FOR SALE to offer sth for sale ○ *The house contents were put up for auction.* **8.** *vt.* PILE HAIR ON TOP OF HEAD to fix long hair in a style that is coiled or piled on the top of the head and then secured, usually with hairpins **9.** *vti.* OFFER SB AS CANDIDATE to offer sb as a candidate **10.** *vt.* RETURN WEAPON TO HOLDER to return a weapon taken out for use to its holder (*archaic*) **11.** *vt.* SCARE GAME BIRD INTO AIR to scare a game bird out from its hiding place and up into the air ◇ **put up or shut up** used to indicate that sb should either do sth about sth or else stop talking about it (*informal*)

WORD KEY: SYNONYMS

See Synonyms at ***build***.

put upon *vt.* to treat sb badly or take advantage of sb

put up to *vt.* to encourage or persuade sb to do sth unpleasant or destructive

put up with *vt.* to tolerate or accept sb or sth calmly

putamen /pyoo táy men/ (*plural* **-tamina** /-támminə/) *n.* the stone inside a peach, plum, apricot, or other similar fruit (*technical*) [Mid-19thC. From Latin, 'shell, peel', from *putare* 'to prune' (see PUTATIVE).]

putative /pyo͞otətiv/ *adj.* **1.** GENERALLY ACCEPTED generally believed to be or regarded as being sth **2.** THOUGHT TO EXIST believed to exist now or to have existed at some time [15thC. From French *putatif* or late Latin *putativus*, formed from *putare* 'to prune, think over' (source of English *computer* and *amputate*).] —**putatively** *adv.*

WORD KEY: ORIGIN

The Latin word *putare*, from which ***putative*** is derived, is also the source of English *account, amputate, compute, count, deputy, dispute, impute, recount*, and *reputation*.

putdown /po͝ot down/ *n.* a critical or scornful remark intended to make sb appear ridiculous or unimportant (*informal*)

put-in *n.* RUGBY in rugby, an act of using the hands to send the ball into a scrum to restart play

putlog /po͝ot log/ *n.* CONSTR a short horizontal bar or beam that helps to support the planks forming the floor of a scaffold [Mid-17thC. Origin uncertain: perhaps from *put*, past participle of PUT + LOG.]

put-on *adj.* FALSE assumed or adopted for effect or in order to deceive ○ *a put-on accent* ■ *n.* (*informal*) **1.** ACT OF TEASING SB the act of intentionally deceiving or giving sb the wrong impression, especially for humorous effect **2.** PRANK an instance of teasing sb, especially as a joke

put out *adj.* having been inconvenienced, upset, annoyed, or offended by sb or sth ○ *I do feel a little put out not to have been invited.*

putout /po͝ot òwt/ *n.* BASEBALL a play in which a batter or base runner is retired

put-put /pút put/ *n.* (*informal*) **1.** SOUND OF SMALL ENGINE the sound made by a small petrol engine, especially an old or broken one **2.** PETROL ENGINE a small petrol engine **3.** VEHICLE WITH PETROL ENGINE a vehicle, especially a boat, fitted with a small petrol engine ■ *vi.* (**put-puts, put-putting, put-putted**) MOVE SLOWLY UNDER LITTLE POWER to move slowly or hesistantly under the power of a small petrol engine (*informal*) [An imitation of the sound]

putrefy /pyo͞otri fī/ (**-fies, -fying, -fied**) *vti.* to decay or make sth decay with a foul smell [15thC. From Latin *putrefacere*, from *putr-*, the stem of *puter* 'putrid' (see PUTRID) + *facere* 'to make'.] —**putrefaction** /-fáksh'n/ *n.* —**putrefactive** /pyo͞otri fáktiv/ *adj.* —**putrefiable** *adj.* —**putrefier** *n.*

putrescent /pyoo tréss'nt/ *adj.* **1.** DECAYING decaying or rotting **2.** RELATING TO DECAY relating to the process of decay [Mid-18thC. From Latin *putrescent-*, present participle stem of *putrescere*, literally 'to begin to rot', from, ultimately, *putr-*, the stem of *puter* 'rotten'.] —**putrescence** *n.*

putrescible /pyoo tréssəb'l/ *adj.* capable of decaying or rotting [Late 18thC. Formed from Latin *putrescere* 'to become rotten', ultimately from *putr* (see PUTRID).]

putrescine /pyoo trésseen, -tréssin/ *n.* a colourless crystalline compound (**ptomaine**) found during the decay of flesh. Formula: $C_4H_{12}N_2$. [Late 19thC. Formed from Latin *putrescere* 'to become rotten', ultimately from *putr-* (see PUTRID).]

putrid /pyo͞otrid/ *adj.* **1.** DECAYING WITH DISGUSTING SMELL rotting and giving off a foul smell **2.** DISGUSTING physically or morally disgusting **3.** WORTHLESS worthless or contemptible (*informal*) [15thC. From Latin *putridus*

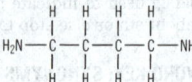

Putrescine

'rotten', from, ultimately, *putr-*, stem of *puter*. Ultimately from an Indo-European word that is also the ancestor of English *filth* and *potpourri*.] —**putridity** /pyoo tríddəti/ *n.* —**putridly** /pyoótridli/ *adv.* —**putridness** /pyoótridnəss/ *n.*

putsch /pooch/ *n.* a sudden planned attempt to overthrow a government using military force [Early 20thC. From Swiss German, 'thrust, blow'.] —**putschist** *n.*

putt /put/ *vti.* (**putts, putting, putted**) GOLF HIT GOLF BALL WITH TAPPING STROKE to hit a golf ball with a gentle tapping stroke along the ground on a green, aiming for the hole ■ *n.* GOLF TAPPING GOLF STROKE a gentle tapping stroke that hits a golf ball along the ground on a green, aiming for the hole [Mid-18thC. Variant of PUT.]

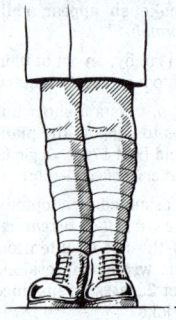

Puttee

puttee /pútti/ *n.* **1.** CLOTH STRIP WOUND ROUND LOWER LEG a strip of cloth wrapped round the lower leg from the ankle to the knee, especially one worn as part of a military uniform **2.** LEATHER COVERING FOR LOWER LEG a leather legging or gaiter that covers the lower leg [Late 19thC. From Hindi *patti*, from Sanskrit *pattika* 'bandage, strip of cloth'.]

putter[1] /púttər/ *n.* **1.** GOLF CLUB FOR USE ON GREEN a golf club with a flat-faced metal head, for hitting a golf ball with a gentle tapping stroke on a green **2.** PUTTING GOLFER a golfer who is in the process of putting

putter[2] /púttər/ (**-ters, -tering, -tered**) *vi.* US = **potter** [Late 19thC. Variant of POTTER.]

putting green *n.* **1.** = **green** *n.* **8 2.** LAWN FOR PRACTISING PUTTING STROKES a lawn with holes for practising putting strokes

Puttnam /pútnəm/, **David, Baron Puttnam of Queensgate** (*b.* 1941) British film producer. He helped revive the British film industry with *Chariots of Fire* (1981) and *The Killing Fields* (1984).

putto /poóttō/ (*plural* **-ti** /poótti/) *n.* in art especially of the baroque period, an infant boy or cherub, often portrayed with wings [Mid-17thC. Via Italian from Latin *putus* 'boy'.]

putty /pútti/ *n.* **1.** PASTE USED IN GLAZING WINDOWS a paste with the consistency of dough made from linseed oil and powdered chalk, used to fix glass into wooden window frames and to fill holes in wood **2.** PASTE FORMING TOP COAT ON PLASTER a thin paste of lime, water, and sand or plaster of Paris, used as a finishing coat on plaster **3.** COLOURS LIGHT GREY COLOUR a light grey colour tinged with yellow ■ *adj.* COLOURS LIGHT GREY of a light grey colour with a tinge of yellow ■ *vt.* (**-ties, -tying, -tied**) FIX OR REPAIR STH WITH PUTTY to fix windows into wooden frames, or fill holes in wood, using putty [Mid-17thC. From French *potée*, originally

'potful', from *pot* 'pot' (see POT[1]).] ◇ **be putty in sb's hands** to be easily influenced and controlled by sb

putty knife *n.* a tool similar to a knife with a blunt wide flexible blade, especially one used by glaziers to spread putty onto wooden window frames

putty powder *n.* a powder consisting of tin oxide or a mixture of tin and lead oxides that is used for polishing metal and glass

puttyroot /pútti root/ *n.* A North American orchid that has only one leaf and a brown or purplish-brown flower. Latin name: *Aplectrum hyemale*. [Mid-19thC. So called because of the substance found in the plant's corm that resembles cement.]

put-up *adj.* fraudulently, dishonestly, or deviously planned or organized (*informal*) ○ *Was the fire a put-up job?*

put-upon *adj.* treated badly, especially by being taken advantage of or being asked to do an excessive amount of work

putz /puts/ *n.* **1.** US, Can UNINTELLIGENT PERSON a very unintelligent and unpleasant person (*informal insult*) **2.** US OFFENSIVE TERM an offensive term for a penis (*offensive slang*) [Early 20thC. From Yiddish *potz* 'fool, penis'.]

Puy de Sancy /pwee də saaN see/ mountain in central France. It is the highest peak in the Massif Central. Height: 1,886 m/6,188 ft.

puzzle /púzz'l/ *vt.* (**-zles, -zling, -zled**) CONFUSE SB to confuse sb by being difficult or impossible to understand ■ *n.* **1.** DIFFICULT PROBLEM OR SITUATION a problem that is difficult or impossible to solve or a situation that is difficult to resolve **2.** SB MYSTERIOUS sb whose behaviour or motives are difficult to understand **3.** GAME OF SKILL OR INTELLIGENCE a game or toy designed to test skill or intelligence [Late 16thC. Origin uncertain.]

———— **WORD KEY: SYNONYMS** ————
See Synonyms at *problem*.

puzzle out *vt.* to use logic or reasoning to reach an understanding of sth confusing or complicated
puzzle over *vt.* to spend time thinking about and trying to understand sth confusing or complicated

puzzlement /púzz'lmənt/ *n.* a state of confusion resulting from an inability to understand or to deal with sth

puzzler /púzz'lər/ *n.* **1.** STH CONFUSING OR CHALLENGING sth confusing, mystifying, or testing skill or intelligence **2.** SOLVER OF PUZZLES sb who enjoys solving puzzles

PVA *n.* a colourless resin used in adhesives and paints. Full form **polyvinyl acetate**

PVC *n.* a hard-wearing synthetic resin made by polymerizing vinyl chloride, used for making flooring, piping, and clothing. Full form **polyvinyl chloride**

PVS *abbr.* **1.** postviral syndrome **2.** persistent vegetative state

Pvt. *abbr.* private

PW *abbr.* Policewoman

p.w. *abbr.* per week

PWA *abbr.* person with Aids

PWC *abbr.* US personal watercraft

PWR *abbr.* pressurized-water reactor

pwt *abbr.* pennyweight

PX *n.* MIL a store in a United States military base selling goods to military personnel and their families, as well as to some authorized civilians. Full form **Post Exchange**

py- *prefix.* = **pyo-** (*used before vowels*)

pya /pyaa/ *n.* **1.** MINOR UNIT OF MYANMAR CURRENCY a minor unit of currency in Myanmar, 100 of which are worth a kyat. See table at **currency 2.** COIN EQUIVALENT TO PYA a coin worth a pya, 100 of which are worth a kyat [Mid-20thC. From Burmese.]

pycnidium /pik níddi əm/ (*plural* **-a** /-di ə/) *n.* an asexual flask-shaped structure in some fungi [Mid-19thC. From modern Latin, where it was formed from Greek *puknos* 'dense'.]

pycno- *prefix.* dense, density ○ *pycnometer* [From Greek *puknos* 'strong, thick, dense']

pycnogonid /pik nóggənid/ *n.* = **sea spider** [Late 19thC. From modern Latin *Pycnogonida* from *pycnogonum*, the genus name of these arthropods, from *pycno-* + Greek *gonu* 'knee'.]

pycnometer /pik nómmitər/ *n.* a standard container of accurately defined volume used to determine the relative density of liquids and solids —**pycnometric** /píknō méttrik/ *adj.*

pye-dog /pí-/ *n.* a stray, half-wild dog found in villages in Asia [Mid-19thC. *Pye* of uncertain origin: probably a contraction of *pariah*(*-dog*), or from Hindi *pahi* 'outsider'.]

pyel- *prefix.* = **pyelo-** (*used before vowels*)

pyelitis /pí ə lítiss/ *n.* inflammation of the part of the kidney (**pelvis**) from which urine drains into the tube leading to the bladder, sometimes caused by a bacterial infection that may occur during pregnancy —**pyelitic** /-líttik/ *adj.*

pyelo- *prefix.* kidney, pelvis of the kidney ○ *pyelonephritis* [From Greek *puelos* 'basin, trough']

pyelogram /pí əlō gram/ *n.* an X-ray of the urine-collecting part of the kidney. The X-ray is taken following the introduction of a contrast medium either into the bloodstream or directly into the kidney in order to highlight the internal structures

pyelography /pí ə lóggrəfi/ *n.* the branch of radiography dealing with the kidneys and surrounding tissue, usually involving introduction of a contrast medium to highlight the internal structures —**pyelographic** /pí əlō gráffik/ *adj.*

pyelonephritis /pí əlō ni frítiss/ *n.* inflammation of the kidney, including both the urine-forming and urine-collecting parts [Mid-19thC. From PYELITIS + NEPHRITIS.]

pyemia *n.* US = **pyaemia**

pygidium /pī jíddiəm/ (*plural* **-a** /pī jíddiə/) *n.* **1.** HINDMOST PART OF INVERTEBRATE the hindmost part of the body in some insects, worms, and other invertebrates **2.** COVERING FOR PART OF INVERTEBRATE ABDOMEN a protective covering of the anal portion of the abdomen of some invertebrates [Mid-19thC. Coined from Greek *puge* 'rump' + -IDIUM.] —**pygidial** /pī jíddi əl/ *adj.*

Pygmalion /pig máyli ən/ *n.* a king of Cyprus in Greek mythology who fell in love with the goddess Aphrodite and made a statue of her that she brought to life as Galatea

pygmy /pígmi/, **pigmy** *n.* (*plural* **-mies**) **1.** SB SHORTER THAN AVERAGE sb who is of shorter than average height (*often considered offensive*) **2.** OFFENSIVE TERM an offensive term that insults sb's importance, especially in a particular field (*offensive*) ■ *adj.* OF SMALL BREED belonging to a small breed (*offensive in some contexts*) ○ *a pygmy hippopotamus* [14thC. Via Latin *pygmaei* (plural) from, ultimately, Greek *pugmaios* (singular) 'dwarfish', from *pugmē* 'distance from the elbow to the knuckles'.]

Pygmy /pígmi/ (*plural* **-mies**), **Pigmy** (*plural* **-mies**) *n.* **1.** = **Negrillo 2.** = **Negrito**

pygmy chimpanzee *n.* a species of chimpanzee from West Africa that is smaller than other chimpanzees, with a lighter build and darker colour. Latin name: *Pan paniscus*.

pyinkado /pying kaadō/ (*plural* **-dos**) *n.* **1.** ASIAN TREE WITH HARD WOOD an Asian tree that is a source of very hard wood used in the construction industry. Latin name: *Xylia xylocarpa*. **2.** WOOD OF PYINKADO TREE the very hard wood of the pyinkado tree, used in the construction industry [Mid-19thC. From Burmese.]

pyjama cricket *n.* ANZ one-day cricket that takes place partly or wholly at night, on floodlit pitches, with players in brightly-coloured outfits rather than in the traditional whites (*informal humorous*)

pyjama party *n.* a party at which the guests wear pyjamas for fun or, especially in the case of children, bring their pyjamas so that they can stay the night

pyjamas /pə jáaməz/ *npl.* **1.** SLEEPING CLOTHES a light loose pair of trousers and a matching loose-fitting shirt for wearing in bed **2.** LOOSE TROUSERS WORN IN EASTERN COUNTRIES loose-fitting trousers made of silk or lightweight cotton tied at the waist, worn by both men and women in India, Turkey, and other Eastern countries **3.** WOMAN'S LOOSE-FITTING TROUSER SUIT a woman's suit consisting of a loose blouse and flared trousers [Early 19thC. Plural of *pajama*, from Persian and Urdu *pāy-jāmah*, literally 'leg garment'.]

Pylon

pylon /pílən/ *n.* **1.** METAL TOWER SUPPORTING HIGH-VOLTAGE CABLES a tall metal tower typically made of criss-crossing steel bars that supports high-voltage cables across a long span **2.** AIRFIELD TOWER TO GUIDE PILOT a tower erected at an airfield to mark a course for pilots, e.g. in a race **3.** BRACKET FIXING STH TO AIRCRAFT BODY a rigid metal bracket that attaches an external aircraft part such as an engine, fuel tank, or armament to the main body of the aircraft **4.** TALL VERTICAL PART OF STRUCTURE a tall vertical structure on or forming part of a building or other construction, especially an ancient structure, e.g. a decorative gateway or a monumental pillar [Mid-19thC. From Greek *pulōn* 'gateway', from *pulē* 'gate'.]

pylorectomy /pílaw réktəmi/ (*plural* **-mies**) *n.* the surgical removal of all or part of the pylorus, sometimes including the removal of part of the stomach [Late 19thC. Coined from PYLORUS + -ECTOMY.]

pylorus /pī láwrəss/ (*plural* **-ri** /-rī/) *n.* the thick muscular ring (**sphincter**) surrounding the outlet of the stomach into the duodenum. It closes to prevent unduly large lumps of food from leaving, thus enabling stomach acid and enzymes to break them down further. [Early 17thC. Via late Latin from Greek *puloros* 'gatekeeper', from *pulē* 'gate'.] —**pyloric** /pī lórrik/ *adj.*

Pym /pim/, **John** (1583?–1643) English parliamentary leader. He was one of the five members Charles I tried to arrest (1642), and was active in events leading up to the Civil War.

PYO *abbr.* pick your own

pyo- *prefix.* pus ◦ *pyoderma* [From Greek *puon*. Ultimately from an Indo-European word meaning 'to rot', which is also the ancestor of English *foul*, *putrid*, and *purulent*.]

pyoderma /pí ō dúrmə/ *n.* a skin infection causing the development of pus or pustules

pyogenesis /pí ō jénnəssiss/ *n.* the formation or production of pus —**pyogenic** *adj.*

Pyongyang /pyóng yang/, **P'yŏngyang** capital city of North Korea, situated on the Taedong River in the western part of the country. It is thought to be the oldest city on the Korean Peninsula. Population: 2,000,000 (1994).

pyorrhea *n. US* = **pyorrhoea**

pyorrhoea /pí ə reè ə/ *n.* inflammation of the gums with a loosening of the teeth and a discharge of pus from the tooth sockets [Early 19thC. From modern Latin, literally 'flowing of pus', from Greek *puon* 'pus' (see PYO-).] —**pyorrhoeal** *adj.* —**pyorrhoeic** *adj.*

pyr- *prefix.* = **pyro-** (*used before vowels or h*)

pyracantha /pírə kánthə/ *n.* a European and Asian evergreen shrub of the rose family that has spiky branches and leaves, clusters of white flowers, and red or yellow berries. Latin name: *Pyracantha coccinea*. US term **firethorn** [Early 17thC. Via modern Latin from Greek *purakantha*, an unidentified plant, from *pur* 'fire' + *akantha* 'thorn'.]

pyralid /pírrəlid/ *n.* a small or medium-sized, slender, widely distributed moth with long triangular forewings. Family: Pyralidae. [Late 19thC. From modern Latin *Pyralidae*, from Greek *puralis* 'mythical fly said to live in fire', from *pur* 'fire'.] —**pyralid** *adj.*

Pyramid: Chephren Pyramid, Giza, Egypt

pyramid /pírrəmid/ *n.* **1.** EGYPTIAN STONE TOMB a huge stone tomb of ancient Egyptian royalty with a square base and triangular walls that slope to meet in a point at the top **2.** SOLID SHAPE WITH SLOPING TRIANGULAR SIDES a solid shape or structure that has triangular sides that slope to meet in a point and a base that is often, but not necessarily, a square. The volume of a pyramid is one-third of the product of the area of the base and the height of the vertex. **3.** SYSTEM WITH GRADUALLY EXPANDING STRUCTURE an arrangement or system that has a small number of elements at one point and expands gradually to have a large number of elements at the opposite point **4.** POINTED BODY PART a pointed or cone-shaped body part, e.g. either of two bundles of fibres located in the brain **5.** INVESTMENT METHOD SPREADING RISK a financial risk structure that spreads investments between high, medium, and low risk **6.** CRYSTALLINE FORM WITH MULTIPLE NONPARALLEL FACES a crystalline form in which three or more nonparallel faces intersect all three axes of the crystal ■ *vi.* (**-mids, -miding, -mided**) TAKE ON PYRAMID SHAPE to take on the shape of a pyramid, with few elements at one point or level and gradually increasing numbers of elements towards the opposite point or level [Mid-16thC. Via the Latin stem *pyramid-* from Greek *puramis*, of uncertain origin: probably an alteration of Egyptian *pimar* through the exchange of the letters *m* and *r*.] —**pyramidal** /pi rámmid'l/ *adj.* —**pyramidally** /pi rámmid'li/ *adv.* —**pyramidic** /pírrə míddik/ *adj.* —**pyramidical** *adj.* —**pyramidically** /-míddikli/ *adv.*

pyramidal peak *n.* a high mountain peak formed by the walls of three or more adjacent steep-sided glacial basins, e.g. the Matterhorn

pyramidal tract *n.* either of two bundles of nerve fibres, shaped like inverted pyramids, running from either hemisphere of the cerebral cortex down the spinal cord to all voluntary muscles of the body. In the brain, they are susceptible to stroke damage that can lead to inability to move one side of the body.

pyramid selling *n.* a method of distributing goods in bulk to a number of distributors, who in turn sell the goods in batches to a number of subdistributors, and so on

Pyramus and Thisbe /pírəməs ənd thízbi/ *n.* two young Babylonian lovers in an ancient love story who were forbidden to marry. Pyramus, thinking Thisbe has been killed by a lion, kills himself, and Thisbe, on finding his body, kills herself.

pyran /pí ran/ *n.* either of two isomers of a crystalline cyclic compound with a ring consisting of five carbon atoms and an oxygen atom with two double bonds. It is best known for its benzene derivatives, which are naturally occurring dyes that produce the colours of flowers. Formula: C_5H_6O. [Early 20thC. Coined from *pyrone* + -AN.]

pyrargyrite /pī raárjə rīt/ *n.* a deep-red to black mineral with a metallic lustre consisting of silver antimony sulphide. An important source of silver, it is commonly found associated with other silver ores. [Mid-19thC. Coined from PYRO- + Greek *arguros* 'silver' + -ITE.]

pyrazole /pírrəzōl/ *n.* a crystalline cyclic compound with a ring consisting of three carbon atoms and two nitrogen atoms with two double bonds. The ring system does not occur naturally, and pyrazole and its derivatives are exclusively synthetic com-

pounds. Formula: $C_3H_4N_2$. [Late 19thC. Coined from PYRROLE + AZO-.]

pyre /pīr/ *n.* a pile of burning material, especially a pile of wood on which a dead body is ceremonially cremated [Mid-17thC. Via Latin *pyra* from Greek *pura*, from *pur* 'fire'. Ultimately from an Indo-European word that is also the ancestor of English *fire*.]

pyrene[1] /pí reen/ *n.* the stone inside some types of fruit such as cherries (*technical*) [Mid-19thC. From modern Latin *pyrena*, from Greek *purēn*.]

pyrene[2] *n.* a solid, colourless to yellow, crystalline, multiple-ringed hydrocarbon compound obtained from coal tar that has been shown to be carcinogenic. Formula: $C_{16}H_{10}$. [Mid-19thC. Coined from Greek *pur* 'fire' + -ENE.]

Pyrenean mountain dog /pírrəneeən-/ *n.* a large bulky dog with a thick shaggy white coat, originally bred to protect sheep from wild animals in mountain areas [Named after the PYRENEES]

Pyrenees /pírrə neéz/ mountain range in southwestern Europe, forming a natural boundary between France and Spain. Length: 435 km/270 mi. Area: 55,374 sq. km/21,380 sq. mi.

pyrethrin /pī reéthrin/ *n.* either of two oily liquid complex organic compounds obtained from pyrethrum flowers and used as a contact insecticide. Despite their quick lethal action on insects, pyrethrins are valued for their relative nontoxicity to humans and other animals. Formula: $C_{21}H_{28}O_3$ or $C_{22}H_{28}O_5$. [Early 20thC. Coined from PYRETHRUM + -IN.]

pyrethroid /pī reéth royd/ *n.* COMPOUND WITH SIMILAR PROPERTIES TO PYRETHRIN a synthetic complex organic compound with insecticidal properties similar to those of pyrethrin ■ *adj.* WITH PROPERTIES SIMILAR TO PYRETHRIN belonging to the class of organic compounds with properties similar to those of pyrethrin [Mid-20thC. Coined from PYRETHRUM + -OID.]

pyrethrum /pī reéthrəm/ *n.* **1.** TYPE OF CHRYSANTHEMUM a chrysanthemum cultivated for its ornamental flowers. Genus: *Chrysanthemum*. **2.** INSECTICIDE IN POWDER FORM a mixture of pyrethrins extracted from the flowerheads of various chrysanthemums and used as an insecticide. It has low toxicity to warm-blooded animals and degrades rapidly in the environment, but has now been superseded by synthetic pyrethrins. [Mid-16thC. Via Latin from Greek *purethron* 'feverfew', of uncertain origin: perhaps formed from *puretos* 'fever'.]

pyretic /pī réttik/ *adj.* RELATING TO FEVER relating to, producing, or having a fever ■ *n.* FEVER-CAUSING AGENT an agent that causes fever [Mid-19thC. From modern Latin *pyreticos*, from Greek *puretos* 'fever'.]

Pyrex /pī reks/ *tdmk.* a trademark for a type of borosilicate glass that is resistant to heat and chemicals and is used in household kitchenware and laboratory apparatus

pyrexia /pī réksi ə/ *n.* fever (*technical*) [Mid-18thC. Via modern Latin from Greek *purexis*, from *puressein* 'to be feverish', from *pur* 'fire'.] —**pyrexial** *adj.* —**pyrexic** *adj.*

pyrheliometer /pīr heéli ómmitər/ *n.* an instrument that measures the intensity of the Sun's radiation received at the Earth's surface [Mid-19thC. Coined from Greek *pur* 'fire' + *helios* 'sun' + -METER.] —**pyrheliometric** /pīr heéli ə méttrik/ *adj.*

pyric /pírik/ *adj.* relating to burning, or produced as a result of burning [Mid-20thC. From French *pyrique*, from Greek *pur* 'fire'.]

pyridine /pírri deen/ *n.* a toxic, flammable, colourless

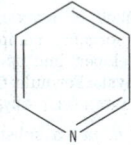

Pyridine

to yellow liquid with a noxious smell, used in the manufacture of chemicals, pharmaceuticals, and paints, and in textile dyeing. It occurs naturally in bone oil and coal tar. Formula: C_5H_5N. [Mid-19thC. Coined from Greek *pur* 'fire' + -IDINE.]

pyridoxal /pírri dóks'l/ *n.* a crystalline aldehyde of the vitamin B_6 group that is a derivative of pyridoxine and acts as an active coenzyme in amino acid synthesis. Formula: $C_8H_9NO_3$. [Mid-20thC. Formed from PYRIDOXINE.]

pyridoxamine /pírri dóksə meen/ *n.* a crystalline amine of the vitamin B_6 group that is a derivative of pyridoxine and acts as a coenzyme in protein metabolism. Formula: $C_8H_{12}N_2O_2$. [Mid-20thC. Coined from PYRIDINE + OXY- + -AMINE.]

pyridoxine /pírri dók seen/ *n.* a crystalline derivative of pyrimidine, found in cereals, yeast, liver, and fish. In an organism, pyridoxine is metabolically changed to pyridoxal and pyridoxamine. Formula: $C_{18}H_{11}NO_3$. [Mid-20thC. Coined from PYRIDINE + OXY-.]

pyriform /pírri fawrm/ *adj.* shaped like a pear [Mid-18thC. From modern Latin *pyriformis*, from Latin *pyrum* 'pear'.]

pyrimethamine /pírə méthə meen/ *n.* a drug used as a preventive in the treatment of malaria [Mid-20thC. From *pyrimidine* + ETHYL-AMINE.]

pyrimidine /pī rímmi deen/ *n.* **1.** CRYSTALLINE ORGANIC COMPOUND a strong smelling, weakly basic crystalline organic compound with a six-sided ring structure that includes two nitrogen atoms. Formula: $C_4H_4N_2$. **2.** PYRIMIDINE DERIVATIVE a biologically significant derivative of pyrimidine, especially the bases cytosine, thymine, and uracil found in RNA and DNA [Late 19thC. From PYRIDINE + IMIDE.]

pyrite /pír īt/ *n.* a cubic iron sulphide mineral with a brassy metallic lustre that is used as an iron ore, as a source of sulphur, and in the production of sulphuric acid. It is the commonest of the sulphide minerals and is widely distributed geographically. [Mid-19thC. From French or Latin (see PYRITES).] —**pyritic** /pī ríttik/ *adj.*

pyrites /pī rī teez/ (*plural* **-tes**) *n.* = **pyrite** [Mid-16thC. Via Latin from Greek *purites (lithos)* 'fire (stone), flint', from *pur* 'fire'.]

pyro- *prefix.* **1.** fire, heat ○ *pyromania* **2.** produced by fire or heat ○ *pyroligneous* **3.** fever ○ *pyrogenic* **4.** derived from an acid by loss of a molecule of water ○ *pyrophosphate* [From Greek *pur* 'fire' (source also of English *pyre*). Ultimately from the Indo-European word that is also the the ancestor of English *fire*.]

pyrocatechol /pírō kátti chol, -kol/ *n.* = **catechol**

pyrocellulose /pírō séllyoolōss/ *n.* a highly nitrated cellulose used in the manufacture of explosives, particularly smokeless powder

pyrochemical /pírō kémmik'l/ *adj.* relating to or resulting from chemical changes that take place at very high temperatures —**pyrochemically** *adv.*

pyroclastic /pírō klástik/ *adj.* used to describe sedimentary rock that is composed of fragments of volcanic rock produced by the explosion of a volcanic eruption

pyroconductivity /pírō kon duk tívvəti/ *n.* the capacity to conduct electricity created in a solid substance by heating it to a high temperature

pyroelectricity /pírō i lek tríssəti, -əllek-/ *n.* the production of electric charges on opposite faces of some crystals by a change in temperature —**pyroelectric** /pírō i lék trik/ *adj.*

pyrogallic acid /pírō galik-/ *n.* = **pyrogallol**

pyrogallol /pírō gállol/ *n.* a toxic, bitter, lustrous, white crystalline organic compound used as a photographic developer, and as an absorbent for oxygen in gas analysis. Formula: $C_6H_6H_3$. [Late 19thC. Coined from PYROGALLATE + -OL.] —**pyrogallic** *adj.*

pyrogen /pírō jen/ *n.* MED a substance that causes fever, especially a substance introduced into sb's bloodstream

pyrogenic /pírō jénnik/ *adj.* **1.** MED CAUSING FEVER causing fever or produced as a result of fever **2.** GEOL IGNEOUS produced by igneous activity

pyrography /pī róggrəfi/ (*plural* **-phies**) *n.* **1.** BURNING DESIGNS INTO WOOD AND LEATHER the creation of designs on wood and leather using heated tools that burn away some of the surface **2.** DESIGN CREATED BY BURNING a design burned into wood or leather using a heated tool —**pyrographer** *n.* —**pyrographic** /pírō gráffik/ *adj.*

pyroligneous /pírō lígni əss/ *adj.* produced by the destructive distillation of wood

pyroligneous acid *n.* a reddish-brown liquid, produced by the destructive distillation of wood, that was once a commercial source of acetic acid, which is its primary constituent. Among its impurities may be acetone, methanol, wood oils, and tars.

pyrolusite /pírō lóo sīt/ *n.* a black or grey powdery mineral with high mass and a metallic sheen, that is an important source of manganese. It is found associated with other manganese ores, e.g. manganite, and as nodules on the sea bed. Formula: MnO_2. [Early 19thC. Coined from PYRO- + Greek *lousis* 'washing' (from its use in decolourizing glass) + -ITE.]

pyrolysate /pírō lī sayt/ *n.* a product of a chemical change caused by heating

pyrolyse /pírō līz/ (**-yses, -ysing, -ysed**) *vt.* to make a complex chemical substance decompose into simpler substances by heating it [Early 20thC. From PYROLYSIS by analogy with ANALYSE.] —**pyrolyser** *n.*

pyrolysis /pī róllәssiss/ *n.* the use of heat to break down complex chemical substances into simpler substances —**pyrolytic** /pírō líttik/ *adj.*

pyrolyze /pírō līz/ (**-yzes, -yzing, -yzed**) *vt.* to make a complex chemical substance decompose into simpler substances by heating it [Early 20thC. From *pyrolysis* by analogy with *analyse*.] —**pyrolyzer** *n.*

pyromancy /pírō manssi/ *n.* attempting to tell the future by using fire or flames [14thC. Via Old French *pyromancie* from late Latin *pyromantia*, from Greek *puromanteia*, from *pur* 'fire'.] —**pyromancer** *n.* —**pyromantic** /pírō mántik/ *adj.*

pyromania /pírō máyni ə/ *n.* the uncontrollable urge to set fire to things —**pyromaniac** /-ni ak/ *n.* —**pyromaniacal** /pírōmə nī ək'l/ *adj.*

pyrometallurgy /pírō me tállərji/ *n.* the treatment of ores and metals using high-temperature processes, or the study of these processes, which include alloying, casting, distilling, roasting, refining, sintering, smelting, and heat treating

pyrometer /pī rómmitər/ *n.* an instrument that measures high temperatures, typically by converting brightness, radiation, or electric current measurements into temperature readings —**pyrometric** /pírō méttrik/ *adj.* —**pyrometrical** /-méttrik'l/ *adj.* —**pyrometrically** /-métrikli/ *adv.* —**pyrometry** /pī rómmətri/ *n.*

pyromorphite /pírō máwr fīt/ *n.* a minor ore of lead found as brown, green, grey, white, and yellow crystals of lead chlorophosphate

pyrone /pírōn/ *n.* either of two six-membered organic ring compounds containing five carbon atoms and an oxygen atom, with a second oxygen atom attached to one of the carbon atoms. The benzene derivative is used as a pharmaceutical. Formula: $C_5H_4O_2$.

pyronine /pírə neen/ *n.* a red dye used in biological tests, especially a test to detect the presence of RNA [Late 19thC. From German, of uncertain origin: probably coined from PYRO- + -INE.]

pyrope /pírōp/ *n.* a deep red garnet containing magnesium and aluminium, frequently used as a gemstone [Early 19thC. Via Old French *pirope* from Latin *pyropus*, from Greek *puropos* literally 'fiery-eyed', from *pur* 'fire'.]

pyrophobia /pírō fōbi ə/ *n.* an irrational fear of fire

pyrophoric /pírō fórrik/ *adj.* **1.** CHEM IGNITING SPONTANEOUSLY bursting into flames spontaneously when exposed to air **2.** METALL PRODUCING SPARKS WHEN STRUCK giving off sparks when struck or scraped [Mid-19thC. Formed from Greek *purophoros* 'fire-bearing', from *pur* 'fire'.]

pyrophosphate /pírō fós fayt/ *n.* a salt or ester produced when pyrophosphoric acid reacts with some metals or metallic compounds [Mid-19thC. Coined from *pyrophosphic* + -ATE.]

pyrophosphoric acid /pírō fosfórrik-/ *n.* a viscous liquid, formed when orthophosphoric acid is heated and loses a water molecule, used as a catalyst. Formula: $H_4P_2O_7$.

pyrophotometer /pírō fō tómmitər/ *n.* an instrument that determines the temperature of an incandescent body as a function of the light it emits

pyrophyllite /pírō fíllīt/ *n.* a silvery-white or greenish hydrous aluminium silicate mineral that resembles talc and is found in metamorphic rock [Early 19thC. From German *Pyrophyllit*, from Greek *pur* 'fire' + *phullon* 'leaf'; so called because it exfoliates when exposed to flame.]

pyrosis /pī róssiss/ *n.* heartburn (*technical*) [Late 18thC. Via Greek *purōsis* 'burning' from, ultimately, *pur* 'fire' (see PYRO-).]

pyrostat /pírō stat/ *n.* a thermostat that is suitable for use at very high temperatures [Formed from PYRO- on the model of 'thermostat'] —**pyrostatic** /pírō státtik/ *adj.*

pyrotechnic /pírō téknik/, **pyrotechnical** /-téknik'l/ *adj.* **1.** RELATING TO FIREWORKS relating to, used in, or involving fireworks **2.** BRILLIANT showing brilliance, e.g. in style or technique [Early 19thC. Formed from modern Latin *pyrotechnia*, from Greek *pur* 'fire' + *tekhnē* 'craft'.] —**pyrotechnically** *adv.* —**pyrotechnist** *n.*

pyrotechnics /pírō tékniks/ *n.* CRAFT OF MAKING FIREWORKS the craft or skill of making and using fireworks (*takes a singular verb*) ■ *npl.* (*takes a singular or plural verb*) **1.** FIREWORK DISPLAY a display of fireworks **2.** SHOWY DISPLAY an extravagant display of brilliance, virtuosity, or strong emotion

pyroxene /pī rók seen/ *n.* a silicate mineral, usually dark green, brown, or black, that contains varying amounts of calcium, iron, magnesium, and sodium and is widely distributed in igneous and metamorphic rocks [Early 19thC. From French *pyroxène*, from Greek *pur* 'fire' + *xenos* 'stranger'; so called because it was originally thought to be a foreign substance in igneous rock.] —**pyroxenic** /pī rok sénnik/ *adj.*

pyroxylin /pī róksəlin/ *n.* a highly flammable substance used to make plastics and lacquers. It is a form of cellulose nitrate. [Mid-19thC. Coined from PYRO- + XYLO- + -IN.]

pyrrhic /pírrik/ *n.* POETIC UNIT a unit of poetic rhythm that has two short or unaccented syllables ■ *adj.* IN PYRRHICS relating to or written in pyrrhics [Early 17thC. Via Latin from, ultimately, Greek *purrikhē*, named after the chorist *Pyrrhikhos*, who is supposed to have invented it.]

Pyrrhic victory *n.* a victory won at such great cost to the victor that it is tantamount to a defeat [Late 19thC. Named after PYRRHUS.]

Pyrrhonism /pírrōnizəm/ *n.* **1.** PHILOS SCEPTICAL PHILOSOPHY OF PYRRHO the doctrine of the ancient Greek philosopher Pyrrho, who believed that it was impossible to be certain about anything and therefore suspended judgment on everything **2.** COMPLETE SCEPTICISM scepticism to an extreme or excessive degree [Late 17thC. Formed from Greek *Purrhōn* 'Pyrrho', (360?–272? BC), the Greek philosopher who founded philosophical scepticism.] —**Pyrrhonist** *n.*, *adj.*

pyrrhotite /pírrō tīt/, **pyrrhotine** /-teen/ *n.* a widely occurring yellow-brown lustrous iron sulphide mineral, found in igneous rocks and used as an iron ore. Formula: FeS. [Mid-19thC. Alteration of German *Pyrrhotin*, from Greek *purrotēs* 'fiery redness', from *pur* 'fire' (see PYRO-).]

pyrrhuloxia /pírrə lóksi ə/ (*plural* **-as** *or* **-a**) *n.* a bird of the southwestern United States, Mexico, and Central America that is related to and resembles the cardinal but with mostly grey plumage touched with red. Latin name: *Cardinalis sinuatus.*

Pyrrhus /pírrəss/, **King of Epirus** (318?–272 BC). The king of a Greek province (307–272 BC), he invaded Italy and defeated the Roman army at Heraclea (280 BC) and Asculum (279 BC), but sustained huge losses to his troops.

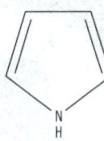

Pyrrole

pyrrole /pírrōl/ *n.* a colourless toxic liquid compound containing carbon, hydrogen, and nitrogen. It is found in many important biological substances, e.g. chlorophyll, haemoglobin, and bile pigments. Formula: C_4H_5N. [Mid-19thC. Coined from Greek *purros* 'fiery red' (from *pur* 'fire') + -OLE.] —**pyrrolic** /pi róllik/ *adj.*

pyruvic acid /pī roŏvik-/ *n.* a colourless acid that is formed as an intermediate compound during the metabolism of carbohydrates and proteins. Formula: $C_3H_4O_3$. [Mid-19thC. Coined from PYRO- + Latin *uva* 'grape'; so called because it was obtained by dry distillation from racemic acid.]

Pythagoras /pī thággərəss/ (582?–500? BC) Greek philosopher and mathematician. He or his followers made important discoveries about number and proportion, which they believed underlay everything in the universe. They also proposed that the Earth is a globe, and that the planets orbit the Sun. Known as **Pythagoras of Samos**

Pythagoras' theorem *n.* a proved geometric proposition stating that the square of the longest side (**hypotenuse**) of a right-angled triangle is equal to the sum of the squares of the other two sides [Named after *Pythagoras*, who formulated it]

Pythagorean /pī thággə reé ən/ *adj.* MATH, PHILOS **RELATING TO PYTHAGORAS** relating or belonging to the ancient Greek philosopher and mathematician Pythagoras, his theories, or his followers ■ *n.* **FOLLOWER OF PYTHAGORAS** a follower of Pythagoras and his theories

Pythagoreanism /pī thággə reé ənizəm/ *n.* the theories and teachings of Pythagoras, especially those that apply mathematics to the workings of the universe

Pytheas /píthi əss/ (*fl.* 300 BC) Greek mathematician, astronomer, and explorer. He explored the Atlantic coast of Europe, possibly reaching Norway, and sailed around Britain.

Pythian /píthi ən/, **Pythic** /píthik/ *adj.* **1.** OF DELPHI relating to the ancient Greek city of Delphi, especially to Apollo's temple there, the site of Apollo's oracle **2.** OF PYTHIAN GAMES relating to the athletic games held in Delphi [Late 16thC. Via Latin from, ultimately, Greek *Puthō*, the ancient name of Delphi.]

Pythian Games *npl.* a series of athletic contests held every four years in Delphi in ancient Greece in honour of the god Apollo

Python

python /píth'n/ *n.* a nonvenomous constricting snake native to Asia, Africa, and Australia. Pythons kill their prey through suffocation and can reach lengths of over 6 m/19ft. Family: Pythonidae. [Mid-19thC. Directly or via French from Latin, name of a mythical serpent killed by Apollo, from Greek *Puthōn.*]

Pythonesque /píthə nésk/ *adj.* absurdly or surreally comical in a way that is reminiscent of the 1970s British TV comedy show 'Monty Python's Flying Circus' [Late 20thC]

pythoness /píthə ness/ *n.* in Greek mythology, a woman believed to be possessed by the spirit of an oracle, especially Apollo's priestess at Delphi [14thC. From late Latin *pythonissa*, feminine of *python*, from Greek *Puthōn*, named after the serpent that Apollo killed near Delphi.]

pyuria /pī yoŏri ə/ *n.* the presence of pus in the urine [Early 19thC. Coined from PYO- + -URIA.]

pyx /piks/, **pix** *n.* **1.** CHR **BOX FOR COMMUNION WAFERS** a container in which the consecrated wafers for the Communion are placed so that they can be taken to those who cannot leave home **2.** CONTAINER FOR COINS AT MINT a chest in which newly minted coins are placed before being tested [14thC. Via Latin from Greek *puxis* 'box' (see PYXIS).]

pyxidium /pik síddi əm/ (*plural* **-a** /-di ə/) *n.* BOT = **pyxis** *n.* 1 [Mid-19thC. Via modern Latin from Greek *puxidion*, 'small box', from *puxis* (see PYXIS).]

pyxie /píksi/ (*plural* **-ies** *or* **-ie**) *n.* a low-growing evergreen shrub native to the eastern United States with small pink or white star-shaped flowers. Latin name: *Pyxidanthera barbulata.* [Late 19thC. Shortening of modern Latin *Pyxidanthera*, genus name, from *puxidium* 'little box' + *anthera* 'pollen'.]

pyxis /píksiss/ (*plural* **-ides** /-si deez/) *n.* **1.** BOT **SEED CAPSULE** a seed capsule with a cap that falls off to release the seeds **2.** SMALL BOX a small container for medicines, toiletries, or similar items (*archaic*) [Late 17thC. Via Latin from Greek *puxis* 'box' (source of English box^1), from *puxos* 'boxwood' (source of box^3 and bush), of unknown origin.]

Pyxis /píksiss/ *n.* a small inconspicuous constellation of the southern hemisphere lying partly in the Milky Way, located between Puppis and Antlia

pzazz *n.* = pizzazz

Qq

q[1] /kyoo/ (*plural* **q's**), **Q** (*plural* **Q's** *or* **Qs**) *n.* **1.** 17TH LETTER OF ENGLISH ALPHABET the 17th letter of the modern English alphabet **2.** SPEECH SOUND CORRESPONDING TO LETTER 'Q' the speech sound that corresponds to the letter 'Q' **3.** LETTER 'Q' WRITTEN a written representation of the letter 'Q'

q[2] *symbol.* PHYS **1.** electric charge **2.** heat *n.* 1.

Q *abbr.* **1.** CHESS queen **2.** MONEY quetzal

q. *abbr.* **1.** quart **2.** quarter **3.** quarterly **4.** quarto **5.** question **6.** query **7.** quire **8.** MEASURE quintal

Q. *abbr.* **1.** quartermaster **2.** quarto **3.** Quebec **4.** queen

Qadaffi = Muammar al- Gadaffi

qadi *n.* = cadi

q & a *abbr.* question and answer

Qatar

Qatar /kataár, káttar, kúttər/ independent state in the Middle East, on a peninsula in the Persian Gulf, north of Saudi Arabia and the United Arab Emirates. Language: Arabic. Currency: Qatar riyal. Capital: Doha. Population: 125,665 (1991). Area: 11,437 sq. km/4,416 sq. mi. Official name **State of Qatar** —**Qatari** *adj.*, *n.*

Qattara depression /kə taárə-/ desert basin in northwestern Egypt. Its lowest point is 133 m/435 ft below sea level. Area: 19,400 sq. km/7,500 sq. mi.

Qayrawan, Al- /kî'rə waán/ city in northern Tunisia, capital of al-Qayrawan Governorate. Called the 'City of 100 Mosques', it is one of the holiest Muslim cities. Population: 102,600 (1992).

QB *symbol.* CHESS queen's bishop

Q.B. *abbr.* LAW Queen's Bench

Q-boat *n.* = Q-ship

QBP *symbol.* CHESS queen's bishop's pawn

QC, Q.C. *abbr.* Queen's Counsel

QCD *abbr.* quantum chromodynamics

q.e. *abbr.* which is (*used in doctors' prescriptions*) [Latin, *quod est*]

QED *abbr.* **1.** quod erat demonstrandum **2.** PHYS quantum electrodynamics

QEF *abbr.* which was to be done [Latin, *quod erat faciendum*]

QF *abbr.* ARMS quick-firing

Q fever *n.* an infectious disease caused by rickettsial bacteria and characterized by fever, chills, and muscle pain [Mid-20thC. Origin uncertain: probably a

shortening of QUEENSLAND, where the disease was first described.]

qi, Qi *n.* = chi[2] *n.*

Qiblah *n.* = Kiblah

q.i.d. *abbr.* four times per day (*used in doctors' prescriptions*) [Latin, *quater in die*]

Qin /chin/, **Ch'in** *n.* a dynasty in ancient China that ruled from 221–206 BC, during which the first unified Chinese empire emerged and much of the Great Wall of China was built [Late 18thC. From Chinese *Qín.*]

Qing /ching/, **Ch'ing** *n.* the last of the Chinese dynasties, founded by the conquering Manchu who ruled from 1644 until 1912, when the nationalist revolutionaries overthrew it [Late 18thC. From Chinese *Qīng.*]

Qingdao /chíng dów/ city on the Yellow Sea, in Shandong Province, eastern China, between Beijing and Shanghai. Population: 2,060,000 (1991).

Qinghai /chíng hî/ province of western China bounded by Xinjiang Uygur, Gansu, Sichuan, and Tibet. Capital: Xining. Population: 4,740,000 (1994). Area: 720,999 sq. km/278,378 sq. mi.

Qinghai Hu /chíng hî hoo/ lake in northeastern Qinghai Province, China

Qiqiha'er /cheé chee haár/ city and port in Heilongjiang Province, China, situated on the left bank of the River Nen 274 km/170 mi. northwest of Harbin. Population: 1,260,000 (1986).

qiviut /keévi ət/ *n.* the soft wool that grows beneath the long outer coat of the musk ox, used to make yarn [Mid-20thC. From Inuit.]

QKt *symbol.* CHESS queen's knight

QKtP *symbol.* CHESS queen's knight's pawn

ql *abbr.* quintal

QL *abbr.* COMPUT query language

q.l. *abbr.* as much as you like (*used in doctors' prescriptions*) [Latin, *quantum libet*]

Qld *abbr.* Queensland

qlty *abbr.* quality

qm *abbr.* every morning (*used in doctors' prescriptions*) [Latin, *quaque mane*]

QM *abbr.* quartermaster

QMC *abbr.* quartermaster corps

QMG *abbr.* Quartermaster General

QMS *abbr.* Quartermaster Sergeant

qn *abbr.* question

q.n. *abbr.* every night (*used in doctors' prescriptions*) [Latin, *quaque nocte*]

qoph /koóf, kof/ *n.* see table at **alphabet**. = **koph** [From Hebrew *qōph*, from a Semitic word meaning 'eye of a needle']

QP *symbol.* CHESS queen's pawn

qq. *abbr.* questions

qqv *abbr.* which (things) see (*used as a cross reference to more than one item*) [Latin, *quae vide*]

QR *symbol.* CHESS queen's rook

qr. *abbr.* **1.** quarter **2.** quarterly **3.** quire

QRP *symbol.* CHESS queen's rook's pawn

qs *abbr.* quarter section (*used of land*)

QS *abbr.* quarter sessions

q.s. *abbr.* as much as suffices (*used in doctors' prescriptions*) [Latin, *quantum suffict*]

Q-ship *n.* an armed ship disguised as a merchant ship, used to decoy or destroy enemy vessels [From the naval designation for this type of vessel]

QSO *abbr.* ASTRON quasistellar object

qt *abbr.* **1.** quart **2.** quantity

q.t. *abbr.* quiet (*informal*) [Shortening of *quiet*] ◇ **on the q.t.** quietly and secretly (*informal*)

Q-Tips *tdmk.* a trademark for cotton-tipped swabs

qto *abbr.* quarto

qty *abbr.* quantity

qu. *abbr.* **1.** queen **2.** query **3.** question

qua /kway, kwaa/ *prep.* in the capacity or function of ○ *'Restrictions on trade, or on production for purposes of trade, are indeed restraints; and all restraint, qua restraint, is an evil'.* (John Stuart Mill, *On Liberty*; 1859) [Mid-17thC. From Latin *qua*, from *qui* 'who' (source also of English *quorum* and *quibble*).]

quack[1] /kwak/ *n.* SOUND MADE BY A DUCK the harsh sound typically made by a duck ■ *vi.* (**quacks, quacking, quacked**) **1.** MAKE THE SOUND OF A DUCK to make the harsh sound that is characteristic of a duck **2.** SPEAK IRRITATINGLY to speak loudly and endlessly in an irritating manner (*slang*) [Early 17thC. An imitation of the sound.]

quack[2] /kwak/ *n.* **1.** FAKE DOCTOR sb who practises medicine without training or qualifications (*often used before a noun*) **2.** DOCTOR a doctor (*dated informal*) **3.** SB WHO IS A FRAUD sb who makes false claims to skills and qualifications in fields other than medicine ■ *vi.* (**quacks, quacking, quacked**) BE A QUACK to practise medicine without training or qualifications, or to make false claims of expertise in any field [Early 17thC. Shortening of QUACKSALVER.] —**quackish** *adj.*

quackery /kwákəri/ *n.* the practices or methods of sb who makes false claims about medical or other skills or qualifications [Early 18thC. From QUACK[2].]

quack grass *n.* = couch grass

quacksalver /kwák salvər/ *n.* sb who falsely claims to have medical or other skills or qualifications (*archaic*) [Late 16thC. From obsolete Dutch, literally 'salve-hawker', from Dutch *kwaken*, 'to quack, prattle' + *zalf* 'salve'.]

quad[1] /kwod/ *n.* a quadruplet (*informal*) [Late 19thC. Shortening.]

quad[2] /kwod/ *n.* a quadrangle (*informal*) [Early 19thC. Shortening.]

quad[3] /kwod/ *adj.* quadraphonic (*informal*) [Late 20thC. Shortening.]

quad[4] /kwod/ *n.* PRINTING a piece of blank type metal used for spacing [Late 19thC. Shortening of QUADRAT.]

quad[5] /kwod/ *n.* a quadriceps (*informal*) [Mid-20thC. Shortening.]

quad[6] *abbr.* **1.** quadrangle **2.** quadrant **3.** quadrilateral

quadr- *prefix.* = **quadri-** (*used before vowels*)

quadra- *prefix.* = **quadri-** (*used before consonants*)

quadragenarian /kwódrōjə náiri ən/ *n.* PERSON IN 40S sb between the ages of 40 and 49 (*formal*) ■ *adj.* IN YOUR 40S between the ages of 40 and 49 (*formal*) [Mid-19thC. Via late Latin *quadragenarius* from, ultimately, *quadraginta* 'forty' (source of English *quarantine*).]

Quadragesima /kwóddrə jéssimə/ *n.* **1.** FIRST SUNDAY IN LENT in the Christian liturgical calendar, the first Sunday in Lent **2.** LENT the 40 days of Lent (*archaic*) [14thC. Via late Latin *quadragesima (dies)*, 'fortieth (day)' (before Easter), from *quadraginta* 'forty'.]

quadragesimal /kwóddrə jéssim'l/ *adj.* CHR relating to Lent

quadrangle /kwód rang g'l/ *n.* **1.** FOUR-SIDED SHAPE a two-dimensional figure that consists of four points connected by straight lines, especially a rectangle **2.** OPEN AREA SURROUNDED BY BUILDINGS an open rectangular yard that is surrounded on all four sides by buildings **3.** BUILDINGS SURROUNDING YARD the buildings that surround an open rectangular yard [15thC. Via Old French from, ultimately, Latin *quadrangulus*, 'having four corners'.] —**quadrangular** /kwod ráng gyōōlər/ *adj.*

quadrant /kwóddrənt/ *n.* **1.** GEOM QUARTER OF CIRCUMFERENCE OF CIRCLE a 90-degree arc representing one fourth of the circumference of a circle **2.** GEOM QUARTER OF AREA OF CIRCLE the area bounded by a quadrant and the two perpendicular lines that connect it to the centre of the circle **3.** GEOM QUARTER OF PLANE SURFACE any of the four sections into which the perpendicular axes of a coordinate system divide a two-dimensional surface **4.** GEOM QUARTER OF AREA OR SURFACE any of the four approximately equal parts into which an area or a surface is divided by two real or imaginary perpendicular lines **5.** ASTRON DEVICE FOR MEASURING ANGLE OF STAR an instrument with a movable sighting mechanism attached to a 90-degree arc, formerly used in astronomy and navigation to measure the angles and altitudes of stars **6.** DEVICE SHAPED LIKE QUARTER CIRCLE a mechanical device or machine part in the shape of a quarter of a circle [14thC. From Latin *quadrant-*, the stem of *quadrans* 'fourth part, quarter'.]

quadraphonic /kwóddrə fónnik/, **quadrophonic** *adj.* using a four-channel system to record and reproduce sound. The four separate signals may be fed to individual loudspeakers placed in the corners of a room. —**quadraphonics** *n.* —**quadraphony** /kwo dróffəni/ *n.*

quadrat /kwódrət/ *n.* **1.** PRINTING = **quad**[4] **2.** ECOL AREA OF LAND FOR ECOLOGICAL STUDY a small plot of land set aside for plant and animal population studies [Late 17thC. Variant of QUADRATE.]

quadrate *n.* /kwód rayt/ **1.** SQUARE OR CUBE a square or cube or a square or cubic area, space, or thing **2.** ZOOL JAW JOINT OF SOME VERTEBRATES in birds, fish, reptiles, and amphibians, a bony or cartilaginous part of the upper jaw that articulates with the lower jaw at the side of the skull. In mammals, this structure has evolved into the incus, a small bone of the middle ear. ■ *adj.* **1.** ZOOL OF THE VERTEBRATE QUADRATE relating to the quadrate in vertebrates **2.** SQUARE OR RECTANGULAR with four sides and four right angles ■ *v.* /kwo dráyt/ (**-rates, -rating, -rated**) **1.** *vt.* to make sth square or rectangular **2.** *vti.* CONFORM OR CORRESPOND WITH STH to conform or correspond with sth or to make one thing conform or correspond with another [14thC. Via Latin *quadratum* from, ultimately, *quadrum* 'square' (source of English *square* and *cadre*). Ultimately from an Indo-European word meaning 'fourfold', which is also the ancestor of *quadrant*.]

quadratic /kwo dráttik/ *adj.* MATH relating to or containing terms with powers no higher than the power of two [Mid-17thC. Formed from QUADRATE.] —**quadratically** *adv.*

quadratic equation *n.* an equation containing one or more terms raised to the power of two but no higher

quadratics /kwo dráttiks/ *n.* the branch of algebra that deals with quadratic equations (*takes a singular verb*)

quadrature /kwódrəchər/ *n.* **1.** MAKING STH SQUARE making sth square or dividing sth into squares **2.** MATH MATHEMATICAL TECHNIQUE FOR EQUATING AREAS the construction of a square with an area equal to that of a specified surface **3.** ASTRON 90-DEGREE SEPARATION OF CELESTIAL BODIES the relative position of two celestial bodies with a separation of 90 degrees as seen from a third, especially the Sun and Moon as seen from the Earth

quadrennia plural of **quadrennium**

quadrennial /kwo drénni əl/ *adj.* **1.** HAPPENING EVERY FOUR YEARS occurring every fourth year **2.** LASTING FOUR YEARS lasting for four years ■ *n.* FOUR-YEAR PERIOD a period of four years —**quadrennially** *adv.*

quadrennium /kwo drénni əm/ (*plural* **-ums** or **-a** /-ni ə/) *n.* a period of four years [Mid-19thC. From Latin, from *quadri-* 'four' + *annus* 'year'.]

quadri- *prefix.* **1.** four, fourth ○ *quadripartite* ○ *quadricentennial* **2.** square ○ *quadric* [From Latin. Ultimately from the Indo-European word for 'four', which is also the ancestor of English *quadrant*, *tetra-*, and *fourth*.]

quadric /kwóddrik/ *adj.* MATH = **quadratic** *adj.* ■ *n.* MATH STH DEFINED BY QUADRATIC EQUATION a surface or curve specified by a second degree equation [Mid-19thC. Formed from Latin *quadra*, feminine of *quadrum* 'square' (see QUADRATE).]

quadricentennial /kwóddri sen ténni əl/ *n.* 400TH ANNIVERSARY a 400th anniversary or a celebration of it ■ *adj.* MARKING 400TH ANNIVERSARY marking or relating to a 400th anniversary

quadriceps /kwóddri seps/ (*plural* **-ceps** or **-cepses**) *n.* ANAT a large four-part muscle at the front of the thigh that acts to extend the leg [Mid-19thC. From Latin, 'four-headed'.] —**quadricipital** /kwóddri síppit'l/ *adj.*

quadriga /kwo dréegə/ (*plural* **-gae** /-dréejee/) *n.* a two-wheeled chariot in ancient Greece or Rome that was drawn by four horses harnessed alongside each other [Early 18thC. Via Latin from, ultimately, *quadrijuga* 'team of four', from *quadri-* 'four' + *jugum* 'yoke'.]

quadrilateral /kwóddri láttərəl/ *n.* FOUR-SIDED FIGURE a two-dimensional geometric figure with four sides ■ *adj.* FOUR-SIDED with four sides

quadrille[1] /kwə dríl/ *n.* **1.** SQUARE DANCE OF FRENCH ORIGIN a French square dance popular in the 18th and 19th centuries, danced by four or more couples together **2.** MUSIC MUSIC FOR QUADRILLE the music for a quadrille, often taken from a popular source and usually in a lively duple metre [Mid-18thC. Via French from Spanish *cuadrilla*, 'troop, company', from *cuadro* 'square', from Latin *quadrum* (see QUADRATE).]

quadrille[2] /kwə dríl/ *n.* a card game for four players that uses a deck of 40 cards. It was popular in the 18th century [Early 18thC. From French, of uncertain origin: probably from Spanish *cuartillo*, from *cuarto* 'fourth', from Latin *quartus* (see QUART).]

quadrillion /kwo drílli ən/ (*plural* **-lions** or **-lion**) *n.* **1.** ONE FOLLOWED BY 15 ZEROS the number equal to 10^{15}, written as 1 followed by 15 zeros **2.** ONE FOLLOWED BY 24 ZEROS the number equal to 10^{24}, written as 1 followed by 24 zeros (*dated*) [Late 17thC. Formed from QUADRI-, on the model of 'billion'.] —**quadrillion** *adj.*, *pron.* —**quadrillionth** *adj.*, *n.*

quadripartite /kwóddri paár tīt/ *adj.* **1.** IN FOUR PARTS made up of four parts or divided into four **2.** INVOLVING FOUR PARTICIPANTS involving the participation of four individuals or groups

quadriplegia /kwóddri pleéji ə/ *n.* the inability to move all four limbs or the entire body below the neck —**quadriplegic** *n.*, *adj.*

quadrivalent /kwóddri váylənt/ *adj.* **1.** = **tetravalent 2.** WITH FOUR VALENCIES with four different valencies —**quadrivalency** *n.*

quadrivial /kwo drívvi əl/ *adj.* **1.** FOUR ROADS MEETING with four roads or ways going in different directions and meeting at the same point **2.** OF THE QUADRIVIUM relating to the quadrivium

quadrivium /kwo drívvi əm/ *n.* four of the seven liberal arts taught in medieval universities, consisting of arithmetic, geometry, music, and astronomy. The three lower arts (**trivium**) were grammar, rhetoric,

and logic. [Early 19thC. Via late Latin from Latin, 'crossroads', from *quadri-* 'four' + *via* 'road'.]

quadroon /kwo droón/ *n.* an offensive term for sb with one black and three white grandparents (*offensive*) [Mid-17thC. Via Spanish *cuarterón* from, ultimately, Latin *quartus* 'quarter' (see QUART).]

quadrophonic /kwóddrə fónnik/ *adj.* = **quadraphonic**

quadru- *prefix.* = **quadri-** (*used before consonants*)

quadrumanous /kwo droómənəss/ *adj.* with four feet that can also be used as hands, each having an opposable first digit. Most primates, apart from human beings, are quadrumanous. [Late 17thC. Formed from QUADRU- + Latin *manus* 'hand'.]

quadrumvirate /kwo drúmvərət/ *n.* a group of four people sharing power, especially forming a government [Mid-18thC. Formed from QUADRI-, on the model of 'triumvirate'.]

quadruped /kwóddrŏŏ ped/ *n.* FOUR-FOOTED ANIMAL an animal such as a lion or lizard with four limbs and feet, all of which are used for walking ■ *adj.* FOUR-FOOTED with four feet —**quadrupedal** /kwo droópid'l/ *adj.*

quadruple /kwóddroóp'l, kwo droóp'l/ *vti.* (**-ples, -pling, -pled**) INCREASE FOURFOLD to multiply sth by four or become four times as great ■ *adj.* **1.** MULTIPLIED BY FOUR four times as great **2.** WITH FOUR PARTS made up of four parts **3.** MUSIC WITH FOUR BEATS PER BAR used to describe a time or metre consisting of four beats to a bar ■ *n.* QUANTITY FOUR TIMES AS GREAT a number or amount that is four times as great as another [14thC. Via French from Latin *quintuplus*, literally 'fourfold', from *quadri-* 'four' (see QUADRI-).] —**quadruply** *adv.*

quadruplet /kwóddroóplət/ *n.* **1.** ONE OF FOUR BABIES any of four babies born to the same mother from one pregnancy **2.** FOUR SIMILAR THINGS a set of four identical or very similar things **3.** MUSIC FOUR NOTES PLAYED FASTER THAN NORMAL a group of four notes performed in the time usually occupied by three [Late 18thC. Formed from QUADRUPLE.]

quadruplicate *vti.* /kwo droópli kayt/ (**-cates, -cating, -cated**) INCREASE FOURFOLD to multiply sth by four or to be multiplied by four ■ *adj.* /kwo droóplikat/ WITH FOUR PARTS consisting of four identical or corresponding parts ■ *n.* /kwo droóplikat/ ONE OF FOUR any of a set of four identical things or copies [Mid-17thC. Formed from Latin *quadri-* 'four', on the model of 'duplicate'.] —**quadruplication** /kwo droópli káysh'n/ *n.*

quaere /kwéeri/ *n.* QUERY a query or question (*archaic*) ■ *interj.* INTRODUCING QUESTIONS used to introduce a query (*formal*) [Mid-16thC. From Latin (see QUERY).]

quaestor /kwéestər/ *n.* in ancient Rome, a magistrate responsible chiefly for financial administration [14thC. From Latin, formed from *quaest-*, the past participle stem of *quaerere* 'to inquire' (see QUERY).] —**quaestorial** /kwee stáwri əl/ *adj.* —**quaestorship** /kwéestər ship/ *n.*

quaff /kwof/ *vti.* (**quaffs, quaffing, quaffed**) DRINK QUICKLY OR HEARTILY to drink sth in large gulps or with great enjoyment (*literary or humorous*) ■ *n.* HEARTY DRINK a long deep drink (*literary or humorous*) [Early 16thC. Origin uncertain.] —**quaffer** *n.*

quag /kwag, kwog/ *n.* = **quagmire**. **1** [Late 16thC. Origin uncertain.]

quagga /kwággə/ (*plural* **-gas** or **-ga**) *n.* an extinct mammal of the horse family, related to the zebra, with yellowish-brown colouring and stripes on the head, neck, and shoulders. It was found in southern Africa until the late 19th century. Latin name: *Equus quagga*. [Late 18thC. From Afrikaans, of Nguni origin, said to be an imitation of the animal's call.]

quaggy /kwággi/ (**-gier, -giest**) *adj.* **1.** MARSHY soft and wet like a marsh or bog **2.** FLABBY lacking in firmness —**quagginess** *n.*

quagmire /kwág mīr, kwóg-/ *n.* **1.** BOG OR SWAMP a soft marshy area of land that gives way when walked on **2.** DIFFICULT SITUATION an awkward, complicated, or dangerous situation from which it is difficult to escape [Late 16thC. Formed from QUAG + MIRE.]

quahog /kwaá hog/, **quahaug** *n.* a thick-shelled edible clam of the North Atlantic coast of the United States. The shells were formerly used as money by Native North Americans. Latin name: *Mercenaria mercenaria*. [Mid-18thC. From Narragansett *poqua hock*.]

quaich /kwaykh/, **quaigh** *n. Scotland* a shallow drinking vessel with two handles, usually made from wood or metal [Mid-17thC. Via Scottish Gaelic from Old Irish *cúach*, which was borrowed from medieval Latin *caucus* 'drinking cup' (possible source of English *caucus*).]

Quai d'Orsay /káy dáw say/ *n.* **1.** LOCATION OF FRENCH FOREIGN OFFICE the street along the south bank of the Seine in Paris on which the French foreign office is located **2.** FRENCH FOREIGN OFFICE the French foreign office itself ○ *The Quai d'Orsay chose to make no immediate comment on the crisis.*

Quail

quail[1] /kwayl/ (*plural* **quails** *or* **quail**) *n.* **1.** BIRD WITH MOTTLED BROWN PLUMAGE a small game bird of Europe, Asia, and Africa with a rounded body, mottled brown plumage, and a short tail. Genus: *Coturnix*. **2.** NEW WORLD GAME BIRD any of several small New World game birds related to the quail, including the bobwhite [14thC. Via Old French from medieval Latin *coacula*, from a Germanic word that is ultimately an imitation of the bird's call.]

quail[2] /kwayl/ (**quails, quailing, quailed**) *vi.* to tremble or shrink with fear or apprehension [Early 19thC. Of uncertain origin: possibly from Middle Dutch *qualen* 'to suffer'.]

——————— **WORD KEY: SYNONYMS** ———————
See Synonyms at *recoil*.

quaint /kwaynt/ *adj.* **1.** ATTRACTIVELY OLD-FASHIONED with a charming old-fashioned quality ○ *a quaint little shop* **2.** PLEASANTLY STRANGE strange or unusual, especially in a pleasing or interesting way **3.** ECCENTRICALLY OUTDATED amusingly or irritatingly inappropriate to modern circumstances [12thC. Via Old French *cointe, queinte* 'clever' from Latin *cognit-*, the past participle stem of *cognoscere* 'to learn' (see COGNITION).] —**quaintly** *adv.* —**quaintness** *n.*

quake /kwayk/ *vi.* (**quakes, quaking, quaked**) **1.** TREMBLE WITH FEAR to shake or tremble, especially with fear **2.** SHAKE to shake or rock, e.g. from instability or a geological disturbance ■ *n.* **1.** EARTHQUAKE an earthquake (*informal*) **2.** SHAKING a tremor or shake [Old English *cwacian*, of unknown origin] —**quaky** *adj.*

Quaker /kwáykər/ *n.* a member of the Society of Friends, a Christian denomination founded in England in the 17th century that rejects formal sacraments, ministry, and creed, and is committed to pacifism. At meetings members are encouraged to speak when they feel moved to do so. [Late 17thC. Formed from QUAKE, probably because founder George Fox (1624–91) admonished that they should 'tremble at the word of the Lord'.] —**Quakerism** *n.* —**Quakerly** *adj.*

Quaker gun *n.* a dummy gun or cannon, usually made of wood, used in military training or to deceive an enemy [From the Quakers' refusal to fight in wars]

quaking aspen (*plural* **quaking aspens** *or* **quaking aspen**), **quaker** *n.* an aspen tree, native to the northern United States and Canada, with rounded flat leaves that tremble in the wind. Latin name: *Populus tremuloides.*

quale /kwaá li/ (*plural* **-lia** /kwaá li ə/) *n.* a property of sth, e.g. its feel or appearance, rather than the thing itself [Mid-17thC. From Latin, neuter of *qualis* 'of what kind' (see QUALITY).]

qualification /kwólifi káysh'n/ *n.* **1.** ESSENTIAL ATTRIBUTE a skill, quality, or attribute that makes sb suitable for a particular job, activity, or task **2.** OFFICIAL REQUIREMENT a condition or requirement, e.g. passing

an examination, that must be met by sb who is to be eligible for a position or privilege (*often used in the plural*) **3.** MEETING OF REQUIREMENTS the meeting of a condition or requirement to become eligible for a position or privilege **4.** STH RESTRICTIVE sth that modifies, limits, or restricts **5.** RESTRICTING OR CHANGING STH the modification or limitation of sth, e.g. in meaning, scope, or strength

qualified /kwólli fīd/ *adj.* **1.** OFFICIALLY ELIGIBLE having met a condition or requirement to become legally eligible for or entitled to a position or privilege **2.** SUITABLE OR ELIGIBLE TO DO STH with the necessary skills, qualities, or attributes to do a particular thing ○ *She's well qualified to comment on international affairs.* **3.** RESTRICTED OR CHANGED modified or limited in some way —**qualifiedly** *adv.*

qualifier /kwólli fī ər/ *n.* **1.** QUALIFYING PERSON OR TEAM an individual or team that is successful in the preliminary part of a competition and earns the right to take part in the next stage **2.** EARLY ROUND a preliminary round of a competition **3.** SB WITH A RIGHT OR SKILLS sb who meets the requirements of or has the qualifications for sth **4.** GRAM MODIFIER a word or phrase that restricts or modifies the meaning of another word or phrase, e.g. the word 'fairly'

qualify /kwólli fī/ (**-fies, -fying, -fied**) *v.* **1.** *vti.* BE OR MAKE SB SUITABLE to have or give sb a skill or attribute necessary for a particular activity **2.** *vti.* HAVE OR GIVE SB ELIGIBILITY to become legally eligible or make sb legally eligible for a position or privilege ○ *Did your exam results qualify you for the job?* **3.** *vi.* WIN FIRST ROUND OF COMPETITION to complete the preliminary part of a competition successfully and earn the right to go on to the next stage **4.** *vt.* RESTRICT OR CHANGE to modify or limit sth in meaning, scope, or strength **5.** *vt.* MODERATE to make sth less strong or extreme **6.** *vt.* DESCRIBE AS STH to attribute a particular quality or characteristic to sth **7.** *vt.* GRAM MODIFY OR RESTRICT MEANING to modify or restrict the meaning of a word [Mid-16thC. Via French *qualifier* from medieval Latin *qualificare* 'to attribute a quality to', from Latin *qualis* (see QUALITY).] —**qualifiable** *adj.* —**qualificatory** /kwóllifi kaytəri/ *adj.*

qualitative /kwóllitətiv/ *adj.* relating to or based on the quality or character of sth, often as opposed to its size or quantity [Early 17thC. Via late Latin *qualitativus* from Latin *qualitas* (see QUALITY).] —**qualitatively** *adv.*

qualitative analysis *n.* the identifying of the components in a mixture

quality /kwóllǝti/ (*plural* **-ties**) *n.* **1.** DISTINGUISHING CHARACTERISTIC a distinctive characteristic of sb or sth **2.** ESSENTIAL PROPERTY an essential identifying nature or character of sb or sth **3.** STANDARD the general standard or grade of sth ○ *goods of a pretty dubious quality* **4.** EXCELLENCE the highest or finest standard (*often used before a noun*) ○ *quality products* **5.** UPPER SOCIAL CLASS high social position or aristocratic breeding (*dated informal*) **6.** PEOPLE OF UPPER SOCIAL CLASS people of high social position or aristocratic breeding (*dated informal*) ○ *quality manners* **7.** PHON CHARACTER OF VOWEL SOUND the character of a vowel sound that depends on such factors as the shape of the mouth and position of the tongue when it is uttered **8.** MUSIC TONE OF NOTE the distinctive tone of a musical note **9.** LOGIC AFFIRMATIVE OR NEGATIVE CHARACTERISTIC the positive or negative nature of a logical proposition [13thC. Via French *qualité* from the Latin stem *qualitat-*, from *qualis* 'of what kind'. Ultimately from an Indo-European word that is also the ancestor of English *what, how,* and *quantity*.]

quality circle *n.* COMM a group of employees from different levels of a company who meet regularly to discuss ways of improving quality and to resolve any problems related to production

quality control *n.* a system for achieving or maintaining the desired level of quality in a manufactured product by inspecting samples and assessing what changes may be needed in the manufacturing process

quality factor *n.* a number by which a given dose of absorbed radiation is multiplied to determine the radiation's biological effect

quality of life *n.* the degree of enjoyment and satisfaction experienced in everyday life as opposed to financial or material well-being

quality time *n.* time spent with loved ones in enjoyable activities that enhance the relationship ○ *working parents determined to spend quality time with their kids*

qualm /kwaam/ *n.* **1.** DOUBT ABOUT PROPRIETY OF BEHAVIOUR an uneasy conscience about an action or conduct **2.** SICK FEELING a sudden pang of nausea **3.** FEELING OF UNEASE a sudden feeling of uncertainty or apprehension [Early 16thC. Of uncertain origin.] —**qualmish** *adj.* —**qualmishly** *adv.* —**qualmishness** *n.*

quamash /kwaá mash, kwə másh/ (*plural* **-ashes** *or* **-ash**) *n.* = camas *n.* 1

Quanah /kwaá anə/ (1845?–1911) US Native North American leader. He led the Comanche in raids against Caucasian settlers in the southwest during the early 1870s. Known as **Chief Quanah**. Full name **Parker Quanah**

quandary /kwóndəri/ (*plural* **-ries**) *n.* a state of uncertainty or indecision as to what to do in a particular situation [Late 16thC. Of uncertain origin.]

quandong /kwón dong/ (*plural* **-dongs** *or* **-dong**) *n.* **1.** TREES SMALL AUSTRALIAN TREE a small Australian tree that bears a large edible red fruit with an edible kernel. Latin name: *Santalum acuminatum.* **2.** FRUIT OF QUANDONG the large red edible fruit of the quandong, or its edible kernel, used to make jam **3.** TREES LARGE AUSTRALIAN TREE a large Australian tree with a wide buttressed trunk that bears shiny blue fruits containing edible seeds and yields a light-coloured wood used as timber. Latin name: *Elaeocarpus grandis.* [Mid-19thC. From Wiradhuri *guwandhāng.*]

quango /kwáng gō/ (*plural* **-gos**) *n.* an organization that is able to act independently of the government that finances it [Late 20thC. Acronym of Quasi-Autonomous Non-Governmental Organization.]

quant[1] /kwont/ *n.* POLE FOR PROPELLING BOAT a long pole for pushing against the bottom of a river or lake to propel a boat ■ *vti.* (**quants, quanting, quanted**) PROPEL BOAT WITH LONG POLE to move a punt or other boat along with a quant [15thC. Origin uncertain: perhaps via Latin *contus* from Greek *kontos*.]

quant[2] /kwont/ *n.* sb skilled in computing and the analysis of quantitative data, employed by a company to make financial predictions (*slang*) [Late 20thC. Shortening of QUANTITATIVE.]

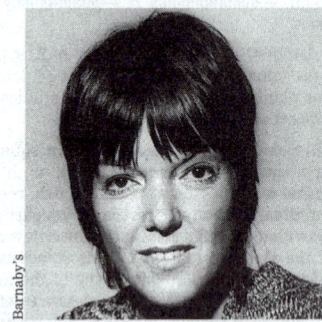

Barnaby's

Mary Quant

Quant /kwont/, **Mary** (*b.* 1934) British fashion designer. A leader of 1960s London style, she created the miniskirt and hotpants, and later expanded her business into cosmetics and textiles.

quant. /kwont/ *abbr.* quantitative

quanta plural of **quantum**

quantal /kwónt'l/ *adj.* **1.** PHYS RELATING TO QUANTUM relating to a quantum or to a system that has been quantized **2.** SCI IN ONE OF TWO POSSIBLE STATES used to describe sth that at a given instant can be found in one of two possible states [Mid-20thC. Formed from QUANTUM.] —**quantally** *adv.*

quantic /kwóntik/ *n.* a mathematical expression with more than one variable that contains terms raised to the same power with respect to all the variables [Mid-19thC. Formed from Latin *quantus* 'how much' (see QUANTITY).]

quantifier /kwónti fī ər/ *n.* a word such as 'all', 'some', or 'most', or a logical symbol with this meaning, that indicates the range of individuals or items referred to

quantify /kwónti fī/ (**-fies, -fying, -fied**) *vt.* **1.** DETERMINE NUMBER OR EXTENT OF STH to calculate or express the number, degree, or amount of sth **2.** LOGIC SHOW RANGE OF REFERENCE OF STH to use a quantifier to limit the range of individuals or items referred to in a sentence or proposition [Mid-19thC. From medieval Latin *quantificare*, from Latin *quantus* (see QUANTITY).] —**quantifiable** /kwónti fī əb'l/ *adj.* —**quantification** /kwóntifi káysh'n/ *n.*

quantitate /kwónti tayt/ (**-tates, -tating, -tated**) *vt.* to estimate or determine precisely the number, degree, or amount of sth [Mid-20thC. Back-formation from QUANTITATIVE.] —**quantitation** /kwónti táysh'n/ *n.*

quantitative /kwóntitətiv/ *adj.* **1.** RELATING TO QUANTITY relating to, concerning, or based on the amount or number of sth **2.** MEASURABLE capable of being measured or expressed in numerical terms **3.** POETRY BASED ON LENGTH OF SYLLABLES relating or belonging to a metrical system based on the length of syllables rather than on stress. Classical Latin and Greek verse uses a quantitative system. [Late 16thC. From medieval Latin *quantitativus*, from Latin *quantitas* (see QUANTITY).] —**quantitatively** *adv.* —**quantitativeness** *n.*

quantitative analysis *n.* the determining of the relative amounts of the components in a mixture

quantitative digital radiography *n.* a method of detecting thinning of the bones (**osteoporosis**) by assessing the levels of calcium present, usually in the spine and hip

quantity /kwóntəti/ (*plural* **-ties**) *n.* **1.** AMOUNT an amount or number of sth **2.** MEASURABLE PROPERTY the measurable property of sth **3.** LARGE AMOUNTS a large amount or number ○ *Foodstuffs were imported in quantity.* **4.** MATH MATHEMATICAL ENTITY WITH NUMERICAL VALUE a mathematical entity that has a numerical value or magnitude **5.** PHYS SPECIFIED MAGNITUDE OF STH the product of a measurable phenomenon such as electric current or radiation intensity and the time during which the phenomenon is measured **6.** LOGIC UNIVERSAL OR PARTICULAR NATURE OF PROPOSITION the characteristic of a logical proposition that distinguishes it as universal or particular **7.** PHON RELATIVE DURATION OF SOUND the length of a vowel sound or syllable [13thC. Via French *quantité* from the Latin stem *quantitat-*, from *quantus* 'how much'. Ultimately from an Indo-European word that is also the ancestor of English *what, how,* and *quality.*]

quantity surveyor *n.* sb who assesses the cost of a construction job based on the amount of labour and materials required to complete it

quantity theory *n.* the theory that prices vary with the amount of money in circulation and the rate at which it circulates

quantize /kwón tīz/ (**-tizes, -tizing, -tized**), **quantise** (**-tises, -tising, -tised**) *vt.* **1.** EXPRESS IN QUANTUM NUMBERS to express sth in terms of quantum numbers **2.** APPLY QUANTUM MECHANICS TO to divide sth into tiny discrete increments applying the rules of quantum mechanics [Early 20thC. Formed from QUANTUM.] —**quantization** /kwón tī záysh'n/ *n.*

Quantock Hills /kwóntək hílz/ ridge of hills in Somerset, England, and a designated Area of Outstanding Natural Beauty. Its highest point is Will's Neck, 385 m/1,262 ft.

quantum /kwóntəm/ *n.* (*plural* **-ta** /kwóntə/) **1.** PHYS SMALLEST QUANTITY OF ENERGY the smallest discrete quantity of a physical property, e.g. electromagnetic radiation or angular momentum **2.** QUANTITY a quantity or amount of anything **3.** SPECIFIC AMOUNT a specific quantity or portion ■ *adj.* MAJOR sudden, dramatic, and significant [Early 17thC. From Latin, formed from *quantus* 'how much' (see QUANTITY).]

quantum chromodynamics *n.* a quantum field theory of elementary particles that states that the colour properties of quarks are bound together by gluons

quantum electrodynamics *n.* a quantum field theory that describes the properties of electromagnetic radiation and its interaction with electrically charged particles

quantum field theory *n.* a theory developed from quantum mechanics based on the assumption that elementary particles interact through the influence of fields around them and the exchange of energy

quantum jump *n.* **1.** PHYS SUDDEN CHANGE OF ENERGY STATE the sudden transition of an atom or particle from one energy state to another **2.** = **quantum leap**

quantum leap *n.* a sudden, dramatic, and significant change or advance ○ *a quantum leap in our understanding of molecular science*

quantum mechanics *n.* the study and analysis of the interactions of atoms and elementary particles based on quantum theory. The study evolved in an effort to explain the behaviour of atoms and subatomic particles, which do not obey the laws of classical Newtonian mechanics. (*takes a singular verb*) —**quantum mechanical** *adj.*

quantum number *n.* any of the set of integers or half integers that characterize the properties and energy states of an elementary particle or system

quantum theory *n.* a theory describing the behaviour and interactions of elementary particles or energy states based on the assumptions that energy is subdivided into discrete amounts and that matter possesses wave properties

Qu'Appelle /kwə pél/ river in southern Saskatchewan, which joins the Assiniboine River east of the Manitoba border. Length: 435 km/270 mi.

quar. *abbr.* **1.** quarter **2.** quarterly

quarantine /kwórrən teen/ *n.* **1.** ISOLATION TO PREVENT SPREAD OF DISEASE enforced isolation of people or animals that may have been exposed to a contagious or infectious disease, e.g. when entering a country (*often used before a noun*) **2.** PLACE OF ISOLATION a place in which people or animals spend a period of isolation to prevent the spread of disease **3.** TIME OF ENFORCED ISOLATION the period of time during which people or animals are kept in isolation to prevent the spread of disease **4.** STATE OR PERIOD OF ISOLATION enforced isolation, e.g. for social or political reasons, or a period of such isolation **5.** 40 DAYS a period of 40 days (*archaic*) ■ *vt.* (**-tines, -tining, -tined**) **1.** ISOLATE TO AVOID SPREAD OF DISEASE to isolate a person or animal that may have been exposed to a contagious or infectious disease in order to prevent the possible spread of that disease **2.** DETAIN to isolate or detain sb, e.g. for social or political reasons [Early 17thC. Via Italian *quarantina* from, ultimately, Latin *quadraginta* 'forty'; so called because ships suspected of carrying disease were refused entrance to port for 40 days.] —**quarantinable** *adj.*

quark[1] /kwaark/ *n.* any elementary particle with an electric charge equal to one-third or two-thirds that of the electron. Quarks are believed to be the constituents of baryons and mesons. There are six types (**flavours**) of quark, each paired with an antiquark, and three properties (**colours**) that determine their role in interactions. [Mid-20thC. Coined by American physicist Murray Gell-Mann (b. 1929), alluding to the phrase 'three quarks for Mr. Mark' in James Joyce's *Finnegans Wake*; because originally there were thought to be three quarks.]

quark[2] /kwaark/ *n.* a type of soft cheese of German origin made from skimmed milk [Mid-20thC. From German, ultimately of Slavic origin.]

quarrel[1] /kwórrəl/ *n.* **1.** ARGUMENT BETWEEN PEOPLE an angry dispute between two or more people **2.** REASON TO ARGUE a reason for a disagreement or dispute between people ○ *I have no quarrel with their proposals.* ■ *vi.* (**-rels, -relling, -relled**) **1.** ARGUE VEHEMENTLY to engage in an angry dispute **2.** DISAGREE WITH STH to dispute or disagree with sth such as a decision **3.** FIND FAULT to complain about sth [14thC. Via Old French from Latin *querela* 'complaint', from *queri* 'to complain' (source of English *querulous*).] —**quarreller** *n.*

quarrel[2] /kwórrəl/ *n.* **1.** CROSSBOW BOLT a short square-headed bolt or arrow used in a crossbow **2.** SQUARE GLASS PANE any of several small square or diamond-shaped panes of glass in a window [12thC. Via Old French from assumed Vulgar Latin *quadrellus*, literally 'small square', from Latin *quadrum* (see QUADRATE).]

quarrelsome /kwórrəlsəm/ *adj.* having a tendency to argue with people —**quarrelsomely** *adv.* —**quarrelsomeness** *n.*

quarrier /kwórri ər/ *n.* sb who works in a stone quarry

quarry[1] /kwórri/ *n.* (*plural* **-ries**) **1.** OPEN AREA FOR MINING an open excavation from which stone or other material is extracted by blasting, cutting, or drilling **2.** SOURCE a rich source of sth ■ *v.* (**-ries, -rying, -ried**) **1.** *vti.* MINING OBTAIN STH FROM QUARRY to extract stone or other material from a quarry **2.** *vt.* USE PLACE FOR EXTRACTING STONE to make a quarry in a particular place such as a hillside and remove material from it ○ *The area was extensively quarried last century.* **3.** *vti.* EXTRACT LABORIOUSLY to obtain sth, such as facts or information, by searching laboriously and carefully [14thC. Via medieval Latin *quarreia* from Old French *quarriere*, from assumed *quarre* 'square-cut stone', from Latin *quadrum* 'square' (see QUADRATE).]

quarry[2] /kwórri/ (*plural* **-ries**) *n.* **1.** HUNTED ANIMAL OR BIRD an animal or bird that is hunted by sth or sb **2.** OBJECT OF PURSUIT sb or sth that is chased or hunted by another [15thC. Via Anglo-Norman *couree* 'entrails of an animal given to the hounds' from assumed Vulgar Latin *corata*, from Latin *cor* 'heart' (see CORDATE).]

quarry[3] /kwórri/ (*plural* **-ries**) *n.* **1.** SQUARE SHAPE a square or diamond shape **2.** STH SQUARE OR DIAMOND-SHAPED sth with a square or diamond shape, e.g. a pane of glass in a latticed window [Mid-16thC. Alteration of QUARREL[2].]

quarry tile *n.* a tile with a square or diamond shape, especially a hardwearing unglazed clay tile used for flooring [From QUARRY[3]]

quart[1] /kwawrt/ *n.* **1.** QUARTER OF GALLON a unit of measurement for liquids equal to two pints **2.** ONE-EIGHTH OF PECK a unit of measurement for dry substances equal to two pints **3.** CONTAINER OR CONTENTS a container that holds one quart or its contents [13thC. Via Old French *quarte* from, ultimately, Latin *quartus* 'fourth'. Ultimately from an Indo-European word that is also the ancestor of English *fourth* and *farthing*.]

quart[2] /kawrt/ *n.* **1.** CARDS SEQUENCE OF FOUR CARDS a sequence of four cards in piquet and some other card games **2.** FENCING = **quarte** [Mid-17thC. Via French, literally 'fourth', from Latin *quartus* (see QUART[1]).]

quartan /kwáwrt'n/ *adj.* used to describe a fever that recurs every fourth day, e.g. in some types of malaria [13thC. Via Old French *quartaine* from, ultimately, Latin *quartus* 'fourth' (see QUART[1]).]

quarte /kaart/, **quart, carte** *n.* FENCING the fourth of the eight parrying or attacking positions in fencing [Mid-17thC. Via French, 'fourth', from, ultimately, Latin *quartus* (see QUART[1]).]

quarter /kwáwrtər/ *n.* **1.** ONE OF FOUR PARTS any of four equal or approximately equal parts into which sth is divided **2.** ONE-FOURTH a number that is equal to one divided by four, represented by the symbol $\frac{1}{4}$ **3.** PERIOD OF THREE MONTHS any of the three-month periods into which the year is divided, especially for accounting purposes **4.** 25 CENTS in the United States and Canada, the sum of 25 cents **5.** COIN WORTH 25 CENTS in the United States and Canada, a coin worth 25 cents or one quarter of a dollar **6.** 15 MINUTES BEFORE OR AFTER HOUR either of the points in time 15 minutes before or after the hour, marked on a traditional clock face at 3 and 9 **7.** MEASURE 28 LB IN WEIGHT in the UK, a unit of weight equal to 12.71 kg/28 lb or one quarter of a hundredweight **8.** MEASURE 25 LB IN WEIGHT in the United States, a unit of weight equal to 11.35 kg/25 lb or one quarter of a hundredweight **9.** MEASURE 8 BUSHELS a unit of capacity for grain and similar substances equal to approximately 8 bushels **10.** MEASURE 4 OZ OF STH an amount of sth weighing 113.4 g/4 oz or a quarter of a pound (*informal*) **11.** QUARTER OF SQUARE MILE one quarter of a square mile of rural land **12.** **quarter, Quarter** DISTRICT OF TOWN an area in a town of a particular type or inhabited by a particular group of people ○ *We visited the French Quarter while we were in New Orleans.* **13.** UNSPECIFIED PERSON OR GROUP an unspecified person or group of people ○ *They're looking for help from any quarter.* **14.** MERCY mercy offered to a defeated enemy **15.** ASTRON MOON PHASE either of the two phases of the Moon in which half of its illuminated surface can be seen from the Earth **16.**

ASTRON **QUARTER OF MOON'S ORBIT** one fourth of the Moon's orbital period about the Earth **17.** SPORTS **PART OF SPORTING CONTEST** one of the four equal parts into which games are divided in some sports **18.** NAUT **SIDE OF REAR HALF OF VESSEL** either side of the rear half of a boat or ship, usually behind the rearmost mast **19.** GEOG **NORTHEAST, SOUTHEAST, SOUTHWEST, OR NORTHWEST** any one of the four compass points that lie midway between north, east, south, and west **20.** HERALDRY **ANY SECTION OF HERALDIC SHIELD** any one of the four sections into which a heraldic shield may be divided **21. PART OF ANIMAL OR BIRD** any one of the four parts into which the body of an animal or bird may be divided, with a leg or wing forming part of each quarter **22. SIDE OF HOOF** the side of a horse's hoof **23. SHOE PART** the part of a shoe between the heel and the front part of the upper ■ **quarters** *npl.* **ACCOMMODATION** living or sleeping accommodation provided for sb, e.g. military personnel and their families, household employees, or members of a ship's crew ■ *adj.* **DIVIDED BY FOUR** used to describe one fourth part of sth ■ *v.* (**-ters, -tering, -tered**) **1.** *vt.* **DIVIDE STH INTO FOUR** to divide sth into four equal or approximately equal parts **2.** *vt.* HIST **CUT BODY INTO FOUR** to cut a human body into four parts following an execution **3.** *vt.* **GIVE SB LODGINGS** to assign accommodation to sb ○ *The soldiers were quartered in an old barn.* **4.** *vt.* HERALDRY **DIVIDE SHIELD INTO FOUR SECTIONS** to divide a heraldic shield into four sections **5.** *vi.* **CROSS IN ZIGZAG COURSE** to cover all parts of an area of land, sea, or air by ranging from side to side while moving forward, e.g. while searching for sb or sth **6.** *vi.* NAUT **COME FROM REAR PART OF SIDE** to come from a direction at approximately 45 degrees to the stern of a boat or ship **7.** *vt.* **POSITION STH AT 90 DEGREES** to locate or position a machine part at right angles to another [13thC. Via Old French *quartier* from, ultimately, Latin *quartus* 'fourth' (see QUART[1]).]

quarterage /kwáwtərij/ *n.* a sum of money paid or received every three months

quarterback /kwáwrtər bak/ *n.* in American football, a player positioned behind the centre who directs the play by calling signals

quarter-bound *adj.* used to describe a book that is bound in one material, usually leather, on the spine and another on the covers

quarter day *n.* one of four days in a year regarded as the beginning or end of a quarter, when particular payments are due (*archaic*)

quarterdeck /kwáwrtər dek/ *n.* NAUT the rear part of the upper deck of a ship, where official ceremonies traditionally take place on a vessel

quarterfinal /kwáwrtər fín'l/ *n.* any one of four contests in a tournament or competition, the winners of which go on to play each other in the semifinals [Early 20thC. Modelled on SEMIFINAL.] —**quarterfinalist** *n.*

quarter horse *n.* a strong horse formerly bred to run short races in the United States [From 'quarter-race', a race over a quarter mile]

quarter hour *n.* **1. 15 MINUTES** a period of 15 minutes **2. 15 MINUTES BEFORE OR AFTER HOUR** either of the points on a clock face that indicate a time 15 minutes before or after the hour ○ *The clock chimes on the quarter hour.*

quarterlight /kwáwrtər līt/ *n.* a small triangular window in the side of some cars and other vehicles that can be pivoted open for ventilation [Late 19thC. Formed from QUARTER 'side' + LIGHT 'window'.]

quarterly /kwáwrtərli/ *adj.* **1. HAPPENING EVERY THREE MONTHS** happening, produced, or published four times a year, at three-month intervals **2.** HERALDRY **DIVIDED INTO FOUR SECTIONS** used to describe a heraldic shield that is divided into four sections ■ *adv.* **EVERY THREE MONTHS** once every three months ■ *n.* (*plural* **-lies**) **JOURNAL PUBLISHED EVERY THREE MONTHS** a magazine or journal published four times a year, at three-month intervals

quartermaster /kwáwrtər maastər/ *n.* **1. ARMY OFFICER** an army officer responsible for providing soldiers with food, clothing, equipment, and living quarters **2. NAVAL OFFICER** in the navy, a petty officer or ship's mate with some responsibilities for navigation and signals

quartern /kwáwrtərn/ *n.* **1. ONE FOURTH** a fourth part of sth, especially of some old weights and measures **2. quartern, quartern loaf** (*plural* **quartern loaves**) **SMALL LOAF** a loaf of bread 10 cm/4 in square, used especially for making sandwiches **3. quartern, quartern loaf** (*plural* **quartern loaves**) **LARGE LOAF** a loaf of bread weighing 1.6 kg/4 lb [13thC. From Anglo-Norman *quartrun*.]

quarter note *n.* *US* = **crotchet**

quarter-phase *adj.* ELEC ENG = **two-phase** [So called because the two currents are 90 degrees out of phase]

quarter round *n.* a moulding that, in cross-section, is the shape of a quarter of a circle

quarters /kwáwrtərz/ *npl.* a building or set of rooms where people live, especially military personnel or servants ◇ **at close quarters** from very near

quartersawn /kwáwrtər sawn/ *adj.* used to describe wooden boards sawn from a log cut into quarters lengthwise so as to show off the grain of the wood

quarter section *n.* *US, Can* a tract of land measuring 800 metres/half a mile on each side, equal to 65 hectares/160 acres or one fourth of a section

quarter sessions *npl.* formerly in England and Wales, a local court sitting quarterly with limited authority to try civil and criminal cases

quarterstaff /kwáwrtər staaf/ (*plural* **-staves** /-stayvz/ *or* **-staffs**) *n.* a long heavy wooden stick tipped with iron, formerly used in hand-to-hand fighting [Mid-16thC. *Quarter* is of uncertain origin: possibly because it was made from a tree of a certain size cut into quarters.]

quarter tone *n.* a difference in pitch between two tones (**interval**) that is equal to half a semitone

quartet /kwawr tét/, **quartette** *n.* **1. MUSICAL GROUP** a group of four singers or musicians (*takes a singular or plural verb*) **2. PIECE OF MUSIC** a piece of music written for four voices or instruments **3. GROUP OF FOUR** a group or set of four people or things (*takes a singular or plural verb*) [Late 18thC. Via French *quartette* from Italian *quartetto*, from *quarto* 'fourth', from Latin *quartus* (see QUART).]

quartic /kwáwrtik/ *adj.* MATH of or relating to the fourth degree. A quartic equation has the general form $ax^4 + bx^3 + cx^2 + dx + e = 0$. [Mid-19thC. Formed from Latin *quartus* (see QUART).]

quartile /kwáwr tīl/ *n.* **1. STATISTICAL DIVISION** any one of the four equal groups into which a statistical sample can be divided **2. STATISTICAL VALUE** in statistics, any one of the three values that divide a frequency distribution into four parts, each containing a quarter of the sample population **3. DISTANCE BETWEEN PLANETS** the astrological aspect of planets that are distant from each other by 90 degrees, or one fourth of the zodiac [Early 16thC. Via Old French *quartil* from, ultimately, Latin *quartus* (see QUART).]

quarto /kwáwrtō/ (*plural* **-tos**) *n.* **1. PAGE SIZE** the page size created by folding a single sheet of standard-sized printing paper in half twice to create four leaves or eight pages **2. BOOK WITH QUARTO PAGES** a book with quarto pages [Late 16thC. From Latin *(in) quarto*, 'in a fourth', from *quartus* (see QUART).]

quartz /kwawrts/ *n.* a usually colourless transparent crystalline mineral widely distributed in rocks of all types. Coloured varieties are used as gemstones. Its hardness makes it a valuable industrial component, e.g. as a frequency control in electronic communications and timing devices. [Mid-18thC. From German *Quarz*, ultimately from a western Slavic word meaning 'hard'.]

quartz clock *n.* a clock in which the time-keeping mechanism is accurately controlled by a quartz crystal that vibrates at a fixed frequency in an oscillating electric circuit

quartz crystal *n.* a small piece of quartz cut so that it vibrates at a known frequency. In an oscillating electric circuit, it produces a constant signal for accurate timekeeping.

quartz glass *n.* a clear glass made from melted silica. It can withstand high or rapidly changing temperatures and is unusually transparent to ultraviolet radiation. It is made in both transparent and translucent forms, the latter being clouded by minute gas bubbles trapped within it.

quartz heater *n.* a portable electric heater with heating elements sealed in quartz glass tubes

quartziferous /kwawrt síffərəss/ *adj.* containing or consisting of quartz

quartz-iodine lamp *n.* a very bright lamp with a bulb made of quartz glass that has a tungsten filament and usually contains iodine vapour. It is used in car headlights and film projectors.

quartzite /kwáwrts īt/ *n.* a pale metamorphic rock composed mainly of quartz, formed by the action of heat and pressure on sandstone. It is an important building material used, e.g. for high-quality paving blocks and the facades of buildings. —**quartzitic** /kwawrt síttik/ *adj.*

quartz lamp *n.* a mercury vapour lamp with a bulb made from quartz glass that produces light rich in ultraviolet radiation and is used for street lighting and sun lamps

quartz watch *n.* a watch in which the time-keeping mechanism is accurately controlled by a quartz crystal that vibrates at a fixed frequency in an oscillating electric circuit

quasar /kwáy zaar, -saar/ *n.* a remote compact object in space that usually has a large red shift and emits radio waves at high intensity [Mid-20thC. Contraction of *quasi-stellar object*.]

quash[1] /kwosh/ (**quashes, quashing, quashed**) *vt.* **1. PUT A STOP TO STH** to put a stop to sth forcibly **2. STIFLE** to prevent feelings from developing or being expressed [14thC. Via Old French *quasser* from medieval Latin *quassare* 'to shake to pieces', from *quatere* 'to shake' (source of English *squash*[1] and *concussion*).]

quash[2] (**quashes, quashing, quashed**) *vt.* to declare formally that sth such as a law or a court's verdict is not valid [13thC. Via Old French *quasser* from, ultimately, Latin *cassare*, from *cassus* 'empty, void'.]

quasi /kwáy zī, kwáy sī, kwaázi/ *adj.* **ALMOST BUT NOT QUITE** resembling sb or sth in some ways, but not exactly the same ■ *adv.* **SO TO SPEAK** so to speak (*archaic*) ○ *'under this roof, which is quasi mine'* (Sir Walter Scott, *Waverley*; 1814) [15thC. Via Old French from Latin, 'as if', from *quam* 'as' + *si* 'if'.]

quasi- *prefix.* as if, resembling [Via Old French from Latin *quasi*, literally 'as if', from *quam* 'as' + *si* 'if']

quasijudicial /kwáy zī joo dísh'l/ *adj.* used to describe decision-making powers that are similar to those of a court judge, or to describe any arbitrator or inquiry with such powers [Mid-19thC] —**quasijudicially** *adv.*

quasilegislative /kwáy zī léj islətiv/ *adj.* used to describe regulations that are not regarded as laws proper but have the force of law, or to describe bodies that have the right to make such regulations [Mid-20thC]

quasi-stellar object *n.* = **quasar**

quassia /kwóshə/ *n.* **1. TREE YIELDING FINE-GRAINED TIMBER** a tropical American shrub or small tree with scarlet flowers that yields fine-grained timber from which an insecticide can be extracted. Genus: *Quassia.* **2. WOOD OF QUASSIA TREE** the fine-grained pale wood of the quassia tree, used for making furniture **3. INSECTICIDE DERIVED FROM QUASSIA WOOD** a bitter substance obtained from the bark and wood of the quassia tree, formerly used in medicine and now used as an insecticide [Origin uncertain]

quatercentenary /kwáttər sen téenəri/ (*plural* **-ries**) *n.* a four hundredth anniversary [Late 19thC. 'quater' from Latin, 'four times' (see QUATERNARY).]

quaternary /kwə túrnəri/ *adj.* **1. OCCURRING IN FOURS** consisting of four parts, or occurring in sets of four **2. HAVING FOUR-ATOM BONDS** bonded to four other non-hydrogen atoms or groups of atoms, or containing atoms bonded in this way ■ *n.* (*plural* **-ies**) **SET OF FOUR OR FOURTH MEMBER** a set of four, or the fourth member of a set [15thC. From Latin *quaternarius*, from *quaterni* 'by fours', from *quater* 'four times'.]

Quaternary /kwə túrnəri/ *adj.* **BELONGING TO PRESENT GEOLOGICAL PERIOD** belonging to or dating from the most recent geological period, spanning the last 2 million years ■ *n.* **MOST RECENT GEOLOGICAL PERIOD** the current period of geological time and the second period of the Cenozoic era. It is characterized by the appearance and dominance of humans.

quaternary ammonium compound *n.* a nitrogen compound regarded as a derivative of ammonium. Some are used as solvents and disinfectants.

quaternion /kwə túrni ən/ *n.* **1.** = **quaternary** *n.* **2.** GENERALIZED COMPLEX NUMBER a generalized complex number that contains four terms, one real and three imaginary, and is the sum of a real number and a vector [14thC. From the late Latin stem *quaternion-*, from Latin *quaterni* (see QUATERNARY).]

quaternity /kwə túrnəti/ (*plural* **-ties**) *n.* a set of four, especially the four beings that, in some religions, are unified in God [Early 16thC. From late Latin *quaternitas*, from Latin *quaterni* (see QUATERNARY).]

quatrain /kwó trayn/ *n.* a verse of poetry consisting of four lines, especially one with lines that rhyme alternately [Late 16thC. From French, formed from *quatre* 'four', from Latin *quattuor*. Ultimately from the Indo-European word for 'four' that is also the ancestor of English *four*, *quarter*, and *tetra-*.]

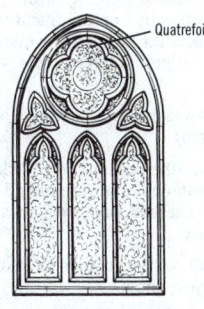

Quatrefoil

quatrefoil /káttrə foyl/ *n.* **1.** FLOWER OR LEAF SYMBOL a design or symbol in the shape of a flower with four petals, or a leaf with four parts. It is often used in heraldry. **2.** ARCHITECTURAL ORNAMENT an architectural decoration consisting of four arcs radiating from a centre like flower petals [15thC. From Anglo-Norman, literally 'four-leaf'.]

quattrocento /kwáttrō chéntō/ *n.* the 15th century in Italy, especially with reference to art and literature [Late 19thC. From Italian, shortening of *mil quattrocento* 'one thousand four hundred'.]

quaver /kwáyvər/ *v.* (**-vers, -vering, -vered**) **1.** *vi.* TREMBLE SLIGHTLY to tremble because of nervousness or fear **2.** *vti.* SAY TREMBLINGLY to say sth or speak in a trembling voice because of nervousness or fear **3.** *vi.* SING WITH TRILL to sing in a trilling voice ■ *n.* **1.** TREMBLING SOUND a tremble in the voice caused by nervousness or fear **2.** LENGTH OF NOTE a musical note equal in length to one eighth of a semibreve. US term **eighth note** **3.** TRILL an alternation of a musical tone with the tone just above it [15thC. Formed from earlier *quave* 'to tremble', of prehistoric Germanic origin.] —**quaveringly** *adv.* —**quavery** *adj.*

quaver rest *n.* a rest equal in length to an eighth note. US term **eighth rest**

quay /kee/ *n.* a platform that runs along the edge of a port or harbour, where boats are loaded and unloaded [14thC. Via Old North French *cai* from Gaulish *caio* 'rampart'. Ultimately from an Indo-European base denoting a fence that is also the ancestor of English *hedge*.]

quayage /kée ij/ *n.* **1.** FEE FOR USING QUAY a charge that ship owners must pay to dock at a quay in order to load and unload there **2.** QUAY SPACE the space available on a quay for ships to load and unload **3.** QUAY SYSTEM a system of quays

Quayle /kwayl/, **Sir Anthony** (1913–89) British actor and director. He was cofounder of the Royal Shakespeare Memorial Theatre Company, and set up his own touring company in 1984.

quayside /kée sīd/ *n.* the edge of a quay, where it meets the water

Que. *abbr.* Quebec

quean /kween/ *n.* an offensive term that deliberately insults a woman's morality (*archaic offensive*) [Old English *cwene* 'woman' (see QUEAN)]

queasy /kwéezi/ (**-sier, -siest**) *adj.* **1.** NAUSEOUS feeling ill in the stomach, as if on the point of vomiting **2.** CAUSING NAUSEA causing a feeling of nausea **3.** EASILY MADE NAUSEOUS easily made to feel nauseous **4.** CAUSING UNEASINESS causing a feeling of uneasiness [15thC. Origin unknown.] —**queasily** *adv.* —**queasiness** *n.*

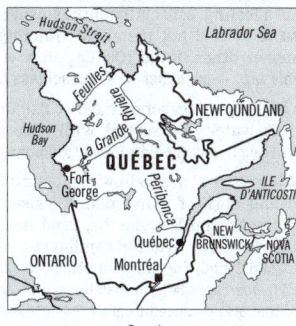

Quebec

Quebec[1] /kwi bék, ki-/ **1.** **Québec, Quebec City** capital city of the province of Quebec, Canada, situated on the St Lawrence River. Population: 671,889 (1996). **2.** the largest province in Canada, situated between Ontario and Newfoundland, with French-based social institutions, language, and culture. Capital: Quebec. Population: 7,138,795 (1996). Area: 1,540,680 sq. km/594,858 sq. mi. —**Quebecer** /kwi békər, ki-/ *n.*

Quebec[2] /kwi bék, ki-/ *n.* the NATO phonetic alphabet code word for the letter 'Q', used in international radio communications

Québécois /kwi békwaa, kay-/, **Québecois, Quebecois** *adj.* OF QUEBEC relating to or typical of Quebec, especially its French-speaking inhabitants or their culture ■ *n.* (*plural* **-cois**) SB FROM QUEBEC sb who was born or brought up in Quebec, especially sb who is French-speaking [French, 'from Quebec']

quebracho /kay braachō/ (*plural* **-chos**) *n.* **1.** TREE WITH MEDICINAL BARK a tree native to Chile and Argentina whose bark yields a medicine used in treating respiratory ailments. Latin name: *Aspidosperma quebracho-blanco*. **2.** TREE WITH TANNIN-RICH WOOD a tree of southern South America whose hard tannin-rich wood is used in the leather industry. Genus: *Schinopsis*. **3.** BARK OF QUEBRACHO TREE the bark of the quebracho tree that yields a medicine used in treating respiratory ailments **4.** WOOD OF QUEBRACHO TREE the hard tannin-rich wood of the quebracho tree that is used in the leather industry [Late 19thC. From Spanish, an alteration of *quiebrahacha*, literally 'axe-breaker', from *quebrar* 'to break' + *hacha* 'axe'.]

Quechua /kéchwə/ (*plural* **-ua** *or* **-uas**), **Kechua** (*plural* **-ua** *or* **-uas**), **Quichua** /kíchwə/ (*plural* **-ua** *or* **-uas**) *n.* **1.** MEMBER OF NATIVE S AMERICAN PEOPLE a member of any of several Native South American peoples, including the Incas, living in the Andes **2.** QUECHUA LANGUAGE a Native South American language spoken in the Andes, from southern Colombia through Chile and Argentina. It belongs to the Andean branch of Andean-Equatorial languages. Quechua is spoken by about 10 million people. [Mid-19thC. From Spanish, of uncertain origin: probably from Quechua *kkechúwa* 'plunderer'.] —**Quechua** *adj.* —**Quechuan** *adj.*, *n.*

queen /kween/ *n.* **1.** FEMALE RULER a woman who rules over a country, usually by right of birth **2.** KING'S WIFE the wife of a king **3.** ADMIRED WOMAN, PLACE, OR THING a greatly admired woman who stands out above all others, or a place or thing considered the best of its kind and personified as a woman **4.** CHESS MOST POWERFUL CHESS PIECE the most powerful piece in chess, able to move over any number of squares forwards, backwards, sideways, and diagonally **5.** FACE CARD a playing card with a picture of a queen on it, ranking above a jack and below a king **6.** EGG-LAYING BEE, ANT, OR TERMITE a large, fully developed female that lays eggs in a colony of social insects, such as bees or ants. She is usually the only fertile female member of the colony. **7.** OFFENSIVE TERM an offensive term for a homosexual man (*offensive*) **8.** GAY MAN a word used in the gay community to refer to a homosexual man who behaves in a flamboyantly effeminate way (*slang*) ■ *vti.* (**queens, queening, queened**) MAKE PAWN

INTO QUEEN to promote a pawn to the rank of queen by managing to take it to the opponent's end of the board, or to become promoted from pawn to queen [Old English *cwēn* 'woman'. Ultimately from an Indo-European word that is also the ancestor of English *gyno-* and *banshee*.] ◊ **queen it** to behave in a domineering, arrogant way (*informal*)

Queen Anne *n.* a style of furniture popular in the early 18th century, characterized by the use of simple curves and cabriole legs [Early 19thC. Named after Queen ANNE.]

Queen Anne's lace *n.* = **cow parsley** [Late 19thC. Named after Queen ANNE, perhaps from the resemblance of the plant's flowers to delicate embroidery.]

queen bee *n.* **1.** FERTILE FEMALE BEE a large, fully developed female bee that lays eggs continually. She is usually the only fertile female in the colony. **2.** IMPORTANT WOMAN a woman who is treated as the most important member of her group, or who behaves as if she is (*informal*)

queencake /kween kayk/ *n.* a small currant cake, usually heart-shaped

Queen Charlotte Islands group of 150 islands in Canada, off the western coast of British Columbia. Area: 9,596 sq. km/3,705 sq. mi. Population: 3,368 (1986).

queen consort (*plural* **queens consort**) *n.* a woman married to a reigning king

queen cup *n.* a stemless plant of western North America that produces a single white flower and a blue berry. Latin name: *Clintonia uniflora*.

queen dowager *n.* a widow of a king

Queen Elizabeth Islands /-i lízzəbəth-/ group of islands in northern Canada, in the Arctic Archipelago, shared between Nunavut and the Northwest Territories. Area: 425,000 sq. km/164,000 sq. mi.

queenly /kwéenli/ *adj.* **1.** REGAL having the qualities typical of a queen, especially grace and dignity **2.** RELATING TO QUEEN relating to a queen or suitable for a queen ■ *adv.* REGALLY in a way thought fitting for or typical of a queen, especially with grace and dignity —**queenliness** *n.*

Queen Maud Gulf /-máwd/ gulf in the Arctic Ocean, between southeastern Victoria Island and the mainland of Nunavut, Canada

queen mother *n.* the mother of a reigning king or queen and the widow of a former king

queen of puddings *n.* a pudding made of breadcrumbs and milk, often with a layer of meringue on top

Queen of the May (*plural* **Queens of the May**) *n.* = **May Queen**

queen-of-the-prairie *n.* a plant that bears small pink flowers and grows in grasslands of the central and eastern United States. Latin name: *Filipendula rubra*.

queen olive *n.* a large edible olive with a long flat stone

queen post *n.* either of two vertical posts forming part of the triangular framework that supports a roof. They support the rafters and the horizontal tie beam. Queen posts are used where the central support provided by a king post would be insufficient because of the width of the frame. ◊ **king post** [Modelled on 'king post']

queen regent (*plural* **queens regent**) *n.* a queen reigning on behalf of another person, especially one too young to take the throne

queen regnant (*plural* **queens regnant**) *n.* a queen who reigns in her own right, as distinct from the wife of a king

Queens /kweenz/ the largest borough in New York City, on western Long Island. Population: 1,951,598 (1990). Area: 282 sq. km/109 sq. mi.

Queen's Bench *n.* a division of the High Court of Justice in England. It is called the King's Bench when the reigning British monarch is a king. ◊ **King's Bench**

Queensberry rules /kwéenzbəri-/ *npl.* **1.** BOXING RULES the rules that govern boxing, drawn up in 1867

under the supervision of the Marquess of Queensberry **2.** FAIR PLAY accepted standards of fairness or courteousness in any situation (*informal*)

Queen's Counsel *n.* a senior barrister in England, entitled to wear a silk gown and sit inside the bar of the court. The title is King's Counsel when the reigning British monarch is a king.

Queen's English *n.* standard written or spoken British English, regarded as the most correct form of the language. It is called the King's English when the reigning British monarch is a king.

Queen's evidence *n.* evidence for the prosecution given by sb who took part in a crime, usually in exchange for leniency. It is called King's evidence when the reigning British monarch is a king.

Queen's Highway *n.* a public road, regarded as belonging ultimately to the Queen. It is called the King's Highway when the reigning British monarch is a king. (*formal or humorous*)

queenship /kweén ship/ *n.* the rank or position of queen

queenside /kweén sīd/ *n.* the side of a chessboard on which the queen is located at the beginning of a game

queen-size *adj.* larger than the standard size but smaller than king-size (*refers to beds and bedclothes*) [Modelled on 'king-size']

Queensland /kweénzlənd, kweénz land/ state in northeastern Australia. Originally part of New South Wales, it became a separate colony in 1859. Capital: Brisbane. Population: 3,339,000 (1996). Area: 1,727,200 sq. km/666,876 sq. mi. —**Queenslander** *n.*

Queen's shilling *n.* in former times, a coin given to new military recruits as a symbol of enlistment. It was called the King's shilling when the reigning British monarch was a king. (*literary or humorous*)

Queen's speech *n.* **1.** SPEECH OPENING PARLIAMENT a speech given by the Queen at the opening of Parliament each year, setting out the government's proposed legislation **2.** QUEEN'S CHRISTMAS BROADCAST in the UK, a speech by the Queen to the nation and the Commonwealth broadcast on Christmas Day

Queenstown /kweénz town/ town in the southwest of the South Island, New Zealand. Situated on the shore of Lake Wakatipu, it is a major tourist resort. Population: 3,500 (1996).

queen substance *n.* a pheromone secreted by a queen bee and consumed by worker bees in the same hive that prevents the worker bees from becoming fully developed and reproducing

queer /kweer/ *adj.* **1.** NOT USUAL not usual or expected (*dated*) **2.** ECCENTRIC eccentric or unconventional (*dated informal*) **3.** SUSPICIOUS arousing suspicion (*dated informal*) **4.** NAUSEOUS slightly unwell, especially nauseous or faint (*dated*) **5.** OFFENSIVE TERM an offensive term meaning homosexual (*offensive*) ■ *n.* OFFENSIVE TERM an offensive term for a homosexual person, especially a man (*offensive*) ■ *vt.* (**queers, queering, queered**) **1.** THWART to spoil or thwart sth, especially sb's plans (*dated informal*) **2.** COMPROMISE SB to put sb in an awkward situation [Early 16thC. Origin uncertain: probably from Low German *quer* 'oblique, crooked'. Ultimately from an Indo-European base meaning 'to twist' that is also the ancestor of English *thwart* and *contort*.] —**queerish** *adj.* —**queerly** *adv.* —**queerness** *n.*

queer bashing *n.* an offensive term for the practice or an instance of committing unprovoked acts of violence against homosexuals (*informal offensive*) —**queer basher** *n.*

queercore /kweér kawr/ *n.* (*slang*) **1.** GAY YOUTH MOVEMENT a gay youth movement that rejects the stereotype of the gay person as persecuted victim by confidently and assertively proclaiming homosexuality, especially in punk-style music **2.** GAY YOUTH MUSIC a style of music similar to punk rock with lyrics that proclaim homosexuality confidently and assertively [Late 20thC. Coined from QUEER + HARD-CORE.]

queer fish *n.* sb with unusual habits or beliefs (*dated informal*)

quell /kwel/ (**quells, quelling, quelled**) *vt.* **1.** PUT STOP TO to bring sth to an end, usually by means of force **2.** SUPPRESS FEELING to suppress or allay a feeling [Old English *cwellan* 'to kill'. Ultimately from an Indo-European word meaning 'to stab, kill' that is also the ancestor of English *kill* and *quail*[2].]

quench /kwench/ (**quenches, quenching, quenched**) *vt.* **1.** SATISFY THIRST to satisfy a thirst by drinking sth **2.** EXTINGUISH FIRE to put out a fire or light **3.** SUBDUE FEELING to subdue a feeling, especially enthusiasm or desire **4.** COOL METAL to cool hot metal by plunging it into cold water or other liquid [Old English *ācwencan*] —**quenchable** *adj.* —**quencher** *n.* —**quenchless** *adj.*

quenelle /kə nél/ *n.* a seasoned meat or fish dumpling poached in water and served with a sauce [Mid-19thC. Via French from German *Knödel* (dumpling).]

quercetin /kwúrssitin/ *n.* a yellow compound found in the rind and bark of many plants, especially the bark of the oak and Douglas fir, used medicinally to treat abnormally fragile capillaries. Formula: $C_{15}H_{10}O_7$. [Mid-19thC. Formed from Latin *quercetum* 'oak-forest', from *quercus* 'oak'. Ultimately from an Indo-European word that also produced English *fir* and *cork*.]

quercitron /kwúrssitrən/ *n.* **1.** OAK BARK the bright orange inner bark of the black oak tree, used in tanning and dyeing **2.** YELLOW DYE yellow dye made from quercitron [Late 18thC. Blend of Latin *quercus* 'oak' and CITRON (from the colour of its bark).]

querist /kweérist/ *n.* sb who asks questions (*formal*) [Mid-17thC. Formed from an early variant of QUERY.]

quern /kwurn/ *n.* a simple stone mill used for grinding grain by hand [Old English *cweorn*. Ultimately from an Indo-European base meaning 'heavy' that is also the ancestor of English *grave*[2], *baro-*, *brute*, and *guru*.]

querulous /kwérrŏŏləss, -ryŏŏ-/ *adj.* **1.** TENDING TO COMPLAIN inclined to complain or find fault **2.** WHINING whining or complaining in tone [15thC. Via late Latin *querulosus* from, ultimately, Latin *queri* 'to complain' (source of English *quarrel*).] —**querulously** *adv.* —**querulousness** *n.*

query /kweéri/ *n.* (*plural* **-ries**) **1.** QUESTION a request for information **2.** DOUBT a doubt or criticism **3.** = **question mark** ■ *vt.* (**-ries, -rying, -ried**) **1.** QUESTION STH to express doubts about, or objections to, sth **2.** INQUIRE to ask a question [Mid-17thC. Anglicization of earlier *quere*, from Latin *quaere* 'ask', from *quaerere* 'to seek, ask' (source also of English *question*, *inquire*, and *conquer*.)] —**querier** *n.*

ques. *abbr.* question

quest /kwest/ *n.* **1.** SEARCH a search for sth, especially a long or difficult one **2.** ADVENTUROUS EXPEDITION a journey in search of sth, especially one made by knights in medieval tales **3.** STH SOUGHT the object or goal of a quest (*literary*) ■ *v.* (**quests, questing, quested**) **1.** *vti.* SEEK STH to seek or go in search of sth (*literary*) **2.** *vi.* TRACK ANIMALS to follow the track of a bird or animal that is being hunted (*refers to hunting dogs*) [14thC. Via Old French *queste* from, ultimately, Latin *quaesta*, the feminine past participle of *quaerere* 'to seek' (see QUERY).] —**quester** *n.* —**questingly** *adv.*

question /kwéschən/ *n.* **1.** WRITTEN OR SPOKEN INQUIRY a request for information or for a reply, which usually ends with a question mark if written or on a rising intonation if spoken ○ *Does anyone have any questions?* **2.** DOUBT a doubt or uncertainty about sb or sth **3.** ISSUE a matter that is the subject of discussion, debate, or negotiation **4.** EXAMINATION PROBLEM a problem to be discussed or solved in an examination ■ *v.* (**-tions, -tioning, -tioned**) **1.** *vti.* INTERROGATE to ask sb questions, especially formally or officially, about a particular topic **2.** *vt.* DOUBT STH to raise doubts about sth, especially about its truth, genuineness, or usefulness [13thC. Via French from the Latin stem *quaestion-* 'inquiry', from *quaest-*, the past participle stem of *quaerere* (see QUERY).] —**questioner** *n.* ◇ **beg the question 1.** to take for granted the very point that needs to be proved, and so fail to address an issue properly **2.** to give rise to sth else that should be answered or explained ◇ **be out of the question** to be impossible or unacceptable ◇ **call sth into question** to raise doubts about sth ◇ **in question** used to indicate the person or thing under discussion ◇ **pop the question** to propose marriage to sb (*informal*)

WORD KEY: SYNONYMS

question, quiz, interrogate, grill, give the third degree to

CORE MEANING: asking for information

question the process of asking sb for information on a particular subject, for example about sth sb has done or as part of a formal or official investigation; **quiz** persistent questioning in an ordinary situation; **interrogate** a formal or official systematic intensive questioning of a suspect or witness with a view to making him or her reveal information; **grill** an informal word similar in use to 'interrogate' but suggesting an even greater degree of intensiveness or pressure; **give sb the third degree to** an informal phrase for sustained intensive questioning, especially by police or the military in order to elicit a confession or information. It can also be used to suggest that sb in an ordinary situation is questioning another person in an unnecessarily harsh or persistent manner.

questionable /kwéschənəb'l/ *adj.* **1.** DUBIOUS open to doubt or disagreement **2.** IMMORAL not respectable or morally proper ○ *questionable motives* —**questionability** /kwéschənə bíllәti/ *n.* —**questionably** /kwéschənəbli/ *adv.*

questioning /kwéschəning/ *n.* INTERROGATION a situation in which sb is asked a lot of questions, especially formally or officially, or an instance of this ■ *adj.* EXPRESSING QUESTION expressing a question without using words ○ *a questioning glance* —**questioningly** *adv.*

questionless /kwéschənləss/ *adj.* **1.** = **unquestionable 2.** = **unquestioning**

question mark *n.* the punctuation mark (?) placed at the end of a sentence or phrase intended as a direct question ◇ **a question mark over** an area of doubt and uncertainty

question master *n.* sb who asks questions on a radio or television quiz show

questionnaire /kwéschə náir, késchə náir/ *n.* a set of questions used to gather information in a survey, or the printed paper that contains the questions [Late 19thC. From French, formed from *questionner* 'to ask', from *question* (see QUESTION).]

question tag *n.* a short phrase at the end of a statement that changes it into a question. In English, some examples are the phrases 'isn't it?' and 'have you?'

question time *n.* in Parliament, a period of time every day during which members of parliament may address questions to government ministers

Quetta /kwéttə/ capital city of Baluchistan Province, in west-central Pakistan. Population: 285,719 (1981).

Quetzal

quetzal /kéts'l/ (*plural* **-zals** *or* **-zales** /ket saá layss/) *n.* **1.** CENTRAL AMERICAN BIRD WITH BRIGHT PLUMAGE a Central American bird with brilliant green and red plumage and, in the male, long streaming tail feathers. Latin name: *Pharomachrus mocino.* **2.** UNIT OF GUATEMALAN CURRENCY the main unit of currency in Guatemala worth 100 centavos. See table at **currency 3.** NOTE WORTH A QUETZAL a note worth one quetzal [Early 19thC. Via American Spanish from, ultimately, Nahuatl *quetzalli* 'brilliantly coloured tail feather'.]

Quetzalcoatl /kéts'l kō átt'l/ *n.* a Toltec and Aztec god and the legendary ruler of Mexico, represented as a feathered serpent. For the Toltecs, he was a god of soil fertility, while for the Aztecs, he was a sun god and also the god of death and resurrection. [Via Spanish from Nahuatl *Quetzalcōātl*, from *quetzal(li)* 'brightly coloured tail feather' + *cōātl* 'snake']

queue /kyoo/ *n.* **1.** LINE OF PEOPLE WAITING a line of people or vehicles waiting for sth, especially waiting for their turn to do sth. US term **line**[1] *n.* 34 **2.** COMPUT SET OF COMPUTER TASKS a series of messages or jobs waiting to be processed automatically one after the other by a computer system **3.** COMPUT LIST OF DATA ELEMENTS a list of computer data constructed and maintained so that the elements are inserted at one end and deleted from the other in first in, first out fashion **4.** HIST MAN'S PIGTAIL IN FORMER TIMES a short plait of hair worn at the back of the neck by soldiers and sailors in the late 18th and early 19th centuries ■ *v.* (**queues, queueing** *or* **queuing, queued**) **1.** *vt.* COMPUT ADD TO COMPUTER'S TASKS to add a job or message to the list of tasks being held in storage by a computer, awaiting automatic dispatching **2.** *vi.* FORM WAITING LINE to form a line while waiting for sth **3.** *vi.* WAIT IN LARGE NUMBERS to be waiting for or eagerly anticipating sth along with a lot of other people (*informal*) ○ *the most eminent critics queueing up to review her latest book* [Late 16thC. Via French from Latin *cauda* 'tail' (source also of English *coda*).] ◇ **jump the queue** to push in or move ahead of others unfairly in a queue

queue-jump (**queue-jumps, queue-jumping, queue-jumped**) *vt.* to push in or move ahead of others unfairly in a queue or in a situation where people should wait their turn —**queue-jumper** *n.*

Quezón y Molina /káyz on ee mo léenə, ke thón-/, **Manuel Luis** (1878–1944) Philippine statesman. He worked for Philippine independence, and was the first president of the Commonwealth of the Philippines (1935–44).

quibble /kwíbb'l/ *vi.* (**-bles, -bling, -bled**) MAKE TRIVIAL OBJECTIONS to argue over unimportant things and make petty objections ■ *n.* **1.** PETTY OBJECTION an unimportant distinction or petty objection **2.** PUN a pun (*archaic*) [Early 17thC. Origin uncertain: probably formed from obsolete *quib* 'pun, equivocation', from Latin *quibus* 'to whom, for whom', often used in legal documents and thus associated with dubious legal proceedings and practices.] —**quibbler** *n.* —**quibblingly** *adv.*

quiche /keesh/ *n.* a savoury tart filled with an egg-and-cream mixture and various meat or vegetable ingredients [Mid-20thC. Via French from German dialect *Küche* 'small cake', from German *Kuchen* 'cake' (see CAKE).]

quiche Lorraine /-lə ráyn/ *n.* a quiche made with cheese and bacon [Mid-20thC. Named after its place of origin, the French region of *Lorraine*.]

Quichua /kíchwə/ *n., adj.* = **Quechua**

quick /kwik/ *adj.* **1.** DOING STH FAST moving or doing sth fast **2.** ALERT demonstrating alertness or sharp perception ○ *She has a very quick mind.* **3.** NIMBLE moving swiftly and with skill ○ *quick fingers* **4.** DONE WITHOUT DELAY doing sth without delay ○ *They promised a quick delivery.* **5.** EASILY ANGERED used to describe a temper that is easily roused **6.** BRIEF taking or lasting only a short time ○ *We stopped to have a quick chat.* **7.** HASTY tending to be hasty ○ *Don't be too quick to blame others.* **8.** ALIVE living (*archaic*) ■ *n.* **1.** FLESH UNDER NAIL the sensitive flesh under a fingernail or toenail **2.** SENSITIVE AREA sb's deepest feelings or most private emotions ○ *criticisms that cut him to the quick* **3.** THE LIVING the living (*archaic*) ○ *the quick and the dead* ■ *adv.* FAST in a speedy manner (*informal*) ○ *Come quick!* [Old English *cwic(u)* 'alive, lively'. Ultimately from an Indo-European base meaning 'to live' that is also the ancestor of English *vital*, *bio-*, *zoo-*, and *whisky*.] —**quickly** *adv.* —**quickness** *n.* ◇ **quick and dirty** produced to meet an immediate or pressing need, rather than in accordance with high standards of research or design

WORD KEY: SYNONYMS

See Synonyms at ***intelligent***.

quick assets *npl.* cash along with other assets that can readily be converted into cash

quick bread *n.* bread leavened with baking powder or soda, as opposed to yeast, and ready to bake as soon as it is mixed

quick-change artist *n.* a performer who is skilled at changing quickly from one costume or character to the next

quicken /kwíkən/ (**-ens, -ening, -ened**) *v.* **1.** *vti.* BECOME OR MAKE STH FASTER to become faster or make sth faster **2.** *vti.* STIMULATE OR BE STIMULATED to stimulate sth, e.g. interest or enthusiasm, or to be stimulated **3.** *vi.* BEGIN TO COME TO LIFE to begin a period of development **4.** *vi.* MOVE IN WOMB to begin to move and be felt moving in the womb (*used to refer to a foetus*)

quick-fire /kwík fīr/ *adj.* US term **rapid-fire 1.** FIRING SHOTS RAPIDLY designed to fire shots in quick succession **2.** OCCURRING IN RAPID SUCCESSION coming one after another in rapid succession (*informal*) ○ *a round of quickfire questions*

quick fix *n.* a speedily or hastily contrived solution to a problem, often one that fails to resolve long-term issues (*informal*)

quick-freeze *vt.* to freeze food rapidly in an effort to keep its full flavour and nutritional value

quickie /kwíki/ *n.* sth that is done hurriedly, especially a hurried act of sex or a speedily consumed alcoholic drink (*informal*)

quicklime /kwík līm/ *n.* calcium oxide [14thC. Translation of Latin *calx viva*, literally 'living lime'.]

quick march *n.* MARCH IN QUICK TIME a march at the standard military pace known as quick time ■ *interj.* ORDER TO MARCH IN QUICK TIME an order to march in quick time

quicksand /kwík sand/ *n.* **1.** DANGEROUS SAND a deep mass of loose wet sand that sucks down any heavy object falling onto its surface **2.** DANGEROUS SITUATION a hidden trap from which escape is difficult or impossible [15thC. From QUICK.]

quickset /kwík set/ *n.* **1.** PLANT CUTTING a plant cutting, especially a cutting of hawthorn, planted with others to make a hedge **2.** HEDGE a hedge, especially of hawthorn, grown from cuttings [15thC. Formed from QUICK in the sense 'alive' + SET.]

quicksilver /kwík silvər/ *n.* MERCURY mercury (*archaic*) ■ *adj.* CHANGING UNPREDICTABLY tending to change rapidly and unpredictably [Pre-12thC. Translation of Latin *argentum vivum*, literally 'living silver', from the way it moves when in its fluid state at room temperature.]

quickstep /kwík step/ *n.* **1.** FAST BALLROOM DANCE a ballroom dance with fast steps **2.** MUSIC DANCE MUSIC a piece of dance music in quadruple time for dancing the quickstep **3.** MIL MARCHING STEP the marching step used in the fastest marching pace (**quick time**)

quick study *n.* *US* sb who is able to learn new things or pick up new skills quickly and easily ○ *She's a quick study.*

quick-tempered *adj.* having a short temper

quickthorn /kwík thawrn/ *n.* a thorny plant, especially hawthorn, planted and cut to form a hedge [Early 17thC. From its rapid growth.]

quick time *n.* a fast military marching pace, approximately 120 paces per minute. It is the fastest of all marching paces.

quick trick *n.* in bridge, a high-ranking card, or a combination of high-ranking cards, that make it possible to win a trick on the first or second round of the suit

quick-witted *adj.* able to think quickly and inventively —**quick-wittedly** *adv.* —**quick-wittedness** *n.*

quid[1] /kwid/ (*plural* **quid**) *n.* a pound sterling (*informal*) [Late 17thC. Origin uncertain: perhaps from Latin *quid* 'what, sth', possibly inspired by the phrase *quid pro quo*.] ◇ **be quids in** to have made a profit or be in a financially advantageous position (*informal*) ◇ **not the full quid** *Aus* unintelligent (*slang insult*)

quid[2] /kwid/ *n.* a piece of chewing tobacco [Early 18thC. Alteration of CUD.]

quidditch /kwíddich/ *n.* fictional game [Late 20thC. Coined by J. K. Rowling in her novel, *Harry Potter and the Philosopher's Stone* (1997).]

quiddity /kwíddəti/ (*plural* **-ties**) *n.* (*formal*) **1.** ESSENCE the real nature or essential character of sth **2.** TRIFLING DISTINCTION an unimportant or trifling distinction [Mid-16thC. From medieval Latin *quidditas*, from Latin *quid* 'what'. Ultimately from an Indo-European base that is also the ancestor of English *what* and *who*.]

quidnunc /kwíd nungk/ *n.* sb who is nosy or gossipy (*literary*) [Early 18thC. From Latin, literally 'what now'.]

quid pro quo /kwíd prō kwṓ/ (*plural* **quid pro quos**) *n.* **1.** STH DONE IN EXCHANGE sth given or done in exchange for sth else **2.** RETURNING OF FAVOUR the giving of sth in return for sth else, often in a spirit of co-operation [Mid-16thC. From Latin, literally 'sth for sth'.]

quiescent /kwi éss'nt/ *adj.* inactive or at rest (*formal*) [Early 17thC. From Latin *quiescere* 'to come to rest' (see QUIET).] —**quiescence** *n.* —**quiescently** *adv.*

quiet /kwī ət/ *adj.* **1.** MAKING LITTLE NOISE making little or no noise **2.** PEACEFUL free from noise or commotion ○ *in a quiet corner of the room* **3.** DONE IN PRIVATE carried out in private, with voices not raised, so as not to be overheard ○ *I'd like a quiet word with you.* **4.** FREE FROM TROUBLE free from trouble or disturbance ○ *a quiet life* **5.** RELAXING relaxing, peaceful, and free from excitement ○ *a quiet evening at home* **6.** NOT SHOWY not grand, showy, or pretentious ○ *a quiet wedding* **7.** DISPLAYING CALMNESS displaying calmness and self-control **8.** NOT EXPRESSED IN WORDS not expressed in words ○ *a sense of quiet optimism* **9.** NOT FLOURISHING not busy, active, or flourishing ○ *Business is a little too quiet.* **10.** CALM OR MOTIONLESS marked by very little motion ○ *a quiet sea* ■ *n.* ABSENCE OF NOISE the absence of noise or disturbance ○ *the quiet of the forest* ■ *vt.* (**-ets, -eting, -eted**) LAW SECURE LEGAL CLAIM to make a legal claim secure by resolving all possible challenges to it [14thC. Via Old French from Latin *quietus*, the past participle of *quiescere* 'to come to rest', from *quies* 'rest, quiet' (source also of English *coy*).] —**quietly** *adv.* —**quietness** *n.* ◇ **on the quiet** secretly

WORD KEY: SYNONYMS

See Synonyms at ***silent***.

quieten /kwī ət'n/ (**-ens, -ening, -ened**) *v.* US term **quiet 1.** *vti.* MAKE OR BECOME QUIET to become calm and quiet, or make sb calm and quiet **2.** *vt.* ALLAY to calm sb's feelings, such as doubts or fears

quietism /kwī ətizəm/ *n.* **1.** CHRISTIAN MYSTICISM a system of Christian mysticism that requires a withdrawal from the world, a renunciation of the individual will, and passive contemplation of God and divine things **2.** CALMNESS a state of calmness, especially one arising from noninvolvement in sth (*literary*) [Late 17thC. From Italian *quietismo*, from *quieto*, from Latin *quietus* (see QUIET).] —**quietist** *adj., n.* —**quietistic** /kwī ə tístik/ *adj.*

quietude /kwī ə tyood/ *n.* the state of being quiet, peaceful, or tranquil (*literary*) [Late 16thC. Directly or via French *quiétude* from medieval Latin *quietudo*, from Latin *quietus* (see QUIET).]

quietus /kwī éetəss, -áy-/ *n.* (*literary*) **1.** DEATH death, especially when viewed as a welcome release from life **2.** RELEASE a release from a debt or duty **3.** CHECK sth that brings an activity to an end [Mid-16thC. From medieval Latin *quietus (est)* '(it is) at rest', a formula acknowledging receipt or discharge of an obligation.]

quiff /kwif/ *n.* part of a man's hairstyle in which the hair at the front is brushed upwards and backwards [Late 19thC. Origin unknown.]

quill /kwil/ *n.* **1.** ZOOL LARGE FEATHER a large, stiff feather from a bird's wing or tail, or the hollow shaft of one of these feathers **2.** PEN MADE FROM FEATHER SHAFT an old-fashioned pen made from the shaft of a feather. The split and sharpened end was dipped in ink. **3.** ZOOL SPINE a sharp hollow spine on the body of a porcupine or hedgehog **4.** TEXTILES SPINDLE OR BOBBIN a spindle or bobbin onto which thread or yarn is wound **5.** HOLLOW SHAFT in a mechanical device, a hollow shaft in which a second independently rotating shaft is enclosed ■ *vt.* (**quills, quilling, quilled**) **1.** TEXTILES WIND THREAD to wind thread or yarn onto a spindle or bobbin **2.** SEW MAKE FOLDS IN to make small rounded ridges or folds in fabric, e.g. to make a ruff [15thC. Origin uncertain.]

quillback /kwíl bak/ (*plural* **-backs** *or* **-back**), **quillback carpsucker** /kwíl bak kaárp sukər/ *n.* a North American freshwater fish of the sucker family that has a long ray projecting from its dorsal fin. Latin name: *Carpiodes cyprinus.*

Quiller Couch /kwíllər kooch/, **Sir Arthur** (1863–1944) British author. Editor of the *Oxford Book of English Verse* (1900) and other anthologies, he also wrote novels under the pseudonym 'Q'. Full name **Sir Arthur Thomas Quiller Couch**

quill pen *n.* = **quill** *n.* 2

quillwort /kwíl wurt/ *n.* a nonflowering water plant that produces a rosette of tubular leaves, at the bases of which are spore-forming organs. Genus: *Isoetes*.

quilt /kwilt/ *n.* **1.** BEDCOVER a bedcover made of two layers of fabric stitched together, with interior padding of cotton or feathers held in place by decorative intersecting seams **2.** DUVET a duvet (*informal*) **3.** STH SIMILAR TO QUILT sth that resembles a quilt or is quilted ■ *vt.* (**quilts, quilting, quilted**) MAKE FABRIC ARTICLE to make a fabric article, especially a bedcover, by sewing two layers of fabric together with a filling, especially using decorative stitching [13thC. Via Anglo-Norman from Latin *culcita* 'cushion, mattress' (source of English *counterpane* and *quoit*), of unknown origin.] —**quilter** *n.*

quilting /kwílting/ *n.* **1.** MAKING QUILTS the sewing of quilted bedcovers or other quilted work **2.** QUILTED MATERIAL material that has been quilted or that is used to make quilts

Quimper /kaN pér/ city and administrative centre of Finistère Department, in Brittany Region, western France. Population: 62,540 (1990).

quin /kwin/ *n.* a quintuplet (*informal*) US term **quint** *n.* 2 [Mid-20thC. Shortening.]

quin- *prefix.* = **quino-** (*used before vowels*)

quinacrine hydrochloride /kwínnə kreen-/ *n.* a drug used to treat malaria [*Quinacrine* is a blend of QUININE and ACRIDINE]

quinalizarin /kwínnə lízzərin/ *n.* a red crystalline organic compound with a green metallic lustre, used especially to dye cotton. Formula: $C_{14}H_8O_6$. [Coined from QUINO- + ALIZARIN.]

quinary /kwínəri/ *adj.* OCCURRING IN FIVES consisting of five parts, or occurring in sets of five (*formal*) ■ *n.* (*plural* **-ies**) SET OF FIVE OR FIFTH MEMBER a set of five, or the fifth member of a set (*formal*) [Early 17thC. From Latin *quinarius*, from *quini* 'five each', from *quinque* 'five' (see QUINQUE-).]

quinate /kwí nayt/ *adj.* BOT used to describe leaves that occur in clusters of five [Early 19thC. From modern Latin *quinatus*, from *quini* (see QUINARY).]

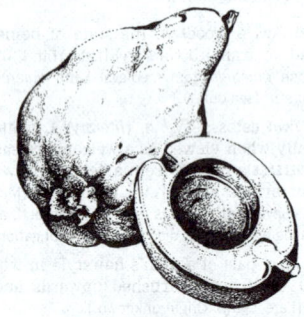

Quince

quince /kwinss/ *n.* **1.** ASIAN FRUIT TREE a small tree native to western Asia but widely cultivated that bears white flowers and hard pear-shaped fruit. Latin name: *Cydonia oblonga*. **2.** FRUIT OF QUINCE TREE the fruit of the quince tree, edible only when cooked [14thC. Via Old French *cooin* from Latin (*malum*) *cotoneum*, from Greek (*mēlon*) *kudōnion*, literally 'apple of Cydonia' (Canea), by folk etymology from a Lydian name for the fruit.]

quincentenary /kwín sen teénəri, -ténnəri/ (*plural* **-ries**), **quincentennial** /-ténni əl/ *n.* a 500th anniversary [Late 19thC. 'quin' from Latin *quinque* (see QUINQUE-).] —**quincentenary** *adj.*

quincunx /kwín kungks/ *n.* an arrangement of five objects in a square, with four at the corners and one in the centre [Mid-17thC. From Latin, literally 'five-twelfths' (from the use of this pattern on a Roman coin worth five-twelfths of an as), from *quinque* 'five' + *uncia* 'a twelfth' (see OUNCE[1]).] —**quincuncial** /kwin kúnsh'l/ *adj.*

Quincy /kwínssi/ **1.** city and port in western Illinois, on the eastern bank of the Mississippi River on the Illinois-Missouri border. Population: 40,545 (1996). **2.** city in eastern Massachusetts on Massachusetts Bay. It is a southeastern suburb of Boston and the birthplace of US presidents John Adams and John Quincy Adams. Population: 85,532 (1996).

quindecagon /kwin dékəgən/ *n.* a flat geometric shape with fifteen angles and fifteen sides [Late 16thC. Coined from Latin *quindecim* 'fifteen' + -GON.]

quindecennial /kwíndi sénni əl/ *adj.* **1.** HAPPENING EVERY 15 YEARS happening once every 15 years **2.** LASTING 15 YEARS lasting for 15 years ■ *n.* 15TH ANNIVERSARY a 15th anniversary [20thC. Formed from Latin *quindecim* 'fifteen', on the model of CENTENNIAL.]

quinella /kwi néllə/ *n.* a bet in which the punter picks the first two finishers in a race but does not have to place them [Early 20thC. From American Spanish *quiniela*, from Spanish *quina* 'keno', from French *quine* (see KENO).]

quinic acid /kwínnik-/ *n.* a white crystalline organic compound found in cinchona bark, coffee beans, and the leaves of many plants. It is used in medicine. Formula: $C_6H_7(OH)_4COOH$. [From Spanish *quina* 'cinchona bark' (see QUINO-).]

quinidine /kwínni deen/ *n.* a colourless crystalline organic compound related to quinine that is used in medicine to treat malaria and heart disorders. It is found in cinchona bark. Formula: $C_{20}H_{24}N_2O_2$. [Mid-19thC. Coined from QUINO- + -IDINE.]

Quinine

quinine /kwi neén, kwínneen/ *n.* a bitter-tasting drug made from cinchona bark, used to treat forms of malaria resistant to chloroquine [Early 19thC. Formed from Spanish *quina* 'cinchona bark' (see QUINO-).]

quinine water *n.* US = **tonic water**

quinnat salmon /kwínnat-/ *n.* = **Chinook salmon** [From Chinook *ikwanat*]

quino- *prefix.* **1.** cinchona, cinchona bark ○ *quinone* **2.** quinone ○ *quinoid* [Via Spanish *quina* 'cinchona bark' from Quechua *kina*]

quinoa /kwi nó ə/ *n.* a plant of the goosefoot family that is native to the Andes and cultivated for its seeds, which are ground and eaten. Latin name: *Chenopodium quinoa*. [Early 17thC. Via Spanish from Quechua *kinoa*.]

quinoline /kwínnə leen, -lin/ *n.* an oily colourless substance obtained from coal tar and used in making antiseptics and dyes. Formula: C_9H_7N. [Mid-19thC. Formed from QUINOL.]

quinone /kwi nón, kwínnōn/ *n.* **1.** = **benzoquinone 2.** PLANT PIGMENT OR ANIMAL VITAMIN an organic compound found as a yellow, orange, or red pigment in plants, fungi, and bacteria and also as vitamins in animals. Vitamin A is a quinone. [Late 19thC. Formed from QUININE.]

quinonoid /kwínnə noyd, kwi nó noyd/ *n.* STH RESEMBLING QUINONE a substance that contains quinone or resembles it in chemical structure or physical properties ■ *adj.* RESEMBLING QUINONE resembling quinone in chemical structure or physical properties [Late 19thC. Formed from QUINONE.]

quinquagenarian /kwíngkwəjə náiri ən/ *adj.* 50 YEARS OLD 50 years old, or between the ages of 50 and 59 (*formal*) ■ *n.* SB 50 YEARS OLD sb who is 50 years old or between the ages of 50 and 59 (*formal*) [Early 19thC. Via Latin *quinquagenarius*, from, ultimately, *quinquaginta* 'fifty'.]

Quinquagesima /kwíngkwə jéssimə/ *n.* in the Christian liturgical calendar, the Sunday before Lent, seven weeks or the fiftieth day before Easter [14thC. From medieval Latin, literally 'fiftieth (day)', from Latin *quinquagesimus*, *quinquaginta* 'fifty'.]

quinque- *prefix.* five ○ *quinquepartite* [From Latin *quinque* 'five'. Ultimately from the Indo-European word for 'five', which is also the ancestor of English *five*, *pentad*, *finger*, and *fist*.]

quinquennium /kwing kwénni əm/ (*plural* **-a** /-ni ə/) *n.* a period of five years [Early 17thC. From Latin, from *quinque* 'five' + *annus* 'year'.] —**quinquennial** *adj.* —**quinquennially** *adv.*

quinquereme /kwíngkwi reém/ *n.* an ancient Greek or Roman galley ship propelled by five banks of oars on each side [Mid-16thC. From Latin *quinqueremis*, from *quinque* 'five' + *remus* 'oar'.]

quinquevalent /kwíngkwi váylənt/ *adj.* = **pentavalent**

quinsy /kwínzi/ *n.* a severe inflammation of the throat near a tonsil that sometimes leads to the formation of an abcess that may require surgery [14thC. Via Old French *quinencie* and medieval Latin *quinancia* from Greek *kunagkhē*, literally 'dog-strangling', from *kuōn* 'dog' + *ankhein* 'to squeeze'.]

quint /kwint/ *n.* **1.** SET OF FIVE CARDS in the card game piquet, a sequence of five cards of the same suit **2.** US = **quin** (*informal*) [Late 17thC. Via French, literally 'fifth', from Latin *quintus*. Ultimately from an Indo-European word that is also the ancestor of English *fifth*.]

quintain /kwíntin/ *n.* a medieval knight's target for jousting practice [15thC. Via Old French from Latin *quintana (via)*, 'fifth (street)' (in a Roman camp), possibly so called because this street was used for military exercises.]

quintal /kwínt'l/ *n.* **1.** METRIC UNIT OF WEIGHT in the metric system, a unit of weight equal to 100 kilograms **2.** HUNDREDWEIGHT a hundredweight (*archaic*) [15thC. Via Old French, medieval Latin *quintale*, and Arabic *kintār* from, ultimately, Latin *centenarius* 'containing one hundred' (see CENTENARY).]

quintan /kwíntən/ *adj.* OCCURRING EVERY FIFTH DAY flaring up every fifth day ■ *n.* FEVER a fever that flares up every fifth day [Mid-17thC. Via medieval Latin *quintana* from Latin *quintus* 'fifth' (see QUINT).]

quinte /kwint, kaNt/ *n.* the fifth in the series of eight standard positions used to teach fencing [Early 18thC. From French, feminine of *quint* (see QUINT).]

quintessence /kwin téss'nss/ *n.* **1.** EMBODIMENT the purest or most perfect example of sth **2.** CHEM EXTRACT the purest extract or essence of a substance. It contains the substance's properties in their most concentrated form. **3.** PHILOS FIFTH ELEMENT in ancient and medieval philosophy, the fifth element after earth, air, fire, and water. Heavenly bodies were said to be made of it. [15thC. Via French from medieval Latin *quinta essentia*, literally 'fifth essence', a translation of Greek *pemptē ousia*.] —**quintessential** /kwínti sénsh'l/ *adj.* —**quintessentially** /-sénsh'li/ *adv.*

quintet /kwin tét/, **quintette** *n.* **1.** MUSICIANS a group of five singers or musicians (*takes a singular or plural verb*) **2.** MUSIC a piece of music written for five voices or instruments **3.** GROUP OF FIVE a group or set of five people or things [Late 18thC. Via French *quintette* from Italian *quintetto*, from *quinto* 'fifth', from Latin *quintus* (see QUINT).]

quintic /kwíntik/ *adj.* relating to the fifth power in a mathematical expression or equation [Mid-19thC. Formed from Latin *quintus* (see QUINT).]

quintile /kwín tīl/ *n.* **1.** STATISTICAL DIVISION any one of the five equal populations into which a statistical sample can be divided **2.** STATISTICAL VALUE in statistics, any one of the values that divide a frequency distribution into five parts, each containing a fifth of the sample population **3.** DISTANCE BETWEEN PLANETS the astrological aspect of planets that are distant from each other by 72 degrees, or one fifth of the zodiac [Early 17thC. From Latin *quintilis*, from *quintus* 'fifth' (see QUINT).]

quintillion /kwin tíllyən/ *n.* **1.** ONE FOLLOWED BY 18 ZEROS the number equal to 10^{18}, written as 1 followed by 18 zeros **2.** ONE FOLLOWED BY 30 ZEROS the number equal to 10^{30}, written as 1 followed by 30 zeros (*dated*) —**quintillion** *adj., pron.* —**quintillionth** *adj., n., pron.*

quintuple /kwíntyoōp'l, kwin tyoōp-/ *adj.* **1.** BEING FIVE TIMES AS MUCH being five times as much or as many **2.** CONSISTING OF FIVE PARTS made up of five parts **3.** MUSIC HAVING FIVE BEATS TO BAR having five musical beats to the bar ■ *vti.* (**-ples, -pling, -pled**) MULTIPLY BY FIVE to multiply sth by five or to be multiplied by five [Late

16thC. Via French from medieval Latin *quintuplus*, literally 'fivefold', from *quintus* 'fifth' (see QUINT).]

quintuplet /kwín tyŏŏplət, kwin tyŏŏp-/ *n.* **1.** ONE OF FIVE OFFSPRING one of five offspring born to one mother from a single pregnancy **2.** GROUP OF FIVE a group of five things, especially five of the same kind **3.** MUSIC GROUP OF FIVE MUSICAL NOTES a group of five musical notes to be played in the time usually occupied by three or four notes [Late 19thC. Formed from QUINTUPLE.]

quintuplicate *adj.* /kwin tyŏŏplikit/ MULTIPLIED BY FIVE multiplied by five ■ *n.* /kwin tyŏŏplikit/ **1.** ONE OF FIVE one of a set of five identical things **2.** GROUP OF FIVE a group of five usually identical things ■ *vt.* /kwin tyŏŏpli kayt/ (**-cates, -cating, -cated**) MAKE FIVE COPIES to make five copies of sth [Mid-17thC. Formed from Latin *quintus* 'fifth' (see QUINT) on the model of 'duplicate'.] — **quintuplication** /kwin tyŏŏpli káysh'n/ *n.*

quip /kwip/ *n.* **1.** WITTICISM a witty remark, especially one made on the spur of the moment **2.** PETTY DISTINCTION a small and unimportant distinction (*archaic*) **3.** STH STRANGE sth odd or strange (*archaic*) ■ *vti.* (**quips, quipping, quipped**) SAY STH WITTILY to make a witty remark [Mid-16thC. Origin uncertain: perhaps from Latin *quippe* 'indeed, really' (used sarcastically), from *quid* 'sth, what'.]

quipster /kwípstər/ *n.* sb who makes witty remarks

quipu /keé pŏŏ/ (*plural* **-pus**) *n.* a device consisting of a set of coloured and knotted cords used by the Incas for conveying messages and for record-keeping [Early 18thC. Via Spanish from Quechua *kipu*, literally 'knot'.]

quire /kwīr/ *n.* **1.** PAPER MEASURE a set of 24 or 25 sheets of paper of the same size and quality, equalling one twentieth of a ream **2.** PAPER FOLDED FOR BINDING a bundle of sheets of paper folded together for binding into a book, especially a four-sheet bundle, folded once to make eight leaves or sixteen pages [15thC. Via Old French *qua(i)er* 'copybook', literally 'set of four (sheets)', from Latin *quaterni* (see QUATERNARY).]

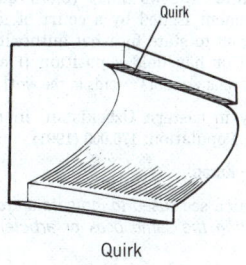

Quirk

quirk /qwurk/ *n.* **1.** ODD EVENT a strange and unexpected turn of events ○ *a strange quirk of fate* **2.** ODD MANNERISM a peculiar habit, mannerism, or aspect of sb's character **3.** CURVED SHAPE a curved shape, pattern, or decoration, e.g. a flourish in handwriting **4.** ARCHIT GROOVE a continuous groove running along a moulding or separating a moulding from adjoining members [Mid-16thC. Origin unknown.] — **quirkily** *adv.* — **quirkiness** *n.* — **quirky** *adj.*

quirt /kwurt/ (**quirts, quirting, quirted**) *n.* US a riding whip with a short handle and a braided leather lash [Mid-19thC. From Mexican Spanish *cuarta* 'whip'.]

quisling /kwízzling/ *n.* a traitor, especially sb who collaborates with an occupying force (*dated*) [Mid-20thC. Named after Vidkun *Quisling*.] — **quislingism** *n.*

─── WORD KEY: ORIGIN ───
Vidkun *Quisling* was a Norwegian politician who from 1933 led the National Union Party, the Norwegian fascist party. (*Quisling* was not his real name – he was originally Abraham Lauritz Jonsson.) When the Germans invaded Norway in 1940 he gave them active support, urging his fellow Norwegians not to resist them, and in 1942 he was installed by Hitler as a puppet premier. In 1945 he was shot for treason.

quit /kwit/ *v.* (**quits, quitting, quitted** *or* **quit**) **1.** *vti.* RESIGN to give up, leave, or resign from a position or organization (*informal*) **2.** *vti.* US STOP DOING STH to stop

doing sth, especially sth bad or irritating (*informal*) ○ *Quit moaning.* **3.** *vt.* LEAVE to depart from a place (*archaic*) ○ *'No, he would sooner quit Kellynch Hall at once, than remain in it on such disgraceful terms'.* (Jane Austen, *Persuasion*; 1818) **4.** *vti.* COMPUT EXIT FROM PROGRAM to exit from a computer program using the required exit procedure, so that the data and program configuration are saved **5.** *vti.* MOVE OUT to move out of rented property ○ *He gave his tenants notice to quit.* **6.** *vt.* PAY OFF to settle a debt (*archaic*) **7.** *vt.* UNBURDEN to free sb from sth burdensome (*archaic*) **8.** *vt.* = acquit (*archaic*) ■ *adj.* UNBURDENED no longer troubled with a problem or difficult situation (*formal*) ○ *'it would be easier to die than to live, and so be quit of all the trouble'* (Bram Stoker, *Dracula*; 1897) [13thC. Via Old French *quiter* 'to release, set free' from, ultimately, Latin *quietus* (see QUIET).]

quitch grass /kwitch-/, **quitch** *n.* = couch grass [Old English *cwice*]

quitclaim /kwít klaym/ *n.* RENUNCIATION OF CLAIM a formal statement renouncing a legal claim previously made ■ *vt.* (**-claims, -claiming, -claimed**) **1.** RENOUNCE CLAIM formally to withdraw a legal claim previously made **2.** FREE OF LIABILITY formally to declare sb to be no longer legally liable for sth [13thC. From Anglo-Norman *quiteclamer* 'to proclaim (someone) free', from *quite* 'free' + *clamer* 'to proclaim'.]

quite /kwīt/ *adv.* **1.** SOMEWHAT to some degree, but not to a great degree ○ *The film was quite good, but I wouldn't bother seeing it again.* **2.** ENTIRELY in the highest degree, or to the fullest extent ○ *I was quite sure I'd met him before.* **3.** NEARLY used with a negative to indicate that sth is almost in a particular state or condition ○ *The dress is not quite finished.* **4.** EMPHASIZING EXTENT used with expressions of quantity to emphasize the great extent of sth ○ *They spent quite some time considering the problem.* **5.** EMPHASIZING EXCEPTIONAL QUALITY used to emphasize the exceptional or impressive nature of sb or sth ○ *That was quite a celebration we had yesterday.* **6.** EXPRESSING AGREEMENT used on its own or with 'so' to express agreement or understanding ○ *'I didn't want to mention it until I was sure'. 'Quite'.* [14thC. Originally a variant of QUIT 'unburdened, free', the modern meaning evolved via the sense 'clearly, thoroughly'.] ◇ **be quite sth** to be remarkably good, fine, attractive, or otherwise admirable or impressive (*informal*)

Quito /keé tō/ capital city of Ecuador, situated in the north of the country. Population: 1,100,847 (1990).

quitrent /kwít rent/ *n.* in the feudal system, a rent paid by a tenant to a feudal lord in exchange for being released from certain feudal obligations [15thC. From QUIT 'unburdened'.]

quits /kwits/ *adj.* on even terms, especially following the repayment of a debt (*informal*) [Mid-17thC. Origin uncertain: probably formed from QUIT 'unburdened', influenced by medieval Latin *quittus* 'freed'.] ◇ **call it quits 1.** to agree with sb that neither owes the other money, a favour, or an act of vengeance **2.** to agree or decide to stop doing work or an activity (*informal*) **3.** to agree that an argument or dispute is over and that both parties are equal (*informal*)

quittance /kwítt'ns/ *n.* **1.** EXEMPTION release from a debt or obligation **2.** EXEMPTING DOCUMENT a document or statement that releases sb from a debt or obligation [13thC. Via Old French from *quiter* (see QUIT).]

quitter /kwíttər/ *n.* sb who gives up easily (*informal*)

quittor /kwíttər/ *n.* an infectious disease that affects the feet of horses and donkeys, causing inflammation [13thC. Origin uncertain: possibly via Old French *quiture* 'boiling' from, ultimately, Latin *coquere* 'to cook'.]

quiver[1] /kwívvər/ *vi.* (**-ers, -ering, -ered**) TREMBLE to shake rapidly with small movements ■ *n.* TREMBLING MOVEMENT a repeated light and fast shaking movement [15thC. Origin uncertain: probably from assumed Old English *cwifer* 'active, nimble', thought to suggest rapid movement, in which case related to English *quick*.] — **quiverer** *n.* — **quivery** *adj.*

quiver[2] /kwívvər/ *n.* **1.** ARROW CASE a long narrow case for holding arrows **2.** ARROWS the arrows contained in a quiver [14thC. Via Anglo-Norman *quiveir* from, ultimately, medieval Latin *cucurum* (of Hunnish origin).]

quiverful /kwívvərfŏŏl/ (*plural* **-erfuls** *or* **-ersful**) *n.* **1.** ARROWS IN QUIVER the full complement of arrows in a quiver **2.** LARGE NUMBER a large number of things or people, especially the full number of children in a large family (*literary*)

qui vive /kwée veev/ ['Qui vive' from French, literally 'long live who?', a phrase used by sentries to challenge someone approaching their post] ◇ **on the qui vive** alert and vigilant

quixotic /kwik sóttik/ *adj.* **1.** ROMANTIC tending to take a romanticized view of life **2.** IMPRACTICAL motivated by an idealism that overlooks practical considerations **3.** IMPULSIVE tending to act on whims or impulses [Late 18thC. Formed from the name Don *Quixote*, the hero of the novel of the same name, written by Miguel de Cervantes.] — **quixotically** *adv.* — **quixotism** /kwíksətizəm/ *n.*

quiz /kwiz/ *n.* (*plural* **quizzes**) **1.** TEST OF KNOWLEDGE a test of knowledge in the form of a short or rapid series of questions (*often used after a noun*) **2.** TRICK a hoax, joke, or other trick (*archaic*) **3.** ODD PERSON sb who is regarded as eccentric by others (*archaic*) ○ *'I could make out that he was at once the quiz of the wardroom'* (Robert Louis Stevenson, *The Wrecker*; 1896) ■ *vt.* (**quizzes, quizzing, quizzed**) **1.** INTERROGATE SB to subject sb to a round of sustained close questioning ○ *She was again called in and quizzed about the disappearance of the money.* **2.** RIDICULE to make fun of sb (*archaic*) **3.** PEER AT SB to look quizzically at sb (*archaic*) [Late 18thC. Origin unknown: originally in the sense 'odd person', the main modern meaning evolved via 'to ridicule'.] — **quizzer** *n.*

─── WORD KEY: SYNONYMS ───
See Synonyms at *question*.

quizmaster /kwíz maastər/ *n.* the presenter of a quiz show, who puts the questions to the contestants

quiz show *n.* a television or radio programme in the form of a game in which contestants compete against each other for prizes by answering questions that test their general or specialist knowledge

quizzical /kwízzik'l/ *adj.* expressing a question or expressing puzzlement or doubt, especially in a mocking or amused way ○ *a quizzical glance* — **quizzicality** /kwízzi kálləti/ *n.* — **quizzically** /kwízzikli/ *adv.*

quizzing glass *n.* a monocle (*archaic*)

quod /kwod/ *n.* a prison (*slang*) [Late 17thC. Origin uncertain: possibly a shortening and alteration of QUADRANGLE.]

quod erat demonstrandum /kwód érrat démmən strándəm/ *adv.* used in a formal conclusion to indicate that a particular fact is proof of the theory that has just been been advanced. Full form of **QED** [From Latin, literally 'which was to be shown']

quodlibet /kwóddli bet/ *n.* **1.** PHILOSOPHY THEOLOGICAL DISCUSSION POINT a theological question put forth as an exercise for discussion **2.** MUSIC MEDLEY OF TUNES a musical performance composed largely of familiar tunes [14thC. Via medieval Latin *quodlibetum* from Latin *quodlibet*, literally 'whatever pleases'.]

quo-he *npl.* Ireland a word used to disparage country people as unintelligent or uninformed (*insult*)

Quoin

quoin /koyn, kwoyn/, **coign**, **coigne** *n.* **1.** OUTER CORNER the outer corner of a wall **2.** BLOCK FORMING CORNER a stone block used to form a quoin, especially when it is different, e.g. in size or material, from the other blocks or bricks in the wall **3.** = **keystone** *n.* **1** ■ *vt.* (**quoins, quoining, quoined**) **BUILD CORNER WITH DISTINCTIVE BLOCKS** to build an outer corner of a wall using blocks that are different, e.g. in size or texture, from the other blocks or bricks used to build the wall [Mid-16thC. Variant of COIN.]

Quoit

quoit /koyt, kwoyt/ *n.* a ring used in the game of quoits [14thC. Origin uncertain: probably via Old French *coite* 'flat stone, quoit' from Latin *culcita* 'cushion' (source of English *quilt*).]

quoits /koyts, kwoyts/ *n.* a game in which players attempt to throw rings over or near a small post (*takes a singular verb*) [14thC. Plural of *quoit*, originally 'flat disc', of uncertain origin: perhaps from Old French.]

quokka /kwóka/ *n.* a small short-tailed wallaby that lives in large colonies. It is now found mainly on islands off the coast of Western Australia. Latin name: *Setonix brachyurus*. [Mid-19thC. From Australian Aboriginal Nyungar *kwaka*.]

quondam /kwón dam, -dəm/ *adj.* of an earlier time (*archaic or literary*) ○ '... *now torn and rent by their quondam allies*' (Jack London, *The Iron Heel*; 1907) [Mid-16thC. From Latin, from *quom* 'when'.]

Quonset /kwónsət/ *tdmk. US* a trademark for a prefabricated structure that has a semicircular roof curving downwards to form walls, often used to house military personnel

quorate /kwáw rayt/ *adj.* used to describe a meeting attended by at least the minimum number of members that the rules state are needed in order for business to be conducted

Quorn /kworn/ *tdmk.* a trademark for a vegetable protein used in cooking as a meat substitute.

quorum /kwáwrəm/ *n.* a fixed minimum number of members of a legislative assembly, a committee, or other organization who must be present before the members can conduct valid business [15thC. From Latin, literally 'of whom', from the words used in requests for people to serve on committees.]

quot. *abbr.* quotation

quota /kwóta/ *n.* **1.** **PROPORTIONAL SHARE** a proportional share of sth that sb should contribute or receive ○ *You haven't done your quota of night shifts.* **2.** **MAXIMUM PERMITTED NUMBER OR AMOUNT** a maximum number or quantity that is permitted or needed ○ *European fishing quotas* [Early 17thC. Via medieval Latin *quota (pars)*, literally 'how large (a part)?', the feminine of *quotus* (see QUOTE).]

quotable /kwótəb'l/ *adj.* **1.** **WORTH QUOTING** worthy of being quoted **2.** **ON THE RECORD** able to be quoted in a publication such as a newspaper because the person speaking or writing has given permission —**quotability** /kwóta bílləti/ *n.*

quotation /kwō táysh'n/ *n.* **1.** **STH QUOTED** a piece of speech or writing quoted somewhere, e.g. in a book or magazine ○ *a quotation from Henry James* **2.** **QUOTING OF WHAT SB HAS SAID** the quoting of what sb else has said or written **3.** **BUSINESS ESTIMATE FOR WORK** an estimated price for a job or service **4.** **STOCK EXCH SHARE PRICE** the prevailing price at which a stock, bond, or commodity may be purchased or sold **5.** **STOCK EXCH QUOTING OF PRICES** the quoting of prevailing stock, bond, or commodity market prices **6.** **ARTS RE-USE OF ARTISTIC MATERIAL** the use in an artistic work, especially music, of material taken from or alluding to sb else's work —**quotational** *adj.* —**quotationally** *adv.*

quotation mark *n.* either of a pair of punctuation marks, either in single ('...') or double ("...") form, used in printed or written English to mark the beginning and end of a quotation

quote /kwōt/ *v.* (**quotes, quoting, quoted**) **1.** *vti.* **REPEAT SB'S EXACT WORDS** to repeat or copy the exact words spoken or written by sb **2.** *vti.* **REFER TO STH FOR PROOF** to refer to sth as an example in support of an argument ○ *He quoted some recently published statistics.* **3.** *vti.* **PRINTING PUT PUNCTUATION AROUND QUOTATION** to place quotation marks around a passage of speech or writing that is being quoted **4.** *vti.* **BUSINESS GIVE ESTIMATE FOR COST** to give an estimate of the price of providing sb with a product or service **5.** *vt.* **STOCK EXCH GIVE CURRENT MARKET PRICE** to state the current market price of a share, bond, or commodity **6.** *vt.* **BETTING GIVE BETTING ODDS** to give sb or sth, e.g. a racehorse, betting odds (*usually passive*) **7.** *vt.* **ARTS REPEAT FROM ARTISTIC WORK** to repeat an excerpt from an artistic work created by sb else, especially a piece of music ■ *n.* **1.** **QUOTATION** sth that is repeated exactly (*informal*) **2.** **PRINTING QUOTATION MARK** one of a pair of quotation marks (*often used in the plural*) **3.** **BUSINESS** = **quotation** ■ *interj.* **INTRODUCING QUOTATION** used to show that the following words are a quotation (*often used with 'unquote'*) ○ *She told me she is, quote, 'too good for him', unquote.* [14thC. Via medieval Latin *quotare* 'to number chapters' from, ultimately, Latin *quot* 'how many?' (source of English *quotient*.)] —**quoter** *n.*

quoth /kwōth/ *vt.* said, when used with direct speech (*archaic or literary*) ○ *quoth he* [Old English *cwað*, the past tense of *cweþan* 'to say' (source of English *bequeath*)]

quotha /kwóthə/ *interj.* used after quoting another person to express contempt, sarcasm, or surprise (*archaic*) ○ *Love, quotha; what manner of love is this?* [Early 16thC. Shortening and alteration of 'quoth he'.]

quotidian /kwō tíddi ən/ *adj.* **1.** **COMMONPLACE** of the most ordinary everyday kind (*formal*) **2.** **DAILY** done or experienced on a daily basis (*formal*) **3.** **MED RECURRING DAILY** recurring or flaring up every day ■ *n.* **quotidian, quotidian fever** **MED FEVER RECURRING DAILY** a fever, especially malaria, in which attacks of the illness recur daily [14thC. Via Old French *cotidien* from Latin *quotidianus*, from *cotidie* 'every day'.]

quotient /kwósh'nt/ *n.* **1.** **MATH RESULT OF DIVISION** the number that results from the division of one number by another **2.** **MATH RATIO** a ratio of two numbers or quantities **3.** **MATH WHOLE NUMBER RESULT OF DIVISION** the whole number element of the result of dividing one number by another. ◊ **remainder** **4.** **AMOUNT OF QUALITY** a scale, or a point on a scale indicating the amount, degree, or level of sth (*informal*) [15thC. From Latin *quotiens* 'how many times?', from *quot* (see QUOTE).]

quo warranto /kwó wə rántō/ (*plural* **quo warrantos**) *n.* a document issued by a court of law formally requiring sb to state by what authority he or she has acted or has held a position [From Law Latin, literally 'by what warrant?', words in the writ]

Qŭqon city in eastern Uzbekistan, in the Fergana Province. Population: 175,000 (1991).

Qur'an *n.* = Koran

qv *abbr.* which see (*used to indicate a cross reference to sth within the same book or article*) [Latin, quod vide]

Qwaqwa /kwaákwə/ former homeland in South Africa. It was abolished in 1994 and incorporated into Free State Province.

qwerty keyboard /kwúrti-/, **QWERTY keyboard** *n.* a typewriter or computer keyboard with the standard arrangement of keys for the Roman alphabet, with the top row of alphabetic characters beginning with the letters q,w, e, r, t, and y

qy *abbr.* query

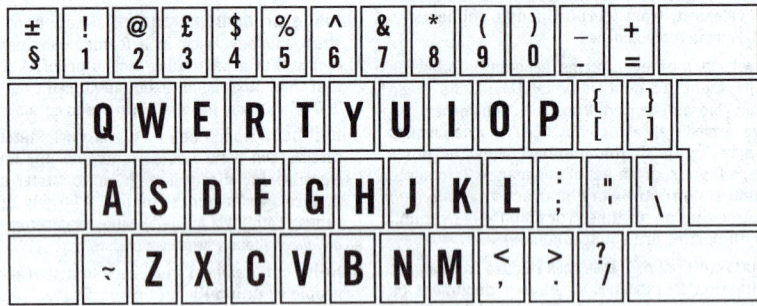

Qwerty keyboard

r[1] /aar/ (plural **r's**), **R** (plural **R's** or **Rs**) n. **1.** 18TH LETTER OF ENGLISH ALPHABET the 18th letter of the modern English alphabet **2.** SOUND CORRESPONDING TO LETTER 'R' the speech sound that corresponds to the letter 'R' **3.** LETTER 'R' WRITTEN a written representation of the letter 'R' ◊ **the three R's** the basic skills of reading, writing, and arithmetic

r[2] symbol. **1. r, r.** MATH radius n. **1. 2. r, R** ELEC. ENG resistance

R[1] symbol. **1.** PHYS gas constant **2.** CHEM radical **3.** Réaumur scale **4.** ELEC ENG resistance

R[2], **R.** abbr. CHR response (in Christian liturgy)

R[3] /aar/ n. in Australia, a censorship classification indicating that a film or video can only be seen by people over the age of 18 years of age. Full form **restricted**

R[4] abbr. **1.** MATH radius **2.** MONEY rand **3.** Regina (used after the name of a queen) **4.** CHR response (in Christian liturgy) **5.** Rex (used after the name of a king) **6.** CARS Romania (international vehicle registration)

r. abbr. **1. r., R.** railway **2.** rare **3.** recto **4. r., R.** right **5. r., R.** river **6. r., R.** road **7.** MEASURE rod **8. r., R.** MONEY rouble **9.** CRICKET runs **10. r., R.** MONEY rupee

R. abbr. **1.** JUDAISM rabbi **2.** GEOG range **3.** CHR rector **4.** POL republican **5.** royal

Ra[1] /raa/, **Re** /ray/ n. in ancient Egyptian mythology, the sun god, creator and controller of the universe, represented as having a human body and a hawk's head. ◊ **Osiris, Isis** [From Egyptian r']

Ra[2] symbol. CHEM ELEM radium

RA abbr. **1.** NAVY Rear Admiral **2.** CARS Argentina (international vehicle registration) **3.** ASTRON right ascension **4.** Royal Academician **5.** Royal Artillery

RAA abbr. Royal Academy of Arts

RAAF abbr. Royal Australian Air Force

Rabat /rə baát/ capital city of Morocco, situated in the northwest of the country, at the mouth of the River Bou Regreg, on the Atlantic coast. Population: 1,386,000 (1994).

rabbet /rábbit/ n. = **rebate**[2] n. ■ vt. (**-bets, -beting, -beted**) = **rebate**[2] v. 1 [15thC. From Old French rab(b)at 'recess', from rabattre (see REBATE).]

rabbi /rábbī/ (plural **rabbis** or **Rabbis**) n. **1.** JEWISH RELIGIOUS LEADER the leader of a Jewish congregation, or the chief religious official of a synagogue **2.** JEWISH SCHOLAR a scholar qualified to teach or interpret Jewish law [Pre-12thC. Via late Latin and Greek from Hebrew rabbī, literally 'my master'.]

rabbinate /rábbinət/ n. **1.** RABBI'S POSITION the post or term of office of a rabbi **2.** RABBIS COLLECTIVELY rabbis considered as a group

rabbinic /rə bínnik/, **rabbinical** /-nik'l/ adj. relating to rabbis or to their beliefs, language, teachings, or writings —**rabbinically** adv.

Rabbinic Hebrew n. the form of Hebrew used by rabbis between the 5th and 16th centuries. It contains much of the Aramaic language and was influenced by the language of the Talmud.

Rabbit

rabbit /rábbit/ n. (plural **-bits** or **-bit**) **1.** ZOOL SMALL FURRY MAMMAL a small burrowing mammal with long ears, soft fur, and a short tail. Rabbits are commonly kept as pets. Family: Leporidae. **2.** INDUST RABBIT'S FUR the fur of a rabbit, used to make hats and other accessories **3.** FOOD RABBIT'S FLESH the meat of a rabbit ○ rabbit pie **4.** NOVICE a beginner or an unskilful player of a game or sport (dated informal) ■ vi. (**-bits, -biting, -bited**) **1.** HUNT RABBITS to go hunting for wild rabbits **2.** CHATTER to talk for a long time about unimportant things (informal) ○ He spent over an hour rabbiting to his mother on the phone. [14thC. Origin uncertain: probably via Old French from, ultimately, Middle Dutch or Low German robbe.] —**rabbiter** n.

—————— **WORD KEY: CULTURAL NOTE** ——————

Rabbit, Run, a novel by US writer John Updike (1960). It depicts the disastrous attempts of Harry Rabbit Angstrom to flee an unhappy marriage and the responsibilites of adulthood. Updike continued Harry's story in three subsequent novels, *Rabbit Redux* (1971), *Rabbit is Rich* (1981), and *Rabbit at Rest* (1990), creating a tetralogy that highlights sexual and moral confusion in late 20th century American society.

rabbit fever n. = tularaemia

rabbit food n. an offensive term that deliberately dismisses a vegetarian diet, especially as providing insufficient nutrition for a human being (informal offensive)

rabbit-foot clover n. a variety of clover native to Europe, Asia, and Africa. Its leaves bear a superficial resemblance to rabbits' paws. Latin name: Trifolium arvense.

rabbiting /rábbiting/ n. the activity of hunting for wild rabbits

rabbit-proof fence n. Aus a boundary between Australian states (informal) ○ the daftest scheme hatched this side of the rabbit-proof fence ○ I found this opal on the other side of the rabbit-proof fence. [Because fences were formerly erected along state boundaries to limit the spread of rabbits]

rabbit punch n. a short sharp blow to the back of the neck —**rabbit-punch** vt.

rabbitry /rábbitri/ (plural **-tries**) n. a place where rabbits are bred to be sold as pets

rabbit warren n. a system of underground tunnels burrowed by wild rabbits, traditionally regarded as complex and extensive ○ Once you get beyond the front doors, the place is like a rabbit warren.

rabble[1] /rább'l/ n. **1.** UNRULY CROWD a noisy and unruly crowd of people **2.** OFFENSIVE TERM an offensive term that deliberately insults people lacking in wealth and status (insult) (takes a singular or plural verb) **3.** OFFENSIVE TERM an offensive term that deliberately insults the abilities or significance of a group of people (insult) [14thC. Origin uncertain. Originally used for 'pack of dogs'.]

rabble[2] /rább'l/ n. FURNACE TOOL a device for stirring or skimming molten metal in a furnace ■ vt. (**-bles, -bling, -bled**) STIR STH WITH RABBLE to stir or skim molten metal with a rabble [Mid-19thC. Via French râble 'fire rake', from, ultimately, Latin rutabulum, from ruere 'to rake up'.] —**rabbler** n.

rabble-rouser n. sb who stirs up anger, violence, or other strong feelings in a crowd, especially for political reasons (disapproving) —**rabble-rousing** n., adj.

Rabelais /rábbə láy/, François (1493?–1553) French humanist and writer. His greatest works, *Pantagruel* (1532) and *Gargantua* (1534), satirized medieval scholasticism and are notable for their exuberance and earthy humour. —**Rabelaisian** /rábbə láyziən, rábbə láyzh'n/ adj., n.

Rabia /rə beé ə/, **Rabi** /raábi/ n. **1. Rabia, Rabi, Rabia I, Rabi I** 3RD MONTH OF ISLAMIC CALENDAR in the Islamic calendar, the third month of the year, made up of 30 days **2. Rabia, Rabi, Rabia II, Rabi II** 4TH MONTH OF ISLAMIC CALENDAR in the Islamic calendar, the fourth month of the year, made up of 29 days [Mid-18thC. From Arabic rabī'.]

rabid /rábbid/ adj. **1.** MED, VET HAVING RABIES infected with rabies **2.** FANATICAL having extremist views, especially about politics (disapproving) **3.** FURIOUS extremely angry or violent **4.** INTENSE extremely intense and unceasing ○ a rabid lust for power [Early 17thC. From Latin rabidus, from rabere (see RABIES).] —**rabidity** /rə bíddəti/ n. —**rabidly** /rábbidli/ adv. —**rabidness** n.

rabies /ráy beez/ n. an often fatal viral disease that affects the central nervous systems of most warm-blooded animals and is transmitted in the saliva of an infected animal. It causes convulsions, inability to move, and strange behaviour. [Late 16thC. From Latin, 'fury', from rabere 'to rave, be mad' (source of English rage).] —**rabic** adj. —**rabietic** /ráybi éttik/ adj.

Rabin /rə béen/, Yitzhak (1922–95) Israeli statesman. He served as prime minister from 1974 to 1977 and from 1992 until he was assassinated in 1995. He received the Nobel Peace Prize (1994).

RAC abbr. **1.** Royal Armoured Corps **2.** Royal Automobile Club

raccoon /rə koón, ra-/ (plural **-coons** or **-coon**), **racoon** (plural **-coons** or **-coon**) n. **1.** SMALL RING-TAILED MAMMAL a small mammal native to the forests of North and Central America that has greyish-black fur, black patches around the eyes, and a long bushy ringed tail. Genus: Procyon. **2.** RACCOON FUR the fur of the raccoon [Early 17thC. From Virginia Algonquian aroughcun.]

raccoon dog n. a small wild dog, native to woodland areas of eastern Asia, with facial markings similar to a raccoon's and a thick yellow-brown coat. Latin name: Nyctereutes procyonoides.

race[1] /rayss/ n. **1.** SPORTS CONTEST OF SPEED a contest, e.g. between or among runners or horseriders, to decide who is the fastest **2.** CONTEST BETWEEN RIVALS a contest

Raccoon

between two or more people seeking to do or reach the same thing, or do or reach it first **3.** OCEANOG, GEOG **WATER CURRENT** a strong localized current in the sea or a river **4.** CIV ENG **WATER CHANNEL** a channel that carries water from one place to another, especially from a stream to a millwheel **5.** TECH **GROOVE GUIDING SLIDING OBJECT** a groove along which sth, e.g. a ball-bearing, slides **6.** **NARROW PASSAGE** any narrow track or passage, e.g. one leading sheep from their enclosure to a dip **7.** **REGULAR COURSE** the fixed course regularly followed or travelled by sth, especially the Sun or the Moon (*archaic or literary*) **8.** **JOURNEY** a single passage along a fixed course, especially the course that sb's life follows (*archaic or literary*) ■ **races** *npl.* HORSERACING **HORSE RACES OR HORSERACING** horse races, the racetrack at which they are run, or horse-racing as a spectator sport ○ *We spent the day at the races.* ■ *v.* (**races, racing, raced**) **1.** *vti.* SPORTS **COMPETE AGAINST IN RACE** to compete with sb in a contest of speed **2.** *vt.* **ENTER STH IN RACE** to enter, ride, or drive sth, e.g. a horse or car, in a race **3.** *vti.* **MOVE VERY FAST** to move somewhere with great speed or haste, or make sb or sth move or be transported in this way **4.** *vi.* **BEAT FAST** to beat much faster than usual, e.g. out of nervousness or excitement (*refers to the heart*) **5.** *vti.* AUTOMOT **IDLE FAST** to run or make an engine or motor run at a high speed [13thC. From Old Norse *rás* 'rush, running'. Ultimately from an Indo-European word meaning 'to be in motion', which is also the ancestor of English *err* and *error*.]

race off *vt. Aus* to take sb away with the intention of having sex with him or her (*slang offensive*)

race[2] /rayss/ *n.* **1.** **GROUP OF HUMANS** any one of the groups into which the world's population can be divided on the basis of physical characteristics such as skin or hair colour **2.** **FACT OF BELONGING TO A GROUP** the fact of belonging to a group of humans who share the same physical features such as skin colour ○ *an attempt to end discrimination on grounds of race* **3.** **HUMANKIND** humanity considered as a whole ○ *the fate of the race* **4.** BIOL **STRAIN OF ORGANISM** a breed, strain, or subspecies of an organism **5.** WINE **WINE'S DISTINCTIVE TASTE** the distinctive taste of a particular wine, by which its grape variety or region of origin can be identified [Early 16thC. Via French from Italian *razza*, of unknown origin.]

racecar /rayss kaar/ *n. US* = **racing car**

racecard /rayss kaard/ *n.* the programme of events at a race meeting

racecourse /rayss kawrss/ *n.* **1.** **TRACK FOR HORSE RACES** a track around which horses race, or the grounds in which the track is sited. US term **racetrack** *n.* ι **2.** *US* = **racetrack**

racegoer /rayss gō ər/ *n.* sb attending a race meeting or sb who regularly goes to race meetings

racehorse /rayss hawrss/ *n.* a horse bred and trained to run in races

racemate /rayssə mayt/ *n.* a chemical compound that does not deflect any of the light passing through it [Mid-19thC. Formed from RACEMIC.]

raceme /rásseem/ *n.* a flower cluster (**inflorescence**) in which the flowers are borne on short stalks along a long main stem, as they are in the lily of the valley [Late 18thC. From Latin *racemus* 'bunch of grapes' (source of English *raisin*).]

race meeting *n.* a series of horse races held on the

same course on a single day or over consecutive days

racemic /rə seémik, -sémmik/ *adj.* used to describe a chemical compound that does not deflect or absorb any of the light passing through it. This is due to its consisting of a precise mixture of dextrorotatory and levorotatory isomers. [Late 19thC. Formed from Latin *racemus* 'bunch of grapes', because the compound was originally derived from grapes.]

racemic acid *n.* a form of tartaric acid that does not deflect or absorb any of the light passing through it. It is found in grape juice.

racemization /rássi mī záysh'n/, **racemisation** *n.* the process of converting from an optically active compound or mixture to one that is racemic —**racemize** /rássə mīz/ *vt.*

racemose /rássimōss, -mōz/ *adj.* **1.** BOT **WITH FLOWERS CLUSTERED ALONG STEM** used to describe a flower cluster (**inflorescence**) in which the flowers are borne on short stalks on a long main stem, as they are in the lily of the valley **2.** ANAT **CLUSTERED LIKE BUNCH OF GRAPES** used to describe glands that resemble a bunch of grapes in their structure —**racemosely** *adv.* —**racemously** *adv.*

racer /ráyssər/ *n.* **1.** **SB OR STH THAT RACES** a person, animal, or vehicle competing in a race **2.** **TRACK FOR MOVABLE ARTILLERY GUN** a circular rail on which the travelling platform of a heavy artillery gun is mounted **3.** **THIN FAST-MOVING SNAKE** a slender fast-moving nonvenomous North American snake. Genus: *Coluber*.

racerunner /ráyss runnər/ *n.* a fast-moving lizard found in North and Central America. Genus: *Cnemidophurus*.

racetrack /ráyss trak/ *n.* **1.** **TRACK FOR CARS OR RUNNERS** a track around which cars or runners race, or the grounds in which such a track is sited. US term **racecourse 2.** *US* = **racecourse**

race-walk *vi.* to compete in the sport of race walking

race walking *n.* the sport of racing at a fast walking pace, with rules that require walkers to keep at least one foot on the ground at all times —**race walker** *n.*

raceway /ráyss way/ *n. US* **1.** CIV ENG = **race**[1] *n.* **4 2.** SPORTS **RACETRACK** a track on which races, especially harness races, are held, or the grounds in which the track is sited

Rachel /ráchəl/ *n.* in the Bible, the daughter of Laban, wife of Jacob, and mother of Joseph and Benjamin (Genesis 29–35)

rachilla /rə kíllə/ (*plural* **-lae** /-lee/), **rhachilla** (*plural* **-lae**) *n.* a side branch of a compound leaf, e.g. on a fern that bears the individual leaflets [Mid-19thC. From modern Latin, literally 'little rachis', from *rachis* (see RACHIS).]

rachio- *prefix.* spine ○ *rachiotomy* [Via modern Latin from Greek *rhakhis* 'spine']

rachis /ráykiss/ (*plural* **rachises** *or* **rachides** /ráyki deez/), **rhachis** (*plural* **rhachises** *or* **rhachides**) *n.* **1.** BOT **PLANT STEM** the main stem of a flower cluster or a compound leaf **2.** BIRDS **FEATHER SHAFT** the main shaft of a feather **3.** ANAT **SPINE** the spine of a vertebrate animal (*technical*) [Late 18thC. Via modern Latin from Greek *rhakhis* 'spine, ridge'.] —**rachial** /ráyki əl/ *adj.* —**rachidial** /rə kíddi əl/ *adj.*

rachitis /rə kítiss/ *n.* the disease rickets (*technical*) [Early 18thC. From Greek *rhakhitis* 'disease of the spine', from *rhakhis* 'spine'.] —**rachitic** /rə kíttik/ *adj.*

Rachmaninoff /rak mánni nof/, **Sergey** (1873–1943)

AKG London

Sergey Rachmaninoff

Russian-born composer and pianist. His symphonies and compositions for piano are considered the last major musical expression of the Romantic era. Full name **Sergey Vasilyevich Rachmaninoff**

rachmanism /rákmənizəm/, **Rachmanism** *n.* exploitation or intimidation by a landlord of tenants living in slum property [Mid-20thC. Named after Peter *Rachman* (1919–62), a London landlord.]

racial /ráysh'l/ *adj.* **1.** **EXISTING BETWEEN RACES** existing or taking place between different races ○ *racial harmony* **2.** **RELATING TO RACE** relating to or characteristic of races or a particular race of people — **racially** *adv.*

racialism /ráysh'lizəm/ *n.* **1.** **SKIN COLOUR AS POSITIVE ATTRIBUTE** the attitude that skin colour distinguishes people in terms of positive attributes but not in terms of the negative attributes of worth or value of a race **2.** **RACISM** racism (*dated*) —**racialist** *n.*, *adj.* —**racialistic** /ráyshəlístik/ *adj.*

Racine /ra seén/, **Jean Baptiste** (1639–99) French playwright. Considered to be the greatest French classical tragedian, he adapted Greek and Roman plays in works such as *Bajazet* (1672) and *Phèdre* (1677).

racing /ráyssing/ *n.* the sport of taking part in races, e.g. as a runner, on a horse, or in a sports car

racing car *n.* a car used, designed, or adapted for racing. US term **racecar**

racism /ráyssizəm/ *n.* (*disapproving*) **1.** **ANIMOSITY TOWARDS OTHER RACES** prejudice or animosity against people who belong to other races ○ *'I am a Muslim and ... my religion makes me against all forms of racism'.* (Malcolm X, *Speech, Prospects for Freedom*; 1965) **2.** **BELIEF IN RACIAL SUPERIORITY** the belief that people of different races have different qualities and abilities, and that some races are inherently superior or inferior

racist /ráyssist/ *adj.* (*disapproving*) **1.** **BASED ON RACISM** based on notions and stereotypes related to race **2.** **PREJUDICED AGAINST OTHER RACES** prejudiced against all people who belong to other races ○ *'Black power ... a call to reject the racist institutions and values of this society'* (Stokley Carmichael [Kwame Toure] and Charles Vernon Hamilton, *Black Power!*; 1967) ■ *n.* **RACIST PERSON** sb who is racist (*disapproving*)

rack[1] /rak/ *n.* **1.** **FRAMEWORK FOR HOLDING THINGS** a framework or stand for carrying, holding, or storing things ○ *a wine rack* **2.** AGRIC **FEED-HOLDING FRAMEWORK** a framework containing hay or other fodder for livestock **3.** AIR FORCE **BOMB-HOLDING FRAMEWORK** a bomb- or rocket-carrying framework attached to an aircraft **4.** MECH ENG **TOOTHED BAR** a bar with notches, designed to engage the teeth of a pinion or worm gear and convert rotary motion to linear motion, e.g. in a vehicle's steering system **5.** **INSTRUMENT OF TORTURE** a torture device used to stretch the body of a victim strapped horizontally onto it **6.** *US, Can* CUE GAMES = **frame** ■ *vt.* (**racks, racking, racked**) **1.** **CAUSE SB PAIN** to cause sb great pain or stress ○ *the coughing spasms that racked his body* **2.** **SHAKE STH** to shake or strain sth with violent force ○ *The high winds racked villages all along the coast.* **3.** **STRAIN STH** to stretch sth with extreme force or mental effort ○ *I racked my memory trying to think where I'd seen him before.* **4.** **TORTURE SB ON RACK** to torture sb on a rack **5.** **PUT STH IN RACK** to place sth in or on a rack **6.** MECH ENG **MOVE STH WITH RACK** to move a device or part using a rack-and-pinion system [14thC. From Dutch *rak*, which evolved from Middle Dutch *rec* 'framework'.] —**racker** *n.* ◇ **on the rack** experiencing great mental anguish (*informal*)

rack off *vi. Aus* used to tell sb to go away in a slightly offensive way (*slang*) ○ *I told him to rack off and leave me alone.*

rack up *vt.* to accumulate sth, usually points (*informal*) ○ *The company racked up sales of $8 million in its first year of trading.*

rack[2] /rak/ *n.* a joint of meat, usually lamb, consisting of one or both sides of the front ribs prepared for roasting, often joined end to end in a circle [Late 16thC. Origin uncertain: possibly from RACK[1].]

rack[3] /rak/ (**racks, racking, racked**) *vt.* to siphon clear wine or beer out of a barrel, leaving the sediment behind [15thC. From Provençal *arracar*, from *raca* 'dregs', of unknown origin.]

rack[4] /rak/ *n.* SHOWY WALKING PACE FOR HORSE in dressage, a fast walking pace for a horse in which each foot is lifted off the ground in turn ■ *vi.* WALK AT RACK to walk at a fast pace, lifting each foot off the ground in turn (*refers to horses*) [Late 16thC. Origin unknown.]

rack[5] /rak/ *n.* MOVING CLOUD MASS a mass of broken cloud blown fast by the wind (*literary*) ■ *vi.* (**racks, racking, racked**) RACE ACROSS SKY to be blown fast by the wind (*literary*) (*refers to clouds*) [14thC. Origin uncertain: possibly from Old Norse.]

rack[6] /rak/ *n.* a state of ruin or destruction (*archaic*) [Late 16thC. Variant of WRACK.] ◇ **go to rack and ruin** to deteriorate into a state of neglect or ruin

rack-and-pinion *adj.* using or relating to a mechanical system in which a toothed wheel (**pinion**) engages a notched bar (**rack**) to convert rotary motion into linear motion

Racket

racket[1] /rákit/, **racquet** *n.* **1.** SPORTS SPORTS BAT a lightweight bat with a network of strings, used in badminton, squash, tennis, and similar games. The frame is usually made of a substance such as wood, aluminium, or graphite, and the strings of gut or nylon. **2.** SNOWSHOE a snowshoe in the shape of a racket [Early 16thC. Via French *raquette* from, ultimately, Arabic *rāhat* 'palm of the hand'.]

racket[2] /rákit/ *n.* **1.** NOISE a loud noise, especially when it disturbs people (*informal*) **2.** CRIMINOL ILLEGAL SCHEME an illegal or dishonest money-making scheme, involving activities such as bribery, fraud, or intimidation (*informal*) **3.** BUSINESS a business, job, or activity of any kind (*informal*) ○ *He's in the advertising racket.* **4.** EASY LIVING an easy and very profitable way of earning a living (*informal*) **5.** PARTY an uproarious party (*dated*) ○ *We had a fine old racket in the commandant's office*. (John Buchan, *Greenmantle*) **6.** MUSIC FORMER WOODWIND INSTRUMENT a woodwind instrument of the renaissance and baroque periods, consisting of a long tube coiled and enclosed in a cylinder **7.** MUSIC ORGAN STOP an organ stop that imitates the sound of the racket ■ *vi.* (**-ets, -eting, -eted**) **1.** MOVE AROUND NOISILY to make a lot of noise while moving around (*informal*) ○ *We could still hear them racketing around downstairs.* **2.** LIVE DEBAUCHED LIFE to lead a riotous life devoted to pleasure (*dated*) [Mid-16thC. Origin unknown: perhaps thought to suggest loud noise.]

racketeer /ráki teér/ *n.* CRIMINAL SCHEMER sb who makes money from illegal activities such as bribery, fraud, or intimidation ■ *vi.* (**-ets, -eering, -eered**) RUN CRIMINAL RACKET to make money from illegal activities, or operate a racket —**racketeering** *n.*

rackets /rákits/, **racquets** *n.* a fast game similar to squash played by two to four people on a four-walled indoor court using long-handled rackets and a small hard ball. It is derived from the old game of real tennis. US term **racquets**

racket-tail *n.* a name given to various birds of the hummingbird family that have racket-shaped tail feathers

rackety /rákiti/ *adj.* **1.** WITH LIVELY SOCIAL LIFE leading a lively but sometimes rather dissipated social life **2.** ROWDY noisy and boisterous (*dated*)

Rackham /rákəm/, **Arthur** (1867–1939) British illustrator and watercolour painter. He created fanciful illustrations for editions of literary classics, as well as for children's books.

rack railway *n.* a mountain railway that has locomotives with a central cogwheel that engages with a toothed rack between the rails in order to pull the train up steep slopes. US term **cog railway**

rack-rent *n.* EXCESSIVE RENT an unreasonably high rent ■ *vti.* (**rack-rents, rack-renting, rack-rented**) CHARGE TENANT EXCESSIVE RENT to charge tenants an unreasonably high rent [From RACK[1], in the sense 'to torture'] —**rack-renter** *n.*

raclette /ra klét/ *n.* **1.** DISH OF MELTED CHEESE WITH POTATOES a Swiss dish consisting of slices of melted cheese served on boiled potatoes or bread. The cheese is traditionally melted over a fire but electric raclette machines are now available. **2.** CHEESE USED FOR RACLETTE a hard-crusted type of Swiss cheese that melts easily, traditionally used for raclette [Mid-20thC. From French, from *racler* 'to scrape', because the cheese is melted and scraped onto a plate.]

racon /ráy kon/ *n.* = **radar beacon** [Mid-20thC. Blend of RADAR and BEACON.]

raconteur /rá kon túr/ *n.* sb who tells stories or anecdotes in an interesting or entertaining way [Early 19thC. Via French from, ultimately, Old French *raconter* 'to recount, retell'.]

racoon *n.* = **raccoon**

racquet *n.* = **racket**[1]

racquetball /rákit bawl/ *n.* a game played on a four-walled indoor court by two, three, or four players using short-handled rackets and a ball larger than the ball used in squash or rackets

racquets *n.* = **rackets** [Mid-18thC. From French *raquette* (see RACKET).]

racy /ráyssi/ (**-ier, -iest**) *adj.* **1.** MILDLY INDECENT mildly shocking because of references to or descriptions of sex **2.** LIVELY full of energy or spirit ○ *'the peculiar mixture of accurate knowledge and of racy imagination which gave them their fascination'* (Arthur Conan Doyle, *The Lost World*; 1912) **3.** DISTINCTIVE with a distinctive quality or flavour **4.** PUNGENT sharp or piquant in taste or smell [Mid-17thC. Formed from RACE[1]. Originally in the sense 'having a distinctive flavour'.] —**racily** *adv.* —**raciness** *n.*

rad[1] /rad/ *n.* the unit formerly used to measure the level of ionizing radiation absorbed by sth, equal to 0.01 joule per kilogram of irradiated material [Early 20thC. Acronym of 'radiation absorbed dose'.]

rad[2] /rad/ (**radder, raddest**) *adj.* US very good, desirable, admirable, or fashionable (*slang*) ○ *a totally rad idea* [Early 19thC. Shortening of RADICAL.]

rad[3] *symbol.* MATH radian

rad. *abbr.* **1.** radiator **2.** MATH radical **3.** radio **4.** MATH radius **5.** MATH radix

RADA /ráadə/ *abbr.* Royal Academy of Dramatic Art

radar /ráy daar/ *n.* **1.** OBJECT-LOCATING SYSTEM the use of reflected radio waves to determine the presence, location, and speed of distant objects. The system has military, policing, and navigational applications. Examples of its uses include the locating of enemy aircraft or ships and the monitoring of vehicle speeds. **2.** OBJECT-LOCATING EQUIPMENT the electronic equipment that transmits and receives high-frequency radio waves to detect, locate, and track distant objects [Mid-20thC. Acronym formed from 'radio detection and ranging'.] ◇ **be on sb's radar screen** US to be a focal point of interest to sb (*informal*) ○ *This issue of bank fraud has been on the district attorney's radar screen for at least six months.*

radar astronomy *n.* the use of radar techniques to study and map celestial bodies in the solar system

radar beacon *n.* a ground-based fixed position radar receiver-transmitter whose signals can be received by an aircraft or ship's navigator to determine bearing and range

radar gun *n.* a small hand-held radar device used to determine the speed of nearby objects

radarscope /ráy daar skóp/ *n.* the display screen on radar equipment, displaying the reflected radio signal as a dot of light. In sophisticated screens, textual data such as speed, direction, and altitude are also shown.

radar trap *n.* = **speed trap**

raddle[1] /rádd'l/ (**-dles, -dling, -dled**) *vt.* to twist or weave things together [Late 17thC. Via Anglo-Norman *reidele* 'wooden pole' from Old French *reddalle*, perhaps of Middle High German origin. Used for 'strip of wood twisted between stakes to make a fence'.]

raddle[2] /rádd'l/ *n., vt.* = **ruddle** ■ *vt.* MARK STH WITH RED DYE to mark or paint sth with a red dye or colour (*archaic*)

raddled /rádd'ld/ *adj.* with a worn-out appearance that suggests long life or a life of indulgence [Late 17thC. Origin uncertain.]

radial /ráydi əl/ *adj.* **1.** RUNNING FROM CENTRE OUTWARDS spreading out from a common centre like the spokes of a wheel ○ *petals in a radial arrangement* **2.** OF RADIUS relating to a radius, especially moving along a radius **3.** ZOOL WITH BODY PARTS IN CIRCULAR ARRANGEMENT used to describe the arrangement of the bodies of invertebrate marine animals such as the starfish and sea anemone that have parts spreading out from a single centre **4.** ANAT OF FOREARM BONE relating to the radius bone of the forearm ■ *n.* CARS = **radial tyre** —**radially** *adv.*

radial drilling machine *n.* a machine with a drilling head mounted on an arm that can be freely rotated to allow a given workpiece to be drilled at any point

radial engine *n.* an internal-combustion engine that has its cylinders arranged around a central crankshaft like the spokes of a wheel, instead of in one or two straight rows. ◊ **rotary engine**

radial keratotomy *n.* a surgical procedure for correcting short-sightedness, using a series of small radial incisions to change the shape of the cornea

radial-ply *adj.* used to describe a tyre in which the fabric cords that make up the foundation of the tyre run at right angles to the circumference of the tyre

radial symmetry *n.* symmetry in which sth can be divided into two identical halves by a line or plane passing through a central point or axis at any angle —**radially symmetrical** *adj.*

radial tyre *n.* a tyre in which the fabric cords that make up the foundation of the tyre run at right angles to the circumference of the tyre

radial velocity *n.* the velocity of a star or other celestial body measured along the observer's line of sight

radian /ráydi ən/ *n.* a unit of angular measurement equivalent to the angle between two radii that enclose a section of a circle's circumference (**arc**) equal in length to the length of a radius. There are 2π radians in a circle. Symbol **rad** [Late 19thC. Formed from RADIUS.]

radiance /ráydi ənss/ *n.* **1.** HAPPINESS OR ENERGY joy, energy, or good health discernible in sb's face or demeanour **2.** PHYS MEASURE OF RADIANT ENERGY a measure of the amount of radiant energy emitted or received per unit area of a surface over a specified time. Symbol L_e

radiant /ráydi ənt/ *adj.* **1.** SHOWING HAPPINESS expressing joy, energy, or good health in a pleasing way **2.** SHINING lit with a bright or glowing light **3.** PHYS IN RAY FORM used to describe light, heat, or other energy emitted in the form of waves or rays ○ *radiant heat* **4.** PHYS EMITTING RADIANT ENERGY emitting light, heat, or other energy in the form of waves or rays ■ *n.* **1.** ELEC ENG HEATING ELEMENT an element in a heater that gives out radiant heat **2.** ASTRON METEOR SHOWER'S POINT OF ORIGIN a point in space from which a meteor shower appears to originate [15thC. From Latin *radiant-*, the present participle stem of *radiare* (See RADIATE).] —**radiantly** *adv.*

radiant energy *n.* energy emitted as waves, usually electromagnetic waves, through space or some other medium. Symbol Q_e

radiant flux *n.* the rate of flow of radiant energy. Symbol Φ_e

radiant heat *n.* heat transmitted by infrared radiation from a heat source, as distinct from heat transmitted by conduction or convection

radiant heating *n.* heating by means of heaters such as radiators, baseboard heaters, and electric coils rather than by forced hot air

radiata /ráydi áatə/ (*plural* **-tas**) *n. ANZ* the Monterey pine [Mid-20thC. Via modern Latin, the species name, from, ultimately, Latin *radiare* (see RADIATE), because its cones grow in rings.]

radiate *v.* /ráydi ayt/ (**-ates, -ating, -ated**) **1.** *vti.* PHYS **SEND OR BE SENT IN RAYS** to send out energy, e.g. heat or light, in the form of rays or waves, or be sent out in this form **2.** *vti.* **SHOW A FEELING OR QUALITY** to clearly show a feeling or quality through looks, speech, behaviour, or content ○ *a popular speech that radiated goodwill and commitment* **3.** *vti.* **SPREAD FROM CENTRE** to spread out, or cause sth to spread out, from a central point like rays **4.** *vi.* BIOL **DEVELOP AND SPREAD** to develop into several different forms capable of exploiting different resources or of living in different environments (*refers to animal and plant species*) ■ *adj.* /ráydi ət, -ayt/ **1.** **WITH RADIATING PARTS** with, or in the form of, parts spreading out from a common centre **2.** BOT **WITH PETALS RADIATING FROM CENTRE** used to describe a flowerhead that has petals radiating from a centre, e.g. that of a daisy **3.** ZOOL **WITH RADIALLY SYMMETRICAL BODY** used to describe the bodies of starfish and other vertebrate marine organisms with body parts radiating from a common centre **4.** **WITH RAYS** surrounded or decorated with rays [Early 17thC. From Latin *radiat-*, the past participle stem of *radiare* 'to emit rays', from *radius* 'ray' (source of English *ray*[1]).] —**radiately** /ráydi ətli/ *adv.* —**radiative** /-ətiv/ *adj.*

radiation /ráydi áysh'n/ *n.* **1.** PHYS **PARTICLES EMITTED BY RADIOACTIVE SUBSTANCES** energy emitted in the form of particles by substances, e.g. uranium and plutonium, whose atoms are not stable and are spontaneously decaying. This energy can be converted into electrical power, but it also causes severe or fatal health problems to people who are exposed to it. **2.** PHYS **ENERGY EMITTED IN RAYS OR WAVES** any kind of energy that is emitted from a source in the form of rays or waves, e.g. heat, light, or sound **3.** PHYS **RADIATING OF ENERGY** the emission of energy in the form of waves **4.** **EFFECT OF RADIATING** the feeling of sth being radiated, e.g. heat from a hot oven **5.** MED = **radiotherapy 6.** BIOL **ADAPTIVE RADIATION** adaptive radiation —**radiational** *adj.*

radiational cooling *n.* loss of heat from the Earth's surface and from air near the Earth's surface, occurring mainly at night

radiation biology *n.* = **radiobiology**

radiation chemistry *n.* the branch of chemistry concerned with chemical changes caused by the impact of radiation

radiation physics *n.* the branch of physics that is concerned with the interaction between radiation and matter (*takes a singular verb*)

radiation sickness *n.* a medical condition caused by overexposure to X-rays or to emissions from radioactive material. Symptoms include fatigue, headache, vomiting, diarrhoea, loss of hair and teeth, and in severe cases, haemorrhaging.

radiation therapy *n.* = **radiotherapy**

radiator /ráydi aytər/ *n.* **1.** **ROOM HEATER WITH PIPES** a room-heating device that emits heat from pipes through which hot water, steam, or hot oil circulates, especially one connected to a central boiler-fed system **2.** CARS **ENGINE-COOLING DEVICE** a device that prevents a vehicle's engine from overheating, consisting of tubes through which heated water from the engine circulates to be cooled. Cool air is usually circulated around the tubes by means of a fan. **3.** ANZ **ELECTRIC HEATER** an electric fire or heater **4.** TECH **DEVICE EMITTING RADIANT ENERGY** a device that emits radiant energy, e.g. a light bulb or a television transmitter

radical /ráddik'l/ *adj.* **1.** **BASIC** relating to or affecting the basic nature or most important features of sth ○ *a radical difference between the two* **2.** **PERVASIVE** far-reaching, searching, or thoroughgoing ○ *a radical reorganization of the company* **3.** **FAVOURING MAJOR CHANGES** favouring or making economic, political, or social changes of a sweeping or extreme nature ○ *radical policies* **4.** MED **REMOVING DISEASE'S SOURCE** used to describe medical treatment that is intended to remove the source of a disease, rather than simply treat the symptoms **5.** BOT **GROWING FROM ROOT** growing from a root of a plant or from the base of a stem **6.** MATH **OF A MATHEMATICAL ROOT** relating to the roots of

numbers **7.** LING **OF WORD ROOTS** relating to the roots of words **8.** *US* **EXCELLENT** very good, desirable, admirable, or fashionable (*slang*) ■ *n.* **1.** POL, SOC SCI, ECON **SB WITH RADICAL VIEWS** sb with radical views on political, economic, or social issues ○ *the radicals in the party* **2.** MATH **MATHEMATICAL ROOT** a mathematical root of another number or quantity **3.** CHEM **FREE RADICAL** a free radical **4.** CHEM **CHEMICAL GROUP** a chemical group that behaves as a single entity in reactions (*dated*) **5.** LING = **root**[1] *n.* **7** [14thC. From late Latin *radicalis* 'of roots' (the original sense in English), from *radix* 'root' (source of English *radish*).] —**radically** *adv.* —**radicalness** *n.*

radical chic *n.* the fashionable adoption of radical left-wing views by rich or famous people (*disapproving*) ○ *'Radical chic invariably favors radicals who seem primitive, exotic, and romantic'.* (Tom Wolfe, *Radical Chic*; 1970)

radicalise *vti.* = **radicalize**

radicalism /ráddik'lizəm/ *n.* **1.** POLITICS **ADVOCATING MAJOR CHANGES** political policies that advocate more sweeping political, economic, or social change than that traditionally supported by the mainstream political parties **2.** **POLITICALLY RADICAL ATTITUDES** support for radical political policies **3.** **SIGNIFICANT CHANGE** sweeping change in any context, or the attitudes of people who favour sweeping change —**radicalistic** /ráddikəlístik/ *adj.* —**radicalistically** *adv.*

radicalize /ráddikəlīz/ (**-izes, -izing, -ized**), **radicalise** (**-ises, -ising, -ised**) *vti.* **1.** **CHANGE FUNDAMENTALLY** to undergo fundamental change, or introduce sweeping change in sth **2.** **MAKE OR BECOME POLITICALLY RADICAL** to adopt, or cause sb to adopt, politically radical views ○ *The experience of war radicalized the younger generation.* —**radicalization** /ráddikə līzáysh'n/ *n.*

radical sign *n.* the sign √ placed before a mathematical expression to denote the extraction of a square root or higher root. Roots higher than a square root are indicated by a superscript number preceding the sign.

radicand /ráddi kand/ *n.* a mathematical quantity from which a square root or higher root is to be extracted [Late 19thC. Formed from Latin *radicandus*, from *radicare* 'to take root'.]

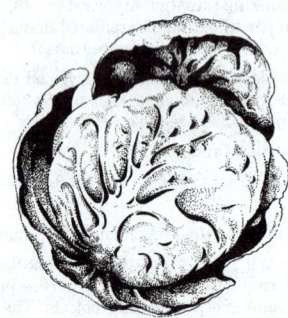

Radicchio

radicchio /ra díki ō/ (*plural* **-os**), **radichio** (*plural* **-os**) *n.* an Italian variety of chicory with reddish-purple and white leaves, usually eaten raw in salads [Late 20thC. Via Italian, 'chicory', from, ultimately, Latin *radicula* (see RADICLE).]

radices plural of **radix**

radicle /ráddik'l/ *n.* **1.** BOT **EMBRYONIC ROOT** the part of a plant embryo that forms the root of the young plant **2.** ANAT **BODY PART LIKE ROOT** a small body part such as a branch of a nerve that superficially resembles the root of a plant [Late 17thC. From Latin *radicula*, literally 'little root', from *radix* 'root' (source of English *radish*).] —**radicular** /ra díkyoolər/ *adj.*

radio /ráydi ō/ *n.* (*plural* **-os**) **1.** **USE OF ELECTROMAGNETIC WAVES FOR COMMUNICATION** the use of electromagnetic waves to transmit and receive information, as in sound broadcasts or two-way communication, without the need for connecting wires **2.** **COMMUNICATION USING RADIO WAVES** communication that takes place by means of radio waves **3.** **DEVICE RECEIVING SOUND BROADCASTS** an electronic device for receiving sound broadcasts transmitted via radio signals **4.** **TWO-WAY**

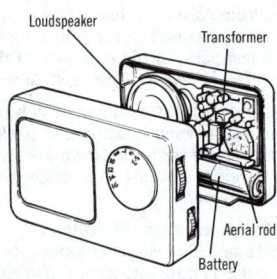

Radio

COMMUNICATION DEVICE an electronic device used to send and receive radio signals, used for two-way communication **5.** **RADIO BROADCASTS** sound broadcasts transmitted by means of radio waves **6.** **BROADCASTING OF PROGRAMMES BY RADIO** the broadcasting by radio of programmes for the public **7.** **RADIO BROADCASTING STATION OR ORGANIZATION** a station for transmitting radio broadcasts or an organization involved in radio broadcasting ○ *Radio 1* **8.** **SOUND BROADCASTING** radio broadcasting as an industry or profession ○ *She works in radio.* ■ *vti.* (**-os, -oing, -oed**) **COMMUNICATE BY RADIO** to communicate by radio or send sb a message by radio ■ *adj.* PHYS **OF ELECTROMAGNETIC WAVES** relating to electromagnetic waves or electromagnetic phenomena with frequencies between 10 kHz and 300,000 MHz [Early 20thC. Shortening of *radiotelegraph*.]

radio- *prefix.* **1.** radiation ○ *radiocarbon* **2.** radio ○ *radiolocation* [Shortening of words such as RADIATION and RADIOACTIVE]

radioactive /ráydi ō áktiv/ *adj.* **1.** **EMITTING RADIATION** used to describe a substance such as uranium or plutonium that emits energy in the form of streams of particles, owing to the decaying of its unstable atoms. This energy can be damaging or fatal to the health of people exposed to it. **2.** **OF OR USING RADIOACTIVE SUBSTANCES** relating to or making use of radioactive substances or the radiation they emit —**radioactively** *adv.*

radioactive decay *n.* = **decay** *n.* **4**

radioactive series *n.* a series of related atom types (**nuclides**) of radioactive isotopes, each of which is transformed into the next by the emission of an elementary particle until a stable nuclide results. There are three such sequences, the thorium, the uranium-radium, and the actinium, and almost all naturally occurring radioactive isotopes belong to one of them.

radioactive tracer *n.* a chemical substance that has a radioactive isotope attached, making it detectable when introduced into the body. Such tracers are used medically to diagnose diseases and biologically to study biochemical processes.

radioactive waste *n.* waste material that is radioactive, particularly the waste from nuclear reactors and medical treatment and research

radioactivity /ráydi ō ak tívvəti/ *n.* **1.** **RADIOACTIVE NATURE** the radioactive nature of a substance such as uranium or plutonium **2.** **RADIATION** the high-energy particles emitted by radioactive substances

radio alarm *n.* an electronic device that combines a radio with the functions of an alarm clock. It can be set not only to sound an alarm, but also to turn on the radio at a particular time.

radio astronomy *n.* a branch of astronomy that deals with the detection and analysis of radio waves received from space —**radio astronomer** *n.*

radio beacon *n.* a fixed ground-based radio transmitter that sends out a distinctive signal to help aircraft and shipping to identify their position

radio beam *n.* a beam of radio signals transmitted by a radio beacon for navigation purposes

radiobiology /ráydi ō bī ólləji/ *n.* a branch of biology that deals with the effects of radiation on living tissues and organisms —**radiobiologic** *adj.* —**radiobiological** /ráydi ō bī ə lójjik'l/ *adj.* —**radiobiologically** *adv.* —**radiobiologist** /ráydi ō bī ólləjist/ *n.*

radio button *n.* in a computer dialogue box, any one of several circles or rectangles, each with text next to it, representing a fixed set of choices, one of which must be selected

radio car *n.* **1.** CAR WITH TWO-WAY RADIO a car, especially a police car, equipped with a two-way radio **2.** VEHICLE FOR RADIO INTERVIEWS a vehicle from which radio broadcasts are made, especially interviews

radiocarbon /ráydi ō kaárbən/ *n.* a radioactive form of carbon, especially the isotope of carbon that has a mass number of 14

radiocarbon dating *n.* = carbon dating

radio cassette, **radio-cassette player** *n.* a radio and a cassette player combined in a single, usually portable machine

radiochemistry /ráydi ō kémmistri/ *n.* a branch of chemistry that deals with radioactive elements and their applications —**radiochemical** *adj.* —**radiochemically** *adv.* —**radiochemist** *n.*

radio compass *n.* a navigation device that uses incoming radio signals from radio beacons to determine a ship's or aircraft's position

radio-controlled *adj.* used to describe a device whose operation or movement is controlled from a distance using a transmitter, often hand-held, that sends radio signals to the device

radioelement /ráydi ō éllimənt/ *n.* a chemical element that is radioactive

radio frequency *n.* **1.** PHYS FREQUENCY USED FOR RADIO TRANSMISSIONS any of the frequencies of electromagnetic radiation in the range between 10 Khz and 300 MHz, including those used for radio and television transmission **2.** BROADCAST RADIO STATION'S FREQUENCY a frequency on which a radio station broadcasts its programmes

radio galaxy *n.* a galaxy that is a strong source of radio-frequency waves

radiogenic /ráydi ō jénnik/ *adj.* **1.** CREATED BY RADIOACTIVE DECAY used to describe a substance created as a result of the spontaneous decaying of the unstable atoms of another substance ○ *a radiogenic isotope* **2.** FROM RADIOACTIVE DECAY emitted as a result of radioactive decay ○ *radiogenic heat*

radiogram /ráydi ō gram/ *n.* **1.** TELECOM TELEGRAM a telegram sent by radio **2.** MED = **radiograph** *n.* **3.** RADIO AND RECORD PLAYER COMBINED a radio and a record player combined in a single unit (*dated*)

radiograph /ráydi ō graaf, -graf/ *n.* X-RAY PHOTOGRAPH an image produced on film or another sensitive surface by radiation, e.g. X-rays or gamma rays, passing through an object ■ *vt.* (-**graphs**, -**graphing**, -**graphed**) TAKE X-RAY OF STH to make a radiograph of sth, especially a part of the body —**radiographer** /ráydi ógrəfər/ *n.* —**radiographic** /ráydi ō gráffik/ *adj.* —**radiographically** *adv.* —**radiography** /ráydi óggrəfi/ *n.*

radioimmunoassay /ráydi ō ímmyōonō ássay/ *n.* the technique of measuring the levels of antibodies in the blood by introducing into the bloodstream a substance that has a radioactive tracer attached to it —**radioimmunoassayable** /ráydi ō ímmyənō ássay əb'l/ *adj.*

radioiodine /ráydi ō í ə deen/ *n.* a radioactive form of iodine, often used in medicine as a tracer

radioisotope /ráydi ō íssətōp/ *n.* a particular form of a chemical element (**isotope**) that is radioactive —**radioisotopic** /ráydi ō íssə tóppik/ *adj.*

radiolabel /ráydi ō láyb'l/ *n.* RADIOACTIVE SUBSTANCE ATTACHED TO ANOTHER a radioactive substance attached to another substance as a means of tracing the location or tracking the movement of that substance. The technique is used in medicine, e.g. to monitor the distribution of a drug throughout the body. ■ *vt.* (-**labels**, -**labelling**, -**labelled**) TAG SUBSTANCE WITH A RADIOLABEL to attach a radiolabel to a substance —**radiolabelled** *adj.* —**radiolabelling** *n.*

radiolarian /ráydi ō láiri ən/ *n.* a single-celled marine organism with a round silica-containing shell that has the organs of movement radiating around it. Amoebas are radiolarians. [Late 19thC. Formed from modern Latin *Radiolaria*, the class name, from *radiolus*, literally 'little staff, stick', from *radius* (see RADIUS).]

radiolocation /ráydi ō lō káysh'n/ *n.* the use of radar to detect distant objects

radiology /ráydi ólləji/ *n.* **1.** BRANCH OF MEDICINE USING X-RAYS a branch of medicine dealing with the use of X-rays and radioactive substances, such as radium, in the diagnosis and treatment of diseases **2.** SCIENCE OF RADIATION AND RADIOACTIVE SUBSTANCES the science of radiation and radioactive substances and their applications, such as in structural analysis —**radiologic** /ráydi ə lójjik/ *adj.* —**radiological** /-lójjik'l/ *adj.* —**radiologically** /-lójjikəli/ *adv.* —**radiologist** /ráydi ólləjist/ *n.*

radiolucent /ráydi ō lo͞oss'nt/ *adj.* interfering very little or not at all with the passage of X-rays and other forms of electromagnetic radiation —**radiolucency** /ráydi ō lo͞oss'nsi/ *n.*

radiolysis /ráydi ō ólississ/ *n.* the breakdown of sth into its chemical components by means of X-rays or other radiation —**radiolytic** /ráydi ō líttik/ *adj.*

radiometer /ráydi ómmitər/ *n.* a device used to detect and measure radiant energy, especially an instrument used to demonstrate the conversion of such energy into mechanical work —**radiometric** /ráydi ə métrik/ *adj.* —**radiometrically** /-métrikəli/ *adv.* —**radiometry** /ráydi ómmitri/ *n.*

radiometric dating *n.* any method of determining the age of objects or material using the decay rates of radioactive components, such as potassium-argon

radiomimetic /rádi əmi méttik/ *adj.* exerting effects similar to those of ionizing radiation ○ *the radiomimetic effects of certain chemicals, such as urethane*

radionuclide /ráydi ə nyo͞oklīd/ *n.* a radioactive nuclide

radiopaque /ráydi ō páyk/ *adj.* blocking the passage of X-rays and other forms of electromagnetic radiation —**radiopacity** /rádi ō pássiti/ *n.*

radiopharmaceutical /ráydi ō faarmə syo͞otik'l/ *n.* a radioactive drug or substance used in medicine to diagnose or treat a disease —**radiopharmaceutical** /ráydi ō faarmə syo͞otik'l/ *adj.*

radiophoto /ráydi ō fṓ tō/ (*plural* -**tos**) *n.* = **radiophotograph**

radiophotograph /ráydi ō fṓtə graaf, -graf/ *n.* a photograph or another image that is sent from one location to another by means of radio waves

radioprotective /ráydi ō prə téktiv/ *adj.* protecting or helping to protect against the harmful effects of X-rays and other radiation —**radioprotection** /ráydi ō prə téksh'n/ *n.*

radioscopy /ráydi óskəpi/ *n.* the use of X-rays or some other form of electromagnetic radiation to study the internal structure of sth —**radioscopic** /ráydi ə skóppik/ *adj.* —**radioscopical** /-skóppik'l/ *adj.*

radiosensitive /ráydi ō sénsitiv/ *adj.* sensitive to the biological effects of radiant energy such as X-rays —**radiosensitivity** /ráydi ō sensitívity/ *n.*

radiosonde /ráydi ō sond/ *n.* an instrument carried aloft by a balloon and used to measure and transmit meteorological data by radio [Mid-20thC. From RADIO + SONDE.]

radio spectrum *n.* the range of radio frequencies used for radio, television, and other electromagnetic communications, between 10 Khz and 300 Mhz

radio telescope *n.* an astronomical instrument used to detect and analyse radio waves from celestial objects. It consists of an antenna, often in the form of a large dish, a detector, and an amplifier.

radioteletype /ráydi ō téllitīp/ *n.* **1.** RADIO TELEPRINTER a teleprinter that transmits and receives by radio rather than along a cable **2.** RADIOTELETYPE SYSTEM a receiving and transmitting system that uses radioteletypes

radiotherapy /ráydi ō thérrəpi/ *n.* the treatment of disease using radiation X-rays or beta rays directed at the body from an external source or emitted by radioactive materials placed within the body —**radiotherapeutic** /ráydi ō therə pyo͞otik/ *adj.* —**radiotherapist** /ráydi ō thérrəpist/ *n.*

radiothorium /ráydi ō tháwri əm/ *n.* a radioactive

isotope of the element thorium, with a mass number of 228

radiotoxic /ráydi ō tóksik/ *adj.* relating to the toxic effects of radiation or radioactive substances

radiotracer /ráydi ō tráyssər/ *n.* a radioactive substance introduced into the body as a tracer, e.g. to observe the steps in a chemical or biochemical process or locate diseased cells or tissue

radio wave *n.* an electromagnetic wave whose frequency falls within the radio spectrum

Radish

radish /ráddish/ *n.* **1.** PLANTS PLANT WITH EDIBLE ROOT a Eurasian plant of the mustard family that has white to purple flowers and an edible root. Latin name: *Raphanus sativus*. **2.** FOOD EDIBLE ROOT the crisp pungent root of the radish plant, usually white with a red skin, eaten raw [Pre-12thC. Formed from Latin *radic-*, the stem of *radix* (see RADIX), perhaps modelled on French *radis* 'radish'.]

radium /ráydi əm/ *n.* a white highly radioactive metallic element found in minerals such as pitchblende and carnotite. It emits alpha particles as it decays to radon and is used in luminous coatings and the treatment of cancer. Symbol **Ra** [Late 19thC. Formed from Latin *radius* (see RADIUS), from the rays emitted by radium, which penetrate certain opaque materials.]

radium therapy *n.* the medical use of radium to treat cancer and other diseases with radiation

radius /ráydi əss/ (*plural* -**i** /-di ī/ *or* -**uses**) *n.* **1.** MATH, GEOM LINE FROM CENTRE a straight line extending from the centre of a circle to its edge or from the centre of a sphere to its surface. Symbol **r 2.** MATH, GEOM LENGTH OF RADIUS the length of a radius. Symbol **r 3.** CIRCULAR AREA an area enclosed by a circle that has a radius of a specified length ○ *all the houses within a radius of 2 miles of the explosion* **4.** RANGE OF EFFECTIVENESS OR INFLUENCE the area or range within which sb or sth can act, work, or exert influence effectively ○ *beyond the radius of the UN's influence* **5.** ANAT, ZOOL BONE IN ARM OR FORELIMB the shorter and thicker of the two bones in the human forearm, the one on the thumb side, or the equivalent bone in the lower forelimbs of animals **6.** RADIATING PART a radiating line, part, or structure [Late 16thC. From Latin, 'staff, spoke, ray, beam of light' (source also of English *ray*[1]).]

radius of action *n.* **1.** MIL AREA OF OPERATION a broadly circular area in which a military unit can operate or bring force to bear on an enemy **2.** TRANSP DISTANCE FROM WHICH RETURN IS POSSIBLE the distance a vehicle, ship, or aircraft can go out to and return safely to base without refuelling

radius of curvature *n.* the radius of the circle whose curvature matches that of a curve at a particular point

radius vector *n.* **1.** MATH LINE JOINING POINTS a line connecting a fixed point or origin and a variable point, or the length of such a line **2.** ASTRON IMAGINARY LINE CONNECTING CELESTIAL BODIES a line connecting the centre of a celestial body and the centre of another in orbit around it

radix /ráydiks/ (*plural* **radices** /ráydi seez/ *or* **radixes**) *n.* **1.** MATH BASE NUMBER the base of a number system or system of logarithms **2.** BIOL ROOT a root part or point where a plant or animal part begins [Late 16thC. From Latin, literally 'root, radish, foundation'. Ultimately from an Indo-European base that is also the ancestor of English *root* and *wort*.]

RADM, **RAdm** *abbr.* rear admiral

radome /ráy dōm/ *n.* a dome-shaped protective enclosure for a radar antenna, made from materials that do not interfere with the transmission and reception of radio waves [Mid-20thC. Blend of RADAR and DOME.]

radon /ráy don/ *n.* a heavy gaseous radioactive chemical element formed from the decay of radium that is used in radiotherapy and found in small quantities in rock and soil. The radon in rock and soil accounts for most of normal background radiation. In heavier concentrations, however, sometimes detected inside houses, it is thought to pose a risk of cancer. Symbol **Rn** [Early 20thC. Coined from RADIUM + -ON.]

radula /ráddyŏŏlə/ (*plural* **-lae** /-lee/) *n.* a band of tissue in the mouth of some molluscs (**gastropods**) containing rows of small teeth, used in scraping off particles of food and bringing them into the mouth [Mid-18thC. From Latin, 'scraper', from *radere* 'to scrape' (source of English *abrade, erase, rail,* and *rash*).] —**radular** *adj.*

radwaste /rád wayst/ *n.* radioactive waste (*informal*) [Late 20thC. Contraction of RADIOACTIVE WASTE.]

Raeburn /ráybərn/, **Sir Henry** (1756–1823) Scottish painter. A portraitist, especially of the Scottish upper classes, he is noted especially for *The Rev. Robert Walker Skating* (1784).

RAEC *abbr.* Royal Army Educational Corps

RAF *abbr.* Royal Air Force

RAFDS *abbr.* Royal Australian Flying Doctor Service

Rafferty /ráffərti/, **Chips** (1909–71) Australian actor. His films include *The Sundowners* (1960) and *Wake in Fright* (1971). Real name **John William Pilbean Goffage**

raffia /ráffi ə/, **raphia** *n.* **1.** INDUST **FIBRE OF PALM TREE** fibre in the form of flexible straw-coloured ribbons, obtained from the leaves of the raffia palm, used in making mats, baskets, and other products **2.** TREES = **raffia palm** [Late 19thC. From Malagasy *rafia.*]

raffia palm *n.* a palm tree that grows in Madagascar and has large leaves that yield a strong fibre used to make mats and baskets and other products. Latin name: *Raphia ruffia.*

raffinate /ráffi nayt/ *n.* the remaining or refined part of a liquid mixture, left after other substances dissolved in it have been extracted [Early 20thC. From French *raffinat,* from *raffiner* 'to refine'.]

raffinose /ráffi nōz, -nōss/ *n.* a white crystalline slightly sweet sugar present in many plant products and obtained commercially from cottonseed meal, sugar beet, and molasses. Formula: $C_{18}H_{32}O_{16}$. [Late 19thC. Coined from French *raffiner* (see RAFFINATE) + -OSE.]

raffish /ráffish/ *adj.* **1.** **CHARMINGLY UNCONVENTIONAL OR DISREPUTABLE** displaying a charming, free-spirited disregard for the conventions of society or for approved behaviour ○ *a raffish politician whose engaging antics never alienated the voters* **2.** **SHOWY** displaying an exaggerated or obtrusive showiness ○ *a raffish hotel* [Early 19thC. Formed from earlier *raff* 'common people', of unknown origin.] —**raffishly** *adv.* —**raffishness** *n.*

raffle[1] /ráff'l/ *n.* **LOTTERY WITH OBJECTS AS PRIZES** an event in which numbered tickets are sold, some of which are drawn at random to win prizes. The prizes in a raffle are usually objects rather than money and raffles are usually held in order to raise money for some cause or organization. ○ *I won this vase in a raffle.* ■ *vt.* (**-fles, -fling, -fled**) **AWARD STH IN RAFFLE** to offer or give away sth as a prize in a raffle [14thC. Via Old French, 'act of plundering', of uncertain origin: perhaps from Middle Dutch *raffel* 'game of dice', the original meaning in English.] —**raffler** *n.*

raffle[2] /ráff'l/ *n.* **1.** **RUBBISH** unwanted items or debris **2.** NAUT **TANGLE** tangled ropes or other bits and pieces on a ship [Late 18thC. Origin uncertain: perhaps from Old French *ne rafle* 'nothing at all'.]

Raffles /ráff'lz/, **Sir Stamford** (1781–1826) British colonial administrator. He was lieutenant-governor of Java (1811–16) and Bengkulu (1818–24), and founder of the city of Singapore (1819). Full name **Thomas Stamford Raffles**

rafflesia /ra fleézi ə/ *n.* a leafless tropical Asian plant that is a parasite of other plants and has large foul-smelling flowers pollinated by carrion flies. One species has the largest flower of all plants, measuring up to 1 m/40 in across. Genus: *Rafflesia.* [Early 19thC. From modern Latin, genus name, named after Sir Stamford *Raffles,* (1781–1826), British colonial administrator in Southeast Asia, who obtained the type specimen.]

raft[1] /raaft/ *n.* **1.** NAUT **FLAT BOAT** a flat floating structure made of wooden planks, logs, barrels, or similar materials, used as a boat or anchored in the water as a dock or diving platform **2.** LEISURE **INFLATABLE BOAT OR MAT** an inflatable flat-bottomed rubber or plastic boat used for drifting along on a river, or an inflatable rectangular mat used for surfing or lounging in the water **3.** *US* **COLLECTION OF FLOATING OBJECTS** a group of animals, especially wildfowl, or a mass of things floating or travelling together on water ○ *a raft of ducks* **4.** **BASE SLAB FOR BUILDING** a thick concrete slab laid down as a foundation for a building that is being constructed on soft ground ■ *v.* (**rafts, rafting, rafted**) **1.** *vt.* **MOVE STH BY RAFT** to transport sth by raft **2.** *vi.* NAUT **SAIL ON A RAFT** to travel on a raft **3.** *vt.* **FORM A RAFT** to form sth into a raft, or make sth gather together into a raft ○ *The lumberjacks rafted the logs together before sending them downstream.* [13thC. From Old Norse *raptr* 'log, beam'.]

WORD KEY: CULTURAL NOTE

The Raft of the Medusa, a painting by French artist Théodore Géricault (1819). This monumental work is a harrowing depiction of the suffering of the survivors of an infamous 1816 shipwreck. Géricault's treatment of a contemporary subject in an epic style more traditionally associated with classical or historical themes was seen as a significant development in European art.

raft[2] /raaft/ *n.* a very large number or amount of sth (*informal*) ○ *a whole raft of proposals* [Mid-19thC. Alteration of earlier *raff,* probably modelled on RAFT[1].]

rafter[1] /raáftər/ *n.* any of the sloping supporting timbers, beams, or boards that run from the ridge beam of a roof to its edge [Old English *ræfter,* of prehistoric Germanic origin] —**raftered** *adj.* —**raftering** *n.*

rafter[2] /raáftər/ *n.* **1.** **SAILOR ON RAFT** sb who travels on a raft **2.** **MAKER OF LOG RAFT** a lumberjack who ties logs into a raft to transport them downstream

rafting /raáfting/ *n.* the outdoor leisure pursuit of floating on a lake or sailing on a river in a raft

rafty /raáfti/ *adj. N England* rancid (*informal*)

RAFVR *abbr.* Royal Air Force Volunteer Reserve

rag[1] /rag/ *n.* **1.** **SMALL PIECE OF CLOTH** a small piece or scrap of usually old or unwanted cloth taken, e.g., from torn-up old clothing, often used for cleaning, polishing, or applying liquid substances **2.** **SMALL TATTERED PIECE** a small, irregular, or tattered scrap or piece of sth **3.** **PIECE OF CLOTHING** an item of clothing, thought of as being worn or tattered and not really fit to wear (*informal; often used ironically*) ○ *This? Oh, this is just some old rag I pulled out of the wardrobe.* **4.** **INFERIOR NEWSPAPER** a newspaper with low journalistic standards, or any newspaper regarded with contempt (*informal*) ○ *That rag prints nothing but lies and gossip.* **5.** **CLOTH FOR PAPERMAKING** cloth or cloth fibres that are used in making paper ■ **rags** *npl.* **WORN-OUT CLOTHES** clothes that are tattered, frayed, or torn [14thC. Origin uncertain: probably from assumed Old Norse *rogg* 'shaggy tuft'.] ◇ **be (like) a red rag to a bull (to sb)** to be certain to make sb angry ◇ **go from rags to riches** to start off in poverty and then become very wealthy ◇ **in rags** in a worn-out, tattered, and torn condition ◇ **lose your rag** to lose your temper (*slang*)

rag[2] /rag/ *v.* (**rags, ragging, ragged**) **1.** *vti.* **TEASE OR TAUNT SB** to subject sb to persistent teasing or taunting (*dated*) ○ *His friends ragged him about his new haircut.* **2.** *vt.* **PLAY PRANKS ON SB** to play pranks or jokes on sb, often to the point of tormenting him or her (*dated*) **3.** *vi.* **BEHAVE BOISTEROUSLY** to take part in good-humoured, boisterous activity (*dated*) **4.** *vt.* **SCOLD SB** to scold sb persistently or vehemently ■ *n.* **1.** UNIV **CHARITY FUND-RAISING AT UNIVERSITY** an activity or a set of activities conducted by university students in order to raise money for charity while having a good time **2.** **PRACTICAL JOKE** a prank or practical joke, especially by a student on a fellow student (*dated*) [Mid-18thC. Origin unknown.] —**ragging** *n.*

rag[3] /rag/ *n.* MUSIC **RAGTIME MUSIC** a type of jazz in which a syncopated rhythm in the melody is accompanied by a steady beat, or a piece of music in this style ■ *vt.* (**rags, ragging, ragged**) **WRITE RAGTIME** to compose or perform ragtime music [Late 19thC. Origin uncertain: perhaps a shortening of RAGGED, from the syncopation of the music.]

rag[4] /rag/ *n.* **1.** = **ragstone 2.** **ROOFING SLATE** a roofing slate that has a rough surface on one side [13thC. Origin unknown.]

rag[5] *n.* = **raga**

raga /raágə/, **rag** /raag/, **raag** *n.* any of a body of scales, melodies, or rhythmic patterns that form the basis of the classical music of the Indian subcontinent. Particular ragas are associated with different times of the day, and are intended to create different moods. Performances may be partly or completely improvised. [Late 18thC. From Sanskrit *rāga* 'colour, musical colour, harmony'.]

ragamuffin /rággə mufin/ *n.* **1.** **NEGLECTED CHILD** a child dressed in worn or tattered clothes, often one allowed to roam the streets (*dated*) **2.** *Carib* = **ragga** [14thC. Origin uncertain: perhaps from RAG[1] + Middle Dutch *muffe, moffe* 'mitten' (source of English *muff*).]

rag-and-bone man *n.* sb who travels the streets buying and selling unwanted clothes and household items and other discarded things. US term **junkman**

ragbag /rág bag/ *n.* **1.** **MISCELLANY** a collection of miscellaneous things (*informal*) **2.** **BAG OF RAGS** a bag in which unwanted clothes and bits of cloth are kept for use as rags

rag doll *n.* a floppy stuffed cloth doll

rage /rayj/ *n.* **1.** **EXTREME ANGER** sudden and extreme anger, or an outburst of strong anger **2.** **FORCE OR INTENSITY** extreme or unrelenting intensity **3.** **OBJECT OF FAD** sth that is the object of a short-lived fascination, fashion, or enthusiasm shared by many people ○ *Those toys are all the rage for kids at the moment.* **4.** *ANZ* **PARTY** a party or celebration ○ *The kids are planning a bit of a rage this weekend to celebrate the end of term.* **5.** **STRONG PASSION OR ENTHUSIASM** a strong and sometimes overpowering desire or enthusiasm ■ *vi.* (**rages, raging, raged**) **1.** **ACT WITH OR FEEL RAGE** to speak or do sth with sudden, extreme anger, or feel such strong anger ○ *She was raging against the injustice of the situation.* **2.** **OCCUR WITH VIOLENCE** to occur, continue, move, or spread with great force and violence ○ *The battle raged for three days.* **3.** *ANZ* **HOLD PARTY** to have a party to celebrate sth or to socialize ○ *We were out raging all weekend.* [13thC. Via Old French, from Vulgar Latin *rabia,* an alteration of Latin *rabies* (see RABIES).]

WORD KEY: SYNONYMS

See Synonyms at ***anger***.

ragee *n.* = **ragi**

ragfish /rágfish/ (*plural* **-fishes** *or* **-fish**) *n.* a scaleless deep-sea fish with a cartilaginous skeleton that makes it so flexible it flops like a rag when taken out of the water. Latin name: *Icosteus aenigmaticus.*

ragga /rággə/ *n.* a style of reggae characterized by long rap monologues and repetitive beats

ragged /rággid/ *adj.* **1.** **TATTERED** frayed or torn into irregular shapes or pieces, especially along the edge **2.** **WEARING RAGS** dressed in torn, tattered, or frayed clothes **3.** **WITH UNEVEN EDGE OR SURFACE** with a surface, edge, or outline that is rough, uneven, or jagged **4.** **UNKEMPT** rough and irregular in appearance and suggesting neglect and a lack of grooming ○ *a ragged beard* **5.** **NOT FIRM OR REGULAR** done in an uncoordinated, hesitant, or irregular way, especially by a group who do not manage to do sth all together or in unison **6.** **OF VARYING QUALITY** of unequal quality, some parts being less good than others ○ *He gave a rather ragged performance as Othello.* **7.** **EXHAUSTED** extremely tired or anxious ○ *speaking with a ragged voice* [13thC. Formed from RAG[1].] —**raggedly** *adv.* —**raggedness** *n.*

ragged robin *n.* a perennial plant of the pink family that has narrow leaves and pink or, less commonly, white flowers with ragged lobed petals. Latin name: *Lychnis floscuculi.*

raggedy /rággidi/ *adj.* (*informal*) **1.** TATTERED having been torn and worn excessively **2.** BADLY DRESSED wearing worn-out torn clothes **3.** ROUGH OR UNEVEN having rough untidy ends or edges

raggee *n.* = **ragi**

raggle-taggle /rágg'l tágg'l/ *adj.* consisting of a mixture of strange or very different kinds, often with an element of untidiness or scruffiness ○ *a raggle-taggle collection of animals in a small zoo* [Early 20thC. Alteration of RAGTAG.]

ragi /rággi/, **ragee, raggee** *n.* **1.** CEREAL GRASS a cereal grass cultivated for its edible grain in southern Asia and parts of Africa. Latin name: *Eleusine coracana.* **2.** GRAIN USED AS FOOD the grain of ragi used as food [Late 18thC. From Hindi *rāgī*.]

raging /ráyjing/ *adj.* **1.** VERY ANGRY out of control or angry **2.** VERY STRONG done or happening with great force or intensity **3.** VERY SEVERE OR PAINFUL very severe and causing great pain or distress ○ *a raging toothache* **4.** VERY GOOD very good or great ○ *The play was a raging success.*

raglan /rágglən/ *adj.* **1.** EXTENDING TO COLLAR used to describe a sleeve extending to the collar of a garment instead of ending at the shoulder, attached with slanting seams running from under the arm to the neck **2.** HAVING RAGLAN SLEEVES made with raglan sleeves ■ *n.* GARMENT WITH RAGLAN SLEEVES an overcoat, jumper, or other garment that has raglan sleeves [Mid-19thC. Named after Field Marshal Lord *Raglan* (1788–1855), British soldier, who favoured overcoats in this style.]

ragman /rág man/ (*plural* **-men** /-mən/) *n.* sb who buys and sells old cloth and clothes as a business

ragnail /rág nayl/ *n. Scotland* a hangnail

Ragnarök /raágnə rok/ *n.* in Norse mythology, the final destruction of the gods in a great battle against the forces of evil, after which a new world will arise [Mid-18thC. From Old Norse *ragnarök*, literally 'fate of the gods', from *regin* 'gods' + *rok* 'fate'.]

ragout /ra goó/ *n.* a rich slow-cooked stew of meat and vegetables [Mid-17thC. From French, from *ragoûter* 'to renew the appetite', from *goût* 'taste', from Latin *gustus* (source of English *disgust* and *gusto*).]

ragpicker /rág pikər/ *n.* sb who makes money by collecting old clothes and other discarded items and selling them

rag-rolling *n.* the decorative technique of using a crumpled cloth to dab paint that has been applied to a wall or other surface, in order to produce an irregularly patterned effect

rag rug *n.* a rug made by knotting or hooking short strips of waste fabric through an openweave base to form a shaggy pile

ragstone /rág stōn/ *n.* a hard sandstone or limestone that tends to break up into slabs and is used as a building material

ragtag /rág tag/ *adj.* **1.** MIXED AND OFTEN DUBIOUS made up of a wide-ranging mix of people or things, often ones that are of questionable quality (*disapproving*) ○ *a ragtag crowd of exiles* **2.** UNTIDY untidy, unkempt, or ragged in appearance [Late 19thC. From RAG[1].]

ragtag and bobtail *n.* people who are members of the lowest social classes, especially when considered as dissatisfied with their lives and likely to be disorderly or rebellious (*dated insult*)

ragtime /rág tīm/ *n.* a style of US popular music of the late 19th and early 20th centuries characterized by distinctive syncopated right-hand rhythms against a regularly accented left-hand beat. Ragtime was widely popularized by the pianist and composer Scott Joplin.

rag trade *n.* the clothing industry and the various professions involved in the design, manufacture, and sale of clothing (*informal*)

ragweed /rág weed/ *n.* **1.** PLANT CAUSING HAY FEVER a weedy, chiefly North American plant that has small green flower heads and large amounts of pollen that is a cause of hay fever in many people. Genus: *Ambrosia.* **2.** = **ragwort** [From the raggedness of the leaves]

ragworm /rág wurm/ *n.* a marine worm often used as fishing bait. Latin name: *Nereis diversicolor.* US term **clamworm** [From the ragged appearance of its appendages]

ragwort /rág wurt/ *n.* a plant with clusters of small yellow flowers with radiating petals like those of daisies. Genus: *Senecio.* [From the raggedness of the leaves]

rah /raa/ *interj.* used to express approval or encouragement (*informal*) [Mid-19thC. Shortening of HURRAH.]

Rahman /rəmaán/, **Sheikh Mujibur** (1920–75) Bangladeshi statesman. The founding father of Bangladesh, he served as the country's first prime minister (1972–75). Soon after becoming president (1975) he was assassinated.

Rahman, Ziaur (1935–81) Bangladeshi statesman. As president of Bangladesh (1977–81), he ended martial law but was assassinated in an attempted military coup.

rah-rah /raá raa/ *adj. US* spiritedly and often unthinkingly enthusiastic (*slang*) ○ *the rah-rah attitude of the project's supporters*

rah-rah skirt, **ra-ra skirt** *n.* a short full skirt usually layered or with rows of frills, popular in the 1980s and inspired by the costumes of US cheerleaders [RAH-RAH because originally worn by cheerleaders]

rai /rī/ *n.* a form of music popular in Algeria that combines elements of Algerian traditional music with western rock [Late 20thC. From Arabic.]

raid /rayd/ *n.* **1.** SUDDEN ATTACK a sudden attack made by soldiers, aircraft, police, bandits, or any other force in an attempt to seize or destroy sth **2.** STOCK EXCH ATTEMPT TO BUY CONTROL the buying of a large number of shares in a company in an attempt to gain control of it ○ *The company beat off the raid but took on debt to buy its own shares.* **3.** STOCK EXCH ILLEGAL ATTEMPT TO LOWER STOCK PRICE the illegal coordinated selling of shares in a company's stock by a group of speculators in an attempt to make the stock price fall **4.** *US* BUSINESS LURING PEOPLE AWAY in the business world, an attempt by an organization to lure away a competitor's employees, members, or clients ○ *a raid by one advertising agency on another's clients* ■ *v.* (**raids, raiding, raided**) **1.** *vti.* MAKE SURPRISE ATTACK to make or participate in a raid on sb or sth **2.** *vt.* STEAL STH FROM SOMEWHERE to take sth secretly or stealthily because it is illegal or forbidden ○ *The bank's funds had been raided by its former president.* **3.** *vt. US* BUSINESS LURE SB AWAY to lure sb away from another organization, usually from a competitor ○ *The new league began to raid players from its rival.* [15thC. Scots dialect form of Old English *rād* 'expedition, riding, road' (source of English *road*).] —**raider** *n.*

rail[1] /rayl/ *n.* **1.** LONG PIECE OF WOOD OR METAL a long horizontal or sloping piece of wood, metal, or other material that is used as a barrier, support, or place to hang things **2.** FENCE OR RAILING a structure made of a rail or rails and their supports, e.g. a fence or railing (*often used in the plural*) **3.** STEEL BAR OF RAILWAY TRACK a narrow steel bar, or a series of connected bars laid in two parallel lines, supporting and guiding the wheels of railway engines and carriages or anything similar. ◊ **third rail 4.** TRANSP RAILWAY the railway as a means or form of transport ○ *rail travel* ■ *vt.* (**rails, railing, railed**) PUT RAIL ON OR ROUND STH to put a rail or railing on or around sth to provide a guard, barrier, or support ○ *They ought to rail off the children's play area.* [13thC. Via Old French *reille* 'bar' from Latin *regula* 'straight stick, rod' (source also of English *rule*). Ultimately from a Latin base that also produced English *regal* and *royal*.] —**railless** *adj.* ◇ **go off the rails 1.** to begin to behave in an unacceptable, irresponsible, or illegal way **2.** to begin to go wrong and lose direction

rail[2] /rayl/ (**rails, railing, railed**) *vi.* to denounce, protest against, or attack sb or sth in bitter or harsh language ○ *Some people rail against the injustice of the system.* [15thC. Via French *railler* 'to mock, tease' from Old Provençal *ralhar* 'to chat, joke', from, ultimately, late Latin *ragere* 'to neigh, roar'.] —**railer** *n.*

rail[3] /rayl/ (*plural* **rails** *or* **rail**) *n.* a small or medium-sized bird with a short tail, short wings, long legs, and long toes. Rails are usually found near water or marshy ground. Family: Rallidae. [15thC. Via Old French *raale* from, ultimately, assumed Vulgar Latin *rasclare*, *rasiculare* 'to scrape' (from the bird's harsh-sounding call), from Latin *ras-*, the past participle stem of *radere* (see RADULA).]

railbus /ráyl buss/ *n.* a lightweight, self-propelled, usually diesel-powered passenger railway carriage with four wheels, used on branch lines (*dated*) [Mid-20thC]

railcar /ráyl kaar/ *n.* **1.** COACH WITH OWN ENGINE a self-propelled, usually diesel-powered passenger railway coach, more substantial than a railbus, for use on branch lines **2.** *US* RAILWAY CARRIAGE a railway carriage

railcard /ráyl kaard/ *n.* an identity card allowing the holder, e.g. a student, senior citizen, or family group, to buy rail tickets at reduced rates, usually restricted to off-peak travel times

railhead /ráyl hed/ *n.* **1.** END OF RAILWAY LINE the farthest point to which the track of a railway line runs **2.** DISTRIBUTION POINT FOR RAILWAY a place where supplies, often military materials, are unloaded from railway wagons for distribution to other points

railing /ráyling/ *n.* **1.** STRUCTURE WITH RAILS AND POSTS a structure consisting of one or more rails and their supports, used to provide a barrier or support in walking or climbing, or the upper rail of such a structure **2.** METAL FENCE an often ornamental fence of vertical metal poles held in position by one or more narrow horizontal bars, providing a barrier round sth such as a park (*usually used in the plural*) ○ *ivy growing up the railings* **3.** RAILS rails for making a railing

raillery /ráyləri/ (*plural* **-ies**) *n.* **1.** GOOD-HUMOURED TEASING humorous, playful, or friendly ridiculing of sb or sth **2.** JOKING REMARK a remark that ridicules sb or sth jokingly and with good humour

raillink /ráyl lingk/ *n.* a short connecting railway line, usually between a city centre and an airport

railroad /ráyl rōd/ *n. US* = **railway** ■ *v.* (**-roads, -roading, -roaded**) **1.** *vt.* FORCE STH THROUGH QUICKLY WITHOUT DISCUSSION to push sth through a legislature, committee, or other decision-making body quickly so that there is not enough time for objections to be considered ○ *The changes to the proposal were railroaded through the subcommittee.* **2.** *vt.* FORCE SB TO ACT HASTILY to force a person or group to make a decision or take action quickly, without time for consideration or discussion (*informal*) **3.** *vt.* CONVICT SB TOO QUICKLY to convict sb on the basis of flimsy or false evidence (*informal*) **4.** *vt. US* TRANSP TRANSPORT STH BY RAIL to transport or send sth by rail **5.** *vi. US* WORK ON RAILWAY to work on a railway ○ *She used to railroad for the Southern Pacific.* —**railroader** *n.*

railslide /ráyl slīd/ (**-slides, -sliding, -slid**) *vi.* in skateboarding, to slide along the top or upper edge of a ramp or obstacle with the bottom of the board in contact with the ground rather than the wheels [Late 20thC]

railtour /ráyl toor/ *n.* an excursion on a chartered or special train intended for railway enthusiasts

Railtrack /ráyl trak/ *n.* a statutory company that owns and operates the track, stations, signals, and other plant in the UK railway system, but does not run trains

railway /ráyl way/ *n.* US term **railroad 1.** TRACK MADE OF RAILS a track consisting of steel rails usually fastened to wood or concrete sleepers, designed to carry the engine and carriages of a train or anything similar **2.** RAIL SYSTEM a network of railway lines, together with the trains, buildings, equipment, and staff needed to operate a rail transport system, or the organization or company that owns or runs this

railwayman /ráyl waymən/ (*plural* **-men**) *n.* a worker on the railways, especially any worker who is not a driver

raiment /ráymənt/ *n.* clothing (*formal*) [14thC. Shortening of *arrayment*.]

rain /rayn/ *n.* **1.** WATER FALLING FROM CLOUDS water condensed from vapour in the atmosphere and falling in drops from clouds **2.** PERIOD OF WET WEATHER any storm, shower, or other quantity of water falling from the sky **3.** RAINY WEATHER weather marked by heavy or persistent rainfall **4.** GREAT NUMBER OR FLOW a great number of small individual things coming in a steady flow or anything else flowing or falling like rain ○ *A rain of dust fell from the crumbling ceiling.* ■ **rains** *npl.* RAINY SEASON in some countries, a season of the year when a lot of rain falls ■ *v.* **(rains, raining, rained) 1.** *vi.* DROP RAIN to fall from the sky or release water in the form of rain ○ *It's raining again.* **2.** *vti.* COME IN A GREAT NUMBER to come or fall, or drop or deliver sth, in the form of a great number of units arriving separately but in very quick succession, or in a continuous stream ○ *They rained blows on the poor man's head.* ○ *Missiles rained down on us from the defenders on the battlements.* **3.** *vt.* GIVE STH GENEROUSLY to give sb sth in large quantities, continuously, and over a considerable period of time ○ *Generous to a fault, they positively rained gifts on all their friends.* [Old English *regn, rēn,* of prehistoric Germanic origin] —**rainless** *adj.* ◇ **rain or shine, come rain or shine, come rain or come shine** whatever the weather or the circumstances ○ *The picnic will be held, rain or shine.* ◇ **(as) right as rain** perfectly all right (*informal*)

rain off *vt.* to cause an event such as a sporting fixture to be cancelled or postponed because of rain (*usually passive*) US term **rain out**

rainbird /ráyn burd/ *n.* a bird, e.g. the green woodpecker or certain members of the cuckoo family, thought to call before rainstorms

rainbow /ráynbō/ *n.* **1.** MULTICOLOURED ARC IN SKY an arc of light separated into bands of colour that appears when the sun's rays are refracted and reflected by drops of mist or rain. The colours of the rainbow are conventionally said to be red, orange, yellow, green, blue, indigo, and violet. **2.** ARC OF BANDS OF COLOUR multicoloured arc similar to a rainbow **3.** BRIGHT MULTICOLOURED SIGHT an arrangement, display, or sight containing many bright colours or bright multicoloured objects ○ *Her makeup box was a rainbow of colours.* **4.** FALSE HOPE a goal, hope, or ideal that is unlikely to be achieved or realized **5.** VARIED ASSORTMENT a wide range or varied assortment of things, usually coexisting without clashing ■ *adj.* **1.** WITH VARIED COLOURS having the colours of the rainbow or colours as varied as those of a rainbow **2.** WITH MANY DIFFERENT THINGS comprising a wide variety of types or elements, especially made up of people of different ethnic groups or from a variety of minority groups ○ *a rainbow coalition*

WORD KEY: CULTURAL NOTE

The Rainbow, a novel by D. H. Lawrence (1915). Set in the English Midlands between 1840 and 1905, it describes the impact of contemporary social developments on the lifestyles and attitudes of succeeding generations of a provincial family, the Brangwens. The latter part of the book focuses on Ursula, the family's first independent woman, whose story is continued in a subsequent novel *Women in Love* (1920).

rainbow fish *n.* a brightly coloured fish such as the guppy or parrot fish

rainbow lorikeet *n.* a colourful Australian bird of the parrot family with a blue head, orange breast, and green wings and back. The rainbow lorikeet feeds on nectar, fruit, and seeds, and is common in northern and eastern forests and woodlands. Latin name: *Trichoglossus haematodus.*

rainbow runner *n.* a large colourful fish found in tropical Indian and Pacific waters. Latin name: *Elagatis bipinnulatus.*

rainbow trout *n.* a freshwater food and game fish, originally from North America, with a reddish or pinkish band along either side of its body and numerous black spots. Latin name: *Salmo gairdneri.*

rain check *n.* *US* **1.** TICKET FOR RESCHEDULED EVENT a ticket or ticket stub entitling sb to attend an event cancelled because of rain at a later rescheduled time **2.** GUARANTEE OF OFFER a promise or voucher guaranteeing that an offer that cannot be fulfilled or accepted at present will be fulfilled or accepted at a later time ◇ **take a rain check (on sth)** *US* to delay doing sth until a later date or time (*informal*)

raincoat /ráyn kōt/ *n.* a coat designed to keep the wearer dry when worn in the rain, with a water-resistant or waterproof surface or coating

rainfall /ráyn fawl/ *n.* **1.** AMOUNT OF RAIN FALLEN OVER TIME the amount of rain that falls in a particular location over a particular period of time ○ *the annual rainfall in a city* **2.** OCCURRENCE OF RAIN a rain shower or rainstorm

rainforest /ráyn forist/ *n.* a thick evergreen tropical forest found in areas of heavy rainfall and containing trees with broad leaves that form a continuous canopy

rain gauge *n.* a device used to measure the amount of rain that falls in a particular location

Rainier III /ráyni ay/, **Prince of Monaco** (*b.* 1923). He acceded to the throne in 1949, and in 1962 agreed to a new constitution reducing the power of the monarchy.

rain lily *n.* = **zephyr lily**

rainmaker /ráyn maykər/ *n.* **1.** SB WHO CAUSES RAIN sb who causes rain to fall, e.g. by seeding clouds with chemicals such as silver iodide, or who is believed to do so by magic **2.** *US* ACHIEVER sb who achieves outstanding results in business or politics (*informal*) —**rainmaking** *n.*

rainout /ráyn owt/ *n.* **1.** GEOG POLLUTION IN RAIN atmospheric pollution such as radioactive fallout that is carried down to earth in rain **2.** *US* CANCELLATION BECAUSE OF RAIN an event that is cancelled or postponed because of rainy weather, or the cancellation or postponement of an event because of rain ○ *There was a rainout at the ballpark today.*

rainproof /ráyn proof/ *adj.* IMPERVIOUS TO RAIN designed or treated to prevent rain from soaking into it or passing through it ■ *vt.* **(-proofs, -proofing, -proofed)** MAKE STH IMPERVIOUS TO RAIN to treat sth such as an item of clothing so that it becomes rainproof

rain shadow *n.* an area on the side of a mountain barrier that is sheltered from prevailing winds and rain-bearing clouds, resulting in relatively dry conditions

rainstorm /ráyn stawrm/ *n.* a storm with heavy or steady rain

rainwash /ráyn wosh/ *n.* rock and soil washed away and deposited elsewhere by rainwater, or the process of erosion by rainwater

rainwater /ráyn wawtər/ *n.* water that has fallen as rain, which usually has relatively small amounts of minerals dissolved in it

rainwear /ráyn wair/ *n.* clothing, mainly outerwear, that is waterproof and is designed to keep the wearer dry in rainy weather

rainy /ráyni/ **(-ier, -iest)** *adj.* characterized by or bringing rain, especially long or frequently recurring periods of rainfall —**rainily** *adv.* —**raininess** *n.*

rainy day *n.* a possible time of need in the future

Rais /rayss/, **Gilles de, Baron** (1404–40) French politician and marshal of France. In his pursuit of riches he turned to alchemy and Satanism, and was executed for heresy and child murder.

raise /rayz/ *v.* **(raises, raising, raised) 1.** *vt.* MOVE STH HIGHER to cause sb or sth to move upwards or to a higher level or position ○ *She was too weak to raise her head from the pillow.* **2.** *vt.* STAND OR SIT UP to move yourself or sb else to a standing or sitting position ○ *I raised myself with difficulty and staggered to the door.* **3.** *vt.* DIRECT STH AT HIGHER ANGLE to direct sth upwards, or make sth point at a higher angle ○ *She answered without raising her eyes from the book.* **4.** *vt.* CONSTR PUT STH UP to set up, erect, or build sth **5.** *vt.* STRETCH STH OUT to make sth such as a crest or frill stretch out and become more visible **6.** *vt.* CAUSE STH TO SWELL UP to make sth rise up or swell up, e.g. on sb's skin **7.** *vt.* MAKE STH LARGER OR GREATER to increase sth in size, amount, value, or scope ○ *They've raised the ticket prices yet again.* **8.** *vt.* INTENSIFY STH to increase sth in degree, strength, or pitch ○ *raised voices* **9.** *vt.* IMPROVE STH to make sth better in some way ○ *You can't raise educational standards unless you train and motivate the teachers better.* **10.** *vt.* IMPROVE SB'S CONDITION to improve sb's situation or condition, or move sb to a higher rank or status ○ *helping the downtrodden to raise themselves* **11.** *vt.* AGRIC, GARDENING GROW OR BREED STH to grow vegetables or breed and care for animals, usually for profit or personal satisfaction **12.** *vt.* ACT AS PARENT OR GUARDIAN TO SB to look after sb as or like a parent, while he or she is growing up (*often passive*) ○ *After my parents died, I was raised by my grandfather.* **13.** *vt.* OFFER STH FOR CONSIDERATION to put sth forward for consideration or discussion ○ *I'd like to raise a number of points that I think need clarification.* **14.** *vt.* COLLECT STH TOGETHER to gather sth together, collect sth, or ask for sth and be given it ○ *raising money for the local orphanage* **15.** *vt.* CAUSE STH to cause sth to appear, arise, form, or occur ○ *The strict new rules raised a storm of protest.* **16.** *vt.* GIVE SIGN OF FEELING to produce a response such as a smile or cheer, or cause sb else to produce one ○ *She obviously felt awful, but still managed to raise a faint smile.* **17.** *vt.* START STH NOISY to start sth that involves a lot of loud noise or boisterous activity ○ *Raise the alarm!* **18.** *vt.* ROUSE SB to rouse sb from sleep, or bring a dead person back to life ○ *They were shouting loud enough to raise the dead.* **19.** *vt.* PARANORMAL CALL STH UP to attempt to cause a supernatural being to appear, e.g. by special ceremonies or magic **20.** *vt.* PUT SB IN AUTHORITY to place sb in a position of power or authority (*literary*) **21.** *vt.* COMMUNICATION CONTACT SB BY RADIO to get into contact with sb by radio ○ *Air traffic control was still trying to raise the missing plane.* **22.** *vt.* MATH MULTIPLY A NUMBER to multiply a term or number by itself a specified number of times ○ *2 raised by the power of 4 is 16.* **23.** *vti.* CARDS INCREASE BET OR BID in poker and other games, to increase a bet or bet more than another player, often specifying the amount of the increase **24.** *vt.* INCREASE PARTNER'S BID in bridge, to make a higher bid in the suit bid by your partner **25.** *vt.* MIL END SIEGE to end a siege by withdrawing the besieging force or forcing it to withdraw **26.** *vt.* POL, COMM END STH to bring a ban or restriction imposed on sb to an end ○ *finally raised the arms embargo* **27.** *vt.* NAUT SEE LAND APPEAR ON HORIZON to have approached near enough to land after a sea voyage for it to make its first appearance on the horizon ○ *The ship raised Bermuda two days after leaving New York.* **28.** *vt.* *US* FIN FRAUDULENTLY INCREASE STH'S VALUE to increase the face value of sth, especially a cheque, in an attempt to defraud sb ○ *The embezzler was caught raising cheques.* **29.** *vt.* COOK MAKE DOUGH RISE to make dough rise and swell by using yeast or a similar agent **30.** *vt.* PHON REPLACE VOWEL BY HIGHER VOWEL to replace a vowel by one formed with the tongue higher in the mouth **31.** *vi.* *US* RISE to rise (*nonstandard*) ○ *'Jimmy gazed at her in such consternation that he felt his hair begin to raise!'* (George Randolph Chester, *The Jingo*; 1912) ■ *n.* **1.** *Aus, Can, US* PAY INCREASE a pay increase **2.** ACT OF INCREASING the raising of sb or sth, or the amount by which sb or sth is raised, e.g. in cards [12thC. From Old Norse *reisa.* Ultimately from a prehistoric Germanic base that also produced English *rise* and the verb *rear.*] —**raisable** *adj.* —**raiser** *n.*

WORD KEY: SYNONYMS

raise, elevate, lift, hoist, uplift

CORE MEANING: to place sth in a higher position

raise to move sth to a higher position, usually by means of physical effort. It does not suggest great physical effort; **elevate** a formal word meaning the same as 'raise'; **lift** to raise sth either by means of physical effort or using a mechanism; **hoist** to raise sth by mechanical means, sometimes by heavy manual effort; **uplift** used in Scotland, South Africa, and New Zealand to mean 'to collect or pick up sth such as a parcel'.

raised beach *n.* a former beach found above the present shoreline of a sea or lake following a fall in water level or a rise in land level. Raised beaches are common in areas once glaciated, which rise as the land surface readjusts to the removal of the weight of a former icecap.

raised work *n.* embroidery stitches that produce a raised surface on the fabric or that are worked over a piece of padding

raisin /ráyz'n/ *n.* a sweet grape that has been dried in the sun or by being processed with heat, usually to prevent spoiling and permit long-term storage [14thC. Via French, 'grape', from Latin *racemus* 'bunch, cluster' (source also of English *raceme*).]

raison d'état /ráy zoN day taá/ (plural **raisons d'état** /ráy zoN-/) n. an overriding concern, usually the interests of the country concerned, that justifies political or diplomatic action that might otherwise be considered reprehensible [From French, literally 'reason of state']

raison d'être /ráy zoN déttra/ (plural **raisons d'être** /ráy zoN-/) n. sth that gives meaning or purpose to sb's life, or the justification for sth's existence [From French, literally 'reason for being']

raita /ráytə, rī éetə/ n. an Indian dish served with curries, consisting of yoghurt usually mixed with finely chopped ingredients such as cucumber, mint, or garlic [Mid-20thC. From Hindi *rāytā*.]

Raj /raaj/ n. the British rule of the Indian subcontinent, now the countries of India, Pakistan, and Bangladesh, from 1757 to 1947 [Late 18thC. Via Hindi *rāj* from Sanskrit *rājya* 'kingdom, rule'. Ultimately from an Indo-European base that is also the ancestor of English *regal*, *rich*, and *rule* and German *Reich* 'empire'.]

Rajab /rə jáb/ n. in the Islamic calendar, the seventh month of the year, made up of 30 days [Late 18thC. From Arabic.]

rajah /raájə/, **raja** n. a king, prince, or chief in India or among the Malay, Javanese, and other peoples of Southeast Asia [Mid-16thC. Via Hindi *rājā* from Sanskrit *rājan* 'king', from the same base as produced English *Raj*.]

Rajasthan /raájə staan/, **Rājasthān** state in northwestern India, bordering Pakistan. Capital: Jaipur. Population: 48,040,000 (1994). Area: 342,239 sq. km/132,139 sq. mi.

Rajasthani /raájə staáni/ n. 1. INDIAN LANGUAGE a group of Indic languages spoken in northwestern India and neighbouring parts of Pakistan that form a subgroup of the Indo-Iranian branch of Indo-European languages. About 25 million people speak one of the Rajasthani languages. 2. SB FROM RAJASTHAN sb who lives in or was born or brought up in Rajasthan [Early 20thC. From Hindi, from *Rajasthan*, state in northwestern India.] —**Rajasthani** adj.

Rajkot /raáj kōt/ city and administrative headquarters of Rajkot District, in Gujarat State, west-central India. Population: 556,137 (1991).

Rajneesh /raaj neésh/, **Bhagwan Shree** (1931–90) Indian spiritual teacher. As founder of the Neo-Sannyas Movement in the late 1960s, he established meditation centres in India, Europe, and the United States. Real name **Rajneesh Chandra Mohan**

Rajput /raáj pŏŏt/ n. a Hindu belonging to a fierce warrior caste, the second-highest caste after the Brahmins. Many kings and princes were Rajputs. [Late 16thC. From Hindi *rājpūt*, literally 'king's son', from Sanskrit *rājan* 'king' + *putra* 'son'.]

Rajya Sabha /raáyjə súbbə/ n. the upper house of India's national parliament [From Sanskrit, literally 'State assembly']

Rakaia /rə kí ə/ river in the South Island, New Zealand. It rises in the Southern Alps and flows into the Pacific Ocean west of the Banks Peninsula. Length: 145 km/90 mi.

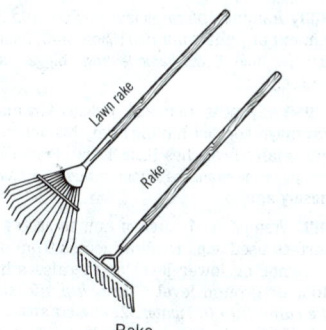

Lawn rake

Rake

Rake

rake[1] /rayk/ n. 1. GARDENING LONG-HANDLED TOOTHED GARDENING TOOL a tool with a long handle and a head with long teeth, used for gathering leaves or cut grass or for smoothing or loosening the surface of the soil 2. TOOL RESEMBLING A GARDEN RAKE any tool that is broadly

---

similar to a garden rake but is used for a different purpose, e.g. digging clams or gathering money at a gambling table 3. CLEARING, GATHERING, OR SMOOTHING an act of clearing, gathering, or smoothing sth with a rake or similar implement 4. SEARCH a search through sth ■ v. (**rakes, raking, raked**) 1. vti. MOVE WITH A RAKE to gather sth together, remove, or clear sth using a rake or similar implement ○ *raked up the dead leaves* 2. vti. GARDENING WORK WITH A RAKE to make sth neat, smooth it out, or loosen it using a rake or similar tool 3. vti. SEARCH to search through or examine sth thoroughly, or to make a search for sth 4. vt. USE STH LIKE A RAKE to draw or move sth through or across sth else like a rake ○ *She raked her fingers through her hair.* 5. vti. SCRAPE OR SCRATCH STH to claw, scrape, or scratch sb or sth with a dragging movement like the action of sb using a rake 6. vti. PASS ACROSS STH to pass across the whole length or extent of sth in a continuous sweeping movement, or cause sth to do this ○ *The spotlight raked around the perimeter fence.* 7. vti. SHOOT ALONG THE LENGTH OF STH to aim shots from a gun or guns in quick succession over the whole length or extent of sth ○ *The ship's cannon raked the land battery.* [Old English *raca*, *racu*. Perhaps ultimately from an Indo-European base meaning 'to direct' (ancestor of English *regal*, *rich*, and *rule*), in which case the underlying idea is 'stretching out, collecting'.]

rake in vt. to take in large quantities of sth, especially money gained or earned with relatively little effort (informal)

rake over vt. = **rake up** v. 1 (informal)

rake together vt. to gather people or things together with difficulty (informal)

rake up vt. (informal) 1. BRING STH TO MIND to mention or bring up for discussion sth unfortunate or undesirable that happened in the past 2. = **rake together**

rake[2] /rayk/ n. 1. NAUT SLANT OR SLOPE a slant away from an upright or perpendicular position, or an incline upwards from a flat or horizontal position such as that on a ship or a stage 2. AEROSP ANGLE OF WING OR PROPELLER the angle that a wing or propeller blade of an aircraft makes with a perpendicular or line of symmetry ■ vti. (**rakes, raking, raked, raked**) ANGLE to design or build sth, or be designed or built, with a slant or slope away from the vertical or horizontal ○ *a jet with wings that rake sharply back* [Early 17thC. Origin unknown.]

rake[3] /rayk/ n. sb who indulges without restraint in physical pleasures and vices such as drinking and gambling [Mid-17thC. Shortening of RAKEHELL.]

─── **WORD KEY: CULTURAL NOTE** ───
The Rake's Progress, a series of paintings by English artist William Hogarth (1735?). These eight satirical scenes, which were much influenced by contemporary theatre, depict the moral decline of a young city gent who inherits a fortune and squanders it on vice. Hogarth created engravings of the same images, which were immensely popular. In 1951, Stravinsky turned the story into an opera with a libretto by W.H. Auden.

rake[4] /rayk/ n. a distinct break or shallow gully that slants obliquely across a rock face [14thC. From Old Norse *rák* 'stripe, streak'.]

rakee n. = **raki**

rakehell /ráyk hell/ n. sb who indulges without restraint in physical pleasures and vices such as drinking and gambling (archaic) [Mid-16thC. By folk etymology from Middle English *rakel* 'hasty, rash' (of unknown origin), by association with RAKE[1] and HELL.]

rake-off n. a portion or share of a profit, fee, or sth similar, especially as a bribe or other illegal or morally dubious payment (informal)

raki /ráki, raa keé/, **rakee** n. any of various alcoholic drinks from the eastern Mediterranean, especially a brandy made in Turkey and the Balkans from grapes, plums, or grain and flavoured with aniseed [Late 17thC. Via Turkish *rāqī* from Arabic *arak̄*.]

rakish[1] /ráykish/ adj. 1. DASHINGLY STYLISH stylish in a dashing or sporty way ○ *a hat worn at a rakish angle* 2. NAUT MAKING A BOAT LOOK FAST having a streamlined look that suggests rapid movement through the water ○ *a rakish yacht* [Early 19thC. Formed from RAKE[2].] —**rakishly** adv. —**rakishness** n.

---

rakish[2] /ráykish/ adj. having or showing a strong concern for presenting a stylish self-confident appearance [Early 18thC. Formed from RAKE[3].] —**rakishly** adv. —**rakishness** adv.

raku /raákoo/ n. a pottery technique in which pots are raw-glazed at a low temperature then taken red-hot from the kiln and plunged in water or sawdust for reduction or carbonizing [Late 19thC. From Japanese, literally 'ease, enjoyment'.]

rale /raal/, **râle** n. a symptomatic intermittent crackling or bubbling sound produced by the lungs and heard via a stethoscope. It indicates fluid in the air passages and air sacs. [Early 19thC. From French *râle*, from *râler* 'to make a rattling sound in the throat', of uncertain origin: probably from assumed Vulgar Latin *rasclare* (see RAIL[3]).]

Raleigh /raáli, ráwli/ capital city of North Carolina, located in the centre of the state. Population: 236,707 (1994).

Raleigh, Sir Walter (1554–1618) English navigator and writer. A favourite of Queen Elizabeth I, he led three expeditions to the Americas, founding the first English settlement in North America at Jamestown, Virginia (1585). He wrote his *History of the World* (1614) while imprisoned for treason (1603–13).

rall. abbr. MUSIC rallentando

rallentando /rállən tándō/ adv. MUSIC with a gradual slowing of pace (used as a musical direction) [Early 19thC. From Italian, the present participle of *rallentare* 'to slow down'.]

rally[1] /ráli/ v. (**-lies, -lying, -lied**) 1. vti. GATHER TOGETHER FOR STH to come together, uniting for a common purpose or in a common cause, or to call on people to come together and unite ○ *The instinct of the party faithful was to rally behind the leader in a crisis.* 2. vti. MIL FORM TOGETHER AGAIN to reorganize, or reorganize forces, after a setback and restore order and morale, especially to stop troops retreating further ○ *The captain rallied his retreating troops and formed a defensive line.* 3. vti. REVIVE OR RECOVER to recover or improve after a setback, crisis, or period of illness, inactivity, or deterioration, or to bring about a recovery or improvement in sth ○ *Our spirits rallied once we had our first success.* 4. vi. STOCK EXCH INCREASE IN VALUE to increase sharply in value or price owing to renewed buying by investors 5. vi. STOCK EXCH BEGIN BUYING STOCKS AGAIN to be involved in renewed buying of stocks after a period of selling 6. vi. RACKET GAMES EXCHANGE SHOTS to exchange a series of shots before scoring a point ■ n. (plural **-lies**) 1. GATHERING a large meeting or gathering of people, usually organized by a movement or political party and intended to inspire and generate enthusiasm among those present 2. RECOVERY OR IMPROVEMENT a sudden recovery or improvement after a setback, crisis, or period of illness, inactivity, or deterioration 3. MIL REASSEMBLY OF TROOPS a regrouping of a disorganized military force and the re-establishment of command over it, or the signal calling for this ○ *The retreating hussars made a rally and drove the attackers back.* 4. STOCK EXCH RENEWED BUYING OF STOCKS a renewed buying of stocks after a period of selling, leading to a rise in stock prices ○ *a rally in the industrial sector of the stock market* 5. RACKET GAMES EXCHANGE OF SHOTS an exchange of several shots between two opponents or sides before a point is scored 6. MOTOR SPORTS CAR RACE a car race that is held on public roads using a route not known in advance by the drivers and having special rules for speed or time [Late 16thC. From French *rallier* 'to reunite', from *alier* (see ALLY).] —**rallier** n.

rally round vi. to come to the aid of sb in difficulty or need, offering either practical or moral support

rally[2] /ráli/ (**-lies, -lying, -lied**) vt. to tease or ridicule sb in a friendly or good-humoured way ○ *She rallied him about his cooking skills.* [Mid-17thC. From French *railler* (see RAIL[2]).]

rallycross /ráli kross/ n. motor racing on a circuit partly on roads and partly across country [Mid-20thC. Blend of RALLY and AUTOCROSS.]

rallying /ráli ing/ n. car racing on public roads using a route not known in advance by the drivers and with special rules for speed or time

---

ralph /ralf/ (**ralphs, ralphing, ralphed**) *vi. US* to vomit (*slang*) [Late 20thC. Origin uncertain: probably from the male first name *Ralph*, chosen for a supposed resemblance to the sound of vomiting.]

ram /ram/ *n.* **1.** AGRIC **MALE SHEEP** a male sheep **2.** TECH **BATTERING OR CRUSHING DEVICE** a device designed to batter, crush, press, or push sth, e.g. a projecting underwater part of a boat's prow or the weight dropped by a pile driver **3.** TECH **HYDRAULIC RAM** a hydraulic ram **4.** NAUT **WARSHIP WITH A RAM** a former type of warship equipped with a projecting underwater part on the prow that was designed to make a hole in the hull of an enemy warship ■ *v.* (**rams, ramming, rammed**) **1.** *vti.* **STRIKE STH WITH GREAT FORCE** to hit or collide with sth, or make sth hit sth else, with great force or violence ○ *She swerved, almost ramming into a wall.* **2.** *vt.* **COLLIDE WITH STH DELIBERATELY** to collide with another ship or vehicle deliberately in order to sink, disable, or damage it ○ *The police car rammed the getaway vehicle and pushed it off the road.* **3.** *vt.* **FORCE STH INTO PLACE** to press, force, or push sth into place ○ *He quickly rammed another charge down the barrel and took aim* **4.** *vt.* **FORCE ACCEPTANCE OF STH** to force the passage of a bill or acceptance of a suggestion, usually despite strong objection ○ *rammed the legislation through Congress.* **5.** *vt.* **PRESENT STH VERY FORCEFULLY** to present sth forcefully in order to impress and convince people ○ *Former addicts appeared on television to try to ram warnings home.* [Old English *ram(m)*] —**rammer** *n.*

Ram /ram/ *n.* ZODIAC = **Aries**

RAM /ram/ *abbr.* **1.** COMPUT random-access memory **2.** ENG rocket-assisted motor **3.** MUSIC Royal Academy of Music

r.a.m. *abbr.* relative atomic mass

Rama /ra'amə/ *n.* an incarnation (**avatar**) of the god Vishnu

Ramadan /rammə da'an, rammə dan/ *n.* in the Islamic calendar, the ninth month of the year, made up of 30 days. During Ramadan, Muslims fast between dawn and dusk. [Late 16thC. From Arabic, literally 'the hot month', from *ramaḍ* 'dryness'.]

Ramakrishna /raamə krishnə/, **Sri** (1834–86) Indian religious teacher. He taught that all mystical religious experiences are equally valid, and was instrumental in bringing about the 19th-century Hindu revival in India. His followers founded the Ramakrishna Mission. Real name **Gadadhar Chatterji**

Raman /ra'amən/, **Sir Chandrasekhara Venkata** (1888–1970) Indian physicist. His work on molecular diffraction of light won him a Nobel Prize in physics (1930).

Raman effect *n.* PHYS the change in wavelength and phase exhibited by monochromatic light passing through a transparent medium. The scattering that results is used in Raman spectroscopy to obtain information about the structure of molecules. [Early 20thC. Named after Sir Chandrasekhara Venkata RAMAN, who discovered it.]

ramate *adj.* BIOL = **ramose**

Ramayana /raa mī' ənə/ *n.* a great epic of the Hindu religion and of classical Sanskrit literature that tells of the adventures of Rama, an incarnation (**avatar**) of the god Vishnu

Dame Marie Rambert

Rambert /raam báir/, **Dame Marie** (1888–1982) Polish-born British ballet dancer and teacher. She founded the Ballet Rambert (1926), later called the Rambert

Dance Company, which promoted the work of British choreographers. Real name **Miriam Rambach**

ramble /rámb'l/ *vi.* (**-bles, -bling, -bled**) **1.** WALK FOR PLEASURE to go for a walk for pleasure, usually in the countryside and sometimes without a fixed route in mind ○ *He had spent a week rambling about among the villages of the Apennines.* **2.** FOLLOW A CHANGING COURSE to have, follow, or proceed along a winding or often changing course ○ *The path rambled though the fields down to the river.* **3.** BOT GROW IN RANDOM WAY to grow in random directions, usually covering a sizable area in the process ○ *Vines rambled all over the low stone wall.* **4.** TALK OR WRITE AIMLESSLY to talk, write, or continue for a long time, not always keeping to the intended subject or tending to change the subject ○ *The speaker rambled on for over an hour.* ■ *n.* WALK a walk for pleasure, usually in the countryside and less strenuous than a hike ○ *a ramble through the woods on a spring holiday* [15thC. Origin uncertain.]

rambler /rámblər/ *n.* **1.** WALKER sb who goes walking in the countryside for pleasure **2.** PLANTS CLIMBING ROSE a hybrid climbing rose with long flexible canes and clusters of small double flowers **3.** SB WHO TALKS TOO MUCH sb who talks or writes for too long and does not keep to the subject

rambling /rámbling/ *adj.* **1.** NOT TO THE POINT continuing for too long and with many changes of subject ○ *a long, rambling story* **2.** SPREAD OUT built or spread over a large area and not clearly organized or regular in shape ○ *a rambling old house* **3.** PLANTS, BOT GROWING AS RAMBLER growing with long straggling shoots **4.** MEANDERING not following a direct course ○ *a narrow rambling path through the hills* **5.** PREFERRING TO ROAM preferring to move from place to place rather than stay in one place or settle down —**ramblingly** *adv.*

——— **WORD KEY: SYNONYMS** ———

See Synonyms at **wordy**.

Rambo /rámbō/ (*plural* **-bos**) *n.* sb who is extremely aggressive or readily resorts to violence, willingly breaking rules, laws, or other generally accepted regulations to achieve what he or she believes to be right (*slang*) [Late 20thC. Named after John *Rambo*, the aggressive protagonist in the film *First Blood* (1982).] —**Ramboesque** /rám bōésk/ *adj.* —**Ramboism** /rám bōizəm/ *n.*

——— **WORD KEY: CULTURAL NOTE** ———

Rambo is a character who appeared in a series of films including *First Blood* by director Ted Kotcheff (1982), *Rambo: First Blood, part II* by director George Pan Cosmatos (1985), and *Rambo III* by director Peter Macdonald (1988). Played by Sylvester Stallone, Rambo is a vengeful Vietnam Vet, hired by the authorities to rescue fellow fighters still trapped in Southeast Asia, and, subsequently, to fight Communist oppression in Afghanistan. The terms *Rambo, Ramboism, Rambo cop*, and *Rambo driver/motorist* have entered the general language, meaning respectively 'an overly aggressive person', 'great aggressiveness in actions', 'an overly zealous police officer prone to unnecessary force', and 'a motorist who engages in acts of aggression and road rage while behind the wheel'.

Rambouillet[1] /rámboo'yay/ *n.* a large sturdy sheep belonging to a breed developed in France from the merino and bred for wool and meat [Early 20thC. Named after *Rambouillet*, a town in northern France where the breed was developed.]

Rambouillet[2] /rámboo'yay/ town in Yvelines Department, north-central France, southwest of Paris. The town's chateau is the French president's summer residence and is used for international conferences, e.g. the talks that tried to find a peaceful settlement to the Balkan crisis in Kosovo in spring, 1999. Population: 24,343 (1990).

rambunctious /ram búngkshəss/ *adj.* noisy, very active, and hard to control, usually as a result of excitement or youthful energy [Mid-19thC. Origin uncertain: perhaps an alteration of RUMBUSTIOUS.] —**rambunctiously** *adv.* —**rambunctiousness** *n.*

rambutan /ram boot'n/ *n.* **1.** MALAYSIAN TREE a Malaysian tree with red spiny edible fruit. Latin name: *Nephelium lappaceum*. **2.** FRUIT OF THE RAMBUTAN TREE the

oval fruit of the rambutan tree [Early 18thC. From Malay, from *rambut* 'hair', from the hairy skin of the fruit.]

RAMC *abbr.* Royal Army Medical Corps

ramekin /rámmikin/, **ramequin** *n.* **1.** SMALL BAKING DISH a small ovenproof dish with vertical fluted sides designed to hold a single serving of a prepared food, especially one that is baked **2.** FOOD SERVED IN A RAMEKIN a portion of food cooked and served in a ramekin [Early 18thC. Via French *ramequin* from Middle Dutch *rameken*, literally 'little cream', from *ram* 'cream'.]

ramen /ráymən/ *n.* a Japanese dish of thin white noodles in small dried cakes, served in a thin well-flavoured soup or stock [Late 20thC. Via Japanese *rāmen* from Chinese *lāmiàn*, literally 'pulled noodles'.]

ramequin *n.* = **ramekin**

Rameses II /rámmə seez/, **Ramses II** (*fl.* 13th century BC) Egyptian pharaoh. His long and prosperous reign (1279–12 BC), which marked the pinnacle of Egypt's power, saw the building of numerous monuments including the sandstone temples at Abu Simbel. The Jewish exodus from Egypt is thought to have occurred during his rule. Known as **Rameses the Great**

Rameses III, **Ramses III** (*fl.* 12th century BC) Egyptian pharaoh. As pharoah (1182–51 BC) he was a great military leader who repeatedly saved the country from invasion, notably by the Libyans.

ramet /ráymət/ *n.* BIOL any individual in a clone [Early 20thC. Formed from Latin *ramus* (see RAMUS).]

rami plural of **ramus**

ramie /rámmi/ *n.* **1.** BOT ASIAN SHRUB a perennial Asian shrub of the nettle family that has broad leaves and small flowers. It yields a tough fibre resembling flax. Latin name: *Boehmeria nivea*. **2.** INDUST STRONG FIBRE a strong lustrous fibre obtained from the stem of the ramie shrub, used in fabric and rope **3.** TEXTILES CLOTH cloth made from ramie fibre [Early 19thC. From Malay *rami*.]

ramification /rámmifi káysh'n/ *n.* **1.** COMPLICATING RESULT a usually unintended consequence of an action, decision, or judgment that may complicate the situation or make the intended result more difficult to achieve ○ *an unexpected ramification of a new law* **2.** BRANCHING DIVISION the process of dividing or spreading out into branches **3.** BRANCH a branch or arrangement of branches

ramiform /rámmi fawrm/ *adj.* spreading out like branches or having the form of a branch or branches [Mid-19thC. Coined from Latin *ramus* (see RAMUS) + *-iform* (see -FORM).]

ramify /rámmi fī/ (**-fies, -fying, -fied**) *vi.* **1.** BIOL BRANCH to divide into branches or similar parts **2.** HAVE COMPLICATING RESULTS to have unforeseen results or effects that will cause complications or interfere with the purpose intended ○ *Their difficulties ramified after they made the suggested changes.* [Mid-16thC. Via Old French *ramifier* from medieval Latin *ramificare*, from Latin *ramus* (see RAMUS).]

ramjet /rám jet/ *n.* a jet engine in which fuel is burned in a duct with air compressed by the forward motion of the aircraft

rammy /rámmi/ (*plural* **-mies**) *n. Scotland* a noisy argument or fight (*informal*) [Mid-20thC. Origin uncertain: perhaps from Scots *rammle* 'row, binge', a variant of RAMBLE.]

ramose /ráy mōss, ra móss/, **ramous** /ráy məss/, **ramate** /ráy mayt/ *adj.* BIOL having many branches or divided into many branches [Late 17thC. From Latin *ramosus* 'having many branches', from *ramus* (see RAMUS).] —**ramosely** *adv.*

ramp[1] /ramp/ *n.* **1.** SLOPING PATH OR ACCESS a sloping surface used, e.g., to allow access from one level to a higher or lower level or to raise sth up above floor or ground level ○ *The ship slid slowly down the ramp into the water.* **2.** MOVABLE STAIRS a movable set of stairs used for boarding or disembarking from an aircraft **3.** CURVED BEND IN A HANDRAIL a curved bend or slope in a handrail or coping where it changes direction, e.g. on a stair landing **4.** ROAD RIDGE a raised part of a road constructed to make traffic slow down ■ *vt.* (**ramps, ramping, ramped**) BUILD STH WITH A SLOPE to build sth with a sloped surface, or provide sth with a ramp ○ *The entrance must be ramped for wheelchair access.* [Late 18thC. From French *rampe*, from *ramper* (see RAMP²).] —**ramped** *adj.*

ramp up *vt.* to increase a level of activity or cause the level of activity of sth to increase ○ *'As business ramps up to manage greater responsibility for its social and environmental impacts...'* (*Marketing Week*; December 1998)

ramp² /ramp/ (**ramps, ramping, ramped**) *vi.* **1.** ACT THREATENINGLY to act in a threatening manner or assume a threatening stance, e.g. rearing with the forelegs ready to strike **2.** MOVE VIOLENTLY OR THREATENINGLY to move or rush violently, threateningly, or furiously **3.** HERALDRY BE SHOWN REARED UP IN PROFILE to be in the rampant position ○ *an old seal marked with a ramping lion on a shield* [14thC. From French *ramper* 'to crawl, creep, rear up'.]

rampage *vi.* /ram páyj/ (**-pages, -paging, -paged**) ACT VIOLENTLY OR RIOTOUSLY to engage in uncontrolled violent or riotous behaviour, or to commit a series of violent or riotous acts ○ *This weather system has rampaged up the coast, with blizzards and howling winds causing severe damage.* ■ *n.* /rám payj, ram páyj/ VIOLENT BEHAVIOUR an outburst of uncontrolled violent or riotous behaviour or a series of violent or riotous actions [Early 18thC. Origin uncertain: probably formed from RAMP².] —**rampageous** *adj.* —**rampageously** *adv.* —**rampageousness** *n.* —**rampager** *n.* —**rampaging** *adj.* ◇ **on the rampage** behaving in a wild and uncontrolled manner

rampant /rámpənt/ *adj.* **1.** OCCURRING UNCHECKED happening in an unrestrained manner, usually so as to be regarded as a menace ○ *rampant inflation* **2.** BOT GROWING WILDLY growing strongly and to a very large size, or spreading uncontrollably **3.** FIERCE exhibiting ferocious behaviour or fierceness of spirit **4.** HERALDRY ON HIND LEGS used to describe a heraldic beast depicted reared up, in profile, and with its forelegs raised, the right one above the left **5.** BUILDING WITH UNEQUAL SUPPORTS having a support or an abutment that is higher on one side than the other [14thC. From French, the present participle of *ramper* (see RAMP².)] —**rampancy** *n.* —**rampantly** *adv.*

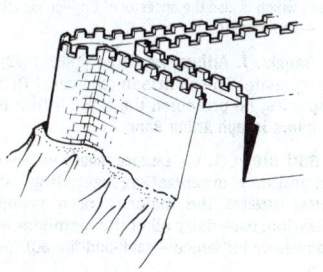

Rampart

rampart /rám paart/ *n.* FORTIFIED EMBANKMENT a defensive fortification made of an earthen embankment, often topped by a low protective wall ■ *vt.* (**-parts, -parting, -parted**) FORTIFY OR PROTECT STH to protect sb or sth with ramparts or sth similar ○ *walls ramparting a town* [Late 16thC. From French *rempart*, from *remparer*, literally 'to defend again', from Old French *emparer* 'to defend', from, ultimately, assumed Vulgar Latin *parare* 'to prepare' (source of English *prepare*).]

rampike /rám pīk/ *n.* a dead tree that is still standing, especially one reduced by fire to little more than a trunk [Late 16thC. Origin unknown.]

rampion /rámpi ən/ *n.* **1.** EURASIAN PLANT WITH BLUISH FLOWERS a plant of Europe and Asia with clusters of bluish flowers and a white edible root used in salads. Latin name: *Campanula rapunculus.* **2.** BLUE-FLOWERED PLANT any plant related to the rampion, typically with blue flowers. Genus: *Phyteuma.* [Late 16thC. Origin uncertain: probably an alteration of Old French *raiponce*, from Old Italian *raponzo*, from Latin *rapum* 'turnip' (source of English *rape* 'plant').]

Rampur /rám poŏr/ city and administrative headquarters of Rampur District, Uttar Pradesh State, northern India. Population: 243,000 (1991).

ram-raid *n.* SMASHING WINDOW WITH CAR a theft carried out by driving a stolen car through a shop window and stealing the goods inside ■ *vti.* (**ram-raids, ram-raiding, ram-raided**) SMASH WINDOW WITH CAR to carry out a ram-raid on sth —**ram-raider** *n.* —**ram-raiding** *n.*

ramrod /rám rod/ *n.* **1.** ARMS ROD FOR LOADING GUNS a rod for loading a charge into a muzzle-loading musket, cannon, or other gun **2.** ARMS CLEANING ROD a rod for cleaning the barrel of a firearm **3.** *US* STERN OR STRICT OVERSEER a stern or strict boss, commander, or other person in a position of authority ■ *vt.* (**-rods, -rodding, -rodded**) *US* **1.** PUSH STH THROUGH BY FORCE to push through or achieve sth by force or threat ○ *tried to ramrod the bill through the legislature* **2.** CONTROL SB STRICTLY to exert strict control over sb or enforce strict discipline on sb

Ramsay/, Sir Alf (1922–99) British footballer and manager. He was manager of the England team (1963–74), which he led to a World Cup (1966). Full name **Alfred Ramsay**

Ramses II ▸ Rameses II

Ramses III ▸ Rameses III

Ramsey Island /rámzi-/ islet in Wales, off the coast of Pembrokeshire. Area: 2.6 sq. km/1 sq. mi.

Ramsgate /rámz gayt, rámzgit/ town on the eastern coast of Kent, in southeastern England. Population: 37,895 (1991).

ramshackle /rám shak'l/ *adj.* poorly maintained or constructed and seeming likely to fall apart or collapse [Mid-19thC. Back-formation from earlier *ramshackled*, from, ultimately, ransack.]

ram's horn *n.* JUDAISM = shofar

ramsons /rámzə'nz/ *n.* a wild garlic of Europe and Asia with a bulbous root eaten in salads. Latin name: *Allium ursinum.* (takes a singular verb) [Mid-16thC. Formed from Old English *hram(e)san*, plural of *hramsa*, later erroneously regarded as singular.]

ramtil /rámtil/ *n.* an Ethiopian plant with yellow flowers, grown for its oil-rich seeds. Latin name: *Guizotia abyssinica.* [Mid-19thC. From Bengali *rāmtil*, literally 'pleasing sesame'.]

ramulose /rámmyoŏ lōss/ *adj.* BIOL having many small branches [Mid-18thC. From Latin *ramulosus* 'full of branching veins', from, ultimately, *ramus* (see RAMUS).]

ramus /ráyməss/ (plural **-mi** /-mī/) *n.* a small branching body part such as a stem, bone, or nerve [Early 18thC. From Latin, 'branch'.]

ran past tense of **run**

Ran /ran/ *n.* in Norse mythology, the goddess of the sea

RAN *abbr.* **1.** Royal Australian Navy **2.** request for authority to negotiate

Rance /raaNss/ river in Brittany, in northwestern France. Length: 100 km/60 mi.

ranch /raanch/ *n.* **1.** LIVESTOCK FARM ON OPEN LAND a farm where cattle, sheep, horses, or other livestock are raised on large tracts of open land, especially in North and South America and Australia **2.** FARM FOR RAISING A PARTICULAR SPECIES a large farm devoted to keeping a single species of animal or growing a single type of crop **3.** = ranch house *n.* 1, ranch house *n.* 2 **4.** FOOD = ranch dressing ■ *v.* (**ranches, ranching, ranched**) **1.** *vi.* WORK ON A RANCH to own, manage, or work on a ranch ○ *ranching animals in western Texas* **2.** *vt.* RAISE ON A RANCH to breed, raise, or tend animals on a ranch [Early 19thC. Via American Spanish *rancho* from Spanish, 'group of people who eat together', from, ultimately, French *ranger* 'to arrange in position', from *rang* 'row, line' (source of English *rank*).] —**ranching** *n.*

ranch dressing *n.* *US* a creamy salad dressing that has a mixture of mayonnaise and buttermilk or milk as its base

rancher /ráanchər/ *n.* **1.** RANCH OWNER sb who owns or manages a ranch **2.** *US* = ranch house *n.* 2

ranchero /raan cháirō/ (plural **-ros**) *n. Southwest US* AGRIC sb who owns or manages a ranch, particularly a rancher in the southwestern United States and Spanish-speaking countries of Latin America [Early 19thC. From American Spanish, formed from *rancho* (see RANCH).]

ranch house *n.* *US* **1.** HOUSE ON A RANCH the building on a ranch where the owner or manager lives, typically having one storey, a spread-out floor plan, and a roof that is not steeply pitched **2.** SINGLE-STOREY HOUSE a single-storey house built in a style similar to a traditional ranch house, especially one located in a suburban housing development

Ranchi /ránchi/ city and administrative headquarters of Ranchi District, in Bihar State, northeastern India. Population: 599,000 (1991).

rancho /ráanchō/ (plural **-chos**) *n. Southwest US* **1.** RANCH a ranch **2.** RANCH WORKER'S HUT a hut where a ranch worker lives, or a group of such huts [Early 19thC. From American Spanish (see RANCH).]

rancid /ránssid/ *adj.* **1.** WITH A DISAGREEABLE TASTE having the strong disagreeable smell or taste of decomposing fats or oils **2.** CAUSING DISGUST causing disgust or greatly offensive [Mid-17thC. From Latin *rancidus* 'stinking, rank', from *rancere* 'to stink'.] —**rancidity** /ran síddəti/ *n.* —**rancidness** /ránssidnəss/ *n.*

rancor *n.* *US* = rancour

rancour /rángkər/ *n.* bitter, deeply held, and long-lasting ill will or resentment [12thC. Via Old French from Latin *rancor* 'stinking smell or offensive flavour, bitterness', from *rancere* 'to stink'.] —**rancorous** *adj.* —**rancorously** *adv.* —**rancorousness** *n.*

rand /rand/ (plural **rand**) *n.* **1.** UNIT OF S AFRICAN CURRENCY the standard unit of currency in the Republic of South Africa, worth 100 cents. See table at currency **2.** COIN WORTH A RAND a coin worth one rand [Mid-20thC. Named after the *Rand*, a gold-mining district in the Transvaal, from Afrikaans *rand* 'ridge of ground', from Dutch, 'edge'.]

randan¹ /ran dán, rán dan/ *n.* a noisy and boisterous celebration (*informal*) [Early 18thC. Origin uncertain: perhaps an alteration of French *randon* 'random'.]

randan² /ran dán, rán dan/ *n.* **1.** ROWING BOAT a type of boat designed to be rowed by three people **2.** METHOD OF ROWING the method of rowing a randan, with one person using two oars and the other two one oar each [Early 19thC. Origin unknown.]

R & B *abbr.* rhythm and blues

R & D *abbr.* research and development

randem /rán dem/ *adv.* WITH THREE HORSES with a team of three horses harnessed one behind another ■ *n.* THREE HORSES OR CARRIAGE a team of three horses harnessed one behind another, or a carriage pulled by such a team [Late 19thC. Origin uncertain: probably an alteration of RANDOM, modelled on TANDEM.]

random /rándəm/ *adj.* **1.** WITHOUT A PATTERN done, chosen, or occurring without a specific pattern, plan, or connection ○ *random testing for drugs* **2.** LACKING REGULARITY without a pattern or in sizes that are not uniform or regular ○ *a wall constructed of random stones* **3.** STATS EQUALLY LIKELY relating or belonging to a set in which all the members have the same probability of occurrence ○ *a random sampling* **4.** STATS HAVING DEFINITE PROBABILITY relating to or involving variables that have undetermined value but definite probability [Mid-17thC. From Old French *randon* 'impetuosity, rush' (the original sense in English), from *randir* 'to run'. Ultimately from a prehistoric Germanic base (probably also the ancestor of English *run*).] —**randomly** *adv.* —**randomness** *n.* ◇ **at random** with no set plan, system, or connection

random-access *adj.* COMPUT relating to the capability of a computer to obtain information from any memory location without having to begin its search at the memory's starting-point and work through it in sequence ○ *random-access input/output*

random-access memory *n.* **1.** COMPUT COMPUTER STORAGE MEDIUM a computer storage medium on which data items are stored in an arbitrary fashion but can be accessed directly because each has a unique address. Because each data item can be addressed independently of any other item, the time it takes to access any memory location on a given medium is the same. **2.** PRIMARY WORKING MEMORY OF A COMPUTER the primary working memory in a computer used for the temporary storage of programs and data and in which the data can be accessed directly and modified

randomize /rándə mīz/ (-izes, -izing, -ized), **randomise** (-ises, -ising, -ised) *vti.* to arrange or select items so that no specific pattern or order determines the resulting arrangement or the selection process —**randomization** /rándə mī záysh'n/ *n.* —**randomizer** /rándə mīzər/ *n.*

random number *n.* any of a series of numbers that have no pattern in their progression

random sample *n.* a sample of subjects that is randomly selected from a group and is therefore assumed to be representative of that group

random variable *n.* STATS a variable that can have any of a range of values that occur randomly but can be described probabilistically

random walk *n.* MATH a model applicable to various processes such as diffusion in which the direction and sometimes the magnitude of successive steps are determined by chance

R and R, **R & R** *abbr.* **1.** MIL rest and recreation **2.** rest and relaxation

randy /rándi/ (-dier, -diest) *adj.* having a strong desire for sex (*informal*) [Late 17thC. Formed from *rand* 'to rant', an earlier Scots variant of RANT. Originally in the sense 'aggressive, rude'.] —**randily** *adv.* —**randiness** *n.*

rang past tense of **ring**[2]

rangatira /rúng gə teérə/ *n.* NZ a Maori chief or noble [Early 19thC. From Maori.]

range /raynj/ *n.* **1.** VARIEDNESS the number and variety of different things that sth includes or can deal with ○ *The range of her reading is extraordinary.* **2.** NUMBER OF SIMILAR THINGS a number or set of different things belonging to the same general category ○ *The range of courses this year is greater than ever.* **3.** COMM PRODUCTS PRODUCED OR SOLD all the products produced or sold by sb considered as a set, often ranked according to price and degree of sophistication ○ *the best-selling product in its range* **4.** CATEGORY DEFINED BY LIMITS a category defined by an upper and a lower limit ○ *the age range 25 to 45* **5.** AREA OF EFFECTIVE OPERATION the area within which, or the distance over which, sth can operate effectively ○ *out of range of the radar* **6.** MIL FARTHEST DISTANCE FOR AN EFFECTIVE OPERATION the farthest distance at which sth can operate effectively, e.g. the farthest distance to which a gun can shoot a bullet or shell **7.** ARMS DISTANCE BETWEEN WEAPON AND TARGET the distance between sth, especially a gun or a tracking device and the object it is aimed at **8.** SPORTS PRACTICE AREA a place where an activity is practised or performed **9.** TRANSP DISTANCE TRAVELLED WITHOUT REFUELLING the farthest distance that a vehicle or aircraft can travel without refuelling **10.** MUSIC PRODUCIBLE NOTES the notes, from the highest to the lowest, that sb's voice or a musical instrument is capable of producing **11.** MUSIC REGISTER OF MUSICAL PASSAGE the register of a musical passage, from the highest to the lowest note it contains **12.** GEOG ROW OF MOUNTAINS a number of mountains or hills forming a connected row or group **13.** US, Can AGRIC OPEN LAND FOR GRAZING FARM ANIMALS a large area of open land on which farm animals can graze **14.** ECOL AREA WHERE ORGANISM IS NORMALLY FOUND a geographical area in which a species of organism normally lives or grows **15.** MOVEMENT OVER AREA movement over or within an area **16.** HOUSEHOLD STOVE a cooking stove with one or more ovens and with hotplates or burners on top, especially a large old-fashioned one heated with solid fuel and often kept constantly burning **17.** MATH SET OF VALUES the set of values that can be taken by a function or a variable **18.** STATS EXTENT OF FREQUENCY DISTRIBUTION the difference between the smallest and the largest value in a frequency distribution **19.** TWO-SIDED BOOKCASE a large free-standing bookcase in a library that is built to hold books on both sides ■ *v.* (ranges, ranging, ranged) **1.** *vi.* VARY BETWEEN LIMITS to vary between a particular upper and lower limit ○ *prices ranging from £1.50 to £10.00* **2.** *vi.* DEAL WITH A NUMBER OF THINGS to include, cover, or deal with a number of different things, usually within a particular context ○ *Her interests range from parapsychology to parachuting.* **3.** *vt.* ARRANGE THINGS IN LINE to arrange things in a particular way, especially in a line or row (*usually passive*) ○ *Jars of pickles were ranged along the kitchen shelf.* **4.** *vt.* ALIGN OR CLASSIFY SB OR STH to put sth or sb into a particular group or category **5.** *vr.* GIVE PERSONAL SUPPORT to support or side with sb **6.** *vti.* TRAVEL FREELY AND EXTENSIVELY to move freely across, through, or back and forth within a particular area ○ *She allowed her thoughts to range freely over the events of the previous week.* **7.** *vt.* ARMS TRAVEL CERTAIN DISTANCE to be able to travel a particular distance (*refers to bullets or missiles*) **8.** *vti.* POINT OR AIM STH AT STH to point or aim sth such as a gun, missile, or telescope at a specific object, or to be pointed at a specific object **9.** *vi.* ECOL LIVE OR GROW to live or grow in a particular geographical area (*refers to animals or plants*) ○ *Buffalo once ranged over the plains.* **10.** *vt.* AGRIC PUT LIVESTOCK OUT TO GRAZE to put livestock out to graze on a large open area [13thC. From Old French *rangier* 'to put in order', from *ranc* (see RANK[1]).]

rangefinder *n.* **1.** DISTANCE-FINDING INSTRUMENT an instrument used to estimate the distance between the user and an object, especially one that is to be shot at or photographed **2.** = tachymeter

rangeland /ráynj land/ *n.* = **range** *n.* 13

range pole *n.* CONSTR = **ranging pole**

ranger /ráynjər/ *n.* **1.** WANDERER sb who wanders **2.** OFFICIAL OVERSEEING A FOREST OR COUNTRYSIDE AREA sb whose job is to oversee, protect, and patrol a forest or an area of natural beauty **3.** US MEMBER OF RURAL POLICE UNIT a member of an armed law-enforcement unit in certain parts of the United States, especially Texas

Ranger /ráynjər/ *n.* **1.** SENIOR GUIDE a member of the senior branch of the Guides for girls between 14 and 19 years old **2.** US COMMANDO a member of a military unit of the United States Army specially trained for commando raids

ranging pole, **ranging rod**, **range pole** *n.* a pole, usually held vertically, used to mark a specific position when surveying a plot of land

rangiora /rángji áwrə/ *n.* a small evergreen tree native to New Zealand that has large oval leaves and small greenish-white flowers. Latin name: *Brachyglottis repanda*. [Mid-19thC. From Maori.]

Rangitaiki /ráng gə tī́ ki/ river in the centre of the North Island, New Zealand. It flows northwards into the Bay of Plenty. Length: 193 km/120 sq. mi.

Rangitata /rángi taátə/ river in the east of the South Island, New Zealand, formed by the confluence of the rivers Clyde and Havelock , and emptying into Canterbury Bight. Length: 121 km/75 mi.

Rangitikei /ráng gə teé kay/ river in the centre of the North Island, New Zealand. It rises in the Kaimanawa Mountains and flows south into South Taranaki Bight. Length: 241 km/150 mi.

Rangitoto Island /ráng gə tótó-/ uninhabited volcanic island in the Hauraki Gulf, off the northeastern coast of the North Island, New Zealand. Area: 23 sq. km/9 sq. mi.

Rangoon /rang goón/ former name for **Yangon** (until 1989)

rangy /ráynji/ (-ier, -iest) *adj.* tall and lean with long legs —**ranginess** *n.*

rani /raáni, raa neé/, **ranee** *n.* a queen or princess, or the wife or widow of a rajah in India or a neighbouring country [Late 17thC. Via Hindi from, ultimately, Sanskrit *rājñī*, from *rājan* (see RAJAH).]

Ranjit Singh /rúndjit síng/ (1780–1839) Indian warrior. He founded the Sikh Kingdom of the Punjab, which he built up from a small confederacy. It was annexed by the British in 1849.

rank[1] /rangk/ *n.* **1.** MIL OFFICIAL STATUS WITHIN ORGANIZATION an official title or category that shows the holder's relative importance or seniority within an organization, especially a military force **2.** STATUS RELATIVE TO OTHERS the degree of importance or excellence of sb or sth relative to other members of a group ○ *a political journalist of the first rank* **3.** HIGH STATUS high status or importance, especially in the military or among the wealthy **4.** LINE OF PEOPLE OR THINGS a line of people, especially soldiers, or things standing side by side **5.** TRANSP PLACE FOR TAXIS TO WAIT a place where taxis wait for passengers **6.** CHESS HORIZONTAL LINE OF SQUARES ON A CHESSBOARD any of the horizontal lines of squares on a chessboard **7.** MATH LINEARLY INDEPENDENT ROWS the largest number of linearly independent rows in a matrix **8.** MUSIC SET OF ORGAN PIPES a set of organ pipes linked to a particular stop ■ **ranks** *npl.* **1.** ORDINARY PEOPLE members of the armed forces who are not officers, or the ordinary members or personnel of any organization who do not hold high office **2.** PEOPLE OF A PARTICULAR GROUP OR CATEGORY the people belonging to a specified group or category, considered collectively and usually with the understanding that there are large numbers of them ○ *among the ranks of her supporters* ■ *v.* (ranks, ranking, ranked) **1.** *vti.* HAVE OR GIVE STH A SPECIFIC RATING to have, or to give sb or sth, a particular rating, position, or importance relative to other people or things in a group ○ *This ranks fairly high on my list of desirable improvements.* **2.** *vti.* POSITION OR STAND IN ROWS to place people or things in a row or rows or to stand or form in rows (*usually passive*) **3.** *vt.* US OUTRANK SB to have a higher rank than and take precedence over sb or sth else in a group, especially in a hierarchy ○ *A colonel ranks a major.* [14thC. From Old French *ranc* 'row', from a prehistoric Germanic word that is also the ancestor of English *range* and *ring*.] ◇ **break ranks 1.** to fall out of an ordered line of soldiers, especially when being attacked **2.** to stop supporting the policy of a group of which you are a member ◇ **close ranks 1.** to form into tight disciplined lines in preparation for an expected attack (*refers to soldiers*) **2.** to unite closely, especially when taking some kind of defensive action ◇ **pull rank (on sb)** to assert authority over other people in a hierarchy, especially in order to obtain personal advantage ◇ **rise (up) through the ranks** to reach a senior position in an organization by gradual promotions from an originally low position

rank[2] *adj.* **1.** SHOWING VIGOROUS GROWTH growing and spreading in a particularly vigorous way (*refers to vegetation*) ○ *'the rank ailanthus of the April dooryard'* (T.S. Eliot, *The Dry Salvages*; 1941) **2.** UTTER of the most extreme and obvious kind ○ *a rank amateur* **3.** FOUL foul-smelling or foul-tasting (*literary*) ○ *'O, my offence is rank! It smells to heaven'.* (Shakespeare, *Hamlet* 3.ii; 1604) [Old English *ranc* 'haughty, full-grown', of uncertain origin: perhaps ultimately from an Indo-European word meaning 'to move straight ahead', which is also the ancestor of English *right*] —**rankly** *adv.* —**rankness** *n.*

Rank /rangk/, **J. Arthur, 1st Baron** (1888–1972) British film magnate. The chairman of several British film companies, he promoted the British film industry. Full name **Joseph Arthur Rank**

rank and file *n.* **1.** MIL ENLISTED TROOPS enlisted troops in a military organization, excluding officers **2.** ORDINARY MEMBERS the majority of a group or organization, especially all of the members who have no power or influence —**rank-and-file** *adj.* —**rank and filer** *n.*

rank correlation *n.* assessment of the extent to which different ways of ranking the members of a set correlate with one another

ranker /rángkər/ *n.* **1.** PRIVATE a private in the army **2.** OFFICER RISEN FROM THE RANKS a commissioned army officer who has previously served as a private

Rankine scale /rángkin-/ *n.* an absolute temperature scale in which each degree equals one degree on the Fahrenheit scale, with the freezing point of water being 491.67°, and its boiling point 671.67° [Mid-19thC. Named after the British physicist and engineer W. J. M. *Rankine* (1820–72).]

ranking /rángking/ *n.* POSITION RELATIVE TO OTHERS the position or status held by or allocated to sb or sth relative to others in a particular group ■ *adj.* US **1.** HOLDING HIGH RANK holding a high rank in military or other organization ○ *the ranking diplomat at the reception* **2.** FOREMOST considered to be the most eminent or important of the members of a particular group

rankle /rángk'l/ (-kles, -kling, -kled) *vi.* to cause persistent feelings of bitterness, resentment, or anger ○ *It still rankles after all these years.* [14thC. From Old French *raoncler*, from *raoncle* 'festering sore', literally 'little snake (bite)', from, ultimately, Latin *dracunculus*, from *draco* (see DRAGON).]

ransack /rán sak/ (**-sacks, -sacking, -sacked**) *vt.* **1. ROB AND DESPOIL STH** to go through a place stealing some things and usually destroying or spoiling everything else **2. SEARCH STH VERY THOROUGHLY** to search sth very thoroughly but handling things carelessly ○ *I ransacked the drawers but couldn't find my keys.* [13thC. From Old Norse *rannsaka*, from *rann* 'house' + *-saka* (related to English *seek*) 'to search'.] —**ransacker** *n.*

ransom /ránsəm/ *n.* **1. MONEY DEMANDED FOR RELEASING CAPTIVE** a sum of money demanded or paid for the release of sb who is being held prisoner **2. RELEASE OF PRISONER** the release of a prisoner in return for the payment of money **3. DELIVERANCE** the act of saving sb from an oppressed condition or dangerous situation through self-sacrifice (*literary*) ■ *vt.* (**-soms, -soming, -somed**) **1. PAY MONEY FOR SB'S RELEASE** to release sb from captivity by paying money to the captors **2. RELEASE CAPTIVE ON RECEIPT OF MONEY** to set a captive free or release sth being held on the receipt of money **3. RESCUE OR REDEEM SB** to rescue or redeem sb, especially by a self-sacrificing act, and especially from sin or its punishment (*literary*) [13thC. Via Old French *ransoun* from the Latin stem *redemption-* (see REDEMPTION).] —**ransomer** *n.* ◇ **a king's ransom, a queen's ransom** a very large amount of money ◇ **hold sb to ransom 1.** to use threats to try to make sb do what you want **2.** to hold sb captive until a sum of money is paid for his or her release

rant /rant/ *vti.* (**rants, ranting, ranted**) **SPEAK IN LOUD EXAGGERATED MANNER** to speak in a very loud, aggressive, or bombastic way, usually at length and repetitively ○ *He ranted for hours about how ungrateful we were.* ■ *n.* **LOUD AND THREATENING SPEECH** speech or language that is very loud and threatening but also monotonous or unconvincing [Late 16thC. From Dutch *ranten*.] —**ranter** *n.* —**ranting** *adj.* —**ranting** *n.* —**rantingly** *adv.*

ranula /rányoōlə/ *n.* a cyst that forms on the underside of the tongue when the duct of a salivary or mucous gland is blocked [Mid-17thC. From Latin, literally 'little frog', from *rana* 'frog'.]

ranunculus /rə núngkyoōləss/ (*plural* **-luses** *or* **-li** /-lī/) *n.* a plant that has divided leaves and flowers with five petals such as the buttercup, clematis, and columbine. Genus: *Ranunculus.* [Late 16thC. From modern Latin, genus name, from Latin, literally 'little frog', from *rana* 'frog'.] —**ranunculaceous** /rə núngkyoō láyshəss/ *adj.*

RAOC *abbr.* Royal Army Ordnance Corps

rap[1] /rap/ *v.* (**raps, rapping, rapped**) **1.** *vti.* **HIT STH SHARPLY** to strike sth with a quick sharp blow ○ *The teacher rapped on the desk to get the students' attention* **2.** *vt.* **SAY STH QUICKLY** to say sth in a quick sharp way ○ *The sergeant rapped out an order.* **3.** *vt.* **REBUKE SB** to criticize or reproach sb harshly ■ *n.* **1. SHARP BLOW** a sharp quick blow **2. SOUND OF KNOCKING** a quick sharp knocking sound **3. REBUKE** a harsh rebuke or criticism (*slang*) [13thC. Origin uncertain: perhaps an imitation of the sound.] —**rapper** *n.* ◇ **take the rap (for sth)** to take the blame or punishment for sth, whether or not it was your fault (*slang*) ◇ **not give a rap** to not care at all

rap[2] /rap/ *n.* **1.** *US* **INFORMAL TALK** an informal talk or discussion (*slang*) **2.** MUSIC **POPULAR MUSIC WITH RHYMING VERSES** popular music characterized by spoken rhyming vocals and often featuring a looped electronic beat in the background ■ *v.* (**raps, rapping, rapped**) **1.** *vt. US* **TALK INFORMALLY** to talk or discuss sth informally (*slang*) ○ *We rapped till dawn.* **2.** *vi.* MUSIC **PLAY RAP** to perform rap music [13thC. Origin uncertain: perhaps an imitation of the sound.] —**rapper** *n.*

rapacious /rə páyshəss/ *adj.* **1. GRASPING** greedy and grasping, especially for money, and sometimes willing to use unscrupulous means to obtain what is desired **2. DESTRUCTIVE AND VICIOUS** engaging in violent pillaging and likely to harm or destroy things **3.** ZOOL **PREDATORY** living by eating live prey [Mid-17thC. From Latin *rapac-*, stem of *rapax* 'tearing, grasping', from *rapere* (see RAPE[1]).] —**rapaciously** *adv.* —**rapaciousness** *n.*

rape[1] /rayp/ *n.* **1.** CRIMINOL **FORCING OF SB INTO SEX** the crime of forcing sb to have sex **2.** CRIMINOL **INSTANCE OF RAPE** an instance of the crime of rape **3. VIOLENT DESTRUCTIVE TREATMENT** violent, destructive, or abusive treatment of sth ○ *the rape of a beautiful stretch of countryside* **4. ABDUCTION** an act of seizing sb and carrying him or her away by force (*archaic*) ■ *vt.* (**rapes, raping, raped**) **1. FORCE SB TO HAVE SEX** to force sb to have sex **2. VIOLATE STH** to treat sth in a violent, destructive, or abusive way ○ *rape the land for its resources* **3. ABDUCT SB** to seize and carry off sb or sth by force (*archaic*) [14thC. Via Anglo-Norman *raper* from Latin *rapere* 'to seize'.]

WORD KEY: ORIGIN

The Latin word *rapere* from which ***rape*** is derived is also the source of English *rapacious, rapine, rapid, rapture, ravage, ravenous, ravine, ravish, surreptitious,* and *usurp.*

rape[2] /rayp/ *n.* PLANTS an annual plant of the cabbage family that has bright yellow flowers and is grown commercially for its oil-bearing seeds and as a fodder crop. Latin name: *Brassica napus.* [14thC. From Latin *rapa* 'turnip'.]

rape[3] /rayp/ *n.* WINE the skins and stalks of grapes after their juice has been extracted for use in wine-making [Early 17thC. From French *râpe* 'grape stalk', from Old French, from *rasper* (see RASP).]

rape oil *n.* oil extracted from the seeds of the rape plant, used as a lubricant, in making soap, and in cooking

rapeseed /ráyp seed/ *n.* the seeds of the rape plant

rapeseed oil *n.* = **rape oil**

Raphael /ráffay əl/ *n.* in Hebrew tradition, one of the seven archangels, and the angel of healing

Raphael /ráffay əl/ (1483–1520) Italian artist. A master of the Italian High Renaissance, he is best known for his religious paintings. Real name **Raffaello Sanzio**

raphe /ráyfi/ (*plural* **-phae** /-fee/) *n.* **1. CONNECTING RIDGE** a connecting ridge or seam between two similar parts of an organ of the body, e.g. between the two halves of the medulla oblongata or along the scrotum **2.** BOT **RIDGE ALONG SOME SEEDCOATS** a ridge along the coat of some seeds formed by fusion of the connecting stalk (**funiculus**) with the outer layer of the developing ovule **3.** BOT **LONGITUDINAL GROOVE** a longitudinal groove on the valve of a diatom [Mid-18thC. Via modern Latin from Greek *rhaphē* 'seam', from *rhaptein* 'to sew'.]

raphide /ráy fīd/, **raphis** /ráyfiss/ (*plural* **raphides** /ráffi deez/) *n.* any one of a bundle of needle-shaped crystals, usually of calcium oxalate, that develop in some plant cells as a by-product of their metabolism [Mid-19thC. Via French from the Greek stem *raphid-* 'needle', from *rhaptein* 'to sew'.]

rapid /ráppid/ *adj.* **SWIFT** acting, moving, or happening very quickly ○ *a rapid increase in turnover* ■ **rapids** *npl.* **TURBULENT PART OF A RIVERBED** a part of a riverbed where the water moves very fast, usually over rocks or round boulders ○ *crossed the rapids in a small canoe* [Mid-17thC. From Latin *rapidus* 'seizing', from *rapere* (see RAPE[1]).] —**rapidly** *adv.* —**rapidness** *n.*

rapid eye movement *n.* jerky movements of the eyeballs while the eyes are closed, characteristic of sb who is dreaming while asleep, especially during REM sleep

rapid eye movement sleep *n.* = **REM sleep**

rapid-fire *adj.* ARMS = **quick-fire**

rapid prototyping *n.* a method of quickly creating mechanical components, especially those with complex shapes, from a computer-based drawing that can be used to check the validity of a design

rapid transit *n. US* high-speed urban public transport system using underground or elevated railways or a combination of both

rapier /ráypi ər/ *n.* a sword with a cup-shaped hilt and a long slender blade that can have two cutting edges or only a sharply pointed tip for thrusting [Early 16thC. Origin uncertain: probably via Dutch or Low German *rappir* from French *(espee) rapière* 'rapier (sword)', of unknown origin.]

rapine /ráppīn, -pin/ *n.* the use of force to seize sb else's property (*archaic or formal*) [14thC. Directly or via French from Latin *rapina.*]

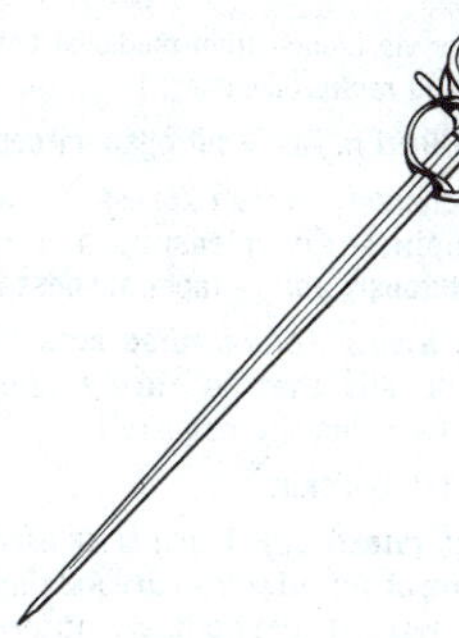

Rapier

rapini /ra peéni/ *npl.* the leaves of immature turnip plants, used especially in Italian and Chinese cooking [Late 20thC. From Italian.]

rapist /ráypist/ *n.* a man who forces sb to have sex with him

rappee /ra peé/ *n.* a moist, strongly flavoured snuff made from dark coarse tobacco (*archaic*) [Mid-18thC. From French *tabac râpé*, literally 'rasped tobacco', from *râper* 'to rasp', from Old French *rasper* 'to scrape' from, ultimately, prehistoric Germanic.]

rappel /ra pél/ *vi.* (**-pels, -pelling, -pelled**), *n. US* = **abseil** [Mid-20thC. From French, from Old French *rapeler* 'to recall', from *apeler* 'to call'.]

rappen /rápp'n/ (*plural* **-pen**) *n.* a Swiss centime [Mid-19thC. From German, from Middle High German *rappe* 'raven', referring to the depiction of a bird on a coin of the Middle Ages.]

rapport /ra páwr/ *n.* an emotional bond or friendly relationship between people based on mutual liking, trust, and a sense that they understand and share each other's concerns ○ *She manages to strike up a rapport with audiences as soon as she steps onto the platform.* [Mid-17thC. From French, from Old French *raporter*, literally 'to bring back', from *aporter* 'to bring', ultimately from Latin *portare* (see PORT[5]).]

rapporteur /ráppawr túr/ *n.* sb who is appointed to investigate a subject and deliver a report on it (*formal*) [Late 15thC. From French, from, ultimately, Old French *raporter* (see RAPPORT).]

rapprochement /ra próshmoN/ *n.* the establishment or renewal of friendly relations between people or nations that were previously hostile or unsympathetic towards each other (*formal*) [Early 19thC. From French, from *rapprocher*, literally 'to bring together', from *approcher* (see APPROACH).]

rapscallion /rap skálli ən/ *n.* a mischievous and annoying child or disreputable and dishonest person (*archaic or humorous*) [Late 17thC. Alteration of earlier *rascallion*, of uncertain origin: probably formed from RASCAL.]

rapt /rapt/ *adj.* **1. COMPLETELY ENGROSSED** involved in, fascinated by, or concentrating on sth to the exclusion of everything else ○ *staring with rapt attention at the speaker* **2. BLISSFULLY HAPPY** showing or suggesting deep emotions of joy or ecstasy **3. rapt, wrapped** *Aus* **PLEASED** extremely pleased (*informal*) [14thC. From Latin *raptus* 'seized', past participle of *rapere* (see RAPE[1]).] —**raptly** *adv.* —**raptness** *n.*

raptor /ráptər/ *n.* a bird of prey [14thC. From Latin, 'robber', from *rapere* (see RAPE[1]).]

raptorial /rap táwri əl/ *adj.* **1. LIVING BY PREDATION** able to live by catching prey **2. ADAPTED FOR CATCHING PREY** specially adapted for seizing prey, as are the feet of birds of prey with their sharp talons **3. OF PREDATORY BIRDS** typical of or relating to birds of prey

rapture /rápchər/ *n.* **1. OVERWHELMING HAPPINESS** a euphoric transcendent state in which sb is overwhelmed by happiness or delight and unaware of anything else **2.** CHR **MYSTICAL TRANSPORTATION** a mystical experience of being transported into the spiritual realm, sometimes applied to the second coming of Jesus Christ when true believers are expected to rise up to join him in heaven ■ **raptures** *npl.* **STATE OF GREAT HAPPINESS OR ENTHUSIASM** a state of great happiness or enthusiasm about sth, or words and gestures that express this ○ *went into raptures about the meal they'd had* [Late

16thC. Directly or via French from medieval Latin *raptura* 'seizure', from Latin *raptus* (see RAPT).]

rapture of the deep *n.* MED = **nitrogen narcosis**

rapturous /rápchərəss/ *adj.* expressing great enthusiasm, happiness, or pleasure ○ *a rapturous welcome* —**rapturously** *adv.* —**rapturousness** *n.*

rara avis /ráirə áyviss/ (*plural* **rarae aves** /ráir ee áy veez/) *n.* sb or sth that is rarely encountered (*literary*) [From Latin, literally 'rare bird']

ra-ra skirt *n.* = **rah-rah skirt**

rare[1] /rair/ (**rarer, rarest**) *adj.* **1.** NOT OFTEN HAPPENING not often happening or found ○ *It's rare for them to miss a meeting.* **2.** VALUABLE particularly interesting or valuable, especially to collectors or scholars, because only a few exist ○ *a collection of rare 18th-century porcelain* **3.** GREAT unusually great or excellent ○ *a rare gift for languages* **4.** CONTAINING LITTLE OXYGEN thin in density and containing so little oxygen that breathing is difficult [15thC. From Latin *rarus* 'having a loose texture, scarce'.] —**rareness** *n.*

rare[2] /rair/ (**rarer, rarest**) *adj.* used to describe meat that is cooked quickly and lightly so as to remain raw and juicy inside [Mid-17thC. Alteration of dialect *rear* 'underdone' (of eggs), from Old English *hrēr*, of uncertain origin: possibly originally 'lightly stirred'.]

rarebit /ráir bit/ *n.* = **Welsh rarebit** [Late 19thC. Alteration of *rabbit* in *Welsh rabbit* (see WELSH RAREBIT).]

rare earth *n.* an oxide of a rare-earth element

rare-earth element *n.* a member of the lanthanide series, which contains 15 elements that have atomic numbers from 57 to 71 and share closely related chemical properties

raree show /ráiri-/ *n.* (*archaic*) **1.** PEEPSHOW a peepshow **2.** CARNIVAL a street show or spectacle with unusual or outlandish items on view [Alteration of *rare show*]

rarefaction /ráiri fáksh'n/, **rarefication** /ráirifi káysh'n/ *n.* the process of becoming or of making sth such as a gas less dense [Early 17thC. From the medieval Latin stem *rarefaction-*, from Latin *rarefacere* (see RAREFY).] —**rarefactional** *adj.*

rarefied /ráiri fīd/ *adj.* **1.** PHYS WITH LOW DENSITY having a low density, especially owing to a low oxygen content **2.** ESOTERIC OR ELITE seemingly distinct or remote from ordinary reality and common people, and often purged of elements perceived as coarse or tasteless **3.** ABOVE THE ORDINARY existing or showing very high quality in character or style (*literary*) ○ *Milton's rarefied prose*

rarefy /ráiri fī/ (**-fies, -fying, -fied**) *v.* **1.** *vti.* BECOME OR MAKE STH LESS DENSE to make sth, especially a gas, less dense, or to become less dense **2.** *vt.* MAKE STH MORE REFINED to make sth less connected with or typical of the ordinary [14thC. Directly or via French from medieval Latin *rareficare*, from Latin *rarefacere*, literally 'to make rare', from *rarus* (see RARE[1]) + *facere* (see FACT).] —**rarefiable** *adj.*

rare gas *n.* CHEM = **noble gas**

rarely /ráirli/ *adv.* **1.** ALMOST NEVER almost never or not very often **2.** THOROUGHLY in a thorough way or to an unusual extent (*archaic*) **3.** WELL exceptionally well (*regional*) ○ *wrote rarely on the final essay*

rareripe /ráir rīp/ *adj.* US RIPENING EARLY that ripens early ■ *n.* US STH THAT RIPENS EARLY a fruit or vegetable that ripens early [Early 18thC. *Rare* 'early' is a variant of RATHE.]

rarify *v.* ♦ **rarefy**

raring /ráiring/ *adj.* very enthusiastic and eager to start doing sth ○ *They were raring to go.* [Early 20thC. Present participle of *rare*, variant of REAR[1].]

rarity /ráirəti/ (*plural* **-ties**) *n.* **1.** INFREQUENCY the fact of happening very seldom or of being very unusual **2.** RARE OBJECT OR EVENT sth that happens rarely or that is particularly interesting or valuable because it is so unusual

RAS *abbr.* **1.** Royal Agricultural Society **2.** Royal Astronomical Society

rasbora /raz báwrə/ *n.* a tropical freshwater fish found in East Africa and Asia, several species of which are brightly coloured and often kept in home aquariums. Genus: *Rasbora.* [Mid-20thC. From modern Latin, of unknown origin.]

rascal /raásk'l/ *n.* **1.** SB WHO BEHAVES MISCHIEVOUSLY sb who behaves in a teasing mischievous way, especially a child (*humorous*) **2.** DISHONEST PERSON sb, especially a man, who is dishonest or otherwise unethical [14thC. From Old French *rascaille* 'mob, rabble', of uncertain origin: probably ultimately via *rasche* 'scurf, scab' from Latin *radere* (see RAZE).] —**rascally** *adj.*

rase *vt.* = **raze** (*dated*)

rash[1] /rash/ *adj.* acting with, resulting from, or typical of thoughtless impetuous behaviour [14thC. Origin uncertain: probably via assumed Old English *ræsc* from a prehistoric Germanic word meaning 'quick' that is also the ancestor of English *rathe*.] —**rashly** *adv.* —**rashness** *n.*

rash[2] /rash/ *n.* **1.** MED SKIN ERUPTION an outbreak on the skin's surface that is often reddish and itchy **2.** SEVERAL INSTANCES a series of events that happen in a brief period and are considered to be unusual or rare ○ *a rash of burglaries* [Early 18thC. Origin uncertain: perhaps from obsolete French *rache* 'a sore', from, ultimately, Latin *rasus*, past participle of *radere* (see RAZE).]

rasher /ráshər/ *n.* a slice of bacon or ham, cooked or uncooked [Late 16thC. Origin unknown.]

rasorial /rə sáwri əl/ *adj.* used to describe a bird that is capable of or adapted for scratching the ground to look for food [Mid-19thC. Formed from late Latin *rasor* 'scraper', from Latin *rasus* (see RASH[2]).]

Rasp

rasp[1] /raasp/ *n.* **1.** TYPE OF FILE a tool used for scraping or smoothing wood or metal, similar to a file but with larger teeth on its cutting surface **2.** ACT OF SMOOTHING STH the act of smoothing the surface of sth such as wood or metal with a rasp **3.** HARSH GRATING SOUND a harsh grating sound, similar to that of a rasp or saw cutting into wood ■ *v.* (**rasps, rasping, rasped**) **1.** *vt.* SAY STH IN HARSH VOICE to say sth, especially to give an order, in a harsh voice **2.** *vti.* FILE OR SCRAPE STH to use a rasp to file or scrape a surface in order to remove unevenness **3.** *vt.* IRRITATE SB to irritate or annoy sb [13thC. From Old French *rasper* 'to scrape', from, ultimately, prehistoric Germanic.] —**rasper** *n.* —**rasping** *adj.* —**raspingly** *adv.* —**raspy** *adj.*

rasp[2] /raasp/ *n.* Scotland a raspberry [Mid-16thC. Shortening of obsolete *raspis* 'raspberry', of unknown origin.]

raspatory /raáspətəri/ (*plural* **-ries**) *n.* a surgical instrument similar to a rasp, used to smooth the ends of a bone [15thC. From medieval Latin *raspatorium*, from *raspare* 'to scrape', from, ultimately, prehistoric Germanic.]

raspberry /raázbəri/ (*plural* **-ries**) *n.* **1.** SMALL CUP-SHAPED FRUIT a small red or black cup-shaped fruit with a sweet taste that grows around a pithy stalk and is made up of many tiny juicy globes (**drupelets**) **2.** BUSH a shrubby plant of the rose family that has a straight prickly stem on which raspberries grow. Genus: *Rubus.* **3.** RUDE NOISE a rude noise meant to imitate the sound of passing wind, made by blowing air through pursed lips and intended as an insult or a gesture of disapproval or defiance (*slang*) **4.** RED COLOUR a deep pink colour with a purplish tinge to it [Early 17thC. From RASP[2] + BERRY.]

raspings /raáspingz/ *npl.* fine breadcrumbs, often toasted, used to coat fish or other foods before frying or baking

Rasputin /ra spyoótin/, **Grigory Yefimovich** (1872–1916) Russian peasant and self-proclaimed holy man. His friendship with Russia's last emperor and empress wrecked the Romanov dynasty's prestige and contributed to the coming of the Russian Revolution (1917).

Grigory Yefimovich Rasputin

rasse /rássi, rásś/ *n.* a small carnivorous mammal that is similar to a cat in appearance. It has anal scent glands and is native to South and Southeast Asia. Latin name: *Viverricula indica.* [Early 19thC. From Javanese.]

Rasta /rástə/ *n.* RASTAFARIAN a Rastafarian (*informal*) ■ *adj.* OF RASTAFARIANS relating to Rastafarians or Rastafarianism (*informal*) [Mid-20thC. Shortening.]

Rastafarian /rástə fáiri ən/ *n.* a member of an Afro-Caribbean religious group that venerates the former emperor of Ethiopia, Haile Selassie, forbids the cutting of hair, and stresses Black culture and identity [Mid-20thC. Formed from Amharic *Ras Tafari*, the name by which Haile Selassie was known prior to his coming to power, literally 'prince to be feared'.] —**Rastafarianism** *n.*

raster /rástər/ *n.* the pattern of horizontal scanning lines made by an electron beam on the surface of a cathode-ray tube that create the image that appears on a television or computer screen [Mid-20thC. Via German, 'screen', from Latin *rastrum* 'rake', from *radere* (see RAZE).]

rasterize /rástə rīz/ (**-izes, -izing, -ized**) *vt.* to convert digitized image into a format suitable for display on a computer monitor or printout

Rat

rat /rat/ *n.* **1.** ZOOL LONG-TAILED RODENT a long-tailed rodent, larger than a mouse. Genus: *Rattus.* **2.** ANIMAL LIKE A RAT an animal that resembles a rat **3.** SB UNTRUSTWORTHY a mean sneaky deceitful person, especially sb who betrays friends or confidences (*slang*) ■ *v.* (**rats, ratting, ratted**) HUNT HUNT RATS to hunt and kill rats ■ *interj.* **rats** EXPRESSION OF ANNOYANCE used to express annoyance or contempt [Old English *ræt*.] ◇ **smell a rat** be suspicious that sth is not right (*informal*)
rat on *vt.* (*informal*) **1.** TREAT SB UNTRUSTWORTHILY to betray sb's trust, especially by revealing sth told in confidence **2.** FAIL SB OR DEFAULT ON STH to abandon sb or sth or fail to do sth

rata /raátə/ *n.* a large New Zealand tree that belongs to the same family as the eucalyptus and myrtle and has hard red wood and crimson flowers. Genus: *Metrosideros.* [Late 18thC. From Maori.]

ratable /ráytəb'l/, **rateable** *adj.* **1.** ABLE TO BE RATED able to be estimated or have a value placed on it **2.** TAXABLE liable for a tax —**ratability** /ráytə bíllət i/ *n.* —**ratably** /ráytəbli/ *adv.*

ratafia /ráttə fee ə/ *n.* **1.** LIQUEUR a liqueur made from fruit juices or softened fruit in liquor, especially brandy, and often flavoured with almonds or with peach or apricot kernels **2.** **ratafia, ratafia biscuit** BISCUIT a small biscuit similar to a macaroon, flavoured with almond or ratafia. ◊ **macaroon** [Late 17thC. Via French from Caribbean Creole.]

Ratana, Tahupotiki Wiremu (1870–1939) New Zealand religious leader. He founded the Ratana Church (1920), a Maori revivalist movement that formed a lasting political alliance with the Labour Party.

rataplan /ráttə plan/ *n.* a noise like the rapid beating of a drum, the sound of horses' hooves striking the ground, or machine-gun fire, made up of a series of short repeated sounds [Mid-19thC. From French, an imitation of the sound.]

rat-arsed /-aarst/ *adj.* extremely drunk (*slang*)

ratatat-tat /ráttə tat tát/, **rat-a-tat** /ráttə tát/, **rat-tat, rat-tat-tat** *n.* SOUND OF KNOCKING AT DOOR the distinctive rhythmic pattern of short loud sounds made by sb knocking at a door ■ *interj.* IMITATION OF A KNOCKING SOUND an imitation of the sound of sb knocking on a door [Late 17thC. An imitation of the sound.]

ratatouille /ráttə too̅i/ *n.* a dish of stewed vegetables, originally from southern France, usually consisting of tomatoes, onions, peppers, aubergines, and courgettes cooked slowly in olive oil [Late 19thC. From French, an alteration of *touiller* 'to stir', from Old French *tooiller* (see TOIL).]

ratbag /rát bag/ *n.* (*slang insult*) **1.** SB UNPLEASANT sb unpleasant, or who the speaker dislikes, disapproves of, or feels angry with for any reason **2.** *ANZ* UNINTELLIGENT PERSON sb perceived as lacking intelligence or common sense

ratbite fever /rát bīt-/ *n.* an infectious disease in humans caused by the bite of a rat infected with either of two bacteria, *Streptobacillus moniliformis* or *Spirillum minus*

rat-catcher *n.* sb whose job is to rid buildings of rats and other vermin

ratchet /ráchit/ *n.* **1.** TURNING DEVICE MOVING IN ONE DIRECTION a mechanism, used especially in lifting devices and some hand tools, consisting of a metal wheel operating with a catch that permits motion in only one direction **2.** RATCHET WHEEL OR PAWL either of the main parts of a ratchet device, the toothed wheel or bar, or the pawl ■ *v.* **(-ets, -etting, -etted)** *US* **1.** *vti.* MOVE WITH RATCHET to move, or to move sth gradually up or down by means of a ratchet **2.** *vt.* FORCE STH UP OR DOWN to force sth such as prices or political rhetoric to rise or fall in level or intensity by deliberately applying pressure in successive and irreversible stages [Mid-17thC. Via French *rochet* 'spool' from, ultimately, a prehistoric Germanic word that is also the ancestor of English *rocket*.]

ratchet wheel *n.* a toothed wheel in a ratchet mechanism

rate /rayt/ *n.* **1.** SPEED the speed at which one measured quantity happens, runs, moves, or changes compared to another measured amount such as time ○ *We'll have to step up our work rate if we're going to finish on schedule.* **2.** AMOUNT IN RELATION TO STANDARD FIGURE the amount, frequency, or speed of sth expressed as a proportion of a larger figure or in relation to a whole ○ *The drop-out rate at the end of the first year is around one in three.* **3.** COMM CHARGE the amount of money charged per unit, e.g. per hour, per page, or per thousand, for a particular job, service, or commodity ○ *I'm charging you the going rate for the job.* ■ **rates** *npl.* FORMER LOCAL TAX a tax formerly levied by local authorities in the United Kingdom on all properties in their areas of jurisdiction, based on a fixed ratable value for each property ■ *v.* **(rates, rating, rated) 1.** *vt.* SET A VALUE ON STH to calculate or appraise the value of sth ○ *How would you rate this gem collection?* **2.** *vti.* ASSESS to have or to be regarded as having a particular value, position, or importance relative to other people or things ○ *This rates as undoubtedly the worst film I have ever seen.* **3.** *vt.* DESERVE STH to deserve or be worthy of sth ○ *Her latest book didn't even rate a review.* **4.** *vt.* CLASSIFY STH to give a particular classification or rating to sth such as a machine, that identifies its performance capabilities and limits **5.** *vt.* FIN VALUE STH FOR TAX PURPOSES to value sth, especially a property, for tax purposes **6.** *vt.* THINK HIGHLY OF SB OR STH to like, approve of, or regard sb or sth as good or excellent (*informal*) ○ *My friends really rate him, but I think his work is amateur.* [15thC. Via Old French from medieval Latin *(pro) rata (parte)*, literally '(according to a) fixed (part)', from Latin *ratus*, past participle of *reri* 'to calculate'.] ◇ **at any rate** used to indicate that an important point is true, whatever other considerations there may be

WORD KEY: ORIGIN

The Latin word *reri* from which *rate* is derived is also the source of English *ratify, ration,* and *reason.*

rateable *adj., n.* = **ratable**

rate-cap **(rate-caps, rate-capping, rate-capped)** *vt.* to set an upper limit on the amount of money that a local authority can raise by means of rates —**rate-capping** *n.*

ratel /ráyt'l/ *n.* ZOOL a carnivorous animal with short thick legs, a strong body with a thick furry coat, dark underneath and whitish on top, and a head similar to a badger's. Ratels are found in Asia and Africa, live on honey and small animals, and are noted for being very aggressive. Latin name: *Mellivora capensis.* [Late 18thC. From Afrikaans, of unknown origin.]

rate of change *n.* the ratio of the difference in values of a variable during a time period to the length of that time period

rate of exchange *n.* = **exchange rate**

rate of return *n.* the amount of income generated in a year by capital invested, expressed as a percentage of the total sum

ratepayer /ráyt payər/ *n.* sb who formerly paid a tax to a local authority, based on the value of his or her dwelling

ratfink /rát fingk/ *n.* *US* an offensive term for sb regarded as obnoxious or despicable (*insult*)

ratfish /rát fish/ (*plural* **-fish** *or* **-fishes**) *n.* a cartilaginous deep-sea fish with a long narrow tail, found worldwide. Family: Chimaeridae.

rath /rath/ *n.* a circular enclosure built in ancient Ireland, surrounded by an earth wall and used as a fort or dwelling place [14thC. From Irish.]

ratha /rut/ *n.* *S Asia* a four-wheeled carriage, drawn by horses or oxen and used in India [From Sanskrit, 'wagon, chariot']

rathe /rayth/ *adj.* ripening or appearing early (*archaic*) [Old English *hræþ* 'quick', from a prehistoric Germanic word that is perhaps also the ancestor of English *rash*]

Rathenau /raátə noir/, **Walther** (1867–1922) German political economist and public servant. As foreign minister, he represented Germany at reparations conferences after World War I. He was assassinated by German nationalists.

rather /raáthər/ *adv.* **1.** SOMEWHAT to some extent or degree ○ *rather disappointing* **2.** CONSIDERABLY to a great extent or degree ○ *I think the irises are rather lovely.* **3.** MORE WILLINGLY more readily or willingly ○ *You go to the cinema; I'd rather stay in tonight.* **4.** WITH MORE JUSTIFICATION with more logic, evidence, precision, or justification ○ *You should praise rather than blame them.* **5.** ON THE CONTRARY in contrast or opposition to what has been stated or expected ○ *You think she's snobbish? Rather, I'd say she's shy.* ■ *interj.* *UK* MOST CERTAINLY used to express complete or enthusiastic agreement with what has just been said (*dated*) [Old English *hræþor*, originally the comparative form of *hraep* (see RATHE, and so meaning 'more quickly', hence 'earlier, sooner']

Rathlin Island /ráthlin-/ island in Northern Ireland, off the northern coast of County Antrim. It is home to three lighthouses. Length: 10 km/6 mi.

rat hole *n.* the entrance to a rat's nest

rathskeller /raát skelər/ *n.* *US* a beer hall or restaurant that serves German dishes, usually located below street level [Early 20thC. From obsolete German, literally 'council cellar' (cellar of the town hall), from *Rat* 'council' + *Keller* 'cellar'.]

ratify /rátti fī/ **(-fies, -fying, -fied)** *vt.* to give formal approval to sth, usually an agreement negotiated by sb else, in order that it can become valid or operative [14thC. Via French *ratifier* from medieval Latin *ratificare*, literally 'to make fixed', from Latin *ratus* (see RATE).] —**ratifiable** *adj.* —**ratification** /ráttifi káysh'n/ *n.* —**ratifier** /rátti fī ər/ *n.*

ratiné /rátti nay/, **ratine** /ra teén/ *n.* a loosely woven cloth with a coarse knobbly texture [Early 20thC. From French, past participle of *ratiner* 'to raise a nap', from *ratine* (see RATTEEN.]

rating /ráyting/ *n.* **1.** ASSESSMENT an assessment or classification of sth on a scale according to how much or how little of a particular quality it possesses ○ *On a scale of one to ten, their rating would be about six* **2.** COMM CREDIT STANDING an assessment of the financial status and creditworthiness of a company or an individual **3.** NAVY ORDINARY SEAMAN a serving member of a navy, especially the Royal Navy, who is not an officer **4.** SAILING HANDICAP IN YACHT RACING a classification of a racing yacht, based on factors such as its size, weight, and area of sail **5.** MECH ENG PERFORMANCE LIMIT OF A MACHINE a stated performance limit of a machine or system, expressed as capacity, range, or working capability ■ **ratings** *npl.* TV, RADIO LIST SHOWING SIZE OF AN AUDIENCE a list or lists showing the estimated number of people who tuned in to a particular TV or radio programme, used as an indication of its relative popularity

ratio /ráyshi ō/ (*plural* **-tios**) *n.* **1.** PROPORTIONAL RELATIONSHIP a proportional relationship between two different numbers or quantities **2.** MATH ONE NUMBER DIVIDED BY ANOTHER a quotient of two numbers or expressions arrived at by dividing one by the other [Mid-17thC. From Latin, 'calculation', formed from *ratus* (see RATE).]

ratiocinate /rátti óssi nayt/ **(-nates, -nating, -nated)** *vi.* to think or put forward an argument about sth in a strictly logical way (*formal*) [Mid-17thC. From Latin *ratiocinat-*, past participle stem of *ratiocinari* 'to compute', from *ratio* (see RATIO).] —**ratiocination** /rátti óssi náysh'n/ *n.* —**ratiocinative** /rátti óssinətiv/ *adj.* —**ratiocinator** /-naytər/ *n.*

ration /rásh'n/ *n.* **1.** FIXED AMOUNT ALLOCATED TO AN INDIVIDUAL a fixed and limited amount of sth, especially food, given or allocated to sb or a group from the stocks available, especially during a time of shortage or a war **2.** ADEQUATE AMOUNT the amount of anything that it seems normal or desirable for an individual to have ○ *rather more than your ration of good luck* ■ **rations** *npl.* AMOUNT OF FOOD OFFICIALLY ALLOCATED food, especially an amount of food allocated to sb, e.g. a soldier or hiker, from a limited stock ○ *The campers had to carry their own rations.* ■ *vt.* **(-tions, -tioning, -tioned) 1.** RESTRICT AVAILABLE AMOUNT OF STH to restrict the amount of sth, usually a commodity in short supply, that an individual is allowed to buy, consume, or use ○ *Petrol was rationed, so long journeys were out of the question.* **2.** LIMIT QUANTITY AVAILABLE TO SB to allow sb only a limited quantity of sth ○ *I'm trying to ration myself to one drink a day.* [Early 18thC. Via French from Spanish *ración*, from Latin *ratio* (see RATIO). The modern meaning developed from 'amount of provisions calculated for a soldier'.]

ration out *vt.* to distribute sth, especially sth that is in short supply, in fixed or strictly limited quantities

rational /rásh'nəl/ *adj.* **1.** REASONABLE AND SENSIBLE governed by, or showing evidence of, clear and sensible thinking and judgment, based on reason rather than emotion or prejudice **2.** IN ACCORDANCE WITH REASON AND LOGIC presented or understandable in terms that accord with reason and logic or with scientific knowledge and are not based on appeals to emotion or, prejudice **3.** ABLE TO REASON endowed with the ability to reason, as opposed to being governed solely by instinct and appetite **4.** MATH EXPRESSIBLE AS RATIO OF POLYNOMIALS able to be expressed exactly as the quotient of two whole numbers or polynomials ○ *a rational function* ■ *n.* MATH RATIONAL NUMBER a rational number [14thC. From Latin *rationalis*, from *ratio* (see RATIO).] —**rationally** *adv.* —**rationalness** *n.*

rational choice theory *n.* the hypothesis, derived from game theory, that there is a rational, definable, and calculable basis to human decision-making

rationale /ráshə naál/ *n.* the reasoning or principle that underlies or explains a particular course of action, or a statement setting out these reasons or principles [Mid-17thC. From modern Latin, from Latin *rationalis* (see RATIONAL).]

rational-emotive behaviour therapy, **rational-emotive therapy** *n.* a form of cognitive-behavioural therapy in which the client is encouraged to examine and change irrational thought patterns and beliefs in order to reduce dysfunctional behaviour

rationalisation *n.* = rationalization

rationalise *vti.* = rationalize

rationalism /rásh'nəlizəm/ *n.* **1.** REASONING AS BASIS OF ACTION the belief that thought and action should be governed by reason **2.** REASON AS SOURCE OF TRUTH the belief that reason and logic are the primary sources of knowledge and truth and should be relied on in searching for and testing the truth of things — **rationalist** *n.* —**rationalistic** /rásh'nə lístik/ *adj.* —**rationalistically** *adv.*

rationality /rásha nálləti/ (*plural* -**ties**) *n.* **1.** FACT OF BEING RATIONAL thinking or behaving in a rational way, or having the ability to think rationally **2.** STH RATIONAL a rational belief, opinion, or action (*often used in the plural*)

rationalization /rásh'nə īt záysh'n/, **rationalisation** *n.* **1.** PROCESS OF RATIONALIZING the process of rationalizing sth, or an effect of rationalizing sth **2.** PSYCHOANAL DEFENCE MECHANISM in psychoanalytic theory, a defence mechanism whereby people attempt to hide their true motivations and emotions by providing reasonable or self-justifying explanations for irrational or unacceptable behaviour

rationalize /rásh'nə līz/ (-**izes**, -**izing**, -**ized**), **rationalise** (-**ises**, -**ising**, -**ised**) *v.* **1.** *vt.* MAKE STH MORE LOGICAL OR RATIONAL to make sth rational, logical, or consistent **2.** *vt.* INTERPRET STH LOGICALLY to interpret sth from a logical or rational perspective **3.** *vti.* OFFER A REASONABLE EXPLANATION to attempt to justify behaviour normally considered irrational or unacceptable by offering an apparently reasonable explanation **4.** *vt.* MATH ELIMINATE RADICALS to eliminate irrational numbers from an expression or an equation **5.** *vti.* MAKE STH MORE EFFICIENT AND PROFITABLE to make sth more efficient and profitable, especially by getting rid of staff, equipment, or parts of the business that are considered to be inefficient or unprofitable —**rationalizable** *adj.* —**rationalizer** *n.*

rational number *n.* a whole number or the quotient of any whole numbers, excluding zero as a denominator

ratio scale *n.* a scale for measuring data that makes it possible to compare different values and to state the difference between them in the form of a ratio

Rat Islands /rát-/ group of islands in Alaska, in the western Aleutian Islands, including Kiska, Amchitka, Semisopochnoi, and Rat Island

ratite /ráttīt/ *n.* a flightless bird such as the ostrich or emu that has a flat breastbone without the keel that flying birds have [Late 19thC. From Latin *ratitus* 'having the figure of a raft', from *ratis* 'raft'.]

rat kangaroo *n.* small kangaroo found in Australia and Tasmania that resembles a rat and has long hind legs for jumping. Genera: *Potorus* and *Bettongia.*

ratline /ráttlin/, **ratlin** *n.* any of the small ropes fastened horizontally between the shrouds in the rigging of a sailing ship to make a ladder for the crew going aloft [15thC. Origin unknown.]

RATO /ráytō/ *abbr.* rocket-assisted takeoff

ratoon /ra toón/, **rattoon** *n.* **1.** SHOOT AT THE BASE OF A CROP PLANT a shoot growing up from the base of a crop plant such as sugar cane or bananas after the previous growth has been cut back **2.** CROP PRODUCED ON RATOONS a crop, e.g. sugar cane, bananas, or pineapple, that is produced on ratoons ■ *vti.* (-**toons**, -**tooning**, -**tooned**) PRODUCE RATOONS to propagate by inducing the formation of ratoons, or to send up ratoons [Mid-17thC. Via Spanish *retoño* 'shoot' from, ultimately, Latin *autumnus* 'autumn'.]

rat pack *n.* a group of people who have close ties or common interests and aims, whose activities are sometimes regarded with suspicion or disapproval (*slang insult*)

rat race *n.* the struggle of individuals to survive and make progress in the competitive environment of modern life, seen as a dehumanizing and ultimately futile activity (*informal*) ○ *I'd like to get out of this rat race and retire to an isolated farm.*

ratshit /rátshit/ *adj.* Aus lacking in quality or excellence (*slang offensive*)

rat snake *n.* a large nonvenomous snake of North America and Asia that eats rodents. Genera: *Elaphe* and *Ptyas.*

rattail /rát tayl/ *n.* HAIRLESS TAIL a hairless tail on a horse ■ *adj.* **rattail, rat-tail** LIKE A RAT'S TAIL looking like or having a part that resembles a rat's tail ○ *a rat-tail comb*

rattan /ra tán/ *n.* **1.** INDUST STEMS OF A TROPICAL PLANT the stems of a tropical plant, used in wickerwork and for making furniture and canes **2.** PLANTS TROPICAL ASIAN CLIMBING PALM a tropical Asian climbing palm that has long thin jointed and pliable stems. Genera: *Calamus* and *Daemonorops* and *Plectomia.* **3.** WALKING STICK a walking stick or cane made from the stem of a rattan plant [Mid-17thC. From Malay *rotan*, of uncertain origin: probably formed from *raut* 'to trim, to strip'.]

rat-tat *n.*, *interj.* = ratatat-tat

ratted /ráttid/ *adj.* drunk (*slang*) [Late 20thC. Formed from RAT, probably on the model of RAT-ARSED.]

ratteen /ra teén/ *n.* ratiné (*archaic*) [Mid-17thC. From French *ratine*, of uncertain origin: perhaps ultimately from Latin *radere* 'to scrape'.]

ratter /ráttər/ *n.* an animal, especially a cat or dog, that is good at catching rats

rattle[1] /rátt'l/ *v.* (-**tles**, -**tling**, -**tled**) **1.** *vti.* MAKE SHORT SHARP KNOCKING SOUNDS to make short sharp knocking or jangling sounds in quick succession, especially as a result of being moved or shaken, or to shake sth so as to produce such sounds ○ *He picked up the box and rattled it.* ○ *The windows and doors rattled in the wind.* **2.** *vi.* MOVE WITH RATTLING SOUND to move while making a rattling sound ○ *The old car rattled noisily down the street.* **3.** *vt.* DISCONCERT SB to make sb lose his or her composure and feel frightened, worried, confused, or annoyed ○ *Reporters shouting questions rattled her.* ■ *n.* **1.** SHORT SHARP KNOCKING OR JANGLING SOUNDS a succession of short sharp knocking or jangling sounds, usually caused by sth shaking or being shaken **2.** BABY'S TOY a baby's toy consisting of a hollow shape with small objects inside, usually attached to a handle, that makes a rattling noise when shaken **3.** NOISEMAKER an object such as a musical instrument or a Shaman's implement that produces a loud rattling sound **4.** ZOOL TIP OF RATTLESNAKE'S TAIL a set of loosely attached horny segments at the end of a rattlesnake's tail that produce a buzzing or rattling sound when shaken **5.** PLANTS PLANT WITH RATTLING SEEDS any of various European plants whose seeds make a rattling noise inside the seed capsule **6.** MED RATTLING NOISE IN THE THROAT a raspy or rattling noise made in the throat caused by obstructed breathing and heard especially near death [14thC. Origin uncertain: probably from Middle Low German *ratelen*, an imitation of the sound.]

rattle around *vi.* to be in a room, house, or building that is bigger than it needs to be (*informal*) ○ *There's just the two of us rattling around in this place.*

rattle off *vt.* to say, read aloud, or perform sth very rapidly or with no apparent effort

rattle on *vi.* to talk rapidly and at length about sth that is of little interest or importance to the listener

rattle through *vt.* to do sth very quickly and often in a perfunctory way ○ *He rattled through the agenda, scarcely pausing for breath.*

rattle[2] /rátt'l/ *vt.* (-**tles**, -**tling**, -**tled**) to attach ratlines to the shrouds in the rigging of a ship [Early 18thC. Back-formation from *rattling*, a variant of RATLINE.]

Rattle /rátt'l/, **Sir Simon** (*b.* 1955) British conductor. He was principal conductor of the City of Birmingham Symphony Orchestra (1980–97), and became a leading interpreter of 20th-century music. Full name **Simon Denis Rattle**

rattlebox /rátt'l boks/ *n.* a tropical plant that has inflated seed pods containing seeds that make a rattling noise when the stem moves. Genus: *Crotalaria.*

rattler /rátt'lər/ *n.* **1.** = rattlesnake **2.** RATTLING THING sb or sth that rattles **3.** US a freight train (*informal*)

Rattlesnake

rattlesnake /rátt'l snayk/ *n.* a large venomous snake of the pit viper family, found in North and South America, whose tail has loosely attached horny segments that buzz or rattle when vibrated. Genus: *Crotalis* and *Sistrurus.*

rattlesnake plantain *n.* an orchid with striped or mottled leaves that resemble a rattlesnake's skin and spikes of white or yellow flowers. Genus: *Goodyera.*

rattletrap /rátt'l trap/ *n.* an old noisy worn-out car or other vehicle (*informal*)

rattling /rátt'ling/ *adj.* MOVING OR TALKING BRISKLY moving or talking at a very fast or lively pace ○ *a rattling TV debate* ■ *adv.* VERY extremely (*dated informal*) ○ *tells a rattling good story* —**rattlingly** *adv.*

rattly /rátt'li/ (-**tlier**, -**tliest**) *adj.* making a lot of noise, usually because of being in very bad condition or not firmly fixed ○ *a rattly air conditioner*

rattoon *n.* = ratoon

rat-trap *n.* **1.** TRAP FOR RATS a trap designed to catch rats **2.** TYPE OF BICYCLE PEDAL a bicycle pedal with an all-metal footrest with serrated edges and a toe clip on the front (*informal*)

ratty /rátti/ (-**tier**, -**tiest**) *adj.* **1.** IRRITABLE irritable or annoyed (*informal*) ○ *Don't get ratty, it won't take very long.* **2.** OF RATS relating to or believed to be characteristic of rats **3.** INFESTED WITH RATS full of or overrun with rats **4.** MESSY having an appearance that is messy and generally unkempt (*informal*) **5.** US, Can DILAPIDATED in an unsafe, rundown condition and unfit for human habitation (*informal*) **6.** Aus OFFENSIVE TERM appearing to be or behaving as if mentally ill (*slang offensive*) —**rattily** *adv.* —**rattiness** *n.*

raucous /ráwkəss/ *adj.* loud and hoarse or unpleasant-sounding, or characterized by loud noise, shouting, and ribald laughter [Mid-18thC. Formed from Latin *raucus* 'hoarse'.] —**raucity** /ráwssəti/ *n.* —**raucously** *adv.* —**raucousness** *n.*

raunch /rawnch/ *n.* (*slang*) **1.** SEXUAL EXPLICITNESS sexual explicitness or suggestiveness of an earthy or vulgar kind, especially as part of a performer's material or act **2.** SEXUALLY EXPLICIT MATERIAL sexually explicit or lewd material or language **3.** US MESSINESS lack of cleanliness or neatness [Mid-20thC. Back-formation from RAUNCHY.]

raunchy /ráwnchi/ (-**chier**, -**chiest**) *adj.* **1.** SEXUALLY EXPLICIT OR OBSCENE sexually explicit or obscene in a coarse vulgar way (*informal*) **2.** US DIRTY lacking neatness or cleanliness (*slang*) [Mid-20thC. Origin unknown.] —**raunchily** *adv.* —**raunchiness** *n.*

Rauschenberg /rówsh'n burg/, **Robert** (*b.* 1925) US

Robert Rauschenberg

artist. His hybrid three-dimensional works such as *Monogram* (1955–59) had a strong influence on the pop art movement of the 1960s.

rauwolfia /raw wŏolfi ə, row-/ *n.* **1.** TROPICAL SE ASIAN TREE a tropical Southeast Asian tree or shrub belonging to the dogbane family. Latin name: *Rauwolfia serpentina.* **2.** ROOT USED TO MAKE SEDATIVE DRUGS the root of the rauwolfia, used to make various sedative drugs, including reserpine [Mid-18thC. From modern Latin, genus name, named after Leonhard *Rauwolf* (died 1596), a German botanist and physician.]

ravage /rávvij/ *v.* (**-ages, -aging, -aged**) **1.** *vti.* COMPLETELY WRECK OR DAMAGE STH to wreck or utterly destroy sth through a violent onslaught of some kind (*often passive*) ○ *a once-beautiful landscape ravaged by development* **2.** *vt.* WRECK AND PLUNDER A PLACE to plunder or sack a place or area ■ *n.* ACT OR HABIT OF DESTRUCTION the act or habit of destroying or plundering sth ■ **ravages** *npl.* DAMAGING EFFECTS the damaging or disfiguring effects of sth [Early 17thC. From French *ravager*, alteration of *ravine* 'rushing of water', from, ultimately, Latin *rapere* (see RAPE[1]).] **—ravagement** *n.* **—ravager** *n.*

RAVC *abbr.* Royal Army Veterinary Corps

rave /rayv/ *v.* (**raves, raving, raved**) **1.** *vti.* SPEAK WILDLY AND INCOHERENTLY to speak in a loud or angry way that suggests lack of rationality or loss of self-control **2.** *vi.* GIVE HIGH PRAISE to praise sth in a very enthusiastic way (*informal*) ○ *All the critics raved about her performance.* **3.** *vi.* STORM to be very stormy and make a loud roaring noise (*literary*) **4.** *rave, rave it up vi.* HAVE A GOOD TIME to have a good time, especially at a party, in a wild uninhibited way (*dated slang*) ■ *n.* **1.** ACT OF RAVING an act or instance of raving **2.** ENTHUSIASTIC PRAISE sth, especially a review, that expresses extremely enthusiastic praise for sth (*informal; used before a noun*) ○ *gave the novel rave reviews* **3.** LARGE-SCALE PARTY a large-scale party or club event at which pop music is played, lasting sometimes all night (*slang*) ■ *adj.* CRAZE a craze or fad (*dated slang*) [14thC. From Old Northern French *raver*, of uncertain origin.]

ravel /rávv'l/ (**-els, -elling, -elled**) *v.* **1.** *vti.* TANGLE to become tangled, or cause threads or fibres of some kind to tangle ○ *My fishing line has ravelled.* **2.** *vti.* FRAY to come, or cause threads to come, loose from a knitted or woven fabric **3.** *vt.* RESOLVE STH to clarify or resolve sth complicated **4.** *vt.* BREAK UP ROAD SURFACE to break up a road surface or begin to break into fragments [Late 16thC. Origin uncertain: probably from Dutch *ravelen.*] **—raveler** *n.* **—ravelment** *n.*

AKG London

Maurice Ravel

Ravel /rə vél/, **Maurice** (1875–1937) French composer. A master of orchestration, he wrote impressionistic pieces that are classics of the 20th-century repertoire. His works include *Boléro* (1928) and *Daphnis et Chloé* (1912). Full name **Maurice Joseph Ravel**

ravelin /rávvlin/ *n.* a small outwork in fortifications consisting of two embankments shaped like an arrowhead that point outwards in front of a larger defence work [Late 16thC. Via French from Italian *ravellina*, of unknown origin.]

raven[1] /ráyv'n/ *n.* LARGE BLACK BIRD OF CROW FAMILY a large bird belonging to the crow family with glossy black plumage, a wedge-shaped tail, and a large beak. It is found throughout the northern hemisphere, chiefly in upland regions, and is a subject of legend and folklore, being often perceived as a bad omen. Latin name: *Corvus corax.* ■ *adj.* COLOURS SHINY BLACK of a deep lustrous black (*literary*) [Old English *hræfn.*

Raven

Ultimately from a prehistoric Germanic word, thought to be an imitation of its croaking.]

─────── **WORD KEY: CULTURAL NOTE** ───────

The Raven, a poem by US writer Edgar Allen Poe (1845)This melancholy tale of lost love gained Poe national fame. As a young student mourns the death of his lover, a raven–a traditional symbol of doom–appears at his window. To every question that the student poses about his future and his lover, the bird responds 'Nevermore'.

raven[2] /rávv'n/ (**-ens, -ening, -ened**) *vti.* **1.** EAT GREEDILY to eat sth voraciously or greedily **2.** TAKE STH AWAY BY FORCE to take sth away by force, especially prey or plunder [15thC. Via Old French *raviner* 'to seize' from, ultimately, Latin *rapere* (see RAPE[1]).] **—ravener** *n.*

ravening /rávv'ning/ *adj.* living by hunting prey, especially in a greedy voracious way **—raveningly** *adv.*

Ravenna /rə vénnə/ capital city of Ravenna Province, Emilia-Romagna Region, northeastern Italy. An ancient Roman city, it contains several early Christian churches. Population: 134,000 (1994).

ravenous /rávv'nəss/ *adj.* **1.** HUNGRY extremely hungry **2.** GREEDY FOR STH hungry or greedy for sth, especially for the gratification of wants or desires **—ravenously** *adv.* **—ravenousness** *n.*

raver /ráyvər/ *n.* (*informal*) **1.** SB WHO ENJOYS PARTIES sb who has a busy and exciting social life, especially sb who enjoys going to parties and behaving in an uninhibited way **2.** SB FREQUENTING RAVES sb who goes to raves

rave-up *n.* a wild noisy party with a lot of music, drinking, and dancing (*dated slang*)

ravine /rə véen/ *n.* a deep narrow valley, especially one formed by running water [15thC. From Old French *ravine* 'rapine, violent rush', from, ultimately, Latin *rapere* (see RAPE[1]).]

raving /ráyving/ *adj.* **1.** IRRATIONAL wildly irrational, angry, or insulting **2.** STUNNING used to emphasize the sense of admiration and excitement felt for sth (*informal*) ○ *a raving review of the play* ■ **ravings** *npl.* WILDLY IRRATIONAL SPEECH wildly irrational, angry, or insulting utterances ○ *the ravings of a person cheated* **—ravingly** *adv.*

ravioli /rávvi óli/ *n.* a food made from small squares of pasta sealed around a meat, fish, vegetable, or other filling [Mid-19thC. From Italian, the plural of dialectal *raviolo* 'small turnip'.]

ravish /rávvish/ (**-ishes, -ishing, -ished**) *vt.* **1.** OVERWHELM SB EMOTIONALLY to overwhelm sb with deep and pleasurable feelings or emotions (*usually passive*) **2.** RAPE SB to force sb to engage in sexual intercourse (*literary*) **3.** CARRY STH OFF to carry off sth by violent force (*archaic or literary*) [13thC. From the French stem *raviss-* 'to seize', from, ultimately, Latin *rapere* (see RAPE[1]).] **—ravisher** *n.* **—ravishment** *n.*

ravishing /rávvishing/ *adj.* extremely delightful or beautiful **—ravishingly** *adv.*

raw /raw/ *adj.* **1.** UNCOOKED not cooked **2.** UNPROCESSED not processed, refined, or treated in any way **3.** HURT AND SORE cut, scraped, or inflamed, often painfully so **4.** INEXPERIENCED lacking training or experience with sth **5.** COLD extremely cold and harsh **6.** NOT SUBTLE not subtle, restrained, or refined ○ *the raw power of the music* **7.** BRUTALLY REALISTIC factual and realistic, especially in connection with unpleasant matters ○ *a raw portrayal of a model's life* **8.** NOT CHANGED OR

INTERPRETED in an original state and not yet subjected to correction or analysis [Old English *hrēaw.* Ultimately from an Indo-European word that also produced Latin *crudus* 'raw' (source of English *crude* and *cruel*).] **—rawly** *adv.* **—rawness** *n.* ◇ **touch sb on the raw** to upset sb or to make sb uncomfortable by referring to sth that he or she is very sensitive about ◇ **in the raw 1.** not wearing clothes (*informal*) **2.** in a natural state, without embellishment or refinement

Rawalpindi /ráwl píndi/, **Rāwalpindi** city of Punjab Province, northern Pakistan. Population: 1,290,000 (1995).

rawboned /ráw bōnd/ *adj.* having a lean body with prominent bones

raw deal *n.* an arrangement, situation, or treatment that is unfair

rawhide /ráw hīd/ *n.* **1.** UNTANNED HIDE untanned animal hide **2.** WHIP OR ROPE a whip or rope made of rawhide

rawhide hammer *n.* a hammer designed to avoid damage to finished surfaces, with a head made from a tight roll of hide held in a metal tube

rawinsonde /ráywin sond/ *n.* a balloon carrying meteorological instruments (**radiosonde**) that has a trackable radar target and is used to observe the velocity and direction of upper-air winds [Mid-20thC. A blend of RADAR, WIND, and *radiosonde.*]

Rawlings /ráwlingz/, **Jerry** (*b.* 1947) Ghanaian soldier and statesman. He was elected president of Ghana (1992) and was chair of the Economic Community of West African States (1994–96). Full name **Jerry John Rawlings**

raw material *n.* **1.** NATURAL UNPROCESSED MATERIAL a natural unprocessed material that is used in a manufacturing process **2.** STH POTENTIALLY USEFUL sth or sb considered to have potential for use or development

raw sienna *n.* **1.** COLOURS YELLOWISH-BROWN a yellowish-brown colour **2.** INDUST PIGMENT a natural yellowish-brown substance that is used as a pigment

raw silk *n.* **1.** UNTREATED SILK FIBRES silk fibres reeled from silkworm cocoons and left untreated **2.** SILK FABRIC fabric or yarn made from raw silk

Rawsthorne /ráws thawrn/, **Alan** (1905–71) British composer. His symphonies, concertos, and chamber and orchestral works follow traditional principles of tonality.

rax /raks/ (**raxes, raxing, raxed**) *v.* Scotland **1.** *vti.* STRETCH to stretch or reach out **2.** *vt.* PASS STH to pass sth with an outstretched hand [Old English *raxan.* Ultimately from a prehistoric Germanic word that also produced German *recken* 'to stretch'.]

ray[1] /ray/ *n.* **1.** BEAM OF LIGHT a narrow beam of light from the sun or an artificial light source **2.** TRACE OF STH POSITIVE a slight indication of sth positive in a difficult or worrying situation **3.** PHYS BEAM OF ENERGY a thin beam of radiant energy or particles **4.** MATH LINE EXTENDING FROM POINT a straight line that extends from a point infinitely in one direction **5.** ZOOL ARM OF STARFISH any of the arms of a starfish or other animal with body parts radiating from the centre **6.** ASTRON BRIGHT STREAK FROM LUNAR CRATER any of the bright streaks on the lunar surface that radiate from some craters **7.** BOT RADIAL STRAND OF PLANT PITH a distinct strand of tissue running radially through the conducting tissues in the stem of a plant ■ **rays** *npl.* SUNSHINE hot or warm sunshine, especially when thought of as a tanning agent (*slang*) ○ *catch some rays* ■ *v.* (**rays, raying, rayed**) **1.** *vti.* EMIT LIGHT to shine or emit rays, e.g. of light or electromagnetic particles **2.** *vi.* EXTEND IN LINES to extend in radiating lines from a point [14thC. Via French *rai* from Latin *radius* (see RADIUS).] **—rayed** *adj.*

ray[2] /ray/ *n.* a fish with a cartilage skeleton, a flat head and body, broad pectoral fins, and a tapering tail. It lives near the sea floor, feeding on shellfish. The gill inlets are on top of the head behind the eyes, while the outlets are on the underside. Order: Rajiformes. ◊ **stingray** [14thC. Via French *raie* from Latin *raia.*]

ray[3] /ray/ *n.* MUSIC a syllable that represents the second note in a scale, used for singing exercises (**solfeggio**). US term **re** [15thC. Alteration of REZZ.]

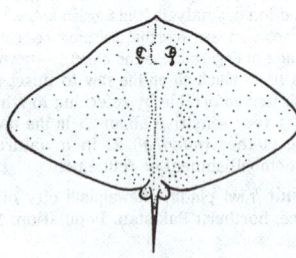

Ray

AKG London

Man Ray

Ray /ray/, **Man** (1890–1976) US artist. Founder of the New York Dada movement, he is known for his avant-garde photographs and paintings. Real name **Emanuel Rudnitsky**

Popperfoto

Satyajit Ray

Ray, Satyajit (1921–92) Indian film director. His *Apu* (1955–9) and *Calcutta* (1970–75) film trilogies won him international acclaim.

ray flower, **ray floret** *n.* any of the radiating parts of the flower of a composite plant such as the dandelion or daisy, comprising either the whole flower head or only its margin

ray gun *n.* in science fiction, a gun capable of firing rays of energy that stun or destroy

Rayleigh /ráyli/, **John William Strutt, 3rd Baron** (1842–1919) British physicist. He performed research into resonance and vibration and, with Sir William Ramsay, discovered argon (1894).

Rayleigh scattering /ráyli-/ *n.* the scattering of electromagnetic radiation into different wavelengths by very small particles of matter, responsible for red sunrises and sunsets as well as the blue of the daytime sky. The particles must be very small relative to the wavelength of the radiation, and while there is no frequency change there is a phase change and a separation of colours. [Mid-20thC. Named after John William Strutt RAYLEIGH, who first described it.]

rayless /ráyləss/ *adj.* **1.** WITHOUT LIGHT dark, gloomy, or lacking light (*literary*) **2.** BOT LACKING RAY FLOWERS lacking the ray flowers that typically form part of the flower heads of plants in the daisy family — **raylessly** *adv.* —**raylessness** *n.*

Raymond Terrace /ráymənd-/ town in eastern New South Wales, Australia, located at the junction of

the rivers Hunter and Williams. Population: 12,332 (1996).

Raynaud's disease /ráy nōz-/ *n.* a disorder of the blood vessels in which sb is affected by Raynaud's phenomenon without any identifiable underlying cause [Late 19thC. Named after the French physician Maurice *Raynaud* (1834–81), who first described it.]

Raynaud's phenomenon *n.* spasms of the arteries of the fingers and toes, typically brought on by cold, causing the hands and feet to become pale, cold, numb, and sometimes painful. Causes include diseases of the arteries, rheumatoid arthritis, and repeated trauma to the fingers. [Mid-20thC (see RAYNAUD'S DISEASE)]

rayon /ráy on/ *n.* **1.** SYNTHETIC TEXTILE FIBRE a synthetic textile fibre made from cellulose **2.** SYNTHETIC FABRIC a synthetic fabric or yarn made from rayon fibres [Early 20thC. Coined from RAY[1], perhaps influenced by French *rayon* 'ray'; from its sheen.]

raze /rayz/ (**razes, razing, razed**), **rase** (**rases, rasing, rased**) *vt.* **1.** COMPLETELY DESTROY PLACE to destroy or level a building or settlement completely **2.** US SCRAPE STH to scrape or shave sth off sth else **3.** ERASE STH to erase sth (*archaic*) [Mid-16thC. Via Old French *raser*, literally 'to shave off', from, ultimately, Latin *radere* 'to scrape, scratch' (source also of English *abrade*, *erase*, and *rash*).] — **razer** *n.*

razoo /rə zóó/ (*plural* **-zoos**) *n.* ANZ an imaginary coin that has little or no value (*informal; always used in negative sentences*) [Mid-20thC. Origin unknown.]

razor /ráyzər/ *n.* INSTRUMENT FOR SHAVING an instrument with a blade or powered cutting head that is used for shaving hair off the face or body ▪ *vt.* (**-zors, -zoring, -zored**) SHAVE OR CUT HAIR to shave or cut hair using a razor [13thC. From Old French *rasor*, from *raser* (see RAZE).]

razorback /ráyzər bak/ *n.* **1.** MARINE BIOL = finback **2.** US FERAL PIG a feral pig of the southeastern United States that has a narrow body, ridged back, and long legs **3.** US = hogback

Razorbill

razorbill /ráyzər bil/, **razor-billed auk** *n.* a seabird of the auk family, with black-and-white plumage and a sharp hooked beak. It inhabits coastal regions of the North Atlantic, feeding underwater on fish and shellfish. Latin name: *Alca torda.*

razor blade *n.* a flat blade designed to be used in a safety razor

razor clam *n.* US = razor-shell

razor cut *n.* HAIRCUT WITH RAZOR a haircut that is done using a razor rather than scissors ▪ *vt.* CUT HAIR WITH RAZOR to cut or style hair with a razor rather than scissors

razor-shell *n.* any of various bivalve molluscs, found near Atlantic and Pacific coasts, that have a long narrow tubular shell with squared ends. They burrow rapidly downwards into the sand by extending a muscular foot. Family: Solenidae. US term **razor clam**

razor wire *n.* wire with sharp pieces of metal fixed along its length, used for fences and barriers

razz /raz/ *vt.* (**razzes, razzing, razzed**) US, Can TEASE SB to tease or make fun of sb (*informal*) ▪ *n.* US, Can RASPBERRY a raspberry noise (*informal*) [Early 20thC. Shortening and alteration of RASPBERRY.]

razzle /rázz'l/ *n.* = **razzle-dazzle** *n.* **2** [Early 20thC. Shortening.] ◇ **on the razzle** enjoying a spell of unrestrained partying or heavy drinking (*informal*)

razzle-dazzle *n.* **1.** SHOWINESS THAT ASTONISHES an often gaudy showiness that is designed to impress and excite people **2.** SPREE a spell of unrestrained partying or heavy drinking [Late 19thC. Rhyming compound formed from DAZZLE.]

razzmatazz /rázmə táz/ *n.* showiness that is designed to impress and excite people, especially in the context of a stage show or other spectacle [Late 19thC. Origin uncertain: perhaps an alteration of RAZZLE-DAZZLE.]

Rb *symbol.* rubidium

rbc, **RBC** *abbr.* red blood (cell) count

RBE *abbr.* relative biological effectiveness

rc *abbr.* reinforced concrete

RC *abbr.* **1.** Red Cross **2. RC, R.C.** Roman Catholic **3.** Reserve Corps **4.** Republic of China (Taiwan) (*international vehicle registration*)

RCA *abbr.* **1.** Central African Republic (French *République Centrafricaine*) (*international vehicle registration*) **2.** Royal College of Art

rcd *abbr.* received

RCM *abbr.* Royal College of Music

RCMP *abbr.* Royal Canadian Mounted Police

RCN *abbr.* **1.** Royal Canadian Navy **2.** Royal College of Nursing

r-colour *n.* in phonetics, the effect of an 'r' sound uttered simultaneously with a vowel by constricting the oral cavity with the tongue

RCP *abbr.* Royal College of Physicians

rcpt *abbr.* receipt

RCS *abbr.* **1.** Royal College of Surgeons **2.** Royal Corps of Signals **3.** Royal College of Science

rct *abbr.* recruit

RCT *abbr.* Royal Corps of Transport

RCVS *abbr.* Royal College of Veterinary Surgeons

rd *abbr.* **1.** rendered **2.** road **3.** MEASURE rod **4.** round

Rd *abbr.* Road (*in addresses*)

RD *abbr.* **1.** refer to drawer (*on cheques*) **2.** MAIL Rural Delivery

R/D *abbr.* refer to drawer (*on cheques*)

RDF *abbr.* RADIO radio direction finder

RDO *n. Aus* a day off given by some employers in lieu of extra hours worked, sometimes on a regular basis (*informal*) [Shortening of *rostered day off*]

RDS *n.* a system for tuning radio receivers automatically by sending digital signals with normal radio programmes [Shortening of *radio data system*]

re[1] /ray/ *n.* MUSIC = **ray**[1] *n.* **2** [15thC. Shortening of medieval Latin *resonare* (see GAMUT).]

re[2] /ree, ray/ *prep.* with reference to [Early 18thC. From Latin, literally 'on the matter of', a form of *res* 'thing, matter'.]

Usage: The use of *re* meaning 'with reference to' is largely restricted to the language of business, but it is also used informally as a convenient short form standing for 'regarding, concerning': *Re your invitation, I'll be pleased to come.*

're *contr.* are ○ *They're planning to come.*

Re[1] /ray/ *n.* MYTHOL = **Ra**

Re[2] *symbol.* **1.** CHEM ELEM rhenium **2.** MONEY rupee **3.** Reynolds number

RE *abbr.* **1.** Religious Education **2.** Reformed Episcopal **3.** Right Excellent **4.** Royal Engineers

re- *prefix.* **1.** again, anew ○ *rebuild* **2.** back, backward ○ *recall* [Via Old French from Latin]

reach /reech/ *v.* (**reaches, reaching, reached**) **1.** *vti.* EXTEND to stretch out physically or extend as far as a particular place or point ○ *I can't reach the top shelf without a chair.* **2.** *vi.* MOVE TOWARDS STH TO TOUCH IT to move towards sth to touch or grasp it ○ *She reached for her coat.* **3.** *vt.* ARRIVE AT PARTICULAR PLACE to arrive or come to a particular place or point

○ *We reached home before midnight.* **4.** *vt.* **ARRIVE AT PARTICULAR STATE** to get into a particular state or condition ○ *I had reached desperation point.* **5.** *vti.* **INFLUENCE PEOPLE** to have an influence or impact on people or on a group ○ *This campaign will reach millions of people.* **6.** *vt.* **CONTACT SB** to communicate with sb ○ *I'll try to reach you at home.* **7.** *vt.* **PASS STH** to pass or hand sb sth (*informal*) ○ *Just reach me down that file, would you.* **8.** *vi.* **STRIVE FOR STH** to strive too much to achieve or acquire sth, especially without success **9.** *vi.* SAILING **SAIL WITH WIND TO THE SIDE** to sail on a tack with the wind blowing from the side ■ *n.* **1. ACT OF STRETCHING OUT** the act of stretching out or extending **2. EXTENT OF REACHING** the extent or range that sb or sth is able to reach ○ *The top shelf is just beyond his reach.* **3. RANGE OF POWER** the extent of the power or influence exercised by sb or sth ○ *beyond the reach of the law* **4. STRETCH OF WATER** a stretch of open water, e.g. on a river **5.** SAILING **TACK SAILED BY VESSEL** a tack sailed by a vessel with the wind blowing from the side **6. NUMBER OF VIEWERS** the number of viewers who visit a website or watch a particular television program (*informal*) ○ *Reach is one factor determining whether companies invest in the Web.* ■ **reaches** *npl.* **AREA OR LEVEL** an area or level of sth ○ *the upper reaches of the Amazon* [Old English *rǣcan*. Ultimately from a prehistoric Germanic word that also produced German *reichen* 'to reach'.] —**reachable** *adj.* —**reacher** *n.*

react /ri ákt/ (**-acts, -acting, -acted**) *vi.* **1. RESPOND EMOTIONALLY** to respond to sth by showing the feelings or thoughts it arouses **2. RESPOND BY TAKING ACTION** to respond to sth by taking action **3. RESPOND PHYSICALLY** to respond to the physical effects of sth, e.g. a medication or air pollutants **4.** CHEM **CHANGE CHEMICALLY** to undergo a chemical reaction

reactance /ri áktənss/ *n.* opposition to the flow of alternating current caused by the inductance and capacitance in a circuit, measured in ohms. The total opposition to the flow of current in the circuit is the impedance, which is the sum of the reactance and the resistance in the circuit. Symbol *X*

reactant /ri áktənt/ *n.* a substance that reacts with another in a chemical reaction

reaction /ri ákshʹn/ *n.* **1. EMOTIONAL RESPONSE** an emotional or intellectual response that sth arouses **2. ACTIVE RESPONSE** a response to sth that involves taking action, or an action taken in response to sth **3. PHYSICAL RESPONSE** a response to the physical effects of sth such as heat, cold, or pollution **4.** MED **BODILY RESPONSE TO SUBSTANCE** a response by the body to a foreign substance, especially to an infection, medication, food, or sth that causes an allergy **5.** PHYS **FORCES ACTING ON A BODY** an equal but opposite force exerted by a body when a force acts upon it **6.** POL **STRONG CONSERVATISM** strong opposition to social or political changes that the speaker considers liberal or progressive (*disapproving*) **7.** PHYS **NUCLEAR PROCESS** a nuclear process resulting in a change in structure of atomic nuclei ■ **reactions** *npl.* **SB'S ABILITY TO REACT QUICKLY** sb's ability to respond quickly to an unexpected situation, especially one of danger ○ *His quick reactions saved us from certain death.* —**reactional** *adj.*

reactionary /ri ákshʹnəri/ *adj.* **OPPOSED TO LIBERAL OR PROGRESSIVE CHANGE** opposed to social or political changes that the speaker considers liberal or progressive (*disapproving*) ■ *n.* (*plural* **-ies**) **OPPONENT OF LIBERAL OR PROGRESSIVE CHANGE** an opponent of social and political changes that the speaker considers liberal or progressive (*disapproving*)

reaction engine *n.* an engine that produces thrust by ejecting a stream of gas at high velocity, as do jet engines and rocket engines

reaction formation *n.* in psychoanalysis, a defence mechanism in which sb condemns sth that has an unconscious appeal

reaction time *n.* **1.** PHYSIOL **TIME BETWEEN STIMULUS AND RESPONSE** the interval of time between the application of a stimulus and the first indication of a response **2.** COMPUT = **access time**

reactivate /ri ákti vayt/ (**-vates, -vating, -vated**) *vti.* to make sth active again, or to become active again —**reactivation** /ri ákti váyshʹn/ *n.*

reactive /ri áktiv/ *adj.* **1. REACTING TO EVENTS AND SITUATIONS** reacting to events, situations, and stimuli, especially when doing so spontaneously as they occur **2.** CHEM **REACTING CHEMICALLY** taking part in chemical reactions **3.** PSYCHOL **CAUSED BY STIMULI OR EVENTS** used to describe a psychiatric condition caused by particular situations or stimuli, e.g. the behaviour of other people or the death of a loved one —**reactively** *adv.* —**reactiveness** *n.* —**reactivity** /rée ak tívvəti/ *n.*

reactor /ri áktər/ *n.* **1. STH THAT REACTS** sb or sth that reacts or takes part in a reaction **2.** PHYS **DEVICE IN WHICH NUCLEAR REACTION OCCURS** a device in which self-sustained controlled nuclear fission or experimental nuclear fusion takes place, producing heat energy. Reactors are usually characterized by their fuel, moderator, and coolant, although sometimes their function, power, or size are employed. **3.** INDUST **CONTAINER IN WHICH CHEMICAL REACTION OCCURS** a vessel or other equipment in which an industrial chemical reaction takes place **4.** ELEC **COMPONENT IN ELECTRICAL CIRCUIT** a component in an electrical circuit used to create reactance, e.g. a capacitor or an inductor **5.** MED **SB SENSITIVE TO MEDICATION** a person or animal that displays a reaction to a medication, vaccine, or other substance, especially one that shows a positive reaction to a skin test for latent infection

read /reed/ *v.* (**reads, reading, read** /red/) **1.** *vti.* **INTERPRET WRITTEN MATERIAL** to interpret the characters in written or printed material, understanding the sense of what is written **2.** *vti.* **UTTER WRITTEN WORDS** to say the words of written or printed material either internally or out loud **3.** *vti.* **LEARN STH BY READING** to find sth out by studying written or printed material ○ *I read it in a book.* **4.** *vt.* **INTERPRET NONWRITTEN MATERIAL** to interpret the information conveyed by movements, signs, or signals ○ *We could no longer read the trail.* **5.** *vti.* **INTERPRET PRINTED SIGNS** to interpret the meaning of signs and symbols in printed material, some of which may not be in verbal form ○ *to learn to read music* **6.** *vt.* **BE ABLE TO READ IN FOREIGN LANGUAGE** to know a foreign language well enough to be able to read in it ○ *Can you read French?* **7.** *vt.* EDUC **TAKE UNIVERSITY COURSE** to pursue a particular course of study at a university **8.** *vt.* **UNDERSTAND STH INTUITIVELY** to have an understanding of sth by experience or intuitive means ○ *claiming to be able to read the future* **9.** *vti.* PUBL **PROOFREAD STH** to read through sth in order to find poor grammar, misprints, and other errors **10.** *vti.* **INTERPRET STH IN PARTICULAR WAY** to interpret or understand sth, or be interpreted or understood, in a particular way ○ *I read this passage as being extremely optimistic.* **11.** *vi.* **HAVE QUALITIES THAT AFFECT UNDERSTANDING** to have particular characteristics that affect the way sth is understood ○ *In the original it reads as poetry rather than prose.* **12.** *vi.* **HAVE PARTICULAR WORDS** to have a particular wording ○ *a sign that reads DANGER* **13.** *vti.* RADIO **HEAR STH ON TWO-WAY RADIO** to receive and understand a message sent by sb on a two-way radio **14.** *vt.* **INDICATE DATA** to indicate or display data, e.g. a temperature ○ *What does the thermometer read?* **15.** *vt.* PUBL **SUBSTITUTE WORD** to substitute a word or words for others that were printed incorrectly ○ *For 'peasant' read 'pheasant'.* **16.** *vti.* COMPUT **TRANSFER DATA INTO COMPUTER MEMORY** to transfer program instructions or data from a storage device into a computer's main memory ■ *n.* **1. STH PRODUCING PARTICULAR REACTION** sth that produces a particular reaction in the reader when read ○ *a thrilling read* **2. TIME SPENT READING** a period devoted to reading ○ *She settled down for a long read.* [Old English *rǣdan*. Ultimately from an Indo-European word that is also the ancestor of English *riddle*.] ◇ **take sth as read** to assume sth to be the case

read into *vt.* to detect meanings in speech or written text that were not necessarily intended by the speaker or writer

read out *vt.* **1. READ STH ALOUD** to read sth out loud **2.** COMPUT **RETRIEVE INFORMATION FROM COMPUTER** to retrieve data from the memory or a disk or other storage device of a computer **3.** *US* **EXPEL SB FROM ORGANIZATION** to expel sb formally from a political party, organization, or other group

read up *vti.* to learn a lot about a subject by reading about it or researching it

Read /reed/, **Sir Herbert** (1893–1968) British art historian. A prominent advocate in his day of contemporary British art, he founded the Institute of Contemporary Arts (1947). Full name **Herbert Edward Read**

readable /réedəbʹl/ *adj.* **1. LEGIBLE** able to be read easily **2. ENJOYABLE TO READ** having a style that makes reading enjoyable and interesting —**readability** /réedə bílləti/ *n.* —**readableness** *n.* —**readably** *adv.*

readdress /rée ə dréss/ (**-dresses, -dressing, -dressed**) *vt.* **1. PUT NEW ADDRESS ON LETTER** to put a new address on a letter, especially if the existing address is wrong or if the letter has to be forwarded **2. ATTEND TO AGAIN** to return to a problem or issue, especially with the intention of resolving it

reader /réedər/ *n.* **1. SB WHO READS** sb who reads or who reads in a particular manner **2.** COMPUT **READING DEVICE** a device that reads, especially one connected to a computer for reading media **3.** EDUC **EDUCATIONAL BOOK** an educational book intended as an aid in learning to read or learning a foreign language **4.** LITERAT **ANTHOLOGY** a collection of literary works by a single author or by several authors linked, e.g. by their period or style **5.** PUBL **SB WHO READS FOR PUBLISHER** sb who reads manuscripts for a publisher to assess whether they are publishable **6.** CHR = **lay reader 7.** JUDAISM = **cantor 8.** UNIV **LECTURER AT UNIVERSITY** a lecturer at university who ranks above a senior lecturer and below a professor

readership /réedər ship/ *n.* **1.** PRESS **PEOPLE WHO READ PARTICULAR NEWSPAPER** the group or number of people who read a particular newspaper, magazine, or journal **2.** UNIV **POSITION OF READER IN UNIVERSITY** the position of reader in a British university, ranking above a senior lectureship

readily /réddili/ *adv.* **1. WITHOUT HESITATION** promptly and without any hesitation **2. EASILY** with little difficulty

reading /réeding/ *n.* **1. IDENTIFYING OF WRITTEN OR PRINTED WORDS** the identifying of combinations of written or printed letters or characters as words in a language and understanding their meaning **2. MATERIAL THAT IS READ** printed or written material that can be read **3. OCCASION OF READING STH** an occasion when sb reads sth, especially a poem or a piece of literature, to an audience **4. TEXT READ TO AUDIENCE OR CONGREGATION** a piece of literature that is read to an audience, or a passage from a sacred text that is read to a congregation **5. INTERPRETATION OF STH** an interpretation or understanding of a situation or of sth that has been written or said **6.** TECH **INFORMATION TAKEN FROM EQUIPMENT** information or a measurement taken from a piece of equipment or with the help of equipment **7. RECITAL OF PARLIAMENTARY BILL** the formal recital of a bill as part of the procedure in Parliament after which it has to pass through three other stages before it can become law **8. ONE OF BILL'S THREE PARLIAMENTARY STAGES** one of the three stages that a bill passes through in parliament before it becomes law

Reading /rédding/ **1.** county town of Berkshire, southern England. Population: 135,455 (1996). **2.** city in northeastern Massachusetts, southeast of Andover and northwest of Boston. Population: 22,956 (1996). **3.** city in southeastern Pennsylvania. Population: 78,380 (1990).

reading age *n.* a child's competence in reading, measured against the average competence of children of the same age

readjust /rée ə júst/ (**-justs, -justing, -justed**) *v.* **1.** *vi.* **GET USED TO STH AGAIN** to get used to sth after a period of absence from it **2.** *vt.* **REARRANGE** to rearrange or make small changes to sth —**readjustable** *adj.* —**readjuster** *n.* —**readjustment** *n.*

README file /rééd mee-/ *n.* a computer text file supplied with the software for a program and containing information that a user may need in order to install or operate the program

read-only *adj.* used to describe computer files that can be retrieved and displayed but cannot be changed or deleted

read-only memory *n.* a small computer memory for storing data permanently. Once data has been written onto it, the data cannot be altered or added to and can only be read. Because read-only memory retains its contents when the power is turned off, most personal computers use it to store essential programs such as the one that boots the computer.

read-out *n.* **1.** DATA RETRIEVAL the retrieving of data from a computer's memory, disk, or other storage device **2.** DATA RETRIEVED BY COMPUTER the data retrieved from a computer's memory, disk, or other storage system **3.** DEVICE DISPLAYING INFORMATION a part of a piece of equipment that displays information

readthrough /réed throo/ *n.* a reading of a play without acting, allowing actors to familiarize themselves with the dialogue before full rehearsals begin

read-write head *n.* a magnetic device that can both read from and write data to a magnetic medium such as a computer floppy or hard disk. The head moves linearly between the hub and the rim of the disk to store and retrieve data from the disk's surface while the disk rotates beneath it.

ready /réddi/ *adj.* (**-ier, -iest**) **1.** PREPARED FOR STH prepared for sth that is going to happen ○ *Are you ready to leave?* **2.** FINISHED AND AVAILABLE FOR USE finished or completed and so able to be used immediately ○ *When will dinner be ready?* **3.** ON THE POINT OF DOING STH on the point of doing sth or liable to do sth ○ *This old roof is ready to cave in.* **4.** PREPARED IN ADVANCE prepared or blended in advance, and able to be used with very little additional preparation (*often used in combination*) ○ *available ready-sliced in small packets* **5.** WILLING TO DO STH eager, willing, or prepared to do sth ○ *Don't be so ready to give in!* **6.** QUICKLY PRODUCED quickly and easily given, provided, or available ○ *a ready response to questions about wrongdoing* **7.** INTELLIGENT intelligent, alert, and quick-witted ○ *a ready wit* ■ *vt.* (**-ies, -ying, -ied**) PREPARE to prepare sth, especially so that it is in a condition for sth to happen to it ■ *n.* = **ready money** (*informal*) [12thC. Formed from Old English *rǣde* 'prompt'. Ultimately from a prehistoric Germanic word meaning 'arranged'.] —**readiness** *n.* ◇ **at the ready** prepared for immediate use or action ◇ **ready to hand** positioned so that it can easily be reached or retrieved

ready cash *n.* = **ready money**

ready-made *adj.* **1.** ALREADY PREPARED already prepared or made for convenience **2.** PRECONCEIVED thought out in advance ■ *n.* READY-TO-WEAR GARMENT an item of clothing that is offered for sale in a standard size and completely finished, as opposed to clothing that is made to the customer's specifications

ready-mix *n.* a correct mixture of ingredients that is preblended and able to be used with very little additional preparation —**ready-mixed** *adj.*

ready money *n.* money that is available to be spent immediately, usually as notes and coins

ready reckoner *n.* a table that shows at a glance frequently used arithmetic calculations for easy reference

ready-to-wear *adj.* MADE IN STANDARD SIZES AND DESIGNS already made in standard sizes, designs, and colours, rather than being specially made or designed for an individual ■ *n.* ITEM OF READY-MADE CLOTHING an item of clothing that is already made in standard sizes and designs, rather than being specially designed or tailored for an individual

reafforest /rée ə fórrist/ *vt.* = **reforest** —**reafforestation** /rée ə fórri stáysh'n/ *n.*

The White House
Ronald Reagan

Reagan /ráygən/, **Ronald** (*b.* 1911) US statesman and 40th president of the United States. After a career as a film actor, he served as Republican president twice (1981–89). Full name **Ronald Wilson Reagan**

Reaganomics /ráygə nómmiks/ *n.* the free-market economic approach espoused by US President Ronald Reagan, involving cuts in taxes and social spending together with deregulation of domestic markets [Late 20thC. A blend of REAGAN and ECONOMICS.]

reagent /ri áyjənt/ *n.* a substance taking part in a chemical reaction, especially one used to detect, measure, or prepare another substance

reagin /rée əjin/ *n.* a type of antibody involved in allergic reactions such as hay fever. Reagins are produced following an initial exposure to an allergenic substance, and interact with allergenic substances to trigger the release of histamines, causing inflammation, swelling, and other symptoms. [Early 20thC. From German, formed from *reagieren* 'to react'.] —**reaginic** /rée ə jínnik/ *adj.*

real[1] /rée əl, reel/ *adj.* **1.** PHYSICALLY EXISTING having actual physical existence **2.** VERIFIABLE AS ACTUAL FACT verifiable as actual fact, e.g. legally or scientifically ○ *What is his real name?* **3.** NOT IMAGINARY existing as fact, rather than as a product of dreams or the imagination **4.** NOT ARTIFICIAL genuine and original, and so not artificial or synthetic **5.** TRADITIONAL AND AUTHENTIC prepared or made in a traditional or authentic way, rather than being mass-produced or artificial ○ *looking for some real food* **6.** SINCERE honest or sincere, not feigned or affected ○ *express your real feelings* **7.** EMPHASIZING TRUTH used to emphasize the accuracy or appropriateness of a particular thing ○ *He's a real professional.* **8.** UNDISPUTED based on fact, observation, or experience and so undisputed ○ *The real success of the evening was the comedy act.* **9.** ESSENTIAL of basic, essential, or critical importance **10.** ECON IN TERMS OF PURCHASING POWER regarded in terms of purchasing power rather than the actual amount **11.** PROPERTY LAW RELATING TO FIXED PROPERTY relating to land and the fixed property associated with it **12.** MATH INVOLVING ONLY REAL NUMBERS involving, relating to, or having elements of the set of rational or irrational numbers only **13.** PHILOSOPHY ABOUT EXISTENCE concerned with independent objective existence ■ *adv. US* VERY very or extremely (*informal*) ○ *I'm real tired.* ■ *n.* **1.** = **real number 2.** REALITY everything that exists in the actual world [15thC. Directly or via Old French from late Latin *realis*, literally 'related to things (in law)', from Latin *res* 'thing, fact'.] —**realness** *n.* ◇ **for real** *US* seriously, not as a joke or as a practice (*informal*) ◇ **get real!** used to indicate strongly that what sb said or thought is unrealistic, untrue, or out of date (*slang*) ◇ **(in) real life** in the course of normal life as opposed to imagined or fictional representations of life, e.g. in books and films ◇ **the real thing, the real McCoy** sth that is authentic and not an imitation

real[2] /ray áal/ (*plural* **-als** *or* **-ales** /ray áales/) *n.* **1.** UNIT OF BRAZILIAN CURRENCY the unit of currency in Brazil. See table at **currency 2.** COIN OR NOTE WORTH A REAL a coin or note worth a real **3.** FORMER CURRENCY IN SPANISH-SPEAKING COUNTRIES in the past, a silver coin used as a unit of currency in several Spanish-speaking countries [Late 16thC. Via Spanish from Latin *regalis* (see ROYAL).]

real[3] /ray áal/ (*plural* **reals** *or* **reis** /rays/) *n.* a coin that was used as a unit of currency in Portugal [Mid-20thC. Via Portuguese from Latin *regalis* (see ROYAL).]

real ale *n.* any beer that is allowed to ferment in the cask and does not have carbon dioxide added to it when it is served [From the traditional brewing method used]

real estate *n. US, ANZ* land including all the property on it that cannot be moved and any attached rights

real-estate agent *n. ANZ, US* a person who buys, sells, and leases property on behalf of sb else. = **estate agent**

real focus *n.* a point from which light diverges or at which it converges

realgar /ri álgər/ *n.* a soft orange-red arsenic ore consisting of crystalline arsenic sulphide, used in tanning, as a pigment, and to make fireworks [14thC. Via medieval Latin *realger* from, ultimately, Arabic *rahj al-ġār*, literally 'powder of the cave'.]

realign /rée ə lín/ (**-ligns, -ligning, -ligned**) *v.* **1.** *vt.* STRAIGHTEN AGAIN to readjust or manipulate sth so that it is in a straight line or is correctly oriented **2.** *vti.* CHANGE STH TO FIT SITUATION to alter or change sth to fit particular circumstances **3.** *vti.* MAKE NEW ALLIANCES to form, or cause people or groups to form, new alliances or associations ○ *The party has realigned itself with several former ideological opponents.* —**realignment** *n.*

real image *n.* an optical image of sth that is produced by reflection or refraction and can be transferred onto a surface such as the film inside a camera

realism /rée əlizəm/ *n.* **1.** UNDERSTANDING OF NATURE OF REAL LIFE a practical understanding and acceptance of the actual nature of the world, rather than an idealized or romantic view of it **2.** ACCURACY OF SIMULATION the simulation of sth in a way that accurately resembles real things ○ *the increasing realism of computer graphics* **3.** ARTS, LITERAT LIFELIKE ARTISTIC REPRESENTATION in artistic and literary works, lifelike representation of people and the world, without any idealization **4.** PHILOSOPHY THEORY THAT THINGS EXIST OBJECTIVELY the theory that things such as universals, moral facts, and theoretical scientific entities exist independently of people's thoughts and perceptions **5.** PHILOSOPHY THEORY THAT PEOPLE PERCEIVE INDEPENDENT WORLD the theory that although there is an objectively existing world, not dependent on our minds, people are able to understand aspects of that world through perception **6.** PHILOSOPHY THEORY THAT STATEMENTS HAVE TRUTH VALUES the theory that every declarative statement is either true or false, regardless of whether this can be verified

realist /rée əlist/ *n.* **1.** PRAGMATIST sb who is sensible, practical, and not concerned with abstract theories or idealistic views of life **2.** ADHERENT OF REALISM sb who practises realism in the arts or believes in philosophical theories of realism

realistic /rée ə lístik/ *adj.* **1.** PRACTICAL seeking what is achievable or possible, based on known facts ○ *set realistic goals when looking for a new job* **2.** SIMULATING REALITY simulating real things or imaginary things in a way that seems real ○ *computer games with realistic graphics* **3.** REASONABLE not priced or valued too low or high **4.** ARTS, LITERAT REPRESENTING REAL LIFE in the arts and literature, representing life as it really is, rather than an idealized picture of it **5.** PHILOSOPHY RELATING TO PHILOSOPHICAL REALISM relating to philosophical theories of realism —**realistically** *adv.*

reality /ri állәti/ (*plural* **-ties**) *n.* **1.** REAL EXISTENCE actual being or existence, as opposed to an imaginary, idealized, or false nature **2.** ALL THAT ACTUALLY EXISTS OR HAPPENS everything that actually does or could exist or happen in real life **3.** STH THAT EXIST OR HAPPENS sth that has real existence and must be dealt with in real life ○ *a vision that ignores the realities of the business world* **4.** TYPE OF EXISTENCE a kind of existence or universe, either connected with or independent from other kinds ○ *fantastic notions of alternative realities* **5.** PHILOSOPHY TOTALITY OF REAL THINGS the totality of real things in the world, independent of people's knowledge or perception of them ◇ **in reality** in actual fact

reality check *n. US* an action taken to reconcile sb's ideas or desires with reality (*informal*)

reality principle *n.* in Freudian theory, the ego's ability to postpone gratification to avoid unpleasant consequences or to gain greater reward

realization /rée ə lī záysh'n/, **realisation** *n.* **1.** REALIZING OF STH the realizing of sth **2.** STH REALIZED sth that has been realized

realize /rée ə līz/ (**-izes, -izing, -ized**), **realise** (**-ises, -ising, -ised**) *v.* **1.** *vti.* KNOW AND UNDERSTAND STH to know, understand, and accept sth ○ *doesn't realize how lucky he is* **2.** *vti.* BE OR BECOME AWARE OF STH to be aware or conscious of sth, or to become aware of sth ○ *Do you realize the problems you've caused?* **3.** *vt.* ACHIEVE STH HOPED FOR to achieve in actuality sth that has been hoped or worked for **4.** *vt.* TURN WORK INTO PERFORMANCE to turn sth such as a play or novel into a stage or film performance **5.** *vt.* COMM TRANSLATE STH INTO MONEY to translate sth into a particular amount of money, usually by selling it **6.** *vt.* CONVERT GAIN OR LOSS INTO CASH to convert a paper gain or loss into a cash gain or loss by closing out the original transaction **7.** *vt.* MUSIC INTERPRET PIECE OF MUSIC to interpret a musical composition, especially the figured bass of a baroque composition [Early 17thC. Formed from REAL[1] on the model of French *réaliser*.] —**realizable** *adj.* —**realizer** *n.*

——— **WORD KEY: SYNONYMS** ———
See Synonyms at ***accomplish***.

real-life *adj.* actual or true, as opposed to fictional or imaginary

real-live *adj.* not artificial, imagined, or invented ○ *face-to-face with a real-live gangster*

really /reé əli, reéli/ *adv.* **1.** IN FACT in fact or in reality, especially as distinct from what has been believed until now ○ *She's really going to Paris, not Bangkok.* **2.** GENUINELY used to emphasize the truthfulness or accuracy of what is being said ○ *She really is going to Paris next year.* **3.** UNDOUBTEDLY truly and without any doubt ○ *That's really interesting.* **4.** PROPERLY in order to act in the correct or proper manner ○ *You should really apply in writing.* ■ *interj.* EXCLAMATION OF SURPRISE used to express surprise, doubt, or exasperation ○ *You're getting married? Really! Well really, how rude!*

realm /relm/ *n.* **1.** SCOPE OF STH a particular or stated area, range, or domain ○ *Here the scenario enters the realms of fantasy.* **2.** AREA OF INTEREST a defined area of interest or study ○ *the realm of pure mathematics* **3.** KINGDOM a country ruled by a monarch [13thC. Via Old French *realme* from Latin *regimen* 'government', from *regere* 'to rule' (source of English *rector*, *regent*, and *register*); the *l* was due to the influence of Old French *reiel* 'royal'.]

real number *n.* a number that is either rational or irrational rather than imaginary. ◊ **imaginary number**

real part *n.* the part of a complex number that does not have an imaginary factor, e.g. the number 3 in the complex number 3 + 5i

realpolitik /ray aál polli teek/ *n.* politics based on pragmatism or practicality rather than on ethical or theoretical considerations [Early 20thC. From German, literally 'real politics'.] —**realpolitiker** /ray aál po líttikər/ *n.*

real presence *n.* the doctrine that the body and blood of Jesus Christ are actually present in the elements of Communion

real property *n.* land together with all the property on it that cannot be moved and any attached rights. ◊ **real estate**

real tennis *n.* a form of tennis played on an indoor court with a sloping roof against which the ball can be hit [*Real* because it was the original game of tennis]

real time *n.* COMPUT the actual time in which a computer-controlled calculation or process takes place

real-time *adj.* **1.** COMPUT RELATING TO IMMEDIATE DATA PROCESSING relating to the ability of certain computer systems to process and update data as soon as it is received from some external source, e.g. an air traffic control or antilock brake system. The time available to receive the data, process it, and respond to the external process is dictated by the time constraints imposed by the process. **2.** HAPPENING NOW happening at the very present time ○ *real-time coverage of the crisis*

Realtor /reé əltər/ *tdmk.* US a trademark for a real-estate agent who is a member of the National Association of Realtors

realty /reé əlti/ *n.* = **real property**

real-world *adj.* relevant or practical in terms of everyday life

ream[1] /reem/ *n.* QUANTITY OF PAPER a quantity of paper, formerly 480 sheets but now usually 500 sheets ■ **reams** *npl.* LARGE QUANTITY a large quantity of material, especially written material [14thC. Via Old French *raime* from, ultimately, Arabic *rizma* 'bundle'.]

ream[2] /reem/ *vt.* (**reams, reaming, reamed**) *vt.* **1.** FORM HOLE WITH REAMER to form, enlarge, or shape a hole with a reamer **2.** US SQUEEZE CITRUS JUICE to squeeze the juice from a citrus fruit with a reamer **3.** US CHEAT to cheat or swindle sb (*slang*) **4.** US REPRIMAND to reprimand sb severely (*slang*) **5.** US OFFENSIVE TERM a highly offensive term meaning to have anal intercourse with

sb (*taboo offensive*) [Mid-18thC. Origin uncertain: perhaps from Old English *rȳman* 'to widen'.]

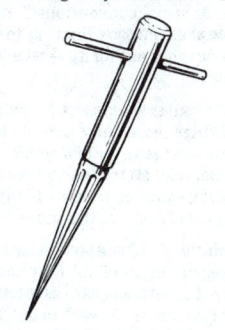

Reamer

reamer /reémər/ *n.* **1.** TOOL FOR FORMING OR ENLARGING HOLES a tool that is used to form, enlarge, or shape holes **2.** US COOK = **lemon squeezer**

reap /reep/ (**reaps, reaping, reaped**) *vt.* **1.** GATHER CROP to cut and gather a crop, especially a grain crop, from the land where it is growing **2.** OBTAIN AS RESULT to obtain sth, especially as a consequence of previous effort or action [Old English *rīpan*. Origin uncertain: perhaps ultimately from an Indo-European word meaning 'to tear'.] —**reapable** *adj.*

reaper /reépər/ *n.* sb or sth that reaps, especially, formerly, a machine for harvesting grain crops ◊ **the grim reaper, the reaper** death, or a personification of death

rear[1] /reer/ (**rears, rearing, reared**) *v.* **1.** *vt.* RAISE YOUNG ANIMALS OR CHILDREN to bring up and care for young animals or children until they are fully grown **2.** *vt.* GROW A PLANT to raise a plant to full growth **3.** *vi.* RISE ON HIND LEGS to rise up on the hind legs (*refers to animals*) **4.** *vi.* RISE HIGH to rise high into the air ○ *tall office buildings rearing into the night sky* [Old English *rǣran*. Ultimately from an Indo-European word that is also the ancestor of English *raise* and *rise*.] —**rearer** *n.*

rear[2] /reer/ *n.* **1.** BACK OF STH the back of sth, or the area near the back of sth **2.** MIL PART OF ARMY FARTHEST FROM FRONT the part of an army or a procession that is farthest from the front **3.** BUTTOCKS sb's buttocks, or the similar part of an animal (*informal*) ■ *adj.* BACK situated at the back ○ *Do not join the rear four carriages.* [Late 16thC. Via Old French *rere* from Latin *retro* (see RETRO-).] ◊ **bring up the rear** to be at the back, particularly in a race or procession

rear admiral *n.* a rank in the Royal Navy or US Navy or Coast Guard that is above captain or commodore and below vice admiral, or an officer holding this rank

rear end = **rear**[2] *n.* 1, **rear**[2] *n.* 3

rear-end (**rear-ends, rear-ending, rear-ended**) *vt.* US to collide with the back of another vehicle

rear-ender *n.* US an accident in which one vehicle collides with the back of another (*informal*)

rearguard /reér gaard/ *n.* **1.** MIL TROOPS ACTING IN RETREAT a body of troops designated to delay the enemy during a retreat or withdrawal **2.** CONSERVATIVES members of a political party or other organization who are strongly conservative and opposed to change and progress (*disapproving*)

rearm /ree aárm/ (**-arms, -arming, -armed**) *vti.* to equip people, an organization, or a nation with weapons and ammunition again, or to become so equipped —**rearmament** *n.*

rearmost /reér mōst/ *adj.* farthest towards the back

rearrange /ree ə ráynj/ (**-ranges, -ranging, -ranged**) *vt.* **1.** CHANGE ORDER OF STH to change the order or position of sth **2.** CHANGE TIME OF STH to reschedule the time of sth such as an event —**rearrangement** *n.*

rearview mirror /reér vyoo-/ *n.* a mirror attached to the inside of the windscreen or the outside of a front door of a vehicle, allowing the driver to see behind the vehicle

rearward /reérwərd/ *adv.* **rearwards** TOWARDS REAR towards or in the rear or back ■ *adj.* LOCATED IN REAR located in or near the rear or back

reason /reéz'n/ *n.* **1.** JUSTIFICATION an explanation or justification for sth ○ *refused to give a reason for her behaviour* **2.** MOTIVE a motive or cause for acting or thinking in a particular way ○ *His only reason for going was that she would be there.* **3.** POWER OF ORDERLY THOUGHT the power of being able to think in a logical and rational manner ○ *use reason rather than force* **4.** CAUSE THAT EXPLAINS STH a cause that explains a particular phenomenon ○ *What's the reason for grass being green?* **5.** ABILITY TO THINK CLEARLY the ability to think clearly and coherently **6.** PHILOSOPHY INTELLECT AS BASIS FOR KNOWLEDGE the ability to think logically regarded as a basis for knowledge, as distinct from experience or emotions ■ *v.* (**-sons, -soning, -soned**) **1.** *vi.* THINK IN LOGICAL WAY to think logically or use rational faculties **2.** *vi.* USE RATIONAL ARGUMENT TO PERSUADE to try to reason or influence sb by means of rational argument ○ *I tried to reason with him but he insisted on going ahead.* **3.** *vt.* RESOLVE BY RATIONAL MEANS to formulate or resolve sth using rational means ○ *reason out a maths problem* [13thC. Via Old French *reisun* from, ultimately, Latin *ratio* 'calculation, thought' (source of English *rate* and *rational*), from *reri* 'to think'.] —**reasoner** *n.* ◊ **it stands to reason** used to emphasize that sth seems obvious or logical ◊ **within reason** within reasonable limits

——— **WORD KEY: USAGE** ———
the reason is that or **the reason is because**? Particularly in writing, **reason** is more correctly followed by *that* than by *because* in sentences of the type *The reason I left is that* [not *because*] *I was bored.* Informally, however, and especially in conversation, *because* does occur.

——— **WORD KEY: SYNONYMS** ———
See Synonyms at ***deduce***.

reasonable /reéz'nəb'l/ *adj.* **1.** RATIONAL sensible and capable of making rational judgments ○ *He did what any reasonable person would have done in that situation.* **2.** IN ACCORD WITH COMMON SENSE acceptable and according to common sense ○ *hoping to arrive at a reasonable time* **3.** NOT EXPECTING MORE THAN IS POSSIBLE not expecting or demanding more than is possible or achievable ○ *Come on, be reasonable!* **4.** FAIRLY GOOD fairly good but not excellent ○ *The food was reasonable.* **5.** FAIRLY LARGE large enough but not excessive ○ *He earns a reasonable amount of money.* **6.** NOT EXORBITANT fairly priced and not too expensive ○ *Three bottles for £7.50 is very reasonable.* —**reasonableness** *n.* —**reasonably** *adv.*

——— **WORD KEY: SYNONYMS** ———
See Synonyms at ***valid***.

reasoned /reéz'nd/ *adj.* rational and carefully thought out

reasoning /reéz'ning/ *n.* **1.** LOGICAL THINKING the use of logical thinking in order to find results or draw conclusions **2.** ARGUMENT an argument or other example of logical thinking ○ *Her reasoning was based on the available facts.*

reassure /ree ə shoór, -sháwr/ (**-sures, -suring, -sured**) *vt.* **1.** PUT SB'S MIND AT EASE to make a person feel less anxious or worried **2.** = **reinsure** —**reassurance** *n.* —**reassurer** *n.*

reassuring /ree ə shooring, -sháwring/ *adj.* having the effect of making people feel less anxious or worried —**reassuringly** *adv.*

Réaumur /ráy ə myoor/ *adj.* using or measured on the Réaumur scale [Early 19thC. Named after the French physicist René Antoine Ferchault de *Réaumur* (1683–1757), who developed the scale.]

Réaumur scale *n.* an obsolete temperature scale on which water freezes at 0 degrees and boils at 80 degrees under normal atmospheric conditions [Late 18thC. Named after the French physicist and inventor René Antoine Ferchault de *Réaumur* (1683–1757), who introduced it.]

reave[1] /reev/ (**reaves, reaving, reaved** *or* **reft** /reft/, **reaved** *or* **reft**) *vt.* (*archaic*) **1.** TAKE STH FORCIBLY to plunder sth or carry sth off by force **2.** DEPRIVE SB to rob sb or deprive sb of sth [Old English *rēafian*. Ultimately from a prehistoric Germanic word that is also the ancestor of English *rob*.] —**reaver** *n.*

reave[2] /reev/ (**reaves, reaving, reaved** *or* **reft** /reft/, **reaved**

or **reft** /reft/ *vt.* to tear sth apart (*archaic*) [13thC. Alteration of RIVE.] —**reaver** *n.*

reb /reb/, **Reb** *n.* US = **Johnny Reb** (*informal*) [Mid-19thC. Shortening of REBEL.]

Reb /reb/ *n.* JUDAISM a title of respect that is roughly equivalent to 'Mister' (*used with a man's first name*) [Late 19thC. From Yiddish, shortening of *rebbe* (see REBBE).]

rebarbative /ri baárbətiv/ *adj.* unpleasant, annoying, or forbidding (*formal*) [Late 19thC. From French *rebarbatif*, from *rebarber*, literally 'to face beard to beard', from *barbe* 'beard'.] —**rebarbatively** *adv.*

rebate[1] *n.* /reé bayt/ MONEY PAID BACK money that is paid back, e.g. because sb has overpaid tax or is entitled to a refund ■ *vt.* /ri báyt/ (**-bates, -bating, -bated**) GIVE REBATE TO SB to give sb a rebate [15thC. From French *rabattre*, literally 'to beat down again', from *abattre* 'to beat down' (source of English *abate* and *abattoir*), from Latin *battuere* 'to beat'.] —**rebatable** /ri báytəb'l/ *adj.* —**rebater** /ri báytər/ *n.*

rebate[2] *n.* /reé bayt/ GROOVE CUT FOR WOOD JOINT a groove or step cut along the length of the edge of a piece of wood that is to be joined to another with a corresponding tongue or ledge cut into it. US term **rabbet** ■ *vt.* /ri báyt/ (**-bates, -bating, -bated**) US term **rabbet** 1. CUT REBATE IN STH to cut a rebate in a piece of wood 2. JOIN PIECES WITH REBATE to join two pieces of wood at their edges by means of a rebate [Late 17thC. Alteration of RABBET.]

rebbe /rébbə/, **Rebbe** *n.* a rabbi or spiritual leader of a Hasidic Jewish community [Late 19thC. Via Yiddish from Hebrew *rabbī*, literally 'my teacher'.]

rebbetzin /rébbətsən/, **rebbitzin** *n.* the wife of a rabbi [Late 19thC. From Yiddish, formed from *rebbe* (see REBBE).]

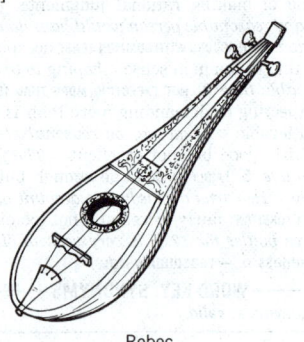

Rebec

rebec /reé bek/, **rebeck** *n.* a two- or three-stringed medieval instrument that looks like a lute and is played with a bow. It is one of the earliest bowed stringed instruments. [Early 16thC. Via French from, ultimately, Arabic *rabāb*.]

Rebecca /ri békə/, **Rebekah** *n.* in the Bible, the wife of Isaac, and mother of Jacob and Esau

rebel *n.* /rébb'l/ 1. PROTESTER sb who protests against sth by defying authority ○ *The rebels in the party voted against their leaders.* 2. UNCONVENTIONAL PERSON sb who refuses to conform to the codes and conventions of society ○ *always something of a rebel* 3. SOLDIER WHO OPPOSES GOVERNMENT IN POWER a soldier who belongs to a force seeking to overthrow a government or ruling power ■ *vi.* /ri bél/ (**rebels, rebelling, rebelled**) 1. REVOLT AGAINST A GOVERNMENT to fight to overthrow a government or ruling power 2. PROTEST BY DEFYING AUTHORITY to protest sth by defying a government or other form of authority ○ *students rebelling against education funding cuts* 3. REFUSE TO CONFORM to refuse to conform to the usual codes and conventions of society 4. HAVE DISLIKE FOR STH to experience or express an intense dislike or distaste for sth [13thC. Via French *rebelle* from Latin *rebellis* from *bellum* 'war' (source of English *belligerent*). The underlying idea is of the defeated 'making war again' against their conquerors.]

rebellion /ri béllyən/ *n.* 1. ATTEMPT TO OVERTHROW GOVERNMENT an organized attempt to overthrow a government or other authority by the use of violence 2. DEFIANCE OF AUTHORITY opposition or defiance of authority, accepted moral codes, or social conventions

rebellious /ri béllyəss/ *adj.* 1. OPPOSING OR DEFYING AUTHORITY opposing or defying authority, accepted moral codes, or social conventions 2. FIGHTING TO OVERTHROW GOVERNMENT OR AUTHORITY fighting to overthrow a government or other authority —**rebelliously** *adv.* —**rebelliousness** *n.*

rebid *n.* /reé bid/ FURTHER BID IN BRIDGE a further bid in an auction at bridge, especially one of the same suit as a previous one ■ *vi.* /ri bíd/ (**-bids, -bidding, -bid** *or* **-bade** *or* **-bid, -bid**) BID FURTHER to make a bid in an auction at bridge after previously bidding no trump or a suit, especially one in the same suit

rebirth /reé búrth/ *n.* 1. REGENERATION OF STH DEAD OR DESTROYED the regeneration of sth that has died or has been destroyed 2. REVIVAL OF IDEAS OR FORCES the revival of important ideas or forces, usually as part of broad and significant change 3. RELIG REINCARNATION the act or process of reincarnation

reblochon /rə blósho N/ *n.* a soft delicately flavoured washed-rind cheese with a pale pinkish skin, made in the Savoy region of France [Early 20thC. From French, from *reblocher* 'to milk for a second time'.]

reboot *vti.* /reé bóot/ (**-boots, -booting, -booted**) RESTART COMPUTER to restart a computer or an operating system, or to be restarted ■ *n.* /reé boot/ RESTART OF COMPUTER a restart of a computer or an operating system

rebore *vt.* /reé báwr/ (**-bores, -boring, -bored**) BORE OUT CYLINDERS AND FIT PISTONS to enlarge the bore hole of a cylinder in a car's engine and fit it with new pistons ■ *n.* /reé bawr/ PROCESS OF REBORING the process of reboring a cylinder, or all the cylinders in an engine

reborn /reé bawrn/ *adj.* recreated or regenerated, especially in order to be more effective or modern, or renewed spiritually

rebound *vi.* /ri bównd/ (**-bounds, -bounding, -bounded**) 1. SPRING BACK to spring back or recoil 2. MOVE BACK TO PREVIOUS LEVEL to recover from a setback and move back to a previous or higher level or position ■ *n.* /reé bownd/ 1. UPWARD MOVEMENT an upward movement or a recovery, especially after a setback 2. SPORTS BALL THAT BOUNCES a ball that bounces back, particularly off a backboard or rim of the basket in basketball or off a goalkeeper or goalpost in hockey, football, or a similar sport —**rebounder** *n.* ◇ **on the rebound** starting sth new in the wake of a disappointment or setback, often the ending of a relationship, and therefore feeling uneasy or vulnerable

—— **WORD KEY: USAGE** ——

rebound or **redound**? In its figurative use, **rebound** is a metaphor based on the image of an object bouncing and returning. Just as a ball that **rebounds** affects the person who threw it, so an action or statement **rebounds** on its creator when it affects him or her directly, usually in an unpleasant or unwelcome way: *The council's decision to cut library services rebounded on councillors when they were unable to get the information they needed.* **Redound** does not have any physical meaning and is therefore not a metaphor. It is sometimes used in the same way as **rebound**, but in its primary meaning it is followed by *to* and means 'to contribute or lead to', with sth good or creditable as the object (the opposite connotation to **rebound**): *The individual performances redounded to the benefit of the team as a whole.* Note that only **rebound** can be used as a noun.

rebuff /ri búf/ *vt.* (**-buffs, -buffing, -buffed**) 1. REJECT OR SNUB STH to reject or snub an offer, advance, or approach made by sb 2. REPEL ATTACK to beat back or repel an attack or an attacking force ■ *n.* 1. REJECTION a blunt rejection or snub of an offer, advance, or approach made by sb else 2. SETBACK a sudden severe setback to progress [Late 16thC. Via obsolete French *rebuffer* and Italian *ribuffare* 'to scold' from, ultimately, *buffo* 'puff', originally an imitation of the sound.]

rebuild /reé bíld/ (**-builds, -building, -built** /-bílt/, **-built**) *vt.* 1. BUILD STRUCTURE AGAIN to construct a building or other structure again because it has been damaged or destroyed 2. RESTORE STH to work to restore sth that has been weakened, damaged, or ruined 3. MAKE MAJOR CHANGES TO STH to make major alterations or improvements to sth ○ *to rebuild society for the information age*

rebuke /ri byoók/ *vt.* (**-bukes, -buking, -buked**) TELL SB OFF to criticize or reprimand sb, usually sharply ■ *n.* A TELLING OFF a reprimand or expression of criticism or disapproval [14thC. From Anglo-Norman and Old Northern French *rebuker*, literally 'to chop wood', from, ultimately, Old French *busche* 'log', of prehistoric Germanic origin.] —**rebuker** *n.*

Rebus

rebus /reé bəss/ (*plural* **-buses**) *n.* 1. WORD PUZZLE a puzzle in which the syllables of words and names are represented either by pictures of things that sound the same, or by letters 2. HERALDRY HERALDIC EMBLEM a heraldic emblem showing a picture that represents the name of the bearer, e.g. a picture of a lion for sb named Lyon [Early 17thC. Via French from Latin, literally 'by things', from *res* 'thing'. Perhaps from the phrase *non verbis sed rebus* 'not by words but by things'.]

rebut /ri bút/ (**-buts, -butting, -butted**) *vti.* to deny the truth of sth, especially by presenting arguments that disprove it [13thC. Via Anglo-Norman *rebuter* from Old French *reboter*, from *boter* (see BUTT[1]).] —**rebuttable** *adj.* —**rebuttal** *n.*

rebutter /ri búttər/ *n.* 1. LAW DEFENDANT'S ANSWER the defendant's answer in the third round of pleading in a legal action 2. SB WHO REBUTS sb who rebuts sth

rec /rek/ *n.* (*informal*) 1. RECREATION recreation (*often used before a noun*) ○ *rec room* 2. RECREATION GROUND a recreation ground [Early 20thC. Shortening.]

rec. *abbr.* 1. receipt 2. received 3. recipe 4. recommended 5. MAIL recorded 6. recorder 7. recording 8. recreation

recalcitrant /ri kálssitrənt/ *adj.* 1. RESISTING CONTROL stubbornly resisting the authority or control of another 2. HARD TO DO OR HANDLE difficult to deal with or operate ○ *struggling in front of the mirror with a recalcitrant tie* ■ *n.* STUBBORN OPPONENT sb who stubbornly resists authority or control by another ○ *A few recalcitrants refused to submit.* [Mid-19thC. Directly or via French from Latin *recalcitrant-* present participle stem of *recalcitrare*, literally 'to kick back' (used of horses), from *calcitrare* 'to kick (with the heels)', from the stem of *calc-* 'heel'.] —**recalcitrance** *n.*

—— **WORD KEY: SYNONYMS** ——
See Synonyms at **unruly**.

recalculate /reé kálkyoo layt/ (**-lates, -lating, -lated**) *vti.* to calculate sth again in order to make sure it is correct, or to incorporate new information —**recalculation** /reé kálkyoo láysh'n/ *n.*

recalesce /reékə léss/ (**-lesces, -lescing, -lesced**) *vi.* to exhibit or undergo a sudden increase in temperature [Late 19thC. Back-formation from RECALESCENCE.]

recalescence /reékə léss'ns/ *n.* a sudden increase in the temperature and brightness of a cooling metal, caused by the release of latent heat as the metal undergoes a change in crystalline structure [Late 19thC. Formed from Latin *calescere* 'to grow warm', from *calere* 'to be warm' (source of English *nonchalant*).] —**recalescent** *adj.*

recall /ri káwl/ *v.* (**-calls, -calling, -called**) 1. *vti.* REMEMBER STH to remember sth or bring sth back to mind ○ *I don't recall what she was wearing.* 2. *vt.* ORDER SB OR STH BACK to order sb or sth to come back or be sent back 3. *vt.* REVOKE STH to revoke or cancel a previous decision or instruction 4. *vt.* BRING ATTENTION BACK to bring sb's attention or thoughts back to an ongoing matter 5. *vt.* RESEMBLE SB OR STH to remind another person of sb or sth familiar or previously seen ○ *Her face recalls that of her grandmother.* ■ *n.* **1. RECALLING OF STH** the remembering of sth or the calling back of sb or sth **2. MEMORY** sb's memory or ability to remember ○ *a vague recall of the actual events* **3. REVOCATION** a revocation or cancellation of a previous decision or instruction **4.** MIL **SIGNAL TO RETURN** a signal, especially a bugle call, ordering troops to return to their positions or to a rallying point **5.** COMM **MANUFACTURER'S REQUEST TO RETURN PRODUCT** a request by a manufacturer to return a product because of a defect or contamination [Late 16thC. Formed from CALL on the model of French *rappeler* or Latin *revocare*.] —**recallability** /ri káwlə bílləti/ *n.* —**recallable** /ri káwləb'l/ *adj.* —**recaller** *n.*

recamier /ray kámmi ay/ *n.* a couch with a high headrest and low footrest, often without a back [Early 20thC. Named after Jeanne *Récamier* (1777–1849), French hostess, portrayed reclining on a couch in a painting.]

recanalization /ree kánnə lī záysh'n/, **recanalisation** *n.* the surgical unblocking of an obstructed vessel within the body or the reconnection of a tube or duct

recant /ri kánt/ (**-cants, -canting, -canted**) *vti.* to deny believing in sth or withdraw sth previously said ○ *She stands by what she said and refuses to recant.* [Mid-16thC. From Latin *recantare*, literally 'to sing back' (modelled on Greek *palinōidein* 'to recant'), from *cantare* 'to sing'.] —**recantation** /rée kan táysh'n/ *n.* —**recanter** /ri kántər/ *n.*

recap[1] /ree káp/ *vti.* (**-caps, -capping, -capped**) **RESTATE MAIN POINTS** to go over the main points of sth such as an argument or a proposal again ■ *n.* **SUMMARY** a summing-up of the main points of sth previously put forward, e.g. a proposal [Mid-20thC. Shortening.]

recap[2] /rée kap/ *n.* *ANZ, US* TRANSP **RETREAD** a retread ■ *vt.* (**-caps, -capping, -capped**) *ANZ, US* **RETREAD A TYRE** to retread a tyre [Mid-20thC. Formed from CAP. Originally in the sense 'to put a cap on sth again'.] —**recappable** /ree káppəb'l/ *adj.*

recapitalize /ree káppitə līz/ (**-izes, -izing, -ized**), **recapitalise** (**-ises, -ising, -ised**) *vt.* to supply a business with new capital or change the way in which its capital is held —**recapitalization** /ree káppitə lī záysh'n/ *n.*

recapitulate /rée kə píchoo layt/ (**-lates, -lating, -lated**) *v.* **1.** *vti.* **RECAP** to recap (*formal*) **2.** *vt.* BIOL **REPEAT EVOLUTIONARY STAGES AS EMBRYO** to repeat stages from the evolution of the species during the embryonic period of an animal's life [Late 16thC. Partly from Latin *recapitulat-*, past participle stem of *recapitulare*, literally 'to restate by chapters', from *capitulum* 'chapter' (source of English *chapter*); partly a back-formation from RECAPITULATION.] —**recapitulative** /-píchoo lətiv/ *adj.* —**recapitulatory** /-píchələtəri/ *adj.*

recapitulation /rée kə píchoo láysh'n/ *n.* **1. RECAP** a summing-up of the main points of sth (*formal*) **2.** BIOL **REPEATING EVOLUTIONARY STAGES DURING EMBRYONIC PERIOD** the theoretical process of going through successive stages during the embryonic period of an animal's life that duplicate the evolutionary stages the species experienced **3.** MUSIC **REPETITION OF THEMES** the repetition of earlier themes in a piece of music, especially in sonata form at the end of a movement [14thC. Directly or via French from the late Latin stem *recapitulation* from Latin *recapitulat-* (see RECAPITULATE).]

recaption /ree kápsh'n/ *n.* LAW the taking back, by peaceful means, of property from sb who has unlawfully taken it, or of a spouse or child from sb who has unlawfully detained him or her [Early 17thC. From the Anglo-Latin stem *recaption-* 'capturing back', from Latin *captio* 'capturing' Originally in English, 'second legal seizure of another's goods'.]

recapture /ree kápchər/ *vt.* (**-tures, -turing, -tured**) **1. CAPTURE SB OR STH AGAIN** to capture again or take back sb or sth that has escaped or that has been taken away **2. EXPERIENCE STH AGAIN** to have, show, or experience again sth that existed in the past or has been lost ○ *a failed attempt to recapture their youth* ■ *n.* **1. TAKING BACK OF STH** the capture of sb or sth that has escaped or that has been taken away ○ *the information that led to his recapture* **2. EXPERIENCING OF STH AGAIN** the having, showing, or experiencing again of sth that is in the past or has been lost ○ *the recapture of youthful joys*

recast /ree kaast/ (**-casts, -casting, -cast**) *vt.* **1. CAST OBJECT AGAIN** to repeat the casting process for an object formed in a mould **2. CHANGE STH** to change the form of sth ○ *The experience led him to recast his philosophy of life.* **3. GIVE ROLES TO DIFFERENT ACTORS** to assign roles in sth such as a play or film to different actors ○ *recast the play for a road tour*

recce /réki/ *n.* **RECONNAISSANCE** a reconnaissance (*slang*) ○ *He's gone for a recce along the beach.* ■ *vt.* (**-ces, -ceing, -ced**) **RECONNOITRE STH** to reconnoitre sth (*slang*) [Mid-20thC. Shortening and alteration.]

recd, rec'd *abbr.* received

recede /ri seed/ (**-cedes, -ceding, -ceded**) *vi.* **1. GO BACK** to go back or down from a certain point or level ○ *waiting for the flood waters to recede* **2. GET FURTHER AWAY** to become more distant or unlikely ○ *As the ship gathered speed, the island receded in the distance.* **3. SLOPE** to slope backwards **4. GO BALD** to gradually go bald from the front of the head backwards **5. BECOME LESS** to become less in value or quality ○ *The value of her shares receded sharply.* **6. WITHDRAW** engage in a retreat [15thC. Directly or via Old French *receder* from Latin *recedere*, literally 'to go back', from *cedere* (see CEDE).]

receipt /ri seet/ *n.* **1. ACKNOWLEDGMENT OF RECEIVING** a written or printed acknowledgment that sth such as money or goods has been given to the person who issues the acknowledgment ○ *The shop will exchange goods if you have a receipt.* **2. ACT OF RECEIVING** the receiving of sth ○ *The balance is payable on receipt of the goods.* **3.** COOK **RECIPE** a recipe (*old*) ■ **receipts** *npl.* **AMOUNT RECEIVED** the amount of money or goods received, especially in business ○ *Receipts are down on last month.* ■ *v.* (**-ceipts, -ceipting, -ceipted**) **1.** *vt.* **ACKNOWLEDGE PAYMENT BY SIGNING** to acknowledge, with a signature, that a bill has been paid **2.** *vti.* **GIVE RECEIPT** to give a receipt for money or goods [14thC. From Anglo-Norman or Old Northern French *receite* '(medicinal) recipe, receipt', from, ultimately, Latin *recipere* (see RECEIVE).]

receivable /ri seevəb'l/ *adj.* **1. SUITABLE TO BE RECEIVED** suitable to be received, especially as payment ○ *receivable notes* **2. AWAITING PAYMENT** used to describe a bill or account that is due to be paid ■ **receivables** *npl.* **MONEY OWED** business assets consisting of amounts of money that a company is owed

receive /ri seev/ (**-ceives, -ceiving, -ceived**) *v.* **1.** *vti.* **GET STH** to take or accept sth given ○ *It is better to give than to receive.* **2.** *vti.* **CONVERT ELECTRONIC SIGNALS** to pick up electronic signals and convert them into sound or pictures ○ *This radio is able to transmit and receive.* **3.** *vt.* **TAKE DELIVERY OF MESSAGE** to take delivery of a message, e.g. a letter or telephone call ○ *We've received a few complaints.* **4.** *vt.* **LEARN INFORMATION** to learn of sth such as news or information **5.** *vt.* **MEET WITH STH** to meet with or experience sth ○ *We received a warm reception from the crowd.* **6.** *vt.* **BEAR STH** to bear or sustain sth such as a burden ○ *The bridge is reinforced to receive the weight of heavy traffic.* **7.** *vt.* **CATCH STH** to hold or take sth ○ *A water butt receives the overflow from the guttering.* **8.** *vt.* **BE HURT BY STH** to be subjected to sth such as an injury, blow, or pressure ○ *The parachutist received the full force of the earth's gravity upon landing.* **9.** *vt.* **ACQUIRE STH** to come to have sth, e.g. through effort **10.** *vti.* **ENTERTAIN VISITORS** to be at home or available to entertain visitors ○ *Find out the hours during which patients can receive visitors.* **11.** *vt.* **GREET GUESTS** to greet and admit guests ○ *We were received by the duke himself.* **12.** *vt.* **ADMIT SB** to allow a person entry ○ *A knight had to prove himself worthy before being received into their fellowship.* **13.** *vt.* **REACT TO STH** to react to sth in a specified way ○ *The proposals were not well received by the members.* **14.** *vt.* **HEAR AND ACKNOWLEDGE STH** to hear and acknowledge sth formally ○ *The priest received her confession.* **15.** *vti.* LAW **ACCEPT STOLEN GOODS** to accept or deal in stolen goods **16.** *vi.* CHR **TAKE COMMUNION** to partake of Holy Communion **17.** *vti.* SPORTS **PLAY BALL SENT BY OPPONENT** to catch, hit, or kick a ball played by an opponent [14thC. Via Old French *receivre* from, ultimately, Latin *recipere*, literally 'to take back', from *capere* 'to take' (source of English *captive*, *capture*, and *conceive*).]

received /ri seevd/ *adj.* generally accepted as true ○ *The received wisdom in these matters is seldom wrong.*

Received Pronunciation *n.* the accent of British English that educated people from the southern part of England traditionally use, widely regarded as the least regionally modified of all British accents

receiver /ri seevər/ *n.* **1. SB WHO RECEIVES STH** sb who takes or accepts sth given or takes delivery of sth sent **2.** TELECOM **PART OF A PHONE** the part of a telephone that contains the earpiece and mouthpiece and receives and converts electronic signals into sound **3.** ELECTRON ENG **DEVICE FOR PICKING UP SIGNALS** an electrical device that receives and converts electronic signals into sound or pictures **4.** FIN **SB COURT APPOINTS TO RUN BUSINESS** sb appointed by a court to manage a business or property that is involved in a legal process such as bankruptcy **5.** LAW **SB DEALING IN STOLEN GOODS** sb who knowingly buys and sells stolen goods **6.** CHEM **COLLECTING VESSEL IN CHEMISTRY** a vessel used during distillation to collect the distillate **7.** FOOTBALL US **PLAYER CATCHING FORWARD PASS** an American football player on the attacking side who is eligible to catch a forward pass **8.** BASEBALL **CATCHER** a catcher

receivership /ri seevərship/ *n.* LAW **1. OFFICE OF RECEIVER** the office or duties of sb appointed by a court to manage a business or property that is involved in a legal process such as bankruptcy **2. BEING IN HANDS OF RECEIVER** management by a receiver of a business or property that is involved in a legal process such as bankruptcy ○ *The company is now in receivership.*

receiving end *n.* the position of having to endure sth ○ *We were on the receiving end of some harsh criticism.*

receiving order *n.* a court order that appoints a receiver to take charge of a business involved in a legal proceeding such as bankruptcy

recension /ri sénsh'n/ *n.* **1. CRITICAL REVISION** a critical revision carried out on a literary text **2. REVISED TEXT** a literary text that has been given a critical revision [Mid-17thC. From the Latin stem *recension-* 'review', from *recensere*, literally 'to reassess', from *censere* 'to appraise, assess'.]

recent /reess'nt/ *adj.* **1. HAVING HAPPENED NOT LONG AGO** having happened or appeared not long ago ○ *the recent birth of her child* **2. MODERN** from current times or the very near past ○ *recent political trends* [15thC. Directly or via French from Latin *recent-*, the stem of *recens*, of uncertain origin: perhaps related to Greek *kainos* 'new'.] —**recency** *n.* —**recently** *adv.* —**recentness** *n.*

Recent /reess'nt/ *adj.*, *n.* = **Holocene**

receptacle /ri séptək'l/ *n.* **1. CONTAINER** a container that holds, contains, or receives a liquid or solid **2.** BOT **FLOWER-BEARING PART OF PLANT** the end of a flower stalk, bearing the parts of a flower or the florets of a composite flower **3.** BOT **PLANT PART BEARING REPRODUCTIVE ORGANS** in a plant that reproduces through spores, e.g. an alga or liverwort, the part that bears the reproductive organs [14thC. Directly or via French from Latin *receptaculum*, literally 'place in which to store sth received', from, ultimately, *recipere* (see RECEIVE).]

reception /ri sépsh'n/ *n.* **1. ACT OF RECEIVING** the receiving of sth given or sent **2. WAY SB OR STH IS RECEIVED** the way in which sb or sth is received or greeted ○ *The audience gave her a warm reception.* **3. FORMAL PARTY** a formal party to welcome sb or celebrate an event, e.g. a wedding **4. PLACE WHERE VISITORS ARE RECEIVED** a place in a hotel, office, or public building where visitors are first received ○ *I'll be waiting for you in reception.* **5.** ELECTRON ENG **CONVERSION OF ELECTRONIC SIGNALS** the receiving and conversion of electronic signals **6.** BROADCAST **QUALITY OF SIGNAL** the quality of the signal received by a radio or television set ○ *We don't get very good reception on this channel.* **7.** = **reception room** **8.** FOOTBALL US **CATCHING OF FORWARD PASS** in American football, the catching of a pass made towards the opponent's goal **9.** EDUC **FIRST CLASS AT INFANT SCHOOL** the class of children beginning their first year of full-time education [14thC. Directly or via French from the Latin stem *reception-*, from, ultimately, *recipere* (see RECEIVE).]

reception centre *n.* **1. TEMPORARY HOME** a place that accommodates people in need of shelter, e.g. homeless people, refugees, or victims of natural disasters, until more permanent accommodation can be found **2.** CHILDREN'S HOME a children's home run by a local authority to house children whose families cannot look after them, either temporarily or for a longer period

receptionist /ri sépsh'nist/ *n.* an employee who greets visitors, customers, or patients, answers the telephone, and makes appointments

reception room *n.* **1.** ROOM FOR ENTERTAINING GUESTS a room used for entertaining guests in a house ○ *The house has four bedrooms and two reception rooms.* **2.** ROOM IN HOTEL FOR ENTERTAINING a room used for a party or reception in a hotel

receptive /ri séptiv/ *adj.* **1.** WILLING TO ACCEPT ready and willing to accept sth, e.g. new ideas ○ *The city's art collectors were highly receptive to the new wave in painting.* **2.** ABLE TO RECEIVE able to receive sth ○ *countries that were not immediately receptive to the refugees* **3.** QUICK TO LEARN quick to take in new information **4.** PHYSIOL ABLE TO RECEIVE STIMULI capable of transmitting and receiving stimuli (*refers to a sensory organ*) [15thC. Directly or via French from medieval Latin *receptivus*, from, ultimately, Latin *recipere* (see RECEIVE).] —**receptively** *adv.* —**receptiveness** *n.* —**receptivity** /reé sep tívvəti/ *n.*

receptor /ri séptər/ *n.* **1.** PHYSIOL SENSITIVE NERVE ENDING a nerve ending that is sensitive to stimuli and can convert them into nerve impulses **2.** ELECTRON ENG RECEIVING DEVICE a device designed to receive electronic signals **3.** CHEM SPECIFIC CELL BINDING SITE OR MOLECULE a molecule, group, or site that is in a cell or on a cell surface and binds with a specific molecule, antigen, hormone, or antibody **4.** ENVIRON RECEIVER OF POLLUTION sb or sth adversely affected by a pollutant [15thC. Directly or via Old French *receptour* 'person who harbours criminals or stolen goods' (the original English sense) from Latin *receptor*, from, ultimately, *recipere* (see RECEIVE).]

recess /ri séss, reé sess/ *n.* **1.** ARCHIT INDENTED OR HOLLOWED-OUT SPACE an area such as an alcove or niche, set into a wall or other flat surface ○ *a recess large enough to take a bed* **2.** REMOTE PLACE a remote or secluded place (*often used in the plural*) ○ *A distant memory haunted the recesses of her mind.* **3.** POL BREAK FROM BUSINESS a time during which no work or business is done, specifically a long period in which a legislative body is not sitting **4.** *US, Can* EDUC BREAK FROM SCHOOL a break from classes during the school day or year ○ *played hopscotch during recess* **5.** LAW PERIOD WHEN COURT DOES NOT SIT a period of time of varying length when a court of law does not sit ○ *The court will stand in recess until noon on Friday.* **6.** ANAT BODY CAVITY a concave area or cavity in a part of the body ■ *vt.* (**-cesses, -cessing, -cessed**) **1.** PUT STH IN ALCOVE to put sth in a recess, especially in a wall ○ *a chapel recessed in a transept of the cathedral* **2.** MAKE INDENTATION IN STH to make a recess in sth, especially a wall ○ *The north wall of the chamber has been recessed to form an alcove.* [Mid-16thC. Directly or via Old French *reces* from Latin *recessus*, literally 'going back', from *recedere* (see RECEDE).]

recession /ri sésh'n/ *n.* **1.** ECON DEPRESSION IN ECONOMIC ACTIVITY a period, shorter than a depression, during which there is a decline in economic trade and prosperity **2.** CHR WITHDRAWAL OF SB IN CEREMONY the withdrawal of the participants in a ceremony, e.g. the clergy and choir after a church service **3.** RECEDING a going back or becoming more distant

recessional /ri sésh'nəl/ *adj.* RELATING TO RECESSION involving or typical of a recession ■ *n.* CHR TYPE OF HYMN a hymn sung as the clergy and choir withdraw from a church after a service

recessive /ri séssiv/ *adj.* **1.** RECEDING tending to go backwards or to recede ○ *recessive flood waters* **2.** GENETICS PRODUCING EFFECT IN CERTAIN CONDITIONS ONLY used to describe a gene that produces an effect in an organism only when its matching allele is identical. The effect is masked when the matching allele is nonidentical. **3.** GENETICS CONTROLLED BY RECESSIVE GENE used to describe a characteristic or trait determined by a recessive gene **4.** LING FALLING AT BEGINNING OF WORD used to describe stress that is placed at or near the beginning of a word ■ *n.* GENETICS **1.** RECESSIVE GENE OR TRAIT a recessive gene or trait **2.** ORGANISM WITH RECESSIVE GENE OR TRAIT an organism that has a recessive gene or trait —**recessively** *adv.* —**recessiveness** *n.*

Rechabite /rékə bīt/ *n.* sb who abstains totally from alcoholic drink, especially a member of the Independent Order of Rechabites, an organization of such abstainers founded in 1835 [14thC. From ecclesiastical Latin *Rechabita* 'descendants of Rechab', a translation of Hebrew *rēkābīm*, from *rēkāb* 'Rechab' (the Bible, *Jeremiah* 35:6), whose descendants refused to drink wine.]

recharge /ree chaárj/ (**-charges, -charging, -charged**) *vt.* **1.** REPLENISH ELECTRICITY IN STH to replenish the amount of electric power in sth, especially a battery **2.** RENEW STH to renew sth, e.g. sb's energy ○ *We felt recharged after the weekend.* [15thC. Partly formed from *charge*; partly modelled on French *recharger*. Originally in English, 'to reload (a vessel)'.] —**rechargeable** *adj.* —**recharger** *n.*

réchauffé /ray shō fay/ *n.* **1.** REHEATED FOOD a dish of reheated leftovers **2.** REUSED MATERIAL a piece of work, e.g. a piece of writing, that is merely a reuse of old material [Early 19thC. From French, the past participle of *réchauffer* 'to reheat'.]

recherché /rə sháir shay/ *adj.* **1.** RARE AND EXQUISITE marked by such rare and exquisite quality that it is known only to connoisseurs **2.** APPRECIATING FINE THINGS having a deep appreciation of unusual or choice things ○ *a recherché taste in sculpture* **3.** AFFECTED marked by excessive refinement or exaggerated importance ○ *Some of his ideas are a little recherché for my taste.* [Late 17thC. From French, the past participle of *rechercher*, literally 'to seek thoroughly', from *chercher* 'to seek'.]

recidivism /ri síddivizəm/ *n.* the tendency to relapse into a previous undesirable type of behaviour, especially crime [Late 19thC. Formed from *recidivist*, which came via French *récidiviste* from, ultimately, Latin *recidivus* 'falling back', from *recidere* 'to fall back', from *cadere* 'to fall'.] —**recidivist** *n., adj.* —**recidivistic** /ri síddi vístik/ *adj.*

Recife /re seéfə/ capital city of Pernambuco State, northeastern Brazil, and the major city of the region. It is a port on the Atlantic Ocean. Population: 1,342,877 (1996).

recip. *abbr.* **1.** reciprocity **2.** MATH reciprocal

recipe /réssəpi/ *n.* **1.** COOK INSTRUCTIONS FOR MAKING FOOD a list of ingredients and instructions for making sth, especially a food dish **2.** METHOD a method of doing sth or a combination of circumstances likely to bring sth about ○ *Hard work is the recipe for success.* **3.** MED PRESCRIPTION a prescription for a therapeutic preparation (*archaic*) [14thC. Directly or via French from Latin, 'take!' (the original sense in English), a form of *recipere* (see RECEIVE).]

recipience /ri síppi ənss/, **recipiency** /-ənssi/ *n.* **1.** ACT OF RECEIVING the receiving of sth **2.** RECEPTIVENESS the tendency or ability to receive

recipient /ri síppi ənt/ *n.* RECEIVER sb or sth that receives sth ■ *adj.* RECEIVING tending or able to receive [Mid-16thC. Directly or via French from Latin *recipient-*, the present participle stem of *recipere* (see RECEIVE).]

reciprocal /ri sípprək'l/ *adj.* **1.** GIVEN BY EACH SIDE given or shown by each of two sides or individuals to the other ○ *reciprocal compliments* **2.** IN RETURN given or done in return for sth else ○ *a reciprocal attack on the aggressor* **3.** MATH MULTIPLIED TO GIVE ONE used to describe a number or quality that is related to another by the fact that when multiplied together the product is one **4.** MATH COMPLEMENTING serving to complement one another ■ *n.* **1.** STH MUTUAL sth that is mutual or done in return **2.** MATH NUMBER MULTIPLIED TO GIVE ONE a number or quantity that is related to another by the fact that when multiplied together the product is one ○ *4 and $\frac{1}{4}$ are reciprocals* [Late 16thC. Formed from Latin *reciprocus*, literally 'that goes backwards and forwards', from, ultimately, *re-* 'backwards' + *pro-* 'forwards'.] —**reciprocality** /ri sípprə kálləti/ *n.* —**reciprocally** /ri sípprəkli/ *adv.* —**reciprocalness** *n.*

reciprocal pronoun *n.* a word or phrase such as 'each other' representing two or more things that mutually correspond to one another

reciprocate /ri sípprə kayt/ (**-cates, -cating, -cated**) *v.* **1.** *vti.* GIVE MUTUALLY to give or feel sth mutually or in return ○ *I couldn't accept such a generous gift without reciprocating.* **2.** *vti.* ENG MOVE BACKWARDS AND FORWARDS to move backwards and forwards in an alternating motion, or move sth in this way **3.** *vi.* BE COMPLEMENTARY to be the same or complementary [Late 16thC. From Latin *reciprocat-*, the past participle stem of *reciprocare* 'to move back and forth, reciprocate', from *reciprocus* (see RECIPROCAL).] —**reciprocation** /ri sípprə káysh'n/ *n.* —**reciprocative** /ri sípprəkətiv/ *adj.* —**reciprocator** /-kaytər/ *n.*

reciprocating engine *n.* an engine with one or more cylinders in which pistons move backwards and forwards

reciprocity /réssi próssəti/ (*plural* **-ties**) *n.* **1.** RECIPROCAL RELATIONSHIP OR ACT sth done mutually or in return **2.** RELATIONSHIP INVOLVING MUTUAL EXCHANGE a relationship between people involving the exchange of goods, services, favours, or obligations, especially a mutual exchange of privileges between trading nations ○ *the long-standing tariff reciprocity between our two countries* [Mid-18thC. From French *réciprocité*, from, ultimately, Latin *reciprocus* (see RECIPROCAL).]

reciprocity failure *n.* in photography, the failure of light intensity and exposure time to act reciprocally when their values are extremely high or low, sometimes affecting the colour characteristics of the resulting photograph

recision /ri sízh'n/ *n.* the cancellation or rescinding of sth [Early 17thC. Via the Latin stem *recision-*, literally 'cutting back', from, ultimately, Latin *recidere*, literally 'to cut back', from *caedere* 'to cut' (source of English *circumcise*).]

recit. *abbr.* MUSIC recitative

recital /ri sít'l/ *n.* **1.** ARTS SOLO PERFORMANCE a performance given by a solo musician or dancer, or a series of solo performances by a group of musicians or dancers **2.** ARTS PERFORMANCE BY MUSIC OR DANCE STUDENTS a performance given by music or dance students to demonstrate the progress they have made **3.** RECITING OF STH the reading aloud or reciting from memory of sth such as a poem ○ *a lively recital of a poem by Burns* **4.** DETAILED ACCOUNT a detailed account or report of sth ○ *his recital of the events of the day* **5.** LAW DETAILED PRESENTATION OF FACT a statement in a judgment laying out jurisdictional facts, or a deed's preliminary part laying out the circumstances leading to its existence (*often used in the plural*) —**recitalist** *n.*

recitation /réssi táysh'n/ *n.* **1.** READING ALOUD the public reading aloud of sth or reciting of sth from memory, especially poetry **2.** MATTER READ ALOUD material read aloud or recited from memory in public, especially poetry **3.** REPORTING OF STH the listing or reporting of sth [15thC]

recitative[1] /réssitə teév/, **recitativo** /-teévō/ (*plural* **-vos**) *n.* **1.** SINGING LIKE SPEECH a style of singing that is close to the rhythm of natural speech, used in opera for dialogue and narration **2.** PASSAGE SUNG LIKE SPEECH a passage in a musical composition that is sung in the form of recitative [Mid-17thC. Formed from Italian *recitativo*, from Latin *recitat-*, the past participle stem of *recitare* (see RECITE).]

recitative[2] /ri sítətiv/ *adj.* relating to recital or recitation [Mid-17thC. Via Italian *recitativo* from, ultimately, Latin *recitare* (see RECITE).]

recite /ri sít/ (**-cites, -citing, -cited**) *v.* **1.** *vti.* REPEAT OR READ ALOUD to read sth aloud or repeat sth from memory, especially for an audience **2.** *vt.* EDUC REPEAT STH LEARNT to repeat aloud sth learnt, e.g. a lesson in school **3.** *vt.* GIVE DETAILED ACCOUNT OF STH to give a detailed account of an occurrence or event ○ *There's no need to recite every detail of your weekend.* **4.** *vt.* LIST STH to give a list of sth ○ *He then recited all my faults.* [15thC. Directly or via French *réciter* from Latin *recitare*, literally 'to summon again', from *citare* (see CITE).] —**reciter** *n.*

reck /rek/ (**recks, recking, recked**) *vti.* (*archaic*) **1.** CARE to care or mind about sth **2.** MATTER to matter to, or matter to sb [Old English *rēcan* (recorded only in the past tense), *reccan* 'to care, take care of, be interested in'. From a prehistoric Germanic base that also produced English *reckless*.]

reckless /rékləss/ *adj.* marked by a lack of thought about danger or other possible undesirable consequences ○ *with a reckless disregard for the established safety procedures* [Old English *rec(c)elēas*. From a prehistoric Germanic word (ancestor also of German *ruchlos* 'dastardly' and Dutch *roekeloos* 'reckless') formed from the base that produced English *reck*.] —**recklessly** *adv.* —**recklessness** *n.*

reckon /rékən/ (**-ons, -oning, -oned**) *v.* **1.** *vti.* COUNT to count or calculate sth ○ *I reckon the total at 200.* **2.** *vt.* REGARD SB OR STH AS STH to consider sb or sth to be sth (*often passive*) ○ *She's reckoned the best in her field.* **3.** *vt.* INCLUDE SB OR STH to include or class a person or thing as being part of a particular group ○ *I reckon him among my friends.* **4.** *vt.* THINK OR BELIEVE STH to suppose sth to be true (*regional*) ○ *I reckon we're finished now.* **5.** *vt.* THINK HIGHLY OF STH OR SB to rate sth or sb highly (*informal*) ○ *This kid really reckons his chances of winning.* **6.** *vi.* DEPEND to expect with confident assurance (*informal*) ○ *You can reckon on my support.* [Old English *gerecenian* 'to explain, recount, tell'. From a prehistoric Germanic word (ancestor also of German *rechnen* 'to work out, calculate, estimate').]

WORD KEY: USAGE

I reckon you're right: The use of ***reckon*** meaning 'think, believe' and followed by a clause (with the word *that* present or suppressed) occurs occasionally in informal use only.

reckon with *vt.* **1.** BE FACED WITH SB to deal or come to terms with sb powerful ○ *If he lets you down he'll have me to reckon with.* **2.** ALLOW FOR SB OR STH to take sb or sth into account ○ *We didn't reckon with the strength of the tide.*

reckon without *vt.* to fail to take sth into account ○ *The government reckoned without the strength of public feeling against the new measure.*

reckoner /rékənər/ *n.* a book of tables of calculations that are already worked out and are used as an aid in calculation [12thC. Originally in the sense 'person who reckons'.]

reckoning /rékəning/ *n.* **1.** CALCULATION calculation of an aircraft's, a spacecraft's, or a vessel's position in the air, in space, or on the sea **2.** SETTLEMENT OF AN ACCOUNT the settlement of an account **3.** FIN ACCOUNT OR BILL a statement of debts owed or repaid **4.** TIME TO ACCOUNT FOR WRONGS a time to account for or be punished for wrongs ○ *day of reckoning*

reclaim /ri kláym/ *vt.* (**-claims, -claiming, -claimed**) **1.** CLAIM STH BACK to claim back sth that has been taken away or temporarily given to another **2.** CONVERT WASTELAND to convert unusable land, e.g. desert or marsh, into land suitable for farming or other use **3.** EXTRACT USEFUL SUBSTANCES to extract useful substances from waste or refuse **4.** MAKE SB VIRTUOUS AGAIN to make sb stop doing things regarded as immoral and return to virtue **5.** TAME A BIRD to tame a hawk or falcon ■ *n.* RECOVERY OR CONVERSION the reclaiming of sth, or the state of being reclaimed ○ *polluted land beyond reclaim.* [14thC. Via the Old French stem *reclaim-* from Latin *reclamare* 'to cry out against', from *clamare* (see CLAIM).] —**reclaimable** *adj.* —**reclaimant** *n.* —**reclaimer** *n.*

reclamation /réklə máysh'n/ *n.* **1.** ENVIRON CONVERSION OF LAND the conversion of unusable land, e.g. desert or marsh, into land suitable for farming or other uses **2.** ENVIRON EXTRACTION FROM WASTE the extraction of useful substances from waste or refuse **3.** RECLAIMING OF STH the claiming back of sth taken or given away [Early 16thC. Directly or via French from the Latin stem *reclamation-*, from, ultimately, *reclamare* (see RECLAIM).]

réclame /ray klaám/ *n.* **1.** FAME public attention or fame **2.** CAPACITY TO ATTRACT NOTORIETY the capacity or gift for attracting public attention or fame [Late 19thC. From French, literally 'advertisement', formed from *réclamer* (see RECLAIM).]

reclinate /rékli nayt/ *adj.* BOT used to describe a leaf or stem that is bent or curved backward or down [Mid-18thC]

recline /ri klín/ (**-clines, -clining, -clined**) *v.* **1.** *vi.* LIE BACK to lean back into a supported sloping or horizontal position, usually in order to rest or relax ○ *She was reclining on a chaise longue.* **2.** *vti.* TILT BACK to tilt back from an upright position, or make sth tilt back ○ *These seats are more comfortable because they recline.* [15thC. Directly or via Old French *recliner* from Latin *reclinare*, literally 'to bend back or against', from *clinare* 'to bend' (source of English *incline*).] —**reclinable** *adj.* —**reclination** /rékli náysh'n/ *n.*

recliner /ri klínər/ *n.* **1.** RECLINING CHAIR a chair that tilts back to a sloping or almost horizontal position, often with a footrest that can be raised, allowing the person sitting in it to rest more comfortably **2.** SB WHO RECLINES sb who lies back

recluse /ri klóoss/ *n.* **1.** SB LIVING APART FROM OTHERS sb who lives alone and deliberately keeps away from other people **2.** SB LIVING A LIFE OF PRAYER sb who lives a solitary life devoted to prayer and meditation ■ *adj.* RECLUSIVE reclusive (*archaic*) [12thC. Via French *reclus*, the past participle of Old French *reclure* 'to shut up', from Latin *recludere*, literally 'to shut again', from *claudere* 'to shut' (source of English *close*).] —**reclusion** /ri klóozh'n/ *n.*

reclusive /ri klóossiv/ *adj.* solitary and withdrawn from the rest of the world ○ *lead a reclusive existence* [Late 16thC. Formed from earlier English *recluse* 'to shut up', from Latin *reclus-*, the past participle stem of *recludere* (see RECLUSE).] —**reclusively** *adv.* —**reclusiveness** *n.*

recognise *vt.* = **recognize**

recognition /rékəg nísh'n/ *n.* **1.** RECOGNIZING OF STH OR BEING RECOGNIZED the perception that sb or sth has been seen before or an identification based on such perception **2.** APPRECIATION appreciation or fame earned by an achievement ○ *His pioneering work never got the recognition it deserved.* **3.** ACKNOWLEDGMENT acknowledgment of validity ○ *They'll need recognition from the committee in order to proceed.* **4.** POL ACCEPTANCE OF A COUNTRY'S EXISTENCE the formal acceptance by one country of the independent and legal status of another **5.** TOKEN OF ACKNOWLEDGMENT sth given or awarded as a token of acknowledgment or gratitude **6.** COMPUT SENSING OF DATA BY A COMPUTER the sensing and conversion of data into machine-readable form by a computer **7.** BIOL COMPATIBILITY OF MOLECULES the ability of molecules with complementary shapes to attach to one another [15thC. Directly or via Old French from the Latin stem *recognition-*, from *recognit-*, the past participle stem of *recognoscere* (see RECOGNIZE).] —**recognitive** /ri kógnətiv/ *adj.* —**recognitory** /-nətəri/ *adj.*

recognizance /ri kógnizənss/, **recognisance** *n.* **1.** LAW FORMAL BOND a formal agreement made by sb before a judge or magistrate to do sth, e.g. to appear in court at a set date ○ *He was released on his own recognizance.* **2.** FIN, LAW MONEY PLEDGED a sum of money pledged by sb making a recognizance, to be forfeited if the agreed act is not carried out **3.** RECOGNITION recognition (*archaic*) [14thC. From Old French *recon(u)issance*, an alteration (influenced by medieval Latin *recognizare* 'to recognize') of *reconoissance*, from the stem of *reconoistre* (see RECOGNIZE).] —**recognizant** *adj.*

recognize /rékəg nīz/ (**-nizes, -nizing, -nized**), **recognise** (**-nises, -nising, -nised**) *vt.* **1.** IDENTIFY SB OR STH SEEN BEFORE to identify a thing or person because of having perceived him, her, or it before ○ *If you saw him again, would you recognize him?* **2.** ACKNOWLEDGE SB'S ACHIEVEMENT to show appreciation of or give credit to another's achievement ○ *I hope you recognize their contribution to the success of the campaign.* **3.** ACCEPT STH to accept the validity or truth of sth ○ *I recognize that I am at fault.* **4.** ACCEPT STATE'S INDEPENDENCE to accept formally the independent and legal status of a country or regime ○ *refused to recognize the military government* **5.** ALLOW SB TO SPEAK to allow a person to speak to a meeting ○ *The chair recognizes the representative.* **6.** SHOW ACKNOWLEDGEMENT to show in some way that sb is personally known ○ *She recognized old friends in the crowd with a smile and a wave.* **7.** REWARD SB to give or award sth to a person as a token of acknowledgment or of gratitude ○ *The government recognized his services to industry with a knighthood.* **8.** BIOL BIND ANOTHER MOLECULE to bind another molecule that has a complementary structure [15thC. Via Old French *recon(n)iss-*, the stem of *reconnaistre*, from Latin *recognoscere* 'to know again', from *cognoscere* 'to know' (source of English *cognition* and *quaint*).] —**recognizability** /rékəg nīzə bílləti/ *n.* —**recognizable** /rékəg nīzəb'l/ *adj.* —**recognizably** *adv.* —**recognizer** *n.*

recognized /rékəg nīzd/, **recognised** *adj.* generally accepted as being true, valid, worthy, or rightful ○ *a recognized teaching qualification*

recoil *vi.* /ri kóyl/ (**-coils, -coiling, -coiled**) **1.** MOVE BACK SUDDENLY to move back suddenly and violently, e.g. after impact **2.** MOVE BACK IN HORROR to move back or away from sth in horror or disgust **3.** FAIL to go wrong and, as a consequence, hurt the perpetrator **4.** PHYS CHANGE MOMENTUM to experience a change in momentum as a result of a nuclear collision or the emission of an elementary particle ■ *n.* /ri kóyl, rée koyl/ **1.** SUDDEN BACKWARD MOVEMENT a sudden and violent backward movement, especially that of a firearm when it is fired **2.** MOVEMENT AWAY IN HORROR a movement back or away from sth, especially in horror or disgust ○ *his rapid recoil from the cockroach* **3.** PHYS CHANGE IN MOMENTUM a change in the momentum of an atom, nucleus, or elementary particle as a result of a nuclear collision or the emission of an elementary particle [12thC. Via French *reculer* from assumed Vulgar Latin *reculare*, literally 'to withdraw (your) backside', from Latin *culus* 'backside'. Originally in English, 'to force back'.] —**recoiler** /ri kóylər/ *n.*

WORD KEY: SYNONYMS

recoil, flinch, quail, shrink, wince

CORE MEANING: to draw back in fear or distaste

recoil is to draw back suddenly in fear, horror, disgust, or distaste. It can also mean to react mentally to sth with fear or disgust, causing reluctance to do or deal with that thing; **flinch** is to draw back physically because of fear or pain. It can also mean to react mentally to sth with fear or disgust, resulting in reluctance to do or deal with that thing; **quail** is to cower in fear. It also means to feel very reluctant to confront or face sth repellant or frightening; **shrink** is to move away physically from sth because of fear or disgust. It can also mean to indicate reluctance to do sth because of fear or disgust; **wince** is to move the body slightly in an involuntary reaction to a stimulus such as pain or great embarrassment.

recoilless /ri kóyl ləss/ *adj.* relating to a heavy firearm, e.g. an antitank gun, whose recoil is reduced by venting the blast to the rear

recoil-operated *adj.* using the movement caused by the recoil of a firearm to operate part of its mechanism

recollect /rékə lékt/ (**-lects, -lecting, -lected**) *vti.* to bring sth back to mind ○ *Can you recollect what she was wearing?* [Early 16thC. From Latin *recollect-*, the past participle stem of *recolligere* 'to gather again' (later 'to recall'), from *colligere* (see COLLECT).] —**recollective** *adj.* —**recollectively** *adv.*

re-collect (**re-collects, re-collecting, re-collected**) *vt.* **1.** REGAIN CONTROL OF STH to regain control, especially of the self **2.** COLLECT STH AGAIN to collect again sth that has been scattered or dispersed

recollection /rékə léksh'n/ *n.* **1.** REMEMBERING OF STH the remembering of sth, or the ability to remember ○ *That's not the way it happened, according to my recollection.* **2.** MEMORY sth that a person remembers ○ *a recollection of having met him before*

recombinant /ri kómbinənt/ *adj.* **1.** OF GENETIC RECOMBINATION relating to or involved in genetic recombination ○ *a recombinant chromosome* **2.** RELATING TO RECOMBINANT DNA relating to recombinant DNA or produced by recombinant DNA technology ■ *n.* **1.** RESULT OF GENETIC RECOMBINATION a cell or organism exhibiting genetic recombination **2.** GENETIC MATERIAL FROM GENE-SPLICING genetic material resulting from the splicing of DNA fragments

recombinant DNA *n.* DNA extracted from two or more different sources, e.g. genes from different organisms, and joined together to form a single molecule or fragment

recombination /rée kombi náysh'n/ *n.* GENETICS any process that gives rise to offspring that have combinations of genes different to those of either parent, such as crossing-over and independent assortment of chromosomes during gamete formation —**recombinational** *adj.*

recombine /réekəm bín/ (**-bines, -bining, -bined**) *vti.* **1.** JOIN AGAIN to become combined again or combine things again **2.** GENETICS EXPERIENCE OR CAUSE GENETIC RECOMBINATION to undergo or cause sth to undergo genetic recombination

recommend /rékə ménd/ (**-mends, -mending, -mended**) *vt.* **1.** SUGGEST STH AS BEST IDEA to suggest sth as worthy of being accepted, used, or done ○ *We recommend that you consider the consequences of your actions.* **2.** ENDORSE SB OR STH to endorse a person or thing as being the most worthy or pleasing ○ *recommended him for the promotion* **3.** **MAKE STH APPEALING OR ATTRACTIVE** to make sth worth doing or having because it is beneficial or pleasing ○ *The film has little to recommend it other than its special effects.* **4.** **ENTRUST SB TO ANOTHER** to entrust a person or thing to the care of another (*formal*) ○ *She was recommended to our care until her family returned.* [14thC. From medieval Latin *recommendare*, literally 'to commit thoroughly', from Latin *commendare* (see COMMEND).] —**recommendable** *adj.* —**recommendatory** *adj.* —**recommender** *n.*

WORD KEY: SYNONYMS

recommend, advise, advocate, counsel, suggest

CORE MEANING: to put foward ideas to sb deciding on a course of action

recommend is to put forward a person or thing as being particularly suitable in the circumstances; **advise** is used in a similar way to 'recommend', but usually suggests giving advice in a less forceful or definite way; **advocate** is a formal word meaning to recommend sth in a forceful way; **counsel** is a fairly formal word meaning the same as 'advise'; **suggest** is to recommend sth in a tentative way without putting pressure on anybody to do what is recommended.

recommendation /rékə men dáysh'n/ *n.* **1.** **RECOMMENDING OF STH** the suggestion or endorsement of sth as the most worthy **2.** **STH THAT RECOMMENDS** a favourable reference about sb or sth, or other endorsement of desirability ○ *You come to us with many recommendations.* **3.** **STH RECOMMENDED** the best course of action recommended ○ *My recommendation would be to leave on the next train.* [15thC]

recommit /reékə mít/ (**-mits, -mitting, -mitted**) *vt.* **1.** **SEND STH BACK** to return sth, usually a bill, to a committee for more discussion **2.** **COMMIT STH AGAIN** to commit sth or sb again —**recommittal** *n.* —**recommitment** *n.*

recompense /rékəm penss/ *vt.* (**-penses, -pensing, -pensed**) **1.** **PAY OR REWARD SB** to pay another for doing work or for performing a service **2.** **GIVE COMPENSATION** to give compensation to another for an injury or loss ○ *The state will recompense you for the accidental destruction of your property.* ■ *n.* **1.** **REMUNERATION** payment for services or work performed **2.** **COMPENSATION** compensation for a loss or injury [14thC. Directly or via French *récompenser* from late Latin *recompensare*, literally 'to balance out again', from Latin *compensare* 'to balance out' (source of English *compensate*).]

recompose /reékəm pṓz/ (**-poses, -posing, -posed**) *vt.* **1.** **CAUSE SB TO REGAIN COMPOSURE** to return to a calm or composed state of mind **2.** **CHANGE ARRANGEMENT** to change the arrangement or composition of a thing or group —**recomposition** /reékompə zísh'n/ *n.*

reconcile /rékən sīl/ (**-ciles, -ciling, -ciled**) *v.* **1.** *vt.* **MAKE PEOPLE FRIENDLY** to bring about a friendly relationship between disputing people or groups (*often passive*) **2.** *vt.* **END CONFLICT** to solve a dispute or end a quarrel ○ *reconciled their differences* **3.** *vt.* **MAKE SB ACCEPT STH** to make sb accept that sth undesirable cannot be changed ○ *He reconciled himself to the fact that his sporting career was over.* **4.** *vti.* **MAKE CONSISTENT OR COMPATIBLE** to make two or more apparently conflicting things consistent or compatible, or to become consistent or compatible ○ *trying to reconcile fitness with a penchant for fast food* [14thC. Directly or via French *réconcilier* from Latin *reconciliare*, literally 'to make friendly again', from *conciliare* 'to make friendly' (source of English *conciliate*), from *concilium* 'meeting' (source of English *council*).] —**reconcilability** /rékən sīlə bílləti/ *n.* —**reconcilable** /rékən sīləb'l/ *adj.* —**reconcilableness** *n.* —**reconcilably** *adv.* —**reconcilement** *n.* —**reconciler** *n.*

reconciliation /rékən sili áysh'n/ *n.* **1.** **RECONCILING OF PEOPLE** the ending of conflict or renewing of a friendly relationship between disputing people or groups ○ *a series of quarrels and reconciliations* **2.** **ACHIEVEMENT OF CONSISTENCY OR COMPATIBILITY** the making of two or more apparently conflicting things consistent or compatible ○ *the reconciliation of such action with his pacifist principles* **3.** CHR **SACRAMENT OF PENANCE** the sacrament in the Roman Catholic Church whereby an individual's sins are absolved through confession and penance [14thC. Directly or via French from the Latin stem *reconciliation-*, from, ultimately, *reconciliare* (see RECONCILE).] —**reconciliatory** /rékən sílli ətəri/ *adj.*

recondite /rékən dīt, ri kón-/ *adj.* **1.** **UNDERSTOOD ONLY BY EXPERTS** requiring special detailed knowledge in order to be understood ○ *the recondite lore of the ancient Persians* **2.** **DEALING WITH DIFFICULT MATERIAL** dealing with material that is too difficult to be understood by those without special knowledge ○ *recondite learning* **3.** **HIDDEN** hidden from view or knowledge (*archaic*) [Mid-17thC. From Latin *reconditus*, the past participle of *recondere*, literally 'to store away', from *condere* 'to store, hide' (source of English *condiment*).] —**reconditely** *adv.* —**reconditeness** *n.*

WORD KEY: SYNONYMS

See Synonyms at ***obscure***.

recondition /reékən dísh'n/ (**-tions, -tioning, -tioned**) *vt.* to bring sth back into good condition, especially by repairing it and replacing worn-out parts

WORD KEY: SYNONYMS

See Synonyms at ***renew***.

reconfirm /reékən fúrm/ (**-firms, -firming, -firmed**) *vt.* **1.** **CONFIRM STH AGAIN** to confirm sth such as an airline or hotel reservation again **2.** **STRENGTHEN COMMITMENT TO STH** to strengthen a commitment to or a belief in sth ○ *reconfirmed their wedding vows* —**reconfirmation** /reé konfər máysh'n/ *n.*

reconnaissance /ri kónniss'ns/ *n.* **1.** MIL **EXPLORATION TO GATHER INFORMATION** the exploration or examination of an area, especially to gather information about the strength and positioning of enemy forces ○ *We will make a final reconnaissance before dawn.* **2.** GEOG, GEOL **PRELIMINARY SURVEY** a preliminary inspection of a given area to obtain data concerning geographic, hydrographic, or similar information prior to a detailed or full survey [Early 19thC. From French, from *reconnaiss-*, the stem of *reconnaître* 'to reconnoitre', from Latin *recognoscere* (see RECOGNIZE).]

reconnect /reékə nékt/ (**-nects, -necting, -nected**) *vt.* to connect again sth that has been disconnected or cut off, e.g. a telephone communication or an electricity supply —**reconnection** *n.*

reconnoiter *n., vti.* US = **reconnoitre**

reconnoitre /rékə nóytər/ *vti.* (**-tres, -tring, -tred**) MIL **EXPLORE TO GATHER INFORMATION** to explore an area in order to gather information, especially about the strength and positioning of enemy forces ○ *reconnoitre the drop zone* ■ *n.* MIL **RECONNOITRING OF AREA** an exploration of an area in order to gather information [Early 18thC. Via obsolete French *reconnoître* from Latin *recognoscere* (see RECOGNIZE).] —**reconnoitrer** *n.*

reconsider /reékən síddər/ (**-ers, -ering, -ered**) *vti.* to think about sth again, usually with the possibility or intention of changing a previous decision —**reconsideration** /reékən sidə ráysh'n/ *n.*

reconstitute /reé kónsti tyoot/ (**-tutes, -tuting, -tuted**) *vt.* **1.** **BRING STH BACK TO ORIGINAL STATE** to bring specified matter or a material back to its original state, usually by adding water to a concentrated, dried, or powdered form **2.** **GIVE NEW FORM TO STH** to alter the form of sth ○ *reconstitute the government* —**reconstituent** /reékən stíttyoo ənt/ *adj., n.* —**reconstitution** /reé konsti tyoósh'n/ *n.*

reconstruct /reékən strúkt/ (**-structs, -structing, -structed**) *vt.* **1.** **PUT STH BACK TOGETHER** to put sth back together from its component parts, pieces, or remains **2.** **ESTABLISH PLAUSIBLE SCENARIO** to create a plausible scenario of the details of sth based on the known evidence ○ *reconstruct the culture of an ancient society* —**reconstructible** *adj.* —**reconstruction** *n.* —**reconstructive** *adj.* —**reconstructor** *n.*

Reconstruction /reékən strúksh'n/ *n.* the period of US history from 1865 to 1877, during which the states that had seceded during the Civil War were reorganized under federal control and later restored to the Union

Reconstructionism /reékən strúksh'nizəm/ *n.* **1.** JUDAISM **REFORMING MOVEMENT IN JUDAISM** a movement in the United States, begun in the 1920s by Mordechai Kaplan, emphasizing the idea that Judaism is a worldwide religious civilization and advocating continuous adaptation to contemporary conditions **2.** HIST **SUPPORT FOR RECONSTRUCTION** support of the policies of the Reconstruction in the southern United States after the Civil War [Mid-20thC] —**Reconstructionist** *n., adj.*

reconstructive surgery *n.* the use of surgery to restore the appearance or use of a damaged body part

reconvene /reékən veén/ (**-venes, -vening, -vened**) *vti.* to convene sth again or be convened again ○ *The hearing will reconvene tomorrow morning.*

reconvey /reékən váy/ (**-veys, -veying, -veyed**) *vt.* to transfer sth, e.g. property, back to a former owner or location —**reconveyance** *n.*

record /rékawrd/ *n.* **1.** **LASTING ACCOUNT** an account of sth, preserved in a lasting form, e.g. in writing or on film ○ *Some people use a diary to keep a record of their daily lives.* **2.** **ACCOUNT OF PROCEEDINGS** a written account of the proceedings of sth ○ *the records of the Pickwick Society* **3.** LAW **WRITTEN ACCOUNT OF COURT PROCEEDINGS** an official written account of the proceedings of a court, available for use as evidence ○ *His remarks were struck from the record.* **4.** **DOCUMENT CONTAINING HISTORY** the document or book that bears the history of sth ○ *The records are stored in the basement.* **5.** **BODY OF INFORMATION** a body of information or statistics, gathered over a period of time, about a particular subject (*often used in the plural*) ○ *the hottest summer since records began* **6.** **EVIDENCE** sth that acts as evidence or a memorial ○ *The Egyptian pyramids are a record of human engineering expertise.* **7.** **BEST ACCOMPLISHMENT** sth that represents the greatest attainment so far, especially in sports ○ *a world record* **8.** **MUSIC DISC** sth on which sound is copied, especially a plastic disc with a groove that can be played using a gramophone **9.** **COPY OF MUSIC** a piece of music in a format that can be listened to repeatedly (*informal*) ○ *Their new record is only available on CD.* **10.** **PAST PERFORMANCE** a person's accomplishments or performance to date **11.** CRIMINOL **PAST CRIMES** a background of criminal convictions, or a list of the crimes committed by a person **12.** COMPUT **COLLECTION OF DATA** a collection of related items of information treated as a unit by a computer, e.g. in a database ■ *v.* (**records, recording, recorded**) **1.** *vt.* **MAKE A LASTING ACCOUNT OF STH** to make a lasting account of sth, e.g. in writing or on film ○ *Her journal records the last days of the Empire.* **2.** *vt.* **NOTE STH** to make a note of sth, often for official purposes or for subsequent consultation ○ *The clerk recorded their names in the register.* **3.** *vti.* **INDICATE MEASUREMENT** to register or show sth, usually on a scale of a measurement **4.** *vti.* **COPY SOUNDS OR IMAGES** to make a copy of sounds or pictures, e.g. on magnetic tape ○ *I recorded my grandmother reminiscing about the war.* ■ *adj.* **GREATEST YET** representing the greatest extreme yet accomplished ○ *A record crowd turned up for the game.* [12thC. Via French, from *recorder* 'to bring to mind', from Latin *recordare, recordari*, literally 'to bring back to the heart', from the stem of *cor* 'heart, (metaphorically) mind'.] —**recordable** /ri káwrdəb'l/ *adj.* ◇ **off the record** said informally or privately and not intended to be recorded or made public ◇ **on the record** said formally or publicly with the knowledge that it may be recorded or disseminated ◇ **set the record straight** to put right a mistake or misunderstanding

recorded /ri káwrdid/ *adj.* **1.** **NOT LIVE** copied to a record, tape, CD, or other form of permanent copy, rather than listened to or performed live ○ *recorded music* **2.** **SENT BY RECORDED DELIVERY** sent through the mail by recorded delivery ○ *a recorded parcel* [Mid-16thC]

recorded delivery *n.* a method of postage in which an official record is kept of the sending and delivery of the item concerned

recorder /ri káwrdər/ *n.* **1.** **MACHINE FOR RECORDING** a machine that makes a permanent copy of sounds or pictures, e.g. a tape recorder or a video recorder **2.** **PERSON NOTING STH** sb who makes a record of sth, especially an official record **3.** MUSIC **TYPE OF FLUTE** a wind instrument of the flute family that has finger holes and is blown through a whistle-shaped mouthpiece at one end **4.** **recorder, Recorder** LAW **TYPE OF JUDGE** a barrister or solicitor in England and Wales who acts as a part-time judge in the crown court [15thC. Partly from Anglo-Norman *recordour*, Old French *recordeur* 'person who records', from *recorder* (see RECORD); partly formed from RECORD.] —**recordership** *n.*

a at; aa father; aw all; ay day; air hair; ə about, edible, item, common, circus; e egg; ee eel; hw when; i it, happy; ī ice; 'l apple; 'm rhythm; 'n fashion; o odd; ō open; oo good; oo pool; ow owl; oy oil; th thin; th this; u up; ur urge;

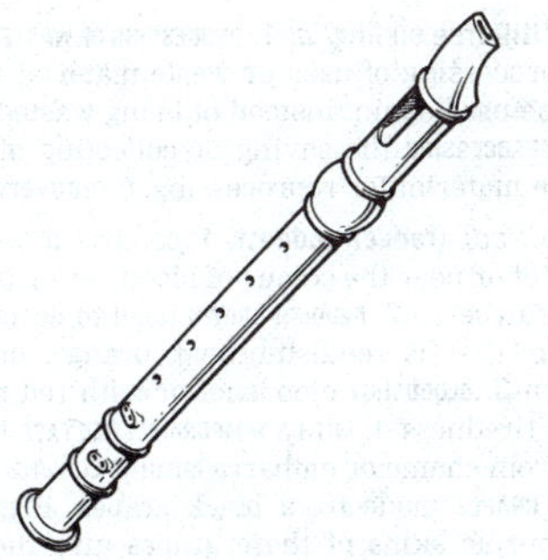

Recorder

recording /ri káwrding/ *n.* **1. MAKING OF RECORD** the making of a record, especially a permanent copy of sounds or images **2. COPY OF MUSIC** a permanent copy of sounds or images, e.g. a tape, CD, or video ○ *She was eager to buy the band's latest recording.* **3. BROADCAST THAT IS NOT LIVE** a broadcast that is not live but has been recorded on an earlier occasion ○ *I watched a recording of the opera on TV.* [14thC. The original sense was 'remembrance, recollection'.]

Recording Angel *n.* an angel believed to keep an account of every person's good and bad deeds

recordist /ri káwrdist/ *n.* sb who records the sound during the making of a film or broadcast

record of achievement *n.* a document that details the personal and educational development of a school pupil

record player *n.* a machine for reproducing the sounds recorded on records, consisting of a turntable on which the disc revolves and a needle that follows the groove to pick up sound

recount /ri kównt/ (**-counts, -counting, -counted**) *vt.* to tell the story or details of sth ○ *a tale recounting the deeds of King Arthur* [15thC. From Anglo-Norman, Old Northern French *reconter*, literally 'to relate again, count again', from *conter* (see COUNT).] —**recountal** *n.* —**recounter** *n.*

re-count /reé kownt/ *n.* **REPEAT COUNTING** a second counting of the votes cast in an election, usually done because the first counting indicated a very close result ■ *vti.* (**re-counts, re-counting, re-counted**) **COUNT AGAIN** to count sth, especially the votes cast in an election, a second time

recoup /ri kóop/ (**-coups, -couping, -couped**) *v.* **1.** *vt.* **GET STH BACK** to regain sth lost or an equivalent **2.** *vt.* **REIMBURSE ANOTHER** to give another party sth to make up for that which has been lost ○ *We were adequately recouped for our losses.* **3.** *vt.* LAW **DEDUCT STH** to deduct legally part of what is due to a claim **4.** *vi.* **MAKE UP FOR A LOSS** to make up for sth lost ○ *It will take us years to recoup.* [Early 17thC. From Old French *recouper* 'to cut back', from *couper* 'to cut', from *coup* 'blow'. Earlier also in the sense 'to cut short, interrupt'.] —**recoupable** *adj.* —**recoupment** *n.*

recourse /ri káwrss/ *n.* **1. CHANCE TO SEEK ASSISTANCE** a turning to another for assistance ○ *Can we resolve our financial problems without recourse to further borrowing?* **2. SOURCE OF HELP OR SOLUTION** sb, sth, or a course of action to which a person turns for help or to solve a problem ○ *She felt she had no recourse but to sue.* **3.** FIN, LAW **RIGHT TO DEMAND PAYMENT** the right to demand payment of a bill of exchange from the person who draws or endorses it, when the person who accepts it fails to pay [14thC. Directly or via French *recours* from Latin *recursus*, literally 'a running back' (the original English sense), from *cursus* (see COURSE).]

recover /ri kúvvər/ (**-ers, -ering, -ered**) *v.* **1.** *vt.* **REGAIN STH** to get back sth previously lost **2.** *vi.* **RETURN TO NORMAL** to return to a previous state of health, prosperity, or equanimity **3.** *vr.* **BRING SELF BACK TO NORMAL** to bring the self back to a normal condition ○ *He soon recovered himself enough to feign a friendly welcome.* **4.** *vi.* **RETURN TO THE RIGHT POSITION** to return to a suitable or correct state or position ○ *The goalkeeper stumbled, but recovered enough to save the goal.* **5.** *vt.* **COMPENSATE FOR STH** to make up for that which is lost ○ *They'll have to work hard in order to recover their losses.* **6.** *vt.* LAW **OBTAIN STH THROUGH A COURT** to obtain sth by the ruling of a court **7.** *vt.* **RECLAIM STH FROM WASTE** to extract useful substances from waste or refuse **8.** *vi.* LAW **SUCCEED IN LITIGATION** to be successful in a lawsuit [13thC. Via Anglo-Norman *recoverer*, Old French *recovrer* from Latin *recuperare* (see RECUPERATE).] —**recoverability** /ri kúvvərə bílləti/ *n.* —**recoverable** /ri kúvvərəb'l/ *adj.* —**recoverer** *n.*

re-cover /reé kúvvər/ (**re-covers, re-covering, re-covered**) *vt.* **1. GIVE STH A NEW COVER** to put a new cover on sth **2. COVER STH AGAIN** to cover sth again

recoverable error *n.* a program error that can be corrected without causing a computer program to fail. For example, if a user enters obviously wrong data, the program might request a different entry.

recovery /ri kúvvəri/ (*plural* **-ies**) *n.* **1. RETURN TO HEALTH** the return to normal health of sb who has been ill or injured **2. RETURN TO A NORMAL STATE** the return of sth to a normal or improved state after a setback or loss ○ *an economic recovery* **3. GAINING BACK OF STH LOST** the regaining of sth lost or taken away ○ *The arrests led to the recovery of large amounts of stolen property.* **4.** ENVIRON **RECLAMATION FROM WASTE** the extraction of useful substances from waste or refuse **5.** LAW **OBTAINING STH THROUGH A COURT** the obtaining of sth by the ruling of a court **6.** GOLF **SHOT OUT OF AN OBSTACLE** a shot played out of the rough or an obstacle onto the green or fairway **7.** FENCING **RETURN TO GUARD** a return to the guard position after making an attack **8.** ROWING, SWIMMING **BRINGING THE ARM FORWARD** the bringing forward of the arm to make another stroke [14thC. The original English sense was 'help, means of recovering'.]

recovery room *n.* a hospital room equipped for the care of patients who have just undergone surgery and are recovering from anaesthesia

recreant /rékri ənt/, **recreance** /-ənss/, **recreancy** /-ənssi/ *adj.* (*archaic*) **1. DISLOYAL** disloyal to a cause or duty **2. COWARDLY** cowardly ■ *n.* (*archaic*) **1. DISLOYAL PERSON** sb who is disloyal or deserts a cause **2. COWARD** a coward [13thC. Via Old French, the present participle of *recroire* 'to surrender' from, ultimately, Latin *credere* 'to entrust'. Originally in English, 'surrendering oneself (to an adversary)'.] —**recreantly** *adv.*

recreate /rékri ayt/ (**-ates, -ating, -ated**) *v.* **1.** *vt.* **REFRESH SELF** to refresh sb, especially the self, mentally or physically (*archaic*) **2.** *vi.* **TAKE PART IN RECREATION** to take part in activities that are mentally or physically refreshing [15thC. From Latin *recreat-*, the past participle stem of *recreare*, literally 'to bring forth again', from *creare* (see CREATE); also, later, a back-formation from RECREATION.] —**recreative** *adj.* —**recreator** *n.*

re-create /reé kri áyt/ (**re-creates, re-creating, re-created**) *vt.* to create sth again or reproduce it ○ *The decor aims to re-create a 19th-century interior.* —**re-creatable** *adj.* —**re-creation** *n.* —**re-creative** *adj.*

WORD KEY: SYNONYMS

See Synonyms at ***copy***.

recreation /rékri áysh'n/ *n.* **1. REFRESHMENT** the refreshment of the mind and body after work, especially by engaging in enjoyable activities ○ *after-work recreation* **2. AMUSEMENT** an activity that a person takes part in for pleasure or relaxation rather than as work ○ *She took up sketching as a recreation.* [14thC]

recreational *adj.* **1. NOT FOR WORK** done or used for pleasure or relaxation rather than work **2.** DRUGS **NOT FOR MEDICAL PURPOSES** used to describe controlled drugs taken illegally —**recreationally** *adv.*

recreational vehicle *n.* *US* a large motor vehicle, usually with facilities for sleeping and eating, used for recreational activities such as camping

recreation ground *n.* a public area for sports and games, often incorporating a children's playground

recreation room *n.* **1. ROOM FOR SOCIAL EVENTS** a room set aside for games, social events, and other kinds of recreation in a public building **2.** *US* **ROOM IN HOUSE FOR RELAXATION** a room used by the occupants of a house for relaxation and recreational activities ○ *a new TV for the recreation room*

recriminate /ri krímmi nayt/ (**-nates, -nating, -nated**) *vi.* to accuse sb who has already brought an accusation [Early 17thC. From medieval Latin *recriminat-*, the past participle stem of *recriminari*, literally 'to accuse back or again', from Latin *criminari*, *criminare* 'to accuse'.] —**recriminative** /-nətiv/ *adj.* —**recriminator** *n.* —**recriminatory** /-nətəri/ *adj.*

recrimination /ri krímmi náysh'n/ *n.* **1. ACCUSING OF SB IN RETURN** an accusation made against sb who has brought a previous accusation ○ *It started out as a calm discussion and ended in tears and recriminations.* **2.** LAW **COUNTERCHARGE** an accusation that sb accused of a crime makes against the accuser [Early 17thC]

rec room *n.* *US* = **recreation room** *n.* 1

recrudesce /reé kroo déss/ (**-desces, -descing, -desced**) *vi.* to break out or become active again after a dormant period [Mid-17thC. Back-formation from *recrudescence*, from Latin *recrudescere*, literally 'to become raw again', from, ultimately, *crudus* 'raw, bloody' (source of English *crude*).] —**recrudescence** *n.* —**recrudescent** *adj.*

recruit /ri kroót/ *v.* (**-cruits, -cruiting, -cruited**) **1.** *vti.* MIL **ENLIST SB** to enlist sb in a military force, or take part in enlisting people for a military force ○ *She was recruited by the Marines.* **2.** *vti.* **ENROL OR TAKE ON SB** to enrol sb as a worker or member, or to take on people as workers or members ○ *The company has stopped recruiting.* **3.** *vt.* MIL **RAISE AN ARMY** to put together a military force **4.** *vti.* **RECOVER** to recover in health or strength, or recover one's own health or strength (*archaic*) ■ *n.* **1.** MIL **NEW SOLDIER** a member of a military force who has joined recently **2. NEW MEMBER** a new member, worker, player, or supporter [Mid-17thC. Via French *recruter* from, ultimately, French *recrue*, literally 'new growth', a noun use of the feminine past participle of *recroître* 'to increase again', from, ultimately, Latin *crescere* 'to grow'.] —**recruiter** *n.* —**recruiting** *n.* —**recruitment** *n.*

recrystallize /ree krístə līz/ (**-lizes, -lizing, -lized**), **recrystallise** (**-lises, -lising, -lised**) *vti.* to crystallize sth or become crystallized again —**recrystallization** /ree krístə lī záysh'n/ *n.*

rec. sec. *abbr.* recording secretary

rect, rec't *abbr.* receipt

rect. *abbr.* rectangle

Rect. *abbr.* **1.** Rector **2.** Rectory

recta plural of **rectum**

rectal /rékt'l/ *adj.* relating to, involving, or in the rectum —**rectally** *adv.*

rectangle /rék tang g'l/ *n.* a four-sided plane figure in which each angle is a right angle, especially one with adjacent sides of different length [Late 16thC. Directly or via French from medieval Latin *rect(i)angulum*, a noun use of the neuter of late Latin *rectiangulus*, literally 'straight angle', from Latin *rectus* 'straight' + *angulus* 'angle'.]

rectangular /rek táng gyóolər/ *adj.* **1. SHAPED LIKE A RECTANGLE** with four sides, usually with adjacent sides of different length, and four right angles ○ *The yard is rectangular rather than square.* **2. WITH OR AT RIGHT ANGLES** involving, having, or meeting at right angles [Early 17thC. Formed from ANGULAR on the model of French *rectangulaire*.] —**rectangularity** /rek táng gyoo lárrəti/ *n.* —**rectangularly** /rek táng gyóolərli/ *adv.*

rectangular coordinate *n.* a Cartesian coordinate used in a system of axes that meet at right angles

rectangular hyperbola *n.* MATH a hyperbola with asymptotes that are at right angles

recti plural of **rectus**

rectifier /rékti fī ər/ *n.* **1.** ELECTRON ENG **ELECTRONIC DEVICE** an electronic device that converts alternating current to direct current, e.g. a set of semiconductor diodes connected in a bridge circuit **2.** CHEM **CONDENSING APPARATUS** an apparatus that condenses vapour to liquid during distillation **3. SB OR STH THAT RECTIFIES** sb or sth that puts sth right

rectify /rékti fī/ (**-fies, -fying, -fied**) *vt.* **1. CORRECT STH** to put sth right **2.** CHEM **PURIFY** to purify a substance, especially by distillation **3.** ELECTRON ENG **CONVERT A CURRENT** to convert alternating current to direct current **4.** MATH **FIND THE LENGTH OF A CURVE** to find the length of a curve [14thC. Directly or via French *rectifier* from medieval Latin *rectificare*, literally 'to make right', from *rectus* 'right' (source of English *rectangle* and *rectum*).] —**rectifiability** /rékti fī ə bílləti/ *n.* —**rectifiable** /rékti fī əb'l/ *adj.* —**rectification** /réktifi káysh'n/ *n.*

rectilinear /rékti línni ər/, **rectilineal** /-ni əl/ *adj.* **1.** WITH STRAIGHT LINES formed or consisting of straight lines **2.** IN A STRAIGHT LINE moving in a straight line [Mid-17thC. Formed from late Latin *rectilineus*, from Latin *rectus* 'straight' + *linea* 'line' (source of English *line*).] —**rectilinearly** *adv.*

rectitude /rékti tyood/ *n.* **1.** RIGHTEOUSNESS strong moral integrity in character or actions **2.** CORRECTNESS correctness in judgment (*formal*) ○ *the admirable rectitude of her assessments* **3.** STRAIGHTNESS straightness in form or shape (*formal*) [15thC. Directly or via French from late Latin *rectitudo*, from Latin *rectus* 'straight, correct'.] —**rectitudinous** /rékti tyóodinəss/ *adj.*

recto /réktō/ (*plural* **-tos**) *n.* ◊ **verso 1.** FRONT OF PRINTED SHEET the front side of a printed sheet **2.** RIGHT-HAND PAGE the right-hand page of an open book [Early 19thC. From modern Latin *(folio) recto* '(the page) being on the right', a form of Latin *rectus* 'straight, correct', the underlying idea being 'right, proper'.]

rector /réktər/ *n.* **1.** CHR CLERIC IN CHARGE OF AN ANGLICAN PARISH a member of the clergy of the Church of England who is in charge of a parish **2.** CHR CLERIC IN CHARGE OF A CATHOLIC CONGREGATION a member of the Roman Catholic clergy who is in charge of a congregation, a college, or a religious community **3.** CHR CLERIC IN CHARGE OF AN EPISCOPAL PARISH a member of the Episcopal clergy who is in charge of a parish **4.** EDUC HEAD OF A SCHOOL the head of certain schools, colleges, or universities **5.** OFFICER ELECTED BY STUDENTS in certain Scottish universities, sb elected by students to represent them on the University Court [14thC. Directly or via Old French, 'captain (of a ship), head of a university', from Latin, 'ruler, governor' (the original English sense), from, ultimately, *regere* 'to rule'.] —**rectorate** *n.* —**rectorial** /rek táwri əl/ *adj.* —**rectorship** /réktər ship/ *n.*

rectory /réktəri/ (*plural* **-ries**) *n.* **1.** RECTOR'S HOUSE the house that a rector lives in, provided by the church **2.** RECTOR'S POST the post of rector and the income that goes with it [Late 16thC. Via Old French *rectorie* or medieval Latin *rectoria* from, ultimately, Latin *rector* (see RECTOR).]

rectrix /rék triks/ (*plural* **-trices** /-tri seez, -trí seez/) *n.* any of a bird's long stiff tail feathers that help to control direction during flight [Mid-18thC. From Latin, feminine of *rector* (see RECTOR).]

rectum /réktəm/ (*plural* **-tums** *or* **-ta** /-tə/) *n.* the lower part of the large intestine, between the colon and the anal canal [15thC. From Latin *(intestinum) rectum* 'straight (intestine)', from *rectus* (see RECTUS).]

rectus /réktəss/ (*plural* **-ti** /-tī/) *n.* any straight muscle, e.g. any of the muscles in the abdomen or the thigh [Early 18thC. From Latin, 'straight' (source of English *rectify* and *correct*). Ultimately from an Indo-European base meaning 'to go straight' (ancestor also of English *right*, *rich*, *rule*, and *regular*).]

recumbent /ri kúmbənt/ *adj.* **1.** LYING lying back or lying down (*literary*) ○ *a colossal recumbent statue* **2.** BIOL RESTING OR LEANING used to describe a plant or animal part that rests or leans against sth else **3.** GEOL HORIZONTAL used to describe a fold whose axis is more or less horizontal [Early 18thC. From Latin *recumbere* 'to lie back', from *-cumbere* 'to lie down'.] —**recumbence** *n.* —**recumbently** *adv.*

recuperate /ri kóopə rayt/ (**-ates, -ating, -ated**) *v.* **1.** *vi.* MED REGAIN HEALTH to recover from an illness or injury **2.** *vt.* GET BACK to recover sth lost, especially a sum of money [Mid-16thC. From Latin *recuperare*, literally 'to take back', from *capere* (see CAPTURE).] —**recuperation** /ri kóopə ráysh'n/ *n.* —**recuperative** /ri kóopərətiv, -raytiv/ *adj.* —**recuperatory** /-rətəri/ *adj.*

WORD KEY: USAGE

Meaning trap ***Recuperate*** is normally used intransitively, that is, without an object, as in *She needed several weeks to recuperate.* When used transitively, with a noun such as *health* as the object, *recover* is a better choice: *She needed several weeks to recover her health.*

WORD KEY: USAGE

Spelling trap The word is sometimes mistakenly spelled *recouperate*, by confusion with the unrelated verb *recoup*.

recuperator /ri kóopə raytər/ *n.* **1.** CHEM ENG HEAT EXCHANGER a device used to recover energy that would otherwise be lost, especially one that takes heat from exhaust gases and uses it to preheat incoming combustion air **2.** ARMS RESETTING DEVICE IN GUN a device in a gun that returns it to its firing position following recoil

recur /ri kúr/ (**-curs, -curring, -curred**) *vi.* **1.** OCCUR AGAIN to happen or appear once again or repeatedly **2.** MATH BE REPEATED INDEFINITELY to occur as an infinitely repeated digit or series of digits at the end of a decimal fraction **3.** RETURN to return to a subject in speech, writing, or thought (*archaic or literary*) **4.** RESORT to turn to sth as an option after considering or trying other options (*archaic or literary*) [Early 16thC. From Latin *recurrere*, literally 'to run back', from *currere* (see CURRENT).]

WORD KEY: USAGE

Redundancy trap: The sense of *again* being an integral part of the meaning of ***recur***, it is redundant to say things like 'The disease recurred again'. Simply say 'recurred'.

recurrent /ri kúrrənt/ *adj.* **1.** OCCURRING AGAIN happening or appearing again, especially repeatedly **2.** ANAT TURNING ROUND used to describe a blood vessel or nerve that turns back on itself and runs in the opposite direction —**recurrence** /ri kúrrənss/ *n.* —**recurrently** *adv.*

recurrent fever *n.* = **relapsing fever**

recurring decimal *n.* a decimal number in which one or more digits repeat indefinitely after the decimal point, e.g. 3.77777.... or 8.691691691....

recursion /ri kúrsh'n/ *n.* **1.** RETURN OF STH the return of sth, often repeatedly **2.** LOGIC, MATH REPETITION OF STEPS TO GIVE RESULT the use of repeated steps, each based on the result of the one before, to define a function or calculate a number [Early 17thC. Via the late Latin stem *recursion-*, literally 'a running back', from Latin *recurs-*, the past participle stem of *recurrere* (see RECUR).]

recursive /ri kúrssiv/ *adj.* **1.** SELF-REPEATING repeating itself, either indefinitely or until a specified point is reached **2.** MATH, LOGIC REPEATEDLY APPLYING FUNCTION TO ITSELF involving the repeated application of a function to its own values [Late 18thC. Formed from Latin *recurs-*, the past participle stem of *recurrere* (see RECUR).] —**recursively** *adv.* —**recursiveness** *n.*

recurvate /ri kúrvət, -vayt/ *adj.* curved backwards, inwards, or downwards

recurve /ri kúrv/ (**-curves, -curving, -curved**) *vti.* to curve backwards, inwards, or downwards, or cause sth to curve in this way [Late 16thC. From Latin *recurvare*, literally 'to curve back', from *curvus* (see CURVE).] —**recurvation** /rée kur váysh'n/ *n.* —**recurved** /ri kúrvd/ *adj.*

recusant /rékyóoz'nt, ri kyóo-/ *n.* **1.** CHR DISSENTING ROMAN CATHOLIC a Roman Catholic who broke the law by refusing to attend Church of England services in England between the 16th and 18th centuries **2.** SB DISOBEYING AUTHORITY sb who refuses to obey authority ■ *adj.* DISOBEYING AUTHORITY refusing to obey authority —**recusance** *n.*

recuse /ri kyóoz/ (**-cuses, -cusing, -cused**) *vti.* to disqualify sb from judging or participating in sth because of bias or personal interest, or withdraw for that reason [Early 19thC. From Latin *recusare* 'to refuse', from *re-* 'back' + *causa* 'cause, case'.] —**recusal** *n.*

recycle /ree sík'l/ *v.* (**-cles, -cling, -cled**) **1.** *vti.* PROCESS FOR RE-USE to process used or waste material so that it can be used again **2.** *vti.* SAVE FOR RE-USE to save or collect used or waste material for reprocessing into sth useful **3.** *vti.* USE AGAIN DIFFERENTLY to adapt or convert sth to a new use **4.** *vt.* RE-USE STH to use sth again for the same purpose **5.** *vt.* USE AGAIN UNIMAGINATIVELY to use sth abstract again in the same form, often at the expense of freshness or originality **6.** *vti.* REPEAT A PROCESS to repeat a process, or pass sth through a process again ■ *n.* RECYCLING OF MATERIAL the recycling of material, especially used or waste materials —**recyclable** *adj.* —**recycler** *n.*

recycled /ree sík'ld/ *adj.* **1.** MADE FROM WASTE manufactured from used or waste materials that have been reprocessed **2.** USED AGAIN used again or repeatedly, often at the expense of freshness or originality

recycling /ree síkling/ *n.* **1.** PROCESSING OF WASTE FOR RE-USE the processing of used or waste material so that it can be used again, instead of being wasted **2.** SAVING FOR REPROCESSING the saving or collecting of used or waste material for reprocessing. ◊ **recovery, re-use**

red /red/ *adj.* (**redder, reddest**) **1.** COLOURS OF THE COLOUR OF BLOOD of or near the colour of blood, or a ripe tomato or strawberry **2.** REDDISH-BROWN used to describe hair or fur that is reddish-brown, orange, or golden-brown **3.** BLOODSHOT bloodshot or with red rims, e.g. from tiredness **4.** WITH A TEMPORARILY RED FACE blushing, e.g. from shame or embarrassment **5.** WINE MADE FROM BLACK GRAPES made from black grapes. Pigments in the purple skins of these grapes give the wine a deep red colour. **6.** ACCT REPRESENTING DEBT representing debt or financial loss **7. red, Red** POL SOCIALIST socialist or communist (*informal disapproving*) ◊ **white 8. red, Red** POL SOVIET relating or belonging to the former Soviet Union (*informal*) ■ *n.* **1.** COLOURS COLOUR OF BLOOD a colour such as that of blood, or of a ripe tomato or strawberry. It lies at the far end of the visible spectrum and is one of the three primary colours of light and pigment. **2.** RED COLOURING a pigment or dye that is of or near to the colour of blood, or a ripe tomato or strawberry **3.** RED FABRIC OR CLOTHES fabric or clothing that is red in colour **4.** STH RED a red object **5.** WINE RED WINE wine made from black grapes (*informal*) **6.** GAMBLING SECTION OF GAMBLING TABLE in roulette and other gambling games, one of the two coloured areas on the table on which players may place bets. The other is black. **7.** ARCHERY PART OF AN ARCHERY TARGET a red ring immediately outside the gold disc at the centre of a target **8.** CUE GAMES RED BALL in billiards, snooker, and other cue games, a red ball **9. red, Red** POL A SOCIALIST OR COMMUNIST sb with socialist or communist views (*informal disapproving*) [From Old English *rēad*. Ultimately from an Indo-European base that is also the ancestor of *ruddy*, *rouge*, and *erythro-*.] —**redly** *adv.* —**redness** *n.* ◇ **in the red** in debt, e.g. to a bank ◇ **see red** to suddenly become very angry (*informal*)

red. *abbr.* **1.** reduced **2.** reduction **3.** redeemable

redact /ri dákt/ (**-dacts, -dacting, -dacted**) *vt.* **1.** DRAFT STH to compose or draft sth for publication or for an announcement (*formal*) **2.** EDIT STH to edit or revise sth in preparation for publication ○ *formerly classified documents that were redacted before release to protect still confidential material* [Mid-19thC. From Latin *redact-*, the past participle stem of *redigere* 'to reduce', literally 'to bring down', from *agere* (see ACT).] —**redaction** *n.* —**redactional** *adj.* —**redactor** *n.*

red admiral *n.* a brightly coloured butterfly with broad orange-red bands on its forewings. It is native to Europe and North America. Latin name: *Vanessa atalanta*.

red alert *n.* a warning or alarm that indicates a situation of the highest priority or greatest urgency, especially an imminent attack, or the state of readiness to deal with such a situation

red algae *npl.* marine algae, e.g. dulse, laver, and carrageen, that contain a red pigment as well as chlorophyll. Family: Rhodophyceae.

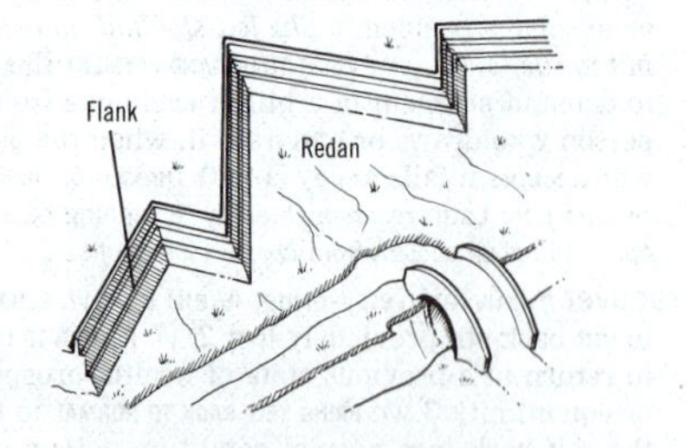

Redan

redan /ri dán/ *n.* a pair of parapets that form a V-shaped projection from the wall of a castle or other fortification [Late 17thC. From French, a variant of *redent*, from *dent* 'tooth', from Latin *dens* (see DENTAL).]

Red Army *n.* the military organization put into place by Leon Trotsky at the time of the Russian revolution. Its members were recruited from the worker and peasant classes.

redback /réd bak/, **redback spider** *n.* a small venomous dark brown or black spider native to Australia and New Zealand. The female has a red stripe or patch on the back of the abdomen. Latin name: *Latrodectus hasselti.*

red-backed shrike *n.* a small bird, native to Europe, Asia, and Africa, the male of which has a chestnut-coloured back and tail and a black-and-white face. Latin name: *Lanius collurio.*

red bay *n.* a small tree that has red-stalked fruit and red heartwood and is widely grown as an ornamental plant. It is native to the southern United States. Latin name: *Persea borbonia.*

red-bellied black snake *n.* a large poisonous snake that is glossy black with an orangish-red underside. It is found in eastern Australian woodlands and can grow to almost 2.5 m/8 ft in length. Latin name: *Pseudechis porphyriacus.*

red biddy *n.* a strong cheap alcoholic drink made by mixing red wine with methylated spirits (*dated informal*)

red blood cell *n.* any of the red-coloured cells in blood that contain haemoglobin and carry oxygen to the tissues

red-blooded *adj.* behaving in ways stereotypically associated with men, e.g. by showing strength or active sexual desire

redbreast /réd brest/ (*plural* **-breasts** *or* **-breast**) *n.* **1.** BIRD WITH RED CHEST a bird with a reddish breast, especially the robin **2.** FISH WITH RED BELLY a freshwater sunfish with a reddish belly, found in the eastern United States. Latin name: *Lepomis auritus.*

redbrick /rédbrik/ *adj.* **1.** UNIV OF 19C BRITISH UNIVERSITY relating to British universities that were founded in the late 19th and early 20th centuries, e.g. Manchester and Leeds. The term was originally intended to emphasize their modernity in contrast to the older British universities such as Oxford and St Andrews, and now also distinguishes them from newer universities. **2.** BUILT OF RED BRICKS constructed of red bricks

Red Brigades *npl.* a left-wing urban organization that was active in Italy during the 1970s and was responsible for the kidnapping and murder of the Italian statesman Aldo Moro in 1978 [Translation of Italian *brigate rosse*]

redbud /réd bud/ (*plural* **-buds** *or* **-bud**) *n.* a North American tree that has heart-shaped leaves and small pale pink flowers. Genus: *Cercis.*

redbug /réd bug/ *n.* a stout red-and-black insect found throughout the tropics and subtropics. Some redbugs, such as the cotton stainer are pests. Family: Pyrrhocoridae.

redcap /réd kap/ *n.* **1.** MIL MILITARY POLICE OFFICER an officer in the military police (*slang*) **2.** US TRANSP PORTER in the United States, a porter at an airport or railway station (*informal*) [From the red caps traditionally worn by such personnel]

red card *n.* **1.** REFEREE'S CARD FOR DISMISSING PLAYER in soccer, a red card displayed by the referee when dismissing a player from the field for a serious infringement of the rules. ◊ **yellow card 2.** DISMISSAL any dismissal or rejection, e.g. from a job (*informal*) ○ *Even his girlfriend has threatened to give him the red card.*

red carpet *n.* **1.** VIP'S CARPET a strip of red-coloured carpet laid on the ground for an important visitor to walk on when arriving or departing **2.** VIP TREATMENT attentive or deferential treatment given to a dignitary, celebrity, or other important person (*hyphenated when used before a noun*)

red cell *n.* = **red blood cell**

red cent *n.* US the smallest amount of money (*informal*) [From the fact that the one-cent coin is made of copper]

Red Cloud

Red Cloud /red klówd/ (1822–1909) US Oglala Sioux leader. He resisted the US government's occupation of Native North American territory in present-day Wyoming and Montana, but his defeat in the Sioux War (1875–76) resulted in the relocation of his people to South Dakota.

red clover *n.* a variety of clover with fragrant red flowers, often grown as a forage crop for horses or cattle. It is native to Europe, Asia, and North America. Latin name: *Trifolium pratense.*

redcoat /réd kōt/ *n.* **1.** HISTORY BRITISH SOLDIER a British soldier serving overseas in former times, especially during the American War of Independence **2.** HOLIDAY CAMP ATTENDANT a uniformed attendant at a Butlin's holiday camp [From their bright-red uniform coats]

red coral *n.* any coral whose hard pinkish-red skeletons are used to make ornaments and jewellery. Genus: *Corallium.*

red corpuscle *n.* = **red blood cell**

Red Crescent *n.* the name under which any branch of the Red Cross functions in Islamic countries

Red Cross *n.* an international organization founded in 1864 and dedicated to the medical care of the sick or wounded in wars and natural disasters

redcurrant /red kúrrənt/ *n.* **1.** FOOD SHARP-TASTING RED BERRY a small round red fruit with a tart flavour that grows in northern regions. It is often used to make jam or jelly. **2.** PLANTS FLOWERING SHRUB a flowering shrub that grows in northern temperate regions and bears redcurrants. Latin name: *Ribes rubrum.*

redd[1] /red/ *vti.* (**redds**, **redding**, **redd** *or* **redded**) TIDY STH to tidy sth, or tidy things generally (*regional*) ■ *n.* TIDYING SESSION a spell of tidying (*regional*) [Early 16thC. From Old Norse *ryðja* (see RID), with the sense influenced by an obsolete verb meaning 'to rescue', from Old English *hreddan.*] —**redder** *n.*

redd[2] /red/ *n.* a hollow that is scooped out in the sand or gravel of a river bed for spawning by fish such as trout and salmon [Early 19thC. Origin unknown.]

red deer *n.* a large deer that has spreading antlers and a reddish-brown summer coat. It is native to Europe and Asia and has been introduced to Australia, New Zealand, and South America. Latin name: *Cervus elaphus.*

redden /rédd'n/ (**-dens**, **-dening**, **-dened**) *v.* **1.** *vti.* MAKE OR BECOME RED to become red or redder, or make sth red or redder **2.** *vi.* BECOME FLUSHED to go red in the face, e.g. with embarrassment, anger, or exertion

Otis Redding

Redding /rédding/, **Otis** (1941–67) US singer and songwriter. He won popular and critical acclaim for his

Southern soul rhythm-and-blues style, an emotional blend of gospel, country, and traditional blues.

reddish /réddish/ *adj.* of a colour that is a shade of red or strongly tinged with red —**reddishness** *n.*

Redditch /réddich/ town in Worcestershire, in western England. It was designated a new town in 1964. Population: 77,900 (1995).

reddle *n.*, *vt.* = **ruddle**

red-dog *vt.* in American football, to charge directly at the quarterback the moment the ball is put into play (*informal*)

rede /reed/ *n.* (*archaic*) **1.** ADVICE advice **2.** EXPLANATION a story, account, or explanation ■ *vt.* (**redes**, **reding**, **reded**) (*archaic*) **1.** ADVISE SB to advise or counsel sb **2.** INTERPRET STH to explain, understand, or interpret sth in a particular way [The noun is from Old English *ræd*; the verb from Old English *rædan* (see READ).]

red earth *n.* a clayey soil found in tropical grasslands, coloured red by the presence of iron compounds

redecorate /ree déka rayt/ (**-rates**, **-rating**, **-rated**) *vti.* to change or renew the interior decoration of a building or room

redeem /ri déem/ (**-deems**, **-deeming**, **-deemed**) *vt.* **1.** MAKE STH ACCEPTABLE to make sth acceptable or pleasant in spite of its negative qualities or aspects **2.** RESTORE REPUTATION to restore yourself to favour or to sb's good opinion **3.** BUY STH BACK to buy back an item given, e.g. to a pawnbroker, as security for a loan **4.** KEEP A PROMISE to fulfil a pledge or promise **5.** EXCHANGE STH FOR MONEY to exchange or convert sth such as a voucher for money or its equivalent **6.** FIN PAY STH OFF to pay off the outstanding portion of a debt **7.** ATONE FOR HUMAN SIN to pay for the sins of humanity with death on the Cross [15thC. Directly or via French *rédimer* from Latin *redimere*, literally 'to buy back', from *emere* (see EXAMPLE).]

redeemable /ri déeməb'l/ *adj.* able to be exchanged for money —**redeemability** /ri déemə bílləti/ *n.* —**redeemably** /ri déeməbli/ *adv.*

redeemer /ri déemər/ *n.* sb who redeems sb or sth, especially sb who saves sb else from unpleasantness or danger

Redeemer *n.* CHR Jesus Christ regarded as the saviour of humanity through his death on the Cross

redeeming /ri déeming/ *adj.* compensating for faults or flaws

redefine /réedi fín/ (**-fines**, **-fining**, **-fined**) *vt.* to change the nature, appearance, or position of sth consciously and sometimes arbitrarily

redemption /ri démpsh'n/ *n.* **1.** IMPROVING OF STH the saving or improving of sth that has declined into a poor state **2.** REDEEMED STATE the improved state of sb or sth saved from apparently irreversible decline **3.** BUYING BACK OF STH the buying back of sth given, e.g. to a pawnbroker, as security for a loan **4.** FIN ENDING OF FINANCIAL OBLIGATION the removal of a financial obligation, e.g. the repayment of a loan or promissory note **5.** CHR ATONEMENT FOR HUMAN SIN deliverance from the sins of humanity by the death of Jesus Christ on the Cross [14thC. Via French *rédemption* from, ultimately, Latin *redempt-*, the past participle stem of *redimere* (see REDEEM).] —**redemptional** *adj.*

redemptioner /ri démpsh'nər/ *n.* an emigrant from Europe in the 18th and 19th centuries who worked as a servant on arriving in North America, to pay for the cost of the voyage

redemptive /ri démptiv/ *adj.* bringing about the redemption of sb or sth [15thC. Formed from Latin *redempt-*, the past participle stem of *redimere* (see REDEEM).] —**redemptively** *adv.*

Redemptorist /ri démptərist/ *n.* a member of the Congregation of the Most Holy Redeemer, a Roman Catholic order specializing in preaching and missionary work, founded in Italy in 1732 [Mid-19thC. Via French *rédemptoriste* from Latin *redemptor* 'redeemer', from *redempt-*, the past participle stem of *redimere* (see REDEEM).]

red ensign *n.* a red flag with the Union Jack in the upper corner of the vertical edge near the staff. It is flown by British merchant ships and pleasure craft.

redeploy /reedi plóy/ (-ploys, -ploying, -ployed) vti. to move people or equipment from one area or activity to another —**redeployment** n.

redesign /reedi zín/ vt. (-signs, -signing, -signed) CHANGE DESIGN OF to change or revise the design of sth ▪ n. NEW DESIGN a new or revised design

redevelop /reedi véllap/ (-ops, -oping, -oped) vt. to improve an area that has become run down by renovating buildings, making better use of wasteland, and encouraging inward investment —**redevelopment** n.

redeye /rédî/ n. 1. PHOTOGRAPHY PHOTOGRAPHIC DEFECT red pupils in the eyes of a subject in flash photography, a common defect in photographs taken with simple cameras (informal) 2. US AIR NIGHT FLIGHT a late night or overnight airline service (informal) 3. US BEVERAGES CHEAP WHISKY cheap inferior whisky (slang)

red-faced adj. blushing, especially with embarrassment

red fescue n. a grass plant that has creeping roots and green, reddish, or bluish-green flower clusters. It is native to Europe, Asia, and North America. Latin name: Festuca rubra.

redfin (plural -fins or -fin), **redfin shiner** n. a small freshwater fish with reddish fins that is native to central North America and is a popular aquarium fish. Genus: Notropis.

red fire n. a chemical mixture, especially one containing strontium salts, that burns with a vivid red flame and is used in fireworks and flares

redfish /réd fish/ (plural -fishes or -fish) n. 1. REDDISH ROCKFISH any reddish North Atlantic rockfish, especially any species used as food 2. = channel bass 3. SALMON a male salmon that has recently spawned

red flag n. 1. FLAG SYMBOLIZING COMMUNISM OR SOCIALISM a plain red flag or banner used as an international symbol of communism or socialism 2. US = red rag 3. WARNING SIGNAL a flag waved as a danger signal or a command to stop

red fox n. the common fox of Europe, Asia, and North America, found in fields and open woods. It has sharply pointed ears, a reddish-orange to reddish-brown coat, and a white-tipped tail. Latin name: Vulpes vulpes.

red giant n. a red-coloured star with a relatively low surface temperature and a diameter much greater than that of the sun

Redgrave /réd grayv/, **Sir Michael** (1908–85) British actor. One of the outstanding actors of his generation, he played both classical and contemporary roles in films and on stage. Full name **Michael Scudamore Redgrave**

Redgrave, Vanessa (b. 1937) British actor. The daughter of Michael Redgrave, she is acclaimed for her sensitive and intelligent portrayals of strong-willed independent women.

Red Guard n. 1. CHINESE COMMUNIST YOUTH MOVEMENT the 1960s Chinese Communist youth movement that attempted to bring about the Cultural Revolution of Mao Zedong 2. YOUNG CHINESE COMMUNIST a member of the Red Guard

red gum n. 1. EUCALYPTUS TREE an Australian eucalyptus tree with aromatic leaves and distinctive red wood. Latin name: Eucalyptus camaldulensis. 2. = sweet gum

red-handed adj. in the act of committing a crime or doing sth wrong ○ caught red-handed [From the notion of having blood on the hands]

red hat n. 1. CARDINAL'S HAT the broad-brimmed crimson hat that a Roman Catholic cardinal wears on ceremonial occasions 2. CARDINAL'S RANK the rank or position of cardinal in the Roman Catholic Church

redhead /réd hed/ n. 1. SB WITH RED HAIR sb, especially a woman, who has reddish-coloured hair 2. BIRDS AMERICAN DIVING DUCK a North American diving duck, the male of which has a bright chestnut head. Latin name: Aythya americana.

redheaded /réd héddid/ adj. 1. WITH RED HAIR with reddish-coloured hair 2. ZOOL WITH RED HEAD used to describe an animal, especially a bird, with a red head

red heat n. the temperature at which sth is red-hot, or the state of being at such a temperature

red herring n. 1. MISLEADING CLUE sth introduced, e.g. into a crime or mystery story, in order to divert attention or mislead 2. FOOD SMOKED HERRING a herring salted and smoked to a reddish-brown colour [From the practice of dragging smoked fish across a scent trail to teach hounds not to be distracted]

red-hot adj. 1. GLOWING RED WITH HEAT heated to such a high temperature as to glow red 2. VERY HOT extremely hot 3. EXTREMELY POPULAR in great demand (informal) 4. VERY RECENT very recent and up to date (informal) 5. PASSIONATE feeling or expressing intense enthusiasm, passion, or anger (informal)

red-hot poker n. a tall perennial plant with spikes of drooping red or orange flowers. It is native to South Africa and cultivated elsewhere as a garden plant. Genus: Kniphofia.

redia /reedi ə/ (plural -ae /-ee/) n. one of the forms that the larvae of trematode worms can take. Rediae are found as parasites in the gut of snails. [Late 19thC. From modern Latin, formed from the name of the Italian biologist Francesco Redi (1626–98).]

redial /ree dî əl/ vti. (-als, -alling, -alled) DIAL TELEPHONE NUMBER AGAIN to dial a particular telephone number again, e.g. because the line was engaged when the number was dialled earlier ▪ n. DIALLING OF NUMBER AGAIN the function that permits automatic redialling of a telephone number

redid past tense of **redo**

Rediffusion /reedi fyoozh'n/ tdmk. a trademark for a broadcasting system that relays radio and television programmes from a local receiver to individual customers by cable

Red Indian n. a highly offensive term formerly used to refer to a Native North American (dated offensive)

Redingote

redingote /rédding gōt/ n. 1. WOMAN'S DRESS OR COAT a belted woman's dress or coat of the 18th century that was open at the front to show a petticoat or dress 2. MAN'S OVERCOAT a man's double-breasted coat of the 18th century that had wide flat cuffs and flared out below the waist [Late 18thC. From French, an alteration of English riding-coat.]

redirect /reedi rékt, -dī-/ (-rects, -recting, -rected) vt. 1. SEND STH ELSEWHERE to send sth received to a different location, e.g. because the intended recipient has moved 2. REROUTE TRAFFIC to send traffic along a different route 3. CHANGE FOCUS to focus actions or activities on a different objective —**redirection** n.

rediscover /reedi skúvvər/ (-ers, -ering, -ered) vt. to experience sth again, especially finding a new source of pleasure in it —**rediscovery** n.

redistribute /reedi strí byoot/ (-utes, -uting, -uted) vt. 1. DISTRIBUTE STH AGAIN to distribute more of sth previously distributed 2. APPORTION STH DIFFERENTLY to divide sth up or share sth out in a different way, e.g. in more equal proportions or among a wider range of people —**redistribution** /reedistri byoosh'n/ n. —**redistributive** /reedi strí byootiv/ adj.

redivivus /réddi vívəss, -vee-/ adj. revived, reborn, or brought back to life (literary) [Late 16thC. From Latin, literally 'alive again', from vivus (see VIVID).]

red kangaroo n. a kangaroo of the largest species, varying in colour from brick red to grey. It is found

in arid areas of Australia. Latin name: Megaleia rufa.

red lead n. a bright red poisonous oxide of lead, used as a pigment in paints. Formula: Pb_3O_4.

redleg /réd leg/ n. 1. BIRDS RED-LEGGED BIRD a bird with red legs, e.g. the redshank 2. VET FROG DISEASE a bacterial disease of frogs that produces a red flush on the hind legs 3. Carib OFFENSIVE TERM an offensive term for a poor white person (slang offensive) 4. US MIL ARTILLERYMAN an artilleryman (slang)

red-letter day n. a very special day or occasion [From the marking of feast days in red on church calendars]

red light n. 1. TRANSP WARNING SIGNAL a red warning signal, especially an instruction to drivers to stop 2. REJECTION a sign of disapproval or rejection, e.g. an instruction not to proceed with sth (informal)

red-light adj. relating to the part of a town or city where brothels and other commercial sex-based activities are concentrated [From the red lights traditionally displayed in the doors and windows of brothels]

redline /réd līn/ (-lines, -lining, -lined) v. 1. vti. POL, ECON REFUSE FINANCIAL SERVICES to refuse loans, insurance, or other financial services to individuals or businesses in a supposedly high-risk area 2. INDUST SELECT FOR REMOVAL to select sth such as an aircraft for removal from service [From the traditional use of red ink to cross out deleted items in a budget]

red marrow n. the reddish bone marrow where red blood cells and some white blood cells are formed

red mass n. a special Roman Catholic mass celebrated in red vestments for the opening of a court or congress

red meat n. meat such as beef or lamb that is relatively dark red in colour when raw

Redmond /rédmund/, **John** (1856–1918) Irish politician. The leader of the Irish Nationalist Party, he campaigned for home rule for Ireland and served in the Constitutional Convention that led to the establishment of the Irish Free State (1922). Full name **John Edward Redmond**

red mullet n. a smallish orange-red edible marine fish found throughout Europe. Latin name: Mullus surmuletus. US term **goatfish**

redneck /réd nek/ n. (informal insult) 1. OFFENSIVE TERM an offensive term for a white farm worker in the southern United States, especially one regarded as uneducated or aggressively prejudiced 2. OFFENSIVE TERM an offensive term for sb who is opposed to liberal social changes, especially sb regarded as prejudiced [From the sunburnt necks of those who work outdoors in sunny climates] —**rednecked** adj.

redo /ree doó/ (-does, -doing, -did /-díd/, -done /-dún/) vt. 1. REPEAT STH to do sth again, e.g. in order to correct mistakes in an earlier effort 2. DO STH DIFFERENTLY to change the appearance of sth such as a hairstyle or the interior decoration of a room

red oak n. a North American oak tree that has bristly lobed leaves and acorns with small cups. Genus: Quercus.

red ochre n. 1. REDDISH EARTH a reddish earth that is rich in iron oxide and used as a red pigment in paints 2. REDDISH PAINT a rich reddish-brown colour used in painting

redolent /rédd'lənt/ adj. 1. SUGGESTING suggestive or reminiscent of sth ○ a report redolent of bias 2. AROMATIC with a strong pleasant aroma (literary) 3. SMELLING with a particular scent or odour ○ old oak furniture redolent of beeswax [15thC. Via Old French from, ultimately, Latin redolere 'to smell strongly', from olere (see OLFACTORY).] —**redolence** n. —**redolently** adv.

redone past participle of **redo**

red osier n. 1. REDDISH WILLOW a willow tree whose reddish branches are used in basketry 2. red osier, **red osier dogwood** DOGWOOD PLANT a North American dogwood plant with red branches and white fruits. Genus: Cornus.

redouble /ridúbb'l/ vti. (-bles, -bling, -bled) 1. INCREASE to increase sth considerably, especially the amount of effort expended on sth, or to become much greater 2. ECHO to echo or re-echo, or cause sth to echo or re-echo 3. CARDS DOUBLE A DOUBLE BID to double an opponent's double as a bid in bridge ■ *n.* CARDS **DOUBLING OF A DOUBLE BID** a redoubling of a bid in bridge [15thC. From French *redoubler*, literally 'to double again', from *double* (see DOUBLE).]

redoubt /ri dówt/ *n.* **1.** **STRONGHOLD** a castle, fortress, or other stronghold (*literary*) **2.** MIL **TEMPORARY FORTIFICATION** a temporary fortification built to defend a position such as a hilltop [Early 17thC. Alteration (influenced by *redoubtable*) of French *redoute*, via Italian *ridotto* from medieval Latin *reductus* 'refuge', from Latin, the past participle of *reducere* (see REDUCE).]

redoubtable /ri dówtəb'l/ *adj.* with personal qualities worthy of respect or fear [14thC. Via French *redoutable* from, ultimately, *douter* (see DOUBT).] —**redoubtably** *adv.*

redound /ri dównd/ (**-dounds, -dounding, -dounded**) *vi.* **1.** **HAVE A PARTICULAR RESULT** to have a particular consequence, usually sth good or positive ○ *All the effort can only redound to her credit.* **2.** **HAVE A CONSEQUENCE FOR SB** to return to affect sb as a repercussion or consequence (*formal*) ○ *His attempts at revenge redounded upon his own head.* [14thC. Via French *redonder* from Latin *redundare* (see REDUNDANT).]

WORD KEY: USAGE

See Usage note at ***rebound***.

redout /réd owt/ *n.* sudden headache and reddening of the field of vision experienced by pilots or astronauts during rapid deceleration and other manoeuvres. It is caused by blood being forced into the vessels of the head.

redowa /réddəvə, -wə/ *n.* a Bohemian folk dance similar to a waltz or a polka [Mid-19thC. Via French or German from Czech *rejdovák*, from *rejdovat* 'to whirl around'.]

redox /réé doks/ *n.* = **oxidation-reduction** [Early 20thC. Coined from REDUCTION + OXIDATION.]

red panda *n.* a reddish-brown mammal that resembles a raccoon in appearance and lives in forests in the Himalayas and nearby areas of eastern Asia. Latin name: *Ailurus fulgens.*

red-pencil *vt.* to revise, correct, or censor written material

red pepper *n.* **1.** **EDIBLE RED POD** any red pod that belongs to the capsicum family of vegetables, especially a ripe sweet pepper. ◊ **green pepper 2.** = **cayenne pepper**

red pine *n.* **1.** **REDDISH PINE TREE** a pine tree that has reddish bark and needles in clusters of two. It is native to northeastern North America. Latin name: *Pinus resinosa.* **2.** **NEW ZEALAND TREE** a coniferous tree of New Zealand with narrow pointed leaves. Latin name: *Dacrydium cupressinum.*

red planet *n.* the planet Mars (*informal*)

redpoll /réd pōl/ *n.* a small bird of the finch family with a red crown and a pink breast that breeds in the far northern regions of North America, Europe, and Asia. Genus: *Carduelis.*

Red Poll *n.* a hornless cow with short reddish hair belonging to a breed originating in England and bred for beef and milk

redraft /réé draaft/ *n.* **SECOND DRAFT** a second or further draft or rewriting ■ *vt.* (**-drafts, -drafting, -drafted**) **DRAFT STH AGAIN** to rewrite sth

red rag *n.* sth that provokes or infuriates sb. US term **red flag** *n.* 2 [From the notion that bulls are enraged at the sight of red objects]

red rattle *n.* a European plant with a seed capsule that rattles. Latin name: *Pedicularis palustris.*

redraw /ree dráw/ (**-draws, -drawing, -drew** /-dróo/, **-drawn** /-dráwn/) *vt.* **1.** **DRAW STH AGAIN** to draw sth another time, usually making changes **2.** **REPOSITION BOUNDARY** to change the position of the boundaries of a region **3.** **REDESIGN STH** to redesign sth, changing its shape or the positions of its constituent parts

redress /ri dréss/ *n.* **1.** **COMPENSATION** compensation or reparation for a loss or wrong sb has experienced **2.** **ACT OF COMPENSATING** the compensating of sb for a loss or wrong experienced ■ *vt.* (**-dresses, -dressing, -dressed**) **1.** **MAKE UP FOR STH** to provide compensation or reparation for a loss or wrong experienced **2.** **IMPOSE FAIRNESS OR EQUALITY ON** to adjust a situation in order to make things fair or equal [14thC. From Old French *redrecier*, from *drecier* (see DRESS).] —**redresser** *n.*

redrew past tense of **redraw**

Red River /red/ **1.** river in southeastern Asia. It rises in southern China and flows through northern Vietnam before emptying into the Gulf of Tonkin. Length: 800 km/500 mi. **2.** river in North America, rising in Minnesota, United States, and emptying into Lake Winnipeg, Canada. Length: 877 km/545 mi.

redroot /réd root/ *n.* **1.** **N AMERICAN BOG PLANT** a perennial bog plant with red roots and woolly yellow flowers, belonging to the bloodwort family. It grows in eastern North America. Latin name: *Lachnanthes caroliana.* **2.** **PLANT WITH RED ROOTS** a plant with red roots, e.g. the bloodroot or pigweed

red route *n.* a major urban road where loading and parking is restricted by a system of red lines and signs at the kerb, enforced by patrols, in order to maintain traffic flows

red salmon *n.* = **sockeye**

Red Sea inland sea between the Arabian peninsula and northeastern Africa. It is linked to the Mediterranean in the north by the Suez Canal. Area: 437,700 sq. km/169,000 sq. mi.

red setter *n.* = **Irish setter**

redshank /réd shangk/ *n.* a large wading bird of slender build with long red legs and red feet. Redshanks are native to Europe and Asia and belong to the sandpiper family. Genus: *Tringa.*

red shank *n.* an annual plant with red stems and spikes of pink flowers. It grows in northern temperate regions. Latin name: *Polygonum persicaria.* US term **lady's thumb**

red shift *n.* a shift in the spectrum of a celestial body towards longer wavelengths, or towards the red end of the spectrum, caused by its motion away from the Earth —**redshifted** *adj.*

Red Sindhi *n.* a small reddish-brown dairy cow belonging to a breed developed in India. It is often used for crossbreeding with European stock in tropical countries.

red siskin *n.* a bright red finch whose head, wings, and tail are black. It is native to northern parts of South America. Latin name: *Carduelis cucullata.*

redskin /réd skin/ *n.* a highly offensive term formerly used to refer to a Native North American (*dated offensive*)

red snapper *n.* a large reddish-coloured food fish found in the warm Atlantic coastal waters off North, South, and Central America. Genus: *Lutjanus.*

red snow *n.* fallen snow that is reddish in colour, either from the presence of airborne dust or from red algae growing in it. It is commonly seen in Arctic and Alpine regions.

red spider, **red spider mite** *n.* = **spider mite**

Red Spot *n.* a large reddish oval and variable marking in the southern hemisphere of Jupiter. It does not rotate at the same rate as the planet and is thought to be an atmospheric phenomenon.

red spruce *n.* a spruce tree that has reddish-brown bark and cones and a light soft wood. It is native to eastern North America. Latin name: *Picea rubens.*

Red Square *n.* a large square in central Moscow, bordered by the Kremlin and Lenin's tomb. It was the site of military parades on public holidays in the former Soviet Union.

red squill *n.* a squill plant whose red bulbs are used as a source of rat poison. It belongs to the lily family. Latin name: *Urginea maritima.*

red squirrel *n.* **1.** **EUROPEAN SQUIRREL** a reddish-brown squirrel with tufted ears that is native to Europe and Asia. Latin name: *Sciurus vulgaris.* **2.** **N AMERICAN SQUIRREL** a squirrel with reddish fur found in coniferous forests of North America. It is smaller than the grey squirrel. Latin name: *Tamiasciurus hudsonicus.*

redstart /réd staart/ *n.* **1.** **THRUSH WITH REDDISH TAIL** a bird of the thrush family that is native to Europe, Asia, and Africa. The male has a black throat and a reddish-brown tail. Genus: *Phoenicurus.* **2.** **AMERICAN WARBLER** a flycatching warbler native to North and South America. The male has reddish-orange patches on black and white plumage. Latin name: *Setophaga ruticilla.* [*Start* is an obsolete word for 'tail' (from Old English *steort*)]

red steenbras *n.* = **dentex**

red tape *n.* official procedure regarded as unnecessary, over-complicated, or obstructive (*informal*) [From the red tape once widely used to seal official documents]

red tide *n.* a brownish-red discoloration in seawater, caused by the increased presence of plant-based plankton. It sometimes leads to the poisoning of fish and, consequently, of those who eat fish.

redtop /réd top/ *n.* a grass plant that has clusters of red flowers and is used in North America for lawns and forage. Genus: *Agrostis.*

red-top /réd top/, **redtop** *n.* a tabloid newspaper (*informal*) ○ *'There is now a debate about whether the red-tops should 'go up-market' to find their audiences'.* (*The Guardian*; November 1998) [Late 20thC. From the red masthead of such a newspaper.]

reduce /ri dyóoss/ (**-duces, -ducing, -duced**) *v.* **1.** *vti.* **DECREASE** to become or make sth smaller in size, number, extent, degree, or intensity **2.** *vt.* **WORSEN STATE OF SB OR STH** to bring sb or sth into a particular undesirable state ○ *The dreadful news reduced them all to tears.* ○ *Bombing had reduced the town to rubble.* **3.** *vt.* **MAKE STH CHEAPER** to lower the price or cost of an item for sale **4.** *vt.* **SIMPLIFY STH** to make sth simpler, especially by extracting or summarizing essential elements **5.** *vt.* **ANALYSE STH SYSTEMATICALLY** to analyse sth in terms of a system or rule, usually as an aid to explaining or understanding it **6.** *vt.* **DEMOTE SB** to place sb officially in a lower rank or grade, e.g. as a punishment for breaking rules **7.** *vt.* **TAKE CONTROL OF PLACE OR PEOPLE** to bring a place or people under a particular authority using force **8.** *vti.* COOK **THICKEN** to make a sauce or stock thicker by boiling off some of the liquid, or to become thicker in this way **9.** *vt.* PHOTOGRAPHY **DECREASE THE DENSITY OF A NEGATIVE** to lessen the density of a photographic negative using a chemical substance **10.** *vt.* METALL **REFINE ORE** to remove the impurities from an ore in order to obtain the pure metal **11.** *vti.* BIOL **UNDERGO CELL DIVISION** to undergo, or cause cells to undergo, a type of cell division (**meiosis**) **12.** *vti.* CHEM **UNDERGO CHEMICAL REACTION** to undergo, or cause a substance to undergo, a chemical reaction in which there is a gain in hydrogen or a loss of oxygen. ◊ **oxidize** *v.* 1 **13.** *vti.* CHEM **GAIN ELECTRONS** to undergo, or cause a substance to undergo, a chemical reaction in which there is an increase in the number of electrons. ◊ **oxidize** *v.* 2 **14.** *vt.* MATH **SIMPLIFY AN EQUATION** to simplify an expression or equation without changing its value [14thC. From Latin *reducere*, literally 'to bring back', from *ducere* (see DUCT).] —**reducibility** /ri dyóossə bílləti/ *n.* —**reducible** /ri dyóossəb'l/ *adj.*

reducer /ri dyóossər/ *n.* **1.** PHOTOGRAPHY **PHOTOGRAPHIC CHEMICAL** a chemical solution that lessens the density of a photographic negative by oxidizing it **2.** CONSTR **PIPE FITTING** a pipe fitting that connects two pipes of different diameters

reducing agent, **reductant** /ridúktənt/ *n.* a chemical substance that reduces the amount of oxygen in another substance and becomes oxidized in the process

reductase /ri dúk tayz, -tayss/ *n.* an enzyme that catalyses the reduction of an organic compound [Early 20thC. Formed from REDUCTION.]

reductio ad absurdum /ri dúkti ō ad ab súrdəm/ (*plural* **reductiones ad absurdum** /-ő neez-/) *n.* **1.** **TAKING STH TO ABSURD LENGTHS** the application of a rule or principle so strictly or literally that the result is ridiculous **2.** PHILOSOPHY **LOGICAL DISPROOF** the disproving of a logical argument by showing that its ultimate conclusion is absurd **3.** PHILOSOPHY **LOGICAL PROOF** the proving of a logical argument indirectly, by showing that the contradictory argument is absurd [Mid-18thC. From Latin, 'reduction to the absurd'.]

reduction /ri dúksh'n/ *n.* **1.** **REDUCING OF STH** the decreasing of sth in size, number, extent, degree, or intensity **2.** **AMOUNT BY WHICH STH IS REDUCED** the amount by which sth is made smaller or less **3.** **SIMPLIFICATION** a simplification or condensation of sth **4.** **SMALLER COPY** a copy of sth made on a smaller scale, e.g. a reduced photocopy **5.** COOK THICKENED SAUCE a sauce or stock that has been thickened by boiling off some of the liquid **6.** MATH MAKING FRACTION SIMPLER the cancelling of common factors in the numerator and denominator of a fraction **7.** MATH DECIMALIZATION OF FRACTION the converting of a fraction into decimal form **8.** BIOL = **meiosis** n. 1 **9.** CHEM CHEMICAL REACTION a chemical reaction that brings about a gain in hydrogen, a loss of oxygen, or an increase in electrons [15thC. Via French from, ultimately, Latin *reducere* (see REDUCE).] —**reductional** *adj.*

reduction division *n.* BIOL = **meiosis** n. 1

reduction firing *n.* the firing of pottery in an oxygen-starved atmosphere in order to change the nature of the glaze applied. It is achieved either by restricting the air intake or by introducing a substance that combines with oxygen.

reduction gear *n.* a set of gears in an engine used to reduce output speed relative to that of the engine while providing greater turning power when, e.g., climbing a hill

reductionism /ri dúksh'nizəm/ *n.* **1.** SIMPLIFICATION the analysis of sth into simpler elements or organized systems, especially with a view to explaining or understanding it **2.** OVERSIMPLIFICATION the over-simplifying of sth complex, or the misguided belief that everything can be explained in simple terms —**reductionist** *n., adj.* —**reductionistic** /ri dúkshə nístik/ *adj.*

reductive /ri dúktiv/ *adj.* **1.** ANALYSING IN SIMPLE TERMS seeking to explain complex things in terms of simple structures and systems **2.** OVERSIMPLIFYING over-simplifying complex things and ignoring their subtleties or important details [Mid-16thC. Via medieval Latin *reductivus* from, ultimately, Latin *reducere* (see REDUCE).] —**reductively** *adv.* —**reductiveness** *n.*

redundancy /ri dúndənssi/ (*plural* -**cies**) *n.* **1.** DISMISSAL FROM WORK dismissal from employment because the job or the worker has been deemed no longer necessary ○ *There may be more redundancies if sales do not improve.* **2.** SUPERFLUOUSNESS the state or fact of not being or no longer being needed or wanted **3.** ELEC ENG DUPLICATION OF COMPONENTS the fitting of duplicate electronic or mechanical components or backup systems that are designed to come into use to keep equipment working if their counterparts fail **4.** TELECOM DUPLICATION OF MESSAGE duplication of information in telecommunications in order to reduce the risk of error **5.** USE OF SUPERFLUOUS WORDS the use of a word whose meaning is already conveyed elsewhere in a passage, without a rhetorical purpose

redundancy payment *n.* a one-off payment given to a worker who has been made redundant, often calculated in relation to length of employment

redundant /ri dúndənt/ *adj.* **1.** DISMISSED FROM WORK dismissed from employment because the job or the worker has been deemed no longer necessary ○ *The companies merged and half the workers were made redundant.* **2.** SUPERFLUOUS not needed or no longer needed **3.** ELEC ENG BACKUP fitted as a backup component or system **4.** LING REPEATING MEANING with the same meaning as a word used elsewhere in a passage and without a rhetorical purpose [Late 16thC. From Latin *redundare* 'to overflow', from *undare* 'to rise in waves', from *unda* (see UNDULATE).] —**redundantly** *adv.*

redupl. *abbr.* reduplicate

reduplicate /ri dyóopli kayt/ *v.* (-**cates**, -**cating**, -**cated**) **1.** *vti.* REPEAT OR DOUBLE to repeat or double sth, or be repeated or doubled **2.** *vt.* LING REPEAT SPEECH SOUND to repeat a vowel, syllable, or word in order to create a new word or linguistic element. For example, the first elements are reduplicated in the words 'wishy-washy' and 'goody-goody'. ■ *adj.* **1.** LING REPEATED repeated in order to create a new word or other linguistic element **2.** BOT CURVING INWARDS used to describe leaves or petals that have their edges curved inwards [Late 16thC. From late Latin *reduplicare*, from Latin *duplicare* (see DUPLICATE).] —**reduplication** /ri dyóopli káysh'n/ *n.* —**reduplicative** /ri dyóoplikətiv/ *adj.* —**reduplicatively** *adv.*

reduviid /ri dyóovi id/ *n.* = **assassin bug** [Late 19thC.

From modern Latin *Reduviidae*, family name, from Latin *reduvia* 'hangnail'.]

redux /ree dúks/ *adj.* brought back, especially in being restored to former importance or prominence (*literary*) [Late 19thC. From Latin, formed from *reducere* (see REDUCE).]

red valerian *n.* a bushy plant with fragrant red or white flowers, native to Europe and Asia. Latin name: *Centranthus ruber.*

redware[1] /réd wair/ *n.* MARINE BIOL = **kelp** n. 1 [*Red* because of its reddish-brown colour; *ware* a northern dialect word meaning 'seaweed' (from Old English *wār*)]

redware[2] /réd wair/ *n.* CRAFT reddish earthenware pottery made from clay with a high iron oxide content

red water *n.* a cattle disease characterized by the passage of reddish urine

redwing /réd wing/ *n.* a bird of the thrush family that has reddish feathers under its wings and a spotted breast. It is native to Europe and Asia. Latin name: *Turdus iliacus.*

red wolf *n.* a small reddish-grey wolf found in south-eastern North America, nearly eliminated by overhunting and hybridization with the coyote. Attempts at reintroduction are now in place. Latin name: *Canis rufus.*

redwood /réd wood/ *n.* a very tall sequoia, with fibrous reddish bark. It grows in coastal California and can reach a height of over 100 m/330 ft. Latin name: *Sequoia sempervirens.*

REE *abbr.* rare-earth element

reebok *n.* = **rhebok**

re-echo /ree ékō/ (**re-echoes**, **re-echoing**, **re-echoed**) *v.* **1.** *vi.* ECHO BACK to resound or echo back **2.** *vt.* REPEAT STH AGAIN to repeat again sth that has already been repeated

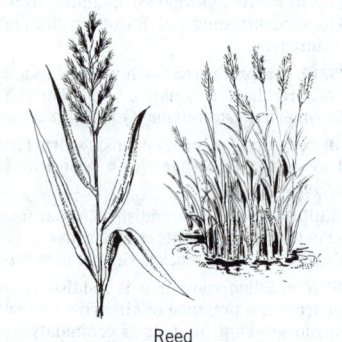

Reed

reed /reed/ *n.* **1.** BOT GRASS PLANT a tall slender grass plant with jointed stalks that grows in marshes and other wet areas. Genus: *Phragmites.* **2.** CRAFT STALK OF REED the stalk of a reed, or a number of such stalks, used for thatching, basketmaking, and other crafts **3.** MUSIC VIBRATING PART OF MUSICAL INSTRUMENT a thin piece of cane, metal, or plastic fitted inside some musical instruments that vibrates to produce sound, usually when the player blows into the instrument. Some woodwind instruments such as the clarinet have single reeds in the mouthpiece, whilst others such as the oboe and bassoon have double reeds. **4.** MUSIC MUSICAL INSTRUMENT a wind instrument such as an oboe or a clarinet, fitted with a reed (*informal*) **5.** TEXTILES WIRES ON A LOOM a series of parallel wires on a loom, used to separate the threads of the warp evenly **6.** MEASURE UNIT OF LENGTH an ancient Hebrew unit of length equal to six cubits [Old English *hrēod*, of prehistoric Germanic origin]

Reed /reed/, **Sir Carol** (1906–76) British film director. His films include *The Third Man* (1949) and *Our Man in Havana* (1959), both written by Graham Greene, and *Oliver!* (1968), for which he won an Academy Award.

reedbuck /réd buk/ *n.* a tawny African antelope with long horns that curve slightly forwards. Reedbucks live near rivers and lakes south of the Sahara. Genus: *Redunca.* [Mid-19thC. Translation of Afrikaans *rietbok*.]

reed bunting *n.* a small bird with brown streaked plumage found near reed beds throughout Europe and Asia. The male has a black head with a white moustache. Latin name: *Emberiza schoeniclus.*

reed grass *n.* a tall grass plant that grows in rivers and ponds in Europe, Asia, and North America. Latin name: *Glyceria maxima.*

reeding /réeding/ *n.* **1.** ARCHIT MOULDING a set of small convex decorative mouldings on a building **2.** COINS COIN GROOVES the narrow vertical grooves on the edge of a coin

reedling /réedling/ *n.* a small brownish-orange songbird with a long tail that lives in reed beds in Europe and Asia. The male has a black patch extending from the eye down the throat. Latin name: *Panurus biarmicus.*

reed mace *n.* a tall slender marsh plant whose flowers grow in brown tube-shaped spikes. Latin name: *Typha latifolia.*

reedman /réedmən/ (*plural* -**men** /-mən/) *n.* a musician who plays a reed instrument, especially a jazz clarinettist or saxophonist (*informal*)

reed organ *n.* a musical instrument such as the harmonium, harmonica, or accordion, in which sound is produced by air passing over a set of reeds

reed pipe *n.* an organ pipe containing a reed that vibrates to make the pipe sound

reed stop *n.* an organ stop that controls a set of reed pipes

re-educate *vt.* **1.** TEACH SB AGAIN to teach sb again, especially in order to change or update knowledge **2.** RETRAIN SB to train or teach sb again who has lost knowledge or a skill —**re-educative** *adj.*

reed warbler *n.* a small brown European bird of the warbler family, commonly found in marsh reeds, and best distinguished by its song. Latin name: *Acrocephalus scirpaceus.*

reedy /réedi/ (-**ier**, -**iest**) *adj.* **1.** FULL OF REEDS full of or thickly planted with reeds ○ *a reedy pond* **2.** HIGH-PITCHED thin and high-pitched, rather than deep or full-toned ○ *reedy voice* **3.** THIN long, thin, or flexible, like a reed —**reedily** *adv.* —**reediness** *n.*

reef[1] /reef/ *n.* **1.** OCEANOG UNDERWATER RIDGE a ridge of coral or rock in a body of water, with the top just below or just above the surface **2.** MINING VEIN OF ORE a lode or vein of ore [Late 16thC. From Dutch *rif*, of uncertain origin: perhaps from Old Norse *rif* 'rib, ridge'.] —**reefy** *adj.*

reef[2] /reef/ *n.* SAILING PART OF SAIL a section of a sail that can be gathered in and tied down to reduce the sail's surface ■ *vt.* (**reefs**, **reefing**, **reefed**) SAILING **1.** MAKE SAIL SMALLER BY GATHERING to reduce the area of a sail by gathering part of it in **2.** SHORTEN RIGGING PIECE to shorten or bring in one of the pieces that support rigging on a ship [14thC. Via Dutch *reef* from Old Norse *rif* 'reef (of a sail)', of uncertain origin: probably from *rif* 'ridge' (see REEF[1]).] —**reefable** *adj.*

reefer[1] /réefər/ *n.* **1.** US CLOTHES = **reefer jacket 2.** NAUT SAILOR WHO REEFS SAILS sb who reefs the sails on a sailing ship [Early 19thC. Formed from REEF[2].]

reefer[2] /réefər/ *n.* DRUGS a marijuana cigarette (*slang*) [Mid-20thC. Origin uncertain: perhaps from Mexican Spanish *grifo* 'marijuana, drug addict', or from REEF[2], from the similarity of furling a sail and rolling such a cigarette.]

reefer[3] /réefər/ *n.* US TRANSP a refrigerated railway wagon or truck trailer (*informal*) [Early 20thC. From REFRIGERATOR.]

reefer jacket *n.* a heavy double-breasted woollen jacket or coat, usually dark blue and hip-length, originally worn by sailors. US term **reefer**[1] n. 1

reef knot *n.* a symmetrical knot that will not slip after tying, made by passing one end of rope over and around another first in one direction, then again in the opposite direction. US term **square knot**

reek /reek/ *v.* (**reeks**, **reeking**, **reeked**) **1.** *vti.* HAVE A VERY STRONG UNPLEASANT SMELL to have a very strong and unpleasant smell, or give off such a smell ○ *The room reeked of smoke.* **2.** *vti.* GIVE CLEAR EVIDENCE OF STH UNPLEASANT to show very strong evidence of an unpleasant quality ○ *The whole document reeks of* *double standards.* **3.** *vi.* **GIVE OFF SMOKE** to give off smoke, steam, or fumes ○ *a reeking pile of old burning tyres* **4.** *vt. US* **TREAT STH WITH SMOKE** to process or treat sth with smoke ■ *n.* **1. UNPLEASANT SMELL** a very strong and unpleasant smell ○ *a reek of disinfectant* **2. VISIBLE VAPOUR** smoke, steam, or other visible vapour (*regional*) [Old English *rēocan*. Ultimately from an Indo-European word that is related to Latin *ructare* 'to belch, vomit' (source of English *eructate*).] —**reeker** *n.* —**reeky** *adj.*

WORD KEY: SYNONYMS

See Synonyms at ***smell***.

reel[1] /reel/ *n.* **1. REVOLVING STORAGE DEVICE** a usually revolving wheel-shaped device around which sth such as thread, film, or wire can be wound for storage **2. A REELFUL** the amount of a material that a reel can hold **3.** CINEMA **SECTION OF CINEMA FILM** the amount of cinema film stored on one reel **4.** ANGLING **WINDER ON FISHING ROD** a winding device attached to a fishing rod that holds the fishing line and enables it to be cast and wound back ■ *vt.* **(reels, reeling, reeled) WIND STH ONTO A REEL** to wind sth such as thread or fishing line onto or off a reel [Old English *hrēol* 'spool (for winding thread)', of unknown origin] —**reeler** *n.*

reel in *vt.* **1. BRING STH CLOSER** to draw sth, especially a fish, in by winding it in with a reel **2. BRING SB OR STH IN** to bring in or acquire sb or sth by using the appropriate skills or offering suitable inducements

reel off *vt.* to list things in rapid succession and with no apparent effort

reel[2] /reel/ *vi.* **(reels, reeling, reeled) 1. STAGGER BACKWARDS** to move in a sudden and uncontrolled fashion, especially backwards as if struck by a blow ○ *reeled back in horror* **2. MOVE UNSTEADILY** to move about unsteadily, staggering or swaying from side to side **3. FEEL GIDDY OR CONFUSED** to feel giddy or shocked and confused ○ *still reeling from the shock of his resignation* **4. WHIRL ROUND AND ROUND** to move or whirl round in circles ■ *n.* **STAGGERING MOTION** an unsteady or circling movement [14thC. Origin uncertain: probably from REEL[1].]

reel[3] /reel/ *n.* **1.** DANCE **SCOTTISH DANCE** a lively Scottish folk dance for sets of two, three, or four couples **2. DANCE MUSIC** a piece of music for a reel, written in quick two-four time ■ *vi.* **(reels, reeling, reeled)** DANCE **DANCE REEL** to dance a reel [Late 16thC. Origin uncertain: probably from REEL[2].]

re-elect *vt.* to elect sb to the same office for another term —**re-election** *n.*

reel mower *n. US* = **cylinder mower**

reel-to-reel *adj.* **HAVING TWO REELS** used to describe magnetic tape that must be wound off a full source reel, threaded through the heads of the machine, and rewound on an empty take-up reel ■ *n.* **TAPE RECORDER WITH TWO REELS** a tape recorder or player that uses reel-to-reel tape

re-enact *vt.* to act out an event that took place in the past, sometimes using the same people who originally took part in it —**re-enactment** *n.*

re-enter *v.* **1.** *vti.* **RETURN** to come back into a place again ○ *The rocket re-entered the atmosphere.* **2.** *vt.* **ENTER DATA AGAIN** to key or write sth in again **3.** *vti.* **GO IN FOR AGAIN** to decide to take part in sth again

re-entrant angle, **re-entrant** *n.* MATH an inward-pointing angle in a polygon that is greater than 180° when viewed or measured from inside the polygon

re-entry *n.* **1. ENTERING AGAIN** the act of entering again **2.** SPACE TECH **RETURN TO EARTH'S ATMOSPHERE** the penetration of the earth's atmosphere by a spacecraft or missile returning from space (*often used before a noun*) ○ *re-entry vehicle* **3.** LAW **REPOSSESSION OF LAND** the repossession of land or other property under the terms of a previous agreement, e.g. where the terms of a lease have not been complied with **4.** CARDS **TAKING OF LEAD IN A CARD GAME** in some card games such as bridge, the regaining of control by taking a trick, or the card played to take the trick

Rees /reess/, **Lloyd Frederic** (1895–1988) Australian painter. His lyrical landscape paintings often incorporate large, bold forms.

re-evaluate *vt.* to think again, or from a different point of view, about the nature, purpose, or value of sth, especially after changes have taken place. ◊ **revalue** —**re-evaluation** *n.*

reeve[1] /reev/ *n.* **1.** *US* **DISTRICT OFFICIAL** an administrative officer in a local district or parish who usually has the responsibility of enforcing the regulations connected with a particular area of activity **2. CANADIAN TOWN COUNCIL PRESIDENT** in Ontario and some western provinces of Canada, the elected president of a town or village council **3.** HIST **REPRESENTATIVE OF THE KING** in Anglo-Saxon times, the representative of the monarch in a shire **4.** HIST **STEWARD OF A FEUDAL MANOR** in medieval times, a steward responsible for running the everyday affairs of a feudal manor [Old English *gerēfa*, literally 'official over an assembly of soldiers', from assumed *rōf* 'array, number']

reeve[2] /reev/ **(reeves, reeving, reeved** *or* **rove** /rōv/) *vt.* NAUT **1. THREAD STH THROUGH AN OPENING** to thread a rope or rod through a ring or other opening **2. FASTEN STH BY REEVING** to fasten a line or rope by passing it around or through some solid object [Early 17thC. Origin uncertain: possibly from Dutch *reven* 'reef' (sail).]

reeve[3] /reev/ *n.* BIRDS the female ruff sandpiper [Mid-17thC. Origin uncertain: perhaps a variant of RUFF[1].]

Reeves /reevz/, **William Pember** (1857–1932) New Zealand politician and writer. As a government minister, he introduced important reforms in industrial relations. He wrote a history of New Zealand, *The Long White Cloud* (1898).

re-examine *vt.* **1. EXAMINE SB OR STH AGAIN** to subject sb or sth to careful further consideration, scrutiny, or checks **2.** LAW **QUESTION SB AGAIN AFTER CROSS-EXAMINATION** to question a witness in court again after he or she has been cross-examined by the other side —**re-examination** *n.*

re-export *vt.* **EXPORT STH AFTER IMPORTING** to export goods that were previously imported from another country, especially after reprocessing them ■ *n.* **1. PROCESS OF RE-EXPORTING** the business or process of re-exporting imported goods **2. STH RE-EXPORTED** sth that is re-exported —**re-exportation** *n.*

ref /ref/ *n.* **REFEREE** a sports referee (*informal*) ■ *vti.* **(refs, reffing, reffed) REFEREE A GAME** to referee a sport or game (*informal*) [Late 19thC. Shortening of REFEREE.]

ref. *abbr.* **1.** reference **2.** refining **3.** reformed **4.** refunding

reface /ree fáyss/ **(-faces, -facing, -faced)** *vt.* **1.** CONSTR **RESTORE EXTERIOR OF BUILDING** to restore or replace the exterior surface of a building or monument **2.** SEW **SEW NEW FACING ON GARMENT** to replace the facing of a garment

Ref. Ch. *abbr.* Reformed Church

refection /ri féksh'n/ *n.* (*literary*) **1. REFRESHMENT** refreshment, especially in the form of food and drink **2. LIGHT MEAL** a portion of food or a light meal [14thC. From the Latin stem *refection-* 'restoration', from *reficere* (see REFECTORY).]

refectory /ri féktəri/ (*plural* **-ries**) *n.* a dining hall, especially in a monastery, convent, or college [15thC. From late Latin *refectorium*, literally 'place where one is restored', ultimately from Latin *reficere* 'to remake', from *facere* 'to make'.]

refectory table *n.* a long narrow dining table with straight heavy legs

refer /ri fúr/ **(-fers, -ferring, -ferred)** *v.* **1.** *vi.* **MENTION** to make a comment in speech or writing that either specifically mentions sb or sth, or is intended to bring sb or sth to mind ○ *referred to the subject only once in his speech* **2.** *vi.* **GIVE A DESCRIPTION** to describe sb or sth in a particular way ○ *tried to be respectful when referring to her colleague's thesis* **3.** *vi.* **BE RELATED** to relate to sth or be connected with it ○ *This clause refers to your responsibilities as the homeowner.* **4.** *vi.* **CONSULT FOR INFORMATION** to consult a source in order to find information or assistance ○ *refer to the manual* **5.** *vt.* **DIRECT SB TO SOURCE OF HELP** to direct sb to sth or sb else for information, help, treatment, or judgment ○ *referred me to a specialist* **6.** *vt.* **ATTRIBUTE STH TO A CAUSE** to attribute the cause or source of sth to sth else ○ *They referred the high gains to the timing of their investment.* **7.** *vt.* EDUC **FAIL AN EXAM CANDIDATE** to fail an examination candidate or ask him or her to retake the exam **8.** *vt.* EDUC **RETURN THESIS FOR REVISION** to return a thesis to a student for further work or revision before it can be accepted [14thC. From French *référer*, from Latin *referre* 'to carry back', from *ferre* 'to carry' (source of English *fertile*).] —**referable** /réffərəb'l, ri fúrəb'l/ *adj.* —**referrer** /ri fúrər/ *n.*

WORD KEY: USAGE

Is **refer back** redundant? Some people think that *refer back* is redundant, because one of the implicit meanings of *re-* is 'back'. But a person may *refer* a problem or request, for example to a new authority for a decision, or *refer* it *back* to the original decision-maker for reconsideration. If the meaning of *refer* is bringing an issue forward to a higher authority, use *refer forward* or *refer ahead* to avoid ambiguity. If the meaning of *refer* is 'to make a mention or reference to sth already mentioned', such as a text quoted, for example in a class lecture, it is better to say *In referring* [not *back*] *to page 321 of my book, I might add the following information not mentioned in Tuesday's lecture.* There, context and meaning determine inclusion or exclusion of *back*.

referee /réffə rée/ *n.* **1.** SPORTS **OFFICIAL OVERSEEING SPORT** an official who oversees the play in a sport or game, judges whether the rules are being followed, and penalizes fouls or infringements **2. ARBITRATOR** sb not directly involved in a matter who is called in to settle disputes, make decisions, or pass judgements concerning the matter **3.** COMM **PERSON WHO GIVES INFORMATION ABOUT SB** sb who is asked to comment on the character or qualifications of another person, especially when that person is applying for a job. US term **reference** *n.* 10 **4.** LAW **SB WHO REVIEWS CASE** sb appointed by a court to review and make a report or judgement on a case ■ *vti.* **(-rees, -reeing, -reed) ACT AS A REFEREE** to act as a referee in a sport, in a dispute, or for an applicant [Early 17thC]

reference /réffərəns/ *n.* **1. MENTION** a spoken or written comment that either specifically mentions or calls attention to sb or sth, or is intended to bring sb or sth to mind **2. PROCESS OF MENTIONING** the process of mentioning or alluding to sb or sth ○ *The document makes reference to three methods for filing a complaint.* **3. APPLICABILITY** applicability or relevance to, or connection with, a particular subject or person ○ *Does what you're saying have any reference at all to the matter in hand?* **4. SOURCE OF INFORMATION** a source of information such as a dictionary or an encyclopedia (*often used before a noun*) ○ *the reference section of the library* **5.** PUBL **SOURCE REFERRED TO** a source of information referred to by a footnote or citation **6.** PUBL **FOOTNOTE OR BIBLIOGRAPHICAL CITATION** a note directing a reader's attention to a particular section of a work or to another source of information **7.** PUBL = **reference mark 8.** COMM **IDENTIFYING CODE** sth, usually a set of letters or figures, that serves to identify sb or sth, e.g. a customer, client, business letter, or a spot on a map (*often used before a noun*) ○ *asked for a customer reference number* **9.** COMM **STATEMENT OF CHARACTER AND QUALIFICATIONS** a statement concerning sb's character or qualifications, given, e.g. to a potential employer **10.** *US* COMM = **referee** *n.* 3 ■ *vt.* **(-ences, -encing, -enced) 1.** PUBL **COMPILE REFERENCES FOR BOOK** to compile a list of references for a book, essay, or thesis **2. USE STH AS A SOURCE** to use or refer to sb or sth as a source in the writing of sth ○ *The author referenced some rather obscure works.* ■ *prep.* **WITH REFERENCE TO** in connection with ○ *Reference our discussion of 5 June, I believe our prior decision stands.*

reference book *n.* **1. INFORMATION SOURCE-BOOK** a book that is intended to be used for looking up facts, definitions, or other information **2.** *S African* = **passbook**

reference mark *n.* a typographical symbol, such as an asterisk or number used to draw the attention of a reader to a note or bibliographic entry

referendum /réffə réndəm/ (*plural* **-dums** *or* **-da** /-də/) *n.* a vote by the whole of an electorate on a specific question or questions put to it by a government or similar body [Mid-19thC. From Latin, literally '(sth) to be referred (to the Senate)', a form of the gerundive of *referre* (see REFER).]

referent /réffərənt/ *n.* the thing or idea that a symbol, word, or phrase denotes

referential /réffə rénsh'l/ *adj.* **1.** RELATING TO REFERENCE relating to references or in the form of a reference **2.** REFERRING TO OTHER WORKS used to describe a work of art that imitates other works or contains oblique references or homages to them, often at the expense of original content or style —**referentiality** /réffə renshi álləti/ *n.* —**referentially** /réffə rénsh'li/ *adv.*

referral /ri fúrəl/ *n.* **1.** PROCESS OF REFERRING the act or process of referring sb or sth to sb else, especially of sending a patient to consult a medical specialist **2.** SB OR STH REFERRED sb or sth that has been referred, especially a patient who has been sent to a medical specialist

referred pain *n.* pain that is felt not at its source but in another part of the body

reffo /réffō/ (*plural* **-fos**) *n.* *Aus* an offensive term for an immigrant to Australia, especially one from Europe, during the period after World War II (*dated informal offensive*) [Mid-20thC. Formed from shortening of REFUGEE + -O.]

refill *vti.* /ree fíl/ (**-fills, -filling, -filled**) FILL AGAIN to fill a container again, or become filled again ■ *n.* /rée fil/ **1.** STH THAT FILLS AGAIN a sufficient amount of sth to fill a container again after it has been emptied **2.** BEVERAGES ANOTHER DRINK another drink to refill an empty glass or cup **3.** COMM REPLACEMENT FOR CONTENTS OF CONTAINER an amount of a product packaged as a replacement for the used up contents of a previously purchased product **4.** *US* MED FURTHER AMOUNT OF A PRESCRIBED MEDICINE a further amount of a medication prescribed on a previous occasion —**refillable** /ree fílləb'l/ *adj.*

refinance /rée fī nánss, réefi nánss, rée fī nanss/ (**-nances, -nancing, -nanced**) *vti.* to obtain new financing for sth on different terms, often involving the paying off of an existing high-interest loan by means of a new lower-interest one —**refinancer** *n.*

refine /ri fīn/ (**-fines, -fining, -fined**) *vti.* **1.** INDUST REMOVE IMPURITIES to produce a purer form of sth by removing the impurities from it, or to become pure through such a process **2.** MAKE OR BECOME MORE ELEGANT to make sb or sth more cultured or elegant by eliminating less acceptable habits and tastes, or become more cultured in this way **3.** MAKE STH MORE EFFECTIVE to improve sth through small changes that make it more effective or more subtle [Late 16thC. Literally 'to make fine again', formed from *fine* (see FINE).] —**refinable** *adj.* —**refiner** *n.*

refined /ri fīnd/ *adj.* **1.** CULTURED AND POLITE cultured and polite in habits, tastes, or appearance **2.** SOPHISTICATED AND EFFECTIVE developed to or possessing a high degree of sophistication and effectiveness **3.** INDUST PURIFIED made purer by an industrial refining process

refinement /ri fīnmənt/ *n.* **1.** ELEGANCE elegance, politeness, and good taste **2.** IMPROVEMENT an addition or alteration that improves sth by making it more sophisticated or effective **3.** INDUST PROCESS OF REFINING the process of refining sth **4.** SUBTLE, PRECISE POINT a subtle or precise distinction in language or point in an argument

refinery /ri fīnəri/ (*plural* **-ies**) *n.* an industrial site where substances such as oil or sugar are processed and purified

refit /ree fít/ *vti.* (**-fits, -fitting, -fitted**) REPAIR AND RE-EQUIP to make sth, especially a ship, ready for further use by repairing and re-equipping it, or to undergo such a process ■ *n.* THOROUGH OVERHAUL a thorough overhaul of sth, especially a ship, in which it is repaired and re-equipped

refl. *abbr.* **1.** MATH reflection **2.** ANAT reflective **3.** MED reflex **4.** reflexive

reflag /ree flág/ (**-flags, -flagging, -flagged**) *vt.* to register a ship or plane with a different national authority

reflation /ree fláysh'n/ *n.* the process of bringing an economy out of recession by increasing the amount of money in circulation within it [Mid-20thC. Coined from *-flation* (as in DEFLATION and INFLATION).] —**reflate** *vti.*

reflect /ri flékt/ (**-flects, -flecting, -flected**) *v.* **1.** *vti.* SEND STH BACK to redirect sth that strikes a surface, especially light, sound, or heat, usually back towards its point of origin ○ *The Moon reflects light from the Sun towards the Earth.* **2.** *vti.* SHOW A MIRROR IMAGE OF to show a reverse image of sb or sth on a mirror or other reflective surface **3.** *vt.* SHOW STH to express or be an indicator of sth ○ *The election results reflect discontent among voters.* **4.** *vi.* THINK SERIOUSLY to think seriously, carefully, and relatively calmly ○ *The retreat will give us time to reflect.* **5.** *vi.* SAY TO SELF THOUGHTFULLY to have a particular thought which may or may not be voiced ○ *That, he reflected, was the only positive thing one could say about the matter.* **6.** *vti.* BRING CREDIT OR DISCREDIT to bring credit, discredit, or another judgement on sb or sth ○ *His current success reflects real credit on the school.* **7.** *vti.* BEND BACK to bend backwards or bend sth back (*archaic*) [14thC. Via Old French *reflecter* from Latin *reflectere* 'to bend back', from *flectere* 'to bend'.]

reflectance /ri fléktənss/ *n.* PHYS = **reflectivity**

reflecting telescope /ri flékting-/ *n.* a telescope in which light from the object is initially focused by a concave mirror

reflection /ri fléksh'n/, **reflexion** *n.* **1.** PHYS ACT OF REFLECTING STH the process or act of reflecting sth, especially light, sound, or heat **2.** REFLECTED IMAGE the image of sb or sth that appears in a mirror or other reflecting surface **3.** CAREFUL THOUGHT careful thought, especially the process of reconsidering previous actions, events, or decisions **4.** CONSIDERED IDEA an idea or thought, especially one produced by careful consideration of sth **5.** INDICATION a clear indication or the result of sth ○ *This award is a reflection of your hard work.* **6.** CAUSE OF BLAME OR CREDIT a cause of blame or credit to sb or sth ○ *Of course, it's no reflection on you that the project failed.* **7.** ANAT BENDING BACK OF A STRUCTURE the bending back upon itself of a membrane or other anatomical structure **8.** MATH SYMMETRICAL TRANSFORMATION a symmetrical transformation in which a figure is reversed along an axis so that the new figure produced is a mirror image of the original one —**reflectional** *adj.*

reflective /ri fléktiv/ *adj.* **1.** THOUGHTFUL characterized by deep careful thought **2.** PHYS ABLE TO REFLECT able to reflect light, sound, or other forms of energy **3.** BY REFLECTION produced by reflection —**reflectively** *adv.* —**reflectiveness** *n.*

reflectivity /rée flek tívvəti/ (*plural* **-ties**) *n.* the ratio of the energy of a wave reflected from a surface to the energy of the incident wave. Symbol ρ

reflectometer /rée flek tómmitər/ *n.* an instrument used to measure the ratio of the energy of a wave after reflection to the energy of the wave before reflection

reflector /ri fléktər/ *n.* **1.** STH THAT REFLECTS LIGHT an object, usually glass, plastic, or metal, that reflects light **2.** ASTRON = **reflecting telescope**

reflet /ri fláy/ *n.* a shiny or iridescent effect, especially in ceramic finishes [Mid-19thC. Via French *reflet*, earlier *reflès*, from Italian *riflesso* 'reflection'.]

reflex *adj.* /rée fleks/ **1.** PHYSIOL AUTOMATIC AND INVOLUNTARY occurring automatically and involuntarily as a result of the nervous system's reaction to a stimulus **2.** EXTREMELY FAST very fast in reacting **3.** PRODUCED AUTOMATICALLY produced automatically, unthinkingly, and totally predictably in response to events ○ *reflex opposition* **4.** MATH BETWEEN 180° AND 360° used to describe an angle of between 180° and 360° **5. reflex, reflexed** BOT BENT BACK bent or folded back ○ *reflex leaves* **6.** PHYS REFLECTED involving a reflection of energy, e.g. of light or a stream of electrons ○ *reflex light* ■ *n.* /rée fleks/ **1.** PHYSIOL INVOLUNTARY BODILY REACTION an involuntary physiological reaction such as a sneeze, triggered by a nerve impulse sent from a nerve centre in response to a nerve receptor's reaction to a stimulus **2.** PHYS STH REFLECTED a reflected image, or a reflection of light, sound, or heat **3.** LING WORD DEVELOPED FROM AN EARLIER FORM a later form of a word or other linguistic element that has developed from an earlier one ■ *vti.* /rifléks/ (**-flexes, -flexing, -flexed**) BEND BACK to bend back, or cause sth to bend back on itself [Early 16thC. From Latin *reflexus* 'bent back', past participle of *reflectere* (see REFLECT).] —**reflexly** /rée fleksli, ri fléksli/ *adv.*

reflex arc *n.* a nerve pathway that is responsible for triggering a reflex action

reflex camera *n.* a camera with an internal mirror that reflects the actual image from the lens into the viewfinder so that the photographer can check the composition and focus exactly. ◊ **single-lens reflex**

reflexed *adj.* BOT = **reflex** *adj.* 5

reflexion *n.* = **reflection**

reflexive /ri fléksiv/ *adj.* **1.** GRAM REFERRING TO PREVIOUS NOUN referring to the same person or thing as another noun or pronoun in the same sentence. The reflexive pronouns in English end in '-self' or '-selves', e.g. 'myself', 'yourself', 'ourselves'. **2.** GRAM DENOTING SELF-DIRECTED ACTION taking a reflexive pronoun as an object, thereby indicating an action that the subject does to or for itself ○ *a reflexive verb* **3.** OF OR BY REFLEX relating to, or being the product of, a reflex **4.** WITHOUT THINKING automatic and involuntary or unthinking **5.** LOGIC, MATH BEING THE SAME used to describe an association between pairs of logical objects or numbers (**relation**) that are the same or of the same size ■ *n.* GRAM REFLEXIVE VERB OR PRONOUN a reflexive verb or pronoun —**reflexively** *adv.* —**reflexiveness** *n.*

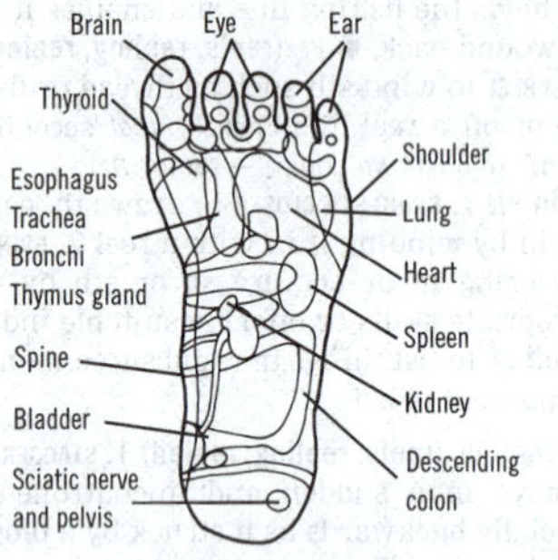

Reflexology

reflexology /rée flek sóllәji/ *n.* **1.** ALTERN MED MASSAGE THERAPY a form of massage in which pressure is applied to certain parts of the feet and hands in order to promote relaxation and healing elsewhere in the body **2.** PHYSIOL STUDY OF REFLEXES AND BEHAVIOUR the scientific study of physiological reflexes and their relation to behaviour **3.** PSYCHOL BEHAVIOURAL THEORY a theory that explains human behaviour as complex chains of conditioned and unconditioned reflexes

refluent /rέffloo ənt/ *adj.* flowing back [Late 17thC. From Latin *refluent-*, present participle stem of *refluere* 'to flow back', from *fluere* 'to flow'.]

reflux /rée fluks/ *n.* **1.** BACKWARD FLOW a returning flow of sth **2.** MED REGURGITATION OF STOMACH FLUID a backflow of liquid in the opposite direction to its normal movement such as the regurgitation of stomach and peptic juices associated with acid indigestion and hiatal hernia **3.** PHYS HEATING WHILE CONDENSING VAPOUR a method of heating liquid so that escaping vapour is condensed and returned to the liquid ■ *vt.* (**-fluxes, -fluxing, -fluxed**) PHYS HEAT STH WHILE CONDENSING VAPOUR to heat a liquid in a container with a condenser that catches and returns escaping vapour [15thC. Coined from RE- + FLUX.]

refocus /ree fókəss/ (**-cuses, -cusing, -cused**) *vti.* **1.** CHANGE FOCUS OF CAMERA to change or adjust the focus of sth such as a camera or telescope **2.** FOCUS ON STH DIFFERENT to concentrate attention or efforts on sth different ○ *We need to refocus our marketing strategies.*

reforest /ree fórrist/ (**-ests, -esting, -ested**), **reafforest** /ree ə fórrist/ (**-ests, -esting, -ested**) *vti.* to replant an area with trees after its original trees have been cut down —**reforestation** /rée forri stáysh'n/ *n.*

reform /ri fáwrm/ *v.* (**-forms, -forming, -formed**) **1.** *vt.* IMPROVE STH BY REMOVING FAULTS to change and improve sth by correcting faults, removing inconsistencies and abuses, and imposing modern methods or values ○ *reform the law* **2.** *vti.* GET RID OF UNACCEPTABLE HABITS to adopt a more acceptable way of life and mode of behaviour or persuade or force sb else to do so **3.** *vt.* INDUST CHANGE THE MOLECULAR STRUCTURE OF PETROLEUM to subject petroleum to a chemical process such as catalytic cracking, in order to convert it into petrol ■ *n.* **1.** REORGANIZATION AND IMPROVEMENT the reorganization and improvement of sth, especially a political institution or system, that is considered to be faulty, ineffective, or unjust ○ *electoral reform*

○ *the reform candidate* **2.** IMPROVING CHANGE a particular change and improvement, especially in the social or political sphere ○ *reforms designed to prevent fraud* **3.** CHARACTER IMPROVEMENT the adoption by sb of a more acceptable way of life [14thC. Directly or via French *réformer* from Latin *reformare*, literally 'to form again', ultimately from *forma* 'form'.] —**reformability** /ri fáwrmə bílləti/ *n.* —**reformable** /ri fáwrməb'l/ *adj.* —**reformative** /-fáwrmətiv/ *adj.*

Reform *adj.* OF REFORM JUDAISM relating or belonging to Reform Judaism ■ *n.* = **Reform Judaism**

re-form /ree fáwrm/ *vti.* to return to or cause sth to return to a previous form —**re-formation** /ree fáwr máysh'n/ *n.*

reformation /réffər máysh'n/ *n.* **1.** ACT OF REFORMING the act or process of reforming sb or sth **2.** REFORMED STATE a reformed state, especially a general improvement in sb's behaviour —**reformational** *adj.*

Reformation *n.* the 16th-century religious movement in Europe that set out to reform some of the doctrines and practices of the Roman Catholic Church and resulted in the development of Protestantism

reformatory /ri fáwrmətəri/ *n.* (*plural* **-ries**) INSTITUTION FOR YOUNG OFFENDERS formerly, a penal institution for young offenders ■ *adj.* INTENDED TO REFORM intended for the reform of sb or sth (*formal*)

Reform Bill *n.* any of a number of 19th-century acts of parliament, especially those of 1832 and 1867, that gave the vote to wider sections of society and redistributed parliamentary seats

reformed /ri fáwrmd/ *adj.* **1.** IMPROVED improved by the removal of outdated, ineffective, or unjust qualities **2.** IMPROVED IN CHARACTER no longer behaving in an unacceptable way

Reformed *adj.* relating or belonging to a Protestant Church, especially one based on the teachings of John Calvin rather than those of Martin Luther

reformer /ri fáwrmər/ *n.* a person or movement that reforms or tries to reform others

Reformer *n.* sb who was deeply involved in the Reformation that resulted in the development of Protestantism

reformism /ri fáwrmizəm/ *n.* a philosophy or movement that advocates the reform of an existing institution

Reform Judaism *n.* the branch of Judaism that seeks to adapt religious practice to modern times and rejects the belief that Moses was literally given the Torah by God. It was established in 19th-century Germany.

refract /ri frákt/ (**-fracts, -fracting, -fracted**) *vt.* **1.** PHYS ALTER COURSE OF WAVE OF ENERGY to alter the course of a wave of energy that passes into sth from another medium, as water does to light entering it from the air **2.** OPHTHALMOL MEASURE DEGREE OF REFRACTION IN STH to measure the degree of refraction in a lens or eye **3.** SHOW STH THROUGH A DIFFERENT MEDIUM to alter the appearance of sth by viewing or showing it through a different medium [Early 17thC. From Latin *refractus*, perfect participle of *refringere* 'to break off, break back', from *frangere* 'to break'.]

refracting telescope *n.* a telescope in which a lens receives and focuses light that is then viewed through a second, magnifying lens in the eyepiece

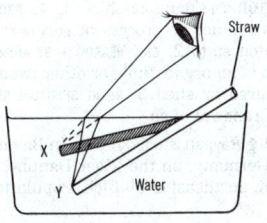

Refraction

refraction /ri fráksh'n/ *n.* **1.** PHYS CHANGE OF DIRECTION OF A WAVE the change in direction that occurs when a

wave of energy such as light passes from one medium to another of a different density, e.g. from air to water **2.** PHYS DEGREE OF WAVE REDIRECTION the degree to which a wave of energy is refracted **3.** ASTRON DISTORTION OF A CELESTIAL BODY'S LOCATION the degree to which the apparent position of a celestial body is distorted by the redirection of its light as it passes through the Earth's atmosphere **4.** OPHTHALMOL EYE'S ABILITY TO BEND LIGHT the ability of the eye to change the direction of light in order to focus it on the retina **5.** OPHTHALMOL MEASURING OF EYE'S REFRACTIVE CAPACITY the process of measuring the eye's ability to refract light —**refractional** *adj.*

refractive /ri fráktiv/ *adj.* PHYS relating to, involving, or capable of refraction —**refractively** *adv.* —**refractiveness** *n.* —**refractivity** /reè frak tívvəti/ *n.*

refractive index *n.* PHYS the ratio of the speed of refracted light in a vacuum or reference medium to its speed in the medium under examination. US term **index of refraction**. Symbol *n*

refractometer /reè frak tómmitər/ *n.* an instrument that measures the refractive index of a medium —**refractometric** /ri fráktə métrik/ *adj.* —**refractometry** /reè frak tómmətri/ *n.*

refractor /ri fráktər/ *n.* **1.** = **refracting telescope 2.** PHYS LIGHT-REFRACTING DEVICE a device that alters the direction of a beam of light by passing it between two transparent materials of different density

refractory /ri fráktəri/ *adj.* **1.** UNCONTROLLABLE stubborn, rebellious, and uncontrollable **2.** PHYS HEAT-RESISTANT resistant to high temperatures, and therefore not easily melted or worked **3.** MED UNRESPONSIVE TO TREATMENT unresponsive to medical treatment ○ *a refractory infection* **4.** MED RESISTANT TO INFECTION resistant to infection or disease **5.** UNRESPONSIVE TO STIMULUS not able to respond to a stimulus ■ *n.* (*plural* **-ries**) INDUST, PHYS HIGHLY HEAT-RESISTANT MATERIAL a material that is able to withstand high temperatures without melting, e.g. the fire clay used to line furnaces [Early 17thC. Variant of earlier 'refractary', from Latin *refractarius* 'stubborn', from *refractus* (see REFRACT).] —**refractorily** *adv.* —**refractoriness** *n.*

refractory period *n.* the time after receiving a stimulus during which a nerve or muscle cell cannot respond to further stimuli

refrain[1] /ri fráyn/ (**-frains, -fraining, -frained**) *vi.* to avoid or hold yourself back from doing sth [14thC. Via Old French *refrener* from Latin *refrenare* 'to hold back, curb', from *frenum* 'bridle'.] —**refrainment** *n.*

refrain[2] /ri fráyn/ *n.* **1.** POETRY RECURRING PIECE OF VERSE a line or group of lines that recurs at regular intervals in a poem, especially at the ends of verses **2.** MUSIC CHORUS the chorus in a song, or the music that accompanies it **3.** MUSIC MELODY a melody or tune **4.** STH REPEATED OFTEN sth that is frequently repeated, such as a saying or an idea [14thC. From Old French, past participle of *refraindre* 'to repeat', from assumed Vulgar Latin *refrangere*, alteration of Latin *refringere* (see REFRACT).]

refrangible /ri fránjəb'l/ *adj.* able to be refracted [Late 17thC. From modern Latin *refrangibilis*, from *refrangere*, alteration of Latin *refringere* (see REFRACT).] —**refrangibility** /ri fránjə bílləti/ *n.*

refresh /ri frésh/ (**-freshes, -freshing, -freshed**) *v.* **1.** *vt.* RENEW SB'S ENERGY to make sb feel more energetic, especially with rest, food, or drink ○ *feel refreshed after a nap* **2.** *vt.* MAKE SB FRESH AND COOL to make sb feel fresh and cool or clean **3.** *vt.* REACTIVATE MEMORY to prompt or reactivate the memory with a piece of information ○ *Just refresh my memory.* **4.** *vt.* MAKE STH FRESH OR BRIGHT AGAIN to bring the freshness or the brightness and colour back to sth that is stale, wilting, or faded ○ *Plunge the carrots in ice water to refresh them.* **5.** *vt.* REPLENISH STH to replenish the supplies of sth ○ *Can I refresh your drink?* **6.** *vi.* FOOD HAVE REFRESHMENTS to have or partake of refreshment, especially food or drink (*archaic*) **7.** *vt.* COMPUT UPDATE ELECTRONIC DEVICE WITH DATA to update an electronic device, especially a VDU or active memory chip, with data **8.** *vti.* COMPUT UPDATE INFORMATION to update the information on a particular World Wide Web site, or to be updated ○ *This page refreshes every two minutes.* [14thC. From Old French *refreschir*, literally 'to make fresh again', from *freis* 'fresh'.]

refresher /ri fréshər/ *n.* **1.** STH REFRESHING sth that refreshes **2.** EXTRA PAYMENT FOR A LAWYER an additional payment made to a lawyer during a lengthy case

refresher course *n.* a course of instruction designed to bring sb's knowledge and skills up to date

refreshing /ri fréshing/ *adj.* **1.** RESTORING ENERGY serving to restore energy and vitality **2.** PLEASING AND RATHER EXCITING pleasingly different and exciting

refreshment /ri fréshmənt/ *n.* **1.** STH REFRESHING sth that refreshes, especially food and drink **2.** ACT OF REFRESHING the process of refreshing sb or sth, or a refreshing quality in sth ■ **refreshments** *npl.* STH TO EAT AND DRINK sth to eat and drink, usually snacks or a light meal and drinks

refresh rate *n.* the number of times per second that an image displayed on a screen needs to be regenerated to prevent flicker when viewed by the human eye. The refresh rate is dependent upon the persistence of the material used on the screen and the retina's retentivity.

refried beans /reè fríd-/ *npl.* a Mexican dish of beans cooked with spices, mashed, then fried

refrigerant /ri fríjjərənt/ *n.* **1.** COOLING SUBSTANCE a substance used to cool or freeze, especially the liquid that circulates in a refrigerator **2.** MED FEVER-REDUCING MEDICATION a medication that alleviates fever or reduces body heat ■ *adj.* **1.** COOLING having a cooling or freezing effect **2.** MED REDUCING BODY HEAT reducing fever or body heat [Late 16thC. From Latin *refrigerant-*, present participle of *refrigerare* (see REFRIGERATE).]

refrigerate /ri fríjjə rayt/ (**-ates, -ating, -ated**) *vt.* to cool food or other heat-sensitive products to prevent deterioration in quality [Mid-16thC. From Latin *refrigerare*, 'to chill again, cool', from *friger-*, an obsolete stem of *frigus* 'cold'.] —**refrigeration** /ri fríjjə ráysh'n/ *n.* —**refrigerative** /ri fríjjərətiv/ *adj.*

refrigerated /ri fríjjə raytid/ *adj.* **1.** KEEPING ITS CONTENTS AT LOW TEMPERATURE designed to keep its contents or cargo at a low temperature in order to preserve them, e.g. during a journey **2.** KEPT AT LOW TEMPERATURE kept or preserved at a low temperature in a refrigerator

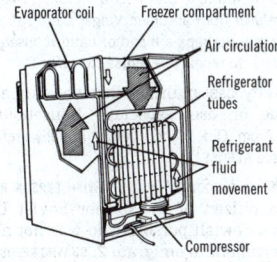

Refrigerator: Cross-section of a refrigerator

refrigerator /ri fríjjə raytər/ *n.* an electrical appliance in the form of an insulated cabinet that keeps items cool through artificial means, or an insulated walk-in chamber artificially cooled for this purpose

refringent /ri frínjənt/ *adj.* refractive [Late 18thC. From Latin *refringent-*, present participle stem of *refringere* (see REFRACT).] —**refringence** *n.*

reft[1] past tense, past participle of **reave**[1]

reft[2] past tense, past participle of **reave**[2]

refuel /ree fyoo əl, ree fyoól/ (**-els, -elling, -elled**) *vti.* **1.** REFILL WITH FUEL to refill a vehicle's tank with fuel **2.** PROVIDE NEW MATERIAL FOR STH to provide additional material for or give a renewed impetus to sth

refuge /réff yooj/ *n.* **1.** SHELTER OR PROTECTION a sheltered or protected state safe from sth threatening, harmful, or unpleasant **2.** SHELTERING PLACE a place, or sometimes a person, offering protection or safe shelter from sth **3.** SAFE ACCOMMODATION FOR BATTERED WOMEN a place offering accommodation to women who are victims of violence, especially in the home **4.** TRANSP = **traffic island** [14thC. Via Old French from Latin *refugium*, literally 'place to flee back to', ultimately from *fugere* 'to flee' (source of English *fugitive*).]

refugee /réffyoo jée/ *n.* sb who is seeking or taking refuge, especially from war or persecution, by going to a foreign country (*often used before a noun*)

refugium /ri fyóoji əm/ (*plural* **-a** /-ji ə/) *n.* an area whose climate remains habitable for particular species, especially rare or endangered ones, when that of the surrounding areas has changed [Mid-20thC. From Latin (see REFUGE).]

refulgent /ri fúljənt/ *adj.* shining brilliantly or splendidly (*literary*) [Early 16thC. From Latin *refulgent-*, present participle stem of *refulgere* 'to shine back, reflect', from *fulgere* 'to shine, flash'.] —**refulgence** *n.* —**refulgently** *adv.*

refund *vt.* /ri fúnd/ (**-funds, -funding, -funded**) RETURN MONEY TO SB to return money to sb, usually because he or she paid too much or did not receive what was paid for ■ *n.* /rée fund/ **1.** RETURNED MONEY an amount of money that is returned to sb **2.** PROCESS OF REPAYMENT the act or process of returning money [14thC. Via Old French *refunder* from Latin *refundere* 'to pour back', from *fundere* 'to pour'.] —**refundable** /ri fúndəb'l/ *adj.*

re-fund *vt.* **1.** FUND STH ANEW to fund sth again **2.** BORROW TO REPAY A DEBT to pay off a debt by new borrowing **3.** REPLACE BOND ISSUE WITH NEW ISSUE to replace an existing issue of bonds with a new issue

refurbish /ree fúrbish/ (**-bishes, -bishing, -bished**) *vt.* to restore sth to a cleaner, brighter, or more functional state —**refurbishment** *n.*

refusal /ri fyóoz'l/ *n.* **1.** UNWILLINGNESS TO DO STH a declaration or an attitude of unwillingness to do or accept sth **2.** FIRST OFFER OF STH the chance to accept or reject sth before it is offered to others **3.** EQU HORSE'S REFUSAL TO JUMP AN OBSTACLE a horse's stopping and not attempting to jump an obstacle in a race or competition

refuse[1] /ri fyóoz/ (**-fuses, -fusing, -fused**) *v.* **1.** *vti.* INDICATE UNWILLINGNESS to declare or make known a decision or intention not to do sth **2.** *vt.* NOT ACCEPT STH to decline to accept sth offered ○ *refused the promotion* **3.** *vt.* DENY STH to be unwilling to give, allow, or agree to sth asked for by sb ○ *I refused them the use of my tools.* **4.** *vti.* EQU BALK AT JUMP to stop and not jump over an obstacle (*refers to a horse*) [14thC. Via Old French *refuser* from assumed Vulgar Latin *refusare*, of uncertain origin: perhaps a blend of Latin *recusare* 'to refuse' and *refutare* 'to repel'.] —**refusable** *adj.*

refuse[2] /réffyooss/ *n.* things thrown away as being of no value or use, especially household rubbish [14thC. From Old French *refus*, literally 'refusal', from *refuser* (see REFUSE[1]).]

refusenik /ri fyóoznik/ *n.* **1.** JEWISH PERSON REFUSED EMIGRATION a citizen of the former Soviet Union, especially a Jewish person, who was not allowed by the government to emigrate **2.** SB WHO REFUSES sb who refuses to agree to, take part in, or cooperate with sth, especially on grounds of principle (*informal*) [Late 20thC. Origin uncertain: perhaps a partial translation of Russian *otkaznik*, from *otkazat'* 'to refuse'.]

refutation /réffyoo táysh'n/ *n.* **1.** PROOF AGAINST STH an argument, statement, or evidence that proves a claim to be wrong **2.** PROCESS OF REFUTING the act or process of refuting sth

refute /ri fyóot/ (**-futes, -futing, -futed**) *vt.* **1.** PROVE STH WRONG to prove sth to be false or sb to be in error through logical argument or by providing evidence to the contrary **2.** DENY STH to deny an allegation or contradict a statement without disproving it [Early 16thC. From Latin *refutare* 'to drive back, rebut', from the stem *-futare* 'to beat'.] —**refutability** /ri fyóotə bílləti, réffyootə-/ *n.* —**refutable** /réffyootəb'l, ri-/ *adj.* —**refutably** *adv.*

WORD KEY: USAGE

refute, dispute, reject, repudiate? The main area of confusion lies between ***refute*** and ***repudiate***. One of the most common mistakes encountered in newspapers and current affairs broadcasting is the use of ***refute***, which properly means 'prove by argument to be false' instead of ***repudiate*** or *deny*, which should be used when a claim or allegation is simply rejected without argument: *He refuted the suggestions point by point* is correct, but *They refuted the allegation and promised a full explanation* needs ***reject*** or *deny* since the *refuting* comes later. ***Repudiate*** is also a valid alternative and conveys rather more force of meaning. To ***dispute*** has a meaning somewhere between ***refute*** and ***repudiate***; it involves rather more than plain rejection without implying a basis in detailed argument.

reg[1] /rej/ *n.* a vehicle's registration number, especially the first or last letter that indicates the vehicle's age (*informal*) ○ *an H-reg hatchback* [Late 20thC. Shortening.]

reg[2] /reg/ *n.* a regulation (*informal*) ○ *rules and regs* [Early 20thC. Shortening.]

reg. *abbr.* **1.** GEOG region **2.** registered **3.** EDUC registrar **4.** registry **5.** regular **6.** regularly **7.** GENETICS regulation **8.** regulator **9.** regulo

Reg. *abbr.* **1.** Regent **2.** Regina

regain /ri gáyn/ (**-gains, -gaining, -gained**) *vt.* **1.** GET STH BACK to recover sth after losing it **2.** REACH SOMEWHERE AGAIN to reach a place again ○ *She regained her seat and sat down.*

regal /reég'l/ *adj.* typical of or suitable for a king or queen, especially in splendour and magnificence [14thC. Via Old French from Latin *regalis*, from *reg-*, stem of *rex* 'king' (source of English *reign* and *royal*).] —**regality** /ree gálləti/ *n.* —**regally** /reég'li/ *adv.*

regale /ri gáyl/ *vt.* (**-gales, -galing, -galed**) **1.** ENTERTAIN SB to entertain or amuse sb, especially by telling stories ○ *regaled us with stories from the early days* **2.** GIVE SB PLENTY TO EAT AND DRINK to give sb plenty of good things to eat and drink ■ *n.* FEAST a feast or a special delicacy (*archaic*) [Mid-17thC. From French *régaler* 'to entertain', literally 'to give pleasure again', from Old French *gale* 'merriment, pleasure'.]

regalia /ri gáyli ə/ *n.* ROYAL INSIGNIA the ceremonial and symbolic objects and clothing used and worn by royalty or other holders of high office on formal occasions (*takes a singular or plural verb*) ■ *npl.* (*takes a singular or plural verb*) **1.** DISTINCTIVE CLOTHING the distinctive clothing or trappings worn by a particular group of people, especially on formal occasions **2.** SPLENDID ATTIRE splendid attire for a formal occasion ○ *The general appeared in full regalia.* [Mid-16thC. From medieval Latin *regalia* 'royal privileges, royal residence', originally a form of Latin *regalis* (see REGAL).]

regard /ri gaárd/ *vt.* (**-gards, -garding, -garded**) **1.** CONSIDER SB OR STH to think of sb or sth as having a particular nature or quality, or a particular role or function ○ *I regard his gift as an apology.* **2.** HAVE FEELINGS IN RELATION TO STH to have a particular feeling towards sb or sth ○ *At first they regarded the idea of early retirement with horror.* **3.** JUDGE SB OR STH to have an opinion as to the quality or worth of sb or sth ○ *I regard her highly.* **4.** LOOK AT SB OR STH to look at sth or sb steadily or attentively ○ *regarded the photograph with interest* **5.** BE ABOUT STH to be about or concerned with sth ○ *This memo regards your performance review.* ■ *n.* **1.** ATTENTION attention to or concern for sb or sth ○ *with no regard for my feelings* **2.** FAVOURABLE OPINION respect, often coupled with affection ○ *I hold her in the highest regard.* **3.** GAZE a look, or sb's gaze (*formal*) ■ **regards** *npl.* FRIENDLY GREETINGS friendly good wishes and greetings ○ *Give my regards to your father.* [14thC. From Old French *regarder*, literally 'to look at fully', from *garder* (see GUARD).] ◇ **as regards** as far as sb or sth is concerned ◇ **in this** *or* **that regard** as far as this or that is concerned, or from this or that point of view (*formal*) ◇ **with** *or* **in regard to** concerning or in connection with sb or sth

WORD KEY: SYNONYMS

regard, admiration, esteem, favour, respect, reverence, veneration

CORE MEANING: referring to the recognition of the worth of sb or sth

regard a mixture of liking and appreciation of sb or sth; **admiration** a warm approval and appreciation of sb or sth, often suggesting a desire to copy or resemble sb or to own sth; **esteem** a high opinion and appreciation of sb; **favour** a liking and preference for sb or sth; **respect** a strong acknowledgement and appreciation of sb's abilities and achievements without necessarily suggesting a liking for the person; **reverence** a mix of strong feelings of admiration and respect that produces a slight sense of awe for the person or thing revered; **veneration** a formal word for profound feelings of the deepest admiration and highest awe.

regardant /ri gaárd'nt/ *adj.* used to describe a heraldic figure that is looking backwards over its shoulder ○ *three lions regardant* [15thC. From Old French, present participle of *regarder* (see REGARD).]

regardful /ri gaárdf'l/ *adj.* **1.** MINDFUL paying due attention **2.** FULL OF ESTEEM full of esteem and often deferential respect for sb —**regardfully** *adv.* —**regardfulness** *n.*

regarding /ri gaárding/ *prep.* about or on the subject of ○ *I'd like a word with you regarding the schedule.*

regardless /ri gaárdləss/ *adv.* IN SPITE OF EVERYTHING in spite of or ignoring setbacks, hindrances, or problems ■ *adj.* INDIFFERENT paying no attention, especially failing to pay proper attention —**regardlessly** *adv.*

WORD KEY: USAGE

See Usage note at ***irregardless***.

regatta /ri gáttə/ *n.* a sports event consisting of a series of boat or yacht races [Mid-17thC. From (Venetian) Italian, 'gondola race (on the Grand Canal)', originally 'contest for mastery', from *regattare* 'to compete', of unknown origin.]

regd *abbr.* registered

regelation /reéji láysh'n/ *n.* **1.** GEOG REFREEZING UNDER GLACIER the process by which water, melted by pressure beneath a glacier, is refrozen **2.** CHEM PRESSURE-INDUCED CHANGE IN FREEZING reduction of the freezing point of water by force of pressure

regency /reéjənssi/ (*plural* **-cies**) *n.* **1.** GROUP SUBSTITUTING FOR MONARCH a group of people ruling on behalf of a monarch who is unable to rule because of youth, illness, or absence **2.** RESPONSIBILITIES OR RULE OF REGENT the authority and responsibilities or period in office of a regent

Regency *n.* **1.** 1811–20 IN GREAT BRITAIN the period from 1811–20 in Great Britain during which George, Prince of Wales, ruled as regent for his father King George III **2.** 1715–23 IN FRANCE the period from 1715–23 in France during which Philip, Duke of Orleans, ruled as regent on behalf of King Louis XV ■ *adj.* IN STYLE OF REGENCY in the style prevalent and fashionable during either of the Regency periods

regenerate *v.* /ri jénnə rayt/ (**-ates, -ating, -ated**) **1.** *vti.* RECOVER FROM DECLINE to return or bring sth back from a state of decline to a revitalized state ○ *regenerating an inner city housing area* **2.** *vti.* FORM AGAIN to form or become formed again **3.** *vti.* BIOL REPLACE BY NEW GROWTH to replace lost tissue or a lost limb or organ with a new growth ○ *Some amphibians can regenerate limbs.* **4.** *vt.* RELIG RESTORE SB SPIRITUALLY to restore and renew sb morally or spiritually **5.** *vt.* ELECTRON ENG RESTORE STH TO ORIGINAL WAVE SHAPE to restore digital electrical signals to their original wave shape after transmission over long distances ■ *n.* /rə jénnə rayt/ **1.** RELIG SB SPIRITUALLY REFORMED sb who is spiritually reborn or renewed **2.** BIOL REPLACEMENT TISSUE tissue that has grown to replace lost tissue, or a regenerated part, organ, or organism ■ *adj.* /rə jénnə rayt/ **1.** RELIG SPIRITUALLY REBORN OR RENEWED spiritually reborn, renewed, or restored to health **2.** BIOL NEWLY FORMED OR GROWN newly formed or grown as a replacement for sth lost —**regenerable** *adj.* —**regeneracy** *n.* —**regenerateness** *n.* —**regenerative** *adj.* —**regenerator** *n.*

regeneration /ri jénnə ráysh'n/ *n.* **1.** PROCESS OF REGENERATING the act or process of regenerating, or a regenerated state **2.** BIOL REGROWTH BY ANIMAL OR PLANT regrowth of an organ, limb, or other tissue that has been injured or shed **3.** RELIG SPIRITUAL RENEWAL the spiritual renewal of sb

Regensburg /ráygənss boork/ town in Bavaria, south-eastern Germany, on the River Danube, about 105 km/65 mi. northeast of Munich. Population: 126,000 (1995).

regent /reéjənt/ *n.* POL SUBSTITUTE FOR MONARCH sb who rules on behalf of a monarch who is unable to rule because of youth, illness, or absence ■ *adj.* ACTING AS REGENT ruling as a regent ○ *the prince regent* [14thC. Via Old French from Latin *regent-*, present participle stem of *regere* 'to rule'.] —**regental** *adj.*

WORD KEY: ORIGIN

The Latin word *regere*, from which **regent** is derived, is also the source of English *address, correct, direct, dirge, dress, erect, escort, realm, régime, regiment, region,* and *resurrect.*

reggae /rég gay/ *n.* popular music, originally from Jamaica, that combines elements of rock, calypso, and soul and is characterized by heavy accentuation of the second and fourth beats of a four-beat bar (*often used before a noun*) ○ *a reggae beat* [Mid-20thC. Origin uncertain: perhaps from Jamaican English *reggay*, alteration of *rege* 'ragged fellow', from RAG¹.]

Reggio di Calabria /réji ō dee ka laábrya/ city and administrative centre of Reggio di Calabria Province in Calabria Region, southern Italy. Population: 178,312 (1992).

Reggio nell'Emilia /-nel ay meélya/ capital city of Reggio nell'Emilia Province in Emilia Romagna Region, northern Italy. Population: 133,191 (1992).

regicide /réjji sīd/ *n.* **1.** MURDER OF KING the killing of a king **2.** KING KILLER sb who kills a king [Mid-16thC. Formed from Latin *reg-*, the stem of *rex* 'king' + -CIDE.] —**regicidal** /réjji sīd'l/ *adj.*

regime /ray zheém, re-/, **régime** *n.* **1.** POL FORM OF GOVERNMENT a system or style of government **2.** POL OPPRESSIVE GOVERNMENT a particular government, especially one that is considered to be oppressive **3.** CONTROLLING GROUP any controlling or managing group, or the system of control and management adopted by it **4.** ESTABLISHED SYSTEM an established system or way of doing things **5.** CHARACTERISTIC CONDITIONS FOR A PROCESS the characteristic conditions under which a natural, scientific, or industrial process occurs **6.** MED = **regimen** *n.* 1 [15thC. Via French from Latin *regimen* (see REGIMEN).]

regimen /réjjimən, -men/ *n.* **1.** MED PROGRAMME TO IMPROVE HEALTH a prescribed or recommended programme of medication, diet, exercise, or other measures intended to improve health or fitness, or stabilize a medical condition **2.** POL GOVERNMENT a government or form of government (*archaic*) **3.** = **regime** *n.* 5 [14thC. From Latin *regimen* 'rule, government', from *regere* 'to rule'.]

regiment *n.* /réjjimənt/ **1.** MIL ARMY UNIT a permanent military unit usually consisting of two or three battalions of ground troops divided into smaller companies or troops and under the command of a colonel **2.** LARGE NUMBER OF PEOPLE OR THINGS a large number of people or things, especially an orderly group **3.** POL GOVERNMENTAL RULE governmental rule or administration (*archaic*) ■ *vt.* /réjjiment/ (**-ments, -menting, -mented**) **1.** CONTROL SB OR STH STRICTLY to impose strict control or discipline on sb or sth, often to the extent of stifling flexibility, individuality, or imagination **2.** GROUP STH SYSTEMATICALLY to organize sth systematically into groups **3.** MIL GROUP SOLDIERS INTO REGIMENTS to form regiments out of a group of soldiers [14thC. Via Old French from late Latin *regimentum*, from Latin *regere* 'to rule' (see REGENT).] —**regimented** /réjji mentid/ *adj.*

regimental /réjji mént'l/ *adj.* **1.** MIL OF REGIMENTS belonging or relating to a military regiment **2.** RIGID marked by strict or excessive discipline ■ **regimentals** *npl.* MIL **1.** REGIMENT'S UNIFORM AND INSIGNIA the uniform and insignia worn by the members of a particular regiment **2.** MILITARY DRESS military dress and insignia, especially as worn for ceremonial occasions —**regimentally** *adv.*

Regina¹ /ri jīnə/ *n.* **1.** QUEEN the reigning queen **2.** LAW CROWN AS LEGAL ENTITY the Crown as the prosecuting authority in lawsuits when the ruling monarch is a queen ○ *the case of Regina versus Higgins* [Early 18thC. From Latin, literally 'queen'.]

Regina² /ri jīnə/ capital city of Saskatchewan Province, Canada. Population: 193,652 (1996).

region /reéjən/ *n.* **1.** GEOG GEOGRAPHIC AREA a large land area that has particular geographic, political, or cultural characteristics that distinguish it from others, whether existing within one country or extending over several **2.** PUBLIC ADMIN ADMINISTRATIVE UNIT a large separate political or administrative unit within a country **3.** ECOL ECOLOGICAL AREA an area of the world with particular animal and plant life **4.** LARGE INDEFINITE AREA any large indefinite area of a surface **5.** AREA OR ASPECT an imprecisely defined area or part of sth such as a sphere of activity **6.** RANGE WITHIN WHICH FIGURE FALLS the range within which sth such as a figure, sum, or price might fall ○ *in the region of £1,000* **7.** ANAT AREA OF THE BODY an area of the body, usually an area surrounding a specific organ or part ■ **regions** *npl.* THE PROVINCES the rest of a country outside its capital, or the rest of an area outside its main city [14thC. Via Old French from the Latin stem *region-* 'boundary, district', literally 'area that is ruled', from *regere* (see REGENT).]

regional /reéjən'l/ *adj.* **1.** GEOG RELATING TO REGION belonging to or typical of a particular geographical region **2.** POL CONNECTED WITH ADMINISTRATIVE REGION serving or connected with one of the administrative regions of a country ○ *a regional authority* **3.** TYPICAL OF PARTICULAR AREA typical of or limited to a particular area of a country, especially typical of the speech and usage of a particular area and different from standard speech and usage —**regionally** *adv.*

regionalism /reéjənəlizəm/ *n.* **1.** POL DIVISION INTO ADMINISTRATIVE AREAS the policy of dividing a political territory into areas with separate administrations, or support for such a policy **2.** LOYALTY TO HOME REGION loyalty to or prejudice in favour of a particular region **3.** LING LINGUISTIC FEATURE RESTRICTED TO ONE AREA a linguistic feature such as a word, pronunciation, or expression that is only found in a particular region —**regionalist** *n., adj.*

regionalize /reéjənə līz/ (**-izes, -izing, -ized**), **regionalise** (**-ises, -ising, -ised**) *vt.* **1.** DIVIDE STH INTO REGIONS to divide an area into administrative regions **2.** ALLOCATE STH TO REGIONS to allocate sth to regional administrations —**regionalization** /reéjənə lī záysh'n/ *n.*

régisseur /rézhi súr/ *n.* a director who is responsible for staging a theatrical work, especially a ballet [Early 19thC. From French, literally 'agent, manager', from *régir* 'to manage, rule'.]

register /réjjistər/ *n.* **1.** OFFICIAL LIST an official record, often in the form of a list **2.** BOOK FOR OFFICIAL RECORDS a book in which a register of names, attendance, or events is kept **3.** ITEM IN OFFICIAL LIST an item recorded in an official register **4.** MEASURE MEASURING DEVICE THAT RECORDS a device that automatically records numbers, degrees, or quantities **5.** = **cash register 6.** CORRECT ALIGNMENT correct alignment or positioning with respect to sth else **7.** HEATING GRATE a closable grill or grate through which warm or cool air is forced in a household heating system **8.** COMPUT COMPUTER MEMORY LOCATION a memory location in a processor or microprocessor that has a particular storage capacity, is usually intended for a particular purpose, and is accessible at very high speeds **9.** MUSIC MUSICAL RANGE the range of a voice or instrument, or a part of this range **10.** MUSIC ORGAN STOP one of a group of organ stops that are similar in tonal quality **11.** LING SITUATION-SPECIFIC LANGUAGE VARIETY language of a type that is used in particular social situations or when communicating with a particular set of people ■ *v.* (**-ters, -tering, -tered**) **1.** *vti.* WRITE IN REGISTER to enter sth in a register, or to have sth entered there by an official ○ *They registered at the hotel.* **2.** *vti.* ENROL to record a name with an organization in order, e.g. to enrol sb for an academic course or fulfil a legal requirement ○ *register for the course in September* **3.** *vt.* MAKE A RECORD OF STH to make a record of sth, or have sth recorded ○ *I want to register a complaint with the manager.* **4.** *vt.* MEASURE SHOW STH AS MEASUREMENT to indicate or record a measurement on a device or scale **5.** *vti.* DISPLAY FEELING OR THOUGHT to be visible in sb's facial expression or body language, or to display sth in this way ○ *Their expressions registered the relief they felt.* **6.** *vt.* NOTE STH MENTALLY to make a mental note of sth ○ *I registered the time before moving on.* **7.** *vi.* BE UNDERSTOOD to be understood or remembered by sb ○ *The implications finally registered with me.* **8.** *vt.* ACHIEVE STH to achieve or accomplish sth (*formal*) ○ *The team registered several notable successes last season.* **9.** *vt.* MAIL SEND STH BY REGISTERED POST to send a letter or package by registered post **10.** *vi.* BE ALIGNED to be correctly aligned [14thC. Via Old French *regestre* from medieval Latin *registrum*, alteration of late Latin *regesta* 'list', literally 'things collected or brought back', ultimately from *gerere* 'to bring'.] —**registrable** *adj.*

registered /réjjistərd/ *adj.* **1.** CERTIFIED officially qualified as or for sth and entered on an official list **2.** ENROLLED WITH BREEDERS' ASSOCIATION enrolled with a breeders' association as a pedigree animal **3.** SENT BY REGISTERED POST sent by registered post

Registered General Nurse *n. UK* a nurse who is qualified to practise, having undergone a three-year course of study and clinical training attached to a university

registered mail *n. US* = **registered post**

registered nurse *n. US, ANZ* a nurse who has passed a qualifying examination in order to be licensed to practice. = **Registered General Nurse**

registered post *n.* a service provided by post offices for an additional fee to ensure safe delivery of valuable items, providing certified delivery and compensation in case of loss. US term **registered mail**

registered trademark *n.* = **trademark** *n.* 1

register office *n.* in the UK, an office where civil marriages are performed and births, marriages, and deaths are recorded (*the official name, not used in everyday language, for registry office*)

register ton *n.* = **ton**¹ *n.* 5

registrant /réjjistrənt/ *n.* sb who registers himself or herself, another person, or sth such as a patent or trademark

registrar /réjji straár, réjji straar/ *n.* **1.** PUBLIC ADMIN SB WHO KEEPS OFFICIAL RECORDS sb who is responsible for keeping official records **2.** PUBLIC ADMIN RECORDER OF BIRTHS, MARRIAGES, AND DEATHS a public official who is in charge of the records of local births, marriages, and deaths **3.** EDUC OFFICIAL RESPONSIBLE FOR STUDENT RECORDS the most senior administrative officer in a university, or any university, college, or school official responsible for keeping records of such things as student enrolments and examination results **4.** MED SENIOR HOSPITAL DOCTOR a senior doctor in a hospital, lower in rank than a consultant, who specializes in a particular branch of medicine or surgery and may train junior doctors **5.** *US* BUSINESS OFFICIAL RESPONSIBLE FOR SHARE RECORDS a company official responsible for keeping records of shares issued **6.** LAW LAW COURT OFFICIAL in the United Kingdom, an official responsible for the administration of justice in the High Court and other courts **7.** *US* MED HOSPITAL ADMINISTRATOR an administrative officer in a hospital responsible for admitting patients —**registrarship** *n.*

Registrar General (*plural* **Registrars General**) *n.* a senior civil servant responsible for population records and censuses

INTERNATIONAL VEHICLE REGISTRATION CODES

Australia **AUS**	Malaysia **MAL**
Bangladesh **BD**	New Zealand **NZ**
Canada **CDN**	Pakistan **PK**
Ghana **GH**	Singapore **SGP**
Hong Kong **HK**	South Africa **ZA**
India **IND**	United Kingdom **GB**
Ireland **IRL**	United States **USA**
Jamaica **JA**	Zimbabwe **ZW**

registration /réjji stráysh'n/ *n.* **1.** ACT OF REGISTERING OR BEING REGISTERED the act or an instance of registering sb or sth, or the process of being registered **2.** ENTRY IN REGISTER an entry in a register, or sb or sth whose name or designation is entered in a register **3.** EDUC TIME OF REGISTERING STUDENTS the act of recording school students as present or absent at the beginning of the school day, or the time or session at which this takes place **4.** EDUC ENROLMENT PROCESS the process of enrolling at a college or university, choosing courses, and paying fees at the beginning of an academic term **5.** CARS LETTER SHOWING VEHICLE'S AGE a letter that identifies the year or part of a year in which a vehicle was registered and put on the road, forming part of its registration number **6.** *US* CARS LEGAL PROOF FOR VEHICLE a certificate showing that a motor vehicle has been properly registered with a state's department of motor vehicles **7.** PEOPLE REGISTERING TOGETHER the number of people who register for a particular thing or at a particular place at one time **8.** MUSIC COMBINATION OF ORGAN STOPS a particular combination of organ stops used to play a piece of music **9.** MUSIC CHOICE OF COMBINATIONS OF ORGAN STOPS the art of choosing combinations of organ stops appropriate for a particular piece or passage

registration document *n.* an official document stating the name of the owner of a motor vehicle and giving details by which it can be identified

registration number *n.* a sequence of letters and numbers by which a motor vehicle can be identified, usually printed on plates (**number plates**) fastened to the front and back of the vehicle

registration plate *n. ANZ* a number plate

registry /réjjistri/ (*plural* **-tries**) *n.* **1.** PUBLIC ADMIN RECORDS OFFICE a place where registers and other records are kept **2.** REGISTERING OF STH the act of registering sb or sth **3.** SHIPPING SHIP'S REGISTRATION IN PARTICULAR COUNTRY the nationality of a ship, as defined by where it is registered not by the nationality of its owner or its usual place of operation

registry office *n.* in the UK, an office where civil marriages are performed and births, marriages, and deaths are recorded (*the term used in everyday speech for register office*)

regius professor /réeji əss-, réejəss-/ *n.* a professor whose professorship was established by a king or queen, especially Henry VIII, and who is officially appointed by the current king or queen [*Regius* from Latin, 'royal', from *rex* 'king']

reglet /régglit/ *n.* **1.** ARCHIT FLAT MOULDING a flat narrow architectural moulding, or a narrow strip separating mouldings or panels **2.** PRINTING PIECE OF WOOD FOR SPACING TYPE a piece of wood used to separate lines of type in traditional hot-metal printing [Late 16thC. From Old French *régelet*, literally 'small rule'.]

regmaker /rékh maakər/ *n. S Africa* a drink taken to relieve the symptoms of a hangover [Mid-20thC. From Afrikaans, from *reg* 'right' + *maker* 'maker'.]

regnal /régn'l/ *adj.* relating to a king or queen's reign, calculated from the date when he or she became the sovereign (*formal*) ○ *the third regnal year* [Early 17thC. Via Anglo-Latin *regnalis*, from Latin *regnum* 'kingdom'.]

regnant /régnənt/ *adj.* (*formal*) **1.** REIGNING actually reigning, usually as opposed to having a royal title by marriage ○ *queen regnant* **2.** WIDESPREAD widespread, predominant, or especially fashionable at a particular time ○ *according to the regnant custom* [Early 17thC. From Latin *regnant-*, present participle stem of *regnare* 'to reign'.]

rego /réjjō/ (*plural* **regos**) *n. Aus* in Australia, the annual reregistration of a motor vehicle, usually including a roadworthiness check (*informal*) [Shortening]

Rego /ráygō/, **Paula** (*b.* 1935) Portuguese-born British painter. She was appointed first associate artist of the National Gallery, London, in 1990. An exhibition of her 'Nursery Rhymes' etchings (1989) received international acclaim.

regolith /réggə lith/ *n.* the layer of loose rock particles that covers the bedrock of most land on Earth and the Moon [Late 19thC. From Greek *rhēgos* 'blanket' + -LITH.]

regorge /ree gáwrj/ (**-gorges, -gorging, -gorged**) *v.* **1.** *vt.* DISGORGE STH to bring up sth that has been swallowed **2.** *vi.* FLOW BACK to flow or gush back along a channel or out of a pit [Early 17thC. Either from Old French *regorger*, ultimately from *gorge* (see GORGE), or coined from RE- + GORGE.]

Reg. Prof. *abbr.* Regius Professor

regress *v.* /ri gréss/ (**-gresses, -gressing, -gressed**) **1.** *vi.* RETURN TO EARLIER, WORSE CONDITION to return to an earlier and less advanced, less healthy, or generally worse state from a more advanced, healthier, or generally better one **2.** *vi.* GO BACK to move backwards ○ *regress in time* **3.** *vi.* STATS TEND TOWARDS MEAN to tend towards a statistical mean **4.** *vti.* PSYCHOL GO BACK TO EARLIER PERIOD PSYCHOLOGICALLY to go back to or cause sb to reenact an earlier emotional state and exhibit the type of behaviour associated with it **5.** *vt.* PARAPSYCHOL SUPPOSEDLY MAKE SB RECALL EARLIER LIVES to cause sb to think of and describe supposed earlier lifetimes while under hypnosis ■ *n.* /rée gress/ **1.** MOVEMENT BACKWARDS a going backwards, especially from a more advanced or better state to a less advanced or worse one **2.** LOGIC REASONING FROM EFFECT TO CAUSE a process of reasoning backwards from effects to their causes [Early 16thC. From Latin *regress-*, past participle stem of *regredi* 'to move backwards', from *gradi* 'to walk'.] — **regressor** *n.*

regression /ri grésh'n/ *n.* **1.** MOVEMENT BACKWARDS a going backwards or a backward movement or progress, especially through the earlier stages or forms of sth **2.** REVERSION TO EARLIER STATE a return to an earlier or less developed condition or way of behaving **3.** PSYCHOL REVERSION TO LESS MATURE STATE reversion to an earlier, less mature, and less adaptive emotional or mental level, often involving the appearance of forms of behaviour associated with childhood **4.** STATS ASSOCIATION BETWEEN VARIABLES a process for determining the statistical relationship between a random variable and one or more independent variables that is used to predict the value of the random variable **5.** BIOL RETURN TO EARLIER PHYSICAL TYPE the recurrence of an earlier, less complicated physical type among the later generations of a particular population **6.** ASTRON RETROGRADE MOTION the apparent backward motion of a celestial body, caused by the differing orbital periods of the Earth and the body being observed **7.** ASTRON MOVEMENT OF MOON'S ORBIT the slow movement around the ecliptic of the two points where the orbit of the Moon crosses it. A complete revolution happens once in about every 19 years.

regressive /ri gréssiv/ *adj.* **1.** RETURNING TO PREVIOUS CONDITION reverting to an earlier, less developed condition or way of behaving **2.** FIN TAXING POORER PEOPLE MORE HARSHLY used to describe a tax system in which those with low incomes pay proportionally higher taxes than the wealthy —**regressively** *adv.* —**regressiveness** *n.*

regret /ri grét/ *vt.* (**-grets, -gretting, -gretted**) **1.** FEEL SORRY FOR STH to feel sorry and sad about sth previously done or said that now appears wrong, mistaken, or hurtful to others **2.** USED POLITELY WHEN GIVING BAD NEWS used as a polite expression of sorrow when making an apology or delivering a piece of bad or unwelcome news ○ *We regret to inform you that this service is no longer available.* **3.** MOURN FOR SB OR STH to feel sadness about sth, or feel a sense of loss and longing for sb or sth that is no longer there (*formal*) ■ *n.* **1.** SAD OR DISAPPOINTED FEELING a feeling or expression of sorrow and guilt for a past action or event that you now wish had not happened or had happened differently **2.** FEELING OF SADNESS a feeling of sadness, disappointment, or of longing for sb or sth that is no longer there ○ *I let them go with regret, knowing that the visit would not be soon repeated.* ■ **regrets** *npl.* EXPRESSION OF SADNESS a polite expression of real or pretended sadness, used especially when refusing sth such as an invitation ○ *Do give them my regrets. I won't be able to come on Saturday.* [15thC. From Old French *regreter*, of uncertain origin: perhaps literally 'to weep much', from a prehistoric Germanic word meaning 'to weep' that is also the ancestor of English *greet*.] —**regretter** *n.*

regretful /ri grétf'l/ *adj.* feeling or showing regret for sth —**regretfully** *adv.* —**regretfulness** *n.*

WORD KEY: USAGE

regretful or **regrettable**? ***Regrettable*** is used of sth that is a cause for regret, whereas ***regretful*** describes sb who has feelings of remorse or sadness about sth: *These mistakes are regrettable. They felt regretful at missing the opportunity.* The adverbs *regrettably* and *regretfully* are even more vulnerable to confusion, but again *regrettably* relates to the cause of regret and *regretfully* to the feeling of regret: *The exam results are regrettably poor. She regretfully turned down the invitation.*

regrettable /ri gréttəb'l/ *adj.* unfortunate or blameworthy, and causing feelings of regret, embarrassment, or even shame ○ *It was a regrettable lapse by a person of otherwise exemplary character.* —**regrettableness** *n.* —**regrettably** *adv.*

WORD KEY: USAGE

See Usage note at ***regretful.***

regroup /ree gro͞op/ (**-groups, -grouping, -grouped**) *v.* **1.** *vti.* MIL FORM INTO ORGANIZED BODY AGAIN to re-form, or re-form troops, into organized units or an effective fighting force, especially after their being dispersed or defeated **2.** *vi.* REORGANIZE to recover, reorganize, and prepare for a further effort after receiving a setback **3.** *vt.* ARRANGE THINGS IN NEW GROUPS to arrange people or things in new or different groups — **regroupment** *n.*

Regt *abbr.* **1.** Regent **2.** Regiment

regular /réggyo͝olər/ *adj.* **1.** HAVING EQUAL TIMES OR SPACES BETWEEN occurring in a fixed, unvarying, or predictable pattern, with equal amounts of time or space between each one ○ *the regular tick-tock of the clock* **2.** HAPPENING FREQUENTLY occurring or doing sth frequently enough over a period of time to establish a pattern, though not necessarily a strict one ○ *Ice storms are becoming a regular occurrence round here.* **3.** USUAL normally expected, or most often used or done ○ *Following our regular practice, we'll start the meeting at noon.* **4.** FOLLOWING ROUTINE carried out according to an established routine or schedule ○ *keep very regular hours* **5.** PHYSIOL MENSTRUATING OR DEFECATING AT PREDICTABLE TIMES menstruating or having bowel movements at predictable times **6.** STANDARD OR MEDIUM of a standard or medium size or strength, as opposed, e.g., to sth of a larger size or greater strength ○ *I'll have the regular fries.* **7.** SYMMETRICAL evenly and pleasingly shaped and symmetrical ○ *a regular facial profile* **8.** PROPER conforming to the normal or accepted rules or standards ○ *It may not be the regular way of doing long division but it works.* **9.** PROFESSIONAL officially or properly qualified to perform a specific job ○ *not a regular doctor* **10.** MIL FORMING PART OF PROFESSIONAL FORCE belonging to or constituting a full-time professional military or police force ○ *an officer in the regular army* **11.** COMPLETE AND UTTER thoroughly deserving a particular description (*informal*) ○ *a regular tyrant in the office* **12.** *US* NICE pleasant, reliable, and thoughtful (*informal*) ○ *a regular guy* **13.** GRAM FOLLOWING NORMAL GRAMMATICAL PATTERNS following the normal or common grammatical patterns of a language. ◊ **irregular 14.** CHR OF RELIGIOUS ORDER belonging to a religious or monastic order ○ *the regular clergy* **15.** *US* POL LOYAL TO PARTY OFFICIALS connected with or loyal to a particular political party **16.** GEOM HAVING EQUAL SIDES AND ANGLES having both equal sides and angles ○ *a regular polygon* **17.** GEOM COMPOSED OF IDENTICAL POLYGONS having faces that are congruent identical polygons and that make equal angles with each other ○ *a regular polyhedron* **18.** BOT HAVING RADIAL SYMMETRY having flower parts that are similar in size and shape and are arranged symmetrically ■ *n.* **1.** FREQUENT VISITOR sb who visits a place frequently (*informal*) **2.** STH USUALLY ASKED FOR sth such as a drink that sb usually asks for or buys (*informal*) **3.** MIL PROFESSIONAL SOLDIER a full-time professional soldier (*often used in the plural*) **4.** STH STANDARD OR MEDIUM sth of a medium or standard size or strength, as opposed to sth larger, smaller, stronger, or weaker **5.** CHR MEMBER OF RELIGIOUS ORDER sb who belongs to a religious or monastic order **6.** *US* POL SB POLITICALLY LOYAL sb who is loyal to a particular political party ○ *strong support from the party regulars* ■ *adv.* FREQUENTLY most or all of the time (*informal*) ○ *We come here regular, don't we?* [14thC. Formed from Latin *rēgula* 'rule' (source of English *rule*). Ultimately from an Indo-European word that is also the ancestor of English *royal* and *correct*.] — **regularity** /réggyo͝o lárrəti/ *n.* —**regularly** /réggyo͝olərli/ *adv.*

regularize /réggyo͝olə rīz/ (**-izes, -izing, -ized**), **regularise** (**-ises, -ising, -ised**) *vt.* to make sth fit in with or conform to usual or accepted standards or practice —**regularization** /réggyo͝olə rī záysh'n/ *n.* —**regularizer** /réggyo͝olə rīzər/ *n.*

regulate /réggyo͝o layt/ (**-lates, -lating, -lated**) *vt.* **1.** ENG CONTROL STH to control sth and bring it to the desired level, e.g. by adjusting the output of a machine or by imposing restrictions on the flow of sth **2.** MECH ENG ADJUST MACHINERY OR SELECT OUTPUT to adjust a piece of machinery or a control device on it so that the machinery works correctly **3.** POL, LAW CONTROL STH BY

RULES OR LAWS to organize and control an activity or process by making it subject to rules or laws (*formal*) **4.** MAKE STH REGULAR to cause sth to occur at predictable intervals or in a regular way [15thC. From late Latin *regulat-*, past participle stem of *regulare*, from Latin *regula* (see REGULAR).] —**regulative** /-lətiv/ *adj.* —**regulatory** /réggyŏŏlətəri/ *adj.*

regulation /réggyŏŏ láysh'n/ *n.* **1.** RULE OR ORDER an official rule, law, or order stating what may or may not be done or how sth must be done (*often used in the plural*) **2.** LAW GOVERNMENT ORDER WITH FORCE OF LAW an order issued by a government department or agency that has the force of law **3.** REGULATING OF STH the adjusting, organizing, or controlling of sth, or the state of being adjusted, organized, or controlled **4.** BIOL ABILITY OF EMBRYO TO GROW NORMALLY the process or mechanism by which an embryo restores its ability to develop normally after being damaged or altered without creating new tissue **5.** LAW DIRECT EU LAW a European Union law that automatically applies in all member states without the need for domestic legislation in the member states ■ *adj.* **1.** OFFICIALLY APPROVED FOR USE officially approved for use, or conforming to the official guidelines for sth **2.** STANDARD AND UNADVENTUROUS like everyone has or does, and completely standard and unadventurous

regulator /réggyŏŏ laytər/ *n.* **1.** ENG CONTROL MECHANISM a mechanism that controls sth such as pressure, temperature, speed, or voltage (*often used in combination*) **2.** CONTROLLING OFFICIAL an official who controls an activity and makes certain that regulations are complied with (*often used in combination*) **3.** TIME VERY ACCURATE TIMEPIECE a very accurate watch or clock, used as a standard by which others are set **4.** GENETICS = **regulator gene**

regulator gene, **regulatory gene** *n.* a gene that regulates the expression of one or more structural genes, thereby controlling the synthesis of their corresponding proteins. In the simplest case, the regulator gene encodes a repressor molecule that binds to a site adjacent to the structural gene, so preventing transcription of the latter.

reguli plural of **regulus**

regulo /réggyŏŏlō/ (*plural* **-los**) *n.* any of the various temperature levels a gas oven can be set at [Early 20thC. Coined from a shortening of REGULATE + -O.]

regulus /réggyŏŏləss/ (*plural* **-luses** *or* **-li** /-lī/) *n.* METALL **1.** IMPURE MASS OF METAL the semipurified mass of metal that forms beneath the slag in the smelting of ore **2.** IMPURE METAL an impure intermediate metal product created by the smelting process [Late 16thC. From Latin, diminutive of *rex* 'king'. Originally found in *regulus of antimony*, a metallic antimony so called because it combined readily with gold, a kingly metal.] —**reguline** /réggyŏŏlin, -līn/ *adj.*

Regulus *n.* ASTRON a bright double star of the first magnitude in the constellation Leo

regurgitate /ri gúrji tayt/ (**-tates, -tating, -tated**) *v.* **1.** *vt.* ZOOL BRING FOOD UP FROM STOMACH to bring undigested or partially digested food up from the stomach to the mouth, as some birds and animals do to feed their young **2.** *vt.* REPEAT INFORMATION MECHANICALLY to repeat or reproduce what has been heard, read, or taught, in a purely mechanical way, with no evidence of personal thought or understanding **3.** *vi.* FLOW OUT to flow out or be ejected, especially from the mouth (*formal*) **4.** *vi.* MED FLOW IN OPPOSITE DIRECTION TO NORMAL to flow in the opposite direction to the normal or usual direction, especially through a defective heart valve [Late 16thC. From medieval Latin *regurgitat-*, past participle stem of *regurgitare*, literally 'to flood back', ultimately from *gurges* 'whirlpool' (source of English *gorge*).] —**regurgitant** /ri gúrjitənt/ *n., adj.* —**regurgitation** /ri gúrji táysh'n/ *n.* —**regurgitative** /ri gúrjitətiv/ *adj.*

rehab /rée hab/ *n.* (*informal*) **1.** *US* SOC WELFARE REHABILITATION the period or process of rehabilitation, e.g. for sb addicted to a chemical substance (*often used before a noun*) ○ *a rehab clinic* **2.** CONSTR STH RECONSTRUCTED sth that has been rehabilitated, especially a rehabilitated building ■ *vt.* (**-habs, -habbing, -habbed**) *US* RESTORE BUILDING to restore sth, especially a building (*informal*) [Mid-20thC. Shortening.] —**rehabber** *n.*

rehabilitate /rée ə bíllī tayt, rée hə-/ (**-tates, -tating, -tated**) *vt.* **1.** SOC WELFARE HELP SB RETURN TO NORMAL LIFE to help sb to return to good health or a normal life by providing training or therapy **2.** RESTORE SB TO RANK OR RIGHTS to restore sb to a former position or rank and grant rights and privileges once more (*often passive*) **3.** RESTORE SB'S REPUTATION to restore sb's good reputation and standing after he or she has been disgraced or neglected **4.** CONSTR RESTORE PLACE TO GOOD CONDITION to restore a building, or part of a town, to its former good condition [Late 16thC. From medieval Latin *rehabilitat-*, past participle stem of *rehabilitare*, literally 'to habilitate again' (see HABILITATE).] —**rehabilitatable** *adj.* —**rehabilitative** /-tətiv/ *adj.* —**rehabilitator** /-taytər/ *n.*

rehabilitation /rée ə bíllī táysh'n, rée hə-/ *n.* **1.** SOC WELFARE HELP FOR RECOVERY training, therapy, or other help given to sb, e.g. sb who has survived a serious injury or illness or an addiction, that will enable him or her to live a healthy and productive life **2.** CONSTR RESTORING OF OLD BUILDINGS the restoration of a building, or part of a town, to its former good condition **3.** RESTORATION OF LOST POSITION OR REPUTATION the restoration of sb's former position, rank, rights and privileges, influence, or good reputation

rehash *vt.* /ree hásh/ (**-hashes, -hashing, -hashed**) REPEAT OR REUSE STH to repeat sth or reuse and rework old material, making some changes but without introducing anything new ■ *n.* /rée hash/ REUSE OF OLD IDEAS a tiresome reuse of ideas or material to which nothing new or significant has been added

rehear /ree héer/ (**-hears, -hearing, -heard, -heard** /-húrd/) *vt.* **1.** HEAR STH AGAIN to hear or, especially, listen to sb or sth again **2.** LAW CONSIDER STH AGAIN to hear a case again in the same court —**rehearing** *n.*

rehearsal /ri húrss'l/ *n.* **1.** PRACTICE PERFORMANCE a session or series of sessions in which sth that is to be done later, especially a public performance, is practised **2.** TEDIOUS REPETITION a detailed listing or repetition of sth (*formal*)

rehearse /ri húrss/ (**-hearses, -hearsing, -hearsed**) *v.* **1.** *vti.* PRACTISE STH BEFORE PERFORMING to practise sth before doing it, especially to practise sth such as a play, speech, or piece of music before performing it for the public **2.** *vt.* TRAIN SB FOR PERFORMANCE to train or instruct sb who is practising before doing sth, especially before giving a public performance **3.** *vt.* GO OVER LIST to go over a list of items, often reasons, complaints, or troubles **4.** *vti.* REPEAT STH to tell or repeat sth such as a story (*literary*) [13thC. From Old French *rehercer*, literally 'to rake over', from *herce* (see HEARSE).] —**rehearser** *n.*

reheat /ree héet/ (**-heats, -heating, -heated**) *v.* **1.** *vti.* HEAT STH AGAIN to heat sth up again after cooling, or be heated up again **2.** *vt.* AEROSP INJECT FUEL INTO JET ENGINE to inject fuel into the exhaust gases in the outlet pipe of a jet engine in order to obtain greater heat and thrust —**reheater** *n.*

rehoboam /rée ə bō əm/ *n.* a large wine bottle, six times the size of a normal bottle [Mid-19thC. Named after *Rehoboam*, who 'fortified the strongholds, and put captains in them...and stores of oil and wine' (2 Chronicles 11:11).]

Rehoboam *n.* in the Bible, the son of Solomon and king of ancient Judah (922? BC-915? BC). His reign was marked by conflict with the rival kingdom of the northern tribes of Israel (1 Kings 11–14).

rehouse /ree hówz/ (**-houses, -housing, -housed**) *vt.* to provide a person or a group of people with a new or different place to live in, often one that is better than the previous dwelling

rehydrate /rée hī drayt, rée hī dráyt/ (**-drates, -drating, -drated**) *v.* **1.** *vt.* RETURN WATER TO STH to add water to sth that has been dried in order to return it to its natural state **2.** *vt.* MED REPLENISH SB'S BODY FLUID to restore the body fluids of sb to a normal or healthy level **3.** *vi.* ABSORB WATER to absorb water after dehydration —**rehydratable** *adj.* —**rehydration** /rée hī dráysh'n/ *n.*

Reibey, Mary (1777–1855) British-born Australian entrepreneur. Transported to New South Wales at the age of 15, she subsequently became one of the colony's leading business figures. Born **Molly Haydock**

Reich /rīk, rīkh/ *n.* the German state or empire, especially the Holy Roman Empire (926–1806) or First Reich, the German Empire (1871–1919) or Second Reich, or the Nazi state (1933–45) or Third Reich [Early 20thC. From German, 'kingdom, state, empire'.]

reichsmark /rīks maark, rīkhs-/ (*plural* **-mark** *or* **-marks**), **Reichsmark** (*plural* **-mark** *or* **-marks**) *n.* the basic unit of German currency from 1923 to 1948 [Mid-20thC. From German, from *Reich* 'empire, kingdom' + *Mark* 'mark'.]

Reichstag /rīks taag, rīkhs-/ *n.* **1.** HIST GERMAN LEGISLATIVE ASSEMBLY 1867–1919 the legislative assembly of both the North German Confederation, from 1867 to 1871, and the German Empire, from 1871 to 1919 **2.** HIST LEGISLATIVE ASSEMBLY OF WEIMAR REPUBLIC the sovereign legislative assembly of the Weimar Republic, from 1919 to 1933 **3.** PARLIAMENT BUILDING IN BERLIN the building in Berlin in which the Reichstag formerly met, destroyed by fire in 1933, and now rebuilt to house the parliament of the reunified German federal state [Mid-19thC. From German, from *Reich* 'empire, kingdom' + *Tag* 'diet, legislative assembly'.]

Reid /reed/, **Sir George Houston** (1845–1918) Scottish-born Australian statesman. He served as prime minister of Australia (1904–05).

reify /rée i fī/ (**-fies, -fying, -fied**) *vt.* to think of or treat sth abstract as if it existed as a real and tangible object [Mid-19thC. Coined from Latin *re-* (stem of *res* 'thing') + -FY.] —**reification** /rée ifi káysh'n/ *n.* —**reificatory** /-káytəri/ *adj.* —**reifier** /rée i fī ər/ *n.*

Reigate /ríg ayt, rígit/ market town in Surrey, in southeastern England. Population: 21,800 (1994).

reign /rayn/ *n.* **1.** PERIOD OF RULE the period of time during which sb, especially a king or queen, rules a nation **2.** CONTROL OR INFLUENCE the fact of being the dominant or controlling power or factor in sth, or the period of time during which this dominance persists ■ *vi.* (**reigns, reigning, reigned**) **1.** RULE A NATION to exercise sovereign power or a controlling influence over sth, especially to rule a country as its king or queen **2.** BE TITULAR SOVEREIGN to hold a royal title and be head of state while possessing only limited powers, as in a constitutional monarchy **3.** BE MOST IMPORTANT FEATURE to be the main or most noticeable feature of a situation, place, or period of time [13thC. Via Old French *reignier* from Latin *regnare* 'to be king', from *regnum* 'kingship'.]

reign of terror *n.* a time when systematic violence is used by a government, individual, or group to intimidate other people and obtain or maintain dominance over them

Reign of Terror *n.* the period of the French Revolution between September 1793 and July 1794, during which thousands of people were executed as enemies of the revolution

reiki /ráy ki/ *n.* a treatment in alternative medicine in which healing energy is channelled from the practitioner to the patient to enhance energy and reduce stress, pain, and fatigue [Late 20thC. From Japanese, 'universal life force energy'.]

reimagine /rée i májjin/ (**-ines, -ining, -ined**) *vt.* **1.** CREATE STH ANEW to recreate sth, or plan to recreate sth, in a fundamentally different way ○ *to reimagine the Shakespearean corpus for television* **2.** REINVENT YOURSELF to create a new and improved image or lifestyle for yourself

reimburse /rée im búrss/ (**-burses, -bursing, -bursed**) *vt.* to pay sb back money spent for an official or approved reason or taken as a loan, or give sb money as compensation for loss or damage [Early 17thC. Formed from obsolete *imburse* 'to pay, put in a purse', ultimately from Old French *borse* 'purse', from medieval Latin *bursa* (source of English *purse*).] —**reimbursable** *adj.* —**reimbursement** *n.* —**reimburser** *n.*

reimport *vt.* /rée im páwrt/ (**-ports, -porting, -ported**) IMPORT GOODS MADE FROM EXPORTED MATERIALS to bring back into a country finished goods made from raw materials that were originally exported from that country ■ *n.* /ree impawrt/ **1.** IMPORTING OF GOODS USING EXPORTED MATERIALS the business of bringing into a country goods made from raw materials originally exported from it **2.** REIMPORTED ITEM sth that has been reimported —**reimportation** /rée im pawr táysh'n/ *n.*

reimpression /re͞e im présh'n/ *n.* a reprint of a book without any changes in the text

Reims /reemz/ city in Marne Department, Champagne-Ardenne Region, northeastern France. Population: 185,164 (1990).

rein /rayn/ *n.* (*often used in the plural*) **1.** EQU **STRAP FOR CONTROLLING HORSE** a strap, or either half of a strap, by which a horse is controlled by its rider or by the driver of a coach or cart it is pulling **2. EXERCISE OF POWER** any means of guiding, controlling, or restraining sb or sth ■ **reins** *npl.* **STRAP FOR GUIDING CHILD** a harness that fits around the body of a very young child, with straps attached by means of which the child can be controlled and guided, especially when walking out ■ *vt.* (**reins, reining, reined**) **CONTROL SB OR STH** to guide, control, or restrain sb or sth [13thC. From Old French *rene*, earlier *resne*, of uncertain origin: perhaps ultimately from Latin *retinere* 'to hold back'.] — **reinless** *adj.* ◇ **give (free) rein to sb** *or* **sth to** allow sb or sth complete freedom, imposing no restraints or limitations ◇ **have a (tight) rein on sb** *or* **sth, keep a (tight) rein on sb** *or* **sth** to maintain strict control over sb or sth

rein back *vt.* to subject sth or sb to stricter control, often to reduce the amount of sth or restrict sb's freedom of action

rein in *v.* **1.** *vti.* RIDING **STOP OR SLOW HORSE** to make a horse stop or slow down by pulling on the reins **2.** *vt.* **CONTROL SB OR STH** to bring sb or sth under control

reincarnate *vt.* /ree in kaar nayt, re͞e in ka̅ar-/ (**-nates, -nating, -nated**) **1.** RELIG **GIVE NEW BIRTH** in some systems of belief, to return sb to Earth to live another life in a different body (*often passive*) **2. PUT INTO NEW FORM** to present sth again in a new form after it has been abandoned or discontinued ■ *adj.* /re͞e in ka̅arnət, -nayt/ **1.** RELIG **REBORN** in some systems of belief, returned to Earth in a new body after death **2. REPACKAGED** embodied or presented in a new form

reincarnation /re͞e in kaar náysh'n/ *n.* **1.** RELIG **REBIRTH OF SOUL** in some systems of belief, the cyclical return of a soul to live another life in a new body **2.** RELIG **BODY IN WHICH SB IS REBORN** in some systems of belief, a person or animal in whose body sb's soul is born again after he, she, or it has died **3. APPEARANCE IN NEW GUISE** a reappearance of sth in a new form — **reincarnationism** *n.* —**reincarnationist** *n.*

reindeer /ráyn deer/ (*plural* **-deer** *or* **-deers**) *n.* a large deer with large branched antlers in both males and females, found in northern and Arctic regions of Europe and Asia, and in North America. Reindeer are domesticated by Sami and other Arctic peoples and used as beasts of burden and a source of food and materials. Latin name: *Rangifer tarandus.* [14thC. From Old Norse *hreinn* 'reindeer' (perhaps of Finnish-Lappish origin) + *dýr* 'animal'.]

Reindeer Lake lake in Canada, on the Saskatchewan-Manitoba border, discharging into the Reindeer River. Area: 6,651 sq. km/2,568 sq. mi.

reindeer moss, **reindeer lichen** *n.* a grey lichen found in subarctic and Arctic regions that grows in large, erect, and branching tufts and provides food for reindeer and other animals. Latin name: *Cladonia rangiferia.*

reindustrialize /re͞e in dústri ə līz/ (**-izes, -izing, -ized**), **reindustrialise** (**-ises, -ising, -ised**) *vti.* to undergo a process of renewal, usually involving government help in the modernization of factories and equipment, or subject an industry or industrial society to such a process —**reindustrialization** /re͞e in dustri ə lī záysh'n/ *n.*

reinforce /re͞e in fáwrss/ (**-forces, -forcing, -forced**), **reenforce** (**-forces, -forcing, -forced**), **re-enforce** (**re-enforces, re-enforcing, re-enforced**) *vt.* **1. STRENGTHEN STH** to make sth stronger by providing additional external support or internal stiffening for it **2. GIVE STH SUPPORT** to give additional strength, force, or conviction to sth such as an idea, opinion, or feeling, e.g. by providing further evidence to support it **3.** MIL **MAKE MILITARY FORCE STRONGER** to make a military force stronger by providing it with more troops or weapons **4.** PSYCHOL **INFLUENCE BEHAVIOUR BY REWARD OR PUNISHMENT** to reward a particular action or type of behaviour to increase the probability that it will be repeated, or punish an action in order to discourage it [15thC. Formed from ENFORCE, probably on the model of Italian *rinforzare*.] —**reinforceable** *adj.*

reinforced concrete *n.* concrete made with metal wire or rods embedded in it to increase its strength

reinforced plastic *n.* plastic with carbon or similar fibres embedded in it to make it stronger

reinforcement /re͞e in fáwrssmənt/ *n.* **1. ADDED SUPPORT** the addition of strengthening or supporting material to make sth stronger or more durable **2. STH ADDED TO INCREASE STRENGTH** sth that is added to strengthen or support sth else **3.** PSYCHOL **REWARD OR PUNISHMENT** the rewarding (**positive reinforcement**) or punishing (**negative reinforcement**) of particular actions, especially in an experimental situation, for the purpose of changing a subject's behaviour ■ **reinforcements** *npl.* MIL **ADDITIONAL TROOPS OR WEAPONS** additional troops, police, or weapons provided to make an existing force stronger

reinforcer /re͞e in fáwrssər/ *n.* in behavioural psychology, a reward or stimulus used to encourage a particular action in order to increase the probability that it will be repeated

Reinga, Cape /ri ángə/ cape at the northwestern tip of the North Island, New Zealand. In Maori folklore, it is the departure point for the souls of the dead returning to the spiritual homeland of Hawaiki.

Reinhardt /rīn haart/, **Django** (1910–53) Belgian musician. He is generally regarded as the finest jazz guitarist of all time. He often performed with Stephane Grappelli. Real name **Jean Baptiste Reinhardt**

Reinhardt, Max (1873–1943) Austrian-born US theatre director. His productions were known for their elaborate settings and costumes and highly disciplined actors. He founded a music and dance festival in Salzburg. Real name **Max Goldmann**

reins /raynz/ *npl.* the kidneys or lower abdomen, formerly thought to be the seat of human passions (*archaic*) [Pre-12thC. Via French from Latin *renes*.]

reinsman /ráynzmən/ (*plural* **-men** /-mən/) *n.* *ANZ* the driver of a gig in trotting races

reinstate /re͞e in stáyt/ (**-states, -stating, -stated**) *vt.* **1. GIVE SB FORMER JOB BACK** to give sb back a job or position of influence that he or she once had and from which he or she was dismissed or deposed **2. REINTRODUCE STH** to bring sth back into use or force again after it has been out of use —**reinstatement** *n.* —**reinstator** *n.*

reinsure /re͞e in sho͝or, -sháwr/ (**-sures, -suring, -sured**) *vt.* to insure sth again, especially to obtain, as an insurer, additional cover from another insurer for a risk that a customer has been insured against — **reinsurance** *n.* —**reinsurer** *n.*

reinswoman /ráynz wo͝omən/ (*plural* **-en** /-wimin/) *n.* *ANZ* a woman who drives a gig in trotting races

reintegrate /ree ínti grayt/ (**-grates, -grating, -grated**) *vt.* **1. BRING SB BACK INTO GROUP** to bring sb or sth back into a group or a larger entity after a period of exclusion from it **2. MAKE STH WHOLE AGAIN** to restore sth to a state of wholeness or unity (*formal*) —**reintegration** /ree ínti gráysh'n/ *n.*

reinterpret /re͞e in túrprit/ (**-prets, -preting, -preted**) *vt.* to interpret sth again or in a different way, especially to find a new and different meaning in sth —**reinterpretation** /re͞e in túrpri táysh'n/ *n.*

reinvent /re͞e in vént/ (**-vents, -venting, -vented**) *vt.* **1. INVENT STH AGAIN** to invent sth again, or bring sth back into existence, use, or popularity after a period of neglect or obscurity ○ *The party claims to have reinvented genuine popular democracy* **2. CREATE NEW VERSION OF STH** to change radically the appearance, form, or presentation of sth or sb —**reinvention** *n.* ◇ **reinvent the wheel 1.** to waste time recreating sth that already exists in a perfectly usable and acceptable form (*disapproving*) **2.** to produce a new version of sth very basic and familiar (*disapproving*)

reinvest /re͞e in vést/ (**-vests, -vesting, -vested**) *vti.* **1.** STOCK EXCH **BUY MORE SECURITIES WITH PROFIT** to invest money again, especially to buy more shares with the income made on a previous investment **2.** BUSINESS, FIN **INVEST IN IMPROVING BUSINESS** to put income back into a business instead of distributing it as profit — **reinvestment** *n.*

reinvigorate /re͞e in víggə rayt/ (**-rates, -rating, -rated**) *vt.* to imbue a person, organization, or idea with new strength, energy, dynamism or appeal —**reinvigoration** /re͞e in víggə ráysh'n/ *n.* —**reinvigorator** /re͞e in víggə raytər/ *n.*

reis plural of **real**[2] *n.* 2

reissue /ree íssyoo, -íshoo/ *vt.* (**-sues, -suing, -sued**) **PRODUCE STH AGAIN** to produce, distribute, or make sth available again, especially sth such as a book or recording, sometimes in a different form ■ *n.* **STH PRODUCED AGAIN** sth, especially a book or recording, that is reissued

reiterate /ree ítti rayt/ (**-ates, -ating, -ated**) *vt.* to say or do sth again, once or several times, sometimes in a tiresome way —**reiterant** *adj.* —**reiteration** /ree íttə ráysh'n/ *n.* —**reiterative** /ree íttərətiv, -raytiv/ *adj.* — **reiteratively** *adv.* —**reiterator** /ree íttə raytər/ *n.*

WORD KEY: USAGE

Redundancy trap: The use of *again*, *once more*, *yet again*, and other such expressions with *reiterate*, whose innate meaning subsumes all of them, is a redudancy to be avoided.

Reiter's syndrome /rítərz-/, **Reiter's disease** *n.* a disease that begins as an infection in genetically predisposed people and is characterized by recurring bouts of arthritis, conjunctivitis, and urethritis [Early 20thC. Named after Hans *Reiter* (1881–1969), German bacteriologist.]

Reith /reeth/, **John, 1st Baron** (1889–1971) British administrator. He was the first general manager (1922–27) and director (1927–38) of the BBC. Full name **John Charles Walsham Reith**

reject *vt.* /ri jékt/ (**-jects, -jecting, -jected**) **1. NOT ACCEPT STH** to refuse to accept, agree to, believe in, or make use of sth **2. TURN SB DOWN** to decide not to give sb sth asked or applied for, e.g. a job or membership of an organization **3. BE UNKIND TO SB** to behave in an unkind and unfriendly way towards sb who expects, or has a right to expect, love, kindness, and friendship **4. NOT KEEP OR ACCEPT STH** to put sth aside, throw it away, or refuse to accept it because it is not good enough or not the right thing **5.** MED **BRING UP FOOD** to be unable to keep food down and vomit it up again **6.** MED **NOT ACCEPT TRANSPLANT** to fail to accept foreign tissue or an organ transplant because of immunological incompatibility ■ *n.* /re͞e jekt/ **STH OR SB NOT WANTED** sb who or sth that is rejected as not meeting a required standard of quality, or as being generally unsuitable [15thC. From Latin *reject-*, past participle stem of *rejicere*, literally 'to throw back', from *jacere* 'to throw'.] — **rejectable** *adj.* —**rejecter** *n.* —**rejective** *adj.* —**rejector** /ri jéktər/ *n.*

WORD KEY: USAGE

See Usage note at ***refute.***

rejection /ri jéksh'n/ *n.* **1. ACT OF REJECTING** the rejecting of sth or sb, or the fact of being rejected **2.** MED **FAILURE OF TRANSPLANT** the destruction by immune mechanisms of transplanted tissue or a transplanted organ from another individual

rejectionist /ri jéksh'nist/ *n.* sb who refuses to accept a policy, proposal, or peace plan that other people have agreed to

rejection slip *n.* an official note stating that sth has been rejected, e.g. a book submitted to a publisher or a painting submitted for exhibition

rejig /ree jíg/ (**-jigs, -jigging, -jigged**) *vt.* **1. ALTER, REARRANGE, OR READJUST STH** to alter, rearrange, or readjust sth, or set it up differently, sometimes with the intention of deceiving a purchaser or user (*informal*) US term **rejigger 2. RE-EQUIP FACTORY** to re-equip a factory so that it can do a different kind of work

rejoice /ri jóyss/ (**-joices, -joicing, -joiced**) *v.* **1.** *vi.* **BE HAPPY** to feel very happy or show great happiness about sth (*literary*) **2.** *vt.* **MAKE SB HAPPY** to fill sb with happiness (*archaic*) [14thC. Via Old French *rejoir* 'to be most joyful' from, ultimately, Latin *gaudere* 'to rejoice' (source of English *joy*).] —**rejoicer** *n.* —**rejoicing** *n.* — **rejoicingly** *adv.*

rejoice in *vt.* to be lucky enough to have or own sth (*often used ironically*)

rejoin[1] /ree jóyn/ (**-joins, -joining, -joined**) *vti.* **1. RETURN TO SB AFTER BEING APART** to meet up again with sb, or go back to sb or sth, after a usually brief period of being away or apart **2. BECOME MEMBER AGAIN** to become a member again of an organization or group you formerly belonged to **3. JOIN TOGETHER AGAIN** to join two things together again, or become joined together or merged with sth again [Formed from RE- + JOIN]

rejoin[2] /ri jóyn/ (**-joins, -joining, -joined**) *v.* **1.** *vti.* **REPLY** to say sth in reply, especially to reply with a sharp, critical, angry, defensive, or clever remark (*formal*) **2.** *vi.* LAW **RESPOND TO PLAINTIFF'S REPLY** to respond to a plaintiff's reply or replication [15thC. From French *rejoign-*, stem of *rejoindre* 'to join again', from *joindre* (see JOIN).]

rejoinder /ri jóyndər/ *n.* **1. RETORT** a reply to sth said, especially one that is sharp, critical, angry, defensive, or clever (*formal*) **2.** LAW **DEFENDANT'S RESPONSE** the answer that a defendant makes during pleading to the plaintiff's reply or replication [15thC. Via Anglo-Norman from Old French (see REJOIN[2]).]

WORD KEY: SYNONYMS

See Synonyms at ***answer***.

rejuvenate /ri jóovi nayt/ (**-nates, -nating, -nated**) *vt.* **1. MAKE SB YOUNG AGAIN** to make sb become, feel, or appear young again **2. RETURN STH TO ORIGINAL CONDITION** to restore sth to its condition when new, or make it more vigorous, dynamic, and effective **3.** GEOL **CAUSE RIVER TO ERODE MORE** to cause a river to start eroding the land it runs over again, usually as a result of the land being uplifted **4.** GEOL **MAKE AREA DEVELOP TOPOGRAPHICALLY YOUNG FEATURES** to cause, through increased erosion of a landscape, the redevelopment of younger topographical features, that is, the more rugged ones typical of an early geological stage [Early 19thC. Formed from RE- + Latin *juvenis* 'young' (source of English *juvenile*) + -ATE.] —**rejuvenation** /ri jóovi náysh'n/ *n.* —**rejuvenative** /ri jóovinətiv, -aytiv/ *adj.* —**rejuvenator** /ri jóovi naytər/ *n.*

rejuvenesce /ri jóovi néss/ (**-nesces, -nescing, -nesced**) *vti.* to become, or make sb feel or look, young again (*formal*) [Late 19thC. From late Latin *rejuvenescere*, from Latin *juvenis* 'young'.] —**rejuvenescence** *n.* —**rejuvenescent** *adj.*

rekey /ree kée/ (**-keys, -keying, -keyed**) *vt.* to reenter lost text or data into a computer, or input text or data in a different form, using a keyboard

rekindle /ree kínd'l/ (**-dles, -dling, -dled**) *vt.* **1. MAKE FIRE BURN AGAIN** to set a fire burning again **2. REVIVE STH** to revive or renew sth, e.g. a feeling or interest

rel. *abbr.* **1.** relating **2.** relative **3.** relatively **4.** released **5.** religion **6.** religious

relapse *vi.* /ri láps/ (**-lapses, -lapsing, -lapsed**) **1. GO INTO FORMER STATE** to fall back into a former mood, state, or way of life, especially a bad or undesirable one, after coming out of it for a while **2.** MED **BECOME ILL AFTER RECOVERY** to become ill again after seeming to have made a recovery ■ *n.* /ri láps, rée laps/ **1. ACT OF RETURNING TO PREVIOUS CONDITION** a return to a former mood, state, or way of life, especially a bad or undesirable one, after coming out of it for a while **2.** MED **WORSENING OF HEALTH** a sudden worsening in the condition of a patient who was ill but who seemed to have made a recovery from the illness [15thC. From Latin *relaps-*, past participle stem of *relabi* 'to slip again', from *labi* 'to slip'.] —**relapser** *n.*

relapsing fever *n.* an infectious disease, characterized by chills and recurring fever, caused by a bacterium transmitted to people by ticks and lice

relate /ri láyt/ (**-lates, -lating, -lated**) *v.* **1.** *vi.* **HAVE A CONNECTION WITH STH** to have a significant connection or bearing on sth ○ *How does this story relate to our conversation?* **2.** *vt.* **CONNECT PEOPLE OR THINGS** to find or show a connection between two or more people or things **3.** *vi.* **INVOLVE SB OR STH** to concern, involve, or apply to sb or sth specifically ○ *These regulations relate only to imported goods.* **4.** *vi.* **FORM FRIENDLY ASSOCIATION** to have a friendly relationship with or friendly feelings towards sb, based on an understanding of the person or on shared views or concerns **5.** *vi.* **RESPOND TO SB OR STH** to understand and respond favourably to sth, or feel that it has a personal meaning or relevance (*informal*) ○ *I just can't seem to relate to the cynicism of that generation.* **6.** *vt.* **TELL OR DESCRIBE STH** to tell a story or describe an event [15thC. Via French *relater* 'to report' from Latin *relatus* (source of English *translate*), use as past participle of *referre* (see REFER).] —**relatable** *adj.* —**relater** *n.*

WORD KEY: USAGE

Jargon trap: The use of ***relate*** in the context of personal dealings between people is much used in the language of sociology but in general use has acquired the reputation of being an example of jargonistic, vague expression. The latter refers to the use of ***relate*** when it is not followed by *to* and a phrase, as in *Children who haven't learned to relate tend to be inadequately socialized.* A clearer way to express this would be *Children who haven't learned to relate to their peers tend to be inadequately socialized.*

related /ri láytid/ *adj.* **1. ASSOCIATED** connected by similarities or a common source **2. BELONGING TO THE SAME FAMILY** belonging to the same family by birth or through adoption or marriage **3.** MUSIC **HAVING CLOSE HARMONIC CONNECTION** used to describe a musical key or chord that, harmonically speaking, is closely connected with another, e.g. by having particular notes in common with it —**relatedly** *adv.* —**relatedness** *n.*

relation /ri láysh'n/ *n.* **1. CONNECTION BETWEEN THINGS** a meaningful connection or association between two or more things, based, e.g., on the similarity or relevance of one thing to another **2. MEMBER OF FAMILY** sb who belongs to the same family as sb else, by birth or through adoption or marriage **3. CONNECTION BY FAMILY** connection by birth, adoption, or marriage **4. NARRATION OF STH** the narration of a story or description of sth that has happened, or what is conveyed in the narration or description (*formal*) **5.** LAW **TAKING OF STH AS DONE EARLIER** a procedure whereby an act done at a particular time is, for legal purposes, deemed to have been done at an earlier time **6.** LOGIC, MATH **SHARED PROPERTY OF ASSOCIATION** a property of association, e.g. 'greater than' or 'less than', shared by ordered pairs of terms or objects ■ *npl.* **1. relations CONTACTS BETWEEN GROUPS OR PEOPLE** contacts or dealings between two or more people or groups **2. SEXUAL ACTS** sexual activities carried out by people (*used euphemistically*) ◇ **in** *or* **with relation to** with reference or regard to, or in comparison with sth

relational /ri láysh'nəl/ *adj.* **1. INVOLVING A RELATIONSHIP** involving or expressing a relationship **2.** GRAM **CONVEYING SYNTACTIC RELATION** expressing or relating to a syntactic relation between elements in a phrase or sentence ○ *Prepositions are relational words.* **3.** COMPUT **OF ORGANIZATION OF DATABASE** used to describe a way of organizing and presenting information in a database so that the user perceives it as a set of tables —**relationally** *adv.*

relationship /ri láysh'nship/ *n.* **1. CONNECTION** a significant connection or similarity between two or more things, or the state of being related to sth else **2. BEHAVIOUR OR FEELINGS TOWARDS SB ELSE** the connection between two or more people or groups and their involvement with each other, especially as regards how they behave and feel towards each other and communicate or cooperate **3. FRIENDSHIP** an emotionally close friendship, especially one involving sexual relations **4. CONNECTION BY FAMILY** the way in which two or more people are related by birth, adoption, or marriage, or the fact of being related by birth, adoption, or marriage **5.** LOGIC, MATH = **relation** *n.* 6

relative /réllətiv/ *adj.* **1. COMPARATIVE** measured or considered in comparison with each other or with sth else ○ *discussing the relative merits of various methods of transport* **2. CHANGING WITH CIRCUMSTANCES** not permanently fixed, but having a meaning or value that can only be established in relation to sth else and will change according to circumstances or context ○ *'Big' and 'small' are relative terms.* **3. DEPENDENT ON STH** depending on or in proportion to sth else ○ *Payment will be relative to the value of the work done rather than the time taken to do it.* **4. CONNECTED WITH STH** connected with or referring to sth ○ *The lawyers now have most of the data relative to the case.* **5.** GRAM **REFERRING TO PREVIOUSLY USED WORD** used to describe words, especially pronouns (**relative pronouns**) or clauses (**relative clauses**) that refer to another word previously used in the same sentence **6.** MUSIC **HAVING IDENTICAL KEY SIGNATURES** used to describe a key that has the same key signature as another, usually a minor key with the same sharps and flats as a major key, or vice versa ■ *n.* **1. MEMBER OF FAMILY** sb who belongs to the same family by birth or through adoption or marriage **2. THING RELATED TO STH ELSE** one thing that is related to sth else, especially a species that has developed from the same origin as another species **3.** GRAM **RELATIVE WORD** a relative word, especially a pronoun, or a relative clause —**relativeness** *n.*

relative atomic mass *n.* the ratio of the average mass per atom of an element to one twelfth of the mass of a carbon-12 atom. Symbol A_r

relative clause *n.* a clause that refers to and provides additional information about a preceding noun or pronoun, often beginning with a relative pronoun such as 'who','which', or 'that'

relative humidity *n.* the ratio of the amount of water vapour in the air at a given temperature to the maximum amount air can hold at the same temperature, expressed as a percentage

relatively /réllətivli/ *adv.* in comparison with other things ○ *a relatively cool day, given the summer weather*

relative permittivity (*plural* **relative permittivities**) *n.* PHYS measure of resistance of a substance to an applied electric field to the ratio of the permittivity of a substance divided by that of free space. Symbol υ_r

relative pitch *n.* **1. TONE'S PITCH COMPARED TO OTHER TONES** the pitch of a tone, determined by its position in a scale with respect to other tones **2. ABILITY TO PRODUCE TONE BY COMPARISON** the ability to identify or produce a tone by mentally comparing it to another tone recently heard

relative pronoun *n.* a pronoun such as 'that','which', or 'who' that refers to a previously used noun and introduces a relative clause

relativise *vti.* = **relativize**

relativism /réllətivizəm/ *n.* the belief that concepts such as right and wrong, goodness and badness, or truth and falsehood are not absolute but change from culture to culture and situation to situation —**relativist** *n.*

relativistic /rélləti vístik/ *adj.* **1.** PHYS **MOVING CLOSE TO SPEED OF LIGHT** moving at a velocity approaching the speed of light, the point at which certain properties such as mass act in accordance with the theory of relativity **2.** PHYS **RELATING TO RELATIVITY** relating to or characterized by relativity **3.** PHILOS **RELATING TO RELATIVISM** involving or characterized by relativism —**relativistically** *adv.*

relativity /rélla tívvəti/ (*plural* **-ties**) *n.* **1.** PHYS **EQUIVALENCE OF MASS AND ENERGY** the first of Einstein's two theories describing the relationship of matter, time, and space, showing that mass and energy are equivalent, and that mass, length, and time change with velocity. The theory is based on two assumptions: that the speed of light in a vacuum is constant, and that physical laws have the same mathematical form throughout the universe. **2.** PHYS **THEORY OF GRAVITATION AND ACCELERATION** the principle put forward in the second of Einstein's two theories extending the principles of the first to gravitation and phenomena related to acceleration **3. DEPENDENCE ON CONTEXTUALLY VARIABLE FACTOR** dependence on a factor that varies according to context **4. FACT OF BEING RELATIVE** the fact or state of being relative to sth else

relativize /rélləti vīz/ (**-izes, -izing, -ized**), **relativise** (**-ises, -ising, -ised**) *vti.* to make sth relative to sth else, or regard sth as relative to sth else

relator /ri láytər/ *n.* **1. SB WHO RELATES STH** sb who tells a story or gives an account of sth **2.** LAW **SB WHO PROVIDES RELEVANT INFORMATION** sb who provides the information used by the Attorney General to bring a court action

relaunch *vt.* /ree láwnch/ (**-launches, -launching, -launched**) **1. INTRODUCE STH INTO MARKET AGAIN** to introduce sth such as a company, product, or service into the market again, sometimes in a new form **2. SET STH GOING AGAIN** to set sth in motion or embark on sth again ■ *n.* /reè lawnch/ **REINTRODUCTION OF STH** the act or process of relaunching sth

relax /ri láks/ (**-laxes, -laxing, -laxed**) *v.* **1.** *vti.* **BECOME OR MAKE STH LOOSER** to slacken sth that is tensed or tight, e.g. a muscle or a grip on sth, or become looser, less tense, or less tight **2.** *vi.* **SPEND TIME DOING STH ENJOYABLE** to spend time resting or doing things for pleasure, especially in contrast to or as a relief from the effort and stress of everyday life **3.** *vti.* **MAKE OR BECOME LESS TENSE** to become, or make sb or sth, less anxious, hostile, defensive, or formal **4.** *vti.* **MAKE OR BECOME LESS STRICT** to make sth such as a rule less strict or less severe, or become less strict **5.** *vti.* **MAKE OR BECOME LESS INTENSE** to become, or make sth, less intense and concentrated **6.** *vt.* HAIR **STRAIGHTEN HAIR** to weaken or remove the curl from hair, usually by chemical means [14thC. From Latin *relaxare* 'to loosen', ultimately from *laxus* 'loose' (source of English *lax*).] —**relaxable** *adj.* —**relaxer** *n.* —**relaxing** *adj.*

relaxant /ri láks'nt/ *n.* **DRUG THAT RELAXES** a drug that reduces tension and strain, particularly in muscles ■ *adj.* **RELAXING** causing sth such as a muscle to become less tense

relaxation /reè lak sáysh'n/ *n.* **1. ENJOYABLE ACTIVITY** a form of activity that provides a change and relief from effort, work, or tension, and gives pleasure **2. LOOSENING OF STH** the process of becoming or of making sth less firm, rigid, or tight **3. LESSENING OF SEVERITY** a lessening of the strictness or severity of regulations, restrictions, or controls **4. REDUCTION IN INTENSITY** a lessening or weakening of sth that was previously concentrated or intense **5.** PHYS **RETURN OF SYSTEM TO EQUILIBRIUM** the return of a system to equilibrium after it has been displaced or changed **6.** MATH **WAY OF SOLVING EQUATIONS** a way of solving equations using a series of approximate solutions, each of which reduces the number of errors contained in the previous one, until the errors fall within acceptable limits [14thC. Originally meaning 'a rupture of a body part'; the sense of 'enjoyable activity' was not recorded until mid-16thC.]

relaxed /ri lákst/ *adj.* **1. WITHOUT STRAIN OR TENSION** under no strain or tension, and not exerting much strain or force on anything else **2. NOT FEELING ANXIOUS OR WORRIED** feeling no anxiety, tension, pressure, or sense of threat **3. ENCOURAGING INFORMALITY** encouraging informality and casual unhurried behaviour —**relaxedly** /ri láksidli/ *adv.* —**relaxedness** *n.*

relaxin /ri láksin/ *n.* a polypeptide hormone that relaxes the pelvic ligaments of female mammals during pregnancy and is produced by the corpus luteum

relay *n.* /reè lay/ **1. PASSING OF STH TO SB** the passing on of sth, especially a message or information received, to sb else, or the process of being passed on **2.** SPORTS **RELAY RACE** a relay race (*informal*) **3.** SPORTS **SECTION OF RELAY RACE** a section or lap of a relay race, run or swum by an individual athlete **4. REPLACEMENT TEAM** one of two or more teams of people or animals that relieve or replace each other in turn, e.g. as the previous team tires **5.** ELECTRON ENG **DEVICE THAT REGULATES ANOTHER** an electronic or electromechanical switching device, typically operated by a low voltage, that controls a higher-voltage circuit and switches it on or off **6.** TELECOM **APPARATUS THAT RECEIVES AND TRANSMITS SIGNALS** an apparatus consisting of a receiver and a transmitter, used to receive and retransmit signals **7.** TELECOM **SIGNAL** a message or broadcast passed on by an apparatus that receives and retransmits signals ■ *vt.* /ri láy/ (**-lays, -laying, -layed**) **1. PASS STH ON TO SB** to pass information or a message on to sb **2.** TELECOM **RETRANSMIT SIGNAL** to receive and retransmit a signal **3. REPLACE TEAM WITH FRESH PEOPLE** to replace or relieve a team, squad, or crew with a new one **4. ARRANGE PEOPLE INTO TEAMS** to organize sb or sth, especially workers, into relays [14thC. Via Old French *relayer* 'to exchange tired horses', from, ultimately, Latin *relaxare* (see RELAX).]

re-lay /ree láy/ (**re-lays** /ree láyd/, **re-laying, re-laid**) *vt.* to lay sth such as a carpet again [Formed from RE- + LAY[1]]

relay race *n.* a race between teams of competitors in which each member of a team runs or swims only part of the total distance to be covered. There are usually four people in a relay-race team. In a running race, the current runner must pass a baton to the person running the next section.

release /ri leéss/ *vt.* (**-leases, -leasing, -leased**) **1. LET SB OR STH GO** to set free a person or animal who is imprisoned, trapped, or confined in some way **2. STOP CLUTCHING STH** to stop gripping or holding sth **3. LET STH OUT** to let out sth that has been contained or confined within sth or pent up or latent inside sb **4. FREE SB FROM OBLIGATION** to make sb free of a debt, obligation, promise, or task **5. MAKE STH AVAILABLE** to make sth available, e.g. by putting it on sale, distributing it to the press or public, or allowing access to it **6. OPERATE CATCH TO LET MECHANISM WORK** to take the tension off a mechanism such as a spring, brake, or catch and so allow sth to move, open, or operate **7.** LAW **RELINQUISH STH** to relinquish sth, e.g. a right or claim, to another party ■ *n.* **1. LIBERATION** the act of setting sb or sth free, or the fact of being freed, from imprisonment, restraint, an obligation, or anything burdensome and oppressive **2. AUTHORIZATION FOR FREEDOM** a document or message stating that sb is to be set free **3. REMOVAL OF BURDEN** the removal of sth that makes sb feel trapped, restricted, or burdened **4. ACT OF MAKING STH AVAILABLE** the act of making sth available for the first time, or the fact of being made available in this way ○ *His latest film is expected to be on general release in the autumn.* **5. STH MADE AVAILABLE TO PUBLIC** sth such as a film, recording, or item of information that is made available to the public, put on show, or put on sale **6. EMISSION** the emission of sth such as heat or radioactivity from the place where it is generated into the atmosphere or the environment **7.** ENG **CONTROL MECHANISM** a mechanism, catch, or handle that is moved or pressed so that sth it controls can be used or allowed to operate **8. OPERATING OF DEVICE** the moving or pressing of a mechanism so that what it controls can be used or allowed to operate **9.** HR **LEAVE OF ABSENCE** leave of absence from a place, especially the workplace, or the granting of leave of absence, to enable sb to do sth else, e.g. attend an educational course **10.** LAW **RELINQUISHING OF CLAIM TO STH** the relinquishment of a right or claim to another party **11.** LAW **DOCUMENT CONFIRMING SURRENDER OF STH** a document stating that sb has surrendered sth, e.g. a claim or right [13thC. From Old French *relaisser* 'to let go', from Latin *relaxare* (see RELAX).] —**releasability** /ri leéssə bílləti/ *n.* —**releasable** /ri leéssəb'l/ *adj.* —**releasably** *adv.* —**releasee** /ri leè seé/ *n.* —**releaser** /ri leéssər/ *n.*

re-lease (**re-leases, re-leasing, re-leased, re-leased**) *vt.* to lease sth such as a flat again [Formed from RE- + LEASE]

released time *n. US* time given to sb by an authority or manager to allow personal matters or interests to be attended to

release print *n.* the version of a film released for distribution to commercial cinemas

releasing factor *n.* a hormone produced by the hypothalamus that causes the pituitary gland to secrete other hormones

relegate /rélli gayt/ (**-gates, -gating, -gated**) *vt.* **1. DEMOTE SB OR STH** to move sb or sth to a less important position, category, or status **2.** SPORTS **TRANSFER TEAM TO LOWER DIVISION** to transfer a sports team from a higher to a lower division in a competition, usually as a result of its being one of the least successful teams in the higher division (*often passive*) **3. HAND STH ON** to pass sth on to sb for the person to deal with it or provide information about it (*formal*) **4. EXILE SB** to banish sb from a country or community [15thC. From Latin *relegat-*, past participle stem of *relegare* 'to send away, refer', from *legare* (see LEGATE).] —**relegation** /rélli gáysh'n/ *n.*

relent /ri lént/ (**-lents, -lenting, -lented**) *vi.* **1. BECOME LESS RIGID OR STRICT** to become more sympathetic or amenable and do sth previously ruled out or allow sth previously forbidden **2. BECOME LESS INTENSE** to slacken or become less intense ○ *At last my headache relented.* [14thC. Formed from RE- + Latin *lentare* 'to bend, soften', from *lentus* 'flexible' (source of English *lento*).]

relentless /ri léntləss/ *adj.* **1. CEASELESS AND INTENSE** never slackening, but continuing always at the same intense, demanding, or punishing level **2. PERSISTENTLY HOSTILE** pursuing, attacking, or opposing sb or sth persistently and without mercy —**relentlessly** *adv.* —**relentlessness** *n.*

relevance /rélləvənss/, **relevancy** /-vənsi/ *n.* **1. CONNECTION** the sensible or logical connection that one thing has with another, e.g. a matter being discussed or investigated **2. APPLICABILITY TO CURRENT ISSUES** applicability to or connection with real-world issues, present-day events, or the current state of society **3.** COMPUT **ABILITY TO FIND RELEVANT DATA** the ability of an information retrieval system to find and retrieve data that fit a user's requirements

relevant /rélləvənt/ *adj.* **1. CONNECTED** having some sensible or logical connection with sth else, e.g. a matter being discussed or investigated **2. HAVING SOCIAL SIGNIFICANCE** having some bearing on or importance for real-world issues, present-day events, or the current state of society **3.** LING = **distinctive** *adj.* 2 [Early 16thC. From medieval Latin *relevant-*, present participle stem of Latin *relevare* 'to relieve' (later, 'to take possession of', hence the modern meaning of 'connected with').] —**relevantly** *adv.*

WORD KEY: USAGE

Spelling trap: The misspelling and mispronunciation 'revelant' for *relevant* is increasingly common and should be avoided.

reliable /ri lí əb'l/ *adj.* **1. DEPENDABLE** able to be trusted to do what is expected or has been promised ○ *She is extremely reliable and a hard worker.* **2. LIKELY TO BE ACCURATE** able to be trusted to be accurate or correct or to provide a correct result ○ *I don't think that clock's very reliable.* —**reliability** /ri lí ə bílləti/ *n.* —**reliableness** /ri lí əb'lnəss/ *n.* —**reliably** *adv.*

reliance /ri lí ənss/ *n.* **1. DEPENDENCE** dependence on another person or on, e.g. a service or a device, and the need for sth that he, she, or it provides **2. CONFIDENCE** trust or confidence in the eventual fulfilment of a promise or in the eventual success of a plan **3. PRIMARY SUPPORT** sb or sth needed or depended on

reliant /ri lí ənt/ *adj.* depending on or needing sb or sth —**reliantly** *adv.*

relic /réllik/ *n.* **1. OLD THING SURVIVING FROM PAST** sth that has survived from a long time ago, often a part of sth old that has remained when the rest of it has decayed or been destroyed **2. OLD CUSTOM** a tradition, practice, or rule that dates from some time in the past, especially one that is considered out of date or inappropriate at the present time **3. KEEPSAKE** sth that is kept for its interesting associations, e.g. with sb famous or with a historic event **4.** RELIG **STH FROM DEAD HOLY PERSON** sth that is kept and venerated because it once belonged to a saint, martyr, or religious leader, especially a part of his or her body **5. OFFENSIVE TERM** an offensive term that deliberately insults sb's advanced age or sb's or sth's relevance to modern conditions (*informal insult*) ■ **relics** *npl.* **CORPSE** the corpse of a deceased person (*archaic*) [13thC. Via Old French *relique*, from Latin *reliquiae* 'remains' (particularly of a dead saint), a plural form of *reliquus* 'remaining'.]

relict /réllikt/ *n.* **1.** BIOL **SURVIVING SPECIES** a species of organism surviving long after the extinction of related species, or a once widespread natural population surviving only in isolated localities because of environmental changes **2.** GEOL **REMNANT OF PRE-EXISTING FORMATION** a remnant of a pre-existing land or rock formation left behind after a destructive event has taken place **3.** GEOL **MINERAL UNALTERED BY METAMORPHISM** a mineral that did not change when the rock in which it occurs underwent metamorphosis **4. WIDOW** the widow of sb (*archaic*) ■ *adj.* BIOL **SURVIVING UNCHANGED** surviving in its original form when other related organisms have become extinct or its environment has changed completely [15thC. From Latin *relictus* 'left behind', from *relinquere* 'to relinquish'. Originally meaning 'widow'.]

reliction /ri líksh'n/ *n.* the gradual withdrawal of water from land, leaving it permanently dry

relief /ri leéf/ *n.* **1. FREEING OF SB FROM ANXIETY** a release from anxiety or tension, or the feeling of release, lightness, and cheerfulness that accompanies this **2. FACTOR THAT ENDS ANXIETY** a factor that ends a painful or stressful experience such as pain, hunger, or

Relief: 9th-century Roman relief sculpture

boredom **3.** SOC WELFARE **AID TO THOSE IN NEED** public help in the form of money, food, clothing, shelter, or medicine, provided to people who are temporarily unable to care for themselves **4.** FIN **PAYMENT REDUCTION OR FINANCIAL HELP** a reduction sb is entitled to in tax or other payments, or money given to him or her to help pay for sth **5.** HR **REPLACEMENT** a person who takes over a task or duty when a previous person completes his or her shift or spell of work, or one person who replaces another who is unable to work **6. DIVERTING CONTRAST** a factor forming a contrast to the general character of sth else, especially sth that breaks the monotony or tension of a longer experience **7.** TRANSP **EXTRA TRANSPORT** a train, bus, or other public transport vehicle that is brought in to provide extra places for passengers when the regular, scheduled service is full **8.** TRANSP = **relief road 9.** MIL **FREEING FROM SIEGE** the freeing of a besieged town, castle, fort, or strategic position by soldiers belonging to the same side as those under siege **10. PROMINENCE CAUSED BY CONTRAST** uniqueness or prominence caused by contrast ○ *to bring out the differences in clear relief* **11.** ARTS **PROJECTION FROM SURFACE** the elevation of figures or shapes from a flat surface, as seen in sculpture, or their apparent elevation, as seen in painting. ◊ **bas-relief 12.** ARTS **WORK OF ART** a work of art with figures or shapes in relief. ◊ **bas-relief 13.** GEOG, MAPS **ELEVATIONS OF LAND** the variations in height of a land surface and its being shaped into hills and valleys **14.** PRINTING **PRINTING PROCESS** a printing process such as engraving that uses raised surfaces to apply ink to the paper **15.** LAW **REDRESS AWARDED BY COURT** compensation or redress for a wrong or hardship, awarded to a party by a court **16.** HIST **PAYMENT TO LORD** a payment made to a feudal lord by the descendant of a tenant in order to inherit a fief [14thC. From Old French *relief*, from *relever* (see RELIEVE). The sense 'projection of a figure from a surface' was first recorded in the early 17thC.]

relief map *n.* a map that shows variations in land height, usually by means of contour lines or different colours

relief road *n.* a road built to divert heavy traffic round an urban area and stop it having to go through the town. US term **loop**

relieve /ri lee̍v/ (**-lieves, -lieving, -lieved**) *v.* **1.** *vti.* **STOP STH UNPLEASANT** to end, lessen, or provide a temporary break from sth unpleasant such as pain, hunger, tension, or boredom **2.** *vt.* SOC WELFARE **HELP SB** to provide help to people who are temporarily unable to care for themselves **3.** *vt.* HR **REPLACE SB** to replace sb on a shift or at a job **4.** *vt.* **EASE SB'S BURDEN** to remove sth such as a burden or difficulty from the one on which it is imposed **5.** *vt.* **REMOVE SB'S LOAD OR BURDEN** to take sth from sb, usually sth that the person is carrying or wearing **6.** *vt.* HR **FIRE EMPLOYEE** to dismiss or suspend sb from a job or position (*formal*) ○ *After the collision, the skipper was relieved of command.* **7.** *vt.* MIL **SAVE STH FROM MILITARY SIEGE** to free a besieged town, castle, fort, or strategic field position **8.** *vr.* PHYSIOL **URINATE** to empty the urinary bladder **9.** *vt.* **MAKE STH PROMINENT** to make sth stand out by contrast (*formal*) [14thC. Via Old French *relever* from Latin *relevare* 'to raise again, help', literally 'to make light again', ultimately from *levis* 'light' (source of English *lever*).] —**relievable** *adj.* —**reliever** *n.*

relievo /ri lee̍ vō/ (*plural* **-vos**), **rilievo** (*plural* **-vos**) *n.* the elevation of figures or shapes from a flat surface, as seen in sculpture, or their apparent elevation, as seen in painting [Early 17thC. From Italian *rilievo*, from *rilevare* 'to raise', from Latin *relevare* (see RELIEVE).]

relig. *abbr.* religion

religion /ri líjjən/ *n.* **1.** RELIG **BELIEFS AND WORSHIP** people's beliefs and opinions concerning the existence, nature, and worship of God, a god, or gods, and divine involvement in the universe and human life **2.** RELIG **PARTICULAR SYSTEM** a particular institutionalized or personal system of beliefs and practices relating to the divine **3. PERSONAL BELIEFS OR VALUES** a set of strongly-held beliefs, values, and attitudes that sb lives by **4. OBSESSION** an object, practice, cause, or activity that sb is completely devoted to or obsessed by ○ *The danger is that you start to make fitness a religion.* **5.** CHR **MONK'S OR NUN'S LIFE** life as a monk or a nun, especially in the Roman Catholic Church [12thC. Via Anglo-Norman *religiun*, from Old French *religion*, from the Latin stem *religion-* 'obligation, reverence', of uncertain origin: probably formed from *religare* (see RELY).] —**religionless** *adj.* ◇ **get religion 1.** to become a believer or join a religious organization, and, usually, start to lead a life that follows its teachings (*informal*) **2.** *US* to conform to the rules, regulations, customs, or expectations of sb or sth (*informal*)

religionism /ri líjjənizəm/ *n.* excessive or affected religious enthusiasm —**religionist** *n.*

religiose /ri líjji ōss/ *adj.* excessively, sentimentally, or affectedly pious (*disapproving*) [Mid-19thC. From Latin *religiosus*.] —**religiosely** *adv.* —**religiosity** /ri líjji óssəti/ *n.*

religious /ri líjjəss/ *adj.* **1. RELATING TO RELIGION** relating to belief in religion, the teaching of religion, or following the practices of a religion ○ *religious freedom* **2. BELIEVING IN A HIGHER BEING** believing in, and showing devotion or reverence for, a deity or deities ○ *a religious family* **3. THOROUGH** very thorough or conscientious ○ *a religious attention to detail* **4.** CHR **BELONGING TO MONASTIC ORDER** used to describe Christians who have committed themselves to a monastic order. The vows taken when doing this include dedication to poverty, chastity, and obedience. ■ *n.* (*plural* **-ious**) **MONK OR NUN** sb who belongs to a monastic order —**religiousness** *n.*

religiously /ri líjjəssli/ *adv.* **1. CONSCIENTIOUSLY** carefully and conscientiously **2. INVOLVING RELIGION** in a way that relates to religion or to a particular religion

relinquish /ri língkwish/ (**-quishes, -quishing, -quished**) *vt.* **1. CEDE STH** to renounce or surrender sth **2. ABANDON STH** to give sth up or put sth aside **3. LET STH GO** to let go of sth physically [15thC. Via the Old French stem *relinquiss-* from Latin *relinquere* 'to leave behind', from *linquere* 'to leave'.] —**relinquisher** *n.* —**relinquishment** *n.*

Reliquary: Reliquary bust of Charlemagne

reliquary /réllikwəri/ (*plural* **-ies**) *n.* a container or shrine where relics, e.g. the remains of a saint, are kept

relique /réllik, rə lee̍k/ *n.* sth from an older time, kept for its religious, historical, or sentimental value (*archaic*) [13thC (see RELIC)]

reliquiae /ri líkwi ee/ *npl.* the remains of sth, especially fossil remains of plants or animals [Mid-17thC. From Latin (see RELIC).]

relish /réllish/ *vt.* (**-ishes, -ishing, -ished**) **1. ENJOY STH** to enjoy or take great pleasure in an experience ○ *relished every minute of their trip* **2. ENJOY EATING STH** to enjoy the taste of a particular food or drink ■ *n.* **1. ENJOYMENT** a liking or appreciation of food or of an experience ○ *a relish for Spanish food* **2.** FOOD **SPICY SIDE DISH OR ACCOMPANIMENT** a spiced side dish or accompaniment to food, e.g. pickled or fresh vegetables with chilli **3. STRONG TASTE** a pleasing sensation of strong taste or flavour **4. INTEREST OR EXCITEMENT** interest or excitement, especially when it makes sth more enjoyable ○ *The incident added relish to an otherwise dull weekend.* [Early 16thC. From Old French *relais*, literally 'remainder'.] —**relishable** *adj.*

relive /ree lív/ (**-lives, -living, -lived**) *vt.* to experience sth again, especially as a result of thinking about it

rellies *npl.* *ANZ* sb's relatives (*informal*) ○ *We'll be seeing all the rellies again at Christmas.* [Late 20thC. Shortening.]

reload /ree lṓd/ (**reloads, reloading, reloaded**) *vti.* to put a new load in sth, e.g. film in a camera or fresh ammunition in a gun

relocate /ree̍ lō káyt/ (**-cates, -cating, -cated**) *vti.* to move or be moved to a new place on a long-term basis, especially to change the location of a business —**relocation** *n.*

relucent /ri lo͞oss'nt/ *adj.* brightly shining or reflecting light (*archaic*) [Early 16thC. Via Old French *reluisant* from Latin *relucere* 'to shine back'.]

reluct /ri lúkt/ (**-lucts, -lucting, -lucted**) *vi.* to offer opposition or resistance (*archaic*) [Early 16thC. From Latin *reluctari* 'to struggle against', from *luctari* 'to struggle'.]

reluctance /ri lúktənss/ *n.* **1. LACK OF ENTHUSIASM** unwillingness or lack of enthusiasm **2.** PHYS **MEASURE OF MAGNETIC RESISTANCE** a measure of the resistance of a closed magnetic circuit to a magnetic flux. It is equal to the ratio of the magnetic potential difference to the magnetic flux.

reluctant /ri lúktənt/ *adj.* **1. NOT KEEN** feeling no willingness or enthusiasm to do sth ○ *I am reluctant to drive in this weather.* **2. UNCOOPERATIVE** showing unwillingness to do sth or cooperate ○ *a reluctant swimmer* **3. OPPOSED** opposing or resisting sb or sth (*archaic*) [Mid-17thC. From Latin *reluctant-*, the present participle stem of *reluctari* 'to struggle against', from *luctari* 'to struggle'.] —**reluctantly** *adv.*

WORD KEY: USAGE

See Usage note at ***reticent***.

WORD KEY: SYNONYMS

See Synonyms at ***unwilling***.

relume /ri lo͞om/ (**-lumes, -luming, -lumed**), **relumine** /ri lo͞omin/ (**-lumines, -lumining, -lumined**) *vt.* to light or light sth up again [Early 17thC. Formed from ILLUME.]

rely /ri lī/ (**-lies, -lying, -lied**) *vi.* **1. DEPEND** to be dependent on sb or sth **2. TRUST** to have faith or confidence in sb or sth [14thC. Via Old French *relier* from Latin *religare* 'to tie back', from *ligare* 'to bind' (source of English *ally* and *religion*).]

rem /rem/ (*plural* **rem**) *n.* a unit for measuring amounts of radiation, equal to the effect that one roentgen of X-rays or gamma-rays would produce in a human being. It is used in radiation protection and monitoring. Full form **roentgen equivalent man**

REM /rem, aar ee ém/ *abbr.* rapid eye movement. ◊ **REM sleep**

remade past tense, past participle of **remake**

remain /ri máyn/ (**-mains, -maining, -mained**) *v.* **1.** *vi.* **STAY** to stay behind or wait somewhere **2.** *vti.* **CONTINUE IN A STATE** to continue in a particular state without changing **3.** *vi.* **BE LEFT** to be left after everything else has gone **4.** *vi.* **REQUIRE MORE WORK** to continue to need to be taken care of after everything else has been dealt with [14thC. Via Old French *remaindre, remanoir* from Latin *remanere*, from *manere* 'to stay' (source of English *permanent*).]

remainder /ri máyndər/ *n.* **1. WHAT IS LEFT OF STH** the part of sth that is left after other parts have gone or been used up **2.** MATH **AMOUNT LEFT OVER AFTER DIVISION** the amount left over when a number or quantity cannot be divided exactly by another **3.** PUBL **UNSOLD BOOKS** the unsold copies of a book, sold by a publisher at a reduced price after demand has fallen off **4.** LAW **INTEREST IN SB ELSE'S ESTATE** an interest in an estate that passes to sb only after a prior interest terminates, e.g. when the current holder of the estate dies ■ *vt.* (**-ders, -dering, -dered**) PUBL **SELL BOOK AT REDUCED PRICE** to sell copies of a book at a reduced price after demand has fallen off [14thC. Via Anglo-Norman from Old French *remaindre* (see REMAIN).]

remainderman /ri máyndər man/ (*plural* **-men** /-men/) *n.* the person who is entitled to a particular estate once everything has been resolved

remaining /ri máyning/ *adj.* still left or still existing

remains /ri máynz/ *npl.* **1.** **WHAT IS LEFT** all that is left of sth ○ *the remains of the barn after the fire* **2.** **CORPSE** a dead body, or what is left of a body **3.** **ANCIENT RUINS** the parts of sth old that are still left ○ *the remains of ancient Roman baths* **4.** **DEAD AUTHOR'S UNPUBLISHED WRITINGS** all of an author's work that was still unpublished at the time of the author's death

remake *n.* /rée mayk/ **NEW VERSION OF STH** sth that has been made again or differently, especially a new version of an old film ■ *vt.* /ree máyk/ (**-makes, -making, -made** /-máyd/, **-made**) **PRODUCE STH AGAIN** to produce a remake of sth

remand /ri maánd/ *vt.* (**-mands, -manding, -manded**) **1.** LAW **RETURN PRISONER TO CUSTODY** to return a prisoner or accused person to custody, or arrange for sb to be released on bail when a court case is adjourned ○ *The judge ordered the prisoner to be remanded in custody.* **2.** **SEND SB BACK** to send or order sb back ■ *n.* LAW **RETURNING OF SB UNTRIED TO PRISON** the return of a prisoner or accused person to custody, or the arrangement of bail for sb, while waiting for trial [15thC. Via Old French *remander* from late Latin *remandare* 'to send word back', from Latin *mandare* 'to command'.] —**remandment** *n.*

remand centre *n.* a place where accused people are detained while awaiting criminal trial

remand home *n.* an institution to which juvenile offenders between the ages of 8 and 14 are remanded or sent for detention. US term **detention home**

remanence /rémmənənss/ *n.* the magnetic inductance that remains in a substance after the magnetizing field has been removed [Mid-16thC. From Latin *remanent-*, the present participle stem of *remanere* (see REMAIN).]

remanent magnetism /rémmənənt-/ *n.* magnetism shown by ferromagnetic minerals, which preserve the sense and direction of the earth's magnetic field from the time of their formation [*Remanent* from Latin, the present participle stem of *remanere* (see REMAIN)]

remark /ri maárk/ *n.* **1.** **CASUAL COMMENT** a casual or brief observation **2.** **ACT OF COMMENTING** the act of making a remark about sth, or an occasion on which this takes place ○ *They consumed their meal without remark.* **3.** COMPUT = **comment** *n.* 4 **4.** **ACT OF NOTICING** an act or instance of noticing sth, especially sth that deserves attention (*formal*) ○ *How could such a major change take place without remark?* ■ *v.* (**-marks, -marking, -marked**) **1.** *vti.* **MAKE COMMENT ON STH** to make a casual comment or observation about sth **2.** *vt.* **OBSERVE STH** to notice or observe sth (*formal*) [Late 16thC. From French *remarquer*, from *marquer* 'to mark'.] —**remarker** *n.*

remarkable /ri maárkəb'l/ *adj.* **1.** **WORTHY OF NOTICE** worth noticing or commenting on **2.** **UNUSUAL** unusual or exceptional, and attracting attention because of this —**remarkableness** *n.*

remarkably /ri maárkəbli/ *adv.* **1.** **TO A REMARKABLE DEGREE** to an extent or degree that is remarkable **2.** **IN A REMARKABLE WAY** used to emphasize that sth is worth noticing or commenting on ○ *Remarkably, no one was arrested.*

remarque /ri maárk/ *n.* **1.** **ENGRAVER'S MARK** a mark in the margin of an engraved plate, made to indicate its stage of production and removed before final printing, or the plate with the mark itself **2.** **PROOF OF ENGRAVING** a proof of an engraving made from a plate with a remarque [Late 19thC. From French, formed from *remarquer* (see REMARK).]

Remarque /ri maárk/, **Erich Maria** (1898–1970) German-born US writer. After he was wounded fighting for Germany in World War I, he wrote *All Quiet on the Western Front* (1929), which became a classic war novel. He lived in the United States after 1939.

remaster /ree maástər/ (**-ters, -tering, -tered**) *vt.* to make a new master copy of an earlier audio recording or film to improve its quality of reproduction

rematch /rée mach/ *n.* **SECOND MATCH** a second or return contest between opponents ■ *vt.* (**-matches, -matching, -matched**) **MATCH OPPONENTS AGAIN** to arrange for opponents to meet in a second or return contest

Rembrandt van Rijn

Rembrandt van Rijn /rém brant von rín/ (1606–69) Dutch artist. A major painter of the Dutch Golden Age, he imbued his portraits and religious and historical works with a moving spirituality. Full name **Rembrandt Harmenszoon van Rijn**

REME /rée mee/ *abbr.* Royal Electrical and Mechanical Engineers

remedial /ri meédi əl/ *adj.* **1.** **ACTING AS REMEDY** acting as a remedy or solution to a particular problem **2.** EDUC **HELPING TO IMPROVE SKILLS** designed to help people with learning difficulties to improve their skills or knowledge, or relating to education designed to do this **3.** MED **INTENDED TO IMPROVE HEALTH** intended to cure or relieve the symptoms of sb who is ill or has a physical disability ○ *remedial exercises* —**remedially** *adv.*

remediation /ri meédi áysh'n/ *n.* the use of remedial teaching or therapy to improve skills or health

remedy /rémmədi/ *n.* (*plural* **-dies**) **1.** MED **TREATMENT FOR DISEASE** a medication or treatment that cures a disease or disorder, or relieves its symptoms **2.** ALTERN MED **HOMEOPATHIC TREATMENT** a substance prescribed by a homeopath, and taken in minute quantities **3.** **WAY OF PUTTING STH RIGHT** a means of setting sth right or getting rid of sth undesirable ○ *no easy remedy for society's ills* **4.** LAW **LEGAL REDRESS** a legal means of enforcing a right or of providing redress **5.** COINS **PERMITTED VARIATION IN COINS** the legally permitted variation from an established standard in the weight or quality of a coin ■ *vt.* (**-dies, -dying, -died**) **1.** MED **CURE A DISEASE** to cure or relieve a disease or disorder **2.** **PUT STH RIGHT** to set sth right, or get rid of sth undesirable [13thC. Via Anglo-Norman *remedie* from, ultimately, Latin *remedium* 'medicine'.] —**remediable** /ri méedi ab'l/ *adj.* —**remediably** /ri méedi əbli/ *adv.*

remember /ri mémbər/ (**-bers, -bering, -bered**) *v.* **1.** *vti.* **RECALL STH FORGOTTEN** to recall sth to mind or become aware of sth that had been forgotten **2.** *vti.* **KEEP STH IN MEMORY** to retain an idea in the memory without forgetting it **3.** *vt.* **KEEP SB IN MIND** to keep sb in mind for attention or consideration **4.** *vt.* **GIVE SB A GIFT** to give sb a gift, money, or a tip ○ *She always remembered him on his birthday.* **5.** *vt.* **SEND SB'S GREETINGS** to mention sb to sb else as a greeting to yet another person ○ *Remember me to your Dad.* **6.** *vr.* **BECOME POLITE AGAIN** to resume behaving in a mannerly way after having briefly acted badly ○ *I was about to make a hurtful comment but I remembered myself just in time.* **7.** *vt.* **COMMEMORATE SB OR STH** to commemorate sb or sth, e.g. in a ceremony or funeral service [14thC. Via Old French *remembrer* from late Latin *rememorari*, from Latin *memor* 'mindful' (source of English *memory*).] —**rememberer** *n.*

remembrance /ri mémbrənss/ *n.* **1.** **REMEMBERING** the act or process of remembering people, things, or events **2.** **BEING REMEMBERED** the state of being remembered, or of remaining in people's minds ○ *We hold her name in fond remembrance.* **3.** **ACT OF HONOURING** the act of honouring the memory of a person or event ○ *a remembrance service* **4.** **STH REMEMBERED** sth that is remembered **5.** **EXTENT OF MEMORY** the period of time over which memory extends **6.** **MEMENTO** sth that reminds sb of a thing, event, or another person **7.** **GREETING** a greeting, gift, or other expression of affection and friendship

WORD KEY: CULTURAL NOTE

Remembrance of Things Past, a series of novels by French writer Marcel Proust (1913–27). Regarded as one of the greatest works of 20th-century literature, this remarkable meditation on time and memory describes the narrator's childhood encounters with his aristocratic neighbours and his subsequent introduction to Parisian society. A series of unconscious recollections triggers the realization that the past is not lost but can be retrieved by memory and preserved as art.

Remembrance Day *n.* 11 November, observed in Canada as a public holiday and with a two-minute silence in remembrance of those who died in World Wars I and II and subsequent conflicts

remembrancer /ri mémbrənssər/ *n.* (*archaic*) **1.** **SB WHO REMINDS SB ELSE** sb who reminds sb else about sth **2.** **MEMENTO** a reminder or memento

Remembrancer *n.* **1.** **OFFICIAL OF EXCHEQUER** a British official of the Exchequer, the Queen's or King's Remembrancer, who collects debts owed to the Crown **2.** **OFFICIAL OF CITY OF LONDON** the City Remembrancer, appointed by the Corporation of the City of London to represent its interests

Remembrance Sunday *n.* the Sunday nearest to 11 November (**Armistice Day**), on which those who died in World Wars I and II and subsequent conflicts are remembered, especially in church services

remex /rée meks/ (*plural* **remiges** /rémmi jeez/) *n.* any of the flight feathers of a bird's wing (*technical*) [Late 17thC. From Latin, literally 'oarsman', formed from *remus* 'oar'.] —**remigial** /ri míjji əl/ *adj.*

remind /ri mínd/ (**-minds, -minding, -minded**) *vt.* to cause a person to remember or think of sth or sb else ○ *Remind me to collect the dry-cleaning.* ○ *He reminds me of his grandfather.*

reminder /ri míndər/ *n.* **1.** **STH USED TO REMIND SB** sth that is used to remind sb about sth, e.g. a letter or message ○ *If they don't settle the bill next week, send them a reminder.* **2.** **STH THAT REMINDS** sb who or sth that makes sb remember or think of another person or thing ○ *The monument is a reminder of their bravery.*

reminisce /rémmi níss/ (**-nisces, -niscing, -nisced**) *vi.* to talk or write about events remembered from the past [Early 19thC. Back-formation from REMINISCENCE.] —**reminiscer** *n.*

reminiscence /rémmi níss'nss/ *n.* **1.** **RECOLLECTION OF THE PAST** the recollection of past experiences or events in speech or writing, or the act of recalling the past **2.** **STH REMEMBERED** an experience or event remembered from the past **3.** **REMINDER** sth that recalls or suggests sth similar **4.** PHILOS **IDEA FROM PLATO** the Platonic doctrine that anything we encounter is an imperfect recollection of an idea that our souls have encountered in a previous disembodied existence **5.** PSYCHOL **ABILITY TO PERFORM TASK BETTER** the ability to perform a task or remember information better some time after it has been learnt than was possible immediately after it was learnt

reminiscent /rémmi níss'nt/ *adj.* **1.** **LIKE STH OR SB ELSE** suggesting similarities or comparisons with sth or sb else **2.** **SUGGESTING MEMORIES OF THE PAST** characterized by or containing recollections of the past ○ *scenes reminiscent of her childhood* **3.** **RECALLING THE PAST** given to reminiscing about the past [Mid-18thC. From Latin, the present participle stem of *reminisci* 'to recollect'.] —**reminiscently** *adv.*

remise /ri méez/ *n.* FENCING **SECOND THRUST** in fencing, a further thrust made on the same lunge to follow up a first thrust that has missed ■ *vi.* (**-mises, -mising, -mised**) FENCING **MAKE REMISE** to make a remise when a first thrust has missed [15thC. Via French from, ultimately, Latin *remittere* (see REMIT).]

remiss /ri míss/ *adj.* careless or negligent about doing sth that is expected [15thC. From Latin *remissus*, the past participle of *remittere* (see REMIT).]

remissible /ri míssəb'l/ *adj.* worthy of forgiveness —**remissibility** /ri míssə bíllәti/ *n.*

remission /ri mísh'n/ *n.* **1.** MED **SLOWING OF DISEASE** a lessening of the symptoms of a disease, or their temporary reduction or disappearance **2.** LAW **REDUCTION IN A PRISON TERM** the reduction of sb's prison sentence for good conduct **3. LESSENING OF STH** a lessening or a reduction in the severity of sth ○ *The afternoon sun beat down without remission.* **4. RELEASE** a release from a debt, penalty, or obligation **5. FORGIVENESS** pardon or forgiveness **6. ACT OF REMITTING** an instance or the action of remitting sth

remit *v.* /ri mít/ (**-mits, -mitting, -mitted**) **1.** *vti.* **SEND PAYMENT** to send money to pay for goods or services, especially by post **2.** *vt.* LAW **SEND CASE BACK TO LOWER COURT** to send a case back to a lower court for further action to be taken **3.** *vt.* **CANCEL STH** to cancel or hold back from enforcing sth **4.** *vti.* **REDUCE INTENSITY OF STH** to reduce or allow the reduction in the intensity of sth **5.** *vt.* **DEFER STH** to postpone or defer sth **6.** *vt.* **PARDON STH** to pardon or forgive sth (*archaic*) ■ *n.* /réemit, ri mít/ **1. AREA OF RESPONSIBILITY** the scope or area of responsibility belonging to a particular person, group, or investigation ○ *This matter is beyond the remit of the committee.* **2.** LAW **TRANSFER OF LEGAL CASE** the transfer of a legal case from a higher to a lower court for further action to be taken **3. STH REMITTED** sth sent to another person or authority for consideration **4.** *NZ* **PROPOSAL** an item submitted by a person or organization for consideration at a conference [14thC. From Latin *remittere* 'to send back', from *mittere* (see ADMIT).] —**remittable** *adj.* —**remittal** *n.* —**remitter** *n.*

remittance /ri mítt'nss/ *n.* **1. ACT OF PAYING** the sending of money to pay for goods or services **2. MONEY** money sent as payment for goods or services **3. REMITTING** the act of remitting sth

remittance man *n.* a man who lives abroad, especially, in the past, somewhere in the British Empire, and is dependent on money sent from home (*dated*)

remittee /ri mít ée, ri míttee/ *n.* sb to whom payment is sent

remittent /ri mítt'nt/ *adj.* lessening and then intensifying again at intervals ○ *slowed down by a remittent fever* —**remittence** *n.* —**remittency** *n.* —**remittently** *adv.*

remix *vt.* /ree míks/ (**-mixes, -mixing, -mixed**) **PRODUCE NEW VERSION OF MUSIC** to produce a new version of a piece of music by altering the emphasis of the sound and, in pop music, often adding new tracks in place of existing ones ■ *n.* /réemiks/ **NEW RECORDING** a recording that has been remixed

remnant /rémnənt/ *n.* **1. SMALL PART STILL LEFT** a small part of sth that remains after the rest has gone **2. SMALL AMOUNT OF CLOTH OR CARPET** a small amount of unsold cloth or flooring material left at the end of a roll, often sold at a reduced price **3. TRACE OF STH** a small amount or trace of sth such as a feeling or emotion **4. SMALL SURVIVING GROUP OF PEOPLE** a small isolated group of people surviving from a particular culture or group [14thC. From Old French *remanant*, the present participle of *remanoir* (see REMAIN).]

remodel /ree módd'l/ (**-els, -elling, -elled**) *vt.* to renovate or alter the structure or style of sth, e.g. a building, room, or design

remonetize /ree múnni tīz/ (**-tizes, -tizing, -tized**), **remonetise** (**-tises, -tising, -tised**) *vt.* to reinstate sth as valid currency or legal tender —**remonetization** /ree múnni tī záysh'n/ *n.*

remonstrance /ri mónstrənss/ *n.* **1. ARGUMENT** a forceful argument in favour or against sth, or the act of making such an argument **2. FORMAL PROTEST** a formal protest, usually in the form of a document or petition

Remonstrance *n.* **1.** HIST = **Grand Remonstrance 2.** CHR **STATEMENT OF ARMINIAN PROTESTANT PRINCIPLES** the statement expressing Arminian Protestant principles, drawn up in 1610 in Gouda, the Netherlands. The doctrines of Jacob Arminius rejected Calvinist predestination and supported the notion of free will, and had a profound effect on Wesleyan and Methodist theology.

remonstrant /ri mónstrənt/ *n.* **PROTESTER** sb who remonstrates ■ *adj.* **PROTESTING** involved in or used for a protest (*formal*) [Early 17thC. From medieval Latin, the present participle stem of *remonstrare* (see REMONSTRATE).]

Remonstrant *n.* a Dutch dissenter and supporter of the Remonstrance of 1610

remonstrate /rémmən strayt/ (**-strates, -strating, -strated**) *vi.* to reason or argue forcefully with sb about sth [Late 16thC. From the past participle stem of medieval Latin *remonstrare* 'to demonstrate', from *monstrare* 'to show'.] —**remonstration** /rémmən stráysh'n/ *n.* —**remonstrative** /ri mónstrətiv/ *adj.* —**remonstratively** /-tivli/ *adv.* —**remonstrator** /rémmən straytər/ *n.*

WORD KEY: SYNONYMS

See Synonyms at ***object***.

remontant /ri móntənt/ *adj.* **FLOWERING MORE THAN ONCE** blooming or bearing fruit more than once in a season ■ *n.* **PLANT FLOWERING MORE THAN ONCE** a plant that blooms or bears fruit more than once a season [Late 19thC. From French, the present participle of *remonter* 'to rise again'.]

remora /rémmərə/ *n.* a bony salt water fish with a suction disc on the top of its head that it uses to attach itself to a larger fish or a ship's hull. Family: Echeneidae. [Mid-16thC. From Latin, literally 'hindrance'; from the belief that it slowed ships down when attaching itself to them.]

remorse /ri máwrss/ *n.* **1. GUILT** a strong feeling of guilt and regret **2. PITY** compassion or pity (*archaic*) [14thC. Via Old French *remors* from, ultimately, Latin *remordere* 'to torment', from *mordere* 'to bite'.] —**remorseful** *adj.* —**remorsefully** *adv.* —**remorsefulness** *n.*

remorseless /ri máwrssləss/ *adj.* **1. WITHOUT COMPASSION** showing no pity or compassion **2. RELENTLESS** continuing without lessening in strength or intensity —**remorselessly** *adv.* —**remorselessness** *n.*

remortgage /ree máwrgij/ *vt.* (**-gages, -gaging, -gaged**) **1. CHANGE MORTGAGE TERMS** to revise the terms of a mortgage on a property **2. MORTGAGE STH AGAIN** to mortgage sth again after the original mortgage has been paid off ■ *n.* **NEW MORTGAGE** a revised or second mortgage taken out on sth

remote /ri mṓt/ *adj.* **1. FAR AWAY** situated a long way away **2. OUT-OF-THE-WAY** far away from civilization, society, or any other populated area **3. DISTANTLY RELATED** distantly related by blood, adoption, or marriage ○ *a remote relative on my father's side* **4. LONG AGO** distant in time **5. SLIGHT** faint or slight ○ *not the remotest possibility of her coming here* **6. DISTANT** distant in connection, relevance, or effect **7. ALOOF** distant in manner or behaviour **8. SEPARATED** operated or performed from a distance ○ *a remote camera* ○ *a remote shopping service* ■ *n.* **1.** HOUSEHOLD **REMOTE CONTROL** a remote control for an electronic device (*informal*) **2.** COMPUT **COMPUTER FAR FROM CENTRAL COMPUTER** a device or computer system that is situated at a distance from a central computer and that can be accessed via a network **3.** *US* BROADCAST = **outside broadcast** [15thC. From Latin *remotus*, the past participle of *removere* 'to remove'.] —**remoteness** *n.*

remote access *n.* access that is gained to a computer by means of a separate terminal

remote control *n.* **1.** HOUSEHOLD **HAND-HELD CONTROL** a hand-held device used to operate a television set, video cassette recorder, or other electronic device from a distance **2. OPERATION FROM DISTANCE** the control of a device, system, or activity from a distance, usually by radio signals (*hyphenated when used before a noun*) ○ *a remote-control transmitter*

remotely /ri mṓtli/ *adv.* **1. SLIGHTLY** in a slight or tenuous way ○ *The two events were only remotely connected.* **2. IN THE LEAST** in the least possible way or to the least possible extent ○ *I am not even remotely interested in what they say.* **3. BY REMOTE CONTROL** using remote control **4. IN A DETACHED WAY** in a distant or aloof manner **5. DISTANTLY** far in the future or past ○ *looking to a remotely future epoch* **6. IN A DISTANT WAY** distantly in terms of family or biological connection ○ *We are remotely related.* **7. FAR AWAY** at a distance or far away

remote sensor *n.* an instrument, e.g. a radar or photographic device, that gathers information about the Earth or another astronomical body from an airborne platform or from space

rémoulade /rémmoo la̅ad, rémmə láyd/ *n.* mayonnaise with herbs, mustard, capers, and gherkin added, and sometimes chopped hard-boiled egg [Mid-19thC. From French, of uncertain origin: perhaps, ultimately, from Latin *armoracea* 'wild radish'.]

remould *n.* /rée mōld/ **TYRE WITH NEW TREAD** a second-hand tyre with a new tread bonded to it. US term **retread** ■ *vt.* /ree mṓld/ (**-moulds, -moulding, -moulded**) **1. CHANGE STH** to change or remodel sth such as an idea or principle **2. FIT TYRE WITH NEW TREAD** to bond a new tread onto an old tyre. US term **retread**

remount *v.* /ree mównt/ (**-mounts, -mounting, -mounted**) **1.** *vt.* **PUT STH ON AGAIN** to mount sth again or anew **2.** *vti.* **GET BACK INTO SADDLE** to get back on a horse or bicycle ■ *n.* /rée mownt/ **SUBSTITUTE HORSE** a replacement horse to ride

removable /ri mo͞ovəb'l/ *adj.* designed in a way that allows it to be taken off and put back on again —**removability** /ri mo͞ovə bíllǝti/ *n.* —**removableness** /ri mo͞ovə b'lnəss/ *n.* —**removably** *adv.*

removal /ri mo͞ov'l/ *n.* **1. REMOVING OF STH** the taking away or getting rid of sth **2. CHANGE OF LOCATION** a change in location, or in the place where sb lives **3.** HR **DISMISSAL** dismissal from office or from a position

removalist /ri mo͞ovəlist/ *n. ANZ* a person or company that transports people's belongings from one house to another

remove /ri mo͞ov/ *v.* (**-moves, -moving, -moved**) **1.** *vt.* **TAKE STH AWAY** to take sth away from sb or from a place **2.** *vti.* **RELOCATE** to transfer sb or sth to another place, or change a place of residence **3.** *vt.* **TAKE STH OFF** to take off an article of clothing **4.** *vt.* **GET RID OF STH** to make sth go away or disappear ○ *a detergent that can remove stains even more quickly* **5.** *vt.* HR **DISMISS SB** to dismiss sb from office ■ *n.* **1. DISTANCE** the degree of distance or closeness between people or things ○ *He has only experienced war at one remove.* **2.** EDUC **CLASS** a class or form in some British secondary schools, especially public schools (*dated*) **3. CHANGE OF LOCATION** a change of residence or business (*formal*) **4.** FOOD **INDIVIDUAL DISH IN MEAL** a dish that is taken away during a formal meal to make way for another (*dated formal*)

removed /ri mo͞ovd/ *adj.* **1. DISTANT** separate or distant in space, time, or character from sth or sb else **2. DISTANTLY RELATED** separated from sb to a specified degree by birth, adoption, or marriage ○ *a cousin twice removed* —**removedness** /ri mo͞ovidnəss, ri mo͞ovdnəss/ *n.*

REM sleep *n.* a stage of sleep that recurs several times during the night and is marked by dreaming, rapid eye movements under closed lids, and elevated pulse rate and brain activity

remunerate /ri myo͞onə rayt/ (**-ates, -ating, -ated**) *vt.* to pay sb for goods or services, or compensate sb for losses sustained or inconvenience caused in money [Early 16thC. Via Latin *remunerat-*, the past participle stem of *remunerari* 'to reward', from, ultimately, *munus* 'gift'.] —**remunerability** /ri myo͞onərə bíllǝti/ *n.* —**remunerable** /ri myo͞onərəb'l/ *adj.* —**remunerator** /-raytər/ *n.* —**remuneratory** /-rətəri/ *adj.*

remuneration /ri myo͞onə ráysh'n/ *n.* **1. PAY** a payment or reward for goods or services or for losses sustained or inconvenience caused **2. PAYING** the paying or rewarding of sb for goods or services or for losses sustained or inconvenience caused

WORD KEY: SYNONYMS

See Synonyms at ***wage***.

remunerative /ri myo͞onərətiv/ *adj.* paying sb or rewarding sb with money —**remuneratively** *adv.*

Remus /réeməss/ *n.* in Roman mythology, the son of Mars and twin brother of Romulus, the founder of the city of Rome. ◊ **Romulus**

renaissance /ri náys'nss/, **renascence** *n.* a rebirth or revival, e.g. of culture, skills, or learning forgotten or previously ignored [Late 19thC. From French, formed from *renaître* 'to be reborn', from Latin *renasci* (see RENASCENT).]

Renaissance: Detail of the bronze doors of the Baptistery, Florence, Italy, by Lorenzo Ghiberti

Renaissance *n.* **1. END OF MIDDLE AGES** the period in European history from about the 14th to 16th centuries regarded as marking the end of the Middle Ages and featuring major cultural and artistic change **2. CLASSICAL REVIVAL** the cultural and religious spirit that characterized the Renaissance, including the decline of Gothic architecture, the revival of classical culture, the beginnings of modern science, and geographical exploration. The new emphasis on individualism and secularism in this time led to the Reformation. ■ *adj.* **1. RELATING TO THE RENAISSANCE** relating to the history and culture of the Renaissance **2.** ARCHIT **IN ARCHITECTURAL STYLE OF RENAISSANCE** in the architectural style of classical revival that characterized the Renaissance

Renaissance man *n.* a man who has a wide range of accomplishments and intellectual interests

Renaissance woman *n.* a woman who has a wide range of accomplishments and intellectual interests

renal /réen'l/ *adj.* relating to or affecting the kidneys [Mid-17thC. Via French from, ultimately, Latin *renes* 'kidneys'.]

renal clearance *n.* a measure of the removal of waste products from the blood by the kidneys, expressed as the volume of blood cleared of one particular substance in one minute

renal pelvis *n.* the cavity in the kidney where urine collects before passing into the ureter

renascence /ri náss'nss, -náy-/ *n.* = **renaissance**

renascent /ri náss'nt, ri náyss'nt/ *adj.* showing new life or activity [Early 18thC. From Latin, the present participle stem of *renasci* 'to be reborn'.]

renature /ree náychər/ (**-tures, -turing, -tured**) *vt.* to restore the physical and chemical properties of an organic molecule, e.g. a denatured protein

rencounter /ren kówntər/ (**-ters, -tering, -tered**) *n.* (*archaic*) **1. HOSTILE MEETING** a hostile meeting between adversaries **2. CASUAL MEETING** an unexpected casual meeting [Early 16thC. From French *rencontrer* 'to have a (hostile) meeting', from *encontrer* (see ENCOUNTER).]

rend /rend/ (**rends, rending, rent** /rent/, **rent**) *v.* **1.** *vti.* **TEAR STH APART** to tear sth apart violently, or be torn apart in this way ○ *The hurricane rent the flimsy houses in pieces.* **2.** *vt.* **TEAR CLOTHES** to tear or pull clothes or hair out of rage, frustration, or grief **3.** *vt.* **TAKE SB OR STH AWAY FORCIBLY** to tear or wrest sth or sb away **4.** *vt.* **MAKE A PIERCING SOUND** to disturb the silence or pierce the air with a loud sound ○ *a scream rent the air* **5.** *vt.* **DISTRESS SB** to cause pain or distress to the heart or emotions [Old English. Ultimately, from a prehistoric Germanic word that is also the ancestor of English *rind*.]

WORD KEY: SYNONYMS

See Synonyms at ***tear***.

Rendell /rénd'l/, **Ruth** (*b.* 1930) British novelist. Her popular crime novels include the Chief Inspector Wexford series.

render /réndər/ *v.* (**-ders, -dering, -dered**) **1.** *vt.* **GIVE HELP** to give help or provide a service (*formal*) **2.** *vt.* **TRANSLATE STH** to translate sth into another language (*formal*) ○ *fragments of poetry, hastily rendered into English* **3.** *vt.* ARTS **PORTRAY STH ARTISTICALLY** to portray sth or sb in art, literature, music, or acting (*formal*) ○ *a scene of utter desolation, skilfully rendered without sentiment* **4.** *vt.* **GIVE DECISION** to deliver a verdict or decision officially (*formal*) **5.** *vt.* **SUBMIT STH FOR ACTION** to submit sth for consideration, approval, or payment (*formal*) ○ *render all passports for inspection* **6.** *vt.* **PAY RESPECT** to give what is due or appropriate to sb who has authority or power (*formal*) ○ *'Render therefore unto Caesar the things which are Caesar's'* (Matthew 22:21, *The Bible*) **7.** *vt.* **PUT SB OR STH IN PARTICULAR STATE** to make sb or sth be or become sth (*formal*) ○ *His actions rendered her powerless.* **8.** *vt.* **PURIFY FAT** to purify or extract sth by melting, especially to heat solid fat slowly until as much liquid fat as possible has been extracted from it, leaving small crisp remains **9.** *vt.* BUILDING **COVER WALL WITH PLASTER** to cover masonry with a thin coat of plaster **10.** *vti.* **GIVE UP STH** to surrender sth (*formal or literary*) **11.** *vt.* **TRADE STH** to give sth in exchange for sth else (*formal or literary*) **12.** *vt.* **RETURN STH** to give sth back (*formal or literary*) ■ *n.* **1.** BUILDING **COAT OF PLASTER** the first thin coat of plaster applied to masonry **2.** HIST **TENANT'S PAYMENT** a payment in goods, services, or money made by a tenant to a feudal lord [14thC. Via Old French *rendre* from, ultimately, Latin *reddere* 'to give back', from *dare* 'to give' (source of English *date*).] —**renderable** *adj.* —**renderer** *n.*

rendering /réndəring/ *n.* **1.** ARTS **ARTISTIC PORTRAYAL** a portrayal of sb or sth in art, music, literature, or drama **2.** LITERAT **TRANSLATION** a translation of a literary work **3.** INDUST **HEATING ANIMAL REMAINS TO EXTRACT FAT** the process or business of separating fat from meat or animal remains by slow heating **4.** BUILDING **COAT OF PLASTER** a coat of plaster applied to masonry **5.** ARCHIT **ARCHITECT'S PERSPECTIVE DRAWING** an architect's representation of the inside and outside of a finished building, drawn in perspective

rendezvous /róndi voo, -day-/ *n.* (*plural* **-vous**) **1. MEETING** a meeting arranged for a specified time and place **2. PLACE OF MEETING** the location of a prearranged meeting **3. PLACE WHERE PEOPLE MEET** a popular meeting place for people ■ *vti.* (**-vouses, -vousing, -voused**) **MEET SB** to meet, or meet sb, at a specified time and place, or cause this to happen [Late 16thC. From French, literally 'present yourself'.]

rendition /ren dísh'n/ *n.* **1.** ARTS **VERSION OF MUSICAL OR THEATRICAL PIECE** an interpretation or performance of a piece of music or drama **2.** LITERAT **TRANSLATION** a translation of a literary work **3. TRANSLATING** the act of translating sth into another language (*formal*) **4. SURRENDER** a surrender (*archaic*) [Early 17thC. From French, formed from *rendre* (see RENDER).]

rendzina /ren dzéenə/ *n.* a dark rich soil that develops beneath grassland above a layer of limestone or chalk [Early 20thC. From Polish *rędzina*.]

Rene, Roy (1892–1954) Australian actor. He created the music-hall act Mo the clown, and starred in the film *Strike Me Lucky* (1935). Real name **Henry van der Sluys Rene**

renegade /rénni gayd/ *n.* **1. TRAITOR** sb who abandons previously held beliefs or loyalties **2. REBEL** sb who chooses to live outside of the laws or conventions of a group [From Spanish *renegado*, from medieval Latin *renegatus*, from the past participle of Latin *renegare* (see RENEGE)]

renege /ri néeg, ri náyg/ (**-neges, -neging, -neged**) *vi.* **1. BREAK A PROMISE** to go back on a promise or commitment **2.** CARDS **NOT FOLLOW SUIT** in cards, to fail to follow suit when able and required to do so [Mid-16thC. From medieval Latin *renegare* 'to deny', from Latin *negare* (source of English *negate*).] —**reneger** *n.*

renegotiate /reeni góshi ayt/ (**-ates, -ating, -ated**) *vti.* to negotiate an agreement again in order to change the terms

renew /ri nyóo/ (**-news, -newing, -newed**) *v.* **1.** *vti.* **RETURN TO DOING STH** to begin sth again, or return to doing sth **2.** *vti.* **EXTEND STH** to make sth such as a contract, lease, or licence effective for a longer period ○ *You'll need to renew your lease at the end of the year.* **3.** *vt.* **REPLACE STH WORN** to replace sth that is worn out or no longer suitable for use **4.** *vt.* LIBRARIES **BORROW LIBRARY BOOK FOR LONGER** to extend the period of time a book or other item is borrowed from a library **5.** *vt.* **REPEAT PROMISE** to reaffirm or restate a promise or commitment ○ *renewed their marriage vows* **6.** *vt.* **GIVE SB OR STH NEW ENERGY** to give sb or sth new energy, strength, or enthusiasm ○ *I felt quite renewed after the weekend.* **7.** *vt.* **GET NEW SUPPLY** to get a new a supply of sth **8.** *vt.* **MAKE STH NEW AGAIN** to make sth new or as if new again —**renewer** *n.*

WORD KEY: SYNONYMS

renew, recondition, renovate, restore, revamp

CORE MEANING: to improve the condition of sth

renew to replace sth worn or broken; **recondition** to bring sth such as a machine or appliance back to a good condition or working state by means of repairs or replacement of parts; **renovate** to bring sth such as a building back to a former better state by means of repairs, redecoration, or refurbishment; **restore** to bring sth back to an original state after it has been damaged or fallen into a bad condition; **revamp** an informal word, to improve the appearance or condition of sth.

renewable /ri nyóo əb'l/ *adj.* **1. ABLE TO BE RENEWED** capable of being renewed **2. NOT LIKELY TO RUN OUT** able to be sustained or renewed indefinitely, either because of inexhaustible supplies or because of new growth ○ *renewable resources* —**renewability** /ri nyóo ə bíllәti/ *n.* —**renewably** /ri nyóo əbli/ *adv.*

renewable energy *n.* = **alternative energy**

renewable resource *n.* **1. RESOURCE THAT CAN BE SUSTAINED** a resource such as timber that can be renewed as quickly as it is used up so that it can, in theory, last indefinitely, unlike mineral resources **2. NATURAL RESOURCE THAT REPLACES ITSELF** a natural resource that replaces itself unless overused, e.g. animal or plant life or fresh water **3. RENEWABLE FORM OF ENERGY** a source of energy, e.g. sunlight, wind, or tidal power, that can be used indefinitely to generate electricity because it does not involve burning fuel or damaging the environment

renewal /ri nyóo əl/ *n.* **1. ACT OF RENEWING STH** the act or process of renewing sth, or the state of being renewed **2. STH RENEWED** sth that is being or has been renewed

Renfrew /rén froo/ town near the River Clyde, near Glasgow, in Scotland. Population: 20,764 (1991).

Renfrewshire /rén frooshər, rén froo sheer/ council area in Scotland. Paisley is the administrative centre. Population: 178,550 (1995).

reniform /rénni fawrm, réeni fawrm/ *adj.* shaped like or suggestive of a kidney

renin /réenin/ *n.* an enzyme released by the kidneys that breaks down proteins and plays an important role in regulating blood pressure

renitent /ri nít'nt, rénnitənt/ *adj.* (*formal*) **1. RIGID IN STRUCTURE** resisting physical pressure, rather than being flexible or pliant **2. RIGID IN ATTITUDE** reluctant to have a change of mind or concede to others [Early 18thC. From Latin, the present participle stem of *reniti* 'to struggle against'.] —**renitence** *n.* —**renitency** *n.*

Rennes /ren/ capital city of Ile-Vilaine Department, Brittany Region, western France. It is situated about 97 km/60 mi. north of Nantes. Population: 203,533 (1990).

rennet /rénnit/ *n.* **1.** ANAT **STOMACH LINING OF CALVES** the inner lining of the fourth stomach or abomasum of calves and other young ruminants **2.** FOOD, MANUF **SUBSTANCE FOR CURDLING MILK** a preparation made from rennet that contains the enzyme rennin and is used to curdle milk in making cheese **3.** BIOCHEM = **rennin** [15thC. Origin uncertain: probably from an Old English word.]

rennin /rénnin/ *n.* an enzyme that is found in the gastric juice of the fourth stomach of calves and other young ruminants and is the constituent in rennet that curdles milk [Late 19thC. Formed from RENNET.]

renogram /réenə gram/ *n.* **1. RECORD OF KIDNEY FUNCTION** a photographic record of kidney function, showing how quickly a radioactive substance injected into the bloodstream is removed when it passes through the kidneys **2. KIDNEY X-RAY** an X-ray image of a kidney [Early 20thC. *Reno-* formed from Latin *renes* 'kidneys'.]

Renoir /rén waar, rən waár/, **Jean** (1894–1979) French film director. The son of Pierre Auguste Renoir, he was a technical innovator known for the fluidity of his work. His greatest film is *The Rules of the Game* (1939). He lived in the United States after 1941.

AKG London

Pierre Auguste Renoir

Renoir, Pierre Auguste (1841–1919) French painter and sculptor. One of the leading Impressionists, he is noted for the harmony of his lines, the brilliance of his colours, and the intimate charm of his wide variety of subjects.

renounce /ri nównss/ *v.* **(-nounces, -nouncing, -nounced) 1.** *vt.* GIVE UP CLAIM TO STH formally to give up a claim, title, position, or right **2.** *vt.* REJECT BELIEF to reject or disavow a belief or theory **3.** *vt.* GIVE STH UP to give up a habit, pursuit, or practice **4.** *vi.* CARDS NOT FOLLOW SUIT in cards, to be unable to follow suit and be forced to play a card from a different suit ■ *n.* CARDS ACT OF NOT FOLLOWING SUIT a failure to follow suit [14thC. Via French *renoncer* from Latin *renuntiare* 'to report', from *nuntiare* 'to announce'.] —**renouncement** *n.* —**renouncer** *n.*

renovascular /reénō váskyŏŏlər/ *adj.* relating to the blood vessels of the kidneys [Mid-20thC. Coined from Latin *ren* 'kidney' + VASCULAR.]

renovate /rénnə vayt/ *(-vates, -vating, -vated) vt.* **1.** MAKE STH LIKE NEW AGAIN to restore sth to good condition **2.** REFRESH SB OR STH to give new vigour to sb or sth [15thC. From Latin *renovare*, from *novus* 'new'.] —**renovation** /rénnə váysh'n/ *n.* —**renovative** /rénnə vaytiv/ *adj.* —**renovator** /-vaytər/ *n.*

WORD KEY: SYNONYMS

See Synonyms at *renew*.

renown /ri nówn/ *n.* widespread fame or honour [14thC. From Old French *renon*, from *renomer* 'to make famous', from *nomer* 'to name', from Latin *nominare* (source of English *nominate*).]

renowned /ri nównd/ *adj.* well known or famous, especially for a skill or expertise

rent[1] /rent/ *n.* **1.** PAYMENT BY TENANT a regular payment made by a tenant to an owner or landlord for the right to occupy or use property **2.** PAYMENT TO USE EQUIPMENT a regular payment to the owner for the right to use equipment or personal property **3.** PROFIT FROM CULTIVATED LAND the financial return from cultivated land after production costs have been deducted **4.** INCOME OF LANDOWNERS the portion of the national income that is earned by landowners **5.** ECON = **economic rent** ■ *vti.* **(rents, renting, rented) 1.** PAY TO USE SB'S PROPERTY to occupy sb else's property or use sb else's equipment in return for regular payments **2.** ALLOW USE OF PROPERTY FOR PAYMENT to allow sb to occupy property or use equipment in return for regular payment [12thC. Via French *rente* from, ultimately, Latin *reddere* (see RENDER).]

WORD KEY: SYNONYMS

See Synonyms at *hire*.

rent[2] /rent/ *n.* **1.** HOLE MADE BY TEARING an opening or hole made by tearing sth **2.** RELATIONSHIP RIFT a rift in a relationship or breach in friendly relations [Mid-16thC. From the past participle of REND.]

rent[3] past tense, past participle of **rend**

rental /rént'l/ *n.* **1.** RENT PAYMENT the amount paid in rent **2.** RENT INCOME the amount received in rent **3.** ACT OF RENTING STH the renting of property or equipment **4.** *US* STH RENTABLE sth rented or available to rent **5.** *US* RENTING BUSINESS a business that rents out property or equipment ■ *adj.* RELATING TO RENT relating to property for rent or with rent payments

rent boy *n.* a young male prostitute (*slang*)

rent control *n.* government regulation of the amount charged for housing rental and sometimes of eviction procedures —**rent-controlled** *adj.*

renter /réntər/ *n.* **1.** SB WHO RENTS FROM SB sb who rents property or equipment from sb else **2.** SB WHO RENTS TO SB sb who rents property or equipment to sb else **3.** CINEMA FILM DISTRIBUTOR a film distributor renting films to cinemas

rentier /raaN tyay, rónti ay/ *n.* sb whose income is primarily from rent and securities [Mid-19thC. From French, formed from *rente* (see RENT[1]).]

rent strike *n.* an organized refusal by tenants to pay their rent

renunciation /ri núnssi áysh'n/ *n.* **1.** DENIAL OR REJECTION a denial or rejection of sth, usually for moral or religious reasons **2.** DECLARATION GIVING STH UP an official declaration giving up a title, office, claim, or privilege —**renunciatory** /ri núnsi ətəri/ *adj.*

renvoi /ren vóy/ *n.* the referral of a case or dispute from the country in which it arose to the laws of another [Late 19thC. From French, formed from *renvoyer* 'to send back'.]

reorder /ree áwrdər/ *v.* **(-ders, -dering, -dered) 1.** *vti.* REQUEST NEW SUPPLY to order the same goods again **2.** *vt.* REARRANGE STH to arrange sth differently **3.** *vt.* ARRANGE STH AGAIN to put sth in order again ■ *n.* ANOTHER ORDER another order for the same goods from the same supplier

reorganization /ree áwrgə nī záysh'n/ *n.* **1.** CHANGE IN STH a change in the way sth is organized, arranged, or done **2.** BUSINESS RESTRUCTURING OF ORGANIZATION the thorough physical or financial restructuring of a business or organization —**reorganizational** *adj.*

reorganize /ree áwrgə nīz/ **(-izes, -izing, -ized), reorganise (-ises, -ising, -ised)** *vti.* **1.** ORGANIZE STH AGAIN to impose organization on sth again after its being disturbed **2.** ORGANIZE STH DIFFERENTLY to change the way that sth is organised —**reorganizer** *n.*

reorient /ree áwri ənt/ **(-ents, -enting, -ented), reorientate (-tates, -tating, -tated)** *vti.* **1.** ADAPT TO NEW SITUATION to change your behaviour or ideas to deal with a new situation **2.** GET BEARINGS to find out where you are or where you are going after being lost —**reorientation** /ree áwri ən táysh'n/ *n.*

reovirus /reé ō vīrəss/ *n.* a virus that contains double-stranded RNA and is associated with various infections in plants and animals. Reoviruses are often found in people with breathing and stomach disorders. [Mid-20thC. *Reo-*, an acronym formed from *respiratory enteric orphan*.]

rep[1] /rep/, **repp** *n.* a ribbed or corded fabric made from silk, wool, rayon, or cotton [Mid-19thC. From French *reps*, of uncertain origin: probably from English *ribs*, plural of RIB.]

rep[2] /rep/ *n.* repertory theatre, or a repertory company (*informal*) [Early 20thC. Shortening.]

rep[3] /rep/ *n.* SALES REPRESENTATIVE a sales representative (*informal*) ■ *vi.* **(reps, repping, repped)** BE A SALES REPRESENTATIVE to work as a sales representative (*informal*) [Late 19thC. Shortening.]

rep[4] /rep/ *n.* a reputation (*informal*) [Early 18thC. Shortening.]

rep[5] /rep/ *n.* a repetition of a fitness exercise (*informal*)

rep. *abbr.* **1.** repair **2.** report **3.** reported **4.** reporter **5.** reprint

Rep. *abbr.* **1.** *US* Representative **2.** Republic **3.** *US* Republican

repackage /ree pákij/ **(-ages, -aging, -aged)** *v.* **1.** PUT PRODUCT IN NEW PACKAGING to package a product in a new and differently designed container or wrapping **2.** *vt.* GIVE SB NEW IMAGE to give sb such as a political leader or celebrity a new public image

repaid *v.* past tense, past participle of **repay**

repair[1] /ri páir/ *vt.* **(-pairs, -pairing, -paired) 1.** FIX OR MEND STH to restore sth broken or damaged to good condition ○ *repair a flat tyre* **2.** RESTORE RELATIONSHIP to restore a relationship or friendship by resolving a difficulty or disagreement **3.** ATONE FOR STH to make amends for sth wrong ○ *How can I repair this wrong?* ■ *n.* **1.** JOB OF MENDING STH the process of mending sth, or the job that is done in order to achieve this ○ *carry out repairs* **2.** REPAIRED ITEM sth that has been repaired **3.** CONDITION OF STH the condition of sth with respect to whether it needs mending or fixing ○ *an air conditioner no longer in good repair* [14thC. Via Old French *réparer* from Latin *reparare*, from *parare* 'to make ready' (source of English *prepare*).] —**repairability** /ri páirə bílləti/ *n.* —**repairable** *adj.* —**repairer** *n.*

repair[2] /ri páir/ *v.* **(-pairs, -pairing, -paired)** (*formal*) **1.** *vi.* GO SOMEWHERE to go to a particular place ○ *repaired to the library after dinner* **2.** *vt.* CONSULT SB to go to sb for help or advice ■ *n.* (*archaic*) **1.** ACT OF GOING SOMEWHERE the act of going to a particular place **2.** MEETING PLACE a meeting place or a place where a person or animal is found [14thC. Via French *repairer* from late Latin *repatriare* (see REPATRIATE).]

repairman /ri páir man/ (*plural* **-men** /-men/) *n.* a man whose job is making repairs to equipment or machinery

repairwoman /ri páir wŏŏmən/ (*plural* **-en** /-wimin/) *n.* a woman whose job is making repairs to equipment or machinery

repand /ri pánd/ *adj.* BOT with a wavy edge ○ *a repand leaf* [Mid-18thC. Via Latin *repandus*, literally 'curving back', from, ultimately, *pandere*, 'to become curved'.]

reparable /réppərəb'l/ *adj.* able to be repaired, recovered, or put right —**reparability** /réppərə bílləti/ *n.* —**reparably** /réppərəbli/ *adv.*

reparation /réppə ráysh'n/ *n.* **1.** AMENDS compensation for a wrong, or sth that is done to achieve this **2.** REPAIR restoration of sth to good condition, or the process of doing this (*formal*) ■ **reparations** *npl.* COMPENSATION FOR WAR compensation demanded of a defeated nation by the victor in a war, especially that demanded of Germany by the Treaty of Versailles after World War I —**reparative** /ri párrətiv/ *adj.* —**reparatory** /-párrətəri/ *adj.*

repartee /réppaar teé/ *n.* **1.** WITTY TALK conversation consisting of witty remarks **2.** WIT skill in making witty remarks or conversation **3.** WITTY REMARK a witty remark or reply [Mid-17thC. From French *repartie*, from *repartir*, literally 'to set out again', from *partir* (see PART).]

repartition /reé paar tísh'n/ *n.* **1.** DISTRIBUTION distribution or division of sth **2.** DIVIDING OF STH AGAIN the act of dividing or distributing sth again, either in the same way or differently ■ *vt.* **(-tions, -tioning, -tioned)** DIVIDE STH UP AGAIN to divide sth up again, either in the same way or differently

repast /ri paást/ *n.* FOOD a meal, or the food eaten at a meal (*archaic or literary*) ■ *vi.* **(-pasts, -pasting, -pasted)** EAT to eat or feast on food (*formal or literary*) [14thC. From Old French, formed from *repaistre* 'to feed', from, ultimately, Latin *pascere* (source of English *pasture*).]

repatriate *vt.* /ree páttri ayt/ **(-ates, -ating, -ated) 1.** SEND SB BACK to send sb back to his or her country of birth, the country of which he or she is a citizen, or the country from which he or she arrived **2.** FIN SEND BACK MONEY to send money that has been invested abroad back to its country of origin ■ *n.* /ree páttri ət/ SB REPATRIATED sb who has been repatriated [Early 17thC. From Latin *repatriare* 'to go back home', from *patria* 'homeland'.] —**repatriation** /ree páttri áysh'n/ *n.*

repay /ri páy/ **(-pays, -paying, -paid** /ri páyd/, **-paid)** *vt.* **1.** PAY BACK MONEY TO SB to pay back money that is owed to sb **2.** RETURN FAVOUR to reward sb for that his or her effort, aid, or success **3.** RETURN IN KIND to return sth in kind —**repayable** *adj.*

repayment /ri páymənt/ *n.* **1.** SUM PAID BACK TO LENDER a sum of money, especially one of a series of instalments, paid back by a borrower to a lender **2.** REPAYING OF STH the act or an instance of repaying sth

repeal /ri peél/ *vt.* **(-peals, -pealing, -pealed) 1.** LAW UNDO LAW to officially revoke or abolish sth such as a law **2.** BRING SB BACK FROM EXILE to recall sb from exile (*archaic*) ■ *n.* LAW ABOLITION OF LAW the act of repealing sth such as a law [14thC. From Anglo-Norman *repeler*, a variant of Old French *rapeler*, from *re-* 'again, back', + *apeler* (see APPEAL).] —**repealable** *adj.* —**repealer** *n.*

repeat /ri peét/ *v.* **(-peats, -peating, -peated) 1.** *vt.* SAY STH AGAIN to say or write sth again **2.** *vti.* DO OR UNDERGO STH AGAIN to do, produce, or experience sth again or several times ○ *She repeated the exercises every day.*

3. *vti.* ECHO SB'S WORDS to say again what sb else has said **4.** *vt.* TELL WHAT HAS BEEN HEARD to tell another person sth that was told to you, especially when it was done in confidence ○ *I'll tell you, but you mustn't repeat it to anyone else.* **5.** *vt.* SAY STH MEMORIZED to recite sth that has been learned **6.** *vr.* SAY THE SAME THING OVER AGAIN to do or say sth again, especially more than once ○ *You get tired of repeating yourself after a while.* **7.** *vr.* HAPPEN AGAIN AS BEFORE to happen again in the same way as previously **8.** *vti.* BROADCAST BROADCAST AGAIN to broadcast a television or radio programme again, or be broadcast again **9.** *vi.* FOOD BE TASTED AGAIN to be tasted again after having been eaten, through wind or partial regurgitation (*informal*) ○ *Those spicy meatballs are repeating on me.* **10.** *vi.* TIME SIGNAL TIME to make a sound signalling the latest hour, or sometimes quarter hour when sb presses a spring (*refers to a clock or watch*) ■ *n.* **1.** RECURRING EVENT OR SITUATION an event or situation that is the same as a previous one **2.** BROADCAST STH SHOWN AGAIN sth that is broadcast, shown, or performed again **3.** MUSIC RECURRING MUSICAL PASSAGE OR ITS NOTATION a passage of music played again within a single piece, or the notation indicating that this is to be done. If a passage is to be repeated, the notation '·∶' or '∶·' is placed before or after it in a musical score. **4.** UNIFORMLY REPRODUCED PATTERN a pattern reproduced uniformly across a surface ○ *upholstery fabric with a large floral repeat* **5.** ACT OF REORDERING STH a reorder of the same goods or by the same customer [14thC. Via French *répéter* from Latin *repetere*, literally 'to demand again', from *petere* 'to demand' (source of English *petition*).] —**repeatability** /ri peềtə bílləti/ *n.* —**repeatable** /ri peềtəb'l/ *adj.*

repeated /ri peềtid/ *adj.* happening or done again and again

repeatedly /ri peềtidli/ *adv.* again and again, or on several occasions

repeater /ri peềtər/ *n.* **1.** SB OR STH REPEATING sb who or sth that repeats **2.** ARMS GUN FIRING SEVERAL SHOTS WITHOUT RELOADING a firearm such as a rifle with a magazine that can fire several shots before it has to be reloaded **3.** TIME TIMEPIECE THAT REPEATS CHIMES a clock or watch that can be made to repeat its latest chime when sb presses a spring **4.** ELEC ENG DEVICE FOR AMPLIFYING SIGNALS an electrical device that boosts and amplifies incoming communications signals and retransmits them. Such boosting is needed as the quality and strength of the analog signal decays over distance.

repeating decimal *n.* = recurring decimal

repeating firearm *n.* = repeater *n.* 2

repeat performance *n.* an event that is the same as one that happened before

repeat prescription *n.* UK, Can a prescription for a regularly needed medicine that has been prescribed before and can be renewed without the doctor having to see the patient

repechage /réppə shaâzh/ *n.* a heat within a competition such as a fencing, rowing, or cycling competition, during which runners-up in earlier heats have a final chance to qualify for the next round [Early 20thC. From French, from *repêcher*, literally 'to fish out'.]

repel /ri pél/ (**-pels, -pelling, -pelled**) *v.* **1.** *vti.* CAUSE GREAT DISTASTE to make sb feel intense aversion, disgust, or revulsion **2.** *vt.* MIL RESIST ATTACK to ward off or force back an attack or invasion **3.** *vt.* KEEP STH AWAY to ward sth off or keep sth away ○ *a cream that is effective in repelling mosquitoes* **4.** *vti.* FAIL TO MIX to fail to mix or blend with sth else ○ *Oil and water repel each other.* **5.** *vti.* PHYS EXERT OPPOSING FORCE to exert a force that tends to push sth away ○ *Particles of like charge repel each other.* **6.** *vt.* SPURN SB OR STH to reject or refuse to accept sth or sb [15thC. Via Old French *repeler* from Latin *repellere*, literally 'to drive back', from *pellere* 'to drive' (source of English *pulse*).] —**repeller** *n.*

— **WORD KEY: USAGE** —
See Usage note at *repulse.*

repellent /ri péllənt/, **repellant** *adj.* **1.** CAUSING DISGUST making sb feel intense dislike, disgust, or revulsion **2.** RESISTANT TO STH resistant or impervious to sth (*often*

used in combination) ○ *water-repellent material* **3.** PUSHING AWAY pushing sth away or driving sth back ■ *n.* **1.** STH THAT REPELS INSECTS a substance that drives away insects **2.** SUBSTANCE THAT RESISTS STH HARMFUL a substance that is applied to a surface of sth to resist water, mould, or mildew —**repellence** *n.* —**repellently** *adv.*

— **WORD KEY: USAGE** —
repellent or **repulsive**? Both words mean 'causing disgust or revulsion', but **repulsive** is rather stronger in effect than **repellent**, corresponding to the difference in strength between the root verbs *repulse* and *repel.* **Repellent** is common in combinations such as *insect-repellent* and *water-repellent*, denoting substances that repel or resist the things specified. **Repulsive** does not have a literal meaning corresponding to this, except in technical use in physics.

— **WORD KEY: USAGE** —
Spelling trap Note that the adjective is usually spelled *-ent* and not *-ant*. The *-ant* form is somewhat more common for the noun, but *-ent* is still preferable.

repent[1] /ri pént/ (**-pents, -penting, -pented**) *vti.* **1.** BE SORRY to recognize the wrong in sth you have done and be sorry about it **2.** RELIG CHANGE WAYS to feel regret about a sin or past actions and change your ways or habits [13thC. From French *repentir*, from *pentir*, from, ultimately, Latin *paenitere* (source also of English *penitent*).] —**repenter** *n.*

repent[2] /ri pént/ *adj.* growing or lying along the ground [Mid-17thC. From Latin *repent-*, the present participle stem of *repere* 'to creep' (source also of English *reptile*).]

repentance /ri péntənss/ *n.* a feeling of regret or contrition for having done sth wrong

repentant /ri péntənt/ *adj.* feeling or showing regret about having done sth wrong —**repentantly** *adv.*

repercussion /reépər kúsh'n/ *n.* **1.** RESULT OF ACTION sth, especially an unforeseen problem, that results from an action (*often used in the plural*) **2.** REBOUND the rebounding of a force after impact **3.** PHYS REFLECTION the reflection of light or sound **4.** MUSIC POINT OF REAPPEARANCE IN FUGUE in a fugue, the return of the theme after an episode [Mid-16thC. Directly or via French from Latin *repercuss-*, the past participle stem of *repercutere*, literally 'to strike back through', from *percutere* 'to strike through'.] —**repercussive** *adj.*

repertoire /réppər twaar/ *n.* **1.** MATERIAL AVAILABLE FOR PERFORMANCE a stock of musical or dramatic material that is known and can be performed **2.** BODY OF ARTISTIC WORKS the entire body of works in a specific area of the arts **3.** RANGE OF RESOURCES THAT SB HAS the range of techniques, abilities, or skills that sb or sth has ○ *the surgeon's repertoire* [Mid-19thC. Via French from late Latin *repertorium* (see REPERTORY).] ◇ **in repertoire** used to refer to performances of different plays or ballets given on different days

repertory /réppərtəri/ (*plural* **-ries**) *n.* **1.** THEATRE SYSTEM OF PRESENTING PLAYS a system by which a permanent theatre company presents a set of works during a season, usually in its own theatre. US term **stock 2.** THEATRE GROUP OR THEATRE USING REPERTORY SYSTEM a theatre or company that uses the repertory system **3.** ARTS = repertoire *n.* 1, repertoire *n.* 2 **4.** COLLECTION OF AVAILABLE THINGS a store or stock of available items ○ *a comedian with a large repertory of jokes* [Late 16thC. From late Latin *repertorium* 'inventory', from, ultimately, Latin *reperire* 'to get completely', from *parire* 'to get' (source of English *parent*).] —**repertorial** /réppər táwri əl/ *adj.*

repertory company *n.* a theatre company that performs different plays on different days in the same theatre. US term **stock company**

repetend /réppi tend, réppi ténd/ *n.* **1.** MATH REPEATED PART OF DECIMAL the part of a repeating decimal that is repeated infinitely, e.g. '37' in '0.373737' **2.** STH REPEATED sth that is repeated [Early 18thC. From Latin *reperendum* 'thing to be repeated', from *repetere* (see REPEAT).]

répétiteur /ray pétti túr, ri-/ *n.* a musician in an opera company who coaches the singers and accompanies them on the piano in rehearsal [Mid-20thC. From French, literally 'sb who repeats'.]

repetition /réppə tísh'n/ *n.* **1.** REPEATING OF STH an act of doing sth again **2.** STH THE SAME AS BEFORE an event or situation that is the same as one that happened previously **3.** PROCEDURE OF STATING STH AGAIN the act or process of saying or writing sth again **4.** REPEATED WORDS sth that is repeated, especially unnecessary words **5.** REPLICA a replica or duplicate of sth (*archaic*) [Early 16thC. Via French from, ultimately, Latin *repetere* (see REPEAT).]

repetitious /réppə tíshəss/ *adj.* full of things that are said or written over and over again, especially in an unnecessary or tiresome way —**repetitiously** *adv.* —**repetitiousness** *n.*

repetitive /ri péttətiv/ *adj.* full of or involving things that are done over and over again ○ *a boring, repetitive task* —**repetitively** *adv.* —**repetitiveness** *n.*

repetitive strain injury, **repetitive stress injury** *n.* full form of **RSI**

rephrase /ree fráyz/ (**-phrases, -phrasing, -phrased**) *vt.* to say or write sth again using different words as a clarification or for variety

repine /ri pín/ (**-pines, -pining, -pined**) *vi.* to feel dissatisfied or fretful about sth and complain or grumble about it (*formal*) [Early 16thC. Formed from PINE[2] 'to fret', on the model of *repent*.] —**repiner** *n.*

replace /ri pláyss/ (**-places, -placing, -placed**) *vt.* **1.** SUBSTITUTE FOR STH to take the place of or substitute for sb or sth ○ *The new ways rapidly replaced the old.* **2.** SUPPLANT SB OR STH to fill the place of sth or sb with sth or sb else ○ *You can be replaced.* **3.** PUT STH IN ANOTHER'S PLACE to provide or find a substitute for sth ○ *can't afford to replace his car* **4.** PUT STH BACK IN ITS PLACE to put an object back in its usual place ○ *She replaced the receiver slowly.* [Late 16thC. Formed from PLACE 'to put', on the model of French *remplacer*.] —**replaceable** *adj.* —**replacer** *n.*

— **WORD KEY: USAGE** —
See Usage note at *substitute.*

replacement /ri pláyssmənt/ *n.* **1.** SUBSTITUTION OF SB OR STH the act or process of taking the place of or substituting for sb or sth **2.** FILLING OF SB'S OR STH'S PLACE the filling of the place of sb or sth with sb or sth else **3.** SUBSTITUTE sb who or sth that replaces another **4.** CHEM CHANGE OF ONE MINERAL TO ANOTHER the partial or complete transformation of one mineral into another in response to changing conditions such as the presence of water **5.** US MIL SB FILLING MILITARY VACANCY sb who fills a vacancy in a military force

replant /ree pláant/ (**-plants, -planting, -planted**) *vt.* **1.** GARDENING TRANSFER PLANT TO NEW PLACE to transfer a plant or part of a plant into new soil or a new area **2.** GARDENING PROVIDE PLACE WITH NEW PLANTS to put new plants in a place or container to replace previous plants ○ *replant the flower boxes every spring* **3.** MED, DENT REATTACH OR REINSERT BODY PART to reattach or reinsert a severed body part such as a limb or tooth —**replantation** /rée plaan táysh'n/ *n.*

replay *vt.* /ree pláy/ (**-plays, -playing, -played**) **1.** SPORTS, GAME PLAY MATCH AGAIN to play a game, match, or contest again **2.** RECORDING PLAY RECORDING AGAIN to play again sth that has been recorded on tape, video, or film ■ *n.* /rée play/ **1.** SPORTS, GAME CONTEST PLAYED AGAIN a contest, match, or game that is played again **2.** RECORDING RECORDED MATERIAL REPLAYED sth recorded on tape, video, or film that is played again **3.** REPEAT OF PREVIOUS EVENT an event that repeats or appears to repeat in the past ○ *The latest business failure was a replay of the previous one.*

replenish /ri plénnish/ (**-ishes, -ishing, -ished**) *vt.* **1.** NOURISH SB OR STH to fill sb or sth with needed energy or nourishment **2.** REPLACE USED ITEMS to restock depleted items or material ○ *time for the campers to replenish their supplies* **3.** FURNISH NEW FUEL FOR FIRE to resupply a fire with fuel [Early 17thC. From Old French *repleniss-*, the stem of *replenir*, from *plenir* 'to fill', from, ultimately, Latin *plenus* (source of English *full*).] —**replenisher** *n.* —**replenishment** *n.*

replete /ri pleét/ *adj.* **1.** AMPLY OR FULLY EQUIPPED amply, completely, or fully supplied with sth ○ *a kitchen replete with all the latest gadgets* **2.** FULL UP having eaten enough to be fully satisfied [14thC. Directly or via French from Latin *repletus*, the past participle of *replere*, literally 'to fill up', from *plere* 'to fill' (source of English *complete*).] —**repleteness** *n.*

repletion /ri pléesh'n/ *n.* **1.** STATE OF BEING GORGED a condition of being overfull after eating too much **2.** STATE OF BEING SATISFIED the condition of being fully satisfied

replevin /ri plévvin/ *n.* ACTION BY CLAIMANT TO RECOVER GOODS an act or writ to recover goods by sb who claims to own them and who promises to have the claim later tested in court ■ *vt.* (-ins, -ining, -ined) = **replevy** *v.* [14thC. From Anglo-Norman, from *replevir* (see REPLEVY).]

replevy /ri plévvi/ *vt.* (-ies, -ying, -ied) SEIZE CLAIMED GOODS BEFORE LEGAL TEST to seize goods on the grounds of ownership after promising to test the claim in court ■ *n.* (*plural* -ies) SEIZURE OF CLAIMED GOODS a seizure of claimed goods after a promise that the claim will be tested in court later [Late 16thC. Via Anglo-Norman *replevir*, literally 'to recover thoroughly', from *plevir* 'to recover'. Ultimately from a prehistoric Germanic word (ancestor also of English *pledge*).] —**repleviable** *adj.*

replica /répplikə/ *n.* **1.** FAITHFUL COPY OF STH an accurate reproduction of an object **2.** ARTS FAITHFUL COPY OF ARTWORK a scrupulous copy of a work of art, especially one made, authorized, or supervised by the original artist [Early 19thC. Via Italian, 'repeat', from, ultimately, Latin *replicare* (see REPLICATE).]

replicant /répplikənt/ *n.* an imaginary being, especially in science fiction, that has been constructed from organic and computerized components to look like a human being. ◊ **cyborg**

replicate *v.* /réppli kayt/ (-cates, -cating, -cated) **1.** *vt.* DO STH AGAIN to do sth again or copy sth **2.** *vi.* BE DONE AGAIN to undergo a repetition or reproduction **3.** *vt.* BIOL COPY CELLULAR OR GENETIC MATERIAL to reproduce exactly an organism, genetic material, or a cell ■ *adj.* /répplikət, réppli kayt/ BOT BENT BACK folded back on itself [Mid-16thC. From Latin *replicare*, literally 'to fold back' (source also of English *reply*), from *plicare* 'to fold'. The underlying idea is of 'going over again'.] —**replicative** /répplikətiv/ *adj.*

WORD KEY: SYNONYMS

See Synonyms at *copy*.

replication /réppli káysh'n/ *n.* **1.** PROCESS OF REPEATING the process of repeating, duplicating, or reproducing sth **2.** BIOL MAKING OF CELLULAR OR GENETIC COPY the production of exact copies of molecules, genetic material, or cells **3.** LAW REPLY a reply (*dated*) **4.** BOT FOLD a fold or folding back

replicon /répli kon/ *n.* a segment of DNA or RNA that replicates itself as a unit, distinct from adjacent segments in a chromosome or other genetic element [Mid-20thC. Coined from REPLICATION + ON.]

reply /ri plī/ *v.* (-plies, -plying, -plied) **1.** *vti.* RESPOND TO WHAT SB SAYS to say or write sth in response to what sb else has said or written ○ *replied that she wouldn't be available to take the job* **2.** *vi.* RESPOND WITH ACTION OR GESTURE to respond to sb's action with a countering action or gesture **3.** *vi.* LAW ANSWER DEFENDANT'S PLEA to speak in response to the plea of a defendant **4.** *vi.* ECHO to echo or return a sound ■ *n.* (*plural* -plies) **1.** SPOKEN OR WRITTEN RESPONSE sth said or written as a response to sth else **2.** ACTION PERFORMED AS RESPONSE sth done as a response to sb else's action ○ *Her only reply was to turn on her heel and leave.* **3.** LAW ANSWER TO DEFENDANT'S PLEA a statement made in response to the plea of a defendant [14thC. Via Old French *replier* from Latin *replicare* (see REPLICATE).] —**replier** *n.*

WORD KEY: SYNONYMS

See Synonyms at *answer*.

reply-paid *adj.* with postage paid by the sender so that it costs nothing to reply

repoint /ree póynt/ (-points, -pointing, -pointed) *vt.* to repair a brick wall by putting new mortar or cement between the bricks

report /ri páwrt/ *v.* (-ports, -porting, -ported) **1.** *vti.* TELL ABOUT WHAT HAPPENED to give information about sth that has happened ○ *reported that negotiations were proceeding slowly* **2.** *vti.* BROADCAST, PRESS TELL PEOPLE NEWS USING MEDIA to find out facts and tell people about them in print or a broadcast **3.** *vt.* INFORM AUTHORITIES ABOUT STH OR SB to inform sb in authority about sth that has happened, especially a crime or an accident, or about sb who has done sth wrong ○ *reported him missing two days ago* ○ *reported the break-in to the police* **4.** *vti.* TELL ABOUT RESEARCH OR INVESTIGATION to give detailed information about research or an investigation ○ *The committee will report their findings early next week.* **5.** *vti.* MAKE FULL OFFICIAL STATEMENT to make a formal statement regarding sth **6.** *vt.* LAW RECORD COURT PROCEEDINGS to record the proceedings of a court **7.** *vi.* INFORM ABOUT ARRIVAL to let sb know you have arrived ○ *Guests should report to reception on arrival.* **8.** *vi.* DECLARE STATE OF HEALTH to declare that you are in a specified condition of health ○ *another worker reporting sick* **9.** *vi.* BE UNDER SB'S AUTHORITY to be subordinate and responsible to sb or sth ○ *You'll be reporting to me from now on.* ■ *n.* **1.** ACCOUNT OF STH an account of an event, situation, or episode **2.** PRESS, BROADCAST NEWS ITEM OR BROADCAST an account of news presented by a journalist **3.** DOCUMENT GIVING INFORMATION ABOUT STH a document that gives information about an investigation or a piece of research, often put together by a group of people working together **4.** UNCONFIRMED ACCOUNT OF STH a widely-known account of sth that may be true but has not been confirmed ○ *Report had it that the company was approaching bankruptcy.* **5.** BUSINESS PERIODIC STATEMENT OF COMPANY'S FINANCES a detailed periodic account of a company's activities, financial condition, and prospects that is made available to shareholders and investors ○ *a quarterly report* **6.** EDUC WRITTEN ACCOUNT OF CHILD'S SCHOOLWORK a record of a child's academic performance at school over a specified period, prepared by teachers and given to the child's parents. US term **report card** **7.** LAW SHARP LOUD NOISE a very sharp loud noise, especially that of an explosion or gunshot **8.** REPUTATION reputation or character ■ **reports** *npl.* LAW ACCOUNTS OF CASE AT LAW written accounts of a court's adjudication, summarizing arguments and findings [14thC. Via Old French from Latin *reportare*, literally 'to carry back', from *portare* 'to carry'. The underlying idea is of 'bringing back news'.] —**reportable** *adj.*

reportage /ri páwr tij, réppawr taázh/ *n.* **1.** PROCESS OF TELLING NEWS the use of print and electronic media to inform people about news and current events **2.** THINGS REPORTED a body of reported news **3.** WAY OF GIVING NEWS a particular way of gathering and presenting news [Late 19thC. Formed from REPORT, in the model of French *reportage*.]

report card *n.* US = **report** *n.* 6

reportedly /ri páwrtidli/ *adv.* according to an unconfirmed report ○ *Reportedly he lost all his money.*

reported speech *n.* = **indirect speech**

reporter /ri páwrtər/ *n.* **1.** BROADCAST, PRESS SB WHO REPORTS NEWS sb whose job is to find out facts and use the print or broadcast media to tell people about them **2.** SB WHO REPORTS sb who makes a report of any kind **3.** LAW COMPILER OF COURT PROCEEDINGS sb who compiles summarized records of court proceeding **4.** POL SB WHO COMPILES LEGISLATIVE PROCEEDINGS an official who compiles the proceedings of a legislature —**reportorial** /réppawr táwri əl/ *adj.* —**reportorially** *adv.*

report stage *n.* a phase in the passage of a piece of legislation in the British Parliament, following the report of a committee and preceding a third reading

repose[1] /ri pṓz/ *n.* **1.** REST a state of rest or inactivity **2.** RELIG REST AFTER DEATH eternal or heavenly rest **3.** TRANQUILLITY a condition of peacefulness and tranquillity, e.g. in a place **4.** COMPOSURE calmness and composure of manner ■ *v.* (-poses, -posing, -posed) (*formal*) **1.** *vti.* LIE RESTING to lie or lay sth at rest **2.** *vi.* BE DEAD to lie dead (*used euphemistically*) **3.** *vi.* LIE RESTING ON TOP OF STH to lie while resting on or supported by sth **4.** *vr.* SETTLE SELF AT REST to settle yourself in a relaxed or restful position **5.** *vi.* TAKE SUPPORT FROM STH to be supported or based on sth ○ *Your argument reposes on false analogies.* [15thC. Via French *reposer* from Latin *repausare*, literally 'to rest completely', from *pausare* 'to rest' (source of English *pause*).] —**reposal** *n.* —**reposer** *n.*

repose[2] /ri pṓz/ (-poses, -posing, -posed) *vt.* to place faith, confidence, or trust in sb or sth (*formal*) ○ *reposed a great deal of confidence in him* [Mid-16thC. Formed from Latin *repos-*, the stem of *reponere*, literally 'to place again', from *ponere* 'to place' (source of English *position*).]

reposeful /ri pṓzf'l/ *adj.* showing or giving rise to restfulness or calm —**reposefully** *adv.* —**reposefulness** *n.*

reposit /ri pózzit/ (-its, -iting, -ited) *vt.* to put or store sth somewhere (*formal*) [Mid-17thC. From Latin *reposit-*, the past participle stem of *reponere* (see REPOSE[2]).]

reposition /réepə zísh'n/ (-tions, -tioning, -tioned) *vt.* **1.** PUT STH SOMEWHERE DIFFERENT to put sth in a new position **2.** MARKETING CHANGE MARKETING OF STH to change the marketing strategy of a company or product so as to have a wider or different appeal

repository /ri pózzitəri/ (*plural* -ries) *n.* **1.** PLACE OR RECEPTACLE FOR STORAGE a place or container in which sth is stored **2.** SB WITH EXTENSIVE KNOWLEDGE sb with, or sth such as a book that contains, extensive detailed knowledge of sth ○ *She was a repository of information about the history of the island.* **3.** SB ENTRUSTED WITH STH sb in whom sth is confided **4.** COMM WAREHOUSE FOR COMMODITIES a place where goods are stored prior to sale **5.** TOMB a burial vault or sepulchre

repossess /rée pə zéss/ (-sesses, -sessing, -sessed) *vt.* to take back goods or property from a buyer who has failed to keep up payments on them —**repossession** *n.* —**repossessor** *n.*

repot /ree pót/ (-pots, -potting, -potted) *vt.* to take a plant out of one pot and put it in another, usually larger one —**repotting** *n.*

repoussé /rə poóssay/ *adj.* **1.** FORMING PATTERN IN RELIEF formed as a raised pattern on a thin piece of metal by having been hammered through from the reverse side **2.** DECORATED WITH HAMMERED PATTERN decorated with a raised pattern that has been hammered through from the reverse side ■ *n.* **1.** HAMMERED DESIGN ON METAL a raised design on a piece of metal made by hammering the design through from the reverse side **2.** TECHNIQUE OF HAMMERING A DESIGN the technique of producing a raised design on a thin piece of metal by hammering it through from the reverse side [Mid-19thC. From French, the past participle of *repousser*, literally 'to push back', from *pousser* 'to push' (source of English *push*).]

repp *n.* = **rep**[1]

repr. *abbr.* **1.** representative **2.** represented **3.** representing **4.** reprint

reprehend /réppri hénd/ (-hends, -hending, -hended) *vt.* to criticize or reprove sb or sth [14thC. From Latin *reprehendere*, literally 'to seize again', from *prehendere* 'to seize' (source of English *prison*).] —**reprehendable** *adj.* —**reprehender** *n.*

reprehensible /réppri hénssəb'l/ *adj.* highly unacceptable and deserving censure [14thC. From late Latin *reprehensibilis*, from, ultimately, *reprehendere* (see REPREHEND).] —**reprehensibility** /réppri hénssə bílləti/ *n.* —**reprehensibly** /réppri hénssəbli/ *adv.*

reprehension /réppri hénsh'n/ *n.* reproof or criticism for wrongdoing [14thC. Formed from Latin *reprehension-*, the past participle stem of *reprehendere* (see REPREHEND).] —**reprehensive** *adj.* —**reprehensively** *adv.*

represent /réppri zént/ (-sents, -senting, -sented) *v.* **1.** *vt.* ACT OR SPEAK FOR ANOTHER to act or speak on behalf of sb or sth **2.** *vt.* GO SOMEWHERE ON BEHALF OF ANOTHER to go or be present somewhere on behalf of sb or sth **3.** *vt.* ACT FOR ANOTHER OFFICIALLY to speak and act for sb else in an official way ○ *Who will be representing France at the conference?* **4.** *vt.* BE PRESENT SOMEWHERE to be somewhere in large or small numbers **5.** *vt.* BE EQUIVALENT OF STH to be a sign or equivalent of sth **6.** *vt.* SYMBOLIZE STH to symbolize sth, especially as a sign on a map showing the position of sth ○ *On the map a blue line represents a river.* **7.** *vt.* DEPICT STH OR SB to portray or present an image of sb or sth as being sth in particular **8.** *vr.* UNTRUTHFULLY CLAIM TO BE STH to describe yourself as sth you are not ○ *He was arrested at the airport despite trying to represent himself as a tourist.* **9.** *vt.* THEATRE DEPICT SB ON STAGE to portray or perform a character or role on stage [14thC. Directly or via French from Latin *repraesentare*, literally 'to show back', from *praesentare* 'to show' (source of English *present*[2]).] —**representability** /réppri zéntə bílləti/ *n.* —**representable** /réppri zéntəb'l/ *adj.* —**representer** *n.*

re-present /reē pri zént/ (**re-presents, re-presenting, re-presented**) *vt.* to send, offer, or present sth again

representation /réppri zen táysh'n/ *n.* **1.** FACT OF BEING SERVED BY REPRESENTATIVE the fact or right of being represented by sb, especially of having a member in a legislature with power to vote or speak for an electorate **2.** VOTING SYSTEM OR BODY OF ELECTORS the system by which electors vote for people to represent them as legislators, administrators, or judges, or the group of people so elected **3.** PICTURE a visual depiction of sb or sth **4.** STH SPOKEN OR DONE FOR ANOTHER action or speech on behalf of another, especially as an agent or deputy **5.** STH DESCRIBED OR STATED a description, account, or statement of sth real or alleged, especially one meant to induce a response from authority (*often used in the plural*) **6.** LAW STATEMENT INDUCING SB TO MAKE CONTRACT a statement, real or implied, that encourages sb to make an agreement **7.** THEATRE PERFORMANCE a theatrical performance or production

representational /réppri zen táysh'nəl/ *adj.* **1.** CHARACTERIZED BY REPRESENTATION relating to or characterized by representation **2.** ARTS PORTRAYING RECOGNIZABLE OBJECTS depicting sth in a physically recognizable form, especially in art ○ *representational painting* —**representationally** *adv.*

representationalism /réppri zen táysh'nəlizəm/, **representationism** /-táysh'nizəm/ *n.* **1.** PHILOS THEORY OF DIRECT APPREHENSION OF OBJECTS the theory that the mind directly apprehends external objects only through ideas or data provided by the senses **2.** ARTS REALISTIC DEPICTION OF OBJECTS the practice or principle of depicting objects in recognizable form, especially in art —**representionalist** *n.* —**representationalistic** /réppri zen táysh'nə lístik/ *adj.*

representative /réppri zéntətiv/ *n.* **1.** SB WHO SPEAKS FOR OTHERS sb who votes or speaks on behalf of others **2.** POL MEMBER OF LEGISLATURE a member of a legislative assembly **3. representative, Representative** *US* MEMBER OF HOUSE OF REPRESENTATIVES a member of the House of Representatives, the lower chamber in the US Congress, or of one of the state legislatures **4.** COMM COMMERCIAL AGENT OR SALESPERSON an agent or salesperson for a company **5.** EXAMPLE an example or type of sth **6.** *NZ* FOOTBALL PLAYER REPRESENTING PROVINCE a rugby or football player who represents a province during interprovincial competition ■ *adj.* **1.** TYPICAL typical of sth, especially of a class or kind **2.** MADE UP OF ELECTED PEOPLE composed of elected or authorized people ○ *a representative assembly* **3.** POL LETTING PEOPLE ELECT SB allowing people to vote for sb to represent them in a legislative body such as the Congress in the United States or the House of Commons in the United Kingdom ○ *a representative form of government* **4.** MADE UP OF ALL TYPES including a complete range of examples of sth ○ *a representative sample* **5.** ACTING ON SB'S BEHALF acting as sb's agent, deputy, or delegate —**representatively** *adv.* —**representativeness** *n.*

repress /ri préss/ (**-presses, -pressing, -pressed**) *vt.* **1.** CURB ACTIONS THAT SHOW FEELINGS to check or restrain an action that would reveal feelings ○ *He had to repress a smile.* **2.** USE AUTHORITY TO CONTROL PEOPLE'S FREEDOM to control people's freedom by force or military means ○ *repress an uprising* **3.** PSYCHOL BLOCK STH FROM MIND to block unacceptable or painful impulses, desires, or memories from the conscious mind [14thC. From Latin *repress-*, the past participle stem of *reprimere*, literally 'to press back', from *premere* 'to press' (source of English *press*).] —**repressibility** /ri préssə bíllәti/ *n.* —**repressible** /ri préssəb'l/ *adj.*

re-press (**re-presses, re-pressing, re-pressed**) *vt.* to press sth again, especially to manufacture another issue of a recording

repressed /ri prést/ *adj.* **1.** WITH CURBED EMOTIONS not allowing personal experience of strong feelings, particularly of anger or sexual desire **2.** PSYCHOL BLOCKED FROM CONSCIOUSNESS in Freudian psychology, blocked from the conscious mind and relegated to the unconscious **3.** SUBDUED FORCIBLY kept under control by force ○ *the repressed peoples of the invaded islands*

represser *n.* = **repressor 2**

repression /ri présh'n/ *n.* **1.** PSYCHOL PSYCHOLOGICAL PROTECTIVE MECHANISM in Freudian psychology, a mechanism by which individuals protect themselves from threatening thoughts by blocking them out of the conscious mind. ◊ **denial 2.** BEING KEPT DOWN BY FORCE the process of suppressing sb or the condition of having political, social, or cultural freedom controlled by force

repressive /ri préssiv/ *adj.* exerting strict control on the freedom of others —**repressively** *adv.* —**repressiveness** *n.*

repressor /ri préssər/ *n.* **1.** BIOCHEM PROTEIN BLOCKING TRANSCRIPTION OF MESSENGER RNA a protein that binds to an operator gene and blocks transcription by messenger RNA. It is produced in the translation of a regulatory gene. **2. repressor, represser** REPRESSING PERSON OR THING sb or sth that represses

reprieve /ri préev/ *vt.* (**-prieves, -prieving, -prieved**) **1.** STOP OR POSTPONE SB'S PUNISHMENT to halt or delay sb's punishment, especially when the punishment is death (*often passive*) **2.** OFFER RESPITE TO SB to provide sb with temporary relief from sth harmful, especially danger or pain ■ *n.* **1.** STOPPING OR POSTPONEMENT OF PUNISHMENT the halting or delay of sb's punishment, especially when the punishment is death **2.** WARRANT HALTING OR POSTPONING PUNISHMENT a warrant giving the authority to stop or postpone sb's punishment, especially when the punishment is death **3.** RESPITE FROM STH HARMFUL a relief from sth harmful, especially danger or pain [Mid-17thC. Alteration of earlier *repry* 'to take back to prison' (hence 'to escape the death sentence'), via Old French *repris* 'taken back', from, ultimately, Latin *reprehendere* (see REPREHEND).] —**reprievable** *adj.* —**repriever** *n.*

reprimand /réppri maand/ *vt.* (**-mands, -manding, -manded**) TELL SB OFF to rebuke sb for a wrongdoing ■ *n.* REBUKE a rebuke given for having done sth wrong [Mid-17thC. Via French *réprimande* from, ultimately, Latin *reprimenda* 'that is to be suppressed', from, ultimately, *reprimere* (see REPRESS).]

reprint *vt.* /ree prínt/ (**-prints, -printing, -printed**) PRINT STH AGAIN to print sth again, especially with few or no changes ■ *n.* /reē print/ **1.** COPY OF STH ALREADY PUBLISHED a printed copy of sth that has already been in print **2.** = **offprint 3.** REISSUE OF PRINTED WORK a book or other printed work that is the same as, or has only minor changes from, one that was previously issued —**reprinter** /ree príntər/ *n.*

reprisal /ri prīz'l/ *n.* **1.** MIL RETALIATION IN WAR a violent military action such as the killing of prisoners or civilians, carried out in retaliation for an enemy's action **2.** STRONG OR VIOLENT RETALIATION a strong or violent retaliation for an action that sb has taken **3.** RETALIATORY SEIZURE FROM ANOTHER COUNTRY the forcible seizure of property or people from another country as retaliation for some injury [15thC. Via Anglo-Norman *reprisaille* from, ultimately, Latin *reprehendere* (see REPREHEND).]

reprise /ri préez/ *n.* **1.** MUSIC REPEAT OF MUSICAL PASSAGE a repeated passage of music, or a return to an earlier musical theme **2.** MUSIC = **chorus** *n.* 1 **3.** REPETITION a repetition or recurrence of sth ■ *vt.* (**-prises, -prising, -prised**) **1.** MUSIC REPEAT MUSIC to repeat a passage of music or return to an earlier theme **2.** REPEAT ACTION to repeat an action or performance ○ *reprised her role as Gertrude in the New York production* [Mid-20thC. Via French, the past participle of *reprendre*, literally 'to take again', used as a noun, from *prendre* 'to take', from Latin *prehendere*.]

reprivatize /ree prívətīz/ (**-tizes, -tizing, -tized**), **reprivatise** (**-tises, -tising, -tised**) *vt.* to return sth from public to private ownership —**reprivatization** /ree prívə tī záysh'n/ *n.*

repro /reē prō/ *n.* (*informal*) **1.** REPRODUCTION a reproduction, especially of a painting or piece of furniture **2.** PRINTING REPRODUCTION PROOF a reproduction proof [Mid-20thC. Shortening.]

reproach /ri prōch/ *v.* (**-proaches, -proaching, -proached**) **1.** *vt.* CRITICIZE SB to criticize sb for doing sth wrong **2.** *vr.* FEEL BLAMEWORTHY to feel ashamed because you know you have done sth wrong ○ *There's no reason to reproach yourself, because there was nothing you could do.* **3.** *vt.* DISGRACE SB OR STH to bring disgrace upon sb or sth (*archaic*) ■ *n.* **1.** CRITICISM criticism or disapproval for having done sth wrong, or an expression of this **2.** STH DISGRACEFUL sth that reflects badly on sb who has failed to improve or deal with it **3.** DISCREDIT shame or disgrace that sb or sth incurs ○ *actions that brought reproach upon his family* [15thC. Via Old French *reprochier* from assumed Vulgar Latin *repropiare* 'to bring back near' (hence 'to force to face up to things'), from Latin *prope* 'near'.] —**reproachable** *adj.* —**reproachableness** *n.* —**reproachably** *adv.* —**reproacher** *n.* —**reproachingly** *adv.* ◇ **above** *or* **beyond reproach** so good that no criticism can be made

reproachful /ri prōchf'l/ *adj.* expressing disapproval or blame —**reproachfully** *adv.* —**reproachfulness** *n.*

reprobate /rέpprō bayt/ *n.* **1.** SB IMMORAL a disreputable or immoral person **2.** RELIG SB DAMNED sb whose soul is believed to be damned ■ *adj.* **1.** DISREPUTABLE disreputable or immoral **2.** RELIG DAMNED with a soul that is damned ■ *vt.* (**-bates, -bating, -bated**) **1.** CENSURE SB to censure or condemn sb (*formal*) **2.** RELIG DENY SALVATION TO SB to condemn sb to supposed eternal damnation [Mid-16thC. Via late Latin *reprobatus*, from Latin, the past participle of *reprobare* (see REPROVE).] —**reprobacy** /-bəssi/ *n.* —**reprobater** *n.* —**reprobative** /-bətiv/ *adj.*

reprobation /réprrō báysh'n/ *n.* **1.** DISAPPROVAL strong condemnation or disapproval of sb or sth **2.** RELIG DIVINE REJECTION the supposed condemnation of sb's soul to eternal damnation [15thC. Directly or via French from, ultimately, Latin *reprobare* (see REPROVE).] —**reprobationary** *adj.*

reproduce /reēprə dyōōss/ (**-duces, -ducing, -duced**) *v.* **1.** *vti.* MAKE DUPLICATE OF STH to duplicate sth, or be duplicated, by photographing, scanning, printing, or another process **2.** *vt.* REPEAT STH to do sth in the same way as before **3.** *vi.* BIOL PRODUCE OFFSPRING to produce offspring or new individuals through a sexual or asexual process **4.** *vt.* REMEMBER STH to remember or imagine sth again —**reproducer** *n.* —**reproducibility** /reēprə dyōōssə bílləti/ *n.* —**reproducible** /reēprə dyōōssəb'l/ *adj.* —**reproducibly** *adv.*

WORD KEY: SYNONYMS

See Synonyms at ***copy***.

reproduction /reēprə dúksh'n/ *n.* **1.** COPY OF OBJECT a copy of sth in an earlier style, especially a painting or a piece of furniture **2.** REPRODUCING OF STH the act or process of reproducing sth **3.** PRINT, ELECTRONIC, OR PHOTOGRAPHIC DUPLICATE a copy of sth printed, scanned, photographed, or produced by other means **4.** RECORDING RECORDING OF SOUND the recording of sound or the quality of recorded sound **5.** BIOL PRODUCTION OF OFFSPRING the production of young plants and animals of the same kind through a sexual or asexual process [Mid-17thC. Formed from REPRODUCE, on the model of *production*.]

reproduction proof *n.* a printed proof, usually on glossy paper, of such high quality that it can be photographed for making a printing plate

reproductive /reēprə dúktiv/ *adj.* relating to, taking part in, or enabling the production of new offspring or individuals ○ *reproductive organs* [Mid-18thC. Formed from REPRODUCE, on the model of *productive*.] —**reproductively** *adv.* —**reproductiveness** *n.*

reproductive system *n.* the combination of bodily organs and tissues used in the process of producing offspring

reprography /ri próggrəfi/ *n.* the reproduction of sth printed, e.g. by offset printing, microfilming, photography, or xerography [Mid-20thC. From German *Reprographie*, a blend of *Reproduktion* 'reproduction' + *Photographie* 'photography'.] —**reprographic** /réppra gráffik/ *adj.*

reproof /ri prōōf/, **reproval** /ri prōōv'l/ *n.* the act of criticizing sb for having done sth wrong, or sth stated as a rebuke [14thC. From Old French *reprove*, from *reprover* (see REPROVE).]

reprove /ri prōōv/ (**-proves, -proving, -proved**) *vt.* to speak to sb in a way that shows disapproval of sth he or she has done [14thC. Via Old French *reprover* from Latin *reprobare*, literally 'to prove to be unworthy', from *probare* 'to prove' (source of English *prove*).] —**reprovable** *adj.* —**reprover** *n.* —**reprovingly** *adv.*

rept *abbr.* 1. receipt 2. report

reptant /réptənt/ *adj.* creeping or lying along the

ground [Mid-17thC. From Latin *reptare*, literally 'to keep creeping', from *repere* (see REPTILE).]

reptile /rép tīl/ *n.* **1.** COLD-BLOODED SCALY VERTEBRATE an air-breathing cold-blooded egg-laying vertebrate such as the crocodile, tortoise, snake, or lizard, with an outer covering of scales or plates and a bony skeleton. Class: Reptilia. **2.** OFFENSIVE TERM an offensive term that deliberately insults sb whose behaviour or character is regarded as suspicious, untrustworthy, or sickeningly ingratiating (*informal insult*) ■ *adj.* BEING A REPTILE belonging to the class of reptiles [14thC. Via French from, ultimately, late Latin *reptilis* 'creeping', from *rept-*, the past participle stem of *repere* 'to creep'.]

reptilian /rep tílli ən/ *adj.* **1.** OF REPTILES relating to reptiles **2.** MEAN OR GROVELLING displaying any of the characteristics traditionally attributed to or suggestive of reptiles, e.g. coldness and lack of emotion, or creeping, grovelling behaviour ■ *n.* = **reptile** *n.* 1

Repton /répt'n/, **Humphry** (1752–1818) British landscape architect. He designed many parks of country houses, working in the picturesque style.

Repub. *abbr.* **1.** Republic **2.** Republican

republic /ri púbblik/ *n.* **1.** POLITICAL SYSTEM WITH POWERFUL ELECTORATE a political system or form of government in which people elect representatives to exercise power for them **2.** STATE WITH POWERFUL ELECTORATE a state or other political unit with a form of government in which the supreme power is in the hands of representatives elected by the people **3.** GROUP OF EQUALS WITH COLLECTIVE INTERESTS a group of people who are considered to be equals and who have a collective interest, objective, or vocation (*formal*) ○ *the republic of letters* [Late 16thC. Via French *république* from Latin *res publica*, literally 'public matter'.]

WORD KEY: CULTURAL NOTE

The Republic, a political treatise by the Greek philosopher Plato (early 4th century BC). Presented in the form of a series of dialogues between Socrates and his pupils, it begins with a discussion of the nature of justice that leads in turn to an attempt to define the ideal society. For Plato, this would consist of an aristocracy run by a class of legislators groomed for leadership by a state education system.

republican /ri púbblikən/ *n.* SUPPORTER OF REPUBLIC AS GOVERNMENT sb who believes that the best government is one in which supreme power is vested in an electorate ■ *adj.* OF A REPUBLIC relating to, belonging to, or characteristic of a republic

Republican *adj.* **1.** DESIRING UNITED IRELAND supporting the idea that Northern Ireland should be united politically with the Republic of Ireland and should cease to form part of the United Kingdom **2.** OF REPUBLICAN PARTY belonging to or supporting the Republican Party in the United States ■ *n.* **1.** SUPPORTER OF UNITED IRELAND sb who wants Northern Ireland to be united politically with the Republic of Ireland **2.** *US* REPUBLICAN PARTY MEMBER a member or supporter of the Republican Party in the United States

republicanise *vt.* = **republicanize**

republicanism /ri púbblikənizəm/ *n.* **1.** BELIEF IN REPUBLIC AS POLITICAL SYSTEM the belief that the supreme power of a country should be vested in an electorate **2.** THEORY OF REPUBLICAN GOVERNMENT the theory and principles of republican government

Republicanism *n.* **1.** SUPPORT FOR UNITED IRELAND support for the idea of uniting Northern Ireland politically with the Republic of Ireland **2.** REPUBLICAN PARTY SUPPORT support for the Republican Party in the United States

republicanize /ri púbblikə nīz/ (**-izes, -izing, -ized**), **republicanise** (**-ises, -ising, -ised**) *vt.* to make a state or other political unit into a republic —**republicanization** /ri púbblikə nī záysh'n/ *n.*

Republican Party *n.* a political party at state and national level in the United States, founded in 1854–56

republication /reé púbbli káysh'n/ *n.* **1.** REPUBLISHING OF STH the act or process of publishing sth again **2.** STH PUBLISHED AGAIN sth published again, especially in an unchanged form

republish /reé púbblish/ (**-lishes, -lishing, -lished**) *vt.* to reissue a publication, especially in an unchanged form —**republisher** *n.*

repudiate /ri pyóodi ayt/ (**-ates, -ating, -ated**) *vt.* **1.** DISOWN STH to disapprove of sth formally and strongly and renounce any connection with it ○ *She repudiated the committee's actions.* **2.** DENY STH to state that sth is untrue **3.** REJECT STH to reject sth that is offered **4.** DISOWN LOVED ONE to disown a family member or lover **5.** REJECT STH AS INVALID to refuse to accept the validity of sth **6.** REFUSE TO PAY DEBT to refuse to acknowledge or pay a debt [Mid-16thC. Via Latin *repudiare* 'to divorce' (the original meaning in English) from *repudium* 'divorce'.] —**repudiable** *adj.* —**repudiation** /ri pyóodi áysh'n/ *n.* —**repudiative** /ri pyóodi ətiv/ *adj.* —**repudiator** /ri pyóodi aytər/ *n.*

WORD KEY: USAGE

See Usage note at ***refute***.

repugn /ri pyóon/ (**-pugns, -pugning, -pugned**) *vt.* to oppose or resist sth (*archaic*) [14thC. Directly or via Old French from Latin *repugnare*, literally 'to fight back', from *pugnare* 'to fight' (source of English *pugnacious*).]

repugnance /ri púgnənss/, **repugnancy** /ri púgnənssi/ *n.* a very strong dislike or distaste

WORD KEY: SYNONYMS

See Synonyms at ***dislike***.

repugnant /ri púgnənt/ *adj.* **1.** OFFENSIVE offensive and completely unacceptable **2.** REVOLTING making sb feel physically repelled ○ *a repugnant odour* [Late 18thC. Via Old French, 'contrary', from, ultimately, Latin *repugnare* (see REPUGN).] —**repugnantly** *adv.*

repulse /ri púlss/ *vt.* (**-pulses, -pulsing, -pulsed**) **1.** MIL FORCE BACK MILITARY ATTACK to force back an attacking military force **2.** SPURN SB to reject or rebuff an approach from sb ■ *n.* **1.** REJECTION a refusal or rejection of sb **2.** MIL ACT OF FORCING BACK ATTACK the forcing back of an attacking military force [Mid-16thC. From Latin *repuls-*, the past participle stem of *repellere* (see REPEL).]

WORD KEY: USAGE

repulse or **repel**? ***Repulse*** is a much stronger word than ***repel*** in all its meanings, physical and abstract. To ***repel*** people physically is to drive them back from the immediate vicinity; and its figurative equivalent is 'to ward off' or 'to be distasteful to'. To ***repulse*** people physically is to drive them away with great force or strength, and it is normally used with reference to battles and warfare. The corresponding figurative meaning here is 'to disgust'.

repulsion /ri púlsh'n/ *n.* **1.** REVULSION a feeling of disgust or very strong dislike **2.** PHYS REPELLING FORCE a force between two bodies of like electric charge or magnetic polarity that tends to repel or separate them. It is this repulsive force between atoms and molecules at very short distances that tends to keep them separated.

repulsive /ri púlssiv/ *adj.* **1.** VERY UNPLEASANT making sb feel disgust or very strong dislike **2.** REPELLENT tending to repel —**repulsively** *adv.* —**repulsiveness** *n.*

WORD KEY: USAGE

See Usage note at ***repellent***.

reputable /réppyŏŏtəb'l/ *adj.* known to be honest, reliable, or respectable [Late 17thC. Directly or via French from medieval Latin *reputabilis*, from Latin *reputare* (see REPUTE).] —**reputability** /réppyŏŏtə bíllәti/ *n.* —**reputably** /réppyŏŏtəbli/ *adv.*

reputation /réppyŏŏ táysh'n/ *n.* **1.** GENERAL OPINIONS ABOUT SB OR STH the views that are generally held about sb or sth **2.** GOOD OPINION a high opinion that people hold about sb or sth [14thC. From the Latin stem *reputation-* 'consideration', from *reputare* (see REPUTE).]

repute /ri pyóot/ *n.* (*formal*) **1.** REPUTATION estimation or character according to what people in general think **2.** GOOD REPUTATION good reputation or standing [Mid-16thC. Directly or via French *reputer* from Latin *reputare*, literally 'to think repeatedly', formed from *putare* 'to think'. The underlying idea is 'to think well or badly of'.]

reputed /ri pyóotid/ *adj.* widely believed, although not necessarily established as fact [Late 16thC. Formed from REPUTE, used as a verb.]

reputedly /ri pyóotidli/ *adv.* according to popular belief

req. *abbr.* **1.** request **2.** require **3.** required **4.** requirement **5.** requisition

request /ri kwést/ *vt.* (**-quests, -questing, -quested**) **1.** ASK POLITELY FOR STH to ask formally or courteously for sth to be given or done ○ *requested that he be excused* ○ *requested her favourite song* **2.** ASK SB FOR STH to ask sb to do sth ○ *requested Father Peter to perform their marriage ceremony* ■ *n.* **1.** EXPRESSION OF A POLITE WISH OR DESIRE an act of politely or formally asking that sth be done or given **2.** MUSIC THAT HAS BEEN ASKED FOR a piece of music played on a radio programme, at a live performance, or at a disco because sb asks for it ○ *We'll be taking several requests tonight.* **3.** ACT OF EXPRESSING A WISH the act of asking or petitioning for sth to be done or given [14thC. Via Old French from, ultimately, Latin *requisitus*, the past participle of *requirere* (see REQUIRE).] —**requester** *n.*

request stop *n.* a bus stop at which the bus does not halt unless sb at the stop signals for it to do so or if sb wants to get off there. US term **flag stop**

requiem /rékwi əm, -wi em/, **Requiem** *n.* **1.** CHR ROMAN CATHOLIC SERVICE FOR THE DEAD a Roman Catholic mass held to offer prayers for sb who has died **2.** MUSIC, CHR MUSIC FOR A REQUIEM a piece of music written to accompany a requiem mass **3.** MUSIC SAD COMMEMORATIVE MUSIC a piece of music written to commemorate sb who has died [14thC. From Latin, 'rest', in a line of a prayer *Requiem aeternam dona eis Domine* 'Grant them eternal rest, O Lord'.]

requiem shark *n.* a voracious shark of tropical waters. Hammerheads, tiger sharks, and soupfins are all requiem sharks. Family: Carcharhinidae. [By folk etymology from French *requin* 'shark']

requiescat /rékwi éss kat/ *n.* a prayer asking that the soul of a dead person might be at rest [Early 19thC. From Latin, 'may he or she rest'.]

require /ri kwír/ (**-quires, -quiring, -quired**) *vt.* **1.** NEED STH OR SB to be in need of sth or sb for a particular purpose ○ *The recipe requires a cup of milk.* **2.** MAKE STH NECESSARY to have sth as a necessary precondition ○ *A password is required for entry to the system.* **3.** DEMAND STH BY LAW to demand sth by a law or regulation (*often passive*) ○ *Notification was required by law.* **4.** INSIST ON STH to insist that sb do sth ○ *All applicants are required to pass a medical exam.* [14thC. From Old French *requ(i)er-*, the stem of *requere*, from, ultimately, Latin *requirere*, literally 'to seek in return', from Latin *quaerere* 'to seek' (source of English *query*).] —**requirable** *adj.* —**requirer** *n.*

required /ri kwírd/ *adj.* **1.** NEEDED necessary or appropriate ○ *He lacks the required degree of expertise.* **2.** COMPULSORY insisted upon or imposed as a condition ○ *required reading for a course*

requirement /ri kwírmənt/ *n.* **1.** STH NEEDED sth that is needed for a particular purpose (*often used in the plural*) **2.** STH INSISTED UPON sth that is obligatory or demanded (*often used in the plural*) ○ *a requirement for the job* **3.** FACT OF REQUIRING STH an act or process of requiring sth

requisite /rékwizit/ *adj.* ESSENTIAL necessary or indispensable for sth (*formal*) ○ *the requisite skills for the job* ■ *n.* STH ESSENTIAL sth that is necessary or indispensable [15thC. From Latin *requisitus*, the past participle of *requirere* (see REQUIRE).] —**requisitely** *adv.* —**requisiteness** *n.*

WORD KEY: SYNONYMS

See Synonyms at ***necessary***.

requisition /rékwi zísh'n/ *n.* **1.** DEMAND FOR STH a demand for sth that is required **2.** OFFICIAL FORM a written or printed request for sth that is needed **3.** FACT OF MAKING A FORMAL DEMAND the act or process of making a formal demand for sth **4.** POL REQUEST FOR THE RETURN OF A FUGITIVE a request by a government that another government return a fugitive from the law ■ *vt.* (**-tions, -tioning, -tioned**) **1.** DEMAND AND TAKE STH OFFICIALLY to demand and take sth that is needed, especially for official or military use **2.** REQUIRE AND OBTAIN SB FOR A JOB to require and obtain the services of sb to do sth ○ *requisitioned a few friends for the weekend to help paint the house* [Mid-16thC. Directly or via French from, ultimately, Latin *requisit-*, the past participle stem of *requirere* (see REQUIRE).] —**requisitionary** *adj.*

zh vision In foreign words: kh German Bach; aN French vin; aaN French blanc; ö German schön, French feu; oN French bon; öN French un; ü French rue Stress marks: ´ as in secret \seék rət\; academic \àkə démmik\

requital *n.* **1.** ACT DONE IN RESPONSE an act done in response, repayment, or retaliation (*formal*) **2.** REPAYMENT OR RETALIATION response, repayment, or retaliation

requite /ri kwít/ (-quites, -quiting, -quited) *vt.* **1.** PAY STH BACK to return in kind a kindness or hurt that sb has done **2.** RECOMPENSE SB to pay sb back for a service performed [Early 16thC. Formed from an earlier form of QUIT, in the meaning 'to pay up'.] —**requitable** *adj.* —**requitement** *n.* —**requiter** *n.*

reradiate /ree ráydi ayt/ (-ates, -ating, -ated) *vt.* to emit radiation after absorbing incident radiation —**reradiation** /rèe raydi áysh'n/ *n.*

reread /ree réed/ (-reads, -reading, -read, -read /-réd/) *vt.* to read sth again

reredorter /reèr dawrter/ *n.* a latrine or privy at the back of a dormitory in a medieval monastery

Reredos

reredos /reér doss/ *n.* **1.** CHR DECORATION FOR THE REAR OF AN ALTAR an artistic decoration behind the altar in a church, e.g. a wood or stone screen or a wall-hanging **2.** BACK OF A FIREPLACE the back of an open fireplace [14thC. Via Anglo-Norman from Old French *areredos*, from *arere* 'behind' + *dos* 'back' (from Latin *dorsum*).]

rerelease /rèe ri leéss/ *vt.* (-leases, -leasing, -leased) DISTRIBUTE STH AGAIN to release a music recording or a film again for distribution to the public ■ *n.* RE-RELEASED RECORDING OR FILM a music recording or a film that has been released again to the public

reroute /ree róot/ (-routes, -routing, -routed) *vt.* to direct people or vehicles along an alternative route, e.g. because of an accident, road construction, or for security reasons

rerun *vt.* /ree rún/ (-runs, -running, -ran /-rán/, -run) **1.** CINEMA, TV SHOW RECORDED ENTERTAINMENT AGAIN to show or broadcast a TV series, video, or film again **2.** SPORTS REPEAT A RACE to run a race again, or cause a race to be run again, after the result on the first occasion has been disallowed because of an infringement ■ *n.* /ree rún/ (*plural* -runs) **1.** CINEMA, TV REPEAT SHOWING OF RECORDED ENTERTAINMENT a repeat showing of recorded entertainment, especially a TV series **2.** SPORTS REPEAT RUNNING OF RACE the repeat running of a race after an infringement

res /rayz, rayss/ (*plural* **res**) *n.* in law, a matter or thing [From Latin, 'thing, legal matter']

RES *abbr.* **1.** renewable energy source **2.** renewable energy system **3.** reticuloendothelial system **4.** Royal Entomological Society

res. *abbr.* **1.** research **2.** reservation **3.** reserved **4.** reservoir **5.** residence **6.** resident **7.** resigned **8.** resolution

res adjudicata *n.* LAW = res judicata

resale /ree sayl, ree sáyl/ *n.* **1.** SELLING AGAIN the selling of sth again ○ *Not for resale.* **2.** SELLING SECOND-HAND the selling of sth second-hand —**resalable** /ree sáylə bílləti/ *n.* —**resale** /ree sáyləb'l/ *adj.*

resale price maintenance *n.* the setting by the manufacturer of a minimum price at which its goods are to be sold at retail

rescale /ree skáyl/ (-scales, -scaling, -scaled) *vt.* to modify the scale of sth, especially to reduce it ○ *rescale a budget* ○ *rescale a drawing*

reschedule /ree shéddyool, -skédd-/ (-ules, -uling, -uled) *vt.* **1.** CHANGE THE TIME FIXED FOR STH to arrange a

new time slot for sth **2.** FIN EXTEND A LOAN to extend the payment schedule of a loan

rescind /ri sínd/ (-scinds, -scinding, -scinded) *vt.* **1.** CANCEL STH to remove the validity or authority of sth **2.** REVOKE CONTRACT to revoke a contract and return the parties to their former positions before the contract **3.** REPEAL A DECISION OR ENACTMENT to declare a decision or enactment null and void [Mid-16thC. From Latin *rescindere*, literally 'to cut back', from *scindere* 'to cut'.] —**rescindable** *adj.* —**rescinder** *n.* —**rescindment** *n.*

rescission /ri sízh'n/ *n.* the act of rescinding sth [Early 17thC. Via the late Latin stem *rescission-* from, ultimately, Latin *rescindere* (see RESCIND).]

rescissory /ri síssəri/ *adj.* relating to rescission or having the power to rescind (*formal*) [Early 17thC. Via late Latin *rescissorius* from, ultimately, Latin *rescindere* (see RESCIND).]

rescore /ree skáwr/ (-scores, -scoring, -scored) *vt.* to write new instrumentation for a piece of music

rescript /reé skript/ *n.* **1.** CHR ECCLESIASTICAL RULING a formal reply by the pope or some other high dignitary of the Roman Catholic Church on a matter of doctrine or discipline **2.** HIST, LAW ROMAN EMPEROR'S LEGAL RULING a formal reply by an ancient Roman or Holy Roman emperor on a point of law **3.** REWRITE an act of rewriting sth [14thC. From Latin *rescriptum*, the neuter past participle of *rescribere*, literally 'to write back', from *scribere*.]

rescue /réss kyoo/ *v.* (-cues, -cuing, -cued) **1.** *vt.* REMOVE SB OR STH FROM DANGER to save sb or sth from a dangerous or harmful situation ○ *The boys had to be rescued from the rocks by helicopter* **2.** SAVE STH to prevent sth from being discarded, rejected, or put out of operation ○ *At the last minute the factory was rescued from closure.* **3.** *vt.* LAW GET SB OUT OF JAIL to release sb from legal custody by force **4.** *vt.* LAW TAKE FORCIBLE POSSESSION OF STH to seize property or goods by force ■ *n.* REMOVAL FROM DANGER OR HARM an act or instance of saving sb or sth from a dangerous or harmful situation (*often used before a noun*) ○ *a daring rescue attempt* ○ an instance of helping sb in an awkward or difficult situation ○ *I couldn't think what to say, but luckily he came to my rescue.* ■ *n.* LAW **1.** RELEASE FROM JAIL the release of sb from legal custody by force **2.** SEIZURE OF GOODS the seizure of property or goods by force [14thC. From Old French *rescourre*, literally 'to shake loose', from *escourre* 'to shake', from Latin *escutere*, from *ex-* 'out'+ *quatere* 'to strike'.] —**rescuable** *adj.* —**rescuer** *n.*

research /ri súrch, reé surch/ *n.* ORGANIZED STUDY methodical investigation into a subject in order to discover facts, to establish or revise a theory, or to develop a plan of action based on the facts discovered ■ *vti.* (-searches, -searching, -searched) STUDY STH METHODICALLY to carry out research into a subject [Late 16thC. Via obsolete French *recherche* from Old French *recercher*, literally 'to search closely', from *cerchier* (see SEARCH).] —**researchable** *adj.* —**researcher** *n.* —**researchist** *n.*

— **WORD KEY: USAGE** —

Pronunciation trap The traditional pronunciation is with the stress on the second syllable, both for the noun and the verb. More recently, a pronunciation with the stress on the first syllable (reesurch) has become common, especially in broadcasting, although this is widely disliked, especially for the noun.

research and development *n.* the work in a company of investigating improved processes, products, and services and of developing new ones

reseat /ree seét/ (-seats, -seating, -seated) *vt.* **1.** SEAT SB ELSEWHERE to seat sb in another place **2.** SEAT SB AS BEFORE to return sb to the seat previously occupied **3.** REPLACE THE SEATS IN BUILDING to fit new seats in an auditorium or hall **4.** PROVIDE A NEW SEAT FOR to replace the material on a seat **5.** REPLACE VALVE SEATING to return the seating of a valve to good condition

reseau /rézzō/ (*plural* -seaux /rézzō, rézzōz/ *or* -seaus) *n.* **1.** CRAFT NET FOR MAKING LACE a mesh foundation on which lace is made **2.** ASTRON PHOTOGRAPHIC REFERENCE PLATE a grid of lines photographed onto or cut into a glass plate and used as a reference for astronomical observations [Late 16thC. Via French *réseau* 'network'

from Old French *reseuil*, literally 'little net', from *raiz* 'net', from Latin *rete* 'net'.]

resect /ri sékt/ (-sects, -secting, -sected) *vt.* to cut through and surgically remove part of an organ, bone, or other body part [Mid-17thC. From Latin *resect-*, the past participle stem of *resecare*, literally 'to cut back', from *secare* 'to cut'.]

resection /ri séksh'n/ *n.* **1.** SURG PARTIAL SURGICAL REMOVAL the surgical removal of part of an organ, bone, or other body part **2.** CIV ENG ESTABLISHMENT OF LOCATION OF POINT the establishment of the location of a point when surveying by sighting from that point to two other points whose locations are known

resectoscope /ri séktə skōp/ *n.* a surgical instrument that allows a resection to be made without a bigger incision than that caused by the instrument itself

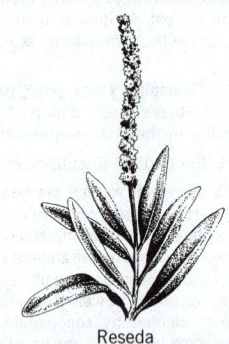

Reseda

reseda /réssidə, ri seédə/ *n.* (*plural* -das *or* -da) **1.** PLANTS MEDITERRANEAN PLANT WITH GREYISH-GREEN FLOWERS a Mediterranean plant that has small dense spikes of greyish-green flowers with divided petals. Genus: *Reseda.* **2.** COLOURS GREYISH-GREEN a greyish-green colour ■ *adj.* GREYISH-GREEN IN COLOUR of a greyish-green colour [Mid-18thC. Via modern Latin, genus name, from Latin, of unknown origin.]

reseed /ree seéd/ (-seeds, -seeding, -seeded) *v.* **1.** *vt.* PLANT LAND WITH SEEDS AGAIN to plant seeds on an area of land again **2.** *vti.* START A PLANT FROM ITS SEED to grow a plant or to grow from seed dropped by the previous generation

reselect /reé si lékt/ (-lects, -lecting, -lected) *vt.* to select sb or sth again, especially an existing officeholder for re-election —**reselection** *n.*

resemblance /ri zémblənss/ *n.* **1.** SIMILARITY TO SB OR STH similarity in appearance or quality to sb or sth else **2.** DEGREE OF SIMILARITY the extent to which sb or sth resembles sb or sth else ○ *the resemblance between them is striking* **3.** POINT OF SIMILARITY a respect in which sb or sth resembles sb or sth else **4.** STH SIMILAR sth that resembles sth else

resemble /ri zémb'əl/ (-bles, -bling, -bled) *vt.* to be similar to sb or sth in appearance or behaviour [14thC. From Old French *resembler*, literally 'to be very like', from *sembler* 'to seem' (source of English *semblance*), from Latin *simulare* 'to simulate').] —**resembler** *n.*

resend /ree sénd/ (-sends, -sending, -sent, -sent /-sént/) *vt.* to send sth again

resent /ri zént/ (-sents, -senting, -sented) *vt.* to feel aggrieved about sth or towards sb often because of a perceived wrong or injustice [Late 16thC. From obsolete French *ressentir*, literally 'to feel strongly', from *sentir* 'to feel', from Latin *sentire* 'to feel'.]

resentful /ri zéntf'l/ *adj.* **1.** ANNOYED feeling aggrieved and ill-used **2.** RESULTING FROM RESENTMENT characterized by feelings of annoyance or ill-use ○ *a resentful silence* —**resentfully** *adv.* —**resentfulness** *n.*

resentment /ri zéntmənt/ *n.* aggrieved feelings about sth or towards sb, usually as a result of ill-usage or insult, or an instance of these [Early 17thC. From obsolete French *ressentiment* 'strong feeling', from *ressentir* (see RESENT).]

reservation /rézzər váysh'n/ *n.* **1.** ARRANGEMENT MADE BEFOREHAND an advance booking, e.g. of a seat, table, hotel room, or a ticket on a plane, train, or coach **2.** PLACE ARRANGED BEFOREHAND sth such as a seat, table, hotel room, or ticket booked in advance **3.** ARRANGING OF STH BEFOREHAND the act of booking sth in advance **4.** LAND SET ASIDE an area of land set aside for a particular purpose, especially in North America for the use of a Native North American people **5.** TRANSP = **central reservation 6.** KEEPING STH BACK the act of withholding sth, or an instance of so doing **7.** LIMITING CONDITION a limiting condition to an agreement **8.** LAW LEGAL INTEREST RETAINED IN STH GRANTED a clause in a deed by which sb retains an interest in sth being granted or leased, or such an interest itself **9.** CHR PRESERVATION OF CONSECRATED ELEMENTS FOR LATER the practice of retaining part of the consecrated bread and wine after celebrating Communion, in order to use it later, e.g. when visiting the sick ■ **reservations** *npl.* MISGIVINGS THAT CAUSE HESITATION doubts that prevent wholehearted agreement to or approval of sth —**reservationist** *n.*

WORD KEY: SYNONYMS

See Synonyms at ***doubtful***.

reserve /ri zúrv/ *vt.* (**-serves, -serving, -served**) **1.** SET STH ASIDE to keep sth back for future use or for some specific purpose **2.** BOOK A PLACE BEFOREHAND to make arrangements in advance to secure a place such as a seat, ticket, table, or hotel room **3.** RETAIN STH FOR YOUR OWN BENEFIT to retain the option of future action on sb's or your own behalf ○ *I reserve the right to change my mind.* **4.** POSTPONE A DECISION to defer making a decision until all the issues have been considered ○ *reserve judgement* ■ *n.* **1.** EMERGENCY SUPPLY sth kept back for later use, especially in an emergency **2.** WILDLIFE CONSERVATION AREA an area of land set aside for conserving wildlife. US term **preserve 3.** COOLNESS OF MANNER emotional restraint, resulting in a reticent or composed manner **4.** SPORTS SUBSTITUTE PLAYER a team member called to play when a member of the original team withdraws, either before or during a game **5.** MIL INACTIVE PART OF THE ARMED SERVICES the part of a country's armed services that is not on active service at a given time **6.** MIL REINFORCEMENT FORCE the part of an armed force that is not initially committed during a military engagement but supplies reinforcements as necessary **7.** MIL MEMBER OF A RESERVE a member of a military reserve **8.** FIN MONEY RETAINED FOR FUTURE USE an amount of capital or revenue retained by a company or financial institution to meet future contingencies (*often used in the plural*) **9.** ECON NATIONAL FUNDS a country's supply of gold and foreign currency that is held by the central bank against future liabilities or to support the currency when the exchange rates fluctuate **10.** GEOL UNEXPLOITED NATURAL RESOURCE a supply of a natural resource such as a mineral or petrochemical that is estimated to exist from geological data but is not yet utilized **11.** *ANZ* LAND FOR PUBLIC RECREATION an area of government-owned land set aside for public recreation **12.** *Can* LAND USED AS A RESERVATION an area of land set aside as a reservation for use by a Native North American people **13.** NEXT RUNNER-UP a competitor or exhibit such as an animal at an agricultural show that places immediately after the prizewinners and will receive a prize if a prizewinner is disqualified **14.** = **reserve price** ■ **reserves** *npl.* EXTRA STAMINA, USABLE IN AN EMERGENCY additional personal resources of energy or strength that can be called upon in an emergency [14thC. Directly and via French *réserver* from Latin *reservare*, literally 'to keep back', from *servare* 'to keep'.] —**reservable** *adj.* —**reserver** *n.* ◇ **have** *or* **keep sth in reserve** to use only part of sth, keeping some of it back in case it is needed at a later time

reserve bank *n.* **1.** BANK IN US FEDERAL RESERVE SYSTEM one of the 12 banks in the US Federal Reserve system **2.** CENTRAL BANK OF AUSTRALIA the central bank of Australia responsible for the issuing of currency, banking for federal and state governments, and regulating Australian financial systems

reserve clause *n.* formerly, a clause in the contract of a professional sportsperson stating that the club, not the sportsperson, has the exclusive right to renew the contract

reserve currency *n.* foreign currency that is acceptable for settling international transactions and that is held in reserve for that purpose by a central bank

reserved /ri zúrvd/ *adj.* **1.** BOOKED booked in advance **2.** EARMARKED FOR A SPECIFIC USE kept or set aside for a particular purpose **3.** HAVING A COOL MANNER having a tendency to emotional restraint and so appearing reticent or composed —**reservedly** /ri zúrvidli/ *adv.* —**reservedness** /-zúrvidnəss/ *n.*

reserved list *n.* a list of officers retired from the armed forces who are willing and available to be recalled to active service in an emergency

reserved occupation *n.* an occupation of such national importance in wartime that those working in it are exempted from military service

reserve-grade *adj. Aus* relating to or made up of players at the reserve level

reserve price *n.* the lowest price that a seller is willing to accept for sth being sold at auction. ◊ **upset price**

reservist /ri zúrvist/ *n.* a member of a military force not on active service at a given time

reservoir /rézzər vwaar/ *n.* **1.** ENVIRON LAKE OR TANK FOR STORING WATER a large tank or natural or artificial lake used for collecting and storing water for human consumption or agricultural use **2.** LARGE BACKUP SUPPLY a substantial reserve supply of sth intangible **3.** BIOL ORGANISM ACTING AS A PARASITE CARRIER an organism in which a parasite lives and develops without damaging it, but from which the parasite passes to another species that is damaged by it **4.** ANAT = **cisterna 5.** LIQUID STORE IN A DEVICE a part of a machine or device where liquid is stored for use by the machine or device **6.** GEOL, INDUST UNDERGROUND SUPPLY OF GAS OR OIL a natural chamber in porous rock where a supply of natural gas or crude oil collects [Mid-17thC. From French, formed from *réserver* (see RESERVE).]

reset[1] /ree sét/ (**-sets, -setting, -set**) *vt.* **1.** SET STH AGAIN to set sth again **2.** PUT STH BACK TO ZERO to change the reading of dial or counter to zero or a different number —**resettable** *adj.* —**resetter** *n.*

reset[2] *vti.* /ree sét/ (**-sets, -setting, -set**) *Scotland* RECEIVE to receive stolen goods ■ *n.* /reé set/ *Scotland* RECEIVING the crime of receiving stolen goods [14thC. Via Old French *recet(t)er* from Latin *receptare*, from *recept-*, the past participle stem of *recipere* (see RECEIVE).] —**resetter** *n.*

resettle /ree sétt'l/ (**-tles, -tling, -tled**) *vt.* to provide a group or population with a new place to live and transfer it there —**resettlement** *n.*

res gestae /-gést ī, ráyss jésti/ *npl.* circumstances and facts that may be admitted as evidence in a lawsuit because they shed light on the matters in question [From Latin, literally 'things done']

resh /raysh/ *n.* the 20th letter of the Hebrew alphabet, represented in the English alphabet as 'r' [Early 19thC. From Aramaic *rēš* 'head'.]

reshape /ree sháyp/ (**-shapes, -shaping, -shaped**) *vt.* **1.** CHANGE OR RESTORE SHAPE OF STH to alter or restore the shape of sth **2.** CHANGE THE ORGANIZATION OF STH to change the form or organization of sth

reshuffle *n.* /reé shuff'l/ **1.** POL REDISTRIBUTION OF JOBS a reorganization of the jobs of a group of people, especially a change by a prime minister or president of the posts or personnel of a cabinet **2.** CARDS SHUFFLING OF CARDS AGAIN an act of shuffling sth, especially cards, again ■ *vt.* /ree shúff'l/ (**-fles, -fling, -fled**) **1.** POL REDISTRIBUTE JOBS to carry out a reshuffle of jobs **2.** CARDS SHUFFLE CARDS AGAIN to shuffle sth, especially cards, again

reside /ri zíd/ (**-sides, -siding, -sided**) *vi.* **1.** LIVE SOMEWHERE to have a home in a particular place **2.** BE PRESENT to be present in or belong to sb or sth **3.** BE VESTED to be vested or placed in sb or sth [15thC. Origin uncertain: probably via French *résider* from Latin *residere*, literally 'to remain behind', from *sedere* 'to sit'.]

residence /rézzidənss/ *n.* **1.** HOME the house, flat, or other dwelling in which sb lives **2.** LARGE HOUSE a grand and imposing dwelling **3.** HIST COLONIAL GOVERNOR'S HOUSE the governor's official house in a colony or former colony **4.** LIVING SOMEWHERE the fact of living in a particular place **5.** TIME LIVED IN PLACE the period of time that sb lives in a particular place **6.** *US* MED = **residency** ◇ **in residence 1.** living in a place at a particular time **2.** employed as a creative artist by an educational or other institution to foster interest in a subject

residency /rézzidənsi/ (*plural* **-cies**) *n.* **1.** ARTS PERFORMING AND TEACHING ENGAGEMENT an engagement at a university or conservatory for a performer or group of performers, usually for at least a term, that involves performance, teaching, and master classes **2.** HIST OFFICIAL RESIDENCE OF AN INDIAN GOVERNOR formerly, the official residence of a governor in India **3.** POL, HIST TERRITORY ADMINISTERED BY RESIDENT AGENT formerly, a territory such as the East Indies that was administered by the resident agent of a protecting state **4.** *US* MED MEDICAL TRAINING FOLLOWING INTERNSHIP a period of specialized training in clinical medicine or surgery in a US hospital on completion of an internship

resident /rézzidənt/ *n.* **1.** SB LIVING IN A PARTICULAR PLACE sb who lives permanently or for a considerable period in a particular place **2.** *US* MED DOCTOR COMPLETING A RESIDENCY a doctor or surgeon engaged in a residency **3.** MED DOCTOR LIVING IN HOSPITAL a junior doctor who lives in the hospital where he or she is working **4.** SOC WELFARE SB WHO LIVES IN A RESIDENTIAL SITUATION sb who lives in a nursing home, children's home, retirement home, or other communal housing **5.** HIST, INTERNAT REL BRITISH COLONIAL REPRESENTATIVE a representative of the British government in a British colony or protectorate **6.** POL DIPLOMAT a diplomatic official based in a foreign country **7.** ZOOL NONMIGRATING BIRD OR OTHER ANIMAL a bird or other animal that does not migrate seasonally ■ *adj.* **1.** LIVING IN A PARTICULAR PLACE living permanently or for a considerable period in a particular place **2.** LIVE-IN living somewhere as part of a particular job **3.** BELONGING TO GROUP forming part of a group of people **4.** INHERENT present or inherent in sth **5.** ZOOL NONMIGRATING not migrating seasonally **6.** COMPUT PERMANENTLY INSTALLED IN A COMPUTER'S MEMORY used to describe a computer program or data intentionally retained in random-access memory after being loaded, even if another program is executing, so that it can be accessed quickly —**residentship** *n.*

resident commissioner *n. US* a representative from a dependency who is allowed to speak but not vote in the US House of Representatives

residential /rézzi dénsh'l/ *adj.* **1.** RELATING TO HOUSING relating to or consisting of private housing rather than offices or factories **2.** USED FOR LONG-TERM LIVING used as a place to live for the long term **3.** WITH LIVING ACCOMMODATION providing living accommodation [Mid-17thC. Formed from RESIDENCE.] —**residentially** *adv.*

residential care *n.* a supervised home environment provided by a welfare agency for people unable to live alone, e.g. children in care or adults with severe learning disabilities

residential school *n.* **1.** SCHOOL FOR CHILDREN WITH DISABILITIES a government-run school providing education and living accommodation for children with disabilities **2.** *Can* CANADIAN BOARDING SCHOOL formerly, a boarding school provided by the Canadian government and run by Christian organizations for the education and assimilation of Aboriginal children from thinly populated areas

residentiary /rézzi dénshəri/ *adj.* **1.** LIVE-IN requiring the incumbent to live in an official residence **2.** LIVING IN AN OFFICIAL RESIDENCE residing in official residence

residents' association *n.* an association of people living in the same building or neighbourhood that deals with matters of common interest such as vandalism, traffic problems, or changes in local bylaws

residual /ri zíddyoo əl/ *adj.* **1.** LEFT OVER remaining after completion of a process that involves the removal of part of the original ○ *residual damp* **2.** GEOL RELATING TO RESIDUE FROM ROCK WEATHERING relating to the material left after weathering of a rock and removal of its soluble constituents ■ *n.* **1.** STH LEFT OVER sth that remains after completion of a process that involves the removal of part of the original **2.** STATS DIFFERENCE BETWEEN ACTUAL AND THEORETICAL RESULTS the difference between results obtained through theoretical calculation and those obtained through observation **3.** CINEMA, TV REPEAT FEE a payment to performers, directors, or writers when their filmed work is shown again, especially on television —**residually** *adv.*

residual oil *n.* the low-grade hydrocarbons that remain after the process of petroleum distillation, used e.g. in asphalt or as a furnace fuel

residual unemployment *n.* the remaining unemployment during times of full employment consisting of people unable to work because of poor physical or mental health

residuary /ri zíddyoŏ əri/ *adj.* **1.** LAW **ENTITLED TO THE REMAINDER OF AN ESTATE** entitled to the residue of a deceased person's estate after debts have been paid and bequests distributed **2. LEFTOVER** remaining after a process has been gone through [Early 18thC. Formed from RESIDUUM.]

residue /rézzi dyoo/ *n.* **1. STH LEFT OVER** sth that remains after a process involving the removal of part of the original has been completed **2.** LAW **REMAINDER OF AN ESTATE** the remainder of a deceased person's estate after debts have been paid and bequests distributed **3. REMAINDER AFTER PROCESSING** sth remaining after a chemical or physical process such as combustion, distillation, evaporation, or filtration removes part of the original [14thC. Via Old French from Latin *residuum* 'sth remaining', from *residere* (see RESIDE).]

residuum /ri zíddyoŏ əm/ (*plural* **-a** /-ə/) *n.* LAW = **residue** *n.* 2 [Late 17thC. From Latin (see RESIDUE).]

resign /ri zín/ (**-signs, -signing, -signed**) *v.* **1.** *vti.* **LEAVE A JOB** to give up a paid or unpaid post voluntarily **2.** *vr.* **ACCEPT STH RELUCTANTLY** to come to terms with sth and acquiesce in it reluctantly ○ *He resigned himself to giving up work.* **3.** *vt.* **RELINQUISH A CLAIM** to give up a right or claim to sth [14thC. Via Old French *resigner* from Latin *resignare* 'to unseal, cancel, give back', from *signare* 'to seal', from *signum* 'mark'.] —**resigner** *n.*

re-sign (**re-signs, re-signing, re-signed**) *v.* **1.** *vti.* SPORTS **SIGN ANOTHER CONTRACT** to sign or cause a player to sign another contract **2.** *vt.* **SIGN STH AGAIN** to sign a document again

resignation /rézzig náysh'n/ *n.* **1. NOTIFICATION OF LEAVING A JOB** a formal notification of leaving a paid or unpaid post ○ *I've handed in my resignation.* **2. DEPARTURE FROM JOB** an instance of leaving a paid or unpaid post **3. UNPROTESTING ACCEPTANCE OF STH** agreement to sth, usually given reluctantly but without protest

resigned /ri zínd/ *adj.* acquiescing in sth reluctantly, but without protest —**resignedly** /ri zínidli/ *adv.* —**resignedness** /-zíndnəss/ *n.*

resile /ri zíl/ (**-siles, -siling, -siled**) *vi.* (*formal*) **1. SPRING BACK INTO THE SAME SHAPE** to spring back into the same shape or position **2. JUMP BACK** to jump or leap back [Early 16thC. Directly or via obsolete French *resilir* from Latin *resilire* (see RESILIENT).]

resilience /ri zílli ənss/, **resiliency** /-ənssi/ *n.* **1. SPEEDY RECOVERY FROM PROBLEMS** the ability to recover quickly from setbacks **2. ELASTICITY** the ability of matter to spring back quickly into shape after being bent, stretched, or deformed

resilient /ri zílli ənt/ *adj.* **1. RECOVERING QUICKLY** able to recover quickly from setbacks **2. ELASTIC** able to spring back quickly into shape after being bent, stretched, or deformed [Mid-17thC. From Latin *resilient-*, the present participle stem of *resilire*, literally 'to jump back', from *salire* (see SALIENT).] —**resiliently** *adv.*

resin /rézzin/ *n.* **1.** PLANTS **ORGANIC SUBSTANCE FROM PLANTS** a solid or semisolid natural organic substance secreted in the sap of some plants and trees that has a transparent or translucent quality and a yellow or brown colour. It is used in varnishes, paints, adhesives, inks, and medicines. **2.** CHEM **SYNTHETIC COMPOUND RESEMBLING RESIN** a synthetic polymeric compound physically resembling natural resin, e.g. polyvinyl, polystyrene, or epoxy, used in the petrochemical and plastics industries ■ *vt.* (**-ins, -ining, -ined**) **TREAT STH WITH RESIN** to coat or rub sth with resin [14thC. Via Old French *resine* and Latin *resina* from, ultimately, Greek *rhētinē*, of unknown origin (source also of English *rosin*).] —**resinous** *adj.* —**resinously** *adv.* —**resinousness** *n.*

resinate /rézzi nayt/ (**-ates, -ating, -ated**) *vt.* to impregnate, saturate, or flavour sth with resin

resin canal *n.* a tubular space between cells of woody vascular seed plants that is lined with resin-secreting cells

resiniferous /rézzi níffərəss/ *adj.* producing, yielding, or secreting resin

resinoid /rézzi noyd/ *adj.* **OF RESIN** relating to or containing resin ■ *n.* **SYNTHETIC RESIN** a resinous, usually synthetic, substance

res ipsa loquitur /-ípsə lókwitər/ *n.* a rule of evidence that allows that mere proof that an accident occurred is enough to prove negligence on the part of the defendant [From Latin, literally 'the thing speaks for itself']

resist /ri zíst/ *v.* (**-sists, -sisting, -sisted**) **1.** *vti.* **FIGHT AGAINST SB OR STH** to oppose and stand firm against sb or sth **2.** *vt.* **REFUSE TO GIVE IN TO STH** to refuse to accept or comply with sth ○ *resisted all attempts to force them out of their homes* **3.** *vt.* **BE UNHARMED BY STH** to remain unaltered by the damaging effect of sth ○ *ability to resist infection* **4.** *vti.* **SAY NO TO STH TEMPTING** to refrain from sth in spite of being tempted ○ *I couldn't resist having a peek.* ■ *n.* TECH **PROTECTIVE COATING** a protective coating, especially one used to prevent corrosion or oxidation, provide electrical insulation in a printed circuit, or prevent part of a fabric from accepting dye [14thC. Directly and via French *résister* from Latin *resistere*, literally 'to stand against', from *sistere* 'to make stand', from *stare* 'to stand'.] —**resistibility** /ri zístə bílləti/ *n.* —**resistible** *adj.* —**resistibly** /ri zístəbli/ *adv.*

resistance /ri zístənss/ *n.* **1. OPPOSITION** opposition to sb or sth **2. REFUSAL TO GIVE IN** refusal to accept or comply with sth **3.** MED, PHYSIOL **ABILITY TO WITHSTAND DAMAGING EFFECT** the ability to remain unaltered by the damaging effect of sth, e.g. an organism's ability not to succumb to disease or infection **4. ABILITY TO SAY NO TO TEMPTATION** the ability to refrain from sth in spite of being tempted **5.** PHYS **FORCE OPPOSING ANOTHER FORCE** a force that opposes or slows down another force. Symbol *R* **6.** ELEC **OPPOSITION TO AN ELECTRIC CURRENT** the opposition that a circuit, component, or substance presents to the flow of electricity. Symbol *R* **7.** ELEC **SOURCE OF RESISTANCE** sth such as a resistor that is a source of opposition to the flow of electricity. Symbol *R* **8.** PSYCHOANAL **REPRESSION OF THOUGHTS** the process by which the ego keeps repressed thoughts and feelings from the conscious mind

Resistance *n.* an illegal secret organization that fights for national freedom against an occupying power, especially one that fought in France, the Netherlands, Denmark, or Italy during World War II

resistant /ri zístənt/ *adj.* **1. RESISTING** offering resistance to sth ○ *resistant to change* **2. NOT DAMAGED BY STH** unaltered by or impervious to the damaging effect of sth (*often used in combination*) ○ *moisture-resistant* ■ *n.* **SB OR STH THAT RESISTS** sb or sth that offers resistance

resistive /ri zístiv/ *adj.* **1.** = **resistant 2.** ELEC **ELECTRICALLY RESISTANT** having the property of electrical resistance —**resistively** *adv.* —**resistiveness** *n.*

resistivity /reézi stívvəti/ *n.* **1.** ELEC **ELECTRICAL RESISTANCE OF A STANDARD-LENGTH SUBSTANCE** the electrical resistance of a substance of a standard length and cross section. Symbol *ρ* **2. ABILITY TO RESIST** capacity to resist

resistless /ri zístləss/ *adj.* (*archaic*) **1. IRRESISTIBLE** not able to be resisted **2. UNABLE TO RESIST** not able to resist sth

resistor /ri zístər/ *n.* a component of an electrical circuit that has resistance and is used to control the flow of electric current

resit *vti.* /ree sít/ (**-sits, -sitting, -sat**) **TAKE EXAMINATION AGAIN** to take an examination again after failing the first time ■ *n.* /reé sit/ **EXAMINATION TAKEN AGAIN** a later examination in the same subject for those who failed the first time

resize /ree síz/ (**-sizes, -sizing, -sized**) *vt.* to make sth a different size, e.g. a dress pattern or graphics on a computer screen

res judicata /-joódi kaátə/, **res adjudicata** /-ə-/ *n.* an issue already decided by a court [From Latin, literally 'judged matter']

Resnais /rénnay/, **Alain** (*b.* 1922) French film director. Among his noted films are *Hiroshima Mon Amour* (1959) and *Last Year at Marienbad* (1961).

resole /ree sṓl/ (**-soles, -soling, -soled**) *vt.* to put a new sole on a shoe

resoluble /ri zóllyoŏb'l/ *adj.* able to be resolved or analysed [Early 17thC. Directly or via French from Latin *resolubilis*, from *resolvere*, literally 'to loosen up'.] —**resolubility** /ri zóllyoŏ bílləti/ *n.* —**resolubleness** /ri zóllyoŏb'lnəss/ *n.*

re-soluble /ree sóllyoŏb'l/ *adj.* able to be dissolved again [15thC. Formed from SOLUBLE.] —**re-solubility** /ree sóllyoŏ bílləti/ *n.* —**re-solubleness** /ri zóllyoŏb'lnəss/ *n.* —**re-solubly** *adv.*

resolute /rézzə loot/ *adj.* **1. HAVING DETERMINATION** possessing determination and purposefulness **2. CHARACTERIZED BY DETERMINATION** motivated by or displaying determination and purposefulness [15thC. From Latin *resolutus*, the past participle of *resolvere* (see RESOLVE).] —**resolutely** *adv.* —**resoluteness** *n.*

resolution /rézzə loósh'n/ *n.* **1. RESOLVING OF STH** the process of resolving sth ○ *the resolution of a difficulty* **2. DECISION** a firm decision to do sth **3. DETERMINATION** firmness of mind or purpose **4. SOLUTION** an answer to a problem **5. JOINT FORMAL EXPRESSION OF OPINION** a formal expression of the consensus at a meeting, arrived at after discussion and usually as the result of a vote **6.** ELECTRON ENG **REPRODUCTION OF DETAIL IN AN IMAGE** the level of reproduction of detail offered by a TV or computer screen or a film image **7.** PHYS, CHEM **SEPARATION INTO CONSTITUENT PARTS** the process or act of separating sth such as a chemical compound or a source of light into its constituent parts **8.** MED **SUBSIDING** the disappearance or coming to an end of symptom or condition such as fever or inflammation **9.** MUSIC **SATISFACTORY CONCLUSION OF A HARMONIC PATTERN** the movement from a dissonant to a consonant chord or note **10.** MUSIC **FINAL NOTE IN A HARMONIC PROGRESSION** the note or chord to which the harmony moves when progressing from dissonance to consonance **11.** THEATRE **PART OF A STORY WHEN CONFLICT IS RESOLVED** the point in a dramatic work when the conflict is resolved **12.** PHYS = **resolving power 13.** POETRY **SYLLABLE REPLACEMENT** the substitution of a long syllable for two short ones in the rhythm of a line of poetry [14thC. Directly and via Old French from, ultimately, Latin *resolut-*, the past participle stem of *resolvere* (see RESOLVE).] —**resolutioner** *n.*

resolve /ri zólv/ *v.* (**-solves, -solving, -solved**) **1.** *vti.* **MAKE A DECISION** to come to or cause sb to come to a firm decision about sth ○ *He resolved to leave.* **2.** *vt.* **SOLVE A DIFFICULTY** to find a solution to a problem **3.** *vt.* **DISPEL DOUBTS** to dispel doubts or anxieties **4.** *vt.* **SETTLE AN ARGUMENT** to bring a disagreement to an end **5.** *vr.* **CHANGE** to change into sth else **6.** *vt.* **EXPRESS A JOINT OPINION FORMALLY** to express the opinion of a meeting formally as a consensus, after discussion and usually as the result of a vote **7.** *vti.* MED **MAKE OR BECOME LESS SWOLLEN** to subside or to cause an inflammation, swelling, or tumour to subside **8.** *vti.* **SPLIT INTO CONSTITUENT PARTS** to cause sth to separate into its constituent elements, or to become separated into constituent parts **9.** *vt.* CHEM **SEPARATE A RACEMIC MIXTURE** to separate a racemic compound or mixture into its two components **10.** *vti.* MUSIC **MOVE FROM DISSONANT TO CONSONANT** to move, or cause a chord or note to move, from dissonant to consonant **11.** *vt.* PHYS **MAKE PARTS OF AN IMAGE DISTINCT** to make parts of an image distinct, e.g. in a microscope or telescope **12.** *vt.* MATH **SPLIT A VECTOR INTO DIRECTIONAL COMPONENTS** to separate a vector into its directional components ■ *n.* **1. DETERMINATION** firmness of purpose **2. DECISION** a firm decision to do sth [14thC. Directly and via Old French from Latin *resolvere*, literally 'to loosen up', from *solvere* (see SOLVE).] —**resolvability** /ri zólvə bílləti/ *n.* —**resolvable** /ri zólvəb'l/ *adj.* —**resolvableness** *n.* —**resolver** *n.*

resolved /ri zólvd/ *adj.* determined in purpose —**resolvedly** /ri zólvidli/ *adv.* —**resolvedness** /-zólvidnəss/ *n.*

resolvent /ri zólvənt/ *adj.* **1.** SCI **CAUSING SEPARATION INTO CONSTITUENT ELEMENTS** causing or capable of causing sth to separate into its constituent elements **2.** MED **ANTI-INFLAMMATORY** able to cause reduction in inflammation or swelling ■ *n.* **1.** SCI **STH CAUSING SEPARATION INTO CONSTITUENT ELEMENTS** a substance that causes or is capable of causing sth to separate into its constituent elements **2.** MED **ANTI-INFLAMMATORY MEDICINE** a medicine that reduces inflammation or swelling

resolving power *n.* the ability of an optical system such as a telescope or microscope to distinguish objects separated by small angular distances

resonance /rézzənənss/ *n.* **1. RESONANT QUALITY** the quality or state of being resonant **2. UNDERLYING MEANING** the effect of an event or work of art beyond its immediate or surface meaning **3.** ACOUSTICS **AMPLIFIED SOUND** an intense and prolonged sound produced by sympathetic vibration **4.** ACOUSTICS, MUSIC **RINGING QUALITY OF AN INSTRUMENT OR VOICE** an amplification of a sound, e.g. that of an instrument or the human voice, caused by sympathetic vibration in a chamber such as an auditorium or a singer's chest **5.** PHYS **LARGE OSCILLATION AT A NATURAL FREQUENCY** increased amplitude of oscillation of a mechanical system when it is subjected to vibration from another source at or near its own natural frequency **6.** ELEC **OSCILLATION IN AN ELECTRICAL CIRCUIT** a state of oscillation that occurs at a very specific frequency in an electrical circuit consisting of inductive and capacitive components **7.** MED **SOUND WHEN A BODY CAVITY IS TAPPED** the sound heard during tapping (**percussion**) of a healthy chest or abdomen **8.** CHEM **PROPERTY OF CERTAIN CHEMICAL COMPOUNDS** the property of some chemical compounds of having characteristics of two or more electronic structures simultaneously

resonant /rézzənənt/ *adj.* **1. DEEP IN SOUND** deep and rich in sound **2. RESOUNDING** continuing to sound for some time **3.** ACOUSTICS **CAUSING ECHOES** producing or increasing amplification of sound or echoes, usually by sympathetic vibration [Late 16thC. Directly or via French from, ultimately, Latin *resonare* (see RESONATE).] —**resonantly** *adv.*

resonate /rézzə nayt/ (**-nates, -nating, -nated**) *v.* **1.** *vti.* **RESOUND** to resound or echo, or cause sth to resound or echo **2. HAVE EXTENDED EFFECT** to have an effect or impact beyond that which is immediately apparent **3.** *vti.* MECH ENG, ELEC, CHEM **PRODUCE OR MAKE STH PRODUCE RESONANCE** to produce or exhibit chemical, mechanical, or electrical resonance, or to cause a chemical compound or a electrical system to produce or exhibit resonance **4.** *vi.* **BE FAMILIAR** to produce a response in sb, especially by reminding that person of sth [Late 19thC. From Latin *resonare* 'to resound', from *sonare* 'to sound'.] —**resonation** /rézzə náysh'n/ *n.*

resonator /rézzə naytər/ *n.* **1.** ELEC **RESONATING DEVICE** a device or part that resonates, especially one that produces sound or microwaves **2.** MUSIC **RESONATING PART OF AN INSTRUMENT** a part of a musical instrument designed to produce resonance, e.g. the hollow body of a violin or the tubes in a vibraphone

resorb /ri-/ (**-sorbs, -sorbing, -sorbed**) *vt.* to absorb sth again [Mid-17thC. From Latin *resorbere*, literally 'to drink in again', from *sorbere* (see ABSORB).] —**resorbent** *adj.*

resorcinol /ri záwrssi nol/ *n.* a colourless crystalline phenol used in making dyes, resins, and drugs and in tanning. Formula: $C_6H_6O_2$. [Late 19thC. Coined from RESIN + *orcin* + -OL.]

resorption /ri sáwrpsh'n/ *n.* **1. RESORBING OR BEING RESORBED** the process or state of resorbing or being resorbed **2.** GEOL **PARTIAL FUSION OF A CRYSTAL IN A MAGMA** the partial fusion of a crystal in a magma in response to changing conditions of temperature and pressure [Early 19thC. Formed from RESORB, on the model of *absorption*.] —**resorptive** *adj.*

resort /ri záwrt/ *n.* **1. HOLIDAY PLACE** a place that is popular for recreation and holidays and provides accommodation and entertainment **2. SOURCE OF HELP** a person, place, or course of action seen as a source of help in dealing with a problem ○ *As a last resort we could sell the car.* **3. ACT OF HAVING RECOURSE TO** the act of turning to sb or sth for help in dealing with a problem **4. FREQUENT VISITING** the act of going somewhere frequently or in large numbers **5. MUCH-VISITED PLACE** a place frequently visited [14thC. From Old French *resortir*, literally 'to come back', from *sortir* 'to go out' (source of English *sortie*).]

resort to *vt.* **1. HAVE RECOURSE TO STH** to turn to sth, sometimes sth extreme, for help in dealing with a problem **2. GO SOMEWHERE FREQUENTLY VISITED** to go somewhere that is frequently visited, or go somewhere in large numbers

re-sort (**re-sorts, re-sorting, re-sorted**) *vt.* to sort sth again

resound /ri zównd/ (**-sounds, -sounding, -sounded**) *vi.* **1. MAKE A REVERBERATING SOUND** to produce a long reverberating sound **2. SOUND CLEARLY** to sound loudly and clearly **3. BE FILLED WITH A REVERBERATING SOUND** to be filled with a long reverberating sound ○ *The hall resounded to the cheers of the audience.* **4. BE EXTREMELY WELL KNOWN** to be extremely well known, especially over a long period or a wide area [14thC. Alteration of Old French *resoner* (under the influence of SOUND), from Latin *resonare* (see RESONATE).]

resounding /ri zównding/ *adj.* **1. CLEAR AND EMPHATIC** clear and unequivocal ○ *a resounding defeat* **2. ECHOING LOUDLY** making a loud noise that echoes —**resoundingly** *adv.*

resource /ri záwrss, -sáwrss/ *n.* **1. SOURCE OF HELP** sb who or sth that can be used as a source of help or information **2. BACKUP SUPPLY** a reserve supply of sth such as money, personnel, or equipment **3. ABILITY TO FIND SOLUTIONS** adeptness at finding solutions to problems **4.** = **natural resource** ■ *npl.* **1. resources TALENT DRAWN ON WHEN NECESSARY** an inner ability or capacity that is drawn on in time of need **2. NATION'S NATURAL, ECONOMIC, OR MILITARY ASSET** a natural, economic, political, or military asset enjoyed by a nation, e.g. mineral wealth, labour, capital, or military personnel **3.** COMM **COMPANY'S ASSET** a source drawn on by a company for making profit, e.g. personnel, capital, machinery, or stock ■ *vt.* (**-sources, -sourcing, -sourced**) **PROVIDE STH WITH RESOURCES** to provide sth with monetary or other resources [Early 17thC. Via French, from, ultimately, Latin *resurgere* 'to rise again, be replenished', from *surgere*, literally 'to rise up from below'.] —**resourceless** *adj.*

resourceful /ri záwrsf'l, -sáwrs-/ *adj.* full of initiative and good at problem-solving, especially in difficult situations —**resourcefully** *adv.* —**resourcefulness** *n.*

resp. *abbr.* **1.** respective **2.** respectively **3.** respiration **4.** respondent

respect /ri spékt/ *n.* **1. ESTEEM** a feeling or attitude of admiration and deference towards sb or sth ○ *won the respect of her colleagues* **2. STATE OF BEING ADMIRED** the state of being admired deferentially **3. THOUGHTFULNESS** consideration or thoughtfulness **4. CHARACTERISTIC** an individual characteristic or point ○ *satisfactory in all respects* ■ **respects** *npl.* **REGARDS** polite greetings offered to sb ■ *vt.* (**-spects, -specting, -spected**) **1. ESTEEM SB OR STH** to feel or show admiration and deference towards sb or sth **2. NOT GO AGAINST OR VIOLATE STH** to pay due attention to and refrain from violating sth ○ *respect the law* ○ *respect another's privacy* **3. BE CONSIDERATE TOWARDS SB OR STH** to show consideration or thoughtfulness in relation to sb or sth [14thC. Via Old French from Latin *respectus*, the past participle of *respicere* 'to regard', literally 'to look back at', from *specere* 'to look at'.] —**respecter** *n.*

WORD KEY: SYNONYMS

See Synonyms at ***regard***.

respectable /ri spéktəb'l/ *adj.* **1. MORALLY ABOVE REPROACH** in accordance with accepted standards of correctness or decency ○ *a respectable district* **2. SATISFACTORY** meeting an adequate standard ○ *a respectable salary* **3. WORTHY OF RESPECT** deserving or receiving respect **4. LARGE ENOUGH** sufficiently large **5. ACCEPTABLE IN APPEARANCE** tidy and fit to be seen in public (*informal*) —**respectability** /ri spéktə bílləti/ *n.* —**respectableness** /ri spéktəb'lnəss/ *n.* —**respectably** *adv.*

respected /ri spéktid/ *adj.* held in high regard by equals as well as subordinates

respectful /ri spéktf'l/ *adj.* showing appropriate deference and respect —**respectfully** *adv.* —**respectfulness** *n.*

respecting /ri spékting/ *prep.* regarding or concerning sb or sth

respective /ri spéktiv/ *adj.* varying according to each of the people or things concerned ○ *They returned to their respective homes.* —**respectiveness** *n.*

respectively *adv.* matching one list with another in the order given for both ○ *Joe and his wife are aged 52 and 51 respectively.*

respell /ree spél/ (**-spells, -spelling, -spelt** *or* **-spelled**) *vt.* to spell sth again or in a different way, especially using a different alphabet in order to give guidance on pronunciation —**respelling** *n.*

respirable /réspərəb'l, ri spírəb'l/ *adj.* fit or able to be breathed —**respirability** /réspərə bílləti, ri spírə bílləti/ *n.*

respiration /réspə ráysh'n/ *n.* **1. BREATHING** the act of breathing air in and out **2.** BIOL **DISTRIBUTION OF OXYGEN** the complete chemical and physical process in which oxygen is delivered to tissues or cells of the body and carbon dioxide and water are given off **3.** BIOL **OXIDATION PROCESS IN CELLS** an energy-producing oxidation process in cells —**respirational** *adj.*

respirator /réspə raytər/ *n.* **1. MACHINE PROVIDING ARTIFICIAL RESPIRATION** a machine used in hospitals to maintain breathing **2. PROTECTIVE MASK THROUGH WHICH TO BREATHE** a device placed over the nose and mouth to filter out noxious particles and fumes from inhaled air or to warm chilled air before it is inhaled

respiratory /ri spírrətəri, réspərətəri/ *adj.* relating to or used in breathing or the system in the body that takes in and distributes oxygen

respiratory distress syndrome *n.* a respiratory disease of newborns, especially premature infants, caused by the inability of the lungs to take in oxygen and marked by cyanosis and difficult breathing

respiratory pigment *n.* a protein such as haemoglobin found in any of several colours in the cells of living organisms and serving to transfer oxygen atoms among some molecules active in cellular respiration

respiratory quotient *n.* the ratio of the volume of carbon dioxide released to the volume of oxygen absorbed by an organism, cell, or tissue over a given time period

respiratory system *n.* the system of organs in the body responsible for the intake of oxygen and the expiration of carbon dioxide. In mammals it consists of the lungs, bronchi, bronchioles, trachea, diaphragm, and nerve supply.

respire /ri spír/ (**-spires, -spiring, -spired**) *v.* **1.** *vti.* **BREATHE** to breathe air in and out **2.** *vi.* **BREATHE NORMALLY AFTER ANXIETY OR EXERTION** to breathe again in a normal way after anxiety or exertion (*literary*) [14thC. Directly or via French from Latin *respirare*, literally 'to breathe again', from *spirare* 'to breathe'.]

respirometer /réspə rómmitər/ *n.* an instrument for measuring and studying the process in which oxygen is taken into the body, delivered to tissues and cells, and used by them [Late 19thC. Coined from RESPIRATION + -METER.] —**respirometric** /réspərō méttrik/ *adj.* —**respirometry** /réspə rómmətri/ *n.*

respite /résplt, réspit/ *n.* **1. BRIEF INTERVAL OF REST** a brief period of rest and recovery between periods of exertion or after sth disagreeable **2. DELAY** a temporary delay **3.** LAW **REPRIEVE** a temporary stay of execution of a criminal [13thC. Via Old French, 'refuge', from Latin *respectus*, the past participle of *respicere* 'to look back'.]

respite care *n.* temporary residential care for patients that provides relief for the permanent carers

resplendent /ri spléndənt/ *adj.* having a dazzlingly impressive appearance ○ *resplendent in his dress uniform* [15thC. From Latin *resplendere*, literally 'to shine brightly', from *splendere* 'to shine'.] —**resplendence** *n.* —**resplendently** *adv.*

respond /ri spónd/ *v.* (**-sponds, -sponding, -sponded**) **1.** *vti.* **PROVIDE AN ANSWER** to reply sth or to sth in spoken or written words **2.** *vi.* **REACT** to act or do sth in reaction to sth else ○ *was unsure of how to respond to his moods* **3.** *vi.* MED **HAVE A POSITIVE MEDICAL REACTION** to react positively to medical treatment ■ *n.* **1.** ARCHIT **PILASTER OR PILLAR SUPPORTING ARCH** a pilaster or pillar that supports an arch **2.** CHR, MUSIC **CHORAL PART OF AN ANTHEM** the choral part in an anthem for priest and choir following a lesson in a church service [Mid-16thC. Via Old French *respondre* from Latin *respondere*, literally 'to promise in return', from *spondere* 'to pledge'.] —**respondence** *n.*

respondent /ri spóndənt/ *n.* **1.** LAW **DEFENDANT** the person against whom a divorce petition or an appeal is brought **2. ANSWERER** sb who replies to sth ■ *adj.* **1. RESPONDING** giving a response **2.** LAW **BEING A RESPONDENT** being a defendant in a divorce petition or appeal

responsa plural of **responsum**

response /ri spónss/ *n.* **1. REPLY GIVEN TO A QUESTION** sth said or written in reply to a statement or question from sb else **2. REACTION** sth done in reaction to sth else **3.** CARDS **BID IN BRIDGE** a bid in bridge that is in reply to a partner's bid or double **4.** CHR **REPLY MADE BY CHURCH CHOIR** a phrase sung or spoken by the choir or congregation in reply to the officiant during a church service **5.** MED **BODY'S REACTION TO STIMULUS** the reaction of an organism or any of its parts to a stimulus [14thC. Directly or via Old French from Latin *responsum*, from the past participle of *respondere* (see RESPOND).] —**responseless** *adj.*

WORD KEY: SYNONYMS

See Synonyms at ***answer***.

responsibility /ri spónssə bílləti/ (*plural* **-ties**) *n.* **1. ACCOUNTABILITY** the state, fact, or position of being accountable to sb or for sth ○ *The responsibilities of parenthood* **2. STH TO BE RESPONSIBLE FOR** sb or sth for which a person or organization is responsible **3. BLAME** the blame for sth that has happened ○ *took full responsibility for the mixup* **4. AUTHORITY TO ACT** authority to take decisions independently

responsible /ri spónssəb'l/ *adj.* **1. ANSWERABLE TO SB** accountable to sb for an action or for the successful carrying out of a duty **2. IN CHARGE OF SB OR STH** expected to deal with sth or take care of sb **3. BEING TO BLAME FOR STH** being the cause of sth, usually sth wrong or disapproved of ○ *Who's responsible for this mess?* **4. IMPORTANT** conferring the authority to take decisions independently and requiring conscientiousness and trustworthiness ○ *in a responsible position* **5. RELIABLE** able to be counted on owing to qualities of conscientiousness and trustworthiness **6. RATIONAL AND ACCOUNTABLE FOR YOUR ACTIONS** capable of taking rational or moral decisions, and therefore accountable for your actions **7. HAVING AUTHORITY TO ACT** having the authority to take decisions independently **8.** FIN **FINANCIALLY SOUND** having adequate means to meet financial obligations [Late 16thC. Via obsolete French, 'corresponding', from Latin *respons-*, the past participle stem of *respondere* (see RESPOND).] —**responsibleness** *n.* —**responsibly** *adv.*

responsive /ri spónssiv/ *adj.* **1. DONE IN RESPONSE** serving to respond to sth **2. SHOWING A POSITIVE RESPONSE** reacting quickly, strongly, or favourably to sth, especially a suggestion or proposal **3. REACTING TO STIMULUS** showing reaction to a stimulus **4.** CHR **CONSISTING OF A CHOIR'S OR CONGREGATION'S RESPONSES** consisting of responses by a choir or congregation in a church service —**responsively** *adv.* —**responsiveness** *n.*

responsory /ri spónssəri/ (*plural* **-ries**) *n.* an anthem consisting of short verses sung or spoken by the officiant and responses sung or spoken by the choir, especially after the lesson in a church service —**responsorial** /ri spón sáwri əl/ *adj.*

responsum /ri spónssəm/ (*plural* **-sa** /-sə/) *n.* a definitive written reply by a rabbinic authority to a question on religion [Late 19thC. From Latin, 'reply', from the past participle of *respondere* (see RESPOND).]

res publica /-póobli kaa, -púbblikə/ *n.* **1.** POL **CONCEPT OF THE STATE** the state, a republic, or the commonwealth as a concept **2. PUBLIC GOOD** the public or common good [From Latin, literally 'public matter']

rest[1] /rest/ *n.* **1. CESSATION OF LABOUR** a state or period of refreshing freedom from exertion ○ *a period of rest and recreation* **2. REFRESHING REPOSE OF SLEEP** the repose of sleep that is refreshing to body and mind and is marked by a reduction in metabolic activity **3. CESSATION OF MOVEMENT** the cessation of movement or action **4. REPOSE OF DEATH** death perceived as freedom from earthly toil **5. FREEDOM FROM ANXIETY** freedom from mental or emotional anxiety ○ *I put her mind at rest.* **6.** MUSIC **PAUSE IN MUSIC** a rhythmic pause between musical notes, or the mark indicating a musical pause **7.** POETRY = **caesura 8. PLACE TO STOP AND RELAX** a stopping place for shelter and relaxation **9. SUPPORT** sth used for support, especially on a piece of furniture **10.** CUE GAMES **SUPPORT TOOL IN POOL** a tool used to support the cue in pool ■ *v.* (**rests, resting, rested**) **1.** *vti.* **SLEEP OR RELAX** to restore energy to sb or sth by means of relaxation or sleep ○ *rest the sled dogs* ○ *Put your feet up and rest.* **2.** *vi.* **BE TRANQUIL** to be in a state of tranquillity **3.** *vi.* **BE DEAD** to be dead, and so free from earthly concerns **4.** *vti.* **STOP MOVING** to cease activity, or cause sth to cease activity **5.** *vi.* **BE LEFT ALONE** to be subject to no further discussion or attention ○ *Let the matter rest.* **6.** *vi.* **LIE FALLOW** to lie unfarmed **7.** *vti.* **SUPPORT OR BE SUPPORTED** to support sth, or to be supported, on or against sth ○ *The ornament was resting on a narrow ledge.* **8.** *vi.* **COME TO STOP** to allow the eyes to come to a stop on sb or sth **9.** *vi.* **BE VESTED** to be vested or placed in sb or sth **10.** *vi.* **DEPEND ON SB OR STH** to depend on sb or sth for action or as a burden or responsibility **11.** *vi.* **BE BASED ON STH** to rely on sth for proof or explanation **12.** *vti.* LAW **CONCLUDE A LEGAL CASE** to conclude the presentation of evidence in a case ○ *I rest my case.* [The verb is from Old English *ræstan*; the noun from Old English *ræst*, both of prehistoric Germanic origin] —**rester** *n.*

rest[2] /rest/ *n.* **REMAINDER** sth left as a remainder (*takes a singular or plural verb*) ■ *vi.* (**rests, resting, rested**) **CONTINUE TO BE** to remain or continue to be (*usually used as a command*) ○ *Rest assured that we're doing everything possible.* [15thC. From French *reste* 'remnant', from *rester* 'to remain', from Latin *restare* 'to stay behind', literally 'to stand back', from *stare* (see STATION).]

rest area *n.* *US, ANZ* an area at the side of a major road where motorists can rest. These areas may be equipped with picnic tables, light refreshments, or toilet facilities.

restart (**-starts, -starting, -started**) *vti.* /ree staárt/ **1. RESUME STH** to begin doing sth again after it was stopped or suspended **2. GET STH WORKING AGAIN** to start sth or get it working again —**restart** /reé staart/ *n.* —**restartable** *adj.*

restate /ree stáyt/ (**-states, -stating, -stated**) *vt.* to say sth again, especially in order to clarify or summarize what has already been said ○ *time to restate our goals*

restaurant /réstə ront, -roN, -rənt/ *n.* a place where meals and drinks are sold and served to customers [Early 19thC. From French, the present participle of *restaurer* (see RESTORE).]

restaurant car *n.* a railway carriage in which meals are served to passengers. US term **dining car**

restaurateur /réstərə túr/ *n.* sb who owns or manages a restaurant [Late 18thC. From French, literally 'restorer', from *restaurer* (see RESTORE).]

WORD KEY: USAGE

Spelling trap: Note that there is no *-n-* in this word as there is in *restaurant.*

rest cure *n.* a treatment involving complete rest, e.g. as a remedy for stress

rested /réstid/ *adj.* refreshed and relaxed following a period of rest

restful /réstf'l/ *adj.* **1. PROVIDING REST** giving, promoting, or involving rest ○ *a restful holiday* **2. CALM** at rest or tranquil —**restfully** *adv.* —**restfulness** *n.*

restharrow /rést harō/ *n.* a pod-bearing plant of Europe and Asia that has three-lobed leaves, woody stems and roots, and clusters of white, purple, or pink flowers. Latin name: *Ononsis repens* and *Ononsis spinosa.* [So called because its tough roots can stop, or arrest, the progress of a harrow]

rest home *n.* a place where infirm senior citizens and chronically ill people are housed and cared for (*dated*)

restiform /rési fawrm/ *adj.* shaped like a rope or cord [Mid-19thC. From modern Latin *restiformis*, from Latin *restis* 'cord'.]

resting /résting/ *adj.* **1.** BIOL **IMMOBILE** used to describe organisms that are not moving or active **2.** CELL BIOL **NOT DIVIDING** not undergoing cell division **3.** BOT **DORMANT** used to describe spores, seeds, and eggs that are dormant before germination **4. UNEMPLOYED** not currently employed as an actor (*informal*) (*used euphemistically*)

restitution /résti tyóosh'n/ *n.* **1. GIVING BACK** the return of sth to its rightful owner **2. PAYING BACK** compensation for a loss, damage, or injury **3. RESTORATION** the return of sth to the condition it was in before it was changed [13thC. Directly or via French from the Latin stem *restitution-*, ultimately from *restituere* 'to restore', from *statuere* (see STATUE).] —**restitutive** /résti tyootiv/ *adj.* —**restitutory** /résti tyóotəri/ *adj.*

restive /réstiv/ *adj.* **1. UNEASY** uneasy and on the verge of resisting control ○ *The people soon grew restive under the rule of the occupying force.* **2. IMPATIENT** having little patience and unwilling to tolerate annoyances **3. OBSTINATE OR AWKWARD** unwilling to be guided or controlled ○ *a restive horse* [Late 16thC. An alteration of earlier *restiff*, from Old French *restif*, from, ultimately, Latin *restare* 'to rest'.] —**restively** *adv.* —**restiveness** *n.*

restless /réstləss/ *adj.* **1. CONSTANTLY MOVING** constantly moving, or unable to be still ○ *Some waited patiently but others were restless.* **2. DISCONTENTED** seeking a change because of discontent ○ *He began to feel restless after only a few weeks in the job.* **3. SLEEPLESS** lacking rest or sleep ○ *She spent a restless night worrying.* —**restlessly** *adv.* —**restlessness** *n.*

rest mass *n.* the mass a body has when it is not moving, as opposed to the additional mass it gains as a result of its movement, according to the theory of relativity

restock /ree stók/ (**-stocks, -stocking, -stocked**) *vti.* to replace or refill sth after it has been used or its contents emptied

restoration /réstə ráysh'n/ *n.* **1. RESTORING OF STH** the return of sth that was removed, or the restoring of sth to a former condition ○ *calls for the restoration of curfews* **2. THING RESTORED** sth, especially a building, that has been brought back to an earlier and usually better condition **3. MODEL** a model made to resemble or represent sth in its original condition ○ *a restoration of a Neanderthal dwelling*

Restoration *n.* the re-establishment of monarchy in Great Britain under Charles II in 1660, or the period of his reign

restorative /ri stáwrətiv/ *adj.* **GIVING NEW STRENGTH** tending or meant to give sb new strength or vigour ○ *a restorative tonic* ■ *n.* **STH THAT RESTORES** sth that gives sb new strength or vigour, especially an activity or medication —**restoratively** *adv.* —**restorativeness** *n.*

restore /ri stáwr/ (**-stores, -storing, -stored**) *vt.* **1. GIVE STH BACK** to return sth to its proper owner or place **2. RETURN STH TO PREVIOUS CONDITION** to bring sth back to an earlier and better condition ○ *techniques used to restore old oil paintings* **3. MAKE SB FEEL BETTER** to give sb new strength or vigour ○ *I felt restored after my weekend away.* **4. RETURN SB TO PREVIOUS POSITION** to return sb to a previously held rank, office, or position ○ *restore her to the throne* **5. PUT STH BACK** to re-establish or put back sth that was once but is no longer there ○ *restore order in the capital* [13thC. Via Old French *restorer* from Latin *restaurare*, literally 'to set upright again', from the stem *-staurare*.] —**restorable** *adj.* —**restorer** *n.*

WORD KEY: SYNONYMS

See Synonyms at ***renew***.

restrain /ri stráyn/ (**-strains, -straining, -strained**) *vt.* **1. HOLD SB BACK** to prevent sb or yourself from doing sth ○ *I couldn't restrain myself from calling out.* **2. CONTROL STH** to keep sth under control or within limits ○ *trying to restrain his desire to flee* **3. CONTROL SB** to physically control the movements of a person or animal ○ *Restrain him before he hurts someone.* **4. IMPRISON SB** to put sb in prison or otherwise take away his or her freedom [14thC. Via Old French *restreindre* from Latin *restingere* 'to bind fast, confine', from *stringere* (see STRAIN).] —**restrainable** *adj.*

restrained /ri stráynd/ *adj.* characterized by control, especially in not being excessively emotional or aggressive ○ *the artist's restrained use of colour* —**restrainedly** /-idli/ *adv.*

restraining order *n.* *US* a court order that commands sb to stop doing sth until the issuing court can determine its legality

a at; aa father; aw all; ay day; air hair; ə about, edible, item, common, circus; e egg; ee eel; hw when; i it, happy; ī ice; 'l apple; 'm rhythm; 'n fashion; o odd; ō open; ŏŏ good; oo pool; ow owl; oy oil; th thin; th this; u up; ur urge;

restraint /ri stráynt/ *n.* **1.** HOLDING BACK an act or the quality of holding back, limiting, or controlling sth ○ *Although severely provoked, she showed admirable restraint in not retaliating.* **2.** RESTRAINING THING sth that controls or limits sb or sth ○ *His poverty was no restraint on his ambition.* **3.** HOLDING DEVICE sth that is fastened to limit sb's freedom of movement [14thC. From Old French *restreinte*, the feminine past participle of *restreindre* (see RESTRAIN).]

restraint of trade *n.* the limiting of commercial competition by means such as price-fixing or monopolistic practices

restrict /ri stríkt/ (**-stricts, -stricting, -stricted**) *vt.* to keep sth within fixed limits ○ *Entry is restricted to members only.* [15thC. From Latin *restrictus*, the past participle of *restringere* (see RESTRAIN).]

restricted /ri stríktid/ *adj.* **1.** LIMITED limited or made smaller or less than might be desired ○ *It's difficult to turn the vehicle in such a restricted space.* **2.** SUBJECT TO CONTROLS subject to controls or limits, e.g. of time or availability ○ *restricted use of the facilities* **3.** REQUIRING AUTHORIZATION intended only for authorized people ○ *You are entering a restricted area.* —**restrictedly** *adv.*

restriction /ri stríksh'n/ *n.* **1.** STH THAT LIMITS sth that limits or controls sth else ○ *There are restrictions on the use of the photocopier.* **2.** ACT OR STATE OF RESTRICTING a restricting of sth, or the condition of being restricted ○ *the restriction of a person's freedom*

restriction enzyme *n.* an enzyme that can be used to break down DNA into segments at precise locations for use in genetic engineering

restriction fragment *n.* a portion of a larger DNA molecule that has been separated at precise locations by a restriction enzyme

restrictive /ri stríktiv/ *adj.* **1.** TENDING TO LIMIT acting as a limit or control on sth **2.** GRAM LIMITING A MEANING limiting the range of reference or application of a word, phrase, or clause —**restrictively** *adv.* —**restrictiveness** *n.*

restrictive covenant *n.* a stipulation on a party buying or leasing land to refrain from uses or activities that would lessen its value

restrictive practice *n.* **1.** WORKING CUSTOM THAT LIMITS OTHERS sth done customarily by a group of workers, especially a trade union, that places limits on the work of others or the freedom of operation of employers **2.** TRADE AGREEMENT AGAINST PUBLIC INTEREST sth done by companies in trade that is against the public interest, e.g. price-fixing

restrike /rée strīk/ *n.* a coin struck at a later date from a die that has already been used to produce the original issue —**restrike** /ree strīk/ *vt.*

rest room *n.* a room that includes a toilet, especially in a building used by the public

restructure /ree strúkchər/ (**-tures, -turing, -tured**) *v.* **1.** *vti.* CHANGE STH'S BASIC STRUCTURE to change the way in which sth is organized or arranged ○ *restructure the firm* **2.** *vt.* FIN REORGANIZE A DEBT to alter the terms of a loan, especially to relieve its burden on the debtor

restructuring /ree strúkchəring/ *n.* the process or an instance of changing the way in which sth is organized or arranged

result /ri zúlt/ *n.* **1.** CONSEQUENCE sth that follows as a consequence of a particular action, condition, or event **2.** SCORE an outcome, especially the final score in a sporting competition or the grade awarded to sb who has sat an examination ○ *The results were in Saturday's paper.* **3.** NUMBER a number arrived at by a calculation **4.** SUCCESS a successful outcome to sth, especially a sporting competition (*informal*) ○ *If the lads play like this next week they'll definitely get a result.* ■ **results** *npl.* DESIRED OUTCOME the desired outcome from an action ○ *The new policy is already showing results.* ■ *v.* (**-sults, -sulting, -sulted**) **1.** *vi.* CAUSE AN OUTCOME to produce a particular outcome ○ *Overgrazing results in soil erosion.* **2.** *vi.* FOLLOW AS CONSEQUENCE to follow as a consequence of a particular action, condition, or event ○ *This kind of error results from inattention.* **3.** *vt.* = **revert** *v.* 5 [15thC. From Latin *resultare* 'to spring back, reverberate' ('to result' in medieval Latin), from *saltare* 'to jump' (source of English *sauté*).]

resultant /ri zúlt'nt/ *adj.* RESULTING FROM happening as a consequence of sth else ■ *n.* PHYS, MATH SINGLE VECTOR EQUIVALENT TO OTHERS ADDED a single vector that is equivalent to two or more other vectors

resultant tone *n.* a tone that is created by the sounding together of two other tones but is different from both of them

resulting /ri zúlting/ *adj.* happening as a consequence ○ *the heavy snowfall and the resulting chaos on the roads*

resume /ri zyóom/ (**-sumes, -suming, -sumed**) *v.* **1.** *vti.* CONTINUE STH to continue with sth after a temporary halt **2.** *vt.* TAKE STH AGAIN to take, assume, or occupy a position again ○ *She came in and resumed her place at the head of the table.* [15thC. Directly or via French *résumer* from Latin *resumere* 'to take up again', from *sumere* 'to take' (source of English *assume*).] —**resumable** *adj.*

résumé /rézzyoo may, ráy-/ *n.* **1.** SUMMARY a summary of sth such as events that have happened ○ *a résumé of the afternoon's activities* **2.** *US, Can, ANZ* CV a curriculum vitae [Early 19thC. From French, the past participle of *résumer* (probably influenced by Old French *sommer* 'to find the sum of') (see RESUME).]

resumption /ri zúmpsh'n/ *n.* the act or an instance of continuing with sth that has been stopped for a while ○ *hoping for a resumption of negotiations* [15thC. Directly or via French *résumption* from Latin *resumpt-*, the past participle stem of *resumere* (see RESUME).]

resupinate /ri syóopinit/ *adj.* used to describe a plant part, especially the flower of an orchid, that grows upside down or appears to do so [Late 18thC. From Latin *resupinatus*, the past participle of *resupinare* 'to bend back', ultimately from *supinus* 'turned upwards'.] —**resupination** /ri syóopi náysh'n/ *n.*

resurface /ree súrfiss/ (**-faces, -facing, -faced**) *v.* **1.** *vi.* COME TO SURFACE AGAIN to come back to the surface of a body of water after having submerged **2.** *vi.* APPEAR AGAIN to appear again after having disappeared or been absent ○ *He resurfaced in Bangkok after the war.* **3.** *vt.* PUT NEW SURFACE ON STH to put a new surface on sth, especially a road

resurfacing /ree súrfissing/ *n.* the process of putting a new surface on sth, especially a road ○ *The main road is closed for resurfacing.*

resurge /ri súrj/ (**-surges, -surging, -surged**) *vi.* to rise or grow strong again (*literary*) [Late 16thC. From Latin *resurgere*, from *surgere* (see SURGE).]

resurgence /ri súrjənss/ *n.* the act or process of rising again or becoming stronger again ○ *a resurgence of patriotism*

resurgent /ri súrjənt/ *adj.* rising or becoming stronger again [Late 18thC. From Latin *resurgere* (see RESURGE).]

resurrect /rézzə rékt/ (**-rects, -recting, -rected**) *v.* **1.** *vti.* RAISE SB FROM DEAD to come or bring sb back to life after apparent death **2.** *vt.* REINSTATE STH to bring back into use sth that had been stopped or discarded ○ *resurrect an old argument* [Late 18thC. Back-formation from RESURRECTION.]

resurrection /rézzə réksh'n/ *n.* **1.** RISING FROM DEAD in some systems of belief, a rising from or raising of sb from the dead, or the state of having risen from the dead **2.** REVIVAL the revival of sth old or long disused ○ *the resurrection of a youthful dream* [13thC. Via Old French *résurrection* from, ultimately, Latin *resurrect-*, the past participle stem of *resurgere* (see RESURGE).] —**resurrectional** *adj.*

Resurrection *n.* **1.** JESUS CHRIST'S RISING FROM THE DEAD in Christian belief, the rising of Jesus Christ from the dead after his crucifixion and entombment **2.** RISING OF DEAD ON JUDGMENT DAY the rising of the dead on Judgment Day, as anticipated by Christians, Jews, and Muslims

resurrection plant *n.* a plant that survives well in hot dry conditions e.g. the Rose of Jericho

resuscitate /ri sússi tayt/ (**-tates, -tating, -tated**) *vti.* to revive sb or be revived from unconsciousness or apparent death [Early 16thC. From Latin *resuscitare*, from *suscitare* 'to raise', literally 'to move from under', from *citare* (see CITE).] —**resuscitable** *adj.* —**resuscitative** *adj.*

resuscitation /ri sússi táysh'n/ *n.* the revival of sb who is unconscious or near death, especially by cardiac massage and artificial respiration

resuscitator /ri sússi taytər/ *n.* sb who resuscitates sb else, or more commonly, a machine used to re-establish normal breathing or heartbeat

ret /ret/ (**rets, retting, retted**) *vti.* to soak or moisten plant fibres such as flax or hemp so that they become easier to separate [15thC. From Middle Dutch *reeten*.]

ret. *abbr.* **1.** LAW retain **2.** retired **3.** LAW return **4.** COMM returned

retable /ri táyb'l/ *n.* a shelf or setting behind an altar for holding candles, flowers, or religious images [Early 19thC. Via French *rétable* from, ultimately, Latin *retro-* 'back' + *tabula* 'table'.]

retail /rée tayl/ *n.* SALE TO CONSUMERS the selling of goods in small amounts directly to customers, e.g. in shops ○ *She works in retail.* ■ *adv.* IN SMALL, NOT BULK, AMOUNTS from an ordinary shop or at the normal customer price and in small amounts rather than in bulk ○ *I bought it retail.* ■ *v.* (**-tails, -tailing, -tailed**) **1.** *vti.* SELL GOODS to sell goods, or be sold, to customers in small amounts and without a discount ○ *This item usually retails at a much higher price.* **2.** *vt.* REPEAT STH HEARD to regularly repeat what is heard, especially gossip [14thC. From Old French *retaille* 'piece cut off', ultimately from *taillier* 'to cut' (source of English *tailor*), the underlying idea being to sell in small quantities, not wholesale.]

retailer /rée taylər/ *n.* a person, shop, or business that sells goods directly to the public ○ *You can buy these at any local retailer.*

retail price index *n.* a list of the prices of essential consumer goods that is published each month by the government to show how much prices in general have risen or fallen

retain /ri táyn/ (**-tains, -taining, -tained**) *vt.* **1.** KEEP STH to keep possession of sth ○ *Despite losing the court case he retains all rights to the magazine article.* **2.** REMEMBER THINGS to be able to keep ideas or information in mind or memory **3.** KEEP STH IN POSITION to keep or hold sth in a place or position ○ *water retained by a dam* **4.** HOLD STH WITHIN to be able to hold or accumulate sth, especially liquid **5.** PAY SB TO DO WORK to pay sb regularly to do work **6.** HIRE PROFESSIONAL PERSON to pay a preliminary fee to reserve the services of a barrister, accountant, or other professional person whenever needed [14thC. Via the Anglo-Norman stem *retaign-* from, ultimately, Latin *retinere* 'to hold back' (source of English *rein*), from *tenere* 'to hold' (see TENANT).] —**retainability** /ri táynə bílləti/ *n.* —**retainable** /ri táynəb'l/ *adj.* —**retainment** *n.*

retained object *n.* the direct or indirect object of a passive verb, e.g. 'letter' in 'She was sent a letter by her brother'

retained profits *npl.* the part of the after-tax profits of a business that is not distributed to shareholders

retainer[1] /ri táynər/ *n.* **1.** HOLDER a device for holding sth in place **2.** DENT DEVICE HOLDING TEETH IN POSITION a device for holding a tooth or teeth in position after orthodontic treatment **3.** HR SERVANT a paid servant, especially one who has been employed for many years ○ *She gave the cottage to one of her old family retainers.* **4.** FOLLOWER in the past, a soldier or other person who supported or was dependent on sb of high rank

retainer[2] /ri táynər/ *n.* **1.** FEE RESERVING PROFESSIONAL SERVICES a fee paid to reserve the services of a professional person, especially a barrister or accountant, whenever needed **2.** FEE RESERVING ACCOMMODATION a fee paid by sb who rents accommodation to reserve it while they are temporarily away ◇ **on (a) retainer** paid regularly in order to be consulted whenever necessary, rather than being paid for each job

retaining wall *n.* a wall built to keep earth or water from moving

retake *vt.* /ree táyk/ (**-takes, -taking, -took** /-tóok/, **-taken** /-táykən/) **1.** MIL RECAPTURE STH to recapture a place that has been captured by an enemy **2.** RECORDING, CINEMA FILM STH AGAIN to record, photograph, or film sth again in order to get it right **3.** SPORTS TAKE SHOT AGAIN to take a shot in a game again because of some infringement during the first attempt ○ *The referee ordered him to retake the penalty.* ■ *n.* /rée tayk/

ACT OF RECORDING STH AGAIN an instance of recording, photographing, or filming sth again, or the product that results from this

retaliate /ri tálli ayt/ (**-ates, -ating, -ated**) *vi.* to deliberately harm sb in response or revenge for a harm he or she has done [Early 17thC. From Latin *retaliare* 'to pay back in kind', from *talio* 'punishment in kind'.] —**retaliative** /ri tálli ətiv/ *adj.* —**retaliatory** /-ətəri/ *adj.*

retaliation /ri tálli áysh'n/ *n.* infliction of deliberate harm on sb in response or revenge for a harm he or she has done

retard *vt.* /ri taárd/ (**-tards, -tarding, -tarded**) **SLOW STH DOWN** to slow or delay the progress of sth ■ *n.* /reé taard/ *US* **OFFENSIVE TERM** an offensive term that deliberately insults sb with a learning disability or sb regarded as unintelligent (*slang insult*) [15thC. Via French *retarder* from Latin *retardare*, from *tardus* 'slow' (source of English *tardy*).] —**retardative** /ri taárdətiv/ *adj.* —**retardatory** /-ətəri/ *adj.*

retardant /ri taárd'nt/ *n.* **SLOWING AGENT** sth designed to slow down a particular process or change, especially a chemical substance that inhibits change (*often used in combination*) ■ *adj.* **ABLE TO SLOW STH** capable of making sth move or happen more slowly ○ *flame-retardant fabric*

retardation /reé taar dáysh'n/ *n.* **1. SLOWING** the process or fact of slowing down **2.** PSYCHOL = **developmental disability** (*dated offensive*) **3. DELAY** sth that acts as a delay or obstacle to progress **4. DECELERATION** deceleration, or the rate of deceleration

retarded /ri taárdid/ *adj.* **1. UNDERDEVELOPED** not fully developed ○ *the retarded growth of the plant* **2.** PSYCHOL **MENTALLY CHALLENGED** mentally challenged (*dated offensive*)

retardment /ri taárdmənt/ *n.* = **retardation** *n.* 1

retch /rech/ *v.* (**retches, retching, retched**) **1.** *vi.* **EXPERIENCE A VOMITING SPASM** to experience a spasm of vomiting without actually bringing anything up **2.** *vti.* **VOMIT** to vomit, or vomit sth ■ *n.* **VOMITING SPASM** a spasm of vomiting without bringing anything up [Mid-16thC. Variant of obsolete *reach* 'to spit, vomit', from Old English *hrǣcan*, from prehistoric Germanic; originally an imitation of the sound.]

retd *abbr.* **1.** retained **2.** retired **3.** COMM returned

rete /reéti/ (*plural* **-tia** /reéshi ə, -ti ə/) *n.* a network of veins, arteries, or nerve fibres in the body [14thC. From Latin, 'net'. Originally in the meaning of 'astrolabe'.] —**retial** /reéshi əl/ *adj.*

retell /ree tél/ (**-tells, -telling, -told** /-tṓld/, **-told**) *vt.* to tell sth such as a story or joke again, especially in a different form or to sb who has not heard it

retelling /ree télling/ *n.* a repeating of an account or story that has been told before ○ *a modern retelling of an ancient fable*

retene /reé teen, ré-/ *n.* a yellow crystalline hydrocarbon that occurs in pine tar and in some fossil resins. Formula: $C_{18}H_{18}$. [Mid-19thC. Coined from Greek *rhētinē* 'resin' + -ENE.]

retention /ri ténsh'n/ *n.* **1. HOLDING IN OF STH** the act of retaining sth or the condition of being retained **2. MEMORY** the ability to remember things **3.** PHYSIOL **ABNORMAL HOLDING OF WASTE** the abnormal holding in the body of waste that is normally excreted **4.** FIN **AMOUNT OF MONEY HELD BACK** an amount of money that is part of a sum agreed to be paid to sb but which is not paid until a condition has been satisfied ○ *a mortgage of £80,000 with a retention of £10,000 pending major repairs* [14thC. Directly or via French from the Latin stem *retention-*, ultimately from *retinere* (see RETAIN).]

retentive /ri téntiv/ *adj.* **1. ABLE TO RETAIN STH** able to or tending to hold sth ○ *a soil that is highly retentive of rainwater* **2. WITH GOOD MEMORY** able to remember a great deal of information [14thC. Via Old French *retentif* or medieval Latin *retentivus* from Latin *retent-*, the past participle stem of *retinere* (see RETAIN).] —**retentively** *adv.* —**retentiveness** *n.*

retentivity /reé ten tívvəti/ *n.* **1. POWER TO RETAIN** the power or condition of retaining sth **2.** PHYS **MAGNETIZATION CAPACITY** the capacity of a material to remain magnetized after the force that magnetized it has been taken away

rethink /ree thíngk/ *vti.* (**-thinks, -thinking, -thought** /-tháwrt/, **-thought**) **RECONSIDER STH** to think about sth again, especially using new information or in order to produce a better result ■ *n.* **RECONSIDERATION** an attempt to rethink sth, or an occasion on which sth is rethought ○ *Let's have a rethink before we proceed.*

retia plural of **rete**

retiarius /reéti áiri əss, reéshi-/ (*plural* **-ii** /-áiri ī/) *n.* an ancient Roman gladiator who fought using a net and a trident [Mid-17thC. From Latin, from *rete* 'net'.]

reticence /réttiss'nss/ *n.* the tendency not to communicate very much or not reveal everything [Early 17thC. From Latin *reticentia*, from *reticere* 'to keep silent', from *tacere* 'to be silent' (source of English *taciturn*).]

reticent /réttis'nt/ *adj.* unwilling to communicate very much, talk a lot, or reveal all the facts ○ *rather reticent on the subject of her finances* —**reticently** *adv.*

WORD KEY: USAGE

Extended senses: In its traditional sense, ***reticent*** means a reluctance to speak. Thus it is more nearly a synonym for *silent* than it is for *reluctant*: *He was never reticent about wanting the job.* It is, however, increasingly seen in contexts in which it conveys other kinds of reluctance: *He was reticent to travel so much.* Many regard this as a misuse, and in fact such usages tend to convey nothing that *reluctant* would not convey better.

WORD KEY: SYNONYMS

See Synonyms at ***silent***.

reticle /réttik'l/ *n.* a grid of fine lines in the focus of an optical instrument, used for determining the scale or position of what is being looked at [Mid-17thC. From Latin *reticulum* (see RETICULUM).]

reticula plural of **reticulum**

reticular /ri tíkyŏŏlər/ *adj.* relating to, involving, or structurally resembling a net or network [Late 16thC. From modern Latin *reticularis*, from Latin *reticulum* (see RETICULUM).]

reticular formation *n.* a formation of neurons in the brainstem that regulates many body functions, including respiration, blood pressure, sleeping and waking, and transmission of stimuli

reticulate *adj.* /ri tíkyŏŏ lət, -layt/ = **reticular** *adj.* ■ *vti.* /ri tíkyŏŏ layt/ (**-lates, -lating, -lated**) **HAVE A NETWORK STRUCTURE** to form a network, or be formed into a network [Mid-17thC. From Latin *reticulatus*, from *reticulum* (see RETICULUM).] —**reticulately** /ri tíkyŏŏlətli/ *adv.* —**reticulation** /ri tíkyŏŏ láysh'n/ *n.*

reticule /rétti kyool/ *n.* **1.** ACCESSORIES **WOMAN'S HANDBAG** a small handbag made of netting or lightweight fabric, usually closed with a drawstring, carried by women in the late 18th and early 19th centuries (*archaic*) **2.** OPTICS = **reticle** [Early 18thC. Via French *réticule* from Latin *reticulum* (see RETICULUM).]

reticulocyte /ri tíkyŏŏlə sīt/ *n.* an immature red blood cell containing a network of fibres of ribosomal remains that show up with laboratory staining [Early 20thC. Coined from RETICULUM + -CYTE.] —**reticulocytic** /ri tíkyŏŏlə síttik/ *adj.*

reticulum /ri tíkyŏŏləm/ (*plural* **-la** /-y-lə/) *n.* **1. NETWORK** a network or sth resembling a network in structure **2.** ANAT **SECOND STOMACH** the second stomach or stomach compartment in cows, sheep, and other ruminants [Mid-17thC. From Latin *reticulum*, literally 'little net', from *rete* 'net'.]

Reticulum /ri tíkyŏŏləm/ *n.* a small constellation of the southern hemisphere lying between Dorado and Horologium near to the Large Magellanic Cloud

retin- *prefix.* = **retino-** (*used before vowels*)

retina /réttinə/ (*plural* **-nas** *or* **-nae** /-nee/) *n.* a light-sensitive membrane in the back of the eye containing rods and cones that receive an image from the lens and send it to the brain through the optic nerve [14thC. From medieval Latin, formed from Latin *rete* 'net', from the network of blood-vessels.] —**retinal** *adj.*

retinaculum /rétti nákyŏŏləm/ (*plural* **-la** /-lə/) *n.* an anatomical structure of insects that holds small body parts together like a hook or clasp [Mid-18thC. From Latin, 'band', literally 'little thing that holds back', from *retinire* (see RETAIN).] —**retinacular** *adj.*

retinae plural of **retina**

retinene /rétti neen/, **retinal** /réttin'l/ *n.* an aldehyde derived from vitamin A that combines with proteins to form visual pigments in the eye. Formula: $C_{20}H_{28}O$.

retinite /rétti nīt/ *n.* a fossil resin, especially one in which the plant matter has not formed a hard coal [Early 19thC. From French, formed from Greek *rhētinē* 'resin'.]

retinitis /rétti nītiss/ *n.* inflammation of the retina

retinitis pigmentosa /-pígmən tṓzə/ *n.* an inherited disorder of the eye involving progressive disintegration of the retina and optic nerve and leading eventually to tunnel vision or inability to see [*Pigmentosa* from modern Latin, 'pigmented']

retino- *prefix.* retina ○ *retinoblastoma* [From RETINA]

retinoblastoma /réttinō bla stṓmə/ (*plural* **-mata** /-mətə/ *or* **-mas**) *n.* a malignant tumour of the eye, usually resulting from a genetic disorder and appearing in early childhood

retinol /rétti nol/ *n.* **1.** = **vitamin A 2.** = **rosin oil** [Mid-20thC. Formed from RETINA.]

retinopathy /rétti nóppəthi/ (*plural* **-thies**) *n.* a disease of the retina, especially one that is noninflammatory and usually associated with damage to the blood vessels of the retina ○ *diabetic retinopathy* —**retinopathic** /réttinō páthik/ *adj.*

retinoscope /réttinə skōp/ *n.* an instrument for identifying refractive errors in the eye by measuring the angle of a beam of light reflected from the retina and back out through the pupil

retinoscopy /rétti nóskəpi/ (*plural* **-pies**) *n.* a method of measuring refractive errors in the eye using a retinoscope —**retinoscopic** /réttinə skóppik/ *adj.* —**retinoscopically** *adv.* —**retinoscopist** /réttin óskəpist/ *n.*

retinue /rétti nyoo/ *n.* a body of people who travel with and attend an important person [14thC. From Old French, literally 'retained (in service)', from the past participle of *retenir* 'to retain', from Latin *retinere* (see RETAIN).]

retiral /ri tírəl/ *n.* *Scotland* retirement from a job or post ○ *He's due for retiral next year.*

retire /ri tír/ (**-tires, -tiring, -tired**) *v.* **1.** *vi.* HR **STOP WORKING WILLINGLY** to leave a job or career voluntarily, at or near the usual age for doing so **2.** *vi.* **GO TO BED** to stop engaging in daily activities and go to bed **3.** *vi.* **WITHDRAW** to leave a place, position, or way of life and go to a place of less activity ○ *retire from public life* **4.** *vt.* **MAKE SB STOP WORKING** to stop a person or an animal performing some activity because of illness or an inability to continue ○ *injuries so extensive that the horse was retired* **5.** *vt.* **WITHDRAW STH FROM SERVICE** to take a machine or piece of equipment out of service **6.** *vti.* MIL **GO BACK OR MOVE TROOPS BACK** to fall back, or move troops away from a position, action, or danger **7.** *vti.* SPORTS **WITHDRAW FROM SPORTS CONTEST** to withdraw or withdraw sb from a sports contest, because of an inability to continue **8.** *vt.* FIN **WITHDRAW STH FROM CIRCULATION** to take a loan, stock, bond, or other financial instrument out of circulation by paying for it [Mid-16thC. From French *retirer* 'retreat', from *tirer* 'to draw' (source of English *tier* and *tirade*).] —**retirer** *n.*

retired /ri tírd/ *adj.* **1. NO LONGER WORKING** having given up working, typically after having worked many years ○ *a retired bus driver* **2. HAVING WITHDRAWN** having withdrawn from a busy way of life ○ *a retired lifestyle*

retiree /ri tī reé/ *n.* sb who has retired from a job or career

retirement /ri tírmənt/ *n.* **1. LEAVING OF JOB OR CAREER** the act of leaving a job or career at or near the usual age for doing so **2. TIME AFTER HAVING STOPPED WORKING** the time that follows the end of sb's working life **3. BEING AWAY FROM BUSY LIFE** a state of being withdrawn from the rest of the world or a former busy life ○ *He lives in retirement in the country.*

retirement pension *n.* a pension paid to a retired person, usually by the state

retiring /ri tíring/ *adj.* **1. SHY AND RESERVED** avoiding social contact with other people **2. UNDERGOING RETIREMENT** at, involving, or undergoing retirement from a job or

retool /ree tóol/ (-tools, -tooling, -tooled) v. 1. vti. REFIT EQUIPMENT to replace the tools or machinery in a factory, or to obtain new tools or machinery 2. vt. US REORGANIZE STH to reorganize sth in order to make it more efficient or powerful ○ *The company will have to retool if it's to remain competitive.*

retorsion /ri táwrsh'n/ n. an act of retaliation by a government against citizens of another country for a similar offence committed by the other country [Mid-17thC. Via French *rétorsion* from, ultimately, Latin *retort-*, the past participle stem of *retorquere* (see RETORT[1]).]

retort[1] /ri táwrt/ vt. (-torts, -torting, -torted) 1. RESPOND SHARPLY to say sth sharp, angry, witty, or insulting in quick response to sth sb else has said 2. ARGUE STH IN REPLY to put forward sth as an argument in reply to sb else's argument ■ n. SHARP ANSWER sth sharp, angry, witty, or insulting said quickly in response to sth sb else has said [15thC. From Latin *retort-*, the past participle stem of *retorquere*, literally 'to twist again', from *torquere* (see TORQUE).] —**retorter** n.

WORD KEY: SYNONYMS
See Synonyms at **answer**.

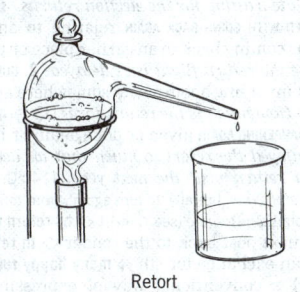

Retort

retort[2] /ri táwrt/ n. 1. GLASS VESSEL a glass vessel with a long downwards-pointing tapering spout, used for distilling by heat 2. CLOSED CONTAINER FOR HEATING SUBSTANCES a closed container in which large quantities of a substance are heated to extract sth, e.g. metal from ore ■ vt. (-torts, -torting, -torted) HEAT STH IN RETORT to heat or distil sth in a retort [Early 17thC. Via French *retorte* from medieval Latin *retorta*, from Latin *retorquere* 'to twist back' (see RETORT[1]), from the shape of the neck.]

retortion n. 1. ACT OF RETORTING an act or the process of saying sth as a retort to sb else 2. INTERNAT REL = **retorsion**

retouch vt. /ree túch/ (-touches, -touching, -touched) 1. IMPROVE STH to make small finishing, correcting, or improving changes to sth 2. PHOTOGRAPHY ALTER PHOTOGRAPH to alter a photographic negative or print by removing imperfections or adding details ■ n. /ree túch/ 1. ACTIVITY OF RETOUCHING the process of retouching sth, or the occasion on which sth is retouched 2. PHOTOGRAPHY STH ALTERED sth that has been retouched, especially a photograph 3. IMPROVING CHANGE a small, finishing, correcting, or improving change to sth — **retoucher** n.

retrace /ri tráyss/ (-traces, -tracing, -traced) vt. 1. FOLLOW ROUTE AGAIN to go back over a path or route again 2. REVIEW STH to review sth in the mind, e.g. an argument, account, or series of events ○ *retraced the events leading up to the war* —**retraceable** adj.

retract /ri trákt/ (-tracts, -tracting, -tracted) v. 1. vti. MOVE, OR MOVE STH, BACK INSIDE to draw sth in from an extended position, or be able to be drawn in ○ *Cats can retract their claws but dogs can't.* 2. vti. WITHDRAW STATEMENT to withdraw or deny sth previously said, published, or promised ○ *She has since retracted her earlier statement.* 3. vi. MOVE BACK to move back from sth 4. vt. PHON CHANGE VOWEL SOUND to alter a vowel sound by drawing the tongue inwards from the lips [15thC. From Latin *retract-*, the past participle stem of *retrahere* 'to draw back', from *trahere* 'to pull' (see TRACTOR).] —**retractability** /ri tráktə bílləti/ n. —**retractable** /ri tráktəb'l/ adj. —**retractation** /ree trak táysh'n/ n.

retractile /ri trák tīl/ adj. capable of being retracted — **retractility** /ree trak tílləti/ n.

retraction /ri tráksh'n/ n. 1. ACT OF RETRACTING the act of retracting sth or the condition of being retracted 2. RETRACTING STATEMENT a statement, sometimes formal, that withdraws or denies a previous statement

retractor /ri tráktər/ n. 1. SURG SURGICAL INSTRUMENT a surgical instrument used to hold back skin or tissue during surgery 2. ANAT MUSCLE THAT RETRACTS BODY PART a muscle that retracts a body part, e.g. one that closes the jaw

retrain /ree tráyn/ (-trains, -training, -trained) vti. to teach sb or learn new skills ○ *decided to retrain as a systems analyst*

retraining /ree tráyning/ n. the process or activity of learning new skills or of updating existing skills

retransmit /ree tranz mít, -transs-t, -traanz-, -traanss-/ (-mits, -mitting, -mitted) v. 1. vt. TRANSMIT STH AGAIN to transmit or broadcast sth again, or transmit sth onwards to another place 2. TRANSMIT A BROADCAST BY CABLE to transmit a television broadcast by cable — **retransmission** n.

retread vt. /ree tréd/ (-treads, -treading, -treaded) = **remould** v. 1 ■ n. /ree tred/ 1. = remould n. 2. US RETURNING WORKER sb who returns to a line of work previously given up (*informal*)

re-tread /ree tréd/ (re-treads, re-treading, re-trod /ree tród/, re-trodden /ree tród'n/) vt. to walk again on a route that has already been walked over

retreat /ri treet/ n. 1. MOVEMENT BACK a movement away from danger or a confrontation, back along the original route ○ *The bear had the hunters in full retreat.* 2. MIL TROOP WITHDRAWAL a withdrawal of military forces following a defeat or preceding a change of position 3. MIL SIGNAL TO MOVE BACK a signal, usually a bugle call or drumbeat, telling soldiers to perform a retreat 4. WITHDRAWAL FROM POSITION a withdrawal from a particular position or point of view to one intended to lessen conflict ○ *their retreat from a previously inflexible position* 5. QUIET TIME a period of quiet rest and contemplation in a secluded place 6. QUIET PLACE a quiet, secluded place where people go for rest and privacy 7. SAFE PLACE a place where people or animals go to avoid danger or capture 8. RELIG PERIOD OF SECLUSION a period away from normal activities, devoted to prayer and meditation, often spent in a religious community 9. SPECIAL HOSPITAL a place for the long-term care and treatment of people who are incapable of caring for themselves (*dated*) 10. MIL FLAG-LOWERING CEREMONY the ceremony of lowering the flag at a military institution, or the signal given to lower the flag ■ v. (-treats, -treating, -treated) 1. vi. MOVE BACK to move back away from danger or a confrontation 2. vi. MIL MAKE MILITARY WITHDRAWAL to withdraw following a defeat or prior to a change of position 3. vi. WITHDRAW FROM POSITION to withdraw from a particular position or point of view to one intended to lessen conflict 4. vi. RECEDE to recede or fall back from a previous position 5. vt. CHESS MOVE PIECE BACK to move a chesspiece back to an earlier position [13thC. From Old French *retret*, from the past participle of *retraire*, from Latin *retrahere* (see RETRACT).] ◇ **beat a (hasty) retreat** to leave, especially in a hurry

retreatant /ri treet'nt/ n. sb who takes part in a spiritual or religious retreat

retrench /ri trénch/ (-trenches, -trenching, -trenched) v. 1. vti. ECONOMIZE to reduce sth such as costs 2. vt. CUT STH OUT to cut out, cut back, or omit sth [Late 16thC. From French *retrancher* 'to recut', from *trenchier* 'to cut' (source of English *trench*).]

retrenchment /ri trénchmənt/ n. the cutting back of expenses

retrial /ree trī əl, ree trī əl/ n. a second trial in a court of law that replaces a prior one that was flawed or ended in a hung jury

retribution /réttri byoósh'n/ n. sth done or given to sb as punishment or vengeance for sth he or she has done ○ *a just retribution for their crime* [14thC. From the Latin stem *retribution-*, ultimately from *retribuere* 'to hand back, repay', from *tribuere* 'to allot' (source of English *tribute*).] —**retributive** /ri tríbbyōōtiv/ adj. —**retributively** adv. —**retributory** adj.

retrieval /ri treev'l/ n. 1. RECOVERY OF STH the act of getting sth back, or a particular occasion on which this is done 2. POSSIBILITY OF BEING RESTORED the possibility of sth being brought back, saved, or restored to an original condition ○ *Their business seemed beyond retrieval.* 3. COMPUT DATA ACCESS the process of reading data from a storage device and returning it to the program or device that requested it

retrieve /ri treev/ v. (-trieves, -trieving, -trieved) 1. vt. GET STH BACK to get sth back 2. vt. SAVE STH to save sth from being lost, damaged, or destroyed 3. vt. REMEDY STH to set sth right or make it better ○ *attempt to retrieve the situation before it worsens* 4. vt. RESTORE STH to restore or restore sth to its original condition ○ *She quickly retrieved her sense of humour.* 5. vt. REMEMBER STH to recall sth from memory 6. vt. COMPUT GET DATA to read data from a storage device and return it to the program or device that requested it 7. vti. RACKET GAMES RETURN SHOT to return a difficult shot in a game such as tennis or badminton 8. vti. HUNT FETCH GAME to fetch small game that has been shot by a hunter ■ n. RETRIEVING OF STH the act of retrieving sth ○ *a successful retrieve* [15thC. From Old French *retroev-*, the stem of *retrover* 'to find again', from *trover* 'to find'.] —**retrievability** /ri treevə bílləti/ n. —**retrievable** /ri treevəb'l/ adj. —**retrievably** adv.

Retriever

retriever /ri treevər/ n. 1. ZOOL LARGE DOG THAT RETRIEVES GAME a large strong-bodied dog originally bred to retrieve game for a hunter 2. SB OR STH THAT RETRIEVES any person who or thing that retrieves sth

retro adj. MODELLED ON STH FROM PAST modelled on sth from the past, e.g. a style of fashion or music ○ *retro clothing* ■ n. (plural -ros) 1. USE OF PAST STYLES the practice of modelling things such as clothes or music on styles from the past, or an example of such a practice ○ *The band is heavily into sixties retro.* 2. AEROSP = **retrorocket** [Late 20thC. From French *rétro*, a shortening of *rétrograde* 'retrograde', from Latin *retrogradus* (see RETROGRADE); influenced by RETRO-.]

retro- prefix. 1. back, backward, after ○ *retrorocket* ○ *retrofit* 2. behind ○ *retrochoir* [From Latin *retro*]

retroact /réttrō ákt/ (-acts, -acting, -acted) vi. 1. BE IN OPPOSITION to act in a way that opposes sth else 2. APPLY TO PAST to apply to things that have happened in the past

retroaction /réttrō áksh'n/ n. 1. APPLICABILITY TO THE PAST the applicability of sth to past circumstances or events 2. ACTION REACTING TO PAST SITUATION an action that responds or reacts to sth in the past 3. COUNTEREFFECT an action that goes against or balances a previous action

retroactive /réttrō áktiv/ adj. relating or applying to things that have happened in the past as well as the present ○ *a pay increase retroactive to the beginning of the year*

retroactive inhibition n. the tendency of recently gained knowledge or skills to degenerate when new learning in a similar area is acquired

retrocede /réttrō seéd/ (-cedes, -ceding, -ceded) v. 1. vi. GO BACK to go back or return 2. vt. GIVE STH BACK to give back sth such as land or a territory [Mid-17thC. From French *rétrocéder*, from *céder* (see CEDE).] — **retrocedent** adj. —**retrocession** /-sésh'n/ n. —**retrocessive** /-séssiv/ adj.

retrochoir /réttrō kwīr/ n. the area behind the high altar in a large church or cathedral [Mid-19thC. From medieval Latin *retrochorus*, literally 'back choir', from *chorus* (see CHOIR).]

re-trod past tense of **re-tread**

re-trodden past participle of **re-tread**

retro-engine *n.* = **retrorocket**

retrofire /réttrō fīr/ *vt.* (**-fires, -firing, -fired**) IGNITE RETROROCKET to fire a retrorocket to decelerate ■ *n.* IGNITION OF RETROROCKET the process of firing a retrorocket, or an occasion of doing this

retrofit /réttrō fit/ *vt.* (**-fits, -fitting, -fitted**) **1.** MODIFY STH WITH NEW PARTS to modify sth such as a machine or a building by adding parts or devices of types not originally included ○ *older cars retrofitted with catalytic converters* **2.** INSTALL NEW PARTS to install new parts or devices of types not originally included in existing equipment, machinery, or buildings ○ *retrofit a microchip in the alarm system* ■ *n.* **1.** NEW PART OR STH WITH ONE sth that has been equipped with a newly developed component, or such a component designed for sth that is already in use **2.** PROCESS OF ADDING NEW PART the process or an instance of modifying sth such as a machine or a building by adding new parts or devices

retroflection *n.* = **retroflexion**

retroflex /réttrō fleks/, **retroflexed** /-flekst/ *adj.* **1.** BENT BACKWARDS bent or curved backwards **2.** PHON WITH TIP OF TONGUE BENT BACKWARDS used to describe speech sounds that are pronounced with the tip of the tongue raised and bent backwards [Late 18thC. From Latin *retroflex-*, the past participle stem of *retroflectere* 'to bend back', from *flectere* 'to bend'.]

retroflexion /réttrō fléksh'n/, **retroflection** *n.* **1.** BENT CONDITION the condition of bending or being bent backwards **2.** PHON PRONUNCIATION WITH TONGUE BENT BACK the pronunciation of a letter or sound with the tongue raised and bent backwards **3.** PSYCHOL INABILITY TO EXTERNALIZE DIFFICULT EMOTION in Gestalt therapy, the act of directing a difficult emotion such as anger at yourself rather than at sb who has provoked the emotion [Early 19th C. Coined from RETRO- on the model of REFLECTION.]

retrograde /réttrō grayd/ *adj.* **1.** MOVING BACKWARDS moving backwards in space or time **2.** INVERSE in writing, inverse or reversed, especially in syntactic order **3.** GETTING WORSE worsening or returning to an earlier worse condition **4.** ASTRON HAVING A CONTRARY ORBIT orbiting in a direction opposite to that of the Earth's orbit around the Sun or of the Moon's orbit around the Earth **5.** ASTRON MOVING EAST TO WEST moving or appearing to move from east to west in the sky, counter to the direction of most astronomical bodies **6.** MUSIC REVERSING NOTES reversing the sequence of notes of an earlier version of a musical composition ■ *vi.* (**-grades, -grading, -graded**) **1.** GO BACKWARDS to go back or appear to be moving backwards in space or time **2.** = **retrogress** *v.* 1 [14thC. From Latin *retrogradus* 'going backwards', from *gradus* 'step'.] —**retrogradation** /réttrō gray dáysh'n/ *n.* —**retrogradely** /réttrō graydli/ *adv.*

retrogress /réttrō gréss/ (**-gresses, -gressing, -gressed**) *vi.* **1.** REVERT OR DEGENERATE to return to an earlier and usually worse condition **2.** GO BACKWARDS to move or travel backwards **3.** BIOL HAVE LESS COMPLEX FEATURES to show or develop the less complex features of simpler organisms [Early 19thC. Formed from RETRO- on the model of PROGRESS.] —**retrogressive** *adj.* —**retrogressively** *adv.*

retrogression /réttrō grésh'n/ *n.* **1.** RETURN TO WORSE CONDITION the process of returning to an earlier and usually worse condition **2.** BIOL DEVELOPMENT OF LESS COMPLEX FEATURES the development of less complex features usually associated with simpler organisms

retrolental /réttrō lént'l/ *adj.* located behind the lens of the eye, or the lens of an optical instrument [Mid-20thC. Coined from RETRO- + modern Latin *lent-*, the stem of *lens* (see LENS).]

retronym /réttrō nim/ *n. US* a term that distinguishes a subclass from members of a superclass, e.g. 'snail mail' is a retronym coined by those for whom 'mail' is likely to mean 'e-mail' [Combination of RETRO- + SYNONYM]

retropack /réttrō pak/ *n.* an array of retrorockets on a spacecraft, used for slowing down or for changing direction

retropulsion /réttrō púlsh'n/ *n.* a tendency to walk backwards involuntarily, associated with Parkinson's disease [Late 18thC. Blend of RETRO- and PROPULSION.]

retrorocket /réttrō rokit/ *n.* a small rocket engine on a spacecraft or missile that produces thrust to act against the main engines and is used for decelerating

retrorse /ri tráwrss/ *adj.* used to describe plant parts that are turned back or down [Early 19thC. From Latin *retrorsus*, a contraction of *retroversus* 'turning backwards', from *versus* 'turning'.] —**retrorsely** *adv.*

retrospect /réttrō spekt/ *n.* the remembering of past events [Early 17thC. Formed from RETRO- on the model of PROSPECT.] ◇ **in retrospect** thinking about or reviewing the past, especially from a new perspective or with new information

retrospection /réttrō spéksh'n/ *n.* the act of looking back over things in the past, especially personal memories

retrospective /réttrō spéktiv/ *adj.* **1.** LOOKING TO THE PAST looking back over things in the past **2.** ARTS CONTAINING PAST WORKS containing examples of work from many periods of an artist's life ○ *a retrospective exhibition* **3.** APPLYING TO PAST EVENTS applying to things that have happened in the past as well as the present ○ *a retrospective ruling* ■ *n.* ARTS EXHIBITION OF ARTIST'S PAST WORK an exhibition of the work of a particular artist or artistic movement, showing examples from all periods or styles ○ *a Degas retrospective* —**retrospectively** *adv.*

retroussé /rə troo say/ *adj.* turned up at the end ○ *a retroussé nose* [Early 19thC. From French, literally 'turned up'.]

retroversion /réttrō vúrsh'n/ *n.* **1.** TURNING BACKWARDS the act or condition of being turned backwards **2.** MED BACKWARDS TILT OF BODY PART the abnormal turning or tilting backwards of a body part, e.g. the uterus, but without folding [Late 16thC. Formed from Latin *retroversus* (see RETRORSE).] —**retroverse** *adj.* —**retroverted** *adj.*

retrovirus /réttrō vīrəss/ *n.* a type of virus whose genetic information is contained in RNA rather than DNA. Some retroviruses cause Aids and cancer and they contain the enzyme reverse transcriptase for generating DNA from RNA. —**retroviral** /réttrō vīrəl/ *adj.*

retry *v.* /ree trī/ (**-tries, -trying, -tried**) **1.** *vt.* LAW TRY SB AGAIN to try a person or case again in a court of law **2.** *vti.* ATTEMPT STH AGAIN to try to do sth again ■ *n.* /rée trī/ (*plural* **-tries**) SECOND ATTEMPT another attempt to do sth

retsina /ret séenə/ *n.* a Greek wine flavoured with pine resin [Early 20thC. Via modern Greek from, ultimately, Greek *rhētinē* 'pine resin'.]

return /ri túrn/ *v.* (**-turns, -turning, -turned**) **1.** *vi.* COME OR GO BACK to come or go back to a place after leaving it or to a former condition **2.** *vi.* GO BACK to go back to sth that has already been mentioned or considered, especially in order to deal with it more thoroughly or conclusively ○ *Let's return to the matter in hand.* **3.** *vi.* APPEAR AGAIN to appear or happen again **4.** *vt.* REPLY TO SB to answer or reply to sth sb has said ○ *'Do it yourself!' she returned.* **5.** *vt.* PUT STH BACK to put, bring, send, or take sth back to where it came from **6.** *vt.* REPAY STH to give back sth of equivalent value ○ *I hope that one day I'll be able to return your kindness.* **7.** *vt.* YIELD PROFIT to yield sth as a profit on an investment ○ *returns 6% per annum* **8.** *vt.* RE-ELECT SB TO OFFICE to re-elect sb to an office or position ○ *returned her to Parliament for a second term* **9.** *vt.* REFLECT STH to send back or reflect sth such as an echo ○ *The cliff wall returned the sound of their laughter.* **10.** *vt.* LAW PRODUCE VERDICT to give a particular verdict in a court of law ○ *return a guilty verdict* **11.** *vt.* SUBMIT OFFICIAL REPORT to give an official report, usually in response to a request or legal requirement **12.** *vt.* COMPUT GIVE RESPONSE to give a particular response to a command, routine, or subroutine ○ *returns zero if the condition is false* **13.** *vt.* ARCHIT BUILD STH TO FACE OPPOSITE DIRECTION to construct part of a building, e.g. a wall or decoration, so that it turns away from its original direction **14.** *vti.* SPORTS HIT BALL BACK to hit a ball, especially a service, back to an opponent in various games **15.** *vt.* CARDS LEAD SAME SUIT to lead the same suit as a partner in various card games, including bridge and whist ■ *n.* **1.** GOING OR COMING BACK a going or coming back to a place after having left it or to a former condition **2.** REPLACEMENT a putting, taking, sending, or bringing back of sth to where it came from **3.** STH GIVEN BACK sth that has come or been brought back, especially unsold merchandise ○ *Returns go in that bin over there* **4.** REAPPEARANCE a reappearance or recurrence of sth **5.** RECIPROCATION a response to sth done or given ○ *If you are kind to your puppy it will give you love in return* **6.** ANSWER sth said in response to sth else ○ *If you ask her an absurd question you can expect an angry return* **7.** FIN PROFIT a profit made on an investment or business venture (*often used in the plural*) **8.** TRANSP = **return ticket 9.** FIN TAX RETURN a tax return **10.** FINANCIAL REPORT a periodic financial report of an organization **11. return, return key** COMPUT = **enter key 12.** ARCHIT ANGLED PART part of a building, e.g. a wall or decoration, built so that it turns away from its original direction **13.** SPORTS BALL PLAYED BACK an instance of hitting or playing the ball back to an opponent in various games **14.** LAW LEGAL REPORT a report on a legal document previously issued, e.g. a subpoena or writ, by an officer of that court of law **15.** CARDS LEAD OF SAME SUIT an instance of leading the same suit as a partner in various card games **16.** *Northern Ireland* ARCHIT BUILDING EXTENSION a rearward extension to a building ■ **returns** *npl.* ELECTION RESULTS the results from an election or election district ○ *We sat up late waiting for the election returns.* ■ *adj.* **1.** CONNECTED WITH GOING BACK AGAIN relating to an act of going or coming back to an earlier place or position ○ *I hope the return flight isn't delayed.* **2.** GOING THERE AND BACK involving a journey to somewhere and back again ○ *How much is the return fare?* US term **round-trip 3.** HAPPENING AGAIN given or done again or in order ○ *We enjoyed the resort so much that we decided to make a return visit the next year.* [14thC. Via Old French *reto(u)rner*, literally 'to turn again', from *to(u)rner* 'to turn', from Latin *tornare* (see TURN).] ◇ **by return (of post)** by the next post back to the sender ◇ **in return (for sth)** as an exchange for sth ◇ **many happy returns (of the day)** a conventional way of expressing good wishes to sb whose birthday it is, often as an exclamation

returnable /ri túrnəb'l/ *adj.* **1.** ABLE TO BE RETURNED capable of being returned ○ *a returnable deposit* **2.** REQUIRING RESPONSE requiring a response to a formal document, usually within a particular period of time, as do e.g., some court writs

Returned Services League *n.* full form of **RSL**

returnee /ri túr née/ *n.* sb who comes back, especially from military service or some other long absence

returning officer *n.* an official who is responsible in a constituency for overseeing the count and announcing the result in an election

return key = **return** *n.* 11

return ticket *n.* a ticket that entitles a passenger to travel both to and back from a particular destination. US term **round-trip ticket**

retuse /ri tyóoss/ *adj.* used to describe leaves that have a blunt notched apex [Mid-18thC. From Latin *retusus*, past participle of *retundere* 'to beat back', from *tundere* 'to beat'.]

Reuben /róobin/ *n.* in the Bible, a Hebrew patriarch and the eldest son of Jacob and Leah. He was the ancestor of one of the tribes of Israel.

reunify /ree yóoni fī/ (**-fies, -fying, -fied**) *vti.* to come together or bring people or factions together again, after they have been divided —**reunification** /ree yóonifi káysh'n/ *n.*

reunion /ree yóonyən/ *n.* **1.** GATHERING a gathering of old friends, relatives, or people who were colleagues at one time ○ *a high-school class reunion* **2.** A COMING TOGETHER AGAIN the coming together again of things or people that have been divided, or the condition of having come together in this way

reunionist /ree yóonyənist/ *n.* a supporter of reunion between divided groups or parties, especially sb who seeks reunion between the Anglican and Roman Catholic churches —**reunionism** *n.* —**reunionistic** /-nístik/ *adj.*

reunite /rée yoo nīt/ (**-nites, -niting, -nited**) *vti.* to bring people together, or come together, after a separation

reupholster /reè up hṓlstər/ (**-sters, -stering, -stered**) *vt.* to replace the worn or damaged upholstery on a chair or sofa

reuse *vt.* /ree yoóz/ (**-uses, -using, -used**) USE STH AGAIN to use sth again, often for a different purpose and usually as an alternative to throwing it away ■ *n.* /ree yoóss/ USE OF STH AGAIN the using of sth again, often for a different purpose and usually as an alternative to throwing it away —**reusability** /-bíllәti/ *n.* —**reusable** /ree yoózәb'l/ *adj.*

Reuter /róytər/, **Paul Julius, Baron von** (1816–99) German-born British journalist. In 1851 he established the pioneer Reuters Telegrams, now Reuters, the first news agency in the world. Real name **Isreal Beer Josaphat**

Reuters /róytərz/ *n.* a London news agency providing international news reports [Mid-19thC. Named after Paul Julius, Baron von REUTER.]

rev /rev/ *vti.* (**revs, revving, revved**) MAKE VEHICLE ENGINE GO FASTER to increase a vehicle's engine speed by pressing down on the accelerator or advancing the throttle, especially while the vehicle is stationary ■ *n.* ENGINE REVOLUTION a single revolution of a vehicle's engine (*informal*) (*usually plural*) [Early 20thC. Shortening of 'revolutions per minute'.]

rev up *vt.* (*informal*) **1.** INTENSIFY STH to increase the tempo, intensity, or amount of sth ○ *We'd better rev up production if we're to meet our deadline.* **2.** IMPASSION SB to stir up intense feelings in sb, usually feelings of excitement, desire, or anger

rev. *abbr.* **1.** revenue **2.** reverse **3.** MIL review **4.** PUBL revised **5.** EDUC revision **6.** revolution **7.** ARMS revolver **8.** revolving

Rev. /rev/ *abbr.* Reverend

revalue /reè vállyoo/ (**-ues, -uing, -ued**), **revaluate** /reè vállyoo ayt/ (**-ates, -ating, -ated**) *vt.* **1.** FIN RAISE VALUE OF CURRENCY to increase the value of a nation's currency. ◊ **re-evaluate 2.** COMM REASSESS THE PRESENT VALUE to assign a new value to sth such as assets

revamp *vt.* /ree vámp/ (**-vamps, -vamping, -vamped**) ALTER STH FOR THE BETTER to alter sth in order to improve the way it looks or works ■ *n.* /reè̇vamp/ ALTERATION FOR THE BETTER a change made in sth in order to improve its appearance or functioning [The word meant originally 'to furnish a shoe with a new vamp']

WORD KEY: SYNONYMS

See Synonyms at ***renew***.

revanche /ri vánch/ *n.* a nation's or an ethnic group's policy of regaining lost territory [Mid-19thC. Via French from Old French *revancher* 'to revenge', from *vengier* (see REVENGE).] —**revanchism** *n.* —**revanchist** *adj., n.* —**revanchistic** /ri ván chístik/ *adj.*

rev counter *n.* a tachometer (*informal*)

Revd *abbr.* Reverend

reveal[1] /ri veél/ (**-veals, -vealing, -vealed**) *vt.* **1.** MAKE STH KNOWN to disclose sth that was unknown or secret **2.** EXPOSE STH to make sth visible that had been hidden or covered **3.** RELIG MAKE KNOWN DIVINE TRUTH to make sth known by divine or supernatural means [14thC. Via French *révéler* from Latin *revelare*, literally 'to unveil', from *velum* (see VEIL).] —**revealer** *n.*

reveal[2] /ri veél/ *n.* the vertical section of wall that lies between a doorframe or window frame and the outer wall [Late 17thC. Alteration of earlier *revale* 'to lower', from Old French *revaler*, from *val* 'valley' (see VALE).]

revealed religion *n.* a religion based on what its adherents believe to be the word of a supreme deity

revealing /ri veéling/ *adj.* **1.** SHOWING BODY exposing part of the body that would normally be kept covered **2.** DISCLOSING INFORMATION giving away new, surprising, or valuable information —**revealingly** *adv.*

revegetate /ree véjji tayt/ (**-tates, -tating, -tated**) *vti.* to provide eroded or otherwise barren land with new plant life —**revegetation** /-táysh'n/ *n.*

reveille /ri válli/ (*plural* **-les**) *n.* **1.** WAKE-UP CALL the sounding of a bugle to awaken and summon military personnel in a camp **2.** TIME OF REVEILLE the time of day at which reveille is sounded **3.** EARLY-MORNING MILITARY FORMATION the military formation that begins the day **4.** SIGNAL TO AWAKE any signal that it is time to get out of bed [Mid-17thC. Alteration of French *réveillez* 'wake up!', from Old French *resveiller* 'to awaken', from *esveiller*, via assumed Vulgar Latin *exvigilare* from, ultimately, Latin *vigil* (see VIGIL).]

revel /révv'l/ *vi.* (**-els, -elling, -elled**) **1.** ENJOY to take great pleasure in sth **2.** BE AT A PARTY to have an enjoyable time in the company of others, especially at a party ■ *n.* NOISY CELEBRATION an uproarious party or celebration (*often used in the plural*) [14thC. Via Old French *reveler* 'to rebel, carouse' from Latin *rebellare* (see REBEL).] —**reveller** *n.*

revelation /révvə láysh'n/ *n.* **1.** INFORMATION REVEALED information that is newly disclosed, especially surprising or valuable information **2.** SURPRISING THING a surprisingly good or valuable experience **3.** DISCLOSURE the revealing of sth previously hidden or secret **4.** CHR DEMONSTRATION OF DIVINE WILL a showing or revealing of divine will or truth [14thC. Via French from, ultimately, Latin *revelare* (see REVEAL).] —**revelational** *adj.*

Revelation, Revelations *n.* a book of the Bible that includes a description of the end of the world

revelator /révvə laytər/ *n.* sb or sth believed to reveal divine will or truth [15thC. From late Latin, formed from Latin *revelare* (see REVEAL).]

revelatory /révvə láytəri/ *adj.* disclosing sth not previously known

reveller /révv'lər/ *n.* sb enjoying a noisy party or celebration

revelry /révvəlri/ (*plural* **-ries**) *n.* lively enjoyment or celebration, usually involving eating, drinking, dancing, and noise (*often used in the plural*)

revenant /révvənənt/ *n.* a dead person believed to have come back as a ghost (*literary*) [Early 19thC. From French, the present participle of *revenir* (see REVENUE).]

revenge /ri vénj/ *n.* **1.** RETALIATORY PUNISHMENT the punishing of sb in retaliation for harm done **2.** STH DONE IN REVENGE sth done to get even with sb else who has caused harm **3.** DESIRE FOR REVENGE the desire or urge to get even with sb ■ *vt.* (**-venges, -venging, -venged**) **1.** PUNISH SB FOR HARM DONE to punish sb in retaliation for harm or injury done **2.** SECURE REVENGE FOR SB to avenge yourself or sb else who has been harmed [14thC. From Old French *revengier*, from *vengier* 'to avenge', from late Latin *vindicare* (see VINDICATE).] —**revengeful** *adj.* —**revengefully** *adv.* —**revenger** *n.*

revenue /révvə nyoo/ *n.* **1.** BUSINESS INCOME FROM BUSINESS money that comes into a business from the sale of goods or services **2.** POL GOVERNMENT INCOME the income of a government from all sources, used to pay for a nation's expenses **3.** FIN PERSONAL INCOME income or salary received from employment **4.** FIN YIELD ON INVESTMENT the total return produced by an investment **5.** TAX-COLLECTING DEPARTMENT the department of a nation's government that is responsible for collecting taxes. ◊ **Inland Revenue** [15thC. From French *revenu*, the past participle of *revenir* 'to return', from Latin *revenire*, literally 'to come back', from *venire* (see VENUE).]

revenue bond *n.* a bond issued by a US government agency in order to build or improve a public property. The income from the property pays for the bond.

revenue cutter *n.* a small lightly armed boat used to patrol coastlines, enforce customs regulations, and prevent smuggling

revenuer /révvə nyoo ər/ *n.* POL a US government agent who is in charge of stopping the illegal manufacture of alcoholic beverages (*informal*)

revenue tariff *n.* a tax or duty imposed to produce public revenue, as distinct from one imposed to protect a domestic economy

reverb *n.* /reè vurb/ **1.** ECHO IN MUSIC an echoing effect produced in live or recorded music by electronic means **2.** ECHO-PRODUCING DEVICE an electronic device used to produce an echoing effect in live or recorded music ■ *vi.* /ri vúrb/ (**-verbs, -verbing, -verbed**) PRODUCE ELECTRONIC ECHO to produce an echoing effect in live or recorded music [Early 17thC. Shortening of REVERBERATE; earliest as verb meaning 'to reverberate'.]

reverberant /ri vúrbərənt/ *adj.* making an echoing sound —**reverberantly** *adv.*

reverberate /ri vúrbə rayt/ (**-ates, -ating, -ated**) *v.* **1.** *vi.* ECHO to echo repeatedly **2.** *vi.* HAVE CONTINUING EFFECT to have a far-reaching or lasting impact, especially as a result of being circulated widely **3.** *vi.* PHYS BOUNCE BACK to be reflected repeatedly off different surfaces (*refers to heat, light, or sound waves*) **4.** *vt.* CAUSE SOUND TO ECHO to cause sound to bounce back from a surface **5.** *vt.* METALL HEAT OR REFINE METAL to treat metal in a furnace (**reverberatory furnace**) that reflects flame or heat [15thC. From Latin *reverberare*, literally 'to beat again', from *verberare* 'to beat', from *verber* 'scourge'.] —**reverberation** /ri vúrbə ráysh'n/ *n.* —**reverberative** /ri vúrbərətiv/ *adj.*

reverberation time *n.* the time it takes for a sound in a room to be reduced by 60 decibels

reverberatory /ri vúrbərətəri/ *adj.* produced or functioning by the process of deflection of sound, light, or heat

reverberatory furnace *n.* a furnace in which material is heated by heat reflected from above

revere /ri veér/ (**-veres, -vering, -vered**) *vt.* to regard sb with admiration and deep respect [Mid-17thC. Via French *révérer* from Latin *revereri*, from *vereri* 'to be in awe of'.]

reverence /révvərənss/ *n.* **1.** RESPECT FELT feelings of deep respect or devotion **2.** RESPECT GAINED the respect or devotion that others show sb or sth **3. reverence, Reverence** CHR USED TO ADDRESS CHRISTIAN CLERGY used as a form of address for some members of the Christian clergy ■ *vt.* (**-ences, -encing, -enced**) RESPECT SB OR STH DEEPLY to regard sb or sth with deep respect (*formal*)

WORD KEY: SYNONYMS

See Synonyms at ***regard***.

reverend /révvrənd/ *adj.* **1.** RESPECTED deserving to be shown respect (*formal*) **2.** CHR OF CLERGY relating or belonging to the Christian clergy ■ *n.* CHR CHRISTIAN PRIEST a member of the Christian clergy (*informal*) [15thC. Directly or via French from Latin *reverendus* 'to be revered', from *revereri* (see REVERE).]

WORD KEY: USAGE

reverend or **reverent**? Care should be taken in distinguishing between ***reverend***, which refers to a member of the clergy, and ***reverent***, which is a descriptive adjective, meaning 'showing reverence', applicable to anyone who merits it.

Reverend *n.* used as a title and form of address for some members of the clergy in many Christian churches

Reverend Mother *n.* CHR used as a title of respect to address the nun in charge of a convent

reverent /révvərənt/ *adj.* feeling or expressing profound respect or awe [14thC. From Latin *revereri* (see REVERE).] —**reverently** *adv.*

WORD KEY: USAGE

See Usage note at ***reverend***.

reverential /révvə rénsh'l/ *adj.* **1.** RESPECTFUL feeling or expressing deep respect or awe **2.** DESERVING RESPECT worthy of deep respect or awe —**reverentially** *adv.*

reverie /révvəri/ (*plural* **-ies**) *n.* a state of idle and pleasant contemplation [Early 17thC. From French, formed from *rêver* 'to dream', of unknown origin.]

revers /ri veér/ (*plural* **-vers**) *n.* a part of a garment such as a lapel, turned back so that the reverse side shows [Mid-19thC. From French, (see REVERSE).]

reversal /ri vúrss'l/ *n.* **1.** CHANGE TO OPPOSITE DIRECTION a change to an opposite direction or state **2.** PROBLEM an unfortunate experience or setback, particularly in business or financial affairs **3.** REVERSING OF STH the changing of sth to an opposite direction or state **4.** LAW CHANGE OF JUDICIAL DECISION a ruling made by a higher court that sets aside the decision of a lower court

reverse /ri vúrss/ *v.* (**-verses, -versing, -versed**) **1.** *vt.* CHANGE STH TO OPPOSITE to change sth to the opposite direction, order, or position ○ *reversing the trend of population growth* **2.** *vti.* GO BACKWARDS to go backwards, or move sth in a backwards direction ○ *reverse the car* **3.** *vt.* TURN STH INSIDE OUT to change sth so that the opposite side or part shows ○ *You can reverse the cloak and wear it with the lining on the outside.* **4.** *vt.* LAW REVOKE RULING to overturn a previous ruling made by a lower court **5.** *vt.* PRINTING PRINT STH WHITE AGAINST DARK BACKGROUND to print text or graphics in white against a dark or colour background **6.** *vt.* MIL **TURN WEAPON UPSIDE DOWN** to turn a weapon upside down, especially as a sign of mourning ■ *n.* **1. THE OPPOSITE** the contrary of sth ○ *She always does the reverse of what I tell her.* **2. BACK SIDE** the rear or back side of sth ○ *The names are written on the reverse of the photo.* **3.** MONEY **BACK SIDE OF COIN** the side of a coin, medal, or seal on which the primary design does not appear ○ *The reverse of some coins carries the national motto.* ◊ **obverse 4. CHANGE TO OPPOSITE DIRECTION** a change or turn to the opposite direction, position, or condition **5. SETBACK** a change for the worse ○ *a military reverse* **6.** MECH ENG **GEAR FOR BACKWARDS MOVEMENT** the gear in a vehicle or machine that makes it run backwards ○ *It's easier to get out of here in reverse.* **7.** AMERICAN FOOTBALL **OFFENSIVE PLAY IN AMERICAN FOOTBALL** in American football, a move in which a back receives the handoff from the quarterback and then hands the ball to another back running in the opposite direction ■ *adj.* **1. OPPOSITE TO USUAL OR PREVIOUS ARRANGEMENT** opposite to what is usual or what was previously said or arranged ○ *announce the results in reverse order* **2. ON BACK SIDE** on the other side or the back side of sth **3. FOR BACKWARDS MOVEMENT** used to make a machine or vehicle go backwards ○ *reverse gear* [14thC. Via Old French *revers* 'reversed' from Latin *reversus*, the past participle of *revertere*, literally 'to turn back', from *vertere* (see VERSE).] —**reversely** *adv.* —**reverser** *n.*

reverse-charge *adj.* TELECOM used to describe a telephone call paid for by the person receiving it. US term **collect**

reverse commuting *n.* the practice of travelling regularly between a home in a city and a job in the suburbs —**reverse commuter** *n.*

reverse discrimination *n.* *US* discrimination against a member of a social group generally regarded as dominant or privileged, e.g. in employment or admission to university

reverse engineering *n.* the pirating of a competitor's technology by dismantling an existing product and reproducing its parts and construction to manufacture a replica —**reverse-engineer** *vt.* —**reverse-engineered** *adj.*

reverse mortgage *n.* a financial instrument in the United States and Canada in which a residential mortgage is transferred to a bank, which then pays an annuity to the homeowner

reverse osmosis *n.* a process of purifying water or other liquids such as fruit juices by passing them through a semipermeable membrane that filters out unwanted substances

reverse takeover *n.* the sale of a company to another company in order to avoid takeover by an unwanted predatory company

reverse transcriptase *n.* an enzyme that assists in the formation of DNA using RNA as a template, used in genetic engineering because it reverses the natural flow of genetic information

reverse video *n.* the reversal of the usual character and background colour combination on a computer display, used as a highlighting tool

reversi /ri vúrssi/ *n.* a board game for two players, played on a draughtboard, in which captured pieces are transferred to the capturer [Early 19thC. From French, an alteration of *reversin*, via Italian *rovescina* 'reversal' from, ultimately, Latin *reversus* (see REVERSE).]

reversible /ri vúrssəb'l/ *adj.* **1. ABLE TO BE REVERSED** able to be changed or undone **2.** CLOTHES **USABLE INSIDE OUT** made so that either side can be used as the outer or upper side **3.** CHEM **UNDERGOING A REACTION AND REVERSING IT** capable of going through a stage such as a chemical reaction and then reversing the process —**reversibility** /ri vúrssə bíllәti/ *n.* —**reversibleness** /ri vúrssəb'lnəss/ *n.* —**reversibly** /-əbli/ *adv.*

reversing light *n.* either one of the white lights on the rear of a vehicle that shine when the vehicle is being reversed

reversion /ri vúrsh'n/ *n.* **1. RETURN TO FORMER CONDITION** a return to an earlier condition often perceived as less desirable or inferior **2. REVERSAL** a change to the opposite direction **3.** GENETICS **RETURN TO ORIGINAL CHARACTERISTICS** the restoration of the normal genetic constitution in a mutant organism, e.g. by means of a second mutation that cancels out the effects of an earlier one **4.** GENETICS **REVERTED ORGANISM** an organism that has reverted to ancestral genetic characteristics **5.** LAW **RETURN TO FORMER OWNER** the return of property to its former owner or his or her heirs at the end of a specified period, usually when the present owner dies **6.** LAW **PROPERTY RETURNED TO FORMER OWNER** property that has been returned to its former owner or his or her heirs **7.** LAW **RIGHT TO INHERIT PROPERTY** the right to succeed to property, granted to sb by the former owner —**reversional** *adj.* —**reversionally** *adv.* —**reversionary** *adj.*

reversioner /ri vúrsh'nər/ *n.* sb to whom ownership of property will be returned after a specified period of time

revert /ri vúrt/ (**-verts, -verting, -verted**) *vi.* **1. GO BACK TO PREVIOUS STATE** to return to a former state, often one perceived as less desirable or inferior **2. RETURN IN DISCUSSION** to return to an earlier topic in the course of a discussion **3.** GENETICS **REACQUIRE ORIGINAL FEATURES** to acquire or develop original genetic features again **4. RETURN TO OLD HABITS** to return to a former pattern of behaviour, usually sth less acceptable **5.** LAW **BE RETURNED TO OWNER** to become once again the property of the former owner or his or her heirs [14thC. Via Old French *revertir* from, ultimately, Latin *revertere*, literally 'to turn back', from *vertere* (see VERSE).] —**reverter** *n.* —**revertible** *adj.*

WORD KEY: USAGE

See Usage note at *refer.*

revertant /ri vúrt'nt/ *adj.* **HAVING REACQUIRED ORIGINAL FEATURES** used to describe an organism or part of an organism that has reacquired features that are original or simpler ■ *n.* **REVERTANT ORGANISM** a revertant organism or part

revest /ree vést/ (**-vests, -vesting, -vested**) *vt.* **1. REINSTATE SB** to reinstate sb in a position or office **2. RESTORE STH TO SB** to restore power or property to sb

revet /ri vét/ (**-vets, -vetting, -vetted**) *vti.* to give a structure additional support by adding a facing of bricks, stone, or concrete [Early 19thC. Via French *revêtir* from late Latin *revestire*, literally 'to clothe again', from *vestire* 'to clothe', from *vestis* (see VEST).]

revetment /ri vétmənt/ *n.* **1.** BUILDING **SUPPORTING FACING ON STRUCTURE** a facing added to a structure such as a wall or building that provides additional support **2.** MIL **BARRICADE** a barricade constructed to protect against damage or injury from explosives

revhead /rév hed/ *n.* *Aus* sb whose main interest is fast cars or motor racing (*informal*)

review /ri vyóo/ *v.* (**-views, -viewing, -viewed**) **1.** *vt.* **LOOK AT STH CRITICALLY** to examine sth to make sure that it is adequate, accurate, or correct ○ *They need to review their sales strategy.* **2.** *vt.* ARTS **GIVE OPINION ON QUALITY OF STH** to write a journalistic report on the quality of a new play, book, film, concert, or other public performance ○ *He reviews films for a newspaper.* **3.** *vt.* **CONSIDER STH AGAIN** to consider, study, or check sth again **4.** *vi.* *US* EDUC = **revise** *v.* 4 **5.** *vt.* **LOOK BACK ON STH** to discuss or examine sth again ○ *She's writing an article reviewing the company's history.* **6.** *vt.* LAW **RECONSIDER DECISION JUDICIALLY** to re-examine a judicial decision made in a lower court in order to consider whether it should be overturned **7.** *vt.* MIL **SUBJECT TROOPS TO MILITARY INSPECTION** to make a formal inspection of a military force ■ *n.* **1. SURVEY OF PAST** a report or survey of past actions, performance, or events ○ *a review of the stock market for the past five years* **2.** ARTS **JOURNALISTIC ARTICLE GIVING OPINION** a journalistic article giving an assessment of a book, play, film, concert, or other public performance ○ *The book got unexpectedly bad reviews.* **3.** PUBL **PUBLICATION FEATURING REVIEWS** a magazine or journal that publishes reviews ○ *the Literary Review* **4. RE-EXAMINATION OF STH** another look at or consideration of sth **5.** *US* = **revision** *n.* 4 **6.** MIL **MILITARY INSPECTION** a formal military inspection **7.** MIL **FORMAL MILITARY CEREMONY** a formal military ceremony staged to honour a person or an occasion **8.** LAW **JUDICIAL RE-EXAMINATION** a critical examination by a higher court of a decision taken by a lower court **9.** THEATRE = **revue** [15thC. From obsolete French *reveue* 'inspection', from *revoir* 'to inspect', from Latin *revidere*, literally 'to see again', from *videre* (see VISION).] —**reviewable** *adj.*

review copy *n.* a copy of a new book that a publisher sends to potential critics and reviewers to encourage published reviews

reviewer /ri vyóo ər/ *n.* sb who writes journalistic articles giving opinions on plays, books, films, concerts, and other events or works in the arts

revile /ri víl/ (**-viles, -viling, -viled**) *v.* **1.** *vt.* **ATTACK SB OR STH VERBALLY** to make a fierce or abusive verbal attack on sb or sth **2.** *vi.* **USE ABUSIVE LANGUAGE** to use insulting or abusive language [14thC. From Old French *reviler*, from *vil* (see VILE).] —**revilement** *n.* —**reviler** *n.*

revise /ri víz/ *v.* (**-vises, -vising, -vised**) **1.** *vt.* **RETHINK STH** to come to different conclusions about sb or sth after thinking again **2.** *vt.* **GIVE UPDATED VERSION OF STH** to change a previous estimate in order to make it more accurate or realistic **3.** *vt.* **ALTER STH FOR CORRECTION OR UPDATING** to amend a text in order to correct, update, or improve it **4.** *vti.* EDUC **STUDY FOR EXAM** to study for a test by looking over notes and course materials. US term **review** *v.* 4 ■ *n.* **1. STH REVISED** sth that has been revised **2.** PUBL **LATE STAGE OF PRINTED PROOF** a late stage of a printed proof that incorporates corrections to earlier proofs (*often used in the plural*) [Mid-16thC. Via French *réviser* from Latin *revisere*, literally 'to look over again', from *visere* 'to keep watching', from *videre* (see VISION).] —**revisable** *adj.* —**reviser** *n.*

Revised Standard Version *n.* a modern US revision of the American Standard Version of the Bible, published in full in 1953

Revised Version *n.* a 19th-century British revision of the Authorized Version of the Bible

revision /ri vízh'n/ *n.* **1. CHANGING OF TEXT** the amending of a text in order to correct, update, improve, or adapt it **2. CHANGING OF STH** the changing of a decision, estimate, statistic, or set of figures in order to correct it or make it more realistic **3.** PUBL **NEW EDITION** a revised and republished version of a text **4.** EDUC **STUDY FOR EXAM** study that involves looking over notes and course materials, in preparation for a test. US term **review** *n.* 5 —**revisionary** *adj.*

revisionism /ri vízh'nizəm/ *n.* **1. RECONSIDERING OF ACCEPTED TRUTHS** the reconsidering of long-established practices, views, or beliefs **2.** POL, HIST **ANTI-MARXIST SOCIALIST MOVEMENT** a socialist movement arguing against revolutionary Marxist theory and believing in the peaceful achievement of social progress through reforms —**revisionist** *adj., n.*

revisit /ree vízzit/ *vt.* (**-its, -iting, -ited**) **1. GO TO PLACE AGAIN** to visit a place again **2. RECONSIDER STH** to reconsider sth such as an issue of public policy or a course of action, especially when additional facts indicate that an earlier decision was inappropriate ■ *n.* **SUBSEQUENT VISIT** another visit to a place

revisory /ri vízəri/ *adj.* carrying out a revision, or given the authority to revise sth

revitalize /ree vítə līz/ (**-izes, -izing, -ized**), **revitalise** (**-ises, -ising, -ised**) *vt.* to give new life or energy to sb or sth —**revitalization** /ree vítə lī záysh'n/ *n.*

revival /ri vív'l/ *n.* **1. RENEWAL OF INTEREST** a renewal of interest in sth that results in its becoming popular once more **2.** THEATRE, MUSIC **NEW PRODUCTION** a new production of a play or opera that has not been performed recently **3. REVIVING OF SB** the process of bringing sb back to life, consciousness, or full strength **4. RECOVERY** the recovering of life, consciousness, or full strength **5.** RELIG **RENEWED RELIGIOUS INTEREST** a new interest in religion, or the reawakening of such interest **6.** CHR **EVANGELICAL CHRISTIAN MEETING** a meeting or a series of meetings of evangelical Christians intended to awaken religious fervour in those who attend **7.** LAW **RE-ESTABLISHING OF LEGAL VALIDITY** the renewal of the validity of a contract or the effect of a judicial decision

revivalism /ri vívəlizəm/ *n.* **1. DESIRE TO FOSTER NEW INTEREST** a desire or tendency to renew interest in sth old, e.g. old customs or beliefs **2.** RELIG **EVANGELICAL RELIGIOUS MOVEMENT** the efforts of a religious movement, especially an evangelical Christian movement, to reawaken religious commitment

revivalist /ri vívəlist/ *n.* **1. SB ADVOCATING RENEWED INTEREST** sb who wishes to revive old customs, ideas, or institutions 2. RELIG EVANGELIST sb who promotes, organizes, or preaches at a religious revival meeting, especially one for evangelical Christians ■ *adj.* RELIG REAWAKENING RELIGIOUS FAITH dedicated to reawakening or stimulating religious fervour in evangelical Christians —**revivalistic** /ri vīvə lístik/ *adj.*

revive /ri vív/ (**-vives, -viving, -vived**) *v.* **1.** *vti.* RECOVER CONSCIOUSNESS to come, or bring sb, back to life, consciousness, or full strength **2.** *vti.* FLOURISH AGAIN to become, or make sth, active, accepted, or popular once more **3.** *vt.* CAUSE EXPERIENCE TO RETURN to cause sth to be experienced again as a memory or feeling **4.** *vt.* THEATRE, MUSIC STAGE AGAIN to stage a new production of an old play or opera [15thC. Directly or via French *revivre* from late Latin *revivere*, literally 'to make live again', from *vivere* (see VIVID).] —**revivable** *adj.* —**reviver** *n.*

revivify /ree vívvi fī/ (**-fies, -fying, -fied**) *vt.* to impart new life, energy, or spirit to sth or sb —**revivification** /ree vívvifi káysh'n/ *n.*

revocable /révvəkəb'l, ri vṓk-/ *adj.* able to be revoked or cancelled —**revocability** /révvəkə bílləti, ri vṓkə bílləti/ *n.* —**revocably** /révvəkəbli, ri vṓkəbli/ *adv.*

revocation /révvə káysh'n/ *n.* the cancellation or withdrawal of sth such as a law or licence —**revocatory** /révvəkətəri/ *adj.*

revoke /ri vṓk/ *v.* (**-vokes, -voking, -voked**) **1.** *vt.* LAW FORMALLY CANCEL STH to make sth null and void by withdrawing, recalling, or reversing it **2.** *vt.* SUMMON SB BACK to call sb back, e.g. from exile or from an overseas position **3.** *vi.* CARDS NOT FOLLOW SUIT IN CARDS in a card game, to fail to follow suit though able to do so ■ *n.* CARDS FAILURE TO FOLLOW SUIT IN CARDS failure to follow suit in a card game when able to do so [14thC. Via French *révoquer* from Latin *revocare*, literally 'to call back', from *vocare* (see VOCAL).] —**revoker** *n.*

revolt /ri vṓlt/ *v.* (**-volts, -volting, -volted**) **1.** *vi.* REBEL AGAINST THE STATE to try to overthrow an existing government **2.** *vi.* DEFY AUTHORITY to resist authority or rules **3.** *vti.* FEEL DISGUST to feel, or cause sb to feel, disgust or repulsion ■ *n.* **1.** UPRISING AGAINST GOVERNMENT an uprising that attempts to overthrow a government **2.** DEFIANCE OF AUTHORITY a protest against authority or rules [Mid-16thC. Via French *révolter* from, ultimately, assumed Vulgar Latin *revolvitare* 'to overturn', from Latin *revolvere* (see REVOLVE).] —**revolter** *n.*

revolting /ri vṓlting/ *adj.* **1.** PROVOKING DISGUST arousing feelings of disgust, nausea, or repulsion **2.** NASTY unattractive or otherwise unpleasant (*informal*) —**revoltingly** *adv.*

revolute /révvə loot/ *adj.* used to describe leaves and other plant parts that are rolled backwards and downwards from the tip or edge [Mid-18thC. From Latin *revolutus*, the past participle of *revolvere* (see REVOLVE).]

revolution /révvə lóosh'n/ *n.* **1.** POL OVERTHROW OF GOVERNMENT the overthrow of a ruler or political system **2.** MAJOR CHANGE a dramatic change in ideas or practice **3.** COMPLETE CIRCULAR TURN one complete circular movement made by sth round or cylindrical, e.g. a wheel, around a fixed point **4.** CIRCLE ROUND STH a complete circle made round sth, e.g. the orbit made by a planet or satellite round another body **5.** GEOL PERIOD OF MAJOR GEOLOGICAL CHANGE a period during which the Earth's crust changes considerably and major features such as mountain ranges may emerge [14thC. Via French from, ultimately, Latin *revolut-*, the past participle stem of *revolvere* (see REVOLVE).]

revolutionary /révvə lóosh'nəri/ *adj.* **1.** POL OF A POLITICAL REVOLUTION relating to or involving a political or social revolution **2.** POL STIRRING REBELLION causing, supporting, or advocating revolution **3.** NEW AND DIFFERENT so new and different as to cause a major change in sth ■ *n.* (*plural* **-ies**) POL REBEL sb committed to a political or social revolution —**revolutionarily** *adv.* —**revolutionariness** *n.*

Revolutionary *adj.* **1.** *US* OF THE AMERICAN WAR OF INDEPENDENCE relating to the war with Great Britain fought by the American colonists **2.** OF PARTICULAR NATIONAL REVOLUTION relating to a particular revolution that has taken place such as the Russian Revolution or the French Revolution

Revolutionary Calendar *n.* = **French Republican Calendar**

revolutionise *vt.* = **revolutionize**

revolutionist /révvə lóosh'nist/ *n.* = **revolutionary**

revolutionize (**-izes, -izing, -ized**), **revolutionise** (**-ises, -ising, -ised**) *vt.* **1.** CHANGE STH RADICALLY to cause a radical change in sth such as a method or approach **2.** POL INCITE PEOPLE TO REBELLION to inspire people with revolutionary ideas **3.** POL CAUSE REBELLION IN COUNTRY to bring about a revolution in a country —**revolutionizer** *n.*

revolve /ri vólv/ *v.* (**-volves, -volving, -volved**) **1.** *vti.* MOVE IN CIRCULAR FASHION to move, or send sth, in a circular movement, either around an object or on a central axis **2.** *vi.* BE FOCUSED to have sth as a primary focus or theme **3.** *vi.* RECUR to happen in cycles or regular periodic intervals ■ *n.* THEATRE TURNING STAGE a circular part of a stage that can be turned mechanically in order to change a scene [14thC. From Latin *revolvere*, literally 'to roll back', from *volvere* (see VOLUTE).] —**revolvable** *adj.*

revolver /ri vólvər/ *n.* a handgun with a revolving cylinder of chambers, allowing several shots to be fired without reloading

revolving credit *n.* a credit scheme that imposes regular repayments and a predetermined spending limit

revolving door *n.* **1.** DOOR THAT GOES ROUND a door, usually in a large building, consisting of four panels that intersect at right angles and turn on a central pivot **2.** HR CIRCULAR SYSTEM any system in which people frequently enter and leave, e.g. a corporation that repeatedly hires and fires staff or a criminal justice system that returns offenders to society (*hyphenated when used before a noun*)

revolving fund *n.* a fund that can be drawn upon and repaid as desired, established for a particular purpose

revue /ri vyóo/ (*plural* **-vues**) *n.* a musical variety show consisting of skits, dance routines, and songs that often satirize current events and personalities [Late 19thC. From French, formed from *revoir* (see REVIEW).]

revulsion /ri vúlsh'n/ *n.* **1.** FEELING OF DISGUST a sudden and violent feeling of extreme loathing **2.** WITHDRAWAL a pulling or turning back (*formal*) **3.** MED DIVERSION OF BLOOD the diversion of blood or disease from one part of the body to another [Mid-16thC. Via French from, ultimately, Latin *revuls-*, the past participle stem of *revellere*, literally 'to pull back', from *vellere* 'to tear, pull'.] —**revulsive** /-ssiv/ *adj.*

Rev. Ver. *abbr.* Revised Version

reward /ri wáwrd/ *n.* **1.** THING GIVEN IN RETURN sth desirable given in return for what sb has done **2.** MONEY OFFERED IN RETURN money offered for information about the whereabouts of a criminal or the return of sth lost or stolen **3.** BENEFIT RECEIVED a benefit obtained as a result of an action taken or a job done **4.** PSYCHOL STH REINFORCING DESIRED BEHAVIOUR sth positive that follows a desired response and acts to encourage desired behaviour ■ *vt.* (**-wards, -warding, -warded**) **1.** GIVE SB STH AS REWARD to give sb sth in return, especially in thanks for kindness or help **2.** REPAY EFFORT to be worth the effort or attention that is given [14thC. From Anglo-Norman, a variant of Old French *reguard* (see REGARD).] —**rewardable** *adj.* —**rewarder** *n.*

rewarding /ri wáwrding/ *adj.* **1.** SATISFYING providing sb with personal satisfaction or great pleasure **2.** GIVEN AS REWARD intended as a reward for sth —**rewardingly** *adv.*

rewind *vt.* /ree wínd/ (**-winds, -winding, -wound** /-wównd/) WIND STH BACK to wind sth such as video or audio tape back onto its original spool or back to an earlier point ■ *n.* /rée wīnd/ **1.** REWINDING PROCESS the process of rewinding sth **2.** REWINDING FUNCTION a function, e.g. on a camera or video recorder, that rewinds film or tape

rewire /ree wír/ (**-wires, -wiring, -wired**) *vt.* to install new electrical wiring in a building, vehicle, or electrical device

reword /ree wúrd/ (**-words, -wording, -worded**) *vt.* to change the wording of sth written or spoken

rework *vt.* /ree wúrk/ (**-works, -working, -worked**) **1.** MAKE IMPROVEMENTS TO STH to alter or revise sth in order to improve or update it **2.** AMEND STH FOR REUSE to alter sth in order to reuse it in a different context ■ *n.* /rée wurk/ = **reworking**

reworking /rée wúrking/ *n.* a new version of sth, especially a spoken or written text. US term **rework**

rewrite *vt.* /ree rít/ (**-writes, -writing, -wrote** /-rṓt/, **-written** /-rítt'n/) **1.** AMEND WORDING OF TEXT to redraft a text by changing the wording or structure **2.** PRESS EDIT FOR PUBLICATION to edit a reporter's copy for publication in a newspaper or magazine **3.** ALTER FACTS ABOUT STH to change the way the past is perceived or known about ■ *n.* /rée rīt, ree rít/ AMENDED TEXT an amended version of a written document —**rewriter** /ree rítər/ *n.*

Rex /reks/ *n.* a word used in the formal title of a reigning king, especially on coins and official documents (*formal*) [Early 17thC. From Latin, 'king' (source of English *regal*, *royal*, *viceroy*, and *reign*). Ultimately from an Indo-European word that is also the ancestor of *rich*, *Reich*, and *rajah*.]

Rexburg /réks burg/ city in northeastern Idaho, northeast of Idaho Falls. Population: 14,204 (1996).

Rexine /rék seen/ *tdmk.* a trademark for a type of artificial leather

Reye's syndrome /rīz-, ráyz-/ *n.* a rare and serious childhood disease, usually following a respiratory infection, causing vomiting, fatty deposits in the liver, disorientation, and swelling of the kidneys and brain [Named after the Australian paediatrician Ralph Douglas *Reye* (1912–78), who first described the condition]

Reykjavik /ráykyə vik/ capital city of Iceland, situated on Faxaflói Bay, in the southwest of the country. Population: 103,000 (1994).

Reynolds /rénn'ldz/, **Henry** (*b.* 1938) Australian historian. He wrote works on the relationships between Aboriginal peoples and European settlers, including *The Other Side of the Frontier* (1981).

Reynolds, Sir Joshua (1723–92) British painter. He painted portraits of many notable people of his day, and was the founding president of the Royal Academy of Arts (1768).

Reynold's number /rénn'ldz-/ *n.* a number used to indicate the flow of fluid through a pipe or around an obstruction. Symbol *Re* [Named after the Irish physicist Osborne *Reynolds* (1842–1912)]

Rf[1] *symbol.* CHEM ELEM rutherfordium

Rf[2] *abbr.* MONEY rufiyaa

RF[1] *abbr.* **1.** RADIO radio frequency **2.** MIL reconnaissance fighter **3.** MIL regular forces **4.** GENETICS releasing factor **5.** MAPS representative fraction **6.** République française **7.** MIL Reserve Force **8.** CHEM retention factor **9.** BASEBALL right fielder **10.** MIL Royal Fusiliers

RF[2] MONEY symbol **Rwanda franc**

rf. *abbr.* **1.** reef **2.** COMM refund

r.f. *abbr.* **1.** RADIO radio frequency **2.** MIL rapid fire **3.** TELECOM reception fair **4.** PAPER rough finish

R factor *n.* a combination of genes that makes some bacteria resistant to antibiotics. It can be transferred to other bacteria through conjugation. [*R* abbreviation of *resistance*]

RFC *abbr.* **1.** MIL Royal Flying Corps **2.** SPORTS Rugby Football Club

RFD *abbr.* **1.** RADIO radio-frequency device **2.** MIL reporting for duty

Rfn *abbr.* Rifleman

r.g., RG *abbr.* right guard

RGB *abbr.* red, green, blue (*used to describe a colour monitor or colour value*)

RGN *abbr.* Registered General Nurse

RGS *abbr.* Royal Geographical Society

Rgt *abbr.* regiment

rh *abbr.* **1.** METEOROL relative humidity **2.** right hand

Rh[1] *symbol.* rhodium

Rh[2] *abbr.* rhesus factor

RH *abbr.* **1.** METEOROL relative humidity **2.** right hand **3.** Royal Highness

RHA *abbr.* **1.** Regional Health Authority **2.** Royal Horse Artillery

rhabdom /rábdəm/ *n.* a transparent rod-shaped part of the compound eye of insects, spiders, and other arthropods [Late 19thC. From late Greek *rhabdōma*, from *rhabdos* 'rod'.]

rhabdomancy /rábdō manssi/ *n.* the use of a divining rod to locate underground water or mineral ores [Mid-17thC. From Greek *rhabdomanteia*, from *rhabdos* 'rod' + -*manteia* (see -MANCY).] —**rhabdomancer** *n.* —**rhabdomantist** *n.*

rhabdovirus /rábdō vīrəss/ *n.* a rod-shaped virus that contains RNA such as the virus that causes rabies [Mid-20thC. Coined from Greek *rhabdos* 'rod' + VIRUS.]

Rhadamanthus /ráddə mánthəss/ *n.* in Greek mythology, the son of Zeus and Europa, and brother of Minos. According to Homer, he dwelt in Elysium, the home of the blessed dead. Later legend states that he was one of the three judges of the dead in the underworld.

Rhaetian /reesh'n/ *n.* = **Rhaeto-Romance** ■ *adj.* **1.** LANG OF RHAETO-ROMANCE relating or belonging to Rhaeto-Romance **2.** OF RHAETIA relating to Rhaetia, an alpine province of ancient Rome, or the section of the Alps in this area [Late 16thC. Formed from *Rhaetia*, an alpine province of ancient Rome.]

Rhaeto-Romance /reétō rō mánss/ *n.* a group of Romance dialects, sometimes considered to be separate languages, spoken in some Alpine regions of Switzerland and Italy. The group comprises Romansch, Ladin, and Friulian. —**Rhaeto-Romance** *adj.*

rhamnose /rámnōss, -nōz/ *n.* a crystalline sugar found in the cells of most plants. Formula: $C_6H_{12}O_5$. [Late 19thC. Formed from modern Latin *rhamnus*, genus name of the buckthorn (in whose berries the substance is found), from Greek *rhamnos*.]

rhapsode /rápsōd/ *n.* = **rhapsodist** *n.* **2** [Mid-19thC. From Greek *rhapsōidēs*, from *rhapsōidein* 'to recite' (see RHAPSODY).]

rhapsodic /rap sóddik/, **rhapsodical** /-ik'l/ *adj.* **1.** MUSIC OF A RHAPSODY relating to a rhapsody, or with the emotional and improvisational qualities of a rhapsody **2.** ENTHUSIASTIC joyfully enthusiastic or ecstatic about sth —**rhapsodically** *adv.*

rhapsodise *vti.* = **rhapsodize**

rhapsodist /rápsədist/ *n.* **1.** ENTHUSIASTIC PERSON sb who is joyfully enthusiastic or ecstatic about sth (*literary*) **2.** HIST ANCIENT GREEK RECITER an ancient Greek poet who recited epic poetry professionally

rhapsodize /rápsə dīz/ (**-dizes, -dizing, -dized**), **rhapsodise** (**-dises, -dising, -dised**) *v.* **1.** *vi.* EXPRESS ENTHUSIASM to speak or write in an enthusiastic or ecstatic manner **2.** *vti.* POETRY RECITE RHAPSODY to write or recite a rhapsody

rhapsody /rápsədi/ (*plural* **-dies**) *n.* **1.** MUSIC FREE-FORM MUSICAL COMPOSITION a composition that is often irregular in form, emotional in effect, and improvisational in nature **2.** ENTHUSIASTIC TALK an expression of intense enthusiasm (*often used in the plural*) **3.** POETRY ANCIENT GREEK RECITED POEM in ancient Greece, an epic poem recited by a professional reciter **4.** LITERAT EXALTED LITERARY COMPOSITION any literary work written in an intense or exalted style [Mid-16thC. Via Latin from Greek *rhapsōdia*, from *rhapsōidein* 'to recite poems', from *rhaptein* 'to stitch together' + *ōidē* 'song' (see ODE).]

WORD KEY: CULTURAL NOTE

Rhapsody in Blue, a musical composition by US composer George Gershwin (1924). Originally written for piano and jazz band, it was later rearranged for orchestra by Ferde Grofé. One of the first classical works to incorporate jazz influences such as syncopated rhythms, it was inspired by the vibrancy of contemporary urban life, particularly that of New York City.

rhatany /ráttəni/ (*plural* **-ny** *or* **-nies**) *n.* **1.** S AMERICAN SHRUB a South American shrub with two-sided symmetrical flowers, spiny globular fruits, and thick roots. Genus: *Krameria*. **2.** DRIED RHATANY ROOT the dried root of the rhatany, formerly used as an astringent but now commonly used in dental products, including toothpaste and mouthwash [Early 19thC. Via modern Latin *rhatania*, ultimately, Quechua *ratánya*.]

rhd *abbr.* right-hand drive

rhea /reé ə/ (*plural* **-as** *or* **-a**) *n.* a large flightless bird that looks like an ostrich but is slightly smaller. It is native to South America and lives in open country. Rheas have long legs and can run at high speeds. Family: Rheidae. [Early 19thC. From modern Latin, genus name, of uncertain origin: probably from RHEA[1].]

Rhea[1] /reé ə/ *n.* in Greek mythology, a Titan who was the wife of Cronus and mother of the gods. Roman equivalent **Cybele**

Rhea[2] /reé ə/ *n.* the second-largest natural satellite of Saturn, discovered in 1672. It is 1,528 km in diameter and occupies an intermediate orbit.

rhebok /reé bok/ (*plural* **-boks** *or* **-bok**), **reebok** (*plural* **-boks** *or* **-bok**) *n.* a straight-horned antelope that lives in upland meadows and rocky outcrops in southern Africa. It has brownish-grey woolly hair. Rheboks are related to reedbucks. Latin name: *Pelea capreolus*. [Late 18thC. From Dutch *reebok* 'roebuck'.]

rheme /reem/ *n.* the part of a sentence, often the predicate, that adds the greatest amount of new information to what is already available in the discourse. ◊ **theme** [Late 19thC. From Greek *rhēma* 'what is said'. Ultimately from an Indo-European base meaning 'to speak', which is also the ancestor of English *word, verb,* and *irony.*]

Rhenish /rénnish, reé-/ *adj.* coming from or relating to the Rhineland area of Germany [14thC. Via Anglo-Norman *reneis*, from, ultimately, Latin *Rhenus* 'Rhine'.]

rhenium /reéni əm/ *n.* a rare heavy silvery-white metallic chemical element that has a high melting point and is used as a catalyst and with tungsten in thermocouples. Symbol **Re** [Early 20thC. Via German, which was coined by its discoverers, from Latin *Rhenus* 'the Rhine'.]

rheo- *prefix.* flow, current ○ *rheometer* [From Greek *rheos* 'stream, current', which was formed from *rhein* 'to flow'. Ultimately from an Indo-European word that is also the ancestor of English *stream.*]

rheobase /reé ō bayss/ *n.* the minimum electrical nerve impulse necessary to cause a twitch in a muscle

rheology /ri óllə ji/ *n.* a branch of physics dealing with the way matter flows and changes shape —**rheological** /reé ə lójjik'l/ *adj.* —**rheologically** /-lójjikli/ *adv.* —**rheologist** /ri ólləjist/ *n.*

rheometer /ri ómmitər/ *n.* an instrument that measures the flow of thick liquids such as blood —**rheometric** /reé ə méttrik/ *adj.*

rheomorphism /reé ə máwrfizəm/ *n.* the liquefying of rock

rheostat /reé ə stat/ *n.* a resistor designed to allow variation in resistance without breaking the electrical circuit of which it is a part. An example is the volume control of a radio. —**rheostatic** /reé ə státtik/ *adj.*

rheotaxis /reé ə táksiss/ *n.* the motion of an organism towards or away from a current of water or air —**rheotactic** /-táktik/ *adj.*

rheotropism /reé ə trópizəm/ *n.* growth of a plant, or of an immobile animal such as a coral, in the direction of a flow of water

Rhesus /reéssəss/ *n.* in Greek mythology, one of the kings of Thrace

rhesus baby (*plural* **rhesus babies**) *n.* a baby born with a serious condition requiring blood transfusion because the baby's Rh-positive blood has been attacked by antibodies in the blood of its Rh-negative mother. ♦ **Rh factor** [See RHESUS FACTOR]

Rhesus factor *n.* = **Rh factor** [From the fact that the antigens were first discovered in the blood of rhesus monkeys]

rhesus monkey *n.* a brownish monkey of the macaque family, found in southern Asia and used in medical research. It is the most common monkey in India. Latin name: *Macaca mulatta*. [*Rhesus* from modern Latin genus name, arbitrarily after RHESUS]

Rhesus negative *adj.* = **Rh negative**

Rhesus positive *adj.* = **Rh positive**

rhetoric /réttərik/ *n.* **1.** PERSUASIVE SPEECH OR WRITING speech or writing that communicates its point persuasively **2.** PRETENTIOUS WORDS complex or elaborate language that only succeeds in sounding pretentious **3.** SKILL WITH LANGUAGE the ability to use language effectively, especially to persuade or influence people **4.** STUDY OF WRITING OR SPEAKING EFFECTIVELY the study of methods employed to write or speak effectively and persuasively [14thC. Via Old French *rethorique*, from, ultimately, Greek *rhētorikē (tekhnē)* '(art) of public speaking', from *rhētōr* 'speaker'.]

rhetorical /ri tórrik'l/ *adj.* **1.** BOMBASTIC relating to or using language that is elaborate or fine-sounding but insincere **2.** OF EFFECTIVE USE OF LANGUAGE relating to the skill of using language effectively and persuasively —**rhetorically** *adv.*

rhetorical question *n.* a question asked for effect that neither expects nor requires an answer

rhetorician /réttə rísh'n/ *n.* **1.** EDUC RHETORIC TEACHER sb who teaches the art of using language effectively and persuasively **2.** SKILLED SPEAKER OR WRITER a skilled and effective speaker or writer **3.** PRETENTIOUS SPEAKER OR WRITER sb who speaks or writes using elaborate or fine-sounding but insincere language

rheum /room/ *n.* watery discharge coming from the eyes, nose, or mouth [14thC. Via Old French *reume* from, ultimately, Greek *rheuma* 'flow, bodily humour'.]

rheumatic /roo máttik/ *adj.* relating to or affected with rheumatism ■ *n.* SB WITH RHEUMATISM sb who is affected with rheumatism —**rheumatically** *adv.*

rheumatic fever *n.* an acute infectious disease that causes a sore throat, fever, pain, swelling in the joints, and often damage to the heart valves. It affects children particularly.

rheumatic heart disease *n.* damage to the valves or muscular tissue of the heart caused by rheumatic fever

rheumatics /roo máttiks/ *npl.* rheumatism (*informal*)

rheumatism /róomətizəm/ *n.* **1.** STIFFNESS IN JOINTS OR MUSCLES any painful condition of the joints or muscles that is not caused by infection or injury **2.** RHEUMATOID ARTHRITIS a popular name for rheumatoid arthritis

rheumatoid /róomə toyd/ *adj.* relating to or affected with rheumatism or rheumatoid arthritis —**rheumatoidally** /róomə tóyd'li/ *adv.*

rheumatoid arthritis *n.* a chronic disease of the joints that causes stiffness, swelling, weakness, loss of mobility, and eventual destruction and deformity of the joints

rheumatoid factor *n.* an antibody found in the blood serum of many people who have rheumatoid arthritis. It is used to diagnose the disease.

rheumatology /róomə tólləji/ *n.* a branch of medicine dealing with the study and treatment of rheumatic diseases —**rheumatologist** *n.*

Rh factor *n.* a group of antibody-producing substances (**antigens**) present in most people's red blood cells. Rh compatibility is important in matching blood for transfusions and between pregnant women and their foetuses. ◊ **Rh negative, Rh positive** [Rh from *rhesus*]

RHG *abbr.* Royal Horse Guards

rhin- *prefix.* = **rhino-** (*used before vowels*)

rhinal /rín'l/ *adj.* relating to the nose

Rhine /rīn/ river and major economic waterway in western Europe, flowing through Switzerland, Austria, Liechtenstein, France, Germany, and the Netherlands. Length: 1,320 km/820 mi.

rhinencephalon /rín en séffə lon/ (*plural* **-lons** *or* **-la** /-lə/) *n.* the area of the forebrain that controls the sense of smell —**rhinencephalic** /rín enssə fállik/ *adj.*

rhinestone /rín stōn/ *n.* a small piece of paste or glass used as an imitation diamond [Late 19thC. Translation of French *caillou du Rhin*, so called because the stones were first made in the city of Strasbourg, on the Rhine.]

rhinitis /rī nítiss/ *n.* inflammation of the mucous membranes of the nose, usually accompanied by a discharge of mucus

rhino[1] /rī́nō/ (*plural* **-nos** *or* **-no**) *n.* a rhinoceros (*informal*) [Late 19thC. Shortening.]

rhino[2] /rī́nō/ *n.* money (*archaic slang*) [Early 17thC. Origin unknown.]

rhino- *prefix.* nose, nasal ○ *rhinoplasty* [From Greek *rhin-*, the stem of *rhis* 'nose', of unknown origin]

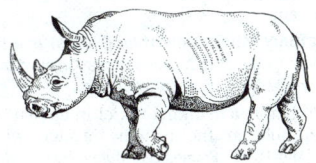

Rhinoceros

rhinoceros /rī nóssərəss/ (*plural* **-oses** *or* **-os**) *n.* a very large herbivorous mammal with very thick skin and one or two horns on its snout. It is native to Africa and Asia. Family: Rhinocerotidae. [13thC. Via Latin from Greek *rhinokerōs*, from *rhin-*, the stem of *rhis* 'nose' + *keras* 'horn' (see KERATO-).] —**rhinocerotic** /rī́nō sə róttik/ *adj.*

rhinoceros beetle *n.* any large tropical scarab beetle that has horns on its head and thorax

rhinoceros bird *n.* = oxpecker

rhinology /rī nólləji/ *n.* the branch of medicine dealing with conditions and structures of the nose

rhinopharyngitis /rī́nō fárrən jī́tiss/ *n.* inflammation of the mucous membranes in the nose and pharynx

rhinoplasty /rī́nō plasti/ (*plural* **-ties**) *n.* plastic surgery performed on the nose, whether for medical or cosmetic reasons —**rhinoplastic** /rī́nō plástik/ *adj.*

rhinoscope /rī́nō skōp/ *n.* a device used by doctors to examine the nasal passages —**rhinoscopy** /rī nóskəpi/ *n.*

rhinovirus /rī́nō vīrəss/ *n.* a virus containing RNA that causes infections of the upper respiratory system, including the common cold

rhiz- *prefix.* = rhizo- (used before vowels)

rhizo- *prefix.* root ○ *rhizosphere* [From Greek *rhiza* 'root' (source also of English *licorice*). Probably ultimately from an Indo-European word that is also the ancestor of *root*, *wort*, and *radical*.]

rhizobium /rī zṓbi əm/ (*plural* **-a** /-ə/) *n.* a soil bacterium that forms nodules on the roots of legumes such as beans and clover and takes up nitrogen from the atmosphere. Genus: *Rhizobium.* [Early 20thC. From modern Latin, genus name, from Greek *rhiza* 'root' + *bios* 'life'.]

rhizocarpous /rī́zō kaárpəss/ *adj.* used to describe plants that produce their fruit underground

rhizocephalan /rī́zō séffələn/ *n.* a small crustacean that lives in water as a parasite on crabs. Order: Rhizocephala. [Late 19thC. Formed from modern Latin *Rhizocephala*, order name, from Greek *rhiza* 'root' + *kephalē* 'head'.] —**rhizocephalous** *adj.*

rhizogenic /rī́zō jénnik/, **rhizogenetic** /rī́zōjə néttik/, **rhizogenous** /rī zójjənəss/ *adj.* used to describe plant cells and tissues from which roots develop

rhizoid /rī́ zoyd/ *n.* a slender outgrowth on mosses, liverworts, and the reproductive cells of ferns that absorbs nourishment in much the same way as a root —**rhizoidal** /rī zóyd'l/ *adj.*

rhizome /rī́zōm/ *n.* a thick underground horizontal stem that produces roots and has shoots that develop into new plants. In some plants such as the iris it is fleshy and survives the winter. [Mid-19thC. Via Greek *rhizōma* 'mass of roots' from, ultimately, *rhiza* 'root' (see RHIZO-).] —**rhizomatous** /rī zómmətəss/ *adj.*

rhizomorph /rī́zō mawrf/ *n.* a structure in some pathogenic fungi that allows them to move from host to host —**rhizomorphous** /rī́zō máwrfəss/ *adj.*

rhizophagous /rī zóffəgəss/ *adj.* feeding on roots

rhizoplane /rī́zō playn/ *n.* the part of a plant's root that lies at the surface of the soil, where many microorganisms adhere to it

rhizopod /rī́zō pod/ *n.* a single-celled organism (**protozoan**) that moves and eats by means of filaments that it can extend temporarily. Subphylum: Rhizopoda. —**rhizopodous** /rī zóppədəss/ *adj.*

rhizopus /rī́zōpəss/ *n.* a mould that causes decay such as the common bread mould. Genus: *Rhizopus.* [Late 19thC. From modern Latin, genus name, from Greek *rhiza* 'root' + *pous* 'foot'; so called because of its shape.]

rhizosphere /rī́zō sfeer/ *n.* the area of soil that immediately surrounds and is affected by a plant's roots

rhizotomy /rī zóttəmi/ (*plural* **-mies**) *n.* surgery in which spinal nerves are cut in order to relieve pain or high blood pressure

Rh negative *adj.* lacking the Rh factor in the blood. ◊ **Rh factor, Rh positive**

rho /rō/ (*plural* **rhos**) *n.* the 17th letter of the Greek alphabet, represented in the English alphabet as 'r'. See table at **alphabet** [14thC. From Greek *rhō*, of Phoenician origin.]

rhod- *prefix.* = rhodo- (used before vowels)

rhodamine /rṓdə meen/ *n.* a red or pink fluorescent dye used to colour wool and silk, and also used as a biological stain [Late 19thC. Coined from Greek *rhodon* 'rose' + -AMINE.]

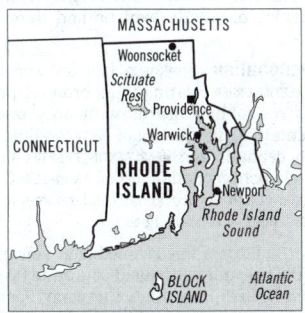

Rhode Island

Rhode Island /rōd/ *n.* state in the northeastern United States, bordered by Massachusetts, Connecticut, and the Atlantic Ocean. The country's smallest state, its territory was bought from Native North American peoples by religious dissidents from Massachusetts in the 1630s. Capital: Providence. Population: 987,429 (1997). Area: 3,188 sq. km/1,231 sq. mi. Official name **State of Rhode Island and Providence Plantations** —**Rhode Islander** *n.*

Rhodes /rōdz/ **1.** island in Greece, the largest of the Dodecanese Islands. Population: 87,831 (1981). Area: 1,400 sq. km/540 sq. mi. **2.** city in Greece, the capital of the island of Rhodes. Population: 40,656 (1981).

Rhodes, Cecil (1853–1902) British colonial statesman. He made a fortune mining diamonds in South Africa, where he formed De Beers Consolidated Mining Company (1888). He was prime minister of Cape Colony (1890–96) and helped to develop Rhodesia after 1889. Full name **Cecil John Rhodes**

Rhodesia /rō deéshə, -zhə/ former name for **Zimbabwe** —**Rhodesian** /rō deésh'n/ *adj., n.*

Rhodesian man *n.* an early human being sharing features with the Neanderthals and with modern human beings and living in Africa in the late Pleistocene period. Latin name: *Homo sapiens rhodesiensis.* [Early 20thC. Named after RHODESIA, where the fossils were found.]

Rhodesian ridgeback *n.* a large dog with a ridge of hair growing down its back, belonging to a breed originally developed in Africa

Rhodes scholarship *n.* a sum of money awarded annually to students from the United States, South Africa, and several Commonwealth countries to help pay for studies at Oxford University [Early 19thC. Named after Cecil RHODES.] —**Rhodes scholar** *n.*

rhodinal /rōdin'l/ *n.* = citronellal

rhodium /rṓdi əm/ *n.* a hard silvery-white metallic chemical element that is resistant to corrosion. It is found in platinum and nickel ores and is used with platinum in alloys and in plating other metals. Symbol **Rh** [Early 19thC. Formed from Greek *rhodos* 'rose', from the pink colour of its compounds.]

rhodo- *prefix.* red, rosy ○ *rhodolite* [From Greek *rhodon* 'rose'. Ultimately related to Latin *rosa* (source of English *rose*).]

rhodochrosite /rṓdō krṓ sīt/ *n.* a pink, red, brown, or grey mineral that is an ore of manganese. It consists of manganese carbonate. [Mid-19thC. Formed from Greek *rhodokhrōs* 'rose-coloured'.]

Rhododendron

rhododendron /rṓdə déndrən/ *n.* an evergreen shrub of the heath family that is native to southern Asia but is widely grown in temperate regions for its clusters of brightly coloured flowers. Genus: *Rhododendron.* [Early 17thC. Via Latin, 'oleander', from Greek, from *rhodon* 'rose' + *dendron* 'tree'.]

rhodolite /róddə līt/ *n.* a variety of garnet, used as a gem, with a colour ranging from pink to rose red [Late 19thC. Coined from RHODO- + -LITE.]

rhodonite /róddə nīt/ *n.* a pink to brown mineral that consists mainly of manganese silicate. It is found in metamorphic rock and is used as an ornamental stone. [Early 19thC. Formed from Greek *rhodon* 'rose'.]

Rhodope Mountains /róddəpi-/ mountain range in the Balkan peninsula, situated predominantly in southwestern Bulgaria. Its highest point is Musala, 2,925 m/9,596 ft.

rhodopsin /rō dópsin/ *n.* a reddish light-sensitive pigment found in the rod cells of the retina of the eye. Light splits the pigment's molecule into its two components, retinal and opsin, triggering nerve impulses to the brain. [Late 19thC. Coined from RHODO- + Greek *opsis* 'sight' + -IN.]

rhodora /rō dáwrə/ *n.* a shrub of the rhododendron family, native to marshy regions of northeastern North America, with deep pink flowers that bloom in spring before the leaves emerge. Latin name: *Rhododendron canadense.* [Late 18thC. From modern Latin, former genus name, of uncertain origin: possibly an alteration of Latin *rodarum*, a kind of plant, or formed from Greek *rhodon* 'rose'.]

rhomb /rom, romb/ *n.* = rhombus

rhombencephalon /rómb en séffə lon/ *n.* = hindbrain [Late 19thC. Coined from RHOMBUS + ENCEPHALON.]

rhombi plural of **rhombus**

rhombohedron /rómbō heédrən/ *n.* a prism with six faces, each one a rhombus [Mid-19thC. Coined from RHOMBUS, on the model of *polyhedron*.]

rhomboid /róm boyd/ *n.* **PARALLELOGRAM WITH UNEQUAL ADJACENT SIDES** a parallelogram with adjacent sides that are not equal ■ *adj.* **1. RHOMBOID-SHAPED** shaped like a rhomboid **2. RELATING TO RHOMBUS** relating to or characteristic of a rhombus [Late 16thC. From Greek *rhomboeidēs* 'lozenge-shaped', from *rhombos* (see RHOMBUS).]

rhombus /rómbəss/ (*plural* **-buses** *or* **rhombi** /-bī/) *n.* a parallelogram that has four equal sides and oblique angles [Mid-16thC. Via Latin from Greek *rhombos*. Ultimately, from an Indo-European word meaning 'to bend', which is also the ancestor of English *warp*.] —**rhombic** *adj.*

rhonchus /róngkəss/ (*plural* **-chi** /-kī/) *n.* a harsh rattling or whistling sound heard through a stethoscope on examination of the chest, caused by partial obstruction of the airways [Early 19thC. Via Latin, 'snoring', from, ultimately, Greek *rhegkhos*, from *rhegkein* 'to snore'.] —**rhonchal** *adj.*

Rhône /rōn/ major river in southern Europe, flowing through Switzerland and France. Length: 813 km/505 mi.

rhotacism /rṓtəsizəm/ *n.* unusual pronunciation of the letter 'r', or too much emphasis on this sound [Mid-19thC. Via modern Latin *rhotacismus*, from, ultimately, Greek *rhōtakizein* 'to make wrong use of the letter r', from *rhō*.]

rhotic /rótik/ *adj.* pronouncing the letter 'r' when it occurs after a vowel or at the end of a syllable ○ *a rhotic accent* [Mid-20thC. Formed from RHOTACISM.]

r.h.p. *abbr.* rated horsepower

Rh positive *adj.* containing the Rh factor in the blood or having blood that contains the Rh factor. ◊ **Rh factor, Rh negative**

RHS *abbr.* Royal Horticultural Society

Rhubarb

rhubarb /roö baarb/ *n.* **1.** PLANTS PLANT WITH EDIBLE STALKS a perennial plant, found in the wild and cultivated, with green or pink leaf stalks that are edible when cooked. The leaves are toxic. Genus: *Rheum*. **2.** FOOD RHUBARB STALKS AS FOOD the pink stalks of the common rhubarb plant, cooked and eaten as fruit **3.** PHARM MEDICINAL ASIAN PLANT a rhubarb plant found in central and eastern Asia whose underground stems may be dried and used as a laxative **4.** US, Can QUARREL a serious disagreement, quarrel, or fight (*informal*) **5.** THEATRE APPARENT CONVERSATION IN PLAY the word 'rhubarb' used repeatedly by several actors at once to give the impression that they are talking to one another [14thC. Via Old French *reubarbe*, from, ultimately, Latin *rha barbarum* 'barbarian rhubarb', from Greek *Rha*, the ancient name of the river Volga, because rhubarb was once grown on its banks.]

——— **WORD KEY: ORIGIN** ———

The Greeks had two words for *rhubarb*: 'rheon' (which evolved into Latin 'rheum', now the plant's scientific name) and *rha*, which is said to have come from *Rha*, an ancient name of the river Volga, in allusion to the fact that *rhubarb* was once grown on its banks (*rhubarb* is native to China, and was once imported to Europe via Russia). In medieval Latin *rhubarb* became known as *rha barbarum* 'barbarian rhubarb, foreign rhubarb', again with reference to the plant's exotic origins; and in due course association with Latin *rheum* altered this to *rheubarbarum*.

rhumb /rum/ *n.* **1.** NAVIG = **rhumb line** n **2 2.** COMPASS POINT any of the 32 points of a compass

rhumba *n.* = rumba

rhumb line *n.* **1.** GEOG IMAGINARY GEOMETRIC LINE an imaginary line on the surface of the Earth intersecting all meridians at the same angle **2.** NAVIG STEADY COURSE a steady course along one compass setting taken by a ship or aircraft

rhyme /rīm/, rime *n.* **1.** SIMILARITY IN SOUND similarity in the sound of word endings, especially in poetry **2.** WORD SOUNDING SAME AS ANOTHER a word with an ending that sounds similar to the ending of another word **3.** POEM a poem, or poetry generally, of a lighthearted kind with a pattern of similar sounds at the ends of the lines ■ *v.* (**rhymes, rhyming, rhymed; rimes, riming, rimed**) **1.** vti. SOUND SIMILAR to have an ending that sounds similar to another word or line of poetry ○ *'Rough' rhymes with 'cuff'.* **2.** vt. CHOOSE RHYMING WORD to find or choose a word with an

ending that sounds similar to another **3.** vti. WRITE POETRY to write rhyming poetry or express sth in rhyme [12thC. Alteration (influenced by RHYTHM) of earlier *rime*, from Old French, of Germanic origin. Ultimately from an Indo-European base meaning 'to put in order' that is also the ancestor of English *arithmetic* and *rite*.] ◊ **without rhyme or reason** without any rational explanation or apparent sense

rhymer, rimer *n.* = rhymester

rhyme royal *n.* a form of poetry using verses with seven lines of iambic pentameter with a rhyme scheme ababbcc, or one of these verses [Mid-19thC. From the use of the form by James I of Scotland.]

rhyme scheme *n.* the pattern of rhyming lines in a poem or verse of a poem often indicated with matching letters to show which lines rhyme. For example, ababcc means the first and third, second and fourth, and fifth and sixth lines rhyme with each other.

rhymester, rimester *n.* sb who writes poems with rhyming lines, especially lighthearted or poor quality verse

rhyming /rī́ming/ *adj.* with lines that end in similar sounding words, forming a pattern

rhyming slang *n.* a form of slang that replaces a word with an expression that rhymes with the word but has no meaningful connection with it, used especially in Cockney. Sometimes the rhyming part of the original expression is eventually dropped, e.g.'whistle', originally 'whistle and flute', means 'suit'.

rhynchocephalian /ríngkōssə fálli ən/ *adj.* OF NEARLY EXTINCT REPTILE ORDER relating to an order of primitive reptiles resembling lizards with only one living representative, the tuatara of New Zealand. Order: Rhynchocephalia. ■ *n.* NEARLY EXTINCT REPTILE a member of the rhynchocephalian order [Mid-19thC. Formed from modern Latin *Rhyncocephalia*, order name, from Greek *rhugkhos* 'snout' + *kephalē* 'head'.]

rhyolite /rī́ ə līt/ *n.* a fine-grained acid volcanic rock that is the volcanic equivalent of granite [Mid-19thC. Coined from Greek *rhuax* 'stream (of lava)' (formed from *rhein* 'to flow') + -LITE.] —**rhyolitic** /rī́ ə líttik/ *adj.*

Rhys /reess/, Jean (1894–1979) West Indian-born British writer. Her work reflects her West Indian background and often reveals a pessimistic view of the world. Pseudonym of **Ellen Gwendolen Rees Williams**

rhythm /rí́thəm/ *n.* **1.** MUSIC PATTERN OF BEATS IN MUSIC the regular pattern of beats and emphasis in a piece of music ○ *The audience clapped in rhythm as we sang.* **2.** MUSIC PARTICULAR MUSIC PATTERN a particular pattern of beats in a piece or kind of music **3.** POETRY PATTERN OF STRESS IN POETRY in poetry, the pattern formed by stressed and unstressed syllables **4.** POETRY PARTICULAR POETRY PATTERN a particular pattern of stress in a poem or kind of poetry **5.** REGULAR PATTERN any regularly recurring pattern of activity such as the cycle of the seasons, night and day, or repeated functions of the body **6.** CHARACTERISTIC PATTERN the characteristic pattern of a particular activity **7.** ARTS PATTERN IN ART a pattern of elements suggesting movement or pace in sth such as a work of art **8.** LANG SOUND PATTERN the pattern of sound that characterizes a language, dialect, or accent **9.** CINEMA, LITERAT PATTERN FROM REPEATED ELEMENTS a mood or effect in a book, play, or film created from repeated elements [Mid-16thC. Via Latin from Greek *rhuthmos*. Ultimately from an Indo-European word meaning 'to flow' that is also the ancestor of English *stream* and *haemorrhoid*.]

rhythm and blues *n.* a style of music combining elements of blues and jazz, originally developed by African American musicians

rhythm guitar *n.* chordal accompaniment from a guitar that does not play the melody

rhythmic /rí́thmik/, rhythmical /rí́thmik'l/ *adj.* **1.** WITH RECURRING PATTERN with a regularly recurring pattern or beat **2.** OF RHYTHM relating to rhythm —**rhythmically** *adv.* —**rhythmicity** /rith míssəti/ *n.*

rhythmic gymnastics *n.* gymnastics that makes use of apparatus such as ribbons and hoops

rhythmics /rí́th miks/ *n.* the study of rhythms and rhythmic forms (*takes a singular verb*)

rhythm method *n.* a method of contraception in which sexual intercourse is avoided at the times when a woman is most likely to conceive

rhythm section *n.* the instruments in a band such as the drums, bass, piano, or guitar that provide the basic rhythm

rhythm stick *n.* either of a pair of wooden sticks, often with notches, used as a simple percussion instrument

rhytidectomy /rī́tidéktəmi/ (*plural* -**mies**) *n.* a face-lift (*technical*) [Mid-20thC. Coined from Greek *rhutid-*, the stem of *rhutis* 'wrinkle' + -ECTOMY.]

rhyton /rī́ ton/ *n.* a drinking vessel in ancient Greece with a hole in the bottom through which to drink [Mid-19thC. From Greek *rhuton*, from *rhutos* 'flowing'.]

RI *abbr.* **1.** religious instruction **2.** Queen and Empress **3.** King and Emperor **4.** Royal Institution **5.** Rhode Island

ria /rée ə/ *n.* a narrow inlet running inland from the coastline, formed when a valley is permanently flooded as a result of a rise in sea-level. Rias are a feature of the coastlines of southwestern England and southwestern Ireland. [Late 19thC. From Spanish *ría* 'estuary', feminine of *río* 'river', from Latin *rivus* 'stream' (see RIVAL).]

RIA *abbr.* **1.** Royal Irish Academy **2.** radioimmunoassay

rial /ri áal/, ryal *n.* **1.** UNIT OF MIDDLE EASTERN CURRENCY the main unit of currency in Iran, Oman, Qatar, Saudi Arabia, and Yemen. See table at **currency 2.** COIN WORTH ONE RIAL a coin worth one rial [Mid-20thC. Via Persian and Arabic *riyāl* from Spanish *real* (see REAL²).]

rialto /ri ált ō/ (*plural* **rialtos**) *n.* COMM **1.** MARKETPLACE a market or marketplace **2.** EXCHANGE a place where securities or commodities such as grain or raw materials are traded [Mid-16thC. Named after *Rialto*, the district of Venice in which the Exchange was located.]

riata /ri áatə/ *n.* a lasso or lariat [Mid-19thC. From Spanish *reata* (source of English *lariat*), from *reatar*, literally 'to retie', from *atar* 'to tie', via Latin *aptare* 'to join' from, ultimately, *apere* 'to tie'.]

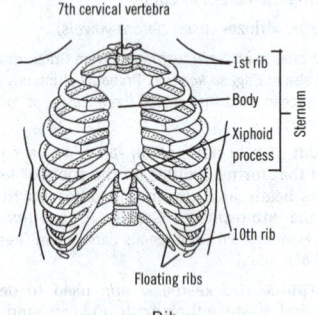

7th cervical vertebra

1st rib
Body
Sternum
Xiphoid process

10th rib

Floating ribs

Rib

rib /rib/ *n.* **1.** ANAT CURVED BONE OF CHEST any of the curved bones extending from the vertebrae and in some cases meeting the sternum, forming a cavity housing vital organs in many vertebrates **2.** FOOD MEAT a cut of meat that contains ribs **3.** KNITTING RIDGED KNITTING a portion of knitted material with raised vertical lines of stitches, made by alternating purl stitches with plain stitches **4.** BOT LEAF VEIN a raised vein on a leaf **5.** ARCHIT MOULDING ON VAULT a ridge or moulding on the underside of a vault or arched ceiling **6.** NAUT PART OF A SHIP'S HULL any of the beams extending from the keel to the top of the hull of a ship, giving it its shape **7.** AIR PART OF AIRCRAFT WING a part of an aircraft wing crossing from the leading to the trailing edge of the wing **8.** PIECE RESEMBLING RIB a bar, rod, or other supporting part that has the shape or function of a rib ○ *a broken rib on the umbrella* **9.** TEASING COMMENT a comment or action meant as a joke or to tease sb (*informal*) ■ **ribs** *npl.* RIBS WITH LITTLE MEAT ribs of an animal from which most of the meat has been removed, eaten as food ■ *v.* (**ribs, ribbing, ribbed**) **1.** vti. TEASE to make playful teasing remarks to sb about sth (*informal*) ○ *They* ribbed me about my haircut. **2.** *vti.* KNITTING **KNIT PLAIN AND PURL STITCHES** to knit plain stitches alternately with purl stitches to make raised lines in knitting **3.** *vt.* **PROVIDE WITH RIBS** to provide or strengthen sth with ribs [Old English *ribb*, from a prehistoric Germanic word meaning 'covering (of the chest cavity)']

RIBA *abbr.* **1.** Royal Institute of British Architects **2.** Member of the Royal Institute of British Architects

ribald /ríbb'ld/ *adj.* **COARSE AND FUNNY** humorous but rude and vulgar, often involving jokes about sex ■ *n.* **RIBALD PERSON** sb who often uses ribald language [14thC. From Old French *ribau(l)t*, from *riber* 'to sleep around', of Germanic origin.] —**ribaldly** *adv.*

ribaldry /ríbb'ldri/ *n.* language or behaviour that is humorous but rude and vulgar, often involving jokes about sex

riband, **ribband** *n.* **1.** **RIBBON** a ribbon, especially one that is presented to sb as an award or prize **2.** **RAIL OF PALISADE** a rail attached to the upright posts in a defensive fence (**palisade**) [14thC. Variant of *riban* (see RIBBON).]

ribavirin /ríbə vírin/ *n.* a synthetic antiviral agent that is used to treat certain viral diseases, notably Lassa fever. It inhibits the synthesis of DNA and RNA. [Late 20thC. Coined from *riba-*, of uncertain origin: probably from *rib(onucleic) a(cid)* + VIRUS + -IN.]

ribband *n.* = riband

ribbed /ribd/ *adj.* **1.** **HAVING RIBS** with structural support or decoration in the form of ribs **2.** KNITTING **KNITTED INTO PATTERN OF VERTICAL LINES** knitted to form a pattern of raised vertical lines, giving a stretchy fabric **3.** **STRIPED** with a surface marked by raised, roughly parallel bands

Ribbentrop /ríbbən trop/, **Joachim von** (1893–1946) German government official. As ambassador to Britain (1936) and foreign minister (1938–43), he helped promote the expansionist programme of the Nazis. After World War II he was tried at Nuremberg and executed.

ribbing /ríbbing/ *n.* **1.** KNITTING **SECTION OF RIB IN KNITTING** a section of knitting in a pattern of raised vertical lines, making a stretchy fabric **2.** **RIB FRAMEWORK** a supporting structure or framework of ribs, e.g. in the hull of a boat **3.** **TEASING** playful or friendly teasing (*informal*)

Ribble /ríbb'l/ river in Yorkshire and Lancashire, in northwestern England. Length: 120 km/75 mi.

ribbon /ríbbən/ *n.* **1.** TEXTILES **DECORATIVE STRIP OF FABRIC** a strip of fabric, often in a bright colour, used for tying hair, trimming gifts, and other decorative purposes **2.** COMM **STRIP OF INKED MATERIAL** a strip of material with ink on it, used in some printers and typewriters **3.** COMPUT **FLAT CABLE** a flat cable in which all the wires are parallel to one another in a single plane **4.** **RIBBON AS AWARD OR BADGE** a decorative strip of fabric given to sb as an award or worn as a sign of rank or membership **5.** **LONG NARROW STRIP** sth that is long, narrow, and thin, in the shape of a ribbon **6.** CONSTR = ledger board ■ **ribbons** *npl.* **BADLY DAMAGED STATE** a damaged state in which sth is cut or torn very badly ○ *My shirt was in ribbons.* ■ *vt.* (-bons, -boning, -boned) **1.** **DECORATE WITH RIBBONS** to decorate sth by attaching ribbons to it **2.** **TEAR INTO STRIPS** to tear sth into strips [Early 16thC. Variant of earlier *riban*, from Old French, a variant of *ruban*, of uncertain origin: probably from a Germanic source.] —**ribbony** *adj.*

ribbon development *n.* a planning scheme or development with houses built in a single row on each side of main roads leading out of a town or city centre

ribbonfish /ríbbən fish/ (*plural* **-fish** *or* **-fishes**) *n.* a marine fish that has a long tapering ribbon-shaped body and, typically, a dorsal fin extending from head to tail. Some species can exceed 10 m/32 ft in length. Family: Trachypteridae.

ribbon grass *n.* a grass that is grown as an ornamental in northern temperate regions for its drooping cream-striped leaves. Latin name: *Phalaris arundinacea picta.*

ribbon snake *n.* a nonvenomous North American snake with longitudinal reddish or yellow stripes extending the full length of its body. It bears live young and feeds on frogs and worms. Latin name: *Thamnophis sauritus.*

ribbonwood /ríbbən wŏŏd/ *n.* a small evergreen tree native to New Zealand that bears clusters of small white flowers. Its bark has traditionally been used to make cord. Latin name: *Hoheria populnea.*

ribbon worm *n.* = nemertean

rib cage *n.* the ribs as a whole, forming a protective bony enclosure surrounding the heart and lungs

ribo- *prefix.* ribose ○ *riboflavin* [From RIBOSE]

riboflavin /ríbō fláyvin/, **riboflavine** *n.* an orange-yellow crystalline pigment in the vitamin B complex, essential for normal growth in humans and an important component of many of the body's enzymes. It is found in foods such as spinach, eggs, milk, and liver. Formula: $C_{17}H_{20}N_4O_6$.

ribonuclease /ríbō nyŏŏkli ayz, -ayss/ *n.* any enzyme that catalyses the breakdown of RNA

ribonucleic acid /ríbō nyŏŏ kleé ik-/ *n.* full form of RNA

ribonucleoprotein /ríbō nyŏŏkli ō prṓ teen/ *n.* a conjugated protein found in chromosomes, made up of RNA molecules together with protein molecules

ribonucleoside /ríbō nyŏŏkli ō síd/ *n.* a nucleoside in which the sugar group is ribose. Ribonucleosides are important in living organisms as precursors of ribonucleotides.

ribonucleotide /ríbō nyŏŏkli ō tíd/ *n.* a nucleotide that contains the sugar ribose and makes up many important cellular molecules including RNA and energy coenzymes such as ATP

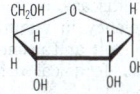

Ribose

ribose /ríbōz/ *n.* a five-carbon sugar found in all living cells as a constituent of RNA and many other metabolically important compounds, including ribonucleotides, nucleic acids, and riboflavin. Formula: $C_5H_{10}O_5$. [Late 19thC. Via German, from ARABINOSE.]

ribosomal RNA /ríbə sṓm'l-/ *n.* an RNA that is a structural and functional component of ribosomes

ribosome /ríbə sōm/ *n.* a submicroscopic cluster of proteins and RNA, occurring in great numbers in the cytoplasm of living cells, that takes part in the manufacture of proteins. Ribosomes bind to messenger RNA molecules, which carry encoded transcripts of the cell's genes, and direct the assembly of amino acids into proteins according to the code. [Mid-20thC. Coined from RIBONUCLEIC ACID + -SOME.] —**ribosomal** /ríbə sṓm'l/ *adj.*

ribozyme /ríbō zīm/ *n.* a strand of RNA that attaches to and catalyses site-specific cleavages of other strands of RNA. Ribozymes are the only nonenzyme biological catalysts known. [Late 20thC. Coined from RIBONUCLEIC ACID + ENZYME.]

rib-tickler *n.* a very funny joke or story (*informal*)

ribwort /ríb wurt/, **ribwort plantain** *n.* a weed-like Eurasian plant with long slender ribbed leaves and a dense rounded spike of small white flowers. Latin name: *Plantago lanceolata.* [14thC. Because the leaves resemble ribs.]

Riccio /rée chee ō/, **David** (1533?–66) Italian courtier. As adviser to Mary, Queen of Scots, he arranged her marriage with Lord Darnley, who later plotted his murder.

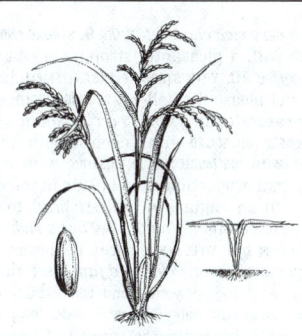

Rice

rice /ríss/ (*plural* **rices** *or* **rice**) *n.* **1.** BOT **TALL GRASS** an annual grass probably native to India but long cultivated for its grain in tropical and warm regions of the world. Latin name: *Oryza sativa.* **2.** FOOD **EDIBLE GRAINS** the edible grains obtained from the rice plant, served hot or cold after cooking in water or other liquid [13thC. Via Old French *ris* and Italian *riso* from, ultimately, Greek *oruza*, of Iranian origin.]

Anne Rice

Rice /ríss/, **Anne** (*b.* 1941) US writer. She is best known for the Vampire Chronicles, beginning with *Interview with the Vampire* (1976). Born **Howard Allen O'Brien**

rice leafhopper *n.* a small hopping insect that is a severe pest in India and other rice-growing regions. Genus: *Nephotettix.*

rice paper *n.* **1.** FOOD **EDIBLE PAPER** thin brittle edible paper made from plant sources, used to undercoat baked foods such as almond macaroons that would otherwise stick to the tin during baking. The paper bakes into the mixture providing an edible, slightly crisp base. **2.** INDUST **PAPER FROM RICE-PAPER PLANT** thin paper made from the rice-paper plant

rice-paper plant *n.* a Chinese shrub grown for its fibre that is used to make rice paper. Latin name: *Tetrapanax papyriferus.*

rice pudding *n.* a hot dessert made by baking rice slowly in milk and sugar

rice rat *n.* a rat that inhabits the marshes of the southern United States and Central and South America where rice fields are located. Genus: *Oryzomys.*

ricercare /reéchər kaá ray/ (*plural* **ricercari** /-ree/) *n.* a fugal composition for musical instruments, analogous to a motet for voices, involving lines of melody interwoven in an often complicated pattern [Late 18thC. From Italian, literally 'to seek out'.]

rice weevil *n.* an insect of the weevil family that infests stored rice, wheat, and other grains. Latin name: *Sitophilus oryzae.*

rich /rich/ *adj.* **1.** **WEALTHY** owning a lot of money or expensive property **2.** **WORTH MUCH** worth a great deal **3.** **COSTLY AND FINE** made from or consisting of things of the highest quality ○ *rich fabrics* **4.** **WITH GOOD SUPPLY OF STH** with a good supply of a resource or substance ○ *an area rich in minerals* **5.** **PLENTIFUL** existing in large quantities in plentiful supply ○ *a rich supply of conscripts* **6.** **PRODUCTIVE** productive and so potentially very profitable **7.** AGRIC **FERTILE** very fertile and able to produce strong healthy plants **8.** FOOD **WITH HIGH PROPORTION OF FATTY FOODS** containing a high proportion of foods such as cream, eggs, or butter, that are full of fat ○ *a very rich chocolate cake* **9.** **STRONG AND SMOOTH-FLAVOURED** with a pleasantly strong, smooth flavour ○ *rich coffee* **10.** **WITH STRONG PLEASANT SMELL** having a strong and pleasant smell **11.** **STRONGLY COLOURED** deep or fully saturated in colour ○ *a rich shade of brown* **12.** **WITH DEEP FULL SOUND** with a deep smooth full sound **13.** CARS **WITH TOO MUCH FUEL IN MIXTURE** with a higher than normal proportion of fuel to air in the mixture supplied to an engine **14.** **UNLIKELY** hard to believe because ridiculous (*informal*) ○ *That's rich, coming from her!* ■ *npl.* **WELL-OFF** wealthy people in general ○ *a playground for the rich and famous.* ◊ **riches** [Old English *rīce* 'strong, powerful' and Old French *riche*, of Germanic origin. Ultimately, from an Indo-European word meaning 'king' that is also the ancestor of English *royal*, *rajah*, and *bishopric*.] —**richness** *n.*

Richard I /ríchərd/, **King of England** (1157–99). He spent most of his reign (1189–99) overseas, fighting in the Third Crusade and against Philip II of France. Known as **Richard the Lionheart**

Richard II, King of England (1367–99). His reign (1377–99) was marked by national disunity and civil strife that culminated in his being deposed.

Richard III, King of England (1452–85). He usurped the throne while protector of the young Edward V (1483), but was defeated at the Battle of Bosworth Field (1485) in a rebellion led by the future King Henry VII.

Richards /ríchərdz/, **Mark** (*b.* 1957) Australian surfer. He won the world championship for four consecutive years (1979–82).

Richards, Vivian (*b.* 1952) Jamaican cricketer. A powerful batsman and skilled fielder, he was captain of the West Indies (1985–91). Full name **Isaac Vivian Alexander Richards**

Richardson /ríchərdss'n/, **Henry Handel** (1870–1946) Australian novelist. She wrote the trilogy *The Fortunes of Richard Mahony* (1917–29). Pseudonym of **Ethel Florence Robertson**. Born **Ethel Florence Lindsay Richardson**

Richardson, Sir Ralph (1902–83) British actor. He appeared in many Shakespearean and classical stage roles, and in numerous films. Full name **Sir Ralph David Richardson**

Richardson, Samuel (1689–1761) British novelist. He wrote *Pamela* (1740), *Clarissa* (1747–48), and other novels in epistolary form, and had a major influence on the early development of the English novel.

Richardson's ground squirrel /ríchərdsənz-/ *n.* a ground squirrel found in the northwestern United States and Canadian prairies that can be a pest of grain crops. Latin name: *Citellus richardsoni*. [Mid-20thC. Named after the Scottish naturalist Sir John *Richardson* (1787–1865), who first collected it.]

Richelieu /réesh lyö/, **Armand Jean du Plessis, Duc de** (1585–1642) French cardinal and statesman. He was named a cardinal in 1622. As chief minister to Louis XIII after 1624, he wielded supreme power in France. He strengthened the monarchy and made France the pre-eminent military power in Europe. Known as **Cardinal Richelieu**

riches /ríchiz/ *npl.* **1.** **GREAT WEALTH** great wealth or many valuable possessions **2.** **PLENTIFUL NATURAL THINGS** things occurring naturally in abundance ○ *enjoy the riches of the forest* [12thC. Originally singular, misunderstood as plural; variant of *richesse*, from Old French *richeise*, from *riche* 'rich', from the prehistoric Germanic ancestor of English *rich* (see RICH).]

richly /ríchli/ *adv.* **1.** **ELABORATELY** beautifully and elaborately ○ *richly decorated* **2.** **WITH DEEP COLOUR** with a deep, fully saturated colour **3.** **COMPLETELY** completely and suitably ○ *a richly deserved award* **4.** **PLENTIFULLY** plentifully or very fully [Old English *rīclīce*]

Richmond /ríchmənd/ **1.** market town in North Yorkshire, northern England, on the banks of the River Swale. Population: 7,862 (1991). **2.** capital city of the state of Virginia, situated in the eastern part of the state. Population: 201,108 (1994). **3.** town in eastern New South Wales, Australia, on the River Hawkesbury. Population: (including Windsor) 21,317 (1996).

Richmond-upon-Thames town in southeastern England, on the River Thames. It is now part of Greater London.

Richter /rík<u>h</u>tər/, **Johann Paul Friedrich** (1763–1825) German novelist and humorist. He wrote *Hesperus* (1795), *Titan* (1800–03), and other romances and satirical works. Pseudonym **Jean Paul**

Richter scale /ríktər-, rík<u>h</u>tər-/ *n.* a scale from 1 to 10 used to measure the severity of earthquakes according to the amount of energy released, with a higher number indicating stronger tremors. Each increment of the scale is a 32-fold increase over the previous one. ◊ **Mercalli scale** [Mid-20thC. Named after the US seismologist Charles Francis *Richter* (1900–85), who devised it.]

Richthofen /rík<u>h</u>t hōfən/, **Manfred, Baron von** (1882–1918) German military aviator. As the leader of a squadron during World War I, he shot down 80 Allied aircraft. Known as **the Red Baron**

ricin /ríssin/ *n.* a white poisonous protein extracted from the beans of the castor plant for use as a biochemical reagent that acts in the body to clump red blood cells [Late 19thC. Formed from Latin *ricinus* 'castor oil plant', of unknown origin.]

ricinoleic acid /ríssinō lée ik-/ *n.* an unsaturated fatty acid that is the main constituent of castor oil and is used in making soap, plastics, and in textile finishing. Formula: $C_{18}H_{34}O_3$. [Coined from Latin *ricinus* 'castor oil plant' + OLEIC]

rick[1] /rik/ *n.* **STACK OF HAY OR STRAW** a large quantity of hay or straw stacked into a rectangular shape for storage and covered at the top to protect it from the weather ■ *vt.* (**ricks, ricking, ricked**) **FORM A RICK** to stack hay or straw to form a rick [Old English *hrēac*, of unknown origin]

rick[2], **wrick** *vt.* (**ricks, ricking, ricked; wricks, wricking, wricked**) **STRAIN A JOINT** to wrench or sprain a joint of the body slightly ■ *n.* **SLIGHT INJURY** a slight injury to a joint caused by wrenching or spraining it [Late 18thC. Origin uncertain: perhaps of Low Dutch or Low German origin.]

rickets /ríkits/ *n.* a disease, especially of children, caused by a deficiency in vitamin D that makes the bones become soft and prone to bending and structural change. Technical name **rachitis** [Mid-17thC. Origin unknown.]

rickettsia /ri kétsi ə/ (*plural* **-ettsiae** /ri kétsi ee/ *or* **-ettsias**) *n.* a parasitic bacterium that typically lives inside ticks and can be transmitted to humans, causing Rocky Mountain spotted fever, certain forms of typhus, and other diseases. Order: Rickettsiales. [Early 20thC. From modern Latin, genus name, named after the US pathologist H. T. *Ricketts* (1871–1910).] —**rickettsial** *adj.*

rickety /ríkiti/ (**-ier, -iest**) *adj.* **1.** **UNSTABLE** in bad condition, unstable, and likely to collapse ○ *a rickety chair* **2.** **INFIRM** weakened by the ageing process or illness **3.** MED **WITH RICKETS** affected by rickets **4.** MED **RELATING TO RICKETS** relating to or resembling rickets [Late 17thC. Formed from RICKETS, from the unsteadiness that the disease causes.] —**ricketiness** *n.*

rickey /ríki/ (*plural* **-eys**) *n.* a cocktail made from soda water, lime or lemon juice, sugar, and gin or vodka [Late 19thC. Origin uncertain: probably from the name *Rickey*.]

rickrack /rík rak/, **ricrac** *n.* a narrow decorative braid in a zigzag shape [Late 19thC. Doubling of RACK[1].]

rickshaw /rík shaw/, **ricksha** *n.* **1.** **TWO-WHEELED PASSENGER VEHICLE** a small vehicle with two wheels and a seat for passengers, pulled along by sb walking in front of it, used especially in Asia **2.** **THREE-WHEELED PASSENGER VEHICLE** a small three-wheeled vehicle, like a tricycle with a seat at the back for passengers, that is driven by sb sitting at the front and pedalling [Late 19thC. Shortening of Japanese *jinrikisha*, from *jin* 'man' + *riki* 'strength' + *sha* 'vehicle'.]

ricochet /ríkə shay/ *vi.* (**-chets, -cheting** *or* **ricochetting, -cheted** *or* **ricochetted**) **REBOUND** to hit a surface and bounce, travelling away in a different direction ■ *n.* **REBOUNDING ACTION** the rebounding action of sth that hits a surface and bounces off in a different direction [Mid-18thC. From Old French, 'give-and-take, repetition', of unknown origin.]

ricotta /ri kóttə/ *n.* a soft white mild-tasting Italian cheese made from whey and used mostly in cooking, or a cheese made to resemble this [Late 19thC. Via Italian, literally 'recooked', from Latin *recocta*, the feminine past participle of *recoquere* 'to recook', from *coquere* (see COOK).]

RICS *abbr.* Royal Institution of Chartered Surveyors

rictus /ríktəss/ (*plural* **-tus** *or* **-tuses**) *n.* **1.** **STRANGE GRIN OR GRIMACE** a fixed open-mouthed grin or grimace, especially an expression of horror **2.** ZOOL **GAPE OF BIRD'S BEAK** the gape of a bird's beak [Mid-18thC. From Latin, from the past participle of *ringi* 'to gape', of unknown origin.] —**rictal** *adj.*

rid /rid/ (**rids, ridding, rid** *or* **ridded** *archaic*) *vt.* **1.** **EMPTY OF STH** to free, relieve, or empty a place or thing of sth, usually sth undesirable ○ *an attempt to rid the town of crime* **2.** **FREE YOURSELF FROM STH** to free sb or yourself from sth undesirable ○ *trying to rid myself of the habit* [12thC. From Old Norse *ryðja* 'to clear land', from *hrjóða* 'to strip'.] —**ridder** *n.* ◇ **be** *or* **get rid of 1.** to make sb or sth burdensome, unpleasant, or unnecessary go away **2.** to throw sth out

rid up *vti.* *N England or Scotland* to tidy up a place (*informal*)

riddance /rídd'nss/ *n.* the removal or destruction of sth unwanted ◇ **good riddance (to sb** *or* **sth)** used to show that you are glad to be free of sb or sth

ridden past participle of **ride**

riddle[1] /rídd'l/ *n.* **1.** **WORD PUZZLE** a puzzle in the form of a question or rhyme that contains clues to its answer **2.** **PUZZLING THING** sth that is difficult to understand or presents a problem that needs to be solved ■ *v.* (**-dles, -dling, -dled**) **1.** *vti.* **ANSWER RIDDLE** to find or explain the answer to a riddle **2.** *vi.* **TALK IN RIDDLES** to speak in a deliberately obscure way [Old English *rædels*. Ultimately from an Indo-European word that is also the ancestor of English *read*, *reason*, and *rathskeller*.] —**riddler** *n.*

WORD KEY: SYNONYMS

See Synonyms at ***problem***.

riddle[2] /rídd'l/ *vt.* (**-dles, -dling, -dled**) **1.** **MAKE HOLES IN STH** to damage sth by making a large number of small holes in it **2.** **AFFECT EVERY PART** to affect every part of sth, e.g. by spreading throughout **3.** **SIEVE SOIL OR STONES** to put soil or stones through a sieve to separate the large pieces from the small ones **4.** **SHAKE ASHES FROM FIRE** to shake ashes from the bottom of a fire by poking it with a metal rod or moving a mechanism under the grate ■ *n.* **SIEVE** a large flat shallow sieve for sifting soil or stones [Old English *hriddel* 'sieve', an alteration of *hridder*. Ultimately from an Indo-European word meaning 'to sort' that is also the ancestor of English *discriminate*, *criterion*, and *crime*.] —**riddler** *n.*

ride /rīd/ *v.* (**rides, riding, ridden** /rídd'n/ *or* **rode** /rōd/) **1.** *vti.* EQU **SIT ON AND CONTROL HORSE** to sit on a horse or other animal and control it as it moves along **2.** *vti.* TRANSP **TRAVEL ON BIKE** to travel mounted on a bicycle or motorcycle **3.** *vt.* SPORTS **USE SPORTS EQUIPMENT** to use any of various kinds of gliding or rolling sports equipment such as a skateboard or surfboard **4.** *vti.* **TRAVEL AS PASSENGER** to travel as a passenger in a vehicle **5.** *vti.* *US* **TRAVEL IN A LIFT** to travel in a lift **6.** *vt.* **TRAVEL OVER AREA** to travel across an area of land ○ *ride the range* **7.** *vt.* SPORTS **BE IN RACE** to take part in a race or other event on a horse or bike **8.** *vi.* *US* CARS **HANDLE WELL OR BADLY** to function in a particular way while moving ○ *a car that rides well over rough ground* **9.** *vi.* *S Africa* CARS **DRIVE CAR** to drive a car **10.** *vt.* **TO CARRY SB ALONG** to carry or take sb along ○ *His mother rode him around on her bicycle.* **11.** *vi.* **APPEAR TO BE FLOATING** to appear to be floating in the sky or moving like a floating object ○ *Birds soared above our heads, riding the currents.* **12.** *vi.* **DO STH EFFORTLESSLY** to do sth successfully and apparently effortlessly, as if carried along by a wave ○ *riding on a tide of sympathy* **13.** *vi.* **DEPEND ON STH** to depend on sth for success ○ *Her future is riding on the outcome of the interview.* **14.** *vi.* **BE ALLOWED TO CONTINUE** to continue without intervention or alteration ○ *let it ride for a few days* **15.** *vt.* **DEAL WITH PROBLEM AND SURVIVE** to manage to deal with a difficult situation successfully and survive without too much harm ○ *to ride the storm* **16.** *vt.* *US* **TEASE OR TORMENT** to tease or torment sb with criticism or mockery (*informal*) ○ *My sister always rides me about my hair.* **17.** *vt.* SAILING **RISE ON TOP OF WAVE** to rise up on a wave and move forward with it **18.** *vti.* NAUT **ANCHOR** to be moored with the anchor down, or to moor a ship by dropping its anchor ○ *a ship riding at anchor* **19.** *vi.* ENG **BE SUPPORTED BY STH** to be supported by sth such as a pivot or an axle ○ *Most of the weight rides on the central shaft.* **20.** *vt.* CARS **PARTIALLY DEPRESS CLUTCH OR BRAKE** to put your foot on the clutch or brake, partially depressing it, while driving **21.** *vt.* **OVERLAP** to overlap or encroach on sth such as another part **22.** *vt.* **YIELD TO BLOW** to move in the direction of sth forceful such as a blow, in order to lessen the impact ■ *n.* **1.** TRANSP **JOURNEY BY VEHICLE OR ANIMAL** a journey or outing in a motor vehicle or on an animal ○ *to go for a ride* **2.** *US* TRANSP **MEANS OF TRANSPORT** transportation as a passenger in a vehicle, especially when this is offered to sb who would otherwise have to walk or use public transport ○ *Do you want a ride?* **3.** CARS **QUALITY OF TRAVEL** the quality of travel in a motor vehicle ○ *The new model offers a very smooth ride.* **4.** LEISURE **FAIRGROUND ENTERTAINMENT** an entertainment such as a rollercoaster at an amusement park or fairground, offering a thrilling experience **5.** EQU **PATH FOR HORSES** a broad grassy path where horses can be ridden **6.** MUSIC **JAZZ CYMBAL** one of the three cymbals in a drum set, used to keep time and mark rhythmic accents in jazz [Old English *rīdan*. Ultimately from an Indo-European base that is also the ancestor of English *road, raid, ready,* and *array*.] —**ridable** *adj.* ◇ **be riding high** to be enjoying a period or feeling of success ◇ **ride herd on sb** to keep a close eye on or control over sb ◇ **ride roughshod over sb** to treat sb very arrogantly without regard to that person's feelings ◇ **ride roughshod over sth** to disregard a rule, law, or agreement ◇ **take sb for a ride** to cheat or deceive sb

ride down *vt.* **1. TRAMPLE** to hit and knock down sb while riding, especially on horseback **2. CATCH UP WITH OR OVERTAKE** to catch up with or overtake sb

ride out *vti.* to manage to deal with a difficult situation successfully and survive without too much harm ○ *ride out the storm*

ride up *vi.* to gradually move upward out of the correct position ○ *Her skirt was riding up.*

rider /rídər/ *n.* **1.** TRANSP **SB ON HORSE OR BIKE** sb who rides or is riding on an animal or vehicle **2. ADDITIONAL COMMENT** an extra comment or clause added to a document or statement **3.** LAW **ADDITIONAL CLAUSE TO BILL** an extra clause added to a parliamentary or legislative bill, often not directly related to the main issue **4.** LAW **ADDITIONAL STATEMENT BY JURY** a secondary statement made by a jury, giving a comment in addition to the verdict **5. STH RESTING ON OR STRENGTHENING STH** sth that rests on or strengthens sth else, e.g. the horizontal rail of a fence or additional timbers in the frame of a ship **6. SLIDING ADJUSTMENT** a small sliding weight on the arm of a chemical balance, used for adjusting the scales **7.** GEOL **THIN SEAM** a thin seam of a mineral lying above a thicker one

ridesharing /ríd shairing/ *n. US* an arrangement in which commuters take turns using their cars for going to work, taking one another as passengers to cut down the number of cars on the roads

ridge /rij/ *n.* **1. RAISED STRIP** a long narrow raised area of sth **2.** GEOG **RAISED LAND FORMATION** a long narrow hilltop or range of hills **3.** GEOG **RIDGE ON OCEAN FLOOR** an elevation on the ocean floor resembling a ridge on land and resulting from volcanic eruption along the fissures between tectonic plates **4.** METEOROL **AREA OF HIGH PRESSURE** a long area of high pressure in a weather system **5.** ANAT **RAISED BIT ON BONE** a long narrow protuberance or crest, e.g. on a bone **6.** ZOOL **BACKBONE OF ANIMAL** the backbone of an animal, especially a whale **7.** CONSTR **TOP OF ROOF** the line along the top of a roof or a tent where the two sloping sides meet ■ *vti.* (**ridges, ridging, ridged**) **FORM RIDGES** to mark, form, or provide sth with ridges, or make sth into the shape of a ridge [Old English *hrycg*. From a prehistoric Germanic word meaning 'back, spine' that is also the ancestor of English *rucksack*.] —**ridgy** *adj.*

ridgeback /ríj bak/ *n.* = **Rhodesian ridgeback**

ridgel /ríjj'l/ *n.* = **ridgeling**

ridgeline /ríj līn/ *n.* = **ridge** *n.* 2

ridgeling /ríjling/, **ridgling** *n.* a male animal in which one or both testes fail to descend into the scrotum at the usual time. The condition is most common in horses and pigs. [Mid-16thC. Formed from earlier *ridgel*, of uncertain origin.]

ridgepole /ríj pōl/, **ridgetree** /ríj tree/ *n.* **1.** BUILDING **BEAM ALONG RIDGE OF ROOF** a long beam of wood that runs along the ridge of a roof, supporting the upper ends of the rafters **2.** CAMPING **HORIZONTAL TENT POLE** the horizontal pole supporting the top of a ridge tent

ridge tent *n.* a tent with rectangular sides that stands chiefly by suspension from a supported ridgepole

ridgetree /ríj tree/ *n.* = **ridgepole**

ridgeway /ríj way/ *n.* a track, usually of ancient origin, running along the top of a ridge of hills [Old English *hrycgweg*]

ridicule /ríddi kyool/ *vt.* (**-cules, -culing, -culed**) **MOCK** to make fun of or mock sb or sth in a contemptuous way ■ *n.* **MOCKING LAUGHTER, BEHAVIOUR, OR COMMENTS** mocking laughter, mimicry, or comments intended to make fun of sb in a contemptuous way [Late 17thC. Directly or via French from Latin *ridiculum* 'joke', from *ridiculus* (see RIDICULOUS).] —**ridiculer** *n.*

WORD KEY: SYNONYMS

ridicule, deride, laugh at, mock, send up

CORE MEANING: to belittle or make fun of sb or sth

ridicule to belittle sb or sth in a cruel contemptuous way in order to make that person or thing an object of fun; **deride** a formal word used to talk about ridiculing sb or sth in strong harsh terms; **laugh at** to ridicule sb in an amused or contemptuous way; **mock** to treat sb or sth with scorn or contempt, often involving cruel mimicking. It is often used to suggest sth more subtle than *ridicule* or *deride*; **send up** an informal phrase meaning to make fun of or mock sb or sth, usually by means of parody or mimicking.

ridiculous /ri díkyōōləss/ *adj.* **1. UNREASONABLE** completely unreasonable and not at all sensible or acceptable **2. COMPLETELY SILLY** silly and funny [Mid-16thC. Formed from Latin *ridiculus* 'laughable', from *ridere* 'to laugh' (source of English *risible*), of unknown origin.] —**ridiculously** *adv.* —**ridiculousness** *n.*

riding[1] /rīding/ *n.* **1.** EQU **BEING ON A HORSE** the sport or hobby of sitting on a horse and controlling it as it moves along **2.** TRANSP **TRAVELLING ON ANIMAL OR VEHICLE** the act of travelling on an animal or vehicle ■ *adj.* EQU **USED ON HORSEBACK** used while riding a horse ○ *riding breeches*

riding[2] /rīding/ *n.* **1. riding, Riding AREA OF YORKSHIRE** one of the three administrative districts into which Yorkshire was formerly split **2.** *Canadian* **CANADIAN CONSTITUENCY** a constituency represented by either a federal member of parliament or a member of the provincial legislature **3.** *NZ* **RURAL LOCAL GOVERNMENT ELECTORATE** a rural electorate for local government [Pre-12thC. From Old Norse *þriðungr* 'third part', from *þriði* 'third'.]

riding coat *n.* a coat with cutaway front and tails worn in the 19th century for riding

riding crop *n.* a straight short riding whip with a loop at the end

riding habit *n.* a jacket with a matching skirt worn by women for riding from the late 17th to the early 20th century

Riding Mountain National Park /rīding-/ national park in Canada, in southwestern Manitoba. Area: 2,973 sq. km/1,148 sq. mi.

ridley /rídli/ (*plural* **-leys**) *n.* **1.** a small turtle, especially the grey-shelled Kemp's ridley found in the Atlantic, or the larger greenish olive ridley found in the Pacific **2.** = **olive ridley**

ridotto /ri dóttō/ (*plural* **ridottos**) *n.* a musical entertainment with dancing, popular in the 18th century [Early 18thC. Via Italian, 'retreat, entertainment', from medieval Latin *reductus*, from the past participle of Latin *reducere* (see REDUCE).]

riebeckite /rée bek īt/ *n.* a blue-black silicate mineral of the amphibole group, found in acidic igneous rocks and metamorphic schists. Tiger's eye is a mixture of riebeckite and silica. [Late 19thC. Named after the German explorer Emil *Riebeck* (died 1885).]

Riefenstahl /réef'n shtaal/, **Leni** (*b.* 1902) German film director and photographer. Her documentary films of a Nazi rally and of the 1936 Berlin Olympic Games glorified the Nazis, but are nevertheless masterpieces of cinematic technique. Born **Helena Bertha Amalie**

Riemann /réemən/, **Georg Friedrich Bernhard** (1826–66) German mathematician. He studied function theory and developed a system of geometry relevant to modern theoretical physics.

Riemannian geometry /ree mánni ən-/ *n.* a type of non-Euclidean geometry in which it is assumed that in a plane all pairs of straight lines intersect [Early 20thC. Named after G. F. B. *Riemann* (1826–66), the German mathematician who founded it.]

riempie /rímpi, réémpi/ *n. S Africa* a strip of leather used for weaving chair seats [Mid-19thC. Via Afrikaans from Dutch *riempje*, literally 'small thong', from *riem* 'thong'.]

riesling /réezling/, **Riesling** *n.* **1. WHITE WINE** a fruity dry to sweet white wine produced from a white grape grown mainly in Germany, Austria, Alsace, and Australia **2. RIESLING GRAPE** the grape used to make riesling [Mid-19thC. From German, alteration of obsolete *Rüssling*.]

rifampicin /ri fámpissin/ *n.* an antibiotic derived from soil bacteria and used to treat various bacterial infections, including tuberculosis. It works by interfering with RNA synthesis in the infecting bacteria. US term **rifampin** [Mid-20thC. Blend of RIFAMYCIN and PIPERAZINE.]

rifamycin /reéfə mīssin/ *n.* an antibiotic produced by a soil bacterium *Streptomyces mediterranei* and used to treat various bacterial infections, including leprosy and tuberculosis [Mid-20thC. Origin uncertain: probably coined from Italian *riformare* 'to reform', from *formare* 'to form' from Latin (see REFORM) + -MYCIN.]

rife /rīf/ *adj.* **1. WIDESPREAD AND PLENTIFUL** occurring everywhere in plentiful supply ○ *areas where poverty is rife* **2. FULL OF STH** full of or severely affected by sth undesirable ○ *an organization rife with corruption* [Old English *rȳfe*] —**rifely** *adv.* —**rifeness** *n.*

WORD KEY: SYNONYMS

See Synonyms at ***widespread***.

riff /rif/ *n.* MUSIC **SERIES OF NOTES** a short, often repeated series of notes in pop music or jazz that forms a distinctive part of the accompaniment ■ *vi.* (**riffs, riffing, riffed**) **USE RIFFS** to play riffs [Early 20thC. Origin uncertain: possibly a shortening of RIFFLE, or perhaps an alteration of REFRAIN.]

Riffian /ríffi ən/ *n.* a dialect of Berber spoken in Morocco, especially in the Riff Mountains of northern Morocco —**Riffian** *adj.*

riffle /ríff'l/ *v.* (**-fles, -fling, -fled**) **1.** *vti.* **FLICK THROUGH PAGES** to flick through the pages of a book, magazine, or newspaper, glancing casually at the contents **2.** *vt.* CARDS **SHUFFLE CARDS** to shuffle playing cards by halving the pack, lifting the corners, and flicking the cards so that they overlap as they fall **3.** *vi.* **BECOME CHOPPY** to become rough and choppy when passing over submerged rocks ○ *Water riffles over the rocks.* ■ *n.* **1.** *US* OCEANOG **SUBMERGED ROCKS OR SANDBAR** an area of rocks or a sandbar lying just below the surface of the water **2.** *US* OCEANOG **ROUGH WATER** an area of rough water caused by submerged rocks or a sandbar **3. QUICK LOOK AT BOOK** a quick flick through the pages of a book, magazine, or newspaper **4.** CARDS **SHUFFLING** the shuffling of playing cards **5.** MINING **GROOVED PART OF SLUICE** the bottom part of a sluice that has grooves for collecting gold or other mineral particles [Mid-18thC. Origin uncertain: perhaps a blend of RIPPLE and RUFFLE[1].]

riffler /rífflər/ *n.* a curved file for smoothing concave surfaces [Late 18thC. From French *rifloir*, from *rifler* 'to scratch' (see RIFLE[2]).]

riffraff /ríf raf/ *n.* **1. OFFENSIVE TERM** an offensive term that deliberately insults sb's social status, importance, and manners (*insult*) **2. WORTHLESS THINGS** rubbish or worthless objects (*informal*) [15thC. From French *rif et raf* 'pieces of plunder of small value', from *rifler* 'to plunder' and *raffler* 'to snatch'.]

rifle[1] /ríf'l/ *n.* **1. GUN** a gun with a long barrel that is fired from the shoulder. Spiral grooves inside the barrel make the bullet spin, improving its accuracy over a long distance. **2. CANNON** a large cannon with spirals cut into the bore ■ **rifles, Rifles** *npl.* ARMY **UNIT OF ARMED SOLDIERS** a unit of soldiers carrying rifles ■ *vt.* (**-fles, -fling, -fled**) **1.** ARMS **CUT GUN BARREL** to cut the inside of a gun barrel with spiral grooves **2.** SPORTS **THROW FAST BALL** to hit or throw a ball hard, making it travel very fast [Late 17thC. From French *rifler* 'to scratch' (see RIFLE[2]).]

rifle[2] /rĭf'l/ (**-fles, -fling, -fled**) *v.* **1.** *vti.* **SEARCH THROUGH VIGOROUSLY** to search vigorously through sth such as a drawer or room, often leaving things in disorder and sometimes with the intent to steal **2.** *vt.* **ROB** to rob or plunder sb or sth [14thC. From French *rifler* 'to plunder, scratch', of uncertain origin: probably from prehistoric Germanic.] —**rifler** *n.*

riflebird /rĭf'l burd/ *n.* a bird of paradise found in parts of Australia and New Guinea, the male of which performs an elaborate courtship dance. Genus: *Ptiloris.* [Mid-19thC. *Rifle* of uncertain origin: probably from RIFLE[1], either an imitation of the sound of the bird's cry, or because its plumage resembles a military uniform.]

rifle green *adj.* of a dark green colour, like the uniform of a private in the British army's rifle regiment —**rifle green** *n.*

rifle grenade *n.* a grenade propelled to its target by a rifle-fired bullet, requiring special adapting hardware

rifleman /rĭf'lmən/ (*plural* **riflemen** /-mən/) *n.* **1.** ARMY **SOLDIER WITH RIFLE** a soldier who has been trained to use a rifle **2.** ARMS **RIFLE USER** sb skilled in the use of a rifle **3.** BIRDS **NEW ZEALAND WREN** a tiny wren found in bush areas of New Zealand with a short tail, round wings and a broad head. Latin name: *Acanthisitta chloris.*

rifle range *n.* an area with targets where people can practise shooting rifles

riflery /rĭf'lri/ *n.* *US* **1.** **FIRING RIFLES** the skill or practice of firing rifles **2.** **RIFLE FIRE** fire from rifles

riflescope /rĭf'l skōp/ *n.* a telescopic sight designed to be used on a rifle [Mid-20thC. Coined from RIFLE + TELESCOPE.]

rifling /rĭfling/ *n.* **1.** **CUTTING GROOVES** the cutting of spiral grooves in the barrel of a gun **2.** **SPIRAL GROOVES** a series of spiral grooves cut in the barrel of a gun

rift /rift/ *n.* **1.** **GAP OR BREAK** a gap or break in sth where it has split apart **2.** **DISAGREEMENT** a serious disagreement that disrupts good relations **3.** GEOL = **fault** *n.* 6 ■ *vti.* (**rifts, rifting, rifted**) **SPLIT** to split or make sth split apart [14thC. Of Scandinavian origin.]

rift valley *n.* a valley formed by geological faulting, where the land between two parallel faults drops down to give a broad central plain with steep sides

rift zone *n.* an area of the earth's surface, often associated with the margins of continental plates, that is especially heavily faulted and may be subject to earth tremors

rig[1] /rig/ *vt.* (**rigs, rigging, rigged**) **1.** SAILING **EQUIP VESSEL WITH RIGGING** to fit a boat or its mast with sails and rigging **2.** **EQUIP** to equip or fit out sth so it is ready to use **3.** **MAKE** to make sth temporary and serviceable, usually done in haste and lacking the proper materials **4.** AIR **PREPARE AIRCRAFT FOR USE** to make an aircraft ready for use by making sure that all the parts are correctly adjusted **5.** CLOTHES **DRESS** to dress or adorn sth or sb (*usually passive*) ○ *rigged in striped pyjamas* ■ *n.* **1.** INDUST **DRILLING STRUCTURE FOR OIL** a structure and apparatus used for drilling for oil and gas **2.** SAILING **ARRANGEMENT OF SAILS AND MASTS** the arrangement of sails and masts on a boat **3.** CLOTHES **OUTFIT OF CLOTHING** an outfit that sb is wearing (*informal*) **4.** TRANSP **LORRY** an articulated lorry or lorry with a trailer (*informal*) **5.** *US* TRANSP **HORSE CARRIAGE** in former times, a carriage or cart pulled by one or more horses [15thC. Origin uncertain: probably from a Scandinavian source.]

rig out *vt.* (*informal*) **1.** **DRESS SB UP** to put a special kind of clothing on sb ○ *rigged himself out for a heavyweight bout* **2.** **PROVIDE EQUIPMENT FOR SB OR STH** to fit a person, place, or object with proper or necessary equipment ○ *rigged out for a trekking expedition*

rig[2] /rig/ *vt.* (**rigs, rigging, rigged**) **ARRANGE OUTCOME DISHONESTLY** to affect the outcome of sth by intervening dishonestly or unfairly to gain an advantage ■ *n.* **TRICK** a trick or swindle [Early 18thC. Origin unknown.]

rig[3] /rig/ *n.* a male animal in which one or both testes fail to descend into the scrotum at the usual time. The condition is most common in horses and pigs. (*informal*) [15thC. Variant of RIDGE.]

Riga /réegə/ capital city of Latvia, on its eastern coast. Population: 839,675 (1995).

rigadoon /rìggə do͞on/, **rigaudon** /ri gaw dáwN/ *n.* in former times, a lively couple dance, or the music for it, with two or four beats to the bar. Traditionally from the Provence region of France, in the 17th and 18th centuries it was popular in the French court where it was danced in a more dignified manner. [Late 17thC. From French *rigaudon*, of uncertain origin: perhaps named after *Rigaud*, a dancing-master in Marseilles who is said to have invented it.]

rigatoni /rìggə tṓni/ *n.* short rounded tubes of pasta with narrow ridges running along them [Mid-20thC. From Italian, from *rigato* 'ridged', the past participle of *rigare* 'to draw a line', from *riga* 'line'.]

rigaudon *n.* = **rigadoon**

Rigel /rīg'l/ *n.* a blue-white double star of the first magnitude in the constellation Orion [From Arabic *rijl*, literally 'foot', because it appears at the base of the constellation]

rigger /ríggər/ *n.* **1.** ROWING **BRACKET ON ROWING BOAT** a bracket supporting a rowlock on a rowing boat **2.** SAILING **SB WHO RIGS BOATS** sb whose job is to rig a boat **3.** SAILING **SHIP** a ship, especially one with a specific kind of rigging **4.** CONSTR **SCAFFOLDING WORKER** sb whose job is to erect and maintain scaffolding and lifting equipment **5.** INDUST **OIL-RIG WORKER** sb who works on an oil or gas rig

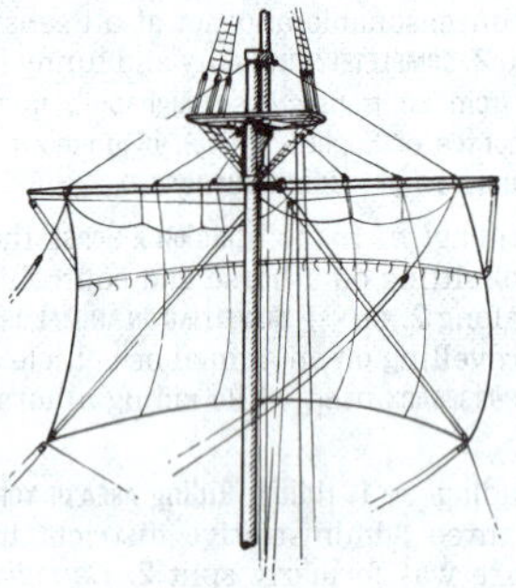

Rigging

rigging /rígging/ *n.* **1.** SAILING **ROPES, WIRES, AND PULLEYS** the ropes, wires, and pulleys that support the masts and control the sails of a boat **2.** THEATRE **THEATRE EQUIPMENT** the system of ropes, pulleys, and other equipment used to shift scenery on a stage **3.** **SUPPORTING EQUIPMENT** any system of ropes, pulleys, or other equipment used as a support for sth, e.g. construction scaffolding **4.** CLOTHES **SPECIAL-PURPOSE CLOTHING** clothing, especially when designed for a special purpose

rigging loft *n.* **1.** SHIPPING **RAISED AREA IN BOATYARD** a raised area or gallery in a boatyard where workers stand while fitting rigging **2.** THEATRE **AREA ABOVE STAGE** an area above a stage equipped with lifting gear for raising and lowering scenery

right /rīt/ *adj.* **1.** **TRUE** consistent with facts or belief ○ *gave the right answer* **2.** **SOCIALLY APPROVED** adhering to or consistent with conventional ideas of morality, propriety, or decorum ○ *right conduct between nations* **3.** **USUAL** conforming to what is usual or expected ○ *Something didn't seem right when I walked in.* **4.** **PROPER** proper with regard to use, function, or operation ○ *You're not holding the thing by the right end.* **5.** **BEST** most suitable or desirable ○ *waiting for the right offer to come along* **6.** **SUPERIOR** holding a view or position that is superior, more proper, or more moral ○ *hard to tell who's right in this situation* **7.** **HEALTHY** in good physical and mental health ○ *hasn't felt right in weeks* **8.** **IN A SATISFACTORY CONDITION** being in a satisfactory condition or proper state, or going into one ○ *make things right for them* **9.** **PROMINENT** prominent in business, society, or some other sphere ○ *knows all the right people* **10.** **EAST WHEN FACING NORTH** on the side of the body that is east when you face north **11.** **MAIN** main or most prominent ○ *has to be stored right side up* **12.** GEOM **PERPENDICULAR** being perpendicular or forming an angle of 90 degrees ■ *adv.* **1.** **PROPERLY** in the proper or conventional way, or a way that will be successful ○ *You didn't do it right.* **2.** **IMMEDIATELY OR EXACTLY** used to emphasize immediacy or exactness ○ *right at that moment* **3.** **STRAIGHT** without deviating from a course ○ *went right to work from the hospital* **4.** **CORRECTLY** in conformity with fact or expectation ○ *If you'd answered right you would have won £100.* **5.** **MORALLY AND APPROPRIATELY** in conformity with conventional morality, propriety, or justice ○ *I want to do right by my children.* **6.** **DESIRABLY** desirably or advantageously ○ *afraid that it won't turn out right* **7.** **TOWARDS EAST WHEN FACING NORTH** in or towards the east when you are facing or moving north, and correspondingly for other directions ○ *turn right at the church* **8.** **VERY** very (*regional*) ○ *a right good deal* **9.** **INTENSELY** used to intensify the meaning of another term ○ *He just kept right on going and didn't even think about anyone else.* **10.** **USED AS PART OF TITLE** used as part of a title of respect ○ *Right Reverend* ■ *n.* **1.** **MORALLY APPROPRIATE THING** that which is conventionally moral or appropriate ○ *She's too young to know right from wrong.* **2.** **ACCURATE OR TRUE** sth that is correct, completely true, and accurate **3.** **ENTITLEMENT** an entitlement, freedom, or privilege to do sth (*often used in the plural*) ○ *human rights* **4.** **ENTITLEMENT UNDER LAW** an entitlement granted under law ○ *the right to an appeal* **5.** LAW **CLAIM** sb's interest in a property (*often used in the plural*) **6.** FIN **SECURITIES OPTION** the entitlement or option to purchase or receive securities not offered for sale openly, or the certificate indicating this (*often used in the plural*) **7.** **Right, right** **CONSERVATIVES** political conservatives generally, or the opinions they hold **8.** **EAST WHEN FACING NORTH** the side of sth that lies east when you are facing north **9.** **RIGHT-HAND TURN** a turn to the right **10.** CLOTHES **ONE OF PAIR** the member of a pair designed for the right hand or foot **11.** **BLOW WITH RIGHT HAND** a blow delivered with the right hand ■ *v.* (**rights, righting, righted**) **1.** *vti.* **MAKE OR BECOME UPRIGHT** to put sth upright, or to return to an upright position ○ *I righted the vase and mopped up the water.* **2.** *vt.* **BRING JUSTICE** to bring justice or proper results to a situation **3.** *vt.* **CORRECT MISTAKE** to change sth that is wrong so that it is correct **4.** *vt.* **MAKE AMENDS FOR WRONG** to redress an error or misdeed ■ *interj.* **1.** **USED TO AGREE** used to indicate assent or understanding (*informal*) **2.** **SEEKING CONFIRMATION** used to solicit confirmation of a statement ○ *You just got here, right?* [Old English *riht*. Ultimately, from an Indo-European word meaning 'to go straight', which is also the ancestor of English *direct* and *rectify*.] —**righter** *n.* —**rightness** *n.* ◇ **be in the right** to be correct in what you say or do ◇ **have** *or* **catch sb bang to rights** to catch a criminal in the act of committing a crime (*informal*) ◇ **in sb's own right** because of sb's birth, ability, or other entitlement, without reference to anyone else ◇ **set** *or* **put sth to rights** to put sth into a correct or ordered state

WORD KEY: REGIONAL NOTE

Right is used as an intensifier meaning 'very' in such phrases as *right tasty, right tidy.* Intensifiers are often region specific. Northern Ireland speakers use 'right and' and 'brave and' to mean 'quite', as in *right and tall, brave and tricky*, and there is a growing tendency in England to use 'well', as in *well happy.*

rightable /rítəb'l/ *adj.* designed to be able to be restored to an upright position

rightabout /rítə bowt/ *n.* **TURN THROUGH 180°** a turn through 180° to face in the opposite direction ■ *adj., adv.* **FACING OPPOSITE** facing in the opposite direction

right angle *n.* an angle of 90° —**right-angled** *adj.*

right-angled triangle *n.* a triangle with one right angle. US term **right triangle**

right ascension *n.* one of the two reference points in the equatorial coordinate system for specifying the position of an astronomical object on the celestial sphere. Corresponding to longitude on the earth, it is measured in hours, minutes, and seconds eastwards from the vernal equinox, the point where the ecliptic intersects the celestial equator.

right atrioventricular valve *n.* = **tricuspid valve**

right away *adv.* immediately, without waiting or any delay

right-brain *adj.* relating to or involving emotions or creative ability that are believed to be associated with the right half of the cerebrum

right circular cone *n.* = **cone** *n.* 2

righteous /rīchəss/ *adj.* 1. STRICTLY OBSERVANT OF MORALITY always behaving according to a religious or moral code 2. JUSTIFIABLE considered to be correct or justifiable 3. RESPONDING TO INJUSTICE arising from the perception of great injustice or wrongdoing ○ *righteous indignation* ■ *n.* MORALLY UPRIGHT GROUP righteous people viewed as a group ○ *believing that the righteous will prevail* [Alteration of Old English *rihtwīs*, from earlier forms of RIGHT + -WISE] —**righteously** *adv.* —**righteousness** *n.*

rightful /rītf'l/ *adj.* 1. HAVING CLAIM with a legal or moral claim to sth ○ *the rightful owner* 2. OWNED BY SB WITH RIGHT owned by sb who has a right to it ○ *rightful property* 3. FAIR considered to be right and fair ○ *a rightful objection* —**rightfully** *adv.* —**rightfulness** *n.*

right hand *n.* 1. RIGHT SIDE the side of sth that lies east when you are facing north 2. SB INVALUABLE sb who is of invaluable assistance to another

WORD KEY: SYNONYMS

See Synonyms at ***assistant***.

right-hand *adj.* 1. ON OR TO THE RIGHT on the right or bending to the right 2. FOR THE RIGHT HAND designed for or done with the right hand 3. MOST IMPORTANT AND TRUSTED most important and trusted, and relied upon to the greatest extent

right-handed *adj.* 1. PREFERRING TO USE RIGHT HAND using the right hand in preference to the left for writing, throwing, and other activities that require skill and careful control 2. DONE WITH RIGHT HAND carried out with the right hand 3. DESIGNED FOR RIGHT HAND designed to be done with or used by the right hand 4. TOWARDS THE RIGHT turning towards the right in a clockwise direction ■ *adv.* 1. WITH RIGHT HAND using the right hand 2. TOWARDS THE LEFT with a swing or direction towards the left ○ *hit a ball right-handed* —**right-handedly** *adv.* —**right-handedness** *n.*

right-hander *n.* 1. SB RIGHT-HANDED a right-handed person, especially a sportsperson 2. BLOW WITH RIGHT HAND a blow delivered with the right hand

Right Honourable *n.* 1. USED WHEN REFERRING TO MP a title used in the British House of Commons when referring to, but not talking directly to, a member of parliament 2. TITLE OF PRIVY COUNCILLOR OR JUDGE a title used in Britain when referring to, but not talking directly to, a member of the Privy Council or a judge who presides over an appeal court 3. TITLE OF RESPECT a title used in Britain when referring to, but not talking directly to, a baron, viscount, or earl, and to lord mayors and lord provosts of some cities 4. *Can* CANADIAN TITLE OF RESPECT a title of respect used to refer to the governor general, prime minister, or chief justice of Canada, and some other eminent Canadians

rightio *interj.* = **righto** (*dated informal*)

rightist /rītist/ *adj.* RELATING TO CONSERVATISM favouring or relating to political conservatism ■ *n.* POLITICAL CONSERVATIVE sb with politically conservative views —**rightism** *n.*

rightly /rītli/ *adv.* 1. CORRECTLY correctly, properly, and appropriately 2. UNDERSTANDABLY with very good reason 3. CERTAINLY certainly or positively (*informal*)

right-minded *adj.* with opinions and attitudes considered to be sensible and fair —**right-mindedly** *adv.* —**right-mindedness** *n.*

rightmost /rīt mōst/ *adj.* in the position that is farthest to the right

righto /rī tó/, **right oh, rightio** /rīti ó/ *interj.* used to say that you acknowledge what sb has just said and that you will do what is suggested (*dated informal*) [Late 19thC. Formed from RIGHT + HO.]

right off *adv.* immediately, without waiting or any delay

right of search *n.* the right of a country at war to stop and search the merchant ships of neutral nations to determine if they are carrying forbidden goods that may be seized

right of way *n.* 1. TRANSP PERMISSION TO GO FIRST the legal or accepted right of a vehicle or craft to proceed ahead of another 2. LAW RIGHT TO CROSS PROPERTY the right to cross sb else's property by a specific route, e.g. as a means of accessing your own property 3. LAWFUL ROUTE ACROSS SB'S PROPERTY a lawful route that may be taken across sb else's property 4. *US, Can* TRANSP LAND USED FOR ROAD OR LINE a narrow length of land used for the route of a railway, electric power line, or public road

right on *interj.* *US* used to show enthusiastic agreement with sth said or done (*dated informal*)

right-on *adj.* (*informal*) 1. UP-TO-DATE socially and politically fashionable and forward-looking, particularly in a way that corresponds to the attitudes of the political left 2. *US* TRUE perfectly true

Right Reverend *n.* a form of address for a Roman Catholic, Anglican, or Episcopal bishop, or for a Roman Catholic abbot or monsignor

right shoulder arms *n.* the command or act of bringing a weapon to rest on the right shoulder during a military drill

rights issue *n.* an instance of an organization offering shares to existing holders on favourable terms so that they can maintain their percentage share of ownership

right-size (**right-sizes, right-sizing, right-sized**) *vi.* to achieve an optimal size appropriate to a particular company, usually an effort considered to require dismissal of employees

right stuff *n.* exactly the psychological and physical characteristics called for by a task (*informal*)

right-thinking *adj.* = **right-minded**

right-to-die *adj.* having or concerned with the right to cease living by obliging others not to intervene and thereby let nature take its course ○ *the right-to-die question*

right-to-life *adj.* = **pro-life**

rightward /rītwərd/ *adj.* moving towards or positioned on the right

rightwards /rītwərdz/ *adv.* towards the right

right whale *n.* a large-headed whale of the northern Atlantic and Pacific oceans with a deeply curved jawline and notched tail. Family: Balaenidae.

right wing *n.* 1. POL CONSERVATIVE MEMBERS the conservative membership of a group or political party 2. SPORTS PLAYER OR POSITION AT RIGHT in certain team games, the player or position occupying the right-hand part of a playing area when facing an opponent 3. MIL RIGHT-HAND MILITARY FORCE OR POSITION the right-hand part or position of a military force while facing the enemy

right-wing *adj.* 1. POL CONSERVATIVE conservative in conviction or temperament 2. SPORTS ON RIGHT WHILE FACING OPPONENT occupying the right-hand part of a playing area when facing an opponent 3. MIL OCCUPYING RIGHT DURING MILITARY ENGAGEMENT occupying the right-hand part or position of a military force when it is facing the enemy —**right-winger** *n.*

rigid /rījjid/ *adj.* 1. FIRM AND STIFF not bending or easily moved into a different shape or position ○ *lengths of rigid plastic pipe* 2. INFLEXIBLE applied or carried out strictly, with no allowances or exceptions ○ *a rigid set of rules* 3. HELD INFLEXIBLY inflexibly adhered to ○ *rigid opinions* 4. REFUSING TO CHANGE unchanging in behaviour, opinions, or attitudes ○ *Despite arguments to the contrary, she remained rigid in her stand.* [15thC. From Latin *rigidus*, from *rigere* 'to be stiff' (source of English rigour).] —**rigidity** /ri jíddəti/ *n.* —**rigidly** *adv.* —**rigidness** /rījjidnəss/ *n.*

rigid designator *n.* in philosophy, a name that stands for the same thing in every possible world as opposed to a description that could stand for sb or sth else in some possible world

rigidify /ri jíddi fī/ (**-fies, -fying, -fied**) *vti.* to become or cause sth to become stiff and inflexible

rigmarole /rígmərōl/ *n.* 1. OVERELABORATE ACCOUNT OF STH a tediously long, complicated, or unhelpful explanation 2. RIDICULOUSLY COMPLICATED PROCESS an irritating, tedious, or confusing sequence of tasks, especially tasks that seem unnecessary or absurd [Mid-18thC. Origin uncertain: probably an alteration of earlier *ragman roll*, a parchment scroll used in the gambling game of *ragman*.]

WORD KEY: ORIGIN

A *ragman roll* was a parchment scroll used in a medieval gambling game. The roll had things such as names written on it, with pieces of string attached to them, and participants had to select a string at random. The word *ragman* may have been a contraction of *ragged man*, perhaps in allusion to the appearance of the scroll, with all its bits of string hanging from it. *Ragman roll* eventually came to be used for any list or catalogue, and *ragman* itself denoted a 'long rambling discourse' in 16th-century Scottish English – a meaning that seems to have transferred itself eventually to ***rigmarole***.

rigor *n.* *US* = **rigour**

rigorism /rígərizəm/ *n.* 1. SEVERITY great strictness or severity 2. CHR ADOPTION OF STRICT MORALITY in Roman Catholic philosophy, the theory that in matters of moral choice the stricter course should be taken —**rigoristic** /rìggə rístik/ *adj.*

rigor mortis /rìggər máwrtiss/ *n.* the progressive stiffening of the body that occurs several hours after death, due to the coagulation of protein in the muscles. It usually starts to wane after about 24 hours. [From Latin, literally 'stiffness of death']

rigorous /ríggərəss/ *adj.* 1. STRICT harsh, strict, or difficult in nature ○ *a rigorous training programme* 2. EXACTING extremely precise and exacting ○ *rigorous standards of cleanliness* 3. SEVERE severe and extreme to experience ○ *climbing in rigorous conditions* 4. LOGIC PRECISE precise and formalized ○ *a rigorous proof* —**rigorously** *adv.* —**rigorousness** *n.*

rigour /ríggər/ *n.* 1. LACK OF TOLERANCE severity, strictness, or harshness in dealing with sb 2. USE OF DEMANDING STANDARDS the application of precise and exacting standards in the doing of sth 3. METEOROL SEVERE WEATHER harshness of weather or climate 4. HARDSHIP great hardship or difficulty 5. MED RIGIDITY OF BODY stiffness and lack of response to stimuli in body organs or tissues 6. MED SUDDEN FEELING OF CHILLINESS an abrupt attack of shivering and coldness, typically marking a rise in body temperature, e.g. at the onset of fever 7. BOT INERTIA IN PLANTS insensitivity of a plant due to unfavourable conditions [14thC. Directly and via Old French from Latin *rigor* 'stiffness', from *rigere* 'to be stiff' (source also of English *rigid*).]

Rig-Veda /ríg váydə/ *n.* a large collection of Hindu hymns dating from 2000 BC or earlier [Late 18thC. From Sanskrit *ṛgvedaḥ*, from *ṛc* 'verse' + *vedaḥ* 'knowledge' (see VEDA).]

Rijeka /ri éka/ city and port in northwestern Croatia, situated on the Gulf of Kvarner, on the Adriatic Sea. Population: 167,964 (1991).

rijsttafel /ríss taaf'l/, **rijstafel** *n.* a Dutch meal of Indonesian origin based on rice with many small side dishes, e.g. Indonesian-style curry, seafood, satay, soups, sauces, and condiments [Late 19thC. From Dutch, from *rijs* 'rice' + *tafel* 'table'.]

Riksdag /réeks dag/ *n.* the parliament of Sweden [Late 19thC. From Swedish, from *rike* 'realm' + *dag* 'day' (equivalent to German *Reichstag*).]

rile /rīl/ (**riles, riling, riled**) *vt.* 1. GET SB ANGRY to irritate sb enough that it provokes anger (*informal; often passive*) 2. *US, Can* MAKE WAVES IN WATER to stir up water or other liquid violently [Early 19thC. Variant of ROIL.]

Riley /rīli/ [Early 20thC. Origin uncertain: probably from a popular late 19th-century song.] ◇ **the life of Riley** a comfortable well-off life with no worries

Riley /rīli/, **Bridget** (*b.* 1931) British painter. She was a leading figure in the 1960s art movement known as op art. Full name **Bridget Louise Riley**

rilievo *n.* = **relievo**

rill /ril/ *n.* 1. STREAM a little stream or brook 2. GEOG GROOVE IN SOIL a small channel cut in soil 3. **rill, rille** ASTRON TRENCH ON MOON a long narrow valley on the

Moon's surface ■ *vt.* (**rills, rilling, rilled**) GEOG FORM CHANNELS IN FIELD to form small channels in a ploughed field as a result of the runoff of rainwater [Mid-16thC. From Low German *rille*. Ultimately from an Indo-European word meaning 'to run', which is also the ancestor of English *run* and *rivulet*.]

rillet /ríllit/ *n.* **1.** TINY STREAM a little rill **2.** ASTRON SHORT VALLEY ON MOON a short narrow valley on the moon's surface

rillettes /ri léts/ *n.* seasoned pork or goose cooked in its own fat until very tender and potted as a type of soft spreadable pâté (*takes a singular or plural verb*) [Late 19thC. From French, literally 'small pieces of pork', from *rille* 'piece of pork', a variant of *reille* 'board', from Latin *regula* (see RULE).]

rim /rim/ *n.* **1.** OUTER EDGE OF STH CIRCULAR an outer edge, often slightly raised, that runs along the outside of sth curved or circular **2.** LIMIT the farthest limit of sth (*literary*) **3.** TRANSP PART AROUND A WHEEL'S EDGE the curved outer edge of a wheel of a motor vehicle or bicycle **4.** PART OF GLASSES FRAME a usually curved part that holds and forms an edge to lenses in a pair of glasses **5.** BASKETBALL METAL HOOP FOR BASKETBALL NET the metal hoop to which a basketball net is attached ■ *vt.* (**rims, rimming, rimmed**) FORM STH'S OUTER EDGE to form an edge, usually a slightly raised edge, along the edge of sth curved or circular [Old English *rima* 'border, coast', of unknown origin] —**rimless** *adj.*

RIM *abbr.* Mauritania (*international vehicle registration*)

rimaye /ri máy/ *n.* GEOG = **bergschrund** [Early 20thC. From French, literally 'group of fissures', from Latin *rima* (see RIMOSE).]

Rimbaud /rámb ō/, **Arthur** (1854–91) French poet. Although he stopped writing at only 19 years of age, his poems were an important influence upon symbolism. Full name **Jean Nicholas Rimbaud**

rim-brake *n.* a brake that acts on the rim of a wheel

rime[1] /rīm/ *n.* FROST COATING a thin coating of frost formed on cold objects exposed to fog or cloud ■ *vt.* (**rimes, riming, rimed**) COAT STH WITH THIN FROST to cover sth with a thin frost or with sth resembling it (*often passive*) [Old English *hrīm*, from a prehistoric Germanic word of unknown origin]

rime[2] /rīm/ *n.* POETRY a rhyme (*archaic*)

rimfire /rím fīr/ *adj.* designed for or using a cartridge with its primer located in the rim of the base, rather than in the centre

Rimini /rímməni/ city and port in Forli Province, Emilia-Romagna Region, northern Italy, on the Adriatic Sea. Population: 129,876 (1992).

rim job *n.* an offensive term for the use of the lips and tongue on or in the anus of a sexual partner (*slang taboo*)

rimmed /rimd/ *adj.* made with an outer rim or border, sometimes of a different material, substance, or colour

rimose /rī mṓss/ *adj.* covered with cracks, fissures, or crevices [Early 18thC. From Latin *rimosus*, from *rima* 'fissure'. Ultimately from an Indo-European word meaning 'to scratch', which is also the ancestor of English *row*[1].] —**rimosely** *adv.* —**rimosity** /rī móssəti/ *n.*

Rimouski /ri moóski/ city in Canada, in Quebec State, on the St Lawrence River, northeast of Quebec City. Population: 48,104 (1996).

rimple /rímp'l/ *n.* WRINKLE a wrinkle (*regional archaic*) ■ *vti.* (**-ples, -pling, -pled**) TO WRINKLE to wrinkle, rumple, or crease sth (*regional archaic*) [Old English *hrympel*. From a prehistoric Germanic word that is also the ancestor of English *rumple*.]

rimrock /rím rok/ *n.* a layer of rock that forms a vertical boundary to a plateau, valley, or deposit of gravel

Rimsky-Korsakov /rímski káwssə kof/, **Nikolay** (1844–1908) Russian composer. He was renowned as a consummate orchestrator. His works, often inspired by Russian folk music, include *Scheherazade* (1888). Full name **Nikolay Andreyevich Rimsky-Korsakov**

rimu /ree moo/ *n.* = **red pine** [Mid-19thC. From Maori.]

rimy /rími/ (**-ier, -iest**) *adj.* with a thin coating of frost (*literary*)

rind /rīnd/ *n.* **1.** TOUGH OUTSIDE LAYER OF FRUIT the thick tough outer skin of a fruit **2.** FOOD HARD OUTER LAYER OF FOOD a tough outer protective layer of a food product, e.g. a cheese **3.** TREES BARK the bark of a tree or shrub [Old English *rind(e)*, literally 'sth torn off'. Ultimately from an Indo-European word meaning 'to tear', which is also the ancestor of English *rend*.]

rinderpest /ríndər pest/ *n.* a sometimes fatal viral disease mainly affecting cattle, sheep, and goats that occurs chiefly in central Africa and Asia and is marked by fever, haemorrhage, and diarrhoea. Animals can be vaccinated against rinderpest, and importation of animals from affected regions is strictly controlled. [Mid-19thC. From German, from *Rinder* 'cattle' + *Pest* 'plague'.]

rinforzando /reen fawr tsándō/ *adj., adv.* loud and with emphasis (*used as a musical direction*) [Early 19thC. From Italian 'getting stronger'.]

ring[1] /ring/ *n.* **1.** SMALL BAND OF STH a durable circular band of sth, especially a small band made of a particular material or for some special use **2.** ACCESSORIES SMALL CIRCULAR PIECE OF JEWELLERY a band, usually made of metal, worn as an ornament on a part of the body, especially round a finger. Rings are made in a variety of decorative designs, sometimes with mounted gemstones on the outer part of the band. **3.** ENCIRCLING MARK an outline, mark, or figure in the shape of a circle (*often used in the plural*) **4.** CIRCLE OF STH a circular arrangement of people or objects ○ *a ring of chairs* **5.** CIRCULAR MOTION a movement of steps, especially by people skipping or dancing, that goes round in a continuous circle ○ *dancing in a ring* **6.** ROUND COOKING SURFACE a circular device on a stove designed to stand a pan on so that heat may be turned on and adjusted for cooking **7.** CRIMINOL GROUP OF PEOPLE OPERATING DISHONESTLY an organized group of people who work together in a dishonest or unethical way ○ *a gambling ring* **8.** ARTS CIRCULAR AREA FOR PERFORMANCE a round stage or piece of ground, usually surrounded by seating, on which a spectator event such as a circus or a theatrical performance takes place ○ *a three-ring circus* **9.** BOXING, WRESTLING PLATFORM FOR BOXING OR WRESTLING a raised square roped platform on which a boxing or wrestling match takes place **10.** BOXING BOXING the sport of boxing ○ *choose the ring as a career* **11.** ASTRON BAND OF MATTER CIRCLING PLANET a band of dust, particles, and small bodies revolving around a planet. Such bands are known to circle Saturn, Jupiter, Uranus, and Neptune. **12.** TREES = **growth ring 13.** SPORTS = **bullring 14.** GAMBLING BETTING ENCLOSURE an enclosed area in which bets are taken at a racecourse **15.** CONTEST a competition or contest, especially a political one **16.** AGRIC ENCLOSURE FOR LIVESTOCK AT FAIR an enclosure at a market or agricultural show in which livestock are shown, paraded, or auctioned **17.** TURN OF SPIRAL a single turn of a spiral **18.** MATH SET OF MATHEMATICAL ELEMENTS a set of elements that is associative under multiplication and distributive under addition **19.** CHEM CLOSED LOOP OF ATOMS a collection of bound atoms represented graphically in cyclic form **20.** GEOM SPACE BETWEEN CIRCLES a space between two concentric circles ■ **rings** *npl.* SPORTS GYMNASTIC APPARATUS a pair of wooden rings that are suspended from a ceiling and used to perform gymnastic routines ■ *v.* (**rings, ringing, ringed**) **1.** *vt.* WRITE CIRCLE ROUND STH to draw or mark a circle round sth, e.g. a word or number **2.** *vti.* ENCIRCLE to encircle sth, or be encircled by sth ○ *We were ringed by the herd of cattle.* **3.** *vt.* ZOOL, VET, GAME IDENTIFY AN ANIMAL WITH TAG to attach a ring-shaped tag to an animal, especially to the leg of a bird, for subsequent identification **4.** *vt.* FORESTRY = **girdle** [Old English *hring*. Ultimately from an Indo-European base meaning 'to curl', which is also the ancestor of English *shrink* and *curve*.]

——— **WORD KEY: CULTURAL NOTE** ———

The Ring of the Nibelung, a series of musical dramas by German composer Richard Wagner (1813–83). Based on Teutonic legends, this massive tetralogy — *The Rhinegold* (1869), *The Valkyrie* (1870), *Siegfried* (1876), and *The Twilight of the Gods* (1876) — a full performance of which lasts up to 15 hours, recounts the complex chain of events triggered by the theft of a magical gold ring. It represents Wagner's most successful attempt to create a new form of theatre in which poetic drama is set to a musical score unified by recurring themes or leitmotifs.

ring back *vti.* to make a return telephone call to sb (*informal*) ○ *I left several messages but she never rang back.*

ring in *v.* **1.** *vti.* = **phone in 2.** *vt.* CELEBRATE THE BEGINNING OF STH to make bells ring in celebration of the beginning of sth **3.** *vt.* Aus FRAUDULENTLY SUBSTITUTE STH to substitute sth fraudulently, especially a horse in a race

ring off *vi.* to finish speaking on the telephone and to break the connection, usually by replacing the receiver

ring out *v.* **1.** *vi.* SOUND LOUDLY to be heard loudly and clearly **2.** *vt.* CELEBRATE THE END OF STH to make bells ring in celebration of the end of sth

ring up *v.* **1.** *vti.* PHONE to telephone sb **2.** *vt.* COMM ENTER SUM PAID FOR STH to press keys on a cash register to record the amount of money being paid for sth (*dated*)

ring[2] /ring/ *v.* (**rings, ringing, rang** /rang/, **rung** /rung/) **1.** *vti.* MAKE THE SOUND OF A BELL to make, or cause sth such as a bell to make, a metallic sound when struck or played **2.** *vti.* MAKE A SOUND TO ALERT SB to produce or make sth produce a continuous or regular high-pitched sound to alert sb **3.** *vti.* UTIL TELEPHONE to telephone sb ○ *He rang me to cancel the appointment.* **4.** *vi.* ECHO LOUDLY to be full of a loud, high-pitched, or reverberating sound, especially laughter or applause ○ *The hall rang with applause.* **5.** *vi.* MAKE CALL FOR STH to call for sb or sth by sounding a bell or buzzer **6.** *vi.* IMPRESS SB AS STH to make a particular impression on sb ○ *His excuse didn't ring true.* **7.** *vi.* HAVE SENSATION OF HIGH-PITCHED SOUNDS to have a sensation of a repeated or continuous high-pitched sound ○ *It made my ears ring.* ■ *n.* **1.** ACT OF SOUNDING BELL the act of making a bell sound **2.** BELL SOUND the sound of a bell or sth like a bell **3.** UTIL PHONE CALL a call on the telephone (*informal*) ○ *She gave us a ring about noon.* **4.** GENERAL IMPRESSION a general impression made by sb or sth ○ *It had a familiar ring to it.* **5.** REPEATED SOUND a loud continuous repeated or reverberating sound **6.** SET OF BELLS IN TOWER a set of bells in a tower or belfry [Old English *hringan*, of uncertain origin: probably from a prehistoric Germanic word meaning 'to make a noise', which is also the ancestor of English *raven* and *cricket*[1]] ◇ **ring down the curtain on sth** to bring an end to sth (*informal*)

ring-a-ring-a-roses /-rṓziz/ *n.* a young children's game in which players sing while moving round in a circle and abruptly squat when the words 'all fall down' are sung [Late 19thC. Origin uncertain: popularly thought to refer to the 'rosy' (rash) of the bubonic plague, but probably originally simply a singing game with a curtsy at the end.]

ring-around-the-rosey *n.* US = **ring-a-ring-a-roses**

ringbark /ríng baark/ *vt.* = **girdle**

ring-bill *n.* = **ring-necked duck**

ring-billed gull *n.* a white gull that nests by inland lakes of North America, lives on the coast in winter, and has a black ring round its bill. Latin name: *Larus delawarensis.*

ring binder *n.* a stiff cover with metal rings inside the spine that snap open for insertion or removal of punched looseleaf paper

ring-bolt *n.* a bolt with a ring fitted through the eye at its head

ringbone /ríng bōn/ *n.* **1.** HORSE'S BONE DISORDER a condition of a horse's pastern bone in which bony outgrowths develop, sometimes leading to pain and lameness. It is treated with rest, medication, or surgery. **2.** BONY OUTGROWTH a bony outgrowth characteristic of ringbone [So called because the outgrowths encircle the bone]

ring buoy *n.* a buoy in the shape of a ring

ring circuit *n.* a wiring arrangement in which electrical power is distributed to sockets and appliances through a single loop of cable that begins and ends in a fusebox

ring dance *n.* = **round dance**

ringdove /ríng duv/ *n.* **1.** = **wood pigeon 2.** BLACK-COLLARED PIGEON a domesticated variety of the collared dove that has a semicircular black collar. Latin name: *Streptopelia risoria.*

ring-dyke *n.* a system of volcanic outcrops of magma (**dykes**) that form a ring-like structure

ringed /ringd/ *adj.* **1.** WEARING RING wearing one or more rings **2.** ENCIRCLED encircled by a ring **3.** ZOOL WITH MARKS THAT FORM RING with markings that form a ring round the neck, bill, or other body part

ringed plover *n.* a plover of sandy or shingle shores of Europe, Asia, and Africa with a grey back and wings, white undersides, a black breast band, and a black-tipped orange bill. Latin name: *Charadrius hiaticula.*

ringed seal *n.* a seal of Arctic and subarctic regions that has a dark greyish coat with lighter markings that encircle the body. Latin name: *Pusa hispida.*

ringent /rínjənt/ *adj.* with an opening bordered by parts resembling the lips of a gaping mouth, as has, e.g. the flower of an antirrhinum [Mid-18thC. From Latin *ringent-*, the present participle stem of *ringi* 'to gape' (source of English *rictus*).]

ringer[1] /ríngər/ *n.* **1.** US term **bander.** AUS term **stockman 2.** *Aus* AGRIC FAST SHEARER the fastest shearer in a shed **3.** *Aus* FASTEST the fastest or best at anything **4.** *US* CRIMINOL FRAUDULENT ENTRY sb or sth fraudulently substituted in a competition (*informal*) **5.** LEISURE GAME OF MARBLES a game in which marbles are formed like a cross inside a circle and each player uses a marble to shoot the laid out marbles outside the circle

ringer[2] /ríngər/ *n.* **1.** SB WHO RINGS A BELL sb who rings a bell **2.** STH THROWN AT AND ENCIRCLING PEG a quoit thrown skilfully so that it encircles a peg or stake

ringers /ríngərz/ *n.* = **ringer**[1] *n.* 5 (*takes a singular verb*)

Ringer's solution /ríngərz-/, **Ringer solution** *n.* a solution of inorganic salts used to sustain cells, tissues, or organs outside the body [Late 19thC. Named after Sydney *Ringer* (1834–1910), the British physician who introduced this type of solution.]

ring-fence *vt.* (**ring-fences, ring-fencing, ring-fenced**) SPECIFY USE OF MONEY to specify that money be used for a specific purpose ■ *n.* **1.** FIN AGREEMENT RESTRICTING USE OF MONEY an agreement in which money is reserved for a particular purpose **2.** AGRIC FENCE ENCLOSING AREA a fence that encircles a large area or a whole estate within one enclosure

ring finger *n.* the third finger of the hand, especially the left hand, on which an engagement or wedding ring is traditionally worn

ringhals /ríng halss/ (*plural* **-hals** *or* **-halses**) *n.* a southern African snake related to the cobra that has a small rough-skinned black or brown body and can spit jets of venom from its fangs at an aggressor. Latin name: *Hemachatus hemachatus.* [Late 18thC. From Afrikaans, literally 'ring-neck', from the one or two white rings across the snake's neck.]

ring-in *n. Aus* an outsider brought into a team or group, usually to replace sb or make up the numbers (*informal*)

ringing /ríngíng/ *n.* CONTINUING SOUND a clear continuing usually high-pitched sound ■ *adj.* STATED LOUDLY AND UNMISTAKABLY expressed in a definite and unrestrained way —**ringingly** *adv.*

ringing tone *n.* a sequence of paired sounds heard in a telephone receiver when a number has been dialled successfully to a phone that is not already engaged

ringleader /ríng leedər/ *n.* the member of a circle or gang who organizes and encourages others to do sth unlawful or rebellious [From the phrase *lead the ring* 'to go first']

ringlet /rínglət/ *n.* **1.** HAIR CURLY LOCK OF HAIR a spiral curl of hair **2.** ZOOL BROWN EUROPEAN BUTTERFLY a southern European brown butterfly with dark eyespots on the wings, found in hedges, wood margins, and other shady places. Genus: *Erebia.* **3.** SMALL RING a small ring or circle

ringleted /ringlətid/ *adj.* wearing the hair in ringlets

ring main *n.* a wiring circuit in which a number of outlet sockets are connected in parallel to a ring circuit which starts and finishes at a mains supply point

ringmaster /ríng maastər/ *n.* sb who presides over a circus show from a ring, announcing and commenting on the events

Ring Nebula *n.* a nebula in the constellation Lyra that has a ring-shaped appearance

ring-necked /ríng nékt/, **ringneck** /-nek/ *adj.* with markings resembling a ring round the neck in a colour that contrasts with adjacent feathers, scales, or hair

ring-necked duck *n.* a North American diving duck found on woodland ponds that has coppery ring neck markings and two white rings on the bill. The males are mainly black, the females mostly brown. Latin name: *Aythya collaris.*

ring-necked pheasant *n.* an Asian pheasant widely introduced elsewhere as a game bird. Males have a white neck collar, a red head, and lustrous coppery-red and green plumage; females are mottled brown. Latin name: *Phasianus colchicus.*

ringneck snake /ríng nek-/, **ring-necked snake** *n.* a small nonvenomous North American snake that has a yellowish or orange neck band. Genus: *Diadophis.*

ring ouzel *n.* = **ousel**

ring-porous *adj.* with annual rings marked by prominent bands of large pores. These rings are readily apparent when a cross section of a trunk or branch is examined.

ring-pull *n.* a ring or tab of metal on the top of a drinks can that is pulled in order to open it. US term **pull-tab**

ring road *n.* a main road designed and built to take traffic round the edge of an urban area so that the urban centre can be kept free of traffic congestion. US term **beltway**

ringside /ríng sīd/ *n.* **1.** AREA NEXT TO RING the row of seats or area directly in front of a boxing, wrestling, or circus ring **2.** PLACE OFFERING GOOD VIEW OF STH a place or location offering a clear and close view of sth (*informal*) —**ringsider** *n.*

ring-spot *n.* **1.** ROUND PLANT DISCOLORATION a pale or yellowish ring-shaped discoloration occurring in plants infected with a virus disease **2.** FUNGAL DISEASE OF CABBAGE a fungus disease affecting members of the cabbage family, with brown spots appearing on the leaves

ringster /ríngstər/ *n.* sb who belongs to an illegal or unethical business or political group that manipulates sth to its own advantage (*dated*)

ringtail /ríng tayl/ *n.* **1.** RING-TAILED ANIMAL a ring-tailed mammal, especially a member of the family that includes the cacomistle and raccoon. Family: Procyonidae. **2.** = **ringtail possum**

ring-tailed *adj.* with a tail encircled by coloured bands or markings in a colour that contrasts with adjacent feathers, scales, or hair

ring-tailed lemur *n.* a lemur with a grey coat and a long tail with black and white bands. Latin name: *Lemur catta.*

ringtail possum /ríng tayl-/ *n.* a possum found in Australasia and New Guinea that has a curly-tipped striped tail that it uses for grasping branches and carrying objects. Family: Pseudocheiridae.

ringworm /ríng wurm/ *n.* a fungal disease of the skin, scalp, or nails in which intensely itchy ring-shaped patches develop. Infection is transmitted to humans from pets or livestock, or from infected bedding.

rink /ringk/ *n.* **1.** ICE SKATING AREA OF ICE USED FOR SPORTS a smooth, enclosed, and often artificially prepared ice surface used for ice-skating, ice hockey, or curling **2.** SPORTS SURFACE USED FOR ROLLER-SKATING a smooth, enclosed, usually wooden surface used for roller-skating **3.** SPORTS BUILDING FOR ICE SPORTS a building or arena in which ice-skating, ice hockey, or curling takes place **4.** BOWLS PART OF BOWLING GREEN FOR MATCH an area of a bowling green on which a single match takes place **5.** SPORTS PLAYING SIDE a team of players in curling, bowls, or quoits [14thC. Origin uncertain: perhaps ultimately from Old French *renc* 'line, row' (see RANK[1]). The English word originally meant 'racecourse'.]

rinky-dink /ríngki dingk/ *adj. US* (*informal*) **1.** OUT-OF-DATE broken down or no longer useful **2.** OLD-FASHIONED old-fashioned or outmoded **3.** INSIGNIFICANT small and insignificant [Late 19thC. Origin uncertain: perhaps an alteration of RICKETY.]

rinse /rinss/ *vt.* (**rinses, rinsing, rinsed**) **1.** LIGHTLY CLEAN STH IN LIQUID to wash sth lightly by dipping it in a liquid, especially clean water, or by running liquid over it **2.** FLUSH MOUTH WITH WATER to flush the mouth or teeth with clean water **3.** TEXTILES DIP STH INTO DYE to dip fabrics or garments into a dye solution ■ *n.* **1.** GENTLE WASH the act of washing sth lightly by running a liquid, usually clean water, over or around it **2.** HAIR COSMETIC TREATMENT FOR HAIR a solution that is applied to sb's wet hair to alter or enhance its colour or condition temporarily **3.** CLEANSING LIQUID a liquid, usually water or a water-based solution, used to wash away sth lightly [13thC. Via Old French *reincier*, of uncertain origin: possibly via assumed Vulgar Latin *recentiare* 'to freshen', from Latin *recens* (see RECENT).] —**rinsable** *adj.* —**rinser** *n.* —**rinsible** *adj.*

rinsing /rínssing/ *n.* the process or action of washing sth quickly, gently, or finally in clean water or a cleaning solution

Rio de Janeiro /reé ō də zhə neér ō, -day-, -di-/ city and port in Brazil, in the southeast of the country. It is the capital of Rio de Janeiro State, and the former capital of the country. Population: 5,533,011 (1996).

Rio Grande /reé ō gránd, -grándi/ river of North America, rising in Colorado, flowing through New Mexico and along the Texas-Mexico boundary, and emptying into the Gulf of Mexico. Length: 3,034 km/1,885 mi.

Rioja /ri óhə, ri ókhə/ *n.* a dry red or white wine with a distinctive flavour, produced in northern Spain [Early 20thC. Named after *Rioja*, the district in northern Spain where the wine is produced.]

Río Muni /reé ō mooni/ mainland region of Equatorial Guinea, in western-central Africa. Population: 240,804 (1983). Area: 26,017 sq. km/10,045 sq. mi.

riot /rí ət/ *n.* **1.** VIOLENT DISTURBANCE a public disturbance during which a group of angry people becomes noisy and out of control, often damaging property and acting violently. In law, a riot is typically defined as a group of three or more persons disturbing the public peace for private purposes. **2.** STH EXTREMELY ENJOYABLE a social occasion, event, or experience that people enjoy in a wild, noisy, and energetic way (*informal*) **3.** FUNNY PERSON sb who is highly amusing (*informal*) **4.** GREAT DISPLAY a spectacular visual display **5.** UNCONTROLLED WAY OF LIFE behaviour that shows complete lack of control, especially financially or sexually (*archaic*) ■ *vi.* (**-ots, -oting, -oted**) **1.** TAKE PART IN PUBLIC DISTURBANCE to act as part of a crowd in an unruly, violent, and unrestrained way **2.** BE WILD AND SELF-INDULGENT to behave without any personal control, especially financially or sexually (*archaic*) [12thC. From Old French, 'quarrel', from *rioter* 'to quarrel', of uncertain origin.] ◇ **run riot 1.** to behave in a wild and uncontrolled way **2.** to grow in profusion

Riot Act *n.* an English law, passed in 1713, providing that persons making a public disturbance had to disperse within one hour of having had the act read to them by a magistrate ◇ **read (sb) the riot act** to reprimand sb severely for doing sth, often including a threat of punishment if the offending behaviour does not stop

riot gun *n.* a short-barrelled gun used to disperse crowds. It fires plastic or rubber bullets, or CS gas cartridges.

riotous /rí ətəss/ *adj.* **1.** UNRESTRAINED loud, conspicuous, and unrestrained **2.** RIOTING OR LIKELY TO RIOT involved in or taking part in serious public unrest (*formal*) —**riotously** *adv.* —**riotousness** *n.*

riot police *n.* a police reserve specially equipped for controlling a rioting crowd

riot shield *n.* a large oblong transparent shield used to protect the face and upper body of a police officer attempting to disperse a riot

rip[1] /rip/ *v.* (**rips, ripping, ripped**) **1.** *vti.* TEAR OR BE TORN to tear sth or become torn with a sudden or rough splitting action, especially occurring accidentally and usually accompanied by a distinct tearing noise **2.** *vt.* **USE FORCE TO REMOVE STH** to remove sth from a place where it had been firmly fixed, especially by tearing it out forcibly without taking time or care ○ *Most of the original features of the house were ripped out.* **3.** *vi.* **MOVE WITH EXTREME SPEED** to move with dangerous or violent speed ○ *The tornado ripped through northern Nebraska.* **4.** *vt.* WOODWORK **DIVIDE TIMBER LENGTHWAYS** to make a split along the grain of a piece of wood using a saw or chopping tool ■ *n.* **1.** **ROUGHLY TORN PLACE** a rough tear or split, especially one that is caused suddenly and forcefully **2.** **RIPSAW** a ripsaw (*informal*) [14thC. Origin uncertain. Ultimately from an Indo-European base meaning 'to snatch away', which is also the ancestor of English *rob* and *bereave*.] ◇ **let rip** to speak rapidly and without restraint, especially with a series of curses (*informal*)

—— **WORD KEY: SYNONYMS** ——
See Synonyms at **tear**.

rip into *vt.* to attack sb or sth, especially with a sudden and damaging criticism (*informal*)
rip off *vt.* (*informal*) **1.** **TREAT SB UNFAIRLY OVER MONEY** to charge sb an unfair price or cheat sb financially **2.** **STEAL STH** to rob sb or steal sth
rip up *vt.* to tear sth up with the hands into pieces or strips

rip² /rip/ *n.* **1.** **ROUGH WATER** an area of rough water caused by winds or opposing currents **2.** = **rip current, riptide** [Late 18thC. Origin uncertain: probably from RIP¹.]

rip³ /rip/ *n.* (*archaic informal*) **1.** **DISSOLUTE PERSON** sb considered to be corrupt and dissolute **2.** **STH OLD AND WORTHLESS** sth, especially a horse, that is old and of no value [Late 18thC. Origin uncertain: perhaps an altered shortening of REPROBATE.]

RIP *abbr.* rest in peace [Latin *requiescat in pace* or *requiescant in pace*]

riparian /rī paíri ən, ri-/ *adj.* **ALONG RIVERBANK** situated or taking place along or near the bank of a river ■ *n.* **LAND OWNER BY RIVER** sb who owns land along a river [Mid-19thC. Formed from Latin *riparius* (source of English *river*), from *ripa* 'riverbank'. Ultimately from an Indo-European word meaning 'to cut', which is also the ancestor of *rift*.]

ripcord /ríp kawrd/ *n.* **1.** **CORD TO OPEN PARACHUTE** a cord that, when pulled, opens a parachute **2.** **CORD RELEASING GAS IN BALLOON** a cord used to release gas from a hot air balloon during an emergency

rip current *n.* a narrow current strongly flowing from the shore to the sea, visible as a band of agitated water [From RIP²]

ripe /rīp/ (**riper, ripest**) *adj.* **1.** **READY AND PLEASANT TO EAT** ready to be picked and eaten because it is mature and has reached optimum flavour **2.** BOT, AGRIC **READY TO HARVEST** having developed to the stage for harvesting and subsequent storage or sale **3.** FOOD **MATURE AND MELLOW** matured enough to have developed the best flavour and body ○ *ripe cheese* **4.** **IMPOLITE OR LEWD** full of rude words, swearwords, sexual references, or outrageous opinions (*informal*) **5.** **EXACTLY READY** at the most suitable stage of preparation or development ○ *The occasion was ripe for asking for a pay rise.* **6.** **ADVANCED IN YEARS** representing or constituting a long life **7.** **EXPERIENCED AND KNOWLEDGEABLE** showing plenty of experience and knowledge accumulated gradually over time **8.** **SMELLY** giving off a strong and unpleasant smell, especially caused by sweat from part of the body (*informal*) **9.** **FULL AND RED** full and ruddy, suggesting ripe fruit [Old English *rīpe*. Ultimately from a prehistoric Germanic word that is also the ancestor of English *reap* and *ripple²*.] —**ripely** *adv.* —**ripeness** *n.*

ripen /rípən/ (**-ens, -ening, -ened**) *vti.* **1.** **MAKE OR BECOME READY TO EAT** to reach, or cause fruit or other food to reach, a ripe or mature condition **2.** **REACH RIGHT CONDITION** to become or make sth fully developed, mature, or ready (*often passive*) —**ripener** *n.* —**ripening** *adj.*, *n.*

ripieno /ríppi áyn ō/ *n.* in a baroque concerto, the full ensemble, as contrasted with the soloist or group of soloists (**concertino**) [Mid-18thC. From Italian, literally 'filled up', from *pieno* 'full'.]

---

rip-off *n.* (*informal*) **1.** **UNFAIRLY PRICED ITEM** sth that is not worth the price asked or paid **2.** **ACT OF BEING DISHONESTLY TREATED** an act or example of being cheated, tricked, or exploited **3.** **IMITATION OF STH** an imitation of sth more inventive, successful, or famous perpetrated in order to make a financial gain based on the other's reputation

Ripon /ríppən/ city in North Yorkshire, England, on the River Ure. Population: 13,806 (1991).

riposte /ri póst/ *n.* **1.** **SMART ANSWER** sth said or done quickly and effectively in response **2.** FENCING **QUICK FENCING THRUST** a quick deft thrust made after parrying the lunge of a fencing opponent [Early 18thC. Via French from Italian *risposta*, the past participle of *rispondere* 'to respond', from Latin *respondere* (see RESPOND).]

—— **WORD KEY: SYNONYMS** ——
See Synonyms at **answer**.

ripper /ríppər/ *n.* (*informal*) **1.** **MURDERER USING KNIFE** a murderer who uses a knife to kill and mutilate people **2.** Aus **EXCELLENT THING** sth or sb outstandingly good ○ *a ripper of a shot* ■ *interj.* Aus **EXCLAMATION OF ENTHUSIASM** used to express enthusiasm or delight (*informal*)

ripping /rípping/ *adj.* wonderful or excellent (*dated informal*) —**rippingly** *adv.*

ripple¹ /rípp'l/ *v.* (**-ples, -pling, -pled**) **1.** *vti.* **FLOW IN TINY GENTLE WAVES** to flow with, or be lightly disturbed by, a succession of tiny waves moving quickly and gently ○ *a breeze rippled the water* **2.** *vti.* **SHAPE STH INTO GENTLE WAVY PATTERN** to take on or give sth an appearance of very small wavy shapes across its surface or length **3.** *vi.* **MAKE LAPPING SOUND** to make a gentle lapping sound **4.** *vi.* **BE HEARD BRIEFLY AMONG CROWD** to begin as a sound made by a few people, spreading and briefly becoming slightly louder before dying away ○ *Laughter rippled round the room.* ■ *n.* **1.** **TINY WAVE OR SERIES OF WAVES** a small wave or series of gentle waves across a surface **2.** **GENTLE WAVY SHAPE OR MARK** sth that resembles a ripple in its smooth undulating shape **3.** **GENTLE PATTERN OF SOUND** a sound that starts quietly and then spreads, becoming slightly louder for a few seconds before dying away ○ *a ripple of scorn* **4.** GEOL **SHALLOW BROKEN RIVER WATER** an area of shallow water in a river broken by rocks or sand bars **5.** ELEC **OSCILLATION OF CURRENT** a small oscillation of electrical current ■ **ripples** *npl.* **CONSEQUENCES** a series of repercussions or consequences ○ *The ripples of the sector's downturn continue to be felt.* ■ *adj.* FOOD **WITH SECOND FLAVOUR MIXED IN** with a second flavour partly combined or marbled through ○ *raspberry ripple ice cream* [Late 17thC. Origin unknown.] —**rippler** *n.* —**ripply** *adj.*

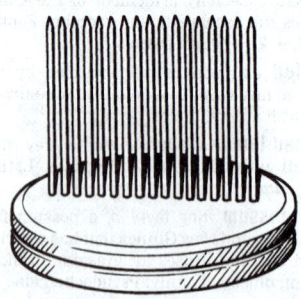

Ripple

ripple² /rípp'l/ *vt.* (**-ples, -pling, -pled**) **REMOVE PLANT'S SEEDS** to use a comb-shaped tool to remove seeds from a plant ■ *n.* **TOOL TO REMOVE PLANT'S SEEDS** a comb-shaped tool used to remove seeds from a plant [Mid-17thC. Origin uncertain.]

ripple effect *n.* a spreading series of effects or consequences caused by a single event [From the ripples that spread across the surface of a pool when sth is dropped into the water]

ripple mark *n.* a series of small wavy ridges created in sand or silt by wind or water. Ripple marks can be preserved in sedimentary rocks. —**ripple-marked** *adj.*

---

ripplet /ríplit/ *n.* a small ripple (*literary*)

rippling /rípp'ling/ *adj.* **1.** **IN SMOOTH GENTLE WAVES** moving in or resembling the flow of small gentle waves **2.** **SOUNDING LIKE SOFTLY FLOWING WATER** moving with a gentle lapping or soothingly liquid sound ■ *n.* **SOUND OF SOFTLY FLOWING WATER** the gentle lapping sound that shallow or lightly disturbed water makes as it flows

riprap /ríp rap/ *n.* **1.** **BROKEN STONE USED IN CONSTRUCTION** broken stone used in making protective foundations and embankments for riverbeds and riverbanks **2.** **STH BUILT OF BROKEN STONE** a protective foundation or embankment made from broken stone loosely or irregularly combined ■ *vt.* (**-raps, -rapping, -rapped**) **CONSTRUCT STH WITH BROKEN STONE** to build or strengthen a riverbed or riverbank with broken stone [Late 16thC. Doubling of RAP¹.]

rip-roaring /-ráwring/ *adj.* full of boisterous excitement or energy (*informal*) [Mid-19thC. Formed from RIP¹ + UPROARIOUS.] —**rip-roaringly** *adv.*

ripsaw /ríp saw/ *n.* a saw with coarse teeth used to cut wood along the grain of wood

ripsnorter /ríp snawrtər/ *n.* US sth or sb exceptionally impressive (*informal*) [Mid-19thC. Formed from RIP¹ + SNORT 'sth big and impressive'.]

ripstop /ríp stop/ *adj.* woven with extra threads to make tearing less likely ○ *ripstop nylon*

riptide /ríp tīd/ *n.* a strong narrow tide that opposes other currents and produces turbulence, especially sea water that rushes seawards after incoming waves mount up on the shore [From RIP²]

Ripuarian /ríppyoo aíri ən/ *adj.* belonging or relating to the Frankish people who lived beside the Rhine in the 4th century BC [Late 18thC. Formed from medieval Latin *Ripuarius*, of unknown origin.]

RISC /risk/ *abbr.* reduced-instruction-set computer

rise /rīz/ *v.* (**rises, rising, rose** /rōz/, **risen** /rízz'n/) **1.** *vi.* **STAND UP** to assume a standing or nearly vertical position after sitting, kneeling, or lying **2.** *vi.* **ASCEND** to go up to a higher position or location ○ *Disturbed by our footsteps, the birds rose above the trees.* **3.** *vi.* **GET HIGHER** to gain a greater height or level ○ *After heavy rains the river rose dangerously.* **4.** *vi.* **GROW LARGER** to increase in amount, degree, or quantity ○ *Prices are rising.* **5.** *vi.* **ACHIEVE GREATER SOCIAL PROMINENCE** to achieve higher wealth, status, or importance ○ *He rose steadily through the ranks.* **6.** *vi.* **EXTEND UPWARDS** to become elevated or extend upwards ○ *The church tower rose above the village.* **7.** *vi.* **GROW LOUDER OR MORE INTENSE** to increase in volume or intensity of sound ○ *Their voices rose.* **8.** *vi.* **BECOME MENTALLY MORE INTENSE** to become more intense or powerful in the mind ○ *Her spirits rose.* **9.** *vi.* **GROW OR INTENSIFY** to grow or intensify, especially until a particular state is reached ○ *When we woke, the wind had risen.* **10.** *vi.* **BECOME LARGER AND PUFFIER** to swell and puff out, e.g. in the manner of dough containing yeast ○ *The bread is rising.* **11.** *vi.* **REBEL OR REVOLT** to make an organized rebellion against sth or sb ○ *They rose against the government.* **12.** *vi.* **END A MEETING** to adjourn after a meeting or assembly **13.** *vi.* **BECOME ERECT** to become stiff and erect ○ *He felt the hair rise on the back of his neck.* **14.** *vi.* **BECOME GREATER** to become stronger or more stimulated ○ *Her temper rose.* **15.** *vi.* **ORIGINATE** to have an origin or beginning ○ *The stream rises a few miles back.* **16.** *vi.* **GROW** to spring up or grow **17.** *vi.* **BECOME APPARENT** to become visible or apparent ○ *After many days at sea, Africa rose before their astonished eyes.* **18.** *vi.* **BUILDING BE BUILT** to become larger during the process of building **19.** *vi.* ASTRON **APPEAR OVER HORIZON** to appear above the horizon ○ *The sun was rising when we went to bed.* **20.** *vt.* NAUT = **raise** *v.* 26 **21.** *vi.* ANGLING **MOVE UP TO TAKE BAIT** to move up to the surface of water to take an angler's bait ○ *The trout rose to my fly.* **22.** *vi.* **BE RESURRECTED** to become resurrected ○ *rise from the dead* ■ *n.* **1.** **INCREASE** an increase in amount ○ *a rise in prices* **2.** **SALARY INCREASE** an increase in salary or wages **3.** **PROCESS OF BEING NOTICED** the process of becoming noticed and successful ○ *the rise of a new talent* **4.** **INCREASE IN SOCIAL IMPORTANCE** an increase in wealth, status, or importance ○ *the rise and fall of the empire* **5.** **UPWARD SLOPE** an upward slope or gradient ○ *a rise in the road* **6.** **HIGHER GROUND** a hill or piece of raised or rising ground **7.** **UPWARDS MOVEMENT**

an ascent or upwards movement **8.** INCREASE IN A QUALITY an increase in degree, intensity, or force ○ *a rise in her fever* **9.** INCREASE OF SOUND an increase in loudness or pitch **10.** HEIGHT the vertical extent of sth **11.** ASTRON APPEARANCE ABOVE HORIZON the appearance of sth above the horizon **12.** ORIGIN a beginning or origin of sth **13.** REBELLION a rebellion against authority **14.** ANGLING APPEARANCE ON WATER SURFACE the appearance of sth, especially a number of feeding fish, at the surface of the water ○ *There was a good rise of trout this evening.* **15.** CLOTHES DISTANCE BETWEEN CROTCH AND WAIST the length between the crotch and the waist of a pair of trousers [Old English *rīsan*. Ultimately from a prehistoric Germanic word that is also the ancestor of English *raise* and *rear*[1].] ◇ **give rise to sth** to cause sth ◇ **take** *or* **get a rise out of sb** to produce a desired response, usually anger or annoyance, by teasing or taunting sb (*informal*)

rise above *vt.* to overcome sth unpleasant by not letting it become too important

rise to *vt.* (*informal*) **1.** PERFORM WELL IN RESPONSE TO STH to behave well in response to a challenge or difficulty ○ *rose to the occasion* **2.** RESPOND TO STH EMOTIONALLY to react to sth angrily or excitedly

riser /rízər/ *n.* **1.** SB WHO RISES FROM BED sb who gets up in a particular way after sleeping for the night ○ *We are late risers at the weekend.* **2.** VERTICAL PART OF STEP the vertical part of a step or stair **3.** CONSTR VERTICAL PIPE a vertical pipe, duct, or conduit **4.** SB RISING sb who or sth that rises

risibility /rízzi bílləti/ (*plural* **-ties**) *n.* **1.** ABILITY TO LAUGH an ability or tendency to laugh (*formal*) ○ *'I believe that the humorous peculiarities of my countenance excited the infant's risibilities; at any rate, the young mother assured me that he smiled when he looked at me'.* (George van Schaick, *A Top-Floor Idyl*; 1917) **2.** LUDICROUSNESS laughable or ludicrous quality

risible /rízzəb'l/ *adj.* **1.** LUDICROUS causing or capable of causing laughter **2.** INCLINED TO LAUGH able or inclined to laugh (*formal*) [Mid-16thC. From late Latin *risibilis*, from Latin *ris-*, the past participle stem of *ridere* 'to laugh' (source of English *ridiculous*).]

rising /rízing/ *adj.* **1.** GETTING MORE IMPORTANT becoming increasingly respected or significant in an occupation or activity **2.** BECOMING POWERFUL becoming more influential and powerful **3.** GETTING HIGHER going up or becoming higher ■ *adv.* CLOSE TO AGE getting close to a particular age (*dated informal*) ○ *rising sixty* ■ *n.* **1.** REVOLT a rebellion or revolt **2.** STH GETTING HIGHER sth that rises in height **3.** UPWARDS MOVEMENT the action of sth that moves upwards or to a higher level **4.** ACTION OF STANDING UP the action of assuming a standing or nearly vertical position after sitting, kneeling, or lying **5.** FOOD LEAVENING PROCESS the process of leavening bread

rising damp *n.* moisture that is absorbed from the ground into walls, resulting in structural damage

rising diphthong *n.* a diphthong in which the second of two sounds has more stress or sonority than the first

rising rhythm *n.* a rhythmic pattern produced by a succession of metrical feet, each foot having an accented syllable preceded by one or more syllables that are unaccented

rising trot *n.* a horse-riding technique used at the trot, in which the rider rises from the saddle every second beat. ◊ **sitting trot**

risk /risk/ *n.* **1.** CHANCE OF STH GOING WRONG the danger that injury, damage, or loss will occur **2.** SB OR STH HAZARDOUS sb or sth likely to cause injury, damage, or loss **3.** INSUR CHANCE OF LOSS TO INSURER the probability, amount, or type of possible loss incurred and covered by an insurer **4.** FIN POSSIBILITY OF INVESTMENT LOSS the possibility of loss in an investment or speculation **5.** STATISTICAL ODDS OF DANGER the statistical chance of danger from sth, especially from the failure of an engineered system ■ *vt.* (**risks, risking, risked**) **1.** PUT STH IN DANGER to place sth valued in a position or situation where it could be damaged or lost, or exposed to damage or loss **2.** DO STH DESPITE DANGER to incur the chance of harm or loss by taking an action [Mid-17thC. Via French *risque* from Italian *rischo*, from *rischiare* 'to run into danger', of uncertain origin.] —**risker** *n.* ◇ **at risk 1.** in danger of damage or loss **2.** SOC SCI in danger of being harmed or of harming others ◇ **run** *or* **take a risk** to do sth that involves the possibility of injury, damage, or harm

risk arbitrage *n.* the technique of using price discrepancies in a market in order to profit, e.g. by buying shares in a company being acquired while selling shares in the acquiring company —**risk arbitrageur** *n.*

risk-benefit *adj.* studying or testing whether the benefits of a procedure, process, or treatment outweigh the risks involved

risk capital *n.* = **venture capital**

risk factor *n.* a feature of sb's habits, genetic makeup, or personal history that increases the probability that disease or harm to health will occur

risk management *n.* the profession or technique of determining, minimizing, and preventing accidental loss in a business, e.g. by taking safety measures and buying insurance

risk society *n.* a society exposed to harm as a consequence of human activities, e.g. environmental damage or nuclear accidents, rather than naturally occurring events such as earthquakes or volcanic eruptions

risky /ríski/ (**-ier, -iest**) *adj.* likely to cause damage, injury, or loss —**riskily** *adv.* —**riskiness** *n.*

Risorgimento /ri sáwrji méntō/ *n.* the movement for, and period of, political unification in Italy beginning about 1750 and culminating in the occupation of Rome by Italian troops in 1870 [Late 19thC. From Italian, literally 'resurgence'.]

risotto /ri zóttō/ (*plural* **-tos**) *n.* a moist Italian dish of short-grained rice and other ingredients cooked gently in stock [Mid-19thC. From Italian, formed from *riso* (see RICE).]

risqué /rísk ay, ree skáy/ *adj.* alluding to sexual conduct in a way that is close to being indecent or in bad taste [Mid-19thC. From French, the past participle of *risquer* 'to risk', from *risque* (see RISK).]

Riss /riss/ *n.* one of the four major glacial periods in Europe, at its peak 150,000 years ago [Early 20thC. Named after the river *Riss*, a tributary of the Danube in Germany where signs of the glaciation were observed.]

rissole /ríssōl/ *n.* a small fried cake of minced seasoned meat or poultry, often coated or mixed with breadcrumbs [Early 18thC. Via French from assumed Vulgar Latin *russeola (pasta)* 'reddish (pastry)', from Latin *russus* 'red'.]

Risso's dolphin /ríssōz-/ *n.* = **grampus**

risus sardonicus /reéssəss saar dónnikəss/ *n.* a distorted grinning expression caused by involuntary prolonged contraction of the facial muscles, especially as a result of tetanus [From modern Latin, literally 'sardonic grin']

rit. *abbr.* **1.** ritardando **2.** ritenuto

Ritalin /ríttəlin/ *tdmk.* a trademark for methylphenidate

ritardando /ríttaar dándō/ *adj., adv.* becoming gradually slower (*used as a musical direction*) [Early 19thC. From Italian, the present participle of *ritardare* 'to slow down', from Latin *retardare* (see RETARD).]

rite /rīt/ *n.* **1.** CEREMONIAL ACT a solemn and ceremonial act or procedure that follows the rule customary to a community, especially a religious group (*often used in the plural*) ○ *the rite of baptism* **2.** FORMAL PROCEDURE a formal, customary observance or procedure (*often used in the plural*) ○ *rites of courtship* **3.** CEREMONIAL WAY OF PROCEEDING a system of ceremonial procedure ○ *Roman rite* **4. rite, Rite** CHR LITURGICAL PROCEDURE a liturgy or version of a liturgy, especially of a Communion service **5. rite, Rite** CHR DIVISION OF CHURCHES a historical division of Christian churches based on their liturgies [14thC. Directly or via French from Latin *ritus*. Ultimately from an Indo-European base meaning 'to fit together', which is also the ancestor of English *arithmetic* and *rhyme*.]

ritenuto /rìttə nyóotō/ *adj., adv.* played slightly slower than the rest of a piece of music (*used as a musical direction*) [Early 19thC. From Italian, 'held back'.]

rite of passage *n.* **1.** SIGNIFICANT TRANSITIONAL EVENT an event or act that marks a significant transition in a human life **2.** ANTHROP CEREMONY MARKING CHANGED STATUS a ceremony that marks sb's passage from one stage of life to another, e.g. from childhood to puberty or from unmarried to married life [Translation of French *rite de passage*]

ritornello /ríttər néllō/ (*plural* **-los** *or* **-li** /-lee/) *n.* **1.** MUSICAL REFRAIN a short musical passage used as an orchestral refrain between verses of a song or aria **2.** RETURN OF ORCHESTRAL MUSIC AFTER SOLO in a concerto grosso, the return of full orchestral music after a solo [Late 17thC. From Italian, literally 'little return'.]

ritual /ríchoo əl/ *n.* **1.** ESTABLISHED FORMAL BEHAVIOUR an established and prescribed pattern of observance, e.g. in a religion **2.** ACTIONS DONE FORMALLY AND REPEATEDLY the performance of actions or procedures in a set, ordered, and ceremonial way (*often used before a noun*) ○ *a ritual dance* **3.** UNCHANGING PATTERN a formalized pattern of actions or words followed regularly and precisely (*informal*) ○ *the weekend car-washing ritual* **4.** BIOL SET FORM OF COMMUNICATION a set sequence of actions that an animal uses to communicate information or to reinforce social cohesion ○ *mating rituals* **5.** PSYCHOL REPETITIVE BEHAVIOUR an inflexible, stylized, and often repetitive sequence of actions, e.g. repeated hand-washing, that may indicate an obsession **6.** BOOK OF CEREMONIES a book containing rites or ceremonial procedures, especially religious rites ■ *adj.* CONCERNED WITH RITE concerned with or practising a rite ○ *ritual observance* [Late 16thC. From Latin *ritualis*, from *ritus* (see RITE).] —**ritually** *adv.*

ritual abuse *n.* the alleged physical abuse of children by adults taking part in supposed satanic rituals

ritualism /ríchoo əlizəm/ *n.* a devotion or adherence to rituals

ritualistic /ríchoo ə lístik/ *adj.* forming part of or adhering to a ritual —**ritualistically** *adv.*

ritualization /ríchoo ə lī záysh'n/, **ritualisation** *n.* **1.** TURNING STH INTO RITUAL the act of making sth into a ritual **2.** ETHNOL PROCESS OF MODIFYING BEHAVIOUR INTO RITUALS the process in which different forms of behaviour are modified and combined to form a ritual

ritualize /ríchoo ə līz/ (**-izes, -izing, -ized**), **ritualise** (**-ises, -ising, -ised**) *v.* **1.** *vt.* MAKE STH A RITUAL to make a ritual of sth **2.** *vi.* PROMOTE RITUALS to promote the use of rituals

ritualized /ríchoo ə līzd/, **ritualised** *adj.* **1.** MADE INTO RITUAL made into a ritual **2.** CONCERNED WITH RITUAL concerned with a ritual

ritual murder *n.* **1.** RELIG OFFERING OF HUMAN LIFE a human sacrifice, especially to appease a deity **2.** CRIMINOL MURDER WITH RITUALISTIC APPEARANCE a murder performed in a methodical, formalized, or ritualistic way

ritz /rits/ [Early 20thC. Back-formation from RITZY.] ◇ **put on the ritz** to make a show of wealth and extravagance (*dated informal*)

ritzy /rítsi/ (**-ier, -iest**) *adj.* expensively stylish and elegant (*informal*) [Early 20thC. Formed from *Ritz*, name of the luxurious hotels established by the Swiss-born entrepreneur César *Ritz* (1850–1918).] —**ritzily** /rítsili/ *adv.* —**ritziness** *n.*

riv. *abbr.* river

rivage /rívvij/ *n.* a shore, coastline, or bank (*archaic literary*) [13thC. From French, formed from *rive* 'bank', from Latin *ripa* (see RIPARIAN).]

rival /rív'l/ *n.* **1.** COMPETING PERSON OR GROUP a person or group competing with another for sth or sb **2.** SB EQUAL OR BETTER sb who or sth that can equal or surpass another in a particular respect ■ *v.* (**-vals, -valling, -valled**) **1.** *vt.* EQUAL OR SURPASS to equal or better sb or sth in a particular respect **2.** *vti.* COMPETE to compete with sb **3.** *vt.* TRY TO EQUAL to try to equal or surpass sb or sth in a particular respect ■ *adj.* COMPETING competing with sb or sth [Late 16thC. From Latin *rivalis*, literally 'using the same stream', from *rivus* 'stream' (source of English *derive*). Ultimately from an Indo-European word that is also the ancestor of English *run*.] —**rivalrous** *adj.*

WORD KEY: CULTURAL NOTE

The Rivals, a play by Irish dramatist Richard Brinsley Sheridan (1775). This lively comedy of manners portrays the attempts of Captain Jack Absolute to woo Lydia Languish, the idealistic niece and ward of Mrs Malaprop. The latter's habit of misusing similar-sounding words created one of the most memorable characters in English drama and gave rise to a new term: *malapropism*.

rivalry /rívəlri/ (*plural* **-ries**) *n.* **1.** CONDITION OF COMPETITIVENESS the condition or fact of competing with sb or sth **2.** COMPETITIVE ACTION an act of competitiveness

rive /rīv/ (**rives, riving, rived,** *or* **riven** /rívv'n/) *v.* **1.** *vt.* TEAR STH APART to tear sth apart (*archaic*) **2.** *vti.* SPLIT to split or become split (*literary*) [12thC. From Old Norse *rífa*. Ultimately from an Indo-European base meaning 'to cut', which is also the ancestor of English *rift* and *river*.]

riven *adj.* torn apart (*literary*) ○ *a political party riven by dissent* [Past participle of RIVE]

WORLD'S LONGEST RIVERS

1	Nile	
Length	[4,160 mi. / 6,695 km]	
Location	*Africa*	
2	Amazon	
Length	[4,000 mi. / 6,400 km]	
Location	*South America*	
3	Yangtze (Chang Jiang)	
Length	[3,900 mi. / 6,300 km]	
Location	*Asia*	
4	Mississippi-Missouri	
Length	[3,710 mi. / 5,970 km]	
Location	*North America*	
5	Huang He (Yellow River)	
Length	[3,395 mi. / 5,464 km]	
Location	*Asia*	
6	Ob'-Irtysh	
Length	[3,362 mi. / 5,410 km]	
Location	*Asia*	
7	Congo	
Length	[2,710 mi. / 4,374 km]	
Location	*Africa*	
8	Amur	
Length	[2,700 mi. / 4,345 km]	
Location	*Asia*	
8	Lena	
Length	[2,700 mi. / 4,400 km]	
Location	*Asia*	
10	Mekong	
Length	[2,600 mi. / 4,200 km]	
Location	*Asia*	
10	Niger	
Length	[2,600 mi. / 4,200 km]	
Location	*Africa*	

river /rívvər/ *n.* **1.** GEOG LARGE NATURAL CHANNEL OF WATER a natural formation in which fresh water forms a wide stream that runs across the land until it reaches the sea or another area of water **2.** FLOW a large flow or stream of sth (*often used in the plural*) ○ *a river of mud* [13thC. Via Anglo-Norman *rivere* from, ultimately, Latin *riparius* (see RIPARIAN).] ◇ **sell sb down the river** to betray or desert sb, usually for a selfish or mercenary motive (*informal*)

Diego Rivera

Rivera /ree vérraa/, **Diego** (1886–1957) Mexican artist. He is known for his murals portraying Mexican social issues, influenced by Native American art.

riverbank /rívvər bangk/ *n.* a piece of sloping ground at the edge of a river

river basin *n.* a large area of land that drains exclusively to a particular river

riverbed /rívvər bed/ *n.* the ground or part of the ground covered by a river along its course and between its banks

river blindness *n.* = onchocerciasis

riverboat /rívvər bōt/ *n.* a boat built with a flat bottom or shallow draft, used for travelling on rivers

river catchment *n.* = river basin

riverfront /rívvər frunt/ *n.* the area of a town, property, or built-up area directly facing a river

river gum *n.* = river red gum

riverhead /rívvər hed/ *n.* the upstream source of a river or the area of land around it

Riverina /rívvə reenə/ region in southern New South Wales, Australia. It is heavily irrigated and predominantly agricultural.

riverine /rívvə rīn/ *adj.* **1.** OF A RIVER relating to or produced by a river **2.** BESIDE A RIVER located beside a river

river red gum *n.* a large eucalyptus tree, widespread along inland waterways of Australia, that has pale smooth bark and durable dark red timber. Latin name: *Eucalyptus camaldulensis*.

riverside /rívvər sīd/ *n.* LAND BY RIVER the area of land beside a river ■ *adj.* BY A RIVER located beside a river

riverweed /rívvər weed/ *n.* a small many-branched freshwater plant that clings to rock with roots that function as suckers. Genus: *Podostema*.

rivet /rívvit/ *n.* SHORT METAL FASTENING a fastening in the form of a short metal rod with a head. The shaft is passed through holes in materials and flattened into a second head on the other side. Rivets are commonly used in aircraft, building, and bridge construction. ■ *vt.* (**-ets, -eting, -eted**) **1.** FIRMLY FIX ATTENTION to fix or hold the attention completely (*informal; often passive*) **2.** FASTEN WITH RIVET to fasten sth using a rivet or rivets **3.** PULL AND HOLD ONTO STH FIRMLY to draw and hold people's eyes or attention in a powerful, absorbing way (*informal*) ○ '*Old Grannis dared not move, but sat rigid, his eyes riveted on his empty soup plate*'. (Frank Norris, *McTeague – A Story of San Francisco*; 1899) **4.** FIX STH FIRMLY to fix or secure sth firmly [14thC. From Old French, formed from *river* 'to fasten', of unknown origin.]

riveting /rívviting/ *adj.* completely fixing and holding the attention (*informal*) —**rivetingly** *adv.*

riviera /rívvi áirə/ *n.* a stretch of coastland where the climate and beaches are good and there are fashionable resort towns

Riviera /rívvi áirə/ coastal region in southern Europe, extending from Cannes, in France, to La Spezia, in Italy

rivière /rívvi áir/ *n.* a necklace made of a string of diamonds or other gemstones that gradually increase in size up to a large centred gem [Mid-19thC. Via French, literally 'river', from, ultimately, Latin *riparius* (see RIPARIAN).]

rivulet /rívvyoolət/ *n.* **1.** LITTLE STREAM a small stream of flowing water (*literary*) **2.** SMALL FLOW a small quick-flowing stream of sth [Late 16thC. Origin uncertain: perhaps via Italian *rivoletto*, literally 'little stream', from, ultimately, Latin *rivus* (see RIVAL).]

rix-dollar /ríks-/ *n.* any of several silver coins formerly used in Denmark, the Netherlands, and Germany [Late 16thC. From obsolete Dutch *rijksdaler* 'dollar of the realm'.]

Riyadh /ree aád/ capital city of Saudi Arabia, located in the eastern-central part of the country. Population: 2,500,000 (1994).

riyal *n.* MONEY = rial

RJ *abbr.* road junction

RK *abbr.* religious knowledge

RL *abbr.* **1.** Rugby League **2.** (Republic of) Lebanon (*international vehicle registration*) **3.** real life (*used in e-mail and Internet chat*)

Rls *symbol.* rial

rly *abbr.* railway

rm *abbr.* **1.** ream **2.** room

Rm *abbr.* BIBLE Romans

RM *abbr.* **1.** Madagascar (*international vehicle registration*) **2.** MIL Royal Marines **3.** Royal Mail **4.** Registered Midwife

RMA *abbr.* **1.** Royal Military Academy (Sandhurst) **2.** Royal Marine Artillery

r.m.m. *abbr.* relative molecular mass

rms *abbr.* root mean square

RMS *abbr.* **1.** Royal Mail Ship **2.** Royal Mail Service

RMT *abbr.* National Union of Rail, Maritime, and Transport Workers

Rn *symbol.* radon

RN *abbr.* **1.** NAVY Royal Navy **2.** Republic of Niger (*international vehicle registration*)

RNA *n.* a nucleic acid that contains the sugar ribose, is found in all living cells, and is essential for the manufacture of proteins according to the instructions carried by genes. RNA also acts instead of DNA as the genetic material in certain viruses. Full form **ribonucleic acid**

RNA polymerase *n.* a polymerase, found in living cells, that catalyses the synthesis of RNA from its constituent nucleotides, using DNA or RNA as a template

RNAS *abbr.* **1.** Royal Naval Air Service(s) **2.** Royal Naval Air Station

RNase /áar en ayz, -ayss/ *abbr.* ribonuclease

RNA virus *n.* a virus in which the core of nucleic acid consists of RNA

R'n'B, **R & B** *abbr.* rhythm and blues

rnd *abbr.* round

RNIB *abbr.* Royal National Institute for the Blind

RNLI *abbr.* Royal National Lifeboat Institution

RNP *abbr.* ribonucleoprotein

RNR *abbr.* Royal Naval Reserve

rns *abbr.* CRICKET runs

RNVR *abbr.* Royal Naval Volunteer Force

RNZAF *abbr.* NZ Royal New Zealand Air Force

RNZN *abbr.* NZ Royal New Zealand Navy

RO *abbr.* Romania (*international vehicle registration*)

ro. *abbr.* MEASURE rood

roach[1] /rōch/ (*plural* **roach** *or* **roaches**) *n.* **1.** FOOD FISH a northern European freshwater fish of the carp family that has an olive-green or grey-green back and reddish fins. It is a popular game fish. Latin name: *Rutilus rutilus*. **2.** SMALL N AMERICAN FISH a small sunfish of eastern North America that resembles a European roach. Latin name: *Hesperoleucus symmetricus*. [12thC. From Old French *roche*, of unknown origin.]

roach[2] /rōch/ *n.* **1.** INSECTS COCKROACH a cockroach (*informal*) **2.** DRUGS MARIJUANA CIGARETTE BUTT the end of a marijuana cigarette after the rest of it has been smoked (*slang*) [Mid-19thC. Shortening of COCKROACH.]

roach[3] /rōch/ *n.* SAILING CURVE OF SAIL the upward curve at the foot of a square sail ■ *vt.* (**roaches, roaching, roached**) EQU CUT HORSE'S MANE to cut a horse's mane short so that the hairs stand up [Late 18thC. Origin uncertain: perhaps from ROACH[1], perhaps from the shape of its back.]

road /rōd/ *n.* **1.** HARD TRACK FOR USE OF VEHICLES a long surfaced route broad enough for vehicles to be driven on it (*often used in placenames*) **2.** COURSE OF ACTION a route or way that heads towards some predictable outcome ○ *the road to financial success* **3.** US RAIL = railroad **4.** MINING MINE TUNNEL a tunnel used for hauling coal or ore in a mine **5.** SHIPPING = roadstead (*often used in the plural*) **6.** N England, Scotland PATH the route to somewhere (*informal*) ○ *I went the wrong road.* ○ *Get out of my road!* [Old English *rād* 'a riding' (source also of English *raid*). Ultimately from an Indo-European word meaning 'to ride', which is also the ancestor of English *ride* and *ready*.] ◇ **one for the road** an alcoholic drink taken just before leaving (*informal*) ◇ **on the road** travelling from place to place ○ *The band have been on the road all summer.*

WORD KEY: CULTURAL NOTE

On the Road, a novel by US writer Jack Kerouac (1957). A thinly disguised and rapidly composed memoir, it describes a series of cross-country journeys undertaken by a group of people united by their quest for new experiences and disregard for traditional values. It is both an engaging chronicle of the Beat generation and a lyrical evocation of the energy and passion of youth.

roadbed /rŏd bed/ *n.* a foundation of soil, cinders, or crushed rock that supports a road or railway

roadblock /rŏd blok/ *n.* **1.** BARRIER ACROSS ROAD TO STOP TRAFFIC a temporary barrier used to prevent vehicles from continuing along a road so that they can be checked or their drivers questioned, usually by police or military personnel **2.** OBSTACLE a hindrance or obstacle to sth

road book *n.* a publication for road-users showing maps and an index for all the routes in an area

road company *n. US* a group of actors who tour with a show, usually performing a play that has been successful in a large city

road-fund licence *n.* a disc affixed to a motor vehicle to show that its road tax has been paid (*dated or formal*)

road hog *n.* sb who drives in an inconsiderate and dangerous way, usually by refusing to let other motorists overtake or go first, or by forcing them to move out of the way (*informal*)

roadholding /rŏd hōlding/ *n.* the ability of a motor vehicle to remain controlled and safely positioned on the road, especially in bad conditions or on sharp corners

roadhouse /rŏd howss/ (*plural* **-houses** /-howziz/) *n.* a hotel or pub located beside a main road (*dated*)

road hump *n.* = speed bump

roadie /rŏdi/ *n.* sb who loads, unloads, and sets up the equipment used by a musical or theatrical group on tour, especially a rock band

roadkill /rŏd kil/ *n. US* a bird or animal that has been hit and killed by a motor vehicle on the road

road map *n.* a motorists' map or atlas that shows routes, mileage, and often other features of interest to travellers

road metal *n.* the cinders, crushed rock, and other materials used in the construction of roads

road movie *n.* a film that depicts the adventures of a person or people who leave home and travel from place to place by road, often to find or escape from sth

road pricing *n.* a system for controlling road use in which drivers of road vehicles pay a charge to use their cars in certain conditions, e.g. at peak periods

road racing *n.* a race for motor vehicles or bicycles that takes place on a public road temporarily reserved for the purpose, or on a racing course resembling a public road

roadroller /rŏd rōlər/ *n.* a machine with wide heavy wheels used to roll flat a new or repaired road

Roadrunner

roadrunner /rŏd runnər/ *n.* a swift-running bird of the cuckoo family, found in deserts of the western United States and Mexico. It has streaked brown-and-white plumage, a head crest, small, round

wings, and a long tail. Latin name: *Geococcyx californianus.*

road show *n.* **1.** BROADCAST TRAVELLING RADIO BROADCAST a live open-air radio show that travels to a series of locations, usually during the summer months. The following venue is announced in advance to ensure an audience. **2.** TRAVELLING PROMOTIONAL GROUP a group of people who travel from place to place in order to broadcast, publicize, or promote sth, or to conduct a political campaign **3.** THEATRE PERFORMANCE BY TRAVELLING ACTORS a show staged by a touring company of entertainers, or the company performing such a show

roadside /rŏd sīd/ *n.* an area along or bordering a road

roadstead /rŏd sted/ *n.* a partly sheltered area for anchored vessels

roadster /rŏdstər/ *n.* **1.** US CARS SPORTS CAR a small open-topped car with a single seat in front and often with an additional folding seat (**rumble seat**) at the back (*dated*) **2.** EQU HORSE FOR RIDING ON ROAD a sturdy horse for riding on a road (*archaic*)

road tax *n.* a tax paid for the right to drive a motor vehicle on the roads. When the tax is paid, a tax disc is issued that must be displayed on the vehicle's windscreen.

road test *n.* **1.** CARS TEST OF VEHICLE OR TYRE PERFORMANCE a test of a motor vehicle or tyre under actual operating conditions **2.** US CARS PRACTICAL DRIVING TEST an offical test on the road to determine whether a driver of a motor vehicle is competent to be issued a licence to drive **3.** MANUF TEST OF HOW WELL STH WORKS a series of tests carried out on a new product or design to determine how well it performs during actual use

road-test *vt.* to carry out a test of a vehicle or other product under actual operating conditions

road-train *n. Aus* a truck that pulls several large articulated trailers, often to transport livestock or bulk goods over long distances

roadway /rŏd way/ *n.* the main part of a road area meant to be driven on

roadwork /rŏd wurk/ *n.* SPORTS a form of exercise consisting of long runs on roads, chiefly used as part of training for boxers

roadworks /rŏd wurks/ *n.* construction or repair work being carried out on a section of public road, or on the utilities located beneath it, creating a temporary obstruction for road users. US term **roadwork**

roadworthiness /rŏd wurthinəss/ *n.* the condition of a motor vehicle in terms of whether it can be driven safely on public roads

roadworthy /rŏd wurthi/ *adj.* in a safe condition to be driven on public roads [Early 19thC. Modelled on 'seaworthy'.]

roam /rōm/ *vti.* (**roams, roaming, roamed**) WANDER AIMLESSLY to move about a large area, especially without any particular purpose or definite destination ■ *n.* AIMLESS WANDER an act of roaming [14thC. Origin unknown.] —**roamer** *n.*

roan /rōn/ *adj.* WITH LIGHT SPECKLES IN DARK COAT having a reddish-brown, brown, or black coat speckled with white or grey hairs ■ *n.* **1.** ROAN HORSE an animal, especially a horse, that has a roan coat **2.** COLOURS ROAN COLOUR the colour of a roan animal **3.** INDUST FINE-GRAINED LEATHER a soft pliable kind of sheepskin leather used in bookbinding. It has a close grain resembling that of morocco. [Early 16thC. Via French from Old Spanish *roano*, of uncertain origin: possibly from Germanic.]

Roanoke /rŏ ə nōk/ city in southwestern Virginia, on the Roanoke River. Population: 96,397 (1990).

roar /rawr/ *v.* (**roars, roaring, roared**) **1.** *vi.* GROWL LOUDLY to make a loud natural growling noise, e.g. as a lion makes **2.** *vti.* SHOUT LOUDLY to make a loud shouting noise, or utter sth with a loud shouting noise, especially in anger **3.** *vi.* LAUGH LOUDLY to give a loud, prolonged, and unrestrained laugh **4.** *vi.* BURN NOISILY to burn noisily while giving off a lot of heat ○ *a roaring fire* **5.** *vi.* CRASH LOUDLY to make a loud crashing or blowing noise, e.g. as wind, waves, and other natural phenomena do **6.** *vi.* VET BREATHE NOISILY to breathe with difficulty, making a rasping or wheezing noise, as some diseased horses do **7.** *vi.* MOVE

NOISILY to move quickly and with a loud mechanical noise, especially a harsh or droning noise **8.** *vr.* BECOME BY ROARING to cause the voice to be in a particular condition through shouting, cheering, or making some other loud vocal noise ○ *roared themselves hoarse* ■ *n.* **1.** LOUD SHOUT a loud, often prolonged, shout or cry, especially one made by a person or crowd that is cheering, angry, or upset **2.** LOUD LAUGH a loud, prolonged, and unrestrained laugh **3.** LOUD GROWL a loud growling noise made by a large animal, especially a lion **4.** NOISE OF STH BURNING a loud continuous noise made by sth burning intensely **5.** LOUD CRASHING NOISE a loud crashing or blowing noise made by waves, the wind, or some other natural phenomenon **6.** LOUD MECHANICAL NOISE a loud, harsh or droning mechanical noise made by sth as it moves or functions [Old English *rārian*, of uncertain origin: possibly an imitation of the sound] —**roarer** *n.*

roaring /rawring/ *adj.* **1.** WITH FAST SALES selling vigorously and making a good profit ○ *It's a hot day and the ice-cream sellers are doing a roaring trade.* **2.** HUGE conspicuously great ○ *Her new novel proved a roaring success.* ◇ **rip-roaring** ■ *n.* VET BREATHING DIFFICULTIES IN HORSES noisy breathing in horses, especially when caused by paralysis of the recurrent laryngeal nerve ■ *adv.* EXCEEDINGLY to an extreme degree —**roaringly** *adv.*

Roaring Forties *npl.* the area of the ocean in the southern hemisphere lying between 40° and 50° latitude that is noted for its strong winds, storms, and difficult sailing conditions

Roaring Twenties *npl.* the 1920s, especially when thought of as being a time of exuberance, hedonism, and prosperity in contrast to the hardship of World War I

roast /rōst/ *v.* (**roasts, roasting, roasted**) **1.** *vti.* COOK COOK IN OVEN to cook sth, especially meat or vegetables, by dry heat, usually in an oven or over an open fire, basting it with fat, or be cooked in this way **2.** *vti.* COOK, INDUST PREPARE BY DRYING OR BROWNING to heat sth until it is dry or brown, especially coffee beans or nuts, as part of a manufacturing process, or be heated in this way **3.** *vt.* METALL HEAT ORE IN FURNACE to heat ore in a furnace without fusing in order to concentrate, dehydrate, or purify it or to cause a chemical change that will facilitate smelting. When sulphide ores are roasted to covert them to oxides, the escaping sulphur-laden gases are often used to make sulphuric acid. **4.** *vti.* OVERHEAT to become too warm or make sth or sb too warm at a source of heat such as the sun or a fire ○ *roast in front of the log fire* **5.** *vt.* DISPARAGE to criticize sb or sth harshly (*informal*) **6.** *vt. US* MOCK to make fun of sb (*informal*) ■ *n.* **1.** COOK, FOOD OVEN-COOKED MEAT sth such as a piece of meat that is suitable for roasting, or that has been roasted **2.** *US* OPEN-AIR MEAL an outside gathering or party with food cooked on open fires **3.** *US* PARTY FOR SB a gathering, party, or other celebration where the guest of honour is the subject of speeches that alternate between praise and humorous criticism ■ *adj.* OVEN-COOKED cooked by dry heat, usually in an oven or over an open fire, and basted with fat [13thC. From Old French *rostir*, of prehistoric Germanic origin.]

roaster /rōstər/ *n.* **1.** STH FOR ROASTING FOOD a pan, dish, or oven for roasting food in **2.** ROASTED CHICKEN an item of food, especially a chicken, that is suitable for roasting **3.** SB OR STH THAT ROASTS sb who or sth that roasts a food or ore

roasting /rōsting/ *adj.* VERY HOT feeling or causing sb to feel very hot (*informal*) ■ *n.* HARSH CRITICISM a harsh criticism of sb (*informal*) ■ *adv.* EXTREMELY to a high degree of temperature (*informal*) ○ *roasting hot*

rob /rob/ (**robs, robbing, robbed**) *v.* **1.** *vt.* DEPRIVE SB ILLEGALLY to take sth illegally from a person or place, especially by using force, threats, or violence **2.** *vt.* DEPRIVE SB UNFAIRLY to deprive sb of sth unfairly or harmfully ○ *The wet weather robbed her of her holiday.* **3.** *vi.* COMMIT ROBBERY to commit robbery, especially habitually **4.** *vt.* STEAL STH to steal sth (*nonstandard*) ○ *They broke in and robbed the TV and video.* [12thC. From Old French *rober*, from a prehistoric Germanic word that is also the ancestor of English *bereave* and *rover*.]

robalo /róbbəlō, ró-/ (*plural* **-los** *or* **-lo**) *n.* any fish in a large diverse family that ranges from large ocean fish such as the snook to the tiny glass fish popular with aquarists. Family: Centropomidae. [Late 19thC. From Spanish *robalo*, of uncertain origin: probably from assumed *lobaro* 'wolflike fish', from *lobo* 'wolf', from Latin *lupus*.]

roband /róbbənd, ró-/, **robbin** /róbbin/ *n.* a piece of rope used to attach a sail to a spar [15thC. Origin uncertain: probably from Dutch *raband*, from *ra* 'sailyard' + *band* 'band'.]

Robbe-Grillet /rob griyé/, **Alain** (*b.* 1922) French novelist and screenwriter. He was one of the leading experimental writers in France in the 1950s and wrote the screenplay of *Last Year in Marienbad* (1961).

robber /róbbər/ *n.* sb who commits robbery

robber baron *n.* **1.** UNSCRUPULOUS 19C US INDUSTRIALIST in the United States, a wealthy industrialist or businessman of the late 19th century who used unscrupulous business practices **2.** MEDIEVAL NOBLEMAN STEALING FROM TRAVELLERS a land-holding nobleman who, in feudal Europe, habitually stole from people travelling through his lands

robber fly *n.* a predatory fly that catches other insects in its long bristly legs and pierces them with its sharp mouthparts. Family: Leptidae.

robbery /róbbəri/ (*plural* **-ies**) *n.* the act or an instance of illegally taking sth that belongs to sb else, especially by using force, threats, or violence

────── **WORD KEY: SYNONYMS** ──────
See Synonyms at *theft.*

robbin *n.* = roband

robe /rōb/ *n.* **1.** CLOTHES CEREMONIAL DRESS a long loose outer garment worn on ceremonial occasions or as a symbol of authority, especially by the peerage, judiciary, academics, and members of the clergy (*often used in the plural*) **2.** CLOTHES DRESSING GOWN OR BATHROBE a loose garment for wear at home, especially a dressing gown or bathrobe **3.** CLOTHES, CHR = **christening robe 4.** CLOTHES, HIST WOMAN'S OUTER DRESS in the 17th and 18th centuries, a woman's outer dress, especially a heavy brocade and ornately decorated one worn over a plainer one ■ *vti.* (**robes, robing, robed**) DRESS IN ROBE to dress sb in a robe, or be dressed in a robe [13thC. From Old French, literally '(clothes taken as) booty, spoil', ultimately from a prehistoric Germanic word that is also the ancestor of English *rob*.]

robe de chambre /rób də shaámbra, rób-/ (*plural* **robes de chambre**) *n.* = **dressing gown** [Mid-18thC. From French, literally 'chamber robe, dressing gown'.]

Robert I /róbbərt/, **King of Scotland** (1274–1329). He fought successfully for Scottish independence from the English, whom he defeated at the Battle of Bannockburn (1314). Known as **Robert the Bruce**

Robert II, King of Scotland (1316–90). The grandson of Robert I, he founded the Stuart dynasty.

Robert III, King of Scotland (1337–1406). The son of Robert II and father of James I of Scotland, he ruled Scotland (1390–1406) during a time of civil strife and war with England.

Roberts /róbbərts/, **Tom** (1856–1931) English-born Australian painter. He was a pioneer of Australian impressionism, and was one of the founders of the Heidelberg School. Full name **Thomas William Roberts**

Robertson /róbbətsən/, **George** (1860–1933) English-born Australian publisher. He was one of the founders of the Australian publishing company Angus and Robertson.

Robeson /róbsən/, **Paul** (1898–1976) US singer and actor. He acted in both musicals and Shakespeare, and gave recitals of spirituals. His openly communist sympathies and opposition to racial discrimination forced him from public life. Full name **Paul Bustill Robeson**

Robespierre /róbz pyair/, **Maximilien** (1758–94) French lawyer and revolutionary. He was elected as first deputy for Paris to the National Convention after the fall of the monarchy in 1792. As commissioner of public safety (1793) he instituted the Reign of

Paul Robeson

Terror and was later guillotined. Full name **Maximilien François Marie Isidore de Robespierre**

Robey /róbi/, **Sir George** (1869–1954) British comedian. He appeared in musicals and was celebrated for his role as the Shakespearean character Falstaff. Real name **George Edward Wade**. Known as **The Prime Minister of Mirth**

Robin

robin /róbbin/ *n.* **1.** EUROPEAN SONGBIRD a small thrush, native mainly to Europe, the adult male of which has an reddish-orange breast and head. Latin name: *Erithacus rubercula*. **2.** LARGE N AMERICAN THRUSH a large North American thrush with a rust-coloured breast and dark grey or brown upper parts. Latin name: *Turdus migratorius*. **3.** BIRD WITH REDDISH BREAST LIKE ROBIN a bird with a reddish breast that is similar to the European or North American robin, especially numerous Australian species [Mid-16thC. Shortening of ROBIN REDBREAST, from the name *Robin*, a diminutive of *Robert*.]

Robin Goodfellow /róbbin good fellō/ *n.* = **Puck**

robing room *n.* a room set aside, e.g. in a court, church, parliament, or other building, for putting on ceremonial or official robes

robin redbreast *n.* = **robin** *n.* 2, **robin** *n.* 1

robin's-egg blue *n.* a pale greenish-blue colour — **robins' egg blue** *adj.*

Robinson /róbbinss'n/, **Jackie** (1919–72) US baseball player and civil rights activist. He broke baseball's colour barrier, stole home 19 times, and was elected to the Baseball Hall of Fame (1962). Full name **Jack Roosevelt Robinson**

Mary Robinson

Robinson, Mary (*b.* 1944) Irish lawyer and politician. After her tenure as president of the Republic of Ireland (1990–97), the first woman to serve in that

role, she became the United Nations High Commissioner for Human Rights in 1997. Born **Mary Bourke**

Robinson, William Heath (1872–1944) British cartoonist. His humorous drawings of elaborate machinery designed to perform simple tasks gave rise to the term 'Heath Robinson contraption'.

Robinson Crusoe /róbbins'n kroóssō/ *n.* the eponymous hero of Daniel Defoe's novel of 1719, in which the ingenuity, loneliness, survival, and eventual rescue of the ship-wrecked sailor on a desert island are chronicled. The novel, which is often regarded as the first English novel, is based on the true story of Alexander Selkirk's five-year stay on the uninhabited island of Juan Fernandez.

Robin's plantain /róbbinz-/ *n.* a plant of eastern North America with rayed purple flower heads. Latin name: *Erigeron pulchellus*. [Late 18thC. Origin unknown.]

roble /ró blay/ *n.* an oak, native to California, that has a short trunk, leathery leaves, and thin tapering acorns. Latin name: *Quercus lobata*. [Mid-19thC. Via Spanish and Portuguese from Latin *robur* 'oak tree, hardness, strength'.]

roborant /róbərənt, róbbə-/ *adj.* FORTIFYING OR STRENGTHENING used to describe medications or other remedies that have the effect of restoring sb's strength or vigour ■ *n.* STRENGTHENING SUBSTANCE a medication or other remedy that restores strength or vigour [Mid-17thC. From Latin *roborant-*, present participle stem of *roborare* 'to strengthen', from *robur* 'oak tree, hardness, strength'.]

Robot: Part of an automated car assembly line

robot /ró bot/ *n.* **1.** MECHANICAL DEVICE PROGRAMMED TO PERFORM TASKS any machine that can be programmed to carry out instructions and perform particular duties, especially one that can take over tasks normally done by people. These mechanical devices are best suited to sensing, gripping, and moving objects or to performing repetitive tasks such as welding. ◊ **automaton 2.** IMAGINARY MACHINE LIKE HUMAN a machine that resembles a human in appearance and can function like a human, especially in science fiction. ◊ **android 3.** PERSON LIKE A MACHINE sb who works or behaves mechanically, showing little or no emotion and often responding to orders without question **4.** S Africa TRAFFIC LIGHT a set of automatic traffic lights (*informal*) [Early 20thC. Via German from Czech, from *robota* 'forced labour'; coined by Karel Čapek in his play *R.U.R.* (Rossum's Universal Robots) (1920).] —**robotic** /ró bóttik/ *adj.* —**robotically** /-tikli/ *adv.* —**robotism** /ró botizəm/ *n.* —**robotistic** /ró bo tístik/ *adj.* —**robot-like** /ró bot līk/ *adj.* —**robotry** /róbotri/ *n.*

robot bomb *n.* a jet-propelled bomb whose flight to a target is governed by a gyroscopic guidance system, e.g. the V-1 used by Germany against London in World War II

robot dancing, robotic dancing *n.* a style of dancing characterized by stiff, jerky body movements, popular in the 1980s

robotics /ró bóttiks/ *n.* **1.** DESIGN AND USE OF ROBOTS the science and technology relating to computer-controlled mechanical devices, e.g. the automated tools commonly found on automobile assembly lines (*takes a singular verb*) **2.** = **robot dancing**

robotize /ró bo tīz/ (**-izes, -izing, -ized**), **robotise** (**-ises, -ising, -ised**) *vt.* **1.** AUTOMATE STH to introduce automation into sth, especially a factory or factory process **2. MAKE BEHAVE LIKE ROBOT** to make sb act in an automated and unemotional or insensitive fashion —**robotization** /rṓ bo tī záysh'n, -bə-/ *n.*

Rob Roy /rób róy/ (1671–1734) Scottish brigand. Forced into life as an outlaw by debts, he led raids against both the English and the Scots. His life was romanticized in a novel by Sir Walter Scott. Real name **Robert MacGregor**

Robson /róbsən/, **Dame Flora** (1902–84) British actor. She performed in classical and contemporary roles, in both films and plays. Full name **Dame Flora McKenzie Robson**

robust /rō búst/ *adj.* **1. STRONG AND HEALTHY** strong, healthy, and hardy in constitution **2. STRONGLY CONSTRUCTED** built, constructed, or designed to be sturdy, durable, or hard-wearing **3. NEEDING PHYSICAL STRENGTH** involving or requiring great physical strength and stamina ○ *Rugby is a robust sport.* **4.** FOOD **FULL-FLAVOURED** rich, strong-tasting, and full-bodied **5. DETERMINED** characterized by firmness and determination and a refusal to make concessions **6. STRAIGHTFORWARD** showing clear thought and common sense **7. BLUNT OR CRUDE** rough and direct or crude **8.** COMPUT **CAPABLE OF RECOVERY** able to recover from unexpected conditions during operation ○ *a robust operating system* [Mid-16thC. From Latin *robustus* 'oaken, hard, strong', from *robur* 'oak tree, hardness, strength'.] —**robustly** *adv.* —**robustness** *n.*

robusta /rō bústə/ *n.* **1. AFRICAN COFFEE PLANT** a coffee plant, native to western central Africa, that has white flowers and red berries. Latin name: *Coffea canephora.* **2. COFFEE** beans from the robusta coffee plant, or coffee made from them [Early 20thC. From Latin, feminine of *robustus* 'robust'.]

robustious /rō búschəss/ *adj.* **1. HEALTHY** strong, healthy, and hardy in constitution (*archaic*) **2. VULGAR** vulgar or crude (*archaic*) —**robustiously** *adv.* —**robustiousness** *n.*

roc /rok/ *n.* in Arabian legend, a large bird of prey strong enough to lift and fly with an elephant in its talons [Late 16thC. Via Arabic *rukk* from Persian *ruk*, source of English *rook*[2].]

ROC *abbr.* Royal Observer Corps

rocaille /ro kī́, rō kī́/ *n.* **1. DECORATIVE STONEWORK** decorative rococo stonework or shellwork, especially scrollwork **2.** = **rococo** [Mid-19thC. From French, literally 'pebble work, rock work', from *roc* 'rock' (see ROCK).]

rocambole /rókəm bōl/ *n.* a leek of Europe and Asia grown for its bulb that resembles garlic and used to flavour food. Latin name: *Allium scorodoprasum.* [Late 17thC. Via French from German *Rockenbolle* 'distaff bulb' (from its shape), formed from *Rocken* 'distaff' + *Bolle* 'bulb'.]

Rochdale /róch dayl/ town in Lancashire, northwestern England. Population: 207,100 (1994).

Roche /rōch/, **Tony** (*b.* 1945) Australian tennis player. He was runner-up at Wimbledon in 1968 and four times Wimbledon doubles champion with John Newcombe. He was coach of the Australian Davis Cup team from 1994. Full name **Anthony Roche**

Roche limit /rósh-/ *n.* the closest a satellite can come to the celestial body it is orbiting before being torn apart by tidal forces generated by the gravitational attraction of the celestial body. The distance varies with relative density but is approximately 2.45 times the radius of the primary for bodies of similar density. [Late 19thC. Named after Édouard *Roche* (1820–83), French astronomer who first made the calculation.]

Rochelle salt /ro shél-/ *n.* a white powder used in medicine as a mild laxative, as a food preservative, and in electronics. Formula: $KNaC_4H_4O_6$. [Mid-18thC. Named after *La Rochelle*, a French seaport, at which the salt is mined.]

roche moutonnée /rósh mootónnay/ *n.* an elongated mound of bare rock, modified by glacial erosion, that is smooth and striated on one side and shattered rubble on the other [Mid-19thC. From French, literally 'fleecy rock' (that is, rounded like a sheep's back).]

Rochester /róchistər/ **1.** city on the River Medway, in Kent, England. Population: 145,000 (1994). **2.** city and port in western New York State, south of Lake Ontario and northeast of Buffalo. Population: 221,594 (1996).

rochet /róchit/ *n.* a white linen garment, similar to a surplice but with tight-fitting sleeves, worn on ceremonial occasions by bishops and other high-ranking members of the clergy [14thC. From Old French, 'little mantle', from *roc* 'mantle', of prehistoric Germanic origin.]

rock[1] /rok/ *n.* **1. HARD MINERAL AGGREGATE** any consolidated material such as granite or limestone, or unconsolidated material such as sand or mud, consisting of more than one mineral and sometimes organic material **2. PROJECTING MASS OF ROCK** a large mass of mineral material, especially an isolated or projecting one (*often used in placenames*) **3. BOULDER** a large stone or boulder **4. SB DEPENDABLE** sb who or sth that is considered to be stable, dependable, or supportive, especially in times of trouble **5. HARD SWEET** a hard, often brightly coloured, sweet made from boiled sugar, usually in the form of a long cylindrical stick, sometimes with the name of a seaside resort through it ○ *a stick of Blackpool rock* **6. DIAMOND** a large gemstone, especially a diamond (*informal*) **7. CRACK COCAINE** crack cocaine, or a small piece of crack cocaine (*slang*) **8.** = **rockfish** *n.* 2 ■ **rocks** *npl.* **1.** *US* **MONEY** money (*informal*) **2. OFFENSIVE TERM** an offensive term for the testicles (*slang offensive*) [14thC. Via Old French *ro(c)que* from assumed Vulgar Latin *rocca*, of unknown origin.] ◇ **between a rock and a hard place** *US* faced with a choice between two equally unpleasant or undesirable alternatives ◇ **get your rocks off 1.** an offensive term meaning to have an orgasm (*slang offensive; refers to a male*) **2.** to get a great deal of pleasure or excitement from some activity (*slang offensive*) ◇ **on the rocks 1.** in great difficulties and heading for ruin or disaster, especially financially or emotionally (*informal*) **2.** served with ice cubes

rock up *vi. Aus* to turn up or arrive, especially unannounced (*informal*)

rock[2] /rok/ *v.* (**rocks, rocking, rocked**) **1.** *vti.* **SWAY TO AND FRO** to swing or sway, or cause sth or sb to swing or sway, backwards and forwards or from side to side, especially with a slow gentle rhythm **2.** *vti.* **SHAKE OR TREMBLE** to move or shake, or cause sb or sth to move or shake, violently ○ *An earth tremor rocked the city.* **3.** *vt.* **SHOCK** to disturb, upset, or shock sb (*informal*) ○ *The ruling rocked the legal profession.* **4.** *vi.* **PLAY OR DANCE TO ROCK MUSIC** to sing, play, or dance to music, especially to rock music (*informal*) **5.** *vi.* **BE FILLED WITH ROCK MUSIC** to contain people performing or enjoying music, especially rock music (*informal*) ○ *The joint was really rocking.* **6.** *vi.* MUSIC **HAVE STRONG BEAT** to have or play music with a strong solid beat (*informal*) **7.** *vi.* **TRAVEL** to advance steadily or quickly (*informal*) ○ *rocking along at 60 miles an hour* **8.** *vti.* MINING **WASH ORE IN CRADLE** to wash gold-bearing or gem-bearing sands or gravel in a pivoting cradle (**rocker**) **9.** *vt.* ARTS **ROUGHEN COPPER PLATE** in engraving a mezzotint, to prepare a copper plate with a tool with a short, curved, jagged blade (**rocker**) ■ *n.* **1. ACT OF ROCKING** an act or the process of rocking sb or sth **2.** MUSIC **TYPE OF POP MUSIC** a style of pop music, derived from rock and roll, usually played on electric or electronic instruments and equipment [Old English *roccian*, of uncertain origin: probably from a prehistoric Germanic word meaning 'to move']

Rock /rok/ *n.* the Rock of Gibraltar (*informal*)

rockabilly /rókə billi/ *n.* a style of pop music, originating in the late 1950s, that combines elements of rock and roll with elements of country music [Mid-20thC. Blend of ROCK AND ROLL + HILLBILLY.]

rockabye /rókə bī/, **rockaby** *interj.* used to encourage a baby or child to go to sleep [Early 19thC. Blend of ROCK[2] + LULLABY.]

Rockall /rók awl/ rocky islet in the Atlantic Ocean, 354 km/220 mi. west of the Outer Hebrides. Area: 743 sq. m./8,000 sq. ft.

rock and roll /rókən rṓl/, **rock'n'roll** *n.* **1.** MUSIC **POP MUSIC WITH HEAVY BEAT** a style of pop music that has its roots mainly in blues music and is characterized by heavily stressed beats. It is played on electric instruments, and has simple, often repetitive, lyrics. **2.** DANCE **DANCE DONE TO ROCK AND ROLL** a style of dancing done to rock and roll music ■ *vi.* (**rocks and rolls, rocking and rolling, rocked and rolled; rock'n'rolls, rock'n'rolling, rock'n'rolled**) **DANCE TO ROCK AND ROLL** to do a rock and roll dance —**rock and roller** *n.*

rock bass /rók bass/ *n.* a sunfish with a dark olive back, white undersides, and red eyes. It is a freshwater food and game fish native to eastern and central North America. Latin name: *Ambloplites rupestris.*

rock bottom *n.* the lowest level or price possible —**rock-bottom** *adj.*

rockbound /rók bownd/ *adj.* **1. SURROUNDED BY ROCKS** entirely, or almost entirely, surrounded by rocks **2. TOO ROCKY TO GET AT** being so rocky as to be inaccessible

rock brake *n.* a fern that has compound fronds and grows on rocky ground. Genus: *Crytogramma.*

rock cake, rock bun *n.* a small individual cake containing dried fruit and sometimes spices and candied peel. It gets its name because of its lumpy, uneven, crusty surface.

rock candy *n. US* a hard sweet consisting of dissolved sugar that is cooled to form large crystals. It is sometimes made on a piece of string or a stick.

rock climb *n.* **1. ACT OF CLIMBING ROCK FACE** an act or instance of scaling a rock face, usually using ropes and other specialized equipment **2. ROCK CLIMB ROUTE** the route followed on a rock climb

rock climbing *n.* the activity of scaling rock faces, usually using ropes and other specialized equipment and often in a team —**rock-climb** *vi.* —**rock climber** *n.*

rock cod (*plural* **rock cod** *or* **rock cods**) *n. NZ* = **blue cod**

rock crab *n.* a crab found in rocky coastal areas of North America. Genus: *Cancer.*

rock crystal *n.* a colourless transparent variety of quartz, used in electronic and optical instruments

rock dove *n.* a bluish-grey dove of Europe and Asia from which domestic and wild pigeons are descended. Latin name: *Columba livia.*

rock elm *n.* **1.** TREES **EASTERN N AMERICAN ELM TREE** a deciduous tree of eastern North America with corky branches. Latin name: *Ulmus thomasii.* **2.** INDUST **TIMBER** the wood of the rock elm tree

rocker /rókər/ *n.* **1. ROCKING DEVICE** a device that functions by way of a rocking movement **2. FURNITURE STAND** an upwardly curved piece of wood or metal that allows sth such as a rocking chair or baby's cradle to move backwards and forwards or from side to side **3.** FURNITURE = **rocking chair 4.** HOUSEHOLD = **rocker switch 5.** MINING = **cradle** *n.* 8 **6.** ARTS **ENGRAVER'S TOOL** a tool with a short, curved, jagged blade used in the engraving of mezzotints for roughening the copper plates **7.** ICE SKATING **TYPE OF ICE SKATE** an ice skate with a curved blade, or the curved blade itself (*often used in the plural*) **8.** MUSIC **ROCK MUSICIAN** a rock singer or musician (*informal*) **9.** MUSIC **ROCK FAN** a fan of rock music or rock and roll (*informal*) **10.** HIST **MEMBER OF 60S YOUTH GROUP** a follower of a youth group in 1960s Britain who rode motorcycles, liked rock and roll, wore leather jackets, and sometimes fought with smart youths on motor scooters (**mods**) ◇ **be off your rocker** an offensive phrase that deliberately insults sb's mental balance (*informal or offensive*)

rocker arm *n.* a pivoted lever, e.g. in an internal-combustion engine, that transmits motion from a cam or pushrod at one end to open and close a valve at the other

rocker cam *n.* a cam that oscillates or rocks but does not revolve

rocker panel *n.* on a passenger vehicle, the exterior panel located below the doorsill of the passenger compartment

rocker switch *n.* a switch on a central pivot, especially one that operates between an 'on' and 'off' position on an electrical appliance

rockery /rókəri/ (*plural* **-ies**) *n.* a garden or area of a garden that has large stones in it with plants, especially low-growing colourful hardy ones such as edelweiss, gentian, and heathers growing in between them. US term **rock garden**

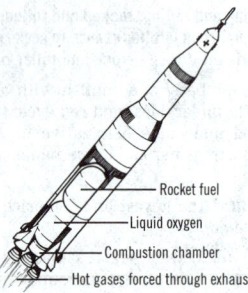

Rocket

rocket[1] /rókit/ *n.* **1.** SPACE TECH **SPACE VEHICLE** a device or vehicle designed for space travel, propelled by a device that carries both fuel and oxidizer and produces thrust by expelling expanding hot gases (**rocket engine**) **2.** = **rocket engine** **3.** MIL **ROCKET-PROPELLED WEAPON** a weapon consisting of an explosive, nuclear, or other warhead that is propelled by a rocket engine **4.** SELF-PROPELLED FIREWORK OR FLARE a firework, flare, or similar device containing combustible propellants. Rockets are usually cylindrical in shape with a lightable fuse at the bottom. **5.** TELLING OFF a stern reprimand or rebuke (*informal*) ■ *v.* (**-ets, -eting, -eted**) **1.** *vi.* MOVE FAST to move or begin to move at great speed **2.** *vti.* ATTAIN OR MAKE ATTAIN STH QUICKLY to get to, or cause sb or sth to get to, a particular condition or position very quickly (*informal*) **3.** *vi.* INCREASE QUICKLY to increase very quickly and dramatically (*informal*) **4.** *vt.* MIL, AEROSP POWER STH USING ROCKET ENGINE to send sth, especially a spacecraft, warhead, or missile, into the air or atmosphere by means of a rocket engine or rocket engines **5.** *vt.* BOMBARD WITH ROCKET to fire a rocket at a target **6.** *vi.* FLY UP QUICKLY to fly up vertically at speed (*refers to game birds*) [Early 17thC. From Italian *rocchetta* 'small distaff' (from its shape), from *rocca* 'distaff', of prehistoric Germanic origin.]

rocket[2] /rókit/ *n.* **1.** SALAD PLANT a Mediterranean plant with leaves that are used as salad leaves. Latin name: *Eruca vesicaria*. US term **arugula** **2.** YELLOW-FLOWERED FAST-GROWING PLANT a fast-growing plant with pale yellow flowers, typically growing on waste ground. Genus: *Sisymbrium*. **3.** = **dame's violet** **4.** = **sea rocket** [Early 16thC. Via French *roquette* from Italian *ruchetta*, literally 'small ruca' (a cabbage), ultimately from Latin *eruca* 'caterpillar, cole'.]

rocketeer /róki teer/ *n.* **1.** SB WHO DESIGNS SPACE ROCKETS a scientist or engineer who designs space rockets **2.** SB TRAVELLING IN SPACE ROCKET sb who launches, operates, or travels in a space rocket

rocket engine *n.* a device that carries both fuel and oxidizer that it burns in a combustion chamber, producing thrust by expelling the expanding hot gases through a nozzle. The fuel and oxidizer may be liquefied gases, such as oxygen and hydrogen, or solids, such as powdered aluminium and ammonium perchloride.

rocket plane *n.* an aircraft that is designed to carry and launch rockets, missiles, or warheads

rocketry /rókitri/ *n.* the science and technology of the design, construction, operation, flying, and maintenance of rockets

rocket salad *n.* = **rocket**[2] *n.* 1

rocket science *n.* a complex and intellectually demanding activity (*informal*) ○ *Using the Internet isn't exactly rocket science.* [Late 20thC. From the idea that rocket science is the province of a few highly qualified specialists.]

rocket scientist *n.* (*informal*) **1.** INTELLIGENT PERSON sb who is highly intelligent ○ *It doesn't take a rocket scientist to figure that one out!* **2.** STOCK EXCH EXPERT IN QUANTITATIVE ANALYSIS sb highly skilled in quantitative analysis who studies the capital markets

rocket sled *n.* a rocket-propelled vehicle that runs on a rail or rails and can be accelerated rapidly to high speeds, used in aeronautical applications such as crash and G-force tolerance testing

rocketsonde /rókit sond/ *n.* an instrument transported by rocket to the upper atmosphere to carry out weather observations

rockfall /rók fawl/ *n.* **1.** FALLEN ROCKS a collection or mass of fallen rocks **2.** FALLING ROCKS an avalanche of falling rocks

rockfish /rók fish/ (*plural* **-fish** *or* **-fishes**) *n.* **1.** FOOD FISH LIVING AMONG ROCKS a fish that lives among rocks. Many are important food fishes. **2.** DOGFISH OR CATFISH AS FOOD the dogfish or catfish when sold by fishmongers for use as food

rock flour *n.* fine powdery rock produced by grinding or abrasion, e.g. by the movement of a glacier

Rockford /rókfərd/ city in northern Illinois, south of the Wisconsin border, east of Freeport and northwest of Chicago. Population: 143,531 (1996).

rock garden *n.* a garden in which large stones or rockeries are a prominent feature

Rockhampton /rok hámptən/ city in eastern Queensland, Australia, on the River Fitzroy. Population: 57,770 (1996).

rockhopper /rók hopər/ *n.* a small penguin, native to Antarctica, New Zealand, and the Falkland Islands, that has a stout bill and a yellow crest. Latin name: *Eudyptes crestatus*.

rock hound *n.* US (*informal*) **1.** ROCK COLLECTOR sb who has an interest in, or whose hobby is, collecting rocks and minerals **2.** GEOL a geologist —**rock-hounding** *n.*

rock hyrax *n.* a small plant-eating African hyrax that lives in large colonies in rocky outcrops. Genus: *Procavia*.

Rockies /rókiz/ = **Rocky Mountains**

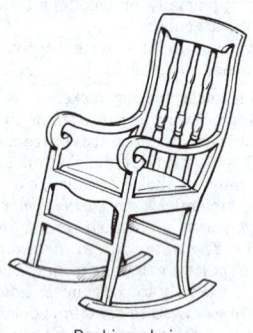

Rocking chair

rocking chair *n.* a chair that is set on a pair of curved pieces of wood so that sb sitting in it can be rocked backwards and forwards

Rockingham /rókingəm/ coastal town in southwestern Western Australia, near Perth. Population: 49,917 (1996).

Rockingham, Charles Watson-Wentworth, 2nd Marquess (1730–82) British statesman. As prime minister of Great Britain (1765–66 and 1782), he took a sympathetic attitude towards Britain's colonies in America.

rocking horse *n.* a small model horse fitted with reins and a saddle and set on a pair of rockers on which a child can sit and rock backwards and forwards

rocking stone *n.* a large stone or boulder that is so finely balanced, e.g. on another stone or stones, that it can be made to rock backwards and forwards with little effort

rockling /rókling/ (*plural* **-lings** *or* **-ling**) *n.* any of various small North Atlantic fishes of the cod family. Family: Gadidae.

rock lobster *n.* = **spiny lobster**

rock mechanics *n.* the study of the physical properties of rocks, e.g. density, elasticity, and strength, especially with relation to their behaviour in tunnels and mines and when subjected to environmental forces (*takes a singular verb*)

rock melon *n.* ANZ a cantaloupe

rock'n'roll *n., vi.* = **rock and roll**

rock oil *n.* = **petroleum**

rock pigeon *n.* = **rock dove**

rock plant *n.* a plant that has adapted to living on rocks or rocky ground

rock rabbit *n.* = **rock hyrax**

rock-ribbed *adj.* characterized by rocks or rocky outcrops

rockrose /rók rōz/ *n.* a woody shrub or plant grown for its small light-yellow or reddish flowers that are shaped like roses. Genera: *Cistus* and *Helianthemum*.

rock salmon *n.* = **rockfish**

rock salt *n.* = **halite**

rockslide /rók slīd/ *n.* **1.** ROCKS THAT HAVE SLID DOWNWARDS a collection or mass of rocks that have slid downwards **2.** SLIDING AVALANCHE OF ROCKS an avalanche of rocks as a result of surface movement

rock snake *n.* a large snake native to Australia and Asia. Genus: *Liasis*.

rock-solid *adj.* **1.** COMPLETELY SOLID firm and unshakable **2.** UNLIKELY TO BREAK extremely hard and unlikely to break

rock steady *n.* a type of reggae popular in Jamaica in the early 1960s and designed to be danced to

rock-steady *adj.* firm, unshaking, and calm

rockumentary /rókyoo méntəri/ (*plural* **-taries**) *n.* a film documentary about rock music in general or a particular rock band or musician, containing film footage of relevant performances (*informal*) [Late 20thC. Formed from ROCK AND ROLL + DOCUMENTARY.]

rock wallaby *n.* a medium-sized Australian marsupial that is found in open rocky country and has large well-padded hind feet with stiff hairs to prevent it from slipping on the rocks. Genus: *Petrogale*.

rockweed /rók weed/ *n.* any of various coarse brown seaweeds that grow on coastal rocks. Genera: *Fucus* and *Ascophyllum*.

rock wool *n.* = **mineral wool**

rockwork /rók wurk/ *n.* **1.** DECORATIVE STONEWORK artificial or decorative stonework designed to resemble the irregularity of natural rocks **2.** MASS OF STONES a collection or mass of large stones or rocks

rock wren *n.* a grey wren of western North America, commonly found in rocky areas. Latin name: *Salpinctes obsoletus*.

rocky[1] /róki/ (**-ier, -iest**) *adj.* **1.** WITH ROCKS consisting of or covered with rocks **2.** HARD resembling rock in its hardness or firmness **3.** COMPLETELY STEADY unyielding, unwavering, or lacking in human emotions —**rockiness** *n.*

rocky[2] /róki/ (**-ier, -iest**) *adj.* **1.** DIFFICULT characterized by difficulties, obstacles, or troubles **2.** UNSTEADY wobbly and unsteady **3.** UNWELL unwell, especially feeling sick or dizzy (*informal*) —**rockily** *adv.* —**rockiness** *n.*

Rocky Mountain goat *n.* = **mountain goat**

Rocky Mountains /róki-/ major mountain system of North America. Its highest point is Mount Elbert, at 4,399 m/14,433 ft. Length: 4,800 km/3,000 mi.

Rocky Mountain spotted fever *n.* an acute infectious disease transmitted by the bite of ticks infected with the microorganism *Rickettsia rickettsi*. Symptoms include chills, fever, muscle and joint pain, skin rash, and prostration. [Because first reported in the area of the ROCKY MOUNTAINS]

rococo /rə kókō/ *n.* **1.** rococo, Rococo ARTS ORNATE 18C ART

Rococo: Detail of stuccowork at Wies church, Bavaria, Germany (1745–54)

STYLE a style of architecture and the decorative arts characterized by intricate ornamentation that was popular throughout Europe in the early 18th century **2. rococo, Rococo** MUSIC ORNATE 18C MUSIC STYLE a style of music characterized by the use of ornamentation and embellishment that was popular in the 18th century **3.** ORNATE STYLE any excessively ornate or fancy style ■ *adj.* **1. rococo, Rococo** ARTS, MUSIC IN STYLE OF ROCOCO belonging to, relating to, or in the style of 18th-century rococo **2.** ORNATE excessively ornate or fancy [Mid-19thC. From French, a fanciful alteration of ROCAILLE.]

rod /rod/ *n.* **1.** THIN STICK a narrow, usually cylindrical, length of wood, metal, plastic, or other material **2.** ANGLING = **fishing rod 3.** WHIPPING STICK a stick, or bundle of sticks tied together, used for whipping sb as a punishment **4.** BUILDING SURVEYING POLE a graduated pole used by surveyors for sighting with a levelling instrument to determine elevation differences **5.** MEASURE = **measuring rod 6.** POL STAFF OF OFFICE a staff, especially one that indicates sb's standing, office, authority, or power **7.** POWER WIELDED tyrannical or oppressive power **8.** BOT PLANT STEM a straight stem or shoot that has been cut from, or that is growing on, a woody plant **9.** JOINERY BOARD MARKED WITH FULL-SCALE JOINERY PATTERN a board on which the dimensions of a joinery assembly, e.g. a window or door frame, are marked in full scale **10.** ANAT RECEPTOR CELL IN EYE a rod-shaped receptor in the retina of the eye that is sensitive to dim light but not colour **11.** MICROBIOL BACTERIUM a rod-shaped bacterium **12.** *US* FREIGHT, RAIL METAL BAR SUPPORTING RAILWAY CARRIAGE one of the metal bars that form the framework of the underside of a railway carriage, especially one on a goods carriage (*often used in the plural*) **13.** MEASURE UNIT OF LENGTH a unit of length equal to 5.03 m/5½ yd, now largely obsolete **14.** MEASURE UNIT OF AREA a unit of area equal to 25.3 m^2/30¼ sq. yd, now largely obsolete **15.** OFFENSIVE TERM a penis (*slang offensive*) **16.** PISTOL a gun, especially a pistol (*slang*) ■ *vt.* **(rods, rodding, rodded)** TECH CLEAR STH OUT USING ROD to use a rod to clear an obstruction from sth [Old English *rodd* 'pole, rod', of uncertain origin] —**rodless** *adj.* —**rodlike** *adj.*

rode[1] past tense of **ride**

rode[2] /rōd/ *n.* a rope or chain, especially one attached to an anchor [Early17thC. Of uncertain origin.]

rode[3] /rōd/ **(rodes, roding, roded)** *vi.* **1.** GO TO ROOST to fly to roost at nightfall (*refers to wildfowl*) **2.** FLY AS MATING DISPLAY to fly at nightfall as a mating display (*refers to male woodcock*) [Mid-18thC. Origin unknown.] —**roding** *n.*

rodent /rṓd'nt/ *n.* a small mammal such as a mouse, rat, squirrel, or marmot with large gnawing incisor teeth that continue growing throughout the animal's life. Rodents make up more than a third of all living mammal species and are adapted to all terrestrial habitats. Order: Rodentia. [Mid-19thC. From modern Latin *Rodentia*, order name, from Latin *rodent-*, the present participle stem of *rodere* 'to gnaw'.]

rodenticide /rō dénti sīd/ *n.* a substance designed to kill rodents, especially rats and mice

rodent ulcer *n.* a persistent, usually cancerous ulcer of the skin, especially of the face [*Rodent* literally 'gnawing' (see RODENT)]

rodeo /rō dáy ō, rṓdi-/ (*plural* **-os**) *n.* **1.** COMPETITION IN COWBOY SKILLS a competition or display of lassoing, riding unbroken horses, calf-roping, and cattle-wrestling **2.** MOTORCYCLING COMPETITION a competition or display of motorcycle riding that often includes stunts **3.** AGRIC CATTLE ROUND-UP an occasion when cattle are rounded up, especially so that they can be branded, counted, or have their health checked **4.** AGRIC CATTLE PEN a pen for rounded-up cattle [Mid-19thC. From Spanish, literally 'cattle ring', from *rodear* 'to go round, surround', from Latin *rotare* (see ROTATE).]

Rodin /rō dáN/, **Auguste** (1840–1917) French sculptor. Among his bronze sculptures are *The Thinker* (1880), *The Kiss* (1880), and *The Burghers of Calais* (1886). Full name **François Auguste René Rodin**

rodman /ródmən, -man/ (*plural* **-men** /-mən, -men/) *n.* *US* = **staffman**

rodomontade /róddə mon táyd, -taád/ *n.* BOASTFULNESS pretentious, self-important, or self-indulgent boasting, speech, or behaviour (*literary*) ■ *vi.* **(-tades, -tading, -taded)** BOAST to boast, speak, or behave in a pretentious, self-important, or self-indulgent way (*literary*) ■ *adj.* BOASTFUL boastful in a pretentious, self-important, or self-indulgent way (*literary*) [Early 17thC. Via French from obsolete Italian *rodomontada*, from *rodomonte* 'braggart', from *Rodomonte*, a boastful Saracen king in Boiardo's *Orlando Innamorato* and Ariosto's *Orlando Furioso*.]

Auguste Rodin: Bronze portrait bust (1888–89) by Camille Claudel

roe[1] /rō/ *n.* **1.** ZOOL, FOOD FISH EGGS a mass of mature fish eggs, especially when still inside the ovarian sac, sometimes eaten cooked **2.** ZOOL FISH SPERM a mass of mature fish sperm, especially when it is still inside the testicular sac **3.** ZOOL CRUSTACEAN EGGS a mass of mature eggs of certain crustaceans, e.g. the lobster, especially when still inside the ovarian sac [15thC. From Middle Dutch or Middle Low German *roge*, of unknown origin.]

roe[2] /rō/ (*plural* **roes** *or* **roe**) *n.* = **roe deer** [Old English *rā*, from prehistoric Germanic]

roebuck /rṓ buk/ (*plural* **-bucks** *or* **-buck**) *n.* a male roe deer, especially an adult one

Roedean /rṓ deen/ *n.* a public school for girls in southern England. It was founded in 1885.

roe deer *n.* a medium-sized reddish-brown European and Asian deer found in deciduous woodlands. Latin name: *Capreolus capreolus.*

Roeg /rṓ əg/, **Nicolas** (*b.* 1928) British film director. He is noted especially for *Performance* (1970), which he made with Donald Cammell, and for *Don't Look Now* (1973). Full name **Nicolas Jack Roeg**

roentgen /róntgən/, **röntgen** *n.* a unit of radiation, used to measure the exposure of sb or sth to X-rays and gamma rays, defined in terms of the ionization effect on air. It is equal to the quantity of radiation that produces ionization equal to one electrostatic unit of charge at 0° and standard atmospheric pressure. Symbol **R** [Late 19thC. Named after W.C. ROENTGEN.]

Roentgen /róntgən/, **Wilhelm Conrad** (1845–1923) German physicist. He was awarded a Nobel Prize in 1901 for his discovery of X-rays, originally known also as Roentgen rays.

roentgen- *prefix.* = **roentgeno-** (*used before vowels*)

roentgen equivalent physical *n.* full form of **rep**

roentgeno- *prefix.* X-ray ○ *roentgenotherapy* [From ROENTGEN]

Roeslare /rṓossə laarə/ city in West Flanders Province, western Belgium, 29 km/18 mi. south of Bruges. Population: 53,706 (1996).

rogallo /rō gálō/ (*plural* **-los**), **rogallo wing** *n.* a fabric covered delta-shaped wing that can be folded compactly, used for hang gliding and in microlight aircraft [Mid-20thC. Named after Francis M. *Rogallo*, American engineer.]

rogation /rō gáysh'n/ *n.* **1.** CHR SOLEMN PRAYER in the Christian church, a solemn prayer or supplication, especially one made as part of the observation of the three days preceding Ascension Day **(Rogation Days)** (*often used in the plural*) **2.** HIST SUBMISSION OF LAW FOR APPROVAL in ancient Rome, the submission of a law by a consul or tribune to the people for their approval, or a law so submitted [14thC. From the Latin stem *rogation-*, from *rogare* 'to ask, beg'.]

Rogation Day *n.* any of the three days preceding Ascension Day on which Christians are expected to pray (*often used in the plural*)

Rogation Sunday *n.* **1.** SUNDAY BEFORE ASCENSION DAY the Sunday before the Christian festival of Ascension Day, falling five weeks after Easter **2.** Sunday before Ascension Day: the Sunday before the Christian festival of Ascension Day, falling five weeks after Easter

rogatory /róggətəri, rṓgətəri/ *adj.* requesting information, especially information that might be pertinent to a court case [Mid-19thC. Via French *rogatoire* from medieval Latin *rogatorius*, from Latin *rogare* 'to ask, beg'.]

roger /rójjər/ *interj.* **1.** TELECOM AS CODEWORD IN TELECOMMUNICATIONS used in telecommunications to indicate that the speaker has received and understood a transmitted message **2.** OK used to indicate the speaker's agreement to sth (*informal*) ■ *vti.* **(-ers, -ering, -ered)** OFFENSIVE TERM an offensive term meaning to have sexual intercourse with a woman (*slang offensive*) [Mid-20thC. From the name *Roger*, used in radio communications for the letter *r* and meaning *received*.]

Roger II /rójjər/, **King of Sicily** (1095–1154) French monarch. His sovereignty also extended over southern Italy, and his domain was called the Kingdom of the Two Sicilies.

Rogers /rójjərz/, **Sir Richard George, Baron Rogers of Riverside** (*b.* 1933) British architect. A prominent exponent of postmodernism, he developed a high-tech style, exemplified by the Lloyd's Building, London (1986).

Roget /rō zháy/, **Peter Mark** (1779–1869) British scholar and doctor. He compiled the *Thesaurus of English Words and Phrases* (1852), now known as Roget's Thesaurus.

rogue /rōg/ *n.* **1.** SB DISHONEST sb who is unscrupulous or dishonest, especially sb who is nevertheless likable **2.** SB MISCHIEVOUS sb who is mischievously playful, especially a naughty child **3.** PLANTS, ZOOL BIOLOGICALLY INFERIOR VARIANT a plant or animal that is a biologically inferior variant as compared to the rest of its species **4.** ZOOL DANGEROUS SOLITARY ANIMAL a vicious or uncontrolled animal that lives apart from the rest of its herd or group, especially an elephant **5.** TRAMP a tramp or vagrant (*archaic*) ■ *adj.* **1.** ZOOL DANGEROUS AND SOLITARY vicious and uncontrolled and living apart from the rest of the herd or group **2.** MAVERICK acting independently and using unorthodox methods that often cause trouble **3.** STRAY different and unwanted, and often dangerous or destructive ■ *v.* **(rogues, roguing, rogued) 1.** *vt.* AGRIC, PLANTS CLEAR AWAY PLANTS FROM LAND to remove inferior plants from a piece of land or a group of plants **2.** *vt.* DEFRAUD to swindle or defraud sb **3.** *vi.* BE A ROGUE to be a rogue [Mid-16thC. Originally 'vagrant', of uncertain origin: possibly from *roger* ('g' pronounced hard) 'beggar posing as an impoverished student', from Latin *rogare* 'to beg'.]

Rogue /rōg/ river in southwestern Oregon, rising in the Cascade Mountains and emptying into the Pacific Ocean. Length: 320 km/200 mi.

roguery /rṓgəri/ (*plural* **-ies**) *n.* **1.** DISHONEST ACTION an act or behaviour that is unscrupulous or dishonest **2.** MISCHIEVOUS ACTION an act or behaviour that is mischievously playful

rogues' gallery *n.* a set of photographs of known criminals that the police show to witnesses to crimes for possible identification (*archaic*)

rogue site *n.* a World Wide website that redirects users to its site by having a similar domain name as a popular site

roguish /rṓgish/ *adj.* **1.** DISHONEST unscrupulous or dishonest in the manner of a rogue **2.** MISCHIEVOUS mischievously playful —**roguishly** *adv.* —**roguishness** *n.*

Röhm /rōm/, **Ernst** (1887–1934) German Nazi leader. Commander of the stormtroopers, he advocated that they take control of the German army. He was murdered on Adolf Hitler's orders.

ROI *abbr.* **1.** region of interest **2.** return on investment

roil /royl/ **(roils, roiling, roiled)** *v.* **1.** *vti.* PHYS MAKE OR BECOME OPAQUE to stir up a liquid so that the sediment becomes dispersed through the liquid and makes it cloudy, or become cloudy with sediment by being stirred **2.** *vt.* MAKE SB ANGRY to anger or annoy sb. ◊ **rile 3.** *vi.* BE BOISTEROUS to behave in a loud, rowdy way (*regional*) [Late 16thC. Origin uncertain: perhaps from

French *rouiller* 'to make muddy, rust', from assumed Vulgar Latin *robicula*, alteration of Latin *robigo* 'rust'.] —**roily** *adj.*

Roisín Dubh /ro shéen dóov/ *n. Ireland* Ireland personified as a woman (*literary*) [From Irish Gaelic, literally 'black rose']

roister /róystər/ (**-ters, -tering, -tered**) *vi.* **1.** **CELEBRATE ROWDILY** to take part in loud rowdy partying or celebrations **2.** **BRAG LOUDLY** to behave in a loud bragging manner [Mid-16thC. Origin uncertain: probably from Old French *ru(i)stre* 'boor, churl', ultimately from Latin *rusticus* 'rustic'.] —**roisterer** *n.* —**roisterous** *adj.* —**roisterously** *adv.*

ROK *abbr.* Republic of Korea (*international vehicle registration*)

Roland /rólənd/ ◇ **a Roland for an Oliver** an equally good retort, response, or retaliation

role /rōl/, **rôle** *n.* **1.** ARTS **ACTING PART** an individual part in a play, film, opera, or other performance played by an actor, singer, or other performer **2.** **SPECIFIC FUNCTION** the usual or expected function of sb or sth, or the part sb or sth plays in a particular action or event **3.** PSYCHOL, SOCIOL **PART PLAYED IN SOCIAL CONTEXT** the part played by sb in a given social context, with any characteristic or expected pattern of behaviour that it entails [Early 17thC. From French *rôle* '(paper) roll on which an actor's part is written', from Old French *rol(l)e* (see ROLL).]

role model *n.* sb who is regarded as sb to look up to and often as an example to emulate

role-play *n.* **ACTING OUT OF PART** role-playing, or an instance of it ■ *vti.* **ACT OUT PART** to engage or act out a part in role-playing

role-playing, rôle-playing *n.* the acting out of a part, especially that of sb with a particular social role, in order to understand the role or person better. This process is used in psychotherapy and in training people in interpersonal skills.

Rolfing /rólfing/ a service mark for a type of therapy using vigorous massage to alleviate physical or psychological tension

roll /rōl/ *v.* (**rolls, rolling, rolled**) **1.** *vti.* **TURN OVER AND OVER** to move or cause sth to move with repeated turning or rotating motions **2.** *vti.* **MOVE ON WHEELS** to move, or cause sth to move, on wheels or rollers **3.** *vti.* **FORM INTO ROUND SHAPE** to form sth, or be formed, into a ball, tube, cylinder, or other rounded shape, or form sth with such a shape **4.** *vt.* **WRAP STH INTO CYLINDER** to make sth into a cylinder shape, especially by wrapping sth over and over on itself **5.** *vt.* **TURN BETWEEN OR ON STH** to revolve sth between two surfaces or on a coating material **6.** *vti.* **MOVE WITH UNDULATIONS** to move, or cause sth to move, in a steady flowing motion **7.** *vi.* **STRETCH OUT OR AWAY IN UNDULATIONS** to have or take the form of a succession of gentle slopes ○ *green hills rolling away into the distance* **8.** *vi.* **DRIVE IN VEHICLE** to move in a wheeled vehicle **9.** *vi.* **ELAPSE** to go by or elapse, especially uneventfully or imperceptibly (*refers especially to time*) **10.** *vti.* **ROTATE** to turn or cause sth to turn in a complete or partial rotation **11.** *vt.* **FLATTEN STH WITH ROLLER** to flatten or spread sth, especially by using a roller or rolling pin **12.** *vi.* **REVERBERATE LOUDLY** to make a low prolonged rumbling noise **13.** *vi.* MUSIC, MIL **BEAT DRUM** to make a series of quick beats on a drum **14.** *vt.* PHON **TRILL SOUND** to pronounce a sound, especially an 'r', with a trill **15.** *vi.* ZOOL **WRITHE** to lie on the back and move about or from side to side, but without moving very far, often with a writhing motion (*refers to animals*) **16.** *vti.* AIR **ROTATE AIRCRAFT** to cause an aircraft to perform a single complete rotation about its lengthwise axis while maintaining the same altitude and direction, or perform such a rotation **17.** *vti.* NAUT **ROCK FROM SIDE TO SIDE** to move with a sideways swaying or rocking motion on waves or a swell, or cause sth, especially a ship, to move in this way **18.** *vi.* **MOVE AS CROWD** to move or arrive in large numbers or in a crowd **19.** *vi.* ASTRON **ORBIT** to revolve in an orbit (*refers to celestial bodies*) **20.** *vi.* **WALK UNSTEADILY** to walk with an unsteady or staggering motion **21.** *vi.* **WALK WITH A SWAY** to sway rhythmically in walking **22.** *vti.* **OPERATE STH** to function or cause sth, especially a movie camera or printing press, to function **23.** *vti.* CINEMA, TV **SEND OR GO UP ON SCREEN** to cause credits, titles, or other captions to move in a continuous upwards direction on a cinema or television screen, or move in this way **24.** *vt.* PRINTING **INK STH WITH ROLLER** to apply ink to type or a plate with a roller **25.** *vi.* **TRAVEL AROUND** to travel from place to place **26.** *vi.* **CARRY ON** to proceed or continue successfully (*informal*) ○ *Now this project is finally rolling.* **27.** *vti.* **OVERTURN CAR** to overturn a motor vehicle, especially a car, or be overturned **28.** *vti.* GAME **THROW DICE** to throw a die or dice **29.** *vt.* GAME **SCORE NUMBER BY THROWING DICE** to achieve a specified number, position, or score by throwing a die or dice **30.** *vi.* **BE CARRIED BY RIVER** to be transported by river **31.** *vt.* MUSIC **PLAY CHORD WITH SPREAD NOTES** to play a chord with its notes in rapid succession (**arpeggio**) rather than simultaneously **32.** *vt.* CRIMINOL **ROB SB** to take money or belongings from sb who cannot offer any resistance (*informal*) **33.** *vti.* **HAVE SEX** to have sexual intercourse or engage in sexual foreplay with sb (*informal; offensive in some contexts*) ■ *n.* **1.** **STH TUBE-SHAPED** a tube, cylinder, or coil of sth, especially sth that is wrapped around itself **2.** FOOD **INDIVIDUAL LOAF** a small individual-sized loaf of bread, usually round or long in shape, or a sandwich made from one **3.** **OFFICIAL LIST** an official register or list of names, especially of school pupils, members of a club, or of people entitled to vote **4.** **TOTAL ON OFFICIAL LIST** the total number of people registered on a school, club, or electoral roll **5.** **ROUNDED LAYER** a thick rounded layer of sth, especially of flesh **6.** FOOD **FILLED FOOD** a food made by wrapping pastry around a filling or by spreading a filling on sth, e.g. sponge cake, and wrapping it around itself (*usually used in combination*) **7.** **RUMBLING NOISE** a low prolonged rumbling noise **8.** MUSIC, MIL **DRUM BEATS** a series of quick beats on a drum **9.** **STH UNDULATING** a gentle rounded hump on a surface, often one of a series **10.** **SINGLE TURN** a complete or partial rotation **11.** **REPEATED TURN** a repeated turning or rotating motion **12.** AIR **ROTATION OF AIRCRAFT** a midair flight manoeuvre in which an aircraft maintains the same height and direction while doing a single complete rotation about its lengthwise axis. ◊ **pitch, yaw** **13.** GYMNASTICS **SOMERSAULT** a gentle somersault **14.** **ACT OF FLATTENING** an act of flattening or spreading sth, especially by using a roller or rolling pin **15.** **MOVEMENT ON WHEELS** a movement on wheels or rollers **16.** **WRITHING MOTION** an action that involves writhing while turning backwards and forwards or from side to side, but without moving very far **17.** **MOVEMENT FROM SIDE TO SIDE** a swaying or rocking motion, especially by a ship. ◊ **pitch, yaw** **18.** **SWAYING WALK** a rhythmical sway in walking **19.** **UNDULATING MOVEMENT** a steady, flowing, undulating movement **20.** **RHYTHMICAL STREAM OF WORDS** a continuous stream of words with a rhythmical quality **21.** **EQUIPMENT HOLDER WITH POCKETS** a length or belt of fabric or leather that has pockets to hold tools, medical instruments, or other equipment and can usually be wrapped around itself and tied up **22.** INDUST **ROLLER FOR METAL** a cylinder or roller used for pressing, shaping, or flattening sth, especially one used for shaping metal in a rolling mill **23.** CRAFT **BOOKBINDER'S TOOL** a bookbinder's tool for embossing book covers **24.** **TRILLING SOUND** a trilling noise, especially the sound of a trilled 'r' or the song of a canary **25.** MUSIC **CHORD WITH SPREAD NOTES** a chord played with its notes in rapid succession (**arpeggio**) rather than simultaneously **26.** ARCHIT **SPIRAL SCROLL** in Greek architecture, a spiral scroll on an Ionic column **27.** **WAD OF MONEY** a cylindrical wad of banknotes formed by coiling the wad around itself (*informal*) **28.** GAME **TOSS OF DICE** a throw of a die or dice **29.** CRIMINOL **ACT OF ROBBERY** an act or the process of taking money or belongings from sb who cannot offer any resistance (*informal*) **30.** **SEX ACT** an act of sexual intercourse or foreplay (*informal; offensive in some contexts*) [12thC. Via Old French *rolle* 'scroll', from the Latin stem *rotul-* 'little wheel', ultimately from Latin *rota* 'wheel'.] ◇ **on a roll** enjoying a period of good luck or of doing sth well (*informal*) ◇ **rolled into one** forming a single unit consisting of a number of different aspects or qualities

roll back *vt.* **1.** *US* **DECREASE STH** to cause sth, especially prices or wages, to decrease **2.** **PUT STOP TO STH** to reduce or nullify the influence or effectiveness of sth

roll in *vi.* **1.** **ARRIVE LATE** to come home or arrive at a destination, especially in a leisurely way, often later than expected **2.** **ARRIVE IN LARGE NUMBERS** to arrive or attend in large numbers or quantities

roll off *vi.* **1.** **MOVE EASILY OR IN QUANTITY** to flow, especially with ease or in large numbers **2.** **REDUCE AMPLITUDE-FREQUENCY RESPONSE** to display a gradually decreasing response in the upper and lower portions of the amplitude-frequency range of an electronic system or transducer

roll on *vi.* used to express a wish that a time or occasion may arrive soon (*informal*)

roll out *vt.* **1.** **FLATTEN PASTRY** to flatten pastry, dough, or other uncooked food by shaping it with a rolling pin **2.** **UNCOIL** to unfold or uncoil sth **3.** AEROSP **SHOW NEW AIRCRAFT TO PUBLIC** to put a new aircraft or spacecraft on public display for the first time **4.** MARKETING **LAUNCH PRODUCT GRADUALLY** to launch a new product or service by gradually increasing the number of outlets where it is available to the public

roll over *v.* **1.** *vi.* **CAPSIZE** to capsize, tip over, or overturn **2.** *vti.* **ADD ON JACKPOT** to add the prize funds from a previous jackpot of the National Lottery that no one has won to the jackpot for the next draw **3.** *vt.* FIN **REINVEST FUNDS** to transfer funds from one investment to a similar investment **4.** *vt.* FIN **EXTEND LOAN** to allow a loan to be paid at a later date **5.** *vt.* FIN **NEGOTIATE NEW FINANCIAL TERMS FOR STH** to achieve new terms for a financial contract through discussion **6.** *vt.* **DEFEAT SB** to defeat a person or team overwhelmingly

roll up *v.* **1.** *vi.* **ARRIVE** to come to a place or destination, often in a vehicle and especially when later than expected or when not expected at all **2.** *vt.* **PRODUCE CYLINDER SHAPE** to turn sth into a cylindrical form

rollaway /rólə way/ *adj.* fitted with wheels or castors so as to be easily moved or stored

rollback /rōl bak/ *n.* **1.** **MONEY CUT** a decrease in sth, especially in sth such as prices and wages involving money **2.** **REDUCTION OF INFLUENCE OR EFFECTIVENESS** a reduction or nullification of the influence or effectiveness of sth

rollbar /rōl baar/ *n.* a reinforcing bar across the top of a vehicle, especially an open-top sports car or rally car, to protect the occupants if the vehicle overturns

roll call *n.* **1.** **ATTENDANCE CHECK** a check on attendance, especially in a school or military establishment, by calling out the names of those expected to be present, with each of those present responding **2.** **TIME FOR ROLL CALL** a time when a roll call is read out, especially one that is fixed at a regular time of day

rolled gold *n.* a base metal, e.g. brass, that has been covered with a very thin layer of gold applied by a rolling method. It is used in the manufacture of inexpensive and costume jewellery. US term **filled gold**

rolled oats *npl.* oats that have had the husks removed and been flattened. They are especially used in making porridge.

rolled paperwork *n.* a form of decorative covering for boxes and other small objects that consists of curls of paper laid in a pattern

rolled steel *n.* steel produced to a desired thickness by being passed through a set of rollers

rolled steel joist *n.* a beam made of rolled steel with a cross-section shaped like the letter H

roller /rólər/ *n.* **1.** **DEVICE FOR APPLYING PAINT** a painting tool in the form of a revolving tube with a soft absorbent covering and a handle, used for applying paint to large surface areas **2.** GARDENING **DEVICE FOR FLATTENING LAWNS** a large heavy revolving cylinder or pair of cylinders with a handle, used for flattening a lawn or green **3.** HAIR **HAIR CURLER** a short tube around which hair is wrapped in order to make it curly or wavy **4.** **HEAVY WAVE** a long heavy wave that does not break until it reaches the shoreline **5.** **SPOKELESS WHEEL** a small wheel without spokes, especially on a skate or piece of heavy furniture **6.** **TUBE WRAPPED IN STH** a long tube with a particular material, e.g. a section of window blind or length of towel, wrapped around it **7.** MED **COILED BANDAGE** a long bandage that is rolled up tightly upon itself to form a dense cylinder. The required amount is then cut off for use. **8.** ENG **CYLINDER THAT TRANSMITS FORCE AND MOTION** a cylindrically shaped rotating device that transmits force and motion via its rotation and is often used in sets or pairs and machine-operated **9.** PRINTING **INKED TUBE** a hard tube, usually of compressed rubber, on which ink is spread. It is used for inking type or a plate. **10.** BIRDS **BRIGHTLY COLOURED BIRD KNOWN FOR TUMBLING FLIGHT** a brightly coloured European bird with a hooked bill that performs rolling dives and erratic flight during the breeding season as a courtship display. Family: Coraciidae. **11.** EQU **BELT FOR HORSE BLANKET** a strap around the belly of a horse to hold a blanket in place **12. SB OR STH THAT ROLLS** sb who or sth that rolls **13.** *US* BASEBALL **BALL HIT WITH LITTLE FORCE** in baseball, a batted ball that rolls along the ground slowly

rollerball /rṓlər bawl/ *n.* a pen with a writing tip in the form of a small moveable metal or plastic ball

roller bearing *n.* a set of rotating cylindrically shaped parallel steel rollers contained within a closed track, used to prevent friction between machine parts

Rollerblade /rṓlər blayd/ *tdmk.* a trademark for a type of roller skate on which the wheels are arranged in one straight line

roller blind *n.* a blind consisting of a length of fabric rolled around a pole and fitted to the top of a window. It unrolls when lowered and rolls up when raised.

roller chain *n.* a driving or power transmission chain consisting of freely rotating hollow cylindrical rollers mounted on pins that connect the sideplates that link adjacent rollers

roller coaster *n.* **1.** LEISURE **FAIRGROUND RIDE** an amusement park ride consisting of a narrow rail track on a metal framework shaped into extreme peaks and troughs and sharp bends **2. SITUATION WITH EXTREME HIGHS AND LOWS** a situation that is characterized by sudden, extreme, and often repeated, changes (*hyphenated when used before a noun*)

roller derby *n.* competition between two teams of roller skaters

roller hockey *n.* hockey played on a roller-skating rink or other hard surface by players wearing roller skates

roller skate *n.* **1. SET OF WHEELS ATTACHED TO SHOE** a metal or plastic frame with wheels attached, usually one pair at the front and another at the back, fastened onto a shoe and used for skating **2. SHOE FOR ROLLER-SKATING** a specially designed shoe or boot to which a roller skate is attached —**roller skater** *n.* —**roller skating** *n.*

roller-skate /rṓlər skáyt/ (**roller-skates, roller-skating, roller-skated**) *vi.* to travel on roller skates

roller towel *n.* a continuous roll of material, usually linen or towelling, housed inside a metal box and used, especially in public toilets, for drying the hands. Each user pulls down a fresh section of towel.

roll film *n.* a length of film rolled around a spool and put inside a protective case ready to be loaded into a camera

rollick /róllik/ *vi.* (**-licks, -licking, -licked**) **DISPLAY BOISTEROUS HIGH SPIRITS** to have fun, especially in a loud, rowdy way ■ *n.* **DISPLAY OF BOISTEROUS HIGH SPIRITS** a loud, rowdy session of having fun [Early 19thC. Origin uncertain: probably a blend of ROLL or ROMP and FROLIC.] —**rollick** *n.* —**rollicksome** *adj.* —**rollicky** *adj.*

rollicking[1] *adj.* loud and rowdy —**rollickingly** *adv.*

rollicking[2] /rólliking/ *n.* a severe reprimand or scolding (*informal*)

rolling /rṓling/ *adj.* **1. GRADUALLY DEVELOPING** proceeding in successive phases and usually gaining in momentum, intensity, or effectiveness **2. CONSTANTLY UPDATED** responsive to change and constantly updated **3. RICH** rich or very well-off (*informal*) **4. FOLDABLE UP OR DOWN** able to be turned up or down ■ *adv.* **EXTREMELY** to the extent of staggering (*informal*) ◇ *rolling drunk* ◇ **be rolling in it** *or* **sth** to have plenty of sth, especially money, assets, or wealth (*informal*)

rolling bearing *n.* a bearing in which the rolling action of components such as balls or cylinders reduces friction

rolling launch *n.* a way of introducing a new product or service onto a market by gradually increasing the number of outlets where it is available to the public

rolling mill *n.* **1. METAL-PRESSING FACTORY** a factory, or part of a factory, where metal, usually in ingot form, is processed by being rolled into sheets or bars of the desired shape and size **2. METAL PRESS EMPLOYING ROLLERS** a machine with rollers that press metal into sheets or bars of the desired shape and size

rolling paper *n.* a small piece of fine paper used for rolling a handmade cigarette (*often used in the plural*)

rolling pin *n.* a cylinder, sometimes with small handles at either end, used for rolling out and flattening dough, pastry, or other uncooked food

rolling stock *n.* **1. RAILWAY VEHICLES** railway vehicles such as locomotives, passenger carriages, and goods wagons thought of collectively, especially those belonging to a particular company **2.** *US* **ROAD VEHICLES** road vehicles thought of collectively, especially those belonging to a particular company

rolling stone *n.* sb who is unable to stay in the same job, or live in the same place, for any length of time [Originally in the proverb, *a rolling stone gathers no moss*]

Rolling Stones /rṓling stṓnz/ British rock group, formed in 1962, that rivalled the popularity of the group's early contemporaries, the Beatles. The group was formed by Mick Jagger, Keith Richards, Brian Jones, Charlie Watts, and Bill Wyman, who left the band in late 1992. After Jones' death (1968), Mick Taylor replaced him until 1975, when Ron Wood took his place.

rollmop /rṓl mop/ *n.* a fillet of raw herring wrapped around a slice of onion or a pickle and left to marinate in spiced vinegar. It is usually served as an hors d'oeuvre. [Early 20thC. From German, from *rollen* 'to roll' + *Mops* 'pug dog'.]

rollneck /rṓl nek/ *n.* = **polo neck** —**rollnecked** *adj.*

roll-neck *n.* a garment, especially a sweater, with a roll-neck

Rollo /róllō/ (860?–932?). Viking leader. An ancestor of William the Conqueror, he founded the duchy of Normandy (911?).

roll of honour *n.* **1. LIST OF DISTINGUISHED NAMES** a list of names of people who have all excelled in some way **2. LIST OF WAR DEAD** a list of names of people who have died during a battle or war in the service of their country, especially people from one area

roll-on *adj.* **WITH ROTATING-BALL APPLICATOR** that is applied to the skin by means of a rotating ball in the top of the container ■ *n.* **1. DEODORANT WITH ROTATING-BALL APPLICATOR** a deodorant, cosmetic, or other product that comes in a container with a rotating ball in its top **2. WOMAN'S UNDERGARMENT** a woman's elasticated girdle that is pulled on rather than fastened down the front

roll-on roll-off *adj.* **DRIVEN STRAIGHT THROUGH** designed so that vehicles are driven on one end of a vessel, especially a ferry, and, on arrival at their destination, are driven off the other end ■ *n.* **ROLL-ON ROLL-OFF VESSEL** a roll-on roll-off vessel, especially a ferry

roll-out *n.* **1.** AEROSP **SHOWING OF NEW AIRCRAFT** the first public display of a new aircraft or spacecraft **2.** MARKETING **GRADUAL LAUNCH OF NEW PRODUCT** a launch of a new product that involves gradually increasing the number of outlets where it is available to the public

rollover /rṓl ōvər/ *n.* **1. CAPSIZING INCIDENT** an act or the process of capsizing, tipping over, or overturning **2. LOTTERY DRAW WITH DOUBLE PRIZE MONEY** a National Lottery draw to which the prize fund from the previous draw has been added because no one won the jackpot on that occasion **3.** FIN **TRANSFER OF FUNDS** a transfer of funds from one investment to another similar investment, often without taking possession of the funds

roll-top desk, **roll-top** *n.* a desk with a rounded cover consisting of connected parallel wooden slats that can be pulled down over the writing area and, usually, locked

roll-up *n.* a hand-rolled cigarette made using a cigarette paper and loose tobacco (*informal*)

rollway /rṓl way/ *n.* **1. SLOPE FOR LOGS** a natural or artificial sloping area along which cylindrical objects are rolled, especially a slope used by lumberjacks to move felled timber to water for transportation **2. SET OF ROLLERS** a series of parallel rollers used to facilitate the transportation of heavy loads

roll-your-own *n.* = **roll-up** (*informal*)

roly-poly /rṓli pṓli/ *adj.* **OVERWEIGHT** of greater body weight than is desirable (*insult*) ■ *n.* **1. roly-poly, roly-poly pudding JAM SUET PUDDING IN ROLL** a hot pudding made with suet pastry spread with jam or fruit, rolled to form a coil, and baked or steamed **2.** *Aus* = **tumbleweed** (*informal*) [Early 17thC. Origin uncertain: probably a rhyming compound of ROLL and POLL, originally meaning 'rascal', and the name of several games of rolling balls.] —**roly-poly** *n.*

Rom /rom/ (*plural* **Roma** /rómmə/) *n.* a member of the Romany people, especially a Romany man [Mid-19thC. From Romany, literally 'married man'.]

ROM /rom/ *abbr.* COMPUT read-only memory

rom., **rom** *abbr.* PRINTING roman

Rom. *abbr.* **1.** GEOG Roman **2.** BIBLE Romans **3.** LANG Romance **4.** Romania **5.** LANG Romanian

Roma plural of **Rom**

Romaic /rō máy ik/ *n.*, *adj.* modern Greek (*archaic*) [Early 19thC. From Greek *Rhōmaïkos* 'Roman' (in reference to the Eastern Roman Empire).]

romaine /rō máyn/, **romaine lettuce** *n.* *US, Can* = **cos** [Early 20thC. From French, feminine of *romain* 'Roman'; perhaps because this lettuce was introduced into France during the Avignon papacy (1309–77).]

romaji /rṓ maaji/ *n.* the Roman alphabet as used for transliterating Japanese [Late 19thC. From Japanese, from *roma* 'Roman' + *ji* 'character'.]

roman[1] /rṓmən/ *adj.* **IN OR OF UPRIGHT TYPE** relating to a type with upright as opposed to slanting characters that is the standard type used in printing books, newspapers, and magazines ■ *n.* **ROMAN TYPE** roman type or characters [Early 16thC. So called because it imitates the style of Roman inscriptions.]

roman[2] /rō máaN, rōmaàn/ *n.* **1. NOVEL** a novel, especially a French one or one in a French genre (*literary*) **2. MEDIEVAL FRENCH POEM** a medieval French narrative poem, especially one that has heroic exploits as its main theme [Mid-18thC. From French, literally 'romance, novel'.]

Roman /rṓmən/ *adj.* **1. OF MODERN ROME** relating to or belonging to the modern city of Rome and its inhabitants **2.** HIST **OF ANCIENT ROME** belonging to or characteristic of the ancient city of Rome and its territories and inhabitants **3.** ARCHIT **IN ANCIENT ROMAN ARCHITECTURAL STYLE** relating to, belonging to, or built in a style characteristic of the buildings of ancient Rome, especially in having rounded arches, vaults, and domes **4.** CHR **OF THE ROMAN CATHOLIC CHURCH** belonging to or characteristic of the Roman Catholic church ■ *n.* **1. SB FROM MODERN ROME** sb who was born in or is a citizen of the modern city of Rome **2.** HIST **SB FROM ANCIENT ROME** sb who was born in or was a citizen of ancient Rome **3.** CHR **OFFENSIVE TERM** an offensive term for a member of the Roman Catholic church (*offensive*) [Pre-12thC. From Latin *Romanus* 'Roman, a Roman', from *Roma* 'Rome'; later reinforced by French *Romain*.]

roman à clef /rō máaN a kláy, rō maán aa-/ *n.* a novel in which some or all of the characters are based on real people and that usually includes clues to the characters' true identities [From French, literally 'novel with a key']

Roman alphabet *n.* the writing system that represents sounds by the letters A-Z and is used for the languages of most Western European countries and many elsewhere. It is based on the alphabet developed in ancient Rome and now has 26 letters.

roman à thèse /rō maáN a téz, rō maán aa-/ (*plural* **romans à thèse**) *n.* a novel in which the author focuses on an injustice and suggests how this might be rectified, especially by putting forward a particular political or social theory or message [From French, literally 'novel with a thesis']

Roman calendar *n.* the lunar calendar, comprising 10 months and an intercalated month, that was used by the ancient Romans until the introduction of the Julian calendar in 46 BC. ◊ **Julian calendar, Gregorian calendar**

Roman candle *n.* a short cylindrical firework that when placed on the ground and lit produces showers of sparks and occasional coloured balls or stars of fire

Roman Catholic *adj.* OF THE CATHOLIC CHURCH relating to the Roman Catholic Church, its members, or its beliefs ■ *n.* MEMBER OF THE CATHOLIC CHURCH a member of the Roman Catholic Church

Roman Catholic Church *n.* a Christian church that has a pope as the head of a hierarchy of bishops and priests and is administered from the Vatican City in Rome

Roman Catholicism *n.* the system of beliefs, practices, and organization of the Roman Catholic Church

romance /rō mánss, rṓ manss/ *n.* **1.** LOVE AFFAIR a love affair, especially a brief and intense one ○ *This is more than just a holiday romance.* **2.** LOVE sexual love, especially when the other person or the relationship is idealized or when it is exciting and intense ○ *The secret of a happy marriage is to keep the romance alive.* **3.** SPIRIT OF ADVENTURE a spirit or feeling of adventure, excitement, the potential for heroic achievement, and the exotic ○ *the romance of cruising down the Nile* **4.** FASCINATION WITH STH a particular fascination or enthusiasm for sth, especially of an uncritical or inexplicable kind ○ *his lifelong romance with football* **5.** STORY OF LOVE a novel, film, or play with a love story as its main theme ○ *a writer of cheap romances* **6.** LOVE STORIES COLLECTIVELY love stories considered as a genre **7.** LITERAT MEDIEVAL ADVENTURE STORY a story of the adventures of chivalrous heroes written in verse or prose in a vernacular language in the Middle Ages **8.** LITERAT MEDIEVAL ADVENTURE STORIES COLLECTIVELY the genre of medieval adventure stories ○ *Arthurian romance* **9.** NARRATIVE OF ADVENTURES a fictional narrative dealing with exciting and extravagant adventures ○ *a romance of piracy on the high seas* **10.** FICTITIOUS ACCOUNT an extravagant or absurd fictitious account of sth **11.** MUSIC SHORT LYRICAL PIECE a short lyrical song or instrumental composition, usually expressing or evoking tender emotions ■ *v.* (-mances, -mancing, -manced) **1.** *vi.* TELL ROMANTIC OR ADVENTUROUS STORIES to tell or write extravagant or idealized fictitious accounts **2.** *vi.* TELL LOVE STORIES to tell or write stories about love **3.** *vi.* THINK ROMANTICALLY to think or behave in a romantic way **4.** *vt.* TREAT SB ROMANTICALLY to treat sb in a special way during a love relationship or with a view to entering on one **5.** *vt.* HAVE AN AFFAIR WITH SB to have a love affair with sb [13thC. From Old French *romanz* '(work composed) in French', from assumed Vulgar Latin *romanice* 'in the vernacular', a form of Latin *romanicus* 'Roman', ultimately from ROME.] —**romancer** *n.*

Romance /rō mánss, rṓ manss/ *n.* the Italic branch of the Indo-European group of languages that includes French, Italian, Portuguese, Romanian, and Spanish, all of which are descended from Latin. About 500 million people speak one of the Romance languages. —**Romance** *adj.*

Roman collar *n.* = clerical collar

Roman Empire *n.* **1.** TERRITORY RULED BY ROMAN EMPERORS the territories ruled by ancient Rome under its emperors, from 27 BC to AD 395. In 395, these territories were split into the Byzantine or Eastern Roman Empire and the Western Roman Empire. ◊ **Holy Roman Empire 2.** RULE OF ROMAN EMPERORS the rule or form of government of ancient Rome under its emperors

Romanesque /rōmə nésk/ *adj.* **1.** TYPICAL OF AN EARLY EUROPEAN ARCHITECTURAL STYLE relating to or built in the style of European architecture that combines Roman and Byzantine elements, prevalent from the 9th century to the 12th and featuring rounded arches and barrel vaults **2.** RELATING TO THE PERIOD OF ROMANESQUE ARCHITECTURE characteristic of or relating to the style of European painting, sculpture, or decorative arts contemporary with Romanesque architecture. Romanesque works of art show a Byzantine influence and often feature elaborate or-

Romanesque: Carved stone capital (1127–45) from Pamplona Cathedral, Spain

CORBIS/ Andrea Jemolo

namentation. ■ *n.* ROMANESQUE STYLE the Romanesque style in architecture or art

roman-fleuve /rō maáN flṓv, rō mán-/ *(plural* **romans-fleuves** /rō maáN flṓv, rō mán-/) *n.* a long novel or series of novels telling the stories of a linked group of people over many years [From French, literally 'river-novel']

Roman holiday *n.* **1.** ENTERTAINMENT INVOLVING CRUELTY a type of entertainment in which people are killed, e.g. a gladiatorial contest **2.** PLEASURE IN WATCHING BLOODSHED a feeling of pleasure derived from watching others be maimed or killed

Romani *n.* = Romany [See ROMANY]

Romania

Romania /roo máyni ə, rō máyni ə/ republic in southeastern Europe, bordered by Ukraine, Moldova, the Black Sea, Bulgaria, Yugoslavia, and Hungary. Language: Romanian. Currency: Romanian leu. Capital: Bucharest. Population: 22,600,000 (1997). Area: 237,500 sq. km/91,700 sq. mi.

Romanian /roo máyni ən, rō-/ *n.* **1.** PEOPLES SB FROM ROMANIA sb who was born or brought up in Romania, or who has Romanian citizenship **2.** LANG LANGUAGE OF ROMANIA the official language of Romania, belonging to the Romance group of Indo-European languages that developed from Latin —**Romanian** *adj.*

Romanic /rō mánnik/ *adj.* **1.** HIST OF ANCIENT ROME belonging or relating to ancient Rome or the ancient Romans **2.** LANG OF ROMANCE LANGUAGES belonging or relating to the Romance family of languages ■ *n.* LANG ROMANCE LANGUAGES COLLECTIVELY the Romance family of languages as a group

Romanise *vti.* = Romanize

Romanism /rṓmənizəm/ *n.* an offensive term for Roman Catholicism, especially its ritual

Romanist /rṓmənist/ *n.* **1.** SB INFLUENCED BY CATHOLICISM a member of a church, especially the Church of England, who is sympathetic to or influenced by Roman Catholicism **2.** OFFENSIVE TERM an offensive term for a member of the Roman Catholic Church (*offensive*) **3.** STUDENT OF ANCIENT ROME sb who studies or is an expert in ancient Roman history or law ■ *adj.* **1.** OFFENSIVE TERM an offensive term meaning belonging or relating to the Roman Catholic Church (*disapproving*) **2.** OF ANCIENT ROMAN HISTORY relating to or involving ancient Roman history or law —**Romanistic** /rṓmə nístik/ *adj.*

Romanize /rṓmə nīz/ (-izes, -izing, -ized), **Romanise** (-ises, -ising, -ised) *v.* **1.** *vt.* CHR MAKE STH ROMAN CATHOLIC

to make sth such as a service take on a Roman Catholic character or influence **2.** *vti.* CHR CONVERT TO ROMAN CATHOLICISM to become a Roman Catholic, or convert sb to Roman Catholicism **3.** **romanize, Romanize, romanise, Romanise** *vt.* LANG TRANSCRIBE STH INTO THE ROMAN ALPHABET to transcribe sth such as a language or text in the characters of the Roman alphabet **4.** *vti.* HIST MAKE OR BECOME ROMAN to take on Roman characteristics, or make sb or sth take on Roman characteristics ○ *the Romanized Celts* —**Romanization** /rōmə nī záysh'n/ *n.*

Roman law *n.* **1.** LAW OF ANCIENT ROME the system of law established in ancient Rome, forming the basis of many modern legal systems **2.** = **civil law** *n.* 3

Roman mile *n.* a measure of distance used in ancient Rome, approximately equal to 1,481 metres/1,620 yards

Roman nose *n.* a nose with a high and prominent bridge

Roman numeral *n.* any of the letters or sequences of letters used by the ancient Romans to represent cardinal numbers, including I for 1, V for 5, and X for 10

Romans /rṓmənz/ *n.* in the Bible, a letter from St Paul to the Church at Rome. Written in about AD 58, it is an exposition of his theory of religious thinking. See table at Bible

Romansch /rō mánsh/, **Romansh** *n.* one of the official languages of Switzerland, belonging to the Romance group of Indo-European languages and existing in several dialectal forms. Romansch is spoken by about 50,000 people. [Mid-17thC. From Romansch, via medieval Latin *romanice* from assumed Vulgar Latin (see ROMANCE).] —**Romansch** *adj.*

romans-fleuves plural of **roman-fleuve**

romantic /rō mántik/ *adj.* **1.** INVOLVING SEXUAL LOVE involving or characteristic of a love affair or sexual love, especially when the relationship is idealized or exciting and intense ○ *I don't think there's any romantic attachment between them.* **2.** SUITABLE FOR LOVE characterized by or suitable for lovemaking or the expression of tender emotions ○ *a romantic candlelit dinner for two* **3.** INVOLVING ENTHUSIASM relating to or characterized by a fascination or enthusiasm for sth, especially of an uncritical or indefinable kind ○ *a romantic attachment to the mountains* **4.** INVOLVING ADVENTURE relating to or characterized by adventure, excitement, the potential for heroic achievement, and the exotic ○ *a romantic tale about life in the Outback* **5.** IDEALISTIC characterized by or arising from idealistic or impractical attitudes and expectations ○ *a romantic dreamer* **6.** IMAGINARY imaginary or fictitious in an extravagant or glamorizing way ○ *a romantic version of the events of her life* **7.** ARTS = **Romantic** *adj.* ■ *n.* **1.** ROMANTIC PERSON sb who has a romantic personality or outlook **2.** ARTS = **Romantic** *n.* [Mid-17thC. Formed from *romaunt* Mid-16thC. From Old French, variant of *romanz* (see ROMANCE).] —**romantically** *adv.*

Romantic /rō mántik/, **romantic** *adj.* OF AN 18C ARTISTIC MOVEMENT relating to the movement in late 18th- and early 19th-century music, literature, and art that departed from classicism and emphasized sensibility, the free expression of feelings, nature, and the exotic ■ *n.* ARTS ARTIST INVOLVED IN THE ROMANTIC MOVEMENT a writer, composer, or artist who was involved in the Romantic movement during the late 18th and early 19th centuries

romanticise *vti.* = romanticize

romanticism *n.* the quality of being romantic or having romantic inclinations

Romanticism /rō mántissizzəm/ *n.* in the arts, the style and theories of the Romantic movement, or the movement itself —**Romanticist** *n.*

romanticize /rō mánti sīz/ (-cizes, -cizing, -cized), **romanticise** (-cises, -cising, -cised) *v.* **1.** *vt.* MAKE STH APPEAR GLAMOROUS to make sth seem or believe sth to be more glamorous or ideal than it really is ○ *The film tends to romanticize a rather sordid period in history.* **2.** *vi.* THINK ROMANTICALLY to think or express sth in an amorous, idealistic, or sentimental way —**romanticization** /rō mánti sī záysh'n/ *n.*

Romany /rṓmənі, rómmənі/ (*plural* **-nies**), **Romani** *n.* **1.** PEOPLES **MEMBER OF A NOMADIC PEOPLE** a member of a nomadic people who probably originated in northwestern India. They appeared in Western Europe in the fifteenth century and there are now Romany communities throughout the world. **2. Romany, Romani** LANG **LANGUAGE OF THE ROMANIES** the Indic language spoken by the Romany people. It belongs to the Indo-European family of languages and is spoken by around 250,000 people. [Early 19thC. From Romany *Romani*, a form of *Romano* 'Romany' (adjective), from *Rom* 'man'.]

Rome /rōm/ capital city of Italy, located in the centre of the country. The former capital of the Roman Empire, it includes within its boundaries the independent state of the Vatican City. Population: 2,687,881 (1993). ◇ **fiddle while Rome burns** to occupy yourself with unimportant things when there are extremely important things requiring to be done ◇ **when in Rome (do as the Romans do)** used to indicate the advisability of adopting the behaviour and customs of the place or circumstances in which you find yourself

Romeldale /rómm'l dayl/ *n.* an American breed of sheep that produces fine wool and high-grade lamb [Mid-20thC. Blend of ROMNEY MARSH, RAMBOUILLET, and CORRIEDALE.]

Romeo /rṓmi ō/ (*plural* **-os**) *n.* **1. AMOROUS MAN** a man with a reputation for having or seeking romantic or sexual involvement with a large number of women ○ *the office Romeo* **2.** COMMUNICATION **CODE WORD FOR THE LETTER 'R'** the NATO phonetic alphabet code word for the letter 'R', used in international radio communications [Mid-18thC. Named after *Romeo*, lover of Juliet in William Shakespeare's play *Romeo and Juliet* 1594.]

Romish /rṓmish/ *adj.* an offensive term meaning belonging to, characteristic of, or influenced by the Roman Catholic Church (*disapproving*) —**Romishly** *adv.* —**Romishness** *n.*

Rommel /rómməl/, **Erwin** (1891–1944) German military leader. He is renowned for his victories in the African deserts during World War II. Known as **the Desert Fox**

Romney /rómni, rúmni/, **George** (1734–1802) British painter. He is noted for his portraits of British aristocracy in neoclassical settings, especially Emma Hamilton, whom he depicted in more than 50 portraits.

Romney Marsh[1] /rómni-/ *n.* a sheep of a breed that has long wool and is bred for mutton, originally from the Romney Marsh area in southern England

Romney Marsh[2] /rómni-, rúmni-/ region in southern Kent, England. It is protected from the sea by a seawall. Area: 176 sq. km/68 sq. mi.

romp /romp/ *vi.* (**romps, romping, romped**) **1. PLAY BOISTEROUSLY** to run around or play in a boisterous way ○ *kids romping in the playground* **2. WIN** to win a contest easily (*informal*) ○ *The horse romped home* **3. MAKE EASY PROGRESS** to progress swiftly and effortlessly ○ *romped through her final exam* ■ *n.* **1. BOISTEROUS ACTIVITY** boisterous or playful activity ○ *The dogs had a romp in the park.* **2. LIGHTHEARTED WORK** a book, play or film that is lighthearted and lively as opposed to serious or weighty (*informal*) ○ *The novel is an exhilarating romp through the pages of recent history.* **3. CASUAL SEX** a casual or lighthearted sexual encounter (*informal*) **4. EASY VICTORY** a victory that is remarkably or unexpectedly easy (*informal*) **5. SB PLAYFUL** a playful or boisterous person, especially a woman (*archaic*) [Early 18thC. Origin uncertain: perhaps an alteration of RAMP[2] in the sense 'to stand menacingly'.]

rompers /rómpərz/ *npl.* **1. BABY SUIT** a one-piece suit of trousers, often short, and a bib held up by shoulder straps, worn by babies and small children **2.** *NZ* **GIRL'S ATHLETIC COSTUME** a one-piece garment worn by schoolgirls when they engage in games and gymnastics

Romulus /rómmyōōləss/ *n.* in Roman mythology, the founder of the city of Rome. He was the son of Mars and twin brother of Remus, whom he is said to have killed. ◊ **Remus**

Romulus Augustulus /-aw gústyōōləss/ (461?–476) Roman emperor. He was the last Roman emperor in the West, and his deposition by Odoacer in 476 marked the end of the Western Roman Empire.

rondavel /ron daavəl/ *n. S Africa* in southern Africa, a circular hut or other building, usually with a conical thatched roof [Late 19thC. From Afrikaans *rondawel*.]

rondeau /róndō/ (*plural* **-deaux** /-dōz/) *n.* **1.** LITERAT **POEM WITH A REFRAIN** a poem of 13 or 10 lines in three stanzas, with two rhymes and with the opening phrase repeated twice as an unrhyming refrain **2.** MUSIC **MEDIEVAL FRENCH SONG** a medieval French song, especially a trouvère song with a two-part refrain [Early 16thC. From French, later form of *rondel* (see RONDEL).]

rondel /rónd'l/, **rondelle** /ron dél/ *n.* a poem, similar to a rondeau, that has 13 or 14 lines in 3 stanzas, with 2 rhymes and with the opening 2 lines repeated as a refrain [14thC. From Old French, literally 'small round' (from the repetition of the opening two lines), from *rond* 'round', from, ultimately, Latin *rotundus* (see ROUND).]

rondelet /róndə let, -lay/ *n.* a short form of rondeau, with five or seven lines and the first line repeated as a refrain. The first line is of four syllables and is repeated as line three and, in the longer form, line seven, while the other lines have eight syllables.

rondo /róndō/ (*plural* **-dos**) *n.* an instrumental piece or movement in which the principal theme is repeated between at least two sections that contrast with it, often forming the last movement of a sonata [Late 18thC. Via Italian from French *rondeau* 'rondeau', a later form of Old French *rondel* (see RONDEL).]

rondure /rón dyoor/ *n.* sth that has a circular, curved, or round shape (*literary*) [Late 16thC. From French *rondeur* 'roundness', from *rond* (see RONDEL).]

rone /rōn/ *n. Scotland* **1. GUTTER** a gutter at the edge of a roof, for channelling rain away **2. rone, ronepipe DRAINPIPE** a drainpipe that channels rainwater down the side of a building away from a roof gutter [Late 16thC. Origin unknown.]

röntgen *n.* = **roentgen**

roo /roo/ (*plural* **roos**) *n. Aus* a kangaroo (*informal*) [Early 20thC. Shortening.]

roo bar *n. Aus* a metal bar on the front of a car or truck that prevents the vehicle being damaged in the event of a collision with an animal

rood /rood/ *n.* **1.** ARCHIT **CRUCIFIX** a crucifix, especially one mounted at the entrance to the choir or chancel of a church **2. JESUS CHRIST'S CROSS** the cross on which Jesus Christ was crucified (*archaic*) **3.** MEASURE **QUARTER OF AN ACRE** a unit of area equal to 0.10117 hectares/0.25 acre [Old English *rōd* 'cross, pole']

rood screen *n.* a partition with a cross mounted on it and often decorated, separating the choir or chancel of a church from the nave or main part

roof /roof/ *n.* **1. UPPER COVERING OF A BUILDING** the outside covering of the top of a building, or the framework supporting this **2. TOP PART** the top part of sth, forming a covering, e.g. the top of a vehicle ○ *a blue car with a black roof* **3. TOP OF INSIDE CAVITY** the top of the inside of a hollow structure ○ *the roof of the cave* **4. STRUCTURE COVERING A BODY CAVITY** the upper covering structure of a body part, especially one with a vaulted structure such as the mouth **5. HIGHEST POINT** the highest point or upper limit of sth ○ *a mountain range known as the roof of the world* ■ *vt.* (**roofs** /roovz/, **roofing, roofed**) **FIX ROOF ON STH** to fix a top covering onto sth, especially a building ○ *The house is roofed with slate tiles.* [Old English *hrōf* 'roof, ceiling, top', from prehistoric Germanic] —**roofless** /róofləss/ *adj.* —**rooflike** /roof līk, ro͝of-/ *adj.* ◇ **hit the roof** to be extremely angry

WORD KEY: CULTURAL NOTE

Cat on a Hot Tin Roof, a play by US dramatist Tennessee Williams (1955). Set in the US South, it depicts the Pollitt family gathering to celebrate the 65th birthday of patriarch Big Daddy. The simmering conflicts between Daddy and sons Gooper and Buck and their wives reflect the lies and deceit that underpin many family relationships. It was made into a film by Richard Brooks in 1958. One of its most famous lines is the last one from Act III: 'Nothing's more determined than a cat on a tin roof–is there? Is there, baby?'.

roofer /róofər/ *n.* sb whose job is to build or repair the roofs of buildings

roof garden *n.* a garden on the flat roof of a building

roofing /róofing/ *n.* **1.** CONSTR **MATERIAL FOR A ROOF** material used to make a roof **2. TOP OF STH** sth forming a top or roof **3. OCCUPATION OF MAKING OR REPAIRING ROOFS** the business or occupation of making or repairing roofs

roof rack *n.* a frame attached to the top of a motor vehicle, used for carrying things, especially luggage. US term **luggage rack** *n.* 1

rooftop /róof top/ *n.* the outer surface of the roof of a building

rooftree /róof tree/ *n.* = **ridgepole** *n.* 1

rooinek /ró͝o i nek, róy nek/ *n. S Africa* an offensive term for a British person, or an English-speaking South African (*slang insult*) [Late 19thC. From Afrikaans, literally 'red neck', from *rooi* 'red' + *nek* 'neck'.]

rook[1] /ro͝ok/ *n.* **1. BIRD OF THE CROW FAMILY** a large bird of the crow family found in Europe and Asia that has black plumage and a pale area at the base of its bill. It nests in colonies in treetops. Latin name: *Corvus frugilegus.* **2. SWINDLER** sb who swindles or cheats, especially at cards (*slang*) ■ *vt.* (**rooks, rooking, rooked**) **CHEAT SB** to overcharge, swindle, or cheat sb (*slang*) ○ *If you paid that amount you've been rooked.* [Old English *hrōc*, from a prehistoric Germanic word of uncertain origin: probably an imitation of the sound] —**rooky** *adj.*

rook[2] /ro͝ok/ *n.* any one of four chess pieces that begin a game in the corner squares and that can move in a straight line in any direction over any number of unoccupied squares [13thC. From Old French *rok*, ultimately from Arabic *rukk* (of unknown original meaning).]

rookery /ro͝okəri/ (*plural* **-ies**) *n.* **1. COLONY OF ROOKS** a colony of nesting rooks **2. ROOKS' BREEDING PLACE** a place, especially in the tops of trees, where rooks breed **3. ANIMALS' COLLECTIVE BREEDING PLACE** a breeding or living area for large numbers of animals, especially birds or mammals that come together in colonies to nest or breed **4. SLUM** a slum or overcrowded group of run-down houses, especially tenements (*archaic*)

rookie /ro͝oki/ *n. US* sb who is new to an activity or job, e.g. a new recruit to the army (*informal*) [Late 19thC. Origin uncertain: perhaps an alteration of RECRUIT, influenced by ROOK[1] in the obsolete sense 'dupe, person easily cheated'.]

room /room, ro͝om/ *n.* **1. USABLE SPACE** space that may or may not be filled with sth ○ *There's room for another passenger in my car.* **2. PART OF A BUILDING** an area within a building that is enclosed by a floor, walls, and a ceiling ○ *a hotel room* **3. PEOPLE IN A ROOM** the people in a room considered as a group ○ *Her entrance silenced the room.* **4. SCOPE** the scope, opportunity, or possibility for sth to exist, happen, or be done ○ *there's room for improvement* ■ **rooms** *npl.* **ACCOMMODATION** part of a house or hotel that may be rented as separate accommodation ○ *I managed to find myself rooms in town.* ■ *vi.* (**rooms, rooming, roomed**) *US* **SHARE LIVING QUARTERS WITH SB** to occupy or share living quarters with one person or several people [Old English *rūm*, from a prehistoric Germanic word meaning 'spacious', of uncertain origin: perhaps ultimately from an Indo-European word that is also the ancestor of English *rural*]

roomer /róomər, ro͝omər/ *n. US* = **lodger**

roomette /roo mét, ro͝o-/ *n. US, Can* a private single compartment in a railway sleeping car

roomful /róom fo͝ol, ro͝o-/ *n.* **1. CONTENTS OF A FULL ROOM** as many people or things as a room can hold ○ *a roomful of desks* **2. THOSE IN A ROOM** all the people or things in a room

roommate /róom mayt, ro͝o-/ *n.* sb with whom a person shares a room

room service *n.* a service providing food and drinks served to hotel guests in their rooms ○ *Room service is available throughout the day.*

room temperature *n.* the average normal temperature of a living room, usually thought of as around 68°F/20°C or slightly above ○ *This wine should be served at room temperature.*

Gable   Gable + valley   Hipped

Sloped turret   Pavilion   Conical   Helm

Imperial   Dome   Bell   Lean-to

Mansard   Gambrel   Jerkin-head or half hip

Roof

Theodore Roosevelt

rooster /roöstər/ *n. US* an adult male bird, especially a domestic fowl

root[1] /root/ *n.* **1.** BOT **UNDERGROUND BASE OF A PLANT** the part of a plant that has no leaves or buds and usually spreads underground, anchoring the plant and absorbing water and nutrients from the soil **2.** BOT **UNDERGROUND STEM OF A PLANT** an underground plant part that behaves like a root, e.g. a rhizome or tuber, especially a fleshy edible one such as that of a carrot or turnip **3.** ANAT **EMBEDDED BODY PART** the portion of a body part such as a tooth or hair that is embedded in tissue **4.** BASE OF STH the bottom or base of sth, or the part by which sth is attached to the body ○ *the root of the tongue* **5.** CAUSE the fundamental cause, basis, or essence of sth, or the source from which sth derives ○ *the roots of discontent* **6.** ANCESTOR an ancestor or progenitor, especially one from whom many people are descended **7.** MATH **NUMBER MULTIPLIED BY ITSELF** a number that when multiplied by itself a given number of times equals another number ○ *2 is the square root of 4.* **8.** MATH **NUMBER SUBSTITUTABLE FOR A VARIABLE** a number that can take the place of the variable in an equation and solve the equation **9.** LING **BASIC PART OF A WORD** in linguistics, the basic meaningful part of a word that is left when any affixes are removed and that cannot be analysed further into other meaningful elements **10.** LING **ORIGINAL FORM OF A WORD** in historical linguistics, the original reconstructed form from which a recorded word is derived, e.g. by phonetic change or the addition of affixes **11.** MUSIC **FOUNDATION OF A CHORD** the note that forms the foundation of a chord **12.** ANAT **END OF A NERVE** the end of a nerve that is nearer to the centre of the body **13.** *vti. ANZ* **OFFENSIVE TERM** a sexual partner, especially of a man (*slang offensive*) ■ **roots** *npl.* **1.** **FEELING OF BELONGING** a feeling of belonging in a particular place or culture ○ *I live in the city but my roots are in the country.* **2.** SB'S GENETIC ORIGIN sb's origins or ancestry ■ *v.* (**roots, rooting, rooted**) **1.** *vti.* GROW ROOTS to develop a root or roots or cause a plant to grow roots **2.** *vti.* BE FIXED to become fixed, embedded, or immobile or to cause sb or sth to become fixed, embedded, or immobile ○ *news that rooted me to the spot* **3.** *vi.* BE BASED to have a basis or origin in sth ○ *herbal remedies that are rooted in folk medicine* **4.** *vti. ANZ* OFFENSIVE TERM to have sexual intercourse with sb, especially a woman (*slang offensive*) [Pre-12thC. From Old Norse *rót*. Ultimately from an Indo-European word meaning 'branch, root', which is also the ancestor of English *eradicate*, *radical*, and *wort*.] — **rooter** *n.* ◇ **root and branch** in every respect or to the fullest extent ○ *reformed the system root and branch* ◇ **take root** to become established and accepted

— **WORD KEY: SYNONYMS** —
See Synonyms at *origin*.

root out *vt.* **1.** ERADICATE STH to eradicate or remove sb or sth completely ○ *He ruthlessly rooted out all opposition.* **2.** FIND STH EVENTUALLY to find or remove sth after rummaging for it ○ *I'll root out some old photos of him.*

root up *vt.* to pull or dig up a whole plant, including its roots

root[2] /root/ (**roots, rooting, rooted**) *v.* **1.** *vti.* DIG IN THE GROUND WITH THE SNOUT to dig in the surface of the ground with the snout or nose out of curiosity or in search of food ○ *The pigs were rooting for beech nuts.* **2.** *vi.* RUMMAGE to move things about unsystematically while looking for sth ○ *rooting in the drawer for a pencil* [Mid-16thC. Alteration (influenced

Rook

roomy /roõmi, roõ-/ (**-ier, -iest**) *adj.* having plenty of space in which to move around —**roomily** *adv.* — **roominess** *n.*

Eleanor Roosevelt

Roosevelt /rõzə velt/, **Eleanor** (1884–1962) US first lady, social activist, and writer. As the first lady of President Franklin D. Roosevelt, her national broadcasts and syndicated newspaper column established her reputation as a campaigner for progressive social causes. She was a US delegate to the United Nations

(1945–53) and chaired the commission that drafted the Universal Declaration of Human Rights. Born **Anna Eleanor Roosevelt**

Franklin D. Roosevelt

Roosevelt, Franklin D. (1882–1945) US statesman and 32nd president of the United States. He served longer than any other president (1933–45), with an unprecedented election to four terms. He held office during the Great Depression of the 1930s and World War II. Full name **Franklin Delano Roosevelt**

Roosevelt, Theodore (1858–1919) US statesman and 26th president of the United States During his presidency (1901–09) he expanded US involvement in world affairs, established domestic reforms, and promoted conservation. Known as **Teddy Roosevelt**

roost /roost/ *n.* **1.** PLACE WHERE BIRDS SLEEP a place where a bird rests or sleeps such as a perch or a building with perches for domestic fowl **2.** TEMPORARY ACCOMMODATION a place where sb may rest or sleep temporarily **3.** BIRDS SHARING A ROOST a group of birds sharing a roost ■ *vi.* (**roosts, roosting, roosted**) GO TO SLEEP to rest or sleep on or in a roost ○ *Starlings were roosting in the trees.* [Old English *hrōst*] ◇ **come home to roost** to result in undesirable or negative effects, usually after a fairly long period of time ◇ **rule the roost** to be the person who is in charge and who must be obeyed by ROOT¹) of *wroten*, from Old English *wrōtan*.] —**rooter** *n.*

root³ /root/ (**roots, rooting, rooted**) *vi.* **1.** SUPPORT SB OR STH NOISILY to cheer, shout, or applaud in support of a contestant or team **2.** LEND SUPPORT TO SB to provide support to or be actively in favour of sb or sth [Late 19thC. Origin uncertain: perhaps an alteration of *rout* 'to low loudly'.] —**rooter** *n.*

rootage /rootij/ *n.* **1.** PLANTS PLANT ROOTS a system of plant roots **2.** PLANTS GROWTH OF ROOTS the developing of roots **3.** ACT OR PROCESS OF BECOMING FIXED the act or process of becoming rooted or established

root ball *n.* the tightly packed mass of roots and soil produced by a plant, especially when grown in a container

root beer *n.* a sweet fizzy soft drink made from the extracts of various roots and herbs

root canal *n.* the cavity in the root of a tooth, containing pulp, nerves, and blood vessels

root cap *n.* a thick protective mass of cells that covers the growing tip of the root of a plant

root climber *n.* a vine such as an ivy that climbs up a structure by developing small roots on its stems that grip the structure

root crop *n.* a crop grown for its edible roots, e.g. turnips, potatoes, or sugar beets

rooted /rootid/ *adj.* **1.** HAVING ROOTS on which strong roots have developed ○ *a rooted plant* **2.** WELL ESTABLISHED arising from firmly held beliefs or long-standing traditions or practices ○ *a rooted conviction* **3.** US UNABLE TO MOVE unable to move because of shock or fear **4.** HAVING STRONG TIES having strong emotional or cultural roots **5.** ANZ TIRED OR NOT FUNCTIONING exhausted, or unable to function (*slang*) —**rootedness** *n.* ◊ **get rooted** ANZ used when angry or irritated to tell sb to go away (*slang vulgar*)

root hair *n.* a fine growth from the outer cells of a plant root that resembles a hair and absorbs nutrients. Root hairs are elongated epidermal cells that increase the surface area of roots to improve absorption of water and minerals.

roothold /root hōld/ *n.* the anchoring of a plant in the soil by the spreading of its roots

root knot *n.* a disease of plants caused by nematodes in which the roots become enlarged and plant growth is stunted

rootle /root'l/ (**rootles, rootling, rootled**) *vi.* to root about or around [Early 19thC. Formed from ROOT².]

rootless /rootlass/ *adj.* **1.** PLANTS WITHOUT ROOTS with roots cut off or underdeveloped **2.** LACKING A BOND WITH PEOPLE lacking close ties to people or places —**rootlessly** *adv.* —**rootlessness** *n.*

rootlet /rootlat/ *n.* a small root or part of a root

root mean square *n.* the square root of the mean of the squares of a set of numbers. Sometimes the root mean square is a more useful measure of central tendency than the mean or the median.

root nodule *n.* a swelling on the roots of leguminous plants such as alfalfa, soybeans, and peas, caused by symbiotic bacteria that can fix nitrogen in the soil

root pressure *n.* the pressure that forces water upwards through the conducting tissues of a plant, caused by the water potential in the stem being lower than in the root. Root pressure causes exudation of sap from cut stems and secretion of water droplets from leaves.

root rot *n.* a disease of plants that causes the roots to break or decay, often caused by fungi

roots music *n.* world music (*dated*)

rootstock /root stok/ *n.* **1.** PLANTS = rhizome **2.** PLANTS ROOT USED IN GRAFTING a root or piece of root used as a stock in propagation by grafting. ◊ **stock** *n.* 12 **3.** SOURCE OF STH a source or origin of sth

root system *n.* the network of roots that a plant develops

root vegetable *n.* a vegetable such as a carrot, turnip, or beet that is grown for its fleshy edible root or tuber. Some are also used for their young leaves.

rooty /rooti/ (**-ier, -iest**) *adj.* **1.** HAVING MANY ROOTS full of

or having many roots **2.** SIMILAR TO A ROOT resembling a root or roots —**rootiness** *n.*

ropable /rōpab'l/, **ropeable** *adj.* **1.** ABLE TO BE ROPED able to be caught or restrained using a rope **2.** ANZ ANGRY extremely angry (*informal*)

rope /rōp/ *n.* **1.** STRONG CORD a strong cord made by twisting together strands of hemp or other fibres or wire **2.** STRING OF STH a row of things strung or twisted together ○ *a rope of pearls* **3.** STRAND OF STICKY MATERIAL a stringy strand of a sticky substance ○ *a rope of saliva* **4.** CORD FOR HANGING SB a cord with a noose at one end, used to execute people by hanging **5.** DEATH BY HANGING execution by hanging **6.** FREEDOM TO DO STH freedom or latitude to do sth ■ *ropes npl.* **1.** BOXING CORDS OF A RING USED FOR FIGHTING the cords used to enclose a boxing or wrestling ring **2.** HOW TO DO STH the appropriate means and procedures for doing sth or for functioning in an environment (*informal*) ○ *Her task was to show the new employee the ropes.* ■ *v.* (**ropes, roping, roped**) **1.** *vt.* SECURE STH WITH A ROPE to tie, link, or bind sb or sth with rope ○ *the two climbers were roped together for the ascent* **2.** *vt.* ENCLOSE AN AREA to enclose or partition an area using ropes as barriers ○ *Museum staff had roped off the area.* **3.** *vt.* CATCH AN ANIMAL WITH A LASSO to catch an animal with a lasso ○ *rope a steer* **4.** *vi.* FORM STRANDS SIMILAR TO ROPE to form strands that resemble rope in shape or texture [Old English *rāp* (source of English *stirrup*)] —**roper** *n.* ◊ **give sb enough rope to hang himself** *or* **herself** to give sb enough freedom to make mistakes or reveal his or her shortcomings ◊ **on the ropes** in a desperate or hopeless position and likely to fail (*informal*)

rope in *vt.* to involve sb in an activity, especially if he or she was initially reluctant or unwilling ○ *We got roped in to help with the cleaning up.*

ropedancer /rōp daanssar/ *n.* an acrobat who dances or performs feats on a rope, especially a tightrope, stretched above the ground —**ropedancing** *n.*

Roper /rōpar/ river in northern Australia, in the Northern Territory. Length: 400 km/250 mi.

ropewalk /rōp wawk/ *n.* a long shed or covered walk where ropes are made

rope-walker *n.* an acrobat who performs on a rope stretched above the ground, especially a tightrope walker

ropeway /rōp way/ *n.* a system of cables strung from high supports and used to carry heavy objects such as logs from one place to another through the air

ropy /rōpi/ (**-ier, -iest**), **ropey** (**-ier, -iest**) *adj.* **1.** INFERIOR not meeting an acceptable standard (*informal*) ○ *a rather ropy performance* **2.** ILL slightly unwell (*informal*) **3.** FORMING STICKY THREADS forming into sticky, stringy strands **4.** SIMILAR TO ROPE resembling a rope or ropes —**ropily** *adv.* —**ropiness** *n.*

roque /rōk/ *n.* a US game developed from croquet and played on a hard court with a surrounding wall from which the ball can rebound and still be in play [Late 19thC. Alteration of CROQUET.]

Roquefort /rōk fawr/ *n.* a moist, strongly flavoured, blue-veined cheese made from ewes' milk and matured in caves [Mid-19thC. Named after ROQUEFORT-SUR-SOULZON, where it was first made.]

Roquefort-sur-Soulzon /rōk fawr syoor sóo zoN/ town in Aveyron Region, in southwestern France, famous for its blue cheese. Population: 880 (1998).

roquelaure /rōkə lawr/ *n.* a knee-length hooded cloak worn by men in Europe in the 18th and 19th centuries [Early 18thC. Named after Antoine-Gaston (1656–1738), Duc de *Roquelaure* and Marshal of France.]

roquet /rōki/ *vti.* (**-quets, -queting, -queted**) STRIKE AN OPPONENT'S CROQUET BALL in croquet, to strike another player's ball with your own ball ■ *n.* CROQUET STROKE HITTING ANOTHER BALL in croquet, a stroke that makes the player's ball strike that of another player [Mid-19thC. Origin uncertain: probably an alteration of CROQUET.]

roquette *n.* = rocket² **1** [Early 20thC. From French (see ROCKET).]

ro-ro *abbr.* roll-on roll-off

rorqual /rawrkwəl/ *n.* any large streamlined baleen whale that has a small pointed dorsal fin and longitudinal grooves on the throat, e.g. the blue whale

or the humpback whale. Genus: *Balaenoptera*. [Early 19thC. Via French from Norwegian *røyrkval*, from Old Norse *reyðarhvalr*, from *reyðr* 'rorqual' (which was formed from *rauðr* 'red') + *hvalr* 'whale'; from its reddish colour.]

Rorschach test /ráwr shaak-, -shakh-/ *n.* a projective test of personality or mental state based on sb's interpretation of a series of standard inkblots. ◊ **projective test** [Early 20thC. Named after its inventor, Hermann Rorschach (1884–1922), a Swiss psychiatrist.]

rort /rawrt/ *n.* Aus DISHONEST SCHEME a dishonest scheme or practice (*informal*) ■ *vt.* (**rorts, rorting, rorted**) Aus FALSIFY STH to manipulate sth to personal advantage dishonestly or fraudulently (*informal*) ○ *accused of rorting their travel expenses* [Mid-20thC. Back-formation from *rorty* 'boisterous, rowdy', of unknown origin.] —**rorter** *n.*

rosace /rōz ayss/ *n.* **1.** ROSE WINDOW a rose window **2.** ROSETTE a rosette [Mid-19thC. Via French from Latin *rosaceus* 'made of roses', from *rosa* 'rose' (see ROSE).]

rosacea /rō záyshə/ *n.* a recurring inflammatory disorder of the skin of the nose, cheeks, and forehead that is characterized by swelling, dilation of capillaries, pimples, and a reddened appearance [Late 19thC. Via modern Latin (*acne*) *rosacea* 'rose-coloured' (*acne*) from Latin *rosacea*, feminine of *rosaceus*.]

rosaceous /rō záyshəss/ *adj.* **1.** OF ROSES belonging or relating to the rose family (**Rosaceae**) of flowering plants **2.** SIMILAR TO A ROSE resembling a rose flower [Mid-18thC. From Latin *rosaceus*.]

Rosalind /rózzə lind/ *n.* a small inner natural satellite of Uranus, discovered in 1986 by the Voyager 2 planetary probe. It is approximately 58 km in diameter.

rosaniline /rō zánnə leen, -līn/, **rosanilin** /rō zánnə lin/ *n.* a brownish-red crystalline compound derived from aniline and used as a dye, in the preparation of other dyes, as an antifungal drug, and in Schiff's reagent. Formula: $C_{20}H_{21}N_3O$. [Mid-19thC. From ROSE + ANILINE.]

rosarian /rō záiri ən/ *n.* sb who cultivates roses or who is an expert on their cultivation [Mid-19thC. Formed from Latin *rosarium* 'rose garden', a form of *rosarius* 'of roses', from *rosa* (see ROSE).]

Rosario /rō sáari ō/ city in east-central Argentina, situated on the River Parana. Population: 894,645 (1991).

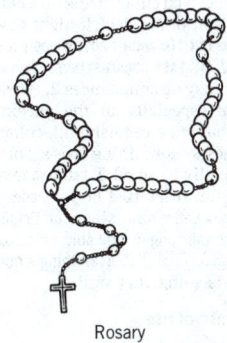

Rosary

rosary /rōzəri/ (*plural* **-ries**) *n.* **1.** SERIES OF PRAYERS a series of Roman Catholic prayers, usually made up of 5 or 15 decades of Hail Marys, each decade beginning with an Our Father and ending with a Gloria **2.** CATHOLIC PRAYER BEADS a string of beads used in counting the prayers said in a rosary **3.** rosary, rosary bead NON-CATHOLIC PRAYER BEADS a string of beads used in praying by members of religions or denominations other than Roman Catholicism [15thC. From Latin *rosarium* and Anglo-Latin *rosarius* 'rose garden' (see ROSARIAN).]

─────── **WORD KEY: ORIGIN** ───────

It was a common stylistic device in the Middle Ages to name collections of verse or similar short pieces after bunches of flowers (*anthology* comes from the Greek word for 'flower', and a similar inspiration underlies *florilegium*). This was the background against which a collection of Roman Catholic prayers came to be known as a *rosary*. The metaphor was probably encouraged by the symbolic association of roses and rose gardens with, respectively, the Virgin Mary and paradise.

ROSCO /róskō/ (*plural* **ROSCOs**) *n.* a rolling stock operating company, a company that leases trains to train operating companies under the arrangements by which the UK national railway system was privatized [Late 20thC. Acronym.]

Roscommon /ross kómmən/ **1.** county in Connacht province, west-central Republic of Ireland. Population: 51,897 (1997). Area: 2,463 sq. km/951 sq. mi. **2.** town and administrative centre of County Roscommon, in the Republic of Ireland. Population: 1,363 (1986).

Rose

rose[1] /rōz/ *n.* **1.** PLANTS **PRICKLY SHRUB WITH ORNAMENTAL FLOWERS** a prickly shrub or bush with compound leaves that is cultivated in many varieties and hybrids for its flowers. Genus: *Rosa*. **2.** PLANTS **FLOWER OF A ROSE SHRUB** the flower of the rose shrub. Roses are usually red, pink, yellow, or white and are often fragrant. The wild rose has five petals, but cultivated varieties are usually double or partly double. **3.** PLANTS **PLANT SIMILAR TO A ROSE** a member of the family of flowering plants that includes the rose, or a plant that resembles it, especially in having similar flowers. Family: Rosaceae. **4.** COLOURS **REDDISH COLOUR** a reddish-pink colour **5.** ORNAMENT RESEMBLING A ROSE a representation of a rose flower as an emblem or decoration, or an ornament or design resembling a rose flower **6.** MINERALS **FORM OF VARIOUS MINERALS** a mineral form that is round and resembles a rose **7.** SPRINKLER NOZZLE a perforated nozzle on a watering can or hose for producing a spray **8.** CEILING FITMENT FOR WIRES a circular fitting on a ceiling through which the lead of an electric light passes **9.** CRAFT, INDUST = **rose cut 10.** ARCHIT **ROSE WINDOW** a rose window ■ **roses** *npl.* **1.** EASY CIRCUMSTANCES favourable, comfortable, or easy circumstances **2.** PINK COLOURING pink colouration, especially in the cheeks ■ *adj.* **1.** REDDISH-PINK having a reddish-pink colour **2.** HAVING OR RESEMBLING ROSES containing roses or resembling roses, especially in smell **3.** RELATING TO ROSES relating to or used for roses [Old English *rōse*, via prehistoric Germanic from Latin *rosa* (source of English *rosary*, and *rosé*), of uncertain origin: probably ultimately from Greek *rhodon*, of Iranian origin] ◇ **everything's coming up roses** everything is going very well

rose[2] past tense of **rise**

rosé /rṓ zay/ *n.* a pink-coloured wine, especially one made by fermenting red grapes and removing the skins from the juice before all the colour has been extracted [Late 19thC. From French, from *(vin) rosé* 'pink (wine)'.]

Rose /rōz/, **Murray** (*b.* 1939) English-born Australian swimmer. He won gold medals at the 1956 and 1960 Olympics. Full name **Iain Murray Rose**

rose apple *n.* an evergreen tree of Southeast Asia that is widely grown for its decorative flowers and edible fruit. Latin name: *Eugenia jambos* and *Syzygium jambos*.

roseate /rṓzi ət/ *adj.* **1.** ROSE-COLOURED of the reddish-pink colour of roses **2.** OPTIMISTIC optimistic or idealistic, especially to an absurd degree [15thC. Formed from Latin *roseus* 'rosy', from *rosa* 'rose' (see ROSE).] —**roseately** *adv.*

roseate spoonbill *n.* an American wading bird that has rosy plumage and a spoon-shaped bill. Latin name: *Ajaia ajaja*.

rosebay /rōz bay/ *n.* **1.** = rosebay willowherb **2.** = oleander

rosebay willowherb *n.* a perennial plant of northern temperate regions that has spikes of pink flowers. Latin name: *Chamaenerion angustifolium*. US term **fireweed**

rose beetle *n.* = rose chafer

Rosebery /rōz berri/ lake in the centre of the North Island, New Zealand, originally formed by a volcanic eruption. It is a major tourist centre. Area: 80 sq. km/31 sq. mi.

Rosebery, Archibald Philip Primrose, 5th Earl of (1847–1929) British statesman. He succeeded W. E. Gladstone as Liberal Party leader and prime minister (1894–95) before retiring from a long political career.

rosebud /rōz bud/ *n.* the unopened flower of a rose

rosebush /rōz boŏsh/ *n.* any variety of rose that grows as a bush

rose campion *n.* a plant that has white woolly down on its stems and leaves and is grown for its pink flowers. It is native to Europe and Asia but naturalized in northeastern North America. Latin name: *Lychnis coronaria*.

rose chafer *n.* a greenish-gold beetle that feeds on the roots, leaves, and flowers of roses and other garden plants. Latin name: *Cetonia aurata*.

rose-coloured *adj.* **1.** COLOURS REDDISH PINK a reddish-pink colour **2.** OPTIMISTIC optimistic or idealistic, especially to an unjustifiable degree

rose cut *n.* a way of cutting gemstones that gives them a flat base and a hemispherical crown with facets rising to a low point —**rose-cut** *adj.*

rosefish /rōz fish/ (*plural* **-fish** *or* **-fishes**) *n.* **1.** N ATLANTIC FISH a spiny-finned red food fish of the North Atlantic. Latin name: *Sebastes marinus*. **2.** = redfish *n.* 1

rose geranium *n.* a shrub grown for its pink flowers and fragrant leaves that are used for scenting cosmetics and for flavouring. Latin name: *Pelargonium graveolens*.

rosehip /rōz hip/ *n.* the fleshy fruit of a rose, resembling a berry and used to make jelly, herbal tea, or a medicinal syrup [Mid-19thC]

rosella /rō zéllə/ *n.* an Australian parrot with bright colourful plumage and a long graduated tail, sometimes kept as a cage bird. Genus: *Platycercus*. [Early 19thC. Origin uncertain: probably an alteration of *Rose-hiller*, which was named after *Rose-hill*, Parramatta, near Sydney in Australia.]

rose mallow *n.* **1.** MARSH PLANT a tall plant that grows in marshy areas of eastern North America and has downy leaves and pink or white flowers. Genus: *Hibiscus*. **2.** US = hollyhock

Rosemary

rosemary /rṓzməri/ (*plural* **-ies**) *n.* a southern European aromatic shrub of the mint family grown for its fragrant grey-green needle-shaped leaves and used as a flavouring in cooking and in making perfume. Latin name: *Rosmarinus officinalis*. [14thC. By folk etymology from *rosmarine*, ultimately from Latin *rosmarinus*, from *ros* 'dew' + *marinus* 'of the sea', from its growth near sea coasts and its blossom's resemblance to dew.]

rose moss *n.* a low-growing fleshy-leaved Brazilian plant that is widely grown for its bright flowers. Latin name: *Portulaca grandiflora*.

Rosenberg /rṓz'n burg/, **Julius** (1917–53) US convicted spy. He and his wife Ethel Rosenberg (1916–53), both members of the Communist Party, were convicted in 1951 of passing nuclear weapons information to the Soviets during World War II. They were the first US civilians to be executed for espionage (1953).

rose of Jericho *n.* a plant of desert regions that curls up into a ball in dry conditions and unfolds and grows in wet conditions. One variety is found in North Africa and southwest Asia, and the other in southwest North America and northern South America. Latin name: *Anastatica hierochuntica* and *Selaginella lepidophylla*. [Named after JERICHO]

rose of Sharon /-shárən/ *n.* **1.** EUROPEAN SHRUB WITH YELLOW FLOWERS a creeping southern European shrub, widely grown as ground cover and for its large yellow flowers. Latin name: *Hypericum calycinum*. **2.** HIBISCUS a Syrian shrub that is widely grown for its large red, purple, or white flowers. Latin name: *Hibiscus syriacus*. [Early 17thC. Translation of the Hebrew name in the *Song of Solomon*; *Sharon* refers to the fertile plain south of Mount Carmel in Israel.]

rose oil *n.* an essential oil made from rose flowers, used in perfumes, flavourings, and medicines

roseola /rō zee ələ, rōzi ṓlə/ *n.* a red rash on the skin, seen in diseases such as measles, scarlet fever, and syphilis [Early 19thC. Formed on the model of RUBEOLA from Latin *roseus* 'rosy', from *rosa* (see ROSE).] —**roseolar** *adj.*

roseola infantum /rō zee ələ in fántəm, rōzi ṓlə/ *n.* a mild disease of young children, typically involving a three-day fever and the eruption of pink spots

rose quartz *n.* a pink translucent variety of quartz used as a gemstone and for ornaments

roseroot /rōz root/ *n.* a perennial mountain plant of Europe and Asia with yellow flowers, fleshy leaves, and a pinkish underground stem. Latin name: *Sedum rosea*. [Late 16thC. *Rose* from its root, which smells of roses when bruised.]

rose topaz *n.* a pink form of topaz made by applying heat to yellowish-brown topaz

Rosetta /rō zéttə/ town in Egypt, on the Mediterranean coast. Population: 52,014 (1986).

Rosetta stone /rō zéttə-/ *n.* a stone tablet found in 1799 near Rosetta in Egypt that contained the same text repeated in Egyptian hieroglyphics, Egyptian demotic script, and Greek, thereby supplying the key to deciphering hieroglyphics

rosette /rō zét/ *n.* **1.** ROSE-SHAPED BADGE a circular badge made from gathered loops of ribbon or pleated material, worn to demonstrate support for a team or political party or to indicate having won a prize **2.** ORNAMENT RESEMBLING A ROSE a carved or painted ornament resembling the open flower of a rose **3.** ZOOL MARKING RESEMBLING A ROSE a patch of colour or a marking resembling the open flower of a rose, especially a cluster of spots on the fur of a leopard **4.** BOT CLUSTER OF LEAVES a circular or spiral cluster of leaves at the base of the stem of a plant [Mid-18thC. From French, literally 'small rose', from *rose* 'rose', from Latin *rosa* (see ROSE).]

Rosewall /rōz wawl/, **Ken** (*b.* 1934) Australian tennis player. He won the Australian, French, and US championships, and was also a successful doubles player. Full name **Kenneth Robert Rosewall**

rose water, **rose-water** *n.* a fragrant liquid made by distilling or steeping rose petals in water, used as toilet water and in cooking

rose window, **rose** *n.* a round window with tracery radiating from the centre in a pattern that resembles a rose. Often made of stained glass, rose windows are a feature of the Gothic style of church architecture.

rosewood /rōz woŏd/ *n.* **1.** DARK WOOD OF TROPICAL TREES a dark, heavy, rose-scented wood used in cabinetmaking that is obtained from various tropical trees, especially blackwood. Genus: *Dalbergia*. **2.** ROSEWOOD TREE a tree that yields rosewood

Rosh Chodesh /rósh khóddəsh/ *n.* the first day of a new month in the Jewish religious calendar [From Hebrew *rō'shŏdeš*, literally 'head of the month']

Rose window

Rosh Hashanah /rósh hə shaánə/, **Rosh Hashana** *n.* the festival that celebrates the Jewish New Year, observed on the first and second days of Tishri in the autumn. It marks the beginning of the Days of Awe, a period concerned with confessions of sin and redemption. [Mid-18thC. From Hebrew *rō'š haš-šānāh*, literally 'head of the year'.]

Rosicrucian /rózi krōōsh'n/ *n.* a member of an international organization concerned with esoteric wisdom derived from ancient mystical and philosophical doctrines [Early 17thC. Formed from modern Latin *rosa crucis* 'rose of the cross', translation of German *Rosenkreuz*, named after the organization's reputed founder, Christian *Rosenkreuz*.] —**Rosicrucianism** *n.*

rosin /rózzin/ *n.* HARD RESIN a hard translucent resin ranging in colour from amber to dark brown that is derived from the sap, stumps, or other parts of pine trees. It is used in making varnishes and other products and to increase friction, e.g. between the bow and strings of some stringed instruments. ■ *vt.* (**-ins, -ining, -ined**) TREAT STH WITH ROSIN to treat sth with rosin, in particular to rub rosin on the bow of a stringed instrument to increase friction [13thC. Alteration of Old French *raisine*, variant of *resine*, from Latin *resina* (source of English *resin*); also via Anglo-Latin *rosina* from, ultimately, Latin *resina*.] —**rosiny** *adj.*

Rosinante /rózzi nánti/ *n.* **1.** DON QUIXOTE'S HORSE the bony old horse that belongs to Don Quixote, the hero of the novel by Cervantes published in 1605 **2.** OLD HORSE any worn-out old horse (*literary*)

rosin oil *n.* a thick yellowish sticky liquid distilled from rosin and used in making varnishes, inks, and other products

rosinweed /rózzin weed/ *n.* a North American plant that smells of resin or has resinous juice, e.g. the compass plant. Genera: *Silphium* and *Grindelia*.

Roskilde /róss killə/ city in Denmark, in eastern Sjaelland, situated about 24 km/15 mi. west of Copenhagen. Population: 49,080 (1990).

RoSPA /róspə/ *abbr.* Royal Society for the Prevention of Accidents

Diana Ross

Ross /ross/, **Diana** (b. 1944) US pop singer. Known for her seductive vocal style and glamorous appearance, she helped her 1960s female group the Supremes become one of the most successful acts in the history of popular music before pursuing a solo career. Real name **Diane Ernestine Ross**

Ross, Sir James Clark (1800–62) British explorer. He determined the position of the magnetic North Pole (1831) and discovered Victoria Land, Ross Island, and the Ross Sea (1839–43).

Rossellini /rossə leéni/, **Roberto** (1906–77) Italian film director. He directed several neorealist films after World War II, including *Rome, Open City* (1945) and historical films for television.

AKG London
Christina Rossetti

Rossetti /rə zétti/, **Christina** (1830–94) British lyric poet. She wrote in a variety of styles and forms, often exploring the themes of religion and death. She was the sister of Dante Gabriel Rossetti. Full name **Christina Georgina Rossetti**

Rossetti, Dante Gabriel (1828–82) British painter and poet. A founder of the Pre-Raphaelite Brotherhood (1848), he brought medieval and Italianate influences to bear on idealized, emotionally charged paintings such as *The Annunciation* (1850) and *Proserpina* (1874). His last volume of verse was *Ballads and Sonnets* (1881). He was the brother of Christina Rossetti. Full name **Gabriel Charles Dante Rossetti**

Rossini /ro seéni/, **Gioacchino Antonio** (1792–1868) Italian composer. The most successful operatic composer of his time, he was a master of the bel canto style and excelled in comedy. His 37 operas, all written before 1831, include *The Barber of Seville* (1816) and *William Tell* (1829).

Rosslare /róss láir/ town in County Wexford, on the southeastern coast of Ireland

Ross River virus *n.* Aus in Australia, a virus that is transmitted by mosquitoes and causes fever, headaches, lethargy, rashes, and muscle and joint pains. The illness tends to recur. [Mid-20thC. Named after *Ross River*, a river near Townsville in northeastern Australia, near which the virus was first isolated.]

Ross Sea southern extension of the Pacific Ocean, bordering Antarctica. A large part of its surface is frozen, forming the Ross Ice Shelf. Ross Island, in the Ross Sea, is the location of the volcano Mt Erebus.

rostellum /ro stélləm/ (*plural* **-la** /-lə/) *n.* a part of an animal or plant that resembles a beak, e.g. the hooked projection from the head of a tapeworm [Mid-18thC. From Latin, 'small beak', from *rostrum* (see ROSTRUM).] —**rostellar** *adj.* —**rostellate** *adj.*

roster /róstər/ *n.* **1.** LIST OF NAMES a list, especially of employees, athletes, or members of the armed forces, often detailing their duties and the times when they are to be carried out **2.** PEOPLE ON A LIST the people listed on a roster ■ *vt.* (**-ters, -tering, -tered**) PUT SB ON A ROSTER to put sb's name on a roster [Early 18thC. From Dutch *rooster*, originally 'gridiron', hence (from the resemblance of its pattern to lines on paper) 'list', from *roosten* 'to roast'.]

rösti /rósti/ *n.* a Swiss fried potato cake made from thinly sliced or grated potatoes, sometimes with added onions and bacon [Mid-20thC. From Swiss German.]

Rostock /róst ok/ city and port in northeastern Germany, in the state of Mecklenburg-Western Pomerania, on the Baltic Sea. Population: 236,100 (1994).

Rostov /rós tov/ city in southwestern European Russia, on the River Don. Population: 1,027,100 (1992).

rostra plural of **rostrum**

rostrate /rós trayt/ *adj.* having a part that is shaped like a beak

rostrum /róstrəm/ (*plural* **-trums** or **-tra** /-trə/) *n.* **1.** PLATFORM FOR PUBLIC SPEAKING a platform or raised area where sb stands to address an audience **2.** MUSIC CONDUCTOR'S PLATFORM a platform on a stage or in front of an orchestra where the conductor stands **3.** PLATFORM FOR CAMERA a platform, stand, or raised area supporting a film or television camera **4.** HIST PROW OF ROMAN SHIP the beak-shaped prow of an ancient Roman ship, especially a war galley **5.** BEAK-SHAPED PART a beak or beak-shaped part of sth [Mid-16thC. From Latin, 'beak, ship's prow', in plural, 'platform' (because ships' prows decorated the orator's platform in the Forum), from *rodere* 'to gnaw'.] —**rostral** *adj.* —**rostrally** *adv.*

rosy /rózi/ (**-ier, -iest**) *adj.* **1.** ROSE-COLOURED of the reddish-pink colour of roses ○ *the sunset turning the sky a rosy hue* **2.** HAVING A PINKISH COMPLEXION having a pinkish complexion that is regarded as indicating good health in white people **3.** PROMISING likely to be characterized by success or happiness ○ *predicts a rosy future for the business* **4.** OPTIMISTIC optimistic, especially to an unreasonable degree ○ *takes a rosy view of things* **5.** LIKE A ROSE resembling roses, characteristic of roses, or full of roses —**rosily** *adv.* —**rosiness** *n.*

rosy pastor *n.* BIRDS = **pastor** *n.* 4

rot /rot/ *v.* (**rots, rotting, rotted**) **1.** *vti.* DECOMPOSE to be broken down or to break sth organic down by the action of bacteria or fungi ○ *rotting vegetation* **2.** *vti.* CHANGE BY DECOMPOSITION to be reduced, damaged, or broken by the action of bacteria or fungi, or to affect sth organic in this way ○ *allow the compost to rot down* **3.** *vi.* LANGUISH to endure the effects of complete neglect ○ *thrown into prison and left to rot* ■ *n.* **1.** PROCESS OF DECAYING the process or condition of decaying or a decayed area **2.** NONSENSE irrelevant or ridiculous talk (*informal*) **3.** FUNGAL DISEASE disease caused by fungi, e.g. foot rot of sheep, dry rot of timber and plants, and wet rot of timber **4.** ZOOL ANIMAL DISEASE infestation with liver flukes **5.** BOT BACTERIAL PLANT DISEASE a plant disease in which the tissue is broken down by the action of bacteria ■ *interj.* EXPRESSION OF DISAGREEMENT used to disagree with what sb has said or to express annoyance or exasperation (*informal*) [Old English *rotian* (verb), ultimately of uncertain origin: perhaps from an Indo-European word that is also the ancestor of English *rude*. The noun perhaps came from Scandinavian.]

rot. *abbr.* MATH rotation

rota /rótə/ *n.* a list of people's names and the order in which they are to carry out specified duties [Mid-17thC. From Latin, 'wheel'.]

─────── **WORD KEY: ORIGIN** ───────
The Latin word *rota* from which **rota** is derived is also the source of English *control, rodeo, roll, rondo, rotate, rotund, roué,* and *round.*
─────────────────────────

Rota *n.* the supreme ecclesiastical tribunal of the Roman Catholic Church

Rotameter /rótə meetər/ *tdmk.* a trademark for an instrument for measuring a fluid's rate of flow by indicating the height reached in a tube by a small float supported by the flowing liquid

Rotarian /rō táiri ən/ *n.* sb who belongs to a Rotary Club —**Rotarianism** *n.*

rotary /rótəri/ (*plural* **-ries**) *n.* **1.** ROTATING PART a machine or part of a machine that rotates around an axis or a fixed point **2.** TRANSP US = **roundabout** [Mid-18thC. From medieval Latin *rotarius*, from Latin *rota* 'wheel'.]

Rotary Club *n.* a local club that is a member of Rotary International, an international organization of business and professional people originally formed in the United States to encourage service to the community [*Rotary* from the organization's early practice of holding meetings in rotation at members' business premises]

rotary cultivator *n.* AGRIC = **rotary plough**

rotary engine *n.* **1.** INTERNAL-COMBUSTION ENGINE WITH ROTATING CYLINDERS an internal-combustion engine with cylinders that rotate about a fixed crankshaft **2.** ENGINE POWERING A ROTATING PART an engine that produces torque or power entirely by a rotating mechanism rather than a crankshaft and reciprocating piston arrangement. ◊ **radial engine**

rotary mower *n.* a lawn mower with a single blade attached in the middle and sharpened at both ends that rotates as the mower is moved

rotary plough *n.* AGRIC a machine for breaking up and tilling soil, consisting of a series of blades mounted on a revolving power-driven shaft

rotary press *n.* a printing press that prints from curved plates mounted on a revolving cylinder, often onto a continuous roll of paper

rotary pump *n.* a pump that imparts motion by internal sets of rotating vanes or screws, used to move water or other fluids

rotary tiller *n.* AGRIC = rotary plough

rotary-wing aircraft *n.* an aircraft, especially a helicopter, that is lifted or propelled by rotating aerofoils

rotate /rō táyt/ *v.* (**-tates, -tating, -tated**) **1.** *vti.* TURN AROUND AN AXIS to turn like a wheel around an axis or a fixed point, or make sth turn around an axis or a fixed point ○ *The earth rotates around the axis through its poles.* ○ *The windmill's sails are rotated by the wind.* **2.** *vti.* AGRIC VARY THE CROP GROWN to vary the crops grown on the same piece of ground so as not to exhaust the soil or make it susceptible to disease **3.** *vti.* FOLLOW IN ORDER to follow in a sequence, taking turns, or make things follow in such a sequence ○ *Rotate the plates in the pile so that they all get used.* **4.** REPLACE PERSONNEL to be replaced by sb else, or replace one person or group by another, e.g. in a sports team or military unit ○ *The manager rotates first-team players with promising newcomers in less important games.* ■ *adj.* WHEEL-SHAPED having parts that radiate from a central point [Late 17thC. Origin uncertain: either from Latin *rotat-*, past participle stem of *rotare*, from *rota* 'wheel'; or a back-formation from ROTATION.] —**rotatable** *adj.*

rotation /rō táysh'n/ *n.* **1.** TURNING MOTION a turning motion like that of a wheel around an axis or a fixed point, or the act or process of turning in such a way ○ *the rotation of the earth* **2.** SINGLE REVOLUTION a single turn of sth around an axis or a fixed point ○ *one full rotation of the wheel* **3.** REGULAR VARIATION a regular or planned recurrent sequence of events or changes of position ○ *The families use the holiday cottage by strict rotation.* **4.** AGRIC CROP ROTATION crop rotation **5.** MATH MATHEMATICAL TRANSFORMATION a mathematical transformation in which axes are rotated by a fixed angle while the origin remains unchanged —**rotational** *adj.*

rotative *adj.* = rotatory —**rotatively** *adv.*

rotator /rō táytər/ *n.* **1.** SB OR STH ROTATING sb who or sth that rotates or causes rotation **2.** (*plural* **-tores**) ANAT MUSCLE FOR ROTATION a muscle that rotates part of the body on an axis

rotator cuff *n.* the deep muscles of the shoulder and their tendons, which connect the arm to the shoulder joint, encircle it, and provide strength and stability while permitting rotation of the arm

rotatory /rō táytəri/, **rotative** /rō táytiv/ *adj.* **1.** ROTATING LIKE A WHEEL involving, characterized by, or causing rotation around an axis or a fixed point **2.** VARYING REGULARLY involving, characterized by, or causing rotation of people or things in sequence

rotavate /rótə vayt/ (**-vates, -vating, -vated**), **rotovate** (**-vates, -vating, -vated**) *vt.* to break up or till soil using a rotary plough

Rotavator /rótə vaytər/, **Rotovator** *tdmk.* a trademark for a type of rotary plough

rotavirus /rótə vīrəss/ *n.* a wheel-shaped RNA virus that causes gastroenteritis, especially in infants. It is the most common cause of viral gastroenteritis. [Late 20thC. From modern Latin, literally 'wheel-virus', from Latin *rota* 'wheel' + *virus* 'poison, virus'.]

rote[1] /rōt/ *n.* mechanical repetition of sth so that it is remembered, often without real understanding of its meaning or significance ○ *learned it by rote* [13thC. Origin uncertain: perhaps from Old French *ro(u)te* (see ROUTE) or Latin *rota* 'wheel'.]

rote[2] /rōt/ *n.* a medieval stringed instrument played by plucking [14thC. From Old French, of uncertain origin: probably ultimately from late Latin *chrotta* 'British musical instrument', from Welsh *crwth* '(type of) Celtic stringed instrument' or Old Irish *crot* 'harp, cithara'.]

rotenone /rótə nōn/ *n.* a white crystalline insecticide extracted from the roots of derris. Formula:

$C_{23}H_{22}O_6$. [Early 20thC. Formed from Japanese *roten* 'derris'.]

ROTFL *abbr.* rolling on the floor laughing (*used in e-mail messages*)

rotgut /rót gut/ *n.* cheap and rough alcoholic drink (*informal*)

Rother /róthər/ river in East Sussex and Kent, England. Length: 50 km/31 mi.

Rotherham /róthərəm/ town in Yorkshire, northern England. Population: 251,637 (1994).

Rothermere /róthəmir/, **Harold Sydney, 1st Viscount Harmsworth** (1868–1940) British newspaper magnate. Brother of Alfred Harmsworth, his newspaper empire included the *Daily Mail* and *Sunday Dispatch.*

Rothesay /róthsi, -say/ town in Argyll and Bute Council Area, Scotland. Population: 5,264 (1991).

Rothschild /róths chīld/, **Lionel Nathan** (1808–79) British financier. The eldest son of Nathan Mayer Rothschild, he was manager of the London branch of the family business and the first Jewish MP.

Rothschild, Mayer Amschel (1743–1812) German financier. The father of Nathan Mayer Rothschild, he was financial adviser to William IX and financial agent of the British government.

Rothschild, Nathan Mayer (1777–1836) German financier. The son of Mayer Amschel Rothschild and father of Lionel Nathan Rothschild, he founded the British branch of the family firm.

roti /róti/ (*plural* **-tis**) *n.* a type of unleavened bread originally from the northern parts of the Indian subcontinent, also eaten in the Caribbean [Early 20thC. From Hindi *roṭī*.]

rotifer /rótifər/ *n.* a microscopic invertebrate animal that has a wheel-shaped crown of projecting threads (**cilia**) at the anterior end and lives mostly in fresh-water habitats. The cilia aid in locomotion and food ingestion. Phylum: Rotifera. [Late 18thC. From modern Latin, literally 'wheel-bearing, wheel-bearer', from, ultimately, Latin *rota* 'wheel'.] —**rotiferal** /rō tíffərəl/ *adj.* —**rotiferous** /-fərəss/ *adj.*

rotisserie /rō tíssəri/ *n.* **1.** ROASTING SPIT a cooking appliance for roasting meat using a rotating spit **2.** PLACE ROASTING MEAT a shop or restaurant where meat is roasted and sold [Mid-19thC. From French *rôtisserie*, from *rôtir* 'to roast', from Old French *rostir*, from a prehistoric Germanic word that is also the ancestor of English *roster*.]

rotl /rótt'l/ *n.* a unit of weight used in many Islamic countries, varying from approximately 0.45 to 2.25 kg/1 to 5 lbs [Early 17thC. From Arabic *raṭl*, of uncertain origin: perhaps an alteration of Greek *litra* 'pound (unit of weight)' (source of English *litre*).]

rotogravure /rő tōgrə vyoor/ *n.* **1.** PRINTING PROCESS WITH A ROTARY PRESS a printing process in which images are etched photomechanically onto copper cylinders mounted in a rotary press, from which they are printed onto a moving web of paper **2.** STH PRINTED BY ROTOGRAVURE PROCESS sth printed using rotogravure, e.g. a magazine or a photographic section of a newspaper [Early 20thC. From German *Rotogravur*, company name, of uncertain origin: perhaps a blend of the company names *Rotophot* and (*Deutsche*) *Photogravur*.]

rotor /rótər/ *n.* **1.** AIR ROTATING AEROFOILS an assembly of aerofoils that rotates about a hub to give lift to an aircraft, especially a helicopter **2.** AIR ROTOR BLADE a blade or aerofoil of a rotor (*informal*) **3.** ROTATING PART OF MACHINE a rotating part of an electrical apparatus, e.g. the armature of a generator, or of a mechanical device [Late 19thC. Contraction (perhaps modelled on VECTOR) or ROTATOR.]

Rotorua /rótə roo ə/ city in the centre of the North Island, New Zealand, noted for its volcanic activity and thermal springs. Population: 56,928 (1996).

Rotorua, Lake lake in the centre of the North Island, New Zealand, originally formed by a volcanic eruption. It is a major tourist centre. Area: 80 sq. km/31 sq. mi.

rototiller /rótə tillər/ *n.* US = rotary plough [Early 20thC. From, ultimately, Latin *rota* 'wheel' (see ROTA) + TILLER.]

rotovate *vt.* = rotavate

Rotovator *tdmk.* = Rotavator

rotten /rótt'n/ *adj.* **1.** DECAYED affected by rot or decay ○ *a rotten apple* **2.** FOUL extremely unpleasant, unfortunate, or nasty (*informal*) ○ *rotten weather* **3.** INFERIOR below the acceptable standard (*informal*) ○ *He's a rotten driver.* **4.** NOT FEELING WELL feeling unwell, usually without a specific complaint (*informal*) **5.** UNHAPPY feeling unhappy or uncomfortable, especially through guilt or embarrassment (*informal*) ○ *I feel rotten about letting you down.* **6.** UNETHICAL lacking ethical principles in the treatment of other people or animals **7.** DRUNK very drunk (*regional*) ■ *adv.* TO A GREAT DEGREE to a great degree, especially so much as to be disapproved of (*informal*) ○ *The grandmother spoils those kids rotten.* ○ *She fancies you rotten.* [13thC. From Old Norse *rotinn*, of uncertain origin: probably the past participle of an assumed verb.] —**rottenly** *adv.* —**rottenness** *n.*

rotten borough *n.* HIST a political constituency with few electors but the same right to elect a representative as a more populous constituency, especially any of various parliamentary constituencies in England before 1832

rottenstone /rótt'n stōn/ *n.* a form of silica-rich limestone that has been decomposed by weathering and is used in powdered form for polishing metal

rotter /róttər/ *n.* sb who behaves in a nasty or unpleasant way (*informal dated*) [Early 17thC. Originally in the sense 'causer of rotting'.]

Rotterdam /róttər dam/ city and port in Zuid-Holland Province, southwestern Netherlands. Population: 1,074,387 (1994).

Rottweiler *n.* a large powerful dog of a breed that has a black smooth coat with tan markings. Rottweilers are often used as guard dogs.

rotund /rō túnd/ *adj.* **1.** OVERWEIGHT with a greater body weight than is advisable **2.** RICH IN SOUND having a full, rich sound [15thC. Directly or via Italian *rotondo* from Latin *rotundus* 'round', from *rotare* 'to rotate', from *rota* 'wheel'.] —**rotundity** *n.* —**rotundly** *adv.* —**rotundness** *n.*

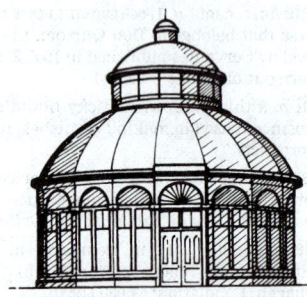

Rotunda

rotunda /rō túndə/ *n.* **1.** ROUND BUILDING a round building, usually covered with a dome **2.** ROUND ROOM a large round hall or room **3.** Can, US OPEN AREA IN A PUBLIC BUILDING a large open area at an airport, railway station, or other public building [Early 17thC. Alteration (modelled on Latin *rotundus* 'round') of Italian *rotonda*, from *rotunda*, the feminine of *rotundus* 'round'.]

roturier /rō toōri ay, -tyoōri-/ *n.* a commoner or peasant [Late 16thC. From French, from *roture* 'land tenure by sb of low social class', hence 'newly cultivated land', from Latin *ruptura* 'breaking' (source of English *rupture*).]

ROU *abbr.* Republic of Uruguay

Rouault /roo ṓ/, **Georges Henri** (1871–1958) French painter and engraver. A member of the Fauves, his work is characterized by glowing colours, impasto, and heavy outlines.

Roubaix /roo bé/ city in Nord Department, Nord-Pas-de-Calais Region, northern France, situated northeast of Lille. Population: 98,179 (1990).

rouble /roob'l/, **ruble** *n.* **1.** UNIT OF RUSSIAN CURRENCY the main unit of currency in Russia, Belarus, and some other former republics of the USSR. See table at **currency** **2.** COIN WORTH ONE ROUBLE a coin worth one rouble

roué /ro͞o ay/ *n.* a man who regularly engages in drinking, gambling, and womanizing (*literary*) [Early 19thC. From French, noun use of the past participle of *rouer* 'to break on the wheel' (a medieval instrument of torture), from, ultimately, Latin *rotare* (see ROTATE).]

WORD KEY: ORIGIN

The term ***roué*** is thought to stem from Philip II, Regent of France (1715–23), who humorously designated his debauched companions as *roués*, either to suggest that they deserved to be broken upon the wheel or because their behaviour was so exhausting that they felt they had undergone this torture.

Rouen /ro͞o aaN/ capital of Seine-Maritime Department, Haute-Normandie Region, northwestern France. Population: 105,470 (1990).

rouge /roo*zh*/ *n.* **1. REDDISH MAKEUP FOR THE CHEEKS** red or pink makeup in powder or cream form used to add colour to the cheeks or lips or to accentuate the shape of the cheekbones (*dated*) **2. POLISH IN POWDER FORM** any of various kinds of polish in powder form containing metallic oxides, especially a polish for metal called jeweller's rouge that contains ferric oxide ■ *v.* **(rouges, rouging, rouged) 1.** *vt.* **COLOUR STH WITH ROUGE** to put rouge on the cheeks or lips (*dated*) **2.** *vti.* **BLUSH** to blush or cause sb to blush (*archaic*) [Mid-18thC. Via French from Latin *rubeus* 'red'.]

rouge et noir /-ay-/ *n.* a card game in which gamblers place their stakes on a table marked with two red and two black diamonds and all betting is against the house at even money [From French, literally 'red and black']

rough /ruf/ *adj.* **1. NOT SMOOTH OR FLAT** having a bumpy, knobbly, or uneven surface rather than being smooth, flat, and regular **2. NOT SOFT** not soft and smooth, but rather coarse in texture ○ *a dog with a rough, bristly coat* **3. WINDY OR TURBULENT** stormy, or unpleasantly turbulent as a result of stormy conditions ○ *The weather had been rough for days.* **4. WILD AND UNCULTIVATED** not cleared, flattened, and cultivated, but in a natural state with wild vegetation, or else allowed to fall into a derelict, disused state ○ *marching over rough terrain* **5. NOT GENTLE** done with or using a lot of force or violence ○ *toys that will stand up to rough handling* **6. NOT POLITE** not refined or polite in manner and behaviour ○ *rough talk* **7. SOUNDING OR TASTING HARSH** harsh on the ears or to the taste **8. NOT DETAILED** not exact, precise, or detailed, but broadly correct ○ *a rough estimate* **9. JUST BARELY SERVICEABLE** made quickly or without using proper or good-quality materials, or reaching only the most basic standard ○ *used branches to build a rough shelter* **10. LACKING FINISH OR REFINEMENT** hastily or incompletely made ○ *a rough wooden carving* **11. SEVERE OR UNPLEASANT** severe, unfair, or generally unpleasant (*informal*) ○ *received rough treatment at the hands of the judge* **12. SLIGHTLY UNWELL** rather unwell, especially as a result of tiredness or overindulgence rather than because of illness (*informal*) ○ *She felt a bit rough the next morning.* **13. ROWDY** tending to noisy, rowdy, or violent ○ *a rough crowd* **14. FREQUENTED BY UNSAVOURY PEOPLE** frequented or inhabited by people who tend to be noisy, rowdy, or violent (*informal*) ○ *a rough part of town* ■ *n.* **1.** GOLF **UNMOWED PART OF A GOLF COURSE** that area of a golf course on which grass and other vegetation is allowed to grow higher than on the fairway **2. PRELIMINARY OUTLINE** a preliminary version of sth, e.g. a sketch giving the broad layout of an artwork **3. VIOLENT PERSON** a violent or brutal person, especially a hired thug (*regional*) **4. SIDE OF RACQUET** the side of a tennis or other racquet where the binding of the strings is not smooth ■ *vt.* **(roughs, roughing, roughed) ROUGHEN STH** to make sth rough [Old English *rūh*. Ultimately from a prehistoric Germanic word that is also the ancestor of Dutch *ruw* and German *rauh*.] —**roughish** *adj.* —**roughness** *n.* ◇ **a bit of rough** a person, usually a man, whose rough-and-ready nature is found sexually attractive by sb from a higher social class (*slang*) ◇ **in the rough** in a crude, unfinished, or uncultivated state ◇ **rough it** to live in a less comfortable or less sophisticated way than usual (*informal*) ◇ **rough or smooth** RACKET GAMES used as a call when spinning a racquet in a game of tennis or squash to decide which player should serve first or choose the end to serve from ◇ **take the rough with the smooth** to accept the disadvantages of a situation with the advantages

rough out *vt.* to prepare a rough model, plan, or sketch of sth ○ *The scriptwriters meet to rough out a scene-by-scene narrative long before a word of dialogue is written.*

rough up *vt.* **1. BEAT SB VIOLENTLY** to subject sb to a violent beating (*informal*) **2. GIVE STH AN UNTIDY LOOK** to make sth such as sb's hair look untidy by rubbing it to make it stick up or stick out

roughage /rúffij/ *n.* MED = **fibre** *n.* 7 [Late 19thC. Originally in the sense 'rough grass, weeds'.]

rough-and-ready *adj.* **1. CRUDE BUT SERVICEABLE** not elegant or stylish but practical or usable ○ *rough-and-ready accommodation in a hostel* **2. LACKING POLITENESS BUT NOT FRIENDLINESS** not polite or well-mannered but friendly or kind-hearted

rough-and-tumble *n.* a situation characterized by a lack of restraint and a ruthless disregard for rules and conventions —**rough-and-tumble** *adj.*

rough breathing *n.* in ancient Greek, a sound like that of the English 'h', occurring with an initial vowel or the letter ρ and indicated by the symbol (ʽ). ◊ **smooth breathing**

roughcast /rúf kaast/ *n.* **1. PEBBLED SURFACE ON WALLS** a surface of coarse plaster covered with pebbles on the outside walls of a building (*often used before a noun*) ○ *roughcast walls* **2. ROUGH MODEL** a preliminary form or model of sth ○ *made a roughcast in clay before starting to work the marble* ■ *vt.* **(-casts, -casting, -cast) 1. COVER A WALL WITH ROUGHCAST** to cover the surface of a wall or the walls of a building with roughcast **2. FORM STH ROUGHLY** to shape or form sth in a crude fashion or as a preliminary to more polished work —**roughcaster** *n.*

rough collie *n.* a long-haired collie dog that is black and white or black, white, and tan and has a band of thick hair round its neck and shoulders

rough cut *n.* the preliminary version of a cinema film, with only basic editing done to put the scenes together in sequence

rough diamond *n.* **1. UNCUT AND UNPOLISHED DIAMOND** a diamond in its natural state, before it has been cut into shape and polished **2. UNREFINED BUT LIKEABLE PERSON** sb who does not care about good manners or formality but is likeable or trustworthy. US term **diamond in the rough**

rough-dry *vt.* to dry washed laundry but not iron it —**rough-dry** *adj.*

roughen /rúff'n/ **(-ens, -ening, -ened)** *vti.* to make sth rough, or become rough

rough fish *n.* a species of fish that is neither caught for food nor fished for by anglers

rough-hew **(rough-hews, rough-hewing, rough-hewed, rough-hewed** *or* **rough-hewn)** *vt.* **1. CUT STH ROUGHLY, WITHOUT SMOOTHING** to cut or carve sth roughly without smoothing the surface or edges ○ *He rough-hewed the wood to make a crude table.* **2. MAKE STH CRUDELY** to shape or form sth crudely

rough-hewn *adj.* **1. CUT NOT SMOOTHED** cut or shaped only roughly, with the surface and the edges not smoothed ○ *blocks of rough-hewn sandstone* **2. CRUDELY MADE** crudely shape or formed **3. RUGGED** rugged or rough and unrefined in character

roughhouse /rúf howss/ *n.* **ROWDINESS** rough behaviour or excessively boisterous play (*informal*) ○ *The party turned into a roughhouse.* ■ *vti.* **(-houses, -housing, -housed) BEHAVE OR TREAT SB ROUGHLY** to behave or treat sb in a rough boisterous way (*informal*) [Late 19thC. From the idea of an establishment such as a bar or brothel where disorderly behaviour occurs.]

rough-legged buzzard /-léggid-/ *n.* a large Arctic hawk that has a dark body, feathers covering its legs, and a white tail with a broad dark band at the end. Latin name: *Buteo lagopus.* US term **rough-legged hawk**

rough-legged hawk *n.* *US* = **rough-legged buzzard**

roughly /rúf li/ *adv.* **1. CRUDELY** in a crude or incomplete way ○ *shape the minced beef roughly into balls* **2. VIOLENTLY OR RUDELY** in a violent way or a manner lacking in gentleness and politeness **3. APPROXIMATELY** as a guess without any claim to exactness ○ *Roughly one third of the funding comes from government.*

roughneck /rúf nek/ *n.* **1. HIRED THUG** sb who is violent, especially a hired thug (*informal*) **2. COARSE PERSON** sb who behaves in a rough, bad-mannered way (*informal*) **3.** INDUST **OIL-FIELD WORKER** an unskilled worker on an oil rig or at an oil well (*slang*) [Mid-19thC. *Neck* used here for 'person'.]

roughrider /rúf rīdər/ *n.* sb who breaks wild horses, or who is skilled at riding horses that have not been trained

roughshod /rúf shod/ *adj.* **1. WEARING SPIKED HORSESHOES** fitted with horseshoes that have short spikes to prevent slipping in wet weather **2. BRUTAL** displaying great forcefulness and a lack of consideration ◇ **ride roughshod over sb** to treat sb with no justice or consideration

rough shooting *n.* shooting game on moorland without using beaters

rough stuff *n.* violent behaviour or acts (*informal*)

rough trade *n.* an offensive term for a tough or sometimes violent sexual partner for a gay man (*slang offensive*)

rouille /roo ée/ *n.* a sauce made from chillies, garlic, and olive oil served as an accompaniment to many Provençal foods, especially bouillabaisse and other fish soups [Mid-20thC. Via French, literally 'rust' (from its colour), from, ultimately, Latin *robigo*.]

roulade /roo laád/ (*plural* **-lades**) *n.* **1.** FOOD **FOOD IN THE FORM OF A ROLL** a dish in which a piece of food is coated with a sauce or filling and rolled up before being cooked, so that each slice has a spiral appearance **2.** MUSIC **VOCAL MUSICAL ORNAMENT** a run of several musical notes sung rapidly to one syllable [Early 18thC. Via French, from *rouler* 'to roll', from, ultimately, Latin *rota* 'wheel' (source of English *rota* and *rotate*).]

rouleau /ro͞olō/ (*plural* **-leaux** /-lō/ *or* **-leaus** /-lōz/) *n.* **1. ROLL OF COINS** a stack of coins wrapped in a paper cylinder **2.** SEW **PIPING** rolled or folded ribbon used as decorative piping or trimming [Late 17thC. Via French, literally 'small roll', from, ultimately, Latin *rotula* 'small wheel', from *rota* (see ROULADE).]

roulette /roo lét/ *n.* **1.** GAMBLING **GAMBLING GAME WITH A SPINNING WHEEL** a game in which a ball is rolled onto a spinning horizontal wheel divided into compartments, with players betting on which compartment the ball will come to rest in (*often used before a noun*) **2. TOOL WITH A TOOTHED WHEEL** a tool with a toothed wheel used for making dots, e.g. in engraving, or for making perforations in paper, e.g. on a sheet of postage stamps **3. SLITS CUT IN PAPER** a line of slits or perforations made by a cutting tool on a sheet of paper ■ *vt.* **(-lettes, -letting, -letted) MARK STH WITH DOTS OR PERFORATIONS** to use a roulette to mark a surface with a line of dots or make perforations in a sheet of paper [Mid-18thC. Via French, literally 'small wheel' (the original sense in English), from, ultimately, late Latin *rotella*, from Latin *rota* 'wheel' (source of English *rota*).]

Roumanian *n., adj.* Romanian (*dated*)

round[1] /rownd/ CORE MEANING: a grammatical word used to indicate that a circle of people, a place, or an object surrounds or encloses sth ○ (prep) *She sat clasping her hands round her knees.* ○ (prep) *an area of green belt round the town* ○ (adv) *a crowd soon gathered round*

1. *prep., adv.* **IN DIFFERENT PARTS OF** situated at various points in, or moving to various places in ○ (prep) *newspapers and books scattered round the room* ○ (adv) *We managed to find someone to show us round.* ○ (adv) *She keeps moving things round and I can't find anything!* **2.** *prep., adv.* **IN ALL DIRECTIONS** situated or moving in all directions from a central point of reference ○ (prep) *gazing round him at the strange sights of this new country* ○ (adv) *They could see nothing but green fields for 10 miles round.* ○ *driving round for hours looking for them* **3.** *prep.* **IN A PARTIAL CIRCUIT** to move to the other side of a corner or obstacle in a partial circuit, or be reached by such a movement ○ *The lorry came round the bend at breakneck speed.* **4.** *prep., adv.* **TURNING ON AN AXIS** revolving round a centre or axis ○ (prep) *the movement of the planets round the sun* ○ (adv) *cylinders going round at 1,000 revolutions per minute.* **5.** *adv.* **IN THE OPPOSITE DIRECTION** to turn so as to be facing in the opposite direction ○ *She turned round when he called* *her name.* **6.** *prep., adv.* **IN CIRCUMFERENCE** on or outside the circumference or perimeter ○ (prep) *I measure 25 inches round the waist.* ○ (adv) *The tower was 60 feet tall and 30 feet round.* **7.** *prep., adv.* **TO EVERYONE** to all members in a group, from person to person ○ (adv) *She handed round the drinks.* ○ (prep) *News of the closure was passed round the factory.* **8.** *adv.* **VISIT** to visit a particular place ○ *She went round to give them the news.* **9.** *adv.* **IN A CURVE** in a curved shape or by a circuitous route ○ *After the pedestrian crossing, the road bends round to the left.* **10.** *prep.* **HAVING A BASIS IN** used to indicate the thing that is the basis for sth such as a concept or a storyline ○ *The plot is centred round the relationship between two brothers.* [13thC. Via Old French *ro(u)nd-*, the stem of *ro(o)nt*, from, ultimately, Latin *rotundus* (source of English *rotund*, *rondo*, and *roundelay*).]

round off *vt.* **1. MAKE STH MORE ROUNDED** to make the edges, sides, or corners of sth less straight or angular and more rounded **2. FINISH STH IN PLEASING WAY** to bring sth to a pleasant or satisfactory end by doing or adding one last thing

round on *vt.* to attack sb suddenly, either physically or verbally, in a fit of anger

round out *vti.* to achieve or cause sth to achieve a more complete or satisfactory form

round up *vt.* to gather people or animals together in one place

round[2] /rownd/ *adj.* **1. CIRCULAR OR SPHERICAL** shaped like a circle or a ball ○ *a big, perfectly round bowl* **2. CURVED** curved rather than square or angular ○ *round hips and a small waist* **3. IN A CIRCULAR MOTION** done with or involving a circular motion **4. COMPLETE** not less or more than ○ *I'll have a round 100 of them.* **5.** MATH **EXPRESSED BY AN INTEGER** expressed as an approximate value, especially to the nearest integer or power of ten ○ *use 1500 as a round number* **6. CONSIDERABLE** large in amount or size ○ *a round sum* **7. FULLY DEVELOPED** fully developed in terms of personality, or fully depicted, as in a character in a book ○ *His heroes are always very round and colourful.* **8. RATHER PLUMP** full and plump, especially in facial features ○ *kindly eyes surrounded by a round face* **9. SONOROUS** mellow and rich in tone **10. BRISK** lively and rather fast ○ *We set off at a round pace.* **11. STRAIGHTFORWARD** plain and outspoken ○ *'I said in good round English, "I'm going to knock the stuffing out of you".'* (John Buchan, *Greenmantle*) **12.** PHON **PRONOUNCED WITH ROUNDED LIPS** articulated with the lips forming an oval opening ○ *a round vowel sound*

round[3] /rownd/ *n.* **1. ROUND SHAPE** a round shape or object ○ *little rounds of cheese* **2. SESSION** a session or instance of a particular event, usually in a series of similar or related events ○ *the Uruguay round of global talks* ○ *the dreary round of fruitless calls* **3.** SPORTS **STAGE OF A COMPETITION** a game or series of games in a competition ○ *He beat last year's champion in the first round of the competition.* **4.** WRESTLING, BOXING **PERIOD OF BOXING OR WRESTLING** a time period, usually three minutes, during which boxers or wrestlers fight **5.** GOLF **GAME OF GOLF** a playing of all the holes on a golf course constituting one game **6.** LEISURE **TURN OF PLAY** a single turn of play, as in a game of cards **7.** ARCHERY **ARROWS SHOT** a specified number of arrow shot from a specified distance **8.** ARMS **CHARGE OF AMMUNITION** a bullet, blank cartridge, or other charge of ammunition ○ *a city that has received more than its share of mortar rounds* **9.** ARMS **GUN DISCHARGE** a single discharge by a gun or guns ○ *loose off a few rounds* **10. SERIES OF VISITS** a series of visits made on a regular basis to different places or people (*often used in the plural*) **11. DRINKS BOUGHT** a number of drinks bought for each member of a group of people **12.** FOOD **SLICE OF BREAD** a slice of bread or toast, or a sandwich made from two slices of bread **13. APPLAUSE** an outburst of applause or cheering ○ *She entered the hall to a huge round of applause.* **14.** MUSIC **PARTSONG** a song sung by several people whereby each person sings a different part of the song at the same time **15. MOVEMENT IN A CIRCLE** movement in a circle or around an axis **16.** MUSIC **BELLS RUNG** a sequence of bells rung in order of treble to tenor **17.** DANCE **CIRCULAR DANCE** a dance involving a sequence of movements in a circle **18.** FOOD **CUT OF BEEF** a cut of beef from between the rump and the shank ◇ **the rounds 1.** to circulate and become widespread ○ *a new rumour making the rounds* **2.** to go from place to place in a regular pattern ◇ **in the round 1.** THEATRE visible or viewed from all sides **2.** with full detail and perspective from all sides

round[4] /rownd/ (**rounds, rounding, rounded**) *v.* **1.** *vt.* **MOVE PAST AN OBSTACLE** to move in a curve past the edge or corner of sth ○ *as they rounded the corner* **2.** *vti.* MATH **EXPRESS AS A ROUND NUMBER** to express a number containing several units as the nearest significant number above or below it, e.g. treating 5,753 as 6,000, or 6.375 as 6 ○ *The estimate was rounded to the nearest pound.* **3.** *vt.* **PRONOUNCE SOUNDS** to pronounce a sound with rounded lips ○ *Try to round your vowels.* **4.** *vt.* **PURSE LIPS** to purse the lips

round down *vt.* to express a number as a smaller and less exact number for ease of calculation

round up *vt.* to express a number containing several units as the nearest significant number above it, regarding, e.g. 5,924 as 6,000, or 7.57 as 8

roundabout /równdə bowt/ *n.* **1.** LEISURE **REVOLVING RIDE IN PLAYGROUND** a piece of playground equipment in the form of a revolving structure for children to sit on and push or be pushed round and round. US term **merry-go-round 2.** TRANSP **CIRCULAR ROAD JUNCTION** a road junction with a central island around which traffic moves in one direction. US term **traffic circle** ■ *adj.* **CIRCUITOUS** indirect and not straightforward ○ *went by a roundabout route* ○ *answered in a roundabout way* —**roundaboutness** *n.*

round-arm *adj.* **1. WITH OUTWARD ARM SWING** made with a near-horizontal swing of the arm **2.** CRICKET **WITH NEAR-HORIZONTAL ARM MOVEMENT** in cricket, with the bowler's arm coming over the shoulder at an angle nearer horizontal than vertical ○ *a round-arm action*

round clam *n.* = **quahog** [From its rounded shell]

round dance *n.* **1.** DANCING **FOLK DANCE IN A CIRCLE** any folk dance in which several dancers or couples come together to form a circle **2.** DANCING **BALLROOM DANCE WITH A REVOLVING MOTION** any ballroom dance in which couples revolve as they move round the room, as they do in a waltz **3.** ZOOL **BEE'S SEQUENCE OF MOVEMENTS** a more or less circular sequence of movements that a honey bee performs in or near the hive to show others that food is nearby

rounded /równdid/ *adj.* **1. CURVED, OR WITH CURVED PARTS** having curved, not straight or angular, surfaces or edges ○ *a rounded lawn* **2. COMPLEX OR DIVERSE** having many different features or aspects that together form a whole that is complete and interestingly complex or diverse ○ *received a very rounded education* **3.** PHON **PRONOUNCED WITH PURSED LIPS** pronounced with the lips pursed to form a round shape — **roundedness** *n.*

roundel /równd'l/ *n.* **1. ROUND PART** a round part or piece such as a round section in a stained-glass window or a round panel in a section of wood panelling **2. IDENTIFYING DISC ON AIRCRAFT WING** a coloured disc on a military aircraft wing identifying the aircraft's country of origin **3. ROUND PIECE OF ARMOUR** a circular section of armour that protects the wearer's armpit **4.** POETRY **MODIFIED FORM OF RONDEAU** an English form of the rondeau that has eleven lines arranged in three stanzas of three lines and a one-line refrain after the first and third stanzas **5.** POETRY **TYPE OF RONDEL** a modified form of the rondel that has ten lines arranged in two stanzas of three lines and one of four lines, with the opening line repeated as a refrain **6.** DANCE = **roundelay** [13thC. From Old French *rondel*, literally 'small circle', from *ro(u)nd-*, the stem of *ro(o)nt* (see ROUND[1]).]

roundelay /równdə lay/ *n.* **1.** MUSIC **SONG WITH A VERSE REPEATED AS A CHORUS** a simple song in which the chorus consists of one of the verses repeated, or the music for this song **2.** DANCE **MEDIEVAL DANCE WITH DANCERS IN A CIRCLE** a slow medieval dance performed by a group arranged in a circle [15thC. Anglicization of French *rondelet* 'small roundel', from *rondel*, literally 'small circle', from *ro(u)nd-*, the stem of *ro(o)nt* (see ROUND[1]).]

rounder /równdər/ *n.* **1.** SPORTS **COMPLETE CIRCUIT IN ROUNDERS** a score in the game of rounders made when the batter runs round all four bases after a single hit of the ball **2. TOOL MAKING THINGS ROUND** a tool that makes edges or surfaces round **3.** *US, Can* **SB LIVING A DEBAUCHED LIFE** sb who lives a life of crime or debauchery (*informal*) [Early 17thC. Originally in the sense 'sb who makes the rounds of sentries'.]

rounders /równdərz/ *n.* a ball game in which batters score a point, or rounder, if they run round all four marked fielding positions or bases after a single hit of the ball

round hand *n.* handwriting with broad rounded letters as opposed to, e.g. copperplate

Roundhead /równd hed/ *n.* sb who supported Oliver Cromwell and the parliamentary party against King Charles I during the English Civil War of 1642 to 1649. ◊ **Cavalier** [Mid-17thC. From their close-cropped hair (contrasted with that of the Cavaliers).]

round herring *n.* a small silvery fish that is similar and related to the herring but does not have its sharp keeled abdomen. Family: Dussumieriidae.

roundhouse /równd howss/ (*plural* **-houses** /-howziz/) *n.* **1.** RAIL **BUILDING FOR RAILWAY ENGINES** a circular building in which railway engines are stored or serviced, consisting of a central turntable with several sections of track radiating from it **2.** SHIPPING **CABIN ON A SAILING SHIP** a large cabin or set of cabins at the rear of an old-fashioned sailing ship **3.** BOXING **PUNCH DELIVERED WITH A CIRCULAR SWING** a punch made with a wide circular swing of the arm (*slang*) **4.** CARDS **PINOCHLE MELD** a meld of four kings and four queens in all suits in the card game pinochle [Late 16thC. Originally in the sense 'prison'.]

roundlet /równdlət/ *n.* a small circular or disc-shaped object (*literary*)

round lot *n.* STOCK EXCH a regular number of stocks or bonds as a trading unit, usually 100 shares of stock or 5 bonds

roundly /równdli/ *adv.* **1. SEVERELY** forcefully and thoroughly ○ *They were roundly criticized for their failure.* **2. AS A CIRCLE OR SPHERE** so as to form a circle or sphere (*dated*)

round robin *n.* **1.** SPORTS **TOURNAMENT WITH EVERYONE PLAYING ONE ANOTHER** a tournament in which each player or team plays against every other player or team in turn (*hyphenated before a noun*) ○ *a round-robin contest* **2. PETITION WITH SIGNATURES IN A CIRCLE** a letter, especially a petition or letter of protest, on which the signatures are arranged in a circle in order to hide the identity of the first person to sign **3. DOCUMENT EACH PERSON PASSES ON** a letter or other document circulated in turn to all members of a group, with each of them adding comments if they wish [From the male first name *Robin*]

round-shouldered *adj.* with the shoulders hunched or drooping and the upper back bent forward slightly

roundsman /równdzmən/ (*plural* **-men** /-mən/) *n.* **1. SB DOING THE ROUNDS OF PLACES** sb who makes regular visits to places on a set route, e.g. to make deliveries or carry out inspections **2.** *US* **POLICE OFFICER SUPERVISING A PATROL** a police officer, especially a sergeant, in charge of all the officers patrolling a particular area **3.** *ANZ* **REPORTER COVERING FIXED AREA OR SUBJECT** a journalist employed to cover stories in a particular topic or field of interest

round table *n.* a discussion or negotiation between several parties or groups who all take part on equal terms (*hyphenated when used before a noun*) [From ROUND TABLE]

Round Table *n.* **1. KING ARTHUR'S TABLE** the legendary table at which King Arthur and his knights sat, made round so that no one would appear to have precedence **2. KING ARTHUR'S KNIGHTS** the knights of King Arthur as a group **3. INTERNATIONAL ASSOCIATION UNDERTAKING CHARITABLE WORK** an international association of businessmen set up in 1927 to carry out charitable work in local communities worldwide, or a local branch of the association

round-the-clock *adj.* lasting or operating throughout the day and night ○ *mounted round-the-clock surveillance on the house*

round trip *n.* **1.** TRANSP **JOURNEY THERE AND BACK** a journey to a place and back again, usually returning by the same route (*hyphenated before a noun*) ○ *the round-trip fare* **2.** CARDS = **roundhouse** *n.* 4

round-trip *adj.* *US* = **return** ○ *How much is the return-trip fare?*

round-trip ticket *n.* *US* = **return ticket**

round-up *n.* **1.** GATHERING OF PEOPLE OR ANIMALS a gathering together of people or animals, e.g. suspects in a criminal investigation or livestock on a farm or ranch **2.** SUMMARY a gathering together of things of any kind, especially information or news ○ *a news round-up on the hour*

roundworm /równd wurm/ *n.* a parasitic round-bodied worm (**nematode**) that infests the intestine of people and some animals. Latin name: *Ascaris lumbricoides.*

roup /roop/ *n.* an infectious respiratory disease that affects poultry [14thC. Origin uncertain: probably from a Scandinavian source. Originally in the sense 'to shout, croak'.]

rouse /rowz/ (**rouses, rousing, roused**) *v.* **1.** *vti.* WAKE, OR WAKE SB to wake up, or wake sb from sleep or unconsciousness **2.** *vt.* SHAKE SB OUT OF APATHY to stir sb into action or a more active state, or to become more active ○ *Anger roused her to write a letter of complaint.* **3.** *vt.* PROVOKE FEELING IN SB to cause sb to feel a particular emotion ○ *the feelings of guilt that the whole affair roused in us* **4.** *vt.* SCARE HUNTED ANIMAL INTO THE OPEN to scare a hunted animal or bird out of its hiding place [15thC. Origin uncertain: perhaps via Old French *r(e)user* 'to repel', from, ultimately, Latin *recusare*, literally 'to cause to go back', formed from *causa* 'cause' (source of English *cause*).] —**rouser** *n.*

rouseabout /rówzə bowt/ *n.* *ANZ* an unskilled worker who carries out menial tasks, especially on a sheep or cattle station (*dated*) [Mid-18thC. Originally in the sense 'bustling or active person'.]

rousing /rówzing/ *adj.* **1.** INCITING EMOTION filling people with passion, emotion, and enthusiasm ○ *a rousing speech* **2.** LIVELY suggesting energy and vigour, especially by its fast pace —**rousingly** *adv.*

Rous sarcoma /rówss-/ *n.* a cancerous tumour found in chickens, caused by a specific tumour-producing RNA virus [Early 20thC. Named after Francis Peyton *Rous* (1879–1970), the US physician who first described it.]

Rousseau /roos ṓ/, **Jean Jacques** (1712–78) French philosopher and writer. He was one of the great authors of the Age of Enlightenment. His works include *The Social Contract* (1762), *The New Heloise* (1761), and *Émile* (1762).

roust /rowst/ *vt.* (**rousts, rousting, rousted**) **1.** FORCE SB TO GET UP to make sb get up, make a move, or take action, especially abruptly or roughly **2.** *US* HARASS SB to bother, annoy, or jostle sb (*slang*) ■ *n.* *US* HARASSING a harassing of sb (*slang*) [Mid-17thC. Origin uncertain: probably an alteration of ROUSE.]

roustabout /rówstə bowt/ *n.* **1.** *US, Can* UNSKILLED LABOURER an unskilled labourer, especially on an oil rig, on a ship or wharf, or in a circus **2.** *ANZ* = **rouseabout** (*dated*)

rout[1] /rowt/ *n.* **1.** DEFEATED ARMY'S RETREAT a swift and disorderly retreat by a defeated army **2.** CRUSHING DEFEAT any severe and humiliating defeat ○ *the rout suffered at the general election* **3.** RABBLE a noisy and disorganized group of people ■ *vt.* (**routs, routing, routed**) **1.** FORCE AN ARMY TO RETREAT to defeat an army completely and force it to make a swift and disorderly retreat **2.** DEFEAT SB THOROUGHLY to subject an opponent to a thorough and humiliating defeat [13thC. Via Anglo-Norman *rute* and Old French *route* 'dispersed group', from, ultimately, Latin *rumpere* 'to break' (source of English *rupture*).]

rout out *vt.* **1.** FORCE SB OUT to drive a person or animal from a place, especially by the use of force **2.** REVEAL STH AFTER SEARCHING to reveal or uncover sth, especially after a search ○ *routed out his true motives*

rout[2] /rowt/ (**routs, routing, routed**) *v.* **1.** *vt.* CONSTR MAKE A GROOVE IN STH to cut a groove in wood or metal, especially with a router **2.** *vti.* SEARCH BY POKING to search for sth by poking about, as pigs do with their snouts [Mid-16thC. Variant of ROOT[2].]

route /root/; *in military usage also* /rowt/ *n.* **1.** WAY TO TRAVEL a way, path, or road for travelling from one place to another **2.** GENERAL COURSE STH FOLLOWS the course that sth follows, or the way it progresses or develops ○ *My career might have taken an entirely different route.* **3.** REGULAR JOURNEY OR SEQUENCE OF CALLS a journey sb regularly makes, especially a set sequence of calls or stops made, e.g. by sb delivering sth ○ *Their store wasn't on my usual route.* ■ *vt.* (**routes, routeing, routed**) SEND SB OR STH ALONG A ROUTE to direct or arrange for sb or sth to follow a particular course ○ *All phone calls were routed through my office.* [12thC. Via Old French *route* from assumed Vulgar Latin *rupta*, literally 'broken' (from frequent use), the feminine past participle of Latin *rumpere* 'to break' (source of English *rupture*).]

route march *n.* a long march over rough ground, often used as training in physical endurance for soldiers, in which discipline is often relaxed and route step is allowed —**route-march** *vti.*

router[1] /róotər/ *n.* COMPUT a computer switching program that transfers incoming messages to outgoing links via the most efficient route possible, e.g. over the Internet

router[2] /rówtər/ *n.* CONSTR a tool that cuts shaped grooves and hollows in wood or metal, originally a hand tool but now usually driven by electricity

route step *n.* a mode of marching in formation where there is no requirement to keep in step and talking and singing are allowed

routine /roo teén/ *n.* **1.** USUAL SEQUENCE OF ACTIVITIES the usual way tasks or activities are arranged **2.** STH REPETITIVE sth that is unvarying or boringly repetitive ○ *a life of mindless routine* **3.** REGULAR PATTERN OF BEHAVIOUR a typical pattern of behaviour that sb adopts in particular circumstances, especially insincere or affected behaviour (*informal*) ○ *The salesman went into his routine about the car's unique reliability and performance.* **4.** REHEARSED PERFORMANCE a rehearsed set of movements, actions, or speeches that make up a performance ○ *her gymnastic routine on the parallel bars* **5.** COMPUT PART OF A COMPUTER PROGRAM a part of a computer program that performs a particular task ○ *a dump routine* ■ *adj.* **1.** USUAL OR STANDARD regular or standard and nothing out of the ordinary ○ *carrying out routine inquiries* **2.** REPETITIVE boringly predictable, monotonous, and unchanging ○ *found the work pretty routine* [Late 17thC. From French, from *route* (see ROUTE).] —**routinely** *adv.*

WORD KEY: SYNONYMS

See Synonyms at ***habit***.

routinize /roo teén īz, róotin īz/ (**-izes, -izing, -ized**), **routinise** (**-ises, -ising, -ised**) *vt.* to arrange or plan sth so that it follows a regular or unchanging pattern —**routinization** /roo teén ī záysh'n, róoti nī-/ *n.*

roux /roo/ (*plural* **roux** /rooz/) *n.* a mixture of flour and fat that is cooked briefly and used as the thickening base of a sauce or soup [Early 19thC. Via French, 'browned', which evolved from Old French *rous* 'reddish brown', from Latin *russus* 'red' (source of English *russet* and *rissole*).]

rove[1] /rōv/ (**roves, roving, roved**) *v.* **1.** *vti.* WANDER OR TRAVEL AIMLESSLY to wander or travel about with no definite purpose, often over a wide area **2.** *vi.* MOVE IN CHANGING DIRECTIONS to move, especially to look, in changing directions ○ *The officer's trained gaze roved around the room, taking it all in.* [Early 16thC. Origin uncertain: perhaps originally a dialect word meaning 'to wander', probably of Scandinavian origin. Originally, 'to shoot at random targets'.]

rove[2] /rōv/ *vt.* (**roves, roving, roved**) TEXTILES TWIST FIBRES PRIOR TO SPINNING to twist fibres slightly before they are spun into yarn or thread ■ *n.* TEXTILES FIBRES TWISTED FOR SPINNING wool, cotton, or other fibres twisted slightly in preparation for spinning [Late 18thC. Origin unknown.]

rove[3] NAUT past tense, past participle of **reeve**

rove beetle *n.* a carnivorous or scavenging beetle with a long body and short wing covers. Family: Staphylinidae. [Origin uncertain: perhaps from ROVE[1]]

rover[1] /rṓvər/ *n.* **1.** WANDERER sb who wanders from place to place, never settling anywhere for long **2.** ARCHERY ARCHERY TARGET a mark or object selected randomly as a target in archery **3.** SPORTS CROQUET BALL a ball in croquet that has been through all the hoops but has not yet hit the final peg **4.** *ANZ* AUSTRALIAN RULES PLAYER in Australian Rules football, a player, usually smaller than the others, who plays alongside the two ruckmen, and who gathers and clears the ball when it emerges from a ruck **5.** SPACE TECH VEHICLE FOR EXPLORING A PLANET a small vehicle launched from a lander and used to explore the surface of the moon or a planet

rover[2] /rṓvər/ *n.* a pirate or pirate ship (*archaic*) [14thC. From Middle Low German or Middle Dutch *rōver*, from *rōven* 'to rob'.]

rover[3] /rṓvər/ *n.* TEXTILES a machine or attachment for twisting fibres slightly in preparation for spinning [Mid-18thC. Originally in the sense 'sb who twists fibres for spinning'.]

Rover Scout *n.* the former name for a Venture Scout, a senior member of the Scout Movement, aged 16 or over

roving /rṓving/ *adj.* **1.** MOVING ABOUT moving or travelling from one place or thing to another ○ *a bulletin from our roving reporter* **2.** ERRATIC OR FICKLE tending to wander or waver rather than settle or concentrate on one thing

roving eye *n.* a wide and often promiscuous sexual interest

row[1] /rō/ *n.* **1.** LINE OF THINGS things or people that are arranged in a line that is usually straight, or the line itself ○ *cabbages planted in a row* **2.** LINE OF SEATS a line of seats in a theatre, cinema, lecture hall, or similar public place ○ *the second row in the balcony* **3.** NARROW STREET BETWEEN LINES OF HOUSES a narrow street that is lined with houses or other buildings on both sides **4.** STREET WITH A PARTICULAR CHARACTER a street where a particular occupation or type of person predominates ○ *lawyer's row* **5.** MUSIC = **tone row** [Old English *rāw*] ◇ **in a row** one after the other in succession ◇ **a hard row to hoe** sth that is difficult to do

row[2] /rō/ (**rows, rowing, rowed**) *v.* **1.** *vti.* PROPEL A BOAT WITH OARS to propel a boat across water by using oars **2.** *vi.* ROW AS SPORT to take part in the sport of rowing [Old English *rōwan*. Ultimately from a prehistoric Germanic base meaning 'to steer'.] —**rower** *n.*

row[3] /row/ *n.* **1.** LOUD FIGHT a noisy quarrel or dispute **2.** RACKET an unpleasant or excessively loud noise ■ *vi.* (**rows, rowing, rowed**) ARGUE NOISILY to have a noisy argument [Mid-18thC. Origin unknown.]

rowan /rṓ ən, rów ən/ *n.* **1.** EUROPEAN TREE WITH RED BERRIES a slim smallish deciduous tree found throughout northern Europe with long thin leaves and cream-coloured flowers that are followed by bright red berries. Latin name: *Sorbus aucuparia.* **2. rowan, rowanberry** (*plural* **-ries**) BERRY OF ROWAN a red to orange berry from a rowan tree [Early 19thC. From a Scandinavian source. Ultimately from an Indo-European base meaning 'red'. Originally a Scots and northern English dialect word.]

rowboat /rṓ bōt/ *n.* *US* = **rowing boat**

rowdy /rówdi/ *adj.* (**-dier, -diest**) UNRULY noisy and disorderly ○ *The debate was a pretty rowdy affair.* ■ *n.* (*plural* **-dies**) HOOLIGAN sb who is rough and noisy and often causes disturbances ○ *a bar full of local rowdies* [Early 19thC. Origin uncertain: probably formed from ROW[3].] —**rowdily** *adv.* —**rowdiness** *n.* —**rowdyism** *n.*

rowel /rów əl/ *n.* SPIKED WHEEL ON A SPUR a small spiked revolving wheel on the end of a horse-rider's spur ■ *vt.* (**-els, -elling, -elled**) SPUR A HORSE ON to urge a horse on by digging rowels into its sides [14thC. Via Old French *roel(e)* 'small wheel' (the original English sense), from late Latin *rotella* (source of English *roulette*), formed from Latin *rota* 'wheel' (source of English *rota*).]

rowen /rów ən/ *n.* *New England* a second mowing of hay or grass in the same season [14thC. From Old Norman French, a variant of French *regain*, literally 'to till again', formed from Old French *gaignier* 'to till' (source of English *gain*[1]).]

row house *n.* *US* = **terraced house**

rowing /rṓ ing/ *n.* the propelling of a small boat through the water using oars, especially the sport of racing in specially designed lightweight boats (*often used before a noun*) ○ *a member of the rowing team* [Old English *rōwing*]

rowing boat *n.* a small lightweight boat designed to be propelled through the water by one or more people rowing with oars. US term **rowboat**

rowing machine *n.* a fitness machine that imitates the action of rowing a boat

Rowlandson /rólǝndsǝn/, **Thomas** (1756–1827) British painter and caricaturist. He created satirical illustrations of life in Georgian and Regency England.

Rowling /róling/, **Bill** (1927–95) New Zealand statesman. He was a Labour Party politician, and prime minister of New Zealand (1974–75). Full name **Sir Wallace Edward Rowling**

rowlock /róllǝk, rúllǝk/ *n.* a more or less U-shaped pivoting metal rest fitted to the side of a rowing boat, in which an oar rests. US term **oarlock** [Mid-18thC. Alteration of OARLOCK by substituting ROW for OAR.]

Rowntree /równ tree/, **Benjamin Seebohm** (1871–1954) British manufacturer and philanthropist. He was chairman of the chocolate firm founded by his father Joseph Rowntree, and was noted for his concern for social welfare.

Arundhati Roy

Roy /roy/, **Arundhati** (*b.* 1961) Indian writer. She achieved success with her first novel, *The God of Small Things* (1997), which won the Booker Prize.

royal /róy ǝl/ *adj.* **1.** OF KINGS AND QUEENS relating to, belonging to, or consisting of a king, queen, or other member of a monarch's family ○ *members of the royal household* **2.** ENJOYING ROYAL PATRONAGE a word used in the titles of organizations and societies established by a monarch or a member of a monarch's family, or given his or her formal approval and support **3.** LARGEST OR BEST of the largest size or of the highest standard **4.** EXCELLENT of the most excellent kind ○ *given a royal welcome* **5.** EXTREMELY BAD used to emphasize how extremely bad sth is (*informal*) ○ *a right royal pain in the neck* **6.** SAILING ABOVE THE TOPGALLANT located in the area of rigging that is above the topgallant ■ *n.* **1.** MONARCH OR MEMBER OF MONARCH'S FAMILY a monarch or a member of a monarch's family, especially his or her immediate family (*informal*) **2.** HUNT STAG WITH LARGE ANTLERS a stag with large antlers that have 12 or more points on them **3.** SAILING SAIL ABOVE TOPGALLANT SAIL the sail above the topgallant sail on a full-rigged ship **4.** PRINTING SIZE OF PAPER a size of paper, especially a British size of writing paper 483 x 610 mm/19 x 24 in or a size of printing paper 508 x 635 mm/20 x 25 in [13thC. Via Old French *roial* from Latin *regalis* (source of English *regal* and *regalia*), from *reg-*, the stem of *rex* 'king' (source of English *regicide*).]

Royal Air Force *n.* the Air Force of the United Kingdom

Royal Assent, **royal assent** *n.* the British monarch's formal signing of an act of parliament, making it law

royal blue *adj.* of a bright, deep blue colour (*hyphenated before a noun*) —**royal blue** *n.*

Royal British Legion *n.* a charitable organization in Britain that provides help for former members of the armed forces

Royal Canadian Mounted Police *n.* a police force that operates throughout Canada except in cities and provinces with their own police forces

Royal Commission *n.* a committee set up by the monarch on the prime minister's advice to inquire into a particular issue ○ *set up a Royal Commission to investigate environmental pollution*

royal fern *n.* a deep-rooted fern with branched stems, found throughout the world. Latin name: *Osmunda regalis.*

royal flush *n.* in poker, a hand that consists of a ten, jack, queen, king, and ace of the same suit

Royal Flying Doctor Service *n.* a medical service operated in remote parts of Australia that involves doctors and emergency medical services travelling to patients by light aircraft

Royal Highness *n.* a title used when speaking or referring to a member of a royal family other than a king or queen

royal icing *n.* a firm crisp icing made by mixing icing sugar with egg whites instead of with water

royalist /róy ǝlist/ *n.* sb who supports the monarchy or who thinks a country should keep its king or queen rather than become a republic (*often used before a noun*) —**royalism** *n.*

Royalist /róy ǝlist/ *n.* **1.** CAVALIER a Cavalier, or supporter of Charles I during the English Civil War **2.** = **Tory** *n.* 5 **3.** FRENCH LOYALIST in France, a supporter of the Bourbon dynasty after the Revolution

royal jelly *n.* a protein-rich substance that worker bees secrete and feed to larvae in the early stages of their development and to the larvae of queen bees in all stages of their development

Royal Leamington Spa ▶ Leamington Spa

royally /róy ǝli/ *adv.* with impressive generosity and hospitality ○ *royally entertained*

royal mast *n.* the highest section of a mast that is immediately above the topgallant

royal palm *n.* a palm tree with a tall naked trunk, found in the tropical regions of the Americas. Genus: *Roystonea.*

royal poinciana *n.* a tropical tree native to Madagascar but widely grown in other tropical regions for its bright red flower clusters. Latin name: *Delonix regia.*

royal purple *adj.* of a deep vivid reddish-purple colour (*hyphenated before a noun*) —**royal purple** *n.*

royal road *n.* the route or method by which progress or a particular result is guaranteed, often by virtue of special privileges ○ *a young singer on the royal road to stardom*

royal standard *n.* the flag of the British monarch, flown from the place he or she is staying in at the time

royalty /róy ǝlti/ (*plural* **-ties**) *n.* **1.** ROYAL PERSON OR PEOPLE a king, queen, or other member of a monarch's family, or members of a royal family generally ○ *mixing with royalty at garden parties* **2.** ROYAL PERSON'S STATUS the status or authority of a king, queen, or other member of a monarch's family **3.** KINGLY OR QUEENLY QUALITIES the personal qualities conventionally ascribed to a king or queen, especially great dignity **4.** MONARCH'S PERMISSION TO HAVE STH the right to have or take sth, especially minerals, granted by a king or queen to a person or company **5.** PERCENTAGE OF INCOME PAID TO CREATOR a percentage of the income from a book, piece of music, or invention that is paid to the author, composer, or inventor (*often used in the plural*) ○ *still living on the royalties from her first novel* **6.** MINING COMPANY'S PAYMENT TO LANDOWNER money paid to a landowner by a company taking minerals, oil, or gas from his or her land (*often used in the plural*)

royal warrant *n.* a king's or queen's official authorization to a company to supply goods to a royal household

rozzer /rózzǝr/ *n.* a member of a police force (*dated slang*) [Late 19thC. Origin unknown.]

RP *abbr.* **1.** Received Pronunciation **2.** Regius Professor **3.** Republic of the Philippines

RPB *abbr.* Recognized Professional Body

RPG *n.* a high level computer language used primarily to produce business reports. Full form **report program generator**

RPI *abbr.* retail price index

rpm *abbr.* revolutions per minute

RPM *abbr.* resale price maintenance

RPO *abbr.* Royal Philharmonic Orchestra

rps *abbr.* revolutions per second

RPS *abbr.* Royal Photographic Society

rpt *abbr.* **1.** repeat **2.** report

RPV *abbr.* MIL remotely piloted vehicle

RQ *abbr.* MED respiratory quotient

RR *abbr.* **1.** railroad **2.** Right Reverend

-rrhagia *suffix.* abnormal or excessive flow or discharge ○ *metrorrhagia* [From Greek, formed from *rhag-*, the stem of *rhēgnunai* 'to burst forth']

-rrhoea, **-rrhea** *suffix.* flow, discharge ○ *pyorrhoea* [Via modern Latin from, ultimately, Greek *rhein* 'to flow' (see RHEO-)]

rRNA *abbr.* ribosomal RNA

RRP *abbr.* recommended retail price

Rs *symbol.* rupees

RS *abbr.* **1.** recording secretary **2.** right side **3.** Royal Society

RSA[1] *abbr.* **1.** Republic of South Africa **2.** Returned Services Association (New Zealand) **3.** Royal Scottish Academician **4.** Royal Scottish Academy **5.** Royal Society of Arts

RSA[2] *n.* COMPUT a system of encryption based on the difficulty of factoring very large numbers

RSC *n.*, *abbr.* Royal Shakespeare Company ■ *abbr.* Royal Society of Chemistry

RSFSR *abbr.* Russian Soviet Federated Socialist Republic

RSI *n.* a painful condition affecting some people who overuse muscles as a result of, e.g. regularly operating a computer keyboard and mouse or playing the piano. Full form **repetitive strain injury.** ◊ **tenosynovitis**

RSL *abbr.* **1.** Returned Services League (Australia) **2.** Royal Society of Literature

RSM *abbr.* **1.** regimental sergeant major **2.** Republic of San Marino **3.** MED Royal Society of Medicine

RSPB *abbr.* Royal Society for the Protection of Birds

RSPCA *abbr.* Royal Society for the Prevention of Cruelty to Animals

RSV *abbr.* BIBLE Revised Standard Version

RSVP used on an invitation to request a response to it. Abbr of **please reply** [French, *répondez s'il vous plaît*]

rt *abbr.* right

RT *abbr.* **1.** radio telegraph **2.** radio telegraphy **3.** radio telephone **4.** radio telephony **5.** room temperature

RTDS *abbr.* COMPUT real-time data system

rte *abbr.* route

RTE *abbr.* Radio Telefís Éireann [Gaelic, 'Irish Radio and Television']

rtf *suffix.* COMPUT used after the dot in a computer file name to show that the file contains codes identifying different fonts, layouts and other presentational features. Full form **rich text format**

RTFM COMPUT an offensive term used as a response in e-mail communications to an obvious technical question (*slang offensive*) Abbr of **read the fucking manual**

Rt Hon. *abbr.* Right Honourable

Rt Rev. *abbr.* Right Reverend

RTW *abbr.* ready-to-wear

Ru *symbol.* ruthenium

RU *abbr.* **1.** Republic of Burundi **2.** Rugby Union

RU-486 *tdmk.* a trademark for a drug that blocks the body's use of progesterone and is used to induce early-term abortion

Ruahine Range /roo ǝ hee nay-/ mountain range in the south of the North Island, New Zealand. Its highest point is Mount Mangaweka, 1,733 m/5,686 ft.

Ruapehu /roo ǝ páy hoo/ active volcano in the central North Island, New Zealand, and have various ski resorts. It last erupted in 1996. Height: 2,797 m/9,177 ft.

rub /rub/ *v.* **(rubs, rubbing, rubbed) 1.** *vt.* **PRESS AND MOVE HAND ON STH** to move the hand or an object over the surface of sth, pressing down with a repeated circular or backwards and forwards motion ○ *rubbing ointment into his skin* **2.** *vi.* **TOUCH STH WITH DRAGGING PRESSURE** to make dragging contact with a surface ○ *metal parts rubbing against one another* **3.** *vti.* **CLEAN STH WITH REPEATED STROKES** to clean, dry, or polish sth, or be able to be cleaned, dried, or polished, by moving a cloth, sponge, or other implement over the surface repeatedly ○ *Rub the flaking paint off with sandpaper.* **4.** *vti.* **CAUSE DISCOMFORT ON SKIN BY SCRAPING** to cause discomfort or pain by repeatedly scraping the skin ○ *These shoes are rubbing my heels.* **5.** *vt.* **ANNOY SB** to cause annoyance to sb (*informal*) ○ *Her brusqueness was beginning to rub me.* **6.** *vi.* BOWLS **BE SLOWED DOWN IN BOWLS** in bowls, to be slowed by an uneven patch on the green ■ *n.* **1. RUBBING ACTION** a rubbing motion, or a rubbing of sth with or against sth else **2. MASSAGE** a massaging of part of the body ○ *a soothing back rub* **3. DIFFICULTY** a problem or difficulty ○ *That's the rub: too little time.* **4. IRRITATING THING** sth that sb does or says that irritates or offends sb else **5.** BOWLS **UNEVEN PATCH IN BOWLS** in bowls, an uneven patch of grass in the green [14thC. Origin uncertain: perhaps from Low German *rubben*, of unknown origin.] ◇ **rub sb up the wrong way** to irritate or annoy sb

rub along *vi.* to have a friendly enough relationship or existence together (*informal*)

rub down *vt.* **1. MAKE SURFACE SMOOTH FOR PAINTING** to prepare a surface for painting or varnishing by smoothing it or removing the old paint or varnish with sandpaper or some other abrasive **2. MASSAGE SB** to massage sb or part of the body vigorously **3. DRY BODY WITH VIGOROUS RUBBING** to dry a person's or animal's body by vigorous rubbing with a towel

rub in *v.* **1. MENTION STH REPEATEDLY TO ANNOY** to keep reminding sb of sth that person does not want to be reminded of, usually because it is embarrassing (*informal*) **2.** *vt.* **MIX FAT WITH FLOUR USING FINGERTIPS** to mix fat, usually butter, into flour in small pieces between the fingertips

rub off *vi.* to be passed to sb or be an influence on sb who is exposed to it

rub out *v.* **1.** *vti.* **REMOVE WITH A RUBBER** to remove sth written, or to be removed, with a rubber **2.** *vt. US, Can* **KILL** to murder sb (*slang*)

rub up *v.* **1.** *vt.* **POLISH STH** to polish sth by vigorous rubbing ○ *Let the polish soak into the leather before you rub them up.* **2.** *vti.* **REFRESH OLD KNOWLEDGE OR SKILL** to refresh old knowledge of sth, or to bring a skill back up to its former standard ○ *rubbing up on his French*

Rub al-Khali /ro͝ob al kaálí/ desert in the Arabian Peninsula. Also called the Empty Quarter, it extends from central Saudi Arabia into Yemen, the United Arab Emirates, and Oman. Area: 2,300,000 sq. km/900,000 sq. mi.

rubato /roo baátō/ *n.* **DIVERGENCE FROM STRICT BEAT** rhythmic freedom in musical performance, often against a steady accompaniment ■ *adj., adv.* **WITH RUBATO** performed with rubato [Late 18thC. From Italian *(tempo) rubato*, literally 'robbed (time)', the past participle of *rubare* 'to rob'.]

rubber[1] /rúbbər/ *n.* **1.** INDUST **NATURALLY OCCURRING ELASTIC SUBSTANCE** a strong elastic material made by drying the sap from various tropical trees, especially the rubber tree **2.** INDUST **ELASTIC SYNTHETIC SUBSTANCE** a strong elastic synthetic substance made either by improving the qualities of natural rubber or by an industrial process using petroleum and coal products **3.** *US* CLOTHES **WATERPROOF OVERSHOE** a waterproof overshoe worn over normal shoes to protect them in wet weather (*usually used in the plural*) **4.** BASEBALL **SPOT PITCHER STANDS ON** the rectangle of hard rubber on the mound that the pitcher stands on to throw the ball in baseball **5.** FURNITURE **RUBBING OR POLISHING CLOTH** a cloth or pad used for rubbing or polishing sth, especially the pad that a cabinetmaker uses to apply varnish or French polish **6. DEVICE THAT RUBS STH** any machine or device that rubs a surface **7. DEVICE FOR ERASING** a piece of rubber used for erasing writing US term **eraser 8. CONDOM** a condom (*informal*) [Mid-16thC. Formed from RUB.] ◇ **burn rubber** to drive very fast (*informal*)

rubber[2] /rúbbər/ *n.* **1.** CARDS **BRIDGE MATCH OF THREE GAMES** a match of three or five games in cards, especially bridge and whist **2.** CARDS **DECIDING GAME IN CARDS MATCH** in some card games, an extra game played to decide a tied match **3.** CARDS **SESSION OF PLAY IN CARD GAME** a match or session of playing in a card game (*informal*) **4.** SPORTS **SET OF GAMES** a set or series of games in some sports (*informal*) [Late 16thC. Origin uncertain: perhaps from RUBBER[1].]

rubber band *n.* a loop of thin rubber that is wrapped round objects to hold them together

rubber bridge *n.* a form of contract bridge in which a new hand is dealt for each round

rubber bullet *n.* a cylindrical block of hard rubber fired by police officers or troops during crowd-control operations, designed as a deterrent but capable of inflicting serious injury

rubber cement *n.* an adhesive made by dissolving rubber in an organic solvent

rubber cheque *n.* a cheque that is returned by a bank because the person who wrote it has insufficient funds in his or her account to cover it (*informal humorous*) [Because it bounces]

rubber-chicken circuit *n. US* a series of events that people feel obliged to attend, especially lunches or dinners for politicians or other public figures (*informal*) [Because the food served is usually unappetizing]

rubber goods *npl.* a euphemism for condoms (*informal*)

rubberize /rúbbə rīz/ **(-izes, -izing, -ized), rubberise (-ises, -ising, -ised)** *vt.* to coat or impregnate sth, especially fabric, with rubber

rubberneck /rúbbər nek/ *n.* **GAWKING PERSON** sb who stares in an over-inquisitive or insensitive way (*informal*) ■ *vi.* **(-necks, -necking, -necked) GAWK AT STH** to stare at sb or sth in an over-inquisitive or insensitive way (*informal*) [Late 19thC. From craning or turning the neck as if it were made of rubber. Originally a US word.] —**rubbernecking** *n.*

WORD KEY: SYNONYMS

See Synonyms at ***gaze***.

rubbernecked /rúbbər nekt/ *adj.* staring insensitively or in an over-inquisitive way (*informal*) ○ *a crowd of rubbernecked onlookers*

rubbernecker /rúbbər nekər/ *n.* = **rubberneck** (*informal*)

rubber plant *n.* **1. TROPICAL PLANT GROWN AS HOUSEPLANT** a tropical plant with thick glossy leaves and a rubbery sap, widely grown as a houseplant but growing as a full-size tree in Southeast Asia. Latin name: *Ficus elastica.* **2. PLANT WITH RUBBERY SAP** any plant that produces a rubbery sap

rubber stamp *n.* **1. STAMPING DEVICE** a device for stamping words or numbers on paper, consisting of an embossed flat rubber pad that is inked **2. AUTOMATIC AUTHORIZATION** authorization or approval that is given automatically **3. SB GIVING APPROVAL AUTOMATICALLY** a person or group who gives authorization or approval automatically, without thinking, questioning, or dissenting

rubber-stamp (rubber-stamps, rubber-stamping, rubber-stamped) *vt.* **1. GIVE STH AUTOMATIC APPROVAL** to authorize or approve sth automatically, without thinking, questioning, or dissenting **2. TO STAMP STH WITH IMPRINT** to mark a document with an imprint from a rubber stamp

rubber tree *n.* **1. TROPICAL AMERICAN TREE SUPPLYING RUBBER** a tropical American tree whose sap is the world's largest commercial source of natural rubber. Latin name: *Hevea brasiliensis.* **2. ANY TREE PRODUCING RUBBER** any tree that produces a sap from which rubber is made

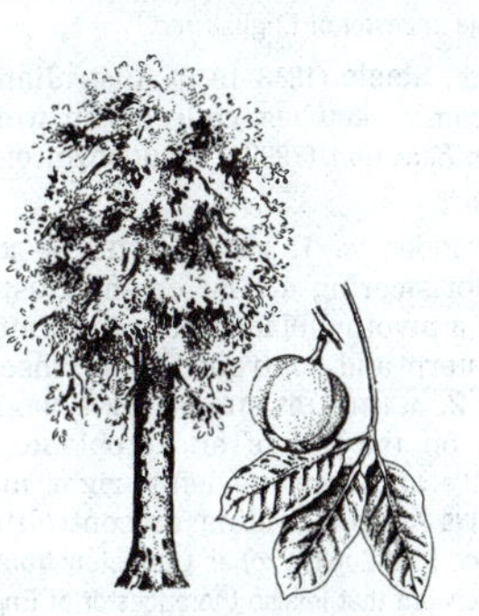

Rubber tree

rubbery /rúbbəri/ *adj.* with the elastic or tough texture of rubber

rubbing /rúbbing/ *n.* an impression of a textured surface, e.g. a raised design on a tombstone, made by placing paper over the surface and rubbing with a drawing implement [14thC. Originally in the sense 'action of rubbing'.]

rubbing alcohol *n.* a liquid, usually consisting of 70% denatured ethanol or isopropanol, used for massaging and as an antiseptic

rubbish /rúbbish/ *n.* **1. MATERIAL** things that are thrown away as unwanted, usually the remains of things that have been used or used up (*often used before a noun*) **2. WORTHLESS THINGS** things that are worthless or of very poor quality ○ *Most of what he's written is utter rubbish.* **3. NONSENSE** foolish things said or written, or things dismissed as wrong or not to be believed ○ *Don't talk rubbish!* ■ *vt.* **(-bishes, -bishing, -bished) DISMISS STH OR CRITICIZE SB** to dismiss sth as worthless or to criticize sb severely (*informal*) ○ *The scheme has been rubbished in the national press.* [14thC. From Anglo-Norman *rubbous*, of uncertain origin: perhaps from, ultimately, Old French *robe* 'stolen objects' (source of English *robe*), from Vulgar Latin *rauba*).] —**rubbishy** *adj.*

rubbish bin *n.* a large lidded usually cylindrical container for household rubbish, kept outdoors

rubble /rúbb'l/ *n.* **1. FRAGMENTS OF BROKEN BUILDINGS** broken stones, bricks, and other materials from buildings that have fallen down or been demolished **2.** CONSTR **ROUGH STONES AS FILLER OR BULK** rough unfinished stones used to fill space between walls or to build the bulk of a wall that will have a finishing surface of dressed stone **3. rubble, rubblework** CONSTR **MASONRY OF ROUGH STONES** masonry that is constructed using rough unfinished stones [14thC. Origin uncertain: perhaps from Anglo-Norman, an alteration of Old French *robe* (see RUBBISH).] —**rubbly** *adj.*

Rubbra /rúbbrə/, **Edmund** (1901–86) British composer. In his symphonies, chamber music, and choral compositions, he made much use of counterpoint and polyphony.

rubdown /rúb down/ *n.* a brisk rubbing down, usually of a person's or animal's body after exercising

rubefacient /ro͞obi fáysh'nt/ *adj.* **REDDENING THE SKIN** causing the skin to become red (*formal*) ■ *n.* **STH THAT MAKES SKIN RED** a substance that causes the skin to become red, particularly a cream or ointment used as a counterirritant [Early 19thC. From Latin *rubefacient-*, the present participle stem of *rubefacere* 'to make red', from *rubeus* 'red' + *facere* 'to make'.] —**rubefaction** /ro͞obi fáksh'n/ *n.*

rubefy /ro͞obi fī/ **(-fies, -fying, -fied)** *vti.* MED to use a rubefacient on skin [14thC. Formed from Old French *rube-*, the stem of *rubifier* from, ultimately, Latin *rubeus* 'red'.]

Rube Goldberg /roob gōld burg/ *adj. US, Can* = **Heath Robinson** [Mid-20thC. Named after *Reuben Goldberg* (1883–1970), a US cartoonist known for his depictions of complex devices performing elementary tasks.]

rubella /roo béllə/ *n.* = **German measles** [Late 19thC. From modern Latin, 'rash', noun use of the neuter plural of Latin *rubellus* 'reddish', from *rubeus* 'red' (source of English *rubeola*).]

rubellite /ro͞obi līt, roo béllīt/ *n.* a red variety of the glassy mineral tourmaline, used in jewellery [Late 18thC. Formed from Latin *rubellus* (see RUBELLA).]

Rubens /ro͞obənz/, **Peter Paul** (1577–1640) Flemish painter. He is considered one of the most important artists of the 17th century, and his style has come to define the sensuous aspects of baroque painting.

rubeola /roo bée ələ, ro͞obi ṓlə/ *n.* measles (*technical*) [Late 17thC. From modern Latin, noun use of the neuter plural of assumed *rubeolus* 'reddish', from Latin *rubeus* 'red' (source of English *rubella*).] —**rubeolar** *adj.*

rubescent /roo béss'nt/ *adj.* turning red or reddish, e.g. by blushing (*literary*) [Mid-18thC. From Latin *ru-*

bescent-, the present participle stem of *rubescere* 'to redden', from, ultimately, *ruber* 'red'.] —**rubescence** *n.*

Rubicon[1] /róobikən, -kon/, **rubicon** *n.* a point at which any action taken commits the person taking it to a further particular course of action that cannot be avoided [Early 17thC. Named after the RUBICON[2].] ◇ **cross the Rubicon** to do sth that commits you to a particular course of action

WORD KEY: ORIGIN

The ***Rubicon*** was a stream in northern Italy that formerly constituted part of the boundary between Cisalpine Gaul and Italy. By crossing it with his army en route to Rome in 49 BC, Julius Caesar broke a law forbidding a general to lead an army out of his own province and so committed himself to civil war against the Senate and Pompey. The expression *crossing the Rubicon* has come to mean making an irrevocable step that commits you to a course of action.

Rubicon[2] /róobikən/ stream in northeastern Italy that in ancient times marked the frontier between Italy and Cisalpine Gaul. Now called the Rubicone, it empties into the Adriatic Sea just north of Rimini. See Origin note above.

rubicund /róobikənd/ *adj.* with the reddish skin colour that is widely regarded as a sign of good health in people with white skin (*literary*) [15thC. From Latin *rubicundus*, from, ultimately, *ruber* 'red' (source of English *rubescent*).] —**rubicundity** /róobi kúndəti/ *n.*

rubidium /roo bíddi əm/ *n.* a soft silvery-white radioactive chemical element of the alkali metal group that reacts strongly with water, bursts into flame when exposed to air, and is used in photocells. Symbol **Rb** [Mid-19thC. From modern Latin, from Latin *rubidus* 'red', from *rubere* 'to be red'; from the two red lines in its spectrum.]

rubiginous /roo bíjjinəss/ *adj.* reddish-brown, like the colour of rust (*formal*) [Mid-17thC. Formed from Latin *rubigin-*, the stem of *rubigo* 'rust', a variant of *robigo* (source of English *rouille*). Originally in the sense '(of a plant) affected by blight'.]

Rubik's cube /róobiks-/, **Rubik cube** *tdmk.* a trademark for a puzzle that is a cube composed of smaller rotating coloured cubes, the aim being to rotate them to make each of the large cube's faces a uniform colour

rubious /róobi əss/ *adj.* dark red, like the colour of rubies (*literary*) [Early 17thC. Formed from RUBY.]

ruble *n.* = **rouble**

rubric /róobrik/ *n.* **1.** TITLE OR HEADING a printed title or heading, usually distinguished from the body of the text in some way, especially the heading of a section of a legal statute, originally underlined in red **2.** SET OF PRINTED INSTRUCTIONS a set of printed rules or instructions, e.g. the rules governing how Christian services are to be conducted, often printed in red in a prayer book **3.** ESTABLISHED CUSTOM a well-established custom or tradition that provides rules for conduct **4.** CATEGORY a class or category of things ■ *adj.* IN RED printed or marked in red [13thC. Directly or via Old French from Latin *rubrica* 'red ochre', from the base of *rubeus*, *ruber* 'red' (source of English *ruby*).] —**rubrical** *adj.* —**rubrically** *adv.*

rubricate /róobri kayt/ (**-cates, -cating, -cated**) *vt.* (*formal*) **1.** ADD HEADINGS TO TEXT to add titles or heading to a text, or to print them in red **2.** MARK STH IN RED to print or mark sth in red **3.** REGULATE STH to apply a set of rules to sth —**rubrication** /róobri káysh'n/ *n.* —**rubricator** /róobri kaytər/ *n.*

rubrician /roo brísh'n/ *n.* sb who is an authority on the way religious services should be conducted

ruby /róobi/ *n.* (*plural* **-bies**) **1.** MINERALS RED GEMSTONE a glassy red stone that is a variety of corundum, highly valued for its use in jewellery as well as in the making of watches and other precision instruments (*often used before a noun*) ○ *a ruby ring* **2.** COLOURS DEEP RED a deep glowing red colour tinged with dark purple, like that of a ruby ■ *adj.* COLOURS DEEP RED IN COLOUR of a deep glowing red colour tinged with purple, like that of a ruby [14thC. Via Old French from, ultimately, Latin *ruber*, *rubeus* 'red' (source also of English *rubella* and *rubric*).]

ruby port *n.* a port that is matured for a minimal period in the barrel and then bottled for immediate drinking

ruby spinel *n.* a red transparent variety of the mineral spinel, used in jewellery

ruby-throated hummingbird /-thrōtid-/ *n.* the most common hummingbird in North America, with a red throat and a shiny green back. Latin name: *Archilochus colubris.*

ruby wedding *n.* the 40th anniversary of a married couple's wedding

RUC *abbr.* Royal Ulster Constabulary

ruche /roosh/ *n.* GARMENT'S FRILLY EDGING a strip of gathered, pleated, or frilled fabric used as a decorative edging on a garment ■ *vt.* (**ruches, ruching, ruched**) TRIM GARMENT WITH RUCHES to decorate the edges of a garment with ruches [Early 19thC. Via French from medieval Latin *rusca* 'tree bark', of Celtic origin.]

ruching /róoshing/ *n.* decorative edges of gathered, pleated, or frilled fabric

ruck[1] /ruk/ *n.* **1.** LARGE NUMBER a large number of people or things **2.** ORDINARY PEOPLE OR THINGS the great mass of unexceptional people or things **3.** FOLLOWERS the group of competitors behind the leader in a race **4.** RUGBY LOOSE SCRUM in rugby, a loose scrum formed around the ball when it is on the ground **5.** FOOTBALL GROUP OF ROVING PLAYERS in Australian Rules football, three players who have no fixed positions but follow play, trying to win possession of the ball for their team ■ *vi.* (**rucks, rucking, rucked**) RUGBY FORM A RUCK in rugby, to form a loose scrum around the ball on the ground [13thC. Origin uncertain: probably from a Scandinavian language. Originally in the meaning 'pile of combustible material'.]

ruck[2] /ruk/ *vti.* (**rucks, rucking, rucked**) WRINKLE to become wrinkled or creased, or cause sth, especially fabric, to become wrinkled or creased ○ *The carpet is rucked up under your chair.* ■ *n.* UNWANTED FOLD a crease or wrinkle, especially in a fabric [Late 18thC. From Old Norse *hrukka* 'wrinkle'.]

rucksack /rúk sak, róok-/ *n.* a large bag, usually with two straps and often with a supporting frame, carried on the back and used especially by walkers and climbers [Mid-19thC. From German, literally 'back-sack'.]

ruckus /rúkəss/ *n.* a noisy and unpleasant disturbance [Late 19thC. Origin uncertain: perhaps a blend of RUCTION and RUMPUS.]

ruction /rúksh'n/ *n.* QUARREL OR FIGHT a noisy, often violent, quarrel or fight ■ **ructions** *npl.* HEATED ARGUMENTS angry reactions, protests, or arguments ○ *There'll be ructions if the boss finds out!* [Early 18thC. Origin uncertain: perhaps an alteration of INSURRECTION.]

rudbeckia /rud békі ə/ (*plural* **-as** *or* **-a**) *n.* a North American plant with showy yellow flowers that have green or black centres. It has alternate leaves and belongs to the composite family of flowering plants. Genus: *Rudbeckia.* [Mid-19thC. From modern Latin, named after the Swedish botanists Olof *Rudbeck* the elder (1630–1702) and the younger (1660–1740).]

rudd /rud/ (*plural* **rudds** *or* **rudd**) *n.* a European freshwater fish of the carp family with a thin greenish-brown body and red fins. Latin name: *Scardinius erythrophthalmus.* [Early 16thC. Variant of obsolete *rud* 'redness'. Ultimately from a prehistoric Germanic word that is also the ancestor of English *red.*]

Rudd /rud/, **Steele** (1868–1935) Australian writer. He wrote comic sketches, collected in works such as *On Our Selection* (1899). Pseudonym of **Arthur Hoey Davis**

rudder /rúddər/ *n.* **1.** MEANS OF STEERING BOAT OR SHIP a means of steering a boat or ship, usually in the form of a pivoting blade under the water, mounted at the stern and controlled by a wheel or handle (**tiller**) **2.** AEROFOIL FOR STEERING AEROPLANE an aerofoil, usually on the tail of an aeroplane, that pivots vertically and controls left-to-right movement **3.** CONTROLLING FORCE a guiding or controlling force or influence [Old English *rōþer*. Ultimately from a prehistoric Germanic word that is also the ancestor of English *row.*] —**rudderless** *adj.*

rudderfish /rúddər fish/ (*plural* **-fish** *or* **-fishes**) *n.* a small-to-medium oval fish known for its habit of following oceangoing ships in schools. Family: Kyphosidae.

ruddle /rúdd'l/, **reddle** /rédd'l/, **raddle** /rádd'l/ *n.* COLOURING SUBSTANCE a type of red ochre used as a dye. It was formerly used to mark sheep. ■ *vt.* (**-dles, -dling, -dled**) COLOUR STH WITH RUDDLE to dye or mark sth such as a sheep with ruddle [Mid-16thC. Formed from obsolete *rud* (see RUDD).]

ruddy /rúddi/ *adj.* (**-dier, -diest**) **1.** ROSY WITH HEALTH with a healthy reddish glow ○ *ruddy cheeks* **2.** REDDISH red or reddish in colour ○ *ruddy sky* ■ *adj.* (**-dier, -diest**), *adv.* SWEARWORD used as a mild swearword to emphasize how good, bad, or severe sth is (*slang*) (*offensive in some contexts*) [Old English *rudig*. Ultimately from a prehistoric Germanic word that is also the ancestor of English *red.*] —**ruddily** *adv.* —**ruddiness** *n.*

ruddy duck *n.* a North American duck with a broad bill, upright tail, and white cheeks. During the mating season the male is brownish-red with a black crown and blue bill. Latin name: *Oxyura jamaicensis.*

rude /rood/ (**ruder, rudest**) *adj.* **1.** ILL-MANNERED disagreeable or discourteous in manner or action ○ *Don't be rude!* **2.** INDECENT offensive to accepted standards of decency ○ *rude words* **3.** UNREFINED lacking refinement or social skills **4.** SUDDEN AND UNPLEASANT happening with unexpected suddenness and unpleasantness ○ *a rude awakening* **5.** ROUGHLY MADE in a rough or incomplete state ○ *a rude wooden bench* **6.** UNSKILLED showing a lack of skill or training ○ *rude paintings* **7.** INEXPERIENCED without schooling or experience ○ *a rude youth raised in the wilderness* **8.** RAW in a raw or unprocessed state ○ *rude fibres* **9.** VAGUE lacking precision ○ *a rude guess* **10.** UNDEVELOPED technologically or economically undeveloped **11.** ROBUST strong and energetic ○ *in rude health* [13thC. Via French from Latin *rudis* 'raw, rough' (source of English *rudiment* and *erudite*).] —**rudely** *adv.* —**rudeness** *n.*

ruderal /róodərəl/ *adj.* GROWING IN RUBBISH growing in wasteland, rubbish, or disturbed ground ■ *n.* RUDERAL PLANT a plant that grows in wasteland, rubbish, or disturbed ground [Mid-19thC. Formed from the Latin stem *ruder-* 'rubble'.]

rudiment /róodimənt/ *n.* **1.** STH BASIC TO SUBJECT a basic principle or skill, especially in a particular field or subject (*often used in the plural*) ○ *the rudiments of computer programming* **2.** BEGINNING an early stage in the development of sth such as a plan (*often used in the plural*) **3.** BIOL UNDEVELOPED BODY PART a body part that does not develop fully and performs no useful function. The mammary gland in males is a rudiment. **4.** BIOL EMBRYO OF ORGAN an embryonic stage of an organ or body part [Mid-16thC. Directly or via French from, ultimately, Latin *rudis* (see RUDE).]

rudimentary /róodi méntəri/, **rudimental** /-mént'l/ *adj.* **1.** BASIC existing at an elementary or basic level **2.** DEVELOPING in an early or partially developed stage **3.** BIOL UNDEVELOPED not fully developed ○ *a rudimentary tail* **4.** BIOL IN FORM OF EMBRYO in an embryonic state — **rudimentarily** *adv.* —**rudimentariness** *n.*

Rudolf /róo dolf/, **Archduke and Crown Prince of Austria** (1858–89). The son of Franz Josef of Austria, he was a well-travelled patron of the arts. He was found dead with his lover, Baroness Marie Vetsera.

Rudolf I, King of Germany and Holy Roman Emperor (1218–91). His acquisition of Bohemian territories in 1278 greatly strengthened the house of Habsburg. He is considered the founder of the Habsburg dynasty.

Rudolf, Lake former name for **Turkana, Lake**

rue[1] /roo/ *vti.* (**rues, ruing, rued**) FEEL REGRET FOR to feel regret or sorrow for sth in the past ○ *I rue the day I offered to help.* ■ *n.* FEELING OF REGRET a feeling of regret or sorrow (*archaic*) [Old English *hrēowan*. Ultimately from a prehistoric Germanic word that also produced German *reuen* 'to repent'. Originally in the meaning 'to induce pity'.]

rue[2] /roo/ (*plural* **rues** *or* **rue**) *n.* a woody plant with small yellow flowers, native to Europe and Asia. Its bitter, strongly scented leaves yield an oil formerly used as a narcotic and stimulant. Latin name: *Ruta graveolens.* [14thC. Via French and Latin *ruta* from Greek *rhutē.*]

rueful /roóf'l/ adj. **1.** REGRETFUL feeling, showing, or causing regret **2.** INDUCING PITY causing people to feel pity —**ruefully** adv. —**ruefulness** n.

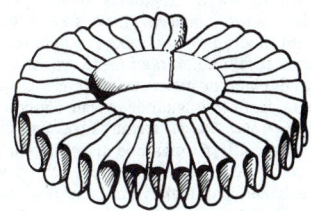

Ruff

ruff[1] /ruf/ n. **1.** FANCY PLEATED COLLAR a separate collar of starched pleated linen or lace worn by men and women from the middle of the 16th century to the early 17th century **2.** ZOOL NECK HAIR OR FEATHERS a growth of long, colourful, or bushy hair or feathers on the neck of a bird or other animal **3.** (plural **ruffs** or **ruff**) BIRDS BIRD WITH ELABORATE RUFF a bird of the sandpiper family, the male of which has a ruff of feathers that are erected during courtship displays. It is native to Europe and Asia. Latin name: *Philomachus pugnax*. [Early 16thC. Origin uncertain: probably a variant of ROUGH, or perhaps a shortening of RUFFLE.] —**ruffed** adj.

ruff[2] /ruf/ n. **1.** PLAYING OF TRUMP CARD in bridge or whist, the act of playing a trump card **2.** CARDS CARD GAME an old card game similar to whist ■ vti. (**ruffs, ruffing, ruffed**) PLAY TRUMP ON DIFFERENT SUIT in bridge or whist, to play a trump card on a card from a different suit [Late 16thC. From Old French *roffle*, a card game, of uncertain origin: perhaps from *renfler* 'to rise' (from, ultimately, Latin *inflare* 'to inflate'), or from Italian *trionfo* 'trump'.]

ruffe (plural **ruffes** or **ruffe**), **ruff** (plural **ruffs** or **ruff**) n. a small European freshwater fish of the perch family with a single spiny dorsal fin. Latin name: *Acerina cernua*. [15thC. Origin uncertain: probably a variant of ROUGH (from its rough scales).]

ruffian /rúffi ən/ n. ROUGH PERSON sb who behaves in a rough, bullying, or violent way, often a member of a gang of criminal thugs (dated) ■ adj. VIOLENT behaving in a rough, bullying, or violent way [15thC. Via French from, ultimately, Italian *ruffiano*, of Germanic origin.] —**ruffianism** n. —**ruffianly** adj.

ruffle[1] /rúf'l/ v. (**-fles, -fling, -fled**) **1.** vti. MAKE WAVES IN A SURFACE to disturb or ripple sth, especially a surface, or to become disturbed or rippled **2.** vti. ANNOY SB to bother or fluster sb, or to become bothered or flustered ○ gets ruffled so easily **3.** vt. MAKE FEATHERS ERECT to erect feathers, e.g. in defence, as a display, or for warmth or grooming **4.** vt. GLANCE QUICKLY THROUGH STH to flick rapidly through the pages of a book or magazine (dated) **5.** vt. SEW GATHER OR PLEAT to draw a strip of material into pleats or gathers to use as trim **6.** vt. CARDS SHUFFLE CARDS to shuffle playing cards (dated) ■ n. **1.** WAVE IN SURFACE a disturbance or ripple in sth, especially a surface **2.** IRRITATING THING a source of irritation or annoyance **3.** SEW TRIM OF PLEATED FABRIC a strip of closely pleated or gathered material used as trim **4.** ZOOL = **ruff**[1] n. 2 [14thC. Origin uncertain: perhaps thought to suggest the action.] —**ruffled** adj. —**ruffly** adj.

ruffle[2] /rúff'l/ n. LOW DRUMBEAT a low continuous drumbeat ■ vt. (**-fles, -fling, -fled**) BEAT RUFFLE ON A DRUM to play a ruffle on a drum [Early 18thC. Origin uncertain: probably an imitation of the sound.]

ruffle[3] /rúff'l/ (**-fles, -fling, -fled**) vi. to behave in an ostentatiously arrogant or boastful way (archaic) [15thC. Origin unknown. It disappeared by 1700 but was revived in the 19thC by Sir Walter Scott.]

rufiyaa /roo fèe yaa/ (plural **-yaa**) n. **1.** UNIT OF CURRENCY OF MALDIVES the main unit of currency in the Maldive Islands, worth 100 laari. See table at **currency 2.** NOTE WORTH ONE RUFIYAA a note worth one rufiyaa [Late 20thC. Via Maldivian from Hindi *rupiya* (see RUPEE).]

rug /rug/ n. **1.** FABRIC FLOOR COVERING a thick heavy fabric covering for a floor, especially one that is smaller than a carpet **2.** ANIMAL SKIN MAT an animal skin used as a mat or small carpet **3.** BLANKET a thick blanket, especially one formerly used by car or carriage passengers to cover their legs and feet **4.** HAIRPIECE a toupee or wig (informal) [Mid-16thC. Origin uncertain: probably from a Scandinavian word.]

ruga /roógə/ (plural **-gae** /roó jee, roó gī/) n. a natural crease or ridge in a body part, especially in the internal organs (often used in the plural) [Late 18thC. From Latin, 'wrinkle'.] —**rugate** /roó gayt/ adj.

Rugby: A player attempts a kick

rugby /rúgbi/, **rugby football** n. a team sport in which players run with an oval ball, pass it laterally from hand to hand, and kick it (often used before a noun) [Mid-19thC. Named after RUGBY School, where it was reputedly invented.]

Rugby /rúgbi/ town in Warwickshire, central England. Rugby School, a leading independent school, is located there. Population: 84,300 (1991).

Rugby League n. a form of rugby that has teams of 13 players

Rugby Union n. a form of rugby that has teams of 15 players

rugged /rúggid/ adj. **1.** WITH IRREGULAR SURFACE with a sharply rising and falling, rough, or jagged surface ○ over rugged terrain **2.** STRONG-FEATURED with furrowed facial features thought to suggest physical strength or strength of character, especially in men ○ their rugged faces **3.** PHYSICALLY RESILIENT physically strong enough to endure harsh conditions, or used to enduring them **4.** SEVERE IN MANNER harsh and forbidding in manner **5.** METEOROL STORMY affected by violent and dangerous storms **6.** LACKING REFINEMENT coarse or unrefined in behaviour **7.** TESTING requiring strength, skill, or endurance **8.** ENG STRONGLY BUILT designed and manufactured to withstand hard use or harsh environments [13thC. Origin uncertain: probably from a Scandinavian word. The underlying idea is of a bristled surface.] —**ruggedly** adv. —**ruggedness** n.

ruggedize /rúggi dīz/ (**-izes, -izing, -ized**), **ruggedise** (**-ises, -ising, -ised**) vt. to make sth such as a piece of equipment capable of withstanding rough treatment —**ruggedization** /rúggidī záysh'n/ n.

rugger /rúggər/ n. rugby (informal) [Late 19thC. Alteration of RUGBY. Originally upper-class slang.]

rugosa rose /roo gốssə-/ n. a common hedge rose that has not been cultivated. It is thorny with fragrant pink or white blossoms and is found across eastern North America. Latin name: *Rosa rugosa*. [Rugosa from Latin, the feminine form of *rugosus* (see RUGOSE).]

rugose /roó gōss, roó-, roo gốss/, **rugous** /roógəss/ adj. **1.** CREASED with creases, wrinkles, or ridges **2.** BOT WITH RIDGED SURFACE used to describe a leaf or other plant part that has a surface of alternating depressions and ridges [15thC. From Latin *rugosus*, from *ruga* 'wrinkle'.] —**rugosely** adv. —**rugosity** /roo gốssəti/ n.

rug rat n. an offensive term for a young child, especially an infant or toddler (slang offensive)

Ruhr /roor/ river in western Germany. The Ruhr valley contains the largest coalfield and industrial region in western Europe. Length: 235 km/146 mi.

ruin /roó in/ n. **1.** BROKEN REMAINS the physical remains of sth such as a building or city that has decayed or been destroyed (often used in the plural) **2.** COMPLETE DEVASTATION a state of complete destruction, decay, collapse, or loss ○ The buildings had gone to ruin. **3.** COMPLETE FAILURE complete moral, social, or economic failure ○ facing financial ruin **4.** SB OR STH DESTROYED sb or sth completely lost or destroyed **5.** CAUSE OF DESTRUCTION a cause of complete loss or destruction ○ Alcohol was their ruin. **6.** LOSS OF VIRGINITY a woman's loss of virginity to a man other than her husband (archaic) ■ **ruins** npl. COMPLETE DEVASTATION a state of complete destruction, decay, collapse, or loss ○ Her dreams lay in ruins. ■ v. (**-ins, -ining, -ined**) **1.** vt. DESTROY STH to cause sth to be destroyed or lost **2.** vt. DESTROY SB FINANCIALLY to bring about sb's financial demise **3.** vt. DAMAGE STH BEYOND REPAIR to spoil sth so severely that it cannot be restored **4.** vi. DECLINE to fall into a state of complete destruction or loss (literary) **5.** vt. SEDUCE THEN ABANDON A WOMAN to induce a woman to engage in sex before marriage, then abandon her (archaic) [14thC. Via French *ruine* from Latin *ruina*, from *ruere* 'to fall'.] —**ruined** adj. —**ruiner** n.

ruination /roó i náysh'n/ n. **1.** LOSS the destruction or loss of sth **2.** CAUSE OF LOSS sth that brings about destruction or loss

ruinous /roó inəss/ adj. **1.** DAMAGING causing severe damage or complete destruction or loss **2.** DECAYED decayed or deteriorated beyond repair —**ruinously** adv. —**ruinousness** n.

rule /rool/ n. **1.** PRINCIPLE GOVERNING CONDUCT an authoritative principle set forth to guide behaviour or action ○ the rules of the game **2.** NORM sth regarded as customary or normal **3.** USUAL CONDITION a prevailing condition or quality **4.** GOVERNING POWER a governing or reigning power ○ under Communist rule **5.** REIGN OR GOVERNMENT a period during which a person or group reigns or governs **6.** RELIG RELIGIOUS PRINCIPLES a body of principles governing a religious order or group ○ the Benedictine rule **7.** MATH METHOD OF CALCULATING a mathematical procedure for performing an operation or solving a problem **8.** = **ruler** n. 2 **9.** PRINTING LINE BETWEEN PRINTED COLUMNS a thin strip or design used for borders or for separating columns of type **10.** LAW LAW GOVERNING COURT PROCEDURE a law made to govern procedure in court **11.** LAW COURT ORDER an order issued by a court of law or by a judge ■ v. (**rules, ruling, ruled**) **1.** vti. GOVERN to exercise controlling authority over sb or sth ○ She ruled for almost 50 years. **2.** vti. DOMINATE to prevail or be the prevailing influence over sth ○ He let his heart rule his head. **3.** vt. MARK WITH LINES to make a straight line or mark sth with straight lines **4.** vt. CONTROL STH to subject sth to control or to restrain sth **5.** vti. LAW MAKE LEGAL DECISION to issue a legal decision or order ○ The judge ruled against the plaintiff. [13thC. Via French *riule* from, ultimately, Latin *regula* 'straight stick, standard' (source of English *regular* and *regulate*).] —**rulable** adj. —**ruleless** adj.

rule out vt. **1.** EXCLUDE STH to exclude sth or take a decision not to consider sth **2.** PREVENT STH to make sth impossible

rule of thumb n. **1.** COMMON PRACTICE a way of proceeding based on experience or sound judgment **2.** GENERALLY RELIABLE METHOD any practical, though not entirely accurate, method that can be relied on for an acceptable result [Said to derive from the workman's practice of using the thumb as a rough measure] —**rule-of-thumb** adj.

ruler /roólər/ n. **1.** SB WHO RULES sb such as a sovereign who governs a state or nation **2.** STRAIGHT TOOL FOR MEASURING AND DRAWING a strip of plastic, wood, or metal with at least one straight edge and units of length marked on it. It is used for measuring and for drawing straight lines.

ruling /roóling/ adj. **1.** IN POWER exercising controlling or governing authority ○ the ruling party **2.** MOST POWERFUL exerting the strongest influence ○ a ruling passion ■ n. LAW DECISION BY AUTHORITY an official or binding decision made, e.g., by a court or judge

rum[1] /rum/ n. **1.** SPIRIT MADE FROM SUGAR CANE an alcoholic spirit made from sugar cane or molasses. It can be clear but is usually coloured brownish-red by storage in oak casks or by the addition of caramel. **2.** US LIQUOR any intoxicating liquor [Mid-17thC. Shortening of obsolete *rumbullion*, of unknown origin.]

rum[2] /rum/ (**rummer, rummest**) *adj.* out of the ordinary (*dated informal*) [Late 18thC. Origin unknown.] —**rumly** *adv.* —**rumness** *n.*

Rum /rum/ island in the Inner Hebrides, northwestern Scotland. Area: 109 sq. km/42 sq. mi.

rumba /rúmbə, rŏŏm-/, **rhumba** *n.* **1. CUBAN DANCE** a rhythmically complex Cuban dance **2. RHYTHMIC BALLROOM DANCE** a ballroom dance based on the Cuban rumba. It is danced more or less on the spot, with exaggerated swinging of the hips. **3. MUSIC FOR RUMBA** a piece of music for or in the rhythm of a rumba ■ *vi.* (**-bas, -baing, -baed**) **DANCE RUMBA** to dance a rumba [Early 20thC. Via American Spanish and Spanish *rumbo* 'course, direction' from, ultimately, Latin *rhombus* 'rhombus'.]

rumble /rúmb'l/ *v.* (**-bles, -bling, -bled**) **1.** *vi.* **MAKE DEEP SOUND** to make a deep rolling sound ○ *thunder rumbling in the distance* **2.** *vi.* **MOVE NOISILY** to travel, e.g. along a road, with a deep rolling sound ○ *Trucks rumbled past.* **3.** *vt.* **UTTER WITH A RUMBLE** to say sth with a deep rolling voice **4.** *vt.* **FIND OUT ABOUT SB OR STH** to discover the truth about sb or sth (*informal*) ○ *We've been rumbled!* **5.** *vi. US, NZ* **BE IN A FIGHT** to be involved in a street fight, especially one between members of rival gangs (*slang*) **6.** *vt.* MINERALS, MECH ENG **TO CLEAN STONES OR METAL** to polish stones or metal in a rotating drum (**tumbler**) ■ *n.* **1. DEEP SOUND** a deep rolling sound **2. MURMUR OF DISSATISFACTION** a feeling of dissatisfaction quietly expressed by several people (*informal*) **3.** *US, NZ* **STREET FIGHT** a street fight, especially one fought by members of rival gangs (*slang*) **4.** MINERALS, MECH ENG = **tumbler** [14thC. Origin uncertain: probably from obsolete Dutch *rommelen*, an imitation of the sound.] —**rumbler** *n.* —**rumbly** *adj.*

rumble seat *n. US* = **dicky**

rumble strip *n.* a strip of textured road surface that alerts drivers by vibration or tyre noise to an approaching a junction, speed restriction or hazard

rumbling /rúmbling/ *n.* **1. DEEP SOUND** a deep rolling sound **2. FIRST INDICATION** an early sign of growing discontent, or an indication of an unpleasant event that is about to happen (*often used in the plural*) ■ *adj.* **MAKING DEEP SOUND** making a deep rolling sound ○ *rumbling stomach*

rumbustious /rum bússchəss/ *adj.* full of noisy uncontrollable exuberance [Late 18thC. Origin uncertain: probably an alteration of ROBUSTIOUS.] —**rumbustiously** *adv.* —**rumbustiousness** *n.*

rumen /rŏŏ men, rŏŏmən/ (*plural* **-mens** *or* **-mina** /rŏŏminə/) *n.* the large first chamber of a ruminant animal's stomach in which microorganisms break down plant cellulose before the food is returned to the mouth as cud for additional chewing [Early 18thC. From Latin.] —**ruminal** /rŏŏminəl/ *adj.*

ruminant /rŏŏminənt/ *n.* ZOOL **HOOFED ANIMAL THAT CHEWS CUD** any cud-chewing hoofed mammal with an even number of toes and a stomach with multiple chambers. Cattle, camels, and giraffes are ruminants. Suborder: Ruminantia. ■ *adj.* **1.** ZOOL **OF RUMINANTS** relating or belonging to the suborder of animals that chew the cud **2. THOUGHTFUL** inclined to be thoughtful and reflective [Mid-17thC. From the present participle stem of Latin *ruminare* (see RUMINATE).] —**ruminantly** *adv.*

ruminate /rŏŏmi nayt/ (**-nates, -nating, -nated**) *v.* **1.** *vi.* ZOOL **CHEW PARTIALLY DIGESTED FOOD** to regurgitate partially digested food and chew it again (*refers to ruminants*) **2.** *vti.* **MULL STH OVER** to think carefully and at length about sth [Mid-16thC. From Latin *ruminat-*, the past participle stem of *ruminare*, from *rumen* 'rumen'.] —**rumination** /rŏŏmi náysh'n/ *n.* —**ruminative** /rŏŏminətiv/ *adj.* —**ruminatively** *adv.*

rummage /rúmmij/ *v.* (**-mages, -maging, -maged**) **1.** *vti.* **GO THROUGH THINGS LOOKING FOR STH** to make a rapid search for or through sth by carelessly moving and disarranging things **2.** *vt.* **FIND STH** to find sth by searching ■ *n.* **1. THOROUGH SEARCH** a thorough search for or through sth **2.** *US* = **jumble 3. GROUP OF THINGS** a miscellaneous collection of items [15thC. Via Old French *arrumage* 'arrangement of cargo in a ship' from, ultimately, *run* 'ship's hold', from Dutch *ruim* 'space'.] —**rummager** *n.*

rummage sale *n. US* = **jumble sale**

rummer /rúmmər/ *n.* a large drinking glass, especially one with a short stem [Mid-17thC. Directly or via German *Römer* from Dutch *roemer*, from *roemen* 'to praise'.]

rummy[1] /rúmmi/ *n.* a card game in which the players try to get three or more cards of the same rank or a sequence of three or more cards of the same suit [Early 20thC. Origin unknown.]

rummy[2] /rúmmi/ *n.* (*plural* **-mies**) *Can, US* **DRUNKARD** a drunkard (*slang*) ■ *adj.* **OF OR LIKE RUM** tasting or smelling of rum, or similar to rum in smell or taste

rumor *n., vt. US* = **rumour**

rumour /rŏŏmər/ *n.* **1. UNVERIFIED REPORT** a generally circulated story, report, or statement without facts to confirm its truth **2. IDLE SPECULATION** general talk or opinion of uncertain reliability **3. UPROAR** a loud noise or disturbance (*archaic*) ■ *vt.* (**-mours, -mouring, -moured**) **TO PASS ON RUMOURS** to pass along information by rumour (*usually passive*) ○ *It is rumoured that they are leaving the company.* [14thC. Via Old French *rumur* from Latin *rumor* 'noise, rumour'.]

rumourmonger /rŏŏmər mung gər/ *n.* **SB SPREADING RUMOURS** sb who habitually spreads rumours ■ *vi.* (**-gers, -gering, -gered**) **SPREAD RUMOURS** to participate actively in spreading rumours

rump /rump/ *n.* **1.** ZOOL **ANIMAL'S HINDQUARTERS** the fleshy hindquarters of a four-legged mammal, not including its legs **2.** FOOD **BEEF FROM THE HINDQUARTERS** a cut of beef that is tender and contains some fat, taken from the rump ○ *rump steak* **3. BUTTOCKS** sb's buttocks (*informal*) **4.** LAW **REMAINS OF LEGISLATURE** the remnant of a legislative body after the majority of its members have resigned or been expelled **5.** BIRDS **BIRD'S TAIL END** the lower part of a bird's back, nearest the tail. It is sometimes coloured distinctively. [15thC. Origin uncertain: probably from a Scandinavian language.]

rumple /rúmp'l/ *vti.* (**-ples, -pling, -pled**) **MAKE OR BECOME UNKEMPT** to take on a dishevelled appearance, or to make clothes or hair untidy, e.g. by creasing clothes or pulling hair out of style ■ *n.* **A CREASE** a wrinkle or crease [Early 16thC. Origin uncertain: perhaps from Dutch *rumpelen*.]

rumpus /rúmpəss/ *n.* an outcry or noisy disturbance [Mid-18thC. Origin unknown.]

rumpus room *n. Can, ANZ, US* a room in a house for recreational activities such as parties and children's play

run /run/ *v.* (**runs, running, ran** /ran/, **run**) **1.** *vi.* **GO AT FAST PACE** to move rapidly on foot so that both feet are momentarily off the ground in each step **2.** *vi.* **GALLOP** to go at a fast pace in which all four feet are momentarily off the ground in each stride (*refers to four-footed animals*) **3.** *vt.* **TRAVEL DISTANCE BY RUNNING** to cover a particular distance while running **4.** *vti.* **PARTICIPATE IN RACE** to compete in a race on foot, or on a horse or other animal **5.** *vt.* **ENTER ANIMAL IN RACE** to enter a horse or other animal in a race **6.** *vti. Can, US* **BE A CANDIDATE** to be a candidate, or enter sb as a candidate, in an election ○ *running for president* **7.** *vi.* **BE IN RELATIVE POSITION** to be or end in a particular position, e.g. in a race, election, or contest ○ *running behind until the last lap* **8.** *vt.* **PERFORM STH** to carry out or accomplish sth ○ *run a test* **9.** *vi.* **LEAVE QUICKLY** to leave a place quickly or in a hurry, usually in order to escape notice or capture ○ *take the money and run* **10.** *vi.* **MOVE FREELY** to move around without restraint ○ *allow the cats to run* **11.** *vt.* **SPEED ACROSS STH** to travel quickly across, over, or through sth ○ *running the rapids* **12.** *vt.* **TRANSPORT SB OR STH** to take or transport sb or sth, usually by motor vehicle ○ *ran me into town* **13.** *vi.* **GO TO FOR HELP** to turn to sb for assistance, especially in desperation or as a dependant to a protector ○ *He always runs to his brother for money.* **14.** *vi.* **VISIT** to make a brief trip or visit somewhere ○ *ran out to the mountains for the weekend* **15.** *vti.* **MOVE SMOOTHLY** to pass, or cause sth to pass, quickly or smoothly through or over sth ○ *ropes running easily through the pulleys* **16.** *vi.* **COME INTO PARTICULAR STATE** to enter into a particular state or condition ○ *Supplies were running low.* **17.** *vti.* **OPERATE** to be functioning, or to put or leave sth in a functioning mode ○ *Let the engine run.* **18.** *vt.* **CONTROL STH** to direct the activities, affairs, or operation of sth ○ *responsible for running the whole department* **19.** *vti.* **POUR OR FLOW** to flow, or cause water or another liquid to flow from or to sth ○ *run a tap* **20.** *vi.* MED **RELEASE MUCUS** to discharge a fluid such as pus or mucus ○ *a nose that was constantly running* **21.** *vti.* **GO BACK AND FORTH** to travel, or cause sb or sth to travel, regularly over a set route ○ *running a shuttle between stations* **22.** *vi.* **ROLL FREELY** to roll unhindered or unchecked ○ *could only stand and watch it run down the hill* **23.** *vti.* **GO OR TAKE OFF COURSE** to deviate, or allow sth such as a ship or car to deviate, from the usual or proper course ○ *run a car off the road* **24.** *vi.* **SPREAD OR LEAK UNDESIRABLY** to spread as a result of unwanted dissolving or mixing ○ *The red stripes ran into the white.* **25.** *vi.* **RANGE** to range between particular limits ○ *The work ran from difficult to impossible.* **26.** *vi.* **KEEP COMPANY** to associate with a particular person or group **27.** *vti.* **EXTEND STH** to route sth or be routed in a particular direction or for a particular distance ○ *They plan to run the cable under the road.* **28.** *vi.* **CONTINUE A TIME** to continue for a particular length or period ○ *a report running to ten pages* **29.** *vti.* PUBL, BROADCAST **SHOW PUBLICLY** to print, broadcast, or exhibit sth, or to be printed, broadcast, or exhibited ○ *run a news story* **30.** *vt.* **EXPERIENCE STH** to experience, undergo, or be subject to sth ○ *a child running a high temperature* **31.** *vti.* **BE COVERED WITH STH** to be covered or flowing with sth ○ *The valley ran lava.* **32.** *vti.* **TOTAL** to total a particular amount ○ *The bill runs to four figures.* **33.** *vt.* **BREACH STH** to break through a barrier of some kind ○ *run a checkpoint* **34.** *vi.* **BE WORDED** to be worded in a particular way ○ *in a statement that runs as follows* **35.** *vi.* **EXHIBIT TENDENCY** to tend or be inclined in a particular direction ○ *His tastes in art run towards abstractions.* **36.** *vi.* **BE RECURRENT** to appear recurrently as a feature or quality ○ *Stubbornness runs in the family.* **37.** *vi.* **BE COMMUNICATED** to be communicated from person to person ○ *a story running round the office* **38.** *vti.* **SUSTAIN DAMAGE THROUGH UNRAVELLING STITCHES** to come undone, causing damage to a garment (*refers to stitches*) **39.** *vi.* **REMAIN LEGALLY VALID** to continue to have force in law ○ *The contract has a year to run.* **40.** *vt.* **TRADE GOODS ILLEGALLY** to import or export goods illegally ○ *running guns to the rebels* **41.** *vi.* ZOOL **GO UPSTREAM TO SPAWN** to migrate in large numbers, usually upstream, to spawn (*refers to fish*) **42.** *vti.* AMERICAN FOOTBALL **CARRY FOOTBALL DOWNFIELD** to advance the football while running as opposed to passing **43.** *vt.* METALL **PRODUCE METAL BY CASTING** to cast or mould molten metal ■ *n.* **1. FAST PACE** a rapid pace faster than a walk or jog **2. GALLOPING PACE** an animal's fastest pace **3. SPELL OF RUNNING** a spell of running, especially for pleasure or exercise **4. RACE** a race in which the competitors run **5. REGULAR TRIP** a regular or scheduled trip or route ○ *the run to work each day* **6. TRIP FOR PLEASURE** a trip in a vehicle, especially for pleasure ○ *went for a run along the coast road* **7. DISTANCE OR TIME COVERED** a distance or period covered while travelling or running **8. ERRAND** a brief trip made in order to get sth **9. FREE USE OF A PLACE** unrestricted access to, use of, and movement around a place ○ *given the run of the whole house* **10. UNINTERRUPTED PERIOD** an extended period during which a particular condition or circumstance prevails ○ *a run of bad luck* **11.** MANUF, PRINTING **QUANTITY MANUFACTURED** an amount of sth produced in a period of continuous operation of a machine or factory ○ *an initial print run of five thousand copies* **12.** MANUF **OPERATING PERIOD** a period of continuous operation of a machine or factory **13.** CARDS **SEQUENCE OF CARDS** in card games, a sequence of playing cards in one suit **14.** CUE GAMES **SUCCESSIVE SHOTS** a series of successful shots in some games such as billiards **15.** ARTS **SERIES OF PERFORMANCES** a series of continuous showings or performances **16. URGENT REQUIREMENT** a sudden large demand for sth such as goods or payment ○ *Rumours of a shortage led to a run on coffee.* **17. FLOW** a flow of liquid **18. PIPE FOR LIQUID** a channel or pipe in which a liquid flows **19. PERIOD OF FLOW** a period during which a liquid flows **20. AMOUNT OF LIQUID** an amount of liquid in a flow **21.** SPORTS **STEEP ROUTE** a sloping course or track for a particular activity ○ *a ski run* **22.** SPORTS **PASSAGE DOWN TRACK** a single trip along a course or down a slope **23. DIRECTION STH LIES IN** the natural direction of a pattern in sth, e.g. wood grain **24. TENDENCY** the general direction in which things or events are moving ○ *the usual run of things* **25. STH ORDINARY** an average or typical kind of person or thing ○ *the general run of merchandise* **26. UNRAVELLING OF STITCHES** a damaged section of a stocking or other knitted garment caused by unravelling stitches **27.** AGRIC **ANIMAL ENCLOSURE** an outdoor enclosure for domestic animals, often one attached to or used as a temporary break from a standard enclosure that allows less freedom of movement **28.** ZOOL **ANIMAL TRAIL** a trail followed regularly by a group or herd of animals **29. REPORTER'S TERRITORY** a media reporter's regular territory **30.** MUSIC **RAPID MUSICAL PASSAGE** a rapid musical scale or melodic passage, especially one for the piano **31.** CRICKET **POINT SCORED IN CRICKET** a point scored in cricket, usually when one or both batsmen run between the wickets **32.** BASEBALL **SCORE IN BASEBALL** a score in baseball made by travelling round all the bases to home plate ■ **runs** *n.* MED **DIARRHOEA** an attack of diarrhoea (*informal; takes a singular or plural verb*) ○ *have the runs* ■ *adj.* **1. MELTED** in a melted state **2. WORN OUT** exhausted or out of breath, especially from running [Old English *rinnan*. Ultimately from a prehistoric Germanic word that is also the ancestor of English *runnel*.] ◇ **be on the run** to be fleeing from sth, especially the law ◇ **give sb a run for his** *or* **her money** to provide sb with some serious, sometimes unexpected, competition ◇ **run yourself** *or* **sb ragged** to work yourself or sb else to the point of exhaustion

run about *vi.* to move hurriedly from place to place

run across *vt.* to meet sb or find sth unexpectedly

run after *vt.* **1. PURSUE SB OR STH** to chase after sb or sth **2. PURSUE SB ROMANTICALLY** to pursue sb romantically or sexually (*informal*)

run along *vi.* to go away (*usually used as a command*)

run around *vi.* (*informal*) **1. BE PROMISCUOUS** to behave promiscuously **2. ASSOCIATE** to spend a lot of time with sb ○ *running around with a bad crowd*

run away *vi.* to escape or flee from sb or sth

run away with *vt.* **1. TAKE STH AND LEAVE** to steal sth and escape with it **2. ELOPE WITH SB** to leave secretly with a lover, especially in order to marry **3. TAKE CONTROL OF SB** to cause sb to lose self-control ○ *His excitement ran away with him.* **4. WIN EASILY** to win a competition, contest, or election easily

run by, run past *vt.* to tell sb about sth in order to find out his or her opinions or ideas about it ○ *Could I run these figures by you before I send them out?*

run down *v.* **1.** *vti.* **STOP FUNCTIONING** to lose power and cease to function, or allow a device to lose its power **2.** *vt.* **HIT SB WITH A VEHICLE** to knock sb or sth to the ground with a vehicle **3.** *vti.* **REDUCE** to shrink in size or amount, or reduce the size or amount of sth **4.** *vt.* **BELITTLE SB** to speak of sb in a disparaging or critical manner **5.** *vt.* **CATCH SB EVENTUALLY** to find or capture sb after a long search or chase **6.** *vt.* US **TRACE STH** to find the source of sth ○ *run down a lead* **7.** *vt.* **READ STH QUICKLY** to read or review sth quickly **8.** *vt.* SHIPPING **CAUSE SHIP TO SINK** to collide with a ship and cause it to sink **9.** *vt.* BASEBALL **REMOVE BASEBALL PLAYER** to chase and tag out a base runner trapped between two bases

run in *v.* **1.** *vt.* **TREAT VEHICLE CAREFULLY WHILE STILL NEW** to operate a new vehicle or engine carefully until it is functioning efficiently **2.** *vt.* **ARREST SB** to take sb into police custody (*informal*) **3.** *vi.* US **VISIT** to pay sb a casual visit (*informal*) **4.** *vt.* PRINTING **ADD STH AS TEXT** to insert additional text in printed matter

run into *v.* **1.** *vt.* **MEET SB BY CHANCE** to meet sb unexpectedly **2.** *vti.* **COLLIDE WITH STH** to have, cause, or allow a collision between people or things **3.** *vt.* **ENCOUNTER STH** to encounter sth unanticipated, usually problems or trouble **4.** *vt.* **AMOUNT TO STH** to add up to sth or be approximately equal to sth ○ *left debts running into millions*

run off *v.* **1.** *vi.* **LEAVE IN HASTE** to leave quickly without notifying anyone **2.** *vt.* **MAKE COPIES** to produce or print copies, e.g. on a photocopier **3.** *vt.* **FORCE SB TO LEAVE** to force trespassers off property **4.** *vt.* **SETTLE TIED CONTEST** to settle a tied competition or election by running a final deciding contest

run off with *vt.* **1.** **STEAL STH** to steal and escape with sth **2.** **ELOPE WITH SB** to leave secretly with a lover, especially in order to marry

run on *v.* **1.** *vi.* **TALK AT LENGTH** to talk at length, especially about trivial things **2.** *vi.* **CONTINUE** to continue without interruption, often boringly or frustratingly **3.** *vt.* PRINTING **PRINT TEXT WITHOUT PARAGRAPH BREAK** to print or typeset following text without a paragraph break

run out *v.* **1.** *vi.* **COME TO AN END** to be consumed completely ○ *Time is running out.* **2.** *vi.* **EXHAUST SUPPLIES** to consume all of a supply of sth ○ *We've run out of milk.* **3.** *vi.* **BECOME INVALID** to become invalid because of time restrictions **4.** *vt.* US **CHASE SB AWAY** to expel sb using force **5.** *vt.* CRICKET **DISMISS RUNNING BATSMAN** in cricket, to dismiss a player who is trying to complete a run by breaking the wicket with the ball at the end he or she is running to

run out on *vt.* to leave sb or sth in a helpless state or at a time when support is needed (*informal*)

run over *v.* **1.** *vt.* **KNOCK SB DOWN WITH VEHICLE** to hit sb or sth with a vehicle while driving it **2.** *vi.* **OVERFLOW** to overflow the limits or capacity of a container **3.** *vti.* **TAKE LONGER THAN PLANNED** to go beyond a limit or time previously set **4.** *vt.* **REVIEW STH** to examine or consider sth again, especially reviewing its main points

run through *vt.* **1.** **USE STH UP** to exhaust a supply of sth, especially money, quickly and without much consideration **2.** **REVIEW STH** to examine or consider sth again, especially reviewing its main points **3.** ARTS **REHEARSE STH QUICKLY** to read or perform at speed the whole or part of a play, script, piece of music, lecture or other prepared text in order to rehearse it **4.** ARMS **STAB SB WITH SWORD** to push a sword all the way through sb's body (*literary*)

run to *vt.* **1.** **BE SUFFICIENT FOR** to be or have sufficient resources for sth ○ *finances might run to two holidays this year* **2.** **AMOUNT TO** to have the specified length

run up *vt.* **1.** FIN **INCUR AS EXPENSE** to amass or accumulate a large expense **2.** SEW **SEW** to make sth, usually a garment, by means of fast sewing **3.** **RAISE ON FLAGPOLE** to hoist a flag on a flagpole

run up against *vt.* to suddenly encounter an unexpected problem

runabout /rúnnə bowt/ *n.* **1. SMALL VEHICLE** a small car, motorboat, or aircraft, especially one used for short trips **2. WANDERER** sb who moves from place to place

runaround /rún ə rownd/ *n.* **1. DELAYING OR MISLEADING TACTICS** inconvenience deliberately engineered in order to mislead or delay sb (*informal*) ○ *They've been giving me the runaround.* **2.** PRINTING **ARRANGEMENT OF TYPE ROUND A PICTURE** an arrangement of printed type in which lines are shortened to leave room for an illustration or symbol

runaway /rúnnə way/ *n.* **SB WHO ESCAPES** sb who leaves a place, e.g. to escape confinement or harm (*often used before a noun*) ■ *adj.* **1. OUT OF CONTROL** moving too fast to be stopped or controlled **2. EASILY WON** won by an overwhelming margin (*informal*)

Runaway, Cape /rúnnə way/ *cape on the northeastern coast of the North Island, New Zealand, situated at the eastern end of the Bay of Plenty

runcible spoon /rúnssib'l-/ *n.* a fork with three curved prongs, one of which is sharp ['Runcible' is a nonsense word coined by Edward Lear in *The Owl and the Pussy Cat* (1871)]

Runcorn /rún kawrn/ town and port in Cheshire, England, on the River Mersey. It was designated a new town in 1964. Population: 65,100 (1993).

rundown /rún down/ *n.* **1. REVIEW** a summary of the main points of a subject **2. CONTROLLED REDUCTION** a deliberate and controlled decrease in size, amount, or production (*often used before a noun*)

run-down *adj.* **1. EXHAUSTED** tired out, e.g. from overwork or poor health **2. SHABBY** in poor repair from neglect or hard use **3. OUT OF POWER** depleted of energy or power and unable to operate

Rundstedt /rúnt shtet/, **Karl Rudolf Gerd von** (1875–1953) German military commander. He led the German offensives on the Western Front (1942–44) during World War II.

rune /roon/ *n.* **1. LANGUAGE OLD GERMANIC ALPHABET CHARACTER** a character in any of several ancient Germanic alphabets used from about the 3rd to the 13th centuries. The earliest Anglo-Saxon texts and inscriptions were written in runes. **2. MAGICAL SYMBOL OR SPELL** a mysterious symbol, inscription, or incantation, especially one believed to have magical power **3.** POETRY **POEM IN FINNISH** a Finnish poem or stanza [Old English *rūn*. From a prehistoric Germanic word that also produced German *raunen* 'to whisper'. Its 'runic

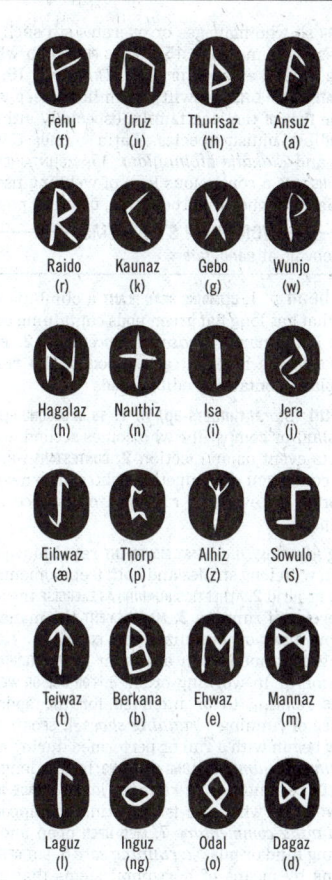

Rune

character' sense, once obsolete, was reintroduced from Old Norse *rún* in the 17thC.] —**runic** *adj.*

rung[1] /rung/ *n.* **1. LADDER STEP** any of the steps of a ladder **2. CROSSPIECE OF CHAIR** a horizontal bar used to strengthen the legs of a chair or stool **3. LEVEL IN HIERARCHY** a position in a hierarchy, e.g. of a profession **4. CUDGEL** a staff or cudgel (*regional*) **5.** NAUT **PART OF SHIP'S WHEEL** a spoke or handle on the wheel of a ship by which the wheel is turned [Old English *hrung*. Ultimately from a prehistoric Germanic word that also produced German *Runge* 'rung'.]

rung[2] past participle of **ring**

run-in *n.* **1. ARGUMENT** a heated argument or quarrel (*informal*) **2.** PRINTING **ADDITION TO PRINTED TEXT** a section of text added to a page that has already been typeset or printed

runnel /rúnn'l/ *n.* **1. STREAM** a small brook or stream **2. WATER CHANNEL** any narrow channel for water such as a gutter [Late 16thC. Alteration of obsolete *rindle*. Ultimately from a prehistoric Germanic word that is also the ancestor of English *run*.]

runner /rúnnər/ *n.* **1. RACER** sb or sth that runs, especially an athlete or a horse in a flat race **2.** POL **CANDIDATE** sb entered as a candidate in an election **3. STRIP UNDER A SLEDGE** either of the long blades beneath a sledge or sleigh, on which it rides **4. SKATE BLADE** the blade of an ice skate **5. CARPET STRIP** a long narrow piece of carpet **6. FABRIC STRIP** a strip of fabric, often linen or lace, used to protect or decorate the top of a piece of furniture such as a dressing table **7. DOOR OR DRAWER SLIDE** a guide on which a drawer or door slides **8. MESSENGER** sb who carries messages or does errands for a bank, brokerage firm, or other business **9.** BOT **CREEPING STEM THAT GROWS ROOTS** a thin horizontal stem that grows roots from nodes at regular intervals **10.** BOT **PLANT GROWING FROM STEM NODES** a plant such as a strawberry that has runners or grows by runners **11.** BOT **CLIMBING PLANT** a plant that climbs and twists, e.g. a bean plant **12. SMUGGLER** sb involved in smuggling (*often used in combination*) ○ *gun runner* **13.** SHIPPING **SMUGGLER'S VESSEL** a boat or ship used for smuggling (*often used in combination*) **14.**

OPERATOR sb who manages or operates sth such as a business or a machine **15.** FLEEING PERSON sb who is fleeing, e.g. an escaped prisoner (*informal*) **16.** ZOOL DEEP-WATER MARINE FISH a swift streamlined deep-water marine fish of the jack family, especially either of two edible bluish species. Latin name: *Caranx crysos* and *Elagatis bipinnulata.* **17.** MOUNTAINEERING ANCHORING LOOP a continuous loop of webbing used to provide an anchor to a rock, tree, or other point

WORD KEY: SYNONYMS

See Synonyms at ***candidate***.

runner bean *n.* **1.** CLIMBING BEAN PLANT a climbing bean plant that has long flat green pods containing edible seeds. Latin name: *Phaseolus coccineus.* **2.** POD OF RUNNER BEAN the long flat green pod of the runner bean plant, containing edible seeds

runner-up (*plural* **runners-up**) *n.* **1.** SB IN SECOND PLACE a contestant or competitor who comes second, e.g. in a sports event or an election **2.** CONTESTANT WHO DOES WELL a contestant or competitor who comes near the winner in an event or race and often receives a small prize

running /rúnning/ *n.* **1.** FAST MOVEMENT rapid movement on foot, with long strides and both feet momentarily off the ground **2.** ATHLETICS RUNNING AS EXERCISE the sport or exercise of running **3.** MANAGEMENT the managing of a business or organization ■ *adj.* **1.** FLOWING flowing continuously in a stream **2.** FUNCTIONING in operation or in working order **3.** FOR USE OR WEAR BY RUNNERS relating to or intended for the sport or exercise of running ○ *running shoes* **4.** SPORTS WHILE RUNNING begun with a run or performed during a run ○ *a running jump* **5.** LONG-STANDING begun long ago and still continuing ○ *a running joke* **6.** MADE DURING AN EVENT made while sth is operating or happening ○ *a running commentary* **7.** MED OPEN open and discharging fluid or pus ○ *a running sore* **8.** BOT CREEPING growing by means of horizontal stems that creep along the ground **9.** AMERICAN FOOTBALL GAINING YARDS WHILE RUNNING advancing the ball while running rather than passing ■ *adv.* CONSECUTIVELY in succession ○ *for five days running* [Old English] ◇ **be in** *or* **out of the running** to have or not have a chance of success

running board *n.* a narrow step beneath the doors of some motor vehicles, typically vintage cars

running hand *n.* handwriting done without lifting the pen or pencil from the writing surface

running head, **running title** *n.* a heading printed on every page or every other page of a book

running light *n.* a light displayed on a ship or aircraft at night to show its location and size

running mate *n.* **1.** *US* POL NOMINEE FOR LESSER OFFICE a candidate for the lesser of two associated political offices, e.g. a vice-presidential candidate **2.** HORSE-RACING PACESETTING HORSE in horseracing, a horse that is entered in a race for the purpose of setting the pace for a stronger horse from the same stable

running stitch *n.* a simple sewing stitch that goes down and up evenly through cloth without being looped

running title *n.* PUBL = **running head**

runny /rúnni/ (**-nier, -niest**) *adj.* **1.** OF A LIQUID CONSISTENCY of a liquid or semiliquid consistency that pours or flows **2.** WATERY of a consistency that is too thin **3.** RELEASING MUCUS producing excessive flowing mucus ○ *a runny nose*

Runnymede /rúnni meed/ meadow on the southern bank of the River Thames, near Windsor, south-eastern England. King John granted Magna Carta there in 1215.

runoff /rún of/ *n.* **1.** GEOG WATER NOT ABSORBED BY SOIL rainfall that does not soak into the soil but flows into surface waters **2.** ENVIRON, MANUF, AGRIC WATER POLLUTION agricultural or industrial waste products that are carried by rainfall and melting snow into surface waters **3.** SPORTS, POL SECOND CONTEST TO DETERMINE THE WINNER an election, race, or other contest held after an earlier one that produced no clear winner

run-of-the-mill *adj.* with no exceptional or distinguishing qualities

run-on *adj.* PRINTING ON THE SAME LINE added to a line of text without a line break ■ *n.* **1.** PRINTING TEXT ADDED WITHOUT A LINE BREAK an added section of text that continues a line, without a line break **2.** LING WORD UNDERSTOOD BUT UNDEFINED an undefined word appearing at the end of a dictionary entry, whose meaning can be understood from the previous defined senses (*often used before a noun*)

run past *vt.* = **run by**

runrig /rúnnrig/ *n. Scotland* SHARED LAND USE IN SCOTLAND formerly in Scotland, a system of land-sharing in which tenants each worked several separate strips (**rigs**) of land allocated by lot each year ■ *adv.* ON RUNRIG SYSTEM using a runrig system [15thC. From RUN + *rig*.]

runt /runt/ *n.* **1.** SMALLEST ANIMAL an animal that is considerably smaller than others of the same kind, especially the smallest or weakest animal in a litter **2.** OFFENSIVE TERM an offensive term for a short person or sb regarded as lacking physical strength (*informal insult*) **3.** PIGEON a large domestic pigeon [Mid-16thC. Origin uncertain: perhaps from Dutch *rund* 'bull, cow, small ox'.] —**runtiness** *n.* —**runtish** *adj.* —**runty** *adj.*

run-through *n.* **1.** REHEARSAL a practice or rehearsal of sth, especially a dramatic performance **2.** BRIEF SURVEY a brief review of sth such as an agenda or report

run time *n.* **1.** = **execution time 2.** RUNNING TIME OF PROGRAM the time during which a program runs **3.** PROGRAM VERSION WITH LIMITED FUNCTIONS a version of a computer program that allows a user to perform some, but not all, of the program's functions (*hyphenated when used before a noun*) ○ *a run-time module*

run-up *n.* **1.** RUN PRECEDING STH a run taken to gather momentum, e.g. for a jump or kick in an athletics or sports event **2.** TIME IMMEDIATELY BEFORE STH the period of time that leads up to an important event

runway /rún way/ *n.* **1.** STRIP FOR AIRCRAFT LANDINGS AND TAKEOFFS a long wide level roadway or other strip of land on which aircraft land and take off **2.** EXTENSION OF STAGE INTO AUDIENCE a narrow ramp or platform that is part of a stage and extends into the auditorium of a theatre or nightclub **3.** *US* CHUTE FOR LOGS a chute down which logs are slid **4.** TRACK a track, passageway, or channel along which sth runs

Damon Runyon

Runyon /rúny'n/, **Damon** (1884–1946) US journalist and short story writer. His writings, mainly about low life, are distinguished by their use of slang and colourful characterizations. Full name **Alfred Damon Runyon**

rupee /roo pée/ *n.* **1.** CURRENCY OF INDIA AND PAKISTAN the standard unit of currency in India, Pakistan, the Maldive Islands, Mauritius, Nepal, Bhutan, the Seychelles, and Sri Lanka. See table at **currency 2.** NOTE WORTH A RUPEE a note worth a rupee [Early 17thC. From Hindi *rūpiyā*, from Sanskrit *rūpya*, 'wrought silver', from *rūpa*, 'shape'.]

Rupert (of the Rhine) /róopət/, **Prince** (1619–82) German prince. A nephew of Charles I of England, he took part in the English Civil War and was a founder of the Hudson's Bay Company.

Rupes Recta /róopez réktə/ *n.* a fault on the surface of the Moon running north – south for 120 km/75 mi. along the eastern edge of Mare Nubium

rupiah /roo pée ə/ (*plural* **-ahs** *or* **-ah**) *n.* **1.** UNIT OF INDONESIAN CURRENCY the standard unit of currency in Indonesia. See table at **currency 2.** NOTE WORTH A RUPIAH a note worth one rupiah [Mid-20thC. Via Malay from Hindi *rūpiyā* (see RUPEE).]

rupicolous /roo píkələss/ *adj.* used to describe organisms that live or grow on or among rocks [Mid-19thC. Formed from Latin *rupi-* 'rock, cliff' + -COLOUS.]

rupture /rúpchər/ *n.* **1.** BROKEN STATE OF STH a break in or breaking apart of sth ○ *a rupture in the fabric of the balloon* **2.** TORN TISSUE a tear in or tearing of bodily tissue ○ *the rupture of a blood vessel* **3.** = **hernia 4.** BREACH IN RELATIONS a breakdown in a friendly or peaceful relationship ■ *vti.* (**-tures, -turing, -tured**) **1.** BREAK, BURST, OR TEAR STH to break, burst, or tear sth or to become broken, burst, or torn **2.** CAUSE RIFT IN RELATIONSHIP to cause or undergo a breakdown in a friendly or peaceful relationship **3.** TEAR TISSUE to cause or suffer a tearing of bodily tissue **4.** PRODUCE OR HAVE HERNIA to cause or suffer a hernia [15thC. Via Old French from Latin *ruptura*, from *rumpere* 'to break'.] —**rupturable** *adj.*

WORD KEY: ORIGIN

Latin *rumpere*, from which ***rupture*** is derived, is also the source of English *corrupt, disrupt, erupt, rout, route,* and *routine.*

rural /róorəl/ *adj.* **1.** OUTSIDE THE CITY found in or living in the country **2.** TYPICAL OF COUNTRY relating to or characteristic of the country or of country living **3.** AGRICULTURAL relating to, characteristic of, or involving farming [15thC. Via Old French from Latin *rural-*, from *rur-*, stem of *rus* 'country, countryside' (source of English *rustic*).] —**rurality** /roor rálləti/ *n.* —**rurally** /róorəli/ *adv.*

rural dean *n.* a clergyman with authority over the clergy of a number of parishes

rural district *n.* formerly, an administrative division of a county in England, Wales, and Northern Ireland, abolished in the 1970s

ruralise *vti.* = **ruralize**

ruralist /róorəlist/ *n.* **1.** SB LIVING IN COUNTRY sb who lives in the country **2.** SB FAVOURING RURAL LIFE sb who supports or promotes a rural lifestyle and rural interests

ruralize /róorə līz/ (**-izes, -izing, -ized**), **ruralise** (**-ises, -ising, -ised**) *v.* **1.** *vt.* MAKE STH RURAL to make sth rural in character or habit **2.** *vi.* LIVE IN COUNTRYSIDE to live or pass time in the country after having lived in a city or town —**ruralization** /róorə lī záysh'n/ *n.*

Rurik /róorik/ *n.* a Scandinavian leader who died in AD 879 after establishing the first kingdom and royal dynasty of Russia, which continued until 1598

Ruritania /róori táyni ə/ *n.* a place of romance, adventure, and intrigue [Late 19thC. Named after *Ruritania*, fictional central European kingdom in the novels *The Prisoner of Zenda* 1894 and *Rupert of Hentzau* 1898 by Anthony Hope.] —**Ruritanian** *adj.*, *n.*

rurp /rurp/ *n.* a small piton used by mountain climbers [Mid-20thC. Acronym formed from *realized ultimate reality piton*.]

ruse /rooz/ *n.* a clever trick or plot used to deceive others [15thC. Originally 'doubling of hunted game in its tracks', from Old French *ruser* 'to repulse, retreat, dodge' (source of English *rush*[1]).]

Ruse /róoss ay/ city in Ruse Province, northern Bulgaria. Population: 168,000 (1996).

Ruse, James (1760–1837) English-born Australian farmer. He was transported to New South Wales for burglary in 1788, and went on to become the first self-sufficient farmer in the colony.

rush[1] /rush/ *v.* (**rushes, rushing, rushed**) **1.** *vi.* MOVE FAST to move, act, or proceed quickly **2.** *vt.* HURRY SB OR STH ALONG to make sb or sth move, act, or proceed quickly ○ *Don't rush me.* **3.** *vt.* TAKE SB OR STH URGENTLY to take or send sb or sth to a place quickly and urgently ○ *We rushed him to the airport to catch his flight.* **4.** *vt.* DO STH HASTILY to do sth in a hurry and without careful thought ○ *rush a job* **5.** *vi.* GO RECKLESSLY to proceed in a quick and reckless way ○ *We mustn't rush into things.* ○ *'For fools rush in where angels fear to tread'.* (Alexander Pope, *An Essay on Criticism*; 1711) **6.** *vi.* FLOW FAST to flow somewhere quickly **7.** *vt.* CAPTURE AN ENEMY QUICKLY to seize a position or overcome an enemy by a sudden quick attack **8.** *vt.* CHEAT SB cheat sb, especially by overcharging for sth (slang) ○ *How much did they rush you for that jacket?* **9.** *vt.* **PASS RUGBY BALL UP PITCH** in rugby, to move the ball up the field by giving it short kicks and running after it in a loose group ■ *n.* **1. HURRY** a hurry or need for hurry **2. SUDDEN FAST MOVEMENT BY A CROWD** a sudden and quick movement of a person or group of people towards a place or objective ○ *there was a rush to the door* **3. BUSY TIME** a very busy period, e.g. a time when large numbers of people try to do sth at the same time ○ *a rush during the store's sale* **4. GREAT DEMAND** a sudden and high demand for sth **5. SUDDEN ATTACK** a sudden quick forward movement in an attack **6. SUDDEN FLOW** a sudden quick flow or movement of sth **7. SUDDEN FEELING** a sudden powerful onset of an emotion **8. SUDDEN PLEASURABLE SENSATION** a sudden feeling of elation and pleasure (*informal*) **9. RUGBY ACT OF RUSHING RUGBY BALL** in rugby, the act or an instance of rushing the ball **10.** *npl.* **rushes** CINEMA **UNEDITED PRINTS OF FILM SCENES** the first unedited prints of a scene or scenes shot for a film ■ *adj.* **1. DONE QUICKLY** done or needing to be done quickly ○ *a rush job* **2. VERY BUSY** very busy, especially with many people travelling at the same time [14thC. From Old French *re(h)usser* 'to repel', of uncertain origin: perhaps from Latin *recusare* 'to object to'; or from assumed Vulgar Latin *rusare*, from Latin *rursus* 'backwards'.] —**rusher** *n.*

rush into *vt.* to do or agree to sth or to cause sb to do or agree to sth quickly, with little consideration of the consequences

rush through *vt.* **1. GET STH APPROVED QUICKLY** to get sth approved or put in place hurriedly, often without allowing time for full consideration ○ *The government hoped to rush the bill through Parliament before the election.* ○ *The plans for the new building were rushed through.* **2. DO STH QUICKLY** to do sth quickly and with little thought or preparation

rush² /rush/ *n.* **1. PLANT GROWING IN WET AREAS** a marsh plant with a cylindrical stem that is sometimes hollow and leaves that resemble blades of grass. Genus: *Juncus.* **2. STEM OF THE RUSH PLANT** the stem of a rush plant, used in weaving baskets and mats and in bottoming chairs (*often used before a noun*) ○ *a rush mat* **3. STH UNIMPORTANT** sth of very little importance or value (*archaic*) **4.** = **rush light** [Old English *rysc*, from prehistoric Germanic]

Rush /rush/, **Geoffrey** (*b.* 1951) Australian actor. In 1997 he won an Academy Award for his role in *Shine* (1996).

rush candle *n.* = **rush light**

Rushdie /rúshdi/, **Salman** (*b.* 1947) Indian-born British novelist. A master of the magic realist style, his novels include *Midnight's Children* (1981), which won the Booker Prize, *The Satanic Verses* (1988), and *The Ground Beneath Her Feet* (1999).

rushed /rusht/ *adj.* **1. DONE IN A HURRY** done very quickly, usually too quickly **2. VERY BUSY** feeling a need or obligation to do sth quickly

rush hour *n.* a period of heavy traffic in the morning and evening during which people are travelling to and from work (*hyphenated when used before a noun*)

rush light *n.* a candle made from pith of the stem of a rush that has been dipped in tallow

Mount Rushmore

Rushmore, Mount /rúsh mawr/ mountain in the Black Hills, western South Dakota, carved with the faces of presidents George Washington, Thomas Jefferson, Theodore Roosevelt, and Abraham Lincoln. Height: 1,700 m/5,600 ft.

rushy /rúshi/ (**-ier, -iest**) *adj.* overgrown with, made of, or resembling rushes

rusk /rusk/ *n.* a sweet crisp golden-brown biscuit, often given to children and babies and made from bread that is baked, sliced, left to dry out, and then baked again [Late 16thC. Alteration of Portuguese or Spanish *rosca* 'screw, coil, bread twist', of uncertain origin.]

Ruskin /rúskin/, **John** (1819–1900) British art and social critic. He argued for the moral and religious significance of art in works such as *Modern Painters* (1843–60) and *The Stones of Venice* (1851–53).

Russ. *abbr.* **1.** Russia **2.** Russian

Russell /rúss'l/, **Bertrand, 3rd Earl Russell** (1872–1970) British philosopher and mathematician. A pacifist and winner of a Nobel prize in literature (1950), he wrote many highly influential philosophical works. Full name **Bertrand Arthur William Russell**

Russell, Ken (*b.* 1927) British film director. His vivid adaptations of the novels of D. H. Lawrence and biographies of composers often attracted controversy. Full name **Henry Kenneth Alfred Russell**

Russell's paradox /rúss'lz-/ *n.* the contradiction in set theory resulting from assuming that it is possible to form any set whatsoever, contradicted by the set of all and only things that are not members of themselves [Early 20thC. Named after Bertrand RUSSELL, who formulated the paradox.]

Russell's viper *n.* a venomous snake common in India. Latin name: *Vipera russelli*. [Early 20thC. Named after Patrick *Russell* (1727–1805), Scottish naturalist and physician.]

russet /rússit/ *n.* **1. COLOURS REDDISH BROWN** a reddish-brown colour **2. russet, russet apple** BOT **APPLE WITH ROUGH SKIN** an apple with a rough brownish skin, a deep sweet-sharp flavour, and a firm texture **3.** TEXTILES **HOMESPUN FABRIC** a coarse homespun fabric with a reddish-brown colour ■ *adj.* **REDDISH-BROWN** of a reddish-brown colour [13thC. From Old French *rousset*, literally 'small red', from *rous* 'red', from Latin *russus* (source of English *roux*).]

Russia

Russia /rúshə/ republic in eastern Europe and northern and western Asia. In the past the term referred to the Russian Empire, a state that included several republics that are now independent. Language: Russian. Currency: rouble. Capital: Moscow. Population: 147,501,000 (1997). Area: 17,075,400 sq. km/6,592,850 sq. mi. Official name **Russian Federation**

Russia leather *n.* a smooth brownish-red leather impregnated with oil from birch bark, used for binding books

Russian /rúsh'n/ *n.* **1.** PEOPLES **SB FROM RUSSIA** sb who was born or brought up in Russia or who has Russian citizenship **2.** LANG **OFFICIAL LANGUAGE OF RUSSIA** the official language of Russia, also spoken by people of Russian descent in other parts of the world. It belongs to the Balto-Slavic branch of Indo-European languages. There are about 160 million native speakers of Russian and approximately another 110 million people use it as a second language. ■ *adj.* **1.** PEOPLES **OF RUSSIA** relating to Russia, or its people or culture **2.** LANG **OF RUSSIAN** relating to the Russian language **3.** PEOPLES **OF THE FORMER SOVIET UNION** relating to the former Soviet Union, or its peoples or cultures (*dated*)

Russian blue *n.* a cat belonging to a breed of short-haired domestic cats with a slender body and bluish-grey fur

Russian doll *n.* a hollow painted wooden doll made in Russia. The top and bottom come apart to reveal a smaller, similar doll inside that similarly comes apart, and so on.

Russian dressing *n.* a salad dressing with a mayonnaise or vinaigrette base and sometimes with added chilli sauce or pickles

Russianize /rúshə nīz/ (**-izes, -izing, -ized**), **Russianise** (**-ises, -ising, -ised**) *vti.* to become or make sb or sth become Russian in style, character, or appearance —**Russianization** /rúshə nī záysh'n/ *n.*

Russian Orthodox Church *n.* the national church of Russia, an independent section of the Eastern Orthodox Church with the Patriarch of Moscow at its head

Russian roulette *n.* **1. DEADLY GAME USING A REVOLVER** a deadly game in which people take turns to fire a revolver loaded with only one bullet at their own heads, after spinning the cylinder **2. STH DANGEROUS** a dangerous or reckless action or activity [*Russian* because it was reportedly played by Russian officers in Romania in 1917, except that only one bullet was removed from the revolver]

Russian salad *n.* a mixed salad of cooked diced vegetables in a mayonnaise or Russian dressing

Russian tea *n.* tea served with lemon, without milk, and usually in a glass

Russian wolfhound *n.* = **borzoi**

Russki /rúski/, **Russky** (*plural* **-skies**) *n. US* an offensive term referring to a Russian person (*slang offensive*) [Mid-19thC. From Russian *russkiĭ*.]

Russo- *prefix.* Russia, Russian ○ *Russophile* [From RUSSIA]

Russo-Japanese War /rússō jáppə neez-/ *n.* a war fought in 1904–05 between Russia and Japan, mainly over control of Korea, in which Russia was unexpectedly defeated

Russophile /rússō fīl/, **Russophil** *n.* sb who likes or admires Russia, its people, or its culture —**Russophile** *adj.*

Russophobe /rússō fōb/ *n.* sb who dislikes or is afraid of Russia, its people, or its culture —**Russophobia** /rússō fōbi ə/ *n.* —**Russophobic** *adj.*

russula /rússyoōlə/ (*plural* **-sulae** /-yoō lee/ *or* **-sulas**) *n.* a common genus of mushroom found widely in Europe and North America. Genus: *Russula*. [Mid-20thC. From modern Latin *Russula*, the genus name.]

rust /rust/ *n.* **1. REDDISH-BROWN COATING ON METAL** a reddish-brown coating of iron oxide on the surface of iron or steel that forms when the metal is exposed to air and moisture **2. STH RESEMBLING RUST** sth that resembles rust, especially in colour, e.g. another type of corrosion or a stain **3. COLOURS REDDISH BROWN** a reddish-brown colour **4. BOT PLANT DISEASE** a disease of plants caused by rust fungus, in which reddish-brown spots form on the leaves and stems **5. BOT** = **rust fungus** ■ *v.* (**rusts, rusting, rusted**) **1.** *vti.* **CORRODE WITH RUST** to cause sth to corrode with rust or to become corroded with rust **2.** *vi.* **BOT DEVELOP A PLANT DISEASE** to become infected with a disease caused by rust fungus **3.** *vi.* **DETERIORATE** to deteriorate from neglect or lack of use ○ *His knowledge of German had rusted over the years.* ■ *adj.* **REDDISH-BROWN** of a reddish-brown colour [Old English *rūst*, from a prehistoric Germanic word that is also the ancestor of English *red*]

rust bucket *n.* a car that is badly affected by rust (*informal humorous*)

rust fungus *n.* a fungus that lives as a parasite on many plants, causing reddish-brown spots on the plant parts. Order: Uredinales.

rustic /rústik/ *adj.* **1. RELATING TO A COUNTRY LIFESTYLE** relating to, characteristic of, or appropriate to the country or country living **2. PLAIN AND SIMPLE** lacking excessive refinement or elegance **3. MADE OF ROUGH BRANCHES** made of rough wood, especially branches with the bark left on them **4.** CONSTR **HAVING A ROUGH SURFACE** with a rough finish ○ *rustic bricks* ■ *n.* **1. SB LIVING IN COUNTRY** sb who lives in the country, especially sb who is considered to be unsophisticated (*offensive in some contexts*) **2. BRICK WITH ROUGH FINISH** brick or stone with a rough finish [15thC. From Latin *rusticus*, from *rus* 'country' (see RURAL).] —**rustically** *adv.* —**rusticity** /ru stíssəti/ *n.*

rusticate /rústi kayt/ (**-cates, -cating, -cated**) *v.* **1.** *vi.* **MOVE TO THE COUNTRY** to go to the country to live **2.** *vt.* **SEND SB TO THE COUNTRY** to send sb to the country to live **3.** *vt.* **MAKE SB OR STH APPEAR RUSTIC** to become or to cause sb or sth to become rustic in appearance or quality **4.** *vt.* **SUSPEND STUDENT FROM UNIVERSITY** to suspend a student from university for a set time as a punishment **5.** *vt.* CONSTR **FINISH A WALL WITH ROUGH MASONRY** to finish the outside of a wall with large blocks of masonry that are left with a rough surface, bevelled, and have deep joints between them —**rustication** /rústi káysh'n/ *n.* —**rusticator** /rústi kaytər/ *n.*

rusticwork /rústik wurk/ *n.* = **rustic** *n.* 2

rustle[1] /rúss'l/ *v.* (**-tles, -tling, -tled**) **1.** *vti.* **MAKE SWISHING SOUND** to make or cause sth to make a swishing or soft crackling sound, e.g. that made by dry leaves rubbing together **2.** *vi.* **MOVE WITH RUSTLING SOUND** to move with a swishing or soft crackling sound ■ *n.* **RUSTLING SOUND** a swishing or soft crackling sound ○ *the rustle of paper money* [14thC. An imitation of the sound.] —**rustlingly** *adv.*

rustle up *vt.* (*informal*) **1. PREPARE FOOD QUICKLY** to prepare a meal or snack quickly using any food that is immediately available **2. GET THINGS OR PEOPLE TOGETHER** to quickly find and bring together things or people

rustle[2] /rúss'l/ (**-tles, -tling, -tled**) *v.* **1.** *vti.* US, Can **STEAL LIVESTOCK** to steal livestock, especially cattle or horses **2.** *vi.* US **MOVE QUICKLY AND ENERGETICALLY** to move or work quickly and energetically [Early 20thC. From RUSTLE[1].]

rustler /rússlər/ *n.* US, Can sb who steals livestock, especially cattle or horses

rust mite *n.* a gall mite that produces brown spots on leaves and fruit by burrowing into them

rustproof /rúst proof/ *adj.* **TREATED TO INHIBIT RUST** not susceptible to rust or treated so as not to be susceptible to rust ■ *vt.* (**-proofs, -proofing, -proofed**) **MAKE METAL RUSTPROOF** to treat metal to prevent it rusting —**rustproofing** *n.*

rusty /rústi/ (**-ier, -iest**) *adj.* **1. CORRODED** covered with or corroded by rust **2. OUT OF PRACTICE** out of practice or impaired because of old age, neglect, or lack of use ○ *My German is very rusty.* **3. RUST-COLOURED** of the colour of rust **4.** BOT **INFECTED WITH RUST FUNGUS** affected by rust fungus **5. DISCOLOURED** faded and threadbare from wear and age **6. OLD** old or old-fashioned ○ *rusty ideas* **7. ROUGH-SOUNDING** croaking or rough-sounding ○ *a rusty voice* [Old English] —**rustily** *adv.* —**rustiness** *n.*

rut[1] /rut/ *n.* **1. NARROW GROOVE** a narrow channel or groove in sth, especially one made by the wheels of vehicles **2. BORING SITUATION** a routine procedure, situation, or way of life that has become uninteresting and tiresome ○ *I felt I was in a rut.* ■ *vt.* (**ruts, rutting, rutted**) **MAKE RUTS IN STH** to make ruts in a road, track, or similar surface [Late 16thC. Origin uncertain: probably from Old French *rote* 'route'.]

rut[2] /rut/ *n.* **SEXUAL EXCITEMENT IN MALE DEER** a period of sexual excitement that recurs annually in male ruminants, especially deer ■ *vi.* (**ruts, rutting, rutted**) **BE IN RUT** to be in a state of sexual excitement (*refers to male ruminants*) [12thC. From Old French, 'bellowing', from Latin *rugitus* 'roaring', from Latin *rugire* 'to roar'.] —**ruttish** *adj.*

rutabaga /roota baygə, -báygə/ *n.* US, Can = **swede** [Late 18thC. Anglicization of Swedish dialect *rotabagge*, literally 'baggy root', from *rot* 'root' + *bagge* 'bag' (source of English *bag*).]

ruth /rooth/ *n.* (*archaic*) **1. SADNESS FOR ANOTHER** pity for another person's troubles **2. SORROW** sorrow or remorse for having done sth wrong [12thC. Formed by adding *-th* (on the model of words like TRUTH) from RUE.]

Ruth /rooth/ *n.* **1. WOMAN IN THE BIBLE** in the Bible, a Moabite widow who left her own people to live with her mother-in-law Naomi, married Boaz, and was an ancestor of King David **2. BOOK OF BIBLE** the book of the Bible that tells the story of Ruth

Babe Ruth

Popperfoto

Ruth /rooth/, **Babe** (1895–1948) US baseball player. While playing for the New York Yankees in the 1920s and 1930s, his legendary home run hitting dominated the sport and made him one of the most popular players in the history of baseball. Real name **George Herman Ruth**.

Ruthenia /roo théeni ə/ former region of Czechoslovakia, corresponding to modern-day Zakarpats'ka Oblast, Ukraine

Ruthenian /roo théeni ən/ *n.* **1. SB FROM RUTHENIA** sb who was born or brought up in the former region of Ruthenia, or who was a citizen of Ruthenia **2. UKRAINIAN DIALECT** a dialect of Ukrainian spoken in the former region of Ruthenia —**Ruthenian** *adj.*

ruthenic /roo thénnik, -théenik/ *adj.* relating to or containing ruthenium, especially with a high valency [Mid-19thC. Formed from RUTHENIUM + -IC.]

ruthenious /roo théeni əss/ *adj.* relating to or containing ruthenium, especially with a low valency [Mid-19thC. Formed from RUTHENIUM + -OUS.]

ruthenium /roo théeni əm/ *n.* a brittle white metallic chemical element found in platinum ores and used to harden platinum and palladium alloys. Symbol **Ru** [Mid-19thC. Named after RUTHENIA, where the ore was first found.]

Rutherford /rúthər furd/, **Ernest, 1st Baron Rutherford of Nelson and Cambridge** (1871–1937) New Zealand-born British physicist. He discovered the nuclear structure of the atom (1909), and was awarded a Nobel Prize in chemistry (1908).

Dame Margaret Rutherford

National Screen Service Ltd

Rutherford, Dame Margaret (1892–1972) British actor. A character and comic actor in films and on stage, she is best known for her role as Miss Marple in film adaptations of the novels by Agatha Christie.

rutherfordium /rúthər fáwrdi əm/ *n.* US CHEM ELEM a radioactive chemical element that does not occur naturally but is produced artificially in high-energy atomic collisions. Symbol **Rf**

ruthful /roothf'l/ *adj.* feeling or causing sb to feel sorrow or pity (*archaic*) —**ruthfully** *adv.* —**ruthfulness** *n.*

ruthless /roothləss/ *adj.* having or showing no pity or mercy —**ruthlessly** *adv.* —**ruthlessness** *n.*

rutile /roo tīl/ *n.* a dark reddish-brown or lustrous black form of titanium dioxide that occurs widely in igneous and metamorphic rocks as needle-shaped crystals and is used as a source of titanium [Early 19thC. Via French and German from Latin *rutilus* 'reddish'.]

Rutland /rútlənd/ county in the eastern Midlands, England. Between 1974 and 1997 it was part of Leicestershire. Population: 35,000 (1997). Area: 394 sq. km/152 sq. mi.

rutty /rútti/ (**-tier, -tiest**) *adj.* with a surface marked by ruts —**ruttiness** *n.*

Ruwenzori Range /roo ən záwri-/ mountain range in central Africa, on the northeastern border of the Democratic Republic of the Congo and the southwestern border of Uganda, between lakes Edward and Albert

rv *abbr.* random variable

RV *abbr.* **1.** US recreational vehicle **2.** re-entry vehicle **3. RV** BIBLE Revised Version

Rv. *abbr.* Revelation

RW *abbr.* **1.** Right Worshipful **2.** Right Worthy

Rwanda[1] /roo andə/ *n.* LANG one of the official languages of Rwanda, also spoken in other parts of east-central Africa. It is a Bantu language belonging to the Benue-Congo branch of Niger-Congo languages and is spoken by about 15 million people. [Early 20thC. From Bantu.]

Rwanda

Rwanda[2] /roo ándə/ republic in east-central Africa bordered by Uganda, Tanzania, Burundi, Lake Kivu, and the Democratic Republic of Congo. Language: Rwanda, French. Currency: Rwanda franc. Capital: Kigali. Population: 6,727,000 (1996). Area: 26,338 sq. km/10,169 sq. mi. Official name **Rwandese Republic** —**Rwandan** *n.*, *adj.* —**Rwandese** *n.*, *adj.*

rwd *abbr.* TRANSP rear-wheel drive

rwy, Rwy *abbr.* railway

ry, Ry *abbr.* railway

-ry *suffix.* = -ery

rya /rée ə/ *n.* **1. HANDWOVEN SCANDINAVIAN RUG** a type of handwoven Scandinavian rug with a deep pile and a colourful pattern **2. WEAVING PATTERN USED FOR A RYA** the weaving pattern or style used in making a rya [Mid-20thC. Named after *Rya*, a city in Sweden where the craft originated.]

rye[1] /rī/ *n.* **1.** BOT **HARDY ANNUAL GRASS** a tall hardy annual cereal grass that has bluish-green leaves and is widely cultivated for its light brown grain. Latin name: *Secale cereale*. **2. RYE GRAIN** the grain of the rye plant, used to make flour and whisky and also as fodder **3.** = **rye whisky** [Old English *ryge*]

—— **WORD KEY: CULTURAL NOTE** ——

Catcher in the Rye, a novel by US writer J. D. Salinger (1951). A moving and realistic account of a young boy's attempt to come to terms with encroaching adulthood, it describes two days in the life of disaffected teenager Holden Caulfield. Holden absconds to New York, then resolves to leave home for good; his failure to accomplish this results in his mental collapse.

---

rye[2] /rī/ n. a word used by Romany people to mean gentleman [Mid-19thC. From Romany *rai*, from Sanskrit *rājan* 'rajah'.]

Rye /rī/ historic market town in East Sussex, southeastern England, and a Cinque Port since 1350. Population: 3,708 (1991).

rye bread n. a dark or light bread made using rye flour, often flavoured with caraway seed

Rye

rye-grass n. a European grass that is widely cultivated as forage, as a cover crop, and for lawns. Latin name: *Lolium perenne*.

rye whisky n. whisky distilled from fermented rye

Ryle /rīl/, **Sir Martin** (1918–84) British astronomer. As Astronomer Royal (1972–82) he received the Nobel Prize in physics (1974) for his development of aperture synthesis in radio astronomy.

ryot /rī ət/ n. a peasant in India [Early 17thC. Via Persian and Urdu *ra'īyat*, ultimately from Arabic *ra'īyya(t)* 'subjects', literally 'herd, flock', from *ra'ā* 'pasture'.]

Ryukyu Islands /ri oʹo koo-/ chain of islands in southwestern Japan, between Kyushu and Taiwan. Population: 1,222,458 (1990). Area: 2,260 sq. km/870 sq. mi.

Ss

s¹ /ess/ (*plural* **s's**), **S** (*plural* **S's** *or* **Ss**) *n.* **1.** 19TH LETTER OF ENGLISH ALPHABET the 19th letter of the modern English alphabet **2.** SPEECH SOUND CORRESPONDING TO LETTER 'S' the speech sound that corresponds to the letter 'S' **3.** LETTER 'S' WRITTEN a written representation of the letter 'S'

s² *symbol.* TIME, GEOM second

s³ *abbr.* **1.** MEASURE stere **2.** QUANTUM PHYS strange quark

S¹, s *symbol.* PHYS siemens

S² *symbol.* **1.** QUANTUM PHYS entropy **2.** MONEY schilling **3.** sulphur **4.** MONEY sucre

S³ *abbr.* **1.** BIBLE Samuel **2.** EDUC satisfactory **3.** QUANTUM PHYS strangeness **4.** South **5.** Sweden (*international vehicle registration*) **6.** small

s. *abbr.* **1.** semi- **2.** MUSIC solo **3.** shilling **4.** GRAM singular **5.** MUSIC soprano **6.** sire **7.** sister **8.** son **9.** stock **10.** GRAM substantive

S. *abbr.* **1.** Sabbath **2.** Saturday **3.** Saxon **4.** September **5.** Saint **6.** Sea **7.** Socialist **8.** Sunday

SA *abbr.* **1.** South Africa **2.** South America **3.** South Australia **4.** Salvation Army **5.** Sturmabteilung **6.** limited company

s.a. *abbr.* **1.** semiannual **2.** without date **3.** COMM subject to approval

SAA *abbr.* COMPUT systems application architecture

Saarbrücken /sá brŏokən, za brýkən/ capital city of Saarland State, in southwestern Germany. Population: 189,900 (1994).

Saarinen /sáarinən/, **Eero** (1910–61) Finnish-born US architect. He is known for his innovative and elegant buildings such as the TWA terminal at New York's Kennedy International Airport (1962). He was the son of Eliel Saarinen.

Saarinen, Eliel (1873–1950) Finnish-born US architect, whose most admired work was the Helsinki Railway Station (1915). He emigrated to the US (1923), where he headed the Cranmore Academy of Art (1932–48). He often worked in collaboration with his son, Eero Saarinen. Full name **Gottlieb Eliel Saarinen**

sab /sab/ *vti.* (**sabs, sabbing, sabbed**) OBSTRUCT FOX HUNT to obstruct a fox hunt because of opposition to blood sports (*slang*) ■ *n.* SB OBSTRUCTING FOX HUNT sb who obstructs a fox hunt because of opposition to blood sports (*slang*) [Late 20thC. Shortening of SABOTEUR.]

Sab. *abbr.* Sabbath

sabadilla /sábbə díllə/ (*plural* **-las** *or* **-la**) *n.* **1.** MEXICAN PLANT a Mexican plant of the lily family with long flower spikelets and bitter brown seeds. Latin name: *Schoenocaulon officinale*. **2.** SEEDS OF SABADILLA PLANT the seeds of the sabadilla plant, used in insecticides and the source of the toxic compound veratrine [Early 19thC. From Spanish *cebadilla*, a diminutive of *cebada* 'barley', ultimately from Latin *cibatus* 'food, fodder', from *cibus* 'food'.]

Sabah /sáa baa/ the second largest state in Malaysia, on the northeast of the island of Borneo. Capital: Kota Kinabalu. Population: 1,736,902 (1991). Area: 73,711 sq. km/28,800 sq. mi. Former name **North Borneo** (until 1963)

Sabatier /saa baa tyáy/, **Paul** (1854–1941) French chemist. His research on the catalytic hydrogenation of oils made possible the manufacture of margarine. He shared the Nobel Prize in chemistry (1912).

sabayon /sábay yón/ *n.* a light frothy dessert sauce made by whisking together egg yolks, sugar, and wine over a gentle heat [Early 20thC. Via French from Italian dialect *zabaione* (source of English *zabaglione*).]

sabbat /sábbət/ *n.* = **witches' Sabbath** [Via French from Latin *sabbatum* (see SABBATH)]

Sabbatarian /sábbə táiri ən/ *n.* **1.** STRICT OBSERVER OF THE SABBATH sb who believes in the strict observance of Sunday, in most Christian denominations, or Saturday, in Judaism and some Christian denominations, as a day of worship and rest **2.** OBSERVER OF SATURDAY AS SABBATH sb who observes Saturday as the Sabbath, e.g. in Judaism ■ *adj.* OF SABBATH OR SABBATARIANS relating to the Sabbath, its observance, or to Sabbatarians [Early 17thC. Formed from late Latin *Sabbatarius*, from Latin *sabbatum* (see SABBATH).] —**Sabbatarianism** *n.*

Sabbath /sábbəth/ *n.* **1.** SUNDAY AS DAY OF RELIGIOUS WORSHIP Sunday, observed by most Christians as the day of worship and rest from work **2.** SATURDAY AS DAY OF RELIGIOUS WORSHIP Saturday, observed as a day of religious worship and rest from work in Judaism and some Christian denominations **3.** = **witches' Sabbath** [Pre-12thC. Via Latin *sabbatum* from Greek *sabbaton*, from Hebrew *šabbāt* 'rest', from *šābat* 'to rest'.]

sabbath school, **Sabbath School** *n.* in the tradition of the Seventh-Day Adventists, a school for religious teaching held on Saturday

sabbatical, **sabbatic** *n.* LEAVE FROM WORK a period of leave from work for research, study, or travel, often with pay and usually granted to university lecturers every seven years ■ *adj.* OF SABBATICAL relating to a sabbatical [Late 16thC. Ultimately from Greek *sabbatikos* 'of the sabbath', from *sabbaton* (see SABBATH).]

Sabbatical, **Sabbatic** *adj.* OF SABBATH relating to or suitable for the Sabbath ■ *n.* = **Sabbatical Year**

sabbatical year, **sabbatical leave** *n.* = **sabbatical** *n.*

Sabbatical Year *n.* every seventh year, during which the ancient Israelites allowed their land to lie fallow

SABC *abbr.* South African Broadcasting Corporation

saber *n.*, *vt.* US = **sabre**

sabin /sáybin/ *n.* a unit of sound absorption equal to the absorption of one square foot of a perfectly absorbing surface [Mid-20thC. Named after Wallace Clement Ware *Sabine* 1868–1919, US physicist who established the discipline of architectural acoustics.]

Sabin /sáybin/, **Albert** (1906–93) Russian-born US microbiologist and immunologist. Best known for developing an oral, live-virus polio vaccine (1957), he also developed vaccines against dengue and sandfly fever. Full name **Albert Bruce Sabin**

Sabine¹ /sábbīn/ *n.* **1.** PEOPLES MEMBER OF ANCIENT ITALIAN PEOPLE a member of an ancient people that occupied lands in central Italy, to the northeast of Rome. By the 3rd century BC, after centuries of rivalry and fighting, the Romans had defeated them. **2.** LANG SABINE LANGUAGE the Italic language of the Sabines [14thC. From Latin *Sabinus*.] —**Sabine** *adj.*

Sabine² /sə béen/ river rising in Texas, forming the Texas-Louisiana border, flowing into the Gulf of Mexico. Length: 612 km/380 mi.

Sabin vaccine /sáybin-/ *n.* an oral vaccine used to immunize against poliomyelitis and containing live poliovirus [Mid-20thC. Named after Albert SABIN who developed the vaccine.]

sabji /súbji/ *n.* S Asia a raw or cooked vegetable [Early 19thC. From Urdu *sabzī* 'greenness', from *sabz* 'green', from Persian *sebz*.]

sable /sáyb'l/ *n.* (*plural* **-bles** *or* **-ble**) **1.** ZOOL NORTHERN ASIAN MARTEN a marten of northern Asia that has soft dark fur. Latin name: *Martes zibellina*. **2.** FUR OF SABLE the fur of the sable, which is highly valued **3.** SABLE GARMENT a garment made of sable fur **4.** ARTS ARTIST'S BRUSH an artist's brush made with the hairs of a sable **5.** COLOURS BLACK COLOUR a black colour, the colour of sable fur (*literary*) **6.** HERALDRY COLOUR BLACK IN HERALDRY in heraldry, the colour black ■ **sables** *npl.* MOURNING CLOTHES black clothes worn in mourning (*archaic*) ■ *adj.* **1.** COLOURS OF A BLACK COLOUR of a black colour, like that of sable fur (*literary*) **2.** DARK very dark or gloomy (*literary*) **3.** HERALDRY OF HERALDIC BLACK COLOUR in heraldry, of a black colour [15thC. Via Old French from medieval Latin *sabelum*, from a Baltic (Lithuanian *sàbalas*) or a Slavic (Russian *sobol*) source.]

sable antelope *n.* a large African antelope with long backward-curving horns. The male has a black coat. Latin name: *Hippotragus niger*.

sabot /sábbō/ *n.* **1.** WOODEN SHOE a wooden shoe, or a shoe with a wooden sole, formerly worn in Belgium, France, the Netherlands, and Germany **2.** SUPPORT FOR PROJECTILE IN WEAPON a sleeve placed around a projectile so that it can be fired from a weapon with a larger bore. The sabot drops away shortly after the projectile is fired. [Early 17thC. Via French from Old French *çabot*, the source of English *sabotage*, a blend of *savate* 'old shoe', of unknown origin, and *bot* (source of English *boot*).]

sabotage /sábbə taazh/ *n.* **1.** DELIBERATE DESTRUCTION the deliberate damaging or destroying of property or equipment, e.g. by resistance fighters, enemy agents, or disgruntled workers **2.** ACTION TO HINDER an action taken to undermine or destroy sb's efforts or achievements ■ *vt.* (**-tages, -taging, -taged**) **1.** DAMAGE STH to damage, destroy, or disrupt sth deliberately, especially in a war **2.** HINDER STH to undermine or destroy sb's efforts or achievements [Mid-19thC. From French from *saboter* 'to clatter in clogs', hence 'to act clumsily, work badly, ruin', from *sabot* (see SABOT).]

saboteur /sábbə túr/ *n.* sb who carries out an act of sabotage [Early 20thC. From French, from *sabot* (see SABOTAGE).]

sabra /sáabrə/ *n.* a Jewish person who was born in Israel [Mid-20thC. Directly or via colloquial modern Hebrew *ṣābrāh* from Arabic *ṣabr* 'prickly pear' (widespread in the Negev).]

sabre /sáybər/ *n.* **1.** HEAVY SWORD WITH CURVED BLADE a heavy cavalry sword with a slightly curved blade that is sharp on one edge **2.** FENCING SWORD WITH TAPERING BLADE a light sword with a guard to cover the hand and a tapering flexible blade, used in fencing **3.** FENCING WITH SABRE the sport or technique of fencing with a sabre **4.** CAVALRY SOLDIER a soldier in a cavalry regiment ■ *vt.* (**sabres, sabring, sabred**) INJURE SB WITH SABRE to jab, injure, or kill sb with a sabre [Late 17thC. Via French *sabre* from obsolete German *Sabel*, of uncertain origin: perhaps from Slavic (Polish *szabla* or Russian *sablya*) or from Hungarian *szablya*.]

sabre rattling *n.* an aggressive display or threat of force, especially military force

sabretache /sábbər tash/ *n.* a small leather case worn on a cavalryman's belt [Early 19thC. From French, a translation of German *Säbeltasche*, literally 'sabre pocket'.]

sabre-toothed tiger, **sabre-toothed cat** *n.* an extinct animal of the cat family that lived in the Oligocene and Pleistocene epochs and had long curving upper canine teeth. Genus: *Smilodon*.

sabulose /sábbyoŏ lōss/, **sabulous** /-ləss/ *adj.* **1. SANDY** having a gritty texture like sand **2. GROWING IN SAND** growing in sand or sandy soil [Mid-19thC. Formed from Latin *sabulum* 'sand'.] —**sabulosity** /sábbyoŏ lóssəti/ *n.*

sac /sak/ *n.* a small bag or pouch, especially one that contains a fluid, formed by a membrane in an animal or plant ○ *amniotic sac* [Mid-18thC. Via French from Latin *saccus*. See SACK[1].]

Sac /sak/ (*plural* **Sacs** or **Sac**) *n.* PEOPLES, LANG = **Sauk**

sacaton /sákə tōn/ *n.* a coarse perennial grass grown in the southwestern United States and Mexico and used for hay and pasture in dry alkaline areas. Latin name: *Sporobolus wrightii*. [Mid-19thC. From American Spanish *zacatón*, literally 'large coarse grass' from *zacate* 'coarse grass', from Nahuatl *zacatl* 'straw'.]

saccade /sa kaád, -káyd/ *n.* **1. EYE MOVEMENT** a rapid irregular movement of the eye as it changes focus moving from one point to another, e.g. while reading **2. PULL ON HORSE'S REINS** a sudden brief pull by a rider on a horse's reins in order to check the horse [Early 18thC. From French, literally 'twitch' (literally 'pulling as if drawing a sack closed violently'), ultimately from *sac* 'sack', from Latin *saccus* (see SACK[1]).] —**saccadic** *adj.* —**saccadically** *adv.*

saccate /sákayt/ *adj.* enclosed in or resembling a sac [Early 19thC. From modern Latin *saccatus*, a derivative of *saccus* (see SACK[1]).]

sacchar- *prefix.* = **saccharo-** (*used before vowels*)

saccharate /sákə rayt/ *n.* a chemical compound that is a salt or ester of saccharic acid [Early 19thC. Formed from SACCHARIC ACID + -ATE.]

saccharic acid /sə kárrik-/ *n.* a white soluble solid formed by the oxidation of sugar or starch. Formula: COOH(CHOH)₄COOH.

saccharide /sákə rīd/ *n.* a water-soluble carbohydrate with a sweet taste and a chemical structure comprising a ring of four or five carbon atoms and one oxygen atom

saccharify /sə kárri fī/ (**-fies**, **-fying**, **-fied**) *vt.* to convert a complex substance such as starch into simple sugars —**saccharification** /sə kárrifi káysh'n/ *n.*

saccharimeter /sákə rímmitər/ *n.* an instrument, e.g. a polarimeter, used to measure the concentration of sugar in a solution —**saccharimetry** *n.*

Saccharin

saccharin /sákərin/ *n.* a white crystalline compound that is several hundred times sweeter than sugar, used as a sugar substitute. Formula: C₇H₅NO₃S.

saccharine /sákə reen, -rīn, -rin/ *adj.* **1. OF OR LIKE SUGAR** relating to, resembling, or containing sugar **2. TOO SWEET** excessively sweet and ingratiating ○ *a saccharine smile* **3. TOO SENTIMENTAL** excessively sentimental and cloying —**saccharinely** *adv.* —**saccharinity** /sákə rínnəti/ *n.*

saccharo- *prefix.* sugar ○ *saccharometer* [Via Latin and Greek from, ultimately, Sanskrit *śarkarā* 'sugar']

saccharoid /sákə royd/, **saccharoidal** /sákə róydl/ *adj.* used to describe rocks and minerals that have a texture resembling loaf sugar

saccharometer /sákə rómmitər/ *n.* a hydrometer used to determine the strength of a sugar solution by measuring its density

saccharomycete /sákərō mí seet/ (*plural* **-cetes**) *n.* a single-celled yeast that has no mycelium, reproduces asexually, and ferments sugar. Genus: *Saccharomyces*. [Late 19thC. Coined from SACCHARO- + Greek *mukēs* 'mushroom, fungus'.]

saccharose /sákə rōss, -rōz/ *n.* = **sucrose** [Late 19thC. Formed from SACCHARO- + -OSE.]

saccular /sákyoōlər/ *adj.* resembling a sac or saccule [Mid-19thC. Formed from Latin *sacculus* (see SACCULE).]

sacculate /sákyoōlət, -layt/, **sacculated** /-laytid/ *adj.* containing or resembling a saccule or saccules [Late 19thC. Formed from Latin *sacculus* (see SACCULE).] —**sacculation** /sákyoō láysh'n/ *n.*

saccule /sákyool/, **sacculus** /sákyoōləss/ (*plural* **-li** /-yoō lī/) *n.* **1. SMALL SAC** a small membranous bag or pouch in an animal or plant **2. SAC IN INNER EAR** the smaller of two sacs in the vestibule of the inner ear [Mid-19thC. From Latin *sacculus*, literally 'little sack' from *saccus* (see SACK[1]).]

sacerdotal /sássər dṓt'l, sákər-/ *adj.* relating to or characteristic of a priest or the priesthood [14thC. Via Old French from Latin *sacerdotalis* 'priestly', from the stem *sacerdot-* the stem of *sacerdos* 'priest'.] —**sacerdotally** *adv.*

sacerdotalism /sássər dṓt'lizəm, sákər-/ *n.* **1. PRINCIPLES OF PRIESTHOOD** the beliefs or methods of priests **2. BELIEF IN PRIEST'S POWER AS MEDIATOR** the belief that a priest is able to mediate between God and human beings **3. PRIEST'S POWER OVER ORDINARY PEOPLE** power that a priest has over ordinary people, especially when this is seen as excessive or dishonestly achieved —**sacerdotalist** *n.*

SACEUR *abbr.* Supreme Allied Commander, Europe

sac fungus *n.* = **ascomycete**

sachem /sáychəm/ *n.* **1. NATIVE N AMERICAN CHIEF** a chief of a Native North American tribe or confederation, especially of Algonquian people **2.** *US* POL **LEADER OF TAMMANY SOCIETY** a leader or official of the Tammany Society [Early 17thC. From an Algonquian word.] —**sachemic** /say chémmik/ *adj.*

sachertorte /sákər tawrt, zaákhər tawrtə/ *n.* a dark rich chocolate cake, sometimes with a filling of apricot jam, covered with glossy chocolate icing [Early 20thC. From German, named after Franz *Sacher*, the pastry chef who invented the cake.]

sachet /sásh ay/ *n.* **1. SMALL ENVELOPE** a small flat sealed packet that contains a powder, cream, or liquid **2. PERFUMED BAG TO SCENT CLOTHES** a small bag containing perfumed powder or potpourri, used to scent clothes in wardrobes or drawers [15thC. From Old French, literally 'little sack', a diminutive of *sac* 'bag' from Latin *saccus* (see SACK[1]).]

sack[1] /sak/ *n.* **1. LARGE BAG** a large bag, especially one that is made from hessian, other coarse cloth, or thick heavy-duty paper **2. AMOUNT IN SACK** the amount that a sack will hold **3. JOB DISMISSAL** dismissal from a job (*informal*) ○ *to get the sack* **4. BED** bed (*informal*) **5. WOMAN'S DRESS** a woman's loose-fitting dress that narrows below the knee **6. 18TH-CENTURY WOMAN'S GOWN** a gown worn by women in the 18th century that had a bodice with loose pleats at the back ■ *vt.* (**sacks**, **sacking**, **sacked**) **1. FIRE SB** to dismiss sb from a job (*informal*) **2. PUT STH IN A SACK** to put sth into a sack, e.g. for storage or transport [Pre-12thC. Via Latin *saccus* 'sack, bag, wallet' from Old French *sac*, also from Latin *saccus* from Greek *sakkos* 'packing material', from a Semitic word.] —**sacker** *n.* ◇ **hit the sack** to go to bed (*informal*)

sack out *vi. US* to go to sleep or to bed (*informal*)

sack[2] /sak/ *vt.* (**sacks**, **sacking**, **sacked**) **DESTROY AND PLUNDER PLACE** to destroy a captured town or city and plunder its goods and valuables ■ *n.* **DESTRUCTION AND PLUNDERING** the destruction of a captured town or city and the plundering of its goods and valuables [Mid-16thC. Via Old French (*a*) *sac*, call to plunder, literally '(to the) bag', from, ultimately, Italian *saccomano* 'plunderer',

literally 'bag-man', via German from, ultimately, Latin *saccus* 'sack'.]

sack[3] /sak/ *n.* dry white wine from Spain, Portugal, or the Canary Islands (*archaic*) [Mid-16thC. An alteration of earlier *wine seck*, a partial translation of French (*vin*) *sec* 'dry (wine)', from Latin *siccus* 'dry' (source of English *desiccate*).]

sackbut /sák but/ *n.* a wind instrument with a long slide like a trombone, played in medieval times [Early 16thC. From Old French *saqueb(o)ute* 'hooked lance for pulling riders from their horses', of uncertain origin: perhaps from *saquer* 'to pull' + assumed Vulgar Latin *bottare* 'to push against'.]

sackcloth /sák kloth/ *n.* **1. CLOTH FOR SACKS** coarse cloth used to make sacks **2. MOURNING CLOTHES** clothes made from the type of coarse cloth usually used for sacks, which were worn in the past as a sign of mourning or penitence ◇ **sackcloth and ashes** a show of mourning or repentance

sacking /sáking/ *n.* coarse cloth used for making sacks, usually woven from hemp or jute

sack race *n.* a race in which each competitor stands in a sack and jumps towards the finish line while holding up the sack

Sackville /sákvil/, **Thomas, 1st Earl of Dorset** (1536–1608) English poet, playwright, and diplomat. He was the co-author (with Thomas Norton) of *Gorboduc* (1565), the first blank-verse tragedy in English. He served at the court of Elizabeth I.

Vita Sackville-West

Sackville-West /sák vil wést/, **Vita** (1892–1962) British writer. She is remembered for poems such as 'The Land' (1926) and novels including *The Edwardians* (1930). Virginia Woolf celebrated their friendship in her novel *Orlando* (1928). Full name **Victoria Mary Sackville-West**

Saco /sáykō/ city in southwestern Maine, on the northern shore of the Saco River, opposite Biddeford. Population: 15,681 (1996).

sacra *plural of* **sacrum**

sacral[1] /sáykrəl, sák-/ *adj.* relating to or near the sacrum

sacral[2] /sáykrəl, sák-/ *adj.* relating to or used in sacred rites [Late 19thC. From Latin *sacr-*, the stem of *sacer* 'sacred' (source of English *sacred*).]

sacrament /sákrəmənt/ *n.* **1. RELIGIOUS RITE OR CEREMONY** in Christianity, a rite that is considered to have been established by Jesus Christ to bring grace to those participating in or receiving it. In the Protestant Church, the sacraments are baptism and Communion. The Roman Catholic and Eastern Churches also include penance, confirmation, holy orders, matrimony, and the anointing of the sick. **2. sacrament, Sacrament CONSECRATED ELEMENTS OF COMMUNION** the bread and wine consecrated at Communion **3. STH SACRED** sth considered to be sacred or have a special significance [12thC. Via Old French from Late Latin *sacramentum* 'rite, mystery, (gospel) revelation, sacrament' from Latin, 'soldier's oath of loyalty, solemn obligation' (see SACRED).]

sacramental /sákrə mént'l/ *adj.* **1. USED IN SACRAMENT** relating to or used in a sacrament **2. SACRED** bound by a sacrament or in a way considered inviolable ■ *n.* **RITUAL ACTION OR SIGN** in the Roman Catholic Church, an object, act, or ritual such as the sign of the cross that is used to show religious devotion —

sacramentality /sákrə men tálləti/ *n.* —**sacramentally** /-méntəli/ *adv.* —**sacramentalness** /-mént'lnəss/ *n.*

sacramentalism /sákrə mént'lizəm/ *n.* in Christianity, the belief in the necessity of the sacraments to attain salvation and God's grace —**sacramentalist** *n.*

Sacramentarian /sákrə men táiri ən/ *n.* **1.** BELIEVER IN THE SYMBOLIC NATURE OF COMMUNION sb who believes that the consecrated bread and wine of the Communion are only symbolic of the body and blood of Jesus Christ **2.** SACRAMENTALIST sb who believes in sacramentalism ■ *adj.* OF SACRAMENTARIANS relating to or characteristic of Sacramentarians —**Sacramentarianism** *n.*

Sacramento /sákrə méntō/ capital city of California, at the confluence of the Sacramento and American rivers. Population: 369,365 (1990).

sacrarium /sa kráiri əm/ (*plural* **-a** /-ri ə/) *n.* **1.** SANCTUARY OR SACRISTY a Christian church's sanctuary or sacristy **2.** = **piscina** *n.* 1 [Early 18thC. From Latin, literally 'place for keeping sacred things, shrine', from *sacer* 'holy, sacred'.]

sacred /sáykrid/ *adj.* **1.** DEVOTED TO DEITY dedicated to a deity or religious purpose **2.** OF RELIGION relating to or used in religious worship **3.** WORTHY OF WORSHIP worthy of or regarded with religious veneration, worship, and respect **4.** DEDICATED TO SB dedicated to or in honour of sb **5.** INVIOLABLE not to be challenged or disrespected [14thC. Originally the past participle of archaic *sacre* 'to consecrate', via Old French *sacrer* from Latin *sacrare*, from *sacr-*, the stem of *sacer* 'holy, sacred'.] —**sacredly** *adv.* —**sacredness** *n.*

WORD KEY: ORIGIN

The Latin word *sacer*, from which ***sacred*** is derived, is also the source of English *consecrate*, *execrate*, *sacrament*, *sacrifice*, *sacrilege*, *sacristan*, and *sexton*.

sacred baboon *n.* = **hamadryas baboon** [Late 19thC. From its being held sacred by the ancient Egyptians.]

sacred cow *n.* sb or sth exempt from any criticism by, or interference from, others [Early 20thC. From the sacrosanctity of cattle for Hindus.]

Sacred Heart *n.* **1.** HEART OF JESUS CHRIST in the Roman Catholic Church, the heart of Jesus Christ, seen as a symbol of his love **2.** IMAGE OF SACRED HEART an image representing the Sacred Heart, often shown as bleeding

sacred ibis *n.* a large wading bird of sub-Saharan Africa and Arabia with bold black-and-white plumage, a large downward-curving beak, and decorative plumes on its back. Latin name: *Threskiornis aethiopica.* [*Sacred* from its being held sacred by the ancient Egyptians]

sacred mushroom *n.* a hallucinogenic American mushroom eaten in the past in Native American rituals. Genus: *Psilocybe.*

sacred thread *n.* a cotton thread worn by Brahmin males to symbolize initiation into adulthood

sacrifice /sákri fīss/ *n.* **1.** GIVING UP OF STH VALUED a giving up of sth valuable or important for sb or sth else considered to be of more value or importance **2.** STH VALUED AND GIVEN UP sth valuable or important given up as a sacrifice **3.** OFFERING TO GOD an offering to honour or appease a god, especially of a ritually slaughtered animal or person **4.** SYMBOLIC OFFERING a symbolic offering made to a god **5.** LOSS IN GIVING UP STH VALUED a loss incurred by giving away or selling sth below its value **6.** CHESS STRATEGIC GIVING UP OF CHESS PIECE in chess, an act or instance of allowing or forcing an opponent to take one of your pieces or pawns so that you can gain an advantage position ■ *v.* (**-fices, -ficing, -ficed**) **1.** *vt.* GIVE UP SB OR STH VALUED to give up sb or sth important or valued in exchange for sb or sth else that is considered more important or valuable **2.** *vt.* ABANDON SB OR STH FOR ADVANTAGE to allow sb or sth to be hurt, killed, or destroyed for your own advantage **3.** *vti.* MAKE OFFERING TO GOD to make an offering of a ritually slaughtered animal or person to a god **4.** *vt.* STRATEGICALLY GIVE UP CHESS PIECE in chess, to allow or force one of your pieces or pawns to be taken by an opponent so that you can gain an advantage in position [13thC. Via Old French from Latin *sacrificium*, literally 'making sacred', from *sacr-*, stem of *sacer* 'sacred'.] —**sacrificeable** *adj.* —**sacrificer** *n.*

sacrificial /sákri físh'l/ *adj.* relating to, used in, or offered as a sacrifice —**sacrificially** *adv.*

sacrilege /sákrilij/ *n.* **1.** TREATING HOLY THING WITHOUT RESPECT the violation, desecration, or theft of sth considered holy or sacred **2.** DISRESPECT the disrespectful or irreverent treatment of sth others consider worthy of respect or reverence [14thC. Via Old French from Latin *sacrilegium* 'temple robbery', from *sacrilegus*, literally 'collector of sacred things', from *sacr-* the stem of *sacer* 'sacred'.] —**sacrilegist** /sákri léejist/ *n.*

sacrilegious /sákri líjjəss/ *adj.* relating to, involving, or committing sacrilege —**sacrilegiously** *adv.* —**sacrilegiousness** *n.*

sacristan /sákristən/, **sacrist** /sákrist, sáy-/ *n.* **1.** SB RESPONSIBLE FOR CHRISTIAN CHURCH CONTENTS sb who looks after the contents of a Christian church, especially those kept in the sacristy **2.** SEXTON a sexton (*dated*) [14thC. From medieval Latin *sacristanus*, from *sacrista* 'keeper of sacred things', from *sacer* 'sacred'.]

sacristy /sákristi/ (*plural* **-ties**) *n.* a room in a Christian church in which sacred objects such as vessels and vestments are kept [15thC. Via French from medieval Latin *sacristia*, from *sacrista*. See SACRISTAN.]

sacroiliac /sáykrō ílli ak, sák-/ *adj.* RELATING TO SACRUM AND ILIUM relating to the sacrum and the upper portion of the hip bone (**ilium**), or to the joint between the sacrum and ilium ■ *n.* JOINT WHERE SACRUM AND ILIUM MEET the joint in the back where the sacrum and the ilium meet [Mid-19thC. Coined from *sacrum* + ILIUM.]

sacrosanct /sákrō sangkt/ *adj.* **1.** SACRED very holy and sacred **2.** INVIOLABLE not to be criticized or tampered with [Early 17thC. From Latin *sacrosanctus*, from *sacro sanctus* 'made holy through religious rites', from *sacer* 'sacred'.] —**sacrosanctity** /sákrō sángktəti/ *n.* —**sacrosanctness** /-sangktnəss/ *n.*

sacrum /sáykrəm, sák-/ (*plural* **-crums** *or* **-cra** /-krə/) *n.* a triangular bone at the base of the spine that joins to a hip bone on either side and forms part of the pelvis. In human beings it consists of five fused vertebrae. [Mid-18thC. From Latin *(os) sacrum*, a translation of Greek *hieron (osteon)* 'sacred (bone)' (from the belief that the soul resided there).]

sad /sad/ (**sadder, saddest**) *adj.* **1.** UNHAPPY feeling or showing unhappiness, grief, or sorrow ○ *a sad expression* **2.** CAUSING UNHAPPINESS causing or containing unhappiness ○ *sad news* **3.** REGRETTABLE unfortunate, or to be deplored ○ *The sad fact is that there are not enough funds available to support this project.* **4.** PITIABLE OR CONTEMPTIBLE uninteresting and pitiable or contemptible, especially because lacking taste and style (*slang informal*) ○ *wearing a really sad shirt* **5.** DULL IN COLOUR dull or dark in colour **6.** COOK NOT HAVING RISEN PROPERLY doughy, or not having risen properly [Old English *sæd* 'weary, heavy, sated'. Ultimately from an Indo-European word that is also the ancestor of English *satisfy.* The meaning 'unhappy' developed in the 14thC.] —**sadly** *adv.* —**sadness** *n.*

SAD *abbr.* seasonal affective disorder

Anwar al-Sadat

Sadat /sə dát/, **Anwar al-** (1918–81) Egyptian statesman. As president of Egypt (1970–81), he was the first Arab leader to recognize Israel, and he shared the Nobel Peace Prize with Israeli prime minister Menachem Begin in 1978 for the negotiations that culminated in the signing of their historic peace treaty in 1979. He was assassinated by members of his own army.

sadden /sádd'n/ (**-dens, -dening, -dened**) *vti.* to become sad or to cause sb to become sad (*often passive*)

saddhu *n.* = **sadhu**

saddle /sádd'l/ *n.* **1.** SEAT FOR RIDING AN ANIMAL a seat, usually made of leather, used by a rider on the back of an animal such as a horse or donkey **2.** SEAT ON A BICYCLE OR MOTORCYCLE a padded seat for a rider on a vehicle such as a bicycle, motorcycle, or tractor **3.** PART OF AN ANIMAL'S BACK the part of an animal where a saddle is placed **4.** PART OF A HARNESS a pad that forms part of a harness and fits across the back of an animal carrying or pulling sth **5.** STH RESEMBLING A SADDLE sth that looks like or is used like a saddle **6.** GEOG LOW POINT OF A RIDGE a low point of a ridge connecting two peaks **7.** CUT OF MEAT a cut of meat that includes part of the backbone and both loins **8.** BACK PART OF A CHICKEN the back part of a chicken or other fowl nearest its tail ■ *v.* (**-dles, -dling, -dled**) **1.** *vt.* STRAP A SADDLE ONTO AN ANIMAL to put a saddle onto a horse or other animal **2.** *vi.* MOUNT AN ANIMAL to mount a horse, or other animal, that has a saddle on it [Old English *sadol.* Ultimately from an Indo-European word meaning 'to sit', which is also the ancestor of English *sit.*] —**saddleless** *adj.* ◇ **in the saddle** in control of sth

saddle up *vti.* to put a saddle on a horse in readiness for riding it

saddle with *vt.* to give sb an unwelcome or unpleasant task or responsibility

saddleback /sádd'l bak/ *n.* **1.** ANIMAL WITH A SADDLE-SHAPED MARKING an animal such as a bird, fish, or other vertebrate that has a saddle-shaped marking on its back **2.** ARCHIT = **saddle roof 3.** GEOG = **saddle** *n.* 6

saddle-backed *adj.* **1.** HAVING BACK LIKE A SADDLE with its back curved into a shape like a saddle **2.** HAVING SADDLEBACK with a saddle-shaped marking on its back

saddlebag /sádd'l bag/ *n.* a bag, sometimes one of a pair, carried near or attached to an animal's saddle or attached to a frame over a wheel of a bicycle or motorcycle

saddlebill /sádd'l bil/ (*plural* **-bills** *or* **-bill**) *n.* a stork of sub-Saharan Africa that has black-and-white plumage, long black legs with red joints, and a red bill with a black band. Latin name: *Ephippiorhynchus senegalensis.*

saddle blanket *n.* a blanket or other pad placed under a saddle to prevent it from chafing the animal's back

saddlebow /sádd'l bō/ *n.* the high arch or raised part (**pommel**) at the front of a horse's saddle [Old English]

saddlecloth /sádd'l kloth/ *n.* **1.** CLOTH UNDER SADDLE TO PREVENT CHAFING a cloth placed under a saddle to prevent it from chafing the horse's back **2.** CLOTH IDENTIFYING A RACEHORSE a cloth placed under or over a racehorse's saddle that shows the horse's number

saddle horse *n.* a horse that is used or trained for riding

saddler /sáddlər/ *n.* sb who makes, sells, or repairs saddlery

saddle roof *n.* a roof that has two gables and a ridge

saddlery /sáddləri/ (*plural* **-ies**) *n.* **1.** EQUIPMENT FOR HORSES saddles, harnesses, and other equipment for horses **2.** JOB OF SADDLER the work done by a saddler **3.** SADDLER'S SHOP a shop that sells equipment for horses **4.** PLACE FOR STORING SADDLES a room in or near a stable used for making, repairing, or storing equipment for horses

saddle soap *n.* a mild soap containing neat's-foot oil, used for cleaning, softening, and preserving leather

saddle sore *n.* **1.** SORE ON A RIDER a sore on the buttocks, groin, or inner thighs of a rider, caused by the rubbing of the saddle **2.** SORE ON A HORSE a sore on a horse's body, caused by the rubbing of an ill-fitting saddle

saddle-sore *adj.* **1.** SORE FROM RIDING sore from having ridden sth with a saddle such as a horse or bicycle **2.** SORE FROM HAVING WORN A SADDLE sore, or affected by sores, from the wearing of a saddle

saddle stitch *n.* **1. RUNNING STITCH** a long running stitch, usually made with a contrasting colour for ornamentation **2. BINDING BY STITCHING ON A FOLD** in bookbinding, a method of binding the pages of a small book or magazine together by folding it in half and stitching along the line of the fold

saddle-stitch (**saddle-stitches, saddle-stitching, saddle-stitched**) *vti.* to sew sth using a saddle stitch

saddletree /sádd'l tree/ *n.* the frame of a saddle

saddo /sáddō/ *n.* sb who is uninteresting and pitiable or contemptible, especially because of a lack of taste and style (*slang*) [Late 20thC. Formed from SAD.]

Sadducee /sáddyōō see/ *n.* a member of an ancient Jewish group of priests and aristocrats who accepted the literal interpretation of the Torah but rejected Oral Law and belief in the afterlife. Sadducees favoured accommodation with the Roman occupiers of Palestine. [Pre-12thC. Via late Latin from late Greek *Saddoukaios*, from post-Biblical Hebrew *Ṣĕḏūqī* 'follower of Zadok', from *Ṣāḏōq* 'Zadok' (the high priest who supposedly founded the group), literally 'righteous'.] —**Sadducean** /sáddyōō sée ən/ *adj.* —**Sadduceeism** /-see izəm/ *n.*

Sade /saad/, **Marquis de** (1740–1814) French philosopher and novelist. His own cruel sexual practices, for which he was imprisoned, were reflected in such novels as *Juliette* (1797). Full name **Donatien Alphonse François, Comte de Sade**

sadhe /saádi/, **sade, tsade** *n.* the 18th letter of the Hebrew alphabet, represented in the English alphabet as 's' or 'ts'. See table at **alphabet** [Late 19thC. From Hebrew *ṣāḏhē*.]

sadhu /saá doo/, **saddhu** *n.* a Hindu holy man who lives by begging [Mid-19thC. From Sanskrit *sādhu* 'good, holy', literally 'straight'.]

sadiron /sád ī ərn/ *n.* a heavy iron that curves to a point at both ends, has a removable handle, is heated on an external source, and is used for pressing clothes and linens [Mid-18thC. From SAD in the obsolete sense 'solid, heavy' + IRON.]

sadism /sáydizəm/; *formerly also* /sáddizəm/ *n.* **1.** PSYCHOL **HURTING OTHERS FOR SEXUAL PLEASURE** the gaining of sexual gratification by causing physical or mental pain to other people, or the acts that produce such gratification **2. BEING CRUEL FOR FUN** the gaining of pleasure from causing physical or mental pain to people or animals **3. CRUELTY** great physical or mental cruelty [Late 19thC. From French *sadisme*, named after the Marquis de SADE.] —**sadist** *n.* —**sadistic** /sə dístik/ *adj.* —**sadistically** *adv.*

sadomasochism /sáydō mássəkizəm/ *n.* PSYCHOL **1. SEXUAL PRACTICES INVOLVING SADISM AND MASOCHISM** the gaining of sexual gratification by alternately or simultaneously enduring pain and causing pain to sb else, or the acts that produce such gratification **2. COMBINATION OF SADISTIC AND MASOCHISTIC TENDENCIES** a combination of sadistic and masochistic sexual tendencies within an individual, who may derive sexual pleasure both from inflicting and from enduring pain and cruelty [Mid-20thC. From SADISM + MASOCHISM.] —**sadomasochist** *n.* —**sadomasochistic** /sáydō mássə kístik/ *adj.*

sad sack *n.* US sb, especially a soldier, who means well but is hopelessly inept (*informal*) [Mid-20thC. From the name of a melancholy cartoon GI created by the US cartoonist George Baker during World War II.]

s.a.e., **SAE** *abbr.* **1.** self-addressed envelope **2.** stamped addressed envelope

SAEF *n., abbr.* Stock Exchange Automatic Execution Facility

Safar /sə faár/, **Saphar** *n.* CALENDAR in the Islamic calendar, the second month of the year, made up of 29 days [Late 18thC. From Arabic *safar*.]

safari /sə faári/ *n.* **1. CROSS-COUNTRY EXPEDITION** a journey across a stretch of land, especially in East Africa, for the purpose of hunting or observing wild animals ○ *go on safari* **2. PEOPLE ON EXPEDITION** a group of people on a safari, together with the animals or vehicles that transport them [Late 19thC. Via Swahili from Arabic *safar* 'journey'.]

safari jacket *n.* a casual jacket, usually made of tough light-coloured fabric, with four large pockets and a belt

safari park *n.* a large enclosed area of land where wild animals wander relatively freely and people pay to drive around and observe them

safari suit *n.* a short-sleeved safari jacket in a light-coloured fabric, with matching trousers, shorts, or skirt

Safavid dynasty /sa faávid-/ *n.* a Persian dynasty, originally part of a Turkic nomadic group, that ruled from 1500 to 1722 and established the Shiite branch of Islam as the state religion [Early 20thC. Formed from Arabic *ṣafaw ī*, from *Ṣ ī al-Din Isḥ aq*, the name of the dynasty's founder.]

safe /sayf/ *adj.* **1. NOT DANGEROUS** unlikely to cause or result in harm, injury, or damage ○ *Is it safe to open the window?* **2. NOT IN DANGER** in a position or situation that offers protection, so that harm, damage, loss, or unwanted tampering is unlikely ○ *You'll be safe with me.* ○ *It's hidden in a safe place.* **3. UNHARMED OR UNDAMAGED** in an unharmed, uninjured, or undamaged condition ○ *They're safe, but the car's beyond repair.* **4. SURE TO BE SUCCESSFUL** certain to be successful or profitable, and not at risk of failure or loss ○ *a safe investment* ○ *This investment is as safe as houses.* **5. UNLIKELY TO CAUSE TROUBLE** unlikely to cause trouble or controversy ○ *Is it safe to talk about politics with them?* **6. PROBABLY CORRECT** unlikely to be wrong ○ *It's safe to assume that the weather will be good.* **7. CAUTIOUS AND CONSERVATIVE** cautious with regard to risks or unforeseen problems, conservative with regard to estimates, or unadventurous with regard to choices and decisions ○ *The safe option is just to put the money in the bank.* **8. DEPENDABLE** able to be trusted or depended on ○ *Don't worry, your child's in safe hands.* **9.** BASEBALL **HAVING REACHED BASE SUCCESSFULLY** having reached a base or home plate without being put out ■ *n.* **1. CONTAINER FOR VALUABLES** a strong metal container, often with a complex locking system, for the storage of money and other valuables **2. STORAGE CONTAINER** a container for storage or protection, especially a ventilated box or small cupboard for keeping food cool or fresh (*dated*) **3.** US **CONDOM** a condom (*slang*) [13thC. Via Old French *sauf* from Latin *salvus*.] —**safely** /sáyfli/ *adv.* —**safeness** *n.* ◇ **be on the safe side** to take as few risks, or eliminate as many risks, as possible

safeblower /sáyf blō ər/ *n.* sb who uses explosives to open a safe in order to steal the contents

safebreaker /sáyf braykər/ *n.* a person who breaks into a safe, with or without the use of force, in order to steal the contents. US term **safecracker** —**safebreaking** *n.*

safe-conduct *n.* **1. GUARANTEE OF TRAVELLER'S SAFETY** official protection from harm or immunity from arrest for sb passing through a dangerous area, such as enemy territory in wartime **2. STH GUARANTEEING TRAVELLER'S SAFETY** a document or escort providing safe-conduct

safecracker /sáyf krakər/ *n.* = **safebreaker** —**safecracking** *n.*

safe-deposit *n.* a place where money and other valuables can be stored without risk of loss or damage by fire or theft, e.g. a bank vault or strongroom

safe-deposit box *n.* a strong metal container for valuables, e.g. jewellery or documents, usually kept in a bank vault or strongroom

safeguard /sáyf gaard/ *n.* **1. PROTECTIVE MEASURE** sth intended to prevent undesirable consequences from happening, e.g. a safety device or measure, or a proviso in a legal document **2. SAFE-CONDUCT DOCUMENT** a document providing safe-conduct ■ *vt.* (**-guards, -guarding, -guarded**) **KEEP STH SAFE** to prevent sth or sb from being harmed, damaged, or lost [14thC. From Anglo-Norman *salve garde* and French *sauve garde*, from *sauf* 'safe' (see SAFE) + *garde* (see GUARD).]

WORD KEY: SYNONYMS

safeguard, protect, defend, guard, shield

CORE MEANING: to keep safe from actual or potential injury, danger, or attack

safeguard a fairly formal word, often used to talk about preventative or precautionary planning, usually against potential harm or damage; **protect** a general word, used to talk about working to prevent harm, or sth that is intended to prevent harm; **defend** to take measures to ward off defeat or an actual or threatened attack; **guard** to work to prevent harm, damage, or attack by being vigilant and taking defensive measures; **shield** to prevent harm, damage, or attack by doing sth that forms a barrier between the person or thing being defended and the source of the threat.

safe house *n.* a house or other place of refuge where people in danger can hide or meet in secret

safekeeping /sayf kéeping/ *n.* protection from harm, damage, loss, or theft ○ *I put the documents in my desk for safekeeping.*

safelight /sáyf līt/ *n.* a type of light used in darkrooms that filters out the rays that are harmful to sensitive film and photographic paper

safe seat *n.* a parliamentary seat that is likely to continue to be held by the same party after an election

safe sex *n.* sexual activity in which precautions are taken to avoid spreading sexually transmitted diseases, e.g. by using a condom

safety /sáyfti/ (*plural* **-ties**) *n.* **1. FREEDOM FROM DANGER** protection from or nonexposure to the risk of harm or injury ○ *a safety device* ○ *The captain is responsible for the safety of the crew.* **2. LACK OF DANGER** inability to cause or result in harm, injury, or damage ○ *People are beginning to question the safety of the medication.* **3. SAFE PLACE** a place or situation where harm, damage, or loss is unlikely ○ *She led the passengers to safety.* **4. BEING UNHARMED OR UNDAMAGED** the fact of being or remaining unharmed, uninjured, or undamaged ○ *There are fears for their safety.* **5. SAFETY DEVICE** a safety catch or other device intended to prevent harm, injury, or damage **6.** FOOTBALL **DEFENSIVE BACK** in American football, a player defending the back of the field **7.** US **CONDOM** a condom (*slang*) [14thC. Via French *sauveté* from medieval Latin *salvitas*, from Latin *salvus* (see SAFE).]

safety belt *n.* **1.** = **seat belt 2. STRAP TO PREVENT SB FALLING** a strong strap attached to a fixed point, worn by a person in danger of falling, such as sb working in a high place

safety catch *n.* a device designed to prevent a mechanism from being operated unintentionally, e.g. one that stops a gun from being fired or a hoisting device from falling

safety curtain *n.* a fireproof curtain that can be lowered at the front of the stage in a theatre to isolate the auditorium from the stage in the event of fire

safety-deposit *n.* = **safe-deposit**

safety-deposit box *n.* = **safe-deposit box**

safety film *n.* nonflammable cinema film made with a cellulose acetate or polyester base. Formerly, film was made with cellulose nitrate and was prone to catch fire upon aging.

safety glass *n.* **1. SHATTERPROOF GLASS** a type of strong laminated glass designed not to shatter, made with a layer of clear plastic sandwiched between two glass sheets **2. SPLINTERPROOF GLASS** a type of glass that, if it breaks, forms rounded fragments rather than sharp splinters

safety lamp *n.* a miner's lamp in which the flame is enclosed in fine wire gauze to prevent the combustion of flammable gases

safety match *n.* a match that will only produce a flame if it is struck against a specially prepared surface

safety net *n.* **1. NET TO CATCH FALLING PERSON** a net installed below a high place, such as a circus tightrope or trapeze from which sb might fall or jump **2. PROTECTION FOR PEOPLE IN DIFFICULTY** sth intended to help people in the event of hardship or misfortune, especially sth providing financial security, such as insurance or welfare payments

safety pin *n.* **1. PIN WITH COVERED POINT** a loop-shaped pin that fastens into itself with its point under a protective cover to prevent accidental opening or injury **2.** ARMS **PIN PREVENTING DETONATION** a pin, e.g. in a grenade, that when properly seated prevents accidental or premature detonation

safety razor *n.* a razor in which the blade is partially covered to minimize the risk of accidental injury

safety valve *n.* **1.** ENG FLUID RELEASE VALVE a valve that will automatically open and release a fluid when the pressure in a chamber, e.g. a steam engine or a boiler, approaches a dangerous level **2.** PSYCHOL MEANS OF RELEASING EMOTION OR ENERGY sth that enables people to get rid of strong feelings such as anger, grief, anxiety, or excitement without harming themselves or others

saffian /sáffi ən/ *n.* hides of sheep or goats tanned with sumach and often dyed in bright colours [Late 16thC. Via Russian *saf'yan* from, ultimately, Persian *saktiyān*.]

safflower /sá flow ər/ *n.* **1.** PLANTS PLANT YIELDING OIL AND DYE an annual composite plant with orange or red flowers, native to the Indian subcontinent, from which dye and an oil used in cooking, paints, and medicine are obtained. Latin name: *Carthamus tinctorius*. **2.** DRIED FLOWERS the dried flowers of the safflower plant, used to make a red dye **3.** RED DYE a red dye made from the dried flowers of the safflower plant, used to colour fabric, food, and cosmetics [15thC. Via Dutch or German from Old French *saffleur*, ultimately Italian *asfiore* from, ultimately, Arabic *asfar* 'yellow plant'; influenced by SAFFRON and FLOWER.]

saffron /sáffrən/ *n.* (*plural* **-frons** *or* **-fron**) **1.** SPICE-PRODUCING CROCUS a crocus introduced into Europe from Asia Minor, with showy purple or white flowers bearing stigmas that are used as spice. Latin name: *Crocus sativus*. **2.** COOKING SPICE the deep orange-coloured stigmas of the saffron plant, or an orange or yellow powder obtained from these, used to colour and flavour food **3.** COLOURS BRIGHT ORANGE-YELLOW COLOUR a bright orange-yellow colour ■ *adj.* COLOURS ORANGE-YELLOW of a bright orange-yellow colour [Pre-12thC. Via Old French *safran* and medieval Latin *safranum* from, ultimately, Arabic *za'farān*.]

Saffron Walden /sáffrən wáwldən/ market town in Essex, England. The first part of the name comes from the saffron crocuses that were once grown there. Population: 14,445 (1994).

Safi /saa feé/ capital city of Safi Province and a port on the Atlantic Ocean, in western Morocco. Population: 278,000 (1993).

S. Afr. *abbr.* South Africa

safranine /sáffrə neen/, **safranin** /sáffrə nin/ *n.* red organic dye derived from phenazine, used to colour textiles and as a biological stain [Mid-19thC. From French, formed from *safran* (see SAFFRON).]

Safrole

safrole /sáffrōl/ *n.* a colourless or yellow poisonous oily liquid found in sassafras oil and used in making perfumes and soap. Formula: $C_{10}H_{10}O_2$. [Mid-19thC. Coined from SASSAFRAS + -OLE.]

sag /sag/ *v.* (**sags**, **sagging**, **sagged**) **1.** *vti.* BEND UNDER WEIGHT to bend downwards in the middle, or to hang or droop instead of remaining firm or level, or to make sth bend in this way, usually through having to support excessive weight ○ *My cakes always sag in the middle.* **2.** *vi.* BECOME WEAKER OR LOSE INTENSITY to become weaker or lose intensity or enthusiasm **3.** *vi.* FALL IN VALUE to decrease in value **4.** *vi.* NAUT DRIFT LEEWARD to drift to leeward ■ *n.* **1.** PLACE WHERE STH SAGS a bend, depression, or slackness in sth where it has sagged **2.** DECLINE IN STRENGTH a decline in strength,

intensity, or value ○ *a sag in the stock market* **3.** NAUT LEEWARD DRIFT a tendency to drift to leeward [14thC. Origin uncertain: possibly from a Scandinavian source or from Middle Low German *sacken* 'to sink'.] —**saggy** *adj.*

saga /sáagə/ *n.* **1.** NORSE LITERARY GENRE an epic tale in Old Norse literature, usually in prose, recounting events in the lives of historical and mythological figures from medieval Iceland and Norway **2.** LONG NOVEL OR SERIES OF NOVELS a long story or novel, or a series of stories or novels, often following the lives of a family or community over several generations **3.** SERIES OF EVENTS a complicated series of events or personal experiences stretching over a considerable period of time, or a detailed account of such a series of events or experiences (*informal*) ○ *Have you heard the saga of our house move?* [Early 18thC. From Old Icelandic *saga* 'saga, story' (see SAW).]

─────── **WORD KEY: CULTURAL NOTE** ───────
The Forsyte Saga, a series of novels by John Galsworthy (1906–22). Set in early 20th-century England, it charts the decline of Victorian values in upper-middle-class society through the story of three generations of the Forsyte family. It was made into a popular television series in 1967.

sagacious /sə gáyshəss/ *adj.* having or based on a profound knowledge and understanding of the world combined with intelligence and good judgment (*formal*) [Early 17thC. Formed from Latin *sagac-*, the stem of *sagax* 'of quick perception'. Ultimately from an Indo-European word meaning 'to seek', which is also the ancestor of English *seek*.] —**sagaciously** *adv.* —**sagaciousness** *n.*

sagacity /sə gássəti/ *n.* profound knowledge and understanding, coupled with foresight and good judgment [15thC. Via Old French *sagacité* from Latin *sagacitas*, from the stem *sagac-* (see SAGACIOUS).]

sagamore /sággə mawr/ *n.* among the Native North American Algonquian people, a subordinate chief [Early 17thC. From Algonquian (Abnaki) *sangman* literally 'he overcomes' or 'chief'.]

AKG London
Françoise Sagan

Sagan /saa gaán/, **Françoise** (*b.* 1935) French writer. Among her best known novels are *Bonjour Tristesse* (1954) and *A Certain Smile* (1956). Pseudonym of **Françoise Quoirez**

saga novel *n.* = roman-fleuve

sag bag *n.* = beanbag

sage[1] /sayj/ *n.* WISE PERSON sb who is regarded as knowledgeable, wise, and experienced, especially a man of advanced years revered for his wisdom and good judgment (*literary*) ■ *adj.* WISE having or showing great wisdom, especially that gained from long experience of life (*literary*) [14thC. Via Old French from, ultimately, Latin *sapere* 'to be wise, have taste' (source of English *savour* and *savvy*).] —**sagely** *adv.* —**sageness** *n.*

sage[2] /sayj/ (*plural* **sages** *or* **sage**) *n.* **1.** PLANT WITH AROMATIC LEAVES a plant or shrub with blue, purple, or white flowers and aromatic greyish-green leaves that are used as a flavouring. Latin name: *Salvia officinalis*. **2.** LEAVES USED AS COOKING HERB the fresh or dried leaves of the sage plant used in cookery as a flavouring for savoury dishes and in sage and onion stuffing **3.** = sagebrush **4.** = sage green [14thC. Via Old French *sauge* from Latin *salvia* 'healing plant', from *salvus*.]

sagebrush /sáyj brush/ (*plural* **-brushes** *or* **-brush**) *n.* a bushy composite plant native to dry regions of

North America that has silvery wedge-shaped leaves and large clusters of small white flowers. Genus: *Artemisia*.

sage Derby *n.* a type of Derby cheese that is flavoured with sage and marbled with a green colour

sage green, **sage** *adj.* of a greyish-green colour, like sage leaves —**sage green** *n.*

sage grouse *n.* a large grouse of western North America that has mottled plumage, a black belly, and a long pointed tail that it spreads during courtship. Latin name: *Centrocercus urophasianus*.

sage thrasher *n.* a greyish-brown bird of the mockingbird family found in western North America that nests in sagebrush and other low-growing desert plants. Latin name: *Oreoscoptese montanus*.

saggar /sággər/, **sagger** *n.* a clay box into which delicate ceramic objects are placed to protect them in the kiln during firing. It is seldom used now that fuels are cleaner. [Mid-18thC. Origin uncertain: probably a contraction of SAFEGUARD.]

Sagitta /sə gíttə/ *n.* a small but conspicuous constellation in the sky of the northern hemisphere lying in the Milky Way between Aquila and Vulpecula

sagittal /sájjit'l/ *adj.* **1.** ZOOL RELATING TO MEDIAN PLANE relating to or situated on the imaginary plane that divides a human or animal body into right and left halves **2.** RESEMBLING ARROW resembling an arrow or an arrowhead in shape [Mid-16thC. From medieval Latin *sagittalis*, from Latin *sagitta* 'arrow'.] —**sagittally** /sájjitli/ *adv.*

Sagittarian /sájji táiri ən/ *adj.* BORN UNDER SIGN OF SAGITTARIUS born between 22 November and 21 December ■ *n.* SB BORN UNDER SIGN OF SAGITTARIUS sb born between 22 November and 21 December. US term **Sagittarius**

Sagittarius /sájji táiri əss/ *n.* **1.** ASTRON CONSTELLATION IN THE SOUTHERN HEMISPHERE a large zodiacal constellation in the sky of the southern hemisphere between Scorpius and Capricornus, crossed by the Milky Way and lying in the direction of the centre of the galaxy **2.** NINTH SIGN OF ZODIAC the ninth sign of the zodiac, represented by an archer and lasting from approximately 22 November to 21 December. Sagittarius is classified as a fire sign and its ruling planet is Jupiter. ■ *n.*, *adj.* = **Sagittarian** [Pre-12thC. From Latin, 'archer', from *sagitta* 'arrow'.]

sagittate /sájji tayt/, **sagittiform** /sá jítti fawrm/ *adj.* used to describe a leaf that is shaped like an arrowhead [Mid-18thC. Formed from Latin *sagitta* 'arrow'.]

sago /sáygō/ *n.* a powdery substance obtained from the pith of the sago palm, used in cookery and for stiffening textiles. Sago was traditionally used in cookery as a thickener, e.g. in soups, but is now more widely used to make a sweet milk pudding similar to rice pudding. [Mid-16thC. From Malay *sagu*.]

sago palm *n.* a tall Asian palm tree that yields sago. Genus: *Metroxylan*.

saguaro /sə gwaárō, sə waárō/ (*plural* **-ros** *or* **-ro**), **sahuaro** /sə waárō/ (*plural* **-ros** *or* **-ro**) *n.* a large cactus of the southwestern United States and northern Mexico growing up to 18 m/60 ft tall with upward-curving branches, white nocturnal flowers, and edible red fruit. Latin name: *Carnegiea gigantea*. [Mid-19thC. From Mexican Spanish, of uncertain origin: probably from Uto-Aztecan.]

Sahara /sə haárə/ the largest desert in the world, covering much of northern Africa between the Atlantic Ocean and the Red Sea. Area: 9,100,000 sq. km/3,500,000 sq. mi.

Saharan /sə haárən/ *n.* GROUP OF LANGUAGES SPOKEN IN CHAD a group of languages spoken in parts of Chad and neighbouring countries. It is thought to be a branch of the Nilo-Saharan family. ■ *adj.* **1.** RELATING TO SAHARA relating to or found in the Sahara **2.** BELONGING TO SAHARAN GROUP OF LANGUAGES relating to or belonging to the Saharan group of languages

saheb *n.* = sahib

Sahel /sə hél/ semiarid zone, extending from Sudan in the east to Senegal in the west, and separating the Sahara from the tropical regions of western and central Africa

sahib /saab, saá hib, saá ib/, **saheb** /saab, saá heb/ *n.* *S Asia* a respectful form of address for men in the Indian subcontinent, formerly widely used to Caucasian men during the colonial period. The term is also used as a title, placed after the man's name. [Late 17thC. Via Hindi from Arabic 'friend'.]

Sahitya Akademi /sə hítyə ə kaddəmi/ *n.* an institute set up by the Indian government to promote literature in the Indian languages and in English

saice *n.* = **syce**

said[1] *v.* past tense, past participle of **say** ■ *adj.* LAW **PREVIOUSLY MENTIONED** previously named or mentioned ○ *The said car was later found abandoned.*

said[2] *n.* = **sayyid**

saiga /sáygə/ (*plural* **-gas** *or* **-ga**) *n.* an antelope of central Asia, with a thick tawny coat and enlarged snout, considered a genetic link between the antelope and the sheep. Genus: *Saiga.* [Early 19thC. From Russian, of uncertain origin: probably from a Finnic language.]

sail /sayl/ *n.* **1. FABRIC CATCHING WIND ON BOAT** a large piece of strong fabric, usually triangular or rectangular in shape, fixed by rigging, masts, and booms to catch the wind and propel a vessel forward **2. JOURNEY IN VESSEL** a trip or voyage in a boat or ship, especially a sailing vessel ○ *a pleasant sail across the bay* **3.** (*plural* **sail**) **VESSEL WITH SAILS** a boat or ship with sails, or such vessels considered collectively ○ *go by sail* **4. SAILS OF VESSEL** the sails of a boat or ship considered collectively ○ *a ship under full sail* **5. THING OR PART RESEMBLING SAIL** sth that resembles a sail of a boat or ship in form, function, or position **6. BLADE OF WINDMILL** any of the long flat structures on the outside of a windmill that are turned by the wind **7.** NAUT **PART OF SUBMARINE** the conning tower of a submarine ■ *v.* (**sails, sailing, sailed**) **1.** *vti.* **GO BY VESSEL ON WATER** to travel in a boat or ship across a stretch of water **2.** *vti.* **MOVE ON WATER** to move across the surface of water, or across a particular stretch of water, driven by wind or engine power ○ *pirate ships that sailed the high seas* **3.** *vt.* **DRIVE BOAT OR SHIP** to control the movement of a boat or ship, especially one with sails ○ *She sailed the boat into the harbour.* **4.** *vi.* **BEGIN SEA JOURNEY** to depart in a boat or ship, or to leave a harbour, mooring, or anchorage ○ *The ferry sails at noon.* **5.** *vi.* **MOVE SMOOTHLY** to move smoothly or swiftly and usually in a graceful way ○ *The ball sailed over the fence.* [Old English *segl*, from a prehistoric Germanic word perhaps meaning 'cut cloth'] —**sailable** *adj.* —**sailless** *adj.* ◇ **set sail** to depart in a boat or ship, or to leave a harbour, mooring, or anchorage ◇ **under sail** with sails hoisted, and not propelled by an engine

sail into *vt.* (*informal*) **1. ATTACK SB VIOLENTLY** to make a violent physical or verbal attack on sb ○ *She sailed into me for forgetting to post the letter.* **2. GET ON WITH STH** to tackle sth with vigour and enthusiasm ○ *He sailed into the task of redesigning the building.*

sail through *vti.* to do sth, especially to pass a test, with ease ○ *He sailed through the exam.*

sailboard /sáyl bawrd/ *n.* **SURFBOARD WITH A SAIL** a large surfboard with a keel and a mast and a sail mounted on it that is operated by one person standing up in the sport of windsurfing ■ *vi.* **RIDE ON SAILBOARD** to ride on a sailboard or take part in the sport of windsurfing —**sailboarder** *n.*

sailboarding /sáyl bawrding/ *n.* = **windsurfing**

sailboat /sáyl bōt/ *n.* *US* = **sailing boat**

sailcloth /sáyl kloth/ *n.* **1. FABRIC FOR SAILS** any strong fabric used to make sails, originally a heavy cotton canvas **2. FABRIC FOR CLOTHES** a lightweight cotton fabric with a texture like that of canvas, used to make clothes

sailer /sáylər/ *n.* a boat or ship, especially a sailing vessel, that has particular sailing characteristics

sailfish /sáyl fish/ (*plural* **-fish** *or* **-fishes**) *n.* a warm-water marine fish with a large high dorsal fin resembling a sail and an elongated upper jaw that projects forward like a spear. Genus: *Istiophorus.*

sailing /sáyling/ *n.* **1. TRAVELLING IN A VESSEL WITH SAILS** the sport, leisure activity, or occupation of travelling in or operating a boat or ship propelled by sails **2. SKILL OF OPERATING VESSEL** the art or a method of controlling a boat or ship, especially one with sails ○ *Expert sailing is required in such conditions.* **3. SHIP'S DEPARTURE OR DEPARTURE TIME** the departure of a ship, or the time at which a ship is scheduled to leave port ○ *The next sailing is at noon.* [Old English *segling*]

sailing boat *n.* a boat with one or more masts and sails that is propelled by the wind, chiefly used for sport and leisure. US term **sailboat**

sailing ship *n.* a ship with masts and sails that is propelled by the wind, formerly used for transporting passengers and goods

sailor /sáylər/ *n.* **1. SB WHO WORKS ON SHIP** sb who works aboard a boat or ship, especially a low-ranking member of the crew of a merchant or naval ship **2. SB TRAVELLING ON WATER** sb who frequently sails or travels on a boat or ship, especially with reference to his or her susceptibility to seasickness ○ *I'm not a good sailor.*

sailor blouse *n.* a pull-on top with a collar that is large and square at the back and comes to a V in the front, of the type often worn by sailors

sailor collar *n.* a collar that is V-shaped in front and has a broad square shape at the back, traditionally worn by sailors

sailor hat *n.* a hat with a flat top, a low crown, and wide brim that is either straight or rolled upwards all around

sailor's-choice *n.* a small fish of Atlantic coastal regions of North America such as the pinfish or pigfish

sailor suit *n.* an outfit for children resembling the traditional sailor uniform, made up of a top with a sailor collar and trousers or a skirt, usually in dark blue and white

sailplane /sáyl playn/ *n.* **LIGHT GLIDER** a light glider particularly well adapted to making use of rising air currents, used for soaring ■ *vi.* (**-planes, -planing, -planed**) **TRAVEL BY SAILPLANE** to travel in a sailplane —**sailplaner** *n.*

Saimaa, Lake /sīmaa-/ lake in southeastern Finland. Area: 1,300 sq. km/500 sq. mi.

sain /sayn/ (**sains, saining, sained**) *vt.* to make the sign of the cross over sb or sth as a blessing or protection against evil (*archaic*) [Pre 12thC. From Latin *signare* 'to mark (with the cross)', from *signum* 'mark' (source of English *sign*).]

sainfoin /sán foyn/ (*plural* **-foins** *or* **-foin**) *n.* a plant of the pea family that is grown as forage. It has clusters of pink flowers and is native to Europe and Asia. Latin name: *Onobrychis viciifolia.* [Early 17thC. From obsolete French, from modern Latin *sanctum foenum*, literally 'holy hay', alteration of *sanum foenum* 'wholesome hay'.]

saint *stressed* /saynt/; *unstressed* /sənt, sən/; *in French names often* /saN/ *n.* **1. SB HONOURED BY CHURCH AFTER DEATH** sb who has been particularly holy in life and after death is declared by a Christian church to have a privileged place in heaven and be worthy of veneration **2. MEMBER OF CHOSEN PEOPLE** sb chosen by God because of personal righteousness or the nature of his or her faith, sometimes used by particular religious groups to refer to their own members (*often used in the plural*) **3. VIRTUOUS PERSON** a particularly good or holy person, or one who is kind and patient in dealing with difficult people or situations ■ *vt.* (**saints, sainting, sainted**) **RECOGNIZE SB AS SAINT** to declare sb officially to be a saint of a Christian church [Pre-12thC. From Latin *sanctus* 'holy', literally 'consecrated', past participle of *sancire* 'to confirm, consecrate'.] —**saintdom** *n.*

St Agnes's Eve /sənt ágnəssəz-/ *n.* CALENDAR 20 January, the eve of St Agnes's Day, on which, according to British folklore, people dream of their future partners if they have performed particular rituals before going to sleep

St Albans /sənt áwlbənz/ city in Hertfordshire, south-eastern England. Nearby are the ruins of the Roman town of Verulamium. Population: 128,700 (1994).

St Andrews /sənt ándrooz/ university town in Fife, Scotland. It is famous for its historic connections with the game of golf. Population: 11,136 (1991).

St Andrew's cross *n.* a diagonal cross with arms of equal length, especially a white one on a blue background as on the flag of St Andrew and Scotland

St Anthony's cross /sənt ántəneez-/ *n.* = **tau cross**

St Anthony's fire *n.* any acutely painful inflammatory skin disorder such as cellulitis, shingles, or erysipelas (*archaic*)

St Austell /sənt óstəl/ market town in Cornwall, England. It is a centre of the china clay industry. Population: 21,200 (1994).

St Bartholomew's Day Massacre /sənt baar thóllə myooz-/ *n.* a massacre of Huguenots that began in Paris on St Bartholomew's Day, 24 August, 1572

St Bernard /sənt búrnərd/ *n.* a very large working dog belonging to a breed developed in Switzerland to rescue lost mountain travellers [Mid-19thC. Named after the Hospice of the Great ST BERNARD PASS.]

St Bernard Pass either of two mountain passes running between Italy and Switzerland

St-Brieuc /sáN bri ő/ city and administrative centre of Côtes-du-Nord Department, Brittany Region, northwestern France. Population: 44,752 (1990).

St Catharines /sənt káthərənz/ city in Ontario, Canada, on the Welland Ship Canal, across Lake Ontario from Toronto. Population: 129,300 (1996).

St Croix /sənt króy/ the largest island of the US Virgin Islands, situated in the West Indies. Population: 50,139 (1990). Area: 218 sq. km/84 sq. mi.

St David's /sənt dáyvədz/ village in Pembrokeshire, Wales, that was granted the status of city in 1994. Its cathedral was a pilgrimage centre in the Middle Ages. Population: 1,460 (1991).

St David's Day *n.* CALENDAR 1 March, the Christian saint's day commemorating St David, the patron saint of Wales

St-Denis /sáN də neé/ city in north-central France, in Seine-St-Denis Department, on the River Seine. It is a northern suburb of Paris. Population: 90,806 (1990).

sainted /sáyntid/ *adj.* **1. RECOGNIZED AS SAINT** officially declared to be a saint of a Christian church **2. IN HEAVEN** dead and thought to be in heaven **3. VIRTUOUS** good, virtuous, or holy (*literary*)

St Elias, Mount /sənt ə líəss/ the second highest mountain in Canada, in the St Elias Range, on the Alaska-Yukon Territory border. Height: 5,489 m/18,008 ft.

St Elmo's fire /sənt élmōz-/ *n.* a luminous region of electrical discharge that appears during stormy weather around a narrow pointed object, such as a church spire or the mast of a ship [Early 19thC. Named after *St Elmo* (died AD 303), patron saint of sailors.]

St-Émilion /sánt e méeli on/ *n.* a red wine produced in the area around St-Émilion in the Bordeaux region of France

St-Étienne /sáNt eti én/ city and administrative centre of Loire Department, Rhône-Alpes Region, east-central France. Population: 201,695 (1990).

Saint-Exupéry /sánt eg zóope ree/, **Antoine Marie Roger de** (1900–44) French aviator and writer. He wrote novels, essays and autobiographical works, but is chiefly remembered for his much-loved children's story, *The Little Prince* (1943).

St Gallen, St Gall /sənt gaálən, -gáll/ capital of St Gallen Canton, northeastern Switzerland, situated about 64 km/40 mi. east of Zürich. Population: 75,541 (1990).

St George's Channel /sənt jáwrjəz-/ sea passage between southeastern Ireland and southwestern Wales

St George's cross *n.* a red cross on a white background, as on the flags of St George and England

St George's Day *n.* CALENDAR 23 April, the Christian saint's day commemorating St George, the patron saint of England

St Gotthard Pass /sənt góttərd-/ pass through the central Alps between southern Switzerland and Italy. Length: 26 km/16 mi.

St Helens /sənt héllənz/ town in Lancashire, north-western England. Population: 179,900 (1995).

St Helens, Mount active volcano in southwestern Washington State, in the Cascade Range. Its last major eruption was in 1980. Height: 2,550 m/8,365 ft.

St Helier /sənt hélli ər/ port and chief town of Jersey, in the Channel Islands. Population: 28,123 (1991).

sainthood /sáynt hŏŏd/ *n.* **1.** STATUS OF BEING SAINT the condition or status of being a saint or saintly **2.** SAINTS COLLECTIVELY saints regarded as a group

St Ives /sənt ívz/ town and fishing port in Cornwall, southwestern England. Population: 9,700 (1994).

St Johns /sənt jónz/ river flowing in eastern Florida to Jacksonville, emptying into the Atlantic Ocean. Length: 444 km/276 mi.

St John's /sənt jónz/ **1.** capital city and principal port of Newfoundland, Canada, situated on the Atlantic Ocean. Population: 174,051 (1996). **2.** capital city of Antigua and Barbuda. It is situated in the north-western part of Antigua, on an inlet of the Caribbean Sea. Population: 21,514 (1991).

St John's bread *n.* = carob

St John's wort *n.* a herb or shrub with showy five-petalled yellow flowers. Genus: *Hypericum*. [*St John's* from its being said to flower on the feast of St John the Baptist]

St Kilda /sənt kíldə/ group of small, now uninhabited islands in the Outer Hebrides, Scotland. They are home to a seabird sanctuary and a National Nature Reserve.

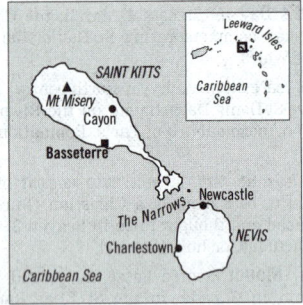
St Kitts and Nevis

St Kitts and Nevis /sənt kíts ənd néeviss/ independent state in the West Indies, comprising two islands that are part of the Leeward Islands group. Language: English. Currency: East Caribbean dollar. Capital: Basseterre. Population: 39,400 (1996). Area: 269 sq. km/104 sq. mi. Official name **Federation of St Kitts and Nevis**

St Lawrence /sənt lórrənss/ major river of North America, linking the outflow from the Great Lakes with the Atlantic Ocean. Length: 1,300 km/800 mi.

St Lawrence, Gulf of deep inlet of the Atlantic Ocean between Newfoundland and the Canadian mainland

St Lawrence Seaway system of canals bypassing unnavigable sections of the St Lawrence River and allowing oceangoing vessels to reach the Great Lakes sometimes also including the canals between the Great Lakes

St Leger /sənt léjjər/ *n.* a horse race run annually since 1776 at Doncaster

St-Lô /saN lố/ city and administrative centre of Manche Department, Basse-Normandie Region, northwestern France. Population: 22,819 (1990).

St Louis /sənt lŏŏ iss, -lŏŏ i/ city in eastern Missouri, extending along the western bank of the Mississippi River. It is one of the principal industrial and cultural centres of the Midwest. Population: 368,215 (1994).

St-Louis /saN loo ée/ town and port in northwestern Senegal, situated 177 km/110 mi. northeast of Dakar. Population: 132,444 (1994).

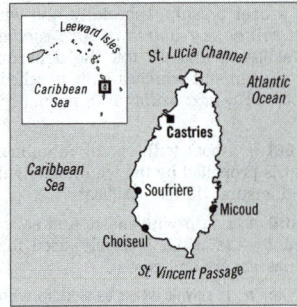
St Lucia

St Lucia /sənt lŏŏshə/ independent island state in the West Indies. It is one of the Windward Islands. Language: English. Currency: East Caribbean dollar. Capital: Castries. Population: 143,000 (1995). Area: 617 sq. km/238 sq. mi.

St Luke's summer /sənt lŏŏks-/ *n.* a period of warm weather occurring in the autumn, around 18 October, the festival of St Luke (*archaic*)

saintly /sáyntli/ (**-lier, -liest**) *adj.* **1.** OF CHRISTIAN SAINT characteristic of or associated with a saint of a Christian church **2.** VERY VIRTUOUS very good, virtuous, or holy —**saintlily** *adv.* —**saintliness** *n.*

St Martin /sənt maártin/ island in the West Indies, one of the Leeward Islands, between the islands of Anguilla and Saint-Barthélemy. It is a dependency of Guadeloupe. Area: 52 sq. km/20 sq. mi.

St Martin's summer *n.* a period of warm weather occurring in the autumn, around 11 November, the festival of St Martin (*archaic*)

St Matthews /sənt máth yooz/ city in northern Kentucky, south of the Illinois border. It is an eastern suburb of Louisville. Population: 16,562 (1996).

St Michael's Mount /sənt míkəlz-/ granite island off the coast of Cornwall, in southwestern England. A causeway links it to the mainland at low tide. Population: 25 (1991).

St Moritz /sáN mə ríts/ spa town in southeastern Switzerland, situated 14 km/9 mi. from the Italian border. Population: 5,600 (1996).

St-Nazaire /sáN na záir/ city and port in Loire-Atlantique Department, Pays de la Loire Region, western France. Population: 66,087 (1990).

St Neots /sənt née əts/ market town in Huntingdonshire, England. Population: 25,540 (1991).

St Patrick's Day /sənt pátt riks-/ *n.* CALENDAR 17 March, the Christian feast day of St Patrick, the patron saint of Ireland

St Paul /sənt páwl/ capital city of Minnesota, in the southeastern part of the state on the banks of the Mississippi River. Population: 262,071 (1994).

saintpaulia /sənt páwli ə/ (*plural* **-lias** *or* **-lia**) *n.* = **African violet** [Late 19thC. Named after the German explorer Baron Walter von *Saint-Paul* (1860–1910).]

St Paul's Cathedral *n.* a large, domed, baroque cathedral in the City of London, designed by Christopher Wren and completed in 1710

St Peter Port /sənt péetər-/ port and chief town of Guernsey, in the Channel Islands. Population: 16,648 (1991).

St Peter's /sənt péetərz/ *n.* a large Baroque basilica

St Peter's, Vatican, Rome, Italy

in the Vatican City, Rome, that was completed in 1612. It is one of the largest churches in the world.

St Petersburg /sənt péetərz burg/ the second largest city in Russia, located in the northwestern part of the country. Situated at the head of the Gulf of Finland, an arm of the Baltic Sea, it is also the country's largest port. It was the capital of Russia for two centuries, from 1712 until 1918. Population: 4,672,000 (1997). Former name **Leningrad** (1924–90)

St-Pierre /sənt pyáir/ town and tourist centre in the French West Indies, on Martinique Island in the Caribbean Sea, near the base of the volcano, Montagne Pelée. Population: 5,007 (1990).

St-Pierre and Miquelon /-mée kloN/ overseas territory of France, in the North Atlantic Ocean, off the coast of Newfoundland, Canada. It consists of two small groups of islands. Population: 6,392 (1990). Area: 242 sq. km/93 sq. mi.

Saint-Saëns /sáN sóNss, -sóN/, **Camille** (1835–1921) French composer. His works, including symphonies, church music, concertos, songs, and operas, are in the classical French tradition. Full name **Charles Camille Saint-Saëns**

saint's day *n.* a day of the year on which a particular saint is remembered or honoured. Some saint's days are marked by traditional festivities or associated with popular superstitions.

St Swithin's Day /sənt swíthinz-/ *n.* CALENDAR 15 July, the Christian saint's day commemorating Saint Swithin. If it rains on this day, according to superstition, it will rain on the next 40 days, and if not, it will stay dry for 40 days.

St Thomas /sənt tómməss-/ island of the US Virgin Islands, situated in the West Indies. Population: 48,166 (1990). Area: 73 sq. km/28 sq. mi.

St-Tropez /sáN trō páy/ resort town on the Mediterranean coast, southern France. It is situated 155 km/60 mi. east of Marseille. Population: 5,790 (1990).

St Valentine's Day *n.* CALENDAR = **Valentine's Day**

St Vincent, Cape /sənt vínsənt-/ cape at the south-westernmost point of Portugal

St Vincent, Gulf of gulf in southern Australia, located between the Yorke and Fleurieu peninsulas

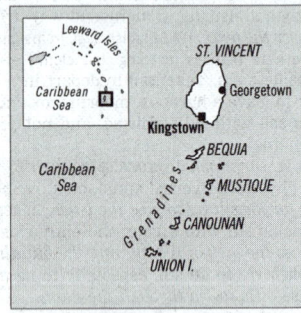
St Vincent and the Grenadines

St Vincent and the Grenadines /-grénnə deenz/ independent state in the West Indies comprising the island of St Vincent and 32 of the islands of the Grenadine group. Language: English. Currency: East Caribbean dollar. Capital: Kingstown. Population: 112,000 (1995). Area: 389 sq. km/150 sq. mi.

St Vitus's dance /sənt vítəssiz-/ *n.* Sydenham's chorea (*no longer in technical use*) [Early 17thC. Named after *St Vitus* (3rdC), patron saint of those affected by this condition.]

saith /seth/ 3rd person present singular of **say** (*archaic*)

Saiva /sívə, shívə/ *n.* a member of a Hindu religious group that worships Shiva [Late 18thC. From Sanskrit *-saiva-* 'sacred to Shiva'.] —**Saiva** *adj.* —**Saivism** *n.* —**Saivite** *n.*

sakai /sákī/ *n.* a member of an aboriginal people who live in the forests of Malaysia [Mid-19thC. From Malay, 'dependent, subject'.]

Sakai /saa kí/ town south of Osaka, situated on Osaka bay in Osaka Prefecture, on western Honshu, Japan. Population: 807,765 (1990).

a at; aa father; aw all; ay day; air hair; ə about, edible, item, common, circus; e egg; ee eel; hw when; i it, happy; ī ice; 'l apple; 'm rhythm; 'n fashion; o odd; ō open; ŏŏ good; oo pool; ow owl; oy oil; th thin; th this; u up; ur urge;

sake[1] /sayk/ *n.* **1.** SB'S OR STH'S INTEREST the good, benefit, or welfare of sb or sth ○ *I hope you're right, for all our sakes!* **2.** MOTIVE OR OBJECTIVE the purpose of doing, obtaining, achieving, or maintaining sth ○ *It's not worth risking your life for the sake of getting there a few minutes earlier.* [Old English *sacu*, from a prehistoric Germanic word meaning 'seeking', hence 'accusation, cause', which is also the ancestor of English *seek*]

sake[2] /saáki/, **saki, saké** *n.* a Japanese alcoholic beverage made from fermented rice and usually served warm [Late 17thC. From Japanese.]

saker /saykər/ *n.* a large falcon from central Asia and eastern Europe with brown body plumage and a pale-coloured head, used in falconry. Latin name: *Falco cherrug*. [15thC. Via (Old) French *sacre* from Arabic *sakr* 'hawk, falcon'.]

saki *n.* = **sake**

Sakkara /sə kaárə/ village near Cairo, Egypt. It is the site of a stepped pyramid built by King Zoser between 2737 and 2717 BC, the first monumental royal tomb, and one of the oldest stone structures in Egypt.

Sakta /shaáktə/, **Shakta** *n.* INDIAN RELIG a member of a Hindu religious group who particularly worship the female principle or the female gods

Sakti /sákti/, **Shakti** /shúkti/ *n.* in Hinduism, the vital generative and creative principle at work in the universe, typically associated with the feminine component of the divine, often embodied as a goddess [Early 19thC. From Sanskrit *śaktih*, literally 'power', from *śak-* 'to be strong' (source of English *Sikh*).]

Sakyamuni /saákyə moóni/ *n.* one of the names of the Buddha, deriving from Sakya, the name of his clan

sal /sal/ *n.* PHARM used in pharmacology to denote salt (*usually used in combination*) ○ *sal ammoniac* [14thC. From Latin, 'salt'.]

salaam /sə laám/ *n.* **1.** DEEP BOW WITH HAND ON FOREHEAD a deeply respectful or deferential gesture of greeting or acknowledgment, used especially in Islamic countries, made by bowing low with the palm of the right hand against the forehead **2.** RESPECTFUL GREETING the word 'salaam', meaning 'peace', used as a respectful greeting ■ *vti.* (**-laams, -laaming, -laamed**) MAKE SALUTATION OR GREETING OR RESPECT to perform a salaam, or to greet sb with a salaam [Early 17thC. From Arabic *salām* 'peace'.]

salable *adj.* = **saleable**

salacious /sə láyshəss/ *adj.* **1.** WITH SEXUAL CONTENT intended to titillate or arouse people sexually, usually by having an explicit erotic content **2.** EXPLICITLY SEXUAL having or showing explicit or crude sexual desire or interest [Mid-17thC. Formed from the Latin stem *salac-*, from *salire* 'to leap' (source of English *salient*).] —**salaciously** *adv.* —**salaciousness** *n.* —**salacity** /sə lássəti/ *n.*

salad /sáləd/ *n.* **1.** MIXTURE OF RAW VEGETABLES a cold dish consisting mainly of a mixture of raw vegetables, whole, sliced, chopped, or in pieces, usually served with a dressing for moisture and flavour. Many other ingredients may be incorporated into a salad, which can be served as a separate course or as an accompaniment to other food. **2.** DISH OF COLD INGREDIENTS a cold dish consisting of a particular type of food, e.g. a single vegetable or a selection of fruit, cut into pieces or slices, and served usually with a dressing ○ *potato salad* **3.** COLD MEAL a dish consisting of cold meat, fish, cheese, or egg served with a salad of lettuce, tomato, cucumber, and other vegetables ○ *chicken salad* **4.** LEAFY VEGETABLES any of the leafy vegetables commonly used to make a green salad, typically the many types of lettuce, watercress, chicory, endive, mustard, and cress **5.** CONFUSED MIXTURE a confused or varied mixture ○ *a salad of ideas* [14thC. Via French *salade* from assumed Vulgar Latin *salata* 'salted', ultimately from Latin *sal* 'salt' (source of English *salami*).]

salad bar *n.* a counter in a restaurant or shop where salads of various types are available, often set up as a buffet where customers can choose their own ingredients

salad cream *n.* a ready-made creamy white dressing with a flowing consistency for eating with salad

salad days *npl.* the period of a person's life when he or she is young, innocent, naive, and inexperienced (*dated*) [From the words of Cleopatra in Shakespeare's *Antony and Cleopatra*: 'My salad days, When I was green in judgement, cold in blood']

salad dressing *n.* a well-seasoned sauce poured over or mixed with the ingredients of a salad, e.g. a vinaigrette made from oil and vinegar

salade niçoise /sáləd nee swáaz/ *n.* a cold dish originally from the region around Nice in France, containing anchovies, tuna fillets, olives, green beans, and sometimes other ingredients, served with a dressing of olive oil and garlic [Early 20thC. From French, named after NICE.]

Saladin /sáladin/, **Sultan of Egypt and Syria** (1137–93). During his sultanate (1174–93), he led the Muslims successfully against the Christian crusaders in Palestine until he was defeated and captured at Acre (1191). Full name **Salah ed-din Yussuf ibn Ayub**

salal /sə lál/ (*plural* **salals** or **salal**) *n.* an evergreen shrub of the heath family native to the west coast of North America, with leathery leaves, clusters of pink or white flowers, and edible purple berries. Latin name: *Gaultheria shallon*. [Early 19thC. From Chinook jargon *sallal*.]

Salam /saa laám/, **Abdus** (1926–96) Pakistani physicist. He was noted for his study of the interactions of elementary particles, in particular his formulation of the electroweak theory. He shared the Nobel Prize in physics (1979).

Salamanca /salə mángkə/ city in the autonomous region of Castile-León, west-central Spain. It is the site of the University of Salamanca, founded in 1218. Population: 167,316 (1995).

Salamander

salamander /sálə mandər/ *n.* **1.** SMALL ANIMAL RESEMBLING LIZARD an amphibian that resembles a lizard but has porous moist skin instead of scales, and that lives in water as a larva and on land as an adult. Order: Caudata. **2.** MYTHOL MYTHICAL REPTILE LIVING IN FIRE a mythical lizard that can live in fire **3.** COOK, HOUSEHOLD HOT METAL PLATE FOR BROWNING FOOD a cooking utensil most often in the form of a metal plate with a handle, designed to be heated until very hot then held over food to produce a browned or caramelized surface **4.** BUILDING PORTABLE STOVE a stove that is used on construction projects to heat or dry out buildings or to thaw frozen water pipes [14thC. Directly and via Old French from Latin and Greek *salamandra*.] —**salamandrine** /sálə mándrin/ *adj.*

salami /sə laámi/ *n.* a large thick highly seasoned sausage, Italian in origin and very often cured, usually served cold in thin slices [Mid-19thC. From Italian, plural of *salame*, from, ultimately, Latin *sal* 'salt' (source of English *sauce*).]

Salamis /sáləməss/ island in eastern Greece 13 km/8 mi. west of the port of Piraeus. It was the location of a major sea battle in 480 BC in which the Greeks defeated the Persians. Population: 28,574 (1981). Area: 10 sq. km/39 sq. mi.

sal ammoniac /sál ə móni ak/ *n.* = **ammonium chloride** [From Latin *sal ammoniacus*, literally 'salt of Ammon' (see AMMONIA)]

salary /sáləri/ (*plural* **-ies**) *n.* a set sum of money paid at regular intervals to an employee, especially for professional or clerical work [13thC. Via Old French *salaire* and directly from Latin *salarium* 'money given to a Roman soldier to buy salt']

salaried /sálərid/ *adj.* receiving a regular salary for employment, e.g. as opposed to being paid by the hour

salbutamol /sal byoótə mol/ *n.* a bronchodilating drug used as a component in inhalers to relieve asthma, emphysema, and chronic bronchitis. Formula: $C_{13}H_{21}NO_3$. [Mid-20thC. Coined from *salicylic acid* + BUTYL + AMINE +-OL.]

salchow /sálkō/ *n.* a jump in figure skating in which the skater takes off from one skate, does a complete rotation in the air, and lands on the opposite skate [Early 20thC. Named after the Swedish figure-skater Ulrich *Salchow* (1877–1949).]

sale /sayl/ *n.* **1.** SELLING OF STH the exchanging of goods or services for an agreed amount of money, or a single transaction of this nature **2.** OPPORTUNITY TO BUY GOODS AT DISCOUNT a period of time when a shop sells goods at reduced prices, often in order to clear stocks ○ *I never go shopping during the sales.* **3.** OPPORTUNITY TO BUY SECOND-HAND GOODS an event at which personal possessions or other second-hand items are sold, usually at low prices, sometimes to raise money for a charitable or other cause **4.** AUCTION an event at which goods are sold to the highest bidder **5.** MARKET OR DEMAND demand that creates an opportunity to sell sth **6.** AMOUNT SOLD OR RATE OF SELLING a quantity of things sold, or the rate at which they are sold ■ **sales** *npl.* **1.** DEPARTMENT SELLING THINGS the department of a company involved with selling its products or services **2.** THINGS SOLD the total number or value of items sold ○ *Sales fell by 10 per cent last month* [Pre-12thC. From Old Norse *sala*, from a prehistoric Germanic word that is also the ancestor of English *sell*.] ◇ **for sale** available for purchase ◇ **on sale** available for purchase, usually from a shop or other commercial organization

Sale /sayl/ **1.** town on the River Mersey in Cheshire, England, near Manchester. Population: 56,052 (1991). **2.** city in southeastern Victoria, Australia. It is a supply and processing centre. Population: 13,366 (1996).

saleable, **salable** *adj.* suitable for selling or capable of being sold —**saleability** /sáylə bílləti/ *n.* —**saleableness** /sáyləb'lnəss/ *n.* —**saleably** /-əbli/ *adv.*

sale and leaseback *n.* the sale of an asset that the vendor rents back from the buyer immediately after the sale, thereby raising cash and allowing a tax deduction

sale and return *n.* = **sale or return**

Saleh /saa lékh/, **Ali Abdullah** (*b.* 1942) Yemeni soldier and statesman. He became president of North Yemen in 1978 and in 1990 unified the country with South Yemen as the Republic of Yemen.

Salem /sáyləm/ **1.** city in northeastern Massachusetts, on Massachusetts Bay, northeast of Boston. It was the site of witchcraft trials and executions in 1692. Population: 38,008 (1996). **2.** capital city of Oregon, on the Willamette River, in the northwest of the state. Population: 107,786 (1990).

sale of work *n.* an event at which home-made goods are sold, usually to raise money for a church or other charitable cause

sale or return, **sale and return** *n.* an agreement between a supplier and a purchaser or retailer whereby the latter returns any unused or unsold goods, only paying for those that have been used or sold

salep /sáləp/ *n.* the dried ground tubers of various orchids used as food and formerly in medicine [Mid-18thC. Via French from Turkish *sālep*, from Arabic *ta'lab* 'fox', a shortening of *kuşa* 't-ta'lab'orchid', literally 'fox's testicles'.]

saleratus /sálə ráytəss/ *n.* US baking soda (*archaic*) [Mid-19thC. From modern Latin *sal aeratus*, literally 'aerated salt'.]

Salerno /sə lúrnō/ capital city and port in Salerno Province, Campania Region, southern Italy. Population: 147,564 (1994).

saleroom /sáyl room, sáyl roóm/ *n.* a large room where goods are sold by auction. US term **salesroom**

sales assistant *n.* sb who is employed to assist and

sell goods to customers in a retail shop. US term **salesclerk**

salesclerk /sáylz klaark/ n. US = **sales assistant**

sales force n. the body of salespeople employed by a company to sell its goods and services

salesgirl /sáylz gurl/ n. a young woman employed to sell goods to customers in a shop (dated or offensive)

Salesian /sə léezi ən, -léezh'n/ n. a member of the Roman Catholic order of Saint Francis de Sales founded in Turin, Italy, in 1845 and dedicated to educational and missionary work —**Salesian** adj.

salesman /sáylzmən/ (plural **-men** /-mən/) n. a man who sells goods or services, either in a shop or by contacting potential customers within a particular area

--- **WORD KEY: CULTURAL NOTE** ---

Death of a Salesman, a play by US dramatist Arthur Miller (1949). The tragic story of Willi Loman, an ageing salesman tormented by an overwhelming sense of failure, highlights the false values of contemporary consumer society and questions traditional ideas of success and failure. It was made into a film by Volker Schlöndorff in 1985. As a result of the power of the play, the term *Willi Loman* came to mean a man who has tragically sacrificed or sold his own life, and that of his family, in pursuit of the so-called American Dream.

---

salesmanship /sáylzmən ship/ n. the skills, techniques, and tactics involved in persuading people to buy goods or services

salesperson /sáylz purss'n/ (plural **-people** /-peep'l/ or **-persons**) n. sb who sells goods or services, usually in a shop or by contacting customers within a particular area

sales pitch n. the statements made, arguments used, and assurances given by sb trying to sell sth

sales rep n. a sales representative (informal) [Shortening]

sales representative n. sb employed by a company to visit prospective customers with a view to selling them the company's products

sales resistance n. reluctance or refusal to buy, especially when aggressive selling techniques are used

salesroom /sáylz room, -roöm/ n. **1.** PLACE DISPLAYING GOODS FOR SALE a large room where goods for sale are put on display **2.** US = **saleroom**

sales team n. = **sales force**

saleswoman /sáylz woomən/ (plural **-en** /-wimin/) n. a woman who sells goods or services, usually in a shop or by contacting customers within a particular area

salet /sállit/ n. = **sallet**

Salford /sáwlfərd/ city in Lancashire, northwestern England. It is adjacent to Manchester, from which it is separated by the River Irwell. Population: 230,700 (1994).

Salian /sáyli ən/ n. a member of the branch of Frankish people, the Salii, who invaded and then settled in an area of the Rhine valley in the Netherlands during the 4th century AD. They subsequently spread into and conquered large parts of Northern Gaul. [Early 17thC. Formed from late Latin *Salii* 'Salian Franks'.]

Salic /sáylik, sállik/, **Salique** adj. **1.** PEOPLES RELATING TO SALIANS relating to or typical of the Salians, or their culture **2.** HIST RELATING TO SALIC LAW relating to Salic Law [Mid-16thC. Via French *salique* or medieval Latin *Salicus* from late Latin *Salii* (plural) 'Salian Franks'.]

salicaceous /sálli káyshəss/ adj. used to describe trees or woody shrubs that have catkins, e.g. the willow and poplar. Family: Salicaceae. [Mid-19thC. Formed from modern Latin *salicaceus*, from Latin *salic-*, stem of *salix* 'willow'.]

salicin /sállissin/, **salicine** n. a colourless crystalline substance obtained from the bark of certain poplar and willow trees and formerly used as an analgesic. Formula: $C_{13}H_{18}O_7$. [Mid-19thC. Via French *salicine* from Latin *salic-* the stem of *salic* 'willow'.]

salicional /sə lísh'nəl/ n. a stop and pipes on an organ that produce a soft, gentle tone [Mid-19thC. Via German from Latin *salic-*, the stem of *salix* 'willow'.]

Salic law n. a law excluding women from the right to succeed to the throne that formerly applied in France and some other European monarchies. The prohibition was supposedly founded on a law of the Salians that prevented women from inheriting land in some areas.

salicylate /sə líssi layt/ n. a salt or ester of salicylic acid [Mid-19thC. Via French *salicyle* from Latin *salictum*, from *salic-*, the stem of *salix* 'willow'.]

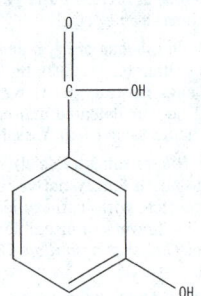

Salicylic acid

salicylic acid /sálli síllik-/ n. a white crystalline acid used in making aspirin and dyes and to preserve foods. Formula: $C_7H_6O_3$. [Formed from French *salicyle* (see SALICYLATE)]

salience /sáyli ənss/, **saliency** /-ənssi/ (plural **-cies**) n. **1.** BEING IMPORTANT the quality of being particularly important or striking **2.** IMPORTANT OR STRIKING FEATURE a particularly important or striking feature

salient /sáyli ənt/ adj. **1.** NOTICEABLE OR STRIKING particularly noticeable, striking, or relevant **2.** PROJECTING sticking out from a surface **3.** GEOM PROJECTING OUTWARDS used to describe an angle that projects outwards from a polygon **4.** HERALDRY JUMPING represented as a jumping or leaping animal ■ n. **1.** MIL PROJECTING PART OF DEFENSIVE ALIGNMENT a part of a front, line, or fortification that projects outwards into enemy-held territory or towards the enemy **2.** GEOM SALIENT ANGLE a salient angle [Mid-17thC. From Latin *salient-*, present participle stem of *salire* 'to jump' (source of English *salacious*).] —**saliently** adv.

--- **WORD KEY: ORIGIN** ---

The Latin word *salire*, from which **salient** is derived, is also the source of English *assail*, *assault*, *desultory*, *insult*, *salacious*, *sally*, and *sauté*.

---

salientian /sáyli énshi ən/ adj. = **anuran** [Mid-20thC. Formed from modern Latin *Salentia* from the Latin stem *salient-* (see SALIENT).]

Salieri /sálli áiri/, **Antonio** (1750–1825) Italian composer. As a successful writer of operas and church music in Vienna, he was a rival of Mozart.

saliferous /sə lífferəss/ adj. used to describe a geological formation that contains or produces salt [Early 19thC. Coined from Latin *sal* 'salt' + -FEROUS.]

salimeter /sa límmitər/ n. = **salinometer** [Mid-19thC. Coined from Latin *sal* 'salt' + -METER.] —**salimetric** /sálli méttrik/ adj. —**salimetry** /sa límmətri/ n.

salina /sə línə, sə leenə/ n. a salt marsh, lake, pond, or spring [Late 16thC. Via Spanish from medieval Latin, 'salt pit'.]

Salinas /sə leenəss/ river in western California, rising in the Santa Lucia Mountains and flowing into Monterey Bay. Length: 241 km/150 mi.

saline /sáy līn/ adj. **1.** CONTAINING SALT containing salt or impregnated with salt **2.** CHEM CONTAINING SALTS relating to or containing alkali metal salts or magnesium salt ■ n. MED SOLUTION OF SALT AND DISTILLED WATER a solution of common salt (**sodium chloride**) and distilled water, especially one having the same concentration as body fluids. It is used as a diluent for drugs and as a plasma substitute. [15thC. From Latin *salinum* 'salt cellar', from *sal* 'salt' (source of English *salad*).] —**salinity** /sə línnəti/ n.

Salinger /sállinjər/, **J. D.** (b. 1919) US writer. After great success with such works as *The Catcher in the Rye* (1951), in the mid-1960s he became a complete recluse. Full name **Jerome David Salinger**

salinize /sálli nīz/ (**-nizes, -nizing, -nized**), **salinise** (**-nises, -nising, -nised**) vt. to treat or contaminate sth with salt —**salinization** /sálli nī záysh'n/ n.

salinometer /sálli nómmitər/ n. an instrument used to measure the concentration of salt in salt solutions —**salinometric** /sállinə méttrik/ adj. —**salinometry** /sálli nómmətri/ n.

Salique adj. = **Salic**

Salisbury /sáwlzbəri, -bri/ city in Wiltshire, southwestern England. Salisbury Cathedral dates from the 12th century and has the highest spire in the country at 125 m/404 ft. Population: 39,700 (1994).

Salisbury Plain area of rolling, chalky downs in Wiltshire, southwestern England. Stonehenge is located there. Area: 775 sq. km/300 sq. mi.

Salish /sáylish/ n. **1.** Salish, Salishan LANG FAMILY OF NATIVE N AMERICAN LANGUAGES a family of Native North American languages spoken in the northwestern United States and British Columbia. Around 2,000 people speak one of the remaining 20 Salish languages. **2.** PEOPLES NATIVE N AMERICANS SPEAKING SALISH LANGUAGES the group of Native North American peoples who speak the Salish languages (takes a plural verb) [Mid-19thC. From Salish *sə'liš* 'Flatheads'.] —**Salishan** adj.

saliva /sə lívə/ n. the clear liquid secreted into the mouth by the salivary glands, consisting of water, mucin, protein, and enzymes. It moistens food and starts the breakdown of starches. [15thC. Via French *salive* and directly from Latin *saliva* 'spittle'.]

salivary /sə lívəri, sállivəri/ adj. relating to saliva or the salivary glands

salivary gland n. any of the glands in mammals that produce and secrete saliva into the mouth

salivate /sálli vayt/ (**-vates, -vating, -vated**) v. **1.** vi. PRODUCE SALIVA to produce saliva in the mouth, especially at an increased rate, e.g. when food is seen, smelled, or expected **2.** vt. CAUSE ANIMAL TO SALIVATE to cause an animal, e.g. an animal in an experiment, to produce large amounts of saliva **3.** vi. LONG FOR to feel or show an immense desire for or appreciation of sth (informal) ○ *salivating over the magnificent range of fitted kitchens* [Mid-17thC. Back-formation from *salivation*, directly and via French from, ultimately, Latin *saliva* 'saliva'.] —**salivation** /sálli váysh'n/ n.

AKG London

Jonas Salk

Salk /sawk/, **Jonas** (1914–95) US physician and epidemiologist. He developed the first vaccine against poliomyelitis. Full name **Jonas Edward Salk**

Salk vaccine n. a vaccine against poliomyelitis containing a form of the virus that causes it, which has been made inactive by treatment with a solution of formaldehyde. ◊ **Sabin vaccine** [Mid-20thC. Named after Jonas *Salk*.]

sallet /sállit/, **salet** n. a light helmet protecting the head and the back of the neck, worn in the late Middle Ages [15thC. Via French *salade* from, ultimately, Latin *caelata* 'engraved (helmet)', from *caelum* 'chisel'.]

sallow[1] /sállō/ adj. UNNATURALLY YELLOW unnaturally pale and yellowish ○ *a sallow complexion* ■ vt. (**-lows, -lowing, -lowed**) MAKE STH SALLOW to make sth unnaturally pale and yellowish ○ *The illness had sallowed her skin.* [Old English *salo* 'dark, dusky', from prehistoric Germanic] —**sallowish** *adj.* —**sallowly** *adv.* —**sallowness** *n.*

sallow[2] /sállō/ (*plural* **-lows** *or* **-low**) *n.* a small European willow tree with broad leaves and large catkins that yields a hard wood used to produce charcoal. Latin name: *Salix caprea.* [Old English *salh.* Ultimately from an Indo-European word meaning 'willow', which is also the ancestor of English *salicaceous.*] —**sallowy** *adj.*

Sallust /sálləst/ (86–35? BC) Roman historian. His histories of Catiline's conspiracy and a Roman war in Africa, written after he retired from holding colonial governorships, influenced the work of later historians. Full name **Gaius Sallustius Crispus**

sally /sálli/ *n.* (*plural* **-lies**) **1.** MIL **ATTACK FROM DEFENSIVE POSITION** an offensive thrust from a defensive position, especially, formerly, a sudden attack by the defenders of a besieged position on the people besieging them **2. SUDDEN RUSH FORWARD** a sudden rush or spring forward **3. SUDDEN ACTION** a sudden burst of activity or springing into action **4. SUDDEN EXPRESSION** a sudden outburst of speech or expression of emotion **5. WITTY REMARK** a witty remark, reply, or retort **6. EXPEDITION** an expedition or excursion ■ *vi.* (**-lies, -lying, -lied**) **1.** MIL **MAKE SALLY** to make an offensive thrust from a defensive position **2. SET OUT** to go out after being indoors or set out on a journey or excursion **3. RUSH OUT SUDDENLY** to rush or spring out suddenly [Mid-16thC. From French *saillie*, from the past participle of *saillir* 'to leap', ultimately from Latin *salire* (source of English *salient*).] —**sallier** *n.*

Sally Army /sálli-/ *n.* the Salvation Army (*informal*) [*Sally* a shortening and alteration of *Salvation*]

Sally Lunn /sálli lún/ *n.* a sweet bread leavened with yeast that is typically baked in a tin and served warm in slices with butter. It is particularly popular in the southern United States. [Late 18thC. Origin uncertain: perhaps named after the woman in Bath who first sold these cakes.]

sallyport /sálli pawrt/ *n.* an opening in a fortification from which the defenders can make sallies [Mid-17thC]

salmagundi /sálmə gúndi/ *n.* **1. MIXED SALAD** a mixed salad of many ingredients, such as meat, poultry, fish, and vegetables, arranged in rows on a platter **2. MIXTURE** a mixture or miscellany (*literary*) [Late 17thC. From French *salmagondis*, originally 'seasoned salt meats', of uncertain origin.]

Salmanazar /sálmə názzər/, **salmanazar** *n.* a large wine bottle that holds the equivalent of 12 standard bottles, used especially for champagne [Mid-20thC. From late Latin *Salmanasar*, a variant of *Shalmaneser*, a king of Assyria in the Bible.]

salmi /sálmi/, **salmis** (*plural* **-mis**) *n.* a dish made from pieces of partly roasted game stewed with mushrooms and served with a rich wine sauce [Mid-18thC. Shortening of French *salmagondis* (see SALMAGUNDI).]

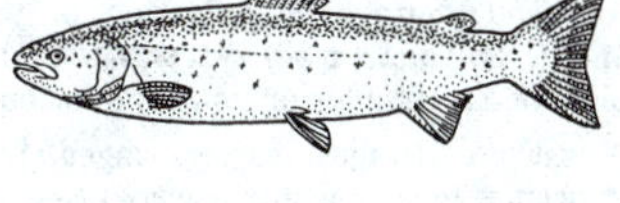

Salmon

salmon /sámmən/ (*plural* **-on** *or* **-ons**) *n.* **1.** ZOOL **LARGE ATLANTIC FOOD AND GAME FISH** a large North Atlantic fish, popular for fishing and eating, that has soft fins and pink flesh and migrates up freshwater rivers to spawn. Family: Salmonidae. **2.** ZOOL **LARGE PACIFIC FOOD AND GAME FISH** a food fish of the salmon family found in the North Pacific, e.g. the Chinook, sockeye, coho, or chum. Genus: *Oncorhynchus.* **3.** FOOD **SALMON AS FOOD** the red or pink flesh of the salmon eaten as food **4.** COLOURS = **salmon pink** [13thC. Via French *saumon* from Latin *salmon-*, stem of *salmo*, of uncertain origin: perhaps from *salire* 'to leap'.]

Salmon /sámmən/ river in Idaho flowing into the Snake River on the Washington border. Length: 676 km/420 mi.

salmonberry /sámmənbəri/ (*plural* **-ries** /sámmən beri/) *n.* **1.** PLANTS **N AMERICAN RASPBERRY** a raspberry plant from the Pacific coast of North America that has showy red flowers and salmon-pink fruit. Latin name: *Rubus spectabilis.* **2.** FOOD **FRUIT OF SALMONBERRY** the edible salmon-pink fruit of the salmonberry

salmonella /sálmə néllə/ (*plural* **-lae**) *n.* **1.** BIOL **BACTERIUM CAUSING FOOD POISONING** a rod-shaped bacterium found in the intestine that can cause food poisoning, gastroenteritis, and typhoid fever. Genus: *Salmonella.* **2.** MED = **salmonellosis** [Early 20thC. From modern Latin, named after Daniel Elmer *Salmon* (1850–1914), the US veterinary surgeon who isolated a strain of these bacteria.]

salmonellosis /sálmə ne lṓsiss/ *n.* food poisoning caused by infection with salmonella organisms, usually characterized by gastrointestinal upset, diarrhoea, fever, and occasionally death. It is usually contracted by eating undercooked contaminated food.

salmonid /sálmənid/ *n.* a bony soft-finned fish belonging to the family that includes salmon, trout, whitefish, and char. Family: Salmonidae.

salmon pink *n.* a pale orange-pink colour, like the flesh of a salmon —**salmon-pink** *adj.*

Salome /sə lṓmi/ *n.* in the New Testament, the daughter of Herodias who demanded and received John the Baptist's head as reward for her dancing before her stepfather, Herod Antipas (Matthew 14:6–11 and Mark 6:21–28)

salometer /sa lómmitər/ *n.* = **salinometer** [Mid-19thC. Coined from Latin *sal* 'salt' + -METER.]

salon /sáll on/ *n.* **1. GRAND SITTING ROOM** an elegantly furnished room in a large house where guests are received and entertained **2. SOCIAL GATHERING OF INTELLECTUALS** a regular gathering of prominent people from the worlds of literature, art, music, or politics, especially one held at the home of a wealthy woman. Salons were especially popular in the 17th, 18th, and 19th centuries. **3. PLACE FOR HAIRDRESSING OR BEAUTY TREATMENTS** a commercial establishment where hairdressers or beauticians work, sometimes part of a larger shop or department store or a hotel **4.** FASHION **EXPENSIVE CLOTHES SHOP** a shop selling elegant or fashionable women's clothes, especially expensive designer clothes **5.** ARTS **ART EXHIBITION OR GALLERY** an art exhibition, especially one devoted to the work of living artists, or the hall in which the exhibits are displayed [Late 17thC. Via French from Italian *salone* 'large hall', from *sala*, ultimately from prehistoric Germanic.]

Salonika /sə lónnikə/ = **Thessaloniki**

salon music *n.* light classical music for easy listening

saloon /sə lóon/ *n.* **1. DRINKING PLACE** in North America, a commercial establishment serving alcoholic drinks to the general public **2.** = **lounge bar 3.** *UK* CARS **CLOSED CAR WITH BOOT** a car with two or four doors, four to six seats, a fixed roof, and a separate boot. ◊ **sedan 4.** RAIL **PART OF SHIP OR TRAIN** a large room on a ship or, formerly, a carriage on a train where passengers can sit and relax **5. LARGE PUBLIC ROOM** a large public room used for any of various purposes, e.g. receptions, dances, entertainment, or sport **6.** *S Asia* **BARBER'S SHOP** a men's barber's shop [Early 18thC. Anglicization of SALON.]

saloon bar *n.* = **lounge bar**

saloop /sə lóop/ *n.* a hot drink prepared from aromatic herbs or plant parts such as salep or sassafras, formerly used for medicinal purposes (*archaic*) [Early 18thC. Alteration of French *salep* (see SALEP).]

salopettes /sállə péts/ *npl.* a garment worn by skiers, comprising a pair of usually padded, water-resistant trousers that reach up to the chest with straps passing over the shoulders [Late 20thC. From French.]

salp /salp/, **salpa** /sálpə/ (*plural* **-pae** /-pee/ *or* **-pas**) *n.* a tiny free-swimming organism (**tunicate**) that inhabits warm seas and has a transparent barrel-shaped body. Genus: *Salpa.* [Mid-19thC. Via French from modern Latin *salpa* from, ultimately, Greek *salpe* 'fish'.] —**salpiform** /sálpi fawrm/ *adj.*

salpicon /sálpikən/ *n.* a mixture of chopped ingredients, such as meat, fish, or vegetables, bound together by a thick sauce and used to make croquettes or as a filling for pastries [Early 20thC. Via French from, ultimately, Spanish *salpicar* 'to sprinkle with salt'.]

salpiglossis /sálpi glóssiss/ (*plural* **-ses** /-seez/ *or* **-sis**) *n.* a Chilean plant of the nightshade family, often grown for its large showy funnel-shaped flowers. Genus: *Salpiglossis.* [Early 19thC. From modern Latin, from Greek *salpigx* 'trumpet' + *glossa* 'tongue', from the plant's shape.]

salpingectomy /sálpin jéktəmi/ (*plural* **-mies**) *n.* the severing or surgical removal of a fallopian tube [Late 19thC. Coined from Greek *salpigg-*, the stem of *salpinx* 'trumpet' + -ECTOMY.]

salpingitis /sálpin jítiss/ *n.* inflammation of a fallopian tube [Mid-19thC. Coined from the Greek stem *salpigg-* 'trumpet' + -ITIS.] —**salpingitic** /sálpin jíttik/ *adj.*

salsa /sálssə/ *n.* **1.** MUSIC **LATIN AMERICAN DANCE MUSIC** a type of Latin American dance music combining elements of jazz and rock with rhythmic African-Cuban melodies **2.** DANCING **DANCE TO SALSA MUSIC** a dance performed to salsa music **3.** FOOD **SPICY MEXICAN SAUCE** a spicy sauce of finely chopped vegetables including tomatoes, onions, and chillis, eaten with tortilla chips and other Mexican foods [Late 20thC. Via Spanish, 'sauce', from Latin, 'salted', from the past participle of *sallere* 'to salt', from *sal* 'salt' (source of English *sauce*).]

salsify /sálssəfi/ (*plural* **-fies** *or* **-fy**) *n.* **1.** PLANTS **EUROPEAN HERB WITH EDIBLE ROOT** a European composite plant that has leaves resembling grass, purple flowers, and a long edible root. Latin name: *Tragopogon porrifolius.* **2.** FOOD **ROOT EATEN AS VEGETABLE** the long pale edible root of the salsify plant, which can be eaten boiled or fried as a vegetable [Early 18thC. Via French *salsifis* from Italian *salsefica*, of unknown origin.]

sal soda *n.* = **washing soda**

salt /sawlt, solt/ *n.* **1.** FOOD **WHITE CRYSTALS USED IN FOOD PREPARATION** a substance, usually in the form of small white crystals, with a sharp tangy taste that is used to season or preserve food. Salt consists mainly of sodium chloride and is abundant in sea water. ◊ **sodium chloride 2.** CHEM **CRYSTALLINE CHEMICAL COMPOUND** a crystalline chemical compound formed as a result of the neutralization of an acid by a base containing a metal or group acting like a metal **3. STH THAT ADDS ZEST** sth that adds zest, piquancy, liveliness, or vigour **4. DRY WIT** sharp or dry wit **5.** = **old salt 6.** HOUSEHOLD = **saltcellar** ■ **salts** *npl.* **SUBSTANCE RESEMBLING SALT** a chemical or crystalline solution used for a particular purpose ○ *smelling salts* ■ *adj.* **1. PRESERVED WITH SALT** preserved with salt or a salt solution ○ *salt cod* **2. CONTAINING SALT** containing or consisting of salt ○ *salt tears* **3. CONTAINING OR ASSOCIATED WITH SALT WATER** containing, covered with, or growing near salt water **4. TASTING OF SALT** tasting or smelling of salt ■ *vt.* (**salts, salting, salted**) **1. SEASON FOOD WITH SALT** to add salt to food, during or after preparation, to emphasize its flavour **2. PRESERVE FOOD WITH SALT** to preserve food by treating it with salt or a salt solution **3. PUT SALT ON COLD GROUND** to scatter salt over a road or pavement to melt ice or prevent it from forming **4. ADD ZEST TO STH** to add a more lively or entertaining quality to sth ○ *She salted her speech with jokes.* **5.** MINING **ENRICH ORE SAMPLE** to enrich a mining area or sample with a valuable ore artificially introduced in order to increase its apparent value [Old English *sealt.* Ultimately from an Indo-European word meaning 'salt'.] —**saltness** *n.* ◇ **rub salt in the wound** to add to sb's distress, embarrassment, or sense of shame, often deliberately ◇ **take sth with a grain** *or* **pinch of salt** to listen to sth without fully believing it ◇ **the salt of the earth** a very good, worthy person or group of people ◇ **worth your salt** efficient and doing the job well

WORD KEY: ORIGIN

The Indo-European ancestor of ***salt*** is also the ultimate source of English *halogen, salad, salami, salary, saline, sauce, saucer, sausage, silt,* and *souse,* and also of the *cellar* of saltcellar.

salt away *vt.* to hoard or save money for future use, often secretly or illegally [Origin uncertain: probably from the practice of preserving food in salt]

salt out *vt.* to cause a dissolved substance to come out of solution by adding a salt

SALT /sawlt, solt/ *abbr.* Strategic Arms Limitation Talks (or Treaty)

salt-and-pepper *adj.* = **pepper-and-salt**

saltarello /sáltə réllō/ (*plural* **-los** *or* **-li** /-rélli/) *n.* **1.** DANCE **QUICK DANCE WITH MEDIEVAL ORIGINS** a quick dance in triple time dating from the medieval period and especially popular in Spain and Italy **2.** MUSIC **MUSIC FOR SALTARELLO DANCE** a piece of music for a saltarello [Late 16thC. Via Italian from, ultimately, Latin *saltare* 'to dance', (see SALTATION).]

Saltash /sáwlt ash, sólt-/ town in Cornwall, England, on the estuary of the River Tamar. Population: 14,139 (1991).

saltation /sal táysh'n, sawl-/ *n.* **1. JUMPING OR JUMP** leaping or jumping, or a sudden jump or leap (*formal*) **2. SUDDEN CHANGE** development or transition that takes place in jumps or leaps (*formal*) **3.** BIOL **ABRUPT EVOLUTIONARY DEVELOPMENT** the abrupt evolutionary development of a new species or property, especially as a result of genetic mutation **4.** GEOL **JUMPING MOTION OF PARTICLES** the transportation of particles of soil or sand in the wind or in running water, characterized by bouncing movements [Early 17thC. From the Latin stem *saltation-*, from *saltare* literally 'to keep leaping', from *salire* 'to leap' (source of English *salient*).]

saltatorial /sáltə táwri əl, sáwltə-, sóltə-/, **saltatory** /sáltətəri, sáwltətəri/ *adj.* **1.** ZOOL **RELATING TO JUMPING** relating to or adapted for jumping ○ *an insect with saltatorial legs* **2. ASSOCIATED WITH JUMPING OR DANCING** associated with or involving jumping, leaping, or dancing **3. DEVELOPING IN JUMPS OR LEAPS** involving or characterized by sudden change rather than gradual transition

saltbox /sáwlt boks, sólt-/ *n.* **1. BOX FOR SALT** a box in which salt is stored, especially one with a sloping lid **2.** *US* ARCHIT **FRAME HOUSE DESIGN** a wood-frame house that has two floors at the front but only one at the back, and with a long sloping roof on the rear side

saltbush /sáwlt bŏosh, sólt-/ (*plural* **-bushes** *or* **-bush**) *n.* = **orach**

salt cake *n.* an impure form of sodium sulphate used in the manufacture of glass, paper pulp, soap, and ceramic glazes

saltcellar /sáwlt selər, sólt-/ *n.* **1. SALT DISPENSER** a small container for salt, especially one used at the table to season food after it is served **2. HOLLOW ABOVE COLLARBONE** one of two depressions above the collarbone, at either side of the neck, especially prominent in very slim people (*informal*)

saltchuck /sáwlt chuk, sólt-/ *n. Can* a stretch of salt water flowing into a freshwater lake or river

saltchucker /sáwlt chukər, sólt chukər/ *n. Can* an angler who fishes in salt water

salt depletion *n.* the dangerous loss of salt from the body by excessive sweating, diarrhoea, and vomiting, causing muscular weakness and cramps

salt dome *n.* a dome-shaped structure formed in sedimentary rock when buried salt deposits move up through overlying rocks, owing to their low density and high buoyancy

salted /sáwltid, sóltid/ *adj.* **1. TREATED WITH SALT** with salt added for seasoning, preservation, or some other purpose **2. HARDENED OR EXPERIENCED** hardened or experienced, e.g. in a trade or profession

salter /sáwltər, sól-/ *n.* **1. DEALER IN SALT** sb who produces or sells salt **2. SB TREATING FOOD WITH SALT** sb who treats food with salt to preserve it

saltern /sáwltərn, sól-/ *n.* **1.** INDUST **SALTWORKS** a place where salt is produced commercially **2.** GEOG **SOURCE OF SALT PRODUCED BY EVAPORATION** a place where salt is produced naturally when pools of sea water evaporate [Old English, from *sealt* (see SALT) + *ærn* 'building' (source of English *barn*)]

saltfish /sáwlt fish, sólt fish/ *n. Carib* cod or other fish preserved with salt

salt flat *n.* a broad flat area in hot deserts encrusted with salt left after the evaporation of water from shallow saline lakes (*often used in the plural*)

salt gland *n.* a gland in certain marine animals, e.g. birds or reptiles, used to excrete excess ingested salt

salt glaze *n.* a glaze formed by throwing salt into a kiln during the firing process

salt grass *n.* any grass native to salt marshes or alkaline regions

salt hay *n.* hay produced from salt grass, used as fodder

Saltillo /sal tēel yō/ capital of Coahuila State in northern Mexico, founded in 1575. Population: 420,845 (1990).

saltimbocca /sáltim bókə/ *n.* a dish consisting of thin slices of veal rolled up with prosciutto ham and fresh sage leaves, lightly fried and braised in white wine [Mid-20thC. From Italian, from *saltare* 'to leap' + *in* 'into' + *bocca* 'mouth'.]

saltine /sawl tēen, sol-/ *n. US* a thin crisp cracker sprinkled with salt

salting /sáwlting, sól-/ *n.* a low-lying area of land regularly flooded with salt water (*often used in the plural*)

saltire /sáwl tīr, sál-/ *n.* one of the basic designs used on coats of arms consisting of a diagonal cross [15thC. Via Old French *sau(l)toir* 'stirrup, style' from, ultimately, Latin *saltare* (see SALTATION).]

salt-kind *n. Carib* salted meat or meat soaked in brine, including pig's feet and oxtails, used in making soup or cooking beans

salt lake *n.* a lake with no outlet and having a high salt content as a result of evaporation, e.g. the Dead Sea

Salt Lake City /sáwlt layk-, sólt-/ capital city of Utah, located in the northern-central part of the state, 24 km/15 mi. east of the Great Salt Lake. Population: 171,849 (1994).

salt lick *n.* **1. PLACE WHERE ANIMALS LICK SALT DEPOSITS** a place where animals go to lick salt deposits that occur naturally **2. SALT FED TO FARM ANIMALS** a block of salt or other preparation that livestock lick in order to supplement their salt intake. It may also contain other essential minerals such as magnesium or iodine.

salt marsh *n.* a marshy grassland area regularly flooded with salt water

saltpan /sáwlt pan, sólt-/ *n.* a basin in a semiarid region where salts are precipitated after saline floodwaters evaporate

saltpeter *n.* US = **saltpetre**

saltpetre *n.* **1.** = **Chile saltpetre 2.** = **potassium nitrate** [14thC. Alteration, influenced by SALT, of *salpetre*, from, ultimately, Latin *sal* 'salt' + *petra* 'rock', from its appearance as a crust on rock.]

salt pork *n.* a fat cut of pork from the belly, back, or sides, cured by salting

saltwater /sáwlt wawtər, sólt-/ *adj.* **1. OF SALT WATER** containing or involving salt water **2.** BIOL **LIVING IN SALT WATER** living or growing in salt water

salt water *n.* **1. WATER CONTAINING SALT** water containing a lot of salt **2. SEAWATER** the water of the sea and coastal inlets

saltwater crocodile *n.* a large crocodile that inhabits the coastal waterways of northern Australia and Southeast Asia and feeds on fish, birds, reptiles, and small mammals. Latin name: *Crocodylus porosus.*

saltworks /sáwlt wurks, sólt-/ *n.* a place or factory where salt is produced commercially (*takes a singular or plural verb*)

saltwort /sáwlt wurt, sólt-/ (*plural* **-worts** *or* **-wort**) *n.* a plant of the goosefoot family with prickly leaves and small flowers that is native to seashores. Genus: *Salsosa.*

salty /sáwlti, sólti/ (**-ier, -iest**) *adj.* **1. TASTING OF SALT** containing or tasting of salt **2. OF SEA OR SAILORS** associated with the sea or with nautical life **3. LIVELY AND AMUSING** lively, amusing, and sometimes mildly indecent ○ *salty jokes* —**saltily** *adv.* —**saltiness** *n.*

salubrious /sə lóobri əss/ *adj.* **1. GOOD FOR THE HEALTH** beneficial to or promoting health or well-being (*formal*) **2. PLEASANT** decent, respectable, or generally pleasant (*informal humorous*) ○ *advised to avoid the less salubrious parts of the old quarter* [Mid-16thC. Formed from Latin *salubris,* from *salus* 'health' (source of English *salutary* and *salute*).] —**salubriously** *adv.* —**salubriousness** *n.* —**salubrity** *n.*

Saluda /sə lóodə/ river in South Carolina, rising in the Blue Ridge Mountains and flowing into the Congaree River. Length: 322 km/200 mi.

saluki /sə lóoki/ *n.* a tall slender dog belonging to a breed originally developed in Arabia and Egypt. It has a smooth coat and long fringes on the ears and tail. [Early 19thC. From Arabic *salūķī*, from *Salūķ*, a town in Yemen.]

salutary /sállyŏotəri/ *adj.* **1. USEFUL** of value or benefit to sb or sth ○ *We asked if military service had been a salutary experience for him.* **2. HEALTHFUL** promoting good health (*formal*) [15thC. Directly or via French *salutaire* from Latin *salutaris,* from *salus* 'health' (source of English *salubrious*).] —**salutarily** *adv.* —**salutariness** *n.*

salutation /sállyŏo táysh'n/ *n.* **1. SIGN OF GREETING** a gesture or phrase that is used to greet, welcome, or recognize sb **2. ACT OF GREETING SB** the expression of greetings, welcome, or recognition **3. OPENING GREETING** the opening phrase of a letter or speech, used to address the recipient or audience, e.g. 'Dear Sir or Madam' or 'Ladies and Gentlemen' ■ *interj.* **salutations** *npl.* **GREETINGS** greetings or regards (*formal*) ○ *Salutations from us all!* —**salutational** *adj.*

salutatory /sə lóotətəri/ (*plural* **-ries**) *adj.* expressing or conveying greetings

salute /sə lóot/ *v.* (**-lutes, -luting, -luted**) **1.** *vti.* MIL **GIVE FORMAL SIGN OF RESPECT** to formally signal respect to another member of the armed forces or to a flag, usually by raising the right hand to the forehead or by presenting arms **2.** *vt.* **GREET SB** to greet, welcome, or acknowledge sb, either with a gesture or in words **3.** *vt.* **FORMALLY PRAISE OR HONOUR SB** to praise or honour sb for sth, especially in a formal ceremony ○ *We salute you for your contribution.* ■ *n.* **1. GESTURE OF RESPECT** a gesture used by members of the armed forces and some other organized groups as a formal sign of respect **2. FIRING GUNS AS MILITARY HONOUR** a military display of honour for a dignitary or on a special occasion, e.g. the firing of guns into the air at the funeral of an officer ○ *a 21-gun salute* **3. ACT OF SALUTING** an act or an occasion of saluting [14thC. From Latin *salutare,* from *salut-,* stem of *salus* 'health' (source of English *salubrious*).] —**saluter** *n.*

salvable /sálvəb'l/ *adj.* capable of being saved or salvaged (*formal*) [Mid-17thC. Formed from late Latin *salvare* 'to save' (see SALVAGE).]

Salvador /sálvədawr/ port and capital city of Bahia State in eastern Brazil, on the Atlantic Ocean. Population: 2,209,465 (1996).

Salvador, El ◆ **El Salvador**

Salvadoran /sálvə dáwrən/, **Salvadorian** /sálvə dáwriən/, **Salvadorean** *n.* **SB FROM EL SALVADOR** sb who was born or brought up in El Salvador, or who is a citizen of El Salvador ■ *adj.* **OF EL SALVADOR** relating to or typical of El Salvador or its people or culture

salvage /sálvij/ *vt.* (**-vages, -vaging, -vaged**) **1. SAVE STH FROM DESTRUCTION** to save a ship, cargo, crew, or other property or goods from destruction or loss (*often passive*) ○ *They salvaged what they could from the wreckage.* **2. SAVE STH FOR FURTHER USE** to save used, damaged, or rejected goods for recycling or further use ○ *Maybe we can salvage some spare parts from your old car.* **3. RESCUE STH FROM BAD SITUATION** to save sth of worth or merit from a situation or event that is otherwise a failure ■ *n.* **1. RESCUE OF PROPERTY FROM DESTRUCTION** the rescue of property or goods from destruction or loss, e.g. because of a flood or fire **2.** SHIPPING **RESCUE OF SHIP FROM SEA** the rescue of a ship, its cargo, or crew from loss at sea **3. RESCUED GOODS** sth such as a ship or goods that have been saved from destruction or loss **4. STH REUSED** sth that would otherwise be destroyed or discarded but is recycled or put to further use **5.** PAYMENT TO RESCUERS payment made to volunteers who help in the rescue of ships, property, or goods from destruction or loss **6.** MONEY FROM SALE OF RESCUED GOODS money from the sale of goods or property that have been saved from destruction or loss [Mid-17thC. Via French from, ultimately, late Latin *salvare* 'to save', from Latin *salvus* 'safe'.] —**salvageability** /sálvijə bílləti/ *n.* —**salvageable** /sálvijəb'l/ *adj.* —**salvager** *n.*

salvation /sal váysh'n/ *n.* **1.** ACT OF SAVING FROM HARM the saving of sb or sth from harm, destruction, difficulty, or failure ○ *The business was clearly beyond salvation.* **2.** MEANS OF SAVING SB OR STH sb or sth that protects or delivers sb or sth else from harm, destruction, difficulty, or failure ○ *Those long walks were my salvation.* **3.** CHR DELIVERANCE FROM SIN THROUGH JESUS CHRIST in the Christian religion, deliverance from sin or the consequences of sin through Jesus Christ's death on the cross **4.** CHRISTIAN SCIENCE PHILOSOPHY OF LIFE in the Christian Science religion, belief in the supremacy of life, truth, and love, and in their destruction of such illusions as sin, illness, and death [13thC. Via Old French *salvacion* from, ultimately, Latin *salvare* 'to save' (see SALVAGE).] —**salvational** *adj.*

Salvation Army *n.* a worldwide evangelical Christian organization that provides aid to those in need. It was founded by William Booth in London in 1865.

salvationist /sal váyshˈnist/ *n.* a Christian who preaches the doctrine that Jesus Christ died on the cross to save people from sin or the consequences of sin —**salvationism** *n.*

Salvationist *n.* a member of the Salvation Army

salve¹ /salv/; *old fashioned* /saáv/ *n.* **1.** SOOTHING OINTMENT an ointment for soothing or healing wounds or sores **2.** STH THAT SOOTHES OR CALMS anything that eases pain or anxiety ○ *Her forgiveness was a salve to my conscience.* ■ *vt.* (**salves, salving, salved**) EASE PAIN OR WORRY to soothe or ease pain or anxiety ○ *salve your wounded pride* [Old English *sealf*, of prehistoric Germanic origin]

salve² /salv/ (**salves, salving, salved**) *vt.* to save sth from destruction or loss [Early 18thC. Back-formation from SALVAGE.] —**salvor** *n.*

salver /sálvər/ *n.* a tray, especially a silver one, used to serve food or drinks, or to present things such as letters or visiting cards [Mid-17thC. Via French *salve* 'tray for presenting things to the king' from, ultimately, late Latin *salvare* 'to save' (see SALVAGE).]

salverform /sálvər fawrm/ *adj.* used to describe the corolla of a flower with joined petals that is long and tube-shaped with a spreading upper part

salvia /sálvi ə/ (*plural* **-as** *or* **-a**) *n.* an ornamental plant of the mint family with opposite leaves and whorled red flowers, each of which has a two-lipped corolla and two anthers. Latin name: *Salvia splendens.* [Mid-19thC. Via modern Latin *Salvia*, genus name, from Latin *salvia* 'sage', from *salvus* 'safe'.]

salvific /sal víffik/ *adj.* having the power or desire to bring salvation (*formal*) [Late 16thC. From late Latin *salvificus*, from Latin *salvus* 'safe'.]

salvo¹ /sálvō/ (*plural* **-vos** *or* **-voes**) *n.* **1.** SIMULTANEOUS DISCHARGE OF WEAPONS the firing of several weapons simultaneously, especially at a formal military ceremony **2.** HEAVY BURST OF FIRING OR BOMBING a concentrated burst of firing or bombing from several different sources during a battle **3.** NUMBER OF BOMBS RELEASED AT ONCE a number of bombs or projectiles released simultaneously **4.** OUTBURST a sudden burst of applause or cheering ○ *a salvo of applause* **5.** VERBAL ATTACK a vigorous written or spoken attack ○ *a blistering salvo* [Late 16thC. Via French *salve* or Italian *salva* 'greeting, salutation' from, ultimately, Latin *salvus* 'safe'.]

salvo² /sálvō/ (*plural* **-vos**) *n.* sth that is used to save a reputation or soothe sb's conscience or wounded pride [Early 17thC. From Latin, a form of *salvus* 'safe'.]

Salvo /sálvō/ (*plural* **-vos**) *n. Aus* a member of the Salvation Army (*informal*) [Late 19thC. Shortening.]

sal volatile /sál və láttəli/ *n.* **1.** = **ammonium carbonate** **2.** SMELLING SALTS a solution of ammonium carbonate in alcohol and ammonia in water, often mixed with aromatic oils, that is used as smelling salts [Mid-17thC. From modern Latin, literally 'volatile salt'.]

salwar /shál vaar/ *n.* loose-fitting trousers worn by women in Northern India and Pakistan, especially in the Punjab region [Early 19thC. From Persian *šalwār*.]

Salween /sálween/ river in Southeast Asia, flowing through China, including Tibet, and Myanmar (Burma). Length: 2,900 km/1,800 mi.

Salzburg /sáltsburg, zaáltsboo erg/ capital city of Salzburg Province in western Austria. The Salzburg Festival, which concentrates on the music of Mozart, who was born in the city, is held there annually. Population: 143,978 (1991).

Salzgitter /zaálts gitər/ city in Lower Saxony State, northern-central Germany, situated 169 km/105 mi. south of Hamburg. Population: 117,700 (1994).

SAM /sam, éss ay ém/ *abbr.* surface-to-air missile

Sam. *abbr.* BIBLE Samuel

Samaria /sə máiri ə/ ancient city and state in Palestine, located north of present-day Jerusalem, east of the Mediterranean Sea —**Samarian** *n., adj.*

Samaritan /sə márritən/ *n.* **1.** PEOPLES SB FROM SAMARIA sb who was born in or was a citizen of Samaria **2.** SB WHO HELPS THOSE IN NEED sb who helps others who are in difficulty, without expecting any reward or recognition. = **Good Samaritan** **3.** WORKER FOR SAMARITANS ORGANIZATION a volunteer who works for the Samaritans organization ■ **Samaritans** *npl.* ORGANIZATION HELPING PEOPLE IN CRISIS a charitable organization that runs a telephone helpline for people in crisis [Pre-12thC. Via late Latin *Samaritanus* from, ultimately, Greek *Samareia* 'Samaria'.] —**Samaritanism** *n.*

samarium /sə máiri əm/ *n.* a silvery-grey metallic chemical element that is found in monazite and bastnaesite and is used particularly in making strong magnets. It is also used in carbon-arc lighting, as a dopant for laser materials, and as a neutron absorber. Symbol **Sm** [Late 19thC. Coined from SAMARSKITE + -IUM.]

Samarkand /sámmaar kánd, sámmər kand/, **Samarqand** capital city of Samarkand Oblast, central Uzbekistan. Located in the valley of the River Zeravshan, it is the oldest city in central Asia. Population: 371,000 (1991).

samarskite /sə maár skīt/ *n.* a black mineral that contains uranium and a mix of rare-earth elements and is found in pegmatites [Mid-19thC. Named after the Russian mining engineer V. E. Samarskii-Vykhovets (1803–70).]

Sama-Veda /saámə váydə/ *n.* one of the four collections of chants (**Veda**) used during Hindu sacrifices. It contains songs based on the Rig-Veda with instructions on their recitation. [Late 18thC. From Sanskrit, formed from *sāman* 'chant' + *vedaḥ* 'knowledge' (see RIG-VEDA).]

samba /sámbə/ *n.* **1.** DANCE BRAZILIAN DANCE a lively Brazilian ballroom dance with strong African influences **2.** MUSIC MUSIC FOR SAMBA a piece of music in 4/4 time written for the samba ■ *vi.* (**-bas, -baing, -baed**) DANCE DANCE THE SAMBA to dance the samba [Late 19thC. From Portuguese, of uncertain origin: perhaps from an African language.]

sambal /sám bal/, **sambol** /sám bol/ *n.* a spicy condiment or relish of Southeast Asia made of chilli, spices, vinegar, tomato, onion, and other vegetables [Early 19thC. From Malay.]

sambar /sámbər/ (*plural* **-bars** *or* **-bar**), **sambur** (*plural* **-burs** *or* **-bur**) *n.* a large deer that has a reddish-brown coat and three-pronged antlers. It is native to Southeast Asia. Latin name: *Cervus unicolor.* [Late 17thC. Via Hindi *sāmbar* from Sanskrit *śambaraḥ*.]

sambo¹ /sámbō/ *n.* a highly offensive term used for a Black person (*dated taboo insult*)

sambo² /sámbō/, **sambo wrestling** *n.* a form of wrestling based on judo that originated in the former Soviet Union and is now practised internationally [Mid-20thC. An acronym from Russian *samozashchita bez oruzhiya*, literally 'unarmed self-defence'.] —**sambo wrestler** *n.*

sambol *n.* = **sambal**

Sam Browne belt /sám brówn-/, **Sam Browne** *n.* a wide belt supported by a diagonal strap that passes from the left-hand side over the right shoulder, worn as part of military or police uniforms [Named after the British military commander Sir *Samuel Browne* (1824–1901), who invented it]

sambuca /sam bóokə/ *n.* an Italian liqueur made from elderberries and flavoured with liquorice or aniseed [Late 20thC. Via Italian from Latin *sambucus* 'elder tree'.]

sambur *n.* = **sambar**

same /saym/ CORE MEANING: a word indicating that one thing or person is involved rather than two or more different things or people ○ (adj.) *I can't drive and talk at the same time.* ○ (adj.) *He lives in the same street as I do.*

1. *adj., pron.* PREVIOUSLY MENTIONED previously mentioned, or as previously described (*used as pronoun without 'the' in business contexts*) ○ (adj.) *She left because she was bored, and I left two months later for the same reason.* ○ (pron.) *Wool should always be washed carefully. The same applies to silk.* **2.** *adj., pron., adv.* IDENTICAL resembling sth exactly ○ (adj.) *They turned up at the party wearing the same dress.* ○ (adj.) *All the houses looked exactly the same.* ○ (adj.) *Look – their curtains are the same as ours!* ○ (pron.) *All the experts say the same.* **3.** *adj.* UNCHANGED unchanged or unchanging ○ *After the accident, he just wasn't the same person.* ○ *The house looked the same as always.* ○ *I want things to stay the same.* [12thC. From Old Norse *samr.* Ultimately from an Indo-European base meaning 'one', which is also the ancestor of English *simple* and *homo-*.] ◇ **the same as** in the identical way that (*informal*) ○ *He wants to win, the same as I do.*

WORD KEY: USAGE

We have received your order and have pleasure in completing same. This use of **same** as a pronoun is characteristic of commercial language and is not normally suitable for general use, except for special or humorous effect: *She poured out a large glass of water and drank same.*

samekh /saá mek, -mekh/ *n.* the 15th letter of the Hebrew alphabet, represented in the English alphabet as 's'. See table at **alphabet** [Early 19thC. From Hebrew *sāmekh*, literally 'a support'.]

sameness /sáymnəss/ *n.* **1.** QUALITY OF BEING THE SAME the quality or condition of being very similar or the same ○ *There was a sameness about the two accounts.* **2.** LACK OF VARIETY a lack of variety or change ○ *There's a certain sameness about all his paintings.*

same-sex *adj.* homosexual or lesbian ○ *involved in a same-sex relationship*

samey /sáymi/ *adj.* boringly repetitive or unchanging (*informal*)

Sami /saámi/ (*plural* **-mi** *or* **-mis**) *n.* **1.** SB FROM LAPLAND a member of the indigenous people of Lapland who are traditionally nomadic herders of reindeer **2.** SAMI LANGUAGE the Finno-Ugric language of the Sami. Sami is spoken by about 80,000 people. [Late 18thC. From Sami.]

Samian /sáymi ən/ *n.* PEOPLES sb who was born or brought up on the Greek island of Samos —**Samian** *adj.*

Samian ware *n.* reddish-brown or black earthenware pottery found in large quantities at Roman archaeological sites

samiel /sám yel/ *n.* METEOROL = **simoom** [Late 17thC. From Turkish *samyeli*, literally 'poisonous wind'.]

samisen /sámmi sen/ *n.* a Japanese three-stringed musical instrument that has a long fretless neck and is played with a plectrum [Early 17thC. Via Japanese from Chinese *sānxián* literally 'three strings'.]

samite /sámm īt, sáy-/ *n.* a heavy silk fabric, often interwoven with gold or silver threads, that was used for clothing in the Middle Ages [12thC. Via Old French *samit* and medieval Latin *examitum* from, ultimately, Greek *hexamiton* literally 'six threads'.]

samiti /súmmiti/, **samithi** *n.* a committee in the Indian subcontinent, especially one that is formed to organize political activity [Mid-20thC. From Sanskrit 'meeting'.]

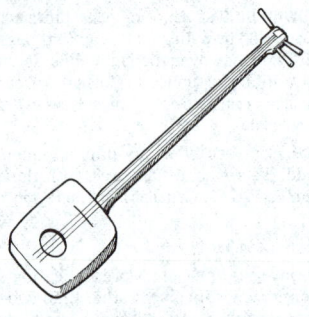
Samisen

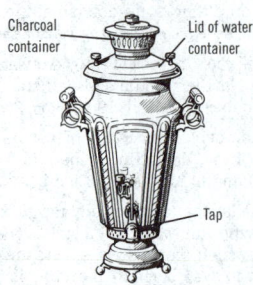
Charcoal container — Lid of water container — Tap
Samovar

samizdat /sámmiz dát/ n. **1.** UNDERGROUND PUBLISHING IN FORMER USSR in the former Soviet Union, the printing and distribution of secret or banned literature **2.** BANNED LITERATURE literature produced by the samizdat system **3.** SECRET PRINTING PRESS a secret printing press, especially in the former Soviet Union [Mid-20thC. From Russian, formed from sam- 'self' + izdatel'stvo 'publishing house'.]

sammy /sámmi/ (plural **-mies**) n. S AFRICA in South Africa, an offensive term for an Indian person, especially a greengrocer who sells door-to-door (dated offensive slang) [Late 19thC. Formed from the second element of common Indian names such as Ramsamy.]

Samnite /sám nīt/ n. MEMBER OF PEOPLE IN ANCIENT ITALY a member of an ancient people who occupied an area of central and southern Italy known as Samnium. They repeatedly tried to spread into territory held by Rome during the 4th and 3rd centuries BC and were eventually defeated by the Romans around 290 BC. ■ adj. OF THE SAMNITES relating to the Samnites, or their culture or empire ○ the Samnite Wars [14th C. From Latin Samnites 'the Samnites'.]

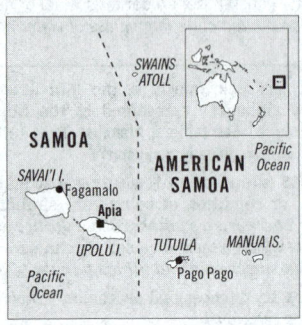
SWAINS ATOLL / SAMOA / SAVAI'I I. / Fagamalo / Apia / UPOLU I. / Pacific Ocean / AMERICAN SAMOA / Pacific Ocean / TUTUILA / Pago Pago / MANUA IS.
Samoa

Samoa /sə mṓ ə/ independent island state in the southern Pacific Ocean, situated west of American Samoa. Language: Samoan, English. Currency: tala. Capital: Apia. Population: 167,400 (1996). Area: 2,831 sq. km/1,093 sq. mi. Official name **Independent State of Samoa**. Former name **Western Samoa**

Samoan /sə mṓ ən/ n. **1.** PEOPLES SB FROM SAMOA sb who was born or brought up in Samoa or is a citizen of American Samoa or the Independent State of Samoa **2.** LANG LANGUAGE OF SAMOA the language of Samoa, belonging to the Polynesian family of languages. About 300,000 people speak Samoan. —**Samoan** adj.

Samos /sáymoss/ Greek island in the Aegean Sea, separated from the southwestern coast of Turkey by the narrow Samos Strait. Population: 41,965 (1991). Area: 505 sq. km/195 sq. mi.

samosa /sə mṓssə, -mṓzə/ (plural **-sas** or **-sa**) n. a savoury Indian snack consisting of a thin pastry case filled with spiced vegetables or meat and then deep-fried [Mid-20thC. From Urdu.]

Samothrace /sámmə thrayss/ Greek island in the northeastern Aegean Sea, situated 40 km/25 mi. from mainland Greece. Population: 2,871 (1981). Area: 178 sq. km/69 sq. mi.

samovar /sámmə vaar/ n. a large and often ornate Russian tea urn. In older models the water was heated by a built-in charcoal burner, but many modern models are electrically operated. [Mid-19thC. From Russian, formed from samo- 'self' + varit 'to boil'.]

Samoyed /sámmə yed/ n. **1.** (plural **-yeds** or **-yed**) PEOPLES MEMBER OF A SIBERIAN PEOPLE a member of a people living traditionally as reindeer herders in far northeastern European Russia and western Siberia **2.** LANG SAMOYED LANGUAGE the group of languages spoken by the Samoyed peoples. They belong to the Uralic family of languages, are related to Finno-Ugric, and are sometimes classified as belonging to the Ural-Altaic group. **3.** ZOOL SIBERIAN DOG a dog belonging to a Siberian breed that has a thick creamy-white coat, distinctive ruff, and tightly-curled tail [Late 16thC. From Russian.] —**Samoyed** adj.

Sampan

sampan /sám pan/ n. a small flat-bottomed boat (**skiff**) propelled by two oars or a single rear-mounted oar (**scull**) [Early 17thC. From Chinese sānbǎn, literally 'three-board (boat)'.]

samphire /sám fīr/ (plural **-phires** or **-phire**) n. **1.** EUROPEAN PLANT WITH WHITE FLOWERS a European coastal plant that has small white flowers, and fleshy leaves that are used in pickles. Latin name: Crithmum maritimum. **2.** = **glasswort** [Mid-16thC. Contraction of French herbe de Saint Pierre.]

sample /sáamp'l/ n. **1.** EXAMPLE OF STH a small amount of sth, used as an example of more general character, features, or quality ○ a free sample of the new shampoo **2.** SPECIMEN FOR ANALYSIS a small part or quantity of sth, e.g. blood or soil, for scientific or medical examination or analysis ○ took a blood sample **3.** RECORDING PIECE OF RECORDED SOUND a piece of recorded sound or a musical phrase taken from an existing recording, especially in digital form, used as part of a new recording ○ a CD of drum samples **4.** STATS GROUP SELECTED FOR TESTING a representative selection of a population that is examined to gain statistical information about the whole ■ vti. (**-ples**, **-pling**, **-pled**) **1.** GET A SAMPLE OF STH to take a sample of sth, especially to determine its character, features, or quality ○ sample the river water **2.** RECORDING TAKE SAMPLE OF STH FOR RECORDING to take a sample of recorded music, especially in order to use it in another recording ○ sampled whatever albums happened to be lying around **3.** RECORDING CONVERT SOUND INTO DIGITAL INFORMATION to convert sound into digital information in order to store or manipulate it electronically [13thC. Shortening of Norman French assample 'example'.]

sampler /sáamplər/ n. **1.** SB WHO ANALYSES SAMPLES sb who samples small quantities of sth, especially in order to determine quality **2.** DEVICE FOR TAKING SAMPLES a machine or device used to take and analyse samples

3. STATS REPRESENTATIVE SELECTION a selection that is intended to represent what is available in a particular range **4.** SEW EMBROIDERED CLOTH a piece of embroidered cloth containing rows of different stitches, either as a practice piece or, originally, as a demonstration of the embroiderer's skill **5.** RECORDING ELECTRONIC EQUIPMENT FOR SAMPLING MUSICAL PHRASES an electronic device that can record sounds or take short musical phrases from an existing recording, and allow them to be manipulated digitally before being used to make a new recording **6.** RECORDING MACHINE CONVERTING SOUND TO DIGITAL INFORMATION an electronic device that converts sound to digital information for electronic storage or manipulation

sample space n. the set of all possible outcomes of a statistical experiment, represented by points

sampling /sáampling/ n. **1.** PROCESS OF SELECTING SAMPLE GROUP the process of selecting a group of people or products to be used as a representative or random sample **2.** STH USED AS A SAMPLE a small part, number, or quantity of sth that has been taken or selected as a sample **3.** RECORDING REUSE OF RECORDED MUSICAL PHRASES the process of taking a short musical phrase from one recording and using it in another recording, often in repeated sequences and sometimes in an adapted or edited form ○ recent advances in sampling technology

sampling frame n. a list of the people or items from which a statistical sample is taken

Popperfoto
Pete Sampras

Sampras /sámprəss/, **Pete** (b. 1971) US tennis player. At 19, he became the youngest player to win the US Open championship. He was ranked the world's number one player in 1993 and 1994. Full name **Peter Sampras**. Known as **Pistol Pete**

samsara /səm saará/ n. **1.** HINDU CYCLE OF DEATH AND REBIRTH in Hinduism, the endless cycle of birth, life, death, and rebirth **2.** REBIRTH in Buddhism, sb's rebirth [Late 19thC. From Sanskrit saṃs araḥ, from sam 'together' + sarati 'it flows'.]

samshu /sám shoo/ n. a Chinese alcoholic drink made from fermented rice [Late 17thC. From Pidgin English, of uncertain origin.]

Samson /sámssən/ n. **1.** BIBLICAL WARRIOR in the Bible, an Israelite judge and warrior. He used his enormous strength to fight the Philistines, to whom he was ultimately betrayed by his mistress, Delilah (Judges 13–16). **2.** STRONG MAN any very strong man —**Samsonian** /sam sṓni ən/ adj.

Samuel n. in the Bible, the leader of the Israelites in the 11th century BC. He was the first prophet after Moses.

samurai /sámmoŏ rī, sámmyoŏ-/ (plural **-rai** or **-rais**) n. **1.** FORMER JAPANESE WARRIOR CLASS the powerful class of Japanese warriors that dominated the military aristocracy from the 11th to the 19th centuries **2.** ARISTOCRATIC JAPANESE WARRIOR an aristocratic Japanese warrior of a class that dominated the military aristocracy from the 11th to the 19th centuries [Early 18thC. From Japanese.]

san /san/, **-san** n. used in Japanese after sb's first name, last name, or title, as a polite form of address [Late 19thC. From Japanese, contraction of sama.]

San[1] /san/ n. used as a title, usually in place names, before the name of a man who has been made a saint. ◊ **Santo, Santa** [Via Spanish and Italian, 'Saint', from Latin sanctus 'sacred' (see SAINT)]

San[2] /saan/ (*plural* **San** *or* **Sans**) *n.* **1. MEMBER OF SOUTHERN AFRICAN PEOPLE** a member of a people living in southern Africa. The San traditionally live in small nomadic groups as hunters and gatherers. **2. SAN LANGUAGE** the group of Khoisan languages spoken by the San people [Late 19thC. From Nama *san*.]

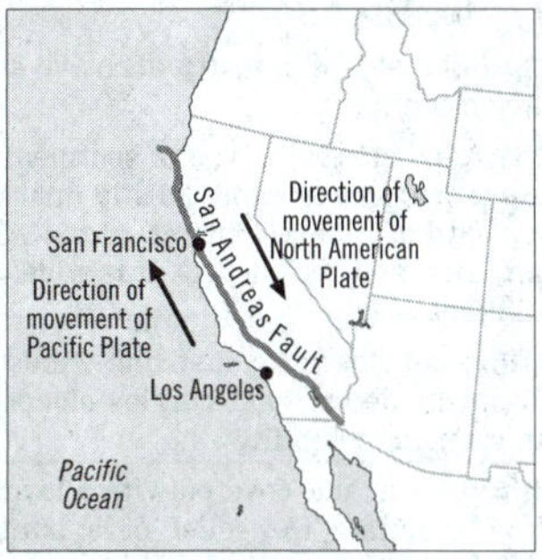

San Andreas Fault

San Andreas Fault /sán an dráyəss-/ *n.* a geological fault zone between two tectonic plates that runs from San Francisco south to San Diego in California. It is an area of frequent earthquakes caused by the plates sliding past each other. Length: 970 km/600 mi. [So called because it runs along the San Andreas valley]

sanative /sánnətiv/ *adj.* able to restore health (*archaic formal*) [15thC. Directly, or via Old French *sanatif*, from late Latin *sanativus*, from Latin *sanare* 'to heal'.]

sanatorium /sánnə táwri əm/ (*plural* **-ums** *or* **-a** /-táwri ə/) *n.* **1. MEDICAL FACILITY FOR LONG-TERM ILLNESS** a medical facility where people affected by long-term illnesses can receive treatment and those recovering from severe illnesses can recuperate **2. HEALTH RESORT** a resort for maintaining or improving health (*dated*) **3. MEDICAL ROOM IN BOARDING SCHOOL** a room or unit in a boarding school where pupils who are ill can receive treatment and recuperate [Mid-19thC. From modern Latin, from Latin *sanat-*, the past participle stem of *sanare* 'to cure', from *sanus* 'healthy' (source of English *sane*).]

sanbenito /sánbə neéto/ (*plural* **-tos**) *n.* a sackcloth garment worn by those declared heretics by the Spanish Inquisition. Penitent heretics wore a yellow one with a red cross on it and impenitent heretics wore a black one decorated with flames and devils. [Mid-16thC. From Spanish *sambenito*, an alteration of *San Benito* 'St Benedict', because it resembles the scapular of a Benedictine monk.]

San Bernardino Mountains /san búrnər deénō-/ mountain range in southern California. The highest peak is San Gorgonio Mountain, 3,506 m/11,485 ft. Length: 160 km/100 mi.

sancoche /sang kóch, -kósh, -kóchee/ *n. Carib* a Caribbean soup made with a variety of vegetables, split peas, and salted meat, or sometimes with chicken or beef [Mid-20thC. Via American Spanish *sancocho* from, ultimately, Spanish *sancochar* 'to parboil'.]

San Cristobal /san krístə baal/ one of the Galapagos Islands, off the coast of Ecuador. Area: 505 sq. km/195 sq. mi.

San Cristóbal /sang kri stō bal/ capital city of Táchira State, western Venezuela. Population: 238,670 (1992).

sancta plural of **sanctum**

sancta sanctorum plural of **sanctum sanctorum**

sanctify /sángkti fī/ (**-fies, -fying, -fied**) *vt.* **1.** RELIG **BLESS STH** to make sth holy **2.** RELIG **FREE SB FROM SIN** to free sb from sin, e.g. by a ritual act of purification **3.** RELIG **BLESS STH THROUGH RELIGIOUS VOW** to give a religious blessing to sth, e.g. a marriage, usually through an oath or vow **4. OFFICIALLY APPROVE STH** to give social, moral, or official approval to sth **5.** RELIG **MAKE STH ROUTE TO HOLINESS** to make sth a means of achieving holiness or a source of grace **6. CAUSE STH TO BE REVERED** to designate sth an object of reverence (*archaic*) [14thC. Via Old French *saintifier* from, ultimately, Latin *sanctus* 'sacred' (see SAINT).] —**sanctifiable** *adj.* —**sanctification** /sángktifi káysh'n/ *n.* —**sanctifier** /sángkti fī ər/ *n.*

sanctimonious /sángkti mṓni əss/ *adj.* making an exaggerated show of holiness or moral superiority (*disapproving*) [Early 17thC. Formed from Latin *sanctimonia* 'sanctity', from *sanctus* 'sacred' (see SAINT).] —**sanctimoniously** *adv.* —**sanctimoniousness** *n.* —**sanctimony** /sángktiməni/ *n.*

sanction /sángksh'n/ *n.* **1. AUTHORIZATION** official permission or approval for a course of action ○ *unable to proceed without the sanction of the board* **2. SUPPORT** sth that serves as approval or encouragement, e.g. social acceptance or custom **3. LAW** a law or rule that leads to a penalty being imposed when it is disobeyed **4. PENALTY IMPOSED FOR BREAKING RULE** a punishment imposed as a result of breaking a law or rule **5.** INTERNAT REL **PUNITIVE MEASURE TO PRESSURE A COUNTRY** a measure taken by one or more nations to apply pressure on another nation to conform to international law or opinion. Such measures usually include restrictions on or withdrawal of trade rights, diplomatic ties, and membership of international organizations or forums. (*often used in the plural*) ○ *to impose trade sanctions* **6.** ETHICS **PRINCIPLE DETERMINING BEHAVIOUR** an ethical principle or consideration that determines or influences sb's conduct ■ *vt.* (**-tions, -tioning, -tioned**) **1. AUTHORIZE STH** to grant official approval or permission for sth ○ *The town council refused to sanction the proposed design of the new building.* **2. APPROVE OF STH** to allow sth to be tolerated or accepted ○ *The school's inaction further sanctions this behaviour.* [15thC. Via Old French from, ultimately, Latin *sanctus* 'sacred' (see SAINT).] —**sanctionable** *adj.* —**sanctioner** *n.* —**sanctionless** *adj.*

sanctity /sángktəti/ (*plural* **-ties**) *n.* **1. SACREDNESS** the condition of being considered sacred or holy, and therefore entitled to respect and reverence **2. HOLY THING** sth considered holy or sacred (*formal*) [14thC. Directly and via Old French *saincteté* from Latin *sanctitas*, from *sanctus* 'sacred' (see SAINT).]

sanctuary /sángkchoo əri/ (*plural* **-ies**) *n.* **1. REFUGE** a safe place, especially for people being persecuted **2. SAFETY PROVIDED BY REFUGE** the safety and protection afforded by a place of refuge ○ *immigrants seeking sanctuary in the United States* **3. PLACE WHERE WILDLIFE IS PROTECTED** a place or area of land where wildlife is protected from predators and from being destroyed or hunted by human beings ○ *a bird sanctuary* **4.** CHR **CHURCH PROTECTING FUGITIVES** in medieval times, a holy place, usually a church, that provided immunity from the law **5.** CHR **CHURCH PROTECTION FOR FUGITIVES** the immunity from arrest, violence, or execution provided to fugitives under medieval church law **6.** RELIG **HOLY PLACE** a holy place such as a church, mosque, or temple **7.** RELIG **MOST SACRED PART OF HOLY BUILDING** the most sacred part of a consecrated building, e.g. the area around the altar in a Christian church **8.** JUDAISM, HIST **ISRAELITE HOLY OF HOLIES** the holy of holies in the Israelite temple at Jerusalem [14thC. Via Anglo-Norman *sanctuarie* from, ultimately, Latin *sanctus* 'sacred' (see SAINT).]

sanctum /sángktəm/ (*plural* **-tums** *or* **-ta** /-tə/) *n.* **1.** RELIG **SACRED INNER PLACE** a sacred place inside a church, temple, or mosque **2. QUIET PRIVATE PLACE** a quiet private place where sb is free from interference or interruption [Late 16thC. Via late Latin from Latin *sanctus* 'sacred' (see SAINT).]

sanctum sanctorum /sángktəm saángk táwrəm/ (*plural* **sancta sanctorum** /sángktə-/ *or* **sanctum sanctorums**) *n.* **1.** = **holy of holies** *n.* 1 **2. PRIVATE, QUIET PLACE** a very private, quiet place in which to be alone or relax [14thC. From late Latin, literally 'holy of holies'.]

Sanctus /sángktəss, -tooss/ *n.* in some Christian churches, a musical setting that forms part of the Mass and praises the power and holiness of God [14thC. Via late Latin from Latin *sanctus* 'sacred' (see SAINT), the first word of the hymn.]

Sanctus bell *n.* in the Roman Catholic Church, a bell rung at the beginning of the Sanctus and at other times during Mass, e.g. at the elevation of the consecrated elements

sand /sand/ *n.* **1. MATERIAL MADE OF TINY GRAINS** a substance consisting of fine loose grains of rock or minerals, found on beaches, in the desert, and in soil, and also used as a building material. Sand is a sedimentary material, usually quartz fragments, that is finer than gravel but coarser than silt, with particle sizes between 0.06 mm and 2 mm. **2.** GEOG **AREA OF SAND** an area covered with or made up of sand, e.g. a beach or a desert ○ *playing on the sand and swimming in the sea* **3.** COLOURS **BROWNISH-YELLOW** a brownish-yellow colour like that of sand **4. PARTICLES IN HOURGLASS** the tiny grains in an hourglass **5.** *US* **DETERMINATION** courage and determination (*dated informal*) ■ **sands** *npl.* **TIME REMAINING** remaining or allotted portion of time (*literary*) ○ *the sands of time* ■ *v.* (**sands, sanding, sanded**) **1.** *vt.* **SMOOTH STH USING SANDPAPER** to rub a surface with sandpaper or sand to make it smoother **2.** *vt.* **SPRINKLE STH WITH SAND** to cover or sprinkle sth such as an icy road with sand **3.** *vt.* **ADD SAND TO STH** to add sand to sth, e.g. to a mixture of building materials when making mortar **4.** *vti.* **FILL WITH SAND** to become filled with sand, or fill sth with sand ■ *adj.* COLOURS **OF THE COLOUR OF SAND** of a brownish-yellow colour, like sand [Old English, of prehistoric Germanic origin] —**sandlike** *adj.* ◇ **kick sand in sb's face** to show contempt for or dominance over sb less strong or powerful, especially sb already in a weak position

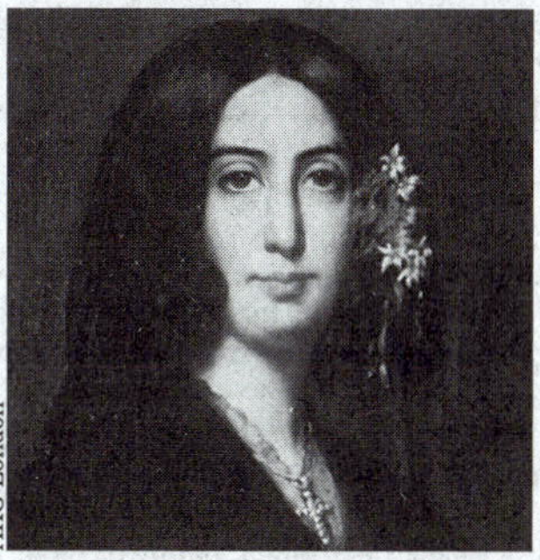

George Sand: Portrait (1839) by Auguste Charpentier

Sand /saan, saaN/, **George** (1804–76) French writer. She wrote many volumes of essays, novels, and plays, which reflect her feminist and libertarian ideals. Pseudonym of **Amandine Aurore Lucille, Baronne Dudevant**

sandal /sánd'l/ *n.* **1. LIGHT SHOE WITH STRAPS** a light open shoe that is held on by straps across the instep or around the heel or ankle, usually worn during warm weather **2. STRAP FOR FASTENING SHOE** a strap for going around the ankle or across the instep to keep a shoe on a foot [14thC. Via Latin *sandalium* from, ultimately, Greek *sandalon*, of uncertain origin: probably from an Asian language.] —**sandalled** *adj.*

sandalwood /sánd'l wŏŏd/ *n.* **1.** TREES **TROPICAL EVERGREEN TREE** a tropical evergreen tree native to southern Asia and Australia that has a fragrant wood. Genus: *Santalum*. **2.** INDUST **WOOD OF SANDALWOOD TREE** the wood of the sandalwood tree, used extensively in the manufacture of furniture, and burnt as incense **3. AROMATIC OIL OF SANDALWOOD TREE** the aromatic oil that is extracted from the wood of sandalwood trees and used in perfumes and incense and as an essential oil in aromatherapy **4.** TREES **TREE RESEMBLING SANDALWOOD TREE** any tree native to southern Asia and Australia that resembles the sandalwood and that is harvested for wood. Genera: *Adenanthera* and *Myroporum* and *Pterocarpus*.

sandarac /sándə rak/, **sandarach** *n.* **1. EVERGREEN TREE OF AFRICA AND SPAIN** a coniferous tree that is native to northwestern Africa and Spain and has flat branches, leaves with overlapping scales, and dark hard aromatic wood. Latin name: *Tetraclinis articulata*. **2. RESIN FROM SANDARAC TREE** a brittle yellowish translucent resin that oozes from the bark of the sandarac and is used in varnishes and incense **3. WOOD FROM SANDARAC TREE** the wood from the sandarac, used as a building material [Mid-17thC. Via Latin *sandaraca* from Greek *sandarakē*.]

sandbag /sánd bag/ *n.* **1. SACK OF SAND** a sealed bag full of sand, used in building defences against gunfire or flooding, or as ballast in hot air balloons **2. BAG OF SAND USED AS WEAPON** a small bag filled with sand and used as a weapon in the same way as a cosh ■ *v.* (**-bags, -bagging, -bagged**) **1.** *vt.* **PROTECT STH WITH SANDBAGS** to put sandbags in or around sth as protection **2.** *vt.* **KNOCK SB OR STH DOWN** to attack or hit sb or sth with a sandbag (*informal*) **3.** *vti.* **DELAY NEGOTIATIONS** to delay negotiations or a business deal in the hope of receiving a more favourable offer from sb else (*slang*) —**sandbagger** *n.*

sandbank /sánd bangk/ *n.* a mound or bank of sand, especially one that is submerged at most states of the tide

sandbar /sánd baar/ *n.* a long ridge of sand formed in a body of water by currents or tides

sandblast /sánd blaast/ *n.* **1.** **JET OF SAND FIRED UNDER PRESSURE** a jet of pressurized air or steam mixed with sand or grit that is fired through a fine nozzle, used to clean, polish, or mark glass, metal, or stone surfaces **2.** **MACHINE FOR FIRING SANDBLAST** a machine that is used to fire a sandblast ■ *vti.* (**-blasts**, **-blasting**, **-blasted**) **POLISH WITH SAND** to clean, polish, or mark glass, metal, or a stone surface with a sandblast — **sandblaster** *n.*

sand-blind *adj.* having reduced ability to see (*archaic or literary*) [15thC. Alteration of Old English *samblind*, from *sam-* 'half' + *blind* 'blind'. Ultimately from an Indo-European word meaning 'half', which is also the ancestor of English *semi-* and *hemi-*.] —**sand-blindness** *n.*

sandbox /sánd boks/ *n.* **1.** **CONTAINER ON LOCOMOTIVE THAT RELEASES SAND** a container on a railway locomotive that releases sand onto the track to increase traction **2.** *US* = **sandpit**

sandbox tree *n.* a tropical American tree with spiny bark, milky sap that can irritate the skin, and woody seed capsules that explode when ripe. Latin name: *Hura crepitans*. [So called because the seed capsules formerly served as boxes for sand]

sandboy /sánd boy/ [Early 19thC. Origin obscure: perhaps originally meaning 'a boy selling sand'.] ◊ **(as) happy** *or* **jolly as a sandboy** extremely happy or cheerful

sand-cast *vt.* to make a casting by pouring molten metal into a sand mould

sand casting *n.* a casting made by pouring molten metal into a sand mould

sand crack *n.* a crack in a horse's hoof that starts at the top (**coronet**) and extends vertically towards the sole

sand dab *n.* a small flatfish that is native to North American Pacific coastal waters and is caught for food. Genus: *Citharichthys*.

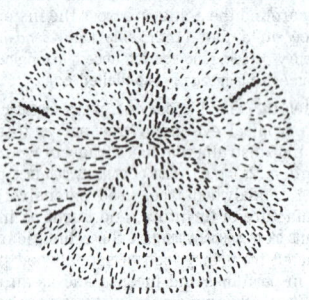

Sand dollar

sand dollar *n.* a flat circular animal (**echinoderm**) related to the starfish and sea urchin, found in shallow sandy North American coastal waters. Its shell looks like a white disc with an imprint that resembles a flower. Genus: *Citharichthys*.

sand eel *n.* a small slender marine fish that resembles an eel. It travels in large schools, and burrows in sand or shingle. Genus: *Ammodytes*. US term **sand lance**

sander /sándər/ *n.* **1.** **POWER TOOL FOR SMOOTHING SURFACES** an electric power tool that is used to smooth wooden or metal surfaces **2.** **SB WHO SANDS STH** sb who sands sth or operates a sander

sanderling /sándərling/ (*plural* **-lings** *or* **-ling**) *n.* a small bird, found in coastal regions worldwide, that is similar to but smaller than a sandpiper and has grey and white plumage. Latin name: *Calidris alba*. [Early 17thC. Origin uncertain: perhaps formed from SAND + -LING.]

Sanderson /saándərssən/, **Tessa** (*b.* 1956) British javelin thrower, who was a gold medallist in the 1984 Olympic Games and winner of the 1992 World Cup. She later pursued a career in the media. Real name **Teresa Ione Sanderson**

sand flea *n.* = **chigoe**

sandfly /sánd flī/ *n.* a hairy fly that resembles a moth and lives in tropical regions. Bloodsucking females transmit several tropical diseases. Genus: *Phlebotomus*.

sandfly fever *n.* a mild viral illness transmitted by the bite of a female sandfly. It causes fever, headaches, eye pain, and general discomfort.

sandglass /sánd glaass/ *n.* = **hourglass**

sandgrouse /sánd growss/ (*plural* **-grouses** *or* **-grouse**) *n.* a bird related to the pigeon that is native to the arid and semiarid regions of Europe and Asia. Sandgrouse have long pointed wings and tails, and short feet and bills. Genus: *Pterocles*.

sandhi /sándi/ *n.* the modification of the sound or form of a word under the influence of a preceding or following sound. The variation between 'a' and 'an' for the indefinite article in English is a form of sandhi. [Early 19thC. From Sanskrit *saṃdhiḥ* 'combination'.]

sandhog /sánd hog/ *n.* *US*, *Can* sb who works inside a caisson in underwater building projects such as tunnels (*slang*)

sand hopper *n.* a tiny jumping crustacean that lives on sandy tidal beaches. Genus: *Orchestia*. US term **sand flea**

San Diego /san di áygō/ city in southwestern California, on San Diego Bay. It is the second largest city in California, and the sixth largest in the United States. Population: 1,151,977 (1994).

Sandinista /sándi neésta/ *n.* a member of a socialist movement in Nicaragua that successfully overthrew the government of President Anastasio Somoza in 1979 and fought a United-States-backed insurgent force in the 1980s [Early 20thC. Named after the Nicaraguan revolutionary leader Augusto César *Sandino* (1893–1934).]

S & L *abbr.* savings and loan association

sand leek *n.* a Eurasian plant that has reddish-pink flowers and a bulb shaped like that of garlic. Rocambole is a cultivated variety. Latin name: *Alium scorodoprasum*.

sand lizard *n.* a small greyish-brown lizard that is native to Europe and is found among sand dunes. It has long clawed digits and a bright green underbelly in the male. Latin name: *Lacerta agilis*.

sandlot /sánd lot/ *n.* *US* a vacant lot or area of land used by children for playing games, especially baseball (*informal*) —**sandlotter** *n.*

S & M *abbr.* sadomasochism

sandman /sánd man/ *n.* a character from folklore and fairy tales, personifying drowsiness, who makes children go to sleep by sprinkling sand in their eyes

sand martin *n.* a small songbird related to the swallow and native to Europe that nests in burrows in sand or river banks. It is brown with a white underbelly. Latin name: *Riparia riparia*.

sand painting *n.* **1.** **NATIVE N AMERICAN CEREMONIAL PRACTICE USING SAND** a ceremonial practice of the Navajo and Pueblo peoples, in which different colours of sand are distributed over a flat surface to create symbolic pictures and designs **2.** **DESIGN MADE BY SAND PAINTING** a picture or design made by sand painting

sandpaper /sánd paypər/ *n.* **STRONG PAPER COATED WITH ABRASIVE MATERIAL** strong paper coated on one side with sand or another abrasive, used for smoothing surfaces ■ *vt.* (**-pers**, **-pering**, **-pered**) **SMOOTH STH USING SANDPAPER** to rub a surface, e.g. a piece of wood or a wall, with sandpaper —**sandpapery** *adj.*

sandpiper /sánd pīpər/ (*plural* **-pers** *or* **-per**) *n.* a wading shore bird with a long slender sensitive bill that it uses to catch insects, worms, and soft molluscs in sand and mud. Family: Scolopacidae. [*Piper* from its piping voice]

sandpit /sánd pit/ *n.* **1.** **CONTAINER OF SAND FOR CHILDREN** an area of sand for children to play in, often contained in a box or frame. US term **sandbox 2.** **PIT FOR EXCAVATING SAND** a large deep pit from which sand is excavated

sand shark *n.* a shark that lives mainly in the shallow coastal waters of the central and southern Atlantic and western Pacific. Although it has very sharp teeth, it is not generally considered dangerous. Genus: *Carcharias*.

sandshoe /sánd shoo/ *n.* a light low-cut canvas shoe with a rubber sole

sandsoap /sánd sōp/ *n.* a gritty abrasive soap used for heavy cleaning

sandstone /sánd stōn/ *n.* a type of sedimentary rock made up of particles of sand, mostly quartz, bound together with a mineral cement, along with some feldspar, mica, and rock debris. It is widely used as a building material.

sandstorm /sánd stawrm/ *n.* a strong windstorm, especially in the desert, that carries clouds of sand or dust, reducing visibility

sand table *n.* **MIL** a table covered with a layer of sand moulded to imitate the relief of a battleground terrain, used to plan military tactics

sand trap *n.* *US* a depression on a golf course that is partly filled with sand, usually located near a green as a hazard

sand viper *n.* **1.** = **horned viper 2.** **SOUTHERN EUROPEAN VIPER** a viper that is native to southern Europe and has a yellowish-brown zigzag pattern along its back. Latin name: *Vipera ammodytes*.

sand wedge *n.* a golf club with a face angle of more than 50° that is used for chipping the ball out of a bunker

sandwich /sánwij, -wich/ *n.* **1.** **FOOD BREAD SLICES WITH FILLING IN BETWEEN** a snack or light meal usually made of two slices of bread or a split roll with a filling, or a single slice of bread with a topping. ◊ **club sandwich 2.** = **sandwich cake 3.** **STH LIKE A SANDWICH** sth resembling a sandwich, especially sth in which various things are squashed together or arranged in layers ■ *vt.* (**-wiches**, **-wiching**, **-wiched**) **PLACE SB OR STH BETWEEN THINGS** to fit sth or sb tightly between two other things or people in space or time ○ *I'll see if I can sandwich you in on Tuesday.* [Mid-18thC. Named after John Montague, fourth Earl of *Sandwich* (1718–92).]

― WORD KEY: ORIGIN ―
The Earl of *Sandwich* is said to have been so addicted to the gambling table that in order to sustain him through an entire 24-hour session uninterrupted, he had a portable meal of cold beef between slices of toast brought to him. The idea was not new, but the earl's patronage ensured that it became a vogue, and by the early 1760s we have the first evidence of his name being attached to it: the historian Edward Gibbon recorded in his diary in 1762 how he dined at the Cocoa Tree and saw 'twenty or thirty of the best men in the kingdom ... supping at little tables ... upon a bit of cold meat, or a **Sandwich**.'

Sandwich /sán wich/ market town in southern Kent, England. It was one of the original Cinque Ports. Population: 4,164 (1991).

sandwich board *n.* **1.** **NOTICES HANGING FROM SHOULDERS** a pair of boards, usually displaying advertisements or notices, joined by straps and hung from the shoulders with one displayed in front and one behind **2.** **ONE BOARD OF A SANDWICH BOARD** either of the two boards that make up a sandwich board [So called because the boards sandwich the person wearing them]

sandwich cake *n.* a cake with two or more layers separated by a filling such as jam or cream

sandwich course *n.* an educational course in which work experience or practical training alternates with periods of study

sandwich man *n.* a man who carries a sandwich board

sandwich tern *n.* a European tern with white plumage, a forked tail, and a black yellow-tipped bill. It nests in colonies on beaches and cliffs. Latin name: *Sterna sandvicensis*. [Named after the town of Sandwich in Kent]

sandworm /sánd wurm/ *n.* a segmented worm living in coastal sand or mud, often used as fishing bait. Genera: *Nereis* and *Anicola*.

sandwort /sánd wurt/ (*plural* **-worts** *or* **-wort**) *n.* a plant that grows in thick tufts close to the ground on sandy soil and has single white or pink flowers. Genus: *Arenaria*.

sandy /sándi/ (**-ier, -iest**) *adj.* **1. FULL OF SAND** made up of, covered in, or full of sand **2. LIKE SAND** having a grainy texture or consistency similar to that of sand **3. OF THE COLOUR OF SAND** of a yellow colour tinged with red or brown —**sandiness** *n.*

sand yacht *n.* a small light boat fitted with a sail and wheels that allow it to be propelled by the wind over flat land, especially beaches

sane /sayn/ (**saner, sanest**) *adj.* **1. MENTALLY BALANCED** mentally healthy and able to make rational decisions **2. REASONABLE** based on sensible, reasonable, or rational thinking ○ *a sane and practical solution to the problem* **3. HEALTHY** in good health (*archaic*) [Early 17thC. From Latin *sanus* 'healthy' (source of English *sanatorium*).] —**sanely** *adv.* —**saneness** *n.*

San Fernando Valley residential and industrial region in southern California, north of Los Angeles. It is bounded by the Transverse Range on the north, the Santa Susana Mountains on the west, and the Santa Monica Mountains on the south. Population: 1,300,000 (1998).

Sanforized /sánfə rīzd/ *tdmk.* a trademark used to describe fabric preshrunk by a patented process

San Francisco /san frən sískō/ city in western California, in a spectacular location on San Francisco Bay. Population: 723,959 (1990). —**San Franciscan** *n., adj.*

sang past tense of **sing**

sangar /sángər/ *n.* a small low temporary defensive work (**breastwork**), usually built of stone around an existing hollow in the ground [Mid-19thC. From Persian and Pashto, of uncertain origin: probably formed from Persian *sang* 'stone'.]

sangaree /sáng gə reé/ *n.* a chilled drink of wine mixed with fruit juice, nutmeg, and sometimes other spirits [Mid-18thC. Alteration of Spanish *sangría* (see SANGRIA).]

sanger /sángə/ *n. Aus* a sandwich (*informal*)

Sanger /sángər/, **Frederick** (*b.* 1918) British biochemist. He was noted for his work on insulin, the structure of proteins, and the nucleotide sequence of nucleic acids. He twice won the Nobel Prize in chemistry (1958, 1980).

Margaret Sanger

Sanger, Margaret (1883–1966) US social reformer. She founded and led the US birth control movement in the 1910s and 1920s. Born **Margaret Louise Higgins**

sang-froid /song frwaá, sang-/ *n.* self-possession or calmness, especially in a dangerous or stressful situation (*formal*) [Mid-18thC. From French, literally 'cold blood'.]

sangoma /sang gṓmə/ *n. S Africa* in South Africa, a traditional healer (**shaman**) or herbalist [Late 19thC. From Nguni.]

Sangrail /sang grɑ́yl/, **Sangraal, Sangreal** /san gri əl/ *n.* CHR = **Grail** *n.* [15thC. From Old French *saint graal* 'Holy Grail'.]

Sangre de Cristo Mountains /sáng gri də krístō-/ range of the Rocky Mountains. Its highest point is Blanca Peak, 4,372 m/14,345 ft. Length: 354 km/220 mi.

sangria /sang greé ə, sáng gri ə/ *n.* a chilled Spanish drink of red wine, fruit juice, lemonade or soda water, and brandy or another spirit, usually served

in a jug with pieces of fruit [Mid-20thC. Via Spanish, literally 'a bleeding', from, ultimately Latin *sanguis* 'blood' (source of English *sanguine*).]

sanguinaria /sáng gwi náiri ə/ *n.* MED the dried rhizome and roots of the bloodroot plant, formerly used internally as a medicine, now used as an antiplaque agent in toothpaste [Early 19thC. Via modern Latin *Sanguinaria*, order name, from, ultimately, Latin *sanguis* 'blood'.]

sanguinary /sáng gwinəri/ *adj.* (*formal*) **1. INVOLVING BLOODSHED** involving death or bloodshed **2. BLOODTHIRSTY** bloodthirsty or eager to kill **3. BLOODIED** consisting of or stained with blood —**sanguinarily** *adv.* —**sanguinariness** *n.*

sanguine /sáng gwin/ *adj.* **1. CONFIDENT** cheerfully optimistic **2. RUDDY** flushed with a healthy rosy colour **3. COLOURS BLOOD-RED** of a blood-red colour **4. BLOODTHIRSTY** eager to shed blood (*archaic*) **5. PHYSIOL, HIST HAVING BLOOD AS DOMINANT HUMOUR** in medieval physiology, having blood as the dominant humour and therefore characterized by a ruddy complexion and a courageous, optimistic, and romantic temperament. ◊ **phlegmatic, melancholic, choleric** ■ *n.* **RED CRAYON** a red crayon that contains ferric oxide, used for drawing [14thC. Via French from, ultimately, Latin *sanguin-*, the stem of *sanguis* 'blood'.] —**sanguinely** *adv.* —**sanguineness** *n.* —**sanguinity** /sang gwínnəti/ *n.*

sanguineous /sang gwínni əss/ *adj.* **1. MED CONTAINING BLOOD** relating to or containing blood, especially mixed with other fluids (*often used in combination*) ○ *a sero-sanguineous discharge* **2. COLOURS BLOOD-COLOURED** of the colour of blood **3. BLOODTHIRSTY** involving or enjoying bloodshed (*literary*) [Early 19thC. Formed from Latin *sanguineus*, from *sanguin*, the stem of *sanguis* 'blood'.] —**sanguineousness** *n.*

Sanhedrin /sánnədrin/ *n.* the supreme Jewish judicial, ecclesiastical, and administrative council in ancient Jerusalem before AD 70, having 71 members from the nobility and presided over by the high priest [Late 16thC. Via Hebrew from Greek *sunedrion* 'council', from *sun* 'together' + *hedra* 'seat'.]

sanicle /sánnik'l/ *n.* a widely distributed plant with clusters of small, variously coloured flowers, oval fruits, and hooked bristles. It was formerly used as an astringent. Genus: *Sanicula*. [15thC. Via Old French from medieval Latin *sanicula*, of uncertain origin: probably formed from Latin *sanus* 'healthy'.]

sanidine /sánnidin/ *n.* a glassy high-temperature form of the potassium feldspar variety of orthoclase, found in lava deposits. When translucent it is known as moonstone. Formula: KAlSi₃O₈. [Early 19thC. From Greek *sanid-*, stem of *sanis* 'board', from the shape of the mineral's crystals.]

sanitarian /sánni táiri ən/ *adj.* OF PUBLIC HEALTH relating to public health and hygiene, especially public health sanitation (*formal*) ■ *n.* PUBLIC HEALTH OFFICIAL a public health official or inspector, especially one involved in sanitation (*formal*)

sanitary /sánnitəri/ *adj.* **1. CONNECTED WITH PUBLIC HEALTH** relating to public health, especially general hygiene and the removal of human waste through the sewage system **2. CLEAN AND HYGIENIC** clean and free from agents that cause disease or infection [Mid-19thC. Via French *sanitaire* from, ultimately, Latin *sanus* 'healthy' (source of English *sane*).] —**sanitarily** *adv.* —**sanitariness** *n.*

sanitary engineering *n.* the branch of civil engineering concerned with the building, maintenance, and development of water and sewage systems and other public health services —**sanitary engineer** *n.*

sanitary pad, sanitary napkin *n. US* = **sanitary towel**

sanitation /sánni táysh'n/ *n.* **1. STUDY OF WATER AND SEWAGE SYSTEMS** the study and maintenance of public health and hygiene, especially the water supply and sewage systems ○ *sanitation laws* **2. SEWAGE AND REFUSE COLLECTION AND DISPOSAL** conditions or procedures related to the collection and disposal of sewage and refuse [Mid-19thC. Formed from SANITARY.]

sanitize /sánni tīz/ (**-tizes, -tizing, -tized**), **sanitise** (**-tises, -tising, -tised**) *v. t.* **1. CLEAN STH BY DISINFECTING OR STERILIZING** to clean sth thoroughly by disinfecting or sterilizing it **2. MAKE STH LESS LIKELY TO OFFEND** to make

sth more likely to be acceptable by removing anything that might be considered offensive or controversial (*usually passive*) ○ *a sanitized version of the article* [Mid-19thC. Formed from SANITARY.] —**sanitization** /sánni tī záysh'n/ *n.*

sanity /sánniti/ *n.* **1. STATE OF GOOD MENTAL BALANCE** the condition of being mentally healthy and able to make rational decisions **2. GOOD SENSE** common sense, reasonableness, and predictability ○ *to restore a little sanity to the situation* [Early 17thC. via Old French *sanite* from, ultimately, Latin *sanus* 'whole, sound'.]

San José /san hō sáy/ capital city of Costa Rica, and of San José Province, situated in the centre of the country. It is the country's largest city and its economic and political centre. Population: 324,011 (1996).

San Jose scale /san hō sáy-/ *n.* a scale insect that originated in Asia and is destructive to fruit trees and other fruit-bearing plants. Latin name: *Quadraspidiotus perniciosus*. [Late 19thC. Named after the city of *San Jose* in California, where it was first identified in the United States.]

sank past tense of **sink**

——— WORD KEY: USAGE ———
See Usage note at **sink**.

Sankhya /sángkyə/ *n.* one of six systems of orthodox Hindu philosophy, based on the perpetual interaction of spirit and matter [Late 18thC. From Sanskrit *sāṃkhya*, literally 'relating to number'.]

San Marino

San Marino /san mə reénō/ small independent republic entirely surrounded by Italy. It has been independent since AD 885 and a republic since the 14th century. Language: Italian. Currency: Italian lira. Capital: San Marino. Population: 24,521 (1996). Area: 61 sq. km/24 sq. mi. Official name **Republic of San Marino** —**Sammarinese** /sa márri neéz/ *n., adj.* —**San Marinese** *n., adj.*

San Miguel de Tucumán /san mi gél də too koo maán/ capital city of Tucumán Province, northwestern Argentina, on the Río Salí. Population: 626,143 (1990).

sannyasi /sun yaássi/, **sannyasin** /-yaássin/ *n.* in Hinduism, a Brahmin who has reached the fourth and final stage of life as a mendicant and will be absorbed into the Universal Soul instead of being reborn [Early 17thC. From Sanskrit *saṃnyāsī*, literally 'sb who renounces'.]

S-A node *abbr.* sinoatrial node

San Pedro Sula /san péddrō soó laa/ capital city of Cortés Department, northwestern Honduras, in the Sula Valley. Population: 353,800 (1993).

San Remo /san reémō/ town and port in Imperia Province, Liguria Region, northwestern Italy. Population: 59,600 (1990).

sans /sanz/ *prep.* without (*archaic or literary or humorous*) ○ *looking forward to a well-earned break sans children* [13thC. Via Old French *sanz* from, ultimately Latin *sine* 'without', influenced by *absentia* 'absence'.]

San Salvador /san sálvədawr/ **1.** capital city of El Salvador and of San Salvador Department, located in central El Salvador. Population: 422,520 (1992). **2.** island of the Bahamas, in the Atlantic Ocean, near Cat Island. Population: 465 (1990). Area: 155 sq. km/60 sq. mi.

Library of Congress

sans-culotte /sánz kyoò lót/ *n.* **1.** REVOLUTIONARY IN FRENCH REVOLUTION during the French Revolution, a revolutionary either from the poorer classes or with extreme republican sympathies **2.** REVOLUTIONARY EXTREMIST a revolutionary in any country who has extremist views (*formal*) [Late 18thC. From French, literally 'without breeches'.] —**sans-culottic** *adj.* —**sans-culottism** *n.* —**sans-culottist** *n.*

San Sebastián /san sə bástien/ city and administrative centre of Guipúzcoa Province in the Basque Country, northern Spain. It is the site of an annual international film festival. Population: 178,470 (1995).

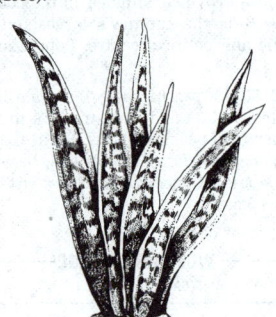
Sansevieria

sansevieria /sánssi veéri ə/ (*plural* **-as** *or* **-a**) *n.* a plant, native to tropical Africa and Asia, with thick variegated blade-shaped leaves. It is commonly grown as a houseplant or as a source of bowstring hemp. Genus: *Sansevieria*. [Early 19thC. Named after the Italian patron of horticulture, Raimondo de Sangro, Prince of *Sanseviero* (1710–70).]

Sanskrit /sánskrit/ *n.* the extinct Indo-European language of ancient India. Sanskrit was spoken between the fourteenth and fifth centuries BC, and survives as the language of classical Indian literature and Hindu religious texts. [Early 17thC. From Sanskrit *saṃskṛta* 'perfected'.] —**Sanskritic** /san skríttik/ *n., adj.* —**Sanskritist** /sánskritist/ *n.*

sans serif /sán sérrif/, **sanserif** *n.* any style of typeface in which there are no fine lines (**serifs**) at the ends of the main strokes of the characters

Santa[1] /sántə/ *n.* used as a title, usually in place names, before the name of a woman who has been made a saint. ◊ **San, Santo** [From Spanish and Italian, a form of *San* 'Saint']

Santa[2] /sántə/ *n.* Santa Claus (*informal*) [Early 20thC. Shortening.]

Santa Barbara Islands /sántə baárbərə-/ group of eight US islands in the Pacific Ocean, off the southern coast of California

Santa Cruz /sántə kroóz/ **1.** river in southern Argentina that flows eastwards out of Lake Argentino in western Santa Cruz Province, and empties into the Atlantic Ocean at the port of Santa Cruz. Length: 400 km/250 mi. **2.** city in Santa Cruz Department, central Bolivia, on the River Piray, in the tropical plains region east of the Andes Mountains. Population: 694,616 (1992). **3.** city and tourist centre in Santa Cruz County, western California, on Monterey Bay. Population: 49,040 (1990).

Santa Cruz de Tenerife /sántə krooz də tenə reéf/ capital city and port of Tenerife Island and of Santa Cruz de Tenerife Province, in the Canary Islands, Spain. Population: 204,948 (1995).

Santa Fe /sántə fáy/ **1.** capital city of Santa Fe Province in northeastern Argentina. It is a port on the Salado River. Population: 342,796 (1991). **2.** capital city of New Mexico, on the Santa Fe River, in the north of the state. Population: 66,522 (1996).

Santa Fe Trail *n.* an important route from Independence, Missouri, to Santa Fe in what is now New Mexico for wagons and stagecoaches prior to the opening of the railway during the 19th century. ◊ **Route 66**

Santa Gertrudis /-gər troòdis/ (*plural* **Santa Gertrudises** *or* **Santa Gertrudis**) *n.* a large red cow belonging to a breed developed in Texas from Brahman and shorthorn cattle and bred for beef. It is highly resistant to heat and insects. [Named after a section of the King Ranch in Kingsville, Texas, where the breed was developed]

Santamaria /sántə mə reé ə/, **B.A.** (1915–98) Australian writer and political activist, who was active in various Roman Catholic organizations, and as a staunch anticommunist helped establish the Democratic Labor Party. Full name **Bartholomew Augustine Santamaria**

Santa Marta /sántə maártə/ port and capital city of Magdalena Department in northern Colombia, on the Caribbean Sea. Population: 309,372 (1995).

Santa Monica /sántə mónnikə/ city near Los Angeles in southwestern California, on Santa Monica Bay. It is chiefly a resort and residential city. Population: 86,905 (1990).

Santander /sántən dáir/ port and capital city of Santander Province in the autonomous region of Cantabria, northern Spain. Population: 194,837 (1995).

Santería /sántə reé ə/, **santería** *n.* a religion that combines the West African Yoruba religion with Roman Catholicism. The religion recognizes a supreme God as well as other spirits. Originally developed in Cuba by West African enslaved labourers, it is now practised in the Caribbean and the United States. [Mid-20thC. Via Spanish *santería* 'holiness' from, ultimately, Latin *sanctus* 'sacred' (see SAINT).]

Santiago /sánti aágo/ capital and largest city of Chile, on the River Mapocho, in the central part of the country. Population: 4,295,593 (1992).

Santiago de Compostela /santi aágo day kompo stáylə/ capital city of the autonomous region of Galicia, northwestern Spain. Its cathedral has been a major place of pilgrimage since medieval times. Population: 94,057 (1995).

Santiago de Cuba /santi aágo day koóbə/ the second largest city in Cuba, situated in the southeast of the country. It is a major port. Population: 440,084 (1993).

santim /sán teem/ *n.* **1.** SUBUNIT OF LATVIAN CURRENCY a subunit of currency in Latvia, 100 of which are worth one lat. See table at **currency 2.** COIN WORTH A SANTIM a coin worth a santim

Santo /sántō/ (*plural* **-tos**) *n.* used as a title, usually in place names, before the name of a man who has been made a saint. ◊ **San, Santa** [Via Spanish and Italian from Latin *sanctus* (see SAINT)]

Santo Domingo capital and largest city of the Dominican Republic, situated in the south of the country. Population: 2,100,000 (1993).

santolina /sántə leénə/ (*plural* **-nas** *or* **-na**) *n.* a evergreen plant native to the Mediterranean that is grown for its distinctive silvery-grey velvety foliage. Latin name: *Santolina chamaecyparissus*. [Late 16thC. From modern Latin, perhaps an alteration of SANTONICA.]

santonica /san tónnikə/ (*plural* **-cas** *or* **-ca**) *n.* **1.** WORMWOOD PLANT WITH ABUNDANT FLOWERS a shrubby wormwood plant native to Europe and Asia that has twin needle-shaped leaves and abundant flower heads. Genus: *Artemisia*. **2.** SOURCE OF SANTONIN the dried unopened flower heads of the santonica plant which contain santonin [Mid-17thC. Via modern Latin from, ultimately, Latin *santonicus* 'of the Santoni', a tribe of the Gauls.]

santonin /sántənin/ *n.* a white crystalline compound that is extracted from the dried flower heads of the santonica plant, formerly used to eradicate parasitic worms. Formula: $C_{15}H_{18}O_3$. [Mid-19thC. Coined from SANTONICA + -IN.]

Santorini /sánto rí ni/ = **Thera**

Santos /sántooss/ city and port in São Paulo State, in southeastern Brazil, situated on the Atlantic island of São Vicente. Population: 412,288 (1996).

San Yu /sán yoó/ (*b.* 1919) Myanmar soldier and statesman, who was secretary-general of the Burmese Socialist Programme Party (1973–81) and president of Myanmar (1981–88).

São Miguel /sow mi gél/ the largest island of the Azores, located in the North Atlantic Ocean 1,200 km/740 mi. from the western coast of Portugal.

Population: 126,388 (1991). Area: 746 sq. km/288 sq. mi.

Saône /sōn/ river in east-central France. It is a tributary of the Rhône. Length: 431 km/268 mi.

São Paulo /sow pówlō/ capital of São Paulo State in southeastern Brazil. It is the largest city in South America, and an industrial and commercial metropolis. Population: 9,811,776 (1996).

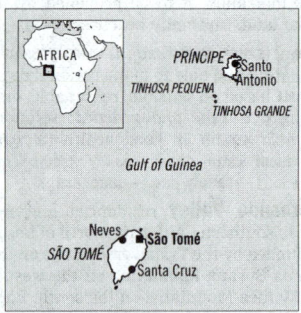
São Tomé and Príncipe

São Tomé and Príncipe /sow tō máy ənd prínchə pay/ island republic in the Gulf of Guinea, approximately 290 km/180 mi. west of Gabon, western Africa. Formerly Portuguese, the territory became an independent republic in 1975. Language: Portuguese. Currency: dobra. Capital: São Tomé. Population: 134,000 (1996). Area: 964 sq. km/372 sq. mi. Official name **Democratic Republic of São Tomé and Príncipe**

sap[1] /sap/ *n.* **1.** PLANT FLUID a watery liquid containing mineral salts, sugars, and other nutrients that circulates through the conducting tissues of a plant **2.** BOT = sapwood **3.** BODY FLUID any essential body fluid **4.** ENERGY bodily strength or vitality ○ *feel the sap rising* **5.** OFFENSIVE TERM an offensive term that deliberately insults sb's intelligence and ability to recognize the truth (*informal insult*) **6.** US COSH a weapon such as a cosh or blackjack ■ *vt.* (**saps, sapping, sapped**) **1.** DRAIN PLANT OF SAP to drain a plant of sap **2.** US HIT SB WITH A SAP to hit or knock sb out with a sap [Old English *sæp*. From a prehistoric Germanic word that is also the ancestor of German *Saft* 'juice'.] —**sapless** *adj.*

sap[2] /sap/ *n.* COVERED TRENCH LEADING TO ENEMY TERRITORY a deep narrow covered trench, dug to approach or get inside enemy territory, especially during a siege ■ *v.* (**saps, sapping, sapped**) **1.** *vti.* DIG A SAP to dig a sap, or undermine the foundations of an enemy fortification by digging a tunnel **2.** *vt.* TAKE AWAY SB'S ENERGY to gradually weaken or reduce sth, especially sb's strength or energy ○ *The long hours were sapping his strength.* [Late 16thC. Via obsolete French *sappe* and Italian *zappa* from late Latin *sappa*, of uncertain origin: perhaps from Arabic *sarab* 'burrow'.]

sapajou /sáppə joo/ (*plural* **-jous** *or* **-jou**) *n.* = capuchin [Late 17thC. From French, of uncertain origin: perhaps from Tupi.]

sapanwood *n.* = sappanwood

sapele /sə peéli/ (*plural* **-les** *or* **-le**) *n.* **1.** TREES WEST AFRICAN TREE WITH HARD WOOD a tree native to western Africa that produces a hard wood. Genus: *Entandrophragma*. **2.** INDUST WOOD FROM SAPELE TREE the wood from the sapele tree, which is similar to mahogany and is used for making furniture [Early 20thC. Named after *Sapele*, a port on the Benin River in Nigeria.]

saphead /sáp hed/ *n.* an offensive term that deliberately insults sb's intelligence or cunning (*slang insult*) —**sapheaded** *adj.*

saphenous vein /sə feénəss/ *n.* either of two major veins in the leg that run from the foot to the thigh near the surface of the skin [From medieval Latin, 'vein']

sapid /sáppid/ *adj.* (*formal*) **1.** FLAVOURFUL having a strong and pleasant taste **2.** PLEASANT TO THINK ABOUT engaging or pleasant to think about [Early 17thC. From Latin *sapidus*, from *sapere* 'to taste' (source of English *insipid*).] —**sapidity** /sə píddəti/ *n.* —**sapidness** /sáppidnəss/ *n.*

sapient /sáypi ənt/ *adj.* wise or learned [15thC. Via Old French from Latin *sapiens-*, the present participle stem of *sapere* 'to be wise, taste'.] —**sapience** *n.* —**sapiently** *adv.*

sapiential /sáypi énsh'l/ *adj.* having or giving wisdom (*formal*) —**sapientially** *adv.*

sapindaceous /sáppin dáyshəss/ *adj.* belonging to an order of trees and shrubs that includes the soapberry. Order: Sapindaceae. [19thC. Formed from modern Latin *Sapindaceae*, order name, from *Sapindus*, literally 'Indian soap', from *sapo* 'soap' + *Indus* 'India'.]

Sapir-Whorf hypothesis /sə péer wáwrf-/ *n.* the theory that the structure of a language helps determine how its native speakers perceive and categorize experience. It was proposed by Edward Sapir in 1929 and further developed by Benjamin Lee Whorf.

sapling /sáppling/ *n.* **1.** TREES **SMALL TREE** a young tree with a slender trunk **2. YOUNG PERSON** a young person (*literary*)

sapodilla /sáppə díllə/ *n.* **1.** TREES **TROPICAL EVERGREEN TREE** an evergreen tree of Mexico, Central America, and the Caribbean that yields chicle and has a brown rough-skinned fruit with sweet yellowish pulp **2.** FOOD **SAPODILLA FRUIT** a small round edible fruit with a brown skin that grows on the sapodilla tree [Late 17thC. From Spanish *zapotillo*, from *zapote*, from Nahuatl *tzapotl*.]

saponaceous /sáppə náyshəss/ *adj.* with the consistency of soap (*formal*) [Early 18thC. Formed from modern Latin from Latin *sapon- saponaceus*, from 'hair dye' (see SAPONATED).] —**saponaceousness** *n.*

saponated /sáppə naytid/ *adj.* treated or mixed with soap [Mid-18thC. Formed from Latin *sapon-*, the stem of *sapo* 'hair dye', from a prehistoric Germanic word.]

saponify /sə pónni fī/ (**-fies, -fying, -fied**) *vti.* to be converted into soap or to convert a fat into soap, especially by reaction with an alkali [Early 19thC. Via French *saponifier* from, ultimately, Latin *sapo-* 'hair dye' (see SAPONATED).] —**saponifiable** *adj.* —**saponifier** *n.*

saponin /sáppənin/ *n.* any of a group of chemical substances (**glucosides**) extracted from plants that form a soapy lather when mixed with water and are used to make detergents [Mid-19thC. Via French *saponine* from, ultimately, the Latin stem *sapon-* 'hair dye' (see SAPONATED).]

saponite /sáppə nīt/ *n.* a soft soapy clay mineral found in the veins and cavities of certain rocks that have undergone hydrothermal alteration [Mid-19thC. Formed from the Latin stem *sapon-* 'hair dye' (see SAPONATED).]

sapor /sáy pawr/ *n.* taste or flavour as a characteristic of sth (*formal*) [15thC. From Latin (also the source of English *savour*), formed from *sapere* 'to taste'.] —**saporific** /sáypə ríffik/ *adj.* —**saporous** /sáypərəss/ *adj.*

sapota /sə pṓtə/ (*plural* **-tas** *or* **-ta**) *n.* **1.** = **sapodilla** *n.* 1 **2.** = **sapote** *n.* 1

sapotaceous /sáppə táyshəss/ *adj.* belonging to an order of trees that includes the balata tree. Order: Sapotaceae. [Mid-19thC. From modern Latin, formed from *sapota* (see SAPOTA).]

sapote /sə pṓtə/ *n.* **1.** TREES **TROPICAL AMERICAN TREE** a Mexican and Central American tree that has a sweet brown fruit. Latin name: *Poulteria sapota*. **2.** FOOD **FRUIT OF SAPOTE TREE** an oval brown edible fruit that grows on the sapote tree [Mid-16thC. Via modern Latin from Spanish *zapote*, from Nahuatl *tzapotl*.]

sappanwood /sáppən wòod/, **sapanwood** *n.* **1.** TREES **TROPICAL ASIAN TREE** a tropical Asian tree. Latin name: *Caesalpina sappan*. **2.** INDUST **TROPICAL WOOD** the wood of the sappanwood tree, which yields a red dye [Late 16thC. Via Dutch from Malay *sapang*.]

sapper /sáppər/ *n.* **1. SPECIALIST IN TRENCHES AND TUNNELS** a military engineer who specializes in fortifications, especially tunnels dug under enemy territory **2. SPECIALIST IN MINES** a military engineer who lays, detects, and disarms mines **3. PRIVATE IN ROYAL ENGINEERS** in the British Army, a private in the Royal Engineers [Early 17thC. Formed from SAP^2.]

Sapphic /sáffik/ *adj.* **1. RELATING TO SAPPHO'S POETRY** relating to the Greek poet Sappho or her poetry, largely written in 11-syllable lines, with stanzas of three such lines and a shorter fourth line **2. LESBIAN** lesbian (*literary*) ■ *n.* **GREEK POEM** a Sapphic line, stanza, or poem

sapphire /sáff īr/ *n.* **1.** MINERALS **DEEP BLUE JEWEL** a clear hard precious stone that is a variety of the mineral corundum and is usually deep blue in colour **2.** COLOURS **BRILLIANT BLUE COLOUR** a brilliant blue colour like that of a sapphire ■ *adj.* **1. WITH A SAPPHIRE** made of or set with a sapphire **2.** COLOURS **OF BRILLIANT BLUE** of a brilliant blue colour like that of a sapphire [13thC. Via Old French *safir* and Latin *sapphirus* from Greek *sappheiros*.]

sapphirine /sáffə reen/ *adj.* **LIKE A SAPPHIRE** resembling a sapphire, especially in being a brilliant blue colour ■ *n.* **KIND OF MINERAL** a rare blue or green mineral that is a silicate of aluminium and magnesium

sapphism /sáffizzəm/ *n.* lesbianism (*literary*) [Late 19thC. Named after the Greek poet SAPPHO.]

Sappho /sáffō/ (*fl.* 7th century BC) Greek poet. She wrote odes, wedding songs, and hymns notable for their depth of feeling. Few fragments of her work remain.

Sapporo /sáppōrō, sa pṓrō/ commercial centre and capital of Hokkaido Prefecture, on western Hokkaido Island, Japan. Population: 1,748,000 (1995).

sappy /sáppi/ (**-pier, -piest**) *adj.* **1.** PLANTS **FULL OF SAP** full of sap **2. OFFENSIVE TERM** an offensive term describing sb as thoughtless or unintelligent (*informal insult*) —**sappily** *adv.*

sapr- *prefix.* = **sapro-** (*used before vowels*)

sapro- *prefix.* **1.** death, decay, putrefaction ○ *saprozoic* **2.** dead or decaying organic matter ○ *saprophagous* [From Greek *sapros* 'rotten']

saprobe /sáp prōb/ *n.* an organism that gets its nourishment from inorganic or decaying organic matter [Mid-20thC. Formed from SAPRO-, on the model of *microbe*.] —**saprobic** /sə prṓbik/ *adj.*

saprobiology /sáp prō bī óllәji/ *n.* the study of environments that support organisms (**saprobes**) that feed on decaying organic matter —**saprobiological** /sáp prō bī ə lójjik'l/ *adj.* —**saprobiologist** /-bī óllәjist/ *n.*

saprogenic /sáp prō jénnik/ *adj.* causing or resulting from decay —**saprogenicity** /sápprojә nissәti/ *n.*

saprolite /sáp prō līt/ *n.* soft disintegrating igneous rock that remains where it was located when solid, formed by heavy weathering in a humid environment —**saprolitic** /sáp prō líttik/ *adj.*

sapropel /sápprə pel/ *n.* a soft black layer of decaying organic matter at the bottom of a body of water [Early 20thC. From German, from Greek *sapros* 'rotten' (see SAPRO-) + *pēlos* 'mud'.] —**sapropelic** /sáprə péllik/ *adj.*

saprophagous /sa próffəgəss/ *adj.* feeding on or obtaining food from decaying organic matter

saprophyte /sáp prō fīt/ *n.* a plant, especially a fungus, or bacterium that obtains food from dead or decaying organic matter —**saprophytic** /sáp prō fíttik/ *adj.* —**saprophytically** *adv.*

saprozoic /sáp prō zṓ ik/ *adj.* getting nourishment by absorbing dissolved organic matter and salts

sapsago /sápsəgō/ (*plural* **-gos** *or* **-go**) *n.* a hard green Swiss cheese made with sour skimmed milk and flavoured with sweet clover [Mid-19thC. Alteration of German *Schabzieger*, from *schaben* 'to scrape' and *zieger* 'curd cheese'.]

sapsucker /sáp sukər/ *n.* a small North American woodpecker that drills holes in trees in order to drink the sap and eat insects attracted by the sap. Genus: *Sphyrapicus*.

sapwood /sáp wòod/ *n.* the soft wood of a tree between the inner bark and the heartwood. It is lighter in colour than the heartwood and more active in conducting water.

saraband /sárrə band/, **sarabande** *n.* **1.** DANCE **SPANISH COURT DANCE** a slow and dignified dance in triple time, favoured by the Spanish nobility in the 17th and 18th centuries **2.** MUSIC **MUSIC FOR SARABAND** music for the saraband, written in triple time with an accent on the second beat of the bar [Early 17thC. Via French from Spanish *zarabanda*.]

Saracen /sárrəs'n/ *n.* **1. MUSLIM OPPOSING CHRISTIAN CRUSADES** a Muslim who fought against the Christian Crusaders in the Middle Ages **2. MEMBER OF ANCIENT DESERT PEOPLE** a member of an ancient nomadic desert people of Syria and Arabia living on the fringes of the Roman Empire. They resisted periodic Roman attempts to incorporate their territories. **3. ARAB** an Arab (*archaic*) ■ *adj.* **1. RELATING TO SARACENS** relating to or typical of the ancient or medieval Saracens or their culture **2. ISLAMIC OR ARAB** relating to Muslims or Arabs or their cultures (*archaic*) [Pre-12thC. Via Old French *sarazin* from, ultimately, late Greek *sarakēnos*, of uncertain origin: perhaps from Arabic *sarki* 'eastern'.] —**Saracenic** /sárrə sénnik/ *adj.* —**Saracenical** *adj.*

Saragossa /sárrə góssə/ = **Zaragoza**

Sarah /sáirə/ *n.* in the Bible, the wife and half-sister of Abraham, and mother of Isaac (Genesis 17:15–22)

Sarajevo /sárrə yáyvō/ capital city of Bosnia-Herzegovina, in the eastern-central part of the country. Population: 415,631 (1991).

saran /sə rán/ *n.* a thermoplastic resin created from a vinyl compound and used to make fabrics, plastic wrap, and other articles [Mid-20thC. Originally a trademark.]

sarangi /saa rúng gi/ (*plural* **-gis**) *n.* a musical instrument of the Indian subcontinent that is similar to a violin with a rectangular soundbox and three strings with additional sympathetic strings [Mid-19thC. From Sanskrit *sāraṅgī*.]

Sarawak /sə ráawək/ state in Malaysia, in the northwestern portion of the island of Borneo. Capital: Kuching. Population: 1,648,217 (1990). Area: 124,449 sq. km/48,050 sq. mi.

sarc- *prefix.* = **sarco-** (*used before vowels*)

sarcasm /saár kazzəm/ *n.* remarks that mean the opposite of what they seem to say and are intended to mock or deride [Mid-16thC. Via French from, ultimately, Greek *sarkazein* 'to tear flesh', from *sarx* 'flesh' (source of English *sarcoma* and *sarcophagus*).]

sarcastic /saar kástik/ *adj.* **1. MOCKING** characterized by words that mean the opposite of what they seem to say and make fun of sth or sb or express irritation **2. FOND OF SARCASM** fond of or habitually using sarcasm —**sarcastically** *adv.*

WORD KEY: SYNONYMS

sarcastic, ironic, sardonic, satirical, satiric, caustic

CORE MEANING: used to describe remarks that are designed to hurt or mock

sarcastic used to describe remarks that are contemptuous, scornful, or mocking and that are intended to hurt or belittle the person or thing they are directed at; **ironic** used to describe remarks that deliberately state the opposite of the truth, usually with the intention of being amusing rather than contemptuous or mocking; **sardonic** used to describe remarks or behaviour that are mocking and cynical or disdainful. It does not suggest such deliberate hurtfulness as does ***sarcastic***; **satirical** used to describe writing, drama, drawing, or any other form of expression that uses ridicule and irony to criticize sb's or sth's faults; **satiric** a more formal word used in the same way as *satirical*; **caustic** used to describe remarks that are harsh and bitter and intended to mock, offend, or belittle the person or thing they are directed at.

sarcenet /saárssnət/, **sarsenet** *n.* a soft delicate silk cloth once widely used for veils, linings, and ribbons [15thC. From Old French *sarzinet*, of uncertain origin: perhaps formed from *Sarazin* (see SARACEN).]

sarco- *prefix.* **1.** striated muscle ○ *sarcolemma* **2.** flesh ○ *sarcoid* [From Greek *sark-*, the stem of *sarx* 'flesh'. Ultimately from an Indo-European word meaning 'to cut, tear', which is also the ancestor of English *sarcasm* and *sarcophagus*.]

sarcodinian /sáarkə dínni ən/ *adj.* **OF AMOEBA CLASS OF PROTOZOANS** belonging to the class of protozoans that includes amoebas ■ *n.* **SARCODINIAN PROTOZOAN** a protozoan that belongs to the same class as amoebas [Formed from modern Latin *Sarcodina*, superclass name, from Greek *sarkōdēs*, 'fleshy', from *sarx* 'flesh']

sarcoid /saár koyd/ *n.* **INFECTED AREA** a small area of chronic infection in the body of a person affected by

sarcoidosis ■ *adj.* **LIKE FLESH** relating to or resembling flesh

sarcoidosis /saar koy dṓssiss/ *n.* a disease in which lumps of fibrous tissue and collections of cells (**granulomas**) appear on the skin and internal organs

sarcolactic acid /saárkō láktik-/ *n.* a form of lactic acid produced by muscle tissue during anaerobic activity

sarcolemma /saárkō lémmə/ (*plural* **-colemmas** *or* **-colemmata** /-mətə/) *n.* a thin clear membrane that covers a striated muscle fibre

sarcoma /saar kṓmə/ (*plural* **-mas** *or* **-mata** /-mətə/) *n.* a malignant tumour that begins growing in connective tissue such as muscle, bone, fat, or cartilage. Sarcomas may occur in any part of the body, and are typically fast-growing and quick to spread. —**sarcomatoid** *adj.* —**sarcomatous** *adj.*

sarcomatosis /saar kṓmə tṓssiss/ *n.* a disease marked by the growth of sarcomas in various parts of the body

sarcomere /saárkō meer/ *n.* any of the tiny segments that make up a fibril of striated muscle

sarcophagus /saar kóffəgəss/ (*plural* **-gi** /-gī/ *or* **-guses**) *n.* an ancient stone or marble coffin, often decorated with sculpture and inscriptions [Early 17thC. Via Latin from Greek *sarkophagos*, literally 'flesh-eater'. The word originally referred to a kind of limestone used for making coffins in which bodies were thought to decompose quickly.]

sarcoplasm /saárkō plazzəm/ *n.* the cytoplasm of a striated muscle fibre —**sarcoplasmic** /saárkō plázmik/ *adj.* —**sarcoplasmous** /-plázməss/ *adj.*

sarcoplasmic reticulum *n.* the endoplasmic reticulum of a striated muscle fibre

sarcoptic mange /saar kóptik-/ *n.* a form of mange caused by a parasitic mite that burrows into the skin [Formed from modern Latin *Sarcoptes*, genus name of the mite that causes the disease, from Greek *sarx* 'flesh' + *koptein* 'to cut'.]

sarcostyle /saárkō stīl/ *n.* = **myofibril**

sarcous /saárkəss/ *adj.* consisting of or relating to flesh or muscle tissue

sard /saard/ *n.* a deep orange-red variety of chalcedony used in making jewellery [15thC. Via Latin *sarda* from Greek *sardios*, of uncertain origin: perhaps from SARDIS.]

Sardanapalus /saárdə náppələss/ (*fl.* 7th century BC) legendary Assyrian ruler, who was the last Assyrian king and who died in a fire in his palace during an enemy siege. He is probably an amalgam of several Assyrian kings.

sardar *n.* = **sirdar** [Late 16thC. From Persian, literally 'holding the position of chief'.]

sardine /saar deén/ *n.* a small marine fish related to the herring, especially the European pilchard. Sardines are netted in large numbers for food and preserved in cans, packed tightly in oil. Latin name: *Sardinia pilchardus*. [15thC. Via French from, ultimately, Greek *Sardō* 'Sardinia'.] ◇ **be packed like sardines** to be crowded closely together

Sardinia /saar dínni ə/ Italian island in the Mediterranean Sea. It is the second largest island in the Mediterranean after Sicily. Capital: Cagliari. Population: 1,659,466 (1995). Area: 23,813 sq. km/9,194 sq. mi.

Sardinian /saar dínni ən/ *n.* **1.** PEOPLES SB FROM SARDINIA sb who was born in or who lives in Sardinia **2.** LANG SPOKEN LANGUAGE OF SARDINIA the language spoken in Sardinia. It belongs to the Romance family of languages and is regarded by some linguists as a dialect of Italian. ■ *adj.* RELATING TO SARDINIA relating to Sardinia, or its people or culture

Sardis /saárdiss/ ancient city of Asia Minor, in present-day Turkey. It was the capital city of Lydia and an early seat of Christianity.

sardius /saárdi əss/ *n.* = **sard** [15thC. From Latin, formed from *sarda* (see SARD).]

sardonic /saar dónnik/ *adj.* disdainfully or ironically mocking [Mid-17thC. Via French *sardonique* from, ultimately, Greek *sardanios* 'scornful'. Originally meaning 'Sardinian', its later meaning derives from the 'Sardinian plant',

which caused facial contortions resembling a scornful grin.] —**sardonically** *adv.* —**sardonicism** /-sizzəm/ *n.*

— **WORD KEY: SYNONYMS** —
See Synonyms at *sarcastic*.

sardonyx /saárdəniks/ *n.* a variety of onyx with alternating bands of light orange-brown sard and white chalcedony, once widely used in making cameos [14thC. Via Latin from Greek *sardonux*, from *sardios* (see SARD) + *onux* (see ONYX).]

saree *n.* = **sari**

sargasso /saar gássō/, **sargasso weed** *n.* = **gulfweed** [Late 16thC. From Portuguese *sargaço*, of unknown origin.]

Sargasso Sea /sar gássō-/ section of the North Atlantic Ocean, between the West Indies and the Azores. It is noted for its predominantly still waters.

sargassum /saar gássəm/ *n.* = **gulfweed** [Early 20thC. From modern Latin, from SARGASSO.]

sarge /saarj/ *n.* a sergeant in the armed forces or police (*informal*) [Mid-19thC. Shortening of SERGEANT.]

Library of Congress

John Singer Sargent

Sargent /saárjənt/, **John Singer** (1856–1925) Italian-born US artist. Possessing a brilliant technique, he was known for oil portraits of well-known people such as *Madame Gautreau* (1882–83). He later turned to watercolours.

Sargeson /saárjəss'n/, **Frank** (1903–82) New Zealand writer. His short story collections include *A Man and His Wife* (1940). Pseudonym of **Norris Frank Davey**

Sargodha /saar gṓdə/ city in Punjab Province, Pakistan, about 177 km/110 mi. northwest of Lahore. Population: 291,361 (1981).

Sari

sari /saári/, **saree** *n.* a traditional garment worn by women in or from the Indian subcontinent, consisting of a long rectangle of fabric reaching the feet, wrapped and pleated around the waist over an underskirt and choli, and draped over the shoulder [Late 18thC. Via Hindi *sari* from, ultimately, Sanskrit *sati* 'garment'.]

sarin /saárin, sárrin/ *n.* an extremely toxic gas that attacks the central nervous system, causing convulsions and death. It has been used for chemical warfare. Formula: $C_4H_{10}FO_2P$. [Mid-20thC. From German, of unknown origin.]

Sark /saark/ one of the Channel Islands, in the English Channel, forming a dependency of Guernsey. It comprises Great Sark and Little Sark that are linked by a narrow isthmus. Population: 575 (1991). Area: 5 sq. km/2 sq. mi.

sarking /saárking/ *n.* Scotland, N England, NZ planks of wood nailed to the rafters of a building to support a slate roof

sarky /saárki/ (**sarkier, sarkiest**) *adj.* sarcastic (*informal*) [Early 20thC. Shortening of SARCASTIC.]

sarmentose /saar mént ōss/, **sarmentous** /-təss/ *adj.* producing long slender stems that reach out and take root along the ground [Mid-18thC. Formed from Latin *sarmentosus* 'full of twigs', from *sarmentum* 'twig'.]

Sarnia /saárniə/ city at the southern tip of Lake Huron, on the St Clair River, Ontario, Canada. Population: 86,480 (1996).

sarnie /saárni/ *n.* a sandwich (*informal*) [Mid-20thC. Origin uncertain: probably an alteration of the first element of SANDWICH.]

sarod /sa rṓd/ *n.* a stringed instrument of northern India that resembles a lute with two resonating gourds but is played with a bow [Mid-19thC. Via Urdu from Persian *sar ud*.]

Sarong

sarong /sə róng/ *n.* **1.** TRADITIONAL MALAYSIAN GARMENT a traditional garment of Java and the Malay archipelago, consisting of a length of fabric wrapped and tied around the body at the waist or under the arms. It is worn by men and women. **2.** CLOTHES FASHION VERSION OF SARONG a fashion version of the sarong worn by a woman as a wrapped skirt, often for the beach **3.** CLOTH FOR MALAYSIAN GARMENTS cloth for a sarong, often brightly coloured [Mid-19thC. From Malay 'covering'.]

Saronic Gulf /sə rónnik-/ gulf of the Aegean Sea, on the coast of southeastern Greece

saros /sáir oss/ *n.* the cycle of 6,585.32 days, or approximately 18 years 11 days, after which a sequence of eclipses of the sun and moon repeats itself. It was known to the Babylonians and some other ancient civilizations. [Early 19thC. Via Greek from Babylonian *sāru* 'the number 3600'. The modern sense, 'eclipse cycle', derives from a 19thC misunderstanding of the Babylonian word.] —**saronic** /sə rónnik/ *adj.*

sarpanch /sər púnch/ *n.* the head of a village council (**panchayat**) in India [Mid-20thC. From Urdu, formed from *sar* 'head' + *panch* 'five'.]

sarracenia /sárrə seéni ə/ (*plural* **-as** *or* **-a**) *n.* any of the pitcher plants that are native to eastern North America and have hollow tubular leaves that trap insects. Genus: *Sarracenia*. [Mid-18thC. From modern Latin, named after the 17thC Canadian botanist D. *Sarrazin*.]

sarrusophone /sə rṓozə fōn/ *n.* a woodwind musical instrument similar to a bassoon but made of brass [Late 19thC. Named after M. *Sarrus*, the 19thC French bandmaster who invented the instrument.]

sarsaparilla /saárspə ríllə/ (*plural* **-las** *or* **-la**) *n.* **1.** TROPICAL VINE tropical American vine with aromatic roots and heart-shaped leaves. Genus: *Smilax*. **2.** PLANT SIMILAR TO SARSAPARILLA a plant similar to sarsaparilla, especially American sarsaparilla and Australian sarsaparilla **3.** MEDICINAL ROOT the dried root of any sarsaparilla plant, used in traditional or herbal medicine to make a soft drink **4.** BEVERAGES KIND OF FIZZY DRINK a carbonated drink flavoured with sarsaparilla root [Late 16thC. From Spanish *zarzaparilla*, from *zarza* literally 'little bramble vine'.]

sarsen /saársn/ *n.* any of the many large sedimentary rocks that have been broken into blocks by frost action and are found scattered across the chalk downs of southern England [Late 17thC. Alteration of SARACEN. The association is unclear.]

sarsenet *n.* = sarcenet

sartor /saártər/ *n.* a tailor (*literary*) [Mid-17thC. From Latin, formed from *sart-*, the past participle stem of *sarcire* 'to patch'.]

sartorial /saar táwri əl/ *adj.* **1.** CLOTHES OF TAILORING relating to tailoring or clothing in general **2.** ANAT OF SARTORIUS MUSCLE relating to the sartorius muscle in the thigh

sartorius /saar táwri əss/ (*plural* **-i** /-ri ī/) *n.* a flat narrow muscle that extends from the hip to the inner thigh and helps rotate the leg to a cross-legged position. It is the longest muscle in the human body. [Early 18thC. From modern Latin *musculus sartorius* 'tailor's muscle', from *sartor* (see SARTOR). The term derives from the cross-legged seating posture tailors traditionally assumed when sewing.]

AKG London
Jean-Paul Sartre

Sartre /saártrə/, **Jean-Paul** (1905–80) French philosopher, playwright, and novelist. The principal exponent of existentialism, he wrote *Being and Nothingness* (1943) and the novel *Nausea* (1938).

Sarvodaya /saar vṓdəyə/ *n.* the name that Mohandas K. Gandhi and his followers gave to the new social order that they sought to establish in India. [Early 20thC. From Sanskrit, literally 'prosperity for all'.]

SAS *n.* a British military force that is specially trained to undertake dangerous clandestine operations. Full form **Special Air Service**

sash /sash/ *n.* **1.** FABRIC BELT a strip of cloth tied around the waist, e.g. as part of ceremonial dress **2.** WIDE RIBBON WORN ACROSS THE CHEST a band of cloth draped over one shoulder and across the chest as a symbol of rank or office **3.** FRAME FOR GLASS a frame holding the glass panes of a window or door [Late 17thC. From Arabic 'muslin'.]

sashay /sásh ay/ *vi.* (**-shays, -shaying, -shayed**) **1.** FLOUNCE GRACEFULLY to walk in a way that is intended to attract attention, especially by swaying the hips or swinging the elbows (*informal*) **2.** PERFORM STEPS IN SQUARE DANCING to dance a sequence of steps in square dancing ■ *n.* **1.** = chassé **2.** PATTERN IN SQUARE DANCING a figure in square dancing in which partners circle each other using sideways steps [Mid-19thC. From French *chassé*, literally 'chasing, chase'.]

sash cord *n.* a weighted cord that runs through a groove on either side of a window frame, to provide balance as the window is raised and lowered

sashimi /sáshimi/ *n.* a Japanese dish consisting of slices of raw fish, usually served with a dipping sauce such as a seasoned soy sauce. Small quantities of other ingredients, e.g. finely shredded white radish or selected pickles, may also be added as garnishes and palate-refreshing accompaniments. [Late 19thC. From Japanese.]

sashing /sáshing/ *n.* strips of fabric used to separate blocks in a patchwork

sash saw *n.* a small saw with a thin blade, used in making window sashes

sash weight *n.* a small metal weight attached to the sash cord on either side of a window frame to provide balance so that the window can be raised and lowered smoothly

sash window *n.* a window that consists of two frames, one above the other in vertical grooves,

allowing either to be opened or shut by sliding it up or down

sasin /sássin/ *n.* = blackbuck

Sask. *abbr.* Saskatchewan

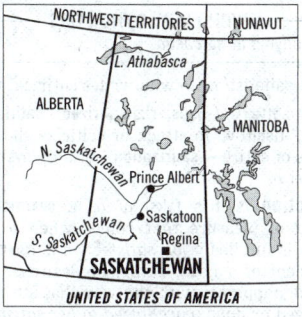
Saskatchewan

Saskatchewan¹ /səs káchəwən/ the central Prairie province of Canada, along with Alberta and Manitoba. Capital: Regina. Population: 990,237 (1996). Area: 652,330 sq. km/251,865 sq. mi. —**Saskatchewanian** *n.*, *adj.*

Saskatchewan² river in Canada, rising in central Saskatchewan and flowing into Lake Winnipeg, in Manitoba. Length: 547 km/340 mi.

saskatoon /sáskə toón/ *n.* the sweet purple-black fruit of the saskatoon [Early 19thC. From Cree *misaaskwatoomin*, 'amelanchier berry'.]

Saskatoon /sáskə toón/ the second largest city in Saskatchewan, Canada, 242 km/150 mi. northwest of Regina. Population: 219,056 (1996).

sasquatch /sásk wach/ *n.* a large hairy humanoid creature said to live in the mountains of western Canada [Early 20thC. From Salish.]

sass /sass/ *n.* US BACKCHAT disrespectful or impudent remarks, especially in reply to an older person or sb in authority (*informal*) ■ *vt.* (**sasses, sassing, sassed**) US TALK BACK TO SB to talk disrespectfully or impudently, especially to sb who is older or in authority (*informal*) [Mid-19thC. Alteration of SAUCE.]

sassaby /sássəbi/ (*plural* **-bies**) *n.* = topi¹ *n.* [Early 19thC. Alteration of Tswana *tsessébi*.]

sassafras /sássə frass/ (*plural* **-fras**) *n.* **1.** N AMERICAN TREE an eastern North American tree with aromatic bark, unevenly lobed leaves, and small bluish fruits. Latin name: *Sassafras albidum*. **2.** FLAVOURED BARK the dried root bark of the sassafras tree, used for flavouring and in perfumes and medicines [Late 16thC. From Spanish *sasafrás*, of uncertain origin: perhaps from Latin *saxifraga* (see SAXIFRAGE).]

sassafras oil *n.* a clear oil made from the root of the sassafras tree

Sassanid /sássənid/ *n.* a member of a Persian dynasty that ruled from AD 224–651. The dynasty superseded the Parthian Empire, and challenged Roman power in the East. It was the last line of Persian kings before the Arab conquests. [Late 18thC. Named after the Persian monarch *Sasan*, grandfather of the first Sassanian king.] —**Sassanian** /sə sáyni ən/ *adj.*

Sassari /sássəri/ capital of Sassari Province, Sardinia, Italy, situated near the northwestern coast of the island. Population: 121,961 (1992).

Sassenach /sássə nak, -nakh/ (*plural* **-nachs**) *n.* Scotland, Ireland an English person (*humorous or offensive*) [Early 18thC. Via Gaelic *Sassunach* from Latin *Saxones* 'Saxons', of Germanic origin.]

Sassoon /sə soón/, **Siegfried** (1886–1967) British poet and novelist. He is known for his searing poems about the horrors of World War I and for his semi-autobiographical fictional trilogy, collected as *The Memoirs of George Sherston* (1928–36). Full name **Siegfried Lorraine Sassoon**

sasswood /sáss woŏd/ *n.* = sassy²

sassy¹ /sássi/ (*plural* **-sies**, *comparative* **-sier**, *superlative* **-siest**) *adj.* US **1.** IMPUDENT impudent or disrespectful **2.** HIGH-SPIRITED lively and high-spirited ○ *The show has refreshingly sassy hoedown-style*

choreography. **3.** STYLISH stylish or fashionable ○ *a sassy look for spring* [Mid-19thC. Alteration of SAUCY.]

sassy² /sássi/ (*plural* **-sies**) *n.* a western African tree with poisonous bark and hard insect-resistant wood used for building. Latin name: *Erythrophleum suaveolens*. [Mid-19thC. Origin uncertain: perhaps from Twi *sese* 'plane tree'.]

sassy wood *n.* **1.** = sassy² **2.** W AFRICAN POISON a drink made with the poisonous extract of the sassy tree. In West African tradition it was used as a poison in trial by ordeal, and the ability to drink it and survive was thought to be a proof of innocence.

sastra *n.* = shastra

sastruga /sə stroŏgə/ *n.* a long wave-shaped ridge of hard snow formed by the wind and common in polar regions [Mid-19thC. Via German from Russian *zastruga*.]

sat past tense, past participle of **sit**

SAT /sat/ *abbr.* standard assessment task ■ *n.* US HIGH SCHOOL TEST in the United States, a test of performance given to high school students, used to determine eligibility for admission to a college or university. Full form **Scholastic Aptitude Test**

sat. *abbr.* **1.** saturated **2.** saturation **3.** satellite

Sat. *abbr.* CALENDAR Saturday

Satan /sáyt'n/ *n.* in Christianity, the enemy of God, the lord of evil, and the tempter of human beings. He is sometimes identified with Lucifer, the leader of the fallen angels. [Pre-12thC. Via Latin from, ultimately, Hebrew *śāṭān* 'to accuse'.]

satang /sa táng/ (*plural* **-tang**) *n.* **1.** SUBUNIT OF THAI CURRENCY a subunit of currency in Thailand, 100 of which are worth one baht. See table at **currency 2.** COIN WORTH A SATANG a coin worth a satang

satanic /sə tánnik/ *adj.* **1.** RELATING TO SATAN WORSHIP relating to Satan or the worship of Satan **2.** EXTREMELY EVIL extremely evil or cruel —**satanically** *adv.* —**satanicalness** *n.*

Satanism /sáyt'nizzəm/ *n.* the worship of Satan, especially as a parody of Christian rites

satay /sáttay/ *n.* a dish popular in Indonesia and Malaysia, consisting of marinated well-seasoned pieces of meat, chicken, or fish grilled on wooden skewers and served with peanut sauce [Mid-20thC. From Malay.]

SATB *abbr.* soprano, alto, tenor, bass

satchel /sáchəl/ *n.* a small bag, often with a shoulder strap, used for carrying books and personal belongings [14thC. Via Old French *sachel* from Latin *sacellus*, from *saccus* 'bag' (source of English sack).]

sate /sayt/ (**sates, sating, sated**) *vt.* **1.** FULLY GRATIFY DESIRE to satisfy completely sb's hunger or some other desire **2.** GLUT SB to provide sb with more than enough, to the point of exhaustion or disgust [Old English *sadian*. Ultimately from an Indo-European word that is also the ancestor of English sad, satisfy, and asset.]

sateen /sə teén/ (*plural* **-teens** *or* **-teen**) *n.* a cotton or polyester fabric with a shiny side intended to look like satin [Late 19thC. Formed from SATIN, on the model of 'velveteen'.]

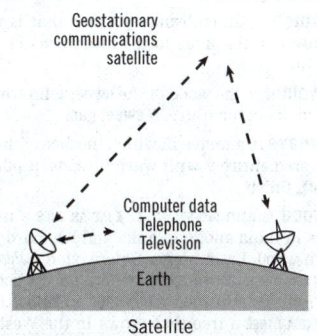
Geostationary communications satellite

Computer data
Telephone
Television

Earth

Satellite

satellite /sáttə līt/ *n.* **1.** TELECOM DEVICE THAT ORBITS A PLANET an object put into orbit around Earth or any other planet in order to relay communications signals or transmit scientific data **2.** ASTRON MOON ORBITING OTHER BODY a celestial body that orbits a larger one **3.** COUNTRY DEPENDENT ON ANOTHER COUNTRY a nation or political unit that is dependent economically and politically on another more powerful nation **4.** GEOG **SUBURB** a town or small city located near and dependent on a larger city **5.** **ATTENDANT** sb who attends a person of importance, often obsequiously [Mid-16thC. Via French from Latin *satelles* 'attendant'.]

satellite broadcasting *n.* the global transmission of television programmes via satellite

satellite cell *n.* one of the cells forming the capsule that encloses the nerve cells in many spinal ganglia

satellite dish *n.* a dish-shaped device for receiving television signals broadcast via satellite

satellite DNA *n.* a component of an animal's DNA that differs in density from surrounding DNA, consists of short repeating sequences of nucleotide pairs, and does not undergo transcription

satellitium /sáttə lítti əm/ *n.* in astrology, a group of planets in one sign of the zodiac (*archaic*)

satem /saátəm/ *adj.* relating to Indo-European languages in which the consonant sounding like 'k' developed into the sound 's' or 'sh' [Early 20thC. From Avestan *satem* 'hundred'.]

sati *n.* = **suttee**

satiable /sáyshəb'l/ *adj.* able to be satisfied [Late 16thC. Formed from Latin *satiare* 'to satisfy' (see SATIATE).] —**satiability** /sáyshə bílləti/ *n.* —**satiably** /sáyshəbli/ *adv.*

satiate /sáyshi ayt/ *vt.* (**-ates, -ating, -ated**) **1.** **GLUT SB** to provide sb with too much of sth desirable, to the point of overindulgence (*often passive*) **2.** **GRATIFY DESIRE** to satisfy hunger or another appetite completely ■ *adj.* **HAVING TOO MUCH** having had enough or too much [15thC. From Latin *satiat-*, the past participle stem of *satiare*, from *satis* 'enough' (source of English *satisfy*).]

Satie /saa tí/, **Erik** (1866–1925) French composer His light, innovative ballets, dramas, and piano pieces influenced Ravel, Debussy, and the composers known as Les Six. Full name **Erik Alfred Leslie Satie**

satiety /sə tí̄ əti/ *n.* a state in which sb has had enough or too much [Mid-16thC. Via French *satiété* from, ultimately, Latin *satis* 'enough'.]

satin /sáttin/ *n.* **GLOSSY SILK OR RAYON FABRIC** a fabric woven of silk or rayon, with a smooth glossy finish and a dull back ■ *adj.* **1.** **OF SATIN** made of satin fabric **2.** **GLOSSY LIKE SATIN** smooth and glossy like satin [14thC. Via Old French from Arabic *zaytūnī* 'of the town of Zaytun', of uncertain location: probably the Chinese city of Tsinkiang.] —**satiny** *adj.*

satin bowerbird *n.* a large bowerbird found in the eastern rainforests of Australia. The male is a glossy blue-black and is renowned for its elaborate courtship display involving the construction of a bower made of twigs, which it surrounds with a variety of blue objects. Latin name: *Ptilinorhynchus violaceus.*

satinet /sátti nét/, **satinette** *n.* **1.** **IMITATION SATIN** an imitation satin made from cotton and wool **2.** **INFERIOR SATIN** thin or inferior satin

satin spar *n.* a variety of sulphate or carbonate of calcium. ◊ **gypsum**

satin stitch *n.* an embroidery stitch that is worked in close parallel lines to fill in an area or form a solid line

satin walnut *n.* the wood of the sweet gum tree, often used to make furniture. ◊ **sweet gum**

satin weave *n.* a weave in which the face of the fabric is covered entirely with warp threads, producing a smooth finish

satinwood /sáttin wŏŏd/ *n.* **1.** **E INDIAN TREE** a tree that grows in India and Sri Lanka and has hard yellow-brown wood. Latin name: *Chloroxylon swietenia.* **2.** **WOOD FROM SATINWOOD TREE** the smooth hard wood of the East Indian satinwood tree, used in fine carpentry **3.** **W INDIAN TREE** a tree that grows in the West Indies and has smooth lustrous wood. Latin name: *Zanthoxylum flavum.*

satire /sáttīr/ *n.* **1.** **USE OF WIT** the use of wit, especially irony, sarcasm, and ridicule, to attack the vices and follies of humankind **2.** **LITERARY WORK USING SATIRE** a literary work that uses satire, or the branch of literature made up of such works [Early 16thC. Directly or via French from Latin *satira* 'poetic medley, satire', of uncertain origin: perhaps a variant of *satura* 'a mixed dish'.]

satirical /sə tírrik'l/ *adj.* relating to satire or the use of wit to attack the vices and follies of humankind —**satirically** *adv.*

WORD KEY: SYNONYMS

See Synonyms at ***sarcastic***.

satirist /sáttərist/ *n.* sb who writes satirical works

satirize /sáttə rīz/ (**-rizes, -rizing, -rized**), **satirise** (**-rises, -rising, -rised**) *vt.* to attack or criticize sb or sth by means of satire —**satirization** /sáttə rī záysh'n/ *n.* —**satirizer** *n.*

satisfaction /sáttiss fáksh'n/ *n.* **1.** **GRATIFICATION** the feeling of pleasure that comes when a need or desire is fulfilled ○ *job satisfaction* **2.** **FULFILMENT** the fulfilment of a need, claim, or desire **3.** **HAPPINESS WITH STH** happiness with the way that sth has been arranged or done ○ *organized to her satisfaction* **4.** **FREEDOM FROM DOUBT** the assurance that sth has been fully explained or settled ○ *a solution that was never explained to my satisfaction* **5.** **COMPENSATION** compensation for an injury or loss ○ *demanded satisfaction for their mistreatment* [14thC. Via French from, ultimately, Latin *satisfacere*, from *satis* 'enough' + *facere* 'to make'.]

satisfactory /sáttiss fáktəri/ *adj.* good enough to meet a requirement or to be considered acceptable [15thC. Via French *satisfactoire* from, ultimately, Latin *satisfacere* 'to satisfy' (see SATISFACTION).]

satisfied /sáttiss fīd/ *adj.* **1.** **CONTENT WITH STH** contented or pleased with what has happened **2.** **FULLY CONVINCED** fully convinced that sth is right, proper, or true **3.** **FULLY PAID** paid in full

satisfy /sáttiss fī/ (**-fies, -fying, -fied**) *v.* **1.** *vt.* **MAKE SB FEEL CONTENT** to do or offer enough to make sb feel pleased or content **2.** *vti.* **FULFIL NEED** to fulfil a need or gratify a desire **3.** *vt.* **RESOLVE DOUBTS** to convince sb by resolving questions or doubts **4.** *vt.* **BE GOOD ENOUGH TO MEET CONDITION** to achieve or be of sufficient standard to meet a requirement or condition **5.** *vt.* MATH **SOLVE MATHEMATICAL PROBLEM** to make both sides of an equation equal by finding the quantities of the unknown variables **6.** *vt.* LAW **PAY DEBT** to pay a debt in full **7.** *vt.* **COMPENSATE SB** to compensate sb for an injury or loss [15thC. Via Old French *satisfier* from Latin *satisfacere* 'to satisfy' (see SATISFACTION).] —**satisfier** *n.*

satori /sə táwri/ *n.* in Zen Buddhism, a state of spiritual enlightenment that is a spiritual objective [Early 18thC. From Japanese 'awakening'.]

satrap /sáttrap/ *n.* **1.** **PERSIAN GOVERNOR** the governor of a province in ancient Persia **2.** **POLITICAL HENCHMAN** a subordinate official, especially a self-important one [15thC. Via French and Latin from, ultimately, Old Persian *kšatrapāvan*, literally 'protector of the country'.]

satrapy /sáttrəpi/ (*plural* **-pies**) *n.* the province or territory ruled by a satrap

satsuma /sat sŏŏmə/ *n.* **1.** FOOD **KIND OF TANGERINE** a citrus fruit with a thin orange skin **2.** TREES **JAPANESE CITRUS TREE** a small Japanese tree that bears satsumas. Latin name: *Citrus reticulata.* [Late 19thC. Named after a province in the island of Kiusiu, in Japan.]

Satsuma ware, **Satsuma** *n.* a kind of cream-coloured Japanese pottery

saturable /sáchərəb'l/ *adj.* capable of being saturated, or of reaching the point where nothing more can be absorbed [Late 16thC. Formed from Latin *saturat-*, the past participle stem of *saturare* 'to saturate' (see SATURATE).] —**saturability** /sáchərə bílləti/ *n.*

saturant /sáchərənt/ *n.* **STH THAT SATURATES** a substance that is used to saturate another substance ■ *adj.* **SATURATING** causing saturation [Mid-18thC. From Latin *saturant-*, the present participle stem of *saturare* 'to saturate' (see SATURATE).]

saturate *vt.* /sáchə rayt/ (**-rates, -rating, -rated**) **1.** **MAKE STH WET** to make sth soaked with liquid **2.** **FILL STH COMPLETELY** to fill sth with so many people or things that no more can be added **3.** COMM **SUPPLY MARKET FULLY** to supply a market fully, so that all existing demand for a product is met **4.** CHEM **FILL SOLUTION WITH ANOTHER SUBSTANCE** to add a liquid, solid, or gas to a solution until it reaches the point where nothing more can be absorbed **5.** MIL **BOMB ENEMY HEAVILY** to overwhelm an enemy with intensive bombing ■ *adj.* /sáchərət/ **SATURATED** saturated with liquid (*archaic*) [Mid-16thC. From Latin *saturat-*, the past participle stem of *saturare*, from *satur* 'satiated' (probable source of English *satire*).]

saturated /sáchə raytid/ *adj.* **1.** **WET** soaked with liquid **2.** CHEM **CONTAINING MAXIMUM SOLUTE** containing the maximum amount of absorbed solute **3.** **PACKED FULL** completely packed or full so that no more can be added **4.** FOOD **CONTAINING FATTY ACIDS** containing a relatively large number of fatty acids

saturated fat *n.* a kind of fat, often found in meat and other animal products, that cannot incorporate any additional hydrogen atoms. A diet heavy in saturated fat is thought to raise cholesterol in the bloodstream.

saturation /sáchə ráysh'n/ *n.* **1.** **STATE OF TOTAL WETNESS** a state in which sth is completely soaked with liquid **2.** **STATE OF BEING PACKED FULL** a state in which sth is so full or packed that no more can be added **3.** MIL **HEAVY BOMBING** intensive bombing of a military target in order to overwhelm an enemy **4.** COMM **FULL SUPPLYING OF MARKET** the full supplying of a market, to the point where all existing demand for a product is met **5.** CHEM **MAXIMUM ABSORPTION** the absorption of the greatest possible amount of a liquid, solid, or gas by a solution **6.** PHYS **STATE OF MAGNETIZATION** a state of complete magnetization **7.** METEOROL **100 PER CENT HUMIDITY** the condition of the atmosphere when it contains as much water vapour as it can hold at a specific temperature **8.** PHYS **COLOUR INTENSITY** the intensity of a colour **9.** ELECTRON ENG **CONDITION OF STABLE OUTPUT CURRENT** a condition where the output current of an electronic device is substantially constant and no longer increases as a function of increasing input ■ *adj.* **COMPREHENSIVE** comprehensive in the use of outlets or other resources ○ *The event had saturation coverage in the press.*

saturation diving *n.* a method of diving in which the diver's bloodstream is saturated with an inert gas so that the time required for decompression is unaffected by the duration of the dive

saturation point *n.* **1.** **LIMIT TO SCOPE FOR EXPANSION** the point at which no more can be added **2.** CHEM **LIMIT TO ABSORPTION** the point at which the greatest possible amount of a substance has been absorbed in a solution

saturation zone *n.* the zone below the water table that is saturated with groundwater

Saturday /sáttər day, -di/ *n.* CALENDAR the day of the week after Friday and before Sunday [Pre-12thC. Translation of Latin *Saturni dies*, literally 'day of Saturn' (see SATURN).]

Saturday night special *n.* *US* a small cheap handgun that is easy to obtain and conceal [Because the guns are most often used in urban attacks, fights and robberies, the types of crime that typically occur on a Saturday night]

Saturdays /sáttər dayz, -diz/ *adv.* CALENDAR every Saturday

Saturn /sáttərn/ *n.* **1.** **ROMAN GOD OF AGRICULTURE** in Roman mythology, the god of agriculture and ruler of the universe during the Golden Age. Greek equivalent **Cronus** **2.** **PLANET 6TH FROM SUN** the second largest planet in the solar system and the sixth planet from the sun. Saturn has bright rings made up of orbiting fragments of rock. It takes 10 hours and 39 minutes to rotate on its axis and 29.5 years to orbit the Sun. Its mass is 95 times that of Earth. [Old English. From Latin *Saturnus*, of uncertain origin: perhaps from Etruscan.]

saturnalia /sáttər náyli ə/ (*plural* **-as** *or* **-a**) *n.* a wild celebration or orgy [Late 18thC. Generalized use of SATURNALIA.]

Saturnalia *npl.* an ancient Roman festival of feasting and revelry held in mid-December in celebration of the god Saturn and the winter solstice [Late 16thC. From Latin, formed from *Saturnus* 'Saturn' (see SATURN).]

Saturnian /sa túrni ən/ *adj.* **1.** **OF THE PLANET SATURN** relating to the planet Saturn **2.** **OF GOD SATURN** relating to the Roman god Saturn or the Golden Age of his reign

saturniid /sa túrni id/ *n.* a large brightly coloured moth that has a stout hairy body. Family: Saturniidae. [Late 19thC. From modern Latin *Saturniidae*, from Latin *Saturnus* 'Saturn' (see SATURN).]

saturnine /sáttər nīn/ *adj.* gloomy and morose [15thC. Directly or via French from medieval Latin *saturninus*, from Latin *Saturnus* 'Saturn' (see SATURN).] —**saturninely** *adv.*

satyagraha /sut yáagrəhə/ *n.* the doctrine of non-violent resistance originated by Mohandas K. Gandhi and used in the opposition to British rule in India. [Early 20thC. From Sanskrit *satyāgrahaḥ*, literally 'force born out of truth'.]

satyagrahi /sut yáagrəhi/ *n.* sb who practises non-violent resistance or satyagraha [Early 20thC. From Sanskrit (see SATYAGRAHA).]

satyr /sáttər/ *n.* **1.** MYTHOL HALF-MAN, HALF-GOAT in Greek mythology, a wood-dwelling creature with the head and body of a man and the ears, horns, and legs of a goat. Roman equivalent **faun 2.** MAN DISPLAYING INAPPROPRIATE SEXUAL BEHAVIOUR a man who displays inappropriate or excessive sexual behaviour **3.** ZOOL BUTTERFLY a brown or grey butterfly with spotted wings. Family: Satyridae. [14thC. Via French from Latin *satyrus*, from Greek *saturos*.] —**satyric** /sə tírrik/ *adj.* —**satyrical** *adj.*

satyriasis /sáttə rí əssiss/ *n.* PSYCHIAT excessive and uncontrollable sexual desire in a man

satyrid /sə téerid/ *n.* a small brown butterfly. Family: Satyridae.

satyr play *n.* in ancient Greece, a comic play that mocked a mythological subject and included a chorus of satyrs

sauce /sawss/ *n.* **1.** FLAVOURING LIQUID FOR FOOD a thick liquid that is served with food to add extra flavour **2.** IMPUDENT REMARKS impudent or disrespectful remarks (*informal*) **3.** US, Can STEWED FRUIT stewed fruit served with a meal ○ *cranberry sauce* **4.** ZEST sth that adds zest or excitement **5.** US LIQUOR alcoholic liquor (*slang*) ■ *vt.* (**sauces, saucing, sauced**) **1.** SPEAK TO SB DISRESPECTFULLY to make impudent or disrespectful remarks to sb (*informal*) **2.** ADD SAUCE TO FOOD to add flavour to food using a sauce **3.** ENLIVEN STH to add zest or interest to sth [14thC. Via Old French from, ultimately, Latin *salsus*, past participle of *sallere* 'to salt', from *sal* 'salt'.]

Sauce boat

sauce boat *n.* a low boat-shaped jug used for serving sauce or gravy

saucepan /sáwspən/ *n.* a cooking pot with a handle, used on top of a cooker

saucer /sáwssər/ *n.* **1.** SMALL CIRCULAR DISH a small shallow dish designed to hold a matching cup **2.** ROUND FLAT OBJECT anything circular and shallow like a saucer

sauce suprême *n.* = suprême sauce

saucy /sáwssi/ (**-ier, -iest**) *adj.* **1.** CHEEKY showing a lack of respect **2.** PERT cheerfully pert ○ *a hat at a saucy angle* **3.** SEXUALLY EXPLICIT intended to be amusingly vulgar, especially in sexual innuendo ○ *a range of saucy postcards* [Early 16thC.] —**saucily** *adv.* —**sauciness** *n.*

Saudi /sówdi, sáwdi/ *n.* SB FROM SAUDI ARABIA sb who was born or brought up in Saudi Arabia, or who is a citizen of Saudi Arabia ■ *adj.* RELATING TO SAUDI ARABIA relating to or typical of Saudi Arabia, or its people or culture [Mid-20thC. Named after *Sa'ūd*, founder of the dynasty that has ruled Saudi Arabia since 1932.]

Saudi Arabia

Saudi Arabia /sówdi ə ráybi ə/ monarchy in the Middle East, on the Arabian Peninsula. Language: Arabic. Currency: riyal. Capital: Riyadh. Population: 18,426,000 (1996). Area: 2,240,000 sq. km/864,869 sq. mi. Official name **Kingdom of Saudi Arabia** —**Saudi Arabian** *n., adj.*

sauerbraten /sówər braat'n/ *n.* a German dish of beef marinated and cooked in a vinegar mixture [Late 19thC. From German, literally 'sour roast meat'.]

sauerkraut /sówər krowt/ *n.* a German dish of shredded cabbage fermented in its own juice with salt [Mid-17thC. From German, literally 'sour cabbage'.]

sauger /sáwgər/ *n.* a North American freshwater fish similar to but smaller than a walleyed pike and valued in sport fishing. Latin name: *Stizostedion canadense*. [Late 19thC. Origin unknown.]

Sauk /sawk/ (*plural* **Sauk** *or* **Sauks**), **Sac** (*plural* **Sac** *or* **Sacs**) *n.* **1.** MEMBER OF NATIVE N AMERICAN PEOPLE a member of a Native North American people that originally occupied lands in Wisconsin, Illinois, and Iowa, and whose members now live mainly in Oklahoma. The Sauk joined with the Fox to fight in the Black Hawk War of 1832, following US attempts to move the Fox from their lands in Illinois. **2.** SAUK LANGUAGE the Algonquian language of the Sauk, related to Fox [Early 18thC. Via Canadian French *Saki* from Ojibwa *osáki*.]

Saul /sawl/ (*fl.* 11th century BC) Israeli monarch, mentioned in 1 Samuel 8–15. He defeated the Philistines but later died in battle against them. He was succeeded by his son-in-law, David.

sault /soo, sō/ *n.* US, Can a waterfall or rapids [14thC. Via Old French from Latin *saltus* 'leap', from *salire* 'to leap' (source of English *somersault* and *insult*).]

Sault Sainte Marie /soo saynt mə rée/ **1.** city in Ontario, Canada, between Lakes Superior and Huron, on the St Mary's River. Population: 83,619 (1996). **2.** city in northern Michigan, opposite Sault Sainte Marie, Ontario. Population: 14,689 (1990).

sauna /sáwnə/ *n.* **1.** STEAM BATH a kind of bath involving a spell in a hot steamy room followed by a plunge into cold water or a light brushing with birch or cedar boughs **2.** ROOM FOR SAUNA a room designed or prepared for having a sauna [Late 19thC. From Finnish.]

saunter /sáwntər/ *vi.* (**-ters, -tering, -tered**) STROLL to walk at an easy unhurried pace ■ *n.* **1.** EASY PACE an easy unhurried pace ○ *walk at a saunter* **2.** SLOW WALK a slow leisurely walk ○ *go for a saunter round the grounds* [Mid-17thC. Origin unknown.] —**saunterer** *n.*

saurel /sáwrəl/ *n.* US = horse mackerel [Late 19thC. Via Latin *saurus* from Greek *sauros* 'lizard, horse mackerel' (source of English *dinosaur*).]

saurian /sáwri ən/ *n.* LIZARD any of a former suborder of reptiles that included all lizards. Suborder: Sauria. ■ *adj.* OF LIZARDS relating to or resembling a lizard [Early 19thC. Formed from modern Latin *Sauria*, name of the suborder, from Latin *saurus* 'lizard', from Greek *sauros*.]

saurischian /saw ríski ən/ *n.* KIND OF DINOSAUR a dinosaur that had a pelvis like that of a modern lizard. Order: Saurischia. ■ *adj.* OF SAURISCHIANS relating to the saurischians [Late 19thC. Formed from modern Latin *Saurischia*, name of the order, literally 'lizard hip-joint'.]

sauropod /sáwrō pod/ *n.* KIND OF DINOSAUR a gigantic plant-eating dinosaur that had a long neck and tail

and a small head. Suborder: Sauropoda. ■ *adj.* OF SAUROPODS relating to the sauropods [Late 19thC. Formed from modern Latin *Sauropoda*, name of the suborder, literally 'lizard foot'.] —**sauropodous** /saw róppədəss/ *adj.*

saury /sáwri/ (*plural* **-ries**) *n.* a small offshore tropical or temperate marine fish that resembles a needlefish but has shorter jaws and a series of finlets behind the dorsal and anal fins. Family: Scomberosocidae. [Late 18thC. Formed from modern Latin *saurus* 'lizard', from Greek *sauros*.]

sausage /sóssij/ *n.* **1.** SPICY MEAT IN A CASING seasoned pork or other meat chopped fine and stuffed into a tube of animal intestine or another tube-shaped skin **2.** = sausagemeat [15thC. Via Old French *saussiche* from medieval Latin *salsicius* 'made by salting', from Latin *salsus* 'salted'.] ◇ **not a sausage** nothing at all (*informal*)

sausage dog *n.* = dachshund (*informal*)

sausagemeat /sóssij meet/ *n.* seasoned minced pork, usually mixed with fat and bread or cereal. It can be encased in pastry in a sausage roll or encase an egg in a Scotch egg.

sausage roll *n.* a short length of sausagemeat wrapped in pastry and baked

sausage tree *n.* a tropical African tree with clusters of scarlet flowers and long fruits with hard shells. Latin name: *Kigelia pinnata*.

Saussure /sō syoor, -soor/, **Ferdinand de** (1857–1913) Swiss linguist. His masterwork, *Cours de linguistique générale* (1916), was assembled from his students' lecture notes. He is considered the founder of structural linguistics, structuralism, and semiotics.

sauté /só tay/ *vt.* (**-tés, -téing, -téed**) FRY STH LIGHTLY to cook food quickly and lightly in a little butter, oil, or fat ■ *n.* SAUTÉED DISH a dish consisting of food, usually meat, that has been sautéed and prepared with a sauce ■ *adj.* BEING COOKED LIGHTLY cooked by being sautéed [Early 19thC. From French, the past participle of *sauter* 'to leap', from, ultimately, Latin *salire*.]

sauternes /sō túrn/ *n.* a sweet white wine made from grapes grown in the Sauternes region of France [Early 18thC. Named after the French region of *Sauternes* where the wine is produced.]

sauve qui peut /sóv kee pő/ *n.* a disordered or panicked escape [Early 19thC. From French, literally 'save who can'.]

Sauvignon blanc /só veen yon-/ *n.* a variety of grape from which white wine is made [Mid-20thC. From French, literally 'white Sauvignon'.]

sav /sav/ *n.* Aus a saveloy sausage (*informal*) [Mid-20thC. Shortening.]

savage /sávvij/ *adj.* **1.** VIOLENT unrestrained, violent or vicious **2.** BRUTAL brutal and severe ○ *savage cuts in funding* **3.** UNDOMESTICATED living wild, beyond the control of people ○ *savage beasts* **4.** OFFENSIVE TERM an offensive term referring to a culture perceived as inferior to one's own (*offensive*) ■ *n.* **1.** VICIOUS OR VIOLENT PERSON sb who enjoys treating other people and animals in a cruel violent way **2.** OFFENSIVE TERM an offensive term referring to a member of a people considered inferior or not as advanced as your own group (*offensive*) ■ *vt.* (**-ages, -aging, -aged**) **1.** ATTACK SB OR STH VIOLENTLY to attack sb or sth violently, viciously, and without restraint **2.** CRITICIZE SB OR STH CRUELLY to criticize sb or sth cruelly and unrestrainedly ○ *The same critics who praised her first book savaged her second.* [13thC. Via French *sauvage* from, ultimately, Latin *silvaticus* 'wild', from *silva* 'forest' (source of English *sylvan*).] —**savagely** *adv.* —**savageness** *n.*

WORD KEY: USAGE

Sensitivity trap: The use of *savage* to refer to primitive peoples was a feature of 19th-century and earlier English (*Vouchsafe to show the sunshine of your face, that we, like savages, may worship it*, Shakespeare, *Love's Labour's Lost* Act 5, scene 2), but is regarded as inappropriate and offensive in current use.

savagery /sávvijəri/ *n.* **1.** VIOLENT CRUELTY barbarity or violent cruelty **2.** OFFENSIVE TERM an offensive term referring to a culture perceived to be inferior to or less advanced than your own (*offensive*)

savanna /sə vánnə/, **savannah** n. a flat grassland, sometimes with scattered trees, in a tropical or subtropical region [Mid-16thC. Via Spanish *zavana* from Taino.]

savant /sávvənt/ n. a wise or scholarly person [Early 18thC. From French, the present participle of *savoir* 'to know', from, ultimately, Latin *sapere* 'to be wise'.]

savate /sə vát/ n. a form of boxing in which kicking as well as hitting is allowed [Mid-19thC. From French, originally a kind of shoe.]

save[1] /sayv/ v. (**saves, saving, saved**) **1.** *vt.* RESCUE SB OR STH to rescue sb or sth from harm or danger ○ *The entire crew were saved.* **2.** *vti.* ACCUMULATE MONEY to set aside money for later use, often adding to the sum periodically ○ *She's saving for a new computer.* **3.** *vt.* CONSERVE STH to avoid wasting sth or using it unnecessarily ○ *take a shortcut to save time* **4.** *vt.* KEEP STH BACK FOR LATER to set sth aside, keep sth back, or protect sth so that it can be used later ○ *Save some of the pie for tomorrow.* **5.** *vti.* REDUCE EXPENSE to reduce or limit the expense of sth ○ *Extra insulation helps us to save on fuel.* **6.** *vt.* COLLECT ITEMS FOR LATER to collect as many items of a particular kind as possible, usually in order to do sth with them later ○ *She saves old jam jars for when she makes marmalade.* **7.** *vt.* SPARE STH FROM STH to make it possible for sb to be spared from a situation or activity ○ *It will save me from having to decide.* **8.** *vt.* PRESERVE STH to treat sth carefully or stop using it in order to keep it from being used up or worn out ○ *Switch the radio off to save the batteries.* **9.** *vt.* SPORTS PREVENT GOAL to prevent an opponent from scoring a goal **10.** *vti.* COMPUT COPY DATA FOR STORAGE to store a copy of a data file on a storage medium such as a hard drive or disk **11.** *vt.* RELIG REDEEM SB to free sb from the consequences of sin ■ n. SPORTS BLOCK an action that keeps an opponent from scoring [13thC. Via Old French *salver* from late Latin *salvare*, which was formed from Latin *salvus* 'safe'.]

save[2] /sayv/ prep., conj. except ○ *Everyone agreed save one.*

save-all n. **1.** CONTAINER FOR SALVAGING WASTE a receptacle for catching waste products so that they can be reused **2.** STH PREVENTING WASTE sth that prevents waste or loss

save as you earn n. a savings plan in the United Kingdom in which monthly deposits are made over a five-year period. The savings are tax-free and they accumulate interest as well as earning a bonus at the end of five years.

saveloy /sávvə loy/ n. a spicy smoked pork sausage [Mid-19thC. Via French *cervelas* from Italian *cervellata* 'sausage'.]

saver /sáyvər/ n. **1.** FIN SB WHO SAVES MONEY sb who sets aside money for later use, especially in a bank or buliding society account ○ *The fall in interest rates is not such good news for savers.* **2.** STH THAT CONSERVES RESOURCES sth that avoids wasting resources or using them unnecessarily (*used in combinations*) ○ *E-mail is a great time-saver.* **3.** TRANSP CHEAP TRAVEL TICKET an airline, coach, or train ticket that is cheaper than the normal price and usually places a number of restrictions on the date and time of travel ○ *A weekend saver to Leeds, please.*

Savernake Forest /sávvər nayk-/ ancient beech forest near Marlborough, Wiltshire, England. It was formerly a royal hunting ground. Area: 18 sq. km/7 sq. mi.

Savery /sáyvəri/, **Thomas** (1650?–1715) English engineer and inventor. He patented a method of paddle-wheel propulsion for vessels and a steam pump, and with Thomas Newcomen developed a steam piston engine.

Save the Children Fund n. an organization that provides international aid directed towards children's well-being

Savimbi /sə vímbi/, **Jonas** (b. 1934) Angolan soldier and revolutionary. He was a founder and leader of the independence movement UNITA, and a fighter for Angolan independence. He declined the vice presidency of Angola and continued to fight the government (1995). Full name **Jonas Malheiro Savimbi**

savin /sávvin/, **savine** n. an evergreen shrub found in Europe, northern Asia, and North America that yields an oil formerly used as a medicine and in perfumes. Latin name: *Juniperus sabina*. [Pre-12thC. Via Old French *savine* from Latin *herba Sabina* 'Sabine plant'.]

saving /sáyving/ n. **1.** STH KEPT FROM BEING WASTED an amount of time or money that is reduced or not spent or used **2.** RESCUE FROM DANGER rescue of sb or sth from harm or danger **3.** LAW LEGAL EXCEPTION an exception or reservation in law ■ **savings** npl. MONEY SET ASIDE money set aside for future use ■ prep., conj. EXCEPT except (*literary*)

saving grace n. a quality or feature that redeems a person or situation

savings account /sáyvingz-/ n. a bank or building society account that earns interest on money saved

savings and loan association n. US a financial institution that issues shares to members who deposit savings and invests the money mainly in home mortgage loans. Members receive interest on their savings in the form of dividends.

savings bank n. a bank that invests the savings of individual depositors and pays interest on the deposits

savings bond n. **1.** US GOVERNMENT BOND a registered bond issued by the US government in denominations of $50 to $10,000. It allows people to earn interest on the savings they entrust to the government in exchange for the bond. **2.** Can CANADIAN GOVERNMENT-ISSUED BOND a bond issued by the Canadian government in denominations of $100 to $100,000. The bond is offered to most working Canadians through a payroll deduction scheme.

savings method n. US a method of testing memory by assessing how much faster sb can learn information already previously learned, seen, or read

savings ratio n. the ratio of national disposable income to consumer spending, used as a measure of national saving

savior n. US = saviour

Savior n. US = Saviour

saviour /sáyvyər/ n. sb who rescues sb or sth from harm or danger [13thC. Via Old french *sauveour* from, ultimately, late Latin *salvare* 'to save' (see SAVE).]

Saviour /sáyvyər/ n. a name used by Christians for the teacher and prophet Jesus Christ

savoir-faire /sáv waar fáir/ n. the ability to act appropriately and adroitly in any situation [Early 19thC. From French, literally 'to know how to do'.]

savoir-vivre /-veévrə/ n. the ability to behave appropriately in society [Mid-18thC. From French, literally 'to know how to live'.]

savor n., vti. US = savour

savory[1] adj., n. (*plural* -ies) US = savoury

savory[2] /sáyvəri/ n. **1.** KIND OF MINT a Mediterranean herb with pale lavender and white flowers and aromatic leaves used for seasoning. Latin name: *Satureja hortensis*. **2.** SAVORY LEAVES the leaves of savory used as a herb [14thC. From Latin *satureia*.]

savour /sáyvər/ v. (**savours, savouring, savoured**) **1.** *vt.* ENJOY STH UNHURRIEDLY to enjoy sth with unhurried appreciation ○ *savour the moment* **2.** *vi.* SHOW TRACES to show traces of sth ○ *something in his manner that savoured of deceit* **3.** *vt.* RELISH STH to enjoy the taste or smell of sth **4.** *vi.* HAVE TASTE OR SMELL to have a specific taste or smell (*old*) **5.** *vt.* SEASON STH to add flavour or scent to, especially by seasoning (*archaic*) ■ n. **1.** ENJOYMENT enjoyment and relish **2.** TASTE OR SMELL STH HAS the way that sth tastes or smells **3.** DISTINCTIVE QUALITY a quality that identifies or distinguishes sth [12thC. Via Old French *savour* from Latin *sapor* 'taste', from *sapere* 'to have a taste'.] —**savourless** adj. —**savorous** adj.

savoury /sáyvəri/ adj. **1.** NOT SWEET salty or sharp-tasting rather than sweet **2.** APPETIZING having an appetizing taste or smell **3.** RESPECTABLE respectable or morally acceptable ○ *not a very savoury character* ■ n. (*plural* **savouries**) FOOD DISH THAT ADDS RELISH a light dish served before or at the end of a meal [13thC. Via Old French *savoure*, the past participle of *savourer* 'to taste'

from, ultimately, Latin *sapor* (see SAVOUR).] —**savourily** /sáyvərili/ adv. —**savouriness** n.

savoy /sə vóy/, **savoy cabbage** n. a winter cabbage with crinkled leaves [16thC. Named after the *Savoy* region of southeast France.]

Savoyard /sə vóy aard, sávvoy aárd/ n. **1.** SB FROM SAVOY sb who was born or lives in the French region of Savoy **2.** MUSIC DEVOTEE OF GILBERT AND SULLIVAN a performer, producer, or admirer of the operettas of W. S. Gilbert and Arthur Sullivan. [Early 17thC. From French, formed from *Savoie* 'the region of Savoy'.]

savoy cabbage n. = savoy

Savoy opera n. an operetta by Gilbert and Sullivan or a work composed in the same style

savvy /sávvi/ n. SHREWDNESS shrewdness and practical knowledge (*informal*) ■ adj. SHREWD shrewd and well informed (*informal*) ■ vti. (-**vies, -vying, -vied**) COMPREHEND STH to understand sth, especially what sb has said (*informal*) [Late 18thC. Originally an African American dialect form of Spanish *sabe usted*, literally 'you know'.]

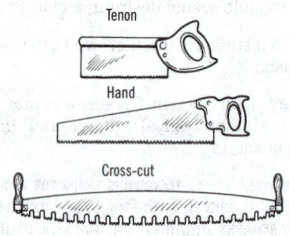

Tenon
Hand
Cross-cut
Saw

saw[1] /saw/ n. TOOL FOR CUTTING WOOD a hand-operated or power-driven tool with a toothed metal blade, used to cut wood or other hard materials ■ v. (**saws, sawing, sawed, sawed** *or* **sawn** /sawn/) **1.** *vti.* CUT STH USING SAW to cut sth using a saw **2.** *vt.* MOVE FORWARD AND BACK to make back-and-forth motions, as if using a handsaw [Old English *saga*. Ultimately from an Indo-European word that is also the ancestor of English *section* and *sickle*.]

saw[2] /saw/ n. an old saying, especially a cliché [Old English *sagu*. Ultimately from a prehistoric Germanic word that is also the ancestor of English *say*.]

saw[3] /saw/ past tense of **see**

SAW abbr. surface acoustic wave

sawbill /sáw bil/ n. = merganser

sawbones /sáw bōnz/ (*plural* -**bones** *or* -**boneses**) n. a surgeon or physician (*slang*) [Mid-19thC. From early surgeons' role as amputators.]

sawbuck /sáw buk/ n. US **1.** = sawhorse **2.** 10 DOLLARS a ten-dollar bill (*slang*) [Mid-19thC. From Dutch *zaagbok*; in sense 2, from the resemblance between the X-shaped end of a sawhorse and the roman numeral for 'ten'.]

sawder /sáwdər/ n. FLATTERY persuasive talk or flattery (*informal*) ■ vt. (-**ders, -dering, -dered**) FLATTER SB to flatter or cajole sb (*informal*) [Mid-19thC. Origin uncertain: probably a variant of SOLDER.]

saw doctor n. **1.** MACHINE GIVING EDGE TO SAW a machine that gives a saw a serrated edge **2.** NZ SAW SHARPENER sb who sharpens the blades in a sawmill

sawdust /sáw dust/ n. tiny particles of wood produced when wood is sawn

sawed-off adj. US = sawn-off

sawfish /sáw fish/ (*plural* -**fish** *or* -**fishes**) n. a ray that inhabits tropical seas and is characterized by a long snout with projections resembling teeth that it uses as a weapon. Family: Pristidae.

sawfly /sáw flī/ (*plural* -**flies**) n. an insect in which the female has a prominent, often serrated appendage at the tip of its abdomen, for boring holes and laying eggs in wood and plants. Family: Tenthredinidae.

saw grass n. any of various sedges that have serrated leaves. Genus: *Cladium*.

Sawfish

sawhorse /sáw hawrss/ n. a support for wood during sawing

sawine /sáa wīn/ n. *Carib* a Trinidadian dessert consisting mostly of milk with fried vermicelli, spiced with cinnamon, raisins, and other additions, usually made and shared with others during the Muslim festival of Eid-ul-Fitr

Saw Maung /sow maa óong/ (*b.* 1928) Myanmar general, who was dictatorial premier of Burma (1988–92). In 1989 he oversaw its renaming as Myanmar.

sawmill /sáw mil/ n. **1. FACTORY WHERE WOOD IS SAWN** a factory in which wood is sawn into planks or boards by machine **2. SAWING MACHINE** a powerful sawing machine

sawn past participle of **saw**

sawn-off *adj.* **1. CUT SHORT** relating to a shotgun with the barrel cut short. This increases the gun's field of fire as well as making it less cumbersome or obtrusive. **2. SHORT** of small stature (*slang offensive*)

saw palmetto n. a small palm tree of the southeastern United States that has spiny-toothed leafstalks. Latin name: *Serenoa repens*.

saw-scaled viper n. a small venomous snake of arid North Africa and Central Asia that is believed to have the most powerful venom of all the vipers. Latin name: *Echis carinaus.*

saw set n. an instrument that bends alternating teeth of a saw in opposite directions

Sawtell /saw tél/ coastal town in northeastern New South Wales, Australia. Population: 13,240 (1996).

sawtooth /sáw tooth/ n. (*plural* **-teeth** /-teeth/) **TOOTH OF A SAW** any one of the teeth of a saw ■ *adj.* **sawtooth, sawtoothed ZIGZAG** in a zigzag shape, like the teeth of a saw

saw-toothed *adj.* **1. WITH TEETH LIKE A SAW'S** having notched teeth like a saw **2.** = **sawtooth** *adj.*

saw-toothed grain beetle n. a tiny red beetle with prominent teeth on either side of the front of the middle part of its body. It is a common pest in grain warehouses and processing plants. Latin name: *Oryzaephilus surinamensis.*

saw-whet owl n. a small North American owl with a call that is a long series of short whistles. Latin name: *Aegolius acadicus.* [*Saw-whet* because its call was considered to resemble the sound of a saw being sharpened]

saw-wort n. a European plant of the daisy family with serrated leaves that yield a yellow dye. Latin name: *Serratula tinctoria.*

sawyer /sáw yər/ n. **1. SB WHO SAWS WOOD** sb who saws wood for a living **2. HORNED BEETLE** a horned beetle whose larvae bore into coniferous trees. Genus: *Monochamus*. **3.** *NZ* **HORNED GRASSHOPPER** a wingless horned grasshopper whose larvae bore into trees [13thC. Formed from SAW + -*yer*, a variant of -IER.]

sax /saks/ n. a saxophone (*informal*) [Early 20thC. Shortening.]

Sax. *abbr.* **1.** Saxon **2.** Saxony

saxatile /sáksə tīl/ *adj.* growing on or living in rocks [Mid-17thC. Directly or via French from Latin *saxatilis*, from *saxum* 'rock, stone'.]

saxe blue /sáks-/ *adj.* of a light blue colour with a tinge of grey [*Saxe* via French from German *Sachsen* 'Saxony', because the colour is produced from SAXON BLUE] —**saxe blue** n.

saxhorn /sáks hawrn/ n. any of a family of valved brass wind instruments, often used in military brass bands [Mid-19thC. Named after the Belgian instrument makers Charles Joseph *Sax* 1791–1865, who invented these instruments, and his son Antoine Joseph *Sax* 1814–94 (known as 'Adolphe'), who improved them.]

saxicolous /sak síkələss/, **saxicoline** /-līn/ *adj.* = **saxatile** [Mid-19thC. From modern Latin *saxicola*, from Latin *saxum* 'rock, stone' + *colere* 'to inhabit'.]

saxifrage /sáksi frayj/ (*plural* **-frages** *or* **-frage**) n. a plant growing on rocky ground that has small white, yellow, purple, or red flowers. Genus: *Saxifraga*. [14thC. Directly or via French from Latin *saxifraga* 'rock-breaking', from *saxum* 'rock, stone' (because the plants often grow in rock crevices).]

saxitoxin /sáksi tóksin/ n. a strong neurotoxin that is produced by certain organisms found in plankton (**dinoflagellates**) and accumulates in shellfish feeding on them, causing food poisoning in humans. It is found in red tides. [Mid-20thC. From modern Latin *Saxodomus*, genus of clams (from Latin *saxum* 'rock' + *domus* 'home') + TOXIN.]

Saxon /sáks'n/ n. **1. MEMBER OF ANCIENT GERMANIC PEOPLE** a member of a West Germanic people that originally came from the southern part of the Jutland Peninsula, and who started to spread west during Roman times. During the 5th century AD, they made incursions into Gaul and Britain and by the 7th century they had settlements in southern Britain, where, with the Angles, they established powerful kingdoms. ◊ **Angle, Jute 2. LANGUAGE OF ANCIENT SAXONS** the group of West Germanic dialects spoken by the ancient Saxons. ◊ **Anglo-Saxon 3. SB FROM SAXONY** sb who was born or who lives in the region of Saxony in Germany [12thC. Via French from Latin *Saxones* (plural), from a prehistoric Germanic word perhaps meaning 'to cut' (perhaps because they were armed with swords).] — **Saxon** *adj.*

Saxon blue n. a dye made from a solution of indigo in sulphuric acid

Saxonism /sáks'nizəm/ n. a word, phrase, or idiom in English supposedly from an Anglo-Saxon rather than Latin source

saxony /sáksəni/ n. **1. FINE YARN** a fine three-ply knitting yarn **2. FINE WOOLLEN FABRIC** a fine woollen fabric used for coats [Mid-19thC. Originally 'fine kind of wool', named after the state of SAXONY in Germany, where it was first made.]

Saxony /sáksəni/ state in eastern Germany. It was a kingdom until 1918, although part of the North German Confederation from 1866. Between 1945 and 1989 the area was part of East Germany. Population: 5,000,000 (1990).

saxophone /sáksə fōn/ n. a metal wind instrument with keys and a reed that comes in several sizes and registers, the alto and tenor saxophones being the most popular. It is particularly associated with jazz. [Mid-19thC. Named after Adolphe Sax (see SAXHORN), who invented it.] —**saxophonic** /sáksə fónnik/ *adj.* —**saxophonist** /sak sóffənist/ n.

saxtuba /sáks tyoobə/ n. a large bass saxhorn [Mid-19thC. Blend of SAXHORN and TUBA.]

say /say/ v. (**says, saying, said** /sed/, **said**) **1.** *vt.* **UTTER STH** to utter sth in a normal voice, not singing, shouting, or whispering **2.** *vti.* **EXPRESS VERBALLY** to convey information or express feelings in spoken words **3.** *vt.* **STATE STH** to utter sth as a matter of fact, belief, or prediction ○ *said to be the largest in captivity* **4.** *vt.* **INDICATE STH** to convey information in written or printed words, numbers, or symbols ○ *The clock said midnight.* ○ *The rules say that you should not kick your opponent.* **5.** *vt.* **MAKE CASE FOR OR AGAINST STH** to utter sth by way of argument, explanation, or excuse ○ *There's much to be said for being rich.* **6.** *vt.* **COMMAND STH** to utter sth as an instruction ○ *She said to buy some wine for tonight.* **7.** *vt.* **SUPPOSE STH** to assume sth for the sake of argument, or take sth as a suitable example ○ *Let's say that it will cost you £500.* **8.** *vt.* **RECITE STH** to utter sth that has a formula or set form of words ○ *says his prayers* **9.** *vt.* **CONVEY STH INDIRECTLY** to convey sth over and above the immediate words or superficial sound or appearance ○ *The finale says that we can all triumph in the end.* **10.** *vt.* **CONVEY STH IMPORTANT** to convey sth substantial or significant in what is said or written ○ *We talked for hours but didn't really say anything.* ■ n. **1. CHANCE TO SPEAK** a chance or turn to say sth, especially to give an opinion ○ *You've already had your say.* **2. RIGHT TO GIVE OPINION** the right to express an opinion and have it considered by others ○ *The junior staff appeared to have no say in the way things were done.* ■ *interj. US, Can* (*informal*) **1. EXPRESSING SURPRISE** used to express surprise, admiration, or protest **2. ATTRACTING ATTENTION** used to attract sb's attention [Old English *secgan*, from a prehistoric Germanic word that is also the ancestor of English *saga* and *scold*] —**sayer** n. ◇ **enough said** used to indicate that nothing more need be said for a situation to be understood ◇ **I say 1.** used to express surprise, admiration, or protest (*dated*) **2.** used to attract sb's attention (*dated*) ◇ **it goes without saying** used to emphasize that there should be no doubt concerning sth ◇ **say when** used to ask sb to indicate when enough drink has been poured or food served (*informal*) ◇ **that is to say** used to indicate that you are repeating sth more clearly or in other words ◇ **you can say that again!** used to indicate complete agreement with what has just been said (*informal*)

SAYE *abbr.* save as you earn

Dorothy L. Sayers

Sayers /sáy ərz/, **Dorothy L.** (1893–1957) British writer. She wrote detective stories, including *Whose Body?* (1923) and *Gaudy Night* (1935). Full name **Dorothy Leigh Sayers**

sayest /sáy əst/, **sayst** 2nd person present singular of **say** (*archaic*)

sayid n. = **sayyid**

saying /sáy ing/ n. a frequently offered piece of advice or information, or a frequently heard reflection on the way things are

sayonara /sí ə naárə/ n. goodbye [Late 19thC. From Japanese, literally 'if it be so'.]

say-so n. (*informal*) **1. AUTHORIZATION** permission or authorization from sb **2. ASSERTION** a mere assertion by sb that sth is so

sayyid /sí yid/, **sayid, said** n. **1. DESCENDANT OF MUHAMMAD'S GRANDSON** a Muslim who claims to be descended from Muhammad's grandson Husain **2. ISLAMIC TITLE** an Islamic title of respect for a man [Mid-17thC. From Arabic, literally 'prince'.]

Sazerac /sázzə rak/ *tdmk. US* a trademark for a cocktail of bourbon, bitters, Pernod, and sugar, with a twist of lemon

Sb *symbol.* antimony [Shortening of Latin *stibium* 'antimony']

SB *abbr.* simultaneous broadcast

SBA n. a system of radio navigation that provides an aircraft with lateral guidance and marker beam indicators at set points during its landing approach. Abbr of **standard beam approach**

SbE *abbr.* south by east

S-bend n. an S-shaped bend in a road or a pipe

SBS *abbr.* **1.** MIL Special Boat Service **2.** *Aus* Special Broadcasting Service

SBU *abbr.* strategic business unit

SbW *abbr.* south by west

sc, s.c. *abbr.* small capital

Sc *symbol.* scandium

SC *abbr.* **1.** Security Council **2.** South Carolina **3.** Signal Corps **4.** *ANZ* School Certificate

sc. *abbr.* **1.** that is to say **2.** scene **3.** MEASURE scruple

Sc. *abbr.* **1.** Scots **2.** Scottish

s/c *abbr.* self-contained (*used in advertisements*)

scab /skab/ *n.* **1.** CRUST OVER HEALING WOUND a hard crust of dried blood, serum, or pus, that forms over a wound during healing **2.** OFFENSIVE TERM an offensive term for sb who continues to work during a strike, or who does a striker's job during a strike (*insult offensive*) **3.** VET SKIN DISEASE OF SHEEP a skin disease of sheep and other animals that resembles mange **4.** BOT PLANT DISEASE CAUSING CRUSTY SPOTS a fungal plant disease causing crusty spots on the affected parts **5.** BOT CRUSTY SPOT ON A PLANT a crusty spot on a plant caused by a fungal disease **6.** DISLIKABLE PERSON a despicable or dislikable person (*slang insult*) ■ *vi.* **(scabs, scabbing, scabbed) 1.** BECOME COVERED WITH SCAB to become covered with a scab during healing **2.** WORK DURING STRIKE to continue to work during a strike, or do a striker's job during a strike (*disapproving*) [13thC. From Old Norse *skabb*; ultimately 'sth that is scratched', from an Indo-European word meaning 'to scrape', which is also the ancestor of English *scabies* and *shabby*.]

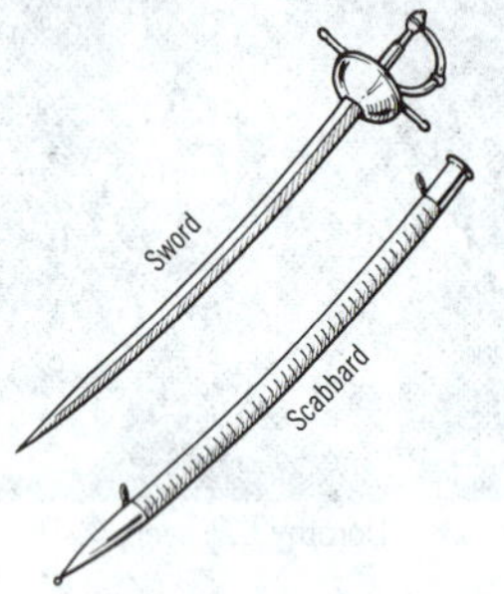

Scabbard

scabbard /skábbərd/ *n.* SHEATH FOR SWORD a sheath, hanging from a belt, for a sword, dagger, or bayonet ■ *vt.* **(-bards, -barding, -barded)** PUT SWORD INTO SHEATH to put a sword, dagger, or bayonet into a sheath [13thC. From Anglo-Norman *escauberge*, of uncertain origin: probably originally 'blade protector', from prehistoric Germanic.]

scabbard fish *n.* any of various marine fishes that have an elongated body and long sharp teeth. Family: Trichiuridae.

scabble /skább'l/ **(-bles, -bling, -bled)** *vt.* to give a rough shape to stone [Early 17thC. Alteration of Middle English *scapple*, from Old French *escapeler* 'to shape timber', from *capler* 'to cut'.]

scabby /skábbi/ **(-bier, -biest)** *adj.* **1.** WITH SCABS having or covered in scabs **2.** DISLIKABLE despicable or dislikable (*slang*) —**scabbily** *adv.* —**scabbiness** *n.*

scabies /skáy beez/ *n.* a contagious skin disease marked by intense itching, inflammation, and red papules. It is caused by the itch mite, which burrows into the skin. [14thC. From Latin, from *scabere* 'to scratch' (see SCAB).] —**scabietic** /skáybi éttik/ *adj.*

scabious /skáybi əss/ *n.* (*plural* **-ouses** *or* **-ous**) PLANT WITH DOME-SHAPED FLOWERS a plant with blue, pink, or white dome-shaped flowers. Genera: *Scabiosa* and *Knautia*. ■ *adj.* COVERED IN SCABS having scabs or scabies [14thC. Directly and via French *scabieux* from Latin *scabiosus*, from *scabies* (see SCABIES); the plant was formerly used in cures for skin diseases.]

scablands /skábbləndz/ *npl.* tracts of elevated land with bare rock, thin soil, and sparse vegetation, crossed by dry channels formed by glacial floodwaters

scabrous /skáybrəss, skább-/ *adj.* **1.** WITH A ROUGH SURFACE having a rough surface because of scales or short stiff hairs **2.** REQUIRING TACT requiring sth to be handled with tact and care **3.** OBSCENE dealing with sex or referring to sex in an obscene way (*literary*) [Late 16thC. Directly or via French *scabreux* from late Latin *scabrosus*, from Latin *scaber* 'scurfy, scaly, rough'.] —**scabrously** *adv.* —**scabrousness** *n.*

scad /skad/ (*plural* **scad** *or* **scads**) *n.* **1.** FISH WITH LONG BODY a fish that has a long body and sharp bony plates on either side of the narrow point of the tail, found in tropical and subtropical seas. Family: Caringidae. **2.** = **horse mackerel** [Early 17thC. Origin unknown.]

scads /skadz/ *npl.* large numbers or quantities (*informal*) ○ *scads of money* [Mid-19thC. Origin uncertain: earlier also 'money'; perhaps from Scandinavian.]

Scafell Pike /skáw fel-/ the highest mountain in the Lake District in Cumbria, England. Height: 978 m/3,209 ft.

scaffold /skáffōld, -f'ld/ *n.* **1.** FRAMEWORK TO SUPPORT WORKERS a temporary framework of poles and planks that is used to support workers and materials during the erection, repair, or decoration of a building **2.** PLATFORM FOR EXECUTIONS a raised platform on which sb is executed by hanging or beheading **3.** DEATH BY HANGING death by hanging or beheading as a form of punishment **4.** SUPPORT any supporting framework ■ *vt.* **(-folds, -folding, -folded)** ERECT SCAFFOLD AROUND BUILDING to put up a scaffold around or against a building [13thC. Via Old French *(e)schaffaut* from, ultimately, assumed Vulgar Latin *catafalcum* (source of English *catafalque*).] —**scaffolder** *n.*

scaffolding /skáffōlding, -f'lding/ *n.* **1.** SYSTEM OF SCAFFOLDS a scaffold or a system of scaffolds **2.** MATERIALS FOR BUILDING SCAFFOLD the poles and planks used to build a scaffold

scag /skag/, **skag** *n.* = **heroin** (*slang*) [Early 20thC. Origin unknown.]

scagliola /skal yṓlə/ *n.* imitation marble made of gypsum mixed with glue with a polished surface of marble or granite dust [Late 16thC. From Italian, literally 'tiny scale, small chip of marble', ultimately from a prehistoric Germanic word that is also the ancestor of English *scale*[1].]

scalable /skáyləb'l/ *adj.* **1.** CLIMBABLE able to be climbed up or over **2.** VARIABLE used to describe computer graphics fonts generated by an algorithm that permits the size to vary proportionately over a wide range **3.** EXPANDABLE used to describe a computer, component, or network that can be expanded to meet future needs —**scalability** *n.* —**scalableness** *n.* —**scalably** *adv.*

scalage /skáylij/ *n.* *US* **1.** COMM PERCENTAGE OFF COST FOR SHRINKAGE an allowance in the form of a percentage deducted from the cost of goods to reflect loss in amount or size during storage or shipping **2.** FORESTRY ESTIMATED LUMBER YIELD the estimated yield of lumber from a log

scalar /skáylər/ *n.* QUANTITY WITH MAGNITUDE BUT NOT DIRECTION a quantity, e.g. mass or time, that has magnitude but no direction ■ *adj.* WITH MAGNITUDE BUT NOT DIRECTION used to describe a quantity that has magnitude but no direction [Mid-17thC. From Latin *scalaris*, from *scala* (see SCALE[2]).]

scalare /skə láari/ (*plural* **-re** *or* **-res**) *n.* = **angelfish** [Early 20thC. From Latin, a form of *scalaris* 'of a ladder' (from its parallel markings), from *scala* (see SCALE[2]).]

scalariform /skə láari fawrm/ *adj.* used to describe the walls of a cell that have parallel structural formations resembling the rungs of a ladder [Mid-19thC. Formed from Latin *scalaris* 'of a ladder', from *scala* (see SCALE[2]).]

scalar product *n.* a number (**scalar**) equal to the product of the magnitudes of any two vectors and the cosine of the angle formed between them

scalawag *n.* = **scallywag**

scald /skawld/ *v.* **(scalds, scalding, scalded) 1.** *vt.* BURN SB WITH HOT LIQUID to burn sb or a part of the body with hot liquid or steam **2.** *vt.* STERILIZE STH WITH BOILING LIQUID to subject sth to the action of boiling liquid or steam in order to clean or sterilize it **3.** *vt.* HEAT LIQUID TO NEAR BOILING POINT to heat a liquid to just below the boiling point **4.** *vt.* TREAT FRUIT WITH BOILING WATER to plunge a fruit or vegetable into boiling water or pour boiling water over it and leave it briefly before draining to prevent cooking. Scalding is used to loosen skin on fruit and to stop naturally present enzymes working on fruit and vegetables during freezing. **5.** BREW TEA to pour boiling water on to tea and leave it to brew (*informal*) ■ *n.* **1.** BURN CAUSED BY LIQUID a burn caused by hot liquid or steam **2.** PLANT DISEASE any of various plant diseases or conditions that produce brownish discoloration of leaves and fruit ■ *v.* **(scalds, scalding, scalded)** brew tea (*regional informal*) [12thC. Via Anglo-Norman *escalder* from, ultimately, late Latin *excaldere* 'to bathe in hot water', literally 'to be very hot', from *calidus* 'hot' (see CAULDRON).]

scalding /skáwlding/ *adj.* **1.** EXTREMELY HOT extremely hot, especially hot enough to scald sb **2.** SCATHING severely critical

scale[1] /skayl/ *n.* **1.** BONY PLATE ON FISH any one of the small flat bony or horny overlapping plates that cover the bodies of fish and some reptiles and mammals **2.** FLAKE a thin flat piece or flake of sth such as dead skin **3.** ZOOL COVERING OF BUTTERFLY WING any of the small overlapping structures that cover the wings of butterflies and moths **4.** METALL BLACK OXIDE ON HEATED IRON a flaky oxide that forms on the surface of some metals undergoing heat treatment, especially the black oxide that forms on iron or steel at high temperatures **5.** HOUSEHOLD DEPOSIT INSIDE A KETTLE OR BOILER a white deposit sometimes formed on the inside of a kettle or boiler by the action of heat on the water **6.** DENT = **tartar** *n.* 1 **7.** BOT = **scale leaf 8.** INSECTS = **scale insect 9.** BOT PLANT DISEASE the diseased condition of plants caused by scale insects ■ *v.* **(scales, scaling, scaled) 1.** *vt.* CLEAN SCALES OR SCALE FROM STH to remove the scales or scale from sth **2.** *vi.* FLAKE OFF to come off in scales **3.** *vi.* ZOOL SHED SCALES to shed scales **4.** *vi.* *Aus* DODGE FARE to travel by public transport without paying (*informal*) [13thC. Via Old French *escale* from, ultimately, a prehistoric Germanic word that is also the ancestor of English *shield*, *shell*, and *skill*.] —**scaleless** *adj.*

scale[2] /skayl/ *n.* **1.** MEASURING SYSTEM a system of measurement based on a series of marks laid down at regular intervals and representing numerical values **2.** CLASSIFICATION SYSTEM a system of classification based on differing quantity or value, e.g. one used in paying employees **3.** LEVEL the extent or relative size of sth **4.** SIZE RATIO a ratio representing the size of an illustration or reproduction, especially a map or a model, in relation to the object it represents ○ *The scale of the map is 1:50,000.* **5.** MEASURING INSTRUMENT an instrument or apparatus with graduated markings for measuring sth **6.** MUSIC SERIES OF MUSICAL NOTES a series of musical notes, usually sequential, arranged in ascending or descending order of pitch ■ *v.* **(scales, scaling, scaled) 1.** *vt.* CLIMB STH to climb up sth, especially a steep incline, often using a ladder **2.** *vt.* MAKE STH TO SCALE to make a model or draw a map in a regular proportion to the size of the original **3.** *vi.* RISE IN STAGES to go upward in stages or steps [14thC. From Latin *scala* 'staircase, ladder'.] ◇ **to scale** with the same proportion of reduction or enlargement throughout, e.g. in a map or model

scale down *vt.* to reduce sth in size, amount, or extent

scale[3] /skayl/ *n.* **1.** WEIGHING MACHINE a device on which sth or sb can be weighed (*often used in the plural*) **2.** PAN OF BALANCE either of the dishes or pans of a balance ■ *vt.* **(scales, scaling, scaled) 1.** WEIGH STH OR SB to weigh sth or sb with a scale **2.** WEIGH SO MUCH to have a particular weight when put on a scale [12thC. From Old Norse *skál* 'bowl' (plural 'pair of scales'), from a prehistoric Germanic word that is also the ancestor of English *scale*[1].] ◇ **tip the scales at sth** to weigh a particular amount

scaleboard /skáyl bawrd/ *n.* **1.** THIN BOARD FOR BACKING PICTURES very thin board used to back a picture or mirror **2.** STRIP FOR JUSTIFYING TYPE a thin strip of wood used to justify hand-set type

scale insect, **scale** *n.* any of various plant-sucking insects found worldwide that cover themselves with a waxy secretion resembling scales. They are extremely destructive, especially to fruit trees. Superfamily: Coccoidea.

scale leaf, **scale** *n.* a kind of leaf that protects a plant bud before the bud expands

scale moss *n.* any of various liverworts with leaves resembling scales. Order: Jungermanniales.

scalene /skáyl een/ *adj.* used to describe a triangle in which each side is a different length [Mid-17thC. Via Latin *scalenus* from Greek *skalenos* 'uneven, unequal'.]

scaler /skáylər/ *n.* an electronic circuit that produces an output pulse for every specified number of input pulses received. It is typically used in counting applications and the implementation of electronic counters.

Scales /skaylz/ *npl.* = **Libra**

scaling /skáyling/ *n.* the creation of a measurement device for such things as attitudes and strength of feeling, where there is no existing scale. These devices are used in social research.

scaling ladder *n.* a ladder used to climb high walls, especially those of a besieged fortress.

scallion /skálli ən/ *n.* any onion with a small bulb and long green leaves, e.g. spring onions and shallots [13thC. From Anglo-Norman *scal(o)un*, variant of Old French *escalo(i)gne* (source of English *shallot*) from, ultimately, Latin *Ascalonia (caepa)*, literally '(onion) of Ascalon' from *Ascalon*, port in ancient Palestine.]

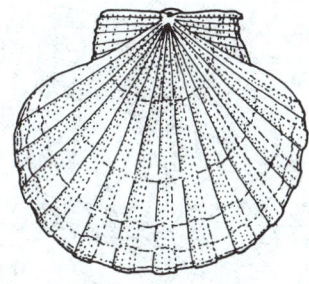

Scallop

scallop /skólləp, skáll-/, **scollop** *n.* **1. MARINE MOLLUSC** a marine bivalve mollusc that has a fan-shaped shell with radial ribs and wavy edges. Scallops move by opening and closing the valves. Family: Pectinidae. **2. SCALLOP AS FOOD** the round white edible muscle of a scallop, often with bright red roe around one side **3.** = scallop shell **4. DISH SHAPED LIKE SCALLOP SHELL** a dish shaped like a scallop shell, used for cooking and serving food in **5. PILGRIM'S BADGE** a representation of a scallop shell worn as a badge by pilgrims in the Middle Ages **6. FABRIC EDGING** an ornamental undulating edging in fabric **7.** *US* = **escalope 8.** *Aus* **FRIED POTATO CAKE** a slice of potato deep-fried in batter ■ *v.* (-lops, -loping, -loped) **1.** *vt.* **MAKE EDGE WAVY** to decorate the edge of a fabric or object with an undulating pattern **2.** *vt.* **COOK FOOD IN SCALLOP SHELL** to cook food in a scallop shell or in a dish shaped like a scallop shell **3.** *vi.* **COLLECT SCALLOPS** to gather or dredge for scallops [14thC. From Old French *escalope*, of uncertain origin.] —**scalloped** *adj.* —**scalloper** *n.* —**scalloping** *n.*

scallop shell *n.* either of the fan-shaped shell valves of the scallop, with radial ribs and a wavy edge. Scallop shells are used for cooking and serving seafood dishes in.

scally /skálli/ (*plural* **scallies**) *n.* *N England* a mischievous or naughty person (*informal*) [Late 20thC. Shortening of SCALLYWAG.]

scallywag /skálli wag/, **scalawag** /skálla wag/ *n.* **1. MISCHIEVOUS PERSON** sb who behaves in inappropriate or disruptive ways (*dated informal*) **2. SOUTHERNER WHO COLLABORATED WITH GOVERNMENT** in the United States, a white person in the South who worked with the federal government during the Reconstruction period after the Civil War [Mid-19thC. Origin uncertain: perhaps an alteration of Scottish *scallag* 'farm servant', from Old Scottish *scolloc* 'tenant of church land', originally 'monastery student', from Latin *schola* (see SCHOOL).]

scalogram /skálə gram/ *n.* a test of attitudes or opinions in which the questions are ranked so that the answer to one implies the same answer to all questions lower on the scale [Mid-20thC. Formed from SCALE², probably modelled on CARDIOGRAM.]

scalp /skalp/ *n.* **1. SKIN ON TOP OF HEAD** the skin and underlying tissues covering the dome of the skull **2. SCALP CUT OFF AS TROPHY** the scalp of an enemy cut off as a trophy **3. TROPHY** a trophy or achievement belonging to sb that sb else wants to win or take away ■ *vt.* (**scalps, scalping, scalped**) **1. CUT OFF SB'S SCALP** to cut off the scalp of an enemy as a trophy **2.** *US* **RESELL STH FOR QUICK PROFIT** to resell sth quickly or at an inflated price in order to make a quick profit [14thC. Origin uncertain: probably from a Scandinavian language.] —**scalper** *n.*

scalpel /skálp'l/ *n.* a surgical knife with a short, very sharp blade [Mid-18thC. Directly or via French from Latin *scalpellum* 'small cutting tool'.]

scalp lock *n.* a tuft or plait of hair left on the otherwise shaven scalp by the men among some Native North American peoples

scaly /skáyli/ (**-ier, -iest**) *adj.* covered in scales or flakes —**scaliness** *n.*

scaly anteater *n.* = pangolin

scam /skam/ *n.* **DISHONEST SCHEME** a scheme for making money by dishonest means (*slang*) ■ *vt.* (**scams, scamming, scammed**) **TRICK SB** to obtain money from sb by dishonest means (*slang*) [Mid-20thC. Origin unknown.] —**scammer** *n.*

scammony /skámməni/ (*plural* **-nies** *or* **-ny**) *n.* **1. TWINING PLANT** a twining Asian plant that has arrow-shaped leaves and white, pink, or purple funnel-shaped flowers. Latin name: *Convulvulus scammonia.* **2. PURGATIVE FROM SCAMMONY ROOT** a resin obtained from the roots of the scammony or similar plants and used as a purgative [Pre-12thC. Via Old French *escamonie* or Latin *scammonia* from Greek *skammōnia*.]

scamp¹ /skamp/ *n.* **1. MISCHIEVOUS CHILD** a mischievous person, especially a child who misbehaves in harmless or humorous ways (*informal*) **2. ROGUE** a rascally or dishonest person (*dated informal*) [Mid-18thC. Origin uncertain: probably via Middle Dutch *schampen* 'to slip away, decamp' from Old French *esc(h)amper*, ultimately from Latin *campus* 'field' (source of English *camp*, *campus*, and *champion*).] —**scampish** *adj.*

scamp² /skamp/ (**scamps, scamping, scamped**) *vt.* to do sth hastily, carelessly, or in a perfunctory manner [Mid-19thC. Origin uncertain: perhaps from SCAMP¹; or related to SKIMP.]

scamper /skámpər/ *vi.* (**-pers, -pering, -pered**) **RUN PLAYFULLY** to run quickly or playfully ■ *n.* **PLAYFUL RUN** a quick or playful run [Late 17thC. Origin uncertain: probably from Middle Dutch *schampen* (see SCAMP¹).] —**scamperer** *n.*

scampi /skámpi/ *npl.* pieces of tail meat from Dublin Bay prawns, usually fried in batter or breadcrumbs (*takes a singular or plural verb*) [Mid-20thC. From Italian, plural of *scampo*, a kind of lobster, from Greek *kampē* 'bending'; from its shape.]

scan /skan/ *v.* (**scans, scanning, scanned**) **1.** *vt.* **EXAMINE STH IN DETAIL** to subject sth to a thorough examination **2.** *vt.* **LOOK THROUGH STH QUICKLY** to look through or read sth quickly **3.** *vt.* **LOOK AT STH INTENTLY** to look over and around sth intently **4.** *vi.* **CONFORM TO VERSE RULES** to conform to the rules of metre **5.** *vt.* **ANALYSE VERSE** to analyse verse according to the rules of metre **6.** *vt.* **EXAMINE STH WITH BEAM OF LIGHT** to direct a light-sensitive device over a surface in order to convert an image into digital or electronic form for further storage, retrieval, and transmission **7.** *vt.* **EXAMINE STORED DATA** to make an automatic search of a computer storage medium such as a magnetic disk or tape for data in anticipation of retrieving that data **8.** *vt.* **OBTAIN IMAGE OF BODY** to obtain an image of internal organs with any of various devices, especially in order to make a diagnosis without the need for exploratory surgery. ◊ **CT scan, MRI 9.** *vti.* **SEARCH AREA USING RADAR** to search a region for specific objects, such as aircraft, by systematically sweeping a radar or sonar beam across it ■ *n.* **1. BRIEF PERUSAL** a quick look at or through sth **2. IMAGE OF BODY** an image of an internal body part taken using a scanner, or the process involved in obtaining one [14thC. From late Latin *scandere* 'to scan a verse' from 'to climb'. Originally, in English, 'to mark off a verse into metrical feet', hence 'to analyse'.] —**scannable** *adj.*

Scan., **Scand.** *abbr.* **1.** Scandinavia **2.** Scandinavian

scandal /skánd'l/ *n.* **1. STH CAUSING PUBLIC OUTRAGE** a situation or event that causes public outrage or censure **2. PUBLIC OUTRAGE** an outburst of public outrage or censure as a consequence of some event **3. MALICIOUS TALK** malicious talk, especially about other people's private lives [12thC. Via French *scandale* (later form of *escandle*, source of English *slander*) from, ultimately, Greek *skandalon* 'trap, temptation'.]

scandalize /skándə līz/ (**-izes, -izing, -ized**), **scandalise** (**-ises, -ising, -ised**) *vt.* to shock people by outrageous or improper behaviour —**scandalization** /skándə līzáysh'n/ *n.* —**scandalizer** /-līzər/ *n.*

scandalmonger /skánd'l mung gər/ *n.* sb who indulges in malicious talk about other people's private lives

scandalous /skándələss/ *adj.* **1. SHOCKING** causing or deserving to cause public outrage or censure **2. DEFAMATORY** causing or having the potential to cause damage to sb's reputation —**scandalously** *adv.* —**scandalousness** *n.*

scandal sheet *n.* a periodical publication that features scandalous stories about people's private lives (*disapproving*)

scandent /skándənt/ *adj.* used to describe a plant that climbs as it grows [Late 17thC. From Latin *scandent-*, present participle stem of *scandere* 'to climb'.]

scandic /skándik/ *adj.* containing the element scandium

Scandinavia /skán də náyviə/ region in northern Europe comprising Norway, Sweden, Denmark, Finland, Iceland, and the Faroe Islands —**Scandinavian** *n., adj.*

scandium /skándi əm/ *n.* a rare silvery-white metallic chemical element found in various minerals in association with rare-earth elements. Symbol **Sc** [Late 19thC. Formed from Latin *Scandia*, shortening of SCANDINAVIA, because it is found in various minerals in Scandinavia.]

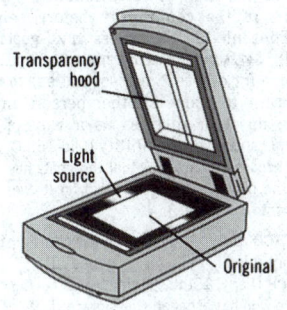

Scanner

scanner /skánnər/ *n.* **1. BODY-SCANNING DEVICE** a device used to obtain information about the internal parts of the body without the need for surgery, or the contents of sth without the need for opening it. ◊ **CT SCANNER 2. DATA-SCANNING DEVICE** a device for examining written or recorded data, e.g. for reading a product bar code for inventory and pricing purposes **3. DEVICE PUTTING STH INTO DIGITAL FORM** a device used to convert an image into digital form for storage, retrieval, and transmission **4. RADAR SEARCHING DEVICE** a rotating directional radar antenna that emits a beam to search for or locate objects **5. SB WHO SCANS TEXTS** sb who scans texts, e.g. for errors or in poetic analysis

scanning electron microscope *n.* a microscope that uses a beam of electrons to scan an object and produce an enlarged image of it on a cathode-ray tube. It can work at much greater magnifications than a light microscope whilst avoiding depth of field problems. —**scanning electron microscopy** *n.*

scansion /skánsh'n/ *n.* **1. ANALYSIS OF VERSE** analysis of verse according to the rules of metre **2. METRICAL**

STRUCTURE the way that a line, verse, or poem scans [Late 17thC. From late Latin *scansion-*, the stem of *scansio*, from Latin, 'act of climbing', from *scandere* 'to climb', the underlying idea being 'moving along in steps'.]

scant /skant/ *adj.* **1.** INADEQUATE not sufficient **2.** ONLY OR NOT QUITE only just at or just below the amount stated ○ *a scant twenty votes* ■ *vt.* (**scants, scanting, scanted**) NOT PROVIDE ENOUGH OF STH to provide an insufficient supply of sth (*archaic*) [14thC. From Old Norse *skamt*, a form of *skammr* 'short, brief'.] —**scantly** *adv.*

scantling /skántling/ *n.* **1.** THIN PIECE OF TIMBER a piece of timber with a small cross-section, e.g. a rafter **2.** SIZE the dimension of a building material or a structural part of a ship **3.** SMALL AMOUNT a small amount or quantity [Early 16thC. Alteration of obsolete *scantillon* 'gauge', via Old French *escantillon* 'sample' from, ultimately, late Latin *scandaculum* 'ladder, gauge', from Latin *scandere* 'to climb'.]

scanty /skánti/ (**-ier, -iest**) *adj.* **1.** INADEQUATE not much and less than is needed **2.** MEAGRE only just enough **3.** REVEALING not covering much of the part of the body that it is worn on —**scantily** *adv.* —**scantiness** *n.*

Scapa Flow /skaàppə-/ anchorage in the Orkney Islands, Scotland. It was used as a base for Britain's Home Fleet during both World Wars. Area: 310 sq. km/120 sq. mi.

scape[1] /skayp/ *n.* **1.** BOT LEAFLESS FLOWER STALK a leafless flower stalk rising directly from the root **2.** ZOOL PART OF FEATHER OR ANTENNA a shaft of a feather or other animal part, or a segment of an antenna **3.** ARCHIT ARCHITECTURAL COLUMN the shaft of an architectural column [Early 17thC. Via Latin *scapus* from Greek *skapos* 'rod'.] —**scapose** /skáppōss/ *adj.*

scape[2] /skayp/ (**scapes, scaping, scaped**) *vti.* to escape (*archaic*) [13thC. Shortening of ESCAPE.]

-scape *suffix.* a scene or view ○ *seascape* ○ *lunarscape* [From LANDSCAPE]

scapegoat /skáyp gōt/ *n.* **1.** SB MADE TO TAKE THE BLAME sb who is made to take the blame for others **2.** PSYCHOL SB WRONGLY BLAMED sb who is unjustly blamed for causing upset or distress by another person who is unwilling or unable to take personal responsibility for his or her own actions **3.** BIBLE GOAT GIVEN SINS IN JEWISH RITUAL on the Jewish Day of Atonement, a goat on which the high priest symbolically loaded all the sins of the community before sending the animal out into the wilderness ■ *v.* (**-goats, -goating, -goated**) **1.** *vt.* MAKE SB TAKE THE BLAME to force sb to take the blame for others **2.** PSYCHOL BLAME SB TO AVOID TAKING RESPONSIBILITY to blame another person unjustly for causing upset or distress as a way of avoiding taking personal responsibility [Mid-16thC. *Scape* from SCAPE[2], because in Jewish ritual the goat, having had the sins of the people symbolically laid on it, was allowed to 'escape' into the desert.]

scapegrace /skáyp grayss/ *n.* a lazy, mischievous, or irresponsible person, especially a child (*archaic*) [Early 19thC. From SCAPE[2] + GRACE; literally 'someone who has escaped God's grace'.]

scaphoid /skáffoyd/ *adj.* ANAT navicular (*archaic*) [Mid-18thC. Via modern Latin *scaphoides* from Greek *skaphoeidēs*, from *skaphē* 'boat'.]

scapolite /skáppō līt/ *n.* any of a group of variously coloured aluminosilicate minerals found in metamorphic rocks and as weathering products of basic igneous rocks. They include semiprecious gemstones. [Early 19thC. From Greek *skapos* 'rod' + *lithos* 'stone'.]

scapula /skáppyŏŏlə/ (*plural* **-lae** *or* **-las**) *n.* **1.** BONE FORMING BACK OF SHOULDER either of two large flat triangular bones that form the back of the shoulder in humans. Each forms a joint with the respective upper arm and provides attachment for muscles. **2.** SHOULDER BLADE IN VERTEBRATES a bone in vertebrates that corresponds to the human shoulder blade [Late 16thC. From late Latin, singular of Latin *scapulae* 'shoulder blades'.]

scapular[1] /skáppyŏŏlər/ *n.* BIRD'S SHOULDER FEATHER any one of the feathers on a bird's shoulder ■ *adj.* OF SHOULDER BLADE relating to or associated with the shoulder blade

scapular[2] /skáppyŏŏlər/, **scapulary** /-ləri/ (*plural* **-ies**) *n.* **1.** MONK'S GARMENT a loose sleeveless garment worn by monks **2.** CLOTHS SHOWING AFFILIATION TO RELIGIOUS ORDER two pieces of cloth joined together and worn over the shoulder and back underneath other garments to signify membership in a particular religious order or some other devotional purpose [15thC. From late Latin *scapulare*, from *scapula* 'shoulder' (see SCAPULA), because it covers the shoulders.]

scar[1] /skaar/ *n.* **1.** MARK ON SKIN AFTER WOUND HEALS a mark left on the skin after a wound, burn, or sore has healed over **2.** MENTAL EFFECT OF DISTRESSING EXPERIENCE a lasting effect left on sb's mind by a personal misfortune or unpleasant experience **3.** MARK ON SURFACE a mark on a surface caused by damage **4.** MARK OF FORMER ATTACHMENT ON PLANT the mark on a plant indicating the place where a part such as a leaf was formerly attached ■ *v.* (**scars, scarring, scarred**) **1.** *vt.* MARK SB OR STH WITH SCARS to leave sb or sth with a physical or emotional scar **2.** *vi.* FORM A SCAR to form or become marked by a scar [14thC. Via Old French *escharre* 'scar, scab', from, ultimately, Greek *eskhara* 'hearth, brazier, scab formed after a burn'.]

scar[2] /skaar/ *n.* **1.** STEEP CRAGGY ROCK FORMATION a steep bare rocky cliff, typically in the limestones of the Yorkshire Dales **2.** ROCK SUBMERGED IN SEA a rock submerged or partly submerged in the ocean [14thC. From Old Norse *sker* 'low reef', from a prehistoric Germanic word that is also the ancestor of English *shear*.]

scarab /skárrəb/ *n.* **1.** SACRED BEETLE any of several beetles regarded as sacred by the ancient Egyptians. Many scarabs roll dung into balls to provision their larvae. Family: Scarabaeidae. **2.** REPRESENTATION OF A BEETLE a representation of a beetle used on amulets and signets by the ancient Egyptians [Late 16thC. Via Latin *scarabaeus* from Greek *karabos* 'crab, beetle'.]

scarabaeid /skárrə bée id/, **scarabaean** /-ən/ *n.* = **scarab** *n.* 1 [Mid-19thC. Via modern Latin *Scarabaeidae*, family name, from Latin *scarabaeus* (see SCARAB).]

scarabaeus /skárrə bée əss/ (*plural* **-uses** *or* **-i** /-ī/) *n.* = **scarab** *n.* 2 [Late 16thC. Via Latin (see SCARAB).]

Scaramouch /skárrə mooch, -moosh, -mowch/, **Scaramouche** *n.* a boastful and cowardly man (*archaic*) [Mid-17thC. Directly or via French *Scaramouche* from Italian *Scaramuccia*, character in the commedia dell'-arte, literally 'skirmish' (see SKIRMISH).]

Scarborough /skaàrbərə/ town in North Yorkshire, northern England, on the North Sea. A market centre in the Middle Ages, it is now primarily a resort. Population: 107,800 (1991).

scarce /skairss/ *adj.* **1.** INSUFFICIENT being in insufficient supply **2.** RARE rarely found or rarely occurring ■ *adv.* SCARCELY scarcely (*archaic or literary*) [13thC. Via Anglo-Norman *(e)scars* from, ultimately, Latin *excerpere* 'to pick out' (source of English *excerpt*), from *carpere* 'to pluck' (source of English *carpet*).] —**scarceness** *n.* ◇ **make yourself scarce** to go or stay away, often in order to avoid some kind of trouble or difficulty (*informal*)

scarcely /skáirssli/ *adv.* **1.** HARDLY AT ALL only to the slightest degree ○ *I scarcely slept all night.* **2.** SURELY NOT surely or almost certainly not ○ *That is scarcely a good reason for taking the day off.*

WORD KEY: USAGE

See Usage note at ***hardly***.

scarcement /skáirssmənt/ *n.* a ledge in a wall [Early 16thC. Formed from obsolete *scarce* 'to make scarce'.]

scarcity /skáirssəti/ (*plural* **-ties**) *n.* **1.** INSUFFICIENT SUPPLY an insufficient supply of sth **2.** RARITY an infrequency of occurrence of sth

scare /skair/ *v.* (**scares, scaring, scared**) **1.** *vt.* FRIGHTEN SB to make sb afraid or alarmed **2.** *vi.* BE FRIGHTENED to be or become frightened ■ *n.* **1.** FRIGHT a sudden fright or feeling of fear **2.** STH THAT FRIGHTENS a situation causing general fear or alarm [12thC. From Old Norse *skirra* 'to frighten, to avoid', from *skjarr* 'timid, shy'.] —**scarer** *n.*

scare off, scare away *vt.* to frighten a person or an animal into going away

scare up *vt. US, Can* to manage to find sth or put sth together from whatever is available (*informal*)

scarecrow /skáirkrō/ *n.* **1.** OBJECT FOR SCARING BIRDS AWAY an object in the shape of a person dressed in old clothes, set up in a field to scare birds away from the crops **2.** POORLY DRESSED PERSON sb who wears ragged clothes (*informal*) **3.** STH FRIGHTENING BUT NOT DANGEROUS sb or sth that may have a frightening effect but is not dangerous

scared /skaird/ *adj.* feeling full of worry or fear —**scaredly** *adv.* —**scaredness** *n.*

scaredy-cat /skáirdi-/ *n.* sb who is unusually timid and frightened (*informal; usually used by or to children*) US term **fraidy-cat**

scaremonger /skáir mung gər/ *n.* sb who deliberately spreads alarming rumours —**scaremongering** *n.*

scarf[1] /skaarf/ *n.* (*plural* **scarfs** *or* **scarves** /skaarvz/) **1.** CLOTH WORN ROUND THE NECK a piece of cloth of various shapes, worn round the neck or on the head for warmth or decoration **2.** MILITARY SASH an official sash, usually indicating military rank ■ *vt.* (**scarfs, scarfing, scarfed**) WRAP STH IN SCARF to wrap a scarf round sth (*literary*) [Mid-16thC. Via Old Northern French *escarpe* from Old French *escherpe* 'pilgrim's bag hung around the neck', from assumed Frankish *skirpja* 'bag woven from rushes', from Latin *scirpus* 'rush'.]

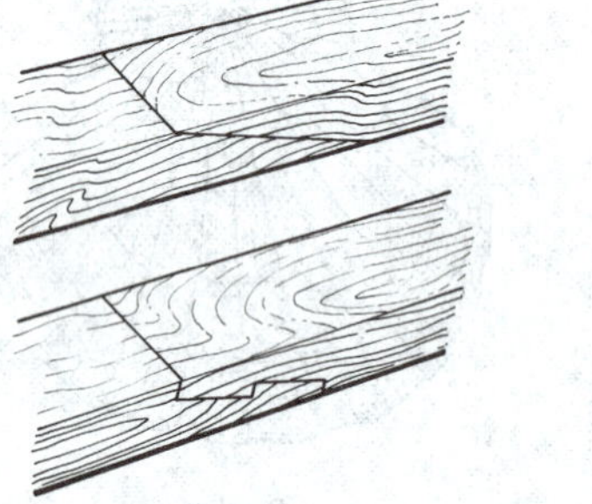

Scarf

scarf[2] /skaarf/ *n.* **1.** **scarf, scarf joint** JOINT MADE BETWEEN NOTCHED ENDS a joint made by joining two notched boards together **2.** NOTCHED END either of the notched ends of a scarf joint ■ *vt.* (**scarfs, scarfing, scarfed**) JOIN BOARDS USING NOTCHES to join boards together by means of a scarf joint [13thC. Origin uncertain: probably via Old French from a Scandinavian language.]

scarf[3] /skaàrf-/, **scarf down** *vt. US* to eat or drink sth greedily or noisily (*slang*) ['Scarf': variant of SCOFF]

scarf joint *n.* = **scarf**[2] *n.* 2

scarfskin /skaàrf skin/ *n.* the outermost layer of skin, especially the cuticle of a nail [Early 16thC. 'Scarf' from SCARF[1], with the underlying sense of a light outer covering.]

scarificator /skárrifi kaytər, skáiri-/ *n.* a surgical instrument formerly used to make superficial incisions in the skin

scarify[1] /skárri fī, skáiri-/ (**-fies, -fying, -fied**) *vt.* **1.** MAKE SCRATCHES ON SKIN to make scratches on or superficial incisions in the skin, done in the past, e.g. to promote an improved blood supply in the underlying tissues **2.** LOOSEN SOIL to break up and loosen the surface of soil **3.** SCRATCH SEEDS to break the outer cover of hard seeds to aid germination [14thC. Via French *scarifier* from, ultimately, Greek *skarisphasthai* 'to scratch an outline, sketch lightly', from *skariphos* 'stylus'.] —**scarification** /skárrifi káysh'n, skáiri-/ *n.* —**scarifier** /skárri fī ər, skáiri-/ *n.*

scarify[2] /skáiri-/ (**-fies, -fying, -fied**) *vt.* to make sb afraid or alarmed (*informal*) [Late 18thC. Formed from SCARE, perhaps modelled on TERRIFY.] —**scarifyingly** *adv.*

scarious /skáiri əss/, **scariose** *adj.* used to describe parts of plants that have a thin dry membranous appearance [Late 18thC. Via French *scarieux* from modern Latin *scariosus*.]

scarlatina /skaàrlə téenə/ *n.* = **scarlet fever** (*technical*) [Early 19thC. Via modern Latin from Italian *scarlattina* 'little scarlet things', from *scarlatto* 'scarlet', from, ultimately, Arabic *siqillāt* (see SCARLET).] —**scarlatinal** *adj.*

Scarlatti /skaar látti/, **Alessandro** (1659–1725) Italian composer. The father of Domenico Scarlatti, he was a major contributor to the establishment of the Neapolitan style of opera. He also wrote over 700 works of church music. Full name **Pietro Alessandro Gaspare Scarlatti**

Scarlatti, Domenico (1685–1757) Italian composer. The son of Alessandro Scarlatti, he composed operas and church music, but is best known for over 550 sonatas for harpsichord.

scarlet /skaárlət/ *n.* **1.** BRIGHT RED COLOUR a bright red colour tinged with orange **2.** SCARLET CLOTH scarlet clothing or cloth, especially the traditional red uniforms of the British army ■ *adj.* BRIGHT RED IN COLOUR of a bright red colour tinged with orange ○ *scarlet lipstick* [13thC. Via Old French *escarlate* from Arabic *siqillāt*, a rich cloth (scarlet being its usual colour), from Latin *sigillatus* 'decorated with raised figures', ultimately from *signum* 'sign'.]

scarlet fever *n.* a contagious bacterial infection marked by fever, a sore throat, and a red rash, mainly affecting children

scarlet hat *n.* CHR = **red hat**

scarlet ibis *n.* BIRDS an ibis that is bright red when mature. It nests in swamps and is the national bird of Trinidad and Tobago, displayed on the national coat-of-arms. Latin name: *Eudocimus ruber*.

scarlet letter *n.* a scarlet letter A that a woman convicted of adultery was formerly made to wear, especially among the Puritans of 17th-century New England

WORD KEY: CULTURAL NOTE

The Scarlet Letter, a novel by US writer Nathaniel Hawthorne (1850). The title of this eloquent plea for tolerance refers to the red letter A that Hester Prynne, a woman living in mid-17th-century New England, is forced to wear as punishment for an adulterous affair. While her husband and lover are consumed by anger and guilt respectively, Hester's honesty and strength of character help her to survive the scandal. The term *scarlet letter*, used generically to denote adultery or evidence of it, derives from this novel.

scarlet pimpernel *n.* a common pimpernel that has small scarlet, purple, or white flowers that close in cloudy weather. Latin name: *Anagallis arvensis*.

scarlet runner *n.* = **runner bean**

scarlet tanager *n.* a medium-sized songbird of the eastern United States. The male is bright red with black wings and tail during the breeding season. Latin name: *Piranga olivacea*.

scarlet woman *n.* an offensive term referring to a woman believed to be an adulterer or prostitute or to engage excessively in sexual activity, especially a prostitute (*disapproving*) [From the Bible, *Revelations* 17:1–6, in which a whorish woman, representing the Roman Church, appears 'in purple and scarlet colour']

scarp /skaarp/ *n.* **1.** GEOG STEEP CLIFF a steep slope or cliff, formed by erosion or faulting. ◊ **escarpment 2.** MIL STEEP SLOPE IN A FORTIFICATION a steep slope, e.g. the inner wall of a ditch, in front of a fortification [Late 16thC. From Italian *scarpa* (source of English *escarp*), of uncertain origin.]

scarper /skaárpər/ (**-ers, -ering, -ered**) *vi.* to leave a place quickly (*slang*) [Mid-19thC. Origin uncertain: probably from Italian *scappare* 'to escape', influenced by rhyming slang 'Scapa Flow', 'go'.]

scart /skaart/ (**scarts, scarting, scarted**) *vti. Scotland* to scratch sth or the self (*nonstandard*) [14thC. Alteration of dialect *scrat*, of unknown origin.]

Scart /skaart/, **SCART** *n.* a device for making an electrical connection that has a socket and plug with 21 pins. It is used to connect video equipment. ○ *a Scart lead* [Late 20thC. From French, an acronym formed from *Syndicat des Constructeurs des Appareils Radiorécepteurs et Téléviseurs*, the committee that designed the connector.]

scar tissue *n.* dense fibrous tissue that forms the scar over a healed wound

scarves plural of **scarf**

scary /skáiri/ (**-ier, -iest**) *adj.* (*informal*) **1.** FRIGHTENING causing fear or alarm **2.** TIMID easily frightened —**scarily** *adv.* —**scariness** *n.*

scat[1] /skat/ (**scats, scatting, scatted**) *vi.* to leave immediately and quickly (*informal; usually used as a command*) [Mid-19thC. Origin unknown.]

scat[2] /skat/ *n.* JAZZ VOCAL STYLE a style of jazz singing that uses nonsense syllables to approximate the sound of a solo instrument. Ella Fitzgerald and Mel Tormé are considered consummate scat singers. ■ *vi.* (**scats, scatting, scatted**) SING SCAT to sing in scat style [Early 20thC. Origin uncertain: probably an imitation of the sound.]

scat[3] /skat/ (*plural* **scats** *or* **scat**) *n.* a small tropical Indo-Pacific marine fish, popular for aquariums because of its bright colour. Family: Scatophagidae. [Mid-20thC. Shortening of modern Latin *Scatophagidae*, family name, from Greek *scatophagos*, 'dung-eating', because it frequents sewage outlets.]

scat[4] /skat/ *n.* a faecal dropping of an animal [Mid-20thC. From the Greek stem *skat-* (see SCATOLOGY).]

scathe /skay*th*/ *vt.* (**scathes, scathing, scathed**) **1.** CRITICIZE SB to subject sb to severe criticism (*literary*) **2.** DAMAGE STH BY BLASTING to damage sth by blasting or scorching it (*archaic*) ■ *n.* HARM injury or harm (*archaic*) [12thC. From Old Norse *skaða* 'to harm or damage'.] —**scatheless** *adj.*

scathing /skáy*th*ing/ *adj.* severely critical and scornful —**scathingly** *adv.*

scato- *prefix.* excrement ○ *scatology* [Formed from Greek *skat-*, the stem of *skōr* 'excrement'. Ultimately from an Indo-European word meaning literally 'sth cut off', which is also the ancestor of English *dreck*.]

scatology /ska tólləji/ *n.* **1.** OBSESSION WITH EXCREMENT preoccupation with excrement or obscenity **2.** STUDY OF EXCREMENT the scientific study of excrement, especially for diagnostic purposes —**scatological** /skáttə lójjik'l/ *adj.* —**scatologist** /ska tóllə jist/ *n.*

scatter /skáttər/ *v.* (**-ters, -tering, -tered**) **1.** *vt.* THROW THINGS ABOUT to throw things about so that they land with an irregular distribution over a relatively wide area **2.** *vt.* SCATTER STH OVER AN AREA to cover an area by throwing things about over it ○ *scatter seed* **3.** *vti.* DISPERSE to separate and move suddenly in different directions, or cause people or animals to move in this way **4.** *vti.* PHYS DEVIATE to cause waves or a beam of particles to be irregularly deflected, dispersed, or reflected, or to be turned aside in such a fashion ■ *n.* THINGS SCATTERED ABOUT a number of things spread untidily about an area (*literary*) [12thC. Origin uncertain: probably a variant of SHATTER.] —**scatterable** *adj.* —**scatterer** *n.*

WORD KEY: SYNONYMS

scatter, broadcast, distribute, disseminate

CORE MEANING: to spread around

scatter to spread things around physically, especially in a random widespread manner; **broadcast** used in old-fashioned or formal English with the meaning to scatter seeds. It is now commonly used with the meaning to spread or transmit information, especially by means of radio or television; **distribute** to allocate sth or give it out in a structured or organized way. It can also be used in formal English in a similar way to **scatter**, to talk about physically spreading sth over a surface or area; **disseminate** a formal word with the meaning to spread abstract things such as ideas, information, or good will.

scatterbrain /skáttər brayn/ *n.* sb who is incapable of serious or organized thought, or of remembering important things —**scatterbrained** *adj.*

scatter cushion *n.* a small moveable cushion placed on a sofa or armchair (*often used in the plural*) US term **throw pillow**

scatter diagram *n.* a graph that represents the joint relationship of two variables by depicting the data as points along two axes at right angles to each other. The smoother the curve that can be drawn through the points, the greater the relationship between the variables.

scattered /skáttərd/ *adj.* **1.** DISPERSED in a number of different places far away from each other ○ *scattered communities* **2.** INFREQUENT OR ISOLATED few in number and far apart in distance or time ○ *scattered showers*

scattergood /skáttər gŏŏd/ *n.* sb who spends money wastefully

scatter-gun *n. US* a shotgun

scattering /skáttəring/ *n.* **1.** SMALL AMOUNT OR NUMBER a small amount or number of things irregularly spread over a large area **2.** PHYS DEFLECTION OF PARTICLES the deflection of a wave or beam of particles caused by collisions with other particles

scattering layer *n.* an undersea zone where there is a high concentration of plankton that causes sound waves to become scattered. This makes strong acoustic echoes possible.

scatter pin *n.* a small decorative pin typically worn as part of a cluster on clothing

scatter rug *n.* a small decorative rug

scattershot /skáttər shot/ *adj.* indiscriminate and lacking in focus ○ *a scattershot approach to the operation*

scatty /skátti/ (**-tier, -tiest**) *adj. UK, Can* (*informal*) **1.** FORGETFUL OR ECCENTRIC lacking in serious or organized thought, forgetful, and often eccentric in behaviour **2.** ANNOYED OR CONFUSED extremely muddled, irritated, or angry ○ *These children are driving me scatty.* [Early 20thC. Origin uncertain: probably formed from a shortening of *scatterbrained*.] —**scattily** *adv.* —**scattiness** *n.*

scaup /skawp/ (*plural* **scaups** *or* **scaup**), **scaup duck** *n.* a diving duck native to Europe and North America. The male has a black-and-white body. Genus: *Aythya*. [Late 17thC. Variant of *scalp* 'shellfish-bed', of uncertain origin: perhaps because it feeds on shellfish.]

scauper /skáwpər/ *n.* an engraving tool used to clear away lines or other unwanted areas on wood [Mid-19thC. Variant of scalper from SCALP.]

scaur /skawr/ *n. Scotland* a steep eroded hill or precipice (*often used in placenames*) [Early 18thC. Variant of SCAR[2].]

scavenge /skávvinj/ (**-enges, -enging, -enged**) *vti.* **1.** LOOK FOR STH USABLE to search for or through discarded material in order to find sth usable **2.** FEED ON CARRION OR SCRAPS to feed on dead and rotting flesh or discarded food scraps **3.** CLEAN UP to remove waste material and dirt from an area **4.** CHEM GET RID OF IMPURITIES to neutralize or remove impurities in a chemical reaction or mixture [Mid-17thC. Back-formation from SCAVENGER.]

scavenger /skávvinjər/ *n.* **1.** ANIMAL FEEDING ON CARRION OR SCRAPS an animal, bird, or other organism that feeds on dead and rotting flesh or discarded food scraps **2.** SB LOOKING FOR STH USABLE sb who searches for or through discarded material in order to find sth usable **3.** CHEM SUBSTANCE REMOVING IMPURITIES sth that is added to a chemical reaction or mixture to neutralize or remove impurities **4.** STREET CLEANER sb who works as a street cleaner or refuse collector (*archaic*) [Mid-16thC. Alteration of *scavager* 'tax collector', from Anglo-Norman *scawager*, from, ultimately, Flemish *scauwen* 'to look at'.] —**scavengery** *n.*

WORD KEY: ORIGIN

The term *scavager* was originally, in the Middle Ages, an official who collected taxes levied on overseas merchants. Later the term came to denote a street-cleaner, and by the time it had metamorphosed into ***scavenger*** (by the same process as produced *messenger* from *messager* and *passenger* from *passager*) it had completed its descent to its modern meaning.

scavenger beetle *n.* a dark oval-shaped beetle that lives in water and feeds on decaying vegetation. Family: Hydrophilidae.

scavenger hunt *n.* a game in which people must obtain items on a list within a time limit and without buying them

scavenger moth *n.* a small moth that is commonly found scavenging stored food, e.g. grains and oils. The clothes moth is a kind of scavenger moth. Family: Tineidae.

ScB *abbr.* Bachelor of Science (*an academic title sometimes used in place of BSc*) [Latin, *Scientiae Baccalaureus*]

SCC *abbr.* storage connecting circuit

ScD *abbr.* Doctor of Science [Latin, *Scientiae Doctor*]

SCE *n.* in Scotland, any of three levels of examinations in a wide range of subjects taken in the last three years of secondary school. Standard Grades are usually taken at the age of 16, Highers at 17, and Sixth Year Studies at 18. Full form **Scottish Certificate of Education**

scena /sháynə/ (*plural* **-ne**) *n.* **1.** **SCENE IN OPERA** a division of an opera that is equivalent in length or structure to a scene in a play **2.** **DRAMATIC CONCERT PIECE** a dramatic concert piece written and performed in the style of an operatic scena [Early 19thC. Via Italian from Latin *scaena* (see SCENE[1]).]

scenario /si naári ō/ (*plural* **-os**) *n.* **1.** **POSSIBLE SITUATION** an imagined sequence of possible events ○ *the worst-case scenario* **2.** **PLOT OUTLINE** an outline of the plot of a play or opera **3.** CINEMA **SCREENPLAY** a screenplay [Late 19thC. From Italian, formed from *scena* 'scene', from Latin *scaena* (see SCENE[1]).]

WORD KEY: USAGE

Meaning trap The use of **scenario** in a generalized way to denote a projected or imagined sequence of events or set of circumstances (*an alternative scenario if the vote goes the other way*) is widely deprecated in dictionaries and books on usage, although it is hard to see why this figurative use of a word is to be rejected when so many others (such as *scene*) are accepted without comment. It is a useful word when the imagined events or circumstances can be regarded as a whole and are therefore directly comparable to the elements of a film or theatre plot.

scenarist /seénərist, sə naárist, si-/ *n.* sb who writes film scripts

scend /skend/, **send** *n.* **SHIP'S UPWARD PITCH** the upward movement of a ship that is pitching in heavy seas ■ *vi.* **(scends, scending, scended)** **RISE HIGH ON WAVE** to rise up high under the force of a strong wave (*refers to ships*) [15thC. Origin uncertain: probably an alteration of DESCEND or ASCEND.]

scene[1] /seen/ *n.* **1.** ARTS **DIVISION OF AN ACT OF A PLAY** any of the divisions of an act of a play or opera, presenting continuous action in one place **2.** ARTS **SHORT SECTION OF A PLAY OR FILM** a short section of a play, film, opera, or work of literature that presents a single event ○ *the love scene* **3.** ARTS **SETTING IN A DRAMATIC WORK** a setting for the whole or a part of a play, film, opera, or work of literature **4.** **PLACE WHERE STH HAPPENS** a location at which an event or action happens ○ *the scene of many battles* **5.** ARTS **SCENERY FOR DRAMATIC WORK** the backgrounds, sets, or props for a play, film, or opera (*often used before a noun*) ○ *a couple of quick scene changes* **6.** **VIEW OR PICTURE** a view of a place or an activity, especially one presented in a painting or photograph **7.** **EMBARRASSING PUBLIC DISPLAY** an embarrassing or disconcerting public display of emotion ○ *Don't make a scene, but I think they've lost your coat.* **8.** **MILIEU** the characteristic environment in which an activity or pursuit is carried out ○ *new to the fashion scene* **9.** *US* **SITUATION** a set of circumstances of any kind (*informal*) ○ *We seem to have stumbled into a bad scene.* [Mid-16thC. Via Latin *scaena* from Greek *skēnē* 'tent, stage'. The underlying idea is of sth that gives shade.] ◇ **behind the scenes 1.** out of sight of the audience at a performance or spectacle **2.** in private and away from public view ◇ **it's not my** *or* **your** *or* **his** *or* **her etc scene** it is not the kind of thing that sb likes to do or takes an interest in ◇ **set the scene 1.** to describe a situation or the background to an event **2.** to create the circumstances in which sth can or does happen

scene[2] plural of **scena**

scenery /seénəri/ *n.* **1.** ARTS **THEATRICAL BACKDROP** the set or decorated background for a play, film, or opera **2.** **SURROUNDINGS** landscape or natural surroundings, especially when regarded as picturesque ○ *admired the scenery from the hotel balcony* [Mid-18thC. Alteration of *scenary*, from Italian *scenario* (see SCENARIO).]

sceneshifter /seén shiftər/ *n.* sb who moves sets or props in a theatre or opera house

scene-stealer *n.* a performer who, by his or her performance or personal qualities, takes the audience's attention away from another performer who is supposedly the focus of the scene

scenic /seénik/ *adj.* **1.** **PICTURESQUE** with attractive or impressive natural scenery **2.** **OF NATURAL SCENERY** relating to the natural scenery of an area ○ *famous for its scenic beauty* **3.** ARTS **OF DRAMATIC SCENES** relating to scenes in a play, film, or opera **4.** THEATRE **OF STAGE SCENERY** relating to stage scenery —**scenically** *adv.*

scenic railway *n.* **1.** **MINIATURE RAILWAY IN A PARK** a miniature railway that carries customers past artificial scenery in a theme park or other place of entertainment **2.** **ROLLER COASTER** a roller coaster (*dated*)

scenography /see nóggrəfi/ *n.* **1.** PAINTING **PAINTING OR DRAWING IN PERSPECTIVE** the artistic representation of objects according to the rules of perspective **2.** THEATRE **SCENERY-PAINTING** the painting of theatrical scenery —**scenographer** *n.* —**scenographic** /seénə gráffik/ *adj.* —**scenographical** /-gráffik'l/ *adj.* —**scenographically** /-gráffikli/ *adv.*

scent /sent/ *n.* **1.** **CHARACTERISTIC PLEASANT SMELL** a distinctive odour, especially a pleasant one ○ *the scent of jasmine* **2.** **SMELL USED AS TRAIL** a smell left behind by a person or animal and used especially for tracking ○ *They followed the scent deep into the forest.* **3.** **PERFUME** cosmetic fragrances, especially women's perfume **4.** **SMELLING SENSE** the sense of smell **5.** **ABILITY TO SENSE STH** an ability to sense or detect sth as likely to happen **6.** **HINT** a faint indication that sth is likely to happen ○ *There was the scent of danger in the air.* ■ *v.* **(scents, scenting, scented) 1.** *vti.* **SMELL SB OR STH** to perceive sb or sth by smelling **2.** *vt.* **DETECT STH AS IMMINENT** to sense that sth is likely to happen ○ *They could scent victory.* **3.** *vt.* **IMBUE STH WITH A PLEASANT SMELL** to fill sth with a distinctive odour, especially a pleasant one ○ *Roses scented the room.* [14thC. Via French *sentir* from Latin *sentire* 'to feel' (source of English *sense* and *sentiment*).] ◇ **put** *or* **throw sb off the scent** to divert sb from finding or discovering sth

WORD KEY: SYNONYMS

See Synonyms at ***smell***.

scented orchid *n.* a wild orchid that has fragrant pink flowers. Latin name: *Gymnadenia conopsea.*

scent gland *n.* a specialized skin gland that enables an animal to secrete a scent designed to send social or sexual signals or serve as a deterrent

scent strip *n.* a strip of perfumed paper used to advertise a commercially available perfume to potential customers

scepter *n., vt.* US = **sceptre**

sceptic /sképtik/ *n.* **1.** **SB WHO DOUBTS STH IS TRUE** sb who questions the validity or truth of things that most people accept **2.** **SB WHO DOUBTS RELIGIOUS TEACHINGS** sb who is not willing to accept the doctrines and principles that form the basis of a religion [Late 16thC. Via French *sceptique* or directly from Latin *scepticus* 'follower of the Greek philosopher Pyrrho', from Greek *skeptikos*, from *skeptesthai* 'to look about'.]

Sceptic /sképtik/ *n.* **SB DENYING KNOWLEDGE IS POSSIBLE** a member of an ancient Greek school of philosophy holding the doctrine that real knowledge is impossible, or a later follower of this doctrine ■ *adj.* **RELATING TO SCEPTICS** relating to an ancient Greek school of philosophy or its members, who believed that knowledge is impossible [Late 16thC] —**Skeptic** *adj.*

sceptical /sképtik'l/ *adj.* **1.** **DOUBTFUL** tending not to believe things but to question them **2.** **SHOWING DOUBT** marked by a doubting attitude —**scepticalness** *n.* —**sceptically** *adv.*

WORD KEY: SYNONYMS

See Synonyms at ***doubtful***.

scepticism /sképtisizəm/ *n.* **1.** **DOUBTING ATTITUDE** an attitude marked by a tendency to doubt what others accept to be true **2.** RELIG **DOUBT OF RELIGION** a doubting attitude toward religious beliefs **3. scepticism, Scepticism** PHILOS **DOCTRINE THAT KNOWLEDGE IS IMPOSSIBLE** the doctrine that holds that true knowledge is not possible [Mid-17thC]

sceptre /séptər/ *n.* **1.** **STAFF USED AS A ROYAL EMBLEM** a ceremonial staff, rod, or wand used as an emblem of a monarch's authority **2.** **ROYAL AUTHORITY** royal or imperial power or authority ■ *vt.* **(-tres, -tring, -tred)** **GIVE SB ROYAL AUTHORITY** to endow sb with royal power or authority [13thC. Via Old French *sceptre* from, ultimately, Greek *skēptron* 'staff, sceptre', from *skēptein* 'to lean on'.] —**sceptred** *adj.*

SCF *abbr.* Save the Children Fund

sch. *abbr.* school

schadenfreude /shaád'n froydə/, **Schadenfreude** *n.* malicious or smug pleasure taken in sb else's misfortune [Late 19thC. From German, formed from *Schaden* 'harm' + *Freude* 'joy'.]

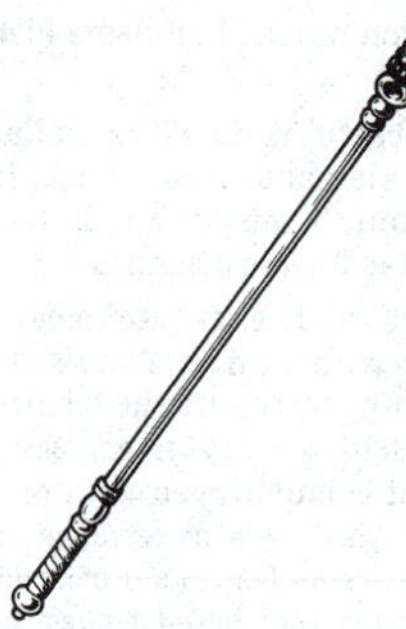

Sceptre

Schaffhausen /shaaf hówzən/ capital of Schaffhausen Canton, in northern Switzerland. Population: 34,396 (1983).

schappe /shápp ə/ *n.* yarn or fabric made from the waste products of silk [Late 19thC. From German.]

schechita /shə keétə/ *n.* = **shechita**

schedule /shéddyool, skéd-/ *n.* **1.** **WORK PLAN** a plan of work to be done in a specified order and by specified times **2.** **LIST OF MEETINGS, COMMITMENTS, OR APPOINTMENTS** an outline description of the things sb is to do and the times at which they are to be done ○ *Her schedule was full from daylight to dark.* **3.** = **timetable 4.** *US* EDUC **STUDENT'S TIMETABLE** a list of the classes that are the responsibility of a student or a teacher in a given period **5.** **LIST OF ITEMS** a table of items of information ○ *a schedule of tariffs* **6.** LAW **SUPPLEMENTARY LIST** a list of details, often in the form of an appendix to a legal or legislative document ■ *vt.* **(-ules, -uling, -uled) 1.** **PLAN STH FOR A PARTICULAR TIME** to plan sth to happen at a particular time ○ *They are scheduled to arrive at midday.* **2.** **MAKE A LIST OF THINGS** to put together a table of items of information, or place an item in the table **3.** **PROTECT BUILDING BY LAW** to put a building on a list of officially protected buildings [14thC. Via Old French *cēdule* from late Latin *schedula* 'small piece of paper', from, ultimately, Greek *skhedē* 'page'.] —**schedular** *adj.* —**scheduler** *n.*

scheduled castes *npl.* castes in India that are officially considered disadvantaged and granted special treatment

scheduled territories *npl.* = **sterling area**

scheelite /sheé līt/ *n.* a variously coloured mineral that occurs in veins and is the chief ore of tungsten [Mid-19thC. Named after Karl Wilhelm *Scheele* (1742–86), the German-born Swedish chemist who first isolated tungstic acid from this mineral.]

schefflera /shéfflərə/ (*plural* **-ras** *or* **-ra**) *n.* a tropical tree or shrub with glossy leaves, often cultivated as a house plant. Genus: *Schefflera.* [Mid-20thC. From modern Latin, named after German botanist J. C. *Scheffler* (1742–86).]

Schelte /skéltə/ river in Europe that flows through France, Belgium, and the Netherlands. Length: 435 km/270 mi.

schema /skeémə/ (*plural* **-mata** /skeémətə/) *n.* **1.** **DIAGRAM** a diagram or plan showing the basic outline of sth **2.** PSYCHOL **MENTAL PATTERN** an organizational or conceptual pattern in the mind **3.** PHILOS **KANTIAN PHILOSOPHICAL PRINCIPLE** in the philosophy of Kant, a method that allows the understanding to apply concepts to the evidence of the senses **4.** LOGIC **DUMMY EXPRESSION IN LOGIC** in logic, a dummy expression indicating where certain words should appear, e.g. in 'S and R', 'S' and 'R' are schemata for sentences [Late 18thC. Via German from Greek *skhēma* (see SCHEME).]

schematic /skee máttik, ski-/ *adj.* **SHOWING LAYOUT** showing the basic form or layout of sth ○ *a schematic drawing* ■ *n.* **DIAGRAM** a diagram, especially of electrical circuits

schematise *vt.* = **schematize**

schematism /skeémətizəm/ *n.* the basic arrangement or layout of parts in a complex object or system [Mid-17thC]

schematize /skéemə tīz/ (**-tizes, -tizing, -tized**), **schematise** (**-tises, -tising, -tised**) *vt.* to arrange or organize sth according to a system —**schematization** /skéemə tī záysh'n/ *n.*

scheme /skeem/ *n.* **1. SECRET PLOT** a secret and cunning plan, especially one designed to cause damage or harm **2. PLAN** a systematic plan of action **3. SYSTEM** a systematic and coherent arrangement of parts **4. DIAGRAM** a diagram, chart, or map **5. GOVERNMENT OR BUSINESS PROGRAMME** a plan, policy, or programme carried out by a government or business ○ *training scheme* ○ *pension scheme* **6. ASTRON ASTROLOGER'S CHART** an astrological chart of the sky **7. *Scotland*** = **housing scheme** ■ *v.* (**schemes, scheming, schemed**) **1.** *vi.* **MAKE A SECRET PLAN** to devise a secret and cunning plan, especially one intended to cause damage or harm **2.** *vt.* **PLAN STH SYSTEMATICALLY** to devise a systematic plan for sth [Mid-16thC. Via Latin *schema* (stem *schemat-*) 'form', from Greek *skhēma*. Ultimately from an Indo-European word meaning 'to hold', which is also the ancestor of English *school*.]

scheming /skéeming/ *adj.* making secret and cunning plans, especially to do damage or cause harm — **schemingly** *adv.*

Schenectady /skə néktədi/ city in eastern New York State, on the Mohawk River, northwest of Albany. Population: 62,893 (1996).

Schepisi /shéppissi, she peéssi/, **Fred** (*b.* 1939) Australian filmmaker. He directed *The Chant of Jimmie Blacksmith* (1978). After the 1980s he made films for Hollywood including *Six Degrees of Separation* (1994). Full name **Frederick Alan Schepisi**

scherzando /skairt sándō/ *adj., adv.* **IN PLAYFUL STYLE** performed in a playful musical style and tempo (*used as a musical direction*) ■ *n.* (*plural* **-di** /-di/ *or* **-dos**) **SCHERZANDO PIECE** a scherzando piece or passage of music [Early 19thC. From Italian, formed from *scherzare* (see SCHERZO).]

scherzo /skáirtsō/ (*plural* **-zos** *or* **-zi** /-si/) *n.* **1. LIGHTHEARTED MUSICAL MOVEMENT** a rapid, playful, or humorous movement, usually the third of four, in a musical work **2. LIGHTHEARTED MUSICAL PIECE** an independent musical work in a rapid, playful, or humorous style [Mid-19thC. From Italian, formed from *scherzare* 'to joke', of uncertain origin: probably of Germanic origin.]

Scheveningen /skáyvən ingə/ resort town in the western Netherlands, on the North Sea. It is now a district of The Hague.

· Elsa Schiaparelli

Schiaparelli /skee aápə rélli, skáppə-/, **Elsa** (1896–1973) Italian fashion designer. Her designs were often extravagant with deliberately overstated effects.

Schick test /shík-/ *n.* an injection of nontoxic diphtheria under the skin, used to determine whether a patient is immune to diphtheria. A patch of reddened skin at the point of injection indicates no immunity. [Early 20thC. Named after Bela Schick (1877–1967), the Hungarian-born US paediatrician who devised the test.]

Schiele /sheélə/, **Egon** (1890–1918) Austrian painter. His depictions of the human figure, in the expressionist style, have a strongly erotic quality.

Schiff's reagent /shífs-/, **Schiff reagent** *n.* an acid solution of fuchsine used to test for the presence of aldehydes [Late 19thC. Named after the German chemist Hugo Schiff (1834–1915).]

schiller /shíllər/ *n.* a metallic iridescent lustre in some minerals [Early 19thC. From German, 'iridescence'.]

Schiller /shíllər/, **Friedrich von** (1759–1805) German poet, dramatist, historian, and philosopher. Regarded as Germany's greatest playwright, he wrote works in praise of the freedom of the human spirit, including the dramas *Wallenstein*, *Maria Stuart* (both 1800), and *William Tell* (1804). Full name **Johann Christoph Friedrich von Schiller**

schilling /shílling/ *n.* **1. AUSTRIAN UNIT OF CURRENCY** a unit of currency in Austria worth 100 groschen. See table at **currency 2. COIN WORTH SCHILLING** a coin worth one schilling [Mid-18thC. From German.]

Schipperke

schipperke /shíppərki, skíp-/ (*plural* **-kes** *or* **-ke**) *n.* a small black tailless dog of a breed with pointed ears and a thick coat [Late 19thC. From Dutch dialect, a diminutive of Dutch *schipper* 'skipper' (see SKIPPER[1]). From the use of the dog as a watchdog on boats.]

schism /skízzəm, sízzəm/ *n.* **1. SPLITTING INTO FACTIONS** the division of a group into mutually antagonistic factions **2. FACTION** a faction formed as a result of a schism **3. RELIG DIVISION IN OR FROM A RELIGIOUS DENOMINATION** a division within a religious denomination or a breaking away from it, usually on the grounds of differing beliefs or practices [14thC. Via Old French *scisme* from late Latin *schisma* from, ultimately, Greek *skhizein* (see SCHIZO-).]

schismatic /skiz máttik, siz-/, **schismatical** /-máttik'l/ *adj.* **OF A SCHISM** relating to, involved in, or causing schism ■ *n.* **MEMBER OR PROMOTER OF A SCHISM** sb who is involved in a schism or who causes a schism — **schismatically** *adv.* —**schismaticalness** *n.*

schist /shist/ *n.* any rock whose minerals have aligned themselves in one direction in response to deformation stresses, with the result that the rock can be split in parallel layers [Late 18thC. Via French *schiste* from Latin (*lapis*) *schistos* 'fissile (stone)', from Greek *skhistos*, from *skhizein* (see SCHIZO-).] —**schistose** /shístōss, -tōz/ *adj.* —**schistosity** /shiss tóssəti/ *n.*

schistocyte /shístō sīt/ *n.* a red blood cell undergoing fragmentation, or any of the fragments that are formed as a result

schistosome /shístō sōm/ *n.* a tiny flatworm that often lives as a parasite in the blood of birds and mammals. In humans, it causes the disease schistosomiasis.

schistosomiasis /shístō sō mī əssiss/ *n.* an often chronic illness that results from infection of the blood with a parasitic flatworm (**schistosome**). It causes debilitation and can cause liver and intestinal damage. It is most common in Asia, Africa, and South America, especially in areas where the water is contaminated by freshwater snails that carry the parasite.

schiz- *prefix.* = **schizo-** (*used before vowels*)

schizanthus /skit sánthəss, ski zánth-/ (*plural* **-thus**) *n.* a Chilean plant with small flowers that resemble orchids. Genus: *Schizanthus*. [Early 19thC. From modern Latin, name of the genus; coined from SCHIZO- + Greek *anthos* 'flower'.]

schizo /skítsō/ *n.* (*plural* **-os**) **AN OFFENSIVE TERM** an offensive term for sb who has schizophrenia (*slang offensive*) ■ *adj.* **OFFENSIVE TERM** an offensive term referring to characteristics often erroneously thought of as symptomatic of schizophrenia (*slang offensive*) [Mid-20thC. Shortening of SCHIZOPHRENIC.]

schizo- *prefix.* **1.** split, cleft ○ *schizocarp* **2.** cleavage, fission ○ *schizogenesis* **3.** schizophrenia ○ *schizoaffective* [Via modern Latin from Greek *skhizein* 'to split'. Ultimately from an Indo-European base that is also the ancestor of English *schism* and *rescind*.]

schizocarp /skítsōh-/ *n.* a dry fruit that splits into individually seeded parts (**carpels**) when ripe — **schizocarpic** /skítsō kaárpik, skízō-/ *adj.* —**schizocarpous** /-kaárpəss/ *adj.*

schizogony /skit zóggəni, shī-/ *n.* a form of asexual reproduction that occurs in certain single-celled organisms (**protozoans**), in which the nucleus of an individual divides many times before the cytoplasm divides to form the daughter cells. This process enables certain parasites, including the malaria parasite, to undergo rapid proliferation in the body tissues of an infected host.

schizoid /skít soyd/ *adj.* **1. PSYCHIAT TENDING TOWARDS SCHIZOPHRENIA** with some of the symptoms of schizophrenia, e.g. withdrawal into the self and a tendency to fantasize ○ *exhibits a schizoid personality* **2. OFFENSIVE TERM** an offensive term describing a personality that suggests inner conflicts and exhibits outer contradictions (*offensive*)

schizont /skítsont, shíz-/ *n.* a cell formed during the asexual phase of the life cycle of certain single-celled organisms (**protozoans**)

schizophrenia /skítsō freéni ə/ *n.* **1. PSYCHIATRIC DISORDER AFFECTING THE COHERENCE OF THE PERSONALITY** a severe psychiatric disorder with symptoms of emotional instability, detachment from reality, often with delusions and hallucinations, and withdrawal into the self **2. OFFENSIVE TERM** an offensive term for contradictory or conflicting attitudes, behaviour, or qualities (*offensive*) [Early 20thC. Coined from SCHIZO- + Greek *phrēn* 'mind' (see PHRENO-).]

schizophrenic /skítsō frénnik/ *adj.* **1. PSYCHIAT OF SCHIZOPHRENIA** relating to schizophrenia or resulting from schizophrenia **2. OFFENSIVE TERM** an offensive term meaning characterized by conflicts and contradictions (*offensive*)

schizophyte /skítsō fīt, shízə-/ *n.* a microorganism that reproduces by fission. Bacteria and bluish-green algae are schizophytes. —**schizophytic** /skítsə fíttik, shízə-/ *adj.*

schizopod /skítsə pod, shízə-/ (*plural* **-pods** *or* **-pod**) *n.* any of numerous kinds of crustacean that resemble shrimp, including krill. Order: Mysidacea and Euphausiacea.

schizothymia /skítsō thími ə/ *n.* an introverted psychiatric condition that resembles a mild form of schizophrenia [Mid-20thC. Ultimately from Greek *skhizein* 'to split' + *thumos* 'soul, mind'.] —**schizothymic** *adj.*

schizy /skítsi/ (**-ier, -iest**) *adj.* offensive term meaning emotionally sensitive or moody to a degree that makes others feel uneasy (*slang offensive*) [Mid-20thC. Shortening of SCHIZOPHRENIC or SCHIZOID with alteration.]

schlemiel /shlə meél/, **schlemihl** *n.* US an offensive term referring to sb regarded as bungling, inept, or unlucky (*insult slang*) [Late 19thC. From Yiddish *shlemiel*, of uncertain origin: probably from *Shelumiel*, biblical figure identified in the Talmud with a prince who was killed while committing adultery.]

schlep /shlep/ *v.* (**schleps** *or* **shleps, schlepping** *or* **shlepping, schlepped** *or* **shlepped**) (*informal*) **1.** *vt.* **MOVE STH WITH DIFFICULTY** to lug or haul sth from one place to another **2.** *vi.* **GO WITH DIFFICULTY** to move slowly, clumsily, or tediously ■ *n.* (*plural* **schleps** *or* **shleps**) **1. TEDIOUS JOURNEY** a long, tedious, or difficult journey (*informal*) ○ *It's such a schlep all the way across town.* **2. OFFENSIVE TERM** an offensive term referring to sb who is regarded as unintelligent or clumsy (*insult*) [Early 20thC. Via Yiddish *shlepn* from German *schleppen* 'to drag'.] —**schlepper** *n.*

Schleswig-Holstein /shléz vig hólstīn/ state in northern Germany occupying the southern part of the Jutland peninsula. Capital: Kiel. Population: 2,708,000 (1994). Area: 15,710 sq. km/6,066 sq. mi.

schlieren /shleérən/ *npl.* **1. PHYS STREAKS IN FLUID** zones of different density and refraction in a transparent fluid, visible as streaks and caused by pressure or temperature variations **2. GEOL LINEAR FEATURES IN ROCKS**

a texture observed in some igneous rocks where the darker, more basic minerals form linear aggregates in the paler host rock [Late 19thC. Via German, 'streaks', from, ultimately, Middle High German *slier* 'mud', of uncertain origin.]

schlieren photography *n.* a form of flash photography that records schlieren present in a fluid

schlock /shlok/ *n. US* JUNK sth that has no value and is shoddily made (*slang*) ■ *adj. US* LACKING IN SUBSTANCE cheap and lacking any redeeming quality (*slang*) ○ *a schlock horror film* [Early 20thC. Origin uncertain: possibly from Yiddish *shlak* 'stroke, evil', from Middle High German *slag*.] —**schlocky** *adj.*

schmaltz /shmawlts, shmolts/, **schmalz, shmaltz** *n.* cloying or exaggerated sentimentality (*informal*) [Mid-20thC. Via Yiddish *shmalts*, literally 'melted fat', from German *Schmalz*.] —**schmaltzy** *adj.*

schmatte /shmáttə/, **shmatte** *n. US* a rag or worthless thing (*informal*) [Late 20thC. Via Yiddish from Polish *szmata* 'rag'.]

Schmeling /shmáyling/, **Max** (*b.* 1905) German boxer, who was holder of the world heavyweight title (1930–32 and 1936–38). After serving in the German army, he retired in 1945 to pursue a business career. Full name **Maximilian Schmeling**

Schmidt /shmit/, **Helmut** (*b.* 1918) German statesman. He was chancellor of West Germany (1974–82), a prominent leader of the European Union, and, from 1983, publisher of *Die Zeit*. Full name **Helmut Heinrich Waldemar Schmidt**

Schmidt camera *n.* = **Schmidt telescope**

Schmidt system *n.* an optical system that uses a special concave spherical mirror to correct optical aberrations [Mid-20thC. Named after Bernhard Voldemar *Schmidt* (1879–1935), an Estonian-born German specialist in optics.]

Schmidt telescope *n.* a wide-angle photographic telescope used in astronomy. It has a special internal mirror to correct optical aberrations. [Mid-20thC (see SCHMIDT SYSTEM)]

Schmitt trigger /shmít-/ *n.* an electronic circuit that produces an output when the input exceeds a predetermined turn-on or threshold level. The output is maintained until the input falls below the threshold level. [Mid-20thC. Named after Otto H. *Schmitt* (b. 1913), US biophysicist and electronics engineer.]

schmo /shmō/ (*plural* **schmoes**), **shmo** (*plural* **shmoes**) *n. US* an offensive term referring to sb regarded as boring, easily deceived, or having otherwise objectionable qualities (*slang insult*) [Mid-20thC. Alteration of SCHMUCK.]

schmooze /shmooz/ *v.* (**schmoozes, schmoozing, schmoozed**) 1. *vi.* CHAT INFORMALLY to chat socially and agreeably (*slang*) 2. *vt.* BE INGRATIATING TOWARDS SB to talk persuasively to sb, often to gain personal advantage ■ *n.* A CHAT an informal chat about trivial matters (*slang*) [Late 19thC. Via Yiddish *schmuesn* 'to talk' from, ultimately, Hebrew *šĕmū'āh* 'rumour'.] —**schmoozer** *n.*

schmuck /shmuk/, **shmuck** *n. US* an offensive term referring to sb who is regarded as being unworthy of respect (*slang insult*) [Late 19thC. From Yiddish *shmok* 'penis', of unknown origin.]

schnapps /shnaps/ (*plural* **schnapps**), **schnaps** (*plural* **schnaps**) *n.* 1. ALCOHOLIC DRINK a strong alcoholic spirit made in Germany and the Netherlands 2. GLASS OF SCHNAPPS a glass or measure of schnapps [Early 19thC. Via German from Low German or Dutch *snaps*, 'mouthful' (of uncertain origin).]

schnauzer /shnówtsər/ *n.* a wiry-coated dog with bushy eyebrows and whiskers that grow like a beard, belonging to any of three breeds that originated in Germany. They are bred in giant, standard, and miniature sizes. [Early 20thC. From German, formed from *Schnauze* 'snout'.]

schnitzel /shníts'l/ *n.* a piece of meat, typically veal, beaten flat and served fried, usually coated in egg and breadcrumbs [Mid-19thC. From German, formed from, ultimately, Old High German *snidan* 'to cut'.]

Schnitzler /shnítslər/, **Arthur** (1862–1931) Austrian doctor, playwright, and novelist. He was a founder of the Young Vienna group (1891). His works, inspired by psychoanalysis and focusing on human relationships, include *Reigen* (1900), later staged and filmed as *La Ronde*.

schnozzle /shnózz'l/, **schnoz** /shnoz/ (*plural* **schnozes**) *n. US* a nose, especially a large one (*slang*) [Mid-20thC. From Yiddish *shnoytsl*, a diminutive of *shnoyts* 'snout', from German *Schnauze*.]

Schoenberg /shúrn burg, shōn bòork/, **Arnold** (1874–1951) Austrian composer. He is known for his revolutionary 12-tone, or serial, system and the discordant works it produced. Full name **Arnold Franz Walter Schoenberg**

schola cantorum /skṓlə kan táwrəm/ (*plural* **scholae cantorum** /skṓlee-/) *n.* a choir, or choir school, housed in a church or cathedral [Late 18thC. From medieval Latin, literally 'school of singers'.]

scholar /skóllər/ *n.* 1. LEARNED PERSON sb who has a great deal of knowledge, especially an academic who specializes in a particular arts subject 2. SCHOLARSHIP STUDENT a student who receives a scholarship 3. PUPIL a school pupil (*formal*) [Pre-12thC. From late Latin *scholaris*, from Latin *schola* (see SCHOOL).]

scholarly /skóllərli/ *adj.* 1. LEARNED with a great deal of knowledge, especially knowledge of an academic subject 2. OF SCHOLARS relating to scholars or to formal study ○ *scholarly journals* 3. ACCORDING TO PRINCIPLES OF FORMAL STUDY in keeping with a rigorous and systematic approach to acquiring knowledge or to setting out the results of formal study —**scholarliness** *n.*

scholarship /skóllər ship/ *n.* 1. FINANCIAL HELP FOR A STUDENT a sum of money awarded to a student on the basis of academic merit, to help with living expenses, study, or travel 2. FORMAL STUDY academic learning or achievement 3. ACADEMIC WORKS a body of learning on an academic subject ○ *a review of German scholarship on the topic*

scholastic /skə lástik/ *adj.* 1. OF SCHOOLS OR STUDYING relating to students, schools, or studying 2. PEDANTIC too concerned with details or fine distinctions and too ready to criticize minor errors 3. HIST OF SCHOLASTICISM relating to the medieval movement of religious and philosophical learning known as scholasticism ■ *n.* 1. HIST STUDENT OR TEACHER UNDER SCHOLASTICISM a student or teacher in the medieval intellectual movement known as scholasticism 2. PEDANT sb who is quibbling or pedantic 3. CHR SB UNDERGOING ROMAN CATHOLIC SCHOLASTICATE sb who is undergoing a scholasticate at a Roman Catholic seminary [Late 16thC. Via Latin *scholasticus* from Greek *skholastikos* 'learned', from, ultimately, *skholē* (see SCHOOL).] —**scholastically** *adv.*

scholasticate /skə lástikət/ *n.* 1. PERIOD OF STUDY AT A SEMINARY a probationary period of study for a Jesuit student at a Roman Catholic seminary 2. JESUIT SEMINARY a seminary where a scholasticate is undertaken

scholasticism /skə lástissizəm/ *n.* 1. HIST MEDIEVAL THEOLOGY AND PHILOSOPHY a medieval theological and philosophical system of learning based on the authority of St Augustine and other leaders of the early Christian Church, and on the works of Aristotle. It sought to bridge the gap between religion and reason. 2. TRADITIONAL LEARNING narrowly traditional learning, or adherence to traditional educational methods

scholia plural of **scholium**

scholiast /skṓli ast/ *n.* a medieval scholar who wrote commentaries on ancient Greek and Latin texts [Late 16thC. From medieval Greek *skholiastēs*, from, ultimately, *skholion* (see SCHOLIUM).] —**scholiastic** /skṓli ástik/ *adj.*

scholium /skṓli əm/ (*plural* **-a** /-li ə/) *n.* a medieval annotation or commentary written on an ancient Greek or Latin text [Mid-16thC. From Greek *skholion* 'interpretation', from *skholē* (see SCHOOL).]

school[1] /skool/ *n.* 1. EDUC BUILDING FOR TEACHING CHILDREN a building or institution in which children and teenagers are taught, usually up to the age of 16 or 18 (*often used before a noun*) 2. *US* UNIV COLLEGE OR UNIVERSITY any college or university 3. UNIV DEPARTMENT SPECIALIZING IN AN ACADEMIC SUBJECT a faculty, department, or institution that offers specialized instruction in an academic subject ○ *medical school* 4. INSTITUTION TEACHING A NONACADEMIC SKILL an institution that specializes in teaching a specific skill, especially a practical or sports skill ○ *tennis school* 5. STAFF AND STUDENTS all the staff and students of an educational institution (*often used before a noun*) 6. DAY AT SCHOOL the part of a day spent teaching or being taught in a school ○ *School was over for another day.* 7. YEARS SPENT AT SCHOOL the part of sb's life spent being taught in a school ○ *After school, he went abroad for two years.* 8. INSTRUCTIVE PLACE OR PERIOD any place or period of activity regarded as providing knowledge or experience ○ *the school of life* 9. ARTISTS OR WRITERS SHARING SAME APPROACH a group of people, especially artists, writers, or philosophers, who share the same principles, methods, ideals, or style ○ *the Impressionist school* ○ *the Aristotelian school* ■ *vt.* (**schools, schooling, schooled**) 1. INSTRUCT SB to train or instruct sb in a specific skill ○ *schooled in the art of debate* 2. EDUCATE SB IN SCHOOL to educate a child or teenager formally in a school 3. DISCIPLINE SB to exert control or discipline over sb or yourself 4. EQU TRAIN A HORSE to train a horse, especially for riding and dressage [Pre-12thC. Via Latin *schola* from Greek *skholē* 'leisure, learned discussion, school'. Ultimately from an Indo-European base meaning 'to hold', which is also the ancestor of English *epoch*.]

WORD KEY: SYNONYMS

See Synonyms at ***teach***.

school[2] /skool/ *n.* SHOAL OF AQUATIC ANIMALS a group of fish, whales, porpoises, or other aquatic animals of a single type ■ *vi.* (**schools, schooling, schooled**) FORM OR SWIM IN A SCHOOL to congregate in a school or swim in a school [14thC. From Middle Dutch *schole*, from prehistoric West Germanic, perhaps from a base meaning 'to divide' (ancestor also of English *scale*[2]), in which case the underlying meaning is 'division'.]

school age *n.* the age at which a child is required legally to attend school —**school-age** *adj.*

school board *n.* in Britain, between 1870 and 1902, an elected committee that supervised local elementary schools

schoolboy /skóol boy/ *n.* YOUNG MALE SCHOOL PUPIL a boy who attends school ■ *adj.* IMMATURE at a level of maturity typical of, or designed to appeal to, male children of school age ○ *schoolboy humour*

school bus *n.* a large motor vehicle that takes children to and from school or on school-related trips

school captain *n. Aus, Scotland* a boy or girl appointed or elected to be the senior representative of a school's pupils

School Certificate *n.* in New Zealand, and from 1917 to 1951 in England and Wales, a certificate awarded to students who pass or passed a public examination

schoolchild /skóol chīld/ (*plural* **-children** /-childrən/) *n.* a child who attends school

school crossing patrol *n.* sb employed to stop traffic to allow schoolchildren to cross a road (*formal*) ◊ **lollipop man, lollipop lady**

school day *n.* any day on which school is conducted, or the hours of instruction in that day ◇ **school days** the period of time in sb's life spent attending school

schoolfellow /skóol fellō/ *n.* a schoolmate (*dated*)

school figure *n.* any one of a number of basic movements in figure-skating that are performed in competition (*often used in the plural*)

schoolgirl /skóol gurl/ *n.* a girl who attends school

schoolhouse /skóol howss/ (*plural* **-houses** /-howziz/) *n.* 1. BUILDING USED AS A SCHOOL a building that houses a school, especially a rural primary school 2. TEACHER'S HOUSE ATTACHED TO A SCHOOL a house attached to a school where a teacher lives, often the head teacher

schoolies week /skóoleez week/ *n. Aus* the week after the final-year school examinations, when school pupils traditionally congregate in holiday resorts to celebrate leaving school (*informal*)

schooling /skóoling/ *n.* 1. EDUC EDUCATION AT SCHOOL the education or instruction that is acquired at school 2. INSTRUCTION instruction or training in anything, carried out systematically and in a disciplined way 3. EQU TRAINING OF A HORSE the training of a horse, especially for riding and dressage

school inspector *n.* an official appointed by the government to check on the standards of education in state-funded schools

schoolkid /skool kid/ *n.* a child or teenager who attends school (*informal*)

school-leaver *n.* a pupil who has left school or is about to do so, especially one who leaves at the minimum age and does not go on to further or higher education

Schoolman /skoolman/ (*plural* **-men**) *n.* sb who taught or studied as part of the medieval intellectual movement known as a scholasticism

schoolmarm /skool maarm/ *n.* **1.** OFFENSIVE TERM an offensive term for a woman schoolteacher, especially one considered too proper and old-fashioned (*dated insult*) **2.** OFFENSIVE TERM an offensive term for a woman thought to live in a way regarded as old-fashioned (*informal insult*) —**schoolmarmish** *adj.*

schoolmaster /skool maastər/ *n.* (*plural* **-ters** *or* **-ter**) ZOOL TROPICAL FOOD FISH a Caribbean and tropical Atlantic food fish with yellow fins. It belongs to the snapper family. Latin name: *Lutjanus apodus.* ▪ *vi.* (**-ters, -tering, -tered**) BE A SCHOOLMASTER to be a schoolmaster by profession (*dated*) —**schoolmasterish** *adj.* —**schoolmasterly** *adj.* —**schoolmastership** *n.*

schoolmate /skool mayt/ *n.* a friend or companion at school

school milk *n.* a third of a pint of milk formerly provided free to British schoolchildren

schoolmistress /skool mistrəss/ *n.* a woman schoolteacher, especially in a private school —**schoolmistressy** *adj.*

school of arts *n. Aus* a building used for adult education classes in a rural town

school of hard knocks *n.* difficult or challenging experiences that are considered to be instructive

School of the Air *n. Aus* an education service provided for children living in remote parts of Australia. Lessons are carried out by radio as well as through video, tape, fax, and computer networks.

school of thought *n.* a way of thinking about sth, or a group of people who share the same attitude or opinion

school psychologist *n.* a psychologist who visits a group of schools to give teachers and parents advice on the psychological and developmental problems of individual schoolchildren

schoolroom /skool room, -room/ *n.* a classroom in a school

Schools /skoolz/ *npl.* MEDIEVAL UNIVERSITIES OR SCHOLASTICS the universities of medieval Europe, or the scholastics who taught in them ▪ *n.* (*takes a singular or plural verb*) **1.** OXFORD UNIVERSITY EXAMINATIONS BUILDING at Oxford University, the university building in which examinations are held **2.** OXFORD UNIVERSITY FINAL EXAMINATIONS at Oxford University, the final examinations for the degree of BA that are held in the Examination Schools [Old English]

schoolteacher /skool teechər/ *n.* sb who teaches in a school —**schoolteaching** *n.*

schoolwork /skool wurk/ *n.* the work that a pupil does in or after school

schoolyard /skool yaard/ *n. US* = **playground**

school year *n.* **1.** TWELVE-MONTH EDUCATIONAL PERIOD a period of twelve months, beginning usually in late August or early September, throughout which pupils are assigned to the same class **2.** PERIOD WHEN SCHOOLS ARE OPEN the months during which instruction is given at a school

schooner /skoonər/ *n.* **1.** SAILING SAILING VESSEL a fast sailing ship with at least two masts and with sails set lengthways (**fore and aft**) **2.** SHERRY GLASS a large glass for sherry **3.** *US, Aus* BEER GLASS a tall slim glass for beer **4.** HIST = **prairie schooner** [Early 18thC. Origin unknown.]

schooner rig *n.* an arrangement of masts and sails (**rig**) in which the mainmast is taller than the foremast —**schooner-rigged** *adj.*

Schopenhauer /shópən hówər/, **Arthur** (1788–1860) German philosopher. His atheistic, deeply pes-

Schooner

simistic philosophy was most fully expounded in *The World as Will and Idea* (1819).

schorl /shawrl/ *n.* a black opaque form of the mineral tourmaline, often occurring in needle-shaped radiating crystals [Late 18thC. From German *Schörl*, of unknown origin.] —**schorlaceous** /shawr láyshəss/ *adj.*

schottische /sho teesh/ *n.* **1.** GERMAN FOLK DANCE a round dance of German origin, resembling a slow polka **2.** MUSIC FOR A SCHOTTISCHE a piece of music for a schottische [Mid-19thC. From German (*der*) *Schottische(tanz)*, literally 'the Scottish dance'.]

Schottky effect /shótki-/ *n.* a reduction in the energy needed to remove an electron from a solid surface caused by the application of an electric field [Mid-20thC. Named after Walter *Schottky* (1886–1976), the German physicist who described the phenomenon.]

Schrödinger /shrúrdingər, shród-, shrôd-/, **Erwin** (1887–1961) Austrian physicist. His mathematical analysis of the wave mechanics of orbiting electrons made a major contribution to quantum theory. He shared the Nobel Prize in physics (1933).

schtick *n.* = **shtick**

Franz Schubert

Schubert /shoobərt/, **Franz** (1797–1828) Austrian composer. He is particularly noted for his songs and chamber works, although he also wrote choral and orchestral music. Full name **Franz Peter Schubert**

schul *n.* = **shul**

Schultz /shoolts/, **Charles** (*b.* 1922) US cartoonist. He created the successful *Peanuts* comic strip (1950), featuring Snoopy and Charlie Brown. Full name **Charles Monroe Schultz**

Schumacher /shoo makər/, **E.F.** (1911–77) German-born British economist and conservationist. He was the author of *Small is Beautiful* (1973), and an advocate of intermediate technology and the preservation of natural resources. Full name **Ernst Friederich Schumacher**

Schumacher, Michael (*b.* 1969) German racing driver. He was Formula One world champion (1994 and 1995) and winner of the British Grand Prix (1998).

Schumann /shoomən/, **Robert** (1810–56) German composer. He was a major exponent of the romantic style, noted for his songs, piano music, and orchestral and chamber works. Full name **Robert Alexander Schumann**

schuss /shooss/ *vi.* (**schusses, schussing, schussed**) SKI DOWNHILL to ski straight downhill at high speed ▪ *n.* DOWNHILL RUN IN SKIING a straight fast downhill run on skis [Mid-20thC. From German *Schuß* 'shot'.]

schussboomer /shooss boomər/ *n.* a skier adept at making fast straight downhill runs (*informal*)

schwa /shwaa/, **shwa** *n.* an unstressed vowel, e.g. 'a' in 'above' or 'e' in 'sicken'. It is represented in the International Phonetic Alphabet by the symbol ə. [Late 19thC. Via German from Hebrew *šĕwā*, of uncertain origin: probably an alteration of *šēwā* 'emptiness'.]

Schwann cell /shwon-, shván-/ *n.* a cell of the peripheral nervous system that wraps around a nerve fibre and forms the myelin sheath [Early 20thC. Named after Theodor *Schwann* (1810–82), the German physiologist and histologist who described the structure.]

Schwarzenegger /shvaártsə negər, swáwrtsə-/, **Arnold** (*b.* 1947) Austrian-born US body builder and film actor. He has appeared in action films such as *The Terminator* (1984).

Schwarzkopf /shvaárts kopf, swáwrts kopf/, **Dame Elisabeth** (*b.* 1915) German soprano. She was noted for her operatic roles, especially in operas by Mozart and Richard Strauss, and for her interpretation of *lieder*. Full name **Olga Maria Elisabeth Friederike Schwarzkopf**

Schwarzschild radius /shwáwrts shild-/ *n.* the critical radius within which the gravitational force of a gravitationally collapsing celestial body becomes so great that neither matter nor energy can escape, creating a black hole [Mid-20thC. Named after the German astronomer Karl *Schwarzschild* (1873–1916).]

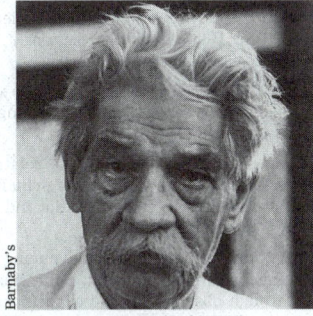
Albert Schweitzer

Schweitzer /shwítsər/, **Albert** (1875–1965) German-born theologian, musicologist, and missionary. He wrote important works on J.S. Bach and New Testament theology before setting up a hospital in 1913 at Lambáréné, in present-day Gabon, where he spent most of the rest of his life. He was awarded a Nobel Peace Prize (1952).

Schwitters /shvíttərz/, **Kurt** (1887–1948) German artist, who was noted for his collages, in which ephemera are a prominent element, and his sculpture composed from junk.

sci *abbr.* PRINTING single column inch

sci. *abbr.* **1.** science **2.** scientific

sciaenid /sī eénid/ *n.* a carnivorous tropical or subtropical fish that produces loud sounds by snapping muscles attached to its air bladder. Croakers, drums, and grunts are all members of the family. Family: Sciaenidae. [Early 20thC. Via modern Latin *Sciaenidae* from *Sciaena*, name of the genus, from Greek *skiaina*, a kind of fish.] —**sciaenid** *adj.*

sciamachy /sī ámməki/ (*plural* **-chies**), **skiamachy** (*plural* **-chies**) *n.* (*literary*) **1.** SHADOW-BOXING practice fighting with a shadow or with an imaginary opponent **2.** FUTILE FIGHTING fighting with an imagined foe or against a foe who cannot be defeated, or an instance of this [Early 17thC. From Greek *skiamakhia*, literally 'shadow fight', from *makhia* 'fight'.]

sciatic /sī áttik/ *adj.* **1.** OF THE HIP OR SCIATIC NERVE relating to or affecting the back of the hip or the sciatic nerve **2.** OF SCIATICA causing sciatica or caused by sciatica [Early 16thC. Via French *sciatique* from, ultimately, Greek *iskhion* 'hip joint'.]

sciatica /sī áttikə/ *n.* pain and tenderness extending from the back of the hip down to the calf, usually caused by a protrusion of vertebral disc substance pressing on the roots of the sciatic nerve [15thC. From medieval Latin, the feminine of *sciaticus* (see SCIATIC).]

sciatic nerve *n.* either of two nerves that run from the back of the hip down the thigh to the calf

SCID *abbr.* severe combined immunodeficiency

science /síˈənss/ *n.* **1.** STUDY OF THE PHYSICAL WORLD the study of the physical world and its manifestations, especially by using systematic observation and experiment (*often used before a noun*) **2.** BRANCH OF SCIENCE a branch of science of a particular area of study ○ *the life sciences* **3.** KNOWLEDGE GAINED FROM SCIENCE the knowledge gained by the study of the physical world **4.** SYSTEMATIC BODY OF KNOWLEDGE any systematically organized body of knowledge about a specific subject ○ *the social sciences* **5.** STH STUDIED OR PERFORMED METHODICALLY any activity that is the object of careful study or that is carried out according to a developed method ○ *treated me to a lecture on the science of dressing for success* [14thC. Via Old French from Latin *scientia*, from *scient-*, present participle stem of *scire* 'to know', ultimately 'to discern', from an Indo-European word meaning 'to cut'.] ◇ **blind sb with science** to confuse or overwhelm sb by giving an impenetrable explanation using technical terms and concepts

science fiction *n.* a form of fiction, usually set in the future, that deals with imaginary scientific and technological developments and contact with other worlds (*often used before a noun*)

science park *n.* an area, usually associated with a university, where scientific research is carried out by commercial companies

scienter /sī éntər/ *adv.* LAW with full knowledge or awareness [Early 19thC. From Latin, 'knowingly', formed from the stem *scient-* (see SCIENCE).]

sciential /sī énsh'l/ *adj.* **1.** OF SCIENCE relating to science or knowledge **2.** KNOWLEDGEABLE possessing considerable knowledge or skill (*formal*)

scientific /sī ən tíffik/ *adj.* **1.** OF SCIENCE relating to, using, or conforming to science or its principles **2.** METHODICAL proceeding in a systematic and methodical way —**scientifically** *adv.*

scientific method *n.* the system of advancing knowledge by formulating a question, collecting data about it through observation and experiment, and testing a hypothetical answer

scientific notation *n.* a way of expressing a given number as a number between 1 and 10 multiplied by 10 to the appropriate power. 5,743.6 expressed in scientific notation is 5.7436×10^3.

scientific revolution *n.* the period of advances in science that was at its height in the 17th century and produced widespread change in traditional beliefs held since the Middle Ages

scientism /sī əntizəm/ *n.* **1.** USE OF THE SCIENTIFIC METHOD the use of the scientific method of acquiring knowledge, whether in the traditional sciences or in other fields of inquiry **2.** RELIANCE ON SCIENCE FOR ANSWERS the belief that science alone can explain phenomena, or the application of scientific methods to fields unsuitable for it (*disapproving*) ○ *'We feel that the attitude that predominates in science at present is arrogance, which has fostered dogmatism and scientism'.* (Brian D. Josephson, Beverly A. Rubik, *The Challenge of Consciousness Research*; 1992) —**scientistic** /sī ən tístik/ *adj.*

scientist /sī əntist/ *n.* sb who has had a scientific training or who works in one of the sciences ○ *a social scientist*

Scientist /sī əntist/ *n.* CHR **1.** JESUS CHRIST in Christian Science belief, Jesus Christ as the paramount spiritual healer **2.** CHRISTIAN SCIENTIST a Christian Scientist

sci-fi /sī fí/ *n.* science fiction (*informal*) [Shortening of SCIENCE FICTION]

scilicet /síli set, síli-, sílə-, skeéli ket/ *adv.* used to introduce a word or phrase of clarification, or a missing word or phrase [14thC. From Latin, a contraction of *scire licet*, literally 'it is permitted to know'.]

scilla /sílə/ (*plural* -**las** *or* -**la**) *n.* a plant of the lily family with flowers shaped like small bells. It is native to Europe and Asia. Genus: *Scilla*. [Early 19thC. Via Latin from Greek *skilla* 'squill'.]

Scilly Isles /síli-/ group of about 150 islands, only four of which are inhabited, in the Atlantic Ocean off the western coast of Cornwall, England. Population: 2,000 (1994). Area: 16 sq. km/6 sq. mi.

Scimitar

scimitar /símmitər, -taar/, **simitar** *n.* an Arab or Turkish sword with a curved blade that broadens out as it nears the point [Mid-16thC. From French *cimeterre* or Italian *scimitarra*, of uncertain origin: perhaps from Persian *šimšir*.]

scindapsus /skin dápsəss/ (*plural* -**suses** *or* -**sus**) *n.* a climbing plant that has heart-shaped, often variegated leaves and is popular as a house plant. It is native to Asia. Genus: *Scindapsus*. [Mid-20thC. Via modern Latin *Scindapsus*, name of the genus, from Greek *skindapsos*, an ivy-like plant.]

scintigram /sínti gram/ *n.* a two-dimensional image of the distribution of a radioactive tracer in a body organ such as the brain or a kidney, obtained using a special scanner (**scintiscanner**) [Mid-20thC. Coined from SCINTILLATION + -GRAM.]

scintilla /sin tíllə/ *n.* a tiny amount of sth ○ *There's not a scintilla of truth in what he said.* [Late 17thC. From Latin, 'spark'.]

scintillate /sínti layt/ (-**lates**, -**lating**, -**lated**) *v.* **1.** *vi.* SPARKLE to give off or reflect light in sparks or flashes **2.** *vi.* BE VERY DAZZLINGLY CLEVER to be dazzlingly lively, clever, or witty **3.** *vt.* PHYS EMIT LIGHT FLASHES to produce sparks of light when hit by particles or photons [Early 17thC. Formed from Latin *scintillat-*, past participle stem of *scintillare*, from *scintilla* 'spark'.] —**scintillant** *adj.* —**scintillantly** *adv.*

scintillating /sínti layting/ *adj.* possessing or displaying dazzling liveliness, cleverness, or wit —**scintillatingly** *adv.*

scintillation /sínti láysh'n/ *n.* **1.** ASTRON TWINKLING OF STARS the twinkling of stars, caused by refraction of light rays from the stars because of different densities in the Earth's atmosphere **2.** PHYS FLASH OF LIGHT a flash of light caused by the impact of particles or photons **3.** LIVELINESS dazzling liveliness, cleverness, or wit (*literary*)

scintillation counter *n.* a device that detects and measures high-energy radiation through flashes of light produced when ionizing radiation impacts on a phosphorescent substance

scintillator /sínti laytər/ *n.* a phosphorescent substance that produces flashes of light when struck by particles or photons

scintiscan /sínti skan/ *n.* MED = scintigram [Mid-20thC. Coined from SCINTILLATION + SCAN.]

scintiscanner /sínti skanər/ *n.* an apparatus used in diagnosing certain diseases that produces an image (**scintigram**) of the distribution in the body of a radioactive tracer that has been administered to the patient

sciolism /sī əlizəm/ *n.* displays of sham learning designed to deceive or impress [Early 19thC. From late Latin *sciolus*, a diminutive of *scius* 'having knowledge', from *scire* (see SCIENCE).] —**sciolist** *n.* —**sciolistic** /sī ə lísstik/ *adj.*

scion /sī ən/ *n.* **1.** BOT PART OF A PLANT FOR GRAFTING a living shoot or twig of a plant used for grafting to a stock **2.** YOUNGER MEMBER OF A FAMILY a child or descendant of a family, especially a rich, famous, or important family [13thC. From Old French *ciun*, of unknown origin.]

sciophyte /sī ə fít/ *n.* a plant that prefers shady conditions [Early 20thC. Coined from Greek *skia* 'shadow' + -PHYTE.] —**sciophytic** /sī ə fíttik/ *adj.*

Scipio /skíppi ō, síppi ō/, **Publius Cornelius** (*d.* 211 BC) Roman general. He was the father of Scipio Africanus the Elder. Although he failed to defeat the Carthaginians in northern Italy and Spain, he helped to check their advances on Rome.

Scipio Africanus (the Elder) /-áffri kaˈanəss/ (234?–183 BC) Roman general. He was the grandfather by adoption of Scipio Africanus the Younger. His defeat of Hannibal in 202 BC ended the Second Punic War. Full name **Publius Cornelius Scipio**

Scipio Africanus (the Younger) (185?–129 BC) Roman general. He was the grandson by adoption of Scipio Africanus the Elder. A successful military commander, he destroyed Carthage to end the Third Punic War (146 BC). As a government official in Rome, he opposed the populist Gracchi brothers. Full name **Publius Cornelius Scipio Aemilianus**

scire facias /síri fáyshi ass/ *n.* LAW the judicial proceeding that produces a writ of scire facias [15thC. From Latin, literally 'you should cause (him) to know'.]

scirocco *n.* = sirocco

scirrhous /sírrəss, skírrəss/ *adj.* used to describe a cancerous tumour (**carcinoma**) that is hard and fibrous [Mid-16thC. Via French from modern Latin *scirrhosus*, ultimately via Latin from Greek *skirros* 'hard coat or covering'.] —**scirrhosity** /si róssəti, ski-/ *n.*

scissel /skíss'l/ *n.* metal clippings left over after discs, especially coins, have been punched out of sheets of metal [Early 17thC. From French *cisaille*, from *cisailler* 'to clip with shears'.]

scissile /síss'l/ *adj.* capable of being easily and smoothly cut, separated, or divided [Early 17thC. From Latin *scissilis*, from the stem *sciss-* (see SCISSION).]

scission /sízh'n, sísh'n/ *n.* the act or process of cutting, separating, or dividing [15thC. Via French or directly from the Latin stem *scission-*, from *sciss-*, past participle stem of *scindere* 'to cut'.]

scissor /sízzər/ (-**sors**, -**soring**, -**sored**) *vti.* **1.** CUT WITH SCISSORS to use scissors to cut sth **2.** MAKE A MOVEMENT LIKE SCISSORS to move the legs, arms, or body in the way that the blades of a pair of scissors open and shut ○ *The swimmer scissored through the water.* [Early 17thC. From the singular of SCISSORS.]

scissors /sízzərz/ *npl.* INSTRUMENT FOR CUTTING STH a hand-held cutting instrument made up of two crossed connected blades, each with a ring-shaped handle, that cut as they slide and pivot ■ *n.* (*plural* -**sors**) **1.** GYMNASTICS GYMNASTICS MOVEMENT in gymnastics, a movement of the legs that resembles the opening and closing of scissors **2.** SPORTS TECHNIQUE IN HIGH-JUMPING in the high jump, a simple technique of clearing the bar sideways on with each leg separately in a fast scissors movement. This technique is now rarely used. **3.** WRESTLING = scissors hold [14thC. Via French *cisoires* from the plural of late Latin *cisorium* 'cutting tool', from Latin *caedere* 'to cut' (source of English *concise* and *decide*).]

scissors-and-paste *adj.* crudely or hastily put together

scissors hold *n.* a wrestling hold in which the legs are wrapped and the feet locked around an opponent's head or body

scissors kick *n.* **1.** SWIMMING SWIMMING MOVEMENT in swimming, a kicking motion that resembles the opening and closing of scissors, used especially when doing the sidestroke **2.** SOCCER SOCCER KICK in soccer, a mid-air kick of the ball with the legs moving in a way that resembles the movement of scissor blades

scissortail /sízzər tayl/ (*plural* -**tails** *or* -**tail**) *n.* any bird with a long forked tail, especially a scissor-tailed flycatcher

scissure /sízhər, síshər/ *n.* a long slit, especially one running lengthways (*archaic*) [14thC. Via French or directly from Latin *scissura*, from the stem *sciss-* (see SCISSION).]

sciurine /sī yoorīn/, **sciurid** /sī yoorid/ *n.* RODENT OF THE SQUIRREL FAMILY any rodent belonging to the family that includes squirrels, marmots, and chipmunks. Family: Sciuridae. ■ *adj.* OF THE SQUIRREL FAMILY relating to or belonging to the squirrel family of rodents [Mid-19thC. Formed from Latin *sciurus* (see SQUIRREL).]

sclaff /sklaf/ *vti.* (**sclaffs, sclaffing, sclaffed**) HIT THE GROUND WITH A GOLF CLUB in golf, to play a faulty stroke in which the clubhead scrapes the ground before coming into contact with the ball ■ *n.* FAULTY GOLF STROKE a golf stroke that is sclaffed [Early 19thC. Origin uncertain: probably an imitation of the sound produced when a club strikes the ground.] —**sclaffer** *n.*

scler- *prefix.* = **sclero-** (*used before vowels*)

sclera /skléerə/ *n.* the dense outer coating of the eyeball that forms the white of the eye [Late 19thC. Via modern Latin from Greek *sklēros* 'hard'.]

sclereid /skléerid/ *n.* any of a group of mainly short thick-walled plant cells that help to make up a plant's supporting tissue (**sclerenchyma**) [Late 19thC. Coined from Greek *sklēros* 'hard' + -ID.]

sclerenchyma /skleer éngkimə/ *n.* strengthening or supporting walls of plant tissue made up of long cells or fibres and short cells (**sclereids**) [Mid-19thC. Formed from SCLERO- on the model of *parenchyma*.] —**sclerenchymatous** /skleer eng kímmətəss/ *adj.*

scleriasis /skleer ī əssiss/ *n.* = **scleroderma**

sclerite /skléer īt/ *n.* a hard plate or layer of chitin or calcium on the outer skeleton of an arthropod —**scleritic** /skleer íttik/ *adj.*

scleritis /skleer ītiss/ *n.* inflammation of the tough outer coat of the eyeball that forms the white of the eye (**sclera**) [Mid-19thC. Formed from SCLERA.]

sclero- *prefix.* **1.** hard ○ *scleroderma* **2.** hardness ○ *sclerometer* **3.** sclera ○ *scleritis* [From Greek *sklēros* 'hard'. Ultimately from an Indo-European base meaning 'dried up, withered', which is also the ancestor of English *skeleton*.]

scleroderma /skléerō dúrmə/ *n.* a disease in which the skin becomes progressively hard and thickened

sclerodermatous /skléerō dúrmətəss/ *adj.* **1.** BIOL SCALY with a hard external covering of scales or plates **2.** MED OF SCLERODERMA relating to or characteristic of the skin disease scleroderma

sclerodermia /skléerō dúrmi ə/ *n.* = **scleroderma**

scleroid /skléeroyd/ *adj.* used to describe tissues or body parts that have become harder than is normal

sclerometer /sklə rómmətər, skli-, skleer rómmitər/ *n.* an instrument that determines the hardness of a metal or mineral by measuring the force required to scratch or pierce it —**sclerometric** /sklérrə méttrik, skléerō-/ *adj.*

sclerophyll /skléerəfil, sklérrəfil/ *n.* any woody plant of arid areas with thick leathery evergreen foliage that retains water —**sclerophyllous** /sklə róffiləss, skleer-/ *adj.*

scleroprotein /skléerō prṓ teen, sklerrō-/ *n.* any one of a group of fibrous insoluble proteins, such as keratin, elastin, and collagen that are found in body tissue

sclerosed /sklə rṓst, skleer-/ *adj.* used to describe tissues and body parts that have become harder and thicker than normal [Late 19thC. Formed from SCLEROSIS.]

sclerosis /sklə rṓssiss, skli-, skleer-/ (*plural* **-ses**) *n.* **1.** MED HARDENING OF BODY TISSUE the hardening and thickening of body tissue as a result of unwarranted growth, degeneration of nerve fibres, or deposition of minerals, especially calcium **2.** BOT HARDENING OF PLANT CELL WALL the hardening and thickening of a plant cell wall that occurs as lignin is deposited, turning young green growth woody —**sclerosal** *adj.*

sclerotia plural of **sclerotium**

sclerotic /sklə róttik, skleer-/ *adj.* **1.** BOT OF PLANT CELL WALL HARDENING relating to the hardening and thickening of plant cell walls that turns young green growth woody **2.** BIOL OF THE WHITE OF THE EYE relating to the dense outer coating of the eyeball that forms the white of the eye (**sclera**) **3.** MED OF SCLEROSIS OF BODY TISSUE relating to or suffering from sclerosis of body tissue **4.** INFLEXIBLE having become unresponsively rigid, especially from longevity ○ *a political party grown sclerotic from too many years in power* ■ *n.* BIOL = **sclera** [Mid-16thC. From modern Latin *sclerotica*, ultimately from Greek *sklēros* 'hard'; or formed from SCLERA.]

sclerotin /skléerōtin, sklérrō-/ *n.* an insoluble protein that hardens and darkens the chitin on the outer skeleton of arthropods [Mid-20thC. Formed from SCLERO- on the model of words such as *keratin*.]

sclerotise *vt.* = **sclerotize**

sclerotium /sklə rṓti əm/ (*plural* **-a** /-ti ə/) *n.* in fungi, a compact hard mass that contains stored food [Mid-19thC. From modern Latin, originally the name of a genus of fungi, formed from Greek *sklērotēs* 'hardness', from *sklēros* (see SCLERA).] —**sclerotial** *adj.* —**sclerotioid** *adj.*

sclerotize /skléerō tīz, sklérrō-/ (**-tizes, -tizing, -tized**), **sclerotise** (**-tises, -tising, -tised**) *vt.* to harden and darken an arthropod's outer skeleton [Mid-20thC. Ultimately from SCLEROTIC.] —**sclerotization** /skléerō tī záysh'n, sklérrō tī-/ *n.*

sclerotomy /sklə róttəmi, skleer-/ (*plural* **-mies**) *n.* a surgical operation in which the outer coat (**sclera**) of the eyeball is cut, e.g. in order to remove an underlying tumour

sclerous /skléerəss, sklérrəss/ *adj.* **1.** ZOOL HARD used to describe animal parts that are bony or scaly **2.** MED HARDENED used to describe body tissue or body parts that have become especially hardened, as a result of the deposition of minerals

SCM *abbr.* **1.** State Certified Midwife **2.** Student Christian Movement

scoff[1] /skof/ *vi.* (**scoffs, scoffing, scoffed**) BE DERISIVE OR SCORNFUL to express derision or scorn about sb or sth ○ *She scoffed at all our suggestions.* ■ *n.* **1.** EXPRESSION OF SCORN an expression of derision or scorn **2.** OBJECT OF SCORN sb or sth that is derided or scorned [14thC. Origin uncertain: probably from Scandinavian.] —**scoffer** *n.* —**scoffing** *adj.* —**scoffingly** *adv.*

scoff[2] /skof/ *vti.* (**scoffs, scoffing, scoffed**) EAT HUNGRILY to eat food quickly and hungrily or greedily (*informal*) ■ *n.* FOOD food (*slang*) [Late 18thC. Variant of dialect *scaff*, of unknown origin.]

Scofield /skṓ feeld/, **Sir Paul** (*b.* 1922) British actor. He won an Academy Award for *A Man for All Seasons* (1966) and is known for his versatility in numerous stage and screen roles, from Shakespeare to contemporary drama. Full name **Sir David Paul Scofield**

scold /skōld/ *v.* (**scolds, scolding, scolded**) **1.** *vt.* TELL SB OFF to rebuke sb angrily **2.** *vi.* SPEAK HARSHLY to use harsh language, especially when complaining or finding fault ■ *n.* **1.** REBUKING PERSON sb who is constantly rebuking others **2.** OFFENSIVE TERM an offensive term for a woman who is said to make a habit of using abusive language, especially when she is constantly reminding a man to do sth (*archaic*) [13thC. Origin uncertain: probably from Old Norse *skáld* 'poet', from the poet's role of satirizing or poking fun at people.] —**scolder** *n.* —**scoldingly** *adv.*

scolecite /skólli sīt, skṓli sīt/ *n.* a white zeolite mineral consisting of hydrated calcium aluminium silicate and found in both crystalline and massive forms [Early 19thC. Formed from Greek *skōlēk-*, stem of *skōlēx* 'worm'.]

scolex /skṓ leks/ (*plural* **-leces** /-li seez/ *or* **-lices**) *n.* the head of a tapeworm, with suckers or hooks that enable the parasitic worm to attach itself to its host [Mid-19thC. Via modern Latin from Greek *skōlēx* 'worm'.]

scoliosis /skṓli ṓssiss/ *n.* an excessive, sideways curvature of the spine. ◊ **kyphosis, lordosis** [Early 18thC. Via modern Latin from Greek *skoliōsis*, from *skolios* 'bent, curved'.] —**scoliotic** /-óttik/ *adj.*

scollop *n.* = **scallop**

sconce[1] /skonss/ *n.* a wall bracket for holding candles or, sometimes, electric light bulbs [14thC. From Old French *esconse* 'hiding place, lantern', or from medieval Latin *absconsa laterna* 'dark lantern', from *abscondere* (see ABSCOND).]

sconce[2] /skonss/ *vt.* (**sconces, sconcing, sconced**) MAKE SB DRINK BEER AS FORFEIT at Oxford or Cambridge universities, to demand that another student drink a large quantity of beer in one go as a punishment for a social faux pas ■ *n.* **1.** DRINKING VESSEL a drinking vessel used in sconcing **2.** SCONCING an act of sconcing [Early 17thC. Originally 'to fine as punishment', of uncertain origin: perhaps from SCONCE[4], associated with 'to have a head', 'to run up a bill'.]

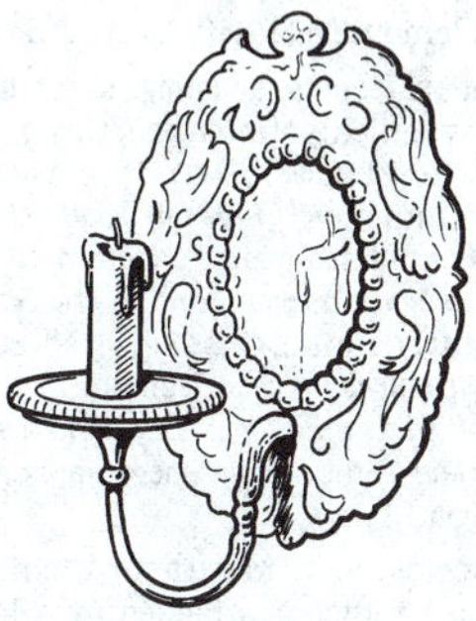

Sconce

sconce[3] /skonss/ *n.* MIL a small defensive fort or earthwork [Late 16thC. From Dutch *schans* 'brushwood, earthwork', of unknown origin.]

sconce[4] /skonss/ *n.* (*archaic*) **1.** HEAD OR SKULL the head or skull of a human being **2.** INTELLIGENCE wit or brains [Mid-16thC. Origin uncertain: perhaps a humorous use of SCONCE[1].]

scone /skon, skōn/ *n.* **1.** SWEET OR SAVOURY UNYEASTED CAKE an individual baked product similar to a sweet or savoury unyeasted cake, usually served split and buttered. Plain scones are served with jam and clotted cream as part of the traditional British cream tea. **2.** *ANZ* HEAD the human head (*informal humorous*) [Early 16thC. Origin uncertain: perhaps from Middle Dutch *schoonbroot* 'fine bread'.]

Scone /skoon/ village in central Scotland, near the River Tay. It is famous for the Stone of Destiny on which Scottish kings were crowned, which was originally located there.

scoop /skoop/ *n.* **1.** SHOVEL a utensil with a short handle and deep rounded sides, used for shovelling or ladling grain, flour, or other dry or semisolid substances **2.** COOK LADLE a utensil with a long handle and round bowl, used for transferring liquids **3.** COOK UTENSIL WITH A BOWL-SHAPED HEAD a utensil with a long handle and a small hemispherical bowl, used for serving such things as ice cream and mashed potato or making melon balls **4.** AUTOMOT DIGGING PART the part of a dredge or digging machine that is used for excavating **5.** QUANTITY LIFTED IN A SCOOP the quantity that is taken by a scoop ○ *three scoops of ice cream* **6.** DIGGING MOTION a curving digging movement of a scoop or the hand **7.** CAVITY a shallow cavity, hole, or other hollow area in sth **8.** BROADCAST, PRESS EXCLUSIVE a news story that is published by a newspaper, magazine, or news programme before its rivals (*informal*) ○ *scoop of the year* **9.** NEWS the latest news or gossip (*informal*) ○ *What's the scoop?* **10.** MUSIC SLIDING UP TO PITCH in vocal and instrumental music, a sliding up to a pitch **11.** QUICK PROFIT a large amount of money made quickly (*informal*) ■ *v.* (**scoops, scooping, scooped**) **1.** *vt.* HOLLOW STH OUT to create a shallow hole in sth with a scoop or similar object, or a curved hand ○ *He scooped out a hole in the earth.* **2.** *vt.* REMOVE STH to remove an amount of a liquid or solid substance with a scoop or similar object, or a curved hand ○ *scooping up water with a ladle* **3.** *vt.* LIFT SB OR STH SWIFTLY to pick sb or sth up swiftly and without ceremony ○ *She scooped him up in her arms.* **4.** *vt.* BROADCAST PUBLISH OR BROADCAST STH FIRST to publish or broadcast an item of news before any other newspaper, magazine, or news programme ○ *The newspaper scooped its rivals for the second time in a week.* ○ *scooping the hottest story of the year* **5.** *vt.* GET A GREAT DEAL OF MONEY to win or otherwise obtain a large amount of money **6.** *vti.* SPORTS HIT A BALL UP IN THE AIR to hit a ball upwards from underneath so that it rises into the air [14thC. From Middle Low German and Middle Dutch *schōpe* 'bucket for bailing, bucket of a waterwheel'.] —**scooper** *n.*

scoop neck *n.* a low curved neckline on an article of women's clothing

scoosh /skoosh/ *vti.* (**scooshes, scooshing, scooshed**) *Scotland* SQUIRT to squirt a liquid, or be squirted (*informal*) ■ *n. Scotland* (*informal*) **1.** SQUIRTING an act of squirting **2.** FIZZY DRINK a sweet fizzy drink, especially lemonade [19thC. An imitation of the sound.]

scoot /skoot/ *v.* (**scoots, scooting, scooted**) **1.** *vi.* LEAVE to go away quickly (*informal*) (*usually used as a command*) **2.** *vi.* MOVE QUICKLY to move, run, or go somewhere quickly (*informal*) **3.** *vt. US* SEND QUICKLY to move or send sth quickly (*informal*) ○ *Scoot that file to me as soon as you can.* **4.** *vti. Scotland* SQUIRT LIQUID to squirt a liquid, or be squirted ■ *n.* (*informal*) **1.** SWIFT MOVEMENT a swift movement or trip ○ *a quick scoot to the supermarket* **2.** *Scotland* A SQUIRT a gush of liquid [Mid-18thC. Origin uncertain: perhaps of Scandinavian origin.]

scooter /skootər/ *n.* **1.** WHEELED TOY a child's toy consisting of a handlebar attached by a long rod to a footboard on two wheels. One foot is placed on the board and the other propels it along. **2.** AUTOMOT = **motor scooter** [Early 19thC. Formed from SCOOT.]

scop /skop/ *n.* a bard or poet in Anglo-Saxon England [Old English *sc(e)op*, from a prehistoric Germanic word that may also be the ancestor of English *scoff*. Obsolete by the 14thC but revived in the 18thC.]

scope[1] /skōp/ *n.* **1.** ROOM TO ACT freedom, space, or capacity to act ○ *not much scope for originality* **2.** RANGE COVERED the range covered by an activity, subject, or topic ○ *a question that is beyond the scope of this lecture* **3.** MENTAL CAPACITY the extent of sb's mental capacity **4.** SHIPPING MOORING CABLE the length of a ship's mooring cable **5.** LOGIC RANGE OF A LOGICAL OPERATOR the range of application or boundaries of a logical operator, usually indicated by parentheses. The scope of 'and' in '(p and q) or r' is limited to 'p' and 'q'. [Mid-16thC. Via Italian *scopo* 'aim, purpose' from Greek *skopos* 'target'. The underlying sense is 'sth aimed at or kept in view', hence 'range of view'.]

scope[2] /skōp/ *n.* any optical device or tool whose name ends in '-scope' such as a telescope, microscope, endoscope, or oscilloscope (*informal*) [Early 17thC. Shortening.]

scope[3] /skōp/ (**scopes, scoping, scoped**) *vt.* to look at or examine sth (*informal*) [Mid-17thC. From SCOPE[1].]

-scope *suffix.* an instrument for viewing or observing ○ *nephroscope* [Via modern Latin *-scopium* from, ultimately, Greek *skopein* 'to look, see'. Ultimately from an Indo-European base that is also the ancestor of English *inspect, specimen*, and *spy*.] —**-scopic** *suffix.* —**-scopy** *suffix.*

scopolamine /skə póllə meen, -min/ *n.* a colourless thick liquid poisonous alkaloid found in some plants of the nightshade family and used as a truth serum, to prevent motion sickness, and as a sedative. Formula: $C_{17}H_{21}NO_4$. [Late 19thC. From modern Latin *Scopolia japonica*, scientific name of the Japanese belladonna, from which scopolamine was first extracted, and which was named after G. A. *Scopoli* (1723–88), Italian naturalist.]

scopula /skóppyoolə/ (*plural* **-las** *or* **-lae** /-lee/) *n.* a tuft of dense hairs on the back of the legs of some insects or spiders [Early 19thC. From late Latin, literally 'little broom'.]

scorbutic /skawr byootik/ *adj.* relating to, affected with, or causing scurvy [Mid-17thC. Via modern Latin *scorbuticus* from medieval Latin *scorbutus* 'scurvy', of uncertain origin: perhaps ultimately from a prehistoric Germanic word that is also the ancestor of English *scurf*.] —**scorbutically** *adv.*

scorch /skawrch/ *v.* (**scorches, scorching, scorched**) **1.** *vti.* BURN STH ON ITS SURFACE to burn the surface of sth, or to be burnt so as to cause pain, injury, or discolouring ○ *scorched the handkerchief with the iron* **2.** *vti.* DRY OUT to dry or parch sth with intense heat, or to become dried out or parched because of intense heat ○ *The plains had been scorched by the sun.* **3.** *vt.* CRITICIZE SB to subject sb to severe criticism (*informal*) **4.** *vi.* DRIVE FAST to drive or travel extremely fast (*informal*) ○ *scorching down the motorway in a Porsche* ■ *n.* **1.** SURFACE BURN a burn, or burn mark on the surface of sth ○ *The iron left a slight scorch on the blouse.* **2.** BOT DISCOLORATION ON PLANTS a brown marking on plants or vegetables caused by disease, insecticide, or heat [12thC. Origin uncertain: probably of Scandinavian origin.]

scorched earth policy *n.* **1.** MIL LEAVING NOTHING FOR AN ENEMY a policy of destroying crops or buildings, especially by burning, or of removing anything that might be useful to an advancing enemy in wartime **2.** BUSINESS TAKEOVER-AVOIDANCE STRATEGY a strategy adopted by a company facing a hostile takeover whereby it makes itself appear a financially less attractive acquisition until the threat has gone

scorcher /skáwrchər/ *n.* **1.** STH THAT BURNS sb or sth that scorches **2.** HOT DAY an extremely hot day (*informal*) ○ *Yesterday was fairly warm but today is a scorcher!* **3.** CRITICAL REMARK a severely critical remark **4.** STH VERY GOOD sth extraordinary or excellent (*informal*)

scorching /skáwrching/ *adj.* extremely hot (*informal*)

score /skawr/ *n.* **1.** SPORTS, GAME POINTS GAINED the total number of points gained by a player or team at the end of or during a match or game **2.** SPORTS, GAME TALLY OF POINTS GAINED a record of the number of points gained by a player or team in a match or game ○ *Who's keeping the score?* **3.** SPORTS, GAME GAINING OF POINT the gaining of a point or points in a match or game **4.** (*plural* **score** *or* **scores**) GROUP OF 20 a group of twenty things or people ○ *A score or more people showed up.* **5.** MUSIC PRINTED MUSIC a written or printed copy of a musical composition ○ *distributed copies of the score to the chorus* **6.** MUSIC MUSIC COMPOSED the music that has been composed for a film, play, or musical ○ *a film with a breathtaking score* **7.** DANCE COPY OF CHOREOGRAPHIC NOTATION a written record of the choreography for a dance or ballet **8.** NOTCH a notch or incision cut into the surface of sth **9.** PARTIAL CUT a crease or superficial cut made in sth, such as a piece of paper to enable it to be folded or separated easily **10.** GRUDGE a grievance that is not resolved and incurs resentment **11.** RECORD OF MONEY OWED a record of an amount of money due for payment **12.** MONEY OWED an amount of money due for payment **13.** PRESENT SITUATION the present state or actual facts of a situation (*informal*) ○ *What's the score, are you coming or not?* **14.** SUCCESS a successful result or achievement, especially one that is significant (*informal*) **15.** DRUGS DRUG DEAL a purchase of illegal drugs (*slang*) **16.** CRIMINOL ROBBERY the successful theft of sth (*informal*) **17.** SEXUAL CONQUEST a successful seduction of sb or the sexual encounter itself (*informal*) **18.** SAILING GROOVE FOR ROPE a groove cut in wood to hold a rope ■ **scores** *npl.* MANY a great many ○ *Scores of members protested at the decision.* ■ *v.* (**scores, scoring, scored**) **1.** *vti.* SPORTS, GAME GAIN POINTS to gain a point or points in a match or game ○ *scored twice in the second half* **2.** *vt.* SPORTS, GAME GAIN A TOTAL OF POINTS IN GAME to gain a total number of points in a match, game, or other competition **3.** *vti.* SPORTS, GAME RECORD POINTS to keep a record of the number of points gained in a match, game, or other competition ○ *Who's scoring?* **4.** *vt.* SPORTS, GAME ASSIGN SB POINTS to award a particular number of points to sb in a match, game, or other competition ○ *Three of the judges scored her a perfect 10.* **5.** *vt.* SPORTS, GAME BE WORTH CERTAIN POINTS IN A GAME to count for a particular number of points in a match, game, or other competition ○ *Hitting the red area scores ten.* **6.** *vt.* CUT LINES IN STH to make notches, cuts, or lines in a surface **7.** *vt.* CUT STH SUPERFICIALLY TO SEPARATE IT to make a superficial cut or crease in sth, such as a piece of paper in order to fold, tear, or break it easily **8.** *vt.* WRITE STH BY MAKING INCISIONS to write sth by means of notches, incisions, or lines cut into a surface ○ *names scored on the back of the bench with a penknife* **9.** *vti.* CROSS STH OUT to draw a line through sth in order to mark it as cancelled or deleted **10.** *vt.* RECORD MONEY OWED to keep a record of an amount of money owed by sb by making a series of marks next to his or her name **11.** *vi.* DO WELL to secure an advantage in a particular field or area of activity ○ *She scores because she can communicate.* **12.** *vt.* MUSIC ORCHESTRATE STH to orchestrate or arrange a piece of music **13.** *vt.* MUSIC COMPOSE THE MUSIC FOR STH to write the music for a film, play, or musical **14.** *vt.* DANCE WRITE THE CHOREOGRAPHY FOR STH to write out the choreography for a dance or ballet **15.** *vt.* GET STH to succeed in getting sth (*informal*) ○ *scored front-row tickets for the concert* **16.** *vti.* DRUGS BUY DRUGS to buy illegal drugs (*slang*) **17.** *vi.* HAVE SEX to succeed in having sex with sb, especially a new sexual partner (*slang*) [Pre-12thC. From Old Norse *skor* 'notch, tally, 20'.] ◇ **on this** *or* **that score** as far as this or that is concerned ○ *Her health is fine, so there's no need to worry on that score.*

scoreboard /skáwr bawrd/ *n.* a board at a sporting venue on which the score of a game, match, or other competition in progress is displayed. Scores of other games in progress elsewhere may also be shown.

scorecard /skáwr kaard/ *n.* **1.** CARD TO KEEP SCORE WITH a small card used by a player to keep a record of his or her own score, e.g. in golf **2.** CARD LISTING PLAYERS IN A MATCH a card listing the players in a game or match that enables a spectator to identify who is who and to keep a record of the progress of play

score draw *n.* a result in a match, especially a soccer match, in which both sides have scored the same number of goals

scorekeeper /skáwr keepər/ *n.* sb who is responsible for keeping a note of the score in a game, match, or other competition —**scorekeeping** *n.*

scoreless /skáwrləss/ *adj.* having no points or goals scored

scoreline /skáwr līn/ *n.* the total number of points gained by players or teams at the end of a match or game

scorer /skáwrər/ *n.* **1.** SPORTS, GAME SB SCORING POINT sb who scores a point or goal in a game or match **2.** SPORTS, GAME = **scorekeeper 3.** TECH CUTTING DEVICE a device for cutting a notch or incision into sth

Scoresby Sound /skáwrzbi-/ arm of the Norwegian Sea touching eastern Greenland. It is the largest fjord in the world. Length: 451 km/280 mi.

scoresheet /skáwr sheet/ *n.* a record of who has scored a point or goal in a game or match, especially in soccer or rugby

scoria /skáwri ə/ (*plural* **-ae** /-ri ee/) *n.* **1.** GEOL POROUS ROCK loose rubbly porous solidified lava that is ejected from a volcano and builds up round the crater **2.** METALL = **slag** *n.* 1 [14thC. Via Latin from Greek *skōria* 'refuse, dross', from *skōr* 'dung'.] —**scoriaceous** /skáwri áyshəss/ *adj.*

scorify /skáwri fī/ (**-fies, -fying, -fied**) *vt.* to purify ore by separating it out into metal and slag —**scorification** /skáwrifi káysh'n/ *n.* —**scorifier** *n.*

scorn /skawrn/ *n.* **1.** DISDAIN a strong feeling of contempt ○ *poured scorn on my attempts at writing* **2.** OBJECT OF CONTEMPT sb or sth that is held in contempt ○ *Their behaviour made them the scorn of the entire community.* ■ *v.* (**scorns, scorning, scorned**) **1.** *vt.* DISDAIN SB OR STH to hold sb or sth in contempt **2.** *vti.* REJECT STH CONTEMPTUOUSLY to reject sth with contempt ○ *They had scorned our attempts at peace.* [12thC. From Old French *escharnir* 'to mock or despise'.] —**scorner** *n.*

scornful /skáwrnf'l/ *adj.* feeling or expressing great contempt for sb or sth —**scornfully** *adv.* —**scornfulness** *n.*

scorpaenid /skawr peénid/ *n.* a marine fish with spiny fins such as the scorpion fish, redfish, or rockfish. Family: Scorpaenidae. [Late 19thC. From modern Latin *Scorpaenidae*, from Latin *scorpaena*, a kind of fish, from Greek *skorpios* (see SCORPION).] —**scorpaenid** *adj.*

Scorpio /skáwrpi ō/ *n.* **1.** ASTRON = **Scorpius 2.** ZODIAC EIGHTH SIGN OF THE ZODIAC the eighth sign of the zodiac, represented by a scorpion and lasting from approximately 23 October to 21 November. Scorpio is classified as a water sign and its ruling planets are Mars and Pluto. **3. Scorpio** (*plural* **-os**), **Scorpian** ZODIAC SB BORN UNDER SCORPIO sb whose birthday falls between 23 October and 21 November [14thC. From Latin, from *scorpio* (see SCORPION).] —**Scorpio** *adj.*

scorpioid /skáwrpi oyd/ *adj.* **1.** BOT WITH A COILED MAIN STEM having the main stem curled at the end ○ *a scorpioid cyme* **2.** ZOOL OF OR LIKE A SCORPION relating to or resembling a scorpion [Mid-19thC. From Greek *skorpioeidēs*, from *skorpios* (see SCORPION).]

scorpion /skáwrpi ən/ *n.* **1.** ARACHNID WITH A POISONOUS STING a nocturnal arachnid of warm dry regions that has a long body with pincers in front and a thin segmented upturned tail tipped with a venomous sting. Order: Scorpionida. **2.** BARBED WHIP in the Bible, a whip with metal barbs [12thC. Via French from, ultimately, Greek *skorpios* 'sea fish, scorpion'.]

Scorpion /skáwrpi ən/ *n.* **1.** ASTRON = **Scorpius 2.** ZODIAC = **Scorpio** *n.* 2

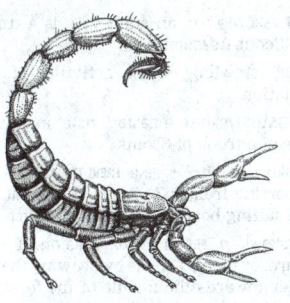

Scorpion

scorpion fish *n.* a small brightly coloured fish with venomous spines in its fins. Family: Scorpaenidae.

scorpion fly *n.* a nonvenomous insect that has downward-pointing mouthparts and a reproductive organ in the male resembling the sting of a scorpion. Order: Mecoptera.

scorpion grass *n.* = forget-me-not

Scorpius /skáwrpi əss/ *n.* a distinctive bright zodiacal constellation between Libra and Sagittarius lying partly in the Milky Way. Scorpius contains the bright red star Antares. [15thC. From Latin *scorpius* (see SCORPION).]

Scorsese /skawr sáyzi/, **Martin** (*b.* 1942) US film director. His films, including *Taxi Driver* (1976) and *Goodfellas* (1990), often depict urban violence.

scot /skot/ *n.* formerly, a type of tax (*archaic*) [Pre-12thC. Partly from Old Norse *skot* 'shot', partly from Old French *escot*.]

Scot /skot/ *n.* **1.** SB FROM SCOTLAND sb who was born or brought up in Scotland, or is of Scottish descent **2.** MEMBER OF ANCIENT BRITISH PEOPLE a member of a people who lived in Ireland and who periodically invaded western Britain from the 3rd century AD, before settling in northern Britain during the 6th century [Pre-12thC. Via medieval Latin from late Latin *Scottus*, of unknown origin.]

─── **WORD KEY: USAGE** ───

Scot, Scotch, or **Scottish**? All these words mean 'of Scotland', but they are used in different ways. **Scottish** is the most generally used word to describe the country and people of Scotland (*Scottish history*; *a Scottish poet*; *Scottish Gaelic*), whereas **Scots** is normally applied to people or to the form of English spoken in Scotland (*Scots Guard*; *a Scots accent*). A **Scot** is a person from Scotland; more specific words are *Scotsman* and *Scotswoman*. **Scotch** is a literary word more closely associated with the writing of Robert Burns and Sir Walter Scott, and has fallen out of general use, usually being considered offensive unless used in fixed expressions such as *Scotch pine* and *Scotch mist*.

Scot. *abbr.* **1.** Scotland **2.** Scottish **3.** Scotch

scot and lot *n.* formerly, a municipal tax. Those paying it qualified to receive the vote. ['Lot' in an earlier sense 'tax or due']

scotch[1] /skoch/ *vt.* (**scotches, scotching, scotched**) **1.** STOP STH to put a stop to sth such as a rumour **2.** DISABLE SB to disable sb by wounding (*archaic*) **3.** GASH STH to make a gash or score in sth (*archaic*) ◼ *n.* (*archaic*) **1.** SCORE IN STH a cut or score in sth **2.** LINE a line drawn on the ground, especially one used to mark out a grid for hopscotch [15thC. Origin uncertain: perhaps from Anglo-Norman *escocher* 'to notch', ultimately from Latin *coccum* 'scarlet oak berry' (that has notches), from Greek *kokkos*.]

scotch[2] /skoch/ *n.* TECH WEDGE a wedge used to prevent sth from moving ◼ *vt.* (**scotches, scotching, scotched**) TECH WEDGE STH to wedge sth in order to prevent it from moving [Early 17thC. Origin uncertain.]

Scotch /skoch/, **Scotch whisky** *n.* **1.** BEVERAGES WHISKY whisky produced in Scotland **2.** LANG = Scots *n.* ◼ *npl.* PEOPLES SCOTTISH PEOPLE people who were born or brought up in Scotland or who are of Scottish descent (*offensive*) ◼ *adj.* **1.** OF SCOTLAND relating to Scotland, its people, or its culture (*offensive*) **2.** FROM SCOTLAND made in Scotland, or typical of a style

prevalent in Scotland ○ *Scotch broth* [Late 16thC. Contraction of SCOTTISH.]

─── **WORD KEY: USAGE** ───

See Usage note at *Scot*.

Scotch broth *n.* a soup made with lamb or beef, mixed root vegetables, and pearl barley

Scotch catch *n.* = Scotch snap

Scotch egg *n.* a hard-boiled egg wrapped in sausagemeat, coated with breadcrumbs, and deep fried. It is served cut in half, either hot or cold.

Scotch-Irish *npl.* US = Scottish-Irish —**Scotch-Irish** *adj.*

Scotchman /skóchmən/ (*plural* -**men** /-mən/) *n.* a Scotsman (*archaic or offensive*)

Scotch mist *n.* **1.** DRIZZLY MIST a fine, damp mist **2.** STH IMAGINED a figment of sb's imagination (*humorous*)

Scotch pancake *n.* = drop scone

Scotch pine *n.* TREES = Scots pine

Scotch snap *n.* in music, a rhythmic figure consisting of a dotted note preceded by a note the value of the dot

Scotch tape *tdmk.* US a trademark for a type of transparent adhesive tape

Scotch terrier *n.* = Scottish terrier

Scotch whisky *n.* = Scotch

Scotchwoman /skóch woomən/ (*plural* -**en** /-wimmin/) *n.* a Scotswoman (*archaic or offensive*)

Scotch woodcock *n.* a snack or light meal of toast spread with an anchovy paste and topped with scrambled eggs [Fanciful name for a meal, thought to originate in Scotland, that is completely different to what its name suggests]

scoter /skótər/ (*plural* -**ters** *or* -**ter**) *n.* a large sea duck of the northern coasts of North America, Asia, and Europe, the male of which has black plumage with white spots on its head. Genus: *Melanitta*. [Late 17thC. Origin unknown.]

scot-free *adv.* without punishment being exacted or payment being made [The original meaning was 'without having to pay SCOT']

scotia /skósha/ *n.* a deep concave moulding, especially on the base of a column [Mid-16thC. Via Latin from Greek *skotia*, from *skotos* 'darkness' (from the shadow inside the moulding).]

Scotia /skósha/ *n.* a former name for Scotland, still sometimes used in literary contexts (*archaic or literary*) [Early 17thC. From medieval Latin *Scotia*.] —**Scotian** *adj.*

Scotism /skótizəm/ *n.* the philosophical tenets of, or school of scholastic philosophy founded by, Duns Scotus, the 13th-century Scottish philosopher and theologian —**Scotist** *adj.* —**Scotistic** /skō tístik/ *adj.*

Scotland /skótlənd/ *n.* one of the four countries that comprise the United Kingdom of Great Britain and Northern Ireland. It consists of the northern third of Great Britain, as well as hundreds of islands. It became united with England in 1707. Capital: Edinburgh. Population: 5,132,400 (1994). Area: 77,080 sq. km/29,750 sq. mi.

Scotland Yard *n.* the headquarters of the Metropolitan Police in London, from which national criminal investigations are coordinated. The headquarters moved to new premises in 1890 and 1967 and is officially known as New Scotland Yard. [Because it was originally located in *Great Scotland Yard*, a street in which the palace used by visiting kings of Scotland in medieval times formerly stood]

Scot Nat /-nát/ *n.* SCOTTISH NATIONALIST a Scottish Nationalist (*informal*) ◼ *adj.* OF SCOTTISH NATIONALISTS relating to the Scottish Nationalists (*informal*) [Shortening]

scotoma /skə tómə/ (*plural* -**mas** *or* -**mata** /-mətə/) *n.* a permanent or temporary area of diminished sight in the field of vision [Mid-16thC. Via late Latin from Greek *skotōma* 'dizziness', ultimately from *skotos* 'darkness'.] —**scotomatous** *adj.*

scotopia /skə tópi ə, skó-/ *n.* the ability to see in poor light or in the dark [Early 20thC. Coined from Greek *skotos* 'darkness' + -OPIA.] —**scotopic** /-tóppik, -/ *adj.*

Scots /skots/ *adj.* OF SCOTLAND relating to Scotland, its people, or its culture ◼ *n.* LANG SCOTTISH DIALECT OF ENGLISH the dialect of English spoken in Scotland [14thC. Contraction of SCOTTISH.]

─── **WORD KEY: WORLD ENGLISH** ───

Scots is the Germanic speech of the Scottish Lowlands, in contrast to Gaelic, the traditional Celtic speech of the Highlands. It is regarded by some as a dialect of English, by others as a distinct language. Many scholars regard Scots of the period before the Union of the Crowns (1603) as a language in its own right and after that date as a more limited vernacular. It is however listed alongside languages such as Basque, Catalan, Gaelic, by the Bureau of Lesser Used European Languages (an institution of the European Union). Scots has its own dialects, from the Borders (linked with the dialects of Northern England) to Orkney and Shetland (mixed with elements of Old Norse). Its literature includes two medieval epic poems, copious 16th-century verse, the works of Robert Burns, and more recent poetry and fiction. Though there has been a massive mixing with English for over 200 years, its major characteristics remain clear-cut, including, first, a strong 'rhotic' pronunciation (i.e., 'r' is pronounced as an 'alveolar tap', or trill, in words such as *art, door,* and *worker*). Second, the pronunciation is marked by use of the 'velar fricative', (as in German 'machen') in words such as *nicht* (night), *sicht* (sight), *ach* (ah), and *och* (oh). Third, verbs like *tell* and *sell* have distinctive past forms: *tellt* and *sellt* (for *told* and *sold*). Fourth, some 'double modal' verbs, as in 'Ah micht could dae it' ('I might could do it'), are used to mean 'I could probably do it'. Fifth, the vocabulary is large and distinctive: e.g., *tae blether* (to talk nonsense), *a blether* (someone who talks nonsense); *tae dicht* (to wipe clean); *tae ken* (to know); *tae lowp* (to leap), *a lowp* (a leap); *an ashet*, (a serving dish, (from French *assiette*); *a dwam* (a hazy mental condition); *a howf(f)*, (a favourite spot, a pub); *glaikit* (stupid-looking); *fantoosh* (flashy); and *tapselteerie* (topsy-turvy). See IRISH ENGLISH, SCOTTISH ENGLISH.

Scots Gaelic *n.* = Scottish Gaelic

Scots Guards *npl.* one of the regiments of the Household Division in the British Army

Scots-Irish *npl., adj.* = Scottish-Irish

Scots Law *n.* the Scottish legal system, different from that of England and based on Roman Law

Scotsman /skótsmən/ (*plural* -**men** /-mən/) *n.* PEOPLES a man who was born or brought up in Scotland, or who has Scottish ancestry

─── **WORD KEY: USAGE** ───

See Usage note at *Scot*.

Scots pine *n.* US term **Scotch pine 1.** EURASIAN PINE WITH HARD YELLOW WOOD a Eurasian pine that has a reddish trunk, twisted bluish-green needles, and hard yellow wood valued as timber. Latin name: *Pinus sylvestris*. **2.** WOOD OF SCOTS PINE the wood of the Scots pine

Scotswoman /skóts woomən/ (*plural* -**en** /-wimin/) *n.* a woman who was born or brought up in Scotland, or who has Scottish ancestry

─── **WORD KEY: USAGE** ───

See Usage note at *Scot*.

Scott /skot/, **Sir Peter** (1909–89) British ornithologist and painter. The son of Robert Falcon Scott, he was the founder of the Severn Wild Fowl Trust (1948) and leader of ornithological expeditions. He was noted for his bird paintings. Full name **Sir Peter Markham Scott**

Scott, Robert Falcon (1868–1912) British naval officer and explorer. On his second expedition to Antarctica (1910–12) he was beaten to the South Pole by Roald Amundsen. He died on the return journey.

Scott, Sir Walter (1771–1832) Scottish novelist and poet. His ballads and historical novels, which mainly dealt with Scottish subjects, made him one of the most popular writers of his day and did much to establish widespread European interest in Scottish history and culture.

Scotticism /skóttissizəm/ *n.* a word, phrase, or idiom that is characteristic of English as spoken in Scotland

Sir Walter Scott

Scottie /skótti/, **Scotty** (plural **-ties**) n. **1.** ZOOL SCOTTISH TERRIER a Scottish terrier (informal) **2.** PEOPLES SCOTSMAN sb, especially a man, who is Scottish (informal offensive)

Scottish /skóttish/ adj. OF SCOTLAND relating to Scotland, or its people or culture ■ npl. PEOPLES PEOPLE OF SCOTLAND people who were born, brought up, or live in Scotland ■ n. (plural **-tish**) LANG = **Scots** n. [12thC. Formed from SCOT.] —**Scottishness** n.

———— WORD KEY: USAGE ————

See Usage note at **Scot**.

Scottish Blackface n. a mountain sheep with horns and a black face, belonging to a breed mainly bred and kept in Scotland

Scottish Certificate of Education n. full form of SCE

Scottish English n. a variety of English spoken in Scotland

———— WORD KEY: WORLD ENGLISH ————

Scottish English is the English language as used in Scotland, considered by some to include traditional (Lowland) Scots, and by others to be distinct from it, despite overlap. A compromise with the English of England began to emerge after the Union of the Crowns in 1707, when many among the upper and middle classes began to adapt towards the pronunciation, grammar, and vocabulary of 'refined' London. The Scottish aristocracy became socially and linguistically indistinguishable from their peers in England, while the middle class developed a shaky compromise.

Scottish Gaelic n. the Celtic language still spoken in parts of the Highlands and Western Isles of Scotland

Scottish-Irish, **Scots-Irish** npl. IRISH PEOPLE OF SCOTTISH DESCENT Irish people of Scottish descent or Americans descended from these people. US term **Scotch-Irish** ■ adj. OF THE SCOTTISH-IRISH relating to or typical of the Scottish-Irish. US term **Scotch-Irish**

Scottish Land Court n. a Scottish court whose jurisdiction covers the various forms of agricultural tenancy

Scottish Nationalist n. MEMBER OF SNP a member or supporter of the Scottish National Party ■ adj. RELATING TO SNP relating to or belonging to the Scottish National Party

Scottish National Party n. a Scottish political party founded in 1934 that advocates independence for Scotland

Scottish terrier, **Scotch terrier** n. a terrier of a breed

Scottish terrier

with short sturdy legs, pointed ears and thick, wiry, usually black hair

Scotty (plural **-ties**) n. ZOOL = **Scottie** (informal)

scoundrel /skówndrəl/ n. sb who behaves dishonourably towards other people [Late 16thC. Origin unknown.] —**scoundrelly** adj.

scour[1] /skowr/ v. (**scours**, **scouring**, **scoured**) **1.** vti. CLEAN BY RUBBING to clean or brighten sth by rubbing it with an abrasive substance or material **2.** vti. REMOVE STH BY RUBBING to remove sth by rubbing with an abrasive substance or material **3.** vt. FREE STH FROM DIRT OR IMPURITIES to remove dirt or impurities from sth by washing **4.** vt. FLUSH STH OUT to clear sth out by using water **5.** vi. VET HAVE DIARRHOEA to be affected by diarrhoea (refers to cattle) ■ n. **1.** SCOURING a scouring of sth **2.** CLEANING SUBSTANCE a substance or tool that can be used for cleaning **3.** PLACE SCOURED a place that has been scoured, especially by water **4.** VET DIARRHOEA diarrhoea affecting cattle and pigs (often used in the plural with a singular or plural verb) [12thC. Via Middle Low German or Middle Dutch from, ultimately, late Latin excurare, literally 'to clean out, take care of', ultimately from Latin cura 'care' (source of English cure).] —**scourer** n.

scour[2] /skowr/ (**scours**, **scouring**, **scoured**) vti. **1.** SEARCH STH CAREFULLY to search sth thoroughly and quickly for sb or sth ○ They scoured the countryside for him, but to no avail. **2.** MOVE ABOUT AT SPEED to move quickly over or through an area [15thC. Origin uncertain: probably from a Scandinavian language.] —**scourer** n.

scourge /skurj/ n. **1.** TORMENTOR sb or sth that is perceived as an agent of punishment, destruction, or severe criticism ○ the scourge of my childhood **2.** WHIP a whip that is used for inflicting punishment ■ vt. (**scourges**, **scourging**, **scourged**) **1.** PUNISH SB to punish or criticize sb severely **2.** WHIP SB to whip sb severely [12thC. From Old French escorgier 'to whip', ultimately from Latin corrigia 'thong, whip'.] —**scourger** n.

scouring rush n. a horsetail that has a rough stem and was, in the past, used for scouring, especially the Dutch rush. Genus: *Equisetum*.

scourings /skówringz/ npl. the material removed or left after scouring sth, especially that left after scouring grain

scouse /skowss/ n. a stew made from leftover meat with potatoes and vegetables (regional) [Mid-19thC. Shortening of LOBSCOUSE (the original meaning).]

Scouse /skowss/ n. (informal) **1.** Scouse, Scouser SB FROM LIVERPOOL sb who was born, brought up, or lives in Liverpool **2.** LIVERPOOL DIALECT the dialect spoken in Liverpool ■ adj. LIVERPUDLIAN relating to Liverpool, or its inhabitants or their English dialect (informal) [Mid-19thC. Shortening of LOBSCOUSE (the original meaning).]

scout[1] /skowt/ n. **1.** MIL SOLDIER SENT TO GATHER INFORMATION sb, especially a soldier, who is sent to gather information about an enemy's position or movements **2.** SPORTS, ARTS = **talent scout 3.** OXFORD COLLEGE SERVANT sb employed to clean students' rooms at Oxford University **4.** MIL RECONNAISSANCE CRAFT OR VEHICLE a ship, aircraft, or vehicle designed and used for reconnaissance purposes **5.** MIL RECONNOITRING a gathering of information concerning an enemy's position or movements **6.** PERSON a boy or man (dated informal) ○ Be a good scout and give me a hand here. ■ v. (**scouts**, **scouting**, **scouted**) **1.** vti. SEARCH AREA to make a search of an area for sb or sth ○ scouting around for a place to camp **2.** vi. GATHER INFORMATION to seek out information about sb or sth, especially about an enemy's position or movements **3.** vti. SPORTS, ARTS SEEK OUT NEW TALENT to look for talented players for a sports team, or for talented performers for a show or group [14thC. Via Old French escouter from, ultimately, Latin auscultare 'to listen'.] —**scouter** n.

scout[2] /skowt/ (**scouts**, **scouting**, **scouted**) vt. to reject sb or sth with scorn or derision (archaic) [Early 17thC. Origin uncertain: probably from a Scandinavian language.]

Scout /skowt/, **scout** n. a member of the Scout Association, an international youth organization founded for boys in 1908 by Lord Baden-Powell. ◊ **Boy Scout**, **Girl Scout** [Early 20thC. From SCOUT[1].]

Scouter /skówtər/ n. an adult who is a troop leader in the Scout Association

Scouting /skówting/ n. the activities of the Scout Association

scoutmaster /skówt maastər/ n. a man who is in charge of a troop of Scouts

scow /skow/ n. **1.** SHIPPING FREIGHT BARGE a barge for transporting freight **2.** SAILING SAILING BOAT a flat-bottomed sailing boat [Mid-17thC. From Dutch schouw.]

scowl /skowl/ n. FROWN an expression of anger, displeasure, or menace made by drawing the eyebrows together towards the middle of the forehead ■ vi. (**scowls**, **scowling**, **scowled**) MAKE A FROWN to draw the eyebrows together towards the middle of the forehead in an expression of anger, displeasure, or menace [14thC. Origin uncertain: probably from a Scandinavian language.] —**scowler** n.

SCPO abbr. Senior Chief Petty Officer

SCPS abbr. Society of Civil and Public Servants

SCR n. (plural **SCRs**), abbr. senior common room

scrabble /skrább'l/ v. (**-bles**, **-bling**, **-bled**) **1.** vi. SCRATCH AT STH to scrape or scratch at sth with small, hurried movements of the fingers, toes, or claws ○ The cat was scrabbling at the door. **2.** vi. FEEL WITH FINGERS to grope about frantically in an effort to find sth ○ She scrabbled around trying to find the torch. **3.** vi. CLIMB OVER STH to climb hastily or clumsily up or over sth **4.** vi. STRUGGLE TO GET STH to struggle desperately to get sth **5.** vt. PRODUCE STH WITH DIFFICULTY to produce sth hastily and with difficulty from scarce resources **6.** vti. SCRIBBLE to scribble sth ■ n. **1.** A SCRATCHING AT STH a scraping or scratching at sth with short hurried movements of the fingers, toes, or claws **2.** A SEARCH WITH FINGERS a frantic groping about in an effort to find sth **3.** A CLIMB OVER STH a climb up or over sth, performed hastily or clumsily **4.** A STRUGGLE TO GET STH a desperate struggle to acquire or gain sth **5.** A SCRIBBLING a scribbling of sth **6.** STH SCRIBBLED sth that sb has scribbled [Mid-16thC. From Middle Dutch schrabbelen, literally 'to scratch repeatedly', from schrabben 'to scratch or scrape'.] —**scrabbler** n.

Scrabble /skrább'l/ tdmk. a trademark for a board game in which the players try to form words by placing tiles, each with a single letter on it, on the squares of a board

scrag /skrag/ n. **1.** = **scrag end 2.** THIN PERSON OR ANIMAL an unattractively thin person or animal **3.** NECK sb's neck (informal) ■ vt. (**scrags**, **scragging**, **scragged**) STRANGLE SB to throttle or strangle sb (informal) [Mid-16thC. Origin uncertain: probably from dialect crag 'neck', from Middle Dutch craghe 'throat'.]

scrag end n. the bony neck joint of a sheep or lamb, usually cut up and used in soup or stew

scraggly /skrággli/ (**-glier**, **-gliest**) adj. untidy in appearance or shape [Mid-19thC. Formed from SCRAG.] —**scraggliness** n.

scraggy /skrággi/ (**-gier**, **-giest**) adj. bony and thin ○ a scraggy little cat [Early 17thC. Formed from SCRAG.] —**scraggily** adv. —**scragginess** n.

———— WORD KEY: SYNONYMS ————

See Synonyms at **thin**.

scram /skram/ v. (**scrams**, **scramming**, **scrammed**) **1.** vi. LEAVE QUICKLY to get out or leave quickly (informal) (usually used as a command) **2.** vti. PHYS SHUT DOWN NUCLEAR REACTOR to shut down a nuclear reactor rapidly in an emergency, or be shut down rapidly ■ n. PHYS REACTOR SHUTDOWN a rapid shutting-down of a nuclear reactor in an emergency [Early 20thC. Origin uncertain: perhaps a shortening of SCRAMBLE.]

scramble /skrámb'l/ v. (**-bles**, **-bling**, **-bled**) **1.** vi. CLAMBER to climb or advance over sth using both hands and feet ○ We managed to scramble over the fence. **2.** vi. HURRY to move in haste and with a sense of urgency **3.** vi. COMPETE FRANTICALLY to struggle or compete frantically in order to get sth ○ Everyone was scrambling for the best seats. **4.** vt. JUMBLE THINGS TOGETHER to mix or gather two or more things together haphazardly **5.** vt. COOK BEAT AND COOK EGGS to beat together and cook eggs, butter, and milk **6.** vt. TELECOM ENCODE TRANSMITTED SIGNALS to render a telecommunications or broadcast signal unintelligible by means of an electronic device **7.** vti. AIR FORCE LAUNCH AIRCRAFT AGAINST ATTACK to launch a large number of aircraft in a short space of time in response to an impending attack, or to be launched in these circumstances ■ *n.* **1.** HARD CLIMB a difficult climb or walk that involves using the hands as well as the feet but no ropes **2.** DASH OR STRUGGLE a hasty, undignified, or disorganized struggle for sth or in order to do sth **3.** MOTORCYCLES MOTORCYCLE RACE a motorcycle race over rough terrain **4.** AIR FORCE LAUNCH OF AIRCRAFT the scrambling of military aircraft **5.** CONFUSED MASS a jumbled mass of people or things [Late 16thC. Thought to suggest the action.]

scrambled eggs *n.* COOKED BEATEN EGGS a dish made by beating eggs, milk, and butter together and cooking them in a pan ■ *npl.* OFFICER'S GOLD BRAID gold braid attached to the peak of the cap of a senior military officer (*slang*)

scrambler /skrámblər/ *n.* **1.** PLANTS STRAGGLING PLANT a plant with long straggling shoots that are held up by adjacent plants **2.** TELECOM DEVICE TO ENCODE TRANSMITTED SIGNALS an electronic device that renders telecommunications or broadcast signals unintelligible without a special receiver **3.** MOTORCYCLES ROUGH-TERRAIN MOTORCYCLE a motorcycle designed for racing across rough terrain

scramjet /skrám jet/ *n.* a ramjet aircraft in which fuel is burned in air that is moving at supersonic speeds [Mid-20thC. From the initial letters of SUPERSONIC and COMBUSTION + RAMJET.]

scran /skran/ *n.* food (*slang*) [Early 19thC. Origin unknown.] ◇ **bad scran to sb** *Ireland* used to wish sb bad luck

scrap[1] /skrap/ *n.* **1.** FRAGMENT a small piece or remnant that has been detached or torn off from a larger piece **2.** WASTE MATERIAL waste material, especially metal awaiting reprocessing **3.** SMALL PIECE a very small piece of sth ○ *There's not a scrap of evidence to prove it.* **4.** BIT OF WRITTEN OR PRINTED MATERIAL a short piece of writing, or a cutting from sth printed ■ **scraps** *npl.* COOK LEFTOVERS pieces of leftover food ○ *table scraps* ■ *vt.* **(scraps, scrapping, scrapped) 1.** GET RID OF STH to discard or discontinue sth because it is considered useless or ineffective **2.** CONVERT STH TO SCRAP to convert sth into scrap material ○ *scrapping old warships* [14thC. From Old Norse *skrap* 'scraps, trifles'.]

scrap[2] /skrap/ *n.* MINOR FIGHT a minor fight or disagreement (*informal*) ■ *vi.* **(scraps, scrapping, scrapped)** FIGHT OR DISAGREE to have a minor fight or disagreement with sb [Late 17thC. Origin uncertain: perhaps a variant of SCRAPE.]

scrapbook /skráp bòòk/ *n.* a blank book or album for pasting in photos, pictures, cuttings, or other material

scrape /skrayp/ *v.* **(scrapes, scraping, scraped) 1.** *vti.* RUB STH ON SURFACE to move sth hard, sharp, or rough across a surface, especially in order to clean it ○ *scraping the wall to remove the paint* **2.** *vt.* TAKE STH OFF to remove sth by applying a hard or sharp edge to it and rubbing with it ○ *My efforts to scrape the paint off failed.* **3.** *vt.* SCRATCH STH to scratch, cut, or damage sth by bringing it into contact with a rough or abrasive surface ○ *fell and scraped my knees* **4.** *vti.* MAKE GRATING NOISE to make a harsh grating sound or cause sth to make such a sound ○ *scraping his chair along the floor* **5.** *vi.* SCRIMP to live economically in an effort to save money ○ *scraping by on a single income* **6.** *vti.* ONLY JUST DO STH to manage only just to do or achieve sth ○ *He just scraped through law school.* **7.** *vt.* DRAW HAIR BACK to draw sth, especially the hair, back tightly ○ *She wore her hair scraped back in a bun.* ■ *n.* **1.** SCRAPING a scraping of sth ○ *I'll give the paint a quick scrape.* **2.** LIGHT SCRATCH a light cut, graze, or area of damage caused by contact with a rough or abrasive surface **3.** GRATING SOUND a sharp, grating sound ○ *the scrape of chairs on the bare floor* **4.** DANGEROUS SITUATION a dangerous, difficult, or awkward situation (*informal*) **5.** MINOR FIGHT a minor fight or disagreement (*informal*) [Old English *scrapian* 'to scratch', from a prehistoric Germanic word that is also the ancestor of English *shear*. Reinforced by related Old Norse *skrapa* or Dutch *schrapen*.] —**scraper** *n.*

scrape together, scrape up *vt.* to manage with difficulty to collect together an amount of sth, especially money, or a number of people or things

scraperboard /skráypər bawrd/ *n.* **1.** CLAY-COVERED DRAWING BOARD a drawing board that is covered with a layer of white clay on top of which is a layer of black that can be scraped away to make white-line drawings. US term **scratchboard 2.** SCRAPERBOARD DRAWING a drawing produced on a scraperboard

scrapheap /skráp heep/ *n.* **1.** RUBBISH PILE a large pile of unwanted or discarded items, especially those being used as scrap material **2.** PLACE FOR DISCARDED THINGS an imagined place to which people and things discarded as worn out and useless are consigned (*informal*) ○ *workers who are relegated to the scrapheap at 50*

scrapie /skráypi/ *n.* a usually fatal disease affecting the nervous system of sheep and goats that is marked by intense itching and loss of muscular control. It is now thought to be one of the diseases caused by a prion, and is similar to BSE in cattle and CJD in humans. [Early 20thC. Formed from SCRAPE, from the animals' rubbing against objects to alleviate itching.]

scrapple /skrápp'l/ *n. US* scraps of pork cooked with cornmeal and seasonings, formed into a loaf, and cooled. It is sliced and fried before serving. [Mid-19thC. Formed from SCRAP[1].]

scrappy[1] /skráppi/ **(-pier, -piest)** *adj.* **1.** IN SCRAPS consisting of scraps or fragments **2.** DISCONNECTED poorly held together or structured —**scrappily** *adv.* —**scrappiness** *n.*

scrappy[2] /skráppi/ **(-pier, -piest)** *adj.* (*informal*) **1.** PLUCKY fighting with enthusiasm and determination **2.** BELLIGERENT too ready to fight or quarrel —**scrappily** *adv.* —**scrappiness** *n.*

scratch /skrach/ *v.* **(scratches, scratching, scratched) 1.** *vt.* MAKE MARK IN STH to scrape or make a slight mark in the surface of sth ○ *He scratched the table top with the knife.* **2.** *vti.* TEAR SKIN to make a thin tear in the surface of the skin of a person or animal ○ *The cat scratched me.* **3.** *vti.* MAKE SCRAPING MOVEMENT to rub or scrape a surface, e.g. with claws or a scraping instrument ○ *The cat was scratching at the door.* **4.** *vi.* MAKE HARSH NOISE to make a scraping sound **5.** *vti.* MUSIC PRODUCE SCRAPING SOUND FROM RECORD to run a record backwards and forwards on a turntable in order to repeat and distort the original sound of the record **6.** *vt.* DRAG STH ALONG SURFACE to drag sth along a rough surface so that the object is scraped **7.** *vti.* RELIEVE ITCHING to rub the skin with nails or claws, especially to relieve itching or discomfort **8.** *vti.* CAUSE ITCHING to irritate the surface of the skin by being rough or prickly **9.** *vt.* WRITE STH WITH SHARP INSTRUMENT to write or draw sth by marking a surface with a pointed or sharp instrument ○ *names scratched on the tree* **10.** *vti.* PEN STH QUICKLY to write or draw sth hastily **11.** *vt.* DELETE STH to delete or erase sth by scraping it off, crossing it out, or rendering it illegible **12.** *vt.* CANCEL STH to cancel or abandon a project, plan, or proposal completely **13.** *vi.* SEARCH AIMLESSLY to search for sth in an unsystematic way by picking through things or looking on the ground ○ *scratching around for evidence* **14.** *vti.* SPORTS WITHDRAW FROM COMPETITION to withdraw an individual or team from a race or competition **15.** *vi.* CUE GAMES INCUR PENALTY to make a billiard shot that incurs a penalty, e.g. by hitting the cue ball into a pocket **16.** *vi.* CUE GAMES MAKE FLUKE SHOT in billiards, to make a mishit that produces a score **17.** *vti.* JUST GET BY to make a barely adequate living ○ *scratching out a living* ■ *n.* **1.** MARK ON SURFACE a slight cut or mark on a surface **2.** TEAR IN SKIN a thin cut or tear in the surface of the skin of a person or animal **3.** SCRAPING SOUND a scraping sound, especially one made with the claws or nails **4.** ACTION TO RELIEVE ITCHING a rubbing of the skin with the nails or claws, especially to relieve itching or discomfort **5.** SCRIBBLY WRITING sth written hastily or illegibly **6.** SPORTS WITHDRAWN COMPETITOR an individual or team withdrawn from a race or competition **7.** GOLF HANDICAP OF ZERO in golf, a zero handicap **8.** CUE GAMES SHOT INCURRING PENALTY a billiard shot that incurs a penalty **9.** FLUKE SHOT in billiards, a mishit that produces a score **10.** MUSIC TYPE OF POP MUSIC music produced by running a record backwards and forwards on a turntable, repeating and distorting the original sound. Scratch is performed especially by disc jockeys in clubs. **11.** MONEY money or cash (*slang*) ■ *adj.* **1.** DONE RANDOMLY done randomly or by chance **2.** FOR JOTTED NOTES used for making quick or preliminary notes ○ *scratch paper* **3.** SPORTS ASSEMBLED HASTILY assembled hastily from available resources ○ *a scratch team* **4.** GOLF WITH NO HANDICAP playing golf with a handicap of zero [14thC. Origin uncertain: probably a blend of 'scrat' (of unknown origin) and 'cratch' (probably from Middle Dutch *kratsen*), both meaning 'to scratch'.] ◇ **from scratch** right from the beginning, or with nothing having been done previously (*informal*) ◇ **up to scratch** of or up to a satisfactory standard (*informal*) ○ *exam results that aren't really up to scratch*

scratch together, scratch up *vt.* = **scrape together**

scratch-and-sniff *adj.* designed to release a smell when scratched, especially as a complement to a visual experience

scratchboard /skrách bawrd/ *n. US* = **scraperboard** *n.* 1

scratch card *n.* a card containing one or more sections covered in an overlay that can be scratched off to reveal a possible prize printed beneath

scratch file *n.* a temporary computer file created in a memory device as a work area or for use when executing a program

scratchie /skráchi/ *n.* a scratch card (*informal*)

scratchings /skráchingz/ *npl.* = **pork scratchings** [14thC. Origin unknown.]

scratch line *n.* **1.** scratch line, scratch STARTING LINE a starting line in a race **2.** LINE NOT TO BE OVERSTEPPED a line that a competitor may not step over without committing a foul

scratchpad /skrách pad/ *n.* **1.** *US* NOTE PAD a pad of paper for making rough notes **2.** COMPUTER MEMORY AREA a high-speed temporary storage area in a computer memory

scratch test *n.* a test to discover if sb is allergic to a substance (**allergen**), in which a small amount of the substance is rubbed into a lightly scratched area of skin. A reaction, e.g. the formation of a weal, indicates an allergy to the substance.

scratch ticket *n. Aus* a scratch card (*informal*)

scratchy /skráchi/ **(-ier, -iest)** *adj.* **1.** ITCHY causing or feeling itchiness on the skin ○ *a scratchy sweater* **2.** SOUNDING LIKE SCRATCHES making a scratching or scraping sound ○ *a scratchy recording* **3.** PENNED QUICKLY written or drawn hastily or illegibly —**scratchily** *adv.* —**scratchiness** *n.*

scrawl /skrawl/ *vti.* **(scrawls, scrawling, scrawled)** WRITE OR DRAW STH MESSILY to write or draw sth untidily or hastily, especially in large letters that are difficult to read ■ *n.* UNTIDY WRITING untidy or hurried-looking handwriting or drawing [Early 17thC. Origin uncertain: perhaps from obsolete *scrawl* 'to gesticulate, sprawl', blend of SPRAWL and CRAWL.] —**scrawler** *n.* —**scrawly** *adj.*

scrawny /skráwni/ **(-nier, -niest)** *adj.* unpleasantly or unhealthily thin and bony [Mid-19thC. Variant of dialect 'scranny', of uncertain origin: probably from a Scandinavian language.] —**scrawnily** *adv.* —**scrawniness** *n.*

WORD KEY: SYNONYMS

See Synonyms at *thin*.

screak /skreek/ *vi.* **(screaks, screaking, screaked)** *US* **1.** TO SCREECH to produce a screech **2.** TO CREAK to produce a creak ■ *n. US* **1.** SCREECH a screeching sound **2.** CREAK a creaking sound [15thC. From Old Norse *skrækja*, an imitation of the sound.] —**screaky** *adj.*

scream /skreem/ *n.* **1.** PIERCING CRY a loud, piercing, high-pitched cry, uttered especially in fear, pain, excitement, or amusement **2.** HIGH-PITCHED NOISE a very loud, high-pitched sound such as that of a siren or jet engine **3.** SB OR STH HIGHLY AMUSING an extremely funny or entertaining person, event, or activity (*informal*) ■ *v.* **(screams, screaming, screamed) 1.** *vi.* CRY to utter a loud, piercing, high-pitched cry, especially in fear, pain, or excitement ○ *He screamed for help.* **2.** *vt.* SHOUT STH IN PIERCING VOICE to utter sth in a loud, piercing, high-pitched voice, especially in fear, panic, desperation, or excitement ○ *'Get out!' he screamed.* **3.** *vi.* LAUGH LOUDLY to laugh shrilly and loudly **4.** *vi.* MAKE HIGH-PITCHED SOUND to make a loud high-pitched sound ○ *The ambulance went by, sirens screaming.* **5.** *vi.* MOVE AT SPEED to move extremely quickly while producing a loud high-pitched sound

○ *The police car screamed by.* **6.** *vi.* **BE OBVIOUS** to be extremely obvious or noticeable ○ *The mistakes just scream out at you.* [13thC. Origin uncertain: perhaps from Middle Dutch *schreem* or Old Norse *scræma*, both imitations of the sound.] —**screamingly** *adv.*

WORD KEY: CULTURAL NOTE

The Scream, a painting by the Norwegian painter Edvard Munch (1893). Painted in a bold, expressionist style, it depicts a panic-stricken human figure standing on a bridge or pier. The skull-like face appears to emit a cry that reverberates through the surrounding landscape. A powerful symbol of despair, it is one of the best-known icons of modern art.

screamer /skreémər/ *n.* **1.** **STH THAT SCREAMS** sb or sth that screams **2.** BIRDS **BIRD RESEMBLING GOOSE** a South American aquatic bird that resembles a goose, but with a smaller bill, and has a harsh call. Family: Anhimidae. **3.** PRINTING **EXCLAMATION MARK** an exclamation mark (*slang*) **4.** **HILARIOUS PERSON OR THING** sb or sth that is extremely funny or entertaining (*informal*)

screaming abdabs /skreéming áb dabz/, **screaming habdabs** /-háb dabz/ *npl.* an attack of nervous anxiety (*dated informal*) US term **screaming meemies** ['Abdabs' of unknown origin]

screaming meemies /-meémiz/ *npl. US* = **screaming abdabs** (*informal*) (*takes a singular or plural verb*) [*Meemies* of unknown origin]

scree /skree/ *n.* **1.** **ROCK DEBRIS AT BASE OF HILL** an accumulation of rock debris at the base of a cliff, hill, or mountain slope, often forming a heap **2.** **SCREE-COVERED SLOPE** a slope covered with a layer of scree [Early 18thC. From Old Norse *skriða* 'landslip'.]

screech /skreech/ *n.* **1.** **SHRILL SCREAM** a high-pitched grating cry or scream, uttered especially in fear, pain, excitement, or amusement ○ *the screech of an owl* **2.** **HIGH-PITCHED SOUND** a loud high-pitched grating sound ○ *a screech of brakes* ■ *v.* (**screeches, screeching, screeched**) **1.** *vi.* **UTTER SHRILL SCREAM** to utter a high-pitched grating cry or scream, especially in fear, pain, excitement, or amusement **2.** *vt.* **SHRIEK STH** to utter sth in a high-pitched and grating tone of voice **3.** *vi.* **MAKE SCREECHING SOUND** to make a loud high-pitched grating sound **4.** *vi.* **PRODUCE SCREECHING SOUND BY MOVING FAST** to move, usually extremely fast, while producing a screeching sound ○ *The car screeched to a stop.* [Mid-16thC. Alteration of archaic *scritch*, ultimately an imitation of the sound.] —**screecher** *n.* —**screechiness** *n.* —**screechy** *adj.*

screech owl *n.* any European owl that has a characteristic screeching cry

screed /skreed/ *n.* **1.** **LENGTHY PIECE OF WRITING** a long and often tedious piece of writing or speech (*often used in the plural*) **2.** CONSTR **GUIDE FOR PLASTERING** a strip of plaster, wood, or other material placed on a surface as a guide to the correct thickness of plaster or concrete to be applied there **3.** CONSTR **BOARD FOR LEVELLING** a board or tool used to level a layer of concrete, sand, or other loose material **4.** CONSTR **TOP LAYER** a smooth top layer on a concrete floor or other surface **5.** *Scotland* **A TEAR** a tear or tearing sound [14thC. Variant of SHRED; originally in the sense 'torn strip'.]

screen /skreen/ *n.* **1.** **PARTITION OR SHELTER** a fixed or movable partition or frame that is used to conceal, divide, separate, or provide shelter ○ *You may get changed behind the screen.* **2.** **STH THAT CONCEALS** anything that serves to conceal, divide, separate, or provide shelter ○ *A screen of leaves protected her from the sun.* **3.** ARCHIT **DECORATIVE FRAME** a decorative frame or partition, e.g. in a church choir ○ *a rood screen* **4.** ELECTRON ENG **ELECTRONIC DISPLAY SURFACE** the broad flat end of a cathode-ray tube or liquid crystal display on which images are displayed, e.g. in a television set or computer monitor **5.** COMPUT **DATA DISPLAYED ON MONITOR** the data displayed on the screen of a computer monitor ○ *to print the screen* **6.** CINEMA, PHOTOGRAPHY **SURFACE FOR PROJECTING FILM ONTO** a large flat white or silver surface onto which a film or slide is projected **7.** CINEMA **FILM** the film industry **8.** **MESH FRAME OR MESH** a frame with a fine wire or plastic mesh designed to prevent the entry of mosquitoes or other insects, or the mesh itself **9.** **WINDSCREEN** a windscreen **10.** **CONCEALMENT** a measure taken to conceal sth ○ *This report is just a screen for the government's inaction.* **11.** **SELECTION SYSTEM** a system for selecting suitable people, e.g. for a post, membership of an organization, or tenancy of property **12.** **SIEVE** a sieve used to filter out fine particles, e.g. of sand or gravel **13.** MIL **ADVANCE DETACHMENT** a military detachment sent in advance of a main force to protect it from the enemy or give warning of enemy approach **14.** PHOTOGRAPHY **CAMERA PLATE FOR FOCUSING** a ground-glass plate in a camera that is used for getting an image properly focused before it is photographed **15.** PRINTING **GLASS PLATE FOR HALF-TONE REPRODUCTIONS** a glass plate marked with very fine lines and used in producing half-tone reproductions **16.** PSYCHOANAL **EMOTIONAL BLOCK** sth that prevents sb from understanding his or her real feelings ■ *v.* (**screens, screening, screened**) **1.** *vt.* **CONCEAL OR SHELTER SB OR STH** to provide shelter, protection, or concealment from sb or sth **2.** *vt.* **PARTITION STH OFF** to partition, separate, or divide sth off from sth else ○ *They had screened the area into cubicles.* **3.** *vt.* **FIT STH WITH SCREEN** to provide sth with a screen **4.** *vt.* **PROTECT SB** to protect sb from sth unpleasant or dangerous **5.** *vti.* CINEMA **SHOW IN CINEMA** to project a film onto a screen in a cinema **6.** *vti.* TV **SHOW ON TELEVISION** to broadcast a film, programme, or other item on television **7.** *vti.* **TEST FOR DISEASE** to test sb or sth for a particular illness or disease **8.** *vti.* **SELECT BY WEEDING OUT** to select sb as being suitable for sth, e.g. a post, membership of an organization, or tenancy of property **9.** *vt.* **SIEVE STH** to filter sth through a sieve **10.** *vt.* PRINTING **PHOTOGRAPH STH FOR HALF-TONE REPRODUCTION** to photograph sth through a glass plate to make a half-tone reproduction [14thC. From Old Northern French *escren*.] —**screenable** *adj.* —**screener** *n.*

screen dump *n.* the process of printing or saving the contents of a computer display screen

screening /skreéning/ *n.* **1.** CINEMA **A SHOWING IN A CINEMA** a projection of a film on a screen in a cinema **2.** TV **A SHOWING ON TELEVISION** a showing of a film, programme, or other item on television **3.** MED **TEST FOR DISEASE** a test or testing carried out routinely on supposedly healthy people in order to establish, as early as possible, whether or not an illness or disease is present **4.** **PROTECTING SCREENS** screens for providing shelter, protection, or concealment, or for separating or dividing **5.** **WIRE MESH** fine wire or plastic mesh used on a door or window to prevent the entry of mosquitoes or other insects ■ **screenings** *npl.* **SIEVED MATERIAL** waste material that has been screened from sth

screen memory *n.* an early childhood memory that is used subconsciously to mask another related, often distressful, memory

screenplay /skreén play/ *n.* a script or scenario for a film

screen-print *n.* a print produced by silk-screen printing —**screen-printing** *n.* —**screen-print** *vti.*

screen saver *n.* a computer utility that automatically makes the screen go blank or display a particular image after a particular period of time. Originally developed to prevent the permanent etching of a pattern on the screen of older monochrome monitors, screen savers now are an adornment with which to personalize a computer.

screen test *n.* an audition for a film role in which an actor is filmed, or the film made of the audition —**screen-test** *vti.*

screenwriter /skreén rītər/ *n.* the writer of a script that is intended to be filmed —**screenwriting** *n.*

screw /skroo/ *n.* **1.** CONSTR **THREADED FASTENER INSERTED INTO MATERIAL** a piece of metal with a tapering threaded body and grooved head by which it is turned into sth in order to fasten things together **2.** CONSTR **SCREW FOR NUT** a screw with a blunt end onto which a nut is fitted to hold two objects together **3.** **DEVICE SIMILAR TO SCREW** anything that has a form similar to a tapering metal screw, e.g. a corkscrew **4.** **TWISTING ACTION** a turn of a screw or of a device like a screw **5.** ENG = **propeller** **6.** CUE GAMES **SHOT IN WHICH CUE BALL REBOUNDS** a shot in billiards or snooker in which the cue ball returns towards the player after hitting the ball it was aimed at **7.** **OFFENSIVE TERM** an offensive

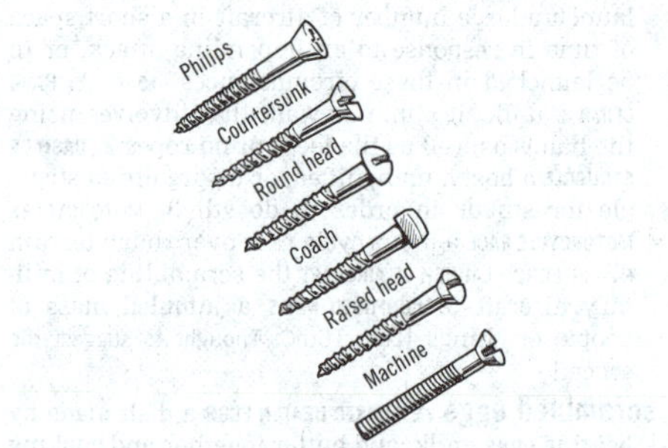

Screw

term for an act or instance of sexual intercourse (*slang offensive*) **8.** **OFFENSIVE TERM** an offensive term for a sexual partner with regard to his or her sexual performance (*slang offensive*) **9.** CRIMINOL **WARDER** a prison warder (*slang*) **10.** **PAPER TWIST** a small twist of paper, especially one containing tobacco (*dated informal*) **11.** **SALARY** a salary or wages earned by sb (*dated informal*) **12.** **MISER** sb who is considered to be miserly with money (*informal*) **13.** **OLD HORSE** a decrepit old horse (*informal*) ■ *v.* (**screws, screwing, screwed**) **1.** *vti.* **FASTEN WITH SCREWS** to fasten or tighten sth with a screw or screws ○ *He screwed the shelf to the wall.* **2.** *vti.* **FASTEN BY ROTATING** to rotate sth along a thread in order to fasten or tighten it ○ *screwed the bulb in carefully* **3.** *vt.* **CRUSH STH** to crumple or crush sth into a tight ball **4.** *vti.* **CONTORT** to contort or crumple a part of or all of the face, or to be contorted or crumpled ○ *She screwed her eyes up against the glare.* **5.** *vt.* CUE GAMES **CAUSE CUE BALL TO REBOUND** in billiards or snooker, to hit the cue ball below its centre of gravity so that, when it strikes a ball it is aimed at, it rolls back on itself **6.** *vti.* **OFFENSIVE TERM** an offensive term meaning to have sexual intercourse with sb (*slang offensive*) **7.** *vt.* **CHEAT SB** to cheat or swindle sb (*informal*) **8.** *vt.* **EXTORT STH** to get sth out of sb with great difficulty (*informal*) ○ *We managed to screw some money out of him in the end.* **9.** *vt.* **OFFENSIVE TERM** an offensive term used to express anger or frustration (*slang offensive*) [15thC. From Old French *escroue*, directly or via prehistoric Germanic from Latin *scrofa* 'sow' (because of its curly tail shaped like a corkscrew).] —**screwable** *adj.* —**screwer** *n.* ◇ **have a screw loose** to be irrational or lack common sense or good judgment (*informal*) ◇ **put the screws on sb** to use force or pressure on sb (*slang*)

screw around *vi.* (*slang offensive*) **1.** **OFFENSIVE TERM** an offensive term meaning to have sex with a number of different people, especially when married or in an established relationship **2.** **OFFENSIVE TERM** an offensive term meaning to waste time in trivial or pointless activities

screw up *v.* **1.** *vti.* **OFFENSIVE TERM** an offensive term meaning to mismanage, disrupt, or make a mess of sth (*slang offensive*) **2.** *vt.* **OFFENSIVE TERM** an offensive term meaning to disturb sb psychologically or emotionally (*slang offensive*) **3.** **MUSTER STH** to gather courage or nerve before doing sth

screwball /skroó bawl/ *n.* **OFFENSIVE TERM** an offensive term for sb who is regarded as behaving in an unconventional, irrational, or strange way (*informal insult*) ■ *adj.* **STRANGE** regarded as unconventional, irrational, or strange (*informal*)

screwball comedy *n.* a film, especially a Hollywood comedy of the 1930s, featuring the amusing antics of appealing characters in a glamorous world. These films often feature an emancipated and strong-willed heroine.

screw bean *n.* **1.** **SHRUB PRODUCING PODS USED AS FODDER** a shrub of the legume family that is native to the southwestern United States and Mexico and produces twisted pods that are used as fodder. Latin name: *Prosopis pubescens.* **2.** **SEED POD** a pod of the screw bean plant

screwdriver /skroó drīvər/ *n.* **1.** TECH **TOOL FOR FASTENING SCREWS** a tool for driving screws that consists of a handle with a metal rod shaped at the tip to fit into the head of a screw **2.** BEVERAGES **VODKA AND ORANGE COCKTAIL** a cocktail made from vodka and orange juice

screwed /skrood/ *adj.* **1. FASTENED WITH SCREW** fastened or tightened with a screw or screws **2. WITH SCREW THREAD** having a screw thread **3. CONTORTED** misshapen or contorted **4. OFFENSIVE TERM** in serious difficulties (*slang offensive*) **5. DRUNK** drunk (*dated slang*)

screwed up *adj.* (*hyphenated when used before a noun*) **1. OFFENSIVE TERM** an offensive term meaning affected by or displaying symptoms of psychological or emotional disorder (*slang offensive*) **2. OFFENSIVE TERM** an offensive term meaning mismanaged, disrupted, or made a mess of (*informal*)

screw eye *n.* a screw with a looped instead of a flat head

screw jack *n.* a jack used for lifting heavy items such as vehicles, operated by a screw mechanism

screw pine *n.* = **pandanus**

screw propeller *n.* = **propeller**

screw tap *n.* a tool for making female screws

screw thread *n.* **1. OUTER RIDGE OF SCREW** the continuous helical outer surface of a screw or the inner surface of a nut **2. TURN OF SCREW THREAD** a full turn of a screw thread

screw top *n.* a lid or cap that screws onto a container (*hyphenated when used before a noun*) ○ *a screw-top jar*

screwup /skróo up/ *n.* an offensive term for a mess, muddle, or bungled event (*slang offensive*)

screwworm /skróo wurm/ *n.* the larva of the screwworm fly that grows under the skin of livestock and other mammals, causing injury and death [Late 19thC. *Screw* from the spiny hairs of the larva, which encircle each segment.]

screwworm fly *n.* a bluish blowfly whose eggs, laid on the skin of livestock and other large mammals, hatch as larvae (**screwworms**) that grow under the skin. Latin name: *Cochliomyia hominivorax.*

screwy /skróo i/ (**-ier, -iest**) *adj.* an offensive term meaning irrational, unconventional, or strange (*informal*) —**screwily** *adv.* —**screwiness** *n.*

scribal /skrīb'l/ *adj.* relating to or done by a scribe

scribble[1] /skríbb'l/ *v.* (**-bles, -bling, -bled**) **1.** *vti.* **WRITE MESSILY** to write sth hastily or untidily, often in smallish letters **2.** *vti.* **MAKE MEANINGLESS MARKINGS** to write or draw meaningless or undecipherable marks on sth ○ *Don't scribble on the wall!* **3.** *vi.* **BE WRITER** to be a writer, especially one of little merit (*humorous*) ■ *n.* **1. MESSY HANDWRITING** untidy or careless handwriting **2. HASTY NOTE** sth written untidily or hastily **3. DOODLES** meaningless marks written or drawn on sth [15thC. Ultimately from Latin *scribere* 'to write' (source of English *scribe*).] —**scribbler** *n.*

scribble[2] /skríbb'l/ (**-bles, -bling, -bled**) *vt.* to card wool roughly [Late 17thC. Origin uncertain.]

scribbly gum /skríbbli-/ *n.* any of a number of eucalyptus trees whose bark is marked with patterns resembling scribbles that are actually created by burrowing insect larvae. Genus: *Eucalyptus.*

scribe /skrīb/ *n.* **1.** HIST **BOOK COPIER** sb who copies or writes out documents, especially sb who copied manuscripts in medieval times **2.** JUDAISM **COPIER OF JEWISH RELIGIOUS DOCUMENTS** sb who copies the Sefer Torah and other religious documents using a quill pen on parchment **3. CLERK** an official public clerk **4. JOURNALIST** a writer, especially a journalist (*humorous*) **5.** TECH = **scriber** ■ *vti.* (**scribes, scribing, scribed**) TECH **MARK LINES ON STH** to mark sth such as wood or metal with a line using a pointed instrument, especially as a guide for cutting [12thC. From Latin *scriba* 'official or public writer', from *scribere* 'to write'.]

scriber /skrībər/ *n.* a sharp instrument for marking lines on wood or other material

scrim /skrim/ *n.* **1.** THEATRE **THEATRICAL CURTAIN** a drop curtain in the theatre that appears opaque to the audience when lit from the front but transparent when lit from behind **2.** TEXTILES **COTTON OR LINEN FABRIC** a durable open-weave cotton or linen fabric used for curtains, clothing, upholstery lining, and in industry [Late 18thC. Origin unknown.]

scrimmage /skrímmij/ *n.* **1. FIGHT** a skirmish or minor battle **2. STRUGGLE** a rough or confused struggle **3.** RUGBY **SCRUM** a scrum (*archaic*) ■ *vti.* (**-mages, -maging, -maged**) **TAKE PART IN SCRIMMAGE** to engage in a scrimmage against sb [15thC. Alteration of SKIRMISH.]

scrimp /skrimp/ (**scrimps, scrimping, scrimped**) *v.* **1.** *vi.* **ECONOMIZE** to economize drastically or be extremely frugal ○ *scrimp on food* **2.** *vt.* **BE STINGY TO SB** to treat sb meanly or limit provision to sb severely **3.** *vt.* **MAKE STH TOO SMALL** to make sth too small or scanty [Mid-18thC. From obsolete *scrimp* 'scant, meagre', of uncertain origin: perhaps ultimately from a Scandinavian source.] —**scrimpily** *adv.* —**scrimpiness** *n.* —**scrimpy** *adj.*

scrimshank /skrím shangk/ (**-shanks, -shanking, -shanked**) *vi.* to shirk work or obligations (*dated slang*) [Late 19thC. Origin unknown.] —**scrimshanker** *n.*

scrimshaw /skrím shaw/ *n.* **1. CARVED WHALE IVORY** a carved or engraved article made originally by North American whalers from the teeth and bones of whales, or such articles collectively **2. MAKING OF SCRIMSHAW** the skill or pastime of making scrimshaw ■ *v.* (**-shaws, -shawing, -shawed**) **1.** *vi.* **MAKE SCRIMSHAW** to make scrimshaw **2.** *vt.* **CARVE OR ENGRAVE STH** to carve or engrave sth into scrimshaw [Mid-19thC. From earlier *scrimshonting* 'carving whale ivory', ultimately of unknown origin: perhaps influenced by the surname *Scrimshaw.*]

scrip[1] /skrip/ *n.* **1. BRIEF PIECE OF WRITING** a list, receipt, or other short piece of writing **2.** *US* **TEMPORARY PAPER CURRENCY** paper currency issued for temporary emergency use, e.g. by an occupying force [Late 16thC. Alteration of SCRIPT, influenced by SCRAP.]

scrip[2] /skrip/ *n.* a document or certificate representing a fraction of a share or stock [Mid-18thC. Shortening of *subscription receipt.*]

scrip[3] /skrip/ *n.* a wallet or small satchel or bag (*archaic*) [14thC. From Old French *escrep(p)e* 'alms purse', from *escherpe* 'scarf'.]

scrip issue *n.* FIN = **bonus issue**

scripophily /skripóffili/ *n.* the hobby of collecting share and bond certificates, especially those of historical interest [Late 20thC. Coined from SCRIP[2] + -PHILY.] —**scripophile** /skrípə fīl/ *n.*

script /skript/ *n.* **1. TEXT OF PLAY OR BROADCAST** the printed version of a stage play, film screenplay, or radio or television broadcast, including the words to be spoken and often also technical directions **2. MANUSCRIPT** an original document or manuscript **3. SYSTEM OF WRITING** any system of characters used in writing **4. HANDWRITING** characters written by hand, especially in cursive form **5. PRINTED TYPE RESEMBLING WRITING** printed type designed to imitate handwriting **6.** EDUC **ANSWER PAPER** an answer paper in an examination ■ *vt.* (**scripts, scripting, scripted**) **WRITE SCRIPT FOR STH** to write or prepare a script for sth [14thC. Via Old French *escri(p)t* from Latin *scriptus*, from *scribere* 'to write' (source of English *description* and *scripture*).]

Script. *abbr.* Scripture

scriptorium /skrip táwri əm/ (*plural* **-ums** *or* **-a** /-ri ə/) *n.* a room in a monastery for storing, copying, illustrating, or reading manuscripts [Late 18thC. From medieval Latin, where it was formed from Latin *scribere* (see SCRIPTURE).]

scriptural /skrípchərəl/ *adj.* **1.** RELIG **OF SACRED WRITINGS** relating to, contained in, or according to sacred writings, especially the biblical scriptures **2. OF WRITING** written or relating to writing [Mid-17thC. From late Latin *scripturalis*, from *scriptura* (see SCRIPTURE).] —**scripturally** *adv.*

scripture /skrípchər/, **Scripture** *n.* **1. BIBLICAL WRITINGS** the sacred writings of the Bible **2. BIBLICAL TEXT** a passage from the Bible **3. SACRED WRITING** any sacred writing or book ○ *Buddhist scripture* **4. AUTHORITATIVE STATEMENT** a statement regarded as authoritative [14thC. From Latin *scriptura* 'that which is written', from the past participle of *scribere* 'to write'.]

scriptwriter /skrípt rītər/ *n.* sb who writes scripts for material to be broadcast

scrivener /skrívvənər/ *n.* **1. PROFESSIONAL COPYIST OR SCRIBE** in former times, sb whose job involved writing or making handwritten copies of documents, books, or other texts **2. NOTARY PUBLIC** a notary public (*archaic*) [14thC. Via Old French *escrivein*, ultimately from Latin *scriba* (see SCRIBE).]

scrobiculate /skrō bíkyŏŏlət, -layt/ *adj.* BIOL with a grooved or pitted surface [Late 19thC. Via *scrobicule* 'small pit or groove', from late Latin *scrobiculus* 'little trench', from *scrobis* 'trench'.]

scrofula /skróffyŏŏlə/ *n.* tuberculosis of the lymph glands, especially of the neck. If untreated, the glands burst through the skin to form running sores. [14thC. From medieval Latin *scrofula* 'swelling of glands', from *scrofa* 'breeding sow', because the glands resemble a pig's back, or because 'scrofula' meant 'swine disease'.]

scrofulous /skróffyŏŏləss/ *adj.* **1. HAVING OR RESEMBLING SCROFULA** affected with or characteristic of scrofula **2. SHABBY IN APPEARANCE** run-down, diseased, or shabby in appearance **3. MORALLY CORRUPT** morally corrupt and degenerate —**scrofulously** *adv.* —**scrofulousness** *n.*

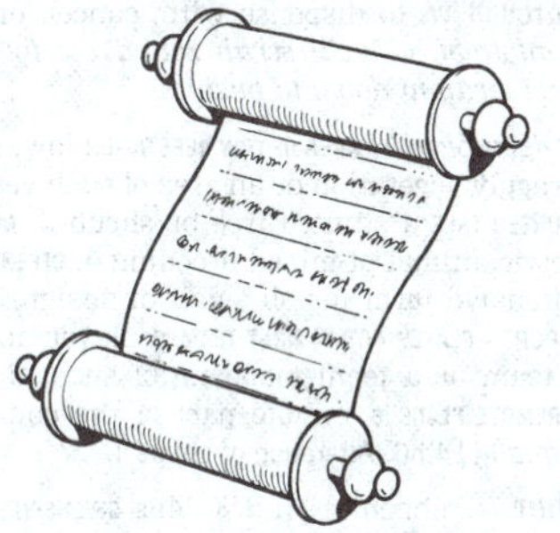

Scroll

scroll /skrōl/ *n.* **1. ROLL OF PARCHMENT** a roll of paper, parchment, leather, or other material for writing a document **2. LIST** a list, roll, or roster **3. ORNAMENTAL DESIGN RESEMBLING ROLL OF PAPER** an ornamental design shaped like a rolled or partially rolled piece of paper **4.** MUSIC **CURVED HEAD OF STRINGED INSTRUMENT** the curved head of a stringed musical instrument such as a violin where the tuning pegs are set **5.** HERALDRY **HERALDIC RIBBON WITH MOTTO** in heraldry, a ribbon with rolled ends inscribed with a motto ■ *vti.* (**scrolls, scrolling, scrolled**) **MOVE TEXT OR GRAPHICS** to cause text or graphics to move up, down, or across a computer display screen, or to be moved in this way [15thC. Alteration of *scrowe*, influenced by ROLL, via Old French *escroe* 'strip of parchment' from medieval Latin *scroda* 'strip', ultimately from a prehistoric Germanic word meaning 'sth cut'.]

scroll bar *n.* a horizontal or vertical bar on a computer display screen containing a box used to make text or graphics move up, down, or across the screen

scroll saw *n.* a saw with a narrow blade used for cutting curved ornamental designs

scrollwork /skrōl wurk/ *n.* ornamental designs characterized by scrolls, especially in wood

scrooge /skrooj/, **Scrooge** *n.* sb who is regarded as very miserly (*informal*) [Mid-19thC. From *Ebenezer Scrooge*, a character in *A Christmas Carol* (1843), by Charles DICKENS.]

scroop /skroop/ *n.* **RUSTLING SOUND OF SILK** a rasping sound like that of rustling silk ■ *vi.* (**scroops, scrooping, scrooped**) **RUSTLE** to make a rustling or rasping noise [Late 18thC. An imitation of the sound.]

scrote /skrōt/ *n.* an offensive term referring to a man who is seen as unpleasant or malicious (*offensive insult*)

scrotum /skrṓtəm/ (*plural* **-tums** *or* **-ta** /-tə/) *n.* the external pouch of skin and muscle containing the testes in mammals. It allows sperm to develop at a temperature lower than that of the body. [Late 16thC. From Latin. Ultimately from an Indo-European word that is also the ancestor of English *shroud.*] —**scrotal** *adj.*

scrouge /skrowj, skrooj/ (**scrouges, scrouging, scrouged**) *vti.* to squeeze, crowd, or press sb or sth (*regional*) [Mid-18thC. Alteration of *scruze*, blend of SCREW and SQUEEZE.]

scrounge /skrownj/ (**scrounges, scrounging, scrounged**) *vti.* (*informal*) **1. BEG OR BORROW** to acquire sth from sb by begging or borrowing without intending to make repayment or return **2. GET FROM ANY AVAILABLE SOURCE** to seek and acquire sth from any available source, e.g.

by foraging [Early 20thC. Alteration of *scringe*, 'to prowl around', from CRINGE.] —**scrounger** *n.*

scrub^{1} /skrub/ *v.* (**scrubs, scrubbing, scrubbed**) **1.** *vti.* **CLEAN BY RUBBING** to clean sth by rubbing hard **2.** *vt.* **REMOVE DIRT BY RUBBING** to remove dirt by rubbing hard, usually with a brush **3.** *vt.* **REMOVE IMPURITIES FROM GAS** to remove impurities from a gas by passing it over or through a liquid **4.** *vi.* **CLEANSE FOR SURGERY** to cleanse the arms and hands in preparation for surgery **5.** *vt.* **CANCEL STH** to cancel or postpone sth (*informal*) ■ *n.* **ACT OF SCRUBBING** the act of cleaning sth by rubbing hard ■ **scrubs** *npl. US* **CLOTHING WORN WHILE PERFORMING SURGERY** the clothing, usually a matching green shirt and trousers, worn by surgeons and nurses in an operating theatre (*informal*) [13thC. Origin uncertain: probably from Middle Low German or Middle Dutch *schrubben*.]
scrub round *vt.* to dispense with, cancel, or ignore sth (*informal*) ○ *We'll scrub round the formalities and get straight down to business.*

scrub^{2} /skrub/ *n.* **1. AREA OF LOW VEGETATION** low, stunted, or straggly vegetation or an area of such vegetation **2. STUNTED TREE** a stunted tree or shrub **3. MONGREL** a domestic animal of mixed breeding **4. OFFENSIVE TERM** an offensive term for sb small or insignificant **5.** *US* SPORTS **PLAYER NOT IN FIRST TEAM** a player not in the first team or a team made up of such players **6.** *Aus* **REMOTE PLACE** a remote part of the countryside (*informal*) [14thC. Alteration of SHRUB.]

scrubber /skrúbbər/ *n.* **1.** *UK, Aus* **OFFENSIVE TERM** an offensive term referring contemptuously to a prostitute or a woman who is considered promiscuous, coarse, or slovenly (*slang offensive*) **2. SB OR STH THAT SCRUBS** sb or sth that cleans by rubbing hard, often with a brush **3. APPARATUS FOR PURIFYING GAS** a device for removing impurities from a gas [Mid-19thC. Formed from SCRUB^{1}; 'promiscuous woman' perhaps also from SCRUB^{2} in the sense 'mongrel'.]

scrubby /skrúbbi/ (**-bier, -biest**) *adj.* **1. STUNTED OR STRAGGLY** inferior in size or quality **2. COVERED WITH LOW TREES** covered with or consisting of low or undersized shrubs or trees **3. SHABBY** shabby, untidy, or wretched in appearance —**scrubbiness** *n.*

scrubland /skrúb land/ *n.* land covered with low trees and shrubs

scrub typhus *n.* a common infectious disease in Asia that is caused by the microorganism *Rickettsia tsutsugamushi* and spread by a biting mite. Symptoms include fever, painful swollen lymph nodes, and a skin rash.

scruff^{1} /skruf/ *n.* the back of the neck, especially when used to seize, drag, or lift a person or animal [Late 18thC. Alteration of earlier *scuff*, from Old Norse *skoft*, 'hair of the head'.]

scruff^{2} /skruf/ *n.* sb who is untidy or is regarded as disreputable (*informal*) [Old English *scruf*, alteration of SCURF]

scruffy /skrúffi/ (**-ier, -iest**) *adj.* untidy, shabby, or rundown in appearance [Mid-17thC. Formed from SCRUFF. The modern meaning, 'shabby', evolved from 'scaly, covered with scurf'.] —**scruffily** *adv.* —**scruffiness** *n.*

scrum /skrum/ *n.* **1. RUGBY FORMATION DECIDING POSSESSION OF BALL** a part of a rugby match in which the two sets of forwards gather around the ball with heads down and arms linked and try to obtain possession of it **2. CONFUSED JOSTLE OR STRUGGLE** a crowd of people jostling or struggling for sth ■ *vi.* (**scrums, scrumming, scrummed**) **FORM RUGBY SCRUM** to form a scrum in rugby [Late 19thC. Shortening of SCRUMMAGE.]

scrum half *n.* in rugby, the halfback who places the ball in the scrum, or the position of this player

scrummage /skrúmmij/ *n., vi.* (**-mages, -maging, -maged**) = **scrum** *n.* 1 [Early 19thC. Alteration of SCRIMMAGE.] —**scrummager** *n.*

scrummy /skrúmmi/ *adj.* very attractive, delicious, or excellent (*dated informal*) [Early 20thC. From a shortening of SCRUMPTIOUS + -Y.]

scrump /skrump/ (**scrumps, scrumping, scrumped**) *vti.* to steal fruit, especially apples, from a garden or orchard (*informal*) [Mid-19thC. From dialect *scrump* 'sth withered, withered apple', of uncertain origin.]

scrumptious /skrúmpshəss/ *adj.* very pleasing, especially to the taste (*informal*) [Mid-19thC. Origin uncertain: probably an alteration of SUMPTUOUS.] —**scrumptiously** *adv.* —**scrumptiousness** *n.*

scrumpy /skrúmpi/ (*plural* **-pies**) *n. W Country* a rough strong dry cider, usually made in the West Country (*informal*) [Early 20thC. Formed from dialect *scrump* (see SCRUMP).]

scrunch /skrunch/ (**scrunches, scrunching, scrunched**) *v.* **1.** *vt.* **SQUEEZE STH** to crumple, crush, or squeeze sth together tightly **2.** *vi.* **MOVE WITH CRUNCHING SOUND** to move with or make a crunching sound [Late 18thC. Thought to suggest the action, or to be an imitation of the sound.]

scrunch-dry (**scrunch-dries, scrunch-drying, scrunch-dried**) *vt.* to dry hair while squeezing it together tightly in your hand to add volume and create a natural curly style

scrunchie /skrúnchi/ *n.* a thick elasticated band loosely covered with fabric, used to hold a bunch of hair, e.g. in a pony tail [Late 20thC. Formed from SCRUNCH, because of its crumpled appearance.]

scruple /skrōōp'l/ *n.* **1. MORAL OR ETHICAL CONSIDERATION** a moral or ethical consideration that tends to restrain action or behaviour **2.** MEASURE **UNIT OF WEIGHT** a unit of apothecaries' weight equal to or about 1.3 g/20 grains **3. VERY SMALL AMOUNT** a minute amount or portion of sth (*archaic*) ■ *vi.* (**-ples, -pling, -pled**) **HESITATE BECAUSE OF MORAL CONSIDERATIONS** to hesitate because of moral or ethical considerations ○ *She wouldn't scruple to cheat.* [15thC. Via Old French *scrupule* from Latin *scrupulus* 'small sharp stone, uneasiness', from *scrupus* 'sharp stone'. The underlying idea is of a sharp stone causing discomfort.]

scrupulous /skrōōpyōōləss/ *adj.* **1. HAVING MORAL INTEGRITY** having or showing careful regard for what is morally right **2. VERY PRECISE** rigorously precise and exact —**scrupulosity** /skrōōpyōō lóssəti/ *n.* —**scrupulously** *adv.* —**scrupulousness** /skrōōpyōōləssnəss/ *n.*

WORD KEY: SYNONYMS

See Synonyms at ***careful***.

scrutable /skrōōtəb'l/ *adj.* capable of being understood by careful observation, examination, or study (*formal or humorous*) [Late 16thC. Back-formation from INSCRUTABLE.] —**scrutability** /skrōōtə bíllәti/ *n.*

scrutineer /skrōōti néer/ *n.* sb who inspects or examines sth very carefully, e.g. votes at an election or vehicles participating in motor sport [Mid-16thC. Coined from SCRUTINY + -EER.]

scrutinize /skrōōti nīz/ (**-nizes, -nizing, -nized**) *vt.* to examine sb or sth closely and carefully [Late 17thC. Formed from SCRUTINY.] —**scrutinizer** *n.*

scrutiny /skrōōti ni/ (*plural* **-nies**) *n.* **1. CAREFUL INSPECTION** close, careful, searching examination or inspection **2. OBSERVATION** careful study or surveillance **3. GAZE** a searching look [15thC. From Latin *scrutinium* 'search, inquiry', from *scrutinari* 'to search, examine', literally 'to pick through rags', which was in turn formed from *scruta* 'rubbish'.]

scry /skrī/ (**scries, scrying, scried**) *vi.* to predict the future using a crystal ball [Early 16thC. Shortening of DESCRY.]

SCSI /skúzzi/ *n.* a specification for a high-speed computer interface used to connect peripheral devices to a computer. Abbr of **small computer systems interface**

scuba /skōōbə/ *n.* an apparatus for breathing underwater consisting of a portable canister of compressed air and a mouthpiece [Mid-20thC. Acronym formed from *Self-Contained Underwater Breathing Apparatus*.]

scuba diver *n.* sb who swims underwater using scuba equipment —**scuba diving** *n.*

scud /skud/ *vi.* (**scuds, scudding, scudded**) **1. MOVE SWIFTLY** to move swiftly and smoothly **2.** SAILING **SAIL BEFORE GALE** to sail with a gale or strong wind blowing from behind ■ *n.* **1. SWIFT MOVEMENT** a swift smooth movement **2.** METEOROL **CLOUDS DRIVEN BY WIND** low clouds that are driven swiftly by the wind **3.** METEOROL **SUDDEN SHOWER OR GUST** a sudden shower of rain or gust of wind [Mid-16thC. Origin uncertain: perhaps literally 'to race like a hare', alteration of SCUT in the obsolete sense 'hare'.]

Scudamore /skyōōdə mawr, skōōdə-/, **Peter** (*b.* 1958) British jockey. In his career, he rode 1,678 winners, the most in National Hunt history. He was eight times champion jockey. Full name **Peter Michael Scudamore**

Scud missile /skud-/ *n.* a surface-to-surface missile that can take a nuclear, conventional, or chemical warhead [*Scud*: a NATO codename, from SCUD]

scudo /skōōdō/ (*plural* **-di**) *n.* a gold or silver coin introduced in the early 16th century and formerly current in various Italian states, now only appearing occasionally as a commemorative coin issued by the republic of San Marino [Mid-17thC. Via Italian from Latin *scutum*, 'shield' (source of *écu* and *escudo*).]

scuff /skuf/ *vti.* (**scuffs, scuffing, scuffed**) **1. SCRAPE OR RUB** to scrape, rub, or wear away the surface of sth, or to become scraped, rubbed, or worn with use **2. SCRAPE FEET WHILE WALKING** to scrape the feet on the ground while standing or walking or to walk in a manner that makes the feet scrape ■ *n.* **1. ACT OF SCUFFING** a scraping or shuffling movement or sound **2. MARK FROM SCRAPING OR RUBBING** a mark or scratch made by scuffing **3. FLAT SHOE** a flat-soled shoe with no strap or back [Late 16thC. Origin uncertain: possibly from Scandinavian, from a prehistoric Germanic base thought to suggest the action. Originally 'to evade', the modern meaning may have evolved via 'sidestep'.]

scuffle^{1} /skúff'l/ *n.* **DISORDERLY FIGHT** a disorderly confused fight or struggle at close quarters ■ *v.* (**-fles, -fling, -fled**) **1.** *vti.* **FIGHT IN CONFUSION** to struggle or fight at close quarters and in confusion **2.** *vi.* **SHUFFLE QUICKLY** to shuffle along hurriedly [Late 16thC. Origin uncertain: probably from SCUFF + *-le*, with the original meaning 'to evade or dodge repeatedly'.] —**scuffler** *n.*

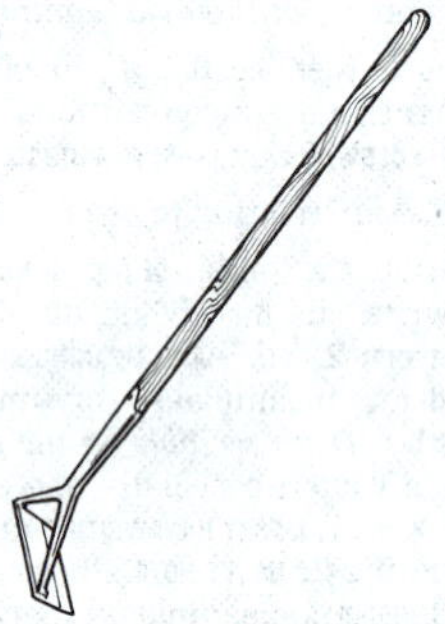

Scuffle

scuffle^{2} /skúff'l/, **scuffle hoe** *n. US* a hoe that is used by pushing it back and forth [Late 18thC. From Dutch *schoffel*.]

scull /skul/ *n.* **1. SINGLE OAR AT BACK OF BOAT** a single oar that is moved from side to side at the stern of a boat to propel the boat forwards **2. EITHER OF A PAIR OF OARS** either of a pair of relatively short oars used by a single rower **3. LIGHT RACING BOAT** a light narrow racing boat propelled by one, two, or four rowers using sculls ■ *vti.* (**sculls, sculling, sculled**) **PROPEL BOAT WITH SCULLS** to propel a boat using a scull or sculls [14thC. Origin unknown.] —**sculler** *n.*

scullery /skúlləri/ (*plural* **-ies**) *n.* a small room for washing and storing dishes and utensils and doing other kitchen chores such as preparing vegetables [15thC. From French *escuelerie* 'duty of servant in charge of plates', from *escuelle* 'dish', from Latin *scutella* 'serving platter' (source of English *skillet*).]

Scullin /skúllin/, **James Henry** (1876–1953) Australian statesman. An Australian Labor Party politician, he was prime minister of Australia (1929–32).

scullion /skúlli ən/ *n.* a servant employed to perform menial kitchen chores [15thC. Via Middle French *escouillon, escouvillon* 'swab, wash-cloth', from *escouve* 'broom', from Latin *scopae* (plural).]

sculp. *abbr.* **1.** sculptor **2.** sculptress **3.** sculpture

sculpin /skúlpin/ (*plural* **-pin** *or* **-pins**) *n.* **1. FLAT-HEADED FISH** a marine and freshwater fish, mostly bottom-dwelling, with a large flat head, large pectoral fins, and spines. Family: Cottidae. **2. SCORPION FISH** a scorpion fish with venomous spines that lives off the southern California coast and is caught for food and for sport. Latin name: *Scorpaena guttata.* [Late 17thC. Origin uncertain: perhaps from *scorpene* 'scorpion-fish', via Spanish *scorpena* or Latin *scorpæna* from Greek *skorpios* 'scorpion'.]

sculpt /skulpt/ (**sculpts, sculpting, sculpted**) *v.* **1.** *vti.* **MAKE SCULPTURE** to carve, model, cast, or otherwise create a three-dimensional representation of sth as a work of art **2.** *vti.* **CARVE OR MODEL MATERIAL** to use a material to create a three-dimensional work of art **3.** *vi.* **BE SCULPTOR** to create three-dimensional works of art as a profession or pastime **4.** *vt.* **CHANGE SHAPE OF STH NATURALLY** to change the shape or contours of sth by natural processes such as erosion [Mid-19thC. Via French *sculpter*, from Latin *sculpere* 'to carve' (see SCULPTURE).]

sculptor /skúlptər/ *n.* an artist who creates three-dimensional works of art, especially by carving, modelling, or casting [Mid-17thC. From Latin, where it was formed from *sculpere*. See SCULPTURE.]

Sculptor /skúlptor/ *n.* a faint constellation in the sky of the southern hemisphere between Grus and Cetus

sculptress /skúlptrəss/ *n.* a woman artist who creates three-dimensional works of art, especially by carving, modelling, or casting

sculpture /skúlpchər/ *n.* **1. CREATION OF THREE-DIMENSIONAL ART** the creation of a three-dimensional work of art, especially by carving, modelling, or casting **2. THREE-DIMENSIONAL WORK OF ART** a work of art created by sculpture, or such works collectively **3.** BOT, ZOOL **NATURAL MARKING ON A PLANT OR ANIMAL** a natural indentation or other marking on a plant or animal, e.g. a ridge on a seashell ■ *v.* (**-tures, -turing, -tured**) **1.** *vt.* **REPRESENT STH IN THREE-DIMENSIONAL ART** to carve, model, cast, or otherwise create a representation of sth as a three-dimensional work of art **2.** *vi.* = **sculpt** *v.* 1 **3.** *vti.* = **sculpt** *v.* 2 **4.** *vt.* = **sculpt** *v.* 4 [14thC. From Latin *sculptura* 'sculpture', from *sculpere* 'to carve, scratch', variant of *scalpere* 'to carve' (source of English *scalpel*).] —**sculptural** *adj.* —**sculpturally** *adv.*

sculpturesque /skúlpchə résk/ *adj.* resembling sculpture —**sculpturesquely** *adv.* —**sculpturesqueness** *n.*

scum /skum/ *n.* **1. FILMY LAYER ON SURFACE OF LIQUID** a filmy layer of extraneous matter or impurities that rises to or is formed on the surface of a liquid **2. OFFENSIVE TERM** an offensive term for a person or group of people regarded as contemptible, vile, or worthless (*insult offensive*) **3. REFUSE** refuse or worthless items **4.** METALL **REFUSE FROM MOLTEN METAL** dross or refuse from molten metals ■ *v.* (**scums, scumming, scummed**) **1.** *vi.* **HAVE SCUM** to become covered with scum **2.** *vt.* **CLEAR STH OF SCUM** to remove scum from sth [14thC. Via Middle Dutch *scūme*, 'foam, froth', ultimately from Germanic. The meaning evolved from 'froth on liquid' through 'film on top of liquid' and 'film of dirt'.] —**scummer** *n.*

scumbag /skúm bag/ *n.* an offensive term referring to sb who is seen as unpleasant or malicious (*slang insult offensive*) [Mid-20thC. From its original US slang meaning '(used) condom'.]

scumble /skúmb'l/ *vt.* (**-bles, -bling, -bled**) **1. SOFTEN STH WITH OPAQUE COLOUR** to soften the colours or outlines of a painting or drawing by covering it with a film of opaque or semiopaque colour **2. SOFTEN COLOURS BY RUBBING** to soften the colours or outlines of a painting or drawing by rubbing ■ *n.* **1. TECHNIQUE OF SCUMBLING** the technique or effect of scumbling **2. SCUMBLING MATERIAL** a material used for scumbling [Late 17thC. Origin uncertain: perhaps literally 'to skim the surface repeatedly', formed from SCUM.]

scunge /skunj/ *vti.* (**scunges, scunging, scunged**) *ANZ* **SCROUNGE** to scrounge sth (*slang*) ■ *n. ANZ* (*slang*) **1. SB SLOVENLY** sb slovenly and messy **2. DIRTY MESS** a sticky and dirty mess [Early 19thC. Origin uncertain.]

scungies /skúnjiz/ *npl. Aus* (*slang*) **1. SWIMMING TRUNKS** close-fitting swimming trunks **2. OLD WORKING CLOTHES** old clothes worn for painting, gardening, or similar activities [Formed from SCUNGY]

scungy /skúnji/ (**-gier, -giest**) *adj. ANZ* messy, shabby, and unattractive (*slang*)

scunner /skúnnər/ *n.* **1. AVERSION** an unreasonable or extreme dislike (*regional informal*) **2.** *Scotland* **SB OR STH DISLIKED** sb or sth that provokes an unreasonable or extreme dislike (*informal*) ■ *vti.* (**-ners, -nering, -nered**) *Scotland* **FEEL OR INSPIRE DISGUST** to feel or show, or to cause sb to feel or show disgusted aversion (*informal*) [14thC. Origin unknown.]

Scunthorpe /skún thawrp/ town in northern Lincolnshire, England. Population: 60,700 (1994).

scup /skup/ (*plural* **scups** *or* **scup**) *n.* a fish of the porgy family that is caught for food along the Atlantic coast of the United States. Latin name: *Stenotomus chrysops.* [19thC. From Narraganset *mishcup*, 'big and close together', because of the shape of the fish's scales.]

scupper[1] /skúppər/ *n.* **1. OPENING FOR DRAINING WATER FROM DECK** an opening in the bulwarks of a ship that allows water on the deck to drain overboard **2. OPENING ALLOWING DRAINAGE FROM BUILDING** an opening allowing water to drain from the roof or floor of a building [15thC. Origin uncertain: perhaps formed from SCOOP, or from Anglo-Norman and Old French *escopir* 'to spit out'.]

scupper[2] /skúppər/ (**-pers, -pering, -pered**) *vt.* **1.** NAUT **SINK SHIP** to sink a ship, especially to sink your own vessel intentionally **2. WRECK OR RUIN STH** to wreck, defeat, or ruin sth [Late 19thC. Origin uncertain: perhaps from SCUPPER[1].]

scuppernong /skúppər nong/ *n.* **1. MUSCADINE GRAPE** a cultivated variety of the muscadine grape that has sweet yellowish-green fruit **2. WINE MADE FROM SCUPPERNONG GRAPES** a sweet amber-coloured wine made from scuppernong grapes [Early 19thC. Named after the *Scuppernong*, a river in North Carolina, where the vine is found.]

scurf /skurf/ *n.* **1. DANDRUFF** thin dry flaking scales of skin, usually as a result of a specific skin condition such as dandruff **2. FLAKY INCRUSTATION** a flaky or scaly incrustation on a surface **3.** BOT **SCALY DEPOSIT ON PLANT** a scaly deposit or covering on a plant **4.** BOT **PLANT DISEASE** a plant disease characterized by a scaly deposit or covering [Old English]

scurrility /skə ríllәti/ (*plural* **-ties**) *n.* **1. COARSENESS** coarseness, vulgarity, or a lack of refinement **2. VULGAR REMARK OR LANGUAGE** language that is coarse and vulgar, or a remark made in coarse vulgar language

scurrilous /skúrriləss/ *adj.* **1. ABUSIVE OR DEFAMATORY** containing abusive language or defamatory allegations **2. FOUL-MOUTHED OR VULGAR** using or containing coarse, vulgar, or obscene language **3. WICKED** behaving in ways thought to be evil or immoral [Late 16thC. Formed from *scurrile*, directly or via French from Latin *scurrilis*, from *scurra* 'buffoon'.] —**scurrilously** *adv.* —**scurrilousness** *n.*

scurry /skúrri/ *vi.* (**-ries, -rying, -ried**) **1. MOVE BRISKLY** to move at a hurried pace, usually with small fast steps **2. MOVE ABOUT AGITATEDLY** to move about in an agitated manner or with a swirling motion ■ *n.* (*plural* **-ries**) **SCURRYING MOVEMENT** a hurried, agitated, or swirling movement [Early 19thC. Origin uncertain: perhaps a shortening of *hurry-scurry* 'to rush about frantically', variant of HURRY.]

scurvy /skúrvi/ *n.* **DISEASE CAUSED BY VITAMIN DEFICIENCY** a disease caused by insufficient vitamin C, the symptoms of which include spongy gums, loosening of the teeth, and bleeding into the skin and mucous membranes ■ *adj.* (**-vier, -viest**) **DESPICABLE** behaving in ways thought to be mean or contemptible [15thC. Coined from SCURF + -Y. 'Disease' evolved from 'covered with scurf, wretched', and was influenced by French *scorbut* andDutch *scheurbuik* 'scurvy'.] —**scurvily** *adv.* —**scurviness** *n.*

scurvy grass *n.* a northern European plant that was formerly used to treat scurvy. Latin name: *Cochlearia officinalis.*

scut /skut/ *n.* a short erect tail such as that of a rabbit [15thC. Origin uncertain: perhaps from obsolete *scut* 'short', or from Scandinavian.]

scuta plural of **scutum**

scutage /skyóotij/ *n.* in feudal times, a tax paid by a knight or vassal to his lord that freed him from military service [15thC. From medieval Latin *scutagium*, literally 'shield tax', from Latin *scutum* 'shield'.]

scutate /skyóo tayt/ *adj.* **1.** BOT **SHIELD-SHAPED** shaped like a shield ○ *a scutate leaf* **2.** ZOOL **COVERED BY BONY PLATES** covered or protected by external bony or horny plates or scales [Early 19thC. Coined from SCUTUM + -ATE.] —**scutation** /skyoo táysh'n/ *n.*

scutch /skuch/ *vt.* (**scutches, scutching, scutched**) **PROCESS FLAX BY BEATING** to beat flax in order to separate the valuable fibres from the woody parts ■ *n.* **TOOL FOR BEATING FLAX** a tool or machine for scutching flax or cotton [Late 17thC. Via Old French *escoucher*, ultimately from Latin *excutere* 'to shake'. The meaning 'to process flax' evolved from 'to remove moss from bark'.]

scutcheon /skúchən/ *n.* an escutcheon (*archaic*) [14thC. From Anglo-Norman *escuchoune* (see ESCUTCHEON).]

scutch grass *n.* **1.** = **Bermuda grass 2. COUCH GRASS** couch grass (*regional*)

scute /skyoot/ *n.* an external bony or horny plate or scale in some animals, especially snakes and other reptiles [14thC. From Latin *scutum*, 'shield'.]

scutellum /skyoo téllәm/ (*plural* **-la** /-téllә/) *n.* **1.** ZOOL **HARD PLATE OR SCALE** a hard plate or scale, e.g. on the thorax of an insect or a toe of a bird **2.** BOT **LEAF OF DEVELOPING GRASS SEED** the shield-shaped embryonic leaf (**cotyledon**) of a grass seed [Mid-18thC. From modern Latin, where it was formed from Latin *scutella* 'platter'; mistaken as literally 'small shield', formation from Latin *scutum* 'shield'.] —**scutellar** *adj.* —**scutellate** /skyóotәlәt, -layt/ *adj.* —**scutellation** /skyóotә láysh'n/ *n.*

scutiform /skyóoti fawrm/ *adj.* shaped like a shield [Mid-17thC. Coined from Latin *scutum* 'shield' + -FORM.]

scutter /skúttәr/ (**-ters, -tering, -tered**) *vi.* to move hastily in a scurrying manner [Late 18thC. Variant of medieval sense of SCUTTLE 'to scamper about'.]

scuttle[1] /skútt'l/ *n.* NAUT **1. SMALL HATCH** a small hatchway with a cover in the deck or hull of a ship **2. SCUTTLE COVER ON SHIP** the cover for a scuttle on a ship ■ *vt.* (**-tles, -tling, -tled**) **1.** NAUT **SINK SHIP BY LETTING WATER IN** to sink a ship by making or opening holes in the bottom **2. DESTROY STH** to destroy or bring sth to an end ○ *had effectively scuttled his plans* [15thC. Via French *escoutille*, or directly from Spanish *escotilla* 'hatchway', from *escotar* 'to cut out', from a prehistoric Germanic word that is the ancestor of English *sheet*.]

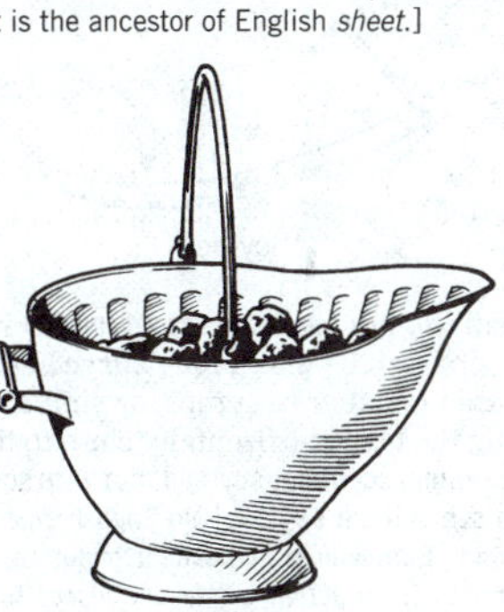

Scuttle

scuttle[2] /skútt'l/ *n.* **1. COAL CONTAINER** a metal container shaped like a wide-rimmed bucket with a lip and a handle, used to carry or store coal indoors **2. SHALLOW BASKET** an open shallow basket used to carry foods or small items **3. TOP PART OF CAR BODY** the part of a motor car behind the bonnet where the windscreen and instrument panel are fixed [15thC. Via Old English *scutel* and Old Norse *skutill* from Latin *scutella* 'dish, tray'.]

scuttle[3] /skútt'l/ *vi.* (**-tles, -tling, -tled**) **MOVE WITH SHORT FAST STEPS** to run or move quickly with short steps ■ *n.* **A RUSH OR RUN** a hurried pace or scuttling movement

scuttlebutt /skútt'l but/ *n.* **1. DRINKING FOUNTAIN ON SHIP** a drinking fountain on a ship **2. CASK OF WATER ON SHIP** a cask on a ship containing a day's supply of fresh water (*archaic*) **3.** *US* **GOSSIP** rumours about sb's activities, often of an intimate and scandalous nature (*slang*) [Early 19thC. From SCUTTLE[2] + BUTT.]

scutum /skyóotәm/ (*plural* **-ta** /-tә/) *n.* **1.** ZOOL = **scute 2.** ARMS **ANCIENT ROMAN SHIELD** a large shield used by legionaries in ancient Rome [Late 18thC. From Latin, 'shield'.]

Scutum *n.* a small faint constellation in the sky of the southern hemisphere lying partly in the Milky Way, located between Sagittarius and Aquila

scuzz /skuz/ *n. US* **1.** STH DISGUSTING sth dirty, disgusting, or disreputable (*slang*) **2. scuzz, scuzzball** OFFENSIVE TERM an offensive term referring to sb regarded as disgusting and contemptible (*slang insult offensive*) [Mid-20thC. Origin uncertain: perhaps a shortening of DISGUSTING, or a blend of SCUM and FUZZ.] — **scuzzily** *adv.* —**scuzziness** *n.* —**scuzzy** *adj.*

scuzzball /skúz bawl/, **scuzzbucket, scuzzbag** /skúz bag/ *n. US* an offensive term that deliberately insults sb regarded as despicable or repellent (*slang insult*)

Scylla /síllə/ *n.* in Greek mythology, a sea monster who attacked sailors. In later times, Scylla was thought to be a rock on the Italian side of the Straits of Messina. ◇ **be between Scylla and Charybdis** to be faced with the necessity of choosing between two equally undesirable or unpleasant things (*formal*)

scyphistoma /sī fístəmə/ (*plural* **-mae** /-mee/ *or* **-mas**) *n.* the form in the life cycle of a marine invertebrate such as a jellyfish that remains fixed in one place and reproduces asexually to produce free-swimming offspring [Late 19thC. Coined from SCYPHUS + STOMA.]

scyphozoan /sífə zṓ ən/ *n.* a marine invertebrate animal such as a jellyfish that is free-swimming and does not have a significant sedentary stage [Early 20thC. From modern Latin, from SCYPHUS and Greek *zōa* 'animals'.]

scyphus /sífəss/ (*plural* **-phi** /-fī/) *n.* **1.** ANCIENT GREEK DRINKING VESSEL a drinking vessel with a deep body, flat bottom, and two small handles near the rim, used by the ancient Greeks **2.** BOT CUP-SHAPED STRUCTURE a cup-shaped enlargement in lichens [Late 18thC. Via Latin, from Greek *skuphos* 'large drinking vessel'.]

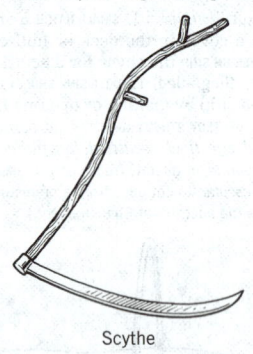

Scythe

scythe /sīth/ *n.* TOOL FOR MOWING OR REAPING an implement with a long handle and a long curved single-edged blade, used to cut grass, crops, or similar plants by swinging the blade horizontally close to the ground ■ *vti.* (**scythes, scything, scythed**) CUT WITH SCYTHE to cut or reap sth with a scythe [Old English *sipe*. Ultimately from an Indo-European word meaning 'to cut' that is also the ancestor of English *section*, *sickle*, and *insect*. Influenced by SCISSORS.]

Scythian /síthi ən, síthi ən/ *n.* INHABITANT OF SCYTHIA a member of an ancient people that lived in Scythia, an area of the present-day Ukraine ■ *adj.* RELATING TO SCYTHIA relating to the ancient region of Scythia, or its people or culture

sd *abbr.* **1.** sine die **2.** STATS standard deviation

SD *abbr.* **1.** South Dakota **2.** STATS standard deviation **3.** Swaziland (*international vehicle registration*)

SDA *abbr.* Scottish Development Agency

S.Dak. *abbr.* South Dakota

SDI *abbr.* Strategic Defense Initiative

SDLP *abbr.* Social Democratic and Labour Party

SDP *abbr.* Social Democratic Party

SDR, **SDRs** *abbr.* ECON special drawing rights

Se *symbol.* selenium

SE *abbr.* **1.** southeast **2.** southeastern **3.** stock exchange

sea /see/ *n.* **1.** SALT WATERS OF EARTH the great body of salt water that covers a large portion of the Earth **2.** PARTICULAR BODY OF SALT WATER a body of salt water that is surrounded by land on all or most sides, or that is part of one of the oceans **3.** LARGE LAKE a large inland body of fresh water **4.** ASTRON = mare² **5.**

TURBULENCE OF OCEAN the motion and disturbance of a large body of water such as the ocean, or the waves themselves **6.** SEAFARER'S JOB OR LIFE the occupation or way of life of a sailor **7.** VAST BODY a large area or great number of sth [Old English *sæ*, from prehistoric Germanic] ◇ **to be at sea 1.** to be travelling on the ocean **2.** to be bewildered and confused

sea anchor *n.* a device such as a conical canvas bag that is thrown overboard and dragged behind a ship to control its speed or heading

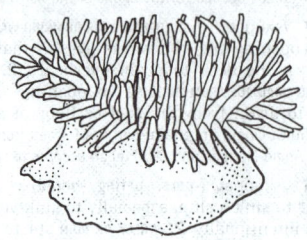

Sea anemone

sea anemone *n.* a solitary and often colourful sea animal with a squat cylindrical body that bears a ring of tentacles and is attached to rock or other nonliving material. Order: Actiniaria.

sea aster *n.* a biennial or perennial plant of the daisy family with narrow fleshy leaves and purple-and-yellow flowers that is found in salt marshes throughout Europe. Latin name: *Aster tripolium.*

sea bass /-bass/ *n.* a bony marine fish with a long body, large mouth, and spiny dorsal fin, caught for food or sport in Atlantic coastal waters of North America. Latin name: *Centropristis striata.*

seabed /see bed/ *n.* the surface of the Earth at the bottom of the sea

Seabee /see bee/ *n.* a member of one of the construction battalions of the United States Navy that builds naval shore facilities in combat zones [Mid-20thC. From the abbreviation CB, 'Construction Battalion', influenced by '(worker) bee'.]

sea beet *n.* a wild beet with leathery leaves and long spikes of inconspicuous green flowers that is found especially on European seashores. Latin name: *Beta vulgaris.*

seabird /see burd/ *n.* a bird such as a gull, albatross, or petrel that frequents the open sea

sea biscuit *n.* = hardtack

seablite /see blīt/ *n.* an annual plant of the goosefoot family that grows in salt marshes. Latin name: *Suaeda maritima.* [Mid-18thC. From SEA + *blite*.]

seaboard /see bawrd/ *n.* land that borders the sea

seaborne /see bawrn/ *adj.* **1.** CARRIED BY SEA carried over, on, or in the sea **2.** TRANSPORTED BY SHIP transported by ship across the sea

sea bream *n.* a marine food fish of European waters. Family: Sparidae.

sea breeze *n.* a cooling breeze that blows inland from the sea during the daytime when the land is warmer than the surface of the water

sea buckthorn *n.* a shrub found on seashores of Europe and Asia that has silvery leaves, greenish flowers, and orange-red edible berries, and yields a yellow dye. Latin name: *Hippophaë rhamnoides.*

sea butterfly *n.* = pteropod

sea captain *n.* the person in charge of a ship, especially a merchant ship

sea change *n.* **1.** GREAT CHANGE a substantial transformation **2.** CHANGE CAUSED BY SEA a change caused by the sea (*archaic*)

sea chest *n.* a large box or trunk in which a sailor's personal belongings are stored

seacoast /see kōst/ *n.* the land that borders the sea

seacock /see kok/ *n.* a valve in the hull of a ship used to let water in or out

sea cow *n.* = sirenian

sea crayfish *n.* = spiny lobster

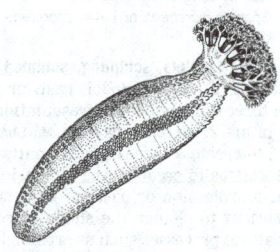

Sea cucumber

sea cucumber *n.* a marine invertebrate (**echinoderm**) that has a long tough muscular body and a mouth encircled by tentacles, and lives on the seabed. Class: Holothuroidea.

sea devil *n.* = devilfish

sea dog *n.* sb who has been a sailor for a long time

seadog /see dog/ *n.* METEOROL = fogbow [Mid-16thC. The original meaning was 'animal like a seal'. The modern meaning evolved through 'experienced sailor' to 'phenomenon recognized by experienced sailors'.]

sea eagle *n.* a fish-eating eagle that lives near the sea

sea-ear (*plural* **sea-ears** *or* **sea-ear**) *n.* MARINE BIOL = abalone

sea elephant *n.* = elephant seal

sea fan *n.* a coral with a fan-shaped skeleton that inhabits the waters of Florida and the West Indies. Genus: *Gorgonia.*

seafarer /see fairər/ *n.* **1.** SEA TRAVELLER sb who travels by sea **2.** SAILOR a sailor (*archaic or literary*)

seafaring /see fairing/ *adj.* **1.** REGULARLY GOING TO SEA regularly travelling by sea or working at sea **2.** OF SEA TRAVEL OR TRANSPORT relating to travel or transport by sea ■ *n.* SAILOR'S WAY OF LIFE the work and way of life of a sailor

sea fire *n.* light that is produced by marine organisms

seafloor /see flawr/ *n.* the surface of the Earth at the bottom of the sea

seafloor spreading *n.* a process in which molten material from the Earth's mantle rises up at ocean ridges, causing volcanic and seismic activity, spreads out, and creates a new seafloor

seafood /see food/ *n.* fish and shellfish from the sea eaten as food

seafowl /see fowl/ (*plural* **-fowl** *or* **-fowls**) *n.* = seabird

seafront /see frunt/ *n.* the part of a town that faces the edge of the sea

sea-girt *adj.* encircled by the sea (*literary*)

seagoing /see gō ing/ *adj.* **1.** FOR OCEAN TRAVEL made or fit for sailing on the open sea **2.** = seafaring *adj.* 1

sea gooseberry *n.* a marine invertebrate (**ctenophore**) resembling a gooseberry in having a round body and fine tentacles like hairs. Genus: *Pleurobrachia.*

sea grape *n.* a tree that grows on sandy shores from Florida to South America and has large rounded leaves and clusters of purple-to-whitish edible berries. Latin name: *Coccoloba uvifera.*

sea green *n.* a blue-green colour in which the green is predominant —**sea-green** *adj.*

seagull /see gul/ *n.* = gull

—— WORD KEY: CULTURAL NOTE ——
The Seagull, a play by the Russian writer Anton Chekhov (1896). The plot centres on the young writer Triplev's love for the aspiring actress Nina, who, to Triplev's dismay, allows herself to be seduced by an older, more famous writer, Trigorin. One of Chekhov's most successful plays, it typically eschews melodrama for social and psychological analysis.

sea hare *n.* a large marine mollusc that has an arched back, a reduced or absent external shell, and two tentacles resembling rabbit ears. Genus: *Aplysia*.

sea heath *n.* a small perennial plant with pink flowers, found in salt marshes of Europe and Asia. Latin name: *Frankenia laevis*.

sea holly *n.* a perennial plant of the carrot family with spiny leaves and blue flowers, found on European seashores. The roots were formerly thought to have aphrodisiac properties. Latin name: *Eryngium maritimum*.

Sea horse

sea horse *n.* **1.** FISH RESEMBLING HORSE a small bony fish with a head shaped like that of a horse, a vertical swimming position, and a prehensile tail that it uses to cling to seaweed. Genus: *Hippocampus*. **2.** MYTHOL MYTHOLOGICAL CREATURE a mythological creature with the head and forelegs of a horse and the body of a fish **3.** WALRUS a walrus (*archaic*)

sea-island cotton *n.* a type of cotton with long silky fibres grown chiefly in the West Indies. Latin name: *Gossypium barbadense*. [Named after the Sea Islands]

sea kale *n.* a plant related to the cabbage that grows along the seashores of Europe and Asia and has edible leaves and shoots. Latin name: *Crambe maritima*.

seakale beet /sée kayl-/ *n.* = **Swiss chard**

sea king *n.* a Norse pirate chief of the early Middle Ages

seal[1] /seel/ *n.* **1.** TIGHT OR PERFECT CLOSURE a closure that prevents the entrance or escape of sth such as air or water, or a substance or device that forms such a closure **2.** SPECIAL CLOSURE THAT REVEALS TAMPERING a closure for sth such as a package or container that must be broken to open it and can thereby reveal tampering **3.** AUTHENTICATING STAMP a ring or stamp with a raised or engraved symbol or emblem that is pressed into wax in order to certify a signature or authenticate a document **4.** WAX MARKED WITH SEAL a piece of wax bearing the mark of a seal **5.** SYMBOL OF OFFICE a device, emblem, or symbol that is a mark of office **6.** ORNAMENTAL ADHESIVE STAMP an ornamental adhesive stamp used to close a letter or package **7.** STH GIVING CONFIRMATION sth that gives confirmation or assurance ○ *Mother gave our plans for the party her seal of approval.* ■ *vt.* (**seals, sealing, sealed**) **1.** CLOSE STH FIRMLY to close sth tightly or securely with a seal, e.g. to prevent tampering **2.** MAKE STH WATERTIGHT OR AIRTIGHT to make sth watertight, airtight, or nonporous, e.g. by filling gaps or applying a special substance to the surface **3.** ATTACH AUTHENTICATING SEAL TO STH to affix a marked piece of wax to sth in order to authenticate or certify it **4.** CONFIRM STH to confirm a decision or come to an agreement on sth **5.** SETTLE STH to determine sth irrevocably ○ *His fate was sealed when his lies were discovered.* **6.** RELIG SOLEMNIZE MARRIAGE OR ADOPTION to solemnize a marriage or adoption in the Church of Jesus Christ of Latter-Day Saints [12thC. Via Anglo-Norman from Latin *sigillum* 'little mark or picture', from *signum* 'sign, token, mark'.] —**sealable** *adj.*

seal off *vt.* to prevent people or things from entering or leaving a place, e.g. by surrounding it or closing it securely ○ *Police sealed off the area.*

Seal

seal[2] /seel/ *n.* **1.** FISH-EATING MARINE MAMMAL a carnivorous marine mammal with a sleek body adapted for swimming and living in cold regions and webbed feet modified as flippers. Families: Otariidae and Phocidae. ◊ **common seal 2.** SEAL'S PELT the pelt or fur of a seal **3.** LEATHER FROM SEAL'S SKIN leather made from the skin of a seal ■ *vi.* (**seals, sealing, sealed**) HUNT SEALS to hunt seals, usually for their skins or blubber [Old English *seolh*]

sea lace *n.* a seaweed with long thin blackish fronds. Latin name: *Chorda filum*.

sea lamprey *n.* a large eel-shaped jawless marine fish that swims up rivers along Atlantic coasts to spawn and is sometimes used as food. It lives as a parasite on other fish as an adult. Latin name: *Petromyzon marinus*.

sea lane *n.* an established and commonly used sea route for large ships

sealant /seelənt/ *n.* a substance used to seal sth, e.g. by filling gaps or making a surface nonporous

sea lavender *n.* a perennial plant of the thrift family with a rosette of slender leaves at the base and branching spikes of bluish-purple flowers, found in temperate salt marshes. Genus: *Limonium*.

sea lawyer *n.* an argumentative sailor, or any contentious person (*informal*)

sealed-beam headlight *n.* a vehicle headlight with a prefocused reflector and lens sealed in one unit

sealed orders *npl.* written instructions not to be opened or read before a particular time, e.g. instructions to the captain of a ship whose destination is not revealed before it leaves harbour

sealed road *n.* ANZ a road with a surface of bitumen or tar

sea legs *npl.* the ability to move with ease on a ship and not feel seasick despite its pitching and rolling motion (*informal*)

sealer[1] /seelər/ *n.* **1.** SB OR STH THAT SEALS a person, substance, or device that seals sth, e.g. a substance used to make a surface nonporous **2.** OFFICIAL WHO CERTIFIES STH an official who inspects and certifies weights and measures

sealer[2] /seelər/ *n.* sb who hunts seals, or a boat used for this purpose

sealery /seeləri/ (*plural* **-ies**) *n.* **1.** REARING OR BREEDING PLACE FOR SEALS a place where seals are reared or where seals congregate and breed **2.** PLACE WHERE SEALS ARE HUNTED a place where seals are hunted **3.** HUNTING OF SEALS the occupation or practice of hunting seals

sea letter *n.* a passport issued to a neutral ship in wartime that entitles the ship to sail under the flag of the nation to which it belongs

sea lettuce *n.* a seaweed sometimes used as food in salads. Genus: *Ulva*.

sea level *n.* the level of the surface of the sea relative to the land, halfway between high and low tide, used as a standard in calculating elevation

sea lily *n.* a marine invertebrate that has a stalk anchored to the seabed and a flower-shaped body. Class: Crinoidea.

sealing wax *n.* a resinous substance that is soft when heated and used for sealing letters, documents, batteries, or jars

Sea lion

sea lion *n.* a large gregarious seal that has external ears and coarse hair with no underfur. Family: Otariidae.

sea loch *n.* = **loch** *n.* 2

Sea Lord *n.* either one of the two most senior serving naval officers on the Admiralty Board of the Ministry of Defence

seal point *n.* a Siamese cat with a cream or fawn body and a dark brown face, paws, and tail. ◊ **blue point**

seal ring *n.* = **signet ring**

sealskin /seel skin/ *n.* the pelt or fur of a seal, or a garment made from this

Sealyham terrier /seeli əm-/ *n.* a dog with short legs, a long head, powerful jaws, and a wiry mostly white coat, belonging to a breed developed in Wales for catching rabbits and similar animals [Late 19thC. Named after the South Welsh village where the dog was first bred.]

seam /seem/ *n.* **1.** PLACE WHERE PIECES JOIN the line along which pieces of cloth or leather are joined by sewing **2.** STITCHES FORMING SEAM the stitches used to form a seam **3.** LINE FORMED BY ADJACENT SECTIONS any line, groove, or ridge formed by joining or fitting together two sections along their edges **4.** LINEAR INDENTATION a scar, wrinkle, or other linear indentation **5.** GEOL THIN LAYER OF ROCK a thin layer of a rock or mineral such as a coal deposit occurring between different strata of bedrock ■ *v.* (**seams, seaming, seamed**) **1.** *vt.* JOIN THINGS ALONG EDGES to join two parts or pieces along their edges, e.g. by sewing them together **2.** *vti.* MARK WITH LINES to mark sth with wrinkles, scars, furrows, or other lines, or to become marked in this way [Old English *sēam*, from a prehistoric Germanic word that is also the ancestor of English *sew*] ◊ **be bulging** *or* **bursting at the seams** to be extremely full ◊ **come** *or* **fall apart at the seams** to enter into a state of collapse

seaman /seemən/ (*plural* **-men** /-mən/) *n.* **1.** = **sailor 2.** SB RANKING BELOW PETTY OFFICER sb enlisted in the US Navy or Coast Guard who ranks below petty officer and above seaman apprentice [Old English]

seamanship /seemən ship/ *n.* the skill of handling, working on, or navigating a boat or ship

seamark /see maark/ *n.* an object on land easily visible from the sea that serves as an aid to navigation

sea mat *n.* = **bryozoan**

seam bowler *n.* CRICKET a fast bowler in cricket who makes the ball bounce on its seam and so deviate from a straight line —**seam bowling** *n.*

seamer /seemər/ *n.* **1.** SB OR STH THAT MAKES SEAMS a person or machine that makes seams or the operator of such a machine **2.** CRICKET = **seam bowler 3.** CRICKET BALL BOWLED BY SEAM BOWLER a ball that bounces on its seam and so deviates from a straight line [Old English]

sea mew *n.* a seagull, especially the common gull

sea mile *n.* = **nautical mile**

sea milkwort *n.* a plant of the primula family with small pink flowers that grows on northern temperate coasts. Latin name: *Glaux maritima*.

seamless /seemləss/ *adj.* **1.** WITHOUT SEAMS having no seams **2.** PERFECTLY SMOOTH free from awkward transitions and creating perfectly smooth continuity —**seamlessly** *adv.* —**seamlessness** *n.*

sea moth *n.* a small tropical marine fish with large wing-shaped pectoral fins, a long snout, and an armour of bony plates. Family: Pegasidae.

seamount /seé mownt/ *n.* an isolated undersea mountain of volcanic origin that rises from the seabed to a height of up to 1,000 m/3,300 ft, usually 1,000 m/3,300 ft to 2,000 m/6,500 ft below the surface of the sea

sea mouse *n.* a large marine worm with a broad flat body that is covered in bristles resembling hair. Genus: *Aphrodite.*

seamstress /sémstrəss, seém-/ *n.* a woman who sews or whose occupation is sewing [Late 16thC. Formed from *seamster* 'tailor, person who sews', from SEAM.]

seamy /seémi/ (**-ier, -iest**) *adj.* having unpleasant qualities associated with a degraded or degenerate way of living [Late 16thC. Coined from SEAM + -Y. The meaning 'degraded' evolved from 'rough side of a garment, where the seams show'.] —**seaminess** *n.*

Seanad Eireann /shánnəth áirən, -nəd-/ *n.* the upper chamber of parliament in the Republic of Ireland [Early 20thC. From Irish, 'Senate of Ireland'.]

seance /sáy oNss, -onss, -aanss/ *n.* **1.** MEETING TO SPEAK WITH DEAD a meeting at which a spiritualist attempts to receive communications from the spirits of the dead **2.** SESSION a sitting, session, or meeting, e.g. of a society or a legislative body [Late 18thC. Via French, 'sitting', and Old French *seoir* 'to sit', from Latin *sedere* 'to sit' (source of English *session, sedentary,* and *sediment*).]

sea nettle *n.* a stinging jellyfish that inhabits Atlantic estuaries from Cape Cod to the West Indies

Sea of Japan *n.* the sea between Korea and Japan that has been the subject of a dispute between the two countries for much of the 20th century

sea onion *n. US* = **sea squill**

sea otter *n.* a marine animal of the weasel family with a thick brown coat that inhabits northern Pacific coasts and feeds mainly on shellfish. Latin name: *Enhydra lutris.*

sea pea *n.* a plant of the pea family that has purple flowers and grows wild along sandy shores of the northern hemisphere. Latin name: *Lathyrus japonicus.* US term **beach pea**

sea pen *n.* a marine organism related to coral that forms feathery colonies in warm seas. Genus: *Pennatula.*

sea pink *n.* = **thrift** *n.* 2

seaplane /seé playn/ *n.* a plane designed in such a way that it can take off from and land on water

sea poacher *n.* a small slender marine fish that has an armour of bony plates and is found near the bottom of the North Pacific and other cold waters. Family: Agonidae.

seaport /seé pawrt/ *n.* a port, town, or harbour that can accommodate seagoing ships

sea power *n.* **1.** NATION WITH NAVAL STRENGTH a nation that has formidable naval strength **2.** NAVAL STRENGTH the military power that a nation can deploy to fight on water

sea purse *n.* the egg pouch of a shark or ray that often has curly tendrils so that it can attach itself to seaweed

SEAQ /seé ak/ *n.* a computerized system for displaying prices and transactions in securities on the Stock Exchange. Abbr of **Stock Exchange Automated Quotation**

seaquake /seé kwayk/ *n.* an earthquake occurring under the sea

sear[1] /seer/ *v.* (**sears, searing, seared**) **1.** *vt.* BURN STH to burn or scorch sth with an application of intense heat **2.** *vt.* HAVE AN UNPLEASANT EFFECT ON to have a sudden painful or unpleasant effect on sb or sth **3.** *vti.* WITHER to wither, shrivel, or dry up, or to cause sth to wither, shrivel, or dry up ■ *n.* BURN OR SCORCH MARK a mark or scar made by searing [Old English *sēarian* 'to wither away', from a prehistoric Germanic word that is also the ancestor of English *sere* 'dried up']

sear[2] /seer/ *n.* the catch that holds a gunlock cocked or at half-cock [Mid-16thC. From French *serre* 'grasp, lock', from *serrer* 'to grasp', ultimately from Latin *sera* 'bar for a door'.]

Sea Ranger *n.* a senior Guide aged between 14 and 20 who specializes in activities at sea

sea raven *n.* a large fish found along the Atlantic coast of North America that swallows air and blows up like a balloon when removed from the water. Latin name: *Hemitripterus americanus.*

search /surch/ *v.* (**searches, searching, searched**) **1.** *vti.* EXAMINE THOROUGHLY to look into, over, or through sth carefully in order to find sb or sth **2.** *vt.* EXAMINE STH FOR CONCEALED ITEMS to examine the clothing, personal effects, or body of sb in order to discover sth such as weapons or illegal drugs that have been deliberately concealed **3.** *vt.* EXAMINE PUBLIC RECORD to examine a public record to find information about sth **4.** *vt.* DISCOVER STH BY EXAMINATION to discover, come to know, or find sth by examination **5.** *vt.* COMPUT EXAMINE COMPUTER FILE to examine a computer file, disk, database, or network for particular information ■ *n.* **1.** THOROUGH EXAMINATION a careful and thorough examination in order to find sb or sth **2.** COMPUT EXAMINATION OF COMPUTER FILE the examination of a computer file, disk, database, or network in order to find particular information **3.** LAW BOARDING OF SHIP TO SEARCH IT the boarding of a ship in accordance with international law in order to search it, especially during wartime [14thC. Via Anglo-Norman *sercher,* and Old French *cerchier* 'to explore', from Latin *circare* 'to go around in circles', from *circus* 'circle' (source of English *circular*).] —**searchable** *adj.* —**searcher** *n.* ◇ **search me** used to emphasize your lack of knowledge about sth (*informal*)

search engine *n.* a computer program that searches for specified keywords and returns a list of documents in which they were found, especially a commercial service that scans documents on the Internet

searching /súrching/ *adj.* observing acutely or examining thoroughly —**searchingly** *adv.* —**searchingness** *n.*

searchlight /súrch līt/ *n.* **1.** APPARATUS FOR PROJECTING LIGHT an apparatus for projecting a high-intensity beam of light in any direction **2.** INTENSE PROJECTED LIGHT the light from a searchlight

search party *n.* a group of volunteers or professionals organized to search for a missing person

search warrant *n.* a court order authorizing entry to sb's property to look for unlawful possessions

sea robin *n.* a marine fish with red or brown colouring, a bony head, and long pectoral fins with finger-shaped extensions that it uses as feelers or for crawling. Family: Triglidae and Peristediidae.

sea rocket *n.* a plant of the mustard family that grows along seashores and has sharp-tasting leaves and white or lavender flowers. Genus: *Cakile.*

searoom /seé room, -rŏom/ *n.* open space at sea in which to turn or manoeuvre a ship

sea rover *n.* a pirate or a pirate ship (*literary*)

sea salt *n.* coarse salt obtained from the evaporation of seawater

seascape /seé skayp/ *n.* a painting or picture of the sea, or a view of the sea [Late 18thC. Formed from SEA, on the model of LANDSCAPE.]

Sea Scout *n.* a member of a scouting organization who learns sailing, boating, canoeing, and other water activities

sea serpent *n.* **1.** MYTHOL MYTHICAL CREATURE a giant creature resembling a snake often reported to have been seen at sea, but never proved to exist **2.** ZOOL = **sea snake** *n.* 1

seashell /seé shel/ *n.* the empty shell of a sea creature, especially a mollusc

seashore /seé shawr/ *n.* **1.** LAND LYING NEXT TO SEA the land lying next to the sea, especially a beach **2.** LAW LAND BETWEEN TIDEMARKS the land lying between the usual high and low water marks

seasick /seé sik/ *adj.* feeling sick or dizzy as a result of the rocking movement of a vessel on water —**seasickness** *n.*

seaside /seé sīd/ *n.* LAND ALONG SEA the area of land bordering the sea, especially as a place for holidays and leisure activities ■ *adj.* AT THE SEASIDE situated or taking place at the seaside ○ *a seaside cottage*

sea slater *n.* a small sea creature that resembles a large woodlouse, lives in cracks in the rocks around the highwater mark, and is active mainly at night. Latin name: *Ligea oceanica.*

sea slug *n.* a marine mollusc without gills that resembles a sea snail with no shell and is often brightly coloured. Order: Nudibranchia.

sea snail *n.* **1.** SEA CREATURE WITH A SPIRAL SHELL a small sea creature such as a whelk or periwinkle with a spiral shell resembling that of a snail. Class: Gastropoda. **2.** = **snailfish**

sea snake *n.* **1.** POISONOUS TROPICAL SNAKE a venomous snake found in tropical seas that swims by means of an oar-shaped tail and bears live young. Family: Hydrophidae. **2.** MYTHOL = **sea serpent** *n.* 1

season /seéz'n/ *n.* **1.** TRADITIONAL DIVISION OF YEAR any one of the periods marked by particular weather conditions into which the year is traditionally divided. In temperate regions, there are four seasons, spring, summer, autumn, and winter, while in tropical countries there are often only two, a dry season and a rainy season. **2.** PERIOD FOR PARTICULAR ACTIVITY a time or period of the year during which a particular activity usually takes place in the human world or among plants and animals ○ *planting season* ○ *mating season* **3.** PERIOD SET ASIDE FOR ACTIVITY a fixed period of every year during which particular activities, especially sports, take place or are permitted ○ *cricket season* **4.** PLAYER'S OR TEAM'S PERFORMANCE the performance of a player or team during a sporting season in relation to others ○ *had his best season ever* **5.** TIME FOR FOOD the time of year when sth, especially a kind of food, is abundant and at its best ○ *asparagus season* **6.** ARTS CONNECTED SERIES OF PERFORMANCES a period of time during which works that are all by or featuring the same person, or are connected by theme or period, are shown or performed **7.** HIGH SEASON AT RESORTS the time of year at which resorts receive most visitors and charge their highest rates **8.** SOCIAL SEASON the time during which the important social events of the year involving members of high society take place **9.** TIME AROUND HOLIDAY the period of time just before, after, and including a holiday ○ *the Christmas season* **10.** VET SEXUAL RECEPTIVENESS the period during which a female animal is sexually receptive and ready to be mated **11.** PERIOD OF TIME a period of time of unspecified length ○ *a brief season* **12.** SUITABLE TIME a fit or appropriate time for sth or to do sth (*literary*) **13.** TRANSP SEASON TICKET a season ticket (*informal*) ■ *v.* (**-sons, -soning, -soned**) **1.** *vti.* ADD FLAVOURINGS to add flavourings such as salt, spices, or herbs to food **2.** *vt.* ENLIVEN STH to liven up sth such as a speech or piece of writing by inserting exciting or amusing material ○ *a speech seasoned with wit* **3.** *vti.* DRY OUT BEFORE USE to allow wood to dry out fully before use, or to become fully dried out before being used **4.** *vt.* PREPARE NEW PAN FOR USE to prepare a new frying pan or wok for use by rubbing vegetable oil into the heated cooking surface **5.** *vt.* CAUSE SB TO GAIN EXPERIENCE to cause or enable sb to gain experience and become more skilled, or to gain toughness and strength ○ *seasoned troops* **6.** *vt.* MODERATE STH to temper sth such as a strong emotion (*literary*) [14thC. Via Old French from the Latin stem *sation-* 'sowing', from *sat-*, past participle stem of *serere* 'to sow'.] —**seasoner** *n.* ◇ **in season 1.** plentifully available and at a peak of quality ○ *Strawberries are in season now.* **2.** allowed to be hunted, caught, or killed **3.** VET sexually receptive to males **4.** at an appropriate time (*literary*) ◇ **out of season 1.** not widely available or not of good quality because of the time of year ○ *Tulips are out of season at this time of year.* **2.** not allowed to be hunted, caught, or killed because of the time of year **3.** at an inappropriate time (*literary*)

WORD KEY: CULTURAL NOTE

The Four Seasons, a violin concerto by the Italian composer Antonio Vivaldi (1725). Vivaldi's best-known work (Opus 8) consists of four movements, each of which describes a season with appropriate music. The section called 'Spring', for example, features birdsong while 'Autumn' incorporates sounds that suggest rustling leaves. Vivaldi provided a commentary on each movement in a series of sonnets he wrote to accompany the concerto.

seasonable /seéz'nəb'l/ *adj.* **1.** TYPICAL OF PARTICULAR SEASON typical of or appropriate for a particular season of the year **2.** OPPORTUNE done, given, or occurring at a time when needed or appropriate — **seasonableness** *n.* —**seasonably** *adv.*

seasonal /seéz'nəl/ *adj.* **1.** DEPENDENT ON SEASON dependent on or determined by the time of year **2.** LIMITED TO PARTICULAR TIMES available or employed only during a particular time or at particular times of the year —**seasonally** *adv.* —**seasonalness** *n.*

seasonal affective disorder, **seasonal affective disorder syndrome** *n.* a type of depression associated with the onset of winter and thought to be caused by decreasing amounts of daylight

seasoning /seéz'ning/ *n.* **1.** FLAVOURING salt, pepper, or any herb or spice used to give additional flavour to food **2.** REMOVING MOISTURE FROM TIMBER the process of treating timber to reduce its moisture sufficiently so that it is suitable for the function for which it will be used

season ticket, **season pass** *n.* a ticket or pass valid for a season or specified period of time for travel on public transport, use of sport or leisure facilities, or attendance at sporting or cultural events

sea spider *n.* a sea creature resembling a spider, with a fairly small body and four to six pairs of long jointed legs. Class: Pycnogonida.

sea squill *n.* a Mediterranean plant of the lily family that bears dense spikes of small white flowers. It has an onion-shaped bulb with medicinal properties. Latin name: *Urginea maritima*. US term **sea onion**

sea squirt *n.* a tiny sea creature that has a transparent sac-shaped body with openings through which water passes in and out. It squirts out a stream of water when disturbed. Class: Ascidiacea.

sea star *n.* = starfish

sea steps *npl.* a set of metal bars fixed to the side of a ship to allow people to climb on or off

sea swallow *n.* a tern, especially the common tern. Latin name: *Sterna hirundo*.

seat /seet/ *n.* **1.** PLACE TO SIT sth for sitting on, especially sth designed for this such as a chair or bench **2.** PART OF CHAIR SAT ON the usually horizontal part of a chair or other seat that takes most of the weight of the person sitting on it **3.** VIEWER'S OR TRAVELLER'S SITTING PLACE a place to sit and watch an event or travel in a vehicle, for which a ticket is usually required ○ *We don't really want seats in the front row.* **4.** PART OF GARMENT COVERING BUTTOCKS the part of a garment that covers the buttocks **5.** MEMBERSHIP IN OFFICIAL GROUP a position as a member of an official body or group, especially in an elected legislature ○ *won a seat in the legislature* **6.** CONSTITUENCY the constituency represented by a Member of Parliament **7.** BASE a place where sth is located or based (*formal*) ○ *the seat of consciousness* **8.** RESIDENCE a residence, especially a large house associated with a particular family **9.** OBJECT ON WHICH STH RESTS an object, part, or space on which sth such as a part of a machine or device rests or into which it fits **10.** RIDER'S POSITION the position in which a rider sits on a horse ■ *v.* (**seats, seating, seated**) **1.** *vt.* PLACE SB IN SEAT to place sb or yourself in a chair or other seat **2.** *vt.* PROVIDE SEATS FOR PEOPLE to have or provide seats for a specified number of people ○ *The hall seats five hundred.* **3.** *vti.* REST OR FIT SECURELY to rest sth securely on or fit sth firmly into sth else, or to be firmly resting on or fitted into sth ○ *The valve isn't seating properly.* **4.** *vt.* INSTALL SB IN POWERFUL POSITION to establish sb in a position of power or authority (*literary*) **5.** *vt.* FIT SEAT ON STH to put or refurbish a seat in or on sth such as a chair or garment [12thC. From Old Icelandic *sæti*; from a prehistoric Germanic word that is also the ancestor of English *sit*.] ◇ **by the seat of your pants 1.** using intuition and guesswork rather than theory or specialized knowledge **2.** without the help of any instruments or technical aids

seatback /seét bak/ *n.* the part of a seat against which the back rests

seat belt *n.* a strong strap or harness designed to keep the wearer securely in a seat, especially in a vehicle or aircraft

seating /seéting/ *n.* **1.** SEATS the places provided for people to sit, especially in a public building or a vehicle **2.** ARRANGEMENT OF SEATS OR SITTERS the way in which seats or people sitting are arranged ○ *a seating plan* **3.** STH OBJECT RESTS ON sth on which an object rests or into which it fits **4.** UPHOLSTERING MATERIAL material for upholstering the seat of a chair

SEATO /seétō/ *abbr.* Southeast Asia Treaty Organization

seat-of-the-pants *adj.* relying on intuition or guesswork rather than mechanical aids, rules and procedures, or planning (*informal*) [The expression comes from pilots' cant, presumably because the intuitive understanding of the plane's motions is rumoured to be located in that spot]

sea trout *n.* **1.** EUROPEAN AND N AFRICAN TROUT a large silvery-coloured European and North African trout that lives mainly in the sea but returns to fresh water to spawn. Latin name: *Salmo trutta*. **2.** N AMERICAN MARINE FISH a North American marine fish of the Atlantic coast that resembles a trout but belongs to the croaker family. Latin name: *Cynoscion regalis*.

SEATS /seets/ *n.*, *abbr.* Stock Exchange Alternative Trading Service

Seattle /si átt'l/ city in west-central Washington State, between Puget Sound and Lake Washington. The most important city in the Pacific Northwest, it is a major port and commercial centre. Population: 516,259 (1990).

sea turtle *n.* a large turtle with limbs shaped like paddles that is usually found in tropical and subtropical seas. Family: Cheloniidae and Dermochelyidae.

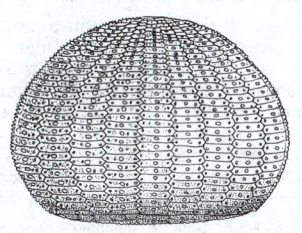

Sea urchin

sea urchin *n.* a small sea animal with a soft body enclosed in a spiny spherical shell. Class: Echinoidea.

sea wall *n.* a wall built to prevent flooding or coastal erosion by the sea

seawards /seéwərd/ *adv.* TOWARDS THE SEA in a direction towards the sea ■ *adj.* **1.** SITUATED TOWARDS THE SEA situated towards the sea **2.** BLOWING FROM SEA used to describe wind that blows in towards the shore from the sea

seaware /seé wair/ *n.* seaweed collected from the shore and used as fertilizer

sea wasp *n.* a jellyfish that has a cube-shaped body with tentacles hanging from the lower corners. Its sting is very venomous and sometimes fatal. Order: Cubomedusae.

seawater /seé wawtər/ *n.* salt water in or from the sea [Old English]

seaway /seé way/ *n.* **1.** INLAND CHANNEL FOR SHIPS an inland canal, passage, or channel large enough for sea-going ships to navigate ○ *the St Lawrence Seaway* **2.** ROUTE ACROSS SEA a shipping route across a sea **3.** SHIP'S PROGRESS the progress of a ship through the sea **4.** ROUGH SEAS seas that are moderate to rough [Old English]

Seaweed

seaweed /seé weed/ *n.* plants such as kelp that grow in the sea

sea whip *n.* a coral that forms long flexible structures with few or no branches and is common on Atlantic reefs

seaworthy /seé wurthi/ *adj.* suitable or in a fit state to sail safely on the sea —**seaworthiness** *n.*

sea wrack *n.* seaweed, especially clumps of the larger varieties, found cast up on the shore

sebaceous /sə báyshəss/ *adj.* relating to or producing a waxy yellowish body secretion (**sebum**) [Early 18thC. Formed from Latin *sebaceus*, from *sebum* (see SEBUM).]

sebaceous gland *n.* a gland that secretes sebum into hair follicles to lubricate the hair and skin. Sebaceous glands are found all over the human body except for the palms of the hands and the soles of the feet.

sebacic acid /sə bássik-, -báyssik-/ *n.* a white crystalline acid that is used in the making of some polyester resins, rubbers, and plasticizers. Formula: $COOH(CH_2)_8COOH$. [*Sebacic* formed from SEBACEOUS]

Sebastian /sə básti ən/, **St** (*fl.* 3rd century) Roman Christian martyr. He is said to have survived execution by archers ordered by the emperor Diocletian, who then had him beaten to death.

Sebastopol /sə bástə pol/, **Sevastopol** city and port on the Black Sea, in the southern Ukraine, on the southern coast of the Crimean Peninsula. Population: 366,200 (1991).

SEbE *abbr.* southeast by east

seborrhea *n.* US = seborrhoea

seborrhoea /sébbə reé ə/ *n.* excessively oily skin caused by heavy discharge from the sebaceous glands [Late 19thC. Coined from SEBUM + -RRHOEA.] —**seborrhoeal** *adj.* —**seborrhoeic** *adj.*

SEbS *abbr.* southeast by south

sebum /seébəm/ *n.* an oily substance secreted by the sebaceous glands that lubricates the hair and skin and gives some protection against bacteria [Late 19thC. From Latin, 'grease, tallow'.]

sec[1] /sek/ *n.* a second (*informal*) [Late 19thC. Shortening.]

sec[2] /sek/ *adj.* used to describe a wine, especially champagne, that is dry in taste [Mid-19thC. Via French from Latin *siccus* 'dry'.]

sec[3] *abbr.* secant

SEC *abbr.* Securities and Exchange Commission

sec. *abbr.* **1.** second **2.** secondary **3.** secretary **4.** section **5.** sector **6.** secundum **7.** security

SECAM /seé kam/ *n.* a broadcasting system for colour television used in France, Russia, and a number of other countries. Full form **séquentiel couleur à mémoire**

secant /seékənt/ *n.* GEOM **1.** STRAIGHT LINE CUTTING CURVE a straight line that intersects with a curve in two or more places **2.** TRIGONOMETRIC FUNCTION the ratio of the hypotenuse to the side adjacent to a given angle in a right-angled triangle [Late 16thC. Via French from, ultimately, Latin *secare* (see SECTION).]

secateurs /sékə turz, -túrz/ *npl.* a gardening tool used for pruning that has two short heavy blades with a spring mechanism [Mid-19thC. From French, from, ultimately, Latin *secare* (see SECTION).]

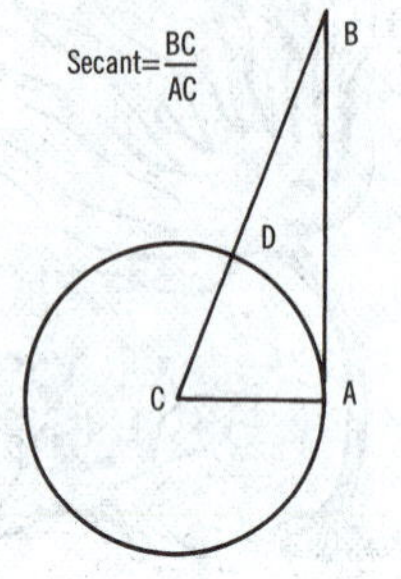

Secant

secco /sékō/ *n.* (*plural* **-cos**) **1.** PAINTING **WALL PAINTING TECHNIQUE** the technique of wall painting on dry plaster using tempera or pigments ground in limewater **2.** PAINTING **PICTURE PAINTED ON WALL** a painting on a wall made by the secco method **3.** MUSIC **RECITATIVE STYLE** a style of vocal recitative in which the natural stress of the words is paramount and, if accompanied at all, is supported only by occasional chords of continuo instruments ■ *adj.* MUSIC **1. ACCOMPANIED ONLY BY CONTINUO INSTRUMENTS** used to refer to vocal recitatives that are unaccompanied or accompanied only by occasional chords of continuo instruments **2. STACCATO** played and released quickly and lacking resonance (*used as a musical direction*) ■ *adv.* MUSIC **IN STACCATO MANNER** with the notes played and released quickly and without resonance (*used as a musical direction*) [Mid-19thC. Via Italian from Latin *siccus* 'dry'.]

secede /si séed/ (**-cedes, -ceding, -ceded**) *vi.* to make a formal withdrawal of membership from an organization, state, or alliance [Early 18thC. From Latin *secedere*, literally 'to go apart', from *cedere* (see CEDE).] —**seceder** *n.*

secern /si súrn/ (**-cerns, -cerning, -cerned**) *vt.* to identify or perceive sth as separate (*archaic*) [Early 17thC. From Latin *secernere*, literally 'to separate apart', from *cernere* 'to separate' (source of English *discern*).] —**secernment** *n.*

secession /si sésh'n/ *n.* a formal withdrawal from an organization, state, or alliance [Mid-16thC. Directly or via French from, ultimately, Latin *secedere* (see SECEDE).] —**secessional** *adj.*

Secession *n.* the withdrawal from the Union of 11 Southern States in 1860–61 that led to the formation of the Confederacy and the beginning of the American Civil War

seclude /si klóod/ (**-cludes, -cluding, -cluded**) *vt.* **1. ISOLATE SB** to remove sb from contact with others **2. MAKE STH PRIVATE** to make a place private and quiet by screening or isolating it [15thC. From Latin *secludere*, literally 'to shut apart', from *claudere* 'to shut' (source of English *conclusive* and *recluse*).]

secluded /si klóodid/ *adj.* **1. PRIVATE AND QUIET** cut off from other places and therefore private and quiet **2. HAVING LITTLE CONTACT** having or involving little or no contact with others —**secludedly** *adv.* —**secludedness** *n.*

seclusion /si kloózh'n/ *n.* **1. CONDITION OF BEING SECLUDED** the condition of being cut off from others, or from other places **2. ACT OF SECLUDING** an act of setting sb or sth apart from others **3. SECLUDED PLACE** a quiet place removed from activity and people [Early 17thC. From Latin *seclusion-*, from *secludere* (see SECLUDE).]

seclusive /si kloóssiv/ *adj.* disposed to be solitary (*literary*) [Mid-19thC. Formed from SECLUDE, on the model of INCLUSIVE.] —**seclusively** *adv.* —**seclusiveness** *n.*

Seconal /sékənəl/ *tdmk.* a trademark for a barbiturate sedative

second[1] /sékənd/ *adj.* **1. COMING AFTER FIRST** coming after the first in a series **2. ANOTHER** additional to, repeating, or following one that came before or was previously mentioned ○ *I need a second look at those figures.* **3. ADDITIONAL AND LESS IMPORTANT** additional to and less important than the first or main one ○ *a second home* **4. SIMILAR TO PREDECESSOR** similar or comparable in many respects to a particular renowned personality or event ○ *a second Watergate* **5. INFERIOR TO** inferior to or less important than sb or sth else ○ *second only to the president* **6.** MUSIC **PERFORMING LOWER OR LESS IMPORTANT PART** singing or playing a lower or less important part ■ *n.* **1. SECOND MEMBER OF SERIES** the second member or item in a series **2. ANOTHER PERSON OR THING** another person or thing of the same kind as one previously mentioned **3. COMPETITOR'S OR DUELLIST'S ASSISTANT** an official assistant to a contestant in a boxing match or a duel **4. SECONDER** a seconder for a proposal, a motion, or nomination in a debate **5. ARTICLE WITH FAULT** an imperfectly manufactured article that is sold at a discount **6.** TRANSP **FORWARD GEAR** a forward gear of a transmission that is higher than first gear and lower than third gear **7.** BASEBALL = **second base** *n.* 1 **8.** UNIV **SECOND CLASS DEGREE** a second class degree from a university or college **9.** MUSIC **INTERVAL OF TWO NOTES** in a standard musical scale, the interval between one note and another that lies one note above or below it. In the scale of C major, C and D form a second. **10.** MUSIC **NOTE A SECOND AWAY FROM ANOTHER** in a standard musical scale, a note that is a second away from another note **11.** BALLET = **second position** ■ **seconds** *npl.* (*informal*) **1.** FOOD **ANOTHER HELPING OR SERVING** another helping or serving of a dish or type of food **2. SECOND COURSE OF A MEAL** the second course of a meal, usually the dessert ■ *vt.* (**-onds, -onding, -onded**) **1. ACT AS SECONDER OF STH** to state support officially for a proposal, motion, or nomination introduced by sb else, so that discussion or voting can take place **2. EXPRESS AGREEMENT AND SUPPORT FOR STH** to express agreement and support for sth that sb has just said (*informal*) ○ *I second that.* **3. ACT AS COMPETITOR'S OR DUELLIST'S SECOND** to act as second to a contestant in a boxing match or duel **4. ASSIST OR SUPPORT** to assist or support sb or sth (*formal*) ○ *seconded her efforts* ■ *adv.* **1. EXCEPT FOR ONE** the one that exceeds all the rest, except for one, in a particular way (*used to qualify a superlative*) ○ *the second highest mountain in the world* **2.** = **secondly** [14thC. Directly or via Old French from Latin *secundus* 'the following, second', from *sequi* 'to follow' (source of English *consequence* and *sequential*).] ◇ **second to none** better than anyone or anything else

second[2] /sékənd/ *n.* **1. GOTH OF MINUTE** a unit of time that is equal to one sixtieth of a minute. Symbol **s** **2.** MEASURE **UNIT OF MEASUREMENT OF ANGLES** a unit of measurement of angles equal to one sixtieth of a minute or one 360th of a degree. Symbol **s** **3. VERY SHORT TIME** a very short period of time [14thC. Via French from medieval Latin *secunda* (see SECOND[1]), from *secunda pars minuta*, literally, 'second diminished part'. The word denotes the second division of an hour by sixty.]

second[3] /si kónd/ (**-conds, -conding, -conded**) *vt.* to transfer an employee, official, or soldier temporarily to other duties [Early 19thC. From French *en second* 'in the second rank'.] —**secondment** *n.*

Second Advent *n.* = **Second Coming**

secondary /sékəndəri/ *adj.* **1. NOT PRIMARY OR MAJOR** less important than or subordinate to sth else ○ *matters of secondary importance* **2. DERIVED FROM STH ORIGINAL** derived from or reliant on sth original ○ *a secondary source* **3.** MED **HAPPENING AS RESULT OF PRIMARY DISORDER** happening as a result of sth else, e.g. an infection starting after a primary illness ○ *secondary tumours* **4.** EDUC **OCCURRING AFTER PRIMARY SCHOOL** intended for students who have completed their primary education, usually for children aged between eleven and eighteen **5.** BIRDS **GROWING ALONG INNER EDGE OF WING** used to describe feathers that grow along the trailing edge of the inner segment of a bird's wing **6.** ELEC **ELECTRICALLY INDUCED** used to describe a circuit or coil that has an electric current produced by induction **7.** INDUST **INVOLVED IN MANUFACTURING** involved in the manufacture of goods from raw materials **8.** CHEM **ORGANIC CARBON COMPOUND** used to describe an organic compound having a carbon atom to which three organic groups of atoms are attached, at least one of which is chemically active **9.** CHEM **RELATING TO ORGANIC NITROGEN COMPOUND** used to describe an amine having two organic groups of atoms and one hydrogen atom attached to a nitrogen atom **10.** BOT **OF RAPIDLY DIVIDING TISSUE** relating to or derived from rapidly dividing tissue (**cambium**) that gives rise to increased girth, not increased length ■ *n.* (*plural* **-ies**) **1. SB OR STH SECONDARY** sb or sth that is secondary or subordinate **2.** MED **SECONDARY TUMOUR** a cancerous growth at a site remote from that of the original malignant tumour **3.** BIRDS **SECONDARY FEATHER** a secondary feather **4.** ELEC **INDUCED COIL OR CIRCUIT** a coil or circuit in which an induced current flows [14thC. Formed from SECOND[1].] —**secondarily** *adv.* —**secondariness** *n.*

secondary accent *n.* **1.** = **secondary stress** **2. STRESS MARK** a mark used to indicate where the secondary accent is placed

secondary cell *n.* an electric cell in which electricity is produced by a reversible chemical reaction. It is therefore rechargeable and able to store electrical energy.

secondary colour *n.* a colour such as orange, green, or purple produced by mixing two primary colours in roughly equal quantities

secondary electron *n.* an electron released by secondary emission

secondary emission *n.* the emission of electrons from the surface of a substance bombarded with electrons or ions

secondary infection *n.* an infection that is acquired during the course of a separate initial infection

secondary modern school, secondary modern *n.* formerly, a secondary school offering a more practical and less academic education than a grammar school and attended by students who did not pass the eleven-plus exam

secondary picketing *n.* the picketing by strikers of premises other than those of the company with which they are in dispute, often those of the suppliers or distributors of their company's products

secondary school *n.* a school for students who have completed their primary education, usually attended by children aged between eleven and eighteen

secondary sexual characteristic *n.* a characteristic that develops at puberty but is not directly concerned with reproduction, e.g. a woman's breasts or a man's facial hair

secondary stress *n.* an accentuation on a syllable that is weaker than that on the syllable receiving the main accent. For example, in the word 'secondary', the main accent falls on the first syllable and the secondary accent on the third. US term **secondary accent**

secondary syphilis *n.* the second, highly infectious stage of syphilis that appears several weeks or months after primary infection and is marked by a faint skin rash, fever, and muscular pain

second ballot *n.* a second round of voting in an election in which no candidate obtained a winning majority in the first round. In a second ballot, the candidates who received the fewest votes in the first round are usually left out.

second base *n.* **1. BASE DIRECTLY OPPOSITE HOME PLATE** the base opposite home plate in the baseball diamond, or the position of the infielder playing nearest to second base on the first-base side **2.** = **second baseman**

second baseman *n.* in baseball, the player positioned closest to second base, on the first-base side of it

second best *adj.* (*hyphenated when used before a noun*) **1. NEXT IN QUALITY TO BEST** next in quality to, or surpassed only by, the best **2. INFERIOR TO BEST** inferior to the best or the favourite ○ *had to make do with a second-best alternative* ■ *n.* **1. SB OR STH NEXT TO BEST** sb or sth that is next in quality to, or surpassed only by, the best **2. SB OR STH INFERIOR TO BEST** sb or sth inferior to the best or the favourite

second chamber *n.* the upper house in a two-chamber legislative assembly, e.g. the House of Lords

second childhood *n.* a condition associated with ageing that manifests itself in behaviour regarded as resembling that of a child (*offensive*)

second class *n.* **1. CATEGORY AFTER BEST** the category or standard of sth, especially of accommodation or travel, that comes immediately below the best **2. MAIL DELIVERY SERVICE** a mail delivery service for letters and packets that is slower but less expensive than first class **3.** SECOND HIGHEST DEGREE the second highest division on the classification of university results, or a degree awarded for a result in this division ■ *adj.* (*hyphenated when used before a noun*) **1.** BELONGING TO SECOND CLASS belonging to or meeting the standards of second class, especially regarding mail service or travel accommodation ○ *second-class accommodation* **2.** INFERIOR inferior to, or less important than sb or sth else ■ *adv.* **second-class** BY SECOND-CLASS MEANS OF TRAVEL by second-class mail delivery service or travel accommodation ○ *travelled second-class*

second-class citizen *n.* sb who does not have or is perceived not to have the same rights, privileges, or opportunities as a full citizen

Second Coming *n.* in Christian belief, the anticipated and prophesied return of Jesus Christ to judge humanity at the end of the world

second cousin *n.* a child of a first cousin of either of your parents

second-degree burn *n.* a burn that causes blistering on the skin, but does not damage the deeper layers of the skin or require grafting

seconde /sə kóNd/ *n.* the second of the eight classic parrying positions in fencing [Early 18thC. From French, a form of *second* (see SECOND[1]).]

Second Empire *n.* **1.** HIST REIGN OF NAPOLEON III the reign or the government of the Emperor Napoleon III of France, lasting from 1852 until 1870 **2.** ARTS STYLE OF SECOND EMPIRE the weighty, grandiose, and highly ornamented style of architecture, furnishing, and decoration typical of the Second Empire

seconder /sékəndər/ *n.* sb who officially states support for a proposal, motion, or nomination introduced by sb else, so that discussion or voting can take place

second estate *n.* the nobility, as one of the three broad traditional classes of people within a monarchical state

second fiddle *n.* a less important or less prominent role or sb or sth in such a role

second floor *n.* (*hyphenated when used before a noun*) **1.** THIRD LEVEL OF A BUILDING the third level of a building, two floors above the floor at ground level. US term **third floor** **2.** *US* = **first floor**

second generation *n.* **1.** CHILDREN OF IMMIGRANTS the children of immigrants to a particular country **2.** LATER STAGE OF DEVELOPMENT a later stage in the development of sth that benefits from what was learned from the first stage of development —**second-generation** *adj.*

second growth *n.* the trees and plants that grow back naturally in an area of forest after the original trees have been removed by cutting or fire

second-guess (**second-guesses, second-guessing, second-guessed**) *vti.* **1.** MAKE A PREDICTION to predict a course of events, outcome, or what someone will do, from a position of relative ignorance ○ *no point in trying to second-guess what they'll do* **2.** *US* CRITICIZE AFTER THE EVENT to criticize, assess, or correct sb or sth after an event is over and the outcome is known —**second-guesser** *n.*

second hand *n.* the hand of a clock or watch that shows time passing second by second and rotates once around the dial in the space of a minute

second-hand *adj.* **1.** PREVIOUSLY OWNED previously owned or used **2.** SELLING USED GOODS selling or dealing in used goods **3.** NOT ORIGINAL received from or reliant on sb or sth other than the original source ○ *second-hand accounts of the incident* ■ *adv.* **1.** IN USED CONDITION after being owned or used by sb else ○ *bought it second-hand* **2.** THROUGH INTERMEDIARY from or through sb or sth else and not by direct experience or personal effort ○ *acquires the information second-hand* ◇ **at second-hand** from or through sb or sth else

secondi plural of **secondo**

second-in-command *n.* sb who is in charge in the absence of the person usually in charge

Second International *n.* an international socialist association established in 1889 in Paris and lasting until World War I

second language *n.* (*hyphenated when used before a noun*) **1.** LANGUAGE LEARNED AFTER FIRST LANGUAGE a language learned by sb after the first language he or she learns at home **2.** LANGUAGE OF SECONDARY IMPORTANCE a language in widespread use in a country that sometimes has official status after the main language of the country

second lieutenant *n.* **1.** OFFICER OF LOWEST COMMISSIONED RANK an officer of the lowest commissioned rank in various military forces such as the US and British armies, the US Marine Corps and Air Force, or the Royal Marines **2.** LOWEST COMMISSIONED RANK the lowest commissioned rank in various military forces, e.g. the US and British armies, the US Marine Corps and Air Force, or the Royal Marines

secondly /sékəndli/ *adv.* used to introduce the second point in an argument or discussion

second man *n.* sb who assists the driver of a railway train

second mate *n.* the officer on a merchant ship next in the line of command after the first mate, usually the third-highest-ranking officer on board

second mortgage *n.* an additional mortgage on a property that has been mortgaged once already and secondary to the main lien for settlement

second name *n.* **1.** SURNAME sb's surname **2.** SECOND FORENAME sb's second forename

second nature *n.* a habit or tendency so well-developed and long-practised that it seems to be done unconsciously

secondo /se kóndō/ (*plural* **-di** /-dí/) *n.* the second or lower part in a piece of music for two players, especially a piano duet [Late 18thC. From Italian, 'second'.]

second opinion *n.* an opinion, especially one of a professional nature, from sb other than the usual or first person consulted

second person *n.* **1.** GRAMMATICAL CLASS OF VERB OR PRONOUN the grammatical class of a verb or pronoun used when addressing sb. In English, the second-person pronoun is 'you'. **2.** ADDRESSING FORM OF VERB OR PRONOUN a form of a pronoun or verb in the second person, e.g. 'you' or 'are'

second position *n.* a position in ballet in which the feet are turned outwards with the feet slightly apart

second-rate *adj.* inadequate in quality or performance ○ *a second-rate pianist* —**second-rater** *n.*

second reading *n.* the second presentation of a bill to a legislature as part of the process of turning the bill into law. In the British Parliament, it precedes a debate on its merits and its submission to committee.

Second Republic *n.* the period of the Republican government in France from 1848 to 1852

second sight *n.* the supposed ability to see things that the physical eye cannot see, especially events taking place in the future or elsewhere —**second-sightedness** *n.*

second-strike *adj.* relating to, involving, or intended for use in, a retaliatory nuclear attack with weapons designed to survive a first nuclear strike by an enemy ○ *second-strike capabilities*

second string *n.* **1.** SUBSTITUTE TEAM a substitute or reserve group of team members **2.** ALTERNATIVE PLAN a fallback plan of action —**second-string** *adj.*

second thought *n.* a reconsideration of sth tentatively decided, e.g. in light of new developments or sth not previously taken into account (*often used in the plural*) ○ *having second thoughts about getting married* ◇ **on second thoughts** after reconsideration

second unit *n.* CINEMA a smaller secondary crew that films locations or crowd scenes in which the main actors do not appear or for which the major production personnel are not required

second wind /-wínd/ *n.* a renewal of energy following a period of effort and exertion

Second World War *n.* = **World War II**

secrecy /séekrəssi/ *n.* **1.** STATE OF CONCEALMENT the state of being concealed or secret ○ *talks held in secrecy* **2.** KEEPING OF SECRETS the keeping of a secret or secrets ○ *sworn to secrecy* **3.** SECRETIVENESS a tendency to keep things secret [Late 16thC. Formed from SECRET.]

secret /séekrət/ *adj.* **1.** NOT WIDELY KNOWN known by only a few people and intentionally withheld from general knowledge **2.** UNDERCOVER working or operating without the knowledge of the general public **3.** UNADMITTED acting or feeling in a particular way without admitting to it ○ *a secret admirer* **4.** PRIVATE AND SECLUDED known to very few people and consequently quiet and secluded **5.** SECRETIVE tending by nature to keep things secret (*informal*) **6.** MYSTERIOUS mysterious and often beyond common understanding ■ *n.* **1.** INFORMATION NOT WIDELY KNOWN a piece of information that is known only to a few people and is intentionally withheld from general knowledge **2.** MYSTERY sth that is unknown, hidden, or not understood **3.** STH ENSURING SUCCESS a little-known technique, approach, or piece of information that is the key to success in a particular endeavour [14thC. Via French from Latin *secretus* 'separate, hidden', from *secernere* (see SECERN).] —**secretly** *adv.* ◇ **in secret** without anyone else's knowledge ○ *meet in secret*

WORD KEY: SYNONYMS

secret, clandestine, covert, furtive, stealthy, surreptitious

CORE MEANING: conveying a desire or need for concealment

secret a general word describing actions or events that are or should be concealed. It can also describe things, places, and information; **clandestine** describes sth such as a meeting between two people that is illicit, unauthorized, or unacceptable, and therefore must be concealed; **covert** a formal word used to describe sth that is done secretly, especially in order to emphasize a lack of honesty or openness; **furtive** the cautious nervous behaviour of a guilty person trying to avoid attention; **stealthy** describes behaviour that is quiet and slow in order to avoid notice, especially when this behaviour is associated with wrongdoing; **surreptitious** describes sth forbidden or unacceptable done at an opportune moment.

Secret, **secret** *n.* a variable prayer said at the conclusion of the Offertory and before the Preface in the Roman Catholic Mass [From ecclesiastical Latin *secreta oratio*, literally, 'concealed speech', from the low voice used]

secret agent *n.* sb engaged in espionage for a government or organization

secretagogue /si kréetə gog/ *n.* a substance such as a hormone that causes or stimulates secretion [Early 20thC. Coined from SECRETE + Greek *agōgos* 'leading, eliciting', from *agein* 'to lead'.] —**secretagogic** /si kréetə gójjik/ *adj.*

secretaire /sékrə táir/ *n.* FURNITURE a large cabinet with a fold-down desktop, usually with drawers below and an enclosed bookcase above. US term **secretary** [Late 18thC. Via French from late Latin *secretarius* (see SECRETARY).]

secretariat /sékrə táiri ət/ *n.* **1.** ADMINISTRATIVE DEPARTMENT a department that carries out the administrative and clerical work of an organization or legislature **2.** SECRETARIAL STAFF the secretarial staff under the direction of a secretary-general **3.** BUILDING HOUSING SECRETARIAT the headquarters or offices of a secretariat [Early 19thC. Via French from medieval Latin *secretariatus*, from late Latin *secretarius* (see SECRETARY).]

secretary /sékritəri/ (*plural* **-ies**) *n.* **1.** CLERICAL WORKER sb who does general clerical and administrative work such as word-processing, filing, and arranging appointments for an individual or an organization **2.** OFFICER OF CLUB, SOCIETY, OR COMMITTEE sb elected or appointed to keep the records of the meetings of an organization such as a club, society, or committee, and to write or answer letters on its behalf **3.** = **company secretary** **4.** = **secretary of state** **5.** CIVIL SERVANT ASSISTING GOVERNMENT MINISTER a senior civil servant who advises a government minister **6.** FURNITURE = **secretaire** [14thC. From late Latin *secretarius* 'confidential officer', from, ultimately, *secretus* (see SECRET).] —**secretarial** /sékri táiri əl/ *adj.* —**secretaryship** /sékri-/ *n.*

secretary bird *n.* a large long-legged African bird of prey that feeds mainly on snakes. It has grey-and-black plumage and a crest projecting from the back of its head. Latin name: *Sagittarius serpentarius.* [*Secretary* from the supposed resemblance of

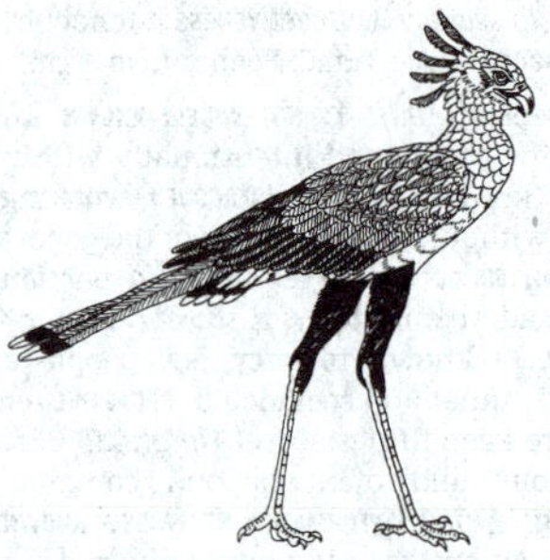

Secretary bird

the bird's crest to quill pens stuck behind a secretary's ear]

secretary-general (*plural* **secretaries-general**) *n.* the chief executive officer of an organization such as the United Nations, who oversees a secretariat

secretary of state *n.* a member of the British government and cabinet who is in charge of a major department such as Education or Defence

Secretary of State *n.* the US government official and cabinet member who is in charge of foreign affairs

secret ballot *n.* a situation in which people cast votes secretly in order to determine the outcome of an election or some other decision

secrete[1] /si kréet/ (**-cretes, -creting, -creted**) *vti.* to produce and discharge a secretion [Early 18thC. From Latin *secret-*, the past participle stem of *secernere* (see SECERN).] —**secretor** *n.*

secrete[2] /si kréet/ (**-cretes, -creting, -creted**) *vt.* **1.** HIDE STH to conceal sb or sth **2.** REMOVE STH SECRETLY to remove or steal sth secretly or without being observed (*archaic*) [Mid-18thC. Alteration (on the model of Latin *secretus* 'hidden') of obsolete *secret* 'to hide', from SECRET.] —**secretion** *n.*

secretin /si kréetin/ *n.* a hormone secreted in the duodenum that stimulates the pancreas and the bowel to produce digestive enzymes and the liver to produce bile [Early 20thC. Formed from SECRETION.]

secretion /si kréesh'n/ *n.* **1.** PROCESS OF SECRETING the process of producing a substance from the cells and fluids within a gland or organ and discharging it **2.** SECRETED SUBSTANCE a substance formed and discharged by a cell, tissue, gland, or organ [Mid-17thC. Via French from, ultimately, Latin *secernere* (see SECERN).] —**secretionary** *adj.*

secretive /séekrətiv/ *adj.* tending to keep information secret —**secretively** *adv.* —**secretiveness** *n.*

secretory /si kréetəri/ *adj.* involved in, producing, or produced by secretion [Late 17thC. Formed from SECRETE[1].]

secret partner *n.* a partner whose involvement in a business is kept secret

secret police *n.* a police force that operates in secret and whose function is to prevent subversion or suppress political opposition to a regime (*takes a plural verb*)

secret service *n.* a government department that carries out secret investigations and covert operations

Secret Service *n.* a branch of the US Treasury Department whose main function is the protection of the president and vice president and their families

secret society *n.* an organization that requires its members to keep all or some of its activities secret from nonmembers

sect /sekt/ *n.* **1.** RELIG NONMAINSTREAM RELIGIOUS GROUP a religious group with beliefs and practices at variance with those of a more established main group **2.** RELIG RELIGIOUS DENOMINATION a denomination of a larger religious group **3.** SOC SCI CLOSE-KNIT GROUP a small close-knit group with strongly held views that are sometimes regarded as extreme by the majority [14thC. Directly or via French from Latin *secta* 'school of thought', originally 'way, road', from *sequi* 'to follow' (source of English *sequence* and *second*).]

sect. *abbr.* **1.** section **2.** sectional

-sect *suffix.* **1.** to cut or divide ○ *quadrisect* **2.** cut, divided ○ *pinnatisect* [From Latin *sectus*, the past participle of *secare* 'to cut' (see SECTION)]

sectarian /sek táiri ən/ *adj.* **1.** RELIG OF RELIGIOUS GROUP relating to or involving relations between religious groups or denominations **2.** RELIG OF SINGLE RELIGIOUS GROUP relating to, involved with, or devoted to a particular religious group or denomination **3.** DOGMATIC AND INTOLERANT rigidly adhering to a particular set of doctrines and intolerant of other views ■ *n.* **1.** MEMBER OF RELIGIOUS GROUP a member of a religious group or denomination **2.** SB DOGMATIC AND INTOLERANT sb who rigidly adheres to a particular set of doctrines and is intolerant of other views —**sectarianism** *n.*

sectarianize /sek táiri ə nīz/ (**-izes, -izing, -ized**), **sectarianise** (**-ises, -ising, -ised**) *vt.* to cause sb or sth to become sectarian

sectary /séktəri/ (*plural* **-ries**) *n.* a member of a religious group or denomination (*archaic*)

sectile /sék tīl/ *adj.* used to describe minerals that can be cut so as to leave a smooth surface [Early 18thC. From Latin *sectilis*, from the stem *sect-* (see SECTION).] —**sectility** /sek tíllәti/ *n.*

section /séksh'n/ *n.* **1.** DISTINCT PART a distinct part that can be separated or considered separately from the whole of sth **2.** UNIT OF PEOPLE a group of people forming a unit within a larger group, e.g. a subdivision of a military unit, or the musicians playing a particular kind of instrument in an orchestra **3.** SUBDIVISION OF DOCUMENT a major subdivision of a written work such as a book or newspaper, or of an official or legal document, often numbered **4.** VIEW OF STH CUT THROUGH a view or representation of sth cut through to show its internal structure or workings **5.** SCI VERY THIN SLICE a very thin slice of sth removed for examination under a microscope ○ *a tissue section* **6.** SURG SURGICAL CUT a surgical incision **7.** CAESAREAN SECTION a caesarean section (*informal*) **8.** RAIL LENGTH OF RAIL TRACK a length of railway track maintained by a single crew or controlled from a single signal box **9.** BOT SEGMENT OF CITRUS FRUIT a segment of an orange, grapefruit, or other citrus fruit **10.** PRINTING = **section mark** **11.** *US* AREA OF ONE SQUARE MILE an area of land, for purposes of land surveying, equal to one square mile, 2.59 square kilometres, or one thirty-sixth of a township **12.** *NZ* RESIDENTIAL BUILDING LOT a residential building lot in a town or city ■ *vt.* (**-tions, -tioning, -tioned**) **1.** DIVIDE STH to divide sth up into separate parts **2.** CUT STH SURGICALLY to make a surgical incision in sth **3.** CONFINE SB TO PSYCHIATRIC HOSPITAL to order sb who is mentally ill to be confined in a psychiatric hospital under the appropriate section of the Mental Health Act [14thC. Directly or via French from the Latin stem *section-*, from *sect-*, past participle stem of *secare* 'to cut'.]

WORD KEY: ORIGIN

The Latin word *secare*, from which ***section*** is derived, is also the source of English *bisect*, *dissect*, *insect*, *intersect*, *secateurs*, *sector*, and *segment*.

sectional /séksh'nəl/ *adj.* **1.** SECTION OF relating to a particular group or section **2.** INVOLVING DIFFERENT SECTIONS involving different groups or sections **3.** CONSISTING OF SECTIONS divided into or made up of sections —**sectionally** *adv.*

sectionalise *vt.* = **sectionalize**

sectionalism /séksh'nəlizəm/ *n.* excessive concern for the interests of a particular group or area to the detriment of the whole —**sectionalist** *n.*, *adj.*

sectionalize /séksh'nə līz/ (**-izes, -izing, -ized**), **sectionalise** (**-ises, -ising, -ised**) *vt.* to divide sth, especially a geographic area, into sections —**sectionalization** /séksh'nə lī záysh'n/ *n.*

section mark *n.* a symbol (§) sometimes used in printing to mark the beginning of a section of a book or one of a series of footnotes, and for various other purposes

sector /séktər/ *n.* **1.** COMPONENT PART a component of an integrated system such as an economy or a society **2.** MIL PART OF AREA OF MILITARY OPERATIONS a part of an area where military forces are operating or in control **3.** GEOM PART OF CIRCLE a part of a circle bounded by two radii and the part of the circumference that lies between them **4.** MEASURING INSTRUMENT a measuring instrument consisting of two arms marked with graduations, hinged together at one end **5.** COMPUT UNIT OF MAGNETIC STORAGE DEVICE the smallest addressable unit of a magnetic storage device ■ *vt.* (**-tors, -toring, -tored**) DIVIDE STH to divide sth into sectors [Late 16thC. From late Latin, 'section of a circle', originally 'cutter', from the stem *sect-* (see SECTION).] —**sectoral** *adj.*

sectorial /sek táwri əl/ *adj.* **1.** OF SECTOR relating to a sector or consisting of sectors **2.** ZOOL USED FOR CUTTING adapted or specialized for cutting ○ *sectorial teeth*

secular /sékyŏŏlər/ *adj.* **1.** NOT CONCERNED WITH RELIGION not controlled by a religious body or concerned with religious or spiritual matters **2.** NOT RELIGIOUS not religious or spiritual in nature ○ *secular music* **3.** NOT MONASTIC not belonging to a monastic order **4.** OCCURRING ONCE A CENTURY occurring only once in the course of an age or century **5.** OCCURRING OVER LONG PERIOD taking place over an extremely or indefinitely long period of time ■ *n.* **1.** MEMBER OF SECULAR CLERGY a member of the secular clergy **2.** LAYPERSON a member of the laity [14thC. Formed from Old French *seculer*, from Latin *saecularis*, from *saeculum* 'world, generation, age'.] —**secularity** /sékyŏŏ lárrəti/ *n.* —**secularly** /sékyŏŏlərli/ *adv.*

secular humanism *n.* a philosophy or world view that stresses human values without reference to religion or spirituality

secularise *vt.* = **secularize**

secularism /sékyŏŏlərizəm/ *n.* **1.** EXCLUSION OF RELIGION FROM PUBLIC AFFAIRS the belief that religion and religious bodies should have no part in political or civic affairs or in running public institutions, especially schools **2.** REJECTION OF RELIGION the rejection of religion or its exclusion from a philosophical or moral system —**secularist** *n.* —**secularistic** /sékyŏŏlə rístik/ *adj.*

secularize /sékyŏŏlə rīz/ (**-izes, -izing, -ized**), **secularise** (**-ises, -ising, -ised**) *vt.* **1.** TRANSFER STH TO CIVIL USE to transfer sth from a religious to a nonreligious use, or from control by a religious body to control by the state or a lay body or person **2.** MAKE STH SECULAR to remove the religious dimension or element from sth, or otherwise make it secular —**secularization** /sékyŏŏlərī záysh'n/ *n.* —**secularizer** /sékyŏŏlə rīzər/ *n.*

secund /si kúnd/ *adj.* arranged on or curving towards only one side of an axis [Late 18thC. From Latin *secundus* (see SECOND).] —**secundly** *adv.*

secure /si kyŏŏr, -kyáwr/ *adj.* **1.** NOT WORRIED untroubled by feelings of fear, doubt, or vulnerability **2.** FIRMLY FIXED firmly fixed or placed in position and unlikely to come loose or give way ○ *made the rope secure* **3.** RELIABLE reliable and unlikely to fail or be lost ○ *a secure investment* **4.** WELL GUARDED AND FORTIFIED well guarded and strongly fortified or protected **5.** SAFE safe, especially against attack or theft **6.** SAFE FOR SECRET COMMUNICATIONS safe to use for secret or confidential communication ○ *a secure line* **7.** ASSURED certain to be achieved or gained ○ *Just when victory seemed secure, we let it slip from our grasp.* ■ *v.* (**-cures, -curing, -cured**) **1.** *vt.* FIX STH FIRMLY to fix sth firmly in position **2.** *vti.* MAKE STH SAFE to make a building or area safe to occupy, usually by ensuring that all internal sources of danger are removed or that it is defended against attack **3.** *vt.* ACQUIRE STH to obtain sth, especially after using considerable effort to persuade sb to grant or allow it ○ *secure an agreement* **4.** *vt.* FIN ENSURE PAYMENT FOR STH to provide security for sth or otherwise guarantee payment ○ *a loan secured against your house* **5.** *vti.* GUARANTEE to guarantee or ensure sth **6.** *vt.* PREVENT SB FROM ESCAPING to ensure that sb cannot escape ○ *secure a prisoner* **7.** *vt.* MAKE STH SAFE FOR SECRET COMMUNICATIONS to ensure that a means of communication can be safely used for secret or confidential messages ○ *secure a telephone line* **8.** *vt.* MAKE THINGS SAFE ON BOARD to make sure that everything on board a ship is safely stowed and that openings are covered ○ *secure a ship* ○ *secure the cargo* [Mid-16thC. From Latin *securus*, literally 'without care', from *cura* 'care' (source of English *cure*).] —**securable** *adj.* —**securely** *adv.* —**securement** *n.* —**secureness** *n.* —**securer** *n.*

── WORD KEY: SYNONYMS ──
See Synonyms at **get**.

secure tenancy *n.* a form of tenancy with a landlord such as a local authority or housing association in which the tenant has security of tenure

Securities and Exchange Commission *n.* an agency of the US government set up to regulate transactions in securities and protect investors against malpractice

Securities and Investment Board *n.* a regulatory body set up in 1986 to oversee financial markets in the City of London. In 1997, it took over the functions formerly exercised by the Bank of England as the guarantor of fair trading and of the soundness of financial institutions in the City.

securitization /si kyoŏri tī záysh'n, -kyáwri-/, **securitisation** *n.* the preparation of readily marketable securities representing an ownership interest in some asset such as credit card loans or forestry land that is not otherwise conveniently traded

security /si kyoŏrəti, -kyáwr-/ (*plural* **-ties**) *n.* **1.** STATE OR FEELING OF SAFETY the state or feeling of being safe and protected **2.** FREEDOM FROM WORRY ABOUT POSSIBLE LOSS the assurance that sth of value will not be taken away **3.** STH GIVING ASSURANCE sth that provides a sense of protection against loss, attack, or harm **4.** SAFETY protection against attack from without or within ○ *a matter of national security* **5.** PRECAUTIONS TO MAINTAIN SAFETY precautions taken to keep sb or sth safe from crime, attack, or danger ○ *security measures* **6.** GUARDS people or an organization entrusted with the job of protecting sb or sth, especially a building or institution, against crime **7.** ASSET DEPOSITED TO GUARANTEE REPAYMENT sth pledged to guarantee fulfilment of an obligation, especially an asset guaranteeing repayment of a loan that becomes the property of the creditor if the loan is not repaid **8.** GUARANTOR sb who guarantees to fulfil an obligation entered into by sb else if that person fails to do so **9.** FINANCIAL INSTRUMENT a tradable document such as a share certificate or bond that shows evidence of debt or ownership

security blanket *n.* **1.** BLANKET THAT CHILD CARRIES AROUND a familiar blanket, toy, or other object that a child carries around for the feeling of security it gives, or any object that fulfils the same function for an adult **2.** POLICY OF WITHHOLDING INFORMATION a policy of withholding information in the interests of security adopted as a temporary measure by the police or any other official body

security clearance *n.* official permission allowing sb to have access to a secure facility or to information that has been classified for reasons of national security

Security Council *n.* the permanent committee of the United Nations that oversees its peacekeeping operations throughout the world. The Security Council has five permanent members: Great Britain, China, France, Russia, and the United States, and ten other members chosen in rotation from among the other member states.

security guard *n.* sb employed by a private organization to guard and protect a building or other property

security of tenure *n.* the right of a tenant to continue occupying a property unless or until the landlord obtains a court order to regain possession of the property or terminate the tenancy

security risk *n.* sb or sth considered a threat to security, especially sb whose behaviour is thought likely to compromise the security of a country

securocrat /sə kyoŏrə krat, -kyáwrə-/ *n.* in South Africa, a military or police officer with power to influence government policy, often from behind the scenes [Blend of SECURITY and BUREAUCRAT]

secy, **sec'y** *abbr.* secretary

SED *n., abbr.* Scottish Education Department

sed. *abbr.* **1.** sediment **2.** sedimentation

sedan[1] /si dán/ *n.* US, Can, ANZ a car with a fully enclosed passenger compartment, a permanent roof, two or four doors, front and rear seats, and a

separate boot [Mid-17thC. Origin uncertain: perhaps via an Italian dialect word from, ultimately, Latin *sedes* 'seat'.]

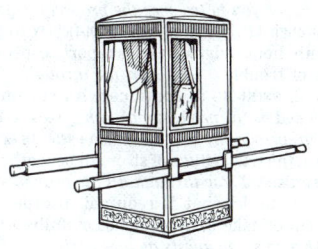

Sedan

sedan[2] **sedan chair** *n.* in the 17th and 18th centuries, an enclosed chair carried by porters at the front and rear on two long poles passed through handles on the sides of the box

Sedan /sə dán, sə doN/ town in Ardennes Department, Champagne-Ardenne Region, northeastern France. It was the location of a decisive French defeat in 1870 during the Franco-Prussian war. Population: 22,407 (1990).

sedan chair *n.* = sedan

sedate[1] /si dáyt/ *adj.* dignified, subdued, and lacking any sense of hurry or urgency [Mid-17thC. From Latin *sedatus*, past participle of *sedare* 'to calm', literally 'to force to sit', from *sedere* 'to sit' (source of English *session*).] —**sedately** *adv.* —**sedateness** *n.*

sedate[2] /si dáyt/ (**-dates**, **-dating**, **-dated**) *vt.* to administer a sedative to sb [Mid-20thC. Back-formation from SEDATIVE and SEDATION.]

sedation /si dáysh'n/ *n.* **1.** STATE OF CALM a state of calm, restfulness, or drowsiness, especially as induced by a sedative or tranquillizing drug **2.** USE OF SEDATIVES the use of a sedative or tranquillizing drug to induce a state of calm, restfulness, or drowsiness

sedative /séddətiv/ *n.* DRUG INDUCING SEDATION a drug or other agent that induces sedation ■ *adj.* INDUCING SEDATION inducing sedation, especially by means of a tranquillizing drug ○ *a sedative effect*

Seddon /sédd'n/, **Richard John** (1845–1906) English-born New Zealand statesman. A Liberal politician, he was New Zealand's longest serving premier (1893–1906). His government was noted for its progressive policies. Known as **King Dick**

sedentary /sédd'ntəri/ *adj.* **1.** INVOLVING SITTING involving a lot of sitting and correspondingly little exercise ○ *sedentary work* **2.** USUALLY SITTING tending to sit most of the time and taking little exercise ○ *a sedentary person* **3.** ZOOL NOT MOVING used to describe shellfish that remain in one place, usually attached to a rock, for most of their lives **4.** BIRDS NONMIGRATORY remaining in the same area throughout the year and not migrating [Late 16thC. Directly or via French *sédentaire* from Latin *sedentarius*, from, ultimately, *sedere* (see SEDATE[2]).] —**sedentarily** *adv.* —**sedentariness** *n.*

Seder /sáydər/ (*plural* **-ders** *or* **-derim** /sə déerim/) *n.* CALENDAR in Judaism, a ceremonial meal eaten on either of the first two nights of Passover, commemorating the exodus of the Jews from Egypt [Mid-19thC. From Hebrew, literally 'order, procedure'.]

sederunt /si déerənt/ *n.* Scotland **1.** LIST OF PEOPLE PRESENT AT SESSION a formula used to introduce the list of those present at a sitting of a body such as an ecclesiastical assembly or a court, or the list itself **2.** SESSION OF COURT OR ASSEMBLY a sitting of a body such as an ecclesiastical assembly or a court (*archaic*) [Early 17thC. From Latin, literally, '(there) they sat', 3rd person plural perfect indicative of *sedere* 'to sit'.]

sedge /sej/ *n.* a wetland plant that resembles grass and has a triangular stem, leaves growing in three vertical rows, and inconspicuous spikes of flowers. Genus: *Carex*. [Old English *secg*. Ultimately from an Indo-European word meaning 'to cut' that is also the ancestor of English *section*. Probably from the plant's sharpness.] —**sedgy** *adj.*

Sedgemoor /séj moor/ former marshland in Somerset, England, where the Duke of Monmouth's rebellion was defeated in 1685

sedge warbler *n.* a European and Central Asian songbird with streaked brownish plumage and a white strip around its eye, found mainly in marshes and reed beds. Latin name: *Acrocephalus schoenobaenus*.

sedge wren *n.* a wren of eastern North America that is similar to a sparrow in coloration and lives in grassy meadows and sedge marshes. Latin name: *Cistothorus platensis*.

Sedgwick /séjjwik/, **Adam** (1785–1873) British geologist. His studies of rock strata contributed to the identification of the Cambrian period, and to a scientific approach to geology, but he opposed Charles Darwin's theory of evolution.

sedilia /si dílli ə/ *npl.* a set of three seats placed near the altar of a church and often recessed into the wall used by priests celebrating Mass or Holy Communion [Late 18thC. From Latin, plural of *sedile* 'seat', from *sedere* 'to sit'.]

sediment /séddimənt/ *n.* **1.** SETTLED MATTER AT BOTTOM OF LIQUID material, originally suspended in a liquid, that settles at the bottom of the liquid when it is left standing for a long time **2.** ERODED MATERIAL material eroded from preexisting rocks that is transported by water, wind, or ice and deposited elsewhere [Mid-16thC. Directly or via French from Latin *sedimentum* 'settling', from *sedere* 'to sit'.] —**sedimentous** /séddi méntəss/ *adj.*

sedimentary /séddi méntəri/ *adj.* **1.** FORMING IN LIQUID forming at the bottom of a liquid **2.** FORMED FROM ERODED MATERIAL used to describe rocks formed from material, including debris of organic origin, deposited as sediment by water, wind, or ice and then consolidated by pressure —**sedimentarily** *adv.*

sedimentation /séddi men táysh'n/ *n.* **1.** FORMATION OF ROCKS the process by which rocks are formed by the accumulation of sediment **2.** PROCESS OF FORMING SEDIMENT IN LIQUID the process by which particles in suspension in a liquid form sediment

sedimentation tank *n.* a tank in which sewage is left in order to allow its solid constituents to separate out

sedimentology /séddi men tólləji/ *n.* the branch of geology concerned with the nature and formation of sedimentary rocks —**sedimentologic** /séddi mentə lójjik/ *adj.* —**sedimentologist** /séddi men tólləjist/ *n.*

sedition /si dísh'n/ *n.* actions or words intended to provoke or incite rebellion against government authority, or such a rebellion [14thC. Directly or via Old French from the Latin stem *sedition-* 'civil disorder', literally, 'a going apart, separation', from, ultimately, *ire* 'to go'.]

seditious /si díshəss/ *adj.* **1.** INVOLVING SEDITION involving or encouraging rebellion against a government or other authority **2.** INVOLVED IN SEDITION taking part in activities that are directed against a government or other authority [15thC Via French *seditieux* from, ultimately, Latin *seditio* 'discord' (see SEDITION)] —**seditiously** *adv.* —**seditiousness** *n.*

seduce /si dyoóss/ (**-duces**, **-ducing**, **-duced**) *vt.* **1.** INDUCE SB TO HAVE SEX to persuade sb to have sex, especially by using a romantic or deceptive approach **2.** LEAD SB ASTRAY to persuade sb into doing sth wrong **3.** WIN SB OVER to persuade sb into giving support or agreement [15thC From Latin *seducere* 'to lead astray', from *ducere* 'to lead' (source of English *educate*)] —**seducer** *n.* —**seducible** *adj.*

seducement /si dyoóssmənt/ *n.* **1.** STH THAT SEDUCES sth that tempts or persuades ○ *'ere any flattering seducement, or vain principle seize them'* (John Milton, *Civil War Polemic, part I*) **2.** SEDUCTION a seduction (*archaic*)

seduction /si dúksh'n/ *n.* **1.** LEADING ASTRAY OF SB the act of persuading sb to do sth wrong ○ *their easy seduction into a life of crime* **2.** LURING OF SB INTO SEX the act of persuading sb to have sex, especially by using a romantic or deceptive approach **3.** TEMPTING THING sth that tempts, persuades, or attracts

seductive /si dúktiv/ *adj.* **1.** SEXUALLY ENTICING aiming to be or regarded as being sexually inviting ○ *his seductive smile* **2.** TEMPTING serving to tempt, persuade, or attract ○ *made me a very seductive offer* —**seductively** *adv.* —**seductiveness** *n.*

seductress /si dúktrəss/ *n.* a woman who seduces others [Early 19thC. Formed from obsolete 'sedutor' + -ESS.]

sedulous /séddyŏŏləss/ *adj.* (*literary*) **1.** WORKING PERSISTENTLY working with great zeal and persistence **2.** PAINSTAKING carried out with great care, concentration, and commitment ○ *sedulous attention to detail* [Mid-16thC. From Latin *sedulus*, from, ultimately, *se* 'without' + *dolus* 'deception'.] —**sedulity** /si dyŏŏləti/ *n.* —**sedulously** /séddyŏŏləssli/ *adv.* —**sedulousness** /-ləssnəss/ *n.*

sedum /seédəm/ *n.* any one of a genus of low-growing herbaceous plants that grow naturally in rocky places and have fleshy leaves and clusters of white, yellow, or pink flowers. Genus: *Sedum.* [Mid-16thC. From Latin, 'houseleek'.]

see[1] /see/ (**sees, seeing, saw** /saw/, **seen** /seen/) *v.* **1.** *vti.* PERCEIVE WITH EYES to perceive, or perceive sth, with the eyes **2.** *vi.* HAVE VISION to be able to perceive things with the eyes ○ *sees fine without his glasses* **3.** *vti.* VIEW OR WATCH to examine, look at, or watch sb or sth using the eyes ○ *He asked to see my passport.* **4.** *vti.* COMPREHEND to have a clear understanding of sth ○ *I'm not sure I see what you mean.* **5.** *vti.* REALIZE BY SEEING to realize that sth is true or exists by using the eyes, e.g. by reading about it ○ *I see from his letter that he's worked here before.* **6.** *vt.* PERCEIVE STH AS PLEASING OR GOOD to perceive or find a trait in sb, especially one that is interesting or pleasing ○ *I don't understand what she sees in him.* **7.** *vt.* MEET OR CONSULT WITH SB to meet sb or spend time with sb, either socially or professionally ○ *I'm seeing an old friend for lunch.* **8.** *vt.* HAVE A RELATIONSHIP WITH SB to meet with sb in a romantic context or have a romantic or sexual relationship with sb ○ *Is he seeing anyone at the moment?* **9.** *vt.* HAVE INTERVIEW WITH SB to meet with sb in order to raise or discuss an issue such as a complaint ○ *She asked to see the customer care manager.* **10.** *vt.* RECEIVE SB FOR INTERVIEW to admit or receive sb who has come for a visit or an interview ○ *The doctor can't see you until next week.* **11.** *vt.* IMAGINE STH to picture sth in the mind ○ *I couldn't see someone like him in a jacket and tie.* **12.** *vt.* BELIEVE STH to regard it as likely that sb will do sth ○ *We couldn't see them agreeing to that.* **13.** *vt.* CONSIDER SB OR STH to regard sb or sth in a particular way ○ *We don't really see them as good friends.* **14.** *vt.* UNDERGO STH to experience sth firsthand ○ *They've seen a lot of unhappiness in their short lives.* **15.** *vt.* ESCORT SB to go somewhere with sb, usually as a guide, for company, or for protection ○ *Would you see me to my car?* **16.** *vt.* MAKE SURE OF STH to remember to do sth or be sure to do it ○ *See that they wipe their feet before they come in.* **17.** *vt.* REFER TO STH to consult sth or refer to sth ○ *See our main advertisement on page 25.* **18.** *vti.* ASCERTAIN to find sth out ○ *See if you can get this book locally.* **19.** *vi.* WAIT UNTIL LATER TO DECIDE to allow time to elapse, either in order to be better able to judge what the outcome will be or in order to delay making a decision ○ *I don't know; we'll have to see.* **20.** *vt.* GAMBLING MATCH BET to match an opponent's bet by staking the same amount [Old English *sēon*. From a prehistoric Germanic base that is also the ancestor of German *sehen*.] —**seeable** *adj.* ◇ **what you see is what you get** used to emphasize that nothing is disguised, hidden, or insincere. ◊ **WYSIWYG**

see about *vt.* to take care of a particular matter

see into *vt.* **1.** PERCEIVE TRUTH ABOUT STH to discern the true nature or content of sth hidden, e.g. sb's thoughts **2.** FORETELL EVENTS to be able to predict future events

see off *vt.* **1.** ATTEND SB'S DEPARTURE to accompany sb to a place of departure and say goodbye **2.** FORCE SB TO GO to make sb leave a place, especially by force (*informal*) ○ *The dogs soon saw them off.* **3.** DEFEAT SB to withstand a challenge, e.g. by beating an opponent in a sporting contest ○ *There's no question that the Brazilians will see off the others in their group.*

see out *vt.* **1.** ESCORT SB OUT to accompany sb who is leaving a room, building, or other place **2.** STAY UNTIL THE END OF STH to stay in a place or stay committed to sth until the end **3.** OUTLIVE SB to last until the end of sb's life and beyond (*informal*) ○ *I reckon this old car will see me out.*

see over, see round *vt.* to make a tour of a place, especially a building, in order to inspect it ○ *We can arrange for you to see over the property.*

see through *vt.* **1.** HELP SB THROUGH DIFFICULTY to provide sb with help, advice, and support, especially in times of trouble ○ *He's seen me through some bad times.* **2.** FINISH STH to continue with sth until it is completed ○ *a professional who sees every job through personally* **3.** PERCEIVE TRUTH BENEATH EXTERIOR to discern the true nature of sb or sth beneath a façade or disguise ○ *I saw through all his bravado.*

see to *vt.* to do what is required in order to deal with sth or take care of sb successfully ○ *We need an usher to see to guests as they arrive.*

see[2] /see/ *n.* **1.** BISHOP'S DIOCESE the area that is under the jurisdiction of a bishop or archbishop **2.** BISHOP'S POWER the position or authority of a bishop or archbishop [13thC Via Old French *se* from, ultimately, Latin *sedere* 'to sit']

Seebeck effect /seé bek-/ *n.* the production of an electric current in a circuit containing junctions between different metals or semiconductors kept at different temperatures. The effect is used in thermocouples. [Early 20thC. Named after Thomas *Seebeck* (1770–1831), the Russian-born German physicist who first discovered the phenomenon.]

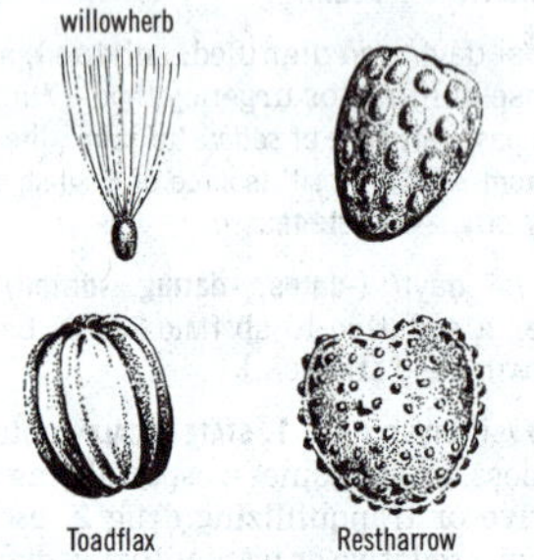
Rosebay willowherb
Figwort
Toadflax
Restharrow
Seed

seed /seed/ *n.* **1.** BOT PLANT PART CONTAINING EMBRYO the body produced by reproduction in most plants that contains the embryo and gives rise to a new individual. In flowering plants, it is enclosed within the fruit. The seed develops from the fertilized ovule, contains a food supply, and is itself enclosed in a protective coat (**testa**). **2.** BOT FRUIT OF GRASS PLANT the small dry hard fruit produced by cereal plants or grasses **3.** BOT PROPAGATIVE PART OF PLANT any compact part of a plant such as a bulb, tuber, or spore that is used for propagation **4.** BOT PROPAGATIVE PLANT PARTS COLLECTIVELY propagative plant parts as a whole, including seeds, tubers, rhizomes, spores, and bulbs ○ *a dry place to store seed* **5.** SOURCE sth that is the source of a significant change in outlook or action ○ *sowing the seeds of doubt in her mind* **6.** STH RESEMBLING SEED sth that resembles a seed in shape, size, or function **7.** CHEM CRYSTAL a small crystal added to a supersaturated or supercooled solution to induce further crystallization **8.** DESCENDANTS descendants (*literary*) ○ *the seed of Abraham* **9.** SPORTS GRADED COMPETITOR a competitor who is graded according to the perceived likelihood of his or her winning a particular tournament **10.** SPERM sperm or semen as a vehicle of reproduction (*literary*) **11.** ZOOL = **seed oyster** ■ *v.* (**seeds, seeding, seeded**) **1.** *vt.* PLANT SEEDS to plant seeds in soil or plant sth by sowing seeds ○ *The lower field was seeded with barley.* **2.** *vi.* DROP SEEDS to shed seeds that develop into new plants (*refers to plants*) ○ *Those poppies have seeded themselves everywhere.* **3.** *vt.* REMOVE SEEDS FROM STH to take the seeds out of a fruit or vegetable before eating or cooking **4.** *vt.* CHEM ADD CRYSTAL TO SOLUTION to add a small crystal to a supersaturated or supercooled solution to induce further crystallization **5.** *vt.* METEOROL SPRINKLE CLOUD WITH CRYSTALS to release silver iodide into clouds to encourage precipitation **6.** *vt.* SPORTS STRUCTURE TOURNAMENT to arrange the draw of a tournament so that the best players meet in the later rounds **7.** *vt.* SPORTS RANK PLAYER to rank a player according to the perceived likelihood of his or her winning a tournament **8.** *vt.* US BUSINESS ENCOURAGE ENTERPRISE to give financial or other assistance to sth such as a business during the early stages of its development ○ *'Big venture capital funds have helped seed a start-up culture...'* (*Newsweek*; November 1998) ■ *adj.* AGRIC RESERVED FOR USE AS SEED reserved for planting to grow the next crop ○ *seed potatoes* [Old English *sǣd*. From a prehistoric Germanic base that is also the ancestor of English *sow*.] —**seedless** *adj.* ◇ **go to seed, run to seed 1.** to reach the stage of producing seeds. At this stage, flowering plants have lost their flowers and the vegetables on vegetable plants have become inedible. **2.** to become shabby or unhealthy from lack of proper care or attention

seedbed /seéd bed/ *n.* **1.** GARDENING GROUND FOR PLANTING a plot of ground in which seeds and seedlings are cultivated before being transplanted **2.** PLACE WHERE STH DEVELOPS a place where conditions encourage the development of a significant change in outlook or action

seedcake /seéd kayk/ *n.* a cake flavoured with seeds, usually caraway seeds. It is usually a madeira cake, often with additional flavourings, e.g. grated lemon rind and nutmeg or mace.

seed capital *n.* money provided to enable a business venture to be developed. US term **seed money**

seed coat *n.* = **testa**

seed corn *n.* **1.** GRAIN KEPT FOR SEED cereal grain that is reserved for use as seed **2.** GOOD INVESTMENTS investments that are expected to yield good profits in the future

seedeater /seéd eetər/ *n.* a bird such as the finch that relies on seeds for its food and usually has a stout conical bill adapted to cracking the seeds open

seeder /seédər/ *n.* **1.** AGRIC MACHINE FOR SOWING SEEDS a mechanical device designed to scatter seed on the surface of the ground, usually either one pulled by a tractor or one with wheels and a handle that is pushed **2.** HOUSEHOLD DEVICE FOR REMOVING SEEDS a kitchen device used to remove the seeds from fruit and vegetables [Old English *sǣdere*]

seed fern *n.* = **pteridosperm**

seedhead /seédhed/ *n.* a fertilized flower or flower cluster that contains numerous seeds

seed leaf *n.* = **cotyledon**

seedling /seédling/ *n.* a young developing plant that is grown from a seed

seed money *n.* *US* = **seed capital**

seed oyster *n.* a small young oyster, especially one that is transplanted to a commercial oyster bed

seed pearl *n.* a very small round pearl, natural or cultured, weighing less than one quarter of a grain

seed plant *n.* = **spermatophyte**

seed pod *n.* = **pod**[1] *n.* 1

seedsman /seédzmən/ (*plural* **-men** /-mən/) *n.* sb who sells seed or produces seed commercially

seed stock *n.* **1.** SEED SUPPLY a supply of seed for planting **2.** SUPPLY OF BREEDING ANIMALS a supply of animals kept or provided for breeding purposes, capable of founding a new population or sustaining an existing population (*hyphenated when used before a noun*)

seed tick *n.* the tiny larva of a tick

seedtime /seéd tīm/ *n.* **1.** SOWING SEASON the time of the year when seeds are sown **2.** DEVELOPMENT PERIOD a period of new development or growth

seed vessel *n.* the part of a plant that contains its seeds, especially a part that is not an edible fruit or vegetable

seed wasp *n.* any of several species of wasp such as the gall wasp that bore into the seeds of plants to lay their eggs. Superfamily: Chalcidoidea.

seed weevil *n.* any one of several species of insect of the weevil family that lays its eggs in seeds, where the larvae then develop

seedy /seédi/ (**-ier, -iest**) *adj.* **1.** UNWELL somewhat ill, especially with a stomach complaint (*informal*) **2.** DINGY shabby, dirty-looking, and often disreputable ○ *He discovered her singing in some seedy bar.* **3.**

HAVING SEEDS containing many seeds ○ *seedy raspberry jam* —**seedily** *adv.* —**seediness** *n.*

seeing /seé ing/ *n.* **1.** VISION vision or perception with the eyes ○ *My seeing isn't too good.* **2.** ASTRON AT-MOSPHERIC CONDITIONS the clarity of the Earth's atmosphere for astronomical observations using an optical telescope, or the quality of the images obtained ■ *conj.* IN VIEW OF used to introduce a statement that takes into account sth mentioned before or after ○ *Seeing that you're an old friend, I can give you a special price.*

WORD KEY: USAGE

Perhaps a bonus on my wages might be an idea, seeing that I shall be doing this out of hours (Paula Marshall, *An American Princess*). The use of ***seeing that*** as a conjunction not grammatically attached to a particular subject is established in current English and conforms to a pattern used also by *given that, granted that,* and others. On the other hand, ***seeing as***, used in the same way, is informal only: *I'll leave now seeing as you look tired.*

seek /seek/ (**seeks, seeking, sought** /sawt/, **sought**) *v.* **1.** *vti.* SEARCH FOR STH to try to find a particular thing or place ○ *journeyed to America to seek their fortune* **2.** *vt.* STRIVE FOR STH to try to achieve or obtain sth ○ *candidates seeking election* **3.** *vt.* HEAD FOR STH to go to or towards a place or thing ○ *As the water rose, they sought higher ground.* **4.** *vt.* ASK FOR STH to consult sb in order to obtain sth such as help or advice ○ *His advice was regularly sought on such matters.* **5.** *vt.* ATTEMPT STH to try to do sth ○ *seeking to exploit the rift between them* [Old English *sécan*. Ultimately from an Indo-European base meaning 'to seek out' that is also the ancestor of English *sagacity*.] —**seeker** *n.*

seek out *vt.* to find sb or sth as a result of active searching

seel /seel/ (**seels, seeling, seeled**) *vt.* to sew up the eyelids of a hawk or falcon in order to make it tame [15thC. Via Old French *siller, ciller* from medieval Latin *ciliare*, from Latin *cilium* 'eyelid'.]

seem /seem/ (**seems, seeming, seemed**) *v.* **1.** *vti.* APPEAR TO BE STH to give a particular impression, either of a quality or of sth happening ○ *It's not as difficult as it seems.* **2.** *vt.* APPEAR TO BE TRUE to appear to exist or be true, used especially to lessen the force of a following statement, usually by suggesting uncertainty or mitigating criticism, often for the sake of politeness ○ *We seem to have a misunderstanding.* [12thC. From Old Norse *sœma* 'to conform to', from *sœmr* 'fitting'. The modern meaning 'to appear to be' evolved via 'to be suitable' and 'to appear to be suitable'.]

seeming /seéming/ *adj.* APPEARING TO EXIST apparent to the senses or to the mind, but not necessarily true or real ○ *her seeming joy at his return* ■ *n.* APPARENT EXISTENCE OF STH appearance to the senses or the mind (*archaic or literary*) —**seemingly** *adv.* —**seemingness** *n.*

seemly /seémli/ *adj.* (**-lier, -liest**) **1.** SUITABLE AND CORRECT in keeping with accepted standards and appropriate to the circumstances **2.** PLEASING pleasing to the eye or to the mind (*archaic or literary*) ■ *adv.* IN SEEMLY WAY in a way that is fitting or appropriate (*archaic*) ○ *He was seemly courteous in his greeting.* [12thC. From Old Norse *sœmiligr*, from *sœmr* 'fitting'.] —**seemliness** *n.*

seen past participle of **see**

seep /seep/ *vi.* (**seeps, seeping, seeped**) **1.** PASS THROUGH to pass or escape through an opening very slowly and in small quantities (*refers to liquids or gases*) ○ *water seeping out of the cracks* **2.** DISAPPEAR to diminish slowly but steadily ○ *with her resistance gradually seeping away* **3.** GO SLOWLY to enter or escape slowly but inexorably ○ *new sensations seeping into his consciousness* ■ *n.* **1.** GEOL PLACE WHERE LIQUID ESCAPES a small pool or spring where liquid escapes from the ground **2.** = **seepage** [Late 18thC. Variant of dialect *sipe*, of uncertain origin: perhaps from Old English *sipian* 'to seep'.]

seepage /seépij/ *n.* the escape of liquid or the amount of liquid that escapes

seer[1] /seer, seé ər/ *n.* **1.** PREDICTER OF FUTURE sb who claims or is assumed to be able to see into the future **2.** OCCULTIST sb who claims to have supernatural powers

seer[2] /seer/ (*plural* **seers** *or* **seer**) *n.* a unit of weight in India approximately equal to 0.9 kg/2 lbs [Early 17thC. Via Hindi *ser* from, ultimately, Greek *statēr*, a unit of weight.]

seersucker /seér sukər/ *n.* a lightweight cotton, linen, or synthetic fabric with a pattern of alternate puckered and smooth stripes [Early 18thC. Via Hindi *śīrśakar* from, ultimately, Persian *shīr o shakar*, literally 'milk and sugar'.]

seesaw /seé saw/ *n.* **1.** PLAYGROUND TOY a playground toy in which two people sit at either end of a bar balanced in the middle and take turns at riding up into the air **2.** SEESAW RIDING the game of riding a seesaw **3.** UP-AND-DOWN MOVEMENT an up-and-down, back-and-forth, or otherwise alternating movement, e.g. in the popularity of one political party over another ■ *vi.* (**-saws, -sawing, -sawed**) **1.** RIDE A SEESAW to ride up and down on a seesaw **2.** MOVE LIKE SEESAW to move in an alternating fashion, especially back and forth or up and down **3.** TO ALTERNATE to change regularly and repeatedly from one thing to another, e.g. one state of mind to another ○ *seesawing between one plan and another* [Mid-17thC. Thought to suggest the repetitive action and sound of using a two-handled saw.]

seethe /seeth/ *v.* (**seethes, seething, seethed**) **1.** *vi.* MAKE BOILING MOVEMENTS to boil or to churn or foam as if boiling **2.** *vi.* BE ANGRY to be in a state of extreme emotion, especially unexpressed anger ○ *I sat in my office quietly seething.* **3.** *vi.* BE BUSY to be full of bustling activity, especially with crowds of people moving in many different directions **4.** *vt. dial* SOAK STH to soak sth in liquid (*archaic*) **5.** *vt.* COOK BOIL STH to cook food by boiling it or boil sth to extract its essence (*archaic*) ■ *n.* SEETHING MOVEMENT OR ACTION an act of seething [Old English *sēothan*]

seething /seéthing/ *adj.* **1.** ANGRY full of anger, especially pent-up anger **2.** BOILING boiling and bubbling or foaming **3.** BUSTLING moving in all directions, busily or frantically ○ *'the seething crowd of Paris'* (Baroness Orczy, *The Scarlet Pimpernel*; 1905) —**seethingly** *adv.*

see-through *adj.* made of transparent material, especially so as to reveal clothes or skin underneath

Sefer Torah /séyffər táwrə/ (*plural* **Sefer Torahs** *or* **Sifrei Torah** /sí fray-/) *n.* a parchment scroll on which the Pentateuch is handwritten [Mid-17thC. From Hebrew *sēpēr tōrāh*, literally 'book of (the) Law'.]

segment /ségmənt/ *n.* **1.** COMPONENT PART any one of the parts or sections into which an object or group is divided **2.** ZOOL ORGANISM'S BODY PART any one of the individual units that make up an animal's body or part of its body. These units can follow a repeated pattern, as with a centipede, or can be variously shaped, as with the mouth parts of a spider. **3.** GEOM PART OF GEOMETRIC FIGURE the portion of a line or curve between any two of its points or the portion of a solid cut by a plane **4.** LING SPEECH SOUND any one of the individual speech sounds that make up a longer string of sounds ■ *vt.* (**-ments, -menting, -mented**) SPLIT STH INTO SEGMENTS to divide an object or group into segments [Late 16thC. From Latin *segmentum*, from *secare* 'to cut'.] —**segmentary** /ségməntəri/ *adj.*

segmental /seg mént'l/ *adj.* **1.** OF SEGMENTS relating to segments or in the form of segments **2.** LING RELATING TO SPEECH SOUNDS relating to individual speech sounds or to the dividing of strings of speech into isolable sounds —**segmentally** *adv.*

segmentation /ség men táysh'n/ *n.* **1.** SPLITTING INTO SEGMENTS the dividing of sth into segments **2.** SEGMENTED STRUCTURE the structure of sth that is made up of a series of similar segments **3.** EMBRYOL = **snow tyre 4.** ZOOL BODY STRUCTURE the structure of the body of an organism such as a worm or centipede that consists of a linear series of similar subunits

segmentation cavity *n.* = **blastocoel**

segno /sénnyō/ (*plural* **segni** *or* **segnos** /-yi/) *n.* a symbol used on sheet music to mark the beginning or end of a repeated section [Early 20thC. Via Italian fromLatin *signum* 'sign'.]

Ségou /sáy goo/ capital city of Ségou Region, in southwestern Mali. Population: 88,877 (1987).

Segovia /sə gốviə/ capital of Segovia Province, in the autonomous region of Castile-León, central Spain. Population: 54,750 (1989).

Segovia /si gốvi ə/, **Andrés** (1893–1987) Spanish guitarist. His successful international career revived interest in the classical guitar. He made many transcriptions for guitar, and a number of contemporary composers wrote works specially for him.

segregant /-gət/ *adj.* HAVING DIFFERENT GENETIC MAKEUP having a genetic makeup that differs from that of either parent because of genetic segregation ■ *n.* DISTINCT ORGANISM an organism having a genetic makeup that differs from that of either parent because of genetic segregation

segregate /séggri gayt/ (**-gates, -gating, -gated**) *v.* **1.** *vt.* SEPARATE PEOPLE OR THINGS to separate one person or group from the rest or to keep different people or groups separate **2.** *vti.* SOCIOL KEEP GROUPS SEPARATE to enforce a policy of keeping different groups within a population separate, especially different ethnic, racial, religious or gender groups **3.** *vti.* GENETICS UNDERGO GENETIC SEGREGATION to undergo or cause cells to undergo genetic segregation [Mid-16thC. From Latin *segregat-*, the past participle stem of *segregare* 'to separate from the flock', from *grex* 'flock'.] —**segregable** /séggrigəb'l/ *adj.* —**segregative** /-gaytiv/ *adj.* —**segregator** /-gaytər/ *n.*

segregation /séggri gáysh'n/ *n.* **1.** SOCIOL ENFORCED SEPARATION OF RACIAL GROUPS the practise of keeping ethnic, racial or religious groups separate especially by enforcing the use of separate schools, transport, housing, and other facilities, and usually discriminating against a minority group **2.** ACT OF SEGREGATING the separating of one person, group, or thing from others or the dividing of people or things into separate groups kept apart from each other **3.** SEGREGATED STATE the state or position of sb or sth kept separate from others **4.** GENETICS GENE SEPARATION the separation of the two versions (**alleles**) of each gene and their distribution to separate sex cells during formation (**meiosis**) of these cells in organisms with paired chromosomes —**segregational** *adj.*

segregationist /séggri gáysh'nist/ *n.* sb who advocates or enforces segregation, especially racial or religious segregation —**segregationist** *adj.*

segue /sé gway/ *vi.* (**-gues, -gueing, -gued**) **1.** MUSIC CONTINUE PLAYING to continue by playing the following piece or passage of music without a pause **2.** MOVE SMOOTHLY to make a smooth, almost imperceptible transition from one state, situation, or subject to another ○ *segued into a discussion of the playoffs without skipping a beat* ■ *n.* **1.** MUSIC CONTINUATION OF MUSIC the act of moving from one musical piece or passage into another, without a pause **2.** MUSIC INSTRUCTION TO CONTINUE an instruction to a musician to begin playing a following piece or passage without a pause **3.** SMOOTH TRANSITION the act of making a smooth transition from one state or situation to another [Mid-18thC. From Italian, the third person singular of *seguire* 'to follow', from Latin *sequi*.]

seguidilla /séggi deélyə/ *n.* **1.** DANCE SPANISH DANCE a Spanish dance in moderate triple time, usually accompanied by castanets and guitars **2.** MUSIC DANCE MUSIC FOR SEGUIDILLA a piece of music written for a seguidilla **3.** POETRY SPANISH VERSE FORM a poem with either four or seven very short verses that makes use of assonance rather than rhyme. It is a popular form in Spanish poetry. [Mid-18thC. Via Spanish, literally 'little sequence', from, ultimately, Latin *sequi* 'to follow'.]

seicento /say chéntō/ *n.* the 17th century, with reference to Italian art and literature [Early 20thC. Shortening of Italian *milseicento*, literally 'one thousand six hundred'.]

seiche /saysh/ *n.* a movement on the surface of an enclosed body of water such as a lake, usually caused by intense storm activity [Mid-19thC. From Swiss French, of uncertain origin: perhaps from German *Seiche* 'sinking'.]

seidel /síd'l, zíd'l/ *n.* a large beer glass [Early 20thC. Via German *Seidel* from Latin *situla* 'bucket'.]

Seidler /zídlər/, **Harry** (*b.* 1923) Austrian-born Australian architect. He was a modernist who studied under Walter Gropius at Harvard. He designed Australia Square in Sydney.

Seidlitz powder /séddlits-/ *n.* a laxative preparation in powder form that contains sodium bicarbonate, tartaric acid, and potassium sodium tartrate (**Rochelle salt**). It is taken dissolved in water. [Late 18thC. Named after the village of *Seidlitz* in Bohemia, which has a mineral spring noted for its laxative properties.]

seif dune /sáyf-, seéf-/ *n.* a sand dune with curved edges, found in hot deserts in a series of parallel ridges and often several miles long and up to 100 m/300 ft in height [Early 20thC. From Arabic *sayf* 'sword' + DUNE. From its shape.]

seigneur /say nyúr/, **Seigneur** *n.* **1.** HIST = SEIGNIOR **2.** FORMER FRENCH CANADIAN ESTATE OWNER in French Canada until 1854, the owner of an estate originally granted by the king of France and farmed by tenants holding a form of feudal tenure over the land [Late 16thC. Via French from Latin *senior* 'older' (the ancestor of English *sire, sir,* and *surly*).]

seigneury /sáynyəri/ (*plural* **-ies**) *n.* **1.** SEIGNEUR'S LAND the estate of a seigneur **2.** SEIGNEUR'S RANK the rank or authority of a seigneur

seignior /sáynyər/ *n.* a feudal lord, especially in England [13thC. Via Old French from Latin *senior* 'older' (source of English *seigneur*).] —**seigniorial** /say nyáwri əl/ *adj.*

seigniorage /sáynyərij/ *n.* **1.** MONARCH'S PERCENTAGE OF BULLION a monarch's right to a percentage of the bullion brought to a mint for the minting of coins **2.** COINING PROFIT the profit represented by the difference between the value of bullion and the face value of the coins minted from it **3.** HIST ARISTOCRAT'S PRIVILEGE a right or privilege claimed by a sovereign or other person of high rank

seigniory /sáynyəri/ (*plural* **-ies**), **signiory** (*plural* **-ies**), **signory** (*plural* **-ies**) *n.* **1.** SEIGNIOR'S LAND the estate of a seignior **2.** SEIGNIOR'S RANK the rank or authority of a seignior **3.** LORDS COLLECTIVELY lords considered as a group, especially English lords under the feudal system

seine /sayn/ *n.* FISHING NET a large commercial fishing net that is weighted so that it hangs vertically in the water. Its ends are then hauled together to form a bag-shaped trap. ■ *vti.* (**seines, seining, seined**) FISH WITH SEINE to catch fish with a seine [Pre-12thC. Via Latin *sagena* from Greek *sagēnē*.] —**seiner** *n.*

Seine /sayn, sen/ river in northern France, flowing from near Dijon into the English Channel. Length: 776 km/482 mi.

seise *vt.* LAW = SEIZE *v.* 9 [Early 17thC. Variant of SEIZE.]

seisin /seézin/, **seizin** *n.* LAW **1.** POSSESSION OF LAND the legal possession of land, or the act of taking possession of it **2.** OWNED LAND land that is wholly and legally owned, especially land taken possession of legally [13thC. Via Anglo-Norman *sesine* or Old French *seisine* from *saisir* (see SEIZE).]

seism /sízəm/ *n.* an earthquake (*technical*) [Late 19thC. From Greek *seismos* 'earthquake', from *seiein* 'to shake'.]

seism- *prefix.* = seismo- (*used before vowels*)

seismic /sízmik/, **seismical** /-mik'l/ *adj.* **1.** RELATING TO EARTHQUAKES relating to or caused by an earthquake or earth tremor **2.** LARGE extremely large or great (*informal*) ○ *This had a seismic impact on the music world.* —**seismically** *adv.*

seismic array *n.* a network of seismometers positioned so as to maximize the sensitivity of each of them and best monitor seismic activity in a particular region of the world

seismicity /síz míssəti/ *n.* the distribution and frequency of seismic events

seismic wave *n.* a shock wave travelling through the Earth from the epicentre of an earthquake

seismogram /sízmə gram/ *n.* a record of an earthquake made by a seismograph

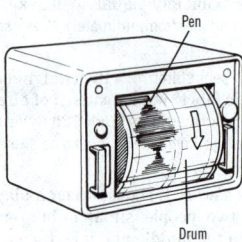

Seismograph

seismograph /sízmə graaf, sízmə graf/ *n.* an instrument that detects the presence of an earthquake and measures and records its magnitude —**seismographer** /sīz móggrəfər/ *n.* —**seismographic** /sízmə gráffik/ *adj.* —**seismography** /sīz móggrəfi/ *n.*

seismology /sīz mólləji/ *n.* the scientific study of earthquakes —**seismological** /sízmə lójjik'l/ *adj.* —**seismologically** /-lójjikli/ *adv.* —**seismologist** /sīz mólləjist/ *n.*

seismometer /sīz mómmitər/ *n.* an instrument used to measure vibrations caused by an earthquake —**seismometric** /sízmə méttrik/ *adj.*

sei whale /sáy-/ *n.* a dark bluish-grey whale similar to the blue whale but smaller and more streamlined. It feeds on tiny marine organisms by filtering them through bony plates on the jaw. It lives in all but the polar oceans and belongs to the rorqual family of whales. Latin name: *Balaenoptera borealis*. [Early 20thC. From Norwegian *sejhval*, from *sei* 'coalfish' + *hval* 'whale'.]

seize /seez/ (**seizes, seizing, seized**) *v.* **1.** *vt.* TAKE HOLD OF STH to take hold of an object quickly and firmly ○ *seized the letter from his hand* **2.** *vt.* EXPLOIT STH IMMEDIATELY to take advantage of sth such as a chance eagerly and immediately ○ *seize an opportunity* **3.** *vt.* AFFECT SB SUDDENLY to overwhelm the mind or emotions suddenly ○ *seized by panic* **4.** *vt.* AFFECT SB PHYSICALLY to overwhelm sb physically ○ *Yet another spasm seized him.* **5.** *vt.* APPROPRIATE STH to take official or legal possession of sth, often sth held illegally such as arms, drugs, or stolen goods ○ *The shipment was seized by customs officials.* **6.** *vt.* ARREST SB to take sb into custody ○ *Attempts to seize the attackers have so far failed.* **7.** *vti.* COMPREHEND STH to understand an idea or concept, especially quickly **8.** *vi.* MECH ENG STOP WORKING to become jammed, especially as a result of great heat, pressure, or friction, often arising from lack of lubrication **9.** *vi.* STIFFEN UP to become painfully stiff and immobile **10.** *vi.* STOP to come to a sudden and sometimes permanent halt ○ *The negotiations seized up after the most recent incident.* **11.** *vt.* LAW GIVE SB LEGAL POSSESSION to make sb the legal owner of property or goods ○ *The families were seized of all the relevant documentation.* **12.** *vt.* SAILING LASH STH WITH THIN ROPE to tie or secure sth by lashing it using several turns of thin rope or wire [13thC. Via Old French *saisir* from medieval Latin *sacire* 'to claim', of Germanic origin.] —**seizable** *adj.* —**seizer** *n.*

——————— **WORD KEY: SYNONYMS** ———————
See Synonyms at *catch*.

seizin *n.* LAW = seisin

seizing /seézing/ *n.* a knot or lashing made using thin rope or wire, e.g. to join two ropes or to secure an item of ship's gear

seizure /seézhər/ *n.* **1.** ACT OF SEIZING STH the seizing of sth, especially the taking of sth by force or the official or legal appropriation of sth **2.** FACT OF BEING SEIZED capture or appropriation ○ *so far managed to avoid seizure* **3.** MED DISEASE ATTACK a sudden attack of an illness or of particular symptoms, especially of the kind experienced by people with epilepsy **4.** EMOTIONAL FIT a sudden and intense rush of emotion ○ *a seizure of panic*

sejant /seéjənt/, **sejeant** *adj.* HERALDRY used to describe a figure on a coat of arms that is in a sitting position [15thC. Variant of French *séant* from, ultimately, Latin *sedere* 'to sit'.]

Sejm /saym/ *n.* the national parliament of Poland. It has a single legislative chamber. [Late 19thC. From Polish, 'Assembly'.]

Sekondi-Takoradi /sekən deé takə raádi/ port and capital of Western Region, southwestern Ghana, situated 193 km/120 mi. southwest of Accra. Population: 116,500 (1990).

selachian /si láyki ən/ *n.* a fish that belongs to the order that includes all sharks, rays, and skates. Order: Selachii. [Mid-19thC. Modelled on French *sélacien*. Via modern Latin *selachii*, from the genus name *selache*, from Greek *selakhē* 'shark'.]

selaginella /si láji néllə, sélləji néllə/ *n.* a mossy plant with branching stems and small leaves bearing spores. It is related to the club mosses. Genus: *Selaginella*. [Mid-19thC. Via modern Latin *Selaginella*, genus name, from, ultimately, Latin *selago*, a herb similar to savin.]

selah /seélə, seé laa/ *interj.* an ancient Hebrew word of unknown meaning and uncertain grammatical status that appears in some books of the Bible and is therefore, when included in English translations, left untranslated. It is used to perform a punctuating function between verses. [Mid-16thC. From Hebrew *selāh*.]

Selby /sélbi/ market town and port on the River Ouse in North Yorkshire, England. Population: 15,292 (1991).

seldom /séldəm/ *adv.* not often [Old English *seldum*. Variant of *seldan*, of Germanic origin.] —**seldomness** *n.*

select /si lékt/ *vti.* (**-lects, -lecting, -lected**) CHOOSE FROM OTHERS to choose sb or sth from among several ○ *select a coffee cream from the box* ■ *adj.* **1.** OF GOOD QUALITY chosen on grounds of particularly high quality **2.** HAVING LIMITED MEMBERSHIP admitting only a few carefully chosen members ○ *one of the more select gentlemen's clubs* **3.** SPECIALLY CHOSEN chosen from several others and given special treatment or a special privilege ○ *advance copies sent to a select few* **4.** DISCRIMINATING showing care and discernment when choosing ○ *'foreign films which generally attract a select audience'* (James Berardinelli, *Review: Deception*; 1993) [Mid-16thC. From Latin *select-*, the past participle stem of *seligere*, from *legere* 'to choose'.] —**selectness** *n.*

select committee *n.* a small group of members of parliament instructed by either the House of Commons or the House of Lords to investigate and report on a particular matter

selectee /si lék teé/ *n.* US sb who is selected, especially for compulsory military service

selection /si léksh'n/ *n.* **1.** SB OR STH CHOSEN sb or sth chosen from among others **2.** AVAILABLE CHOICE the range from which sb or sth can be selected ○ *a fantastic selection of carpets* **3.** ACT OF CHOOSING an act of choosing sb or sth from a wide variety of others **4.** CHOSEN STATE the status of sb or sth chosen from among others **5.** BIOL SURVIVAL OF THE FITTEST the production of more offspring by organisms with particular desirable characteristics, resulting in a better gene pool for the species. This can be a natural process or can be accomplished through human intervention, e.g. when breeding plants or animals for a particular trait. **6.** BETTING GAMBLER'S CHOICE a competitor on whom a bet is placed, especially in horse-racing ○ *always a popular selection here at Goodwood*

selection box *n.* a selection of chocolate bars and other sweets made by a particular manufacturer, packaged in a seasonally decorated box to be used as a gift to a child at Christmas

selectionist /si léksh'nist/ *n.* sb who accepts or promotes the theory that natural selection is the major or only force governing biological development or change

selective /si léktiv/ *adj.* **1.** NOT UNIVERSAL applying to some but not others **2.** DISCERNING tending to make careful choices **3.** ELECTRON ENG RECEIVING ON SOME FREQUENCIES ONLY capable of selecting certain frequencies or frequency bands and blocking out all others, and therefore eliminating interference in reception —**selectively** *adv.* —**selectiveness** *n.*

selective attention *n.* the ability to pay attention to those things that are considered important and to ignore those that are not

selective service *n.* a system for calling up men for US military service

selectivity /si lék tívvəti/ *n.* **1. CHOOSING ONLY SOME** the choosing of only some, not all, and the exercising of judgment in making the choice **2.** ELEC ENG **ABILITY TO DISTINGUISH FREQUENCIES** the degree to which an electronic device or circuit can distinguish a desired frequency from others **3.** PUBLIC ADMIN **WELFARE PRINCIPLE** the principle that government welfare should be given only to those shown to be in greatest need

selector /si léktər/ *n.* a person or device that selects, especially sb responsible for selecting the members of a team ○ *in meetings between the team captain and selectors*

selen- *prefix.* = **seleno-** (*used before vowels*)

selenate /séllə nayt/ *n.* a chemical compound that is a salt or ester of selenic acid [Early 19thC. Coined from SELENIUM + -ATE.]

Selene /sə leé ni/ *n.* in Greek mythology, the goddess of the Moon. Roman equivalent **Luna**

selenic /si leénik/ *adj.* relating to or containing the nonmetallic chemical element selenium, especially in the form in which it has a valency of six [Early 19thC. Coined from SELENIUM + -IC.]

selenic acid *n.* a highly corrosive acid usually found in the form of a whitish solid. Formula: H_2SeO_4.

seleniferous /séllə níffərəss/ *adj.* containing or producing selenium [Early 19thC. Coined from SELENIUM + -FEROUS.]

selenious /si leéni əss/ *adj.* relating to or containing the nonmetallic chemical element selenium, especially in the form in which it has a low valency [Early 19thC. Coined from SELENIUM + -OUS.]

selenite /sélli nīt/ *n.* a transparent colourless variety of gypsum that cleaves in a particular way to reveal lustrous crystal faces [Mid-16thC. Via Latin from Greek *selēnitēs lithos* 'moon stone', from *selēnē* 'moon'. So named because its lustre resembles that of the Moon (see SELENIUM).]

selenium /si leéni əm/ *n.* a nonmetallic chemical element that occurs in several forms ranging from a red powder to grey-black crystals. It is an essential trace element, although toxic in excess, and is used in photocells and photocopiers owing to its light-sensitive properties. Symbol **Se** [Early 19thC. From modern Latin, formed from Greek *selēnē* 'moon', from *selas* 'light'.]

selenium cell *n.* a photoelectric cell based on the light-sensitive properties of selenium and containing a strip of selenium mounted between two metal electrodes

seleno- *prefix.* **1.** the moon ○ *selenography* **2.** selenium ○ *selenite* [From Greek *selēnē* 'moon' (see SELENIUM)]

selenography /seélə nóggrəfi/ *n.* the branch of astronomy that is concerned with mapping the surface features of the Moon —**selenographic** /si leénə gráffik/ *adj.* —**selenographically** *adv.* —**selenographist** /seélə nóggrəfist/ *n.*

selenology /seélə nólləji/ *n.* the branch of astronomy concerned with the origin and physical characteristics of the Moon —**selenological** /si leénə lójjik'l/ *adj.* —**selenologist** /seélə nólləjist/ *n.*

Seles /sél ez, sél esh/, **Monica** (*b.* 1973) Yugoslavian-born US tennis player. She was the winner of the French Open (1990, 1991, 1992), Australian Open (1991, 1992, 1993, 1996), US Open (1991 and 1992), and Canadian Open (1995).

Seleucid /si lóossid/ (*plural* **-cids** *or* **-cidae** /-sidee/) *n.* any of a dynasty of rulers who ruled Asia Minor from 312 to 64 BC, after the death of Alexander the Great [Mid-19thC. Via Latin *Seleucides* from Greek *Seleukidēs*, from *Seleukos*, the name of the founder of the dynasty.] —**Seleucid** *adj.*

self /self/ *n.* (*plural* **selves** /selvz/) **1. PERCEIVED PERSONALITY** sb's personality or an aspect of it, especially as perceived by others ○ *He's not his usual cheery self this morning.* **2. COMPLETE PERSONALITY** a complete and individual personality, especially one that sb recognizes as his or her own and with which there is a sense of ease ○ *A person needs to develop a sense of self.* **3. SELF-INTEREST** sb's own individual interests and welfare, especially when placed before those of other people **4.** IMMUNOL **OWN BODY PARTS** the set of organs and tissues that the body recognizes as its own and does not attack with antibodies **5.** ZOOL **SELF-COLOURED ANIMAL** an animal that is one colour all over, especially a pigeon ■ *pron.* **ONESELF** myself, yourself, himself, or herself (*informal*) ○ *not enough to sustain self and family* ■ *adj.* **1. SELF-COLOURED** having the same colour all over **2. OF SAME FABRIC** made of the same material as the garment it is worn with **3. SAME** same or identical (*archaic*) [Old English. Ultimately from an Indo-European pronoun that is also the ancestor of English *suicide* and *sober*.]

WORD KEY: USAGE

Grammar: The two main uses of **-self** compounds such as *himself, herself,* and *myself* are, first, to serve as a reflexive pronoun when the object of the verb is the same as the subject (*He saw himself in the mirror*) and, second, to reinforce or emphasize a noun (*Jane herself had wanted to go with them*). Compounds with ***-self*** should not be used simply as alternatives for other pronouns, such as *him, her, me,* and *I*: *It was up to her* [not *herself*] *whether she came or not. This is between him and me* [not *myself*].

self- *prefix.* **1.** of, by, for, or in itself ○ *self-assured* **2.** automatic ○ *self-winding* [From SELF]

self-abandoned *adj.* showing little self-control and tending to give in to impulse —**self-abandonment** *n.*

self-abasement *n.* the humbling of yourself in response to feelings of guilt or shame

self-absorbed *adj.* excessively concerned with your own life and interests

self-absorption *n.* **1. PREOCCUPATION WITH SELF** excessive concern with your own life and interests **2.** PHYS **ABSORPTION OF OWN RADIATION** a radioactive material's absorption of part of the radiation that it emits

self-abuse *n.* **1. CRITICISM OF SELF** sb's deprecation or deliberate misuse of his or her talents and abilities **2. MASTURBATION** masturbation when viewed as being detrimental to character (*disapproving or humorous*) —**self-abuser** *n.*

self-acting *adj.* operating itself —**self-action** *n.*

self-actualization, **self-actualisation** *n.* the successful development and use of personal talents and abilities

self-addressed *adj.* **1. ADDRESSED TO SENDER** addressed to the sender for return by post **2. FOR ONESELF** directed by sb towards himself or herself

self-adhesive *adj.* having adhesive on one side and able to be stuck in position without needing to be moistened or to have adhesive applied

self-administer (**self-administers, self-administering, self-administered**) *vt.* to administer sth, especially medical treatment, to yourself —**self-administered** *adj.*

self-advocacy *n.* **1.** SOC WELFARE **LEGAL INDEPENDENCE** the principle and practice of allowing people with psychiatric disorders to assume legal and practical responsibility for their own lives, rather than making them dependent on others **2.** LAW **ACTING AS OWN LAWYER** sb's legal representation of himself or herself, especially in court

self-aggrandizement *n.* the ambitious or ruthless pursuit of increased personal importance, wealth, reputation, or power —**self-aggrandizing** *adj.*

self-annihilation *n.* **1. DETACHMENT FROM SELF** loss of awareness of being an individual, achieved through meditation or other mystical means **2. SUICIDE** an act or instance of suicide

self-appointed *adj.* assuming a role personally, rather than being given it or being regarded as worthy of it by others ○ *a self-appointed arbiter of good taste*

self-assertive *adj.* tending to be aggressively confident in making your views heard and your presence felt —**self-assertively** *adv.* —**self-assertiveness** *n.*

self-assurance *n.* relaxed confidence that your views and abilities are of value

self-assured *adj.* behaving in a relaxed manner that displays confidence that your views and abilities are of value —**self-assuredly** *adv.* —**self-assuredness** *n.*

self-aware *adj.* having a balanced and honest view of your own personality, and often an ability to interact with others frankly and confidently —**self-awareness** *n.*

self-basting *adj.* commercially prepared with added fat to prevent drying out when cooked in an oven ○ *a self-basting turkey*

self-catering *adj.* **NOT PROVIDING FOOD** used to describe accommodation, especially for holidaymakers or students, in which meals are not provided but cooking facilities are ■ *n.* **HOLIDAYS WITHOUT MEALS INCLUDED** holidaying in self-catering accommodation ○ *decided on two weeks self-catering in Corfu*

self-centred *adj.* tending to concentrate selfishly on your own needs and affairs and to show little or no interest in those of others —**self-centredly** *adv.* —**self-centredness** *n.*

self-certification *n.* the system under which employees claim sick pay by making their own formal statement to their employer declaring they were unfit for work, rather than by submitting a doctor's statement. This system was introduced in 1982.

self-cleaning *adj.* designed to stay clean when being used, usually by virtue of being coated with materials that shed dirt ○ *a self-cleaning oven*

self-closing *adj.* used to describe a door, gate, or window fitted with a mechanism that returns it to a closed position after it has been opened

self-coloured *adj.* **1. UNIFORM IN COLOUR** of the same colour all over or throughout **2.** BOT **RETAINING NATURAL COLOUR** used to describe a flower whose colour has not been artificially changed by hybridization **3.** TEXTILES **UNDYED** used to describe cloth that has not been dyed and so retains its natural colour

self-command *n.* the ability to present your ideas and intentions clearly and effectively

self-compatible *adj.* used to describe a plant that is capable of pollinating itself

self-concept *n.* the whole inner picture that sb has of himself or herself, including a complete evaluation of such traits as competence, worth, and attractiveness

self-confessed *adj.* admitting freely to possessing a particular quality or to behaving in a certain way

self-confidence *n.* confidence in yourself and your own abilities

self-confident *adj.* having or showing confidence in yourself and your abilities, usually with a readiness to be assertive —**self-confidently** *adv.*

self-congratulation *n.* the frequent mentioning of personal achievements and the displaying of the smug satisfaction taken in them —**self-congratulatory** *adj.*

self-conscious *adj.* **1. ILL AT EASE** feeling acutely and uncomfortably aware of failings and shortcomings when in the company of others and believing that others are noticing them too ○ *too self-conscious to speak in public* **2. EXCESSIVELY CONCERNED WITH APPEARANCES** highly conscious of the impression made on others and tending to act in a way that reinforces this impression ○ *swinging his car keys in a self-conscious manner* —**self-consciously** *adv.* —**self-consciousness** *n.*

self-contained *adj.* **1. HAVING OWN FACILITIES AND ENTRANCE** used to describe accommodation that has its own kitchen, bathroom, and entrance ○ *self-contained two-bed flat near tube* **2. HAVING EVERYTHING REQUIRED** possessing all the features and facilities required to function independently ○ *a number of self-contained holiday villages* **3. KEEPING FEELINGS PRIVATE** able or tending to keep feelings and opinions private or to control feelings and reactions in front of others **4. INDEPENDENT** not needing the company or support of other people to be a complete and fulfilled person —**self-containedly** *adv.* —**self-containment** *n.*

self-contradiction *n.* **1. LACK OF CONSISTENCY** speech, thoughts, or actions that contradict what their author previously said, thought, or did **2. STH CON-**

TRADICTORY a statement, idea, or theory that contradicts itself —**self-contradictory** adj.

self-control n. the ability to control your own behaviour, especially in terms of reactions and impulses —**self-controlled** adj.

self-correcting adj. 1. CORRECTING ERRORS AUTOMATICALLY used to describe a word processor that automatically corrects typing errors as they occur 2. CORRECTING OWN MISTAKES able or tending to notice personal mistakes and correct them

self-critical adj. tending to notice and dwell on your own shortcomings —**self-criticism** n.

self-deceiving adj. 1. IGNORING TRUTH refusing to recognize the truth, usually because to do so would be painful or difficult 2. TENDING TO GLORIFY SELF cherishing self-indulgent beliefs about yourself —**self-deception** n.

self-defeating adj. defeating the very aim or purpose it is designed to fulfil

self-defence n. 1. LAW LEGAL RIGHT TO DEFEND SELF the use of reasonable force to defend yourself, your family, and your property against physical attack, or the right to do this 2. FIGHTING TECHNIQUES fighting techniques used to defend yourself against physical attack, especially unarmed combat techniques such as any of the martial arts 3. JUSTIFYING OF SELF the defending of your own ideas, principles, or actions —**self-defensive** adj.

self-denial n. the setting aside of your own wishes, needs, or interests, whether voluntary, altruistic, or enforced by circumstances —**self-denying** adj. —**self-denyingly** adv.

self-deprecating, **self-deprecatory** adj. tending to belittle yourself or your achievements

self-destruct vi. (**self-destructs**, **self-destructing**, **self-destructed**) 1. DESTROY ITSELF AUTOMATICALLY to destroy itself by means of a built-in mechanism 2. RUIN OWN LIFE to behave in a way that destroys any chance of your success, credibility, or effectiveness ■ adj. CAUSING DESTRUCTION OF ITSELF causing a device or machine to destroy itself if certain conditions are met

self-destruction n. 1. RUINING OF OWN LIFE the ruining of your own life or an aspect of it such as your health, happiness, or career 2. AUTOMATIC DESTRUCTION OF DEVICE the automatic destruction of a device fitted with a self-destruct mechanism 3. SUICIDE an act or instance of suicide

self-destructive adj. causing or tending to cause harm to yourself

self-determination n. 1. POL RIGHT TO CHOOSE OWN GOVERNMENT the right of a people to determine their own form of government without interference from outside 2. RIGHT TO DECIDE FOR SELF the ability or right to make your own decisions without interference from others

self-discipline n. the ability to do what is necessary or sensible without needing to be urged by sb else —**self-disciplined** adj.

self-discovery n. the process of learning about your true personality and motives

self-doubt n. feelings of doubt about your own worth and abilities

self-drive adj. used to describe a hired car that is driven by the hirer

self-effacing adj. tending to be modest about your achievements and to avoid drawing attention to yourself in company —**self-effacement** n. —**self-effacingly** adv.

self-employed adj. earning a living by working independently of an employer, either freelance or by running a business —**self-employment** n.

self-esteem n. confidence in your own merit as an individual

self-evaluation n. the process of evaluating your own character, work, achievements, or goals

self-evident adj. obvious without explanation or proof —**self-evidence** n. —**self-evidently** adv.

self-examination n. 1. REFLECTION ON OWN CONDITION careful reflection on your own thoughts, beliefs,

behaviour, and circumstances 2. MEDICAL EXAMINATION OF OWN BODY the regular examination of parts of your own body for signs of disease —**self-examining** adj.

self-excited adj. used to describe an electrical device with a field system that is excited by a current the device generates for itself

self-executing adj. legally effective without intervention ○ self-executing clauses in the contract

self-exile /sélIf ék síl/ n. 1. SB WHO LEAVES OWN COUNTRY VOLUNTARILY sb who leaves his or her own country voluntarily to live elsewhere, especially for political reasons 2. VOLUNTARY EXILE a voluntary state of exile —**self-exiled** adj.

self-explanatory adj. clear and easy to understand with no need for explanation

self-expression n. the expressing of your own ideas, emotions, or individuality through behaviour or an activity such as painting, music, or writing

self-feeder n. a machine or device that automatically supplies or replaces materials as they are needed, e.g. a device for feeding animals

self-fertilization n. fertilization of a plant or animal ovum using pollen or sperm from the same individual —**self-fertilized** adj. —**self-fertilizing** adj.

self-financing adj. paid for or run without outside financial support

self-flagellation n. 1. SELF-CRITICISM very strong or harsh self-criticism 2. PUNISHING OF OWN BODY severe self-administered physical punishment. The practice of self-flagellation was formerly used as an act of penance, often in the form of beatings or floggings.

self-flattery n. the exaggerating of positive personal traits while overlooking negative traits

self-focusing adj. focusing automatically rather than manually

self-forgetful adj. putting the interests of others first (archaic) —**self-forgetfully** adv. —**self-forgetfulness** n.

self-fulfilling adj. 1. HAPPENING BECAUSE EXPECTED brought about or proved true because of having been expected or predicted 2. SATISFYING providing satisfaction or pleasure through personal labour, initiative, or talent

self-fulfilment n. contentment or happiness as a result of personal work, initiative, or talent

self-giving adj. willing to act unselfishly for the benefit of others

self-glorification n. promotion of your own qualities and abilities, especially beyond what is true or appropriate

self-governed adj. run by the people who live or work in a particular area or place rather than by external government

self-governing adj. run by its own members, employees, or citizens, rather than being run from outside

self-government n. 1. AUTONOMY the ability or right of the citizens of a region to choose their own government rather than having it imposed from outside 2. SELF-CONTROL the ability to exercise self-control (archaic)

self-gratification n. the satisfying of your own desires for the sake of pleasure

self-hardening adj. becoming harder without special treatment after being heated above a certain temperature

self-harming n. the practice of causing physical harm to yourself, usually as a symptom of a psychiatric disorder

self-hatred, **self-hate** n. hatred or contempt for your own weaknesses

selfheal /sélf heel/ n. a low-growing creeping mint with small spikes of purple-blue flowers that is native to Europe and Asia but grows as a weed in North America. Latin name: *Prunella vulgaris*. [14thC. Applied to various plants believed to have medicinal properties.]

self-help n. 1. GROUP HELP AND SUPPORT the practice of meeting or working with others who share a common problem rather than relying on the gov-

ernment or professionals for help 2. SOLVING PROBLEMS WITHOUT OTHERS' HELP the practice of dealing with your own problems and challenges without seeking outside help

selfhood /sélf hood/ n. 1. INDIVIDUALITY the possession of a unique identity, distinct from others 2. COMPLETE SENSE OF SELF the possession of a fully developed personality and sense of identity 3. SB'S CHARACTER OR PERSONALITY all the qualities and characteristics that make up sb's character or personality

self-hypnosis n. = autohypnosis

self-identity n. 1. INDIVIDUALITY the awareness that an individual or group has of being unique 2. SENSE OF BEING ONE the quality that sth has of being one with itself

self-image n. the opinion that you have of your own worth, attractiveness, or intelligence

self-immolation n. suicide, usually by burning, as an act of sacrifice or protest (formal)

self-importance n. an unrealistically high evaluation of your own importance or worth —**self-important** adj. —**self-importantly** adv.

self-imposed adj. chosen willingly as a burden or limit ○ a self-imposed deadline

self-improvement n. improvement of yourself or advancement in career or status as a result of your own effort

self-incrimination n. speech or action that suggests your own guilt, especially during court testimony —**self-incriminating** adj. —**self-incriminatory** adj.

self-induced adj. 1. RESULTING FROM OWN ACTIONS brought on by your own actions 2. ELECTRON ENG CAUSED BY SELF-INDUCTION produced by the process of self-induction

self-induction n. ELECTRON ENG induction of an electromotive force in a circuit by means of a changing current in that circuit —**self-inductive** adj.

self-indulgence n. 1. PURSUIT OF OWN PLEASURE lack of self-control in pursuing your own pleasure or satisfaction 2. STH SHOWING NO SELF-CONTROL sth that reveals lack of self-restraint —**self-indulgent** adj. —**self-indulgently** adv.

self-inflicted adj. caused or done by your own actions

self-insurance n. the saving of money to protect against a loss instead of buying an insurance policy

self-interest n. 1. SELFISHNESS the placing of your own needs or desires before those of others 2. OWN NEEDS OR DESIRES your own needs and desires —**self-interested** adj. —**self-interestedness** n.

selfish /sélfish/ adj. 1. LOOKING AFTER OWN DESIRES concerned with your own interests, needs, and wishes while ignoring those of others 2. DEMONSTRATING SELFISHNESS showing that personal needs and wishes are thought to be more important than those of other people —**selfishly** adv. —**selfishness** n.

selfish DNA n. a segment of DNA that increases itself, e.g. as repeated sequences, within the total genetic material of a population over successive generations without apparent benefit to the organisms concerned

selfish gene n. a gene that exploits the organism in which it occurs as a vehicle for its self-perpetuation. Posited by the biologist Richard Dawkins in 1976, it overturns the traditional concept of the gene serving as a vehicle of inheritance for the organism.

self-justification n. 1. MAKING OF EXCUSES FOR ACTIONS an attempt to explain your own behaviour or actions by making excuses 2. STH DONE AS JUSTIFICATION sth that sb does or says in an attempt to explain personal behaviour or actions

self-justifying adj. 1. ATTEMPTING TO EXPLAIN making excuses in an attempt to explain your own behaviour or actions 2. AUTOMATICALLY MAKING TEXT UNIFORM ON MARGIN automatically providing an even right or left margin for text printed on a page 3. LOGICALLY COMPLETE used to describe an argument or rule that justifies or explains itself without referring to sth else because of being regarded as completely logical or obvious

a at; aa father; aw all; ay day; air hair; ə about, edible, item, common, circus; e egg; ee eel; hw when; i it, happy; I ice; 'l apple; 'm rhythm; 'n fashion; o odd; ō open; oo good; oo pool; ow owl; oy oil; th thin; th this; u up; ur urge;

self-knowledge *n.* knowledge or understanding of your own motives and behaviour

selfless /sélfləss/ *adj.* putting other people's needs first —**selflessly** *adv.* —**selflessness** *n.*

self-limited, **self-limiting** *adj.* **1.** LIMITED BY OWN NATURE limited by internal or personal characteristics rather than by outside influences **2.** HAVING PARTICULAR LIFESPAN used to describe a disease that lasts for a particular length of time time whether or not it is treated

self-liquidating *adj.* **1.** ABLE TO MAKE MONEY BEFORE DUE used to describe a loan to fund a transaction that is expected to make money before the loan is due to be repaid **2.** PAYING FOR ITSELF used to describe a business transaction that makes enough money to cover its costs

self-loading *adj.* used to describe a firearm that automatically ejects a spent cartridge and puts a new round into the chamber each time it is fired — **self-loader** *n.*

self-loathing *n.* = self-hatred

self-love *n.* concern with only your own wishes and desires

self-made *adj.* **1.** SUCCESSFUL AS A RESULT OF WORK successful or wealthy through your own efforts, rather than through birth or from the work of others **2.** MADE UNAIDED made without the help of others

self-mastery *adj.* control over your own emotions, needs, or desires and their expression

self-medication *n.* the practice of treating illnesses and medical complaints without consulting a doctor, e.g. by buying treatments from a chemist — **self-medicator** *n.*

self-mortification *n.* self-administered punishment, often as prescribed by religious precepts, because of some perceived fault or flaw

self-motivated *adj.* energetic and ambitious, and so able to make plans and get things done without being directed by others —**self-motivation** *n.*

self-murder *n.* suicide (*archaic or disapproving*)

self-mutilation *n.* self-inflicted injury, especially with a sharp object

self-occupied *adj.* busy with your own thoughts or problems

self-opinion *n.* a very high opinion of your own abilities or worth

self-opinionated, **self-opinioned** *adj.* **1.** CERTAIN OF BEING RIGHT confident of holding the correct opinions **2.** VAIN very conceited

self-ordained *adj.* claiming the authority to speak as an expert without qualifications or the support of others

self-parody *n.* unintentional exaggeration or over-emphasis by sb of his or her worst characteristics

self-perpetuating *adj.* continuing because of having the power to preserve or renew itself indefinitely

self-pity *n.* the self-indulgent belief that your life is harder and sadder than everyone else's —**self-pitying** *adj.* —**self-pityingly** *adv.*

self-pollination *n.* pollination that takes place within a flower through the transfer of pollen from its anthers to its stigmas —**self-pollinate** *vi.* —**self-pollinating** *adj.*

self-portrait *n.* a visual image, sculpture, or written description of sb, produced by that person

self-possessed *adj.* confident and in control of your own emotions —**self-possessedly** *adv.*

self-possession *n.* the ability to remain calm and confident, especially in difficult or emotional circumstances

self-preservation *n.* the instinctive need to do what is necessary to survive danger

self-proclaimed *adj.* claiming to be sth, often without justification

self-promotion *n.* behaviour shown or action taken by sb in order to attract attention, especially in relation to work or business

self-pronouncing *adj.* using only letters of the ordinary alphabet to represent a pronunciation, rather than using symbols from the phonetic alphabet

self-propelled *adj.* **1.** MOVING UNDER OWN POWER able to move or travel using its own power source such as a motor or batteries, rather than needing power from an external source **2.** MOUNTED ON VEHICLE relating to a piece of heavy military equipment that is mounted on a vehicle rather than needing to be towed —**self-propelling** *adj.* —**self-propulsion** *n.*

self-protection *n.* action taken to protect against attack on or injury to yourself —**self-protecting** *adj.* —**self-protective** *adj.*

self-published *adj.* published without a publisher, and therefore at the author's own expense

self-raising *adj.* used to describe flour that has a leavening agent added to it, so that baking powder need not be added when baking. US term **self-rising**

self-realization *n.* fulfilment of personal potential

self-reflection *n.* = self-examination *n.* 1

self-regard *n.* **1.** LACKING REGARD FOR OTHERS self-interest rather than concern for the well-being of others **2.** SELF-RESPECT belief in your own worth and dignity — **self-regarding** *adj.*

self-regulating, **self-regulatory** *adj.* **1.** REGULATING ITSELF WITHOUT LAWS regulating its own affairs rather than being regulated by an outside organization or by law **2.** REGULATING SELF AUTOMATICALLY capable of regulating its functions automatically —**self-regulation** *n.*

self-reliance *n.* the ability to make your own decisions confidently and independently —**self-reliant** *adj.* —**self-reliantly** *adv.*

self-renunciation *n.* the giving up of your own rights, claims, or property to benefit others

self-replicating *adj.* used to describe a molecule or bacterium that reproduces on its own by making copies of itself —**self-replication** *n.*

self-reproach *n.* self-criticism or blame —**self-reproachful** *adj.* —**self-reproachfully** *adv.*

self-respect *n.* belief in your own worth and dignity —**self-respecting** *adj.*

self-restraint *n.* self-control over speech, behaviour, or action

self-righteous *adj.* sure of the moral superiority of your own beliefs and actions (*disapproving*) —**self-righteously** *adv.* —**self-righteousness** *n.*

self-righting *adj.* able to right itself after being capsized

self-rising *adj. US* = self-raising

self-rule *n.* = self-government *n.* 1

self-sacrifice *n.* the giving up of personal wants and needs, either from a sense of duty or in order to benefit others —**self-sacrificing** *adj.* —**self-sacrificingly** *adv.*

selfsame /sélf saym/ *adj.* being the very same

self-satisfaction *n.* a feeling of satisfaction in personal achievements and good fortune —**self-satisfied** *adj.*

self-sealing *adj.* **1.** SEALING WITHOUT BEING MOISTENED used to describe an envelope that has a flap coated with adhesive that can be closed without being moistened **2.** ABLE TO SEAL SELF used to describe a tyre that can seal itself after being punctured. The tyre contains a compound that hardens in contact with air.

self-seeded *adj.* = self-sown

self-seeking *adj.* SELFISH interested only in gaining an advantage over others, rather than in sharing or cooperating ■ *n.* SELF-SEEKING BEHAVIOUR behaviour intended to secure an advantage over others —**self-seeker** *n.*

self-selection *n.* **1.** = self-service **2.** SELECTING OF SELF choice of, by, or for yourself —**self-selected** *adj.* —**self-selective** *adj.*

self-service *adj.* used to describe a retail outlet or device used by customers or users helping themselves ○ *a self-service petrol station* ○ *a self-service drinks machine* —**self-service** *n.*

self-serving *adj.* putting personal concerns and interests before those of others

self-sown *adj.* used to describe plants that grow from seeds that reach the soil by themselves, without being carried there by people or animals

self-starter *n.* **1.** SB ENTERPRISING sb with the initiative and motivation to work without needing help or supervision **2.** AUTOMOT ELECTRIC STARTER an electrically operated device for starting an internal-combustion engine —**self-starting** *adj.*

self-styled *adj.* using a particular name or title or professing knowledge of a subject without having training or independent proof

self-sufficient, **self-sufficing** *adj.* **1.** NOT NEEDING THINGS FROM OTHERS able to provide what is needed, e.g. by making enough money or growing enough food, without having to borrow or buy from others **2.** ABLE TO MANAGE ALONE able to live independently of others — **self-sufficiency** *n.* —**self-sufficiently** *adv.*

self-suggestion *n.* = autosuggestion

self-supporting *adj.* **1.** GETTING ALONG FINANCIALLY earning enough money to live or operate without external financial support **2.** STANDING WITHOUT BEING HELD able to stand or stay upright without being supported — **self-support** *n.* —**self-supported** *adj.*

self-sustaining *adj.* able to live or continue existing without outside support

self-talk *n.* the things that an individual says to himself or herself mentally

self-tapping *adj.* used to describe a screw that cuts a thread for itself when it is screwed into a hole in metal

self-taught *adj.* having learned a skill, job, or subject without formal instruction

self-tender *n.* an offer made by a company to buy back shares from its shareholders, e.g. to avoid a hostile takeover bid

self-treatment *n.* an individual's treating of his or her own illnesses or injuries rather than seeking the advice of a doctor

self-will *n.* stubborn determination to hold to personal views and behaviour —**self-willed** *adj.*

self-winding *adj.* not needing to be wound ○ *a self-winding watch*

self-worth *n.* confidence in personal value and worth as an individual

Seljuk /séll jook/ *n.* a member of one of the Turkish dynasties that ruled large areas of Asia during the 11th, 12th, and 13th centuries before the Ottoman Empire [Mid-19thC. From Turkish *Selčük*, the name of the reputed founder of the dynasty.] —**Seljuk** *adj.*

selkie /sélki/ *n. Scotland* a mythological person who is human on land but has the skills of a seal in water

Selkirk /sél kurk/, **Alexander** (1676–1721) Scottish sailor. His solitary life for 52 months on the Juan Fernández Islands 400 miles off Chile is said to have inspired Daniel Defoe's *Robinson Crusoe* (1719).

Selkirk Mountains mountain range in southeastern British Columbia, Canada, west of the Rocky Mountains. The highest point is Mount Sandford, 3,522m/11,555 ft.

sell /sel/ *v.* (**sells**, **selling**, **sold** /sōld/, **sold**) **1.** *vti.* EXCHANGE STH FOR MONEY to exchange a product or service for money **2.** *vt.* OFFER STH FOR SALE to offer a particular product or range of products for sale **3.** *vi.* BE BOUGHT IN QUANTITY to be bought in large numbers ○ *The book is selling well.* **4.** *vt.* MAKE PEOPLE WANT TO BUY STH to increase the sale of or the demand for a particular product ○ *Advertising sells products.* **5.** *vt.* PERSUADE SB TO ACCEPT STH to persuade sb to accept an idea or proposal ○ *You've convinced me but now you have to sell it to the shareholders.* **6.** *vt.* GIVE STH UP FOR MONEY to sacrifice an important personal quality in order to obtain wealth or success ○ *He's sold his integrity for a long-term contract.* **7.** *vt.* CHEAT SB to cheat or trick sb (*informal*) ■ *n.* **1.** PROCESS OF SELLING the activity or process of persuading people to buy a product or service (*informal*) ○ *use an aggressive sell* **2.** TRICK a trick or deception (*informal*) **3.** *Ireland* DISAPPOINTMENT a big disappointment [Old English *sellan* 'to grant, give up, hand over', from a prehistoric Germanic word that is also the ancestor of English *sale*. Current senses developed via 'to betray for money'.] —**sellable** *adj.* ◊ **be sold on sth** be enthusiastic about sth (*informal*) ◊ **sell sb** *or* **sth short 1.** to make an estimate of the quality and worth of sb or sth that is too low **2.** to sell goods or securities without owning them, expecting to buy them at a price lower than the selling price ◊ **sell yourself 1.** to work hard to persuade others that you are talented, pleasant, well-qualified, or suitable for a particular job **2.** to abandon your principles in order to get sth you want or need, e.g. money or success ◊ **sell your soul** to abandon your principles in order to obtain wealth or success

sell off *vt.* to sell sth, especially at a low price, in order to get rid of it

sell-by date *n.* a date displayed on food and pharmaceutical products, after which they should not be sold ◊ **past its** *or* **your sell-by date** thought to be too advanced in years or old-fashioned to be taken seriously any longer (*informal; offensive in some contexts*)

seller /séllər/ *n.* **1.** SB WHO IS SELLING a person, shop, or company that offers sth for sale **2.** ITEM THAT IS SELLING a product that sells in a specified way, especially well or badly **3.** = **selling race**

Sellers /séllərz/, **Peter** (1925–80) British actor. A member of the Goons radio comedy team (1952–60), he was later a screen actor. He played the eccentric detective Inspector Clouseau in the hugely successful Pink Panther films (1963–77).

seller's market *n.* a situation or market in which the demand for sth is greater than the supply, so that its price can be forced up. ◊ **buyer's market**

selling climax *n.* a large volume of trading at the end of a downturn in the stock markets (*informal*)

selling plate *n.* = **selling race**

selling-plater *n.* **1.** HORSE THAT RACES IN SELLING RACE a horse that races in, or is only good enough to race in, a selling race **2.** SB OR STH OF INFERIOR QUALITY sb or sth that is not very good, important, or valuable

selling point *n.* a feature of sth such as a product or an idea that makes people more likely to want to buy or support it

selling race, **selling plate** *n.* a horse race in which the winner is auctioned and sold

Sellotape /séllō tayp/ *tdmk.* a trademark for a type of transparent adhesive tape

sellout /séll owt/ *n.* **1.** EVENT WITH NO TICKETS LEFT a show, concert, or sports event for which all the tickets are sold **2.** BETRAYAL betrayal of personal principles or another person (*informal*)

selsyn /sél sin/ *n.* a system used to transmit angular rotation or position in a generator to a motor [Early 20thC. Blend of SELF and SYNCHRONOUS.]

Seltzer /séltsər/, **Seltzer water** *n.* **1.** NATURALLY FIZZY MINERAL WATER mineral water that contains naturally occurring dissolved gases that make it slightly fizzy, often used for medicinal purposes **2.** SODA WATER soda water (*dated*) [Mid-18thC. Alteration of German *Selterser*, literally 'from Selters', alluding to mineral springs in the village of Nieder-*Selters* near Wiesbaden in Germany.]

selva /sélvə/ *n.* a dense tropical rain forest, especially in the Amazon Basin [Mid-19thC. Via Spanish or Portuguese from Latin *silva* 'wood' (source of English *sylvan* and *savage*).]

selvage /sél vij/, **selvedge** *n.* **1.** NON-FRAYING EDGE OF FABRIC an edge of a piece of fabric that is woven so that it will not fray **2.** STRIP OF MATERIAL an edge or strip of material included when manufacturing sth such as a metal or plastic article or a sheet of postage stamps that allows it to be handled **3.** LOCK PLATE a slotted plate or surface through which the bolt of a lock passes **4.** RUG FRINGE a decorative fringe on the ends of an oriental rug [15thC. Alteration of 'self-edge' (because it 'edges' itself and does not need hemming).] —**selvaged** *adj.*

selves plural of **self**

David O. Selznick

Selznick /sélznik/, **David O.** (1902–65) US film producer. His many classic productions included *Gone With the Wind* (1939). Full name **David Oliver Selznick**

sem. *abbr.* **1.** semester **2.** semicolon **3.** seminary

Sem. *abbr.* **1.** Semitic **2.** Seminary

semanteme /sə mán teem/ *n.* the smallest possible unit of meaning in language [Early 20thC. From French *sémantème*, formed from Greek *semantikos* (see SEMANTIC), on the model of *morphème* (see MORPHEME).]

semantic /sə mántik/ *adj.* **1.** LING RELATING TO WORDS' MEANINGS relating to meaning or the differences between meanings of words or symbols **2.** LING OF SEMANTICS relating to semantics **3.** LOGIC RELATING TO TRUTH relating to the conditions in which a system or theory can be said to be true [Mid-17thC. Via French *semantique* from Greek *semantikos* 'significant', from *se-mainein* 'to show or signify', from *sēma* 'sign, mark'.] —**semantically** *adv.*

semantics /sə mántikss/ *n.* **1.** LING STUDY OF MEANING IN LANGUAGE the study of how meaning in language is created by the use and interrelationships of words, phrases, and sentences **2.** LOGIC STUDY OF SYMBOLS the study of the relationship between symbols and what they represent **3.** LOGIC STUDY OF LOGIC the study of ways of interpreting and analysing theories of logic —**semanticist** /sə mánn tissist/ *n.*

semaphore /sémmə fawr/ *n.* **1.** SYSTEM OF SIGNALLING a system for sending messages using hand-held flags that are moved to represent letters of the alphabet **2.** MECHANICAL SIGNALLING DEVICE a signalling device for sending information over distances using mechanically operated arms or flags mounted on a post, especially on a railway ■ *vti.* (**-phores**, **-phoring**, **-phored**) USE SEMAPHORE TO SIGNAL to send messages using semaphore [Early 19thC. From French *sémaphore*, literally 'sign-bearer', from Greek *sēma* 'mark, sign, signal'.] —**semaphoric** /sémmə fórrik/ *adj.* —**semaphorically** *adv.*

Semarang /sémmə ráng/ *city* and port on the island of Java, Indonesia, located east of Jakarta. Population: 1,250,971 (1990).

semasiology /sə máyzi ólləji/ *n.* = **semantics** *n.* **1**, **semantics** *n.* **2** [Mid-19thC. From German *Semasiologie*, literally 'science of meaning', from Greek *sēmasia* 'meaning', from *sēmainein* (see SEMANTIC).] —**semasiological** /sə máyzi ə lójjik'l/ *adj.* —**semasiologically** *adv.* —**semasiologist** /sə máyzi ólla jist/ *n.*

sematic /sə máttik/ *adj.* used to describe bright colourings on particular animals that act as a warning to predators, e.g. because the animals are poisonous [Late 19thC. Formed from Greek *sēmat-*, stem of *sēma* 'mark, sign'.]

semblable /sémbləb'l/ *n.* SB OR STH LOOKING LIKE ANOTHER sb who or sth that closely resembles sb or sth else (*archaic*) ■ *adj.* **1.** LIKE ANOTHER resembling or similar to sth or sth else (*formal*) **2.** NOT REAL apparent rather than real (*archaic*) [13thC. From Old French, formed from *sembler* (see SEMBLANCE).] —**semblably** *adv.*

semblance /sémblənss/ *n.* **1.** TRACE OF STH a small amount of sth ○ *a semblance of dignity* **2.** LOOK OF BEING STH an outward appearance or imitation of sth ○ *a semblance of competence* **3.** COPY a representation, likeness, or copy (*literary*) [14thC. From Old French, formed from *sembler* 'to seem' (source of English *resemble*), from Latin *simulare* (see SIMULATE).]

semé /sémmay/ *adj.* covered with many small dots or delicate designs [15thC. From French, past participle of *semer* 'to sow', from Latin *semere*.]

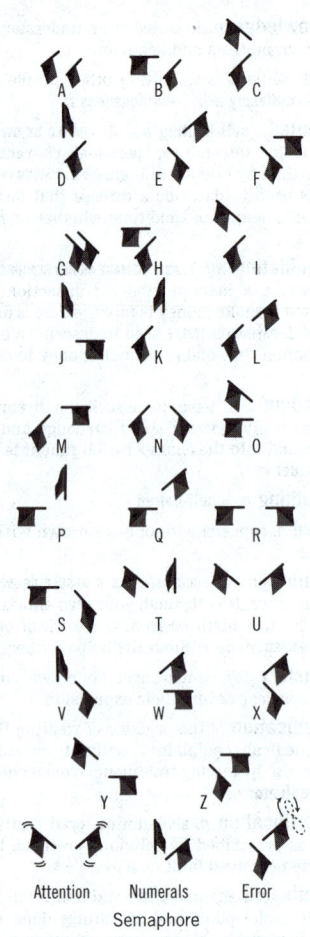

Attention   Numerals   Error

Semaphore

sememe /sée meem/ *n.* the meaning that a morpheme has in a linguistic system [Early 20thC. Formed from Greek *sēma* 'mark, sign'.]

semen /séémən/ *n.* the thick white fluid containing sperm that a male ejaculates [14thC. From Latin, literally 'seed'.]

semester /sə méstər/ *n.* **1.** PERIOD WHEN STUDENTS ARE AT SCHOOL either one of two periods of 15 to 18 weeks into which the academic year is often divided in the United States. ◊ **term 2.** SIX-MONTH GERMAN UNIVERSITY SESSION in German universities, an academic session lasting six months [Early 19thC. Via German from Latin *semestris*, literally 'of six months', from *mensis* 'month' (source of English *menstrual*).] —**semestral** *adj.*

semi /sémmi/ *n.* **1.** SEMIDETACHED HOUSE a house with a wall in common with the next house (*informal*) **2.** SEMIFINAL a semifinal (*informal*) **3.** US = **tractor-trailer** [Early 20thC. Shortening.]

semi- *prefix.* **1.** partial, partially, somewhat ○ *semi-sweet* ○ *semiterrestrial* **2.** half ○ *semiround* **3.** resembling, having some characteristics of sth ○ *semitropical* ○ *semivowel* **4.** occurring twice during a particular period ○ *semiweekly* [From Latin, 'half'. Ultimately from an Indo-European word that is also the ancestor of English *hemi-* and *sand-blind*.]

semiabstract /sémmi áb strakt/ *adj.* used to describe art that has heavily stylized but still recognizable subject matter —**semiabstraction** /sémmi ab straksh'n/ *n.*

semiannual /sémmi ánnyōō əl/ *adj.* **1.** HAPPENING TWICE A YEAR happening or issued every six months or twice a year **2.** LASTING SIX MONTHS lasting for half a year ■ *n.* SEMIANNUAL PLANT a semiannual plant or flower —**semiannually** *adv.*

semiaquatic /sémmi ə kwáttik/ *adj.* growing or living near water as well as in it

semiarid /sémmi árrid/ *adj.* with little rainfall and scrubby vegetation —**semiaridity** /sémmi ə ríddəti/ *n.*

semiautobiographical /sémmi áwtə bī ə gráffik'l/ *adj.* used to describe sth such as a novel or film that is based in part on the life or experiences of its author

semiautomatic /sémmi áwtə máttik/ *adj.* **1.** RELOADING AUTOMATICALLY automatically ejecting a spent shell from a weapon's chamber and replacing it with another round each time the weapon is fired **2.** PARTIALLY AUTOMATED operated partly automatically and partly manually ■ *n.* SEMIAUTOMATIC WEAPON a weapon that is semiautomatic —**semiautomatically** *adv.*

semiautonomous /sémmi aw tónnəməss/ *adj.* **1.** PARTLY SELF-GOVERNING ruled partly by its own citizens or rulers and partly by another country or region **2.** ACTING AS SELF-GOVERNING PART self-governing but remaining within a larger organization of which it is part —**semiautonomously** *adv.* —**semiautonomy** *n.*

semibold /sémmi bṓld/ *adj.* darker than ordinary type but not as dark as bold type

semibreve /sémmi breev/ *n.* the longest musical note in common use, written as an open note-head without a stem or tail, with a duration equivalent to four crotchets or two minims. US term **whole note**

semicentennial /sémmi sen ténni əl/ *adj.* **1.** MARKING 50TH ANNIVERSARY marking the date or year that is 50 years after a particular event **2.** HAPPENING EVERY 50 YEARS happening every 50 years **3.** 50TH ANNIVERSARY OF EVENT the 50th anniversary of an important event

semicircle /sémmi surk'l/ *n.* **1.** HALF CIRCLE half of the area or circumference of a circle **2.** CURVED LINE a curved or crescent-shaped line of things or people in the shape of a semicircle [Early 16thC. From Latin *semicirculus*, from *circulus*, literally 'small circle'.] —**semicircular** /sémmi súrkyŏŏlər/ *adj.* —**semicircularly** *adv.*

semicircular canal *n.* any one of three tubes in the inner ear, semicircular in shape and set at right angles to one another, that help to maintain balance

semiclassical /sémmi klássik'l/ *adj.* classical in musical style, pleasant, easy to listen to, and usually written relatively recently —**semiclassically** *adv.*

semicolon /sémmi kṓlən, -lon/ *n.* a punctuation mark (;) used to separate parts of a sentence or list and indicating a pause longer than a comma but shorter than a full stop

semicoma /sémmi kṓmə/ *n.* a partial or light comatose state from which it is sometimes possible to rouse people by stimulating them

semicomatose /sémmi kṓmətōss/ *adj.* **1.** BEING IN SEMI-COMA bordering on being unconscious but capable of being awakened **2.** NEARLY UNCONSCIOUS almost unconscious or half asleep

semiconductor /sémmi kən dúktər/ *n.* a solid such as silicon or germanium that has electrical conductivity between that of a conductor and an insulator —**semiconducting** *adj.* —**semiconduction** *n.* —**semiconductive** *adj.* —**semiconductivity** /sémmi kon duk tívvəti/ *n.*

semiconscious /sémmi kónnshəss/ *adj.* only partly conscious —**semiconsciously** *adv.* —**semiconsciousness** *n.*

semiconservative /sémmi kən súrvətiv/ *adj.* relating to the replication of a nucleic acid molecule such as DNA in which a double stranded molecule separates into two templates for the formation of complementary strands —**semiconservatively** *adv.*

semidarkness /sémmi daárknəss/ *n.* a state in which it is neither fully dark nor fully light

semidesert /sémmi dézzərt/ *n.* a region that is not completely arid, usually one lying between desert and a more heavily vegetated area

semidetached /sémmi di tácht/ *adj.* SHARING A WALL joined to a neighbouring building by a shared wall ■ *n.* SEMIDETACHED HOUSE a house with a wall in common with the next house

semidiameter /sémmi dī ámmitər/ *n.* half of the angular diameter of the visible disc of a celestial body as measured by an observer

semidiurnal /sémmi dī úrn'l/ *adj.* **1.** LASTING ONE-HALF DAY continuing or happening over half a day **2.** OCCURRING AT 12-HOUR INTERVALS happening approximately once every twelve hours

semidocumentary /sémmi dokyŏŏ méntəri/ (*plural* **-ries**) *n.* a film or TV programme that is fictional but makes use of or is based on factual details or events

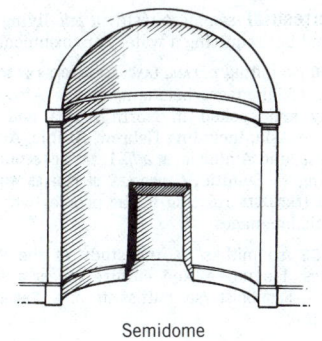

Semidome

semidome /sémmi dṓm/ *n.* a half dome, especially one used as the roof for a semicircular space or recess

semidomesticated /sémmi də méss ti kaytid/ *adj.* still wild but living with and bred by humans for animal products —**semidomestication** /sémmi də méssti káysh'n/ *n.*

semidry /sémmi drī/ *adj.* US used to describe wine that is partially or moderately dry

semielliptical /sémmi i lípptik'l/ *adj.* resembling half an ellipse in shape, especially one that is divided along its major axis

semifinal /sémmi fín'l/ *n.* either one of two matches or games, the winners of which will play each other in the final round of a competition —**semifinal** *adj.* —**semifinalist** *n.*

semifinished /sémmi fínnisht/ *adj.* partially finished, treated, or processed

semifluid /sémmi floo id/ *adj.* having properties between those of a fluid and a solid —**semifluid** *n.* —**semifluidity** /sémmi floo íddəti/ *n.*

semiformal /sémmi fáwrm'l/ *adj.* designed to be worn on moderately formal occasions

semigloss /sémmi glóss/ *n.* a paint or varnish with a finish that is midway between gloss and matt when it dries

semihard /sémmi haárd/ *adj.* used to describe cheese that has a consistency firm enough to slice but that is moist and pliable. Hard cheese is not pliable even when moist.

semi-infinite *adj.* unbounded in one dimension or direction

semilethal /sémmi leéth'l/ *adj.* lethal in more than 50 per cent but fewer than 100 per cent of cases

semiliquid /sémmi líkwid/ *adj.* = **semifluid** —**semiliquid** *n.* —**semiliquidity** /sémmi lí kwìddə ti/ *n.*

semiliterate /sémmi líttərət/ *adj.* unable to read or write properly —**semiliteracy** *n.*

Sémillon /sémmi yoN/ *n.* a late-maturing French grape variety used to produce white wine [Mid-19thC. Via French *Sémillon* from, ultimately, Latin *semen* 'seed'; probably from the grape's high productivity.]

semilunar /sémmi loŏnər/ *adj.* shaped like a crescent or a half moon

semilunar cartilage *n.* either one of two crescent-shaped pieces of cartilage in the knee joint

semilunar valve *n.* either one of two crescent-shaped valves in the heart that prevent blood from flowing back into the ventricles. The two valves are called the aortic valve and the pulmonary valve.

semimonthly /sémmi múnthli/ *adj.* HAPPENING TWICE IN MONTH happening or published twice each month, usually at equal intervals ■ *adv.* TWICE DURING MONTH twice each month, usually at equal intervals ■ *n.* (*plural* **-lies**) PUBL SEMIMONTHLY PUBLICATION a publication that appears twice each month, usually at equal intervals

seminal /sémmin əl/ *adj.* **1.** INFLUENTIAL highly original and influential **2.** CAPABLE OF DEVELOPMENT containing an idea or set of ideas that forms a basis for later developments **3.** BIOL OF SEMEN OR SEEDS relating to, containing, or carrying semen or seeds [14thC. Via French from Latin *seminalis*, from *semin-*, stem of *semen* 'seed' (source of English *seminary* and *disseminate*).] —

seminality /sémmi nálləti/ *n.* —**seminally** /sémminəli/ *adv.*

seminal vesicle *n.* either one of a pair of glands that secrete the fluid component of semen into the ejaculatory duct in males

seminar /sémmi naar/ *n.* **1.** MEETING ON SPECIALIZED SUBJECT a single session or short, often one-day meeting devoted to presentations on and discussion of a particular topic, usually at an advanced or professional level ○ *a seminar on the industrial applications of biotechnology* **2.** MEETING OF STUDENTS AND TUTOR a meeting of university or college students for study or discussion with a tutor, or the group that participates in it **3.** SPECIALIZED EDUCATIONAL CLASS a course of specialized, especially postgraduate study under academic supervision, in which ideas, approaches, and advances are regularly shared among participants [Late 19thC. Via German, 'advanced class', from Latin *seminarium* 'seed plot, breeding ground', ultimately from the stem *semin-* (see SEMINAL).]

seminarian /sémmi naíri ən/, **seminarist** /sémmínərist/ *n.* a student who is training in a seminary to be a priest, minister, or rabbi

seminary /sémmínəri/ (*plural* **-ies**) *n.* **1.** COLLEGE FOR CLERGY a college for the training of priests, ministers, or rabbis **2.** GIRLS' SCHOOL a private residential school for girls (*archaic*) [15thC. From Latin *seminarium* 'seed plot, breeding ground', ultimately from the stem *semin-* (see SEMINAL).]

seminiferous /sémmi nífferəss/ *adj.* **1.** BIOL PRODUCING SEMEN carrying, containing, or producing semen **2.** BOT PRODUCING SEEDS bearing or producing seeds [Late 17thC. Coined from the Latin stem *semin-* (see SEMINAL) + -FEROUS.]

Seminole /sémmi nṓl/ *n.* (*plural* **-nole** or **-noles**) **1.** PEOPLES NATIVE N AMERICAN PEOPLE a member of a Native North American people who originally occupied lands to the east of the Mississippi River, and whose members now live mainly in Oklahoma. The Seminole were one of the Five Civilized Nations who, under the Removal Act of 1830, settled in Indian Territory. **2.** LANG SEMINOLE LANGUAGE either one of the two Muskogean languages spoken by the Seminole ■ *adj.* OF SEMINOLE relating to the Seminole or their languages or culture [Mid-18thC. From Creek *simanó:li*, alteration of *simaló:ni*, alteration of Spanish-American *cimarrón* 'wild, untamed'.]

seminoma /sémmi nṓmə/ (*plural* **-mas** or **-mata** /-mətə/) *n.* a malignant tumour of the sperm-producing tissue in the testicle [Early 20thC. Via French *seminome* from modern Latin *seminoma*, from the Latin stem *semin-* 'seed' + -OMA.]

seminomadic /sémmi nō máddik/ *adj.* belonging or relating to an ethnic group or people who migrate seasonally as well as cultivating crops during periods of settlement

seminude /sémmi nyoŏd/ *adj.* only partly clothed, usually in underclothes or skimpy outer clothing —**seminudity** *n.*

semiochemical /sémmi ō kémmik'l/ *n.* an organic chemical such as pheromone that plays a role in animal communication [Late 20thC. Coined from Greek *sēmeion* 'sign' + CHEMICAL.]

semiofficial /sémmi ə físh'l/ *adj.* with only some degree of authority or official status and therefore not completely reliable —**semiofficially** *adv.*

semiology /sémmi ólləji, seém-/ *n.* = **semiotics** [Late 17thC. Coined from Greek *sēmeion* 'sign' + -LOGY.] —**semiologic** /sémmi ə lójik, seém-/ *adj.* —**semiological** *adj.* —**semiologically** *adv.* —**semiologist** /sémmi ólləjist, seémi-/ *n.*

semiotic /sémmi óttik/ *adj.* **1.** RELATING TO SIGNS OR SYMBOLS relating to signs or symbols, especially in speech or writing **2.** OF SEMIOTICS relating to semiotics **3.** MED RELATING TO SYMPTOMATOLOGY relating to the field of symptomatology [Early 17thC. From Greek *sēmeiōtikos*, from *sēmeiousthai* 'to interpret signs', from *sēmeion* 'sign'.]

semiotics /sémmi óttiks, sémmi-/ *n.* (takes a singular verb) **1.** STUDY OF SIGNS the study of signs and symbols of all kinds, what they mean, and how they relate to the things or ideas they refer to **2.** MED STUDY OF SYMPTOMS OF DISEASES the study of identifying the ways that various symptoms indicate the diseases that underlie them —**semiotician** /sémmi ə tísh'n, seémi-/ n.

semipalmate /sémmi pál mayt/, **semipalmated** /sémmi pál máytid/ adj. with feet or toes that are partially webbed. Some shorebirds have semipalmate feet.

semipermanent /sémmi púrmənent/ adj. set up or arranged to last quite a long time but not indefinitely

semipermeable /sémmi púrmi əb'l/ adj. used to describe a membrane or tissue that allows some types of particle to pass through, but not others —**semipermeability** /sémmi púrmi ə bíllə ti/ n.

semipolar bond /sémmi pōlər-/ n. = **coordinate bond**

semiporcelain /sémmi páwrssəlin, -layn/ n. a durable glazed ceramic material widely used for tableware. It resembles porcelain but is opaque.

semiprecious /sémmi préshəss/ adj. used to describe stones, gems, and minerals that have commercial value but are not valued as highly as those called precious

semipro /sémmi prő/ n. (plural **-pros**) SB SEMIPROFESSIONAL a semiprofessional (informal) ■ adj. SEMIPROFESSIONAL relating to or being semiprofessional (informal)

semiprofessional /sémmi prə fésh'nəl/ adj. **1.** PAID BUT NOT FULL-TIME participating in a sport or artistic activity for pay but not as a full-time professional **2.** FOR SEMIPROFESSIONAL ATHLETES played in or contested by semiprofessional athletes **3.** LIKE A PROFESSIONAL displaying some aspects of a professional ■ n. PART PROFESSIONAL sb, especially an athlete or performing artist, who is intermediate between an amateur and a professional —**semiprofessionally** adv.

semiquaver /sémmi kwayvər/ n. a musical note equivalent to one-sixteenth of a semibreve. US term **sixteenth note**

semiretired /sémmi ri tírd/ adj. working only part-time following the end of a full-time career —**semi-retirement** n.

semirigid /sémmi ríjjid/ adj. **1.** PARTLY RIGID partly rigid or rigid only in some parts **2.** AEROSP WITH RIGID KEEL used to describe an airship with a rigid keel that maintains its shape

semirural /sémmi roóərəl/ adj. intermediate between rural and urban

semisecret /sémmi seékrət/ adj. intended or supposedly intended to be secret but actually known about

semiskilled /sémmi skíld/ adj. with or requiring relatively few skills or little training ○ semiskilled workers ○ a semiskilled job

semi-skimmed adj. with part of the cream removed. Semi-skimmed milk contains less animal fat and fewer calories than full cream milk.

semisoft /sémmi sóft/ adj. softer than most things, especially foods, of its type

semisolid /sémmi sóllid/ adj. HALF SOLID, HALF LIQUID not quite solid or liquid, but somewhere in between, like a gel ■ n. THICK STICKY SUBSTANCE a substance that has most of the qualities of a solid but can also flow, e.g. a gel

semistaged /sémmi stáyjd/ adj. performed without all of the elements of a full stage production such as costumes, props, or minor characters ○ They performed a semistaged version of Faust.

semisubmersible /sémmi səb múrssəb'l/, **semisubmersible rig** n. a self-propelled oil-drilling platform resting on vertical pontoons that can be flooded for stability in deep water

semisynthetic /sémmi sin théttik/ adj. **1.** SYNTHESIZED USING NATURAL INGREDIENTS chemically synthesized from natural ingredients **2.** PART NATURAL made up of some natural and some synthetic ingredients

Semite /seé mīt, sémm-/ n. **1.** MEMBER OF SEMITIC-SPEAKING PEOPLE a member of any of several Semitic-speaking peoples of the Middle East, including the Arab and Jewish peoples, and the ancient Assyrians, Babylonians, Carthaginians, Ethiopians, and Phoenicians **2.** OFFENSIVE TERM an offensive term for a Jewish person (offensive) [Mid-19thC. Ultimately via modern Latin Semita from Greek Sēm 'Shem', son of Noah traditionally believed to be the ancestor of this group.]

semiterrestrial /sémmi tə réstri əl/ adj. living partly on land but requiring a watery environment

Semitic /sə míttik/ n. LANG LANGUAGES SPOKEN BY SEMITES a group of languages belonging to the Afro-Asiatic family and spoken in North Africa and southwestern Asia, including Hebrew, Arabic, Aramaic, Maltese, and Amharic ■ adj. **1.** LANG OF SEMITIC in or relating to Semitic **2.** PEOPLES OF PEOPLES WHO SPEAK SEMITIC LANGUAGES relating to the peoples who speak Semitic languages

Semitics /sə míttiks/ n. the study of the Semitic peoples, languages, and culture (takes a singular verb) —**Semiticist** /sə míttissist/ n. —**Semitist** /sə míttist/ n.

Semitism /sémmətizəm/ n. **1.** SEMITIC CULTURE the customs, traditions, and characteristics of Semitic people, especially Jewish people **2.** LANGUAGE FEATURE OF SEMITIC ORIGIN a word or other language feature of Semitic origin, especially one occurring in a non-Semitic language

semitone /sémmi tōn/ n. the smallest interval of the diatonic scale, half of a whole tone. It is the difference in pitch between adjacent frets on fretted string instruments such as guitars, or between adjacent black or white notes on the piano. [15thC. Directly or via Old French, 'half tone', from medieval Latin semitonus, from tonus (see TONE).] —**semitonal** /sémmi tő n'l/ adj. —**semitonally** adv. —**semitonic** /-tónnik/ adj.

semitrailer /sémmi tráylər/ n. **1.** REAR PART OF ARTICULATED LORRY a large rectangular vehicle with wheels only at the rear and a hitch at the front that attaches to a tractor or other towing vehicle **2.** ARTICULATED LORRY a tractor with an attached semitrailer

semitransparent /sémmi tráns párrənt/ adj. partly, but not completely, transparent

semitropical /sémmi tróppik'l/ adj. = **subtropical** —**semitropics** npl.

semivowel /sémmi vowəl/ n. a sound that is like a vowel in involving no major obstruction of the airflow but that functions as a consonant in preceding vowels that form the nucleus of syllables. Examples in English are initial 'w' and 'y'.

semiweekly /sémmi weékli/ adj. HAPPENING TWICE PER WEEK happening or published twice each week ■ adv. TWICE PER WEEK twice each week

semolina /sémmə leénə/ n. gritty ground-up grains of wheat that are a by-product of flour milling, used in making pasta, couscous, and other foods [Late 18thC. Alteration of Italian semolino, literally 'small bran', formed from semola 'bran', from Latin simila 'fine wheat flour', of uncertain origin: probably from Semitic.]

semper fidelis /sémpər fi dáyliss/ adj. 'always faithful', the motto of the United States Marine Corps [From Latin]

Sempervivum

sempervivum /sémpər veévəm/ n. a widely-grown ornamental garden plant that has rosettes of fleshy leaves and clusters of pink flowers growing on stems. Genus: Sempervivum. [Late 16thC. From Latin, a form of sempervivus 'ever-living', from semper 'ever' + vivus 'living' (see VIVACIOUS).]

sempiternal /sémpi túrn'l/ adj. lasting forever (literary) [15thC. Directly or via Old French from late Latin sempiternalis, from Latin sempiternus, from semper 'always' + -ternus, suffix of time.] —**sempiternally** adv. —**sempiternity** n.

semplice /sémmplichi, -chay/ adv. in a simple manner, without rubato (used in musical directions) [Mid-18thC. From Italian, 'simple'.]

sempre /sémpri, -pray/ adv. to be played or sung throughout in the manner indicated (used in musical directions) ○ sempre largo [Early 19thC. From Italian, 'always, throughout'.]

sempstress /sémpstrəss/ n. a seamstress (archaic) [Mid-17thC. Formed from sempster, variant of seamster.]

Semtex /sém teks/ tdmk. a trademark for a type of plastic explosive of Czech origin

sen /sen/ (plural **sen**) n. **1.** SUBUNIT OF SE ASIAN CURRENCIES a subunit of currency in Cambodia, 100 of which are worth one riel, in Indonesia, 100 of which are worth one rupiah, in Japan, 100 of which are worth one yen, and in Malaysia, 100 of which are worth one ringgit. See table at **currency 2.** COIN WORTH A SEN a coin worth a sen [Early 18thC. From Japanese, ultimately from Mandarin Chinese qián 'money, coin'.]

SEN abbr. EDUC special educational needs ■ n., abbr. (plural **SENs**) MED State Enrolled Nurse (dated)

Sen. abbr. **1.** senior **2.** POL senator **3.** POL senate

Senanayake /se nánnə yaák ay, sénnə ní yə kay/, **D.S.** (1884–1952) Sinhalese statesman. As the first prime minister of Ceylon (1947–52), he presided over the country's transition to independence (1948). Full name **Don Stephen Senanayake**

Senanayake, Dudley (1911–73) Sinhalese statesman. The son of D. S. Senanayake, he was prime minister of Ceylon (1952–53, 1960, and 1965–70). Full name **Dudley Shelton Senanayake**

senary /seénəri, sénn-/ adj. based on six (formal) [Mid-17thC. From Latin senarius 'based on six', from seni 'six each', from sex 'six'.]

senate n. **1.** US STATE LEGISLATURE the higher of two elected legislative bodies in many states of the United States **2.** LEGISLATIVE BODY the sole or upper law-making chamber of government in many countries or states, past or present **3.** HIST ANCIENT ROMAN ASSEMBLY the highest council of the ancient Roman Republic and of the Roman Empire **4.** SENATE BUILDING the building where a senate meets **5.** EDUC UNIVERSITY BODY the main faculty governing body in some universities and colleges [12thC. Via Old French from Latin senatus, literally 'assembly of elders', from senex 'male elder' (source of English senile and senior).]

Senate n. **1.** US LEGISLATURE the higher of the two elected legislative bodies of the United States government. It is made up of two senators from each state. **2.** UPPER HOUSE OF CANADIAN PARLIAMENT the upper chamber of the federal parliament of Canada. It is made up of 104 senators appointed by the ruling government. **3.** UPPER HOUSE OF AUSTRALIAN PARLIAMENT in Australia, the upper house of the federal parliament. It consists of 76 members, 12 from each state plus two each from the Northern Territory and Australian Capital Territory.

senator /sénnətər/ n. an elected or appointed member of a senate, e.g. in the United States, Australia, or ancient Rome

senatorial /sénnə táwri əl/ adj. **1.** OF SENATORS OR A SENATE relating to or characteristic of a senate or with the post of senator ○ senatorial privileges **2.** CONSISTING OF SENATORS made up of senators —**senatorially** adv.

Senatus Academicus /sə naátəss akə démmikəss/ n. in the older Scottish universities, the body, consisting of the Principal, professors, and, more recently, readers and lecturers, that superintends and regulates the teaching and discipline of the university (formal) [From Latin, 'Academic Senate']

send[1] /send/ v. (sends, sending, sent, sent /sent/) **1.** vt. CAUSE SB OR STH TO GO to cause sb or sth to be moved or taken to another place **2.** vt. COMMUNICATE STH to transmit information to sb who is somewhere else **3.** vt. COMMAND SB TO GO to ask or command sb to come or go **4.** vt. ENABLE SB TO GO to enable sb to go somewhere special ○ Let's send the children to camp this summer. **5.** vt. REFER SB SOMEWHERE to suggest that sb go somewhere or see sb, usually for a specific kind of information **6.** vt. BRING STH ABOUT to make sth happen ○ Our blessings were sent by a higher power. **7.** vt. PROPEL STH to make sth move or travel by

ə at; aa father; aw all; ay day; air hair; ə about, edible, item, common, circus; e egg; ee eel; hw when; i it, happy; ī ice; l apple; 'm rhythm; 'n fashion; o odd; ō open; oo good; oo pool; ow owl; oy oil; th thin; th this; u up; ur verge;

pushing it or hitting it ○ *A gust of wind sent the papers swirling round the office.* **8.** *vt.* **DRIVE SB INTO PARTICULAR STATE** to make sb enter a particular condition ○ *The delay is sending her crazy.* **9.** *vt.* **EXCITE SB GREATLY** to excite or thrill sb intensely (*dated slang*) **10.** *vi.* COMPUT **BE TRANSMITTED** to be transmitted or transmittable ○ *This e-mail won't send.* **11.** *vi.* TELECOM **BROADCAST INFORMATION** to transmit information by telecommunication ○ *The operator was still sending when the power was cut off.* ■ *n.* COMPUT **COMMAND TO TRANSMIT COMPUTER DATA** a command, key, or icon on a computer monitor or keyboard that is used to start the transmission of data [Old English *sendan*, from a prehistoric Germanic word meaning 'to cause to go'] ◇ **send flying** to make sb or sth fly through the air by force of impact ◇ **send sb packing 1.** to tell sb to go in a firm, not very polite way (*informal*) **2.** to force or frighten sb into going away (*informal*)

send away for *vt.* to order sth by post or through a mail order catalogue

send down *vt.* **1.** **EXPEL SB** to expel sb from a university, especially Oxford or Cambridge (*often passive*) ○ *He was sent down as a result of this escapade.* **2.** **SENTENCE SB** to imprison sb following conviction (*slang*) ○ *He got sent down for armed robbery.*

send for *vt.* to request the delivery, dispatch, or appearance of sb or sth ○ *send for reinforcements*

send forth *vt.* to give out or produce sb or sth (*archaic or literary*) ○ *sent forth a cry of joy*

send in *vt.* to post sth, e.g. an application form, for processing along with those sent by other people

send off *vt.* **1.** MAIL **DISPATCH STH** to dispatch sth in the post **2.** **SEND SB AWAY** to send sb away, either on an errand, or by way of dismissal ○ *We sent him off to buy some things.* **3.** SPORTS **DISMISS SB FROM GAME** to dismiss a player from a game or competition for breaking the rules, e.g. in football, rugby, or hockey (*often passive*) **4.** **BID SB FAREWELL** to say goodbye or good luck to sb who is leaving ○ *Who was there to send her off?*

send out for *vt.* to order food by telephone, to be delivered to a particular address and paid for when it arrives (*informal*) ○ *Let's send out for a pizza.*

send up *vt.* **1.** **MAKE STH GO UP** to make sth rise or climb, especially a scale or index such as on a thermometer or a listing of stock market values ○ *News of lower interest rates sent the stock market index up 60 points.* **2.** **MOCK SB OR STH BY IMITATION** to make fun of sb or sth by humorous imitation (*informal*) **3.** *US* **SEND SB TO PRISON** to imprison sb following conviction (*informal*) ○ *He was sent up for armed robbery.*

—— **WORD KEY: SYNONYMS** ——
See Synonyms at **ridicule**.

send² *vi.*, *n.* = **scend**

Sendai /sen dí/ capital city of Miyagi Prefecture, on northeastern Honshu Island, Japan. Population: 918,398 (1990).

sendoff /sénnd of/ *n.* an act of showing goodwill towards sb who is leaving or sth that is starting, especially in a group at a place such as an airport or at a farewell party ◇ **give sb a good sendoff** to have a good party after sb's funeral (*informal*)

sendup /sénnd up/ *n.* a parody done as a joke (*informal*)

sene /seen/ (*plural* **-ne**) *n.* **1.** **SUBUNIT OF SAMOAN CURRENCY** a subunit of currency in Samoa, 100 of which are worth one tala. See table at **currency 2.** **COIN WORTH A SENE** a coin worth one sene [Mid-20thC. From Samoan, 'cent'.]

Seneca /sénnikə/ (*plural* **-ca** *or* **-cas**) *n.* **1.** PEOPLES **MEMBER OF NATIVE N AMERICAN PEOPLE** a member of a Native North American people who originally occupied lands in western New York State, and whose members mainly continue to live there and in southern Ontario. The Seneca were one of the five peoples who formed the Iroquois Confederacy, which later became known as the Six Nations. **2.** LANG **SENECA LANGUAGE** the Iroquoian language of the Seneca. It now has few speakers. [Mid-17thC. From Dutch *Sennecaas* (plural) 'the Upper Iroquois peoples', of uncertain origin: possibly from Mahican.] —**Senecan** *adj.*

Seneca /sénnəkə/ (4? BC–AD 65) Spanish-born Roman statesman, philosopher, and dramatist. He was Nero's tutor, and influenced the early years of his

reign, but committed suicide after being condemned for conspiracy against the state. His writings as a dramatist, rhetorician, and Stoic moralist were influential in shaping the thought and literature of the European Renaissance. Full name **Lucius Annaeus Seneca**. Known as **Seneca the Younger**

senecio /sə neéshi ō, -neéssi ō/ (*plural* **senecios**) *n.* = **ragwort** [Mid-16thC. From Latin, 'groundsel', literally 'male elder' (from the plant's white hairs), from *senex* (see SENATE).]

Senegal

Senegal /sénnə gaal, senə gáwl/ republic in western Africa. Formerly a French territory, it became an independent republic in 1960. Language: French. Currency: C.F.A. franc. Capital: Dakar. Population: 8,532,000 (1996). Area: 196,192 sq. km/75,750 sq. mi. Official name **Republic of Senegal** —**Senegalese** /sénnə gaaleéz/ *n.*, *adj.*

senescent /si néss'nt/ *adj.* approaching an advanced age [Mid-17thC. From Latin *senescent-*, present participle stem of *senescere*, ultimately from *senex* 'advanced in age'.] —**senescence** *n.*

seneschal /sénnish'l/ *n.* a steward in medieval times who managed the retainers of a noble house [14thC. Via Old French from medieval Latin *seniscalcus*, from prehistoric Germanic words meaning 'old' and 'servant'.]

Senghor /sáN gawr/, **Léopold Sédar** (b. 1906) Senegalese statesman and writer. He was the first president of Senegal (1960–80) and a leading African intellectual who helped formulate the concept of negritude.

senhor /se nyáw/ (*plural* **-hors** *or* **-hores** /-n yáw ress/) *n.* a Portuguese title equivalent to English 'Mr' [Late 18thC. Portuguese, via medieval Latin *senior* 'lord, superior' from Latin, 'elder, older' (source of English *sir*).]

senhora /sényáwrə/ *n.* a Portuguese title equivalent to English 'Mrs' [Early 19thC. From Portuguese, formed from SENHOR.]

senhorita /sénnyə reétə/ *n.* a Portuguese title equivalent to English 'Miss' [Late 19thC. From Portuguese, literally 'little senhora', formed from SENHORA.]

senile /seé níl/ *adj.* **1.** **MENTALLY LESS ACUTE IN LATER LIFE** forgetful, confused, or otherwise mentally less acute in later life **2.** **RELATING TO LATER LIFE** occurring in or believed to be characteristic of later life, especially the period after the age of 65 years [Mid-17thC. Directly or via French *sénile* from Latin *senilis* 'advanced in age', from *senex* (see SENATE).] —**senilely** *adv.* —**senility** /sə nílla ti/ *n.*

senile dementia *n.* a form of brain disorder marked by progressive and irreversible mental deterioration, memory loss, and disorientation, known to affect some people after the age of about 65 years

senior /seéni ər/ *adj.* **1.** **MORE ADVANCED IN AGE** of a more advanced age **2.** **HIGHER IN RANK** of higher rank or having longer service or employment than another ○ *Everyone on the committee is senior to me* **3. senior, Senior** **RELATING TO EARLIER GENERATION** used to distinguish the elder of two members of the same family with the same name from the younger person of that name ■ *n.* **1.** **SB OF GREATER AGE** sb who is more advanced in age than sb else **2.** **HIGHER-RANKING PERSON** sb who is of a higher rank than sb else or who has worked in the same place longer than another person ○ *She is my only senior in the department.* **3.** *US* EDUC **FINAL-YEAR STUDENT** a student in the last year of high school or college **4.** *Aus* LAW **AUSTRALIAN BARRISTER**

in Australia, a barrister who has qualified as a Queen's Counsel [14thC. From Latin, 'elder, older', the comparative form of *senex* (see SENATE).]

senior aircraftman *n.* sb holding a rank in the Royal Air Force above leading aircraftman, or the rank itself. It is equivalent to that of a private in the army.

senior citizen *n.* sb of retirement age or beyond

senior common room *n.* a common room for the use of academic staff in some colleges and universities in the United Kingdom

senior debt *n.* an indebtedness with no claims ahead of it and the first in line to be paid off

senior high school *n.* *US* a school for the last three or four years of secondary education in the United States, grades 9 or 10 to 12

seniority /seéni órrəti/ (*plural* **-ties**) *n.* **1.** **HIGHER STATUS** status accorded to greater age, higher rank, or longer service or employment ○ *Days off will be awarded on the basis of seniority.* **2.** **STATE OF BEING SENIOR** the state of being of greater age or higher rank than sb else

senior lecturer *n.* a university teacher ranking above a lecturer and below a reader or professor

senior management *n.* the tier of management in an organization that makes important decisions about direction, focus, and general policy

senior service *n.* the Royal Navy, especially as viewed in relation to the Army

seniti /sénni ti/ (*plural* **seniti**) *n.* **1.** **TONGAN SUBUNIT OF CURRENCY** a subunit of currency in Tonga, 100 of which are worth a pa'anga. See table at **currency 2.** **COIN WORTH A SENITI** a coin worth one seniti

senna /sénnə/ *n.* **1.** **FLOWERING PLANT USED AS LAXATIVE** a leguminous plant, usually with clusters of yellow flowers, found widely in temperate regions and sometimes used as a laxative. Genus: *Cassia*. **2.** **DRIED LEAVES OR PODS** the dried leaves or pods of a senna plant used as a purgative or laxative [Mid-16thC. Via modern Latin *sena* from Arabic *sanā*.]

Ayrton Senna

Senna /sénnə/, **Ayrton** (1960–94) Brazilian racing driver. One of the most celebrated Brazilian sportsmen of the 20th century, he won the World Grand Prix Formula One championship three times (1988, 1990, 1991). Full name **Ayrton Senna da Silva**

Sennacherib /sen ákərib/, **King of Assyria** (d. 681 BC). During his reign (705–681 BC) he conquered Babylon (689 BC) and rebuilt Nineveh.

sennet /sénnit/ *n.* a trumpet call that announced the exits and entrances of actors in Elizabethan drama [Late 16thC. Origin uncertain: possibly from assumed Anglo-Norman *senet*, variant of *signet* in the obsolete sense 'signal'.]

sennit /sénnit/ *n.* **1.** **BRAIDED CORD USED ON SHIPS** braided cord in flat strands, used on ships **2.** **BRAIDED STRAW** braided straw, reeds, or leaves, used to make hats [Mid-18thC. Variant of *sinnet*, of unknown origin.]

señor /se nyáw/ (*plural* **-ñors** *or* **-ñores** /-nyáw ress/) *n.* a Spanish title equivalent to English 'Mr' [Early 17thC. From Spanish, via medieval Latin *senior* (see SENHOR).]

señora /se nyáwrə/ *n.* a Spanish title equivalent to English 'Mrs' [Late 16thC. From Spanish, formed from SEÑOR.]

Sennit

señorita /sénnyaw reétə/ *n.* a Spanish title equivalent to English 'Miss' [Early 19thC. From Spanish, literally 'little señora', formed from SEÑORA.]

senryu /sénnri oo/ (*plural* **-ryu**) *n.* a three-line ironic or satirical Japanese poem, similar in structure to a haiku [Mid-20thC. Named after the Japanese poet Karai *Senryu* (1718–90).]

sensate /sén sayt/ *adj.* perceived through any of the senses [15thC. From late Latin *sensatus* 'equipped with senses', from Latin *sensus* (see SENSE).] —**sensately** *adv.*

sensation /sen sáysh'n/ *n.* **1.** PHYSICAL FEELING a physical feeling caused by having one or more of the sense organs stimulated ○ *a burning sensation in my mouth and throat* **2.** POWER TO PERCEIVE the capacity to receive impressions through the sense organs ○ *He has lost all sensation in his legs.* **3.** MENTAL IMPRESSION a vague or general feeling, especially one not attributable to an obvious cause ○ *a sensation of falling* **4.** PUBLIC INTEREST a state of avid public interest in a phenomenon ○ *Her speech caused a sensation.* **5.** INTERESTING PHENOMENON a phenomenon that creates avid public interest [Early 17thC. Directly, or via French, from the medieval Latin stem *sensation-* 'perception', from Latin *sensus* (see SENSE).]

sensational /sen sáysh'nəl/ *adj.* **1.** EXTRAORDINARY attracting a great deal of attention and interest ○ *a sensational defeat* **2.** OUTSTANDING exceptionally good (*informal*) ○ *sensational results* **3.** EMPHASIZING LURID DETAILS giving too much emphasis to the most shocking and lurid aspects of sth ○ *sensational coverage of the murder trial* **4.** SENSORY connected with the senses or sense impressions —**sensationally** *adv.*

sensationalism /sen sáysh'nəlizəm/ *n.* **1.** USE OF SHOCKING MATERIAL the practice of emphasizing the most lurid, shocking, and emotive aspects of anything under discussion or investigation, especially by the media **2.** PHILOS THEORY OF KNOWLEDGE the belief that all knowledge is obtained only through the senses —**sensationalist** *n., adj.* —**sensationalistic** /sen sáysh'nə lístik/ *adj.*

sensationalize /sen sáysh'nə līz/ (**-izes, -izing, -ized**), **sensationalise** (**-ises, -ising, -ised**) *vt.* to place excessive emphasis on the most shocking and emotive aspects of a subject —**sensationalization** /sen sáysh'nə lī záysh'n/ *n.*

sense /senss/ *n.* **1.** PHYSICAL FACULTY one of the faculties by which a person or animal obtains information about the physical world **2.** FEELING DERIVED FROM THE SENSES a feeling derived from multiple or subtle sense impressions ○ *Flying filled him with a sense of insecurity.* **3.** ABILITY TO APPRECIATE STH the faculty whereby sb appreciates a particular quality ○ *She has no sense of humour.* **4.** MORAL DISCERNMENT an ability to perceive and be motivated by moral or ethical principles ○ *instil a sense of right and wrong in the children* **5.** INTELLIGENCE the ability to make intelligent decisions or sound judgments ○ *He's got no sense at all.* **6.** POINT useful purpose or good reason ○ *There's no sense in waiting any longer.* **7.** REASONED OPINION an opinion arrived at through reflection or perception, often as a consensus ○ *The sense of the meeting was clearly against the proposal.* **8.** MAIN IDEA the essence or gist of sth ○ *What was the sense of her argument?* **9.** MEANING a single meaning of a word or phrase that may have many **10.** LOGIC TERM'S MEANING the meaning as opposed to the reference of a term or sentence ■ **senses** *npl.* RATIONAL MIND a sensible, rational state of mind ○ *I must be out of my senses.* ■ *vt.* (**senses, sensing, sensed**) **1.** PERCEIVE SB OR STH to perceive sb or sth with a sense or the senses ○ *I sensed a movement behind me.* **2.** INFER STH to understand sth intuitively ○ *He must have sensed that I was disappointed.* **3.** DETECT AND IDENTIFY CHANGE to detect and identify a change in sth ○ *The device senses when the door is opened and sounds the alarm.* [14thC. Directly, and via Old French, from Latin *sensus* 'feeling, perception', from *sens-*, past participle stem of *sentire* 'to feel'.] ◇ **in a sense 1.** considered from a point of view that may not be the most obvious or the most popular **2.** used when saying that sth could be described in a particular way, but that the description is not complete or accurate ◇ **make sense** to be understandable and consistent with reason ◇ **make sense of sth** to understand sth well enough to be able to act on it or evaluate it

WORD KEY: ORIGIN

The Latin word *sentire*, from which **sense** is derived, is also the source of English *assent, consensus, consent, dissent, resent, sensible, sentence, sentiment*, and *sensual*.

WORD KEY: CULTURAL NOTE

Sense and Sensibility, a novel by Jane Austen (1811). Set in Devonshire, Austen's first novel describes the emotional development of two sisters, Elinor and Marianne Dashwood, who live with their widowed mother in a modest cottage. Outwardly, Elinor appears dull and practical, Marianne sensitive and passionate, but the story of their involvement with two seemingly appropriate suitors warns against simplistic character judgments.

sense datum *n.* in the doctrine of phenomenalism, a sensation

sensei /sen sáy/ (*plural* **-sei**) *n.* **1.** MARTIAL ARTS TEACHER sb who teaches one of the martial arts such as karate or tai-chi **2.** FORM OF ADDRESS used as a title to address sb who is a teacher, especially in the martial arts [Late 19thC. From Japanese, 'teacher, instructor', from *sen* 'previous' + *sei* 'birth'.]

senseless /sénssləss/ *adj.* **1.** WITHOUT INTELLIGENCE demonstrating a lack of reason and intelligence ○ *a senseless decision* **2.** UNCONSCIOUS unconscious, or unable to perceive anything ○ *was knocked senseless by the blow* **3.** WITH NO APPARENT PURPOSE apparently or really without purpose or meaning ○ *a senseless activity*

sense organ *n.* an organ such as an eye or ear that is specialized to receive stimuli from the physical world and transmit them via nerve impulses to the brain. Sense organs include the eye, ear, nose, skin, and taste buds of the tongue, which respond to light, sound, airborne chemicals, touch, and chemicals in food and drink, respectively.

sensibilia /sén sə bílli ə/ *npl.* things that can be sensed, considered collectively [Mid-19thC. From Latin, a plural form of *sensibilis* 'perceptible by the senses', from *sensus* (see SENSE).]

sensibility /sénn sə bíllətí/ *n.* (*plural* **-ties**) **1.** CAPACITY TO FEEL the capacity to perceive or feel **2.** EMOTIONAL RESPONSIVENESS the capacity to respond emotionally or aesthetically ○ *the sensibility of a child* **3.** BOT PLANTS' CAPACITY FOR RESPONSE the sensitivity of plants to external stimuli ■ **sensibilities** *npl.* MORAL SENSE sensitivity about moral or ethical issues ○ *careful not to offend their sensibilities*

WORD KEY: USAGE

sensibility or **sensitivity**? ***Sensitivity*** is used in ways corresponding to the meanings of the adjective *sensitive*, and is mainly concerned with physical or emotional reactions of various kinds: *a sensitivity to bright light.* ***Sensibility*** is less closely related in meaning to *sensible* than ***sensitivity*** is to *sensitive*, and chiefly denotes sb's acute perceptions or finer feelings, corresponding to a particular meaning of *sensible*, as in *poetry that appealed to his sensibility.*

sensible /sénsəb'l/ *adj.* **1.** SHOWING GOOD SENSE having or demonstrating sound reason and judgment ○ *a sensible decision* ○ *She's not very sensible.* **2.** PRACTICAL practical, usually comfortable and hard-wearing, and not worn as an adornment ○ *a pair of sensible shoes* **3.** SUBJECT TO PERCEPTION able to be perceived through the senses ○ *sensible objects in the world around us* **4.** AWARE OF STH aware or conscious of sth (*formal*) ○ *not sensible of the tragic mistake he'd made* **5.** CONSCIOUS awake or conscious, and having the capacity to understand [14thC. Directly, and via French *sensible*, from late Latin *sensibilis* 'perceptible by the senses, able to perceive', from the stem *sens-* (see SENSE).] —**sensibleness** *n.* —**sensibly** *adv.*

WORD KEY: USAGE

sensible or **sensitive**? The two words overlap in meaning to some extent in the sense illustrated by the sentence *I am sensible of your difficult situation* ('I can appreciate your difficult situation'). In this meaning, ***sensible*** is normally used to express emotional or intellectual awareness. In a comparable use, ***sensitive*** is followed by *to* and denotes a more involved and finely attuned feeling about or for sth: *He was always sensitive to their needs.*

WORD KEY: SYNONYMS

See Synonyms at ***aware***.

sensible horizon *n.* ASTRON = **horizon** *n.* **2**

sensillum /sen síllәm/ (*plural* **-la** /-síllә/) *n.* a simple sense organ made up of one or a few cells connected by a nerve cell, often found in insects [Early 20thC. From modern Latin, literally 'little sense', from Latin *sensus* (see SENSE).]

sensitive /sénssətiv/ *adj.* **1.** ACUTELY PERCEPTIVE unusually responsive to stimuli from the physical world ○ *a sensitive nose* **2.** DELICATE easily damaged or irritated physically ○ *a toothpaste for people with sensitive teeth* **3.** AFFECTED BY AN EXTERNAL STIMULUS affected in some way by a particular external stimulus such as an allergen (*often used in combination*) ○ *eyes sensitive to light* ○ *a touch-sensitive screen* ○ *a price-sensitive product* **4.** SUBTLE IN ARTISTIC EXPRESSION subtly expressive in one of the arts **5.** THOUGHTFUL AND SYMPATHETIC tactful and sympathetic in relation to the feelings of others **6.** TOUCHY easily offended or annoyed if sth is spoken about ○ *He's very sensitive about his driving.* **7.** REQUIRING TACTFULNESS needing to be dealt with tactfully to avoid embarrassment ○ *a sensitive issue* **8.** SECRET OR CONFIDENTIAL not to be mentioned or divulged ○ *sensitive matters of national security* **9.** ARTISTICALLY IMPRESSIONABLE susceptible to artistic effects, e.g. in music, writing, or painting **10.** ABLE TO SENSE with the capacity to perceive via the sense organs **11.** ABLE TO MEASURE SMALL DIFFERENCES capable of detecting minute changes in levels, conditions, or amounts ○ *a sensitive scientific instrument* **12.** FIN FLUCTUATING volatile and subject to fluctuation ○ *a sensitive market* **13.** PHOTOGRAPHY RESPONSIVE TO LIGHT extremely responsive to radiation, especially to light of a specific wavelength **14.** ELECTRON ENG RESPONSIVE TO SIGNALS able to respond to transmitted signals ■ *n.* PSYCHIC PERSON sb who has clairvoyant or psychic powers [14thC. Directly, and via French, from medieval Latin *sensitivus*, from the Latin stem *sens-* (see SENSE).] —**sensitively** *adv.* —**sensitiveness** *n.* —**sensitivity** /sénzsə tívvəti/ *n.*

WORD KEY: USAGE

See Usage note at ***sensible***.

sensitive plant *n.* **1.** FLOWERING PLANT SENSITIVE TO THE TOUCH a tropical American shrub with purplish flowers that recoils when touched. Latin name: *Mimosa pudica.* **2.** UNDULY SENSITIVE PERSON sb who is easily upset (*informal*)

sensitize /sénssə tīz/ (**-tizes, -tizing, -tized**), **sensitise** (**-tises, -tising, -tised**) *vt.* **1.** MAKE SB SENSITIVE to make sb sensitive, especially to a situation **2.** MAKE SB ALLERGIC to induce undue sensitivity in sb to a particular substance such as a food ingredient or drug so that subsequent exposure to the substance triggers an allergic reaction **3.** PHOTOGRAPHY MAKE FILM SENSITIVE TO LIGHT to make a film, plate, or other medium sensitive to light by coating it with an emulsion [Mid-19thC. Coined from SENSITIVE + -IZE.] —**sensitization** /sénssə tī záysh'n/ *n.* —**sensitizer** /sénssə tīzər/ *n.*

sensitometer /sénssə tómmitər/ *n.* an instrument for measuring degrees of sensitivity, especially one used on photographic materials [Late 19thC. Coined from SENSITIVE + -METER.] —**sensitometry** *n.*

sensor /sénssər/ *n.* a device capable of detecting and responding to physical stimuli such as movement, light, or heat [Mid-20thC. Coined from SENSE or Latin *sens-*, past participle stem of *sentire* 'to sense', + -OR.]

sensoria plural of **sensorium**

sensorial /sén sáwri əl/ *adj.* relating to sensation and the sense organs [Mid-18thC. Coined from SENSORIUM + -AL.] —**sensorially** *adv.*

sensorimotor /sénssəri mṓtər/ *adj.* **1. SENSORY AND MOTOR** relating to both the motor and sensory functions in the brain or the neurological structures underlying these functions **2. OF MOVEMENT CAUSED BY SENSORY STIMULI** relating to motor functions arising from sensory stimuli

sensorimotor stage *n.* the first major stage in Piaget's theory of cognitive development, from birth to approximately two years, in which children begin to understand their world through sensory and motor experience

sensorineural /sénssəri nyóorəl/ *adj.* involving or relating to sensory nerves

sensorium /sen sáwri əm/ (*plural* **-a** /-ri ə/) *n.* **1. BRAIN AREA THAT RESPONDS TO STIMULI** the sensory components of the brain and nervous system that deal with the receiving and interpreting of external stimuli **2. SENSORY FUNCTIONS** all the sensory functions in the body, considered as a single unit [Mid-17thC. From late Latin *sensorium* 'the seat or organ of sensation', from the stem *sens-* (see SENSE).]

sensory /sénssəri/ *adj.* relating to sensation and the sense organs ○ *heightened sensory awareness* [Mid-18thC. Coined from SENSE or Latin *sens-*, past participle stem of *sentire* 'to feel' + -ORY.]

sensory deprivation *n.* the elimination of or a sharp reduction in sensory stimulation, usually as part of an experiment in psychology or as part of repressive interrogation procedures or brainwashing

sensual /sénssyoo əl, -shoo əl/ *adj.* **1. CARNAL** relating to physical or, especially, sexual pleasure **2. SENSORY** relating to the body and the senses as opposed to the mind or the intellect [15thC. From late Latin *sensualis* 'equipped with feeling or sensation', from Latin *sensus* (see SENSE).] —**sensually** *adv.* —**sensualness** *n.*

WORD KEY: USAGE

sensual or **sensuous**? Both words are connected with gratification of the human senses. ***Sensual*** is the older word, and in the seventeenth century it developed special meanings associated with the bodily appetites, especially eating and above all sexual satisfaction: *Her mouth looked sensual and inviting. They enjoyed the sensual pleasures of the table.* About this time the poet John Milton seems to have invented the word ***sensuous*** to refer more specifically to the aesthetic and spiritual senses (seeing, hearing, thinking), and it was taken up by Samuel Taylor Coleridge in the nineteenth century. In current use, it is almost impossible to keep the two sets of meanings apart, since the senses cannot readily be compartmentalized in this way, but it is prudent to have regard for the main distinction when using these words. ***Sensuous***, for example, is the word to use in connection with music or poetry: *The conductor relished the sensuous parts of Ravel's score.*

sensualism /sénssyoo əlizəm, -shoo əlizəm/ *n.* **1. PLEASURE-SEEKING** devotion to sensual gratification **2.** PHILOS, ETHICS = **sensationalism** *n.* 2 —**sensualist** *n.* —**sensualistic** /sénssyoo ə lístik, -shoo ə lístik/ *adj.*

sensuality /sénssyoo álləti, -shoo álləti/ *n.* **1. BEING SENSUAL** the capacity for enjoying the pleasures of the senses **2. BEING PLEASING TO THE SENSES** the quality of being pleasing to the senses

sensuous /sénssyoo əss, -shoo əss/ *adj.* **1. OF SENSE STIMULATION** relating to stimulation of the senses **2. APPRECIATING STIMULATION** enjoying or appreciating pleasurable stimulation of the senses ○ *a sensuous lover* **3. CAUSING STIMULATION** causing pleasurable stimulation of the senses ○ *a sensuous experience* [Mid-17thC. Coined from Latin *sensus* (see SENSE) + -OUS, apparently by John Milton, in order to avoid the lustful overtones that SENSUAL had at the time.] —**sensuously** *adv.* —**sensuousness** *n.*

WORD KEY: USAGE

See Usage note at ***sensual***.

Sensurround /sénssə rownd/ *tdmk.* a trademark for a film sound effect system emitting low-frequency sound signals that are felt by the audience as vibrations

sent past tense, past participle of **send**[1]

sente /sénti/ (*plural* **lisente** /li sénti/) *n.* **1. LESOTHO SUBUNIT OF CURRENCY** a subunit of currency in Lesotho, 100 of which are worth one loti. See table at **currency** **2. COIN WORTH A SENTE** a coin worth one sente [Late 20thC. From Sesotho, 'cent'.]

sentence /séntənss/ *n.* **1.** GRAM **MEANINGFUL LINGUISTIC UNIT** a group of words or a single word that expresses a complete thought, feeling, or idea. It usually contains an explicit or implied subject and a predicate containing a finite verb. **2.** LAW **JUDGMENT** a judgment by a court specifying the punishment of sb convicted of a crime, or the punishment itself ○ *a sentence of 15 years in prison* **3.** LOGIC **WELL-FORMED EXPRESSION** a well-formed expression in a symbolic language ■ *vt.* (**-tences, -tencing, -tenced**) LAW **ALLOCATE SB PUNISHMENT** to allocate a particular punishment to sb convicted of a crime, usually stating its nature and its duration ○ *was sentenced to two years in prison* [13thC. Via French from Latin *sententia* 'feeling, opinion', from *sentient-*, present participle stem of *sentire* 'to feel'.] —**sentencer** *n.*

sentence adverb *n.* an adverb that modifies an entire sentence. 'Frankly' is a sentence adverb in 'Frankly, I don't care'.

WORD KEY: USAGE

See Usage note at ***clearly***, ***hopefully***, and ***thankfully***.

sentence substitute *n.* a single word that, when used in the proper context, meets all the semantic requirements of a sentence. Words such as 'yes' and 'no' are sentence substitutes.

sentencing /séntənssing/ *n.* the phase of a court trial in which a sentence is arrived at and pronounced, or the act of making such a pronouncement

sententia /sen ténshi ə/ (*plural* **-tiae** /-shi ee/) *n.* a short memorable saying (*formal*) [Early 20thC. From Latin (see SENTENCE).]

sentential /sen ténsh'l/ *adj.* relating to sentences in natural language or logic —**sententially** *adv.*

sentential calculus *n.* LOGIC = **propositional calculus**

sententious /sen ténshəss/ *adj.* **1. FULL OF APHORISMS** tending to use, or full of, maxims and aphorisms **2. OVER-MORALIZING** inclined to moralize more than is merited or appreciated **3. PITHY** expressing much in few words [15thC. Directly, and via Old French *sententieux*, from Latin *sententiosus* 'meaningful, pithy', from *sententia* (see SENTENCE).] —**sententiously** *adv.*

sentience /sénsh'nss, -shi ənss/ *n.* **1. AWARENESS** the condition of being conscious or aware **2. FEELING** the quality of emotional response, distinguished from intellectual processes

sentient /sénsh'nt, -shi ənt/ *adj.* **1. CONSCIOUS** capable of feeling and perception ○ *a sentient being* **2. RESPONDING WITH FEELING** capable of responding emotionally rather than intellectually [Mid-17thC. From Latin *sentient-*, present participle stem of *sentire* 'to feel'.] —**sentiently** *adv.*

sentiment /séntimənt/ *n.* **1. MENTAL FEELING** a thought or idea based on a feeling or emotion **2. GENERAL FEELING** a feeling or opinion prevailing among a group of people ○ *The sentiment emerged that we were acting too soon.* **3. UNDERLYING FEELING** an underlying feeling, as distinct from the action that it brings about ○ *His speech was awkward but the sentiment was right.* **4. APPEAL TO FEELING** a calculated appeal to feeling or emotion, especially one that is excessive and unreasoning ○ *The book ends on a note of cheap sentiment.* **5. DEEP FEELING, ESPECIALLY IN ART** refined or tender feeling, especially when expressed in a work of art (*formal*) ■ **sentiments** *npl.* **OPINION** a point of view or judgment on sth ○ *What are her sentiments on the matter?* [14thC. Via French from medieval Latin *sentimentum* 'opinion, feeling', from Latin *sentire* (see SENSE).]

sentimental /sénti mént'l/ *adj.* **1. MAWKISH IN FEELING** affected acutely by emotional matters, often to the point of mawkishness **2. MAWKISH IN EXPRESSION** displaying too much uncontrolled or self-indulgent emotion **3. APPEALING TO TENDER FEELINGS** appealing to or expressing tender, often romantic, feelings ○ *a sentimental portrait of our town* **4. NOSTALGIC** expressing or experiencing tender sadness or nostalgia **5. EXPRESSING DEEP FEELING** expressing deep, refined feeling (*formal*) —**sentimentally** *adv.*

WORD KEY: CULTURAL NOTE

A Sentimental Journey, a novel by Laurence Sterne (1768). Sterne's second and last novel was intended as a riposte to Tobias Smollett's ill-tempered *Travels Through France and Italy* (1766) and even features a Smollett-like curmudgeon called Smellfungus. A rambling account of a journey through France from Calais to Lyons, it is transformed into an engaging work of art by the author's wit, sensitivity, and sharp social observation. Not surprisingly, the word *smellfungus* came to mean a carping faultfinder in the general parlance.

sentimentalism /sénti méntəlizəm/ *n.* **1. EXCESSIVE DISPLAY OF SENTIMENT** a tendency to express or use obvious or powerful feelings or emotions without appealing to reason **2. STH WITH TOO MUCH EMOTION** sth that expresses excessive emotion, especially sth that is self-indulgent or nostalgic —**sentimentalist** *n.*

sentimentality /sénti men tálləti/ *n.* the tendency or practice of indulging in emotion or nostalgia

sentimentalize /sénti méntə līz/ (**-izes, -izing, -ized**), **sentimentalise** (**-ises, -ising, -ised**) *v.* **1.** *vi.* **BE SENTIMENTAL** to indulge excessively in emotion or nostalgia **2.** *vt.* **TREAT SB OR STH TOO EMOTIONALLY** to treat sb or sth, or express sth, with undue emphasis on feeling —**sentimentalization** /sénti méntə lī záysh'n/ *n.*

sentimental value *n.* a value placed on sth because of its emotional associations rather than its monetary worth

sentinel /séntinəl/ *n.* **SENTRY** sb who is assigned the duty of keeping guard ■ *vt.* (**-nels, -nelling, -nelled**) **1. GUARD STH** to stand guard over sth or a group of people **2. PROVIDE A GUARD FOR STH** to provide a guard for sth or for a group of people [16thC. Via French *sentinelle* from Italian *sentinella*, of uncertain origin: possibly ultimately from Italian *sentire* 'to watch', from Latin, 'to perceive'.]

sentry /séntri/ (*plural* **-tries**) *n.* a member of the armed services who is assigned to keep watch to warn of danger and to guard entrances and exits [Early 17thC. Origin uncertain: perhaps a back-formation from *centrinel*, variant of SENTINEL.]

sentry box *n.* a covered shelter for a sentry, typically at an entrance or crossing

Senussi /se nóossi/, **Senusi** *n.* a member of an Islamic religious group in Arabia and North Africa, founded in the 19th century [Late 19thC. From the name of the founder Sīdī Muḥammad ibn 'Alī as- Sanūsī (d. 1859).] —**Senussian** *adj.*

senza /séntsə, -zə/ *prep.* MUSIC without sth indicated by a following Italian noun (*used in musical directions*) ○ *senza ritenuto* [Early 18thC. From Italian, 'without', of uncertain origin: possibly ultimately from Latin *absentia* 'absence', influenced by *sine* 'without'.]

Seoul /sōl/ capital city of South Korea, on the Han River, in the northwest of the country. Capital of Korea from 1392, it became capital city of the newly formed republic, South Korea, when Korea was partitioned in 1947. Population: 10,229,260 (1995).

sep. *abbr.* **1.** sepal **2.** separate **3.** separation

Sep. *abbr.* **1.** CALENDAR September **2.** Septuagint

sepal /sépp'l/ *n.* a modified leaf in the outermost whorl (**calyx**) of a flower. The sepals enclose the petals and other parts. [Early 19thC. Via French from modern Latin *sepalum*, blend of Greek *skepē* 'covering' (perhaps influenced by Latin *separare* 'to separate') and French *pétale* 'petal'.] —**sepalled** *adj.* —**sepalous** *adj.*

sepaloid /séppə loyd/ *adj.* resembling or functioning as a sepal

-sepalous *suffix.* having a particular number or kind of sepals ○ *trisepalous*

separable /séppərəb'l/ *adj.* capable of being divided, taken apart, or removed, either from each other or from sth else —**separability** /séppərə bílləti/ *n.* —**separableness** /séppərəb'lnəss/ *n.* —**separably** *adv.*

separate *adj.* /séppərət/ **1.** APART not touching or connected, not together, or not in the same place ○ *They slept in separate rooms.* **2.** NOT RELATED TO STH ELSE distinct from or unrelated to sth else ○ *I think we should treat that as a separate issue.* **3.** DIFFERENT not shared with sb or sth else ○ *The book will be sent to you under separate cover.* ■ *v.* /séppə rayt/ (**-rates, -rating, -rated**) **1.** *vt.* MOVE OR KEEP STH APART to move two or more people or things away from each other or prevent them from coming into contact with each other ○ *Somehow we got separated in the crowd.* **2.** *vt.* BE BETWEEN THINGS to stand or lie between one person or thing and another **3.** *vt.* MAKE SB OR STH DIFFERENT to be the factor that makes two people or things different from one another ○ *There was something about her that separated her from the other interviewees.* **4.** *vi.* COME APART to come apart or stop being attached or connected **5.** *vi.* PART COMPANY to leave one another and go off in different directions ○ *A crowd had gathered but it separated as soon as the police arrived.* **6.** *vi.* LAW CEASE LIVING AS A COUPLE to stop living together as a couple **7.** *vt.* CATEGORIZE SB OR STH to put sb or sth into different categories or groups **8.** *vt.* SHOW HOW THINGS DIFFER to see or show that two or more things are different or not ○ *We must separate these two issues in the mind of the public.* **9.** *vti.* DIVIDE to split sth, or to be split, into component parts **10.** *vti.* MAKE OR BECOME INDEPENDENT to leave a larger group and become independent, or to cause part of a larger group to leave and form an independent unit **11.** *vt. US* RELEASE OR FIRE SB to dismiss sb from a job or release sb from military service ■ **separates** *npl.* CLOTHES INDIVIDUAL ITEMS OF CLOTHING articles of women's clothing such as blouses, skirts, jackets, and trousers that can be bought as individual items and worn in various combinations [15thC. From Latin *separare*, literally 'to arrange apart', from *parare* 'to make ready' (source of English *prepare*).] —**separately** /séppərətli/ *adv.* —**separateness** /séppərətnəss/ *n.*

separate off *vt.* to divide sb or sth from sb or sth else

separate out *vti.* to come out of a mixture and form a distinct mass, or to make sth do so

separated /séppə raytid/ *adj.* no longer living together as a couple but still legally married

separating funnel *n.* a large funnel that has a valve in its output tube, used to separate liquids that do not mix

separation /séppə ráysh'n/ *n.* **1.** ACTION THAT SEPARATES OR SEPARATE CONDITION the act of separating things or people **2.** STATE OF BEING APART the state of not being with sb else, or the period of time spent apart **3.** PLACE OF MEETING OR SPACE BETWEEN a place, line, or mark that shows where two things meet, or the gap between them **4.** LAW AGREEMENT NOT TO LIVE TOGETHER the act of stopping living together as husband and wife while remaining married, or a formal agreement to do so, especially one made in a court of law **5.** DIVISION splitting into component parts **6.** *US* DEPARTURE FROM GROUP dismissal from a job or release from military service **7.** DUMPING PART OF ROCKET the act of detaching the rear section of a multistage rocket when it is burnt out, or the time when this happens

separation anxiety *n.* a state of anxiety caused in sb, especially a young child, by the thought or fact of being separated from his or her mother or primary caregiver

separationist /séppə ráysh'nist/ *n., adj.* = **separatist**

separation of powers *n.* in the United States, the constitutional requirement that each of the three branches of government, executive, judicial, and legislative, be autonomous and distinct from the others

separatist /séppərətist/ *n.* **1.** ADVOCATE OF BREAKING AWAY sb who breaks away from or who is in favour of breaking away from a religious group, a country, or a group or organization of any sort **2.** SUPPORTER OF SEPARATION OF DIFFERENT GROUPS sb who is in favour of keeping members of different racial, religious, sexual, or cultural groups separate —**separatism** *n.* —**separatistic** /séppərə tístik/ *adj.*

Separatist *n. Can* sb who is in favour of the secession of a province, especially Quebec, from Canada

separative /séppərətiv/ *adj.* tending to become separate or make sth become separate —**separatively** *adv.* —**separativeness** *n.*

separator /séppə raytər/ *n.* sb or sth that separates one thing from another, e.g. a machine for separating cream from milk

sepd. *abbr. US* separated

Sephardi /se faárdi/ (*plural* **-dim** /si faár dim, sə-, se-/) *n.* a Jewish person of Spanish or Portuguese origin, now used loosely to refer to any Jewish person who is not of German or Eastern European descent. ◊ **Ashkenazi** [Mid-19thC. From modern Hebrew, formed from *sĕpārad*, a land of exile mentioned in the Bible, assumed to be Spain.] —**Sephardic** *adj.*

sepia /seé pi ə/ *n.* **1.** REDDISH-BROWN PIGMENT a deep reddish-brown pigment made from the dark liquid in the ink sacs of various species of cuttlefish, or an artificial form of it, used in painting. The ink is used by the cuttlefish as a means of protection. When disturbed, it ejects a stream of ink, which confuses its attacker. **2.** ARTS SEPIA DRAWING OR PHOTOGRAPH a drawing done in sepia or a photograph with a brownish tone **3.** COLOURS DARK BROWN a dark brown colour with a tinge of yellow or red **4.** PHOTOGRAPHY BROWNISH COLOUR IN PHOTOGRAPHS a brownish tone produced, especially in early photographs, by some photographic processes ■ *adj.* DEEP REDDISH-BROWN of a deep reddish-brown colour [14thC. Via Latin from Greek *sēpia* 'cuttlefish' (the original sense in English).]

sepiolite /seépi ə līt/ *n.* a substance like clay, consisting of hydrated magnesium silicate, formed by hydrothermal alteration of basic igneous rocks. = **meerschaum** *n.* 1 [Mid-19thC. Via German *Sepiolith* from Greek *sēpion* 'cuttlefish bone' (because of its similar texture).]

sepoy /seé poy/ *n.* an Indian soldier under British command, especially one who served in the British East India Company [Early 18thC. From Persian and Urdu *sipāhī* 'horseman, soldier'.]

Sepoy Mutiny, **Sepoy Rebellion** *n.* = **Indian Mutiny**

seppuku /se póokoo/ *n.* = **hara-kiri** [Late 19thC. From Japanese, literally 'to cut the abdomen'.]

sepsis /sépsiss/ *n.* the condition or syndrome caused by the presence of microorganisms or their toxins in the tissue or the bloodstream [Late 19thC. From Greek *sēpsis*, from *sēpein* 'to make rotten'.]

sept /sept/ *n.* **1.** CELTIC CLAN a branch of a Scottish or Irish clan **2.** DIVISION OF A PEOPLE a section of a people that believes itself to be descended from one particular ancestor [Early 16thC. Origin uncertain: probably an alteration of SECT.] —**septal** *adj.*

Sept., **Sept** *abbr.* **1.** CALENDAR September **2.** BIBLE Septuagint

septa plural of **septum**

septal /sépt'l/ *adj.* relating to a septum

septarium /sep táiri əm/ (*plural* **-a** /-ri ə/) *n.* a roughly spherical mass of mineral substance containing cracks that have been filled with a crystalline mineral, usually calcite [Late 18thC. From modern Latin, formed from Latin *septum* (see SEPTUM).] —**septarian** *adj.*

septate /sép tayt/ *adj.* ANAT, BOT, ZOOL divided into sections or compartments by septa

September /sep témbər, səp-/ *n.* CALENDAR in the Gregorian calendar, the ninth month of the year, made up of 30 days [Pre-12thC. Directly or via French *septembre* from Latin *September*, from *septem* 'seven'; September was originally the seventh month of the Roman year.]

September Massacre *n.* the massacre of hundreds of prisoners by Paris mobs in September 1792, during the French Revolution. The killings were caused by fears of a counter-revolution by royalist prisoners, but most of those who were killed were ordinary criminals.

Septembrist /sep témbrist, səp-/ *n.* a member of the Paris mob that carried out the September Massacre in 1792

septenary /séptinəri, sep teénəri/ *adj.* **1.** RELATING TO 7 relating to the number seven **2.** CONTAINING 7 made up of seven people or things **3.** = **septennial** *adj.* **1**, **septennial** *adj.* **2** ■ *n.* (*plural* **-ries**) **1.** NUMBER 7 the number seven **2.** GROUP OF 7 a group of seven people or things **3.** 7 YEARS a period of seven years **4.** POETRY LINE OF VERSE CONTAINING 7 FEET a line of verse that contains seven metrical feet [15thC. From Latin *septenarius*, from *septeni* 'seven each', from *septem* 'seven'.]

septennial /sep ténni əl/ *adj.* **1.** FOR 7 YEARS lasting seven years **2.** HAPPENING EVERY 7 YEARS occurring once every seven years ■ *n.* STH HAPPENING EVERY 7 YEARS sth that happens every seven years [Mid-17thC. Formed from Latin *septennium*.] —**septennially** *adv.*

septennium /sep ténni əm/ (*plural* **-niums** *or* **-nia** /-ni ə/) *n.* a period of seven years (*formal*) [Mid-19thC. From Latin, formed from *septem* 'seven' + *annus* 'year'.]

septet /sep tét/, **septette** *n.* **1.** MUSIC 7 MUSICAL PERFORMERS a group of seven instrumentalists or singers **2.** MUSIC MUSIC FOR 7 PERFORMERS a musical piece composed for seven instrumentalists or singers **3.** GROUP OF 7 a group of seven people or things [Early 19thC. Via German *Septett* from Latin *septem* 'seven'.]

septi- *prefix.* seven ○ *septivalent* [From Latin *septem* (see SEPTET)]

septic /séptik/ *adj.* **1.** POISONED full of or generating pus **2.** INVOLVING SEPSIS relating to, involving, or causing sepsis [Early 17thC. Via Latin *septicus* from Greek *sēptikos*, from *sēpein* 'to make rotten'.] —**septically** *adv.* —**septicity** /sep tíssəti/ *n.*

septicaemia /sépti seémi ə/ *n.* a disease caused by toxic microorganisms in the bloodstream. US term **septicemia** [Mid-19thC. Formed from Latin *septicus* (see SEPTIC).] —**septicaemic** *adj.*

septicemia *n. US* = **septicaemia** —**septicemic** /sépti seémik/ *adj.*

septicidal /sépti sīd'l/ *adj.* used to describe a fruit that splits open along the septa, dividing the component carpels [Early 19thC. Formed from SEPTUM + Latin *-cidere*, from *caedere* 'to cut'.] —**septicidally** *adv.*

septic tank *n.* a tank, usually underground, in which human waste matter is decomposed by bacteria

Sept-Îles /se teél/ city on the northern shore of the St Lawrence River in southeastern Quebec, Canada. Population: 28,005 (1996).

septillion /sep tíllyən/ (*plural* **-lions** *or* **-lion**) *n.* **1.** *US* 10^{24} the number equal to 10^{24}, written as 1 followed by 24 zeros **2.** 10^{42} the number equal to 10^{42}, written as 1 followed by 42 zeros (*dated*) [Late 17thC. From French, formed from *sept* 'seven' + *-illion* as in *million*.] —**septillion** *adj., pron.* —**septillionth** *adj.*

septime /sep teém/ *n.* in fencing, the seventh of eight positions from which a parry or attack can be made [Mid-18thC. From Latin *septimus* 'seventh', from *septem* 'seven'.]

septuagenarian /séptyoo əjə náiri ən/ *n.* SB IN THE 8TH DECADE OF LIFE sb who is between 70 and 79 years old ■ *adj.* BETWEEN 70 AND 79 between 70 and 79 years old [Early 18thC. Formed from Latin *septuaginarius*, ultimately from *septuaginta* 'seventy'.]

Septuagesima /séptyoo ə jéssimə/ *n.* CALENDAR the third Sunday before Lent in the Christian calendar [14thC. From Latin *septuagesima (dies)* 'seventieth (day)', from *septuaginta* 'seventy'. Perhaps because it precedes Sexagesima, or perhaps referring to the seventy days between Septuagesima and the Saturday after Easter.]

Septuagint /séptyoo əjint/ *n.* a Greek translation of the Hebrew Bible made in the 3rd and 2nd centuries BC to meet the needs of Greek-speaking Jewish people outside Palestine. The Septuagint contains some books not in the Hebrew canon. [Mid-16thC. From Latin *septuaginta* 'seventy' (because it is said that about seventy translators worked on it).]

septum /séptəm/ (*plural* **-ta** /-tə/) *n.* **1.** ANAT, BOT THIN PARTITION IN AN ORGANISM a thin partition or membrane dividing sth into two or more cavities such as the tissue separating the nostrils or the internal dividing walls in the seed heads of poppies **2.** ENG PARTITION IN A MACHINE a thin partition that separates components in a machine [Mid-17thC. From Latin, literally 'partition', formed from *sepire* 'to enclose', from *sepes* 'hedge'.]

septuple /séptyòop'l, -tyóop'l/ *adj.* **1.** 7 TIMES AS MUCH seven times as many or as much as sth else **2.** HAVING 7 PARTS consisting of seven parts ■ *vti.* (**-ples, -pling, -pled**) INCREASE BY 7 TIMES to multiply sth by seven, or become seven times as much or as many (*formal*) [Early 17thC. From late Latin *septuplus*, from Latin *septem* 'seven'.]

septuplet /séptyŏŏplət, -tyŏŏplət/ *n.* **1. ONE OF 7 BORN TOGETHER** any one of seven people or animals born to the same mother at one time **2. GROUP OF 7** a group of seven people or things **3.** MUSIC **GROUP OF 7 NOTES** a group of seven notes to be played or sung in the time of four, six, or eight of the same notated value [Late 19thC. Formed from SEPTUPLE, modelled on *triplet*.]

sepulcher *n., vt.* US = **sepulchre**

sepulchral /si-/ *adj.* **1. DISMAL** suggesting or possessing the characteristics associated with the grave, e.g. gloominess **2. OF SEPULCHRES** relating to burial vaults or funerals and burials (*formal*) —**sepulchrally** *adv.*

sepulchre /sépp'lkər/ *n.* **1. BURIAL PLACE** a vault in which sb is buried. US = **sepulcher 2. ALCOVE FOR EUCHARISTIC ITEMS** in medieval churches, an alcove in which the elements of the Eucharist were kept between Good Friday and the Easter rites (*archaic*) ■ *vt.* (**sepulchres, sepulchring, sepulchred**) **PUT A CORPSE IN A BURIAL VAULT** to put a dead body into a sepulchre (*literary*) [12thC. Via Old French *sépulchre* from Latin *sepulc(h)rum*, from *sepult-*, past participle stem of *sepelire* 'to bury'.]

sepulture /sépp'lchər/ *n.* the act of putting a dead body in a grave or tomb (*formal or archaic*) [14thC. Via French from Latin *sepultura*, from *sepult-* (see SEPULCHRE).]

seq. *abbr.* sequel

sequacious /si kwáyshəss/ *adj.* **1. LOGICAL** argued, or developing an argument, in a logically consistent and coherent way (*formal*) **2. UNTHINKINGLY OBEDIENT** too willing to follow a leader uncritically (*archaic*) [Early 17thC. Formed from Latin *sequax*, 'inclined to follow', from *sequi* 'to follow'.] —**sequaciously** *adv.* —**sequaciousness** *n.* —**sequacity** /si kwássəti/ *n.*

sequel /seékwəl/ *n.* **1. CONTINUATION OF A STORY** a film, novel, or play that continues a story begun in a previous film, novel, or play **2. STH FOLLOWING STH ELSE** sth that happens after sth else, especially as a consequence of it [15thC. Directly or via Old French from Latin *sequel(l)a*, from *sequi* 'to follow'.]

sequela /si kweélə/ (*plural* **-ae** /-lee/) *n.* a disease or disorder that is caused by a preceding disease or injury in the same individual [Late 18thC. From Latin (see SEQUEL).]

sequence /seékwənss/ *n.* **1. SERIES OF THINGS** a number of things arranged in a particular order or connected in some way, or a number of actions or events that happen one after another ○ *Can you recall the sequence of events?* **2. ORDER OF THINGS** the order in which things are arranged, actions are carried out, or events happen **3.** CINEMA **SECTION OF FILM** a section of a film showing a single incident or set of related actions or events ○ *a chase sequence* **4.** CARDS **CARDS OF CONSECUTIVE VALUES** three or more consecutive playing cards, usually of the same suit **5.** MUSIC **REPEATED MUSICAL PHRASE** a musical passage or chant consisting of three or more related short phrases repeated several times at successively higher or lower pitch levels **6.** CHR **HYMN** in the Roman Catholic Church, a hymn sung or said between the gradual and the gospel **7.** MATH **ORDERED SET OF ELEMENTS** an ordered set of elements that can be put into a one-to-one correspondence with the set of positive integers **8.** BIOCHEM **ORDER OF MOLECULAR ELEMENTS** the order of the constituent subunits of a large biological molecule, e.g. the order of amino acids in a protein or the order of nucleotides in a nucleic acid. The sequence determines the molecule's biological properties, e.g. its catalytic properties, or the nature of its genetic information. ■ *vt.* (**-quences, -quencing, -quenced**) **1. PUT OR DO THINGS IN ORDER** to arrange things or perform actions in a definite order **2.** BIOCHEM **DETERMINE MOLECULE'S SEQUENCE** to determine the sequence of a biological molecule such as a protein or nucleic acid [14thC. Via late Latin *sequentia* 'what follows' from Latin *sequent-*, present participle stem of *sequi* 'to follow'. The word originally denoted a hymn or chant that followed the gradual.]

WORD KEY: ORIGIN

The Latin word *sequi*, from which ***sequence*** is derived, is also the source of English *consecutive, consequence, ensue, obsequious, persecute, prosecute, pursue, second, sect, sequal, set, subsequent, sue,* and *suit.*

sequence of tenses *n.* the grammatical relationship that causes the tense of a verb in a subordinate clause to be influenced or dictated by the tense of the verb in the related main clause

sequencer /seékwənssər/ *n.* **1.** ELECTRON ENG **DEVICE FOR SORTING DATA** an instrument for sorting information into the correct order for data processing **2.** MUSIC **ELECTRONIC DEVICE FOR STORING MUSIC** an electronic device or software that digitally stores sequences of musical notes, chords, or rhythms that can be transmitted as required to an electronic musical instrument such as a synthesizer **3.** BIOCHEM **DEVICE FOR DETERMINING SEQUENCES** an apparatus for automatically determining the sequence of the constituent subunits of a protein, nucleic acid, or other biological molecule

sequent /seékwənt/ *adj.* **1. CONSEQUENT** following as a consequence or result (*formal*) **2. FOLLOWING** following one after another (*formal or archaic*) ■ *n.* **1. CONSEQUENCE** a consequence or result (*formal*) **2.** LOGIC **FORMAL LOGICAL REPRESENTATION** a formal representation of an argument showing that an element is a theorem [Mid-16thC. Directly or via French from Latin *sequent-* (see SEQUENCE).] —**sequently** *adv.*

sequential /si kwénsh'l/ *adj.* **1. IN SEQUENCE** happening in a particular order or forming a particular sequence **2. RESULTING** being a consequence or result of sth else [Early 19thC. Formed from SEQUENCE, modelled on *consequence, consequential*.] —**sequentiality** /si kwénshi álləti/ *n.* —**sequentially** /si kwénsh'li/ *adv.*

sequential access *n.* a way of accessing and reading a computer file by starting at the beginning. ◊ **direct access**

sequential scanning *n.* a system that scans a television picture using lines in a numerical sequence. ◊ **interlaced scanning**

sequester /si kwéstər/ (**-ters, -tering, -tered**) *vt.* **1. PUT SB INTO ISOLATION** to put sb in an isolated or lonely place away from other people, the pressures of everyday life, or possible disturbances (*formal*) **2.** LAW **TAKE SB'S PROPERTY TO COVER AN OBLIGATION** to take legal possession of sb's property temporarily until a debt that person owes is paid, a dispute is settled, or a court order obeyed **3.** INTERNAT LAW **TAKE AN ENEMY'S PROPERTY** to demand or seize the property of an enemy [14thC. Directly or via French *séquestrer* from late Latin *sequestrare* 'to place in safe keeping', from *sequester* 'trustee', literally 'follower'.] —**sequestrable** *adj.*

sequestrant /si kwés-/ *n.* an agent that removes ions from a chemical solution, often used in horticulture to treat soil that has lime in it

sequestrate /seékwə strayt, si kwé s-/ (**-trates, -trating, -trated**) *vt.* **1. TAKE SB'S PROPERTY TEMPORARILY** to take legal possession of sb's property temporarily until a debt that person owes is paid, a dispute is settled, or a court order obeyed **2.** *Scotland* **DECLARE SB BANKRUPT** in Scottish law, to declare sb bankrupt **3.** *Scotland* **TAKE BANKRUPT'S PROPERTY** in Scottish law, to hand over the property of a bankrupt to a trustee so that it can be used to pay off the bankrupt's debts **4. ISOLATE SB OR STH** to isolate or separate sb or sth (*archaic*) [15thC. From late Latin *sequestrat-*, past participle stem of *sequestrare* (see SEQUESTER).] —**sequestrator** /seékwi straytər/ *n.*

sequestration /seé kwe stráysh'n, sék-/ *n.* **1. CONFISCATING OR BEING CONFISCATED** the act or process of legally confiscating sb's property temporarily until a debt that person owes is paid, a dispute is settled, or a court order obeyed **2.** INTERNAT LAW **SEIZING OR BEING SEIZED** the seizing of an enemy's property, or the fact or process of being seized **3. GOING INTO OR BEING IN ISOLATION** the act of going into or putting sb in an isolated place, away from people or everyday pressures, or the fact of being in such a place (*formal*) **4.** CHEM **ION-BINDING PROCESS** the chemical process of binding an ion, especially a metallic ion, in a coordination complex

sequestrum /si kwéstrəm/ (*plural* **-tra**) *n.* a fragment of dead tissue, usually bone, that separates from surrounding living tissue. It may be seen in X-rays of inflammatory bone disease as a dense region surrounded by a fibrous envelope. [Mid-19thC. From medieval Latin *sequestrum* 'sequestration', from late Latin *sequester* (see SEQUESTER).] —**sequestral** *adj.*

sequin /seékwin/ *n.* **1.** FASHION **SMALL SHINY CLOTHING DECORATION** a small round flat piece of shiny metal or plastic that is sewn onto clothing as a decoration, usually in large numbers **2. sequin, zechin, zecchino** (*plural* **-ni** *or* **-nos**) MONEY **FORMER GOLD COIN** a gold coin that was used in Venice and Turkey between the 16th and 18th centuries [Late 16thC. Via French from Italian *zecchino*, from *zecca* 'mint', from Arabic *sikka* 'coin, die for making coins'.] —**sequined** *adj.*

sequoia /si kwóy ə/ (*plural* **-a** *or* **-as**) *n.* a large coniferous tree of the bald cypress family, native to California. Genus: *Sequoia*. [Mid-19thC. From modern Latin, named after SEQUOYA.]

Sequoia National Park park in south-central California, established in 1890. It includes Mount Whitney, and is noted for its giant sequoia trees. Area: 1629 sq. km/629 sq. mi.

ser. *abbr.* **1.** serial **2.** series **3.** sermon

sera plural of **serum**

serac /sə rák/, **sérac** *n.* a ridge, pinnacle, or block of ice in the crevasses or slope of a glacier [Mid-19thC. From Swiss French *sérac*, originally 'kind of firm white cheese', of uncertain origin: probably from Latin *serum* 'whey' (source of English *serum*).]

seraglio /sə ráali ō/ (*plural* **-glios**) *n.* **1. HAREM** the women's quarters in a Muslim house, or the women themselves **2. PALACE** a Turkish palace, especially the Ottoman sultan's palace at Istanbul [Late 16thC. From Italian *serraglio*, alteration of Turkish *saray* 'palace', from Persian *sarāī* 'inn'; influenced by Italian *serraglio* 'cage', ultimately from Latin *sera* 'bolt'.]

serail /sə rí/ *n.* = **seraglio** [Late 16thC. Via French *sérail* from Italian *serraglio* (see SERAGLIO).]

serape /sə ráapi, -pay/, **sarape** *n.* a usually brightly coloured woollen blanket worn as a cloak by men in Mexico and Central and South America [Early 19thC. From Mexican Spanish *sarape*.]

seraph /sérrəf/ (*plural* **-aphs** *or* **-aphim** /sérrəfim/) *n.* an angel of the highest rank in the traditional medieval hierarchy of nine categories of angels. In the Book of Isaiah they are described as having six wings. [Pre-12thC. Via late Latin *seraphim* (plural) from Hebrew *sĕrāpīm*.] —**seraphic** /sə ráffik/ *adj.* —**seraphically** *adv.*

Serb /surb/ *n.* a member of a Slavic people living mainly in Serbia, where they constitute the largest ethnic group, and other areas of the Balkan region [Early 19thC. From Serbo-Croat *Srb*.]

Serb. *abbr.* **1.** Serbia **2.** Serbian

Serbia /súrbiə/ republic in southeastern Europe that, together with Montenegro, makes up the Federal Republic of Yugoslavia. Capital: Belgrade. Population: 9,979,116 (1996). Area: 88,361 sq. km/34,116 sq. mi.

Serbian /súrbi ən/ *n.* LANG **DIALECT OF SERBO-CROATIAN** the dialect of Serbo-Croatian as it is spoken in Serbia and adjacent areas, written in a Cyrillic alphabet ■ *adj.* **OF SERBIA** relating to Serbia or its people, language, or culture

Serbo-Croatian /súrbō krō áysh'n/, **Serbo-Croat** /súrbō krṓ at/ *n.* **1.** LANG **SLAVIC LANGUAGE** the language spoken by the Serbians and Croatians, which belongs to the Slavic branch of Indo-European **2.** PEOPLES **SPEAKER OF SERBO-CROATIAN** sb whose native language is Serbo-Croatian ■ *adj.* **OF SERBO-CROATIAN** relating to the Serbo-Croatian language or its speakers

SERC *abbr.* Science and Engineering Research Council

sere[1] /seer/, **sear** *adj.* dry and withered (*archaic or literary*) [Old English *sēar* 'withered'. Ultimately from an Indo-European word that is also the ancestor of English *austere*.]

WORD KEY: SYNONYMS

See Synonyms at *dry*.

sere[2] /seer/ *n.* the series of different communities of plants and animals that occupy a given site and create a stable system during the process of ecological succession [Early 20thC. From Latin *serere* 'to join or connect' (source of English *series*).] —**seral** *adj.*

serein /se ráyn, sə ráN/ *n.* in the tropics, a very fine rain that falls from a clear sky at dusk [Late 19thC. Via French from, ultimately, Latin *serum* 'evening', a form of *serus* 'late' (source of English *soirée*).]

serenade /sérrə náyd/ *n.* **1. LOVE SONG** a song or the performance of a song used to court sb, traditionally sung by a man in the evening outside a woman's window **2. INSTRUMENTAL COMPOSITION FOR A SMALL ENSEMBLE** an instrumental work similar to a sonata, designed for evening outdoor performance by a small ensemble of musicians ■ *vti.* (**-nades, -nading, -naded**) **PERFORM A LOVE SONG** to sing or play a serenade ○ *A mockingbird serenades us every evening.* [Mid-17thC. Via French *sérénade* from Italian *serenata* (see SERENATA).] —**serenader** *n.*

serenata /sérrə naátə/ *n.* **1. 18C CHORAL WORK** a choral work popular during the 18th century, often based on a religious text and having solos and duets **2.** = **serenade** *n.* 1, **serenade** *n.* 2 [Mid-18thC. From Italian, formed from *sereno* 'serene', from Latin *serenus* (source of English *serene*). The meaning of the Italian word was influenced by Italian *sera* 'evening'.]

serendipity /sérrən díppəti/ *n.* a natural gift for making useful discoveries quite by accident [Mid-18thC (but rare before the 20thC). From *The Three Princes of Serendip*, an originally Persian story about three princes who had this ability; 'Serendip' is supposedly a former name of Sri Lanka.] —**serendipitous** *adj.* —**serendipitously** *adv.*

WORD KEY: USAGE

Extended senses : The phrase *serendipitous discovery*, which is often seen, manages to suggest that ***serendipity*** is nothing other than good luck. However, the idea of a discovery is necessary to the word, and ***serendipity*** and ***serendipitous*** are nonstandard in senses unrelated to making happy discoveries by chance.

serene /sə réen/ *adj.* **1. CALM AND UNTROUBLED** without worry, stress, or disturbance **2. CLOUDLESS** bright and without clouds [15thC. From Latin *serenus* 'clear, calm'.] —**serenely** *adv.* —**sereneness** *n.* —**serenity** /sə rénnəti/ *n.*

WORD KEY: SYNONYMS

See Synonyms at *calm*.

Serene /sə réen/ *adj.* a word used in the titles of members of certain European royal families, e.g. that of Monaco

Serengeti National Park /sérrəng gétti-/ national park on the plains of western Tanzania. Established in 1941, it is home to many species of large mammals and other wildlife. Area: 14,750 sq. km/5,700 sq. mi.

serf /surf/ *n.* **1. MEDIEVAL FARMWORKER** an agricultural worker, especially in feudal Europe, who cultivated land belonging to a landowner, and who was bought and sold with the land. A serf was little better off than an enslaved labourer. Without the landowner's permission, a serf could not leave his or her plot of land or village, marry, or change occupation. **2. ENSLAVED LABOURER** sb who is, or is like, an enslaved labourer [15thC. Via French from Latin *servus* 'slave'.] —**serfdom** *n.* —**serfhood** *n.*

serge /surj/ *n.* a strong cloth, usually made of wool but sometimes of other fibres, used especially to make coats, jackets, and trousers [14thC. Via Old French *sarge* from, ultimately, Latin *serica lana* 'silken wool', from *sericus* (see SILK).]

sergeant /saárjənt/ *n.* **1. MILITARY RANK** the rank immediately above corporal in the British Army, Royal Air Force, or Royal Marines **2. POLICE RANK** the rank between constable and inspector in the British police force **3. sergeant, serjeant** = **sergeant at arms 4. sergeant, serjeant** = **serjeant at law** (*archaic*) [12thC. Via Old French *sergent* 'servant' (the original sense in English) from Latin *servient-*, present participle stem of *servire* (see SERVE).] —**sergeancy** *n.* —**sergeantship** *n.*

sergeant at arms (*plural* **sergeants at arms**), **serjeant at arms** (*plural* **serjeants at arms**) *n.* **1. SB RESPONSIBLE FOR KEEPING ORDER** sb appointed to keep order within an organization, e.g. a parliament or court of law, and to perform certain other duties, e.g. making arrests **2. ARMED ATTENDANT** in the past, an armed attendant for a noble or monarch

sergeant at law *n.* = **serjeant at law**

sergeant fish *n.* **1.** = **cobia 2.** = **snook** [Said to be so named because of the stripes on its body, like those on a sergeant's arm]

sergeant major (*plural* **sergeants major** *or* **sergeant majors**) *n.* **1. ARMY RANK** in the British armed forces, the second highest rank of noncommissioned officer, immediately below regimental sergeant major, or sb who holds this rank **2.** *US* **MILITARY ADMINISTRATIVE OFFICER** the chief noncommissioned administrative officer at a US Army, Air Force, or Marine Corps headquarters unit **3.** ZOOL **LARGE TROPICAL FISH** a large damselfish of tropical Atlantic waters that ranges from blue-green to yellow in colour with black vertical stripes. Latin name: *Abudefduf saxatilis.*

Sergt *abbr.* sergeant

serial /séeri əl/ *n.* PUBL **1. STORY IN PARTS** a story that is published or broadcast in parts, normally at regular intervals **2. REGULAR NEWSPAPER OR MAGAZINE** a magazine or newspaper published at regular intervals, especially weekly or monthly ■ *adj.* **1. IN A SERIES** in or forming a series, or done or doing sth repeatedly in a series **2. PRODUCED IN PARTS** published or broadcast in parts, usually at regular intervals **3.** COMPUT **SENDING COMPUTER INFORMATION SEQUENTIALLY** used to describe a form of data communication in which the individual bits that comprise each byte or character travel one after another through a single wire. ◊ **parallel 4.** MUSIC **RELATING TO MUSICAL COMPOSITION** used to describe a method of musical composition in which all 12 chromatic tones of the octave appear in strict order with no note repeated before the sequence is completed [Mid-19thC. Formed from SERIES.] —**serially** *adv.*

serialism /séeri əlizəm/ *n.* a method of musical composition in which all 12 chromatic tones of the octave appear in strict order with no note repeated before the sequence is completed —**serialist** *n.*

serialize /séeri ə līz/ (**-izes, -izing, -ized**), **serialise** (**-ises, -ising, -ised**) *vti.* to publish or broadcast a story in parts at intervals, or to be divided into parts suitable for publishing or broadcasting —**serialization** /séeri ə lī záysh'n/ *n.*

serial killer *n.* sb who murders a number of people over a period of time, especially sb who uses the same method each time —**serial killing** *n.*

serial monogamy *n.* the idea or practice of having only one sexual partner at a time and entering another relationship when one comes to an end

serial number *n.* a set of numbers assigned to, and usually marked on, each of a series of identical products, e.g. television sets, cars, paper money, or computers

serial rights *npl.* the right to publish a story or book in parts as a serial

seriate /séeri it/ *adj.* arranged in rows or a series (*formal*) —**seriately** *adv.*

seriatim /séeri áytim, sérri-, -aátim/ *adv.* one after another, or in a series [15thC. From medieval Latin, formed from Latin *series* (see SERIES).]

sericeous /sə ríshəss/ *adj.* **1. COVERED WITH SOFT HAIRS** covered with small soft silky hairs **2. SILKY** having the soft smooth feel of silk (*formal*) [Late 18thC. Formed from Latin *sericus* 'silken', ultimately from Greek *Sēres*, Greek name of the Asian people who originally made silk, thought to be the Chinese.]

sericin /sérris sin/ *n.* a gelatinous protein that binds together the filaments of a silk fibre [Mid-19thC. Formed from Latin *sericum* 'silk', a form of *sericus* (see SERICEOUS).]

sericulture /sérri-/ *n.* the commercial breeding of silkworms for their silk [Mid-20thC. Shortening of French *sériciculture*, from Latin *sericum* 'silk', a form of *sericus* (see SERICEOUS).] —**sericultural** /sérri kúlchərəl/ *adj.* —**sericulturist** *n.*

seriema /sérri éemə/ (*plural* **-ma** *or* **-mas**) *n.* either one of two large, crested, mainly ground-dwelling birds native to South America that have long tails and legs. Family: Cariamidae. [Mid-19thC. Via modern Latin from Tupi *siriema*, probably meaning 'crested'.]

series /séer eez/ (*plural* **-ries**) *n.* **1. THINGS ONE AFTER ANOTHER** a number of similar or related things coming one after another ○ *a series of lectures on modern philosophy* **2.** BROADCAST **SET OF BROADCAST PROGRAMMES** a set of regularly broadcast programmes, each of which is complete in itself **3.** PUBL **SIMILAR PUBLICATIONS FROM ONE ORGANIZATION** a number of books, pamphlets, or periodicals brought out by one company or organization on the same or related topics or in the same format **4.** SPORTS **SET OF MATCHES BETWEEN SAME TEAMS** in some sports, e.g. cricket and baseball, a set of matches between the same teams **5.** COLLECTING **RELATED ITEMS PRODUCED AT ONE TIME** a number of related items, e.g. stamps or coins of different values, brought out at one time **6.** CHEM **RELATED CHEMICALS** a group of related chemical compounds that are similar in structure or properties **7.** MATH **SUM OF SEQUENCE OF TERMS** the indicated sum of a finite or infinite sequence of terms, each term being added to those that precede it. ◊ **geometric series 8.** GEOL **ROCK LAYER** a succession of rock strata deposited during a particular period of geological time **9.** ELECTRON ENG **ARRANGEMENT OF ELECTRIC ELEMENTS** a set of two or more electronic components through which current flows in sequence **10.** MUSIC **SET OF 12 NOTES** a set of 12 notes, the 12 chromatic pitches of an octave, in which no pitch is repeated. This forms the basis for serial composition. **11.** GRAM **TWO OR MORE COORDINATE ELEMENTS** a sequence of two or more elements in a sentence that have the same grammatical structure. ◊ **parallelism** [Early 17thC. From Latin, formed from *serere* 'to join or connect'.] ◇ **in series** connected in a circuit so that the same current flows through each component in sequence

WORD KEY: ORIGIN

The Latin word *serere*, from which ***series*** is derived, is also the source of English *assert*, *insert*, and *serial*.

serif /sérrif/ *n.* a short decorative line at the start or finish of a stroke in a letter [Mid-19thC. Origin uncertain: perhaps from Dutch *schreef* 'dash, line'.]

serigraph /sérri graaf, -graf/ *n.* = **silkscreen** [Late 19thC. Formed from Latin *sericum* 'silk', a form of *sericus* (see SERICEOUS).] —**serigrapher** /sə ríggrəfər/ *n.* —**serigraphy** *n.*

serin /sérrin/ (*plural* **-ins** *or* **-in**) *n.* a yellowish or greyish finch found in North Africa and the Mediterranean region. The best-known serin is the canary. Genus: *Serinus.* [Mid-16thC. From French, literally 'canary' (the original sense in English), of uncertain origin: perhaps ultimately from Greek.]

serine /séer een, sérreen/ *n.* an amino acid that is obtained in the hydrolysis of proteins and is a precursor in the biosynthesis of glycine, choline, and other metabolites. Formula: $C_3H_7O_3N$. [Late 19thC. From German *Serin*, from Latin *sericum* 'silk', a form of *sericus* (see SERICEOUS).]

seringa /sə ríng gə/ *n.* a Brazilian tree that yields rubber. Genus: *Hevea.* [Mid-18thC. Via French and Portuguese from Latin *syringa* (see SYRINGA).]

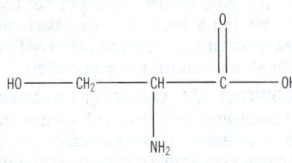

Serine

seriocomic /se͞eri ō kómmik/, **seriocomical** /-kómmik'l/ *adj.* with both serious and comic elements —**serio-comically** *adv.*

serious /se͞eri əss/ *adj.* **1.** VERY BAD OR GREAT very great, bad, dangerous, harmful, or difficult to handle **2.** IMPORTANT important or grave enough to require thought and attention ○ *There are serious arguments against this proposal.* **3.** LIKELY TO SUCCEED having a possibility of success or showing an intention to succeed ○ *Only two of the five applicants can be considered serious candidates for the post.* **4.** THOUGHT-FUL OR THOUGHT-PROVOKING discussing or dealing with matters in a thoughtful or thought-provoking way as opposed to a superficial or merely entertaining manner ○ *a serious discussion of the issues* **5.** NEEDING CAREFUL THOUGHT OR ATTENTION needing careful thought, study, or attention ○ *a serious proposal* **6.** NOT LIGHT-HEARTED quiet, thoughtful, not laughing or making jokes very often, and always being sensible **7.** MEANING STH LITERALLY not joking, pretending, or exaggerating about sth ○ *Do you think she's serious about helping us out?* **8.** SUBSTANTIAL substantial or sustained rather than trivial or insignificant (*informal*) ○ *I've invested serious money in this endeavour.* **9.** DEDICATED TO STH showing great interest in or commitment to an endeavour, skill, or pastime ○ *a serious stamp collector* [15thC. Via French *sérieux* or late Latin *seriosus* from Latin *serius*.] —**seriousness** *n.*

seriously /se͞eri əssli/ *adv.* **1.** BADLY in a great, bad, dangerous, harmful, or problematic way ○ *seriously ill* **2.** GRAVELY in a grave and thoughtful way, without being lighthearted or dismissive ○ *We have to take this threat seriously.* **3.** TRULY in a true or literal way, without exaggeration or deceit ○ *Do you seriously expect me to go along with this?* **4.** EXTREMELY to a great or remarkable extent (*informal*) ○ *I'm getting seriously fed up with her arrogance.*

serious-minded *adj.* earnest and taking an interest in matters that are weighty and important

serjeant *n.* = sergeant (*formal*)

serjeant at arms (*plural* **serjeants at arms**) *n.* = sergeant at arms

serjeant at law (*plural* **serjeants at law**), **sergeant at law** (*plural* **sergeants at law**) *n.* an obsolete term for a high-ranking English barrister (*archaic*)

sermon /súrmən/ *n.* **1.** RELIGIOUS TALK a talk on a religious or moral subject given by a member of the clergy as part of a religious service **2.** LONG LECTURE ON BEHAVIOUR a long and tedious talk, especially one telling sb how or how not to behave [12thC. Via Anglo-Norman *sermun* from Latin *sermo* 'talk, conversation'.] —**sermonic** /sur mónnik/ *adj.*

sermonize /súrmə nīz/ (**-izes, -izing, -ized**), **sermonise** (**-ises, -ising, -ised**) *vti.* to give sb a long tedious talk about how or how not to behave —**sermonizer** *n.*

Sermon on the Mount *n.* a collection of Jesus Christ's religious and moral teachings recorded in Matthew's Gospel in the Bible, much of which Jesus Christ set out in a speech to his disciples from a hillside

sero- *prefix.* serum ○ *serology* [From SERUM]

seroconvert /se͞erō kən vúrt/ (**-verts, -verting, -verted**) *vi.* to produce specific antibodies in response to the presence of an antigen such as a bacterium or virus —**seroconversion** *n.*

serology /seer rólləji/ *n.* the branch of medicine concerned with the study of blood serum and its constituents, especially its role in protecting the human body against disease —**serologic** /se͞eerə lójjik/ *adj.* —**serologist** /seer rólləjist/ *n.*

seronegative /se͞erō néggətiv/ *adj.* after a blood test, showing no immunological evidence of infection, either current or previous, with a particular bacterium, virus, or other infective agent

seropositive /se͞erō pózzitiv/ *adj.* after a blood test, showing immunological evidence of infection, either current or previous, with a particular bacterium, virus, or other agent

seropurulent /se͞erō pyoͦoͦroͦoͦlənt/ *adj.* consisting of a mixture of blood serum and pus

serosa /sə róssə/ (*plural* **-sae** /-səə/ *or* **-sas**) *n.* = **serous membrane** [Late 19thC. From modern Latin (*membrana*) *serosa* 'serous (membrane)'.]

serostatus /se͞erō stáytəss/ *n.* the condition of being either seropositive or seronegative

serotinal /sə rótt'i-, -ró-/ *adj.* = **serotinous** [Late 19thC. Formed from Latin *serotinus* (see SEROTINE).]

serotine /sérrō tīn, séōtin/ *n.* **SMALL BAT** a small brown bat found in Europe and Asia. Genus: *Eptesicus.* ■ *adj.* = serotinous [Late 18thC. Via French *sérotine* from a late Latin sense 'in or of the evening' of Latin *serotinus* 'belated, late flowering', from, ultimately, *serus* 'late'.]

serotinous /sə rótti'nəss, -rō-/, **serotinal** /sə rótt'nəl/, **serotine** /sérrətin, -tīn/ *adj.* developing or blooming during the late part of a growing season [Mid-17thC. From Latin *serotinus* (see SEROTINE).]

serotonergic /sérətō núrjik/, **serotoninergic** /sérrətōni-/ *adj.* used to describe neurons or nerves that are capable of releasing serotonin as a neurotransmitter at their endings

serotonin /sérrə-/ *n.* a chemical derived from the amino acid tryptophan, and widely distributed in tissues. It acts as a neurotransmitter, constricts blood vessels at injury sites, and may affect emotional states. LSD and certain antidepressants work by interfering with serotonin in the brain. Formula: $C_{10}H_{12}N_2O$. [Mid-20thC. Coined from SERO- + TONIC + -IN.]

serous /se͞erəss/ *adj.* relating to, resembling, or producing serum [15thC. From French *séreux* or medieval Latin *serosus*, both formed from Latin *serum* 'whey, watery fluid' (source of English *serum*).]

serous fluid *n.* any bodily fluid that resembles serum

serous membrane *n.* a thin moist transparent membrane that lines the body cavities and surrounds the internal organs, e.g. the peritoneum that lines the abdomen and the pericardium that surrounds the heart. Serous membranes secrete a lubricating fluid that provides for virtually frictionless movement of the internal organs against both the body wall and each other.

serow /sérrō/ (*plural* **serows** *or* **serow**) *n.* a goat antelope that lives in the mountains of tropical and subtropical eastern Asia. Genus: *Capricornus.* [Mid-19thC. Origin uncertain: probably from Lepcha *sā-ro*.]

Serpens /súr penz/ *n.* a constellation of the equatorial region that is unique in being split into two separate parts, the head (**Serpens Caput**) and the tail (**Serpens Cauda**), located either side of Ophiuchus

Serpent

serpent /súrpənt/ *n.* **1.** SNAKE a snake **2.** TREACHEROUS PERSON sb who is sly or treacherous **3.** OLD WIND IN-STRUMENT a woodwind instrument shaped like a curving snake, dating back to the medieval period. The sound is produced as in a brass instrument, but there are key holes instead of valves, as in a wind instrument. [13thC. Via French from Latin *serpent-*, present participle stem of *serpere* 'to creep'.]

Serpent *n.* **1.** BIBLICAL GUISE OF EVIL in the Bible, the reptile said to have tempted Eve **2.** SATAN Satan (*literary*) **3.** ASTRON = Serpens

serpentine /súrpən tīn/ *adj.* **1.** WINDING winding and twisting, with many bends and curves **2.** RESEMBLING SNAKE like a snake in motion or shape (*literary*) **3.** CUNNING untrustworthy and cunning, as a snake is conventionally thought to be (*literary*) **4.** MATH CURVING relating to or being a complex curve that is symmetric about the x-axis and the central part of which is convex ■ *n.* MINERALS GREEN OR BROWN MINERAL a dull green or brownish mineral consisting of hydrous magnesium silicate. It is often used as an ornamental stone. [15thC. In the noun sense, from French *serpentin*; from its being mottled like a snake's skin.]

Serpentine Ridge /súpən tīn-/ *n.* on the moon, a low ridge running north to south across the eastern side of the Mare Serenitatis, or Sea of Tranquillity

SERPS /surps/, **Serps** *n.*, *abbr.* state earnings-related pension scheme

serpulid /súr pyoͦoͦllid/ *n.* a round segmented marine worm that produces a flat, spirally coiled, limy shell, from which it projects a crown of tentacles, typically found on rocks and seaweed. Family: Serpulidae. [Late 19thC. From late Latin *serpula* 'small serpent'.]

serranid /sə ránnid, sérrə-/ *n.* a robust large-mouthed marine fish such as a sea bass or a grouper, living in temperate and tropical seas. Family: Serranidae. [Mid-20thC. From modern Latin *Serranidae*, ultimately from Latin *serra* 'saw' (source of English *serrate*).] —**serranid** *adj.*

serrate /sérrayt/ *adj.* LIKE TEETH OF SAW with notches or projections like the teeth of a saw ■ *vt.* (**-rates** /sə ráyt/, **-rating, -rated**) GIVE STH TOOTHED EDGE to give sth an edge that is notched like the teeth of a saw [14thC. From late Latin *serrat-*, past participle stem of *serrare*, from Latin *serra* 'saw'.]

serrated /sə ráytid/ *adj.* with notches like the teeth of a saw

serration /sə ráysh'n/ *n.* **1.** NOTCHES LIKE SAW TEETH a row of notches like the teeth of a saw **2.** TOOTH OR NOTCH a tooth or notch in a series or row that is like the teeth of a saw **3.** STATE OF BEING NOTCHED the state of having a sharp notched edge like the teeth of a saw

serried /sérrid/ *adj.* crowded together with little space between each (*literary*) [Mid-17thC. Past participle of obsolete *serry* 'to close ranks', from French *serrer* 'to press close together', from, ultimately, Latin *sera* 'bolt'.]

serriform /sérri fawrm/ *adj.* with notches like the teeth of a saw [Early 19thC. Coined from Latin *serra* 'saw' + -FORM.]

serrulate /sérroͦo layt/, **serrulated** /sérroͦo laytid/ *adj.* having an edge with tiny notches like the teeth of a saw [Late 18thC. From modern Latin *serrulatus*, from Latin *serrulus* 'small saw', from *serra* 'saw'.]

serrulation /sérroͦo láysh'n/ *n.* **1.** NOTCH ON EDGE OF STH any of a row of tiny notches around the edge of sth **2.** CONDITION OF HAVING TINY NOTCHES the condition of having tiny notches like the teeth of a saw

Sertorius /sur táwri əss/, **Quintus** (121?–72 BC) Roman general and statesman. He governed Spain virtually independently of Rome and, in the civil wars, led opposition to Sulla in Spain before being assassinated by a lieutenant.

serum /se͞erəm/ (*plural* **-rums** *or* **-ra** /se͞erə/) *n.* **1.** PHYSIOL LIQUID PART OF BLOOD the fluid that separates from clotted blood, similar to plasma but without clotting agents **2.** MED = antiserum **3.** BIOL BODY FLUID any clear watery body fluid, especially that exuded by serous membranes **4.** WHEY whey (*archaic*) [Late 17thC. From Latin, literally 'whey, watery fluid'.] —**serumal** *adj.*

serum albumin *n.* the most abundant protein in blood serum. It helps determine the osmotic pressure of blood, and is used in transfusions to treat shock.

serum globulin *n.* a globular soluble protein or mixture of proteins that can be separated from blood serum and contains most of the blood's antibodies

serum hepatitis *n.* = **hepatitis B**

serum sickness *n.* an illness caused by injection of serum, with symptoms such as swelling, fever, or a rash. It is due to a reaction between the recipient's antibodies and antigens in the injected serum. (*dated*)

serv. *abbr.* **1.** servant **2.** service

serval /súrv'l/ (*plural* **-vals** *or* **-val**) *n.* an African wild cat that has a reddish-brown coat with black spots, long legs, a long neck, and a relatively small head with large ears. The serval lives in the African bush south of the Sahara Desert. It hunts at night, preying on birds and small animals. Latin name: *Felis serval.* [Late 18thC. Via modern Latin or French from Portuguese *lobo cerval* 'lynx' (literally 'deer-like wolf'), ultimately from Latin *cervus* 'deer'.]

servant /súrvənt/ *n.* **1.** SB WHO SERVES ANOTHER sb who serves another, especially sb employed to do household jobs such as cooking, cleaning, and serving meals **2.** SB WORKING FOR PUBLIC sb in the public employ. ◊ **civil servant, public servant** [12thC. From Old French, present participle of *servir* (see SERVE).]

serve /surv/ *v.* (**serves, serving, served**) **1.** *vti.* PREPARE AND SUPPLY FOOD to prepare and supply food or drinks **2.** *vti.* GIVE SB FOOD OR DRINK to bring food or drink to sb **3.** *vt.* PROVIDE CUSTOMERS WITH GOODS to wait on customers in a shop, and provide them with goods, supplies, or services **4.** *vti.* BE OF USE to be useful or helpful for a particular purpose **5.** *vti.* HAVE PARTICULAR EFFECT to have a particular effect or result ○ *This letter will serve to remind you of our appointment.* **6.** *vti.* SPEND TIME IN PRISON to spend a certain length of time in a place, especially in prison **7.** *vi.* BE IN ARMED FORCE to be a member of an armed force, especially in wartime **8.** *vti.* RACKET GAMES PUT BALL OR SHUTTLECOCK IN PLAY to hit a ball or shuttlecock towards an opponent in a racket game as a way of beginning play **9.** *vt.* LAW DELIVER LEGAL DOCUMENT TO SB to deliver to sb a legal document such as a summons, writ, or warrant (*formal*) **10.** *vti.* WORK FOR SB to work, or work for sb **11.** *vti.* WORK AS SERVANT to work as a servant **12.** *vi.* CHR ASSIST DURING MASS to assist a Roman Catholic priest in the celebration of Mass **13.** *vt.* WORSHIP SB OR STH to worship or follow sb or sth (*formal*) **14.** *vt.* COPULATE WITH FEMALE of a male animal, to copulate with a female **15.** *vt.* NAUT BIND ROPE WITH WIRE OR CORD to bind a rope with sth such as fine wire to keep it from wearing or fraying ■ *n.* RACKET GAMES HIT THAT STARTS POINT in racket games, the shot used to begin every point [12thC. Directly or via Old French *servir* from Latin *servire*, from *servus* 'slave'.] —**servable** *adj.* ◇ **serve sb right** to be a deserved punishment for doing sth wrong

WORD KEY: ORIGIN

The Latin word *servire*, from which ***serve*** is derived, is also the source of English *deserve, dessert, sergeant*, and *serviette* (but not of *conserve, observe, preserve*, and *reserve*, which come from the unrelated Latin *servare*).

serve up *vt.* to supply sth, especially food

server /súrvər/ *n.* **1.** SB WHO SERVES sb who serves sth, e.g. food at a meal **2.** RACKET GAMES SB WHO STARTS GAME the player who starts a game in a sport such as tennis or badminton by hitting the ball or shuttlecock across the net to an opponent **3.** DOMESTIC TRAY FOR SERVING STH a tray for serving food or drinks on **4.** DOMESTIC FOOD UTENSIL a utensil for serving food **5.** CHR ASSISTANT AT MASS sb who assists a Roman Catholic priest at Mass. ◊ **acolyte, altar boy 6.** COMPUT = **file server 7.** COMPUT = **print server**

service[1] /súrviss/ *n.* **1.** WORK DONE FOR SB ELSE work done by sb for sb else as a job, a duty, a punishment, or a favour **2.** MEETING OF PUBLIC NEED the system or operation by which people are provided with sth they need, e.g. public transport, or the organization that runs such a system **3.** GOVERNMENT AGENCY an official organization, especially a government department, or the work performed for such an organization ○ *the diplomatic service* **4.** DOMESTIC DOMESTIC SERVANT'S WORK the work done as a servant in a private house **5.** MIL ONE OF THE ARMED FORCES one of a country's armed forces **6.** FOOD SERVING SB FOOD the act of bringing food to sb or the way in which this is done **7.** MAINTENANCE OF MACHINERY the act of cleaning, checking, adjusting, or making minor repairs to a piece of machinery, especially a motor vehicle, to make sure that it works properly **8.** USE OR OPERATION current use or operation **9.** RELIG PUBLIC WORSHIP CEREMONY a religious ceremony usually involving specific forms for worship and prayer **10.** RELIG RELIGIOUS RITUAL a specific religious ritual that is performed according to a prescribed form **11.** RACKET GAMES ACT OF SERVING BALL OR SHUTTLECOCK the act or manner of serving in a racket game, or the right to do so **12.** RACKET GAMES GAME a game in which a player serves **13.** DOMESTIC SET OF DISHES a set of dishes and cups for use in serving a particular meal ○ *dinner service* **14.** LAW SERVING OF LEGAL DOCUMENT TO SB the delivery of a legal document such as a writ or summons **15.** NAUT MATERIAL USED TO BIND ROPE sth such as fine wire or cord used to bind a rope to prevent it from fraying **16.** CHR COLLECTION OF RELIGIOUS MUSICAL SETTINGS a collection of the musical arrangements prescribed for use in the Church of England ■ **services** *npl.* **1.** TRANSP FACILITIES FOR TRAVELLERS facilities such as shops, cafés, and toilets available at certain places along a motorway ○ *There are no services at the next exit.* **2.** COMM WORK THAT DOES NOT MAKE ANYTHING jobs and businesses such as banking and insurance that provide sth for other people but do not produce tangible goods **3.** THINGS PROVIDED BY GOVERNMENT things such as education, healthcare, and roads that are provided by national or local government and paid for by taxation **4.** ARMED FORCES the armed forces of a country ■ *vt.* (**services, servicing, serviced**) **1.** CLEAN AND ADJUST MACHINERY to clean, check, adjust, and make minor repairs to a piece of machinery in order to make sure that it works properly ○ *It's time to have my car serviced.* **2.** PROVIDE STH FOR COMMUNITY to provide a community or organization with sth that it needs ○ *The electric company services all nine counties.* **3.** FIN PAY INTEREST ON DEBT to pay interest on a debt **4.** AGRIC COPULATE WITH FEMALE of a male animal, to copulate with a female ■ *adj.* **1.** USED BY EMPLOYEES OR FOR DELIVERIES intended for employees or deliveries rather than for members of the public (*often used before a noun*) ○ *a service elevator* **2.** PROVIDING A SERVICE NOT GOODS relating to jobs or businesses such as banking and insurance that do sth useful for people but that do not manufacture any goods **3.** FOR MAINTENANCE AND REPAIR providing maintenance and repair for manufactured products [Pre-12thC. Directly or via French from Latin *servitium* 'slavery', from *servus* 'slave'.]

service[2] /súrviss/ *n.* = **service tree** [Mid-16thC. Plural of obsolete 'serve', ultimately from Latin *sorbus*, 'service tree'.]

serviceable /súrvissəb'l/ *adj.* **1.** MADE TO WEAR WELL suitable for everyday use and hard wear **2.** WORKING in working condition **3.** EFFECTIVE useful or effective —**serviceableness** *n.* —**serviceably** *adv.*

service area *n.* **1.** TRANSP FACILITIES FOR MOTORWAY TRAVELLERS a place beside a motorway where there are facilities for travellers such as a restaurant, toilets, and a service station **2.** BROADCAST AREA OF SATISFACTORY SIGNAL the area over which a radio or television broadcasting station can transmit a satisfactory signal for reception

serviceberry /súrviss berri/ (*plural* **-ries**) *n.* **1.** PLANT WITH SMALL EDIBLE BERRIES a small tree or shrub of the rose family, mostly native to North America, that bears clusters of white flowers and produces small, edible, dark blue fruits. Genus: *Amelanchier.* **2.** ROUND FRUIT the round fruit of the serviceberry **3.** FRUIT OF SERVICE TREE the fruit of the service tree [*Service* from SERVICE[2]]

service book *n.* a book containing the correct forms of worship authorized for use in a church

service break *n.* a game won by a player in a racket game when an opponent was serving

service centre *n.* **1.** GARAGE THAT REPAIRS VEHICLES a garage that sells parts and carries out repairs on motor vehicles **2.** RETAIL STORE THAT REPAIRS ITS PRODUCTS a retail store that provides repairs and parts for the items it sells

service charge *n.* **1.** MONEY ADDED TO BILL FOR SERVICE a sum of money, usually calculated as a percentage of a customer's bill, added to the bill in a restaurant or hotel to pay the staff for their service **2.** CHARGE FOR CARRYING BALANCE a fee added to the balance of a bill when it is paid in instalments rather than being paid in one lump sum **3.** COMM MONEY CHARGED FOR PERFORMING SERVICE a sum of money charged by a business or bank for handling a transaction

service contract *n.* **1.** CONTRACT WITH SENIOR EXECUTIVE a contract between a company and a senior employee such as a director or senior executive **2.** REPAIR CONTRACT a contract with a company or manufacturer to maintain equipment in working order at an agreed price over a fixed period

service court *n.* in racket games, the area within which a served ball or shuttlecock must land

service flat *n.* a flat in which some domestic services, e.g. cleaning and laundry, and sometimes also meals, are provided by the management

service industry *n.* an industry that provides a service rather than goods, or such industries as a whole

service line *n.* in racket games and volleyball, a line on a court that the server must not cross before serving

serviceman /súrvissmən/ (*plural* **-men** /-mən/) *n.* **1.** MIL SOLDIER a man serving in the armed forces **2. serviceman, service man** BUSINESS REPAIRMAN a man whose job is repairing and servicing equipment

service mark *n.* a sign or symbol used by people or companies who provide a particular service to identify themselves and set them apart from other companies. For example, in Britain, many independent financial advisers identify themselves by a symbol consisting of a black circle with a £ sign in the middle, surrounded by the words 'Independent Financial Adviser'.

serviceperson /súrviss purss'n/ (*plural* **-people** /-peep'l/ *or* **-persons**) *n.* **1.** MIL SOLDIER sb serving in the armed forces **2. serviceperson, service person** BUSINESS REPAIR PERSON sb whose job is maintaining and servicing equipment

service provider *n.* **1.** BUSINESS THAT CONNECTS PEOPLE TO INTERNET a company that makes money by providing individuals and other businesses with access to the Internet, usually charging a monthly fee **2.** COMPANY THAT PROVIDES SERVICES a company that makes money by providing specific services, e.g. health or life insurance

service road *n.* a minor road that runs alongside a main road, giving access to houses, shops, offices, and other businesses

service station *n.* a place where petrol, oil, and other requirements for motor vehicles can be bought, and that usually also provides other facilities for motorists such as toilets and a shop

service tree, service *n.* a tree, native to central and southern Europe, that has compound leaves of up to 20 toothed leaflets and produces edible fruit. The fruits are fermented with grain to produce an alcoholic beverage. Latin name: *Sorbus domestica.*

servicewoman /súrviss wŏŏmən/ (*plural* **-en** /-wimin/) *n.* **1.** MIL WOMAN SOLDIER a woman serving in the armed forces **2. servicewoman, service woman** BUSINESS REPAIR WOMAN a woman whose job is repairing and servicing equipment

serviette /súrvi étt/ *n.* = **napkin** *n.* 1 [15thC. From French, formed from *servir* 'to serve' (see SERVE).]

servile /súr vīl/ *adj.* **1.** TOO OBEDIENT too willing to agree with sb or to do whatever demeaning thing sb wants **2.** FOR SERVANTS relating to dirty degrading work that is considered fit only for servants or slaves ○ *servile tasks* **3.** RELATING TO SLAVERY relating to slaves or the condition of slavery [14thC. From Latin *servilis*, from *servus* 'slave'.] —**servilely** *adv.* —**servileness** *n.*

serving /súrving/ *n.* an amount of food served to one person

serving hatch *n.* an opening in the wall between a kitchen and a dining area, through which food and dishes may be passed

servitor /súrvitər/ *n.* a servant or attendant (*old*) [14thC. Via Old French from late Latin, formed from Latin *servire* 'to serve' (see SERVE).]

servitude /súrvi tyood/ *n.* **1.** STATE OF SLAVERY the state of being a slave **2.** SUBJECTION the state of being ruled or dominated by sb or sth **3.** WORK IMPOSED AS PUNISHMENT work imposed as a punishment for a crime **4.** LAW RESTRICTION OR OBLIGATION ON PROPERTY a restriction or obligation attached to a property that entitles sb other than the owner to a specified use of it, e.g. the right to cross it [15thC. Via Old French from Latin *servitudo*, from *servus* 'slave'.]

servo[1] /súrvō/ *adj.* RELATING TO SERVOMECHANISM relating to, forming part of, or activated by a servomechanism ■ *n.* (*plural* **-vos**) **1.** = **servomechanism** **2.** = **servomotor** [Late 19thC. Shortening of French *servo-moteur* 'servomotor' (an auxiliary motor); *servo-* from Latin *servus* 'slave'.]

servo[2] /súrvō/ (*plural* **-vos**) *n. Aus* a service station (*informal*) [Late 20thC. Shortening.]

servomechanism /súrvō mekənizəm/ *n.* a closed-circuit device in which a small input power controls a much larger power, as in a radio telescope — **servomechanical** /súrvō mi kánnik'l/ *adj.*

servomotor /súrvō mōtər/ *n.* a motor that supplies the initial power in a servomechanism

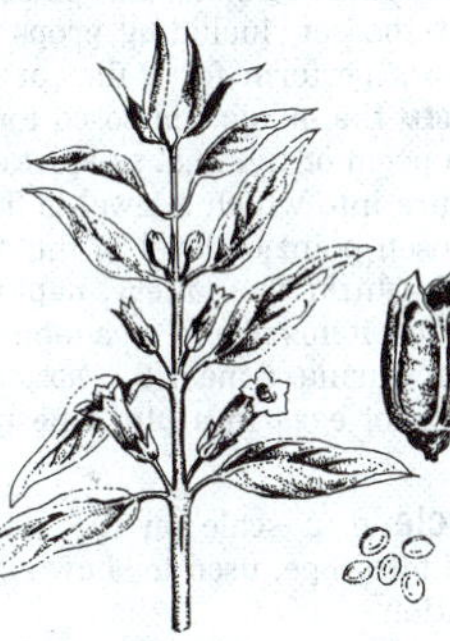

Sesame

sesame /séssəmi/ (*plural* **-mes** *or* **-me**) *n.* **1.** PLANTS TROPICAL PLANT CULTIVATED FOR SEEDS a herbaceous plant of tropical Asia, cultivated for its seeds. Latin name: *Sesamum indicum.* **2.** FOOD SEED OF SESAME PLANT the seed of the sesame plant. Both the seed and its oil are used in cooking. [15thC. Via Latin *sesamum* from Greek *sēsamon*, of Near Eastern origin.]

sesame oil *n.* a strongly flavoured oil from sesame seeds, widely used in Asian and Southeast Asian cooking

sesamoid /séssə moyd/ *n.* SMALL ROUGHLY SPHERICAL BONE a small, roughly spherical bone lying within a tendon to assist in its mechanical action or to bear pressure ■ *adj.* RELATING TO VARIOUS SMALL BONES relating to or being various small bones or cartilages in a tendon or joint such as the knee [Late 17thC. Formed from SESAME.]

Sesotho /si sóotoo/ *n.* the dialect of Sotho spoken by the Basotho in Lesotho [Mid-19thC. From Sesotho.] — **Sesotho** *adj.*

sesqui- *prefix.* one and a half ○ *sesquicentennial* [From Latin, from *semis* 'half' + *-que* 'and']

sesquicentennial /séskwi sen ténni əl/, **sesquicentenary** /séskwi sen teénəri, -ténnəri/ *n.* (*plural* **-ies**) **1.** 150TH ANNIVERSARY a 150th anniversary or the celebration of one **2.** 150 YEARS a period of 150 years ■ *adj.* OCCURRING EVERY 150 YEARS relating to or happening after a period of 150 years —**sesquicentennially** *adv.*

sesquipedalian /séskwi pi dáyli ən/, **sesquipedal** /se skwíppid'l/ *adj.* (*literary*) **1.** USING LONG WORDS characterized by the use of very long words **2.** LONG relating to or being a long word ■ *n.* LONG WORD a word with many letters or syllables (*literary*) [Early 17thC. From Latin *sesquipedalis* 'measuring one and one-half feet', from the stem *ped-* 'foot'.] —**sesquipedalianism** *n.*

sess. *abbr.* session

sessile /séssīl/ *adj.* **1.** BOT LACKING STALK used to describe a leaf or flower that has no stalk but is attached directly to the stem **2.** ZOOL PERMANENTLY ATTACHED used to describe an animal that is permanently attached to sth rather than free-moving, e.g. a barnacle [Early 18thC. From Latin *sessilis* 'lying close to the ground', from *sess-*, past participle stem of *sedere* 'to sit' (source of English *séance, hostage,* and *obsession*).] —**sessility** /sə sílləti/ *n.*

sessile oak *n.* = **durmast oak**

session /sésh'n/ *n.* **1.** MEETING a meeting of an official body, especially a court or legislature **2.** PERIOD OF MEETING a period during which an official body meets or does business **3.** SERIES OF MEETINGS a series of meetings of an official body **4.** EDUC TEACHING PERIOD the time of year or the time of day during which a school or university holds classes **5.** PERIOD OF DOING STH a period of time during which people are involved in doing sth together **6.** PERIOD OF PLAYING MUSIC a period during which musicians play together, especially in a recording studio **7.** CHR GOVERNING BODY OF PRESBYTERIAN CONGREGATION the governing body of a Presbyterian congregation, consisting of the minister and elders ■ **sessions** *npl.* LAW SITTINGS OF JUSTICE OF PEACE the sittings of a justice of the peace in court. ◊ **Court of Session, petty sessions, quarter sessions** ■ *adj.* MUSIC **1.** RELATING TO FREELANCE MUSICIAN relating to or being a musician paid to play or sing on recordings in a studio but not a permanent member of a band **2.** RELATING TO FREELANCE MUSIC relating to playing or singing done by a session musician [14thC. Via Old French from Latin *session-* 'a sitting', from the stem *sess-* (see SESSILE).] — **sessional** *adj.*

WORD KEY: ORIGIN

The Latin word *sedere*, from which ***session*** is derived, is also the source of English *assess, assiduous, assize, insidious, séance, sedentary, size, subsidy,* and *supersede.*

sesterce /sést urss/, **sestertius** /se stúrti əss, -stúrshəss/ (*plural* **-i** /-ti ī, -hi ī/) *n.* an ancient Roman coin, originally silver but later bronze, worth a quarter of a denarius [Late 16thC. From Latin *sestertius* 'two and one-half times as great', literally 'one-half third', from *semis* 'half' + *tertius* 'third'; originally equivalent to two and a half asses.]

sestertium /se stúrti əm, -stúrshəm/ (*plural* **-tia** /-stúrti ə, -stúrshə/) *n.* an ancient Roman unit of currency equal to 1,000 sesterces [Mid-16thC. From the Latin phrase *(mille) sestertium*, literally '(a thousand) of sesterces' (see SESTERCE).]

sestet /se stét/ *n.* a stanza or poem of six lines, especially the last six lines of a Petrarchan sonnet [Early 19thC. From Italian *sestetto*, literally 'little sixth', from *sesto* 'sixth', from Latin *sextus* 'sixth'.]

sestina /se steénə/ *n.* a poem of six six-line stanzas and a three-line envoy, with the last words of the first six lines repeated, in different order, at the ends of the other lines [Mid-19thC. From Italian, formed from *sesto* 'sixth' (see SESTET).]

set[1] /set/ *v.* (**sets, setting, set**) **1.** *vt.* PLACE STH to put sb or sth somewhere ○ *Set the books on the table.* **2.** *vt.* PUT SB INTO CONDITION to get or put sb or sth into a particular condition ○ *set the hostages free* **3.** *vt.* MAKE STH HAPPEN to cause sth to happen ○ *set an unfortunate train of events in motion* **4.** *vt.* FOCUS ON STH to focus on a goal or task ○ *had set his mind on it* **5.** *vt.* ARRANGE FOR USE to arrange, place, or prepare sth to be used ○ *set a trap for them* **6.** *vti.* BECOME OR MAKE SOLID to form or cause sth to be formed in a solid state ○ *Let the concrete set.* **7.** *vt.* ADJUST MEASURING DEVICE to adjust a device such as a clock to a desired time, level, or position ○ *Remember to set the alarm.* **8.** *vt.* DECIDE ON OR IMPOSE STH to decide on a particular time or impose a rule as a condition for sth ○ *We've set a date for the wedding.* **9.** *vt.* BE EXAMPLE to be an example of a type of behaviour ○ *tried to set an example for her younger siblings* **10.** *vt.* DETERMINE PRICE OF STH to determine or state the price of sth ○ *set the price at £20* **11.** *vt.* CONSIDER AS HAVING VALUE to consider sth as having a particular value ○ *set a high value on his own work* **12.** *vt.* DETERMINE COURSE to determine a direction or course to travel ○ *set a course for home* **13.** *vt.* ESTABLISH RECORD to establish a record ○ *set a new 100-metre record* **14.** *vt.* EDUC ASSIGN STH FOR STUDY to assign sth such as a book or subject to be studied **15.** *vt.* HAIR ARRANGE HAIR to arrange hair in a particular style by using styling products or clips **16.** *vt.* PUT GEM IN SETTING to put a gem or stone in a metal setting **17.** *vt.* MED PUT BROKEN BONE IN POSITION to put a broken bone back in its normal position so it can heal properly **18.** *vi.* MED HEAL to heal up and become solid after being broken (*refers to a bone*) **19.** *vt.* MUSIC PROVIDE MUSIC FOR STH to provide the music for sth such as lyrics or a poem ○ *set his words to music* **20.** *vt.* ADORN to adorn sth with decorations ○ *set a gown with sequins* **21.** *vt.* ARTS PORTRAY IN PARTICULAR SETTING to portray sth as happening in a particular place or time period (*usually passive*) ○ *The play is set in the 19th century.* **22.** *vt.* THEATRE PLACE SCENERY ON to place scenery on stage **23.** *vt.* PRINTING ARRANGE TYPE to arrange type for printing **24.** *vti.* SAILING POSITION SAIL to rig a sail to catch the wind, or to be rigged in this way **25.** *vi.* GO BELOW HORIZON to go below the horizon ○ *watched the sun set* **26.** *vi.* CLOTHES FIT WELL OR POORLY to fit in a particular way (*refers to clothes*) ○ *The skirt sets well.* **27.** *vi.* START to begin sth, especially work ○ *set to work with a will* **28.** *vi.* SPORTS GET READY TO START RACE to get into a position ready to start a race ○ *Ready, get set, go!* **29.** *vi.* BECOME PERMANENT to become permanent (*refers to a dye or colour*) **30.** *vt.* COOK LET DOUGH RISE to place dough aside to allow it to rise **31.** *vt.* SHARPEN STH to sharpen a blade **32.** *vt.* DISPLACE TEETH ON SAW to bend the teeth of a saw alternately to either side of the blade **33.** *vt.* DRIVE NAIL HEAD BELOW SURFACE to drive the head of a nail below the surface **34.** *vti.* AGRIC, PLANTS PRODUCE FRUIT OR SEEDS to produce fruit or seeds after being pollinated, or be produced in this way **35.** *vi.* END to come to an end (*literary*) **36.** *vt.* SIT SB to cause sb to sit somewhere (*regional*) ○ *Set yourself here.* **37.** *vt.* AGRIC, GARDENING PLANT to plant sth **38.** *vti.* AGRIC SIT OR MAKE SIT ON EGGS to put a hen on eggs to keep them warm, or to sit on eggs **39.** *vti.* GAME INDICATE GAME to indicate the presence of game by turning towards it and holding that position **40.** *vt.* BRIDGE BEAT IN BRIDGE to prevent an opponent meeting the contract in bridge **41.** *vi.* METALL BECOME BENT to become bent from strain ■ *n.* **1.** CONDITION OF SOLIDITY the condition of being solid **2.** POSTURE the posture or bearing of sb or an animal **3.** CLOTHES FIT OF CLOTHES the way sth hangs when worn **4.** THEATRE, CINEMA THEATRICAL SCENERY scenery for a play or film or the place where this has been put up **5.** PRINTING WIDTH OF PIECE OF TYPE the width of a piece of type **6.** PRINTING WIDTH OF LINE OF TYPE the width of a column or a page of type **7.** SAILING ARRANGEMENT OF SAILS the way the sails and other rigging are arranged on a sailing boat **8.** DIRECTION the direction of a wind, tide, or current **9.** PREFERENCE a preference for or increased ability in a particular activity **10.** PSYCHOL BIAS INFLUENCING REACTION TO STIMULUS the psychological state that causes an organism to react to a stimulus in a particular way **11.** AGRIC, GARDENING SEEDLING READY FOR PLANTING a plant such as a seedling that is ready to be planted **12.** METALL DISTORTION DUE TO STRESS a distortion or bending that occurs in metal as a result of stress **13.** HAIR HAIRSTYLE a way of styling the hair **14.** AGRIC CLUTCH the number of eggs that a hen lays at one time **15.** = **sett** ■ *adj.* **1.** ESTABLISHED previously established such as by tradition, agreement, or authority **2.** INFLEXIBLE being rigid and unwilling to change, especially in the way of doing things ○ *They're so set in their ways, they'll never change.* **3.** READY prepared for sb or sth, or to do sth ○ *We're all set to go.* **4.** STEREOTYPED conforming to an established often conventional formula ○ *a set speech* **5.** DETERMINED determined to do sth ○ *We're set on the idea and won't consider changing.* **6.** EDUC ASSIGNED TO STUDY assigned for students to study ○ *a set text* [Old English *settan*, literally 'to cause to sit'. From a prehistoric Germanic word (ancestor also of German *setzen*) 'to sit'.]

set about *vt.* **1.** BEGIN STH to begin doing sth **2.** ATTACK to attack sb

set against *vt.* **1.** COMPARE to consider one thing in relation to another, especially when the other thing is very important **2.** MAKE PEOPLE FIGHT ONE ANOTHER to make people or groups start to fight with or be hostile to people they used to be on friendly terms with

set apart *vt.* **1.** RESERVE FOR SPECIFIC USE to keep sth for a specific use or purpose **2.** MAKE SB CONSPICUOUS to make sb conspicuous or different ○ *Her knowledge sets her apart.*

set aside *vt.* **1.** RESERVE to keep sth, especially time or money, for a particular purpose **2.** PUT TO ONE SIDE to put sth to one side **3.** REJECT PREVIOUS DECISION to discard, reject, or annul a previous decision or judgment

set back *vt.* **1.** DELAY to block or delay the progress of sth or sb **2. COST SB** to cost sb a lot of money (*informal*)

set down *vt.* **1. PUT DOWN** to put sth down on a surface **2. WRITE DOWN** to write sth down **3. JUDGE** to judge sb or sth as being sth specified ○ *set the whole thing down as a failure* **4. ATTRIBUTE** to attribute an event or quality to sth specified ○ *set his mistake down to inexperience* **5. LET SB GET OFF** to allow a passenger in a vehicle to get off at a specific place **6. SCOLD SB** to snub or rebuke sb **7. LAND AIRCRAFT** to land an aircraft

set forth *v.* **1.** *vi.* **LEAVE** to leave on a journey (*literary*) **2.** *vt.* **STATE** to state or present an argument or a set of figures in speech or writing (*formal*)

set in *v.* **1.** *vi.* **BEGIN** to begin and become established ○ *once the winter snows set in* **2.** *vi.* **MOVE SHOREWARD** to move in a shoreward direction (*refers to a wind, tide, or current*) **3.** *vt.* CLOTHES **ADD ON** to add a separately made part to a garment

set off *v.* **1.** *vi.* **START OUT ON TRIP** to start out on a journey **2.** *vt.* **MAKE STH WORK** to make sth such as an alarm or fireworks operate or explode **3.** *vt.* **MAKE SB START DOING STH** to make sb start doing sth such as laughing, crying, or talking about sth ○ *When she started crying it set us all off too.* **4.** *vt.* **START STH** to make sth start happening ○ *set off a chain of events that eventually led to war* **5.** *vt.* **MAKE STH LOOK ATTRACTIVE** to provide a contrast to sth in a way that makes it look more attractive ○ *The new frame really sets off the painting.* **6.** *vt.* ACCT **COUNTERBALANCE CREDIT** to counterbalance a credit in the accounts of one person or organization against a debit in those of another

set on *vt.* **1. ATTACK** to attack sb or encourage a person or animal to attack sb or sth **2. INCITE SB** to encourage sb to do sth

set out *v.* **1.** *vi.* **BEGIN JOURNEY** to begin sth, especially a journey **2.** *vi.* **INTENTIONALLY START DOING STH** intentionally to start doing sth or planning to do sth ○ *deliberately set out to ruin the performance* **3.** *vt.* **DISPLAY** to arrange, display, or decorate sth ○ *merchants setting out their wares* **4.** *vt.* **LAY OUT** to lay out sth in a planned way ○ *The gardens are beautifully set out.* **5.** *vt.* **PRESENT** to present or explain sth, especially in a full way ○ *a book that clearly sets out the author's philosophy*

set to *vi.* **1. BEGIN TASK** to start doing sth, especially work **2. START FIGHTING** to start fighting

set up *v.* **1.** *vt.* **ERECT** to erect sth or put sth in an upright or usable position ○ *set up road blocks* **2.** *vti.* **PREPARE EQUIPMENT FOR EVENT** to prepare the equipment needed for an event ○ *The band is setting up on stage.* **3.** *vt.* **PUT IN POSITION OF POWER** to put a person or group in a position of power **4.** *vt.* **ORGANIZE** to arrange, establish, or bring about sth ○ *I've set up a meeting for next week.* **5.** *vti.* **CLAIM TO BE STH** to claim to be sth, especially an expert or authority on sth ○ *set herself up as an expert* **6.** *vti.* **START BUSINESS** to start a business or give sb everything needed to start a business ○ *His family set him up in business.* **7.** *vt.* **MAKE HEALTHY** to make sb feel healthy or invigorated, especially after having been ill **8.** *vt.* **PRODUCE STH** to produce or create sth ○ *The spectators set up a howl of protest.* **9.** *vt.* **CAUSE TO BE BLAMED** to cause sb to be caught and blamed for sth (*informal*) ○ *claims he was set up* **10.** *vt.* **GIVE DRINKS** to buy or provide an alcoholic beverage for sb (*informal*) **11.** *vt.* **PLAN** to make necessary arrangements for sth, e.g. a meeting or conference **12.** *vt.* **PROPOSE** to put an idea, theory, or proposal to a group for consideration

set upon *vt.* to attack sb violently

set[2] /set/ *n.* **1. COLLECTION CONSIDERED AS UNIT** a collection of people or things considered together and usually having sth in common **2. SOCIAL GROUP** a group of people who form a social group ○ *They were the first in our set to have kids.* **3.** ELECTRON ENG **DEVICE RECEIVING SIGNALS** a device that receives radio or television signals **4.** RACKET GAMES **PART OF TENNIS MATCH** a part of a tennis match that is won when one player or couple wins a minimum of six games **5. PREFERENCE** a preference for or increased ability in a particular activity **6.** MUSIC **SONGS PLAYED IN ONE SESSION** a number of songs or acts that an entertainer or band performs on a single occasion **7.** SPORTS **NUMBER OF REPETITIONS OF EXERCISE** a number of repetitions of an exercise done at one time **8.** MATH, LOGIC **COLLECTION OF ELEMENTS** a collection of elements in mathematics or logic, e.g. numbers or terms **9.** DANCE **COUPLES REQUIRED FOR DANCE** a number of couples required for certain dances ○ *We need another couple to complete our set.* ■ *vi.* (**sets, setting, set**) DANCE **DANCE FACING PARTNER** to perform a series of moves while facing another dancer [14thC. Via Old French *sette* from Latin *secta* 'sect' (see SECT).]

seta /seetə/ (*plural* **-tae** /-tee/) *n.* a slender, usually rigid bristle or hair [Late 18thC. From Latin, 'bristle'.] —**setal** *adj.*

setaceous /si táyshəss/ *adj.* **1.** BIOL **HAVING BRISTLES** having bristles or made up of bristles **2. RESEMBLING BRISTLES** having the appearance or feel of bristles (*formal*) [Mid-17thC. Formed from modern Latin *setaceus*, from Latin *seta* 'bristle'.]

set-aside *n.* a European Union scheme whereby farmers are paid not to produce crops on particular areas of land as a way of reducing surpluses or controlling prices

setback /sét bak/ *n.* **1. STH THAT DELAYS PROGRESS** sth that reverses or delays the progress of sb or sth **2.** ARCHIT **SHELF OR RECESS IN WALL** a place in the wall of a building where there is a shelf or recess

se tenant /sə tə naàN/ *adj.* **JOINED BUT DIFFERENT** used to describe two stamps that are joined together but have different values or designs ■ *n.* **JOINED PAIR OF DIFFERENT STAMPS** a pair of stamps that are joined together but have different values or designs [Early 20thC. From French, literally 'holding together'.]

SETI /sétti/ *n.* a scientific attempt to detect or communicate with intelligent beings from beyond Earth, especially using radio signals. Full form **Search for Extraterrestrial Intelligence**

setiferous /sə tíffərəss/, **setigerous** /sə tíjjərəss/ *adj.* used to describe a living organism that has bristles or projections that resemble bristles [Early 19thC. *setiferous* coined from SETA + -FEROUS; *setigerous* from Latin *setiger* 'bristly', from *seta* 'bristle'.]

setiform /seéti fawrm/ *adj.* having the shape of a bristle [Early 19thC. Coined from SETA + -FORM.]

setigerous *adj.* = **setiferous**

set-in *adj.* used to describe a part of a garment that is made separately and stitched in

setline /sét līn/ *n.* a fishing line suspended over a stream or between buoys with shorter hooked and baited lines hanging down from it into the water

set-off *n.* **1. COUNTERBALANCE** sth that compensates for sth else **2. STH IMPROVING APPEARANCE** sth that contrasts with sth else in a way that improves its appearance **3.** ARCHIT = **setback** *n.* 2 **4.** PRINTING = **offset** *n.* 6 **5.** ACCT **COUNTERBALANCING CLAIM** a claim brought by a debtor against a creditor that counterbalances the debt owed

Seton /seét'n/, **Ernest Thompson** (1860–1946) British-born US writer and illustrator. He was one of the founders of the Boy Scouts of America (1910). He is known for his stories about animals for young people such as *Wild Animals I Have Known* (1898). Real name **Ernest Seton-Thompson**

setose /seétōss/ *adj.* covered with bristles [Mid-17thC. From Latin *setosus*, formed from *seta* 'bristle'.]

set piece *n.* **1. PLANNED ACTION** a carefully planned and rehearsed performance or action, especially a military or diplomatic operation **2.** ARTS **FORMAL WORK OF ART** a work of art with a formal theme, undertaken to show the artist's skill **3.** SPORTS **PLANNED MANOEUVRE** a planned manoeuvre used by a team in a game, e.g. the way a soccer team takes a corner or free kick (*hyphenated when used before a noun*) **4.** THEATRE **PIECE OF SCENERY** a piece of stage scenery that can stand unsupported **5.** LEISURE **FIXED FIREWORKS IN DISPLAY** a fixed arrangement of fireworks in a display

set point *n.* **1.** TENNIS **POINT TO GAIN SET** a time in a tennis match when a player can win a set by winning the next point, or the point itself **2.** PHYSIOL **NATURAL BODYWEIGHT** the natural weight that sb's body will assume if provided with a balanced diet

setscrew /sét skroo/ *n.* a screw that fixes one part of a mechanism to another and prevents it moving relative to the part to which it is fixed

set square *n.* a flat metal or plastic instrument in the shape of a right-angled triangle, used in technical drawing. US term **triangle**

sett, **set** *n.* **1. PAVING STONE** a rectangular stone paving block **2.** ZOOL **BADGER'S BURROW** the burrow of a badger **3. TARTAN PATTERN** the precise pattern of squares and stripes in a tartan, with particular colours and numbers of threads **4. SQUARE OF TARTAN** an individual square in a tartan pattern [Variant of SET[1]]

settee /se teé, sə-/ *n.* **1. COMFORTABLE SEAT FOR TWO PEOPLE** a comfortable seat for two or more people, with a cushioned back and arms **2.** *US* **BENCH WITH BACK** a long wooden bench with a back [Early 18thC. Origin uncertain: perhaps an alteration of SETTLE.]

setter /séttər/ *n.* **1.** ZOOL **GUN DOG** a long-haired gun dog belonging to various breeds that is trained to crouch in a set position when it finds game **2. SB OR STH THAT SETS** sb or sth that sets sth

set theory *n.* **1.** MATH **MATHEMATICS OF SETS** the branch of mathematics that deals with the properties and relationships of sets **2.** LOGIC **SYSTEM OF SET AXIOMS** the system of axioms for sets

setting /sétting/ *n.* **1. SURROUNDINGS** the surroundings or environment in which sth exists **2.** ARTS **PERIOD OR PLACE OF STORY** the period in time or the place in which the events of a story take place **3.** ARTS **SET FOR PERFORMANCE** the set, including props and scenery, where actors perform for a film or play **4.** MUSIC **MUSIC FOR POEM** the music composed for a particular text, e.g. a poem or hymn **5. SURROUNDINGS OF JEWEL** the metal fixture into which a jewel is fixed **6. LEVEL ON SCALE** a chosen point or level in the operation of a machine **7. CUTLERY** the cutlery, napkin, table mat, and any other items placed on a table to be used by one person during a meal **8.** BIRDS, AGRIC **CLUTCH OF EGGS** a batch of eggs in a bird's nest, especially a hen's

setting circle *n.* a scale on the mounting of an equatorial telescope, used to show right ascension or declination

settle /sétt'l/ *v.* (**-tles, -tling, -tled**) **1.** *vti.* **MAKE SB COMFORTABLE** to make sb feel comfortable in a particular position **2.** *vt.* **PUT IN PLACE** to put sth in a place firmly or permanently **3.** *vi.* **STOP MOVING** to stop moving and come to rest somewhere **4.** *vi.* **MOVE DOWNWARDS** to move downwards and spread over sth ○ *A blanket of mist settled over the field.* **5.** *vi.* **SINK INTO GROUND** to sink slowly to a lower level **6.** *vti.* **SOLVE** to solve a problem or end a dispute **7.** *vt.* **DECIDE ON STH** to decide on sth so that other arrangements can be made **8.** *vti.* **PAY** to pay a bill, debt, or claim **9.** *vt.* **PUT IN ORDER** to put all the details of a piece of business in order or into a desired arrangement **10.** *vti.* **MAKE OR BECOME CALM** to become or cause sb or sth to become calm, quiet, or stable **11.** *vti.* **MAKE OR BECOME RESIDENT** to become or cause sb to become a resident of a place **12.** *vt.* **COLONIZE** to populate an area with permanent residents **13.** *vti.* **ESTABLISH OR BECOME ESTABLISHED** to establish sb or become established in a place, occupation, or way of life **14.** *vti.* **STOP FLOATING** to stop floating and sink to the bottom or the ground, or to cause sth to do this ○ *waited for the dust to settle before opening their eyes* **15.** *vti.* **MAKE OR BECOME CLEAR** to cause a cloudy liquid to become clear after a sediment has sunk to the bottom, or to become clear in this way **16.** *vti.* LAW **END LEGAL DISPUTE** to end a legal dispute by mutual agreement out of court **17.** *vt.* LAW **ASSIGN PROPERTY** to give sth, especially property or money, to sb legally and formally ○ *settled her with a substantial inheritance* **18.** *vti.* **GET REVENGE** to get revenge on sb for an injury or offence **19.** *vi.* **CONCEIVE** of an animal, to become pregnant ■ *n.* FURNITURE **LONG WOODEN SEAT WITH HIGH BACK** a long wooden seat with a high back, and often with storage space inside the box-shaped seat [Old English *setlan*, formed from *setl* 'chair, bench'. Ultimately from an Indo-European base meaning 'to sit' that is also the ancestor of English *saddle* and *Upanishad*.] —**settleable** *adj.*

settle down *v.* **1.** *vti.* **MAKE OR BECOME CALM** to become or cause sb or sth to become calm, quiet, or orderly **2.** *vi.* **LIVE ORDERLY LIFE** to begin a stable, orderly, and often conventional way of life **3.** *vi.* **DO STH DILIGENTLY** to begin doing sth in a diligent and orderly way ○ *settled down to her morning's work*

settle for *vt.* to accept or agree to sth that is not ideal or exactly what was wanted

settle in *v.* **1.** *vti.* **ADAPT** to adapt or cause sb to adapt to a new environment ○ *settling in at a new school*

2. *vi.* **REMAIN SOMEWHERE FOR LONG TIME** to get comfortable in a place because the intention is to stay there for a long time ○ *decided to settle in for the night*

settlement /sétt'lmənt/ *n.* **1. SETTLING** an act of settling or the state of being settled **2. AGREEMENT** an agreement reached after discussion or negotiation **3.** LAW **AGREEMENT OUT-OF-COURT** an agreement reached without completing legal proceedings **4. PAYMENT** the payment of a bill, debt, or claim **5. COLONY** a place that has recently been populated with permanent residents **6. SMALL COMMUNITY** a small community **7. POPULATING** the act of populating a place with permanent residents **8.** BUILDING **SUBSIDENCE** subsidence in a building **9.** SOC WELFARE **WELFARE SERVICES BUILDING** a public building in which social workers provide welfare services in a deprived area **10.** LAW **SETTLING OF PROPERTY ON SB** a conveyance of property to a person or trustees for sb **11.** LAW **CONVEYANCE DOCUMENT** a document recording a conveyance of property

settler /séttlər/ *n.* sb who comes to live in a new place, especially a place that is unpopulated or populated by people of a different race or civilization

settlings /séttlingz/ *npl.* solid material that has sunk to the bottom of a liquid

settlor /séttlər/ *n.* sb who creates a trust or settlement

set-to (*plural* **set-tos**) *n.* a brief and hot-tempered argument or fight (*informal*)

set-top box *n.* a device used with a traditional television set to enable the reception and decoding of satellite, cable, or digital signals

Setúbal /se tóob'l/ city and port in western Portugal, situated 32 km/20 mi. southeast of Lisbon. Population: 83,550 (1991).

setup /sét up/ *n.* **1. ORGANIZATION OF STH** the way that sth is organized or arranged **2. SET OF PREPARED OBJECTS FOR TASK** an assembly of prepared tools or apparatus required for performing a task **3. DISHONEST PLAN OR TRICK** sth that is planned to bring about a desired result dishonestly (*informal*) **4.** CINEMA **POSITION OF CAMERA FOR SCENE** the position of a camera at the beginning of a scene **5.** *US* **TABLE SETTING** a table setting for a single person

set width *n.* = **set**[1] *n.* **5**, **set**[1] *n.* **6**

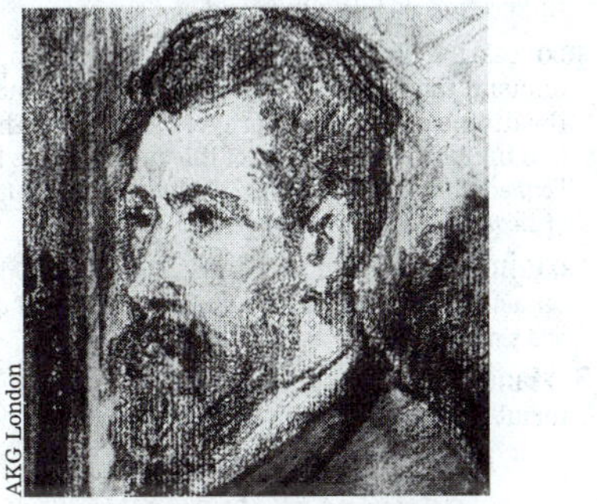

Georges Seurat: Portrait drawing (1890?) by Maximilien Luce

Seurat /súr aa, sör a/, **Georges** (1859–91) French painter. He developed the theory and practice of pointillism, or divisionism, seen in a work such as *Sunday Afternoon at the Grande Jatte (1886).*

Seuss /syooss/, **Dr.** (1904–91) US writer and illustrator. His children's books, replete with fanciful word play and illustrated with his own drawings, include *Horton Hatches the Egg* (1940) and *The Cat in the Hat* (1957). Pseudonym of **Theodor Seuss Geisel**

Sevan, Lake /se vaán-/ the largest lake in Armenia, in the north of the country, in the Caucasus Mountains. It is drained by the River Razdau. Area: 1,397 sq. km/540 sq. mi.

Sevastopol = **Sebastopol**

seven /sévv'n/ *n.* **1. NUMBER 7** the number 7 **2. STH WITH VALUE OF 7** sth in a numbered series, e.g. a playing card, with a value of 7 ○ *the seven of clubs* ○ *to play the seven* **3. GROUP OF 7** a group of seven objects or people **4.** RUGBY **SEVEN-A-SIDE RUGBY** a fast and open form of rugby played by teams of seven players (*takes a singular verb*) [Old English *seofon.* Ultimately from an Indo-European word meaning 'seven', which is also the ancestor of English *septi-* and *hepta-*.] —**seven** *adj., pron.*

seven deadly sins *npl.* = **deadly sins**

sevenfold /sévv'n fōld/ *adj.* **1. BEING SEVEN TIMES AS MUCH** relating to sth that is seven times as much as sth else **2. CONSISTING OF SEVEN PARTS** relating to sth that is made up of seven parts ■ *adv.* **BY SEVEN TIMES** by seven times as much or as many [Old English]

seven seas *npl.* all the oceans of the world. They are the North and South Atlantic, North and South Pacific, Arctic, Antarctic, and Indian Oceans.

Seven Sisters *n.* ASTRON = **Pleiades** (the)

seventeen /sévv'n téen/ *n.* **1. NUMBER 17** the number 17 **2. GROUP OF 17** a group of seventeen objects or people [Old English *seofontīene*, literally 'ten more than seven', from *-tīene* 'ten more than']

seventeenth /sévv'n téenth/ *n.* one of 17 equal parts of sth [Old English] —**seventeenth** *adj., adv.*

seventeen-year locust *n.* a cicada of eastern North America that spends most of its 17 years of life as an underground nymph, living as a winged adult for only a few weeks. In the southern United States the nymph lasts 13 years. Latin name: *Magicicada septendecim.*

seventh /sévv'nth/ *n.* **1. ONE OF 7 PARTS OF STH** one of seven equal parts of sth **2.** = **seventh chord 3.** MUSIC **INTERVAL OF SEVEN NOTES** in a standard musical scale, the interval between one note and another that lies six notes above or below it. In the scale of C major, C and B form a seventh. **4.** MUSIC **NOTE A SEVENTH AWAY FROM ANOTHER** in a standard musical scale, a note that is a seventh away from another note [Old English] —**seventh** *adj., adv.* —**seventhly** *adv.*

seventh chord *n.* a chord with a seventh note above the base note

Seventh-Day Adventist *n.* a member of a Protestant denomination that believes in the imminent Second Coming of Jesus Christ and observes Saturday as the Sabbath

seventh heaven *n.* **1. PERFECT HAPPINESS** a state of extreme happiness **2.** RELIG **HIGHEST HEAVEN** the highest of the seven heavens in Muslim and Talmudic belief

seventieth /sévv'nti əth/ *n.* one of seventy equal parts of sth —**seventieth** *adj., adv.*

seventy /sévv'nti/ *n.* (*plural* **-ties**) **1. NUMBER 70** the number 70 **2. GROUP OF 70** a group of seventy objects or people ■ **seventies** *npl.* **1. NUMBERS 70 TO 79** the numbers 70 to 79, particularly as a range of temperature ○ *in the low seventies* **2. YEARS 1970 TO 1979** the years 1970 to 1979 **3. PERIOD FROM AGE 70 TO 79** the period of sb's life from the age of 70 to 79 [Old English *hundseofontig*, from *hund* (of uncertain origin and lost in Middle English) + *seofon* 'seven' (see SEVEN) + *-tig* 'ten'] —**seventy** *adj., pron.*

seventy-eight, 78 *n.* a gramophone record designed to be played at 78 revolutions per minute, a former standard speed

seventy four *n.* either of two large, colourfully striped South African sea fish related to the seabream. Latin name: *Polysteganus undulosus.* Latin name: *Petrus rupestris.* [Origin uncertain: perhaps because of its many stripes or because the stripes resemble those of an ancient warrior, fancifully imagined to carry seventy-four weapons]

seven-up *n.* a card game in which the first person to reach seven points wins the game

seven-year itch *n.* an inclination towards sexual infidelity, popularly believed to begin after seven years of marriage (*informal*)

Seven Years' War *n.* a war fought from 1756 to 1763 by Prussia, assisted by British subsidies and Hanoverian troops, against France and Austria

sever /sévvər/ (**-ers, -ering, -ered**) *vti.* **1. CUT THROUGH OR OFF** to cut through sth or cut off, or be cut through or off **2. SEPARATE** to separate or put things or people apart, or to become separated or put apart **3. BREAK OFF TIE** to break off a tie, or to become broken off ○ *severed her relationship with him* [14thC. Via Anglo-Norman *severer* from Old French *sevrer* from, ultimately, Latin *separare* 'to separate' (see SEPARATE).]

severable /sévvərəb'l/ *adj.* **1. CAPABLE OF BEING SEVERED** able to be severed **2. LEGALLY SEPARABLE** capable of being legally separated without invalidating what remains, e.g. clauses in an agreement [Mid-16thC] —**severability** /sévvərə bíllәti/ *n.*

several /sévvərəl/ CORE MEANING: a grammatical word indicating a small number ○ (det) *I sent the cheque several days ago.* ○ (pron) *Several of the apples were bruised.*

adj. **1. VARIOUS** various or separate ○ *They all went their several ways.* **2.** LAW **SEPARATE** relating to separate individuals ○ *joint and several liability* [15thC. Via Anglo-Norman from, ultimately, Latin *separ* 'separate', from *separare* 'to separate' (see SEPARATE).]

severalfold /sévvərəl fōld/ *adj.* **1. BEING SEVERAL TIMES AS MUCH** relating to sth that is several times as much as sth else **2. CONSISTING OF SEVERAL PARTS** relating to sth that is made up of several parts ■ *adv.* **BY SEVERAL TIMES** by several times as much or as many

severally /sévvrəli/ *adv.* (*formal or literary*) **1. SEPARATELY** in a separate or individual way **2. RESPECTIVELY** in turn or respectively

severance /sévvərənss/ *n.* **1. ACT OF SEVERING** an act of severing or the state of being severed **2.** = **severance pay 3.** LAW **SPLITTING INTO PARTS** the splitting into separate parts of sth held jointly, e.g. an estate

severance pay, severance *n.* money paid as compensation, on the basis of length of service, to an employee whose job ceases to exist

severe /si véer/ *adj.* **1. HARSH** very harsh or strict **2. STERN** looking stern or serious **3. DANGEROUS** extremely bad or dangerous ○ *severe injuries* **4. EXTREMELY UNPLEASANT** causing great discomfort by being extreme ○ *a severe frost* **5. DIFFICULT TO ENDURE** difficult to do or endure ○ *severe hardship* **6. EXACTING** having standards or other criteria that are difficult to meet ○ *a severe test* **7. PLAIN** plain or austere in style, with little or no decoration ○ *severe clothing* [Mid-16thC. Via French *sévère* or directly from Latin *severus* 'serious', of uncertain origin.] —**severely** *adv.* —**severeness** *n.*

severity /si vérrəti/ *n.* **1. STATE OR EXTENT OF BADNESS** the state of being very bad, or the extent to which sth is bad **2. STRICTNESS OR STERNNESS** the state of being very strict or stern **3. PLAINNESS** the plainness or austerity of sth such as a building or style of dress **4.** (*plural* **-ties**) **HARSH ACT OR CRITICISM** an instance of harsh treatment or censure

Severn /sévvurn/ **1.** the longest river in Britain, rising in Wales and flowing into the Bristol Channel. Its estuary is crossed by two suspension bridges. Length: 338 km/210 mi. **2.** river that originates in lakes in western Ontario, in Canada, and flows northeast into Hudson Bay. Length: 982 km/610 mi.

Severus /si véerəss/, **Lucius Septimus** (146–211) North African-born Roman emperor. As emperor (193–211), he was noted for his civil, judicial, and military reforms, and his military expeditions to maintain his control of the Roman Empire.

Seveso /se vássō/ town situated near Milan, in northern Italy. It was the scene of an industrial accident in 1976, when the poisonous gas dioxin escaped into the atmosphere.

seviche *n.* = **ceviche**

Seville /sə víl/ city and river port in the autonomous region of Andalusia, southwestern Spain. Population: 719,590 (1995).

Seville orange *n.* US term **bitter orange 1.** FOOD **ORANGE FRUIT FOR MAKING MARMALADE** the bitter fruit of the Seville orange tree, often used to make marmalade **2.** TREES **ORANGE TREE** an orange tree of tropical and subtropical regions, grown for its bitter fruit. Latin name: *Citrus aurantium.* [Late 16thC. Named after SEVILLE, known for the quality of its oranges.]

Sèvres /sévvrə/ *n.* a highly decorated French porcelain

sew /sō/ (**sews, sewing, sewed, sewn** /sōn/ *or* **sewed**) *vti.* to join things or repair or make sth by using a needle to pass thread repeatedly through material [Old English *siowan.* Ultimately from an Indo-European word meaning 'to sew' that is also the ancestor of English *hymen* and *suture*.] —**sewable** *adj.*

sew up *vt.* to finish a business or plan successfully

sewage /sóo ij, syóo-/ *n.* human and domestic waste matter from buildings, especially houses, that is carried away through sewers [Mid-19thC. Formed from SEWER.]

sewage farm *n.* a place where sewage is treated to make it nontoxic, and especially to make it into manure. US term **sewage plant**

Sewell /sýoo əl, soo-/, **Anna** (1820–78) British writer. Her only book, *Black Beauty* (1877), was written to advocate humane treatment of animals and became a children's classic.

Sewell, Henry (1807–79) British-born New Zealand statesman. He was the first premier of New Zealand for a brief term (May 1856).

sewellel /sə wélləl/ *n.* = **mountain beaver** [Early 19thC. From Chinook *šwalál* 'robe made of sewellel skin'.]

sewen *n.* = **sewin**

sewer[1] /sóo ər, syoo-/ *n.* DRAIN FOR WASTE a pipe or drain, usually underground, that carries away waste or rainwater ■ *vt.* (-ers, -ering, -ered) PROVIDE WITH SEWERS to provide a place with sewers [15thC. Via Anglo-Norman *sever* from, ultimately, assumed Vulgar Latin *exaquare* 'to remove water, drain', from Latin *ex-* 'out' + *aqua* 'water' (source of English *aquarium*).]

sewer[2] /sóo ər, syoo-/ *n.* a medieval servant who served meals [14thC. From Anglo-Norman *asseour*, from French *asseoir* 'to place a seat for', literally 'to sit to', ultimately from Latin *sedere* 'to sit'.]

sewer[3] /só ər/ *n.* sb or sth that sews

sewerage /sóo ərij, syoo-/ *n.* **1.** SEWER SYSTEM a system of sewers **2.** REMOVAL OF WASTE the removal of waste by means of sewers **3.** = **sewage**

sewin /syoo in/ (*plural* **sewins** *or* **sewin**), **sewen** (*plural* **sewens** *or* **sewen**) *n. Wales, Ireland* a sea trout [Mid-16thC. Origin unknown.]

sewing /só ing/ *n.* **1.** USE OF NEEDLE AND THREAD the act or work of using a needle and thread to join or repair material **2.** MATERIAL BEING SEWN a piece of material that sb is sewing

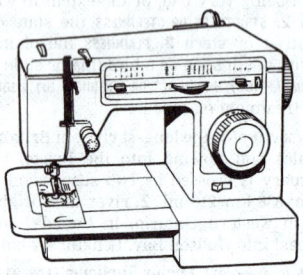

Sewing machine

sewing machine *n.* a machine, now usually electric, for sewing material

sewn past participle of **sew**

sex /seks/ *n.* **1.** MALE OR FEMALE GENDER either of the two reproductive categories, male or female, of animals and plants **2.** INTERCOURSE sexual intercourse **3.** SEXUAL BEHAVIOUR sexual activity or behaviour leading to it **4.** GENITALS the genitals (*literary*) **5.** BIOL REPRODUCTIVE CHARACTERISTICS the set of characteristics that determine whether the reproductive role of an animal or plant is male or female ■ *adj.* OF SEX relating to sexual matters or the sexes ■ *vt.* (**sexes, sexing, sexed**) DETERMINE SEX OF to determine the sex of an animal or plant [14thC. Via French *sexe* or directly from Latin *sexus*. The meaning of 'sexual intercourse' (first recorded in the works of D. H. Lawrence) is a 20thC development.]

──── **WORD KEY: USAGE** ────
See Usage note at *gender*.

sex- *prefix.* six ○ *sexangular* [From Latin *sex* 'six'. Ultimately from the Indo-European word for 'six', which is also the ancestor of English *six* and *hexa-*.]

sexagenarian /séksəjə náiri ən/, **sexagenary** *n.* sb aged between 60 and 69 **—sexagenarian** *adj.*

Sexagesima /séksə jéssimə/ *n.* CALENDAR in the Christian calendar, the second Sunday before Lent, eight weeks before Easter [14thC. From ecclesiastical Latin,

a form of Latin *sexagesimus* 'sixtieth' (see SEXAGESIMAL); probably because the day occurs two Sundays before *Quadragesima*, literally 'fortieth (day)'.]

sexagesimal /séksə jéssim'l/ *adj.* BASED ON 60 relating to or based on the number 60 ■ *n.* FRACTION WITH DENOMINATOR POWER OF 60 a fraction in which the denominator is a power of 60 [Late 17thC. Formed from Latin *sexagesimus* 'sixtieth', from *sexaginta* 'sixty' (see SEXAGENARY).]

sex appeal *n.* the quality of being sexually attractive

sexavalent /séksə váylənt/ *adj.* = **hexavalent**

sex cell *n.* = **gamete**

sexcentenary /sék sen teénəri/ *adj.* **1.** OF 600 relating to the number 600 or a period of 600 years **2.** OF 600TH ANNIVERSARY relating to a 600th anniversary ■ *n.* (*plural* **-ies**) 600TH ANNIVERSARY a 600th anniversary or the celebration of one

sex change *n.* an operation with accompanying hormonal treatment that changes sb's physical characteristics from those of one sex to the other

sex chromatin *n.* = **Barr body**

sex chromosome *n.* a chromosome that determines the sex of an organism such as the X and Y chromosomes in humans and other mammals. In each cell nucleus, a male mammal has one X and one Y chromosome, and a female has two X chromosomes.

sexduction /seks dúksh'n/ *n.* the transfer of a fragment of chromosome from one bacterial cell to another by its incorporation into a special DNA particle (**plasmid**) that initiates sexual conjugation between the cells [Mid-20thC. Blend of SEX and TRANSDUCTION.]

sexed /sekst/ *adj.* **1.** INTERESTED IN SEX having a specified degree of interest in sex ○ *highly sexed* **2.** BIOL HAVING SEXUAL CHARACTERISTICS possessing sexual characteristics [Late 16thC]

sexennial /sek sénni əl/ *adj.* OCCURRING EVERY SIX YEARS happening every six years or over a period of six years ■ *n.* STH OCCURRING EVERY SIX YEARS sth that happens every six years or over a period of six years [Mid-17thC. Formed from Latin *sexennium* 'a period of six years', from *annus* 'year' (see ANNUAL).] **—sexennially** *adv.*

sex factor *n.* a genetic element found in certain bacteria that enables the cell to put out a fine tube to another bacterial cell and transfer some of its genetic material

sex gland *n.* = **gonad**

sex hormone *n.* a hormone that affects the development of the reproductive organs and sexual characteristics

sexism /séksizəm/ *n.* **1.** SEX DISCRIMINATION discrimination against women or men because of their sex **2.** SEXUAL STEREOTYPING the tendency to treat people as cultural stereotypes of their sex

sexist /séksist/ *adj.* **1.** BELIEVING ONE SEX IS INFERIOR believing that one sex is inferior to the other in a variety of attributes **2.** RESULTING FROM SEXIST BELIEF resulting from or relating to the belief that one sex is inferior to the other in a variety of attributes ■ *n.* SB WHO IS SEXIST sb who believes that one sex is weaker to the other in a variety of attributes

sexivalent /séksi váylənt/ *adj.* = **hexavalent**

sex kitten *n.* an offensive term referring to a young woman perceived as sexually appealing (*offensive*)

sexless /séksləss/ *adj.* **1.** NOT SEXY sexually unattractive **2.** WITHOUT SEXUAL ACTIVITY living without sexual intercourse or interest in sex **3.** WITHOUT SEXUAL CHARACTERISTICS used to describe an animal or plant that has no, or no obvious, sexual characteristics **—sexlessly** *adv.* **—sexlessness** *n.*

sex-limited *adj.* used to describe genetically inherited traits or conditions that appear in one sex only, although the genes themselves may be found in either sex

sex-linked *adj.* relating to a gene located on a sex chromosome, typically the X chromosome, or inheritance determined by such a gene **—sex-linkage** *n.*

sex object *n.* sb treated or seen as worthy of notice because of characteristics perceived as sexually appealing

sex offender *n.* sb who commits a crime involving a sexual act

sexology /sek sólləji/ *n.* the study of human sexual behaviour **—sexological** /séksə lójjik'l/ *adj.* **—sexologist** /-sólləjist/ *n.*

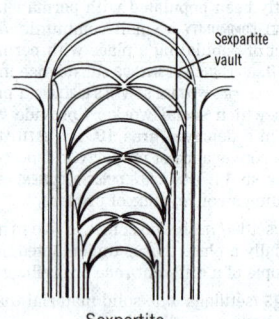

Sexpartite

sexpartite /seks paár tīt/ *adj.* **1.** ARCHIT CONSISTING OF SIX PARTS divided into or made up of six parts ○ *a sexpartite vault* **2.** HAVING SIX PARTICIPANTS involving six participants [Mid-18thC. Formed from SEX- + PARTITE.]

sexploitation /séks ploy táysh'n/ *n.* the deliberate use of sexual material to make a product, especially a film, commercially successful [Mid-20thC. Blend of SEX and EXPLOITATION.]

sexpot /séks pot/ *n.* an offensive term referring to a woman who appears to radiate sexuality (*offensive*)

sex role *n.* a set of behaviours characteristic of or expected of members of one sex or the other

sex shop *n.* a shop that sells items intended to aid sexual arousal or add to the pleasure of sexual intercourse

sex-starved *adj.* lacking sexual activity even though it is desired

sex symbol *n.* sb such as a film star whose fame is linked to a widely perceived sex appeal

sext /sekst/ *n.* in Christianity, especially Roman Catholicism, the fourth of the seven canonical hours of the divine office, or the prayers said then. This was originally the sixth hour of the day, midday. [14thC. Formed from Latin *sexta (hora)* 'sixth (hour)', the feminine of *sextus*.]

sextain /séks tayn/ *n.* = **sestina** [Mid-17thC. Origin uncertain: probably formed from SEX- on the model of *quatrain* and similar forms.]

Sextans /sékstənz/ *n.* a faint constellation of the equatorial region lying between Leo and Hydra

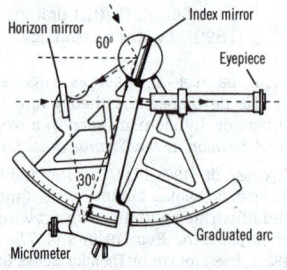

Sextant

sextant /sékstənt/ *n.* a navigational instrument incorporating a telescope and an angular scale that is used to work out latitude and longitude. A celestial body is viewed through the telescope and its angular distance above the horizon is read off the scale. The data is then used to calculate position. [Late 16thC. From the Latin stem *sextant-* 'sixth part (of a circle)' (referring to the arc on which the scale is marked), from *sextus*.]

sextet /sek stét/, **sextette** *n.* **1.** SIX PLAYERS OR SINGERS a group of six musicians or singers, or a piece of music composed for them **2. SIX PEOPLE OR THINGS** any group of six people or things [Mid-19thC. Alteration of SESTET under the influence of Latin *sex* 'six' (see SEX-).]

sex therapy *n.* the treatment of sexual problems through counselling and psychotherapy —**sex therapist** *n.*

sextile /séks tīl/ *n.* **1. STATS STATISTICAL DIVISION** any of the six equal groups into which a statistical sample can be divided **2. STATS STATISTICAL VALUE** any of the five statistical values that divide a frequency distribution into six parts, with each containing a sixth of the sample population **3. ASTRON ANGLE BETWEEN PLANETS** a position of two celestial bodies in which they are 60 degrees apart as viewed from the Earth [Mid-16thC. From Latin *sextilis*, from *sextus* 'sixth'.] —**sextile** *adj.*

sextillion /seks tílli ən/ (*plural* **-lions** *or* **-lion**) *n.* **1. FOLLOWED BY 21 ZEROS** the number equal to 10^{21}, written as 1 followed by 21 zeros **2. 1 FOLLOWED BY 36 ZEROS** the number equal to 10^{36}, written as 1 followed by 36 zeros (*dated*) [Late 17thC. From French, formed from Latin *sex* 'six' (see SEX-) on the model of *million* and similar numerals.] —**sextillion** *adj.*, *pron.* —**sextillionth** *n.*, *adj.*

sextodecimo /sékstō déssimō/ (*plural* **-mos**) *n.* a size of book page obtained by folding a sheet of paper into 16 leaves, producing 32 pages [Mid-17thC. From Latin *sexto decimo*, a form of *sextus decimus* 'sixteenth', literally 'sixth tenth' (*decimus*) source of English *decimal*.]

sexton /sékstən/ *n.* **1. CHR CHURCH CARETAKER** the caretaker of a church and its graveyard whose duties often include ringing the bell and digging graves **2. sexton, sexton beetle INSECTS BEETLE THAT EATS DEAD ANIMALS** a beetle that buries the bodies of dead small animals such as mice by digging beneath them, using the bodies as food for itself and its larvae. Genus: *Necrophorus*. [14thC. Via Anglo-Norman *segerstein* from, ultimately, medieval Latin *sacristanus* 'sacristan' (see SACRISTAN).]

sextuple /sékstyoop'l, sekstyoop'l/ *n.* **MATH NUMBER SIX TIMES ANOTHER** a number or quantity that is six times another number or quantity ■ *adj.* **1. MATH BEING SIX TIMES ANOTHER** relating to or being a number or quantity that is six times another number or quantity **2. CONSISTING OF SIX PARTS** made up of six parts or members **3. MUSIC HAVING SIX BEATS TO BAR** used to describe a time or rhythm in which there are six beats to the bar ■ *vti.* (**-ples, -pling, -pled**) **MULTIPLY BY SIX** to multiply sth by six or be multiplied by six [Early 17thC. From medieval Latin *sextuplus*, from Latin *sex* 'six' (see SEX-) on the model of medieval Latin *quintuplus* 'quintuple'.]

sextuplet /sékstyooplət, seks tyooplət/ *n.* **1. BIOL ONE OF SIX OFFSPRING BORN TOGETHER** one of six offspring born in a single birth **2. GROUP OF SIX** a group of six things **3. MUSIC GROUP OF SIX NOTES** a group of six notes played in a time normally given to four [Mid-19thC. Formed from SEXTUPLE on the model of *triplet*.]

sextuplicate *n.* /-tyooplikət/ **SET OF SIX COPIES** a set of six things, especially identical copies ■ *adj.* /-tyooplikət/ **MATH BEING SIX TIMES ANOTHER** relating to or being six times another number or quantity ■ *v.* /seks tyoopli kayt/ (**-cates, -cating, -cated**) **1.** *vti.* **MATH MULTIPLY BY SIX** to multiply sth by six or be multiplied by six **2.** *vt.* **MAKE SIX COPIES** to make six copies of sth [Mid-17thC. Formed from medieval Latin *sextuplicat-*, the past participle stem of *sextuplicare* 'to increase sixfold', from, ultimately, Latin *sex* 'six' (see SEX-).]

sex-typed *adj.* intended for or conventionally perceived as appropriate for one sex and not the other —**sex-typing** *n.*

sexual /sékshoo əl/ *adj.* **1. OF SEX** relating to sex, sexuality, or the sexual organs **2. RELATING TO EITHER SEX** relating to the two sexes or to either of them **3. BIOL INVOLVING REPRODUCTIVE UNION** relating to the union of male and female gametes in reproduction [Mid-17thC. From late Latin *sexualis*, from Latin *sexus* 'sex'.] —**sexually** *adv.*

sexual assault *n.* an incident that involves sexual contact that is forced on sb or to which sb cannot consent

sexual dimorphism *n.* the existence of differences in the appearance of the male and female of a species

sexual harassment *n.* unwanted sex-related behaviour towards sb, e.g. touching sb or making suggestive remarks, especially by sb with authority to a subordinate

sexual intercourse *n.* an act carried out for reproduction or pleasure involving penetration, especially one in which a man inserts his erect penis into a woman's vagina

sexualise *vt.* = sexualize

sexuality /sékshoo álləti/ *n.* **1. SEXUAL APPEAL** sexual appeal or potency **2. STATE OF BEING SEXUAL** the state of being sexual **3. INVOLVEMENT IN SEXUAL ACTIVITY** involvement or interest in sexual activity

sexualize /sékshoo ə līz/ (**-izes, -izing, -ized**), **sexualise** (**-ises, -ising, -ised**) *vt.* to impose a sexual interpretation or perception on sth or sb

sexually transmitted disease *n.* a disease such as syphilis or genital herpes that is normally passed from one person to another through sexual activity

sexual orientation *n.* the direction of sb's sexual desire, towards people of the opposite sex, or of the same sex, or of both sexes

sexual relations *npl.* = sexual intercourse

sexual reproduction *n.* reproduction that involves the union of male and female gametes, each contributing half of the genetic makeup of the resulting zygote

sexual selection *n.* the choice by a female animal of a mate on the basis of a characteristic, e.g. a bird song or bright plumage

sexvalent /seks váylənt/ *adj.* = hexavalent

sex work *n.* the work of sb in one of the sex industries such as pornography or prostitution —**sex worker** *n.*

sexy /séksi/ (**-ier, -iest**) *adj.* **1. AROUSING DESIRE** arousing or intended to arouse sexual desire **2. AROUSED** sexually aroused **3. APPEALING** appealing especially because of being new, interesting, or trendy (*informal*) —**sexily** *adv.* —**sexiness** *n.*

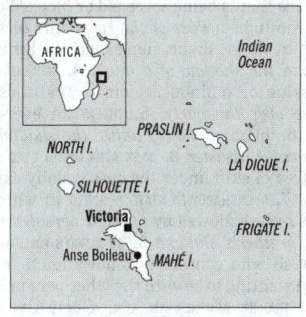

Seychelles

Seychelles /say shélz/ island republic in the Indian Ocean. It contains four main islands and many islets. Language: Creole, English, French. Currency: Seychelles rupee. Capital: Victoria. Population: 76,100 (1996). Area: 455 sq. km/175 sq. mi. Official name **Republic of Seychelles** —**Seychellois** /sáy shel waa/ *adj.*, *n.*

Seyfert galaxy /síffərt-/ *n.* a small spiral galaxy that varies in brightness and emits radio waves and X-rays [Mid-20thC. Named after Carl K. *Seyfert* (1911–60), the US astronomer who first described this type of galaxy.]

Seymour /seém awr/**, Jane, Queen of England and Ireland** (1509?–37). She was the third wife of Henry VIII of England, and died shortly after giving birth to Edward VI, Henry's only male heir.

sf *abbr.* **1.** sforzando **2.** science fiction

SF *abbr.* **1.** science fiction **2.** sinking fund

SFA *abbr.* **1.** Scottish Football Association **2.** Securities and Futures Authority Ltd

Sfax /sfaks/ port and capital city of Safaqis Governorate, east-central Tunisia. Population: 230,900 (1994).

sferics /sférriks/ *npl. US* = spherics

SFO *abbr.* **1.** Superannuation Funds Office **2.** Serious Fraud Office

sforzando /sfawrt sándō/, **sforzato** /zfawrt saátō/ *adv.* **WITH STRONG ACCENT** with a sudden strong accent (*used as a musical direction*) ■ *n.* (*plural* **-dos** *or* **-di** /-dee/; *plural* **-tos** *or* **-ti** /-ti/) **SUDDEN STRONG NOTE** a note or chord that is to be played with a sudden strong accent, or a symbol indicating this [Early 19thC. From Italian, formed from *sforzare* 'to use force', from, ultimately, Latin *fortis* 'strong' (see FORTIS).] —**sforzando** *adj.*

sfumato /sfoo maátō/ *n.* the gradual blending of one area of colour into another without a sharp outline [Mid-19thC. From Italian, past participle of *sfumare* 'to tone down', literally 'to smoke out', from, ultimately, Latin *fumus* 'smoke' (see FUME).]

sfz. *abbr.* sforzando

sg *abbr.* specific gravity

Sg *abbr.* Song of Songs

SG *abbr.* **1.** solicitor general **2.** singular

sgd *abbr.* signed

SGHWR *abbr.* steam-generating heavy-water reactor

SGML *n.* an international standard for the definition of system-independent methods of representing texts in electronic form by describing the relationship between a document's form and its structure. SGML is used widely to manage large documents that are subject to frequent revisions and need to be printed in different formats. Full form **Standard Generalized Markup Language**

SGP *abbr.* Singapore (*international vehicle registration*)

sgraffito /sgraa féetō/ (*plural* **-ti** /-ti/) *n.* **1. DECORATION TECHNIQUE** a technique used to decorate ceramics or plaster walls, in which the top layer has patterns scratched into it, revealing the different-coloured layer beneath **2. DECORATION** a decoration made using the sgraffito technique **3. DECORATED OBJECT** an object decorated using the sgraffito technique [Mid-18thC. From Italian, the past participle of *sgraffire* 'to scratch', from *sgraffio* 'scratch', from *sgraffiare* 'to scratch' from Old Italian, literally 'to scratch completely', from *graffiare* (see GRAFFITO).]

Sgt *abbr.* Sergeant

Sgt Maj. *abbr.* Sergeant Major

sh, shh *interj.* used to tell sb to be silent or quieter [Mid-19thC. A naturally produced interjection.]

sh. *abbr.* **1.** sheep **2.** sheet **3.** shilling **4.** share

SHA *abbr.* sidereal hour angle

Shaanxi /shaa aánshi/ province in China bordering Ningsia Hui, Inner Mongolia, Shanxi, Henan, Hubei, Sichuan, and Gansu. Capital: Xi'an. Population: 34,810,000 (1994). Area: 195,799 sq. km/75,598 sq. mi.

Shaban /shə baán, shaa-/, **Shaaban** *n.* **CALENDAR** in the Islamic calendar, the eighth month of the year [Mid-18thC. From Arabic *ša'bān*.]

Shabbat /shaa baát/ (*plural* **-batot** /shaa baa tót/ *or* **-bes** /shaábəss/) *n.* **CALENDAR** the Jewish Sabbath, celebrated on Saturday [Mid-19thC. From Hebrew *šabbāt*, literally 'day of rest' (source of English *Sabbath*).]

shabby /shábbi/ (**-bier, -biest**) *adj.* **1. WORN AND THREADBARE** worn out, frayed, or threadbare after long use **2. WEARING WORN CLOTHES** wearing worn-out clothing and perceived as being unappealing to the eye **3. INCONSIDERATE** inconsiderate and unfair ○ *won't put up with shabby treatment* **4.** **INFERIOR IN QUALITY** inferior in quality ○ *shabby goods* **5. RUN DOWN** poorly maintained and thus falling apart or dirty ○ *a shabby section of town* [Mid-17thC. Formed from obsolete *shab* 'disreputable person', from Old English *sceabb* 'scab'. Ultimately from a prehistoric Germanic word that is also the ancestor of English *scab*.] —**shabbily** *adv.* —**shabbiness** *adv.*

shabby-genteel *adj.* trying to keep up the appearances that the middle or upper middle class demands, despite not having enough money

Shacharis /shaákhəriss/ *n.* the Jewish morning liturgy [From Hebrew *šaḥărit*, literally 'morning time']

shack /shak/ *n.* a small crude building typically made of boards or sheets of material, usually without a foundation [Late 19thC. Origin uncertain: perhaps via Mexican Spanish *jacal* 'wooden hut' from Nahuatl *xacalli*.]
shack up *vi.* to live with a lover without being

married (*informal disapproving*) [From the practice of military personnel living with local women off base]

Shackle

shackle /shák'l/ *n.* **1.** METAL BRACELET FOR HOLDING PRISONERS a round metal band that can be opened or locked in order to hold the wrist or ankle of a captive, usually attached by chains in pairs or fours (*often used in the plural*) **2.** RIDING BINDER FOR ANIMAL LEGS a device used to hold together the legs of horses and other animals **3.** U-SHAPED FASTENER a U-shaped bar that is fastened with a straight pin or bolt to hold sth securely **4.** RESTRAINT ON FREEDOM an oppressive restraint on sth or sb (*often plural*) ○ *mental shackles* ■ *vt.* (-les, -ling, -led) **1.** RESTRICT FREEDOM to restrict the freedom of sb or sth ○ *felt shackled by the inflexible rules* **2.** RESTRAIN WITH SHACKLES to restrain sb or an animal using shackles **3.** SECURE WITH SHACKLE to connect or secure sth with a shackle [Old English *sceacul.* Ultimately from a prehistoric Germanic word denoting 'a fastening'.] —**shackler** *n.*

shad /shad/ (*plural* **shads** *or* **shad**) *n.* any of various North Atlantic fishes similar to herring, commonly used as food. They leave salt water to spawn upstream in rivers. Genus: *Alosa.* [Old English *sceadd*]

shadberry /shádbəri/ (*plural* -**ries**) *n.* = **serviceberry** *n.* **2** [Mid-19thC. From its flowering when shad appear in the rivers to spawn.]

Shadbolt /shádbōlt/, **Maurice Francis Richard** (*b.* 1932) New Zealand writer. He wrote the short story collection *The New Zealanders* (1959) and novels including *Season of the Jew* (1986).

shadbush /shád boosh/ *n. US* = **serviceberry** *n.* **1**

shadchan /shaad kháan, sha'ádkhən/ (*plural* -**chanim** /shaad kháaním/ *or* -**chans**), **shadkhan** (*plural* -**kanim** *or* -**khans**) *n.* a marriage broker for Jewish couples [Mid-19thC. Via Yiddish *shadkhn* from medieval Hebrew *šadděkān*, from *šiddēk* 'to make marriage proposals'.]

shaddock /sháddək/ *n.* = **pomelo** *n.* **1**, **pomelo** *n.* **2** [Late 17thC. Named after a 17C English ship captain named *Shaddock*, who brought the seed to Barbados.]

shade /shayd/ *n.* **1.** AREA OUT OF DIRECT SUNLIGHT an area of relative darkness where direct sunlight is blocked or obscured **2.** SLIGHTLY DIFFERENT COLOUR a colour that is a variation on a basic colour, e.g. by being more or less bright or dark ○ *a pretty shade of blue* **3.** STH THAT BLOCKS LIGHT sth, e.g. a lampshade, used to block a direct light source **4.** *US* WINDOW DEVICE a flexible piece of material mounted on a window that can be rolled down to block light or up to admit light **5.** ARTS DARK PARTS OF PAINTING the darker parts of a painting, drawing, or photograph **6.** SMALL AMOUNT a slight degree or amount ○ *a shade too close* **7.** VARIATION a slight variation on sth similar ○ *different shades of opinion* **8.** OBSCURITY relative obscurity **9.** PARANORMAL GHOST a ghost or phantom (*literary*) **10.** SHADOW a shadow (*archaic*) ■ **shades** *npl.* SUNGLASSES sunglasses (*informal*) ■ *v.* (**shades, shading, shaded**) **1.** *vt.* PROTECT FROM SUNLIGHT to protect sth or block it off from direct light, particularly from direct sunlight ○ *The awning shades the porch well.* **2.** *vt.* DARKEN PART OF PICTURE to darken part of a drawing or picture using pencil, ink, or some other dark medium ○ *He shaded in the trees in the background.* **3.** *vi.* CHANGE SLIGHTLY GRADUALLY to change imperceptibly into sth slightly different ○ *The cream gradually shades into gold.* **4.** *vt.* DARKEN to make a place or area darker **5.** *vt.* BUSINESS REDUCE PRICE to reduce a price slightly [Old English *sceadu* (source also of English *shadow*). Ultimately

from an Indo-European word meaning 'darkness, shadow'.] ◇ **put sb** *or* **sth in the shade** to make sb or sth seem unimportant by appearing much more special or attractive ◇ **shades of sb** *or* **sth** used to say that sth is reminiscent of sth, especially a time in the past or the work of a writer or other artist ○ *You can take tea on the terrace – shades of E. M. Forster – or ride on an elephant.*

Shades /shaydz/ *npl.* the underworld (*literary*) [Late 16thC. Originally in the meaning 'darkness' (as of the underworld).]

shading /sháyding/ *n.* **1.** DARKENED AREA IN PICTURE an area of relatively dark tone or close lines, dots, or hatching that produces darkness or shadow in a drawing or picture **2.** SLIGHT DIFFERENCE a subtle difference or variation

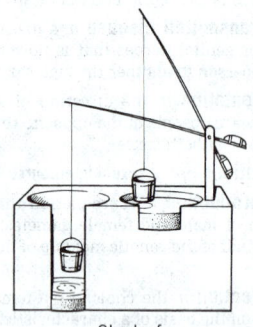

Shadoof

shadoof /shə doof/, **shaduf** *n.* a water-raising device used in ancient Egypt consisting of a suspended pivoting pole with a bucket on one end and a counterweight on the other [Mid-19thC. From Egyptian Arabic *šādūf.*]

shadow /sháddō/ *n.* **1.** DARKENED SHAPE OF STH IN LIGHT a darkened shape on a surface that falls behind sb or sth blocking the light **2.** DARKNESS relative darkness in a place that is being screened or blocked off from direct sunlight ○ *Part of the room was in shadow.* **3.** HINT OF STH a slight suggestion or hint of sth ○ *beyond the shadow of a doubt* **4.** OMINOUS GLOOM a depressing or ominous gloom ○ *The news cast a shadow over the party.* **5.** THREAT an ever-present threat or blight ○ *living under the shadow of environmental disaster* **6.** DARK AREA UNDER EYES a darkened area of skin under the eyes usually caused by fatigue **7.** OVERSHADOWED STATE a state in which sb is always overshadowed by another person ○ *grew up in his brother's shadow* **8.** SB ALWAYS FOLLOWING AFTER ANOTHER sb who constantly follows another person around wanting to be with the other person **9.** PERSON SECRETLY TRAILING ANOTHER sb, e.g. a detective or spy, who secretly follows sb **10.** POL OPPOSITION MINISTER WITH PARTICUAR JOB a politician in an opposition party who speaks on a particular area of policy and would hold a ministerial job if the party were in government **11.** ARTS = **shade** *n.* **5** **12.** PARANORMAL = **shade** *n.* **9** **13.** REFLECTION a reflection of sth in water ○ *the shadow of the stars in the dark lake* **14.** COPY an imitation or copy of sth **15.** INFERIOR REMNANT a remnant of sb or sth formerly greater or more important ○ *now a shadow of her former self* **16.** BUSINESS SB LEARNING JOB BY FOLLOWING WORKER sb who learns a job by following and observing sb else who knows or regularly does the job **17.** MED ABNORMAL AREA IN X-RAY an abnormal area showing up on an X-ray **18.** PSYCHOL JUNGIAN ARCHETYPE in Jungian psychology, the archetype that represents sexual and aggressive instincts inherited from a more primitive stage of humanity **19.** SHELTER sth that provides protection ■ *vt.* (-ows, -owing, -owed) **1.** PROTECT FROM LIGHT to shade sth from the light ○ *Her face was shadowed by a wide-brimmed straw hat.* **2.** FOLLOW to follow sb secretly ○ *The police had been shadowing him for days.* **3.** BUSINESS LEARN JOB BY FOLLOWING WORKER to learn a job by following sb who is actually doing the job **4.** REPRESENT VAGUELY to represent sth vaguely or in outline **5.** SHELTER STH to provide protection from sth (*archaic*) ■ *adj.* POL IN CAPACITY OF OPPOSITION COUNTERPART used to describe a member of an opposition party who speaks on a particular area of policy and would hold a ministerial job if the party

were in government ○ *the shadow cabinet* [Old English *sceaduwe,* a form of *sceadu* (see SHADE)] —**shadower** *n.*

shadow-box (**shadow-boxes, shadow-boxing, shadow-boxed**) *vi.* to practise boxing moves by sparring with an imaginary partner

shadow dance *n.* a dance performance in which the dancers' shadows are seen on a screen

shadowgraph /sháddō graaf, -graf/ *n.* **1.** IMAGE CAST IN SHADOW an image of a shape made by casting a shadow onto a surface, e.g. by shaping the hands so that their shadow resembles the silhouette of an animal **2.** = **radiograph**

shadow mask *n.* a perforated metal sheet mounted close to the rear of the phosphor dot faceplate of a three gun colour picture tube. The shadow mask is used to direct the electron beam to the desired phosphor colour element.

shadow play *n.* a theatrical performance where the audience views a screen on which the shadows of puppets or performers are cast by a light source behind them

shadow price *n.* the estimated price of goods or a service for which no market price exists

shadow senator *n.* a nonvoting representative of the District of Columbia in the US Senate

shadowy /sháddō i/ (-**ier**, -**iest**) *adj.* **1.** FULL OF SHADOWS full of shadows or shade **2.** NOT CLEARLY SEEN not clearly or only vaguely seen **3.** MYSTERIOUS mysteriously little-known or obscure —**shadowiness** *n.*

shaduf *n.* = **shadoof**

shady /sháydi/ (-**ier**, -**iest**) *adj.* **1.** HAVING SHADE having little natural light, often giving shelter from harsh sunlight **2.** DISHONEST probably dishonest or illegal ○ *shady dealings with foreign investors* **3.** PROVIDING SHADE providing shade —**shadily** *adv.* —**shadiness** *n.*

SHAEF /shayf/ *abbr.* Supreme Headquarters Allied Expeditionary Forces

shaft /shaaft/ *n.* **1.** LONG HANDLE the long slender handle on various instruments and tools, e.g. golf clubs and hammers **2.** VERTICAL PASSAGE a vertical passage, especially one in which a lift travels or one that gives access to a mine **3.** PASSAGE FOR VENTILATION IN BUILDING a small passageway in a building, particularly in a wall, ceiling, or floor, to allow for air circulation **4.** MECH ENG ROTATING ROD IN MACHINE a rotating rod that provides motion or power for a machine **5.** LIGHT BEAM a beam of light ○ *a shaft of sunlight* **6.** SHARP COMMENT a sharp or barbed comment directed at sb ○ *a shaft of wit* **7.** POLE FOR HARNESSING HORSE either of the two parallel bars by which an animal is harnessed to a cart or wagon **8.** *US* HARSH TREATMENT unkind or harsh treatment or dismissal (*informal*) ○ *His girlfriend gave him the shaft.* **9.** ARROW an arrow (*literary*) **10.** BODY OF PROJECTILE a long narrow rod that forms the body of a spear, arrow, harpoon, or other projectile **11.** ANAT MIDDLE OF LONG BONE the middle part of a long bone **12.** ANAT BODY OF PENIS the cylindrical body of the penis **13.** ANAT MAIN PART OF HAIR the part of a hair that is visible above the skin **14.** ARCHIT BODY OF COLUMN the main body of a column, between the capital and base **15.** ARCHIT COLUMN a column, especially one of a pair supporting an arch **16.** BIRDS FEATHER RIB the central rib of a feather **17.** TREES TREE TRUNK the trunk of a tree **18.** UPRIGHT PART OF CROSS the upright bar in a cross ■ *vt.* (**shafts, shafting, shafted**) **1.** TREAT UNFAIRLY to cheat sb or treat sb unfairly (*slang*) ○ *She got shafted on her book contract.* **2.** OFFENSIVE TERM to have sexual intercourse with a woman (*slang offensive*) [Old English *sceaft*]

Shaftesbury /sha'áftsbəri, -bri/ market town in Dorset, southwestern England. Population: 6,250 (1994).

shag[1] /shag/ *n.* **1.** TEXTILES LONG PILE ON TEXTILE a long rough nap or pile on a textile **2.** HAIR LAYERED HAIRCUT a hairstyle with layers that are cut progressively shorter from base to crown **3.** DRUGS SHREDDED TOBACCO a strong, coarse tobacco that is finely shredded **4.** MATTED TANGLE OF HAIR a rough matted tangle of hair or wool ■ *v.* (**shags, shagging, shagged**) **1.** *vt.* MAKE ROUGH to cause sth to be rough looking and shaggy **2.** *vi.*

HANG UNTIDILY to hang in an untidy manner **3.** *vt.* PROVIDE WITH SHAFT to provide sth such as a tool with a shaft [Old English *sceacga*]

shag[2] /shag/ *n.* a small crested cormorant mainly found in Europe and North Africa. Latin name: *Phalacrocorax aristotelis*. [Mid-16thC. Origin uncertain: perhaps from SHAG[1], because of the bird's shaggy crest.]

shag[3] /shag/ *vti.* (**shags, shagging, shagged**) OFFENSIVE TERM an offensive term referring to sexual intercourse (*slang taboo*) ■ *n.* OFFENSIVE TERM an act of sexual intercourse (*slang offensive*) [Late 18thC. Origin unknown.] —**shagger** *n.*

shag[4] /shag/ *n.* 1930S DANCE a 1930s dance step involving hopping alternately on each foot ■ *vi.* (**shags, shagging, shagged**) DANCE THE SHAG to dance the shag [Early 20thC. Origin uncertain.] —**shagger** *n.*

shag[5] /shag/ (**shags, shagging, shagged**) *vt. US* **1.** RETRIEVE to run and retrieve sth **2.** CHASE AWAY to chase sb or sth away (*regional*) [Early 20thC. Origin unknown.]

shagbark /shág baark/, **shagbark hickory** *n.* **1.** TREES HICKORY WITH SHAGGY BARK a hickory of eastern North America that has grey shaggy bark. Latin name: *Carya ovata*. **2.** INDUST SHAGBARK WOOD the valuable hard light-coloured wood of the shagbark **3.** FOOD HICKORY NUT the round hard-shelled edible nut of the shagbark

shagged /shagd/, **shagged out** *adj.* extremely tired (*slang*)

shaggy /shággi/ (**-gier, -giest**) *adj.* **1.** LONG AND UNTIDY growing long and untidily **2.** HAVING COARSE LONG FIBRES covered with or resembling coarse, long, and usually uneven hair, wool, or similar fibres **3.** TEXTILES ROUGH NAPPED having a rough, relatively long nap or pile

shaggy cap *n.* = shaggymane

shaggy dog story *n.* a long drawn-out absurd story or joke, often with an ending or punchline that is anticlimactic [From one such anecdote involving a shaggy dog]

shaggymane /shággi mayn/ *n.* a common edible mushroom with shaggy scales on its cap that contain black spores. Latin name: *Coprinus comatus*.

shagreen /shə grēen/ *n.* **1.** ROUGH SHARK SKIN the rough skin of certain sharks and rays, used as an abrasive or as leather **2.** ROUGH, UNTANNED LEATHER rough, untanned leather with a grainy surface, made from the hide of various animals and often dyed green [Late 17thC. Via French *chagrin* 'untanned leather' from Turkish *sağri* 'back of a horse'.]

shah /shaa/ *n.* formerly, the hereditary monarch of certain Middle Eastern nations, especially Iran [Mid-16thC. Via Persian *šāh* from Old Persian *xšāyathiya-* 'king' (source of English *check*).] —**shahdom** *n.*

Shah Jahan /shaa jə haan/, **Emperor of India** (1592–1666). The fifth Mughal emperor (1628–58), he made Delhi the capital of India, and built the Taj Mahal and Pearl Mosque in Agra.

shaitan /shī taan/ *n.* in Islamic countries, an evil spirit or person [Mid-17thC. Via Arabic *šayṭān* from Hebrew *śāṭān*.]

Shaitan /shī taan/ *n.* in Islamic belief, the Devil

Shaka /shaaka/ (1787?–1828) South African ruler. Through conquest he centralized and expanded the Zulu nation, taking control of Natal (now KwaZulu, Natal, South Africa) and initiating the period of warfare and migrations known as the *mfecane*.

shake /shayk/ *v.* (**shakes, shaking, shook** /shŏŏk/, **shaken** /sháykən/) **1.** *vti.* MOVE BACK AND FORTH to move or make sth or sb move back and forth or up and down in short quick movements ○ *I shook my coat to see if my keys were in the pockets.* **2.** *vi.* TREMBLE to tremble uncontrollably ○ *shaking with fright* **3.** *vti.* BECOME BY SHAKING to achieve a particular state by shaking, or shake sth in order to achieve a particular state ○ *The door finally shook free of its hinges* **4.** *vt.* SHAKE TO DISLODGE to shake sth in order to make parts attached to it come off ○ *We shook the apples from the tree.* **5.** *vi.* QUAVER WITH EMOTION to sound uncertain, nervous, angry, or distressed ○ *Her voice was shaking.* **6.** *vt.* SHOCK AND UPSET SB to shock and upset or disturb sb ○ *He was badly shaken by the accident.* **7.** *vt.* MAKE SB LESS CONFIDENT to cause sb to lose confidence or certainty ○ *Nothing could shake his faith.* **8.** *vti.* CLASP HANDS AS GREETING to grasp another person's hand and move it up and down as a greeting or sign of trust **9.** *vt. US* = shake off **10.** *vt.* MIX BY SHAKING to mix ingredients together in a container by shaking the container **11.** *vt.* MOVE HEAD TO EXPRESS 'NO' to move the head from side to side in order to express disagreement, disbelief, commiseration, or sorrow **12.** *vt.* WAVE STH THREATENINGLY to wave sth in the air in a threatening way ○ *She shook her fist at them.* **13.** *vti.* RATTLE DICE BEFORE THROWING to rattle a die or dice in the hand or in a dice cup before throwing **14.** *vti.* MUSIC TRILL to trill a note ■ *n.* **1.** ACT OF SHAKING a shaking of sth ○ *She gave the bag a good shake.* **2.** VIBRATION a trembling motion or vibration ○ *The device moves smoothly along the track without shake.* **3.** MOMENT a brief moment (*informal*) ○ *I'll do it in two shakes.* **4.** BEVERAGES = **milk shake** *n.* **5.** BEVERAGES SHAKEN BEVERAGE a beverage made without milk or ice cream but blended or shaken like a milk shake ○ *a fruit and yogurt shake* **6.** HANDSHAKE an act of grasping sb's hand as a greeting **7.** *US* REASONABLE CHANCE reasonable treatment or a reasonable opportunity to succeed ○ *give everybody a fair shake* **8.** GEOL, FORESTRY FISSURE OR CRACK a fissure or crack in a rock or timber **9.** MUSIC TRILL a trilled note **10.** SEISMOL EARTHQUAKE an earthquake (*informal*) **11.** BUILDING WOODEN SHINGLE a rough wooden shingle cut with a hatchet ■ **shakes** *npl.* UNCONTROLLABLE TREMBLING uncontrollable trembling caused, e.g., by fear or illness [Old English *sceacan*] —**shakable** *adj.* ◇ **be no great shakes** to be not very good or not very important (*informal*)

shake down *v.* **1.** *vt. US* EXTORT MONEY FROM SB to extort money from sb (*slang*) **2.** *vt. US* TAKE STH FOR TRIAL RUN to subject a ship or aircraft to a trial run in order to look for defects or train the crew **3.** *vi.* BECOME ACCUSTOMED to become comfortable in a new setting (*informal*) **4.** *vi.* SLEEP IN MAKESHIFT BED to go to bed in a makeshift bed

shake off *vt.* **1.** GET RID OF STH UNWANTED to get rid of sth unwanted **2.** ESCAPE FROM SB to get away from a following or pursuing person

shake out *vt.* to open sth, spread sth, or dislodge things from sth by holding it and shaking it

shake up *vt.* **1.** MAKE MAJOR CHANGES to make major changes in an organization or institution, especially with the intention of improving or modernizing it **2.** UPSET SB to make sb feel upset and disturbed **3.** MIX BY SHAKING to mix sth by shaking it in a container

shakedown /sháyk down/ *n.* **1.** *US* ACT OF EXTORTION an act of extorting money from sb using threats (*slang*) **2.** TRIAL RUN OF VESSEL a trial run of a ship or aircraft in order to locate and fix problems or to familiarize the crew with their duties **3.** MAKESHIFT BED a makeshift bed such as a pile of blankets on a floor

shaken past participle of **shake**

shaken baby syndrome, **shaken infant syndrome** *n.* in young babies, a series of often life-threatening internal head injuries sustained through being shaken violently

shake-out *n.* a major change in an organization or system resulting in the falling away of some elements ○ *a shake-out in the voluntary sector*

shaker /sháykər/ *n.* **1.** CONTAINER FOR DISPERSING FINE PARTICLES a container with small holes in its lid that can be shaken to disperse the contents **2.** CONTAINER FOR MIXING DRINKS a container with a lid in which drinks are mixed by shaking the container **3.** SB CAUSING CHANGE sb who is active in some field, especially sb who brings about change (*informal*) ○ *a real shaker in the industry* **4.** STH THAT SHAKES sb or sth that shakes or shakes sth

Shaker /sháykər/ *n.* CHR MEMBER OF ASCETIC DENOMINATION a member of a Christian denomination related to the Quakers who live communally, simply, and celibately. The denomination originated in England in the 18th century but settled in the United States. ■ *adj.* **1.** DESIGN SIMPLE AND FUNCTIONAL designed or made in the simple, functional style that originated with the Shakers **2.** Shaker, shaker PARALLEL RIBBED knitted at a large gauge in thin parallel ribs [Late 18thC. From the shaking movements in their ritual dances.]

Shakespeare /sháyks peer/, **William** (1564–1616) English poet and playwright. He is widely recognized as one of the greatest dramatists in the

Shaker: Wooden Shaker box

William Shakespeare

English-speaking world. Although much about his life is obscure, he was born in Stratford-upon-Avon. He was established as an actor-playwright in London by about 1590, and over the next 23 years wrote 36 tragedies, histories, and comedies, including *Hamlet* (1601?), *Richard III* (1595–96?), and *Twelfth Night* (1600?). His poetry includes over 150 sonnets.

Shakespearean /shayk speéri ən/, **Shakespearian** *adj.* RELATING TO SHAKESPEARE relating to or written by William Shakespeare, or typical of his works ■ *n.* STUDIER OF SHAKESPEARE a scholar who studies Shakespeare and his works

Shakespeareana /shayk speéri aánə/, **Shakespeariana** *n.* collectively, things relating to William Shakespeare

Shakespearean sonnet *n.* a sonnet in iambic pentameter composed of three quatrains followed by a couplet. The rhyme pattern is abab cdcd efef gg. This is the form perfected by William Shakespeare.

Shakespearian *adj.* = Shakespearean

Shakespeariana *n.* = Shakespeareana

shake-up, **shakeup** *n.* a major reorganization or change

shaking palsy *n.* Parkinson's disease (*informal dated*) [From its characteristic tremor]

shako /shákō, sháykō/ (*plural* **-os** *or* **-oes**) *n.* a tall cylindrical military hat made of stiff material with a short visor and a plume in front [Early 19thC. Via French *schako* from Hungarian *csákós (süveg)* 'peaked (cap)', of uncertain origin: probably from German *Zacken* 'peak, point'.]

Shakta /shúktə/, **Sakta** *n.* a Hindu who worships Shakti, the female consort of Shiva [Early 19thC. From Sanskrit *śāktaḥ*, from *śaktiḥ* (see SHAKTI).] —**Shaktism** *n.* —**Shaktist** *n.*

Shakti *n.* = sakti

shakuhachi /sháchoo haáchi/ (*plural* **-chis**) *n.* a Japanese bamboo flute [Late 19thC. From Japanese, from *shaku*, a unit of measure + *hachi* 'eight'; so called because it is one and eight-tenths of a 'shaku' in length.]

shaky /sháyki/ (**-ier, -iest**) *adj.* **1.** TREMBLING trembling or unsteady **2.** NOT STURDY not sturdy or firm and likely to collapse **3.** WEAK AND NOT LIKELY TO LAST weak or wavering and unlikely to last long or to be successful ○ *a shaky financial venture* **4.** UNRELIABLE unreliable or uncertain ○ *made us a rather shaky promise* —**shakily** *adv.* —**shakiness** *n.*

shale /shayl/ *n.* a dark fine-grained sedimentary rock composed of layers of compressed clay, silt, or mud [Mid-18thC. Origin uncertain: ultimately from a prehistoric Germanic word meaning 'to split', which is also the ancestor of English *scale* and *shell*.] —**shaly** *adj.*

shale oil *n.* crude oil distilled from heated shale

shall *stressed* /shal/; *unstressed* /sh'l/ CORE MEANING: will happen in the future, or intended to happen ○ *I shall as president promote measures that keep families whole.*

vi. **1.** MUST used especially in formal speech and writing to indicate determination on the part of the speaker that sth will happen or sb will do sth ○ *If you want to behave like that you shall certainly not do it here.* **2.** RULES AND LAWS indicating that sth must happen or sb is obliged to do sth because of a rule or law ○ *The department shall issue an account number to the vehicle owner.* **3.** OFFERS AND SUGGESTIONS used to make offers and suggestions or to ask for advice (*used in questions*) ○ *Shall I arrange it for you?* ○ *What shall I do next?* **4.** CERTAINTY indicating the certainty or inevitability of sth happening in the future (*usually used with 'you'*) ○ *If you want a new outfit that badly then you shall have one.* [Old English *sceal*. From a prehistoric Germanic word meaning 'to owe'.]

───── **WORD KEY: USAGE** ─────

shall or **will**? The traditional rule, often stated in grammars and usage books, is that to express a simple future tense **shall** is used after *I* and *we* and **will** in other cases, and to express intention or wish their roles are reversed; but it is unlikely that this rule has ever been regularly observed, and many examples of written English can be found that contradict it. (The distinction is often difficult to establish, especially in the first person when the speaker is also the performer of the future action and intention must always be involved to some extent.) Although **will** and (occasionally) **shall** are used as auxiliary verbs with reference to future action or state, there are other ways of expressing this that are often preferred as more natural, such as *am going to*. When **shall** and **will** are used in conversation, they are normally contracted to *'ll*, so that the difference between the two words becomes irrelevant. In all parts of the English-speaking world other than England, **shall** has been more or less driven out by **will**. It survives mostly in the contracted negative form *shan't*. In the English of England (note: England, not Britain), **shall** is fighting a rearguard action in such uses as *They shall apologize immediately* (a command) and *Shall you bring the children?* (an inquiry rather than a request), but even these sound very old-fashioned and affected, and **will** is now more common, especially in speech.

shalloon /sha loón/ *n.* a light wool twill, usually used as a garment lining [Mid-17thC. From French *chalon*, of uncertain origin: perhaps named after the French city of *Châlons*-sur-Marne, where it is said to have first been made.]

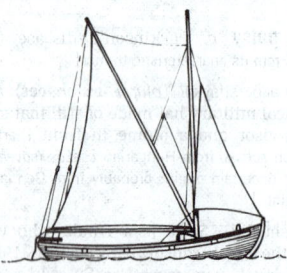
Shallop

shallop /shálləp/ *n.* a light boat with oars, sails, or both, used in shallow waters [Late 16thC. From French *chaloupe*, of uncertain origin: perhaps an alteration of Dutch *sloep* (see SLOOP).]

shallot /shə lót/ *n.* **1.** PLANTS PLANT IN ONION FAMILY a plant of the onion family widely cultivated for use in cooking. Latin name: *Allium ascalonicum*. **2.** FOOD SHALLOT BULB USED AS FOOD the bulb of the shallot that divides into small sections and is used in cooking for its delicate onion flavour [Mid-17thC. From French *échalotte*, an alteration of Old French *esc(h)aloigne*, from assumed Vulgar Latin *escalonia* (see SCALLION).]

shallow /shállō/ *adj.* **1.** NOT DEEP with little space between the bottom and the surface or top **2.** NOT THINKING OR FEELING DEEPLY having or displaying little intellectual or emotional complexity or value **3.** TAKING IN LITTLE AIR characterized by the inhaling and exhaling of an abnormally small amount of air ■ **shallows** *npl.* AREA OF SHALLOW WATER an area of shallow water ■ *vti.* (**-lows, -lowing, -lowed**) MAKE OR BECOME SHALLOW to become less deep or to make water less deep [15thC. Origin uncertain.] —**shallowly** *adv.* —**shallowness** *n.*

shalom /sha lóm/ *interj.* used as a Jewish greeting or leave-taking [Late 19thC. From Hebrew *šālōm* 'peace'.]

shalt /shalt/ *2nd person present singular, 2nd person present plural of* **shall** (*archaic*)

sham /sham/ *n.* **1.** A FAKE sth that is presented as genuine but that is not **2.** IMPOSTER sb who pretends to be a completely different person or different type of person ■ *adj.* NOT GENUINE not genuine and used for deception ○ *sham credentials* ■ *vti.* (**shams, shamming, shammed**) FEIGN to pretend to be experiencing a condition, e.g. illness or an emotion, in order to deceive [Late 17thC. Origin uncertain: probably a northern English variant of SHAME.] —**shammer** *n.*

shaman /shámmən, sháymən, sháamən/ *n.* sb who acts as a go-between for the physical and spiritual realms, and who is said to have particular powers such as prophecy and healing [Late 17thC. Via Russian from Tungus *šaman*, ultimately from Sanskrit *śramanaḥ* 'Buddhist ascetic', from *śramas* 'religious exercise'.] —**shamanic** /shə mánnik/ *adj.*

shamanism /shámmən izəm, sháy-, sháa-/ *n.* **1.** SPIRITUALIST RELIGION OF ASIA a religion of northern Asia, in which shamans can intercede between humanity and powerful good and evil spirits **2.** ANIMISTIC BELIEF SYSTEM any animistic belief system involving shamans

shamash *n.* = shammash

shamateur /shámmətər, shámmə choŏr/ *n.* an athlete who is officially an amateur but who is secretly paid [Late 19thC. Blend of SHAM and AMATEUR.]

shamble /shámb'l/ *vi.* (**-bles, -bling, -bled**) SHUFFLE ALONG CLUMSILY to walk clumsily keeping the feet close to the ground ■ *n.* SHUFFLING WALK a shuffling, awkward walking style [Late 16thC. Origin uncertain: probably from the obsolete expression *shamble legs* 'ungainly legs', alluding to the rickety legs of a meat vendor's stall (see SHAMBLES).]

shambles /shámb'lz/ *n.* **1.** DISORGANIZED FAILURE a failure caused by inadequate planning or organization **2.** MESSY DISORDER a state of messy disorder or chaos **3.** PLACE OF CARNAGE a place of great destruction and carnage **4.** SLAUGHTERHOUSE a slaughterhouse **5.** MEAT MARKET a meat or fish market (*archaic*) [15thC. Formed from obsolete *shamble* 'meat vendor's stall', from, ultimately, Latin *scamellum* 'small bench'.]

───── **WORD KEY: ORIGIN** ─────

The Old English ancestor of *shamble* still meant simply 'stool, table'. It gradually acquired the specialized meaning 'meat table', being applied to meat sellers' stalls at markets (a street in the old butchers' quarter of York is still known as the Shambles). By a natural extension the plural form *shambles* came to denote a 'slaughterhouse', and hence metaphorically any 'scene of bloodshed and slaughter', but the milder modern sense 'scene of disorder or ruin' did not emerge until as recently as the early 20th century.

shambolic /sham bóllik/ *adj.* poorly organized and in a messy or chaotic state (*informal*) [Late 20thC. Formed from SHAMBLES, perhaps on the model of 'symbolic'.]

shame /shaym/ *n.* **1.** NEGATIVE EMOTION a negative emotion that combines feelings of dishonour, unworthiness, and embarrassment **2.** CAPACITY TO FEEL UNWORTHY the capacity or tendency to feel shame ○ *He has no shame.* **3.** STATE OF DISGRACE a state of disgrace or dishonour ○ *bring shame on the family* **4.** CAUSE FOR REGRET a cause for regret or disappointment ○ *It's a shame you couldn't stay for lunch.* **5.** CAUSE OF SHAME sb or sth that causes sb to feel shame ■ *vt.* (**shames, shaming, shamed**) **1.** MAKE SB FEEL ASHAMED to make sb feel ashamed ○ *It shamed her that she had cheated.* **2.** FORCE SB THROUGH SHAME to make sb do sth by exploiting the fact that he or she would be ashamed not to do it ○ *He shamed us into making higher donations to the ministry.* **3.** MAKE SB FEEL INFERIOR to be so much better or more successful than others as to expose their comparative inadequacy ○ *Their exam results shame other local schools.* ■ *interj.* **1.** USED IN SYMPATHETIC REACTION used to react sympathetically to sth disappointing ○ *Shame, man, we would have invited you if we'd known you were free.* **2.** *S Africa* USED TO SHOW SENTIMENTAL APPROVAL used to show that you think that sth or sb is attractive in an endearing way ○ *'Have you seen our new puppy?' 'Oh, shame! Isn't it cute!'* [Old English *sceamu*] ◇ **put sb** *or* **sth to shame** to make sb or sth seem inferior or of inferior quality by comparison

shamefaced /sháym fáyst/ *adj.* **1.** SHOWING SHAME showing a feeling of shame or embarrassment **2.** TIMID timid or easily embarrassed [Mid-16thC. Alteration (influenced by SHAME) of obsolete *shamefast* 'bashful', literally 'held fast by shame', from Old English *sceamfæst*.] —**shamefacedly** /sháym fáyssidli, -fáystli/ *adv.* —**shamefacedness** /sháym fáyssidnəss, -fáystnəss/ *n.*

shameful /sháymf'l/ *adj.* **1.** DISGRACEFUL OR SCANDALOUS bad enough to inspire shame in those responsible **2.** ASHAMED feeling shame (*archaic*) [Old English *sceamful*] —**shamefully** *adv.* —**shamefulness** *n.*

shameless /sháymləss/ *adj.* **1.** NOT FEELING SHAME untroubled or unaffected by shame, especially in situations where others would be shamed **2.** DONE WITHOUT SHAME done without shame, especially where others would feel shame [Old English *sceamlēas*] —**shamelessly** *adv.* —**shamelessness** *n.*

shamiana /shámmi áanə, sháymi-/ *n. S Asia* a decorative circus-style tent used for outdoor entertaining or weddings [Early 17thC. From Persian and Urdu *shāmiyāna*.]

Shamir /sha meér/, **Yitzhak** (*b.* 1914) Polish-born Israeli political leader. He held many government positions, including foreign minister (1980–92), leader of the Likud Party (1983–93), and prime minister (1983–84, 1986–92). Real name **Yitzhak Jazernicki**

shammash /shámməss/ (*plural* **-mashim** /sha móssim/), **shamash** (*plural* **-mashim**), **shammes** (*plural* **-mosim**) *n.* **1.** SYNAGOGUE CARETAKER the beadle of a synagogue **2.** CANDLE USED TO LIGHT OTHERS the candle used to light the candles in the Hanukkah candlestick [Mid-17thC. Via Yiddish *shames* from Hebrew *šammaš* 'attendant', from *šimmēš* 'to serve'.]

shammy /shámmi/ (*plural* **-mies**) *n.* = chamois

shampoo /sham poó/ *n.* **1.** HAIR-CLEANING SOAP soap for cleaning the hair and scalp, usually in liquid or gel form **2.** SUDSY DETERGENT sudsy detergent for cleaning upholstery and carpets **3.** USE OF SHAMPOO a cleaning of the hair with shampoo ■ *vt.* (**-poos, -pooing, -pooed**) CLEAN WITH SHAMPOO to clean sth with shampoo [Mid-18thC. Via Anglo-Indian from Hindi *cāpo*, from *cāpnā* 'to knead, press, massage'.]

Shamrock

shamrock /shám rok/ *n.* a three-leafed clover or a plant similar to clover that serves as the national emblem of Ireland [Late 16thC. From Irish *seamróg* 'small clover', from *seamar* 'clover'.]

shamus /sháyməss, sháaməss/ *n. US* (*slang*) **1.** POLICE OFFICER a police officer **2.** PRIVATE DETECTIVE private detective [Early 20thC. Origin uncertain: possibly an alteration of SHAMMASH, or perhaps from the Irish name *Séamus*, in allusion to the many Irish immigrants who became police officers.]

Shan /shaan, shan/ (*plural* **Shan** *or* **Shans**) *n.* **1. MEMBER OF SOUTHEAST ASIAN PEOPLES** a member of a group of peoples living mainly in the hilly regions of northeastern Myanmar, and also in neighbouring parts of China, Laos, and Thailand **2.** LANG **SHAN LANGUAGE** the tai language of the Shan people. Shan is spoken by 2.5 million people. [Early 19thC. From Burmese.] —**Shan** *adj.*

Shandong /shan dóong/ province on the eastern coast of China, bordered by Hebei, Henan, and Jiangsu. Capital: Jinan. Population: 86,710,000 (1994). Area: 153,300 sq. km/59,200 sq. mi.

shandy /shándi/ (*plural* **-dies**) *n.* a drink made of beer and lemonade [Late 19thC. Shortening of SHANDYGAFF.]

shandygaff /shándi gaf/ *n.* US a drink made of beer and ginger beer [Mid-19thC. Origin unknown.]

Shang /shang/ *n.* a Chinese dynasty that ruled from 1766? to 1027? BC, a period that coincided with the development of China's system of handwriting and bronzework (*often used before a noun*) [Mid-17thC. From Chinese *Shāng*.]

Shangaan /sháng gaan/ (*plural* **-gaan** *or* **-gaans**) *n.* = **Tsonga** [Late 19thC. Of Bantu origin.]

shanghai /sháng hī/ (**-hais, -haiing, -haied**) *vt.* **1.** NAVY **FORCE INTO NAVAL SERVICE** to recruit sb forcibly into a navy **2. TRICK OR FORCE TO DO STH** to trick or force sb to do sth or go somewhere [Late 19thC. Named after SHANGHAI, a typical destination of ships crewed in this way.]

Shanghai /shang hī/ city and port on the River Huang-p'u in eastern China. Population: 8,760,000 (1993). —**Shanghainese** /shang hī néez/ *npl.*

Shango /sháng gō/ *n.* a religious group in the Caribbean characterized by a blend of West African religious practice and Christianity. Rituals involve drumming, dancing, and chanting, as well as the sacrifice of small animals. Some participants enter a state of trance. [Mid-20thC. From Yoruba, name of the god of thunder.]

Shangri-la /sháng gri láa/ *n.* an imaginary and remote paradise on earth [Mid-20thC. From the name given to an imaginary land in the novel *Lost Horizon* (1933) by the English novelist James Hilton.]

shank /shangk/ *n.* **1. LONG, NARROW PART** the long narrowest part of sth such as a key or pipe, especially when it connects two functional parts **2.** FOOD **CUT OF MEAT** a cut of meat from the leg of cattle or sheep **3.** ZOOL **BOTTOM OF ANIMAL LEG** the lower part of an animal's leg, between the bottom and middle joints **4. LOWER LEG** the lower part of the human leg, from ankle to knee **5. LEG** a human leg (*informal*) **6.** MECH ENG **BODY OF PIN OR NAIL** the long, narrow part of a pin, nail, screw, or bolt, between the head and the pointed or threaded part **7.** MECH ENG **PART CONNECTING TOOL HEAD TO HANDLE** a part sticking out from the head of a tool, by which it can be fitted into a handle **8.** ACCESSORIES **RING BAND** the plain band part of a ring, not including the jewels and their settings **9.** ACCESSORIES **NARROW PART OF SOLE** the narrow part of the sole of a shoe, beneath the arch of the foot, or any fitting at this part of a shoe **10.** NAUT **ANCHOR'S STEM** the stem of an anchor **11.** PRINTING **PART OF PRINTING TYPE** the body of a piece of type, between the foot and shoulder **12.** CLOTHES **BUTTON STEM** a loop or stem at the back of a button, by which it is sewn to the cloth **13. HOMEMADE DAGGER** a makeshift dagger, e.g. one made from a shard of glass, and especially one made by a prisoner (*slang*) ■ *v.* (**shanks, shanking, shanked**) **1.** *vt.* GOLF **MISHIT A GOLF BALL** to hit a golf ball with the heel of the club, sending it in the wrong direction **2.** *vi.* BOT **SHOW DISEASE FROM BASE UP** to shrivel, or show other signs of disease spreading upwards from the base of the stem [Old English *sceanca*. 'shinbone'.]

Shankar /shángk aar/, **Ravi** (*b.* 1920) Indian sitarist, composer, and teacher. His international tours popularized Indian music in the West. His compositions include film scores and sitar concertos.

shanking /shángking/ *n.* a disease of plants marked by shrivelling and decay from the base of the stems

shank's mare *n.* US = **shanks's pony** (*dated or informal*)

shanks's pony *n.* the legs or feet, as a means of transportation (*dated informal humorous*) US term **shank's mare**

Ravi Shankar

shannachie /shánna khee/ *n.* Ireland a traditional Irish story-teller [From Irish *seanchaidhe*]

Shannon /shánnən/ the longest river in the British Isles. It rises in northwestern County Cavan, north-central Ireland. Length: 354 km/220 mi.

shanny /shánni/ (*plural* **-nies** *or* **-ny**) *n.* a European fish with a small tapering body and a long dorsal fin that lives in rocky coastal areas. Latin name: *Blennius pholis*. [Mid-19thC. Origin unknown.]

shan't /shaant/ *contr.* contraction of 'shall not'

shantey /shánti/ *n.* = **shanty**[2]

shantung /shán túng/ *n.* **1. NUBBY SILK** heavy silk cloth with a nubby uneven weave **2. FABRIC RESEMBLING SHANTUNG** cotton or synthetic fabric made to resemble silk shantung [Late 19thC. Named after the Chinese province of *Shantung* (Shandong), where it was originally manufactured.]

shanty[1] /shánti/ (*plural* **-ties**) *n.* a crudely built shack or hut [Early 19thC. Origin uncertain: possibly from Canadian French *chantier* 'lumberjack's hut', via French, 'timberyard', from, ultimately, Latin *cant(h)erius* 'rafter'.]

shanty[2] /shánti/ (*plural* **-ties**), **shantey, chanty** *n.* a rhythmical song of a kind originally sung by sailors while they were working in groups

shantytown /shánti town/ *n.* a settlement consisting of crudely built shacks

Shanxi /shánshi/ agricultural province of northeastern China, bordered by Inner Mongolia, Hebei, Henan, and Shaanxi. Capital: Taiyuan. Population: 28,759,014 (1990). Area: 157,099 sq. km/60,656 sq. mi.

shape /shayp/ *n.* **1. OUTLINE OF STH'S FORM** the outline of sth's form ○ *His face has a square shape.* **2. STH NOT CLEARLY SEEN** sth that has bulk but is not clearly seen in outline ○ *She could see a shape through the fog.* **3.** GEOM **GEOMETRIC FORM** a geometric form such as a square, triangle, cone, or cube **4. GENERAL CHARACTER OF STH** the broad character that sth has ○ *the overall shape of the proposals* **5. ORIGINAL FORM** the original or optimal form of sth ○ *The pleats lost their shape in the wash.* **6. HEALTH** the condition of sb's health or fitness ○ *She exercises regularly and is in good shape.* **7. CONDITION OF STH** the condition of sth ○ *The lawn is in great shape.* **8. PHYSIQUE** the figure of a person **9. MOULD** a mould or pattern for making or giving sth its form **10. GHOST** a ghostly form or phantom ■ *v.* (**shapes, shaping, shaped**) **1.** *vt.* **INFLUENCE STH GREATLY** to have a profound or crucial influence over sth ○ *His beliefs were shaped by his upbringing.* **2.** *vt.* **PLAN FOR NATURE OF STH** to plan or decide on what the character of sth should be ○ *They are meeting to shape the nation's future.* **3.** *vt.* **GIVE STH PARTICULAR SHAPE** to mould sth into a different shape ○ *She shapes the clay into little animals.* **4.** *vi.* **HAPPEN** to happen or occur **5.** *vt.* PSYCHOL **TRAIN WITH REWARD AND PUNISHMENT** to change sb's behaviour gradually using reward as the person comes closer to the desired behaviour, and punishment for moving away from it [Old English *gesceap* 'creation', literally 'sth cut out'. From a prehistoric Germanic word meaning 'to cut out', which is also the ancestor of English *-ship* and *-scape*.] ◇ **knock** *or* **lick** *or* **whip sb** *or* **sth into shape** to bring sb or sth to a desired state quickly, roughly, or haphazardly (*informal*) ◇ **take shape** to take a definite form

shape up *vi.* **1. IMPROVE** to improve or develop in the way that is wanted (*informal*) **2. REACH ACCEPTABLE STANDARD** to reach an acceptably high standard of behaviour, skill, or attitude **3. DEVELOP IN PARTICULAR WAY** to seem to be developing in the way specified ○ *It's shaping up to be an environmental disaster.*

SHAPE /shayp/ *abbr.* Supreme Headquarters Allied Powers Europe

shapeless /sháypləss/ *adj.* **1. LACKING PRECISE SHAPE** with an indefinite or imprecise shape **2. LACKING STRUCTURE** put together in a very haphazard way —**shapelessly** *adv.* —**shapelessness** *n.*

shapely /sháypli/ (**-lier, -liest**) *adj.* having a shape that is visually appealing —**shapeliness** *n.*

shape-shifter *n.* sb or sth that is able to change form

shape-up /sháyp up/, **shapeup** *n.* US a method of hiring dock workers in which those seeking work arrive at the docks in the morning and employers select from among them

shard /shaard/, **sherd** /shurd/ *n.* **1. BROKEN PIECE OF GLASS** a sharp broken piece of glass or metal **2.** ARCHAEOL = **potsherd 3.** ZOOL **SCALE OR SHELL** an animal's scales, shell, or other tough outer covering **4.** INSECTS **BEETLE'S OUTER WING** the outer wing covering of a beetle [Old English *sceard* 'cut, notch'. Ultimately from an Indo-European word meaning 'to cut', which is also the ancestor of English *shear, scar, score,* and *short*.]

share[1] /shair/ *v.* (**shares, sharing, shared**) **1.** *vti.* **USE STH ALONG WITH OTHERS** to have or use sth in common with other people ○ *We shared a flat.* **2.** *vti.* **TAKE RESPONSIBILITY TOGETHER** to take equal responsibility for sth along with other people ○ *We shared the blame.* **3.** *vti.* **LET SB USE STH** to allow sb to use sth or have part of sth ○ *I shared my ice cream with him.* **4.** *vt.* **DIVIDE STH EQUALLY BETWEEN PEOPLE** to allocate equal parts of sth to different people or groups ○ *She shared the money out between her six grandchildren.* **5.** *vt.* **HAVE SIMILAR FEELING OR EXPERIENCE** to have sth the same as or in common with sb else ○ *He shared my view that the plan would not work.* **6.** *vt.* **TELL SB STH** to express sth to another person rather than keeping silent ○ *Do you want to share your feelings?* ■ *n.* **1. PART OF STH ALLOTTED** a part of sth that is owned by, paid for by, done by, or set aside for each of several people ○ *He hasn't had his share of the cake.* **2.** FIN **PART OF COMPANY'S STOCK** any of the equal, usually small, parts into which a company's capital stock is divided ○ *She owns shares in several companies* **3. REASONABLE OR APPROPRIATE PORTION** the portion that sb deserves or should be responsible for ○ *She does more than her share of the work.* [Old English *scearu* 'division, portion'. Ultimately from an Indo-European word meaning 'to cut', which is also the ancestor of English *shear, scar, score,* and *shirt*.] —**sharer** *n.*

share[2] /shair/ *n.* = **ploughshare** [Old English *scear*. Ultimately from an Indo-European word meaning 'to cut', which is also the ancestor of *shear* and *share*[1].]

share certificate *n.* a document certifying ownership of shares, issued by a company to an individual who holds shares in that company. US term **stock certificate**

sharecrop /sháir krop/ (**-crops, -cropping, -cropped**) *vti.* US to farm land as a sharecropper [Early 20thC. From SHARE[1], because the crop was shared with the landowner.]

sharecropper /sháir kroppər/ *n.* US a tenant farmer who farms land for the owner and is paid a share of the value of the yielded crop

shared ownership *n.* a form of home ownership in which the resident buys part of the property and rents part of it from a housing association

shareholder /sháir hōldər/ *n.* sb who owns one or more shares of a company's stock

share index *n.* an index showing movement of share prices

share-milker *n.* NZ a person who tends and milks a herd of cows as a tenant on another's farm and shares in the profits of the business [Modelled on 'sharecropper']

share option *n.* a benefit in which an employee of a company can buy its shares at a special price

shareware /sháir wair/ *n.* software made available for free trial with the understanding that users will voluntarily pay a fee to the author or publisher if they continue to use it

sharia /shə ree ə/, **shari'a, shari'ah** n. Islamic religious law, based on the Koran (*often used before a noun*) [Mid-19thC. Via Arabic *šar'īya* 'lawfulness' from, ultimately, *aš-šar'* 'Islamic law'.]

sharif n. = **sherif**

Sharjah /shaárjə/ one of the seven member states of the United Arab Emirates. Population: 125,000 (1995).

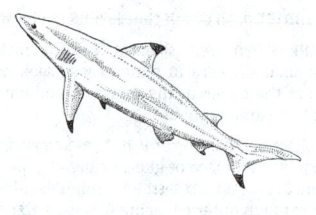

Shark

shark /shaark/ n. 1. ZOOL CARNIVOROUS FISH a carnivorous fish that has a long body, two dorsal fins, sharp teeth, a cartilaginous skeleton, and thick, rough skin. Class: Chondrichthyes. 2. RUTHLESS PERSON a ruthless greedy person (*informal*) 3. LOANSHARK a loan-shark (*informal*) ■ v. (**sharks, sharking, sharked**) 1. vt. GET STH ILLICITLY to get sth illegally or unethically (*archaic*) 2. vi. CHEAT OTHERS PROFESSIONALLY to make a living as a cheater or fraud [Mid-16thC. Origin unknown. Introduced to English in a ballad about the things seen by a group of explorers. In the sense 'ruthless person', perhaps from German *schurke* 'scoundrel'.]

Shark Bay /shaark-/ bay on the coast of Western Australia

shark bell n. Aus = **shark siren**

shark net n. a net strung across a bay to keep sharks out

shark patrol n. Aus a patrol carried out by boat or plane to watch for sharks that may approach public swimming areas

shark siren n. Aus a siren or similar mechanism sounded to warn swimmers and surfers that sharks have been spotted offshore

sharkskin /shaark skin/ n. 1. TEXTILES GLOSSY FABRIC a smooth glossy fabric made from a mixture of acetate and rayon 2. INDUST SHARK LEATHER leather made from shark's skin

sharksucker /shaark sukər/ n. = **remora** [Mid-19thC. From its habit of attaching itself to sharks by means of a sucking disk.]

Helen Sharman

Sharman /shaármən/, **Helen** (b. 1963) British astronaut. With her participation in the Russian scientific space mission Project Juno (1991), she became Britain's first astronaut. Full name **Helen Patricia Sharman**

sharon fruit /shárrən-/ n. = **persimmon** [Named after the Plain of SHARON, where it is grown]

sharp /shaarp/ adj. 1. ABLE TO CUT with an edge or point that is very acute and able to cut or puncture things ○ *a sharp blade* 2. POINTED ending in a point or sharp angle ○ *a sharp nose* 3. ABRUPT IN CHANGING DIRECTION making a change in direction that forms an acute angle ○ *a sharp turn* 4. QUICK-WITTED quick-witted and intelligent or quick to notice and understand 5. CRITICAL critical and unsympathetic ○ *a sharp rebuke* 6. IRRITABLE irritable or angry ○ *a sharp temper* 7. SUDDEN sudden and significant ○ *a sharp rise in prices* 8. SURPRISED abrupt or unexpected ○ *a sharp intake of breath* 9. DISTINCT clearly and definitely distinct ○ *Her soft voice was in sharp contrast to her forbidding expression.* 10. CLEARLY DETAILED with the detail clear and distinct ○ *a sharp image* 11. PIERCING loud, piercing, and abrupt or unexpected ○ *a sharp cry* 12. STRONG IN TASTE strong and slightly bitter in taste ○ *a sharp cheese* 13. INTENSE penetrating and intense ○ *a sharp frost* 14. MUSIC HIGHER BY SEMITONE higher in pitch by a semitone ○ *F sharp* 15. MUSIC TOO HIGH PITCHED a little too high in pitch and therefore slightly out of tune 16. STYLISH neat, stylish, and fashionable ○ *a sharp dresser* 17. FRAUDULENT deceitful or fraudulent ○ *sharp practice* ■ adv. 1. PRECISELY exactly, and not before or after ○ *at 9 o'clock sharp* 2. MUSIC AT SLIGHTLY TOO HIGH A PITCH at higher than the usual pitch and therefore slightly out of tune ○ *She's singing sharp.* ■ n. 1. MUSIC NOTE HIGHER BY SEMITONE a note or tone that is a semitone higher in pitch than the natural or unmodified pitch. Symbol ♯ 2. MUSIC SHARP SYMBOL the symbol for a sharp note. Symbol ♯ 3. SEW LONG SEWING NEEDLE a long thin needle for hand-sewing 4. MED SHARP MEDICAL INSTRUMENT a sharp medical instrument such as a hypodermic or surgical blade that requires careful disposal (*usually used in the plural*) ○ *a container labelled 'sharps only'* 5. SHARPER a sharper (*informal*) 6. EXPERT sb expert at sth (*informal*) ■ interj. S Africa FINE used among South African black male youths as a reply to a greeting (**heita**) (*informal*) [Old English *scearp*. Ultimately from an Indo-European word meaning 'to cut', which is also the ancestor of English *sharp*, *scarf*, and *shard*.] —**sharply** adv. —**sharpness** n.

Sharp /shaarp/, **Cecil** (1859–1924) British musicologist. His collections of folk songs and dances from Britain and the United States reawakened interest in folk song and folk dance. Full name **Cecil James Sharp**

sharpbill /shaarp bil/ n. a small fruit-eating bird of the Central and South American rainforest with a straight sharp bill, green and yellow plumage, and a red crest. Latin name: *Oxyruncus cristatus*.

shar-pei /shaar páy/, **Shar-Pei** n. a medium-sized dog with a squarish snout, blue tongue, short hair, and loose skin that falls in folds over its body, especially when young. It belongs to a breed originating in China. [Late 20thC. From Chinese *shā pi*, literally 'sand skin'.]

sharpen /shaárpən/ (**-ens, -ening, -ened**) v. 1. vti. BECOME OR MAKE SHARPER to become or make sth sharp or sharper 2. vt. MUSIC RAISE PITCH OF NOTE to raise a note in pitch, especially by a semitone 3. vt. IMPROVE STH to improve sth so that it is more efficient or stylish than before

sharper /shaárpər/ n. a skilful cheat, especially in gambling

Sharpeville /shaarp vil/ African township near Vereeniging, South Africa. It was the scene of a massacre of antiapartheid demonstrators in 1960. Population: 42,000 (1972).

sharp-eyed adj. 1. ALERT TO DETAIL alert and able to notice detail 2. HAVING GOOD EYESIGHT with very keen eyesight

sharpie /shaárpi/, **sharpy** (*plural* **-ies**) n. US a sharper (*informal*)

sharpish /shaárpish/ adv. quickly or without delay (*informal*)

sharp-nosed puffer n. any tropical marine fish that can inflate its body like other puffers but also has a characteristic long snout with prominent nostrils. Family: Canthigasteridae.

sharp-set adj. eagerly wanting sth, especially food

sharp-shinned hawk n. a small bird-hunting hawk of North America with short wings, a long square tail, and grey feathers with a brown underside. Latin name: *Accipiter striatus*. [From its slender legs]

sharpshooter /shaarp shootər/ n. sb who is very good at hitting precise targets using firearms

sharp-sighted adj. 1. HAVING GOOD VISION with very good eyesight 2. ALERT TO DETAIL quick to notice detail —**sharp-sightedly** adv. —**sharp-sightedness** n.

sharp-tongued adj. critical or sarcastic and unsympathetic in speech

sharp-witted adj. quick to think, understand, or react —**sharp-wittedly** adv.

sharpy n. = **sharpie**

shashlik /shásh lik, shaásh lik/, **shashlick** n. = **shish kebab** [Early 20thC. Via Russian *shashlyk* from Crimean Turkish *şişlik* 'small skewer', from *şiş* 'skewer'.]

Shasta daisy /shástə-/ n. a chrysanthemum with large white flower heads. Latin name: *Chrysanthemum maximum*. [Early 20thC. Named after Mount Shasta, or the *Shasta* peoples of northern California, where the flower is commonly found.]

shastra /shaástrə/, **sastra** n. in Hinduism, a sacred text [Mid-17thC. From Sanskrit *śāstra* 'lesson', from *śās* 'to instruct'.]

shat past tense, past participle of **shit** (*taboo*)

Shatt al-Arab /shát al árrəb/ river in southwestern Asia. It rises at the confluence of the Euphrates and Tigris rivers, flows along the border between Iran and Iraq, and empties into the Persian Gulf, near Kuwait. Length: 170 km/106 mi.

shatter /sháttər/ v. (**-ters, -tering, -tered**) 1. vti. SMASH INTO PIECES to break or cause sth to break suddenly into many small, brittle pieces 2. vt. DESTROY HOPE OR BELIEF to destroy sth that sb believed in or hoped for 3. vt. SHOCK SB to shock and distress sb badly 4. vt. SCATTER STH to scatter things (*archaic*) ■ **shatters** npl. FRAGMENTS fragments made by shattering sth [Assumed Old English *sceaterian*. Ultimately from an Indo-European word meaning 'to split apart', which is also the ancestor of English *shingle*[1].] —**shatterer** n.

shatter cone n. a cone-shaped rock piece that has stripes running from its point, created by volcanic pressure or meteoric impact

shattered /sháttərd/ adj. thoroughly tired out

shatterproof /sháttər proof/ adj. made to resist shattering

shave /shayv/ v. (**shaves, shaving, shaved, shaved** or **shaven** /sháyvən/) 1. vti. REMOVE HAIR WITH RAZOR to remove hair from the body using a razor 2. vt. REDUCE AMOUNT SLIGHTLY to reduce an amount, price, or time taken by a very slight amount ○ *shaved two seconds off her best time* 3. vt. BARELY TOUCH IN PASSING to barely touch sth when passing 4. vt. REMOVE A THIN LAYER OF to remove a thin layer from sth using a razor, rasp, or similar tool 5. vt. TRIM STH CLOSELY to trim sth closely ■ n. 1. ACT OF SHAVING the act, process, or result of shaving 2. = **shaving** n. 3. SHAVING TOOL any tool for shaving or scraping [Old English *sceafan*. Ultimately from an Indo-European word meaning 'to scrape, scratch', which is also the ancestor of English *scabies*.]

shaven /sháyvən/ v. past participle of **shave** ■ adj. (*often used in combination*) 1. WITH NO BEARD OR HAIR with the beard or the hair shaved off 2. TRIMMED trimmed or cropped

shaver /sháyvər/ n. 1. DEVICE FOR SHAVING a device that is used to shave the beard or hair, especially an electric razor (*often used before a noun*) 2. YOUNG BOY a boy who is not old enough to shave (*dated informal*) [The meaning of 'young boy' developed from 'fellow']

Shavian /sháyvi ən/ adj. 1. BY OR LIKE G. B. SHAW written by or in the style of the work of the playwright George Bernard Shaw 2. OF SHAW relating to or studying Shaw or his works ■ n. ADMIRER OR STUDENT OF SHAW an admirer of Shaw, or a scholar who studies his works [Early 20thC. Formed from *Shavius*, Latinized form of SHAW.]

shaving /sháyving/ n. 1. SHAVED-OFF PIECE a thin slice shaved off 2. HAIR REMOVAL WITH RAZOR the removing of hair or a beard with a razor (*often used before a noun*)

Shavuoth /shə vóo ōth/, **Shavuot** /-ōt/ n. CALENDAR a Jewish festival held on the 6th day of Sivan, in May or June, and commemorating the Law being given by God to Moses on Mount Sinai [Late 19thC. From Hebrew *šābū'ōt*, plural of *šābūā* 'week', alluding to the weeks between Passover and Pentecost.]

shaw /shaw/ *n. UK, Midwest* a thicket of shrubs or small trees [Old English *sceaga*. Ultimately from a prehistoric Germanic word meaning 'sth sticking out', which is also the ancestor of English *shag* 'long coarse pile'.]

George Bernard Shaw

Shaw /shaw/, **George Bernard** (1856–1950) Irish playwright. His plays, including *Pygmalion* (1913) and *Heartbreak House* (1919), established him as the leading English-language playwright of his time. He promoted socialism in works such as *The Intelligent Woman's Guide to Socialism and Capitalism* (1928).

Shaw, Norman (1831–1912) British architect. He was noted for his town and country houses and for New Scotland Yard (1888–90). He formulated the Queen Anne style. Full name **Richard Norman Shaw**

Shawano *n., adj.* = **Shawnee**

Shawinigan /shə wínnigən/ city in southern Quebec, Canada, northwest of Trois Rivières on the St Maurice River. Population: 19,931 (1991).

shawl /shawl/ *n.* GARMENT FOR THE HEAD AND SHOULDERS a fabric square worn by women over the shoulders or head and shoulders or used to wrap a baby in ■ *vt.* (shawls, shawling, shawled) WRAP IN A SHAWL to cover sb or sth with a shawl or with sth performing a similar function [Early 17thC. From Persian and Urdu *šāl*.]

shawm /shawm/ *n.* a woodwind instrument of the Middle Ages and Renaissance that has a double reed and was the predecessor of the modern oboe [14thC. Origin uncertain: probably a back-formation from *schalmys*, plural of *shalemie*, from Old French *chalemie*, ultimately from Latin *calamus* 'reed' (see CALAMUS).]

Shawnee /sháw née/ (*plural* **-nee** *or* **-nees**), **Shawano** /shə waánō/ (*plural* **-no** *or* **-nos**) *n.* **1.** PEOPLES MEMBER OF NATIVE N AMERICAN PEOPLE a member of a Native North American people who originally occupied lands along the Ohio, Cumberland, and Tennessee rivers, and whose descendants now live mainly in Oklahoma **2.** LANG LANGUAGE OF SHAWNEE the language of the Shawnee people, belonging to the Algonquian family. Few people now speak Shawnee. [Late 17thC. From Delaware *ša:wano:w.*] —**Shawnee** *adj.*

Shawwal /shə wól/ *n.* in the Islamic calendar, the tenth lunar month of the year [Late 18thC. From Arabic *shawwāl*.]

she *stressed* /shee/; *unstressed* /shi/ *pron.* (used as the subject of a verb) **1.** PREVIOUSLY MENTIONED FEMALE PERSON OR ANIMAL used to refer to a female person or animal who has been previously mentioned or whose identity is known ○ *Ms Jones continues to enjoy high approval ratings as she starts her third year in office.* **2.** OBJECT PERCEIVED AS FEMALE used to refer to sth previously mentioned or known that has been traditionally thought of as female, e.g. a nation, a car, a machine, a boat, or a ship ○ *Iran stated that she is ready to start talks on the issue.* ○ *She'll have to go to the scrap yard; she can't be repaired any longer.* ■ *n.* STH FEMALE a female animal or person, sometimes used of a new baby ○ *Is it a he or a she?* [12thC. Origin uncertain: probably a variant of Old English *hēo*.]

s/he /shée awr hée/ *pron.* used in writing as a pronoun to mean 'she or he' (*intended to avoid sexism in writing*) ○ *If a student wishes to change courses s/he should consult me before the end of term.*

shea *n.* = **shea tree** [Late 18thC. From Mande *si*.]

shea butter *n.* a white fat obtained from the seeds of the shea tree. It is used as a food and in the manufacture of soap and candles.

sheading /shéeding/ *n.* any of the six administrative districts into which the Isle of Man is divided [Late 16thC. Variant of *shedding* 'division', originally the present participle of SHED in the sense 'to divide'.]

sheaf /sheef/ *n.* (*plural* **sheaves** /sheevz/) **1.** BUNDLE OF HARVESTED GRAIN STALKS a bundle of the harvested stalks of a plant, especially wheat, barley, or another cereal, with the heads still containing their seeds **2.** ANY BUNDLE a bundle of objects gathered or tied together ■ *vt.* = **sheave**[1] *v.* [Old English *sceaf*. Ultimately from a prehistoric Germanic word that is also the ancestor of English *shove*. The underlying idea is of things shoved together.]

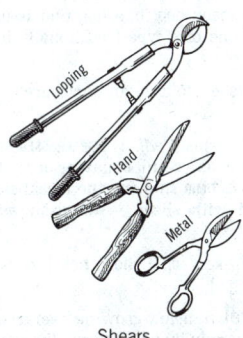
Lopping
Hand
Metal
Shears

shear /sheer/ *v.* (**shears, shearing, sheared, sheared** *or* **shorn** /shawrn/) **1.** *vti.* CUT OFF to remove sth with a sharp tool **2.** *vti.* CUT HAIR, WOOL, OR FOLIAGE FROM to cut hair, fleece, or foliage from the surface of sth using a sharp tool **3.** *vt.* DEPRIVE to take sth valuable or prized away from sb ○ *sheared of all self-respect* **4.** *vti.* MOVE CLEANLY THROUGH STH to move quickly and cleanly through sth **5.** *vti.* DEFORM BY APPLYING TWISTING FORCE to cause sth to deform or break by applying a twisting force ■ *n.* **1.** REMOVAL OF FLEECE a cutting off of a sheep's wool, often used as a measure of the age of a sheep **2.** WOOL CUT OFF a quantity of wool cut off **3.** = **shear strain 4.** = **shear stress** ■ **shears** *npl.* **1.** CUTTING TOOL a tool like a large pair of scissors, used for cutting or trimming **2.** SHEERLEGS a sheerlegs [Old English *sceran*. Ultimately, from an Indo-European word meaning 'to cut' that is also the ancestor of English *score*, *short*, and *curtail*.]

shearer /shéerər/ *n.* a farm worker who shears sheep for a living, especially in Australia and New Zealand

Shearer /shéerər/, **Alan** (*b.* 1970) British footballer. A skilled centre-forward, he played for Blackburn Rovers (1992–96) before joining Newcastle United (1996).

shear force *n.* a force, or a component of a force, that acts parallel to a plane

shearlegs *n.* = **sheerlegs**

shearling /shéerling/ *n.* **1.** YOUNG SHEEP SHORN FOR FIRST TIME a young sheep, usually between six and twelve months old, after its first shearing **2.** TANNED SKIN WITH WOOL ATTACHED the tanned skin of a recently sheared lamb or sheep, with the short wool that remains after shearing still attached

shear modulus *n.* the ratio of the shear stress to the shear strain, taken as an indication of the strength of a material under shear forces

shear pin *n.* a pin inserted in a machine as a safety device. If safe loads are exceeded, the pin breaks and the machine shuts down.

shear strain *n.* the angular deformation of a body, quantitatively taken to be the sideways displacement of two adjacent planes divided by the distance between them

shear stress *n.* the forces acting on a body that produce shear strain

shearwater /shéer waatər/ (*plural* **-ters** *or* **-ter**) *n.* a long-winged dark-coloured sea bird with a short hooked bill. It flies low over the water in search of food. Genus: *Puffinus*. [From the impression given when the bird flies that its wings are shearing the water]

sheath /sheeth/ *n.* (*plural* **sheaths**) **1.** CASE FOR A BLADE a case for the blade of a knife, sword, or other cutting implement **2.** CLOSE-FITTING COVERING a covering or case that fits closely around sth in the way that a sheath covers a blade **3.** CLOSELY FITTING DRESS a woman's closely fitting dress, originally floor-length, but now also knee-length **4.** = **condom 5.** BIOL PROTECTIVE TUBE a tubular covering that protects some body parts and plant parts, e.g. certain nerves and blood vessels in animals or leaf stems in some grasses ■ *vt.* = **sheathe** [Old English *scǣð*. Ultimately from a prehistoric Germanic word that probably meant 'to divide, split' (ancestor also of *shed*[1]), the underlying idea being of sth split open.]

sheathbill /shéeth bil/ *n.* a squat shore bird with a horny sheath on its face, around the bill. It is a gregarious scavenger native to rocky Antarctic and subantarctic coasts. Latin name: *Chionis alba* and *Chionis minor*.

sheathe /sheeth/ (**sheathes, sheathing, sheathed**), **sheath** /sheeth/ (**sheaths, sheathing, sheathed**) *vt.* **1.** PUT INTO A SHEATH to put a knife, sword, or other cutting implement into a sheath **2.** ENCLOSE WITH A COVERING OR CASE to enclose sth in a protective covering or case **3.** RETRACT to retract the claws, in the way that a cat does **4.** THRUST INTO FLESH to thrust a knife or sword into sb's flesh (*literary*) [14thC. Formed from SHEATH.]

sheathing /shéething/ *n.* sth that encloses and protects, e.g. a covering of boards on a building's framework or a protective material applied to the underwater surfaces of a boat's hull

sheath knife *n.* a knife with a fixed blade that is carried in a sheath

shea tree /sháy-/, **shea** *n.* a tropical West African tree with seeds from which shea butter is obtained. Latin name: *Vitellaria paradoxa* and *Butyrospermum parkii*.

sheave[1] /sheev/ (**sheaves, sheaving, sheaved**), **sheaf** /sheef/ (**sheafs, sheafing, sheafed**) *vt.* to gather sth, especially the cut stalks of a cereal crop, into a sheaf [Late 16thC. Back-formation from SHEAVES.]

sheave[2] /sheev/ *n.* a wheel with a grooved rim for a rope, cable, or belt, especially one used as a pulley [13thC. Ultimately from a prehistoric Germanic word meaning 'disc, slice of bread'.]

sheaves plural of **sheaf**

Sheba /shéebə/ ancient kingdom of southwestern Arabia, in present-day Yemen. It reached the height of its wealth and power in the 8th century BC. In the Bible, it is the meeting place of Solomon and the Queen of Sheba (1 Kings 10:1–13).

shebang /shi báng/ [Mid-19thC. Origin uncertain: perhaps a variant of SHEBEEN. Originally used for 'hut, shed'.] ◇ **the whole shebang** the whole of sth (*informal*)

Shebat *n.* CALENDAR, JUDAISM = **Shevat**

shebeen /shi beén/ *n.* a small establishment that sells alcoholic beverages illegally or without a licence, traditionally operating in the poorer regions of Ireland, Scotland, and South Africa [Late 18thC. From Irish *síbín*, literally 'little mug', from *séibe* 'mug'.]

Shechina /shə keénə, -kínə/, **Shechinah, Shekhinah** *n.* in Jewish theology, God's presence in and throughout the world [Mid-17thC. From late Hebrew *šĕkīnāh*, from *šākan* 'to rest, dwell'.]

shechita /shə kheétə/, **schechita** *n.* the prescribed method of slaughter of animals and birds under Jewish dietary laws. The act is performed by a trained and licensed slaughterer (**shochet**) who draws a very sharp knife across the animal's throat and allows the blood to drain out. [Late 19thC. From Hebrew *šĕhītāh*, literally 'slaughter', from *šāhat* 'to slaughter'.]

shed[1] /shed/ *v.* (**sheds, shedding, shed**) **1.** *vt.* CAUSE TO FLOW to cause tears or blood to pour out **2.** *vt.* RADIATE to radiate or disperse sth, especially light **3.** *vti.* LOSE NATURALLY to cast off a growing part, e.g. hair or leaves, as a result of a natural process such as moulting **4.** *vt.* GET RID OF to get rid of sb or sth that is unwanted or unnecessary **5.** *vti.* REPEL OR BE REPELLED to flow off or drop off, or cause sth, especially water, to flow off or drop off **6.** *vt.* LOSE ACCIDENTALLY to have a transported load accidentally fall off onto the road **7.** *vt. Scotland* PART HAIR to part the hair ■ *n. Scotland*

DIVISION IN HAIR a parting in the hair [Old English *scēadan* 'to divide, separate'. Ultimately from a prehistoric Germanic word that is also the ancestor of English *ski* and, probably, *sheath*.]

shed[2] /shed/ *n.* **1. SMALL BUILDING** a small structure, either free-standing or attached to a larger building, used especially for storage or shelter **2. LARGE OPEN BUILDING** a large building with an open interior, used for storage or shelter or as a work area. Some sides often have no walls. [15thC. Origin uncertain: probably a variant of SHADE.]

she'd /sheed/ *contr.* a short form of 'she had' or 'she would'

Shed dormer

shed dormer *n.* a dormer window with a flat roof that slopes in the same direction as the main roof that surrounds it

she-devil *n.* a woman who is perceived as treating people with cruelty or contempt

sheen /sheen/ *n.* **1. GLOSSY APPEARANCE** a bright, softly shining surface or appearance **2. FINE CLOTHING** fine or brightly coloured clothing (*literary*) ■ *vi.* (**sheens, sheening, sheened**) **SHINE** to have a sheen (*regional*) [14thC. From earlier *sheen* 'beautiful', via Old English *scēne* from a prehistoric Germanic word meaning 'to see' (ancestor of English *show*).] —**sheeny** *adj.*

Sheene /sheen/, **Barry** (*b.* 1950) British motorcyclist. He was a world champion at 500cc (1976 and 1977) and winner of 23 Grand Prix (1971–81). He went on to work as a television commentator in Australia.

sheeny /sheeni/ (*plural* **-nies**) *n.* a highly offensive term for a Jewish person (*dated or offensive*)

Sheep

sheep /sheep/ (*plural* **sheep**) *n.* **1. MAMMAL RAISED FOR WOOL AND MEAT** a stocky hooved mammal with ribbed horns that is raised for its wool and meat. Genus: *Ovis.* **2. LEATHER FROM SHEEP** leather made from the skin of a sheep **3. SUBMISSIVE PERSON** sb who is timid, submits readily to others, or is easily led [Old English *scēap.* Ultimately from a prehistoric Germanic word perhaps meaning 'to make', in which case the underlying idea is 'sth made or created'.] ◇ **separate the sheep from the goats** to distinguish good or competent members of a group from the bad or incompetent

sheep-dip *n.* **1. DISINFECTANT FOR SHEEP** a disinfectant in which sheep are immersed to rid them of external parasites such as mites, ticks, and flies **2. BATH CONTAINING SHEEP-DIP** a bath containing a disinfectant in which sheep are immersed to rid them of external parasites

Sheepdog

sheepdog /sheep dog/ *n.* a dog that is used to herd sheep, or one of a type traditionally bred to herd sheep

sheepfold /sheepfōld/ *n.* an enclosure or shelter for sheep

sheepish /sheepish/ *adj.* **1. EMBARRASSED** showing embarrassment as a result of having done sth awkward or wrong **2. TIMID** showing the meekness popularly associated with sheep —**sheepishly** *adv.* —**sheepishness** *n.*

sheep ked /-ked/ *n.* = **sheep tick** [*Ked* 'sheep tick' of unknown origin]

sheep laurel *n.* a low-growing evergreen shrub of the heath family that is native to the eastern United States and Canada and is poisonous to young grazing animals. Latin name: *Kalmia angustifolia.*

sheep's eyes *npl.* shy glances full of love and longing [From the large size and the docile appearance of the eyes of sheep]

sheepshank /sheep shangk/ *n.* a knot used to shorten a rope in which the rope is doubled up upon itself

sheepskin /sheep skin/ *n.* **1. SHEEP LEATHER WITH OR WITHOUT WOOL** the skin of a sheep used as leather, with or without the wool still attached (*often used before a noun*) **2. SHEEPSKIN GARMENT OR RUG** a rug or a garment, especially a coat or jacket, made from sheepskin with the wool attached **3. PARCHMENT** a parchment made from the skin of a sheep (*often used before a noun*) **4. US DIPLOMA** a diploma, traditionally made of sheepskin parchment (*informal*)

sheep tick *n.* a wingless fly that lives as a blood-sucking parasite on sheep and can cause serious skin irritations. Latin name: *Melophagus ovinus.*

sheer[1] /sheer/ *adj.* **1. COMPLETE AND UTTER** used to emphasize the unlimited extent or unmitigated quality of sth ○ *That explanation is sheer nonsense.* **2. EXCLUSIVE OF ANYTHING ELSE** considered by itself without reference to anything else, or acting by itself without help from anything else ○ *She won the race by sheer endurance.* **3. PURE OR UNADULTERATED** free from any impurities, or not mixed with anything else **4. VERTICAL** rising nearly straight up or falling nearly straight down over a long distance ○ *They looked over the edge and there was a sheer drop.* **5. THIN AND ALMOST TRANSPARENT** so thin and fine as to be almost transparent ○ *a sheer summer blouse* ■ *adv.* **1. VERTICALLY** with an almost vertical rise or fall **2. COMPLETELY** completely and utterly ■ *n.* **NEARLY TRANSPARENT FABRIC** a fabric or piece of clothing that is very thin and fine and almost transparent [Mid-16thC. Origin uncertain: perhaps from Old English *scīr* 'bright, shining' from, ultimately, a prehistoric Germanic base that is also the ancestor of English *shimmer*.] —**sheerly** *adv.* —**sheerness** *n.*

sheer[2] /sheer/ *vti.* (**sheers, sheering, sheered**) **SWERVE FROM A COURSE** to swerve from a course, or cause a vehicle or vessel to swerve from its course ■ *n.* **1. CHANGE OF COURSE** an abrupt or sudden change of course **2. NAUT POSITION OF SHIP AT ANCHOR** the position of a ship in relation to its anchor [Early 17thC. Origin uncertain: perhaps from Low German *scheren.*]

sheer[3] /sheer/ *n.* the upward curve of a boat's hull as seen from the side, or the degree to which the hull curves upwards [Late 17thC. Origin uncertain: perhaps from SHEAR.]

sheerlegs /sheer legz/, **shearlegs** *n.* a lifting device consisting of two poles tied together at the top and spread apart at the bottom with a pulley suspended from the apex (*takes a singular or plural verb*)

Sheerness /sheer néss/ town, incorporating a river port and former naval dockyard, on the Isle of Sheppey, Kent, England. Population: 11,653 (1991).

sheet[1] /sheet/ *n.* **1. HOUSEHOLD CLOTH USED ON BED** a large rectangular piece of cloth that is used to cover the mattress of a bed or sb sleeping on the mattress **2. FLAT THIN RECTANGULAR PIECE** a broad flat thin piece of a material, especially a rectangular piece of paper, metal, or glass **3. BROAD THIN EXPANSE** a broad flat thin expanse of a substance, especially ice or water **4. EXPANSE OF STH MOVING** a broad expanse of sth that is in motion, e.g. falling water **5. STAMPS PAGE OF STAMPS** an entire rectangular page of postage stamps that were printed as a unit **6. PUBL NEWSPAPER** a newspaper or periodical, especially one dismissed as trivial ■ *v.* (**sheets, sheeting, sheeted**) **1.** *vt.* **PUT A SHEET OVER** to cover or wrap sth in a sheet **2.** *vt.* **COVER WITH THIN LAYER** to cover sth with a thin layer of a material **3.** *vt.* **MAKE INTO FLAT THIN PIECES** to form sth, especially metal, into broad flat thin pieces **4.** *vi.* **FALL OVER BROAD EXPANSE** to fall, flow, or spread out over a broad area ■ *adj.* **1. BROAD, FLAT, AND THIN** made in broad, flat, thin, usually rectangular pieces **2. COVERING THINLY** covering a broad area thinly [Old English *scēte* 'cloth'. Ultimately from a prehistoric Germanic word meaning 'to project' (ancestor also of English *shoot, shout,* and *scuttle*).]

sheet down *vi.* to fall in torrents (*refers to rain*)

sheet[2] /sheet/ *n.* **ROPE FOR CHANGING SAIL'S POSITION** a rope or line attached to a bottom corner of a sail and used to change the sail's position ■ **sheets** *npl.* **SPACES AT BOW AND STERN** the spaces in the bow and stern of an open boat that are not occupied by the seats [Old English *scēata* 'corner; lower part of a sail']

sheet anchor *n.* **1. LARGE EMERGENCY ANCHOR** a large anchor that is dropped only in emergencies **2. HELP IN EMERGENCY** sb who or sth that is relied on for help in a time of crisis or danger [*Sheet* of unknown origin: perhaps influenced by SHEET[2]]

sheeting /sheeting/ *n.* **1. CLOTH FOR SHEETS** wide cotton or linen cloth used primarily for making bedsheets **2. THIN MATERIAL FOR COVERING** thin material used for covering or lining the surface of sth

sheet lightning *n.* lightning that appears in a broad sheet as a result of being diffused by cloud cover

sheet metal *n.* metal that has been formed into a sheet by being pressed between rollers until it is thinner than plate but thicker than foil

sheet music *n.* music printed on folded or unfolded sheets of paper that have not been bound into a book

sheet pile *n.* a vertical column of steel, wood, or concrete driven into the ground alongside others to form an underground barrier impeding the movement of earth or water

Sheffield /shéffeeld/ city in southern Yorkshire, northern England. It was for many years the centre of the British steel industry. Population: 528,500 (1995).

shegetz /sháygits/ (*plural* **shkotzim** /shkótsim/), **sheygetz** (*plural* **shkotzim**) *n.* an offensive Jewish term for a boy or man who is not Jewish (*taboo insult*) [Early 20thC. Via Yiddish *sheygets* from Hebrew *sheqes* 'abomination, detested thing'.]

sheik /shayk, sheek/, **sheikh, shaikh** *n.* **1. ARAB CHIEF** the leader of an Arab tribe or village **2. ISLAM ISLAMIC RELIGIOUS LEADER** a senior official in an Islamic religious organization **3. PHYSICALLY APPEALING MAN** a handsome and physically appealing man (*dated informal*) [Late 16thC. From, ultimately, Arabic *šayk,* literally 'old man', from *šāka* 'to be old'.]

sheika /sháy kaa/, **sheikha, shaikha** *n.* the wife of a sheik [Mid-19thC. From Arabic *šayka.*]

sheikdom /sháykdəm, sheek-/, **sheikhdom, shaikhdom** *n.* a territory ruled by an Islamic religious leader. The emirates of the United Arab Emirates are sheikdoms.

sheikh *n.* = **sheik**

sheikha *n.* = **sheika**

sheikhdom *n.* = **sheikdom**

sheila /shéelə/ *n. ANZ* a woman, especially a girl or young woman (*informal*) [Mid-19thC. Origin uncertain: perhaps from *Sheila*, female name.]

sheitel /sháyt'l/ *n.* a wig worn by an Orthodox married Jewish woman to avoid showing her natural hair, which she is not supposed to do according to Orthodox belief [Late 19thC. Via Yiddish *sheytl* from Middle High German *scheitel* 'crown of the head'.]

shekel /shék'l/ *n.* **1.** ISRAELI CURRENCY UNIT the main unit of currency of the modern state of Israel, worth 100 agorot. See table at **currency 2.** COIN WORTH A SHEKEL a coin worth one shekel **3.** ANCIENT JEWISH UNIT OF WEIGHT an ancient Jewish unit of weight equivalent to approximately 16g/0.5 oz **4.** ANCIENT JEWISH COIN an ancient Jewish coin that was a unit of currency between 66 AD and 130 AD ■ **shekels** *npl.* MONEY money or cash (*slang*) [Mid-16thC. From Hebrew *šeqel*, from *šaqal* 'to weigh'.]

Shelburne /shélbərn, shél burn/, **William Petty Fitzmaurice, 2nd Earl of** (1737–1805) British statesman. He was prime minister of Great Britain (1782–83). He helped draw up the Treaty of Paris (1783), which granted independence to Britain's North American colonies.

sheldrake /shél drayk/ (*plural* **-drakes** *or* **-drake**) *n.* **1.** LARGE EUROPEAN DUCK a large thick-set often brightly coloured or variegated European duck with a thick bill. Genus: *Tadorna*. **2.** = **merganser** [14thC. Origin uncertain: perhaps from earlier *sheld* 'variegated' + DRAKE.]

shelf /shelf/ (*plural* **shelves** /shelvz/) *n.* **1.** FLAT SURFACE FOR HOLDING OBJECTS a flat usually rectangular board on which things are stored or displayed. It can be attached to a wall or can form part of a cabinet. **2.** CONTENTS OF SHELF the contents of a shelf, or the quantity of sth that a shelf holds **3.** GEOG LEDGE ON THE LANDSCAPE a ledge of rock, ice, or sand **4.** MINING LAYER OF UNDERGROUND ROCK a layer of underground rock encountered when sinking a shaft **5.** ARCHERY HEEL OF HAND the part of the heel of the hand on which the back end of an arrow is supported before being fired from a bow [14thC. From Low German *Schelf* 'shelf, shelves', of uncertain origin: perhaps, ultimately, from a prehistoric Germanic word meaning 'to split', the underlying idea being 'split piece of wood'.] —**shelfful** *n.* ◇ **be (left) on the shelf 1.** to be thought too old to have any chance of marrying (*insult*) **2.** to be no longer wanted, used, or taken account of

shelf ice *n.* a large plate of floating ice that has broken off from an ice shelf

shelf life *n.* **1.** STORAGE TIME OF PRODUCT the length of time a product may be stored before it begins to lose its freshness or effectiveness **2.** PERIOD OF POPULARITY the length of time that sb or sth is popular or lasts (*informal*)

shelf-mark *n.* = **pressmark**

shell /shel/ *n.* **1.** ZOOL COVERING OF TURTLE OR CRAB the hard protective outer covering of turtles, crabs, and other molluscs and crustaceans, or the calcium-based material this covering is made of **2.** INSECTS COVERING OF INSECT'S BODY the hard outer covering (**exoskeleton**) of an insect's body **3.** ZOOL COVERING OF EGG the hard or tough protective outer covering of the eggs of birds, reptiles, and a few mammals **4.** BIOL NUT'S OUTER COVERING the hard or fibrous protective outer covering of some seeds and fruits such as nuts **5.** PROTECTIVE CASING any hard casing or covering that protects or holds its contents, or the material composing it **6.** CONSTR FRAMEWORK OF BUILDING the basic framework of a building, especially while under construction or after damage by fire **7.** SHIPPING SHIP'S HULL the outer hull of a ship **8.** COOK PASTRY CASE a casing of pastry that has a filling put into it **9.** HOLLOW OR EMPTY THING an external form that contains nothing ○ *a mere shell of her former self* **10.** RESERVED MANNER a reserved manner behind which a shy person hides feelings or thoughts ○ *eventually came out of her shell and joined in* **11.** ARMS LARGE EXPLOSIVE PROJECTILE an explosive projectile fired from a large-bore gun such as a field gun or tank gun **12.** ARMS GUN CARTRIDGE a piece of ammunition fired by a gun, especially a shotgun cartridge, which holds the shot and explosive powder **13.** INDUST FIREWORK CARTRIDGE the cartridge that forms the outside of a firework and contains the explosive powder **14.** *US* HOUSEHOLD SMALL GLASS a small beer glass **15.** CLOTHES UNLINED JACKET an unlined usually lightweight jacket **16.** *US* CLOTHES SLEEVELESS BLOUSE a sleeveless blouse or sweater for a woman **17.** BUSINESS = **shell company 18.** ROWING NARROW RACING BOAT a narrow light boat used for racing, rowed by one or more people **19.** PHYS GROUP OF ELECTRONS IN SIMILAR ORBITS a group of electrons orbiting the nucleus of an atom and having the same principal quantum number **20.** COMPUT COMMAND PROGRAM a computer program that simplifies the interface between a user and the operating system by allowing the user to pick from a set of menus instead of entering commands ■ *v.* (**shells, shelling, shelled**) **1.** *vti.* TAKE STH OUT OF A SHELL to take sth out of a shell, or be taken out of a shell ○ *shell peas* **2.** *vti.* SEPARATE KERNELS FROM A COB to separate kernels from a cob, or be separated from a cob ○ *shell sweet corn* **3.** *vti.* MIL BOMBARD TARGET to fire artillery shells at sth **4.** *vi.* FLAKE OFF to fall off in thin scales **5.** *vi. US* COLLECT SEASHELLS to look for and gather shells at the seashore [Old English *scell*, originally 'sth that splits off']

shell out *vti.* to pay out money, especially a great deal of money (*informal*)

she'll /sheel/ *contr.* a short form of 'she will' or 'she shall'

shellac /shə lák, shéllak/ *n.* **1.** PURIFIED RESIN yellowish-orange flakes of a resin (**lac**) secreted by a tropical insect **2.** VARNISH a thin varnish made of purified lac dissolved in alcohol, used, especially formerly, as a coating on furniture and other items made of wood **3.** 78 RPM GRAMOPHONE RECORD an old type of gramophone record originally made from a material containing purified lac, played at 78 rpm ■ *vt.* (**-lacs, -lacking, -lacked**) **1.** APPLY SHELLAC TO STH to coat sth with shellac varnish **2.** *US* HIT REPEATEDLY to beat sb repeatedly with hard blows (*slang*) **3.** *US* DEFEAT EASILY to defeat sb easily or decisively (*slang*) [Mid-17thC. From SHELL + LAC, modelled on French *laque en écailles* 'lac (melted) in thin plates'.]

shellacking /shə láking, shéllaking/ *n. US* (*slang*) **1.** SEVERE BEATING a severe physical beating **2.** DECISIVE DEFEAT an easy or decisive defeat

shellback /shél bak/ *n.* **1.** SAILOR WHO HAS CROSSED EQUATOR a sailor who has crossed the equator, especially one whose crossing was marked by a traditional initiation ceremony **2.** EXPERIENCED SAILOR an old or experienced sailor [From the idea that limpets and barnacles have grown on the sailor's back during the long time at sea]

shellbark /shél baark/ *n.* = **shagbark** *n.* 1

shell company *n.* a company that has no independent assets or operations of its own but is used by its owners to conduct certain business dealings or maintain control of other companies

Popperfoto

Mary Shelley

Shelley /shélli/, **Mary** (1797–1851) British writer. Her most famous work is *Frankenstein* (1818). She was the daughter of Mary Wollstonecraft and the wife of Percy Bysshe Shelley. Born **Mary Wollstonecraft Godwin**

Shelley, Percy Bysshe (1792–1822) British poet. His lyric poetry was at the forefront of the English romantic movement, and included odes such as 'To a Skylark' (1820) and an elegy on Keats, 'Adonais' (1821). He was the husband of Mary Shelley.

shellfire /shél fīr/ *n.* **1.** FIRED ARTILLERY SHELLS artillery shells or projectiles fired at a target **2.** FIRING OF ARTILLERY SHELLS the firing or exploding of artillery shells or projectiles

shellfish /shél fish/ (*plural* **-fish** *or* **-fishes**) *n.* an aquatic invertebrate animal with a shell, especially an edible mollusc or crustacean such as an oyster, shrimp, or lobster

shell jacket *n.* a tight-fitting military jacket that extends only to the waist and is worn on semiformal occasions

shell-like *n.* sb's ear (*informal humorous*)

shell pink *adj.* of a delicate pale pink colour (*hyphenated when used before a noun*) —**shell pink** *n.*

shell shock *n.* a psychiatric disorder caused by exposure to warfare, especially shellfire (*dated*)

shell-shocked *adj.* **1.** STUNNED OR EXHAUSTED stunned, upset, or exhausted as a result of a stressful experience (*informal*) **2.** AFFECTED BY BATTLE FATIGUE experiencing severe psychological effects from exposure to warfare, especially shellfire

shell star *n.* a type of star that is thought to have a surrounding shell of gas

shell suit *n.* a lightweight shiny brightly coloured tracksuit worn casually or for sport. It is usually made of nylon with a soft lining.

shellwork /shél wurk/ *n.* seashells stuck on furniture and other items to give a decorative finish

Shelta /shéltə/ *n.* an ancient secret language used by Romany and other travelling people in Ireland and the United Kingdom. It is based on Gaelic with consonants systematically inverted or changed. [Late 19thC. Origin uncertain: perhaps an alteration of Old Irish *bélre* 'language'.]

shelter /shéltər/ *n.* **1.** STRUCTURE THAT PROTECTS OR COVERS a structure or building that provides cover from weather or protection against danger **2.** REFUGE an establishment providing accommodation and food for people who need to leave a violent or otherwise dangerous situation **3.** PROTECTION OR COVER the protection, cover, refuge, or safety that a shelter provides **4.** DWELLING OR HOUSING a place to live, considered as one of life's necessities **5.** *US* REFUGE FOR ANIMALS an establishment that takes in and looks after lost or unwanted animals ■ *v.* (**-ters, -tering, -tered**) **1.** *vt.* PROVIDE WITH PROTECTION to provide sb or sth with protection, cover, refuge, or safety **2.** *vi.* FIND PROTECTION to find protection, cover, refuge, or safety **3.** *vt.* FIN INVEST TO AVOID TAXES to put money into an investment that is subject to a lower tax rate or is free from taxes [Late 16thC. Origin uncertain: perhaps an alteration of earlier *sheltron* 'troops protected by shields', from Old English *scieldtruma*, from *scield* 'shield' + *truma* 'troop'.]

sheltered /shéltərd/ *adj.* **1.** PROTECTED FROM ELEMENTS protected from the adverse effects of the weather, especially wind **2.** NOT EXPOSED TO RIGOURS OF LIFE protected from the unpleasant, upsetting, or testing experiences of life

sheltered housing, sheltered accommodation *n.* accommodation specially designed for elderly or disabled people. It usually consists of self-contained self-catering units with some communal facilities and live-in staff to help when required.

sheltered workshop *n. US* a workplace specially designed to provide a noncompetitive environment where people who have various limitations can acquire job skills and experience

shelter tent *n. US* a small tent for two people usually made from two similar pieces of waterproof fabric

sheltie /shélti/, **shelty** (*plural* **-ties**) *n.* a Shetland pony or a Shetland sheepdog (*informal*) [Early 16thC. Origin uncertain: probably via Orkney dialect from Old Norse *Hjalti* 'Shetlander'.]

shelve[1] /shelv/ (**shelves, shelving, shelved**) *vt.* **1.** PUT ON SHELF to put or store sth on a shelf **2.** SET ASIDE to put sth off until later, or set sth aside **3.** DISMISS to dismiss or withdraw sb or sth from active service [Late 16thC. Back-formation from SHELVES.]

shelve[2] /shelv/ (**shelves, shelving, shelved**) *vi.* to descend with a flat, usually gradual slope [Late 16thC. Origin uncertain: perhaps from earlier SHELF 'grassy bank'.]

shelves plural of **shelf**

shelving /shélving/ *n.* **1. SHELVES** the shelves in a place, or shelves in general **2. MATERIAL FOR SHELVES** material used for making shelves

Shema /shə máa/ *n.* the confession of faith made in Jewish religious practice [Early 18thC. From Hebrew *šĕma*, from the Bible (Deuteronomy 6:4), literally 'Hear!'.]

shemozzle /shə mózz'l/ *n.* (*dated informal*) **1. MUDDLE** a confused or muddled situation **2. NOISY ROW** a noisy quarrel or argument [Late 19thC. Via Yiddish, literally 'crooked luck', from Middle High German *slim* 'crooked' + *mazzāl* 'luck'.]

Shenandoah National Park /shénnən dō ə-/ national park in the Blue Ridge Mountains of northern Virginia, established in 1935. Area: 788 sq. km/304 sq. mi.

shenanigan /shi nánnigən/ *n.* (*informal*) **1. QUESTIONABLE ACT** sth that is deceitful, underhand, or otherwise questionable (*usually used in the plural*) **2. TRICK OR PRANK** a playful trick, mischievous prank, or other display of high spirits [Mid-19thC. Origin uncertain: perhaps from Spanish *chanada* 'trick, deceit', contraction of *charranada*.]

shend /shend/ (**shends, shending, shent** /shent/, **shent**) *vt.* (*archaic*) **1. PUT TO SHAME** to disgrace sb with a superior performance **2. SCOLD** to scold or reprove sb **3. HURT OR RUIN** to hurt sb, damage sth, or destroy sb or sth [Old English *scendan*. Ultimately from a prehistoric Germanic word that is also the ancestor of English *shame*.]

Shenyang /shən yúng/ city in Liaoning Province, northeastern China. Population: 3,860,000 (1993).

Sheol /shée ol, shée ōl/ *n.* in ancient Hebrew theology, the dwelling place of the dead [Late 16thC. From Hebrew *šĕ'ōl*.]

Shepard /shéppərd/, **Alan, Jr.** (1923–98) US astronaut. He was the first US astronaut in space (5 May, 1961) and the fifth person to walk on the moon (1971). Full name **Alan Bartlett Shepard, Jr**

shepherd /shéppərd/ *n.* **1. SB TENDING SHEEP** sb who looks after sheep **2. SB PROVIDING GUIDANCE** sb who is responsible for caring for and guiding a group of people, especially a Christian minister ■ *v.* (**-herds, -herding, -herded**) **1.** *vti.* **TEND SHEEP** to look after sheep **2.** *vt.* **GUIDE** to guide a group of people somewhere **3.** *vt.* **TAKE CARE OF OTHERS** to look after the well-being of a group of people [Old English *scēaphirde*, from *scēap* (see **SHEEP**) + *hierde* 'herder']

shepherdess /shéppər déss/ *n.* a girl or woman who looks after sheep (*dated*)

shepherding /shéppərding/ *n.* in Australian Rules football, the practice of shielding a teammate by blocking the approach of an opposing player

shepherd's check *n.* (*often used before a noun*) **1. PATTERN OF SQUARES** a pattern of small black and white squares **2. SHEPHERD'S CHECK FABRIC** a fabric in a shepherd's check pattern

shepherd's pie *n.* a baked dish made of cooked minced meat, traditionally lamb or mutton, in gravy with a topping of mashed potato

shepherd's plaid *n.* = **shepherd's check** (*often used before a noun*)

shepherd's purse *n.* an annual plant of the mustard family that has white flowers and heart-shaped seed pods and is commonly found as a weed in gardens. Latin name: *Capsella bursa-pastoris*. [From the pod's resemblance to a bag used by shepherds to carry food]

Sheppard /shéppərd/, **Jack** (1702–24) English robber. Notorious for his repeated escapes, he was hanged in London. His exploits were later romanticized in ballads, plays, and novels. Real name **John Sheppard**

Sheppard, Kate (1848–1934) British-born New Zealand suffragist. She was the leader of a successful campaign for the extension of political suffrage to women, which resulted in New Zealand's being the first country to grant women the vote (1893). Born **Catherine Wilson Malcolm**

Shepparton /shéppərtən/ city in northern Victoria, Australia. It is an industrial, agricultural, and food processing centre. Population: 30,510 (1991).

Sheppey, Isle of /shéppi–/ island off the coast of

northern Kent, England, at the mouth of the River Medway. Area: 91 sq. km/35 sq. mi.

Popperfoto

Sheraton

Sheraton /shérrətən/ *adj.* relating to furniture designed by or in the graceful simple style of Thomas Sheraton, who favoured straight lines, understated classical ornamentation, and light thin legs

Sheraton /shérrətən/, **Thomas** (1751–1806) British cabinetmaker. He wrote *The Cabinet-Maker and Upholsterer's Drawing Book* (1793–94), which was influential in formulating the neoclassical style in English furniture.

sherbet /shúrbət/ *n.* **1. FIZZY POWDER** a fruit-flavoured sweet powder that fizzes when moistened on the tongue and is eaten as a confection or is stirred into water to make a fizzy drink (*often used before a noun*) **2. FRUIT DRINK** a drink made from fruit juice, water, and sugar and served chilled **3. sherbet, sherbert** *US* **FROZEN DESSERT** a frozen dessert made with fruit syrup, milk and the white of an egg, whisked until smooth and opaque **4. sherbet, sherbert** **BEER** beer (*dated humorous slang*) [Early 17thC. Via Turkish *şerbet* and Persian *šerbet* from Arabic *šarbat* 'drink', from *šariba* 'to drink' (source of English *syrup*).]

Sherborne /shúr burn/ market town in Dorset, England, known for its 8th-century abbey. Population: 7,606 (1991).

Sherbrooke /shúr brook/ city situated south of the St Lawrence River in Quebec, Canada, 160 km/100 mi. east of Montreal. Population: 76,429 (1991).

sherd *n.* = **potsherd**

Sheridan /shérridən/, **Richard Brinsley** (1751–1816) Irish-born British playwright. His comedies of manners include *The Rivals* (1775) and *The School for Scandal* (1777). He was a Whig MP (1780–1812).

sherif /she réef/, **sharif** /sha réef/, **shereef** *n.* **1. ISLAM DESCENDANT OF MUHAMMAD** a descendant of the prophet Muhammad through his daughter Fatima **2. GOVERNOR OF MECCA** the governor or chief magistrate of Mecca during the years of Ottoman Turkish rule **3. ARAB RULER** an Arab prince or ruler [Late 16thC. From Arabic *sharif*, literally 'illustrious'.]

sheriff /shérrif/ *n.* **1. SENIOR OFFICIAL OF ENGLISH COUNTY** in England and Wales, the senior representative of the monarch in a county, who performs ceremonial and some judicial duties **2. SCOTTISH JUDGE** in Scotland, a judge who presides over one of the lower courts for civil and criminal cases (**sheriff courts**) **3. US COUNTY LAW ENFORCEMENT OFFICER** in the United States, the chief law enforcement officer for a county, whose duties are sometimes restricted to the enforcement of the orders of the courts **4. CANADIAN COURT OFFICER** in Canada, an officer of the courts who assists with the administration of the justice system, e.g. by serving writs **5. AUSTRALIAN COURT OFFICIAL** in Australia, a court official charged with managing juries and implementing orders from the Supreme Court [Old English *scīrgerēfa*, literally 'reeve of the shire', from *scīr* 'shire' + *gerēfa* 'reeve'.] —**sheriffdom** *n.*

sheriff court *n.* in Scotland, the lower court for civil and criminal cases

sheriff officer *n.* in Scotland, a court official who carries out warrants and serves writs

sherlock /shúr lok/ *n.* **1. MYSTERY SOLVER** sb with exceptional powers of deduction or perception (*humorous; used ironically*) **2. DETECTIVE** a private detective (*informal*) [Early 20thC. From *Sherlock* Holmes,

detective in the stories of Arthur Conan Doyle (1859–1930).]

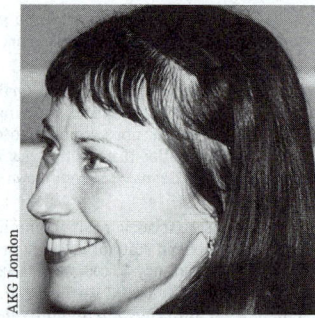
AKG London

Cindy Sherman

Sherman /shúrmən/, **Cindy** (*b.* 1954) US photographer. Her carefully staged and composed photographs, featuring herself in various roles, gained widespread notice in the 1980s.

Sherman, William T. (1820–91) US soldier. A Mexican War veteran, he rejoined the army in 1861 as the Civil War broke out and became one of the Union army's most aggressive and successful generals, marching on Atlanta and then to the sea (1864). Full name **William Tecumseh Sherman**

sherpa /shúrpə/ *n.* **1. TEXTILES FLEECY FABRIC** fabric with a fleecy pile, used as a lining for winter outdoor wear **2. MOUNTAINEERING** = **Sherpa** *n.* **2 3. POL** = **Sherpa** *n.* **3**

Sherpa (*plural* **-pas** *or* **-pa**) *n.* **1. PEOPLES MEMBER OF HIMALAYAN MOUNTAIN PEOPLE** a member of a people originally from Tibet who live on the southern Himalayan slopes in Nepal and Sikkim. Sherpas are noted for their mountaineering skills. **2. MOUNTAINEERING HIMALAYAN MOUNTAIN GUIDE** a Sherpa who works as a guide for mountaineers in the Himalayas **3. POL EXPERT POLITICAL AIDE** an expert who helps a government leader prepare for a summit meeting [Mid-19thC. From Tibetan *sharpa* 'inhabitant of an eastern country'.]

sherry /shérri/ (*plural* **-ries**) *n.* a wine, especially one made near Jerez, Spain, that has a higher alcohol content as a result of adding brandy, and ranges from very sweet to very dry [Alteration of earlier *sherris*, interpreted as plural, named after *Xeres* (now Jerez), Spain, where the wine was produced.]

Sherwood Forest /shúr wood-/ ancient forest in Nottinghamshire, England. According to legend it was the haunt of Robin Hood. Small parts of the forest still remain.

she's /sheez/ *contr.* a short form of 'she is' or 'she has'

Shetland /shétlənd/ *n.* **1. ZOOL** = **Shetland sheepdog 2. TEXTILES** = **Shetland wool 3. CLOTHES GARMENT OF SHETLAND WOOL** an item of clothing made of Shetland wool, especially a sweater ■ *adj.* **MADE OF SHETLAND WOOL** made of Shetland wool

Shetland Islands /shét lənd-/ group of about 150 islands lying 209 km/130 mi. north of mainland Scotland. The islands serve as a base for the North Sea oil industry. Mainland is the chief island. Capital: Lerwick. Population: 23,232 (1996). Area: 1,438 sq. km/555 sq. mi. —**Shetlander** *n.*

Shetland pony *n.* a small sturdy pony with a long

Shetland pony

shaggy mane and tail, belonging to a breed that originated in Shetland

Shetland sheepdog *n.* a small herding dog with a heavy coat that resembles a collie, belonging to a breed that originated in Shetland

Shetland wool *n.* fine wool from sheep raised in Shetland, or a yarn spun from this wool

Shevardnadze /shévvərd naádzi/, **Eduard** (*b.* 1928) Georgian statesman. As foreign minister (1985–90, 1991) during the last years of the Soviet Union, he helped to implement democratic reforms in East European countries and cultivate warmer relations with the West. After his native Georgia became an independent republic, he became its head of state (1992). Full name **Eduard Amvrosiyevich Shevardnadze**

Shevat /shə vót/, **Shebat** /-bót, -vót/ *n.* JUDAISM, CALENDAR the eleventh month of the Jewish religious calendar, covering part of January and February [Mid-16thC. From Hebrew *šəḇaṭ*.]

shew /shō/ (**shews, shewing, shewed, shewed** *or* **shewn** /shōn/) *vti.* to show (*archaic*) [Variant spelling]

shewbread /shṓ bred/ *n.* in the Bible, the twelve loaves of bread placed in the tabernacle every Sabbath by the Hebrew priests of ancient Israel (*archaic*)

sheygets *n.* = **shegetz** (*taboo insult*)

SHF, **shf** *abbr.* superhigh frequency

Shia, **Shi'a**, **Shi'ah** *n.* (*plural* **-a** *or* **-as**; *plural* **-'a** *or* **-'as**; *plural* **-'ah** *or* **-'ahs**) **1. MAJOR BRANCH OF ISLAM** the branch of Islam that considers Ali, the cousin of Muhammad, and his descendants as Muhammad's true successors. ◊ **Sunni 2.** = **Shiite** *n.* ■ *adj.* = **Shiite** *adj.* [Early 17thC. From Arabic *šī'a* 'faction, party' (of Ali, Muhammad's son-in-law and the fourth caliph).]

shiatsu /shi aát soo/, **shiatzu** *n.* a form of healing massage in which the hands are used to apply pressure at acupuncture points on the body in order to stimulate and redistribute energy. Originating in Japan, it is used to treat various conditions, e.g. back pain, migraine, insomnia, depression, and digestive problems. [Mid-20thC. From Japanese, literally 'finger pressure'.]

shibboleth /shíbbə leth/ *n.* **1. CATCHWORD OR SLOGAN** a word or phrase frequently used, or a belief strongly held, by members of a group that is usually regarded by outsiders as meaningless, unimportant, or misguided **2. COMMON SAYING OR BELIEF** a saying that is widely used or a belief that is widely held, especially one that interferes with sb's ability to speak or think about things without preconception **3. IDENTIFYING WORD OR CUSTOM** a unique pronunciation, word, behaviour, or practice used to distinguish one group of people from another and to identify individuals as either members of the group or outsiders [Mid-17thC. From Hebrew *šibbōleṯ* 'stream'.]

WORD KEY: ORIGIN

According to the Bible, the Gileadites used the word *šibbōleṯ* as a password, for they knew their enemies the Ephraimites could not pronounce the 'sh' properly ('And it was so, that when those Ephraimites which were escaped said, Let me go over; that the men of Gilead said unto him, Art thou an Ephraimite? If he said, Nay, then they said unto him, Say now Shibboleth; and he said Sibboleth: for he could not frame to pronounce it right' (Judges 12:5–6).

shidduch /shí da-/ (*plural* **-duchim** /shi dóo-im/) *n.* a prospective Jewish marriage that was formerly usually arranged by a professional matchmaker (**shadchan**) [Late 19thC. Via Yiddish from Hebrew *šiddūḵ* 'negotiation (of an arranged marriage)'.]

Shiel, Loch /sheel/ long narrow lake in western Scotland, linked to the sea by the River Shiel. It is a National Scenic Area. Length: 27 km/17 mi.

shield /sheeld/ *n.* **1.** ARMS **PIECE OF ARMOUR CARRIED ON ARM** a flat or convex piece of armour carried on the arm and used as a protection against weapon blows, arrows, bullets, or projectiles **2. PROTECTION OR DEFENCE** sb or sth that serves as protection or acts as a defence **3.** HERALDRY **COAT OF ARMS** a shield or a shield-shaped insignia that contains sb's coat of arms **4. PRIZE OR TROPHY** a prize or trophy, especially in a sports competition, that is made in the shape

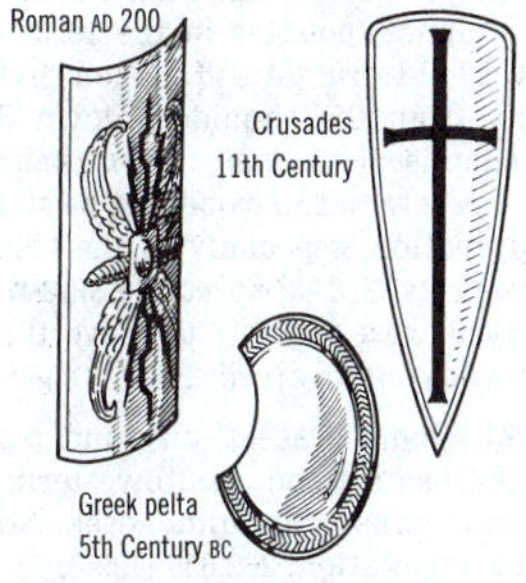
Roman AD 200
Crusades
11th Century
Greek pelta
5th Century BC

Shield

of a shield **5. DECORATIVE OFFICIAL EMBLEM** a decorative device used as an official emblem by a government or organization, usually containing symbolic images associated with the government's territory or the organization's purpose **6.** PUBLIC ADMIN **US POLICE OFFICER'S BADGE** the official badge that a US police officer wears or carries **7.** CLOTHES = **dress shield 8.** ARMS **PROTECTIVE PLATE ATTACHED TO ARTILLERY** a steel plate attached to a piece of artillery to protect those operating the artillery from bullets and shrapnel **9.** MECH ENG **MACHINE'S SAFETY BARRIER** a protective barrier such as a screen or housing around the moving parts of a piece of machinery **10.** ELEC ENG **ANTISTATIC OR ANTIMAGNETIC SCREEN** a screen used to protect equipment or people from unwanted electric or magnetic fields **11.** NUCLEAR PHYS **WALL PROTECTING FROM RADIATION** an encasing structure or wall, usually made of lead or concrete that is put around a nuclear reactor or other source of radiation to prevent the release of radiation **12.** GEOL **FLAT AREA OF ROCK** a broad flat area of exposed Precambrian basement rock that lies at the centre of each continent **13.** ZOOL **ANIMAL'S PROTECTIVE COVERING** the protective covering of an animal, e.g. a shell, scale, or plate **14.** BOT = **apothecium** ■ *v.* (**shields, shielding, shielded**) **1.** *vt.* **PROTECT WITH SHIELD** to defend or protect sb or sth with a shield or by using the body or another object as a shield **2.** *vi.* **ACT AS SHIELD** to serve or act as a protection or defence **3.** *vt.* **HIDE** to conceal or shelter sb or sth from view [Old English *scield*. Ultimately from a prehistoric Germanic word, probably originally used for 'board', from a word meaning 'to split'.] —**shielder** *n.*

WORD KEY: SYNONYMS

See Synonyms at ***safeguard***.

shielding /sheélding/ *n.* the use of material such as lead or concrete around a source of radiation to prevent the harmful release of radiation

Shield of David *n.* = **Star of David**

shieling /sheéling/ *n. Scotland* **1. COWHERD'S MOUNTAIN HUT** a mountain hut used by a cowherd **2. MOUNTAIN PASTURE** a mountain pasture that is used by cattle in the summer [Mid-16thC. Formed from earlier *shiel*, of unknown origin.]

shift /shift/ *v.* (**shifts, shifting, shifted**) **1.** *vti.* **MOVE** to move sb or sth to a different position, or be moved to a different position **2.** *vti.* **CHANGE OR EXCHANGE** to change or exchange sth for sth else of the same group, set, or class ○ *I've shifted jobs three times in the last year.* **3.** *vti.* HOUSEHOLD **REMOVE STAIN** to remove a mark or stain from a material or surface, especially with difficulty, or be removed from a material or surface **4.** *vti.* AUTOMOT **CHANGE GEARS** to change gears in a motor vehicle **5.** *vi.* **PROVIDE FOR OWN NEEDS** to provide personal needs or manage personal affairs ○ *You need to learn to shift for yourself.* **6.** *vi.* **GET BY WITH DECEIT** to get by through the use of deceit, tricks, or underhand methods **7.** *vi.* **MOVE FAST** to move at great speed (*informal*) **8.** *vt.* **EAT OR DRINK QUICKLY OR MUCH** to eat or drink sth quickly or in large amounts (*informal*) **9.** *vt.* **SELL QUICKLY OR IN LARGE AMOUNTS** to sell sth quickly or in large amounts, often when it is stolen or illegal or difficult to sell (*informal*) **10.** *vi.* **PRESS SHIFT KEY** to press the shift key on a computer or typewriter keyboard to produce capital letters and certain other characters **11.** *vti.* LING **ALTER PHONETICALLY** to alter a sound phonetically in the course of the development of a language, or be altered phonetically **12.** *vi. Malaysia, Singapore* **MOVE HOUSE** to move house ○ *We are going to shift to Penang.* ■ *n.* **1. CHANGE MADE** a change in position, direction, makeup, or circumstances **2.** INDUST **PERIOD OF TIME WORKED** a period of working time, especially any of the fixed periods that the day is divided into in workplaces that operate 24 hours a day. There are usually two twelve-hour or three eight-hour shifts. **3. PEOPLE WORKING DURING PERIOD** the group of people who are working during a particular period of time **4. KEY ON COMPUTER KEYBOARD** a key on a computer or typewriter keyboard that is depressed to produce capital letters and certain other characters **5.** CLOTHES **DRESS** a loose-fitting dress that hangs down from the shoulders **6.** CLOTHES **WOMAN'S UNDERGARMENT** a woman's shirt-shaped undergarment of the 17th and 18th centuries **7. PLAN** a tactic or plan required to accomplish sth difficult **8. TRICK** a deceitful or underhand scheme or plan **9.** GEOL **ROCK DISPLACEMENT AT FAULT** a displacement of rocks on a fault line **10.** MUSIC **CHANGE IN HAND POSITION** a change in hand position in order to play a different set of notes in a different register on a keyboard or string instrument **11.** LING **CHANGE IN PRONUNCIATION** a change in the pronunciation of a sound in the course of the development of a language **12.** PHYS **CHANGE IN FREQUENCY** a change in the position of a spectral line representing a change of frequency, e.g. that caused by the Doppler effect [Old English *sciftan* 'to divide, arrange'. Ultimately from prehistoric Germanic. The main modern meanings evolved from 'arrange' via 'change'.]

WORD KEY: SYNONYMS

See Synonyms at ***change***.

shift key *n.* a key on a computer or typewriter keyboard that is pressed to produce capital letters or certain other characters

shiftless /shíftləss/ *adj.* **1. LACKING AMBITION** unwilling to make the effort to be successful or do sth properly **2. INEFFICIENT** lacking the abilities or knowledge required to do sth successfully or properly —**shiftlessly** *adv.* —**shiftlessness** *n.*

shiftwork /shift wurk/ *n.* a system of working in which people work one of a set of usually two twelve-hour or three eight-hour shifts in a 24-hour period (*often used before a noun*)

shifty /shífti/ (**-ier, -iest**) *adj.* **1. UNTRUSTWORTHY** likely to try to deceive or avoid responsibility **2.** *US* **CHANGING DIRECTION OR POSITION** changing direction or position often or quickly, or able to do so **3. RESOURCEFUL** with the abilities and knowledge needed to do sth successfully —**shiftily** *adv.* —**shiftiness** *n.*

shigella /shi géllə/ (*plural* **-lae** /-li/ *or* **-las**) *n.* a rod-shaped bacterium that lives in the intestinal tracts of human beings and animals and causes dysentery. There are four species, all causing dysentery but with varying degrees of severity. Genus: *Shigella.* [Mid-20thC. From modern Latin *Shigella*, genus name, which was named after Kiyoshi *Shiga* (1870–1957), the Japanese bacteriologist who discovered the bacterium.]

shigellosis /shíggə lṓssiss/ (*plural* **-ses** /-seez/) *n.* a highly infectious form of dysentery caused by the shigella bacterium. It occurs mainly in tropical countries, especially under unsanitary conditions and among children and people with weakened immune systems.

shih tzu /shée tsóo/ (*plural* **shih tzus** *or* **shih tzu**) *n.* a small short-legged dog with a short muzzle, long dense coat, and a tail that curls over its back, belonging to a breed developed in Tibet [Early 20thC. From Chinese *shīzigǒu*, literally 'lion dog'.]

Shiism /shée izəm/, **Shi'ism** *n.* = **Shia** *n.* 1 [Late 19thC. Formed from SHIA or SHIITE.]

shiitake /shi taáki/, **shiitake mushroom, shitake, shitake mushroom** *n.* a dark-coloured mushroom with an edible fleshy cap, native to eastern Asia. Latin name: *Lentinus edodes.* [Late 19thC. From Japanese, literally 'oak-tree mushroom'.]

Shiite /shée īt/, **Shi'ite** *n.* **FOLLOWER OF MAJOR BRANCH OF ISLAM** a follower of the Shia branch of Islam, which considers Ali, the cousin of Muhammad, and his descendants as Muhammad's true successors. ◊ **Sunni** ■ *adj.* **OF SHIITES** relating or belonging to Shiites or to the Shia branch of Islam —**Shiitic** /shee íttik/ *adj.*

Shijiazhuang /shəjiə jṓo ung/ industrial centre and capital of Hebei Province, southwest of Beijing, in northeastern China. Population: 1,320,000 (1990).

shikari /shi kaári/, **shikaree** *n. S Asia* a big-game hunter, especially a professional hunter who works as a guide [Early 19thC. Via Urdu from Persian *šikārī* 'of hunting', from *šikār* 'hunting'.]

shiksa /shíksə/, **shikse** *n.* a highly offensive Jewish term for a girl or woman who is not Jewish (*taboo insult*) [Late 19thC. From Yiddish *shikse*, feminine of *sheygets* (see SHEGETZ).]

shill /shil/ *n. US* **1.** **PRETENDED CUSTOMER OR GAMBLER** sb who pretends to be an interested customer or gambler in order to lure others into buying or gambling **2.** **SELF-INTERESTED PROMOTER** sb who promotes sb or makes a sales pitch for sth for reasons of self-interest ■ *v.* **(shills, shilling, shilled)** *US* **1.** *vi.* **BE SHILL** to be or work as a shill **2.** *vt.* **PROMOTE AS SHILL** to promote or sell sth using the tactics of a shill [Early 20thC. Origin uncertain: perhaps a shortening of the name of Benjamin Penhallow *Shillaber* (1814–90), US humorist who was accused of plagiarism.]

shillelagh /shi láylə, -li/, **shillalah** *n. Ireland* a stick or club, traditionally made of oak or blackthorn wood [Late 18thC. Named after *Shillelagh*, town in Co. Wicklow, Ireland, famous for oaks.]

shilling /shílling/ *n.* **1.** **FORMER BRITISH COIN** a former British coin and subunit of currency, in use until 1971, that was equivalent to one-twentieth of a pound **2.** **FORMER US COIN** an old US coin **3.** **UNIT OF CURRENCY IN EAST AFRICA** a unit of currency in Kenya, Somalia, Tanzania, and Uganda. See table at **currency** **4.** **COIN WORTH A SHILLING** a coin worth a shilling in Kenya, Somalia, Tanzania, or Uganda **5.** *Malaysia, Singapore* **COIN** a coin (*informal*) [Old English *scilling*. Ultimately from a prehistoric Germanic word perhaps meaning 'to divide', in which case the underlying idea is 'division of a standard unit of weight or currency'.] ◇ **not the full shilling** extremely unintelligent or affected to some extent by mental illness (*informal humorous*)

Shillong /shi lóng/ capital of Meghalaya State, northeastern India. Population: 132,000 (1991).

Shilluk /shi lóok/ (*plural* **-luk** *or* **-luks**) *n.* **1.** PEOPLES **MEMBER OF NE AFRICAN PEOPLE** a member of a people who live in northeastern Africa, mainly along the western bank of the Nile in Sudan **2.** LANG **SHILLUK LANGUAGE** the language spoken by the Shilluk, belonging to the Nilo-Saharan family of languages. Shilluk is spoken by about 110, 000 people. [Late 18thC. From Shilluk.] —**Shilluk** *adj.*

shilly-shally /shílli shali/ *vi.* **(shilly-shallies, shilly-shallying, shilly-shallied)** **1.** **HESITATE OR VACILLATE** to be unable to make a choice or decision when one is needed **2.** **WASTE TIME** to waste time on unimportant things ■ *adv.* **IRRESOLUTELY** with hesitation or a lack of decision ■ *adj.* **LACKING DECISIVENESS** feeling or showing a lack of decisiveness ■ *n.* (*plural* **shilly-shallies**) **HESITATION** a failure or inability to make a choice or decision [Early 18thC. Alteration (perhaps influenced by DILLY-DALLY) of 'shall I? shall I?'.] —**shilly-shallier** *n.*

shim /shim/ *n.* **THIN WEDGE-SHAPED PIECE** a thin usually wedge-shaped piece of wood, metal, plastic, or other material that is used to help position sth properly, usually by adjusting a level or filling a gap ■ *vt.* **(shims, shimming, shimmed)** **POSITION STH USING SHIM** to position or adjust sth using a shim [Early 18thC. Origin unknown. Originally used for 'piece of iron attached to a tool for scraping soil'.]

shimmer /shímmər/ *vti.* **(-mers, -mering, -mered)** **1.** **SHINE WITH A WAVERING LIGHT** to shine softly with a wavering or flickering light, or cause sth to shine in this way **2.** **BE VISIBLE AS WAVERING IMAGE** to be visible as a wavering or flickering and sometimes distorted image, or make sth visible in this way ■ *n.* **1.** **WAVERING LIGHT OR GLOW** a wavering or flickering soft light or glow **2.** **WAVERING IMAGE OR APPEARANCE** a wavering or flickering and sometimes distorted image, e.g. that caused by hot air rising from the ground [Old English *scymrian*, originally 'to shine repeatedly'. Ultimately from a prehistoric Germanic word meaning 'to shine', which is also the ancestor of English *shine* and *sheer*.] —**shimmery** *adj.*

shimmy /shímmi/ *n.* **1.** AUTOMOT **WOBBLING OF A VEHICLE** a wobbling motion or vibration, especially in the front wheels of a motor vehicle **2.** DANCE **POPULAR 1920S DANCE** a jazz dance, popular in the 1920s in which the body was held straight and shaken rhythmically and rapidly from the shoulders down **3.** CLOTHES **CHEMISE** a chemise (*informal*) ■ *vi.* **(-mies, -mying, -mied)** **1.** AUTOMOT **WOBBLE** to wobble or be shaken with a wobbling motion, especially in the front wheels (*refers to vehicles*) **2.** DANCE **DANCE THE SHIMMY** to dance the shimmy **3.** **MOVE SHAKINGLY** to move the body in shaking or swaying way [Early 20thC. Origin unknown.]

Shimonoseki /shimənō séeki/ city and port in Yamaguchi Prefecture on southwestern Honshu Island, Japan, across the Shimonoseki Strait from Kitakyushu. Population: 262,635 (1990).

shin[1] /shin/ *n.* **1.** ANAT **FRONT OF LOWER LEG** the front portion of the leg from below the knee to above the ankle, or the leg bone (**tibia**) located there **2.** FOOD **CUT OF BEEF** the lower portion of the foreleg in cattle, used as a cut of beef in stews ■ *v.* **(shins, shinning, shinned)** **1.** *vti.* **CLIMB USING ARMS AND LEGS** to climb a rope, tree, or pole with speed and agility by gripping with the arms and legs and then pulling up with the arms and sliding upwards **2.** *vt.* **HIT IN SHIN** to kick or hit sb in the shin [Old English *scinu*. Ultimately from a prehistoric Germanic word probably meaning 'thin piece'.]

shin[2] /shin/ *n.* the 22nd letter of the Hebrew alphabet, represented in the English alphabet as 'sh' [Early 19thC. From Hebrew *šīn*.]

shinbone /shínbōn/ *n.* the flat surface of the bone immediately under the skin on the front of the lower leg. Technical name **tibia** [Old English *scinbān*]

shindig /shíndig/ *n.* **1.** **NOISY PARTY** a noisy and festive party or celebration (*informal*) **2.** = **shindy** *n.* 1 [Late 19thC. Origin uncertain: probably an alteration of SHINDY.]

shindy /shíndi/ (*plural* **-dies**) *n.* **1.** **DISTURBANCE** a disturbance or commotion (*informal*) **2.** = **shindig** *n.* 1 [Early 19thC. Origin uncertain: probably a variant of SHINTY.]

shine /shīn/ *v.* **(shines, shining, shone, shone** /shon/**)** **1.** *vi.* **EMIT LIGHT** to give out light **2.** *vi.* **BE BRIGHT** to be bright or reflect light **3.** *vt.* **DIRECT LIGHT** to direct the light emitted by sth ○ *Shine the torch over here.* **4.** *vi.* **EXCEL** to be very good at or do very well in some form of activity **5.** *vi.* **APPEAR CLEARLY** to appear clearly **6.** *vi.* **HAVE RADIANT QUALITY** to appear to have a specially bright or radiant quality as a result of good health or a strong positive emotion ○ *Her face shone with happiness.* **7.** (*past and past participle* **shined**) *vt.* **POLISH STH** to make sth bright and gleaming by polishing it ■ *n.* **1.** **BRIGHTNESS FROM LIGHT SOURCE** brightness or radiance emitted by a source of light **2.** **BRIGHT SURFACE** the bright or gleaming surface of sth **3.** **ACT OF POLISHING STH** an act of polishing sth to make it shiny **4.** *US* BEVERAGES **MOONSHINE** moonshine (*informal*) [Old English *scīnan*. Ultimately from an Indo-European base meaning 'to glimmer, shine faintly' that is also the ancestor of English *shimmer* and *skiagram*.] ◇ **take a shine to sb** to take a liking to sb (*informal*)

WORD KEY: CULTURAL NOTE

Shine, a film by Australian director Scott Hicks (1996). It tells the true story of pianist David Helfgott's return to performance after a major mental illness and years in psychiatric hospitals. Geoffrey Rush won an Oscar for his portrayal of Helfgott.

shiner /shīnər/ *n.* **1.** **BLACK EYE** a black eye (*informal*) **2.** **SHINY FRESHWATER FISH** a small silvery North American freshwater fish. Genus: *Notropis.* **3.** **STH SHINY** sth that shines or makes sth shine

shingle[1] /shíng g'l/ *n.* **1.** **ROOF OR WALL TILE** a small flat tile, especially one made of wood, used in overlapping rows to cover a roof or wall **2.** **HAIRSTYLE** a short hairstyle for women, popular in the 1920s, in which the back hair was cut to taper at the nape of the neck **3.** *US, Can* **SIGN OR NAMEPLATE** a nameplate or a small sign giving the name of a doctor, lawyer, or other professional person, fixed outside that person's office ■ *vt.* **(-gles, -gling, -gled)** **1.** **COVER STH WITH TILES** to cover sth with small overlapping tiles **2.** **TAPER HAIR AT BACK** to cut hair so that it is tapered at the nape of the neck [12thC. Alteration of late Latin *scindula*, a variant of Latin *scandula*. Ultimately from an Indo-European word meaning 'to split' that is also the ancestor of English *shatter*.] —**shingler** *n.* ◇ **hang out your shingle** *US, Can* to begin working as a professional from your own office (*informal*)

shingle[2] /shíng g'l/ *n.* **1.** **PEBBLES** small round pebbles on a beach **2.** **PEBBLY AREA** an area of beach covered in shingle [Mid-16thC. Origin unknown.] —**shingly** *adj.*

shingle[3] /shíng g'l/ **(-gles, -gling, -gled)** *vt.* to remove the slag from iron by hammering or squeezing it in the process of making wrought iron [Late 17thC. Via French *cingler* from German *zängeln*, from *Zange* 'tongs'.]

shingles /shíng g'lz/ *n.* a disease of adults caused by the reactivation of chickenpox viruses in a nerve ganglion and resulting in inflammation, pain, and a rash of small skin blisters. Technical name **herpes zoster, zoster** [14thC. Alteration of Latin *cingulum* 'girdle' (a translation of Greek *zōstēr*), from *cingere* 'to gird'. So called because the skin eruptions often encircle the body.]

shining /shíning/ *adj.* conspicuously excellent and admirable ○ *a shining example to all* [Old English *scynend*]

shinleaf /shín leef/ (*plural* **-leaves** /-leevz/) *n. US* a plant of the wintergreen family found in Europe, Asia, and North America that has a base of evergreen leaves and white or pink flowers. Family: Pyrolaeceae. [Early 19thC. From its formerly being used to treat shin soreness.]

shinny[1] /shínni/ *n., vi.* US = **shinty**

shinny[2] /shínni/ **(-nies, -nying, -nied)** *vi.* to climb up or down sth using the hands and legs [Late 19thC. Formed from SHIN[1].]

shinplaster /shín plaastər/ *n. US* a piece of low-value paper money, especially one issued in the United States during the Civil War [Early 19thC. From its resemblance to the plaster used for leg plasters.]

shin splints *n.* a painful inflammation of the muscles surrounding the shinbone, often caused by running or jogging on hard roads (*takes a singular or plural verb*)

shintaido /shin tídō/ *n.* a form of exercise based on the movements used in Japanese martial arts, performed by a group [From Japanese]

Shinto /shíntō/ *n.* a Japanese religion in which devotees worship and make offerings to numerous gods and spirits associated with the natural world [Early 18thC. From Japanese *shintō*, literally 'way of the gods'.] —**Shintoism** *n.* —**Shintoist** *n., adj.*

shinty /shínni/ *n.* (*plural* **-ties**) **1.** **GAME RESEMBLING HOCKEY** a Scottish game similar to hockey, played with a small hard ball and curved wooden sticks **2.** **STICK USED IN SHINTY** the stick that is used to play shinty ■ *vi.* **(-ties, -tying, -tied)** **PLAY SHINTY** to play the game of shinty [Late 17thC. Origin uncertain: probably from the phrase *shin (t')ye!*, uttered by players of the game, of unknown origin.]

shiny /shíni/ **(-ier, -iest)** *adj.* **1.** **BRIGHT AND POLISHED** bright and polished or with a glossy or glistening surface **2.** **WORN SMOOTH AND GLOSSY** smooth and glossy on the surface through too much wear ○ *a shiny patch on the seat of his trousers* —**shininess** *n.*

ship /ship/ *n.* **1.** **LARGE BOAT** a large wind-driven or engine-powered vessel designed to carry passengers or cargo over water, especially across the sea **2.** **LARGE SQUARE-RIGGED SAILING VESSEL** a large sailing vessel with three, four, or five square-rigged masts **3.** **SHIP'S CREW** the crew of a ship **4.** **AIRCRAFT OR SPACECRAFT** a large aircraft or spacecraft ■ *v.* **(ships, shipping, shipped)** **1.** *vti.* **TRANSPORT OVER WATER** to transport sth by ship **2.** *vt.* **TRANSPORT OVERLAND OR BY AIR** to send or transport sth overland or by air, using a common carrier **3.** *vt.* **SEND SB** to send sb to a place ○ *shipped the children off to their grandparents for the holidays* **4.** *vi.* **BE SENT TO SHOPS** to be sent to shops and made available for purchase ○ *If all goes well, the new software will be shipping early next year.* **5.** *vt.* **TAKE IN WATER** to take in water over the sides of a ship or boat ○ *We're shipping water.* **6.** *vt.* **BRING OARS INSIDE BOAT** to bring oars inside a boat and lay them down **7.** *vi.* **GO ON SHIP** to travel on a ship **8.** *vi.* **WORK ON SHIP** to take a job aboard a ship [Old English *scip*. From a prehistoric Germanic word that is also the ancestor of English *skipper* and *skiff*.] —**shippable** *adj.* ◇ **desert** *or* **leave a sinking ship** to leave an organization that is having difficulties ◇ **when your ship comes in** when you become rich

WORD KEY: SYNONYMS

See Synonyms at *boat*.

-ship *suffix.* **1.** condition, state, or quality ○ *companionship* **2.** skill, art, craft ○ *musicianship* **3.** office, title, position, profession ○ *governorship* **4.** a group of people collectively ○ *membership* **5.** person holding a particular title ○ *ladyship* **6.** sth showing a particular quality or condition ○ *township* [Old English *-scipe*]

ship biscuit *n.* = **hardtack**

shipboard /shíp bawrd/ *adj.* used, intended for, or occurring on board a ship ◇ **on shipboard** on board a ship

shipborne /shíp bawrn/ *adj.* transported by ship

ship-broker *n.* an agent who acts on behalf of ship owners, organizing cargoes, passengers, and insurance for their ships

shipbuilder /shíp bildər/ *n.* a person or business that constructs ships —**shipbuilding** *n.*

ship canal *n.* a canal that is wide and deep enough for ships to pass through

ship chandler *n.* a person, shop, or company that sells supplies for ships —**ship chandlery** *n.*

Shipley /shíppli/, **Jenny** (*b.* 1952) New Zealand political leader. A Liberal Party politician, she became prime minister of New Zealand in 1997. Full name **Jennifer Mary Shipley**

shipload /shíp lōd/ *n.* the quantity of cargo carried by a ship

shipmaster /shíp maastər/ *n.* the captain or master of a ship

shipmate /shíp mayt/ *n.* a fellow sailor in a ship's crew

shipment /shípmənt/ *n.* **1.** GOODS SHIPPED TOGETHER a quantity of goods that are shipped together as part of the same cargo **2.** ACT OF SHIPPING the act of shipping sth

ship money *n.* a tax levied by English monarchs, especially by King Charles I, to raise money to provide ships for the navy

ship of the line *n.* formerly, a sailing warship large enough to be in the front line of battle

shipper /shíppər/ *n.* a person or company that sends or receives goods by ship, land, or air [Old English *scipere* 'seaman']

shipping /shípping/ *n.* **1.** ACT OF TRANSPORTING GOODS the act or business of transporting goods **2.** GROUP OF SHIPS ships considered collectively, especially those belonging to a single port, country, or industry, and often referred to in terms of their tonnage

shipping agent *n.* a person or company that prepares the documents required for cargoes to be transported, and deals with insurance and customs matters on behalf of ships

shipping articles *npl.* = **ship's articles**

shipping clerk *n.* sb who is employed to prepare, send, receive, and record shipments of goods

shipping forecast *n.* a weather forecast for ships and sailors around the UK coast broadcast at particular times by the BBC

ship rat *n.* = **black rat**

ship-rigged *adj.* used to describe a sailing ship with three, four, or five masts and square sails set at right angles to the hull

ship's articles, **shipping articles** *npl.* the terms of shipboard service agreed to by a sailor

ship's biscuit *n.* = **hardtack** (*dated*)

shipshape /shíp shayp/ *adj.* BEING IN GOOD ORDER neat, tidy, and in good order ■ *adv.* IN ORDERLY WAY in a neat, tidy, and orderly way [Mid-17thC. Shortening of obsolete *shipshapen* 'made appropriate for use aboard ship'.]

shipside /shíp sīd/ *n.* the area, especially at a dock, beside a ship

ship's papers *npl.* documents stating the ownership, nationality, cargo, and destination of a ship, required by international law to be carried by all ships

shipt *abbr.* shipment

shipway /shíp way/ *n.* **1.** STRUCTURE ON WHICH SHIPS ARE BUILT a structure on which a ship is built and down which it slides when it is launched **2.** = **ship canal**

shipworm /shíp wurm/ *n.* a burrowing marine mollusc that drills into wood, damaging wharves and ships. Family: Teredinidae.

shipwreck /shíp rek/ *n.* **1.** SINKING OR DESTRUCTION OF SHIP the sinking, destruction, or damaging of a ship while at sea **2.** SUNKEN SHIP a ship that has been destroyed or sunk **3.** DESTRUCTION the destruction or failure of sth ■ *v.* (**-wrecks, -wrecking, -wrecked**) **1.** *vti.* INVOLVE SB IN SHIPWRECK to experience the sinking or destruction of a ship or cause sb to experience this (*usually passive*) ○ *shipwrecked on a desert island* **2.** *vti.* DESTROY SHIP to sink or destroy a ship, or to be sunk or destroyed, at sea (*usually passive*) **3.** *vt.* RUIN STH to ruin or destroy sth utterly (*literary*) [Old English *scipwræc*]

shipwright /shíp rīt/ *n.* sb who builds or repairs ships [Old English *scipwyrhta*]

shipyard /shíp yaard/ *n.* a place where ships are built or repaired

Shiraz /shi ráz/ *n.* a black grape, grown mainly in Australia and South Africa, used for making red wine [Mid-17thC. Named after the city of SHIRAZ.]

shire[1] /shīr/ *n.* **1.** BRITISH COUNTY a county in Great Britain, especially one with a name ending in '-shire' such as Hertfordshire or Berkshire **2.** **shire, Shire** = **shire horse** [Old English *scīr* 'administrative office, district', of unknown origin]

shire[2] /shīr/ (**shires, shiring, shired**) *vt. Ireland* to clear the head by taking fresh air (*informal*) [Old English *scīr* 'bright, clear']

Shire /shéeray/ river flowing from Malawi to Mozambique in south-central Africa. Length: 402 km/250 mi.

Shire Highlands plateau in southern Malawi, east of the River Shire. Height: 900 m/3,000 ft.

shire horse, **Shire horse** *n.* a large heavy carthorse with long hair growing from its fetlocks, belonging to a breed originating in the Midlands of England

Shires /shīrz/ *npl.* a group of counties in the Midlands of England, especially Northamptonshire and Leicestershire, famous as fox-hunting country

shire town *n.* the administrative capital of a British county, especially whose name ends in '-shire'

shirk /shurk/ (**shirks, shirking, shirked**) *v.* **1.** *vt.* AVOID STH to avoid having to carry out sth such as an obligation, task, or responsibility through lack or initiative, cowardice, or distaste for it **2.** *vi.* AVOID RESPONSIBILITY to lack initiative or deliberately avoid work or duty [Mid-17thC. Origin uncertain: possibly from German *Schurke* 'scoundrel'.] —**shirker** *n.*

Shirley poppy /shúrli-/ *n.* an annual poppy with red, pink, or white single or double flowers [Late 19thC. Named after the district of *Shirley* in Croydon, Surrey, where it was developed.]

shirr /shur/ (**shirrs, shirring, shirred**) *v.* **1.** *vti.* SEW GATHER FABRIC to gather fabric into two or more parallel rows for decoration on a garment such as a skirt, usually using elasticated thread **2.** *vt. US* COOK BAKE EGG IN DISH to bake an egg without its shell, e.g. in a ramekin dish [Mid-19thC. Origin unknown.]

shirt /shurt/ *n.* **1.** CLOTHING FOR UPPER BODY an article of clothing for the upper part of the body usually made of a fairly light material and having a collar, sleeves, and buttons down the front **2.** MAN'S UNDERGARMENT a usually loose linen garment for the upper body with sleeves that was worn by men as underwear until the early 20th century **3.** NIGHTSHIRT a nightshirt [Old English *scyrte*. Ultimately from an Indo-European base meaning 'to cut' that is also the ancestor of English *short* and *cortex*.] ◇ **lose your shirt** to lose everything you have, especially as a result of losing a bet ◇ **keep your shirt on** to keep your temper (*informal; usually used as a command*) ◇ **put your shirt on sth** to bet or risk everything you have on sth (*informal*)

shirtdress /shúrt dress/ *n. US* = **shirtwaister**

shirtfront /shúrt frunt/ *n.* the front part of a shirt, especially the stiffened fabric on the front of a dress shirt

shirting /shúrting/ *n.* fabric used in making men's shirts

shirtsleeve /shúrt sleev/ *n.* the part of a shirt that covers all or part of the arm ◇ **in shirtsleeves** not wearing a jacket

shirt-tail *n.* CLOTHES the lower part of a shirt, usually cut in a curved shape, that extends below the waist at the back and is usually tucked into trousers

shirtwaist /shúrt wayst/ *n. US* a woman's blouse styled like a man's shirt

shirtwaister /shúrt waystər/ *n.* a woman's dress that is tailored to resemble a shirt, with buttons fastening down the front. US term **shirtdress**

shirty /shúrti/ (**-ier, -iest**) *adj.* aggressive or bad-tempered because of being annoyed about sth (*informal*) [Mid-19thC. Origin uncertain: probably from the expression 'get your shirt out' 'to lose your temper'.] —**shirtily** *adv.* —**shirtiness** *n.*

shisha mirror /shíshə-/ *n.* a small mirrored disc used as a surface decoration on textiles [Via Persian *šīša* or Urdu *šīšah* 'mirror']

shish kebab /shísh-/ *n.* a dish of cubes of marinated meat and vegetables grilled and served on a skewer [Early 20thC. Via Armenian from Turkish *şiş kebabıı*, from *şiş* 'skewer' + *kebab* 'roast meat'.]

shit /shit/ *n.* **1.** OFFENSIVE TERM a highly offensive term referring to human or animal excrement (*taboo offensive*) **2.** OFFENSIVE TERM a highly offensive term referring to an act of defecating (*taboo offensive*) **3.** OFFENSIVE TERM a nasty or unpleasant person (*taboo insult*) **4.** OFFENSIVE TERM an offensive term for sth that is unpleasant, of no value, or of inferior quality (*taboo offensive*) **5.** OFFENSIVE TERM a highly offensive term referring to useless or unnecessary things (*taboo*) **6.** OFFENSIVE TERM a highly offensive term referring to nonsense or lies (*taboo offensive*) **7.** OFFENSIVE TERM a highly offensive term referring to difficulty or trouble (*taboo offensive*) **8.** OFFENSIVE TERM a highly offensive term referring to criticism perceived as unhelpful or mean-spirited (*taboo offensive*) **9.** OFFENSIVE TERM a highly offensive term referring to illegal drugs, especially cannabis (*taboo offensive*) ■ **shits** *npl.* OFFENSIVE TERM a highly offensive term referring to diarrhoea (*taboo offensive*) ■ *interj.* OFFENSIVE TERM used as a swearword (*slang offensive*) ■ *v.* (**shits, shitting, shitted** *or* **shit** *or* **shat, shitted** *or* **shit** *or* **shat** /shat/) (*taboo offensive*) **1.** *vti.* OFFENSIVE TERM a highly offensive term meaning to eliminate waste from the body via the rectum **2.** *vr.* OFFENSIVE TERM a highly offensive term meaning to be extremely scared **3.** *vt. US* OFFENSIVE TERM a highly offensive term meaning to tease sb or deceive sb for amusement **4.** *vi.* OFFENSIVE TERM a highly offensive term meaning to behave towards or criticize sb with arrogant contempt and a total disregard for his or her feelings, especially from a position of power ■ *adj.* OFFENSIVE TERM a highly offensive term meaning very bad or inferior (*taboo offensive*) [Old English *scitte*. Ultimately from an Indo-European base meaning 'to cut, split', which is also the ancestor of English *schism* and *science*.] ◇ **get your shit together** *US* a highly offensive phrase meaning to get organized (*taboo offensive*) ◇ **knock** *or* **beat the shit out of sb** to strike or kick sb violently and repeatedly (*taboo*) ◇ **no shit** *US* an offensive exclamation of surprise, disbelief, or sarcasm (*taboo offensive*) ◇ **tough shit** a highly offensive phrase indicating in an unfriendly way that there is no alternative to a difficult or undesirable situation (*taboo offensive*) ◇ **when the shit hits the fan** a highly offensive phrase indicating that trouble is just beginning (*taboo offensive*)

shitake, **shitake mushroom** *n.* = **shiitake**

shite /shīt/ *n.* **1.** EXCREMENT human or animal excrement (*regional taboo*) **2.** UNPLEASANT PERSON a nasty or unpleasant person (*regional taboo insult*) **3.** STH WORTHLESS sth that is or things that are unpleasant, worthless, or of poor quality (*regional taboo*) **4.** NONSENSE nonsense or lies (*regional taboo*) ■ *interj.* SWEARWORD used as a swearword (*slang offensive*)

shitfaced /shít fayst/ *adj.* a highly offensive term describing sb who is completely drunk (*taboo offensive*) [Mid-20thC. From the facial numbness that accompanies extreme drunkenness.]

shithead /shít hed/ *n.* a highly offensive term that deliberately insults sb's intelligence or character (*taboo insult*)

shit hot *adj.* excellent, especially at doing sth (*taboo*)

shithouse /shít howss/ *n.* a highly offensive term referring to a lavatory (*taboo offensive*)

shitless /shítləss/ *adv.* a highly offensive term expressing extreme fear (*taboo offensive*) [Mid-20thC. From the tendency to lose control of the bowels when terror-stricken.]

shitlist /shít list/ *n.* a highly offensive term referring to a list of people who are out of favour, especially in the view of sb in authority (*taboo*)

shitload /shít lōd/ *n.* US a highly offensive term referring to an undesirably large amount or quantity of sth (*taboo offensive*)

shittah /shítta/ (*plural* **-tim** /shíttim/ *or* **-tahs**) *n.* the tree that yielded the shittim wood of the Bible, probably a species of acacia [Early 17thC. From Hebrew *šiṭṭāh*.]

shittim wood /shíttim woóod/ *n.* the wood of the shittah tree that according to the Bible was used to make the Ark of the Covenant

shitty /shítti/ *adj.* 1. OFFENSIVE TERM a highly offensive term describing sth inferior, unpleasant, or unenjoyable (*taboo offensive*) 2. OFFENSIVE TERM a highly offensive term describing a feeling of misery (*taboo*) 3. OFFENSIVE TERM of very poor quality (*taboo*) 4. OFFENSIVE TERM a highly offensive term describing sth covered with excrement (*taboo*) —**shittily** *adv.* —**shittiness** *n.*

shiv /shiv/ *vt., n.* US a flick knife or sharp object used as a weapon [Late 17thC. Alteration of CHIV.]

shiva /she'evə/, **shivah** *n.* seven days of formal mourning observed by close relatives of a deceased Jewish person during which they sit on low stools and do not go out, work, bathe, or shave [Late 19thC. Via Yiddish *shive* from Hebrew *šib'āh* 'seven'.]

Shiva /she'evə/, **Siva** /se'evə/ *n.* an important Hindu deity, worshipped as the god of destruction. Shiva is one of the Trimurti trinity. [Late 18thC. From Sanskrit, literally 'the auspicious one'.]

shivaree /shívvə re'e, shívvəri/ *n.* = **charivari** [Mid-19thC. Alteration of French *charivari*, of uncertain origin.]

shive *n.* = **shiva**

shiver[1] /shívvər/ *v.* (**-ers, -ering, -ered**) 1. *vi.* TO TREMBLE to tremble or shake slightly because of cold, fear, or illness 2. *vti.* FLAP OR MAKE SAIL FLAP to flap, or make a sail flap, when a sailing vessel is too close to the wind ■ *n.* BODY TREMOR a tremor or shudder in the body caused by fear, cold, or illness ■ **shivers** *npl.* ATTACK OF SHIVERING an attack of shivering caused by fear, cold, or illness (*informal*) [13thC. Origin uncertain.] —**shiverer** *n.* —**shiveringly** *adv.*

shiver[2] /shívvər/ *n.* FRAGMENT a very small piece of sth such as glass that has splintered off a larger piece ■ *vti.* (**-ers, -ering, -ered**) SHATTER to splinter into fragments or cause sth to splinter into fragments [12thC. From assumed Old English *scifer*; ultimately from an Indo-European base meaning 'to split' that is also the ancestor of English *schism* and *science*.]

shivery /shívvəri/ *adj.* trembling from cold, fear, or illness

Shizuoka /shee zoo ōkə/ capital city of Shizuoka Prefecture, west of Suruga Bay, on southeastern Honshu Island, Japan. Population: 472,196 (1990).

Shkodër /shkṓdair/ capital city of Shkodër District, northwestern Albania, situated near the southern end of Lake Shkodër. Population: 83,700 (1991).

shkotzim plural of **shegetz**

shlemiel *n.* = **schlemiel** (*informal*)

shlep *vti.* = **schlep** (*slang*)

Shluh /shloo/ (*plural* **Shluh** *or* **Shluhs**) *n.* 1. MEMBER OF NORTH AFRICAN PEOPLE a member of a people that is a subgroup of the Berbers and lives mainly in the Atlas Mountains of Morocco and Algeria 2. SHLUH

LANGUAGE the Berber dialect of the Shluh people [Early 18thC. From Berber.]

SHM *n., abbr.* simple harmonic motion

shmaltz *n.* = **schmaltz**

shmatte *n.* = **schmatte**

shmo (*plural* **shmoes**) *n.* US = **schmo** (*informal*)

shmuck *n.* = **schmuck**

SHO *n., abbr.* Senior House Officer

Shoah /shṓ ə/ *n.* a Hebrew word for the Holocaust [Mid-20thC. From Hebrew *šōāh*, literally 'catastrophe'.]

shoal[1] /shōl/ *n.* 1. GROUP OF FISH a large group of fish or other marine animals swimming together 2. GROUP OF PEOPLE a large group of similar people or things ○ *a shoal of reporters* ■ *vi.* (**shoals, shoaling, shoaled**) FORM SHOAL to group together to form a shoal [Late 16thC. From Middle Dutch *scōle* or Middle Low German *schōle* (see SCHOOL[2]).]

shoal[2] /shōl/ *n.* 1. SHALLOW WATER an area of shallow water in a larger body of water 2. UNDERWATER SANDBANK an underwater sandbank or sandbar that is visible at low water ■ *v.* (**shoals, shoaling, shoaled**) 1. *vti.* MAKE OR BECOME SHALLOW to become shallow or shallower, or to make sth shallow 2. *vi.* ENTER SHALLOWER WATER to enter a shallower area of water ■ *adj.* **shoal, shoaly** SHALLOW shallow [Old English *sceald*]

shoat /shōt/, **shote** *n.* a young pig that has just been weaned [15thC. Origin unknown.]

shochet /shṓkhət/ (*plural* **-etim** /shṓkhətim/) *n.* sb licensed to perform the ritual kosher slaughter of animals for food (**shechita**) [Late 19thC. From Hebrew *šōḥēṭ*, the present participle of *šāḥaṭ* 'to slaughter'.]

shock[1] /shok/ *n.* 1. STH SURPRISING AND UPSETTING an unexpected, intense, and distressing experience that has a sudden and powerful effect on sb's emotions or physical reactions ○ *The news of her death came as a great shock to us all.* 2. DISTRESSING FEELINGS AFTER SHOCK the feeling of distress or numbness experienced by sb who has had a shock 3. MED PHYSIOLOGICAL COLLAPSE a state of physiological collapse, marked by a weak pulse, coldness, sweating, and irregular breathing, and resulting from, e.g., blood loss, heart failure, allergic reaction, or emotional trauma ○ *in shock* 4. PHYSICAL IMPACT a sudden and violent impact, collision, or blow 5. MOVEMENT AFTER IMPACT the movement or violent shaking felt after a collision, explosion, or earthquake 6. STH THREATENING OR DAMAGING an unexpected event that threatens or damages a system, organization, or conventional situation ○ *The economy cannot take any more shocks.* 7. ELECTRIC SHOCK an electric shock 8. US = **shock absorber** ■ *v.* (**shocks, shocking, shocked**) 1. *vt.* UPSET SB to make sb feel suddenly and acutely distressed or upset 2. *vti.* OFFEND OR BE OFFENDED to make sb feel deeply offended or disgusted, or to be likely to feel offended or disgusted ○ *He shocks easily.* 3. *vt.* GIVE SB ELECTRIC SHOCK to give an electric shock to a person or animal 4. *vt.* MED PUT SB INTO SHOCK to cause a state of shock in sb 5. *vti.* COLLIDE to collide, or to cause people or things to collide (*archaic*) [Mid-16thC. The noun is via French *choc*, the verb directly from French *choquer* 'to strike', of uncertain origin.] —**shockability** /shṓkə bílləti/ *n.* —**shockable** /shṓkəb'l/ *adj.*

shock[2] /shok/ *n.* SHEAVES OF DRYING CORN a group of sheaves of corn set upright in a field for drying ■ *vt.* (**shocks, shocking, shocked**) ARRANGE CORN SHEAVES IN SHOCK to arrange sheaves of corn in a shock [14thC. Origin uncertain: perhaps from Middle Dutch or Middle Low German *schok*.]

shock[3] /shok/ *n.* a large amount of thick shaggy hair [Early 19thC. Origin uncertain.]

shock absorber *n.* a device on a vehicle designed to absorb jarring or jolting, e.g. that caused by wheels moving over a rough surface

shocker /shṓkər/ *n.* (*informal*) 1. STH UNPLEASANT a highly unpleasant experience, thing, or person 2. SHOCKING STORY, PLAY, OR FILM a story, play, or film that is particularly lurid and intended to shock people 3. *Aus* BAD SPORTS PERFORMANCE a very poor performance, especially at sport

shockheaded /shṓk héddid/ *adj.* having a large

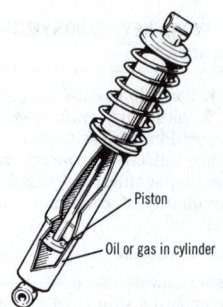

Shock absorber

amount of thick shaggy hair that sticks up or is tousled

shock horror *interj.* used humorously to feign shock about sth that others might really find shocking (*informal*)

shock-horror *adj.* lurid, sensational, and apparently intended to cause a shocked or horrified reaction (*informal; used ironically*)

shocking /shṓking/ *adj.* 1. OUTRAGEOUS provoking a deeply offended or outraged response 2. DISTRESSING emotionally distressing or horrifying 3. VERY BAD very bad or unpleasant (*informal*) ■ *adj., adv.* VERY BRIGHT very bright or glaring in shade of colour —**shockingly** *adv.* —**shockingness** *n.*

shocking pink *adj.* of a bright garish pink colour —**shocking pink** *n.*

shock jock *n.* a disc jockey or radio host who uses provocative language and broadcasts his or her extreme views (*slang*)

shockproof /shṓk proof/ *adj.* designed or able to withstand the effects of jarring or impact

shock tactics *npl.* the use of methods that are likely to shock people in order to achieve sth

shock therapy, **shock treatment** *n.* a method of treating patients affected with psychiatric disorders that involves passing an electric current through the brain

shock troops *npl.* soldiers who are specially trained and equipped to be in the forefront of an attack [Translation of German *Stosstruppen*]

shock wave *n.* 1. WAVE OF HEAT AND AIR PRESSURE a wave of increased temperature or pressure as a result of an explosion or earthquake or the movement of a supersonic body 2. SURPRISED REACTION a widespread reaction of shock or distress caused by an event or piece of news (*often used in the plural*)

shod past participle, past tense of **shoe**

shoddy /shóddi/ *adj.* (**-dier, -diest**) 1. POORLY MADE poorly or carelessly made or done 2. MADE FROM INFERIOR MATERIAL made of inferior material 3. DISHONEST dishonest or disgraceful ○ *shoddy treatment* ■ *n.* (*plural* **-dies**) 1. CLOTH MADE WITH OLD WOOL cloth made using a yarn composed of a mixture of old unravelled woollen cloth and new wool 2. STH INFERIOR sth that is of inferior quality, especially if it is imitating sth better [Mid-19thC. Origin unknown.] —**shoddily** *adv.* —**shoddiness** *n.*

shoe /shoo/ *n.* 1. STIFF OUTER COVERING FOR THE FOOT an outer covering for the foot, usually made of leather, fabric, or plastic, with a stiff sole and usually not reaching above the ankle 2. = **horseshoe** 1 3. PROTECTIVE PART IN AN ENGINE a lining or part in an engine or machine that protects another part from being worn down 4. PLAYING CARD DISPENSER a special box that dispenses playing cards one at a time 5. POWER COLLECTOR ON AN ELECTRIC TRAIN the part of an electric train that connects with the electrified rail from which it draws power 6. METAL STRIP ON SLEDGE a strip of metal along the runner of a sledge 7. PART OF A BRIDGE a base that supports the upper part of a bridge ■ *vt.* (**shoes, shoeing, shod, shod** /shod/) 1. PROVIDE A HORSE WITH HORSESHOES to fix a horseshoe on a horse 2. SUPPLY SB WITH SHOES to provide sb with shoes (*usually passive*) 3. MECH ENG PUT A PROTECTIVE COVERING ON STH to cover sth with a hard, especially metal, plate to

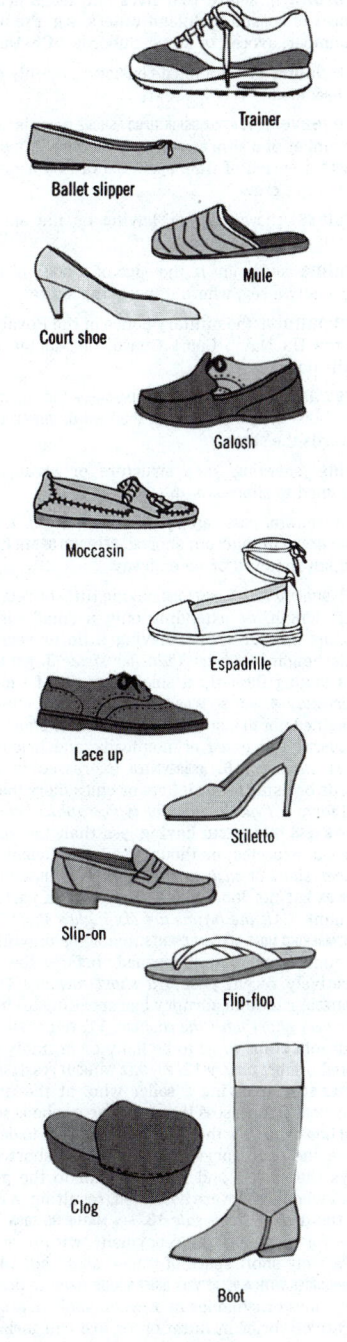

Trainer

Ballet slipper

Mule

Court shoe

Galosh

Moccasin

Espadrille

Lace up

Stiletto

Slip-on

Flip-flop

Clog

Boot

Shoe

protect against wear [Old English *scōh*] ◇ **be in sb's shoes** to be in sb else's position (*informal*)

shoebill /shoóbil/ *n.* a large East African tropical wading bird with shaggy grey plumage, a large head, long black legs, and a broad hooked bill. Latin name: *Balaeniceps rex.*

shoeblack /shoó blak/ *n.* sb who cleans people's shoes in the street (*dated*) US term **bootblack**

shoebox /shoó boks/ *n.* **1.** BOX FOR SHOES a box, usually made of cardboard, in which shoes are packed for sale **2.** CRAMPED SPACE a small and cramped living or working space (*informal*)

shoegazing /shoó gayzing/ *n.* a type of early 1990s guitar music characterized by ambient sounds and static performances [Late 20thC. From the typical stance of the performers and audience, moving only slightly, with heads bent towards the ground.]

shoehorn /shoó hawrn/ *n.* DEVICE TO HELP HEEL INTO SHOE a curved piece of plastic, metal, or horn used to help ease the heel into a tight-fitting shoe or boot ■ *vt.*

(**-horns, -horning, -horned**) SQUEEZE SB OR STH INTO SPACE to squeeze sb or sth into a space that is barely large enough

shoelace /shoó layss/ *n.* a thin cord of leather or fabric used to fasten together the two top flaps of a shoe

shoemaker /shoó maykər/ *n.* sb who makes or repairs boots or shoes —**shoemaking** *n.*

shoeshine /shoó shīn/ *n.* **1.** ACT OF POLISHING SHOES the act of giving a clean or shiny finish to shoes by polishing them **2.** POLISH ON SHOES a polished finish on shoes

shoestring /shoó string/ *adj.* **1.** CONSISTING OF LITTLE MONEY consisting of or running on a very limited amount of money ○ *a shoestring allocation for new class-rooms* **2.** US FOOD LONG AND NARROW cut or made long and narrow in shape ○ *shoestring licorice* ■ *n.* = **shoelace** ◇ **on a shoestring** using very little money

shoetree /shoó tree/ *n.* a wooden or metal block that is inserted into a boot or shoe to stretch it or help it to keep its shape when not being worn

shofar /shố faar/ (*plural* **-fars** *or* **-froth** /shố froth/) *n.* a horn, usually a ram's horn, blown in a synagogue on Rosh Hashanah [Mid-19thC. From Hebrew *šōpār,* literally 'ram's horn'.]

shogi /shố gi/ *n.* a Japanese board game for two players that resembles chess [Mid-19thC. From Japanese *shōgi.*]

shogun /shố gun/ *n.* any one of the hereditary military commanders in feudal Japan who ruled the country under the nominal rule of an emperor between the years 1192 and 1867 [Mid-17thC. Via Japanese *shōgun* from Chinese *jiāng jūn* 'general'.] —**shogunal** *adj.*

shogunate /shố gə nayt/ *n.* the office, period in office, or rule of a shogun

shoji /shố ji/ (*plural* **-ji** *or* **-jis**) *n.* a ricepaper screen in a wooden frame used as a sliding partition or door in traditional Japanese houses [Late 19thC. From Japanese *shōji.*]

Sholapur /shố lə poőr/ city and administrative headquarters of Sholapur District, Maharashtra State, western India. Population: 603,870 (1991).

Shona /shố nə/ (*plural* **-na** *or* **-nas**) *n.* **1.** MEMBER OF CENTRAL AFRICAN PEOPLE a member of a people that live in parts of southern central Africa, mainly in Zimbabwe, where they are the dominant ethnic group, and in Mozambique **2.** SHONA LANGUAGE the Bantu language of the Shona people. Shona is spoken by about eight million people. [Mid-20thC. Of Bantu origin.] —**Shona** *adj.*

shone *v.* past tense, past participle of **shine**

shoneen /shố neen/ *n.* Ireland an Irish person who, in order to seem of a higher social class, imitates an English person, especially in accent [Mid-19thC. From Irish *seoinín,* literally 'little John', from *Seón* 'John, John Bull'.]

shonky /shóngki/ (**-kier, -kiest**) *adj.* Aus unreliable, untrustworthy, or inferior (*informal*) [Late 20thC. Formed from *shonk* 'Jewish person', a shortening of *shonicker,* of unknown origin.]

shoo /shoo/ *interj.* USED TO GET ANIMAL TO LEAVE used to tell a child or animal to go away ■ *vti.* (**shoos, shooing, shooed**) WAVE AWAY to say shoo and gesture to a child or animal to go away [15thC. An instinctive exclamation.]

shoofly pie /shoó flī-/ *n.* US a pie made with a filling of crumbs, butter, and brown sugar or molasses [From its sweet filling, which is apt to attract flies]

shoogle /shoó gg'l/ *vti.* (**-gles, -gling, -gled**) Scotland ROCK RAPIDLY to rock back and forth with small rapid movements, or to cause sth to do this (*informal*) ■ *n.* Scotland RAPID ROCKING MOVEMENT a small, rapid rocking movement (*informal*) [Late 16thC. Variant of *shoggle,* from *shog* 'to shake', of uncertain origin.]

shoogly /shoó ggli/ *adj.* Scotland wobbling or liable to wobble (*informal*)

shoo-in *n.* US, Can sb who is certain to win sth such as an election or be chosen for sth such as a job [Origin uncertain]

shook[1] past tense of **shake**

shook[2] /shook/ *n.* **1.** AGRIC = **stook** **2.** US SET OF TIMBER PARTS FOR BARREL a set of timber parts for assembling a barrel or box [Late 18thC. Origin uncertain: perhaps from the phrase *shook cask,* a cask broken down for shipment, from *shake* in the archaic sense 'to split apart'.]

shook-up *adj.* US disturbed and upset (*informal*)

shoon /shoon, shōn/ Scotland plural of **shoe**

shoot /shoot/ *v.* (**shoots, shooting, shot**) **1.** *vti.* FIRE A WEAPON OR PROJECTILE to fire a projectile such as a bullet, missile, or arrow from a weapon, or make a weapon fire a projectile ○ *Don't shoot!* **2.** *vt.* HIT SB OR STH WITH A BULLET to fire a weapon at and hit, injure, or kill a person or animal ○ *She shot herself.* **3.** *vti.* HUNT ANIMALS WITH A GUN to hunt animals or birds with a gun for sport **4.** *vti.* MOVE FAST to move or cause sth to move quickly and suddenly ○ *She shot out her hand to catch the ball.* **5.** *vi.* DASH to go somewhere quickly and suddenly (*informal*) ○ *He shot off to his interview.* **6.** *vt.* TRAVEL OVER STH FAST to travel quickly over a stretch of water where the current is fast ○ *shoot the rapids* **7.** *vi.* PROGRESS VERY RAPIDLY to make extremely rapid progress or undergo a startlingly rapid change of state ○ *She shot to fame.* **8.** *vi.* MOVE SWIFTLY THROUGH THE BODY to seem to move very swiftly, and usually painfully, through the body ○ *Pain shot up her leg.* **9.** *vti.* SEND STH OUT RAPIDLY to send out sth rapidly or forcefully or in a beam or ray **10.** *vt.* DIRECT STH QUICKLY to direct a look or glance at sth briefly and rapidly ○ *He shot a glance at her.* **11.** *vt.* ASK OR SAY STH RAPIDLY to say sth rapidly or ask a question rapidly **12.** *vti.* RECORD STH ON FILM to record a shot, scene, film, or programme on film with a camera **13.** *vti.* KICK BALL TO GET POINT to kick, hit, or throw a ball in a sport such as football or basketball in an attempt to score a goal or point **14.** *vt.* US, Can SCORE A POINT IN A SPORT to score a goal or point in a sport **15.** *vi.* US STRIVE TO ACHIEVE STH to try to achieve sth difficult (*informal*) ○ *shooting for a five percent increase in productivity* **16.** *vt.* MOVE A BOLT INTO PLACE to move sth such as a bolt into or out of a fastening **17.** *vi.* GERMINATE to germinate or begin to grow **18.** *vt.* DRUGS = **shoot up** *v.* 4 (*slang*) **19.** *vt.* TRAVEL OVER STH FAST to travel quickly over water where the current is fast ○ *shoot the rapids* **20.** *vt.* US CUE GAMES PLAY CUE GAME to play a game of pool or billiards **21.** *vti.* THROW DICE to throw a die or dice **22.** *vt.* MEASURE THE DISTANCE TO HEAVENLY BODY to measure the altitude of a star or other heavenly body ■ *n.* **1.** NEW PLANT GROWTH a newly grown aerial part of a plant, e.g. a leaf bud or branch **2.** OCCASION FOR PHOTOGRAPHING OR FILMING STH an occasion when a professional photographer or filmmaker is photographing or filming sth **3.** ACT OF FIRING an act of firing a weapon **4.** HUNTING EVENT an occasion for hunting animals with guns for sport **5.** HUNTING PARTY a party of people gathered together to hunt animals with guns for sport **6.** HUNTING AREA an area where people shoot animals with guns for sport **7.** GEOL VEIN OF ORE a narrow vein of ore ■ *interj.* (*informal*) **1.** USED TO TELL SB TO START used to tell sb to go ahead and start talking **2.** US USED TO EXPRESS ANNOYANCE used as an exclamation of annoyance or disappointment [Old English *scēotan.* Ultimately from a prehistoric Germanic base that is also the ancestor of English *shot, shut,* and *shuttle.*]

shoot down *vt.* **1.** BRING DOWN AN AIRCRAFT to bring down an aircraft while it is in the air by firing a weapon or missile **2.** KILL SB OR STH BY SHOOTING to fire a weapon at and hit, injure, or kill a person or animal **3.** DESTROY ARGUMENT to destroy sb's argument, theory, or idea by disproving, criticizing, or discrediting it

shoot through *vi.* Aus to leave a place, usually abruptly (*informal*)

shoot up *v.* **1.** *vi.* INCREASE SUDDENLY to increase suddenly by a large amount **2.** *vi.* GET TALLER to grow considerably taller in a short space of time **3.** *vt.* HARM SB OR STH BY GUNFIRE to cause serious injuries to sb or damage to sth with gunfire **4.** *vti.* DRUGS INJECT A DRUG to inject an illegal drug (*slang*)

shoot-'em-up /shoót əm up/ *n.* **1.** US FILM WITH SHOOTING a film or television programme featuring a large amount of shooting and bloodshed (*dated*) **2.** COMPUTER GAME WITH SHOOTING a video or computer game in which a player scores points by shooting at figures on the screen **3.** FAIRGROUND SHOOTING STALL a stall in a fairground where a player shoots a rifle at a sequence of targets in order to win a prize

shooter /shóotər/ n. 1. GUN a pistol or other gun (informal) 2. SB SHOOTING sb or sth that shoots

shooting box n. a house in the country in which guests stay while on a shoot for game

shooting brake n. an estate car (dated)

shooting gallery n. 1. PLACE TO PRACTICE SHOOTING a place used for target practice using guns or rifles 2. PLACE WHERE DRUG ADDICTS SHOOT UP a place such as an abandoned building where addicts inject drugs (slang)

shooting iron n. US a handgun (informal)

shooting lodge n. = shooting box

shooting party n. a group of people who gather together in the country to hunt game with guns for sport

shooting script n. the final screenplay for a cinema or television film that includes directions for shooting and is broken down into scenes with the shots numbered consecutively

shooting star n. 1. = meteor 2. N AMERICAN PRIMROSE a North American plant in the primrose family that has oblong leaves and flowers with petals that curve backwards. Genus: Dodeatheon.

Shooting stick

shooting stick n. a walking stick with handles at one end that fold out to form a small seat, often used by a spectator at an outdoor sporting event

shoot-out n. 1. DECISIVE FIGHT WITH GUNS a fight to the finish with guns 2. = penalty shoot-out

shoot-to-kill adj. relating to or involving the aiming of a gun to kill, not wound, sb

shop /shop/ n. 1. RETAIL BUSINESS a retail business that sells consumer merchandise and sometimes services 2. ACT OF BUYING GOODS the act of going out to buy goods, especially food and household supplies (informal) 3. WORKSHOP a place where goods are manufactured or repaired 4. US INDUSTRIAL ARTS SCHOOL SUBJECT a school subject in which students are taught to work with tools and machinery, especially on wood 5. US SCHOOLROOM FOR LEARNING INDUSTRIAL ARTS a schoolroom or building with tools and equipment for students to learn industrial arts ■ v. (shops, shopping, shopped) 1. vi. BUY GOODS to go to a shop or shops in order to buy things 2. vt. US VISIT PARTICULAR SHOP to buy goods from a particular shop 3. vt. INFORM ON SB to inform on sb to the police or authorities (slang) 4. vt. US TRY TO SELL STH to try to sell sth such as a company or creative work by bringing it to the attention of potential buyers [Old English sceoppa 'booth, peddler's stall' (related to German Schuppen 'shed') ◇ be all over the shop 1. to be scattered or spread out over a wide area, usually untidily (informal) 2. to be in a confused or disorganized state (informal) ◇ shut up shop 1. to stop working or doing sth 2. to close down a business ◇ talk shop to talk about your work or some other specialized activity

shop around vi. 1. LOOK AROUND FOR THE BEST DEAL to look around for the best deal or bargain 2. CONSIDER SEVERAL POSSIBILITIES BEFORE CHOOSING to review a number of possibilities before making a choice

shopaholic /shóppə hóllik/ n. sb who enjoys or compulsively engages in shopping (informal)

shop assistant n. sb who serves customers in a shop. US term **salesclerk**

shop-bought adj. bought ready-made from a shop as opposed to being home-made. US term **store-bought**

shop floor n. 1. MANUFACTURING AREA IN A FACTORY the area in a factory where goods are manufactured 2. MANUAL WORKERS the manual workers in a factory

shopkeeper /shóp keepər/ n. sb who owns or manages a shop. US term **storekeeper**

shoplift /shóplift/ (-lifts, -lifting, -lifted) vti. to steal sth from a shop or store while pretending to shop for goods —**shoplifter** n. —**shoplifting** n.

shoppe /shop/ n. a shop (archaic or humorous) [Early 20thC. Alteration of SHOP.]

shopper /shóppər/ n. 1. SB DOING SHOPPING sb who is looking for things to buy in a shop or store 2. SHOPPING TROLLEY OR BAG a trolley or large bag for putting shopping in 3. US LOCAL NEWSPAPER a usually free newspaper that carries advertising and some local news

shopping /shópping/ n. 1. ACTIVITY OF GOING TO SHOP the activity of visiting shops and stores to look at and buy things 2. GOODS PURCHASED IN SHOPS goods bought in a shop or shops, especially food and household items

shopping bag n. a large strong bag with handles used for carrying purchases when shopping

shopping cart n. US = shopping trolley

shopping centre n. a large enclosed purpose-built area consisting of shops and other facilities, together with a large area for parking. US term **mall**

shopping list n. 1. LIST OF ITEMS TO SHOP FOR a list of all the things sb wants to buy when shopping 2. LIST OF THINGS WANTED a list of demands, requirements, or things wanted

shopping mall n. a pedestrianized shopping area with enclosed walkways in a town

shopping precinct n. UK an pedestrianized area in a town where shops and other facilities are grouped together

shopping trolley n. a small trolley consisting either of a square bag on a frame or a basket on wheels that is pushed or pulled along to carry shopping. US term **shopping cart**

shopsoiled /shóp soyld/ adj. 1. DAMAGED IN SHOP faded, tarnished, or otherwise slightly spoiled from being on display in a shop. US term **shopworn** 2. WORN OUT old, overused, and hackneyed

shop steward n. a worker elected by fellow union members as their representative in dealings with the management

shoptalk /shóp tawk/ n. 1. TALK ABOUT WORK conversation about work or another specialized activity at a time when more lighthearted chat is the norm, especially outside working hours 2. US JOB'S JARGON jargon used in a particular field, job, or profession

shopwalker /shóp wawkər/ n. an employee in a department store who supervises sales staff and assists customers. US term **floorwalker**

shopworn /shóp wawrn/ adj. US = shopsoiled

shoran /shá wran/ n. a short-range navigational system in which a ship's or aircraft's precise location is determined by the time taken for a signal to travel to two fixed stations and back [Mid-20thC. Contraction of short-range navigation.]

shore[1] /shawr/ n. 1. LAND AT EDGE OF WATER the land that runs along the edge of a sea or lake 2. DRY LAND dry land as opposed to water ○ on shore 3. COUNTRY a land or country (literary; often used in the plural) ○ having reached our native shores 4. LAW COAST BETWEEN LOW AND HIGH TIDES the area of land that lies between normal low and high tide marks [Old English scora. Ultimately from an Indo-European base meaning 'to cut' that is also the ancestor of English shear and scarp.]

shore[2] /shawr/ vt. (shores, shoring, shored) 1. PROP UP A STRUCTURE to stop sth such as a wall from falling down or over by propping a support against it 2. HELP TO STOP STH FAILING to give support or help in order to stop sth failing ■ n. PROP TO SUPPORT STH a beam or other prop set at an angle to support sth such as a wall or tree [14thC. From Middle Low German or Middle Dutch schōre 'prop', of unknown origin.]

shore bird n. a bird that lives and feeds near the shores of coastal or inland waters, e.g. the plover, sandpiper, avocet, or snipe. Suborder: Charadrii.

shore dinner n. US a meal consisting mainly of fish and seafood

shore leave n. 1. PERMISSION TO GO ASHORE permission for a member of a ship's crew to go ashore 2. TIME SPENT ASHORE a period of time spent ashore by a member of a ship's crew

shoreless /sháwrləss/ adj. having no flat shore on which a boat can land

shoreline /sháwr līn/ n. the edge of a body of water, especially a sea, where it meets the shore

shore patrol n. the military police of the Royal Navy or the US Navy, Coast Guard, or Marine Corps while on shore

shoreward /sháwrwərd/ adj. FACING SHORE facing or near the shore ■ adv. **shoreward, shorewards** TOWARDS SHORE towards the shore

shoring /sháwring/ n. a structure or arrangement designed to shore sth up

shorn /shawrn/ past participle of shear ■ adj. 1. HAVING SHORT HAIR with hair cut short 2. DEPRIVED OF STH having had sth removed or taken away

short /shawrt/ adj. 1. NOT LONG having little or relatively little length, or extending only a small distance ○ short hair 2. NOT TALL having little or relatively little height ○ shorter than her sister 3. NOT LASTING LONG lasting for only a small amount of time ○ a short stay 4. NOT SEEMING LONG IN DURATION seeming or imagined not to last very long ○ in a few short weeks 5. CONCISE expressed economically and briefly ○ a short summary 6. ABBREVIATED expressed in fewer words or using fewer letters or characters than the full form ○ Typo is short for typographical error. 7. HAVING LESS THAN NEEDED having less than the amount needed, expected, or thought to be sufficient ○ I'm rather short of cash at the moment. 8. INSUFFICIENTLY LONG OR TALL not long or tall enough by a particular amount ○ All the beams are six inches short. 9. NOT REMEMBERING MORE DISTANT EVENTS unable or unwilling to recall events that happened before the comparatively recent past ○ a short memory 10. DISCOURTEOUS rude and abrupt when speaking to sb ○ She was very short with the cashier. 11. FULL OF FAT made with lots of fat so as to be flaky or crumbly when baked ○ short pastry 12. FIN SOLD WITHOUT POSSESSING THE SHARES SOLD involving a seller who, at the time of sale, does not possess the shares he or she is selling and has to borrow them before being able to deliver. Once the share price has fallen, the short seller buys the shares and returns them to the person from whom they were borrowed, resulting in a gain on the deal. ○ short sale 13. FIN MATURING SOON being due for payment or repayment within a comparatively short space of time ○ short bill 14. LING PRONOUNCED WITH A RELATIVELY BRIEF SOUND used to describe phonemes or syllables that, when spoken, are comparatively brief in duration or are categorized as being of this type. The vowel 'a' in the word 'hat' is short compared with the same vowel in the word 'hate'. 15. CRICKET PITCHING CLOSE TO BOWLER pitching comparatively close to the bowler and likely to bounce higher than usual before reaching the batsman ○ short ball 16. BEVERAGES NEAT not diluted with water or a mixer drink ■ adv. 1. ABRUPTLY abruptly and unexpectedly ○ stop short 2. NOT REACHING THE TARGET before reaching a goal, target, or destination ○ The pass fell 3 yards short. 3. FIN WITHOUT ACTUAL POSSESSION without actually possessing the things being sold when the sale is agreed on ○ sell short ■ n. 1. FILM OF SHORT DURATION a film whose running time is approximately 30 minutes or less 2. = short circuit n. 3. SMALL DRINK a drink consisting of a small measure of spirits in a small glass (informal) 4. GARMENT SIZE a size of garment for a short person ■ npl. 1. shorts SHORT TROUSERS trousers that end somewhere between the upper thigh and the knee 2. shorts US UNDERPANTS men's underpants 3. AGRIC MIXTURE OF BRAN AND COARSE FLOUR a mixture of bran and coarse flour left over from the milling of wheat 4. STOCK EXCH SHORT-DATED ITEMS bills or securities that are due to mature within a comparatively short space of time ■ vti. (shorts, shorting, shorted) = short circuit [Old English *sceort*. Ultimately from an Indo-European base meaning 'to cut' that is also the ancestor of English *shirt*, *skirt*, and *curt*.] —**shortness** *n*. ◇ **cut sth short** to end sth earlier than expected or desired ◇ **for short** as an abbreviation or shortened form ◇ **go short** to have insufficient money or food ◇ **in short** used to introduce a rephrasing of sth in a more concise form ◇ **short and sweet** pleasant or bearable because brief ◇ **short of 1.** not having sth, or not having enough of sth **2.** less than **3.** without actually doing sth, usually sth unpleasant or wrong

short-acting *adj*. effective for a short period

shortage /sháwrtij/ *n*. a lack of sth that is needed or required

---
WORD KEY: SYNONYMS

See Synonyms at *lack*.

short black *n*. ANZ a strong black coffee served in a small cup. ◊ **long black**

shortbread /sháwrt bred/ *n*. a rich crumbly biscuit made with a high proportion of butter to flour and a comparatively small proportion of sugar

shortcake /sháwrt kayk/ *n*. **1.** = **shortbread 2.** DESSERT WITH FRUIT AND CREAM a dessert consisting of a shortbread base topped with fruit and cream

shortchange /sháwrt ch-ynj/ (**-changes, -changing, -changed**) *vt*. **1.** GIVE SB TOO LITTLE CHANGE to give sb less change than is due to him or her **2.** TREAT SB UNFAIRLY to behave unfairly towards sb by giving him or her less of sth than he or she deserves or expects — **shortchanger** *n*.

short circuit *n*. a failure in an electrical circuit caused by an accidental connection of low resistance such as when there is a break in the insulation across which an excessive current can flow

short-circuit (**short-circuits, short-circuiting, short-circuited**) *v*. **1.** *vti*. HAVE OR CAUSE FAILURE IN A CIRCUIT to have or cause a failure in an electrical circuit by creating a connection of low resistance across which an excessive current flows **2.** *vt*. USE SHORTCUT TO DO STH to use a much quicker or more direct method to achieve sth **3.** *vt*. US FRUSTRATE OR HINDER PLANS to hinder a plan or project by erecting obstacles

shortcoming /sháwrt kumming/ *n*. a defect or failure in sb's character or in a system or organization (*often used in the plural*)

shortcrust pastry /sháwrt krust-/ *n*. pastry with a crisp crumbly texture made with one measure of fat to every two measures of flour

short cut /sháwrt kut/ *n*. **1.** SHORTER ROUTE a route that is shorter or more direct than the usual one **2.** TIMESAVER a way of saving time and effort in doing sth —**short-cut** *vti*.

short-day *adj*. able to flower only upon exposure to relatively short periods of sunlight, e.g. during spring or autumn

short division *n*. a method of dividing relatively simple numbers without writing down all the steps in the process

shorten /sháwrt'n/ (**-ens, -ening, -ened**) *v*. **1.** *vti*. BECOME OR MAKE SHORTER to make sth shorter or become shorter **2.** *vti*. MAKE ODDS SHORTER to reduce the odds on a bet, or to be reduced in this way **3.** *vt*. REDUCE SAIL AREA to reduce the area of a sail **4.** *vt*. MAKE PASTRY SHORTER to make pastry more crumbly by adding more fat — **shortener** *n*.

shortfall /sháwrt fawl/ *n*. an amount by which sth falls short of what is required

short fuse *n*. a tendency to get angry quickly and with little provocation (*informal*)

shorthair /sháwrt hair/ *n*. a medium-sized muscular domestic cat with a short thick coat

shorthaired /sháwrt haird/, **short-haired** *adj*. having a coat of short hair ○ *a shorthaired cat*

shorthand /sháwrt hand/ *n*. **1.** QUICK WAY OF TAKING NOTES a fast method of writing, using symbols to represent letters, words, or phrases **2.** SHORTER WAY OF SAYING STH a shorter or quicker way of referring to sth

short-handed *adj*. having fewer than the usual or required number of staff, helpers, or players — **short-handedness** *n*.

shorthand typist *n*. sb who takes notes in shorthand, especially from dictation, and types a full version of the text from the notes. US term **stenographer**

short-haul *adj*. travelling or used for travelling a short distance

short head *n*. a distance shorter than the length of a horse's head, used in describing the relative finishing positions of horses in a race

shorthold tenancy /sháwrt hōld-/ *n*. a tenancy that provided only limited security of tenure for the tenant, now made obsolete by legislation

shorthorn /sháwrt hawrn/ (*plural* **-horns** *or* **-horn**) *n*. a reddish-brown or white breed of cattle with short curved horns developed in northern England and used for beef or milk production

short-horned grasshopper *n*. a winged grasshopper with short antennae belonging to the family that includes the locust and many other common crop pests. Family: Acrididae.

short hundredweight *n*. US = **hundredweight** *n*. 2

shortie *n*. = **shorty**

short interest *n*. the number of shares in a particular security that have been borrowed and sold and must eventually be returned to the lender

short leg *n*. **1.** FIELDING POSITION IN CRICKET a fielding position in cricket close to and behind the batsman who is being bowled at **2.** FIELDER IN CRICKET in cricket, a fielder in the short leg position

short list *n*. a list of the best candidates for a position or award after all others have been eliminated

short-list (**short-lists, short-listing, short-listed**) *vt*. to put sb or sth on a final list of candidates for a position or award

short-lived *adj*. lasting or living for only a short period of time

shortly /sháwrtli/ *adv*. **1.** IN SHORT TIME soon or in a short time ○ *The guests will arrive shortly.* **2.** CURTLY in a curt or discourteous manner ○ *'I wish you'd stop interrupting me', he said shortly.* **3.** BRIEFLY using only a few words [Old English]

short odds *npl*. a nearly even chance in betting

short order *n*. Can, US food in a restaurant that is prepared and served quickly (*hyphenated when used before a noun*)

short position *n*. an open position in a security in which the investor borrowed the security from sb, sold it, and promised to replace the borrowed security at a later time

short radius *n*. the perpendicular distance or line from the centre of a regular polygon to one of its sides

short-range *adj*. **1.** FOR SHORT DISTANCE OPERATION designed for or capable of travelling or operating only over a short distance **2.** ABOUT THE NEAR FUTURE concerned with the near future ○ *short-range plans*

short sale *n*. the sale of a borrowed security in anticipation that the security price will fall and can be paid back from the profits earned after repurchasing it at the lower price

short score *n*. a condensed orchestra score omitting some of the less important instruments and often combining several parts on one staff

short shrift *n*. **1.** UNSYMPATHETIC TREATMENT brief and inconsiderate or unsympathetic treatment **2.** BRIEF PERIOD FOR CONFESSION a short period of time before execution during which a condemned prisoner could confess (*archaic*) ◇ **make short shrift of sth** deal with a matter quickly, giving it little attention

short sight *n*. an inability to see distant objects clearly

short-sighted *adj*. **1.** OPHTHALMOL UNABLE TO SEE DISTANT OBJECTS CLEARLY able to see things clearly only if they are very close. US term **nearsighted 2.** FOR SHORT TERM ONLY without taking the future into account —**short-sightedly** *adv*. —**short-sightedness** *n*.

short-spoken *adj*. inclined to speak abruptly

short-staffed *adj*. lacking the normal or required number of staff

shortstop /sháwrt stop/ *n*. **1.** INFIELDER POSITION the position of the infielder in baseball playing closest to second base on the side towards third base **2.** PLAYER AT SHORTSTOP the baseball player playing at shortstop

short story *n*. a work of prose fiction that is shorter than a novel

short subject *n*. US a short film of approximately 30 minutes or less, sometimes a documentary, shown before a full-length feature film

short-tempered *adj*. easily made angry or impatient

short-term *adj*. **1.** NOT LASTING LONG lasting for or affecting a relatively short period of time **2.** FIN MATURING OR DUE SOON maturing or payable within a relatively short period of time **3.** FIN FROM ASSETS HELD BRIEFLY realized from assets held for a short time and then sold

short-termism /-túrmizəm/ *n*. a tendency to disregard long-term consequences in favour of short-term benefits —**short-termist** *adj*., *n*.

short-term memory *n*. the part of the mind used for retaining temporary information over a short period

short time *n*. a situation in which employees work fewer hours than normal for correspondingly reduced pay because of a work shortage

short ton *n*. = **ton**[1] *n*. 1

short-waisted *adj*. unusually short between the shoulders and the waist

short wave *n*. a radio wave with a wavelength that lies between 10 and 100 metres (*hyphenated when used before a noun*) ○ *short-wave radio*

short-winded *adj*. **1.** SHORT OF BREATH experiencing shortness of breath, especially after mild exertion **2.** BRIEF expressed in few words

shorty /sháwrti/ (*plural* **-ies**), **shortie** *n*. sb or sth very short or shorter than average (*informal*)

Shoshone /shō shō ni/ (*plural* **-nes** *or* **-ne**), **Shoshoni** (*plural* **-nis** *or* **-ni**) *n*. **1.** MEMBER OF NATIVE N AMERICAN PEOPLE a member of a Native North American people living mainly in Nevada, Idaho, Wyoming and Utah **2.** SHOSHONE LANGUAGE the Uto-Aztecan group of languages spoken by the Shoshone. Shoshone languages are spoken by about 3,000 people. [Early 19thC. Origin unknown.] —**Shoshonian** *n.*, *adj*.

Shostakovich /shósta kǒvich/, **Dmitry** (1906–75) Russian composer. A major figure in 20th-century music, he wrote prolifically in many different forms despite repeated criticism of his work by the Soviet government. His works include 15 symphonies and an equal number of string quartets. Full name **Dmitry Dmitrievich Shostakovich**

shot[1] /shot/ *n*. **1.** SHOOTING OF GUN a firing of a gun or other weapon **2.** SB WHO SHOOTS sb who shoots in a particular way ○ *a good shot* **3.** SHOOTING OF A PROJECTILE AT A TARGET an aimed discharge of a projectile, e.g. a bullet from a gun **4.** BULLET OR CANNONBALL a single solid metal missile for a gun or cannon, e.g. a bullet or cannonball **5.** SMALL METAL PELLETS small steel or lead pellets used in shotgun shells **6.** SPORTS ATTEMPT TO SCORE an attempt to score points in a sport by throwing, hitting, kicking, or shooting sth ○ *Howells struck a superb shot from just outside the penalty area.* **7.** SPORTS ACT OF HITTING BALL an act of hitting the ball in certain sports such as golf, tennis, or snooker ○ *His shot from the fairway was perfectly placed.* **8.** ATHLETICS = **shot put 9.** PHOTOGRAPHY PARTICULAR VIEW ON FILM a particular view recorded on film with a camera ○ *The cameraman bent down to get a low shot of the damaged wheels.* **10.** CINEMA CONTINUOUS UNINTERRUPTED FILM SEQUENCE a continuous action or image on the screen that appears to be the result of a single uninterrupted operation of the camera **11.** PHOTOGRAPHY CAMERA VIEW the range of, or view from, a camera **12.** ATTEMPT an opportunity to attempt sth ○ *He had a shot at repairing the vacuum cleaner.* **13.** GUESS a wild guess or speculation, usually based on little or no information (*informal*) **14.** MED JAB a jab (*informal*) **15.** BEVERAGES SMALL AMOUNT OF ALCOHOL a small glass or drink of a strong alcoholic beverage (*informal*) 16. **SHARP COMMENT** an angry or critical remark 17. SPACE TECH **ROCKET LAUNCH** the launching of a rocket or probe to a specified destination 18. MINING **BLASTING EXPLOSION** a charge of explosives used in blasting 19. **PROJECTILE FLIGHT PATH** a flight or path of a projectile 20. GAMBLING **CHANCE AT WINNING** sth such as a racehorse to bet on at particular odds (*informal*) ○ *The horse was a 3 to 1 shot.* 21. **SMALL QUANTITY OF STH** a small amount given or taken on one occasion (*informal*) ○ *You need a shot of energy.* 22. **MONEY OWED** an amount due for sth such as a round of drinks (*archaic*) 23. MEASURE **MEASUREMENT IN FATHOMS** a unit of chain length equal to 15 fathoms in the United States and 12.5 fathoms in the United Kingdom [Old English *sceot, gesceot* 'act of shooting', also 'payment'. Ultimately, from a prehistoric Germanic word meaning 'to project', which is also the ancestor of English *shoot* and *shuttle.*] ◇ **a shot in the arm** sth that has a sudden good effect on sb or sth ◇ **a shot in the dark** 1. a guess made without any information 2. an attempt made in desperation but with little hope of success ◇ **deliver** *or* **fire a shot across sb's bows** give sb a warning of what might happen ◇ **get shot of sb** *or* **sth** to get rid of sb or sth (*informal*) ◇ **like a shot** very eagerly and quickly

shot[2] /shot/ past tense, past participle of **shoot** ■ *adj.* 1. **TWO-TONE IN COLOUR** woven of two colours in such a way that when the fabric is viewed from different angles the visible colours change 2. **MARKED WITH VARYING COLOUR** streaked or flecked with a different colour 3. **FILLED WITH PARTICULAR QUALITY** filled with or permeated by an emotion or quality 4. **MADE USELESS** brought to a state of ruin or exhaustion (*informal*) ○ *I've been so busy my nerves are shot.* 5. **USED UP** no longer full or operating properly (*informal*) ○ *This tube of toothpaste is shot.*

shot-blasting *n.* the process of projecting metal shot, usually steel or cast iron, at a surface to remove scale or prepare the surface for further treatment

shote *n.* = **shoat**

shotgun /shót gun/ *n.* 1. **GUN THAT SHOOTS PELLET LOAD** a short-range smoothbore gun that discharges a load of small pellets 2. AMERICAN FOOTBALL **FORMATION IN AMERICAN FOOTBALL** an offensive formation in American football, usually used when passing, in which the quarterback receives the snap a few yards behind the line of scrimmage ■ *adj.* **INVOLVING INTIMIDATION** brought about by pressure, threats, or force

shotgun wedding, **shotgun marriage** *n.* a marriage that takes place at short notice, usually because the bride is pregnant [Because the parties are or feel compelled, as if at gunpoint, to marry]

shot hole *n.* 1. MINING **HOLE FOR EXPLOSIVE CHARGE** a hole bored into rock in which an explosive charge is placed 2. **PARASITE OR INSECT DAMAGE** a small hole made in wood or leaves by insects or parasites (*informal*)

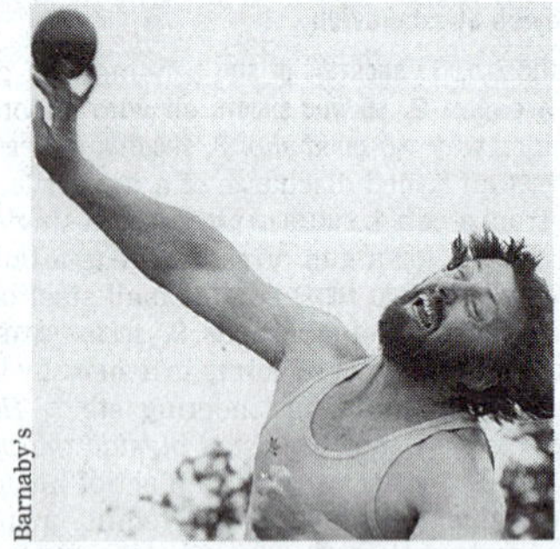

Shot put

shot put *n.* 1. **COMPETITION FOR THROWING BALL** an athletic field event in which contestants compete to throw a heavy metal ball as far as possible 2. **BALL FOR THROWING COMPETITION** a heavy metal ball used in the shot put —**shot-putter** *n.*

shotten /shótt'n/ *adj.* having recently spawned and therefore less valuable as food ○ *a shotten fish* [15thC. From the obsolete past participle of SHOOT.]

shot tower *n.* a tower formerly used for making lead shot, in which molten lead was dropped from the top into water at the bottom in which the drops solidified

should /(stressed) shŏŏd, (unstressed) shəd/ CORE MEANING: modal verb indicating that sth is the right thing for sb to do ○ *You should get more exercise.* ○ *I should have told her I was leaving.* ○ *The report recommended that children should be tested regularly.*

v. 1. **EXPRESSING LIKELIHOOD OR PROBABILITY** to be scheduled or expected to be or do sth ○ *I should be back by 12.* ○ *The scissors should be in the second drawer down.* ○ *They should have arrived at Grandma's by now.* 2. **EXPRESSING CONDITIONS OR CONSEQUENCES** used to express the conditionality of an occurrence and suggest it is not a given, or to indicate the consequence of sth that might happen (*used in conditional clauses*) ○ *If anything should happen to my car, I'd be heartbroken.* ○ *Should you have any questions, our staff will be available to help.* ○ *'If I should die, think only this of me...'* (Rupert Brooke, *The Soldier*; 1887–1915) 3. **WOULD** used to mean the same thing as the verb would (*used with 'I' or 'we'*) ○ *If we spent that much every month, we should soon run out of money.* ○ *I should love to meet her.* 4. **REPORTING PAST VIEWPOINT ABOUT FUTURE** used when reporting sth from a past perspective, e.g. sb's words or thoughts, about a future event ○ *It was intended that the library should be for the use of everyone.* ○ *He was keen that I should meet his publisher friend.* 5. **USED TO SOFTEN HARSH WORDS** used to soften a blunt statement or make one more polite ○ *I should hope you're sorry now.* ◇ **I should** used to advise sb to do sth ○ *I should take him up on his offer, if I were you.*

WORD KEY: USAGE

should or **would**? The same general pattern is true here as for *shall* and *will.* As an auxiliary verb, ***would*** is more usual than ***should*** when stating a condition or proposition and is the only choice when asking a question (*They would like to come. I would think so. Would you like to go to the cinema?*). ***Should*** has the special role of denoting obligation or likelihood (*I should stay until they arrive. Should you be lifting that? That should be our visitors now*) and must be used in inverted constructions expressing a condition: *Should it rain, the party will be held indoors.* ***Would*** has to be used when referring to habitual action in the past: *On Wednesdays I would go to the library.* In conversational English, the contracted form *I'd, you'd,* etc. are regularly used instead of the full forms in making simple statements (*They'd like to come*), but these are not available in place of ***should*** in its sense of obligation or likelihood.

shoulder /shóldər/ *n.* 1. ANAT **PLACE WHERE AN ARM ATTACHES TO THE TRUNK** either one of the two parts of the human body immediately below and at each side of the neck, where the arm joins the trunk 2. ZOOL **JOINT ATTACHING A FORELIMB TO THE TRUNK** the part of the body of a vertebrate animal equivalent to the shoulder, where the forelimb joins the pectoral girdle 3. **PART OF GARMENT FITTING SHOULDER** a part of a piece of clothing that covers the shoulder 4. **MEAT FROM SHOULDER** a fairly fatty cut of meat consisting of the upper part of a foreleg of an animal 5. **STH SLOPED LIKE SHOULDER** sth resembling a shoulder in position or slope, e.g. the part of a stringed instrument between the neck and body or the slope near the top of a hill 6. *US* TRANSP = **hard shoulder** 7. PRINTING **TYPE SURFACE THAT IS NOT LETTER** a flat surface of printers' type below the base of the raised letter or character 8. **WIDER PORTION OF SHAFT** any portion of a shaft or other instrument for transmitting force that has an increase in diameter to withstand thrust 9. LEISURE **OFF-PEAK SEASON** a season preceding or following the peak season, often characterized by lower levels of use as well as lower travel fares and accommodation prices ■ **shoulders** *npl.* 1. ANAT **UPPER AREA OF BACK** the upper back, including both shoulders and the area between them 2. **CAPACITY TO HANDLE RESPONSIBILITY** the capacity to carry responsibility for sth, especially sth unpleasant or worrying ○ *The blame rests on her shoulders.* ■ *v.* (**-ders, -dering, -dered**) 1. *vt.* **CARRY OR PLACE STH ON SHOULDERS** to carry, lift, or place sth on the shoulders 2. *vt.* **ACCEPT RESPONSIBILITY** to accept and bear a burden or responsibility 3. *vti.* **MOVE STH WITH SHOULDER** to push sth or make way using a shoulder ○ *She successfully shouldered her way to the front of the crowd.* [Old English *sculdor.* Ultimately, from a prehistoric West Germanic word meaning 'shoulder blade'.] ◇ **put your shoulder to the wheel** work hard ◇ **rub shoulders with sb** associate with sb of a particular type or social class ◇ **shoulder to shoulder** 1. side by side 2. in a cooperative effort ◇ **straight from the shoulder** in a frank or blunt way

shoulder bag *n.* a bag carried by a long strap hung over the shoulder

shoulder blade *n.* either one of two large flat triangular bones over the upper outer parts of the ribs at the top of the back that joins with the upper arm bone. Technical name **scapula**

shoulder board *n. US* = **shoulder strap**

shoulder flash *n.* = **shoulder patch**

shoulder girdle *n.* an incomplete ring of bones formed by the two shoulder blades (**scapulas**), the two collar bones (**clavicles**), and the upper edge of the breastbone (**sternum**)

shoulder holster *n.* a holster hung from a shoulder strap and worn under the arm, used to hide a gun under a coat or jacket

shoulder knot *n.* a decoration of braided cord worn on the shoulder of a uniform

shoulder pad *n.* a pad inserted into the shoulder of a piece of clothing to improve its shape, often making it appear larger

shoulder patch *n.* a cloth patch with an identifying emblem on it, worn on the upper part of the sleeve of a uniform

shoulder strap *n.* 1. **STRAP TO SUPPORT CLOTHING** a strap that goes over a shoulder for carrying a bag or holding up a garment 2. *US* **CLOTH SHOULDER PATCH SHOWING MILITARY RANK** one of a pair of stiff cloth patches worn on the shoulders of a military uniform to indicate rank. US term **shoulder board**

shouldn't /shŏŏd'nt/ *contr.* should not

shouldst /shoodst/ 2nd person present singular of **should** (*archaic*)

shout /showt/ *v.* (**shouts, shouting, shouted**) 1. *vt.* **SAY STH LOUDLY** to say or utter sth very loudly 2. *vi.* **SPEAK LOUDLY** to speak in a loud or angry voice 3. *vti. ANZ* **PAY FOR FOOD OR DRINK** to buy sth for sb else, especially a drink in a pub or a meal in a restaurant (*informal*) ■ *n.* 1. **LOUD CRY** a loud call or cry 2. **TURN TO PAY** sb's turn to buy sth, especially a drink or meal (*informal*) ○ *'It's my shout. What would you like to drink?'* [14thC. Origin unknown: perhaps from, ultimately, a prehistoric Germanic word meaning 'to project', which is also the ancestor of English *shoot,* or from Old Norse *skúta* 'to taunt'.] —**shouter** *n.* ◇ **be all over bar the shouting** used to say that sth is nearly over, and the outcome is clear ◇ **nothing to shout about** not good enough to speak of with pride (*informal*)

shout down *vt.* to prevent sb from being heard by shouting loudly

shove /shuv/ *vti.* (**shoves, shoving, shoved**) 1. **MOVE STH WITH FORCE** to push sb or sth along or forward with force 2. **PUSH SB OR STH ROUGHLY** to push sb or sth in a rude or careless way ■ *n.* **PUSH** a strong push [Old English *scufan* 'to push away'. Ultimately, from a prehistoric Germanic word that is also the ancestor of English *scuffle.*] —**shover** *n.*

shove off *vi.* 1. **LEAVE** to leave (*informal; sometimes used as a command*) 2. **LEAVE SHORE** to move from shore or a mooring in a boat

shove-halfpenny *n.* a game in which players use the side of the hand to knock coins or discs into ruled scoring areas on a wooden board

shovel /shúvv'l/ *n.* (*plural* **-els** *or* **-els**) 1. **LONG-HANDLED**

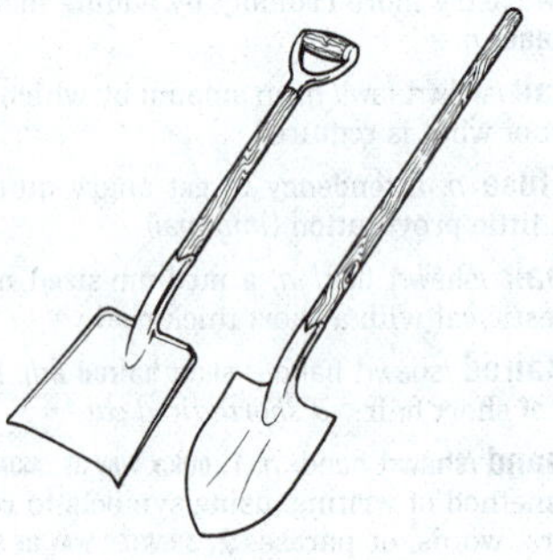
Shovel

SCOOP a hand tool consisting of a broad, usually curved blade attached to a long handle, used for lifting and moving loose material **2. MACHINE FOR EARTH DIGGING** a power-driven machine that operates with a scooping motion, especially one used for digging or moving earth **3. AMOUNT HELD BY SHOVEL** the amount that a shovel is capable of holding ■ *v.* (**-els, -elling, -elled**) **1.** *vti.* **DIG WITH SHOVEL FOR STH** to lift, move, or clear sth with a shovel **2.** *vt.* **THROW STH CARELESSLY** to move large amounts of sth from one place to another in a careless or clumsy way [Old English *scofl.* The underlying sense is 'an implement for shoving'.]

shoveler /shúvvələr/ *n.* **1. SB OR STH THAT SHOVELS** sb or sth that uses a shovel to move or throw sth **2.** BIRDS **BROAD-BILLED DUCK** a small freshwater duck with a broad spoon-shaped bill that inhabits marshes in the northern hemisphere. Latin name: *Anas clypeata.*

shovelful /shúvv'l fòol/ (*plural* **-elfuls** *or* **-elsful**) *n.* an amount that a shovel can hold

shovel hat *n.* a black felt hat with a low crown and a wide brim turned up at the sides, formerly worn by some English clergymen

shovelhead /shóvv'l hed/ (*plural* **-heads** *or* **-head**) *n.* a common hammerhead shark of Atlantic and Pacific waters with a broad shovel-shaped head. It grows to about 1.6 m/6 ft long, is not dangerous to human life, and inhabits shallow waters. Latin name: *Sphyrna tiburo.*

shovelnose /shúvv'l nōz/ *n.* (*plural* **-nose** *or* **-noses**) = **shovel-nosed sturgeon** [Early 18thC. From its broad, flat snout.]

shovel-nosed *adj.* having a broad shovel-shaped head, snout, or bill

shovel-nosed sturgeon *n.* a freshwater sturgeon of North America with a broad shovel-shaped snout. Latin name: *Scaphirhynchus platorhynchus.*

show /shō/ *v.* (**shows, showing, showed, shown** *or* **showed**) **1.** *vti.* **MAKE VISIBLE** to cause or allow sth to come into view ○ *Show me your hand.* **2.** *vti.* **BE VISIBLE** to be visible or allow sth to be seen easily ○ *Does the spot on my shirt show?* **3.** *vti.* **EXHIBIT** to put on an exhibition or performance or to present sth for the public to see ○ *She's showing her paintings all over the world now.* ○ *Several new films are showing this week.* **4.** *vti.* **DISPLAY FOR SALE** to present sth for sale to the public ○ *His work was showing at the Museum of Modern Art.* **5.** *vt.* **GUIDE SB** to guide or accompany sb ○ *Show them to the office.* **6.** *vt.* **POINT STH OUT TO SB** to call sb's attention to sth ○ *She showed him the mistake.* **7.** *vt.* **DEMONSTRATE QUALITIES** to make sb's or sth's fundamental qualities or characteristics evident ○ *He has shown that he is honest.* **8.** *vt.* **ESTABLISH STH USING REASON** to explain, demonstrate, or prove sth in a logical way ○ *The teacher showed them the solution.* **9.** *vt.* **DEMONSTRATE STH FOR INSTRUCTION** to give a demonstration of sth in order to teach others ○ *She showed us how to apply the glaze to the pot.* **10.** *vt.* **GIVE INFORMATION** to register information ○ *This chart shows the sudden increase in temperature.* **11.** *vt.* **DISPLAY ATTITUDE** to display a personal feeling or attitude ○ *She's never shown much interest in art.* **12.** *vi.* **APPEAR IN CERTAIN WAY** to have a particular appearance when being viewed ○ *The horse shows well.* **13.** *vi.* **ARRIVE** to put in an appearance at a place (*informal*) ○ *They never showed.* **14.** *vi. US* **COME IN THIRD** to finish at least third in a race, especially a horse race or a dog race **15.** *vt.* LAW **PLEAD STH IN LAWSUIT** to allege or plead sth in a legal document ■ *n.* **1. DEMONSTRATION** an expression or demonstration of sth ○ *a show of force* **2. PUBLIC PRESENTATION** a public entertainment such as a theatre performance, film, or radio or television programme ○ *Shall we go to a show tonight?* **3. EXHIBITION** an exhibition, e.g. of art, flowers, animals, or an industry's products ○ *a flower show* **4. EVENT WITH FARM COMPETITIONS AND AMUSEMENTS** an annual outdoor event, held especially for a county, with competitions for the best livestock, produce, and prepared foods and with entertainments, rides, and other amusements. US term **fair 5. APPEARANCE** an appearance given, either as an outward display of an emotion or trait, or as a demonstration of falseness and pretence ○ *a show of diligence* **6. SIZABLE VENTURE** an undertaking or task, especially one of some size and complexity (*informal*) ○ *You decide – it's your show!* **7. IMPRESSIVE DISPLAY** an extravagant or impressive display **8. SPECTACLE** a display or exhibition designed to evoke laughter or ridicule **9.** *ANZ, US* **OPPORTUNITY** a chance or opportunity (*informal*) ○ *no show of winning* **10. INDICATION** a trace of sth indicating its presence, e.g. oil in the ground **11.** MED **BLOOD INDICATING START OF LABOUR** a bloody mucous discharge indicating the onset of labour in childbirth ■ **shows** *npl. Scotland, N England* **FUNFAIR** a funfair (*informal*) [Old English *sceawian* 'to look at'. Ultimately, from a prehistoric West Germanic word meaning 'to look', which is also the ancestor of English *sheen.*] —**showable** *adj.* ◇ **get the** *or* **this show on the road** begin an activity or start an event (*informal*) ◇ **good show** used to express approval or to congratulate sb on doing well (*dated*) ◇ **steal the show** attract the most attention or admiration

show off *v.* **1.** *vi.* **ATTRACT THE ATTENTION OF OTHERS** to try to impress others by behaving in a way that attracts attention **2.** *vt.* **PRESENT STH FOR APPROVAL** to display sb or sth proudly for others to admire **3.** *vt.* **PRESENT STH IN AN APPEALING WAY** to display sth in a way that enhances it

show up *v.* **1.** *vi.* **ARRIVE** to arrive or put in an appearance (*informal*) **2.** *vt.* **BRING STH TO LIGHT** to expose or reveal sth, especially an error or personal shortcoming **3.** *vi.* **BE SEEN** to be easily seen **4.** *vt.* **EMBARRASS SB BEFORE OTHERS** to embarrass or humiliate sb publicly **5.** *vt.* **MAKE SB LOOK BAD** to perform in a superior way and make sb look inferior by comparison

show-and-tell, **show and tell** *n.* a classroom activity for children in which each child brings an object to school and tells the other children about it

show bill *n.* a poster advertising or publicizing sth

show biz *n.* show business (*informal*)

showboat /shó bōt/ *n.* a river steamboat equipped with a theatre and carrying an acting company that performs for communities along the river

show business *n.* the entertainment industry, including films, radio, television, theatre, and music recording

showcase /shó kayss/ *n.* **1. GLASS CASE FOR DISPLAYING OBJECTS** a box or case, usually one made of glass, used to display objects, especially in a museum or shop **2. MOST FAVOURABLE SETTING** an event, setting, or medium in which sth or sb is presented to advantage ■ *vt.* (**-cases, -casing, -cased**) **PRESENT STH TO ADVANTAGE** to present sth or sb in a way that is designed to attract attention and admiration

showdown /shó down/ *n.* **1. CONFRONTATION** a confrontation to settle a conflict or dispute **2. PLACING OF CARDS FACE UP** in poker, the moment at the end of a round when the players show their cards to see who has the best hand

shower[1] /shówər/ *n.* **1. BATH UNDER SPRAY** a method of washing in which sb stands upright under a spray of water from a nozzle **2. PLACE AND EQUIPMENT FOR SHOWER** an enclosure or the plumbing apparatus for a shower **3.** METEOROL **PERIOD OF PRECIPITATION** a short period of rain, snow, hail, or sleet **4. STH LIKE RAIN** a sudden spray or fall of sth, e.g. meteors, sparks, or bullets **5. LARGE AMOUNT OF STH** sth that sb receives all at once in quantity **6.** *ANZ, Can, US* **PARTY WITH GIFTS** a party given by friends, especially in honour of a woman who is about to be married or is expecting a baby, at which gifts are given **7.** *UK* **DISAGREEABLE GROUP** a group of people considered unpleasant, worthless, or inferior (*informal*) **8.** PHYS **IONIZING PARTICLES CAUSED BY COSMIC RAY** a large number of ionizing particles and photons caused by the collision of a cosmic-ray particle with the upper atmosphere ■ *v.* (**-ers, -ering, -ered**) **1.** *vi.* **WASH UNDER SHOWER** to wash using a shower **2.** *vti.* **RAIN DOWN ON SB** to fall or make things fall in a spray **3.** *vt.* **GIVE SB STH PLENTIFULLY** to give sb sth in abundance ○ *They were showered with gifts.* [Old English *scūr.* Ultimately from a prehistoric West Germanic word that is also the ancestor of German *schauer* and Dutch *schoer.*] —**showery** *adj.*

shower[2] /shó ər/ *n.* sb or sth that shows, especially an exhibitor at a public exhibition [Old English *scēawere* 'scout, watchman', from *scēawian* 'to look at' (see SHOW)]

shower gel *n.* a liquid soap with the consistency of a gel, used especially when in the shower and often scented

showerhead /shówər hed/ *n.* a spray nozzle that is part of an overhead plumbing fixture used in a shower

showerproof /shówər proof/ *adj.* resistant to light but not heavy rain —**showerproofing** *n.*

shower tea *n. ANZ* a party given by friends for a woman soon to be married at which they give her gifts, usually small items for the kitchen

showgirl /shó gurl/ *n.* a young woman who performs in the chorus of a stage show, usually a musical, as a dancer or singer

showground /shó grownd/ *n.* an area of land where an open-air event such as an agricultural show is held. US term **fairground**

show house *n.* a house decorated and furnished for prospective buyers to view as an example of the type of house for sale on a newly built estate. US term **model home**

showing /shó ing/ *n.* **1. DISPLAY** a presentation or exhibition, e.g. of a film or artwork **2. TYPE OF PERFORMANCE** the way a person, group, or team performs **3. PRESENTATION OF FACTS** a presentation of facts [Old English *scēawung*]

showjumping /shó jumping/ *n.* a competitive sport in which riders on horseback take turns jumping over a series of obstacles on a set course and are judged on speed and ability —**showjumper** *n.*

showman /shómən/ (*plural* **-men**) *n.* **1. GIFTED ENTERTAINER** sb who has a natural talent for dramatic presentation or entertainment **2. PRODUCER OF SHOW** a producer or promoter of commercial entertainment ventures, especially in musical theatre **3. CIRCUS MANAGER** manager or owner of circus or fairground —**showmanship** *n.*

shown past participle of **show**

show-off *n.* sb who behaves in a way that attracts attention and invites admiration (*informal*)

show of hands *n.* a form of voting that involves counting the hands raised by people to vote for or against a proposal

showpiece /shó peess/ *n.* sth considered or offered as a fine example of sth

showplace /shó playss/ *n.* **1. SPECIAL PLACE** a place visited for its beauty or historical significance **2. STH EXCEPTIONALLY BEAUTIFUL** a place that is considered or offered as an example of beauty

show pony *n. Aus* sb who looks and sounds good but lacks substance or depth

showroom /shó room, -ròom/ *n.* a room in which goods for sale, especially cars or electrical appliances, are displayed

showstopper /shó stoppər/ *n.* **1. ACT GETTING PROLONGED APPLAUSE** a performance receiving so much applause from an audience that the show is interrupted **2. STH SO STRIKING IT STOPS ACTION** sb or sth so spectacular as to attract and hold everyone's attention

show trial *n.* a trial with a predetermined verdict held for propaganda purposes

showy /shó i/ (**-ier, -iest**) *adj.* **1. IMPRESSIVE** making an attractive or impressive display **2. OSTENTATIOUS** appearing tasteless and ostentatious —**showily** *adv.* —**showiness** *n.*

shoyu /shó yoo/ *n.* a Japanese variety of soy sauce [Early 18thC. From Japanese.]

shp *abbr.* shaft horsepower

shpilkes /shpílkəss/ *npl.* a state of great nervousness or anxiety

shpt *abbr.* shipment

shr. *abbr.* share

shrank past participle of **shrink**

shrapnel /shrápnəl/ *n.* **1. FRAGMENTS FROM AN EXPLOSIVE DEVICE** metal balls or fragments that are scattered when a shell, bomb, or bullet explodes **2. SHELL THAT SCATTERS METAL FRAGMENTS** an artillery shell designed to explode before impact producing a shower of metal balls and fragments [Early 19thC. Named after General Henry Shrapnel, 1761–1842, the British artillery officer who invented the shell.]

shred /shred/ *n.* **1.** LONG TORN STRIP a ragged scrap or strip cut or torn from sth **2.** SMALL PART a very small amount or fragment of sth ■ *v.* **(shreds, shredding, shredded) 1.** *vt.* TEAR STH INTO SHREDS to cut or tear sth into shreds **2.** *vt.* PUT STH THROUGH SHREDDER to reduce a document to unreadable strips in a shredder **3.** *vti. Aus, US* SPORTS SURF OR SNOWBOARD EXPERTLY to ride a wave on a surfboard or descend a slope on a snowboard with expert skill (*informal*) [Old English *scrēade.* Ultimately, from a prehistoric West Germanic word meaning 'cut', which is also the ancestor of English *scroll.*]

shredded wheat *n.* a breakfast cereal made from cooked dried whole wheat that has been shredded, shaped into cakes, and baked

shredder /shréddər/ *n.* **1.** MACHINE FOR DESTROYING DOCUMENTS an office machine used to destroy documents by cutting them into very small pieces so that they cannot be read **2.** *Aus, US* SPORTS GOOD SURFER an expert surfer or snowboarder (*informal*) [Late 16thC. Originally, 'instrument for shredding'.]

Shreveport /shréev pawrt/ city in northwestern Louisiana, on the western bank of the Red River, east of the Texas border. The city is an important producer of oil, natural gas, and cotton. Population: 191,558 (1996).

Shrew

shrew /shroo/ *n.* **1.** SMALL MAMMAL WITH POINTED NOSE a small nocturnal mammal resembling a mouse but really an insectivore, with velvety fur, a long pointed snout, and small eyes and ears. Family: Soricidae. **2.** OFFENSIVE TERM an offensive term referring to a woman who is regarded as quarrelsome, nagging, or ill-tempered (*offensive*) [Old English *scrēawa,* of unknown origin. The sense 'quarrelsome woman' derives from the belief that the shrew had a poisonous bite.]

─────── **WORD KEY: CULTURAL NOTE** ───────

The Taming of the Shrew (1593–94?), a play by William Shakespeare. The central story of this play within a play is set in Verona and describes Petruchio's attempts to woo the wealthy but haughty and temperamental Katharina (the 'shrew' of the title). The rounded and convincing protagonists make this an intriguing character study as well as a boisterous farce. The expression 'Kiss me, Kate' comes from line 318, scene i, Act II: 'Kiss me, Kate, we will be married o' Sunday'.

shrewd /shrood/ *adj.* **1.** GOOD AT JUDGING PEOPLE OR SITUATIONS showing or possessing intelligence, insight, and sound judgment, especially in business or politics **2.** CLEVER AND PROBABLY ACCURATE based on good judgment and probably correct ○ *a shrewd assessment of the situation* **3.** CRAFTY inclined to deal with others in a clever underhand way **4.** SHARP piercing or sharp (*archaic*) [13thC. From SHREW in the obsolete sense of 'wicked man'. The meaning evolved from 'wicked, dangerous' via 'cunning'.] —**shrewdly** *adv.* —**shrewdness** *n.*

shrewish /shroó ish/ *adj.* with a quarrelsome ill-tempered disposition —**shrewishly** *adv.* —**shrewishness** *n.*

Shrewsbury /shroóozbəri, shrózbəri/ county town of Shropshire, England. Population: 94,600 (1994).

shriek /shreek/ *v.* **(shrieks, shrieking, shrieked) 1.** *vi.* MAKE SHRILL SOUND to make a loud high-pitched piercing sound **2.** *vt.* SAY STH IN LOUD SHRILL VOICE to utter sth in a loud high-pitched piercing voice ■ *n.* LOUD SHRILL CRY a loud high-pitched piercing cry or sound [15thC. From a Scandinavian source, probably of imitative origin.] —**shrieker** *n.*

shrieval /shreév'l/ *adj.* belonging or relating to a sheriff [Late 17thC. Formed from an obsolete variant of SHERIFF.]

shrievalty /shreév'lti/ (*plural* -**ties**) *n.* **1.** SHERIFF'S OFFICE the office or position of sheriff **2.** SHERIFF'S TERM the term of office of a sheriff **3.** SHERIFF'S JURISDICTION the jurisdiction of a sheriff [Early 16thC. Formed from obsolete *shrieve* 'sheriff' + -*alty* (modelled on Old French -*alté* '-ty').]

shrieve /shreev/ *vti.* to shrive or shrive sb (*archaic*) [Alteration of SHRIVE]

shrift /shrift/ *n.* (*archaic*) **1.** SHRIVING SB the act of shriving or of being shriven **2.** CONFESSION confession to a priest **3.** ABSOLUTION absolution granted by a priest [Old English *scrift* from *scrīfan* (to SHRIVE)]

Shrike

shrike /shrīk/ (*plural* **shrikes** *or* **shrike**) *n.* a brown or grey songbird with a screeching call and a hooked bill. It eats insects and small animals that it impales on sharp objects such as thorns. Family: Laniidae. [Mid-16thC. Origin uncertain.]

shrill /shril/ *adj.* **1.** PENETRATINGLY HIGH-PITCHED with a high-pitched penetrating quality **2.** MAKING A SHRILL SOUND making a high-pitched penetrating sound **3.** INSISTENT with an obtrusive insistent quality ■ *v.* **(shrills, shrilling, shrilled) 1.** *vi.* MAKE A SHRILL SOUND to make a high-pitched penetrating sound (*literary*) **2.** *vt.* SAY STH IN A PIERCING VOICE to utter sth in a high-pitched penetrating voice [13thC. Origin uncertain.] —**shrillness** *n.* —**shrilly** /shríl li/ *adv.*

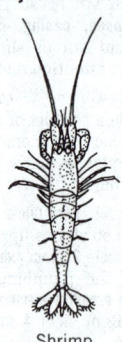

Shrimp

shrimp /shrimp/ *n.* **1.** ZOOL SMALL MARINE CRUSTACEAN WITH TEN LEGS a small mainly marine crustacean with ten legs belonging to a suborder that includes several edible species. A shrimp has a long thin semi-transparent body, five pairs of jointed legs, a tail resembling a fan, and a pair of pincers. Suborder: Natantia. **2.** STH UNDERSIZED sb or sth very small or considered insignificant (*informal*) ■ *vi.* **(shrimps, shrimping, shrimped)** FISH FOR SHRIMPS to fish for shrimps [14thC. Origin uncertain.] —**shrimper** *n.*

shrimp plant *n.* a tropical American plant, grown as a houseplant, with long curving spikes of white flowers that grow out from overlapping pink bracts. Latin name: *Beloperone guttata.*

shrine /shrīn/ *n.* **1.** HOLY PLACE OF WORSHIP a sacred place of worship associated with a holy person or event **2.** CONTAINER FOR HOLY RELICS a case or other container for sacred relics, e.g. the bones of a saint **3.** TOMB OF HOLY PERSON the tomb of a saint or other revered figure **4.** NICHE FOR RELIGIOUS ICON a ledge or alcove for a religious icon, e.g. in a church **5.** STH REVERED an object or place revered for its associations or history ■

vt. **(shrines, shrining, shrined)** ENSHRINE STH to enshrine sth (*literary*) [Pre-12thC. From Latin *scrinium* 'a case for books or papers', of uncertain origin. First used to denote a container.]

shrink /shringk/ *v.* **(shrinks, shrinking, shrank** /shrangk/ *or* **shrunk, shrunk** *or* **shrunken** /shrúngkən/) **1.** *vti.* MAKE OR BECOME SMALLER to become smaller or cause sth to become smaller, e.g. when exposed to cold, heat, or damp **2.** *vti.* REDUCE SIZE to decrease or cause sth to decrease in amount, extent, value, or weight **3.** *vi.* DRAW AWAY FROM STH to move back and away, especially out of disgust, fear, or horror **4.** *vi.* BE DISINCLINED TO DO STH to be unwilling or reluctant to do sth, especially sth difficult or unpleasant ■ *n.* **1.** PSYCHIATRIST a psychiatrist (*slang; considered offensive by some people*) **2.** ACT OF SHRINKING AWAY an act of shrinking away from sth [Old English *scrincan* 'to wither'. Ultimately, from an Indo-European word meaning 'to turn, bend', which is also the ancestor of English *curve.*] —**shrinkable** *adj.* —**shrinker** *n.*

─────── **WORD KEY: SYNONYMS** ───────
See Synonyms at **recoil**.

shrinkage /shríngkij/ *n.* **1.** DECREASE AFTER SHRINKING the amount lost when sth is decreased or reduced, or when it shrinks **2.** ACT OF SHRINKING the shrinking of sth **3.** MERCHANDISE STOLEN OR BROKEN the loss of goods due to theft or breakage **4.** LOSS OF VALUE the decrease in value of sth **5.** AGRIC WEIGHT REDUCTION IN CARCASSES the loss in body weight of livestock carcasses during shipping, storage, and preparation for sale **6.** REDUCED SIZE OF CLAY ITEM the reduction in size of a clay object when it is fired in a kiln, caused by the moisture burning off

shrink fit *n.* the fit of two interlocking parts in which the outer is heated and therefore expands before being put in position, the contraction during cooling ensuring that it is tight

shrinking violet *n.* sb who is very shy or retiring (*informal*)

shrink-wrap *n.* TRANSPARENT PLASTIC PACKAGING MATERIAL a clear thermoplastic film that is wrapped around a product and shrunk to its original smaller size using heat, thereby forming a tightly sealed package ■ *vt.* WRAP STH IN SHRINK-WRAP to wrap goods in shrink-wrap

shrive /shrīv/ **(shrives, shriving, shrove** /shrōv/ *or* **shrived, shriven** /shrívv'n/ *or* **shrived**) *v.* **1.** *vt.* ABSOLVE SB OF SINS in Christianity, to hear sb's confession of sins and give the person absolution **2.** *vt.* IMPOSE PENANCE in Christianity, to impose a penance on a sinner **3.** *vi.* CONFESS to confess sins to a priest (*archaic*) [Pre-12thC. Ultimately, from Latin *scribere* 'to write' (source of English *scribe*). The meaning evolved via the sense 'to prescribe penances'.] —**shriver** *n.*

shrivel /shrívv'l/ **(-els, -elling, -elled)** *vti.* **1.** SHRINK to become or cause sb or sth to become shrunken or wrinkled, especially from drying out or ageing **2.** WEAKEN to become or cause sb to become useless or ineffectual **3.** BECOME OR MAKE SMALLER to become or cause sth to become gradually smaller or less [Mid-16thC. Origin unknown.]

─────── **WORD KEY: SYNONYMS** ───────
See Synonyms at **dry**.

shriven past participle of **shrive**

Shrivijaya /shreévi jay ə/ *n.* a trading empire centred on the Malacca Straits between Malaya and Sumatra with a Buddhist government that opened up Southeast Asia to Muslim conversion when it fell [Late 19thC. From Hindi.]

shroff /shrof/ *n.* **1.** INDIAN BANKER a banker or money-changer in India **2.** EXPERT IN COUNTERFEIT COINS sb employed in eastern Asia to separate counterfeit from real coins ■ *vt.* **(shroffs, shroffing, shroffed)** SEPARATE COUNTERFEIT COINS to separate counterfeit from real coins [Early 17thC. Alteration of Hindi *śarāf,* from Arabic *ṣarrāf.*]

Shropshire /shrópshər/ county on the Welsh border in the Midlands, England. It is mainly agricultural, and was an early centre of the iron industry. Shrewsbury is the county town. Population: 419,900 (1995). Area: 3,490 sq. km/1,348 sq. mi.

shroud /shrowd/ *n.* **1.** BURIAL CLOTH a cloth in which a dead body is wrapped before burial **2.** COVERING sth that covers or conceals sth or sb **3.** PROTECTIVE COVERING a protective covering such as a guard for a piece of machinery **4.** SPACE TECH PROTECTIVE COVERING FOR SPACECRAFT a shield that protects a spacecraft from heat during launch **5.** SAILING MAST STAY any one of the supporting ropes or wires that extend down from the top of a mast **6.** CABLE TO STOP SWAY a supporting cable that extends from the top of a tall structure such as a smokestack to the ground **7.** PART OF AEROFOIL SURFACE a rearward extension of a fixed aerofoil surface covering the leading edge of a movable surface hinged to it **8.** AIR PARACHUTE LINE any one of the lines by which the harness of a parachute is attached to the canopy ■ *v.* **(shrouds, shrouding, shrouded) 1.** *vt.* WRAP CORPSE to wrap a dead body in a cloth **2.** *vt.* COVER OR CONCEAL STH to cover or conceal sb or sth **3.** *vti.* SHELTER to shelter sb or to seek shelter (*archaic*) [Old English *scrūd* 'garment'. Ultimately, from a prehistoric West Germanic word meaning 'to cut', which is also the ancestor of English *shred.*]

shroud-laid *adj.* used to describe a rope that is made up of four twisted strands

shrove past tense of **shrive**

Shrovetide /shrṓv tīd/ *n.* CALENDAR in the Christian calendar, the three-day period preceding Ash Wednesday and the season of Lent

Shrove Tuesday *n.* in the Christian calendar, the last day before the beginning of Lent [From the practice of going to confession at the beginning of Lent]

shrub[1] /shrub/ *n.* any woody plant without a trunk but with several stems growing from the base [Old English *scrybb* 'shrubbery'. Ultimately, from an Indo-European word meaning 'to cut', which is also the ancestor of English *short.*]

shrub[2] /shrub/ *n.* a drink made with fruit juice, sugar, spices, and rum or other alcohol [Early 18thC. From Arabic *surb* 'a drink', which is also the ancestor of English *syrup.*]

shrubbery /shrúbbəri/ (*plural* **-ies**) *n.* **1.** PART OF GARDEN WITH SHRUBS a part of a garden where shrubs grow **2.** SHRUBS COLLECTIVELY shrubs considered collectively

shrubby /shrúbbi/ (**-bier, -biest**) *adj.* **1.** WITH SHRUBS having shrubs or covered with shrubs **2.** LIKE A SHRUB resembling a shrub in size or in having little or no trunk —**shrubbiness** *n.*

shrug /shrug/ *vti.* **(shrugs, shrugging, shrugged)** RAISE AND DROP SHOULDERS BRIEFLY to raise and drop the shoulders briefly, especially to indicate indifference or lack of knowledge ■ *n.* GESTURE OF RAISING AND DROPPING SHOULDERS a gesture of raising and dropping the shoulders briefly [14thC. Origin unknown.]

shrug off *vt.* **1.** DISMISS STH to reject or disregard sth as unimportant **2.** GET FREE OF STH to become free of sth such as a disease **3.** REMOVE CLOTHING to get out of clothing by wriggling

shrunk past tense, past participle of **shrink**

shrunken past participle of **shrink**

sht *abbr.* sheet

shtetl /shtétt'l/ (*plural* **shtetls** *or* **shtetlach** /shtét laak/), **schtetl** (*plural* **schtetls** *or* **schtetlech**) *n.* formerly, a small Jewish town or village in Eastern Europe [Mid-20thC. Via Yiddish, 'little town' from German *Stadt* 'town'.]

shtg. *abbr.* shortage

shtick /shtik/, **schtick, shtik** *n.* **1.** ENTERTAINER'S ROUTINE a comedian's or entertainer's act, routine, or gimmick (*informal*) **2.** SPECIAL ATTRIBUTE OF SB sth, e.g. an interest, talent, trait, job, or hobby, that especially characterizes sb (*slang*) [Mid-20thC. Via Yiddish 'a routine, a piece', from, ultimately, Old High German *stucki* 'piece'.]

shtoom /shtoŏm/, **schtoom, shtum, stumm** *adj.* quiet or silent (*informal*) [Mid-20thC. Via Yiddish from German *stumm.*]

shtuck /shtoŏk/ *n.* trouble resulting from a failing such as an error or misjudgment (*informal*) [Mid-20thC. Origin unknown.]

shuck /shuk/ *n.* **1.** *Can, US* OUTER COVERING OF GRAIN OR FRUIT the husk, pod, or shell of sth such as a nut, pea, or ear of corn **2.** OYSTER OR CLAM SHELL the shell of a clam or oyster ■ *vt.* **(shucks, shucking, shucked)** GET RID OF STH to get rid of or remove sth or throw sth off (*informal*) [Late 17thC. Origin unknown.] —**shucker** *n.*

WORD KEY: REGIONAL NOTE

Shuck, as both noun and verb, is a strong Southern marker that extends from Southern Delaware above Virginia into West Virginia. In the North, it identifies the northern reaches of South Midland territory, from Ohio to Iowa; in the South, the term is virtually unchallenged.

shucks /shuks/ *interj. Can, US* used to express disappointment, bashfulness, or irritation (*informal*) [Mid-19thC. From *shuck* 'sth worthless'.]

shudder /shúddər/ *vi.* **(-ders, -dering, -dered) 1.** SHIVER VIOLENTLY to shake or tremble uncontrollably from a reaction such as cold, fear, or disgust **2.** VIBRATE to vibrate rapidly ■ *n.* **1.** VIOLENT SHAKING MOVEMENT an uncontrolled shaking or trembling movement **2.** VIBRATION a rapid vibrating movement [12thC. Origin uncertain: probably from Middle Low German *schōderen* 'to keep on shuddering' or Middle Dutch *shūderen.*] —**shuddery** *adj.*

Shudra /sho-drə/ (*plural* **-dra**) *n. S Asia* an offensive term referring to a member of the lowest caste in the Hindu system of social stratification (*offensive*) ◊ **Dalit** [Mid-17thC. From Sanskrit *śūdraḥ.*]

shuffle /shúff'l/ *v.* **(-fles, -fling, -fled) 1.** *vi.* WALK WITHOUT LIFTING FEET to walk slowly without picking up the feet **2.** *vti.* DRAG FEET to move the feet without picking them up **3.** *vi.* MOVE AWKWARDLY to move in an awkward clumsy way **4.** *vi.* DANCE DANCE BY SHUFFLING THE FEET to slide the feet in a dance step **5.** *vt.* CHANGE WHERE STH IS LOCATED to move things around from one place to another **6.** *vt.* MIX THINGS UP to mix things together carelessly **7.** *vti.* CARDS REARRANGE ORDER OF PLAYING CARDS to rearrange playing cards randomly so the order is not known **8.** *vt.* AVOID OR HIDE STH to put sth aside in order to avoid or hide it **9.** *vi.* BEHAVE EVASIVELY to be deliberately evasive or shifty in addressing an issue ■ *n.* **1.** FOOT-DRAGGING WALK a slow walk while dragging the feet **2.** DANCE SLIDING DANCE STEP a dance or dance step in which the feet drag or slide on the floor **3.** CARDS REORDERING OF CARDS a random reordering of playing cards **4.** CARDS SB'S CHANCE TO SHUFFLE STH a player's turn to shuffle playing cards **5.** EVASION a deliberate evasion of an issue [Mid-16thC. Origin uncertain: perhaps from Low German *schuffeln* 'to walk with dragging feet'. Ultimately, from a prehistoric Germanic word that is also the ancestor of English *shove.*] —**shuffler** *n.*

shuffleboard /shúff'l bawrd/ *n.* **1.** GAME PLAYED WITH DISCS a game in which players use a long pronged cue to push discs along a smooth hard surface into numbered scoring areas **2.** SURFACE FOR SHUFFLEBOARD the surface on which shuffleboard is played [Mid-19thC. Alteration of *shovelboard*, an alteration of obsolete *shove-board*, an earlier name for the game.]

shufti /shoŏfti/ (*plural* **-ties**), **shufty** (*plural* **-ties**) *n.* a quick look or glance (*informal*) [Mid-20thC. From colloquial Arabic *šuftī* 'have you seen?', from *šāfa* 'to see'.]

shul /shool/, **schul** *n.* a synagogue [Late 19thC. Via Yiddish from German *Schule* 'school'. From its use as a place of learning.]

shun /shun/ **(shuns, shunning, shunned)** *vt.* to avoid sb or sth intentionally [Old English *scunian*, of unknown origin] —**shunner** *n.*

shunt /shunt/ *v.* **(shunts, shunting, shunted) 1.** *vt.* MOVE SB OR STH ELSEWHERE to move sb or sth to a different place, especially for convenience rather than fairness or kindness **2.** *vti.* RAIL CHANGE TRACKS to move rolling railway stock from one track to another, either by using an engine or by means of an automatic switch, especially when assembling trains **3.** *vt.* GET RID OF RESPONSIBILITY to avoid sth by ignoring it or shifting responsibility for it to sb else **4.** *vt.* MOTOR SPORTS CRASH CAR to crash a car (*informal*) **5.** *vt.* ELECTRON ENG DIVERT CURRENT to use an electrical device to divert electrical current from an instrument **6.** *vt.* SURGICALLY DIVERT FLOW to use an artificially created passage to redirect the circulation of blood or cerebrospinal fluid ■ *n.* **1.** DIVERSION OF STH a turning aside or means of turning sth aside **2.** MOTOR SPORTS MINOR CAR CRASH a minor collision between road vehicles in which one runs into the back of another at a relatively low speed (*informal*) **3.** RAIL SORTING OF RAILWAY VEHICLES the act of a locomotive pushing railway vehicles in the process of sorting them **4.** ELECTRON ENG DEVICE FOR DIVERTING ELECTRIC CURRENT a component in an electric circuit that is connected in parallel with an instrument and diverts the majority of current from the instrument **5.** BYPASS FOR BODILY FLUID a passage in the body that diverts the flow of blood or other bodily fluid form one channel to another, created either as a result of disease or injury or artificially by surgery. Artificial shunts are used to facilitate regular connection to a kidney dialysis machine or to relieve the pressure of cerebrospinal fluid on the brain in the condition of hydrocephalus. [13thC. Origin uncertain: perhaps from SHUN.]

shush /shoŏsh, shush/ *interj.* BE QUIET used to tell sb to be quiet ■ *vti.* **(shushes, shushing, shushed)** SILENCE SB to silence sb or to become silent (*informal*) [Early 20thC. Of imitative origin.]

shut /shut/ *v.* **(shuts, shutting, shut) 1.** *vti.* CLOSE OPENING to move sth or move into a position that blocks or covers an opening ○ *leaned over to shut the window* **2.** *vt.* STOP ACCESS OR EXIT to prevent entrance to or exit from sth, e.g. by locking doors ○ *Rising water levels meant that they had to shut the tunnel.* **3.** *vt.* FOLD PARTS CLOSED to close sth by bringing its covering or parts together ○ *had to shut her eyes against the light* **4.** *vt.* LOCK STH to secure sth with a lock or latch ○ *The gate had not been shut properly.* **5.** *vti.* STOP OPERATION to discontinue or cause sth to discontinue operation temporarily or permanently ○ *another factory shut because it was losing money* ■ *adj.* SECURED closed or fastened against entrance or exit ■ *n.* METALL CONNECTION REGION BETWEEN WELDED METAL PIECES the region of connection between pieces of metal that are welded together [Old English *scyttan*. Ultimately, from a prehistoric Germanic word that is also the ancestor of English *shoot*. From the sense of shooting a bolt across a door to fasten it.]

shut down *v.* **1.** *vti.* STOP OPERATION to cease or cause sth to cease operation or activity **2.** *vt.* PHYS CUT REACTOR OUTPUT to reduce the power output of a nuclear reactor by maintaining it at its lowest possible level

shut in *vt.* to confine or enclose sb or sth

shut off *v.* **1.** *vti.* STOP STH WORKING to stop operating or to cause sth to stop operating **2.** *vt.* CUT OFF FLOW to stop the passage, flow, or supply of sth **3.** *vt.* BLOCK STH OFF to impede the flow or progress of sth **4.** *vt.* ISOLATE SB to put sb or sth into a state of isolation

shut out /shút owt/ *vt.* **1.** EXCLUDE SB to exclude sb or sth **2.** STOP SB ENTERING to prevent sb or sth from entering a place **3.** HIDE STH to hide sth from sight **4.** *Can, US* SPORTS KEEP SB FROM SCORING to prevent an opponent from scoring in a game

shut up *v.* **1.** *vi.* STOP TALKING to be quiet or stop talking (*informal*) ○ *I shut up before saying something I would regret.* **2.** *vt.* SILENCE SB to cause sb to be quiet or stop talking (*informal*) ○ *She shot me a look that shut me up instantly.* **3.** *vt.* CONFINE SB to confine or imprison sb or sth ○ *She shut the dog up in the pen.* **4.** *vt.* CLOSE STH to close or prevent entrance to sth ○ *The building is all shut up.*

shutdown /shút down/ *n.* **1.** BUSINESS CLOSING the cessation or suspension of activities at a business, factory, or plant **2.** MAINTENANCE LEVEL OF REACTOR POWER the reduction of power in a nuclear reactor by maintaining the core at the lowest level possible

Shute /shoot/, **Nevil** (1899–1960) British novelist and aeronautical engineer. His experiences during World War II inspired many of his novels. Others, including *A Town Like Alice* (1950), are set in Australia. Real name **Nevil Shute Norway**

shuteye /shút ī/ *n.* a short sleep (*informal*)

shut-off *n.* **1.** DEVICE THAT STOPS STH WORKING a device, usually a valve, that shuts sth off **2.** TEMPORARY STOP an interruption or stoppage, e.g. in flow or supply

shutout *n.* **1.** = **lockout** *n.* **2.** *Can, US* SPORTS GAME SCORELESS ON ONE SIDE a game in which one team does not score

shutter /shúttər/ *n.* **1.** DOOR OR WINDOW COVER a hinged cover for a door or window, often with louvres and usually fitted in pairs **2.** PHOTOGRAPHY CAMERA DEVICE a mechanical part of a camera that opens and closes the lens aperture to expose the film or plate to light ■ *vt.* **(-ters, -tering, -tered) 1.** CLOSE STH USING SHUTTERS to close or protect sth by means of shutters **2. FIT STH WITH SHUTTERS** to equip sth with shutters

shuttering /shúttəring/ n. BUILDING = **formwork**

shuttle /shútt'l/ n. **1. WEAVING DEVICE** a device in weaving that holds the weft thread and is used to pass it between the warp threads **2. SPINDLE OR BOBBIN HOLDING THREAD** a thread holder, e.g. in tatting or netting or for the lower thread in a sewing machine **3. ROUTE TAKEN OR VEHICLE USED** the route taken or the aircraft, bus, or train used to travel frequently between two places, often relatively near each other **4. =** space shuttle **5. GOING BACK AND FORTH** frequent travel by vehicle between two places **6. RACKET GAMES** = **shuttlecock** ■ vti. (-tles, -tling, -tled) **1. GO BACK AND FORTH** to move or cause sb or sth to move between two places frequently **2. TRANSP GO BY SHUTTLE** to transport sb or sth or to be transported by a shuttle [Old English scytel 'arrow, dart'. Ultimately, from a prehistoric Germanic word meaning 'to project', which is also the ancestor of English shoot.]

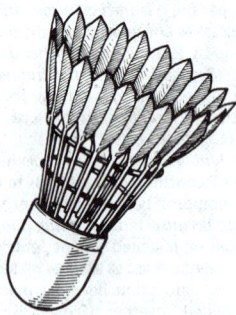

Shuttlecock

shuttlecock /shútt'l kok/ n. **1. OBJECT HIT IN BADMINTON** a small rounded piece of cork or rubber attached to a cone of feathers that is hit back and forth in badminton and in the old game of battledore **2. SUBJECT OF ARGUMENT** sth that is continually argued about by two opposing sides ○ *The sovereignty of the island became a shuttlecock between the two countries.* ■ vt. (-cocks, -cocking, -cocked) **SEND STH BACK AND FORTH** to toss or send sth back and forth [Early 16thC. *Shuttle* probably from its going back and forth, like the shuttle in a loom; *cock* from the feathers, like a bird's crest.]

shuttlecraft /shútt'l kraaft/ (plural **-craft**) n. a reusable spacecraft for carrying astronauts or material between Earth and space or between objects in space

shuttle diplomacy n. diplomatic negotiations carried on between countries by a mediator who travels back and forth between the countries

shwa n. = **schwa**

shy[1] /shī/ adj. (**shier, shiest**) **1. UNCOMFORTABLE WITH OTHERS** reserved, diffident, and uncomfortable in the company of others ○ *She was always shy at parties.* **2. TIMID** easily frightened ○ *The deer were shy and ran when we tried to approach them.* **3. CAUTIOUS** unwilling to trust or put confidence in sb or sth ○ *The children were shy of their new classmates.* **4. RELUCTANT** fearful of making a commitment ○ *Don't be shy of speaking your mind.* **5. DISLIKING** showing a disinclination for sth (*usually used in combination*) ○ *workshy* **6. SHORT OF STH** short of the full or a particular amount ○ *We are £100 shy of the down payment.* **7. BIOL NOT REPRODUCING EASILY** used to describe plants and animals that do not breed readily or freely ■ vi. (**shies, shying, shied**) **1. MOVE SUDDENLY** to move suddenly in fright or alarm ○ *That horse shies at anything in the path.* **2. STAY AWAY** to avoid or evade sth ○ *He always shies away from public speaking.* ■ n. (plural **shies**) **SUDDEN MOVE** a sudden movement in fright or alarm [Old English scéoh. From a prehistoric Germanic base that is also the ancestor of English eschew and skew.] —**shyer** n. —**shyly** adv. —**shyness** n.

shy[2] /shī/ vt. (**shies, shying, shied**) **THROW STH** to toss sth quickly and suddenly ■ n. (plural **shies**) **1. QUICK THROW** a quick sudden throw of sth **2. VERBAL ATTACK** a rude or insulting remark **3. ATTEMPT** an attempt made to do or get sth (*informal*) ○ *We'll have a shy at it.* [Late 18thC. Origin uncertain: perhaps from SHY[1], applied

to timid cockerels, from the custom of throwing sticks at them to make them fight.] —**shyer** n.

shylock /shí lok/ n. a ruthless and demanding money-lender or creditor [Late 18thC. Named after *Shylock*, a moneylender in Shakespeare's play *The Merchant of Venice*.]

shyster /shístər/ n. US an unscrupulous person, especially a lawyer or political representative (*slang insult*) [Mid-19thC. Origin uncertain: perhaps from the name *Scheuster*, a New York lawyer in the 1840s known for his unethical methods. Alternatively from German *Scheisser* 'bastard', formed from *Scheisse* 'excrement'.]

si /see/ n. MUSIC = **te** [Early 18thC. From the initial letters of Latin *Sancte Iohannes* 'St John', which are the words sung to this note in the hymn for St John's day.]

Si symbol. silicon

SI abbr. **1.** NZ South Island **2.** International System of Units [French *Système International (d'Unités)*]

sial /sí əl/ n. a term used in the past for rocks rich in silicon and aluminium that form the crust of the continental masses [Early 20thC. A blend of *silicon* and *aluminium*.] —**sialic** /sí állik/ adj.

sialagogue /sí ál ə gog/, **sialogogue** n. a drug or agent that stimulates the flow of saliva —**sialagogic** /sí ə góg ik/ adj.

sialic acid /sí állik-/ n. an amino acid found in animal blood and tissues

Sialkot /si álkot/ town in Punjab Province, north-eastern Pakistan, situated about 97 km/60 mi. north of Lahore. Population: 302,009 (1981).

sialogogue /sí álə gog/ n. = **sialagogue**

sialoid /sí ə loyd/ adj. resembling saliva

Siam /sī ám/ former name for **Thailand**

Siam, Gulf of former name for **Thailand, Gulf of**

siamang /see ə mang/ n. the largest species of gibbon, found in Sumatra and Malaysia. It has a large throat sac that inflates during calls and webbing between its second and third toes. Latin name: *Hylobates syndactylus*. [Early 19thC. From Malay.]

Siamese /sí ə meez/ adj. PEOPLES = **Thai** (*dated*) ■ n. (plural **-mese**) **1. PEOPLES** = **Thai** (*dated*) **2. =** Siamese **cat** [Late 17thC. The original meaning is 'of Siam'.]

Siamese cat

Siamese cat n. a short-haired domestic cat with blue eyes and a long cream-coloured body with dark ears, paws, face, and tail, belonging to a breed that originated in Thailand (formerly Siam) [Named after its place of origin]

Siamese fighting fish n. a brightly coloured long-finned freshwater fish, native to Thailand and Malaysia. The male of this popular aquarium fish is very aggressive. Latin name: *Betta splendens*.

Siamese twins npl. a term used mainly in the past for twins physically joined together at birth [Named after two twins, Chang and Eng (1811–74), born in Siam (Thailand), who were physically joined together near the waist at birth]

sib /sib/ n. **1. BROTHER OR SISTER** a brother or sister **2. GENETICS INDIVIDUAL WITH SAME PARENTS AS ANOTHER** an individual that has the same parents as another individual **3. ANTHROP GROUP WITH SINGLE COMMON ANCESTOR** a group of people who trace their descent lineally from a single real or presumed ancestor ■ **sibs** npl. **WIDER FAMILY** members of an extended family considered as a group (*takes a plural verb*) ■ adj.

CLOSELY RELATED with the same parents or closely related [Old English *sib(b)*, of unknown origin] —**sibship** n.

SIB abbr. Securities and Investments Board

Sib. abbr. **1.** Siberia **2.** Siberian

AKG London

Jean Sibelius

Sibelius /si báyli əss/, **Jean** (1865–1957) Finnish composer. One of the leading symphonic composers of the 20th century, his works are much influenced by the culture and landscape of his native Finland. Full name **Jean Julius Christian Sibelius**

Siberia /sī beeri ə/ vast region of eastern Russia, extending from the Ural Mountains in the west to the Pacific Ocean in the east, and from the Arctic Ocean in the north, to China, Mongolia, and Kazakhstan in the south. Much of it is frozen for over half the year. Sparsely populated, it was used during Soviet rule (1917–91) as a place of exile, and now has no administrative significance. —**Siberian** /sī beeri ən/ n., adj.

sibilant /síbbilənt/ adj. **1. PRONOUNCED WITH HISSING SOUND** used to describe consonants that are pronounced with a hissing sound **2. PRODUCING HISSING SOUND** producing a hissing sound ○ *the sibilant sound of air escaping from a tyre* ■ n. SIBILANT CONSONANT a sibilant consonant [Mid-17thC. From the present participle stem of Latin *sibilare* 'to hiss', thought to be imitative of the sound.] —**sibilance** n. —**sibilantly** adv.

sibilate /síbbi layt/ (**-lates, -lating, -lated**) vti. to pronounce sounds with a hiss [Mid-17thC. From the past participle stem of Latin *sibilare* (see SIBILANT).]

sibling /síbbling/ n. **1. BROTHER OR SISTER** a brother or sister (*often used before a noun*) **2. ANTHROP MEMBER OF SIB** a member of a group of people who trace their descent from a single real or presumed ancestor [Old English. Formed from *sib(b)* (see SIB). The word disappeared by the end of the 15thC and was re-introduced by anthropologists in the early 20thC.]

sibling species n. a species that closely resembles another in appearance and other characteristics but cannot interbreed with it

sibyl /síbbil, síbb'l/ n. **1. GREEK OR ROMAN PROPHET** a woman of ancient Greece and Rome believed to be an oracle or a prophet **2. FORTUNETELLER** a woman prophet or fortuneteller [13thC. Directly or via Old French *Sibile* from Latin *Sibylla*, which came from Greek *Sibulla*.] —**sibyllic** /si bíllik/ adj. —**sybilline** adj.

sic[1] /sik/ adv. thus or so, used within brackets to indicate that what precedes it is written intentionally or is copied verbatim from the original, even if it appears to be a mistake [Late 19thC. From Latin.] ◇ **sic passim** to show that a particular word or term is used in the same form throughout a printed work (*formal*) ◇ **sic transit gloria mundi** thus passes the glory of the world, used, e.g. when a distinguished person dies or an important era comes to an end

sic[2] /sik/ (**sics, siccing** or **sicking, sicced** or **sicked**), **sick** vt. **1. ATTACK SB** to attack sb physically, usually used as a command to a dog **2. INCITE SB TO ATTACK** to urge a person or animal, especially a dog, to attack sb physically [Mid-19thC. Originally a dialect form of SEEK.]

Sic. abbr. **1.** Sicilian **2.** Sicily

siccar /síkər/, **sicker** adj. Scotland free from doubt or uncertainty [Old English *sicor*. Via prehistoric Germanic from, ultimately, Latin *securus* 'secure' (source of English *secure* and *sure*).]

siccative /síkətiv/ *n.* **DRYING AGENT** a substance added to paints and other liquids to speed drying ■ *adj.* **ABSORBENT** absorbing moisture to promote drying [15thC. From late Latin *siccativus*, from Latin *siccare* 'to dry'.]

sice *n.* = **syce**

Sichuan /sŏ cwaản/ province of southern China bordered by Qinghai, Gansu, Shaanxi, Hubei, Hunan, Guizhou, Yunnan, and Tibet. Capital: Chengdu. Population: 112,140,000 (1994). Area: 569,000 sq. km/219,691 sq. mi.

siciliano /si sílli áanō/ (*plural* **-nos**), **siciliana** /-nə/ *n.* **1.** **SICILIAN DANCE** an old Sicilian folk dance **2.** **MUSIC FOR DANCING** a piece of music for a siciliano, in a minor key with six or twelve beats to the bar [Early 18thC. From Italian, literally 'Sicilian'.]

Sicily /síssəli/ the largest island in the Mediterranean Sea, in southern Italy. Capital: Palermo. Population: 5,082,697 (1995). Area: 25,460 sq. km/9,830 sq. mi. — **Sicilian** /si sílli ən/ *n., adj.*

sick[1] /sik/ *adj.* **1.** **ILL** affected by an illness **2.** **RELATING TO ILLNESS** relating to illness or to people who are ill ○ *sick leave* **3.** **LIKELY TO VOMIT** feeling on the point of vomiting **4.** **OFFENSIVE TERM** an offensive term referring to sb thought to have a psychiatric disorder that makes him or her dangerous to others **5.** **IN BAD TASTE** dealing with subjects regarded by most people as bizarre, gruesome, or otherwise unsuitable for lighthearted treatment (*informal*) **6.** **DISTRESSED** spiritually or emotionally distraught ○ *sick with anxiety* **7.** **VERY BORED WITH STH** utterly tired of sth because of having had too much of it ○ *I am sick of watching television.* **8.** **YEARNING** feeling a deep or passionate longing for sth or sb **9.** **DISGUSTED** filled with disgust or. repulsion ○ *His rudeness makes me sick.* **10.** **IMPAIRED** in need of repair ○ *a sick economy* **11.** **SUGGESTING ILLNESS** pale and unhealthy looking **12.** AGRIC **UNPRODUCTIVE** unable to produce a profitable crop ○ *a sick field* **13.** MED **FORMING UNHEALTHY ENVIRONMENT** used to describe a building or other location that is seen as an unhealthy environment for people ○ *a sick office building* ■ *n.* **1.** **ILL PEOPLE** people who are ill **2.** **VOMIT** vomited stomach contents (*informal*) [Old English *sēoc*, ultimately of unknown origin]

--- **WORD KEY: USAGE** ---

See Usage note at *ill*.

sick up *vti.* to vomit (*informal*)

sick[2] *vt.* = **sic**[2]

sickbag /sík bag/ *n.* a bag made of stiff paper, used for vomiting into by sb who is travel-sick, e.g. on an aircraft (*informal*)

sickbay /sík bay/ *n.* **1.** **SHIP'S HOSPITAL** a hospital and dispensary on a ship **2.** **TREATMENT FACILITY** a place for treating the sick or injured

sickbed /sík bed/ *n.* a bed on which a sick person lies

sick building syndrome *n.* a group of symptoms typically including headaches and respiratory problems that affect workers in usually new or re-modelled office buildings and are attributed to toxic building materials or poor ventilation

sick call *n.* US = **sick parade**

sicken /síkən/ (**-ens**, **-ening**, **-ened**) *vti.* **1.** **MAKE OR BECOME NAUSEOUS** to become ill or nauseous, or make sb feel ill or nauseous ○ *I sicken at the sight of blood.* **2.** **MAKE OR FEEL DISGUSTED** to feel disgust for sth or sb, or inspire disgust in sb **3.** **MAKE OR BECOME BORED** to grow weary of sb or sth, or make sb weary ○ *We soon sickened of their chatter.*

sickener /síkənər/ *n.* **1.** **POISONOUS MUSHROOM** a widely distributed poisonous mushroom with a fragile red cap. Latin name: *Russula emetica* and *Russula fragilis.* **2.** **SEVERE SETBACK** sth that causes great disappointment or discouragement (*informal*) [Early 19thC. Originally in the meaning 'nauseating thing'.]

sickening /síkəning/ *adj.* **1.** **DISGUSTING** inspiring feelings of disgust or repulsion ○ *sickening cruelty* **2.** **VERY DISAPPOINTING** extremely disappointing or annoying (*informal*) **3.** **CAUSING ILLNESS** bringing on illness —**sickeningly** *adv.*

sicker *adj.* Scotland = **siccar**

sick headache *n.* a headache accompanied by feelings of nausea

sickie /síki/ *n.* **1.** **DAY OFF WORK** a day of sick leave, especially one taken for reasons other than genuine sickness (*informal*) **2.** *US* = **sicko** (*offensive*)

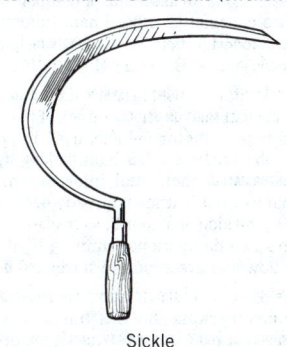

Sickle

sickle /sík'l/ *n.* **1.** **TOOL FOR CUTTING GRASS** a short-handled implement with a curved blade for cutting tall grass or grain **2.** **BLADES OF FARM IMPLEMENT** the cutting mechanism of a combine, reaper, or mower ■ *v.* (**-les**, **-ling**, **-led**) **1.** *vt.* **CUT STH WITH SICKLE** to cut sth using a sickle **2.** *vti.* **DEFORM RED BLOOD CELL** to change a red blood cell into a sickle cell, or become a sickle cell ■ *adj.* **CURVED** curved in shape like a sickle (*literary*) [Old English *sicol.* Via prehistoric Germanic from Latin *secula*, from *secare* 'to cut' (source of English *section* and *insect*).]

sickle leave *n.* absence from work for reasons of illness

sicklebill /sík'l bil/ *n.* a name given to various birds that have long curved bills, e.g. the curlew and the honeycreeper

sickle cell *n.* an abnormal red blood cell that is crescent-shaped as a result of an inherited defect in the cell's haemoglobin

sickle-cell anaemia *n.* a chronic hereditary form of anaemia that occurs mainly in people of African descent. It is caused by a gene inherited from both parents.

sickle cell trait *n.* a hereditary condition of the blood in which some red cells become sickle-shaped, but not enough cells to cause anaemia. This trait, which usually gives some resistance to malaria, occurs when the responsible gene is inherited from only one parent.

sickle feather *n.* a long curving feather in the tail of a cock

sickle medick *n.* a small plant with three-lobed leaves, yellow flowers, and curved pods. It is native to Europe and Asia. Latin name: *Medicago falcata.*

sick list *n.* a list of people who are sick, especially in the military

sickly /síkli/ *adj.* (**-lier**, **-liest**) **1.** **OFTEN ILL** unhealthy or tending to be frequently ill ○ *a sickly child* **2.** **FROM ILLNESS** produced by or related to illness ○ *a sickly complexion* **3.** **BRINGING ILLNESS** causing or conducive to illness ○ *a sickly climate* **4.** **CAUSING DISGUST** provoking feelings of disgust or nausea ○ *a sickly smell* **5.** **FEEBLE** lacking in strength or intensity **6.** **TOO SENTIMENTAL** sentimental to a degree that inspires disgust or scorn ○ *a sickly display of affection* ■ *adv.* **FEEBLY** in a weak or feeble way —**sickliness** *n.*

sickly-sweet *adj.* excessively sweet or sentimental ○ *a sickly-sweet smile*

sickness /síknəss/ *n.* **1.** **ILLNESS** an illness or a disease **2.** **NAUSEA** feelings of nausea **3.** **IMPAIRED CONDITION** an unsound or corrupt condition [Old English]

sickness benefit *n.* **1.** **GOVERNMENT PAYMENT** a weekly payment made by the government to sb who is off work through illness for more than three days and less than six months **2.** *NZ* **PAYMENT COMPENSATING FOR MEDICAL CONDITION** a payment made by a government department to sb who is unable to work owing to a medical condition

sick note *n.* a certification given by an employee to an employer to state that an absence from work for

more than four days is due to illness. US term **excuse** *n.* 4

sicko /síkō/ (*plural* **-os**), **sickie** *n.* an offensive term referring to sb though to have a psychiatric disorder that makes him or her dangerous to others (*offensive*)

sick-out *n.* *US, Carib* an organized absence from work by employees on the pretext of illness in an effort to force an employer to grant demands

sick parade *n.* a daily lineup or formation for military personnel in need of medical attention, or the scheduled time at which they may receive medical attention. US term **sick call**

sick pay *n.* wages paid to an employee who is absent from work owing to illness

sickroom /sík room, -rŏŏm/ *n.* a room to which an ill person is confined

Sarah Siddons

Siddons /sídd'nz/, **Sarah** (1755–1831) British actor. An acclaimed tragic stage actor, she was noted particularly for her role as Lady Macbeth. Born **Sarah Kemble**

siddur /síddər/ (*plural* **-durim** /si d óorim/ *or* **-durs**) *n.* a Jewish daily and Sabbath prayer book [Mid-19thC. From Hebrew *siddūr*, literally 'arrangement, order'.]

side /sīd/ *n.* **1.** **PERIMETER OF FIGURE** a line segment that forms the perimeter of a plane geometric figure ○ *A square has four sides.* **2.** **SURFACE OF FIGURE** a surface of a solid geometric figure ○ *A cube has six sides.* **3.** **SURFACE OF STH FLAT** either of the two surfaces of a flat object **4.** **LEFT OR RIGHT OF STH** the left or right of an object as opposed to the top, bottom, front, or back **5.** **EITHER DIVISION** either of two parts or areas into which sth can be divided relative to the observer ○ *The playing field is on the far side of the park.* **6.** **PLACE RELATIVE TO CENTRE** a location, place, or direction relative to a central point ○ *We live on the east side of the city.* **7.** **PLACE SEPARATED BY BARRIER** a place or area on either side of a barrier or boundary ○ *We live on the south side of the river.* **8.** **VERTICAL SURFACE** a vertical surface of sth ○ *the side of a building* **9.** **EDGE** the area at the edge of sth ○ *the side of the road* **10.** **HALF OF BODY** either half of the body of an animal or person, especially the area of a person's body between the shoulder and the hip ○ *complaining of a pain in her side* **11.** **HALF OF CARCASS** half of a meat carcass ○ *a side of pork* **12.** **NEARBY POSITION** the place next to sb or sth ○ *Come and stand at my side.* **13.** **PARTY IN CONTEST** any one of two or more opposing individuals, teams, groups, or factions **14.** **OPINION IN A DISPUTE** any one of the positions or opinions held in a dispute **15.** **SUPPORTERS** the group of people who support a particular party in a dispute ○ *I'm on your side.* **16.** **ASPECT** an aspect or view of an issue or event ○ *the funny side of a situation* **17.** **PART OF FAMILY** a line of descent ○ *He gets his red hair from his father's side.* **18.** **TELEVISION CHANNEL** a television channel (*dated informal*) ○ *What's on the other side?* **19.** **ARROGANCE** an air of pretentiousness, arrogance, or superiority (*informal*) ○ *You wouldn't think he was a high court judge – there's no side to him.* **20.** **CUE GAMES** **SPIN** spin put on a ball by striking it off-centre with the cue. US term **English** ■ *adj.* **1.** **AT THE SIDE** situated at or on a side ○ *The side door is open.* **2.** **FROM THE SIDE** directed to or from the side ○ *a side blow* **3.** **INCIDENTAL** having only minor or subsidiary importance ○ *a side issue* ■ *v.* (**sides**, **siding**, **sided**) **1.** *vi.* **ALIGN WITH OR AGAINST SB** to align with or against one or other of the individuals, teams, groups, or factions in a contest or dispute

○ *We all sided with the home team.* **2.** *vt.* US, Can FIT BUILDING WITH OUTER WALLS to fit the boards (**siding**) that form the outer skin of a building ○ *side the barn* [Old English *síde*. From a prehistoric Germanic word, of uncertain origin: probably formed from an adjective meaning 'long, deep, low'.] ◇ **get on the right side of sb**, **keep on the right side of sb** to get into or keep in sb's favour ○ **get on the wrong side of sb** to make yourself disliked by sb ◇ **let the side down** to disappoint associates or supporters by not doing as well as expected or by behaving in a way that causes them shame or embarrassment ◇ **on the side 1.** illegally or secretly **2.** in addition to a main job or activity ◇ **on one side, to one side** out of the focus of attention for the moment, to be dealt with later ◇ **side by side** close beside each other ◇ **take sides** to support one person or group against another ◇ **this side of** almost or just short of

side arm *n.* a weapon such as a pistol that is worn at the waist, usually on a belt

sideband /síd band/ *n.* the band of frequencies on either side of the carrier frequency, produced by modulation of a carrier wave

sideboard /síd bawrd/ *n.* a piece of dining room furniture with a flat top and drawers and cupboards to store tableware and linens [14thC. The meaning evolved from 'side table' via 'dining-room table'.]

sideboards /síd bawrdz/ *npl.* hair grown down the side of a man's face in front of his ears. US term **sideburns**

sideburns /síd burnz/ *npl.* US = **sideboards** [Late 19thC. Alteration of *burnsides*, named after the American General Ambrose *Burnside* (1824–81), who wore them.]

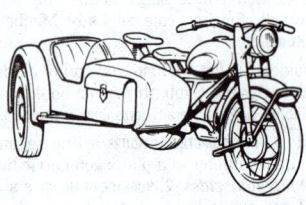

Sidecar

sidecar /síd kaar/ *n.* **1.** VEHICLE ATTACHED TO MOTORCYCLE a one-wheeled passenger vehicle attached to the side of a motorcycle **2.** COCKTAIL a cocktail of brandy, orange liqueur, and lemon juice [Late 19thC. Originally in the meaning 'carriage with lengthwise seats'.]

side chain *n.* a group of atoms attached to an atom in a principal chain or to a ring in a molecule

side deal *n.* a mutually beneficial agreement made between two people aside from an agreement negotiated by them on behalf of the parties or organizations they represent

side dish *n.* accompanying food, e.g. vegetables or salad, served with the main dish of a meal

side-dress *vt.* to fertilize plants by applying nutrients to the soil near the roots

side-dressing *n.* **1.** FERTILIZER ADDED AT ROOTS fertilizer that is put into the soil near the roots of a growing crop **2.** USE OF SIDE-DRESSING the adding of fertilizer near the roots of growing crops

side drum *n.* = **snare drum** [From its place at the drummer's side]

side effect *n.* **1.** SECONDARY MEDICAL EFFECT an undesirable secondary effect of a drug or other form of medical treatment **2.** SECONDARY EFFECT a usually undesirable secondary effect produced by sth

sidefoot /síd foot/ (**sidefoots, sidefooting, sidefooted**) *vt.* to kick a football with the side of the foot (*informal*) ○ *He coolly rounded the keeper and sidefooted the ball into the net.*

side-glance *n.* **1.** SIDEWAYS GLANCE a glance directed sideways **2.** INDIRECT REFERENCE a casual or indirect reference or allusion

side-impact *adj.* relating to or designed to protect sb from an impact from the side

side issue *n.* a matter that tends to distract from the important issue

sidekick /síd kik/ *n.* an associate or companion who is sometimes considered subordinate (*informal*) [Early 20thC. Back-formation from 'side-kicker', which was coined by the American writer O. Henry (1862–1910).]

sidelight /síd līt/ *n.* **1.** LIGHT FROM SIDE light coming from the side **2.** SMALL LIGHT ON VEHICLE either of two small or faint lights on a motor vehicle, used in poor light but not total darkness. US term **parking light 3.** INCIDENTAL INFORMATION incidental information, usually additional to what is known already **4.** SIDE WINDOW a window at the side of a door **5.** NAUT SHIP'S LIGHT either of a ship's two navigational running lights, red on the port bow and green on the starboard bow

sideline /síd līn/ *n.* **1.** SPORTS FIELD'S SIDE BOUNDARY either of two lines marking the side limits of a playing field **2.** SUPPLEMENTARY SOURCE OF INCOME a job or activity that supplements income from a primary job ○ *He does television repairs as a sideline.* **3.** COMM ADDITIONAL RANGE OF MERCHANDISE a supplementary line of merchandise ■ **sidelines** *npl.* **1.** SPORTS AREA OF A PLAYING FIELD the area of a playing field outside the lines marking its limits **2.** PLACE FOR UNINVOLVED PEOPLE a place for people who are not involved in sth, or the condition of being uninvolved ○ *I'm strictly on the sidelines in this affair.* ■ *vt.* (**-lines, -lining, -lined**) EXCLUDE SB to keep sb from participating in an activity

sidelong /síd long/ *adj.* **1.** TO THE SIDE directed to the side **2.** SLOPING slanting to one side **3.** INDIRECT not direct or straightforward ○ *a sidelong remark* ■ *adv.* OBLIQUELY towards an area that lies at the side

sideman /síd mən/ (*plural* **-men** /-mən/) *n.* a member of a jazz or dance band who is neither the leader nor a soloist

side order *n.* a portion of food ordered as an accompaniment to the main dish in a restaurant or other food outlet

sider- *prefix.* = **sidero-** (used before vowels)

sidereal /sī déeri əl/ *adj.* relating to the stars, especially measured with reference to the apparent motion of the stars [Mid-17thC. Directly or via French from Latin *sidereus*, from *sidus* 'star'.]

sidereal day *n.* the time it takes for the Earth to make one complete revolution in relation to a given star, equal to 23 hours, 56 minutes, 4.1 seconds

sidereal hour *n.* a 24th part of a sidereal day

sidereal month *n.* the time it takes for the Moon to make one revolution around the Earth in relation to a given star, equal to 27 days, 7 hours, 43 minutes, 4.5 seconds

sidereal time *n.* time measured by the daily rotation of the Earth in relation to a given star

sidereal year *n.* the time it takes the Earth to make one revolution around the Sun with reference to fixed stars, equal to 365 days, 6 hours, 9 minutes, 9.5 seconds

siderite /síde rīt/ *n.* **1.** ORE OF IRON a yellow-brown mineral that is an important source of iron. It consists mainly of ferrous carbonate and is widespread in sedimentary rock. Formula: $FeCO_3$. **2.** METEORITE a meteorite consisting of dense metallic masses composed chiefly of iron alloyed with nickel [Late 18thC. Coined from Greek *sidēros* 'iron' + -ITE.] —**sideritic** /síde ríttik/ *adj.*

sidero- *prefix.* iron ○ *siderolite* [From Greeek *sidēros* 'iron']

sideroad /síd rōd/ *n.* a secondary road off the main road

siderolite /sídde līt/ *n.* a meteorite that is made up of approximately equal amounts of iron and stone

siderophilin /sídde róffəlin/ *n.* = **transferrin**

siderosis /sídde róssiss/ *n.* **1.** LUNG DISEASE a chronic lung disease caused by inhaling dust particles of iron or other metals. It is a form of pneumoconiosis. **2.** IRON ACCUMULATION IN SB'S BODY an abnormal accumulation of iron in the blood and tissues — **siderotic** /sídde róttik/ *adj.*

siderostat /síddərə stat/ *n.* an astronomical instrument consisting of a plane mirror driven by a clock mechanism that keeps a celestial object within the same field of view of a telescope [Mid-19thC. Coined from *sidero-*, from the Latin stem *sider-* 'star' + -STAT.] —**siderostatic** /síddərə státtik/ *adj.*

sidesaddle /síd sad'l/ *n.* WOMEN'S RIDING SADDLE a saddle designed for women wearing long skirts so that the rider sits with both legs on the same side of the horse ■ *adv.* WITH LEGS ON ONE SIDE seated with both legs on the same side of a horse

sideshow /síd shō/ *n.* **1.** SMALLER SHOW a minor attraction offered in addition to the main entertainment at a circus or fair **2.** MINOR EVENT a subordinate event or spectacle

sideslip /síd slip/ *vi.* (**-slips, -slipping, -slipped**) **1.** SLIDE SIDEWAYS to skid or slide sideways **2.** AIR SLIP SIDEWAYS IN AEROPLANE to move sideways and downwards while banking steeply in an aeroplane **3.** SKIING SLIDE SIDEWAYS DOWN SLOPE to slide at an angle down a slope ■ *n.* **1.** SIDEWAYS SKID a skid sideways ○ *The car went into a sideslip.* **2.** AIR SIDEWAYS MOVEMENT OF AEROPLANE a sideways and downward movement made by a steeply banking aircraft **3.** SKIING ANGLED SLIDE DOWN SLOPE a sideways slide at an angle down a slope

sidesman /síd zmən/ (*plural* **-men** /-mən/) *n.* in the Church of England, an assistant to the parish churchwarden [Mid-17thC. From the idea of being at the side of (and therefore helping) the churchwarden.]

sidesperson /síd z purss'n/ (*plural* **-people** /-peep'l/ *or* **-persons**) *n.* = **sidesman**

sidesplitting /síd splitting/ *adj.* extremely funny [The idea is of bursting with laughter] —**sidesplittingly** *adv.*

—————— WORD KEY: SYNONYMS ——————
See Synonyms at **funny**.

sidestep /síd step/ *vti.* (**-steps, -stepping, -stepped**) **1.** STEP ASIDE to step aside or out of the way of sb or sth ○ *I sidestepped to avoid the running children.* **2.** EVADE STH to avoid saying or discussing sth ○ *good at sidestepping awkward questions* ■ *n.* SIDEWAYS MOVEMENT a movement to one side —**sidestepper** *n.*

side street *n.* a secondary street, often off a main street

sidestroke /síd strōk/ *n.* a swimming stroke performed on the side by thrusting the arms alternately forward and downward while doing a scissors kick

sideswipe /síd swīp/ *n.* **1.** GLANCING BLOW a glancing blow from or on the side **2.** JIBE a critical or insulting remark made in passing (*informal*) ○ *They were all taking sideswipes at my golfing skills.* ■ *vt.* (**-swipes, -swiping, -swiped**) STRIKE SIDE OF STH to strike a glancing blow to or from the side of sth ○ *sideswiped a car in the car park* —**sideswiper** *n.*

side tone *n.* the reproduction of a speaker's voice in a telephone earpiece so that both the speaker's and the other person's voices can be heard in the earpiece

sidetrack /síd trak/ *vt.* (**-tracks, -tracking, -tracked**) DISTRACT SB to divert sb from the original subject or activity ○ *They were sidetracked from their chores when their friends arrived.* ■ *n.* CAUSE OF DIVERSION sth that causes a diversion from the original subject or activity [Mid-19thC. Originally in the meaning 'moving trains off the main line'.]

sidewalk /síd wawk/ *n.* US = **pavement**

sidewall /síd wawl/ *n.* the side surface of a vehicle's tyre, between the edge of the tread and the rim [15thC. Originally any wall forming the side of a structure.]

sideward /síd wərd/ *adj.* AT SIDE towards one side or at one side ■ *adv.* **sideward, sidewards** TOWARDS SIDE towards one side

sideways /síd wayz/ *adj., adv.* **1.** TO ONE SIDE to or towards one side ○ *a sideways jump* **2.** FROM SIDE from one side ○ *a sideways approach* **3.** WITH SIDE FACING FRONT with or into a position with the side towards the front ○ *See if it will fit in sideways.* **4.** INTO NEW BUT EQUAL POSITION into a job or position with the same rank or status as previously held ○ *not a promotion but more of a sideways move into another department*

a at; aa father; aw all; ay day; air hair; ə about, edible, item, common, circus; e egg; ee eel; hw when; i it, happy; ī ice; 'l apple; 'm rhythm; 'n fashion; o odd; ō open; oo good; oo pool; ow owl; oy oil; th thin; th this; u up; ur urge;

sidewheel /sĭd´weel/ n. PADDLE WHEEL either of the paddle wheels on the sides of a sidewheeler ■ adj. WITH PADDLE WHEELS propelled by a paddle wheel on each side ○ a sidewheel steamboat

sidewheeler /sĭd´weelər/ n. a steamboat driven by a paddle wheel on each side

side whiskers npl. sideboards, especially long ones

sidewinder /sĭd´wĭndər/ n. 1. ZOOL RATTLESNAKE a small rattlesnake of the southwestern United States and northern Mexico that moves forward with a diagonal looping motion. Latin name: Crotalus cerastes. 2. MIL AIR-TO-AIR MISSILE an air-to-air missile that uses a heat-seeking device to home in on a target 3. US BOXING PUNCH IN BOXING a hard swinging punch from the side

sidewise /sĭd´wīz/ adj., adv. = sideways

Sidi-bel-Abbès /seedi belə béss/ capital of Sidi-bel-Abbès Province, northwestern Algeria, situated 80 km/50 mi. south of Oran. Population: 152,778 (1995).

siding /sĭd´ing/ n. 1. SHORT RAILWAY TRACK a short stretch of railway track that connects with the main track 2. US, Can MATERIAL FORMING BUILDING'S OUTER SKIN sheets of wood, vinyl, aluminium, or other material used to surface the outside of a building

sidle /sĭd´l/ v. (-dles, -dling, -dled) 1. vi. MOVE FURTIVELY to edge along in a furtive way ○ I sidled to the door in the hope that no one would notice me. 2. vti. MOVE SIDEWAYS to move, or move sth, sidewards ■ n. SIDLING MOVEMENT a sideways or furtive movement [Late 17thC. Origin uncertain: probably a back-formation from earlier sidling 'sideways', modelled on verbs such as paddle and mumble.]

Sidney /sĭd´ni/, **Sir Philip** (1554–86) English soldier, courtier, and poet. He was a favourite of Elizabeth I and an accomplished diplomat and soldier. His Arcadia, posthumously published in 1590, became the model for later English pastoral poetry.

Sidon /sĭd´n/ city and seaport in southwestern Lebanon, on the Mediterranean Sea south of Beirut. It was a Phoenician city-state in the 3rd millennium BC. Population: 38,000 (1988).

Sidra, Gulf of /sĭdrə-/ arm of the Mediterranean Sea that forms a bay on the coast of Libya, northern Africa

SIDS /sidz/ n., abbr. sudden infant death syndrome

siege /seej/ n. 1. MILITARY OPERATION a military or police operation in which an army or the police surround a place and cut off all outside access to force surrender (often used before a noun) ○ siege warfare 2. PROLONGED EFFORT a prolonged effort to gain or overcome sth 3. TIRESOME PERIOD a prolonged and tedious period 4. SEAT a seat, especially a formal or ceremonial seat, e.g. a throne (archaic) ■ vt. (sieges, sieging, sieged) SUBJECT PLACE TO SIEGE to assail or assault an enemy's fortifications militarily ○ a town sieged with troops [12thC. Via Old French sege 'seat' from, ultimately, Latin sedere 'to sit' (source of English session, size, subsidy).] ◇ **lay siege to 1.** to besiege a place 2. to make a persistent attempt to gain sth

Siegfried /seeg´freed/ n. in German legend, a prince who kills the dragon guarding the treasure of the Nibelungs, and wins Brunhild for Gunther

Siegfried line /seeg´freed-/ n. the line of fortifications constructed by Germany before and during World War II on its western frontier, facing the Maginot line in France [Mid-20thC. Named after Siegfried, the (nearly) invincible hero of Germanic legend.]

Sieg Heil /seeg hīl/ interj. hail to victory, a Nazi salute usually accompanied by the right arm raised with the palm facing downward [Mid-20thC. From German.]

siemens /seemənz/ n. (plural -mens) n. the SI unit of electrical conductance equal to one ampere per volt. Symbol **S** [Mid-20thC. Named after the German inventor Werner von Siemens (1816–92).]

Siena /si énnə/ capital of Siena Province, Tuscany Region, in north-central Italy. Population: 58,300 (1990). —**Sienese** n., adj.

sienna /si énnə/ n. 1. EARTH USED AS PIGMENT a kind of iron-rich soil that is used as a pigment in paints. It is brownish-yellow in its natural state (**raw sienna**) and reddish-brown when roasted (**burnt sienna**).

2. PAINT artists' paint made with either colour of sienna, or either colour itself [Late 18thC. Named after Siena, a city in western Italy where the pigment was first produced.] —**sienna** adj.

sierra /sei érrə/ n. a range of mountains with jagged peaks, or the country surrounding such a range [Mid-16thC. Via Spanish from Latin serra 'saw' (source of English serrate).] —**sierran** /sei érrən/ adj.

Sierra /si érrə/ n. the NATO phonetic alphabet code word for the letter 'S', used in international radio communications

Sierra Leone

Sierra Leone /siáirə li ón/ republic in western Africa, situated south of Guinea, northwest of Liberia, and with the Atlantic Ocean on its western coast. Language: English. Currency: leone. Capital: Freetown. Population: 4,630,000 (1996). Area: 71,740 sq. km/27,699 sq. mi. Official name **Republic of Sierra Leone** —**Sierra Leonean** n., adj.

Sierra Madre /si áirrə maá dray/ mountain system in Mexico that stretches southeastwards from the US border in the north to the border with Guatemala in the south. Length: 2,500 km/1,500 mi.

Sierra Nevada /siáirrə nə vaádə/ **1.** mountain range in southeastern Spain. Its highest peak is Cerro de Mulhacén, 3,480 m/11,411 ft. **2.** mountain range in eastern California, extending from the Mojave Desert to the Coast Range. Its highest peak is Mount Whitney, 4,417 m/14,491 ft. Length: 640 km/400 mi.

siesta /si éstə/ n. an early afternoon rest or nap [Mid-17thC. Via Spanish from Latin sexta (hora), literally 'sixth (hour of the day), noon'. From its customary time.]

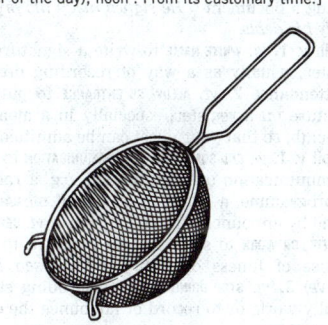

Sieve

sieve /siv/ n. MESHED UTENSIL a utensil consisting of a round frame surrounding a mesh and used to separate solids from liquids, large particles from small particles, or to purée foods ■ vt. (**sieves, sieving, sieved**) PUT STH THROUGH A SIEVE to pass sth through a sieve [Old English sife. From a prehistoric Germanic base that is also the ancestor of English sift.]

sieve plate n. an area of perforations in the end walls of the cells that make up a sieve tube in plants

sievert /seevərt/ n. the SI unit measuring the probability that a stated dose of a particular radiation type will cause a biological effect. 1 sievert is equal to 1 joule per kilogram. Symbol **Sv** [Mid-20thC. Named after the Swedish radiologist R. M. Sievert (1896–1966).]

sieve tube n. a sap-conducting tube within the phloem tissue of a plant. It is composed of numerous cells (**sieve tube elements**) connected end to end and separated by porous sieve plates.

sifaka /si fáakə/ n. a large rare tree-dwelling lemur of Madagascar. It has a black face and long soft fur variously patterned in white, black, or brown. Latin name: Propithecus verreauxi and Propithecus diadema. [Mid-19thC. From Malagasy.]

sift /sift/ (**sifts, sifting, sifted**) v. **1.** vti. SEPARATE PARTICLES to pass a substance through a sieve to separate out or break up coarse particles **2.** vt. TAKE STH OUT to separate sth out with a sieve, or by a process of selection or elimination ○ sift the good from the bad **3.** vt. SCATTER STH to scatter sth with or as if with a sieve ○ We sifted sugar onto the strawberries. **4.** vti. EXAMINE to sort or examine sth carefully ○ sift evidence **5.** vi. PASS THROUGH to pass or fall through or as if through a sieve [Old English siftan. From a prehistoric Germanic base that is also the ancestor of English sieve.] —**sifter** n.

siftings /sĭftingz/ npl. parts or elements separated out using a sieve or by a process of elimination

SIG /sig/ n., abbr. special interest group

sig. abbr. **1.** sig., Sig. signor **2.** sig., Sig. signore **3.** signature

Sig. used on prescriptions before instructions that should be written on the label of the medicine given to a patient. Abbr of **Signa** [Shortening of Latin signa 'mark or label it']

sigh /sī/ v. (**sighs, sighing, sighed**) **1.** vi. BREATHE LONG AND LOUD to take in and let out a deep audible breath in relief or weariness **2.** vi. MAKE EXHALING SOUND to make a sound like the exhalation of a deep breath ○ The wind sighed in the trees. **3.** vi. YEARN to long for sb or sth ○ sigh for simpler times **4.** vt. EXPRESS FEELING IN SIGHS to express an emotion by sighs ○ She sighed her relief when she found us. ■ n. **1.** EXHALATION an audible exhalation of a deep breath **2.** SOUND OF EXHALING a sound like that of sb exhaling a deep breath [13thC. Origin uncertain: probably a back-formation from the past tense form of Old English sīcan 'to sigh', which is of unknown origin.]

sight /sīt/ n. **1.** FACULTY OF SEEING the ability to see using the eyes **2.** SEEING the perception of sth using the visual sense **3.** RANGE OF SEEING the range or field of vision ○ Home is within sight. **4.** STH SEEN sth that sb sees **5.** STH WORTH SEEING sth that is worth seeing, especially the landmarks of a particular place (often used in the plural) ○ the sights of the city **6.** STH UNPLEASANT TO LOOK AT sth or sb that has an unpleasant, distressing, or disarranged appearance (informal) ○ He was a sight after the fight. **7.** ALIGNMENT DEVICE an alignment device on a gun or surveying instrument used to guide the eye in aiming or determining direction **8.** AIM a determination of direction made with a gun or surveying instrument **9.** OPPORTUNITY FOR OBSERVATION an opportunity to observe or inspect **10.** OPINION a point of view ○ In the sight of his followers he was infallible. **11.** INSIGHT expert knowledge or sharp perception (archaic) ■ v. (**sights, sighting, sighted**) **1.** vt. SEE STH to see or notice sb or sth ○ They sighted the plane in the distance. **2.** vti. OBSERVE USING OPTICAL DEVICE to observe sth or take measurements of sth using an optical device **3.** vti. AIM AT STH WITH GUN to take aim at sth with a firearm **4.** vt. ADJUST GUN'S SIGHTS to adjust the sights of a gun **5.** vi. DIRECT THE EYES to look carefully in a particular direction ○ sight down a line [Old English (ge)sih] ◇ **a sight** a great deal or quantity (informal) ○ He's feeling a sight better today. ◇ **a sight for sore eyes** a very welcome sight ◇ **at sight**, **on sight** as soon as sth is able to be seen ◇ **in sight 1.** able to be seen **2.** likely to happen in the near future ◇ **know sb by sight** be able to recognize sb whom you have never actually met or spoken to ◇ **out of sight 1.** no longer able to be seen **2.** used to express approval and surprise (informal) ◇ **set your sights on sth**, **have your sights on sth** to decide to try to get sth ◇ **sight unseen** without seeing or inspecting first ○ buy something sight unseen

sighted /sĭtid/ adj. **1.** ABLE TO SEE having the faculty of sight **2.** WITH SPECIFIED VISION having sight of a particular kind (used in combination) ○ clear-sighted —**sightedness** n.

sighter /sĭtər/ n. a practice shot allowed in a shooting or archery tournament, or a shot used to assess the setting of the sights of a gun

sight gag *n.* a joke or comic episode that depends on it being seen to be funny (*informal*)

sighting /síting/ *n.* an occasion on which sth is seen, usually sth unusual or searched for ○ *sightings of UFOs*

sightless /sítləss/ *adj.* **1. UNABLE TO SEE** without the faculty of sight **2. UNSEEN** invisible (*literary*) ○ *'heaven's cherubim, hors'd upon the sightless couriers of the air'* (William Shakespeare, *Macbeth*; 1623) —**sightlessly** *adv.* —**sightlessness** *n.*

sightline /sít līn/ *n.* a line of vision between a person and an object, especially between a member of an audience and the stage in a theatre

sightly /sítli/ (**-lier**, **-liest**) *adj.* pleasing to look at

sight-read *vti.* to read or perform sth, e.g. music or a foreign language, without having practised or seen it beforehand —**sight reader** *n.*

sight rhyme *n.* = **eye rhyme**

sightscreen /sít skreen/ *n.* a large white screen placed near the boundary of a cricket field behind the bowler to help the batsman see the ball

sightsee /sít see/ (**-sees**, **-seeing**, **-saw** /-saw/, **-seen** /-seen/) *vi.* to visit a place's interesting sights —**sightseer** *n.*

sightseeing /sít see ing/ *n.* visiting places of interest (*often used before a noun*) ○ *a sightseeing tour*

sigil /síjjəl/ *n.* **1. SEAL** a seal or signet **2. MAGICAL SIGN** a sign or image that is supposed to have magical power [16thC. Via late Latin from Latin *sigillum*, literally 'small sign', from *signum* (see SIGN).] —**sigillary** /si jílləri/ *adj.*

Sigismund /síggissmənd/ (1368–1437). As king of Hungary (1387–1437), he conquered much Balkan territory, but was defeated by the Ottoman Turks at Nicopolis (1396). He was Holy Roman Emperor from 1411 to 1437. His rule over Bohemia (1419–37) was constantly challenged by Bohemians opposed to his role in the execution of the religious reformer John Huss (1415).

siglos /síggloss/ (*plural* **-loi** /síggloy/) *n.* a silver coin used in ancient Persia between the sixth and fourth centuries BC [Early 20thC. From Greek.]

sigma /sígmə/ *n.* **1. 18TH GREEK LETTER** the 18th letter of the Greek alphabet, represented in the English alphabet as 's'. See table at **alphabet 2. MATH SYMBOL SHOWING ADDITION** the symbol ' indicating the addition of the numbers or quantities indicated **3. = sigma hyperon** [Early 17thC. Via Latin from Greek.]

sigma hyperon, **sigma**, **sigma particle** *n.* any of three unstable elementary particles of the baryon group, with a mass of 2328 to 2343 times that of an electron, and a positive, negative, or neutral electric charge

sigmate /sígmət/ *adj.* shaped like the Greek letter sigma or the Roman S —**sigmation** /sig máysh'n/ *n.*

sigmoid /síg moyd/ *adj.* **1. S-SHAPED** shaped like the letter S **2. RELATING TO SIGMOID COLON** relating to the sigmoid colon of the large intestine

sigmoid colon *n.* the final S-shaped portion of the large intestine leading to the rectum

sigmoid flexure *n.* **1. = sigmoid colon 2. S-SHAPED CURVE** an S-shaped curve or bend, e.g. in the neck of a bird or turtle

sigmoidoscope /sig móydə skōp/ *n.* a fibre-optic tubular instrument inserted through the anus for examining the interior of the rectum and sigmoid colon —**sigmoidoscopic** /sig móydə skóppik/ *adj.* —**sigmoidoscopy** /síg moy dóskəpi/ *n.*

sign /sīn/ *n.* **1. STH REPRESENTING STH ELSE** sth that indicates or expresses the existence of sth else not immediately apparent ○ *a sign of wealth* **2. STH CONVEYING IDEA** an action or gesture used to convey an idea, information, a wish, or a command ○ *His kick under the table was a sign we should leave.* **3. ADVERTISING NOTICE** a publicly displayed structure, e.g. a painted board or neon lights, carrying lettering or designs intended to advertise a business or product **4. INFORMATION NOTICE** a publicly displayed notice or board bearing directions, instructions, or warnings ○ *a road sign* **5. INDICATION** sth that indicates the presence

of sth or sb ○ *no sign of life* **6. TRACE LEFT BY ANIMAL** a trace of a wild animal, e.g. spoor, scent, or footprints **7. OMEN** sth interpreted as being an omen **8. DIVISION OF ZODIAC** any of the 12 equal parts into which the zodiac is divided, each represented by a symbol **9. EVIDENCE OF DISEASE** an indication of the presence of a disease or disorder, especially one observed by a doctor but not apparent to the patient ○ *Fever is a sign of an infection.* **10. SYMBOL USED IN MATHS OR LOGIC** a symbol indicating an operation or relation in mathematics or logic ○ *the plus sign* **11. MUSICAL NOTATION SYMBOL** a symbol used in musical notation **12. = sign language** ■ *v.* (**signs, signing, signed**) **1.** *vti.* **WRITE NAME** to write a signature on sth **2.** *vti.* **APPROVE DOCUMENT** to affirm or approve a document formally by affixing a signature or seal **3.** *vt.* **EMPLOY SB** to engage sb or sb's services by written agreement ○ *The manager signed two promising young players.* **4.** *vi.* **AGREE TO TAKE JOB** to agree to be employed by writing the signature on a contract ○ *He signed for a year.* **5.** *vti.* **COMMUNICATE IN SIGN LANGUAGE** to use sign language to communicate a message ○ *She signed 'yes'.* **6.** *vti.* **SIGNAL INFORMATION** to convey information using a signal or signals **7.** *vt.* **PORTEND STH** to be an omen of sth to come ○ *That signs danger.* **8.** *vt.* **GIVE BLESSING TO SB** to bless sb or sth by making the sign of the cross [13thC. Via French *signe* from Latin *signum* 'mark', of uncertain origin: perhaps from an Indo-European base, meaning 'to say, tell', which is also the ancestor of English *say*.] —**signer** *n.*

■ WORD KEY: SYNONYMS ———

sign, indication, symptom

CORE MEANING: sth that suggests the presence or occurrence of sth

sign a general word for sth that suggests the presence or occurrence of another thing. It can refer to concrete or abstract things; **indication** used in a similar way to *sign*, but most commonly used to talk about abstract things; **symptom** used to refer to a physical sign that suggests the presence of a particular medical condition. It can also refer to sth that suggests the presence of a particular problem.

——— WORD KEY: ORIGIN ———

The Latin word *signum*, from which **sign** is derived, is also the source of English *assign, consign, design, designate, ensign, insignia, resign, seal, signal, signature, signet,* and *significant.*

---

sign away *vt.* to convey rights or property to sb by signing a document ○ *He signed away his property to pay his debts.*

sign in *v.* **1.** *vi.* **WRITE NAME** to write a signature in a register, usually as a way of recording presence or attendance **2.** *vt.* **ALLOW SB ENTRANCE** to put your signature on a register, especially in a members-only club, so that your guest can be admitted

sign off *v.* **1.** *vi.* **END SOME FORM OF COMMUNICATION** to bring a communication or transmission, e.g. a radio or TV programme, a letter, or an e-mail message, to an end by announcing its conclusion **2.** *vt.* **CERTIFY SB AS UNFIT FOR WORK** to state that sb is not fit to work because of illness or injury (*often used in the passive*) **3.** *vi.* **STOP DOING STH** to stop doing sth, especially work, or to record or announce the end of some activity

sign on *v.* **1.** *vi.* **CONSENT BY SIGNING** to agree to do some activity, especially by signing a contract **2.** *vi.* **REGISTER AS UNEMPLOYED** to register as unemployed in order to receive state benefits **3.** *vt.* **EMPLOY SB** to take sb on as an employee or to do a particular job

sign out *v.* **1.** *vi.* **WRITE NAME ON LEAVING** to write a signature as a record of having left somewhere, especially a workplace **2.** *vt.* **ACKNOWLEDGE RECEIPT** to sign the name as an acknowledgement of having received sth, especially as being temporarily in possession of it

sign over *vt.* to transfer possession of sth to sb else by writing a signature on a document

sign up *vti.* **1. AGREE TO PARTICIPATE** to agree, or get sb to agree, to participate in sth, especially by way of a signature **2. ENLIST** to enlist, or enlist sb, for military service

Signac /sín yak/, **Paul** (1863–1935) French painter. In his earlier years he was a major exponent of divisionism, which he developed to produce a mosaic-like effect.

signage /sínij/ *n.* **1. SIGNS** signs collectively **2. SIGN-DESIGNING** the design and display of signs

signal /sígnəl/ *n.* **1. MEANS OF COMMUNICATION** an action, gesture, or sign used as a means of communication ○ *Yellow is a signal for caution.* **2. COMMUNICATED INFORMATION** a piece of information communicated by an action, gesture, or sign **3. INCITEMENT** sth that incites sb to action ○ *The threat of a shortage was a signal to hoard.* **4. ELECTRON ENG TRANSMITTED INFORMATION** information transmitted by means of a modulated current or an electromagnetic wave and received by telephone, telegraph, radio, television, or radar ■ *adj.* **NOTABLE** of considerable importance ○ *a signal accomplishment* ■ *v.* (**-nals, -nalling, -nalled**) **1.** *vti.* **COMMUNICATE** to communicate a message to sb **2.** *vt.* **SEND MESSAGE USING SIGNAL** to communicate sth by sending a signal of some kind **3.** *vt.* **INDICATE STH** to be a sign that sth has happened or is about to happen ○ *This event signalled the end of the conflict.* [14thC. Via Old French *seignal* from, ultimately, Latin *signum* (see SIGN). The adjective came via French *signalé* and Italian *segnalato* 'made famous'.] —**signaller** *n.*

signal box *n.* a building from which a stretch or system of railway track is controlled, either manually by means of levers, or electrically and semi-automatically. US term **signal tower**

signal generator *n.* a device used to test electronic equipment by generating a signal whose frequency, wave shape, and amplitude are independently adjustable over a wide range of settings

signalize /sígnə līz/ (**-izes, -izing, -ized**), **signalise** (**-ises, -ising, -ised**) *vt.* **1. MAKE STH STAND OUT** to make sth conspicuous or remarkable **2. POINT STH OUT** to indicate sth distinctly —**signalization** /sígnə lī záysh'n/ *n.*

signally /sígnəli/ *adv.* completely and unmistakably

signalman /sígnəlmən/ (*plural* **-men** /-mən/) *n.* **1. SB WHO SENDS AND RECEIVES SIGNALS** a member of the armed forces who sends and receives signals **2. RAILWAY EMPLOYEE** a railway employee who is in charge of operating signals

signal-to-noise ratio *n.* the ratio of the strength of a signal carrying information to unwanted interference in an electronic circuit

signal tower *n. US* = **signal box**

signatory /sígnətəri/ *n.* (*plural* **-ries**) **PARTY TO TREATY OR CONTRACT** a person, government, or organization that has signed a treaty or contract and is bound by it ■ *adj.* **BOUND BY TREATY** bound by the terms of a treaty or contract ○ *a signatory nation*

signature /sígnəchər/ *n.* **1. SIGNED NAME** sb's name signed by him or her or by sb authorized by him or her to sign **2. SIGNING OF NAME** a signing of sb's name **3. DISTINCTIVE CHARACTERISTIC** a distinctive mark, characteristic, or thing that identifies sb (*often used before a noun*) ○ *a signature song* **4. MED DIRECTIONS ON PRESCRIPTION** the part of a doctor's prescription that contains the directions for use **5. MUSIC** = **key signature 6. MUSIC** = **time signature 7. PRINTING MARK INDICATING PAGE ORDER** a letter or mark printed on what will become the first page of a section of a book, indicating its order in binding **8. PRINTING SHEET PRINTED WITH MULTIPLE PAGES** a sheet of paper printed with several pages that, when folded, will become a section of a book **9. PRINTING SECTION OF BOOK** a section of a book consisting of a folded sheet with several pages printed on it [Mid-16thC. Directly or via French from medieval Latin *signatura*, from Latin *signare* (see SIGN).]

signature tune *n.* a piece of music used to introduce or identify a performer, group, or television or radio programme. US term **theme song**

signboard /sín bawrd/ *n.* a board carrying a notice or advertisement

signed /sīnd/ *adj.* **1. HAVING PLUS OR MINUS SIGN** with a positive or negative value, as indicated by a plus or minus sign **2. WITH SIGNATURE ON IT** bearing a signature, e.g. written to authenticate a document or as an autograph

signed-ranks test *n.* = **Wilcoxon test**

signet /sígnət/ *n.* **1. SMALL SEAL** a small seal, e.g. one that is engraved on a ring **2. STAMP FOR DOCUMENTS** a seal used to stamp official documents **3. IMPRESSION**

---

a at; aw father; aw all; ay day; air hair; ə about, edible, item, common, circus; e egg; ee eel; hw when; i it, happy; ī ice; 'l apple; 'm rhythm; 'n fashion; o odd; ō open; oo good; oo pool; ow owl; oy oil; th thin; th this; u up; ur urge;

MADE BY SEAL the impression made on a document with a seal ■ *vt.* (**-nets, -neting, -neted**) STAMP DOCUMENT WITH SEAL to stamp a document with a seal [14thC. Directly or via French from medieval Latin *signetum*, literally 'small seal', from Latin *signum* (see SIGN).]

signet ring *n.* a finger ring containing a small seal

significance /sig níffikənss/, **significancy** /-kənssi/ *n.* **1.** IMPORTANCE the quality of having importance or being regarded as having great meaning **2.** MEANING implied or intended meaning **3.** STATS VALUE AS STATISTICAL POINTER status as a statistical value that is not accidental or random (*often used before a noun*)

significancy *n.* = **significance**

significant /sig níffikənt/ *adj.* **1.** MEANINGFUL having or expressing a meaning **2.** COMMUNICATING SECRET MEANING having a hidden or implied meaning ○ *a significant nod of the head* **3.** MOMENTOUS AND INFLUENTIAL having a major or important effect ○ *a significant idea* **4.** SUBSTANTIAL relatively large in amount ○ *Her work was a significant contribution to the project.* **5.** STATS OCCURRING NOT MERELY BY CHANCE relating to the occurrence of events or outcomes that are too closely linked statistically to be mere chance [Late 16thC. From the present participle stem of Latin *significare* (see SIGNIFY).]

significant digits *npl. US* = **significant figures**

significant figures *npl.* the figures necessary in a decimal number to express accuracy, beginning with the first nonzero figure to the left and ending with the figure farthest to the right. US term **significant digits**

significantly /sig níffikəntli/ *adv.* **1.** GREATLY to a large extent or degree ○ *significantly higher* **2.** IMPORTANTLY in an important or fundamental way ○ *Your ideas will contribute significantly.*

significant other *n.* **1.** HUSBAND, WIFE, PARTNER, OR LOVER a spouse or someone with whom sb has a long-term sexual relationship **2.** SB IMPORTANT an influential or supportive person in sb's life

signification /sígnifi káysh'n/ *n.* **1.** MEANING the meaning of sth, e.g. a word, event, or other phenomenon **2.** SIGNIFYING the signifying or indicating of sth [13thC. Either directly or via Old French from the Latin stem *signification-* 'indication, sign', from *significare* (see SIGNIFY).]

significative /sig níffikətiv/ *adj.* **1.** MEANINGFUL OR IMPORTANT carrying meaning or importance **2.** SIGNIFYING OR INDICATING STH used to describe signs, symbols, or other marks that signify or indicate sth —**significatively** *adv.* —**significativeness** *n.*

signify /sígni fī/ (**-fies, -fying, -fied**) *v.* **1.** *vt.* MEAN STH to have sth as a particular meaning **2.** *vt.* BE SIGN OF STH to be a sign or symbol of sth **3.** *vi.* BE IMPORTANT to be important or significant [13thC. Either directly or via Old French *signifier* from Latin *significare*, from *signum* (see SIGN).] —**signifiable** *adj.* —**signifier** *n.*

signing *n.* = **sign language**

signior *n.* = **signor**

signiory *n.* = **seigniory**

sign language, **sign** *n.* communication, or a system of communication, by gestures as opposed to written or spoken language, especially the highly developed system of hand signs used by or to people who are hearing-impaired

sign manual *n.* sb's signature, especially that of a king or queen on an official document [Translation of Anglo-Latin *signum manuale*, literally 'sign made with the hand']

sign of the cross *n.* in Christianity, a movement of the hand as if tracing a cross in the air or on the body, usually by touching the forehead, chest, and shoulders in turn. The gesture is made, mainly by Roman Catholics, in order to invoke the blessing of God or as a declaration of Christian faith.

signor /seé nyawr/ (*plural* **-gnors** *or* **-gnori** /see nyáwri/), **signior** (*plural* **-gniors** *or* **-gniori**), **Signor** (*plural* **-gnors** *or* **-gnori**), **Signior** (*plural* **-gniors** *or* **-gniori**) *n.* the usual Italian form of title or address for a man. It is the equivalent of English 'Mr'. ◊ **signore, signora, signorina** [Late 16thC. From Italian, a reduced form of *signore*.]

signora /see nyáwrə/ (*plural* **-ras** *or* **-re** /see nyáw ray/), **Signora, Signore** *n.* the usual Italian form of title or address for a married or older woman. It is equivalent to English 'Mrs' or 'madam'. ◊ **signor, signore, signorina** [Mid-17thC. From the Italian feminine form of *signore*.]

signore /see nyáw ray/ (*plural* **-ri** /-ri/) *n.* the Italian form of title or address for a highly respected man or a man of advanced age. It is equivalent to English 'sir'. ◊ **signor, signora, signorina** [Late 16thC. Via Italian from Latin *senior* (source of English *senior*), the comparative form of *senex* 'old'.]

signorina /see nyaw reénə/ (*plural* **signorinas** *or* **signorine** /see nyaw reé nay/) *n.* the usual Italian form of title or address for a young or unmarried woman. It is equivalent to English 'Miss'. ◊ **signor, signore, signora** [Early 19thC. From Italian, literally 'little signora', formed from *signora*.]

signory *n.* = **seigniory**

sign painting *n. US* = **signwriting** —**sign painter** *n.*

signpost /sín pōst/ *n.* **1.** INFORMATION SIGN a pole with a sign on it, especially one that gives directions or other information **2.** STH THAT INDICATES STH sth that gives a clue, indication, hint, or guide ■ *vt.* (**-posts, -posting, -posted**) **1.** DIRECT SB TO PLACE to direct sb or mark the way to a place with signposts or similar indications ○ *a series of notices signposting patients to the X-ray department* **2.** GIVE INDICATION to give a clear indication of sth, especially some future action or decision

signwriting /sín rīting/ *n.* the activity or profession of designing and painting signs, especially for shops, hotels, and other businesses. US term **sign painting** —**signwriter** *n.*

sika /seékə/ *n.* a small deer native to Japan and China that has a brown, often spotted coat with a white patch on the rump. Latin name: *Cervus nippon.* [Late 19thC. From Japanese, 'deer'.]

sike /sīk/ *n. N England, Scotland* **1.** SMALL STREAM a small, usually slow-moving stream, especially one that tends to dry up in summer. ◊ **burn 2.** DITCH a ditch [Old English *sīc*]

Sikh /seek/ *n.* MEMBER OF INDIAN RELIGION a member of a religious group that broke away from Hinduism during the 16th century and advocated a monotheistic doctrine, incorporating some aspects of Islam. ◊ **five Ks** ■ *adj.* OF SIKHS belonging or relating to the Sikhs or their religion, beliefs, customs, or history [Late 18thC. Via Panjabi or Hindi from Sanskrit *śiṣya* 'disciple'.] —**Sikhism** *n.*

Sikkim /síkim/ mountainous state in northeastern India, in the eastern Himalayas, bordered by Tibet, Bhutan, and Nepal. Capital: Gangtok. Population: 406,457 (1991). Area: 7,096 sq. km/2,740 sq. mi. —**Sikkimese** *n., adj.*

Sikorski /si káwrski/, **Władysław** (1881–1943) Polish statesman and soldier. He fought in the Russian-Polish War (1920–21). He was premier of Poland (1922–26) and of the Polish government in exile (1940–43) during World War II. Full name **Władysław Eugeniusz Sikorski**

sila /séelə/ *n.* in Buddhism, morality, one of the three major divisions of the noble eightfold path, which consists of right speech, right action, and right livelihood. ◊ **samadhi, panna** [Mid-20thC. From Pali.]

silage /sílij/ *n.* animal fodder that is made by storing green plant material in a silo where it is preserved by partial fermentation [Late 19thC. Via French *ensilage* from, ultimately, Spanish *ensilar* 'to store in a silo'. The alteration from *ensilage* to 'silage' was probably influenced by SILO.]

silane /sílayn, síllayn/ *n.* a compound containing silicon and hydrogen, analogous to a paraffin hydrocarbon. Formula: Si_nH_{2n+2}. [Early 20thC. Coined from SILICON + -ANE.]

Silbury Hill /sílbəri-/ artificial mound near Avebury, in Wiltshire, England. It was made about 2100 BC. Height: 40 m/130 ft.

sild /sild/ (*plural* **silds** *or* **sild**) *n.* an immature herring, especially one that has been processed and canned. ◊ **sprat, sardine** [Early 20thC. Via Danish and Norwegian from Old Norse *sīld* 'herring'.]

sildenafil citrate /sil dənnəfil sítrayt-/ *n.* a drug used to treat impotence [Late 20thC. *Sildenafil* an invented name.]

silence /sílənss/ *n.* **1.** QUIETNESS the absence or lack of noise **2.** NOT SPEAKING a refusal, failure, or inability to speak **3.** ABSENCE OF ACKNOWLEDGMENT OF STH an absence of notice or acknowledgment of sth ○ *Most remarkable was the statement's silence about the recent policy change.* ■ *vt.* (**-lences, -lencing, -lenced**) **1.** STOP STH OR SB MAKING NOISE to stop sth or sb from making a noise **2.** SUPPRESS STH to suppress the expression of sth or stop a person or group from speaking out ○ *silence criticism* **3.** END SB'S HOSTILE BEHAVIOUR to cause sb to stop hostile or aggressive behaviour [13thC. Via Old French from Latin *silentium*, from the stem of *silens*, the present participle of *silere* 'to be silent'.]

silencer /sílənssər/ *n.* **1.** CARS PART OF EXHAUST SYSTEM the drum-shaped part of a vehicle's exhaust system that is designed to lessen noise. ◊ **muffler 2.** ARMS FIREARM MUFFLER a device that muffles the noise of a gun **3.** SB OR STH IMPOSING SILENCE sb or sth that causes silence or lessens noise

silene /sī leéni/ *n.* a perennial plant often grown for its pink or red flowers. Genus: *Silene.* [Late 18thC. From modern Latin, the genus name, from Latin *Silenus*, name of a woodland satyr, the tutor of Dionysius, from Greek *Silēnos* (see SILENUS).]

silent /sílənt/ *adj.* **1.** UTTERLY QUIET lacking any noise or sound ○ *a silent country lane* **2.** NOT SPEAKING not speaking or communicating, especially through choice ○ *The children all remained silent.* **3.** SAYING LITTLE not inclined to say much ○ *the strong silent type* **4.** UNSPOKEN not expressed or voiced, though felt or believed ○ *rolled her eyes in silent disbelief* **5.** CINEMA WITHOUT SOUNDTRACK relating to films made without sound, typically those made before 1927 **6.** RELIG UNABLE TO SPEAK unable or not allowed to speak ○ *a silent order of monks* **7.** INACTIVE currently inactive or not operating ○ *a silent volcano* **8.** QUIETLY EXPRESSED drawing attention inconspicuously, without making noise ○ *a silent warning* **9.** NOT PRONOUNCED used to describe a letter that appears in a word but is not pronounced, e.g. the 'k' in 'knight' or the 'b' in 'debt' ■ *n.* CINEMA SILENT FILM a film made without sound [15thC. From Latin *silent-*, the stem of *silens* (see SILENCE).] —**silently** *adv.* —**silentness** *n.*

WORD KEY: SYNONYMS

silent, quiet, reticent, taciturn, uncommunicative

CORE MEANING: not speaking or not saying much

silent describes sb who is refraining from speech at a particular time or in a particular situation, or sb who is not disposed to speak much; **quiet** describes sb who is not disposed to speak much, often because of shyness. It can also be used to describe sb who is not speaking much in a particular situation, especially when this seems out of character; **reticent** describes sb who is reluctant to speak on a particular occasion or about a particular subject. It can also describe sb whose disposition is not to reveal much about himself or herself; **taciturn** describes a person who is not inclined to say very much, usually as a matter of disposition, especially when this creates an impression of gruffness or bad-temper; **uncommunicative** describes sb who is deliberately withholding information or refusing to talk about sth. It can also be used in a similar way to *taciturn* to describe sb who tends not to say much.

silent auction *n.* an auction that is conducted by submitting bids in sealed envelopes before the sale

silent cop *n. ANZ* a large metal disc located at an intersection that is designed to prevent drivers cutting corners (*informal*)

silent majority *n.* a significant number of a given population who choose not to express their views, often because of apathy or because they do not believe their views matter

silent partner *n. US* = **sleeping partner**

silenus /sī leénəss/ (*plural* **-ni** /sī leénī/) *n.* in Greek mythology, a woodland god resembling an elderly satyr [Early 18thC. Via Latin from Greek *silenos*, from *Silēnos*, name of a woodland satyr, the tutor of Dionysius.]

Silenus /sī leénəss/ *n.* in Greek mythology, an old woodland god in charge of Dionysus' education. In art, Silenus is often depicted as a drunken old man.

zh vision In foreign words: kh German Bach; aN French vin; aaN French blanc; ö German schön, French feu; oN French bon; öN French un; ü French rue Stress marks: ´ as in secret \seék rət\; academic \àkə démmik\

silesia /sɪˈleezi ə, sɪˈleessi ə, sɪˈleeshə/ *n.* a hard-wearing cotton twill fabric, used especially for pockets and linings of garments [Late 17thC. Named after *Silesia*, where it was manufactured.]

Silesia /sɪˈleeshə/ historic region in east-central Europe, lying mostly within present-day south-western Poland —**Silesian** *n.*, *adj.*

silex /ˈsɪleks/ *n.* **1.** POWDERED SILICA powdered silica or tripoli, used as a filter material **2.** HEAT-RESISTANT GLASS a heat-resistant glass with high quartz content [Late 16thC. From Latin, 'flint'.]

Silhouette

silhouette /ˈsɪlooˌet/ *n.* **1.** SHADOWED CONTOUR an outline of sb or sth filled in with black or a dark colour on a light background, especially when done as a likeness or work of art **2.** STH DARK ON LIGHT BACKGROUND sth lit in such a way as to appear dark but surrounded by light, or the effect produced by such lighting ○ *silhouettes dancing in front of the bonfire* ■ *vt.* (-ettes, -etting, -etted) MAKE STH APPEAR AS A SILHOUETTE to cause sb or sth to appear surrounded by light (*often passive*) ○ *The buildings were silhouetted against the rising sun.* [Late 18thC. Via French, named after Etienne de *Silhouette* (1709–67), French finance minister.]

— WORD KEY: ORIGIN —
As French finance minister in the late 1750s, Étienne de **Silhouette** gained a reputation for stinginess, and **silhouette** came to be used for anything skimped. One account of the application of the word to a 'simple cut-out picture' is that it carries on this notion of 'simplicity' or 'lack of finish', but an alternative theory is that **Silhouette** himself was in the habit of making such pictures.

silic- *prefix.* = **silici-**

silica /ˈsɪlikə/ *n.* silicon dioxide found naturally in various crystalline and amorphous forms, e.g. quartz, opal, sand, flint, and agate [Early 19thC. From modern Latin, from the stem of Latin *silex* 'flint'.]

silica gel *n.* gelatinous silica in a form that readily absorbs water from the air, used as a drying agent, a carrier for catalysts, and an anticaking agent

silicate /ˈsɪlikayt/ *n.* any of the most important and common of the rock-forming minerals, formed from silicon and oxygen combined with various elements, classified by their crystalline structures

siliceous /sɪˈlishəss/, **silicious** *adj.* **1.** OF SILICA OR SILICATES connected with or consisting of silica or a silicate **2.** REQUIRING SILICA used to describe plants that require silica-rich soil in order to grow [Mid-17thC. From Latin *siliceus* 'of flint', from the stem of *silex* 'flint'.]

silici- *prefix.* **1.** silica ○ *silicosis* **2.** silicon ○ *silicate* [From SILICON and SILICA]

silicic /sɪˈlissik/ *adj.* relating to or containing silica or silicon

silicic acid *n.* a weak gelatinous acid obtained by adding an acid to sodium silicate

silicide /ˈsɪliˌsīd/ *n.* a binary compound of silicon with another element

siliciferous /ˌsɪliˈsifərəss/ *adj.* containing or yielding silica

silicify /sɪˈlissifī/ (-fies, -fying, -fied) *vti.* to convert sth or become converted into silica —**silicification** /sɪˌlissifiˈkaysh'n/ *n.*

silicle *n.* = **silicula**

silicon /ˈsɪlikən/ *n.* an abundant brittle nonmetallic chemical element found naturally in sand, granite, clay, and many minerals, and used in alloys, semiconductors, and building materials. Symbol **Si** [Early 19thC. Coined from SILICA + -ON.]

silicon carbide *n.* an extremely hard bluish-black crystalline compound used as an abrasive, refractory, and semiconductor. Formula: SiC.

silicon chip *n.* a small wafer of silicon forming the base on which an integrated circuit is laid out, or such a wafer together with its integrated circuit

silicon dioxide *n.* a colourless transparent solid that melts at a very high temperature. It is an important material in microchip manufacture. Formula: SiO_2.

silicone /ˈsɪliˌkōn/ *n.* a silicon-based synthetic substance in the form of a heat- and water-resistant grease, oil, or plastic. Silicones are used as lubricants, insulators, water-repellents, resins, adhesives, coatings, and paints. ◊ **siloxane** [Mid-20thC. Coined from SILICON + -ONE.]

Silicon Valley region in Santa Clara County, western California, that is an important centre for electronics and computer manufacturing industries

silicosis /ˌsɪliˈkōssiss/ *n.* a lung disease caused by prolonged inhalation of dust containing silica, and marked by the development of fibrous tissue in the lungs resulting in chronic shortness of breath —**silicotic** /ˌsɪliˈkottik/ *adj.*

silicula /sɪˈlikyoōlə/ (*plural* -**lae** /-lee/ *or* -**las**), **silicule** /ˈsɪli kyool/, **silicle** /ˈsɪliklˈl/ *n.* a type of dry fruit, e.g. that of honesty, consisting of a broad flat pod divided by a membrane into two seed chambers [Mid-18thC. From Latin, literally 'little pod', from *siliqua* (see SILIQUE).]

silique /sɪˈleek/, **siliqua** /ˈsɪlikwə/ (*plural* -**quae** /-kwee/ *or* -**quas**) *n.* a long dry seed capsule of plants of the mustard family that has two valves that open, leaving a central partition to which seeds are attached [Late 18thC. Via French from, ultimately, Latin *siliqua* 'seed pod'.] —**siliquaceous** /ˌsɪli ˈkwayshəss/ *adj.* —**siliquose** /ˈsɪlikwōss/ *adj.* —**siliquous** /-kwəss/ *adj.*

silk /sɪlk/ *n.* **1.** THREAD FROM SILKWORMS the fine fibre that silkworms secrete to make their cocoons. Because of its strength and elasticity and soft, shiny appearance, it is used in the manufacture of threads and fabrics. **2.** TEXTILES SILK THREAD OR FABRIC thread or fabric made from the fibre that silkworms secrete **3.** ZOOL THREAD FROM SPIDERS a fine fibre that spiders secrete and use to make their webs, nests, and cocoons **4.** LAW KING'S OR QUEEN'S COUNSEL sb who has the right to practise as a King's or Queen's Counsel (*informal*) **5.** LAW HIGH BARRISTER'S GARMENT the gown worn by a King's or Queen's Counsel ■ **silks** *npl.* HORSERACING JOCKEY'S SILK GARMENTS distinctively coloured clothes made from silk or a similar fabric, worn by a jockey as a mark of identification [Old English *seoloc*. Origin uncertain: probably via a Slavic language, from, ultimately, Chinese.] ◊ **take silk** to become a King's or Queen's Counsel

silkaline /ˈsɪlkə leen/, **silkalene** *n.* a fine cotton fabric with a glossy finish [Late 19thC. Coined from SILK + -OLINE.]

silk cotton *n.* = **kapok**

silk-cotton tree *n.* a tropical tree with large fruit capsules containing seeds coated with silky hairs, the source of kapok. Genera: *Bombax* and *Ceiba*.

silken /ˈsɪlkən/ *adj.* **1.** MADE OF SILK made or consisting of silk **2.** LIKE SILK IN TEXTURE OR APPEARANCE resembling silk, especially in smoothness, softness, or shininess ○ *Spaniels have lovely silken ears.* **3.** IN SILK CLOTHES dressed in garments made of silk **4.** SOFT OR GENTLE pleasingly soft, gentle, or delicate ○ *silken phrases* **5.** LUXURIOUS luxurious or opulent (*dated*)

silk gland *n.* a salivary gland of a cocoon-spinning insect or an abdominal gland of a web-spinning spider that produces a viscous liquid that is expelled in a thread and polymerizes into a filament

silk hat *n.* a man's top hat with an outer covering made of silk or a fabric resembling silk

silkie /ˈsɪlki/ *n. Scotland* = **selkie**

silk-screen *vti.* PRINT DESIGN BY SILK-SCREEN PRINTING to print a design on paper or fabric using the silk-screen printing technique ■ *n.* **1.** = **silk-screen printing 2.** SILK-SCREEN PRINT a print made using the silk-screen printing technique

silk-screen printing, **silk-screen** *n.* a method of printing on paper or fabric in which ink is forced through areas of a silk screen that are not blocked out with an impermeable substance

silk tree *n.* an Asian tree of the mimosa family that is widely cultivated for its showy pink flowers with silky filaments. Latin name: *Albizia julibrissin*.

silkweed /ˈsɪlk weed/ *n.* = **milkweed**

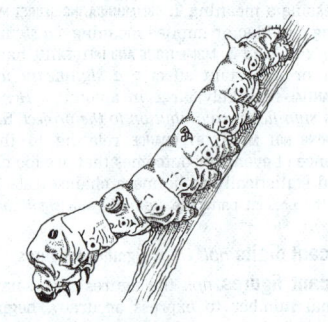
Silkworm

silkworm /ˈsɪlk wurm/ *n.* **1.** MOTH LARVA THAT SPINS SILK a yellowish caterpillar, the larva of an Asian moth, that feeds on mulberry leaves and is a commercial source of silk. Latin name: *Bombyx mori*. **2.** SILK-SPINNING LARVA a moth larva that excretes a substance resembling silk. Family: Bombycidae.

silkworm moth *n.* a moth with larvae that spin silk for cocoons. Family: Bombycidae.

silky /ˈsɪlki/ (-**ier**, -**iest**) *adj.* **1.** LOOKING OR FEELING LIKE SILK resembling silk, especially in smoothness, softness, or shininess ○ *silky hair* **2.** TEXTILES MADE OF SILK made of silk or a similar fibre or fabric ○ *a silky blouse* **3.** SMOOTH IN MANNER smooth, refined, elegant, or sophisticated, often to the extent of being unctuous ○ *a silky manner* **4.** COVERED WITH FINE HAIRS covered with delicate downy hairs or feathers —**silkily** *adv.* —**silkiness** *n.*

silky oak *n.* an Australian evergreen tree grown for its feathery leaves, orange flowers, and smooth silky timber. Latin name: *Grevillea robusta*.

silky terrier *n.* a small slender Australian terrier with a long silky grey or grey-and-tan coat

sill /sɪl/ *n.* **1.** BUILDING WINDOW LEDGE a ledge below a window, especially one on the inside of a building **2.** BUILDING BOTTOM OF FRAME the horizontal part at the bottom of a window or door frame **3.** GEOL LAYER OF IGNEOUS ROCK a more or less horizontal layer of igneous rock forced between layers of sedimentary rock or older volcanic beds [Old English *syll* 'foundation of a wall']

sillabub *n.* = **syllabub**

siller /ˈsɪlər/ *n. Scotland* (*archaic*) **1.** MONEY money **2.** SILVER silver [14thC. Scots variant of SILVER.]

sillimanite /ˈsɪliməˌnīt/ *n.* a white or greenish-brown fibrous mineral consisting of aluminium silicate and found in metamorphic rock [Mid-19thC. Coined from the name of US geologist Benjamin *Silliman* (1779–1864) + -ITE.]

Sillitoe /ˈsɪlitō/, **Alan** (*b.* 1928) British novelist, short story writer, and poet. The theme of social exclusion and of the individual's rebellion against society runs through much of his work, including *Saturday Night and Sunday Morning* (1958).

silly /ˈsɪli/ *adj.* (-**lier**, -**liest**) **1.** RIDICULOUS lacking common sense **2.** TRIVIAL unworthy of serious concern **3.** DAZED OR HELPLESS in or into a stunned, dazed, or helpless condition ○ *be scared silly* **4.** CRICKET NEAR BATSMAN used to describe a fielder or fielding position near the batsman in cricket ○ *silly mid-on* ■ *n.* (*plural* -**lies**) SILLY PERSON sb who lacks sense or acts foolishly (*informal*) [Old English *sælig* 'happy'. Ultimately from a prehistoric West Germanic word meaning 'luck, happiness'.] —**sillily** adv. —**silliness** n.

WORD KEY: ORIGIN

Silly has undergone one of the most astonishing semantic about-faces in the history of the English lexicon. In a thousand years it has gone from 'blessed, happy' to 'foolish'. The transformation began with 'blessed' becoming 'pious'. This led on via 'innocent, harmless', 'pitiable', and 'feeble' to 'feeble in mind, foolish'. The related German *selig* retains its original meaning 'happy, blessed'.

---

silly billy (plural **silly billies**) n. a silly or foolish person (informal)

Silly Putty tdmk. a trademark for a soft coloured modelling material that can be stretched and bounced

silly season n. a period in summer when newspapers print frivolous articles because there is a lack of political news

silo /sílō/ n. (plural **-los**) **1.** CONTAINER FOR GRAIN OR ANIMAL FEED a tall cylindrical tower used for storing grain, animal feed, or other material or for making silage **2.** MISSILE SAFETY CHAMBER a reinforced, protective underground chamber where a missile or missiles can be stored and from which they can be launched ■ vt. (**-los, -loing, -loed**) STORE IN SILO to store sth in a silo [Mid-19thC. Via Spanish from, ultimately, Latin *sirus*, from Greek *siros* 'pit to keep corn in'.]

siloxane /si lók sayn/ n. a compound containing silicon atoms alternating with oxygen atoms and attached to organic groups or hydrogen. ◊ **silicone** [Early 20thC. Coined from SILICON + OXYGEN + METHANE.]

silt /silt/ n. RIVER DEPOSITS fine-grained sediment, especially of mud or clay particles at the bottom of a river or lake ■ vti. (**silts, silting, silted**) CLOG UP to become full or obstructed, or to fill or obstruct sth, with silt [15thC. Origin uncertain: probably from a Scandinavian source.] —**siltation** /sil táysh'n/ n. —**silty** /sílti/ adj.

siltstone /sílt stōn/ n. a form of fine-grained sandstone consisting of compressed silt

Silures /sí lyoŏ reez/ npl. an ancient people that occupied lands in western Britain, especially South Wales, and who put up a strong defence against the invading Romans during the 1st century AD [Late 19thC. From Latin.]

Silurian /s-lyoŏri ən/ n. **1.** GEOL GEOLOGICAL PERIOD the period of geological time when fishes first appeared, 439 to 408.5 million years ago **2.** PEOPLES MEMBER OF SILURES a member of the Silures [Early 18thC. Formed from Latin *Silures*; from the discovery of rocks of this period in southeast Wales, where the Silures lived.] —**Silurian** adj.

silurid /sī loŏrid/ n. EURASIAN FRESHWATER CATFISH a freshwater catfish of Europe and Asia with an elongated scaleless body, a short dorsal fin, and a long anal fin. Family: Siluridae. ■ adj. OF SILURIDS relating or belonging to the silurids [From Latin *silurus* 'type of catfish', which came from Greek *silouros*]

silva, sylva (plural **-vas** or **-vae** /-vee/) n. **1.** REGIONAL FOREST the forests or trees of a particular region **2.** BOOK DESCRIBING TREES a book or treatise on the trees or forests of a particular region

silvan adj. = **sylvan**

Silvanus, Sylvanus n. in Roman mythology, the god of fields and forests, protector of flocks and cattle. He later came to be identified with the gods Pan and Faunus.

silver /sílvər/ n. **1.** SHINY ELEMENT a shiny greyish-white metallic element that has the highest thermal and electric conductivity of any substance and is used in coins, ornaments, jewellery, dental materials, solders, photographic chemicals, and conductors. Symbol Ag **2.** HOUSEHOLD SILVER ARTICLES items of tableware or other household goods that are made of silver, coated with silver plate, or made of a silver-coloured metal **3.** COINS COINS money, especially coins made of silver or a silver-coloured metal **4.** COLOURS LUSTROUS GREYISH-WHITE a pale or lustrous greyish-white colour **5.** SILVER MEDAL a silver medal (informal) **6.** PHOTOGRAPHY SILVER COMPOUND a compound of silver used in photography, e.g. to make paper sensitive to light

■ adj. **1.** MADE OF SILVER made of, plated with, or containing some silver ○ a silver bracelet **2.** COLOURS WITH COLOUR OF SILVER of a pale or lustrous greyish-white colour **3.** SHINY shining like silver ○ silver moonlight **4.** OF 25TH ANNIVERSARY connected with or describing the 25th anniversary of sth ○ silver wedding anniversary **5.** RESONANT pleasingly resonant and clear in tone **6.** FLUENT fluently or persuasively eloquent ○ a silver tongue ■ v. (**-vers, -vering, -vered**) **1.** vt. COAT STH WITH SILVER to coat sth with a layer of silver or a similar shiny material **2.** vti. MAKE OR BECOME LIKE SILVER to become, or cause sth to become, like silver in colour or sheen ○ Frost silvered the trees. [Old English *siolfor*. Probably ultimately from an Asian source.] —**silverer** n. —**silvering** n.

Silver Age n. in classical mythology, the epoch following the Golden Age that was characterized by a refusal to serve the gods and a love of luxury

silverback /sílvər bak/ n. an older adult male gorilla with greyish-white hair on its back

silver beet n. ANZ a type of beet grown in Australia and New Zealand It has large heavily veined leaves and is eaten as a vegetable. Latin name: *Beta vulgaris cicla*. [From its white stalks and midribs]

silverbell /sílvər bel/, **silverbell tree** n. a deciduous tree or shrub of the storax family of the southeastern United States and Asia with toothed leaves and drooping white bell-shaped flowers. Genus: *Halesia*.

silver birch n. a deciduous tree of Europe and Asia that has peeling silvery-white bark. Latin name: *Betula pendula*.

silver bromide n. a yellowish light-sensitive powder that is used in photographic emulsions because it darkens when exposed to light. Formula: AgBr.

silver chloride n. a white light-sensitive powder that is used in photographic emulsions because it darkens when exposed to light. Formula: AgCl.

silver dollar n. COINS **1.** AMERICAN COIN a one-dollar coin with high silver content, minted from time to time in various designs and sizes in the United States **2.** Can COMMEMORATIVE CANADIAN COIN in Canada, a dollar coin issued annually, as a collector's item, to commemorate different subjects

silver dollar fish n. a tropical freshwater fish from Central or South America with a flattened round silver body. It is similar to the piranha but has a more docile nature and plant-eating habits. Genera: *Metynnis* and *Myleus*.

silvereye /sílvər ī/ n. ANZ = **white-eye**

silver fern n. NZ **1.** BOT = **ponga 2.** STYLIZED FROND a stylized depiction of a silver fern leaf on a dark background. It is an emblem of some of New Zealand's sporting teams, especially the All Blacks. [From the colour of its foliage]

silver fir n. a fir tree with leaves that have a white or silvery underside. Genus: *Abies*.

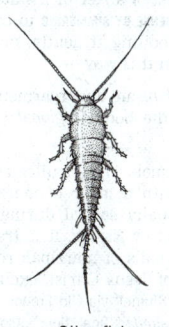

Silverfish

silverfish /sílvər fish/ (plural **-fish** or **-fishes**) n. **1.** INSECTS WINGLESS INSECT a small silvery wingless insect with three long tail bristles and two long antennae that feeds on the starch of books, wallpaper, food, and other materials. Latin name: *Lepisma saccharina*. **2.** ZOOL SILVER-SCALED FISH a silvery fish, e.g. the moonfish, tarpon, or silversides

silver fox n. **1.** ZOOL FOX WITH WHITE-TIPPED FUR an American red fox in the colour phase in which the black

fur is silver-tipped **2.** PELT OF SILVER FOX the pelt of the silver fox, once valued for making fur coats and other articles

silver frost n. = **glaze ice**

silver-gilt n. **1.** SILVER COATED WITH GOLD silver that has been coated with a very thin layer of gold **2.** SILVER COATING a decorative coating of silver leaf

silver-grey adj. PALE LUSTROUS GREY of a pale lustrous grey colour ■ n. PALE LUSTROUS GREY COLOUR a pale lustrous grey colour

silver gull n. a common Australian seagull that has a white head and breast, a grey back, black-tipped wing feathers, and red beak, legs, and eye-ring. Latin name: *Larus novaehollandiae*.

silver hake n. a common fish resembling a cod with silvery scales. It is found in North American Atlantic coastal waters and is an important food fish. Latin name: *Merluccius bilinearis*.

silver iodide n. a yellow light-sensitive powder that is used in photographic emulsions and as an antiseptic. It can also be scattered in clouds to cause rainfall. Formula: AgI.

silver lining n. sth that offers hope or benefit in a situation that is generally adverse [From the proverb 'Every cloud has a silver lining']

silver maple n. **1.** N AMERICAN MAPLE WITH SILVERY LEAVES a common North American maple tree with deeply cut five-lobed leaves that are light green above and silvery-white underneath. Latin name: *Acer saccharinum*. **2.** HARD WOOD the hard wood of the silver maple tree

silver medal n. an award for taking second place in a race or other competition, usually in the form of a silver disc on a ribbon —**silver medallist** n.

silvern /sílvərn/ adj. made of or resembling silver (archaic or literary) [Old English *silfren*, formed from *siolfor* (see SILVER)]

silver nitrate n. a white poisonous light-sensitive compound used in photographic emulsions, as a chemical reagent, and in medicine as an antiseptic and astringent. Formula: AgNO₃.

silver plate n. **1.** THIN LAYER OF SILVER a thin layer of silver, especially one that is used to coat a base metal **2.** ITEMS COATED IN SILVER items, especially of tableware, that are made from a base metal coated with a thin layer of silver

silver-plate (**silver-plates, silver-plating, silver-plated**) vt. to coat sth, especially a base metal, with a thin layer of silver, usually by electroplating

silverpoint /sílvər poynt/ n. **1.** DRAWING TECHNIQUE USING SILVER-TIPPED PENCIL a drawing technique that involves using a silver-tipped pencil on specially prepared paper or parchment **2.** DRAWING IN SILVERPOINT a drawing made using the silverpoint technique

silver salmon n. = **coho salmon**

silver screen n. **1.** CINEMA films or the cinema industry in general **2.** FILM PROJECTION SCREEN the screen that films are projected onto

silver service n. a method of serving food in restaurants that includes correct table settings, changing cutlery to suit dishes ordered, and serving vegetables and other side dishes to diners at table (hyphenated when used before a noun) [From the silver dish and other implements used for serving the food]

silverside /sílvər sīd/ n. **1.** ZOOL SMALL FISH WITH SILVERY BAND a small bony fish with a broad silvery stripe along each side of its body. Family: Atherinidae. **2.** FOOD CUT OF BEEF FOR ROASTING a cut of beef taken from behind and below rump and topside, usually used for roasting or pot-roasting

silversmith /sílvər smith/ n. sb who is skilled in making or repairing silver or silver-plated objects [Old English *seolforsmi*] —**silversmithing** n.

silver spoon n. inherited wealth and high social status [From the expression be born with a silver spoon in your mouth 'to be born advantageously into a wealthy family']

silverspot /sílvər spot/ n. a butterfly of northern temperate areas that has silver-coloured spots. Family: Nymphalidae.

silver standard *n.* a basis for currency consisting of a reserve of silver for which issued bills are redeemable at a fixed rate

silvertail /sílvər tayl/ *n.* *Aus* an affluent and influential member of society (*slang*)

silver-tongued *adj.* having the gift of persuading or complimenting people eloquently and with charm

silverware /sílvər wair/ *n.* **1.** SILVER ITEMS items made of silver or silver plate, especially tableware **2.** *US* METAL TABLEWARE metal knives, forks, and other items of tableware

silverweed /sílvər weed/ *n.* a creeping plant of the rose family that has yellow flowers and leaves with silvery undersides. Latin name: *Potentilla anserina.*

silvery /sílvəri/ *adj.* **1.** LIKE SILVER resembling silver, especially in colour or sheen **2.** WITH SILVER containing some silver or coated with a thin layer of silver **3.** CLEAR AND RESONANT clear and ringing in tone ○ *silvery peals of laughter* —**silveriness** *n.*

silvicolous /sil víkələss/ *adj.* used to describe plants and animals that grow or live in woods or forests [Formed from Latin *silvicola* 'living in woods']

silviculture /sílvi kulchər/, **sylviculture** *n.* the study, cultivation, and management of forest trees [Late 19thC. From French, from Latin *silva* 'a wood' + French *culture* 'cultivation'.] —**silvicultural** /sílvi kúlchərəl/ *adj.* —**silviculturist** /-kúlchərist/ *n.*

sim. *abbr.* similar

sima /símə/ *n.* an area consecrated for the ordination of Buddhist monks, and for other formal monastic activities

simarouba /símmə róobə/, **simaruba** *n.* a tropical American tree of the quassia family with bark that has various medicinal properties. Genus: *Simaruba.*

Simchat Torah /símchass-/, **Simchas Torah** /sím-as-/, **Simchath Torah** *n.* a Jewish festival at the end of Succoth celebrating the end of the annual cycle of reading from the Torah and the beginning of a new one [Late 19thC. From Hebrew *śimḥath tōrā*, literally 'rejoicing of the Torah'.]

Georges Simenon

Simenon /seemə náwN/, **Georges** (1903–89) Belgian-born French writer. He published more than 500 novels under a variety of pseudonyms, but is best known for the 80 crime novels featuring his tough and intuitive sleuth, Inspector Maigret. Full name **Georges Joseph Christian Simenon**

Simferopol /símfə ráwpəl/, **Simferopol'** city on the Crimean Peninsula, in southern Ukraine, situated about 48 km/30 mi. northeast of Sevastopol. Population: 353,000 (1991).

simian /símmi ən/ *adj.* OF OR LIKE MONKEYS AND APES belonging to or characteristic of monkeys or apes, or resembling such animals in appearance or behaviour ■ *n.* MONKEY a monkey or an ape [Early 17thC. Formed from Latin *simia* 'ape', from, ultimately, Greek *simos* 'snub-nosed'.]

similar /símmilər/ *adj.* **1.** ALIKE sharing some qualities, but not exactly identical **2.** GEOM THE SAME PROPORTIONALLY used to describe geometric figures that differ in size or proportion but not in shape or angular measurements **3.** *Malaysia, Singapore* IDENTICAL exactly the same [Late 16thC. Directly or via French *similaire* from medieval Latin *similaris*, from Latin *similis* 'like'.]

similar to In its meaning 'of the same kind, having resemblances', *similar* is followed by *to*: *My own experience has been similar to yours.* Use with *as*, though occasionally found, is incorrect: *I had a similar experience as yours.*

similarity /símmi lárrəti/ (*plural* **-ties**) *n.* **1.** LIKENESS the possession of one or more qualities in common **2.** SHARED CHARACTERISTIC a quality or feature that two or more things or people have in common

similarly /símmilərli/ *adv.* **1.** IN A SIMILAR WAY so as to share some qualities but not exactly identical **2.** CORRESPONDINGLY used to indicate that sth corresponds to or is similar to sth else

simile /símmili/ *n.* a figure of speech that draws a comparison between two different things, especially a phrase containing the word 'like' or 'as', e.g. 'as white as a sheet'. ◊ **metaphor** [14thC. From Latin *simile* 'a like thing', from *similis* 'like'.]

similitude /si mílli tyood/ *n.* **1.** BEING SIMILAR likeness or resemblance (*formal*) **2.** STH OR SB THAT RESEMBLES ANOTHER sth or sb that is like sth or sb else **3.** A SIMILARITY a shared characteristic (*formal*) **4.** FORM OR SEMBLANCE a form or semblance of sb or sth (*formal or literary*) **5.** SIMILE OR ALLEGORY a simile, allegory, or parable (*archaic*) [14thC. Directly or via Old French from Latin *similitudo* 'likeness', from *similis* 'like'.]

simious /símmi əss/ *adj.* simian (*archaic*)

simitar *n.* = scimitar

Simla /símlə/ capital city of Himachal Pradesh State, northwestern India. Population: 81,463 (1991).

Simmental /símmen taal/ (*plural* **-tals** *or* **-tal**), **Simmenthal** (*plural* **-thals** *or* **-thal**) *n.* a large cow with a yellowish-brown or reddish coat, a white head, and white legs. It belongs to a breed originating in Switzerland and is bred for beef and milk. [Early 20thC. Named after the *Simmental* valley in central Switzerland.]

simmer /símmər/ *v.* (**-mers, -mering, -mered**) **1.** *vti.* COOK COOK JUST BELOW BOIL to cook gently or cook sth gently just below boiling point, usually with the occasional bubble breaking on the surface **2.** *vti.* COOK STAY OR KEEP STH BELOW BOIL to stay just below boiling point, or to cause a liquid to stay just below boiling point **3.** *vi.* BE GROWING ANGRY to have anger, or some other strong emotion, building up inside ○ *simmering with rage* **4.** *vi.* BUILD UP to build up or ferment, often without being expressed ○ *'with grief and rage and laughter all simmering within me like a boiling pot'* (Arthur Conan Doyle, *The Lost World*; 1912) ■ *n.* COOK GENTLE COOKING TEMPERATURE a cooking temperature that cooks food or keeps liquid at just below boiling point [Mid-17thC. Alteration of obsolete English *simper* 'to simmer', which may have been an imitation of the sound.] **simmer down** *v.* **1.** *vi.* BECOME CALM to become calm, e.g. after an outburst of anger or a state of excitement **2.** *vti.* COOK CONDENSE BY SIMMERING to condense sth by simmering or boiling it gently, or to reduce the volume of sth in this way

simmet /símmət/ *n.* an undergarment worn on the upper part of the body (*regional regional*) [15thC. From Scots.]

simnel cake /símnəl-/ *n.* a fruitcake covered with marzipan or with a layer of marzipan baked in the middle, usually served during the Christian festivals of Lent or Easter. It is traditionally decorated with 11 balls of marzipan representing the loyal apostles of Jesus Christ, excluding Judas Iscariot. [13thC. 'Simnel' via Old French *simenel* from, ultimately, Latin *simila* 'fine flour' (source of English *semolina*).]

Simon *n.* in the New Testament, one of the 12 apostles, traditionally believed to have been martyred in Persia with St Jude. Known as **Simon the Zealot**

Simon /símən/, **Neil** (*b.* 1927) US playwright. Plays such as *The Odd Couple* (1965) and *Sweet Charity* (1966) made him the country's most successful writer of comedies. He later wrote more serious works including the Pulitzer Prize-winning *Lost in Yonkers* (1991). Full name **Marvin Neil Simon**

Nina Simone

Simone /si mốn/, **Nina** (*b.* 1933) US jazz singer and composer. She wrote and sang protest songs against racism in the 1960s, using her smoky contralto voice to great dramatic effect. Real name **Eunice Kathleen Waymon**

simoniac /si mốni ak/ *n.* SB TRADING IN SACRED THINGS sb who buys and sells sacred things or who has been found guilty of buying and selling sacred things ■ *adj.* **simoniac, simoniacal** CONNECTED WITH SIMONY relating or belonging to the buying or selling of sacred or spiritual things [14thC. From French *simoniaque*, from late Latin *simonia* (see SIMONY).]

simon-pure /símən-/ *adj.* completely genuine or authentic [Late 18thC. From *Simon Pure*, the name of a character in Susannah Centlivre's play *A Bold Stroke for a Wife* (1717).]

Simon's Town town and naval base in Western Cape Province, South Africa, situated about 32 km/20 mi. south of Cape Town. Population: 6,500 (1997).

simony /síməni, símməni/ *n.* in Christianity, the buying or selling of sacred or spiritual things [13thC. Via French *simonie* from late Latin *simonia*, from *Simon Magus*, the name of a Samaritan who tried to buy the power of conferring the Holy Spirit.] —**simonist** *n.*

simoom /si móom/, **simoon** /si móon/ *n.* a hot dry wind that blows across North Africa and the Arabian peninsula, carrying dust and sand particles [Late 18thC. From Arabic *samūm*, from *samma* 'to poison'.]

simp /simp/ *n.* *US* a simpleton (*informal offensive*) [Early 20thC. Shortening.]

simpatico /sim páttikō/ *adj.* sharing similar temperaments or interests and, therefore, able to get on well together [Mid-19thC. Via Spanish *simpático* or Italian *simpatico* 'sympathetic' from, ultimately, Latin *sympathia*.]

simper /símpər/ *v.* (**-pers, -pering, -pered**) **1.** *vi.* SMILE COYLY to smile in an affected, coy, and usually irritating way **2.** *vt.* SAY STH COYLY to say sth while simpering ■ *n.* AFFECTED SMILE a coy and affected smile [Mid-16thC. Origin uncertain: perhaps from Scandinavian source.] —**simperer** *n.* —**simpering** *adj., n.* —**simperingly** *adv.*

simple /símp'l/ *adj.* (**-pler, -plest**) **1.** EASY easy to do, understand, or work out because not complicated ○ *a simple task* **2.** NOT ELABORATE lacking decoration or embellishment and therefore plain in appearance ○ *a simple black dress* **3.** NOT COMPLEX made up of or having only one part or element ○ *a simple organism* **4.** WITHOUT COMPLICATIONS with no complications, luxuries, or embellishments ○ *the simple life* **5.** STRAIGHTFORWARD ordinary or straightforward ○ *It's a simple case of the flu and I should be back to work in a couple of days.* **6.** OFFENSIVE TERM an offensive term referring to sb with an intellectual capacity that does not allow sb to perform higher level cognitive processes (*offensive*) **7.** NAIVE naive and lacking in depth and detail **8.** HUMBLE humble and unsophisticated ○ *simple folk* **9.** GUILELESS direct, sincere, or lacking any form of deceitfulness **10.** CHEM CONTAINING ONE COMPOUND ONLY consisting of a single chemical compound **11.** BIOL NOT DIVIDED not divided, either totally or partially, into separate segments ○ *a simple leaf.* ◊ **compound** ■ *n.* (*archaic*) **1.** NAIVE OR UNINTELLIGENT PERSON a naive, unsophisticated, or unintelligent person **2.** SIMPLE THING sth that has no additions, complications, or separate parts **3.** HERBAL MEDICINE an herbal medicine or an herb that yields medicine [Pre-12thC. Via French from Latin *simplus*. Ultimately from an Indo-European base that is also the ancestor of English *assemble*, *same*, *single*, and *some*.] —**simpleness** *n.*

WORD KEY: USAGE

See Usage note at *simplistic*.

simple closed curve *n.* a plane curve, e.g. a circle or ellipse, that is closed and does not intersect itself

simple equation *n.* = linear equation

simple fraction *n.* a fraction that consists of two whole numbers separated by a horizontal or slanting line, as opposed to a decimal fraction

simple fracture *n.* a fracture of a bone in which the fragments remain in their correct alignment, with little damage to the surrounding tissue

simple fruit *n.* a fruit, e.g. a pea pod or a tomato, that forms from a single pistil

simple harmonic motion *n.* a type of periodic motion in which a body experiences a force proportional to its distance from a fixed point and directed towards the fixed point. US term **harmonic motion**

simple-hearted *adj.* honest, open, and lacking deceit or deviousness

simple interest *n.* interest on an investment that is calculated once per period, usually annually, on the amount of the capital alone and not on any interest already earned

simple machine *n.* any one of the six devices formerly considered to be the elements from which all machines were composed. They were the inclined plane, lever, pulley, screw, wedge, and wheel and axle.

simple-minded *adj.* **1.** LACKING DUE THOUGHT showing a lack of intelligent thinking or proper consideration **2.** OFFENSIVE TERM an offensive term referring to sb whose intellectual ability is limited (*offensive*) **3.** UNSOPHISTICATED without guile or complexity —**simple-mindedly** *adv.* —**simple-mindedness** *n.*

simple protein *n.* a protein such as globulin that yields only amino acids on complete hydrolysis

simple sentence *n.* a sentence that takes the form of a single main clause with no relative or subordinate clause, e.g. 'I read the book'. ◊ **complex sentence**, **compound sentence**

Simple Simon *n.* an offensive term referring to sb, especially a man or boy, who is perceived as lacking intelligence or sophistication (*insult*) [From the name of a character in a nursery rhyme]

simple sugar *n.* = monosaccharide

simple tense *n.* a grammatical form of a verb that expresses a relationship of time without using any auxiliary or modal verbs. In English, there are only two simple tenses, the simple present, as in 'I walk', and the simple past, as in 'I walked'.

simple time *n.* a musical tempo in which the main beats are divisible by two, e.g. 2/2 or 4/4 time

simpleton /símp'ltən/ *n.* an offensive term referring to sb who seems to lack intelligence or common sense (*insult*)

simplex /sím pleks/ *adj.* **1.** SIMPLE containing, using, or designed for a single element or component **2.** TELECOM ALLOWING TRANSMISSION IN ONE DIRECTION allowing transmission of signals or communication in only one direction at a time ■ *n.* **1.** LING ROOT FORM OF WORD a word in its base form, without any inflections, prefixes, or suffixes, and not formed by putting two distinct words together. The words 'book' and 'mark' are simplexes, whereas 'bookmark', 'books', 'marked', and 'remark' are not. **2.** GEOM GEOMETRICAL FIGURE OR ELEMENT a geometrical element in a Euclidean space that exhibits the minimum number of dimensions of the space, e.g. a line in one-dimensional space or a triangle in two-dimensional space **3.** US APARTMENT ON ONE FLOOR an apartment with all rooms on one floor [Late 16thC. From Latin, formed from *simplus* (see SIMPLE).]

simplicity /sim plíssəti/ (*plural* **-ties**) *n.* **1.** BEING SIMPLE lack of complexity, complication, embellishment, or difficulty **2.** SIMPLE THING a simple quality or thing [14thC. Directly or via French *simplicité* from Latin *simplicitas* 'simpleness', from *simplex* (see SIMPLEX).]

simplify /símpli fī/ (**-fies**, **-fying**, **-fied**) *vt.* **1.** MAKE STH EASIER to make sth less complicated or easier to understand **2.** MATH REDUCE MATHEMATICAL EXPRESSION TO SIMPLER TERMS to convert a mathematical expression, e.g. a fraction or equation, to a simpler form by removing common factors or regrouping elements [Mid-17thC. Via French *simplifier* from medieval Latin *simplificare*, from Latin *simplus* (see SIMPLE).] —**simplification** /símplifi káysh'n/ *n.* —**simplificative** /símplifikətiv/ *adj.* —**simplifier** /-fī ər/ *n.*

simplism /símplizəm/ *n.* a tendency to avoid or ignore the complexities of sth —**simplist** *n.*

simplistic /sim plístik/ *adj.* **1.** NAIVELY SIMPLE characterized by naive simplicity **2.** SIMPLIFYING TOO MUCH tending to oversimplify sth, especially by avoiding or ignoring its complexities —**simplistically** *adv.*

WORD KEY: USAGE
---

simple or **simplistic**? *Simplistic* is normally a derogatory word, implying that sth is artificially oversimplified rather than naturally simple: *He argued that it was simplistic to reject these methods as unscientific.* It should not be used as an alternative or supposedly stronger word for **simple**: *A simplistic* [use *simple*] *approach would be helpful here.*

Simplon Pass /sím plon-/ mountain pass in the Swiss Alps, between Brig in Switzerland, and Iselle in northern Italy. Height: 2,009 m/6,590 ft.

simply /símpli/ *adv.* **1.** NOTHING OTHER THAN with nothing else involved ○ *It was simply a misunderstanding.* **2.** PLAINLY in an uncomplicated, straightforward, or plain way ○ *To put it simply, I can't afford it.* **3.** AT ALL OR TOTALLY to any or the fullest degree or extent ○ *simply astonishing* **4.** FRANKLY frankly and without embellishment ○ *It was, quite simply, the best they had in stock.* **5.** NAIVELY without full understanding

Simpson /símps'n/, **Sir James Young** (1811–70) British obstetrician. He was the founder of gynaecology. He pioneered the use of ether in childbirth, then replaced it with chloroform (1847).

Simpson, O.J. (*b.* 1947) US American football player, sportscaster, and actor. He was one of the NFL's greatest running backs in a ten-year career, mostly with the Buffalo Bills. He was acquitted of murdering his wife after a controversial criminal trial (1995), but convicted in a civil trial (1997). Full name **Orenthal James Simpson**

Simpson Desert /símpsən-/ desert in central Australia, centred on the junction of the South Australia, Northern Territory, and Queensland borders. Area: 77,000 sq. km/29,723 sq. mi.

simulacrum /símmyŏŏ láykrəm/ (*plural* **-cra** /-krə/) *n.* **1.** REPRESENTATION OR IMAGE a representation or image of sth **2.** STH VAGUELY SIMILAR sth that has a vague, tentative, or shadowy resemblance to sth else [Late 16thC. From Latin, formed from *simulare* (see SIMULATE).]

simulant /símmyŏŏlənt/ *adj.* SIMULATING serving to imitate or reproduce the essential features of sth (*formal*) ■ *n.* = simulator *n.* 1 [Mid-18thC. From the present participle stem of Latin *simulare* (see SIMULATE).]

simular /símmyŏŏlər/ *n.* SB OR STH FAKE sb or sth that mimics, simulates, or pretends to be another person or thing, especially for deceptive purposes (*archaic*) ■ *adj.* FAKE mimicking, simulating, or pretending to be sb or sth else, especially for deceptive purposes (*archaic*) [Early 16thC. Formed from Latin *simulare* (see SIMULATE), perhaps on the model of SIMILAR.]

simulate /símmyŏŏ layt/ *vt.* (**-lates**, **-lating**, **-lated**) **1.** REPRODUCE FEATURES OF STH to reproduce an essential feature or features of sth, e.g. as an aid to study or training ○ *a computer model simulating the process of continental drift* **2.** FAKE STH to feign sth, or pretend to experience sth ○ *simulating enjoyment* **3.** MIMIC SB OR STH to mimic or imitate sb or sth ■ *adj.* FAKE OR DECEPTIVE mimicking, simulating, or pretending to be sth or sb else (*archaic*) [15thC. From Latin *simulat-*, the past participle stem of *simulare* 'to simulate', from *similis* 'like' (source of English *similar*).] —**simulative** /-lativ/ *adj.* —**simulatively** /-lativli/ *adv.*

simulated /símmyoo laytid, símmyə laytid/ *adj.* **1.** REPRODUCED BY SIMULATION reproduced or realized by simulation, especially computer simulation **2.** NOT GENUINE artificial, especially made in imitation of a genuine article, fabric, or other substance **3.** FALSE feigned or faked

simulation /símmyŏŏ láysh'n/ *n.* **1.** REPRODUCTION OF FEATURES OF STH the reproduction of the essential features of sth, e.g. as an aid to study or training **2.** FALSE APPEARANCE the imitation or feigning of sth **3.** FAKE an artificial or imitation object **4.** COMPUT, STATS CONSTRUCTION OF MATHEMATICAL MODEL the construction of a mathematical model to reproduce the characteristics of a phenomenon, system, or process, often using a computer, in order to infer information or solve problems [14thC]

simulator /símmyŏŏ laytər/ *n.* **1.** DEVICE THAT SIMULATES STH a device, instrument, or piece of equipment designed to reproduce the essential features of sth, e.g. as an aid to study or training. ◊ **emulator** *n.* 2 **2.** SB WHO SIMULATES STH sb who feigns or imitates sth —**simulatory** /símmyŏŏlə təri/ *adj.*

simulcast /símm'l kaast/ *n.* **1.** SIMULTANEOUS TV AND RADIO BROADCAST a programme that is broadcast simultaneously on both television and radio, on multiple channels, or in multiple languages **2.** LIVE BROADCAST a live broadcast of an event on closed-circuit television ■ *vt.* (**-casts**, **-casting**, **-cast**) MAKE SIMULTANEOUS BROADCAST to broadcast a simulcast programme [Mid-20thC. Blend of SIMULTANEOUS and BROADCAST.]

simultaneous /símm'l táyni əss/ *adj.* **1.** AT THE SAME TIME done, happening, or existing at the same time **2.** MATH TAKING SAME VARIABLES used to describe equations that are satisfied by the same values of the variables ■ *n.* CHESS DISPLAY OF CHESS-PLAYING an exhibition of chess-playing skills in which one player is involved in several games at the same time, systematically moving from one board to the next [Mid-17thC. From medieval Latin *simultaneus*, from Latin *simul* 'at the same time', probably on the model of *momentaneus* 'momentary'.] —**simultaneity** /símm'ltə née əti/ *n.* —**simultaneously** /símm'l táyni əssli/ *adv.* —**simultaneousness** /-əessnəss/ *n.*

sin[1] /sin/ *n.* **1.** TRANSGRESSION OF THEOLOGICAL PRINCIPLES an act, a thought, or behaviour that goes against the law or teachings of a particular religion, especially when the person who commits it is aware of this **2.** ESTRANGEMENT FROM GOD in Christian theology, the condition of being denied God's grace because of a sin or sins committed **3.** SHAMEFUL OFFENCE sth that offends a moral or ethical principle ■ *vi.* (**sins**, **sinning**, **sinned**) **1.** KNOWINGLY DO WRONG to commit a sin, especially by knowingly violating a law or the teachings of a particular religion **2.** COMMIT SHAMEFUL OFFENCE to commit any serious moral or ethical offence [Old English *synn*. Ultimately from an Indo-European base that also produced German *Sünde* 'sin' and perhaps Latin *sons* 'guilty'.] ◊ **live in sin** to live together as husband and wife without being married (*dated or humorous*)

sin[2] *abbr.* sine. ◊ **cos**, **tan**

Sinai /sí nī/ peninsula in the Middle East bounded on the east by the Gulf of Aqaba, on the north by the Mediterranean Sea, and on the west by the Gulf of Suez. A sparsely populated wilderness, it has long been the land bridge between Africa and Asia. Area: 60,863 sq. km/23,500 sq. mi.

Sinai, Mount mountain in northeastern Egypt on the south-central Sinai Peninsula, about 2,888 m/7,500 ft high. According to the Bible, it is the place where Moses received the Ten Commandments (Exodus 19).

sinamay /sínnə mī/ *n.* a stiff open-weave fabric spun from the fibres of the banana plant, used in making hats [Mid-20thC. From Tagalog.]

Sinanthropus /sin ánthrəpəss/ *n.* the original scientific name for Peking man [Early 20thC. From modern Latin, coined from late Latin *Sinae* 'the Chinese' + Greek *anthrōpos* 'person'.]

Sinatra /si naátrə/, **Frank** (1915–98) US singer and actor. He won an Academy Award for *From Here to Eternity* (1953), and is generally recognized as the supreme master of the popular song. Full name **Francis Albert Sinatra**

sin bin *n.* an area with a bench beside an ice-hockey rink where penalized players must stay during the

Frank Sinatra

period they have to serve as a time penalty for an offence (*slang*)

since /sinss/ CORE MEANING: a grammatical word used to indicate that a situation has continued from a particular time or event in the past ○ (prep) *Karen has lived in London since 1988.* ○ (adv) *She left the firm in 1980 and has since been self-employed.* ○ (conj) *He has been on a high since he got married in January.*
1. *prep., conj.* HAPPENING AFTER happening at some point or points after the stated period of time or event ○ *The rate of job growth is higher than under any administration since 1920.* ○ *Since Ryland became commissioner in 1994, all complaints are investigated fully.* **2.** *adv.* SUBSEQUENTLY at some point between then and now ○ *even when the department had an engineer, who has since retired* **3.** *conj.* BECAUSE because, seeing that ○ *He recalls that since it was autumn, it was already dark by 6:00 p.m.* [15thC. Contraction of earlier *sithence*, from Old English *siððan*, from *sīð* 'after' + *þām* 'that'.] ◇ **long since** a long time ago

—————— **WORD KEY: USAGE** ——————
See Usage note at *because*.

sincere /sin seer/ (**-cerer, -cerest**) *adj.* **1.** HONEST AND OPEN honest and unaffected in a way that shows what is said is really meant **2.** NOT FEIGNED based on what is truly and deeply felt [Mid-16thC. From Latin *sincerus* 'pure, whole'.] —**sincerely** *adv.* —**sincereness** *n.*

sincerity /sin sérrəti/ *n.* honesty in the expression of true or deep feelings ○ *We had no reason to doubt her sincerity.*

sinciput /sínssi put, -pət/ (*plural* **-ciputs** *or* **-cipita**) *n.* the part of the skull that includes the forehead and the area above it [Late 16thC. From Latin, literally 'half head'.] —**sincipital** /sin síppit'l/ *adj.*

Sinclair /síng klair, sing kláir/, **Sir Clive** (*b.* 1940) British engineer and inventor. He made pocket calculators and digital watches available to the mass market, and developed the C5, an electrically powered vehicle. Full name **Sir Clive Marles Sinclair**

Sind /sind/ historical region of southeastern Pakistan in the lower Indus valley. A province of British India from 1843, it became part of Pakistan after partition in 1947. Capital: Karachi. Population: 21,682,000 (1985). Area: 140,914 sq. km/54,407 sq. mi.

Sindhi /síndi/ (*plural* **-dhi** *or* **-dhis**) *n.* **1.** SB FROM SIND sb who was born or brought up in Sind **2.** SINDHI LANGUAGE the Indic language spoken in Sind and parts of western India. Sindhi is spoken by about 14 million people. [Early 19thC. Via Persian and Urdu *sindī* from *Sind* (see SIND), from Sanskrit *sindhu* 'river', specifically 'the Indus'.]

sine /sīn/ *n.* **1.** TRIGONOMETRIC FUNCTION FOR ANGLES for a given angle in a right-angled triangle, a trigonometric function equal to the length of the side opposite the angle divided by the hypotenuse **2.** MATHEMATICAL FUNCTION ON CIRCLE a mathematical function equal to the vertical coordinate of a circumference point divided by the radius of a circle with its centre at the origin of a Cartesian coordinate system [Late 16thC. From Latin *sinus* 'a curve, fold' (source of English *sinus*) later 'fold in a garment'. From the confusion of Arabic *jiba* 'sine' with *jayb* 'fold in a garment'.]

sinecure /sínni kyoor, sīni-, -kyawr/ *n.* **1.** PAID JOB REQUIRING LITTLE WORK a job or position that provides a regular income but requires little or no work **2.** PAID CHURCH OFFICE WITHOUT DUTIES a church office whose holder is paid but is not required to do pastoral work [Mid-17thC. From the medieval Latin phrase *beneficium sine cura*, literally 'benefice without cure (of souls)'.]

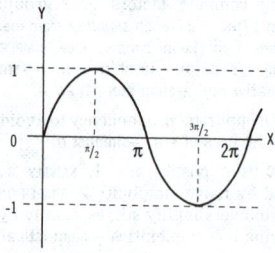
Sine curve

sine curve *n.* a graph of the sine equation 'y = a sin bx', with 'a' and 'b' being constants

sine die /síni dí ee, sínni deé ay/ *adv.* without a day being fixed for a further meeting (*formal*) ○ *The committee was adjourned sine die.* [From Latin, literally 'without day']

sine prole /sínee prṓ lee, sínnay prṓlay/ *adv.* LAW without offspring ○ *She died in 1985, aged 59, sine prole.* [From Latin, literally 'without offspring']

sine qua non /sī nee kway nón, sínnay kwaa nón, sīni kway nón, sínni kwaa nón/ *n.* an essential condition or prerequisite ○ *The suspension of industrial activity is considered a sine qua non for talks to proceed.* [From Latin, literally 'without which (cause) not']

sinew /sínnyoo/ *n.* **1.** = tendon **2.** STRENGTH strength, power, or resilience (*literary*) **3.** SOURCE OF POWER a source of strength or power (*literary*) (*often used in the plural*) ■ *vt.* (**-ews, -ewing, -ewed**) STRENGTHEN SB OR STH to give added strength to sb or sth [Old English *sin(e)we*, *sionwe*. Ultimately from a prehistoric Germanic word that is also the ancestor of Dutch *zenuw* and German *Sehne*.] —**sinewless** *adj.*

sine wave *n.* a waveform with the shape of a sine curve, representing a single frequency indefinitely repeated in time

sinewy /sínnyoo i/ *adj.* **1.** THIN AND STRONG lean, tough, and muscular ○ *a sinewy 20-year-old.* **2.** CONTAINING OR RESEMBLING TENDONS consisting of or containing tendons or stringy parts resembling tendons ○ *a rather sinewy steak* **3.** FORCEFUL vigorous and forceful (*literary*) ○ *rich, sinewy prose* —**sinewiness** *n.*

sinfonia /sínfə née ə, sin fṓni ə/ (*plural* **-as** *or* **-e**) *n.* **1.** OVERTURE OR INTERLUDE a piece of orchestral music used as an overture or interlude in an opera **2.** SYMPHONY OR SYMPHONIC WORK a complex instrumental composition, usually for a group of stringed instruments or an orchestra [Late 18thC. Via Italian from Latin *symphonia* 'sound of instruments, harmony' (source of English *symphony*).]

sinfonietta /sínfōni éttə, sínfəni-/ *n.* **1.** SHORT SYMPHONY an orchestral piece that resembles a symphony but is shorter or written for fewer instruments, often for strings only **2.** SMALL ORCHESTRA a small symphony orchestra, often composed of stringed instruments only [Early 20thC. From Italian, literally 'little sinfonia', from *sinfonia* (see SINFONIA).]

sinful /sínf'l/ *adj.* **1.** COMMITTING OR CHARACTERIZED BY SIN engaging in or characterized by behaviour that goes against the law or teachings of a particular religion **2.** WRONG morally or ethically wrong ○ *a sinful waste of an expensive education* [Old English] —**sinfully** *adv.* —**sinfulness** *n.*

sing /sing/ *v.* (**sings, singing, sang** /sang/, **sung** /sung/) **1.** *vti.* MAKE MUSIC WITH VOICE to use the voice to produce words or sounds in a musical way **2.** *vti.* PERFORM SONGS PROFESSIONALLY to perform songs as a trained or professional singer ○ *The last I heard she was singing with a group in Edinburgh.* **3.** *vti.* MAKE TUNEFUL ANIMAL SOUND to make a melodious sound that is typical of a species (*refers to animals*) **4.** *vi.* MAKE CONTINUOUS MUSICAL SOUND to make a continuous whistling, humming, or ringing sound ○ *a strong wind making the wires sing* **5.** *vi.* MAKE BRIEF SPEEDING SOUND to make a brief whistling or whizzing sound **6.** *vi.* EXPERIENCE RINGING OR HUMMING IN HEAD to experience a continuous ringing or humming sound in the head **7.** *vt.* INTONE STH to chant sth, especially a religious text, on a single note or a small range of notes **8.** *vt.* SING FOR PARTICULAR PURPOSE to bring sth to a particular condition by singing ○ *sing the baby to sleep* **9.** *vi.* CONFESS OR IMPLICATE SB to confess to or implicate others in a crime (*slang*) ○ *McGrath had a reputation for making even the toughest criminals sing.* **10.** *vti.* TELL ABOUT STH to praise sb or proclaim sth, especially in verse **11.** *vi.* BE HAPPY to rejoice in sth ■ *n.* PERFORMANCE OF SONGS a session of singing (*informal*) [Old English *singan*. Ultimately from an Indo-European word that is also the ancestor of English *song*.] —**singable** *adj.* —**singability** /síngə bílləti/ *n.* —**singingly** /síngingli/ *adv.* ◇ **sing from the same hymn-sheet** *or* **song-sheet** to express the same opinion or act in the same way (*informal*)
sing along *vi.* to join in a song that sb else is singing
sing out *vi.* to call out in a loud voice, especially to warn sb ○ *Sing out if you see any rocks ahead.*

sing. *abbr.* singular

sing-along *n. US* = **singsong** *n.* 3

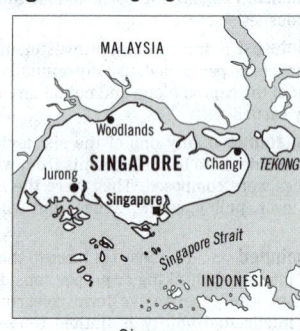
Singapore

Singapore /síngə páwr/ city state in Southeast Asia, comprising one major island and several islets, situated south of Malaysia. Language: Chinese, Malay, Singapore English, Tamil. Currency: Singapore dollar. Population: 2,986,500 (1995). Area: 640 sq. km/247 sq. mi. Official name **Republic of Singapore** —**Singaporean** *n., adj.*

Singapore English *n.* a variety of English spoken in Singapore

————— **WORD KEY: WORLD ENGLISH** —————
Singapore English is the English language as used in the city-state of Singapore, where it has been co-official since 1965 with Mandarin Chinese, Malay, and Tamil, having already been a regional lingua franca since the early 19th century. As the key language of government, business, and education, it has uniquely acquired a large fully native-speaking community of non-Western origin. There are two varieties: educated, more formal usage and a patois influenced by Chinese and Malay (and often referred to pejoratively, humorously, or affectionately as Singlish). Singapore English is 'non-rhotic' (i.e., 'r' is not pronounced in words such as *art*, *door*, and *worker*). It tends to have full vowels in all syllables (e.g., *7* is pronounced 'seh-ven' not 'sevn'). Words ending in *k*, *p*, and *t* are generally pronounced with 'glottal stops', as in 'ki?' (kick), 'sto?' (stop), and 'pu?' (put). Those words ending in clusters such as *-st* and *-ld* are reduced to the vowel and the first of the last two consonants e.g., 'fas' for *fast*, 'sol' for *sold*. Colloquial usage diverges considerably from the standard, as in: 'You come or not?' for 'Are you coming?'; 'My dad, he come from Penang' for 'My dad comes from Penang'; 'This hotel cheap' for 'This hotel is cheap'. Compare MALAYSIAN ENGLISH.

singe /sinj/ *v.* (**singes, singeing, singed**) **1.** *vti.* SCORCH STH SLIGHTLY to burn or cause sth to burn slightly so that only the surface, edge, or tip is affected ○ *The heat from the fire had singed his jacket.* **2.** *vt.* REMOVE FEATHERS OR HAIR WITH FLAME to expose the carcass of a bird or animal to a flame in order to remove unwanted feathers, bristles, or hair **3.** *vt.* BURN ENDS OF CLOTH FIBRES to burn the short fuzzy ends of fibres from cloth in the process of manufacturing it ■ *n.* SCORCH a superficial burn [Old English *sencgan*]

singer /síngər/ *n.* **1.** PERFORMER OF SONGS sb who sings, especially professionally **2.** SINGING BIRD a bird that sings **3.** POET OR VERSIFIER sb who writes poetry or other verse (*literary*)

Singh *n.* a title adopted as a surname by a Sikh boy when he is initiated at puberty into the fraternity of warriors [Early 17thC. Via Panjabi *singh* 'lion' from Sanskrit *siṃha*.]

Singh /síng/, **V.P.** (*b.* 1931) Indian statesman. After falling out with the Congress Party, he became prime minister of India (1989–90) at the head of a coalition that collapsed within a year. Full name **Vishwanath Pratap Singh**

Singh. *abbr.* Singhalese

Singhalese *n., adj.* PEOPLES, LANG = **Sinhalese**

singing /sínging/ *n.* **1.** USE OF VOICE TO PRODUCE SONGS the technique of producing musical sounds with the voice, or the performance of songs **2.** MELODIC SOUNDS the melodic or other sounds made by sb or sth that sings ■ *adj.* MAKING MUSICAL SOUND performing songs or making a melodic, whistling, humming, or ringing sound ◇ **all-singing, all-dancing** elaborate and inclusive (*informal*)

singing telegram *n.* a message sung by a messenger paid to do so, or the service of providing sung messages

single /síng g'l/ *adj.* **1.** ONE only one ○ *We didn't get a single reply.* ○ *in the space of a single day* **2.** CONSIDERED INDIVIDUALLY considered separately as sth distinct or unique ○ *every single time* **3.** UNMARRIED unmarried or characteristic of being unmarried **4.** FOR ONE PERSON suitable or designed for one person ○ *We have a single room on the third floor.* **5.** CONSISTING OF ONE THING consisting of one part, element, or quality **6.** BETWEEN ONLY TWO PEOPLE taking place as a contest or competition between two persons only, one on each side ○ *a single competition* **7.** FORMING ONE UNDIVIDED UNIT forming a whole and left undivided or unbroken ○ *The swan had been carved from a single block of ice.* **8.** UNIFORM sole and the same for all ○ *a single rate for the job* **9.** BOT WITH ONE PETAL ROW used to describe a flower that has only one whorl or row of petals ■ *n.* **1.** ACCOMMODATION FOR ONE a room, cabin, or bed for one person ○ *Do you have any singles left?* **2.** MUSIC RECORDING WITH SONG ON ONE SIDE a record, cassette, or CD with only one song on it, or the song recorded **3.** OUTWARD-BOUND TICKET a ticket that covers the outward-bound part of a journey to a destination but not the return **4.** BASEBALL BASEBALL HIT a hit in baseball that allows the batter to reach first base **5.** CRICKET CRICKET STROKE a stroke in cricket that scores one run **6.** GOLF TWO-PLAYER MATCH a match between two golfers **7.** ONE-POUND NOTE a banknote of the value of one pound (*dated*) **8. singles** RACKET GAMES RACQUET GAME BETWEEN TWO PLAYERS a match between two players in a racquet game ■ **singles** *npl.* UNMARRIED PEOPLE unmarried people considered as a group ■ *vti.* (**-gles, -gling, -gled**) BASEBALL HIT BASEBALL SINGLE to hit a single in baseball or advance a runner by hitting a single [13thC. Via Old French *sengle, single* from Latin *singulus*, from the stem of *simplus* (see SIMPLE).] —**singleness** *n.*

single out *vt.* to select an individual from a group for a particular reason

single-action *adj.* REQUIRING COCKED HAMMER OF FIREARM requiring the hammer of a firearm to be cocked by hand before each shot can be fired ■ *n.* FIREARM REQUIRING COCKED HAMMER a firearm that cannot be fired until the hammer is cocked by hand

single-blind *adj.* used to describe an experiment or clinical trial in which the subjects are not told whether the tested substance or procedure they receive is active, in order to avoid subjective bias in the results. Single-blind experiments are often used to test people's reaction to drugs so as to eliminate the placebo effect.

single bond *n.* a covalent bond between two atoms formed through the sharing of a pair of electrons

single-breasted *adj.* with a small overlap at the front and fastened with a single row of buttons

single-cell protein *n.* a protein derived from one-celled organisms grown in various cultures. It is used as food supplement.

single cream *n. UK* cream that has a butterfat content of 18 per cent and cannot be whipped or frozen. It is used for pouring over desserts or enriching savoury or sweet dishes.

single cross *n.* the first generation of offspring resulting from hybridization between two inbred lines

single currency *n.* a monetary unit that is shared by several countries

single-cut file *n.* a file that has all its teeth pointing in one direction. It is used on soft materials.

single-decker *n.* a bus that has only one passenger deck

single-end *n. Scotland* a flat with one room only

single-ended *adj.* designed for use with an unbalanced electrical signal and having one input and one output permanently earthed

single entry *n.* a system of bookkeeping in which the amounts owed or due are kept in a single account (*hyphenated when used before a noun*)

single file *n.* SINGLE LINE a line of people, animals, or vehicles standing or moving one behind another ○ *We moved along the track in single file.* ■ *adv.* MOVING IN SINGLE LINE moving in a line, one behind another

single-foot *n.* = **rack**[4] *n.* ■ *vti.* (**single-foots, single-footing, single-footed**) = **rack**[4] *v.*

single-handed *adj.* **1.** UNAIDED accomplished alone and unaided ○ *the first single-handed circumnavigation of the world* **2.** WITH ONE-HAND ONLY with only one hand or the use of one hand **3.** FOR ONE HAND ONLY using or requiring only one hand ■ *adv.* WITHOUT HELP without any help from anyone ○ *sailed round the world single-handed* —**single-handedly** *adv.* —**single-handedness** *n.*

single-hearted /-háartəd/ *adj.* sincere, faithful, and straightforward [*Single* in the obsolete sense of 'honest'] —**single-heartedly** *adv.* —**single-heartedness** *n.*

single-lens reflex *n.* a camera in which the light passes through one lens to the film and, by means of a mirror and prism system, to the focusing screen. ◊ **reflex camera**

single-minded *adj.* **1.** WITH SINGLE AIM with only one goal in mind **2.** DEDICATED with the mind fixed on one task or preoccupation —**single-mindedly** *adv.* —**single-mindedness** *n.*

single parent *n.* a parent who brings up a child or children alone, usually because he or she is unmarried, widowed, or divorced (*hyphenated when used before a noun*)

single-phase *adj.* with, generating, or powered by a single alternating voltage

single photon emission computed tomography *n.* a technique used in diagnosing certain diseases that generates a three-dimensional computer-generated image of the distribution of a radioactive tracer in a particular organ

singles bar *n.* a bar frequented by men and women, usually unmarried, who are seeking romance, companionship, or sex

single-serve *adj.* packaged in small amounts intended for one person ○ *available in single-serve sizes*

single-sex *adj.* restricted to either men or to women

single-space (**single-spaces, single-spacing, single-spaced**) *vt.* to type or print text without a blank space between the lines

singlestick /síng g'l stik/ *n.* **1.** FENCING STICK a stick fitted with a handguard, formerly used in fencing **2.** PRACTICE OF FENCING WITH SINGLESTICK the former sport or skill of fencing with a singlestick

singlet /sínglət/ *n.* **1.** SLEEVELESS UNDERGARMENT a sleeveless undershirt **2.** LIGHT SLEEVELESS SHIRT a sleeveless shirt worn with shorts in sports such as basketball or amateur boxing [Mid-18thC. Formed from SINGLE on the model of DOUBLET, because it originally referred to an unlined, one-layered garment.]

singleton /síng g'ltən/ *n.* **1.** SINGLE OCCURRENCE OF SB OR STH sb or sth that occurs singly and not as part of a group, e.g. the only child in a family **2.** CARDS ONE CARD OF A SUIT a playing card that is the only one of its suit in a hand

Singleton /síng gəltən/ town in eastern New South Wales, in Australia. It is a centre for coal mining, agriculture, and light industry. Population: 12,519 (1996).

single-tongue (**single-tongues, single-tonguing, single-tongued**) *vti.* to articulate notes on a wind instrument by raising the tip of the tongue against the palate, temporarily obstructing the flow of air

single-track *adj.* **1.** FIXED ON SINGLE IDEA fixed on one thought or idea only **2.** RAIL WITH ONE TRACK ONLY with only one track and passing places for trains coming from opposite directions **3.** TRANSP WIDE ENOUGH FOR ONE VEHICLE ONLY not wide enough to allow motor vehicles to pass each other

Single Transferable Vote *n.* a system of voting in a multimember constituency in which voters list the candidates in order of preference and any candidate receiving the required number of votes is elected. The excess votes and the votes of the bottom candidate are then redistributed among the other candidates until the required number of members has been chosen.

singly /síng gli/ *adv.* **1.** INDIVIDUALLY IN SEQUENCE one at a time or one by one ○ *They drifted back into camp singly or in small groups.* **2.** WITHOUT HELP alone and by unaided efforts **3.** SEPARATELY solely and separately

singsong /síng song/ *n.* **1.** SINGSONG WAY OF SPEAKING a voice with an intonation that rises and falls regularly in pitch **2.** OCCASION WHEN PEOPLE SING TOGETHER a meeting of a group of people to sing songs together for fun, or an impromptu session of singing ○ *After we've eaten we'll have a singsong.* US term **sing-along** **3.** SINGSONG VERSE RHYTHMS OR RHYMES a singsong rhythm or rhyme in verse, or a verse marked by such monotony ■ *adj.* WITH REPEATEDLY RISING AND FALLING INTONATION with an intonation that regularly rises and falls in pitch

singspiel /síng speel, zíng shpeel/, **Singspiel** *n.* an 18th-century German comic opera consisting of folksongs or classical music performed in a popular or folk style interspersed with spoken dialogue [Late 19thC. From German, literally 'singing play'.]

singular /síng gyōōlər/ *adj.* **1.** LING REFERRING TO ONE PERSON OR THING used to describe a word or form that refers to one person or thing **2.** EXCEPTIONAL remarkably good or admirable **3.** UNUSUAL unusual, odd, or striking ○ *The room had a singular colour scheme.* **4.** LOGIC STANDING FOR INDIVIDUAL THING used to describe a term intended to stand for an individual thing, or a proposition containing such a term ■ *n.* **1.** LING SINGULAR WORD OR FORM the form of a word that is used when referring to one person or thing **2.** LOGIC THING IN ISOLATION sth considered solely by itself [14thC. Via Old French from Latin *singularis* 'alone of its kind', from *singulus* (see SINGLE).] —**singularly** *adv.* —**singularness** *n.*

singularise *vti.* = **singularize**

singularity /síng gyōō lárrəti/ (*plural* **-ties**) *n.* **1.** SINGULAR QUALITY singular, exceptional, or unusual quality **2.** STH UNIQUE OR UNUSUAL sth that is unique, distinctive, or remarkable **3.** CHARACTERISTIC a distinguishing trait **4.** ASTROPHYS HYPOTHETICAL POINT IN SPACE a hypothetical region in space in which gravitational forces cause matter to be infinitely compressed and space and time to become infinitely distorted **5.** MATH FUNCTION THAT IS NOT DIFFERENTIABLE a point at which a complex function is undefined because it is neither differentiable nor single-valued while the function is defined in every neighbourhood of the point [13thC. Via Old French from, ultimately, Latin *singularis* (see SINGULAR).]

singularize /síng gyōōlə rīz/ (**-izes, -izing, -ized**), **singularise** (**-ises, -ising, -ised**) *v.* **1.** *vti.* MAKE OR BECOME SINGULAR to make a word singular or to become singular **2.** *vt.* MAKE CONSPICUOUS to distinguish sb or sth or make sb or sth stand out from the rest (*formal*) —**singularization** /síng gyōōlə rī záysh'n/ *n.*

singular point *n.* MATH = **singularity** *n.* 5

sinh /shīn, sinsh/ *n.* a hyperbolic sine [Late 19thC. Coined from SINE + *h* from HYPERBOLIC.]

Sinhalese /sínhə léez/ (*plural* **-leses** *or* **-lese**), **Singhalese** /síngə léez, síng gə-/ (*plural* **-leses** *or* **-lese**) *n.* **1.** MEMBER OF SRI LANKAN PEOPLE a member of a people who live mainly in Sri Lanka, where they are the dominant ethnic group **2.** SINHALESE LANGUAGE the language of the Sinhalese people and the official language of Sri Lanka. It belongs to the Indic branch of the Indo-European family of languages. [Late 18thC. Via Portuguese *Singhalez* from Sanskrit *Siṁhala*, a variant of *Siṁhala* 'Sri Lanka'.] —**Sinhalese** *adj.*

Sinicise *vti.* = **Sinicize**

Sinicism /sínissizəm, sínni-/ *n.* a custom, usage, or idiom peculiar to or characteristic of the Chinese [Late 19thC. Formed from obsolete English *Sinic* 'Chinese', from late Latin *Sinae* 'the Chinese' (see SINO-).]

Sinicize /síni sīz, sínni-/ (**-cizes, -cizing, -cized**), **Sinicise** (**-cises, -cising, -cised**) *vti.* to acquire, or give sb or sth, a Chinese idiom, form, or cultural trait (*often passive*) [Late 16thC. Formed from obsolete English *Sinic* (see SINICISM).]

Sinification /sínifi-/ *n.* the adoption, imposition, or acquisition of Chinese idioms, forms, or cultural traits [Early 20thC. Formed from English *sinify*, from late Latin *Sinae* (see SINO-).]

sinister /sínnistər/ *adj.* **1.** SUGGESTING EVIL threatening or suggesting malevolence, menace, or harm **2.** HERALDRY ON LEFT PART OF SHIELD on the left side of a heraldic shield as seen by the holder ○ *a bend sinister* [15thC. Directly and via Old French from Latin, 'left', from the superstition that the left side of the body is unlucky.] —**sinisterly** *adv.* —**sinisterness** *n.*

sinistral /sínnistrəl/ *adj.* **1.** OF OR ON LEFT SIDE relating to or located on the left side, especially the left side of the body (*archaic*) **2.** LEFT-HANDED left-handed (*archaic*) **3.** MARINE BIOL COILING CLOCKWISE coiling in a clockwise direction from the apex to the aperture —**sinistrally** *adv.*

sinistrorse /sínni strawrss/ *adj.* growing upward in a clockwise spiral [Mid-19thC. From Latin *sinistrorsus*, from *sinister* (see SINISTER).] —**sinistrorsely** *adv.*

sinistrous /sínnistrəss/ *adj.* sinister or ill-omened (*archaic*) —**sinistrously** *adv.*

Sinitic /sī níttik, si níttik/ *n.* the branch of the Sino-Tibetan language group that includes the Chinese languages [Late 19thC. Formed from late Latin *sinæ* (see SINO-).]

sink /singk/ *v.* (**sinks, sinking, sank** /sangk/ *or* **sunk, sunk** /sungk/ *or* **sunken** /súngkən/) **1.** *vti.* FALL BENEATH SURFACE OF LIQUID to go beneath the surface of a liquid or a soft substance and become partly or wholly submerged ○ *The paper boat began to sink.* **2.** *vi.* APPEAR TO FALL to appear to descend towards or below the horizon ○ *We watched the sun sink in the sky.* **3.** *vi.* FALL TO LOWER LEVEL to become lower in height or depth ○ *The water level in the lake must have sunk six inches.* **4.** *vi.* GO DOWN GRADUALLY to slowly subside or settle at a lower level **5.** *vi.* FALL GENTLY to fall or collapse slowly ○ *He sank to his knees in exhaustion.* **6.** *vt.* DRILL INTO GROUND to drill a well, tunnel, or shaft in the ground **7.** *vt.* DRIVE INTO GROUND to force sth into the ground ○ *We need to sink more piles.* **8.** *vti.* PENETRATE OR MAKE PENETRATE to penetrate sth or cause sth to penetrate sth **9.** *vi.* BE ABSORBED to become absorbed in sth **10.** *vi.* BECOME QUIETER to sound quieter or weaker ○ *voice sank to a whisper* **11.** *vi.* SUBSIDE to diminish in degree, volume, or strength **12.** *vi.* DECLINE PHYSICALLY to deteriorate physically, usually because of fatigue, injury, or ill health ○ *There's a danger he'll sink into a coma.* **13.** *vi.* FEEL DISCOURAGEMENT to pass gradually into a condition of hopelessness, dejection or despair **14.** *vi.* LOSE SOCIAL STATUS to gradually pass from a higher to a lower social status or position **15.** *vt.* INVEST IN STH to invest or lose money in a business or project ○ *He must have sunk millions into these theatres.* **16.** *vi.* DECLINE IN VALUE to decline in value or amount ○ *The pound sank again yesterday.* **17.** *vt.* BRING TO RUIN to defeat, undo, or ruin sb or sth ○ *If they won't accept our offer, we're sunk.* **18.** *vt.* DEFEAT IN CONTEST to defeat an opponent easily in a game or contest (*informal*) **19.** *vt.* SHOOT OR HIT SUCCESSFULLY to take aim at sth and make a successful shot or stroke (*informal*) ○ *sink a critical putt* ■ *n.* **1.** BASIN FOR WASHING STH a basin that is fixed or mounted against a wall, and has a piped water supply and drainage ○ *Just put the pans in the sink.* **2.** CESSPOOL a cesspool, drain, or sewer **3.** BAD OR CORRUPT PLACE a place considered to be wicked and corrupt (*old*) **4.** GEOG POORLY DRAINED LAND WHERE WATER COLLECTS an area of low-lying, poorly drained land in which water collects, sometimes in the form of a salt lake, and evaporates or sinks into the ground **5.** GEOG = **sinkhole** *n.* 1 **6.** PHYS DEVICE ABSORBING ENERGY OR OTHER ENTITY a device or component of a system at which a physical entity such as energy or neutrons is absorbed **7.** MINING MINE SHAFT a shaft in a mine [Old English *sincan*] —**sinkable** *adj.* ◇ **sink or swim** to have no alternative but to succeed or fail without help from anyone else

WORD KEY: USAGE

sank, sunk, or **sunken**? The inflections of the verb ***sink*** have been variable over many centuries of use. In current usage, the preferred past tense is ***sank***, although ***sunk*** is also used and is not incorrect. For the past participle, ***sunk*** is used (*Six enemy ships were sunk on a single day*); the alternative form ***sunken*** is used only as an adjective: *a sunken garden.*

sink in *vi.* to become fully understood ○ *I don't think the news of her death has sunk in yet.*

sinkage /síngkij/ *n.* the process of sinking or the extent to which sth sinks

sinker /síngkər/ *n.* **1.** ANGLING WEIGHT USED IN FISHING a weight used to take a fishing line or net to the bottom **2.** *US* DOUGHNUT a doughnut (*informal*) **3.** BASEBALL DOWNWARD CURVING BASEBALL THROW in baseball, a pitched ball that curves sharply downward as it reaches the plate [Early 16thC. Originally in the meaning 'someone who engraves designs on dies'.]

sinkhole /síngk hōl/ *n.* **1.** GEOG DEPRESSION IN GROUND WITH UNDERGROUND STREAM a natural depression in the land surface, especially in limestone, where a stream flows underground into a passage or cave **2.** SUNKEN AREA a sunken area where waste collects

sinking fund *n.* a fund created by setting aside regular sums for investment, usually in bonds, in order to repay a debt that will fall due at a future date

sinner /sínnər/ *n.* sb who commits a sin or who habitually does wrong

Sinn Féin /shín fáyn/ *n.* a nationalist Irish republican party founded in 1905 [Early 20thC. From Irish *sinn féin*, literally 'we ourselves'.] —**Sinn Féiner** *n.* —**Sinn Féinism** *n.*

sinoatrial /sínō áytri əl/ *adj.* relating to the sinus venosus and the right atrium of the heart [Early 20thC. Coined from SINO-, from SINUS, + *atrial*, from ATRIUM.]

sinoatrial node *n.* a small mass of specialized cardiac muscle fibres located in the wall of the right atrium of the heart. It originates the regular electrical impulses that stimulate the heartbeat.

Sinology /sī nólləji, si-/ *n.* the study of Chinese civilization, literature, and language —**Sinological** /sínə lójjik'l, sínnə-/ *adj.* —**Sinologist** /sī nólləjist, si-/ *n.*

Sinope /si nṓpi/ *n.* the outermost known natural satellite of Jupiter, discovered in 1914. It is 28 km in diameter.

Sinophile /sínə fīl, sínnə fīl/ *n.* sb who admires China or the Chinese

Sinophobe /sínə fōb, sínnə fōb/ *n.* sb who hates or fears China and the Chinese

Sino-Tibetan /sínoti bétt'n/ *n.* a family of languages of East and Southeast Asia. There are two main branches, Chinese (**Sinitic**) and Tibeto-Burman. Over twelve hundred million people speak a Sino-Tibetan language.

sinsemilla /sínssə méelyə, -míllə/ *n.* a very strong form of marijuana obtained from unpollinated female hemp plants [Late 20thC. From American Spanish, literally 'without seed'.]

sinter /síntər/ *vti.* (**-ters, -tering, -tered**) BOND METAL PARTICLES to use pressure and heat below the melting point to bond and partly fuse masses of metal particles, or to be bonded in this way ■ *n.* **1.** BONDED METAL PARTICLES a mass of metal particles bonded and partly fused by the use of pressure and heat below the melting point **2.** POROUS MINERAL SEDIMENT a whitish chemical sediment consisting of porous silica or calcium carbonate deposited by a mineral spring [Late 18thC. From German, 'cinder', from the same prehistoric Germanic word that produced English *cinder*.]

Sintra /síntrə/ city in Portugal, situated 24 km/15 mi. west of Lisbon. Population: 20,000 (1981).

sinuate /sínnyoo ət, -ayt/ *adj.* **sinuate, sinuated** BOT WITH WAVY INDENTED EDGE used to describe a leaf with a wavy indented margin ■ *vi.* (**-ates, -ating, -ated**) WIND SINUOUSLY to wind in and out [Late 16thC. From Latin *sinuat-* the past participle stem of Latin *sinuare*, 'to bend, curve', from *sinus* (see SINUS).] —**sinuately** /sínnyoo ətli, -aytli/ *adv.* —**sinuation** /sínnyoo áysh'n/ *n.*

sinuosity /sínnyoo óssəti/ (*plural* **-ties**) *n.* **1.** SINUOUSNESS the condition of being winding or curving in shape or movement **2.** STH SINUOUS a winding bend or curving movement

sinuous /sínnyoo əss/ *adj.* **1.** MOVING IN GRACEFUL CURVES with graceful winding or curving movements ○ *the sinuous movements of the dancer's arm* **2.** WINDING OR SERPENTINE full of bends and curves ○ *the sinuous course of a hill stream* **3.** DEVIOUS indirect and devious **4.** BOT = **sinuate** [Late 16thC. From Latin *sinuosus*, from *sinus* (see SINUS).] —**sinuously** *adv.* —**sinuousness** *n.*

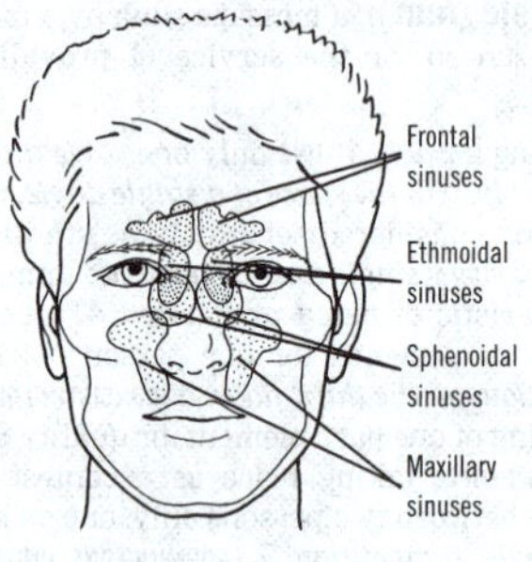

Frontal sinuses
Ethmoidal sinuses
Sphenoidal sinuses
Maxillary sinuses

Sinus

sinus /sínəss/ *n.* **1.** ANAT CAVITY IN BONE OF SKULL a cavity filled with air in the bones of the face and skull, especially one opening into the nasal passages **2.** ANAT CHANNEL FOR BLOOD a widened channel containing blood, especially venous blood **3.** MED CHANNEL LEADING FROM BODY CAVITY an elongated tract leading from a pus-filled region of the body to the exterior or to the cavity of a hollow organ **4.** BOT NOTCH BETWEEN LEAVES a cleft or indentation between the lobes of a leaf or the fused petals of a corolla [15thC. From Latin, 'curve, fold, hollow'.]

Sinus Iridum /sínəss írridəm/ *n.* ASTRON a large half-crater on the Moon adjoining the northwest side of Mare Imbrium. Its walled perimeter forms the Montes Jura and it is approximately 260 km/160 mi. in diameter.

sinusitis /sínə sítiss/ *n.* inflammation of the membrane lining a sinus of the skull

sinus node *n.* = **sinoatrial node**

sinusoid /sínə soyd/ *n.* **1.** SMALL VESSEL IN ORGAN TISSUE a small blood vessel or cavity in the tissue of an organ such as the liver, heart, or pancreas **2.** = **sine curve** ■ *adj.* LIKE SINUS resembling a sinus in shape or function —**sinusoidal** /sínə sóyd'l/ *adj.* —**sinusoidally** /-sóyd'li/ *adv.*

sinusoidal projection *n.* a map projection on which equal areas appear equal, the parallels of latitude are regularly spaced straight lines, and all the lines of longitude except the prime meridian are curved

sinus venosus /-vee nṓssəss/ (*plural* **sinus venosi** /-sī/) *n.* an enlarged pouch attached to the heart of fish, amphibians, and reptiles through which blood from the veins is forced into the atrium [From Latin, literally 'veined sinus']

Siouan /sóo ən/ *n.* **1.** FAMILY OF NATIVE N AMERICAN LANGUAGES a family of Native North American languages that includes Dakota, Omaha, and Choctaw. About 30,000 people speak a Siouan language. **2.** SB SPEAKING SIOUAN LANGUAGE sb who speaks a Siouan language ■ *adj.* PEOPLES RELATING TO SIOUX relating to any of the Sioux peoples or their cultures

Sioux /soo/ (*plural* **Sioux**) *n.* a member of a group of Native North American peoples that originally occupied vast tracts of the Great Plains, and whose members now live mainly in North and South Dakota [Early 18thC. From North American French, shortening of *Nadouessioux*, from Ojibwa (Ottawa dialect) *natowēssiwak*.]

Sioux City /sṓo-/ city in western Iowa, across the Missouri River from South Dakota and Nebraska, and northwest of Council Bluffs. Population: 83,791 (1996).

Sioux Falls city in southeastern South Dakota, on the Big Sioux River, southeast of Mitchell. Population: 113,223 (1996).

sip /sip/ *vti.* (**sips, sipping, sipped**) DRINK SLOWLY IN VERY SMALL AMOUNTS to drink sth slowly, taking only a small amount at a time ■ *n.* SMALL AMOUNT OF DRINK a very small amount of liquid taken into the mouth ○ *a few sips of champagne* [14thC. Origin uncertain: probably a variant of SUP, thought to suggest a less vigorous action.] —**sipper** *n.*

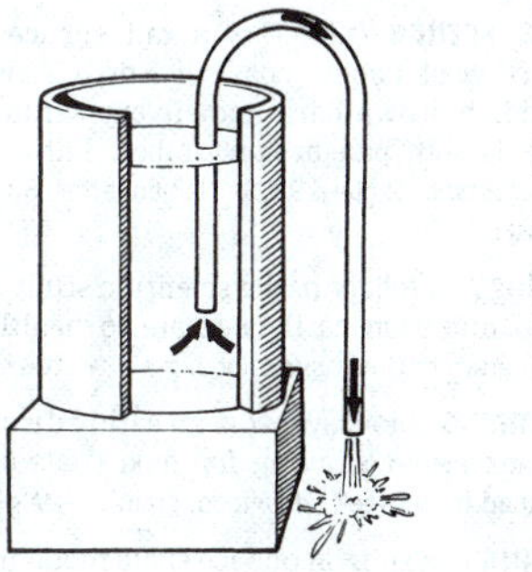

Siphon

siphon /sī́f'n/, **syphon** *v.* (**-phons, -phoning, -phoned**) **1.** *vt.* DRAW LIQUID THROUGH TUBE to transfer liquid from one container to another through a tube using atmospheric pressure to make it flow ○ *Why not siphon some petrol from the tank?* **2.** *vti.* ILLEGALLY TAP FUNDS OR RESOURCES to convey or draw money or resources from sth, especially illegally ○ *It looks as though they were siphoning money from the pension fund.* ■ *n.* **1.** BENT TUBE FOR DRAWING OFF LIQUID a bent tube or pipe used to transfer liquid from one container to another using atmospheric pressure to make it flow **2.** = **soda siphon 3.** MARINE BIOL TUBULAR ORGAN a tubular organ, especially of arthropods and molluscs, by which water is taken in or expelled [14thC. Directly or via French from Latin *sipho*, from Greek *siphōn* 'pipe, tube'.] —**siphonage** *n.* —**siphonal** /sī́fənəl/ *adj.* —**siphonic** /sī fónnik/ *adj.*

siphon bottle *n. US* = **soda siphon**

siphonophore /sī́fənə fawr, sī fónnə-/ *n.* a marine hydrozoan such as the Portuguese man-of-war that forms floating or swimming transparent or lightly-coloured colonies. Order: Siphonophora. [Mid-19thC] —**siphonophorous** /sī̀fə nóffərəss/ *adj.*

siphonostele /sī́fənə steel/ *n.* a type of vascular cylinder (**stele**), found in many ferns, in which the water-conducting vessels of the stem are arranged around a central core of pith [Early 20thC. Coined from Greek *siphōn* + STELE.] —**siphonostelic** /sī̀fənə steélik/ *adj.*

sippet /síppit/ *n.* a small piece of toast or fried bread cut in a triangle or small neat shape and usually eaten with stews or dishes served with sauce (*dated*) [Mid-16thC. Formed from an alteration of SOP, literally 'small sop'.]

sir (*stressed*) /sur/; (*unstressed*) /sər/ *n.* **1.** POLITE FORM OF ADDRESS TO MAN a form of address to a man often used in speech as a sign of respect or as a salutation in a letter ○ *Excuse me, sir, do you know what time it is?* **2.** WAY TO ADDRESS MAN TEACHER a form of address or way of referring to a man teacher, mainly used by his students ○ *Let's ask sir if we can leave early.* [13thC. Variant of SIRE.]

Sir *n.* a title of honour used before the name a knight or baronet ○ *Have you met Sir Robin?*

Siraj-ud-Daula /si raáj ŏŏd dówlə/ (1729?–57) Bengali ruler. His attack on Fort William, Calcutta, led to the Black Hole incident (1756). He was defeated by the British at the Battle of Plassey and executed (1757). Real name **Mirza Muhammad**

sirdar /súr daar/ *n.* **1.** HIGH-RANKING LEADER in India or Pakistan, sb of high rank such as a political or military leader **2.** FORMER BRITISH COMMANDER OF EGYPTIAN ARMY the title formerly given to the British commander of the Egyptian army **3.** TITLE FOR SIKH MAN a title of respect for a Sikh man [Early 17thC. Via Hindi *sardār* from Persian, literally 'head holder'.]

sire /sīr/ *n.* **1. sire, Sire** ADDRESS TO KING OR LORD a respectful form of address for a king or lord (*archaic*) ○ *We are honoured by your presence, Sire.* **2.** MALE PARENT OF FOUR-LEGGED ANIMAL the male parent of a four-legged animal, especially a domesticated animal such as a stallion or bull ■ *vt.* (**sires, siring, sired**) FATHER OFFSPRING to father young, especially animals ○ *A filly sired by the great Man o' War.* [12thC. Via Old French from, ultimately, Latin *senior* 'older' (source of English *senior*).]

siren /sī́rən/ *n.* **1.** STATIONARY WARNING DEVICE a mounted warning device that produces a loud wailing sound when a current of compressed air or steam is forced through a rotating perforated disk ○ *The siren sounded the all clear.* **2.** PORTABLE WARNING DEVICE an electronic warning device, often mounted or placed on a moving vehicle, that produces a loud wailing sound **3.** MYTHOL SEA NYMPH LURING SAILORS ONTO ROCKS a sea nymph, half-woman half-bird, who was believed to sing beguilingly to passing sailors in order to lure them to their doom on the rocks she sat on **4.** OFFENSIVE TERM an offensive term used to refer to a woman who is considered to be attractive in a dangerous way (*offensive*) **5.** BIOL SALAMANDER RESEMBLING EEL a salamander with a long thin body and tail, permanent external gills, lungs, small forelegs, and no hind limbs. Family: Sirenidae. [14thC. Via Old French *sereine* 'sea nymph' and Latin *Siren* from Greek *Seirēn*. The modern meaning evolved from the idea of the sea nymph's cries.]

siren call *n.* = **siren song**

sirenian /sī reéni ən/ *n.* an aquatic herbivorous placental mammal that has forelimbs like paddles, no hind limbs, and a broad flat tail. The dugong and manatee are sirenians. Order: Sirenia. [Late 19thC. Formed from modern Latin *Sirenia*, order name, from Latin *Siren* (see SIREN).] —**sirenian** *adj.*

siren song *n.* an alluring appeal that sth possesses, even though it may have unfortunate effects ○ *She yielded to the siren song of a higher salary.*

siren suit *n.* a long-sleeved one-piece garment that covers the whole body [From its original use as an air-raid shelter garment]

Sirius /sírri əss/ *n.* a binary star in the constellation Canis Major that appears as the brightest star in the sky

sirloin /súr loyn/ *n.* an expensive prime cut of beef used for roasting or steaks, taken from the lower part of the ribs or the upper loin [15thC. From an assumed Old French word, literally 'loin above'.]

WORD KEY: ORIGIN

One of the most persistent of etymological fictions is that the ***sirloin*** got its name because a particular English king found the joint of beef so excellent that he knighted it. The monarch in question has been variously identified as Henry VIII, James I, and Charles II, but none of these is chronologically possible, and in fact the story has no truth in it at all. The spelling *sir-*, which began to replace the original *sur-* (from Old French *sur* 'above') in the 18th century, no doubt owes sth to the 'knighting' story.

sirocco /si rókō/ (*plural* **-cos**), **scirocco** (*plural* **-cos**) *n.* a hot dusty humid southeast wind in southern Europe that begins in the Sahara and picks up moisture as it crosses the Mediterranean [Early 17thC. Via French *sirocco* and Italian *scirocco* from Arabic *sharūq* 'the east', hence 'east wind'.]

sirrah /sírrə/ *n.* a form of address for a man or boy that was used to express contempt (*archaic*) [Early 16thC. Alteration of SIRE, its original second syllable associated with AH, as an expression of contempt.]

sirree /sur reé, sə reé/ [Early 19thC. Extension of SIR, thought to suggest emphasis.] ◇ **yes sirree!, no sirree!** *US* used to emphasize agreement or disagreement (*informal*)

Sir Roger de Coverley /-rójjər də kúvvərli/ *n.* an English country dance, similar to a Virginia reel, that is danced to a traditional tune and performed by two rows of dancers facing each other [Alteration of earlier English *roger of coverley*, probably from *Roger*, the personal name + OF + *Coverley*, a fictitious place name (or perhaps that of *Calverley* in YORKSHIRE)]

sirvente /sər vént/, **sirventes** *n.* a poem in stanza form written by troubadours in Provence that chiefly satirized moral or political matters [Early 17thC. Via French from Provençal *sirventes*, literally 'servant's song' (from the position of a lover in relation to his mistress).]

sis /siss/ *n.* a form of address for a sister (*informal*) [Mid-17thC. Shortening.]

sisal /sī́ss'l, sī́z'l/, **sisal hemp** *n.* **1.** PLANT YIELDING FIBRES a Mexican agave plant widely grown for its large sword-shaped leaves that yield a stiff fibre. Latin name: *Agave sisalana*. **2.** FIBRE FROM SISAL a strong white fibre obtained from the leaves of the sisal plant, used to make rope and rugs [Mid-19thC. Named after Sisal, a town in Yucatán.]

siskin /sískin/ *n.* a yellow-and-black finch of Europe, Asia, and northern Africa that is related to the goldfinch. Latin name: *Carduelis spinus*. [Mid-16thC. From Middle Dutch *siseken* and early Flemish *sijsken*, literally 'little siskin'. Ultimately of Slavic origin.]

Sisley /sízzli, síssli/, **Alfred** (1839–99) French painter. He was one of the early impressionist painters, noted for his landscapes and village scenes of northern France.

sissy /síssi/, **cissy** *n.* (*plural* **-sies**) OFFENSIVE TERM an offensive term used to refer to a boy or man who is considered not to exhibit stereotypical masculine behaviour, especially by other boys or men (*informal offensive*) ■ *adj.* OFFENSIVE TERM an offensive term used to refer to a boy, man, behaviour, or object that is considered not to exhibit or be characteristic of stereotypical masculinity (*informal offensive*) [Mid-19thC. Formed from SIS, originally in the sense 'sister'.] —**sissyish** *adj.* —**sissiness** *n.*

sister /sístər/ *n.* **1.** FEMALE SIBLING a girl or woman who has the same parents as another person **2.** STEPSISTER OR HALF-SISTER a girl or woman who has one parent in common with another person **3.** CHR NUN a female member of a religious community, or a form of address to such a person ○ *Sister Brigit joined us a few weeks ago.* **4.** MED WOMAN SENIOR NURSE a woman who holds the most senior grade of hospital nurse, above staff nurse, often in charge of a ward. ◊ **charge nurse 5.** WOMAN MEMBER OF SAME ORGANIZATION a woman who belongs to the same organization as another **6.** WOMAN SUPPORTER OF FEMINISM a woman who advocates or supports feminist principles **7.** AFRICAN AMERICAN WOMAN a form of address or way of referring to an African American woman, used especially by other African Americans **8.** CLOSE WOMAN FRIEND a close woman friend, especially of another woman ■ *adj.* **1.** CLOSELY LINKED belonging to or closely associated with sth ○ *links with sister organizations in Europe* **2.** GENETICS WITH PAIRED CELL used to describe either of an identical pair of cells or cell components formed by division of a parent cell or component [Old English *sweostor, sweoster*. Ultimately from an Indo-European word that is also the ancestor of English *sorority*.]

WORD KEY: CULTURAL NOTE

The Three Sisters, a play by the Russian dramatist Anton Chekhov (1900). Set in rural Russia, this powerful and compassionate study of the quiet desperation of bourgeois life centers on the three Pozarov sisters. Stifled by the dreariness of local society, they look to the officers of the local garrison for romance and entertainment. But when the army departs, the sisters are left with only their dreams and each other.

sisterhood /sístər hŏŏd/ *n.* **1.** SOLIDARITY AMONG WOMEN the empathy and loyalty that women feel for other women who have shared goals, experiences, or viewpoints **2.** WOMEN'S GROUP a group of women who have shared goals, experiences, or viewpoints (*takes a singular or plural verb*) **3.** STATUS AS SISTER the status of a sister or the relationship of sisters **4.** COMMUNITY OF NUNS a religious community of women

sister-in-law (*plural* **sisters-in-law**) *n.* **1.** SPOUSE'S SISTER the sister of sb's husband or wife **2. BROTHER'S WIFE** the wife of sb's brother

sisterly /sístərli/ adj., adv. relating to, coming from, or characteristic of a sister, especially in an affectionate, kind, or caring way —**sisterliness** n.

Sistine /sís teen, -tīn/ adj. **1. OF POPE SIXTUS** relating to any of the popes named Sixtus, especially Sixtus IV who was pope 1471–84 **2. OF SISTINE CHAPEL** relating to the Sistine Chapel [Late 18thC. From Italian Sistino 'of Sixtus', from Latin Sextus, a Roman personal name, from sextus 'sixth'.]

Sistrum

sistrum /sístrəm/ (plural **-tra** /-trə/) n. an ancient Egyptian percussion instrument consisting of a thin metal frame with rods or loops attached that jingle when shaken [14thC. Via Latin from Greek seistron, from seiein 'to shake'.]

Sisulu /si soóloo/, **Walter** (b. 1912) South African political activist. He served a prison sentence (1963–89) for his membership of the African National Congress, and was later the ANC's deputy president (1991–94).

Sisyphean /síssi feé ən/ adj. involving endless but futile labour [Late 16thC. Formed from Latin Sisypheius, from, ultimately, Greek Sisuphos (see SISYPHUS).]

Sisyphus /síssifəss/ n. in Greek mythology, a cruel king of Corinth who was condemned for eternity to roll a boulder up a hill only to have it roll down again just before it reached the top

sit /sit/ v. (**sits, sitting, sat, sat** /sat/) **1.** vi. **REST WITH WEIGHT ON BUTTOCKS** to assume a position of rest in which the weight is largely supported by the buttocks, usually with the body vertical and the thighs horizontal ○ Where would you like to sit? **2.** vt. **PLACE IN SEAT** to place sb or yourself in a seat or a sitting position ○ They sat us down to hear the whole story. **3.** vi. **REST BODY ON HINDQUARTERS** to rest the body with the weight supported by the lowered hindquarters (refers to four-legged animals) ○ The hound sat in the corner, looking strangely thoughtful **4.** vi. **PERCH, ROOST, OR COVER EGGS** to perch, roost, or cover and warm eggs for hatching ○ A falcon sat on the telephone wire, staring down at us. **5.** vi. **POL, LAW EXERCISE AUTHORITY** to occupy a position of authority while deciding or legislating sth ○ The legislature sat through the night. **6.** vi. **ARTS, PHOTOGRAPHY POSE FOR STH** to pose for a portrait or picture ○ He sat for the country's best-known photographer. **7.** vti. **EDUC TAKE EXAM** to take an examination in sth ○ She sat her finals last week. **8.** vi. **BE IDLE** to be or remain idle ○ They just sit around and do nothing. **9.** vi. **BE PLACED OR SITUATED** to be located or positioned somewhere ○ The dinner dishes were still sitting on the table. **10.** vi. **CLOTHES FIT OR HANG** to fit or hang on sb in a specified way ○ The gown sat beautifully on the model. **11.** vi. **BE IN SPECIFIED WAY** to rest, weigh, or lie as specified ○ Authority sits lightly on his shoulders. **12.** vi. **BE TAKEN AS SPECIFIED** to be accepted or considered in the way specified ○ The news didn't sit well with me. **13.** vi. **BABY-SIT** to baby-sit (informal) **14.** vi. **SET IN SPECIFIED DIRECTION** to be in a specified direction (archaic) ○ The wind sat in the east. **15.** vt. **HAVE SEATING SPACE FOR** to have seats or seating space for a specified number of people ○ We can sit 10 around the dining table. **16.** vi. **BE DIGESTIBLE** to be digestible (informal) ○ The heavy meal didn't sit well with me. **17.** vt. **BE ASTRIDE STH** to sit astride of a horse or similar animal ○ She sat her gelding with great poise. ■ n. **1. TIME SPENT BEING SEATED** a period of being seated, especially while waiting ○ We had a long sit waiting for the dentist. **2.** **CLOTHES WAY GARMENT FITS** the way a garment hangs on sb **3.** **MOUNTED POSITION** a position astride a horse or similar animal [Old English sittan. Ultimately from an Indo-European word that is also the ancestor of English saddle. Related to German sitzen 'to sit'.] ◇ **be sitting pretty** to be in a fortunate or favourable situation (informal) ◇ **sit tight** refrain from moving or acting until the right time (informal)

sit back vi. to take no action ○ sat back and watched the crisis develop

sit down vti. to become seated, or make sb become seated ○ time to sit him down and tell him the truth

sit in vi. **1. ATTEND WITHOUT TAKING PART** to attend sth but not take an active part in it ○ Do you mind if I sit in on your meeting? **2. TEMPORARILY REPLACE SB** to do a job for the person who normally does it ○ sitting in for the regular announcer on the show **3. OCCUPY BUILDING AS PROTEST** to take part in a sit-in

sit on vt. **1. BE PART OF DECISION-MAKING GROUP** to be a member of a group that decides sth **2. SUPPRESS** to suppress sth or delay dealing with it ○ The government sat on the information for weeks.

sit out v. **1.** vt. **STAY UNTIL END OF** to remain until the end of sth, especially sth unpleasant **2.** vt. **NOT PARTICIPATE IN** to remain seated during sth and not join in ○ I think I'll sit this one out. **3.** vi. to lean backwards over the side of a sailing boat to counterbalance the wind in the sails and keep the boat flat in the water. US term **hike out**

sit up vi. **1. SIT STRAIGHT** to sit upright or rise from lying down **2. STAY UP LATE** to stay up past the usual time of going to bed **3. BECOME ALERT** to become alert or interested

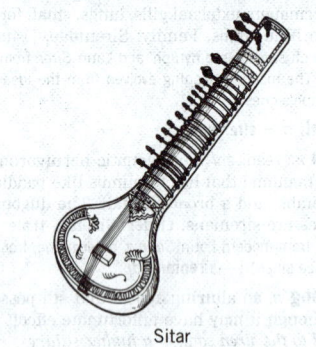

Sitar

sitar /si taár, síttaar/ n. an Indian stringed instrument with a rounded resonating body and a long fretted neck. There are several playing strings and a larger number that vibrate sympathetically. [Mid-19thC. Via Hindi from Persian, literally 'three-stringed', from the original design.] —**sitarist** n.

sitcom /sít kom/ n. a situation comedy (informal) [Mid-20thC. Shortening.]

sit-down n. **1. PERIOD OF RELAXATION BY SITTING** a short spell of sitting in order to relax (informal) ○ After all that shopping I could do with a sit-down. **2. = sit-down strike 3. = sit-in** ■ adj. **SERVED WHILE SITTING DOWN** served to people sitting at a table ○ There's a sit-down dinner before the dancing.

sit-down strike n. a form of protest in which people refuse to leave a place, often sitting or lying down, until their demands are granted or negotiated

site /sīt/ n. **1. PLACE WHERE STH STANDS** an area or piece of land where sth was, is, or will be located ○ The whole area has become one vast building site. **2. PLACE OF SIGNIFICANT EVENT** a place where sth important happened ○ The field was the site of a terrible massacre. **3.** COMPUT **= website** ■ vt. (**sites, siting, sited**) **POSITION STH** to locate sth in a particular place or position ○ The heavy artillery had been sited in the hills. [14thC. Directly or via Anglo-Norman from Latin situs 'place, position', from the past participle of sinere 'to put'.]

sitella /si téllə/ n. a small gregarious songbird found in Australasia, similar to the nuthatch in its stout body, short tail, and habit of hopping up and down trees. Family: Neosittidae. [Mid-19thC. From modern Latin Sittella, former genus name, literally 'little nuthatch', from, ultimately, Greek sittē 'nuthatch'.]

site-specific adj. designed, built, or intended for one particular site

sitfast /sít faast/ n. a sore on a horse's back caused by the rubbing of a saddle

sith /sith/ adv., conj., prep. since (archaic) [Old English Shortening of Old English siðð an 'since' (source also of English since)]

Sithole /si tóli/, **Ndabaningi** (b. 1920) Zimbabwean clergyman and politician. He founded the Zimbabwe African National Union (1963), which he led in a guerrilla war against Rhodesia that was instrumental in gaining majority rule in present-day Zimbabwe (1980).

sit-in n. a form of protest in which people occupy a building or public place and refuse to leave until their demands have been met or negotiated

sitkamer /sít kaamər/ n. S Africa a living room [Early 20thC. From Afrikaans, literally 'sitting room'.]

sitka spruce /sítka-/ n. a tall spruce tree of the northwest Pacific coast of North America. It has reddish-brown bark and silvery-white needles and yields soft, pale-brown timber. Latin name: Picea sitchensis. [Late 19thC. Named after Sitka, a town in Alaska.]

sitology /sī tólləji/ n. the scientific study of food, diet, and nutrition as they relate to health [Mid-19thC. Coined from Greek sitos 'food, grain' + -LOGY.]

sitomania /síta máyni ə/ n. an eating disorder marked by excessive craving for food (dated) [Late 19thC. Coined from Greek sitos 'food, grain' + -MANIA.]

sit spin n. a spin on one ice skate made in a squatting position with one leg stretched out in front of the body

sitter /síttər/ n. **1. HIRED MINDER** sb hired to look after sth (often used in combination) **2. = baby-sitter 3.** MED **SB HIRED TO WATCH PATIENTS** sb hired to watch over patients in order to respond to urgent needs or to prevent them from harming themselves accidentally **4.** ARTS, PHOTOGRAPHY **ARTIST'S OR PHOTOGRAPHER'S MODEL** sb who poses for a portrait **5.** AGRIC **BROODY HEN** a hen or other bird sitting on eggs to hatch them **6. EXTREMELY EASY TASK** sth that is very easy to accomplish, e.g. an effortless catch in cricket (informal)

sitting /sítting/ n. **1. TURN TO EAT** any of the periods when a meal is served in a place where there is insufficient room for everyone to eat at the same time ○ The first sitting is at 12 o'clock. **2.** ARTS, PHOTOGRAPHY **TIME FOR POSING** a period of time during which sb is seated in posing for a portrait ○ I'd like to get another sitting in this afternoon. **3.** POL, LAW **SESSION OF PUBLIC BODY** a meeting or session of an official body such as a legislature or court **4. PERIOD OF BEING SEATED** a period of being seated while engaged in an activity ○ It took him three sittings to read the book. **5.** AGRIC **SET OF EGGS** a clutch of eggs under a brooding bird **6.** AGRIC **INCUBATION OF EGGS** the period of time during which a hen sits on eggs to hatch them ■ adj. **1. SEATED** seated or for being seated ○ a sitting area **2. IN OFFICE** holding office at the present ○ the sitting MP for Southgate

Sitting Bull

Sitting Bull /sítting boól/ (1831?–90) Sioux leader. He defeated General George Custer at the Battle of Little Big Horn in 1876. He was killed during a later outbreak of hostilities.

sitting duck *n.* sb or sth that is defenceless, exposed to danger, and easy to attack or exploit (*informal*) ○ *The company's competitors regarded it as a sitting duck for a takeover.*

sitting room *n.* a room in a house or flat used for relaxing or entertaining guests in comfortable seats. ◊ **living room**

sitting target *n.* = **sitting duck**

sitting tenant *n.* a tenant who has a legal right to continue living in a property when it changes ownership

sitting trot *n.* EQU a slow trot during which the rider does not rise from the horse's saddle. ◊ **rising trot**

situate /síttyoo ayt/ (**-ates, -ating, -ated**) *vt.* to place sth in a context or set of circumstances and show its connections (*formal*) ○ *I shall endeavour to situate these ideas in the early Gnostic tradition.* [15thC. From late Latin *situat-*, the past participle stem of *situare* 'to place', from Latin *situs* 'position' (see SITE).]

situated /síttyoo aytid/ *adj.* (*often used in combination*) **1.** LOCATED located in a place or position ○ *The hotel is situated within the medieval walls of the old town.* ○ *a conveniently situated building* **2.** IN SPECIFIED FINANCIAL STATE in a specified financial condition ○ *comfortably situated, living off their investments*

situation /síttyoo áysh'n/ *n.* **1.** EXISTING CONDITIONS the general conditions that prevail in a place or society ○ *the current political situation in Ireland* **2.** CIRCUMSTANCES OF SB'S LIFE the circumstances that sb is in at a particular moment ○ *In your situation I'd sell my car.* **3.** LOCATION the location of a property ○ *The property is in an idyllic situation on the southern slope of a hill.* **4.** US COMBINATION OF DIFFICULT CIRCUMSTANCES a difficult or problematic set of circumstances **5.** JOB a job or position of employment (*formal*) **6.** ARTS SET OF CIRCUMSTANCES IN PLOT a significant combination of circumstances in a drama, film, or work of literature —**situational** *adj.*

WORD KEY: USAGE

Usage trap In its generalized meaning, **situation** serves a useful purpose when a word that is not too specific is wanted: *We shall have to discuss our financial situation with the bank next week.* In some cases it is superfluous, and such uses are best avoided: *The government is concerned about the unemployment situation* could be expressed equally well as *The government is concerned about unemployment* and *We are facing a crisis situation* as *We are facing a crisis.*

---

situation comedy *n.* a television or radio comedy series in which a regular cast of characters, usually working or living together, respond to everyday situations in a humorous way

situation ethics *n.* a system of ethics in which moral judgments are thought to depend on the context in which they are to be made, rather than on general moral principles (*takes a singular verb*)

situla /síttyoŏlə/ (*plural* **-lae** /-li, -lī/) *n.* an ancient decorated bucket or pottery vessel shaped like a deep bucket, urn, or vase [Late 19thC. From Latin, 'bucket'.]

sit-up *n.* an exercise in which you lie flat on your back with your legs bent and then raise the upper part of your body to a sitting position without using your hands

situs /sítəss/ (*plural* **-tus**) *n.* the position of an organ or part of the body, especially the normal position [Early 18thC. From Latin (see SITE).]

situs inversus /-in vúrtəss/ *n.* an uncommon reversal of organs in the body in which the apex of the heart points to the right and the liver and appendix are on the left side [From Latin, shortening of *situs inversus viscerum* 'inverted position of the internal organs']

Sitwell /sít wel, síttwəl/, **Dame Edith** (1887–1964) British writer. Unconventional in her writing, behaviour, and dress, she is best known for her poetic work *Façade* (1922), which was set to music by Sir William Walton. She was the sister of Osbert and Sacheverell Sitwell. Full name **Dame Edith Louisa Sitwell**

Sitwell, Sir Osbert (1892–1969) British writer. He wrote satirical and serious poetry and five volumes of memoirs (1944–50). He was the brother of Edith and Sacheverell Sitwell.

Popperfoto

Dame Edith Sitwell

Sitwell, Sir Sacheverell (1897–1988) British writer. He was known for his biographies and studies in baroque art, which included *Sacred and Profane Love* (1940). He was the brother of Osbert and Edith Sitwell.

sitz bath /síts-/ *n.* **1.** BATH SHAPED LIKE A CHAIR a bath shaped like a chair in which the bather sits immersed up to the waist in water, to which salts may be added for therapeutic purposes **2.** THERAPEUTIC BATH an act of immersion in a sitz bath, especially for therapeutic purposes [Partial translation of German *Sitzbad*, literally 'sitting bath']

sitzkrieg /síts kreeg/ *n.* a period in a war during which there is little offensive activity or change in the positions of the combatants [Mid-20thC. Coined from German *sitzen* 'to sit' on the model of BLITZKRIEG.]

sitzmark /síts maark/ *n.* a depression in the snow made by a skier who has fallen backwards [Mid-20thC. Partial translation of German *Sitzmarke*, literally 'sitting mark'.]

SI unit *n.* a unit adopted for international use under the Système International d'Unités in science and technology. There are seven fundamental units: the metre, kilogram, second, ampere, kelvin, candela, and mole, and two supplementary units, the radian and steradian.

Siva /sheévə, seévə/ *n.* = **Shiva**

Sivan /sívv'n, see vaán/ *n.* in the Jewish calendar, the third month in biblical reckoning and the ninth month in the civil year, made up of 30 days and usually falling around May [14thC. From Hebrew *sīwān*.]

siwash /sí wosh/ *n.* **1.** Northwest US, Can OFFENSIVE TERM an offensive term for an Aboriginal person (*offensive*) **2.** Can SIWASH SWEATER a siwash sweater (*informal*) ■ *vi.* (**-washes, -washing, -washed**) Northwest US, Can CAMP WITHOUT A TENT to travel and camp out without a tent (*informal*) [Mid-19thC. Via Chinook Jargon from Canadian French *sauvage*, 'savage'.]

six /síks/ *n.* **1.** NUMBER 6 the number 6 **2.** STH WITH VALUE OF 6 sth in a numbered series, e.g. a playing card, with a value of 6 **3.** GROUP OF SIX a group of six objects or people **4.** GROUP OF CUBS OR BROWNIES a division of a Cub Scout pack or Brownie Guide troop **5.** CRICKET BALL CROSSING BOUNDARY a stroke in cricket that clears the boundary without bouncing or the six runs scored by this stroke [Old English *si(e)x*. Ultimately from an Indo-European word that is also the ancestor of English *semester*.] —**six** *adj., pron.* ◊ **at sixes and sevens 1.** disorganized or in disarray (*informal*) **2.** in disagreement (*informal*) ◊ **be six of one and half-a-dozen of the other** used when there is not much difference between two choices ◊ **knock** *or* **hit sb for six** to surprise sb completely (*informal*)

sixain /síks ayn/ *n.* a six-line stanza in poetry [Late 16thC. From French, from *six* 'six'.]

Six Day War *n.* a war between Israel and the states of Egypt, Jordan, and Syria that lasted six days in June 1967. The Six Day War resulted in Israel's occupation of the Gaza Strip, the Sinai Peninsula, the West Bank of the Jordan River, and the Golan Heights.

sixer /síksər/ *n.* a Cub Scout or Brownie Guide who leads one of the divisions of the pack [Early 20thC. From the six members of the division.]

sixfold /síks föld/ *adj.* **1.** SIX TIMES GREATER with six times as much or as many ○ *a sixfold increase in absenteeism* **2.** WITH SIX PARTS with six parts or elements ■ *adv.* MULTIPLIED BY SIX by six times as much or as many ○ *The number of teenagers who enrolled increased sixfold.*

six-footer *n.* sb who is six feet tall or taller (*informal*)

six-gun *n.* US = **six-shooter**

Six Nations *n.* a confederacy of six Native North American peoples, the Cayuga, Mohawk, Oneida, Onondaga, Seneca, and Tuscarora, that lived together in New York State. It was formed in 1722 when the Tuscarora joined the Five Nations of the Iroquois Confederacy.

six-pack *n.* **1.** UNIT OF SIX CANS OR BOTTLES six cans or bottles, usually of beer, sold together in a pack **2.** ANAT ABDOMINAL MUSCLES a well-developed block of abdominal muscles (*informal*)

sixpence /síkspənss/ *n.* a small silver-coloured coin used in the UK between 1550 and 1980, worth 6 old pennies or 2.5 new pence

sixpenny nail /síkspəni-/ *n.* a nail that is 5 cm/2 in long [From the original price of a hundred such nails]

six-shooter *n.* a handgun whose bullets are loaded into a revolving cylinder containing six chambers (*informal*)

sixte /síkst/ *n.* the sixth of the eight basic defensive positions in fencing [Late 19thC. From French, 'sixth'.]

sixteen /síks teén/ *n.* **1.** NUMBER 16 the number 16 **2.** STH WITH VALUE OF 16 sth in a numbered series with a value of 16 **3.** GROUP OF 16 a group of sixteen objects or people [Old English *si(e)xtiene, syxtiene*] —**sixteen** *adj., pron.*

sixteenmo /síks teén mō/ (*plural* **-mos**) *n.* = **sextodecimo** [Mid-19thC. English reading of the symbol *16mo*.]

sixteenth /síks teénth/ *n.* one of 16 equal parts of sth —**sixteenth** *adj., adv.*

sixteenth note *n.* US, Can = **semiquaver**

sixth /síksth/ *n.* **1.** MUSIC INTERVAL OF SIX NOTES in a standard musical scale, the interval between one note and another that lies five notes above or below it. In the scale of C major, C and A form a sixth. **2.** ONE OF 6 PARTS OF STH one of six equal parts of sth **3.** MUSIC NOTE A SIXTH AWAY FROM ANOTHER in a standard musical scale, a note that is a sixth away from another note **4.** HARMONY OF A SIXTH the harmony created by playing two notes a sixth apart **5.** ONE NOTE IN A SIXTH one of the two notes in a sixth —**sixth** *adj., adv.*

sixth chord *n.* a musical chord made up of a note plus a note a third above and a note a sixth above

sixth form *n.* the final optional stage of school education for students in England and Wales aged 16 to 18 in which they study for and sit A-level examinations (*hyphenated when used before a noun*)

sixth-form college *n.* a college for students in England and Wales between the ages of 16 and 18 that offers A-level courses

sixth-former *n.* a student in the sixth form

sixth sense *n.* a supposed special ability to perceive sth not using any of the five senses of sight, hearing, touch, smell, and taste

sixth year *n.* Scotland **1.** FINAL YEAR IN SCOTTISH SCHOOLS the final optional year in Scottish secondary schools during which students can study for Highers and sixth-year studies (*hyphenated when used before a noun*) **2.** SIXTH-YEAR STUDENT a student in the sixth year

sixth-year studies *npl.* Scotland one-year courses of study taken in the final year at Scottish secondary schools after the completion of Highers. These are now generally required for university entrance in Scotland because of competition from students with English A-levels.

sixtieth /síksti əth/ *n.* one of 60 equal parts of sth —**sixtieth** *adj., adv.*

Sixtus V /síkstəss thə fífth/, **Pope** (1521–90). He reformed the church administration, ordered the construction of public buildings in Rome, and supported missions abroad.

sixty /síksti/ *n.* (*plural* **-ties**) **1.** NUMBER 60 the number 60 **2.** GROUP OF 60 a group of sixty objects or people ■

sixties *npl.* **1.** NUMBERS 60 TO 69 the numbers 60 to 69, particularly as a range of temperature ○ *in the low sixties* **2.** YEARS 1960 TO 1969 the years 1960 to 1969 **3.** PERIOD FROM AGE 60 TO 69 the period of sb's life from the age of 60 to 69 [Old English *sixtig*] —**sixty** *adj.*, *pron.*

sixty-fourmo /-fáwrmō/ (*plural* **sixty-fourmos**) *n.* **1.** PAPER SIZE a book or paper size that results from a sheet of paper being folded 64 times **2.** BOOK OF SIXTY-FOURMO SIZE paper or a book that is sixty-fourmo in size [English reading of the symbol 64mo]

sixty-fourth note *n.* US MUSIC = **hemidemisemiquaver**

sixty-nine *n.* an offensive term used to refer to a sexual activity in which two people simultaneously stimulate each other's genitals orally (*slang offensive*) [From the position of the couple, with their heads at opposite ends from each other]

six-yard box *n.* a rectangle of lines on the pitch in front of the goal in association football. It extends six yards from the goal line and goal kicks are taken within it.

sizable /síz əb'l/, **sizeable** *adj.* fairly large —**sizableness** *n.* —**sizably** *adv.*

sizar /sízər/ *n.* an undergraduate student at some universities who receives a grant for expenses from a college [Late 16thC. Coined from SIZE in the obsolete sense 'quantity of bread or ale' (probably because the student's 'sizes' were free) + -AR.] —**sizarship** *n.*

size[1] /sīz/ *n.* **1.** HOW MUCH STH MEASURES the amount, scope, or degree of sth, in terms of how large or small it is **2.** HOW BIG STH IS the large quality or extent of a particular thing **3.** STANDARD MEASUREMENT OF MANUFACTURED ITEM a set of measurements used when making or classifying articles that are produced and sold, such as clothing or shoes. Manufacturers make goods in a fixed set of graduated sizes, with particular dimensions. ■ *vt.* (**sizes, sizing, sized**) **1.** SORT ACCORDING TO SIZE to put things into different groups according to their size **2.** MAKE TO A PARTICULAR SIZE to cut, shape, or manufacture goods so that they have the necessary or chosen measurements **3.** MEASURE to work out or find out the measurements of sth [13thC. From Old French *sise*, an alteration of *assise*, from Latin *assidere* 'to sit beside' (see ASSIZE). Originally 'sitting down to make a judgment (later, on the standardization of amounts)', hence 'dimension'.] ◇ **cut sb down to size** to make sb be less self-important and arrogant ◇ **that's about the size of it** used to indicate that sth describes a situation very well (*informal*) ◇ **try sth (on) for size 1.** to put sth on to see whether it fits you or not **2.** to find out how much you like sth, or how well it suits you
size up *vt.* to assess a person or situation and form a judgment

size[2] /sīz/ *n.* GELATINOUS MIXTURE FOR FILLING POROUS SURFACES a gelatinous mixture made from glue, starch, or varnish that is used to fill the pores in the surface of paper, textiles, or plaster ■ *vt.* (**sizes, sizing, sized**) COAT WITH SIZE to coat a porous surface such as paper, textile, or plaster with size [15thC. Origin uncertain: perhaps the same as SIZE[1].]

sizeable /síz əbəl/ *adj.* = **sizable**

sized /sīzd/, **size** /sīz/ *adj.* having a specified size (*often used in combination*)

sizeism /sízizəm/ *n.* discrimination against sb on the basis of the person's size, especially the person's unusual tallness, shortness, fatness or thinness —**sizeist** *adj.*

sizing /sízing/ *n.* **1.** = **size**[2] *n.* **2.** USE OF SIZE the process of coating sth with size

sizzle /sízz'l/ *v.* (**-zles, -zling, -zled**) **1.** *vti.* MAKE THE NOISE OF FOOD FRYING to make the hissing and spattering sound typical of frying fat, or to cook food so that it makes a hissing sound **2.** *vi.* BE FURIOUS to show or feel great anger (*informal*) **3.** *vi.* BE HOT to be extremely hot (*informal*) **4.** *vi.* BE PHYSICALLY APPEALING to be physically appealing or very popular (*informal*) ■ *n.* HISSING, FRYING NOISE the sound of sth frying, or a sound resembling this [Early 17thC. An imitation of the sound.]

sizzler /sízzlər/ *n.* **1.** STH THAT SIZZLES sth that sizzles **2.** HOT DAY an extremely hot day (*informal*)

sizzling /sízzling/ *adj.* (*informal*) **1.** HOT extremely hot **2.** PHYSICALLY APPEALING physically appealing or very popular —**sizzlingly** *adv.*

SJ *abbr.* Society of Jesus

SJA *abbr.* Saint John Ambulance (Brigade or Association)

Sjaelland /syéllənd/ the main island of Denmark, on which Copenhagen is situated. Population: 2,159,260 (1994). Area: 7,000 sq. km/2,700 sq. mi.

sjambok /shám bok/ *n. S Africa* ANIMAL-SKIN WHIP a sturdy whip or riding crop made from the hide of a rhinoceros or hippopotamus ■ *vt.* (**-boks, -bokking, -bokked**) *S Africa* WHIP WITH SJAMBOK to whip sb or sth with a sjambok [Late 18thC. Via Afrikaans from Malay *chambuk*, from, ultimately, Persian *chābuk* 'whip'.]

SJD *abbr.* Doctor of Juridical Science [Latin, *Scientiae Juridicae Doctor*]

SK *abbr.* Saskatchewan

ska /skaa/ *n.* dance music in 4/4 time originating in Jamaica in the late 1950s, marked by emphasis on the second and fourth beats. It combines traditional Caribbean music and jazz, and was a predecessor of reggae. [Mid-20thC. Origin unknown.]

Skagerrak /skággə rak/ arm of the North Sea between Norway and the Jutland Peninsula, Denmark. Length: 240 km/150 mi.

skald /skawld/ *n.* **scald** *n.* a medieval Scandinavian poet or travelling minstrel (*archaic or literary*) [Mid-18thC. From Old Norse *skáld*. Perhaps ultimately from a prehistoric Germanic word meaning 'to say' that is the ancestor of English *say* and *saga*.] —**skaldic** *adj.*

Skåne /skốnə/ province forming the southern tip of Sweden. It consists of the counties of Kristianstad and Malmöhus. Population: 1,084,755 (1993). Area: 10,984 sq. km/4,241 sq. mi.

skank /skangk/ (**skanks, skanking, skanked**) *vi.* to dance to reggae music, especially in a jerky way [Late 20thC. Origin unknown.]

skat /skat/ *n.* a card game for three players played with 32 cards and involving bids, contracts, and the taking of tricks [Mid-19thC. Via German from Italian *scarto* 'discarded card', from, ultimately, Latin *charta* 'paper' (see CARD).]

skate[1] /skayt/ *n.* **1.** ICE SKATE an ice skate **2.** ROLLER SKATE a roller skate **3.** METAL BLADE FOR AN ICE SKATE a steel runner that is fastened to the sole of a boot or shoe to make an ice skate **4.** TIME SPENT SKATING a period of time spent skating ■ *vi.* (**skates, skating, skated**) **1.** MOVE AROUND ON SKATES to glide along a surface wearing ice skates or roller skates **2.** SLIDE SMOOTHLY to slide along a slippery surface [Mid-17thC. Back-formation from Dutch *schaats* (taken as plural), from Old French *eschasse* 'stilt', probably from prehistoric Germanic.] ◇ **get your skates on** to hurry (*informal*)
skate over *vt.* to mention or deal with sth in a cursory way (*informal*)

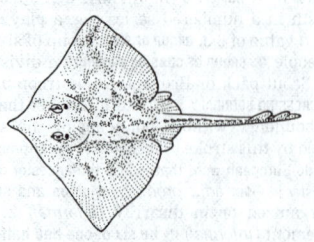

Skate

skate[2] /skayt/ (*plural* **skate** *or* **skates**) *n.* a bottom-dwelling marine cartilaginous fish that has a flattened body, very large flat pectoral fins, two small dorsal fins, a long snout, and short slender tail. Family: Rajidae. [14thC. From Old Norse *skata*.]

skateboard /skáyt bawrd/ *n.* WHEELED BOARD FOR RIDING a short narrow board to which a set of small wheels is fitted on the underside, used to move rapidly or to perform jumps and stunts ■ *vi.* (**-boards, -boarding, -boarded**) RIDE ON SKATEBOARD to ride on a skateboard —**skateboarder** *n.*

skateboarding /skáyt bawrding/ *n.* the sport or pastime of riding a skateboard

skater /skáytər/ *n.* INSECTS = **pond skater**

skating /skáyt ing/ *n.* the pastime or sport of sliding on ice skates or rolling on roller skates

skatole /skáttōl/ *n.* an organic crystalline solid that has a strong faecal odour, is found in faeces, beetroot, and coal tar, and is used as a fixative in making perfumes. Formula: C_9H_9N. [Late 19thC. Coined from the Greek stem *skat-* 'dung' (see SCATO-) + -OLE.]

skean /skeen/ *n. Scotland* a dagger with a double-edged blade used in the past in Scotland and Ireland [Early 16thC. Via Gaelic *scian* from Old Irish. Ultimately from an Indo-European base meaning 'to cut' that is also the ancestor of English *shin* and *schism*.]

skean-dhu /skéen dóo/, **sgian-dhu** *n. Scotland* a small black-hilted dagger tucked into the top of a man's stocking in Highland dress [From Gaelic, literally 'black skean']

skedaddle /ski dádd'l/ *vi.* (**-dles, -dling, -dled**) RUN AWAY to run away quickly (*slang*) ■ *n.* QUICK DEPARTURE a very quick or agitated departure (*slang*) [Mid-19thC. Origin unknown.] —**skedaddler** *n.*

skeet /skeet/, **skeet shooting** *n.* a form of clay-pigeon shooting in which clay targets are tossed into the air [Early 20thC. Said to be from *skeet* (invented as a supposedly archaic form of SHOOT), the winning entry in a contest held to choose a name for this sport.]

skeet shooting *n.* = **skeet**

skeg /skeg/ *n.* **1.** NAUT PART CONNECTING KEEL AND RUDDERPOST a part of the keel of a ship, near the stern, that connects the keel with the rudderpost **2.** FIN ON SURFBOARD the short stabilizing fin on the rear underside of a surfboard or sailboard [Early 17thC. Via Dutch *scheg* from Old Norse *skegg* 'beard, point of a ship's stern'.]

Skegness /skeg néss/ town and seaside resort in Lincolnshire, England. Population: 15,149 (1991).

skein /skayn/ *n.* **1.** TWISTED BUNDLE OF YARN a length of yarn or thread wound loosely and coiled together **2.** BIRDS GROUP OF GEESE IN FLIGHT a flock of geese flying across the sky in a line **3.** A TANGLE tangled or complex mass of material [15thC. From Old French *escaigne*, of unknown origin.]

skeletal /skéll itəl/ *adj.* **1.** OF A SKELETON relating to a skeleton **2.** VERY THIN extremely thin or emaciated —**skeletally** *adv.*

skeleton /skéllitən/ *n.* **1.** ZOOL BONES OF PERSON OR ANIMAL the rigid framework of interconnected bones and cartilage that protects and supports the internal organs and provides attachment for muscles in humans and other vertebrate animals **2.** ZOOL SUPPORTIVE PROTECTIVE STRUCTURE OF INVERTEBRATES sth that provides support, gives protection, or maintains shape in an invertebrate animal, such as the shell of a snail or cuticle of a crab **3.** BASIC FRAME STH IS BUILT AROUND a structure that is needed to support and hold sth together as an internal framework, onto which the connecting or covering parts are attached **4.** STH WITH ONLY ESSENTIAL PARTS LEFT a plan, organization, or structure that has been reduced so that only its most basic and necessary elements are still functioning or in place **5.** OUTLINE OR LAYOUT OF STH a description that gives the main points but no details of sth such as a book or plan **6.** SB VERY THIN an emaciated person or animal (*informal*) [Late 16thC. Via modern Latin from Greek *skeleton* (*sōma*) 'dried up (body)', from *skellein* 'to dry up'.] ◇ **a skeleton in the cupboard** a closely kept secret that is a source of shame or embarrassment

skeletonize /skéllitə nīz/ (**-izes, -izing, -ized**), **skeletonise** (**-ises, -ising, -ised**) *vt.* **1.** CUT BACK TO ABSOLUTE BASICS to reduce sth until only its most basic structure or outline remains **2.** CREATE OUTLINE OF to create sth in basic outline **3.** REDUCE TO A SKELETAL FORM to reduce sth to a skeleton

skeleton key *n.* a key with the usually serrated part that connects with the lever of a lock (**bit**) filed down so that it can open many different unsophisticated locks [From its basic cut-back shape]

skelf /skelf/ *n. N England, Scotland* a thin splinter of wood, especially one that has gone into the

skin [14thC. Origin uncertain: probably from Low German *schelf* 'shelf' (see SHELF).]

skell /skel/ *n. US* sb who has no home or job so must live on the street (*slang*) [Late 20thC. Origin uncertain.]

skelly /skéli/ *adj. Scotland* with a squint or crossed eyes [Late 18thC. From assumed Old Norse *skjelga*, from *skjálgr* 'wry, oblique'.]

Skelmersdale /skélmərz dayl/ town in Lancashire, northwestern England. It was designated a new town in 1961. Population: 42,104 (1991).

skelp /skelp/ *v.* (**skelps, skelping, skelped**) *N England, Scotland* **1.** *vt.* SMACK to slap sb sharply with the hand or with sth flat **2.** *vi.* MOVE AT GREAT SPEED to hustle along quickly and energetically ■ *n.* **1.** *N England, Scotland* A SMACK a slap, usually with the hand **2.** A CRIMINAL a criminal (*slang*) [14thC. Origin uncertain: probably an imitation of the sound of a slap.]

skep /skep/ *n.* **1.** BEEHIVE a beehive made of straw or similar material **2.** BIG WICKER BASKET a large basket woven from straw, reeds, or twigs (*regional*) [Pre-12thC. From Old Norse *skeppa* 'basket, bushel'.]

skeptic *n. US* = **sceptic**

skerrick /skérrik/ *n. Aus, NZ* a tiny scrap or trace of sth (*informal*) [Early 19thC. Originally a dialect form, of unknown origin.]

skerry /skérri/ (*plural* **-ries**) *n. Scotland* a rocky islet or reef [Early 17thC. Via Scots dialect from Old Norse *sker* 'reef'. Ultimately from an Indo-European base meaning 'to cut' that is also the ancestor of English *sharp* and *scrape*.]

sketch /skech/ *n.* **1.** DRAWING PICTURE DONE QUICKLY AND ROUGHLY a drawing or painting that is done quickly without concern for detail. A sketch might be made to capture the general mood of a scene, or to help the artist work out an idea for a finished composition. **2.** ROUGH DESCRIPTION OR EXPLANATION OF STH a short written or spoken account that conveys just a general outline or idea, with little detail **3.** LITERAT SHORT PIECE OF WRITING a short, often descriptive, piece of writing **4.** ARTS SHORT PERFORMANCE a quick comic routine or piece of acting that is part of a variety show or comedy revue **5.** MUSIC SHORT MUSICAL COMPOSITION a short piece of instrumental music, often for piano ■ *vti.* (**sketches, sketching, sketched**) ARTS MAKE A SKETCH to create a sketch of sth [Mid-17thC. Via Dutch *schets* or German *Skizze* from Italian *schizzo*, from, ultimately, Vulgar Latin *schediare* 'to do hastily', from Latin *schedius*, from Greek *skhedios* 'on the spur of the moment'.] —**sketchable** *adj.* —**sketcher** *n.*

sketchbook /skéch book/, **sketchpad** *n.* **1.** ARTIST'S BOOK OF DRAWING PAPER a book of plain paper for making sketches on **2.** BOOK OF LITERARY SKETCHES a book containing a collection of literary sketches

sketchy /skéchi/ *adj.* (**-ier, -iest**) **1.** RESEMBLING A SKETCH giving only the main points with little detail **2.** SUPERFICIAL lacking in substance, clarity, or detail — **sketchily** *adv.* —**sketchiness** *n.*

skew /skyoo/ *v.* (**skews, skewing, skewed**) **1.** *vti.* SLANT OR CAUSE TO SLANT to make sth uneven, sloping, or unsymmetrical, or to be in this state **2.** *vt.* MAKE INCORRECT OR DISTORTED to misrepresent the true meaning or nature of sth **3.** *vi.* SQUINT to look sideways at sth ■ *adj.* **1.** IN A SLANTED POSITION OR LINE being in a slanted or unsymmetrical position **2.** DISTORTING THE TRUTH giving an unfair or untrue account of sth, especially statistics **3.** MATH NOT PARALLEL OR INTERSECTING used to describe a line that is neither parallel nor intersecting ■ *n.* **1.** TILTED OR INACCURATE POSITION a position that is not straight but that slants or twists out of correct alignment **2.** SLANTING DIRECTION a slanting movement, line, or direction [14thC. Shortening of Old Northern French *eskiuer*, a variant of Old French *eschiver* 'to eschew' (see ESCHEW).]

skew arch *n.* an arch, e.g. on a bridge or tunnel, with sides that are not at right angles to the span

skewback /skyoo bak/ *n.* either of the sloping surfaces on which the sides of a segmental arch abut

skewbald /skyoo bawld/ *adj.* WITH WHITE AND BROWN PATCHES used to describe a horse that has a spotted coat consisting of white and another colour other than black, generally brown ■ *n.* SKEWBALD HORSE a skewbald horse [Mid-17thC. Formed from obsolete *skewed* 'having mixed colours', of unknown origin, on the model of PIEBALD.]

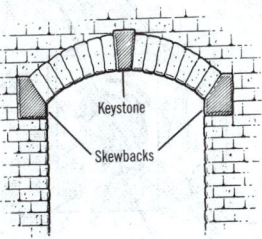

Skewback

skewer /skyoo ər/ *n.* **1.** THIN PIN TO COOK FOOD ON a thin metal or wooden rod with a sharp end used to hold meat or meat and vegetables during cooking **2.** STH SIMILAR TO SKEWER a thin pointed object used to pierce sth or hold it in place ■ *vt.* (**-ers, -ering, -ered**) PIERCE WITH SKEWER to pierce sb or sth with a skewer or with sth else that is thin and sharp [15thC. Origin unknown.]

skewness /skyoo nəss/ *n.* **1.** CROOKEDNESS the way or amount that sth is tilted or distorted from the true or straight position **2.** STATS LACK OF SYMMETRY a lack of symmetry, especially about the mean in a frequency distribution

skewwhiff /skyoo wíf/ *adj.* not level or straight, but crooked, tilted, or lopsided (*informal*) [Mid-18thC. Fanciful formation from SKEW.]

ski /skee/ *n.* (*plural* **skis** or **ski**) **1.** BOARD USED TO SLIDE ACROSS SNOW either of a pair of long thin boards made of wood, metal, or other material that curve up at the front and are used to slide across snow **2.** = **water-ski 3.** RUNNER FOR VEHICLES TRAVELLING ON SNOW a runner fitted to vehicles such as snowmobiles and aeroplanes for landing or travelling on snow and ice ■ *vti.* (**skis, skiing, skied** or **ski'd**) MOVE ALONG ON SKIS to glide over the surface of snow or water wearing skis, as a means of travel or as a leisure pursuit or sport [Mid-18thC. Via Norwegian from Old Norse *skíð* 'piece of split wood, snowshoe'. Ultimately from an Indo-European base meaning 'to cut' that is also the ancestor of English *sheath* and *shiver*.] —**skiable** *adj.* —**skier** *n.*

skibob /skee bob/ *n.* a vehicle similar to a bicycle that has skis instead of wheels and is used to travel over snow [Mid-20thC. *Bob* is a shortening of BOBSLED.] —**skibobber** *n.* —**skibobbing** *n.*

skid /skid/ *n.* **1.** TRANSP UNCONTROLLED SLIDE an uncontrolled slide across a surface in a wheeled vehicle **2.** AIR AIRCRAFT RUNNER a runner on the underside of an aircraft, used as part of its landing gear **3.** TECH PALLET a low pallet on which goods are loaded for handling or transport **4.** MECH ENG BLOCK USED TO PREVENT WHEEL TURNING a shoe or block used to prevent a wheel from turning, e.g. when a vehicle is descending a hill **5.** SHIPPING SHIP'S FENDER a wooden structure hung over the side of a ship to protect the ship in loading and unloading cargo ■ *v.* (**skids, skidding, skidded**) **1.** AUTOMOT SLIDE DANGEROUSLY ACROSS SURFACE to slide or make a vehicle slide across a surface, usually unintentionally, so that the wheels lose their grip and control is lost **2.** *vi.* TRANSP SLIDE OVER SURFACE WITHOUT ROLLING to slide across a surface without turning round and gripping it in the proper way **3.** *vti.* AIR SLIDE SIDEWAYS to slide or make an aircraft slide sideways away from the centre of curvature when it is insufficiently banked in making a turn [Early 17thC. Origin uncertain: perhaps from Old Norse.] —**skiddy** *adj.* ◇ **be on the skids** to be in difficulties and heading for failure (*slang*)

skidlid /skídlid/ *n.* a crash helmet (*dated informal*)

skid marks *npl.* **1.** MARKS MADE ON ROAD BY SKID dark heavy lines marked on a road surface by the wheels of a vehicle that has skidded **2.** FAECAL MARKS traces of excrement on sb's underpants (*slang*)

skidpan /skíd pan/ *n.* an area with a surface that is deliberately made slippery so that drivers can practise dealing with a skidding vehicle

skidproof /skíd proof/ *adj.* designed to prevent skidding

skid road *n.* **1.** *US* = **skid row** (*informal*) **2.** *Can, US* TRACK FOR HAULING LOGS ALONG a road with logs embedded in it, along which timber is hauled to a mill or loading area

skid row *n.* an area of a city that has cheap bars and rundown hotels and is frequented by members of the city's underclass (*informal*) [Alteration of SKID ROAD. The word originally referred to an area of a town that loggers typically frequented.]

skied[1] /skeed/, **ski'd** past tense, past participle of **ski**

skied[2] /skīd/ past participle, past tense of **sky**

skies[1] present tense of **ski**

skies[2] plural of **sky**

skiff /skif/ *n.* a small flatbottomed boat of shallow draft that is usually propelled with oars, a sail, or a motor [Late 15thC. Via French *esquif* from Italian *schifo*, probably from Old High German *schif*. Related to English *ship*.]

skiffle /skíff'l/ *n.* a type of music that was popular in the 1950s, usually played by a small group on guitars as well as improvised instruments such as a washboard used as percussion [Early 20thC. Origin unknown.]

Skiing

skiing /skee ing/ *n.* the activity, sport, or pastime of travelling on skis

skijoring /skee jawring/ *n.* a sport in which a skier is towed across a frozen surface by a horse or vehicle [Early 20thC. From Norwegian *skikjøring*, literally 'ski driving'.] —**skijorer** /skee jawrər/ *n.*

ski jump *n.* **1.** TRACK FOR SKIERS TO JUMP FROM a steep artificial slope with a sharp upturn at the bottom. People ski down this and then leap into the air, competing with one another to travel the longest distance. **2.** JUMP MADE FROM SKI JUMP a jump made by a skier from a ski jump —**ski jumper** *n.*

ski-jump (**ski-jumps, ski-jumping, ski-jumped**) *vi.* to perform a ski jump

Skikda /skik daa/ city and port in northeastern Algeria, situated about 354 km/220 mi. east of Algiers. Population: 128,747 (1987).

skilful *adj.* **1.** PARTICULARLY ADEPT AT STH with a special ability and dexterity in a particular type of work or activity **2.** INVOLVING SPECIAL SKILL requiring or done with specialized techniques and abilities developed over a period of time —**skilfully** *adv.* —**skilfulness** *n.*

ski lift *n.* a motor-driven apparatus consisting of a continuously moving cable with seats, gondolas, or tow bars suspended from it, built to transport skiers to the top of a ski run

skill /skil/ *n.* **1.** ABILITY TO DO STH WELL the ability to do sth well, usually gained through experience and training **2.** STH REQUIRING TRAINING TO DO WELL sth such as an art or trade that requires training and experience to do well [12thC. From Old Norse *skil* 'discernment'. Ultimately from an Indo-European base meaning 'to cut' that is also the ancestor of English *shell* and *scalpel*.] —**skill-less** *adj.* —**skill-lessness** *n.*

—————— **WORD KEY: SYNONYMS** ——————

See Synonyms at *ability*.

Skillcentre /skíl sentər/ *n.* a government-funded agency that provides vocational training and retraining

skilled /skild/ *adj.* **1.** VERY GOOD AT DOING STH having or showing a special ability and competence in a particular type of work or activity **2. REQUIRING TRAINING AND EXPERIENCE** characterized by the need for special abilities developed and practised over time

skillet /skíllit/ *n.* **1.** *US* = **frying pan 2. SMALL FRYING PAN** a small shallow pan with a long handle, used for frying or braising food [15thC. Origin uncertain: probably from Old French *escuelete*, literally 'small platter', from *escuele* 'platter', from Latin *scutella* 'flat dish' (see SCUTTLE).]

skillful /skílf'l, skílfòol/ *adj. US* = **skilful**

skilly /skílli/ (*plural* **-lies**) *n.* a watery type of soup, made from oatmeal or sth similar (*dated*) [Mid-19thC. Shortening of *skilligalee*, 'skilly', a nonsense word.]

skim /skim/ *v.* (**skims, skimming, skimmed**) **1.** *vt.* COOK **SCOOP FROM TOP OF LIQUID** to remove a substance such as a fatty accumulation forming a layer on the surface of a liquid, usually with a large shallow spoon **2.** *vt.* **RID LIQUID OF FLOATING MATERIAL** to rid a liquid of material accumulating on its surface **3.** *vti.* **PASS CLOSELY OVER SURFACE OF STH** to pass or make sth pass quickly across and just above the surface of sth, sometimes touching it lightly and briefly **4.** *vt.* **GLANCE THROUGH A BOOK OR PAPER** to read sth very quickly looking only at occasional lines or words, to get a general idea of its contents **5.** *vt.* **SEND STH BOUNCING ALONG** to throw sth so that it bounces lightly along the surface of water **6.** *vt.* **GIVE LITTLE OR NO ATTENTION TO** to deal with sth in a superficial way **7.** *vti.* **COAT OR BECOME COATED WITH LAYER** to develop a thin surface layer of sth, or coat an object so that its surface is covered in a thin layer of sth **8.** *vt. US* **HIDE PROFITS TO AVOID TAXES** to hide earnings or profits in order to avoid paying taxes on them (*informal*) ■ *n.* **1. THIN FILM** a layer coating a surface **2. CURSORY LOOK** a cursory look at or treatment of sth ○ *a quick skim over the main topics on the agenda* **3. SUBSTANCE REMOVED FROM SURFACE OF STH** the matter that forms a layer on a surface and is skimmed off **4. SKIMMING PROCESS** the process of removing a substance from a surface [15thC. From Old French *escumer*, from *escume* 'scum', from a prehistoric Germanic word that is also the ancestor of English *scum*.]

skim off *vt.* to cull the best people or items from a group

ski mask *n.* a protective covering for the face and sometimes the head, worn by skiers and made of knitted or other material and often having openings for the eyes, nose, and mouth

skimmer /skímmər/ *n.* **1. SB OR STH THAT SKIMS** a person, object, or device that skims **2.** BIRDS **LONG-WINGED MARINE BIRD** a long-winged marine bird that has a bill with the lower half longer than the upper, used for skimming food from the surface of water while in flight. Genus: *Rynchops.* **3.** COOK **UTENSIL USED FOR SKIMMING** a broad flat spoon with small perforations in it used to skim sth such as fat from the surface of a liquid

skim milk *n.* = **skimmed milk**

skimmings /skímmingz/ *npl.* the floating fat or debris skimmed off the surface of a liquid

skimp /skimp/ (**skimps, skimping, skimped**) *v.* **1.** *vti.* **USE TOO LITTLE OF STH** to use or provide hardly enough of sth **2.** *vt.* **DO STH IMPROPERLY** to carry out a piece of work poorly, without spending enough time, trouble, or materials on it **3.** *vt.* **NOT PROVIDE WITH ENOUGH** to give or allow yourself or another person only an inadequate amount of money, food, or other necessary items [Late 18thC. Origin unknown.]

skimpy /skímpi/ (**-ier, -iest**) *adj.* **1. HARDLY ADEQUATE** made or done using barely enough of the necessary materials **2. STINGY** not giving sb enough of sth through meanness —**skimpily** *adv.* —**skimpiness** *n.*

skin /skin/ *n.* **1. NATURAL LAYER COVERING AN ANIMAL'S BODY** the external protective membrane or covering of an animal's body, consisting of the dermis and epidermis and often covered in hair, fur, scales, or feathers **2. SKIN ON FACE** sb's skin, especially on the face, in terms of its colour and appearance **3.** BOT **THIN NATURAL COVERING** a relatively thin but protective layer closely surrounding the flesh of a fruit or vegetable **4.** INDUST **FUR OR LEATHER FROM DEAD ANIMAL** skin or a piece of skin removed from an animal's body, especially once it has been cleaned and treated to use as fur or leather **5. SOLID SURFACE LAYER ON A LIQUID** a thin pliant surface that forms on the top of some liquids, e.g. on hot milk left to cool **6. TIGHT-FITTING**

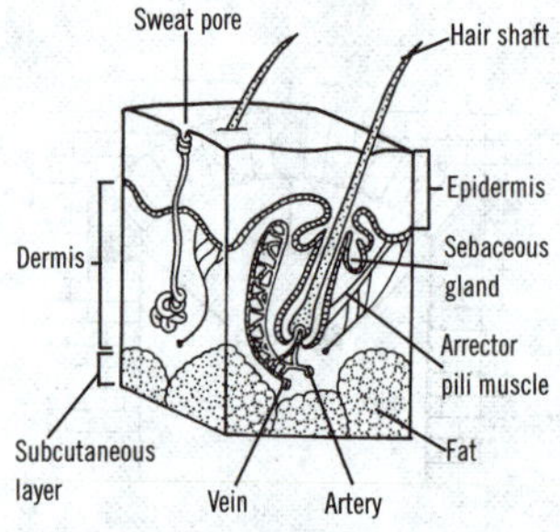

Skin: Cross-section of human skin

COVERING a thin tough casing or cover that fits closely round sth such as a sausage to hold in, protect, or preserve the enclosed material **7. SKINHEAD** a skinhead (*slang informal*) **8. SMALL LEATHER SACK** a bag made from animal hide used to hold liquid such as wine or water **9. OUTER COVERING OF STRUCTURE** the outer protective covering of a structure such as an aircraft **10. CIGARETTE PAPER** a piece of paper used for making marijuana joints or other roll-up cigarettes (*slang*) ■ **skins** *npl.* MUSIC **JAZZ DRUMS** drums, especially in a jazz band (*informal*) ■ *v.* (**skins, skinning, skinned**) **1.** *vt.* **TAKE THE SKIN OFF** to remove the skin from a fruit or vegetable, or from an animal or person, especially by cutting or ripping it **2.** *vt.* MED **SCRAPE THE SKIN** to make the skin on a part of the body red, sore, and broken, especially by falling on it or scraping it **3.** *vt.* **REMOVE OUTSIDE PART OF** to strip off an outer, covering layer that resembles a skin **4.** *vti.* **PUT SKIN ON** to grow or become covered with a skin, or cover sb or sth with a skin **5.** *vt.* CRIMINOL **SWINDLE** to trick sb out of money or property (*slang*) ■ *adj. US* **PORNOGRAPHIC** relating to or containing pornographic material (*informal*) [12thC. From Old Norse *skinn*. Ultimately from an Indo-European word meaning 'to cut' (see SKI). The underlying idea is of sth peeled off (presumably a pelt from a hunted animal).] —**skinless** *adj.* ◇ **be no skin off sb's nose** to be a matter that does not harm you at all and therefore may be of little interest (*informal*) ◇ **by the skin of your teeth** by a very narrow margin, or only just (*informal*) ◇ **get under your skin 1.** to annoy or irritate you (*informal*) **2.** to make you feel great interest or attraction (*informal*) ◇ **save sb's skin** to prevent sb suffering hurt, loss, or punishment by giving vital help (*informal*) ◇ **skin up** *vi.* to roll a marijuana joint or cigarette (*informal*)

skin-deep *adj.* **WITHOUT DEEP MEANING OR IMPORTANCE** appearing to be important, meaningful, or valuable but having little deep or lasting importance ■ *adv.* **NOT DEEPLY** in a superficial way

skin diving *n.* the sport of underwater diving using flippers and a mask and snorkel —**skin-dive** *vi.* —**skin diver** *n.*

skin effect *n.* the tendency of a high-frequency alternating current to flow near the surface of the conductor rather than in its interior

skin flick *n.* a film (*slang*)

skinflint /skínflint/ *n.* sb who hates parting with money, whether by spending it or by giving it to other people [Late 17thC. From the phrase 'skin a flint', used of sb so miserly as to try to remove the skin from a piece of flint.]

skin friction *n.* a frictional force, or drag, acting on the surface of an aerofoil or other object immersed in a large volume of fluid that is in motion relative to the object

skinful /skín fòol/ *n.* **1. LARGE QUANTITY OF ALCOHOLIC DRINK** a large amount of alcoholic drink, especially as much as sb can drink (*informal*) **2. AMOUNT A SKIN HOLDS** the amount of liquid that a skin bag holds [Mid-17thC. From SKIN 'bag for holding an alcoholic beverage'.]

skin game *n.* a confidence trick or scheme used to cheat people of their money (*slang*) [From SKIN 'to swindle']

skin graft *n.* a piece of skin taken from part of the body and used to replace lost or damaged skin

skinhead /skín hed/ *n.* (*slang*) **1. SB WITH SHAVED HEAD** sb whose hair is very short or whose head is shaved **2. YOUNG MAN WITH EXTREME RIGHT-WING VIEWS** a young white man with closely cropped or shaven hair who typically wears jeans, braces, and heavy boots and is associated with aggressive behaviour and extreme right-wing views

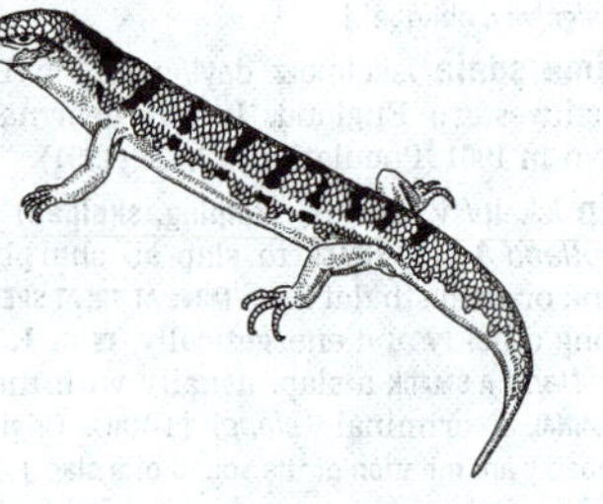

Skink

skink /skingk/ *n.* a small smooth insect-eating lizard with a long thin body and small limbs. It lives in temperate and tropical regions, especially in Asia and Africa. Family: Scincidae. [Late 16thC. Directly or via obsolete French *scinc* from Latin *scincus*, from Greek *skigkos*.]

skinner /skínnər/ *n.* sb who skins animals or deals in animal skins

Skinner /skínnər/, **B. F.** (1904–90) US psychologist. His stimulus-response experiments and behaviourist theories profoundly influenced methods of education and behaviour therapy. His works include *Beyond Freedom and Dignity* (1971). Full name **Burrhus Frederic Skinner** —**Skinnerian** /ski nέəri ən/ *adj., n.*

Skinner box /skínnər-/ *n.* an enclosure for isolating an animal during studies of learning behaviour, or operant conditioning, that contains a device the animal may operate to receive a reward or avoid punishment [Mid-20thC. Named after B. F. SKINNER.]

skinny /skínni/ (**-nier, -niest**) *adj.* **1. VERY THIN** thin, especially in an unappealing or unhealthy way **2. LOW-FAT** made with skimmed milk (*informal*) ○ *One skinny latte to go.* [Mid-16thC. Formed from SKIN.] —**skinniness** *n.*

WORD KEY: SYNONYMS

See Synonyms at *thin*.

skinny-dip *vi.* (**skinny-dips, skinny-dipping, skinny-dipped**) **SWIM NUDE** to go swimming in the nude (*informal*) ■ *n.* **NUDE SWIM** a swim in the nude (*informal*) [From SKINNY in its original sense 'pertaining to the skin'] —**skinny-dipper** *n.* —**skinny-dipping** *n.*

skin-pop (**skin-pops, skin-popping, skin-popped**) *vti.* to take narcotic drugs by inserting the needle under the skin, not straight into a vein (*slang*)

skint /skint/ *adj.* without any money (*informal*) [Early 20thC. Variant of *skinned* (from SKIN) in the sense 'bested'.]

skin test *n.* a test in which a substance is applied to the skin to determine sb's allergic sensitivity or immunity to it

skintight /skín tīt/ *adj.* fitting tightly to the body

skip[1] /skip/ *v.* (**skips, skipping, skipped**) **1.** *vi.* **MOVE WITH SMALL HOPPING STEPS** to move along by hopping from one foot to the other **2.** *vti.* **JUMP REPEATEDLY OVER CIRCLING ROPE** to jump repeatedly over a rope as it is swung round over the head and under the feet **3.** *vt.* **NIMBLY JUMP OVER** to jump nimbly over sth **4.** *vti.* **OMIT** to pass over or leave sth out that should properly follow as part of a sequence or a complete work **5.** *vt.* **DEAL WITH CURSORILY** to deal with or look at sth in a cursory way **6.** *vt.* **NOT ATTEND OR BE AT** to choose or decide to miss an event or activity (*informal*) **7.** *vi.* RECORDING **NOT PLAY CORRECTLY** to fail to play a CD or record properly by jumping from one place to another, or to undergo this kind of faulty playing **8.** *vti.* **LEAVE SOMEWHERE SECRETLY** to make a secret getaway, especially for some dishonest reason, e.g. to avoid being punished for sth (*informal*) **9.** *vti.* **MOVE IN SERIES OF SMALL HOPS** to move lightly across a surface in a series of small hops, or make sth move in this way ■ *n.* **1. SMALL HOPPING STEP** a small forward hopping

step **2.** ACT OF OMITTING STH an act of omitting part of sth [13thC. Origin uncertain: probably from Old Norse.] —**skippable** *adj.*
skip off *vi.* to make a secret getaway, especially for some dishonest reason, e.g. to avoid paying for sth or being punished for sth (*informal*)

skip[2] /skip/ *n.* a large flat-bottomed metal container kept outdoors for putting unwanted materials, furniture, or any bulky refuse in, especially when a building is being renovated or constructed [Early 19thC. Variant of SKEP.]

skip[3] /skip/ *n.* (*plural* **skips**) (*informal*) NAUT SKIPPER a skipper (*slang*) ■ *vi.* (**skips, skipping, skipped**) NAUT BE SKIPPER OF to be the skipper of a vessel (*slang*) [Early 19thC. Shortening.]

ski pants *npl.* **1.** STRETCHY LEGGINGS WITH FOOTSTRAPS women's trousers made of stretchy fabric with elasticated straps that go under the feet **2.** TROUSERS FOR SKIING trousers that are worn for skiing and other cold weather activities and that are often lined, windproof, and water-resistant

skip distance *n.* the shortest distance between a radio transmitter and receiver that permits waves of a particular frequency to be sent and received by reflection from the ionosphere

skipjack /skíp jak/ (*plural* **-jack** /skíp jak/ *or* **-jacks**) *n.* **1.** ZOOL LEAPING MARINE FISH any of various marine fishes that leap out of the water such as the bonito or bluefish **2. skipjack, skipjack tuna** FOOD, ZOOL MARINE FOOD FISH a tropical marine sport and food fish of the tuna family that is blue and silver with dark stripes on its abdomen. Latin name: *Euthynnus pelamus.* **3.** = **click beetle 4.** *US* SAILING SAILING BOAT a sailing boat with straight sides and a V-shaped bottom

skiplane /skeé playn/ *n.* an aircraft equipped with skis for taking off from and landing on snow

ski pole, ski stick *n.* one of a pair of lightweight poles held by skiers for balance and control. The bottom end has a point surrounded by a disc for gaining purchase on the snow.

skipper[1] /skíppər/ *n.* **1.** NAUT SB IN CHARGE OF SHIP sb in charge of a ship or boat **2.** LEADER OF A TEAM sb in charge of a squad or group of others, especially the captain or coach of a sports team (*informal*) ■ *vt.* (**-pers, -pering, -pered**) BE SKIPPER OF to be in charge of a ship, team or aircraft (*informal*) [14thC. From Middle Dutch *schipper*, from *schip* 'ship'.]

skipper[2] /skíppər/ *n.* **1.** SB OR STH THAT SKIPS sb or sth that skips **2.** INSECTS INSECT RESEMBLING MOTH a quick-flying insect that has a stout hairy body and clubbed antennae with hooked tips, and is closely related to true butterflies. Families: Hesperiidae and Megathymidae. **3.** ZOOL = **saury** [Mid-18thC. Formed from SKIP[1]. The word was used to designate these animals because of their jumping and darting movements.]

skipping /skípping/ *n.* the children's pastime or adult exercise in which you skip over a rope as it swings round and round over your head and under your feet

skipping-rope *n.* a piece of rope, often with handles at either end, for skipping over. US term **jump rope**

Skipton /skíptən/ market town in West Yorkshire, England. Population: 13,583 (1991).

skirl /skurl/ *n. Scotland* SHRILL WAILING NOISE the high-pitched wailing sound that bagpipes typically make ■ *vti.* (**skirls, skirling, skirled**) *Scotland* PRODUCE SHRILL WAILING NOISE to produce a high-pitched wailing sound on the bagpipes [14thC. Origin uncertain: probably from a Scandinavian language.]

skirmish /skúrmish/ *n.* **1.** MIL SMALL RELATIVELY UNIMPORTANT BATTLE an incident where fighting breaks out briefly between two small contingents away from the main battlefield in a war **2.** SHORT ARGUMENT a brief fight or disagreement between people ■ *vi.* (**-mishes, -mishing, -mished**) ENGAGE IN MINOR BATTLE to become involved in a skirmish [14thC. From the Old French stem *eskermiss-* 'to fence', from, ultimately, a prehistoric Germanic word meaning 'to defend'; the noun was later reinforced by Old French *escar(a)muche*, from Italian *scaramuccia*.] —**skirmisher** *n.*

WORD KEY: SYNONYMS
See Synonyms at ***fight***.

skirr /skur/ *vti.* (**skirrs, skirring, skirred**) MOVE QUICKLY AND BUSILY to rush along, or rush through an area ■ *n.* WHIR a whirring sound [Mid-16thC. Origin unknown.]

skirret /skírrət/ *n.* a plant cultivated in Europe for its sweetish edible root. Latin name: *Sium sisarum.* [14thC. Earlier *skirwhit*, of uncertain origin: probably by folk etymology (from obsolete *scir* 'pure' + WHITE) from Old French *eschervi*, from Arabic *karawiyā* 'caraway' (see CARAWAY).]

skirt /skurt/ *n.* **1.** CLOTHES GARMENT THAT HANGS FROM THE WAIST a piece of clothing that hangs from the waist and does not divide into two separate legs, usually worn by women and girls **2.** CLOTHES AREA OF FABRIC FALLING FROM WAISTLINE the section from the waist to the hem on a dress, coat, or robe **3.** TECH STH SIMILAR TO SKIRT an attachment shaped like a skirt, or covering the lower part of sth like a skirt **4.** ENG FLAP AROUND BOTTOM OF HOVERCRAFT the lower outer section of a rocket or the flap around the bottom of a hovercraft **5.** FOOD CUT OF BEEF a stewing cut of beef taken from the flank, below the sirloin and rump, and cut from the inside of flank steak **6.** EQU FLAP ON SADDLE one of a pair of leather flaps that hang from a saddle **7.** OFFENSIVE TERM an offensive term used to refer to a girl or woman, or women in general, by suggesting that they are objects (*slang offensive*) ■ *v.* (**skirts, skirting, skirted**) **1.** *vti.* BE AROUND THE OUTSIDE OF STH to form a border along the edge of an area or object **2.** *vti.* MOVE AROUND THE OUTSIDE OF STH to travel along the edge of sth such as an area, structure, or geographical feature **3.** *vt.* AVOID GIVING PROPER ATTENTION TO to avoid dealing with a particular subject in any depth, usually because it is tricky or unpleasant **4.** *vt.* TECH GIVE AN EDGE TO to provide sth with an attachment shaped like a skirt or border [13thC. From Old Norse *skyrta* 'shirt', from a prehistoric Germanic word that is also the ancestor of English *shirt*.] —**skirter** *n.*

skirt-chaser *n.* an offensive term used to refer a man who is regarded as being excessively interested in pursuing women sexually (*slang offensive*) —**skirt-chasing** *n.*

skirting /skúrting/ *n.* **1.** CONSTR = **skirting board 2.** INDUST MATERIAL FOR SKIRTS material used to make skirts ■ **skirtings** *npl. ANZ* PIECES OF FLEECE pieces trimmed from a shorn fleece

skirting board *n.* a narrow board, attached to the base of an interior wall, that covers the joint between the wall and the floor. US term **skirting**

skit /skit/ *n.* **1.** THEATRE SHORT COMIC SKETCH a short, usually comic, dramatic sketch **2.** LITERAT COMIC SATIRICAL WRITING a short piece of comic writing that satirizes sb or sth [Early 18thC. Origin uncertain: perhaps from a Scandinavian language.]

skite[1] /skīt/ *v.* (**skites, skiting, skited**) *Scotland* **1.** *vi.* SLIP to slip on a slippery surface **2.** *vti.* HIT STH SHARPLY to hit sth or sb with a sharp blow, or to hit sth and bounce sharply from it ■ *n. Scotland* **1.** ACT OF SKIDDING OR SLIPPING an instance of sth or sb sliding suddenly across a slippery surface **2.** SHARP KNOCK OR SLAP a sudden forceful glancing blow (*nonstandard*) [Early 18thC. Origin uncertain: perhaps from a Scandinavian language.]

skite[2] /skīt/ *vi.* (**skites, skiting, skited**) *Aus* BOAST to talk with excessive pride about yourself or your accomplishments (*informal*) ■ *n. Aus* **1.** BOASTING TALK talk that exaggerates your own importance and accomplishments **2.** BOASTER an arrogant or boastful person [Mid-19thC. Origin uncertain.]

ski touring *n.* travelling over long distances on skis, especially in wilderness areas

ski tow *n.* an apparatus consisting of a motor-driven rope that skiers hang onto to be towed up a mountain

skitter /skíttər/ *v.* (**-ters, -tering, -tered**) **1.** *vi.* RUN WITH TINY STEPS to move about or run off quickly with small scampering steps **2.** *vti.* SKID LIGHTLY ACROSS STH to pass quickly across sth, touching its surface very lightly and briefly, or to send sth skidding rapidly over the surface of sth ■ *n. Ireland* UNRELIABLE PERSON an unreliable person (*slang*) ■ **skitters** *npl. Ireland, Scotland* DIARRHOEA an attack of diarrhoea (*slang*) [Mid-19thC. Origin uncertain.]

skittish /skíttish/ *adj.* **1.** SILLY AND IRRESPONSIBLE with moods or ideas that constantly change, in a frivolous and unreliable way **2.** NERVOUS easily agitated or alarmed **3.** LIVELY tending to dash about in an energetic or restless way [14thC. Origin uncertain: perhaps formed from an alteration of Old Norse *skjóta* 'to shoot'.] —**skittishly** *adv.* —**skittishness** *n.*

skittle /skítt'l/ *n.* one of the set of wooden or plastic bottle-shaped pins that are stood upright in a group for players to aim at in the game of skittles. US term **ninepin** [Mid-17thC. Origin uncertain: perhaps from a Scandinavian language.]
skittle out *vt.* to put a batting side out quickly in cricket

skive[1] /skīv/ *vti.* (**skives, skiving, skived**) NOT BOTHER DOING YOUR WORK to avoid doing work, studies, or duties (*informal*) ■ *n.* AVOIDANCE OF WORK time spent avoiding work, studies, or duties, or sth that sb uses to disguise doing this (*informal*) [Early 20thC. Origin uncertain: perhaps from French *esquiver* 'to slink away'.]

skive[2] /skīv/ (**skives, skiving, skived**) *vt.* to scrape thin slices off leather in preparing it [Early 19thC. Of Scandinavian origin.]

skiver[1] /skívər/ *n.* sb who tries to avoid doing work (*informal*)

skiver[2] /skívər/ *n.* **1.** THIN SOFT LEATHER a thin soft tanned leather taken from the outer side of a skin **2.** SB OR STH THAT SKIVES sb or sth that skives leather

skivvy /skívvi/ *n.* (*plural* **-vies**) **1.** FEMALE SERVANT a usually female servant who performs menial tasks (*informal insult*) **2.** *ANZ* LONG-SLEEVED COTTON TOP a long-sleeved, usually cotton piece of clothing with a rolled neck worn on the upper part of the body ■ *vi.* (**-vies, -vying, -vied**) PERFORM MENIAL WORK to perform menial tasks for sb else (*informal*) [Mid-20thC. Origin unknown.]

skiwear /skeé wayr/ *n.* clothing designed for skiers to wear

skol /skōl/, **skoal** *interj.* used as a drinking toast [Early 17thC. Via Danish *skaal* and Swedish and Norwegian *skål* from Old Norse *skál* 'bowl' (source of English *scale*).]

skollie /skólli/, **skolly** (*plural* **-lies**) *n. S Africa* a young, usually coloured or Black male who is involved in petty crime and violence and often belongs to a gang (*informal offensive*) [Mid-20thC. From Afrikaans, probably from Dutch *schoelje* 'scoundrel'.]

Skomer /skṓmər/ islet in St Bride's Bay, off the Pembrokeshire coast, Wales

Skopje /skóp yi/ capital of the Republic of Macedonia, situated in the north-central part of the country. Population: 563,102 (1994).

Skr., Skt *abbr.* Sanskrit

skua /skyóo ə/ *n.* a large, brown, predatory seabird with slender wings that chases other birds to make them drop their prey. Genera: *Catharacta* and *Stercorarius.* ◊ **great skua** [Late 17thC. Via modern Latin from a variant of Faeroese *skugvur*, from Old Norse *skufr*, perhaps an imitation of the sound made by the bird.]

skulduggery /skul dúggəri/ *n.* unfair and dishonest practices carried out in a secretive way so as to trick other people (*humorous*) [Mid-19thC. Alteration of *sculduddery* 'sexual impropriety, indecency', of unknown origin.]

skulk /skulk/ *vi.* (**skulks, skulking, skulked**) **1.** MOVE FURTIVELY to move about in a furtive way **2.** HIDE FOR SINISTER PURPOSE to hide, especially in order to do sth sinister **3.** SHIRK to avoid work or responsibilities ■ *n.* **1.** SB WHO SKULKS sb who moves about furtively or conceals a sinister purpose **2.** ZOOL GROUP OF FOXES a pack of foxes [12thC. Of Scandinavian origin.]

skull /skul/ *n.* **1.** ANAT BONY PART OF THE HEAD the skeletal part of the head in humans and other vertebrates, consisting of the cranium, which encases the brain, and the bones of the face and jaws **2.** HEAD a person's head or mind (*informal*) ○ *tried to din the principles of thermodynamics into his skull* [13thC. Origin uncertain: probably from a Scandinavian language.]

skull and crossbones *n.* **1.** SYMBOLIC SIGN REPRESENTING DANGER a representation of a human skull above two

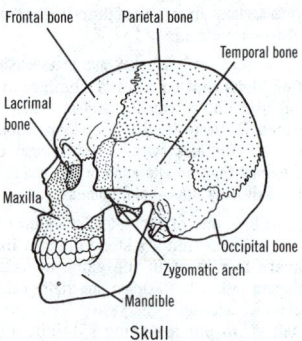

Skull

[Labels: Frontal bone, Parietal bone, Temporal bone, Lacrimal bone, Maxilla, Occipital bone, Zygomatic arch, Mandible]

human thighbones crossed over each other, used as a symbol of danger or death 2. = **Jolly Roger**

skullcap /skúl kap/ n. 1. CLOTHES SMALL ROUND BRIMLESS HAT a simple hat consisting of a small circle of fabric shaped to fit over the crown of the head 2. ANAT TOP OF SKULL the top part of the skull 3. PLANTS PERENNIAL MINT a perennial plant of the mint family. Its blue or pinkish flowers have a calyx shaped like a helmet. Genus: *Scutellaria*.

Skunk

skunk /skungk/ n. (plural **skunk** or **skunks**) 1. ZOOL BLACK-AND-WHITE MAMMAL WITH FOUL-SMELLING SPRAY a North and South American black-and-white mammal of the weasel family that ejects a foul-smelling liquid from an anal gland as a defensive action 2. DESPICABLE PERSON sb who is despised (slang) ■ vt. (**skunks, skunking, skunked**) US, Can DEFEAT SOUNDLY to defeat an opponent soundly, especially by not allowing him or her to score any points in a sporting competition (slang) [Mid-17thC. From Massachusett.]

skunk cabbage, skunkweed (plural **-weeds** or **-weed**) n. 1. FOUL-SMELLING PERENNIAL HERB a foul-smelling perennial herb of swampy areas of eastern North America that has broad leaves and small flowers enclosed in a greenish spathe. Latin name: *Symplocarpus foetidus*. 2. A PLANT SIMILAR TO SKUNK CABBAGE a plant of western North America, similar to skunk cabbage and with a large yellow spathe. Latin name: *Lysichitum americanum*.

sky /skī/ n. (plural **skies**) 1. REGION ABOVE THE EARTH the area high above the trees, buildings, landscape, or horizon. The sky is made up of the various layers of the Earth's atmosphere and the part of space beyond it, as seen from one place on the Earth's surface. 2. WAY SKY APPEARS the way the sky looks in a particular part of the world (often used in the plural) 3. **sky, Sky** HEAVEN the plane, thought of as being high above the Earth, in which immortal powers or beings exist, such as God or immortal souls (literary; often used in the plural) 4. HIGHEST LIMIT the topmost limit or the best and most it is possible to achieve ■ vti. (**skies, skying, skied**) MAKE STH GO VERY HIGH to kick, hit or throw a ball high up into the air [13thC. From Old Norse *ský* 'cloud'. Ultimately from an Indo-European base meaning 'to conceal' that is also the ancestor of English *scum* and *hide*.] ◇ **praise sb to the skies** to praise sb very highly ◇ **the sky's the limit** there is no upper limit on sth (informal)

sky blue adj. PALE BLUE of a pale blue colour like that of the sky on a clear day ■ n. PALE BLUE COLOUR a pale blue colour like that of the sky on a clear day

skydive /skī́ dīv/ (**-dives, -diving, -dived**) vi. to jump from an aeroplane and descend in free fall, sometimes performing acrobatic manoeuvres, before pulling the ripcord of a parachute —**sky diver** n. —**skydiving** n.

Skye /skī/ the largest island in the Inner Hebrides, in Scotland. Portree is the chief town and port. Population: 8,843 (1991). Area: 1,676 sq. km/647 sq. mi.

Skye terrier n. a small terrier with short legs, a long body, and a long straight coat belonging to a breed originating in Scotland [Mid-19thC. Named after the Isle of SKYE, where the dog was bred.]

sky-high adv., adj. EXTREMELY HIGH up to or at the highest level ■ adv. INTO PIECES high into the air or in all directions, forcefully and often in pieces

sky-hook n. 1. IMAGINARY HOOK an imaginary hook conceived as hanging from the sky 2. HEAVY-LIFTING HELICOPTER a helicopter that is specially configured with a hook-and-cable apparatus in its fuselage, used to lift, drop, and transport heavy objects

skyjack /skī́ jak/ (**-jacks, -jacking, -jacked**) vt. to use force to take over control of an aircraft, especially a commercial aircraft, when it is in the air [Mid-20thC. Formed from SKY on the model of HIJACK.] —**skyjacker** n. —**skyjacking** n.

skylark /skī́ laark/ n. BIRDS COMMON LARK a lark that is common in Europe and Asia. It has streaked brown-and-white plumage and is noted for singing melodiously while hanging high in the air. Latin name: *Alauda arvensis*. ■ vi. (**-larks, -larking, -larked**) HAVE BOISTEROUS FUN to take part in lively physical playful behaviour (dated informal) —**skylarker** n.

skylight /skī́ līt/ n. an opening in a roof or ceiling, fitted with glass to let in daylight

skylight filter n. a photographic filter that is slightly pink and is used to filter out ultraviolet light and reduce blueness

skyline /skī́ līn/ n. 1. SHAPE OF OBJECTS AGAINST THE SKY the pattern of shapes made by the various features of a landscape such as hills or buildings against the sky 2. EDGE WHERE SKY AND LANDSCAPE MEET the apparent line where the Earth joins the sky

sky pilot n. an offensive term used to refer to a priest or chaplain, especially in the armed forces (slang offensive) [In supposedly humorous reference to concern with spiritual matters]

skyrocket /skī́ rokit/ n. = rocket[1] n. 4 ■ vti. (**-ets, -eting, -eted**) GO UP DRAMATICALLY AND QUICKLY to rise or make sth rise suddenly to a very high level or value (informal)

Skyros /skeé ross/ the largest and most easterly of the Greek Sporades Islands, in the west-central Aegean Sea. Population: 2,757 (1981). Area: 205 sq. km/79 sq. mi.

skysail /skī́ sayl/ n. a small light square sail that goes above the royal on a square-rigged sailing vessel

skyscape /skī́ skayp/ n. a scene or picture showing chiefly sky, especially an artistic study of a section of sky

skyscraper /skī́ skraypər/ n. a modern building that is extremely tall [Late 18thC. Like *moonraker*, *skyscraper* originally referred to a sail positioned high above the deck (the *skysail*). The meaning 'tall building' first appeared in the early 19thC.]

skyward /skī́wərd/ adv. **skyward, skywards** UPWARDS in the direction of the sky ■ adj. TOWARDS THE SKY heading towards the sky

sky wave n. a radio wave that is transmitted around the curved surface of the Earth by being reflected back to Earth by the ionosphere

skyway /skī́ way/ n. 1. AIR AIRCRAFT ROUTE a route used by aircraft 2. US TRANSP ELEVATED HIGHWAY an elevated highway, supported by tall spans ○ *the Chicago Skyway*

skywriting /skī́ rīting/ n. 1. WRITING WITH AIRCRAFT SMOKE the use of an aircraft releasing coloured smoke to form letters in the sky 2. WRITING MADE WITH AIRCRAFT SMOKE letters or a message formed in the sky by coloured smoke released from an aircraft —**skywrite** vti. —**skywriter** n.

SL abbr. 1. INSUR salvage loss 2. GEOG sea level 3. Solicitor-at-Law 4. LING source language 5. GEOG south latitude

sl. abbr. 1. slightly 2. slow

slab /slab/ n. 1. THICK PIECE a thick flat broad piece of sth, especially when cut or trimmed 2. ARCHIT STONE BASE FOR STH a flat rectangular base or foundation of concrete or stone 3. GEOL SHEET OF ROCK a smooth flat sheet of rock sharply angled to the horizontal 4. MORTUARY TABLE a table on which a body is laid in a mortuary (informal) 5. OFFCUT FROM LOG any of the large outer sections of a log that are sawn off before it is made into planks 6. Aus PACK OF BEER a pack or box of 24 cans or bottles of beer (informal) ■ adj. ANZ made of coarse wooden planks ■ vt. (**slabs, slabbing, slabbed**) 1. MAKE INTO SLABS to cut or make sth into slabs 2. COVER WITH SLABS to cover sth by laying stone or concrete slabs on it 3. TRIM BY SAWING to saw off the rough outer parts of a log [13thC. Origin unknown.]

slabber /slábbər/ vi. TO SLOBBER to slobber (regional) ■ n. SLOBBER slobber (regional) [Mid-16thC. Origin uncertain: probably related to dialect *slab* 'muddy place, puddle', of Scandinavian origin.]

slabbing /slábbing/ n. 1. LAYING OF SLABS the laying of stone or concrete slabs to form a surface such as a pathway 2. SLABS stone or concrete slabs, collectively

slab pottery n. pottery made by hand using rolled-out sheets of clay

slack /slak/ adj. 1. NOT TIGHT not tight or stretched taut, but hanging loosely or having a good deal of give ○ *The reins are too slack.* 2. NOT SHOWING ENOUGH CARE not showing enough care, attention, or rigour ○ *They've been rather slack about keeping to performance targets.* 3. NOT BUSY not busy or active, or less busy than usual ○ *the slack period following the main tourist season* 4. MOVING SLOWLY moving slowly or sluggishly 5. PHON = lax adj. 4 ■ adv. LOOSELY in a loose or limp way ○ *His clothes hung slack on him.* ■ n. 1. LOOSENESS looseness or give in sth such as a rope, or the extra length or fullness in it that needs to be taken in to make it taut 2. UNUSED POTENTIAL productive potential in an organization or system that is not being fully made use of ○ *take in some of the slack in the administrative division* 3. QUIET TIME a period of time that is not busy 4. STILL WATER a stretch of water that is still or moving only slowly ■ vti. (**slacks, slacking, slacked**) 1. AVOID WORK to be lazy, to avoid work, or to work with insufficient vigour or concentration 2. = slacken v. 1 3. CHEM = slake v. 2 [Old English *slæc*. Ultimately from an Indo-European word meaning 'to be loose' that is also the ancestor of English *lax* and *languid*.]

slacken /slákən/ (**-ens, -ening, -ened**) vti. 1. MAKE OR BECOME SLOWER OR QUIETER to become or to make sth become less intense, vigorous, or fast 2. LOOSEN OR RELAX to become or to make sth become looser or more relaxed

slacker /slákər/ n. 1. SHIRKER sb who shirks or avoids doing sth, especially work or military service 2. OFFENSIVE TERM an offensive term used to describe a young educated person who is regarded as being disaffected or apathetic, and underachieving (slang offensive)

slacks /slaks/ npl. casual trousers, especially loose-fitting ones [Early 19thC. From the idea of being loose and slack.]

slack water n. the period of time during which the tide is turning and the water is still or slow-moving because of this

SLADE /slayd/ abbr. Society of Lithographic Artists, Designers, Engravers, and Process Workers

slag /slag/ n. 1. INDUST WASTE MATERIAL FROM SMELTING fused glassy material that is produced when a metal is separated from its ore during smelting 2. MINING COAL WASTE the mixture of coal dust and mineral waste produced after coal has been mined 3. GEOL = scoria n. 2 4. PROMISCUOUS WOMAN an offensive term for a woman who is considered to be sexually promiscuous or generally coarse and sluttish (slang insult offensive) 5. SB DESPISED any individual, especially a man, regarded as despicable (slang insult) ■ v. (**slags, slagging, slagged**) 1. vti. INDUST TURN STH INTO SLAG to convert sth into slag or become slag 2. vt. INSULT OR CRITICIZE to make insulting, mocking, or critical comments about sb or sth (*slang*) ○ *Don't you dare slag off my team!* **3.** *vi. Aus* **SPIT** to spit (*slang*) [Mid-16thC. From Middle Low German *slagge*, from a prehistoric Germanic word meaning 'to strike' that is also the ancestor of English *sledgehammer* and *slay*.]

slagging /slágging/ *n.* a series of insulting, mocking, or critical comments (*slang*) ○ *I took a right slagging over that haircut.*

slag heap *n.* a large mound of waste material from a coal mine or factory

slain past participle of **slay**

slàinte /slaánjə, slaánchə/, **slàinte mhath** *interj. Scotland* used as a drinking toast, meaning 'good health!' [Early 19thC. From Gaelic *slàinte (mhath)* '(good) health'.]

slake /slayk/ (**slakes, slaking, slaked**) *v.* **1.** *vt.* **SATISFY NEED** to satisfy a desire for sth, especially a drink **2.** *vti.* CHEM **MAKE CALCIUM HYDROXIDE** to treat lime with water to produce calcium hydroxide, or to undergo this process [Old English *slacian* 'to relax, slacken', formed from *slæc*, (see SLACK)] —**slakable** *adj.*

slaked lime *n.* = **calcium hydroxide**

Slalom

slalom /slaáləm/ *n.* **1. ZIGZAG SKI RACE** a downhill ski race in which competitors follow a winding course and zigzag through flags on poles or through other obstacles **2. ZIGZAG RACE** any race that involves following a zigzag course through obstacles, e.g. in canoes ■ *vi.* (**-loms, -loming, -lomed**) **FOLLOW ZIGZAG COURSE** to follow a zigzag or winding course, especially in a race [Early 20thC. From Norwegian *slalåm*, literally 'sloping track'.]

slam[1] /slam/ *v.* (**slams, slamming, slammed**) **1.** *vti.* **CLOSE FORCEFULLY** to close sth forcefully and noisily **2.** *vti.* **PUT STH DOWN VIOLENTLY** to put sth down violently and noisily **3.** *vti.* **HIT** to hit with sudden or violent force ○ *The waves slammed into the dock.* **4.** *vt.* **CRITICIZE** to criticize sb or sth forcefully (*informal*) ○ *The press slammed the government's performance.* ■ *n.* **1. IMPACT** a heavy, noisy, or violent blow or impact **2. CRITICISM** a forceful criticism [Late 17thC. Origin uncertain.]

slam[2] /slam/ *n.* CARDS the winning of all, or all but one, of the tricks in a hand of bridge or whist [Mid-17thC. Origin unknown.]

slam-bang *adv. US* (*informal*) **1.** = **slap-bang** *adv.* 1 **2. CARELESSLY** in a careless and reckless way **3. EXCITINGLY** in an exciting and vigorous way ○ *The novel ended slam-bang with a fight to the finish.* ■ *adj. US* (*informal*) **1. SUDDEN AND NOISY** sudden, noisy, or violent ○ *a slam-bang fight* **2. CARELESS AND RECKLESS** careless and reckless ○ *a slam-bang approach to his work* **3. EXCITING** exciting and vigorous ○ *slam-bang action scenes*

slam dancing *n.* boisterous dancing to rock music in which young people hurl their bodies against one another, more out of enthusiasm than aggression —**slam dance** *vi.*

slam-dunk, **slam dunk** *n.* **1.** BASKETBALL **SHOT THROWN DOWN FORCEFULLY INTO BASKET** a shot in basketball in which a player jumps up and throws the ball forcefully down into the basket **2. STH EASILY DONE** sth done without any effective opposition (*informal*) ■ *vt.* (**slam-dunks, slam-dunking, slam-dunked**) **THROW FORCEFULLY INTO BASKET** in basketball, to jump up and throw the ball forcefully down into the basket ■ *adj. US* **CERTAIN OF SUCCESS** without risk and sure to be successful ○ *a slam-dunk scenario*

slammer /slámmər/ *n.* a jail or prison (*slang*) [Mid-20thC. From the idea of the doors slamming shut.]

s.l.a.n. *abbr.* without place, year, or name [Shortening of Latin *sine loco, anno, vel nomine*]

slander /slaándər/ *n.* **1.** LAW **SAYING OF STH FALSE AND DAMAGING** the act of saying sth false or malicious that damages sb's reputation **2. FALSE AND DAMAGING STATEMENT** a false and malicious statement that damages sb's reputation ■ *vt.* (**-ders, -dering, -dered**) **UTTER A SLANDER AGAINST** to make a false and malicious oral statement about sb [13thC. Via Old French *esclandre* from, ultimately, ecclesiastical Latin *scandalum* 'cause of offence' (see SCANDAL).] —**slanderer** *n.* —**slanderous** *adj.* —**slanderously** *adv.* —**slanderousness** *n.*

WORD KEY: SYNONYMS

See Synonyms at ***malign***.

slang /slang/ *n.* **1. VERY CASUAL SPEECH OR WRITING** words, expressions, and usages that are casual, vivid, racy, or playful replacements for standard ones, are often short-lived, and are usually considered unsuitable for formal contexts **2. LANGUAGE OF AN EXCLUSIVE GROUP** a form of language used by a particular group of people, often deliberately created and used to exclude people outside the group ○ *a word that came from surfers' slang* ■ *adj.* **IN SLANG** belonging to, expressed in, or containing slang ○ *a slang dictionary* ■ *vt.* (**slangs, slanging, slanged**) **ATTACK VERBALLY** to use abusive language, usually slang, to attack sb verbally ○ *We'll get nowhere just slanging each other.* [Mid-18thC. Origin unknown.] —**slangily** *adv.* —**slanginess** *n.* —**slangy** *adj.*

slanging match *n. UK, Can* a dispute in which people insult and accuse each other ○ *The level of political debate had deteriorated to a series of slanging matches.*

slant /slaant/ *v.* (**slants, slanting, slanted**) **1.** *vti.* **BE OR SET STH AT AN ANGLE** to be at an angle, or set sth at an angle **2.** *vt.* **CAUSE STH TO HAVE A PARTICULAR APPEAL** to make sth appeal to a particular group of people ○ *a magazine slanted towards the youth market* **3.** *vt.* **PRESENT WITH BIAS** to present sth in a way that is biased towards a particular person, group, or viewpoint ○ *The news report was slanted in favour of the nationalists.* ■ *n.* **1. ANGLED POSITION** an angled position or a direction that is at an angle to sth else ○ *the roof was built on a slant* **2. BIASED PERSPECTIVE** a particular bias, or a perspective on sth that is likely to appeal to a particular group ○ *The news was given a pro-government slant.* **3. POINT OF VIEW** a point of view or way of looking at sth ○ *Her diaries give us a new slant on the events of the time.* ■ *adj.* **slant, slanting, slanty SLOPING** sloping, or at an angle (*informal*) [15thC. Variant of earlier *slent*, of uncertain origin: probably from a Scandinavian language.] —**slanted** *adj.* —**slantingly** *adv.*

slant rhyme *n.* POETRY = **half rhyme**

slantways /slaánt wayz/, **slantwise** /-wīz/ *adv.* at an angle to sth else

slap /slap/ *n.* **1. BLOW MADE WITH THE OPEN HAND** a blow made with the open hand or a flat object **2. NOISE OF A SLAP** the noise made by a slap, or sth that sounds like it ○ *the slap of a wave on the side of the boat* **3. REBUKE** sth that rebukes, insults, or hurts **4. MAKE-UP** make-up, whether for personal everyday use or for the theatre (*slang*) ○ *She said she'd just put some slap on and meet us downstairs.* ■ *v.* (**slaps, slapping, slapped**) **1.** *vt.* **HIT WITH THE OPEN HAND** to hit sb or sth with the open hand or a flat object **2.** *vi.* **STRIKE SHARPLY** to strike sharply and noisily, as if with a slap **3.** *vt.* **PUT DOWN SHARPLY** to put sth down sharply or noisily on sth else ○ *He slapped the money on the table and walked away.* **4.** *vt.* **APPLY CARELESSLY** to put sth on or make sth, quickly and carelessly ○ *I slapped on some makeup and ran for the car.* **5.** *vt.* **APPLY AS A PENALTY** to apply sth as a punishment, penalty, or restriction to sb or sth (*informal*) ○ *The government slapped an embargo on the story.* ■ *adv.* (*informal*) **1. FORCEFULLY** forcefully, and often with the sound or effect of a slap ○ *landed slap on the floor* **2. EXACTLY** exactly, and usually with suddenness and force ○ *slap in the middle of the target* [Mid-17thC. An imitation of the sound.] ◇ **a slap in the face** a rebuke or rebuff (*informal*) ◇ **a slap on the back** congratulations (*informal*) ◇ **a slap on the wrist** a mild rebuke or punishment (*informal*) ◇ **slap and tickle** playful sexual behaviour (*informal*)

slap down *vt.* (*informal*) **1. REBUKE** to rebuke sb sharply or cruelly **2. SUPPRESS** to suppress or check sth thought to be unacceptable ○ *Any disrespect is slapped down immediately.*

slap-bang *adv.* (*informal*) **1. IN SUDDEN, VIOLENT WAY** in a sudden, noisy, or violent way. US term **slam-bang** **2. DIRECTLY** exactly or directly, and usually with suddenness and force ○ *The ball landed slap-bang in the middle of the pond.* US term **smack-dab**

slapdash /sláp dash/ *adj.* **CARELESS** careless, hasty, and unskilful ■ *adv.* **CARELESSLY** in a careless, hasty, and unskilful way ■ *n.* = **roughcast**

slaphappy /sláp happi/ *adj.* (*informal*) **1. CHEERFULLY IRRESPONSIBLE** irresponsible or careless in a cheerful way **2. DAZED** dazed or disoriented, like a boxer who has been hit in the head too many times

slaphead /sláp hed/ *n.* a bald person, especially a man who has gone bald naturally, rather than a man who has shaved his head by fashion choice (*slang insult*) [Late 20thC. From a lighthearted or malicious practice of slapping the heads of bald people.]

slapper /sláppər/ *n.* a woman who is considered sexually promiscuous or generally common and sluttish (*slang insult offensive*) [Late 18thC. Formed from SLAP in an obsolete dialectal sense. Originally used for 'overweight person (usually a woman)'.]

slap shot *n.* a shot in ice hockey in which the player swings the stick with a fast powerful stroke [*Slap* from the loud sound made when the stick hits the ice]

slapstick /sláp stik/ *n.* comedy with the emphasis on fast physical action, farcical situations, and obvious jokes that do not depend on language (*often used before a noun*) ○ *slapstick comedy* [Early 20thC. From earlier *slapstick* 'device made of two flat linked pieces of wood, formerly used in comic performances to simulate the sound of a blow'.]

slap-up *adj.* with lots of good food to eat and served in style (*informal*) ○ *First prize is a slap-up dinner at the restaurant of your choice.*

slash /slash/ *vt.* (**slashes, slashing, slashed**) **1. MAKE CUTS IN** to make long deep cuts in sth **2. ATTACK WITH A SHARP OBJECT** to cut or attack sb with the sharp sweeping strokes of a sword, knife, stick, or whip **3. REDUCE OR SHORTEN** to greatly reduce or shorten sth ○ *All prices slashed!* **4.** CLOTHES **MAKE A SLIT IN CLOTH** to make a slit in fabric or a garment to reveal the lining **5.** FORESTRY **CLEAR A FOREST BY CUTTING** to cut bushes and undergrowth from a wooded area ■ *n.* **1. SHARP SWEEPING STROKE** a sharp sweeping stroke of a sword, knife, stick, or whip **2. LONG AND DEEP CUT** a long deep cut or wound **3. URINATION** an act of urination, usually by a male (*slang*) ○ *Hang on a minute while I go for a quick slash.* **4.** CLOTHES **SLIT IN FABRIC** a slit in fabric or a garment, made to reveal the lining **5.** *US* FORESTRY **DEBRIS FROM CUT TREES** the debris left after trees have been cut down **6.** PRINTING **PRINT CHARACTER** a character, (/), that is used to separate optional items in a list or to express fractions or division, and that has various uses in computer programming. Technical name **solidus** [Late 16thC. Origin uncertain: possibly from French *esclachier* 'to break', variant of Old French *esclater*, from *esclat* 'splinter' (source of English *slat*).] —**slasher** *n.*

slash-and-burn *adj.* **1.** AGRIC **CUTTING, BURNING, AND TILLING** used to describe a form of agriculture characterized by the cutting down and burning of trees and vegetation in order to plant crops **2. TENDING TO DESTROY STH COMPLETELY** having or showing the intention to deal with sb or sth drastically and ruthlessly or to destroy sb or sth completely (*informal*) ○ *her slash-and-burn approach to budget cuts*

slasher movie *n.* a horror film featuring gory effects such as people being slashed with blades (*slang*)

slashing /sláshing/ *adj.* **1. CRITICAL** aggressively critical **2. REDUCING** severely reducing or shortening sth ○ *make slashing cuts to the budget* ■ *n.* **1.** SPORTS **ILLEGAL ACT IN HOCKEY AND LACROSSE** the illegal striking or swinging of a stick at an opposing player in hockey or lacrosse **2. CUTTING ATTACK** an act of attacking and cutting sb with a blade —**slashingly** *adv.*

slash pocket *n.* a pocket in a garment fitted with a diagonal slit for easy access

slat /slat/ *n.* **1.** THIN STRIP a light thin narrow strip of wood or metal **2.** TECH AEROFOIL ON AN AIRCRAFT WING an auxiliary aerofoil fixed to the leading edge of a wing to give extra lift ■ *vt.* **(slats, slatting, slatted)** ADD SLATS TO to put slats in sth [Mid-18thC. From Old French *esclat* 'splinter, piece broken off', of uncertain origin: possibly from prehistoric Germanic.]

slate[1] /slayt/ *n.* **1.** GEOL LAYERED ROCK a fine-grained metamorphic rock that splits easily into layers and is widely used as a roofing material **2.** BUILDING ROOFING TILE a roofing tile made of slate **3.** WRITING TABLET a small square piece of slate used in the past for writing on, especially by school students. It could be wiped clean and reused indefinitely. **4.** COLOURS DARK GREY a dark grey or bluish-grey colour **5.** *US, Can* POL LIST OF CANDIDATES a list of the candidates in an election **6.** CINEMA IDENTIFYING BOARD ON A FILM SET an identifying board used on a film set showing information such as the shot number that is held in front of a camera at the beginning or end of a shot ■ *vt.* **(slates, slating, slated) 1.** COVER A ROOF WITH SLATE to cover a roof with tiles made of slate **2.** *US* POL INCLUDE SB IN LIST OF A CANDIDATES to put sb's name on a list of candidates for election ■ *adj.* COLOURS DARK GREY of a dark grey or bluish-grey colour [14thC. From Old French *esclate*, feminine form of *esclat* 'splinter, piece broken off' (source of *slat*).] ◇ **a clean slate** an imaginary record of sb's past, with no transgressions recorded on it or with all previous transgressions forgotten (*informal*) ◇ **have a slate loose** *UK, Ireland* to be eccentric or very odd (*informal*) ◇ **on the slate** on credit (*informal*) ◇ **wipe the slate clean** to forget about what has happened and make a fresh start (*informal*)

slate[2] /slayt/ **(slates, slating, slated)** *vt.* to criticize severely sb or sth (*informal*) ○ *His last play was slated by the critics.* [Early 19thC. From SLATE[1]. Formerly in the meaning of 'to beat severely' (as if with a slate).]

slate blue, **slate grey** *adj.* of a dark bluish-grey colour —**slate blue** *n.*

slater /sláytər/ *n.* **1.** ROOFING TILE LAYER sb whose job is to lay roofing tiles made of slate **2.** *Scotland, ANZ, US* WOODLOUSE a woodlouse

slather /sláthər/ *vt.* **(-ers, -ering, -ered)** *US, Can* **1.** SPREAD STH THICKLY to spread sth thickly or excessively on sth else **2.** SQUANDER STH to use sth wastefully (*informal*) ■ **slathers** *npl. US* LARGE AMOUNT a large or generous quantity (*informal*) [Mid-19thC. Origin unknown.] ◇ **open slather** *ANZ* a situation in which there are no limits or constraints on behaviour (*informal*) ○ *The government's suggestion that foreign investors be allowed access would lead to open slather in the markets.*

slating[1] /sláyting/ *n.* the process of covering sth with slates, or the slates themselves

slating[2] /sláyting/ *n.* harsh criticism, or a severe reprimand (*informal*)

slattern /sláttərn/ *n.* (*dated insult*) **1.** OFFENSIVE TERM an offensive term referring to a woman regarded as ignoring conventional standards of hygiene and grooming **2.** OFFENSIVE TERM an offensive term referring to a woman regarded as being sexually promiscuous [Mid-17thC. Origin uncertain: possibly from a dialect word meaning 'to slop, be slovenly'.] —**slatternliness** *n.* —**slatternly** *adj.*

slaty /sláyti/ **(-ier, -iest)** *adj.* made of slate or like slate, especially in colour —**slatiness** *n.*

slaughter /sláwtər/ *n.* **1.** KILLING OF ANIMALS the killing of animals for their meat **2.** KILLING OF PEOPLE the brutal killing of a person or large numbers of people **3.** MAJOR DEFEAT an overwhelming defeat (*slang*) ■ *vt.* **(-ters, -tering, -tered) 1.** KILL AN ANIMAL FOR MEAT to kill an animal or animals, usually for their meat **2.** KILL PEOPLE BRUTALLY to kill a person or large numbers of people brutally **3.** DEFEAT SB CONVINCINGLY to defeat a person or a group of people overwhelmingly (*slang*) [13thC. From Old Norse *slátr* 'meat, butchery'.] —**slaughterer** *n.* —**slaughterous** *adj.*

WORD KEY: SYNONYMS

See Synonyms at ***kill***.

slaughterhouse /sláwtər howss/ (*plural* **-houses** /-howziz/) *n.* = **abattoir**

WORD KEY: CULTURAL NOTE

Slaughterhouse 5, a novel by US writer Kurt Vonnegut (1970). In this highly original blend of realism and science fiction, World War II veteran Billy Pilgrim is kidnapped by aliens who enable him to revisit his past. He subsequently relives the Allied firebombing of Dresden in 1945, an event witnessed by Vonnegut himself and here presented as a symbol of the endless cruelty and suffering of humanity.

slaughterman /sláwtərmən/ (*plural* **-men** /-mən/) *n.* sb who is employed to kill and cut up animals in a slaughterhouse

Slav /slaav/ *n.* a member of any of the peoples of Eastern Europe and North Western Asia that speak one of the Slavonic languages [14thC. Via medieval Latin *Sclavus* (source of English *slave*) from medieval Greek *Sklabos*, ultimately of Slavic origin.]

Slav. *abbr.* **1.** Slavic **2.** Slavonic

slave /slayv/ *n.* **1.** PERSON FORCED TO WORK FOR ANOTHER in former times, one person who was forced to work for another person for no payment and was regarded as the property of the person he or she worked for **2.** DOMINATED PERSON sb who is completely dominated by sb or sth **3.** SB ACCEPTING ANOTHER'S RULE sb who meekly accepts being ruled by sb else **4.** VERY HARD WORKER sb who works or has to work very hard, often in bad conditions and for low pay **5.** DEVICE CONTROLLED BY ANOTHER a device that is totally controlled by another (*often used before a noun*) ■ *vi.* **(slaves, slaving, slaved)** WORK VERY HARD to work very hard ○ *I've been slaving away over this manuscript all day.* ■ *adj.* **1.** USING ENSLAVED LABOURERS using or relating to enslaved labourers **2.** HARSH very harsh and unfair ○ *slave conditions* [13thC. Via Old French *esclave* from medieval Latin *sclavus* 'Slav, captive' (see SLAV), because Slavic peoples were widely captured and enslaved during the Middle Ages.]

slave ant *n.* an ant captured and forced to work for an ant colony of another species

slave cylinder *n.* a small, piston-bearing cylinder in a hydraulic system [*Slave* from the fact that its action is linked to a master cylinder]

slave-driver *n.* **1.** SB WHO MAKES PEOPLE WORK HARD sb who makes employees work excessively hard **2.** HIST OVERSEER OF LABOURERS in the past, sb who was employed to make sure that enslaved people worked hard

slave labour *n.* **1.** WORKFORCE OF ENSLAVED LABOURERS a workforce consisting of people who are forced to work against their will ○ *The pyramids were built by slave labour.* **2.** HARD WORK hard or demanding work, in poor conditions, that is not well paid (*informal*) ○ *It's nothing but slave labour in that department.*

slave-making ant, **slave-maker ant** *n.* a species of ant that raids the colonies of other ant species, capturing larvae and pupae to be used in its own colony

slaver[1] /sláyvər/ *n.* HIST **1.** SLAVE OWNER sb who owned or bought and sold slaves in former times **2.** = **slave ship**

slaver[2] /slávvər, sláyvər/ *vi.* **(-ers, -ering, -ered) 1.** DRIBBLE SALIVA to dribble saliva from the mouth **2.** BEHAVE OBSEQUIOUSLY to fawn or behave obsequiously to sb **3.** LUST AFTER to desire or lust after sth or sb greatly ■ *n.* DRIPPING SALIVA saliva that drips from sb's mouth [14thC. Origin uncertain; probably from Scandinavian.]

slavery /sláyvəri/ *n.* **1.** CONDITION OF BEING AN ENSLAVED LABOURER the condition of being forced to work for sb else in past times **2.** SYSTEM BASED ON ENSLAVED LABOUR a system based on using the enforced labour of other people **3.** STATE OF BEING DOMINATED a state of being completely dominated by another **4.** HARD WORK very hard work, especially for low pay and under bad conditions

slave ship *n.* HIST a ship used to carry captured and enslaved people, especially from Africa

Slave State *n.* any of the 15 states in the United States where slavery was legal until the Civil War

slave trade *n.* the business of capturing people and buying and selling them as enslaved labourers

Slavic /slaávik/, **Slavonic** /slə vónnik/ *n.* LANG E EUROPEAN LANGUAGE GROUP a branch of the Indo-European family of languages that includes Bulgarian, Russian, and Polish ■ *adj.* TYPICAL OF SLAVIC LANGUAGES OR PEOPLE relating to the Slavic languages or the people who speak them

slavish /sláyvish/ *adj.* an offensive term comparing sth to the stereotypical traits attributed to an enslaved person —**slavishly** *adv.* —**slavishness** *n.*

Slavism /slaávizəm/ *n.* a feature or characteristic of the Slavs or Slavonic languages

slavocracy /slay vókrəssi/ *n.* slave owners considered collectively as a ruling group, or rule by slave owners

Slavonic *n., adj.* LANG, PEOPLES = **Slavic** [Early 17thC. From medieval Latin *S(c)lavonicus*, from *S(c)lavonia* 'country of the Slavs'.]

Slavophile /slaávō fīl/, **Slavophil** *n.* (*often used before a noun*) **1.** ADMIRER OF SLAVONIC CULTURE OR PEOPLE sb who admires Slavonic culture or people **2.** HIST ADVOCATE OF SLAVONIC SUPREMACY sb who, in 19th-century Russia, asserted the superiority of Slavonic people and worked for their supremacy —**Slavophilism** /slaávōfilizəm/ *n.*

slaw /slaw/ *n. US, Can* FOOD = **coleslaw** [Late 18thC. From Dutch *sla*, a contraction of French *salade* 'salad' (see SALAD).]

slay /slay/ **(slays, slaying, slew** /sloo/, **slain** /slayn/) *vt.* **1.** KILL SB to kill sb or sth (*formal or literary*) **2.** (*past* **slayed**, *past participle* **slayed** *or* **slain**) AMUSE SB to amuse sb very much (*informal*) [Old English *slēan*, from a prehistoric Germanic word meaning 'to strike', which is also the ancestor of English *onslaught* and *sledge*[2]] —**slayer** *n.*

WORD KEY: SYNONYMS

See Synonyms at ***kill***.

slaying /sláy ing/ *n.* a killing or murder

SLBM *abbr.* submarine-launched ballistic missile

SLCM *abbr.* sea-launched cruise missile

sld *abbr.* **1.** sailed **2.** sealed **3.** sold

SLE *abbr.* MED systemic lupus erythematosus

sleaze /sleez/ *n.* **1.** DISHONESTY OR CORRUPTION corruption, dishonesty, or scandal, especially among public figures such as politicians **2.** = **sleazebag** (*slang insult*) [Mid-20thC. Back-formation from SLEAZY.]

sleazebag /sleéz bag/, **sleazeball** *n.* an offensive term referring to sb whose behaviour is perceived as immoral, unethical, or disreputable (*slang insult*)

sleazy /sleézi/ **(-zier, -ziest)** *adj.* **1.** SORDID dirty, disreputable, or sordid in character or appearance **2.** DISHONEST OR IMMORAL dishonest or immoral ○ *You get some pretty sleazy types in here.* [Mid-17thC. Originally 'flimsy in texture', of uncertain origin: perhaps ultimately from SILESIA, region in present-day Poland, where a good linen fabric was made that was later imitated cheaply.] —**sleazily** *adv.* —**sleaziness** *n.*

sled *n., vti.* = **sledge** [14thC. From Middle Low German *sledde*, from a prehistoric Germanic base meaning 'to slip, slide', which is also the ancestor of English *slide, sleigh*, and *sledge*[1].]

sled dog *n.* a dog trained to pull a sledge, especially when part of a dog team

sledge[1] /slej/, **sled** /sled/ *n.* **1.** SMALL VEHICLE SLIDING OVER SNOW a small, low vehicle on ski-style or other runners, designed to be pulled over snow or ice by people or dogs **2.** CHILD'S TOY VEHICLE FOR SNOW a child's toy vehicle on runners, used for sliding down snowy hills ■ *vti.* **(sledges, sledging, sledged; sleds, sledding, sledded)** MOVE USING SLEDGE to ride, travel, or transport sth by sledge [Late 16thC. From Dutch dialect *sleedse*.] —**sledger** *n.*

sledge[2] /slej/ *n.* = **sledgehammer** [Old English *slecg*, from a prehistoric Germanic word meaning 'to strike', which is also the ancestor of English *slay, slaughter*, and *onslaught*]

a at; aa father; aw all; ay day; air hair; ə about, edible, item, common, circus; e egg; ee eel; hw when; i it, happy; ī ice; 'l apple; 'm rhythm; 'n fashion; o odd; ō open; oo good; oo pool; ow owl; oy oil; th thin; th this; u up; ur urge;

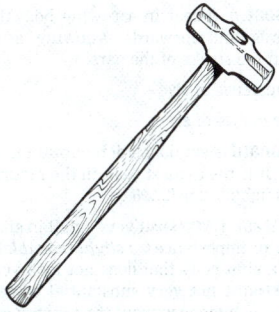

Sledgehammer

sledgehammer /sléj hammər/ *n.* **LARGE HAMMER** a large heavy hammer swung with both hands ■ *vt.* (**-mers, -mering, -mered**) **STRIKE WITH A SLEDGEHAMMER** to hit sth with a sledgehammer or with the force of one ■ *adj.* **VERY FORCEFUL** extremely forceful ○ *sledgehammer blows* [15thC. Coined from SLEDGE² + HAMMER.]

sledging /sléjjing/ *n. Aus* CRICKET the attempt by a cricket fielder or bowler to undermine a batsman's confidence by verbal abuse (*informal*)

sleek /sleek/ *adj.* **1.** **SMOOTH AND SHINY** attractively smooth and shiny **2.** **WELL-GROOMED** well-groomed and healthy looking **3.** **SUAVE** smooth and polished in behaviour or speech, often insincerely or suspiciously so ○ *a sleek sales pitch* ■ *vt.* (**sleeks, sleeking, sleeked**) **MAKE STH SLEEK** to make sth appear smooth or shiny [Late 16thC. Variant of SLICK.] —**sleekly** *adv.* —**sleekness** *n.*

sleekit /sléekit/ *adj. Scotland* superficially charming but cunning and untrustworthy ○ *He's the kind of sleekit character that gets round people.* [14thC. Variant of *sleeked*, past participle of SLEEK (verb).]

sleep /sleep/ *n.* **1.** PHYSIOL **STATE OF NOT BEING AWAKE** a state of partial or full unconsciousness in people and animals during which voluntary functions are suspended and the body rests and restores itself, or a period in this state **2.** **STATE RESEMBLING SLEEP** any state that is inactive or dormant, like sleep **3.** **DEATH** death (*literary; also used euphemistically*) **4.** **MUCUS IN EYES** small amounts of dried mucus that often collect in the eyes during sleep (*informal*) **5.** BOT = **nyctitropism** ■ *v.* (**sleeps, sleeping, slept /slept/**) **1.** *vi.* PHYSIOL **BE IN A STATE OF SLEEP** to go into or be in a state of sleep **2.** *vi.* **BE INACTIVE** to be in an inactive or dormant state ○ *a city that never sleeps* **3.** *vi.* BOT **CHANGE POSITION AT NIGHT** to assume a position at night that is different from the daytime position **4.** *vt.* **PROVIDE BEDS FOR PEOPLE** to provide sleeping accommodation for a particular number of people ○ *The yacht sleeps eight.* **5.** *vi.* **BE DEAD** to be dead (*literary; also used euphemistically*) ○ *He sleeps in the bosom of Abraham.* **6.** *vt.* **SPEND TIME IN SLEEP** to spend a period of time sleeping ○ *We slept the night in a hotel.* [The noun is from Old English *slæp*, the verb from Old English *slæpan*, both from prehistoric Germanic] ◇ **get to sleep, go to sleep** to begin sleeping ◇ **in your sleep 1.** while you are sleeping **2.** with ease, as if not having to be fully awake (*informal*) ○ *I could find my way there in my sleep, I've been so often.* ◇ **not lose (any) sleep over sth** to not worry about sth because it is thought to be trivial or irrelevant ◇ **put sth to sleep** to kill an animal in a humane way, especially because it is ill, injured, or in pain ◇ **sleep on it** to postpone a decision until at least the next day in order to give it more thought ◇ **sleep rough** to sleep outdoors, especially in the street and usually because of being homeless

sleep around *vi.* to have a lot of casual sexual relationships with different people (*informal*)

sleep in *vi.* **1.** **SLEEP LONGER THAN USUAL** to sleep longer than you usually do **2.** *US* = **live in**

sleep off *vt.* to get rid of illness by sleeping until it is gone

sleep out *vi.* **1.** **SLEEP OUTSIDE** sleep out of doors **2.** *US* = **live out**

sleep over *vi.* to sleep at sb else's house as part of a visit

sleep together *vi.* to have sex (*used euphemistically*)

sleep with *vt.* to have sex with sb (*informal; used euphemistically*)

sleep apnoea *n.* a temporary cessation of breathing that happens to some people while they are sleeping

sleeper /sléepər/ *n.* **1.** **SB SLEEPING** sb who is asleep, or sb who sleeps in a particular way ○ *a light sleeper* **2.** RAIL **RAILWAY CARRIAGE WITH BEDS** a railway carriage or compartment with beds for passengers **3.** RAIL **TRAIN WITH BEDS** an overnight train with beds for passengers to sleep in ○ *Should I go down on the sleeper or get an early-morning flight?* **4.** RAIL **BEAM SUPPORTING RAILS** any of the beams of wood or concrete on which the rails of a railway track are laid. US term **tie** *n.* 9 **5.** BUILDING **HEAVY BEAM** a heavy beam used as a sill, footing, or support **6.** **SURPRISING SUCCESS** sb or sth that is not immediately successful but, often surprisingly, becomes so after a while (*informal*) **7.** SPY **INACTIVE UNTIL CALLED INTO ACTION** a spy or secret agent who lives an ordinary life until called into action (*informal*) **8.** **SMALL GOLD EARRING** a small gold stud or ring worn to keep the hole of a pierced ear from closing **9.** ZOOL **TROPICAL FISH** a marine or freshwater tropical fish related to the goby that often lies immobile. Family: Eleotridae. ■ **sleepers** *npl. US* = **sleepsuit**

sleeping bag *n.* a long padded or lined fabric bag for sleeping in, especially when camping

sleeping car *n.* a railway carriage that has bunks or compartments in which passengers can sleep

sleeping draught *n.* a drink containing a drug that is meant to help sb sleep

sleeping partner *n.* BUSINESS a person who puts money into a business but does not play an active part in running it. US term **silent partner**

sleeping pill, **sleeping tablet** *n.* a pill containing a drug that is meant to induce sleep

sleeping policeman *n.* a speed bump (*dated*)

sleeping sickness *n.* **1.** **TROPICAL DISEASE** a disease in tropical Africa caused by parasitic protozoans that are carried by tsetse flies. Affected people and animals experience fever, weight loss, and lethargy. **2.** **ENCEPHALITIS CAUSING LETHARGY** an epidemic form of encephalitis causing lethargy, muscular weakness, and impaired vision

sleep-learning *n.* a method of learning sth that involves the continuous playing of recordings of it to a sleeping learner

sleepless /sléepləss/ *adj.* **1.** **LACKING SLEEP** without sleep, or unable to sleep ○ *a sleepless night* **2.** **AWAKE** always awake, active, or busy —**sleeplessly** *adv.* —**sleeplessness** *n.*

sleep-out *n.* ANZ a part of a veranda or yard that has been turned into an outdoor sleeping area, usually partially or fully enclosed with glass or insect screens

sleepover /sléepōvər/ *n.* an overnight stay at sb else's house after a children's party (*informal*)

sleepsuit /sléep syoot/ *n.* a one-piece sleeping garment for a baby or child, usually covering the feet. US term **sleepers** *npl.*

sleepwalk /sléep wawk/ (**-walks, -walking, -walked**) *vi.* **1.** **WALK WHILE ASLEEP** to walk while you are asleep **2.** **BE INATTENTIVE** to do sth in an inattentive or lethargic way (*informal*) —**sleepwalker** *n.* —**sleepwalking** *n.*

sleepwear /sléep wair/ *n.* = **nightwear**

sleepy /sléepi/ (**-ier, -iest**) *adj.* **1.** **DROWSY** feeling drowsy and wanting to sleep **2.** **QUIET AND WITHOUT MUCH ACTIVITY** quiet and not very lively or exciting ○ *a sleepy mining town* **3.** **CAUSING SLEEP** tending to make sb fall asleep —**sleepily** *adv.* —**sleepiness** *n.*

sleepyhead /sléepi hed/ *n.* sb who has just woken up and is drowsy, or sb who is nearly falling asleep (*informal*) —**sleepyheaded** *adj.*

sleepy sickness *n.* = **sleeping sickness** *n.* 2

sleet /sleet/ *n.* **1.** **RAIN MIXED WITH SNOW** rainfall mixed with snow **2.** *US* **THIN COATING OF ICE** the thin coating of ice formed when rain freezes on sth ■ *v.* (**sleets, sleeting, sleeted**) **FALL AS SLEET** to fall as sleet [13thC. Origin uncertain: probably from an Old English word.]

sleeve /sleev/ *n.* **1.** CLOTHES **COVERING FOR THE ARM** either of the two parts of a garment that wholly or partially cover the arms **2.** ENG **TUBULAR PIECE** a tubular piece designed to fit inside or over a cylinder **3.** RECORDING **RECORD COVER** a decorated protective cover for a record or CD that usually lists the performers and contents. US term **jacket** *n.* 5 ■ *vt.* (**sleeves, sleeving, sleeved**) **FIT WITH A SLEEVE** to provide sth with a sleeve [Old English *slēfe*. Ultimately from an Indo-European word meaning 'to slide, slip', which is also the ancestor of English *slop*, *sloop*, and *lubricate*.] —**sleeveless** *adj.* ◇ **roll up your sleeves** to get ready to do sth vigorously (*informal*) ◇ **up your sleeve** kept hidden or secret but available for use

sleeve board *n.* a small, narrow ironing board used for pressing sleeves

sleeveen /slee veen/ *n. Ireland* sb who is sly, plausible, and good at being ingratiating [Mid-19thC. From Irish *slíbhín* 'sly person, trickster'.]

sleeveless /sléevləss/ *adj.* having no sleeves [Old English]

sleeve notes *npl.* RECORDING information about a record, printed on its cover. Also called **liner notes**

sleeve valve *n.* a valve for an internal-combustion engine, fitted and reciprocating inside a cylinder

sleeving /sléeving/ *n.* flexible, tubular insulation inside which wires that carry electric current can be fitted. US term **spaghetti** *n.* 3

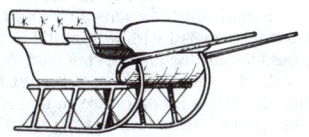

Sleigh

sleigh /slay/ *n.* **SNOW VEHICLE PULLED BY HORSES** an open, usually horse-drawn vehicle on runners, used for travel on snow and ice ■ *vi.* (**sleighs, sleighing, sleighed**) **TRAVEL IN SLEIGH** to move over snow or ice in a sleigh [Early 18thC. Via Dutch *slee* from, ultimately, Middle Dutch *slēde*. From a prehistoric Germanic base meaning 'to slip, slide', which is also the ancestor of English *slide* and *sled*.]

sleighbell /sláy bel/ *n.* one of several small bells attached to a sleigh or to the harness of horses pulling it. Sometimes a number of them are used together as a musical instrument.

sleight /slīt/ *n.* (*archaic*) **1.** **TRICK** a trick or cunning act **2.** **SKILL** dexterity or skill in doing sth **3.** **TRICKERY** cunning or trickery [13thC. From Old Norse *slœgð* 'cunning', from *slœgr* 'crafty' (see SLY).]

sleight of hand *n.* **1.** **SKILL WITH THE HANDS** skill or dexterity with the hands in conjuring, card tricks, or juggling **2.** **DECEPTIVE SKILL** any kind of skill by which sth happens without it being obvious how it is done

slender /sléndər/ *adj.* **1.** **SMALL IN WIDTH** small or slight in width in proportion to height or length ○ *a flower with a slender stem* **2.** **SLIM** thin in a graceful way **3.** **LIMITED** small or limited in degree, extent, or size ○ *The home team won by a slender margin.* [13thC. Origin unknown.] —**slenderly** *adv.* —**slenderness** *n.*

—— **WORD KEY: SYNONYMS** ——
See Synonyms at *thin*.

slenderize /slénda rīz/ (**-izes, -izing, -ized**), **slenderise** (**-ises, -ising, -ized, -ised**) *vti. US* to become slender, or make sb or sth slender (*dated*)

slender loris *n.* a small tailless slow-moving primate found in the rain forests of India and Sri Lanka. Latin name: *Loris tardigradus.*

slept past tense, past participle of **sleep**

Slessor /sléssər/, **Kenneth** (1901–71) Australian poet. His work, mostly written between 1919 and 1939, includes 'Five Bells' (1939). Full name **Kenneth Adolf Slessor**

sleuth /slooth/ *n.* **1. DETECTIVE** a detective (*informal*) **2.** = **sleuthhound** *n.* 1 ■ *v.* **(sleuths, sleuthing, sleuthed) 1.** *vi.* **INVESTIGATE** to investigate as or in a similar way to a detective **2.** *vt.* **TRACK SB** to track or find sb or sth [Early 19thC. Shortening of SLEUTHHOUND.]

sleuthhound /slo͝oth hownd/ *n.* **1. DOG FOR TRACKING PEOPLE** a dog used for tracking people, especially a bloodhound **2.** = **sleuth** *n.* 1 (*informal*) [14thC. *Sleuth* from *sleuth* 'track, trail', from Old Norse *slóð*, of unknown origin.]

S level *n.* an advanced qualification, above and in addition to A level, taken in a subject in England and Wales for the General Certificate of Education. Abbr of **special level**

slew[1] past tense of **slay**

slew[2] /sloo/ *vti.* **(slews, slewing, slewed) TWIST AROUND** to turn or twist sth around, or be turned or twisted around, especially suddenly, violently, or uncontrollably ○ *She jammed on the brakes and the car slewed to a halt.* US term **slue** ■ *n.* **TURN** a forceful or uncontrolled turn or twist around. US term **slue** [Mid-18thC. Origin unknown.]

slew[3] /sloo/ *n. US* a large quantity or number of sth (*informal*) ○ *They hit us with a whole slew of complaints.* [Mid-19thC. Via Irish *sluagh* 'multitude' from Old Irish *slúag* 'host, army' (source of English *slogan*).]

slewed /slood/ *adj.* drunk (*slang*) [Mid-19thC. Formed from SLEW[2].]

slice /slīss/ *n.* **1. PIECE CUT FROM STH** a thin broad piece cut from sth larger ○ *a slice of ham* **2. SHARE** a part, portion, or share of sth ○ *a slice of the profits* **3.** COOK **SERVING UTENSIL** a utensil with a thin, flat, triangular blade, used for cutting and serving food, especially fish or cake **4.** SPORTS **OBLIQUE STRIKE OF A BALL** a stroke in which the ball is hit off-centre so that it follows a curving path **5.** SPORTS **FLIGHT OF A BALL** the flight of a ball that has been sliced **6.** TENNIS **TENNIS SHOT** a tennis shot that makes the ball spin and stay low when it bounces in the opponent's court ■ *v.* **(slices, slicing, sliced) 1.** *vti.* **CUT INTO PORTIONS** to cut sth, or to be cut, into slices or portions **2.** *vti.* **CUT CLEANLY** to cut sth cleanly and effortlessly ○ *The sword sliced the rope in half.* **3.** *vi.* **MOVE SWIFTLY AND CLEANLY** to move swiftly and cleanly, especially through a medium such as air or water **4.** *vti.* **CUT OFF** to cut sth off sth else ○ *The spinning blade sliced off log after log.* **5.** *vt.* SPORTS **SET ON A CURVING PATH** to hit a ball off-centre so that it follows a curving path, whether intentionally or as a result of a bad swing or stroke **6.** *vti.* TENNIS **HIT WITH A CHOPPING ACTION** to hit a tennis shot with a chopping stroke so that the ball spins and stays low when it bounces in the opponent's court **7.** *vt.* ROWING **PUT IN THE WATER SLANTWISE** to put the blade of an oar into the water at an angle [15thC. From Old French *esclice* 'splinter', from *esclicier* 'to splinter', ultimately from a prehistoric Germanic word that is also the ancestor of English *slit*.] —**sliceable** *adj.* —**slicer** *n.*

slice of life *n.* a realistic portrayal of life, especially a harsh or unpleasant life, e.g. in a film (*hyphenated before a noun*) ○ *a slice-of-life drama* [From the idea of cutting into sth to see inside]

slick /slik/ *adj.* **1. POLISHED** done or able to do things with great skill and apparently effortlessly ○ *a slick presentation* **2. CRAFTY** clever and resourceful or suave and sophisticated but not entirely trustworthy (*informal*) **3. GLIB** superficially impressive or persuasive but lacking substance or sincerity ○ *a slick sales pitch* **4.** *US* **SLIPPERY** having a smooth, glossy, or slippery surface ○ *a slick runway* ■ *n.* **1. SLIPPERY PATCH** a thinly spread or slippery patch of sth, especially a quantity of oil floating on top of water **2.** *US* PUBL = **glossy magazine 3.** MOTOR SPORTS **TREADLESS TYRE** a wide treadless tyre used in motor racing ■ *vt.* **(slicks, slicking, slicked) MAKE STH SMOOTH** to make sth smooth, glossy, or presentable [14thC. Ultimately from an Indo-European word denoting 'slippery', which is also the ancestor of English *slime, slip,* and *oblivion*.] —**slickly** *adv.* —**slickness** *n.*

slickenside /slíkən sīd/ *n.* a rock surface that is smooth and marked with fine scratches caused by friction with another rock surface [Early 19thC. Coined from a dialect variant of SLICK + SLIDE.]

slicker /slíkər/ *n.* **1. SOPHISTICATED BUT UNTRUSTWORTHY PERSON** sb who appears to be very sophisticated, stylish, or clever, but is not very honest or trustworthy (*informal*) ◊ **city slicker 2.** *US* **RAINCOAT** a shiny raincoat, often made of a plastic or rubber material **3. SMOOTHING TOOL** a tool used for smoothing sth

slickhead fish *n.* a small slender deep-sea fish with dark colouration and no scales on its head, which gives it a slick appearance. Family: Alepocephalidae.

slide /slīd/ *v.* **(slides, sliding, slid** /slid/, **slid) 1.** *vti.* **MOVE SMOOTHLY** to move or make sth move smoothly across a surface ○ *The car slid for 50 yards when the brakes locked.* **2.** *vti.* **MOVE UNOBTRUSIVELY** to move or move sth unobtrusively ○ *He slid the letter into his pocket.* **3.** *vi.* **SLIP** to lose your grip or secure footing on a surface ○ *I slid on an icy patch and nearly ended up flat on my back.* **4.** *vi.* **TO CHANGE TO A DIFFERENT CONDITION** to change to a different, usually worse, state or condition ○ *unable to stop the economy from sliding into recession* **5.** *vi.* MUSIC **PLAY A GLIDE BETWEEN NOTES** to make a gliding change from one note to another **6.** *vti.* BASEBALL **APPROACH A BASE HORIZONTALLY** to approach a base in baseball or softball while skidding feet first, low to the ground ■ *n.* **1. SLIDING** a sliding movement **2.** LEISURE **STRUCTURE THAT CHILDREN PLAY ON** a structure with a metal slope that children slide down for fun **3.** PHOTOGRAPHY **SMALL POSITIVE PHOTOGRAPH** a positive photograph reproduced on a small piece of film, mounted in a frame or on a plate and viewed by projection on a screen or through a magnifying device **4.** GEOL **FALL OF ROCK, MUD, OR EARTH** a downhill displacement of rock, mud, or earth, often caused by rainfall or erosion **5.** SCI **SPECIMEN HOLDER** a small glass plate on which a specimen is mounted for viewing under a microscope **6.** = **hair slide 7. SLIDING MACHINE PART** a machine part that slides, or the part on which it moves **8.** ROWING = **sliding seat 9.** MUSIC **TROMBONE MECHANISM** the U-shaped tube of a trombone that is pushed in and out to allow for changes in pitch **10.** MUSIC **MUSICAL FEATURE** a sliding change from one note to another [Old English *slīdan*, from a prehistoric Germanic word that is also the ancestor of English *sled* and *sleigh*] ◇ **let things** *or* **sth slide** to let a situation gradually go back to its previous worse state ◇ **on the slide** in the process of becoming worse (*informal*)

slide-action *adj.* used to describe a shotgun or rifle with a lever that ejects the case of a spent round and loads a new one

slider /slídər/ *n.* in Scotland and Northern Ireland, a serving of ice cream between two wafers (*regional informal*)

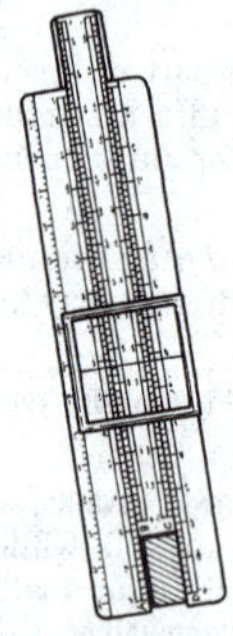

Slide rule

slide rule *n.* a manual calculating device, now largely obsolete, consisting of two rulers marked with graduated logarithmic scales, one sliding inside the other

slide show *n.* a sequence of photographic slides projected on a screen or wall as education or entertainment

slide trombone *n.* a trombone with a slide that is moved to select different pitches as distinct from a trombone fitted with valves

sliding /slíding/ *adj.* **1. VARYING ACCORDING TO STH ELSE** varying according to changing conditions **2. MOVED BY SLIDING** moved by sliding ○ *a sliding door* [Old English]

sliding scale *n.* any scale, e.g. of wages, costs, or fees, that varies according to changes in some other factor

sliding seat *n.* a seat in a rowing boat that slides backwards and forwards, allowing a rower to lengthen the stroke of the oars

slier comparative of **sly**

sliest superlative of **sly**

Slieve Donard /sleev dónnərd/ mountain in Northern Ireland. It is the highest peak in the Mourne Mountains. Height: 852 m/2,796 ft.

slight /slīt/ *adj.* **1. VERY SMALL** very small in size, degree, amount, or importance ○ *a slight resemblance* **2. THIN** having a slim body that does not look very strong **3. INSUBSTANTIAL** not very substantial or convincing ○ *an assertion made without the slightest evidence* ■ *vt.* **(slights, slighting, slighted) 1. SNUB SB** to treat sb rudely, e.g. by deliberately ignoring him or her **2. TREAT STH AS UNIMPORTANT** to think of or treat sth as unimportant **3.** *US* **DO STH CARELESSLY** to handle duties or responsibilities carelessly ■ *n.* **IMPOLITE ACT** an action that shows contempt for sb or sth [14thC. Origin uncertain; possibly from Scandinavian.] —**slightness** *n.* ◇ **(not) in the slightest** (not) at all (*informal*)

slighting /slíting/ *adj.* showing contempt or disrespect ○ *make slighting remarks about it* —**slightingly** *adv.*

slightly /slítli/ *adv.* **1. TO SMALL DEGREE** to a small extent or degree ○ *slightly injured* **2. SLIMLY** slimly and rather delicately ○ *slightly built*

Sligo /slígō/ county in Connacht Province, northwestern Ireland. Capital: Sligo. Population: 55,645 (1996). Area: 1,796 sq. km/693 sq. mi.

slim /slim/ *adj.* **(slimmer, slimmest) 1. SMALLER IN WIDTH THAN HEIGHT** small in width, thickness, or girth and generally long and narrow in shape **2. PLEASINGLY THIN** slender and well-proportioned **3. SMALL** small in degree, quality, or extent ○ *Hopes of their survival were slim.* ■ *v.* **(slims, slimming, slimmed) 1.** *vi.* **LOSE WEIGHT** to lose weight, especially by dieting **2.** *vt.* **REDUCE** to reduce the size or scope of sth ○ *slim down the bloated bureaucracy* [Mid-17thC. Via Dutch, 'inferior, small', from Middle Dutch, 'crooked'. Ultimately from an Indo-European base meaning 'to hang loose', which is also the ancestor of English *lump* and *limp*.] —**slimly** *adv.* —**slimness** *n.*

WORD KEY: SYNONYMS

See Synonyms at ***thin***.

Slim /slim/, **William Joseph, 1st Viscount** (1891–1970) British general. He led the British forces to victory in the Middle East and Burma during World War II and was governor-general of Australia (1952–60).

slime /slīm/ *n.* **1. SLIPPERY LIQUID** a fluid that is thick and slippery, especially one that is unpleasant to touch **2.** BIOL **MUCOUS SECRETION OF SOME LIVING THINGS** a mucous substance secreted by some living things such as fish, snails, and fungi ■ *vt.* **(slimes, sliming, slimed) 1. COVER STH WITH SLIME** to cover or smear sth with slime **2. REMOVE SLIME FROM STH** to remove slime from sth such as a fish before preparing it for cooking [Old English *slīm*. Ultimately from an Indo-European base meaning 'slippery' (see SLICK).]

slimeball /slīm bawl/ *n.* an offensive term that deliberately insults sb regarded as despicable or repellent (*slang insult*) [Late 20thC. Coined from SLIME, on the model of *sleazeball*, variant of SLEAZEBAG.]

slime mould, slime fungus (*plural* **slime fungi** *or* **slime funguses**) *n.* a simple organism that forms a small slimy amoeboid mass, e.g. on fallen logs, and produces spore-bearing reproductive organs similar to those of a fungus

slimline /slim līn/ *adj.* **1. THIN** thinner than the standard ○ *a slimline pocket tape recorder* **2. LOW-CALORIE** designed to help with a weight-reducing diet ○ *slimline tonic and water*

slimmer /slímmər/ *n.* sb who is actively trying to lose weight, especially by dieting. US term **dieter**

slimming /slímming/ *n.* **EFFORT TO LOSE WEIGHT** the process of trying to lose weight, especially by dieting ○ *a slimming club* ■ *adj.* **1. USED IN LOSING WEIGHT** used for losing weight or intended to help with losing weight **2. GIVING SLIM APPEARANCE** tending to make sb look slimmer (*informal*) ○ *That dress is very slimming on you.*

slimsy /slímzi/ (**-sier, -siest**), **slimpsy** *adj. US* both slight and flimsy (*informal*) [Mid-19thC. Blend of SLIM and FLIMSY.]

slimy /slími/ (**-ier, -iest**) *adj.* **1. LIKE SLIME** covered with or resembling slime ○ *a slimy secretion* **2. DISGUSTING** having the semiliquid, sticky consistency of slime ○ *a slimy mess* **3. OFFENSIVE TERM** an offensive term referring to sb thought to behave in an excessively ingratiating way (*insult*) —**slimily** *adv.* —**sliminess** *n.*

sling[1] /sling/ *n.* **1.** MED **SUPPORTING BANDAGE** a wide bandage suspended from sb's neck to support an injured arm or hand **2. CARRYING STRAP** a carrying strap attached to sth such as a rifle ■ *vt.* (**slings, slinging, slung, slung** /slung/) **PASS OR PUT STH CASUALLY** to throw or pass sth or to put or place sth somewhere in a casual or careless way (*informal*) ○ *Sling me that newspaper, will you?* ■ *n.* **LOOP FOR CARRYING STH HEAVY** a loop of rope, leather, chain, or net used to lift, lower, or carry sth heavy ■ *vt.* **USE A CARRYING LOOP ON STH** to attach sth to, carry sth with, or hang sth from a carrying loop ■ *n.* **1. LOOP USED AS WEAPON** a weapon used for throwing a stone or other object, consisting of a loop of leather or other material in which the missile is twirled before being released **2.** NAUT **SUPPORT FOR A YARD** a rope or chain that supports a ship's beam ■ **slings** *npl.* MOUNTAINEERING **ANCHORING LOOP** a fixed loop of webbing used to provide an anchor to a rock, tree, or other point ■ *vt.* **THROW WITH FORCE** to throw sth with a lot of force [13thC. Origin uncertain: the noun is possibly from Low Dutch or Middle Low German *slinge*; the verb partly from Old Norse *slyngva* and partly from the noun.] —**slinger** *n.*

sling off *vi. ANZ* to speak abusively, often while blaming or criticizing ○ *I'm sick of my boss slinging off at me.*

sling[2] /sling/ *n.* a mixed alcoholic drink made with spirits, sugar, lemon or lime juice, and water [Mid-18thC. Origin unknown.]

slingback /slíng bak/ *n.* a woman's shoe that is open at the heel and is held on the foot by a strap (*often used before a noun*)

slingshot /slíng shot/ *n. US* = **catapult**

slink /slingk/ *v.* (**slinks, slinking, slunk, slunk** /slungk/) **1.** *vi.* **MOVE FURTIVELY** to move or behave quietly and secretively ○ *I could see her trying to slink away through the back door.* **2.** *vi.* **MOVE SEXILY** to walk in a sexually alluring way **3.** *vt.* VET **BEAR PREMATURELY** to give birth to young prematurely, especially to a calf ■ *n.* VET **PREMATURE ANIMAL** a prematurely born animal, especially a calf ■ *adj.* VET **BORN EARLY** used to describe an animal, especially a calf, that is born prematurely [Old English *slincan*, from a prehistoric Germanic word meaning 'to slide, throw', which is also the ancestor of English *sling*]

slinky /slíngki/ (**-ier, -iest**) *adj.* **1. SEDUCTIVE** having a seductive appearance or way of moving **2. CLOSE-FITTING** close-fitting and emphasizing the curves of the body ○ *a slinky outfit* —**slinkily** *adv.* —**slinkiness** *n.*

Slinky *tdmk.* a trademark for a spring toy

sliotar /slótər/ *n.* the ball used in the sport of hurling [Early 19thC. From Irish Gaelic.]

slip[1] /slip/ *v.* (**slips, slipping, slipped**) **1.** *vi.* **LOSE YOUR FOOTING** to lose your footing or grip on a slippery surface ○ *I slipped and fell.* **2.** *vi.* **MOVE FROM ITS PROPER POSITION** to slide or move accidentally out of the proper or desired position ○ *This strap keeps slipping off my shoulder.* **3.** *vti.* **MOVE SMOOTHLY** to move or make sth move smoothly and easily and usually with a sliding motion ○ *It slips easily in and out of its case.* **4.** *vi.* **GO QUIETLY** to go somewhere in a quiet, furtive, or unnoticed way ○ *He slipped out while nobody was looking.* **5.** *vt.* **PASS STH SECRETLY** to give sb sth furtively or secretly ○ *I saw the man slip her an envelope* **6.** *vti.* **PUT ON OR TAKE OFF** to put on or take off sth quickly and easily **7.** *vti.* **BE FORGOTTEN** to be forgotten or overlooked by sb ○ *It slipped my mind.* **8.** *vi.* **ERR** to make a mistake or to do sth wrong ○ *You must have slipped up when you were making a note of the number.* **9.** *vi.* **GET WORSE** to decline from a previous standard, e.g., of performance or awareness ○ *He's slipping – two years ago he would have spotted that mistake at once* **10.** *vt.* **DISLOCATE A BONE** to dislocate or displace a bone, especially in the spine **11.** *vti.* AUTOMOT **DISENGAGE THE CLUTCH** to disengage the clutch of a motor vehicle or be disengaged **12.** *vi.* MECH ENG **FAIL TO ENGAGE** to fail to engage properly, usually because of wear (*refers to mechanical parts*) **13.** *vt.* NAUT **LET A RESTRAINING CABLE GO** to let a line or cable that is securing a vessel to a mooring or anchor fall over the side **14.** *vti.* **RELEASE** to release an animal from a restraint, or be released in this way ■ *n.* **1. ACT OF SLIPPING** an act of slipping, especially a sudden slide on a slippery surface **2. ERROR** an error or oversight **3. LAPSE** a moral lapse or instance of misconduct **4. DECLINE** a fall from some previous standard or level **5.** CLOTHES **UNDERGARMENT** a light sleeveless woman's undergarment worn under a dress **6.** NAUT = **slipway** **7.** CRYSTALS **DEFORMATION OF A CRYSTAL** the deformation of a metallic crystal by shearing along a plane **8.** CRICKET **FIELDING POSITION** the position of a fielder behind and near the wicketkeeper, especially on the off side, or the fielder who takes up this position **9. CLOTH COVERING** a cloth covering for sth **10.** = **landslip**. US term **slide** **11.** AIR = **sideslip** *n.* 2 [13thC. Origin uncertain: probably from Middle Dutch or Middle Low German *slippen*.] ◇ **give sb the slip** to get away from sb who is chasing or pursuing you ◇ **let slip 1.** to say sth without meaning to, or reveal sth that should be kept secret **2.** to allow sb or sth to escape ◇ **slip one over on sb** to trick or deceive sb (*informal*)

WORD KEY: SYNONYMS

See Synonyms at ***mistake***.

slip up *vi.* **1. ERR** to make a mistake (*informal*) ○ *Somebody slipped up and forgot to put your name on the guest list.* **2. FALL OVER** to slip and fall while walking or running

slip[2] /slip/ *n.* **1. NARROW PIECE** a narrow strip of sth ○ *a slip of paper* **2. SMALL PIECE OF PAPER** a small piece of paper, especially a small form, document, or record of a transaction ○ *a paying-in slip* **3.** BOT **CUTTING** a stem or branch of a plant broken off and used to start a new plant **4. DELICATE YOUNG PERSON** sb who is both young and slightly built ○ *a slip of a lad* **5.** *US* **NARROW CHURCH PEW** a church pew that is narrow ■ *vt.* (**slips, slipping, slipped**) BOT **REMOVE A SLIP** to remove a slip from a plant in order to grow a new plant

slip[3] /slip/ *n.* a mixture of clay and water, used as a decorative layer on pottery or for casting in moulds to form an actual piece

SLIP /slip/ *n.* the older of two protocols for dial-up access to the Internet using a modem. It has now been largely replaced by a higher-level protocol (**PPP**). Full form **serial line Internet protocol**

slipcase /slíp kayss/ *n.* a box for protecting a book or set of books, usually made of sturdy cardboard, with one or more open ends

slipcover /slíp kuvər/ *n. US, Can* = **loose cover**

slipe /slīp/ *n.* **1.** *Scotland, N England* MINING **SLEDGE USED IN MINE** a sledge or sledge runner used in a mine **2.** *NZ* AGRIC **WOOL FROM SLAUGHTERED SHEEP** wool that is taken from a slaughtered sheep by immersing the pelt in a chemical bath [15thC. From Low German *slīpe*, variant of *slēpe* 'sledge, train'.]

slipknot /slíp not/, **slip knot** *n.* a knot that slips easily along the rope or cord around which it is tied

slip-on *n.* **SHOE WITHOUT FASTENING** a shoe that does not have a fastening ■ *adj.* **WITHOUT FASTENING** used to describe a shoe that does not have a fastening

slipover /slípōvər/ *n.* = **pullover**

slippage /slíppij/ *n.* **1. SLIDE** the process or an instance of slipping, especially from a stable or desired position ○ *Recent thunderstorms have caused slippage in the banks along rivers.* **2. AMOUNT OF SLIPPING** an amount or extent that sth slips **3. DECLINE** a decrease in the quality, performance, or production of sth **4.** MECH ENG **LOSS OF POWER** a loss of power or forward motion caused by the slipping of a mechanical part

slipper /slíppər/ *n.* a flat shoe of soft or lightweight material, usually worn indoors —**slippered** *adj.*

slipper bath *n.* **1. BATH WITH COVERED END** a bath that is covered at one end **2. slipper baths PUBLIC BATH** a place where people can pay to have a bath (*dated*)

slipperwort /slíppər wurt/ *n.* = **calceolaria**

slippery /slíppəri/ (**-ier, -iest**) *adj.* **1. CAUSING SLIDING** likely to cause sb or sth to slip **2. HARD TO HOLD FIRMLY** sliding easily from the grasp or from a position **3. PRECARIOUS** unstable and liable to change ○ *We're in a slippery situation; things could go either way.* **4. UNTRUSTWORTHY** behaving in a devious or deceitful way ○ *a slippery character* —**slipperily** *adv.* —**slipperiness** *n.*

slippery dip *n. Aus* a long children's slide in a playground or funfair

slippery elm *n.* **1.** TREES **N AMERICAN TREE** a deciduous North American hardwood tree with a moist sticky inner bark. Latin name: *Ulmus rubra.* **2.** ALTERN MED **BARK OF SLIPPERY ELM** the inner bark of the slippery elm used as a natural remedy in alternative medicine to relieve inflammation in the digestive tract

slippery slope *n.* a dangerous situation, e.g. in a military, political, foreign-policy, or legal situation, that can lead to ultimate downfall

slippy /slíppi/ (**-pier, -piest**) *adj.* = **slippery** (*informal*)

slip ring *n.* a metal ring in a generator or motor to which current is delivered or from which it is removed by brushes

slip road *n.* a short road for driving onto or off a motorway or fast road

slipsheet /slíp sheet/ *n.* **BLANK PAPER** a sheet of blank paper placed between newly printed sheets to prevent wet ink on the printed sheets from rubbing off or smearing ■ *vt.* (**-sheets, -sheeting, -sheeted**) **INSERT BLANK PAPER BETWEEN PRINTED SHEETS** to place a blank sheet of paper between newly printed papers on which the ink is still wet

slipshod /slíp shod/ *adj.* **1. CARELESS** done in a sloppy way without attention to details **2. UNTIDY** not neat in appearance [Late 16thC. From SLIP 'to slide' + SHOD 'wearing shoes'.] —**slipshodly** *adv.* —**slipshodness** *n.*

slipslop /slíp slop/ *n.* (*archaic*) **1. WATERY FOOD** weak or watery food or drink **2. TRIVIAL TALK OR WRITING** inconsequential speech or writing [Late 17thC. Doubling of SLOP. 'Trivial talk' from the character Mrs Slipslop in *Joseph Andrews* (1742) by Henry Fielding (1707–54).]

slip step *n.* a step performed by moving the left foot one step to the side and then moving the right foot to the left foot, used in Scottish reels and jigs

slip stitch *n.* **HIDDEN SEWING STITCH** a stitch used to connect two layers of fabric in such a way that the stitches are hidden from the right side ■ *vt.* **SEW LAYERS TOGETHER USING SLIP STITCH** to connect two pieces of fabric using a slip stitch

slipstream /slíp streem/ *n.* **1.** AIR **AIR FROM PROPELLER** a stream of air driven backwards by an aircraft's propeller **2. AREA BEHIND FAST-MOVING VEHICLE** an area of reduced air pressure and forward suction that is directly behind and caused by a rapidly moving vehicle ■ *vi.* (**-streams, -streaming, -streamed**) **FOLLOW IN SLIPSTREAM** to follow in another vehicle's slipstream so as to take advantage of the decreased air resistance

slip-up *n.* an accidental mistake or blunder (*informal*)

slipware /slíp wair/ *n.* pottery that has been coated or decorated with slip

slipway /slíp way/ *n.* a sloping surface used to build or repair boats before returning them to the water

slit /slit/ *vt.* (**slits, slitting, slit**) **1. SLICE STH** to make a long straight cut in sth ○ *She slit the bag open with a knife.* **2. CUT STH INTO STRIPS** to cut sth into thin strips ■ *n.* **NARROW CUT OR OPENING** a long narrow cut or opening [12thC, ultimately of prehistoric Germanic origin] —**slitter** *n.*

WORD KEY: SYNONYMS

See Synonyms at ***tear***.

slither /slíthər/ *v.* (**-ers, -ering, -ered**) **1.** *vti.* **SLIDE OR CAUSE STH TO SLIDE** to move along a slippery or uneven surface, or make sth slide along ○ *We slithered down the muddy river bank.* **2.** *vi.* **GLIDE** to slide along easily, using friction to move forward, as a snake does ■ *n.* **GLIDING MOVEMENT** a gliding, effortless movement [12thC. From Old English *slidrian*, literally 'to slide repeatedly', from *slidan*, an earlier form of SLIDE.]

slit trench *n.* a narrow trench dug as protection against shelling during a battle

sliver /slívvər/ *n.* **1. SPLINTER** a thin piece of sth that has been split, cut, or broken off **2. SMALL PIECE** a small narrow portion or piece of sth **3. LOOSE FIBRE** a loose strand of wool, cotton, or some other material prepared for drawing and twisting by carding ■ *vti.* **(-ers, -ering, -ered) BREAK INTO SPLINTERS** to break sth into splinters, or become splintered [14thC. From Old English *slifan* 'to cleave, split', from prehistoric Germanic.]

slivovitz /slívvəvits/ *n.* a dry colourless plum brandy made in eastern Europe [Late 19thC. From Serbo-Croat *sljivovica* 'plum brandy', from *sljiva* 'plum'.]

Sloane Ranger /slṓn-/ *n.* a fashionable and conventional upper-class young person, usually a woman, who lives in London and has a lively social life among people of the same kind (*informal*) [Late 20thC. Facetious pun on *Sloane* Square, London, and the fictional cowboy the Lone *Ranger.*]

slob /slob/ *n.* an offensive term that deliberately insults sb's personal habits, hygiene, and manners (*informal insult*) [Late 18thC. Via Irish *slab* 'mud' from English *slab* 'bog', from Scandinavian, and related to Swedish *slabb* 'slime'.] —**slobbish** *adj.*

slob around *vi.* to spend time being relaxing and doing nothing much (*informal*) ○ *I spent the day slobbing around in my pyjamas.*

slobber /slóbbər/ *v.* **(-bers, -bering, -bered) 1.** *vti.* **DRIBBLE SALIVA** to drool or allow saliva or a liquid to run from the mouth **2.** *vi.* **EXPRESS EXTREME EMOTION** to be overly sentimental or emotional **3.** *vt.* **SMEAR STH WITH SALIVA** to soak or cover sth with saliva or liquid from the mouth ■ *n.* **1. SALIVA** saliva or liquid that has been drooled from the mouth **2. SENTIMENTAL WRITING OR TALK** overemotional or sentimental talk or writing ○ *I can't stand to read such slobber.* [14thC. Origin uncertain: probably from Middle Dutch *slobberen* 'to feed noisily, walk through mud'.] —**slobberer** *n.* —**slobbery** *adj.*

slob ice *n. Can* floating ice in slushy masses

sloe /slō/ (*plural* **sloes** *or* **sloe**) *n.* **1.** = **blackthorn 2. N AMERICAN PLUM TREE** either of two eastern North American plum trees or shrubs that bear dark purple, red, or yellow fruit. Latin name: *Prunus alleghaniensis* and *Prunus americana.* **3. SMALL TART PLUM** the small sour fruit of the blackthorn or either species of sloe [Old English *slāh.* Ultimately from an Indo-European word meaning 'bluish', which is also the ancestor of English *livid* and *slivovitz.*]

sloe-eyed *adj.* with dark almond-shaped eyes [Refers to the blue-black colour of the fruit]

sloe gin *n.* a liqueur made of gin flavoured with sloes

slog /slog/ *v.* **(slogs, slogging, slogged) 1.** *vi.* **PLOD** to walk slowly with great effort ○ *How long did it take us to slog up that mountain?* **2.** *vi.* **WORK LONG AND HARD** to work at sth for a long time with little progress ○ *They've all been down at the office, slogging through endless reams of paperwork.* **3.** *vt.* **MAKE YOUR WAY** to make headway or progress through sth with great difficulty ○ *We had to slog our way through several muddy fields.* **4.** *vt.* **HIT SB OR STH HARD** to hit sb or sth with great force ○ *It was like being slogged by a heavyweight boxer.* ■ *n.* **1. LONG HARD WALK** a long difficult trip or walk ○ *It was quite a slog from the station to the hostel.* **2. HARD WORK** a long period of hard work ○ *Hard slog is the only way you'll pass those exams.* **3. HARD HIT** a hard blow or swipe [Early 19thC. Origin uncertain: perhaps a variant of SLUG[3].] —**slogger** *n.*

slogan /slṓgən/ *n.* **1. MOTTO** a short distinctive phrase used to identify a company or organization or its goals **2. ADVERTISING PHRASE** a short catchy phrase used in advertising to promote sth **3.** *Scotland* **SCOTTISH BATTLE CRY** the battle cry of a Highland clan (*archaic*) [Early 16thC. From Gaelic *sluagh-ghairm*, from *sluagh* 'army' + *gairm* 'cry'. Originally 'a battle cry'.]

sloganeer /slṓgə neer/ *n.* **MAKER OF SLOGANS** sb who creates or frequently uses slogans ○ *the kind of politician who is little more than a clever sloganeer* ■ *vi.* **(-eers, -eering, -eered) MAKE UP SLOGANS** to create or use slogans

sloop /sloop/ *n.* a single-masted sailing boat, rigged fore-and-aft, with one headsail extending from the foremast to the bowsprit [Early 17thC. Via Dutch *sloep* from French *chaloupe*, from Old French *chalupe* 'sloop-rigged boat' (source of English *shallop*).]

sloop of war *n.* a small armed sailing ship that is larger than a gunboat and carries guns on only one deck

slop[1] /slop/ *n.* **1. STH SPILLED** a liquid that has spilled or overflowed ○ *Look at all the slop on the floor!* **2. MUD OR SLUSH** soft mud or slushy snow ○ *How far do we have to wade through this slop?* **3. UNAPPEALING FOOD** poor-quality unappetizing or watery food (*often used in the plural*) **4.** BEVERAGES **MASH** what remains of the mash after an alcoholic beverage has been distilled (*often used in the plural*) **5. HUMAN WASTE** human waste such as urine **6. OVERLY SENTIMENTAL WRITING OR SPEECH** overly emotional or sentimental speech or writing without any literary value (*informal*) ○ *Not all romantic novels are slop.* ■ **slops** *npl.* **PIG FOOD** leftover food, especially kitchen waste, that is fed to pigs ■ *v.* **(slops, slopping, slopped) 1.** *vti.* **SPILL LIQUID** to spill a liquid, or be spilled on or over sb or sth **2.** *vi.* **WALK THROUGH MUD OR WATER** to trudge or splash through water, mud, or slush **3.** *vi.* **WRITE GUSHILY** to write or speak about sth in an overly emotional or sentimental way (*informal*) **4.** *vt.* **SERVE FOOD MESSILY** to serve food in a careless and unappetizing way **5.** *vt.* AGRIC **FEED ANIMALS SLOPS** to feed kitchen waste to pigs and other livestock [14thC. From Old English *sloppe* 'dung', from a prehistoric Germanic word that is also the ancestor of English *slip* 'clay and water'.]

slop out *vi.* to empty a chamber pot as part of prison routine ○ *All prisoners must slop out every morning.*

slop[2] /slop/ *n.* **SMOCK** a loose smock or pair of overalls (*archaic*) ■ **slops** *npl.* **ITEMS SOLD TO SAILORS** clothes and personal articles that are sold from a slop chest to sailors on a merchant ship (*archaic*) [14thC. Origin uncertain: probably from Middle Dutch.]

slop basin *n.* a bowl or other container into which tea or coffee dregs are emptied. US term **slop bowl**

slop bowl *n. US* = **slop basin**

slop chest *n.* a store of merchandise, e.g. tobacco and clothes, kept aboard merchant ships to be sold to the crew

slope /slōp/ *n.* **1. SLANTED GROUND** ground that inclines slightly **2. SIDE OF A HILL OR MOUNTAIN** the part of a hill or mountain that is at an angle ○ *Let's hit the slopes and do some skiing!* **3. SLANT** a slant upwards or downwards, or the degree of such a slant **4. STH SLANTED** a line, surface, direction, or plane that is inclined **5.** MATH **TANGENT** the tangent of the angle between a straight line and the x-axis **6.** MATH **FIRST DERIVATIVE OF CURVE** the first derivative of a curve at a point ■ *v.* **(slopes, sloping, sloped) 1.** *vti.* **GO UP OR DOWN** to ascend or descend, or make sth ascend or descend ○ *From here, the road slopes gently down to the valley.* **2.** *vt.* **TAKE STH UP OR DOWN** to make sth rise or descend gradually ○ *We had a landscaper slope the path through our garden.* **3.** *vi.* **BE AT A SLANT** to be at or have an angle that deviates from horizontal ○ *Does the floor in this room slope?* [Late 16thC. From assumed Old English *aslopen*, past participle of *aslupan* 'to slip away', from *slupan* 'to slip'.] —**sloper** *n.* —**sloping** *adj.*

slope off *vi.* to leave unobtrusively or furtively ○ *I managed to slope off without anyone noticing.*

sloppy /sloppi/ **(-pier, -piest)** *adj.* **1. MESSY** lacking order or tidiness **2. WET** slushy, muddy, or very wet **3. NOT DONE WELL** carelessly or badly done (*informal*) **4. GUSHY** excessively sentimental or emotional (*informal*) **5.** COOK **WATERY** cooked or prepared in a way that results in excessive wateriness **6.** CLOTHES **BAGGY** loose-fitting so as to be casual and comfortable ○ *a big sloppy sweater* **7. DIRTY** splashed or covered with liquid

sloppy joe *n.* a long, baggy, loose-fitting sweater (*informal*) [Origin uncertain: *joe* probably from the name *Joe*]

slopwork /slóp wurk/ *n.* **1. CHEAP CLOTHES OR THEIR MANUFACTURE** clothing or the manufacture of clothing that is cheap and of inferior quality (*dated*) **2. QUICK LOW-QUALITY WORK** any kind of work that has been done quickly and carelessly —**slopworker** *n.*

slosh /slosh/ *v.* **(sloshes, sloshing, sloshed) 1.** *vt.* **SPILL LIQUID CLUMSILY** to spill or splash a liquid on or over sth **2.** *vti.* **STIR STH IN LIQUID** to move or splash sth, or move or splash in a liquid (*informal*) ○ *Slosh the shirt in some warm water before the stain sets.* **3.** *vi.* **WADE IN LIQUID** to wade or splash around in water, mud, or slush (*informal*) **4.** *vt.* **HIT SB** to hit sb very hard (*informal*) ■ *n.* **1. SLUSH** wet snow or mud **2. LIQUID SPLASHING** liquid splashing, or its sound ○ *We could hear the slosh of water against the docks all night because of the storm.* **3. HIT** a heavy blow (*informal*) [Early 19thC. Probably a blend of SLOP 'bog' and SLUSH.] —**sloshy** *adj.*

sloshed /slosht/ *adj.* thoroughly intoxicated (*informal*)

slot[1] /slot/ *n.* **1. OPENING** a narrow vertical or horizontal opening into which sth can be inserted ○ *Put the coin in the slot.* **2. SCHEDULED TIME** an assigned place and time in a sequence or schedule ○ *The station is moving the new comedy to a prime-time slot next month.* **3.** BUSINESS **JOB** a job or a position in a company or other organization **4.** AEROSP **AIR PASSAGE** an air passage in an aerofoil that directs air from the lower to the upper surface **5.** ELEC ENG = **expansion slot** ■ *v.* **(slots, slotting, slotted) 1.** *vti.* **ASSIGN A PLACE TO STH** to put sth in a specific place, position, or time ○ *Slot the shelves into the grooves.* **2.** *vt.* **MAKE SLOT IN STH** to cut a slot or slots in sth [14thC. From Old French *esclot* 'hollow of the breastbone', of unknown origin.]

slot in *vti.* to find a suitable time or place for sb or sth in a plan, organization, or series of events ○ *The doctor is busy this morning but she could slot you in at 2 o'clock.*

slot[2] /slot/ *n.* the track of an animal, especially a deer [Late 16thC. From Old French *esclot* 'horse's hoof-print', of uncertain origin: probably from Old Norse *slōð* 'track' (source of English *sleuth*).]

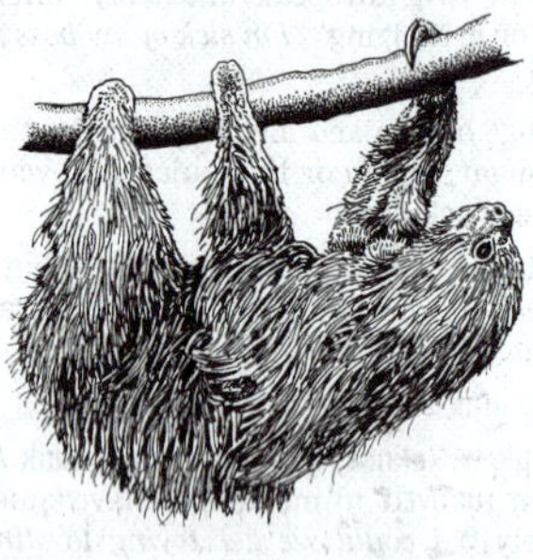

Sloth

sloth /slōth/ *n.* **1. SLOW-MOVING MAMMAL** a slow-moving mammal found in Central and South America that uses its long claws to hang upside down from tree branches. Genera: *Bradypus* and *Choloepus.* **2. LAZINESS** a dislike of work or any kind of physical exertion [12thC. Coined from SLOW + -TH.]

sloth bear *n.* a bear, native to India and Sri Lanka, with long shaggy fur and a long snout that enables it to feed on plants and insects. Latin name: *Melursus ursinus.*

slothful /slṓthf'l/ *adj.* disliking work or any form of physical exertion (*formal*) —**slothfully** *adv.* —**slothfulness** *n.*

slot machine *n.* **1. GAMBLING MACHINE** a gambling machine in which a player inserts coins in a slot and pulls a lever that spins symbols in matching combinations that determine winnings **2. VENDING MACHINE** a coin-operated vending machine

slouch /slowch/ *vti.* **(slouches, slouching, slouched) WALK OR SIT IN A LAZY WAY** to stand, sit, or walk in a careless drooping way or make a part of the body droop carelessly ○ *He slouched his back and shoulders and leaned against the wall.* ■ *n.* **1. EXTREMELY CASUAL POSTURE** an extremely relaxed or ungainly way of sitting, standing, or walking **2. LAZY OR INEPT PERSON** sb who is unwilling or unable to do sth well (*informal; usually used in negative statements*) ○ *very good with children and no slouch around the house, either* [Early 16thC. Origin uncertain: probably from Scandanavian.] —**sloucher** *n.* —**slouchily** *adv.* —**slouchiness** *n.* —**slouchy** *adj.*

slouch hat *n.* a hat made of a soft material, e.g. felt, that has a broad drooping brim, especially an Australian army hat

slough[1] /slow/ *n.* **1. DEEP MUDDY HOLE** a hole or low area in the ground filled with mud or water **2. slough, slue**

US **SWAMPY AREA** a stagnant area of water connected to a larger body of water such as a marsh, inlet, bayou, or backwater **3.** US, Can **ESTUARY** a saltwater estuary **4.** US, Can **HOLE FILLED WITH WATER** on the prairies, a low area filled with water, especially from melting snow **5.** **SPIRITUAL LOW POINT** deep despair or disgrace [Old English *slōh*, ultimately of unknown origin] —**sloughy** adj.

slough[2] /sluf/ n. **1.** ZOOL **DEAD OUTER COVERING** the dead outer skin shed by a reptile or an amphibian **2.** MED **DEAD TISSUE LAYER** a layer of dead skin that separates from healthy skin after an infection or inflammation **3.** **slough, sluff** CARDS **DISCARDED CARD** in card games, a card that has been discarded **4.** STH **CAST OFF** sth discarded or shed ■ v. (**sloughs, sloughing, sloughed**) **1.** vti. **CAST STH OFF** to shed sth, or be shed ○ *Snakes slough off their dead skins.* **2.** vi. MED **SEPARATE FROM HEALED TISSUE** to separate from surrounding healthy skin (*refers to dead skin*) **3.** vt. **DISCARD STH OR SB** to get rid of sb or sth that is no longer wanted or needed ○ *She sloughs off friends when she no longer has a use for them.* **4.** vt. **IGNORE STH** to pay no attention to sth **5.** **slough, sluff** (**sluffs, sluffing, sluffed**) vti. CARDS **DISCARD CARD** to get rid of an unwanted card [14thC. Origin uncertain.]

WORD KEY: REGIONAL NOTE

To *slough* school is a Nevada usage.

Slough /slow/ town in Berkshire, central England. Population: 109,300 (1995).

slough of despond /slow-/ n. a state of extreme despair and depression [Named after the deep bog in *Pilgrim's Progress, Part 1* (1678) by John Bunyan (1628–88) that Christian has to cross to reach the Wicket Gate]

Slovak /slṓ vak/, **Slovakian** /slṓ vá ki ən/ n. **1.** PEOPLES **SB FROM SLOVAKIA** sb who was born or brought up in Slovakia or who is a citizen of Slovakia **2.** LANG **LANGUAGE OF SLOVAKIA** the national language of Slovakia, a member of the Slavic group of Indo-European languages. Slovak is spoken by over five million people. ■ adj. **1.** **OF SLOVAKIA** relating to or typical of Slovakia or its people or culture **2.** LANG **OF SLOVAK** relating to the Slovak language

Slovakia

Slovakia /slō vaáki ə/ republic in eastern-central Europe. It was part of Czechoslovakia until 1993. Language: Slovak. Currency: Slovak koruna. Capital: Bratislava. Population: 5,343,000 (1996). Area: 49,035 sq. km/18,932 sq. mi. Official name **Slovak Republic**

Slovakian n., adj. PEOPLES, LANG = **Slovak**

sloven /slúvv'n/ n. an offensive term that deliberately insults sb who is not concerned about conventional standards of personal hygiene and tidiness (*insult*) [15thC. Origin uncertain: probably from Middle Flemish *slovin* 'a scold'.]

Slovene /slṓ veen/, **Slovenian** /slō veéni ən/ n. **1.** PEOPLES **SB FROM SLOVENIA** sb who was born, brought up in, or is a citizen of Slovenia **2.** LANG **LANGUAGE OF SLOVENIA** the national language of Slovenia, belonging to the Slavic group of Indo-European languages. Slovene is spoken by about two million people. ■ adj. **1.** **OF SLOVENIA** relating to Slovenia or its people or culture **2.** LANG **OF SLOVENE** relating to the Slovene language

Slovenia /slō veéni ə/ republic in eastern Europe, on the Balkan Peninsula. It was part of Yugoslavia until 1991. Language: Slovene. Currency: tolar. Capital: Ljubljana. Population: 1,991,000 (1996).

Slovenia

Area: 20,254 sq. km/7,820 sq. mi. Official name **Republic of Slovenia**

Slovenian n., adj. PEOPLES, LANG = **Slovene**

slovenly /slúvv'nli/ (**-lier, -liest**) adj. an offensive term used to describe sb who is not concerned about conventional standards of personal hygiene and tidiness

Slovo /slóvō/, **Joe** (1926–95) Lithuanian-born South African political leader. He was the leading Caucasian nationalist during South Africa's apartheid era, and served in Nelson Mandela's government (1994–95).

slow /slō/ adj. **1.** **NOT FAST** not moving quickly or at a fast pace **2.** **LENGTHY** taking a long time to do or create sth ○ *Writing software is a slow process.* **3.** **TAKING TOO MUCH TIME** requiring more time than is usual or expected **4.** **NOT KEEPING ACCURATE TIME** showing a time that is earlier than the correct time ○ *I was late for my appointment because my watch was slow.* **5.** **HESITANT** doing sth hesitantly or unwillingly ○ *Why were you so slow to answer my question?* **6.** **SLUGGISH** lacking the usual volume of sales or customers ○ *Business is usually slow during the summer months.* **7.** **OFFENSIVE TERM** an offensive term that deliberately insults sb's imagination or intelligence **8.** **DULL** lacking in interest or activity ○ *The acting was good but the plot was terribly slow.* **9.** COOK **WARM** operating at a low temperature that ensures thorough cooking throughout ○ *Turkey should be cooked in a slow oven.* **10.** SPORTS **REDUCING SPEED OF BALL OR RUNNER** tending to reduce the speed or ability to travel of a ball, runner, or other competitor ○ *That horse usually wins on a slow track.* **11.** **DELIVERING A BALL SLOWLY** in cricket, delivering a ball slowly and with spin ○ *a slow bowler* ■ adv. (**slower** or **slowest**) **1.** **BEHIND** behind the correct time or pace ○ *My watch seems to be running slow.* **2.** **AT A LOW SPEED** at a reduced speed or pace ○ *The law requires motorists to drive slow through residential areas.* ■ vti. (**slows, slowing, slowed**) **1.** **MAKE STH SLOW** to make sb or sth slow or slower, or become slow or slower ○ *Could you slow your speed a little on those sharp turns?* **2.** **DELAY OR BE DELAYED** to reduce the speed or progress of sth, or become reduced in speed or progress [Old English *slaw* 'sluggish'] —**slowly** adv. —**slowness** n. ◇ **go slow** to officially work slower than usual as a form of protest

---
WORD KEY: USAGE
---

slowly or **slow**? The normal adverb is *slowly*: *The car moved slowly up the hill.* *Slow* is used informally as an adverb (*Don't walk so slow*) but this is not regarded as standard. However, in some expressions, such as *go slow*, and *slow-moving*, *slow* is idiomatic and acceptable.

---

slow burn, **slow boil** n. a steadily growing anger (*informal*) ○ *doing a slow burn*

slowcoach /slṓ kōch/ n. sb who moves or does sth too slowly (*informal*) ○ *If you hadn't been such a slowcoach we'd have been on time.* US term **slowpoke**

slowdown /slṓ down/ n. US = **go-slow**

slow-footed adj. happening or proceeding at an extremely slow pace ○ *Congress has been slow-footed in passing the bill.* —**slow-footedness** n.

slow handclap n. a very slow, steady clapping, used by an audience to show its dislike of a performance ○ *You could feel the audience about to break into a slow handclap.*

slow loris n. a small slow-moving primate found in Indonesia that has a rounded, almost tailless body. Latin name: *Nycticebus coucang*.

slow match n. a flameless match or fuse that burns very slowly or at a known rate, used to set off explosives

slow motion n. a method of filming action at a rate faster than the normal projection rate, so that it appears on the screen at a slower-than-normal rate

slow-motion adj. **1.** **SLOWED-DOWN** photographed or shown in slow motion **2.** **HAPPENING SLOWLY** taking place at a slower pace than normal ○ *her slow-motion reaction*

slow neutron n. a relatively slow-moving neutron that possesses less than 100 electronvolts of kinetic energy and is capable of bringing about nuclear fission

slowpoke /slṓ pōk/ n. US = **slowcoach** (*informal*) [Mid-19thC. *Poke* from POKE in the sense 'dawdling person'.]

slow time n. a very slow marching step, used especially in funeral ceremonies

slow virus n. any virus or agent resembling a virus that causes diseases with very long incubation periods. Technical name **lentivirus**

slow-witted adj. an offensive term used to describe sb considered to be slow to understand ideas, events, or situations

slowworm /slṓ wurm/ n. a legless lizard with a smooth body resembling that of a snake. It feeds chiefly on slugs and is found in Europe, northern Africa, and western Asia. Latin name: *Anguis fragilis*. [Old English *slāwyrm* (altered by folk etymology), from *slā* 'slowworm' (of unknown origin) + *wyrm* 'worm']

SLP n., abbr. Scottish Labour Party

SLR abbr. single-lens reflex

slub /slub/ n. **1.** **KNOT IN YARN** a lump in yarn or fabric that is sometimes an imperfection, but is often made to provide a knobby effect **2.** **TWISTED THREAD** a loosely twisted roll of fibre, e.g. of silk or cotton, prepared for spinning ■ vt. (**slubs, slubbing, slubbed**) **PREPARE FIBRE FOR SPINNING** to draw out and twist a strand of fibre to prepare it for spinning [Early 19thC. Origin unknown.]

sludge /sluj/ n. **1.** **SLUSH** wet material, especially watery mud or snow **2.** **SEDIMENT** a solid deposit found at the bottom of a liquid **3.** **BROKEN ICE** a layer of broken or half-formed ice on a body of water, especially the sea **4.** **SOLID WASTE** the solids in sewage that separate out during treatment **5.** MED **MASS OF BLOOD CELLS** a sticky grouping of blood cells that form a mass and hinder the circulation of blood [Mid-17thC. Origin uncertain: possibly from obsolete *slutch* 'mud, mire', or a variant of SLUSH.] —**sludgy** adj.

slue /sloo/ vti. (**slues, sluing, slued**) US = **slew** ■ n. US = **slew** [Variant of SLEW 'alternative for slough' and SLEW 'to turn']

sluff n. = **slough**[2] n. 3 ■ vti. = **slough**[2] v. 5

slug[1] /slug/ n. **1.** ARMS **BULLET** a metal projectile that is fired from a gun or rifle **2.** BEVERAGES **DRINK OF STH** a single drink of a strong alcoholic drink (*informal*) **3.** PRINTING **TYPE-METAL** a strip of type-metal, less than type-high, used for spacing in traditional hot-metal printing **4.** PRINTING **LINE OF TYPE** a strip of cast type in a single strip of metal in traditional hot-metal printing **5.** PRINTING **TEMPORARY TYPE LINE** a temporary type line inserted in copy that carries identifying marks or a compositor's instructions **6.** MANUF **METAL OR GLASS BLANK FOR PROCESSING** a metal or glass blank that will receive further processing **7.** MEASURE **UNIT OF MASS** a foot-pound-second unit of mass equal to 32.17 pounds that will acquire an acceleration of one foot per second per second when acted on by a 1 pound force ■ vt. **1.** **DRINK STH QUICKLY** to gulp down a drink (*informal*) **2.** PRINTING **ADD SLUGS** to add printers' slugs to copy in traditional hot-metal printing [Early 17thC. Originally 'bullet', of uncertain origin: perhaps from SLUG[2], from the similarity in shape. 'Drink' may have come from Gaelic *slog* 'swallow'.]

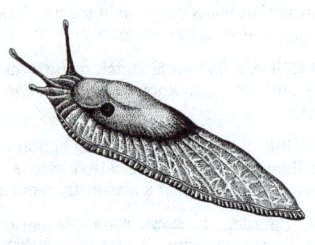

Slug

slug² /slug/ *n.* **1.** ZOOL **MOLLUSC WITHOUT A SHELL** a small slow-moving terrestrial mollusc that resembles a snail but has no shell, or only a rudimentary one. Order: Stylommatophora. **2.** INSECTS **LARVA** a soft smooth larva of some insects, e.g. that of the sawfly **3.** CELL BIOL **CELLS THAT DEVELOP INTO SPORE-BEARING STRUCTURE** a sticky mass of cells from which the sporophore of a slime mould develops **4.** OFFENSIVE TERM an offensive term that deliberately insults sb's level of energy or activity (*insult*) [15thC. Origin uncertain: probably from Scandinavian, and related to Norwegian dialect *slugg* 'large heavy body'.]

slug³ /slug/ *vt.* (**slugs, slugging, slugged**) **1.** HIT SB OR STH **HARD** to strike sb or sth very hard with the fist or a bat **2.** *Aus* CHARGE TOO MUCH to charge sb a price that is unfairly high (*informal*) ■ *n.* HARD HIT a hard strike or blow [Mid-19thC. Origin uncertain: probably ultimately from a prehistoric Germanic word meaning 'to hit', which is also the ancestor of English *slog* and *slay*.] ◇ **slug it out** *US* to fight to a conclusion (*informal*)

slugabed /slúggə bed/ *n.* sb who likes to stay in bed later than other people (*archaic*) [Late 16thC. From SLUG² + ABED.]

sluggard /slúggərd/ *n.* LAZY PERSON sb who avoids work or physical exertion (*archaic*) ■ *adj.* LAZY sluggishly lazy [14thC. Formed from SLUG².] —**sluggardliness** *n.* —**sluggardly** *adj.* —**sluggardness** *n.*

slugger /slúggər/ *n.* sb who delivers very hard blows during a fight [Formed from SLUG³]

sluggish /slúggish/ *adj.* **1.** NOT MOVING MUCH inactive and moving slowly or very little **2.** NOT VERY RESPONSIVE slow to react or to respond to stimulation **3.** LACKING ALERTNESS AND ENERGY not alert and showing little energy or vitality —**sluggishly** *adv.* —**sluggishness** *n.*

Sluice

sluice /slooss/ *n.* **1.** WATER CHANNEL an artificial channel for a flow of water that is controlled by a valve or gate **2.** FLOODGATE a valve or floodgate that controls the water in a sluice **3.** WATER BEHIND FLOODGATE a body of water contained by a floodgate **4.** DRAINAGE CHANNEL a channel for carrying away excess water **5.** TROUGH a long inclined trough used to separate gold ore from sand or gravel **6.** CHANNEL TO MOVE LOGS an artificial stream or channel for floating logs ■ *v.* (**sluices, sluicing, sluiced**) **1.** *vt.* FLUSH STH WITH WATER to flood or clean sth with a sudden heavy flow of water **2.** *vt.* WASH GOLD to wash gold or other minerals in water flowing in a sluice **3.** *vti.* RELEASE STH FROM A SLUICE to flow from or let sth out of a sluice **4.** *vt.* MOVE STH IN SLUICE to float sth, especially logs, down a sluice **5.** *vt.* WASH STH to wash sth in running water ○ *He sluiced his hands under the tap.* [14thC. Via Old French

escluse from Latin *exclus-*, past participle stem of *excludere* 'to shut out' (see EXCLUDE). Altered by folk etymology by association with JUICE.]

sluicegate /slooss gayt/ *n.* = SLUICE *n.* 2

sluiceway /slooss way/ *n.* an artificial channel into which water flows from a sluice

slum /slum/ *n.* POOR AREA an overcrowded area of a city in which the housing is typically in very bad condition (*often used in the plural*) ■ *v.* (**slums, slumming** *or* **slummed, slummed**) **1.** ACCEPT LOWER STANDARDS THAN USUAL to stay in or go to a place that you would usually consider unacceptable (*often used humorously*) ○ *We'll have to slum it and stay here until we can find a better place.* **2.** *vi.* VISIT SLUMS to go into a slum out of curiosity [Mid-19thC. From the earlier expression *back slum* 'street housing poor people' in which *slum* meant 'room' (of unknown origin).] —**slummer** *n.*

slumber /slúmbər/ *vi.* (**-bers, -bering, -bered**) **1.** SLEEP to be asleep **2.** BE IN QUIET STATE to be in a state of inactivity or rest ■ *n.* **1.** SLEEPING the state of being asleep, or a period of sleep ○ *A loud noise disturbed my slumber.* **2.** INACTIVITY a state of being dormant or quiet [14thC. Alteration of obsolete *sloom*, from Old English *slūma* 'light sleep', from prehistoric Germanic.] —**slumberless** *adj.*

slumberous /slúmbərəss/ *adj.* **1.** DROWSY feeling sleepy **2.** INACTIVE characterized by inactivity or sluggishness ○ *A slumberous atmosphere seemed to stifle sound and motion in the town.* **3.** CAUSING SLEEP inducing lethargy or sleep ○ *She dozed in the slumberous heat of the afternoon.* —**slumberously** *adv.* —**slumberousness** *n.*

slump /slump/ *vi.* (**slumps, slumping, slumped**) **1.** COLLAPSE to sink or fall suddenly and heavily **2.** SLOUCH to have a hunched drooping posture ○ *She was slumped over her desk.* **3.** DECREASE to decline suddenly and sharply in value ○ *share prices slumped* ■ *n.* **1.** SLOUCHED POSTURE a drooping or hunched posture **2.** ECONOMIC RECESSION a sudden decline in business, stock prices, or productivity ○ *an economy fluctuating between boom and slump* [Mid-17thC. Origin uncertain: perhaps from Scandinavian.]

slumpflation /slump fláysh'n/ *n.* an economic situation in which an economic depression is accompanied by increasing inflation [Late 20thC. Blend of SLUMP and INFLATION.]

slung past tense, past participle of **sling**

slungshot /slúng shot/ *n.* a weight or weights attached to the end of a cord and used as a weapon

slunk past tense, past participle of **slink**

slur /slur/ *v.* (**slurs, slurring, slurred**) **1.** *vti.* SPEAK INDISTINCTLY to pronounce sounds or words so that they cannot be distinguished **2.** *vt.* DEMEAN SB to speak of sb in an insulting or demeaning way **3.** *vt.* GLOSS OVER STH to ignore sth or treat it superficially ○ *The committee slurred over my protests.* **4.** *vt.* MUSIC PERFORM MUSIC SMOOTHLY to play musical notes in a smooth, uninterrupted way **5.** *vti.* SMEAR OR BE SMEARED to blur or smear wet ink on a page, or be blurred or smeared ■ *n.* **1.** INSULT an insulting or demeaning statement about sb **2.** SLURRED PRONUNCIATION an indistinct pronunciation or sound **3.** MUSIC MUSIC SYMBOL a curved line that connects two or more notes on a score, indicating that they are to be performed smoothly **4.** BLURRED IMAGE an image that has been smeared or blurred [Early 17thC. Origin uncertain.]

slurp /slurp/ *vti.* (**slurps, slurping, slurped**) DRINK STH NOISILY to make a loud sucking sound while drinking or eating sth ○ *Would you stop slurping your milkshake?* ■ *n.* **1.** SUCKING SOUND a loud sucking sound made while drinking or eating **2.** LIQUID MOUTHFUL a mouthful of a liquid (*informal*) ○ *Can I have a slurp of your soda?* [Mid-17thC. From Dutch *slurpen*, of uncertain origin: perhaps an imitation of the sound.] —**slurpingly** *adv.*

slurry /slúrri/ (*plural* **-ries**) *n.* a liquid mixture of water and an insoluble solid material, e.g. cement or clay [15thC. Formed from SLUR.]

slush /slush/ *n.* **1.** MELTING SNOW OR ICE snow or ice that has begun to melt **2.** SEMILIQUID SUBSTANCE a solid substance such as mud that has become wet and sloppy **3.** NAUT GREASE FROM SHIP'S GALLEY the waste grease or

fat produced by a ship's galley **4.** GREASE a greasy substance used to lubricate machine parts **5.** OVERLY SENTIMENTAL EXPRESSION extremely sentimental speech or writing **6.** BEVERAGES ICE DRINK a drink made of finely crushed ice with a flavoured syrup poured over it ■ *v.* (**slushes, slushing, slushed**) **1.** *vt.* ENG GREASE MACHINERY to lubricate the parts of a machine **2.** *vt.* BUILDING PUT MORTAR IN JOINTS to fill masonry joints with mortar, or cover a surface with cement **3.** *vt.* SOAK STH WITH SLUSH to splash or cover sth with mud or slush **4.** *vi.* WALK THROUGH SLUSH to walk through wet snow or mud ○ *It had been raining so hard we had to slush through mud to get there.* **5.** *vi.* MAKE A SPLASHING SOUND to make a splashing or squelching sound [Mid-17thC. Origin uncertain: perhaps an imitation of the sound of splashing, or from Scandinavian.]

slush fund *n.* **1.** CRIMINOL MONEY FOR ILLEGAL ACTIVITIES money set aside by a business or other organization for corrupt activities such as the bribery of public officials **2.** FIN MONEY FOR ENTERTAINMENT money set aside to use for fun or entertainment expenses **3.** NAUT LUXURY FUND FOR SHIP'S CREW money raised by selling refuse and garbage from a ship to pay for small luxuries for the crew [From the money gained from selling a ship's *slush*, the grease collected in a ship's galley. 'Money used for bribes' comes from 'greasing' sb's palm with money.]

slush pile *n.* a pile of unsolicited manuscripts accumulated in a publisher's office (*informal*)

slushy /slúshi/ (**-ier, -iest**) *adj.* **1.** FULL OF SLUSH covered with or full of melting snow and ice **2.** RESEMBLING SLUSH with the consistency of slush **3.** OVERLY SENTIMENTAL filled with or expressing excessive sentiment ○ *a slushy love story* —**slushiness** *n.*

slut /slut/ *n.* **1.** OFFENSIVE TERM a highly offensive term for a woman thought by others to be sexually promiscuous (*insult*) **2.** OFFENSIVE TERM an offensive term for a woman who charges for engaging in sexual activities (*insult*) **3.** OFFENSIVE TERM a highly offensive term for a woman who is not concerned about conventional standards of domestic cleanliness (*insult dated*) [15thC. Origin uncertain.] —**sluttish** *adj.* —**sluttishly** *adv.* —**sluttishness** *n.* —**slutty** *adj.*

SLV *abbr.* standard launch vehicle *or* space launch vehicle

sly /slī/ (**slier, sliest**) *adj.* **1.** CRAFTY cleverly skilful and cunning **2.** EVASIVE lacking honesty or straightforwardness **3.** MISCHIEVOUS full of playful mischief [13thC. From Old Norse *slægr* 'clever, crafty', literally 'able to strike' (source of English *sleight*).] —**slyly** *adv.* —**slyness** *n.* ◇ **on the sly** without the knowledge or permission of others

slyboots /slī boots/ *n.* an offensive term for sb considered to be cunning or devious (*informal insult; takes a singular verb*)

slype /slīp/ *n.* a covered passage in a cathedral or church that joins the transept to a chapter-house [Mid-19thC. Origin uncertain: perhaps a variant of obsolete SLIP, from SLIP; or from Dutch dialect or West Flemish *slijpe* 'secret path'.]

Sm *symbol.* samarium

SM *abbr.* sergeant major

sm. *abbr.* small

S/M, S-M *abbr.* sadomasochism

smack¹ /smak/ *v.* (**smacks, smacking, smacked**) **1.** *vti.* SLAP SB to hit sb with a quick stinging and usually noisy blow with the palm of the hand **2.** *vi.* HIT AGAINST STH NOISILY to strike against, collide with, or land in sth with a sharp loud noise **3.** *vt.* PRESS LIPS TOGETHER to press together and then open the lips with a short loud noise ■ *n.* **1.** SLAP a sharp quick blow with the palm of the hand **2.** NOISY SOUND a sharp loud noise made when one thing strikes another **3.** LOUD KISS a brief noisy kiss ■ *adv.* **1.** WITH A LOUD NOISE with a sharp loud noise or collision **2.** DIRECTLY directly or precisely ○ *I was smack in the middle of getting ready to leave when you called.* [Mid-16thC. From Middle Low German *smacken* 'to open the lips noisily', an imitation of the sound.]

smack² /smak/ *n.* **1.** DISTINCTIVE TASTE a unique flavour or taste of sth **2.** HINT a small amount or trace ■ *vi.* (**smacks, smacking, smacked**) **1.** BE DISTINCTIVELY FLAVOURED to have a unique flavour or taste of sth **2.** EXPRESS STH

INDIRECTLY to suggest or hint at sth ○ *an editorial that smacked of snobbery* [Old English *smæc* 'taste', from prehistoric Germanic]

smack[3] /smak/ *n.* a sailing vessel used for fishing, usually for carrying the catch to market [Early 17thC. From Dutch *smak*, of unknown origin.]

smack[4] /smak/ *n.* heroin (*slang*) [Mid-20thC. Origin uncertain: probably an alteration of *schmeck* 'drug', from Yiddish, 'sniff', ultimately from Middle High German *smecken* 'to smell'.]

smack-dab *adj. US* = **slap-bang** (*informal*)

smacker /smákər/ *n.* (*informal*) **1.** LOUD KISS a noisy smacking kiss **2.** POUND a pound

smacking /smáking/ *adj.* very brisk or lively ○ *a smacking breeze*

small /smawl/ *adj.* **1.** LITTLE of a relatively little size ○ *a small animal* **2.** NOT MUCH little in quantity or value ○ *a small sum of money* **3.** INSIGNIFICANT unimportant or trivial ○ *a small matter* **4.** LIMITED operating on a limited scale ○ *small businesses* **5.** MINOR lacking in power, influence, or status **6.** NOT YET MATURE young or not fully grown ○ *small children* **7.** ORDINARY humble or modest ○ *He came from small beginnings.* **8.** MEAN petty and mean-spirited **9.** LOWER-CASE in lower case rather than capitals ○ *small letters* **10.** WITHOUT SELF-RESPECT humiliated or feeling little self-worth ○ *Her criticisms and ridicule made me feel very small.* **11.** NOT STRONG lacking in strength (*archaic*) ○ *a small sound* ■ *adv.* **1.** IN SMALL PIECES in or into little pieces ○ *Cut it up small.* **2.** IN A SMALL WAY in a moderate or limited way ○ *start out small* **3.** QUIETLY quietly or softly (*archaic*) ■ *n.* **1.** NARROW PART a part of sth that is narrower or smaller than the rest of it ○ *the small of the back* **2.** CLOTHES SIZE FOR SB SMALL a size or a garment in a size that fits sb who is of less than average proportions ■ **smalls** *npl. UK* UNDERGARMENTS items of underwear (*informal or humorous*) [Old English *smæl* 'slender, small', from a prehistoric Germanic word meaning 'small animal'] —**smallish** *adj.* —**smallness** *n.*

small arms *n.* firearms such as pistols and rifles that can be held in one or both hands while firing

small beer *n.* **1.** TRIVIA sth of little or no importance (*informal*) ○ *A thousand pounds is small beer to people like him.* **2.** WEAK BEER weak or inferior beer (*dated*)

small-bore *adj.* used to describe .22-calibre firearms or ammunition.

small calorie *n.* = **calorie** *n.* 1

small capital *n.* a capital letter that is the same height as a lower-case letter

small change *n.* **1.** COINS OF LOW VALUE coins that have a low denomination **2.** STH TRIVIAL sth that is considered to be insignificant, especially when compared with sth else

small claims court *n.* a local court that has jurisdiction to try civil actions involving claims worth only a small sum of money

smallclothes /smáwl klōthz/ *npl.* close-fitting knee breeches worn by men in the 18th century (*archaic*)

small fry *npl.* **1.** TRIVIAL THINGS people, events, or issues that are thought to be of little importance **2.** YOUNG FISH young, immature, or small fish **3.** CHILDREN young children (*informal*)

small game *n.* small animals and birds that are hunted for sport

small goods *npl. ANZ* processed meats such as sausages and salamis

smallholding /smáwl hōlding/ *n.* a piece of farmland that is smaller than the average farm

small hours *n.* the early morning hours after midnight

small intestine *n.* the part of the intestine between the stomach and large intestine, consisting of the duodenum, jejunum, and ileum, where digestion of food and most absorption of nutrients takes place

small-minded *adj.* an offensive term for sb who is considered to be petty and intolerant of the ideas and beliefs of others —**small-mindedly** *adv.* —**small-mindedness** *n.*

smallmouth bass /smáwl mowth báss/ *n.* a greenish-brown freshwater bass of North America that is found in clear streams and lakes and is a popular gamefish. Latin name: *Micropterus dolomieu.*

smallpox /smáwl poks/ *n.* a highly contagious disease caused by a poxvirus and marked by high fever and the formation of scar-producing pustules. A worldwide inoculation programme has virtually eradicated the smallpox virus from the human population. Technical name **variola**

small print *n.* the very fine, hard-to-read print in a contract or other legal document that often contains important information that could be overlooked

small-scale *adj.* **1.** LIMITED limited in scope or size **2.** SMALL IN SIZE made or constructed on a small scale ○ *She built a small-scale replica of the ship.*

small screen *n.* the medium of television, especially as distinct from the cinema (*informal*)

small slam *n.* = **little slam**

small stores *npl.* small items such as clothing sold on a ship or at a naval base

small stuff *n.* light twine or yarn used on a ship

smallsword /smáwl sawrd/ *n.* a light sword used in the 17th and 18th centuries for duelling and fencing (*archaic*)

small talk *n.* polite conversation about matters of little importance, especially between people who do not know each other well

small-time *adj.* of minor importance or influence (*informal*) ○ *He's just a small-time crook.*

smalt /smawlt/ *n.* **1.** BLUE GLASS a kind of silica glass that has been coloured a deep blue by cobalt oxide **2.** PIGMENT a deep blue pigment made by crushing smalt [Mid-16thC. Via French from Italian *smalto* SMALTO.]

smaltite /smáwl tīt/ *n.* a naturally occurring blue-grey arsenide of cobalt and nickel that is an important ore of cobalt

smalto /smaáltō/ *n.* small bits of pottery, glass, and tiles used in mosaics [Early 18thC. From Italian, ultimately from prehistoric Germanic.]

smaragd /smárragd/ (*plural* **-ragds** *or* **-ragdes** /-ragdiz/) *n.* any green gemstone, e.g. an emerald (*archaic*) [13thC. From Latin *smaragdus*, from Greek *smaragdos*, ultimately from Hebrew *bāreqet* 'emerald', from *bāraq* 'flash, sparkle'.] —**smaragdine** /smə rágdin, -dīn/ *adj.*

smaragdite /smə rág dīt/ *n.* a fibrous green amphibole mineral

smarm /smaarm/ *n.* (*informal*) **1.** SELF-SERVING FLATTERY ingratiating or servile flattery **2.** INSINCERE CHARM charm that is distastefully self-conscious or insincere ■ *v.* (**smarms, smarming, smarmed**) (*informal*) **1.** *vi.* FLATTER to make a lot of fuss over sb in order to ingratiate yourself **2.** *vt.* GREASE THE HAIR to flatten hair by smoothing it down with grease [Early 20thC. Origin unknown.]

smarmy /smaármi/ (**-ier, -iest**) *adj.* **1.** EXCESSIVELY INGRATIATING excessively and unpleasantly polite and ingratiating **2.** INSINCERELY CHARMING charming in a distastefully self-conscious or insincere way (*informal*) [Early 20thC. Formed from SMARM.] —**smarmily** *adv.* —**smarminess** *n.*

smart /smaart/ *adj.* **1.** TIDY with a neat and well-cared-for appearance **2.** CLEVER showing intelligence and mental alertness ○ *smart students* **3.** INSOLENT disrespectful or impertinent ○ *Whatever you say to him he has some smart answer.* **4.** WITTY AND AMUSING amusingly clever and possessing a quick wit **5.** KEEN shrewd and calculating in business and other dealings ○ *a smart dealer* **6.** FASHIONABLE fashionable and stylish ○ *smart restaurants* **7.** LIVELY vigorous and brisk ○ *a smart pace* **8.** STINGING causing a sharp stinging sensation ○ *a smart slap* **9.** MIL LASER- OR RADIO-GUIDED used to describe a missile or weapon that is guided to its target by laser or radio beams **10.** ELECTRON ENG ELECTRONIC with a built-in microprocessor ○ *smart traffic lights* ■ *vi.* (**smarts, smarting, smarted**) **1.** CAUSE OR HAVE SHARP PAIN to feel, cause, or be the site of a sharp stinging pain ○ *My hand smarts.* **2.** BE EMBARRASSED to feel acute embarrassment or distress ○ *She still smarted when she remembered his criticism.* **3.** BE PUNISHED to be punished severely ■ *adv.* SMARTLY in a smart manner ■ *n.* **1.** PAIN a sharp stinging localized pain **2.** EMBARRASSMENT OR MENTAL DISCOMFORT a feeling such as embarrassment, remorse, or shame [Old English *smeortan* 'to be painful', ultimately of uncertain origin: perhaps from an Indo-European word meaning 'to harm', which is also the ancestor of English *nightmare* and perhaps *remorse*] —**smartly** *adv.* —**smartness** *n.*

WORD KEY: SYNONYMS

See Synonyms at ***intelligent***.

smart aleck /smaárt alik/, **smart alec** *n.* sb who shows off his or her knowledge or always has the right answer in a way that annoys other people (*informal*) [Mid-19thC. Origin uncertain: perhaps named after an infamous New York pimp and confidence man of the 1840s *Aleck* Hoag.]

smart-aleck /smaárt alik/, **smart-alecky** /smaárt aliki/ *adj.* pretentiously clever and annoyingly self-assertive (*informal*) —**smart-alecky** *adj.*

smartarse /smaárt aarss/ *n.* sb who makes an annoying show of knowledge (*slang*) US term **smartass**

smartass /smaárt ass/, **smart-ass** *n. US* = **smartarse** (*slang*)

smart bomb *n.* a missile that is guided to its target by laser or radio beams

smart card *n.* a small plastic card containing a microchip that can store personal data and bank-account details, enabling it to be used for identification and to pay for purchases

smarten /smaárt'n/ (**-ens, -ening, -ened**) *vt.* **1.** IMPROVE APPEARANCE to improve the appearance of sb or sth **2.** SPEED STH UP to increase the speed of sth

smarten up *vti.* **1.** IMPROVE APPEARANCE to improve your appearance, or the appearance of sb or sth else **2.** MAKE OR BECOME LIVELIER to make sb or sth brighter or livelier, or become brighter or livelier **3.** *US* MAKE OR BECOME WISER to make sb wiser or more knowing, or become wiser or more knowing

smart growth *n.* economic growth that consciously seeks to avoid wastefulness and damage to the environment and communities

smart money *n.* **1.** WISE INVESTMENT OR BET money bet on or invested in sth likely to yield a good profit **2.** WISE INVESTORS those with privileged information to make wise bets or investments **3.** *US* LAW DAMAGES AWARDED TO PUNISH A DEFENDANT damages awarded to a plaintiff in excess of the normal level of compensation to punish a defendant in cases of serious negligence or willful misconduct

smarty-pants /smaárti-/ (*plural* **smarty-pants**), **smarty** (*plural* **smarties**) *n.* sb who is annoying because he or she is always trying to be clever (*informal; takes a singular verb*)

smash /smash/ *v.* (**smashes, smashing, smashed**) **1.** *vti.* BREAK WITH FORCE to break sth, or break through sth, with great force or violence **2.** *vti.* BREAK INTO PIECES to break, or break sth, into many small pieces **3.** *vti.* HIT AGAINST STH to hit sth, or make sth hit sth else, with great force **4.** *vt.* DEFEAT OR DESTROY to ruin, defeat, or put an end to sb or sth completely **5.** *vt.* RACKET GAMES HIT WITH OVERHAND STROKE in games such as tennis and badminton, to hit a ball or shuttlecock with great force, especially with an overhand stroke ■ *n.* **1.** LOUD NOISE the loud sound of sth hitting or being hit by sth else and breaking into pieces ○ *The mirror hit the floor with a smash.* **2.** BLOW a heavy blow **3.** COLLISION a crash or collision ○ *There's been a bad smash on the motorway.* **4.** RACKET GAMES OVERHAND STROKE in games such as tennis and badminton, a strong overhand stroke hit downwards into the opponent's court **5.** BUSINESS, THEATRE GREAT SUCCESS an unqualified success ○ *The new show was a smash hit.* **6.** BUSINESS BIG FAILURE a major failure, especially one involving finances ■ *adv.* WITH A SMASH with the sound of a smash [Late 17thC. Origin uncertain: perhaps a blend of such words as SMACK, SMITE, and others such as BASH, MASH.] —**smashable** *adj.*

smash up *v.* **1.** *vti.* DAMAGE BY COLLISION to damage sth severely, or become badly damaged, because of a collision with sth solid **2.** *vt.* DAMAGE BY BREAKING to damage or destroy sth by breaking

smash-and-grab *adj.* INVOLVING BREAKING WINDOWS AND STEALING relating to a robbery committed by breaking a shop window in order to steal the goods on display ■ *n.* A SMASH-AND-GRAB ROBBERY a smash-and-grab robbery

smashed /smasht/ *adj.* very drunk or under the influence of drugs (*informal*)

smasher /smáshər/ *n.* sth impressive or a person who is physically attractive (*informal*)

smashing /smáshing/ *adj.* extremely good or pleasing

smash-up *n.* a road accident between vehicles in which all those involved are badly damaged

smatter /smáttər/ *n.* = **smattering** *n.* 1, **smattering** *n.* 2 [15thC. Origin uncertain.]

smattering /smáttəring/ *n.* **1.** SLIGHT KNOWLEDGE a slight knowledge of sth such as a subject or language **2.** SMALL AMOUNT a small amount or number ○ *a smattering of rain*

SMATV *abbr.* satellite master antenna television

SME *abbr.* Suriname (international vehicle registration)

smear /smeer/ *v.* (**smears, smearing, smeared**) **1.** *vti.* SPREAD OVER to spread over, or spread sth liquid or greasy over sth ○ *This lipstick is made not to smear.* **2.** *vt.* SPREAD DAMAGING RUMOURS to deliberately spread damaging rumours about sb **3.** *vt. US* DEFEAT to severely defeat a competitor or enemy (*informal; usually passive*) ○ *We got smeared.* ■ *n.* **1.** PATCH OF SMEARED SUBSTANCE an act of smearing, or a smeared patch of sth **2.** MED SAMPLE OF CELLS a sample of cells taken from body tissue or a bodily secretion or discharge and smeared on a microscope slide for examination **3.** MED SMEAR TEST a smear test (*informal*) **4.** HARMFUL RUMOUR a harmful rumour or story about sb [The verb is from Old English *smeirwan*, the noun from *smeoru*, both from a prehistoric Germanic word that is also the ancestor of English *smorgasbord*] —**smearer** *n.*

smear campaign *n.* a concerted effort to diminish sb's reputation by spreading harmful information about him or her

smear test *n.* = **cervical smear**

smeary /sméeri/ (**-ier, -iest**) *adj.* **1.** SMEARED OR LIABLE TO SMEAR smeared on, easily smeared, or likely to smear **2.** COVERED WITH SMEARS having or covered with smears

smectic /sméktik/ *adj.* used to describe materials whose liquid phase consists of elongated molecules arranged in layers and with their axes parallel to each other. Liquid crystals are smectic. [Late 17thC. Via Latin *smecticus*, from Greek *smēktikos*, from *smēkhein* 'to rub, cleanse'.]

smectite /smék tīt/ *n.* any of a group of clay minerals that includes montmorillonite and saponite. These clays swell, or take up liquids between their layers, and are used in ion exchange processes. [Early 19thC. Formed from Greek *smēktis* 'fuller's earth'.]

smeddum /sméddəm/ *n. Scotland* **1.** COMMON SENSE common sense and resourcefulness **2.** FINE DUST fine dust, powder, or flour [Old English *smedena* 'fine flour', of unknown origin]

smegma /smégmə/ *n.* a cheesy secretion of the sebaceous glands that collects under the foreskin or around the clitoris [Early 19thC. Via Latin from Greek *smēgmal* 'soap', from *smēkhein* 'to rub, cleanse'.]

smell /smel/ *v.* (**smells, smelling, smelt** *or* **smelled** /smelt/, **smelt** *or* **smelled**) **1.** *vti.* DETECT BY NOSE to detect or recognize sth by means of sensitive nerves in the nose **2.** *vt.* USE NOSE to use the sensitive nerves in the nose to assess sth ○ *Smell that and see if it's still good.* **3.** *vi.* BE DETECTED WHEN BREATHED IN to seem to be in a particular condition, or give a particular impression, when judged by sb breathing in through the nose ○ *Something smells good.* **4.** *vi.* GIVE UNPLEASANT IMPRESSION to be considered unpleasant when breathed in through the nose **5.** *vi.* GIVE IMPRESSION to give off a suggestion or impression of sth ○ *It smells dangerous.* **6.** *vt.* FEEL OR DETECT to detect the presence or existence of sth, usually sth bad ■ *n.* **1.** SENSE BASED ON NERVES IN NOSE the sense based on the sensitive nerves in the nose that distinguish odours **2.** QUALITY DETECTED BY NOSE the quality of sth that can be detected by the sensitive nerves in the nose **3.** ACT OF SMELLING an act or instance of breathing sth in through the nose in order to make a judgment about it **4.** SUGGESTION OF STH a suggestion or impression of sth [12thC. Origin uncertain.] —**smeller** *n.*

WORD KEY: SYNONYMS

smell, odour, aroma, bouquet, scent, perfume, fragrance, stink, stench, reek

CORE MEANING: the way sth smells

smell is a general word that describes the way sth smells, whether this is neutral, pleasant, or unpleasant; **odour** is a fairly formal word, usually describing either neutral or unpleasant smells; **aroma** is a distinctive pleasant smell, especially one related to cooking or food; **bouquet** is a characteristic pleasant smell, usually associated with fine wines; **scent** is the characteristic smell given off by a particular animal. It is also used to describe a pleasant, sweet smell, for example the smell of flowers; **perfume** is a sweet, pleasant, and heady smell, especially the smell of flowers or plants; **fragrance** is a sweet pleasant smell, especially a delicate or subtle one; **stink** is a strong unpleasant smell; **stench** is a strong unpleasant smell, especially one associated with burning or decay; **reek** is a strong unpleasant smell, especially one associated with people's bodies or homes.

smelling salts *npl.* a mixture of ammonium carbonate and perfume used, especially in the past, to revive sb who felt faint or had become unconscious

smelly /smélli/ (**-ier, -iest**) *adj.* giving off a strong or unpleasant smell —**smelliness** *n.*

smelt[1] /smelt/ (**smelts, smelting, smelted**) *v.* **1.** *vt.* PRODUCE METAL to melt ore in order to get metal from it, or produce metal in this way. The separation of the metal usually requires a chemical change. **2.** *vi.* MELT to undergo fusing or melting in the process of smelting [Mid-16thC. From Middle Low German *smelten*.]

smelt[2] /smelt/ (*plural* **smelts** *or* **smelt**) *n.* a small silvery marine or freshwater fish found in northern waters that has oily flesh and is used extensively for food. Family: Osmeridae. [Old English, of uncertain origin]

smelt[3] past tense, past participle of **smell**

smelter /sméltər/ *n.* **1.** SB WHO SMELTS ORE sb who smelts ore or who owns a factory where ore is smelted **2.** SMELTING APPARATUS OR FACTORY a place where smelting is carried out, or an apparatus used for smelting

smew /smyoo/ (*plural* **smews** *or* **smew**) *n.* a European and Asian duck related to the mergansers that has a hooked serrated bill and, in the male, predominantly white plumage with black markings. Latin name: *Mergus albellus.* [Late 17thC; probably ultimately of prehistoric West Germanic origin]

smidgen /smíjjən/, **smidgin, smidgeon** *n.* a small amount (*informal*) [Mid-19thC. Origin uncertain, perhaps formed from *smitch* 'particle'.]

smilax /smī laks/ *n.* **1.** CLIMBING PLANT a climbing plant of temperate and tropical regions with small white or yellowish flowers, red or bluish-black berries, and in many cases prickly stems. Genus: *Smilax.* **2.** FLORIST'S VINE a South African vine prized by florists for its glossy bright green leaves. Latin name: *Asparagus asparagoides.* [Late 16thC. From Latin, from Greek, 'bindweed'.]

smile /smīl/ *v.* (**smiles, smiling, smiled**) **1.** *vti.* HAVE OR MAKE PLEASANT EXPRESSION to have or make an expression with the corners of the mouth raised, usually expressing amusement, pleasure, or approval **2.** *vi.* HAVE PLEASANT APPEARANCE to appear to be in a state of happiness or enjoying good fortune or pleasure **3.** *vi.* FAVOUR SB to be favourably disposed to sb ○ *Fortune smiled on their journey* **4.** *vt.* EXPRESS STH BY SMILING to express sth by or while smiling ■ *n.* **1.** PLEASANT EXPRESSION a facial expression in which the corners of the mouth are raised, usually expressing amusement, pleasure, or approval **2.** PLEASANT APPEARANCE an appearance of pleasure or approval (*often used in the plural*) **3.** SIGN OF FAVOUR an expression or sign of favour [13thC. Origin uncertain: probably from Scandinavian, from a prehistoric Germanic word that is also the ancestor of English *smirk.*] —**smiler** *n.* —**smilingly** *adv.*

smiley /smíli/ *adj.* (**-ier, -iest**) SMILING smiling or often smiling ■ *n.* (*plural* **-eys**) COMPUT COMPUTER FACE SYMBOL a symbol (**emoticon**), often in the form :-) keyed by a computer user to communicate feelings such as pleasure, approval, or humour

smiley face *n.* **1.** COMPUT = **smiley 2.** CIRCULAR REPRESENTATION OF FACE a round yellow image representing a smiling face, generally consisting of two dots and an upward-curving arc, representing eyes and a mouth

smilodon /smílə don/ *n.* a large sabre-toothed tiger existing during the Pleistocene epoch, between about two million and ten thousand years ago. Genus: *Smilodon.* [Mid-19thC. From modern Latin, literally 'knife-toothed', from Greek *smilē* 'knife'.]

smir /smur/ (**smirs, smirring, smirred**), **smirr** (**smirrs, smirring, smirred**), **smur** (**smurs, smurring, smurred**) *n. Scotland* **1.** FINE RAIN drizzle or very fine rain **2.** *vi.* TO DRIZZLE to be raining very fine rain [Early 19thC. Origin unknown.]

smirch /smurch/ *vt.* (**smirches, smirching, smirched**) **1.** DAMAGE REPUTATION to damage sb's or sth's reputation or good name **2.** DIRTY STH to make sth dirty by smearing or staining it (*archaic or literary*) **3.** SPOIL to spoil or harm sth (*archaic or literary*) ■ *n.* **1.** DIRTY STAIN a dirty stain or smear (*archaic or literary*) **2.** STH DAMAGING sth that damages a reputation [15thC. Origin uncertain: perhaps from Old French *esmorcher* 'to torture'.]

smirk /smurk/ *n.* INSOLENT SMILE an insolent smile expressing feelings such as superiority, self-satisfaction, or conceit ■ *v.* (**smirks, smirking, smirked**) **1.** *vi.* SMILE INSOLENTLY to smile in an insolent, smug, or contemptuous way **2.** *vt.* EXPRESS WITH SMIRK to express sth with a smirk [Old English *smearcian* 'to smile', from a prehistoric Germanic word that is also the ancestor of English *smile*]

smirr *n., vi. Scotland* = **smir**

smit *v.* past tense of **smite** (*archaic or literary*)

smite /smīt/ (**smites, smiting, smote** *or* **smit** /smit/, **smitten** /smítt'n/) *v.* **1.** *vti.* HIT HARD to hit sb or sth hard (*regional archaic or literary*) **2.** *vt.* AFFECT OR AFFLICT to affect sb strongly or disastrously, or afflict sb with sth (*archaic or literary; often passive*) **3.** *vt.* FILL SB WITH LOVE to fill sb with love or longing (*humorous or archaic or literary; usually passive*) [Old English *smītan* 'to smear, pollute', from prehistoric Germanic] —**smiter** *n.*

smith /smith/ *n.* **1.** METAL WORKER sb who repairs and fashions metal objects **2.** = **blacksmith** [Old English *smiþ*, from a prehistoric Germanic word meaning 'coppersmith']

Smith /smith/, **Adam** (1723–90) British philosopher and economist. He articulated his theory of free trade in *The Wealth of Nations* (1776).

Smith, Bernard William (*b.* 1916) Australian art historian. He wrote *European Vision and the South Pacific* (1960).

Smith, Bessie (1894–1937) US singer. The leading blues singer of her day, she recorded widely with major jazz bands. Known as **Empress of the Blues**

Smith, Dick (*b.* 1944) Australian entrepreneur and aviator. In 1983 he became the first person to fly round the world solo by helicopter. Real name **Richard Harold Smith**

Smith, Grace Cossington (1892–1985) Australian painter. She was a modernist artist noted for post-impressionist works such as *The Lacquer Room* (1935).

Smith, Harvey (*b.* 1938) British showjumper. He was many times winner of the British Grand Prix and other championships, and a member of the British Olympic team (1968 and 1972). Full name **Robert Harvey Smith**

Smith, Joseph (1805–44) US religious leader. He was the visionary founder of the Church of the Latter-Day Saints (1830). Amid local controversy, he established communities in Missouri and Illinois. He was killed by a mob opposed to his philosophy.

Smith, Dame Maggie (*b.* 1934) British actor. Her work in classical theatre was complemented by her comedy performances and extensive film appearances. Real name **Dame Margaret Nathalie Smith**

Smith, Stevie (1902–71) British poet and novelist. Her works include the autobiographical *Novel on Yellow Paper* (1936) and collections of sharp, wry verse such as *Not Waving but Drowning* (1957). Her *Collected Poems* (1975) were published posthumously. Real name **Florence Margaret Smith**

Dame Maggie Smith

smithereens /ˌsmíthə reénz/ *npl.* very small broken pieces (*informal*) [Early 19thC. Origin uncertain: probably formed from Irish *smidirín*, literally 'small fragment', from *smiodar* 'fragment'.]

smithery /smíthəri/ (*plural* **-ies**) *n.* **1.** SMITH'S WORK the work or craft of a smith **2.** = **smithy** *n.*

Smithsonian Institution /smith sóni ən-/, **Smithsonian** *n.* a government trust founded in Washington, D.C., by an act of congress in 1846 to promote research and education. It sponsors scientific research and publications and maintains the national collections. The fourteen museums it administers include the National Museum of American History and the National Air and Space Museum in Washington, D.C., and the National Museum of the Native American in New York City. [Early 19thC. Named after James L. M. *Smithson* (1765–1829), British chemist and mineralogist who endowed the institution.]

smithsonite /smíthsə nīt/ *n.* a white or yellow to brown zinc carbonate mineral, an important ore of zinc. The honeycombed variety of smithsonite is also known as dry-bone ore. Formula: $ZnCO_3$. [Mid-19thC. Named after James L. M. *Smithson* (see SMITHSONIAN INSTITUTION).]

smithy /smíthi/ (*plural* **-ies**) *n.* the place where a blacksmith works

smitten past participle of **smite**

smock /smok/ *n.* **1.** LOOSE DRESS a loose dress for a child or woman with the cloth gathered at the chest **2.** OVERSHIRT a loose garment worn to protect the clothes **3.** UNDERGARMENT a woman's loose-fitting undergarment or chemise of a type used until the 18th century ■ *vt.* (**smocks, smocking, smocked**) SEW WITH GATHERING STITCHES to sew or decorate sth with decorative gathering stitches [Old English *smoc*, from a prehistoric Germanic word meaning 'to creep'. The underlying idea is of a garment that you put on by creeping into it.]

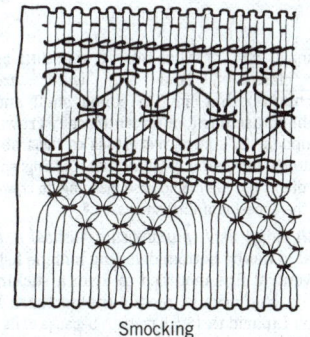

Smocking

smocking /smóking/ *n.* decorative stitching in a honeycomb or zigzag pattern, used to gather fabric evenly

smog /smog/ *n.* a mixture of fog and smoke or other airborne pollutants such as exhaust fumes [Early 20thC. Blend of SMOKE and FOG.] —**smoggy** *adj.*

smoke /smōk/ *n.* **1.** CLOUD OF TINY PARTICLES a mass of tiny particles in the air that rises up from sth burning **2.** VAPOUR RESEMBLING SMOKE sth that resembles smoke, usually consisting of minute particles suspended in a gas ○ *a white, stinging smoke of chemical fumes* **3.** INHALING OF BURNING TOBACCO FUMES an act of smoking a cigarette, cigar, or pipe **4.** CIGARETTE a cigarette or

other tobacco product (*informal*) **5.** SMOKABLE SUBSTANCE sth that can be smoked (*informal*) **6.** STH THAT OBSCURES sth that obscures or obstructs information, understanding, or awareness **7.** STH TRANSIENT sth transient or illusory **8.** COLOURS GREY COLOUR a grey colour with a tinge of blue or brown ■ *v.* (**smokes, smoking, smoked**) **1.** *vti.* USE TOBACCO to have the habit of inhaling the smoke of burning tobacco in cigarettes, cigars or pipes **2.** *vti.* INHALE VAPOURS to inhale the smoke of any substance that can burn and be inhaled **3.** *vi.* GIVE OFF SMOKE to give off smoke, often in a way that indicates some malfunction **4.** *vt.* FOOD CURE FOOD WITH SMOKE to cure or treat food such as meat, fish, or cheese with wood smoke **5.** *vt.* FUMIGATE WITH SMOKE to fumigate, clean, or clear sth with smoke **6.** *vt.* CRAFT DARKEN to darken sth to give it the colour of smoke **7.** *vt.* STUPEFY STH to stupefy sth with smoke ■ *adj.* GREYISH of a grey colour tinged with blue or brown [Old English *smoca*, from prehistoric Germanic. Its use as a verb in connection with tobacco is first recorded in the early 17thC.] —**smokable** *adj.* ◇ **go up in smoke 1.** to be destroyed by burning **2.** to fail completely to happen as planned or hoped

smoke out *vt.* **1.** DRIVE FROM HIDING to drive sb or sth from a hiding place by using smoke **2.** BRING TO LIGHT to bring sth to light by clever or assertive inquiry

smoke alarm *n.* a device intended to give a warning of fire by triggering an alarm when it detects the presence of smoke

smoke bomb *n.* a device that gives off dense clouds of irritating chemical smoke, used to drive people or animals out of a place

smoked rubber *n.* crude rubber prepared by drying coagulated latex sheets in smokehouses before they are packed into bales. The smoking process hinders the formation of bacteria and moulds and aids in the preservation of the rubber against oxidation.

smokehouse /smōk howss/ (*plural* **-houses** /-howziz/) *n.* a small building where meat, fish, or other materials are cured in smoke

smokejack /smōk jak/ *n.* a device that turns a roasting spit and is powered by rising gases in a chimney

smokeless /smōkləss/ *adj.* **1.** PRODUCING NO SMOKE producing little or no smoke **2.** ALLOWING NO SMOKE used to describe an area where smoke, e.g. from coal fires, is not permitted

smokeless powder *n.* a nitrocellulose-based explosive or propellant that produces little smoke

smokeless zone *n.* an area in which only smokeless fuels can be burned

smoker /smōkər/ *n.* **1.** SB WHO SMOKES sb who smokes tobacco or another substance **2.** RAIL RAILWAY CARRIAGE DESIGNATED FOR SMOKING a railway compartment where smoking is permitted **3.** COOK APPARATUS FOR SMOKING FOOD an apparatus for smoking food in **4.** GATHERING OF MEN a social gathering of men

smoker's cough *n.* a hacking cough, often accompanied by phlegm, caused by excessive smoking

smoke screen *n.* **1.** MIL SMOKE HIDING STH a mass of smoke produced to conceal the movements of ships, troops, or equipment **2.** ACTION INTENDED TO OBSCURE an action taken to mislead sb or obscure sth

smokestack /smōk stak/ *n.* **1.** *US* = **chimney 2.** TALL INDUSTRIAL CHIMNEY a tall, often cylindrical industrial chimney, often attached to a factory

smokestack industry (*plural* **smokestack industries**) *n.* any industry characterized by large factories, heavy equipment, high energy consumption, and usually pollution of the environment

smoke tree *n.* a shrub or small tree whose clusters of small flowers resemble puffs of smoke. Genus: *Cotinus.*

smoking compartment *n.* = **smoker** *n.* 2

smoking jacket *n.* a loose-fitting jacket made of a rich fabric such as velvet or silk, worn in the past by men while smoking

smoking room *n.* a room designated for people to smoke in

smoko /smōkō/ (*plural* **-kos**) *n. ANZ* a short break from work to drink, smoke, or have a rest (*informal*) [Mid-19thC. Formed from SMOKE, from the idea of having a cigarette while on a break.]

Smoking jacket

smoky /smōki/ (**-ier, -iest**) *adj.* **1.** FILLED WITH SMOKE filled with smoke, or smelling as if it had been filled with smoke **2.** COLOURS COLOURED LIKE SMOKE of a grey colour, like smoke **3.** FOOD TASTING OF SMOKE having or suggesting a taste imparted by smoke or an open flame **4.** GIVING OFF EXCESSIVE SMOKE giving off smoke, especially excessively **5.** AFFECTED BY SMOKE discoloured or marked with smoke —**smokily** *adv.* —**smokiness** *n.*

smoky quartz *n.* = **cairngorm**

smolder *vi., n.* US = **smoulder**

Smolensk /smo lénsk/ city in western Russia, on the River Dnieper. It is the capital of Smolensk Oblast. Population: 350,000 (1991).

smolt /smōlt/ *n.* a young salmon before it has swum to the sea. It is characterized by physiological changes in preparation for living in salt water, such as silver coloration. [15thC. Origin uncertain.]

smooch /smooch/ *v.* (**smooches, smooching, smooched**) (*informal*) **1.** *vti.* TO KISS to kiss and caress sb **2.** *vi.* DANCE INTIMATELY to dance slowly and closely ■ *n.* (*informal*) **1.** KISS an instance of kissing and cuddling **2.** SLOW DANCING a period of slow, intimate dancing in which a couple hold each other closely [Mid-20thC. An imitation of the sound of kissing.] —**smoochy** *adj.*

smooth /smooth/ *adj.* **1.** NOT ROUGH OR BUMPY not having a rough or uneven surface **2.** WITHOUT LUMPS without lumps or pieces of solid matter ○ *Beat the mixture to a smooth paste.* **3.** WITHOUT UPHEAVAL OR DIFFICULTIES proceeding without interruption, upheaval, or problems **4.** WITHOUT JERKS OR JOLTS in a steady flowing motion, without jolts or interruptions **5.** NOT HARSH without harshness **6.** NOT SHARP OR SOUR not tasting sharp or sour **7.** NOT EASILY UPSET not easily ruffled or upset ○ *a smooth and serene personality* **8.** INSINCERELY CONVINCING using insincere flattery and pleasantness, especially in order to persuade sb to do sth **9.** HAIRLESS without a beard or moustache ○ *a smooth-faced young man* **10.** FRICTIONLESS offering no apparent resistance to sliding **11.** PHON UNASPIRATED spoken without audible breath ■ *vt.* (**smoothes, smoothing, smoothed**) **1.** EVEN OUT ROUGHNESS to remove bumps, unevenness, or roughness **2.** PRESS OUT CREASES to remove lines and creases **3.** MAKE CREAMY to remove lumps from sth **4.** REMOVE DIFFICULTIES to remove obstacles and difficulties ○ *Influential allies smoothed his path to power.* **5.** LESSEN BAD FEELINGS to remove or lessen bad feeling or disagreement between people ○ *I tried to smooth things over with her.* **6.** STATS REMOVE IRREGULARITIES FROM DATA to modify a sequential set of numerical data by reducing the differences in magnitude between adjacent numbers **7.** PHYS, ELEC ENG REMOVE IRREGULARITIES IN CURRENT to remove the slight irregularities (**ripples**) in a rectified current ■ *adv.* WITHOUT PROBLEMS without problems or difficulties ○ *The path of true love never runs smooth.* ■ *n.* **1.** ACT OF SMOOTHING the action of smoothing sth **2.** STH SMOOTH a smooth part of sth [Old English *smōþ*, of unknown origin] —**smoothable** *adj.* —**smoother** *n.* —**smoothly** *adv.* —**smoothness** *n.*

smooth down *vti.* to make sth flat by a smoothing action, or become flat by being smoothed

smooth out *vti.* **1.** MAKE OR BECOME SMOOTH to make sth smooth, or become smooth, by the removal of lines and creases **2.** MAKE OR BECOME EASIER to make sth easier or calmer, or become easier or calmer, after a period of difficulty

smooth over *vt.* to remove or lessen difficulties or tensions

smoothbore /smooth bawr/ *adj.* SMOOTH IN INTERIOR OF BARREL having a barrel with no ridges or grooves in the bore. Early firearms and modern shotguns and mortars are characterized by smooth bores. ■ *n.* SMOOTHBORE GUN a gun with a smooth surface inside its barrel

smooth breathing *n.* a mark " written over some initial Greek vowels to show that they are not aspirated. ◊ **rough breathing**

smooth collie *n.* a dog belonging to a breed of collie with a thick short-haired coat

smoothen /smooth'n/ (-ens, -ening, -ened) *vti.* to make sth smooth, or become smooth

smooth hound *n.* any of several small sharks. Genus: *Mustelus.*

smoothie /smoothi/ *n.* **1.** smoothie, smoothy (*plural* -ies) CHARMING MAN an attractive and charming man perceived as being insincere (*informal*) **2.** BEVERAGES MILK SHAKE a drink similar to a milk shake made with fruit, cream, or milk, and ice cream

smoothing circuit *n.* a circuit used to remove the alternating current component from a direct current power source

smooth muscle *n.* a type of muscle functioning involuntarily and made up of layers of spindle-shaped cells lacking cross striations. It is found in the viscera, e.g. the stomach and bladder. Smooth muscle functions by slow contraction, and is not under voluntary control. It is activated by the autonomic nervous system, hormones, and drugs.

smooth snake *n.* a brownish European snake with dark markings and small, smooth scales. Latin name: *Coronella austriaca.*

smooth-spoken *adj.* speaking or spoken in a gentle and agreeable way

smooth-tongued *adj.* speaking or spoken skilfully and persuasively

smoothy *n.* = **smoothie** *n.* 1 (*informal*)

smorgasbord /smáwrgəss bawrd/ *n.* **1.** BUFFET MEAL a meal served buffet style, consisting of a large variety of hot and cold dishes **2.** VARIETY a wide variety [Late 19thC. From Swedish *smörgåsbord* (see SMEAR).]

smote past tense of **smite**

smother /smúthər/ *v.* (-ers, -ering, -ered) **1.** *vti.* ALLOW OR GET TOO LITTLE AIR to deprive sb or sth of air, or be deprived of air **2.** *vti.* SUFFOCATE to kill sb or sth, or die, by suffocation **3.** *vti.* OVERWHELM WITH AFFECTION to give sb too much love or affection with the effect that he or she feels restricted **4.** *vti.* PUT OUT OR BE PUT OUT to extinguish sth such as a fire, or go out from lack of oxygen **5.** *vt.* SUPPRESS OR HIDE to suppress or hide the expression of sth **6.** *vt.* COVER THICKLY to cover sth with a thick layer of sth else ■ *n.* **1.** DENSE SMOKE dense smoke or gas **2.** THICK COATING a thick coating of sth [12thC. Formed from Old English *smorian* 'to suffocate, choke (with smoke)'.] —**smotherer** *n.* —**smotheringly** *adv.* —**smothery** *adj.*

smothered mate *n.* checkmate resulting when a surrounded king is unable to move and thus escape a threatening knight

smoulder *vi.* (-ders, -dering, -dered) **1.** BURN SLOWLY to burn slowly and gently, usually with some smoke but without a flame **2.** HAVE SUPPRESSED EMOTION to have or show a strong emotion that is suppressed but liable to flare up at any time **3.** EXIST IN BACKGROUND to exist in the background, liable to appear or reappear at any moment ■ *n.* **1.** THICK SMOKE thick smoke from a slow-burning fire **2.** SMOKY FIRE a slow-burning fire [From Old English *smorian* 'to smoke, suffocate']

smout /smowt/, **smowt** *n. Scotland* a small person, especially a young child [Variant of SMOLT]

SMP *abbr.* statutory maternity pay

smriti /smrítti/ *n.* a group of Hindu scriptures giving instruction on social and domestic matters

SMTP *n.* the main protocol used to send electronic mail on the Internet, consisting of rules for how programs sending mail should interact with programs receiving mail. Full form **Simple Mail Transfer Protocol**

smudge /smuj/ *n.* **1.** SMEARED INK OR PAINT a patch of smeared ink or paint blurring what has been written or painted **2.** DIRTY MARK a dirty or greasy mark **3.** INDISTINCT AREA sth visible but blurred or indistinct and not easily identifiable **4.** *US, Can* AGRIC SMOKE OR FIRE smoke produced to protect trees from frost or insect damage, or a fire that produces such smoke ■ *v.* (smudges, smudging, smudged) **1.** *vti.* SMEAR OR BE SMEARED to smear or blur sth by rubbing it, or become smeared or blurred by being rubbed **2.** *vti.* MAKE OR BECOME DIRTY to smear sth, or become smeared, with dirt or grease **3.** *vt. US, Can* AGRIC PROTECT WITH SMOKE to fill an orchard with smoke to protect the trees from frost or insects [15thC. Origin unknown.] —**smudgily** *adv.* —**smudginess** *n.* —**smudgy** *adj.*

smug /smug/ (smugger, smuggest) *adj.* conceited and self-satisfied [Mid-16thC. Origin uncertain: perhaps ultimately from Low German *smuk* 'pretty', from Middle Low German *smucken* 'to adorn'.] —**smugly** *adv.* —**smugness** *n.*

smuggle /smúgg'l/ (-gles, -gling, -gled) *v.* **1.** *vti.* BRING INTO A COUNTRY ILLEGALLY to carry goods into a country secretly because they are illegal or in order to avoid paying duty on them **2.** *vt.* TAKE OR BRING SECRETLY to take, bring, or carry sb or sth secretly into or out of a place [Late 17thC. From Low German *smukkelen* or Dutch *smokkelen*, of uncertain origin: perhaps literally 'to sneak repeatedly', formed from a word.] —**smuggler** *n.*

smurf /smurf/ (smurfs, smurfing, smurfed) *vi.* to route data to a computer or a network of computers in such a way as to flood the target's machine or system with messages, causing a crash (*slang*) [Late 20thC. From *Smurf* the name of a children's tiny blue toy; money laundering sense dates to 1985; computer hacking sense, to 1999.]

smut /smut/ *n.* **1.** OBSCENE MATERIAL obscene jokes, stories, or pictures **2.** SMALL PIECE OF SOOT a speck of dirt or soot **3.** BOT PLANT DISEASE a plant disease, especially of cereals and other grasses, caused by fungi and characterized by sooty black masses of spores forming on leaves and other parts **4.** FUNGUS BEARING DISEASE a parasitic fungus that causes smut. Order: Ustilaginales. ■ *v.* (smuts, smutting, smutted) **1.** *vt.* MAKE DIRTY to mark or dirty sth with smuts **2.** *vi.* BOT BECOME AFFECTED WITH SMUT to become affected with smut [15thC. Ultimately from prehistoric Germanic. Its original meaning was 'to debase, defile'.]

smutch /smuch/ *n.* SMUDGE a smudge of sth dirty or greasy ■ *vt.* (smutches, smutching, smutched) MARK WITH A SMUDGE to mark sth with a smudge of sth dirty or greasy [Mid-16thC. Origin uncertain: perhaps thought to suggest a dirty mark.] —**smutchy** *adj.*

Smuts /smutss, smötss/, **Jan** (1870–1950) South African statesman and general. He was instrumental in forming the Union of South Africa (1910), and as prime minister (1919–24, 1939–48) was sometimes unpopular for his pro-British policies. Full name **Jan Christiaan Smuts**

smutty /smútti/ (-tier, -tiest) *adj.* **1.** OBSCENE obscene or pornographic (*informal*) **2.** MARKED WITH SMUTS covered with sooty marks of dirt **3.** BOT AFFECTED BY SMUT affected by the disease smut —**smuttily** *adv.* —**smuttiness** *n.*

Smyrna /smúrnə/ former name for **Izmir**

Smyth /smith/, **Dame Ethel Mary** (1858–1944) British composer and social reformer. She composed numerous works, and her six operas, written to her own libretti, contributed to the establishment of British opera. She campaigned for women's right to vote.

Sn *symbol.* tin

SN *abbr.* Senegal (international vehicle registration)

SNA *abbr.* COMPUT systems network architecture

snack /snak/ *n.* **1.** SMALL MEAL a small meal of prepared or easy-to-prepare food eaten in place of a regular meal or between regular meals **2.** FOOD FOR SNACK any sort of food suitable for eating between meals or instead of a main meal ■ *vi.* (snacks, snacking, snacked) EAT BETWEEN MEALS to eat between the times that meals are usually served, or eat a snack instead of a main meal ○ *I've been snacking all afternoon.* [15thC. From Middle Dutch *snac* 'bite'.]

snack bar *n.* a small restaurant or food outlet that sells snacks

snaffle /snáff'l/ *n.* **snaffle, snaffle bit** EQU BIT FOR HORSES a bit for a horse that is jointed in the middle and has rings on either end where the reins are attached ■ *vt.* (-fles, -fling, -fled) **1.** STEAL to steal or take sth, usually sth relatively unimportant (*informal*) **2.** EQU FIT WITH BIT to fit a horse or pony with a snaffle bit [Mid-16thC. Formed from a Low Dutch word. The early 18thC meaning 'to steal' may be a different word.]

snafu /sna foo/ *n.* BAD SITUATION CAUSED BY INCOMPETENCE a mishap or mistake generally caused by incompetence and resulting in delay or confusion (*informal*) ■ *vti.* (-fus, -fuing, -fued) *US* SPOIL OR BE SPOILED to cause a situation or process to become confused or delayed, generally by incompetence, or become confused or delayed (*informal*) [Mid-20thC. Originally a US military acronym formed from the initial letters of 'situation normal all fouled up'.]

snag /snag/ *n.* **1.** SMALL PROBLEM a minor problem or obstacle to progress **2.** UNWANTED SHARP POINT a sharp projection on which sth may catch and tear **3.** HOLE IN FABRIC a hole or loose thread in a fabric resulting from catching it on sth sharp **4.** SHIPPING NAVIGATIONAL OBSTRUCTION an object underwater, e.g. a tree stump, that may obstruct boats **5.** *ANZ* SAUSAGE a sausage (*slang*) ■ *v.* (snags, snagging, snagged) **1.** *vti.* CATCH ON A SNAG to catch on or collide with a sharp projection ○ *snagged my sleeve on a nail* **2.** *vt. US* OBSTRUCT to obstruct the progress of sth **3.** *vt. US* OBTAIN to obtain by luck, skilful manoeuvre, or both **4.** *vt. US* CLEAR OF OBSTRUCTIONS to clear a river or lake of underwater obstructions **5.** *vi. US* MEET A PROBLEM to come up against a problem or obstacle that deters progress **6.** *vi.* GET TANGLED to become tangled or entangled [Late 16thC. Origin uncertain: probably from Scandinavian.] —**snaggy** *adj.*

snaggletooth /snágg'l tooth/ (*plural* -teeth /-teeth/) *n.* a broken, projecting, or crooked tooth [Early 19thC. Snaggle: literally 'to snag repeatedly', formed from SNAG.] —**snaggletoothed** *adj.*

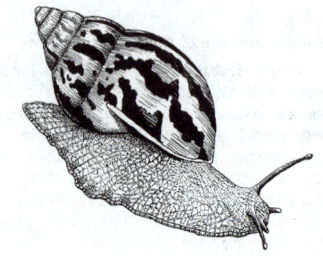

Snail

snail /snayl/ *n.* **1.** CRAWLING CREATURE WITH SHELL any of a large class of land and water creatures (**gastropods**) that have a coiled shell and a retractable muscular foot on which they crawl. Class: Gastropoda. **2.** SLOW-MOVING PERSON OR THING sb or sth that moves very slowly (*informal*) [Old English *snægel*, from a prehistoric Germanic base meaning 'to crawl', which is also the ancestor of English *snake*]

snailfish /snáyl fish/ (*plural* -fish or -fishes) *n.* a small elongated flabby bottom-dwelling marine fish, often with ventral fins modified to form a sucking disc, found in cold oceans, mostly the northern Pacific. Family: Liparidae. [Snail perhaps because of its soft and oily texture]

snail mail *n.* mail sent through the postal service, as distinct from the faster electronic mail (*informal*)

snail's pace *n.* a speed that is thought unbearably or unaccountably slow —**snail-paced** *adj.*

snake /snayk/ *n.* **1.** LEGLESS REPTILE a legless reptile with a scaly tubular body tapering toward the tail, lidless eyes, and often venomous fangs. Suborder: Serpentes. **2.** OFFENSIVE TERM an offensive term that deliberately insults sb's reliability and honesty, especially in personal dealings **3.** PLUMBER'S TOOL a plumber's tool consisting of a long flexible wire that can be inserted into and rotated inside drains to unblock them **4.** FIN EC CURRENCY RESTRICTION a system in the past restricting the amount by which the values of the currencies of EC countries were allowed to vary against each other ■ *v.* (**snakes, snaking, snaked**) **1.** *vi.* MOVE LIKE SNAKE to move or lie like a snake, with many bends or twists **2.** *vt. US* DRAG to drag sth by a rope or chain **3.** *vt. US* TUG to pull or jerk sth suddenly [Old English *snaca*, from a prehistoric Germanic word meaning 'to crawl', which is also the ancestor of English *snail*] ◇ **a snake in the grass** sb who betrays or deceives others

snakebird /snáyk burd/ *n.* = **darter**

snakebite /snáyk bīt/ *n.* **1.** BITE OF A SNAKE the bite of a poisonous snake, or illness resulting from this **2.** ALCOHOLIC DRINK an alcoholic drink that is a mixture of cider and lager

snake charmer *n.* an entertainer who elicits a swaying movement from snakes, especially cobras, by means of music and rhythmic body movements

snake dance *n.* a ritual dance of some Native North American peoples in which live snakes are handled

snake fly *n.* an insect with a small head and long prothorax. Family: Raphidiidae.

snakehead /snáyk hed/ *n.* any of a group of tropical freshwater African or Asian fish that have a protruding lower jaw and are able to breathe air for long periods of time. Family: Channidae.

snake lizard *n.* a legless lizard found in Australia and New Guinea, not easily distinguished from a snake except that its tongue is flat and fleshy like a lizard's. Family: Pygopodidae.

snakeroot /snáyk root/ *n.* a plant with roots used in folk medicine to treat snakebite, or the root of any of these plants used as medicine

snakes and ladders *n.* a game played on a board marked out with squares and with a number of snakes and ladders printed on it, in which players move counters towards the finishing point. Players may climb a ladder to a point closer to the finish, but must go down a snake to a square closer to the starting point.

snake's head *n.* a European plant that grows in damp areas with drooping, purplish, chequered flowers. Latin name: *Fritillaria meleagris.*

snakeskin /snáyk skin/ *n.* **1.** SNAKE'S SKIN the skin of a snake **2.** LEATHER MADE OF SNAKES' SKINS the skin of a snake or snakes made into leather, e.g. for shoes

snakeweed /snáyk weed/ *n.* a plant used in folk medicine to cure snakebite, especially bistort

snaky /snáyki/ (**-ier, -iest**) *adj.* **1.** RESEMBLING A SNAKE resembling a snake in being long and narrow with bends or coils, or like a snake's twisting and turning movements **2.** TREACHEROUS treacherous and deceitful —**snakily** *adv.* —**snakiness** *n.*

snap /snap/ *v.* (**snaps, snapping, snapped**) **1.** *vti.* BREAK WITH SHARP NOISE to break or break sth suddenly with a sharp cracking sound **2.** *vti.* DO STH WITH A SHARP NOISE to move, strike, or operate sth in a way that makes a sharp noise **3.** *vti.* BREAK to break under force or pressure, or break sth by excessive force or pressure **4.** *vi.* LOSE CONTROL to lose control or erupt in anger suddenly **5.** *vti.* SPEAK ANGRILY to say sth or reply in anger or irritation **6.** *vt.* PHOTOGRAPHY TAKE A PHOTOGRAPH to take a photograph of sb or sth, especially in a casual way (*informal*) **7.** *vi.* BITE to bite or try to bite sb or sth with a quick movement or movements **8.** *vti. US* TAKE STH to take or grasp sth eagerly, or take sth away from sb suddenly **9.** *vti.* MOVE SHARPLY to move or be moved quickly and sharply **10.** *vi.* APPEAR ANGRY to flash, especially in anger (*refers to eyes*) **11.** *vt. US* FLICK STH AWAY to flick sth away with a finger coming forward sharply from the thumb **12.** *vt.* FOOTBALL PLAY THE BALL in American football, to put the ball into play by passing it back to the quarterback behind the line of scrimmage ■ *n.* **1.** SHARP SOUND a short sharp sound, e.g. of sth brittle suddenly breaking or of sth clicking shut **2.** SHORT TIME a short period of time, especially one with cold weather ○ *a sudden cold snap* **3.** FOOD SWEET BISCUIT a crisp, thin sweet biscuit **4.** CARDS CARD GAME a game where players lay cards face up in a pile. When two identical cards are played one after the other, the first player to shout 'snap' takes the pile. The object of the game is to win the whole pack of cards. **5.** PHOTOGRAPHY = **snapshot** *n.* 1 **6.** LIVELINESS liveliness and vigour ○ *His campaign needs more snap.* **7.** *US* = **press stud 8.** *US* STH EASY sth easily done ○ *The test was a snap.* **9.** *N England* SNACK a meal or snack, especially a packed lunch (*informal*) **10.** FOOTBALL FOOTBALL PLAY in American football, the action required to start play in football, when the ball is passed to the quarterback behind the line of scrimmage ■ *adj.* **1.** DECIDED WITHOUT REFLECTION arrived at quickly and without reflection ○ *a snap decision* **2.** COMING WITHOUT WARNING coming suddenly and without warning **3.** OPERATING WITH A SHARP SOUND operating with interlocking parts that snap when being shut **4.** *US* EASILY DONE easily done with success ■ *adv.* WITH A SNAP so as to make a sharp sound ■ *interj.* NOTING TWO IDENTICAL THINGS used to acknowledge or draw attention to the simultaneous presence of two identical things or people, and also in the game of snap when attempting to win cards [15thC. Partly an imitation of the sound, and partly from Middle Dutch *snappen* 'to seize' (source of English *snack*).]

snap up *vt.* to quickly buy or take up sth offered or available

snap bean *n. US* an edible bean with long tubular pods that are harvested and eaten when immature [*Snap* either from its crispness, or because the pods are broken into pieces before being cooked]

snap-brim, snap-brim hat *n. US* a man's hat with a flexible brim all around that is usually turned up at the back and down at the front

Snapdragon

snapdragon /snáp dragən/ *n.* a common perennial plant with spikes of flowers of various colours. Genus: *Antirrhinum.* [Late 16thC. So called because the flowers are said to be similar to a dragon's mouth.]

snap link *n.* = **karabiner**

snapper /snáppər/ *n.* **1.** (*plural* **-pers** *or* **-per**) TROPICAL FOOD FISH a carnivorous fish common in tropical waters and caught for food. Family: Lutjanidae. **2.** (*plural* **-pers** *or* **-per**) AUSTRALIAN FOOD FISH a fish found in Australian and New Zealand waters, that has a reddish body with bright blue spots and is much sought after by anglers. Latin name: *Chrysophrys auratus.* **3.** = **snapping turtle 4.** STH THAT SNAPS sb who or sth that snaps

snapping beetle *n. US* = **click beetle**

snapping turtle *n.* a North American freshwater turtle with a large head and powerful hooked jaws. Family: Chelydridae.

snappish /snáppish/ *adj.* **1.** SHOWING IRRITATION showing a sharpness or curtness caused by irritation or impatience **2.** TENDING TO SNAP inclined to snap at things —**snappishly** *adv.* —**snappishness** *n.*

snappy /snáppi/ (**-pier, -piest**) *adj.* **1.** SHOWING IMPATIENCE expressing or showing impatience or irritation **2.** INTERESTING interesting and to the point, or able to write sth interesting and to the point (*informal*) **3.** HASTY done or produced without delay **4.** STYLISH fashionable and stylish (*informal*) ○ *a snappy dresser* —**snappily** *adv.* —**snappiness** *n.* ◇ **make it snappy** to do sth quickly (*informal*)

snap ring *n.* = **karabiner**

snap roll *n.* an aerial manoeuvre in which an aeroplane turns a complete circle longitudinally while maintaining altitude and direction of flight

snapshot /snáp shot/ *n.* **1.** PHOTOGRAPHY PHOTOGRAPH a photograph, especially one taken by an amateur with simple equipment **2.** RECORD OF POINT IN PROCESS a record or view of a particular point in a sequence of events or continuing process [Early 19thC. Originally meaning 'quick shot from a gun', the sense was extended to 'casual photograph' at the end of the 19thC.]

snare[1] /snair/ *n.* **1.** ANIMAL TRAP a trap for small animals that operates like a noose **2.** TRAP FOR UNWARY a situation that is both alluring and dangerous **3.** SURG SURGICAL DEVICE a surgical instrument for removing small polyps and tumours by means of a noose that is tightened by being pulled into a narrow tube ■ *vt.* (**snares, snaring, snared**) **1.** CATCH IN TRAP to catch sb or sth in a snare **2.** ENTRAP SB to entrap sb by alluring deception [Pre-12thC. From Old Norse *snara.* Ultimately from an Indo-European word meaning 'to twist', which is also the ancestor of English *narcotic*.] —**snarer** *n.*

snare[2] /snair/ *n.* any of the gut or wire cords stretched across the bottom skin of a drum to create a rattling sound when the drum is hit (*often used in the plural*) [Late 17thC. Origin uncertain: probably from Dutch *snaar* 'string'.]

snare drum *n.* a drum fitted with snares to produce a rattling effect

Snares Islands /snáirz-/ group of uninhabited islands situated 100 km/62 mi south of Stewart Island, New Zealand. They are home to several large bird colonies. Area: 39 sq. km/15 sq. mi.

snarl[1] /snaarl/ *v.* (**snarls, snarling, snarled**) **1.** *vi.* GROWL to growl threateningly **2.** *vti.* SPEAK ANGRILY to speak or say sth angrily or threateningly ■ *n.* GROWLING NOISE the sound of sb or sth snarling [Late 16thC. Literally 'to 'snar' repeatedly', formed from obsolete *snar* 'to snarl, growl', of uncertain origin: probably ultimately an imitation of the sound.] —**snarler** *n.* —**snarlingly** *adv.*

snarl up *vti.* to become, or make sth such as traffic, complicated, confused, or too congested to move (*often passive*) US term **snarl**

snarl[2] /snaarl/ *n.* **1.** TANGLE a tangled mass of sth such as hair or wool **2.** KNOT IN WOOD a knot in wood **3.** *US* = **snarl-up** ■ *vti.* (**snarls, snarling, snarled**) **1.** TANGLE STH to tangle sth or become tangled **2.** *US* = **snarl up** [14thC. Origin uncertain: probably literally 'small snare', formed from SNARE[1]. Its orginal meaning was 'moral snare, temptation'.]

snarl-up *n.* a tangle of objects, especially a traffic jam. US term **snarl**

snatch /snach/ *vt.* (**snatches, snatching, snatched**) **1.** TAKE QUICKLY to grab or grasp sb or sth hastily **2.** MOVE STH QUICKLY to move or remove sth quickly **3.** TAKE WHEN OPPORTUNITY ARISES to take or get sth while there is an opportunity ○ *snatched a few hours of sleep* **4.** *US* KIDNAP to kidnap sb (*informal*) ■ *n.* **1.** GRABBING an instance of grabbing or grasping sb or sth **2.** SMALL AMOUNT a small, incomplete bit or short period of sth **3.** THEFT an act of stealing (*informal*) **4.** *US* KIDNAPPING an act of kidnapping (*informal*) **5.** LIFTING FEAT a weight-lifting feat in which the barbell is raised from the floor to over the lifter's head in one motion **6.** *US* OFFENSIVE TERM a highly offensive term referring to the outer sexual organs of a woman (*taboo offensive*) [12thC. Origin uncertain: perhaps from Middle Dutch *snacken* 'to snatch, chatter'.] —**snatcher** *n.*

snatch block *n.* a block that can be opened on one side to insert a rope, thereby avoiding the necessity of threading the rope through from one end

snatch squad *n.* a group of soldiers or police officers trained to single out and seize the apparent ringleaders in situations of public disorder

snatchy /snáchi/ (**-ier, -iest**) *adj.* occurring or done in short spells

snath /snath/, **snathe** /snay*th*/ *n.* the handle of a scythe [Late 16thC. Variant of *snead*, from Old English *snǣd*, of unknown origin.]

snazzy /snázzi/ (**-zier, -ziest**) *adj.* attractively new, bright, or fashionable (*informal*) [Mid-20thC. Origin unknown.]

SNCF *n.* Société Nationale des Chemins de Fer, the rail system in France

sneak /sneek/ *v.* (**sneaks, sneaking, sneaked** *or* **snuck** /snuk/) **1.** *vi.* GO STEALTHILY to go or act in a stealthy, secretive way **2.** *vt.* DO STH FURTIVELY to do sth stealthily, furtively, and without being noticed ○ *He sneaked a look over the wall.* **3.** *vt.* BRING STEALTHILY to get or carry sb or sth secretly, furtively, and without being noticed ○ *sneak friends into the house for a surprise party* **4.** *vi.* TELL TALES to tell sb about sth wrong that sb else has done ■ *n.* **1.** UNTRUSTWORTHY PERSON a cunning and deceitful person **2.** SB WHO TELLS TALES sb who tells sb in authority about sth wrong that sb else has done **3.** STEALTHY DEPARTURE a departure intended to be unobserved ■ *adj.* STEALTHILY DONE done stealthily or furtively [Late 16thC. Origin uncertain.]

sneak up on *vt.* **1.** APPROACH SECRETLY to approach stealthily with the intention of surprising or frightening sb or sth **2.** ARRIVE UNEXPECTEDLY to arrive more quickly than expected ○ *The weekend sneaked up on me.*

sneaker /snéekər/ *n. US, Can, ANZ* a shoe with a rubber sole and, usually, a cloth upper (*often used in the plural*)

sneaking /snéeking/ *adj.* **1.** HIDDEN FROM OTHERS unknown to or hidden from others **2.** SLIGHT BUT PERSISTENT slight but persistent ○ *a sneaking suspicion* **3.** DECEPTIVE deceptive or given to cunning and deception —**sneakingly** *adv.*

sneak preview *n.* a public screening of a film prior to its general release, in order to test public reaction to it

sneak thief *n.* a thief who surreptitiously steals unguarded or unsecured articles when the opportunity arises

sneaky /snéeki/ (**-ier, -iest**) *adj.* done, doing sth, or in the habit of behaving, in an underhanded and unfair way —**sneakily** *adv.* —**sneakiness** *n.*

sneck /snek/ *n. N England, Scotland* LATCH OR CATCH a latch on a door or a catch on a door lock that allows it to be left open or fixed closed ■ *vt.* (**snecks, snecking, snecked**) *N England, Scotland* FIX A SNECK to fix or set the sneck on a door or lock [14thC. Origin uncertain.]

sneer /sneer/ *n.* EXPRESSION OF SCORN a facial expression of scorn or hostility in which the upper lip may be raised ■ *v.* (**sneers, sneering, sneered**) **1.** *vi.* FEEL OR SHOW SCORN to feel or show scorn, contempt, or hostility, either in speech or facial expression **2.** *vt.* SAY WITH SCORN to speak or say sth with scorn or contempt [14thC. Origin uncertain: perhaps suggestive of the expression; or an alteration of Old English *fnǣran* 'to snort'.] —**sneerer** *n.* —**sneering** *adj.* —**sneeringly** *adv.*

sneeze /sneez/ *n.* EXPLOSIVE EXPULSION OF AIR a sudden involuntary expulsion of air through the nose and mouth, caused by irritation of the nasal passages ■ *vi.* (**sneezes, sneezing, sneezed**) MAKE A SNEEZE to suddenly, forcefully, and involuntarily expel air through the nose and mouth because of irritation of the nasal passages [15thC. Alteration of *fnesan*, from Old English *fneosan*, an imitation of the sound of breathing or sneezing.] —**sneezer** *n.* —**sneezy** *adj.*

sneezeweed /snéez weed/ *n.* a perennial plant growing wild in North America that makes some people sneeze. Genus: *Helenium.*

sneezewood /snéez wŏŏd/ *n.* a South African tree whose peppery-smelling wood is used for posts and beams. Latin name: *Ptaeroxylon utile.* [Mid-19thC. Probably modelled on Cape Dutch *nieshout*.]

sneezewort /snéez wurt/ *n.* a European and Asian composite plant with small white flowers similar to those of a daisy and silvery leaves that when powdered induce sneezing. Latin name: *Achillea ptarmica.*

snell /snel/ *adj. Scotland* bitingly cold [Old English, from prehistoric Germanic]

Snell /snel/, **Peter George** (*b.* 1938) New Zealand runner. He won Olympic gold medals at the 1960 and 1964 Olympics.

Snell's law /snélz-/ *n.* the law stating that for a light ray passing between two media the ratio of the sines of the angle of incidence and the angle of refraction is a constant [Late 19thC. Named after Willebrord Van Roijen *Snell* 1591–1626, Dutch astronomer and mathematician.]

SNG *n., abbr.* synthetic (or substitute) natural gas

snib /snib/ *n. Ireland, Scotland* BOLT OR CATCH a bolt or catch on a door or a catch on a lock ■ *vt.* (**snibs, snibbing, snibbed**) *Ireland, Scotland* FIX A SNIB to fix or fasten the snib on a door or lock [Early 19thC. Origin uncertain: perhaps from Low German *snibbe* 'beaklike point'.]

snick /snik/ *n.* **1.** SMALL CUT a small cut or notch **2.** CRICKET GLANCING BLOW a glancing blow to the ball off a cricket bat ■ *vt.* (**snicks, snicking, snicked**) **1.** CUT STH to cut sth slightly **2.** CRICKET HIT OBLIQUELY to hit the ball with a glancing blow [Late 17thC. Origin uncertain: probably from obsolete *snick or snee* (see SNICKERSNEE).]

snicker /sníkər/ (**-ers, -ering, -ered**) *vi.* TO NEIGH to neigh or whinny ■ *n.* HORSE'S NEIGH a horse's neigh or whinny [Late 17thC. Origin uncertain: possibly an imitation of the sound.]

snickersnee /sníkər snee/ *n.* a long knife used as a cutting or thrusting weapon (*archaic*) [Early 18thC. Alteration of *snick or snee* 'cut or thrust in knife-fighting', an alteration of *stick or snee*, from Dutch *steken* 'to thrust' + *snee*, variant of *snijden* 'to cut'.]

snide /snīd/ (**snider, snidest**) *adj.* derisively sarcastic [Mid-19thC. Origin unknown. Originally in the meaning of 'counterfeit'.] —**snidely** *adv.*

sniff /snif/ *v.* (**sniffs, sniffing, sniffed**) **1.** *vti.* BREATHE IN THROUGH NOSE to breathe in through the nose, e.g. to see how sth smells **2.** *vt.* SUSPECT STH to have a suspicion of sth, especially sth bad ○ *sniff trouble* ■ *n.* **1.** ACT OR SOUND OF SNIFFING an instance or the sound of inhaling through the nose **2.** SUSPICION a hint or suspicion, especially of sth bad [14thC. An imitation of the sound.]

sniff at *vt.* to show contempt or disdain for sb or sth

sniff out *vt.* to discover sth, especially sth bad, by investigation (*informal*)

sniffer /sníffər/ *n.* sb who sniffs, especially sb who takes drugs by inhaling them through the nose

sniffer dog *n.* a dog trained to detect explosives, drugs, or other contraband by scent

sniffle /sníff'l/ *vi.* (**-fles, -fling, -fled**) **1.** INHALE MUCUS to inhale through the nose to prevent mucus from dripping out of it **2.** WEEP QUIETLY to sniff repeatedly while gently weeping ■ *n.* **1.** ACT OR SOUND OF SNIFFLING an instance or the sound of sniffling **2. sniffles, snuffles** *npl.* SLIGHT COLD a slight cold that causes sniffling (*informal*) [Mid-17thC. An imitation of the sound.] —**sniffler** *n.*

sniffy /sníffi/ (**-ier, -iest**) *adj.* (*informal*) **1.** HAUGHTY behaving in a haughty, disdainful way **2.** SNIFFING tending to sniff a lot, e.g. because of a cold —**sniffily** *adv.* —**sniffiness** *n.*

snifter /sníftər/ *n.* **1.** GLASS FOR SERVING BRANDY a stemmed glass with a bowl that tapers upwards, typically used for brandy **2.** SMALL DRINK a small amount of drink, especially of alcohol (*informal*) [Mid-18thC. Originally in the meaning of 'strong breeze', from archaic *snifter* 'to sniff, snuffle', an imitation of the sound.]

snigger *v.* (**-gers, -gering, -gered**) **1.** *vi.* LAUGH DISRESPECTFULLY to laugh disrespectfully in a covert way **2.** *vt.* SAY DISRESPECTFULLY to speak or say sth while laughing disrespectfully ■ *n.* ACT OR SOUND OF SNIGGERING an instance of or the sound of sniggering [Early 18thC. A later variant of SNICKER.]

sniggle /snígg'l/ *vti.* (**-gles, -gling, -gled**) FISH FOR EELS to fish for eels by putting a baited hook into crevices where they hide, or to catch eels using this method ■ *n.* HOOK a baited hook used for catching eels [Mid-17thC. Formed from *snig* 'young eel', of unknown origin.] —**sniggler** *n.*

snip /snip/ *vti.* (**snips, snipping, snipped**) CUT USING SMALL STROKES to cut with scissors or shears, especially using small strokes, or cut sth using small strokes ■ *n.* **1.** A CUT a short quick cut, made with scissors **2.** SMALL PIECE a small piece of sth that has been snipped off **3.** BARGAIN sth costing less than its real value (*informal*) **4.** EASY THING sth that is a certainty or is easily done (*informal*) **5.** ACT OR SOUND OF SNIPPING the act or sound of using scissors to snip sth ■ *interj.* SOUND OF SNIPPING used to represent the sound that scissors make [Mid-16thC. From Dutch or Low German *snippen*, an imitation of the sound.]

snipe /snīp/ *n.* (*plural* **snipes** *or* **snipe**) **1.** WADING BIRD a wading bird with a long straight bill. It lives in marshy areas and on river banks throughout the northern hemisphere. Latin name: *Gallinago gallinago.* **2.** BIRD RELATED TO SNIPE a bird related to the snipe such as a sandpiper or curlew **3.** SHOT FIRED FROM CONCEALMENT a shot fired from a concealed place ■ *vi.* (**snipes, sniping, sniped**) SHOOT FROM CONCEALED PLACE to shoot at people from a concealed position [14thC. Origin uncertain: probably from Old Norse *snípa*. The verb came from the idea of hunting snipe.]

snipefish /snīp fish/ (*plural* **-fish** *or* **-fishes**) *n.* a fish with a long snout and a spine extending from its dorsal fin to its tail. It lives in tropical and temperate seas and is related to the seahorse. Family: Macrorhamphosidae.

snipe fly *n.* a fly with a long body and long legs that eats other insects. Some also suck the blood of mammals. Family: Leptidae.

sniper /snīpər/ *n.* sb who shoots at people from a concealed position

snipping /snípping/ *n.* = **snip** *n.* 2

snippy /snípp i/ (**-pier, -piest**) *adj.* **1.** SHARP-TONGUED behaving in a curt and irritable way (*informal*) **2.** FRAGMENTARY made up of scraps or fragments **3.** MEAN stingy or mean with money (*regional*) —**snippily** *adv.* —**snippiness** *n.*

snips *npl.* shears used for cutting sheet metal (*takes a singular or plural verb*)

snit /snit/ *n. US* a state of mild irritation or bad temper [Mid-20thC. Origin unknown.]

snitch /snich/ *v.* (**snitches, snitching, snitched**) (*slang*) **1.** *vt.* PILFER STH to steal sth in a sneaky way especially sth of little value **2.** *vi.* INFORM to inform on sb ○ *Friends don't snitch on each other.* ■ *n.* **1.** INFORMER sb who informs on others (*slang*) **2.** NOSE a person's nose (*dated slang*) [Late 17thC. Origin unknown.] —**snitcher** *n.*

snivel /snívv'l/ *vi.* (**-els, -elled, -elling** *or* **-elled**) **1.** SNIFF to sniff audibly **2.** WHINE to behave in a whining, tearful, or self-pitying way **3.** SNIFFLE to have a runny nose ■ *n.* WHINE OR SNIFF an act of snivelling [Assumed Old English *snyflan*] —**sniveller** *n.* —**snivelling** *n., adj.* —**snivelly** *adj.*

snob /snob/ *n.* **1.** SB WHO LOOKS DOWN ON OTHERS sb who admires and cultivates relationships with those considered socially superior, and disdains those considered inferior **2.** SB WHO FEELS SUPERIOR sb who looks down on people considered to have inferior knowledge or tastes [Mid-19thC. Origin unknown. Its meaning developed from 'cobbler's apprentice', through 'lower-class person', to 'sb who tries to imitate those of higher status'.]

WORD KEY: ORIGIN

Snob originally meant 'shoemaker' (a sense that survives in places). Cambridge University students of the late 18th century adopted it as a slang term for a 'townsman, someone not a member of the university', and it seems to have been this usage that formed the basis in the 1830s for the emergence of the new general sense 'member of the lower classes'. The modern sense 'someone who apes social superiors' received a considerable boost when William Thackeray used it in his *Book of Snobs* (1848). As for the origins of the word itself, the suggestion that it comes from *s.nob.*, short for Latin *sine nobilitate* 'without nobility', is ingenious but ignores the word's early history.

snobbery /snóbbəri/ (*plural* **-ies**) *n.* the attitude or behaviour of sb who looks down on those considered inferior, or a particular example of this

snobbish /snóbbish/ *adj.* displaying an offensively superior condescending manner —**snobbishly** *adv.* —**snobbishness** *n.*

snobbism /snóbbisəm/ *n.* = **snobbery**

snobby /snóbbi/ (**-bier, -biest**) *adj.* snobbish (*informal*)

SNOBOL /snó bawl/ *n.* a computer programming language designed for dealing with strings of symbols. Full form **String Oriented Symbolic Language** [Mid-20thC. Modelled on 'COBOL'.]

snob value *n.* worth or desirability arising from being seen as superior (*informal*)

Sno-Cat /snó kat/ *tdmk.* a trademark for a motorized vehicle that has tractor treads for moving easily on snow

snoek /snook/ (*plural* **snoeks** *or* **snoek**) *n.* a long predatory edible fish of Australia, New Zealand, and South Africa that belongs to the snake mackerel family. Latin name: *Thyrsites atun.* [Late 18thC. Via Afrikaans from Middle Dutch *snoec* 'pike' (source of English *snook*).]

snog /snog/ *vti.* (**snogs, snogging, snogged**) *UK* to KISS to kiss and cuddle, especially for a long time (*slang*) ■ *n. UK* A KISS a long kiss or a prolonged kissing and cuddling session (*slang*) [Mid-20thC. Origin unknown.]

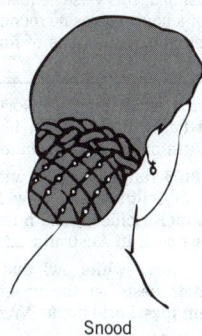
Snood

snood /snood/ *n.* **1.** DECORATIVE HAIR NET a net that holds a woman's hair at the back of her head **2.** RIBBON WORN BY UNMARRIED SCOTTISH WOMEN a hairband or ribbon that unmarried women in Scotland wore in the 17th and 18th centuries ■ *vt.* (**snoods, snooding, snooded**) WEAR A SNOOD OVER THE HAIR to fasten the hair with a snood [Old English *snōd.* Ultimately from an Indo-European base meaning 'to spin, sew', which is also the ancestor of English *needle.*]

snook[1] /snook/ (*plural* **snook** *or* **snooks**) *n.* a large bony fish that lives in warm seas and rivers. Latin name: *Centropomus undecimalis.* [Late 17thC. Via Dutch *snoek* 'pike' from Middle Dutch *snoec.*]

snook[2] /snook, snook/ *n.* a gesture made as a sign of contempt, by putting the thumb to the nose with the fingers outstretched [Late 18thC. Origin unknown.]

snooker /snookar/ *n.* **1.** BALL AND CUE GAME a game played on a table in which a white cue ball is used to hit 15 red balls and 6 balls of different colours into any of 6 pockets **2.** POSITION IN SNOOKER a position in snooker in which a player is forced to play an indirect shot because another ball is between the cue ball and the target ball ■ *vt.* (**-ers, -ering, -ered**) **1.** PUT SB AT DISADVANTAGE IN SNOOKER to put a snooker player in the position of being forced to play an indirect shot because another ball is between the cue ball and the target ball **2.** THWART to thwart sb or put sb in a position of being unable to proceed (*informal*) [Late 19thC. Origin unknown.]

──────── **WORD KEY: ORIGIN** ────────
The most widely canvassed theory of the origins of the word *snooker* is that it is an adaptation of late 19th-century British army slang *snooker* 'new recruit'. The game was invented, as a diversion perhaps from the monotony of billiards, by British army officers serving in India in the 1870s, and the story goes that the term *snooker* was applied to it by Colonel Sir Neville Chamberlain (1856–1944), at that time a subaltern in the Devonshire Regiment stationed in Jubbulpore, in allusion to the inept play of one of his brother officers.

snoop /snoop/ *vi.* (**snoops, snooping, snooped**) PRY to pry into other people's business or affairs, especially in a furtive way (*informal*) ■ *n.* (*informal*) **1.** SB WHO SNOOPS sb who pries into other people's business or affairs, especially in a sneaky way **2.** SNEAKY PRYING INTO SB'S AFFAIRS a furtive search or investigation of sb's private property or affairs [Mid-19thC. From Dutch *snoepen* 'to eat on the sly'.] —**snooper** *n.*

snooperscope /snoopar skōp/ *n.* a device that converts infrared radiation into a visual image and is used for seeing in the dark

snoopy /snoopi/ (**-ier, -iest**) *adj.* tending to pry into the affairs of others

snoot /snoot/ *n.* a nose or snout (*informal*) [Mid-19thC. Variant of SNOUT.]

snooty /snooti/ (**-ier, -iest**) *adj.* (*informal*) **1.** SUPERCILIOUS showing a haughty, condescending manner **2.** EXCLUSIVE excluding some people out of snobbery [Early

20thC. Formed from SNOOT, from the notion of looking down one's nose at others.] —**snootily** *adv.* —**snootiness** *n.*

snooze /snooz/ *vi.* (**snoozes, snoozing, snoozed**) TO NAP to have a short sleep (*informal*) ■ *n.* A NAP a short sleep (*informal*) [Late 18thC. Origin unknown.] —**snoozer** *n.* —**snoozy** *adj.*

snore /snawr/ *vi.* (**snores, snoring, snored**) BREATHE NOISILY IN SLEEP to breathe noisily while asleep because of vibrations of the soft palate ■ *n.* A SOUND MADE BY SNORING a snorting or whistling sound made while sleeping, or an act of snoring [14thC. Origin uncertain: possibly from Old English *fnora* 'sneezing'.] —**snorer** *n.*

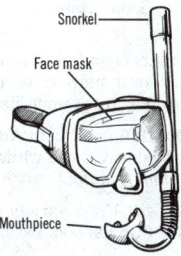
Snorkel

snorkel /snáwrk'l/ *n.* **1.** BREATHING APPARATUS a device allowing sb to swim just below water, consisting of a face mask and a breathing tube held in the mouth while the other end projects above the water **2.** VENTILATOR ON SUBMARINE a ventilation device on a submarine. It projects above the surface while the vessel is submerged, allowing air in and gases out. **3.** DEVICE ON TANK a device on a tank or other vehicle that functions like the snorkel on a submarine and enables the vehicle to go through shallow water ■ *vi.* (**snorkels, snorkelling, snorkelled, snorkeled**) SWIM WITH SNORKEL to swim underwater breathing air through a snorkel [Mid-20thC. From German *Schnorchel*, from a dialect word meaning 'nose'; originally 'intake and exhaust shaft of a submarine'; from its resemblance to a nose.] —**snorkeller** *n.*

snorkelling /snáwrkəling/ *n.* the activity or pastime of swimming with a snorkel

Snorri Sturluson /stúrloossən, stoörloössən/ (1179–1241) Icelandic poet and historian. He wrote a history of the kings of Norway and the *Prose Edda*, a repository of Norse myths.

snort /snawrt/ *v.* (**snorts, snorting, snorted**) **1.** *vi.* FORCE AIR THROUGH NOSE to make a harsh sound by forcing air out through the nostrils **2.** *vi.* SHOW CONTEMPT to express a feeling, especially of contempt or impatience, by snorting **3.** *vti.* DRUGS INHALE DRUG to inhale a powdered drug through the nostrils (*informal*) ■ *n.* **1.** HARSH SOUND a harsh sound made by snorting, or an instance of this **2.** GULP OF ALCOHOL a short drink, especially of alcohol, taken all at once (*informal*) **3.** DRUGS INHALATION OF DRUG an act of inhaling a powdered drug through the nostrils (*informal*) **4.** SUBMARINE SNORKEL the snorkel of a submarine (*slang*) [14thC. Origin uncertain: probably a variant of SNORE.] —**snorter** *n.* —**snorting** *n., adj.*

snot /snot/ *n.* **1.** OFFENSIVE TERM an offensive term referring to mucus produced in the nose (*slang offensive*) **2.** OFFENSIVE TERM an offensive term referring to sb whose behavior is regarded as arrogant or condescending (*slang insult*) [Old English *gesnot.* Ultimately from a prehistoric Germanic word that is also the ancestor of English *snout* and *snoot.*]

snot-nosed *adj.* an offensive term describing sb who is regarded as being young and precocious but not to be taken seriously (*slang offensive*)

snotter /snóttər/ *n.* Scotland SNOT nasal mucus ■ *vi.* (**-ters, -tering, -tered**) *Scotland* **1.** SNUFFLE to breathe through the nose while it is partially blocked up with mucus **2.** SNIVEL to whine and cry messily [Early 18thC. Formed from SNOT.]

snotty /snótti/ (**-tier, -tiest**) *adj.* (*slang offensive*) **1.** OFFENSIVE TERM an offensive term describing sth that is wet or dirty with nasal mucus **2.** OFFENSIVE TERM an offensive term describing sb who is regarded as

behaving in an arrogant and condescending manner **3.** OFFENSIVE TERM an offensive term describing actions that are regarded as mean or rude —**snottily** *adv.* —**snottiness** *n.*

snout /snowt/ *n.* **1.** ZOOL ANIMAL'S NOSE the projecting part of a vertebrate's head, consisting of the nose and mouth **2.** INSECTS PROJECTING PART OF INSECT'S HEAD the projecting part of the head of an insect or other invertebrate such as a weevil **3.** LARGE NOSE sb's nose (*slang*) **4.** PROJECTION SIMILAR TO A SNOUT sth that sticks out like a snout such as the muzzle of a gun **5.** STH TO SMOKE tobacco, or a cigarette (*slang*) **6.** INFORMER sb who gives incriminating information to the police (*slang*) **7.** GEOL STEEP END OF GLACIER the leading face of a glacier, usually heavily loaded with rock debris [13thC.] —**snouted** *adj.*

snout beetle *n.* = **weevil** *n.* **1** ['Snout' from the shape of its head]

snow /snō/ *n.* METEOROL ICE CRYSTAL FLAKES water vapour in the atmosphere that has frozen into ice crystals and then falls to the ground in the form of flakes ■ *npl.* METEOROL FALL OF SNOW an amount of snow that falls at one time ○ *had a heavy snow last night* ■ *n.* **1.** METEOROL SNOW ON GROUND a layer of snow on the ground **2.** STH RESEMBLING SNOW sth that resembles snow in colour or texture **3.** ELEC WHITE SPECKS ON TELEVISION SCREEN random patterns of small white specks on a television or radar screen caused by electrical interference **4.** DRUGS NARCOTIC DRUG cocaine or heroin in the form of a white powder (*slang*) ■ *v.* (**snows, snowing, snowed**) **1.** *vi.* METEOROL TO FALL IN THE FORM OF SNOW to be marked by the falling of snow ○ *It's snowing!* **2.** *vt.* COVER STH WITH SNOW to cover, close in, or block with a fall of snow **3.** *vti.* FALL LIKE SNOW to fall as snow or like snow, or make sth fall in this way **4.** *vt. US, Can* PERSUADE SB WITH GLIB TALK to overwhelm or deceive sb especially with flattery or charm (*slang*) ○ *She actually snowed us into buying worthless stock.* [Old English *snāw.* Ultimately from an Indo-European word meaning 'snow'.] ◇ **be snowed under (with sth)** to be overwhelmed with sth, especially work

snow under (**snows under, snowing under, snowed under**) to inundate sb with sth such as work beyond the point at which the person can deal with it

snowball /snō bawl/ *n.* **1.** BALL OF SNOW a soft lump of snow for throwing at sb or sth, made from handfuls of snow pressed together **2.** ALCOHOLIC DRINK a drink made from advocaat mixed with lemonade ■ *v.* (**-balls, -balling, -balled**) **1.** *vi.* INCREASE RAPIDLY to grow or multiply rapidly or at an accelerating rate ○ *The event snowballed until hundreds of people were involved.* **2.** *vti.* THROW SNOWBALLS to throw snowballs at each other or at sb else ◇ **not have a snowball's chance (in hell)** to have no chance at all (*informal*)

snowberry /snō bəri/ (*plural* **-ries**) *n.* **1.** SHRUB WITH WHITE BERRIES a North American shrub with small pink flowers and white berries. Genus: *Symphoricarpos.* **2.** WHITE BERRY the white berry that grows on the snowberry shrub

snowbird /snō burd/ *n.* any bird that is seen chiefly in winter such as the snow bunting, fieldfare, and junco

snow-blind *adj.* effected with temporary blindness and pain in the eyes caused by bright light reflected from snow and ice

snow blindness *n.* a condition of temporary blindness caused by the bright sunlight and intense radiation reflected from snow or ice, which causes swelling of parts of the eyeball and severe pain

snowblink /snō blingk/ *n.* a white glow in the sky, especially in polar regions, caused by reflection of light from distant snowfields

snowblower /snō blō ər/ *n.* a machine that clears snow from roads by scooping it into a fast-rotating spiral blade and ejecting it to one side

snowboard /snō bawrd/ *n.* **1.** BOARD FOR SLIDING ON SNOW a board that sb stands on to slide down snow slopes. It has bindings for the feet and is used without ski poles. ■ *vi.* (**-boards, -boarding, -boarded**) USE A SNOWBOARD to slide down snow slopes using a snowboard —**snowboarder** *n.* —**snowboarding** *n.*

snowbound /snṓ bownd/ *adj.* prevented from moving or leaving a place by heavy snow

snow bunting *n.* a white finch with dark markings that nests on tundra and winters in coastal regions. Latin name: *Plectrophenax nivalis.*

snowcap /snṓ kap/ *n.* a covering of snow on a mountain peak —**snowcapped** *adj.*

Snowdon, Mount /snṓd'n/ mountain in Gwynedd, northwestern Wales. It is the highest peak in Wales. Height: 1,085 m/3,560 ft.

Snowdonia National Park /snṓ dṓni ə-/ national park incorporating Mount Snowdon, in northwestern Wales, established in 1951. Area: 2,171 sq. km/840 sq. mi.

snowdrift /snṓ drift/ *n.* a bank of snow piled up by the wind

snowdrop /snṓ drop/ *n.* a bulbous plant of Europe and Asia with small white drooping flowers that appear early in spring. Latin name: *Galanthus nivalis.*

snowdrop tree *n.* = **silverbell**

snowfall /snṓ fawl/ *n.* **1.** FALL OF SNOW a period during which snow falls or an instance of snow falling **2.** AMOUNT OF FALLEN SNOW the amount of snow that falls in a particular place or in a given period ○ *What is the average snowfall for the area?*

snow fence *n.* a portable flexible fence made of upright slats, designed to stop snow from drifting onto roads or ski runs

snowfield /snṓ feeld/ *n.* a large area permanently covered in snow

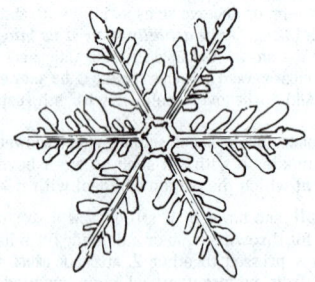

Snowflake

snowflake /snṓ flayk/ *n.* **1.** CRYSTAL OF SNOW any of the individual masses of ice crystals that together fall as snow **2.** PLANT WITH BELL-SHAPED FLOWERS a bulbous garden plant with white flowers like those of a snowdrop but larger. Genus: *Leucojum.* **3.** = **snow bunting**

snow goose *n.* a North American goose that breeds in Arctic regions and migrates to coastal areas in winter. The adults have white plumage and black wingtips. Latin name: *Anser caerulescens.*

snow grass *n.* **1.** AUSTRALIAN GRASS any of several grey-green grasses that grow in upland areas of Australia. Genus: *Poa.* **2.** NEW ZEALAND GRASS any of various grasses that grow in the hills of New Zealand. Genus: *Danthonia.*

snow-in-summer *n.* a perennial European plant with woolly stems, notched silvery-green leaves, and white flowers. Latin name: *Cerastium tomentosum.*

snow job *n.* US, Can an attempt to mislead or persuade sb by insincere talk or flattery (*slang*)

snow leopard *n.* a large cat that lives in mountainous regions of central Asia and has a thick pale-grey or brown coat marked with dark splotches. Latin name: *Panthera uncia.*

snow line *n.* the line of altitude above which there is permanent snow, or the line of latitude that marks the extent of permanent snow in the polar regions

snowman /snṓ man/ (*plural* -**men** /-men/) *n.* a roughly human figure made by piling up and shaping snow

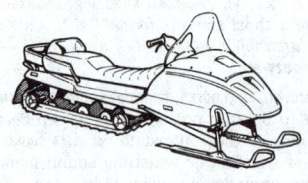

Snowmobile

snowmobile /snṓmə beel, -mō beel/ *n.* a small vehicle used for travelling over snow. It has runners at the front and a caterpillar track underneath.

snow-on-the-mountain *n.* a North American shrub that has white-edged leaves and white bracts. Latin name: *Euphorbia marginata.*

snow pea *n.* US, Can, ANZ a variety of garden pea that has an edible thin flat pod. Latin name: *Pisum sativum.*

snow pellet *n.* a soft white round mass of ice that falls as precipitation (*often used in the plural*)

snow plant *n.* a plant with scarlet flowers and a fleshy reddish stalk. It grows in the mountains of western North America and often flowers before the snow has melted. Latin name: *Sarcodes sanguinea.*

snowplough /snṓ plow/ *n.* **1.** VEHICLE FOR CLEARING SNOW a vehicle or an implement that can be fixed to a vehicle, used for clearing snow from roads or paths **2.** CONTROL TECHNIQUE IN SKIING a technique used in skiing in which the points of the skis are brought together to make a V, enabling the skier to turn or stop ■ *vi.* (-**ploughs**, -**ploughing**, -**ploughed**) SKI IN SNOWPLOUGH POSITION to use the snowplough position to turn or stop in skiing

snowshed /snṓ shed/ *n.* a shelter over an open section of a railway track, especially on a mountainside, to prevent it getting covered in snow

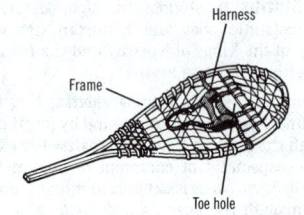

Snowshoe

snowshoe /snṓ shoo/ *n.* SHOE FOR WALKING IN SNOW a metal or wood framework with interwoven straps that is attached to a boot and allows the wearer to walk on snow without sinking ■ *vi.* (-**shoes**, -**shoeing**, -**shoed**) WALK IN SNOWSHOES to walk on snow wearing snowshoes

snowshoe hare, snowshoe rabbit *n.* a North American hare with a white winter coat that turns brown in summer and large heavily furred hind feet that allow it to move quickly in snow. Latin name: *Lepus americanus.*

snowstorm /snṓ stawrm/ *n.* a storm with heavy snow and sometimes strong winds

snow tyre *n.* a tyre with a deep tread pattern or studs to provide extra traction for a vehicle driving in snowy conditions

snow-white *adj.* as white as fresh snow

snowy *adj.* **1.** MARKED BY SNOW characterized by the presence of snow ○ *a snowy day* **2.** LIKE SNOW resembling snow, especially in colour or purity ○ *a snowy beard* —**snowily** *adv.* —**snowiness** *n.*

Snowy /snṓ i/ river in southeastern Australia. It rises in the Snowy Mountains in New South Wales and flows into the Tasman Sea, near the town of Orbost in Victoria. Length: 435 km/270 mi.

─── **WORD KEY: CULTURAL NOTE** ───
The Man From Snowy River, a long poem by Australian writer A.B. Paterson (1895). Set in the high country of southeastern Australia, this verse sequence tells of the heroic exploits of a horseman as he rounds up a mob of wild and escaped horses. It is one of Australia's best-known poems.

snowy egret *n.* a small egret of North and South America that has white feathers, black legs, and yellow feet. Latin name: *Egretta thula.*

Snowy Mountains range of peaks within the Australian Alps, in southeastern New South Wales, Australia. Mount Kosciusko is both its highest peak and the highest peak in Australia, 2,228 m/7,310 ft.

snowy owl *n.* a large white owl that lives in the Arctic. It builds nests on the ground and feeds mainly on lemmings. Latin name: *Nyctea scandiaca.*

SNP *abbr.* Scottish National Party

Snr, snr *abbr.* Senior

snub /snub/ *vt.* (**snubs, snubbing, snubbed**) **1.** TREAT SB RUDELY to treat sb with deliberate coldness or contempt **2.** BRING STH TO A STOP to stop a line from paying out by wrapping it around sth, or to stop sth attached to a line such as a boat or horse from getting away by wrapping the line around sth ■ *n.* HUMILIATING ACTION a remark or act intended to humiliate or insult, e.g. ignoring sb ■ *adj.* SMALL short and flat or turned up at the end [14thC. From Old Norse *snubba*, of uncertain origin: probably from a prehistoric Germanic base of words concerning the nose, which is also the ancestor of English *sniff*.] —**snubber** *n.*

snub-nosed *adj.* **1.** WITH TURNED UP NOSE with a nose that is short and flat or turned up **2.** WITH SHORT BARREL OR BLUNT END having a very short barrel or a blunt end ○ *snub-nosed pliers*

snuff[1] *v.* (**snuffs, snuffing, snuffed**) **1.** *vt.* INHALE STH to inhale sth through the nose **2.** *vti.* SNIFF to sniff, especially noisily, or to examine sth by sniffing it ○ *The hounds snuffed the ground searching for the trail.* ■ *n.* SNIFFING SOUND a sound made by sniffing noisily [Early 16thC. From Dutch *snuffen* 'to snuffle', ultimately from a prehistoric Germanic base concerning the nose (see SNUB).]

snuff[2] *vt.* (**snuffs, snuffing, snuffed**) **1.** EXTINGUISH FLAME to extinguish a flame, e.g. that of a burning candle **2.** TRIM CANDLEWICK to remove the burnt end from the wick of a candle **3.** DESTROY STH to put an end to sb or sth (*informal*) ○ *snuff out enthusiasm* ■ *n.* SOOTY WICK the sooty, charred end of a candlewick [14thC. Origin unknown.] ◇ **snuff it** to die (*informal*)

snuff[3] /snuf/ *n.* **1.** POWDERED TOBACCO tobacco in the form of powder, taken by sniffing it up the nostrils **2.** AMOUNT OF SNUFF a portion of snuff ■ *vi.* (**snuffs, snuffing, snuffed**) TAKE SNUFF to inhale snuff [Late 17thC. From Dutch *snuf*, shortening of *snuftabak*, literally 'sniffing tobacco'. The verb came from Dutch *snuffen* 'to snuffle'.]

snuffbox /snúf boks/ *n.* a small ornamental box for powdered tobacco

snuff-coloured *adj.* of a dark yellowish-brown colour

snuffer /snúffər/ *n.* **1.** LONG-HANDLED CANDLE EXTINGUISHER a device used to extinguish a candle, consisting of a long handle with a cone shape at one end ■ **snuffers** *n.* CANDLE EXTINGUISHER LIKE SCISSORS an instrument resembling a pair of scissors, used for trimming wicks or extinguishing candles or oil lamps (*takes a singular or plural verb*)

snuff film, snuff movie *n.* a pornographic film or video that allegedly ends with the murder of one of the participants in a sex act (*slang*)

snuffle /snúff'l/ *v.* (-**fles, -fling, -fled**) **1.** *vi.* BREATHE NOISILY to breathe noisily through a partially blocked nose **2.** *vti.* SPEAK NASALLY to speak or say sth in a nasal or whining way **3.** *vi.* SNIFF to make repeated sniffing sounds ■ *n.* SOUND OF SNUFFLING the act of snuffling, or the sound made by breathing noisily through the nose ■ **snuffles** *n.* = **sniffle** *n.* 2 [Late 16thC. Origin uncertain: possibly from Dutch *snuffelen*, literally 'to keep sniffing about', from *snuffen* 'to sniff'.] —**snuffler** *n.* —**snuffly** *adj.*

snuffy /snúffi/ (**-ier, -iest**) *adj.* **1.** **LIKE SNUFF** like snuff in colour or smell **2.** **COVERED WITH SNUFF** soiled or marked with snuff **3.** **DISAGREEABLE** in a bad temper and acting irritably —**snuffiness** *n.*

snug /snug/ *adj.* (**snugger, snuggest**) **1.** **COSY** warm and comfortable **2.** **SMALL BUT COMFORTABLE** small in size but offering a comfortable well-arranged space ○ *a snug cottage* **3.** **SHELTERED** protected from the weather ○ *The fishing boats were snug in the harbour.* **4.** **CLOSE-FITTING** fitting comfortably close or too close ○ *The sweater was perhaps a little too snug.* **5.** **CONCEALED** offering a safe and private hiding place ■ *n.* **1.** **SMALL ROOM** a small room or enclosed area in a pub allowing a small number of people to sit in private **2.** **PEG FOR HOLDING A BOLT** a small peg used to hold the head of a bolt in place while a nut is tightened onto the end ■ *v.* (**snugs, snugging, snugged**) **1.** *vt.* **MAKE SNUG** to make sb or sth comfortable and warm **2.** *vti.* **SECURE A BOAT** to make a boat secure to weather a storm [Late 16thC. Origin uncertain: probably from Scandinavian or Low Dutch.]

snuggery /snúggəri/ (*plural* **-ies**) *n.* **1.** **COSY PLACE** a place that is warm and comfortable **2.** = **snug** [Early 19thC. Formed from SNUG.]

snuggle /snúgg'l/ (**-gles, -gling, -gled**) *v.* **1.** *vi.* **CUDDLE UP** to get into a comfortable, cosy position, especially close to another person **2.** *vt.* **GET CLOSE TO SB** to draw close to sb or sth to offer or receive comfort and affection ○ *snuggled in front of the fireplace* [Late 17thC. Formed from SNUG.]

so[1] /sō/ CORE MEANING: a conjunction indicating the reason for an action or situation, or its result ○ *Let's go upstairs and talk, so as to get a bit of privacy.* ○ *Keep your password secret so that others cannot use your user name.* ○ *I had the flu, so I couldn't attend the meeting.*

1. *conj.* **IN ORDER THAT** introduces the reason for doing what has just been mentioned ○ *The poles are joined together so as to enclose an area of about twenty feet in diameter.* ○ *He held her tight so that she wouldn't fall.* **2.** *conj.* **INTRODUCES RESULT** introduces the result of the situation that has just been mentioned ○ *Everything is done on a shoestring, so their prices are very low.* **3.** *adv.* **REFERS BACK** refers back to sth that has just been mentioned ○ *Lunch may be purchased on the island, for those who desire to do so.* **4.** *adv.* **INDICATES IDENTITY** indicates that what is true of one person or thing is also true of another person or thing (*followed by auxiliary or modal, or by the main verb 'do', 'have', or 'be'*) ○ *If you can keep a secret, so can I.* **5.** *adv.* **AS IT IS** indicates that sth is the way it has been described ○ *The city has the potential to be very important, and will soon be so, both politically and commercially.* **6.** *adv.* **TO SUCH AN EXTENT** emphasizes the degree of sth by mentioning its result ○ *He is so busy working at Nathan's, he doesn't have time to take classes.* ○ *He's not so unobservant as to miss seeing the change.* **7.** *adv.* **EMPHASIZES A QUALITY** adds emphasis to the meaning of an adverb or adjective ○ *I was so scared.* ○ *He acts so stubbornly sometimes.* **8.** *adv.* **THEREFORE OR IN CONSEQUENCE** introduces an event in a sequence ○ *It's not working out. So we'll have to go back to the beginning and start again.* ○ *She said she would like to see me again. So I gave her my phone number.* **9.** *adv.* **INTRODUCES COMMENT** introduces a new topic, or a question or comment about sth ○ *So what are we going to do about it?* ○ *So I see you've changed your mind.* **10.** *adv.* **INDICATES POSITION OR DIMENSIONS** indicates the position or dimensions of sth, using actions or gestures ○ *Hold onto the boat like so, and hoist yourself up.* **11.** *conj.* **INDICATES SIMILARITY** indicates that two events or situations are alike in some way ○ *Just as my circumstances have changed, so too have my aims in life.* **12.** *adv.* *US* **INDEED** used to contradict a negative statement (*nonstandard*) ○ *'You never explained what to do'. 'I did so!'* [Old English *swā*. Ultimately from an Indo-European word that is also the ancestor of English *such* and *quasi*.] ◇ **and so on, and so forth** used at the end of a list to indicate that there are other things that could be mentioned ○ *These systems are traditionally used in industries such as insurance, banking, universities and so on.* ○ *Remove any additional hardware from the system (mouse, network card, fax board, modem, and so forth.)* ◇ **or so** approximately ○ *That pair of neutron stars at 1,600 light-years isn't expected to crash for another billion years or so.* ◇ **so be it** expresses agreement or resignation ○ *I wish you'd think again, but never mind – so be it!* ◇ **so much, so many** a certain degree or amount ○ *The government can only do so much.* ○ *I can only take so many insults.* ◇ **so much for 1.** indicates that there is nothing more that can be said or done about sth (*informal*) ○ *So much for the morning. I still had the afternoon to get through.* **2.** indicates that sth has not been successful or helpful (*informal*) ○ *Well, so much for simple fairness!* ◇ **so what?** used to ask rather rudely why sth is important, implying that it is not ○ *You amass all these facts, but the question is, 'so what?'*

so[2] *n.* = **soh**

SO *abbr.* standing order

So., so. *abbr.* **1.** south **2.** southern

s.o. *abbr.* seller's option

soak /sōk/ *v.* (**soaks, soaking, soaked**) **1.** *vti.* **TO STEEP** to immerse sth in liquid or be immersed in liquid for a period of time **2.** *vt.* **MAKE STH WET** to make sth or sb completely wet (*often passive*) ○ *We got soaked in the rain on the way home.* **3.** *vti.* **ABSORB** to draw sth such as moisture in through the pores or other small holes ○ *This sponge soaks up moisture.* **4.** *vti.* **PERMEATE STH** to penetrate sth by saturating it and passing into pores or small holes ○ *The water quickly soaked through her shoes.* **5.** *vti.* **REMOVE STAIN BY SOAKING** to remove sth, especially a mark or a stain from an item of clothing, by leaving it in liquid for a time **6.** *vti.* **GET DRUNK** to drink too much alcohol, or to make sb drunk (*informal*) **7.** *vt.* **OVERCHARGE** to overcharge or tax sb heavily (*slang*) ■ *n.* **1.** **ACT OF SOAKING** an act or the process of immersing sth in liquid ○ *had a long, leisurely soak in the bath* **2.** **SOAKING LIQUID** a solution or liquid for soaking sth in **3.** **HARD DRINKER** sb who habitually drinks too much alcohol (*slang*) [Old English *socian*, from *sūcan*, an earlier form of SUCK] —**soaker** *n.*

soakage /sōkij/ *n.* **1.** **PROCESS OF SOAKING** the process of soaking or the condition of being soaked **2.** **AMOUNT OF LIQUID** the amount of liquid soaking into or out of sth

soakaway /sōkə way/ *n.* a hole where waste water can drain away by filtering down through the soil

soaking /sōking/ *n.* **1.** **STEEPING** an act or the process of steeping sth in liquid **2.** **DRENCHING** an instance of being made very wet (*informal*) ■ *adj.* **VERY WET** very wet, especially because of being rained on (*informal*)

WORD KEY: SYNONYMS

See Synonyms at ***wet***.

so-and-so (*plural* **so-and-sos**) *n.* **1.** **UNNAMED PERSON OR THING** sb or sth not named or specified (*informal*) **2.** **SB UNPLEASANT** sb regarded as annoying or disagreeable (*informal insult*)

Soane /sōn/, **Sir John** (1753–1837) British architect. He was an exponent of the neoclassical style, seen in his churches, private houses, and public buildings, most notably the Bank of England (1795–1827).

soap /sōp/ *n.* **1.** **CLEANSING AGENT** a solid, liquid, or powdered cleaning preparation that is made by potassium or sodium hydroxide reacting with animal or vegetable oils. Soaps are usually used with water and may contain perfumes or other additional ingredients. **2.** **METALLIC SALT COMBINED WITH FATTY ACID** a metallic salt of a fatty acid, often made with calcium, aluminium and lithium, used as a waterproofing agent and as a base for greases **3.** **SOAP OPERA** a soap opera (*informal*) **4.** *US, Can* **MONEY USED TO BRIBE** money, especially when it is used as a bribe or for paying sb secretly (*slang*) ■ *vt.* (**soaps, soaping, soaped**) **PUT SOAP ON** to put soap on sth or sb [Old English *sāpe*, from a prehistoric Germanic word meaning 'soap', which is also the ancestor of Latin *sapo* (source of English *saponaceous*)]

soapbark /sōp baark/ *n.* **1.** **EVERGREEN TREE** a South American evergreen tree of the rose family that has small white flowers and bark high in saponin. Latin name: *Quillaja saponaria.* **2.** **BARK OF SOAPBARK** the bark of the soapbark, which contains saponin and was used in the past as soap

soapberry /sōp beri/ (*plural* **-ries**) *n.* **1.** **TROPICAL AMERICAN TREE** a tropical American tree or shrub that has pulpy fruit containing saponin. Latin name: *Sapindus saponaria.* **2.** **BERRY** the fruit of the soapberry

soap boiler *n.* a soap manufacturer

soapbox /sōp boks/ *n.* **1.** **BOX FOR SOAP** a box in which soap is packed **2.** **PLATFORM FOR SPEAKING** sth, such as a wooden box, used as a platform for making an impromptu speech

soap bubble *n.* **1.** **BUBBLE** a bubble formed with soapy water **2.** **STH ILLUSORY** sth that is beautiful but that does not last

soap opera *n.* a serial on television or radio that deals with the lives of a group of characters, especially in a melodramatic or sentimental way [*Soap* from the fact that they were originally often sponsored by soap manufacturing companies]

soap powder *n.* a detergent in powdered form used in washing machines

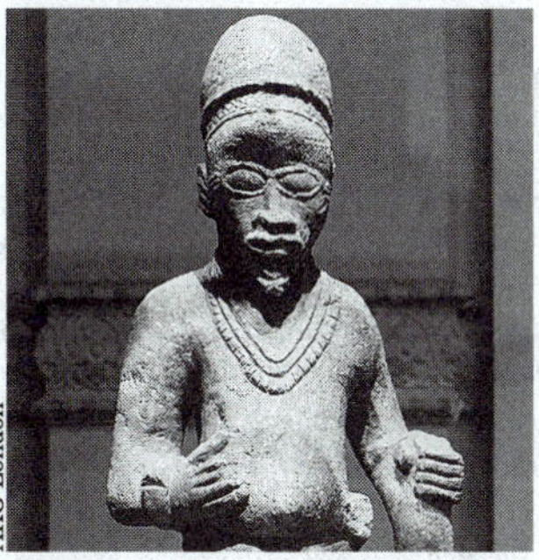

Soapstone: Nigerian carving (12th to 15th centuries)

soapstone /sōp stōn/ *n.* a dark grey or green soft compact variety of talc that has a soapy texture and is used to make objects including ornaments and hearths

soapsuds /sōp sudz/ *npl.* = **suds** *npl.*

soapwort /sōp wurt/ *n.* a European plant with flowers that are pink and white and roots and leaves that yield saponin. Latin name: *Saponaria officinalis.* US term **bouncing Bet**

soapy /sōpi/ (**-ier, -iest**) *adj.* **1.** **WITH SOAP** full of or covered with soap **2.** **LIKE SOAP** with the look or feel of soap ○ *a soapy texture* **3.** **INSINCERE** given to excessive insincere flattery (*slang*)

soar /sawr/ *vi.* (**soars, soaring, soared**) **1.** **FLY** to fly or rise high in the air **2.** **GLIDE HIGH** to glide, on rising currents of air **3.** **INCREASE RAPIDLY** to increase rapidly in number, volume, size, or amount ○ *soaring prices* **4.** **BECOME MORE INTENSE** to rise to a higher, more intense, or exalted level ■ *n.* **ACT OF SOARING** the act of soaring, or the height or range reached by soaring [14thC. Via Old French *essorer* from assumed Vulgar Latin *exaurare*, from Latin *ex-* 'out, up' + *aura* 'air' (see AURA).] —**soarer** *n.*

Soares /swaárish/, **Mário** (*b.* 1924) Portuguese statesman. He was prime minister (1976–78 and 1983–85) and president (1986–96) of Portugal, and re-established democratic government there. Full name **Mário Alberto Nobre Lopes Soares**

Soave /sō aá vay, swaá vay/ *n.* a dry white wine made in Italy [Mid-20thC. Named after the village of *Soave*, near Verona in Italy, where it is produced.]

Soay /sō ay, sóy/ *n.* a small dark brown sheep of a breed found in the Outer Hebrides, especially on the island of Soay

sob /sob/ *v.* (**sobs, sobbing, sobbed**) **1.** *vi.* **GASP WHILE CRYING** to draw in breath while crying, making gasping sounds **2.** *vt.* **UTTER STH WHILE SOBBING** to say sth while sobbing **3.** *vr.* **BECOME BY SOBBING** to get into a particular state by sobbing ○ *to sob yourself to sleep* ■ *n.* **SOUND OF SOBBING** a convulsive breath made while sobbing, or the sound of this breath ○ *stifled a sob* [12thC. Origin uncertain: possibly from Low German or Low Dutch.] —**sobbingly** *adv.*

SOB, s.o.b. *n., abbr. US* son of a bitch (*slang insult*)

sober /sṓbər/ *adj.* **1.** NOT INTOXICATED not under the influence of alcohol **2.** TENDING NOT TO DRINK not in the habit of drinking much alcohol **3.** SERIOUS serious and thoughtful in demeanour or quality ○ *a sober face* **4.** DULL lacking vitality or brightness in appearance ○ *He always dresses in sober colours.* **5.** NOT FANCIFUL OR SPECULATIVE based on facts and rational thinking rather than on speculation ○ *a sober assessment of the situation* ■ *vti.* (-bers, -bering, -bered) LESSEN INTOXICATION to become or make sb become less drunk or completely sober [14thC. Via Old French from Latin *sobrius*. Ultimately from an Indo-European negative prefix and a word meaning 'to drink', which is also the ancestor of English *inebriate*.] —**sobering** *adj.* —**soberingly** *adv.* —**soberly** *adv.* —**soberness** *n.*

sobersides /sṓbər sīdz/ *n.* sb who is solemn and serious —**sobersided** *adj.*

sobriety /sə brī́ əti/ *n.* **1.** ABSTINENCE abstinence from or moderation in the use of alcohol **2.** SERIOUSNESS the quality of being serious and thoughtful [15thC. Via Old French from, ultimately, Latin *sobrius* 'sober' (see SOBER).]

sobriquet /sṓbri kay/, **soubriquet** *n.* an unofficial name or nickname, especially a humorous one [Mid-17thC. From French, literally 'a tap under the chin'.]

sob sister *n.* a journalist who writes or edits sentimental stories or answers problems sent in by readers (*informal*)

sob story *n.* a story told to gain sb's sympathy or pity, especially when offered as an excuse (*informal*)

soc., **Soc.** *abbr.* **1.** society **2.** socialist

soca /sṓkə/ *n.* a style of Caribbean music that combines calypso and soul and has a fast beat [Late 20thC. Blend of SOUL and CALYPSO.]

socage /sókkij/, **soccage** *n.* a feudal system of holding land in which the tenant either paid rent or performed a fixed service, usually agricultural and nonmilitary in nature [14thC. From Anglo-Norman, where it was formed from *soc*, variant of SOKE.] —**socager** *n.*

so-called *adj.* **1.** POPULARLY popularly known as, but not necessarily by the speaker or writer ○ *the so-called Information Superhighway* **2.** INCORRECTLY incorrectly known as ○ *a so-called art expert*

soccer /sókər/ *n.* = **football** [Late 19thC. Formed from *Assoc.*, an abbreviation of *Association football*, because it was played under the rules of the Football Association, as opposed to 'Rugby football'.]

Socceroos /sókə ro͞oz/ *n. Aus* an informal name for the Australian national soccer team (*informal*)

sociable /sṓshəb'l/ *adj.* **1.** GREGARIOUS inclined to seek out the company of other people **2.** FRIENDLY friendly and pleasant to other people **3.** OFFERING OPPORTUNITY FOR SOCIAL INTERACTION allowing people to mix in an informal way ○ *a sociable occasion* [Mid-16thC. Directly or via French from Latin *sociabilis*, from *socius* 'companion' (see SOCIAL).] —**sociability** /sṓshə bíləti/ *n.* —**sociableness** /sṓshəb'lnəss/ *n.* —**sociably** /sṓshəbli/ *adv.*

WORD KEY: USAGE

sociable or **social**? ***Social*** is a neutral word that classifies a person or thing as being concerned in some way with society or its organization. A *social club* is a place provided for people to enjoy themselves, and a *social worker* is involved in work done for people's welfare. ***Sociable***, by contrast, is a judgmental word referring to a person's capacity to deal in social ways with other people, so a *sociable worker* is a worker who enjoys the company of colleagues.

social /sṓsh'l/ *adj.* **1.** RELATING TO SOCIETY relating to human society and how it is organized **2.** RELATING TO INTERACTION OF PEOPLE relating to the way people in groups behave and interact ○ *the social sciences* **3.** LIVING IN A COMMUNITY living or preferring to live as part of a community or colony, rather than alone ○ *social insects such as ants* **4.** OFFERING OPPORTUNITY FOR INTERACTION allowing people to meet and interact with others in a friendly way ○ *a social club* **5.** RELATING TO HUMAN WELFARE relating to human welfare and the organized welfare services that a community provides ○ *social services* **6.** TO DO WITH RANK relating to or thought appropriate to a particular rank in society, especially the upper classes **7.** SOCIABLE tending to seek out the company of others (*informal*) ○ *a very social person* **8.** GROWING IN CLUMPS used to describe plants that grow in clumps or masses ■ *n.* **1.** INFORMAL GET-TOGETHER an informal gathering or party, usually of a particular group of people who meet regularly **2.** **social, Social** SOCIAL SECURITY the Social Security services (*slang*) [Mid-17thC. Via French from Latin *socialis*, from *socius* 'companion'. Ultimately from an Indo-European word meaning 'to follow', which is also the ancestor of English *sequel*.] —**socially** *adv.* —**socialness** *n.*

WORD KEY: USAGE

See Usage note at ***sociable***.

social anthropology *n.* the scientific study of human society or a particular society, including study of kinship systems, traditional political and economic practices, rituals, and beliefs. ◊ **cultural anthropology**

social assistance *n. Can* social security

social capital *n.* the educational, social, and cultural advantages that sb from the upper classes is believed to possess

Social Charter *n.* a declaration that outlines the rights of workers in countries that are part of the European Community

social climber *n.* sb who tries to join a higher social class by setting out to mix with people that belong to it (*disapproving*) —**social climbing** *n.*

social contract, **social compact** *n.* an agreement among individuals in a society or between the people and their government that describes the rights and duties of each party. It derives from the ideas of Hobbes, Locke, and Rousseau and involves individuals giving up certain freedoms in return for benefits such as state protection.

Social Credit *n. Can* a Canadian right-wing political party founded in 1935 —**Social Crediter** *n.*

social democracy, **Social Democracy** *n.* the political belief that a change from capitalism to socialism can be achieved gradually and democratically —**social democrat** *n.* —**social democratic** *adj.*

Social Democratic and Labour Party *n.* a political party in Northern Ireland, many of whose supporters want to unite Northern Ireland and the Republic of Ireland peacefully

Social Democratic Party *n.* **1.** FORMER BRITISH POLITICAL PARTY a British political party existing from 1981 to 1990. Founded by a group who left the Labour Party, many of its members joined the Social and Liberal Democratic Party in 1988. **2.** GERMAN POLITICAL PARTY a German political party advocating gradual reform to socialism

social disease *n.* a venereal disease (*informal; used euphemistically*)

social drinker *n.* sb who only drinks in company and in moderation

social engineering *n.* the use of policies that are based on the findings of social science to deal with social problems

social insurance *n.* state insurance that uses compulsory contributions to pay for benefits for unemployed and retired people

socialisation *n.* = **socialization**

socialise *vti.* = **socialize**

socialism /sṓshəlizəm/ *n.* **1.** POLITICAL SYSTEM OF COMMUNAL OWNERSHIP a political theory or system in which the means of production and distribution are controlled by the people and operated according to equity and fairness rather than market principles **2.** MOVEMENT BASED ON SOCIALISM any of several political movements or theories of the 19th and 20th centuries based on principles of socialism, typically advocating an end to private property and the exploitation of workers **3.** STAGE BETWEEN CAPITALISM AND COMMUNISM in Marxist theory, the stage after the proletarian revolution when a society is changing from capitalism to communism, marked by pay distributed according to work done rather than need

socialist /sṓshəlist/, **Socialist** *n.* BELIEVER IN SOCIALISM sb who believes in and supports socialism or a socialist party ■ *adj.* **1.** ADVOCATING SOCIALISM relating to, based on, or advocating socialism **2.** **socialist, Socialist** RELATING TO SOCIALISTS relating to socialists or a socialist party —**socialistic** /sṓshə lístik/ *adj.* —**socialistically** /-lístikli/ *adv.*

socialist realism *n.* an artistic doctrine officially sanctioned in many Communist countries, especially during the 1930s-50s, that proposed the idea that art and literature should serve to promote and glorify the ideals of a socialist state

socialite /sṓshə līt/ *n.* sb who is well-known in fashionable society

sociality /sṓshi álləti/ (*plural* **-ties**) *n.* **1.** QUALITY OF BEING SOCIAL the quality of being social, or an instance of it **2.** TENDENCY TO FORM SOCIAL GROUPS the tendency to form social groups or live in a community

socialization /sṓshə lī záysh'n/, **socialisation** *n.* the process involved when young children are becoming aware of society and learning how they are expected to behave

socialize /sṓshə līz/ (**-izes, -izing, -ized**), **socialise** (**-ises, -ising, -ised**) *v.* **1.** *vi.* TAKE PART IN SOCIAL ACTIVITIES to take part in social activities or behave in a friendly way to others ○ *a group of friends who like to socialize after work* **2.** *vt.* TRAIN TO BE SOCIAL to teach sb to be a fit member of society ○ *socialize a child* —**socializer** *n.*

socialized medicine, **socialised medicine** *n.* a system of national health care that provides medical care to all and is regulated and subsidized by the government

social mobility *n.* the capacity for individuals in a society to change their class or social status within their lifetimes

social psychology *n.* the area of psychology that deals with how groups behave and how individuals are affected by the group —**social psychologist** *n.*

social realism *n.* the use of realistic portrayals of life in art or literature to make a social or political point

social science *n.* **1.** STUDY OF SOCIETY the study of people in society and how individuals relate to one another and to the group **2.** DISCIPLINE STUDYING SPECIFIC AREA OF SOCIETY any of the disciplines within social science that study a specific area of human society such as sociology, psychology, economics, political science, history, or anthropology —**social scientist** *n.*

social secretary *n.* sb whose job is to arrange social activities and handle correspondence for a person or organization

social security *n.* **1.** **social security, Social Security** GOVERNMENT PROGRAMME PROVIDING ECONOMIC SECURITY a government programme providing for the economic welfare of the individual, e.g. through payments to people who are retired, unemployed, or unable to work **2.** MONEY PAID BY GOVERNMENT TO INDIVIDUAL money paid by a government to an individual through a Social Security programme

social service *n.* SERVICE FOR WELFARE OF COMMUNITY a service provided by a government agency for the welfare of an individual or community. Such services include housing, child protection, free school lunches, or health care. (*often used in the plural*) ■ **social services** *npl.* AGENCY PROVIDING SOCIAL SERVICES a government agency that provides social services to individuals or a community

social studies *n.* an academic subject devoted to the study of society and including geography, economics, and history (*takes a singular or plural verb*)

social welfare *n.* the social services provided by a state or by a private organization

social work *n.* the profession or work of providing people in need with social services —**social worker** *n.*

societal /sə sī́ ət'l/ *adj.* relating to society, especially its organization, structure, or function —**societally** *adv.*

society /sə sī́ əti/ (*plural* **-ties**) *n.* **1.** RELATIONSHIPS AMONG GROUPS the sum of social relationships among groups of humans or animals **2.** STRUCTURED COMMUNITY OF PEOPLE a structured community of people bound together by similar traditions, institutions, or nationality **3.** CUSTOMS OF A COMMUNITY the customs of a community and the way it is organized, e.g. its class structure

○ *the role of women in society* **4.** SUBSET OF SOCIETY a particular section of a community that is distinguished by specific qualities ○ *In those days, the subject was never mentioned in polite society.* **5.** PROMINENT PEOPLE the prominent or fashionable people in a community and their social life **6.** COMPANIONSHIP the state of being with other people **7.** GROUP SHARING INTERESTS an organized group of people who share an interest, aim, or profession [Mid-16thC. Via French from Latin *societas*, literally 'companionship', from *socius* 'companion' (see SOCIAL).]

Society of Friends *n.* the Christian group also known as the Quakers (*formal*)

Society of Jesus *n.* the Roman Catholic religious order also known as the Jesuits (*formal*)

Socinian /sō sínni ən/ *n.* FOLLOWER OF SOCINUS a follower of Laelius and Faustus Socinus, Italian theologians who preached belief in God but rejected other traditional Christian doctrines such as the Trinity and the divinity of Christ ■ *adj.* RELATING TO THE SOCINIANS relating to the Socinians and their beliefs —**Socinianism** *n.*

socio- *prefix.* society, social ○ *sociopath* ○ *sociopsychological* [Via French from, ultimately, Latin *socius* 'companion' (see SOCIAL)]

sociobiology /sṓs si ō bī ólləji, sṓshi-/ *n.* the study of the social behaviour of animals and humans and how this is related to genetics and the survival of species —**sociobiological** /sṓssi ō bí ə lójjik'l, sṓshi ō-/ *adj.*

socioeconomic /sṓsi ō ékkə nómmik, sṓshi ō-, sṓssi ō éekə nómmik, -/ *adj.* involving economic and social factors —**socioeconomically** *adv.*

sociol. *abbr.* sociology

sociolinguistics /sṓssi ō ling gwístiks, sṓshi ō-/ *n.* the study of the relationships between language and the social and cultural factors that affect it —**sociolinguist** /sṓssi ō líng gwist, sṓshi ō-/ *n.* —**sociolinguistic** /sṓssi ō ling gwístik, sṓshi ō-/ *adj.*

sociology /sṓssi ólləji, sṓshi-/ *n.* **1.** STUDY OF SOCIETY the study of the origin, development, and structure of human societies and the behaviour of individuals and groups in society **2.** STUDY OF INDIVIDUAL SOCIAL INSTITUTION the study of a particular social institution and the part it plays in society [Mid-19thC. From French *sociologie*, literally 'science of companions', from Latin *socius* 'companion' (see SOCIO-).] —**sociological** /sṓssi ə lójjikəl, sṓshi ə-/ *adj.* —**sociologically** /-lójjikli/ *adv.* —**sociologist** /sṓssi olləjist, sṓshi-/ *n.*

sociometry /sṓssi ómmətri, sṓshi-/ *n.* the statistical study of behaviour and relationships within social groups, especially expressed in terms of preferences —**sociometric** /sṓssi ō méttrik, sṓshi ō-/ *adj.* —**sociometrist** /sṓssi ómmətrist, sṓshi-/ *n.*

sociopath /sṓssi ō path, sṓshi ō-/ *n.* = **psychopath** [Mid-20thC. Modelled on PSYCHOPATH.] —**sociopathic** /sṓssi ō páthik, sṓshi ō-/ *adj.* —**sociopathy** /sṓssi óppəthi, sṓshi-/ *n.*

sociopolitical /sṓssi ō pə líttik'l, sṓshi ō-/ *adj.* relating to or involving both social and political factors

sociopsychological /sṓssi ō sīkə lójjik'l, sṓshi ō-/ *adj.* **1.** RELATING TO SOCIAL PSYCHOLOGY relating to or involving social psychology **2.** SOCIAL AND PSYCHOLOGICAL relating to or involving both social and psychological factors

sock[1] /sok/ *n.* **1.** SOFT FOOT COVERING a soft, usually knitted covering for the foot and ankle that may reach as high as the knee. It is usually worn inside a shoe. **2.** METEOROL = **windsock 3.** INSOLE a removable inner sole used for warmth or to make a shoe fit better [Old English *socc* 'light shoe, slipper', via prehistoric Germanic from Latin *soccus* (source of English *socle*), from Greek *sukkhos* '(kind of) shoe'] ◇ **pull your socks up** to make an effort to improve (*informal*) ◇ **put a sock in it** used to tell sb to be quiet (*slang*)

sock away *vt. US, Can, NZ* to save money for the future (*informal*) [From the practice of storing savings in a sock]

sock[2] /sok/ *vti.* (**socks, socking, socked**) (*informal*) STRIKE SB to hit sb or sth hard, usually with the fist ■ *n.* HARD HIT OR BLOW a hard hit or blow, usually with the fist [Late 17thC. Origin unknown.] ◇ **sock it to sb sock it to** to speak or behave in a way that makes a strong impression upon sb (*informal*)

socket /sókit/ *n.* **1.** SHAPED HOLE FOR CONNECTION a hole or recess in sth specially shaped to receive a particular object or part, e.g. the hole that receives a light bulb or one that receives a plug on an electrical device **2.** ELEC CONNECTION WITH ELECTRICITY SUPPLY a receptacle, usually mounted on a wall, into which an electric plug is inserted to make a connection to a source of electric power. US term **outlet 3.** HOLLOW IN BODY a bony hollow in the body into which another part fits ■ *vt.* (**-ets, -eting, -eted**) PUT IN SOCKET to insert sth into a socket, or to provide sth with a socket [13thC. From Anglo-Norman *soket*, literally 'small ploughshare', from Old French *sok* 'ploughshare', of uncertain origin: probably ultimately from Gaulish. Originally 'spearhead', later 'socket supporting a spear'.]

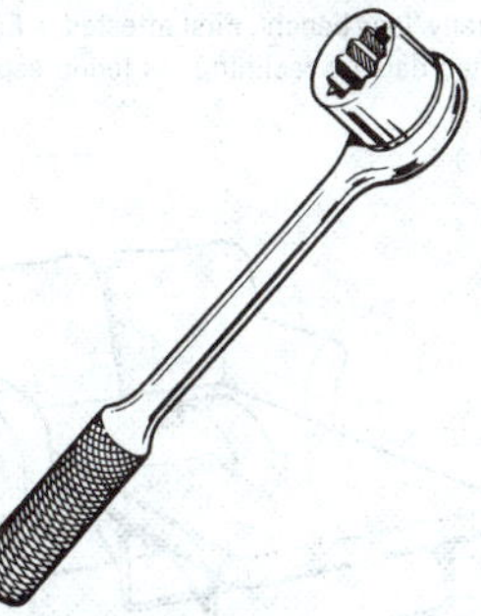

Socket wrench

socket wrench *n.* a long-handled wrench with interchangeable heads that fit over various sized nuts and bolts and a ratchet that makes tightening nuts and bolts easier

sockeye /sók ī/ (*plural* **-eyes** *or* **-eye**), **sockeye salmon** *n.* a Pacific food fish in the salmon family that has red flesh. Latin name: *Oncorhynchus nerka.* [Late 19thC. By folk etymology from Salish *sukai*, literally 'fish of fishes'.]

socle /sók'l/ *n.* a base that sticks out from under the bottom of a wall, or the lowest part of the base of a column or pedestal [Early 18thC. Via French from, ultimately, Latin *socculus* 'small light shoe', from *soccus* (see SOCK[1]).]

Socrates /sókrə teez/ (469–399 BC) Greek philosopher. His philosophy has survived through the writings of his pupils, especially Plato. He employed what became known as the 'Socratic method' to question conventional assumptions about morality, justice, and other social concepts. Charged with atheism and corrupting youth, he was condemned to death.

Socratic /sə kráttik/ *adj.* RELATING TO SOCRATES relating to Socrates, to his philosophy, or to his method of arriving at truth ■ *n.* SB STUDYING SOCRATES a student or follower of Socrates —**Socratically** *adv.* —**Socraticism** /sókrətizəm/ *n.* —**Socratist** /sókrətist/ *n.*

Socratic irony *n.* ignorance feigned in order to elicit explanations from sb whose own ignorance can then be exposed through subsequent clever questioning

Socratic method *n.* a means of arriving at truth by continually questioning, obtaining answers, and criticizing the answers

Socred /sṓkred/ *n. Can* MEMBER OF SOCIAL CREDIT MOVEMENT a member or supporter of a Social Credit movement or political party ■ *adj. Can* OF SOCIAL CREDIT PARTY relating to the Social Credit political party [Mid-20thC. Contraction of SOCIAL CREDIT.]

sod[1] /sod/ *n.* **1.** TURF a surface section or strip of earth with growing grass and roots **2.** GROUND ground or soil (*literary*) ■ *vt.* (**sods, sodding, sodded**) COVER WITH TURF to cover ground with sods [15thC. From Middle Dutch or Low German *sode* 'turf', of unknown origin.]

sod off *vi.* to go away (*slang*) ['Sod' from SOD[2]]

sod[2] /sod/ *n.* **1.** OFFENSIVE TERM an offensive term referring to sb regarded as stupid, annoying, or obnoxious (*slang insult*) **2.** ANY PERSON used, often humorously or affectionately, to refer to a person (*slang; considered offensive in some contexts*) ■ *vt.* DAMN used as a swearword to express anger or defiance (*slang offensive*) [Early 19thC. Shortening of SODOMITE.]

soda /sṓdə/ *n.* **1.** *US* SOFT DRINK a flavoured and carbonated drink, served cold. ◊ **tonic 2.** = **soda water** *n.* 1 **3.** *US* ICE CREAM IN FLAVOURED CARBONATED WATER a refreshment made with flavoured carbonated water and ice cream, usually served in a tall glass **4.** SODIUM sodium that is chemically combined with other elements **5.** = **sodium bicarbonate 6.** = **sodium carbonate 7.** = **sodium hydroxide 8.** CARDS CARD THAT STARTS FARO the card from the top of the pack that is turned face up in the dealing box at the start of the card game faro [15thC. Via Italian 'saltwort' (from which sodium carbonate is obtained) from Arabic *suwwād*.]

soda ash *n.* sodium carbonate when sold commercially, e.g. for use as a manufacturing ingredient in the soap and paper industries

soda biscuit *n.* a biscuit leavened with bicarbonate of soda

soda bread *n.* bread leavened with bicarbonate of soda rather than yeast, associated especially with Irish cooking

soda cracker *n. US* a cracker leavened slightly with baking soda and cream of tartar

soda fountain *n. US* a counter or stand where beverages, ice cream, and snacks are sold (*dated*)

soda lime *n.* a mixture of sodium hydroxide and calcium hydroxide used commercially and industrially to absorb moisture and carbon dioxide

sodalite /sṓdə līt/ *n.* a blue, greyish, or yellow translucent mineral consisting of sodium and aluminium silicates with chlorine. It is found in alkaline igneous rocks. [Early 19thC. Coined from SODA + -LITE.]

sodality /sō dálləti/ (*plural* **-ties**) *n.* **1.** RELIGIOUS SOCIETY a Roman Catholic lay society that is run as a charity or a religious fellowship **2.** ORGANIZED GROUP an association or fellowship of any kind [Early 17thC. Directly or via French *sodalité* from Latin *sodalitas* 'fellowship', from *sodalis* 'fellow, companion'.]

soda nitre *n.* = **Chile saltpetre**

soda siphon *n.* a sealed bottle containing water and carbon dioxide gas under pressure, used to produce soda water. US term **siphon bottle**

soda water *n.* **1.** WATER CHARGED WITH CARBON DIOXIDE carbonated water drunk as a beverage or used as a mixer in alcoholic drinks **2.** DIGESTIVE AID a weak solution of water, bicarbonate of soda, and acid, taken to aid digestion

sodbuster /sódbustə/ *n.* **1.** *US* FARMER sb who farms the land **2.** PLOUGH a plough that is used to break the sod **3.** *Can* HOMESTEADER a prairie homesteader, especially one who raised crops (*informal*)

sodden /sódd'n/ *adj.* **1.** THOROUGHLY WET saturated with moisture **2.** DRUNK with dulled senses from excessive drinking ■ *vti.* (**-dens, -dening, -dened**) MAKE OR BECOME SODDEN to make sth or sb sodden or to become sodden [13thC. The obsolete past participle of SEETHE. Originally 'boiled'; the sense 'thoroughly wet' dates from the 19thC.] —**soddenly** *adv.* —**soddenness** *n.*

WORD KEY: SYNONYMS

See Synonyms at ***wet***.

sodium /sṓdi əm/ *n.* a soft silver-white metallic chemical element that reacts readily with other substances. It is essential to the body's fluid balance and occurs in abundance, especially in common salt. Symbol **Na** [Early 19thC. Coined from SODA (from its being isolated from caustic soda) + -IUM.]

sodium benzoate *n.* a white crystalline powder used as a food preservative, as an antiseptic, and in pharmaceutical preparations. Formula: $C_7H_5O_2Na$.

sodium bicarbonate *n.* a white crystalline slightly alkaline salt used as a leavening agent, in effervescent drinks and fire extinguishers, and medicinally as an antacid. Formula: $NaHCO_3$.

sodium carbonate *n.* **1.** SALT OF CARBONIC ACID a white crystalline salt of carbonic acid used in making glass, ceramics, soap, and paper. It is also used as a water softener, and in cleaning, bleaching, and photography. Formula: Na_2CO_3. **2.** = **washing soda**

sodium chlorate *n.* a colourless crystalline salt used as a weedkiller, a bleaching agent, and in explosives. Formula: $NaClO_3$.

sodium chloride *n.* a colourless crystalline compound, found naturally in sea water and halite and used as a preservative and food seasoning. Formula: NaCl. ◊ **salt**

sodium citrate *n.* a crystalline salt used in photography, and in medicine as an anticoagulant in stored blood. Formula: $Na_3C_6H_5O_7$.

sodium cyanide *n.* a poisonous white salt used in fumigating, in manufacturing steel and dyes, and in extracting gold and silver from ore. Formula: NaCN.

sodium cyclamate *n.* = **cyclamate**

sodium dichromate *n.* a red or orange crystalline salt used in tanning leather, in making dyes and inks, and as an oxidizing agent and corrosion inhibitor. Formula: $Na_2Cr_2O_7$.

sodium fluoride *n.* a poisonous colourless crystalline salt used in small quantities in the fluoridation of water, in preventing tooth decay, in metallurgy, and as a pesticide. Formula: NaF.

sodium fluoroacetate *n.* a white poisonous powder used to kill rodents. Formula: $C_2H_2FNaO_2$. [Mid-20thC. 'Fluoroacetate' coined from FLUORO- + ACETATE.]

sodium glutamate *n.* = **monosodium glutamate**

sodium hydroxide *n.* a brittle white alkaline solid used in making paper, rayon, soap, chemicals, pharmaceuticals, and in petroleum refining. Formula: NaOH.

sodium hypochlorite *n.* a green crystalline salt used in bleaching, disinfecting, and water purification. Formula: NaOCl.

sodium hyposulphite *n.* = **sodium thiosulphate**

sodium nitrate *n.* a white crystalline salt used in curing meat, in rocket propellants, as a fertilizer, and in making explosives, pottery, and glass. Formula: $NaNO_3$.

Sodium Pentothal *tdmk.* a trademark for thiopentone sodium

sodium peroxide *n.* a yellowish odourless powder used in bleaching and as an antiseptic and disinfectant. Formula: Na_2O_2.

sodium phosphate *n.* any of several sodium salts of phosphoric acid that are used in medicine and manufacturing

sodium propionate *n.* a colourless crystalline powder used to kill bacteria and fungi in the preservation of food. Formula: $C_3H_5NaO_2$.

sodium pump *n.* a molecular process by which sodium ions are transported across cell membranes and exchanged with potassium ions

sodium silicate *n.* any of several compounds of silicate glass used as preservatives, in processing textiles, and in cement

sodium sulphate *n.* a bitter white salt used in making glass, wood pulp, rayon, dyes, detergents, ceramic glazes, and in pharmaceuticals as a cathartic. Formula: Na_2SO_4.

sodium thiosulphate *n.* a white crystalline salt used as a fixer in photography and as a bleach. Formula: $Na_2S_2O_3$.

sodium-vapour lamp *n.* an electric lamp containing neon gas and sodium vapour through which a current runs to produce an orange-yellow light used for street lighting

Sodom /sóddəm/ *n.* **1.** CITY OF DEPRAVITY in the Bible, a city full of moral corruption and evil that was destroyed along with Gomorrah by God **2.** CORRUPT PLACE a place that is regarded as corrupt

sodomise *vt.* = **sodomize**

sodomite /sóddə mīt/ *n.* sb who engages in sodomy [14thC. Via French from, ultimately, Greek *Sodomitēs* 'inhabitant of Sodom', from *Sodoma* 'Sodom'.] — **sodomitic** /sóddə míttik/ *adj.*

sodomize /sóddə mīz/ (**-izes, -izing, -ized**), **sodomise** (**-ises, -ising, -ised**) *vt.* to engage in sodomy with sb

sodomy /sóddəmi/ *n.* **1.** ANAL INTERCOURSE anal intercourse engaged in by heterosexual or homosexual partners **2.** INTERCOURSE WITH ANIMALS sexual intercourse with an animal [13thC. Directly or via French *sodomie*

from medieval Latin *sodomia*, which was formed from ecclesiastical Latin *peccatum Sodomiticum* 'sin of Sodom'.]

Sod's law /sódz-/ *n.* one of many humorous variations on the saying that if sth can go wrong it will and at the worst possible moment (*informal*) US term **Murphy's law** [Late 20thC. 'Sod's' from SOD².]

Sod's Law *n.* the law or principle that if anything can go wrong, it will (*informal*) US term **Murphy's Law**

soever /sō évvər/ *adv.* in any way or to any degree possible [13thC. Originally two words (from SO + EVER).]

sofa /sófə/ *n.* a long upholstered seat that has a back and arms and is made to seat more than one person [Early 17thC. Via French from, ultimately, Arabic *suffa*, literally 'long bench'. First attested in English denoting a 'cushioned dais for reclining (as found especially in Arab countries)'.]

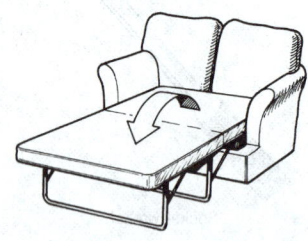

Sofa bed

sofa bed *n.* a sofa that can be temporarily converted into a bed as required, e.g. by unfolding its seat

sofar /só faar/ *n.* a way of locating survivors at sea by measuring the time it takes sound waves to reach three shore locations from an explosion set off underwater by the survivors [Mid-20thC. Acronym formed from *Sound fixing and ranging*.]

soffit /sóffit/ *n.* the underside of a structural component of a building, e.g. the underside of a roof overhang or the inner curve of an arch [Early 17thC. Via French *soffite* or Italian *soffitto* from, ultimately, Latin *suffixus* 'fixed under' (see SUFFIX).]

Sofia /sófi ə/ capital city of Bulgaria, situated in the Sofia basin, about 64 km/40 mi. from the Yugoslavian border. Population: 1,116,000 (1995).

S. of Sol. *abbr.* BIBLE Song of Solomon

soft /soft/ *adj.* **1.** MALLEABLE easily shaped, bent, or cut **2.** YIELDING giving way to externally applied pressure or weight ○ *a soft cushion* **3.** SMOOTH-TEXTURED having a texture that is smooth to the touch ○ *soft fur* **4.** WITH SMOOTH OUTLINE with no sharp or jagged edges ○ *furniture designed with soft lines* **5.** QUIET-SOUNDING quiet and soothing in sound **6.** EASY ON THE EYES without glare or intensity of light or colour **7.** MILD not blowing strongly nor falling heavily ○ *a soft rain* **8.** AFFECTIONATE conveying love and tenderness **9.** EMOTIONAL easily moved to tender emotions **10.** COWARDLY lacking determination or strength of character **11.** LENIENT lenient in treatment or punishment, often too lenient **12.** UNDEMANDING requiring little effort or attention (*informal*) ○ *a soft job* **13.** NOT WELL TONED out of good physical condition **14.** INCAPABLE OF ENDURING HARDSHIP unable or unwilling to put up with hardship or privation, especially from having lived a life of ease **15.** LACKING GOOD SENSE lacking intelligence or sound judgment (*informal*) **16.** NOT EASILY VERIFIABLE dealing with data that is not easily proved or disproved using scientific method **17.** = **soft-core 18.** VULNERABLE unprotected against violent attack **19.** MIL UNARMOURED used to describe military vehicles and sites with little or no protection against military attack **20.** POL NOT POLITICALLY EXTREME holding moderate rather than radical or hardline political views **21.** FIN RELATING TO PAPER MONEY relating to currency or a monetary system that is not backed by gold, and is therefore not easily convertible to a foreign currency **22.** COMM DECLINING ECONOMICALLY exhibiting a downward trend, e.g. in price, demand, or economic activity **23.** PHON SIBILANT OR FRICATIVE used to describe the consonant sounds 'c' and 'g' when pronounced

as a fricative, as in 'dance' and 'age', rather than as a stop, as in 'cat' and 'get' **24.** PHON PALATALIZED used to describe a consonant that is palatalized in a Slavic language **25.** PHYS LOW-ENERGY used to describe radiation that has low energy and lacks penetrating ability ■ *adv.* SOFTLY in a quiet, tender, or lenient way ■ *n.* STH SOFT a soft thing or part of sth [Old English *sōfte* (earlier *sēfte*), from prehistoric Germanic. The underlying idea is perhaps 'fitting, arranged (so as to be pleasing)'.] —**softly** *adv.* —**softness** *n.* ◇ **be soft on sb** to be romantically attracted to sb

softback /sóft bak/ *adj.*, *n.* = **paperback**

softball /sóft báwl/ *n.* **1.** BALLGAME a kind of baseball played on a smaller field with a larger and softer ball that is pitched underhand **2.** BALL USED FOR SOFTBALL the ball used to play softball

soft-boiled *adj.* **1.** WITH SOFT YOLK boiled so that the yolk is soft but the white is firm **2.** TENDING TO SYMPATHIZE with a sympathetic or sentimental nature

soft chancre *n.* = **chancroid** [*Soft* from the softness of the ulcer]

soft coal *n.* = **bituminous coal**

soft commodities *npl.* traded commodities that are not metals, such as cocoa, sugar, cotton, and cereals

soft copy *n.* data stored on a computer disk, as distinct from data that is printed on paper

soft-core *adj.* sexually suggestive or provocative without being explicit

softcover /sóft kuvvər/ *adj.*, *n.* = **paperback**

soft drink *n.* any still or carbonated nonalcoholic beverage served cold

soft drug *n.* any illicit drug that is thought by some to be less addictive and harmful than the narcotic drugs heroin and cocaine

soften /sóff'n/ (**-ens, -ening, -ened**) *vti.* **1.** MAKE OR BECOME LESS HARD to become soft or softer, or to make sth soft or softer **2.** BE KINDER to become gentler or less harsh, or to make sth gentler or less harsh **3.** WEAR SB DOWN to make sb's resolve less firm, or to become less firmly resolved **4.** HARASS ENEMY to weaken an enemy's resistance or morale by continuous bombardment, or to have resistance or morale weakened **5.** REDUCE STH to decline, e.g. in price, demand, or economic activity, or to cause sth such as a market to decline

softener /sóff'nər/ *n.* a substance added to sth such as water or laundry to make it softer

soft focus *n.* a deliberate slight blurring of a photograph or a filmed image giving it a hazy appearance, so as to achieve a special effect such as romance or nostalgia (*hyphenated when used before a noun*)

soft fruit *n.* small stoneless fruit, such as raspberries, strawberries, blackberries, or blackcurrants

soft furnishings *npl.* furnishings made from fabric, such as curtains and rugs, that decorate a house and make it more comfortable. US term **home furnishings**

soft goods *npl.* textiles and the items such as clothing and bedding that are made from them

soft hail *n.* = **graupel**

soft-hearted *adj.* showing sympathy, kindness, or generosity —**soft-heartedly** *adv.* —**soft-heartedness** *n.*

softie *n.* = **softy**

soft-kill *adj.* US intended to disable rather than kill an enemy

soft landing *n.* **1.** SAFE LANDING a landing of a spacecraft, especially on the moon, without enough impact to cause damage **2.** UNCOMPLICATED SOLUTION a resolution of a problem, especially an economic problem, found without undue effort

soft line *n.* a flexible and reasonable approach, especially to a political issue —**soft-liner** *n.*

softly-softly *adj.* characterized by caution or discretion

soft option *n.* the easier or easiest course of action when given a choice

soft palate *n.* the fleshy rear portion of the roof of the mouth, extending from the hard palate at the front and tapering to the hanging uvula at the rear. It elevates to close off the nasal passages when swallowing, sucking, and pronouncing certain sounds.

soft pedal *n.* a pedal on a piano that reduces the usual volume. It either shifts the hammers so that they do not strike all the strings of each note or so that they strike the strings with less force.

soft-pedal (**soft-pedals, soft-pedalling, soft-pedalled**) *vti.* **1. PLAY PIANO'S SOFT PEDAL** to reduce the volume of music played on a piano by operating the soft pedal **2. PLAY STH DOWN** to try to make sth seem less important, noticeable, or objectionable (*informal*)

soft rock *n.* rock music that tends to be slower and more melodic than hard rock, often influenced by folk or country and western music

soft rot *n.* any bacterial or fungal plant disease that causes plant parts, especially fruits and vegetables, to decay into a pulpy mass

soft sell *n.* a method of selling or advertising goods and services that uses subtlety and persuasion, rather than aggressive insistence (*informal*) (*hyphenated when used before a noun*)

soft-shell *adj.* used to describe an aquatic animal with a soft or thin and brittle shell, sometimes as a result of having recently moulted

soft-shelled turtle *n.* a freshwater turtle with sharp claws, a pointed snout, and a soft flat shell covered with leathery skin. Family: Trionychidae.

soft-shoe *n.* a type of tap dancing for which soft-soled shoes without metal taps are worn (*often used before a noun*)

soft soap *n.* **1. TYPE OF SOAP** a liquid or semiliquid soap, usually made with potassium hydroxide **2. MANIPULATIVE FLATTERY** flattery used for the purpose of persuading or distracting sb (*informal*)

soft-soap (**soft-soaps, soft-soaping, soft-soaped**) *vt.* to use flattery to persuade or distract sb (*informal*)

softsore /sóft sawr/ *n.* = **chancroid**

soft-spoken *adj.* speaking or said with a quiet gentle voice

soft spot *n.* a place, position, or area in which sth is weak or vulnerable ◇ **have a soft spot for sb** *or* **sth** to have especially tender feelings or affection for sb or sth

soft top *n.* a car that has a soft roof made of fabric that can be opened and folded back

soft touch *n.* sb who can be easily swayed or imposed upon to do sth

software /sóft wair/ *n.* computer programs and applications, such as word processing or database packages, that can be run on a particular computer system (*often used before a noun*) [Mid-19thC. Originally, in plural, 'soft goods'. The modern sense dates from the mid-20thC.]

software engineering *n.* the application of mathematics and technology to the design, implementation, and testing of computer programs to optimize their production and support

software piracy *n.* the illegal duplication of copyrighted software or the installation of copyrighted software on more computers than authorized under terms of the software licence agreement

soft water *n.* water that contains very low levels of calcium and magnesium salts, either naturally or because they have been removed. Soap lathers easily in soft water.

soft wheat *n.* a type of wheat with soft kernels and weak gluten that is relatively low in protein. It is used mainly for cakes, biscuits, pastries, and as a livestock feed.

softwood /sóft wòod/ *n.* **1. WOOD OF CONIFEROUS TREE** the open-grained wood of a pine, cedar, or other coniferous tree. Many softwoods are, in fact, hard and durable. **2. CONIFEROUS TREE** any tree that yields softwood, such as a pine or cedar

softy /sófti/ (*plural* **-ies**), **softie** *n.* sb who is weak, timid, or sentimental (*informal*)

Sogdian /sógdi ən/ *n.* **1.** PEOPLES **MEMBER OF ANCIENT ASIAN PEOPLE** a member of a people that lived in Sogdiana, an ancient region of central Asia **2.** LANG **SOGDIAN LANGUAGE** the Iranian language of the Sogdian people, now extinct [Mid-16thC. Via Latin from Greek *Sogdianos*, from Old Persian *Suguda*.] —**Sogdian** *adj.*

soggy /sóggi/ (**-gier, -giest**) *adj.* **1. THOROUGHLY WET** soaked through with moisture **2. WITH TOO MUCH LIQUID** unpleasantly wet and heavy in texture **3. UNINTERESTING** lacking animation or vitality [Early 18thC. Formed from obsolete *sog* 'area of marshy ground'.] —**soggily** *adv.* —**sogginess** *n.*

Sogne Fjord /sóngnə-/ inlet of the North Sea in southwestern Norway. Length: 200 km/125 mi.

soh *n.* the fifth note in the sol-fa musical scale. In fixed solfeggio it corresponds to the note 'g'. US term **sol**

Soho /sṓhō/ *n.* **1. AREA IN LONDON** an area of central London well known for its theatres, restaurants and clubs **2. Soho, SoHo AREA IN NEW YORK** an area of the lower west side of Manhattan well known for its art studios and galleries [In sense 2, from the first letters of SOUTH and of *Houston Street*, from its location]

soi-disant /swaa deézaaN, swaádee zaáN/ *adj.* self-styled or so-called (*literary*) [From French, literally 'saying oneself']

soigné /swaán yay/, **soignée** *adj.* **1. WELL GROOMED** neat and smart in dress and appearance **2. WELL FURNISHED** designed or furnished in an elegant style [Early 19thC. From French, past participle of *soigner* 'to care for', from, ultimately, Germanic.]

soil[1] /soyl/ *n.* **1. TOP LAYER OF LAND** the top layer of most of the earth's land surface, consisting of the unconsolidated products of rock erosion and organic decay, along with bacteria and fungi (*often used before a noun*) **2. KIND OF EARTH** earth or ground of a particular kind **3. COUNTRY** sb's country or land (*literary*) **4. FARMING** agricultural life and work (*literary*) **5. NURTURING MEDIUM** any medium in which growth and development takes place (*literary*) [13thC Via Anglo-Norman, 'piece of land', from Latin *solium* 'seat', by association with *solum* 'ground, soil']

soil[2] /soyl/ *vt.* (**soils, soiling, soiled**) **1. MAKE DIRTY** to make sth dirty or stained **2. BRING DISHONOUR ON** to damage sb's reputation, character, or good name ■ *n.* **1. DIRT** dirt or dirty condition ○ *remove soil from linens* **2. MORAL CORRUPTION** immoral behaviour or lack of moral standards (*literary*) [13thC. From Old French *soill(i)er* 'to soil, wallow' (probable source of English *sully*), of uncertain origin: probably from assumed Vulgar Latin *suculare* 'to make dirty', from Latin *sus* 'pig, boar'.]

soil[3] /soyl/ *n.* excrement or sewage ○ *a soil pipe* [15thC. From Old French *souille* 'muddy place', from *soill(i)er* (see SOIL[2]).]

soilure /sóylyər/ *n.* **1. DIRTYING OF STH** the soiling or staining of sth (*literary*) **2. DIRTY MARK** a stain or smudge (*archaic*) [14thC. From Old French *soilleure*, from *soillier* (see SOIL[2]).]

soiree /swaáray/, **soirée** *n.* a party or gathering held in the evening, especially in sb's home (*formal*) [Late 18thC. From *French*, from *soir* 'evening', from Latin *sero* 'at a late hour', from *serus* 'late' (partial source of English *serenade*).]

soixante-neuf /swássont núrf/ *n.* = **sixty-nine** (*slang offensive*) [From French, literally 'sixty-nine']

sojourn /sójjurn, sójjərn/ *n.* **BRIEF VISIT** a short stay at a place (*literary*) ■ *vi.* (**-journs, -journing, -journed**) **STAY FOR TIME** to stay at a place for a time (*literary*) [13thC. Via Anglo-Norman *sujurn* or Old French *sojorn* (noun) from *sojourner* (verb), from assumed Vulgar Latin *subdiurnare* 'to spend the day', from late Latin *diurnum* 'day'.] —**sojourner** *n.*

Sokoto /sṓkətō/ capital city of Sokoto State, northwestern Nigeria, situated about 483 km/300 mi. northwest of Abuja. Population: 207,000 (1995).

sol[1] /sol/ *n. US* = **soh** [14thC. From medieval Latin, being the first syllable of Latin *solve* 'purge!, release!', the word sung to this note in a medieval hymn to St John the Baptist.]

sol[2] /sol/ *n.* a liquid colloidal solution [Late 19thC. Shortening of SOLUTION.]

sol[3] /sol/ *n.* a copper or silver coin formerly used in France, worth 12 deniers [Late 16thC. Via obsolete French from Latin *solidus* (see SOLDIER).]

sol[4] /sol/ (*plural* **soles** /solays/) *n.* MONEY **1. PERUVIAN UNIT OF CURRENCY** the main unit of currency in Peru, worth 100 centimos. See table at **currency 2. COIN WORTH A SOL** a coin worth one sol

Sol /sol/ *n.* **1. SUN PERSONIFIED** the personification of the sun (*literary*) **2. ROMAN SUN GOD** in Roman mythology, the god of the sun. Greek equivalent **Helios** [14thC. From Latin, literally 'sun'.]

sol. *abbr.* **1.** soluble **2.** solution

Sol. *abbr.* **1.** solicitor **2.** BIBLE Solomon

sola[1] /sṓlə/ *adj.* used as a stage direction to indicate that a female character appears alone on stage

sola[2] plural of **solum**

solace /sólləss/ *n.* **1. RELIEF FROM EMOTIONAL DISTRESS** comfort at a time of sadness, grief, or disappointment **2. SOURCE OF COMFORT** sb or sth that provides comfort in times of sadness, grief, or disappointment ■ *vt.* (**-aces, -acing, -aced**) **PROVIDE WITH COMFORT** to comfort sb at a time of sadness, grief, or disappointment [13thC. Via Old French *solas* from Latin *solatium*, from *solari* 'to comfort' (source of English *console*).] —**solacer** *n.*

solan /sṓlən/, **solan goose** *n.* a gannet found in the North Atlantic. Latin name: *Morus bassanus*. [15thC. Origin uncertain: probably from Old Norse *súla* 'gannet' + *and-*, the stem of *ōnd* 'duck'.]

solanaceous /sóllə náyshəss/ *adj.* relating to or belonging to the nightshade family of plants, a family that includes the potato, tomato, and tobacco [Early 19thC. Formed from modern Latin *Solanaceae* (family name), from Latin *solanum* (see SOLANUM).]

solan goose *n.* = **solan**

solanine /sṓlə neen/ *n.* a bitter poisonous alkaloid found in several plants of the nightshade family. It was formerly used to treat epilepsy, bronchitis, and asthma. Formula: $C_{45}H_{73}NO_{15}$.

solanum /sō láynəm, sō láynəm/ (*plural* **solanums** *or* **solanum**) *n.* a plant of the nightshade family. Some species such as the potato and aubergine are cultivated for food. Genus: *Solanum*. [Late 16thC. Via modern Latin, genus name, from Latin, from *sol* 'sun' (see SOLAR).]

solar /sṓlər/ *adj.* **1. FROM THE SUN** relating to or originating from the Sun **2. OPERATING USING ENERGY FROM THE SUN** using the Sun's radiation as a source of energy **3. MEASURED BY THE SUN'S POSITION** measured with reference to the Earth's movement in relation to the Sun [15thC. From Latin *solaris*, from *sol* 'sun' (source of English *parasol*, *solarium*, and *solstice*).]

solar apex *n.* the point in space towards which the Sun appears to be moving. It is in the constellation Hercules.

solar battery *n.* an arrangement of several solar cells for converting solar radiation into electricity

solar cell *n.* an electric cell that converts solar radiation directly into electricity. Solar cells are mounted on solar panels used, e.g. on satellites and spacecraft.

solar cycle *n.* a calendar system based on the solar year, typical of most civilizations. Variations of solar calendars in western civilization are the Julian and Gregorian calendars.

solar day *n.* the time taken for the Earth to make a complete revolution on its axis, measured with respect to the Sun

solar eclipse *n.* an eclipse in which the Moon blocks all or part of the Sun's light from reaching the Earth's surface, because it passes directly between the Earth and the Sun

solar flare *n.* a brief sudden eruption of high-energy hydrogen gas from the surface of the Sun, associated with sunspots. It causes interruptions of communication systems on Earth.

solar furnace *n.* a furnace equipped with a series of concave mirrors that are motorized to follow the Sun and focus its radiation to obtain and maintain extremely high temperatures

solaria plural of **solarium**

solarimeter /sōlə rímmitər/ *n.* an instrument used to measure solar radiation [Early 20thC. Coined from SOLAR + -METER.]

solarise *vt.* = solarize

solarium /sə láiri əm/ (*plural* **-a** /-ri ə/ *or* **-ums**) *n.* **1.** ROOM ENJOYING SUNLIGHT a room built for the purpose of enjoying sunlight, usually with large windows or glass walls, especially a room in a hospital or other healthcare establishment **2.** PLACE TO GET A TAN a room or establishment equipped with sunlamps or sunbeds for acquiring a tan [Mid-19thC. From Latin, 'sundial (the original English sense), sunny roof, terrace', from *sol* 'sun' (see SOLAR).]

solarize /sólə rīz/ (**-izes, -izing, -ized**), **solarise** (**-ises, -ising, -ised**) *vt.* **1.** OVEREXPOSE TO SUNLIGHT to affect or damage sth with solar radiation **2.** PHOTOGRAPHY OVEREXPOSE to overexpose photographic materials to light for deliberate effect, usually in order to exaggerate highlights —**solarization** /sólə rī záysh'n/ *n.*

solar month *n.* one-twelfth of a solar year, equal to 30 days, 10 hours, 29 minutes, 3.8 seconds

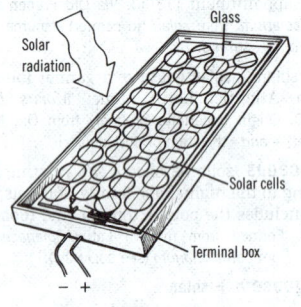
Solar panel

solar panel *n.* a large panel containing solar cells or heat-absorbing plates that convert the sun's radiation into electricity, for use, e.g. in heating buildings and powering satellites and spacecraft

solar plexus *n.* **1.** NERVES IN UPPER ABDOMEN a mass of nerve cells in the upper abdomen behind the stomach, kidneys, and other internal organs **2.** ABDOMINAL AREA a point on the upper abdomen just below where the ribs separate. A sharp blow to this region can cause loss of consciousness. [*Solar* from its radial network of nerves, likened to the sun's rays]

solar system *n.* the Sun and all the planets, satellites, asteroids, meteors, and comets that are subject to its gravitational pull

solar wind *n.* the flow of high-speed ionized particles from the sun's surface into interplanetary space. ◊ **stellar wind**

solar year *n.* the time taken for the Earth to move around the Sun, equal to 365 days, 5 hours, 48 minutes, 45.51 seconds

solation /sō láysh'n/ *n.* the process of changing from a gel to a liquid

solatium /sō láyshi əm/ (*plural* **-a** /-shi ə/) *n.* damages awarded for emotional suffering, as opposed to financial loss or physical injury or suffering [Early 19thC. From Latin (see SOLACE).]

sold past participle, past tense of **sell**

solder /sóldər/ *n.* **1.** ALLOY FOR JOINING METAL an alloy with a low melting point, typically a mixture of tin and lead, used to join electrical components to a circuit board or to join metal objects together **2.** STH THAT UNITES sth that forms a bond or union ■ *vti.* (**-ders, -dering, -dered**) **1.** JOIN THINGS WITH SOLDER to work with solder or to join things using solder **2.** UNITE TO FORM WHOLE to come together in unity, or to establish a bond of unity between people or things [Via Old French from Latin *solidare* 'to fasten together, make solid', from *solidus* 'solid' (see SOLID).] —**solderer** *n.*

soldering iron *n.* a tool with a point that is heated for melting and applying solder

soldier /sóljər/ *n.* **1.** MIL SB SERVING IN ARMY sb who serves in an army or other military service **2.** ARMY ARMY MEMBER BELOW OFFICER RANK a member of an army who ranks below a commissioned officer **3.** DEDICATED WORKER sb who works with dedication for a cause **4.** SKILLED WARRIOR a skilled and experienced fighter or military strategist **5.** INSECTS ANT THAT PROTECTS COLONY a sterile member of an ant or termite colony with a large head and powerful jaws. Its role is to defend the colony. **6.** FOOD PIECE OF BREAD AND BUTTER a thin strip of bread or toast, especially one for dipping into a soft-boiled egg or the yolk of a fried egg (*informal*) ■ *vi.* (**-diers, -diering, -diered**) **1.** BE MEMBER OF AN ARMY to serve as a soldier in an army **2.** PRETEND TO WORK to give the appearance of working while really idling (*archaic slang*) [13thC. From Old French, literally 'sb having pay', from *soulde* '(soldier's) pay', from Latin *solidus (nummus)* 'Roman gold coin', literally 'solid (coin)' (see SOLID).] —**soldierly** *adj.*

soldier on *vi.* to persevere despite difficulties or setbacks

soldier crab *n.* a small pale blue Australian crab, often seen in large groups on rocky shores. Latin name: *Mictyris longicarpus*. ['Soldier' because it resembles a sentry in a sentry box]

soldierfish /sóljər fish/ (*plural* **-fishes** *or* **-fish**) *n.* = **squirrelfish** [*Soldier* from its sharp spines and rough scales]

soldier of fortune *n.* sb who will serve in any army in which there is profit or adventure

soldiery /sóljəri/ *n.* **1.** SOLDIERS COLLECTIVELY soldiers as a group **2.** SOLDIER'S WORK the profession or skill of a soldier

soldo /sóldō/ (*plural* **-di** /-di/) *n.* a copper coin used in the former Italian states until the 19th century, worth one-twentieth of a lira [Late 16thC. Via Italian from Latin *solidus* (see SOLDIER).]

sold-out *adj.* for which all available tickets have been sold

sole[1] /sōl/ *n.* **1.** ANAT BOTTOM OF THE FOOT the underside of the foot, stretching from the toes to the heel **2.** BOTTOM OF A SHOE the underside of a shoe, boot, or other piece of footwear, sometimes excluding the heel **3.** GOLF BOTTOM SURFACE OF A GOLF CLUB the underside of the head of a golf club ■ *vt.* (**soles, soling, soled**) **1.** PUT SOLE ON SHOE to put a sole on a shoe, boot, or other piece of footwear **2.** GOLF PLACE ON THE GROUND to put the sole of a golf club on the ground in preparation for a stroke [14thC. Via Old French from Latin *solea* 'sandal, sole of an animal's foot', from *solum* 'ground, foot, shoe sole'.]

sole[2] /sōl/ *adj.* **1.** ONLY of which there is only one ○ *the sole reason* **2.** EXCLUSIVE belonging to one person or group ○ *has sole responsibility for the department* **3.** UNFETTERED free from the interference of others **4.** LAW UNMARRIED without husband or wife [13thC. Via Old French *soule* from Latin *sola*, the feminine of *solus* (source of English *desolate*, *solitary*, and *sullen*).] —**soleness** *n.*

sole[3] /sōl/ (*plural* **soles** *or* **sole**) *n.* **1.** FISH WITH FLAT BODY a brownish marine fish with a small mouth and both eyes on the upper side of its flat body. It is valued as a food fish. Family: Soleidae. **2.** FOOD FISH LIKE THE SOLE a name used for fishes similar to the sole when they are sold as food [14thC. Via French from, ultimately, Latin *solea* 'sandal' (see SOLE), from its being likened to the sole of a sandal.]

solecism /sólləssizəm/ *n.* **1.** GRAMMATICAL MISTAKE a mistake in grammar or syntax **2.** ERROR sth incorrect, inappropriate, or inconsistent **3.** BREACH OF GOOD MANNERS an action that breaks the rules of etiquette or good manners [Mid-16thC. Ultimately via Latin *soloecismus* from Greek *soloikismos*, from *soloikos* 'speaking incorrectly', literally 'inhabitant of Soloi' (in ancient Cilicia, southern Turkey), whose Attic dialect was considered barbarous.] —**solecist** *n.* —**solecistical** /sóllə sístik'l/ *adj.* —**solecistically** /-sístikli/ *adv.*

solely /sōl li/ *adv.* **1.** ONLY for nothing other than ○ *sold the company solely for commercial reasons* **2.** EXCLUSIVELY to the exclusion of all else or others ○ *He is solely to blame.*

solemn /sólləm/ *adj.* **1.** EARNEST demonstrating sincerity and gravity **2.** HUMOURLESS without joy or humour **3.** FORMAL characterized by ceremony or formality **4.** RELIGIOUS observed with sacred or religious ceremony **5.** AWE-INSPIRING inspiring wonder or reverence [14thC. Via Old French *solemne* from Latin *sol(l)emnis* 'customary, religious', from *sollus* 'whole, entire' (source of English *solicit*) + an element of unknown origin.] —**solemnly** *adv.* —**solemnness** *n.*

solemnify /sə lémni fī/ (**-fies, -fying, -fied**) *vt.* to make sth serious or solemn

solemnise *vt.* = **solemnize**

solemnity /sə lémniti/ (*plural* **-ties**) *n.* **1.** SOLEMN QUALITY the solemn nature or quality of sth **2.** SOLEMN CEREMONY a formal or solemn ceremony held to observe an occasion or event (*often used in the plural*) **3.** LAW LEGAL FORMALITY a formality that must be complied with before a contract or agreement can become effective

solemnize /sólləm nīz/ (**-nizes, -nizing, -nized**), **solemnise** (**-nises, -nising, -nised**) *v.* **1.** *vt.* CELEBRATE WITH CEREMONY to observe an event or occasion with ceremony or formality **2.** *vt.* PERFORM A MARRIAGE CEREMONY to celebrate a marriage with a religious ceremony **3.** *vt.* MAKE DIGNIFIED to bring dignity or formality to sth **4.** *vi.* SPEAK SOLEMNLY to speak or reflect with great seriousness —**solemnization** /sólləm nī záysh'n/ *n.*

solenodon /sə lénnə don/ *n.* a rare nocturnal insect-eating mammal native to the West Indies, with a long snout and a long scaly tail. It looks like a large shrew. Family: Solenodontidae. [Mid-19thC. From modern Latin, genus name, literally 'pipe-tooth', from, ultimately, Greek *sōlēn* 'pipe, channel'.]

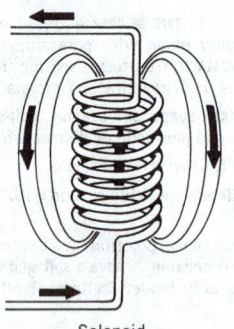
Solenoid

solenoid /sólə noyd/ *n.* a device consisting of a cylindrical coil of wire surrounding a moveable iron core that moves along the length of the coil when an electric current is passed through it. Solenoids are used as switches and relays, e.g. in a motor vehicle to complete the circuit between the battery and starter motor. [Early 19thC. From French *solénoide*, literally 'pipe-shaped', from Greek *sōlēn* 'pipe, channel'.] —**solenoidal** /sólə nóyd'l/ *adj.* —**solenoidally** /-noyd'li/ *adv.*

Solent /sólənt/ arm of the English Channel separating the Isle of Wight from mainland England. Length: 24 km/15 mi.

soleplate /sōl playt/ *n.* **1.** HOUSEHOLD BOTTOM OF AN IRON the underside of an iron for pressing clothes **2.** BUILDING PLATE ON WHICH STUDS REST the plate that supports the bases of the studs used in framing a wall

soleus /sóli əss/ (*plural* **-i** /-li ī/) *n.* a broad flat muscle in the calf of the leg that helps to flex the ankle and depress the sole of the foot [Late 17thC. Via modern Latin from Latin *solea* (see SOLE).]

sol-fa *n.* = tonic sol-fa ■ *vti.* (**sol-fas, sol-faing, sol-faed**) SING USING SOL-FA to sing a tune using the sol-fa syllables

solfatara /sólfə taárə/ *n.* a vent in a volcano through which sulphur-rich gases and steam escape, leaving bright yellow sulphur deposits [Late 18thC. From Italian, 'sulphurous volcano', from *solfo* 'sulphur', from Latin *sulfur* (source of English *sulphur*).] —**solfataric** *adj.*

solfeggio /sol féjji ō/ (*plural* **-gi** /-féjji/ *or* **-gios**), **solfège** /sol fézh/ *n.* an exercise in singing using the sol-fa syllables [Late 18thC. From Italian, from *sol-fa* 'sol-fa'.]

solferino /sólfə reé nō/ *adj.* of a red colour tinged with purple [Mid-19thC. Named after *Solferino*, an Italian town at which a dye of this colour was invented.] —**solferino** *n.*

soli plural of **solo**

solicit /sə líssit/ (**-its, -iting, -ited**) *v.* **1.** *vti.* PLEAD FOR STH to try to get sth by making insistent requests or pleas **2.** *vt.* ASK SB FOR STH to plead with or petition a person or group for sth **3.** *vti.* OFFER SEX FOR MONEY to offer to participate in sexual activities in return for money **4.** *vt.* GET SB TO DO STH WRONG to attempt to draw sb into participating in illegal or immoral acts [15thC. Via French *solliciter* from Latin *sollicitare* 'to disturb', from *sollicitus*, literally 'completely moved', from *sollus* 'whole' + *citus*, past participle of *ciere* 'to move' (source of English *excite*).] —**solicitation** /sə líssi táysh'n/ *n.*

solicitor /sə líssitər/ *n.* a lawyer who gives legal advice, draws up legal documents, and does preparatory work for barristers. A solicitor who holds an advocacy qualification may also represent clients in court. —**solicitorship** *n.*

Solicitor General (*plural* **Solicitors General**) *n.* **1.** LAW OFFICER OF CROWN in England and Wales, the second most senior law officer of the crown, ranking below the Attorney General **2.** *Scotland* LAW OFFICER OF CROWN IN SCOTLAND in Scotland, the second most senior law officer of the crown, ranking below the Lord Advocate **3.** *NZ* NEW ZEALAND'S TOP LEGAL OFFICER in New Zealand, the chief law officer and prosecutor for the Crown

solicitous /sə líssitəss/ *adj.* **1.** CONCERNED expressing an attitude of concern and consideration **2.** READY AND WILLING full of eagerness and anticipation to do sth **3.** METICULOUS paying very careful attention to details **4.** NOT AT EASE troubled by uneasiness or apprehension (*archaic*) [Mid-16thC. Formed from Latin *sollicitus* (see SOLICIT).] —**solicitously** *adv.* —**solicitousness** *n.*

solicitude /sə líssi tyood/ *n.* **1.** EXPRESSED CONCERN concern and consideration, especially when expressed **2.** ANXIETY a state of uneasiness or anxiety (*archaic*) **3.** STH CAUSING CONCERN a cause of concern or uneasiness (*often used in the plural*)

solid /sóllid/ *adj.* **1.** NOT SOFT OR YIELDING consisting of compact unyielding material **2.** NOT HOLLOW having no open interior spaces **3.** UNADULTERATED OR UNMIXED made of the same material throughout **4.** OF STRONG AND SECURE CONSTRUCTION built out of strong substantial material and not likely to break or collapse **5.** UNANIMOUS in complete agreement ○ *Support for the amendment was solid.* **6.** NOURISHING providing ample nourishment **7.** UNINTERRUPTED continuing without breaks or openings ○ *It took a solid two hours to crack the code.* **8.** RELIABLE able to be relied or depended upon **9.** FINANCIALLY SECURE in sound financial condition **10.** GEOM THREE-DIMENSIONAL with the three dimensions of length, breadth, and depth, or relating to geometric figures that have three dimensions **11.** CHEM RETAINING ITS SHAPE with a shape that resists moderate stress or deformation, and therefore distinct from a liquid or a gas **12.** LANG AS SINGLE WORD written as one word without a space or hyphen **13.** PRINTING WITHOUT SPACES without spaces between lines of type in printing **14.** *NZ* EXPENSIVE excessively high in price (*informal*) ■ *n.* **1.** SOLID THING sth that is solid **2.** GEOM SOLID FIGURE a three-dimensional geometric figure or object **3.** CHEM SUBSTANCE THAT RETAINS SHAPE a substance that resists moderate stress and deformation, unlike a liquid or a gas [14thC. Directly or via French *solide* from Latin *solidus* 'firm, whole' (source of English *soldier*).] —**solidity** /sə líddəti/ *n.* —**solidly** /sóllidli/ *adv.* —**solidness** /sóllidnəss/ *n.*

solid angle *n.* a three-dimensional angle formed at the vertex of a cone or the intersection of three planes

solidarity /sólli dárrəti/ *n.* harmony of interests and responsibilities among individuals in a group, especially as manifested in unanimous support and collective action for sth

Solidarity /sólli dárrəti/ *n.* a federation of trade unions in Poland, founded in 1980. Under the leadership of Lech Walesa it challenged the Soviet-backed government of the day. [Late 20thC. Translation of Polish *Solidarność*.]

solid geometry *n.* the branch of geometry dealing with three-dimensional figures

solidi plural of **solidus**

solidify /sə líddi fī/ (**-fies, -fying, -fied**) *vti.* **1.** MAKE OR BECOME SOLID to become compact or firm, or make sth compact or firm **2.** STRENGTHEN to become strong and united, or make sth strong and united —**solidifiable** *adj.* —**solidification** /sə líddifi káysh'n/ *n.* —**solidifier** /sə líddi fīər/ *n.*

solid of revolution *n.* a three-dimensional mathematical figure formed by rotating a plane figure about an axis in its plane

solid solution *n.* a crystalline substance such as glass or an alloy in which certain atoms or molecules have been replaced by others but the structure has not changed

solid-state *adj.* **1.** USING TRANSISTORS OR SEMICONDUCTORS working by means of the flow of electric current through solid material, as happens with semiconductors and transistors. The term is usually used to distinguish modern electronic equipment from earlier devices that made use of valves or heated filaments. **2.** OF ELECTRONICS AND SOLIDS relating to the electronic characteristics of solids, especially at the atomic or molecular level

solidus /sóllidəss/ (*plural* **-di** /-dī/) *n.* **1.** PRINTING SLOPING LINE a line sloping from right to left, used to separate items of information, such as dates, as in '11/11/99', to write fractions, and to indicate alternatives, as in 'and/or'. US term **virgule 2.** MONEY ROMAN GOLD COIN a gold coin used in the Roman Empire from the fourth century BC. It remained in use in Europe until the 12th century AD. [14thC. From Latin (see SOLDIER).]

solifluction /sólli flúksh'n/ *n.* the slow movement of soil downhill as a result of water saturation after rainfall or the melting of ice [Early 20thC. Formed from Latin *solum* 'ground' + *fluct-*, the past participle stem of *fluere* 'to flow' (source of English *fluctuate*).]

Solihull /sóli hul/ town in the Midlands, near Birmingham, England. Population: 94,531 (1991).

soliloquize /sə líllə kwīz/ (**-quizes, -quizing, -quized**), **soliloquise** (**-quises, -quising, -quised**) *vi.* to speak a soliloquy in the course of a play —**soliloquist** *n.* —**soliloquizer** *n.*

soliloquy /sə lílləkwi/ (*plural* **-quies**) *n.* **1.** TALKING WHEN ALONE the act of speaking while alone, especially when used as a theatrical device that allows a character's thoughts and ideas to be conveyed to the audience **2.** SECTION IN PLAY a section of a play or other drama in which a soliloquy is spoken [14thC. From late Latin *soliloquium*, literally 'a speaking alone', from Latin *solus* 'alone' (see SOLE[2]) + *loqui* 'to speak' (source of English *eloquent*).]

Solingen /zṓlingən/ city in North Rhine-Westphalia State, west-central Germany. Population: 166,000 (1994).

solipsism /sóllipsiz'm/ *n.* the belief that the only thing sb can be sure of is that he or she exists, and that true knowledge of anything else is impossible [Late 19thC. Formed from Latin *solus* 'alone' + *ipse* 'self'.] —**solipsist** *n.* —**solipsistic** /sóllip sístik/ *adj.* —**solipsistically** /-sístikli/ *adv.*

solitaire /sólli tair, sólli táir/ *n.* **1.** GAME BOARD GAME FOR ONE a board game for one person, in which pegs are eliminated from the board by being moved into empty spaces, the object being to end with one remaining centre peg **2.** *US* CARDS = **patience 3.** ACCESSORIES SINGLE GEMSTONE a gem, especially a diamond, that is set alone in a ring **4.** BIRDS SONGBIRD a thrush that is native to North and Central America, well known for its attractive song. Genus: *Myadestes.* [14thC. Via French, 'recluse', from Latin *solitarius* (see SOLITARY). The original English sense was 'widow'.]

solitary /sóllitəri/ *adj.* **1.** DONE ALONE done without the company of other people **2.** SHUNNING COMPANY preferring to be or live alone **3.** SECLUDED in a remote location, apart from others **4.** SINGLE existing as the only one of its kind ○ *a solitary boat on the sea* **5.** ZOOL NOT LIVING IN SOCIAL GROUPS used to describe animals that live alone or in pairs rather than in colonies or social groups **6.** BOT GROWING SINGLY used to describe flowers that grow singly rather than as a cluster ■ *n.* (*plural* **-ies**) **1.** RECLUSE sb who lives or prefers to live away from others **2.** = **solitary confinement** [14thC. Directly or via French *solitaire* from Latin *solitarius* (source of English *solitaire*), from *solus* 'alone' (see SOLE[2]).]

solitary bee *n.* a flower-visiting bee that does not live in a colony, but raises its young independently

solitary confinement *n.* confinement of a prisoner in an area or cell isolated from other prisoners, used as a punishment or for protection

solitary wasp *n.* = **hunting wasp**

solitude /sólli tyood/ *n.* **1.** STATE OF BEING ALONE the state of being alone, separated from other people, whether considered as a welcome freedom from disturbance or as an unhappy loneliness **2.** REMOTENESS a quality of quiet remoteness or seclusion in places from which human activity is generally absent **3.** LONELY PLACE a remote or uninhabited place (*literary*) [14thC. Directly or via Old French from Latin *solitudo*, from *solus* 'alone'.] —**solitudinous** /sólli tyoód'nəss/ *adj.*

WORD KEY: CULTURAL NOTE

One Hundred Years of Solitude, a novel by Colombian writer Gabriel Garcia Marquez (1967). It recounts 100 years in the lives of the Buendía family, founders of the town of Macondo in Colombia, a story that mirrors the history of the nation. Marquez's skilful use of fantasy and myth to convey the depth of his characters' experiences make this a key work in the magical realism school of literature.

solitudinarian /sólli tyoodi náiri ən/ *n.* sb who likes to be alone (*literary*)

solleret /sóllə ret/ *n.* a shoe made of steel plates riveted together, forming part of a suit of armour [14thC. Via the diminutive of Old French *soller*, 'shoe' from, ultimately, late Latin *subtel* 'hollow of the foot', from *sub* 'under' + *talus* 'ankle'.]

sollicker /sóllikər/ *n. Aus* sth very large (*slang*) [Late 19thC. Origin unknown.]

solmization /sóllmi záysh'n/ *n.* the assignment of separate syllables to different musical pitches for singing or training the ear, as, e.g. in solfeggio [Mid-18thC. French *solmisation* from *solmiser* 'to sing sol-fa'.]

soln *abbr.* solution

solo /sṓlō/ *n.* (*plural* **-los** *or* **-li** /-lī/) **1.** MUSIC MUSICAL PIECE PERFORMED BY ONE PERSON a piece of music performed by one musician or singer, or a passage for a single player or singer within a longer piece for two or more, a choir, or an orchestra **2.** ARTS PERFORMANCE BY ONE ARTIST a performance by a single artist such as a musician, singer, or dancer with or without accompaniment **3.** ACT DONE BY SINGLE PERSON an action or feat carried out by one person alone, e.g. a flight in an aircraft or a climb up a mountain **4.** MOTORCYCLES MOTORCYCLE WITHOUT SIDECAR a motorcycle without a sidecar **5.** CARDS CARD GAME FOR INDIVIDUAL PLAYERS a card game in which players play on their own, not in pairs or teams, especially solo whist ■ *adj.* **1.** ARTS FOR A SINGLE PERFORMER intended for or executed by sb performing singly, not as one of a group **2.** DONE BY ONE PERSON carried out by one person unaccompanied by anyone else **3.** *ANZ* HAVING NO PARTNER bringing up a child or children alone, without a partner ■ *adv.* ALONE unaccompanied by anyone, or not performing or doing sth as one of a group ■ *vi.* (**-los, -loing, -loed**) DO STH WITHOUT HELP OR ACCOMPANIMENT to do sth alone, without help or accompaniment, especially to fly an aircraft without an instructor or to perform an artistic solo [Late 17thC. Via Italian from Latin *solus* 'alone'.]

soloist /sṓlō ist/ *n.* sb who performs a solo —**soloistic** /sṓlō ístik/ *adj.*

Solo man /sṓlō man/ *n.* an extinct variety of the human species *Homo sapiens* that lived 50,000 years ago during the late Pleistocene epoch and whose fossils were discovered near the River Solo in Java

Solomon /sólləmən/ *n.* sb who is very wise (*informal*)

Solomon /sólləmən/, **King of Israel** (*fl.* 10th century BC) The second son of David and Bathsheba, he ruled Israel from 961 BC to 922 BC. Famed for his wisdom, he is generally acknowledged as the builder of the Temple in Jerusalem. He is credited with writing the biblical *Song of Solomon* and *Proverbs.*

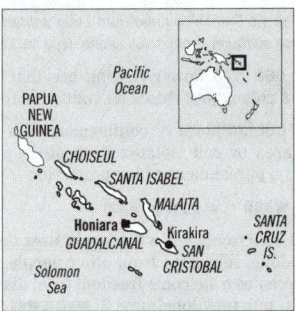

Solomon Islands

Solomon Islands /sóllǝmǝn-/ monarchy comprising over 35 islands and atolls in the southern Pacific Ocean. Language: English. Currency: Solomon Islands dollar. Capital: Honiara. Population: 412,902 (1996). Area: 28,446 sq. km/10,980 sq.mi. —**Solomon Islander** n.

Solomon's seal n. **1.** PLANTS WOODLAND PLANT WITH DROOPING FLOWERS a perennial plant found in woodlands in northern countries that has drooping whitish flowers that grow in pairs. Latin name: *Polygonatum multiflorum.* **2.** SIX-POINTED STAR a six-pointed symbol resembling a star, made up of one triangle laid on top of another facing the other way. Examples are the Star of David that is the symbol of Judaism, and the hexagram that healers of former times believed had the power to cure diseases.

solon /só lon/ n. sb wise, especially an experienced and wise legislator or politician (*literary*) [Early 17thC. Named after *Solon* (638?–558?BC), Athenian statesman, legal reformer, and poet.]

solonchak /sóllǝn chák/ n. an intrazonal soil with a greyish crust that develops in semiarid and desert areas and contains large amounts of soluble salts [Early 20thC. From Russian, literally 'salt marsh, salt lake', from *sol* 'salt'.]

solonetz /sóllǝ néts/, **solonets** n. an intrazonal soil with a blackish crust developed from solonchak soil by leaching of the salts [Early 20thC. From Russian, literally 'salt marsh, salt lake', from *sol* 'salt'.]

so long interj. GOODBYE used to say goodbye (*informal*) ■ adv. S Africa IN THE MEANTIME in the meantime, for the time being (*informal*)

solo stop n. a stop on an organ with a penetrating tone, used in isolated passages of organ pieces to give the effect of a single instrument playing the melody

solo whist n. a version of the card game whist with each of the four players playing on his or her own, instead of in the usual pairs

solstice /sólstiss/ n. **1.** LONGEST OR SHORTEST DAY either of the times when the sun is furthest from the equator, on or about 21 June or 21 December. The summer solstice falls in June in the northern hemisphere but in December in the southern hemisphere, and vice versa for the winter solstice. **2.** POINT ON THE ECLIPTIC either of the two points on the ecliptic when the sun reaches its northernmost or southernmost point relative to the celestial equator [13thC. Via Old French from Latin *solstitium*, from *sol* 'sun' + the past participle stem of *sistere* 'to stand still'.] —**solstitial** /sól stísh'l/ adj.

Solti /shólti/, **Sir Georg** (1912–97) Hungarian conductor. Associated particularly with the music of late romantic composers, he held important posts in Germany, the United Kingdom, and the United States, where he long conducted the Chicago Symphony Orchestra (1969–91).

solubilise vti. = solubilize

solubility /sóllyoŏ bíllǝti/ (*plural* **-ties**) n. **1.** CAPACITY TO DISSOLVE the extent to which one substance is able to dissolve in another **2.** MEASURE OF CAPACITY TO DISSOLVE a measure of one substance's ability to dissolve in a specific amount of another substance at standard temperature and pressure

solubilize /sóllyooŏbǝ līz/ (**-lizes, -lizing, -lized**), **solubilise** /sóllyooŏbi līz/, sóllyǝbi līz/ (**-lises, -lising, -lised**) vti. to make a substance soluble or more soluble, or become soluble or more soluble

soluble /sóllyooŏb'l/ adj. **1.** DISSOLVING IN LIQUID able to be dissolved in another substance. The level of solubility often varies with temperature. (*often used in combination*) ○ *water-soluble* **2.** DESIGNED TO DISSOLVE designed to be dissolved in water **3.** SOLVABLE able to be solved or answered [14thC. Via Old French from Late Latin *solubilis*, from *solvere* 'to loosen, dissolve'.] —**solubly** /sóllyooŏbli/ adv.

soluble glass n. = sodium silicate

soluble RNA n. = transfer RNA

solum /sóllǝm/ (*plural* **-lums** /-lǝ/ or **-la**) n. the upper layers of a soil profile where the formation of new soil takes place and where most plant roots and soil animals are found [Mid-19thC. Via Modern Latin from Latin *solum* 'ground, foundation'.]

solus /sóllǝss/ adj. **1.** ALONE ON STAGE used as a stage direction to indicate that a character appears alone on stage ○ *Enter Hector solus* **2.** MARKETING FEATURED ON OWN in or on which an advertisement appears on its own, rather than alongside advertisements for different products or from competing companies **3.** COMM SELLING ONE COMPANY'S PRODUCTS selling the products of one company only [Late 16thC. From Latin, 'alone'.] —**solus** adv.

solute /so lyoŏt/ n. DISSOLVED SUBSTANCE a substance dissolved in another substance ■ adj. DISSOLVED dissolved in a solution [15thC. From Latin *solutus*, past participle of *solvere* (see SOLUBLE).]

solution /sǝ loŏsh'n/ n. **1.** WAY OF RESOLVING DIFFICULTY a method of successfully dealing with a problem or difficulty **2.** ANSWER TO A PUZZLE the answer to a puzzle or question **3.** FINDING OF A SOLUTION the process of resolving a difficulty or finding the answer to a puzzle or question **4.** FLUID WITH SUBSTANCE DISSOLVED IN IT a substance consisting of two or more substances mixed together and uniformly dispersed, most commonly the result of dissolving a solid, fluid, or gas in a liquid. It is also, however, possible to form a solution by dissolving a gas or solid in a solid or one gas in another gas. **5.** PROCESS OF FORMING A SOLUTION the process of forming a solution or dissolving one substance in another, or the state of being dissolved in another substance **6.** MATH VALUE SATISFYING AN EQUATION a value for a variable that satisfies an equation **7.** LAW TERMINATION OF A DISPUTE the termination of a dispute or payment of a debt **8.** ENDING OF STH the act of ending, breaking, or separating sth (*literary*) [14thC. Via Old French from Latin *solutionem*, from *solvere* (see SOLVE).]

solution set n. the set of values for a variable that satisfy an equation

Solutrean /sǝ loŏtri ǝn/ adj. belonging to a prehistoric culture that existed in Europe between 40,000 BC and 12,000 BC, at the end of the Palaeolithic period, in which people worked with leaf-shaped flint blades [Late 19thC. From French *solutréen*, from *Solutré*, a village in Saône-et-Loire, France, where relics were discovered.]

solvable /sólvǝb'l/ adj. capable of being solved — **solvableness** n.

solvate /sól vayt/ vti. (**-vates, -vating, -vated**) BECOME OR CAUSE TO BECOME SOLUTION to enter into solution with a solvent, or cause a solute to dissolve in solution with a solvent ■ n. AGGREGATE OF SOLUTE AND SOLVENT a compound consisting of an ion or molecule of solute combined with one or more of solvent [Early 20thC. Coined from SOLVENT + -ATE.]

solvation /sól váysh'n/ n. the process by which molecules of a solvent develop a weak bond with molecules or ions of the solute

Solvay process /sól vay prō sess/ n. an industrial process for producing sodium carbonate or washing soda from common salt. A solution of salt is saturated with ammonia and carbon dioxide is passed through it, which causes sodium hydrogen carbonate to precipitate; it is then heated to obtain sodium carbonate. [Late 19thC. Named after the Belgian chemist Ernest *Solvay*, (1838–1922).]

solve /solv/ (**solves, solving, solved**) vt. **1.** DEAL WITH A PROBLEM SUCCESSFULLY to find a way of dealing successfully with a problem or difficulty **2.** FIND ANSWER TO A PUZZLE to find the answer to a question or puzzle **3.** MATH FIND ANSWER TO MATHS PROBLEM to work out the solution to an equation or other mathematical problem [15thC. From Latin *solvere* 'to loosen, dissolve'.]

WORD KEY: ORIGIN

The Latin word *solvere*, from which **solve** is derived, is also the source of English *absolute*, *absolve*, *dissolve*, *resolve*, and *solution*.

---

solvency /sólvǝnsi/ n. the position of having enough money to cover expenses and debts

solvent /sólvǝnt/ adj. **1.** HAVING ENOUGH MONEY having enough money to cover expenses and debts **2.** DISSOLVING STH able to dissolve substances ■ n. SUBSTANCE THAT DISSOLVES THINGS a substance in which other substances are dissolved, often a liquid [Early 17thC. Directly or via French from Latin *solventem*, present participle of *solvere* (see SOLVE).] —**solvently** adv.

solvent abuse n. the inhaling of fumes from solvents such as glues and petrol in order to produce a feeling of euphoria

solvolysis /sol vóllǝsiss/ n. a chemical reaction in which the solute and solvent present in a solution combine to form a new compound

Solway Firth /sól way-/ arm of the Irish Sea separating Dumfries and Galloway in Scotland, from Cumbria in England. Length: 64 km/40 mi.

Aleksandr Isayevich Solzhenitsyn

Solzhenitsyn /sólzhǝ neétsin, sǝlzhǝ nyeétsin/, **Aleksandr Isayevich** (b. 1918) Russian writer. His imprisonment in the Soviet Union for political dissent (1945–53) inspired early novels such as *One Day in the Life of Ivan Denisovich* (1964). He was expelled after the publication of *The Gulag Archipelago* (1974–78), and lived in exile in the United States for 20 years, returning to Russia after the collapse of the Soviet Union. He won a Nobel Prize in literature (1970).

som /sóm/ (*plural* **som**) n. **1.** KYRGYZ UNIT OF CURRENCY the main unit of currency in Kyrgyzstan, worth 100 tiyin. See table at **currency 2. som** UZBEK UNIT OF CURRENCY the main unit of currency in Uzbekistan. See table at **currency 3.** NOTE WORTH A SOM a note worth a som

Som. abbr. **1.** Somalia **2.** Somerset

soma[1] /sómǝ/ (*plural* **-mata** /-mǝtǝ/ or **-mas**) n. **1.** ALL BODY CELLS EXCEPT GERM CELLS all the cells and tissues in the body considered collectively, with the exception of germ cells **2.** BODY AS DISTINCT FROM MIND the body considered separately from the mind or soul [Mid-19thC. Via modern Latin from Greek *sōma* 'body'.]

soma[2] /sómǝ/ n. **1.** BEVERAGES INTOXICATING DRINK IN HINDU SCRIPTURE an intoxicating drink made from plant juice, mentioned in the Vedas, the most ancient

Georg Solti

a at; aa father; aw all; ay day; air hair; ǝ about, edible, item, common, circus; e egg; ee eel; hw when; i it, happy; ī ice; 'l apple; 'm rhythm; 'n fashion; o odd; ō open; oŏ good; oō pool; ow owl; oy oil; th thin; th this; u up; ur urge;

sacred writings of Hinduism **2.** PLANTS **PLANT SOMA IS MADE FROM** the plant that soma is made from, thought to be ephedra, but not identified in the Vedas [Early 19thC. From Sanskrit.]

Somali /sə máali/ (*plural* **-lis** *or* **-li**), **Somalian** /sə máali ən/ *n.* **1.** PEOPLES **MEMBER OF PEOPLE FROM SOMALIA** a member of an Islamic African people living mainly in Somalia **2.** LANG **SOMALI LANGUAGE** the national language of Somalia, also spoken in eastern Ethiopia. It belongs to the Cushitic branch of Afro-Asiatic languages. Somali is spoken by over five million people. [Early 19thC. From Somali.] —**Somali** *adj.*

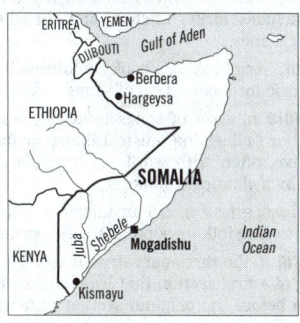

Somalia

Somalia /sə máali ə/ republic in northeastern Africa. Language: Somali. Currency: Somali shilling. Capital: Mogadishu. Population: 6,802,000 (1996). Area: 637,657 sq. km/246,201 sq. mi. Official name **Somali Democratic Republic** —**Somali** *adj.* —**Somalian** /sə máali ən/ *adj.*

Somalian /sə máali ən/ *n., adj.* = **Somali**

Somaliland /sə máali land/ region in northeastern Africa, comprising Somalia, Djibouti, and part of Ethiopia

somat- *prefix.* = **somato-** (*used before vowels*)

somatic /sə máttik/ *adj.* **1.** AFFECTING BODY AS DISTINCT FROM MIND relating to or affecting the body, especially the body as considered to be separate from the mind **2.** ANAT RELATING TO OUTER WALLS OF BODY relating to the outer walls of the body, not the inner organs **3.** OF SOMATIC CELL relating to a somatic cell [Late 18thC. From Greek *sōmatikós* 'bodily', from *sōma* (see SOMA[1]).] —**somatically** *adv.*

somatic cell *n.* any cell of the body with the exception of germ cells

somaticize /sə mátti sīz/ (**-cizes, -cizing, -cized**), **somaticise** (**-cises, -cising, -cised**) *vti.* to believe mistakenly that an emotional pain is a physical symptom

somatic nervous system *n.* the part of the nervous system that serves the sense organs and muscles of the body wall and limbs, and brings about voluntary muscle activity. ◊ autonomic nervous system

somato- *prefix.* body ○ *somatotherapy* [From Greek *sōmat-*, the stem of *sōma*]

somatology /sṓmə tólləji/ *n.* **1.** PHYSIOLOGY AND ANATOMY the study of both the physiology and anatomy of the body **2.** ANTHROPOLOGICAL STUDY OF HUMAN ANATOMY the branch of anthropology that studies human evolution through variation and development in physical characteristics —**somatologic** /sṓmətə lójjik/ *adj.* —**somatological** /-lójjik'l/ *adj.* —**somatologically** /-lójjikli/ *adv.*

somatomedin /sṓmətə méedin/ *n.* a hormone produced in the liver that stimulates the growth of bone and muscle [Late 20thC. Coined from SOMATO- + INTERMEDIARY + -IN.]

somatoplasm /sṓmətə plazəm/ *n.* the protoplasm of body cells as distinct from the protoplasm of germ cells —**somatoplastic** /sṓmətə plástik/ *adj.*

somatopleure /sṓmətə ploor, -plur/ *n.* a fold of embryonic tissue in vertebrates formed by the fusion of ectoderm and mesoderm that gives rise to an embryo's inner and outer membranes —**somatopleural** /sṓmətə plóorəl, -plúrəl/ *adj.* —**somatopleuric** /-plóorik, -plúrik/ *adj.*

somatosensory /sṓmətə sénssəri/ *adj.* used to describe sensory stimuli coming from the skin and internal organs and the perception of these stimuli

somatostatin /sṓmətə státtin/ *n.* a hormone produced in the hypothalamus that inhibits the release of growth hormone [Late 20thC. Coined from SOMATO- + *stat-*, from Latin *stare* 'to stand' + -IN.]

somatotrophin /sṓmətə trófin/, **somatotropin** /sṓmətə trópin/ *n.* = **growth hormone** [Mid-20thC. Coined from SOMATO- + -TROPHIC + -IN.] —**somatotrophic** /sṓmətə tróffik/ *adj.*

somatotype /sṓmətə tīp/ *n.* the type of physical build that a person has

somber *adj.* US = **sombre**

sombre /sómbər/ *adj.* **1.** DARK AND GLOOMY lacking light or brightness and producing a dull, dark, or melancholy atmosphere **2.** DARK IN COLOUR having a colour or tone that is dark, dull, or suitable for a serious mood or occasion **3.** SERIOUS AND MELANCHOLY marked by or conveying strict seriousness combined with sadness or a troubled state of mind [Mid-18thC. Via French, 'gloomy', from, ultimately, late Latin *subumbrare* 'to shadow', from *sub* 'under' + *umbra* 'shade' (source of English *umbrage*).] —**sombrely** *adv.* —**sombreness** *n.*

sombrero /som bráirō/ (*plural* **-ros**) *n.* a straw or felt hat with a very wide upturned brim, originally worn by men in Mexico and some other Spanish-speaking countries [Late 16thC. Via Spanish, 'hat', from *sombra* 'shade', from Vulgar Latin *subombrare* (see SOMBRE).]

sombrous /sómbrəss/ *adj.* sombre (*archaic*) [Early 18thC. From French *sombre* (see SOMBRE) + -OUS.]

some /(stressed) sum, (unstressed) səm/ CORE MEANING: a grammatical word used to indicate an unspecified or unknown quantity of people or things ○ (det) *There is always some risk in any project.* ○ (pron) *There was plenty of food left over, so I took some.* **1.** *det., pron.* A LITTLE used to indicate an unspecified number, quantity, or proportion of a total, generally a fairly small to average or reasonable one ○ *I agree with you to some extent.* ○ *Some of you, I know, will disagree with me.* **2.** *det.* QUITE A FEW used with a slight emphasis to indicate an unspecified but fairly large number or quantity ○ *We have been debating this problem for some months now.* **3.** *det.* PARTICULAR BUT UNSPECIFIED used to indicate an unspecified single person or thing, often in a dismissive way ○ *He was reading some medical book.* **4.** *det.* USED FOR EMPHASIS used to emphasize that sb or sth is impressive or remarkable in a certain way (*informal*) ○ *That was some performance you put on for us!* **5.** *adv.* APPROXIMATELY used to indicate that a number is approximate ○ *for some 30 years* **6.** *adv.* US TO A SMALL EXTENT to a small extent or degree (*informal*) ○ *I do write some, but not as much as I'd like.* **7.** *adv.* US A GREAT DEAL a great deal, at a considerable rate, or vigorously (*informal*) ○ *I'm going to have to study some to get through this exam.* [Old English *sum* 'one, someone'. Ultimately from an Indo-European word meaning 'together with', which is also the ancestor of English *seem* and *similar*.] ◇ **and then some** US used to emphasize that more, often considerably more, has been done than was suggested in a previous statement (*informal*)

-some *suffix.* **1.** characterized by a particular quality, condition, or thing ○ *troublesome* ○ *quarrelsome* **2.** a group containing a particular number of members ○ *foursome* [Old English *-sum*]

-some *suffix.* **1.** body ○ *cytosome* **2.** chromosome ○ *autosome* [From Greek *sōma* 'body']

somebody /súmbədi/, **someone** *pron.* SOME PERSON some unspecified person ■ *n.* (*plural* **-ies**) IMPORTANT PERSON an important or well-known person in society or in a particular place

someday /súm day/ *adv.* at some unknown, unspecified, and usually fairly distant time in the future

—— WORD KEY: USAGE ——
someday, someplace, sometime In British English it is idiomatic to say **someday** (*Someday [or some day] I'll take you away from all this.*) but it is often written as two words, while **someplace** is not used at all except as a conscious Americanism (*I must have left it someplace.*).

Sometime is written as one word as an adjective meaning 'former' (*a sometime president of the Rotary Club*), and as an adverb meaning 'at some time'(*I'll see you again sometime*).

somehow /súm how/ *adv.* **1.** IN SOME WAY in some unspecified or unknown way, often with great effort or difficulty ○ *He somehow managed to scramble back on board.* **2.** FOR AN UNKNOWN REASON for some unknown or inexplicable reason ○ *She somehow forgot to tell anyone where she was going.*

someone *pron., n.* = **sb**

someplace /súm playss/ *adv.* US, Can somewhere (*informal*)

—— WORD KEY: USAGE ——
See Usage note at **someday**.

somersault /-solt/ *n.* **1.** GYMNASTICS ACROBATIC ROLLING OVER OF BODY an acrobatic movement in which the body is rolled over, feet over head, either forwards or backwards, on the ground or in midair, finally returning to an upright position **2.** REVERSAL OF OPINION OR DECISION a complete change of mind or reversal of policy ■ *vi.* (**-saults, -saulting, -saulted**) GYMNASTICS PERFORM SOMERSAULT to perform an acrobatic somersault [Early 16thC. Via Middle French *sombresault*, a variant of *sobresault*, from Latin *super* 'super' + *saltus* 'leap'.]

Somerset /súmmər set/ county in southwestern England that includes Exmoor National Park. Taunton is the county town. Population: 481,000 (1995). Area: 3,458 sq. km/1,335 sq. mi.

Somerset /súmmərssət/, **Edward Seymour, 1st Duke of** (1506?–52) English statesman. The brother of Jane Seymour, he became Protector of England during the minority of the future Edward VI. Rivalry with the duke of Northumberland led to his execution. Known as **Protector Somerset**

Somerset House *n.* a building in London that formerly housed the General Register Office

Somerset Island island in Nunavut, Canada, in the Arctic Archipelago, north of the Boothia Peninsula. Area: 24,786 sq. km/9,570 sq. mi.

somesthetic *adj.* US = **somaesthetic**

something /súm thing/ *pron.* **1.** UNSPECIFIED THING an unspecified or unidentified object, phenomenon, action, utterance, or feeling ○ *Don't just stand there, do something!* ○ *I had a feeling that there was something wrong.* ○ *Would you like something to eat?* **2.** A CERTAIN AMOUNT an unspecified and approximate amount expressed in relation to a specific number or quantity ○ *something over 50* ○ *something between 20 and 30%* **3.** SUGGESTING RESEMBLANCE used to suggest that one thing or person resembles another to a certain extent or has some of the qualities of the other ○ *There's definitely something of the knight errant about him.* **4.** RATHER used to qualify a description of a thing or event and tone it down or make it sound more guarded ○ *It was something of a disappointment.* **5.** STH IMPRESSIVE an impressive or important person or thing ○ *He's really something!* ■ *adv.* **1.** SOMEWHAT slightly or to some degree ○ *It sounds something like what she might have said.* **2.** TO AN EXTREME DEGREE used to intensify the effect of an adjective, especially a strong adjective used as an adverb (*informal*) ○ *It hurts something awful.* **3.** AND A BIT MORE used to indicate that a number is slightly higher than the one mentioned (*informal*) ○ *She's thirty something.* ◇ **sth else** sb or sth really special, remarkable, or extreme (*informal*) ◇ **have sth to do with sb** *or* **sth** to be connected with or involve sb or sth

sometime /súm tīm/ *adv.* **1.** AT SOME TIME at some unspecified or unknown time ○ *They intend to marry sometime soon.* **2.** FORMERLY at one time in the past (*formal*) ○ *our speaker today, sometime a scholar of Lincoln College, Oxford* **3.** OCCASIONALLY occasionally or sporadically (*archaic*) ■ *adj.* **1.** FORMER who at one time in the past had the job, position, or status in question ○ *a sometime student of this university* **2.** OCCASIONAL occasional or sporadic (*old*) ○ *an author and sometime lecturer*

sometimes /súm tīmz/ adv. 1. OCCASIONALLY from time to time, not continually or every time ○ *We go to the theatre sometimes.* 2. FORMERLY at one time in the past (archaic) [Early 16thC. The -s is possessive (genitive) singular, not a plural.]

someway /súm way/ adv. using some means or method that is not yet known or not stated ○ *We'll figure it out someway.*

somewhat /súm wot/ adv. to a certain extent or degree ○ *The hot night had cooled somewhat.*

somewhere /súm wair/ adv. 1. IN SOME UNSPECIFIED PLACE in, to, or at some unspecified place ○ *He lives somewhere in Scotland.* 2. APPROXIMATELY used in giving approximate amounts, numbers, or times ○ *somewhere around three hundred* ○ *somewhere between three and four o'clock* ◇ **get somewhere** to make progress towards achieving sth

somewise /súm wīz/ adv. (archaic) 1. SOMEHOW somehow 2. SOMEWHAT somewhat

somite /só mīt/ n. 1. EMBRYO CELL PAIR FORMING VERTEBRAE one of a series of paired blocks of cells that develop along the back of a vertebrate embryo giving rise to the vertebral column and most of the skeletal muscles 2. BODY SEGMENT a body segment, usually one of several, into which the bodies of certain animals, e.g. earthworms and crayfish, are divided along their length [Mid-19thC. From SOMA + -ITE.] —**somital** /sómīt'l/ adj. —**somitic** /sō míttik/ adj.

Somme /som/ river in northern France, flowing from near St Quentin into the English Channel. The Somme valley was the scene of a major World War I battle in 1916, which resulted in more than one million casualties. Length: 241 km/150 mi.

sommelier /sómm'l yay, sə méliər/ n. a wine waiter in a restaurant, hotel, or other licensed establishment, who supervises the ordering, storing, and serving of wine [Early 20thC. Via a variant of French *sommerier*, *sommier*, 'officer in charge of provisions', from *somme* 'burden', from, ultimately, Greek *ságma*, 'covering, pack-saddle'.]

sommer /sómmər/ adv. S Africa just, only, or somewhat (informal) [Mid-19thC. From Afrikaans *somaar*, *sommer*.]

somn- prefix. = somni- (used before vowels)

somnambulate /som námbyŏŏ layt/ (-lates, -lating, -lated) vi. to sleepwalk (technical) —**somnambulance** n. —**somnambulation** /som námbyŏŏ láysh'n/ n. —**somnambulator** /som námbyŏŏ laytər/ n.

somnambulism /som námbyŏŏliz'm/ n. sleepwalking (technical) —**somnambulist** /som námbyŏŏlist/ n. —**somnambulistic** /som námbyŏŏ lístik/ adj.

somni- prefix. sleep ○ *somnifacient* [From Latin *somnus*]

somnifacient /sómni fáysh'nt/ adj. used to describe a drug designed to induce sleep

somniferous /som nífferəss/ adj. making sb, or designed to make sb, feel sleepy —**somniferously** adv.

somnolent /sómnələnt/ adj. 1. SLEEPY feeling sleepy or tending to fall asleep 2. LACKING ACTIVITY quiet and with little or no activity 3. SLEEP-INDUCING making sb feel sleepy [15thC. Via Old French from Latin *somnolentus*, 'sleepy', from *somnus* 'sleep'.] —**somnolence** n. —**somnolently** adv.

son /sun/ n. 1. MALE CHILD a male child in relation to his parents 2. MALE DESCENDANT a male descendant 3. MALE WITH CONNECTIONS WITH STH a man or boy referred to in terms of his connection with a place, a time in history, or a sphere of interest ○ *the achievements of the sons of the Industrial Revolution* 4. TERM OF ADDRESS an affectionate, or sometimes condescending, way of addressing a boy or man (informal) [Old English *sunu*. Ultimately from an Indo-European word meaning 'to give birth'.] —**sonless** adj. —**sonlike** adj.

Son n. a title that Christians give to Jesus Christ, especially when referred to as the second person in the Holy Trinity

sonant /sónənt/ adj. 1. HAVING SOUND producing or possessing a sound (formal) 2. VOICED made with vi-

bration of the vocal cords 3. SYLLABIC used to describe a consonant that is capable of forming a syllable on its own, without a vowel ■ n. 1. VOICED SOUND a sound made with vibration of the vocal cords 2. SYLLABIC CONSONANT a consonant capable of forming a syllable on its own, without a vowel [Mid-19thC. From Latin *sonans*, present participle of *sonare* 'to sound'.] —**sonance** n. —**sonantal** /sō nánt'l/ adj. —**sonantic** adj.

sonar /só naar/ n. 1. SYSTEM FOR DETECTING UNDERWATER OBJECTS a system that determines the position of unseen underwater objects by transmitting sound waves and measuring the time it takes for their echo to return after hitting the object. Many modern ships, especially warships, are equipped with sonar, as well as many large commercial fishing boats. 2. SONAR DEVICE a device that uses sonar [Mid-20thC. Acronym from *sound navigation ranging*.]

sonata /sə naátə/ n. 1. CLASSICAL COMPOSITION FOR A SOLO INSTRUMENT a piece of classical music for a solo instrument or a small ensemble consisting of several movements, at least one of which is in sonata form 2. ONE-MOVEMENT BAROQUE KEYBOARD COMPOSITION a piece of baroque keyboard music in a single movement [Late 17thC. Via Italian, from *sonare* 'to sound', from Latin *sonare* (see SONANT).]

sonata form n. an important musical form developed in the 18th century consisting of three sections, an exposition, development, and recapitulation, and used especially for the first movement of sonatas, concertos, and symphonies

sonatina /sónnə teénə/ n. a short and usually less technically difficult sonata [Early 18thC. Via Italian, 'little sonata', from *sonata* (see SONATA).]

sondage /son daázh/ n. a deep trench dug in order to study the relative positions of human artefacts in horizontal layers [Mid-20thC. French, literally 'sounding, bore hole' (see SOUND[1]).]

sonde /sónd/ n. a collection of instruments that can be lowered down a borehole or carried into the upper atmosphere by balloon or rocket to transmit information relating to the conditions encountered [Early 20thC. From French, literally 'plumb line, sound' (see SOUND[1]).]

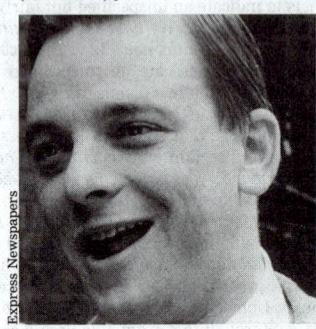

Stephen Sondheim

Sondheim /sónd hīm/, **Stephen** (b. 1930) US composer and lyricist. His innovative musicals include the Pulitzer Prize-winning *Sunday in the Park with George* (1984). Full name **Stephen Joshua Sondheim**

sone /són/ n. a unit measuring the loudness of sound as subjectively perceived, equal to a tone of 1 kilohertz at 40 decibels above the threshold where sounds become audible to the listener [Mid-20thC. From Latin *sonus* 'sound'.]

son et lumière /són ay loomi air/ n. an outdoor nighttime spectacle that combines dramatic lighting effects with recorded sounds and music, usually staged at the site of a famous and historical building, often telling its history [French, literally 'sound and light']

song /song/ n. 1. SET OF WORDS SUNG a usually relatively short musical composition consisting of words set to music 2. SINGING the art or practice of singing 3. INSTRUMENTAL WORK IN STYLE OF SONG an instrumental work written in the style of a vocal song, or, in popular music, any musical work 4. CHARACTERISTIC SOUND OF BIRD OR INSECT the characteristic sound that a bird or insect makes, usually either to attract a mate or to warn off competing members of its species 5. POETRY

poetry or verse (literary) 6. POEM a poem, especially one that rhymes (literary) [Old English *sang*. Ultimately from an Indo-European word meaning 'to sing'.] —**songlike** adj. ◇ **for a song** very cheaply ◇ **on song** performing well or in good form (informal)

Song n. = Sung

song and dance n. (informal) 1. UNNECESSARY FUSS an unnecessary fuss about sth 2. US LONG-WINDED EXPLANATION a long-winded attempt to explain or justify sth

songbird /sóng burd/ n. a bird with a musical call, especially a perching bird belonging to the suborder that includes larks, finches, and thrushes. Suborder: Oscines.

songbook /sóng bŏŏk/ n. a book containing the words and music for a collection of songs

song cycle n. a set of songs linked by a common subject or underlying musical theme or forming a narrative, often with words by a single poet and music by a classical composer

songfest /sóng fest/ n. US an informal gathering of people to sing folk or popular songs together

song form n. the three-part structure of a song consisting of a first section that leads to a contrasting section before the original section returns, either identically or with some variation

songful /sóngfŏŏl, sóngf'l/ adj. resembling song, especially in having a pleasing melody —**songfully** adv. —**songfulness** n.

Songhai[1] /sóng gí/ (plural **-hai** or **-hais**), **Songhay** (plural **-hay** or **-hays**) n. 1. MEMBER OF W AFRICAN PEOPLE a member of a people living in West Africa, mainly in Mali and Niger. The Songhai established a powerful empire in this area during the 7th century AD, and they remained the dominant ethnic group until the 16th century. 2. SONGHAI LANGUAGE the Nilo-Saharan language of the Songhai people. Songhai is spoken by about two million people.

Songhai[2] /sóng gí/ state in western Africa during the 15th and 16th centuries. Its capital was Gao, which stood on the River Niger in what is now Mali.

Song of Solomon, Song of Songs n. a book of the Bible consisting of a set of love poems ascribed to King Solomon. See table at **Bible**

songsmith /sóng smith/ n. = songwriter

song sparrow n. a brown and white North American finch with a musical call. Latin name: *Melospiza melodia*.

songster /sóngstər/ n. 1. SINGER a singer, especially a talented one 2. SONGBIRD a bird with a musical call 3. POET a poet (literary)

songstress /sóngstrəss/ n. a woman singer, songwriter, or poet (dated)

song thrush n. a small common Eurasian bird with brown upper parts and a white breast speckled with brown that has a melodic whistling call. Latin name: *Turdus philomelos*.

songwriter /sóng rītər/ n. sb who writes the words, music, or both for songs, especially popular songs

sonic /sónnik/ adj. 1. RELATING TO SOUND OR SOUND WAVES relating to, using, or producing sound or sound waves 2. AUDIBLE TO HUMAN EAR able to be heard by the human ear 3. RELATING TO SPEED OF SOUND relating to or travelling at the speed of sound in air, approximately 1,220 kilometres per hour/760 mi. per hour at sea level [Early 20thC. Coined from Latin *sonus* 'sound' + -IC.]

sonic barrier n. = sound barrier

sonic boom n. a noise heard as a loud boom at ground level resulting from the shock waves created by an aircraft flying above the speed of sound

sonics /sónniks/ n. the study of sound or, more generally, elastic wave motion (takes a singular verb)

soniferous /so nífferəss/ adj. producing or transmitting sound [Early 18thC. Coined from Latin *sonus* 'sound' + -IFEROUS.]

son-in-law (plural **sons-in-law**) n. the husband of sb's daughter

sonnet /sónnət/ n. FOURTEEN-LINE RHYMING POEM WITH SET STRUCTURE a short poem with fourteen lines, usually ten-syllable rhyming lines, divided into two, three, or four sections. There are many rhyming patterns for sonnets, and they are usually written in iambic pentameter. ■ *vi.* (**-nets, -neting, -neted**) WRITE SONNETS to write sonnets [Mid-16thC. Via French and Italian *sonnetto* from Old Provençal *son* 'poem', from Latin *sonus* 'sound'.]

sonnet cycle *n.* = **sonnet sequence**

sonneteer /sónnə tée̋r/ *n.* **1.** SONNET WRITER a poet who writes sonnets **2.** MEDIOCRE POET a writer of mediocre poems

sonnet sequence *n.* a set of sonnets written by one poet and unified by a single theme or idea

sonny /súnni/ (*plural* **-nies**), **sonny boy** *n.* an affectionate, or sometimes condescending, way of addressing a man or boy (*informal*)

sonobuoy /sṓnə boy, sónnə-/ *n.* a buoy fitted with equipment for detecting underwater noises and transmitting them by radio [Mid-20thC. Coined from Latin *sonus* 'sound' + BUOY.]

son of a bitch *n.* (*plural* **sons of bitches**) *US, Can* **1.** OFFENSIVE TERM an offensive term for sb, usually a man, whom the speaker considers hateful, despicable, or intensely annoying (*slang insult*) **2.** PERSON IN GENERAL used, together with an adjective, as a familiar, humorous, and slightly vulgar term for a person, usually a man, who has the named characteristic (*slang*) ○ *He's a lucky son of a bitch.* ■ *interj. US, Can* SWEARWORD used as a swearword (*slang*)

son of a gun *n.* (*plural* **sons of guns**) *US, Can* PERSON a person, especially a man, and usually sb affectionately or kindly regarded (*informal*) ■ *interj. US, Can* EXCLAMATION used to express mild annoyance or surprise (*informal*) [Perhaps originally for the illegitimate child of a soldier; also influenced by British argot *gun*, meaning 'thief']

son of God *n.* **1.** ANGEL a superhuman, angelic being **2.** CHRISTIAN a believer in the Christian faith

Son of God, **Son of Man** *n.* Jesus Christ, considered as the Messiah

sonogram /sṓnə gram/ *n.* a graphical representation of sound, especially in the three dimensions of frequency, time, and intensity

Sonoran Desert /sə náwrən-/ the largest desert in North America. It is situated in southwestern Arizona, southern California, and northwestern Mexico. Area: 310,000 sq. km/120,000 sq. mi.

sonority /sə nórəti/ (*plural* **-ties**) *n.* **1.** RESONANCE a sonorous quality **2.** RESOUNDING SOUND a sound, especially a rich deep sound [Early 16thC. Via French *sonorité* from medieval Latin *sonoritas*, from Latin *sonorus* (see SONOROUS).]

sonorous /sónnərəss/ *adj.* **1.** PRODUCING SOUND producing or possessing sound **2.** RESONANT sounding with loud, deep, and clear tones **3.** HAVING AN IMPRESSIVE MANNER OF SPEAKING speaking, spoken, or expressed in a rich, full, and impressive manner [Early 17thC. From Latin *sonorus* 'noisy, loud', from *sonor* 'sound', from *sonare* 'to make a sound'.] —**sonorously** *adv.* —**sonorousness** *n.*

Sons of Freedom *npl.* a religious group in western Canada involved in antigovernment terrorism during the 1950s and 1960s

sonsy /sónssi/ (**-sier, -siest**), **sonsie** (**-sier, -siest**) *adj.* (*regional nonstandard*) **1.** BUXOM buxom or chubby **2.** EASY-GOING having a cheerful easy-going nature **3.** LUCKY bringing or having good luck [Mid-16thC. Formed from earlier *sonse* 'abundance, plentifulness' from Gaelic *sonas* 'good fortune'.]

Sontag /són tag/, **Susan** (*b.* 1933) US writer. She is best known for her social commentary such as the article 'Notes on Camp' (1964) and *Illness as Metaphor* (1978). She has also written novels and short stories.

sook /sŏŏk/ (**sooks, sooking, sooked**) *n.* (*informal*) **1.** *Scotland* TOADY sb who flatters sb excessively or blatantly in order to curry favour **2.** *ANZ* SB WEAK OR TIMID sb weak, timid, or cowardly **3.** *NZ* CALF a calf [Late 19thC. Dialect form of SUCK. Probably originally meaning 'calf reared by hand' or 'sucking calf'.]

soon /soon/ *adv.* **1.** AFTER A SHORT TIME within or after a short time ○ *She soon realized that she had made a mistake.* **2.** QUICKLY quickly or without much delay ○ *How soon will you be ready?* ○ *I'll soon see about that!* **3.** EARLY before a reasonable or the desired length of time has elapsed ○ *Do you really have to go so soon?* ○ *It's a bit soon to be thinking of marriage, isn't it?* **4.** WILLINGLY used when expressing a preference for one alternative over another or an equal willingness to accept either, and often in the comparative form 'sooner' ○ *I'd sooner stay in than go out.* ○ *I'd as soon stay in as go out.* [Old English *sōna*. Originally in the sense 'immediately, at once', but current meanings developed in Old English.] ◇ **as soon as** immediately after ◇ **no sooner...than** immediately after one thing had happened, another took place ◇ **sooner or later** inevitably or certainly at some as yet unspecifiable time

Popperfoto

Susan Sontag

soot /sŏŏt/ *n.* BLACK DUST GIVEN OFF BY FIRE a black powdery form of carbon produced when coal, wood, or oil is burned, which rises up in fine particles with the flames and smoke ■ *vt.* (**soots, sooting, sooted**) COVER WITH SOOT to sprinkle or cover sth with soot [Old English *sōt*, literally 'sth that sits'. Ultimately from a prehistoric Germanic word meaning 'sit'.]

sooth /sooth/ *n.* TRUTH truth (*archaic or literary*) ■ *adj.* (*archaic or literary*) **1.** TRUE true **2.** SOFT soft and soothing [Old English *sōþ* 'true'. Ultimately from an Indo-European word meaning 'be', which is also the ancestor of English *is*.] —**soothly** *adv.*

soothe /soo*th*/ (**soothes, soothing, soothed**) *v.* **1.** *vt.* EASE PAIN to make pain or discomfort less severe **2.** *vti.* CALM SB DOWN to make sb less angry, anxious, or upset [Old English *sōþian* 'to prove to be true, verify', from *sōþ* (see SOOTH). The modern meanings evolved from 'prove true' via 'support' and 'encourage'.] —**soother** *n.* —**soothing** *adj.* —**soothingly** *adv.* —**soothingness** *n.*

soothfast /sóoth faast/ *adj.* (*archaic*) **1.** TRUTHFUL truthful **2.** LOYAL loyal

soothsay /sóoth say/ (**-says, -saying, -said**) *vi.* to predict the future [Early 17thC. Back-formation from SOOTHSAYER.] —**soothsaying** *n.*

soothsayer /sóoth sayər/ *n.* sb who attempts to predict the future

sooty /sŏŏti/ (**-ier, -iest**) *adj.* **1.** SOOT-COVERED covered in soot, or lined or blocked with soot **2.** RESEMBLING SOOT resembling soot in its blackness, dirtiness, or powdery texture

sooty mould *n.* **1.** FUNGAL PLANT DISEASE a plant disease characterized by a black velvety fungus **2.** FUNGUS a fungus that causes sooty mould. Genus: *Meliola* and *Capnodium.*

sooty shearwater *n.* a medium-sized dark-grey or brown seabird of the Atlantic and Pacific oceans that rolls its body from side to side as it skims the surface of the water. Latin name: *Puffinus griseus.*

sooty tern *n.* a medium-sized jet-black seabird with white underparts that is found in tropical regions. Latin name: *Sterna fuscata.*

sop /sop/ *n.* **1.** STH GIVEN TO SATISFY DISCONTENTED PERSON sth offered as a concession or gesture to pacify sb who is angry or discontented **2.** FOOD FOOD DIPPED IN LIQUID a piece of food dipped or soaked in liquid before it is eaten **3.** OFFENSIVE TERM an offensive term that deliberately insults sb's, especially a man's, courage (*dated informal insult*) ■ *vti.* (**sops, sopping, sopped**) MAKE OR BECOME SOAKING WET to make sth, or become, thoroughly wet [Old English *sopp* 'bread dipped in liquid', from *sūpan* 'to swallow, taste'. Ultimately from a prehistoric Germanic word meaning 'to take liquid' (ancestor also of English *sip*, *soup*, and *supper*).]

sop up *vt.* to soak up a liquid with sth absorbent

SOP *abbr.* standard operating procedure

sop. *abbr.* soprano

sophism /sóffizəm/ *n.* an argument or explanation that seems very clever or subtle on the surface but is actually flawed, misleading, or intended to deceive [14thC. Via Old French *sophisme* from, ultimately, Greek *sóphisma* 'acquired skill, clever device', ultimately from *sophós* (see SOPHIST).]

sophist /sóffist/ *n.* **1.** **sophist, Sophist** PHILOS ANCIENT GREEK PHILOSOPHER a member of a school of ancient Greek professional philosophers who were expert in and taught the skills of rhetoric, argument, and debate, but were criticized for specious reasoning. The sophists were active before and during the time of Socrates and Plato, who were their main critics. **2.** SB USING CLEVER TALK TO DECEIVE sb who deceives people with clever-sounding but flawed arguments or explanations [Mid-16thC. Via Latin from Greek *sophistēs* 'master of a craft, man clever in practical affairs', also 'cheat', ultimately from *sophós* 'skilled in a craft, clever, wise'.]

sophister /sóffistər/ *n.* formerly, a second-year undergraduate student at a British university [14thC. Via Old French *sophistre* and Latin *sophista* from, ultimately, Greek *sophós* (see SOPHIST).]

sophistic /sə fístik/, **sophistical** *adj.* **1.** CLEVER-SOUNDING BUT FLAWED clever-sounding and plausible but based on shallow or dishonest thinking or flawed logic **2.** PHILOS OF SOPHISTS relating to sophists [Mid-16thC. Via Latin from Greek *sophistikós*, from *sophós* (see SOPHIST).] —**sophistically** *adv.*

sophisticate /sə físti kayt/ *v.* (**-cates, -cating, -cated**) **1.** *vt.* MAKE SB MORE CULTURED OR WORLDLY to make sb more cultured or worldly, especially by educating out or destroying his or her naturalness, naivety, or innocence **2.** *vt.* MAKE STH MORE COMPLEX to make sth more advanced or complex **3.** *vti.* USE SOPHISTRY to use sophistic arguments, or make reasoning or an argument sophistic **4.** *vt.* CORRUPT to make sth impure, false, or adulterated ■ *n.* SB CULTURED OR WORLDLY sb who is knowledgeable about the ways of the world and has cultured taste and refined manners [14thC. From medieval Latin *sophisticatus*, past participle of *sophisticare* 'to deceive with words, disguise', from, ultimately, Greek *sophós* (see SOPHIST).] —**sophisticator** *n.*

sophisticated /sə físti kaytid/ *adj.* **1.** KNOWLEDGEABLE AND CULTURED knowledgeable about the ways of the world, self-confident, and not easily deceived **2.** SUITABLE FOR SOPHISTICATED PEOPLE appealing to or frequented by sophisticated people **3.** ADVANCED complex, advanced, and very up-to-date —**sophisticatedly** *adv.*

sophistication *n.* **1.** KNOWLEDGEABLENESS AND REFINEMENT a combination of worldly wisdom, self-confidence, and refinement in a person **2.** TECHNICAL ADVANCEDNESS technical advancedness and complexity **3.** SOPHISTICATING the process of sophisticating sth or sb

sophistry /sóffistri/ (*plural* **-tries**) *n.* **1.** FLAWED METHOD OF ARGUMENTATION a method of argumentation that seems clever but is actually flawed or dishonest **2.** = **sophism** [14thC. Via Old French *sophistrie* from Latin *sophistria* (see SOPHIST).]

Sophocles /sóffə kleez/ (496?–406? BC) Greek dramatist. The seven tragedies of his 123 plays that survive in complete texts, including *Electra*, *Oedipus Rex*, and *Antigone*, demonstrate the powerful treatment of moral and religious themes that made him one of the greatest dramatists of all time.

sophomore /sóffə mawr/ *n. US, Can* **1.** SECOND-YEAR STUDENT a second-year student at a high school or university **2.** SB IN SECOND YEAR OF STH sb in the second year of a project or activity [Late 17thC. Alteration of earlier *sophumer* (probably influenced by Greek *sophos* 'wise' + *mōros* 'dull'), from obsolete English *sophum* 'sophism', a variant of SOPHISM.]

sophomoric *adj.* **1.** IMMATURE showing the naive lack of judgement that accompanies immaturity **2.** OF SOPHOMORES relating to sophomores

-sophy *suffix.* wisdom, knowledge, science ○ *theosophy* [From Greek *sophia*, from *sophos* 'wise']

sopor /sṓpər/ *n.* an abnormally deep sleep or state of unconsciousness [Mid-17thC. From Latin, 'sleep'.]

soporific /sóppə ríffik/ *adj.* **1. MAKING SB SLEEPY** causing sleep or drowsiness **2. FEELING SLEEPY** experiencing sleepiness or drowsiness **3. TEDIOUS** dull and boring ■ *n.* **SLEEP-INDUCING DRUG** a drug or other substance that induces sleep —**soporifically** *adv.*

sopping /sópping/, **sopping wet** *adj.* thoroughly wet

—— **WORD KEY: SYNONYMS** ——

See Synonyms at **wet**.

soppy /sóppi/ (**-pier, -piest**) *adj.* **1. OVERLY SENTIMENTAL OR AFFECTIONATE** affectionate or sentimental in an excessive way (*informal*) **2. SOAKING** thoroughly wet

sopranino /sópprə neénō/ (*plural* **-nos**) *n.* a musical instrument, usually a wind instrument, that has the highest pitch of all those in its family, being even higher than the soprano [Early 20thC. From Italian, 'little soprano' (see SOPRANO).]

soprano /sə praánō/ (*plural* **-os** or **-i**) *n.* **1. WOMAN OR BOY WITH HIGHEST VOICE** a woman, girl, or a boy with the highest register of singing voice **2. HIGHEST SINGING VOICE** the highest register of singing voice a woman, girl, or boy can have **3. SINGING PART FOR SOPRANO VOICE** a singing part written for sb with a soprano voice **4. MUSICAL INSTRUMENT WITH HIGH PITCH** a musical instrument, especially a wind instrument, with the highest pitch of the instruments in its family, or the second highest, if the family includes a sopranino [Early 18thC. From Italian, from *sopra* 'above', from Latin *supra*.]

soprano clef *n.* a C clef in which middle C is designated by the first line of the staff. It was formerly used for the soprano vocal line.

Sopwith /sóppwith/, **Sir Thomas** (1888–1989) British aircraft designer and yachtsman. His company produced many of the aircraft used during World War I, including the Sopwith Camel. Full name **Sir Thomas Octave Murdoch Sopwith**

SOR, **SoR** *abbr.* sale or return

sora /sáwrə/ *n.* a small greyish-brown North American bird that lives in bogs and swamps, and, though common, is seldom seen. Latin name: *Porzana carolina.* [Early 18thC. Origin unknown: possibly of Native North American origin.]

sorb /sawrb/ *n.* **1.** = service tree **2. sorb, sorb apple BERRY** the berry of the service tree [Early 16thC. Via French *sorbe* from Latin *sorbum* 'service berry'.] —**sorbic** *adj.*

Sorb /sawrb/ *n.* **PEOPLES** a member of a Slavic people living mainly in the upper Spree valley between eastern Germany and southwestern Poland. There are about 150,000 Sorbs, who are descendants of an earlier people known as Wends. [Mid-19thC. Via German *Sorbe*, ultimately from Lusatian *serbje*, related to, or a variant of, SERB.] —**Sorbian** *adj.*

sorbet /sáwr bay, sáwrbit/ *n.* a frozen dessert, usually made with fruit syrup and sometimes egg whites, whisked until smooth [Late 16thC. Via French and Italian *sorbetto* from Turkish *şerbet* 'cool drink' (see SHERBET).]

Sorbian /sáwrbi ən/ *n., adj.* **LANG** = Wendish

sorbic acid /sáwrbik-/ *n.* a white crystalline solid acid obtained from the unripe berries of the mountain ash, or manufactured synthetically, and used as a food preservative and a fungicide. Formula: $C_6H_8O_2$.

sorbitol /sáwrbi tol/ *n.* a white crystalline sweet

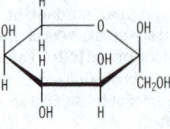

Sorbitol

alcohol extracted from the berries of the mountain ash tree, or manufactured synthetically, and used as a sweetener and in cosmetics, toiletries, and pharmaceuticals. Formula: $C_6H_{14}O_6$.

Sorbonne /sawr bón/ *n.* a part of the University of Paris, founded in 1253, and containing the faculties of science and literature

Sorbo /sáwrbō/ *tdmk.* a trademark for a brand of spongy rubber

sorbose /sáwr bóss/ *n.* a whitish crystalline sugar that is an isomer of fructose and a fermentation product of sorbitol, used in the preparation of vitamin C. Formula: $C_6H_{12}O_6$. [Late 19thC. From SORBITOL + -OSE.]

sorcerer /sáwrssərər/ *n.* sb who is believed or claims to have magical powers [Early 16thC. Via French *sorcier* from, ultimately, Latin *sors* (see SORT).]

sorceress /sáwrsəres/ *n.* a woman who is believed or claims to have magical powers

sorcery /sáwrssəri/ *n.* the supposed use of magic —**sorcerous** *adj.*

sordid /sáwrdid/ *adj.* **1. NASTY** demonstrating the worst aspects of human nature, e.g. immorality, selfishness, and greed **2. SQUALID** dirty and depressing [Late 16thC. Via French *sordide* and Latin *sordidus* from, ultimately, *sordes* 'dirt'.] —**sordidly** *adv.* —**sordidness** *n.*

sordino /sawr deénō/ (*plural* **-ni** /-ni/) *n.* a device used to muffle or soften the tone of a musical instrument, e.g. a mute for a stringed or brass instrument or a damper on a piano [Late 16thC. From Italian, formed from *sordo* 'unable to speak or hear', from Latin *surdus.*]

sore /sawr/ *adj.* (**sorer, sorest**) **1. PAINFUL** painful or tender because of an injury, infection, or unaccustomed exercise **2. ANNOYING** causing annoyance or embarrassment ○ *His dismissal has always been a sore point.* **3. DISTRESSING** causing great worry or distress (*literary*) ○ *Her illness was a sore trial to her husband and children.* **4. URGENT** requiring urgent action to provide relief ○ *The survivors of the flood are in sore need of help.* **5. OFFENDED** angry or irritated, especially because of sth said or done by another person in the recent past (*informal*) ○ *He was still sore because I kidded him about his tie.* ■ *n.* **MED INFECTED SPOT** a painful open skin infection or wound ■ *adv.* **SORELY** sorely (*archaic*) [Old English *sār.* Ultimately from a prehistoric Germanic word that is also the ancestor of English *sorry.*] —**soreness** *n.*

sorehead /sáwr hed/ *n.* *US, Can* sb who is easily offended or angered (*informal*)

sorely /sáwrli/ *adv.* to a great extent or degree (*formal*) ○ *I was sorely tempted to give him the money.*

sorgho *n.* = sorgo

Sorghum

sorghum /sáwrgəm/ (*plural* **-ghums** or **-ghum**) *n.* **1. PLANTS CEREAL CROP** a cereal plant that is resistant to drought, widely cultivated in tropical and warm areas as a grain crop and for animal feed. Genus: *Sorghum.* **2. FOOD SYRUP FROM SORGHUM** a syrup made from the juice of some varieties of sorghum [Late 16thC. Via modern Latin from Italian *sorgo* (see SORGO).]

sorgo /sáwrgō/ (*plural* **-gos**), **sorgho** (*plural* **-ghos**) *n.* any of several varieties of sorghum cultivated as a source of syrup [Mid-18thC. Via Italian from Vulgar Latin *syricum (granum)*, literally 'Syrian (grain)'.]

sori plural of **sorus**

sorites /so rī teez/ (*plural* **-tes**) *n.* an argument consisting of a series of premises arranged so that the predicate of each premise forms the subject of the next. The conclusion unites the subject of the first premise with the predicate of the last. [Mid-16thC. Via Latin from Greek *sōreitēs*, from *sōros* 'heap'.]

Soroptimist /sə róptəmist/ *n.* a member of an international organization (**Soroptimist International**) of professional women and businesswomen that promotes public service. It was founded in California in 1921. [Early 20thC. A blend of Latin *soror* 'sister' and OPTIMIST.]

sororate /sórrə rayt/ *n.* a custom in some societies in which a widower marries a younger sister of his deceased wife [Early 20thC. Formed from Latin *soror* 'sister'.]

sororicide /sə rórissīd/ *n.* **1. MURDER OF SISTER** the murder of a sister **2. KILLER OF SISTER** sb who kills his or her sister [Mid-17thC. Coined from Latin *soror* 'sister' + -CIDE.] —**sororicidal** /sə rórissíd'l/ *adj.*

sorority /sə rór əti/ (*plural* **-ties**) *n.* a social society for women students at an American college or university, with a name made up of Greek letters. ◊ **fraternity** [Mid-16thC. From medieval Latin *sororitas*, from Latin *soror* 'sister'.]

sorption /sáwrpsh'n/ *n.* the taking in or holding of sth, either by absorption or adsorption [Early 20thC. Back-formation from ABSORPTION and ADSORPTION.]

sorrel[1] /sórrəl/ (*plural* **-rels** or **-rel**) *n.* a sharp-tasting plant of the dock family, used for salad greens and in medicines. Genus: *Rumex.* [14thC. From Old French *surele*, from *sur* 'sour'. Ultimately from a prehistoric Germanic word that is also the ancestor of English *sour.*]

sorrel[2] /sórrəl/ *adj.* **COLOURS REDDISH-BROWN** of a reddish-brown colour ■ *n.* **1. COLOURS BROWN WITH RED ADDED** a brown colour with a suggestion of red **2. ZOOL REDDISH-BROWN ANIMAL** a sorrel horse or other animal [15thC. From Old French *sorel*, from *sor* 'yellowish'. Ultimately from a prehistoric Germanic word meaning 'dry'.]

sorrel tree *n.* = sourwood

Sorrento /sə réntō/ town and resort on the southern shore of the Bay of Naples, in Naples Province, Campania Region, in southern Italy. Population: 17,015 (1991).

sorrow /sórrō/ *n.* **1. GRIEF** a feeling of deep sadness caused by a loss or misfortune **2. SADDENING BURDEN** an unfortunate event, experience, or other cause of sorrow ■ *vi.* (**-rows, -rowing, -rowed**) **GRIEVE** to feel or express deep sadness over sth (*literary*) [Old English *sorg.* Ultimately from a prehistoric Germanic word meaning 'care'.] —**sorrower** *n.* ◊ **drown your sorrows** to take alcoholic drink in order to try to forget a source of sadness or disappointment

sorrowful /sórrəf'l/ *adj.* **1. SAD** feeling or expressing sorrow **2. CAUSING SADNESS** characterized by or causing sorrow —**sorrowfully** *adv.* —**sorrowfulness** *n.*

sorry /sórri/ *adj.* (**-rier, -riest**) **1. APOLOGETIC** feeling or expressing regret for an action that has upset or inconvenienced sb, or for a similar future action **2. SYMPATHETIC** feeling or expressing sympathy or empathy, especially because of sth that has happened ○ *I'm sorry you're leaving.* **3. PITIFUL** pitifully bad or neglected **4. VERY BAD** pathetically or contemptibly unsatisfactory ○ *a sorry excuse for a car* ■ *interj.* **1. APOLOGIZING FOR STH** used as an apology for hurting, interrupting, or inconveniencing sb ○ *Sorry – I didn't realize that was your foot.* **2. ASKING SB TO REPEAT STH** used with an interrogative inflexion to ask sb to repeat sth (*informal*) **3. CORRECTING A REMARK** used to introduce a correction in speech ○ *The company employs ten thousand – sorry, twelve thousand workers nationwide.* [Old English *sārig*, formed from *sār* (see SORE)] —**sorrily** *adv.* —**sorriness** *n.*

sort /sawrt/ *n.* **1. CATEGORY** a category of persons or things with shared attributes, to which sb or sth can be assigned ○ *What sort of instrument is that?* **2. PARTICULAR TYPE** a particular type of person (*informal*) ○ *She'll help – she's a good sort.* **3. SIMILAR THING** sth similar to the thing specified ○ *It's a sort of play with dancing.* **4. COMPUT SORTING OF DATA** a process of arranging data in a set order **5. PRINTING LETTER OR SYMBOL** a particular character in a font of type (*often plural*) **6. MANNER** a manner of doing sth (*archaic*) ■

v. (**sorts, sorting, sorted**) **1.** *vt.* **PUT IN CATEGORIES** to place people or things in categories according to shared attributes ○ *clothes sorted into piles* **2.** *vt.* COMPUT **PUT IN SEQUENCE** to arrange things in a set order, especially automatically as some computer programs do with data **3.** *vt.* = **sort out** *v.* 3 **4.** *vi.* **BE COMPATIBLE** to be compatible or in accord with sth (*archaic*) **5.** *vi.* **ASSOCIATE** to associate with sb (*archaic*) [14thC. Via French *sorte* and assumed Proto-Romance *sorta* 'class, order' from Latin *sors* 'lot, fortune' (source of English *sorcerer*).] —**sortable** *adj.* —**sorter** *n.* ◇ **of a sort, of sorts** used to indicate that sth is not very good ○ *We had a meal of sorts at the airport.* ◇ **out of sorts 1.** slightly unwell **2.** not in a very good mood ◇ **sort of** rather (*informal*) ○ *This place is sort of strange.*

WORD KEY: USAGE

See Usage note at ***kind***.

WORD KEY: SYNONYMS

See Synonyms at ***type***.

sort out *vt.* **1. RESOLVE EFFECTIVELY** to deal effectively with a problem ○ *I think we've sorted out our difficulties with the printer.* **2. REACH CONCLUSION** to think and come to a conclusion about a problem or difficulty **3. PUT IN ORDER** to put sth into order, or disentangle sth ○ *It took weeks to sort out the library.* **4. SEPARATE** to separate sth from the mixture it exists in, or from another group of things **5. PUNISH** to deal with or punish sb who has behaved badly (*informal*) ○ *Don't worry about him – I'll soon sort him out.*

sortation /sawr táysh'n/ *n.* the process of sorting items into categories or into a set order, especially when done by machine or computer

sorted /sáwrtid/ *adj.* **1. PUT RIGHT** put to rights, repaired, or dealt with satisfactorily (*informal*) **2. WELL-ADJUSTED** socially or emotionally well-adjusted (*slang*) **3. WELL PREPARED** well prepared for sth or well provided with sth, especially illegal drugs (*slang*)

sortie /sáwrti/ *n.* **1.** MIL **ATTACK ON AN ENEMY** an attack made by a small military force into enemy territory **2.** AIR **AIRCRAFT MISSION** a mission flown by a combat aircraft or group of combat aircraft **3. SHORT TRIP** a brief trip away from home, especially to an unfamiliar place (*humorous*) **4.** MIL **PEOPLE ON SORTIE** the personnel engaged in a military sortie ■ *vi.* (**-ties, -tieing, -tied**) MIL **MAKE A SORTIE** to make a sortie against an enemy position [Late 17thC. From French, the past participle of *sortir* 'to go out', of uncertain origin: perhaps from, ultimately, Latin *sors* (see SORT).]

sortilege /sáwrtilij/ *n.* **1. PROPHECY BY DRAWING LOTS** the supposed foretelling of the future by drawing lots **2. MAGIC** the supposed practice of magic or sorcery [14thC. Via French *sortilège* from, ultimately, Latin *sortilegus* 'prophetic, soothsayer', from *sors* (see SORT) + *legere* 'to read'.]

sorting office *n.* a place where letters and packages for delivery are sorted according to their destinations

sorus /sáwrəss/ (*plural* **-ri** /-rī/) *n.* **1. SPORE CASE CLUSTER** a cluster of spore cases on the underside of some fern fronds **2. SPORE-PRODUCING ORGAN** a spore-producing organ in some algae, fungi, and lichens [Mid-19thC. Via modern Latin from Greek *sōros* 'heap'.]

SOS *n.* **1. DISTRESS SIGNAL** an international radio signal that ships or aircraft in serious distress can use to call for help. It consists of the letters 'SOS' in Morse code (. . . – – – . . .), interpreted as meaning 'save our souls'. **2. CALL FOR HELP** a call or signal requesting help **3. BROADCAST TO CONTACT SB URGENTLY** a radio broadcast attempting to contact sb, whose whereabouts are unknown, in an emergency

sosatie /sə saáti/ *n. S Africa* curried or spicy meat grilled on a skewer [Mid-19thC. Via Afrikaans from, ultimately, Malay *sesate*.]

Sosigenes of Alexandria /so síjjə neez əv állig zaándri ə/ (*fl.* 50 BC) Greek astronomer. He advised Julius Caesar on the adoption of the solar, or Julian, calendar (45 BC).

so-so *adj.* **NEITHER GOOD NOR BAD** neither very good nor very bad (*informal*) ○ *The food was so-so, but the atmosphere was wonderful.* ■ *adv.* **NEITHER WELL NOR BADLY** neither very well nor very badly (*informal*) ○ *feeling so-so*

sostenuto /sóstə noótō/ *adv.* **WITH PROLONGED NOTES** with notes sustained to or beyond the notated value (*used as a musical direction*) ■ *n.* (*plural* **sostenutos**) **SOSTENUTO PIECE OF MUSIC** a piece of music, or a section of a piece, played sostenuto [Mid-18thC. From Italian, the past participle of *sostinere* 'to sustain', from Latin *sustinere*.] —**sostenuto** *adj.*

sot /sot/ *n.* an offensive term for sb who is nearly always drunk (*dated informal insult*) [Pre-12thC. Via Old French, 'fool', from medieval Latin *sottus*.]

soteriology /sō teéri óllәji/ *n.* the Christian doctrine that salvation has been brought about by Jesus Christ [Mid-18thC. Coined from Greek *sōtēria* 'salvation' + -LOGY.] —**soteriologic** /sō teéri ə lójjik/ *adj.*

Sothic cycle *n.* CALENDAR a cycle of 1460 Sothic years in the ancient Egyptian calendar [Early 19thC. *Sothic* formed from Greek *Sōthis*, the star Sirius, used in calendar calculations.]

Sothic year /sṓthik-/ *n.* CALENDAR a year of 365¼ days in the ancient Egyptian calendar, based on the first appearance of the dog star (**Sirius**) above the horizon [See SOTHIC CYCLE]

Sotho /soó too/ (*plural* **-tho** *or* **-thos**) *n.* **1.** PEOPLES **MEMBER OF SOUTHERN AFRICAN PEOPLE** a member of a large group of peoples who live in southern Africa, mainly in Botswana, Lesotho, and South Africa **2.** LANG **SOTHO LANGUAGE** the Bantu language of the Sotho, belonging to the Niger-Congo family. There are several languages in the group, including Tswana and Lesotho. —**Sotho** *adj.*

sottish /sóttish/ *adj.* **1. DRUNKEN** in the habit of drinking far too much alcohol **2. DRUNK** showing the effects of having drunk too much alcohol

sotto voce /sóttō vṓchi/ *adv.* in a soft voice, so as not to be overheard [Mid-18thC. From Italian, literally 'under (the) voice'.] —**sotto voce** *adj.*

sou /soo/ *n.* **1. SMALL FRENCH COIN** a French coin no longer in use, worth only a small amount **2. ANY MONEY** the least amount of money (*informal*) (*used in negative statements*) ○ *I haven't a sou.* [15thC. From French, back-formation from Old French *sous*, the plural of *sout* 'sou', from Latin *solidus* (see SOLIDUS).]

soubrette /soo brét/ *n.* **1. MAIDSERVANT IN COMEDY** a pretty, flirtatious woman's role in a comedy, especially one in which she plays a lady's maid involved in romantic intrigues **2. ACTOR PLAYING SOUBRETTE** an actor who often plays soubrettes **3. DISMISSIVE TERM** a dismissive term for a young woman whose behaviour is interpreted as flirtatious (*dated*) [Mid-18thC. Via French, literally 'maid', and Provençal *soubreto* 'coy' from, ultimately, Latin *superare* 'to surpass', from *super* 'above'.]

soubriquet *n.* = **sobriquet**

souchong /soó chóng/ *n.* black China tea [Mid-18thC. From Cantonese *síu-chúng*, literally 'small kind'.]

souffle /soóf'l/ *n.* a soft blowing sound inside sb's chest, heard through a stethoscope and caused by blood flowing through blood vessels [Late 19thC. From French, literally 'breath', formed from *souffler* (see SOUFFLÉ).]

soufflé /soóf lay/ *n.* a sweet or savoury open-textured dish that has been made light by adding whisked egg whites. Hot soufflés are usually based on a thick milk sauce and are baked, while cold soufflés are made with gelatin and set by chilling. [Early 19thC. From French, the past participle of *souffler* 'to blow, to puff up', from Latin *sufflare*.] —**soufflé** *adj.*

Soufriere Hills Volcano /soófri áir-/ volcano on the island of Montserrat in the Caribbean Sea. It erupted in 1997, leaving large parts of the island uninhabitable. Height: 915 m/3,002 ft.

sough /sow/ *vi.* (**soughs, soughing, soughed**) **TO RUSTLE** to make a soft rustling, sighing, or murmuring sound, like the wind in trees (*archaic or literary*) ■ *n.* **SOUGHING SOUND** a sound like that made by a gentle wind through trees (*archaic or literary*) [Old English *swōgan*, of prehistoric Germanic origin]

sought past tense, past participle of **seek**

sought-after /sáwt aaftər/ *adj.* in high demand because scarce ○ *Blue diamonds are among the most sought-after gems.*

souk /sook/, **suq** *n.* an open-air market in North Africa or the Middle East [Early 19thC. From Arabic *sūḳ*.]

soukous /soó kooss/ *n.* a style of dance music originally from the Congo, combining guitar, drums, and vocals [Late 20thC. Origin uncertain: probably via Lingala from French *secouer* 'to shake'.]

soul /sōl/ *n.* **1. NONPHYSICAL ASPECT OF PERSON** the complex of human attributes that manifests as consciousness, thought, feeling, and will, regarded as distinct from the physical body **2.** RELIG **SPIRIT SURVIVING DEATH** in some systems of religious belief, the spiritual part of a human being that is believed to continue to exist after the body dies. The soul is sometimes regarded as subject to future reward and punishment, and sometimes as able to take a form that allows it to remain on or return to earth. **3. FEELINGS** sb's emotional and moral nature, where the most private thoughts and feelings are hidden ○ *Her soul was in turmoil.* **4.** ARTS **SPIRITUAL DEPTH** evidence of spiritual or emotional depth and sensitivity, either in a person or in sth created by a person ○ *Though technically perfect, the drawing lacked soul.* **5. ESSENCE** the deepest and truest nature of a people or a nation, or what gives sb or sth a distinctive character ○ *In my travels I hoped to discover the soul of the Russian people.* **6. TYPE OF PERSON** sb of a particular type, especially one regarded sympathetically or with familiarity ○ *Poor soul! What will he do now?* **7. ANYONE** anyone at all (*used in the negative*) ○ *You have to promise not to tell a soul.* **8. INDIVIDUAL** an individual person, especially when thought of as making up the number of a particular group (*usually plural*) ○ *a country of some 10 million souls* **9. PERFECT EXAMPLE** sb who is a good example, or personification, of a positive quality ○ *The hotel manager was the soul of discretion.* **10. SB ESSENTIAL TO STH** a leader or the most influential person in a group or movement **11. AFRICAN AMERICAN SPIRIT** the quality that characterizes African American culture, especially as manifested in sb's natural sympathies and in social customs, speech, and music **12.** MUSIC = **soul music** [Old English *sāwol*. Ultimately from a prehistoric Germanic word that is also the ancestor of German *Seele* 'soul'.]

Soul /sōl/ *n.* the name for God in Christian Science

soul brother *n.* a man who is an African American like the person in question

soul-destroying *adj.* extremely boring, repetitive, or unfulfilling

soul food *n.* the traditional foods of African Americans of the American South. Typical dishes are yams, chitterlings, black-eyed peas, and collard greens.

soulful /sṓlf'l/ *adj.* deeply or sincerely emotional —**soulfully** *adv.* —**soulfulness** *n.*

soulless /sṓl ləss/ *adj.* **1. LACKING FEELING** lacking warmth, sensitivity, or feeling ○ *soulless bureaucrats* **2. DEADENING** lacking anything that might stimulate or engage the feelings —**soullessly** *adv.* —**soullessness** *n.*

soul mate *n.* sb with whom sb else naturally shares deep feelings and attitudes

soul music *n.* a style of African American popular music with a strong emotional quality, related to gospel music and rhythm and blues

soul-searching *n.* a thorough examination of personal thoughts and feelings, especially when faced with a difficult problem

soul sister *n.* a woman who is an African American like the person in question (*dated*)

Soult /soolt/, **Nicolas Jean de Dieu** (1769–1851) French marshal and government official. Under Napoleon he led many campaigns in Europe, notably in Spain and Portugal. After the restoration of the monarchy in 1814, he shifted his loyalties and held various high posts, including premier (1833–34, 1839–47).

soum *n.* = **som**

sound[1] /sownd/ *n.* **1. STH AUDIBLE** sth that can be heard ○ *not a sound in the whole house* ○ *the sound of gunfire* **2.** PHYS, ACOUSTICS **VIBRATIONS SENSED BY THE EAR** vibrations travelling through air, water, or some other medium, especially those within the range of frequencies that can be perceived by the human ear. At sea level and freezing point the speed of sound through the air is 1,220 km/760 mi. per hour. **3.** **SENSATION OF VIBRATIONS** the sensation produced in the ear by vibrations travelling through air, water, or some other medium **4.** ELECTRON ENG **REPRODUCED MUSIC OR SPEECH** the music, speech, or other sounds heard through an electronic device such as a television, radio, or loudspeaker, especially with regard to volume or quality ○ *Please turn down the sound.* **5.** BROADCAST **RECORDING MUSIC OR SPEECH** the recording, editing, and replaying of music, speech, or sound effects in the broadcast or entertainment industry **6.** **IMPLICATION** an impression of sb or sth formed from limited but significant information, especially information lately received ○ *From the sound of it she's finally found a job she really likes.* **7.** **NOISE** meaningless noise ○ *I didn't care for the poetry – it had more sound than sense.* **8.** **EARSHOT** the distance or area within which sth can be heard ○ *Our house was within the sound of the church bells.* **9.** LING **ELEMENT OF SPEECH AS HEARD** a basic element of speech formed by the vocal tract and interpreted through the ear, or a combination of such sounds **10.** MUSIC **TYPE OF MUSIC** the distinctive quality that identifies bands or music from a particular place, area, or studio, or belonging to a particular movement or style ■ **sounds** *npl.* **MUSIC** music, especially music that is not classical, such as pop, jazz, or rock (*informal*) ■ *v.* (**sounds, sounding, sounded**) **1.** *vi.* **SEEM** to give a particular impression when mentioned or described ○ *The party sounded awful.* **2.** *vi.* **INDICATE STATUS** to give a particular impression about physical or mental condition via speech or writing ○ *He sounded exhausted when I talked to him on the phone.* **3.** *vi.* **HAVE PARTICULAR QUALITY WHEN HEARD** to give a particular impression to a hearer about the quality of the noise or the identity of the source of the noise ○ *That sounds like the postman.* **4.** *vti.* **MAKE A NOISE** to make a particular noise so as to be heard, or make sth produce such a noise ○ *Somewhere down the corridor, an alarm sounded.* **5.** *vt.* **ANNOUNCE STH** to spread the news of or signal sth by making a noise, or produce a similar effect by saying sth ○ *She sounded a note of caution about the likely result of the election.* **6.** *vt.* PHON **ARTICULATE A SOUND** to pronounce a specific letter or sound, especially in a context in which it might be silent ○ *You don't sound the 'p' in 'psychic'.* **7.** *vt.* MED **TEST BODILY CONDITION BY CAUSING SOUND** to make an organ of the body emit a sound for testing or diagnostic purposes [13thC. Via Anglo-Norman *soun* and French *son* from Latin *sonus* (source of English *consonant, resonant,* and *sonnet*).]

sound off *vi.* **1.** **SPEAK FORCEFULLY** to express strong feelings through speech, or complain loudly about sth (*informal*) ○ *always sounding off about high property taxes* **2.** MIL **COUNT STEPS ALOUD** to chant or count in turn while marching

sound out *vt.* to find out sb's opinions about sth before becoming committed to a course of action

sound[2] /sownd/ *adj.* **1.** **NOT DAMAGED** without any serious damage or decay **2.** **HEALTHY** free from injury, disease, or illness **3.** **SENSIBLE** based on good sense and valid reasoning ○ *a sound argument* **4.** **COMPLETELY ACCEPTABLE** worthy of approval, especially as agreeing with traditional views or conforming to conventional behaviour **5.** **DEEP AND PEACEFUL** unbroken by waking and untroubled by dreams or discomfort ○ *She had a sound night's sleep.* **6.** **COMPLETE** including all necessary aspects and details ○ *sound knowledge of the subject* **7.** **THOROUGH** painful and thorough **8.** FIN **WITH LITTLE FINANCIAL RISK** financially secure and likely to make money **9.** LOGIC **VALID WITH TRUE PREMISES** having a true conclusion that follows from true premises **10.** LAW **LEGALLY VALID** legally valid [12thC. Shortening of Old English *gesund*. Ultimately from a prehistoric Germanic word that also produced German *gesund* 'healthy'.] —**soundly** *adv.* —**soundness** *n.* ◇ **sound asleep** sleeping with no waking or disturbance from dreams or discomfort

WORD KEY: SYNONYMS

See Synonyms at ***valid***.

sound[3] /sownd/ *v.* (**sounds, sounding, sounded**) **1.** *vti.* NAUT **MEASURE DEPTH** to measure the depth of water using a weighted line or sonar **2.** *vi.* ZOOL **DIVE DOWN** to dive suddenly and swiftly downwards **3.** *vt.* MED **EXAMINE WITH A PROBE** to use a surgical probe to examine a bodily cavity or passage, e.g. the bladder, or to dilate an abnormal constriction ■ *n.* MED **SURGICAL PROBE** a surgical probe used to sound bodily cavities [14thC. Via French *sonder* from, ultimately, Vulgar Latin *subundare*, from Latin *sub* 'under' + *unda* 'wave' (source of English *undulate*).]

sound[4] /sownd/ *n.* **1.** GEOG **WIDE CHANNEL** a broad channel between two large bodies of water, or between an island and the mainland **2.** GEOG **OCEAN INLET** a long wide arm of the sea **3.** ZOOL **AIR BLADDER** a fish's air bladder [Old English *sund*. Ultimately from a prehistoric Germanic word that is also the ancestor of English *swim*. The current meaning evolved from 'swimming', influenced by a related Scandinavian word.]

sound-alike *n.* a performer whose voice or musical style closely resembles that of a particular well-known performer

sound barrier *n.* a sudden increase in the force of air opposing an aircraft or other moving body when it approaches the speed of sound, producing a sonic boom

sound bite *n.* a very short comment or phrase intended or suitable for broadcasting in a news programme, especially one by a politician. Their use is often regarded as demonstrating superficiality and glibness. ○ *There's no substance to their policy – it's all sound bites.*

soundboard /sównd bawrd/, **sounding board** /sównding bawrd/ *n.* a thin sheet of wood placed under or above the strings of a musical instrument to increase resonance. On a violin it is the top of the instrument.

sound bow *n.* the thick part of a bell, where the clapper strikes

soundbox /sównd boks/ *n.* the hollow chamber in a stringed instrument that increases its resonance

sound card *n.* a computer circuit board that allows a personal computer to receive sound in digital form and reproduce it through speakers

sound effect *n.* ARTS **SOUND FOR A PERFORMANCE** a recording or imitation of a particular sound used in a film, radio or television programme, play, or other theatrical performance ■ **sound effects** *npl.* **FILM SOUNDS** all the sounds in a film other than dialogue and music. They are generally added after shooting. (*hyphenated when used before a noun*)

sounder /sówndər/ *n.* a device for determining the depth of a body of water

sound hole *n.* an opening near the centre of a hollow stringed instrument that increases resonance

sounding[1] /sównding/ *n.* **1.** NAUT **DEPTH MEASUREMENT** a measurement of the depth of water, taken using sonar or a weighted line **2.** METEOROL **ATMOSPHERIC MEASUREMENT** a measurement of the conditions in the atmosphere at a specific altitude ■ **soundings** *npl.* **1.** **PRELIMINARY INQUIRY INTO OPINION** a sampling of the views of a group of people taken before sb becomes committed to a course of action ○ *taking soundings about the popularity of the council's plans* **2.** NAUT **WATER WHERE SOUNDINGS ARE TAKEN** a place where the water is shallow enough for a sounding line to be used to determine its depth

sounding[2] /sównding/ *adj.* having an impressive or resonant sound (*literary*) —**soundingly** *adv.*

sounding board *n.* **1.** MUSIC = **soundboard** **2.** **SB TO GIVE PRELIMINARY OPINION** a person or group who gives feedback on preliminary ideas before they are considered for further development **3.** ACOUSTICS **STRUCTURE THAT REFLECTS SOUND** a roof-like structure built above a pulpit or platform to direct the speaker's voice to the audience

sounding line *n.* a weighted line with measurements marked on it, used for determining the depth of water

sounding rocket *n.* a rocket used to make scientific observations within the earth's atmosphere

soundless /sówndləss/ *adj.* not making any noise —**soundlessly** *adv.* —**soundlessness** *n.*

sound mixer *n.* a person or machine that combines or balances sounds for a recording, broadcast, or film soundtrack

soundpost /sównd pōst/ *n.* a small piece of wood inside the body of a stringed instrument that supports the bridge and transmits the vibrations to the back

soundproof /sównd proof/ *adj.* **IMPENETRABLE TO NOISE** constructed so that audible sound cannot enter or escape ■ *vt.* (**-proofs, -proofing, -proofed**) **MAKE STH SOUNDPROOF** to line or seal a room so that audible sound cannot enter or escape

sound ranging *n.* a method of locating the source of a sound by measuring the travel time of sound waves to a microphone at a fixed position

sound shift *n.* a systematic change over time in the pronunciation of a set of sounds in a language

sound spectrograph *n.* an electronic instrument that makes a graphic representation of sound qualities

sound stage *n.* a large room or studio, usually soundproof, where film scenes are shot

sound system *n.* electronic equipment for amplifying sound produced by recording, broadcasting, or live at public gatherings

soundtrack /sównd trak/ *n.* **1.** CINEMA, TV **SOUND RECORDING FOR A FILM** the recorded music, dialogue, and sound effects in a film or video production **2.** CINEMA, VIDEO **STRIP CARRYING FILM SOUND** a thin strip at the edge of a film reel or video tape on which sound or the soundtrack is recorded **3.** MUSIC **MUSIC FROM FILM** a commercially released recording of music that has been used in a particular film

sound wave *n.* an audible pressure wave caused by a disturbance in water or air and carried forward in a ripple effect

Souness /sóonəss/, **Graeme** (*b.* 1953) British footballer. A skilled midfield player, he worked in the United Kingdom and with European teams as a player and manager. Full name **Graeme James Souness**

soup /soop/ *n.* **1.** **LIQUID FOOD** a liquid food made by cooking meat, fish, vegetables, and other ingredients in water, milk, or stock **2.** **STH THICK AND SWIRLING** sth with the consistency or appearance of soup, especially a swirling liquid or dense fog ○ *the primordial soup of hydrogen, oxygen, and other gases* **3.** **PHOTOGRAPHIC CHEMICALS** chemicals for developing photographs (*slang*) [Mid-17thC. Via French *soupe* from late Latin *suppa*, formed from assumed *suppare* 'to soak'. Ultimately from a prehistoric Germanic word that also produced English *sop* and *sup*.] ◇ **in the soup** in difficulties or trouble (*informal*)

soup up *vt.* to make changes to a car, motorcycle, engine, or similar machine in order to make it more powerful (*informal*) [From the use of SOUP for 'a drug injected into a horse to increase its speed']

soupçon /-son/ *n.* a very small amount of sth [Mid-18thC. Via French, literally 'suspicion', from, ultimately, the Latin stem *suspicion-* (see SUSPICION).]

soup du jour /sòop dyŏo zhŏor/ (*plural* **soups du jour** /sòop dyŏo zhŏor/) *n.* a soup featured by a restaurant on a particular day [Mid-20thC. From French *soupe du jour.*]

soup kitchen *n.* a place that serves free meals to people who have no money

soupspoon /sóop spoon/ *n.* a large spoon for eating soup

soupy /sóopi/ (**-ier, -iest**) *adj.* **1.** **LIKE SOUP** like soup in appearance or consistency **2.** **DAMP OR FOGGY** unpleasantly damp or foggy (*informal*) **3.** **SENTIMENTAL** highly sentimental (*informal*)

sour /sowr/ *adj.* **1.** **SHARP-TASTING** having a tart or sharp taste that is acidic though not necessarily unpleasant, like the taste of vinegar, lemons, or unripe apples **2.** **BAD THROUGH FERMENTATION** unpleasantly rancid in taste or smell because of fermentation **3.** **DISSATISFIED** characterized by ill temper or feelings of bitterness or dissatisfaction ○ *a sour look* **4.** **UNFRIENDLY** unpleasant, unfriendly, or ill-disposed, having previously been harmonious, friendly, or approving **5.** **UNPLEASANT** causing distaste or discomfort **6.** AGRIC **LACKING LIME** acidic because of a shortage of lime, and so unfavourable to crops **7.** INDUST **SULPHUROUS AND ACIDIC** acidic because of containing sulphur compounds. These make oil or gas foul-smelling, toxic, corrosive to metals, and poisonous to catalysts. ■ *vti.* (**sours, souring, soured**) **1.** BECOME OR MAKE STH SOUR to become, or make sth become, sour in taste, smell, or composition **2.** BECOME OR MAKE SB DISSATISFIED to become, or make sb become, ill-tempered, embittered, or dissatisfied **3.** BECOME OR MAKE SB UNFRIENDLY to become, or make sb or sth become, unpleasant, unfriendly, or ill-disposed towards sb or sth, having previously been harmonious, friendly, or approving ○ *A breach of diplomacy soured relations between the countries.* ■ *n.* **1.** *US* BEVERAGES COCKTAIL WITH LEMON OR LIME a cocktail made with whisky, lemon or lime juice, and often sugar **2.** STH SOUR OR ACID sth sour or acid, especially an acid solution used in bleaching clothes or in curing skins [Old English *sūr.* Ultimately from a prehistoric Germanic word that also produced English *sorrel*[1] and German *sauer* 'sour' (source of English *sauerkraut*).] —**sourly** *adv.* —**sourness** *n.*

source /sawrss/ *n.* **1.** ORIGIN the place where sth begins, the thing from which sth is derived, or the person or group that initiated or created sth **2.** SB OR STH PROVIDING INFORMATION a person, organization, book, or other text that supplies information or evidence ○ *A reliable source* **3.** ARTS WORK ON WHICH ANOTHER IS BASED a creation such as a story or work of art that forms the basis of or inspiration for a later work **4.** GEOG BEGINNING OF RIVER the spring or fountain from which a river or stream first issues from the ground, or the area around this **5.** ELECTRON ENG ELECTRODE REGION a region of a transistor from which charge carriers flow ■ *v.* (**sources, sourcing, sourced**) **1.** *vt.* SPECIFY SOURCES OF STH WRITTEN to list the people and materials used in researching a written work **2.** *vti.* MANUF LOCATE STH FOR USE to get or locate parts, materials, or information from elsewhere [14thC. Via Old French *sourse* 'spring', from, ultimately, Latin *surgere* 'to rise' (source of English *surge*).]

------ **WORD KEY: SYNONYMS** ------
See Synonyms at *origin.*

source book *n.* a document or collection of documents that is the main source of information about a subject of study

source code *n.* computer code written in a recognized programming language that can be converted into machine code. ◊ **object code**

source language *n.* the language from which a translation is made

sour cherry *n.* **1.** TREES FRUIT TREE a Eurasian shrub or small tree with white flowers and edible fruit. Latin name: *Prunus cerasus.* **2.** FOOD FRUIT OF THE SOUR CHERRY the red or blackish fruit of the sour cherry tree. It has a sharp taste, and is used mainly in cooking and preserves.

sour cream *n.* a smooth thick cream that has been soured artificially, used in cooking and baking and as a topping

sourdine /soor deèn/ *n.* **1.** OLD MUSICAL INSTRUMENT a reed instrument with a soft tone similar to a bassoon. It is no longer in use. **2.** = **sordino 3.** ORGAN STOP a stop on an organ that produces a low muted tone [Early 17thC. Via French from Italian *sordina,* the feminine form of *sordino* (see SORDINO).]

sour grapes *n.* the scornful denial that sth is attractive or desirable because it is unobtainable [In allusion to Aesop's fable *The Fox and the Grapes* where the fox disparages some grapes as sour when he cannot reach them]

sour gum *n.* a tree of the eastern United States that has glossy leaves and light wood. Latin name: *Nyssa sylvatica.*

sour mash *n.* **1.** GRAIN MIXTURE FOR DISTILLING a grain mash that is a mixture of new and old batches, used in distilling some kinds of whisky **2.** WHISKY FROM SOUR MASH whisky distilled using sour mash

sourpuss /sówr pŏoss/ *n.* sb who is gloomy or bad-tempered (*informal*)

soursop /sówr sop/ (*plural* -**sops** *or* -**sop**) *n.* **1.** TREES TROPICAL AMERICAN TREE a tropical American tree with spicy fragrant leaves and spiny fruit. Latin name: *Annona muricata.* **2.** FOOD FRUIT OF SOURSOP the spiny fruit of the soursop tree with a tart fibrous pulp

sourwood /sówr woŏd/ (*plural* -**woods** *or* -**wood**) *n.* a tree of the eastern United States with thick bark, small white flowers, and sour-tasting leaves. Latin name: *Oxydendrum arboreum.*

Sousa /soozə/, **John Philip** (1854–1932) US military bandmaster and composer. His rousing patriotic compositions include 'The Stars and Stripes Forever' (1897). Known as **the March King**

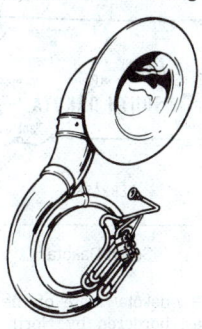

Sousaphone

sousaphone /soozə fōn/ *n.* a large brass instrument with a flaring bell, resembling a tuba. It is used in military marching bands. [Early 20thC. Named after its inventor, John Philip SOUSA.] —**sousaphonist** *n.*

sous-chef /soo-/ *n.* a head chef's assistant and deputy [Late 17thC. *Sous* via French, literally 'under', from Latin *subtus.*]

souse /sowss/ *v.* (**souses, sousing, soused**) **1.** *vt.* PICKLE STH to steep sth in vinegar or brine in order to preserve it (*often passive*) **2.** *vti.* PLUNGE INTO LIQUID to plunge, or plunge sth, into a liquid **3.** *vti.* SOAK to make sth soaking wet, or become soaking wet **4.** *vt.* MAKE SB INTOXICATED to make sb extremely intoxicated (*slang*) (*usually passive*) ■ *n.* **1.** LIQUID USED IN PICKLING the brine or vinegar used in pickling **2.** FOOD PICKLED FOOD pickled food, especially pork trimmings **3.** *Carib* FOOD BROTH MADE WITH PORK broth made with pig's snout, trotters, and sometimes tail, boiled until tender along with sliced cucumbers and various seasonings such as onions, salt, lime, and pepper **4.** HABITUAL ALCOHOL DRINKER sb who habitually consumes alcohol to excess (*slang*) **5.** BINGE a bout of heavy drinking (*slang*) [14thC. From Old French *sous.* Ultimately from a prehistoric Germanic word that is also the ancestor of English *salt* and German *Sülze* 'aspic'.]

souslik *n.* = **suslik**

sou-sou /soo soo/, **susu** *n. Carib* an arrangement for saving money whereby participants pay a certain sum each month for a fixed period of time and take turns borrowing the total amount accumulated [Early 20th C. From Yoruba *eesu* or *esusu* 'fund where several people pool their money, each paying a fixed sum and each drawing out the total in rotation', probably influenced by French *sou* 'coin'.]

Sousse /sooss/ city and port in east-central Tunisia. Population: 125,000 (1994).

soutache /soo tásh/ *n.* a narrow ornamental braid in a herringbone pattern, used for trimming garments [Mid-19thC. Via French from Hungarian *sujtás.*]

soutane /soo taàn, -táàn/ *n.* a priest's robe or cassock, especially one with buttons down the front [Mid-19thC. Via French from Italian *sottana,* from *sotto* 'below', from Latin *subtus.*]

souterrain /soŏtə rayn/ *n.* an ancient underground room or passage [Mid-18thC. From French, literally 'underground'.]

south /sowth/ *n.* **1.** DIRECTION TO THE RIGHT FACING SUN the direction that lies directly to the right of sb facing the rising sun or that is located towards the bottom of a conventional map of the world. **2.** COMPASS POINT OPPOSITE NORTH the compass point that lies directly opposite north **3. south, South** AREA IN THE SOUTH the part of an area, country, or region that is situated in or towards the south **4.** CHR RIGHT-HAND SIDE OF CHURCH the right side of a church as you face the altar from the nave **5.** POSITION EQUIVALENT TO SOUTH the position equivalent to south in any diagram consisting of four points at 90-degree intervals ■ *adj.* **1.** IN THE SOUTH situated in, facing, or coming from the south of a place, region, or country **2.** METEOROL BLOWING FROM THE SOUTH blowing from the south (*refers to winds*) ■ *adv.* TOWARDS THE SOUTH in or towards the south [Old English *sūp.* Ultimately from a prehistoric Germanic word that is probably also the ancestor of English *sun.*]

South /sowth/ *n.* **1.** SOUTHERN ENGLISH COUNTIES the southern region of England, roughly south of the River Severn and the Wash **2.** LESS INDUSTRIALIZED NATIONS the nations of the world with less industrialized economies

South Africa

South Africa republic in southern Africa. It became a fully democratic republic in 1994. Language: Afrikaans, English. Currency: rand. Capital: Pretoria. Population: 42,327,458 (1997). Area: 1,224,691 sq. km/472,731 sq. mi. Official name **Republic of South Africa** —**South African** *n.*, *adj.*

South African Dutch *n.* LANG = **Cape Dutch** *n.* **3** (*not used in South Africa*)

South African English *n.* a variety of English spoken in South Africa

------ **WORD KEY: WORLD ENGLISH** ------
South African English is the English language as used in the Republic of South Africa: since the early 19th century the mother tongue of settlers of British origin and a second language, in varying degrees, of indigenous Afrikaners, Africans, and Asians. Since 1994, the nation has had 11 official languages: English, Afrikaans, Ndebele, Sotho (Northern and Southern), Swati, Tsonga, Tswana, Venda, Xhosa, and Zulu. South African English is generally 'non-rhotic' (i.e., 'r' is not pronounced in words such as *art*, *door*, and *worker*), and, among Africans, tends to have full vowels in all syllables (e.g., *7* is pronounced 'seh-ven' not 'sevn'). Although middle-class British South Africans have traditionally had Received Pronunciation as their ideal, certain distinctive usages are common: e.g., the vowels in *park* and *trap*, heard by outsiders as 'pork' and 'trep', and in *fair hair* as 'fay hay'. Notably, British South Africans pronounce the velar fricative as in Scottish ach and loch, acquired primarily from Afrikaans and used for words from that language. A curiosity of the grammar is the affirmative '*no*', as in 'How are you? – No, I'm fine', probably adopted from Afrikaans. With its parent Dutch, this language has provided the bulk of local borrowings: e.g., *Afrikaner* (South African Caucasian of Dutch or Huguenot origin), *apartheid* (separate racial development, now obsolete), *bakkie* (pickup truck), *braai* (barbecue), *drift* (ford), *kloof* (ravine), the now internationalized *trek* (journey), and *veld* (pronounced 'felt') (open country), with its hybrid extensions *highveld* and *backveld*. Words from African languages include *impala*, *muti* (medicine), *sangoma* (diviner), and *tshwala* (sorghum beer). Distinctive English words are the now-archaic *bioscope* (cinema), *location* (district set aside for a particular group), and *robot* (traffic light).

South America the fourth largest continent in the world, comprising Argentina, Bolivia, Brazil, Chile, Colombia, Ecuador, French Guiana, Guyana, Paraguay, Peru, Suriname, Uruguay, and Venezuela

South American *adj.* relating to any of the countries of South America, or their peoples or cultures

South American trypanosomiasis *n.* = **Chagas' disease**

Southampton /sowth hámptən/ city in Hampshire, southern England. It is one of England's principal ports. Population: 213,400 (1995).

South Asia region comprising the countries of Bangladesh, Bhutan, India, the Maldives, Nepal, Pakistan, and Sri Lanka

South Asian English *n.* a variety of English spoken in South Asia

——WORD KEY: WORLD ENGLISH——

South Asian English is the English language as it has been used since the 17th century in South Asia (the Indian subcontinent), i.e., in Bangladesh, Bhutan, India, the Maldive Islands, Nepal, Pakistan, and Sri Lanka. Usage varies greatly from area to area, primarily because of the influence of local languages on pronunciation, grammar, and vocabulary, e.g., Bengali in Bangladesh and the Indian state of Bengal, Hindi in northern India, Tamil in southern India and Sri Lanka, Urdu in Pakistan and India, and Sinhala in Sri Lanka. At the same time, however, there is considerable uniformity throughout the region as a consequence of British administrative, legal, and commercial usage and the presence of English-language media schools based on British models. South Asian English is 'rhotic' (i.e., 'r' is pronounced in words such as *art*, *door*, and *worker*). It tends to have full vowels in all syllables (e.g., *7* is pronounced 'seh-ven' not *sevn*), and it is widely considered to have a 'singsong' quality often compared to that of English speakers in Wales. Two widespread grammatical features are, first, *Wh*-questions without word-order inversion, as in 'What you would like to buy, please? Where you are coming from? Why you are doing this?' Second is the sentence-final use of *only* for emphasis: 'He is coming once a week only' meaning 'He only comes once a week'. Widely used in the region are adopted local expressions such as: *gherao* (in industrial actions, surrounding people so that they cannot leave a place; also used as a verb, e.g., 'He was gheraoed yesterday'); *wallah* (man, used in compounds like *dhobiwallah* meaning 'laundryman'; and the numbers *lakh* (one hundred thousand), e.g., 'a lakh of rupees', and *crore* (ten million) in 'They have crores of rupees'. Hybridization of English with indigenous usages is common, as in *policewallah* (policeman), and *goondaism* (behaving like a *goonda* or thug, itself a South Asian word). See BANGLADESHI ENGLISH, INDIAN ENGLISH, PAKISTANI ENGLISH, SRI LANKAN ENGLISH.

South Australia state occupying the central part of southern Australia. Founded in 1834, it was the only Australian colony set up as a free settlement rather than a penal colony. Capital: Adelaide. Population: 1,474,000 (1996). Area: 984,377 sq. km/380,070 sq. mi. —**South Australian** /sówth o stráyliən/ *n., adj.*

South Bend city in northern Indiana, on the Kankakee and St Joseph rivers, southwest of Elkhart. Population: 102,100 (1996).

southbound /sówth bownd/ *adj.* leading, going, or travelling towards the south

south by east *n.* the direction or compass point midway between south and south-southeast. —**south by east** *adj., adv.*

south by west *n.* the direction or compass point midway between south and south-southwest —**south by west** *adj., adv.*

South Carolina

South Carolina /-karə línə/ state of the southeastern United States, bordered by North Carolina, the Atlantic Ocean, and Georgia. One of the original 13 colonies, it was admitted as a state in 1788. Capital: Columbia. Population: 3,760,181 (1997). Area: 80,779 sq. km/31,189 sq. mi. —**South Carolinian** *n., adj.*

South China Sea part of the China Sea, surrounded by the Philippines, Borneo, Taiwan, southeastern China, and the Gulf of Thailand. Area: 2,319,086 sq. km/895,400 sq. mi.

South Dakota

South Dakota /-dəkốtə/ state of the north-central United States, bordered by North Dakota, Minnesota, Iowa, Nebraska, Wyoming, and Montana. Capital: Pierre. Population: 737,973 (1997). Area: 199,742 sq. km/77,121 sq. mi. —**South Dakotan** /dəkốtən/ *n., adj.*

Southdown /sówth down/ *n.* a breed of small-to-medium hornless English sheep with short dense wool, usually raised for mutton [Late 18thC. Named after the *South Downs*, where the breed originated.]

South Downs chalk ridge extending along the south coast of England, through Hampshire and Sussex

southeast /sówth eĕst/ *n.* **1.** COMPASS POINT BETWEEN S AND E the direction or compass point midway between south and east. **2.** southeast, Southeast AREA IN THE SOUTHEAST the part of an area, region, or country that is situated in or towards the southeast ■ *adj.* **1.** southeast, Southeast IN THE SOUTHEAST situated in, facing, or lying towards the southeast of a region, place, or country **2.** METEOROL FROM THE SOUTHEAST blowing from the southeast (*refers to winds*) ■ *adv.* TOWARDS THE SOUTHEAST in or towards the southeast [Old English]

Southeast Asia region comprising the countries of Brunei, Cambodia, Indonesia, Laos, Malaysia, Myanmar, the Philippines, Singapore, Thailand, and Vietnam —**Southeast Asian** *n., adj.*

Southeast Asia Treaty Organization *n.* a former alliance of countries for economic cooperation and defence against communism in Southeast Asia and the South Pacific, formed in 1954 and disbanded in 1977. Its members were the United States, the United Kingdom, France, Australia, New Zealand, the Philippines, and Thailand.

southeast by east *n.* the direction or compass point midway between southeast and east-southeast.

southeast by south *n.* the direction or compass point midway between southeast and south-southeast.

southeaster /sówth eĕstər/ *n.* a storm or wind that blows from the southeast

southeasterly /sówth eĕstərli/ *adj.* **1.** IN THE SOUTHEAST situated in or towards the southeast **2.** METEOROL BLOWING FROM THE SOUTHEAST blowing from the southeast (*refers to winds*) ■ *n.* (*plural* -**lies**) WIND FROM THE SOUTHEAST a wind blowing from the southeast

southeastern /sówth eĕstərn/ *adj.* **1.** IN THE SOUTHEAST situated in the southeast of a region or country **2.** FACING SOUTHEAST situated in or facing the southeast **3.** southeastern, Southeastern OF THE SOUTHEAST typical of or native to the southeast of a region or country

southeastward /sówth eĕstwərd/ *adj.* IN THE SOUTHEAST towards or in the southeast ■ *n.* POINT IN THE SOUTHEAST a direction towards or a point in the southeast —**southeastwards** *adv.* —**southeastwardly** *adv., adj.* —**southeastwards** *adv.*

Southend-on-Sea /sówth end ən seĕ/ town in Essex, southeastern England, on the Thames Estuary. Population: 172,300 (1996).

souther /sówthər/ *n.* a strong wind that blows from the south

southerly /sútherli/ *adj.* **1.** IN THE SOUTH situated in or towards the south **2.** METEOROL BLOWING FROM THE SOUTH blowing from the south (*refers to winds*) ■ *n.* (*plural* -**lies**) WIND FROM THE SOUTH a wind blowing from the south

southerly buster *n. Aus* a strong cold southerly wind in southeastern Australia, especially Sydney

southern /súthərn/ *adj.* **1.** IN THE SOUTH situated in the south of a region or country **2.** SOUTH OF EQUATOR lying south of the equator or south of the celestial equator **3.** FACING SOUTH situated in or facing the south **4.** southern, Southern OF THE SOUTH typical of or native to the south of a region or country **5.** METEOROL FROM THE SOUTH blowing from the south (*refers to winds*) [Old English]

Southern Alps mountain range on the South Island, New Zealand. It extends from the far north to the extreme southwest of the island. Its highest peak is Mount Cook, 3,754 m/12,316 ft.

Southern Cross *n.* a constellation near Centaurus in the sky of the southern hemisphere, with four bright stars placed as if at the points of a cross. The smallest of the 88 constellations, it contains the Coalsack, a dark cloud of dust obscuring the stars beyond it in the Milky Way.

southerner /sútharnar/ *n.* sb who lives in or comes from the southern part of a country or region

southern hemisphere *n.* **1.** GEOG SOUTHERN HALF OF EARTH the half of the earth that is south of the equator **2.** ASTRON SOUTHERN HALF OF THE CELESTIAL SPHERE the southern half of an imaginary sphere that contains the universe and is divided horizontally by the celestial equator

Southernism /sútharnizam/ *n.* **1.** LING EXPRESSION CHARACTERISTIC OF SOUTH an expression or pronunciation that is characteristic of the southern United States or southern England **2.** SOC SCI SOUTHERN BELIEF OR PRACTICE an attitude or custom that is characteristic of the South, especially in the United States

southernmost /sútharnmōst/ *adj.* situated farthest south

Southern Paiute *n.* **1.** PEOPLES MEMBER OF NATIVE N AMERICAN PEOPLE a member of a Native North American people who originally occupied lands in Utah, Nevada, Arizona, and California. Most Southern Paiute now live in Utah. **2.** LANG SOUTHERN PAIUTE LANGUAGE the Uto-Aztecan language of the Southern Paiute people —**Southern Paiute** *adj.*

southernwood /sútharn wood/ (*plural* -**woods** *or* -**wood**) *n.* a fragrant European shrub or plant that has cream-coloured flowers and bitter-tasting leaves. Latin name: *Artemisia abrotanum.* [Old English]

South Georgia uninhabited mountainous island in the South Atlantic Ocean, southeast of the Falkland Islands. A dependency of the United Kingdom, it was first visited by Captain James Cook in 1775. Area: 3,755 sq. km/1,450 sq. mi.

South Holland province in the west-central Netherlands. Capital: The Hague. Population: 3,313,193 (1994). Area: 3,333 sq. km/1,287 sq. mi.

southing /sówthing/ *n.* **1.** DISTANCE SOUTH FROM KNOWN LATITUDE how far south a point is from a reference latitude **2.** NAUTICAL PROGRESS TOWARDS SOUTH the distance covered as a ship sails towards the south

South Island the larger and more southerly of the two main islands of New Zealand, in the southwestern Pacific Ocean. Population: 931,566 (1996). Area: 151,215 sq. km/58,368 sq. mi.

South Korea ♦ Korea, South

South Korean SB FROM SOUTH KOREA sb who was born or brought up in South Korea, or who has South Korean citizenship ■ *adj.* OF SOUTH KOREA relating to or typical of South Korea, or its people or culture

Southland /sówthland/ region of New Zealand, occupying the southernmost tip of the South Island. Population: 100,758 (1996). Area: 53,132 sq. km/20,514 sq. mi.

southpaw /sówth paw/ *n.* a left-handed person, especially a boxer who leads with the left hand (*informal*) [Late 19thC. Originally used of left-handed baseball players, from the pitcher's orientation on the mound (since baseball diamonds are traditionally oriented to the same points of the compass).]

South Pole *n.* **1.** SOUTHERN END IN EARTH'S AXIS the southern end of the Earth's axis at the latitude of 90° S **2.** SOUTHERN AXIS INTERSECTION the point where the southern end of the Earth's axis intersects the celestial sphere

Southport /sówth pawrt/ town in Merseyside, in northwestern England. Population: 88,596 (1991).

Southron /súthrən/ *n. Scotland* **1.** ENGLISH PERSON sb from England (*archaic or literary*) **2.** LANG SOUTHERN BRITISH ENGLISH the English language as spoken in England (*archaic*) ■ *adj. Scotland* ENGLISH relating to or typical of England (*dated*) [15thC. Variant of SOUTHERN.]

South Saskatchewan /-sə skáchəwən/ river rising in the Rocky Mountains and flowing north into Lake Winnipeg, Canada. Length: 1,393 km/865 mi.

South Sea Bubble *n.* frenzied speculation in the South Sea Company in early 18th-century Britain. In 1720 the company collapsed, ruining many banks and private investors. The company had taken over much of the national debt in return for sole trading rights in the area.

South Shields /-sheéldz/ town and port in Tyne and Wear County, in northeastern England. Population: 83,704 (1991).

south-southeast *n.* COMPASS POINT BETWEEN S AND SE the direction or compass point midway between south and southeast. ■ *adj., adv.* IN SOUTH-SOUTHEAST in, from, facing, or towards the south-southeast —**south-southeasterly** *adv.*

south-southwest *n.* COMPASS POINT BETWEEN S AND SW the direction or compass point midway between south and southwest. ■ *adj., adv.* IN SOUTH-SOUTHWEST in, from, facing, or towards the south-southwest —**south-southwesterly** *adv.*

South Taranaki Bight /-tárrə náki-/ gulf on the southwestern coast of the North Island, New Zealand. It extends from Otakeho in the west to Kakaramea in the east.

South Vietnam former country in Southeast Asia between 1954 and 1976. It occupied the southern part of modern-day Vietnam. —**South Vietnamese** /sówth vi étnə meéz/ *n., adj.*

southwards /sówthwərd/ *adv.* TOWARDS THE SOUTH in a southerly direction ■ *n.* **southward** POINT IN THE SOUTH a direction towards or a point in the south [Old English] —**southward** *adj.* —**southwardly** *adv., adj.*

——— **WORD KEY: USAGE** ———

southward or **southwards**? *Southward* is the only form available for the adjective: *In a southward direction*, while *southwards* is commonly used as well as *southward* for the adverb *The ship was moving slowly southward/southwards.*

southwest /sówth wést/ *n.* **1.** COMPASS POINT BETWEEN S AND W the direction or compass point midway between south and west. **2.** **southwest, Southwest** AREA IN THE SOUTHWEST the part of an area, region, or country that is situated in or towards the southwest ■ *adj.* IN THE SOUTHWEST situated in, facing, or lying towards the southwest of a region, place, or country ■ *adv.* TOWARDS THE SOUTHWEST in or towards the southwest [Old English]

southwest by south *n.* the direction or compass point midway between southwest and south-southwest. See table at **compass**

southwest by west *n.* the direction or compass point midway between southwest and west-southwest.

Southwest Cape the southernmost point in New Zealand, situated at the southern tip of Stewart Island

southwester /sówth wéstər/ *n.* METEOROL a storm or wind that blows from the southwest

southwesterly /sówth wéstərli/ *adj.* **1.** IN THE SOUTHWEST situated in or towards the southwest **2.** METEOROL FROM THE SOUTHWEST blowing from the southwest (*refers to winds*) ■ *n.* (*plural* -lies) METEOROL WIND FROM THE SOUTHWEST a wind blowing from the southwest

southwestern /sówth wéstərn/ *adj.* **1.** IN THE SOUTHWEST situated in the southwest of a region or country **2.** FACING SOUTHWEST situated in or facing the southwest

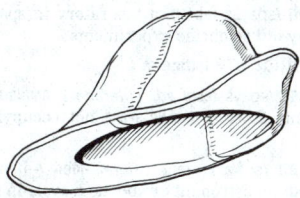

3. southwestern, Southwestern OF THE SOUTHWEST typical of or native to the southwest of a region or country [Old English]

southwestward /sówth wéstwərd/ *adj.* IN THE SOUTHWEST towards or in the southwest ■ *n.* POINT IN THE SOUTHWEST a direction towards or a point in the southwest —**southwestwards** *adv.* —**southwestwardly** *adv., adj.* —**southwestwards** *adv.*

South Yorkshire /-yáwrkshə/ metropolitan county in northwestern England. In 1986 its administrative powers were divided between Barnsley, Doncaster, Rotherham, and Sheffield councils. Area: 1,562 sq. km/603 sq. mi.

souvenir /soóvə neér/ *n.* REMINDER sth bought or kept as a reminder of a particular place or occasion ■ *vt.* (-nirs, -niring, -nired) *Aus* STEAL to steal sth (*informal*) [Late 18thC. Via French, literally 'memory', from, ultimately, Latin *subvenire* 'to come into mind'.]

souvlakia /soov laáki ə/ *npl.* Greek kebabs consisting of pieces of meat, usually lamb, skewered and grilled. The meat is often marinated before cooking. [Mid-20thC. From modern Greek, literally 'small skewers', from *souvla* 'skewer'.]

sou'wester /sow wéstər/ *n.* a waterproof hat with a broad brim covering the back of the neck, originally made of oilskin, now usually of rubber or plastic. Sou'westers were originally worn by sailors and fishermen. [Mid-19thC. Contraction of *southwester*.]

Sov. *abbr.* Soviet

sovereign /sóvvrin/ *n.* **1.** POL MONARCH the ruler or permanent head of a state, especially a king or queen **2.** MONEY OLD BRITISH GOLD COIN a gold coin worth one pound, used in Britain between the early 17th century and the early 20th century ■ *adj.* **1.** INDEPENDENT self-governing and not ruled by any other state **2.** WITH COMPLETE POWER having supreme authority or power **3.** OUTSTANDING outstanding, e.g. in its excellence or effectiveness [13thC. Via Old French *souverein* from Vulgar Latin *superanus*, from Latin *super* 'above'.] —**sovereignly** *adv.*

sovereigntist /sóvvrintist/ *n. Can* a supporter of sovereignty for Quebec

sovereignty /sóvvrənti/ *n.* (*plural* -ties) **1.** TOP AUTHORITY supreme authority, especially over a state **2.** INDEPENDENCE freedom from outside interference and the right to self-government **3.** INDEPENDENT STATE a politically independent state

sovereignty association *n. Can* a proposed type of economic and political association between a sovereign Quebec and the rest of Canada

soviet /sóv i ət, sóv-/ *n.* HIST **1.** COMMUNIST COUNCIL one of the elected government councils that existed at local, regional, and national levels in the former Soviet Union. The highest was the Supreme Soviet. **2.** EARLY RUSSIAN REVOLUTIONARY COUNCIL a council in the early political organization of the Russian Revolution, based on the council of workers formed to seize city government in Petrograd in 1917 [Early 20thC. From Russian *sovet* 'council'.] —**sovietism** *n.*

Soviet /sóviət, sóv-/ *adj.* **1.** TYPICAL OF U.S.S.R. relating to the former Soviet Union, or its people, culture, or political system **2.** COMMUNIST having Communist views similar to those of the former Soviet Union ■ *n.* SB FROM THE U.S.S.R. sb who was born or brought up in or was a citizen of the former Soviet Union

Sovietologist /sóvi ə tólləjist, sóv-/ *n.* a scholar who studies the Soviet Union, especially its government and political history

Soviet Union *n.* a federation of Communist states in eastern Europe and northern and central Asia from 1922 until 1991. Moscow was its capital. Then the largest country in the world, the Soviet Union was the Communist superpower during the Cold War. Official name **Union of Soviet Socialist Republics**

SOW[1] /sō/ (**sows, sowing, sowed, sown** /sōn/ *or* **sowed**) *v.* **1.** *vti.* PLANT SEED to scatter or plant seed on an area of land in order to grow crops **2.** *vt.* INTRODUCE AN IDEA to cause some feeling or belief to arise or become widespread, especially when negative or divisive ○ *Increased competition will only sow discord among the members of the company.* **3.** *vt.* SPREAD THICKLY to spread sth thickly with sth (*often passive*) ○ *a sky sown with stars* [Old English *sāwan*. Ultimately from an Indo-European word that is also the ancestor of English *season, seed,* and *semen.*] —**sowable** *adj.* —**sower** *n.*

SOW[2] /sow/ *n.* **1.** ZOOL FEMALE PIG an adult female pig **2.** ZOOL ADULT FEMALE ANIMAL the adult female of several animals such as the bear, mink, badger, guinea pig, and hedgehog **3.** METALL CHANNEL FOR MOLTEN IRON a channel through which molten iron runs into a mould in the process of casting pig iron **4.** METALL HARDENED IRON a mass of iron that has hardened in a channel or mould in the process of casting pig iron [Old English *sugu*. Ultimately from an Indo-European word that is also the ancestor of English *swine* and Greek *hus* 'pig' (source of English *hyena*).]

Sow. *abbr. S Asia* Sowbhagyawati

sowback /sówbak/ *n.* a long ridge of earth left by a glacier [Late 19thC. From sow[2].]

Sowbhagyawati /sə bági ə wótti/ *n. S Asia* a title used in India before the name of a married woman whose husband is still alive, roughly equivalent to the English term 'Mrs' [From Sanskrit]

sowbread /sów bred/ (*plural* -**breads** *or* -**bread**) *n.* a cyclamen, especially one of a southern European species with a single nodding flower. Genus: *Cyclamen.* [Mid-16thC. So-called because it is supposedly eaten by pigs.]

Soweto /sə wáytō, sə wéttō/ township in southern Johannesburg, Gauteng Province, South Africa. Population: 596,632 (1991).

sown past participle of **sow**[1]

sow thistle /sów-/ *n.* a Eurasian plant with prickly leaves and yellow flowers. Genus: *Sonchus.* [Origin uncertain: perhaps by folk etymology from earlier *thow-thistle*]

soya /sóyə/, **soy** /soy/ *n.* **1.** PLANTS SOYA BEAN PLANT the soya bean plant **2.** FOOD = soy sauce ■ *adj.* FROM SOYA BEANS made or derived from soya beans [Late 17thC. Via Dutch, Malay, and Japanese from Chinese *jiàngyóu*, literally 'soyabean oil'.]

soya bean *n. US* term **soybean 1.** PLANTS PLANT WITH NUTRITIOUS SEEDS a southeastern Asian plant cultivated around the world for its nutritious seeds, for soil improvement, and to provide grazing for animals. Latin name: *Glycine max.* **2.** FOOD SEED OF SOYA BEAN PLANT the edible seeds of the soya bean plant, which are rich in oil and protein

soya milk /sóyə milk/ *n.* a milk substitute made from soya beans, often with vitamins and sugar added

soya sauce *n.* = soy sauce

soybean /sóy been/ *n. US* PLANTS = soya bean

Soyinka /so yíngkə/, **Wole** (*b.* 1934) Nigerian writer and political activist. His plays and novels examine the relationship of traditional and modern African cultures, and include *Poems from Prison* (1969). He won a Nobel Prize in literature (1986). Full name **Akinwande Oluwole Soyinka**

soy sauce, **soy** *n.* a dark, salty liquid made by fermenting soya beans in brine, used to flavour foods

sozzled /sózz'ld/ *adj.* extremely intoxicated (*informal*) [Late 19thC. Formed from English dialect *sozzle* 'to splash', perhaps imitative of the sound.]

sp *abbr.* without children [Latin, *sine prole*]

SP *abbr.* **1.** starting price **2.** NAVY submarine patrol

sp. *abbr.* **1.** special **2.** species **3.** specific **4.** specimen **5.** spelling

Sp. *abbr.* **1.** Spanish **2.** Spain **3.** Spaniard

spa /spaa/ *n.* **1.** RESORT WITH BATHING AND MINERAL WATER a resort with mineral springs (*often used in placenames*) **2.** WHIRLPOOL BATH a bath with a device for aerating or swirling water [Early 17thC. Named after a resort town in eastern Belgium, famous for its mineral springs.]

SpA *abbr.* limited company (*used after the name of a company*) [Italian, *Società per Azioni*]

space /spayss/ *n.* **1.** REGION BEYOND EARTH'S ATMOSPHERE the region that lies beyond the Earth's atmosphere, and all that it contains **2.** REGION BETWEEN ALL CELESTIAL BODIES the region, usually of negligible density, between all celestial bodies in the universe **3.** THREE-DIMENSIONAL EXPANSE WHERE MATTER EXISTS the unbounded three-dimensional expanse in which all matter exists **4.** INTERVAL OF TIME a period or interval of time **5.** AREA SET APART an area set apart or available for use **6.** PRINTING BLANK AREA BETWEEN TYPE a blank area between characters, words, or lines of type, or an interval the width of a single character **7.** MUSIC INTERVAL BETWEEN LINES OF MUSICAL STAFF an interval between the lines of the musical staff **8.** COMMUNICATION TIME OR AREA AVAILABLE FOR USE broadcast time or an area in a publication available for specific use, e.g. by advertisers **9.** MATH SET OF POINTS GOVERNED BY AXIOMS a collection of points that have geometric properties in that they obey set rules (**axioms**), e.g. a Euclidian space that is governed by Euclidian geometry. Each non-Euclidian geometry, having its own axioms, has its own non-Euclidian space containing a collection of points governed by those axioms. **10.** PRINTING PIECE OF TYPE TO CREATE SPACE a piece of type used to create a blank interval in printing **11.** FREEDOM TO ASSERT IDENTITY the freedom or opportunity to assert a personal identity or fulfil personal needs (*informal*) ○ *I need my own personal space in order to live stress-free.* **12.** TECH INTERVAL IN TRANSMISSION OF TELEGRAPHIC MESSAGE an interval during the transmission of a telegraphic message when the key is not in contact ■ *vt.* (**spaces, spacing, spaced**) TO SET THINGS APART to set things some distance apart or arrange them with gaps between [13thC. Via French *espace* from Latin *spatium* 'space, distance'.]

space age *n.* the era marked by the exploration of space, often considered as beginning in 1957 when the Soviet Union launched Sputnik —**space-age** *adj.*

spaceband /spayss band/ *n.* a device used in printing to provide variable but even spacing between words in a justified line

space-bar *n.* a horizontal bar at the bottom of a keyboard or typewriter that is pressed to introduce a space

space blanket *n.* a plastic wrapping with aluminium foil coating that is used to restore body heat in people affected by exposure or exhaustion

spaceborne /spayss bawrn/ *adj.* travelling or operating in outer space

spacebridge /spayss brij/ *n.* a way of communicating internationally by television, using transmissions from orbiting satellites

space cadet *n.* sb who behaves in a forgetful or mildly strange way, especially sb who has taken hallucinogenic drugs (*slang*)

space capsule *n.* a vehicle or cabin designed to support life and used for transporting human beings or animals in outer space or at very high altitudes within Earth's atmosphere

space charge *n.* the net electric charge distributed in a given volume of space

spacecraft /spayss kraaft/ *n.* a vehicle or device designed for travel or use in space

spaced-out *adj.* inattentive, dazed, confused, or lightheaded from or as if from drug use (*slang*)

spacefaring /spayss fairing/ *n.* the use of spacecraft for the exploration of outer space —**spacefaring** *adj.*

spaceflight *n.* flight beyond Earth's atmosphere, or an instance of this

space heater *n.* a small portable appliance used to heat a small area

spacelab /spayss lab/ *n.* a laboratory in space used to carry out scientific experiments

space lattice *n.* = **lattice** 4

spaceless /spayssləss/ *adj.* (*literary*) **1.** BOUNDLESS with no limits **2.** OCCUPYING NO SPACE not occupying any space

spaceman /spayss man/ (*plural* **-men** /-mən/) *n.* **1.** ASTRONAUT an astronaut or sb who travels in space **2.** EXTRATERRESTRIAL a traveller to Earth from outer space, in science fiction

space medicine *n.* a branch of medicine dealing with the effects of space flight on the human body

Space Needle

Space Needle *n.* a tall tower in central Seattle, Washington, United States, with a revolving restaurant and observation deck near the top. It was built for the 1962 World's Fair.

space opera *n.* a science fiction drama involving space travel and, often, extraterrestrial beings

space platform *n.* = **space station**

spaceport /spayss pawrt/ *n.* an installation for launching, testing, landing, and maintaining spacecraft

space probe *n.* a satellite or other spacecraft that is designed to explore the solar system and transmit data back to earth

spacer /spayssər/ *n.* sth inserted between two other things to keep them apart, e.g. a pierced bar threaded on a multistring necklace to prevent the strands from tangling

spaceship /spayss ship/ *n.* a vehicle designed to transport people or materials through outer space

space shuttle *n.* a reusable spacecraft designed to transport people and cargo between earth and space, with two solid rocket boosters and an external fuel tank that are jettisoned after takeoff

space sickness *n.* motion sickness experienced as a result of space flight

space station, **space platform** *n.* a spacecraft or satellite designed to be occupied by a crew for extended periods of time and used as a base for the exploration, observation, and research of space

Spacesuit: Astronaut Buzz Aldrin on the Moon

spacesuit /spayss syoot/ *n.* a sealed pressurized suit designed to support the wearer's life in space

space-time, **space-time continuum** *n.* a four-dimensional system consisting of three spatial co-

ordinates and one for time, in which it is possible to locate events

spacewalk /spayss wawk/ *n.* ASTRONAUT'S EXCURSION OUT OF SPACECRAFT an excursion by an astronaut or cosmonaut outside the spacecraft ■ *vi.* (**-walks, -walking, -walked**) LEAVE SPACECRAFT to go out of a spacecraft in order to perform a task or experiment

spacewoman /spayss woŏmən/ (*plural* **-en** /spayss wimin/) *n.* **1.** WOMAN ASTRONAUT a woman astronaut or cosmonaut who travels in space **2.** FEMALE VISITOR TO EARTH a female who travels to Earth from outer space, in science fiction

space writer *n.* a writer paid according to the area of print taken up by what is written

spacey /spayssi/ *adj.* = **spacy** (*informal*)

spacial /spaysh'l/ *adj.* = **spatial**

spacing *n.* **1.** SPACE OR ITS ARRANGEMENT the space, or the way this is arranged, between several things, e.g. between words or lines in type **2.** ARRANGING IN SPACES the act of arranging things in spaces

spacious /spaysshəss/ *adj.* roomy and containing ample space

spacy /spayssi/ (**-ier, -iest**), **spacey** (**-ier, -iest**) *adj.* spaced-out (*slang*)

spade[1] /spayd/ *n.* DIGGING TOOL a digging tool with a wide shallow blade flattened where it meets the shaft so it can be pushed into the ground with the foot ■ *vti.* (**spades, spading, spaded**) DIG OR REMOVE STH WITH SPADE to dig or remove sth using a spade [Old English *spadu*. Ultimately from an Indo-European word that is also the ancestor of English *spoon* and Greek *spathē* 'broad blade' (source of English *spatula* and *spay*).] — **spader** *n.* ◇ **call a spade a spade** say plainly and bluntly what you mean without being euphemistic in any way

spade[2] /spayd/ *n.* **1.** SUIT WITH SPEAR-SHAPED SYMBOL one of the four suits used in cards, with a black figure shaped like a stylized spearhead as its symbol **2.** CARD OF SPADES SUIT a card of the suit of spades **3.** OFFENSIVE TERM an offensive term referring to sb, especially a man, who is descended from an African people (*slang offensive*) [Late 16thC. Via Italian, the plural of *spada* 'sword' (the sign used on Italian cards), and Latin *spatha* 'broadsword' from Greek *spathē* (see SPADE[1]).] ◇ **in spades** US to a very great degree (*informal*)

spadefish /spayd fish/ (*plural* **-fish** *or* **-fishes**) *n.* a deep-bodied bony fish found in coastal waters of the Atlantic and used as a food fish. Family: Ephippidae. [Early 18thC. From its shape.]

spade guinea *n.* a British gold coin worth 21 shillings issued between 1787 and 1799 [From the spade-shaped shield on its reverse]

spadework /spayd wurk/ *n.* **1.** WORK REQUIRING SPADE work done using a spade **2.** PRELIMINARY WORK preliminary work that is often hard drudgery

spadiceous /spay dishəss/ *adj.* bearing or resembling a spadix [Mid-17thC. Formed from the Latin stem *spadic-* (see SPADIX).]

spadices plural of **spadix**

spadille /spə díl/ *n.* the highest trump card in some card games, e.g. ombre [Late 17thC. Via French and Spanish *espadilla*, literally 'a small sword', from, ultimately, Latin *spatha* (see SPADE[2]).]

spadix /spáydiks/ (*plural* **-dices** /-di seez/) *n.* a fleshy or succulent plant spike bearing tiny flowers and usually enclosed in a leafy sheath (**spathe**) [Mid-18thC. Via Latin, literally 'palm branch torn off with its fruit', from Greek, formed from *span* 'to pull'.]

spaewife /spáy wīf/ (*plural* **-wives** /-wīvz/) *n.* Scotland a woman fortune-teller

spaghetti /spə gétti/ *n.* **1.** STRING-SHAPED PASTA pasta in the shape of long, thin strings **2.** COOKED STRING-SHAPED PASTA a dish of long thin strings of boiled pasta, usually served with a sauce **3.** US = **sleeving** [Mid-19thC. From Italian, literally 'small strings', formed from *spago* 'string', of unknown origin.]

spaghetti junction *n.* a motorway interchange with complex systems of intersections, overpasses, and underpasses

spaghettini /spággə teéni/ *n.* a type of pasta that is thinner than spaghetti but thicker than vermicelli [Mid-20thC. From Italian, literally 'small spaghetti' (see SPAGHETTI).]

spaghetti western *n.* a western made in Europe, usually Spain by an Italian film company, characterized by extreme and melodramatic violence

spahi /spaá hee, -ee/, **spahee** *n.* **1.** TURKISH CAVALRYMAN a cavalryman in the Turkish army in the past **2.** ALGERIAN CAVALRYMAN IN FRENCH SERVICE a member of a corps of Algerian cavalrymen in French service in the past [Mid-16thC. Via French and Turkish from Persian *sipāhī* 'cavalryman', from *sipāh* 'army'.]

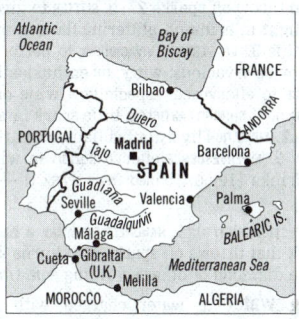
Spain

Spain /spayn/ monarchy in southwestern Europe on the Iberian Peninsula, east of Portugal. Language: Spanish. Currency: peseta. Capital: Madrid. Population: 39,181,114 (1996). Area: 504,782 sq. km/194,897 sq. mi. Official name **Kingdom of Spain**

spake past tense of **speak** (*archaic*)

Spalding /spáwl ding/ market town in Lincolnshire, eastern England. Population: 20,000 (1993).

spall /spawl/ *n.* SMALL CHIP OF STONE OR ORE a small fragment, splinter, or chip of stone or ore ■ *vti.* (**spalls, spalling, spalled**) BREAK INTO CHIPS to break up into small chips, flakes, or splinters [15thC. Origin unknown.]

spallation /spaw láysh'n/ *n.* **1.** NUCLEAR PHYS EMISSION OF NUCLEAR PARTICLES BY BOMBARDMENT a nuclear reaction in which several particles are emitted from the nucleus of an atom after bombardment with high-energy particles or radiation **2.** REMOVAL OF ROCK SURFACE BY METEORITE the removal of the surface layers of a rock by meteorite impact

spalpeen /spál peen/ *n. Ireland* **1.** RASCAL sb who is mischievous and cunning **2.** POOR FARM LABOURER an impoverished farm labourer [Late 18thC. From Irish *spailpín*.]

spam /spam/ *n.* ELECTRONIC JUNK MAIL an unsolicited often commercial message transmitted through the Internet as a mass mailing to a large number of recipients ■ *vti.* (**spams, spamming, spammed**) POST MULTIPLE UNWANTED MESSAGES to post a message many times to a newsgroup, an inappropriate message to multiple newsgroups, or to send an unsolicited message, often an advertisement, to many people [Late 20thC. Origin uncertain: perhaps from a Monty Python sketch in which *Spam* is served whether wanted or not.]

Spam /spam/ *tdmk.* a trademark for tinned chopped meat, mainly of chopped pork, that is pressed into a loaf

span[1] /span/ *n.* **1.** DISTANCE BETWEEN LIMITS the distance or expanse between two extremes or limits **2.** PERIOD FOR MAINTENANCE OF COGNITIVE FUNCTION the period of time during which a mental function or act can be maintained ○ *a short attention span* **3.** CIV ENG DISTANCE BETWEEN BRIDGE SUPPORTS the extent or space between abutments or supports, e.g. on a bridge or arch, or a portion of the structure that is supported in this way **4.** = wingspan **5.** PERIOD OF TIME a period of time, especially the lifetime of an individual **6.** OLD MEASUREMENT an old measurement based on the distance from the end of the thumb to the end of the little finger of a spread hand, approximately 23 cm/nine in ■ *vt.* (**spans, spanning, spanned**) **1.** EXTEND OVER OR ACROSS STH to reach or extend over or across sth **2.** MEASURE STH WITH THE HAND to measure sth by or as if by the hand with fingers and thumb fully extended

3. ENCIRCLE STH WITH THE HANDS to encircle or cover sth with the hands, especially in order to estimate its size [Old English *spann*. Ultimately from a prehistoric Germanic word that also produced German *spannen* 'to stretch' (source of English *spanner*).]

span[2] /span/ (**spans, spanning, spanned**) *n.* EQU a pair of horses or other animals harnessed and driven together [Mid-18thC. From Dutch, formed from *spannen* 'to harness'.]

span[3] past tense of **spin** (*archaic*)

Span. *abbr.* Spanish

spanakopita /spánnə kóppitə, -kə peétə/ *n.* a traditional Greek dish of spinach, feta cheese, and seasonings baked in filo pastry [Mid-20thC. From modern Greek *spanakopēta*, literally 'spinach pie'.]

spancel /spánss'l/ *n.* ROPE USED TO HOBBLE ANIMAL a rope with a noose used to hobble a horse, cow, or other animal ■ *vt.* (**-cels, -celling, -celled**) HOBBLE ANIMAL WITH SPANCEL to hobble a horse, cow, or other animal using a spancel [Early 17thC. From Dutch *spansel*, from *spannen* (see SPAN[2]).]

Spandau /spán dow/ district of Berlin, Germany. It is home to a prison where Rudolf Hess was incarcerated after World War II. Population: 192,895 (1986).

spandex /spán deks/ *n.* a synthetic stretch fabric of fibre made from polyurethane [Mid-20thC. Coined from EXPAND.]

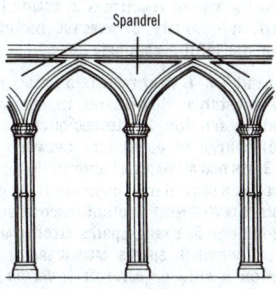
Spandrel

spandrel /spándrəl/, **spandril** *n.* **1.** SPACE BETWEEN ONE ARCH AND ANOTHER the triangular space between the right or left exterior curve of an arch and the framework of another arch **2.** SPACE BETWEEN TWO ARCHES AND CORNICE the area between two arches and a horizontal cornice above them [15thC. Origin uncertain: perhaps via Anglo-Norman *spaundre* from Old French *espandre* (see SPAWN).]

spang /spang/ *adv. US* completely, squarely, or exactly on target or in the middle of sth (*informal*) [Mid-19thC. Origin uncertain: perhaps from a dialect verb meaning 'to leap', or perhaps an alteration of *span-new*.]

spangle /spáng g'l/ *n.* **1.** SMALL SHINY DECORATION a small shiny piece of metal or plastic used for decoration on clothing **2.** SMALL SPARKLING OBJECT a small sparkling spot or object ■ *v.* (**-gles, -gling, -gled**) **1.** *vt.* SPRINKLE STH WITH SPANGLES to sprinkle or adorn sth with spangles **2.** *vi.* GLITTER WITH SPANGLES to sparkle or glitter as if adorned with spangles [15thC. Formed from obsolete *spang* 'glittering ornament', from Dutch *spange* 'clasp'.]

Spaniard /spánnyərd/ *n.* **1.** SB FROM SPAIN sb who was born or brought up in Spain, or who has Spanish citizenship **2.** NEW ZEALAND ROCK PLANT a perennial rock plant with sharp leaves, native to New Zealand [14thC. Via Old French *Espaignart* from, ultimately, Latin *Hispania* 'Spain'.]

spaniel /spánnyəl/ *n.* a small or medium-sized dog characterized by a long wavy silky coat, usually short legs, large drooping ears, and feathering on the legs and tail [14thC. Via Old French *espaigneul*, literally 'Spanish', from, ultimately, Latin *Hispania* 'Spain'. From the breed's Spanish origin.]

Spanish /spánnish/ *n.* ROMANCE LANGUAGE one of the Romance languages, spoken in most of Spain and Central and South America ■ *npl.* PEOPLE OF SPAIN the people of Spain ■ *adj.* **1.** RELATING TO SPAIN relating to

Spaniel

Spain, or its people or culture **2.** RELATING TO SPANISH LANGUAGE relating to the Spanish language

Spanish America parts of America that were colonized by the Spanish from the 16th century and where Spanish is still widely spoken. It includes much of Central and South America and some Caribbean islands.

Spanish-American *n.* **1.** SB FROM SPANISH AMERICA sb who lives in or comes from Spanish America **2.** US CITIZEN OF SPANISH ORIGIN a United States citizen of Spanish descent —**Spanish-American** *adj.*

Spanish bayonet (*plural* **Spanish bayonet** *or* **Spanish bayonets**) *n.* an American plant with stiff pointed leaves, white flowers, and a long woody stem. Genus: *Yucca*. [From its sword-like leaves]

Spanish cedar (*plural* **Spanish cedar** *or* **Spanish cedars**) *n.* a tropical American tree with reddish fragrant wood, used for making cigar boxes. Genus: *Cedrela*.

Spanish chestnut *n.* = chestnut *n.* 1, chestnut *n.* 2

Spanish fly (*plural* **Spanish fly** *or* **Spanish flies**) *n.* **1.** EUROPEAN BEETLE a green European blister beetle, used as a source of the stimulant and irritant cantharides. Latin name: *Lytta vesicatoria* and *Cantharis vesicatoria*. **2.** TOXIC PREPARATION USED AS APHRODISIAC a toxic preparation made from the crushed dried bodies of the Spanish fly, used in the past as an aphrodisiac and to treat skin blisters

Spanish guitar *n.* the classical six-stringed form of guitar

Spanish Inquisition *n.* HIST an ecclesiastical tribunal of the Roman Catholic Church established in Spain in 1542, and finally suppressed in 1834, under which large numbers of supposed heretics were tortured and executed

Spanish mackerel (*plural* **Spanish mackerel** *or* **Spanish mackerels**) *n.* **1.** FOOD FISH OF WESTERN ATLANTIC a large fish in the tuna family that is caught for food and sport, and is found along the Atlantic coast of North and South America. Latin name: *Scomberomorus maculatus*. **2.** ATLANTIC MACKEREL a mackerel found in Atlantic waters of the coasts of Europe and North America. Latin name: *Scomberomorus colias*.

Spanish Main **1.** region of 16th- and 17th-century Spanish America from the isthmus of Panama to the mouth of the Orinoco river **2.** section of the Caribbean Sea crossed by Spanish ships in colonial times

Spanish moss *n.* a plant of the pineapple family that grows on trees in long drooping matted clusters of greyish-green filaments, from the southeastern United States to tropical South America. Latin name: *Tillandsia usneoides*.

Spanish omelette *n.* an omelette filled with a selection of vegetables, usually including tomatoes and cooked potato [Because it contains ingredients typical in Spanish cuisine]

Spanish onion (*plural* **Spanish onion** *or* **Spanish onions**) *n.* an onion with yellow skin and a mild flavour. Latin name: *Allium fistulosum*.

Spanish paprika *n.* a fairly mild but spicy food seasoning made from red peppers

Spanish practices, **Spanish customs** *npl.* irregular practices that are in the interests of workers and are usually imposed on employers by trade unions, e.g. overstaffing and excessive overtime (*dated informal*)

Spanish rice *n.* rice cooked with onion, green pepper, tomato, and seasonings

Spanish Sahara former name for **Western Sahara**

Spanish Town the second largest city in Jamaica, in the southeast of the island on the Cobre River, near Kingston. It was the capital of the island from 1535 until the 1870s. Population: 110,400 (1995).

spank[1] /spangk/ *vt.* (**spanks, spanking, spanked**) SLAP THE BUTTOCKS to strike sb, usually on the buttocks with the open hand in punishment ■ *n.* OPEN-HANDED SLAP an open-handed slap on the buttocks [Early 18thC. Origin uncertain: probably an imitation of the sound.]

spank[2] *vi.* to move briskly, spiritedly, or smartly [Early 19thC. Origin uncertain: probably a back-formation from SPANKING.]

spanker /spángkər/ *n.* the fore-and-aft sail on the sternmost mast of a square-rigged ship [Mid-17thC. Origin uncertain: perhaps formed from SPANK[2].]

spanking[1] *n.* a beating with the flat of the hand on sb's buttocks, given as punishment

spanking[2] /spángking/ *adj.* **1.** EXCEPTIONAL with an unusual quality that makes sth exceptional or remarkable of its kind **2.** BRISK lively, or moving briskly, especially a breeze ■ *adv.* VERY extremely or very [Mid-17thC. Origin uncertain: perhaps from a Scandinavian word.]

spanner /spánnər/ *n.* a tool with fixed or movable jaws, used to seize, turn, or twist objects such as nuts and bolts. US term **wrench** *n.* 3 [Mid-17thC. From German, formed from *spannen* (see SPAN[1].) ◇ **put** *or* **throw a spanner in the works** ruin or impede a plan or system

spar[1] /spaar/ *n.* **1.** NAUT STOUT POLE SUPPORTING RIGGING a stout pole used to support rigging on a ship **2.** AIR LATERAL SUPPORT OF PLANE'S WING one of the principal lateral members supporting the wing of an aeroplane [14thC. Origin uncertain: probably from Old French *esparre* or Old Norse *sperra*.]

spar[2] /spaar/ *vi.* (**spars, sparring, sparred**) **1.** USE LIGHT BLOWS to engage in a practice or exhibition bout of boxing or martial arts using light blows **2.** FIGHT USING FEET AND SPURS to fight using the feet and spurs to strike an opponent (*refers to gamecocks*) **3.** ARGUE to engage in argument ■ *n.* **1.** PRACTICE BOUT a practice or exhibition bout of boxing **2.** PARTICULAR MOTION IN BOXING a motion in boxing for attack or defence [Late 16thC. Origin uncertain: perhaps an alteration of SPUR, or perhaps via Old French *esparer* 'to kick' from, ultimately, Latin *parare* 'to make ready'.]

spar[3] /spaar/ *n.* a light-coloured lustrous nonmetallic flaky mineral that cleaves easily, e.g. feldspar [Late 16thC. From Low German.]

sparable /spaárəb'l/ *n.* a small headless nail used to attach the soles of shoes [Early 17thC. Alteration of *sparrow-bill*. From its resemblance to a sparrow's bill.]

spare /spair/ *v.* (**spares, sparing, spared**) **1.** *vt.* REFRAIN FROM HARMING SB to refrain from killing, punishing, or harming sb **2.** *vt.* TREAT SB LENIENTLY to treat leniently or refrain from treating sb harshly **3.** *vt.* SAVE SB FROM DOING STH to save or relieve sb from the effort or trouble of doing sth **4.** *vt.* WITHHOLD STH to withhold or avoid sth **5.** *vt.* USE STH FRUGALLY to use or dispense sth frugally **6.** *vt.* AFFORD STH to give up or be able to contribute sth from one's resources, especially without inconvenience ○ *I can't spare any time to exercise.* **7.** *vt.* REFRAIN FROM USING STH to refrain from using sth **8.** *vi.* BE FRUGAL to be frugal and thrifty (*archaic*) ■ *adj.* **1.** KEPT IN RESERVE kept in reserve for emergency use **2.** SUPERFLUOUS more than what is needed **3.** LEAN with a muscular physique and no excess fat **4.** SCANTY lacking in quantity or extent ■ *n.* **1.** STH EXTRA sth extra that is kept in reserve **2.** KNOCKING DOWN PINS IN TWO TRIES in tenpin bowling, an instance of knocking down all the pins in two attempts **3.** BOWLING SCORE a score made in tenpin bowling by using two rolls to knock down all ten pins **4.** UNATTACHED MEMBERS OF OPPOSITE SEX unattached members of the opposite sex who are potential sexual partners (*slang*) [Old English *sparian*. Ultimately from a prehistoric Germanic word that also produced German *sparen* 'to save'.] —**sparer** *n.* —**sparely** *adv.* —**spareness** *n.* ◇ **go spare** become upset, especially to lose your

temper (*informal*) ◇ **to spare** more than what is needed

spare part *n.* a replacement for a defective component in a vehicle or machine (*hyphenated when used before a noun*)

spare-part surgery *n.* surgery in which defective organs in the body are replaced by transplanted or artificial organs

sparerib /spáir ríb/ *n.* a rib of pork from which most of the meat has been removed, usually cooked in a barbecue or Chinese sauce [Late 16thC. By folk etymology from Low German *ribbesper* 'pickled pork ribs roasted on a spit', by association with SPARE.]

spare tyre *n.* **1.** EXTRA TYRE an extra tyre, mounted somewhere on a motor vehicle and carried in case of a flat tyre **2.** EXTRA FLESH a roll of extra flesh around sb's waist (*informal humorous*)

sparge /spaarj/ (**sparges, sparging, sparged**) *vt.* to scatter, spray, or sprinkle sth [Late 16thC. Directly or via Old French from Latin *spargere* (see SPARSE.)] —**sparger** *n.*

sparid /spárrid/ (*plural* **-id** *or* **-ids**), **sparoid** /spárroyd/ (*plural* **-oid** *or* **-oids**) *n.* a warm-water marine fish with a compressed body, large head, and sharp teeth. Porgies and breams are sparids. Family: Sparidae. [Late 20thC. Via modern Latin *Sparidae*, family name, from, ultimately, Greek *sparos* 'sea bream'.]

sparing /spáiring/ *adj.* **1.** FRUGAL showing careful restraint in the use of resources **2.** SCANTY limited or restricted in quantity **3.** MERCIFUL inclined to be lenient or merciful —**sparingly** *adv.*

spark[1] /spaark/ *n.* **1.** FIERY PARTICLE a small piece of a burning substance thrown off in combustion or produced in friction **2.** ELECTRIC DISCHARGE a quick bright discharge of electricity between two conductors **3.** STH THAT ACTIVATES a factor or device that sets off or acts as a stimulant, inspiration, or catalyst **4.** STH CAPABLE OF DEVELOPMENT a latent trace of sth capable of development **5.** **spark, sparks** ELECTRICIAN an electrician (*informal*) **6.** **sparks** RADIO OPERATOR the radio operator on a ship or aircraft (*informal*) (*takes a singular verb*) ■ *v.* (**sparks, sparking, sparked**) **1.** *vi.* THROW OFF SPARKS to throw off sparks **2.** *vi.* PRODUCE SPARKS to have an electric ignition working properly so that it generates sparks **3.** *vi.* RESPOND ENTHUSIASTICALLY to respond with lively enthusiasm **4.** *vt.* STIMULATE OR INCITE STH to stimulate or initiate a burst of activity [Old English *spærca*. Origin unknown.]

spark off *vt.* to activate or act as a catalyst for sth

spark[2] /spaark/ *n.* **1.** DANDY a vain young man, especially one concerned with fashion and appearance (*archaic*) **2.** BOYFRIEND a male who courts a woman (*dated informal*) ■ *vti.* (**sparks, sparking, sparked**) WOO to try to persuade sb to become romantically or sexually involved (*archaic*) [Early 16thC. Origin uncertain: probably from SPARK[1].] ◇ **bright spark** a lively and witty person (*informal*)

Dame Muriel Spark
Express Newspapers

Spark /spaark/, **Dame Muriel** (*b.* 1918) British writer. She is best known for her novels, including *Memento Mori* (1959) and *The Prime of Miss Jean Brodie* (1961). Full name **Dame Muriel Sarah Spark**

spark chamber *n.* a device for tracking the path of a subatomic particle, consisting of charged plates that cause the particle to ionize the gas present and create sparks

spark coil *n.* the induction coil that produces the spark discharge to start combustion in an internal combustion engine

spark erosion *n.* a process for shaping metal, similar to conventional machining but using an electric arc from a moving electrode to remove metal

spark gap *n.* a space between two electrodes across which a discharge of electricity occurs, e.g. the gap between electrodes of a spark plug in an internal combustion engine

sparking plug *n.* = spark plug *n.*

sparkle /spaark'l/ *v.* (**-kles, -kling, -kled**) **1.** *vi.* THROW OFF SPARKS to throw off sparks **2.** *vti.* GLITTER to give off or reflect light in brilliant, glittering flashes, or make sth do this **3.** *vi.* PERFORM VIVACIOUSLY to perform brilliantly or be vivacious, witty, or enthusiastic **4.** *vi.* EFFERVESCE to effervesce, especially a wine or other drink ■ *n.* **1.** SHINING PARTICLE a little spark or shining particle **2.** ANIMATION lively or brilliant animation and vivacity **3.** EFFERVESCENCE effervescence in wine and other drinks [12thC. Formed from SPARK[1].] —**sparkly** *adj.*

sparkler /spaárklər/ *n.* **1.** HANDHELD FIREWORK a handheld firework that throws off sparks as it burns **2.** SPARKLING GEM a diamond or other sparkling gem (*informal*)

sparkling water *n.* water charged with carbon dioxide to make it effervescent

sparkling wine *n.* wine that is made effervescent naturally through a second fermentation or artificially through the introduction of carbon dioxide

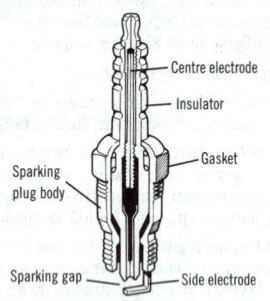

Centre electrode
Insulator
Gasket
Sparking plug body
Sparking gap
Side electrode
Spark plug

spark plug *n.* a device that ignites the fuel mixture in the cylinder in an internal-combustion engine by emitting a spark

spark transmitter *n.* an obsolete form of radio transmitter that used power generated from the discharge of a condenser across a spark gap

sparky /spaárki/ (**-ier, -iest**) *adj.* very lively and enthusiastic

sparling /spaárling/ (*plural* **-lings** *or* **-ling**) *n.* **1.** EUROPEAN SMELT a European smelt. Latin name: *Osmerus eperlanus*. **2.** IMMATURE HERRING a herring that has not yet matured [14thC. From Old French *esperlinge*, of Germanic origin.]

sparoid *n.* = sparid

sparring partner *n.* **1.** SB WHO SPARS WITH A BOXER sb who spars with a boxer to help in training **2.** DEBATING PARTNER sb who is regularly involved in debates or arguments with sb else

sparrow /spárrō/ *n.* **1.** SMALL BROWNISH SONGBIRD a small dull-coloured songbird with a short stout bill for cracking seeds. Family: Passeridae. **2.** US, Can FINCH RESEMBLING SPARROW a finch that resembles the true sparrow [Old English *spearwa*. Ultimately from a prehistoric Germanic word.]

sparrowgrass /spárrō graass/ *n.* US asparagus (*regional*) [Mid-17thC. By folk etymology from ASPARAGUS.]

sparrowhawk /spárrr ō hawk/ *n.* **1.** EUROPEAN AND ASIAN HAWK a small hawk of Europe and Asia that has short broad wings, a long tail, a dark grey to blackish back, and preys on smaller birds. Latin name: *Accipiter nisus*. **2.** N. AMERICAN KESTREL a kestrel native to North America. Latin name: *Falco sparverius*.

sparry /spaári/ *adj.* relating to or resembling a mineral spar

sparse /spaarss/ *adj.* thinly spread, or occurring with many spaces in between [Early 18thC. From Latin *sparsus*, the past participle of *spargere* 'to scatter' (source of English *aspersion* and *sparge*).] —**sparsely** *adv.*

Sparta /spaártə/ town in the southern Peloponnese, Greece. An ancient city-state situated on the site of the modern town was an important military power between the 6th and 4th centuries BC. Population: 14,390 (1981).

Spartacist /spaártəssist/ *n.* a member of a German revolutionary group organized in 1918 and promoting an extreme socialistic agenda [Early 20thC. From German *Spartakist*, from *Spartakus* 'Spartacus', adopted as pen-name by the German socialist leader Karl Liebknecht.]

Spartacus /spaártəkəss/ (*d.* 71 BC) Roman enslaved labourer and rebel leader. He led an uprising that defeated several Roman armies before he was killed in battle against the Roman commander Crassus.

Spartan /spaárt'n/ *n.* **1.** NATIVE OF SPARTA a native or inhabitant of ancient Sparta **2.** SB WITH STRONG CHARACTER sb who has a strong character, marked by self-discipline, courage, and self-restraint ■ *adj.* **1.** RELATING TO ANCIENT SPARTA relating to the ancient Greek city of Sparta, its citizens, or its culture **2.** MARKED BY DISCIPLINE AND AUSTERITY marked by stern discipline, frugality, simplicity, or courage —**Spartanism** *n.*

sparteine /spaárti īn, -in/ *n.* a bitter thick poisonous liquid alkaloid obtained from the common broom plant and used in medicine. Formula: $C_{15}H_{26}N_2$. [Mid-19thC. Formed from modern Latin *Spartium*, broom genus, from, ultimately, Greek *sparton* 'esparto'.]

spasm /spázzəm/ *n.* **1.** INVOLUNTARY MUSCLE CONTRACTION an involuntary sudden muscle contraction **2.** SUDDEN BURST OF ACTIVITY a sudden brief emotion, sensation, or action ○ *a spasm of pain* [14thC. Via French and Latin from Greek *spasmos*, from *span* 'to pull'.]

spasmodic /spaz móddik/ *adj.* **1.** AFFECTED BY SPASMS affected or characterized by spasms **2.** RESEMBLING SPASM resembling a spasm in sudden brief intensity **3.** INTERMITTENT occurring at uneven intervals **4.** EXCITABLE prone to sudden outbursts of emotion [Late 17thC. Via modern Latin *spasmodicus* from Greek *spasmōdēs*, from *spasmos* (see SPASM).] —**spasmodically** *adv.*

spasmolytic /spázmə líttik/ *n., adj.* = **antispasmodic** —**spasmolytic** *adj.*

spastic /spástik/ *adj.* **1.** AFFECTED BY SPASMS relating to or affected by spasms **2.** OFFENSIVE TERM lacking physical coordination or the ability to perform competently (*slang offensive*) ■ *n.* **1.** OFFENSIVE TERM a highly offensive term referring to sb affected by cerebral palsy (*dated insult*) **2.** OFFENSIVE TERM an offensive term that deliberately insults sb's coordination or competence (*slang insult*) [Mid-18thC. Via Latin from Greek *spastikos*, from *span* (see SPASM).] —**spastically** *adv.*

spastic colon *n.* = **irritable bowel syndrome**

spat[1] /spat/ *n.* **1.** PETTY QUARREL a brief quarrel usually concerning petty matters **2.** SLAP a light blow or slap (*archaic*) ■ *v.* (**spats, spatting, spatted**) **1.** *vi. US, Can* QUARREL PETTILY to engage in a petty, brief quarrel **2.** *vt.* SLAP SB OR STH to strike sb or sth with light force (*archaic*) [Early 19thC. Origin unknown.]

spat[2] past tense, past participle of **spit**

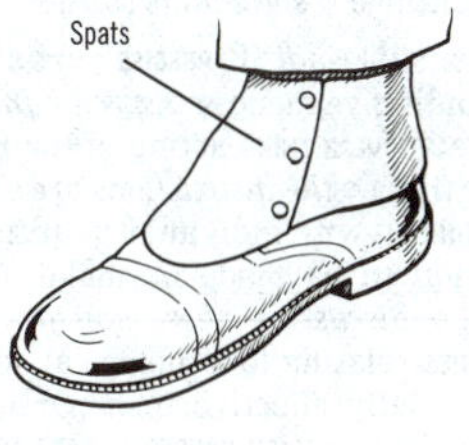

Spat

spat[3] /spat/ *n.* a short cloth or leather gaiter, popular in the late 19th and early 20th centuries, worn over a shoe to cover the instep and the ankle [Early 19thC. Shortening of SPATTERDASH.]

spat[4] /spat/ *n.* an immature bivalve mollusc, e.g. an oyster [Mid-17thC. From Anglo-Norman, of unknown origin.]

spatchcock /spách kok/ *n.* SPLIT BIRD FOR COOKING a chicken or other fowl that is split, dressed, and grilled ■ *vt.* (**-cocks, -cocking, -cocked**) **1.** PREPARE FOWL FOR ROASTING to prepare a chicken or other fowl for roasting by splitting it open **2.** INSERT STH AWKWARDLY to introduce or interpose sth into a piece of writing, especially in a forced or inappropriate way [Late 18thC. Origin uncertain: perhaps an alteration of *spitchcock* 'prepared eel', of unknown origin.]

spate /spayt/ *n.* **1.** FLOOD a flood, or a river overflowing its banks ○ *After the heavy rain the river was in spate.* **2.** OUTBURST a sudden strong outburst **3.** LARGE QUANTITY a large quantity of sth [15thC. Origin uncertain: perhaps via Old French *espoit* from Dutch *spuiten* 'to flood'.]

spathe /spayth/ (*plural* **spathes**) *n.* a leafy sheath (**bract**) that encloses the cluster of flowers (**spadix**) in some plants, e.g. the arum, and sometimes resembles a petal [Late 18thC. Via Latin *spatha* from Greek *spathē* (see SPADE[1]).] —**spathaceous** /spə tháyshəss/ *adj.* —**spathed** /spaythd/ *adj.*

spathic /spáthik/, **spathose** /spáthōss/ *adj.* resembling mineral spar, especially in being easy to split [Late 18thC. Formed from German *Spat(h)* 'spar'.]

spathulate *n.* = **spatulate**

spatial, **spacial** *adj.* relating to, occupying, or happening in space [Mid-19thC. Formed from Latin *spatium* (see SPACE).] —**spatiality** /spáyshi álləti/ *n.* —**spatially** /spásh'li/ *adv.*

spatiotemporal /spáyshi ō témpərəl/ *adj.* **1.** RELATING TO SPACE AND TIME relating to, existing in, or having the qualities of both space and time **2.** RELATING TO SPACE-TIME relating to a four-dimensional space-time system [Early 20thC. Coined from Latin *spatium* (see SPACE) + TEMPORAL.] —**spatiotemporally** *adv.*

spätlese /shpáyt layzə/ (*plural* **-sen** /-layz'n/ *or* **-ses**) *n.* a grade of high-quality German table wine made from late-picked grapes and typically medium sweet [Early 20thC. From German, literally 'late vintage'.]

spatter /spáttər/ *v.* (**-ters, -tering, -tered**) **1.** *vti.* COME OUT IN DROPS to expel sth or come out in small scattered drops or splashes **2.** *vt.* SPLASH WITH LIQUID to splash sth with or as if with a liquid, especially if the liquid leaves a mark or residue **3.** *vti.* SCATTER IN DROPLETS to splash or scatter in droplets **4.** *vt.* DEFAME to defame or sully sb's character ■ *n.* **1.** ACT OF SPATTERING an act of spattering or being spattered **2.** SPATTERING SOUND the sound of spattering **3.** DROPLET OF STH SPATTERED a droplet or splash of sth spattered **4.** SMALL AMOUNT a small amount of sth [Mid-16thC. Origin uncertain: perhaps an imitation of the sound.]

spatterdash /spáttər dash/ *n.* a knee-length cloth or leather legging worn to protect clothing from water or mud spatters

spatula /spáttyoōlə/ *n.* **1.** COOK FLAT UTENSIL WITH HANDLE a flat flexible metal, plastic, or rubber utensil with a handle, used to scoop, lift, spread, or mix **2.** MED TONGUE DEPRESSOR a flat wooden stick used to depress the tongue when the mouth or throat is being examined [Early 16thC. Via Latin, literally 'a small broadsword', from, ultimately, Greek *spathē* (see SPADE[1]).] —**spatular** *adj.*

spatulate /spáttyoōlət/, **spathulate** /spáth-/ *adj.* shaped like a spatula, with a narrow tapering base and a broad rounded tip. = **spathulate**

spavin /spávvin/ *n.* an ailment of horses involving a swelling or enlargement of the hock joint [15thC. From Old French *espavin*, of uncertain origin: perhaps ultimately from a prehistoric Germanic word.]

spavined /spávvind/ *adj.* **1.** WITH SPAVIN having or being lame with a spavin **2.** OLD AND WORN OUT lacking health, vigour, and strength ○ *a spavined horse*

spawn /spawn/ *n.* **1.** BIOL EGG MASS a mass of eggs of a fish, amphibian, or other aquatic animal **2.** OFFSPRING progeny or offspring, especially if numerous **3.** FUNGI MYCELIUM a mass of microscopic fungal threads (**mycelium**), especially when prepared on a growth medium for starting a new culture of the fungus **4.** SEED a seed, germ, or the source of sth ■ *v.* (**spawns, spawning, spawned**) **1.** *vi.* BIOL DEPOSIT EGGS to produce and deposit eggs **2.** *vi.* PRODUCE YOUNG to produce offspring in large numbers **3.** *vt.* GIVE RISE TO STH to generate or give rise to sth **4.** *vt.* START NEW FUNGUS CULTURE to start a new culture of a fungus using spawn [15thC. Via Anglo-Norman *espaundre* 'to shed' and Old French *espandre* from Latin *expandere* 'to spread out' (source of English *expand*).] —**spawner** *n.*

spay /spay/ (**spays, spaying, spayed**) *vt.* VET to surgically remove an animal's ovaries and adjacent parts of the uterus [15thC. From Old French *espeer*, literally 'to cut with a sword', from *espee* 'sword' (source of English *épée*), from, ultimately, Greek *spathē* (see SPADE[1]).]

spaza /spaázə/ *n. S Africa* a small informal shop, often run from a home in a township

SPCK *n., abbr.* Society for Promoting Christian Knowledge

SPD *n., abbr.* Social Democratic Party of Germany [German, Sozialdemokratische Partei Deutschlands]

speak /speek/ (**speaks, speaking, spoke** /spōk/, **spoken** /spōkən/) *v.* **1.** *vti.* TALK to utter words or articulate sounds with the voice **2.** *vi.* EXPRESS THOUGHTS AND OPINIONS to communicate thoughts, opinions, or feelings by uttering with the voice **3.** *vt.* BE ABLE TO USE LANGUAGE to know and be able to converse in a language **4.** *vi.* BE ON GOOD TERMS to be on good and friendly terms with sb ○ *It's sad, but they're not speaking anymore.* **5.** *vi.* DELIVER SPEECH TO AUDIENCE to make a speech or deliver an address **6.** *vti.* EXPRESS IN WRITING to express sth or make a statement in writing **7.** *vti.* COMMUNICATE NONVERBALLY to communicate by other than verbal means ○ *Actions speak louder than words.* **8.** *vi.* MAKE CHARACTERISTIC SOUND to produce or make a sound typical of its kind ○ *The cannon spoke.* **9.** *vt.* NAUT COMMUNICATE WITH ANOTHER SEA-GOING VESSEL to communicate with another vessel at sea [Old English *specan, sprecan*. Ultimately from an Indo-European word that also produced German *sprechen* 'to speak'.] —**speakable** *adj.* ◇ **so to speak** used to indicate that you are expressing sth in an unusual way, e.g. that you are being euphemistic ◇ **speak for itself** have an obvious meaning ◇ **to speak of** significant or worth mentioning

speak for *vt.* to act as an advocate for or speak on behalf of

speak out *vi.* **1.** SPEAK FRANKLY to express opinions boldly, freely, and frankly **2.** TALK LOUDLY to talk loudly or loudly enough to be heard

speak to *vt.* to address a particular issue in a speech or discussion (*formal*) ○ *a speech that spoke to the needs of international students*

speak up *vi.* **1.** TALK LOUDLY to talk loudly enough to be heard **2.** TALK FRANKLY to express opinions freely and frankly

speakeasy /speék eezi/ (*plural* **-ies**) *n. US* a place where alcoholic beverages are sold and consumed illegally, especially during Prohibition in the United States (*dated slang*) [Late 19thC. From the custom of speaking softly so as not to attract attention.]

speaker /speékər/ *n.* **1.** SB WHO SPEAKS a person who speaks **2.** SB WHO MAKES A SPEECH sb who makes a speech or gives a lecture or address **3.** = **loudspeaker**

Speaker *n.* the presiding officer of a legislative body, e.g. the House of Commons or the US or the Australian House of Representatives

speakerphone /speékər fōn/ *n. US* a telephone equipped with a loudspeaker and microphone

speaking /speéking/ *adj.* **1.** INVOLVING SPEECH involving speech or speaking **2.** ELOQUENT capable of communicating in an eloquent or impressive way **3.** APPARENTLY REAL resembling a real person or object ○ *the speaking image of her aunt* **4.** ABLE TO USE SPECIFIED LANGUAGE able to speak a particular language (*usually used in combination*) ○ *French-speaking students*

speaking clock *n.* a telephone service that provides an accurate verbal announcement of the time

speaking in tongues *n.* the making of utterances that are not recognizable as any known language and have no formal linguistic content. It is a normal aspect of worship in many Pentecostal and charismatic churches. ◊ **gift of tongues**

speaking tube *n.* a pipe connecting different parts of sth, e.g. a ship or building, and through which conversation can be conducted

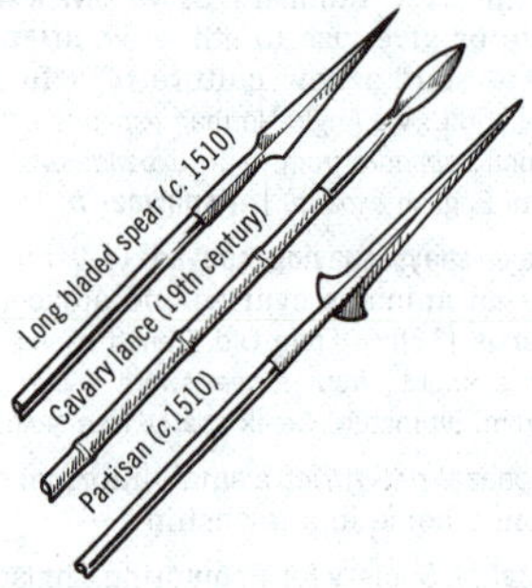
Long bladed spear (c.1510)
Cavalry lance (19th century)
Partisan (c.1510)
Spear

spear[1] /speer/ *n.* **1.** LONG-HANDLED WEAPON WITH BLADE a weapon for throwing or thrusting that has a long handle and a blade or head with a sharpened point **2.** WEAPON FOR SPEARING FISH a weapon with a sharp point and barbs used for catching fish by piercing them **3.** = **spearman** ■ *vti.* **(spears, spearing, speared)** PIERCE STH WITH SPEAR to stab, strike, pierce, or take sb or sth with or as though using a spear [Old English *spere*. Ultimately from a prehistoric Germanic word that also produced German *Speer* 'spear' and is.] —**spearer** *n.*

spear[2] /speer/ *n.* BOT a young blade, shoot, or stalk of a plant such as asparagus or grass [15thC. Alteration of SPIRE.]

spear carrier *n.* **1.** MINOR MEMBER OF CAST a minor member of a cast in a play or opera **2.** SB WHOSE CONTRIBUTIONS ARE UNIMPORTANT sb who contributes little of importance or relevance (*informal*)

spearfish /spe̍er fish/ (*plural* **-fish** *or* **-fishes**) *n.* a large marine swordfish that is related to the marlin and sailfish and has a very long, pointed upper jaw. Genus: *Tetrapturus.*

spear gun *n.* a gun designed to shoot a barbed spear underwater, used to catch fish

spearhead /spe̍er hed/ *n.* **1.** ARMS POINTED HEAD OF SPEAR the pointed head of a spear **2.** MIL LEADING FORCES IN MILITARY ATTACK the leading forces in a military attack **3.** DRIVING FORCE IN EVENT the leading or driving element or force in an undertaking ■ *vt.* **(-heads, -heading, -headed)** ACT AS LEADER OF EVENT to act as the leader or driving force of a military attack, or any event or undertaking

spearman /spe̍ermən/ (*plural* **-men** /spe̍ermən/) *n.* a soldier or other person who is armed with a spear

spearmint /spe̍er mint/ (*plural* **-mint** *or* **-mints**) *n.* a common mint, the leaves and essential oil of which are used for flavouring. Latin name: *Mentha spicata.* [Mid-16thC. From the stem's resemblance to a spear.]

spear side *n.* the male side of a family (*archaic*) ◊ **distaff side** ['Spear' as a symbol of man's domain]

spearwort /spe̍er wurt/ (*plural* **-wort** *or* **-worts**) *n.* a buttercup with spear-shaped leaves and small yellow flowers that grows in Europe, Asia, and the eastern United States [Old English]

spec /spek/ *n.* a detailed description of a particular thing, especially one detailed enough to provide sb with the information needed to make that thing (*informal*) [Late 18thC. Shortening.] ◇ **on spec** with a chance of achieving sth but no certainty of it (*informal*)

spec. *abbr.* **1.** specification **2.** special

special /spésh'l/ *adj.* **1.** UNUSUAL OR SUPERIOR distinct, different, unusual, or superior in comparison to others of the same kind **2.** PRIMARY of the greatest importance **3.** HELD IN ESTEEM regarded with particular esteem or affection **4.** RESERVED unique to or reserved for a specific person or thing **5.** MADE FOR PARTICULAR PURPOSE made or used for a particular purpose or occasion **6.** ARRANGED FOR SPECIFIC PURPOSE planned for a specific occasion **7.** ADDITIONAL in addition to or more than is usual **8.** RELATING TO EDUCATING SPECIAL-NEEDS CHILDREN designed or intended for educating children who are physically or mentally challenged ■ *n.* **1.** STH RESERVED FOR PARTICULAR PURPOSE sth designed or reserved for a particular purpose or occasion **2.** TV TELEVISION PROGRAMME NOT PART OF SCHEDULE a television programme that is not part of a network's normal schedule **3.** *US, Can* TEMPORARY REDUCTION IN PRICE a temporary reduction in the price of an item **4.** FOOD DISH NOT ON USUAL MENU a dish that a restaurant or other food outlet offers in addition to the standard menu, or one that is available for a low price **5.** = **special constable** [12thC. Directly or via Old French *especial* from Latin *specialis*, from *species* (see SPECIES).] ◇ **on special** *ANZ, US* being sold at a reduced price

Special Air Service *n.* full form of **SAS**

Special Boat Service *n.* an elite Royal Marines force that is used to spearhead amphibious operations and to reconnoitre beach landings

Special Branch *n.* the branch of the police force that is the executive arm of the government intelligence agencies and specializes in matters of political security

special constable *n.* sb who acts as a volunteer to supplement the police force, especially on occasions when a large police force is necessary, e.g. emergencies or demonstrations

special delivery *n.* the delivery of mail more quickly than or outside normal delivery times for an extra fee

special drawing rights *n.* a method of settling international debts through the International Monetary Fund in order to stabilize exchange rates

special education *n.* teaching modified to suit students with special educational needs

special effects *npl.* extraordinary visual effects in a film or television programme achieved by technical means, either optically, digitally, or mechanically

special interest group *n.* a group seeking to influence government policy in favour of a particular interest or issue

specialise *vi.* = **specialize**

specialism /spéshəlizəm/ *n.* **1.** CONCENTRATION IN FIELD OF STUDY concentration in a particular field of study ○ *There is a great deal of specialism in their education system.* **2.** = **specialty** *n.* 1

specialist /spéshəlist/ *n.* **1.** SB SPECIALIZING IN PARTICULAR INTEREST sb who is particularly interested in or good at an occupation, interest, or field of study **2.** *US* MIL ENLISTED RANK IN US ARMY an enlisted rank in the US Army from corporal to sergeant first class, and denoting special technical skills **3.** MED TYPE OF PHYSICIAN a medical doctor who practices in a certain field, e.g. surgery, dermatology, or oncology —**specialistic** /spéshə lístik/ *adj.*

speciality /spéshi álləti/ (*plural* **-ties**) *n.* **1.** STH SB SPECIALIZES IN a skill, field of study, interest, or activity in which sb specializes. = **specialty 2.** PRODUCT OF SB'S SPECIALIZATION a product or result of sb's specialization **3.** DISTINCTIVE MARK an unusual, distinctive, or superior mark or quality

WORD KEY: USAGE

speciality or **specialty**? ***Speciality*** is used in British English and ***specialty*** in American English to denote a special interest or ability. Although there are meanings that only occur in American English, for example 'a novelty or new feature', there are no fundamental differences in usage between the two words.

specialization /spéshə lī záysh'n/ *n.* **1.** ACT OF BECOMING SPECIALIZED the act or process of becoming specialized **2.** = **speciality** *n.* 1 **3.** BIOL ADAPTATION OF ORGANISM the adaptation of an organism or a part of an organism to a particular function or condition in response to environmental conditions **4.** BIOL ADAPTED BODY PART an organism or a part of an organism that has been adapted to a particular function or condition

specialize /spéshə līz/ **(-izes, -izing, -ized)**, **specialise** **(-ises, -ising, -ised)** *v.* **1.** *vi.* DEVOTE TIME TO PARTICULAR ACTIVITY to devote time exclusively to a particular interest, skill, or field of study **2.** *vt.* SPECIFY STH to specify or make specific mention of sth **3.** *vt.* ADAPT TO PARTICULAR PURPOSE to adapt sth to suit a specific purpose **4.** *vi.* BECOME ADAPTED to become adapted to a particular function or condition

special licence *n.* a marriage licence that allows a marriage to take place without the usual legal conditions being enforced

special needs *npl.* the particular requirements, especially in education, that some people have because of physical challenges or learning difficulties

Special Olympics *n.* an international athletic competition for athletes who are physically or mentally challenged (*takes a singular or plural verb*)

special pleading *n.* **1.** LAW PLEADING INTRODUCING NEW MATTER pleading that introduces new or special matter and that avoids allegations of matter pleaded by the opposite side, instead of direct denial of those allegations **2.** ARGUMENT PRESENTING ONLY ONE ASPECT an argument that presents only one aspect of an issue and avoids any unfavourable aspects

special relativity *n.* = **relativity** *n.* 1

special school *n.* a school catering to students who have special educational needs, e.g. because of learning difficulties or physical challenges

special session *n.* a session of a legislature, court, or council held in addition to and outside of regularly scheduled sessions

special sort *n.* a character that is not on the usual printing font, e.g. an accented or Greek letter

special theory of relativity *n.* = **relativity** *n.* 1

specialty /spésh'lti/ (*plural* **-ties**) *n.* **1.** *US* = **speciality 2.** MEDICAL SPECIALIZATION an area of medicine in which sb specializes **3.** LAW LEGAL AGREEMENT UNDER SEAL a legal agreement made under seal

speciation /spe̍essi áysh'n/ *n.* the evolutionary formation of new biological species, usually by one species that divides into two or more species that are genetically unique [Early 20thC. Formed from SPECIES.] —**speciate** /spe̍essi ayt/ *vi.*

specie /spe̍eshi/ *n.* money in the form of coins [Mid-16thC. Shortening of Latin *in specie*, literally 'in kind', from *species* (see SPECIES).] ◇ **in specie 1.** in the form of coins **2.** in a similar way or kind **3.** LAW in the form specified

species /spe̍e sheez/ (*plural* **-cies**) *n.* **1.** BIOL TAXONOMIC GROUP a subdivision of a genus considered as a basic biological classification and containing individuals that resemble one another and that may interbreed **2.** BIOL ORGANISMS IN SPECIES the organisms belonging to a particular species **3.** KIND OR SORT a kind, sort, or variety of sth **4.** CHEM ATOM CATEGORY a category of atomic nucleus, ion, molecule, or atom **5.** LOGIC SUBDIVISION OF GENUS a collection of objects or individuals that, on the basis of shared features, form a subdivision of a genus **6.** CHR BREAD AND WINE IN COMMUNION the two elements of the Communion, bread and wine, or their outward form after consecration [14thC. From Latin, 'appearance, kind', (source also of English *spice*), formed from *specere* 'to look' (source of English *spectator* and *spy*).]

WORD KEY: SYNONYMS

See Synonyms at ***type***.

speciesism /spe̍e sheezizəm/ *n.* the belief that the human race is superior to other species, and that exploitation of animals for the advantage of humans is justified

specif. *abbr.* **1.** specific **2.** specifically

specifiable /spéssi fī-əb'l/ *adj.* capable of being explicitly identified ○ *specifiable causes*

specific /spə síffik/ *adj.* **1.** PRECISE particular and detailed, avoiding vagueness ○ *specific instructions* **2.** RELATING TO PARTICULAR THING acting on or relating to a particular thing ○ *the instructions are specific to this task* **3.** DISTINCTIVE with individual qualities that allow a distinction to be made or make a distinction necessary ○ *discussing these specific problems* **4.** BIOL OF SPECIES relating to a biological species **5.** MED EFFECTIVE specially effective in a particular pathological condition **6.** MED CAUSED BY PARTICULAR INFECTIOUS AGENT used to describe a disease caused by a particular infectious agent **7.** PHYS DENOTING PHYSICAL PROPERTY used to indicate that a physical property is being expressed with reference to a particular quantity, such as mass, volume, or length **8.** COMM LEVIED

PER UNIT used to describe taxes or duties levied on a per-unit basis using number, weight, or volume ∎ *n.* **1. DETAIL** a particular item, quality, or detail ○ *didn't go into specifics* **2. PHARM EFFECTIVE DRUG** a medicine that is especially effective against a particular disease [Mid-17thC. From late Latin *specificus*, literally 'making a kind', from Latin *species* 'kind' (see SPECIES).] —**specifically** *adv.* —**specificity** /spéssi físsəti/ *n.*

specification /spéssifi káysh'n/ *n.* **1. DETAILED DESCRIPTION** a detailed description of a particular thing, especially one detailed enough to provide sb with the information needed to make that thing ○ *a look at the engine specification* **2. DETAIL** an item within a specification ○ *The machine's technical specifications are in Appendix A.* **3. SPECIFYING** the specifying of sth **4. COMM LAW INTELLECTUAL PROPERTY DESCRIPTION** a detailed description of intellectual property, as required by law **5. PUBL TYPOGRAPHICAL INSTRUCTIONS** detailed instructions regarding information such as font, point size, and layout that are sent with material to be typeset and printed

specific charge *n.* the ratio of the electric charge of an elementary particle divided by its mass

specific gravity *n.* = relative density (*dated*)

specific heat *n.* US = specific heat capacity

specific heat capacity *n.* the amount of heat needed to raise the temperature of one gram of a substance by one degree, usually measured in joules per kelvin per kilogram. Symbol *c*. US term **specific heat**

specific performance *n.* LAW a court order compelling sb to carry out an obligation, often sth stated in a contract

specific resistance *n.* = resistivity

specify /spéssi fī/ (**-fies, -fying, -fied**) *vt.* **1. STATE EXPLICITLY** to state or identify sth in detail or explicitly **2. STIPULATE** to state sth or make it a condition ○ *The rules specify that pets cannot be kept here.* **3. INCLUDE IN SPECIFICATION** to include or state sth in a specification [13thC. Via French *spécifier* or directly from late Latin *specificare*, from *specificus* (see SPECIFIC).] —**specifiable** *adj.* —**specificative** /spéssifi kaytiv, spə síffi kaytiv/ *adj.* —**specifier** /spéssi fī ər/ *n.*

specimen /spéssimin/ *n.* **1. REPRESENTATIVE THING** sth that is representative because it is typical of its kind or of a whole, especially sth that serves as an example (*often used before a noun*) ○ *a specimen of the candidate's handwriting* **2. TYPE OF PERSON** sb who displays or seems to typify certain characteristics (*informal*) ○ *'turning away with disgust from the loathsome specimen of humanity before him'* (Baroness Orczy, *The Scarlet Pimpernel*; 1905) **3. MED SAMPLE OF BODY MATERIAL** a sample, e.g. of urine or blood used for testing and diagnosis **4. SCI TYPICAL EXAMPLE** an organism or one of its parts preserved as a typical example of its classification [Early 17thC. From Latin, where it was formed from *specere* 'to look at' (source of English *expect*, *despise*, and *conspicuous*).]

specious /spéeshəss/ *adj.* **1. APPARENTLY TRUE BUT ACTUALLY FALSE** appearing to be true but really false **2. DECEPTIVELY ATTRACTIVE** superficially attractive but actually of no real interest or value [14thC. From Latin *speciosus* 'good-looking', from *species* 'appearance' (see SPECIES). Originally in the meaning of 'beautiful'; the modern meaning dates from the 17thC.] —**speciously** *adv.* —**speciousness** *n.*

speck /spek/ *n.* **1. SMALL SPOT** a very small mark or stain **2. PARTICLE** a tiny particle of sth solid ∎ *vt.* (**specks, specking, specked**) **MARK WITH SPECKS** to mark sth with specks (*usually passive*) [Old English *specca*, of uncertain origin]

speckle /spék'l/ *n.* **SMALL COLOURED SPOT** a small spot or mark, often a small irregular patch of contrasting colour, e.g. on plumage or an egg shell ∎ *vt.* (**-les, -ling, -led**) **MARK WITH SPECKLES** to mark sth with speckles (*usually passive*) [15thC. Origin uncertain: probably literally 'little speck'.]

speckled /spék'ld/ *adj.* **1. WITH SMALL SPOTS** with a pattern of many small spots or small irregular patches, often of a contrasting colour **2. WITH CONTRASTS** with parts that contrast distinctly with each other ○ *a speckled career* ○ *speckled shadows*

speckled trout *n.* = brook trout

speckle interferometry /spék'l intər feer rómmətri/ *n.* a technique for reducing distortions in photographic images of celestial objects caused by atmospheric turbulence. A number of images of very short exposure are combined. The technique can also be used to measure the diameter of some stars.

specs /speks/ *npl.* (*informal*) **1. SPECTACLES** eyeglasses **2. SPECIFICATIONS** specifications

SPECT *abbr.* single photon emission computed tomography

spectacle /spéktək'l/ *n.* **1. STH REMARKABLE THAT CAN BE SEEN** an object, phenomenon, or event that is seen or witnessed, especially one that is impressive, unusual, or disturbing **2. LAVISH DISPLAY** an impressive performance or display, especially sth staged as a form of entertainment **3. UNPLEASANT CENTRE OF ATTENTION** sb or sth that attracts attention by being unpleasant or ridiculous ○ *You are making a spectacle of yourself.* [14thC. Via French from Latin *spectaculum*, from *spectare* 'to watch', from *specere* (see SPECIMEN).]

———— **WORD KEY: ORIGIN** ————
The Latin stem *spect-*, from which *spectacle* is derived, is also the source of English *aspect*, *circumspect*, *conspectus*, *expect*, *inspect*, *perspective*, *prospect*, *respect*, *retrospect*, *spectre*, *spectrum*, and *suspect*.

spectacled /spéktək'ld/ *adj.* **1. WEARING SPECTACLES** with eyeglasses on **2. ZOOL WITH MARKINGS LIKE SPECTACLES** with markings on the face that encircle the eyes in a way that resembles spectacles

spectacled bear *n.* a rare South American bear found in the grasslands and forests of the Andes. It is black with white markings around the eyes and is threatened with extinction. Latin name: *Tremarcto ornatus.*

spectacles /spéktək'lz/ *npl.* a pair of glass or plastic lenses worn in a frame in front of the eyes to help correct imperfect vision [15thC. Plural of SPECTACLE. The word was earlier used for various implements of seeing, including windows and mirrors.]

spectacular /spek tákyoólər/ *adj.* **1. VISUALLY IMPRESSIVE** impressive or dramatic to look at or watch **2. REMARKABLE** remarkably large, great, or speedy ∎ *n.* **EXTRAVAGANZA** a lavish celebration or artistic production —**spectacularly** *adv.*

spectate /spek táyt/ (**-tates, -tating, -tated**) *vi.* to watch rather than participate [Early 18thC. Back-formation from SPECTATOR.]

spectator /spek táytər/ *n.* sb who watches or observes, especially sb who watches an event [Late 16thC. Via French *spectateur* or directly from Latin *spectator*, from *spectare* 'to watch' (see SPECTACLE).] —**spectatorial** /spéktə táwri əl/ *adj.* —**spectatorship** /spek táytərship/ *n.*

spectatoritis /spek táytə rítiss/ *n.* the tendency to watch leisure activities, whether live or on television, in preference to actively participating in them [Formed from SPECTATOR]

spectator sport *n.* a sport that attracts spectators in large numbers

specter *n.* US = spectre

spectinomycin /spéktinō mísin/ *n.* an antibiotic used in the treatment of gonorrhoea [Mid-20thC. Formed from modern Latin *spectabilis*, species name, from Latin, 'visible', from *spectare* 'to watch' (see SPECTACLE), modelled on *actinomycin*.]

spectra plural of **spectrum**

spectral /spéktrəl/ *adj.* **1. GHOSTLY** relating to spectres or in the form of a spectre **2. OF SPECTRUM** produced by a spectrum or relating to a spectrum —**spectrality** /spek trálləti/ *n.* —**spectralness** /spéktrəlnəss/ *n.* —**spectrally** /spéktrəli/ *adv.*

spectral class *n.* = spectral type

spectral line *n.* any of the discrete bands of light in a spectrum associated with a specific wavelength. Characteristic spectral lines are emitted by atoms and molecules and may be used to identify substances.

spectral type, **spectral class** *n.* ASTRON a classification system for stars based on an analysis of the light

they emit. This analysis also gives information on a star's temperature and chemical composition.

spectre /spéktər/ *n.* **1. GHOST** a ghostly presence or apparition **2. UNPLEASANT PROSPECT** a threat or prospect of sth unpleasant ○ *the spectre of my performance review* [Early 17thC. Via French or directly from Latin *spectrum* 'image, apparition' (see SPECTRUM).]

spectrin /spéktrin/ *n.* any of a group of fibrous proteins found especially in the membranes of red blood cells [Mid-20thC. Formed from SPECTRE, because the material was first isolated from red blood cells lacking haemoglobin, called 'ghosts'.]

spectro- *prefix.* spectrum ○ *spectroscope* [From SPECTRUM]

spectrogram /spéktrə gram/ *n.* a photograph or representation of a spectrum

spectrograph /spéktrə graaf, spéktrə graf/ *n.* an instrument consisting of a spectrometer and related equipment used to obtain a visual record of a spectrum —**spectrographic** /spéktrə gráffik/ *adj.* —**spectrographically** /-gráffikli/ *adv.* —**spectrography** /spek tróggrəfi/ *n.*

spectroheliogram /spéktrə héeli ə gram/ *n.* an image of the sun produced using a narrow wavelength band of the radiation it emits

spectroheliograph /spéktrō heéli ə graaf/ *n.* an instrument used to obtain images of the sun over a narrow band of wavelengths —**spectroheliographic** /spéktrō heeli ə gráffik/ *adj.* —**spectroheliography** *n.*

spectrohelioscope /spéktrō heéli ə skōp/ *n.* an instrument that is similar to a spectroheliograph but is used for viewing the sun's spectrum, as distinct from recording it —**spectrohelioscopic** /spéktrō heeli ə skóppik/ *adj.*

spectrometer /spek trómmitər/ *n.* an instrument used to disperse radiant energy or particles into a spectrum and measure certain properties such as wavelength, mass, energy, or index of refraction —**spectrometric** /spéktrə méttrik/ *adj.* —**spectrometry** *n.*

spectrophotometer /spéktrōfə tómmitər/ *n.* an instrument used to measure the relative intensities of wavelengths in a spectrum —**spectrophotometric** /spéktrō fōtə méttrik/ *adj.* —**spectrophotometrically** /-méttrikli/ *adv.* —**spectrophotometry** /spéktrōfə tómmətri/ *n.*

spectroscope /spéktrə skōp/ *n.* an instrument for dispersing light, usually light in the visible range, into a spectrum —**spectroscopic** /spktrə skóppik/ *adj.* —**spectroscopically** /-skóppikli/ *adv.*

spectroscopic analysis *n.* the use of spectroscopy to determine the chemical composition, energy levels, and molecular structure of substances

spectroscopy /spek tróskəpi/ *n.* the study of spectra, especially to determine the chemical composition of substances and the physical properties of molecules, ions, and atoms —**spectroscopist** *n.*

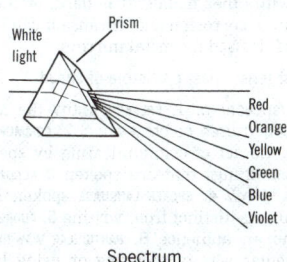

Spectrum

spectrum /spéktrəm/ (*plural* **-tra** /-trə/ *or* **-trums**) *n.* **1. PHYS DISTRIBUTION OF COLOURED LIGHT** a continuous distribution of coloured light produced when a beam of white light is dispersed into its components, e.g. by a prism. ◊ **absorption spectrum, emission spectrum 2. PHYS RADIATION FREQUENCY RANGE WITH SPECIFIED PROPERTY** a range of radiation frequencies that have a specified property. ◊ **electromagnetic spectrum 3. PHYS RECORD OF SUBSTANCE'S RADIATION DENSITY** a visual record of the wavelengths of the radiation or particles emitted by a substance, used as a means of analysing its physical properties, e.g. energy and mass. ◊ **mass spectrum 4. ANY RANGE** any range, especially one with opposite values at its limits ○ *a spectrum of opinions between the two extremes* **5.** PHARM **RANGE OF DRUG TARGETS** the range of organisms that an antibiotic can kill [Late 19thC. From Latin, 'image, apparition', from *specere* 'to see' (see SPECIMEN).]

specula plural of **speculum**

specular /spékyòolər/ *adj.* **1.** OPTICS **OF OR LIKE MIRROR** relating to mirrors or having the characteristics of a mirror **2.** MED **USING SPECULUM** carried out using a speculum [Late 16thC. From Latin *specularis*, from *speculum* (see SPECULUM).]

speculate /spékyòo layt/ (**-lates, -lating, -lated**) *v.* **1.** *vti.* **CONJECTURE** to conjecture sth based on incomplete facts or information **2.** *vi.* **CONSIDER STH** to think over possibilities **3.** *vi.* FIN **MAKE RISKY DEALS FOR PROFIT** to engage in financial transactions such as commodity trading that have an element of risk especially in the short term with the hope of making a profit **4.** *vi.* **TAKE RISKS** to take risks in an attempt to achieve sth or get some benefit **5.** *vi. NZ* RUGBY **KICK AIMLESSLY** in rugby, to kick the ball out of defence hurriedly in order to thwart an attack [Late 16thC. From Latin *speculat-*, the past participle stem of *speculari* 'to observe, spy out', from, ultimately, *specere* (see SPECIMEN).]

speculation /spékyòo láysh'n/ *n.* **1. OPINION BASED ON INCOMPLETE INFORMATION** a conclusion, theory, or opinion based on incomplete information or evidence **2. REASONING BASED ON INCOMPLETE INFORMATION** reasoning based on incomplete information or evidence **3.** FIN **RISKY TRANSACTION** a financial transaction that involves risks but is potentially profitable **4.** FIN **MAKING RISKY TRANSACTIONS** engaging in financial transactions that are risky but also potentially profitable

speculative /spékyòolətiv/ *adj.* **1. USING INCOMPLETE INFORMATION** based on conjecture or incomplete information **2. FORMING CONCLUSIONS NOT BASED ON FACT** given to forming conclusions or opinions that are not based on fact **3.** FIN **RISKY BUT POTENTIALLY PROFITABLE** risky in nature but potentially profitable speculative investments ○ *speculative investments* —**speculatively** *adv.* —**speculativeness** *n.*

speculator /spékyòo laytər/ *n.* **1. SB WHO SPECULATES** sb who speculates, especially financially **2.** *NZ* RUGBY **HURRIED DEFENSIVE KICK FORWARD** in rugby, a hurried forward kick of the ball from a defensive position made in order to thwart a promising attack

speculum /spékyòoləm/ (*plural* **-la** /spékyòolə/ *or* **-lums**) *n.* **1.** OPTICS **MIRROR** a mirror or other reflective surface in an optical instrument such as a telescope **2.** MED **MEDICAL INSTRUMENT** a medical instrument used to hold open a body passage, e.g. the anus or vagina, so that it can be examined **3.** BIRDS **COLOURED PATCH ON BIRD'S WINGS** a patch of colour on the wings of ducks and certain other birds, helpful in identification [Late 16thC. From Latin, 'mirror', formed from *specere* 'to see' (see SPECIMEN).]

speculum metal *n.* an alloy of copper and tin sometimes with other metals. It is hard, brittle, white, resistant to corrosion and, because it can be highly polished, is used for metal mirrors.

sped past tense, past participle of **speed**

speech /speech/ *n.* **1. SPEAKING ABILITY** the ability to speak (*often used before a noun*) **2. COMMUNICATION BY SPEAKING** the act of communicating by speaking **3. THINGS SAID** things that are spoken ○ *recordings of human speech* **4. SPOKEN LANGUAGE** spoken language especially as distinct from writing **5. ADDRESS** a talk given to an audience **6. PARTICULAR WAY OF SPEAKING** a particular way of speaking or using language, especially that of an individual or group **7. RUMOUR** rumour or hearsay (*archaic*) [Old English *spǣc*, from *specan*, an earlier form of SPEAK]

speech community *n.* a group that includes all the speakers of a single language or dialect. They may be widely dispersed geographically.

speech day *n.* an annual event in a school during which speeches are given by staff and guests and pupils are presented with prizes for good work and outstanding achivements

speechify /spéechi fī/ (**-fies, -fying, -fied**) *vi.* (*informal*) **1. TALK SELF-IMPORTANTLY** to talk in a tedious and self-important manner, especially in giving an opinion **2. MAKE SPEECH** to give a speech or speeches —**speechification** /spéechifi káysh'n/ *n.* —**speechifier** /spéechi fī ər/ *n.*

speechless /spéechləss, spéechliss/ *adj.* **1. TEMPORARILY UNABLE TO SPEAK** temporarily not able to speak or not able to think of sth to say, e.g. because of surprise or fear **2. UNABLE TO SPEAK** lacking the power of speech **3. REMAINING SILENT** choosing not to say anything **4. UNSPOKEN** not expressed in words **5. HARD TO EXPRESS** difficult or impossible to put into words [Old English] —**speechlessly** *adv.* —**speechlessness** *n.*

speechmaker /spéech maykər/ *n.* sb who makes a speech, often sb regularly called upon to make speeches —**speechmaking** *n.*

speech pathology *n.* the study, diagnosis, and treatment of speech disorders, including failure of normal speech development in children and language disorders resulting from acquired brain dysfunction —**speech pathologist** *n.*

speech-reading *n.* = **lip-reading**

speech recognition *n.* a system of computer input and control in which the computer can recognize spoken words and transform them into digitized commands or text. With such a system, a computer can be activated and controlled by voice commands or take dictation as input to a word processor or desktop publishing system.

speech synthesis *n.* computer-generated audio output that resembles human speech

speech therapy *n.* the treatment of speech disorders of all kinds —**speech therapist** *n.*

speechwriter /spéech rītər/ *n.* sb who writes speeches for other people often professionally

speed /speed/ *n.* **1. RATE OF MOVEMENT OR HAPPENING** the rate at which sth moves, happens, or functions **2. RAPIDITY** fast movement, progress, or operation **3. RATE OF MOVEMENT IRRESPECTIVE OF DIRECTION** rate of movement irrespective of direction. It is equal either to distance travelled divided by travel time, or to rate of change of distance with respect to time. **4.** DRUGS **AMPHETAMINE** an amphetamine drug (*slang*) **5.** *US* **STH SUITABLE** sth that matches sb's tastes, abilities, or inclinations (*informal*) ○ *The intermediate course will be more my speed.* **6. SUCCESS** success or prosperity (*archaic*) **7.** MECH ENG **GEAR RATIO** a gear ratio in a motor, engine, or driving mechanism ○ *a ten-speed bicycle* ○ *operates at three different speeds* **8.** PHOTOGRAPHY **PHOTOGRAPHIC FILM'S SENSITIVITY TO LIGHT** a measure of the sensitivity of photographic film to light, expressed numerically according to any of various rating systems ■ *v.* (**speeds, speeding, sped** *or* **speeded**) **1.** *vti.* **GO OR MOVE QUICKLY** to go or move quickly, or to make sth or sb go or move quickly **2.** *vi.* **DRIVE FAST** to drive fast, especially exceeding the speed limit **3.** *vi.* **PASS QUICKLY** to pass or happen quickly or more quickly **4.** *vt.* **HASTEN** to make sth happen sooner or more quickly **5.** *vi.* DRUGS **USE AMPHETAMINES** to be under the influence of amphetamines (*slang*) **6.** *vti.* **MAKE OR BE PROSPEROUS** to prosper or cause sb or sth to prosper (*archaic*) [Old English *spēd* 'success, prosperity'. Ultimately from an Indo-European base meaning 'to prosper', which is also the ancestor of English *prosper* and *despair*.] ◇ **be** *or* **get up to speed 1.** to reach the maximum or desirable rate of movement or progress **2.** to be or become fully informed about the latest developments

speedball /spéed bawl/ *n.* **1.** SPORTS **GAME RESEMBLING SOCCER** a team game similar to soccer. The ball can be passed forwards with the hands and caught when in mid-air. **2.** DRUGS **ILLEGAL DRUG MIXTURE** a combination of illegal drugs such as cocaine and heroin taken by injection (*slang*)

speedboat /spéed bōt/ *n.* a motorboat capable of travelling at high speeds

speed brake *n.* a flap on an aircraft wing used to decrease speed in flight before landing

speed bump, **speed hump** *n.* a raised area or ridge on a road surface designed to limit traffic speeds

speed camera *n.* a roadside-mounted camera that automatically photographs a vehicle passing by it at excessive speed. It provides traffic police with concrete evidence of speeding offences.

speed demon *n. US* = **speed merchant** (*informal*)

speed dial *n.* a function on a telephone that enables numbers to be stored in a memory so that they can be dialled by pressing a single button ○ *I have her number on speed dial.*

speedfreak *n.* sb who is addicted to amphetamines or sb who habitually takes them

speed hump *n.* = **speed bump**

speeding /spéeding/ *n.* **DRIVING VEHICLE ABOVE SPEED LIMIT** the offence of driving a vehicle at a speed above the designated speed limit ■ *adj.* **FAST-MOVING** moving or working quickly

speed limit *n.* the maximum permitted speed, usually specified by law, at which a vehicle may travel on a particular stretch of road

speedo /spéedō/ (*plural* **speedos**) *n.* a speedometer (*informal*) [Mid-20thC. Shortening.]

speedometer /spi dómmitər/ *n.* an instrument that continuously measures a vehicle's speed and displays it either numerically or by means of a needle on a dial

speed-read *vti.* to read sth very fast using a learned technique of skimming the text

speed skate *n.* an ice skate designed for racing. It has a blade that is much longer than on a standard skate. —**speed skater** *n.*

speed skating *n.* the sport of racing competitively on speed skates. Two skaters race against each other on a wide oval track divided into two lanes.

speedster /spéedstər/ *n.* (*dated slang*) **1. FAST CAR** a car that goes very fast **2.** *US* **HABITUAL SPEEDER** sb who habitually drives too fast [Early 20thC. Formed from SPEED, on the model of *roadster*.]

speed trap *n.* a stretch of road kept under hidden surveillance by police officers monitoring vehicle speeds, usually using radar equipment

speed walking *n.* = **race walking**

speedway /spéed way/ *n.* **1.** MOTOR SPORT a motor sport in which lightweight motorcycles race against each other on an oval cinder track (*often used before a noun*) **2. SPEEDWAY TRACK** a track or stadium used for speedway

speedwell /spéed wel/ *n.* a perennial European plant of the snapdragon family with opposite leaves and clusters of blue or pinkish flowers. Genus: *Veronica.* [Late 16thC. From SPEED (verb) + WELL.]

speedwriting /spéed rīting/ *n.* a system of shorthand writing that uses combinations of standard letters, as distinct from other systems that use symbols

speedy /spéedi/ (**-ier, -iest**) *adj.* **1. FAST** accomplished or achieved quickly **2. FAST-MOVING** capable of moving very fast —**speedily** *adv.* —**speediness** *n.*

speiss /spīss/ *n.* a compound of arsenic or antimony formed during the smelting of certain ores such as iron, nickel, and copper [Late 18thC. From German *Speise* 'food, speiss'.]

Speke /speek/, **John Hanning** (1827–64) British explorer. Among his African explorations were expeditions to Lake Tanganyika and Lake Victoria (both 1858).

spelaean, **spelean** *adj.* relating to caves, or found in caves [Mid-19thC. Via Latin *spelaeum* from Greek *spēlaion* 'cave'.]

speleology /spéeli ólləji/, **spelaeology** *n.* **1. STUDY OF CAVES** the scientific study of caves **2. EXPLORATION OF CAVES** the sport or pastime of exploring caves. US term **spelunking** —**speleological** /spéeli ə lójjik'l/ *adj.* —**speleologist** *n.*

spell[1] /spel/ (**spells, spelling, spelt** *or* **spelled, spelt** /spelt/ *or* **spelled**) *v.* **1.** *vti.* **NAME OR WRITE LETTERS OF WORD** to name or write in correct order the constituent letters of a word, part of a word, or group of words **2.** *vt.* **FORM WORD** to form a word when arranged in the correct order **3.** *vt.* **SIGNIFY** to be a sign or indication of sth ○ *Increased interest rates could spell trouble for some corporate borrowers.* [13thC. Via Old French *espeller* from, ultimately, a prehistoric Germanic base that is also the ancestor of *spell*[2].]

spell out *vt.* **1. MAKE COMPLETELY CLEAR** to state sth clearly, allowing no room for misunderstanding **2. READ SLOWLY OR WITH DIFFICULTY** to read sth with difficulty or very slowly, especially by reading out words one letter at a time **3. FIGURE OUT** to figure sth out by careful study or analysis

spell[2] /spel/ *n.* **1.** PARANORMAL **WORDS WITH MAGICAL POWER** a word or series of words believed to have magical power, spoken to invoke the magic **2. SPELL'S INFLUENCE** the influence that a spell has over sb or sth **3. FASCINATION** a compelling fascination or attraction ■ *vt.* **(spells, spelling, spelt** *or* **spelled) INFLUENCE USING SPELL** to put sb or sth under the influence of a spell [Old English, from a prehistoric Germanic base that is also the ancestor of English *spell*[1] and *gospel*. Originally in the meaning of 'talk, speech'.]

spell[3] /spel/ *n.* **1. SHORT PERIOD** a period of indeterminate but usually short duration (*informal*) ○ *Let's sit a spell.* **2. PERIOD OF PARTICULAR WEATHER** a period of weather of a particular type ○ *a warm spell* **3. BOUT OF ILLNESS** a period of illness ○ *a fainting spell* **4. PERIOD OF WORK** a period of work or purposeful activity **5. TOUR OF DUTY** sb's turn to work or perform a particular duty **6.** *Scotland, ANZ* **REST PERIOD** a period of rest **7.** *US* **SHORT DISTANCE** a short but unspecified distance (*informal*) ○ *down the road a spell* ■ *v.* **(spells, spelling, spelled, spelt** *or* **spelled** *or* **spelt) 1.** *vt. US, ANZ, Scotland* **RELIEVE** to relieve sb of a task temporarily, especially in order to allow him or her to rest **2.** *vi. US* **TAKE TURNS** to take turns working at a job [Late 16thC. The noun came from the verb, a variant of obsolete *spele* 'to take the place of someone', from Old English *spelian*, of unknown origin.]

spellbinding /spél bīnding/ *adj.* holding attention and interest completely, as if with the influence of a spell —**spellbind** *vt.* —**spellbinder** *n.* —**spellbindingly** *adv.*

spellbound /spél bownd/ *adj.* with attention and interest held completely, as if under the influence of a spell [Late 18thC. Literally 'bound by a spell', formed from SPELL[2].]

spell checker *n.* a computer program usually associated with word processing software that compares words in a text to a file of correctly spelled words in order to detect misspellings —**spell-check** *vt.*

speller /spéllər/ *n.* **1. SB WHO SPELLS** sb who spells words, usually characterized with regard to accuracy **2.** EDUC **BOOK FOR SPELLING** a book for teaching or improving spelling

spellican /spéllikən/ *n.* = **spillikin** [Mid-18thC. Variant.]

spelling /spélling/ *n.* **1. ABILITY TO SPELL** the ability to spell words correctly **2. FORMING WORDS BY ORDERING LETTERS** the forming of words with letters in a conventionally accepted order (*often used before a noun*) **3. SPECIFIC EXAMPLE OF LETTER ORDER** a specific example of how a word is actually spelt

spelling bee *n.* a competition in which the object is to see who can spell the most words correctly

spelling pronunciation *n.* a variant pronunciation of a word that differs from the standard pronunciation and is influenced by the way a word is spelt

spelt[1] past tense, past participle of **spell**

spelt[2] /spelt/ *n.* a hardy variety of wheat of inferior quality, sometimes grown in mountainous regions. Latin name: *Triticum spelta.* [Pre-12thC. From late Latin *spelta*, of uncertain origin: probably from Germanic.]

spelter /spéltər/ *n.* impure zinc often used as a cheap alternative for bronze in cast decorative items [Mid-17thC]

spelunking /spi lúngking/ *n. US* = **speleology** [Mid-20thC. Formed from earlier *spelunk* 'cave', via Old French *spelunque*, from Latin *spelunca*, from Greek *spelunx*.] — **spelunker** *n.*

spencer /spénssər/ *n.* **1. SHORT BOYS' JACKET** a short jacket worn by boys in the late 18th and early 19th centuries **2. WOMEN'S JACKET** a very short jacket worn by women over a high-waisted gown in the late 18th and early 19th centuries [Late 18thC. Named after George John *Spencer*, second Earl Spencer (1758–1834).]

Spencer /spénssər/, **Sir Baldwin** (1860–1929) Australian anthropologist. He was the author of pioneering studies of Australian Aboriginals, including *Native Tribes of Central Australia* (1899). Full name **Sir Walter Baldwin Spencer**

Spencer, Sir Stanley (1891–1959) British painter. Many of his works, such as *The Resurrection, Cookham* (1923–27), place traditional biblical scenes in contemporary settings.

Spencer Gulf /spénsər-/ large coastal inlet in South Australia, flanked by the Eyre and Yorke peninsulas. Length: 322 km/200 mi.

Spencerian /spen séeri ən/ *adj.* used to describe a style of handwriting with perfectly formed letters and ornamentation of capitals [Mid-19thC. Named after Platt Rogers *Spencer* (1800–64), a US calligrapher.]

spend /spend/ *v.* **(spends, spending, spent, spent** /spent/) **1.** *vti.* **PAY MONEY** to pay out money in exchange for goods or services **2.** *vt.* **DEVOTE TIME OR EFFORT** to devote time, energy, or thought to sth ○ *spent a lot of time thinking about it* **3.** *vt.* **PASS TIME** to pass time in a specified place or way ○ *spend a week in Hawaii* **4.** *vt.* **USE UP** to deplete sth totally **5.** *vt.* **SACRIFICE STH** to sacrifice sth, especially for a cause ○ *spent her life working for reform* ■ *n.* **1. SPREE** a time or trip during which things are bought and money is spent, especially a lot of money **2. AMOUNT OF MONEY SPENT** an amount of money spent or set aside for spending ○ *'...is increasing its advertising spend by 40 per cent...'* (*Marketing Week*; December 1998) [Pre-12thC. From Latin *expendere* 'to pay' (see EXPEND), but also in part from Old French *despendre* 'to expend', from Latin *dispendere* 'to distribute by weighing out' (see DISPENSE).]

spender /spéndər/ *n.* sb who spends money, especially in a specified way

Spender /spéndər/, **Dale** (*b.* 1943) Australian writer and feminist. Her books include *Women of Ideas and What Men Have Done to Them* (1982).

Spender, Sir Stephen (1909–95) British poet and editor. He was a prominent member of the left-wing British literary movement in the 1930s, and edited *Encounter* from 1953 to 1967. His works include *Collected Poems* (1986) and *Journals 1939–83* (1986). Full name **Sir Stephen Harold Spender**

spending money *n.* cash used or available for personal expenses, especially expenditure on nonessential items

spendthrift /spénd thrift/ *n.* **EXTRAVAGANT SPENDER** sb who spends money extravagantly and often recklessly ■ *adj.* **WASTEFUL WITH MONEY** tending to spend money extravagantly and wastefully [Late 16thC. From SPEND + THRIFT, in the archaic sense 'savings, earnings'.]

Spenser /spénssər/, **Edmund** (1552?–99) English poet. He wrote the epic romance *The Faerie Queene* (1590–96), a panoramic historical allegory and one of the classics of English Renaissance literature.

Spenserian /spen séeri ən/ *adj.* relating to or characteristic of Edmund Spenser or his literary works —**Spenserian** *n.*

Spenserian sonnet *n.* a sonnet with a rhyme scheme abab, bcbc, cdcd, ee, invented by Edmund Spenser

Spenserian stanza *n.* a stanza devised by Edmund Spenser. It contains eight lines of iambic pentameter and a ninth of iambic hexameter, using the rhyme scheme ababbcbcc. The scheme is used in *The Faerie Queene.*

spent /spent/ past tense, past participle of **spend** ■ *adj.* **1. CONSUMED** used or used up ○ *tossed the spent match into the fire* **2. EXHAUSTED** totally depleted of energy or strength ○ *felt totally spent by the end of the day* **3. FINISHED** at an end **4.** ZOOL **EXHAUSTED OF SPAWN OR SPERM** used to describe a female fish that has deposited all its spawn or a male fish that has used up all its sperm

sperm[1] /spurm/ (*plural* **sperm** *or* **sperms**) *n.* used popularly, but technically incorrectly, to refer to semen [14thC. Via late Latin *sperma* from Greek, 'seed, semen'. Ultimately 'sth scattered', from an Indo-European word meaning 'to scatter', which is also the ancestor of English *spread* and *spore*.]

sperm[2] /spurm/ *n.* **1.** = **spermaceti 2.** = **sperm oil 3.** = **sperm whale** [Mid-19thC. Shortening.]

spermaceti /spúrmə sétti, spúrmə séeti/ *n.* a white waxy solid obtained from oil in the head of sperm whales and other cetaceans, and used in cosmetics, candles, and ointments [Late 15thC. From medieval Latin, from late Latin *sperma* 'semen' (see SPERM[1]) + Latin *ceti* 'of a whale' (see CETUS). From its appearance (it serves no reproductive function).]

spermary /spúrməri/ (*plural* **-ries**) *n.* an organ in which male reproductive cells are developed. The testes are spermaries.

spermat- *prefix.* = **spermato-** (*used before vowels*)

spermatheca /spúrmə théekə/ *n.* a receptacle for storing sperm in the reproductive tracts of certain invertebrates such as insects [Early 19thC. Coined from late Latin *sperma* 'seed, semen' (see SPERM) + THECA.] — **spermathecal** *adj.*

spermatia plural of **spermatium**

spermatic /spur máttik/, **spermic** /spúrmik/ *adj.* **1. OF SEMEN** relating to, carrying, or containing semen **2. OF SPERMARIES OR SPERMATIC CORDS** relating to a spermary or to the spermatic cord —**spermatically** *adv.*

spermatic cord *n.* a cord by which a testis is suspended in the scrotum. It contains the vas deferens as well as nerves, vessels, and veins.

spermatid /spúrmə tid/ *n.* any of the four cells that are formed from a spermatocyte and develop into spermatozoa

spermatium /spur máyshəm/ (*plural* **-a**) *n.* a cell that functions as a male reproductive cell in certain algae, fungi, and lichens [Mid-19thC. Via modern Latin from Greek *spermation*, a diminutive of *sperma* (see SPERM[1]).]

spermato- *prefix.* **1.** sperm, spermatozoon ○ *spermatogenesis* **2.** seed ○ *spermatophyte* [From Greek *spermat-*, the stem of *sperma* (see SPERM[1])]

spermatocide /spur máttō sīd, sp/ *n.* = **spermicide** — **spermatocidal** /spur máttō sīd'l, spúrmətō-/ *adj.*

spermatocyte /spur máttō sīt, sp/ *n.* a cell that develops from a spermatogonium. It divides into four spermatids by means of the kind of cell division known as meiosis.

spermatogenesis /spur mátt-, spúrmətō-/ *n.* the formation and development of spermatozoa in the testes —**spermatogenetic** /spur máttō-, sp/ *adj.*

spermatogonium /spur máttō gṓni əm, spúrmətō-/ (*plural* **-a** /-ni ə/) *n.* a cell in the male testes that develops and divides to form spermatocytes. These subsequently divide to form spermatids, from which spermatozoa finally develop. —**spermatogonial** *adj.*

spermatophore /spur məttō fawr/ *n.* a capsule or mass that encloses spermatozoa in insects and other lower animals and that is transferred to the female during insemination —**spermatophoral** /spur máttə fáwrə, spúrmət-/ *adj.*

spermatophyte /spur máttō fīt/ *n.* any plant that produces seeds, including angiosperms and gymnosperms —**spermatophytic** /spur máttə fíttik, spúrmətō-/ *adj.*

spermatorrhoea /spur mátə rée ə/ *n.* the involuntary emission of semen without orgasm

spermatozoa plural of **spermatozoon**

spermatozoid /spur máttō zṓ id, spúrmətō-/ *n.* a male reproductive cell, resembling a ribbon, produced in algae, ferns, fungi, mosses, and some gymnosperms. It can move by means of flagella. [Mid-19thC. Coined from SPERMATOZOON + -ID.]

spermatozoon /spur máttō zṓ on, spúrmətō-/ (*plural* **-a** /-ə/) *n.* CELL BIOL a male reproductive cell (**gamete**) that has an oval head with a nucleus, a short neck, and a tail by which it moves to find and fertilize an ovum —**spermatozoan** *adj.*

sperm bank *n.* a place that stores semen until it is required for use in artificial insemination

sperm count *n.* **1. CONCENTRATION OF SPERM** the concentration of sperm in a given volume of seminal fluid, taken as an index of male fertility **2. TEST FOR NUMBER OF SPERM** a test to determine a man's sperm count

spermi- *prefix.* = spermo-

spermic *adj.* = spermatic

spermicide /spúrmi sīd/ *n.* a pharmaceutical cream or gel used to kill spermatozoa, especially in conjunction with a birth-control device such as a condom or diaphragm —**spermicidal** /spúrmi sīd'l/ *adj.*

spermiogenesis /spúrmi ō jénnəssiss/ *n.* the stage of spermatogenesis during which a spermatid is transformed into a spermatozoon —**spermiogenetic** /spúrmi ō jə néttik/ *adj.*

spermo- *prefix.* seed, sperm ○ *spermophyte* [From Greek *sperma* 'seed']

sperm oil, **sperm** *n.* a pale yellow oil obtained from the head of the sperm whale and used as an industrial lubricant in delicate mechanisms

spermophyte /spúrmə fīt/ *n.* = spermatophyte

sperm whale, **sperm** *n.* the largest of the toothed whales whose massive square head has a cavity filled with a mixture of sperm oil and spermaceti. Its intestines are the source of ambergris. [Shortening of *spermaceti whale*]

-spermy *suffix.* fertilization ○ *polyspermy* [From Greek *sperma* 'seed' + -Y]

Sperrin Mountains /spérrən-/ mountain range forming the border between the counties of Londonderry and Tyrone, Northern Ireland. Its highest peak is Sawel Peak, 683 m./2,240 ft. Length: 24 km/15 mi.

sperrylite /spérri līt/ *n.* a silvery white mineral and ore of platinum consisting of white crystalline platinum arsenide [Early 20thC. Named after Francis L. *Sperry*, the Canadian chemist who identified the mineral.]

spessartine /spéssər teen/, **spessartite** /spéssər tīt/ *n.* a yellow or reddish-brown garnet consisting of manganese aluminium silicate. It is used as a gemstone. [Mid-19thC. From French, named after *Spessart*, a district in Bavaria, Germany, where it is found.]

spew /spyoo/ *vti.* (**spews**, **spewing**, **spewed**) **1.** VOMIT STH to vomit sth that has been eaten **2.** POUR OR FLOW OUT FORCEFULLY to flow out forcefully, or force sth out in a stream ○ *a volcano spewing ash* **3.** SAY FORCEFULLY to utter sth in an angry, forceful, or relentless way ■ *n.* VOMIT sth ejected from the mouth, especially vomit [Old English *spīwan*. Ultimately from an Indo-European word meaning 'to spit', an imitation of the sound, which is also the ancestor of English *spit*, *spout*, and *sputum*.] —**spewer** *n.*

Spey /spay/ river in northern Scotland, flowing from Loch Lochy to the Moray Firth. Length: 171 km/107 mi.

SPF *n.* the degree to which a sun cream, lotion, screen, or block provides protection for the skin against the sun. Abbr of **sun protection factor**

sp. gr. *abbr.* specific gravity

Spgs *abbr.* Springs (*in place names*)

sphagnum /sfágnəm/ *n.* moss growing in wet, acid, temperate regions that decays and becomes compacted to form peat. Genus: *Sphagnum*. [Mid-18thC. Via modern Latin, genus name, from, ultimately, Greek *sphagnos*, a type of shrub.] —**sphagnous** *adj.*

sphalerite /sfállə rīt, sfáylə rīt/ *n.* a yellow or brownish ore of zinc consisting of crystalline zinc sulphide [Mid-19thC. Formed from Greek *sphaleros* 'slippery, uncertain', because the mineral is easily confused with galena.]

sphen- *prefix.* = spheno- (*used before vowels*)

sphene /sfeen/ *n.* a brown-black mineral composed of calcium titanium silicate that is widely found in low concentrations in coarse-grained igneous rocks [Early 19thC. Via French *sphène* from Greek *sphēn* 'wedge'.]

sphenic /sfeénik/ *adj.* like a wedge in shape

spheno- *prefix.* wedge-shaped ○ *sphenogram* [From Greek *sphēn* 'wedge']

sphenodon /sfeénə don/ *n.* = tuatara [Late 19thC. From modern Latin, genus name, literally 'wedge-toothed', from Greek *sphēn* 'wedge']

sphenogram /sfeénə gram/ *n.* any of the characters with wedge-shaped strokes used in the ancient writing systems known as cuneiform script

sphenoid /sfeé noyd/ *adj.* **1.** WEDGE-SHAPED shaped like a wedge **2.** OF SPHENOID BONE relating to the sphenoid bone

sphenoid bone, **sphenoid** *n.* a bone with prominent wings at the base of the cranium. It forms part of the walls and roof of the nasal cavity.

spher- *prefix.* = sphero- (*used before vowels*)

spheral /sfeérəl/ *adj.* **1.** OF SPHERES relating to a sphere or to spheres in general **2.** SPHERE-SHAPED shaped like a sphere **3.** SYMMETRICAL forming a symmetrical or harmonious shape or whole

sphere /sfeer/ *n.* **1.** GLOBE any object similar in shape to a ball **2.** MATH THREE-DIMENSIONAL SURFACE a three-dimensional closed surface consisting of all points that are a given distance from a centre **3.** MATH ROUND SOLID FIGURE the solid figure bounded by a sphere, or the volume it encloses **4.** FIELD OF KNOWLEDGE OR ACTIVITY a field of knowledge, interest, or activity **5.** AREA OF INFLUENCE an area of control or influence ○ *took no interest in matters beyond her sphere* **6.** GROUP IN SOCIETY a level or group within a society **7.** ASTRON ANY CELESTIAL OBJECT a celestial object, e.g. a planet, moon, or star (*literary*) **8.** ASTRON THE SKY the sky or the heavens (*literary*) **9.** ASTRON FORMER CONCEPT OF CELESTIAL LAYER any of the revolving concentric transparent shells on which, in early astronomy, the Sun, Moon, planets, and stars were thought to be fixed as they moved around the Earth ■ *vt.* (**spheres**, **sphering**, **sphered**) **1.** ENCIRCLE to surround, encircle, or enclose sth (*literary*) **2.** PLACE IN HEAVEN to place in the sky or in heaven, among the celestial spheres (*literary*) **3.** FORM INTO BALL to form sth into the shape of a ball [13thC. Via Old French *espere* from late Latin *sphera*, (which later influenced the English word), from Latin *sphaera*, from Greek *sphaira* 'ball'.] —**sphericity** /sfe ríssəti/ *n.*

sphere of influence *n.* a geographical region or area of activity in which a particular state, organization, or person is dominant

spherical /sférrik'l/, **spheric** /sférrik/ *adj.* **1.** ROUND shaped like a sphere **2.** OF SPHERES relating to a sphere, or to spheres in general **3.** ASTRON OF CELESTIAL BODIES relating to celestial objects **4.** ASTRON OF ANCIENT ASTRONOMY SPHERES relating to the spheres of ancient astronomy —**spherically** *adv.* —**sphericalness** *n.*

spherical aberration *n.* a defect in a lens or curved mirror in which light passing through the edge has a different focal point from light passing through the centre, resulting in blurred images

spherical angle *n.* an angle formed on a sphere at the point at which any two circles of maximum radius intersect

spherical coordinates *npl.* a set of coordinates used for locating a point in space representing its distance from some origin and two angles describing its orientation relative to perpendicular axes extending form that origin

spherical geometry *n.* the geometry of figures formed on the surface of a sphere

spherical polygon *n.* a geometric figure formed on the surface of a sphere, bounded by three or more arcs of great circles

spherical triangle *n.* a spherical polygon that has three sides

spherical trigonometry *n.* trigonometry dealing with spherical triangles

spherics[1] /sférriks/ *n.* **1.** = spherical geometry (*takes a singular verb*) **2.** = spherical trigonometry

spherics[2] /sférriks/ *n.* the study of electromagnetic radiation emanating from natural sources in the atmosphere (*takes a singular verb*) [Mid-20thC. Shortening of ATMOSPHERICS.]

sphero- *prefix.* sphere, spherical ○ *spheroid* [Via Latin *sphaero-* from, ultimately, Greek *sphaira* 'sphere']

spheroid /sférroyd, sfeer oyd/ *n.* a three-dimensional object that is shaped like a sphere but is not perfectly round, e.g. an ellipsoid —**spheroidal** /sfi ródl'l, -ród'li/ *adj.* —**spheroidally** *adv.* —**spheroidicity** /sférroy díssəti, sfeer oy-/ *n.*

spherometer /sfi rómmitər/ *n.* an instrument used to measure the curvature of a surface

spheroplast /sférro plast, -plaast/ *n.* a bacterium or yeast cell that has lost part of its cell wall and is as a result spherical in shape and more sensitive to osmosis

spherule /sférrool/ *n.* a minute sphere or globule [Mid-17thC. From late Latin *spherula*, literally 'small sphere', from Latin *sphaera* (see SPHERE).] —**spherular** *adj.*

spherulite /sférrōō līt/ *n.* a more or less spherical mass of radiating crystal fibres found in some kinds of volcanic rock, e.g. obsidian —**spherulitic** /sférrōō líttik/ *adj.*

sphery /sfeéri/ *adj.* **1.** SPHERE-SHAPED in the shape of a sphere **2.** OF CELESTIAL BODIES relating to or resembling the planets, the stars, and other celestial bodies (*literary*)

sphincter /sfíngktər/ *n.* a circular band of muscle that surrounds an opening or passage in the body and narrows or closes the opening by contracting [Late 16thC. Via Latin from Greek *sphigktēr*, from *sphiggein* 'to bind tight'.] —**sphincteral** *adj.*

sphinges plural of sphinx

sphingosine /sfíng gə seen, -sin/ *n.* a long-chain amino glycol that is part of larger molecules found in nerve tissue, e.g. gangliosides, sphingomyelins, and cerebrosides. Formula: $C_{18}H_{37}O_2N$. [Late 19thC. Coined from Greek *sphiggos* 'of a sphinx' (see SPHINX) + -INE. From the enigmatic character of the material.]

Barnaby's

Sphinx, Giza, Egypt

sphinx /sfingks/ (*plural* **sphinxes** *or* **sphinges** /sfín jeez/) *n.* **1.** GREEK COMPOSITE CREATURE in Greek mythology, a winged creature with a lion's body and a woman's head. It strangled all who could not answer its riddle, but killed itself when Oedipus answered correctly. **2.** EGYPTIAN COMPOSITE CREATURE in Egyptian mythology, a creature with a lion's body and the head of a man, ram, or bird **3.** SPHINX STATUE a statue of a sphinx **4.** MYSTERIOUS PERSON a mysterious or inscrutable person [Late 16thC. Via Latin from Greek *sphigx*, of uncertain origin: probably from *sphiggein* 'to draw tight', because the sphinx that terrorized Thebes often took people by strangulation.]

sphinxlike /sfíngks līk/ *adj.* difficult to understand or find out about

sphinx moth *n.* = hawk moth [*Sphinx* from its appearance, suggestive of a sphinx]

sphragistics /sfrə jístiks/ *n.* the study of seals and signet rings (*takes a singular verb*) [Mid-19thC. Directly or via French *sphragistique* from late Greek *sphragistikos* 'of seals', from *sphragis* 'seal'.] —**sphragistic** *adj.*

sp. ht *abbr.* specific heat

sphygm- *prefix.* = sphygmo- (*used before vowels*)

sphygmic /sfígmik/ *adj.* relating to the pulse [Early 18thC. From Greek *sphugmikos*, from *sphugmos* (see SPHYGMO-).]

sphygmo- *prefix.* pulse ○ *sphygmograph* [From Greek *sphugmos* 'pulsation', from 'sphug-', the stem of *spuzein* 'to throb']

sphygmograph /sfígmō graaf, -graf/ *n.* an apparatus used to make a graphical record (**sphygmogram**) of variations in blood pressure and pulse —**sphygmographic** /sfígmō gráffik/ *adj.* —**sphygmography** /sfig móggrəfi/ *n.*

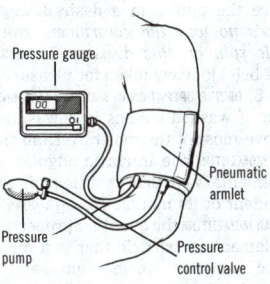

Sphygmomanometer

Labels: Pressure gauge; Pneumatic armlet; Pressure pump; Pressure control valve

sphygmomanometer /sfíg mōmə nómmitər/ *n.* an instrument used to measure blood pressure in an artery. It consists of a pressure gauge, an inflatable cuff placed around the upper arm, and an inflater bulb or pressure pump.

spic /spik/ *n.* a highly offensive term referring to a Spanish or Italian person (*slang taboo*) [Early 20thC. Shortening of *spiggoty*, of uncertain origin: perhaps from a nonstandard pronunciation of '(no) speak the (English)'.]

spica /spíka/ (*plural* **-cae** /-see/ *or* **-cas**) *n.* a bandage applied to a limb in an overlapping figure-of-eight pattern to immobilize it [14thC. From Latin, 'ear of grain'; from its spiralling shape, which is reminiscent of an ear of grain.]

spic-and-span *adj.* = spick-and-span

spicate /spí kayt/ *adj.* growing in the form of a spike, or with flowers growing in spikes [Mid-17thC. From Latin *spicatus*, the past participle of *spicare* 'to furnish with sharp points', from *spica* 'spike'.]

spiccato /spi ka̱ätō/ *n.* (*plural* **-tos**) MUSICIAN'S BOWING TECHNIQUE a technique of playing staccato on stringed instruments, in which the bow is allowed to bounce on the string ■ *adj., adv.* USING SPICCATO BOWING played using a technique of allowing the bow to bounce on the string [Early 18thC. From Italian, the past participle of *spiccare* 'to pick off, detach'.]

spice /spíss/ *n.* 1. AROMATIC PLANT SUBSTANCE USED AS FLAVOURING any of various aromatic plant substance such as nutmeg and ginger used as flavourings 2. FLAVOURINGS FROM PLANTS food flavourings derived from the non leafy parts of plants (*often used before a noun*) 3. EXCITING OR INTERESTING THING a source of excitement or interest 4. US STRONG SMELL a pungent odour or fragrance (*often used before a noun*) 5. TRACE OF STH the tiniest amount of sth ■ *vt.* (**spices, spicing, spiced**) 1. SEASON WITH SPICE to season food or beverages with spice 2. MAKE MORE EXCITING to introduce excitement or interest into sth [13thC. Via Old French *espice* from Latin *species* 'appearance, kind', in late Latin, in plural, 'goods, wares' (see SPECIES).]

spiceberry /spíssberri/ (*plural* **-ries**) *n.* 1. BERRY-PRODUCING SHRUB a name given to various trees and shrubs that produce spicy orange, red, or black berries, e.g. the wintergreen 2. SPICY BERRY a berry from a spiceberry plant

spicebush /spíssbŏŏsh/ *n.* a North American shrub that belongs to the laurel family. It has aromatic leaves and dense clusters of yellow flowers. Latin name: *Lindera benzoin*.

spicey *adj.* = spicy

spick-and-span, **spic-and-span** *adj.* 1. TIDY very clean and tidy (*not hyphenated when used after a verb*) 2. IN PERFECT CONDITION showing not the slightest sign of damage or wear and tear [Late 16thC. Shortening of *spick-and-span-new*, from obsolete *spick*, variant of SPIKE[1] + AND + *span-new*, from Old Norse *spánný*, literally 'new chip', from *spán* 'chip', related to English *spoon*.]

spicule /spíkyool/ (*plural* **spicules** *or* **spiculum**) *n.* 1. BIOL SMALL NEEDLE-SHAPED PART a small hard needle-shaped part, especially any of the calcium- or silicon-containing supporting parts of certain invertebrates such as sponges and corals 2. ASTRON SOLAR PROMINENCE a slender column of relatively cool, high-density gas that rapidly erupts from the solar surface and then falls back. There can be as many as 250,000 spicules rising above the solar surface at any moment. [Late 18thC. From modern Latin *spiculum*, lit-

erally 'small spike', Latin *spica* 'spike', ear of grain (see SPIKE[2]).] —**spicular** /spíkyoŏlar, -lə/ *adj.* —**spiculate** /spíkyoŏlit, -layt/ *adj.*

spicy /spíssi/, **spicey** (**spicier, spiciest**) *adj.* 1. SEASONED WITH SPICE smelling or tasting strongly of spices 2. INVOLVING IMPROPRIETY arousing interest because of its scandalous nature, usually because it deals with sexual impropriety (*informal*) 3. VIVACIOUS with a very lively personality 4. BOT PRODUCING SPICES used to describe plants or plant parts from which spices are obtained —**spicily** *adv.* —**spiciness** *n.*

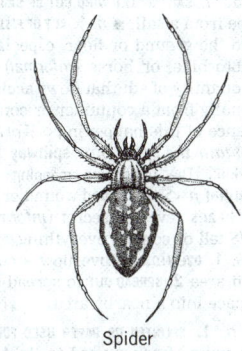

Spider

spider /spídər/ *n.* 1. BIOL EIGHT-LEGGED ANIMAL THAT SPINS WEBS a predatory animal with four pairs of legs and two or more abdominal organs (**spinnerets**) used for spinning webs that serve as nests and traps for prey. It is popularly thought to be an insect, although it is an arachnid. Order: Araneae. 2. US TRIVET a trivet for supporting a pan on a hearth 3. SET OF STRAPS FOR ATTACHING LOADS a bunch of elastic straps joined at a central point, usually with a hook at each free end, used especially for attaching a load to a rack on a vehicle 4. MECH ENG MECHANICAL DEVICE a mechanical device that has radiating arms, spokes, or other parts 5. NAUT FRAME SECURING REDUNDANT ROPES a circular frame at the base of a ship's mast, used to secure ropes when sails are not in use 6. COMPUT PROGRAM SEARCHING INTERNET FOR INFORMATION a computer program that searches the Internet for newly accessible information to be added to the index examined by a standard search tool (**search engine**) 7. CUE GAMES CUE REST a multi-position cue rest with wide legs designed to lift the cue tip over an intervening ball 8. TRANSP = spider phaeton 9. Aus ICE-CREAM SODA an ice-cream soda (*informal*) [Old English *spipra*, from *spinnan* 'to spin'. (see SPIN).]

WORD KEY: REGIONAL NOTE

Spider in the sense 'frying pan' is an old-fashioned New England and Southern term that formerly competed with Midland *skillet*. Today, *frying pan* and *fry pan* are usual throughout the United States.

---

spider beetle *n.* a name given to various wingless beetles, many of which are pests to stored food in households and warehouses. Family: Ptinidae.

spider crab *n.* a marine crab with a small triangular body and long slender legs. Family: Majidae.

spider flower *n.* 1. = cleome 2. AUSTRALIAN FLOWER RESEMBLING SPIDER a name given to various Australian flowering plants whose flowerheads resemble spiders. Genus: *Grevillea*.

spider hole *n.* a concealed sniper position (*informal*)

spider-hunting wasp *n.* a large black or metallic-blue solitary wasp that preys on spiders. Family: Pepsidae.

spider lily *n.* = crinum

spiderman /spídər man/ (*plural* **-men** /-men/) *n.* (*informal*) 1. ERECTOR OF BUILDING'S STEEL FRAME a construction worker who erects the steel frame of a building 2. STEEPLEJACK a steeplejack

spider mite *n.* any tiny web-spinning mite. Some spider mites are garden and crop pests. Family: Tetranychidae.

spider monkey *n.* a tree-dwelling monkey native to Central and South America. It has long slender limbs, a long prehensile tail, and a small head. Genus: *Ateles*.

spider phaeton, **spider** *n.* a high-bodied lightweight fast horse carriage with large wheels

spider plant *n.* a plant of the lily family widely grown as a houseplant for its long narrow variegated leaves, white flowers, and clusters of plantlets. Latin name: *Chlorophytum variegatum*.

spider wasp *n.* = spider-hunting wasp

spiderwort /spídər wurt/ *n.* a plant widely grown as a houseplant for its pink, blue, or violet flowers. Genus: *Tradescantia*. ◊ **tradescantia** [*Spider* from the resemblance of the stamens to a spider's legs]

spidery /spídəri/ *adj.* 1. THIN AND IRREGULAR with thin lines or constituent parts that form irregular angles 2. SPIDER-INFESTED infested with spiders 3. LIKE SPIDER like a spider in shape or movement

spiegeleisen /speég'l īz'n/, **spiegel** /speég'l/ *n.* pig iron containing high concentrations of manganese and carbon. It is added to steel in the late stages of production to adjust the final composition. [Mid-19thC. From German, from *Spiegel* 'mirror' (ultimately from Latin *speculum*; see SPECULUM) + *Eisen* 'iron'.]

spiel /shpeel, speel/ *n.* SPEECH DESIGNED TO CONVINCE an irritatingly long or predictably glib speech, e.g. a rambling apology or a prepared sales patter (*informal*) ■ *vi.* (**spiels, spieling, spieled**) GIVE SPIEL to deliver a spiel (*informal*) [Late 19thC. From German, 'play, game'.]

spiel off *vt.* to say sth very quickly or by rote ○ *spiel off a list of names*

Steven Spielberg

Spielberg /speél burg/, **Steven** (*b.* 1946) US film director and producer. His films include *E.T.* (1982) and the Academy Award-winning *Schindler's List* (1993).

spier /spí ər/ *n.* sb who spies or reconnoitres (*archaic*)

spiffing /spíffing/ *adj.* UK exceptionally good (*dated informal*) [Late 19thC. Origin unknown.]

spiff up (**spiffs up, spiffing up, spiffed up**) *vt.* US to improve sth by adding enhancing features (*informal*) [Late 19thC. Origin unknown.]

spiffy /spíffi/ (**-ier, -iest**) *adj.* US stylish or modern and attractive (*informal*) ○ *'a spiffy collection of supercomputers blinking away in a room of their own'* (Kathleen O'Gorman (*Detroit Free Press*; *1997*) [Mid-19thC. Origin unknown.] —**spiffily** *adv.* —**spiffiness** *n.*

spiflicate /spíffli kayt/ (**-cates, -cating, -cated**), **spifflicate** (**-cates, -cating, -cated**) *vt.* to destroy sth, or beat sb resoundingly (*dated or humorous slang*) [Mid-18thC. Nonsense word.] —**spiflication** /spíffli káysh'n/ *n.*

spigot /spíggət/ *n.* 1. US OUTDOOR TAP tap situated out of doors 2. INDOOR FAUCET an indoor faucet (*regional*) 3. TAP FITTED TO CASK a tap, usually wooden, that is fitted to a cask 4. PLUG FOR CASK HOLE a plug for the vent hole of a cask 5. PIPE END JOINING OTHER the end of a pipe that is joined by insertion into the enlarged end of another pipe [14thC. Origin uncertain: perhaps via Old French from Old Provençal *espiga* 'ear of grain', from Latin *spica* (see SPIKE[2]).]

spike[1] /spík/ *n.* 1. POINTED METAL OR WOODEN PIECE a sharply pointed piece of metal or wood, especially one of a number running along the top of a railing, fence, or wall 2. CONSTR LARGE NAIL a long heavy metal nail 3. CLOTHES METAL POINT ON RUNNING SHOE SOLE a pointed metal stud, part of a set attached to the sole of an athlete's shoe to give better grip (*often used in the plural*) ◊ **cleat** 4. SHARP POINT narrow sharp point 5. ZOOL UNBRANCHED

ANTLER OF DEER the antler of a young deer, straight and without branches **6.** ELEC VARIATION IN VOLTAGE an abrupt temporary surge in the voltage or current in an electrical circuit. The change may be caused by turning off appliances, a lightning strike, or power being restored after a power cut. **7.** IMAGE OF PEAK AND FALL a graphic representation of a sharp rise followed by a sharp fall, especially on a graph or as a reading on an instrument **8.** SPORTS DOWNWARD SMASH OF VOLLEYBALL a hard smash of a volleyball, hit close to the net and straight down into the opponent's court **9.** HOSTEL FOR PEOPLE WITHOUT HOMES a hostel that houses people who have no place to live (*dated slang*) **10.** = **hypodermic needle** (*slang*) **11.** METAL PART FOR GRIPPING AND CLIMBING a sharp pointed metal projection strapped to a boot as an aid in gripping and climbing sth **12.** METAL ROD FOR LOOSE PAPERS a pointed metal rod mounted on a base onto which loose papers are thrust, especially rejected news stories (*dated*) **13.** SUDDEN BRIEF INCREASE a sharp abrupt and brief rise in sth ■ **spikes** *npl.* SPORTS PAIR OF SHOES WITH METAL STUDS a pair of athletic shoes whose soles are equipped with pointed metal studs to give better traction ■ *v.* (**spikes, spiking, spiked**) **1.** *vt.* RENDER USELESS to make sth useless or ineffective (*informal*) **2.** *vt.* SNEAKILY ADD STH TO DRINK to put alcohol, a drug, or a poison into another person's drink surreptitiously **3.** *vt.* PRESS DISCARD POTENTIAL NEWS STORY to reject or decide not to use a news story (*slang*) **4.** *vt.* SPORTS SMASH VOLLEYBALL DOWNWARD to leap high close to the net and hit a volleyball straight down into an opponent's court **5.** *vt.* SPORTS CAUSE INJURY WITH SPIKES ON SHOE to injure another player or competitor with the spikes of an athletic shoe **6.** *vt.* ARMS DISABLE CANNON WITH SPIKE to render a cannon useless by driving a spike into its vent **7.** *vi.* RISE ABRUPTLY to rise sharply and briefly [13thC. Origin uncertain: ultimately from an Indo-European base meaning 'sharp point', which is also the ancestor of English *spit*[2], *spire*, and *spoke*.] —**spiked** *adj.*

spike[2] /spīk/ *n.* **1.** PLANTS FLOWER CLUSTER a long cluster of flowers attached directly to a stem with the newest flowers at the tip. ◊ **inflorescence, raceme 2.** AGRIC EAR OF CORN an ear of corn such as wheat or barley [14thC. From Latin *spica* 'ear of grain'. Ultimately from an Indo-European base meaning 'sharp point', which is also the ancestor of English *spine* and *spike*[1].]

spike heel *n.* a high pointed heel on a woman's shoe, or a shoe with such a heel

spike lavender *n.* a European mint related to lavender that has light purple flowers and yields an oil used in paints. Latin name: *Lavandula latifolia.*

spikelet /spíklət/ *n.* a small flower spike, especially any of the basic units of the flower cluster of a grass or sedge

spikenard /spík naard, spíkə naard/ (*plural* **-nards** *or* **-nard**) *n.* **1.** HIMALAYAN PLANT a perennial aromatic Himalayan plant of the valerian family that has pinkish purple flowers. Latin name: *Nardostachys jatamansi.* **2.** ANCIENT FRAGRANT OINTMENT a fragrant ointment derived from spikenard, used in ancient times **3.** PLANT WITH AROMATIC ROOT a North American plant of the ginseng family that has small whitish flowers, purplish berries, and aromatic roots. Latin name: *Aralia racemosa.* [14thC. From medieval Latin *spica nardi*, literally 'spike of nard' (translation of Greek *nardou stakhus*).]

spike-rush *n.* a perennial plant with narrow leaves and small flowers that grows in temperate regions. Genus: *Eleocharis.*

spiky /spíki/ (**-ier, -iest**) *adj.* **1.** WITH ONE OR SEVERAL SPIKES with one or more narrow sharp points **2.** IRRITABLE easily made angry (*informal*) —**spikily** *adv.* —**spikiness** *n.*

spile /spīl/ *n.* **1.** HEAVY SUPPORTING POST a heavy timber post driven into the ground as a foundation or support **2.** WOODEN PEG a wooden peg, especially used as a plug or stopper **3.** *US, Can* TREE-TAPPING SPOUT a tap for drawing sap from the sugar maple tree ■ *vt.* (**spiles, spiling, spiled**) **1.** SUPPORT WITH POST to provide or support sth with a heavy post driven into the ground **2.** *US, Can* TAP TREE FOR SAP to draw sap from a tree with a spout or spigot [Early 16thC. Via Dutch *spijl* from Middle Dutch or Middle Low German *spile* 'splinter, wooden pin' (see SPILL[2]).]

spill[1] /spil/ *v.* (**spills, spilling, spilt** /spilt/ *or* **spilled, spilt** *or* **spilled**) **1.** *vti.* FLOW FROM CONTAINER to flow or allow sth to flow from a container, especially accidentally and usually resulting in loss or waste **2.** *vi.* COME OUT OF CONFINED SPACE to come out from a building or other confined space in large numbers, often to the wrong place ○ *The fans spilled out onto the pitch* **3.** *vt.* DIVULGE to reveal or divulge sth, often unintentionally (*informal*) ○ *spilled the news* **4.** *vti.* FALL OFF STH to fall off, or make sb fall off, sth onto the ground or floor, especially from a horse, bicycle, or motorbike (*informal*) **5.** *vt.* SAILING LET WIND OUT OF SAIL to let the wind escape from a sail ■ *n.* **1.** ACT OF FALLING FROM STH a tumble to the ground or floor, especially from a bicycle, motorbike, or horse (*informal*) **2.** STH THAT RUNS OVER a quantity of sth that flows accidentally or unintentionally from a container or confined area, or an instance of this happening ○ *Workers fought hard to contain the spill.* **3.** = **spillway** [Old English *spillan* 'to kill'. The underlying meaning is 'to shed blood'.] —**spiller** *n.* ◇ **spill blood** wound or kill people ◇ **spill the beans** reveal a secret (*informal*) ◇ **spill your guts** *US* tell or confess everything

spill over *vi.* **1.** OVERFLOW to overflow a container or an enclosed area **2.** SPREAD OUT to spread out from a confined space into a nearby area

spill[2] /spil/ *n.* **1.** SPLINTER OR PAPER USED FOR LIGHTING a splinter or twist of paper used to light sth, e.g. a pipe or candle **2.** = **spile** *n.* 2 [14thC. From Middle Low German *spile* (source of English *spile*).]

spillage /spíllij/ *n.* **1.** SPILLING OF STH the act of spilling sth **2.** QUANTITY SPILLED a quantity of sth that has been spilled

Spillane /spi láyn/, **Mickey** (*b.* 1918) US writer. He specialized in crime fiction known for its raw energy and violence. Many of his stories featured the detective Mike Hammer. Real name **Frank Morrison Spillane**

spillikin /spílli kin/, **spilikin, spellican** /spéllikən/ *n.* JACKSTRAW any of the thin pieces used in the game of jackstraws (*dated*) ■ **spillikins, spilikins** *npl.* JACKSTRAWS the game of jackstraws (*dated*) (*takes a singular verb*) [Mid-18thC. Formed from SPILL[2], literally 'small spill'.]

spillover /spíl ōvər/ *n.* *US, Can* **1.** SPREAD any spread or expansion of sth **2.** EFFECT an indirect effect of sth

spillway /spíl way/ *n.* a channel for carrying away excess water, e.g. at a reservoir or dam

spilt past tense, past participle of **spill**

spin /spin/ *v.* (**spins, spinning, spun** /spun/ *or* **span, spun**) **1.** *vti.* ROTATE QUICKLY to turn or make sth turn round and round rapidly, as if on an axis ○ *He spun a coin.* ○ *watch the dancers spinning round the room* **2.** *vi.* FACE ABOUT QUICKLY to turn round rapidly to face in the opposite direction **3.** *vti.* TEXTILES CREATE YARN FROM RAW MATERIALS to twist raw fibres, e.g. of wool, silk, or cotton, so that they form a continuous yarn or thread **4.** *vti.* BIOL MAKE WEB OR COCOON to make a web or cocoon from filaments extruded from the body **5.** *vt.* INVENT LONG STORY to make up an extended story or a series of lies **6.** *vti.* SPORTS ROTATE RAPIDLY IN CHANGED DIRECTION to strike, throw, or kick sth in a way that makes it revolve and change direction when it hits sth, or to rotate and change direction in this way **7.** *vi.* ENG ROTATE FREELY to revolve or rotate rapidly around an axis ○ *Our wheels spun on the ice.* **8.** *vti.* AEROSP DIVE STEEPLY to go into a steep spiral dive, or make an aircraft do this **9.** *vi.* BECOME DIZZY to feel dazed, as if whirling round ○ *my head is spinning* **10.** *vi.* ANGLING FISH WITH RAPIDLY MOVING BAIT to fish with a rod, line, and reel, constantly drawing a revolving bait or lure through the water **11.** *vi.* DRIVE FAST AND WELL to drive smoothly and speedily **12.** *vt.* MUSIC PLAY RECORDING to play a piece of recorded music (*informal*) **13.** *vti.* DRY CLOTHES to remove most of the water from washed clothes in a washing machine by rotating them rapidly ■ *n.* **1.** ROTATION a quick rotating movement **2.** SPORTS ROTATION CAUSING CHANGED DIRECTION rotation given to a ball to make it change direction **3.** SPORTS ROTATION WHILE SKATING a stationary rotation during figure skating **4.** AEROSP SPIRALLING DIVE a steep spiral dive in an aircraft **5.** DIZZY STATE a state of mental disorientation or dizziness **6.** MARKETING INTERPRETATIVE POINT OF VIEW a viewpoint, bias, or interpretation, especially one that is presented to influence the public in a desired way (*informal*) ○ *There's no way the government can put a favourable spin on this disaster.* **7.** SHORT JOURNEY IN VEHICLE a brief journey taken for pleasure in a motor vehicle **8.** DRYING OPERATION IN WASHING MACHINE the rapid rotation of washed clothes in a washing machine to remove most of the moisture from them **9.** PHYS ANGULAR MOMENTUM the intrinsic angular momentum of an elementary particle or system of such particles independent of its motion **10.** PHYS QUANTUM PROPERTY OF ANGULAR MOMENTUM the quantum property or number of an elementary particle that is a measure of its intrinsic angular momentum and magnetic moment [Old English *spinnan*. Ultimately from an Indo-European base meaning 'to stretch, spin' that is also the ancestor of English *spider, spindle*, and *span*.] ◇ **in a flat spin** in a state of confusion or panic

spin off *v.* (*informal*) **1.** *vti.* COMM DERIVE STH INCIDENTALLY FROM STH ELSE to derive a new product, material, or service from sth that already exists, or be derived in this way **2.** *vt.* FIN DIVEST A COMPANY OF A SUBSIDIARY to divest a company of a subsidiary by distributing the subsidiary's shares to shareholders in the parent corporation

spin out *v.* **1.** *vt.* PROLONG STH to make an activity last longer than it needs to, usually by adding sth unnecessary **2.** *vt.* MAKE SUPPLIES LAST to make sth last longer than it ordinarily would, usually by careful management **3.** *vi.* LOSE CONTROL OF VEHICLE to skid out of control

spina bifida /spínə bíffidə, spínə bíffidə/ *n.* a congenital condition in which part of the spinal cord or meninges protrudes through a cleft in the spinal column, resulting in partial to total paralysis of the lower body. Spina bifida can sometimes be prevented by taking folic acid from the start of pregnancy. [From modern Latin, 'spine split in two']

spinach /spínich/ *n.* **1.** PLANT WITH EDIBLE LEAVES an annual plant with large, thick, dark-green, edible leaves. It is native to Asia and is widely cultivated in temperate regions. Latin name: *Spinacia oleracea.* **2.** EDIBLE LEAVES OF SPINACH PLANT the dark-green leaves of the spinach plant eaten cooked as a vegetable or raw in salads. They are rich in iron. [14thC. Via Old French *espinache* from, ultimately, Persian *aspānāk*.]

spinal /spín'l/ *adj.* **1.** RELATING TO SPINE on, in, near, or relating to a spine, especially a backbone **2.** LIKE SPINE resembling a spine ■ *n.* MED SPINAL ANAESTHETIC spinal anaesthesia or a spinal anaesthetic (*informal*) —**spinally** *adv.*

spinal anaesthesia *n.* **1.** ANAESTHESIA BY INJECTION INTO SPINE an anaesthesia of the lower half of the body achieved by injecting an anaesthetic into the fluid surrounding the spinal cord. ◊ **epidural 2.** LOSS OF SENSATION FROM SPINAL INJURY the loss of sensation in part of the body caused by injury to the spine

spinal canal *n.* a passage that runs through the opening in the middle of each vertebra of the spinal column and contains the spinal cord, the meninges, nerve roots, and blood vessels

spinal column *n.* the axis of the skeleton of a vertebrate animal, extending from the head and consisting of a series of interconnected vertebrae that enclose and protect the spinal cord

spinal cord *n.* a thick whitish cord of nerve tissue extending from the bottom of the brain through the spinal column and giving rise to pairs of spinal nerves that supply the body. The spinal cord and brain together form the central nervous system.

spin bowler, **spin-bowler** *n.* a bowler in cricket who specializes in bowling balls that spin

spindle /spínd'l/ *n.* **1.** TEXTILES SPECIALLY SHAPED ROD FOR SPINNING THREAD a handheld stick or rod with a notched end through which strands of natural fibres are drawn, then twisted into thread and wound round the rod **2.** TEXTILES THREAD-SPINNING ROD ON SPINNING WHEEL a device similar to the handheld spindle, attached to a spinning wheel **3.** MECHANICAL THREAD-SPINNING DEVICE a device on a spinning machine for spinning thread and winding it onto bobbins **4.** MECH ENG ROTATING ROD FOR DEVICE a rotating rod on a device such as a lathe, turntable, or door handle **5.** SPINDLE-SHAPED PIECE OF WOOD a long thin piece of wood such as a table leg or baluster that is shaped like a spindle **6.** BIOL SPINDLE-

SHAPED CELL STRUCTURE a spindle-shaped structure along which chromosomes are distributed and drawn apart during meiosis and mitosis **7.** SHIPPING **TOPPED METAL ROD USED AS WARNING** a metal rod surmounted by a ball or lantern and fixed to a rock or shoal, used as a warning to approaching vessels ■ *v.* **(-dles, -dling, -dled) 1.** *vt.* **MAKE WITH SPINDLE** to form or equip sth with a spindle **2.** *vi.* BOT **RAPIDLY GROW TALL AND SLENDER** to grow quickly into a high slender stalk or stem [Old English *spinel.* Ultimately from the same prehistoric Germanic base as *spin.*]

spindle-legged, **spindle-shanked** *adj.* with legs that are long and thin

spindle tree *n.* an evergreen tree or shrub of the staff tree family with small flowers and red fruits. Its hard wood was used in the past to make spindles. Genus: *Euonymus.*

spindly /spíndli/ **(-dlier, -dliest)**, **spindling** /spíndling/ *adj.* long or tall, thin, and weak-looking

spin doctor *n.* sb whose job is to present the actions of a person or organization in the best possible light, especially via the news media (*informal*)

spindrift /spín drift/ *n.* **1. SPRAY FROM WAVES** spray that blows from the surface of the sea **2. DRIVING SNOW OR SAND** driving snow or sand in a storm [Early 17thC. Alteration (probably influenced by SPIN) of SPOONDRIFT.]

spin-dry **(spin-dries, spin-drying, spin-dried)** *vt.* to remove most of the water from washed laundry by spinning it in a washing machine or a spin-dryer

spin-dryer, **spin-drier** *n.* a machine that forces most of the water out of wet laundry by spinning it around rapidly in a perforated drum

spine /spīn/ *n.* **1.** ANAT = **spinal column 2.** PRINTING **VERTICAL BACK OF BOOK COVER** the vertical back of a book's cover or a record's sleeve, usually printed with the title and the name of the author or performer **3.** ZOOL **HARD SHARP PROJECTION ON ANIMAL'S BODY** a sharp stiff projection on the body of an animal or a fish, e.g. the quill of a porcupine or the ray of a fish's fin **4.** BOT **SHARP POINT ON PLANT** a stiff sharp pointed plant part that is a modification of part of a leaf, e.g. in holly, or of an entire leaf, e.g. in cacti **5.** GEOG **RIDGE IN MOUNTAINS** a continuous ridge in a range of mountains or hills **6. FLEXIBLE PAY SCALE** a pay scale used by some professions and large organizations that takes into account individual circumstances such as age and location [14thC. Via Old French *espine* from Latin *spina* 'thorn'. Ultimately from an Indo-European base meaning 'sharp point' that is also the ancestor of English *spike*[1] and *spike*[2].]

spine-chiller *n.* sth, especially a book, film, or story, that is meant to frighten people —**spine-chilling** *adj.* —**spine-chillingly** *adv.*

spinel /spi nél/ *n.* a hard crystalline usually red mineral that consists of mixed oxides of magnesium, aluminium, and, in small amounts, iron or manganese. It is sometimes used as a gemstone. [Early 16thC. Via French *spinelle* from, ultimately, Latin *spina* (see SPINE); from its pointed crystals.]

spineless /spínləss/ *adj.* **1. WEAK AND COWARDLY** lacking in willpower, courage, or strength of character **2. WITHOUT SPINE** lacking a vertebral column —**spinelessly** *adv.* —**spinelessness** *n.*

WORD KEY: SYNONYMS

See Synonyms at ***cowardly.***

spinescent /spī néss'nt/ *adj.* having or growing a spine or spines [Late 18thC. From Latin *spinescent-*, the present participle stem of *spinescere* 'to become thorny', from *spina* (see SPINE).]

spinet /spi nét/ *n.* a small harpsichord, popular in the 18th century, that has the strings set at a slant to the keyboard [Mid-17thC. Via French *espinette* from Italian *spinetta*, of uncertain origin: probably formed from *spina* 'quill', from Latin (see SPINE); from the original use of quills resembling thorns to pluck the strings.]

spine-tingling *adj.* causing nervous fear or excitement —**spine-tinglingly** *adv.*

spiniferous /spī nífərəss/ *adj.* having, producing, or bearing spines or needles [Mid-17thC. Coined from Latin *spina* (see SPINE) + -FEROUS.]

spinifex /spínni feks/ (*plural* **-fexes** *or* **-fex**) *n.* **1. AUSTRALIAN GRASS WITH POINTED LEAVES** a perennial Australian grass that has sharp pointed leaves and grows in circular mounds in arid inland areas. Genera: *Plectrachne* and *Triodia.* **2. AUSTRALIAN PLANT GROWING ON SAND DUNES** an Australasian plant that has silvery foliage, globular seed heads, and grows on coastal sand dunes. Genus: *Spinifex.* [Early 19thC. From modern Latin, genus name, literally 'thorn-maker'.]

spinnaker /spínnəkər/ *n.* a large triangular sail set at the front of a racing yacht for running before the wind [Mid-19thC. Origin uncertain: perhaps an alteration of *Sphinx's acre*, from *Sphinx*, the name of the first yacht to carry such a sail.]

spinner /spínnər/ *n.* **1. SB OR STH THAT SPINS** a person, object, or device that spins **2.** ANGLING **FISHING LURE** an angling lure that spins in the water when the line is reeled in **3.** CRICKET = **spin bowler 4.** CRICKET **SPINNING CRICKET BALL** a cricket ball bowled with spin **5.** AIR **COVER FOR AIRCRAFT PROPELLER** a streamlined dome-shaped cap **(fairing)** that fits over the hub of the propeller of an aircraft

spinneret /spínnə ret/ *n.* **1.** BIOL **SILK-PRODUCING ORGAN** a tiny tubular structure, usually one of two pairs, that exudes the fluid produced by the abdominal glands of a silk-producing spider **2.** TEXTILES, INDUST **PERFORATED PLATE FOR MAKING SYNTHETIC FIBRE** a device for making filaments of synthetic fibre, consisting of a finely perforated plate through which viscous liquid is extruded

spinney /spínni/ (*plural* **-neys**) *n.* a small thicket or wood [Late 16thC. Via Old French *espinei* 'thorny hedge' from Latin *spinetum*, from *spina* (see SPINE).]

spinning frame *n.* a machine that draws out fibres, twists them into yarn or thread, and winds them onto spindles

spinning jenny /-jénni/ *n.* a spinning machine invented in the 18th century that was the first practical device to wind yarn onto more than one spindle. Because it allowed one person to spin several yarns at once the spinning jenny was a major invention of the Industrial Revolution.

spinning mule *n.* = **mule**[1] *n.* **5**

spinning top *n.* = **top**[2] *n.*

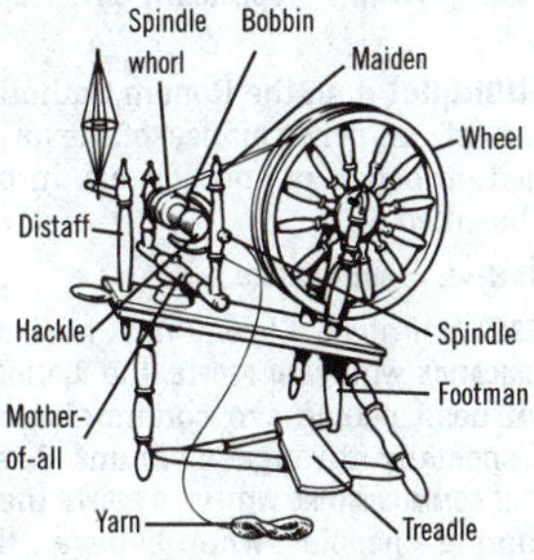
Spindle whorl
Bobbin
Maiden
Wheel
Distaff
Hackle
Spindle
Footman
Mother-of-all
Yarn
Treadle

Spinning wheel

spinning wheel *n.* a machine used at home for twisting fibres into yarn or thread and winding it onto a spindle by means of a large wheel driven by hand or a treadle

spinode /spī nōd/ *n.* MATH = **cusp** *n.* **6** [Mid-19thC. A blend of SPINE and NODE.]

spin-off *v.* **(spin-offs, spin-offing, spin-offed) PRODUCE AS BY-PRODUCT** to derive a new product, material, or service from sth that already exists, or be derived in this way ■ *n.* **1. DERIVATIVE OF STH** a product, material, or service deriving from sth that already exists **2.** BUSINESS **SUBSIDIARY DIVESTED BY DISTRIBUTING SHARES** a subsidiary of a company that is divested by means of a distribution of its shares of stock to shareholders of the parent corporation

spinout /spínnowt/, **spin-out** *n.* a skid, especially in a motor vehicle, that is out of control

Spinoza /spi nṓzə/, **Baruch** (1632–77) Dutch philosopher. Rejecting the Judaism of his cultural background, he developed a philosophy that combined rationalist and pantheistic elements. His major work was his *Ethics* (1674).

Spinozism /spi nṓzizəm/ *n.* the philosophical system developed by Baruch Spinoza, defining God as a unique impersonal deity with an infinite number of attributes and modes —**Spinozist** *n.*

spin stabilization *n.* a method of steadying the flight of a projectile such as a bullet, shell, or rocket by spinning it about its long axis

spinster /spínstər/ *n.* **1. OFFENSIVE TERM** an offensive term for a woman, especially one who is no longer young or is of advanced years who has never married a man (*dated offensive*) **2.** LAW **UNMARRIED WOMAN IN LEGAL DOCUMENTS** in some legal documents, a woman who has never married a man **3. WOMAN SPINNER OF YARN** in former times, a woman whose livelihood was spinning yarn [14thC. Formed from SPIN.]

spinthariscope /spin thárri skōp/ *n.* an instrument used to detect ionizing radiation such as alpha particles that produces flashes of light on a phosphorescent screen [Early 20thC. Coined from Greek *spintharis* 'spark' + -SCOPE.]

spinule /spī nyool/ *n.* BOT a tiny spine or thorn —**spinulose** /spínnyōō lōss/ *adj.*

spiny /spíni/ **(-ier, -iest)** *adj.* **1. WITH SPINES** with or covered with spines **2. THORNY** with thorns or prickles **3. LIKE SPINE** shaped like a spine —**spininess** *n.*

spiny anteater *n.* = **echidna**

spiny-headed worm *n.* a parasitic unsegmented worm that has a proboscis composed of rows of hooked spines, used for attachment to a vertebrate's intestinal wall. Phylum: Acanthocephala.

spiny lobster *n.* a large edible crustacean that is like a lobster but has a spiny shell and lacks enlarged pincers. Family: Palinuridae.

spiracle /spīrək'l/ *n.* **1.** GEOL **VENT IN LAVA FLOW** a small vent in a lava flow that allows the escape of built-up gases **2.** BIOL **BLOWHOLE** a blowhole (*technical*) **3.** INSECTS **SMALL APERTURE IN AN INSECT** a small paired aperture along the side of the thorax or abdomen of an insect or spider through which air enters and leaves **4.** ZOOL **SMALL GILL SLIT** a small gill slit or opening behind the eye area of some fishes, such as skates and rays [Early 17thC. Via Old French from Latin *spiraculum*, from *spirare* 'to breathe' (see SPIRIT).] —**spiracular** /spī rákyōōlər/ *adj.*

spiraea /spī rée ə/, **spirea** *n.* a shrub of the rose family that has dense clusters of small white or pink flowers. Genus: *Spiraea.* [Mid-17thC. Via modern Latin, genus name, from Greek *speiraia* 'privet' (source of English *aspirin*), from *speira* 'coil, twist'.]

spiral /spírəl/ *n.* **1.** GEOM **CONTINUOUS CIRCLING FLAT CURVE** a flat curve or series of curves that constantly increase or decrease in size in circling around a central point **2.** GEOM **HELIX** a helix **3. STH WITH CURVING CIRCULAR PATTERN** sth that has a helical or spiral form **4.** AIR **FLIGHT MANOEUVRE** a manoeuvre in which an aircraft makes a continuous banking turn as it descends **5.** ECON **CHANGE IN ECONOMIC CYCLE** a continuous widening increase or decrease of prices, wages, or interest rates ■ *adj.* **1. CONTINUOUSLY CIRCLING WITH FLAT CURVES** with a flat curve or series of curves that constantly increase or decrease in size in circling around a central point **2. HELICAL** helical in shape ■ *v.* **(-rals, -ralling, -ralled) 1.** *vti.* **SHAPE STH LIKE SPIRAL** to take on or make sth take on a spiral shape **2.** *vti.* **MOVE IN SPIRAL** to move or make sth move in a spiral **3.** *vi.* ECON **CHANGE INCREASINGLY** to increase or decrease with ever-increasing speed [Mid-16thC. From medieval Latin *spiralis* 'coiled', from Latin *spira* (see SPIRE[2]).]

spiral binding *n.* a binding, especially for a notebook or booklet, in which pages are fastened together with a spiral of wire or plastic that coils through a series of punched holes —**spiral-bound** *adj.*

spiral galaxy *n.* a galaxy consisting of an older central nucleus of stars from which extend two spiral arms of gas, dust, and newer stars

spiral staircase *n.* a staircase that winds round a central axis, often made of stone or iron

spirant /spírənt/ *n., adj.* PHON = **fricative** [Mid-19thC. From Latin *spirant-*, the present participle stem of *spirare* 'to breathe' (see SPIRIT).]

spire[1] /spīr/ *n.* **1.** ARCHIT **NARROW TAPERING STRUCTURE TOPPING STH** a tall narrow pointed structure on the top of a

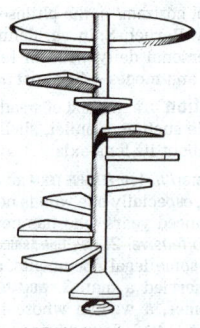

Spiral staircase

Lean spire on parapetted tower | Broach spire | Stone spire

Spire

roof, tower, or steeple **2.** BOT **POINTED SHOOT OF PLANT** a slender, upward-pointing part of a plant such as a blade of grass or the top of a tree **3.** UPWARD-FACING SPIKE the top part of sth narrow and pointed such as a mountain peak ■ *vi.* (**spires, spiring, spired**) RISE TO POINT to rise to a narrow point [Old English *spīr*. Ultimately from an Indo-European base meaning 'sharp point' that is also the ancestor of English *spit¹*, *spike¹*, and *spine*.]

spire² /spīr/ *n.* **1.** SPIRAL a spiral or coil **2.** CONVOLUTION OF SPIRAL a convolution of a spiral or coil [Late 16thC. Via Latin *spira* 'coil' from Greek *speira*.]

spirea *n.* = spiraea

spirillum /spī rílləm/ (*plural* **-la** /-lə/) *n.* a spiral-shaped or curved bacterium with a rigid body requiring oxygen for respiration. Genus: *Spirillum*. [Late 19thC. From modern Latin, genus name, literally 'little spiral', from Latin *spira* (see SPIRE²).] —**spirillar** *adj.*

spirit /spírrit/ *n.* **1.** LIFE FORCE OF INDIVIDUAL a vital force that characterizes a living being as being alive **2.** WILL sb's will, sense of self, or enthusiasm for living **3.** ENTHUSIASM an enthusiasm and energy for living **4.** DISPOSITION sb's personality or temperament **5.** ATTITUDE sb's attitude or state of mind **6.** GROUP LOYALTY a sense of enthusiasm and loyalty that sb feels through belonging to a group **7.** IMPORTANT INFLUENCE sb or sth that is a divine, inspiring, or animating influence **8.** REAL MEANING the intention behind sth such as a rule or decree, rather than its literal interpretation **9.** SHARED OUTLOOK a prevailing mood or outlook characteristic of a place or time **10.** PARANORMAL SUPERNATURAL ENTITY a supernatural being that does not have a physical body, e.g. a ghost, fairy, angel, or demon **11.** PERSON sb who shows a specific quality **12.** SOUL sb's soul, especially that of a dead person **13.** BEVERAGES ALCOHOLIC DRINK a strong alcoholic liquor made by distillation (*often used in the plural*) ○ *We drank a toast with a glass of the local spirit.* **14.** CHEM DISTILLED LIQUID any liquid produced by distillation, especially a distilled solution of ethanol and water (*often used in the plural*) **15.** CHEM ALCOHOLIC SOLUTION an essence or volatile substance in alcohol (*often used in the plural*) ■ **spirits** *npl.* MOOD a particular frame of mind or mood ■ *adj.* BURNING ALCOHOL using alcohol as fuel ○ *a spirit stove* ■ *vt.* (**-its, -iting, -ited**) REMOVE SECRETLY to take sb or sth away quickly in a secret or mysterious way ○ *spirited him out of the room* [13thC. Via Anglo-Norman from Latin *spiritus*, literally 'breath', from *spirare* 'to breathe', of unknown origin. The underlying idea is of the 'breath' of life.] ◇ **out of spirits** sad or dejected

─── WORD KEY: ORIGIN ───
The Latin verb *spirare*, from which *spirit* is derived, is also the source of English *aspire*, *conspire*, *expire*, *inspire*, *perspire*, *respire*, and *transpire*.

Spirit /spírrit/ *n.* in Christianity, the Holy Spirit

spirited /spírritid/ *adj.* **1.** LIVELY lively and vigorous **2.** ANIMATED with great animation **3.** BEHAVING IN SPECIFIED WAY behaving in a way that has a specified feeling, mood, or character (*usually used in combination*) ○ *low-spirited* —**spiritedly** *adv.* —**spiritedness** *n.*

spirit gum *n.* a glue made from a solution of gum in ether, used especially to stick false hair to an actor's skin

spiritism /spírritizəm/ *n.* = spiritualism *n.* 1 —**spiritist** *n.* —**spiritistic** /spírri tístik/ *adj.*

spirit lamp *n.* a lamp that uses methylated spirit as fuel

spiritless /spírritləss/ *adj.* lacking courage or energy —**spiritlessly** *adv.* —**spiritlessness** *n.*

spirit level *n.* a device laid on sth to check whether it is level. If it is, a bubble in a tube filled with alcohol or ether will appear centred between two marks. US term **level** *n.* 11

spiritoso /spírri tóssō/ *adv.* in a lively and vivacious way, or to be played in this way (*used as a musical direction*) [Early 18thC. From Italian, 'spirited'.] —**spiritoso** *adj.*

spiritous /spírritəss/ *adj.* spirituous (*archaic*)

spirits of ammonia *n.* = sal volatile

spirits of turpentine *n.* = turpentine *n.* 3

spirits of wine *n.* alcohol (*archaic*)

spiritual /spírrityoo əl/ *adj.* **1.** OF THE SOUL relating to the soul or spirit, usually in contrast to material things **2.** RELIG OF RELIGION relating to religious or sacred things rather than worldly things **3.** TEMPERAMENTALLY OR INTELLECTUALLY AKIN connected by an affinity of the mind, spirit, or temperament **4.** REFINED showing great refinement and concern with the higher things in life ■ *n.* **1.** MUSIC, CHR FOLK HYMN a religious song, especially one arising from African American culture **2.** THINGS OF THE SPIRIT matters concerning the spirit ○ *He was deeply concerned with anything to do with the spiritual.* —**spiritually** *adv.* —**spiritualness** *n.*

spiritual bouquet *n.* in the Roman Catholic Church, a promise of, or performance of, devotional acts, performed on behalf of another, e.g. in memory of sb who has died

spiritualise *vt.* = spiritualize

spiritualism /spírrityoo ə lizəm/ *n.* **1.** PARANORMAL BELIEF IN COMMUNICATION WITH DEAD PEOPLE the belief that the spirits of dead people can communicate with the living, especially through mediums **2.** PARANORMAL PRACTICES OF COMMUNICATING WITH DEAD PEOPLE the practices used among people who believe that communication occurs between the dead and the living **3.** RELIG BELIEFS EMPHASIZING SPIRITUAL MATTERS a system of belief that emphasizes the spiritual nature of existence **4.** PHILOS PHILOSOPHY EMPHASIZING SPIRITUAL NATURE OF REALITY the philosophical doctrine that all reality is spiritual, not material **5.** SPIRITUAL STATE the quality or state of being spiritual

spiritualist /spírrityoo list/ *n.* **1.** BELIEVER IN COMMUNICATION WITH THE DEAD sb who believes in communication between the living and the dead, especially with the help of a medium **2.** SB WITH SPIRITUAL INTERESTS sb who is interested in spiritual matters —**spiritualistic** /spírrityoo lístik/ *adj.*

spirituality /spírrityoo álləti/ (*plural* **-ties**) *n.* **1.** SPIRITUAL QUALITY the quality or condition of being spiritual **2.** CHR CHURCH PROPERTY OR REVENUE the property or revenue belonging to a church or church official (*often used in the plural*)

spiritualize /spírrityoo līz/ (**-izes, -izing, -ized**), **spiritualise** (**-ises, -ising, -ised**) *vt.* **1.** MAKE SPIRITUAL to give sth a spiritual content **2.** GIVE SPIRITUAL MEANING TO to attribute a spiritual meaning to sth —**spiritualization** *n.* —**spiritualizer** *n.*

spiritualty /spírrityoo álti/ (*plural* **-ties**) *n.* CHR = spirituality *n.* 2

spirituel /spírrityoo él/, **spirituelle** *adj.* showing a refined and graceful intellect [Late 17thC. SPIRITUEL from French (see SPIRITUAL), the masculine form; SPIRITUELLE from French, the feminine form.]

spirituous /spírrityoo əss/ *adj.* containing alcohol or made by distillation (*formal*) —**spirituousness** *n.*

spiritus asper /spírritəss áspər/ *n.* a rough breathing (*technical*) [From Latin, 'rough breath']

spiritus lenis /spírritəss léeniss/ *n.* a smooth breathing (*technical*) [From Latin, 'smooth breath']

spirit varnish *n.* a varnish consisting of a resin dissolved in alcohol

spirketting /spúrkiting/ *n.* a thick planking used to line and reinforce the decks and ports of a wooden ship [Mid-18thC. Formed from *spurket*, 'space between deck and side of a ship', of unknown origin.]

spiro- *prefix.* breathing, respiration ○ *spirograph* [From Latin *spirare* 'to breathe']

spirochaete /spírō keet/, **spirochete** *n.* a coiled rod-shaped bacterium. The causative agents of syphilis and relapsing fever are spirochaetes. Order: Spirochaetales. [Late 19thC. From modern Latin *Spirochaeta*, genus name, from Latin *spira* 'coil' + *chaeta* 'hair'.]

spirochaetosis /spírōki tóssiss/ (*plural* **-ses** /-seez/) *n.* a disease caused by a spirochaete

spirochete *n.* = spirochaete

spirograph /spírə graaf, -graf/ *n.* an instrument that makes a record of the depth and rapidity of sb's breathing [Late 19thC. Coined from Latin *spirare* 'to breathe' + -GRAPH.] —**spirographic** /spírə gráfik/ *adj.* —**spirography** /spí róggrəfi/ *n.*

spirogyra /spírə jírə/ *n.* a multicellular freshwater green alga. Genus: *Spirogyra*. [Late 19thC. From modern Latin, genus name, from Latin *spira* 'coil' + Greek *guros* 'round'.]

spiroid /spí royd/ *adj.* resembling a spiral in shape [Mid-19thC. Formed from Latin *spira* 'coil' (see SPIRE²).]

spirometer /spī rómmitər/ *n.* an instrument for measuring the capacity of the lungs [Mid-19thC. Coined from Latin *spirare* 'to breathe' + -METER.] —**spirometric** /spírə méttrik/ *adj.* —**spirometry** /spī rómmətri/ *n.*

spironolactone /spírōnō láktōn/ *n.* a steroid used with other drugs in treating hypertension. Formula: $C_{24}H_{32}O_4S$. [Mid-20thC. Coined from *spirolactone*, name of a steroid derivative (from Latin *spira* 'coil' + LACTONE) by inserting -ONE.]

spirt /spurt/ *vti.* SPURT to spurt (*dated*) ■ *n.* SPURT a spurt (*dated*) [Mid-16thC. Variant of SPURT.]

spiry¹ /spírī/ *adj.* shaped like a spiral (*literary*) [Late 17thC. Formed from SPIRE².]

spiry² *adj.* shaped like a spire (*literary*) [Early 17thC. Formed from SPIRE¹.]

spit¹ /spit/ *v.* (**spits, spitting, spat** *or* **spit** /spat/, **spat** *or* **spit**) **1.** *vi.* EJECT SALIVA to expel saliva forcefully from the mouth **2.** *vi.* EXPEL SALIVA TO SHOW CONTEMPT to show anger, contempt, or hatred by or as if by expelling saliva **3.** *vt.* EXPEL FROM YOUR MOUTH to eject sth harmful or unpleasant such as blood or food forcefully from the mouth **4.** *vti.* MAKE SOUND OF SPUTTERING to make sputtering sounds, such as those made when a fire shoots out sparks **5.** *vi.* HISS LIKE CAT to make a hissing explosive sound like an angry cat **6.** *vti.* RAIN OR SNOW LIGHTLY to rain lightly or in scattered drops or flakes **7.** *vt.* UTTER ANGRILY to utter sth sharply and angrily ■ *n.* **1.** SPITTLE FROM MOUTH saliva, especially when ejected from the mouth **2.** EXPULSION OF STH FROM THE MOUTH a forceful ejection of saliva or sth else from the mouth **3.** LIKENESS an exact likeness (*informal*) [Old English *spittan*. Ultimately from an Indo-European word that is also the ancestor of English *spew*, *spout*, and *sputum*.] ◇ **spit it out** to say sth at once, especially sth that has been withheld (*informal*) (*usually used as a command*) ◇ **spit chips (tacks)** ANZ to be very angry (*slang*) ◇ **spit up** *vt.* to regurgitate or cough up sth

spit² /spit/ *n.* **1.** COOK THIN ROD FOR ROASTING STH a thin rod on which sth is impaled for roasting over a fire **2.** GEOG LAND PROJECTING FROM SHORE an elongated point of land or shoal projecting into a body of water ■ *vt.* (**spits, spitting, spitted**) IMPALE to impale sb or sth on a roasting spit or on any long sharp pointed thing [Old English *spitu*. Ultimately from an Indo-European base meaning 'sharp point' that is also the ancestor of English *spike*[1], *spire*[1], and *spine*.]

spital /spítt'l/ *n.* a hospital, especially for people with leprosy or others in need (*archaic*) [14thC. Shortening of HOSPITAL.]

spit and polish *n.* meticulous care in presenting a neat appearance, especially in the armed forces (*informal*)

spitchcock /spích kok/ *n.* an eel split and then grilled or fried. ◊ **spatchcock** [Early 17thC. Origin unknown.]

spit curl *n.* *US* = **kiss curl** [From its being fixed in place with saliva]

spite /spīt/ *n.* **PETTY ILL WILL** a malicious, usually small-minded desire to harm or humiliate sb ■ *vt.* **(spites, spiting, spited) ACT MALICIOUSLY TOWARDS** to harm, hinder, or humiliate sb out of small-minded malice [13thC. Shortening of DESPITE.] ◇ **in spite of** notwithstanding, or without taking account of sth

spiteful /spītf'l/ *adj.* full of or showing petty maliciousness —**spitefully** *adv.* —**spitefulness** *n.*

spitfire /spít fīr/ *n.* sb who is very quick-tempered [Late 17thC. The underlying meaning is 'spitting out sparks'.]

Spitfire *n.* a British fighter plane used by the Royal Air Force during World War II

spitter /spíttər/ *n.* sb or sth that spits [14thC. Formed from SPIT[1].]

spitting distance *n.* a short enough distance to seem within reach (*informal*)

spitting image *n.* an exact likeness of sb (*informal*) [Alteration of *spit and image*, from SPIT[1] in the meaning 'an exact likeness']

spitting snake *n.* = **ringhals** [From its spitting of venom]

spittle /spítt'l/ *n.* **1. SALIVA EJECTED FROM MOUTH** saliva, especially that has been or is about to be expelled from the mouth **2. STH RESEMBLING FROTHY SALIVA** sth that looks like frothy saliva, especially the secretions from spittlebugs deposited on plants **(cuckoo spit)** [15thC. Alteration (under the influence of SPIT[1]), of earlier *spattle*, from Old English *spātl* 'spittle', from the same prehistoric Germanic base as *spit*[1].]

spittlebug /spítt'l bug/ *n.* = **froghopper**

spittoon /spi to͞on/ *n.* a container for people to spit into. Spittoons, which used to be common in public places like bars, were especially used by men who chewed tobacco. [Mid-19thC. Formed from SPIT[1].]

spitz /spits/ *n.* a breed of dog with a dense heavy coat, erect pointed ears, and a tightly curled tail. Pomeranians and Samoyeds are spitzes. [Mid-19thC. Shortening of German *Spitzhund*, literally 'pointed dog'.]

spiv /spiv/ *n.* *UK* an offensive term used to refer to a man whose way of dressing is considered ostentatiously smart and whose integrity is doubted (*slang insult*) [Mid-20thC. Origin uncertain.] —**spivvy** *adj.*

splanchnic /splángknik/ *adj.* relating to the intestines (*technical*) [Late 17thC. From modern Latin *splanchnicus*, from, ultimately, Greek *splagkhna* 'entrails'.]

splash /splash/ *v.* **(splashes, splashing, splashed) 1.** *vti.* **SPATTER LIQUID** to make a liquid scatter or fall in drops or larger amounts ○ *The children were splashing in the pool.* ○ *She splashed water over the side of the bath.* **2.** *vi.* **BE SPATTERED ABOUT** to scatter or fly up in drops or larger amounts ○ *The waves splashed against the rocks.* **3.** *vt.* **SPATTER DROPS OF LIQUID ON** to wet or dirty sth by spattering it with liquid ○ *She splashed her blouse with the hot tea.* **4.** *vti.* **MOVE WHILE SPLASHING** to make your way through water or another liquid, scattering it about ○ *They splashed through the puddles.* **5.** *vt.* **ADD CONTRASTS TO** to apply contrasting colour or light to sth **6.** *vt.* **DISPLAY PROMINENTLY** to display sth such as a news headline, story, or photograph conspicuously (*usually passive*) ○ *The story was splashed across the front page.* ■ *n.* **1. NOISE OF WATER SCATTERING** an act or sound of splashing **2. STH SPLASHED** sth that is splashed ○ *The bathroom floor was covered with splashes.* **3. MARK CAUSED BY SPLASH** a mark or stain made by sth splashing or being splashed ○ *The backs of her legs were covered with splashes.* **4. PATCH OF COLOUR** an area of contrasting colour or light, often irregular ○ *The dark forest was dappled with splashes of moonlight.* **5. TINY AMOUNT OF LIQUID** a very small quantity of one liquid added to another (*informal*) ○ *She added a splash of milk to her tea.* **6. PROMINENT DISPLAY** a conspicuous display, e.g. a prominent news headline, story, or photograph [Early 18thC. Origin uncertain: probably a variant of PLASH.] ◇ **make a splash** to attract a great deal of attention or publicity

splash down *vi.* AEROSP to land in the sea after a flight in space

splashback /splásh bak/ *n.* a sheet of sth such as glass or plastic attached to a wall behind a basin or cooker to protect the wall from splashes

splashboard /splásh bawrd/ *n.* **1.** NAUT **PROTECTIVE SCREEN ON BOAT** a screen for preventing water from splashing into a boat **2.** AUTOMOT **PROTECTION AGAINST SPLASHES ON MOTOR VEHICLE** a protective guard that prevents mud or water from splashing the upper part of a motor vehicle and the people travelling in it

splashdown /splásh down/ *n.* the landing of a spacecraft or missile in the sea after a flight

splashguard /splásh gaard/ *n.* *US* AUTOMOT = **mud flap**

splashy /spláshi/ **(-ier, -iest)** *adj.* **1. COLOURFUL** with lots of bright colours **2. ATTRACTING NOTICE** attracting a lot of attention (*informal*) **3. MAKING SPLASHES** with great splashing of liquid —**splashily** *adv.* —**splashiness** *n.*

splat /splat/ *n.* **WET SMACKING SOUND** a sound made when sth soft and wet hits sth hard ■ *adv.* **WITH SMACK** with a wet smacking sound ■ *interj.* **IMITATING IMPACT** used to imitate the sound made when sth soft and wet hits sth hard [Late 19thC. An imitation of the sound.]

splatter /spláttər/ *vti.* **(-ters, -tering, -tered) TO SPATTER** to spatter or splash sth, or to be spattered or splashed ■ *n.* **A SPATTER** a spatter or splash [Late 18thC. Origin uncertain: perhaps a blend of SPATTER and SPLASH.]

splatterpunk /spláttər pungk/ *n.* a form of narrative such as a story, film, or comic strip that contains a lot of gory violence (*slang*)

splay /splay/ *vti.* **(splays, splaying, splayed) 1. SPREAD WIDE AND OUTWARDS** to spread out sth such as the fingers or toes **2. TURN OUT AWKWARDLY** to turn sth awkwardly outwards **3. MAKE SIDES OF STH SLANT** to give sth or have obliquely sloping edges, e.g. an opening in a wall that is bigger on one side than the other ■ *adj.* **1. SPREAD FLAT AND OUTWARDS** sloping, turning, or spread flatly and outwards **2. TURNED AWKWARDLY OUTWARDS** turned awkwardly outwards ■ *n.* **SLANT TO SIDES OF OPENING** an oblique slope given to the edges of sth such as an opening in a wall, so that the opening is bigger on one side than the other [14thC. Shortening of DISPLAY.]

Splayd /splayd/ *tdmk.* *Aus* a trademark for a utensil shaped like a spoon with tines at the end like a fork and a sharp edge on one side like a knife

splayfoot /spláy fo͝ot/ (*plural* **-feet** /-feet/) *n.* **1. FLAT, OUTWARDLY TURNED FOOT** a foot with fallen arches, often with widely spread toes, or the condition that causes this. ◊ **flatfoot 2. OUTSPREAD FOOT** a foot that is excessively turned outwards, or the condition causing it —**splayfooted** /spláy fo͝otid/ *adj.* —**splayfootedly** /-fo͝otidli/ *adv.*

spleen /spleen/ *n.* **1.** PHYSIOL **ORGAN IN ABDOMEN** a vascular ductless organ in the left upper abdomen of humans and other vertebrates that helps to destroy old red blood cells, form lymphocytes, and store blood **2. BAD TEMPER** anger or bad temper [13thC. Via Latin from Greek *splēn*.] —**spleenish** *adj.* —**spleeny** *adj.*

spleenful /spleénf'l/ *adj.* = **splenetic** *adj.* 1 —**spleenfully** *adv.*

spleenwort /spleén wurt/ *n.* an evergreen fern of temperate and tropical regions that has feathery fronds. Genus: *Asplenium*. [Late 16thC. From the former belief that it cured illnesses of the spleen.]

splendid /spléndid/ *adj.* **1. MAGNIFICENT** impressive because of quality or size **2. RADIANT** reflecting light brilliantly **3. EXCELLENT** excellent or highly enjoyable **4. ACCLAIMED** very well known and acclaimed [Early 17thC. From Latin *splendidus*, from *splendere* 'to shine' (source also of English *splendour* and *resplendent*).] —**splendidness** *n.*

splendidly /spléndidli/ *adv.* in a fine or admirable way ○ *The restoration work is coming along splendidly.*

splendiferous /splen díffərəss/ *adj.* magnificent and wonderful (*humorous*) [Mid-19thC. Formed from SPLENDOUR.] —**splendiferously** *adv.* —**splendiferousness** *n.*

splendor *n.* US = **splendour**

splendour /spléndər/ *n.* **1. MAGNIFICENCE** the condition of being magnificent, impressive, or brilliant **2. STH SPLENDID** sth that is magnificent, impressive, or brilliant ○ *the splendours of Ancient Greece* [15thC. Directly and via Old French from Latin *splendor*, from *splendere* 'to shine' (source also of English *splendid*).] —**splendorous** *adj.*

splenectomy /spli néktəmi/ (*plural* **-mies**) *n.* surgical removal of the spleen [Mid-19thC. Coined from Greek *splēn* 'spleen' + -ECTOMY.]

splenetic /spli néttik/ *adj.* **1. BAD-TEMPERED** extremely bad-tempered or spiteful **2. RELATING TO SPLEEN** relating to the spleen (*dated*) ■ *n.* **SB BAD-TEMPERED** sb who is bad-tempered or spiteful [Mid-16thC. From Latin *spleneticus*, from *splen* 'spleen'.] —**splenetically** *adv.*

splenic /splénnik, spleé-/ *adj.* relating to, in, or near the spleen [Early 17thC. Formed from Greek *splēn* 'spleen'.]

splenius /spleéni əss/ (*plural* **-i**) *n.* either of two muscles on each side of the neck that reach from the base of the skull to the upper back and rotate and extend the head and neck [Mid-18thC. Via modern Latin from Greek *splēnion* 'bandage, compress'.] —**splenial** *adj.*

splenomegaly /spleénō méggəli/ *n.* abnormal enlargement of the spleen [Early 20thC. Coined from Greek *splēn* 'spleen' + the Greek stem *megal-* 'great'.]

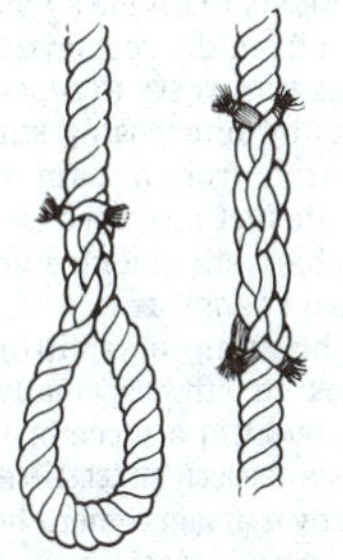

Splice

splice /splīss/ *vt.* **(splices, splicing, spliced) 1.** SAILING, CONSTR **INTERWEAVE STRANDS OF TWO ROPES** to join two pieces of rope or wire by weaving the strands of each into the other **2.** CINEMA, RECORDING **JOIN ENDS OF FILM OR TAPE** to join the ends of two pieces of film or magnetic tape, e.g. in editing **3.** WOODWORK **JOIN PIECES OF WOOD** to join two pieces of wood together by overlapping them and bolting or otherwise attaching them **4.** GENETICS **JOIN GENETIC MATERIAL** to join together or insert pieces of genetic material when altering the genetic structure of sth or when forming a new combination **5. MARRY TWO PEOPLE** to join a couple in marriage (*slang*) (*often passive*) ■ *n.* **1. CONNECTION** a join made by connecting two pieces of sth **2. JUNCTION OF SPLICING** the junction where sth has been spliced **3.** CRICKET **END OF BAT HANDLE** the wedge-shaped end of the handle of a cricket bat where it fits into the striking part [Early 16thC. From Middle Dutch *splissen*. Ultimately from a prehistoric Germanic word meaning 'to split' that is also the ancestor of English *split*, *splint*, and *splinter*.] —**splicer** *n.*

spliff /splif/ *n.* a marijuana cigarette (*slang*) [Mid-20thC. Origin unknown.]

spline /splīn/ *n.* **1. FLAT KEY FORMED IN SHAFT** a flat, relatively narrow key that is integral to a shaft, produced by milling a longitudinal groove **2.** = **slat** *n.* 1 **3. CONNECTING STRIP** a thin narrow piece of wood, metal, or plastic that fits onto or into the edges of tiles or boards and connects them together [Mid-18thC. Origin uncertain: perhaps related to SPLINTER.]

splint /splint/ *n.* **1.** MED **DEVICE TO IMMOBILIZE BROKEN BONE** a strip of rigid material used to keep a broken bone or other injured body part from moving **2.** CRAFT **STRIP OF WOOD USED IN BASKETRY** a thin strip of wood used to weave sth such as a basket or chair seat **3.** = **splinter** *n.* 1 **4. WOOD SLIVER FOR LIGHTING FIRES** a sliver of wood used to carry a flame, e.g. to light a fire or a candle **5.** MIL, HIST **METAL PLATE IN ARMOUR** any of the overlapping metal plates or strips used in making a suit of armour **6.** VET **ENLARGEMENT OF HORSE'S LEG BONE** a condition that occurs in young horses, consisting of painful bony outgrowths in or near the splint bones on the inner sides of the legs ■ *vt.* **(splints, splinting, splinted) 1. IMMOBILIZE INJURED PART** to immobilize a broken bone or injured body part with a rigid support **2. STRENGTHEN** to give support or added strength to sth [13thC. From Middle Low German or Middle Dutch *splinte*.]

splint bone *n.* either of a pair of thin bones on either side of the cannon bone in the lower legs of horses and other hoofed animals

splinter /splíntər/ *n.* **1. THIN SHARP FRAGMENT** a small thin sharp piece of wood, metal, stone, glass, or other material broken from a larger piece **2. BOMB FRAGMENT** a metal fragment thrown from an exploding bomb or shell **3.** = **splinter group** ■ *vti.* **(-ters, -tering, -tered) 1. BREAK INTO SHARP FRAGMENTS** to break sth or be broken into thin sharp fragments **2. DIVIDE GROUP** to split a larger group into factions or independent groups, or to be split in this way [14thC. From Middle Dutch. Ultimately from the same base as *splint*.] —**splintery** *adj.*

splinter group *n.* a group formed by individuals who have dissociated themselves from a larger organization, usually because of disagreement

split /split/ *v.* **(splits, splitting, split) 1.** *vti.* **DIVIDE LENGTHWISE** to divide sth or be divided lengthwise into two or more parts, usually by force **2.** *vti.* **BURST** to burst apart or rip sth apart **3.** *vt.* **AFFECT VIOLENTLY** to disturb or disrupt sth with a violently jarring presence **4.** *vti.* **SEPARATE INTO PARTS** to divide a whole into parts, or to be separated from the rest or from a whole **5.** *vt.* **SEPARATE BY ADDING STH BETWEEN** to separate a whole into its components by interposing sth **6.** *vti.* **DIVIDE INTO FACTIONS** to separate from a main group, or make a group divide into factions, because of disagreement **7.** *vt.* **SHARE** to share sth among a group **8.** *vti.* **DEPART** to leave a place (*slang*) ■ *n.* **1. ACT OF BREAKING APART** the action of breaking or splitting sth **2. CRACK** a crack or break in sth, especially one that runs lengthways **3. FRAGMENT** a piece broken off from the whole **4. DIVISION THROUGH DISAGREEMENT** a breach in a group, caused by a disagreement between members **5. PORTION** a share, especially a share of money (*informal*) **6.** FOOD **ICE CREAM DESSERT** a dessert of fruit with ice cream and a topping of flavoured syrup, nuts, and whipped cream **7.** CRAFT **STRIP OF WOOD FOR BASKETRY** a strip of flexible wood, usually willow, used for basketry **8. LAYER OF ANIMAL HIDE** a single thickness of animal hide other than the outermost layer **9.** INDUST **LEATHER** leather made from a single inner layer of animal hide **10.** SPORTS **ARRANGEMENT OF STANDING BOWLING PINS** in ten-pin bowling, a batch of remaining pins in which the pins are clustered into two groups with a large gap in between ■ **splits** *npl.* **GYMNASTIC ACTION** a gymnastic action in which the legs are fully extended in opposite directions until the body is sitting on or very close to the floor (*takes a singular verb*) ○ *do the splits* ■ *adj.* **1. BROKEN** broken, divided, or separated into parts **2. DISUNITED** divided because of disagreement [Late 16thC. From Dutch *splitten*.] —**splitter** *n.*

split on *vt.* to inform on sb (*informal*)

split up *v.* **1.** *vi.* **END RELATIONSHIP** to end a relationship or a marriage **2.** *vti.* **SEND PEOPLE DIFFERENT WAYS** to go off in a different direction or send individuals off in different directions **3.** *vt.* **DIVIDE INTO PARTS** to divide sth into separate parts

Split /split/ chief city and port of Dalmatia, southern Croatia, on the Adriatic Sea. Population: 189,388 (1991).

split brain *n.* a brain that has the corpus callosum surgically severed or missing from birth, so that the two hemispheres of the brain are not connected

split decision *n.* BOXING in boxing, a win awarded by a majority of judges, rather than by a unanimous decision

split end *n.* **1.** HAIR **HAIR STRAND WITH DAMAGED END** a hair with a damaged end that has separated into strands **2.** AMERICAN FOOTBALL **OFFENSIVE PLAYER** a player at the end of an offensive line that lines up some distance outside the rest of the line

split infinitive *n.* an infinitive in which the 'to' and the verb are separated by another word, as in the phrase 'to seriously think'

WORD KEY: USAGE

What is wrong with a split infinitive? The ***split infinitive*** is a stylistic issue that has been rationalized into a grammatical one. There is no grammatical basis for rejecting split infinitives, since to regard an infinitive with *to* as inseparable has no support in the typical structures of English grammar, which freely separates particles, auxiliary verbs, and other devices from the words to which they belong (e.g. *I have never been to Paris* separates *have* from *been*. The issue is one of style and not of grammar. If splitting an infinitive produces awkwardness, it is better to avoid it, but if the split is natural and supports or clarifies the meaning, there can be no objection to it. The adverb belongs closely with the verb in cases such as *They agreed to flatly forbid such actions* and *They were plotting to secretly copy the files* but can be moved to a more comfortable position in other cases such as *We expect to further modernize our services* (revise as: *... to modernize our services further*) and *I would like to briefly mention a few points* (revise to: *I would like briefly to ...*) It is usually advisable to avoid splitting the infinitive with an adverbial phrase (e.g. *They were trying to in some way improve the situation*). In some cases, however, even an adverbial phrase cannot be separated from its verb: *Prices are likely to more than double* (in which *more than double* is effectively regarded as a set verb phrase). The guiding principle, in sum, is that the split infinitive has a long history of use and is not a cardinal sin; it is acceptable when the rhythm and meaning of the sentence call for it or when its use is that of a set verb phrase. It should be avoided (either by repositioning or by rephrasing) when it seems stilted or awkward, or especially in formal writing where its inclusion may draw criticism.

split-level *adj.* **1. WITH FLOOR ON DIFFERENT LEVELS** used to describe the floor of a room that is on different levels with steps between them **2. WITH SEPARATE OVEN AND HOB** having the oven and hob in separate units (*refers to a cooker*) —**split-level** *n.*

split-new *adj. Scotland* brand-new (*informal*) [*Split* in the sense 'strip of wood', the underlying idea being 'as new as freshly cut wood']

split pea *n.* a pea that has been shelled, dried, and split in half, used especially in soup

split personality *n.* **1.** PSYCHIAT = **multiple personality** **2. TENDENCY TO MOOD SWINGS** a tendency towards erratic mood or temperament changes

split pin *n.* a two-pronged metal pin that holds things together when its prongs are passed through holes on both parts and then bent back

split ring *n.* a small steel ring with two spiral turns, often used as a key ring or as a means of fastening two parts together

split screen *n.* a cinema or television screen frame divided into more than one image

split second *n.* an extremely brief amount of time

split-second *adj.* carried out instantly, or depending on instant skill or judgment

split shift *n.* a single work period that is divided into two or more sessions of work, separated by an interval that is longer than a normal rest or meal break

split stitch *n.* a back stitch in which each new stitch is made through the centre of the previous one

split tin *n.* a long narrow loaf of bread with a shallow lengthwise split along the top [From its being baked in a tin]

splitting /splítting/ *adj.* **PAINFUL** causing intense pain ○ *a splitting headache* ■ *n.* PSYCHIAT **FREUDIAN DEFENCE MECHANISM** a Freudian defence mechanism in which sb separates sth unpleasant such as an idea into parts that are each less threatening than the whole

split-up *n.* an instance or the act of separating, e.g. the ending of a relationship between two people

splodge /sploj/ *n.* **LARGE SPOT** a large irregular spot, stain, or discoloration. US term **splotch** ■ *vt.* **(splodges, splodging, splodged) MARK WITH SPLODGES** to mark or dirty sth with splodges. US term **splotch** [Early 17thC. Origin uncertain: perhaps a blend of SPOT, BLOT, and BOTCH.]

splotch /sploch/ *n.* = **splodge** ■ *vt.* **(splotches, splotching, splotched)** = **splodge** [Early 17thC. Origin uncertain: perhaps a blend of SPOT, BLOT, and BOTCH.]

splurge /splurj/ *v.* **(splurges, splurging, splurged) 1.** *vi.* **INDULGE** to indulge in sth extravagant or expensive (*informal*) **2.** *vt.* **SPEND MONEY EXTRAVAGANTLY** to spend money in an extravagant or wasteful way ■ *n.* (*informal*) **1. BOUT OF EXTRAVAGANCE** a period of indulgence or extravagant spending **2. GRAND DISPLAY** a showy display of sth such as wealth [Early 19thC. Origin uncertain: perhaps a blend of SPLASH and SURGE.]

splutter /splúttər/ *v.* **(-ters, -tering, -tered) 1.** *vi.* **MAKE SPITTING SOUND** to make a spitting or choking sound **2.** *vti.* **SAY INCOHERENTLY** to say sth in a choking incoherent manner **3.** *vti.* **SPIT STH OUT** to scatter saliva, liquid, or particles of food from the mouth ■ *n.* **1. INCOHERENT SPEECH** a burst of choking incoherent speech **2. CHOKING NOISE** a spitting choking noise [Late 17thC. Origin uncertain: perhaps an alteration of SPUTTER.] —**splutterer** *n.* —**spluttering** *n., adj.*

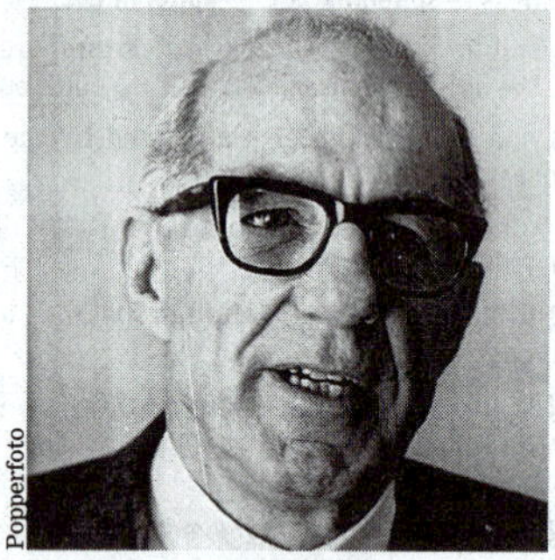

Popperfoto

Dr Spock

Spock /spok/, **Dr** (1903–98) US paediatrician and political activist. His *Book of Baby and Child Care*, first published in 1946, which went through numerous editions and sold tens of millions of copies worldwide, popularized a new, permissive philosophy of parenting. He was a vociferous public opponent of the Vietnam War (1959–75) and of nuclear weapons. Full name **Benjamin McLane Spock**

Spode /spōd/ *tdmk.* a trademark for a high-quality porcelain or bone china

spodumene /spóddyŏŏ meen/ *n.* a greyish-white, greenish, or lilac mineral, found as large translucent crystals, that consists of a silicate of lithium and aluminium and is the chief source of lithium. The green variety, **(hiddenite)**, and the lilac variety, **(kunzite)**, are used as gemstones. [Early 19thC. Via French from Greek *spodoumenos*, literally 'burnt to ashes', from *spodos* 'ashes'; from its greyish colour.]

spoil /spoyl/ *v.* **(spoils, spoiling, spoiled** *or* **spoilt, spoiled** *or* **spoilt** /spoylt/) **1.** *vt.* **IMPAIR** to damage or ruin sth in such a way that a quality such as worth, beauty, or usefulness, is diminished **2.** *vt.* **HARM BY OVERINDULGENCE** to harm a person's character, especially a child's, by repeated overindulgence **3.** *vt.* **TREAT INDULGENTLY** to treat sb with indulgence out of a desire to please ○ *The hotel staff really spoiled us.* **4.** *vt.* **CAUSE TO SEEM UNSATISFACTORY** to be so good by comparison with sth else that what is usually offered no longer seems satisfactory ○ *All that sun spoils you for holidays at home.* **5.** *vi.* **BECOME ROTTEN** to become unfit to eat because of decay **6.** *vt.* **TAKE PROPERTY FROM** to take sb's property by force or violence (*archaic*) ■ *n.* **1. WASTE FROM EXCAVATION** waste material removed from an excavation **2. STEALING** the act of plundering (*archaic*) ■ **spoils** *npl.* **1. PROPERTY SEIZED BY VICTOR** valuables or property seized by the victor in a conflict **2. STH GAINED THROUGH EFFORT** sth valuable or desirable gained through effort, opportunism, or other means [13thC. Via Old French *espoillier* 'to plunder, despoil' from Latin *spoliare*, from *spolium* 'booty'.] ◇ **be spoiling for sth** be eager for sth, usually a conflict or confrontation

spoilage /spóylij/ *n.* **1. DECAYING** the process of decaying or becoming damaged, or such a condition **2. WASTE** waste arising from decay or damage **3. AMOUNT WASTED**

the amount of sth wasted because of decay or damage

spoiled /spoyld/, **spoilt** /spoylt/ *adj.* **1. RUINED** severely or irrevocably impaired, e.g. by damage or decay **2. OVERINDULGED** wilful or selfish because of having been overindulged

spoiled priest *n. Ireland* sb who studied for the priesthood but withdrew or was dismissed

spoiler /spóylər/ *n.* **1. AIR AEROFOIL FOR CONTROLLING LIFT AND DRAG** a narrow hinged aerofoil attached lengthwise to the upper surface of an aircraft wing. It is raised to increase drag and reduce lift during banking and descent. **2. AUTOMOT CAR AIR DEFLECTOR** a fixed air deflector on the rear of a car, designed to keep it on the ground during high speeds **3. SB WHO CAN RUIN ANOTHER'S WIN** a candidate for office, or a competitor in sport, who cannot win but can or does prevent an opponent from doing so **4. PUBL RIVAL PUBLICATION** a newspaper or magazine whose release is calculated to coincide with that of a rival publication in order to divert interest in it and reduce its sales **5. SB WHO WRECKS STH** sb or sth that ruins or wrecks sth **6. ROBBER** sb or sth that robs or pillages

spoilsport /spóyl spawrt/ *n.* sb whose conduct spoils the plans or pleasure of others

spoils system *n.* the practice of a winning political party giving government jobs and public appointments to its supporters

spoilt *adj.* = **spoiled** ■ *v.* past tense, past participle of **spoil**

Spoke

spoke[1] /spōk/ *n.* **1. SUPPORTING ROD FOR WHEEL RIM** any of the bars or rods that extend from the hub of a wheel to support or brace the rim **2. KNOB ON SHIP'S WHEEL** any of the knobs that stick out from the rim of a ship's wheel **3. RUNG** a rung of a ladder [Old English *spāca.* Ultimately from an Indo-European base meaning 'pointed object' that is also the ancestor of English *spike* and *spine.*]
◇ **put a spoke in sb's wheel** to hinder or thwart sb's plans

spoke[2] *v.* past tense of **speak**

spoken /spṓkən/ *v.* past participle of **speak** ■ *adj.* **1. VOCAL** expressed with the voice ○ *the spoken word* **2. SPEAKING IN PARTICULAR WAY** speaking in a stated way, e.g. with a particular voice quality, accent, command of the language, or attitude (*used in combination*) ○ *well-spoken* ◇ **be spoken for 1.** to be already owned or reserved by sb **2.** to be already married, engaged or romantically committed to sb (*dated*)

──── **WORD KEY: SYNONYMS** ────
See Synonyms at *verbal.*

spokeshave /spṓk shayv/ *n.* a small carpenter's plane consisting of a blade with a handle at each end, once used to shape spokes, now used to shape and smooth convex and concave wooden surfaces

spokesman /spṓksmən/ (*plural* **-men** /-mən/) *n.* sb authorized to speak on behalf of another person or other people [Mid-16thC. Formed from SPOKE[2].]

spokesperson /spṓks purss'n/ (*plural* **-people** /-peep'l/) *n.* a spokesman or spokeswoman [Late 20thC. Modelled on SPOKESMAN.]

spokeswoman /spṓks wŏomən/ *n.* a woman authorized to speak on behalf of another person or other people [Mid-17thC. Modelled on SPOKESMAN.]

spoliation /spṓli áysh'n/ *n.* **1. PLUNDERING** the seizing of things by force **2. SEIZURE OF SHIPS** the seizure or plundering of neutral ships at sea by a belligerent power in time of war **3. ALTERATION OF DOCUMENT** the alteration or destruction of a document so as to make it invalid or unusable as evidence **4. LAW TAKING OF POSITION'S PRIVILEGES** the taking of the income or privileges that go with a religious position by sb who is not entitled to them [15thC. From the Latin stem *spoliation-*, from *spoliare* (see SPOIL).] —**spoliatory** /spṓli ətəri/ *adj.*

spondaic /spon dáy ik/ *adj.* **POETRY** relating to spondees or written in spondees [Late 16thC. From French *spondaïque*, from, ultimately, Greek *spondeios* (see SPONDEE).]

spondee /spón dee/ *n.* **POETRY** a unit of rhythm in poetry (**foot**), consisting of two long or stressed syllables [14thC. Via French from, ultimately, Greek *spondeios*, literally 'libational', from *spondē* 'libation'; so called because the spondee was often used in songs accompanying libations.]

spondylitis /spóndi lítiss/ *n.* inflammation of the vertebrae and the attached discs and ligaments [Mid-19thC. Formed from Latin *spondylus* 'vertebra', from Greek *spondulos*, of unknown origin.]

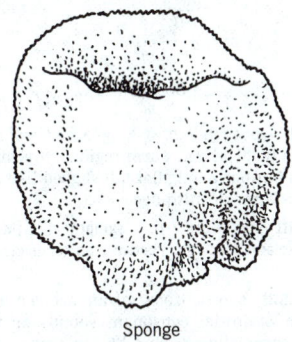

Sponge

sponge /spunj/ *n.* **1. MARINE BIOL MARINE ANIMAL** a chiefly marine invertebrate animal with a porous fibrous skeleton composed of calcium carbonate, silica, and spongin. Sponges live in colonies and attach themselves to underwater objects. Phylum: Porifera. **2. HOUSEHOLD NATURAL MATERIAL USED FOR BATHING** a lightweight porous absorbent piece of the skeleton of some sponges, used for bathing or cleaning **3. HOUSEHOLD SYNTHETIC MATERIAL USED FOR BATHING** a piece of cellulose or synthetic material resembling a true sponge, used for bathing and cleaning **4. MED GAUZE PAD** a folded gauze pad used in surgery or medicine to absorb discharges, to dress wounds, or to apply medications **5.** = **sponger** *n.* 1 (*informal*) **6. HEAVY DRINKER** sb who habitually drinks a lot of alcohol (*informal*) **7. COOK MASS OF RISING YEAST DOUGH** a small amount of yeast dough that is allowed to rise before being kneaded with the rest of the batch **8. FOOD** = **sponge cake 9. PUDDING** a light steamed or baked pudding made from a basic cake mixture. = **sponge pudding 10. ACT OF CLEANING** the act of rubbing or bathing sb or sth with a wet sponge or cloth **11. METALL POROUS METAL** a porous metal capable of absorbing large quantities of gas, obtained by reduction without melting of a metal compound, or by electrolysis ■ *v.* (**sponges, sponging, sponged**) **1.** *vt.* **CLEAN** to wipe sth or clean sb with a wet sponge or cloth **2.** *vt.* **REMOVE** to remove or destroy sth by rubbing **3.** *vt.* **ABSORB** to absorb liquids with a sponge or with the efficiency of a sponge **4.** *vt.* **GET BY IMPOSING** to get sth by imposing on the generosity of others **5.** *vi.* **LIVE OFF OTHERS** to live at the expense of others, repeatedly imposing on them and making no effort to live independently **6.** *vi.* **COLLECT SPONGES** to dive for sponges, especially under the sea [Pre-12thC. Via Latin *spongia* from, ultimately, Greek *sphoggos*. From a pre-Indo-European word that was probably also the source of Latin *fungus.*]

sponge bag *n.* a small waterproof bag used to carry toiletries when travelling

sponge bath *n. US* = **bed bath**

sponge cake *n.* a light open-textured cake made of flour, eggs, sugar, flavouring, and traditionally no fat

sponge mushroom *n.* = **morel**

sponge pudding *n.* a light steamed or baked pudding made from a basic cake mixture

sponger /spúnjər/ *n.* **1. SB WHO LIVES OFF OTHERS** sb who lives off others, habitually imposing on their generosity and making no effort to live independently (*informal*) **2. COLLECTOR OF SPONGES** sb who dives for sponges, or a ship used for gathering sponges

spongiform encephalopathy /spúnji fawrm en keffə lóppəthi/ *n.* any of various brain diseases in humans and animals in which areas of the brain slowly degenerate and take on a spongy appearance

spongin /spúnjin/ *n.* a protein that forms the skeletal framework of sponges [Mid-19thC. Coined from SPONGE + -IN.]

spongioblast /-blast/ *n.* any of the embryonic cells in the brain and spinal cord that develop into supporting connective tissue (**glia**) [Early 20thC. Coined from Latin *spongia* 'sponge' + -BLAST.] —**spongioblastic** /spúnji ō blástik/ *adj.*

spongy /spúnji/ (**-ier**, **-iest**) *adj.* **1. OPEN-TEXTURED** with a light open texture full of holes or cavities **2. ABSORBENT** absorbent and elastic **3. SOFT AND WET** soft and full of water

spongy mesophyll, **spongy parenchyma** *n.* **BOT** a spongy tissue layer of irregularly shaped chlorophyll-bearing cells interspersed with air spaces, sandwiched between the upper and lower epidermal layers of a leaf

sponson /spónss'n/ *n.* **1. NAVY SHIP'S GUN PLATFORM** a gun platform sticking out from the side of a ship. A gun can be mounted in such a way that it can fire both fore and aft. **2. NAUT AIR CHAMBER IN CANOE** an air chamber that runs along each side of a canoe to help keep it afloat **3. AIR STABILIZER FOR SEAPLANE** an air-filled structure or small wing projecting from the lower hull of a seaplane to stabilize it in water **4. ARMY, HIST GUN TURRET** a gun turret mounted on the side of an early tank **5. NAUT SUPPORT FOR PADDLE WHEEL** a structural support for a paddle wheel on a ship [Mid-19thC. Origin uncertain: perhaps an alteration of EXPANSION.]

sponsor /spónssər/ *n.* **1. FIN CONTRIBUTOR TO EVENT'S FUNDING** a person or organization that provides or pledges money to help fund an event, especially an event run by another person or group **2. FIN CONTRIBUTOR TO CHARITY** a person or organization that donates money to a charity on the basis of the performance of a participant in an organized fundraising event **3. POL LEGISLATOR** a legislator who proposes and supports the passage of a bill **4. SUPPORTER** a country, organization, or group that supports or organizes an activity, or one who vouches for the acceptability of another **5. CHR SB ANSWERING AT CHILD'S BAPTISM** sb who answers for a child at baptism and assumes responsibility for the child's religious upbringing (*formal*) **6. US SB RESPONSIBLE FOR ANOTHER** sb who undertakes responsibility for another, especially during a period of education, apprenticeship, or probation **7. BROADCAST RADIO OR TELEVISION ADVERTISER** an individual or a business that pays for radio or television programming by buying advertising time ■ *vt.* (**-sors, -soring, -sored**) **ACT AS SPONSOR TO** to act as a sponsor to sb or sth [Mid-17thC. From late Latin, 'baptismal sponsor', from Latin *spons-*, the past participle stem of *spondere* 'to pledge'.] —**sponsorial** /spon sáwri əl/ *adj.* —**sponsorship** /spónssər ship/ *n.*

──── **WORD KEY: SYNONYMS** ────
See Synonyms at *backer.*

──── **WORD KEY: ORIGIN** ────
The Latin verb *spondere*, from which *sponsor* is derived, is also the source of English *despondent*, *respond*, *riposte*, and *spouse.*

spontaneity /spóntə née əti, -náy-/ *n.* **1. UNCONSTRAINED BEHAVIOUR** behaviour that is natural and unconstrained and is the result of impulse, not planning **2. GENERATION FROM WITHIN** the generating or provoking of activity from within, rather than as a result of external influences

spontaneous /spon táyni əss/ *adj.* **1. ARISING FROM INTERNAL CAUSE** resulting from internal or natural processes, with no apparent external influence **2. ARISING FROM**

IMPULSE arising from natural impulse or inclination, rather than from planning or in response to suggestions from others **3. UNRESTRAINED** naturally unrestrained or uninhibited **4. BOT GROWING UNCULTIVATED** growing without cultivation [Mid-17thC. Formed from late Latin *spontaneus* 'of one's own accord', from Latin *sponte*, of uncertain origin.] —**spontaneously** *adv.* —**spontaneousness** *n.*

spontaneous abortion *n.* = **miscarriage** *n.* 1

spontaneous combustion *n.* the ignition of a combustible material such as hay as a result of internal heat generation usually caused by rapid oxidation

spontaneous generation *n.* BIOL = **abiogenesis**

spontaneous ignition *n.* = spontaneous combustion

spontaneous recovery *n.* PSYCHOL the return of an extinguished conditioned response without reinforcement

spontoon /spon toon/ *n.* a type of halberd used by some infantry officers in the 18th century [Mid-18thC. Via obsolete French *sponton* from Italian *spontone* from, ultimately, *punto* 'point', from Latin *punctum* (see POINT).]

spoof /spoof/ *n.* **1. HOAX** a good-humoured hoax **2. AMUSING SATIRE** a light amusing satire **3.** *Aus* **SEMEN** semen (*slang taboo*) ■ *v.* (**spoofs, spoofing, spoofed**) **1.** *vt.* **DECEIVE** to fool or deceive sb **2.** *vt.* **SATIRIZE** to satirize sb or sth good-naturedly **3.** *vi.* *Aus* **EJACULATE** to ejaculate semen (*slang taboo*) [Late 19thC. Coined by the English comedian Arthur Roberts 1852–1933 as the name for a game of his creation involving hoaxing.] —**spoofer** *n.*

spook /spook/ *n.* (*informal*) **1. GHOST** a ghost or a ghostly figure **2.** *US* **SPY** a spy ■ *v.* (**spooks, spooking, spooked**) **1.** *vt.* **HAUNT** to haunt sb as a ghost **2.** *vt.* *US* **STARTLE SB** to startle or make an animal or person feel uneasy **3.** *vi.* *US* **BE FRIGHTENED** to feel frightened or uneasy [Early 19thC. From Dutch, of unknown origin.]

spooky /spooki/ (**-ier, -iest**) *adj.* **1. FRIGHTENINGLY SUGGESTIVE OF SUPERNATURAL INVOLVEMENT** frightening or unnerving because suggesting the presence of supernatural forces (*informal*) **2. AMAZING** strange or amazing, often because it seems that supernatural influences may have been at work (*informal*) **3.** *US* **EASILY FRIGHTENED** easily frightened or startled —**spookily** *adv.* —**spookiness** *n.*

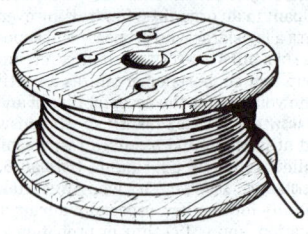

Spool

spool /spool/ *n.* **1. CYLINDER ON WHICH STH IS WOUND** a cylinder around which thread, tape, or film is wound. It has a central hole and a rim at each end. **2. AMOUNT ON SPOOL** the amount of sth wound on a spool ■ *v.* (**spools, spooling, spooled**) **1.** *vti.* **WIND STH ON SPOOL** to wind sth on a spool or on sth similar to a spool such as a reel or bobbin **2.** *vi.* COMPUT **TRANSFER DATA TO STORE** to transfer data for printing into a memory store so that it can be printed later without slowing down the computer's operations [14thC. Directly and via Old French *espole* from Middle Dutch *spoele*.]

spooling /spooling/ *n.* COMPUT the temporary storage of data in the memory of a computer to compensate for the slower operation of a peripheral device such as a printer while processing continues

spoon /spoon/ *n.* **1. HOUSEHOLD EATING UTENSIL** a utensil used for eating or preparing food, consisting of a shallow oval bowl attached to a handle **2. ANGLING SHINY FISHING LURE** a bright oval metal fishing lure with a hook attached **3. GOLF GOLF CLUB** a number three wood, used for hitting long high drives from the fairway (*dated*) **4. DRUGS QUANTITY OF DRUG** a quantity of

hard drugs, especially a two-gram measure of heroin (*slang*) ■ *v.* (**spoons, spooning, spooned**) **1.** *vt.* **EAT FOOD USING SPOON** to eat, scoop, or carry sth with a spoon or with the action of sb using a spoon **2.** *vt.* **HOLLOW OUT** to dig or scrape a hollow in sth, or dig sth out to leave a hollow **3.** *vt.* SPORTS **HIT BALL UP** to hit a ball upwards with a scooping action, often as a result of an imperfect stroke **4.** *vi.* ANGLING **USE SPOON FISHING LURE** to fish with a spoon lure **5.** *vi.* **BE AMOROUS** to indulge in amorous behaviour such as kissing and cuddling (*dated slang*) [Old English *spōn* 'wood chip'. Ultimately from an Indo-European word meaning 'flat piece of wood' that is also the ancestor of English *spade* and *spatula*.]

Spoonbill

spoonbill /spoon bil/ *n.* a long-legged wading bird found in tropical and warm regions. It is similar to the ibis but has a long flat bill shaped like a spoon. Family: Threskiornithidae.

spoondrift /spoon drift/ *n.* = **spindrift** *n.* 2 [Mid-18thC. From obsolete *spoon* 'to run before a sea' (of unknown origin) + DRIFT.]

spoonerism /spoonərizəm/ *n.* an accidental transposition of initial consonant sounds or parts of words, especially one that has an amusing result, e.g. 'half-warmed fish' for 'half-formed wish' [Early 20thC. Named after the British educationalist Reverend William *Spooner* (1844–1930), who was known for such transpositions.]

spooney /spooni/ *adj.* = **spoony**

spoon-feed (**spoon-feeds, spoon-feeding, spoon-fed**) *vt.* **1. FEED WITH SPOON** to feed sb, especially a child or hospital patient, using a spoon **2. GIVE EVERYTHING NEEDED TO** to cater to sb completely, requiring him or her to make no effort at all **3. DEPRIVE OF INDEPENDENT THOUGHT** to provide sb with ideas, opinions, and judgements to an extent that independent thought becomes unnecessary or impossible for that person

spoonful /spoonfool/ *n.* the amount that can be held in a spoon, usually a teaspoon

spoony /spooni/, **spooney** *adj.* (**-ier, -iest**) SENTIMENTAL foolishly sentimental or amorous (*dated*) ■ *n.* (*plural* **-ies**) SB SENTIMENTAL sb foolishly sentimental or amorous (*archaic*)

spoor /spoor, spawr/ *n.* ANIMAL TRAIL the visible trail of an animal, especially an animal that is being hunted for sport ■ *vti.* (**spoors, spooring, spoored**) TRACK ANIMAL to track an animal by following its trail [Early 19thC. Via Afrikaans from Middle Dutch. Ultimately from an Indo-European word meaning 'ankle' that is also the ancestor of English *spur* and *spurn*.] —**spoorer** *n.*

Sporades /spórrədiz/ group of Greek islands in the Aegean Sea, north of the island of Euboea

sporadic /spə ráddik/ *adj.* **1. OCCURRING IRREGULARLY** occurring occasionally at intervals that have no apparent pattern **2.** MED **NOT EPIDEMIC** used to describe a disease that appears in scattered or isolated instances or locations [Late 17thC. Via medieval Latin from, ultimately, Greek *sporad-*, the stem of *sporas* 'scattered'.] —**sporadically** *adv.*

— WORD KEY: SYNONYMS —
See Synonyms at *periodic*.

sporangium /spə ránji əm/ (*plural* **-a** /-ə/) *n.* a hollow spore-producing organ in fungi, ferns, and some other plants [Early 19thC. From modern Latin, literally 'spore-vessel', from Greek *spora* (see SPORE) + *aggeion* 'small vessel' (see ANGIO-).]

spore /spawr/ *n.* BIOL **1. ASEXUAL REPRODUCTIVE STRUCTURE** a small, usually one-celled reproductive structure produced by seedless plants, algae, fungi, and some protozoans that is capable of developing into a new individual **2. DORMANT BACTERIUM** a dormant resistant form taken by some bacteria in response to adverse conditions ■ *vi.* (**spores, sporing, spored**) **PRODUCE SPORES** to produce or release spores [Mid-19thC. Via modern Latin from Greek *spora* 'sowing, seed'. Ultimately from an Indo-European base meaning 'to scatter' that is also the ancestor of English *sprawl, sprout, sperm*, and *diaspora*.]

spore case *n.* = **sporangium**

sporiferous /spə ríffərəss/ *adj.* producing or releasing spores

sporocarp /spórrō kaarp, spáwrō-/ *n.* BOT **1. SPORE-PRODUCING ORGAN OF ALGAE** the spore-producing organ in red algae and some fungi and slime moulds **2. SPORE-PRODUCING ORGAN OF FERN** the hard round spore-producing organ of some aquatic ferns

sporocyte /spórrō sīt, spáwrō-/ *n.* a cell from which spores are produced

sporogenesis /spórrō jénnəssiss, spáwrō jénnəssiss/ *n.* **1. SPORE PRODUCTION** the production or formation of spores **2. REPRODUCTION BY SPORES** reproduction by means of spores —**sporogenous** /spə rójjənəss/ *adj.*

sporogony /spo róggəni, spə róggəni/ *n.* the process in sporozoans by which sporozoites are formed from multiple fission of an encysted zygote

sporophore /spórrə fawr, spáwrə-/ *n.* an organ in fungi that produces spores

sporophyll /spórrə fil, spáwrə-/, **sporophyl** *n.* a leaf or modified leaf that bears spore-producing organs, e.g. the fertile leaf of a fern or club moss

sporophyte /spórrə fīt, spáwrə-/ *n.* in plants that alternate between sexual and asexual phases, a plant in its asexual spore-producing phase —**sporophytic** /spórrə fíttik, spáwrə-/ *adj.*

sporoplasm /spórrə plazəm, spáwrə plazəm/ *n.* an infective mass of protoplasm contained inside a spore that is injected into a host cell by various parasitic organisms

sporopollenin /spórrə póllənin, spáwrə-/ *n.* a polymer that forms the outer layer of pollen and some spores such as bacterial spores [Mid-20thC. Coined from SPORO- + POLLEN + -IN.]

sporotrichosis /spórrə trī kóssiss, spáwrə-/ *n.* a serious infectious disease caused by a fungus *Sporothrix schenckii* that enters the body from soil or wood via a skin wound. It typically produces skin ulcers and nodules on the lymph nodes. [Early 20thC. Formed from modern Latin *Sporotrichum*, former genus name of the fungus, from *spora* (see SPORE) + Greek *thrix* 'hair'.]

sporozoan /spórrə zṓ ən, spáwrə-/ *n.* a parasitic single-celled organism (**protozoan**) that has alternating sexual and asexual generations and reproduces by means of spores. The malaria parasites are sporozoans. Class: Sporozoa. [Late 19thC. Formed from modern Latin *Sporozoa*, class name, from Greek *spora* (see SPORE) + *zōion* 'animal'.]

sporozoite /spáwrə zṓ īt/ *n.* any of the small infectious motile individuals produced in sporozoans by sporogony usually within a host [Late 19thC. Formed from modern Latin *Sporozoa*, class name (see SPOROZOAN).]

sporran /spórrən/ *n.* a leather pouch, sometimes decorated with fur, worn hanging from a belt in front of the kilt in men's traditional Scottish Highland dress [Mid-18thC. Via Scottish Gaelic from Middle Irish *sporán*, of uncertain origin: probably from late Latin *bursa* (see BURSA).]

sport /spawrt/ *n.* **1. COMPETITIVE PHYSICAL ACTIVITY** an individual or group competitive activity involving physical exertion or skill, governed by rules, and sometimes engaged in professionally **2. COMPETITIVE PHYSICAL ACTIVITIES AS A GROUP** competitive physical activities considered collectively as a group **3. PASTIME** an active pastime participated in for pleasure or exercise **4. SB CHEERFUL** sb who remains cheerful when losing or in an unpleasant situation (*informal*) **5. SB WHO PLAYS FAIR** sb noted for abiding by the rules in a game or for generally honourable behaviour (*informal*) **6. GOOD COMPANION** sb who is generally good-natured, easy-going, and good company (*informal*)

7. JOKING good-natured joking (*formal*) ○ *a harmless prank done in sport* 8. DERISION contemptuous mockery (*formal*) 9. OBJECT OF RIDICULE an object of ridicule or mockery (*formal*) 10. SB OR STH MANIPULATED BY OTHERS sb or sth manipulated by external forces (*literary*) 11. GAMBLER a gambler, especially sb who gambles on sporting events (*informal*) 12. *ANZ, US* FORM OF ADDRESS a casual form of address, especially used between men or boys (*informal*) 13. BIOL MUTATED ORGANISM a plant or animal that deviates markedly from its parent stock or type, usually as a result of mutation, especially mutation of somatic tissue 14. BIOL UNUSUAL CHARACTER a mutant character of a mutated organism 15. AMOROUS BEHAVIOUR amorous behaviour such as kissing or cuddling (*archaic*) ■ *v.* (**sports, sporting, sported**) 1. *vt.* WEAR to wear or display sth, usually proudly or with the intention of impressing others (*informal*) 2. *vi.* PLAY HAPPILY to romp and play happily (*formal*) 3. *vi.* ENJOY YOURSELF to enjoy yourself, especially by taking part in outdoor physical activity (*formal*) 4. *vi.* MAKE JOKES to joke or trifle with sb (*formal*) 5. *vi.* BIOL MUTATE to produce or undergo a mutation 6. *vi.* RIDICULE to ridicule sb or sth (*archaic*) [14thC. Shortening of *disport* 'diversion, amusement', from Old French *desport*, from *desporter* (see DISPORT).] —**sporter** *n.* —**sportful** *adj.* —**sportfully** *adv.* —**sportfulness** *n.*

sporting /spáwrting/ *adj.* 1. USED IN SPORTS relating to or used in sports activities ○ *sporting dogs* 2. FAIR in keeping with the principles of fair competition, respect for other competitors, and personal integrity 3. GAMBLING OF GAMBLING relating to gambling, or taking an interest in gambling 4. RISKING willing to take a risk

sporting chance *n.* an even or good chance of succeeding

sportive /spáwrtiv/ *adj.* 1. PLAYFUL playful and frolicsome 2. JOKING done as a joke 3. FOND OF SPORT regularly taking part in sport 4. SEXUALLY ACTIVE frequently indulging in sexual activity or tending to enjoy it (*archaic*) —**sportively** *adv.* —**sportiveness** *n.*

sports /spawrts/ *adj.* 1. FOR SPORTING ACTIVITIES relating to or used in physical or recreational activities ○ *sports equipment* 2. CLOTHES FOR INFORMAL WEAR designed for informal or outdoor wear ○ *sports shirt* ■ *npl.* SPORTS MEETING a meeting for athletics or other sports activities, especially for the pupils of a school ○ *It's the school sports next week.*

sports car *n.* a small car with a low centre of gravity designed for fast acceleration and for handling at high speeds

sportscast /spáwrts kaast/ *n.* a radio or television broadcast of a sports event or of sports news [Mid-20thC. Blend of SPORTS and BROADCAST.] —**sportscaster** *n.*

sports drink *n.* a soft drink that is intended to quench thirst faster than water and replenish the sugar and minerals lost from the body during physical exercise

sports jacket *n.* a man's jacket similar in style to a suit jacket but worn on more informal occasions with trousers of a different material or colour

sportsman /spáwrtsmən/ (*plural* **-men** /-mən/) *n.* 1. MAN ENGAGING IN SPORT a man who participates in and gets pleasure from sport 2. SB FAIR AND HONOURABLE sb who behaves according to principles of fairness, and who observes rules, shows respect for others, and accepts defeat graciously —**sportsmanlike** *adj.*

sportsmanship /spáwrtsmən ship/ *n.* 1. FAIR CONDUCT conduct considered fitting for a sportsperson, including observance of the rules of fair play, respect for others, and graciousness in losing 2. TAKING PART IN SPORTS participation in sports

sports medicine *n.* the branch of medicine concerned with preventing and treating injuries resulting from sport

sportsperson /spáwrts purss'n/ *n.* a sportsman or sportswoman

sports supplement *n.* a dietary supplement used by athletes to enhance bursts of high performance [Late 20thC]

sportswear /spáwrts wair/ *n.* clothes worn for sport or outdoor leisure activities

sportswoman /spáwrts wòomən/ (*plural* **-en** /-wimin/) *n.* 1. WOMAN ENGAGING IN SPORT a woman who participates in and gets pleasure from sport 2. FAIR AND HONOURABLE WOMAN a woman who behaves according to principles of fairness, and who observes rules, shows respect for others, and accepts defeat graciously

sportswriter /spáwrts rītər/ *n.* sb who writes about sport, especially for a newspaper or magazine

sport ute *n.* *US* a sport-utility vehicle (*informal*)

sport-utility (*plural* **sport-utilities**), **sport-utility vehicle** *n.* *US* a four-wheel-drive vehicle used for everyday driving but suitable for rough terrain

sporty /spáwrti/ (**-ier, -iest**) *adj.* 1. FOR SPORT designed or appropriate for sport or leisure activities 2. ENTHUSIASTIC ABOUT SPORT enthusiastic about sports or outdoor activities and regularly taking part in them 3. CARS SIMILAR TO SPORTS CAR with features resembling the style or performance of a sports car

sporulate /spórryòo layt/ (**-lates, -lating, -lated**) *vi.* to produce spores [Late 19thC. Formed from modern Latin *sporula*, literally 'small spore', from *spora* (see SPORE).] —**sporulation** /spórryòo láysh'n/ *n.*

spot /spot/ *n.* 1. SMALL ROUND AREA a small defined area that is different in colour, material, or texture from the surrounding area, especially one that is more or less circular 2. STAIN a dirty mark or stain 3. MARK ON SKIN a mark or blemish on the skin, especially a pimple 4. CHARACTER BLEMISH a blemish on sb's character or reputation 5. PARTICULAR PLACE a particular place or location ○ *find a weak spot in their defences* 6. GEOGRAPHICAL LOCATION a geographical location or area ○ *a local beauty spot* 7. SMALL AMOUNT a small amount, e.g. of liquid to drink or of work to do ○ *What about a spot of lunch?* 8. BROADCAST ANNOUNCEMENT OR ADVERTISEMENT a brief announcement or advertisement inserted between regular radio or television programmes 9. ARTS PERFORMER'S TIME SLOT a performer's appearance in a variety show, or the scheduled or regular time for that appearance 10. AWKWARD SITUATION an awkward or difficult situation (*informal*) 11. ENTERTAINMENT VENUE a place of entertainment (*informal*) ○ *a night spot* 12. *US* POSITION a position in a series or sequence 13. *US* MONEY a piece of paper money worth a certain amount (*informal*) (*usually used in combination*) ○ *She handed me a ten spot.* 14. ARTS = **spotlight** *n.* 1 15. CUE GAMES MARKED WHITE BILLIARD BALL in billiards, the white ball that is marked with a black dot 16. CUE GAMES BILLIARD PLAYER the player in billiards who is using the white ball with the black mark 17. CUE GAMES DOT ON BILLIARD TABLE any of the small black dots on the table in billiards, snooker, and pool that mark where the balls should be placed 18. *US* CARDS SYMBOL ON PLAYING CARD one of the traditional symbols, heart, diamond, spade, or club, on a playing card 19. *US* CARDS PLAYING CARD any playing card from two to ten of any of the four suits ○ *a six spot* 20. *US* LEISURE DOT ON GAME PIECE one of the dots on a domino or dice 21. ELECTRON ENG ILLUMINATED POINT ON CATHODE-RAY TUBE the point on the face of a cathode-ray tube at which the phosphor is illuminated by the impact of an electron beam ■ *adj.* 1. AVAILABLE IMMEDIATELY used to describe goods or currencies that are paid for and delivered immediately after a sale 2. BROADCAST ORIGINATING LOCALLY used to describe a news report that is broadcast from the place where it happens ■ *v.* (**spots, spotting, spotted**) 1. *vt.* SEE to see or detect sth suddenly 2. *vt.* IDENTIFY AS PROMISING to identify sb, especially a performer, as having a promising talent worthy of being developed to a high, often professional standard 3. *vti.* MAKE OR BECOME STAINED to mark or dirty sth with stains, or to become marked or dirtied with stains 4. *vt.* BLEMISH SB'S CHARACTER to blemish sb's character or reputation 5. *vt.* MARK WITH DOTS to mark sth with dots 6. *vti.* MIL ADJUST FIRE to adjust gunfire for accuracy by observation 7. *vi.* FALL LIGHTLY to fall in light drops (*refers to rain*) 8. *vt.* *US* LEND TO OR BUY FOR SB to give or lend money to sb, or pay for sth for sb (*slang*) ○ *Will somebody spot me twenty bucks?* [12thC. Origin uncertain: perhaps from Middle Dutch *spotte*, or perhaps an alteration of Old English *splott* 'spot'. The sense 'to see' comes from the idea of putting a spot on a criminal or suspected person.] ◇ **hit the spot** to be absolutely what is required for total satisfaction, especially in terms of food or drink (*informal*) ◇ **in a spot** in a difficult or embarrassing position (*informal*) ◇ **on the spot** 1. in the exact place where sth is happening 2. immediately 3. in a difficult situation or under pressure ◇ **put sb on the spot** to put sb in a difficult or embarrassing position, especially a position of having to make an instant judgment or decision

spot check *n.* a quick random inspection usually made without prior notice —**spot-check** *vt.*

spotless /spótləss/ *adj.* 1. IMMACULATE impeccably clean ○ *a spotless kitchen* 2. UNBLEMISHED beyond reproach ○ *a spotless reputation* —**spotlessly** *adv.* —**spotlessness** *n.*

spotlight /spót līt/ *n.* 1. FOCUSED BEAM OF LIGHT a strong beam of light that can be directed to illuminate a small area, especially one focusing attention on a stage performer 2. LAMP a lamp that produces a strong narrow beam of light that can be directed at will, e.g. one mounted on a police car 3. FOCUS OF ATTENTION the focus of public attention ■ *vt.* (**-lights, -lighting, -lit** /spót lit/ *or* **-lighted**) 1. ILLUMINATE WITH LIGHT BEAM to direct a beam of light on sb or sth 2. FOCUS ATTENTION ON to focus public attention on sb or sth

spot market *n.* a market in which commodities, securities, or currencies are traded for immediate payment and delivery

spot-on *adj.* (*informal*) 1. CORRECT absolutely correct or perfectly accurate 2. IDEAL exactly what is needed

spot price *n.* the market price for goods, currencies, or securities at a given time

spotted /spóttid/ *adj.* 1. WITH SPOTS with a pattern of spots 2. STAINED stained or soiled with spots of sth

spotted crake *n.* a wading bird of the rail family, found in European and Asian marshes. It has buff speckled plumage and dark brown wings. Latin name: *Porzana porzana.*

spotted dick *n.* a steamed suet pudding containing dried fruit [From its spotted appearance]

spotted fever *n.* any fever accompanied by skin eruptions, e.g. Rocky Mountain spotted fever, typhus, or epidemic cerebrospinal meningitis

spotted-tailed quoll /-kwól/ *n.* a carnivorous marsupial of southeastern Australia and Tasmania that has a brown coat with white spots. Latin name: *Dasyurus maculatus.* [Late 18thC. *Quoll* from an Australian Aboriginal language.]

spotter /spóttər/ *n.* 1. SB WHO MARKS STH sb who puts marks or dots on sth 2. SB WATCHING OUT sb or sth that watches for and locates sth (*often used before a noun*) 3. SB WHOSE HOBBY IS WATCHING sb whose hobby is watching for and noting down sightings of things, especially trains and aircraft (*usually used in combination*) 4. MIL LOCATER OF ENEMY POSITIONS a person or aircraft that locates and reports enemy positions 5. SB LOOKING FOR TALENT sb who watches for new talent or material

spotty /spótti/ (**-tier, -tiest**) *adj.* 1. PIMPLY covered in pimples 2. SPOTTED with a pattern of spots 3. *US* INCONSISTENT inconsistent in quality or character —**spottily** *adv.* —**spottiness** *n.*

spot-weld *vt.* (**spot-welds, spot-welding, spot-welded**) WELD METAL IN SPOTS to join overlapping pieces of metal by making a series of small welds dotted about, rather than by making a large continuous weld. Spot-welding is used when the bond is subject to light temporary stresses but not to structural loads. ■ *n.* JOINT MADE BY SPOT-WELDING a joint between overlapping metal parts, formed using the technique of spot-welding —**spot-welder** *n.*

spousal /spówz'l/ *adj.* 1. OF HUSBAND OR WIFE relating to sb's husband or wife 2. OF MARRIAGE relating to the institution or ceremony of marriage ■ *n.* WEDDING a wedding ceremony (*archaic*) (*often used in the plural*) [13thC. Via Old French *espousaille* 'marriage' from, ultimately, Latin *sponsalia* 'betrothal', from *spons-*, the past participle stem of *spondere* 'to pledge' (see SPONSOR).] —**spousally** *adv.*

spousal equivalent, **spouse equivalent** *n.* *US, Can* sb who acts as or is regarded as the equivalent to a husband or wife, including a same-sex partner, especially for the purposes of tax, pension, or state benefits

spouse /spowss, spowz/ *n.* **HUSBAND OR WIFE** sb's husband or wife ■ *vt.* **(spouses, spousing, spoused) MARRY** to marry sb (*archaic*) [12thC. Via Old French *spous* from Latin *sponsus*, literally 'pledged', the past participle of *spondere* 'to betroth'.]

spouse equivalent *n. US, Can* = **spousal equivalent**

spout /spowt/ *vti.* **(spouts, spouting, spouted) 1. DISCHARGE** to discharge a substance forcibly in a jet or stream **2.** ZOOL **DISCHARGE AIR FROM BLOWHOLE** to discharge air and water through a blowhole (*refers to whales or dolphins*) **3. TALK AT GREAT LENGTH** to talk about sth tediously and at great length, usually with no regard for the listener's interest ■ *n.* **1. TUBE FOR POURING LIQUID** a tube or pipe out of which a liquid is poured **2. CHUTE FOR DISCHARGE OF SOLID SUBSTANCE** a chute through which sth solid such as grain is discharged **3. STREAM OF LIQUID** a continuous and forceful stream of liquid **4.** METEOROL = **waterspout** *n.* 2 **5.** ZOOL **AIR AND WATER FROM BLOWHOLE** a burst of air and water from a whale or other marine animal's blowhole [14thC. From Middle Dutch *spouten* 'to spout'. Ultimately from an Indo-European base, imitative of the sound of spitting that is also the ancestor of English *spew, spit,* and *sputum.*] ◇ **up the spout 1.** ruined or useless (*informal*) **2.** pregnant (*slang*)

spouting /spówting/ *n. NZ, Northeast US* the system of gutters and downpipes that carry rainwater from the roof of a building

spp. *abbr.* species (*plural*)

SPQR *abbr.* the senate and people of Rome [Latin, *Senatus Populusque Romanus*]

Spr. *abbr.* Sapper

sprain /sprayn/ *n.* **INJURY TO LIGAMENTS** a painful injury to the ligaments of a joint caused by wrenching or overstretching ■ *vt.* **(sprains, spraining, sprained) INJURE LIGAMENTS OF** to injure a joint by a sudden wrenching of its ligaments [Early 17thC. Origin uncertain: perhaps, ultimately, from Latin *exprimere* (see EXPRESS).]

sprang *v.* past tense of **spring**

sprat /sprat/ *n.* **1.** (*plural* **sprats** *or* **sprat**) ZOOL **SMALL EDIBLE FISH** a small food fish of the herring family that lives in the northeast Atlantic Ocean and North Sea. Latin name: *Sprattus sprattus.* **2.** ZOOL **SMALL HERRING** a small or young herring or similar fish such as an anchovy **3. SB YOUNG OR UNIMPORTANT** sb who is young, small, or dismissed as insignificant [Old English *sprot*] ◇ **a sprat to catch a mackerel** sth small sacrificed or offered as bait in order to gain sth large

sprawl /sprawl/ *vi.* **(sprawls, sprawling, sprawled) 1. LIE AWKWARDLY** to sit or lie with the arms and legs spread awkwardly in different directions **2. EXTEND DISORDEREDLY** to extend over or across sth in a disordered, awkward, or ugly way ○ *handwritten notes sprawled across the page* ■ *n.* **1. AWKWARD SITTING OR LYING POSITION** a sitting or lying position in which the arms and legs are spread out awkwardly **2. UNCHECKED GROWTH OF URBAN AREA** the scattered, unplanned, and unchecked expansion of a town or city into the surrounding countryside **3. URBANIZED AREAS ON CITY'S EDGE** the urbanized areas on the edge of a town or city that have developed as a result of unplanned and unchecked expansion [Old English *sprēawlian* 'to move convulsively'. Ultimately from an Indo-European base meaning 'to strew' that is also the ancestor of English *spread* and *spray*[1].] —**sprawler** *n.* —**sprawling** *adj.* —**sprawly** *adj.*

spray[1] /spray/ *n.* **1. LIQUID PARTICLES** a moving cloud or mist of water or other liquid particles **2. JET OF LIQUID** a jet of fine particles of liquid from an atomizer or pressurized container **3. CONTAINER FOR RELEASING LIQUID** an atomizer or pressurized container that releases fine particles of a liquid (*often used before a noun*) **4. STH IN PRESSURIZED CONTAINER** a liquid product such as a deodorant, paint, or insecticide that is packaged in an atomizer or pressurized container (*often used before a noun*) ■ *v.* **(sprays, spraying, sprayed) 1.** *vt.* **DISCHARGE FROM PRESSURIZED CONTAINER** to disperse a liquid in the form of fine particles, or apply a liquid in this form to the surface of sth **2.** *vt.* **PAINT WITH PAINT SPRAY** to paint or mark sth using a paint spray ○ *spray the car red* ○ *He sprayed his name on the wall.* **3.** *vi.* **URINATE** to put out a stream of urine, e.g. as a cat does when marking its territory [Early 17thC. From Middle Dutch *sprayen* 'to sprinkle'.]

spray[2] /spray/ *n.* **1. PLANT SPRIG** a shoot or branch of a plant, with flowers, leaves, or berries on it **2. FLOWER ARRANGEMENT** a decorative arrangement of flowers and foliage **3. DECORATION IMITATING FLOWERS AND FOLIAGE** sth decorative such as a brooch, made in imitation of a sprig of flowers and foliage [13thC. From assumed Old English *spræg*, probably related to sprig and Old English *spræc* 'shoot, twig'.]

spray can *n.* a small pressurized container used to disperse liquids in a fine mist

spray gun *n.* a device that uses pressure to apply atomized paint or other liquids, operated by means of a trigger

spread /spred/ *v.* **(spreads, spreading, spread) 1.** *vt.* **OPEN FULLY** to open or extend sth to its fullest area **2.** *vti.* **EXTEND WIDELY** to extend, or cause sth to extend, over a large area **3.** *vti.* **EXTEND IN TIME** to extend sth over a period of time **4.** *vti.* **EXTEND IN RANGE** to extend over a wider range, or cause sth to cover a wider range **5.** *vt.* **SEPARATE THINGS BY STRETCHING** to separate things by stretching or pulling, so that they become far apart **6.** *vti.* **BECOME OR MAKE KNOWN** to become widely known, or make sth widely known **7.** *vt.* **APPLY COATING TO** to coat sth with a layer of a substance, especially one smoothly applied **8.** *vti.* **DISPERSE** to disperse sth over a wide area **9.** *vti.* **SEND OUT IN ALL DIRECTIONS** to send out sth, or to be sent out, in all directions **10.** *vt.* **DISPLAY** to exhibit or display sth in its fullest extent **11.** *vt.* **GET TABLE READY FOR MEAL** to prepare a table for a meal **12.** *vt.* **PUT FOOD ON TABLE** to lay out food or a meal on a table ■ *n.* **1. EXTENSION OF STH** the extension, diffusion, or distribution of sth over an area, range, or time **2. VARIETY** a wide variety of things **3. LIMIT OF EXTENSION** the limit to which sth can be extended **4. DISTANCE BETWEEN THINGS** the distance or range between two points or things **5.** *US* **RANCH** a ranch (*regional*) **6. BED OR TABLE COVER** a covering for a bed or table **7.** FOOD **SPREADABLE FOOD** a food with a soft texture, designed to be spread on bread or crackers **8.** PUBL **PAIR OF FACING PAGES** two facing pages in a newspaper, magazine, or book, often with material printed across the fold **9.** PUBL **EXTENSIVE STORY OR AD** an advertisement or story that occupies two or more columns in a newspaper or magazine **10.** FOOD **MEAL** a large meal laid out on a table (*informal*) **11. WIDENING OF BODY** a widening of the hips and waist owing to weight gain (*informal*) **12.** AIR **PLANE'S WINGSPAN** the wingspan of an aeroplane (*informal*) **13.** FIN **DIFFERENCE BETWEEN BID AND OFFER** the difference between the asking price and the bid price of a security **14. GEMSTONE SIZE** the size of a gemstone when viewed from above, expressed in carats ■ *adj.* **1. EXTENDED** extended or stretched out **2. SHALLOW** used to describe a gemstone that is shallow and flat **3.** PHON **WITH LIPS STRAIGHT** used to describe a speech sound that is pronounced with the lips forming a horizontal line [Old English *sprǣdan*. Ultimately from an Indo-European base meaning 'to strew' that is also the ancestor of English *sprawl, sprout,* and *spray*[1].] —**spreadable** *adj.*

spread eagle *n.* **1. SYMBOLIC IMAGE OF EAGLE** the image of an eagle with its wings and legs outstretched, especially when used as an emblem of the United States. The spread eagle appears on the Great Seal of the United States. **2.** ICE SKATING **SKATING FIGURE** in ice skating, a figure performed with the blades touching heel to heel **3. POSTURE WITH SPREAD LIMBS** a way of standing or lying with arms and legs spread apart

spread-eagle *v.* **(spread-eagles, spread-eagling, spread-eagled) 1.** *vt.* **FORCE INTO SPREAD-OUT POSITION** to force sb to stand or lie with arms and legs spread apart, especially when being arrested or searched **2.** *vi.* ICE SKATING **PERFORM SKATING FIGURE** in ice skating, to perform a spread eagle **3.** *vt.* **STRETCH BODY ACROSS** to stand or lie with limbs spread wide across a gap or an object **4.** *vi.* **ADOPT POSITION WITH SPREAD LIMBS** to stand or lie with arms and legs spread apart ■ *adj. US* = **spread-eagled**

spread-eagled *adj.* standing or lying with arms and legs spread apart. US term **spread-eagle**

spreader /spréddar/ *n.* **1. DEVICE FOR DISTRIBUTING SEED OR FERTILIZER** a machine used by farmers and gardeners to spread manure, fertilizer, seed, or similar material over the ground (*usually used in combination*) **2. IMPLEMENT FOR SPREADING** an implement such as a spatula, trowel, or broad-bladed knife, used for spreading soft substances (*usually used in combination*) **3. DEVICE FOR SEPARATING THINGS** a device such as a bar, used to hold things such as cables or wires apart

spreading factor *n.* = **hyaluronidase**

spreadsheet /spréd sheet/ *n.* **1. COMPUTER PROGRAM FOR NUMERICAL DATA** a computer program that displays numerical data in cells in a simulated accountant's worksheet of rows and columns in which hidden formulas can perform calculations on the visible data. Changing the contents of one cell can cause automatic recalculation of other cells. **2. DISPLAY OR PRINTOUT OF SPREADSHEET** the display or printout of a spreadsheet, showing the many lines and columns of a ledger

sprechgesang /shprékgə zang, shprékh-/, **Sprechgesang** *n.* a style of singing that blends elements of normal nonmusical speech into the voice [Early 20thC. From German, literally 'speech song'.]

sprechstimme /shprék shtimə, shprékh-/, **Sprechstimme** *n.* **1. VOICE SINGING SPRECHGESANG** the voice used to sing sprechgesang **2.** = **sprechgesang** [Early 20thC. From German, literally 'speech voice'.]

spree /spree/ *n.* **1. PERIOD OF EXTRAVAGANT ACTIVITY** a session of extravagant self-indulgent activity, especially of spending or drinking, but also of criminal activity **2. SOCIAL OUTING** a fun-filled sociable outing (*dated*) [Late 18thC. Origin unknown.]

sprier /sprīr/ comparative of **spry**

spriest /sprī əst/ superlative of **spry**

sprig /sprig/ *n.* **1.** BOT **SMALL BRANCH** a shoot, stem, or twig cut or broken from a plant ○ *garnished with a sprig of parsley* **2.** CRAFT **DECORATION** an artistic representation of a sprig that is usually repeated in rows on fabric or wallpaper to produce a decorative pattern **3. YOUTH** a young man (*dated*) **4. SMALL NAIL** a small headless tack that tapers to a point **5.** SPORTS **STUD** a stud or spike in the sole of a boot used for various sports ■ *vt.* **(sprigs, sprigging, sprigged) 1.** CRAFT **PATTERN WITH SPRIGS** to decorate fabric, wallpaper, or pottery with a pattern of sprigs ○ *a dress of sprigged cotton* **2.** BOT **CUT TWIGS FROM PLANT** to cut small twigs or branches from a plant **3.** BUILDING, DIY **NAIL WITH TACKS** to nail sth using brads or tacks [14thC. Origin uncertain: perhaps from Low German *sprick* 'twig', and probably related to *spray*[2] and Old English *spræc* 'shoot, twig'.] —**sprigger** *n.* —**spriggy** *adj.*

sprightful /sprītf'l/ *adj. US* sprightly (*archaic*) [Late 16thC. See SPRIGHTLY.] —**sprightfully** *adv.* —**sprightfulness** *n.*

sprightly /sprītli/ *adj.* **(-lier, -liest) VIGOROUS** full of life and vigour, especially with a light and springy step ■ *adv.* **VIGOROUSLY** in a lively and vigorous way [Early 16thC. Formed from an earlier variant of SPRITE.] —**sprightliness** *n.*

sprigtail /sprig tayl/ *n.* **1.** = **pintail 2.** = **ruddy duck**

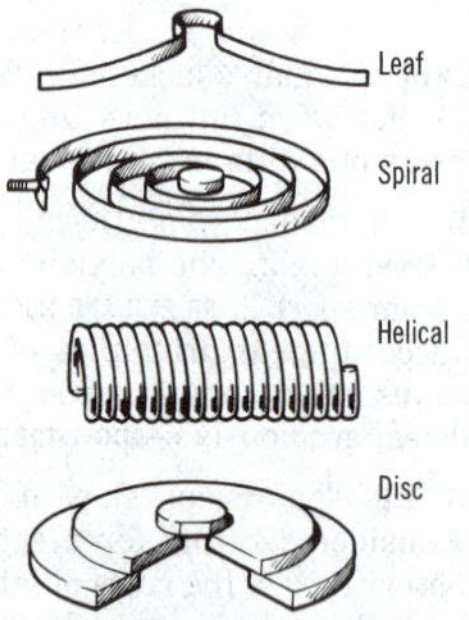
Leaf
Spiral
Helical
Disc

Spring

spring /spring/ *v.* **(springs, springing, sprang** /sprang/, **sprung** /sprung/**) 1.** *vi.* **MOVE SUDDENLY IN SINGLE MOVEMENT** to move rapidly upwards or forwards in a single movement or in a series of rapid movements ○ *He sprang to his feet.* **2.** *vt.* **LEAP OVER** to leap over a barrier **3.** *vi.* **RAPIDLY RESUME ORIGINAL POSITION** to move back rapidly to an original position after being forced in another direction **4.** *vi.* **EMERGE RAPIDLY** to appear or come into existence quickly ○ *new houses springing up* **5.** *vi.* **COME FROM SB'S LIPS** to be uttered, especially as a sudden and almost involuntary reaction to sth **6.** *vi.* **ORIGINATE FROM STH** to originate from a particular source ○ *reform that springs from discontent* **7.** *vi.* **BE DESCENDED** to be descended from a person or family **8.** *vt.* **SUDDENLY REVEAL TO SB** to make sth known to sb unexpectedly or suddenly (*informal*) ○ *You can't just spring a decision like that on me!* **9.** *vt.* **MAKE STH OPERATE** to operate a device or trap by releasing a mechanism that was held in check **10.** *vi.* **JUMP OUT OF PLACE** to move suddenly out of place or come suddenly loose within a mechanism **11.** *vt.* **CRIMINOL GET OUT OF PRISON** to release sb from prison or help sb escape from prison (*slang*) **12.** *vt.* **HUNT MOVE ANIMAL FROM COVER** to move an animal or bird out into the open during a hunting expedition, or be moved in this way **13.** *vti.* **MIL DETONATE MINE** to explode or detonate a mine, or be detonated **14.** *vti.* **TECH WARP OR SPLIT** to crack, split, or warp, or cause wood to do this **15.** *vi.* **ARCHIT EXTEND UPWARDS** to extend upwards from the topmost part of a column **16.** *vi.* **US PAY FOR STH** to pay for sth, usually for another person (*slang*) ○ *I'll spring for lunch.* ■ *n.* **1.** MECH ENG **COIL OF METAL** a resilient metal coil used especially for cushioning and in clockwork **2.** **ABILITY TO REGAIN SHAPE** the ability of an object to revert rapidly to its original position after being extended, compressed, or under tension ○ *a mattress with a lot of spring left in it* **3.** **ONWARD OR UPWARD LEAP** a rapid forward or upward movement **4.** **WATER EMERGING FROM UNDERGROUND** a source of water that flows out of the ground as a small stream or pool **5.** **SOURCE OF STH** the source of sth such as a particular quality or state (*literary*) **6.** **FORCE CAUSING STH** a strong motivation that causes sb to act in a particular way (*formal*) ○ *the springs of her ambition* **7.** **SEASON OF YEAR** the season of the year between winter and summer during which many plants bring forth leaves and flowers **8.** **TIME OF RENEWAL** a time of new growth and regeneration **9.** TECH **WARPING OR BENDING** warping, cracking, or bending, especially when caused by great force **10.** METEOROL = **spring tide** *n.* 1 ■ *adj.* **1.** **HAPPENING IN SPRINGTIME** relating to, occurring in, or appropriate to the season of spring ○ *spring fashions* **2.** **GROWN IN SPRINGTIME** normally grown or growing in the season of spring ○ *spring flowers* **3.** **FULL OF SPRINGS** having or containing springs, especially for cushioning or as part of a clockwork mechanism **4.** **RECOILING** acting like a spring in being held back then quickly releasing energy [Old English *springan*. Ultimately from an Indo-European word meaning 'rapid movement'.]

———— WORD KEY: CULTURAL NOTE ————

The Rite of Spring, a ballet with music by the Russian composer Igor Stravinsky (1913). This one-act work is based on traditional dances performed at pagan festivals in Russia. Its use of dissonance and irregular pulsating rhythms combined with Nijinsky's unorthodox choreography outraged contemporary audiences, resulting in a famous riot at the first performance in Paris on 29 May.

---

spring balance *n.* a device to determine the weight of sth by measuring the tension it creates on a spring

spring beauty *n.* a succulent herb of the purslane family of eastern North America that bears white or pinkish flowers in early spring. Genus: *Claytonia*.

springboard /spríng bawrd/ *n.* **1.** SWIMMING **FLEXIBLE DIVING BOARD** a flexible board secured to a base at one end and projecting over the water at the other, used for diving **2.** GYMNASTICS **GYMNASTIC EQUIPMENT** a flexible board on which gymnasts bounce in order to gain height for vaulting **3.** **EVENT OR FACTOR HELPING ADVANCEMENT** an event, activity, or plan that helps to further sb's career

springbok /spríng bok/ (*plural* **-bok** *or* **-boks**) *n.* a small swift gazelle of the semi-arid regions of southern Africa, noted for its ability to leap high in the air repeatedly when startled. Latin name: *Antidorcas marsupialis*. [Late 18thC. From Afrikaans, literally 'leaping he-goat'.]

Springbok /spríng bok/ *n.* **1.** **S AFRICAN RUGBY PLAYER** a member of the South African national rugby team **2.** **S AFRICAN ATHLETE** in the past, an athlete who has represented South Africa in any of various international sporting competitions (*dated*)

Springbok

springbuck /spríng buk/ (*plural* **-buck** *or* **-bucks**) *n.* = **springbok**

spring chicken *n.* a chicken less than ten months old, formerly available for eating only in spring ◇ **no spring chicken** no longer young, inexperienced, or agile

spring-clean *vti.* (**spring-cleans**, **spring-cleaning**, **spring-cleaned**) **CLEAN THOROUGHLY** to clean a house or room thoroughly, usually including all the contents and furnishings, at the end of the winter or during spring ■ *n.* **THOROUGH CLEAN** a thorough cleaning of a house or room at the end of the winter or during spring —**spring-cleaning** *n.*

springe /sprinj/ *n.* a snare or trap for small animals, consisting of a noose attached to a branch under tension [13thC. From assumed Old English *sprencg*. Ultimately from a prehistoric Germanic word that is also the ancestor of English *spring*.]

springer /spríngər/ *n.* **1.** ARCHIT **WEDGE-SHAPED STONE** the first wedge-shaped stone (**voussoir**) of an arch resting on the top section of the arch's supporting pillar (**impost**) **2.** AGRIC **COW READY TO GIVE BIRTH** a cow that is on the point of giving birth to a calf **3.** ZOOL = **springer spaniel 4.** **SB OR STH THAT LEAPS** a person or animal that springs or leaps

springer spaniel *n.* a hunting dog with a long wavy coat, short legs, and floppy ears, belonging to either an English or a Welsh breed

spring fever *n.* a feeling of restlessness, yearning, lust, or sometimes laziness, believed to be brought on by the coming of spring

Springfield rifle /spríng feeld-/ *n.* a bolt-action .30-calibre rifle developed at the federal arsenal in Springfield, Massachusetts, used by the US Army in World War I.

springfish /spríng fish/ (*plural* **-fish** *or* **-fishes**) *n.* a small North American freshwater fish associated with caves and underground passages in limestone formations, and related to cave fishes. Latin name: *Chlorogaster agassizi*.

springhaas /spríng haass/ (*plural* **-haas**) *n.* a large jumping mammal with hind legs like a kangaroo's and a long black-tufted tail, found in semi-arid regions of southern Africa. It grows to approximately 41 cm/16 in in length excluding the tail. Latin name: *Pedetes capensis*. [Late 18thC. From Afrikaans, literally 'leaping hare'.]

springhalt /spríng hawlt, -holt/ *n.* = **stringhalt** [Early 17thC. Alteration of STRINGHALT.]

springhead /spríng hed/ *n.* **1.** **STREAM SOURCE** the source of a stream **2.** **POINT OF ORIGIN** the source of a particular way of thinking

springhouse /spríng howss/ (*plural* **-houses** /-howziz/) *n.* a storehouse built over a spring, formerly used to keep meat and dairy products fresh and cool

springing /spríngíng/ *n.* the point at which an arch, vault, or dome rises from its support

springlet /sprínglət/ *n.* a small spring of water

spring line *n.* a rope by means of which a sailing vessel is made fast to an anchorage, usually one of two

spring-loaded *adj.* fixed in place or controlled by a spring (*refers to a part of a mechanism*)

spring lock *n.* a lock that is bolted automatically by means of a spring

spring onion *n.* a young onion with a small white bulb and a long green shoot. US term **green onion**

spring peeper *n.* a small brownish tree frog of eastern North America that has an X-shaped marking on its back and makes a shrill peeping call early in the spring. Latin name: *Hyla crucifer*.

spring roll *n.* a hot oriental snack or starter of mixed savoury ingredients formed into a slightly flattened cylindrical shape in a wrapping and fried until crisp and golden. The wrapping is usually thin dough, a pancake mixture, or edible paper. [Translation of Chinese *chūn juǎn*]

Springs /springz/ town in Gauteng Province, South Africa, situated about 40 km/25 mi. east of Johannesburg. Population: 170,000 (1991).

spring scale *n.* = **spring balance**

springtail /spríng tayl/ *n.* a primitive wingless insect with a forked abdominal structure that helps it spring through the air. Order: Collembola.

spring tide *n.* **1.** **TIDE AT NEW AND FULL MOON** a tide that occurs near the times of the new moon and full moon and has a greater than average range **2.** **RUSH OF EMOTION** a great rush of emotion (*literary*)

springtide /spríng tíd/ *n.* springtime (*literary*)

springtime /spríng tím/ *n.* **1.** **SEASON OF SPRING** the season of spring, between winter and summer **2.** **EARLIEST AND BEST PART** the earliest, freshest, and most pleasant stage of sb's life, a relationship, or a period of time (*literary*)

springwood /spríng wŏŏd/ *n.* young relatively soft wood that develops just beneath the bark of trees in spring

springy /spríngi/ *adj.* (**-ier, -iest**) **1.** **BOUNCING BACK INTO SHAPE** springing back strongly to its original shape after being compressed or extended **2.** **MAKING SPRINGING MOTIONS** tending to make a lot of springing movements (*informal*) ■ *n.* (*plural* **-ies**) Aus CLOTHES **WETSUIT** a wetsuit with short sleeves and legs, used in warm conditions (*slang*) —**springily** *adv.* —**springiness** *n.*

sprinkle /spríngk'l/ *v.* (**-kles, -kling, -kled**) **1.** *vt.* **DISTRIBUTE SMALL AMOUNTS OF** to scatter small drops of a liquid or particles of a fine or powdery substance such as sugar, ashes, or flour over the surface of sth **2.** *vt.* **SCATTER OR BE SCATTERED THROUGHOUT THINGS** to scatter things in amongst other things, at random or as though at random, or be scattered amongst other things in this way ○ *hedgerows sprinkled with poppies* **3.** *vt.* **GIVE OUT IN SMALL AMOUNTS** to distribute a substance, emotion, or commodity in small amounts **4.** *vi.* US METEOROL **RAIN VERY SLIGHTLY** to rain very gently in fine drops, usually for a short period ■ *n.* **1.** **ACT OF SPRINKLING** the action of scattering small drops of liquid or particles of a fine or powdery substance **2.** US METEOROL **FINE RAIN** a light rain falling in fine or sporadic drops [14thC. Origin uncertain: perhaps from Dutch *sprenkelen* 'to sprinkle'.]

sprinkler /spríngklər/ *n.* **1.** GARDENING **WATERING APPARATUS** a device that sends a moving spray of water onto a garden or lawn. A sprinkler may be attached to a movable hose or set permanently into a lawn or garden and remotely controlled. ○ *a ban on the use of hosepipes and sprinklers* **2.** GARDENING **NOZZLE** a plastic or metal nozzle perforated with many small holes that fits onto a watering can or hose. It spreads the liquid being distributed so that it falls gently over a larger area. **3.** **PERSON OR DEVICE THAT SPRINKLES** sb who or sth that sprinkles small drops of liquid or particles of a solid on sth

sprinkler system *n.* **1.** ENG **FIRE-EXTINGUISHING SYSTEM** a system for extinguishing fires, designed to release water from overhead nozzles that open automatically when a particular temperature is reached **2.** GARDENING **GARDEN WATERING SYSTEM** a system of sprinklers for watering a garden or lawn, operated by a single control

sprinkling /spríngkling/ *n.* **1.** **SMALL AMOUNT SCATTERED THINLY** a small quantity of a fine or powdery substance such as sugar, snow, dust, or sand scattered on or throughout sth **2.** **MEAGRE AMOUNT** a small, thinly distributed amount of a particular emotion or quality ○ *a sprinkling of wit*

sprint /sprint/ *n.* **1.** SHORT SWIFT RACE a short race run or cycled at a very high speed **2.** FAST FINISHING RUN a burst of fast running or cycling during the last part of a longer race **3.** BURST OF ACTIVITY a sudden burst of activity or speed ■ *vi.* (**sprints, sprinting, sprinted**) GO AT TOP SPEED to run, swim, or cycle as rapidly as possible [Mid-16thC. From Old Norse *spretta* 'to jump'.] —**sprinter** *n.*

sprit /sprit/ *n.* a pole that crosses a fore-and-aft sail diagonally [Old English *sprēot*. Ultimately from a pre-historic Germanic word that is also the ancestor of English *sprout*.]

sprite /sprīt/ *n.* **1.** SUPERNATURAL ELFIN CREATURE in folklore, a small supernatural being like an elf or a fairy, especially one associated with water **2.** SB LIKE AN ELF a small or delicately built person who is likened to an elf or a fairy **3.** GHOST in folklore, a ghost or spirit **4.** COMPUT INDEPENDENT GRAPHIC OBJECT an independent graphic object that moves freely across a computer screen **5.** SOUL a soul (*archaic*) [14thC. Via Old French *esp(i)rit* from Latin *spiritus* (see SPIRIT).]

spritsail /sprít sayl/; *nautical* /spríts'l/ *n.* a sail that is extended by being mounted on a sprit

spritz /sprits/ *vt.* (**spritzes, spritzing, spritzed**) SPRAY LIQUID to spray a fine jet of liquid through a nozzle ■ *n.* FINE SPRAY OF LIQUID a fine spray of liquid squirted through a nozzle [Early 20thC. From German *spritzen* 'to squirt'.]

spritzer /sprítsər/ *n.* a drink consisting of wine, generally white, diluted with sparkling water or lemonade [Mid-20thC. From German, 'splash'.]

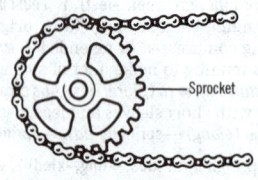

Sprocket

sprocket /sprókit/ *n.* a projecting tooth on a wheel or cylinder that engages with the links of a chain or with perforations in film to make the chain or film move forward [Mid-16thC. Origin unknown.]

sprog /sprog/ *n.* (*slang*) **1.** CHILD a child or baby **2.** AIR FORCE RECRUIT in the RAF, a new recruit [Mid-20thC. Origin unknown.]

sprout /sprowt/ *v.* (**sprouts, sprouting, sprouted**) **1.** *vti.* BOT DEVELOP SHOOTS to develop buds or shoots **2.** *vi.* BOT GERMINATE to begin to grow from a seed **3.** *vti.* GROW to grow or cause sth or sb to grow **4.** *vti.* EMERGE to emerge and grow rapidly, or cause sth to emerge and grow rapidly ■ *n.* **1.** BOT NEW GROWTH ON A PLANT a new growth on a plant, e.g. a bud or shoot **2.** = Brussels sprout **3.** STH LIKE A SPROUT sb who or sth that grows rapidly like a sprout ■ **sprouts** *npl.* US FOOD EDIBLE SHOOTS OF PLANTS newly sprouted seeds or beans, eaten especially in sandwiches, salads, and stir-fries [Old English *-sprūtan*. Ultimately from a prehistoric Germanic word that also produced German *sprießen* 'to sprout'.]

spruce[1] /sprooss/ (*plural* **spruces** *or* **spruce**) *n.* **1.** EVERGREEN TREE an evergreen tree of the pine family with a pyramid shape, short needles, drooping cones, and soft light wood. Genus: *Picea*. **2.** SPRUCE WOOD the soft light wood of a spruce tree [Early 17thC. Shortening of *Spruce fir*, literally 'Prussian fir'; *Spruce* an alteration of *Pruce*, from, ultimately, medieval Latin *Prussia*.]

spruce[2] /sprooss/ *adj.* APPEARING NEAT AND TIDY having a clean, smart, and well-cared-for appearance ○ *a spruce young man* ■ *vti.* (**spruces, sprucing, spruced**) MAKE NEAT to make sth or sb, usually yourself, clean and neat in appearance [Late 16thC. Origin uncertain: perhaps a shortening of *Spruce leather*, a type of fine leather first made in Prussia (see SPRUCE[1]).] —**sprucely** *adv.* —**spruceness** *n.*

Spruce

spruce beer *n.* a fermented drink whose ingredients include spruce leaves and twigs

spruce budworm *n.* a North American moth with destructive larvae that feed on the buds and branch tips of evergreen coniferous trees such as spruce and balsam. Latin name: *Choristoneura fumiferana*.

spruce grouse *n.* a common plump game bird of northern North American coniferous forests that has a black throat and breast. Latin name: *Dendragapus canadensis*.

spruce pine *n.* a tall pine of the southeastern United States with soft wood and needles in pairs. Latin name: *Pinus glabra*.

sprue[1] /sproo/ *n.* INDUST a vertical channel in a mould, used to pour in molten material [Early 19thC. Origin unknown.]

sprue[2] /sproo/ *n.* MED a tropical disease of unknown origin involving deficient absorption of nutrients from the intestine and marked by persistent diarrhoea, weight loss, and anaemia. Treatment with antibiotics and vitamin supplements is often effective. [Late 19thC. From Dutch *spruw* 'the disease thrush'.]

spruik /sprook/ (**-iks, -iking, -iked**) *vi.* Aus **1.** SELL TO PASSERS-BY to promote goods or services by addressing passing members of the public from the door of a shop or similar establishment (*informal*) **2.** PROMOTE to promote goods, services, or a cause by addressing people in a public place (*humorous*) [Early 20thC. Origin unknown.]

spruiker /sprookər/ *n.* Aus **1.** SALESPERSON a salesperson who addresses passing members of the public from the door of a shop, bar, or other establishment (*informal*) **2.** PUBLIC SPEAKER sb who promotes goods, services, or a cause by addressing people in a public place (*humorous*)

sprung past participle of **spring**

sprung rhythm *n.* a system of prosody that always places the accent on the first syllable of any foot in an effort to evoke the rhythms of ordinary speech. The term and practice were originated by the poet Gerard Manley Hopkins.

spry /sprī/ (**spryer** *or* **sprier, spryest** *or* **spriest**) *adj.* markedly brisk and active, especially at an advanced age [Mid-18thC. Origin uncertain: perhaps from a Scandinavian word, or perhaps a shortening of SPRIGHTLY.] —**spryly** *adv.* —**spryness** *n.*

spt *abbr.* seaport

SPUC *abbr.* Society for the Protection of the Unborn Child

spud /spud/ *n.* **1.** FOOD POTATO a potato (*informal*) **2.** GARDENING GARDEN IMPLEMENT a spade with a sharp narrow blade, used for cutting through roots and digging up weeds **3.** FORESTRY TOOL FOR REMOVING BARK FROM TREES a tool resembling a chisel that is used to peel bark from trees ■ *v.* (**spuds, spudding, spudded**) **1.** *vi.* INDUST START DRILLING AN OIL WELL to use a large bit to drill the upper part of the bore of a new oil well **2.** *vt.* FORESTRY REMOVE BARK to remove bark from trees by the use of a tool like a chisel **3.** *vt.* GARDENING DIG WITH A SPUD to use a spud to dig up weeds or cut through roots [15thC. Origin unknown. Originally in the meaning 'dagger', its use for 'potato' seems to have originated in New Zealand English.]

spud-bashing *n.* in the British armed forces, the task of peeling potatoes as a punishment (*slang*)

spume /spyoom/ *n.* FOAM a mass of fine bubbles on the surface of a liquid, especially on the sea (*literary*) ■ *vi.* (**spumes, spuming, spumed**) BE FOAMY to produce or have a mass of fine bubbles on the surface (*literary*) [14thC. Directly or via Old French from Latin *spuma* 'foam'.] —**spumous** *adj.* —**spumy** *adj.*

spumone /spoo mốni/, **spumoni** *n.* **1.** ICE CREAM an Italian ice cream composed of differently coloured and flavoured layers, often containing nuts and candied fruit **2.** LIGHT DESSERT an Italian light mousse dessert [Early 20thC. From Italian, from *spuma* 'foam'.]

spun past tense, past participle of **spin**

spun glass *n.* **1.** = fibreglass **2.** GLASS WITH GLASS THREADS IN IT glass that is blown in such a way as to incorporate slender threads of glass

spunk /spungk/ *n.* **1.** PLUCKINESS spiritedness or eager willingness (*informal*) **2.** OFFENSIVE TERM a highly offensive term for semen (*taboo slang*) **3.** TINDER a combustible material, especially soft wood or twigs, that can be used to kindle fires **4.** Aus SEXUALLY DESIRABLE PERSON sb who is sexually desirable (*informal*) [Mid-16thC. Origin uncertain: perhaps via Irish *sponc* 'tinder' from Latin *spongia* (see SPONGE), or perhaps a blend of SPARK and FUNK. Originally in the meaning 'spark'.]

spunky /spúngki/ (**-ier, -iest**) *adj.* very lively, determined, and courageous (*informal*) —**spunkily** *adv.* —**spunkiness** *n.*

spun silk *n.* inexpensive fabric or yarn made from short-fibred silk combined with silk waste

spun yarn *n.* rope or cord made from several light yarns twisted or spun together

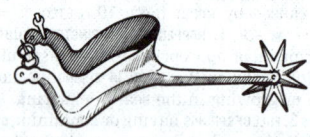

Spur

spur /spur/ *n.* **1.** RIDING DEVICE ATTACHED TO A RIDER'S HEEL a small spike or spiked wheel attached to the heel of a rider's boot that is nudged into the horse's sides to encourage it to go faster **2.** INDUCEMENT sth such as the hope of a reward or the fear of punishment that encourages a person or organization to take action or to make a greater effort **3.** BOT PROJECTING PLANT PART a tubular extension from a flower part, e.g. that in larkspur and columbine **4.** BOT SHORT BRANCH OR SHOOT a short branch or lateral shoot from a stem or branch of a plant **5.** BIRDS HORNY PROJECTION a sharp horny projection on the legs of some male birds, e.g. cocks, above the claws **6.** ZOOL PROJECTING ANIMAL PART a pointed extension or projecting part (**process**) on some animals, e.g. the stiff outgrowth on the legs of some insects and birds **7.** ANAT SHORT BONY OUTGROWTH a bony outgrowth, usually a normal part of the body but sometimes one that develops such as that on the bottom of the heel after an injury **8.** SPIKE FASTENED TO THE LEG OF A GAMECOCK a sharp metal spike attached to the leg of a gamecock **9.** BUILDING PROP a timber or masonry prop or support **10.** GEOG MOUNTAIN RIDGE a ridge that projects outwards from a mountain range and descends towards a valley floor **11.** CIV ENG SHORT JETTY a small jetty extending from a shore to protect a beach against erosion or to trap shifting sands **12.** RAIL PART OF A RAILWAY a short section of railway track leading off a main line **13.** TRANSP ROAD OFF A MAJOR ROAD a short side road leading off a main road **14.** CERAMICS CERAMIC SUPPORT IN A KILN a small ceramic support placed beneath a pot in a kiln ■ *v.* (**spurs, spurring, spurred**) **1.** *vt.* ENCOURAGE SB TO TRY HARDER to stimulate a person or organization to take action or make greater efforts in the hope of a reward or in the fear of punishment ○ '*Public schools are spurred to perform better thanks to new reforms*'. (*US News & World Report*; December 1998)

2. *vt.* RIDING **MAKE A HORSE GO FASTER** to encourage a horse to go faster by nudging spurs into its sides **3.** *vi.* RIDING **RIDE FAST** to ride fast, using spurs (*literary*) **4.** *vi.* **GO QUICKLY** to go or proceed hastily (*literary*) **5.** *vt.* RIDING **CAUSE INJURY TO A HORSE WITH SPURS** to injure a horse by using spurs too strongly and too frequently **6.** *vt.* **PUT SPURS ON SB OR STH** to equip sb or sth with spurs [Old English *spura.* Ultimately from an Indo-European word meaning 'to kick', which is also the ancestor of English *spoor* and *spurn.*] ◇ **win** *or* **gain your spurs 1.** to gain recognition and respect for the first time **2.** HIST in the past, to be given the rank of knight

WORD KEY: SYNONYMS

See Synonyms at ***motive***.

spurge /spurj/ *n.* a herb or shrub that has flowers without petals and a bitter milky juice. Genus: *Euphorbia.* [14thC. From Old French *espurge,* from *espurgier* 'to purge', from Latin *expurgare* 'to cleanse'. From its purgative properties.]

spur gear *n.* a gear whose teeth are arranged along the rim parallel to its axis of rotation

spurge laurel *n.* a low-growing evergreen shrub of Europe and Asia with elongated glossy leaves and yellow flowers. Latin name: *Daphne laureola.*

spurious /spyoóri əs/ *adj.* **1. NOT GENUINE** being different from what it claims to be **2.** BOT **RESEMBLING A PLANT PART** having the outward appearance of another plant part but not its function or origin **3. BORN OUT OF WEDLOCK** born to parents not legally married to each other (*archaic*) [Late 16thC. Formed from Latin *spurius* 'illegitimate child'.] —**spuriously** *adv.* —**spuriousness** *n.*

spurn /spurn/ *v.* (**spurns, spurning, spurned**) **1.** *vti.* **REJECT SB OR STH WITH DISDAIN** to reject a person, offer, gift, or advances with scorn and contempt **2.** *vt.* **THRUST STH AWAY WITH THE FOOT** to reject sth by pushing it away with the foot (*archaic*) ■ *n.* (*archaic*) **1. SCORNFUL REJECTION** a contemptuous or scornful rejection **2. KICK** a kick [Old English *spurnan.* Ultimately from an Indo-European word that is also the ancestor of English *spur* (see SPUR).] —**spurner** *n.*

spurred /spurd/ *adj.* **1.** RIDING **WEARING SPURS** having or wearing spurs **2.** BOT **WITH A PROJECTING PLANT PART** used to describe a flower or plant that has a tubular extension

spurrey /spúrr i/ (*plural* **-reys**), **spurry** (*plural* **-ries**) *n.* a low-growing European plant of the pink family that has linear whorled leaves and small white flowers. Genus: *Spurgula.* [Late 16thC. From Dutch *spurrie.*]

spurt /spurt/ *n.* **1. JET OF LIQUID OR GAS** a sudden stream of liquid or gas, forced out under pressure **2. SUDDEN INCREASE** a short intense burst of energy, interest, action, or speed ○ *I had a spurt of energy as I was digging.* ■ *vt.* (**spurts, spurting, spurted**) **MAKE STH GUSH OUT** to cause a liquid or gas to gush out in a pressurized stream or jet ○ *The burst pipe was spurting water.* [Mid-16thC. Origin uncertain: perhaps ultimately from an Indo-European word thought to be imitative of the sound of spitting.]

spurtle /spúrt'l/ *n. Scotland* a short turned stick, frequently with a decorative end, used for stirring porridge. Spurtles are now more frequently sold as tourist items, often with the decorative top in the design of a thistle. [Early 16thC. Origin unknown.]

spur wheel *n.* MECH ENG = **spur gear**

sputa plural of **sputum**

sputnik /spoótnik, spút-/ *n.* one of a series of ten artificial Earth-orbiting satellites launched by the former Soviet Union starting in 1957. The first launch initiated the space race with the United States. [Mid-20thC. From Russian, literally 'fellow traveller'.]

sputter /spúttər/ *v.* (**-ters, -tering, -tered**) **1.** *vi.* **MAKE POPPING SOUND** to make a popping, spitting sound **2.** *vi.* **SPIT OUT FOOD AND SALIVA** to spray out drops of saliva or food particles, especially when talking or laughing while eating **3.** *vi.* **SPEAK EXPLOSIVELY** to make sounds or pronounce words in an explosive way, especially when angry or excited **4.** *vti.* PHYS **REMOVE SURFACE ATOMS BY ION BOMBARDMENT** to cause or experience the effect in which the atoms of a surface are removed through bombardment by ions, e.g. in cathode evaporation in a discharge tube **5.** *vti.* PHYS **USE A METAL TO COAT STH** to use a metal to coat sth by the process of sputtering, or be coated in this way ■ *n.* **1. NOISE OF SPUTTERING** the noise of a person, fire, candle, or other object sputtering **2. INCOHERENT SPEECH** the confused or incoherent speech of sb who is angry or excited **3. STH EMITTED WHILE SPUTTERING** drops of saliva or food particles sprayed out of the mouth while sputtering [Late 16thC. From Dutch *sputteren* 'to spray', thought to suggest the action.] —**sputterer** *n.*

sputum /spyoótəm/ (*plural* **-ta** /-tə/) *n.* a substance such as saliva, phlegm, or mucus coughed up from the respiratory tract and usually ejected by mouth [Late 17thC. From Latin, 'saliva', from *spuere* 'to spit'.]

spy /spī/ *n.* (*plural* **spies**) **1. SB EMPLOYED TO OBTAIN SECRET INFORMATION** sb who is employed by a government to obtain secret information, particularly regarding military matters, about other hostile countries (*often used before a noun*) ○ *a spy ring* **2. EMPLOYEE WHO OBTAINS INFORMATION ABOUT RIVALS** sb who is employed by a company to obtain secret information about rival organizations **3. SECRET OBSERVER OF OTHERS** sb who watches other people in secret **4. ACT OF A SPY** an instance of acting as a spy **5. CLOSE VIEW** a close view of sth (*archaic*) ■ *v.* (**spies, spying, spied**) **1.** *vi.* **ACT AS A SPY** to work, operate, or function as a spy **2.** *vi.* **ENGAGE IN ESPIONAGE** to maintain a network of spies and gather intelligence in other clandestine ways **3.** *vi.* **OBSERVE IN SECRET** to observe sb or sth secretly ○ *Have you been spying on us again?* **4.** *vt.* **SEE SUDDENLY** to catch sight of sb or sth **5.** *vt.* **DISCOVER BY OBSERVATION** to discover sth by close observation **6.** *vi.* **INVESTIGATE** to investigate sth intensively [13thC. From Old French *espie,* from *espier* 'to spy' (source of English *espy*), of prehistoric Germanic origin; related to Latin *specere* 'to look' (source of English *spectator*).]

spy out *vt.* to discover sth by close and discreet examination

spyglass /spī glaass/ *n.* a telescope that is small enough to be held in the hand

spyhole /spī hōl/ *n.* = **peephole** *n.* 2

spy-in-the-cab (*plural* **spies-in-the-cab**) *n.* a tachograph (*informal*)

spymaster /spī maastər/ *n.* the leader of espionage and intelligence-gathering activities for a country or organization, especially in fictional spy stories

sq. *abbr.* **1.** sequence **2.** sequens **3.** MEASURE square [Latin, 'the one that follows']

Sq. *abbr.* **1.** MIL Squadron **2.** MAIL Square

SQL *n.* a standardized language that approximates the structure of natural English for obtaining information from databases. Full form **structured query language**

Sqn *abbr.* Squadron

sqq. *abbr.* sequentia [Latin, 'those that follow']

squab /skwob/ *n.* (*plural* **squabs** *or* **squab**) **1.** FOOD **YOUNG BIRD** a fledgling bird, especially a pigeon, sometimes cooked as a delicacy **2.** HOUSEHOLD **SOFA** a couch ■ *adj.* (**squabber, squabbest**) **1.** BIRDS **NEWLY HATCHED** newly hatched and not flying yet **2. SHORT AND STOUT** short and somewhat stout [Late 17thC. Origin uncertain: perhaps from a Scandinavian word meaning 'flabby'.] —**squabby** *adj.*

squabble /skwóbb'l/ *n.* **PETTY ROW** a noisy argument over a petty matter ■ *vi.* (**-bles, -bling, -bled**) **ARGUE NOISILY OVER STH UNIMPORTANT** to have a petty argument over a trivial matter [Early 17thC. An imitation of the sound.] —**squabbler** *n.*

squad /skwod/ *n.* **1.** SPORTS **GROUP OF PLAYERS** a number of players from which a team is selected ○ *dropped from the England squad* **2.** MIL **MILITARY FORMATION** a small military formation, especially one that is doing a drill **3.** PUBLIC ADMIN **GROUP OF POLICE OFFICERS** a group of police officers, generally assigned to a particular task **4. TEAM OF PEOPLE** a small group of people engaged in the same activity, especially in a sport ○ *a squad of volunteers* [Mid-17thC. Via French *escouade* and Italian *squadra* or Spanish *escuadra* from assumed Vulgar Latin *exquadra* (see SQUARE From the arrangement of troops in a square formation.]

squad car *n.* a police car linked by radio with police headquarters

squaddie /skwóddi/ *n.* a private soldier (*slang*)

squadron /skwóddrən/ *n.* **1.** NAVY **NAVAL UNIT** a naval unit containing two or more divisions of a fleet **2.** AIR FORCE **AIR FORCE UNIT** an element of a tactical air force belonging to a group and containing two or more flights **3.** MIL **CAVALRY UNIT** an armoured cavalry unit belonging to a regiment and containing two or more troops **4. GROUP** an organized group of people, animals, or objects [Mid-16thC. From Italian *squadrone,* literally 'large squad', from *squadra* (see SQUAD).]

squadron leader *n.* in the RAF, the commander of a squadron of military aircraft

squalene /skwáy leen/ *n.* a colourless hydrocarbon, found primarily in human sebum and shark-liver oil, that is a cholesterol precursor and is used as a bactericide and in the synthesis of some drugs. Formula: $C_{30}H_{50}$. [Early 20thC. Formed from modern Latin *Squalus,* shark genus, from Latin, 'a sea fish'.]

squalid /skwóllid/ *adj.* **1. NEGLECTED AND DIRTY** dirty and shabby because of neglect and lack of money **2. WITHOUT ANY FINE QUALITIES** lacking in honesty, dignity, and morals ○ *a squalid little scandal* [Late 16thC. From Latin *squalidus* 'filthy, rough', from *squalere* 'to be filthy', from *squalus* 'filthy'.] —**squalidly** *adv.* —**squalidness** *n.*

WORD KEY: SYNONYMS

See Synonyms at ***dirty***.

squall[1] /skwawl/ *n.* **1.** METEOROL **WINDSTORM** a sudden strong wind, often with heavy rain or snow **2. BRIEF DISTURBANCE** a short but noisy disturbance **3. SHOW OF TEMPER** a brief but intense outburst of temper ■ *vi.* (**squalls, squalling, squalled**) METEOROL **BLOW STRONGLY** to blow strongly and suddenly (*refers to the wind*) [Late 17thC. Origin uncertain: perhaps from a Scandinavian word.]

squall[2] /skwawl/ *vi.* (**squalls, squalling, squalled**) **YELL** to cry or yell hoarsely ■ *n.* **NOISY CRY** a noisy cry or yell [Mid-17thC. Origin uncertain: perhaps from a Scandinavian word imitative of the sound.] —**squaller** *n.*

squall line *n.* a series of small storms that occur along a cold front

squally /skwáwli/ (**-ier, -iest**) *adj.* **1.** METEOROL **STORMY** occurring in or characterized by strong gusts, often accompanied by rain or snow **2. INVOLVING ARGUMENTS** marked by sudden short noisy arguments

squalor /skwóllər/ *n.* **1. SHABBINESS** shabbiness and dirtiness resulting from poverty or neglect **2. MORAL DEGRADATION** a state of moral degradation [Early 17thC. From Latin, 'dirtiness, roughness', from *squalere* (see SQUALID).]

squama /skwáymə/ (*plural* **-mae** /-mi/) *n.* a scale, or a structure resembling a scale, of the type that make up the covering of fish, reptiles, and some mammals [Early 18thC. From Latin, 'scale'.]

squamate /skwáy mayt/ *n.* **LIZARD OR SNAKE** a reptile of the order that comprises all lizards and snakes and includes about 6,000 species. Order: Squamata. ■ *adj.* **WITH SCALES ON THE BODY** having scales or structures resembling scales of the type that make up the covering of fish, reptiles, and some mammals

squamation /skway máysh'n/ *n.* **1. STATE OF HAVING SCALES ON THE BODY** the state of having a body with scales or plates like scales **2. ARRANGEMENT OF SCALES ON THE BODY** the arrangement of scales on an animal's body

squamiform /skwáymi fawrm/ *adj.* resembling a scale or scales of the type that make up the covering of fish, reptiles, and some mammals

squamosal /skwə mṓss'l/ *n.* a thin plate-shaped bone of the vertebrate skull that forms the forward and upper part of the temporal bone in humans [Mid-19thC. Formed from Latin *squamosus* 'squamous'.]

squamous /skwáyməss/, **squamose** /-mōss/ *adj.* **1.** BIOL **OF SCALES ON THE BODY** covered with, consisting of, or resembling scales or thin plates of the type that make up the covering of fish, reptiles, and some mammals **2.** BIOL **CONSISTING OF SCALE-SHAPED CELLS** used to describe a layer of skin (**epithelium**) made up of small scale-shaped cells **3.** ANAT **OF THE SKULL BONE** relating to the squamosal in the vertebrate skull — **squamously** *adv.* —**squamousness** *n.*

squamous cell carcinoma *n.* a common type of cancer that usually develops in the epithelial layer of the skin but sometimes in various mucous membranes of the body. The cancerous cells often contain keratin, and sometimes intercellular bridges are formed.

squamulose /skwáymyoǒ lōs, -lōz/ *adj.* having or consisting of tiny scales of the type that make up the covering of fish, reptiles, and some mammals [Mid-19thC. Formed from *squamule* 'small scale', from Latin *squamula*, from *squama* 'scale'.]

squander /skwóndər/ *v.* (**-ders, -dering, -dered**) **1.** *vt.* USE STH WASTEFULLY to spend or use sth precious in a wasteful and extravagant way **2.** *vti.* STREW STH to scatter sth, or be scattered (*archaic*) ■ *n.* EXTRAVAGANCE extravagant spending [Late 16thC. Origin unknown.] — **squanderer** *n.*

square /skwair/ *n.* **1.** GEOM EQUILATERAL RECTANGLE a geometric figure with four right angles and four equal sides **2.** RECTANGULAR OBJECT an object in the shape of a square or a rectangle that is nearly a square **3.** GAME DIVISION OF A GAMES BOARD any of the four-sided divisions marked on the board used to play chess, draughts, or other games **4.** ARCHIT OPEN SPACE IN A CITY an open area in a city or town where two or more streets meet, often containing trees, grass, and benches for recreational use **5.** *US* ARCHIT CITY BLOCK a block of buildings surrounded by four streets **6.** MIL MILITARY DRILL AREA an open space within an army barracks where soldiers practise marching and handling weapons **7.** CRICKET PART OF CRICKET PITCH an area in the middle of a cricket pitch where the grass is kept shorter, from which the wicket area is chosen **8.** MATH RESULT OF MULTIPLICATION the product resulting from multiplying a number or term by itself ○ *The square of 7 is 49.* **9.** GEOM DRAWING INSTRUMENT an L- or T-shaped instrument made of plastic, wood, or metal, used for drawing or measuring right angles **10.** MIL BODY OF SOLDIERS formerly, a tactical formation of soldiers in a solid or hollow rectangle, with the soldiers on the sides facing outwards **11.** UNFASHIONABLE PERSON sb who dresses and behaves in an unfashionable way and is out of touch with current popular culture (*slang dated*) **12.** SQUARE MEAL a square meal (*informal*) ■ *adj.* **1.** GEOM SHAPED LIKE A SQUARE having the shape of a square, with four more or less equal sides and angles **2.** GEOM FORMING A RIGHT ANGLE intersecting at, having, or making a right angle **3.** CUBIC in the shape of a cube ○ *a square block of stone* **4.** VAGUELY SQUARE IN SHAPE roughly square or angular in shape, and looking firm and solid **5.** MEASURE OF THE MEASUREMENT OF SURFACE AREA used to describe a measurement of area in which the specified unit refers to the length of each side of a square whose surface area constitutes the measurement. For example one square metre is the surface area of a square all of whose sides are one metre long. ○ *One box contains enough tiles to cover 100 square metres.* **6.** MEASURE WITH SIDES OF A SPECIFIED LENGTH used to describe a square area with sides of a particular length ○ *a room ten feet square* **7.** STRAIGHT OR LEVEL adjusted or made to be perfectly straight, even, level, or lined up with sth ○ *Make sure the picture is square on the wall.* **8.** COMPLETELY FAIR completely fair, honest, and direct ○ *a square deal* **9.** CRICKET AT RIGHT ANGLES TO WICKET in cricket, positioned at right angles to the wicket **10.** BORING AND OLD-FASHIONED dressing and behaving in an unfashionable way and out of touch with current popular culture (*slang dated*) **11.** NOT OWING MONEY with all outstanding debts paid up ○ *She paid me this morning – we're square now.* **12.** CLEAN clean and tidy (*informal*) ○ *The kitchen still needs getting square.* **13.** MUSIC LACKING COMPLEXITY in jazz and popular music, lacking swing or complexity ■ *v.* (**squares, squaring, squared**) **1.** *vt.* MAKE STH SQUARE to make sth into a square or rectangular shape **2.** *vt.* MATH MULTIPLY A NUMBER BY ITSELF to multiply a number or term by itself ○ *Seven squared equals 49.* **3.** *vt.* DIVIDE STH INTO SQUARES to divide a surface, sheet of paper, or other object into squares **4.** *vt.* SET STH STRAIGHT to move an object, item of clothing, or part of the body so that it is straight or level **5.** *vti.* PUT OR BE AT RIGHT ANGLES to adjust sth or be adjusted so that it is at right angles to sth else, or test sth for this alignment **6.** *vt.* SETTLE THINGS FAIRLY to arrive at a fair and equal agreement with sb about sth, especially about paying off money owed ○ *He squared all his bills and left town.* **7.** *vt.* SPORTS BRING SCORES LEVEL to level the scores, especially in a ball game **8.** *vti.* CONCUR OR MAKE STH AGREE to agree with another person, fact, event, or idea, or make two facts, events, or ideas concur ○ *That doesn't square with what we know.* **9.** *vt.* BRIBE SB to bribe another person (*slang*) **10.** *vt.* IMPROVE IMPRESSION to try to improve the impression that sb has of you ■ *adv.* **1.** AT RIGHT ANGLES so as to be even, straight, level, or at right angles to sth **2.** NOT FORWARDS OR BACKWARDS in ball games, to or at another point at the same distance up or down the pitch **3.** DIRECTLY in a direct or forceful way (*informal*) ○ *She drove square into the wall.* **4.** HONESTLY in an honest and straightforward way (*informal*) [13thC. Via Old French *esquare* and assumed Vulgar Latin *exquadra* from, ultimately, Latin *quadrum*, from the Latin stem *quat-* 'four' (source of English *quarter* and *squad*).] —**squarer** *n.* —**squareness** *n.* ◇ **all square 1.** SPORTS in which the scores are even **2.** in which all participants are on equal terms, especially because debts have been settled ◇ **on the square 1.** at right angles to sth, or constructed with right angles **2.** in an honest and direct manner, or direct and honest **3.** done on equal terms, or being on equal terms with sb **4.** being a member of the order of Freemasons ◇ **out of square 1.** not at right angles to sth **2.** not in agreement with each other

square off *vi.* to take the proper stance for beginning to fight

square up *v.* **1.** *vi.* SETTLE DEBTS to pay bills, accounts, or other sums of money owed to sb **2.** *vti.* ARRANGE OR BE ARRANGED SATISFACTORILY to arrange sth or be arranged in an acceptable or pleasing way **3.** *vi.* FACE STH UNPLEASANT to confront sth unpleasant or frightening **4.** *vi.* ADOPT AN AGGRESSIVE POSTURE to put up fists or adopt a similar posture that shows a readiness to fight **5.** *vt.* DESIGN MAKE AN ENLARGEMENT USING A GRID OF SQUARES to enlarge or transfer a drawing using a grid of squares

square-bashing *n.* the training of soldiers in marching and handling arms on a barrack square (*slang*)

square bracket *n.* either of a pair of symbols, [ ], used in keying, printing, or writing to indicate the insertion of special commentary, e.g. that made by an editor. US term **bracket** *n.* 2

square dance *n.* **1.** US COUNTRY DANCE a country dance or style of country dancing featuring dancers in pairs or sets, lively music played on fiddles and other instruments, and a caller who announces the steps. It originated in the United States. **2.** DANCE WHERE FOUR COUPLES FORM SQUARES a country dance in which four couples form a square —**square dancing** *n.*

square knot *n.* = **reef knot**

square leg *n.* CRICKET a fielding position in cricket more or less at right angles to the batsman, or sb who holds this position

squarely /skwáirli/ *adv.* **1.** DIRECTLY in a direct or forceful way ○ *She met my gaze squarely.* **2.** HONESTLY in an honest and straightforward way **3.** AT RIGHT ANGLES in or into a position that is at right angles to sth else

square matrix *n.* a mathematical matrix that has equal numbers of rows and columns

square meal *n.* a filling and nourishing meal

square measure *n.* a unit or system of units for measuring an area, e.g. a hectare or an acre

square-rigged *adj.* having principal sails that are at right angles to the length of the ship

square-rigger *n.* a sailing vessel equipped with square-shaped sails

square root *n.* a number or quantity that when multiplied by itself gives the stated number or quantity. For example, 4 or –4 is the square root of 16.

$$\sqrt{81} = 9$$

$$9^2 = 81$$

Square root

square sail *n.* a sail with four sides that is usually suspended horizontally on the mast

square shooter *n.* *US* sb who is straightforward and honest (*informal*)

squarrose /skwár rōss, skwór-/ *adj.* with many scales or scabs (*dated*) [Mid-18thC. From Latin *squarrosus* 'scurfy'.]

squash[1] /skwosh/ *v.* (**squashes, squashing, squashed**) **1.** *vt.* FLATTEN STH WITH PRESSURE to apply pressure to sth so that its shape is altered ○ *managed to squash it flat before packing it* **2.** *vti.* ENTER OR PUT STH INTO A SMALL SPACE to force your way into a confined space, or force sth into a confined space ○ *people trying to squash into the lift* **3.** *vt.* POL, MIL PUT DOWN A REBELLION to suppress a revolt or uprising completely by using force **4.** *vt.* MAKE SB FEEL SMALL to silence sb with a crushing answer **5.** *vi.* BECOME FLAT to become flat, often making a squelching sound ■ *n.* **1.** BEVERAGES JUICE-BASED DRINK a soft drink made from fruit juice or syrup diluted with water **2.** MANY PEOPLE IN A SMALL SPACE a situation in which a lot of people are crushed into a small space ○ *It was a terrible squash in the back seat.* **3.** ACTION OR NOISE OF SQUASHING the action or noise that results when sth is being squashed **4.** STH SQUASHED a squashed object or number of objects **5.** RACKET GAMES BALL GAME IN A WALLED COURT a game for two or four participants played in an enclosed court with long-handled rackets and a small ball that may be hit off any of the walls **6.** RACKET GAMES GAME LIKE SQUASH WITH TENNIS BALLS a ball game for two players resembling squash rackets but played with a tennis ball and rackets shaped more like conventional tennis rackets [Mid-16thC. Via Old French *esquasser* from assumed Vulgar Latin *exquassare*, from Latin *quassare* (see QUASH).] —**squasher** *n.*

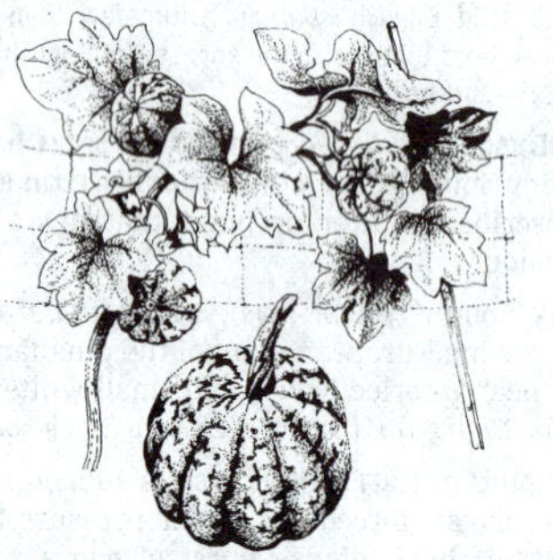

Squash

squash[2] /skwosh/ (*plural* **squash** *or* **squashes**) *n.* **1.** FOOD VEGETABLE OF THE GOURD FAMILY the fruit of any plant of the gourd family, cooked and eaten as a vegetable **2.** PLANTS PLANT BEARING A GOURD any plant yielding or cultivated for its edible gourds. Genus: *Cucurbita.* [Mid-17thC. Shortening of Narragansett *asquutasquash*, literally 'green things that may be eaten raw'.]

squash bug *n.* a large black North American insect that is destructive to plants of the gourd family such as squash and pumpkins. Latin name: *Anasa tristis.*

squash rackets *n.* = **squash**[1] *v.* 5 (*takes a singular verb*)

squash tennis *n.* = **squash**[1] *n.* 1 (*takes a singular verb*)

squashy /skwóshi/ (**-ier, -iest**) *adj.* **1.** EASILY SQUASHED soft and easily squashed **2.** OVERRIPE overripe and full of juice **3.** SOFT AND WET soft and waterlogged **4.** LOOKING SQUASHED having a squashed appearance

squat /skwot/ *vi.* (**squats, squatting, squatted**) **1.** CROUCH DOWN to crouch down with the knees bent and the thighs resting on the calves **2.** CROUCH DOWN LOW to crouch close to the ground like an animal, especially in order to avoid being seen **3.** LAW OCCUPY PROPERTY WITHOUT A LEGAL CLAIM to occupy land or buildings without permission of the owner or other rights holder ■ *adj.* (**squatter, squattest**) **1.** SHORT AND SOLID short and solidly built **2.** IN A CROUCHED POSTURE in a crouched position ■ *n.* **1.** ACTION OF SQUATTING the action of crouching down with the knees bent and the thighs resting on the calves **2.** SQUATTING POSITION a crouched posture with knees bent and thighs resting on calves **3.** SPORTS **WEIGHTLIFTING EXERCISE** an exercise in weightlifting in which the lifter raises a barbell while rising from a crouching position **4.** LAW **PROPERTY OCCUPIED BY SQUATTERS** a piece of property that is occupied by squatters **5.** ZOOL **HARE'S LAIR** the den of a hare [14thC. Via Old French *esquatir* 'to crush', from, ultimately, Latin *coactus*, the past participle of *cogere* 'to force together' (source of English *cogent*).] —**squatness** *n.*

squatly /skwótli/ *adv.* in a solid unyielding manner ○ *The piano stood squatly by the window.*

squatter /skwóttər/ *n.* **1.** LAW **ILLEGAL OCCUPANT OF LAND OR PROPERTY** sb who occupies land or property illegally, especially sb who takes over and lives in sb else's empty house **2.** HIST **HOMESTEADER** an early North American homesteader **3.** HIST **TENANT ON AUSTRALIAN GRAZING LAND** an early Australian settler who farmed supposedly vacant land and subsequently obtained a lease for it from the government **4.** *Aus* **LANDOWNER** a wealthy landowner **5.** HIST **SETTLER IN NEW ZEALAND** an early settler in New Zealand who leased a large area of government-owned land **6. SB OR STH THAT CROUCHES** a person or animal that crouches down

squattocracy /skwo tókrəssi/ *n. Aus* wealthy landowners regarded as a powerful and influential social class (*disapproving*)

squaw /skwaw/ *n.* **1. OFFENSIVE TERM** a highly offensive term for a Native North American woman or wife (*dated offensive*) **2. OFFENSIVE TERM** a highly offensive term for a woman or wife (*slang offensive*) [Mid-17thC. From Narragansett *squaws* 'woman' or Massachusett *squa*.]

squawk /skwawk/ *v.* (**squawks, squawking, squawked**) **1.** *vi.* **UTTER A HARSH CRY** to utter a loud harsh cry **2.** *vti.* **COMPLAIN LOUDLY** to complain or protest about sth noisily and annoyingly (*informal*) **3.** *vi.* **CRY LOUDLY** to cry or wail loudly and annoyingly (*informal*) **4.** *vti.* **SAY STH LOUDLY AND SHRILLY** to say sth in a loud harsh voice (*informal*) ■ *n.* **1. RAUCOUS CRY** a loud raucous cry **2. NOISY COMPLAINT** a noisy and annoying complaint or protest (*informal*) [Early 19thC. An imitation of the sound.] —**squawker** *n.*

squawk box *n.* a public-address system or one of its speakers, originally box-shaped (*dated slang*)

squaw man *n.* a highly offensive term for the husband of a Native North American woman who is himself not Native North American (*slang dated offensive*)

squeak /skweek/ *v.* (**squeaks, squeaking, squeaked**) **1.** *vi.* **MAKE A HIGH-PITCHED SOUND** to make a short high-pitched sound or cry **2.** *vt.* **SAY STH SHRILLY** to say sth in a high-pitched voice **3.** *vi.* **BE AN INFORMER** to give information or evidence about sb to the police (*slang disapproving*) **4.** *vi.* **MANAGE STH WITH NARROW MARGIN** to only just manage to pass, win, or survive sth (*informal*) ○ *squeaked through her final exams* ■ *n.* **HIGH-PITCHED CRY** a short high-pitched sound or cry [14thC. An imitation of the sound.] ◇ **a narrow** *or* **close** *or* **near squeak** an escape from sth by an extremely narrow margin

squeaker /skweékər/ *n.* **1. SB OR STH THAT SQUEAKS** a person, animal, or device that makes a short high-pitched sound or cry **2. INFORMANT** sb who gives information about a criminal to the police (*slang disapproving*) **3.** *US* **NARROWLY WON VICTORY** a competition, election, race, or other event that is won by a very slight margin (*informal*)

squeaky /skweéki/ (**-ier, -iest**) *adj.* **1. TENDING TO SQUEAK** having a tendency to squeak **2. DESIGNED TO SQUEAK** designed to make a squeaking noise when pressed —**squeakily** *adv.* —**squeakiness** *n.*

squeaky-clean *adj.* **1. EXTREMELY CLEAN** so clean that it squeaks when rubbed ○ *His hair was squeaky-clean.* **2. IRREPROACHABLY GOOD** appearing to be almost unnaturally free from general human shortcomings (*informal*)

squeal /skweel/ *n.* **1. SHRILL CRY** a short high cry expressing pain, excitement, delight, or other strong emotion **2. LOUD HIGH SOUND** the screaming sound made by tyres when a vehicle brakes suddenly ■ *v.* (**squeals, squealing, squealed**) **1.** *vti.* **GIVE A SHORT HIGH CRY** to speak or make a sound in a loud high-pitched tone **2.** *vi.* **BECOME AN INFORMER** to give information or evidence against sb to the police (*slang disapproving*) **3.** *vi.* **PROTEST LOUDLY** to protest or complain loudly and annoyingly (*informal*) [13thC. An imitation of the sound.] —**squealer** *n.*

squeamish /skweémish/ *adj.* **1. EASILY MADE TO FEEL SICK** easily sickened by such sights as blood or physical injuries **2. EASILY OFFENDED** easily shocked by such things as violence, the mention of bodily functions, or strong language **3. FASTIDIOUS** excessively scrupulous about manners or behaviour [14thC. From Anglo-Norman *escoymous*, of unknown origin.] —**squeamishly** *adv.* —**squeamishness** *n.*

squeegee /skweé jee/ *n.* **1. IMPLEMENT FOR CLEANING WINDOWS** a T-shaped implement edged with plastic or rubber that is drawn across the surface of windows to remove water after washing **2.** PRINTING, PHOTOGRAPHY **IMPLEMENT TO ELIMINATE LIQUID** an implement, usually a rubber roller, that is used in printing and photography to remove excess water or ink [Mid-19thC. Formed from obsolete *squeege* 'to press', an alteration of SQUEEZE.]

squeegee man *n.* a man or youth, typically one spending time on the streets, who enters stopped traffic without invitation, attempting to wash motorists' windscreens for money (*slang*)

squeeze /skweez/ *v.* (**squeezes, squeezing, squeezed**) **1.** *vt.* **PRESS STH FROM TWO SIDES** to press sth hard in the hand or between two other objects, especially in order to reduce its size or alter its shape **2.** *vt.* **PRESS SB ENCOURAGINGLY** to exert slight pressure on part of sb's body such as the hand, knee, or shoulder, usually as a sign of affection and reassurance **3.** *vti.* **APPLY PRESSURE** to exert pressure on sth ○ *Come on, squeeze harder!* **4.** *vt.* **HUG SB** to hold sb tightly in your arms **5.** *vt.* **PUSH A PERSON OR OBJECT INTO A GAP** to force a person, object, or part of the body into or through a small or narrow space **6.** *vi.* **PUSH INTO OR THROUGH SMALL SPACE** to push into or through a small, narrow, or crowded space ○ *I squeezed through a gap in the hedge.* **7.** *vt.* **PRESS FRUIT TO OBTAIN JUICE** to compress a piece of fruit, especially a citrus fruit, in order to extract its juice **8.** *vt.* **FIND TIME FOR** to find time or space for sb or sth in a busy schedule ○ *I could squeeze you in at 9.30.* **9.** *vt.* **OBTAIN USING PHYSICAL PRESSURE** to extract sth by exerting physical pressure on sb or sth **10.** *vt.* **EXTORT MONEY OR FAVOURS** to obtain sth such as money or favours from sb by means of psychological pressure or threats **11.** *vt.* **DEMAND MONEY FROM** to make excessive financial demands on sb, especially for rent and taxes **12.** *vt.* **PRODUCE WITH DIFFICULTY** to make an effort to produce sth ○ *He managed to squeeze out a timid 'thank you'.* **13.** *vi.* **JUST MANAGE** just narrowly to succeed in winning, passing, or surviving sth ○ *managed to squeeze through the exam with a D* **14.** *vt.* CARDS **PLAY A CARD** to lead a card in bridge or whist that may force an opponent to discard a valuable card **15.** *vi.* **COLLAPSE** to condense or collapse under pressure **16.** *vi.* CRAFT **MAKE AN IMPRESSION OF** to make an impression or mould of an object using a soft material such as wax or plaster of Paris ■ *n.* **1. PHYSICAL PRESSING** a pressing action ○ *gave the sponge a quick squeeze* **2. STH PRESSED OUT** an amount pressed out of sth ○ *Add a squeeze of lemon.* **3. HUG** a hug or close embrace **4. TOUCH THAT SHOWS AFFECTION** the action of briefly clasping sb's hand, arm, knee, or other part of the body, usually as a sign of affection or reassurance **5. CROWD OF PEOPLE OR THINGS** a group of people or objects crowded together **6.** ECON **RESTRICTION IN FINANCIAL CRISIS** a government-imposed restriction on credit and investment to counteract inflation or some other financial crisis **7.** COMM **FINANCIAL PRESSURE TO ACT** an action by business competitors that influences or forces others to make some type of transaction **8. STH EXTORTED** money or goods obtained from sb as a result of threats or the use of force **9.** CARDS **SQUEEZE PLAY** a squeeze play (*informal*) **10.** CRAFT **IMPRESSION OF AN OBJECT** an impression of an object made by using a soft material such as wax or plaster of Paris [Mid-16thC. Alteration of obsolete *quease*, ultimately of unknown origin.] —**squeezability** /skweézə billəti/ *n.* —**squeezable** /skweézəb'l/ *adj.* ◇ **put the squeeze on sb 1.** to exert pressure on sb by means of force and threats in order to extort money or goods or to obtain some other end, e.g. a confession (*slang*) **2.** to place sb in a difficult situation, especially financially, or pressure sb to do sth (*slang*)

squeeze off *vi.* to fire a bullet from a gun

squeezebox /skweéz boks/ *n.* a concertina or small accordion (*informal*)

squeeze play *n.* a play in bridge or whist in which an opponent is forced to discard a valuable and potentially winning card

squelch /skwelch/ *v.* (**squelches, squelching, squelched**) **1.** *vi.* **MAKE A SUCKING SOUND** to move with or make a sucking or gurgling sound like that of sb treading on muddy ground **2.** *vt.* **CRUSH BY TRAMPLING** to crush sth by trampling, or as if by trampling **3.** *vt.* **SILENCE STH** to silence sth such as a rumour or an unwanted remark (*slang*) ■ *n.* **1. SUCKING SOUND** a sucking or gurgling sound like that of sb treading on muddy ground **2. CRUSHING RETORT** a clever or cutting answer to sth sb has said (*slang*) **3.** ELECTRON ENG **ELECTRONIC CIRCUIT** an electronic circuit that automatically reduces the gain of a receiver in response to an input signal that exceeds a predetermined level [Early 17thC. An imitation of the sound.] —**squelcher** *n.* —**squelchy** *adj.*

squeteague /skwi teég/ (*plural* **-teague** *or* **-teagues**) *n.* any one of several large Atlantic fish of the croaker family, especially the Atlantic weakfish. Genus: *Cynoscion.* [Early 19thC. From southern New England Algonquian.]

squib /skwib/ *n.* **1. SMALL FIREWORK** a small firework, especially a banger **2. DUD FIREWORK** a faulty firework that burns without exploding **3.** LITERAT **PIECE OF SATIRE** a short satirical piece of writing or speech **4.** PRESS **SHORT JOURNALISTIC PIECE** a short humorous piece that acts as a filler in a newspaper **5.** AEROSP **DEVICE FOR FIRING A ROCKET ENGINE** a small device for firing a rocket engine **6. SB UNIMPORTANT** sb who is considered to be insignificant or mean-spirited (*archaic*) ■ *v.* (**squibs, squibbing, squibbed**) **1.** *vt.* LITERAT **SATIRIZE SB** to write a satirical squib about sb **2.** *vt.* AMERICAN FOOTBALL **KICK A BALL LOW** in American football, to kick the ball in such a way that it wobbles as it bounces along the ground **3.** *vi.* **SET OFF A FIREWORK** to set off a small firework, especially a banger [Early 16thC. Origin uncertain: perhaps an imitation of the sound made by a faulty firecracker.]

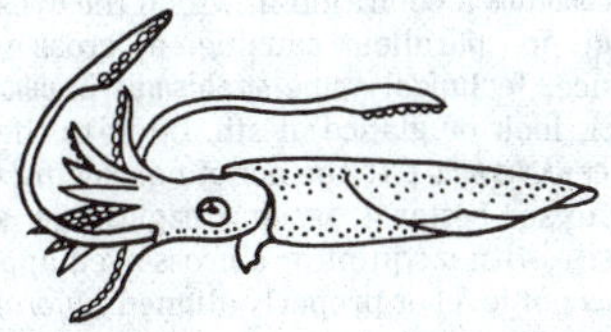

Squid

squid /skwid/ (*plural* **squid** *or* **squids**) *n.* **1.** MARINE BIOL **MOLLUSC WITH TEN ARMS** a marine cephalopod mollusc that has two long tentacles and eight shorter arms, a long tapered body, two triangular fins, and an internal shell. It is often cooked and eaten. Order: Teuthoidea. **2.** FOOD **SQUID AS FOOD** a dish of squid that has been prepared and cooked for eating [Late 16thC. Origin unknown.]

squidgy /skwíjji/ (**-gier, -giest**) *adj.* **1. SOFT AND DAMP** being or feeling soft and damp **2. FEELING SQUASHY** feeling unpleasantly soft and squashy (*informal*) [Late 19thC. Origin uncertain: perhaps from earlier *squidge*, an imitation of the sound made by walking on muddy ground.]

squiffy /skwíffi/ (**squiffier, squiffiest**) *adj.* slightly drunk (*informal*) [Mid-19thC. Origin unknown.]

squiggle /skwígg'l/ *n.* **1. WAVY LINE** a wavy or curly line or movement **2. ILLEGIBLE WORD** an illegible handwritten word or words ■ *vi.* (**-gles, -gling, -gled**) (*informal*) **1. SQUIRM** to twist, squirm, or wriggle **2. DRAW SQUIGGLES** to draw wavy or curly lines [Early 19thC. Origin uncertain: perhaps a blend of SQUIRM and WIGGLE or WRIGGLE.] —**squiggler** *n.* —**squiggly** *adj.*

squill /skwil/ *n.* **1.** PLANTS **PLANT WITH SMALL DROOPING FLOWERS** a bulbous plant native to Europe, Asia, and Africa that has small blue, white, pink, or purple drooping flowers. Genus: *Scilla* and *Pushkinia*. **2.** PLANTS = **sea squill 3.** MED DRIED BULB OF A SEA SQUILL the dried slices of a sea squill's bulb, used medicinally in the past as an expectorant and diuretic [14thC. Via Latin *squilla* 'shrimp, squill' from Greek *skilla*, of unknown origin.]

squilla /skwíllə/ *n.* a burrowing marine crustacean that has eyes on stalks and large grasping appendages. Genus: *Squilla*. [Early 16thC. From modern Latin, genus name, from Latin, 'shrimp' (see SQUILL).]

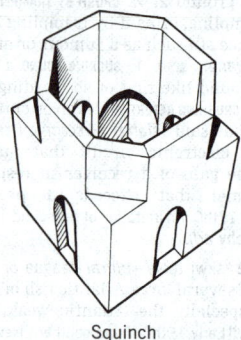

Squinch

squinch[1] /skwinch/ *n.* ARCHIT an arch, corbelling, or lintel built across the upper inside corner of a square tower to support the weight of a spire or other structure above [Mid-19thC. Alteration of *scuncheon*, from Old French *escoinson*, literally 'corner out', from *coin* 'corner' (see COIN).]

squinch[2] /skwinch/ (**squinches, squinching, squinched**) *v.* US **1.** *vt.* SCREW UP THE FACE to screw up the eyes or face **2.** *vti.* CROUCH DOWN to crouch so as to take up less space [Early 19thC. Origin uncertain: probably a blend of SQUINT and PINCH.]

squint /skwint/ *v.* (**squints, squinting, squinted**) **1.** *vi.* PARTLY CLOSE THE EYES to half- close the eyes so as to see better ○ *a photo of them squinting into the camera in bright sunlight* **2.** *vti.* HAVE EYES NOT LOOKING IN PARALLEL to have eyes that are not aligned in parallel **3.** *vi.* GLANCE ASIDE to glance or look at sth sideways **4.** *vi. US* LOOK ASKANCE to regard sth with disapproval (*disapproving*) ○ *Congress clearly is squinting at the prospect of increased funding for the program.* ■ *n.* **1.** EYE CONDITION a condition in which the eyes are not aligned in parallel, causing a cross-eyed appearance. Technical name **strabismus 2.** QUICK GLIMPSE a quick look or glance at sth, often to the side **3.** ACTION OF NARROWING EYES the act of narrowing the eyes to try to see better **4.** ARCHIT = **hagioscope** ■ *adj.* **1.** CROSS-EYED with a squint or a cross-eyed appearance **2.** ASKEW not level or properly aligned (*informal*) [Mid-16thC. Shortening of *asquint*, of uncertain origin: perhaps literally 'on a slant', formed from Low German or Dutch.] —**squinter** *n.* —**squinty** *adj.* ◇ **have** *or* **take a squint at** to have a look at sth (*informal*)

squint-eyed *adj.* **1.** WITH SQUINT with one or both eyes looking slightly inwards or outwards rather than in parallel **2.** LOOKING WITH EYES PARTLY CLOSED looking with the eyes partly closed to see better **3.** ASKANCE looking askance or sidelong

squirarchy /skwír aárki/ *n.* = **squirearchy** [Late 18thC. Coined from SQUIRE + HIERARCHY.]

squire /skwīr/ *n.* **1.** RURAL LANDOWNER a country landowner in England, often the main local landowner **2.** HIST ATTENDANT TO A KNIGHT a young apprentice knight who acted as an attendant to a knight in the Middle Ages **3.** MAN WHO ESCORTS A WOMAN a man who is escorting a woman or going out with her regularly (*dated*) **4.** FORM OF ADDRESS a term used by a man to address another (*informal*) **5.** *US, Can* TITLE GIVEN TO A RURAL DIGNITARY a title of respect given to a magistrate or local dignity, especially in a rural district (*dated*) ■ *vt.* (**squires, squiring, squired**) ESCORT SB to escort or go out with a man or a woman (*dated*) (*often passive*) [13thC. From Old French *esquier* (see ESQUIRE).]

squirearchy /skwír aarki/ (*plural* **-chies**), **squirarchy** (*plural* **-chies**) *n.* the main rural landowners collectively, especially the social, economic, or political class formed by such landed proprietors [Late 18thC. Coined from SQUIRE + HIERARCHY.] —**squirearchal** /skwī raark'l/ *adj.* —**squirearchic** /skwī raark-/ *adj.*

squireen /skwī reén/ *n. Ireland* a rural landowner owning a relatively small amount of land (*archaic*) [Early 19thC. Coined from SQUIRE + the suffix *-een* 'little', from Irish *-ín*.]

squirm /skwurm/ *vi.* (**squirms, squirming, squirmed**) **1.** WRIGGLE FROM DISCOMFORT to wriggle the body, especially because of discomfort or in an attempt to break free from being held **2.** FEEL EMOTIONAL DISTRESS to feel very uncomfortable, especially because of shame, embarrassment, or revulsion ○ *a tough question that made the press office squirm* ■ *n.* WRIGGLING MOVEMENT a wriggling movement, especially from discomfort or as an attempt to break free from being held [Late 17thC. Origin unknown.] —**squirmer** *n.* —**squirmy** *adj.*

Squirrel

squirrel /skwírrəl/ *n.* **1.** SMALL BUSHY-TAILED RODENT a small rodent that has a long bushy tail, lives in trees, and eats nuts and seeds. Family: Sciuridae. ◊ **grey squirrel, red squirrel 2.** RODENT LIKE A SQUIRREL a rodent related to or resembling the squirrel, e.g. the ground squirrel, flying squirrel, or chipmunk **3.** *US* CRIMINAL SUSPECT a person who is a criminal or who is suspected of having committed a crime (*slang*) **4.** HOARDER sb who hoards things (*informal*) ■ *vt.* (**-rels, -relling, -relled**) HOARD STH to hoard or save things [14thC. Via Anglo-Norman *esquirel*, literally 'little squirrel', from, ultimately, Greek *skiouros*, literally 'shady-tail', from *skia* 'shadow' + *oura* 'tail'.]

squirrel cage *n.* **1.** ROTATING FRAMEWORK FOR AN ANIMAL a cage containing a cylindrical framework that goes round when a small pet rodent runs inside it **2.** DULL TASK a dull, repetitive, seemingly purposeless task **3.** MECH ENG WINDING IN INDUCTION MOTORS a rotor of an induction motor consisting of copper bars mounted in slots around the periphery

squirrelfish /skwírrel fish/ (*plural* **-fish** *or* **-fishes**) *n.* a brightly coloured nocturnal fish that lives in the shallow waters of tropical reefs. Family: Holocentridae. [*Squirrel* possibly from their large round eyes and spiny dorsal fin, which is arched like a squirrel's tail]

squirrelly /skwírrəli/ *adj.* **1.** *US* VERY ECCENTRIC very eccentric or odd (*informal offensive*) **2.** CHARACTERISTIC OF SQUIRREL resembling or characteristic of a squirrel ['Eccentric' from the erratic movements of squirrels]

squirrel monkey *n.* a small long-tailed monkey of Central and South America that has soft yellowish-grey, brown, or reddish fur, a white face, and a black muzzle. Genus: *Saimiri*. [*Squirrel* perhaps from its long tail, which is used for balancing]

squirt /skwurt/ *v.* (**squirts, squirting, squirted**) **1.** *vti.* FORCE STH OUT FROM A NARROW OPENING to force sth or be pushed out of a narrow opening in a strong quick stream ○ *The ketchup squirted all over the table.* ○ *managed to squirt the last of the toothpaste out of the tube* **2.** *vt.* SQUIRT LIQUID OVER STH to hit or cover sb or sth with liquid that is forced out of a narrow opening in a strong quick stream ○ *She squirted me with her water bottle.* ■ *n.* **1.** STREAM OF EJECTED LIQUID a small stream of liquid forced out of a narrow opening ○ *a squirt of body lotion* **2.** OFFENSIVE TERM an offensive term that deliberately insults sb's young age or small size, especially in response to perceived impudence (*informal insult*) **3.** INSTRUMENT FOR SQUIRTING LIQUID an instrument such as a syringe that is used to dispense liquid in a thin quick stream [15thC. An imitation of the sound of sth being squirted.]

squirt gun *n. US* = **water pistol**

squirting cucumber *n.* a Mediterranean vine of the gourd family with oblong fruit that burst when ripe, ejecting seeds and juice. Latin name: *Ecballium elaterium.*

squish /skwish/ *v.* (**squishes, squishing, squished**) **1.** *vt.* SQUEEZE to squeeze or crush sth soft **2.** *vi.* MAKE A SOFT SPLASHING NOISE to make a sucking or soft splashing sound when subjected to pressure, as when being walked on or squeezed ■ *n.* **1.** SOFT SPLASHING NOISE a sucking or soft splashing sound **2.** OFFENSIVE TERM an offensive term for sb perceived as weak or cowardly (*slang insult*) [Mid-17thC. Origin uncertain: probably an alteration of SQUASH[1].]

squishy /skwíshi/ (**-ier, -iest**) *adj.* soft and giving under pressure, like mud or a soft fruit

squit /skwit/ *n.* **1.** OFFENSIVE TERM an offensive term that deliberately insults sb's status and importance (*informal insult*) **2.** NONSENSE nonsense (*dated informal*) ■ **squits** *npl.* DIARRHOEA diarrhoea (*slang*) [Early 19thC. Origin uncertain: perhaps from *squitter* 'to squirt, have diarrhoea', an imitation of the sound.]

squiz /skwiz/ (*plural* **squizzes**) *n.* ANZ a quick inquisitive look at sth (*informal*) ○ *Can I have a squiz at your paper?* [Early 20thC. Origin uncertain: possibly a blend of SQUINT and QUIZ.]

sr *symbol.* steradian

Sr[1] *symbol.* strontium

Sr[2] *abbr.* **1.** Sr, sr senior **2.** Señor **3.** Senhor **4.** Sir **5.** sister

Sra *abbr.* **1.** Senhora **2.** Señora

sraddhaa /shráad aal/, **shraddh** /shraad/ *n. S Asia* in the Indian subcontinent, a ceremonial offering of food and water to the dead [Late 18thC. From Sanskrit *śrāddha*, from *śraddhā* 'faith, trust'.]

SRAM *abbr.* static random access memory

Sranantongo /sraánən tóngō/, **Sranan** /sraánən/ *n.* a creole language based on English that is the lingua franca of Suriname [Mid-20thC. From Sranantongo, literally 'Suriname tongue'.]

SRCN *abbr.* State Registered Children's Nurse

S-R connection *n.* the relationship between a stimulus and a response

Srebrenica /srébbrə neétsə/ town in Bosnia-Herzegovina, southeastern Europe, situated between Sarajevo and Tuzla. During the Bosnian-Serbian-Croatian War (1991 to 1995), it was declared a Muslim enclave. Population: 37,211 (1991).

Sri /sree/ *n.* **1.** TITLE FOR A MAN a title of respect for a man in the Indian subcontinent, equivalent to 'Mr' **2.** TITLE FOR A HINDU GOD OR HOLY MAN a title of respect for a Hindu deity or holy man **3.** = **Lakshmi** [Late 18thC. Via Hindi from Sanskrit *śrī* 'lord', literally 'beauty, wealth, majesty'.]

Sri Lanka

Sri Lanka /shri láng kə/ island republic in southern Asia. It became independent from Britain in 1948. Language: Sinhala. Currency: Sri Lankan rupee. Capital: Colombo. Population: 18,318,000 (1996). Area: 65,610 sq. km/25,326 sq. mi. Official name **Democratic Socialist Republic of Sri Lanka.** Former name Ceylon —**Sri Lankan** *n., adj.*

Sriman *n.* = **Sri** *n.* 1

Srinagar /sri núggər, shrínnə gaar/, **Srīnager** capital city of the state of Jammu and Kashmir, northwestern India. Population: 595,000 (1991).

SRN *abbr.* State Registered Nurse

sRNA *abbr.* soluble RNA

SRO *abbr.* **1.** single room occupancy **2.** standing room only **3.** Statutory Rules and Orders **4.** self-regulatory organization

Srta *abbr.* **1.** Senhorita **2.** Señorita

SS *abbr.* **1.** Saints **2.** Social Security **3.** steamship **4.** Sunday school **5.** sworn statement [In sense 4, an abbreviation of German *Schutzstaffel*, literally 'defence squadron']

ss. *abbr.* **1.** sections **2.** scilicet

SSB *abbr.* single sideband (transmission)

SSC *abbr.* **1.** *Scotland* Solicitor to the Supreme Court **2.** Secondary School Certificate

SSD *abbr.* Social Services Department

SSE *abbr.* south-southeast

SSGT, **S., Sgt.** *abbr.* staff sergeant

SSHA *abbr.* Scottish Special Housing Association

SSM *abbr.* surface-to-surface missile

SSP *abbr.* statutory sick pay

ssp. (*plural* **sspp.**) *abbr.* subspecies

SSR *abbr.* HIST Soviet Socialist Republic

SSSI *abbr.* site of special scientific interest

SST *abbr.* supersonic transport

SSW *abbr.* south-southwest

st *abbr.* short ton

ST *abbr.* standard time

st. *abbr.* **1.** stanza **2.** stone **3.** state **4.** stet **5.** statute **6.** CRICKET stumped by **7.** stitch **8.** start **9.** strophe

St. *abbr.* **1.** Saint **2.** Strait **3.** Street

Sta *abbr.* Santa

sta. *abbr.* **1.** station **2.** stationary

stab /stab/ *v.* (**stabs, stabbing, stabbed**) **1.** *vt.* THRUST A KNIFE INTO to thrust a knife or other sharp pointed instrument into sb or sth **2.** *vti.* JAB FINGER OR OBJECT AT to thrust a finger or an object sharply at sth ○ *He stabbed his potato angrily with his fork.* **3.** *vi.* HURT LIKE A KNIFE WOUND to cause a sudden sharp hurting sensation, like that of a knife wound ○ *Pain stabbed at her temples.* ■ *n.* **1.** ACT OF STABBING SB the action or result of thrusting a knife or other sharp implement into sb (*often used before a noun*) ○ *a stab wound* **2.** SEVERE CRITICISM a severe criticism of sb **3.** SUDDEN PAINFUL FEELING a sudden brief sensation, especially of pain ○ *felt a sudden stab of loss* **4.** ATTEMPT an attempt at sth (*informal*) [15thC. Origin unknown.] —**stabber** *n.* ◇ **stab in the back** a betrayal or act of treachery (*informal*) ◇ **stab sb in the back** to betray or harm sb who trusts you (*informal*)

Stabat Mater /stàa bat màatər/ *n.* a Latin hymn that was composed in the 13th century and concerns the grief of the Virgin Mary at the crucifixion of Jesus Christ [Mid-19thC. From Latin *stabat mater dolorosa* 'the mother stood, full of grief', the first words of the hymn.]

stabbing /stábbing/ *n.* ACT OF THRUSTING A KNIFE INTO SB an incident in which sb is deliberately stabbed with a knife or sharp object ■ *adj.* WITH SUDDEN PAIN brief, sharp, and sudden, as if from the thrust of a knife ○ *a stabbing pain in the side*

stabile /stáy bīl/ *n.* SCULPTURE SCULPTURE ATTACHED TO STH an abstract sculpture made of wire, metal, or other materials and attached to fixed supports. ◊ **mobile** ■ *adj.* **1.** STABLE in a fixed position **2.** CHEM NOT CHANGING CHEMICALLY not readily undergoing chemical change [Late 18thC. From Latin *stabilis* (see STABLE[1]).]

stabilisation *n.* = **stabilization**

stabilise /stáybi līz/ *vti.* = **stabilize**

stabiliser /stáybi līzər/ *n.* = **stabilizer**

stability /stə bílləti/ *n.* **1.** STABLE QUALITY the condition of being stable ○ *policies aimed at creating economic stability* **2.** MENTAL FIRMNESS mental or psychological firmness **3.** RESISTANCE TO CHANGE resistance to any sudden change or deterioration **4.** MECH ENG ABILITY TO ADJUST TO LOAD CHANGES a property of a transmission system that allows changes in load to be met without any reduction in performance **5.** METEOROL AIR MASS WITHOUT UPWARD MOVEMENT a condition of no upward movement in an air mass **6.** METEOROL RESISTANCE TO AIR CURRENTS a measure of the tendency of an air mass to be influenced by convection currents **7.** ECOL ABILITY TO MAINTAIN A BALANCE the ability of an ecological community to resist disturbance caused by changes in, e.g., climate, or the ability to return to its original state after disturbance **8.** AEROSP, SHIPPING RESISTANCE TO A CHANGED POSITION the capability of an aircraft, rocket, or ship to maintain a position and to return to it if displaced **9.** CHEM RESISTANCE TO A CHEMICAL CHANGE a resistance to chemical change **10.** PHYS MEASURE OF MAINTAINING EQUILIBRIUM a measure of the difficulty of displacing an object or system from equilibrium

stabilization /stàybilī záysh'n/, **stabilisation** *n.* the act or process of stabilizing sth

stabilization fund *n.* a reserve of money that a country uses to maintain its official exchange rate by buying and selling foreign exchange

stabilize /stáybi līz/ (**-lizes, -lizing, -lized**), **stabilise** (**-lises, -lising, -lised**) *v.* **1.** *vti.* MAKE OR BECOME STABLE to become stable, or make sth stable ○ *The patient's condition has stabilized.* **2.** *vt.* MAINTAIN THE LEVEL OF STH to maintain an unfluctuating level of sth

stabilizer /stáybi līzər/, **stabiliser** *n.* **1.** AEROSP AEROFOIL THAT STABILIZES AN AIRCRAFT an aerofoil or combination of aerofoils, e.g. in the tail assembly of an aeroplane, that keeps an aircraft or missile aligned with the direction of flight. A vertical stabilizer controls yawing, or side-to-side motion, while a horizontal stabilizer controls pitching, or up-and-down motion. **2.** SHIPPING FINS TO CONTROL A SHIP'S ROLLING one or more pairs of submerged fins, often gyroscopically controlled, used to minimize the rolling of a ship in rough waters **3.** CHEM ADDITIVE THAT MAINTAINS CHEMICAL PROPERTIES a chemical compound added to another substance to make it resistant to chemical or physical change **4.** ELEC DEVICE TO PRODUCE A CONSTANT VOLTAGE a device used to maintain a constant voltage from a source of direct current **5.** INDUST STH ADDED TO DISPERSE PAINT a substance added to a fast-drying paint to improve the dispersion of pigment **6.** STABILIZING PERSON OR THING sth that or sb who acts to bring stability ■ **stabilizers, stabilisers** *npl.* EXTRA WHEELS TO BALANCE BICYCLE a pair of small wheels fitted to the back wheel of a bicycle to help balance it while sb is learning to ride. US term **training wheels**

stable[1] /stáyb'l/ *adj.* **1.** NOT CHANGING steady and not liable to change ○ *Prices have remained stable.* **2.** NOT LIKELY TO MOVE steady or firm and not liable to move **3.** NOT EXCITABLE having a calm and steady temperament rather than being excitable or given to apparently irrational behaviour **4.** CHEM NOT READILY UNDERGOING CHANGE not subject to changes in chemical or physical properties **5.** PHYS NOT NATURALLY RADIOACTIVE incapable of becoming a different isotope or element by radioactive decay [13thC. Via Anglo-Norman and Old French from Latin *stabilis* (source of English *establish*). Ultimately from an Indo-European word meaning 'to stand' (see STABLE[2]).] —**stableness** *n.* —**stably** *adv.*

stable[2] /stáyb'l/ *n.* **1.** AGRIC BUILDING FOR HORSES a building in which horses, and sometimes other large types of livestock, are kept **2.** EQU HORSES OWNED BY SB the group of horses, especially racehorses, owned by one person or kept and trained at one establishment **3.** EQU PEOPLE WORKING IN A STABLE the people who work in a stable **4.** GROUP UNDER MANAGEMENT a group of people managed by the same person or organization ○ *a stable of bestselling authors* ■ *vti.* (**stables, stabling, stabled**) PUT OR LIVE IN A STABLE to keep or put a horse or other large animal in a particular building, or be kept in a particular building ○ *We stabled our horses in the barn.* [13thC. Via Old French *estable* from Latin *stabulum*. Ultimately from an Indo-European word meaning 'to stand', which is also the ancestor of English *stand, stem,* and *static*.]

stableboy /stáyb'l boy/ *n.* a youth or man who looks after horses in a racing stable

stable door *n.* a door split into upper and lower sections that can be closed separately. In stables the opened top section allows a confined horse to see out.

stable fly *n.* a biting bloodsucking fly like a housefly that attacks humans and domestic animals. Latin name: *Stomoxys calcitrans*.

stable lad *n.* = **stableboy**

stablemate /stáyb'l mayt/ *n.* **1.** EQU HORSE FROM THE SAME STABLE a horse that belongs to the same owner or is kept and trained at the same racing stable as another **2.** PERSON ASSOCIATED WITH ANOTHER sb who or sth that is associated with another, e.g. an author who shares the same publisher as another author

stabling /stáybling/ *n.* **1.** STABLES a stable or stables **2.** ACCOMMODATION FOR HORSES accommodation for horses, usually but not always in a stable

stab stitch *n.* a very small straight stitch designed to hold two or more pieces of fabric together without showing as more than a dot on the surface

stacc. *abbr.* staccato

staccato /stə kàatō/ *adv.* MUSIC IN QUICK SEPARATE NOTES to be played, as rapid short detached notes (*used as a musical direction*) ■ *adj.* QUICK AND CLIPPED rapid, brief, and clipped in sound ■ *n.* (*plural* **-tos**) MUSIC STACCATO PASSAGE a staccato passage in music [Early 18thC. From Italian, literally 'detached'.]

stachys /stáykiss/ *n.* a plant with spiked whorls of purple, reddish, or white flowers such as lamb's ears or betony. Genus: *Stachys*. [Mid-16thC. Via modern Latin from Greek *stakhus* 'ear of corn'.]

stack /stak/ *n.* **1.** HEAPED PILE OF THINGS a pile of things more or less neatly arranged one on top of another ○ *a stack of chairs* **2.** AGRIC LARGE PILE OF STH STORED OUTDOORS a large pile of hay, straw, or grain often conical in shape, stored outdoors **3.** CHIMNEY OR CHIMNEYS a tall chimney or group of chimneys arranged together. ◊ **smokestack 4.** LARGE NUMBER a large number or amount (*informal*) ○ *She has stacks of money.* **5.** AIR AIRCRAFT WAITING TO LAND a queue of aircraft waiting a turn to land at an airport, circling at different heights **6.** GEOG ROCKY PILLAR RISING FROM COASTAL WATERS a steep-sided pillar of rock that has been isolated from nearby cliffs at the shoreline by the erosion of the waves **7.** COMPUT LIST IN A COMPUTER MEMORY an area in a computer memory where data can be stored temporarily in a list in which the last item entered is the first one removed. A control program uses a stack to save register information and return addresses temporarily so it can restore the environment upon returning from another procedure to which it has jumped. **8.** ARMS ARRANGEMENT OF FIREARMS a group of firearms formed in a pyramid, especially three rifles with their muzzles leaning against each other **9.** VERTICAL PIPE a vertical duct or waste pipe **10.** MEASURE MEASURE FOR COAL OR WOOD a nonmetric measure of coal or firewood equal to 108 cubic feet ■ **stacks** *npl.* BOOK STORAGE IN A LIBRARY an area of a library, usually not open to the public, where books are stored on shelves ■ *v.* (**stacks, stacking, stacked**) **1.** *vti.* PUT IN AN ORGANIZED PILE to put things one on top of another to form a pile, or to be arranged in this way **2.** *vt.* PUT THINGS ON A SHELF to arrange objects on a shelf **3.** *vi.* HEAP WITH PILES OF OBJECTS to load or heap sth with large piles of articles or objects ○ *The bins were stacked with bargains.* **4.** *vt.* MANIPULATE A SITUATION UNETHICALLY to arrange sth underhandedly to ensure a desired outcome **5.** *vti.* AIR KEEP AIRCRAFT WAITING IN A STACK to keep aircraft waiting to land at an airport circling at different heights, or be kept in this position [13thC. From Old Norse *stakkr*, from a prehistoric Germanic word meaning 'stick, pole', which is also the ancestor of English *stagger, stockade,* and *attack*.] —**stackable** *adj.* —**stacker** *n.* ◇ **be stacked against** to amount to an unfair disadvantage ◇ **blow your stack** to become suddenly furious (*slang*) ◇ **stack the deck** *or* **cards 1.** CARDS to arrange playing cards in a deck for the purposes of cheating (*slang*) **2.** to arrange sth dishonestly or unethically so as to gain an unfair advantage (*slang*)

stack up *vi.* **1.** *US* MEASURE UP TO to be measurable against or comparable to sth **2.** *US, Aus* ADD UP TO to add up to a total

stacked /stakt/ *adj.* **1.** *US* OFFENSIVE TERM an offensive term used to describe a woman in terms of her physical characteristics (*slang offensive*) **2.** DISHONESTLY ARRANGED unfairly or dishonestly manipulated or arranged **3.** AIR DISPOSED AT DIFFERENT HEIGHTS disposed at different heights prior to landing

stacked heel *n.* a wide high heel made of different coloured layers of wood or material simulating wood

stacte /stákti/ *n.* a sweet spice mentioned in the Bible as being used by the ancient Jews in making incense [14thC. Via Latin from Greek *staktē*, from *staktos*, the past participle of *stazein* 'to drip, ooze'.]

staddle /stádd'l/ *n.* a supporting base to keep stored hay off the ground (*regional or archaic*) [Old English *stapol*. Ultimately from an Indo-European word meaning 'to stand' (see STABLE[2]).]

stadholder /stád hōldər/, **stadtholder** *n.* **1.** CHIEF MAGISTRATE OF A FORMER DUTCH REPUBLIC the chief magistrate of the Dutch republic from the 16th to 18th centuries **2.** GOVERNOR OF A FORMER DUTCH PROVINCE in the past, a governor or viceroy of a province in the Netherlands [Mid-16thC. Partial translation of Dutch *stadhouder*, literally 'place-holder'.] —**stadholderate** *n.* —**stadholdership** *n.*

stadia[1] plural of **stadium**

stadia[2] /stáydi ə/ *n.* a method of measuring distances or differences in elevation using a telescopic instrument calibrated to correspond to distances from the surveyor [Mid-19thC. Directly or via Italian from Latin, plural of *stadium* (see STADIUM).]

stadimeter /stə dímmitər/ *n.* an optical instrument used for measuring distance from an object of known height such as a ship [Coined from STADIA[2] + METER]

stadiometer /stáydi ómmitər/ *n.* a device for measuring the length of a straight or curved line by tracing its path with a toothed wheel [Mid-19thC. Coined from Greek *stadion* STADIUM + -METER.]

stadium /stáydi əm/ (*plural* **-ums** *or* **-a** /stáydi ə/) *n.* **1.** ARENA WITH TIERED SEATS a place where people watch sports or other activities, usually a large enclosed flat area surrounded by tiers of seats for spectators **2.** HIST ANCIENT GREEK RACECOURSE a racecourse for foot races in ancient Greece that had tiers of seats at each side and one end **3.** MEASURE ANCIENT GREEK MEASUREMENT UNIT a unit of linear measure in ancient Greece equal to about 185 m/607 ft [14thC. Via Latin from Greek *stadion* 'racetrack, unit of measure'.]

stadtholder /stád hōldər/ *n.* = **stadholder**

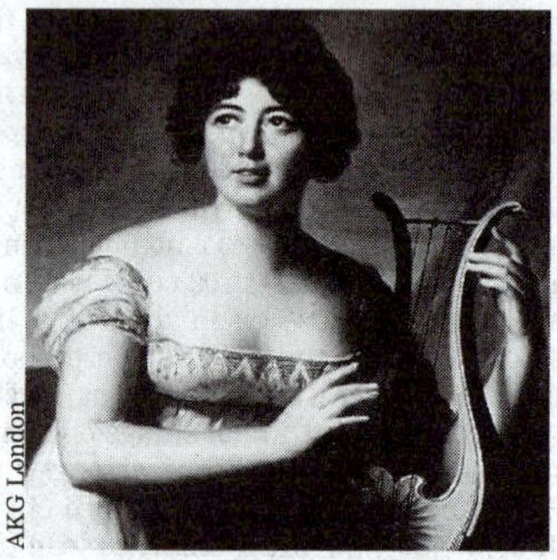

Madame de Staël: Portrait (1808–9) by Elisabeth Vigee-Lebrun

Staël /staal/, **Madame de** (1766–1817) French writer. She is credited with disseminating the theories of romanticism in such works as *Germany* (1810). Full name **Baronne Anne Louise Germaine de Staël-Holstein**. Born **Anne Louise Germaine Necker**

staff[1] /staaf/ *n.* **1.** WORKERS people who are employed by a company or individual **2.** SPECIFIC BODY WITHIN A LARGER GROUP a specific group of employees within a company, institution, or organization **3.** EDUC TEACHERS the teachers in a school or other educational institution, as opposed to the students. US term **faculty 4.** PEOPLE WHO WORK FOR A LEADER a group of people who serve a leader or an executive of a company, organization, or institution **5.** MIL GROUP OF AIDES TO A COMMANDER a group of officers in the armed services who assist a commanding officer or work at headquarters as advisers or planners **6.** *Malaysia, Singapore* HOUSEHOLD, EDUC MEMBER OF STAFF a member of staff working for a company, organization, or school **7.** LARGE HEAVY STICK a stick, rod, or pole, such as a stick used as a support while walking, or a rod used as a symbol of authority in ceremonies **8.** = **flagpole** *n.* **9.** MUSIC SET OF LINES FOR WRITING MUSIC a set of five horizontal lines, together with the four spaces between them, on which the notes of music are written **10.** MEASURE GRADUATED ROD USED FOR MEASURING a graduated rod used for testing or measuring sth, e.g. in surveying ■ *adj.* **1.** EMPLOYED WITH SALARY employed full-time, not on a freelance basis **2.** HOUSEHOLD CONCERNED WITH STAFF for or relating to the staff of a company, institution, or organization ■ *vt.* (**staffs, staffing, staffed**) PROVIDE WITH WORKERS to provide a place or organization with employees (*often passive*) [Old English *stæf* 'stick, rod'. Ultimately from an Indo-European word meaning 'to support', which is also the ancestor of English *step, stampede*, and *stalag*.]

staff[2] /staaf/ *n.* CONSTR a building material of plaster and fibrous material used as a temporary, especially decorative, finish on the outside of a structure [Late 19thC. Origin uncertain: perhaps from German *Stoff* 'material'.]

Staffa /stáffə/ uninhabited island in the Inner Hebrides, Scotland. Its many caverns include Fingal's Cave. Area: 0.5 sq. km/0.2 sq. mi.

staff college *n.* a school in which military officers are prepared for higher positions, e.g. as staff officers or commanders

staffer /staáfər/ *n.* sb who belongs to the staff of an organization (*informal*) ○ *White House staffers*

staffing /staáfing/ *n.* the number of people working in a place or organization, or the act of providing workers

staffman /staáf man/ (*plural* **-men** /-men/) *n.* sb who holds a levelling staff during surveying. US term **rodman**

staff nurse *n.* a fully qualified hospital nurse who ranks next below a team leader

staff of Aesculapius /-éeskyŏŏ láypi əss/ *n.* a symbol for the medical profession consisting of a staff with a single snake entwined round it. ◊ **caduceus**

staff officer *n.* a military officer who assists a commanding officer or works as a planner or adviser at a headquarters

staff of life *n.* bread, or sometimes another food, considered as an essential part of the human diet (*literary*) [*Staff* from STAFF[1], in the sense 'staple, support']

Stafford /stáffərd/ county town of Staffordshire, in central England. Population: 61,885 (1995).

Stafford, Sir Edward William (1819–1901) Irish-born New Zealand statesman. He was prime minister of New Zealand three times (1856–61, 1865–69, 1872).

Staffordshire /stáffərdshər/ county in the Midlands, central England. It includes the Potteries. Stafford is the county town. Population: 1,046,900 (1997). Area: 2,716 sq. km/1,049 sq. mi.

Staffordshire bull terrier, **Staffordshire terrier** *n.* a bull terrier belonging to a breed with a white coat and broad head and often marked or streaked with brown or black [Named after the county of STAFFORDSHIRE where it was developed]

staff rider *n. S Africa* sb, usually a Black youth, who rides a suburban train hanging outside for fun or out of necessity [*Staff* refers to the pole in the doorway of a coach]

staffroom /staáf room, -rŏŏm/ *n.* a room used only by the teachers in a school, e.g. for relaxation between classes

Staffs. /staffs/ *abbr.* Staffordshire

staff sergeant *n.* **1.** US ARMY RANK a noncommissioned officer in the US Army, ranking above sergeant and below sergeant first class **2.** BRITISH ARMY RANK a noncommissioned officer in the British Army, ranking above sergeant and below warrant officer **3.** US AIR FORCE RANK a noncommissioned officer in the US Air Force, ranking above sergeant and below technical sergeant **4.** US MARINE RANK a noncommissioned officer in the US Marines, ranking above sergeant and below gunnery sergeant

stag /stag/ *n.* **1.** ZOOL MATURE MALE DEER an adult male deer, especially a male red deer **2.** *US* UNACCOMPANIED MAN AT A SOCIAL EVENT a man who goes to a social function without a partner (*informal*) **3.** AGRIC CASTRATED ADULT ANIMAL a male animal, e.g. a pig, castrated after it reaches maturity **4.** FIN SPECULATOR IN NEW ISSUES OF SHARES a speculator who applies for a new issue of a security in the hope of making a quick profit when it begins to be traded ■ *adj.* RESTRICTED TO MEN for men only, and usually involving activities that would not be appropriate in mixed company (*informal*) ■ *adv. US* WITHOUT A WOMAN DATE without a woman companion on a social occasion (*informal*) ■ *v.* (**stags, stagging, stagged**) **1.** *vt.* FIN BUY SHARES FOR QUICK PROFIT to buy a new issue of a security in the hope of making a quick profit when it begins to be traded **2.** *vi. US* ATTEND AN EVENT WITHOUT A WOMAN DATE to attend a social event without a woman companion (*informal*) [Old English (assumed) *stagga*. Ultimately from an Indo-European word meaning 'pointed', which is also the ancestor of English *stochastic*, and probably of *sting*.]

stag beetle *n.* a large beetle, the male of which has long extended jaws (**mandibles**) shaped like a stag's antlers. Family: Lucanidae.

stage /stayj/ *n.* **1.** PERIOD OR STEP DURING A PROCESS a step, level, or period in the development or progress of sth ○ *The project is still in its early stages.* **2.** PLATFORM a raised platform, e.g. in a hall or auditorium, where speeches are made and ceremonies are carried out **3.** THEATRE AREA IN A THEATRE the area in a theatre where a performance takes place, especially a platform on which actors perform a play **4.** THEATRE DRAMATIC PROFESSION the profession of acting, drama, or the theatre **5.** SETTING IN WHICH STH HAPPENS the scene of an event or series of events ○ *The summit marks her first appearance on the world stage.* **6.** TRANSP PART OF BUS ROUTE any of the divisions of a bus route that are used to calculate fares **7.** TRANSP PART OF JOURNEY a distinct section of a journey, especially one after which a stop is made **8.** AEROSP DETACHABLE ROCKET UNIT a separable unit of a rocket or spacecraft that contains fuel and can be jettisoned after the fuel is exhausted **9.** *US, Can* CONSTR PLATFORM FOR WORKERS a raised platform, especially a scaffolding for workers during the construction of a building **10.** EDUC SUBJECT STUDIED FOR A YEAR a subject studied for one year at a university or college **11.** PLATFORM FOR DRYING STH a platform used to dry fish or meat **12.** RECORDING = **sound stage 13.** BIOL PERIOD OF DEVELOPMENT OF AN ORGANISM a distinct period of development in the life of an organism when its form is different from earlier or later periods **14.** SIGNIFICANT PHASE an important phase of cultural, economic, or social development **15.** MEASURE ELEVATION OF A RIVER SURFACE a measure of how much the surface of a river or stream rises above a given point **16.** PLATFORM FOR MOUNTING MICROSCOPIC SPECIMEN the small platform of an optical microscope on which a specimen is placed for examination **17.** GEOL PERIOD OF ROCK STRATA a relatively short distinct period, a subdivision of a series, during which rock strata are deposited during an age of geological time **18.** ELEC UNIT OF ELECTRICAL COMPONENTS a group of components that form part of an electronic or electrical system **19.** TRANSP = **stagecoach** ■ *vt.* (**stages, staging, staged**) **1.** ORGANIZE A PERFORMANCE FOR THE PUBLIC to put on a play, concert, exhibition, or similar event for an audience **2.** ORGANIZE EVENT to organize or carry out sth, e.g. an event that will attract attention or publicity **3.** THEATRE SET PLAY IN PLACE OR TIME to set a play in a particular place or time **4.** MED CLASSIFY PHASES OF DISEASE to classify the progress of a disease [13thC. Via Old French *estage* from assumed Vulgar Latin *staticum*, literally 'standing place', from Latin *stat-*, past participle stem of *stare* 'to stand' (see STATION).] —**stageability** /stàyjə bílləti/ *n.* —**stageable** /stáyjəb'l/ *adj.* —**stageably** /stáyjəbli/ *adv.* ◇ **by** *or* **in easy stages** in an unhurried, undemanding way ◇ **hold the stage** to continue to be the centre of attention ◇ **on stage** performing in sth, especially as an actor ◇ **take centre stage** to draw people's or public attention

stage brace *n.* a brace used to support upright pieces of scenery in a play

stage business *n.* THEATRE = **business** *n.* 8

stagecoach /stáyj kōch/ *n.* a large four-wheeled horse-drawn coach used in the past to carry passengers and mail over a regular route

WORD KEY: CULTURAL NOTE

Stagecoach, a film by US director John Ford (1939). Considered the first modern Western, it portrays an encounter between a diverse group of stagecoach pas-

Stagecoach

sengers and an intimidating outlaw, the Ringo Kid (played by John Wayne). Its convincing and intriguing characters, magnificent desert setting, gripping narrative, and exciting climax made it a landmark in US cinema.

stagecraft /stáyj kraaft/ n. the technique or art of writing, adapting, or putting plays on stage

stage direction n. an instruction for an actor in the script of a play

stage door n. a door in the back or side of a theatre that leads directly backstage and is usually used by performers

stage effect n. a special visual or auditory effect created on a theatrical stage by lighting, scenery, or sound

stage fright n. fear or nervousness that sb feels before going in front of an audience to speak or perform

stagehand /stáyj hand/ n. sb who does physical work in a theatre, e.g. setting up and removing stage sets

stage left n. the side of a stage that is to a performer's left when facing the audience. ◊ **stage right**

stage-manage v. 1. vt. TIGHTLY CONTROL EVERY ASPECT OF EVENT to control an organized event, especially in a way that is not public, so that it happens exactly as planned 2. vti. THEATRE BE A STAGE MANAGER to carry out the work of a stage manager, especially on a particular production

stage manager n. sb who assists the director of a play by supervising all backstage activities

stager /stáyjər/ n. an actor (archaic) [Late 16thC. Origin uncertain: possibly a translation of Old French estagier 'long-time resident', from estage 'stage, dwelling' (see STAGE).]

stage right n. the part of a stage that is to the performer's right when facing the audience. ◊ **stage left**

stage-struck adj. loving theatre and intensely wanting to be part of it, especially as a performer

stage wait n. an unintentional pause in the action of a play, especially one caused by an actor's missing a cue

stage whisper n. 1. THEATRE ACTOR'S LOUD WHISPER sth said on stage that for the purposes of the play is supposed to be a whisper but is intended to be heard by the audience 2. CONSPICUOUS WHISPER a loud whisper intended to be overheard

stagflation /stag fláysh'n/ n. a period of rising prices and unemployment but little growth in consumer demand and business activity [Mid-20thC. Blend of STAGNATION and INFLATION.] —**stagflationary** adj.

staggard /stággərd/ n. a male red deer that is in its fourth year [14thC. Formed from STAG.]

stagger /stággər/ v. (-gers, -gering, -gered) 1. vi. MOVE UNSTEADILY, NEARLY FALLING to move or walk unsteadily, almost but not quite falling over 2. vt. MAKE PERSON OR ANIMAL STUMBLE to make a person or animal stumble or nearly fall, especially by a blow 3. vt. ASTONISH SB to completely astonish or amaze sb (often passive) 4. vi. CONTINUE IMPERFECTLY to keep going or operating in a defective or incompetent way 5. vt. ARRANGE ACTIVITIES FOR SEPARATE TIMES to arrange activities so that they do not overlap 6. vt. MAKE INTO AN ALTERNATING OR ZIGZAG PATTERN to arrange things so that they do not form a straight line, especially in an alternating or

zigzag pattern (often passive) 7. vi. HESITATE to hesitate or falter 8. vt. AIR ADJUST THE EDGE OF BIPLANE'S WING to make the leading edge of one wing of a biplane project beyond the leading edge of the other wing ■ n. 1. STUMBLE NEARLY RESULTING IN A FALL an unsteady movement in which a person or animal almost falls 2. AIR ARRANGEMENT OF BIPLANE WINGS a design in which the leading edge of one wing of a biplane is ahead of that of the other wing [Mid-16thC. Alteration of obsolete stacker, from Old Norse stakkra, from staka 'to push', from a prehistoric Germanic word meaning 'pole' (see STACK).] —**staggerer** n.

staggerbush /stággər boosh/ (plural **-bushes** or **-bush**) n. a shrubby deciduous heath of the eastern United States that has clusters of white or pink flowers and leaves that are poisonous to livestock. Latin name: Lyonia mariana.

staggered /stággərd/ adj. 1. SHOCKED shocked or astounded at sth 2. ALTERNATING OR ZIGZAG not arranged in sequence or in a straight line

staggered hours npl. an arrangement in a business in which employees arrive and leave at different times but work hours that overlap for part of the time

staggering /stággəring/ adj. with the effect of shocking or astounding people —**staggeringly** adv.

staggers /stággərz/ n. MED a form of vertigo associated with decompression sickness, with symptoms including dizziness, weakness, and confusion (takes a singular or plural verb)

staghorn /stág hawrn/, **stag's horn** n. 1. PIECE OF STAG'S ANTLER a stag's antler, or a piece of this used as material for carved objects 2. = staghorn fern 3. = staghorn moss ■ adj. MADE FROM STAG'S ANTLER made from a piece of a stag's antlers

staghorn coral n. a form of stony coral branched like a deer's antlers. Genus: Acropora.

staghorn fern n. a fern with broad leaves like antlers and smaller clinging leaves, often cultivated as a houseplant. Genus: Platycerium.

staghorn moss n. a plant with creeping stems like antlers and tiny overlapping leaves. Latin name: Lycopodium clavatum.

staghound /stág hownd/ n. a hound like a large foxhound, used especially in the past in hunting stags

staging /stáyjing/ n. 1. THEATRE TECHNIQUE OF PRESENTING STAGE PLAY the activity, process, or style of presenting a play on a stage 2. CONSTR SCAFFOLDING FOR BUILDING a temporary structure of supports and platforms used in building or working on sth 3. AEROSP TECHNIQUE FOR INCREASING SPACECRAFT'S VELOCITY a technique to increase the velocity achieved by a spacecraft's launch vehicle by using multiple propulsive stages, each being jettisoned after use

staging area n. a place where soldiers and military equipment are gathered for final organization, outfitting, and training before deployment on an operation

staging post n. a place where people on a long journey stop off to take a break from travel, especially on an air route

stagnant /stágnənt/ adj. 1. STILL AND UNMOVING not flowing or moving 2. FOUL OR STALE stale or impure from lack of motion 3. NOT DEVELOPING not developing or making progress 4. INACTIVE not active or lively ○ a stagnant week on the share market [Mid-17thC. From Latin stagnant-, the present participle stem of stagnare (see STAGNATE).] —**stagnancy** n. —**stagnantly** adv.

stagnate /stag náyt/ (-nates, -nating, -nated) vi. 1. STOP FLOWING to stop flowing or moving 2. BECOME FOUL to become stale or impure through not flowing or moving 3. NOT DEVELOP OR MAKE PROGRESS to fail to develop, progress, or make necessary changes 4. BECOME INACTIVE to become listless and inactive [Mid-17thC. From Latin stagnat-, the past participle stem of stagnare, from stagnum 'pool, swamp'.] —**stagnatory** adj.

stagnation /stag náysh'n/ n. a condition of no movement, activity, development, or progress, or the process of becoming like this

stag night, **stag party** n. a social occasion that only men attend, especially an evening of drinking with

his male friends spent by a man about to be married (informal) ◊ **hen night**

stag's horn /stágz hawrn/ n. = staghorn n. 1

stagy /stáyji/ (-ier, -iest), **stagey** (-ier, -iest) adj. exaggerated or artificial in manner, as if in a play (disapproving) —**stagily** adv. —**staginess** n.

staid /stayd/ adj. sedate and settled in habits or temperament, sometimes to the point of dullness [Mid-16thC. An obsolete past participle of STAY[1], literally 'fixed, settled'.] —**staidly** adv. —**staidness** n.

stain /stayn/ n. 1. DISCOLOURED PATCH a discoloured mark made by sth such as blood, wine, or ink 2. FINISH FOR COLOURING STH a liquid that is applied to sth, especially wood, to darken it or change its colour without hiding its texture or grain 3. MICROBIOL DYE USED TO COLOUR MICROSCOPIC SPECIMENS a dye used to colour organic materials, e.g. tissues and cells, to make specimens more distinguishable under a microscope 4. INDUST DYE FOR TEXTILES OR LEATHER a dye that is used in liquid form to colour textiles or leather 5. CHARACTER BLEMISH sth that detracts from sb's good reputation ■ v. (stains, staining, stained) 1. vti. LEAVE MARK ON STH to make a discoloured mark on sth (often passive) 2. vt. DYE STH to dye sth a different or deeper colour using liquid or pigment that penetrates the surface 3. vt. TARNISH STH to disgrace or detract from sth 4. vt. MICROBIOL COLOUR ORGANIC SPECIMENS to colour organic materials with dyes to make specimens more distinguishable under a microscope [15thC. Partly from Old Norse steina 'to paint' (from steinn 'stone, paint') and partly from Old French desteindre, literally 'to discolour' (from Latin tingere 'to dye'; see TINGE).] —**stainability** /stáynə bílləti/ n. —**stainable** adj. —**stainer** /stáynər/ n.

stained glass n. glass that has been coloured so that it can be used to make a mosaic picture, especially in a window. Stained glass may be made by enamelling, burning pigments into the surface, or by fusing metallic oxides with it. (hyphenated when used before a noun)

Staines /staynz/ town in Surrey, England. It was part of Middlesex until 1965. Population: 51,167 (1991).

stainless /stáynləss/ adj. 1. ENTIRELY REPUTABLE without any blemishes, especially of character or reputation 2. WITHOUT STAINS without a stain or discoloured mark 3. RESISTANT TO RUST resisting rust or corrosion ■ n. = stainless steel —**stainlessly** adv.

stainless steel n. a corrosion-resistant steel containing at least 12% chromium that has many domestic and industrial uses, e.g. cutlery, ball bearings, and turbine blades (hyphenated when used before a noun)

stair /stair/ n. 1. SINGLE STEP a step in a series of steps leading from one floor or level to another 2. SERIES OF STEPS a flight of steps leading from one floor or level to another ■ **stairs** npl. SET OF STEPS a set or several sets of steps leading from one floor or level to another [Old English stæger. Ultimately from an Indo-European root meaning 'to step, climb', which is also the ancestor of English stile[1] and stirrup.] ◇ **above stairs** in the upper part of a house, in a large house, formerly occupied by the employers but not the servants (archaic) ◇ **below stairs** in the lower part of a house, in a large house, formerly occupied by the servants (archaic)

staircase /stáir kayss/ n. a set of stairs in a building, usually with bannisters or handrails

stairhead /stáir hed/ n. the landing at the top of a flight of stairs

StairMaster tdmk. a trademark for exercise equipment

stair rod n. a rod laid to hold a carpet in place against the bottom of a riser in a staircase

stairway /stáir way/ n. a passageway from one floor or level of a building to another, consisting of stairs or a staircase

stairwell /stáir wel/ n. the vertical space in a building where stairs are located

stake[1] /stayk/ n. 1. THIN POINTED POST IN THE GROUND a thin wooden or metal post that is driven into the ground to mark or support sth 2. HIST POST TO TIE AND BURN SB a wooden post used in an old form of execution to which the person was tied. Wood was then piled around its base and set alight. **3.** FORM OF EXECUTION the method of execution in which sb was tied to a post and burnt **4.** TRANSP **POST TO RETAIN A LOAD** an independent upright post inserted into sockets of a flat wagon or lorry to keep long loads such as logs in place **5.** RELIG **MORMON CHURCH DISTRICT** an administrative district in the Mormon Church that consists of wards, each governed by a president and two counsellors ■ *v.* **(stakes, staking, staked) 1.** *vt.* **SUPPORT OR STRENGTHEN WITH STAKE** to support or strengthen sth using a stake **2.** *vt.* **TIE OR TETHER TO STAKE** to tie or tether sth to a stake **3.** *vi.* **MARK OR FENCE AREA WITH STAKES** to mark out, confine, or fence off an area using stakes driven into the ground round the boundary **4.** *vt.* **ASSERT RIGHTS OVER STH** to assert sth, usually rights, over sth such as an area of land [Old English *staca*, from a prehistoric Germanic word meaning 'stick, pole' (see STACK)] ◇ **(pull) up stakes** to leave and move to another place ◇ **stake a claim** to claim sth such as an area of land or a deposit of minerals

stake out *vt.* **1. WATCH CONTINUOUSLY** to watch a place continuously from a hidden vantage point (*informal*) **2. ESTABLISH BOUNDARIES** to establish the boundaries of an area intended to be used or controlled **3. ESTABLISH AND CLARIFY POSITION** to establish and clarify a personal position in a situation

stake[2] /stayk/ *n.* **1.** GAMBLING **MONEY RISKED IN GAMBLING** an amount of money risked in a bet or game **2. SHARE OR INTEREST IN STH** a share or interest in sth, particularly through money risked in it **3. PERSONAL INVOLVEMENT** a personal or emotional interest, concern, or involvement ○ *We had a huge stake in his success.* **4.** *US, Can* = **grubstake** ■ **stakes** *npl.* **1. DEGREE OF RISK** the degree of hazard or danger involved in a situation **2. PRIZE AVAILABLE** the prize, reward, or success available in a gamble or competition **3.** GAMBLING **PRIZE MADE UP OF CONTRIBUTIONS** the total of bets made by players in a gambling game that is taken by the winner **4.** CARDS **AMOUNT OF BETS IN POKER** in poker, the cash values assigned to chips, bets, or raises ■ *vt.* **(stakes, staking, staked) 1.** GAMBLING **WAGER STH** to bet sth, especially money, on sth **2. RISK THE LOSS OF STH** to risk the loss of sth valuable **3. SUPPLY SB WITH REQUIREMENTS** to give or lend sb sth needed or wanted **4.** FIN **INVEST IN STH** to put money into sth, especially initial capital [Mid-16thC. Origin uncertain: perhaps from STAKE[1], from a supposed custom of placing a wagered object on a stake.] ◇ **at stake** at risk of being lost

stakeholder /stáyk hōldər/ *n.* **1. SB OR STH WITH DIRECT INTEREST** a person or group with a direct interest, involvement, or investment in sth, e.g. the employees, shareholders, and customers of a business concern ○ *'...demonstrating how to build powerful stakeholder relationships based on trust...'* (*Marketing Week*; December 1998) **2.** GAMBLING **HOLDER AND PAYER OF BETS** sb who holds and pays out bets in a gambling game —**stakeholding** *n.*

stakeholder pension *n.* a type of pension intended to help especially low-paid people to supplement their state pension, administered by the private financial sector but regulated by government

stakeout /stáyk owt/ *n. US* (*informal*) **1. POLICE SURVEILLANCE** hidden surveillance of sb or sth, especially by the police **2. PLACE FOR POLICE SURVEILLANCE** the place from which surveillance is carried out, especially by the police

stakes /stayks/ (*plural* **stakes**) *n.* a horse race in which a prize is offered, especially a sum of money made up of contributions from owners of horses that take part (*takes a singular verb*)

Stakhanovite /stə kánnə vīt/ *n.* **EFFECTIVE SOVIET WORKER** a worker in the former Soviet Union who received a reward for increasing production ■ *adj.* **REWARDING HARD WORK** rewarding people who work very hard, especially in the former Soviet Union [Mid-20thC. Named after the Soviet mine worker Aleksei Grigorevich *Stakhanov* (1906–77), who was held up as a model of productivity.]

stalactite /stálləktīt/ *n.* a conical hanging pillar in a limestone cave that has gradually built up as a deposit from ground water seeping through the cave's roof. ◊ **stalagmite** [Late 17thC. Via modern Latin *stalactites* from Greek *stalaktos* 'dripping', from *stalak-*, the stem of *stalassein* 'to drip', of unknown origin.] —**stalactitic** /stállək títtik/ *adj.* —**stalactitically** /-títtikli/ *adv.*

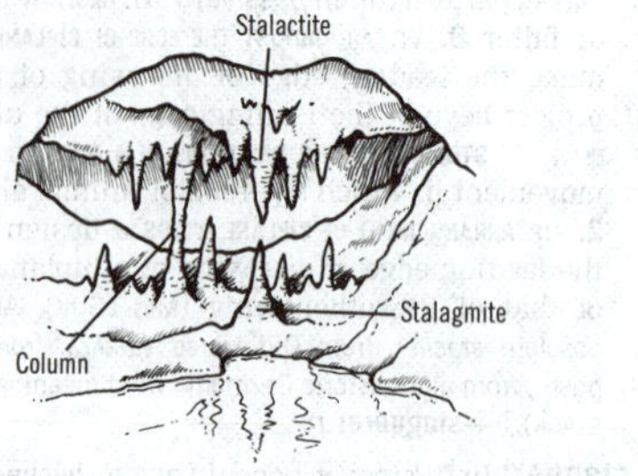

Stalactite and stalagmite

stalag /stálag/ *n.* a German prisoner of war camp in World War II for officers or lower ranks [Mid-20thC. From German, contraction of *Stammlager*, literally 'main camp'.]

stalagmite /stálləg mīt/ *n.* a conical pillar in a limestone cave that is gradually built upwards from the floor as a deposit from ground water seeping through and dripping from the cave's roof. ◊ **stalactite** [Late 17thC. Via modern Latin *stalagmites* from Greek *stalagmos* 'sth dropped', from *stalak-*, the stem of *stalassein* 'to drip' (source also of English *stalactite*).] —**stalagmitic** /stálləg míttik/ *adj.* —**stalagmitically** /-míttikli/ *adv.*

stale[1] /stayl/ *adj.* **(staler, stalest) 1. KEPT TOO LONG** no longer fresh **2. LOW IN OXYGEN** stagnant and low in oxygen owing to lack of circulation or ventilation **3. FREQUENTLY HEARD AND BORING** heard too often before and no longer interesting or amusing **4. OUT OF CONDITION** ineffective, enervated, or bored because of doing too much of the same thing **5.** LAW **LEGALLY EXPIRED** having lost legal force through lack of use or elapse of time **6.** FIN **NOT NEGOTIABLE BECAUSE OF DELAY** used to describe financial statements or cheques that are not negotiable by a bank because a time limit has expired ■ *vti.* **(stales, staling, staled) 1. LOSE FRESHNESS** to become, or make sth become, stale **2. LOSE EFFECTIVENESS** to lose effectiveness or energy **3. BECOME BORING** to become dull and uninteresting over time [13thC. From Old French *estale* 'settled', literally 'standing still', ultimately from *estal* 'standing place', from prehistoric Germanic (see STALL[1]). Originally 'wine or beer with settled sediment'.]

stale[2] /stayl/ *vi.* **(stales, staling, staled) URINATE** to urinate (*refers to livestock*) ■ *n.* **LIVESTOCK URINE** the urine of livestock, especially horses and cattle [14thC. Origin uncertain: perhaps from Old French *estaler* 'to take up a position', from *estal* (see STALE[1]).]

stalemate /stáyl mayt/ *n.* **1. SITUATION WITH NO POTENTIAL WINNERS** a situation in a contest in which neither side can make any further worthwhile action **2.** CHESS **CHESS SITUATION WITH NO WINNER** a situation in chess in which no winner is possible because neither player can move a piece without placing the king in check ■ *vt.* **(-mates, -mating, -mated) PUT INTO STALEMATE** to put sb or sth into a stalemate (*often passive*) [Mid-18thC. Coined from Anglo-Norman *estale* 'fixed position' (from Old French *estaler* 'to take up a position', from *estal*; see STALE[1]) + MATE[2].]

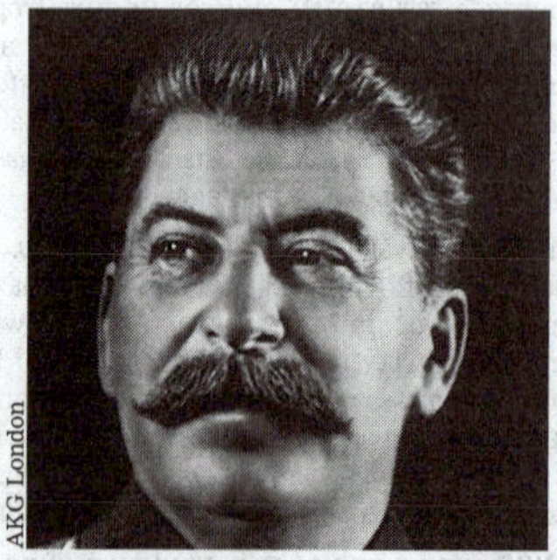

Joseph Stalin

Stalin /staálin/, **Joseph** (1879–1953) Georgian-born Soviet statesman. He was the general secretary of the Soviet Communist Party (1922–53). He ruled the Soviet Union as a dictator after 1930, eliminating political opponents in a series of purges and causing nationwide famine with his collectivist agricultural policy. After World War II, he extended Soviet control over most of eastern Europe. Real name **Iosif Vissarionovich Dzhugashvili**

Stalingrad /staálin grad/ former name for **Volgograd** (1925–61)

Stalinism /staálinizəm/ *n.* the political principles and economic policies developed by Joseph Stalin from Marxist-Leninist thought, which included centralized autocratic rule and total suppression of dissent —**Stalinist** *n., adj.*

stalk[1] /stawk/ *n.* **1.** BOT **STEM OF PLANT** the main stem or axis of a plant that is fleshy rather than woody **2.** BOT **STEM OR STEMLIKE PART OF PLANT** a supporting part of a plant, e.g. a leaf stem **(petiole)** or flower stalk **(pedicel) 3. SLENDER SUPPORTING PART** a thin cylindrical part of sth that acts as a support, e.g. of a glass **4.** ZOOL **SLENDER STRUCTURAL PART OF ANIMAL** a slender supporting structure for an organ or body of an animal [14thC. Origin uncertain: probably an alteration of obsolete *stale* 'stile of a ladder, handle', from Old English *stalu* 'upright piece'.] —**stalked** *adj.* ◇ **eyes out on stalks** wide-eyed in extreme astonishment or shock (*informal*)

stalk[2] /stawk/ *v.* **(stalks, stalking, stalked) 1.** *vt.* **FOLLOW STEALTHILY** to follow or try to get close to a person or animal unobtrusively **2.** *vi.* **WALK STIFFLY AND ANGRILY** to walk in a stiff, angry, or proud way **3.** *vt.* **PROCEED STEADILY AND MALEVOLENTLY** to proceed in a steady and sinister way **4.** *vt.* LAW **PERSISTENTLY HARASS SB** to harass sb by persistent and inappropriate attention, e.g. by constantly following, telephoning, or writing to him or her ■ *n.* **1. STEALTHY PURSUIT** a stealthy pursuit or hunt of sth **2. STIFF WALK** a stiff, angry, or proud walk [Old English (assumed) *stealcian*, from a prehistoric Germanic base meaning 'to steal', which is also the ancestor of English *steal* and *stealth*] —**stalkable** *adj.*

WORD KEY: SYNONYMS

See Synonyms at ***follow***.

stalker /stáwkər/ *n.* **1. STEALTHY PURSUER** sb who follows or tries to approach sb or sth stealthily **2.** LAW **HARASSER** sb who persistently and obsessively harasses sb else with inappropriate attention

stalk-eyed *adj.* with the eyes located on stalks **(pedicels)**, as, e.g. have some crustaceans and dipterans

stalk-eyed fly *n.* a fly mostly found in tropical regions, with eyes that project from the sides of its head on long stalks. Family: Diopsidae.

stalking /stáwking/ *n.* **1. STEALTHY PURSUIT** the act or process of stealthily following or trying to approach sb or sth **2.** LAW **ACT OF STEADY HARASSMENT** the crime of harassing sb with persistent and inappropriate attention —**stalkingly** *adv.*

stalking horse *n.* **1. MEANS TO DISGUISE AN OBJECTIVE** sth used as a means of disguising a real objective **2.** POL **DECEPTIVE CANDIDATE FOR ELECTION** a candidate who is in an election only to conceal the potential candidacy of sb else, to divide the opposition, or to determine how strong the opposition is **3.** HUNT **FAKE HORSE** a horse or figure of a horse that is used as cover in the hunting of game

stalky /stáwki/ **(-ier, -iest)** *adj.* **1. LONG AND THIN** long or tall and thin like a stalk **2. WITH STALKS** with stalks, especially a lot of stalks —**stalkily** *adv.* —**stalkiness** *n.*

stall[1] /stawl/ *n.* **1.** COMM **SMALL AREA SELLING OR DISPENSING GOODS** a booth, table, counter, or compartment set up to display goods for sale or information to give out **2.** AGRIC **COMPARTMENT FOR A LARGE ANIMAL** a compartment in a building where a single large animal lives or is fed or milked **3.** AUTOMOT **SITUATION IN WHICH ENGINE HALTS** a situation in which an engine stops abruptly because of insufficient fuel, being braked too suddenly, or mechanical failure **4.** BUILDING **SMALL ROOM** a very small room, or partitioned area in a room, for a shower or toilet **5.** AIR **SUDDEN DIVE BY AN AIRCRAFT** a situation in which an aircraft suddenly dives because the airflow is so obstructed that lift is lost. The loss of airflow can be caused by insufficient airspeed or by an excessive angle of an aerofoil when the aircraft is climbing. **6.** CHR **SEAT IN A CHURCH** a pew or enclosed seat in a church **7.** MED **SHEATH FOR FINGER** a protective covering for a finger or thumb **8.** HORSERACING **COMPARTMENT OF STARTING GATE** a partitioned compartment at the starting gate of a racecourse that holds a horse before the start of a race ■ **stalls** *npl.* **SEATS CLOSEST TO STAGE** the seats in a theatre or cinema on the ground floor nearest the stage or screen ■ *v.* **(stalls, stalling, stalled) 1.** *vti.* AUTOMOT **STOP OR MAKE AN ENGINE STOP** to stop working suddenly, or make an engine do this **2.** *vti.* AIR **PLUNGE OR CAUSE TO PLUNGE** to go into a sudden dive, or cause a sudden dive in an aircraft **3.** *vt.* AGRIC **PUT LARGE ANIMAL INTO STALL** to put a large animal into a compartment where it will live or be fed or milked **4.** *vti. US* **BECOME STUCK** to cause sth to get stuck, or become immovable ○ *stalled the project* ○ *a project that stalled* [Old English *steall* 'standing place', from a prehistoric Germanic word that is also the ancestor of English *pedestal, stallion,* and *stale*]

stall[2] /stawl/ *vti.* **(stalls, stalling, stalled) DELAY WITH HESITATION OR EVASION** to delay or obstruct sb, or to use delaying tactics ■ *n.* **DECEPTIVE PRETEXT** a pretext or ruse used to delay or deceive sb [Early 19thC. Alteration of obsolete *stale* 'decoy, pickpocket's accomplice', from Anglo-Norman *estale*, literally 'sth set up'.]

stallage /stáwlij/ *n.* the right to use, or the rent paid for, a stall at a fair or market [14thC. Via Anglo-Norman *estalage* from Old French *estal* (see STALL[1]).]

stall angle *n.* AIR = **stalling angle**

stall-feed *vt.* to keep an animal in a stall while fattening it for slaughter

stallholder /stáwl hōldər/ *n.* sb who has a stall at a market or fair

stalling angle *n.* the angle relative to the horizontal at which the flow of air around an aerofoil changes abruptly, resulting in significant changes in the lift and drag of an aircraft

stallion /stályən/ *n.* **1.** ZOOL **UNCASTRATED MALE HORSE** an uncastrated adult male horse, especially one kept for breeding. ◊ **gelding 2. MAN WITH SUPPOSED SEXUAL PROWESS** a man with supposed great sexual prowess (*informal*) [14thC. From Anglo-Norman *estaloun*. Ultimately from a prehistoric Germanic word meaning 'standing place', which is also the ancestor of English STALE[1]; perhaps because stallions were kept confined.]

Stallone /stə lṓn, stə lṓni/, **Sylvester** (*b.* 1946) US actor. He is best known for playing heroes in Hollywood action films, most notably a boxer in the *Rocky* series (1976–90). Full name **Michael Sylvester Stallone**

stalwart /stáwlwərt/ *adj.* **1. DEPENDABLE** dependable and loyal **2. STRONG** sturdy and strong ■ *n.* **HARD-WORKING LOYAL SUPPORTER** sb who is faithful, dependable, and hard-working [15thC. Variant of *stealwurthe*, from Old English *stǣlwierþe* 'good', literally 'having a worthy foundation', from *staþol* 'foundation' (see STADDLE) + *weorþ* (see WORTH).] —**stalwartly** *adv.* —**stalwartness** *n.*

stamen /stáy men, -mən/ (*plural* **-mens** *or* **-mina** /stámminə/) *n.* the male reproductive organ of a flower, typically consisting of a stalk (**filament**) bearing a pollen-producing anther at its tip [Mid-17thC. From Latin, 'thread in the warp of a loom'.] —**staminal** *adj.* —**staminiferous** /stámmi níffərəss/ *adj.*

Stamford /stámfərd/ **1.** market town in Lincolnshire, eastern England. Population: 17,492 (1991). **2.** city in southwestern Connecticut, founded in 1641. Population: 108,056 (1990).

Stamford Bridge /stámfərd-/ village near York, in northern England. Nearby King Harold II defeated an invasion by his brother Tostig and King Harald Hardraada of Norway in 1066. Population: 3,099 (1991).

stamina /stámminə/ *n.* enduring physical or mental energy and strength that allows sb to do sth for a long time [Early 18thC. From Latin, plural of *stamen* 'thread in woven cloth' (see STAMEN). The meaning developed from 'threads of a life', woven by the Fates, to 'innate strength'.] —**staminal** *adj.*

staminate /stámminət/ *adj.* used to describe plants that have stamens, especially flowers with stamens but without female parts (**carpels**)

staminode /stámmi nṓd/, **staminodium** /stámmi nṓdi əm/ (*plural* **-a** /-di ə/) *n.* a sterile or vestigial stamen. It forms a conspicuous part of some flowers, e.g. in the iris. [Early 19thC. From modern Latin *staminodium*, from *stamen* 'thread' (see STAMEN).]

staminody /stámmi nōdi/ *n.* the process by which other organs of a flower are changed into stamens

stammel /stámm'l/ *n.* **1.** TEXTILES **COARSE WOOLLEN CLOTH** a coarse woollen cloth, usually red, used in medieval times to make undergarments **2.** COLOURS **RED COLOUR** a bright red colour, like that of the stammel cloth of medieval times [Mid-16thC. Alteration of earlier *stamin*, via Old French *estamine* from, ultimately, Latin *stamineus* 'consisting of threads', from *stamen* 'thread' (see STAMEN).] —**stammel** *adj.*

stammer /stámmər/ *vti.* **(-mers, -mering, -mered) SPEAK WITH HESITATIONS AND REPETITIONS** to speak, or say sth, with many quick hesitations and repeated consonants or syllables because of a speech condition or a strong emotion ■ *n.* **SPEECH CONDITION** a speech condition that makes sb speak with involuntary hesitations and repetition of consonants or syllables. Stammering will usually respond to treatment from a speech therapist. [Old English *stamerian*, from a prehistoric Germanic base meaning 'to halt, stutter', which is also the ancestor of English *stumble* and *stem*[2]] —**stammerer** *n.*

stamp /stamp/ *n.* **1.** MAIL **GUMMED PAPER PAYING FOR POSTAGE** a small piece of gummed paper that is stuck on an envelope or parcel to show that postage has been paid **2.** MAIL **CANCELLATION ACROSS A POSTAGE STAMP** a mark put across a postage stamp on an envelope or parcel to show that the stamp has been used **3.** PRINTING **SMALL BLOCK FOR PRINTING DESIGN** a small block with a raised design or lettering that can be printed onto paper by inking the block and pressing it to the paper **4. DESIGN PRINTED ONTO PAPER WITH A STAMP** a design printed onto paper using a stamp in order to show that a document has been read, cancelled, or officially approved **5. GUMMED PAPER AS AN OFFICIAL MARK** a piece of printed gummed paper fixed to a document as an official sign of sth, e.g. approval or validity **6. CHARACTERISTIC OF STH** a characteristic or distinguishing sign or impression **7. TYPE OF STH** a class or type of sth **8.** COMM **WAY OF PAYING FOR STH** a piece of paper that can be purchased as a way of redeeming part or all of the amount charged for goods or a service. ◊ **trading stamp 9.** PUBLIC ADMIN **NATIONAL INSURANCE CONTRIBUTION** a contribution to national insurance, recorded in the past by means of a stamp on an official card (*informal*) **10. ACTION OF BANGING DOWN A FOOT** the action of bringing a foot down forcefully on a surface **11.** INDUST **MACHINE FOR CRUSHING ROCKS AND ORES** a machine that crushes rocks and ores, consisting of a freely falling weight lifted and dropped, or the weight in such a machine ■ *v.* **(stamps, stamping, stamped) 1.** *vti.* **BANG A FOOT DOWN FORCIBLY** to bring a foot down forcefully on a surface **2.** *vi.* **WALK FORCEFULLY** to walk by taking short forceful steps **3.** *vt.* **PUT A STAMP ON A DOCUMENT** to press a stamp onto a document leaving a design or lettering on it in order to show that it has been seen, dated, cancelled, or officially approved **4.** *vt.* **HAVE A LASTING EFFECT ON SB** to have a lasting effect or influence on sb **5.** *vt.* MAIL **STICK A POSTAGE STAMP ON STH** to stick a stamp on an envelope or parcel **6.** *vt.* **SUPPRESS STH OR SB** to suppress or eradicate sth or sb ○ *He stamped on any suggestion he should resign.* **7.** *vt.* INDUST **CRUSH ROCKS** to crush or pound rocks and ores [12thC. Origin uncertain: probably from assumed Old English *stampian* 'to pound', from prehistoric Germanic.] —**stampable** *adj.*

stamp out *vt.* **1. ERADICATE STH** to put an end to sth **2. EXTINGUISH STH** to extinguish sth by stamping on it with the feet **3. CUT STH OUT USING A SHARP TOOL** to cut out a shape or object by pressing a sharp-edged machine or tool onto a material

Stamp Act *n.* a law passed in the British parliament in 1765 introducing a tax on legal documents, commercial contracts, licences, publications, and playing cards in the North American colonies. Because of colonial opposition the first Stamp Act was repealed in March 1766 but was later replaced by others.

stamp collecting *n.* the collecting of postage stamps as a hobby or investment. ◊ **philately** —**stamp collector** *n.*

stamp duty *n.* a duty applied to some legal documents. A stamp is fixed to a document to show that the duty has been paid.

stamped /stampt/ *adj.* having or bearing a stamp

stampede /stam peéd/ *n.* **1. HEADLONG RUSH OF ANIMALS** an uncontrolled headlong rush of frightened animals **2. HEADLONG SURGE OF CROWD** an uncontrolled surging rush of a crowd of people **3. SUDDEN RUSH OF PEOPLE DOING STH** a sudden rush of many people all doing or wanting to do sth at the same time ○ *There was a stampede to take advantage of the low prices.* **4.** *US, Can* **FESTIVAL INCLUDING A RODEO** a celebration in the western United States and especially in Canada, usually held annually, that includes a rodeo along with contests, exhibitions, dancing, and entertainment ■ *v.* **(-pedes, -peding, -peded) 1.** *vti.* **RUSH FORWARDS IN FRIGHTENED SURGE** to rush forwards in a frightened headlong surge, or make animals or people surge forward **2.** *vt.* **FORCE SB INTO DOING STH** to force sb to do sth before he or she is ready or has properly thought about it [Early 19thC. From Mexican Spanish *estampida*, from Spanish, 'uproar'. Ultimately from a prehistoric Germanic word that is also the ancestor of English *stamp*.] —**stampeder** *n.*

stamper /stámpər/ *n.* **1. SB OR STH THAT STAMPS** a person or device used for stamping **2.** INDUST **MACHINE FOR STAMPING STH** a tool or machine that stamps sth, especially ore being pulverized **3.** RECORDING **MOULD FOR DISC RECORDINGS** a mould from which disc recordings are pressed

stamping ground *n.* a place where sb or a group of people is habitually found (*informal*)

stamp mill *n.* a machine in which ores and rocks are finely crushed, usually operated by hydraulic power, or a building housing one or more such machines

stance /stanss, staanss/ *n.* **1. ATTITUDE TOWARDS STH** an attitude or view that sb takes about sth **2. WAY OF STANDING** the way a person or an animal stands **3. POSITION OF WHEELS** the position of a vehicle's wheels in relation to its bodywork ○ *The newer model has a wider stance and a taller cab.* **4.** SPORTS **POSITION OF PLAYER** the position in which a player holds the body in attempting to hit a ball, e.g. in cricket or golf **5.** MOUNTAINEERING **PLACE FOR PITCHING AND BELAYING** a place where a mountain climber can pitch and belay **6.** *Scotland* TRANSP **TRANSPORT WAITING PLACE** a place where buses or taxis wait for passengers [Mid-16thC. Via French, 'position', from Italian *stanza* (see STANZA).]

stanch *adj.* = **staunch**

stanchion /staánchən/ *n.* **1. UPRIGHT SUPPORTING POLE** a vertical pole, bar, or beam used to support sth **2.** AGRIC **FRAME FOR CONFINING A COW** an upright frame in which the neck of a cow is loosely fitted, usually to confine the cow for milking ■ *vt.* **(-chions, -chioning, -chioned) SUPPORT STH WITH A POLE** to support sth using a vertical pole, bar, or beam [15thC. From Old French *estanchon*, from *estance* 'prop, support'.]

stand /stand/ *v.* **(stands, standing, stood, stood** /stŏŏd/) **1.** *vti.* **BE OR SET UPRIGHT** to be in an upright position, or put sth in an upright position ○ *I was standing behind him.* ○ *Stand the box in the corner.* **2.** *vi.* **GET UP ON FEET** to get up into an upright position from a sitting or lying position ○ *The newborn foal tried to stand but only collapsed again.* **3.** *vi.* **BE IN PARTICULAR PLACE** to be situated or positioned in a particular place ○ *The castle stands on a headland.* **4.** *vi.* **MEASURE IN HEIGHT** to be of a particular height when upright ○ *He stood six feet tall.* **5.** *vi.* **BE IN PARTICULAR STATE** to be in a particular condition or state ○ *The old place stands in need of a few repairs.* ○ *The document can't be published as it stands.* **6.** *vi.* **REMAIN MOTIONLESS** to remain in a particular place without moving or being used ○ *The car stood outside the office all morning.* **7.** *vi.* **REMAIN VALID** to continue to be in effect or existence ○ *Her world record still stands.* **8.** *vi.* **STOP** to come to a halt ○ *I had to stand and catch my breath.* **9.** *vi.* **GATHER WITHOUT FLOWING AWAY** to gather somewhere and not flow away ○ *rainwater standing in pools* **10.** *vi.* **BE AT PARTICULAR POINT** to be at a particular point while subject to change or fluctuation ○ *The balance of the account stands at four hundred pounds.* **11.** *vt.* **TOLERATE** to accept or put up with sth ○ *He can't stand being kept waiting.* **12.** *vt.* **UNDERGO**

WITHOUT HARM to resist or bear sth without being harmed or damaged ○ *The mechanism is too delicate to stand rough handling.* **13.** *vt.* SUBMIT TO STH to submit or be subjected to sth ○ *I am prepared to stand trial.* **14.** *vi.* POL SEEK ELECTION to enter an election as a candidate ○ *She decided not to stand at the next election.* **15.** *vi.* FIGHT to fight resolutely or give battle, often after having been in retreat ○ *The general was convinced the enemy would not stand if attacked.* **16.** *vt.* BUY STH FOR SB to pay for sth, e.g. a drink, for sb else to have ○ *My uncle offered to stand dinner for all of us.* **17.** *vt.* BENEFIT FROM STH to benefit from sth, or be no worse for sth ○ *I could stand to lose a few more pounds.* ■ *n.* **1.** ACT OF STANDING the act or an example of standing ○ *a long stand in the airport* **2.** ATTITUDE an opinion that sb has or an attitude that sb adopts on a particular subject ○ *Management took a tough stand on absenteeism.* **3.** SUPPORTING STRUCTURE a framework or structure on which sth is supported ○ *a music stand* **4.** FURNITURE PIECE OF FURNITURE a piece of furniture on which clothes or accessories are hung or supported (*often used in combination*) ○ *an umbrella stand* ○ *a hat stand* **5.** SPORTS PLACE FOR SPECTATORS a large covered seating area for spectators in a sports stadium ○ *a ticket for the North stand.* US term **stands** **6.** STATIONARY CONDITION a state of having stopped or being stationary ○ *The runaway vehicle came to a stand in a field.* **7.** COMM PLACE WHERE STH IS SOLD a booth or stall where sth is sold or given out (*often used in combination*) ○ *a refreshment stand* **8.** EXHIBITION AREA one of several places in an exhibition where sth is displayed **9.** BOT AREA OF GROWING THINGS a group of several plants, especially trees, growing together in one place ○ *a stand of trees* **10.** *US* LAW = **witness box** ○ *take the stand* **11.** HALT TO FIGHT a halt made, especially by a force that has been retreating, to give battle ○ *Custer's last stand* **12.** *US* TRANSP PLACE FOR WAITING VEHICLES a place where vehicles, especially taxis, wait to pick up passengers (*usually used in combination*) ○ *a taxi stand* **13.** ARTS STOP FOR PERFORMANCE a halt made to give a performance during a tour by a performer or theatrical company ○ *a three-week stand out of town* **14.** CRICKET TIME AT WICKET a period at a wicket involving two batsmen during which both bat and are not out, or the score they make [Old English *standan.* Ultimately from an Indo-European word meaning 'to stand', which is also the ancestor of English *stem*[1], *stead*, and *stud*.] ◇ **stand fast** to be resolute and refuse to give in ◇ **stand or fall by sth** to succeed or fail depending on particular circumstances

stand by *vi.* **1.** REMAIN READY to wait in a state of readiness to act if required ○ *Stand by for further orders.* **2.** BE PRESENT WITHOUT ACTION to be present while sth is happening but play no part in it ○ *I'm not prepared to stand by and let this go on.* **3.** SUPPORT to support or remain faithful to sb ○ *Her friends all stood by her.* **4.** ADHERE TO STH to continue to assert or believe in sth ○ *I stand by what I said yesterday.*

stand down *v.* **1.** *vi.* RESIGN to resign from office or withdraw from a contest **2.** *vi.* LAW END TESTIMONY to leave a witness box after having been questioned **3.** *vti.* END DUTY to end sb's period of duty, or to go off duty, especially military duty **4.** *vti.* MIL GO OFF ALERT to go off alert or be taken off alert or out of a combat zone

stand for *vt.* **1.** MEAN STH to mean or represent sth else **2.** BELIEVE IN STH to believe in sth strongly and fight for it ○ *To agree with this would go against everything I stand for.* **3.** BECOME A CANDIDATE FOR STH to enter an election as a candidate for a particular office **4.** PUT UP WITH to tolerate or put up with sth ○ *She won't stand for any nonsense.* **5.** NAUT HEAD FOR A PLACE to set a course for a particular destination ○ *The fleet stood for home.*

stand in *vi.* to take the place of sb or sth else as a substitute ○ *Who's going to stand in while you're away?*

stand off *v.* **1.** *vti.* KEEP AWAY to keep at a distance from sth, or to make sb or sth stay at a distance **2.** *vti.* NAUT SAIL AWAY to sail a vessel away from sth such as a shore **3.** *vt.* SUSPEND FROM WORK to suspend sb from work, usually temporarily

stand on *v.* **1.** *vt.* INSIST ON to insist on sth or see it as being important ○ *We don't stand on ceremony in this house.* **2.** *vi.* NAUT MAINTAIN SAILING DIRECTION to continue sailing a vessel on a particular course

stand out *vi.* **1.** BE CONSPICUOUS to be conspicuous or prominent **2.** STICK OUT to project or protrude from sth **3.** REFUSE TO ACCEPT STH to refuse to accept or comply with sth, especially after others have done so

stand to *vti.* to take up position in readiness for military action, or to make sb do this

stand up *v.* **1.** *vti.* RISE to rise to an upright position, or make sth do this **2.** *vi.* RESIST SCRUTINY to be seen as still valid or right despite being closely examined or criticized ○ *I don't think her testimony will stand up in court.*

stand up for *vi.* to defend or act to protect the interests of sb

stand up to *vi.* **1.** RESIST to resist or refuse to be cowed by sb ○ *He'll back down if you stand up to him.* **2.** ENDURE to undergo sth that is potentially damaging without being badly affected ○ *These cars won't stand up to being driven on rough terrain.*

stand up with *vi. US* to act as best man or maid of honour for sb who is getting married

stand-alone *adj.* able to operate as a self-contained unit independently of a computer network or system

standard /stándərd/ *n.* **1.** LEVEL OF QUALITY OR EXCELLENCE the level of quality or excellence attained by sb or sth ○ *I hadn't expected work of such a high standard from trainees.* **2.** LEVEL OF QUALITY ACCEPTED AS NORM a level of quality or excellence that is accepted as the norm or by which actual attainments are judged (*often used in the plural*) ○ *By present-day standards the sound quality of this recording is very poor.* **3.** FLAG a flag with a distinctive design that is the emblem of, and often a focus of loyalty to, a particular nation, person, or group **4.** MIL DEVICE USED AS BATTLE RALLYING POINT a flag or other symbolic device attached to a pole and used as a rallying point for troops in battle **5.** HERALDRY LONG TAPERING FLAG a long tapering flag ending in two points and with heraldic devices on it, used in heraldry as an emblem of a person or corporation. It was formerly carried on ceremonial occasions by or before the nobleman to whom it belonged. **6.** MEASURE AUTHORIZED MODEL OF UNIT OF MEASUREMENT an authorized model used to define a unit of measurement **7.** COINS PROPORTION OF METAL IN COIN the proportion of gold or silver and of nonprecious metal that a coin is legally required to contain **8.** FIN COMMODITY MONEY HAS VALUE BASED ON the commodity or commodities on which the value of a currency or monetary system is based **9.** HOUSEHOLD UPRIGHT POLE OR POST an upright pole or post, usually serving as a support for sth **10.** GARDENING PLANT WITH STRAIGHT BARE STEM a plant, especially a fruit tree or rose, trained so that its leaves and flowers grow at the top of a straight bare stem **11.** MUSIC ITEM IN USUAL REPERTOIRE sth, especially a song or other piece of music, that is very popular or is performed as part of the usual repertoire of sb or sth ○ *played all the old standards* **12.** BOT LARGE UPPER PETAL OF PEA the large upper petal in the flowers of plants of the pea family ■ *adj.* NORMAL constituting or not differing from the norm for a particular thing ○ *This clause is absolutely standard in a contract of this type* ■ **standards** *npl.* PRINCIPLES principles or values that govern sb's behaviour ■ *adj.* **1.** WIDELY USED AND RESPECTED very widely used and generally regarded as authoritative ○ *the standard text in thermodynamics* **2.** GRAM GRAMMATICALLY CORRECT regarded as correct or acceptable by the majority of educated speakers of or authorities on a language **3.** GARDENING TRAINED TO GROW WITH STRAIGHT STEM trained in such a way that the leaves and flowers grow at the top of a straight bare stem [12thC. Via Anglo-Norman *estaundart* 'flag to which troops rally' from Old French *estandart*, of uncertain origin: perhaps from prehistoric Germanic words.]

standard amenities *npl.* the sanitary equipment required as a basic minimum for all dwellings by British housing law, namely a bath or shower, washbasin, sink, and a flush toilet

standard assessment task *n.* a test used to assess the progress of children in a core subject of the national curriculum

standard atmosphere *n.* MEASURE = **atmosphere** *n.* **6**

standard-bearer *n.* **1.** SB WHO CARRIES STANDARD sb who carries a standard or flag, especially for a military unit **2.** LEADER a leader or prominent and inspiring representative of a movement, cause, or party

standard candle *n.* MEASURE = **candela**

standard cell *n.* an electric cell that produces a constant known voltage and can be used to calibrate voltage-measuring equipment

standard cost *n.* the budgeted expenditure of a regular manufacturing process against which the actual cost is measured

standard deviation *n.* a statistical measure of the amount by which a set of values differs from the arithmetical mean, equal to the square root of the mean of the differences' squares

Standard English *n.* the form of the English language used by educated speakers and regarded as representing correct usage in grammar, spelling, vocabulary, and punctuation

standard error *n.* the standard deviation of the sample in a frequency distribution divided by the square root of the number of values in the sample. It is a measure of the variability that a constant would be expected to show during sampling.

standard gauge *n.* the gauge used for most public railway systems worldwide, the distance between the rails being 143.5 cm/4 ft $8\frac{1}{2}$ in

Standard Generalized Markup Language *n.* full form of **SGML**

Standard Grade *n.* **1.** EXAMINATION FOR SCOTTISH CERTIFICATE OF EDUCATION the lower-level examination for the Scottish Certificate of Education, usually taken by school students at the age of 15 or 16 **2.** STH ACHIEVED AT STANDARD GRADE a subject studied, an examination taken, or a pass achieved at Standard Grade

standardize /stándər dīz/ (**-izes, -izing, -ized**), **standardise** (**-ises, -ising, -ised**) *v.* **1.** *vti.* MAKE STANDARD to remove variations and irregularities and make all types or examples of sth the same or bring them into conformity with one another **2.** *vt.* ASSESS STH BY COMPARISON WITH STANDARD to assess sth or determine its properties by comparing it with a standard — **standardizer** *n.*

standard lamp *n.* a tall lamp with a base that stands on the floor. US term **floor lamp**

standard of living *n.* the level of material comfort enjoyed by a person, group, or society

standard operating procedure *n.* a procedure that is usually followed when carrying out a particular operation or dealing with a particular situation

Standards Australia *n.* in Australia, a government-funded independent organization that sets, monitors, and certifies standards in a wide range of fields such as building and manufacturing

standard time *n.* a system of measuring time in relation to the natural day usually based on the mean solar time at the central meridian of a particular time zone

stand-by *n.* **1.** PERSON OR THING READILY AVAILABLE sth or sb that can always be relied on to be available and useful, especially if needed as a substitute or in an emergency **2.** TRANSP UNRESERVED TICKET OR PASSENGER WITHOUT RESERVATION an unreserved ticket or a passenger having no prior reservation on a mode of public transport such as an airline ■ *adj.* **1.** RESERVE able to be used as a replacement **2.** TRANSP UNRESERVED AND SUBJECT TO AVAILABILITY made available, usually at a lower price, shortly before the departure of a flight when there are seats remaining unsold, or using a ticket made available in this way ■ *adv.* TRANSP ON STAND-BY BASIS on the basis of stand-by ○ *flew standby from Washington to Amsterdam* ◇ **be on stand-by** to be available for use or service if necessary

stand-down *n.* a return to normal status after being on alert, or the withdrawal of a military presence ○ *After three weeks on alert in the riot-torn city the UN forces were finally put on stand-down.*

standee /stan dée/ *n.* sb who stands, e.g. on a bus, usually because there are no seats available

stand-in *n.* **1.** TEMPORARY REPLACEMENT sb or sth that acts as a temporary replacement **2.** CINEMA FILM ACTOR'S DOUBLE sb who replaces an actor in a film for preparatory or nonvital work on set or when dangerous stunts are being shot ■ *adj.* ACTING AS REPLACEMENT acting as a temporary replacement for sb or sth

standing /stánding/ *n.* **1.** STATUS AND REPUTATION sb's reputation or position, e.g., in society or business ○ *a person of some standing in computer electronics* **2.** DURATION the period over which sth has been in existence ■ *adj.* **1.** UPRIGHT performed while standing rather than sitting or moving **2.** PERMANENT remaining permanently in existence or in force **3.** NOT FLOWING not flowing, or containing water that cannot flow or run away **4.** AGRIC NOT CUT DOWN growing where planted, having not been cut down

standing army *n.* a permanent professional military force maintained by a country in times of peace as well as war

standing committee *n.* a committee that remains in existence permanently in order to deal with a particular issue

standing crop *n.* the total mass of living things of all kinds or of one particular kind found in a particular area at a particular time

standing order *n.* **1.** ORDER an order or rule, especially one governing military or parliamentary procedures, that remains in force on all relevant occasions until it is specifically revoked **2.** BANKING INSTRUCTION TO BANK an instruction given by an account holder to a bank to pay a specified sum of money at specified intervals to a specified person or account

standing rigging *n.* the wires and ropes holding the masts and spars of a sailing ship that are more or less permanently fixed in place

standing room *n.* space where people can only stand, not sit

standing stone *n.* a large stone set upright in the ground in prehistoric times singly or as part of a larger structure

standing wave *n.* a stationary wave characterized by points of zero vibration and points of maximum vibration, occurring when two waves of equal frequency and intensity travelling in opposite directions combine [Because the points of minimum and maximum vibration remain stationary]

standish /stándish/ *n.* a holder for an ink bottle, pens, and other writing equipment (*archaic*) [14thC. Origin uncertain: probably formed from STAND as a verb.]

standoff /stánd of/ *n.* **1.** DEADLOCK a situation in which no result or conclusion can be reached because the two sides in a contest or dispute are equally matched or are equally intransigent **2.** *US* SPORTS DRAW a draw or tie

stand-off half, **stand-off** *n.* in rugby, a player who plays behind the forwards and the scrum half, provides a link between them and the threequarter backs, and often has control of the team's tactics

standoff insulator *n.* an insulator that supports an electrical conductor and keeps it at a distance from other conducting elements. The insulators supporting power lines are examples of this.

standoffish /stand óffish/ *adj.* reluctant to show friendship or enter into conversation with other people

standoff missile *n.* a guided missile that can be fired from an aircraft at a sufficient distance from its target to be out of range of enemy defences

stand oil *n.* a thick drying oil used in oil enamel paints, made by heating linseed or another oil to a high temperature [Translation of German *Standöl*; it was formerly prepared by allowing linseed oil to stand]

standover man /stánd ōvər-/ *n.* *Aus* sb who intimidates people or threatens them with violence in order to extort money or obtain other services from them

standpipe /stánd pīp/ *n.* **1.** UTIL PIPE FOR EMERGENCY WATER SUPPLY a vertical pipe with a tap on the top, used to enable householders to draw water from a water main in the street when the normal supply is disrupted **2.** ENG VERTICAL PRESSURE-REGULATING PIPE a vertical, open-ended pipe attached to a pipeline to act as a pressure regulator, ensuring that the pressure head at that point cannot exceed the length of the pipe

standpoint /stánd poynt/ *n.* the particular way an individual or a group thinks about or is affected by an event or an issue, usually as opposed to the way others view the same thing ○ *From the ecological standpoint, this is an utter disaster.*

standstill /stánd stil/ *n.* a situation in which all movement or activity ceases and further movement or activity is prevented ○ *Traffic is at a standstill.*

standstill agreement *n.* an agreement that things should remain as they are, especially one between a creditor country and a debtor country that needs extra time to repay its debt

stand-to (*plural* **stand-tos**) *n.* the act of taking up positions ready for action

standup /stánd up/, **stand-up** *adj.* **1.** ERECT standing erect and not folded down **2.** AT WHICH PEOPLE STAND where or at which people stand, especially to eat or drink **3.** NOISY AND INTENSE intense and involving a lot of noise and sometimes violence **4.** ARTS INVOLVING SOLO PERFORMANCE BY COMEDIAN involving a performance by a comedian standing alone on stage telling jokes or stories to an audience **5.** *US* TRUSTWORTHY showing the qualities of honesty, loyalty, and dependability (*informal*) ■ *n.* **1.** ARTS STAND-UP COMEDY comedy in which the performer stands alone on stage telling jokes or stories to an audience **2.** STANDING TO GET WORK standing in a designated place to be hired for a day's work (*informal*) ○ *I'd get in early for the standups*

Stanford /stánfərd/, **Sir Charles Villiers** (1852–1924) British composer and teacher. He wrote operas and symphonies, but is best known for his church music.

Stanford-Binet test /stánfərd bi náy-/ *n.* an intelligence test commonly used with children in the United States [Early 20thC. Named after *Stanford* University, California, + Alfred *Binet*, (1857–1911), a French psychologist who devised the original version.]

stanhope /stán hōp/ *n.* a light open horse-drawn carriage with a single seat and two or four wheels [Early 19thC. Named after Fitzroy H. R. *Stanhope*, (1787–1864), an English clergyman for whom one was first made.]

Stanislavsky /stani slávski/, **Konstantin Sergeyevich Alexeyev** (1863–1938) Russian actor and theatre director. He helped to found the Moscow Arts Theatre (1889), and there adopted methods of training actors that greatly influenced theatre in the 20th century. —**Stanislavskian** /stani slávskiən/ *adj.*

Stanislavsky method, **Stanislavski method** *n.* = **Method**

stank past tense of **stink**

Stanley /stánli/ industrial town in a coal-mining area of Durham, in England. Population: 18,905 (1991).

Stanley /stánnli/, **Sir H. M.** (1841–1904) British journalist and explorer. On his African expeditions he located David Livingstone at Ujiji on Lake Tanganyika (1871), traced the Lualaba and Congo rivers to the sea (1874–77), and helped to found the Congo Free State (1890–95). Full name **Sir Henry Morton Stanley**. Born **John Rowlands**

Stanley knife /stánli-/ *tdmk.* a trademark for a type of knife that is very sharp and has a retractable blade

Stanley Pool former name for **Malebo Pool**

stann- *prefix.* tin ○ *stanniferous*

Stannaries /stánnəriz/ *npl.* a former tin-mining district in Devon and Cornwall

stannary /stánnəri/ (*plural* **-naries**) *n.* a district with tin mines [15thC. Via medieval Latin *stannaria* 'stannaries', from late Latin *stannum* 'tin' (see STANN-).]

stannic /stánnik/ *adj.* containing or relating to tin, especially with a valency of four [Late 18thC. Formed from obsolete *stannum* (see STANN-).]

stannic sulphide *n.* a solid compound of sulphur and tin that is usually found in the form of gold-coloured crystals or a powder

stanniferous /sta nífferəss/ *adj.* containing or yielding tin [Early 19thC. Formed from obsolete English *stannum* (see STANN-).]

stannite /stánnīt/ *n.* a grey mineral with a metallic lustre that is a source of tin. Formula: Cu_2FeSn_4. [Mid-19thC. Formed form obsolete English *stannum* (see STANN-).]

stannous /stánnəss/ *adj.* containing or relating to tin, especially with a valency of two [Mid-19thC. Formed from obsolete English *stannum* (see STANN-).]

stannous fluoride *n.* a white crystalline powder with a bitter salty taste used to fluoridate toothpaste. Formula: SnF_2.

Stansted /stánstəd/ village near Bishop's Stortford, Essex, southeastern England. It is home to London's third airport. Population: 4,943 (1991).

Stanthorpe /stán thawrp/ town in southeastern Queensland, Australia. It is one of the highest towns in the state at 811 m/2,660 ft. Population: 4,154 (1996).

Stanton /stántən/, **Elizabeth Cady** (1815–1902) US social reformer. She worked in the abolitionist and temperance movements, and after 1840 devoted herself to the campaign for women's suffrage and civil rights.

stanza /stánzə/ *n.* a number of lines of verse forming a separate unit within a poem. In many poems each stanza has the same number of lines and the same rhythm and rhyme scheme. [Late 16thC. Via Italian from assumed Vulgar Latin *stantia* 'a standing, stopping place', ultimately from Latin *stare* 'to stand'. From the idea of stopping after a section.] —**stanzaic** /stan záyik/ *adj.*

stapedectomy /stáypi déktəmi/ (*plural* **-mies**) *n.* surgical removal of the stapes of the ear. It is performed in treating some forms of hearing loss. [Late 19thC. Formed from modern Latin *staped-*, stem of *stapes* (see STAPES).]

stapedes plural of **stapes**

stapelia /stə péeli ə/ (*plural* **-as** *or* **-a**) *n.* an African plant that resembles the cactus, has thick fleshy four-angled stems, no leaves, and bears large mottled flowers that give off a foul smell. Genus: *Stapelia*. [Late 18thC. Formed from modern Latin, genus name, named after Jan Bode van *Stapel*, (died 1636), a Dutch botanist.]

stapes /stáy peez/ (*plural* **-pes** *or* **-pedes** /-péedeez/) *n.* a small stirrup-shaped bone in the middle ear of mammals, the innermost of the three small bones that transmit vibration to the inner ear [Mid-17thC. Via modern Latin from medieval Latin, 'stirrup'.] —**stapedial** /stə péedi əl/ *adj.*

staph /staf/ *n.* a staphylococcus (*informal*) [Early 20thC. Shortening.]

staphylococcus /stáffilə kókəss/ (*plural* **-ci** /-kók sī/) *n.* a bacterium that typically occurs in clusters resembling grapes, normally inhabits the skin and mucous membranes, and may cause disease. These bacteria commonly infect the skin, eyes, and urinary tract, and some produce toxins responsible for septicaemia and food poisoning. Genus: *Staphylococcus*. [Late 19thC. Via modern Latin, genus name, from Greek *staphulē* 'bunch of grapes' + *kokkos* 'berry'.] —**staphylococcal** *adj.* —**staphylococcic** /-kóksik/ *adj.*

staple[1] /stáyp'l/ *n.* **1.** COMM BENT WIRE TO FASTEN PAPERS a small thin piece of metal wire bent into the shape of a flattened U with square corners, used to fasten things together, especially sheets of paper. The staple is driven through the material by a device that also bends its two ends inwards and flattens them so that they grip the material firmly. **2.** BUILDING U-SHAPED FASTENER FOR WOOD OR MASONRY a small U-shaped piece of strong metal wire with two sharp points, usually driven into a surface to hold sth such as a bolt or cable in place ■ *vt.* (**-ples, -pling, -pled**) FASTEN WITH STAPLES to fasten sth to sth else or in position with staples [Old English *stapol* 'post, pillar', of prehistoric Germanic origin. The underlying sense is perhaps of 'sth that supports or holds'.]

staple[2] /stáyp'l/ *n.* **1.** COMM MOST IMPORTANT ARTICLE OF TRADE the commodity or product that is most important to the trade of a country, region, or organization **2.** FOOD BASIC INGREDIENT OF DIET a food that forms the basis of the diet of the people of a particular country or region or of a particular animal **3.** PRINCIPAL OR RECURRING INGREDIENT a principal or continually recurring ingredient or feature of sth ○ *I'd hardly describe opera as a staple of the entertainment offered in this theatre.* **4.** MANUF WOOL, COTTON, OR FLAX FIBRE the fibre of wool, cotton, or flax graded according to its length and fineness ■ *adj.* BASIC AND MOST IMPORTANT used or

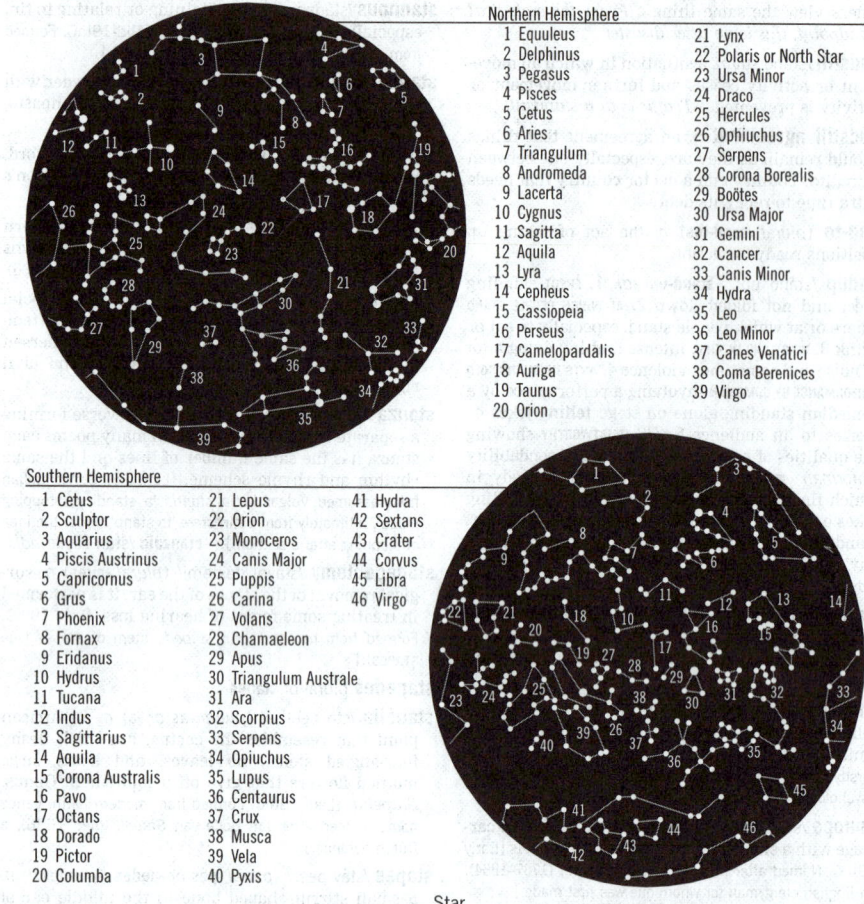

Northern Hemisphere

1 Equuleus		21 Lynx	
2 Delphinus		22 Polaris or North Star	
3 Pegasus		23 Ursa Minor	
4 Pisces		24 Draco	
5 Cetus		25 Hercules	
6 Aries		26 Ophiuchus	
7 Triangulum		27 Serpens	
8 Andromeda		28 Corona Borealis	
9 Lacerta		29 Boötes	
10 Cygnus		30 Ursa Major	
11 Sagitta		31 Gemini	
12 Aquila		32 Cancer	
13 Lyra		33 Canis Minor	
14 Cepheus		34 Hydra	
15 Cassiopeia		35 Leo	
16 Perseus		36 Leo Minor	
17 Camelopardalis		37 Canes Venatici	
18 Auriga		38 Coma Berenices	
19 Taurus		39 Virgo	
20 Orion			

Southern Hemisphere

1 Cetus		21 Lepus		41 Hydra	
2 Sculptor		22 Orion		42 Sextans	
3 Aquarius		23 Monoceros		43 Crater	
4 Piscis Austrinus		24 Canis Major		44 Corvus	
5 Capricornus		25 Puppis		45 Libra	
6 Grus		26 Carina		46 Virgo	
7 Phoenix		27 Volans			
8 Fornax		28 Chamaeleon			
9 Eridanus		29 Apus			
10 Hydrus		30 Triangulum Australe			
11 Tucana		31 Ara			
12 Indus		32 Scorpius			
13 Sagittarius		33 Serpens			
14 Aquila		34 Opiuchus			
15 Corona Australis		35 Lupus			
16 Pavo		36 Centaurus			
17 Octans		37 Crux			
18 Dorado		38 Musca			
19 Pictor		39 Vela			
20 Columba		40 Pyxis			

Star

depended on as the basic and most important element of sth, especially diet or trade ■ *vt.* (**-ples, -pling, -pled**) MANUF GRADE FIBRES to grade the fibres of wool, cotton, or flax according to their length and fineness [14thC. Via Old French *estaple* from Middle Low German and Middle Dutch *stapel* 'shop; pillar', from a prehistoric Germanic word that is also the ancestor of English *staple¹*.]

staple gun *n.* a powerful device used to project heavy metal staples into wood or masonry

stapler /stáyplər/ *n.* a device that fastens paper and other materials together using staples, usually consisting of a flat metal base, a spring-loaded magazine of staples, and a top section

star /staar/ *n.* **1.** ASTRON POINT OF LIGHT IN NIGHT SKY a celestial body usually visible as a small bright point of light in the night sky **2.** ASTRON MASS OF GAS IN SPACE a gaseous mass in space such as the Sun, ranging in size from that of a planet to larger than the Earth's orbit, which generates energy by thermonuclear reactions **3.** STAR SHAPE a shape representing or based on that of a star as seen in the night sky, usually having four or five triangular points radiating from a centre **4.** STAR-SHAPED SYMBOL OF MERIT OR RANK a star-shaped object or symbol used as a sign of merit, quality, or rank **5.** PRINTING = **asterisk 6.** ARTS, SPORTS POPULAR PERFORMER a very famous, successful, and popular performer, especially in the field of entertainment or sport **7.** MOST IMPORTANT OR PROFICIENT PERSON sb who is particularly good at some activity, or who is the most important or most skilful member of a group involved in a particular activity ○ *the star of the French class* **8.** HELPFUL PERSON a very nice or helpful person (*informal*) ○ *Thanks, Ben. You're a star!* **9.** ZODIAC CELESTIAL BODY IN RELATION TO FATE a planet or constellation believed to influence sb's character or fate on Earth ■ **stars** *npl.* ZODIAC DESTINY sb's future, especially as supposedly revealed in a horoscope (*informal*) ■ *v.* (**stars, starring, starred**) **1.** *vt.* CINEMA, THEATRE HAVE AS LEADING ACTOR to have sb as the leading performer or as one of the leading performers **2.** *vi.* CINEMA, THEATRE BE LEADING PERFORMER to be the leading performer or one of the leading

performers in sth such as a film or play **3.** *vt.* PRINTING MARK STH WITH STAR to mark sth with an asterisk or a star-shaped symbol, especially to draw attention to it **4.** *vt.* COVER OR DECORATE STH WITH STARS to cover or decorate sth with stars, or with many brilliant or colourful objects so as to give an effect comparable to that of the stars in the night sky ■ *adj.* OUTSTANDING very or most important, skilful, or successful [Old English *steorra*. Ultimately from an Indo-European word that is also the ancestor of Latin *stella* (source of English *stellar*).]

◇ **see stars** see flashes of light, e.g. after receiving a hard blow to the head

star anise *n.* **1.** CHINESE EVERGREEN TREE a Chinese evergreen tree of the magnolia family that produces purple-red flowers and whose dried seeds and seed pods are used in Chinese cookery and medicine. Latin name: *Illicium verum.* **2.** STAR ANISE SEED POD the star-shaped aniseed-flavoured dried seed and seed pod of the star anise tree, used in Chinese cookery and medicine

star-apple *n.* **1.** TREES TROPICAL AMERICAN EVERGREEN TREE a tropical American evergreen tree that bears purplish-white flowers and produces an apple-shaped fruit with a smooth greenish-purple skin. Latin name: *Chrysophyllum cainito.* **2.** FOOD FRUIT OF THE STAR-APPLE TREE the fruit of the star-apple tree, which is shaped like an apple and when cut open reveals an arrangement of seeds resembling a star

Stara Zagora /stárrə zə górrə/ city in central Bulgaria, situated about 153 km/95 mi. west of the Black Sea port of Burgas. Population: 151,218 (1995).

star billing *n.* the fact of being advertised as the leading performer in sth

starboard /staárbərd/ *n.* RIGHT-HAND SIDE the direction to the right of sb facing the front of a ship or aircraft ■ *adj.* ON RIGHT-HAND SIDE on, towards, or from the right-hand side of sb facing the front of a ship or aircraft ■ *adv.* TOWARDS STARBOARD towards starboard or the starboard side of a ship or aircraft ■ *vt.* (**-boards, -boarding, -boarded**) TURN TOWARDS STARBOARD to turn or move sth, especially the helm, towards starboard [Old English *stēorbord*, from *stēor* 'paddle' + *bord*

'board'. The modern meaning arose from the early Germanic custom of steering boats by means of a paddle on the right side.]

starburst /staár burst/ *n.* a pattern of lines or light rays radiating outwards from a centre

star cactus *n.* a Mexican cactus with yellow flowers and spines arranged in clusters like stars. Genus: *Astrophytum.*

starch /staarch/ *n.* **1.** CARBOHYDRATE SUBSTANCE a carbohydrate substance manufactured by plants and stored in seeds, tubers, fruits, and stems and forming an important source of energy in the diet of human beings and animals. The two main components of starch are amylose and amylopectin. Formula: $(C_6H_{10}O_5)_n$. **2.** HOUSEHOLD STIFFENING SUBSTANCE FOR FABRICS a substance, especially natural starch in the form of a white powder extracted from potatoes and grain, used to stiffen the fabric of clothes before ironing **3.** FOOD STARCHY FOODSTUFF a foodstuff that contains a large amount of starch **4.** STIFF AND FORMAL MANNER behaviour marked by a stiff manner and formality **5.** *US* COURAGE great courage or energy ■ *vt.* (**starches, starching, starched**) HOUSEHOLD STIFFEN WITH STARCH to stiffen fabric with starch [Old English (assumed) *stercan* 'to stiffen', from a prehistoric Germanic base meaning 'to be rigid', which is also the ancestor of English *stare*]

star chamber *n.* a court or tribunal noted for being harsh, arbitrary, and unaccountable in its proceedings

Star Chamber *n.* a court established by King Henry VII of England to try civil and criminal cases, especially those involving the security of the state, in secret. It was noted for its arbitrary proceedings and abolished in 1641. [*Star* because the ceiling of the original courtroom was decorated with stars]

starch syrup *n.* a syrup created through the incomplete hydrolysis of glucose that contains dextrose, maltose, and dextrine

starch wheat *n.* = **emmer**

starchy /staárchi/ (**-ier, -iest**) *adj.* **1.** CONTAINING STARCH containing a large amount of starch, or like starch, especially in consistency **2.** FORMAL very formal and unbending, and apparently lacking in warmth or a sense of humour

star connection *n.* an electrical connection in a polyphase system in which the windings have one end connected to a common junction and the other ends connected to separate load points

star-crossed *adj.* believed to be destined by fate to be unhappy [From the belief in the influence of the stars over human lives]

stardom /staárdəm/ *n.* **1.** STAR STATUS the status of a star performer in sport or entertainment, and the fame and prestige that go with it **2.** STAR PERFORMERS star performers considered as a group

stardust /staár dust/ *n.* **1.** DREAMY ROMANTIC FEELING a dreamy romantic sentimental feeling, or an imaginary substance, usually represented as starry and twinkling, that is supposed to induce this feeling **2.** ASTRON FAR DISTANT STARS far distant stars in a cluster or strewn like a cloud of bright dust in the night sky

stare /stair/ *v.* (**stares, staring, stared**) **1.** *vti.* LOOK FIXEDLY to look directly at sb or sth for a long time without moving the eyes away, usually as a result of curiosity or surprise, or to express rudeness or defiance ○ *'What is this life if, full of care, / We have no time to stand and stare?'* (W. H. Davies *Leisure*; 1911) **2.** *vi.* BE WIDE OPEN WITH SHOCK to look wide open with shock, fear, or amazement (*refers to eyes*) **3.** *vi.* BE OBVIOUS to be obvious or blatant ○ *The answer was staring at you all the time you just couldn't see it.* ■ *n.* **1.** LONG CONCENTRATED LOOK a long concentrated look at sb or sth, often full of curiosity or hostility **2.** FACIAL EXPRESSION a facial expression in which the eyes are wide open with shock or amazement and looking fixedly at sb or sth [Old English *starian*, from a prehistoric Germanic base meaning 'to be rigid', which is also the ancestor of English *stern*. The underlying idea is of 'sth fixed'.] —**starer** *n.*

stare down *vt. US* = **stare out**

stare out *vt.* to look sb directly in the eyes until he or she is forced to look away. US term **stare down**

starets /staárits/ (*plural* **startsy** /staártsi/) *n.* a religious teacher or spiritual adviser in the Eastern Orthodox Church, especially one who is a monk or holy man [Early 20thC. From Russian, 'elderly man, elder'.]

star facet *n.* one of the eight small triangular facets that surround the table of a gem cut in the brilliant style

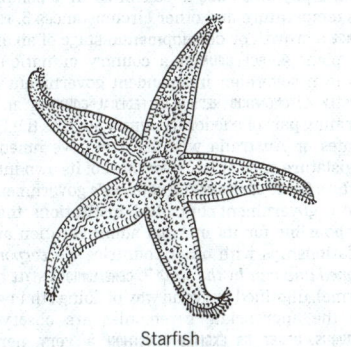

Starfish

starfish /staár fish/ (*plural* **-fish** *or* **-fishes**) *n.* a marine invertebrate animal (**echinoderm**) whose body consists of five or more arms radiating from a central disc. Starfish have a central mouth on the underside and feed on oysters and other molluscs on shores and the seabed. Class: Asteroidea.

starfish flower *n.* = **stapelia**

starflower /staár flowər/ *n.* a plant that has star-shaped flowers, e.g. the star-of-Bethlehem and some plants of northeastern North America

star fruit *n.* = **carambola**

stargaze /staár gayz/ (**-gazes**, **-gazing**, **-gazed**) *vi.* **1.** WATCH STARS AT NIGHT to observe the stars at night **2.** DAYDREAM to engage in daydreaming

stargazer /staár gayzər/ *n.* **1.** DAYDREAMER sb who daydreams **2.** ZOOL TROPICAL MARINE FISH a bottom-dwelling tropical marine fish that has eyes and mouth on the top of its head. Families: Uranoscopidae and Dactyloscopidae.

star grass *n.* a plant of the daffodil family found in tropical and temperate regions that has long leaves that look like grass and star-shaped white or yellow flowers. Genus: *Hypoxis*.

stark /staark/ *adj.* **1.** FORBIDDINGLY BARE AND PLAIN forbidding in its bareness and lack of any ornament, relieving feature, or pleasant prospect ○ *the stark interior of a dungeon cell* **2.** UNAMBIGUOUS AND HARSH presented in plain, unambiguous, and usually rather harsh terms ○ *Faced with the stark choice, we either had to change or go under.* **3.** COMPLETE having reached the fullest extent or degree of sth **4.** WITHOUT CLOTHES completely unclothed and uncovered **5.** RIGID showing or affected by rigor mortis (*archaic*) ■ *adv.* UTTERLY to the utmost degree [Old English *stearc*, from a prehistoric Germanic base meaning 'to be rigid', which is also the ancestor of English *stare* and *starve*] —**starkly** *adv.* —**starkness** *n.*

Stark /staark/, **Dame Freya** (1893–1993) British writer.

Dame Freya Stark

She wrote over 30 travel books describing aspects of the Middle East, especially life in the deserts. Full name **Dame Freya Madeline Stark**

starkers /staárkərz/ *adj.* completely unclothed and uncovered (*informal*) [Early 20thC. Shortening and alteration of STARK-NAKED.]

stark-naked *adj.* completely unclothed and uncovered

starlet /staárlət/ *n.* a young woman actor billed as a possible major film star of the future

starlight /staár līt/ *n.* the light that comes from the stars

starling[1] /staárling/ *n.* a common European bird with glossy greenish-black plumage, a short tail, and pointed wings. Starlings often gather in large noisy flocks to feed and roost. Latin name: *Sturnus vulgaris*. [Old English *stærlinc*, literally 'little starling', from *stær* 'starling'. Ultimately from a prehistoric Germanic word.]

starling[2] /staárling/ *n.* a structure made of piles surrounding a pier of a bridge to protect the pier from floating debris [Late 17thC. Origin uncertain: perhaps an alteration of *staddling* in the obsolete sense 'pier of a bridge'.]

starlit /staár lit/ *adj.* lit by light from the stars

star-nosed mole *n.* a North American mole that has a ring of small pink fleshy tentacles surrounding its nose. Latin name: *Condylura cristata*.

star-of-Bethlehem (*plural* **stars-of-Bethlehem** *or* **star-of-Bethlehem**) *n.* a European perennial plant of the lily family that has long slender leaves and bears clusters of white star-shaped flowers on a central stalk. Genus: *Ornithogalum*. [Late 16thC. From its abundance in Palestine.]

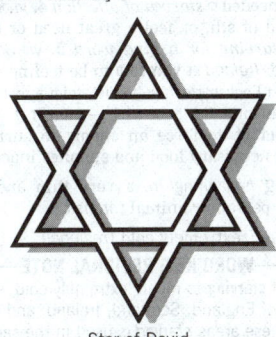

Star of David

Star of David *n.* a symbol of the Jewish faith and of the state of Israel consisting of two equilateral triangles superimposed on each other to form a six-pointed star

Starr /staar/, **Ringo** (b. 1940) British musician. He attained fame as the drummer of the Beatles (1962–70). Real name **Richard Starkey**

star ruby *n.* a ruby with a crystalline structure that reflects light in a shape that resembles a star when it is cut with a convex surface

starry /staári/ (**-rier**, **-riest**) *adj.* **1.** WITH MANY STARS SHINING bright with many shining stars **2.** COVERED WITH STARS covered or decorated with stars **3.** SIMILAR TO STAR relating to or similar in shape or brightness to a star

starry-eyed *adj.* having a happy and enthusiastic or romantic attitude that is naïve and unrealistic

Stars and Bars *n.* the first flag of the Confederacy during the American Civil War, which had two red stripes and one white, and a circle of white stars representing the seceded states (*takes a singular or plural verb*)

Stars and Stripes *n.* the national flag of the United States, which has 13 alternating red and white stripes and one star for each state on a blue field (*takes a singular or plural verb*)

star sapphire *n.* a sapphire with a crystalline structure that reflects light in a star shape when cut with a convex surface

star shell *n.* an artillery shell designed to burst in midair and release a flare or a shower of lights

starship /staár ship/ *n.* a spaceship designed to travel between stars or star systems, and as yet existing only in science fiction

star sign *n.* a sign of the zodiac, especially the sun sign under which sb was born

star-spangled *adj.* **1.** COVERED WITH STARS covered or decorated with stars **2.** FILLED WITH VIPS AND STARS attended by many important people, including politicians, company directors, and film stars

Star-Spangled Banner *n.* **1.** US NATIONAL ANTHEM the national anthem of the United States **2.** NATIONAL FLAG OF US the national flag of the United States

starstruck /staár struk/, **star-struck** *adj.* feeling or showing an awed fascination with stars, especially from the world of entertainment, and stardom

star-studded *adj.* containing many well-known actors or performers

star system *n.* CINEMA the system of deliberately exploiting an individual star, both on screen and off, to sell films

start /staart/ *v.* (**starts**, **starting**, **started**) **1.** *vti.* BEGIN to begin doing sth or begin sth ○ *She started to laugh.* ○ *I'd better start getting ready.* **2.** *vti.* BEGIN HAPPENING to begin happening, or to make sth begin happening ○ *The film starts at 7 o'clock.* **3.** *vt.* CREATE STH to bring sth into being as an entity or operation **4.** *vti.* CARS MAKE ENGINE BEGIN TO WORK to make an engine begin to operate ○ *The car won't start.* ○ *I can't start the car.* **5.** *vt.* BEGIN WORKING to commence work on sth **6.** *vt.* HELP SB BEGIN STH to help sb out in beginning an activity such as a journey or career ○ *It was a university professor who started her on her law career.* **7.** *vti.* SPORTS PLAY FIRST IN A SPORTS MATCH to be or select sb to be in a race or to play at the beginning of a sports match **8.** *vi.* BEGIN ARGUING to begin arguing or making a fuss (*informal*) ○ *Please don't start.* **9.** *vi.* MAKE SUDDEN MOVEMENT to make a sudden movement out of surprise, pain, fear, or anger **10.** *vti.* MOVE SUDDENLY to go or cause a person or animal to go very quickly from being still to moving ○ *start to your feet* **11.** *vt.* ALARM SB to cause sb to be alarmed (*archaic*) **12.** *vi.* GO FROM A PARTICULAR LEVEL to begin at a particular level ○ *Prices start at fifteen pounds.* **13.** *vt.* RAISE STH to raise or care for sth in the early stages of its growth ○ *start some plants in early spring* **14.** *vi.* FLOW VIOLENTLY OUT to flow violently or suddenly out of sth ○ *water starting from the barrel's seams* **15.** *vt.* HUNT CAUSE AN ANIMAL TO APPEAR to cause a hunted animal to appear suddenly from its hiding place or den **16.** *vti.* COME LOOSE to come loose, or cause sth to come loose, from its proper place ○ *timbers starting at the joints* ■ *n.* **1.** BEGINNING the first part of the play **2.** PLACE OR TIME OF START the place or time at which sth starts ○ *The start of the race is scheduled for noon.* **3.** QUICK SUDDEN MOVEMENT a quick sudden movement from being still to moving **4.** SUDDEN INVOLUNTARY MOVEMENT a sudden involuntary movement caused by fear, pain, surprise, or anger **5.** SPORTS INSTANCE OF PARTICIPATING the fact or an instance of participating in a race or game ○ *winning three out of five starts* **6.** POSITION AHEAD OF OTHERS a position of being ahead of other competitors ○ *get a start on the rest* **7.** POSITION AT THE BEGINNING a set of circumstances at the beginning of sth ○ *He needed a better start in life.* **8.** SIGNAL TO BEGIN the signal to begin sth such as a race **9.** STH SURPRISING sth surprising (*informal*) [12thC. Origin uncertain: probably ultimately from Old English *styrtan* 'to jump', from prehistoric Germanic. The meaning 'to begin' would have developed from 'move suddenly' via 'begin a journey'.] ◇ **for a start** used in an argument to indicate that you are making the first point of many ◇ **to start with** at the beginning

start in *vi.* US to begin to scold or criticize sb ○ *As soon as she'd finished tearing a strip off Doreen, she started in on me.* ○ *Don't start on me again.*

start off *v.* **1.** *vti.* BEGIN to begin to do sth, or cause or help sb to begin to do sth ○ *Let's start off by introducing ourselves.* **2.** *vi.* SET OFF to begin moving in a particular direction, or begin a journey ○ *She turned and started off up the hill.* **3.** *vt.* MAKE SB START TALKING OR LAUGHING to do sth that causes sb else to start doing sth such as talking, laughing, crying, or misbehaving (*informal*) ○ *Stop it, or you'll start her off again.*

start on *vt.* **1.** BEGIN TO WORK ON to begin to work on or deal with sth or sb, usually sth that will take a long time to finish ○ *As soon as I've finished cleaning the kitchen, I'm going to start on the bathroom.* **2.** BEGIN TO SCOLD SB to begin to scold, criticize, or attack sb (*informal*) ○ *Look, don't start on me. It's not my fault!*

start out *vi.* **1.** BEGIN JOURNEY to set off on a journey ○ *If we start out at about nine, we should be there in time for lunch.* **2.** BEGIN to do sth at the beginning of a process ○ *He starts out trying to prove she's guilty and ends up convincing everyone she's innocent.* **3.** INTEND to intend to do sth, or have sth as an initial intention ○ *I didn't start out to cause a lot of trouble.* **4.** BEGIN STAGE OF LIFE to make a start in sth such as adult life or a career ○ *young people who are starting out in journalism*

start up *v.* **1.** *vti.* BEGIN TO OPERATE to begin to operate, or make sth begin to operate ○ *start the engine up* **2.** *vti.* OPEN BUSINESS to begin sth such as a business venture ○ *started up her own accountancy firm* **3.** *vi.* BEGIN TO MAKE SOUND to begin to make a sound, especially a characteristic sound, or begin to speak ○ *First a solitary blackbird started up, and soon the whole wood was alive with birdsong.* **4.** *vi.* RISE SUDDENLY to rise suddenly to a standing or upright position ○ *He started up from his chair at the loud sound and rushed to the window.*

START /staart/ *abbr.* Strategic Arms Reduction Talks

starter /staártər/ *n.* **1.** AUTOMOT STARTING DEVICE FOR AN ENGINE a device for starting a machine or engine, especially an electrically operated device that causes the internal-combustion engine in a motor vehicle to fire **2.** SPORTS SB SIGNALLING START OF RACE sb who gives the signal for a race to start **3.** SPORTS COMPETITOR WHO STARTS a horse or competitor who starts in a race **4.** SPORTS PLAYER AT BEGINNING OF A GAME a player who takes the field for a team at the beginning of a game **5.** *US* BASEBALL FIRST PITCHER the pitcher who pitches first for a team, either regularly or in a particular game **6.** FOOD FIRST COURSE OF A MEAL a first course of a meal, or sth suitable to be eaten as a first course of a meal ■ *adj.* USED TO START used to start sth or as an introduction to sth for people with little experience of it ○ *a starter set of paints* ◇ **for starters** as the first thing to be done, considered, or dealt with (*informal*)

starter home *n.* a small property suitable for sb who is buying a home for the first time

star thistle *n.* a plant belonging to the daisy family and native to Europe and Asia that has purple flowers encircled by radiating spines. Genus: *Centaurea.*

starting /staárting/ *adj.* protruding or bulging, or appearing to do so ○ *ran with starting eyes from the horrific scene*

starting block *n.* either of a pair of objects used by runners to brace their feet against at the start of a sprint race. The blocks are made up of a base that can be firmly fixed to the track and angled supports against which the runner places the feet.

starting gate *n.* **1.** STARTING STALLS a line of starting stalls **2.** TAPES RAISED AT START OF HORSERACE a set of tapes spanning the width of a racetrack that are raised by the starter to begin a race **3.** BARRIER CONNECTED TO TIMER a physical barrier or electronic beam that automatically starts a timing device when a competitor passes through it, e.g. at the start of a skiing race

starting grid *n.* a pattern of lines marked on a motor racing track, with numbered starting positions. The cars that recorded the fastest times in practice occupy the front positions.

starting gun *n.* a gun fired as the signal for a race to start

starting line *n.* a line marked across a racetrack to show runners where to start

starting pistol *n.* = starting gun

starting price *n.* the odds being offered by a bookmaker on a particular horse just before the start of the race

starting stalls *npl.* a line of stalls into which racehorses are put at the start of a race that have gates

at the front that spring open simultaneously when operated by the starter

startle /staárt'l/ (**-tles, -tling, -tled**) *vt.* to disconcert or frighten a person or an animal into making an involuntary movement, or become disconcerted or frightened by a sudden shock ○ *gave a startled cry and dropped the plate on the floor* [Old English *steartlian*, from a prehistoric Germanic base that is also the ancestor of English *start*] —**startler** *n.*

startle colour *n.* a patch of bright colour or a bold design on part of an animal's body that is normally hidden and is revealed to scare away predators

startling /staártling/ *adj.* provoking surprise, fright, wonder, or alarm —**startlingly** *adv.*

startsy plural of **starets**

startup /staárt up/, **start-up** *n.* STH JUST BEGINNING sth such as a company that is just beginning operations ■ *adj.* INVOLVED IN STARTING STH UP involved in or used for the establishment of a business venture ■ *n.* COMMENCEMENT OF STH the beginning of an activity such as the construction of a building

star turn *n.* the most striking or popular item or performer in a show

starvation /staar váysh'n/ *n.* **1.** LACK OF FOOD the state of having not enough food, or of losing strength or dying through lack of food **2.** *Scotland, N England* FREEZING extreme cold

starve /staarv/ (**starves, starving, starved**) *v.* **1.** *vti.* WEAKEN OR DIE BECAUSE OF HUNGER to weaken or die through lack of food, or cause sb to do this ○ *The besieged city was starved into submission.* **2.** *vi.* BE HUNGRY to be very hungry (*informal*) ○ *I'm starving! What's for dinner?* **3.** *vt.* DEPRIVE SB to deprive sb or sth of sth vitally needed ○ *starved of affection* **4.** *vi.* NEED to feel deprived of sth, or feel a great need or desire for sth ○ *starving for a kind word* **5.** *vi. Scotland, N England, Ireland* BE VERY COLD to be feeling extremely cold [Old English *steorfan* 'to die', from a prehistoric Germanic base meaning 'to be stiff'] —**starver** *n.*

starve out *vt.* to force an enemy to surrender by making necessary food and supplies inaccessible

starveling /staárvling/ *n.* a very thin and hungry-looking person or animal (*archaic*)

starving *adj.* extremely cold (*regional*)

────── WORD KEY: REGIONAL NOTE ──────

The use of **starving** to mean 'extremely cold' survives in the north of England, Scotland, Ireland, and the Isle of Man. In these areas *starved* is used in the same way.

starwort (*plural* **-worts** *or* **-wort**) *n.* = water starwort

stash /stash/ *n.* **1.** HIDDEN STORE a secret or hidden store of sth such as money or valuables (*informal*) **2.** HIDING PLACE a secret hiding place (*informal*) **3.** DRUGS SECRET STORE OF DRUGS a store of illegal drugs kept for personal consumption (*slang*) ■ *vt.* (**stashes, stashing, stashed**) **1.** HIDE STH to put sth into a secret hidden storage place (*informal*) **2.** *US* PUT STH AWAY to put sth somewhere, e.g. in a convenient place or where it belongs ○ *We'll eat after we've stashed our gear.* [Late 18thC. Origin unknown.]

stasis /stáyssiss/ *n.* **1.** MOTIONLESS STATE a state in which there is neither motion nor development, often resulting from opposing forces balancing each other **2.** MED STOPPAGE OF FLOW OF BODY FLUIDS a condition in which body fluids, such as blood or the contents of the bowel, are prevented from flowing normally through their channels **3.** BIOL STATE OF NO CHANGE a state in which there is little or no apparent change in a species of organism over a long period of time. It is most evident in so-called living fossils, such as the coelacanth, which have remained unchanged for many millions of years. [Mid-18thC. Via modern Latin from Greek, 'standing, stoppage'. Ultimately from an Indo-European word that is also the ancestor of English *stand.*]

stat[1] /stat/ *n.* a statistic (*informal*) [Mid-20thC. Shortening.]

stat[2] /stat/, **stat.** *adv.* MED IMMEDIATELY used in prescriptions to indicate that a drug is to be given immediately ■ *adj.* MED URGENT urgent ○ *The doctor received a stat page while on call.* [Late 19thC. Shortening of Latin *statim* 'immediately'.]

stat. *abbr.* **1.** statue **2.** statute **3.** stationary

-stat *suffix.* **1.** device for stabilizing or regulating ○ *humidistat* ○ *rheostat* **2.** a device for focusing sth in a single direction ○ *siderostat* **3.** a substance or device that inhibits the growth or flow of sth ○ *fungistat* ○ *haemostat* [Via modern Latin *-stata* from Greek *statos* 'standing' and *statēs* 'one that causes to stand']

state /stayt/ *n.* **1.** CONDITION the condition that sth or sb is in at a particular time ○ *What sort of state was he in after hearing the news?* **2.** PHYS FORM OR ENERGY LEVEL any of the various forms such as solid or liquid or quantifiable conditions such as energy levels that a physical substance can be in depending on its temperature and other circumstances **3.** PHYSICAL STAGE a growth or developmental stage of an animal or plant **4.** POL COUNTRY a country or nation with its own sovereign independent government **5.** POL MOSTLY AUTONOMOUS REGION OF FEDERAL COUNTRY an area forming part of a federal country such as the United States or Australia with its own government and legislature and control over most of its own internal affairs **6.** POL GOVERNMENT a country's government and those government-controlled institutions that are responsible for its internal administration and its relationships with other countries ○ *a corporation owned and run by the state* **7.** CEREMONIOUS STYLE a very formal, dignified or grand way of doing sth in which all the appropriate ceremonies are observed **8.** NERVOUS, UPSET, OR EXCITED CONDITION a very nervous, upset, or excited frame of mind or manner of behaving (*informal*) ○ *Don't get into a state worrying about money.* **9.** BAD PHYSICAL CONDITION a very untidy or disreputable condition (*informal*) ○ *The house is in such a state that we'll never get it tidy.* ■ *adj.* **1.** POL RELATING TO GOVERNMENT involving or relating to a state or to its government **2.** POL HELD OR RUN BY A STATE owned, operated, or financed by a state **3.** DONE WITH FULL CEREMONY involving many grand rituals and ceremonies, especially those appropriate to a head of state ■ *vt.* (**states, stating, stated**) **1.** EXPRESS IN WORDS to express sth in spoken or written words, especially to announce sth publicly in a deliberate formal way ○ *We have already stated our position on this issue.* **2.** LAW DECLARE WITH FORCE OF LAW to declare sth officially so that it has the force of a law or regulation ○ *It is expressly stated in your contract that you must not undertake work for another employer.* **3.** MUSIC PLAY MUSICAL THEME FOR FIRST TIME to play a particular musical theme or motif for the first time before it is repeated and developed within a piece of music [12thC. Directly or via Old French *estat* from Latin *status* 'way of standing, condition' (as in *status rei publicae* 'condition of the republic').] ◇ **the state of play** stage reached in a situation or activity

state benefit *n.* money given by the government to people who do not have enough money to live on

state capitalism *n.* an economic system in which the state controls the use of capital and the means of production

statecraft /stáyt kraaft/ *n.* the art of governing or managing the affairs of a country well

stated /stáytid/ *adj.* **1.** OFFICIALLY LAID DOWN laid down by an official agreement or in a legal document **2.** PREVIOUSLY ANNOUNCED announced previously, especially in a public medium

stated case *n.* = case stated

State Department *n.* the department of the United States government that deals with foreign affairs and is headed by a Cabinet secretary and staffed by career foreign service officers

State Enrolled Nurse *n.* a nurse certified as competent to carry out many of the functions of a nurse, but who is less qualified than and junior to a State Registered Nurse

statehood /stáyt hŏŏd/ *n.* the status of a state in a federal union, especially in the United States, as opposed to that of a territory or dependency

statehouse /stáyt howss/ (*plural* **-houses** /-howziz/), **state house, Statehouse** (*plural* **-houses**) *n.* a building in which a state legislature convenes in any of the US state capitals

stateless /stáytləss/ *adj.* not being a citizen of any country and having no nationality

stateless society *n.* a society, e.g. one in Africa, organized around kinship or other forms of obligation and lacking the concentration of political power and authority associated with states

stately /stáytli/ (-lier, -liest) *adj.* **1.** IMPRESSIVELY WEIGHTY AND DIGNIFIED characterized by an impressively weighty and dignified but graceful manner **2.** GRAND AND IMPOSING grand and imposing in appearance

stately home *n.* a large and impressive country house, especially one that is owned by a famous or aristocratic family and is open to the public

statement /stáytmənt/ *n.* **1.** EXPRESSION IN WORDS the expression in spoken or written words of sth such as a fact, intention, or policy, or an instance of this **2.** STH SAID sth that sb says that is not a question or an exclamation and that expresses an idea or facts in definite terms ○ *We were unable to verify the truth of that statement.* **3.** SPECIALLY PREPARED PUBLIC ANNOUNCEMENT a specially prepared announcement or reply that is made public ○ *Has she made a statement to the press?* **4.** CRIMINOL ACCOUNT OF FACTS an account of the facts relating to a crime or case given to the police or in a court of law usually for use as evidence **5.** ARTS WORDLESS EXPRESSION OF IDEA a bold or conspicuous expression of an idea, opinion, or concept made in a nonverbal way ○ *Her art is a powerful statement of her political beliefs.* **6.** FIN PRINTED RECORD OF BANK ACCOUNT a printed record of all transactions that have taken place over a period of time in a bank account and of the amount of the holder's current credit or debt **7.** FIN CUSTOMER'S ACCOUNT an account issued to a customer showing charges made, payments received, and any balance owing **8.** EDUC ASSESSMENT OF CHILD'S SPECIAL EDUCATIONAL NEEDS an official and legally binding assessment made by a local authority of the help required by a child with special educational needs **9.** MUSIC FIRST PRESENTATION OF MUSICAL THEME the first presentation of a theme or idea that is to be developed later in a piece of music **10.** COMPUT COMPUTER INSTRUCTION a computer instruction written in a source language ■ *vt.* (-ments, -menting, -mented) EDUC DRAW UP STATEMENT FOR CHILD to draw up an official statement of a child's special educational needs, thus ensuring that the local education authority will have to make provision for those needs

statement of attainment *n.* a programme of the objectives that school students should be able to attain within their own ability range in a particular subject

statement of case *n.* a formal statement of the facts relating to either of the parties involved in a legal case

statement of claim *n.* = **declaration** *n.* 5

Staten Island /státt'n-/ one of the five boroughs of New York City. It has a regular ferry service to Manhattan and is mainly residential. Population: 378,977 (1990).

State of Origin *n.* in Australia, a policy stating that players must have been born in the state they represent in annual interstate rugby league matches

state of the art *n.* MOST ADVANCED LEVEL OF TECHNOLOGY the most advanced level of knowledge and technology currently achieved in any field at any given time ■ *adj.* **state-of-the-art** MOST ADVANCED representing the most advanced level of knowledge or technology currently achieved in any field at any given time

state of war *n.* **1.** ACTUAL HOSTILITIES armed conflict between states or other groups, with or without a formal declaration of war **2.** LEGAL SITUATION OF DECLARATION OF WAR the situation brought about by a declaration of war, with or without the commencement of actual armed conflict, in which special internationally agreed-on laws apply

state prayers *npl.* the prayers for the Sovereign, the royal family, the clergy, and Parliament, said at services in the Anglican Church

stater[1] /stáytər/ *n.* any of various ancient Greek coins in gold or silver [14thC. Via late Latin from Greek *statēr*, from the base of *histanai* 'to weigh'.]

stater[2] /stáytər/, **Stater** *n.* sb who comes from a particular state, especially of the United States, or from a particular type of state (*usually used in combination*) ○ *Bay Staters are from Massachusetts.*

State Registered Nurse *n.* a nurse who has obtained a higher qualification in nursing than a State Enrolled Nurse and is certified as competent to carry out all the functions of a nurse

stateroom /stáyt room, stáyt ro͝om/ *n.* **1.** TRANSP PRIVATE CABIN OR COMPARTMENT a large and luxuriously furnished private cabin on a ship or a private sleeping compartment on a train **2.** LARGE ROOM USED ON STATE OCCASIONS a large imposing room in a palace or government building, used for large-scale functions and entertaining important guests

States /stayts/ *npl.* **1.** UNITED STATES the United States of America (*informal*) **2.** PARLIAMENT OF CHANNEL ISLANDS the name of the legislative bodies in Jersey, Guernsey, and Alderney in the Channel Islands

state school *n.* a school controlled and financed by a public authority in which education is free

state secret *n.* a piece of information, usually considered important to national security, that is supposed to be known only to certain people authorized by the state

state services *npl.* special forms of service for use in Anglican churches on days of national celebration

state's evidence *n.* evidence given for the prosecution in a criminal trial in the United States and certain other nations, sometimes by one of the accused or by an accomplice to the crime

States General *npl.* **1.** LEGISLATIVE ASSEMBLY OF NETHERLANDS the legislative assembly of the Netherlands **2.** LEGISLATIVE BODY IN FRANCE BEFORE 1789 the legislative body in France before 1789, consisting of representatives of the three estates of the realm

stateside /stáyt sīd/ *adv.* US IN OR TOWARDS UNITED STATES in or towards the continental United States ■ *adj.* US RELATING TO UNITED STATES relating to, in, or towards the continental United States

statesman /stáytsmən/ (*plural* **-men** /-mən/) *n.* **1.** LEADING POLITICIAN a senior male politician who plays an important role in his country's government or in international affairs **2.** RESPECTED IMPARTIAL SENIOR MALE POLITICIAN a senior male politician who is widely respected for his integrity and impartial concern for the public good —**statesmanlike** *adj.* —**statesmanship** *n.*

state socialism *n.* a political and economic system in which the state controls major industries and banks and plans its economic and social welfare programmes in order to bring about an egalitarian society —**state socialist** *n.*

stateswoman /stáyts wo͝ommən/ (*plural* **-men** /-wimmin/) *n.* **1.** LEADING WOMAN POLITICIAN a senior politician who plays an important role in her country's government or in international affairs **2.** RESPECTED IMPARTIAL SENIOR WOMAN POLITICIAN a senior woman politician who is widely respected for her integrity and impartial concern for the public good

state trooper *n.* a member of the highway patrol police of a US state

statewide /stáyt wīd/ *adj.* US AFFECTING ENTIRE STATE affecting or happening throughout an entire state ○ *a statewide search for the escaped prisoner* ■ *adv.* US THROUGHOUT STATE throughout an entire state

static /státtik/ *adj.* **1.** MOTIONLESS not moving or changing, or fixed in position **2.** PHYS OF FORCES NOT CAUSING MOVEMENT relating to forces, weight, or pressure that act without causing movement **3.** PHYS INVOLVING STATICS relating to, involving, or characteristic of statics **4.** ELEC INVOLVING STATIONARY ELECTRIC CHARGES relating to, involving, or characteristic of stationary electric charges **5.** BROADCAST CAUSED BY ELECTRICAL INTERFERENCE relating to or caused by electrical interference in a radio or television broadcast **6.** COMPUT NOT NEEDING TO BE REFRESHED retaining its contents without having to be refreshed by the central processor (*refers to a random-access-memory computer chip*) ■ *n.* **1.** BROADCAST ELECTRICAL INTERFERENCE electrical interference in a radio or television broadcast, causing a random crackling noise or disruption of a picture **2.** ELEC = **static electricity 3.** US OPPOSITION OR INTERFERENCE criticism, opposition, or unwanted interference by sb else (*informal*) ○ *getting a lot of static from the boss* [Mid-19thC. Via modern Latin from Greek *statikos* 'causing to stand', from *statos* 'standing' (see STATO-).] —**statically** *adv.*

statice /státtissi/ *n.* = **sea lavender** [Mid-18thC. Via modern Latin, former genus name, from, ultimately, Greek *statikos* 'causing to stand or stop' (see STATIC), because it stops the flow of blood.]

static electricity *n.* a stationary electric charge that builds up on an insulated object, e.g. on a capacitor or a thundercloud

static line *n.* a rope attached to an aircraft and a parachutist's parachute. When the parachutist jumps from the aircraft the line opens the parachute automatically.

static pressure *n.* pressure not caused by motion at a point on the surface of an object moving freely in a flowing fluid

statics /státtiks/ *n.* a branch of mechanics that deals with forces and systems in equilibrium (*takes a singular verb*)

static tube *n.* a tube used to measure the static pressure present in a moving fluid

station /stáysh'n/ *n.* **1.** STOP ON RAILWAY ROUTE a place along a train or bus route where passengers are picked up or set down, often with amenities such as ticket offices, waiting rooms, refreshments, toilets, and facilities for goods and parcels **2.** LOCAL BRANCH OF AN ORGANIZATION a local branch or headquarters of an official organization such as the police force, fire brigade, or ambulance service **3.** SPECIALLY EQUIPPED BUILDING a building or group of buildings that provides a particular function or service ○ *a pumping station* **4.** BROADCAST BROADCASTING BUILDING a place equipped to make and broadcast radio or television programmes **5.** BROADCAST BROADCASTING CHANNEL a television or radio channel **6.** USUAL PLACE the place or position where sb or sth is usually to be found or is supposed to be found **7.** POSITION FOR PERFORMING TASK a position where sb performs a task, e.g. in a factory, or the equipment used in performing a task **8.** RANK the position sb holds in society or in an organization in terms of rank **9.** MIL MILITARY POSTING a place where military personnel are sent to carry out duties **10.** SHIPPING PLACE ON SHIP FOR CREW MEMBER a place on board a ship where a crew member carries out duties **11.** NAVY PLACE WHERE SHIP IS SENT a place where a naval ship or fleet is sent for a period of duty **12.** *ANZ* SHEEP OR CATTLE FARM a large farm in Australia or New Zealand where sheep or cattle are raised **13.** CIV ENG SURVEYOR'S REFERENCE POINT a fixed point used by surveyors as a reference **14.** CHR STATION OF THE CROSS one of the Stations of the Cross **15.** MILITARY OR GOVERNMENT SETTLEMENT IN INDIA a place where military officers or government officials lived in India while it was under British rule ■ *vt.* (-tions, -tioning, -tioned) PUT IN OR SEND TO A PLACE to assign sb to a particular place, or put sth in a particular place (*often passive*) [Mid-16thC. Via Old French from the Latin stem *station-* 'standing still', from *stare* 'to stand' (source of English *stage* and *obstacle*).]

stationary /stáysh'nəri/ *adj.* **1.** NOT MOVING not moving, especially at a standstill after being in motion **2.** IMMOBILE fixed in position and not able to be moved **3.** UNCHANGING not changing **4.** STAYING IN ONE PLACE showing a tendency to remain in the same place [15thC. Directly or via French *stationnaire* 'motionless' from medieval Latin *stationarius*, from Latin, 'of a military station', from the stem *station-* (see STATION).]

WORD KEY: USAGE

stationary or **stationery**? The two words are distantly related but have quite different meanings. ***Stationary*** is an adjective meaning 'not moving' (normally used of vehicles), whereas ***stationery*** is a noun meaning 'writing materials'. Confusion can be avoided by remembering the connection between ***stationery*** and *stationer*, a trader of ***stationery***.

stationary bicycle *n.* = **exercise bike**

stationary front *n.* a weather condition in which the boundary between a cold air mass and a warm air mass is stationary

stationary orbit *n.* an orbit around a celestial body that has the same period as one revolution of the celestial body. An object in such an orbit appears stationary above the surface.

stationary wave *n.* = standing wave

stationer /stáysh'nər/ *n.* **1.** SELLER OF STATIONERY a person or shop that sells stationery **2.** PUBL BOOK PUBLISHER a person or company that publishes or sells books (*archaic*)

────── **WORD KEY: ORIGIN** ──────

In medieval Latin a *stationarius* was originally a 'trader who kept a permanent stall' (as opposed to an itinerant seller) — the word's source, the Latin stem *station-* (see STATION), meant literally 'standing, keeping still'. Such permanent shops were comparatively rare in the Middle Ages. Of those that did exist, the commonest were bookshops, licensed by the universities, and so English adopted the Latin term. It has since come down in the world somewhat to 'seller of paper, pens, etc'. (a sense first recorded in the mid 17th century), but the earlier application is preserved in the name of the 'Stationers' Company', a London livery company to which booksellers and publishers belong.

stationery /stáysh'nəri/ *n.* paper, envelopes, pens, pencils, and other things used in writing

────── **WORD KEY: USAGE** ──────

See Usage note at *stationary*.

station hand *n.* a worker on a large sheep or cattle farm in Australia

station house *n.* US a building housing a police department or precinct office, or a fire department

stationmaster /stáysh'n maastər/, **station manager** *n.* sb whose job is to oversee the running of a railway station

Stations of the Cross *npl.* **1.** SERIES OF 14 IMAGES a series of 14 images around the inside of a Roman Catholic church, each representing a stage in Jesus Christ's road to Calvary **2.** SERIES OF 14 PRAYERS a Roman Catholic devotion in which a prayer is said before each of the Stations of the Cross

station-to-station *adj.* US CHARGED FROM TIME OF ANSWER charged from the time sb answers the telephone (*dated*) ■ *adv.* US BY STATION-TO-STATION CALL by a station-to-station call

station wagon *n.* US, Can, ANZ an automobile with an extended area behind the rear seats that provides extra seating or carrying capacity, usually with a tailgate [Originally a covered carriage for transporting passengers to and from train stations]

statism /stáytizəm/ *n.* the theory, or its practice, that economic and political power should be controlled by a central government leaving regional government and the individual with relatively little say in political matters [Early 17thC. Formed from STATE.] —**statist** *n.*

statistic /stə tístik/ *n.* **1.** ELEMENT OF DATA a single element of data from a collection **2.** NUMERICAL VALUE OR FUNCTION a numerical value or function, such as a mean or standard deviation, used to describe a sample or population **3.** PIECE OF INFORMATION sb or sth treated as a piece of data or information [Late 18thC. Back-formation from STATISTICS.] —**statistical** *adj.* —**statistically** *adv.*

statistical mechanics *n.* the branch of physics that analyzes macroscopic systems by applying statistical principles to their microscopic constituents (*takes a singular verb*)

statistician /státti stísh'n/ *n.* sb who is skilled in statistics, or who compiles and works with statistics

statistics /stə tístiks/ *n.* BRANCH OF MATHEMATICS a branch of mathematics that deals with the analysis and interpretation of numerical data in terms of samples and populations (*takes a singular verb*) ■ *npl.* COLLECTION OF NUMERICAL DATA a collection of numerical data ○ *this month's sales statistics* [Late 18thC. Via German *Statistik* from, ultimately, Latin *status* (see STATE). The underlying meaning is 'the study of data relating to the state'.]

stative /stáytiv/ *adj.* DEALING WITH STATES, NOT ACTIONS used to describe a verb, e.g. 'know' or 'own', that deals with states, as opposed to one, e.g. 'listen', 'talk' or 'go', that deals with actions ■ *n.* STATIVE VERB a verb dealing with states not actions [Mid-17thC. From Latin

stativus, from *stat-*, past participle stem of *stare* (see STATION).]

stato- *prefix.* **1.** balance, equilibrium ○ *statoscope* **2.** resting ○ *statoblast* [From Greek *statos* 'standing'. Ultimately from an Indo-European base meaning 'to stand', which is also the ancestor of English *stand*, *station*, and *status*.]

statoblast /státtō blast/ *n.* a chitin-encased body that serves as a means of asexual reproduction for freshwater bryozoans. It can withstand climatic extremes and prolonged dormancy.

statocyst /státtō sist/ *n.* a fluid-filled organ of balance in some invertebrates such as the lobster containing suspended bony granules that, along with sensory cells, help it to determine its position

statolith /státtō lith/ *n.* **1.** ZOOL GRANULES WITHIN A STATOCYST any of the tiny bony granules that are suspended in fluid within a statocyst and whose movement is detected by sensory hairs that determine an invertebrate's position **2.** BOT STARCH GRAIN a starch grain or other particle inside plant cells that moves in response to gravity, and is thought to influence the way shoots or other organs grow —**statolithic** /stá ttō líthik/ *adj.*

stator /stáytər/ *n.* a stationary part in a machine, such as a motor or generator, about which or in which a rotor rotates [Late 19thC. From modern Latin, literally 'one that stands', from Latin *stat-*, the past participle stem of *stare* (see STATION).]

statoscope /státtō skōp/ *n.* a sensitive aneroid barometer used to detect small changes in atmospheric pressure, often used in aircraft to determine changes in altitude

statuary /státtyoo əri/ *n.* **1.** STATUES CONSIDERED TOGETHER statues considered collectively **2.** ART OF MAKING STATUES the art and techniques of making statues [Mid-16thC. From Latin *statuarius* 'of a statue', from *statua* (see STATUE).]

statue /státtyoo/ *n.* a three-dimensional image of a human being or animal that is sculpted, modelled, cast, or carved [14thC. Via Old French from Latin *statua*, from *statuere* 'to set up' (see STATUTE).]

Barnaby's

Statue of Liberty

Statue of Liberty *n.* a huge statue of a woman holding a torch and a book inscribed 'July 4, 1776'. It stands in New York Harbour. At 46 m/152 ft high, it is one of the tallest statues in the world. A gift from France to the United States, it was unveiled in 1886.

statuesque /státtyoo ésk/ *adj.* like a statue, especially in having classical beauty, elegance, or proportions —**statuesquely** *adv.*

statuette /státtyoo ét/ *n.* a small usually portable statue

stature /stáchər/ *n.* **1.** HEIGHT the standing height of sb or sth **2.** INDIVIDUAL'S STANDING sb's standing or level of achievement [13thC. Via Old French from *statura*, from *stat-*, the past participle stem of *stare* (see STATION).]

status /stáytəss/ *n.* **1.** RANK the relative position or standing of sb or sth in a society or other group **2.** PRESTIGE high rank or standing, especially in a community, workforce, or organization **3.** CONDITION a condition that is subject to change ○ *What's the current status of the investigation?* **4.** LAW LEGAL STANDING sb's standing in terms of the law [Late 18thC. From Latin (see STATE).]

Status Indian, **status Indian** *n.* Can a member of an indigenous people whom the federal government

recognizes as having special rights and privileges, especially residence on a reserve

status quo /-kwṓ/ *n.* the condition or state of affairs that currently exists [From Latin, literally 'the state in which']

status symbol *n.* a possession that is a sign of wealth or prestige

statutable /státtyootəb'l/ *adj.* **1.** STATUTORY regulated or imposed by statute **2.** COVERED BY STATUTE covered by a statute, and subject to the penalty laid down by that statute —**statutably** *adv.*

statute /státtyoot/ *n.* **1.** LAW LAW ENACTED BY LEGISLATURE a law established by a legislative body, e.g. an Act of Parliament **2.** BUSINESS ESTABLISHED RULE a permanent established rule or law, especially one involved in the running of a company or other organization [13thC. Via Old French from late Latin *statutum*, literally 'sth set up', from Latin *statuere* 'to set up', from *status* 'position' (see STATE).]

statute book *n.* a record of the acts that have been passed by a legislature and remain in force

statute law *n.* the body of law that has been enacted by a legislature, or a specific law so enacted

statute mile *n.* = mile 1 [From the fact that it is fixed by law]

statute of limitations *n.* a statute that lays down the time within which legal proceedings must be started

statutory /státtyootəri/ *adj.* **1.** OF A STATUTE relating to a statute **2.** CONTROLLED BY STATUTE regulated or imposed by statute **3.** SUBJECT TO PENALTY covered by a statute, and subject to the penalty laid down by that statute —**statutorily** *adv.*

statutory declaration *n.* a declaration that sb makes on oath according to statute

statutory order *n.* a statute that augments an existing statute

statutory rape *n.* US the offence under US law of having sexual relations with sb who has not reached the legal age of consent

Stauffenberg /stówfən burg, shtówfən bòórk/, **Claus Schenk**, **Count** (1907–44) German army officer. He was the leader of the unsuccessful July Plot (1944) to assassinate Adolf Hitler.

staunch /stawnch/, **stanch** *adj.* **1.** LOYAL showing loyalty, dependability, and enthusiasm **2.** STURDY solidly built or substantial [15thC. Via Anglo-Norman *estaunche* from, ultimately, Old French *estanchier* 'to stop'.] —**staunchly** *adv.* —**staunchness** *n.*

────── **WORD KEY: USAGE** ──────

stanch or **staunch**? There are two words spelled **staunch** and two others spelled **stanch**. The adjective **staunch** is the most commonly used form in the meaning 'loyal, trustworthy', although **stanch** is also used to mean the same thing. Conversely, **stanch** is more common as a verb meaning 'to stop the flow of', though **staunch** can also occur in this meaning: *The government is trying to staunch the outflow of money*. Note that both **staunch** and **stanch** are pronounced to rhyme with *launch*.

staurolite /stáwrə līt/ *n.* a reddish-brown or black mineral of iron and magnesium that occurs as prismatic crystals in metamorphic rocks, often in a cross shape. It is used as a gemstone. [Late 18thC. Coined from Greek *stauros* 'cross' (because it often forms twin crystals in the shape of a cross) + -LITE.] —**staurolitic** /stáwrə líttik/ *adj.*

Stavanger /stə vángər/ *city and port in southwestern Norway. Population: 103,590 (1995).*

stave /stayv/ *n.* **1.** BAND OF WOOD a long thin piece of wood, one of several fixed together to make the hull of a boat, or the body of a container such as a barrel **2.** RUNG OR BAR OF WOOD a bar or strip of wood or other material, especially one that forms a rung in a ladder or a crosspiece between the legs of a chair **3.** = staff[1] *n.* 7 **4.** MUSIC = staff[1] *n.* 6 **5.** LITERAT POETRY STANZA a stanza of poetry **6.** *Scotland* an injury to a part of the body, e.g. a toe, finger, or elbow, caused by spraining or twisting ■ *v.* (**staves**, **staving**, **stove**) **1.** *vti.* BREAK STAVES to break a barrel, a tub, or a boat's hull by smashing its staves in, or to break by having the staves smashed in **2.** *vti.* BREAK A HOLE

IN AN OBJECT to smash a hole in the side of a boat or a barrel **3.** *vt.* **BREAK INWARDS** to strike sth such as a door or a rib making it break inwards **4.** *vt.* **FIT A STAVE TO** to fit a stave to sth such as a chair or a ladder **5.** *vt. Scotland* **SPRAIN PART OF BODY** to injure a part of the body, e.g. a toe, finger, or elbow, by spraining it or twisting it [14thC. Back-formation from *staves*, the plural of STAFF.]

staves plural of **staff, stave**

stavesacre /stáyvz aykər/ *n.* a delphinium with purple flowers that grows in Europe and Asia. Its poisonous seeds were once used as a cathartic and an emetic. Latin name: *Delphinium staphisagria.* [14thC. Alteration of earlier *staphisagre*, which came via Latin from Greek *staphis agria*, literally 'wild raisin'.]

stay[1] /stay/ *v.* (**stays, staying, stayed**) **1.** *vi.* **REMAIN** to continue to be in the same place, condition, or state **2.** *vi.* **RESIDE FOR A SHORT TIME** to spend some time or live temporarily in a specified place **3.** *vi. Scotland* **RESIDE** to live permanently in a place **4.** *vti.* **PASS SOME TIME** to spend a specified length of time at a place or in doing sth **5.** *vi.* **REMAIN IN CONTENTION** to keep up with sb or sth, especially by going along with the leader or leaders of a race **6.** *vi.* **PERSEVERE** to continue to do sth, especially to support sth, e.g. an idea, plan, or project ○ *stay the course until the task is completed* **7.** *vt.* **UNDERGO** to endure, put up with, or survive sth, especially sth trying, difficult, or unpleasant ○ *The runner had trouble staying the final mile.* **8.** *vi.* **BE AROUND FOR STH** to be present long enough to take part in sth, especially a meal **9.** *vi.* **LINGER** to linger or wait somewhere ○ *Stay a moment.* **10.** *vt.* **STOP** to put a stop to sth **11.** *vt.* **POSTPONE OR HINDER** to postpone, hinder, or delay sth ○ *stay a trip until the weather improves* **12.** *vt.* **ALLEVIATE IN THE SHORT TERM** to relieve or ease sth temporarily, e.g. hunger, thirst, or other physical need **13.** *vt.* **RESTRAIN** to hold sth back or in check **14.** *vt.* LAW **SUSPEND LEGAL PROCESS TEMPORARILY** to suspend a judgment or proceedings temporarily **15.** *vt.* **CRUSH OR STIFLE** to suppress sth unwelcome, such as an uprising or criticism (*archaic*) **16.** *vi.* GAMBLING **STAKE SAME AMOUNT** to stake the same amount of money on a poker hand as the person who last raised the stake ■ *n.* **1. A VISIT** a short spell of being away from home ○ *a weekend stay in the country* **2. CURB OR CHECK** sth that acts to stop or delay sth negative happening **3.** LAW **TEMPORARY HALT** a temporary halt in legal proceedings, or a period during which a judgment may not be carried out [15thC. Via Old French *ester* from Latin *stare* 'to stand' (source of English *stance, stage, distant*, and *constant*).] ◇ **stay put** to remain in a place or position

stay on *vi.* to remain somewhere after others have left or after the expected time of leaving

stay out *vi.* to be away from home, usually for or until a specified time

stay up *vi.* to remain awake and not go to bed at the normal time

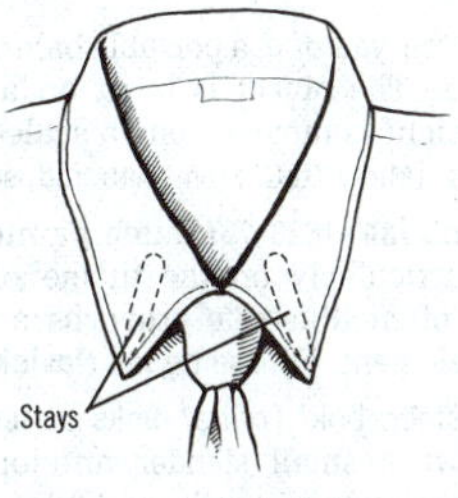

Stay

stay[2] /stay/ *n.* CLOTHES **1. A SUPPORT** sth that gives extra support to sth else, e.g. a brace, prop, or buttress **2. CORSET BONE** a small bone or piece of metal or plastic used as a stiffener in corsets and girdles ■ **stays** *npl.* CLOTHES **STIFFENED CORSET** a corset that is stiffened with strips of whalebone, metal, or other material ■ *vt.* (**stays, staying, stayed**) **1. SUPPORT** to support sth (*archaic*) **2. COMFORT** to give sb comfort or strength (*formal*) [Early 16thC. From Old French *estaye*, of prehistoric Germanic origin.]

stay[3] /stay/ *n.* **1.** SAILING **ROPE SUPPORTING MAST** a rope or cable used to support a mast **2.** BUILDING **STEADYING ROPE** a rope used for steadying or guiding sth, especially on a chimney or flagpole ■ *vti.* (**stays, staying, stayed**) SAILING **TURN ONTO OTHER TACK** to turn onto the other tack, or make a vessel turn [Old English *stæg.* Ultimately from an Indo-European base meaning 'to make stand', which is also the ancestor of English *stay*[2] and *steel*.]

stayer /stáy ər/ *n.* **1. SB WHO STAYS** sb or sth that stays **2. SB PERSISTENT** sb who has plenty of stamina and shows persistence **3. HORSE OR DOG THAT RACES PERSISTENTLY** a racehorse or greyhound that has stamina and competes to the end of a race, even under difficult conditions

staying power *n.* the ability to keep doing sth or keep trying, especially over long periods of time

staysail /stáy sayl/; *nautical* /stáyss'l/ *n.* an extra sail hoisted on one of the stays of a sailing vessel

stay stitching *n.* an extra line of stitches reinforcing a seam, used to prevent stretching and fraying

stay well *interj. S Africa* used when parting company with sb, especially in response when sb has said 'go well' [Translation from Zulu, Xhosa, and Sotho]

stbd *abbr.* starboard

std *abbr.* standard

STD *abbr.* **1.** MED sexually transmitted disease **2.** UTIL subscriber trunk dialling

Ste *abbr.* Sainte [French, '(female) Saint']

stead /sted/ *n.* the position or role of sb or sth else [Old English *stede* 'place'. Ultimately from an Indo-European base meaning 'to stand', which is also the ancestor of English *stand, stud*, and *station*.] ◇ **stand sb in good stead** to be useful to sb, especially at a later time

Stead /sted/, **Christina Ellen** (1902–83) Australian writer. Her short stories and novels include *The Man Who Loved Children* (1941).

Stead, C. K. (*b.* 1932) New Zealand writer. He was the author of the novel *Smith's Dream* (1971) and the verse collection *Poems of a Decade* (1983). Full name **Christian Karlson Stead**

steadfast /stéd faast/, **stedfast** *adj.* **1. FIRM** firm and unwavering in purpose, loyalty, or resolve **2. FIXED** firmly fixed or constant [Old English *stedefæst*, literally 'fixed in place'] —**steadfastly** *adv.* —**steadfastness** *n.*

steading /stédding/ *n.* **1. FARM** a farm, especially a small one **2. FARM OUTBUILDING** a farm outbuilding or all of the outbuildings of a farm [15thC. Formed from STEAD.]

steady /stéddi/ *adj.* (**-ier, -iest**) **1. STABLE** fixed, stable, or not easily moved **2. STAYING THE SAME** showing no tendency to change or fluctuate **3. CONSTANT OR CONTINUOUS** coming in a regular nonstop flow **4. REGULAR OR ORDINARY** reliable, but often rather dull or routine **5. UNRUFFLED** not easily upset or excited **6. STAID OR SERIOUS** having a serious and calm attitude or character **7. REGULAR OR INDUSTRIOUS** regular, habitual, or industrious ■ *adv.* (**-ier, -iest**) **CONTINUOUSLY** in a constant or continuous way (*informal*) ■ *vti.* (**-ies, -ying, -ied**) **MAKE OR BECOME STEADY** to become steady or make sth steady ■ *n.* (*plural* **-ies**) **SB DATED REGULARLY** the person with whom sb regularly goes on dates (*informal*) ■ *interj.* **1. BE CAREFUL** used to tell sb to be careful or be calm **2.** SAILING **KEEP TO PRESENT COURSE** used to tell sb steering a ship or boat to keep to the present course [Mid-13thC. Formed from STEAD. The underlying idea is of being fixed in place.] —**steadier** *n.* —**steadily** *adv.* —**steadiness** *n.* ◇ **go steady** to go out together regularly as a couple (*informal*)

steady state *n.* a condition of stability or equilibrium in a system, e.g. in the energy levels of an atom, in which there is little or no change over time

steady-state theory *n.* a theory in astronomy that the universe has always existed at a uniform density that is maintained because new matter is created continuously as the universe expands

steak /stayk/ *n.* **1. CUT OF BEEF** a thick slice of beef from a lean part of a cow **2. PIECE OF MEAT OR FISH** a piece of meat other than beef, e.g. pork, gammon, venison, or veal, or of a large fish, e.g. cod, salmon, or tuna **3. SERVING OF MINCED MEAT** minced meat formed into a solid shape, usually a flat roundish shape, and served grilled, fried, or barbecued [15thC. From Old Norse *steik* 'meat roasted on a spit'. Ultimately from an Indo-European word meaning 'pointed', which is also the ancestor of English *stick, instigate*, and *instinct*.]

steakhouse /stáyk howss/ (*plural* **-houses** /-howsiz/) *n.* a restaurant that specializes in serving beef steaks

steak knife *n.* a table knife with a sharp usually serrated blade, suitable for cutting steak

steak tartare *n.* freshly minced beef that is served uncooked with raw egg, chopped onions, and seasonings [*Tartare* from French, 'Tartar']

steal /steel/ *v.* (**steals, stealing, stole** /stōl/, **stolen** /stṓlən/) **1.** *vti.* **TAKE UNLAWFULLY** to take sth that belongs to sb else, illegally or without the owner's permission **2.** *vt.* **TAKE FURTIVELY** to take or get sth secretly, surreptitiously, or through trickery ○ *steal a glance* **3.** *vi.* **SNEAK** to move quietly, especially in the hope of not been seen or caught **4.** *vt.* **TAKE AND USE ANOTHER'S IDEAS** to take sth that another person has created, especially ideas, theories, or a piece of writing, and present it as one's own **5.** *vi.* **PASS UNNOTICED** to pass or move without being noticed (*literary*) ○ *Dawn was stealing over the mountaintops.* **6.** *vti.* BASEBALL **GAIN A BASE WITHOUT HIT** to gain a base by running without the ball being hit by the batter and in the absence of an error by the fielding team **7.** *vt.* **SUCCEED AT UNEXPECTEDLY** to win or succeed at sth unexpectedly, luckily, or dishonestly at the expense of another or others (*informal*) ■ *n.* **1. ACT OF STEALING** an act of stealing **2. BARGAIN** sth that does not cost very much or that costs a lot less than would be expected (*informal*) [Old English *stelan*, from a prehistoric Germanic base that is also the ancestor of English *stalk*] —**stealer** *n.*

WORD KEY: SYNONYMS

steal, pinch, nick, filch, purloin, pilfer, embezzle, misappropriate

CORE MEANING: the taking of property unlawfully

steal a general word meaning to take unlawfully another person's property or money; **pinch** an informal word meaning the same as 'steal'; **nick** a slang word meaning the same as 'steal', used especially in British English; **filch** a formal word meaning the same as 'pinch', often suggesting quick casual theft of sth of little value; **purloin** a formal or humorous word meaning the same as 'steal'; **pilfer** meaning to steal things of little value and usually in small amounts, especially when done repeatedly; **embezzle** meaning to take money unlawfully when it has been entrusted to the perpetrator; **misappropriate** a formal word meaning the same as 'embezzle' or 'steal'.

stealth /stelth/ *n.* **1. ACTION TO AVOID DETECTION** the action of doing sth slowly, quietly, and covertly, in order to avoid detection **2. FURTIVENESS** secretive, dishonest, or cunning behaviour or actions ■ *adj.* MIL **VIRTUALLY UNDETECTABLE BY RADAR** designed or constructed in such a way and using requisite technology and materials so as to be invisible to enemy radar ○ *stealth bombers* [13thC. from assumed Old English *stǣlþ*, from a prehistoric Germanic base that is also the ancestor of English *steal*.] —**stealthful** *adj.*

stealth tower *n.* an ecologically friendly and aesthetic, camouflaged wireless telecommunications tower, e.g. one configured as a pine tree, intended to soften the environmental and visual impact of proliferating antenna sites (*informal*)

stealthy /stélthi/ (**-ier, -iest**) *adj.* **1. DONE CAREFULLY** done in a deliberately slow, careful, and quiet way **2. FURTIVE** secretive, furtive, or cunning —**stealthily** *adv.* —**stealthiness** *n.*

WORD KEY: SYNONYMS

See Synonyms at ***secret***.

steam /steem/ *n.* **1. VAPORIZED WATER** the vapour that is formed when water is boiled **2. MIST OF WATER VAPOUR** the visible mist that forms when water vapour condenses in the air **3. VAPOUR** any visible form of vapour **4. POWER** stamina, strength, or speed (*informal*) ○ *running out of steam* ■ *adj.* **1. DRIVEN BY STEAM** driven or powered by steam **2. USING STEAM** using steam to do sth **3. OUTMODED** old-fashioned or obsolete, like the steam engine (*humorous*) ■ *v.* (**steams, steaming, steamed**) **1.** *vi.* **PRODUCE STEAM** to produce or be produced as steam **2.** *vi.* **MOVE BY STEAM** to move or be powered by steam **3.** *vti.* **COOK IN STEAM** to cook sth or be cooked in the steam of boiling water **4.** *vi.* **MOVE FAST** to move very quickly and energetically (*informal*) **5.** *vi.* **GENERATE STEAM** to generate steam (*refers especially to boilers*) [Old English *stēam*] ◇ **get up steam** to gather together enough energy and speed to do sth (*informal*)

steam up *vti.* to become, or make sth become, clouded with condensation

steam bath *n.* a steam-filled room or compartment that people go into to relax and refresh themselves through sweating. A steam bath is often used as a way of temporarily losing weight through sweat loss, especially by boxers and jockeys who need to reach target weights.

steamboat /steem bōt/ *n.* a boat with an engine powered by steam

steam chest *n.* a compartment in a steam engine from which steam is supplied to the valve of the engine

steam engine *n.* an engine powered by steam, typically incorporating a flywheel attached to a reciprocating piston that in turn is driven by the expansive action of steam generated in a boiler

steamer /steemər/ *n.* **1.** SHIPPING **BOAT POWERED BY STEAM** a boat or ship that is powered by a steam engine or engines **2.** COOK **PAN FOR STEAMING FOOD** a covered pan in which food is cooked by steam. It has a perforated base and fits on top of a saucepan in which water is boiled to produce steam. **3.** CONSTR **CONTAINER FOR STEAMING WOOD** a container in which wood is treated with steam to make it pliable **4.** MUGGER a member of a large group of youths who go to crowded areas and do mass muggings (*slang*) **5.** US FOOD **SOFT-SHELL CLAM** a soft-shell clam, especially when steamed and eaten **6.** WETSUIT FOR COLD CONDITIONS a wetsuit with long sleeves and legs, for use in cold conditions (*slang*)

steam-generating heavy-water reactor *n.* a nuclear reactor that uses ordinary water as the coolant, which produces steam, and heavy water as the moderator

steaming /steeming/ *adj.* **1.** VERY ANGRY very angry or upset (*informal*) **2.** DRUNK extremely drunk (*slang*) ■ *n.* MASS MUGGING mass mugging carried out by a large group of youths, in crowded areas such as busy streets or shopping malls, or on trains, buses, or the underground. The group quickly and systematically grab handbags, wallets, watches, and briefcases, and other valuables. (*slang*)

steam iron *n.* an electric iron with a chamber for water. As the iron heats up steam is produced and channelled through holes in the face of the iron to dampen the laundry.

steam jacket *n.* a covering or casing surrounding the cylinders and heads of a steam engine to keep the surfaces hot and dry

steam organ *n.* a musical organ with whistles sounded by steam. It is played manually by keyboard or automatically using a punched card and it used to be a popular fairground attraction. US term **calliope**

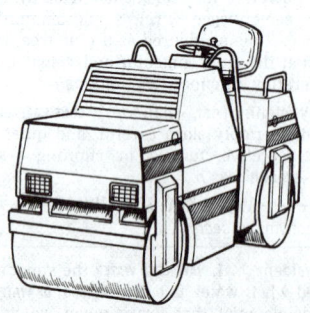

Steamroller

steamroller /steem rōlər/ *n.* **1.** TRANSP **VEHICLE FOR FLATTENING ROADS** a specialized vehicle, originally steampowered, with large heavy rollers for wheels, designed to flatten and compress newly-laid road surfaces **2.** CRUSHING FORCE sb or sth that is a powerful driving force, often crushing or dismissing anybody or anything that might stand in the way ■ *vt.* (**-lers, -lering, -lered**) steamroller, steamroll **1.** TRANSP **FLATTEN**

ROAD to flatten and compress a newly-laid road surface using a steamroller **2.** RUTHLESSLY CRUSH to crush or dismiss anybody or anything that might stand in the way ◇ *steamroller everyone else's ideas* **3.** COMPEL to force sb to do sth

steam room *n.* a room with a steam bath in it, or a room that can be filled with steam and used as a steam bath

steamship /steem ship/ *n.* a ship with an engine powered by steam

steam shovel *n.* a large steam-powered excavating machine, especially an earth-mover that has a bucket on a boom fixed to a jib that can be rotated

steamtight /steem tīt/ *adj.* designed or sealed so that steam cannot escape —**steamtightness** *n.*

steam turbine *n.* a turbine that uses the heat energy of steam to generate the power for mechanical rotation

steam whistle *n.* a large whistle blown by forcing steam through it. Steam whistles were used in the past on steam locomotives, or in factories to signal the end of the working day.

steamy /steemi/ (**-ier**, **-iest**) *adj.* **1.** FULL OF STEAM covered with, full of, affected by, or like steam **2.** OVERTLY SEXUAL with an exaggerated emphasis on sexual relations or sexuality (*informal*) —**steamily** *adv.* —**steaminess** *n.*

steapsin /sti ápsin/ *n.* an enzyme in pancreatic juice that catalyses the hydrolysis of fats [Late 19thC. Blend of Greek *stear* 'fat' (because it helps to break down fats) and PEPSIN.]

stearate /steer ayt/ *n.* a salt or ester of stearic acid [Mid-19thC. Coined from Greek *stear* (see STEATO-) + -ATE.]

stearic /sti árrik/ *adj.* **1.** CONTAINING STEARIN OR FAT relating to, containing, or typical of stearin or fat **2.** DERIVED FROM STEARIC ACID about, derived from, or containing stearic acid [Mid-19thC. Formed from Greek *stear* (see STEATO-).]

stearic acid *n.* a colourless odourless waxy crystalline fatty acid that occurs naturally in animal and vegetable oils and is used in candles, cosmetics, soaps, lubricants, and medicines. Formula: $C_{18}H_{36}O_2$.

stearin /steerin/, **stearine** /steereen/ *n.* **1.** ESTER OF GLYCEROL AND STEARIC ACID a colourless ester of glycerol and stearic acid used in making soap, candles, and adhesives **2.** = **stearic acid 3.** SOLID FORM OF FAT the solid form of fat [Early 19thC. Coined from Greek *stear* (see STEATO-) + -IN.]

steatite /stee ə tīt/ *n.* = **soapstone** [Mid-18thC. Via Latin from Greek *steatitis* (*lithos*) 'tallow-like (stone)', from *stear* (see STEATO-).] —**steatitic** /stee ə títtik/ *adj.*

steato- *prefix.* fat ◇ *steatopygia* [From Greek *steat-*, the stem of *stear* 'solid fat, tallow']

steatopygia /stee ə tō píjhi ə, -pī́ji ə/ *n.* an accumulation of fat on the buttocks [Early 19thC. Coined from STEATO- + Greek *pugē* 'buttocks', of unknown origin.] —**steatopygous** /stee ə tō pī́gəss, stée ə tóppigəss/ *adj.*

steatorrhea *n.* US = **steatorrhoea**

steatorrhoea /stee átə rée ə/ *n.* an unusual condition in which an excess of fat is present in stools

stedfast *adj.* = **steadfast**

steed /steed/ *n.* a horse, especially a lively spirited one (*archaic literary*) [Old English *stēda* 'stallion'. Ultimately from the same prehistoric Germanic base that produced *stud*.]

steel /steel/ *n.* **1.** STRONG ALLOY OF IRON AND CARBON a strong alloy of iron containing up to 1.5% carbon along with small amounts of other elements such as manganese, chromium, and nickel. A wide range of mechanical properties can be produced by varying the composition and treatment. **2.** STH MADE OF STEEL sth made of steel, e.g. a weapon **3.** KNIFE SHARPENER a steel rod, often with a handle, that knives are drawn back and forward along in order to sharpen them **4.** TOUGHNESS determination, toughness, or great strength of character ■ *adj.* STRONG OR HARD like steel, especially in strength or hardness ■ *vt.* (**steels, steeling, steeled**) **1.** TREAT WITH STEEL to coat, plate, edge, or point sth with steel **2.** PREPARE BY HARDENING to make sb unfeeling, or tough enough to withstand a

setback or trial ◇ *steeled myself for the news* [Old English *stēli*. Ultimately from an Indo-European base denoting 'to stand, be solid', which is also the ancestor of English *stay*[2] and *stay*[3].]

steel band *n.* a group of musicians who play steel drums and often specialize in calypsos

steel-blue *adj.* of a cold greyish-blue colour —**steel blue** *n.*

steel drum, **steel pan** *n.* a Caribbean percussion instrument made by hammering an oil drum into a concave shape with flattened areas that make musical notes when struck

Steele, Mount /steel/ peak in the Saint Elias Range, in southwestern Yukon Territory, Canada. Height: 5,073 m/16,644 ft.

steel engraving *n.* **1.** ENGRAVING ON STEEL PLATE the art, technique, or process of engraving on a steel plate **2.** PRINT FROM STEEL PLATE a print made from an engraved steel plate

steel-grey *adj.* of a dark grey colour with a bluish tinge —**steel grey** *n.*

steel guitar *n.* a fretless guitar played on a horizontal stand with a plectrum and a movable metal slide. ◊ **pedal steel guitar**

steelhead /steel hed/ (*plural* **-heads** *or* **-head**) *n.* a rainbow trout that has matured in the North Pacific Ocean and acquired a silver coloration, popular for sport fishing

steel pan *n.* = **steel drum**

steel wool *n.* thin strands of steel tangled together to form an abrasive mass, used for cleaning and polishing

steelwork /steel wurk/ *n.* sth made from steel, especially a structural framework

steelworker /steel wurkər/ *n.* sb who works at making steel

steelworks /steel wurks/ *n.* a factory where steel is made

steely /steeli/ *adj.* **1.** LIKE STEEL like steel, especially in colour or in being tough or determined **2.** MADE OF STEEL made of steel (*dated or literary*) —**steeliness** *n.*

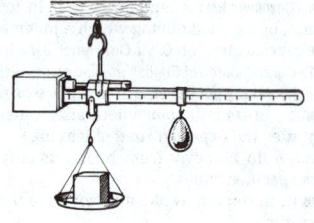

Steelyard

steelyard /steel yaard/ *n.* a portable balance for weighing objects. The object is hung on a hook and a counterweight is moved along a scaled arm to find the weight. [Mid-17thC. From YARD 'rod, spar'.]

Steen /stayn/, **Jan** (1626–79) Dutch painter. His genre scenes, particularly on the theme of eating and drinking, often illustrate proverbs or have an allegorical element. Full name **Jan Havickszoon Steen**

steenbok /steen bok/ (*plural* **-boks** *or* **-bok**), **steinbok** /stīn bák/ *n.* a small slender antelope that lives on the grasslands of southern Africa. It has short straight horns, long legs, and a reddish-brown coat. Latin name: *Raphicerus campestris*. [Late 18thC. Via Afrikaans from Middle Dutch *steenboc*, literally 'stone buck'.]

steep[1] /steep/ *adj.* **1.** ALMOST VERTICAL sloping very sharply, often to the extent of being almost vertical **2.** EXCESSIVE unreasonably or excessively high, especially in cost (*informal*) **3.** UNREASONABLE unreasonable, unfair, or expecting too much (*informal*) **4.** RAPID OR HUGE faster or greater than is usual, or might be expected ◇ *There's been a steep decline in the number of people out of work.* **5.** TAXING very ambitious or difficult [Old English *stēap* 'high'. Ultimately from a prehistoric Germanic base meaning 'lofty, deep', which is also the ancestor of English *steeple* and *stoop*.] —**steeply** *adv.* —**steepness** *n.*

steep[2] /steep/ *v.* (**steeps, steeping, steeped**) **1.** *vti.* IMMERSE IN LIQUID to soak sth, or be soaked, in a liquid, especially for cleaning or softening, or in order to extract sth **2.** *vt.* PERMEATE to permeate sb or sth with a substance or quality, usually over a long period (*usually passive*) ○ *steeped in tradition* ■ *n.* **1.** A SOAKING an act or the process of steeping sth in a liquid **2.** LIQUID FOR SOAKING a liquid that sth is or can be steeped in [14thC. From assumed Old English *stiepan*, from a prehistoric Germanic base that is also the ancestor of English *stoup*.] —**steeper** *n.*

steepen /steepən/ (**-ens, -ening, -ened**) *vti.* to become, or make sth become, steep or steeper

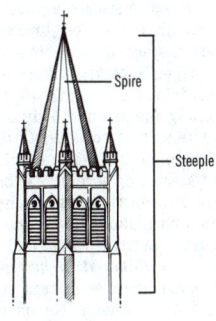

Spire

Steeple

Steeple

steeple /steep'l/ *n.* **1.** CHURCH TOWER a tall ornamental structure, usually a tapering tower with a spire on top of it, found on the roofs of churches and temples **2.** SPIRE a spire [Old English *stēpel*, from a prehistoric Germanic base meaning 'lofty, deep' (see STEEP[1])] —**steepled** *adj.*

steeplebush /steep'l boosh/ *n.* = **hardhack** [Mid-19thC. *Steeple* of uncertain origin: probably from the shape of the flower clusters.]

steeplechase /steep'l chayss/ *n.* **1.** HORSERACING HORSE-RACE WITH JUMPS ON TRACK a horse race, e.g. the Grand National, run over a course that has obstacles, e.g. hedges, ditches, and water jumps, that the horses must jump over. ◊ **flat race 2.** ATHLETICS TRACK EVENT WITH WATER JUMP a track event in which the runners must jump over a water jump as well as hurdles **3.** HORSERACING HORSERACE WITH JUMPS IN OPEN COUNTRY a cross-country horse race that has natural obstacles such as hedges and ditches for the horses to jump over (*archaic*) ■ *vi.* (**-chases, -chasing, -chased**) RUN A STEEPLECHASE to compete in a steeplechase [Late 18thC. From the fact that a church steeple was originally the competitors' goal.] —**steeplechaser** *n.*

steeplejack /steep'l jak/ *n.* sb who builds, works on, or repairs high structures, especially steeples and tall chimneys

steer[1] /steer/ *v.* (**steers, steering, steered**) **1.** *vti.* TRANSP DIRECT to guide sth such as a motor vehicle or ship in a direction using a steering wheel, rudder, or other device **2.** *vt.* INFLUENCE DIRECTION to try to influence people to follow a particular course of action by unobtrusively guiding them towards it **3.** *vi.* FOLLOW PARTICULAR COURSE to follow a specified course **4.** *vi.* TRANSP MANOEUVRE IN A CERTAIN WAY to go or move in a specified way or direction when being driven or propelled ○ *This car steers to the left.* ■ *n.* US PIECE OF ADVICE a piece of information or advice (*informal*) [Old English *stīeran*, from a prehistoric Germanic base meaning 'to steer', which is also the ancestor of English *stern* and *starboard*] —**steerable** *adj.* —**steerer** *n.*

—— **WORD KEY: SYNONYMS** ——
See Synonyms at *guide*.

steer[2] /steer/ *n.* a male of the cattle family that has been castrated before reaching sexual maturity and is raised for beef, especially a young bull [Old English *stēor*]

steerage /steerij/ *n.* **1.** SHIPPING INEXPENSIVE ACCOMMODATION ON SHIPS the cheapest passenger accommodation on board a ship, usually in the area near the rudder and steering gear **2.** NAUT STEERING the act or process of steering a boat

steerageway /steerij way/ *n.* a rate of forward movement that is fast enough to allow a boat to be steered from the helm

steering column *n.* the part in a motor vehicle that connects the steering wheel, or the handlebars on a motorcycle, with the steering gear

steering committee *n.* a group of selected people who decide agendas and topics for discussion, and prioritize urgent business, especially one acting for a legislative body or other assembly

steering gear *n.* the mechanism in a vehicle or ship that allows it to be steered

steering wheel *n.* a wheel in a vehicle or ship that is connected by way of the steering column to the steering gear and is turned to change direction

steersman /steerzmən/ *n.* (*plural* **-men** /-mən/) sb who steers a boat or ship [Old English *stēoresman*, literally 'man for steering', from *stēor* 'steering']

steeve[1] /steev/ *n.* SHIPPING CARGO-STOWING AID a spar with a pulley block at one end that is used for stowing cargo on a boat or ship ■ *vt.* (**steeves, steeving, steeved**) SHIPPING PUT CARGO ON BOARD to stow cargo in the hold of a boat or ship and make it secure [Mid-19thC. Origin uncertain: perhaps via Spanish *estibar* or Catalan *stivar* 'to stow cargo' from Latin *stipare* 'to stuff' (source of English *stevedore* and *constipate*).]

steeve[2] /steev/ *vti.* (**steeves, steeving, steeved**) SAILING INCLINE UPWARDS to incline upwards, or make a bowsprit incline upwards ■ *n.* SAILING ANGLE OF INCLINATION OF BOWSPRIT the angle at which a bowsprit inclines upwards from the horizontal [Mid-17thC. Origin unknown.]

stegosaur /stéggə sawr/, **stegosaurus** /stéggə sáwrəss/ *n.* a plant-eating dinosaur that lived in the Jurassic and Early Cretaceous periods and had tough bony dorsal plates and spikes. Genus: *Stegosauria.* [Early 20thC. From modern Latin *Stegosaurus*, genus name, from Greek *stegos* 'plate' + *sauros* 'lizard'.]

stein /stīn/ *n.* **1.** EARTHENWARE BEER MUG a large beer mug, especially a German earthenware or pewter one, often with a hinged lid **2.** QUANTITY OF BEER the amount of beer or other liquid that a stein holds [Mid-19thC. From German, shortening of *Steinkrug* 'stoneware mug'.]

Gertrude Stein: Photographed by Man Ray (1930)

Stein /stīn/, **Gertrude** (1874–1946) US writer. Her novels and works of fiction are characterized by experimentation with language and style.

Stein /steen/, **Jock** (1922–85) British football manager. He managed Glasgow Celtic during the most successful period in their history (1965–78), and as manager of Scotland (1978–85) took the team to the World Cup Finals. Real name **John Stein**

Steinbeck /stīn bek/, **John** (1902–68) US writer. His fiction includes *Of Mice and Men* (1937) and *The Grapes of Wrath* (1939), and is notable for its social realism. He won a Nobel Prize in literature in 1962. Full name **John Ernst Steinbeck**

steinbok *n.* = **steenbok**

Steinem /stīnəm/, **Gloria** (*b.* 1934) US feminist. A leading member of the women's movement, she was one of the founders of *Ms.* magazine (1972).

Steiner /shtínər, stínər/, **Rudolf** (1861–1925) Austrian philosopher. He founded the Anthroposophical Society (1912) to promote his intellectually-based spirituality. The Waldorf School movement is based on his work.

John Steinbeck

Gloria Steinem

stela /steelə/ (*plural* **-lae** /steé lee/) *n.* = **stele** *n.* 1 [Late 18thC. Via Latin from Greek *stēlē* (see STELE).]

stele /steel, steeli/ (*plural* **-lae** /steé lee/ *or* **-les**) *n.* **1.** ARCHAEOL ANCIENT STONE SLAB an ancient stone slab or pillar, usually engraved, inscribed, or painted, and set upright. Found among the ruins of civilizations as diverse as China, Greece, and Mexico, they are believed to have had religious significance. **2.** BOT CENTRAL PART OF STEMS AND ROOTS the cylindrical core of the stem and roots of a plant that contains the sap-conducting vascular tissues and varying amounts of packing tissue (**pith**) [Early 19thC. From Greek *stēlē* 'standing stone'. Ultimately from an Indo-European word meaning 'post', which is also the ancestor of English *stultify*.] —**stelar** *adj.*

stellar /stéllər/ *adj.* **1.** ASTRON INVOLVING STARS relating to, consisting of, or like a star or stars **2.** US EXCEPTIONAL exceptionally good **3.** INVOLVING FAMOUS PEOPLE about, involving, typical of, or full of famous people, especially those in the film or entertainment industries [Mid-17thC. From late Latin *stellaris*, from Latin *stella* 'star' (source of English *constellation*). Ultimately from the Indo-European word for 'star', which is also the ancestor of English *star* and *disaster*.]

stellar wind *n.* a stream of ionized particles ejected from the surface of a star. ◊ **solar wind**

stellate /stéllət, -ayt/, **stellated** /ste láytid/ *adj.* **1.** STAR-SHAPED shaped like a star **2.** HAVING PARTS RADIATING FROM CENTRE having a central part with smaller parts radiating out from it, like a starfish, some flower heads, and some crystal formations [Mid-17thC. Formed from Latin *stella* (see STELLAR).] —**stellately** *adv.*

stelliform /stélli fawrm/ *adj.* shaped like a star [Late 18thC. Coined from Latin *stella* (see STELLAR) + -FORM.]

Stellite /stéllīt/ *tdmk.* a trademark for a very hard alloy that contains cobalt, chromium, molybdenum, and tungsten

stellular /stéllyoolər/ *adj.* **1.** FULL OF LITTLE STARS full of or covered in little stars **2.** LIKE LITTLE STAR like a little star [Late 18thC. Formed from Latin *stellula*, literally 'small star', from *stella* (see STELLAR).] —**stellularly** *adv.*

stem[1] /stem/ *n.* **1.** BOT MAIN AXIS OF PLANT the main axis of a plant that bears buds and shoots. It is usually above ground, although some plants have underground stems (**rhizomes**). **2.** BOT SECONDARY PLANT BRANCH a slender part of a plant other than its main axis that supports a leaf, flower, or fruit **3.** NARROW CONNECTING PART any long slim part of an object, e.g. the part that connects the base of a wine glass to its bowl, or the hollow tube on a smoker's pipe **4.** GENEALOGICAL LINE the major line of descent in a family tree **5.** CYLINDRICAL WATCH PART a short rod, usually with an expanded crown at the end of it, that is used in winding a watch **6.** LANG BASE OF A WORD the base of a word, to which affixes are added **7.** VERTICAL LETTER PART an upright stroke, especially the main one, in a letter or character **8.** MUSIC VERTICAL PART OF MUSIC NOTE the vertical part that extends from the head of a written musical note **9.** SAILING UPRIGHT BOW TIMBER the main upright timber at the bow of a ship ■ *v.* **(stems, stemming, stemmed) 1.** *vi.* ORIGINATE to derive, originate, or be caused by sth **2.** *vt.* REMOVE STEM OF to take off the stem or part of the stem from sth, especially a flower, fruit, or vegetable **3.** *vt.* GIVE STEM TO to give sth a stem, e.g. a smoker's pipe or a wineglass **4.** *vt.* SAILING MAKE HEADWAY to make headway in a ship or boat against a tide or wind [Old English *stefn*. Ultimately from an Indo-European base meaning 'to stand' (see STATO-).] —**stemmer** *n.* ◇ **from stem to stern** through the whole of a place, especially a ship

stem[2] /stem/ *v.* **(stems, stemming, stemmed) 1.** *vt.* PREVENT FROM FLOWING to hinder, obstruct, or stop sth from flowing, especially by creating a dam or plug **2.** *vt.* STOP UP to plug sth such as a blast or drill hole by packing it **3.** *vti.* SKIING TURN SKI IN to turn the tip of a ski or skis inwards in order to turn or slow down ■ *n.* **stem, stem turn** SKIING TURNING IN OF SKI an act or the technique of turning the tip of a ski or skis inwards to turn or slow down [13thC. From Old Norse *stemma*, from a prehistoric Germanic base meaning 'to halt, stammer', which is also the ancestor of English *stammer* and *stumble*.]

stem cell *n.* an undifferentiated cell from which specialized cells, e.g. blood cells, develop

stem christie /-krísti/ *n.* a skiing turn performed by stemming one ski and then bringing the other parallel to it during the turn [*Stem* from STEM[2]; *christie* a shortening and alteration of CHRISTIANIA]

stem ginger *n.* round portions of the underground stem of a ginger plant, cooked until tender and preserved in syrup

stemma /stémmə/ (*plural* **-mata** /-mətə/) *n.* **1.** FAMILY TREE a family tree **2.** LITERAT DIAGRAM OF TEXTS OF LITERARY WORK a diagram like a family tree, showing the relationships between different texts of a literary work **3.** ZOOL EYE OF ARTHROPOD a simple eye or facet of a compound eye of some arthropods [Mid-17thC. Via Latin from Greek, 'garland'; from the ancient Roman practice of placing garlands on images of their ancestors.]

stemmed /stemd/ *adj.* **1.** HAVING A STEM having a stem, often of a specified kind (*often used in combination*) ○ *long-stemmed lilies* **2.** WITHOUT A STEM having the stem or stems removed

stem rust *n.* a fungal disease of plants in which streaks of dark pustules appear, especially on the stem

stemson /stémss'n/ *n.* a timber attached to the stem and keelson in the bow of a wooden ship [Mid-18thC. Formed from STEM[1], on the model of KEELSON.]

stem turn *n.* = **stem**[2] *n.* ['Stem' from STEM[2]]

stemware /stém wair/ *n.* glasses, goblets, and other glass vessels that have stems

stench /stench/ *n.* a really disgusting smell, especially a strong lingering one [Old English *stenc* 'odour', from a prehistoric Germanic base that is also the ancestor of English *stink*]

WORD KEY: SYNONYMS

See Synonyms at ***smell***.

stench trap *n.* a device used in a sewer to prevent foul-smelling gases from rising, especially one that has a water seal

stencil /sténss'l/ *n.* **1.** PLATE WITH CUT-OUT DESIGN a thin sheet of material with a shape cut out of it that is marked on a surface when paint or ink is applied **2.** PATTERN the design, lettering, or other characters marked using a stencil ■ *vt.* **(-cils, -cilling, -cilled) 1.** MAKE PATTERN USING STENCIL to apply a design, lettering, or other characters to a surface using a stencil **2.** DECORATE USING STENCIL to decorate or mark a surface, e.g. a wall or paper, using a stencil [Early 18thC. Via Old French *estenceler* 'to decorate with bright colours' from, ultimately, Latin *scintilla* 'spark' (source of English *scintillate* and *tinsel*).] —**stenciller** *n.*

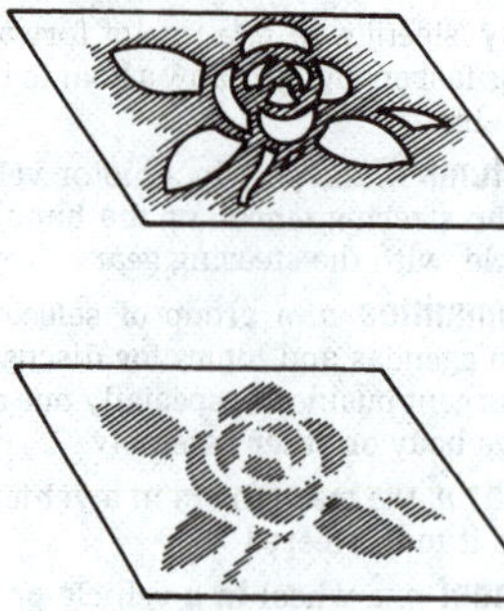

Stencil

stengah /sténg gə/ *n.* = **stinger**[2] *n.* 2 [Late 19thC. From Malay *satĕngah* 'half'.]

Sten gun /stén-/ *n.* a light, cheaply manufactured submachine gun used in the past by the British Army, especially in World War II [*Sten* coined from the first letters of R. V. *Shepherd* and H. J. *Turpin*, who designed it + the district of *Enfield* in Greater London, where it was made (modelled on BREN GUN).]

steno /sténnō/ (*plural* **-os**) *n. US* (*informal*) **1.** STENOGRAPHER a stenographer **2.** STENOGRAPHY stenography [Early 20thC. Shortening.]

steno- *prefix.* narrow, small ○ *stenothermal* [From Greek *stenos*]

stenobathic /sténnō báthik/ *adj.* able to live only within a narrow range of depth of water [Early 20thC. Coined from STENO- + Greek *bathos* 'depth'.] —**stenobath** /sténnō bath/ *n.*

stenograph /sténnə graaf, -graf/ *n.* **1.** SHORTHAND TYPEWRITER a machine like a small typewriter with keys for shorthand characters **2.** SHORTHAND CHARACTER a character in a system of shorthand writing ■ *vt.* **(-graphs, -graphing, -graphed)** WRITE OR TYPE IN SHORTHAND to record sth in shorthand by writing or using a stenograph

stenographer /stə nóggrəfər/ *n.* **1.** SB USING STENOGRAPH sb who uses a stenograph **2.** *US* = **shorthand typist**

stenography /stə nóggrəfi/ (*plural* **-phies**) *n.* **1.** SHORTHAND WRITING OR TYPING the act, process, or skill of recording sth in shorthand by writing or by using a stenograph **2.** STH WRITTEN OR TYPED IN SHORTHAND sth that has been recorded in written shorthand or by using a stenograph —**stenographic** /stənnə gráffik/ *adj.* —**stenographical** /-gráffik'l/ *adj.* —**stenographically** /-gráffikli/ *adv.*

stenohaline /sténnō háy leen, -līn/ *adj.* unable to tolerate wide variations in salinity [Mid-20thC. Coined from STENO- + the Greek stem *hal-* 'salt'.]

stenosis /stə nóssiss/ *n.* an abnormal constriction or narrowing of a duct, passage, or opening in the body [Late 19thC. Via modern Latin from Greek *stenos* 'narrow'.] —**stenosed** /stə nṓzd, -nṓst/ *adj.* —**stenotic** /stə nóttik/ *adj.*

stenothermal /sténnə thúrm'l/ *adj.* able to live only within a narrow temperature range

stenotype /sténnə tīp/ *n.* a machine whose keyboard is used to record speech by means of phonetic shorthand

stenotypy /sténnə tīpi/ *n.* a form of phonetic shorthand that uses combinations of letters to represent sounds and short words —**stenotypic** /sténnə típpik/ *adj.* —**stenotypist** /sténnə tīpist/ *n.*

stentor /stén tawr/ *n.* **1.** SB LOUD sb with a loud powerful voice **2.** ZOOL TRUMPET-SHAPED MICROORGANISM a trumpet-shaped protozoan with a mouth at the broad end. Genus: *Stentor*. [Early 17thC. Named after *Stentor*, a famously strong-voiced Greek herald in the Trojan war.]

stentorian /sten táwri ən/ *adj.* loud, powerful, or declamatory in tone

step /step/ *n.* **1.** SHORT MOVEMENT WITH FOOT a short movement made by raising one foot and lowering it ahead of the other foot **2.** DISTANCE OF STEP the distance travelled in taking a step **3.** SOUND OF FOOTFALL the sound made by moving the foot on a horizontal surface **4.** FOOTPRINT the footprint made by putting down the foot on a surface **5.** WAY OF WALKING a particular manner of walking **6.** SHORT WAY a very short

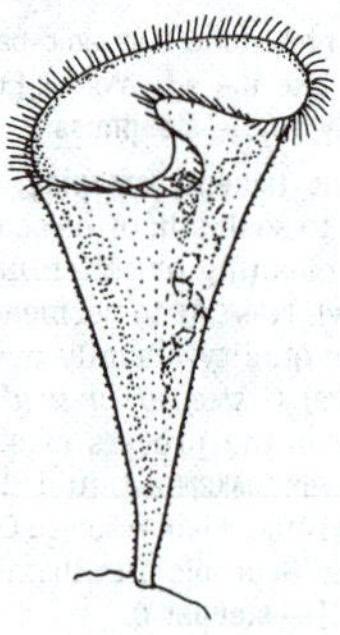

Stentor

distance **7.** RAISED SURFACE a raised surface for the foot, especially in a series going up or down **8.** STAGE IN PROGRESS a stage in a progression towards some goal or target **9.** DEGREE OR GRADE a degree, rank, or grade, especially on a scale **10.** DANCE DANCE MOVES a movement of the feet and body that forms part of a dance **11.** MUSIC DEGREE OR INTERVAL a degree of a musical staff or scale, or the interval between two degrees **12.** STEP AEROBICS step aerobics (*informal*) ○ *a step class* ■ **steps** *npl.* **1.** OUTDOOR STAIRS a flight of stairs, usually outdoors, and made of stone or a similar material **2.** PATH MADE BY SB ELSE a route, path, or course set by sb else ○ *She followed in her mother's steps and became an architect.* ■ *v.* **(steps, stepping, stepped) 1.** *vti.* MOVE FOOT to move a foot on top of sth or in a particular direction ○ *Please step aside.* **2.** *vi.* WALK A FEW STEPS to walk a short distance or to a specific place **3.** *vi.* TO MOVE FORWARD WITH FOOT to move forward by raising one foot and setting it down in front of the other **4.** *vi.* DANCE MOVE IN REGULAR RHYTHM to move at a measured pace, e.g. in a dance **5.** *vi.* TREAT SB WITHOUT RESPECT to show or treat sb with arrogant disregard and unkindness ○ *She is stepping on other people's feelings constantly.* **6.** *vi.* EASILY WALK INTO SITUATION to come into a new situation with ease or with little preparation **7.** *vt.* ARRANGE IN STEPS to arrange or organize sth in steps, or to furnish sth with steps **8.** *vt.* MEASURE BY STEPS to measure sth by walking or pacing its length [Old English *stæpe*, from a prehistoric Germanic base meaning 'to tread', which is also the ancestor of English *stamp*, *stump*, and *stoop*[2]] —**stepped** *adj.* —**stepper** *n.* ◇ **be in** *or* **out of step (with sb** *or* **sth) 1.** to agree or disagree with sb or sth in your attitudes or opinions **2.** to move in unison with other people, or at a different pace and rhythm ◇ **step by step** gradually ◇ **step on it** to hurry (*slang*) ◇ **take steps** to take action ◇ **watch your step 1.** to be careful and cautious **2.** to tread carefully

step down *v.* **1.** *vi.* WITHDRAW FROM POSITION to resign, retire, or withdraw from a position **2.** *vti.* DECREASE IN STAGES to lower or decrease in stages

step in *vi.* to intervene or become involved in sth

step out *vi.* **1.** LEAVE BRIEFLY to leave a place for a brief period **2.** WALK WITH LONG STRIDES to walk fast, with longer strides than usual **3.** DATE SB to go on a date or to a social gathering with sb (*informal*) **4.** TO BE UNFAITHFUL to be unfaithful to a spouse or partner (*informal*)

step up *v.* **1.** *vt.* RAISE IN STAGES to raise or increase sth in stages **2.** *vt.* RAISE VOLTAGE to raise voltage using a transformer **3.** *vi.* TO COME FORWARD to come forward, e.g. to stand for sth or to take responsibility for sth

step- *prefix.* related because of remarriage, not by blood ○ *stepson* [Old English *stēop-*]

step aerobics *n.* an exercise programme done to music that involves performing different movements with the arms and legs while stepping onto and off a small portable platform (*takes a singular or plural verb*)

stepbrother /stép bru*th*ər/ *n.* a boy or man who has brothers or sisters through the remarriage of a parent to sb who has children

stepchild /stép chīld/ (*plural* **-children** /-childrən/) *n.* the son or daughter of a stepparent

stepdaughter /stép dawtər/ *n.* the daughter of sb's spouse by a previous marriage

step-down *adj.* **1.** DECREASING decreasing in quantity, size, or status, especially in stages **2.** ELEC LOWERING VOLTAGE serving to lower voltage —**step-down** *n.*

stepfather /stép faathər/ n. a man who has married sb's mother after the death of or divorce from the person's father

step function n. a mathematical function such as a waveform that remains constant in value over a given interval but changes abruptly in value from one interval to the next

stephanotis /stéffə nótiss/ (plural **-tises** or **-tis**) n. a vine or shrub grown for its fragrant white waxy flowers and leathery leaves. Genus: Stephanotis. [Mid-19thC. From Greek stephanōtis 'fit for a crown', from stephanos 'crown, wreath', from stephein 'to crown'.]

Stephen /steev'n/, **King of England** (1090?–1154). He seized the throne on the death of Henry I (1135), but was engaged in civil war throughout his reign with supporters of Matilda, Henry's daughter.

Stephen, Sir Ninian Martin (b. 1923) British-born Australian lawyer and statesman. He was justice of the High Court (1972–82), and governor-general of Australia (1982–89).

Stephen, St (d. 36) Christian martyr. Condemned to death on a charge of blasphemy, he was the first Christian martyr. Known as **the Protomartyr**

Stephen I, St, King of Hungary (975?–1038). He founded the Hungarian state and established Christianity in Hungary. He is the country's patron saint.

Stephenson /steev'nssən/, **George** (1781–1848) British railway engineer. He built the Liverpool & Manchester Railway (1830) and built the **Rocket**, the first steam locomotive to establish the viability of the railway as a means of passenger transport.

Stephenson, Robert (1803–59) British civil engineer and politician. The son of George Stephenson, he was noted as a builder of bridges in Britain, Egypt, and Canada. He was a MP (1847–59).

step-in adj. PUT ON BY BEING STEPPED INTO without fastenings and put on by stepping into it ■ **step-ins** npl. CLOTHING STEPPED INTO a step-in article of clothing, especially panties with wide legs worn by women in the 1920s and 1930s (dated)

stepladder /stép laddər/ n. a folding ladder that has flat broad steps and a hinged supporting frame

stepmother /stép muthər/ n. a woman who has married sb's father after the death of or divorce from the person's mother

stepparent /stép pairənt/ n. a stepfather or a stepmother —**stepparenting** n.

steppe /step/ n. GEOG an extensive, usually treeless plain, often semiarid and grass-covered [Late 17thC. Via German from Russian step.]

Steppes /steps/ n. the vast grassy plains of Russia and the Ukraine

stepping stone n. **1.** STONE OVER WET AREA one of a series of stones on which sb is able to step, e.g. to cross shallow water **2.** STEP TOWARDS GOAL a stage or step that helps achieve a goal

stepsister /stép sistər/ n. a girl or woman who has brothers or sisters through the remarriage of a parent to sb who has children

stepson /stép sun/ n. the son of sb's spouse by a previous marriage

step stool n. a stool with hinged steps that can be folded

step turn n. a turn in which a skier lifts one ski in a desired direction, brings it down, and then aligns the other ski with it

step-up adj. **1.** INCREASING increasing in quantity, size, or status, usually in stages **2.** ELEC RAISING VOLTAGE serving to raise voltage —**stepped-up** adj. —**step-up** n.

stepwise /stép wīz/ adj. arranged in or resembling steps

ster. abbr. sterling

-ster suffix. **1.** sb who is associated with, or does or makes a particular thing ○ gangster ○ punster **2.** sb who has a particular characteristic ○ youngster [Old English -estre, originally a feminine suffix]

steradian /stə ráydi ən/ n. the basic SI unit of measurement of solid angle. One steradian is the solid angle made at the centre of a sphere by an area on the surface of the sphere equal to the square of the sphere's radius. Symbol **sr** [Late 19thC. Coined from STEREO- + RADIAN.]

stercoraceous /stúrkə ráyshəss/ adj. consisting of or resembling dung or faeces [Mid-18thC. Formed from the Latin stem stercor- 'dung'. Ultimately from an Indo-European word that is also the ancestor of English dreck and scatology.]

stere /steer/ n. a cubic metre, equal to 35.32 cubic ft [Late 18thC. Via French stère from Greek stereos (see STEREO-).]

stere- prefix. = **stereo-** (used before vowels)

stereo /stérri ō, steer-/ (plural **-os**) n. **1.** DEVICE PRODUCING STEREOPHONIC SOUND an audio system or device that reproduces stereophonic sound **2.** STEREOPHONIC REPRODUCTION stereophonic sound reproduction **3.** STEREOSCOPIC PHOTOGRAPHY photography using stereoscopy **4.** PRINTING = **stereotype** n. 3 [Late 19thC. Shortening.]

stereo- prefix. **1.** three-dimensional ○ stereology **2.** solid ○ stereotaxy [From Greek stereos 'solid' (source of English cholesterol). Ultimately from an Indo-European word meaning 'stiff', which is also the ancestor of stern[1], stare, strut, and torpid.]

stereobate /stérri ō bayt, steeri ō-/ n. **1.** SUPPORTING PLATFORM a masonry platform that supports a building **2.** = **stylobate** [Mid-19thC. From Latin stereobates, from Greek stereos 'solid' + -batēs 'walker'.]

stereochemistry /stérri ō kémmistri, steeri ō-/ n. the study of the spatial distribution of atoms in a chemical compound and their effects on the compound's properties

stereochrome /stérri ə krōm, steeri ə-/ n. a wall painting that uses water glass as a medium or preservative [Mid-19thC. From German Stereochrom, from Greek stereos 'solid' + khroma 'colour'.] —**stereochromy** n.

stereogram /stérri ə gram, steeri ə-/ n. **1.** PHOTOGRAPHY = **stereograph 2.** ARTS DIAGRAM GIVING THREE-DIMENSIONAL IMPRESSION a diagram or picture that shows objects as though in relief **3.** RECORDING STEREO RADIOGRAM a stereo radiogram (dated)

stereograph /stérri ə graaf, steeri ə-, -graf, -/ n. a picture with two superimposed images or two almost identical pictures placed side-by-side which when viewed through special glasses or a stereoscope produce a three-dimensional image

stereography /stérri óggrəfi, steeri-/ n. **1.** ILLUSTRATING THREE-DIMENSIONAL FIGURE ON FLAT SURFACE the technique or art of depicting or drawing a three-dimensional object on a flat surface **2.** GEOM STUDY OF SOLID GEOMETRICAL OBJECTS the study and construction of defined geometric objects —**stereographic** /stérri ə gráffik, steeri ə gráffik/ adj. —**stereographically** /stérri ə gráffikli, steeri ə-/ adv.

stereoisomer /stérri ō íssəmər, steeri ō-/ n. one molecule in a group of molecules in which the atoms in the molecules are connected in the same order but have different spatial arrangements

stereoisomerism /stérri ō ī sómmərizəm, steeri ō-/ n. isomerism in which the atoms in the molecules are connected in the same order but have different spatial arrangements —**stereoisomeric** adj.

stereology /stérri ólləji, steeri-/ n. the study of the properties of three-dimensional structures and objects based on two-dimensional views of them —**stereological** adj.

stereometry /stérri ómmətri, steeri-/ n. the measurement of volume —**stereometric** adj.

stereomicroscope /stérri ō míkrəskōp, steeri ō míkrəskōp/ n. a microscope with two optically separate eyepieces to make viewed objects look three-dimensional

stereophonic /stérri ə fónnik, steeri ə-/ adj. using an audio system based on two or more soundtracks to make recorded sound seem more natural when reproduced —**stereophonically** adv. —**stereophony** /stérri óffəni, steeri-/ n.

stereopsis /stérri ópsiss, steeri-/ n. three-dimensional vision

stereopticon /stérri óptikən, steeri-/ n. a type of slide projector able to allow one image to gradually replace another [Mid-19thC. From modern Latin, from Greek stereos 'solid' + optikos 'optic'.]

stereoscope /stérri əskōp, steeri-/ n. a device resembling a pair of binoculars in which two-dimensional pictures of a scene taken at slightly different angles are viewed concurrently, one with each eye, creating the illusion of three dimensions —**stereoscopically** /-skóppikli, -skóppikli/ adv.

stereoscopic /stérri ə skóppik, steeri ə-/ adj. **1.** PRODUCING THREE-DIMENSIONAL EFFECT WHEN SEEN involving, producing, or resembling the effects of seeing sth as three dimensional **2.** RELATING TO STEREOSCOPE produced by or relating to a stereoscope —**stereoscopically** adv.

stereoscopy /stérri óskəpi, steeri-/ n. the visual perception of objects as being three dimensional

stereospecific /stérri ō spə síffik, steeri ō-/ adj. relating to a process in which atoms are in a fixed spatial position

stereotaxis /stérri ō táksiss, steeri ō-/ n. **1.** BIOL = **thigmotaxis 2.** MED TECHNIQUE IN BRAIN SURGERY neurological surgery involving the insertion of delicate instruments that are guided to a specific area by the use of three-dimensional scanning techniques —**stereotactic** /-táktik, -/ adj. —**stereotactically** /-táktikli, -/ adv. —**stereotaxic** /-táksik, -/ adj. —**stereotaxically** /-táktikli, -/ adv.

stereotropism /stérri óttrəpizəm, steeri-/ n. = **thigmotropism** —**stereotropic** /stérri ə tróppik, steeri ə-/ adj.

stereotype /stérri ə tīp, steeri ə-/ n. **1.** OVERSIMPLIFIED CONCEPTION an oversimplified standardized image or idea held by one person or group of another **2.** PSYCHOL = **stereotypy** n. 1 **3.** PRINTING METAL PRINTING PLATE a metal printing plate cast from a mould in another material such as papier-mâché ■ vt. (**-types, -typing, -typed**) **1.** REDUCE TO OVERSIMPLIFIED CATEGORIES to categorize individuals or groups according to an oversimplified standardized image or idea **2.** PRINTING USE STEREOTYPE IN PRINTING to cast or print using a stereotype [Late 18thC. From French stéréotype 'solid-block printing'.] —**stereotyper** n. —**stereotypist** n. —**stereotypical** /stérri ə típpik'l, steeri ə-/ adj. —**stereotypically** adv.

stereotypy /stérri ə tīpi, steeri ə-/ n. **1.** stereotypy, stereotype PERSISTENT INFLEXIBLE BEHAVIOUR a pattern of persistent, fixed, and repeated speech or movement that is apparently meaningless and is characteristic of some mental conditions **2.** PRINTING STEREOTYPES the process of casting or printing stereotypes

steric /stérrik, steer-/ adj. related to the way atoms are spatially arranged [Late 19thC. Coined from STEREO-.] —**sterically** adv.

sterigma /stə rígmə/ (plural **-mata** /-mətə/ or **-mas**) n. a tiny stalk that bears a spore or spores in a fungus [Mid-19thC. Via modern Latin from Greek, 'support', from sterizein 'to support'.]

sterilant /stérrilənt/ n. MED a substance used to sterilize [Mid-20thC. Formed from STERILE.]

sterile /stérrīl/ adj. **1.** ECOL BARREN incapable of supporting vegetation **2.** BIOL INFERTILE incapable of becoming pregnant or of inducing pregnancy **3.** BIOL NOT PRODUCING SEEDS not producing seeds, fruit, or spores **4.** MED FREE FROM INFECTIVE ORGANISMS free from living bacteria and other microorganisms **5.** DULL AND UNCREATIVE unstimulating, uncreative, and lacking in ideas that will lead to any useful outcome [15thC. Via Old French from Latin sterilis.] —**sterilely** adv. —**sterility** /stə rílləti, ste r-/ n.

sterilization /stérri līzáysh'n/, **sterilisation** n. **1.** MED DESTRUCTION OF MICROORGANISMS the destruction of living microorganisms to prevent infection **2.** MED, ZOOL SURGICAL OPERATION PREVENTING REPRODUCTION a surgical procedure that prevents reproduction by total or partial removal of the reproductive organs

sterilize /stérri līz/ (**-izes, -izing, -ized**), **sterilise** (**-ises, -ising, -ised**) vt. **1.** MED DESTROY MICROORGANISMS to kill all living microorganisms in order to make sth incapable of causing infection **2.** ZOOL, MED MAKE INFERTILE to stop a person or animal from reproducing, e.g. by surgical removal or alteration of reproductive organs —**sterilizable** *adj.* —**sterilizer** *n.*

sterlet /stúrlit/ (*plural* **-lets** *or* **-let**) *n.* a small caviar-bearing sturgeon of the Black and Caspian Seas. Latin name: *Acipenser ruthenus.* [Late 16thC. From Russian *sterlyad,* ultimately of prehistoric Germanic origin.]

sterling /stúrling/ *n.* **1.** MONEY BRITISH CURRENCY British money **2.** BRITISH STANDARD FOR COIN METAL PURITY the official standard of purity in terms of precious metal content for gold and silver coins in Britain, being 91.666% (22 carat) or 74.999% (18 carat) for gold and 92.5% for silver **3.** = **sterling silver** ■ *adj.* **1.** OF STERLING SILVER made of sterling silver **2.** ADMIRABLE admirable or valuable ○ *sterling efforts* [13thC. Origin uncertain: probably literally 'small star', from an earlier form of STAR. So called because some early Norman pennies bore such a design.]

sterling area *n.* A group of countries that use British currency, or that link the value of their own currency to that of sterling

sterling silver, **sterling** *n.* an alloy containing at least 92.5% silver with the remainder usually copper

stern[1] /stern/ *adj.* **1.** STRICT rigid, strict, and uncompromising **2.** SEVERE severe and allowing no leeway **3.** FORBIDDING grim, austere, or forbidding in appearance [Old English *styrne.* Ultimately from an Indo-European word meaning 'stiff', which is also the ancestor of English *starch* and *stare.*] —**sternly** *adv.*

stern[2] /stern/ *n.* **1.** NAUT REAR OF SHIP the rear part of a vessel **2.** BACK PART the rear part of sth ■ *adj.* IN REAR located at or resembling the stern [13thC. Origin uncertain: probably from Old Norse *stjórn* 'rudder', from the same prehistoric Germanic base that produced English *steer.*]

sterna plural of **sternum**

stern-chaser, **stern chaser** *n.* a cannon mounted at the stern of a vessel for firing to the rear

Sterne /sturn/, **Laurence** (1713–58) British novelist. His comic masterpiece, *The Life and Opinions of Tristram Shandy* (1759–67), anticipated many of the techniques of the modern novel.

sternite /stúr nīt/ *n.* a ventral shield or cover on the underside of a segment of an arthropod, especially the chitinous sternum of an insect [Mid-19thC. Coined from STERNUM + -ITE.]

Sterno *tdmk.* a trademark for canned liquid cooking fuel

sterno- *prefix.* the sternum ○ *sternotomy* [From Greek *sternon* (see STERNUM)]

sternoclavicular /stúrnōklə víkyōōlər/ *adj.* relating to or connecting the sternum and clavicle

sternocostal /stúrnō kóst'l/ *adj.* situated between or relating to the sternum and ribs [Late 18thC. Coined from STERNO- + Latin *costa* 'rib'.]

sternpost /stúrnpōst/ *n.* the main upright timber in the stern of a vessel

sternsheets /stúrn sheets/ *npl.* the space at the rear of an open boat that is behind the rowers' bench [Mid-17thC. From SHEET[2] 'forward or after section of a boat'.]

sternson /stúrnss'n/ *n.* a reinforcing timber at the joint of a sternpost and keelson at the stern of a wooden vessel [Mid-19thC. Formed from STERN[2], on the model of KEELSON.]

sternum /stúrnəm/ (*plural* **-na** /-nə/ *or* **-nums**) *n.* **1.** ANAT BREASTBONE the breastbone (*technical*) **2.** ZOOL ARTHROPOD'S ABDOMINAL COVERING the chitinous ventral plate covering the abdomen of an arthropod [Mid-17thC. Via modern Latin from Greek *sternon* 'breastbone'. Ultimately from an Indo-European word meaning 'to spread', which is also the ancestor of English *stratus* and *street.*] —**sternal** *adj.*

sternutation /stúrnyōō táysh'n/ *n.* the act of sneezing, or a sneeze (*formal*) [Mid-16thC. From the Latin stem *sternutation-,* from *sternutare,* literally 'to keep sneezing', from *sternuere* 'to sneeze'.]

sternutatory /stur nyóotətəri/ *adj.* CAUSING SNEEZING causing or resulting in sneezing ■ *n.* (*plural* **-ries**) STH THAT CAUSES SNEEZING any substance that causes sneezing [Early 17thC]

sternwards /stúrnwərdz/, **sternward** /-wərd/ *adv.* in the direction of the stern

sternway /stúrn way/ *n.* any backward movement of a vessel

stern-wheeler /stúrn weelər/ *n.* a boat propelled by a large paddle wheel at the rear, especially a river boat

steroid /steér oyd, stérroyd/ *n.* an organic fat-soluble compound composed of four joined carbon rings formed naturally or synthetically, and including bile acids, adrenocortical and sex hormones, sterols, and vitamin D [Mid-20thC. Coined from STEROL + -OID.] —**steroidal** /ste róyd'l/ *adj.*

sterol /steér ol, stérrol/ *n.* a waxy colourless organic solid such as cholesterol or ergosterol, containing an alcohol group and found in animal and plant lipids [Early 20thC. Shortening of CHOLESTEROL.]

-sterone *suffix.* steroid hormone ○ *androsterone* [From STEROL + -ONE]

stertor /stúrtər, stúr tawr/ *n.* noisy or laborious snoring, heard when sb is deeply unconscious or when there are obstructed air passages [Early 19thC. From modern Latin, formed from Latin *stertere* 'to snore'. Ultimately, from an Indo-European base that was originally an imitation of the sound of sneezing or snoring.] —**stertorous** *adj.* —**stertorously** *adv.* —**stertorousness** *n.*

stet /stet/ *vti.* (**stets, stetting, stetted**) RESTORE DELETED TEXT to restore or direct sb to restore sth that has previously been deleted from a printed or written text ■ *n.* INSTRUCTION TO RESTORE DELETED TEXT a word or mark indicating that previously deleted printed or written matter should be restored [Mid-18thC. From Latin, 'let it stand'.]

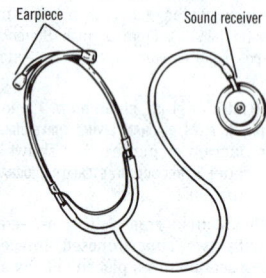

Stethoscope

stethoscope /stéthə skōp/ *n.* a medical instrument used for listening to breathing, heartbeats, and other sounds made by the body [Early 19thC. Coined from Greek *stēthos* 'chest' + -SCOPE.] —**stethoscopic** /stéthə skóppik/ *adj.* —**stethoscopy** /ste thóskəpi/ *n.*

Stetson /stéts'n/ *tdmk.* a trademark for hats having wide brims and high crowns

stevedore /steévə dawr/ *n.* DOCKWORKER sb whose job is to load and unload ships ■ *vti.* (**-dores, -doring, -dored**) DO STEVEDORE WORK to work as a dockworker, loading and unloading ships [Late 18thC. Via Spanish *estibador* or Portuguese *estivador* from, ultimately, Latin *stipare* (see STEEVE[1]).]

stevedore's knot *n.* a knot that forms a lump to prevent a line from passing through a hole

Stevens /steév'nz/, **Siaka Probin** (1905–88) Sierra Leone statesman. Founder of the All-People's Congress (1960), he was the prime minister (1967 and 1968) and first president (1971–85) of Sierra Leone.

Stevens, Wallace (1879–1955) US poet. His poems have a strongly philosophical bent. He won a Pulitzer Prize for his *Collected Poems* (1954).

Stevens-Johnson syndrome /steév'nz jónss'n-/ *n.* a severe inflammation of the skin and mucous membranes, often after a respiratory infection or as an allergic reaction to drugs [Mid-20thC. Named after Albert Mason *Stevens* (1884–1945) and Frank Chambliss *Johnson* (1894–1934), US paediatricians, who identified the disease.]

Stevenson /steévənss'n/, **Robert Louis** (1850–94) Scottish writer. He lived in Europe, the United States, and, after 1889, in Samoa. Among his many books of travel, autobiography, and verse, he is best re-

Wallace Stevens

membered for classic adventure tales such as *Treasure Island* (1883) and *Kidnapped* (1886). Full name **Robert Louis Balfour Stevenson**

stew[1] /styoo/ *n.* **1.** COOK SIMMERED DISH a dish of meat, fish, or vegetables, or a combination of them, that is cooked by slow simmering **2.** MIXTURE any widely assorted mixture **3.** BROTHEL a brothel (*archaic*) ■ *v.* (**stews, stewing, stewed**) **1.** *vti.* COOK COOK BY SIMMERING to cook sth by long slow simmering **2.** *vi.* BE UPSET to be deeply troubled or agitated **3.** *vi.* BE VERY HOT to swelter or become uncomfortably hot **4.** *vti.* MAKE TEA BITTER to cause tea to become bitter by infusing it for too long [14thC. Via Old French *estuve* 'steam bath' from assumed vulgar Latin *extufa* (see STOVE).] ◇ **be** *or* **get in a stew** to be in a difficult situation or to become agitated or anxious (*informal*)

stew[2] /styoo/ *n.* **1.** FISHPOND a fishpond (*archaic*) **2.** OYSTER BED an artificial oyster bed [14thC. Via Old French *estui* 'confinement' from, ultimately, Latin *studium* (see STUDY).]

steward /styoo ərd/ *n.* **1.** TRANSP PLANE OR SHIP ATTENDANT sb who attends to the passengers on an aircraft or ship, or handles food provisions and dining arrangements on a ship **2.** PROPERTY MANAGER sb who manages the property, finances, or household of another **3.** HOTEL OR CLUB MANAGER sb who manages the domestic affairs of a hotel, club, college, or other establishment that provides meals or lodging **4.** = **shop steward 5.** OFFICIAL AT PUBLIC EVENT sb who acts as a marshal or official at a large public event ■ *vti.* (**-ards, -arding, -arded**) WORK AS STEWARD to work as a steward [Old English *stigweard,* from *stig* 'house, hall' (source of English *sty*[1]) + *weard* 'keeper' (see WARD)]

stewardess /styoo ərdiss/ *n.* a woman who attends to the passengers on an aircraft (*dated*)

Stewart /styoo ərt/, **Jackie** (*b.* 1939) British racing driver. He scored 27 Grand Prix wins (1965–73) and was three times world champion (1969, 1971, and 1973). Real name **John Young Stewart**

Jimmy Stewart

Stewart, Jimmy (1908–97) US actor. He was an appealing, drawling presence in dozens of films, and was most closely identified with his roles in *Mr Smith Goes to Washington* (1939) and *It's a Wonderful Life* (1946). Full name **James Maitland Stewart**

Stewart Island island in New Zealand, situated off the south coast of the South Island. Population: 417 (1996). Area: 1,735 sq. km/670 sq. mi.

stewed /styood/ *adj.* **1.** COOK SIMMERED cooked by slow simmering **2.** INTOXICATED very intoxicated (*slang*) **3.** MADE BITTER made bitter by being infused for too long ○ *stewed tea*

St. Ex. *abbr.* Stock Exchange

stey *Scotland* very steep ○ *a stey brae* [14thC. Origin uncertain.]

stg *abbr.* sterling

stge *abbr.* storage

Sth *abbr.* South

sthenia /sthə nī ə, sthe̱ēni-/ *n.* great strength or vitality (*archaic or formal*) [Late 18thC. Formed from Greek *sthenos* 'strength', of unknown origin.] —**sthenic** /sthénnik/ *adj.*

stibine /stíbbeen, -īn/ *n.* a foul-smelling poisonous gas produced by the action of hydrochloric acid on an alloy of antimony and zinc. Formula: SbH_3. [Mid-19thC. Coined from Greek *stibi* 'antimony' + -INE.]

stibnite /stíb nīt/ *n.* MINERALS a soft greyish crystalline mineral that is the chief ore of antimony [Mid-19thC. Coined from STIBINE + -ITE.]

stich /stik/ *n.* a line of poetry [Early 18thC. From Greek *stikhos* 'row, rank, line of verse'.]

Stich /stik, stikh/, **Michael** (*b.* 1968) German tennis player. He won both the Wimbledon Men's Singles (1991) and Men's Doubles (1992), and the ATP World Championship (1993).

stichomythia /stíkō míthi ə/ *n.* a form of dramatic dialogue in which characters speak single lines alternately [Mid-19thC. From Greek *stikhomuthia*, literally 'speaking in lines'.] —**stichomythic** *adj.*

stick[1] /stik/ *n.* **1.** TREES **THIN BRANCH** a thin branch or shoot cut or broken from a tree **2. WOOD USED FOR FUEL OR CONSTRUCTION** wood pieces used as fuel for a fire or as construction material **3. SPECIALLY SHAPED WOOD** a shaped piece of wood used for a specified purpose ○ *a hockey stick* **4. ROD** a rod, wand, or baton **5. CANE** a cane, club, or cudgel **6. SHORT THIN THING** a short slender part or piece ○ *a stick of celery* **7. STH USED TO SECURE COMPLIANCE** sth used to intimidate or coerce sb into compliant behaviour ○ *carrot and stick* **8. PERSON** sb of a particular kind (*dated informal*) ○ *He's a decent old stick.* **9.** *US* **BORING PERSON** sb who is dull or very formal and conventional in manner (*informal*) **10. CRITICISM** strong adverse criticism (*informal*) **11.** FURNITURE **FURNITURE** a piece of furniture (*informal*) ○ *We need a few sticks to furnish the flat* **12.** ARMS **BOMBS FALLING ON TARGET AT INTERVALS** a group of bombs that are arranged to fall on a target at regular intervals **13.** NAUT **SHIP'S MAST** a mast or spar on a ship **14.** PRINTING = **composing stick 15.** AIR **PARACHUTISTS JUMPING TOGETHER** a group of parachutists all jumping at the same time **16.** *Aus* SPORTS **SURFBOARD** a surfboard (*slang*) **17.** *US* DRUGS **CANNABIS CIGARETTE** a marijuana cigarette (*dated slang*) ■ **sticks** *npl.* **REMOTE PLACE** a rural or remote place or district, especially one that is unsophisticated or unfashionable (*informal*) ○ *living out in the sticks* ■ *vt.* (**sticks, sticking, sticked**) **1.** GARDENING **SUPPORT PLANT WITH STICK** to support a plant with a stake or stick **2.** PRINTING **USE COMPOSING STICK** to set type using a composing stick (*dated*) [Old English *sticca* 'peg'. Ultimately from an Indo-European base meaning 'to stick, stab', which is also the ancestor of English *stitch*, *stick*[2], *steak*, *stigma*, and *instigate*.] ◇ **in a cleft stick** in a situation where no possible course of action will bring a good result ◇ **get (hold of) the wrong end of the stick** to misunderstand what sb is saying

stick[2] /stik/ (**sticks, sticking, stuck** /stuk/, **stuck**) *v.* **1.** *vti.* **PENETRATE** to pierce, stab, or puncture sth, or be pierced, stabbed, or punctured **2.** *vt.* **FASTEN WITH POINTED OBJECT** to fasten sth in position by thrusting a pointed object such as a pin or nail through sth **3.** *vti.* **FASTEN WITH ADHESIVE** to fasten or fix sth, or remain attached, by means of an adhesive **4.** *vti.* **PROTRUDE** to protrude or cause sth to protrude ○ *She stuck out her hand.* **5.** *vt.* **PUT SOMEWHERE** to place or put sth in a location or position (*informal*) ○ *Stick it on the shelf.* **6.** *vti.* **BE UNABLE TO MOVE** to be at or cause to be at a standstill or unable to move or proceed ○ *be stuck in traffic* **7.** *vt.* **PUZZLE** to bewilder or perplex (*usually passive*) ○ *stuck for an answer* **8.** *vi.* **STAY IN THE MIND** to remain in the mind ○ *He told me all the facts but they didn't stick.* **9.** *vt.* **BE ABLE TO TOLERATE** to be able to tolerate or put up with a particular thing or person (*informal*) ○ *I can't stick him.* **10.** *vt.* **USE SB** to impose on or exploit sb (*usually passive*) ○ *stuck with the boring jobs* **11.** *vt.* **KILL ANIMAL** to kill an animal by stabbing ○ *stick a pig* [Old English *stician*. Ultimately from the same Indo-European base as *stick*[1].] ◇ **stick it to** to exploit sb or treat sb unfairly (*informal*) ◇ **stick your neck out** to take a risk or make yourself vulnerable (*informal*) ◇ **stick in your craw** *or* **throat** to be extremely distasteful or objectionable (*informal*) ◇ **stick to your guns** to stand firm or maintain an opinion ◇ **stick to your ribs** *US* to be substantial, nourishing, or hearty as a meal (*informal*) ◇ **be stuck on sb** to be infatuated with sb (*slang*) ◇ **stick it out** to persist with sth to the end, even when doing so is difficult

stick around, stick about *vti.* to linger or wait for sb or sth (*informal*)

stick at *vt.* to persist at sth ○ *stick at a job until it's done*

stick by *vt.* to remain loyal to sth or sb ○ *I'll stick by you no matter what.*

stick out *vt.* **1. EXTEND STH** to make sth protrude **2. PUT UP WITH** to endure sth disagreeable ○ *stick out a long wait*

stick to *v.* **1.** *vti.* **ADHERE TO** to adhere to sth, or make sth adhere to sth **2.** *vt.* **BE LOYAL TO** to be loyal or close to sb or sth **3.** *vt.* **PERSIST WITH** to persist with sth **4.** *vt.* **CONTINUE WITH** to keep to without digression

stick together *vi.* to stay close physically or to remain unified ○ *stuck together through thick and thin*

stick up *v.* **1.** *vti.* **BE UPRIGHT** to protrude or point upwards, or to make sth protrude or point upwards **2.** *vt. US* **ROB SB WITH GUNS** to carry out an armed robbery on sb (*informal*)

stick up for *vt.* to defend a belief or a person

stick with *vt.* **1. PERSIST WITH** to continue an enterprise rather than succumb to the temptation to cease **2. STAY LOYAL TO** to remain loyal or faithful to sb or sth

sticker /stíkər/ *n.* **1. STH WITH ADHESIVE** an adhesive label, poster, or paper **2. STH THAT STICKS** sth that or sb who sticks **3. SB PERSISTENT** sb who perseveres

stick-fighting *n. Carib* a highly stylized form of fighting in which two chanting combatants attempt to score points by striking each other with sticks

stick figure *n.* a simple or crude drawing of a person or animal with single lines for the torso, arms, and legs, and a circle for the head

stickhandle /stík hand'l/ (**-dles, -dling, -dled**) *vt.* to control and manoeuvre a ball or puck using a lacrosse or ice hockey stick —**stickhandler** *n.* —**stickhandling** *n.*

sticking plaster *n.* a plaster (*formal*)

sticking point *n.* an issue, detail, or item likely to cause difficulty or prevent progress from being made, e.g. in a negotiation

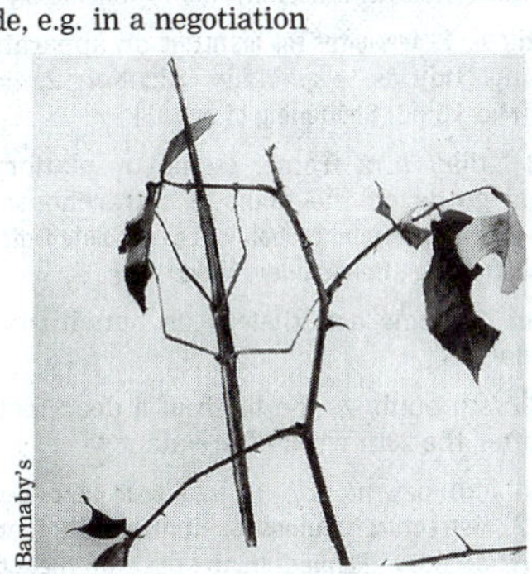

Barnaby's

Stick insect

stick insect *n.* a long brown or green insect that resembles a twig. Family: Phasmidae.

stick-in-the-mud *n.* sb who resists new ideas (*informal*)

stickle /stík'l/ (**-les, -ling, -led**) *vi.* to dispute stubbornly about trivial matters (*archaic*) [Early 17thC. Alteration of obsolete *stightle*, literally 'to keep trying to control things', from Old English *stihtian* 'to arrange, settle'.]

stickleback /stík'l bak/ (*plural* **-backs** *or* **-back**) *n.* **1. SMALL SPINY FISH** a small spiny-backed fish found in both salt and fresh water that has distinctive nest-building and courtship behaviour. Family: Gasterosteidae. **2. MINNOW** a minnow (*regional informal*) [15thC. *stickle*, from Old English *sticel* 'thorn, sting'.]

stickler /stíklər/ *n.* **1. SB FUSSY ABOUT DETAILS** sb who insists on every detail being right **2. PUZZLE** a puzzling or perplexing problem [Mid-16thC. Formed from STICKLE.]

stickseed /stík seed/ *n.* a plant found in Europe, Asia, and North America with prickly seeds that can stick to clothing. Genus: *Lappula.*

stick shift *n. US* a manually operated transmission in a motor vehicle, the gear stick that operates it, or a motor vehicle with a manual transmission

stick tackle *n.* an illegal challenge in hockey when a player hits another player's stick instead of the ball

sticktight /stík tīt/ *n.* a plant with barbed fruits that can stick to clothing or fur

stickup /stík up/, **stick-up** *n. US* an armed robbery (*informal*)

stickweed /stík weed/ (*plural* **-weeds** *or* **-weed**) *n.* a North American plant that has clinging seeds, especially ragweed

sticky /stíki/ *adj.* (**-ier, -iest**) **1. COVERED IN GLUEY STUFF** covered in sth gluey or viscous **2. ADHESIVE** having adhesive qualities **3. HUMID AND HOT** uncomfortably warm and humid ○ *sticky weather* **4.** *US* **SENTIMENTAL** cloying or excessively sentimental (*informal*) ■ *n. ANZ* = **stickybeak** (*informal*) —**stickily** *adv.* —**stickiness** *n.*

stickybeak /stíki beek/ *n. ANZ* (*informal*) **1. SB NOSY** sb who pries or snoops into the affairs of others **2. NOSY LOOK** an inquisitive look ■ *vi.* (**-beaks, -beaking, -beaked**) *ANZ* **SNOOP** to pry or snoop into the affairs of others (*informal*)

sticky end *n.* a nasty or unfortunate outcome (*informal*)

sticky-fingered *adj.* likely to steal things (*informal*)

sticky wicket *n.* **1. AWKWARD CRICKET PITCH** wetted by rain and then dried by sun, that makes the ball bounce awkwardly **2. TRICKY SITUATION** an awkward or difficult situation (*informal*)

stiff /stif/ *adj.* **1. RIGID** rigid, inflexible, or hard to move **2. NOT SUPPLE** painful and not supple ○ *stiff muscles* **3. SEVERE** very harsh or severe ○ *a stiff punishment* **4. TAXING** difficult or demanding ○ *stiff competition* **5. FORCEFUL** having force or power ○ *a stiff breeze* **6. STRONG** strong or potent to the taste or in effect on the body **7. RESOLUTE** showing determination and resolve ○ *stiff resistance* **8. TOO HIGH** higher than is justified or normal ○ *stiff prices* **9. FORMAL** rigidly formal or distant in manner ○ *a stiff manner* **10.** SAILING **NOT LIKELY TO CAPSIZE** relatively stable in the water **11. INTOXICATED** having had too much alcohol to drink (*slang*) ■ *adv.* **1. TOTALLY** totally or utterly ○ *bored stiff* **2. IN A STIFF WAY** in a stiff way or manner ■ *n.* **1.** *US* **PERSON** a person, especially sb of a particular type (*slang*) ○ *a lucky stiff* **2.** *US* **OFFENSIVE TERM** an offensive term referring to sb regarded as unpleasant or overly formal (*slang insult*) **3.** *US* **OFFENSIVE TERM** an offensive term referring to sb who leaves insufficient tips (*slang insult*) **4. CORPSE** a dead body (*slang*) **5. FLOP** sth that is an utter failure (*slang*) ■ *vt.* (**stiffs, stiffing, stiffed**) *US* **RENEGE** to fail to pay sb an amount due or expected (*slang*) ○ *He stiffed me on the tip.* [Old English *stīf*. Ultimately, from an Indo-European word meaning 'to compress, pack', which is also the ancestor of English *constipate* and *stevedore*).] —**stiffish** *adj.* —**stiffly** *adv.* —**stiffness** *n.*

stiffen /stíff'n/ (**-ens, -ening, -ened**) *vti.* **1. BECOME INFLEXIBLE** to become or make sth rigid or inflexible **2. STRENGTHEN STH** to make sth stronger or more effective or to become stronger or more effective ○ *stiffen regulations*

stiffie /stíffi/ *n.* **1. FORMAL INVITATION** a formal invitation card printed on high-quality stiff paper (*slang*) **2. OFFENSIVE TERM** an offensive term for an erect penis (*offensive slang*) [Late 20thC. From the stiff card that they are printed on.]

stiff-necked *adj.* extremely obstinate and arrogant

stifle[1] /stīf'l/ (**-fles, -fling, -fled**) *v.* **1.** *vti.* **SUFFOCATE** to impair sb's breathing or find it hard to breathe **2.** *vt.* **CHECK OR REPRESS** to curb, repress, or prevent the development of sth ○ *stifled the spreading discontent* **3.** *vt.* **REPRESS PHYSICAL ACT** to cut off a physical act, e.g.

a yawn or laugh, before it develops [14thC. Origin uncertain: probably an alteration of Old French *estouffer* 'to smother' (influenced by Old Norse *stífla* 'to stop up'), perhaps of prehistoric Germanic origin.] —**stifler** *n.*

stifle[2] /stíf'l/ *n.* the joint, corresponding to the human knee, in the hind leg of a four-legged animal [14thC. Origin uncertain: perhaps via Old French *estivel* 'leg' from, ultimately, Latin *stipes* 'stick, post'.]

stifling /stífling/ *adj.* **1. TOO HOT** uncomfortably hot and stuffy **2. REPRESSIVE** repressive in not allowing full expression —**stiflingly** *adv.*

stigma /stígmə/ *n.* **1. SIGN OF SOCIAL UNACCEPTABILITY** the shame or disgrace attached to sth regarded as socially unacceptable **2.** BOT **PLANT PART** the part of a flower's female reproductive organ (**carpel**) that receives the male pollen grains. It is generally located at the tip of a slender projecting style. **3. stigma** (*plural* **-mata**) **MARK ON SKIN** a mark on the skin indicating, e.g. a medical condition **4.** ZOOL **SPOT ON BUTTERFLIES** a coloured mark or spot, often resembling an eye, found on certain protozoans and invertebrates, especially butterflies and other lepidoptera [Late 16thC. Via Latin from Greek, 'mark on the skin', from *stig-*, the stem of *stizein* 'to prick'. Ultimately from an Indo-European base that is also the ancestor of English *stick*[1] and *instigate*.]

stigmasterol /stig mástərol/ *n.* a sterol found in soybeans and calabar beans, used in making progesterone. Formula: $C_{29}H_{48}O$. [Early 20thC. Coined from a shortening of *Physostigma* genus name of calabar bean + STEROL.]

stigmata /stígmətə, stig máatə/ *npl.* marks on the hands and feet resembling the wounds from Jesus Christ's crucifixion [Mid-17thC. From Greek, the plural of stigma (see STIGMA).]

stigmatic /stig máttik/ *adj.* **1. SOCIALLY UNACCEPTABLE** socially unacceptable **2.** OPTICS = **anastigmatic** ■ *n.* **SB WITH STIGMATA** sb who bears stigmata [Late 16thC. Formed from Greek *stigmat-*, the stem of *stigma* (see STIGMA). In sense 2, back-formation from ASTIGMATIC.]

stigmatism /stígmətizəm/ *n.* **1.** OPHTHALMOL **PROPERTIES OF AN ANASTIGMATIC LENS** the properties of an anastigmatic lens **2.** MED **BEING ANASTIGMATIC** the condition in which the eye focuses normally **3.** CHR **HAVING STIGMATA** the condition of having stigmata [Mid-19thC. In senses 1 and 2, back-formation from ASTIGMATISM.]

stigmatist /stígmətist/ *n.* = **stigmatic**

stigmatize /stígmə tīz/ (**-tizes, -tizing, -tized**), **stigmatise** (**-tises, -tising, -tised**) *v.* **1.** *vt.* **LABEL AS SOCIALLY UNDESIRABLE** to label sb or sth as socially undesirable **2.** *vti.* **MARK WITH STIGMA** to mark sb or be marked with a stigma or stigmata —**stigmatization** /stígmə tī záysh'n/ *n.* —**stigmatizer** /stígmə tīzər/ *n.*

stilb /stilb/ *n.* a unit of luminescence equal to 1 candela per square centimetre [Mid-20thC. Via French from Greek *stilbein* 'to glitter', of unknown origin.]

stilbene /stíl been/ *n.* a crystalline solid used in making dyes. Formula: $C_{14}H_{12}$. [Mid-19thC. Coined from Greek *stilbein* 'to glitter' + -ENE.]

stilbestrol *n.* = **stilboestrol**

stilbite /stíl bīt/ *n.* a white or yellow mineral consisting of a silicate of aluminium, calcium, and sodium chemically combined with water [Early 19thC. Coined from Greek *stilbein* 'to glitter' + -ITE; from its lustrous crystals.]

stilboestrol /stil béess trol/, **stilbestrol** *n.* = **diethylstilboestrol** [Mid-20thC. Coined from STILBENE + OESTRUS + -OL.]

stile[1] /stīl/ *n.* a step or rung that enables people to climb over a fence or wall [Old English *stigel*. Ultimately from an Indo-European base meaning 'to step, climb', which is also the ancestor of English *stair* and *stirrup*.]

stile[2] /stīl/ *n.* a vertical piece in a door, frame, or panel [Late 17thC. Origin uncertain: probably via Dutch *stijl* 'prop, doorpost' from, ultimately, Latin *stilus* 'column, post' (see STYLUS).]

stilet /stílət/ *n.* **1. WIRE IN CATHETER** a wire inserted in a catheter to give it rigidity **2. WIRE USED AS PROBE** a fine wire used as a probe in surgery [Late 17thC. Via French from Italian *stiletto* (see STILETTO).]

stiletto /sti léttō/ *n.* (*plural* **stilettos** *or* **stilettoes**) **1.** ARMS **SMALL DAGGER** a small dagger with a narrow tapering blade **2. POINTED TOOL** a pointed tool for making holes in fabric or leather **3.** CLOTHES = **stiletto heel** ■ *vt.* (**stilettos, stilettoing, stilettoed**) **TO STAB WITH A STILETTO** to stab sb with a stiletto [Early 17thC. From Italian, literally 'small dagger', from *stilo* 'dagger', from Latin *stilus* (see STYLUS).]

stiletto heel *n.* a high pointed heel on a woman's shoe, or a shoe with such a heel

Stilicho /stíllikō/, **Flavius** (359?–408) Roman general and politician. As guardian of the emperor Flavius Honorius during his minority, he virtually ruled the West Roman Empire.

still[1] /stil/ *adj.* **1. NOT MOVING** motionless and undisturbed **2.** BEVERAGES **NOT CARBONATED** not sparkling or bubbly **3. QUIET** subdued, gentle, or quiet **4.** PHOTOGRAPHY **TAKING STATIC PHOTOGRAPHS** designed for, or relating to the process of, taking photographs as opposed to making films ■ *adv.* **SILENTLY OR WITHOUT MOTION** without sound or movement ■ *n.* **1. PEACE** silence or peace (*literary*) **2.** CINEMA **SCENE FROM A FILM** a photographic print, either made from a single frame of a film or shot independently with a still camera during production ■ *v.* (**stills, stilling, stilled**) **1.** *vti.* **MAKE CALM** to make sb or cause sb to become quiet, calm, soundless, or immobile **2.** *vt.* **RELIEVE** to allay or relieve ○ *stilled our fears* [Old English *stille*. Ultimately from an Indo-European base meaning 'to stay put', which is also the ancestor of English *stall*[2], *stele*, and *apostle*.] —**stillness** *n.*

WORD KEY: SYNONYMS

See Synonyms at ***calm***.

still[2] /stil/ *adv.* **1. EXISTING NOW** an adverb used to indicate that a situation that used to exist has continued, and exists now ○ *The original is still my favourite.* ○ *I still believe it's a mistake.* ○ *It was still light.* **2. EVEN AT THIS TIME** used to emphasize that sth is the case even up to the point mentioned ○ *Her birthday is still a month away.* ○ *He may still be around.* ○ *Still to come...* **3. EVEN MORE** used to emphasize that there is even more of a quality or quantity (*often used with a comparative*) ○ *Profits next year will be larger still.* ○ *The market for flour is equal to almost any in the West, and it will be still better.* **4. NEVERTHELESS** used to emphasize that sth remains the case in spite of the situation mentioned ○ *How am I going to do your work and still have time to do my own?* **5. ALWAYS** always or constantly (*archaic or literary*) [13thC. From STILL[1]. The present-day meanings evolved via 'constantly' from 'motionlessly'.]

still[3] /stil/ *n.* **1. APPARATUS FOR DISTILLING** an apparatus for distilling liquids, especially alcohol **2.** = **distillery** [Mid-16thC. Shortening of DISTIL.]

stillage /stíllij/ *n.* a frame, stand, or platform for keeping goods off the floor in a warehouse [Late 16thC. Origin uncertain: probably from obsolete Dutch *stellagie* 'scaffolding', from *stellen* 'to set up'.]

still and all *adv.* nonetheless or notwithstanding (*informal*)

stillbirth /stíl búrth/ *n.* the birth of a dead foetus or baby after the 28th week of pregnancy

stillborn /stíl bawrn/ *adj.* **1.** MED **BORN DEAD** dead at birth **2. INEFFECTUAL** useless or ineffectual from the start [Mid-16thC. Formed from STILL[1] in the obsolete meaning 'dead'.]

still frame *n.* a single frame from a film or television programme displayed as a photograph

still hunt *n.* *US* a hunt in which game is stalked or ambushed

still-hunt *vt.* *US* to hunt game by stalking or ambushing

still life (*plural* **still lifes**) *n.* **1. PORTRAYAL OF STH INANIMATE** a representation of inanimate objects, e.g. fruit, flowers, or food, often in a domestic setting, in paintings, pictures, and photographs (*hyphenated when used before a noun*) ○ *a still-life class* **2. STYLE OF STILL LIFE PORTRAYALS** the style or genre of still life used in the various arts such as painting and photography

still room *n.* **1.** BEVERAGES **ROOM FOR DISTILLING** a room in which distilling is done **2.** HOUSEHOLD **PANTRY** a pantry or storeroom off the kitchen of a large house

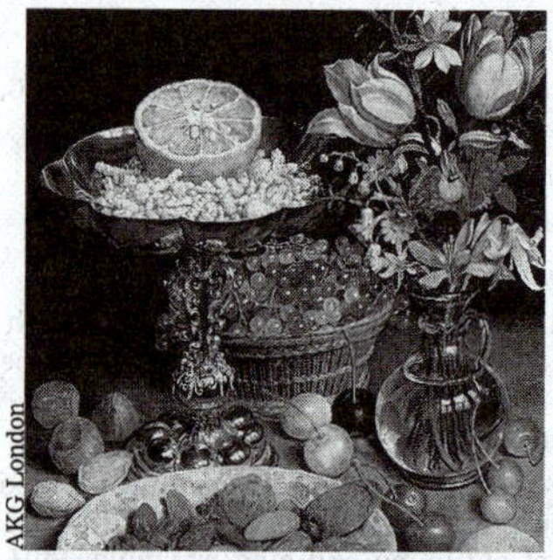

Still life: *Still life with Dessert and Bouquet* (1632) by Georg Flegel

Still's disease /stílz-/ *n.* chronic arthritis that develops in children under the age of 16 [Early 20thC. Named after the English physician Sir George *Still* 1868–1941.]

Stillson /stílss'n-/ *tdmk.* trademark for a monkey wrench whose serrated jaws tighten when pressure is applied to the wrench handle

stilt /stilt/ *n.* **1. POLE FOR WALKING** either of two poles with footrests high off the ground on which sb balances and walks **2.** CONSTR **SUPPORTING POST** a tall post or column that supports a structure above land or water **3.** BIRDS **LONG-LEGGED WADING BIRD** a three-toed, straight-billed, black-and-white shore bird that lives near ponds and marshes. Genera: *Himantopus* and *Cladorhynchus.* ■ *vt.* (**stilts, stilting, stilted**) **RAISE ON STILTS** to place or raise sth up on stilts [14thC. Origin uncertain: probably from Low German; ultimately from an Indo-European base meaning 'to set up', which is also the ancestor of English *stout*, *stalk*[1], and *still*[1].]

stilted /stíltid/ *adj.* **1. NOT FLUENT** lacking fluency in being halting or unnatural in flow **2. FORMAL** pompous or unduly formal **3.** BUILDING **RESTING ON VERTICAL PIECES OF STONE** used to describe an arch that is joined to its supporting impost by vertical pieces of stone [Early 17thC. Originally, 'having stilts'. The sense 'not fluent' evolved via the idea of being unnaturally elevated, hence, 'restrained'.]

Stilton[1] /stíltən/ *n.* either of two strong-flavoured British white cheeses made from whole milk, one veined with blue mould, the other plain [Mid-18thC. Named after the village of STILTON in Cambridgeshire, where the cheese was originally sold.]

Stilton[2] /stíltən/ village near Peterborough, in eastern England. It gave its name to Stilton cheese, made in the surrounding areas. Population: 2,219 (1991).

stimulant /stímmyōōlənt/ *n.* **1. SOURCE OF STIMULUS** sth that provides a stimulus, incentive, or quickening **2.** MED **AGENT PRODUCING INCREASE IN FUNCTIONAL ACTIVITY** a drug or other agent that produces a temporary increase in functional activity of a body organ or part ■ *adj.* **INCREASING ACTIVITY** increasing bodily activity or acting as a stimulus or incentive

stimulate /stímmyōō layt/ (**-lates, -lating, -lated**) *vt.* **1. ENCOURAGE** to encourage sth, e.g. an activity or a process, so that it will begin, increase, or develop **2. MAKE INTERESTED** to cause sb to become interested in or excited about sth **3. CAUSE TO RESPOND** to cause physical activity in sth such as a nerve or an organ [Early 16thC. From Latin *stimulat-*, the past participle stem of *stimulare*, literally 'to goad', from *stimulus* (see STIMULUS).] —**stimulable** *adj.* —**stimulating** *adj.* —**stimulatingly** *adv.* —**stimulation** /stímmyōō láysh'n/ *n.* —**stimulative** /stímmyōōlətiv/ *adj.* —**stimulator** /stímmyōō laytər/ *n.* —**stimulatory** /stímmyōōlətəri/ *adj.*

stimulus /stímmyōōləss/ (*plural* **-li** /stím yōō lī/) *n.* **1. INCENTIVE** sth that encourages an activity or a process to begin, increase, or develop **2. STH AROUSING INTEREST** an agent or factor that provokes interest, enthusiasm, or excitement **3. CAUSE OF A RESPONSE** sth, e.g. a drug or an electrical impulse, that causes a physical response in an organism [Late 17thC. From Latin, 'goad, stake', of uncertain origin.]

sting /sting/ *v.* (**stings, stinging, stung** /stung/) **1.** *vti.* **INJECT WITH TOXIN** to prick the skin and inject a small quantity of a poisonous or irritant substance, causing a sharp pain often followed by itchiness and swelling **2.** *vti.* PRODUCE SHARP PAIN to feel, or cause sb to feel, a sharp pain, usually only for a short period of time ○ *His eyes were stinging with the onions.* **3.** *vt.* UPSET to make sb feel upset, hurt, or annoyed ○ *I was stung by her harsh criticisms.* **4.** *vt.* GOAD to urge sb on, usually with criticism ○ *words that stung them into action* **5.** *vt.* OVERCHARGE to overcharge sb (*informal*) ○ *They stung me £800 for re-painting the wall.* **6.** *vt.* BORROW MONEY FROM to borrow money from sb (*informal*) ○ *I might be able to sting my old man for a tenner.* ■ *n.* **1.** WOUND CAUSED BY STING a skin wound that may hurt, swell up, and itch, caused by an insect, plant, or animal piercing the skin and injecting a small quantity of poison **2.** POISON-INJECTING ORGAN the sharp organ through which an insect or other animal injects poison to immobilize its prey or for defence. US term **stinger**[1] *n.* 3 **3.** SHARP PAIN a short sharp pain, e.g. that caused by the application of an antiseptic to a fresh wound **4.** HURTFULNESS the hurtful nature of sth, e.g. criticism **5.** POWER TO UPSET the power to inflict mental or emotional discomfort ○ *threats that have lost their sting* **6.** = **stinging hair 7.** *US* TRICK an underhand scheme, especially a carefully planned and orchestrated swindle (*slang*) [Old English *stingan*] —**stinging** *adj.* —**stingingly** *adv.*

Sting /sting/ (*b.* 1952) British singer, songwriter, and actor. He formed the group The Police (1978–84), and later pursued a solo singing and acting career. Real name **Gordon Sumner**

stinger[1] /stíngər/ *n.* **1.** STH STINGING sth that stings, especially a hurtful or critical comment **2.** *ANZ* STINGING ANIMAL OR PLANT an animal or plant that stings, especially the box jellyfish **3.** *US* = **sting** *n.* 2 **4.** BLOW a sharp blow or slap that causes a smarting pain (*informal*) **5.** *US* UNDERCOVER OFFICER a law enforcement officer who is taking part in an undercover operation (*informal*)

stinger[2] /stíngər/ *n.* BEVERAGES **1.** *US* COCKTAIL a cocktail consisting of crème de menthe and brandy **2.** WHISKY DRINK a whisky and soda with crushed ice [Early 20thC. Alteration of STENGAH.]

stinging cell *n.* = **cnidoblast**

stinging hair *n.* a glandular plant hair, e.g. on a stinging nettle, that releases an irritant chemical when touched

stinging nettle *n.* = **nettle** *n.* 1

stingless bee /stíngləss-/ *n.* a social bee that has no functional sting, but may bite. Subfamily: Meliponinae.

stingo /stíng gō/ *n.* strong beer, especially an English beer originally made in Yorkshire (*archaic*) [Mid-17thC. Formed from STING; from the beer's sharp taste.]

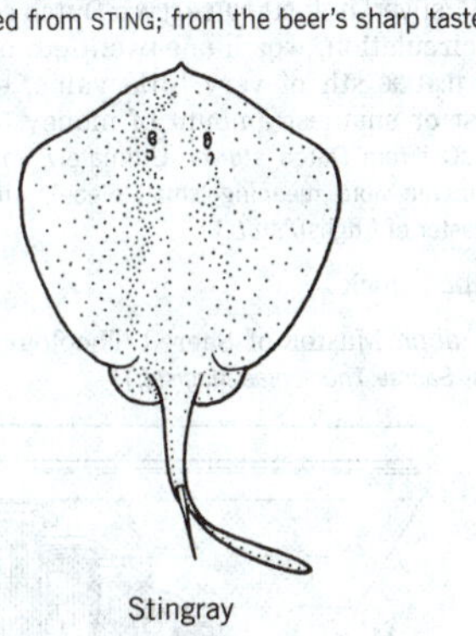

Stingray

stingray /stíng ray/ (*plural* **-rays** *or* **-ray**) *n.* a ray with a flexible tail shaped like a whip with poisonous spines. There are several species, mainly found in shallow warm waters. Family: Dasyatidae.

stingy[1] /stínji/ (**-gier, -giest**) *adj.* (*informal*) **1.** UNGENEROUS not generous in giving or spending money **2.** SMALL OR INADEQUATE ungenerously small or inadequate ○ *a stingy tip* [Mid-17thC. Origin uncertain: perhaps formed from a variant of STING, with an underlying meaning 'irritable, bad-tempered'.] —**stingily** *adv.* —**stinginess** *n.*

stingy[2] /stíngi/ *adj.* (**-ier, -iest**) STINGING stinging or capable of stinging (*informal*) ■ *n.* (*plural* **-ies**) *Wales* NETTLE a nettle (*informal*)

stink /stingk/ *vi.* (**stinks, stinking, stank** /stangk/ *or* **stunk** /stungk/, **stunk**) **1.** SMELL HORRIBLE to have a very strong and extremely unpleasant smell **2.** BE WORTHLESS to be loathsomely bad or worthless (*informal*) ○ *This poetry is so bad it stinks.* **3.** BE CORRUPT to be despicably corrupt or dishonest (*informal*) ○ *The whole admissions process stinks.* **4.** HAVE TOO MUCH to have, or be suspected of having, been assisted by improper influence (*informal*) ○ *a career that stinks of nepotism* ■ *n.* **1.** TERRIBLE SMELL a very strong and unpleasant smell **2.** SCANDAL a scandalous revelation (*informal*) ○ *'even if there was a stink, he had plenty good friends in San Francisco'* (Robert Louis Stevenson, *The Wrecker*; 1896) [Old English *stincan* 'to smell'] —**stinkily** *adv.* —**stinky** *adj.* ◇ **like stink** very hard or fast (*informal*) ◇ **make a stink, kick up a stink, raise a stink** to cause trouble, especially by protesting (*informal*)

WORD KEY: SYNONYMS

See Synonyms at ***smell***.

stink out *vt.* **1.** GIVE FOUL SMELL TO to give sth a very strong and unpleasant smell ○ *The smell of rotting cabbage stank the whole place out.* US term **stink up 2.** DRIVE OUT to drive a person or animal out of a place by introducing a strong and unpleasant smell

stink up *vt. US* = **stink out** *v.* 2

stinkball /stíngk bawl/ *n.* = **stinkpot** *n.* 4

stink bomb *n.* a practical joker's toy in the form of a small glass or plastic capsule that, when smashed, emits a horrible smell

stinkbug /stíngk bug/ *n.* an insect that emits foul-smelling secretions. It typically has a flattish body, and is often camouflaged to blend with its surroundings. Family: Pentatomidae.

stinker /stíngkər/ *n.* (*informal*) **1.** STH UNPLEASANT sth that is very difficult or unpleasant ○ *That last exam was a real stinker.* **2.** BAD BEHAVER sb who behaves in an obnoxious or hateful way **3.** BIRDS SPITTING SEABIRD a fulmar or petrel that spits a foul-smelling oil at aggressors. They feed on offal and carrion.

stinkhorn /stíngk hawrn/ *n.* a fungus with a thick white stalk and a thimble-shaped foul-smelling cap containing spores. The smell attracts flies, which disperse the spores. Order: Phallales.

stinking /stíngking/ *adj.* **1.** SMELLY having or giving off a very strong and unpleasant smell **2.** EXTREMELY BAD used to describe an action or behaviour regarded as unpleasant or contemptible (*informal*) ○ *'This was, of course, a stinking lie'.* (Richard Kadrey, *Metrophage*; 1995) **3.** INTOXICATED very intoxicated (*slang*) ■ *adv.* USED FOR EMPHASIS used to emphasize the contemptible extent of sth (*informal*) —**stinkingly** *adv.*

stinking ash *n.* a deciduous tree with fragrant greenish-white flowers, native to eastern North America. Its fruits have a flavour similar to hops and are used in brewing beer. Latin name: *Ptelea trifoliata.*

stinking badger *n.* = **teledu** [From the foul-smelling secretion that the animal ejects]

stinking camomile *n.* an annual plant, similar to a daisy, with foul-smelling leaves. It grows as a weed on cultivated and waste ground throughout Europe. Latin name: *Anthemis cotula.*

stinking cedar *n.* = **California nutmeg** [From its foul-smelling leaves and wood]

stinko /stíngkō/ *adj.* **1.** INTOXICATED very intoxicated (*dated slang*) **2.** *US* POOR-QUALITY of the poorest quality (*informal*) ○ *a stinko bowl of stew*

stinkpot /stíngk pot/ *n.* **1.** STH WITH HORRIBLE SMELL sb or sth that smells horrible (*informal humorous*) **2.** OFFENSIVE TERM an offensive term referring to sb considered very unpleasant or unpopular (*slang insult*) **3.** ZOOL SMALL N AMERICAN TURTLE a small species of musk turtle found in ponds and sluggish streams in the United States. It emits a foul-smelling secretion from its cloacal glands. Latin name: *Sternotherus odoratus.* **4.** ARMS STINKING WEAPON a military weapon used in former times, consisting of an earthenware pot that released a suffocating vapour when thrown into an enemy position or onto an enemy ship

stinkstone /stíngk stōn/ *n.* rock, especially limestone, that gives off a highly unpleasant odour when rubbed or struck [Early 20thC. Translation of German *Stinkstein.*]

stinkweed /stíngk weed/ (*plural* **-weeds** *or* **-weed**) *n.* **1.** = **wall rocket 2.** FOUL-SMELLING PLANT a plant with unpleasant-smelling flowers or foliage, e.g. mayweed or pennycress

stinkwood /stíngk wŏŏd/ (*plural* **-woods** *or* **-wood**) *n.* **1.** TREE WITH FOUL-SMELLING WOOD a tree with unpleasant-smelling wood, in particular a South African deciduous tree whose hard wood is used for making furniture **2.** WOOD the hard durable wood of any of the stinkwood trees [Mid-18thC. Translation of Dutch *stinkhout.*]

stinky /stíngki/ *adj.* (*informal*) **1.** SMELLING STRONG with a strong and unpleasant smell ○ *one of those stinky cheeses* **2.** NASTY unfair, dishonest, or devious — **stinkily** *adv.*

stint[1] /stint/ *v.* (**stints, stinting, stinted**) **1.** *vi.* BE MISERLY to be ungenerous in offering, providing, or giving ○ *For a really good mousse, you can't stint on the chocolate.* **2.** *vt.* DENY to deny sb sth out of miserliness, or deny sth of the self, usually in an act of sacrifice ○ *'your mother and me economizing and stinting ourselves to give you a University education'* (Thomas Hardy, *Tess of the d'Urbervilles*; 1891) ■ *n.* **1.** ALLOTTED TIME a fixed period of time spent on a particular task or job ○ *do a two-year stint as an apprentice* **2.** LIMITATION limitation or restriction, especially one of time or amount ○ *'I gave him time and thought without stint'* (Willa Cather, *The Professor's House*; 1925) [Old English *styntan* 'to blunt', later reinforced by Old Norse *stytta* 'to shorten'] —**stinter** *n.*

stint[2] /stint/ (*plural* **stints** *or* **stint**) *n.* BIRDS any one of various sandpipers [15thC. Origin unknown.]

stip. *abbr.* **1.** stipend **2.** stipulation

stipe /stīp/ *n.* **1.** BOT FUNGUS OR FERN STALK the stalk of a mushroom or fern **2.** ZOOL = **stipes** *n.* 1 [Late 18thC. Via French from Latin *stipes* (see STIPES).]

stipel /stíp'l/ *n.* a structure shaped like a tiny leaf or scale located at the base of a leaflet of a compound leaf [Early 19thC. Via French from modern Latin *stipella*, literally 'small stipule', from *stipula* (see STIPULE).] —**stipellate** /sti péllət/ *adj.*

stipend /stī pend/ *n.* a fixed amount of money paid at regular intervals as a salary or to cover living expenses, especially one paid to a member of the clergy [15thC. Directly or via Old French from Latin *stipendium* 'soldier's pay', from *stips* 'payment' + *pendere* 'to weigh out' (see PENSIVE).]

WORD KEY: SYNONYMS

See Synonyms at ***wage***.

stipendiary /stī péndi əri/ *adj.* **1.** PROVIDED WITH ALLOWANCE receiving a fixed amount of money on a regular basis as a salary or to cover living expenses **2.** WITH STIPEND paying a stipend or paid for by a stipend ■ *n.* (*plural* **-ies**) SB RECEIVING STIPEND sb who receives a fixed amount of money on a regular basis as a salary or to cover living expenses, e.g. a priest or magistrate

stipes /stī peez/ (*plural* **stipites** /stíppi teez/) *n.* **1.** ZOOL MOUTHPART the second or bottom mouthpart of some insects and crustaceans **2.** ZOOL EYESTALK the eyestalk of a crayfish or crab **3.** BOT = **stipe** *n.* 1 [Mid-18thC. Via modern Latin from Latin, 'post'.] —**stipitiform** /stíppiti fawrm/ *adj.*

stipple /stípp'l/ *vt.* (**-ples, -pling, -pled**) **1.** PAINT BY DABBING to paint, draw, or engrave sth using dots or short dabbing strokes **2.** APPLY WITH DABBING STROKES to apply paint or any other substance in dots or short dabbing strokes **3.** MAKE SURFACE MATERIAL APPEAR GRAINY to give sth, e.g. wet paint or plaster, a rough grainy texture with dabbing strokes **4.** DAPPLE to mark sth with dots or speckles (*literary*) (*usually passive*) ○ *its lime-green weatherboard stippled with sunlight* ■ *n.* **1.** PAINTING ARTISTIC TECHNIQUE the technique of painting, engraving, or drawing using dots or short dabbing strokes **2.** CONSTR DABBED FINISH an irregular or grainy finish in paint or wet plaster, produced using dabbing strokes [Mid-18thC. From Dutch *stippelen*, literally 'to keep pricking', from, ultimately, *stip* 'point, dot'.] —**stippler** *n.* —**stippling** *n.*

stipulate[1] /stíppyoŏ layt/ (-lates, -lating, -lated) v. 1. vt. **SPECIFY** to specify sth such as a condition when making an agreement or an offer ○ *The contract stipulates which expenses will be covered.* 2. vti. **DEMAND** to make a specific demand for sth, usually as a condition in an agreement ○ *stipulate a price* 3. vt. **MAKE FORMAL PROMISE** to promise sth formally or legally 4. vi. **LAW AGREE** to agree, in terms of the conduct of a legal proceeding ○ *We will stipulate to our receipt of all pertinent discovery documents, my lord.* 5. vti. **MAKE ORAL CONTRACT** in Roman Law, to make an oral contract in the form of question and answer [Early 17thC. From Latin *stipulat-*, the past participle stem of *stipulari* 'to demand, bargain', of uncertain origin.] —**stipulable** adj. —**stipulation** /stíppyoŏ láysh'n/ n. —**stipulator** /stíp yoŏ laytər/ n. —**stipulatory** /stíppyoŏlatəri/ adj.

stipulate[2] /stíppyoŏ layt/ adj. used to describe a stem or stalk that has a pair of growths resembling leaves (**stipules**) at the base [Late 18thC. Formed from **STIPULE**.]

stipule /stíppyool/ n. either of a pair of small growths at the base of a leaf stalk or stem that resemble leaves [Late 18thC. Directly or via French from Latin *stipula* 'straw, stalk' (source of English *stubble*), of uncertain origin.] —**stipular** /stíppyoŏlər/ adj.

stir[1] /stur/ v. (**stirs, stirring, stirred**) 1. vt. **MIX INGREDIENTS** to move a spoon, stick, or some other implement through a liquid in order to mix or cool the contents ○ *Slowly stir the cream into the soup.* 2. vi. **BE ABLE TO BE STIRRED** to be of a consistency that allows a spoon or other implement to be moved around 3. vti. **MOVE** to move gently or cause sth to move gently 4. vi. **LEAVE** to move or leave, especially from a favourite or usual place ○ *The guards were told not to stir from their posts.* 5. vi. **MOVE AFTER RESTING** to get up and move about, especially after a rest ○ *anyone stirring at this early hour* 6. vt. **GOAD INTO ACTION** to rouse sb into action 7. vt. **AROUSE FEELING** to arouse sth, e.g. an emotion or a memory (*formal*) 8. vi. **BE FELT** to begin to be experienced as an emotion (*formal*) ○ *Deep-seated bitterness began to stir within him.* 9. vti. **MAKE EMOTIONAL** to arouse strong emotions in sb ○ *music that never fails to stir me* 10. vi. **HAPPEN** to happen or be current (*informal*) ○ *What's stirring this week at Westminster?* ■ n. 1. **ACT OF STIRRING** an act or instance of stirring a liquid 2. **COMMOTION** a fervent reaction, usually either excitement or controversy 3. **SLIGHT MOVEMENT** a gentle movement 4. *Aus* **TROUBLE** trouble (*informal*) 5. *NZ* **NOISY PARTY** a raucous party (*informal*) [Old English *styrian* 'to agitate'. Ultimately from an Indo-European word meaning 'to whirl', which is also the ancestor of English *storm, turbine,* and *disturb*.] —**stirrable** adj. ◇ **for a stir** *Aus* with the aim of making mischief (*informal*)

stir up vt. 1. **CAUSE TROUBLE** to cause trouble or a confrontation deliberately 2. **AGITATE** to cause sth such as dust to rise and swirl around

stir[2] /stur/ n. prison (*slang*) [Mid-19thC. Origin uncertain: perhaps from Romany *sturbin* 'jail'.]

stirabout /stúra bowt/ n. 1. **ACTIVE PERSON** sb who finds it difficult to sit still 2. *Ireland* **PORRIDGE** porridge (*archaic*)

stir-crazy adj. mentally unsettled as a result of spending a long time in a confined space, e.g. a prison cell (*informal or humorous*) [From STIR[2]]

stir-fry vt. **FRY FOOD RAPIDLY** to fry small tender pieces of food rapidly in a small amount of oil over high heat, stirring continuously. This method is used extensively in Chinese cookery. ■ n. **STIR-FRIED DISH** a dish of food prepared by stir-frying

stirk /sturk/ n. a young cow or bullock of varying age (*regional*) [Old English *stirc*, of uncertain origin: probably from a prehistoric Germanic word meaning 'small steer', which is also the ancestor of English *steer*[2]]

Stirling /stúrling/ 1. town in central Scotland, on the River Forth. Population: 30,515 (1991). 2. town in southern South Australia. Population: 16,150 (1996).

Stirling /stúrling/, **Sir James** (1926–92) British architect. His postmodernist style is exemplified by the Staatsgalerie Stuttgart (1977–84) and Clore Gallery, London (1980–86). Full name **Sir James Frazer Stirling**

Stirling engine /stúrling-/ n. an external-combustion engine in which heat generated on the outside of the cylinders causes either air or an inert gas within the cylinders to expand and drive the pistons [Mid-19thC. Named after the Scottish minister and engineer Revd Robert *Stirling* (1790–1878), who invented it.]

Stirling Ranges mountain range in southwestern Western Australia. Its highest peak is Bluff Knoll, 1,073 m/3,520 ft.

Stirling's formula /stúrlingz-/ n. a mathematical formula used to calculate the approximate value of the factorial of a very large number [Mid-20thC. Named after the Scottish mathematician James *Stirling* (1692–1770), who devised the formula.]

stirps /sturps/ (plural **stirpes** /stúr peez/) n. 1. **HERALDRY STOCK** a line of descendants from a common ancestor 2. **BOT PLANT VARIETY** a plant variety in which the characters are fixed through cultivation [Late 17thC. From Latin, 'stem, lineage', of unknown origin.]

stirrer /stúrər/ n. sb who deliberately causes trouble or provokes confrontation, often by spreading rumours or divulging confidences (*informal*)

stirring /stúring/ adj. 1. **CAUSING EMOTIONAL REACTION** causing an emotional or excited reaction 2. **LIVELY** full of energy and vitality ○ *a stirring rendition of a Chopin mazurka* ■ n. 1. **MOVEMENT** a slight movement 2. **AROUSING OF FEELING** the awakening of sth, especially an emotion or memory (*formal*) [Old English *styrend, styring*] —**stirringly** adv.

stirrup /stírrəp/ n. 1. **EQU HORSERIDER'S FOOT SUPPORT** a flat-bottomed metal ring hanging from a strap on each side of a horse's saddle. It provides support for a rider's foot. 2. **STRAP** a loop or strap that supports a foot or passes under a foot, such as the straps supporting a woman's feet in childbirth 3. **NAUT SHIP'S ROPE** one of a set of ropes hanging from a sail-supporting spar (**yard**) on a ship. Loops at the bottom allow another rope for standing on to be threaded through. [Old English *stigrap*, literally 'rope for getting up', from *stigan* 'to go up' (see STY) + *rap* 'rope']

stirrup bone n. the stapes [From its shape]

stirrup cup n. a farewell drink of alcohol, originally one shared with a departing horserider

stirrup leather n. a leather strap that attaches a stirrup to the saddle

stirrup pants npl. *US* = ski pants

stirrup pump n. a portable hand-operated pump, held on the ground with the feet, which draws water from a bucket, and sprays it out. It is used to fight small fires. [From the shape of the foot-piece used to hold the pump in place]

stishie n. *Scotland* = stushie

stishovite /stísha vīt/ n. a rare crystalline form of quartz found in meteor craters. It is formed from common quartz by the tremendous pressure produced on impact. [Mid-20thC. Named after the 20th-century Russian geochemist S. M. *Stishov*, who first synthesized it.]

stitch /stich/ n. 1. **SEW LENGTH OF THREAD IN MATERIAL** a short length of thread that has been passed through one or more pieces of material, either for decoration or to join pieces together 2. **SURG SURGICAL THREAD** a single loop of surgical thread used to close up a wound 3. **KNITTING LOOP OF WOOL** a single loop of wool or similar material, passed around a knitting needle or a crochet hook 4. **CRAFT STYLE OF NEEDLEWORK** a specified style of sewing or knitting ○ *lock stitch* 5. **ACHING PAIN** cramp in the side of the abdomen caused e.g. by exercising or laughing 6. **ARTICLE OF CLOTHING** a single article of clothing (*informal*) ○ *didn't have a stitch on* 7. **AGRIC RIDGE BETWEEN FURROWS** the ridge between two adjacent furrows in a field ■ vt. (**stitches, stitching, stitched**) 1. **SEW** to join, finish, or decorate sth with stitches 2. **SURG CLOSE WOUND** to close a wound with one or more stitches 3. **PRINTING BIND PAGES** to bind the pages of a book, pamphlet, or other publication with thread or staples [Old English *stice* 'prick'. Ultimately from Indo-European, meaning 'to jab' (ancestor also of English *stick*). Sense 7, 'ridge', probably from the same source, the underlying idea being 'cut, divided land'.] —**stitcher** n. ◇ **in stitches** laughing a great deal

stitch up vt. 1. **SEW** to sew fabric or an article, or repair sth by sewing it 2. **CLOSE WOUND** to close wound with stitches ■ 1. **CLOSE SB'S WOUND** to close

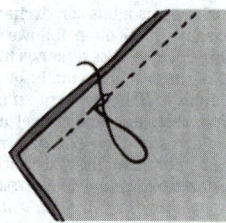

Running stitch

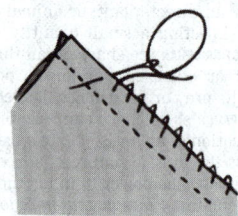

Overcast stitch

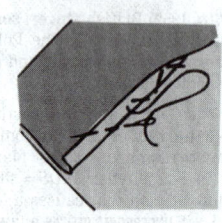

Blindstitch

Stitch

sb's wound with stitches (*informal*) 2. **CAUSE TO APPEAR GUILTY** to deliberately make sb appear guilty when he or she is innocent (*slang*) ○ *He claimed the police had stitched him up.*

stitchery /stíchəri/ n. needlework, especially when it is functional rather than decorative [Early 17thC. Probably coined by Shakespeare.]

stitchwort /stích wurt/ (plural **-worts** or **-wort**) n. a low-growing herbaceous plant with small white star-shaped flowers. There are several species. Genus: *Stellaria.* [Old English *sticwyrt*; from its former use to cure sharp pains in the side]

stiver /stívər/ n. 1. **OLD DUTCH COIN** a Dutch coin, no longer in circulation, worth one-twentieth of a guilder 2. **STH TRIFLING** sth of very little value, especially the least or smallest amount of money (*archaic*) [Early 16thC. From Dutch *stuiver*. Ultimately from a prehistoric Germanic word meaning 'small piece', which is also the ancestor of English *stub*.]

stk abbr. stock

STM abbr. Master of Sacred Theology [Shortening of latin *Sacrae Theologiae Magister*]

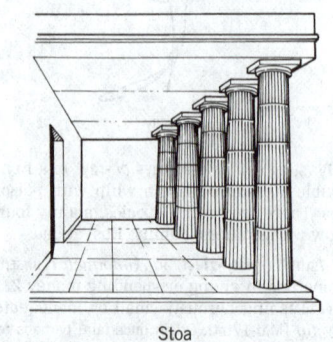

Stoa

stoa /stố ə/ (plural **-as** or **-ae** /stố ee/) n. in ancient Greece, a covered walkway, usually with a row of columns on one side and a wall on the other [Early 17thC. From Greek (source also of English *stoic*).]

stoat /stōt/ (*plural* **stoats** *or* **stoat**) *n.* a small mammal similar to a weasel, with a sleek brown coat. It is native to Europe, Asia, and North America, and feeds on rabbits and other small mammals. Latin name: *Mustela erminea*. ◊ **ermine**. US term **ermine** [15thC. Origin unknown.]

stob /stob/ *n. UK, Southern US* a stake or stump (*regional*) [14thC. Origin uncertain: probably a variant of STUB.]

stochastic /stə kástik/ *adj.* **1.** RANDOM involving or showing random behaviour **2.** INVOLVING PROBABILITY involving or subject to probabilistic behaviour **3.** INVOLVING GUESSWORK involving guesswork or conjecture (*formal*) [Mid-20thC. From Greek *stokhastikos*, from *stokhos* 'target, aim', literally 'pointed stake'. Ultimately from an Indo-European word that is also the ancestor of English *stag*.] —**stochastically** *adv.*

stock /stok/ *n.* **1.** COMM SUPPLY OF SALEABLE GOODS a supply of goods for sale, kept on the premises by a shop or business **2.** SUPPLY a supply held in reserve for future use **3.** AVAILABLE AMOUNT the amount of sth, e.g. a natural resource or a service, available in a particular area ○ *an alarming fall in North Atlantic fish stocks* **4.** FIN MONEY RAISED the amount of money raised by a company through the sale of shares, entitling holders to dividends, certain rights of ownership, and other benefits. US term **capital stock** **5.** FIN INVESTOR'S CAPITAL SHARE the share of capital held by an individual investor (*often used in the plural*) **6.** FIN TOTAL SHARE ISSUE the total number of shares issued by a company or sector **7.** SB'S REPUTATION sb's standing or reputation ○ *Her stock is high in terms of public opinion because of her aid work.* **8.** AGRIC = **livestock** **9.** DESCENT ancestry, usually with reference to race, ethnic group, class, region, or profession **10.** ORIGINAL VARIETY the original variety from which other similar plants, animals, or languages are descended **11.** BIOL RELATED ORGANISMS a race, family, breed, or other related group of animals or plants **12.** COOK BROTH a liquid made by simmering meat, fish, bones, or vegetables with herbs in water, used in soups, stews, and sauces **13.** BOT TRUNK the trunk of a tree or the main stem of a plant **14.** BOT PLANT RECEIVING GRAFT a plant or plant stem onto which a shoot or bud is grafted **15.** BOT PLANT USED FOR CUTTINGS a plant or part of a plant from which cuttings are taken **16.** AGRIC ANIMAL PEN a small pen or frame where a single animal can be confined, e.g. for veterinary examination or treatment (*often used in the plural*) **17.** ARMS PART OF FIREARM the part of a firearm to which the barrel and firing mechanism are attached. It is held in the hand or rested against the shoulder. **18.** ARMS PART OF GUN CARRIAGE the long beam on a field artillery carriage that extends behind it. When placed on the ground, it becomes the piece's third point of contact, along with the two wheels. **19.** AGRIC, HIST PART OF PLOUGH the frame of a horse-drawn plough **20.** HANDLE a handle, e.g. the handle of a fishing rod, whip, or carpentry tool **21.** WOODEN BLOCK a block of wood **22.** SUPPORTING PART any upright supporting part **23.** NAUT ANCHOR PART the crosspiece on certain types of anchor **24.** RAW MATERIAL the basic material from which anything is manufactured **25.** CINEMA UNEXPOSED FILM cinema film that has not yet been exposed **26.** METALL PIECE OF METAL a piece of cut metal ready to be processed, especially by forging **27.** (*plural* **stocks** *or* **stock**) FLOWERING PLANT a plant with clusters of fragrant, brightly coloured flowers. There are several varieties, some of which are widely grown as ornamentals. They are native chiefly to Europe and Asia. Genus: *Matthiola*. **28.** (*plural* **stocks** *or* **stock**) = **Virginia stock** **29.** CHR CLERICAL SHIRT FRONT a broad piece of cloth worn on the chest below a clerical collar by members of the clergy in some denominations of the Christian Church **30.** GAME UNDISTRIBUTED CARDS OR COUNTERS a pile of cards or counters not dealt out at the start of a game, but picked up during it **31.** *US* THEATRE = **repertory** **32.** HUB the hub of a wheel **33.** GEOL ROCK MASS a roughly circular mass of exposed igneous rock **34.** RAIL = **rolling stock** ■ **stocks** *npl.* **1.** PUNISHMENT DEVICE a wooden frame in which, in former times, an offender was secured by the hands and feet or head and hands and left in public to be ridiculed or abused **2.** NAUT CONSTRUCTION STAND a frame that supports a boat or ship while it is being built ■ *adj.* UNORIGINAL typical or familiar and therefore lacking originality ○ *When pushed for an answer, he gave the stock response.* ■ *v.* (**stocks, stocking, stocked**) **1.** *vt.* HAVE PRODUCT IN STOCK to have an item available for sale **2.** *vt.* FILL WITH SUPPLY OF STH to fill sth with goods **3.** *vt.* FILL UP to fill with a plentiful supply of sth ○ *We've stocked the fridge with cold cuts for the big game.* **4.** *vt.* SUPPLY FARM WITH LIVESTOCK to supply a farm with livestock **5.** *vi.* BOT SPROUT to sprout new shoots [Old English *stocc* 'tree trunk'. In sense 27, shortening of earlier *stock-gillyflower*.] —**stocker** *n.* ◇ **take stock 1.** to think carefully about sth so that you can form an opinion about it **2.** COMM make an inventory of the stock, especially at the end of a season in a shop or business. ◊ **stocktaking** *n.* 2

stock up *vti.* to collect a large supply for future use

stockade /sto káyd/ *n.* **1.** DEFENSIVE BARRIER a tall fence or enclosure made of wooden posts driven into the ground side by side, to keep out enemies or intruders **2.** AREA INSIDE STOCKADE an area surrounded by a stockade **3.** *US* MILITARY PRISON a prison on a military base ■ *vt.* (**-ades, -ading, -aded**) SURROUND AREA WITH STOCKADE to enclose an area with a stockade [Early 17thC. Via obsolete French *estocade* from Spanish *estacada*, from *estaca* 'stake', of prehistoric Germanic origin.]

stockbreeder /stók breedər/ *n.* sb who breeds and raises farm animals for a living —**stockbreeding** *n.*

stockbroker /stók brōkər/ *n.* sb who buys and sells stocks, shares, and other securities for clients on a commission basis —**stockbrokerage** *n.* —**stockbrokering** *n.*

stockbroker belt *n.* an affluent residential area outside a city, typically inhabited by middle-class professional people who commute to the city to work

stock car *n.* **1.** MOTOR SPORTS KIND OF RACING CAR a standard passenger car that has been modified for professional racing **2.** *US* RAIL = **cattle truck**

stock certificate *n. US* = **share certificate**

stock company *n. US* **1.** BUSINESS COMPANY ISSUING TRADABLE SHARES a company that has its capital divided into shares that are freely tradable **2.** THEATRE = **repertory company**

stock cube *n.* a small cube of dried and concentrated food extracts that, when added to hot water, makes a stock for use in soups, stews, and sauces. US term **bouillon cube**

stock dove *n.* a greyish dove that is native to Europe. It is slightly smaller than a wood pigeon, and it nests in holes in trees and cliffs. Latin name: *Columba oenas*. [Origin uncertain: probably from STOCK 'tree trunk', from its nesting in trees]

stock exchange *n.* **1.** = **stock market** *n.* 1 **2.** BUILDING a building in which a stock exchange is sited

stock farm *n.* a farm on which animals, e.g. cattle, sheep, and pigs, are bred and raised

stockfish /stók fish/ (*plural* **-fish** *or* **-fishes**) *n.* fish, usually cod or haddock, that has been cured by being split and air-dried without the addition of salt [13thC. Translation of Low German and Middle Dutch *stokvisch*, from *stok* 'stick, tree trunk' + *visch* 'fish'. The reason for the name is unknown.]

Stockhausen /shtók howz'n/, **Karlheinz** (*b.* 1928) German composer. A major figure in the musical avant-garde from the late 1950s, his work incorporates serialism, aleatoric elements, and electronic sound.

stockholder /stók hōldər/ *n.* **1.** *US* FIN OWNER OF COMPANY STOCK sb who owns one or more shares of a company's stock **2.** *Aus* AGRIC LIVESTOCK FARMER a farmer who keeps livestock —**stockholding** *n.*

Stockholm /stók hōm/ capital city of Sweden, on the eastern coast of the country. Population: 711,119 (1996).

Stockholm syndrome /stók hōm-/ *n.* a condition experienced by people who have been held as hostages for some time in which they begin to identify with and feel sympathetic towards their captors [Late 20thC. Named after STOCKHOLM, Sweden, where a bank employee taken hostage in a robbery became attached to one of her captors.]

stockhorse /stók hawrss/ *n. Aus* a horse trained for the herding of livestock

stockinette /stóki nét/, **stockinet** *n.* a stretchy knitted fabric formerly used to make stockings and undergarments, now used for bandages and dishcloths [Late 18thC. Origin uncertain: probably an alteration of *stocking net*.]

stockinette stitch *n. US* = **stocking stitch**

stocking /stóking/ *n.* **1.** COVERING FOR WOMAN'S LEG either of a pair of tightly fitting leg coverings for women, made of silk, nylon, or wool (*often used in the plural*) **2.** SOCK a sock (*dated or formal*) **3.** CHRISTMAS STOCKING a Christmas stocking (*informal*) **4.** DIFFERENTLY COLOURED PART OF ANIMAL'S LEG a differently coloured part of the lower leg of an animal, especially a horse [Late 16thC. From STOCK in the obsolete sense 'stocking', of uncertain origin.] —**stockinged** *adj.*

WORD KEY: ORIGIN

The use of ***stocking*** to mean leg coverings may have arisen in the 15th century from the blackly humorous comparison of the stocks in which one's legs were restrained as punishment with 'leggings, hose'. Until comparatively recently ***stocking*** was a unisex term (as it still is in the expression 'in one's stockinged feet'); the restriction to women's hose is a 20th-century development.

stocking cap *n.* a tightly fitting, cone-shaped knitted cap with a tapering tail that often has a tassel on the end

stocking filler *n.* a small and usually inexpensive Christmas gift, especially one put into a child's Christmas stocking. US term **stocking stuffer**

stocking frame *n.* an early type of knitting machine

stocking mask *n.* a nylon stocking pulled over the head to disguise the features, usually worn by sb committing a crime

stocking stitch *n.* a pattern in knitting that alternates rows of plain and purl stitches. US term **stockinette stitch**

stocking stuffer *n. US* = **stocking filler**

stock-in-trade *n.* **1.** BASIC RESOURCE a resource that sb needs and regularly makes use of, especially at work ○ *Courtesy and composure are the receptionist's stock-in-trade.* **2.** GOODS AND EQUIPMENT the goods and equipment that need to be kept on the premises for a business or shop to run

stockist /stókist/ *n.* a seller or shop that stocks a particular product

stockjobber /stók jobbər/ *n.* **1.** DEALER TRADING WITH BROKERS ONLY formerly, a dealer on the stock exchange who dealt only with brokers, not with members of the public **2.** *US* STOCKBROKER a stockbroker, especially an unscrupulous dealer trading worthless securities (*dated*) —**stockjobbery** *n.* —**stockjobbing** *n.*

stockman /stókmən/ (*plural* **-men** /stókmən/) *n.* **1.** BREEDER OF FARM ANIMALS a man who owns or breeds farm animals, especially cattle **2.** MAN TENDING LIVESTOCK a man who looks after the livestock on a farm

stock market *n.* **1.** FINANCIAL MARKET an organized market where brokers meet to buy and sell stocks and shares **2.** FINANCIAL TRADING the activity of buying and selling stocks and shares, or the global market for stocks and shares (*hyphenated when used before a noun*)

stockpile /stók pīl/ *vti.* (**-piles, -piling, -piled**) AMASS to accumulate large quantities of sth, e.g. food or weapons ■ *n.* LARGE SUPPLY a large supply of sth, e.g. food or weapons, often accumulated in anticipation of future difficulties —**stockpiler** *n.*

WORD KEY: SYNONYMS

See Synonyms at ***collect***.

Stockport /stók pawrt/ town in Cheshire, northwestern England. Population: 132,813 (1991).

stockpot /stók pot/ *n.* a large pot for cooking stock

stockroom /stók room, -ro͝om/ *n.* a room where goods are stored in a shop, office, or factory

stockroute /stók root/ *n. ANZ* a road or track that cattle are herded along

stocks /stoks/ *npl.* **1.** PUNISHMENT DEVICE a wooden frame in which, in former times, an offender was secured by the hands and feet or head and hands and left in public to be ridiculed or abused **2.** CONSTRUCTION STAND a frame that supports a boat or ship while it is being built **3.** RUDDER SHAFT the vertical shaft at the forward edge of a rudder, attached to the steering controls [14thC. From the plural of STOCK in the meaning 'post'.] ◇ **on the stocks** in the process of being made, prepared, or arranged

stock saddle *n. US* = **western saddle** [Originally a Scottish phrase meaning 'saddle with a wooden tree']

stock-still *adv.* absolutely motionless

stocktaking /stók tayking/ *n.* **1.** ASSESSING OF SITUATION evaluating a personal situation, or that of sb else **2.** LISTING MERCHANDISE making an itemized list of all merchandise in a shop or business. US term **inventory**

Stockton-on-Tees /stóktən ən teéz/ town and port in County Durham, northeastern England. Population: 83,576 (1991).

stockwoman /stók woomən/ (*plural* **-men** /stók wimin/) *n.* **1.** WOMAN BREEDER OF FARM ANIMALS a woman who owns or breeds farm animals, especially cattle **2.** WOMAN TENDING LIVESTOCK a woman who looks after the livestock on a farm

stocky /stóki/ (*-ier*, *-iest*) *adj.* **1.** BROAD AND STRONG-LOOKING having a broad strong-looking physique, and usually short in stature **2.** *US* OVERWEIGHT somewhat overweight [Early 14thC. The underlying idea is 'having the form of a tree stump or lump of wood'.] —**stockily** *adv.* —**stockiness** *n.*

stockyard /stók yaard/ *n.* a large enclosed yard with pens or covered stables where livestock are kept before being sold, slaughtered, or shipped on

stodge /stoj/ *n.* **1.** HEAVY FOOD food that is heavy, filling, and usually fairly tasteless (*informal*) **2.** ANYTHING DULL dull or unimaginative matter of any kind, especially writing **3.** SPONGE PUDDING baked or steamed sponge pudding [Late 17thC. Origin uncertain.]

stodgy /stójji/ (*-ier*, *-iest*) *adj.* (*informal*) **1.** FILLING heavy, filling, and usually fairly tasteless **2.** FORMAL OR POMPOUS boringly or laughably conventional, formal, or pompous ○ *another of his stodgy dinner parties* **3.** UNIMAGINATIVE lacking originality, flair, or imagination ○ *another sheaf of stodgy poems* —**stodgily** *adv.* —**stodginess** *n.*

stoep /stoop/ *n. S Africa* a porch or veranda [Late 18thC. Via Afrikaans from Dutch (see STOOP[2]).]

stoic /stó ik/ *n.* SB IMPASSIVE sb who appears unaffected by emotions, especially sb admired for showing patience and endurance in the face of adversity ■ *adj.* **stoic** = **stoical** [Late 16thC. From STOIC.]

— **WORD KEY: SYNONYMS** —
See Synonyms at **impassive**.

Stoic /stó ik/ *n.* ANCIENT PHILOSOPHER a member of an ancient Greek school of philosophy that asserted that happiness can only be achieved by accepting life's ups and downs as the products of unalterable destiny. It was founded around 308 BC by Zeno. ■ *adj.* OF THE STOICS relating to the philosophy of the Stoics [14thC. From Latin *Stoicus*, from, ultimately, Greek *stoa* 'porch', referring to the Painted Porch in Athens, where Zeno taught.]

stoical, **stoic** *adj.* tending to remain unemotional, especially showing admirable patience and endurance in the face of adversity —**stoically** *adv.*

stoichiology /stóyki ólləji/ *n.* the study of the elements or principles of any discipline, especially the chemical principles underlying cell and tissue physiology [19thC. Coined from Greek *stoikheion* 'element' on the model of German *Stöchiologie*.] —**stoichiological** /stóyki ə lójjik'l/ *adj.*

stoichiometry /stóyki ómmətri/ *n.* **1.** BRANCH OF CHEMISTRY the branch of chemistry concerned with measuring the proportions of elements that combine when chemical reactions take place **2.** MEASURE a measure of the relative proportions of the chemical elements that take part in a chemical reaction [Mid-19thC. Coined from Greek *stoikheion* 'element' on the model of German *Stöchiometrie*.] —**stoichiometric** /stóyki ə méttrik/ *adj.* —**stoichiometrically** /-méttrikli/ *adv.*

stoicism /stó isizzəm/ *n.* emotional indifference, especially admirable patience and endurance shown in the face of adversity

Stoicism /stó issizəm/ *n.* an ancient Greek school of philosophy that asserted that happiness can only be achieved by accepting life's ups and downs as the products of unalterable destiny. It was founded around 308 BC by Zeno.

stoke /stōk/ (**stokes**, **stoking**, **stoked**) *vti.* **1.** ADD FUEL to add fuel to a fire and stir it up to make it burn more intensely **2.** TEND BOILER to be responsible for adding fuel to and tending the boiler of a furnace [Mid-17thC. Back-formation from STOKER.]

stoke up *v.* **1.** *vt.* ADD FUEL TO FIRE to add fuel to a fire or a furnace and stir it up so that it burns more intensely **2.** *vt.* INTENSIFY EMOTION to cause an emotion, e.g. anger or fear, to be felt more strongly **3.** *vi.* EAT IN BULK to eat food in large quantities, because or as if food may not be had (*informal*)

stoked /stōkt/ *adj.* **1.** *Aus* DELIGHTED delighted or exhilarated (*informal*) ○ *She said she was stoked about the new job.* **2.** *US* EXHILARATED in an excited or euphoric state, especially from having taken drugs

stokehold /stók hōld/ *n. NAUT* **1.** STEAMSHIP'S BOILER ROOM the boiler room of a steamship **2.** COAL BUNKER a coal bunker for a steamship's boiler

stokehole /stók hōl/ *n.* **1.** MOUTH OF FURNACE the opening through which fuel is added to a boiler or furnace **2.** *NAUT* = **stokehold** [Mid-17thC. Translation of Dutch *stookgat*.]

Stoke-on-Trent /stók ən trént/ city in Staffordshire, central England. It is a major pottery manufacturing centre. Population: 244,600 (1997).

stoker /stókər/ *n.* sb whose job it is to add fuel to and tend a furnace or boiler, e.g. on a steamship or a steam train [Mid-17thC. From Dutch, from, ultimately, Middle Dutch *stoken* 'to poke with a stick'.]

Stokes-Adams syndrome /stóks áddəmz-/ *n.* episodes of temporary dizziness or fainting, due to disruption or extreme slowing of the heartbeat and consequent brief stoppage of blood flow [Early 20thC. Named after the Irish physicians William *Stokes* 1804–75 and Robert *Adams* 1791–1875.]

stokvel /stók fel/ *n. S Africa* an informal savings society in which members contribute regularly and receive payouts in rotation [From Afrikaans, alteration of English *stock-fair* 'livestock market']

STOL /stol, éss tol/ *n.* **1.** FLYING SYSTEM a flying system that gives an aircraft the ability to take off and land on a very short runway. Abbr of **short takeoff and landing 2.** AIRCRAFT an aircraft fitted with the STOL system

stole[1] past tense of **steal**

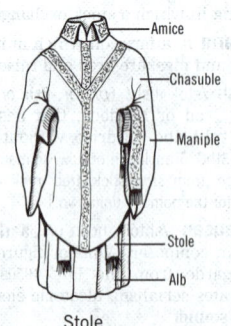
Stole

stole[2] /stōl/ *n.* **1.** CLOTHES WOMAN'S SCARF a woman's scarf or shawl often made of fur or worn as part of evening wear **2.** *CHR* ECCLESIASTICAL SCARF a long, narrow, and usually embroidered scarf made of silk or linen, worn by various members of the clergy [Pre-12thC. Via Latin from Greek *stolē* 'robe, equipment'.]

stolen past participle of **steal**

stolen children *npl. Aus* aboriginal children who, in line with Australian government policy to integrate aboriginals, were taken from their families and placed in state homes or with white foster families. The policy operated from 1910 to 1970.

stolid /stóllid/ *adj.* solemn and showing little or no emotion [Late 16thC. Directly or via French from Latin *stolidus* 'dense, stupid'. Ultimately from an Indo-European word meaning 'standing object, post', which is also the ancestor of English *stele*.] —**stolidity** /stə lídditi/ *n.* —**stolidly** /stólidli/ *adv.* —**stolidness** /stólidnəss/ *n.*

— **WORD KEY: SYNONYMS** —
See Synonyms at **impassive**.

stollen /stóllən/ (*plural* **-len** *or* **-lens**) *n.* a rich sweet German fruit bread made with nuts, raisins, and other dried fruits. It is traditionally served at Christmas. [Early 20thC. Via German from Old High German *stollo* 'post, support'.]

stolon /stó lon/ *n.* **1.** BOT PLANT SHOOT a long stem or shoot that arises from the central rosette of a plant and droops to the ground. It may form new plantlets where it touches the soil. **2.** ZOOL ORGANISM'S ANCHORING PART a budding of the body wall in simple organisms, especially an extension of certain colonial organisms, e.g. hydroids, that anchors the colony to a rock or other substrate [Early 17thC. From the Latin stem *stolon*-. Ultimately from an Indo-European word meaning 'sth standing up', which is also the ancestor of English *stalk*[1].] —**stolonate** /stólənət/ *adj.* —**stoloniferous** /stólə nífferəss/ *adj.*

stoma /stómə/ (*plural* **-mata** /-mətə/) *n.* **1.** BOT PLANT PORE a tiny pore in the outer layer (**epidermis**) of a plant or stem that controls the passing of water vapour and other gases into and out of the plant **2.** ZOOL MOUTH OR SIMILAR STRUCTURE a mouth, or an opening that acts as or is shaped like a mouth **3.** SURG SURGICAL OPENING an artificial opening made in an organ, especially an opening in the colon or ileum made via the abdomen [Late 17thC. Via modern Latin from Greek, 'mouth' (source also of English *stomach*).]

stomach /stúmmək/ *n.* (*plural* **-achs**) **1.** BIOL VERTEBRATES' DIGESTIVE ORGAN an organ resembling a sac in which food is mixed and partially digested. It forms part of the digestive tract of vertebrates and is situated between the oesophagus and the small intestine. **2.** = **abdomen** (*informal*) **3.** ZOOL INVERTEBRATES' DIGESTIVE ORGAN a digestive organ in some invertebrate animals in which food is mixed, stored, and partially digested **4.** COMPARTMENT OF ANIMAL'S STOMACH any of the four digestive chambers that make up the stomach in ruminant animals (*informal*) **5.** SEAT OF UNPLEASANT FEELINGS the part of the body in which disgust, nausea, and fear are experienced ○ *The very idea makes me sick to my stomach.* **6.** RESISTANCE TO UNPLEASANTNESS the ability to withstand disgust, nausea, or fear ○ *This is not a job for someone with a weak stomach.* ■ *vt.* (*-achs*, *-aching*, *-ached*) **1.** TOLERATE to put up with sth ○ *I find their gloating hard to stomach.* **2.** EAT FOOD WITHOUT ILL EFFECTS to eat a particular food without ill effects ○ *for those of you who don't stomach seafood* [14thC. Via Old French *stomaque* from, ultimately, Greek *stomakhos* 'throat, gullet', from *stoma* 'mouth'.]

stomachache /stúmmək ayk/ *n.* a pain in the abdominal region, caused, e.g., by indigestion or an infection

stomach crunch *n.* an exercise in which you lie flat on your back with your legs bent and then raise the upper part of your body a few centimetres off the ground without using your hands

stomacher /stúmməkər/ *n.* a stiff panel of material, often decorated with embroidery or jewels, worn over the chest and abdomen by women in the 17th and 18th centuries, and earlier by both sexes

stomach pump *n.* a popular name for the equipment, consisting of a simple tube, funnel, and bucket, used to flush out the stomach contents of sb who has, e.g., ingested a poison (*informal*)

stomach tooth *n.* either of the first canine teeth in the lower jaw of humans, whose appearance is popularly believed to be hastened by stomach upsets in infants

stomach worm *n.* a parasitic nematode worm that lives in the stomachs of mammals, especially one of those that infest cattle and sheep

stomal /stóm'l/ *adj.* relating to a surgical stoma, or occurring in or near a surgical stoma

stomat- *prefix.* = **stomato-** (*used before vowels*)

stomata plural of **stoma**

stomatal /stómət'l/ *adj.* relating to a stoma, especially in plants and animals [Mid-19thC. Formed from Greek *stomat-*, the stem of *stoma* (see STOMA).]

stomatitis /stómə títiss/ *n.* inflammation of the mucous tissue lining the mouth [Mid-19thC. Coined from Greek *stomat-* (see STOMATAL) + -ITIS.] —**stomatitic** /-títtik/ *adj.*

stomatology /stómə tóllǝji/ *n.* the branch of medicine or dentistry that is concerned with the study of the mouth and diseases of the mouth —**stomatological** /stómətə lójjik'l/ *adj.* —**stomatologist** /stómə tóllǝjist/ *n.*

stomatopod /stómətə pod, stə máttə pod/ *n.* shellfish with abdominal gills and a second pair of claws. They include the squilla. Order: Stomatopoda.

stomatous /stómətəss/ *adj.* resembling a stoma in shape or function

-stome *suffix.* mouth, stoma ○ *peristome* [From Greek *stoma* 'mouth'] —**-stomous** *suffix.*

stomodaeum /stómə dee əm/ (*plural* **-a** /-dee ə/), **stomodeum** (*plural* **-a**) *n.* a depression in the surface of an early embryo that develops into the mouth [Late 19thC. From modern Latin, from Greek *stoma* 'mouth' + *hodaios* 'on the way, becoming' (formed from *hodos* 'way, road').] —**stomodaeal** *adj.*

stomp /stomp/ *vti.* (**stomps, stomping, stomped**) WALK WITH HEAVY STEPS to tread heavily and noisily, often in anger ■ *n.* 1. DANCE JAZZ DANCE a kind of jazz dance with stamping foot movements 2. MUSIC JAZZ MUSIC jazz music accompanying the stomp [Early 19thC. Variant of STAMP.] —**stomper** *n.* —**stompingly** *adv.*

stompie /stómpi/ *n. S Africa* a cigarette or cigarette end (*informal*) [Mid-20thC. From Afrikaans, literally 'little stump', from *stomp* 'stump'.]

-stomy *suffix.* a surgical operation that creates an artificial opening ○ *gastrostomy* [Coined from Greek *stoma* 'mouth, opening' + -Y]

stone /stōn/ *n.* 1. HARD NON-METALLIC MATERIAL the hard solid non-metallic substance that rocks are made of. It is widely used as a building material. 2. ROCK FRAGMENT a small piece of rock of any shape 3. SHAPED ROCK FRAGMENT a piece of rock that has been shaped for a particular purpose, e.g. a gravestone or a paving stone (*often used in combination*) 4. SMALL HARD MASS a small hard mass, e.g. a hailstone (*usually used in combination*) 5. = gemstone 6. HARD MASS INSIDE FRUIT the hard central part of certain fruits, such as cherries, plums, olives, and peaches, that contains the seed 7. (*plural* **stone** *or* **stones**) MEASURE UNIT OF WEIGHT in the United Kingdom, a unit of weight equivalent to 6.35 kg/14lb. It is used especially for expressing sb's weight ○ *He's trying to get down to 12 stone.* 8. MED MINERAL MASS INSIDE ORGAN a small hard mass of mineral material formed in an organ, e.g. the kidney or gall bladder. Technical name **calculus** 9. COLOURS LIGHT GREY OR BEIGE a dull light colour between light grey and beige 10. PRINTING PRINTER'S TABLE a very smooth flat table that is used for arranging printing type 11. SPORTS CURLING BLOCK the shaped and polished mass of granite or iron that is slid along the ice in the game of curling ■ *adj.* 1. STONEWARE made of stoneware 2. COLOURS LIGHT GREY TO BEIGE IN COLOUR of a dull light colour between light grey and beige ■ *adv.* 1. USED FOR EMPHASIS used to emphasize the degree of a quality, usually a quality associated with stone, such as coldness, stillness, or lifelessness 2. USED FOR EMPHASIS used to emphasize the degree of a quality (*slang*) ○ *stone fine* ○ *stone tired* ■ *vt.* (**stones, stoning, stoned**) 1. THROW STONES AT SB to throw stones at sb or sth, especially as a form of punishment, execution, or vandalism 2. REMOVE STONE FROM FRUIT to remove the hard central part from a piece of fruit, e.g. a plum 3. US RUB WITH STONE to polish or sharpen sth on a stone or with a stone [Old English *stān*. Ultimately from an Indo-European word that is also the ancestor of English *tungsten*.] ◇ **be carved** *or* **set** *or* **cast in stone**, **be carved** *or* **set** *or* **cast in tablets of stone** be so firmly established as to make changes impossible or unthinkable ◇ **cast** *or* **throw the first stone** to be the first person to accuse, criticize, or quarrel with sb else ◇ **leave no stone unturned** to be

very thorough in making a search or in carrying out a task

Stone Age *n.* the earliest period of human history, in which tools and weapons were made of stone rather than metal. It is divided into the Palaeolithic, Mesolithic, and Neolithic periods. It extends from around 2.5 million years ago to around 2400 BC.

Stone-Age *adj.* 1. FROM STONE AGE dating from the Stone Age, the earliest period of human history 2. **Stone-Age, stone-age** VERY OLD-FASHIONED hopelessly behind the times

stone bass /-bass/ *n.* a large dark-brown and yellow fish found in Atlantic and Mediterranean waters. It belongs to the perch family and tends to inhabit offshore wreckage. Latin name: *Polyprion americanus.* [From its inhabiting rocky ledges and wrecks]

stone-blind *adj.* an offensive term meaning completely unable to see (*offensive*) —**stone-blindness** *n.*

stone bramble *n.* a prickly herbaceous plant that resembles the wild raspberry. It has white flowers and produces deep-red berries. It is native to Europe and Asia. Latin name: *Rubus saxatilis.* [From its growing in rocky places]

stonecast *n.* = **stone's throw**

stonecat /stōn kat/ (*plural* **-cats** *or* **-cat**) *n.* a slender yellowish-brown North American catfish that inhabits the beds of streams, rivers, and lakes, typically under stones. It has poisonous pectoral spines. Latin name: *Noturus flavus.*

stone cell *n.* BOT a short squat plant cell that performs a strengthening function. It occurs in large numbers in fruits such as the quince and the pear.

stonechat /stōn chat/ (*plural* **-chats** *or* **-chat**) *n.* a small songbird found in the grassy regions and dry plains of Europe and North Africa. Males have a black head, brown back, chestnut breast, and white rump. Latin name: *Saxicola torquata.* [Late 18thC. *Stone* from the resemblance of the bird's call to colliding stones.]

stone-cold *adj.* COMPLETELY COLD completely cold, especially too cold to be palatable ■ *adv.* ABSOLUTELY completely and utterly (*informal*) ○ *stone-cold sober*

stonecrop /stōn krop/ (*plural* **-crops** *or* **-crop**) *n.* 1. PLANT WITH FLESHY LEAVES an annual or perennial flowering plant with fleshy leaves, native mainly to northern temperate regions. Many varieties are grown as ornamentals. Genus: *Sedum.* 2. PLANT SIMILAR TO STONECROP a plant related or similar to the stonecrop [Old English *stāncropp*, from an earlier form of STONE (because the plant grows on rocks) + CROP in the obsolete sense 'flower cluster, ear of grain']

stone curlew *n.* a brownish, mostly nocturnal wading bird that inhabits an open dry stony habitat. It has a large head and eyes, and thick knee joints. Family: Burhinidae.

stonecutter /stōn kuttər/ *n.* 1. SB WHO CUTS STONE sb who is skilled at cutting and carving stone 2. MACHINE FOR CUTTING STONE a machine that is used to cut stone and concrete, especially a hand-held power tool with a circular blade —**stonecutting** *n.*

stoned /stōnd/ *adj.* 1. UNDER THE INFLUENCE OF DRUGS relaxed, excited, or euphoric from taking illegal drugs, especially cannabis (*slang*) 2. INTOXICATED very intoxicated (*informal*)

stone-dead *adj.* definitely or completely lifeless

stone-deaf *adj.* an offensive term meaning completely unable to hear (*offensive*)

stone-faced *adj.* 1. = stony-faced 2. WITH A STONE FACING having a facing of stone

stonefish /stōn fish/ (*plural* **-fishes** *or* **-fish**) *n.* a tropical marine fish whose mottled and knobbly body serves as camouflage in its rocky habitat. It has dorsal spines that can eject poison. Genus: *Synanceja.*

stonefly /stōn flī/ (*plural* **-flies** *or* **-fly**) *n.* an insect that, in its wingless juvenile stage, lives among stones in rivers and streams. The adults have long antennae and usually two pairs of wings. Both larvae and adults are used as fishing bait. Order: Plecoptera.

stone fruit *n.* = **drupe**

stoneground /stōn grownd/ *adj.* ground in the traditional way with millstones rather than with metal rollers

Stoneham /stōnəm/ town in northeastern Massachusetts, east of Woburn. It is a northern suburb of Boston. Population: 22,131 (1996).

stonehearted *adj.* = stony-hearted

Stonehenge

Stonehenge /stōn hénj/ prehistoric monument on Salisbury Plain, southern England, consisting of two concentric circles of large standing stones. It was built between 2800 and 1500 BC and is thought to have been an astronomical calendar or a temple to the sun.

stone lily *n.* a fossil of a sea lily

stone marten *n.* 1. MARTEN OF EUROPE AND ASIA a marten found in the woods of Europe and Asia. It has dark-brown fur with a lighter throat and undersides. It hunts rats and mice. Latin name: *Martes foina.* 2. FUR the fur of the stone marten [From its inhabiting rocky inlets and crevices]

stonemason /stōn mayss'n/ *n.* sb who shapes and prepares stone for use in building work and who is often also skilled at building with stone and repairing stone structures —**stonemasonry** *n.*

stone parsley *n.* a roadside plant found in western Europe and the Mediterranean. It has small white flowers and its leaves, when crushed, smell like a mixture of petrol and nutmeg. [Translation of Greek *petroselinon* (see PARSLEY)]

stone pine *n.* a tall pine tree with an umbrella-shaped crown. It is native to the Mediterranean but is cultivated elsewhere for its seeds, eaten raw or roasted. Latin name: *Pinus pinea.*

stone shoot *n.* a strip of loose stones that extends up a steep hillside or mountainside

stone's throw *n.* not very far away at all

stonewall /stōn wáwl/ (**-walls, -walling, -walled**) *v.* 1. *vti.* REFUSE TO COOPERATE to refuse to cooperate with sb by avoiding answering questions or providing information (*informal*) ○ *All reporters' questions were steadfastly stonewalled.* 2. *vi.* DELIBERATELY CREATE DELAY to create obstructions or employ delaying tactics, especially in order to hinder parliamentary business 3. *vi.* CRICKET PLAY DEFENSIVELY to persistently play defensive batting strokes [Late 19thC. The underlying meaning is 'to put up an immovable barrier'.] —**stonewaller** *n.*

stoneware /stōn wair/ *n.* dense opaque non-porous pottery that is fired at a very high temperature

stonewashed /stōn wosht/ *adj.* washed with small pumice pebbles to give a worn faded look

stonework /stōn wurk/ *n.* 1. STONE PARTS OF BUILDING the parts of a building or other structure that are made of stone 2. BUILDING WITH STONE using stone as a building material —**stoneworker** *n.*

stonewort /stōn wurt/ (*plural* **-worts** *or* **-wort**) *n.* green algae that grow in fresh or slightly salty water. They have jointed branches, often encrusted with lime. Genus: *Chara.*

stoney *adj.* = stony

stonk /stongk/ *vt.* (**stonks, stonking, stonked**) BOMBARD to subject sth, e.g. a building or the enemy, to a heavy artillery bombardment (*dated slang*) ■ *n.* ARTILLERY BOMBARDMENT a heavy artillery bombardment (*dated* *slang*) [Mid-19thC. Origin uncertain: perhaps an imitation of the sound.]

stonker /stóngkər/ *n.* an excellent example of sth, often sth impressively large or powerful (*slang*) ○ *played a stonker of a shot* [Early 20thC. Formed from STONK.]

stonkered /stóngkərd/ *adj.* (*slang*) **1.** OUT OF ACTION exhausted, defeated, or out of action **2.** DEAD DRUNK extremely drunk [Early 20thC. Formed from STONKER.]

stonking /stóngking/ *adj.* EXCELLENT excellent (*slang*) ○ *hit a stonking drive straight down the middle* ■ *adv.* EXTREMELY extremely (*slang*) ○ *a stonking good party* [Late 20thC. Formed from STONK.]

stony /stṓni/ (**-ier, -iest**), **stoney** (**-ier, -iest**) *adj.* **1.** OF OR LIKE STONE made of stone or similar to stone in appearance, texture, or colour **2.** COVERED WITH STONES covered with or having a great many stones **3.** EMOTIONLESS expressing no emotion, especially no friendliness or pity **4.** stony-broke (*slang*) —**stonily** *adv.* —**stoniness** *n.*

stony-broke *adj.* having no money at all (*informal*) US term **stone-broke**

stony coral *n.* a coral with a robust external calcium-based skeleton. It forms reefs and islands. Order: Scleractinia and Madreporaria.

stony-faced, **stone-faced** *adj.* showing not the slightest emotion, especially no sign of friendliness

stony-hearted /-haártid/, **stonehearted** /stṓn haártid/ *adj.* having or showing no compassion or kindness

stony-iron meteorite *n.* a meteorite consisting of metal and stony material

stony meteorite *n.* a meteorite that is composed mainly of rock-forming silicate minerals, especially olivine, plagioclase, and pyroxine

stood past tense, past participle of **stand**

stooge /stooj/ *n.* **1.** COMIC LOSER a comic actor, usually part of a double act, who acts as the butt of most of the jokes **2.** SB EXPLOITED sb whom others take advantage of, especially sb used by criminals in perpetrating their crimes (*slang insult*) **3.** *US* = **stool pigeon** *n.* 1 (*slang*) ■ *vi.* (**stooges, stooging, stooged**) BE TAKEN ADVANTAGE OF to be taken advantage of by another (*informal*) [Early 20thC. Origin unknown.]

stook /stook, stŏŏk/ *n.* AGRIC PILE OF SHEAVES a number of sheaves piled together on their ends in a field to dry ■ *vt.* (**stooks, stooking, stooked**) FORM INTO A STOOK to form sheaves into a stook [14thC. Origin uncertain: perhaps from Middle Low German *stūke*.] —**stooker** *n.*

stookie /stŏŏki/ *n. Scotland* **1.** STUCCO stucco **2.** PLASTER CAST a plaster cast on a broken limb **3.** STATUE a statue ○ *stood there like a stookie* [Late 18thC. Variant of STUCCO.]

stool /stool/ *n.* **1.** SIMPLE SEAT a simple seat with three or four legs and no back or arm rests **2.** MED EXCREMENT a piece of excrement **3.** BOT PLANT BASE the base of a plant, from which shoots or suckers sprout **4.** BOT CLUMP OF SHOOTS a clump of shoots or suckers sprouting from the base of a plant **5.** *US* HUNT HUNTER'S DECOY a real or artificial bird used by hunters as a decoy **6.** AFRICAN CHIEF'S THRONE in West Africa, a chief's throne **7.** TOILET a toilet or toilet seat (*slang*) ■ *vi.* (**stools, stooling, stooled**) **1.** SPROUT SHOOTS to sprout shoots or suckers from a stool **2.** *US* EVACUATE BOWELS to evacuate the bowels **3.** HUNT BE DECOY OR HUNT WITH DECOY to be a decoy for a hunter of wildfowl, or to hunt wildfowl using decoys **4.** *US* BE STOOL PIGEON to provide information to law enforcement agencies about criminals (*slang*) [Old English *stōl* 'chair'. Ultimately from an Indo-European base meaning 'to stand', which is also the ancestor of English *stand* and *stead*. In sense 2, from the idea of sitting to defecate.] ◇ **fall between two stools 1.** to fail to achieve either of two objectives by hesitating between them and failing to take action, or by trying for both and ending up with neither **2.** to be a possible member of two categories but a true member of neither

stool pigeon *n.* **1.** POLICE INFORMER sb who provides information to law enforcement agencies about criminals or their activities (*slang*) **2.** HUNT HUNTER'S DECOY PIGEON a pigeon, or a dummy of a pigeon, used by a hunter as a decoy **3.** DECOY CRIMINAL a criminal working as a decoy for a gang of criminals, with the job of distracting attention or throwing the police off the scent (*slang*) [From the fact that such decoys were originally tied to a wooden platform]

stoop[1] /stoop/ *v.* (**stoops, stooping, stooped**) **1.** *vti.* BEND BODY to bend the top half of the body forwards and downwards **2.** *vi.* WALK OR STAND BENT OVER to walk or stand with the head and shoulders bent forwards and downwards **3.** *vi.* BEHAVE UNETHICALLY to act in an unethical or self-degrading way ○ *I never imagined you would stoop so low.* **4.** *vi.* CONDESCEND to do sth reluctantly and with the attitude of sb who does not normally do sth that is so unworthy ○ *'He could not stoop to love; No lady in the land had power His frozen heart to move'*; (Sir Walter Scott, *Waverley*; 1814) **5.** *vi.* SWOOP DOWN to swoop down with wings folded, e.g. when attacking prey (*refers to birds*) **6.** *vi.* ADMIT DEFEAT to admit defeat (*archaic*) ○ *'as befits mine honour To stoop in such a case'* (William Shakespeare, *Anthony & Cleopatra*; 1606) ■ *n.* **1.** BENT POSTURE a posture in which the head and shoulders are bent forwards and downwards **2.** BIRDS BIRD'S DOWNWARDS SWOOP the downwards swoop of a bird of prey [Old English *stūpian*] —**stooping** *adj.* —**stoopingly** *adv.*

stoop[2] /stoop/ *n. US, Can* a small porch or verandah at the entrance to a house [Mid-18thC. From Dutch *stoep*. Ultimately from a prehistoric Germanic word meaning 'firm support', which is also the ancestor of English *step* and *staple*.]

stoop[3] /stoop/ *n.* a pillar or post (*archaic*) [14thC. Alteration of earlier *stolpe*, from Old Norse *stólpi*.]

stoop[4] *n.* CHR = **stoup**

stoor *n. Scotland* = **stour**

stop /stop/ *v.* (**stops, stopping, stopped**) **1.** *vti.* DISCONTINUE to cease doing sth or make sb cease doing sth ○ *She's trying to stop smoking.* **2.** *vti.* CEASE MOVING to come to a standstill or bring sth to a standstill ○ *Stop the car! I feel sick.* **3.** *vti.* END to come to an end or bring sth to an end ○ *The snow has stopped.* **4.** *vt.* PREVENT FROM HAPPENING to prevent sth from happening or continuing ○ *We couldn't stop the roof from caving in.* **5.** *vt.* PREVENT AN ACTION to prevent sb or sth from doing sth ○ *a way of stopping the children from climbing the fence* **6.** *vi.* PAUSE to pause in order to do sth before continuing ○ *I urge you to stop and think before deciding.* **7.** *vi.* INTERRUPT JOURNEY to interrupt a journey in order to make a brief visit somewhere ○ *Stop at the post office on the way into town.* **8.** *vt.* FILL HOLE to fill or block a hole ○ *We need to stop the cracks in the wall.* **9.** *vt.* BLOCK to block or plug sth, e.g. a pipe or a wound, so that nothing can pass through it ○ *grease stopping up the drain* **10.** *vt.* FIN INTERDICT CHEQUE to instruct a bank not to honour a cheque **11.** *vt.* DEDUCT to deduct money or a payment from sb's salary ○ *have the cost of breakages stopped off your wages* **12.** *vt.* MUSIC PRESS MUSICAL STRING to press a string on a stringed instrument in order to produce a particular note **13.** *vt.* MUSIC COVER HOLE ON INSTRUMENT to use a finger to close a hole on a wind instrument in order to produce a particular note **14.** *vt.* MUSIC PUT HAND INSIDE FRENCH HORN to alter the tone and pitch of a French horn by putting a hand inside the bell **15.** *vt.* BOXING KNOCK OUT to defeat an opponent by a knockout **16.** *vti.* CARDS BLOCK BRIDGE SUIT to block the winning of a suit in bridge **17.** *vt.* BE HIT BY STH to be hit by sth, usually a punch or a bullet (*informal*) **18.** *vt.* DEFEAT SB OR STH to defeat an opponent or competitor or overcome an obstacle (*informal*) ○ *Nothing's going to stop us now.* ■ *n.* **1.** STANDSTILL a complete end or lack of movement **2.** BREAK IN JOURNEY a short break in a journey, e.g. to rest or to visit sb **3.** PLACE VISITED ON THE WAY a place visited while on a journey **4.** PAUSE ON ROUTE a place where a bus or a train regularly pauses on its route ○ *Is this your stop?* **5.** BLOCKAGE a blockage or obstruction **6.** PLUG sth, e.g. a plug or a stopper, that is used to block the flow or passage of sth **7.** DEVICE PREVENTING MOVEMENT a device or control that prevents movement (*often used in combination*) **8.** FULL STOP in punctuation, a full stop (*informal*) ○ *Send help. Stop.* **9.** FIN ORDER INTERDICTING CHEQUE an order to a bank not to honour a cheque ○ *had to put a stop on the lost check* **10.** MUSIC STOPPING ON MUSICAL INSTRUMENT an act of stopping a string or a hole on a musical instrument **11.** MUSIC SUBSET OF ORGAN PIPES a subset of organ pipes or harpsichord strings with a common tone colour that can be played in isolation by silencing the remaining pipes or strings **12.** MUSIC ORGAN CONTROL a knob or lever on an organ or harpsichord that isolates a subset of pipes or strings **13.** PHOTOGRAPHY CAMERA'S APERTURE SETTING one of the graded settings for the size of the aperture of a camera lens **14.** PHOTOGRAPHY CAMERA'S DIAPHRAGM the diaphragm of a camera **15.** SAILING SHORT ROPE a short length of line used to tie up sth, e.g. a sail **16.** PHON SPEECH SOUND a consonant sound made by closing the passage of air through the mouth and then suddenly opening it again. ◊ **continuant 17.** ZOOL PART OF ANIMAL'S FACE the area between the nose and the forehead of a cat or a dog **18.** FENCING COUNTERTHRUST a swift counterthrust made at the time of an opponent's thrust that seeks to make contact first **19.** *Aus* SPORTS BOOT STUD a stud on a football or rugby boot **20.** ARCHIT CARVING a carving that finishes the end of a moulding [Old English *-stoppian* 'to block up'. Via prehistoric Germanic from assumed Vulgar Latin *stuppare* 'to plug up' (source of English *stuff*), from Latin *stuppa* 'plug, stopper', from Greek *stuppē*.] —**stoppable** *adj.* ◇ **pull out all the stops** to make every possible effort in order to accomplish sth ◇ **put a stop to sth** to bring sth to an end, usually quickly and permanently

stop down *vti.* to make the aperture of a camera lens smaller

stop off *vi.* to interrupt a journey briefly in order to do sth or see sb ○ *We stopped off at the supermarket on the way home.*

stop out *vi.* to remain out of the house, or stay out late (*informal*)

stop bath *n.* PHOTOGRAPHY an acid solution in which a negative or print is immersed in order to halt the developing process

stopcock /stóp kok/ *n.* a valve or tap used to turn on, turn off, or regulate the flow of a fluid in a pipe

stope /stōp/ *n.* STEP-SHAPED EXCAVATION an excavation that resembles steps, used especially in the mining of ore ■ *vti.* (**stopes, stoping, stoped**) MAKE STEP-SHAPED EXCAVATIONS to make stopes in a mine, or to extract ore in this way [Mid-18thC. Origin uncertain: possibly from Low German.]

Marie Stopes

Stopes /stōps/, **Marie** (1880–1958) Scottish pioneer advocate of birth control and writer. She wrote prolifically promoting scientific methodology of birth control, and established the first birth control clinic in Britain (1921). Full name **Marie Charlotte Carmichael Stopes**

stopgap /stóp gap/ *n.* TEMPORARY SUBSTITUTE sth used as a temporary substitute for sth that is really needed ■ *adj.* MAKESHIFT used as a temporary substitute for sth that is really needed ○ *a stopgap spending bill*

stop-go *adj.* with deliberate alternation between discouragement and encouragement of development or progress, especially in a government economic policy designed to control inflation

stop light *n. US* **1.** = **traffic light 2.** = **brake light**

stop-loss order *n.* an order to a stock broker to stop selling a stock when its price has fallen below a specified level

stop-off *n.* = **stopover**

stop order *n.* an order to a stock broker to buy or sell a stock when it has risen or fallen to a specified price

stopover *n.* **1.** STOP MADE DURING A TRIP a usually brief halt on a journey **2.** PLACE STOPPED AT a place where sb makes a brief halt on a journey

stoppage /stóppij/ *n.* **1.** STRIKE a strike, especially a brief one **2.** DEDUCTION FROM PAY an amount of money deducted from an employee's pay, e.g. for tax, national insurance, or pension contributions **3.** TIME WHEN PLAY IS HALTED a time during which the play in a game, especially football or rugby, is briefly halted, e.g. because of an injury to a player **4.** ACT OF STOPPING the act of stopping the movement of sth **5.** SITUATION WHERE THINGS ARE STOPPED a situation in which sth has been stopped or blocked ○ *a work stoppage*

stoppage time *n.* extra time played at the end of a game, especially in football or rugby, to make up for time lost in dealing with injured players or through other interruptions

Sir Tom Stoppard

Stoppard /stóppard/, **Sir Tom** (*b.* 1937) Czech-born British dramatist. He had instant success with *Rosencrantz and Guildenstern Are Dead* (1966). Later plays include *Arcadia* (1993). Born **Tom Straussler**

stopper /stóppər/ *n.* **1.** CORK OR PLUG sth that is put into an opening in order to close it **2.** SB OR STH THAT STOPS STH a person or thing that brings sth to a stop **3.** CARDS CARD THAT PREVENTS TAKING OF SUIT a card held by sb that will prevent the opponents from taking all the tricks in that card's suit during a hand of bridge ■ *vt.* (**-pers, -pering, -pered**) CLOSE WITH STOPPER to close or secure sth with a stopper

stopple /stópp'l/ *n.* = **stopper** *n.* 1 [15thC. Formed from STOP.] —**stopple** *vt.*

stop press *n.* **1.** LATE NEWS news that is inserted into an edition of a newspaper after printing has begun (*hyphenated when used before a noun*) **2.** SPACE FOR LATE NEWS a space in a newspaper kept for the insertion of late news

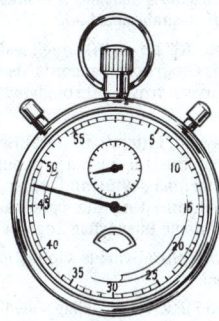

Stopwatch

stopwatch /stópp woch/ (*plural* **-watches**) *n.* a special watch that can be started and stopped instantly and is used to measure the amount of time sb or sth takes, e.g. a runner in a race

stop-work meeting *n. Aus* a meeting held by workers during working hours to discuss wage claims or strike action

storage /stáwrij/ *n.* **1.** STORING OR BEING STORED the act of storing sth, or the condition of being stored **2.** SPACE FOR STORING space in which to store things, especially the amount of such space **3.** FIN PRICE FOR STORING the price charged for storing sth **4.** COMPUT MEDIUM FOR STORING DATA any primary or secondary device or medium used to store data and programs for use by a computer

storage battery *n. US* = **accumulator**

storage cell *n.* = **secondary cell**

storage heater *n.* an electrical device that accumulates energy during off-peak times and later releases it as heat

storax /stáwr aks/ *n.* **1.** SUBTROPICAL TREE WITH WHITE FLOWERS any of various related tropical or subtropical trees or shrubs with hairy leaves and long clusters of drooping white flowers. Genus: *Styrax*. **2.** VANILLA-SCENTED BALSAM a vanilla-scented balsam obtained from a storax tree and used in the past in medicine and perfumery, and as incense. Latin name: *Styrax officinalis*. **3.** FRAGRANT BALSAM a liquid fragrant balsam used as an expectorant and in perfumery, obtained from the bark of an Asian tree. Latin name: *Liquidambar orientalis*. [14thC. From Latin, an alteration of *styrax*.]

store /stawr/ *v.* (**stores, storing, stored**) **1.** *vt.* PUT AWAY to put sth away for use in the future **2.** *vt.* PUT STH INTO SAFEKEEPING to put or hold sth somewhere for safekeeping, e.g. in a warehouse **3.** *vi.* SURVIVE STORAGE to survive or stay fresh while being kept in storage ○ *Apples will store well in a cool, humid building.* **4.** *vt.* STOCK ITEMS to fill or provide sth with other things **5.** *vt.* COMPUT HOLD DATA to enter or save data or programs into a computer memory ■ *n.* **1.** COMM PLACE SELLING GOODS a place where goods are offered for retail sale to customers **2.** QUANTITY SAVED FOR FUTURE USE a quantity or collection put away for future use ○ *a store of grain in a silo* **3.** PLACE WHERE GOODS ARE KEPT a place where goods are kept in quantity, e.g. a warehouse **4.** GREAT QUANTITY a great quantity or large collection ○ *a rich store of memories* **5.** ANIMAL BEING FATTENED an animal that is being fattened for sale ■ **stores** *npl.* SUPPLIES items or materials needed for sth, e.g. a business, expedition, or vessel ■ *adj. US* COMMERCIALLY BOUGHT purchased from a shop [13thC. Via Old French *estorer* 'to build, supply' from Latin *instaurare*. Ultimately from an Indo-European word meaning 'to set up', which is also the ancestor of English *restore* and *stow*.] — **storable** *adj.* ◇ **in store 1.** about to happen in the future ○ *She has a surprise in store for you.* **2.** in a large amount ○ *He has come back with money in store.* ◇ **set** *or* **lay** *or* **put great store by sth** to consider sth to be important, valuable, or worthwhile

store-bought *adj. US* = **shop-bought**

store brand *n. US* = **own brand**

store card *n.* **1.** = **charge card 2.** *US* = **loyalty card**

storehouse /stáwr howss/ (*plural* **-houses** /-howziz/) *n.* **1.** BUILDING WHERE THINGS ARE STORED a place where things are stored **2.** COLLECTION an abundant source, collection, or supply ○ *She's a storehouse of information on local history.*

storekeeper /stáwr keepər/ *n.* **1.** SB IN CHARGE OF SUPPLIES sb who is responsible for overseeing the supplies or stores of a military unit, ship, or organization **2.** *US* = **shopkeeper**

storeroom /stáwr room, -room/ *n.* a room or enclosed space where things are stored

storey /stáwri/ *n.* **1.** FLOOR IN BUILDING any of the different floors or levels in a building **2.** ROOMS ON ONE BUILDING LEVEL a set of rooms, or space, on a particular floor of a building [14thC. Via Anglo-Latin *historia* from Latin (see HISTORY), perhaps because historical scenes were often painted on the façades of medieval buildings.]

Storey /stáwri/, **David** (*b.* 1933) British novelist and playwright. Many of his works, such as *This Sporting Life* (1960), concentrate on ordinary people and draw on his North of England background. Full name **David Malcolm Storey**

storeyed /stáwrid/ *adj.* with stories, usually of a given number (*often used in combination*) [Early 17thC. Formed from STOREY.]

storied[1] /stáwrid/ *adj.* **1.** INTERESTING OR CELEBRATED interesting, famous, or celebrated in stories and books (*literary*) ○ *the storied outlaw Robin Hood* **2.** DECORATED WITH HISTORICAL SCENES decorated with images of scenes from history or legend [14thC. Formed from STORY[1].]

storied[2] *adj. US* = **storeyed**

Stork

stork /stawrk/ (*plural* **storks** *or* **stork**) *n.* large wading bird that is related to heron and ibis and has long legs, a long neck, a long straight bill, and black-and-white plumage. Family: *Ciconiidae*. [Old English *storc.* Ultimately from an Indo-European base meaning 'stiff', which is also the ancestor of English *strut* and *stark*.]

storksbill /stáwrks bil/ *n.* any of various plants of the geranium family that have lobed leaves, clusters of pink or purple flowers, and fruits with a beak-shaped tip. Genus: *Erodium*.

storm /stawrm/ *n.* **1.** METEOROL VIOLENT WEATHER a disturbance in the air above the earth, with strong winds and usually also with rain, snow, sleet, or hail and sometimes lightning and thunder **2.** METEOROL HEAVY RAIN OR SNOW a heavy fall of rain, snow, or sleet, often occurring with strong winds **3.** RAIN OF OBJECTS a heavy bombardment of solid objects **4.** OUTBURST OF FEELING a sudden strong outpouring of feeling in reaction to sth, e.g. of protest or laughter ○ *a storm of anger* **5.** MIL SUDDEN STRONG ATTACK a sudden strong attack on a defended place or position **6.** METEOROL STRONG WIND a gale that has a speed of 103 to 106 km/64 to 72 mi. per hour ■ *v.* (**storms, storming, stormed**) **1.** *vti.* ATTACK VIOLENTLY to attack or capture a place, especially a well defended one, suddenly and with great force ○ *stormed the barricades* **2.** *vti.* BE ANGRY to be violently and noisily angry **3.** *vi.* RUSH WITH VIOLENCE OR ANGER to go somewhere in a rush, violently or angrily ○ *stormed out of the room in a huff* **4.** *vi.* METEOROL BLOW WITH OR WITHOUT PRECIPITATION to blow strongly, to drop large amounts of rain, snow, or sleet, or to do both together [Old English. Ultimately from an Indo-European base meaning 'to whirl', which is also the ancestor of English *stir*[1] and *disturb*.] ◇ **a storm in a teacup** a fuss or row over sth trivial ◇ **take sb** *or* **sth by storm 1.** to capture a place or overwhelm a body of enemies suddenly and with great force **2.** to make a great and immediate impression on sb or sth

storm beach *n.* an accumulation of coarse sand and stones that is built up by storm action on a shore above the high water mark

storm belt *n.* a region on the surface of the earth where there are frequent storms

stormbound /stáwrm bownd/ *adj.* unable to leave, go out, or get in touch with anyone because of a strong storm

storm cellar *n.* a shelter underground used as a refuge during a windstorm

storm centre *n.* **1.** METEOROL CENTRAL AREA OF LOW PRESSURE the central region of a cyclonic storm, with a low barometric pressure and relatively calm conditions **2.** FOCUS OF DISTURBANCE a focus of trouble, disturbance, or controversy

storm cloud *n.* **1.** METEOROL CLOUD INDICATING BAD WEATHER a large dark cloud that is a sign of approaching heavy rain or a storm **2.** SIGN OF WAR a sign that violence, especially war, is soon to break out

storm-cock *n.* = **mistle thrush** (*dated*) [So called because it sings even in bad weather]

storm cone *n.* a cone-shaped canvas signal hoisted on a mast as a warning of approaching high winds

storm door *n.* a door added outside the main door of a house to provide additional protection against extremes of weather

storm drain *n.* a large drain built to carry away excess water from a road during heavy rain. US term **storm sewer**

stormer /stáwrmər/ *n.* a person or thing that is excellent or impressive (*slang*)

storm glass *n.* a glass tube containing a solution that is supposed to indicate weather changes by changes in its appearance

storming /stáwrming/ *adj.* EXCELLENT excellent or impressive (*informal*) ■ *n.* SUDDEN ATTACK the act of suddenly and violently attacking or capturing a place

storm petrel, **stormy petrel** *n.* any of various small seabirds that have black or brown plumage with a white rump, especially a variety that lives in the northern Atlantic and Mediterranean. Latin name: *Hydrobates pelagicus.* [So called because the bird's appearance was thought to forebode a storm]

stormproof /stáwrm proof/ *adj.* able to withstand the wind, rain, or other elements of a storm, or providing protection from them

storm-tossed *adj.* subjected to or disturbed by storms

storm trooper *n.* **1.** MEMBER OF NAZI MILITIA a member of the SA, a private militia of the Nazi party that used tactics of violence and brutality **2.** SOLDIER OF ATTACK FORCE a member of a military shock force specially trained to carry out attacks [Formed from *storm troop*, a translation of German *Sturmabteilung*]

storm window *n.* a window added outside an ordinary house window to provide additional protection against extremes of weather

stormy /stáwrmi/ (**-ier, -iest**) *adj.* **1.** AFFECTED BY OR SUBJECT TO STORMS affected by or experiencing a storm or frequent storms **2.** STRONGLY EMOTIONAL dominated by or subject to strong emotions or disturbances —**stormily** *adv.* —**storminess** *n.*

stormy petrel *n.* **1.** BIRDS = **storm petrel** **2.** SB CAUSING TROUBLE sb who causes trouble or whose appearance is usually followed by trouble

Stornoway[1] /stáwrnə way/ *n. Can* the name of the house that is the official residence of the leader of the political opposition in Canada

Stornoway[2] /stáwrnə way/ town and port on the island of Lewis-with-Harris, in the Outer Hebrides, Scotland. It is the centre of the manufacture of Harris tweed. Population: 5,975 (1991).

Storrier /stórri ər, stáwri ər/, **Tim** (*b.* 1949) Australian painter, noted for his realist landscapes and surrealist-influenced assemblages.

story[1] /stáwri/ *n.* (*plural* **-ries**) **1.** FACTUAL OR FICTIONAL NARRATIVE a factual or fictional account of an event or series of events **2.** LITERAT SHORT FICTIONAL PROSE PIECE a work of fiction in prose that is shorter than a novel **3.** LITERAT, THEATRE PLOT OF FICTION OR DRAMA the plot of a novel, play, film, or other fictional narrative work **4.** ACCOUNT OF FACTS what sb says has happened ○ *changed her story several times* **5.** FALSEHOOD sth that one person tells another that is not true (*informal*) ○ *Don't give me any stories.* **6.** PRESS NEWS REPORT a report in the news of sth that has happened **7.** SUBJECT FOR REPORT a subject or material for a news report **8.** LITERAT LEGEND OR ROMANCE traditional tales and legends, or the literature based on such tales ■ *vt.* (**-ries, -rying, -ried**) **1.** DECORATE WITH LEGENDARY SCENES to decorate sth with images of scenes from history or legend **2.** TELL STH AS STORY to tell sth as or in a story (*archaic*) [13thC. Via Anglo-Norman *estorie* from Latin *historia* (see HISTORY).] ◇ **the same old story** what always happens or is said (*informal disapproving*) ◇ **to cut a long story short** to say sth in a brief rather than a longer and more detailed way

story[2] *n.* US = **storey**

storyboard /stáwri bawrd/ *n.* a set of sketches, arranged in sequence on panels, outlining the scenes that will make up sth to be filmed, e.g. a film, television show, or advertisement

storybook /stáwri book/ *n.* BOOK OF CHILDREN'S STORIES a book of stories for children ■ *adj.* LIKE CHILDREN'S STORIES typical of or like sth found in children's stories rather than the real world

story line *n.* = **story**[1] *n.* 3

storyteller /stáwri tellər/ *n.* **1.** TELLER OR WRITER OF STORIES sb who tells or writes stories **2.** SB WHO FIBS sb who tells lies (*informal*) —**storytelling** *n.*

stoss /stoss/ *adj.* used to describe a mountain, hill, or slope that faces the direction of an oncoming glacier [Late 19thC. From German, 'thrust, push'.]

stot[1] /stot/ (**stots, stotting, stotted**) *v. Scotland* **1.** *vti.* BOUNCE to bounce, or make sth bounce **2.** *vi.* WALK UNSTEADILY to stagger or walk unsteadily [Early 16thC. Origin uncertain: perhaps from, ultimately, a prehistoric Germanic base meaning 'to thrust, push'.]

stot[2] /stot/ *n. Scotland* a bullock (*nonstandard*) [Old English *stott(t)*, of uncertain origin: perhaps from a prehistoric Germanic base meaning 'to thrust, push' (see STOT[1])]

stotin /sto teén/ *n.* a subunit of currency in Slovenia, worth one hundredth of a tolar. See table at **currency** [From Slovene, literally 'hundredth']

stotinka /sto tíngkə/ (*plural* **-ki** /-ki/) *n.* **1.** BULGARIAN SUBUNIT OF CURRENCY a subunit of currency in Bulgaria, worth one hundredth of a lev. See table at **currency** **2.** COIN WORTH A STOTINKA a coin worth a stotinka [Late 19thC. From Bulgarian, literally 'hundredth', from *sto* 'hundred'. Ultimately from an Indo-European word that is also the ancestor of English *hundred, cent, hecto-*, and *satem.*]

stotious /stṓshəss/ *adj. Scotland, Ireland* very drunk (*slang*) [Formed from STOT[1]]

stoup /stoop/, **stoop** *n.* a basin for holy water in a church [14thC. From Old Norse *staup* 'drinking vessel'.]

stour /stowr, stoor/, **stoor** /stoor/ *n.* **1.** TURMOIL confusion, turmoil, or uproar (*regional*) **2.** *Scotland* DUST dust, in a deposit or as a cloud [15thC. Origin uncertain: perhaps from Anglo-Norman *estur* 'tumult'.] —**stoury** *adj.*

Stourbridge /stówrbrij/ town in the western Midlands, England, noted for glassmaking. Population: 55,624 (1991).

stoush /stowsh/ *n. ANZ* a fight or dispute (*informal*) [Early 20thC. Origin uncertain.]

stout /stowt/ *adj.* **1.** THICKSET OR HEAVY thicker and heavier in body than an average person of the same height **2.** COURAGEOUS AND DETERMINED possessing or showing courage and determination **3.** STRONG strong and substantial ■ *n.* BEVERAGES DARK STRONG BEER a strong, very dark, almost black beer made from roasted malted barley [13thC. From Anglo-Norman, of prehistoric Germanic origin.] —**stoutly** *adv.* —**stoutness** *n.*

Stout /stowt/, **Sir Robert** (1844–1930) Scottish-born New Zealand statesman. He was premier of New Zealand (1884–87).

stouten /stówt'n/ (**-ens, -ening, -ened**) *vti.* to become, or make sb or sth, stout or stouter

stouthearted /stówt haártid/ *adj.* having or showing courage and resolution —**stoutheartedly** *adv.* —**stoutheartedness** *n.*

stove[1] /stōv/ *n.* **1.** APPLIANCE FOR COOKING OR HEATING an appliance that uses electricity or burns a fuel to produce heat for cooking or for heating **2.** WOOD-BURNING COOKING APPLIANCE a cooking appliance that runs on solid fuel, e.g. wood **3.** HEAT-PRODUCING CHAMBER OR DEVICE a device or chamber that is used to heat or dry sth, e.g. a kiln ■ *vt.* (**stoves, stoving, stoved**) INDUST HEAT IN A STOVE to treat sth by heating it in a stove in order to coat it with a surface such as enamel [15thC. Origin uncertain: probably from Middle Dutch or Middle Low German, 'heated room'.]

stove[2] past tense, past participle of **stave**

stovepipe /stṓv pīp/ *n.* **1.** PIPE FOR STOVES a pipe used as a chimney for a fuel-burning stove, usually made of sheet steel formed into a tube **2.** = **stovepipe hat**

stovepipe hat *n.* a tall tube-shaped silk hat for a man

stovies /stṓviz/ *npl. Scotland* a dish of sliced potatoes and onions stewed together, sometimes with a little meat

stow /stō/ (**stows, stowing, stowed**) *vt.* **1.** PUT STH AWAY to pack sth or put sth away **2.** FILL STH WITH TIGHTLY PACKED THINGS to fill sth with other things, especially things packed tightly ○ *to stow a boat's hold with cargo* **3.** STORE STH FOR LATER USE to store sth for use in the future **4.** HOLD STH to be capable of containing sth **5.** STOP STH to stop doing sth (*slang*) ○ *Stow this silly chatter.* [14thC. Formed from Old English *stōw* 'place'. Ultimately from an Indo-European word meaning 'to stand', which is also the ancestor of English *stand, stead*, and *store.*]

stow away *vi.* to hide on a ship or aircraft in the hope of being taken somewhere without having to pay

Stow /stō/, **Randolph** (*b.* 1935) Australian writer. His poems and novels include *To the Islands* (1958). Full name **Julian Randolph Stow**

stowage /stṓ ij/ *n.* **1.** STOWING OF THINGS a loading, packing, or storing of sth, or a way of doing this **2.** SITUATION OR ARRANGEMENT OF THINGS PACKED the condition of being stowed, or the way this has been done **3.** THINGS STOWED sth that is stowed somewhere or is to be stowed **4.** PLACE OR SPACE FOR STOWING a place, container, or space for stowing things **5.** FEE FOR STOWING a fee or fees for stowing sth

stowaway /stṓ ə way/ *n.* sb who hides on a ship or aircraft in the hope of being taken somewhere without having to pay

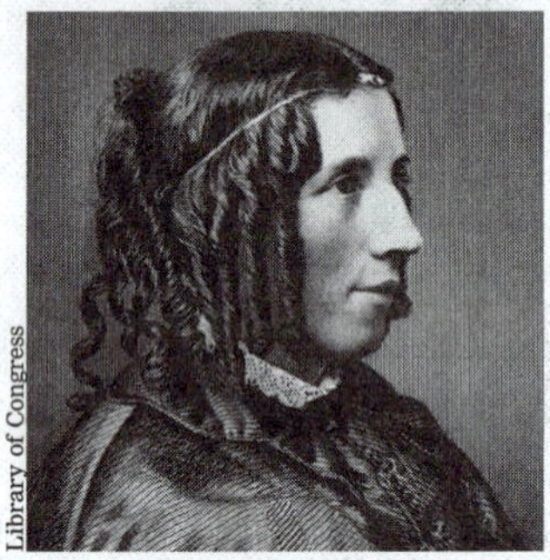

Harriet Beecher Stowe

Stowe /stō/, **Harriet Beecher** (1811–96) US writer and abolitionist. She is best known for her antislavery novel *Uncle Tom's Cabin* (1852). Born **Harriet Elizabeth Beecher**

STP[1] *abbr.* standard temperature and pressure

STP[2] *tdmk.* a trademark for a fuel additive designed to improve the performance of internal-combustion engines

str *abbr.* steamer

str. *abbr.* **1.** **str.**, **Str.** strait **2.** stroke

Strabane /strə bán/ town in County Tyrone, Northern Ireland. Population: 11,981 (1991).

strabismus /strə bízməss/ *n.* a squint (*technical*) [Late 17thC. Via modern Latin from, ultimately, Greek *strabizein* 'to squint', from *strabos* 'squinting'.] —**strabismal** *adj.* —**strabismic** *adj.* —**strabismical** *adj.*

Strabo /stráybō/ (63? BC–AD 24) Greek geographer and historian. His *Geographica* records his observations on his extensive travels throughout the ancient world.

Strachey /stráychi/, **Lytton** (1880–1932) British writer. A member of the Bloomsbury Group, he wrote *Eminent Victorians* (1918) and other biographies known for illuminating the personality of their subjects. Full name **Giles Lytton Strachey**

Strad /strad/ *n.* a Stradivarius violin (*informal*) [Late 19thC. Shortening.]

straddle /strádd'l/ *v.* (**-dles, -dling, -dled**) **1.** *vt.* SIT OR STAND WITH LEGS ASTRIDE STH to sit or stand so that one leg is on one side and the other leg is on the other side of sth or sb **2.** *vt.* BE OVER OR ACROSS STH to be on both sides of sth ○ *The city straddles the river.* **3.** *vt.* APPLY TO MORE THAN ONE THING to exist in, belong to, or apply to more than one situation or category ○ *The rule of the dynasty straddled the end of one century and the beginning of the next.* **4.** *vt.* STRIKE AND NARROWLY MISS TARGET to strike a target as well as miss it on either side **5.** *vt.* SPREAD LEGS APART to spread the legs apart, usually so that each leg is on one side of sth **6.** *vi.* SIT OR WALK WITH LEGS APART to sit, stand, or walk with the legs spread apart or on both sides of sth **7.** *vt.* MIL FIRE SHELLS FOR RANGE to fire artillery shells in front of and behind a target to find the correct range ■ *n.* **1.** POSITION ACROSS OR OVER STH a position in which sth is over or across sth else, or sb's legs are apart or on both sides of sth **2.** ACT OF STRADDLING the act of putting one leg on either side of sth **3.** FIN **STOCK TRANSACTION** the simultaneous holding of options to buy and sell a commodity at a set price during a specific period of time. This ensures a profit for the holder, irrespective of any rises or falls in value. **4.** ATHLETICS **JUMPING TECHNIQUE** a technique used in the high jump, in which the body is held parallel to the bar and the legs straddle it [Mid-16thC. Origin uncertain: probably a variant of obsolete *stridlen*, literally 'to keep striding', from an earlier form of STRIDE.] —**straddler** *n.*

Stradivari /stráddi vaári/, **Antonio** (1644–1737) Italian violin maker. The instruments that he produced, including violas and cellos, are among the most highly prized in the world.

Stradivarius /stráddi váiri əss/ *n.* a violin or other stringed instrument that was made by the Italian violinmaker Antonio Stradivari or his sons [Mid-19thC. Latinized form of STRADIVARI.]

strafe /straaf, strayf/ *vt.* (**strafes, strafing, strafed**) **1.** **ATTACK STH WITH GUNFIRE** to attack a position or troops on the ground with machine gun or cannon fire from a low-flying aircraft **2.** **PUNISH SB** to punish sb, especially severely (*slang*) ■ *n.* **AIR ATTACK** a machine gun or cannon attack by low-flying aircraft on a ground target [Early 20thC. From German *strafen* 'to punish'.] —**strafer** *n.*

Strafford /stráffərd/, **Thomas Wentworth, 1st Earl of** (1593–1641) English statesman. He was principal adviser to Charles I of England and lord lieutenant of Ireland. The Long Parliament ordered his execution.

straggle /strágg'l/ *vi.* (**-gles, -gling, -gled**) **1.** **STRAY FROM PATH** to stray from a path, or wander away from or become separated from a group **2.** **MOVE OR BECOME SPREAD OUT** to move or become spread out over a large area **3.** **COME OR GO IRREGULARLY** to come or go in an irregular or disorganized way **4.** **GROW UNTIDILY** to grow or hang in an untidy or irregular way ■ *n.* **STRAGGLED GROUP OR ARRANGEMENT** a group or arrangement that lacks order, is spread out, or is untidy [15thC. Origin uncertain.] —**straggly** *adj.*

straggler /strágg'lər/ *n.* a person or animal that wanders or becomes separated from a group, especially a soldier who falls behind in a march ○ *fell behind to wait for the stragglers*

straggling /strágg'ling/ *adj.* **1.** **WANDERING** wandering, or having fallen behind or become separated from a group **2.** **SPREAD OUT** spread out over a large area **3.** **GROWING UNTIDILY** growing or hanging in an untidy or irregular way

straight /strayt/ *adj.* **1.** **NOT CURVED** without bends, curves, irregularities, or deviations **2.** **CANDID** making no attempt to deceive or soften the truth ○ *Give a straight answer.* **3.** **LEVEL** level, even, or properly positioned ○ *Your tie isn't straight.* **4.** **ACCURATE** accurate or correct ○ *You can rely on her for the straight figures.* **5.** **HONESTLY STRAIGHTFORWARD** honest, fair and upright ○ *straight dealings* **6.** **CONSECUTIVE** following one after another, without interruption ○ *The team celebrated its tenth straight win.* **7.** BEVERAGES **NOT DILUTED** not diluted or mixed with any other drink **8.** **NEAT AND TIDY** neat and tidy, or in order **9.** **NOT FUNNY** not intended to be funny or unconventional ○ *playing both straight and comic roles* **10.** **CONSISTENT** not leaving or differing from a principle or political party ○ *the straight party line* **11.** **DELIVERED WITH UNBENT ARM** delivered with the arm unbent ○ *a straight left to the body* **12.** **HETEROSEXUAL** heterosexual (*slang*) **13.** **CONVENTIONAL** unremarkable or conventional in outlook, style, or way of life (*slang*) ○ *gave up being a rock musician and got a straight job* **14.** DRUGS **NOT USING DRUGS** not using or addicted to drugs (*slang*) ■ *adv.* **1.** **WITHOUT BENDING** without bending, curving, or diverging from a course **2.** **IMMEDIATELY** without delay or detour ○ *She went straight home.* **3.** **IN A LEVEL POSITION** in a level, even, or proper position ○ *Put your hat on straight.* **4.** **CANDIDLY** without any attempt to deceive or soften the truth ○ *Give it to me straight.* **5.** **WITH NO INTERRUPTION** one after another, without interruption ○ *three nights straight* **6.** **UNDILUTED** without being diluted or mixed with any other drink **7.** **INTO NEAT CONDITION** in or into a neat, tidy, or orderly condition ○ *We'll have to put the place straight after the party.* **8.** **WITHOUT BEING FUNNY** without trying to be funny or unconventional ■ *n.* **1.** **STH STRAIGHT** sth that is straight, e.g. a line **2.** CARDS **FIVE CARDS IN SEQUENCE** a poker hand in which the cards form a continuous sequence but are not all of the same suit **3.** **UNBENDING PART OF RACING TRACK** a part of a racing track that does not bend. US term **straightaway** **4.** **HETEROSEXUAL PERSON** a heterosexual person (*slang*) **5.** **CONVENTIONAL PERSON** sb who is conventional in outlook, style, or way of life (*slang*) **6.** **CIGARETTE WITHOUT ADDED DRUG** an ordinary tobacco-filled cigarette, to which no marijuana or other drug has been added (*dated slang*) [14thC. Originally the past participle of STRETCH.] —**straightly** *adv.* —**straightness** *n.*

straight and narrow *n.* the orthodox and law-abiding way to live life (*informal*)

straight angle *n.* an angle of 180 degrees

straight-arm *adj.* **TACKLE WITH ARM STRETCHED OUT** used to describe a rugby tackle executed with the arm stretched fully out ■ *vt.* (**straight-arms, straight-arming, straight-armed**) **PUSH OPPONENT AWAY WITH OUT-STRETCHED ARM** in rugby football, to push an opponent away with the arm stretched fully out and the hand upturned and stiff

straightaway /stráyt ə wáy/ *adv.* **straight away** immediately and without hesitation

straight chain *n.* an open chain of atoms in a molecule that has no side branches

straightedge /stráyt ej/ *n.* a rigid strip of wood, metal, or plastic that is used in drawing a straight line or checking for straightness

straighten /stráyt'n/ (**-ens, -ening, -ened**) *vti.* to make sth straight, or become straight —**straightener** *n.*

straighten out *vti.* **1.** **MAKE OR BECOME STRAIGHT** to make sth straight, or become straight **2.** **MAKE OR BECOME CLEAR OR SATISFACTORY** to become, or make sth, clear, satisfactory, or less complicated

straighten up *vti.* to become, or make sth, upright or in line

straight face *n.* a serious expression on sb's face that does not betray the fact that he or she really wants to laugh —**straight-faced** *adj.*

straight fight *n.* a contest, especially in politics, between only two opponents

straight flush *n.* a poker hand in which all the cards are of the same suit and form a continuous sequence

straightforward /stráyt fáwrwərd/ *adj.* **1.** **FRANK** truthful and to the point, rather than evasive **2.** **EASY** not complicated, difficult, or hard to understand **3.** **STRAIGHT OR DIRECT** following a straight or direct path ■ *adv.* **straightforwards** **IN STRAIGHTFORWARD WAY** in a straightforward way or direction —**straightforwardly** *adv.* —**straightforwardness** *n.*

straightjacket *n.*, *vt.* = **straitjacket**

straight-line *adj.* with components that are designed to move or make sth move in a straight line, or are arranged in a straight line

straight man *n.* a comedian whose role is to say or do things that allow another comedian to deliver a punch line or make witty or humorous comments in response

straight off *adv.* right away or at once (*informal*)

straight out *adv.* without hesitating or trying to lead up to sth gradually

straight-out *adj.* (*informal*) **1.** **BLUNT OR UNRESTRAINED** showing directness or bluntness rather than restraint ○ *a straight-out refusal* **2.** *US* **COMPLETE AND TOTAL** complete and thoroughgoing, without mitigation ○ *a straight-out jerk*

straight razor *n.* *US* = **cutthroat razor**

straight stitch *n.* a simple stitch that forms a straight line on the surface of the fabric

straight ticket *n.* *US* a ballot where all the candidates selected by the voter are from the same political party

straight up *interj.* used to affirm that sth is definitely true or, as a question, to ask if sth is true (*slang*)

straightway /stráyt way/ *adv.* at once and without delay (*archaic*)

strain[1] /strayn/ *v.* (**strains, straining, strained**) **1.** *vti.* **PULL OR STRETCH TIGHT** to pull or stretch sth until it is tight, or be pulled or stretched until tight **2.** *vi.* **WORK VERY HARD** to work extremely hard or exert yourself to the limit of your power **3.** *vt.* **USE STH TO THE UTMOST** to make the greatest possible use of or demands on sth **4.** *vt.* **INJURE STH** to damage a part of the body through using it too hard or too much **5.** *vti.* **BE OR MAKE STH TENSE** to put sth or sb under stress, or be put under stress **6.** *vti.* **PASS STH THROUGH STRAINER** to pass sth through a filter in order to remove some of its contents, or be passed through a filter **7.** *vt.* **REMOVE STH USING STRAINER** to remove part of sth from the rest of it with a filter **8.** *vt.* **HUG SB** to hold sb closely and tightly **9.** *vt.* PHYS **DEFORM STRUCTURE** to deform a body or material by applying an external force to it **10.** *vt.* **COMPEL SB OR STH** to compel or constrain sb or sth (*archaic*) ○ *'The quality of mercy is not strain'd'* (William Shakespeare, *The Merchant of Venice*; 1596) ■ *n.* **1.** **STRAINING** an act of straining sth ○ *Give the sauce a thorough strain.* **2.** **BEING STRAINED** the state of being strained **3.** **FORCE THAT STRAINS STH** a pulling or stretching force **4.** **MENTAL OR PHYSICAL STRESS** mental or physical stress caused by an intense or extreme pressure or demand **5.** **DEMAND THAT CAUSES STRESS** an intense or extreme demand or pressure that causes mental or physical stress **6.** **GREAT EXERTION** a great, taxing, or extreme exertion or effort **7.** MED **PHYSICAL INJURY** an injury to a part of the body caused by excessive use or by a twisting or stretching of muscles or tendons beyond their normal range **8.** PHYS **DEFORMATION OF STRUCTURE** the deformation of a body or material caused by applying an external force to it [14thC. Via Old French *estreindre* 'to draw tight' from Latin *stringere* (see STRINGENT).]

strain[2] /strayn/ *n.* **1.** **LINE OF ANCESTRY** a line of ancestry or a group of descendants from a common ancestor **2.** ZOOL **VARIETY OF ORGANISM** a subgroup of a species of organism that shows particular characteristics, sometimes developed by breeders for those characteristics **3.** **INHERITED QUALITY OR TRAIT** an inherited tendency, character, or trait **4.** **TRACE** a trace, or small amount of sth mixed in with sth else **5.** **CHARACTER OR MOOD** the style, character, mood, or theme of sth **6.** MUSIC **MUSICAL THEME** a musical theme or melody [Old English *strēon* 'offspring', originally 'gain'. Ultimately from an Indo-European base meaning 'to spread flat', which is also the ancestor of English *strew* and *construct*.]

strained /straynd/ *adj.* **1.** **PASSED THROUGH STRAINER** having been passed through a strainer to remove part of its content **2.** **NOT NATURAL** not natural or spontaneous but produced by an effort **3.** **TENSE** full of tension and often on the verge of hostility

strainer /stráynər/ *n.* a device for removing part of the content of sth, especially lumps or solids from a liquid

strain gauge *n.* a device that measures pressure or stress, using the change of electrical resistance in a wire that is subjected to the same stress as the object being measured

straining beam, **straining piece** *n.* a horizontal beam that connects the tops of two vertical posts (**queen posts**) in a roof truss

strait /strayt/ *n.* (*often used in the plural*) **1.** GEOG **CHANNEL JOINING TWO SEAS** a narrow body of water that joins two larger bodies of water, usually a body of salt water **2.** **DIFFICULT SITUATION** a situation that is difficult or involves hardship ■ *adj.* (*archaic*) **1.** **DISTRESSED OR TRYING** distressed, difficult, or trying **2.** **NARROW OR CONFINED** narrow or with very little room **3.** **STRICT OR RIGID** very strict or severe [14thC. Via Old French *estreit* from Latin *strictus* 'narrow', the past participle of *stringere* 'to draw tight' (see STRINGENT).] —**straitly** *adv.* —**straitness** *n.*

straitened /stráyt'nd/ *adj.* made very difficult, restricted, or narrow ○ *had lost all their money and were living in straitened circumstances*

straitjacket /stráyt jakit/, **straightjacket** *n.* **1.** **CONFINING JACKET-SHAPED GARMENT** a jacket-shaped garment with long sleeves that can be tied, used to restrict the arm movements of a resisting person, e.g. a prisoner **2.** **THING THAT RESTRICTS** sth that limits sb's freedom of action or initiative ○ *a bureaucratic straitjacket of* *regulations* ■ *vt.* (-ets, -eting, -eted) 1. PUT SB INTO STRAITJACKET to put a resisting person into a straitjacket 2. RESTRICT SB to limit sb's freedom of action or initiative

strait-laced *adj.* prudish, or very strict in morals — **strait-lacedly** /stráyt láyssidli, -láystli/ *adv.* —**strait-lacedness** /-láyssidnəss/ *n.*

strake /strayk/ *n.* 1. BAND OF PLANKS OR PLATES a continuous band of wooden planks or metal plates along the hull of a boat or ship 2. PART OF WHEEL a curved metal plate that is part of a rubber tyre or metal wheel rim [15thC. From assumed Old English *straca*; ultimately related to STRETCH.]

stramash /strə másh/ *n.* *Scotland* an uproar, commotion, or rowdy dispute [Late 18thC. Origin unknown.]

stramonium /strə mṓni əm/ *n.* a preparation of dried leaves and flowers of the thorn apple containing alkaloids and formerly used as medicine [Mid-17thC. From modern Latin, of uncertain origin: perhaps ultimately related to Russian *durman*.]

strand[1] /strand/ *n.* LAND AT WATER'S EDGE a strip of land along the edge of a body of water ■ *v.* (strands, stranding, stranded) 1. *vti.* RUN ASHORE OR AGROUND to leave or run a ship or aquatic animal aground, or be left or driven aground 2. *vt.* LEAVE SB IN DIFFICULTY to leave sb in a strange place without the capability or resources to get out of it (*often passive*) ○ *stranded without any means of getting home* [Old English, of uncertain origin]

strand[2] /strand/ *n.* 1. FIBRE, THREAD, WIRE, OR FILAMENT any of the fibres, threads, wires, or other filaments that are twisted or braided together to form a rope, cable, or yarn 2. LONG THIN PIECE a single length of sth long and thin such as wire, string, rope, or wool 3. HUMAN HAIR OR HAIRS a human hair, or a tress of hair 4. LENGTH OF TISSUE RESEMBLING THREAD a length of animal, plant, or mineral fibre or tissue that resembles a thread 5. ACCESSORIES STRING OF BEADS a length of strung pearls or beads, especially when twisted into a rope-like form 6. ELEMENT OF WHOLE any of the elements that together make up a larger complex whole ■ *vt.* (strands, stranding, stranded) MAKE STH BY TWISTING to make sth such as a rope or cable by braiding or twisting threads, wires, or other filaments together ○ *to strand a rope* [15thC. Origin unknown.]

stranded /strándid/ *adj.* left in a strange place without the capability or resources to get out of it [Early 18thC. Formed from STRAND[1].]

stranded cotton *n.* an embroidery cotton made up of six strands of thread loosely twisted together. The strands can be separated and used individually or in combination.

strandline /stránd līn/, **strand line** *n.* a shoreline, usually one that the sea, a lake, or a river had at an earlier point in time and that is higher than the present shoreline

strange /straynj/ *adj.* (stranger, strangest) 1. UNEXPECTED OR EXTRAORDINARY not expected, normal, or ordinary 2. UNFAMILIAR not known or experienced previously 3. HARD TO EXPLAIN difficult to explain or understand 4. EXOTIC coming from a different place or environment, or belonging to a different kind 5. UNACCUSTOMED not yet used to or familiar with sth ○ *strange to these new surroundings* 6. RESERVED reserved or shy, often because of being unfamiliar with people 7. ILL AT EASE uncomfortable, embarrassed, or slightly ill ○ *I've been feeling a little strange since I took the medicine.* 8. PHYS SHOWING QUANTUM CHARACTERISTIC OF STRANGENESS showing or having the quantum characteristic of strangeness ■ *adv.* IN UNUSUAL WAY in a strange way (*nonstandard*) [13thC. Via Old French *estrange* from Latin *extraneus* 'foreign', from *extra*, feminine of *exter* 'outside' (see EXTERIOR).]

strangely /stráynjli/ *adv.* 1. IN UNUSUAL WAY in an unusual or puzzling way 2. ODDLY it is odd or puzzling that ○ *Strangely, they seemed to have no definite plan of action.*

strangeness /stráynjnəss/ *n.* 1. CONDITION OF BEING STRANGE the condition or quality of being strange 2. PHYS QUANTUM CHARACTERISTIC a quantum characteristic of some elementary particles that is conserved in strong and electromagnetic, but not weak, interactions and has a value (**strangeness number**) of zero for most particles

strangeness number *n.* the value of the quantum characteristic of strangeness, equal to the hypercharge minus the baryon number

strange particle *n.* an elementary particle having a strangeness number other than zero [From the fact that such particles' long lifetimes were hard to explain]

strange quark *n.* a quark that has an electric charge equal to $\frac{1}{3}$ that of the electron and a strangeness number of –1

stranger /stráynjər/ *n.* 1. UNFAMILIAR PERSON a person whom sb does not know 2. NEWCOMER sb who is new to a particular place 3. OUTSIDER sb who is not a member of a particular organization or group 4. VISITOR OR GUEST sb who does not live in a particular house or community but is present as a visitor or guest 5. PERSON UNACCUSTOMED TO STH sb who is not accustomed to or acquainted with sth specified ○ *Being a stranger to hard physical work, he found the job exhausting.* 6. ALIENATED PERSON sb who has become distanced or alienated from another, others, or sth ○ *She is a stranger to her former colleagues.* 7. PERSON NOT PRIVY TO TRANSACTION sb who is neither privy nor party to a transaction [14thC. From Old French *estrangier*, from *estrange* 'foreign' (see STRANGE).]

stranger's gallery *n.* a gallery from which members of the public may observe the business of a legislature, especially in the House of Commons

Strangford Lough /strángfərd lókh/ inlet of the sea in County Down, Northern Ireland. Length: 40 km/25 mi.

strangle /stráng g'l/ (-gles, -gling, -gled) *vti.* 1. KILL OR DIE BY CHOKING to kill a person or an animal by squeezing the throat so that air cannot pass through it into the lungs, or die in this way 2. SUPPRESS UTTERANCE to suppress suddenly a sound that is being uttered, or be suppressed suddenly ○ *I managed to strangle my giggles.* 3. STIFLE OR BE STIFLED IN DEVELOPMENT to hinder or stop the growth or development of sth, or be hindered or stopped [13thC. Via Old French *estrangler* from Latin *strangulare* (see STRANGULATE).] —**strangler** *n.*

stranglehold /stráng g'l hōld/ *n.* 1. WRESTLING CHOKING WRESTLING HOLD an illegal hold in wrestling that chokes an opponent 2. COMPLETE POWER power over sth or sb that is complete and prevents any movement or change

strangles /stráng g'lz/ *n.* an infectious disease of horses in which they experience inflammation and abscesses of the mucous membranes of the respiratory tract, causing strangling. It is caused by the bacterium *Streptococcus equi.* (*takes a singular verb*)

strangulate /stráng gyŏŏ layt/ (-lates, -lating, -lated) *v.* 1. *vt.* STRANGLE to strangle a person or animal 2. *vti.* MED OBSTRUCT OR BE OBSTRUCTED to constrict a part of the body, or become constricted, until the natural flow of blood or air is prevented [Mid-17thC. Via Latin *strangulare* from Greek *straggalan*, from *straggalē* 'halter, cord'. Perhaps ultimately from an Indo-European word.] —**strangulation** /stráng gyŏŏ láysh'n/ *n.*

strangury /stráng gyŏŏri/ *n.* painful and slow urination caused by spasms that make urine come out drop by drop [14thC. Via Latin from Greek *straggouria*, from *stragx* 'drop' + *ouron* 'urine'.]

Stranraer /stran ráar/ town and port in Dumfries and Galloway, southwestern Scotland. Population: 11,348 (1991).

strap /strap/ *n.* 1. FLEXIBLE STRIP USED FOR BINDING a narrow flexible strip of leather, nylon webbing, plastic, metal, or other material used to bind or secure sth 2. LOOP OF MATERIAL USED AS HANDLE a loop of flexible material attached to sth so that it can be grasped or slung over a shoulder and used in lifting or carrying sth 3. TRANSP LOOP TO HANG ON TO a loop of leather, rubber, or plastic suspended from the roof inside a bus or train for standing passengers to hold for support 4. RAZOR STROP a strop for a razor 5. LEATHER STRIP FOR FLOGGING a long narrow strip of leather used for flogging or beating ■ *vt.* (straps, strapping, strapped) 1. SECURE WITH STRAP to secure or bind sb or sth with a strap 2. FASTEN STRAPS OF to secure the straps that are used to fasten sth ○ *stood up without strapping her shoes* 3. BEAT WITH STRAP to beat or flog sb with a strap 4. SHARPEN WITH STROP to sharpen sth, e.g. a razor, with a strop [Early 17thC. Originally a Scottish dialect form of STROP.]

straphanger /stráp hangər/ *n.* a passenger who stands in a bus or train and holds onto a strap that is suspended from the roof (*informal*)

strap hinge *n.* a hinge with a flap fastened to the exposed surface of a door, lid, or gate

strapless /strápləss/ *adj.* without straps, other supports, or covering over the shoulders

strapline /stráp līn/ *n.* a subheading in a piece of print, e.g. in a newspaper article

strappado /strə páydō, -paádō/ (*plural* -does) *n.* 1. FORM OF TORTURE a form of torture in which sb is hoisted by a rope around the wrists, which are bound behind the back, and then dropped, but not to the ground 2. APPARATUS USED FOR TORTURE an apparatus or machine that is used to deliver a strappado [Mid-16thC. Alteration of French *(e)strapade*, from Italian *strappata*, from *strappare*, of uncertain origin.]

strapped /strapt/ *adj.* very short of or in need of sth, especially money (*informal*)

strapper /stráppər/ *n.* sb who is big and powerfully built (*informal*)

strapping /strápping/ *adj.* ROBUST tall and powerfully built (*informal*) ■ *n.* 1. STRAPS straps in general, or a set of straps 2. MATERIAL FOR STRAPS material for making straps or for use as straps

strappy /stráppi/ (-pier, -piest) *adj.* with straps, especially when they are an important part of the look or design of sth (*informal*) ○ *strappy sandals*

strap work *n.* decorative work in the form of crossing or interlaced bands on the outside of a building, especially in Tudor architecture

Strasbourg /stráz burg/ capital city of Bas-Rhin Department, Alsace Region, northeastern France. It is the site of the headquarters of the European Parliament and the Council of Europe. Population: 252,338 (1990).

strass /strass/ *n.* = **paste**[1] *n.* 5 [Early 19thC. From German, named after the 18thC. German jeweller Joseph *Strasser*, who invented it.]

strata plural of **stratum**

stratagem /stráttəjəm/ *n.* 1. MIL RUSE FOR DECEIVING ENEMY a military tactic or manoeuvre that is designed to deceive an enemy 2. CLEVER SCHEME clever ruse or scheme that is designed to deceive others or achieve sth 3. USE OF CLEVER SCHEMES the use of stratagems to deceive an enemy or others, or skill in using stratagems [15thC. Via French *stratagème* from, ultimately, Greek *stratēgēma*, from *stratēgos* 'general' (see STRATEGY).]

strata title *n.* *Aus* a system of ownership of space within a block of apartments. Titles are issued for each apartment and for common property, which is managed by a committee of unit owners.

strata unit *n.* *Aus* an apartment whose ownership is registered according to strata title

strategic /strə teéjik/, **strategical** /-teéjik'l/ *adj.* 1. TYPICAL OF STRATEGY relating to involving, or typical of strategy or a strategy ○ *strategic planning* 2. DONE FOR REASONS OF STRATEGY necessary to a strategy, or done because a strategy requires it ○ *a strategic retreat* 3. DISPLAYING SOUND STRATEGY displaying a sound strategy or plan of action ○ *showing strategic timing in selling a stock short* 4. MIL DESTROYING ENEMY'S FIGHTING CAPACITY done to destroy, or having the capability to destroy, an enemy's ability to fight a war ○ *strategic bombing* 5. MIL NECESSARY FOR FIGHTING WAR necessary for fighting a war, or essential to the military forces fighting a war ○ *strategic metals* ○ *strategic air bases*

strategically /strə teéjikli/ *adv.* 1. AS PART OF STRATEGY as part of, or in a way useful to, a strategy 2. IN USEFUL WAY in a clever or useful way

strategics /strə teéjiks/ *n.* the science or art of military strategy (*takes a singular verb*)

strategist /stráttəjist/ *n.* sb who can develop and execute an effective strategy, especially for winning a war

strategy /stráttəji/ (*plural* -gies) *n.* 1. MIL PLANNING OF WAR the science or art of planning and conducting a war or a military campaign 2. PLANNING IN ANY FIELD a carefully devised plan of action to achieve a goal, or the art of developing or carrying out such a plan **3.** BIOL **ADAPTATION IMPORTANT TO EVOLUTIONARY SUCCESS** in evolutionary theory, a behaviour, structure, or other adaptation that improves viability [Early 19thC. Via French *stratégie* from Greek *stratēgia* 'generalship', from *stratēgos* 'general', from *stratos* 'army' + *agein* 'to lead'.]

Stratford-upon-Avon /strátfərd-áyvən/ town in Warwickshire, west-central England. It was the birthplace of William Shakespeare. Population: 22,375 (1991).

strath /strath/ *n. Scotland* a river valley that is wide and flat (*often used in placenames*) [Mid-16thC. Via Scottish Gaelic from Old Irish *srath*. Ultimately from an Indo-European base meaning 'to spread wide', which is also the ancestor of English *strew* and *street*.]

Strathclyde /strath klíd/ former region in southwestern Scotland between 1975 and1996

Strathern /strath úrn/, **Marilyn** (*b.* 1941) Australian anthropologist, noted for her work on gender and identity based on studies of the peoples of Papua New Guinea.

strathspey /strath spáy/ (*plural* **-speys**) *n.* **1.** SCOTTISH DANCE a Scottish dance that is similar to a reel but has a slower tempo **2.** MUSIC FOR STRATHSPEY a piece of music for a strathspey, or one written in a similar style [Mid-18thC. Named after *Strathspey*, the valley of the River Spey in Scotland.]

strati plural of *stratus*

strati- *prefix.* stratum, layer ○ *stratigraphy* [From STRATUM]

straticulate /strə tíkyōōlət, -layt/ *adj.* used to describe a rock formation that is made up of thin layers [Late 19thC. Formed from STRATUM, on the model of *particulate*.] —**straticulation** /strə tíkyōō láysh'n/ *n.*

stratification /stráttifi káysh'n/ *n.* **1.** GEOL FORMATION OF ROCK LAYERS the formation of layers in sedimentary rocks through biological, chemical, or physical changes in the sediments forming them **2.** FORMATION OF LAYERS the formation of layers, castes, classes, or other types of strata **3.** SITUATION WHERE THINGS ARE STRATIFIED a situation or condition where sth is arranged in several strata **4.** GEOL LAYERED ARRANGEMENT OR APPEARANCE a layered arrangement or appearance of successive rock strata **5.** AGRIC SEED STORAGE IN CHILLED MOIST ENVIRONMENT the storing of seeds in a chilled moist environment or material in order to induce germination or to preserve them —**stratificational** *adj.*

stratificational grammar *n.* a form of grammar in which language is analysed in terms of layers linked to one another by rules

stratified charge engine *n.* an internal combustion engine with two layers of fuel density within the cylinder. A rich mixture is adjacent to the spark plug whose combustion assists in the ignition of a lean mixture in the remainder of the cylinder.

stratiform /strátti fawrm/ *adj.* **1.** COMPOSED OF LAYERS composed of layers, or with a layered appearance or arrangement **2.** FORMED AS LAYER forming or formed as a layer **3.** METEOROL LIKE STRATUS CLOUD like or having the form of a stratus cloud

stratify /strátti fī/ (**-fies, -fying, -fied**) *v.* **1.** *vti.* FORM INTO LAYERS to form sth into a layer or layers, or become formed into a layer or layers **2.** *vti.* SOC SCI FORM INTO STATUS GROUPS to form or be formed into castes, classes, or other groups based on status **3.** *vt.* AGRIC STORE SEEDS IN CHILLED MOIST ENVIRONMENT to store seeds in chilled moist sand, peat moss, or other material in order to induce germination or preserve the seeds

stratigraphic /strátti gráffik/, **stratigraphical** /-gráffik'l/ *adj.* relating to stratigraphy —**stratigraphically** *adv.*

stratigraphic column /strátti gráffik-/ *n.* a succession of rocks laid down over a particular period of geologic time

stratigraphic unit *n.* a body of rock defined by its fossil record, physical appearance, or time span

stratigraphy /strə tíggrəfi/ (*plural* **-phies**) *n.* **1.** GEOL STUDY OF ROCK STRATA the study of the origin, composition, and development of rock strata **2.** ARCHAEOL VERTICAL SECTION THROUGH GROUND a section cut vertically through the earth showing its different layers and allowing artefacts to be dated according to the layers in which they are found **3.** GEOL DISPOSITION OF ROCK STRATA the way in which rock strata are arranged, and the chronology of their formation —**stratigrapher** *n.* —**stratigraphist** *n.*

stratocracy /strə tókrəssi/ (*plural* **-cies**) *n.* government by armed forces (*formal*) [Mid-17thC. Coined from Greek *stratos* 'army' (originally 'crowd, people spread out') + -CRACY.] —**stratocrat** /stráttə krat/ *n.* —**stratocratic** /strátta kráttik/ *adj.*

stratocumulus /stráytō kyōomyōōləss, stráttō-/ (*plural* **-li** /-lī/) *n.* a cloud formation in a low-lying extensive layer with large dark round or rolling masses

stratopause /stráttō pawz/ *n.* the boundary layer between the stratosphere and the mesosphere, at around 50 km/30 mi. above the Earth's surface [Mid-20thC. From STRATOSPHERE, modelled on *tropopause*.]

stratosphere /stráttə sfeer/ *n.* **1.** REGION OF THE ATMOSPHERE the region of the Earth's atmosphere between the troposphere and mesosphere, from 10 km/6 mi. to 50 km/30 mi. above the Earth's surface. It has no clouds and is marked by gradual temperature increase. ◊ *ionosphere, mesosphere, troposphere* **2.** VERY HIGH OR HIGHEST POSITION a very high or the highest level or position [Early 20thC. Coined from STRATUM + -SPHERE.]

stratospheric /strátta sférrik/, **stratospherical** /-sférrik'l/ *adj.* **1.** RELATING TO STRATOSPHERE relating or belonging to the stratosphere **2.** VERY HIGH very or excessively high —**stratospherically** *adv.*

stratovolcano /stráytō vol káynō/ (*plural* **-noes** *or* **-nos**) *n.* a volcano consisting of layers of lava alternating with ash or cinder

stratum /stráatəm, stráy-/ (*plural* **-ta** /-, -tə/) *n.* **1.** LAYER any of several parallel layers or levels of sth (*formal*) ○ *We found several strata of archaeological material on the site.* **2.** GEOL = **bed** *n.* 12 **3.** LAYER OF ATMOSPHERE OR SEA a layer of the atmosphere or the sea **4.** BIOL LAYER OF CELLS a layer of living cells **5.** SOC SCI LAYER OF SOCIETY a social class or level of society consisting of people of similar cultural, economic, or educational status **6.** LEVEL WITHIN SYSTEM a layer or level within an ordered system ○ *the various strata of meaning within the text* [Late 16thC. From modern Latin, from Latin, literally 'sth thrown down', from, ultimately, *sternere* (see STREW).] —**stratal** *adj.*

stratus /stráytəss, stráa-/ (*plural* **-ti** /-tī/) *n.* a low-lying flat grey cloud formation [Early 19thC. From modern Latin, which evolved from Latin, the past participle of *sternere* (see STREW).]

Strauss /strówss/, **Johann** (1804–49) Austrian conductor and composer. His compositions include many waltzes and marches. Known as **Johann Strauss the Elder**

Strauss, Johann (1825–99) Austrian composer. The son of Johann Strauss the Elder, he wrote operettas including *Die Fledermaus* (1874) and waltzes and other dance pieces including *The Blue Danube* (1867). Known as **Johann Strauss the Younger**

Strauss /strowss/, **Richard** (1864–1949) German conductor and composer. His late romantic symphonic poems and operas such as *Der Rosenkavalier* (1911) develop the ideas of Richard Wagner and are characterized by rich harmonization.

stravaig /strə váyg/, **stravage** *vi.* (**-vaigs, -vaiging, -vaiged; -ages, -aging, -aged**) *Scotland, Ireland, N England* WANDER AIMLESSLY to wander about in an aimless manner ■ *n. Scotland, Ireland, N England* STROLL an aimless ramble [Late 18thC. Origin uncertain: perhaps a shortening of *extravage*, from medieval Latin *extravagari* (see EXTRAVAGANT).]

Stravinsky /strə vínski/, **Igor** (1882–1971) Russian-born US composer. A major figure in 20th-century music, he experimented widely with musical styles and forms and wrote the music for Sergei Diaghilev's ballets *The Firebird* (1910), *Petrushka* (1911), and *The Rite of Spring* (1913). Full name **Igor Fyodorovich Stravinsky**

straw /straw/ *n.* **1.** STALKS OF THRESHED CEREAL CROPS the stalks of threshed cereal crops such as wheat or barley. It is used as bedding and food for animals, for weaving into objects such as baskets or mats, and for thatching. **2.** BOT DRIED GRASS STALK a single

Igor Stravinsky
AKG London

dried stalk of a cereal crop or grass **3.** CRAFT ITEM MADE OF STRAW sth made of straw, e.g. a hat or basket **4.** THIN TUBE FOR SUCKING UP DRINK a long thin tube, often made of paper or plastic, used for sucking up a drink **5.** STH WORTHLESS anything of little or no importance or value **6.** COLOURS = **straw colour** ■ *adj.* COLOURS OF STRAW COLOUR of the pale brownish-yellow colour of straw [Old English *strēaw*. Ultimately from an Indo-European word meaning 'to spread', which is also the ancestor of English *strew*. The underlying idea is of sth strewn.] —**strawy** *adj.* ◊ **a straw in the wind** a relatively minor incident or thing that gives some indication of what is likely to happen in the future ◊ **clutch** *or* **grasp at straws** to be willing to try anything that may help in a situation that is unlikely to succeed ◊ **draw the short straw** to be chosen from a group of people to do a difficult or unpleasant task

Strawberry

strawberry /stráwbəri/ (*plural* **-ries**) *n.* **1.** PLANTS PLANT WITH EDIBLE RED FRUIT a trailing plant of the rose family that has white flowers and is cultivated for its edible red fruit. Genus: *Fragaria.* **2.** FOOD EDIBLE PART OF STRAWBERRY PLANT a small soft sweet part of the strawberry plant, approximately heart-shaped, with tiny single-seeded fruits on its surface. It may be eaten raw or processed to flavour other foods. [*Straw* perhaps in the obsolete sense 'small piece of chaff' (referring to the external seeds), or perhaps because the plant's runners resemble straws]

strawberry blonde *adj.* REDDISH-BLONDE used to describe hair that is very pale in colour with a reddish or pinkish tinge ■ *n.* SB WITH STRAWBERRY BLONDE HAIR sb who has strawberry blonde hair

strawberry bush *n.* a shrub or small tree of eastern North America with tiny flowers and scarlet pods and seeds. Latin name: *Euonymus americanus.*

strawberry mark *n.* a raised red birthmark, often found on the scalp or face, containing small blood vessels

strawberry roan *n.* a horse that has coat of reddish hairs mixed with white

strawberry tomato *n.* FOOD the round yellow edible fruit of the strawberry tomato plant

strawberry tree *n.* a small evergreen tree of the heath family, native to southern Europe, that has white or pink flowers and small berries resembling strawberries. Latin name: *Arbutus unedo.*

strawboard /stráw bawrd/ *n.* a coarse cardboard made of straw pulp and used in making packaging materials and book covers

straw colour *n.* a pale brownish-yellow colour —**straw-coloured** *adj.*

strawflower /stráw flowər/ *n.* an Australian plant with flower heads that remain colourful when dried. Latin name: *Helichrysum bracteatum.*

straw-hat *adj. US* used to describe or relating to a theatre that operates only in the summer [From the relatively rustic beginnings of these theatres, whose productions were often staged in a converted barn or town hall]

straw man *n.* a straw figure made to resemble a human being

straw mushroom *n.* a small brown or pale-coloured edible mushroom used in Chinese cookery. It has a delicate flavour and a slightly gelatinous texture. Latin name: *Volvariella volvacea.*

straw poll, **straw vote** *n.* an unofficial poll or vote used to discover the likely result of an election or the trend of opinion regarding a particular issue

straw wine *n.* a type of sweet wine made from grapes that have been partially dried in the sun, especially on a bed of straw

strawworm /stráw wurm/ *n.* = **caddis worm** [*Straw* because it infests stalks of grain]

stray /stray/ *vi.* (**strays, straying, strayed**) **1. WANDER AWAY** to leave the correct course or wander away from the correct place, often unintentionally **2. BECOME SEPARATED FROM GROUP** to move away from or become separated from a flock or group **3. WANDER ABOUT AIMLESSLY** to roam or wander without a particular aim or destination **4. DIGRESS FROM SUBJECT** to digress or become diverted from the main subject **5. DEPART FROM ACCEPTED STANDARDS** to depart from traditional or accepted standards of behaviour **6. MEANDER** to take an indirect course ■ *adj.* **1. LOST OR HOMELESS** homeless, lost, or wandering **2. SCATTERED OR SEPARATED** scattered, separated, or happening accidentally or randomly ■ *n.* **1. SB LOST** sb, especially a child, who is lost **2.** AGRIC **LOST OR HOMELESS DOMESTIC ANIMAL** a domestic animal that is lost, has been turned loose, or has wandered away from the place where it lives ■ **strays** *npl.* ELECTRON ENG **ELECTRICAL INTERFERENCE** electrical interference in a radio or television broadcast, causing a random crackling noise or disruption of a picture [13thC. Shortening of *astray*, from Old French *estraier*, of uncertain origin: perhaps ultimately from Latin *extra vagari* 'to wander outside' (source of English *extravagant*).] —**strayer** *n.*

streak /streek/ *n.* **1. THIN STRIPE OF CONTRASTING COLOUR** a long thin stripe or band that is a different colour from its background or surroundings **2. LAYER OF STH** a layer or strip of sth **3. CONTRASTING CHARACTERISTIC** a characteristic of sb or sth, especially one that is only occasionally evident or that contrasts with other characteristics ○ *a happy-go-lucky streak* **4. SHORT PERIOD OR UNBROKEN RUN** a short period or unbroken run, especially of good or bad luck ○ *The team is finally having a winning streak.* **5. RUN IN PUBLIC BY NAKED PERSON** a quick run through a public place by a person with no clothes on, usually as a joke or publicity stunt (*informal*) **6. LIGHTNING FLASH** a flash of lightning **7.** MINERALS **MARK OF MINERAL POWDER** the coloured mark that a mineral makes when scratched on an unglazed porcelain tile. This mark is used to identify the mineral. **8.** BOT **VIRAL PLANT DISEASE** a viral disease of plants such as potatoes or tomatoes that produces discoloured markings on stems and leaves **9.** MICROBIOL **LINEAR GROWTH OF BACTERIA** a linear growth of bacteria on the surface of a culture medium, produced by drawing a contaminated needle across the medium ■ *v.* (**streaks, streaking, streaked**) **1.** *vt.* **MARK WITH STREAKS** to mark or cover sth with streaks **2.** *vt.* HAIR **LIGHTEN HAIR** to lighten strands or sections of hair with a bleach or dye **3.** *vi.* **BECOME STREAKED** to become streaked or form streaks **4.** *vi.* **DASH OR RUSH** to move at great speed **5.** *vi.* **RUN NAKED THROUGH PUBLIC PLACE** to run across or through a public place with no clothes on, usually as a joke or publicity stunt (*informal*) [Old English *strica*. Ultimately from a prehistoric Germanic word meaning 'to touch lightly', which is also the ancestor of English *strike*.] —**streaked** *adj.*

streaker /streékər/ *n.* sb who runs through a public place with no clothes on, usually as a joke or publicity stunt (*informal*)

streaky /streéki/ (**-ier, -iest**) *adj.* **1. MARKED WITH STREAKS** covered or marked with streaks ○ *I cleaned the windows twice but they still looked streaky.* **2. OCCURRING AS STREAKS** occurring in the form of streaks **3. INCONSISTENT** variable and uneven in quality ○ *Her work's a bit streaky.* —**streakily** *adv.* —**streakiness** *n.*

streaky bacon *n.* bacon that consists of alternate layers of meat and fat

stream /streem/ *n.* **1. SMALL RIVER** a narrow and shallow river **2. CONSTANT FLOW** a constant flow of liquid or gas **3. AIR OR WATER CURRENT** a current of air or water **4. CONTINUOUS SERIES** a continuous series or procession of people, things, or events, usually moving in a line or in a certain direction **5. QUICK OR UNBROKEN FLOW** a quick or uninterrupted burst, flow, or succession ○ *a stream of questions* **6. PREVAILING ATTITUDE** a general or prevailing attitude, drift, or trend **7. BEAM OF LIGHT** a steady ray or beam of light **8.** EDUC **GROUP OF PUPILS OF SIMILAR ABILITY** a group or level in which pupils of similar ability are placed and taught together ■ *v.* (**streams, streaming, streamed**) **1.** *vi.* **FLOW IN LARGE QUANTITIES** to flow continuously or quickly in large quantities **2.** *vi.* **MOVE IN QUANTITY IN SAME DIRECTION** to move continuously in large numbers in the same direction **3.** *vti.* **PRODUCE FLOW OF LIQUID** to emit or produce liquid in a continuous flow ○ *His eyes streamed tears.* **4.** *vti.* **FLOAT FREELY** to float or trail freely in air, wind, or water, or cause sth to do this ○ *an advertising banner streaming behind the plane* **5.** *vi.* **POUR OUT IN TRAIL OR BEAM** to issue in a beam or move forward leaving a trail **6.** *vti.* EDUC **PUT PUPILS IN ABILITY GROUPS** to place pupils in groups according to their ability [Old English *strēam*. Ultimately from an Indo-European word meaning 'to flow', which is also the ancestor of English *rhythm, haemorrhoid*, and *maelstrom*.]

streambed /streém bed/ *n.* a channel through which a stream flows or used to flow

streamer /streémər/ *n.* **1. NARROW FLAG** a long narrow flag or banner **2. DECORATIVE PAPER STRIP** a long narrow strip of coloured paper or other material that is used for decoration **3.** ASTRON **LUMINOUS STREAK IN SKY** any one of the luminous streaks that make up the aurora borealis and the aurora australis **4.** PRESS **HEADLINE RUNNING ACROSS A FULL PAGE** a large headline that extends the entire width of a newspaper page

streaming /streéming/ *n.* **1.** EDUC **ABILITY GROUPING OF PUPILS** the practice of placing pupils in groups according to ability. US term **tracking 2.** CELL BIOL = **cyclosis**

streamlet /streémlət/ *n.* a small stream

streamline /streém līn/ *vt.* (**-lines, -lining, -lined**) **1. DESIGN OR BUILD WITH SMOOTH SHAPE** to design or build sth with a smooth shape so that it moves with minimum resistance through air or water **2. MAKE STH MORE EFFICIENT** to make sth such as a business, organization, or manufacturing process more efficient, especially by simplifying or modernizing it ■ *n.* **1. CONTOUR DESIGNED TO MINIMIZE RESISTANCE** a contour of a body, e.g. of a car, boat, or aeroplane, designed to minimize resistance when moving through air or water **2.** PHYS **LINE IN FLUID** a line in a fluid indicating the direction of the velocity of a particle —**streamlined** *adj.* —**streamlining** *n.*

streamline flow *n.* a flow of fluid in which the particles follow continuous paths and the fluid velocity at a particular point either remains constant or varies regularly with time. ◊ **turbulent flow**

stream of consciousness *n.* **1.** LITERAT **LITERARY STYLE** a literary style that presents a character's continuous random flow of thoughts as they arise (*hyphenated when used before a noun*) **2.** PSYCHOL **FLOW OF THOUGHTS** the continuous uninterrupted flow of thoughts and feelings through sb's mind

streamy /streémi/ (**-ier, -iest**) *adj.* **1. HAVING MANY STREAMS** covered with or rich in streams (*literary*) **2. FLOWING** flowing in a steady stream —**streaminess** *n.*

Streep /streep/, **Meryl** (*b.* 1949) US actor. She won Academy Awards for *Kramer vs. Kramer* (1979) and *Sophie's Choice* (1982). Real name **Mary Louise Streep**

street /street/ *n.* **1. PUBLIC ROAD IN TOWN** a public road, especially in a town or city, usually lined with buildings **2. BUILDINGS ON STREET** the buildings on a particular street **3. PART OF ROAD BETWEEN PAVEMENTS** the part of a road that lies between the pavements and is used by vehicles **4. PEOPLE LIVING IN A STREET** the people who live or work in a particular street ■ *adj.* **RELATED TO MODERN URBAN SOCIETY** widely found or used in a modern urban environment or fashionable in its culture, especially among young people or the underworld ○ *Street language has worked its way into the mainstream language.* [Old English *strǣt*. Via prehistoric West Germanic from late Latin *strata* 'paved road', from, ultimately, Latin *sternere* 'to pave, throw down' (source of English *strew*).] ◇ **be on the street** to have nowhere to live ◇ **be right up sb's street** to be exactly suitable or appropriate for sb ◇ **be streets ahead (of sb *or* sth)** to be much better in some way than sb or sth ◇ **go on the streets** to become a prostitute ◇ **the man *or* person *or* woman in the street** the average person

street Arab, **street arab** *n.* an offensive term for a child who has run way from home and lives on the streets (*dated offensive*) [From the perception of Arabs as nomadic]

streetcar /streét kaar/ *n. US, Can* = **tram**

street credibility, **street cred** *n.* popularity and acceptance among fashionable urban people, especially the young —**street-credible** *adj.*

street door *n.* the door of a house or other building that opens onto the street

street fashion *n.* fashion invented and worn by ordinary people rather than by fashion designers, often associated with popular styles of music and dance or with political or class affiliations

street fighter *n.* **1. SB WHO LEARNT FIGHTING ON STREETS** sb whose fighting skills were learnt on the streets rather than through formal training as a boxer **2. SB CUNNING** sb who is tough, cunning, and aggressive (*informal*)

street furniture *n.* objects that are placed in the street for public use, such as pillar boxes, litter bins, benches, and streetlights

streetlight /streét līt/, **streetlamp** /-lamp/ *n.* a light, normally attached to the top of a tall post and one of a series, that illuminates a road or street at night

street name *n.* an informal or colloquial name given to an illegal drug by those who sell or use it ○ *'Smack' has long been used as a street name for heroin.*

Streeton /streétən/, **Sir Arthur Ernest** (1867–1943) Australian painter. He pioneered Australian impressionism and was one of the founders of the Heidelberg School.

streetscape /streét skayp/ *n.* an artistic portrayal of a street and its activities, especially a busy city street

street theatre *n.* dramatic entertainment usually performed outdoors, e.g. in a park or shopping precinct

street value *n.* the price that sth illegal would fetch if sold to a customer

street virus *n.* the natural virulent strain of a virus as distinguished from a less virulent strain of the same organism that has been grown or treated in a laboratory

streetwalker /streét wawkər/ *n.* a prostitute who solicits in the streets (*informal*) —**streetwalking** *n.*

streetwise /streét wīz/ *adj.* shrewd and experienced enough to be able to survive in the often difficult and dangerous environment of a modern city (*informal*)

Strega /stráygə/ *tdmk.* a trademark for an aromatic Italian liqueur flavoured with herbs, spices, and sometimes fruit

Strehlow /stráylō/, **T.G.H.** (1908–78) Australian anthropologist and linguist. He was the author of pioneering studies of Aboriginal languages, myths, and songs. Full name **Theodor George Henry Strehlow**

Streisand /strī sand/, **Barbra** (*b.* 1942) US singer, actor, and film director. The star of musicals, comedies, and dramas, she won an Academy Award for her acting debut in *Funny Girl* (1968). Born **Barbara Joan Streisand**

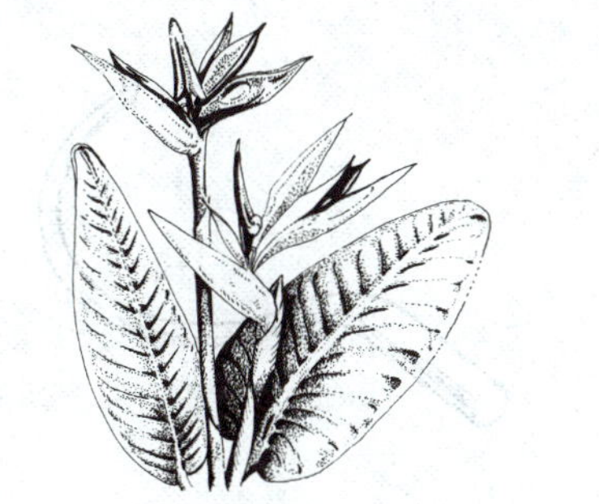

Strelitzia

strelitzia /stre lítsi ə/ (*plural* **-as** *or* **-a**) *n.* a perennial plant of southern Africa that is widely cultivated for its showy flowers that are often unusual or irregular in shape. Genus: *Strelitzia.* [Late 18thC. Named after Charlotte of Mecklenburg-*Strelitz*, queen of George III.]

strength /strength/ *n.* **1.** PHYSICAL OR MENTAL POWER the physical or mental power that makes sb or sth strong **2.** RESISTANCE the ability to withstand force, pressure, or stress **3.** DEFENSIVE ABILITY the ability to resist attack **4.** DEGREE OF INTENSITY degree of intensity, e.g. of colour, light, smell, or sound **5.** FORCE OF FEELING degree of force or effectiveness, e.g. of beliefs or feelings **6.** PERSUASIVE POWER power to convince or persuade, e.g. by argument or suggestion **7.** INTENSITY OF EXPRESSION the intensity of the way sb expresses ideas or feelings **8.** POTENCY the potency of sth such as an alcoholic drink or a drug **9.** NUMBER OF PEOPLE NEEDED FOR STH the number of people required to make sth such as an army, team, or workforce complete, used as a measure of capability **10.** ASSET OR QUALITY an extremely valuable or useful ability, asset, or quality ○ *One of the strengths of this system is its adaptability.* **11.** FIN MAINTENANCE OF PRICES tendency of stock or overall market prices to be stable or rise due to sufficient demand at current prices [Old English *strengþu*. Ultimately from a prehistoric Germanic base meaning 'strong', which is also the ancestor of English *strong*.] ◇ **go from strength to strength** to go on from one success or achievement to another and get progressively better ◇ **in strength** in large numbers ◇ **on the strength of sth** on the basis of sth

strengthen /stréngth'n/ (**-ens, -ening, -ened**) *vti.* to make sth stronger or more powerful, or increase in strength or force —**strengthener** *n.*

strenuous /strénnyoo əss/ *adj.* **1.** TAXING requiring great effort, energy, stamina, or strength **2.** FORCEFUL active, energetic, or determined [Early 17thC. Formed from Latin *strenuus* 'brisk, active', of unknown origin.] —**strenuosity** /strénnyoo óssəti/ *n.* —**strenuously** /strénnyoo əssli/ *adv.* —**strenuousness** /-nəss/ *n.*

WORD KEY: SYNONYMS

See Synonyms at ***hard***.

strep /strep/ *n.* STREPTOCOCCUS a streptococcus (*informal*) ■ *adj.* STREPTOCOCCAL streptococcal (*informal*)

strep throat *n.* an acute sore throat caused by the bacterium *Streptococcus pyogenes* and accompanied by fever and inflammation

strepto- *prefix.* **1.** streptococcus ○ *streptokinase* **2.** twisted chain ○ *streptococcus* **3.** streptomyces ○ *streptothricin* [From Greek *streptos* 'twisted', from *strephein* 'to turn']

streptobacillus /stréptō bə sílləss/ (*plural* **-li** /-lī/) *n.* a rod-shaped bacterium that often causes disease, e.g. rat-bite fever. Individual cells join to form structures resembling chains. Genus: *Streptobacillus.*

streptocarpus /stréptə kaárpəss/ *n.* a subtropical plant with brightly coloured tubular flowers and often only one large leaf. Genus: *Streptocarpus.* [Early 19thC. Via modern Latin, genus name, from Greek *streptos* 'twisted' + *karpos* 'fruit', because its fruit is spirally twisted.]

streptococcus /stréptə kókəss/ (*plural* **-ci** /-kók sī/) *n.* a spherical bacterium that often causes disease, e.g. scarlet fever or pneumonia. The bacteria link together in pairs or chains. Genus: *Streptococcus.* [Late 19thC. Via modern Latin, genus name, literally 'twisted berry', from Greek *streptos* 'twisted' (because the chains are usually twisted) + *coccus* 'berry'.] —**streptococcal** *adj.* —**streptococcic** /-sik/ *adj.*

streptodornase /stréptə dáwr nayz, -nayss/ *n.* an enzyme derived from streptococci and used with streptokinase to liquefy and drain blood clots and purulent discharges, especially during surgery [Mid-20thC. Coined from STREPTOCOCCUS + contraction of *deoxyribonuclease*.]

streptokinase /stréptə kī́ nayz, -nayss/ *n.* an enzyme produced by streptococci that dissolves blood clots [Mid-20thC. Coined from STREPTOCOCCAL + KINASE.]

streptolysin /stréptə lī́ssin/ *n.* a substance that breaks down red blood cells and is produced by streptococci

streptomyces /stréptə mī́ seez/ (*plural* **-ces**) *n.* an aerobic soil bacterium. Some streptomyces produce antibiotics. Genus: *Streptomyces.* [Mid-20thC. From modern Latin, genus name, coined from Greek *strepto-* 'twisted' + *mukēs* 'fungus', because it forms twisted chains and resembles mould.]

streptomycin /stréptə mī́ssin/ *n.* an antibiotic produced by a soil bacterium that is used to treat infections caused by certain bacteria, e.g. tuberculosis. Formula: $C_{21}H_{39}N_7O_{12}$.

streptothricin /stréptə thríssin/ *n.* an antibiotic produced by a soil bacterium that is used against bacteria and certain fungi [Mid-20thC. Coined from modern Latin *Streptothric-*, stem of *Streptothrix*, former genus name, coined from Greek *strepto-* 'twisted' + *thrix* 'hair', because it grows in hair-like filaments.]

Stresemann /stráyssə man, shtráyssə man/, **Gustav** (1878–1929) German statesman. As German chancellor (1923) and minister of foreign affairs (1923–29), he worked for conciliation after World War I and secured Germany's admission to the League of Nations. He shared a Nobel Peace Prize (1926).

stress /stress/ *n.* **1.** STRAIN FELT BY SB mental, emotional, or physical strain, caused, e.g. by anxiety or overwork. It may cause such symptoms as raised blood pressure or depression. **2.** CAUSE OF STRAIN sth that causes mental or emotional strain **3.** SPECIAL IMPORTANCE special emphasis, importance, or significance attached to sth **4.** PHON EMPHASIS ON SYLLABLE the emphasis placed on a particular sound or syllable by pronouncing it more loudly or forcefully than those surrounding it in the same word or phrase **5.** POETRY EMPHASIS IN POETRY the emphasis placed on a particular syllable or word as part of the rhythm of a poem or line **6.** MUSIC ACCENT IN MUSIC the emphasis placed on a particular note as part of the rhythm of a piece of music, or a mark representing this **7.** PHYS FORCE DEFORMING A BODY a force or system of forces exerted on a body and resulting in deformation or strain ■ *vt.* (**stresses, stressing, stressed**) **1.** EMPHASIZE STH to place emphasis on or attach importance to sth **2.** PHON PRONOUNCE FORCEFULLY to pronounce a word or syllable more loudly or forcefully than those surrounding it **3.** LANGUAGE = **accent** *n.* 3 **4.** SUBJECT TO STRESS to cause sb or sth to experience mental or physical stress [14thC. Partly a shortening of DISTRESS, and partly via Old French *estresse* 'narrowness', from Latin *strictus* 'compressed' (source of English *strict*).] —**stressed** *adj.*

WORD KEY: SYNONYMS

See Synonyms at ***worry***.

stress out *vti.* to affect sb with emotional, mental, or physical stress, or be so affected

STRESS *abbr.* structural engineering system solver

stressed out *adj.* unable to relax or function properly as the result of experiencing mental or emotional stress (*informal*) (*hyphenated when used before a noun*)

stress fracture *n.* a small fracture of a bone caused by repeated physical strain, sometimes experienced, e.g. by gymnasts, long-distance runners, or marching soldiers

stressful /stréssf'l/ *adj.* causing or involving mental or physical stress —**stressfully** *adv.* —**stressfulness** *n.*

stress mark *n.* a mark placed before, on, or after a syllable that is to be stressed when the word containing it is pronounced

stressor /stréssər/ *n.* an activity, experience, or other situation that causes stress, e.g. lack of water to a plant or overwork to a person

stretch /strech/ *v.* (**stretches, stretching, stretched**) **1.** *vti.* EXTEND OR BECOME EXTENDED to lengthen, widen, or extend sth, or become lengthened, widened, or extended, especially by force **2.** *vi.* EXPAND AND REGAIN ORIGINAL SHAPE to be capable of expanding and returning to its original shape afterwards **3.** *vti.* EXTEND OR BE EXTENDED EXCESSIVELY to extend sth or be extended excessively so that the shape is permanently altered ○ *The sleeves of this sweater have stretched.* **4.** *vti.* EXTEND BODY TO FULL LENGTH to straighten or extend the body or part of it, especially the limbs, to full length ○ *She woke up, yawned, and stretched.* **5.** *vt.* STRAIN BODY PART to strain a part of the body such as a muscle **6.** *vti.* MAKE STH TAUT to make sth taut or tight, or become taut or tight **7.** *vt.* SUSPEND STH BETWEEN TWO POINTS to suspend sth, or make sth reach, between two points **8.** *vi.* EXTEND IN SPACE to spread out or extend over an area or in a particular direction **9.** *vti.* EXTEND STH OVER TIME to last or continue over a period of time, or prolong sth **10.** *vt.* MAKE SMALL AMOUNT GO FURTHER to make limited supplies or resources go further than usual, planned, or expected **11.** *vi.* BE ENOUGH to be sufficient to allow sth ○ *Will the budget stretch to hiring a temporary assistant?* **12.** *vt.* EXCEED LIMIT OR BREAK RULE to exceed a limit or break a rule that would usually prohibit sth **13.** *vt.* PUSH STH TO LIMIT to strain or push sth to the limit ○ *You're stretching my patience.* **14.** *vt.* PUSH SB TO LIMIT OF ABILITY to cause sb to make full use of abilities or intellect, e.g. with challenging or demanding work **15.** *vt.* EXAGGERATE to make sth sound better or worse than it really is, especially in order to make it seem more impressive (*informal*) ○ *To call his house a mansion is stretching it a bit.* **16.** *vt.* KNOCK SB DOWN to knock sb down with a blow (*informal*) **17.** *vti.* HANG SB to hang or be hanged from a noose (*archaic*) ■ *n.* **1.** STRETCHING EXERCISE the straightening and extending of a part of the body, e.g. as an exercise **2.** EXPANSE a large expanse of sth, especially land or water **3.** PERIOD OF TIME an uninterrupted period of time **4.** PRISON TERM a term of imprisonment (*informal*) **5.** ELASTICITY the ability to expand and return to the original shape afterwards **6.** CHALLENGE sth that is difficult to achieve (*informal*) **7.** HORSERACING, MOTOR SPORTS, ATHLETICS STRAIGHT PART OF RACECOURSE the straight part of a racecourse, especially the final section approaching the finishing line **8.** FINAL STAGE the final stage of an event, task, process, or period of time, especially one that has been difficult or challenging ■ *adj.* EXTENDED TO PROVIDE EXTRA SPACE extended or enlarged in order to prove extra space, e.g. for additional seating [Old English *streccan*, of uncertain origin. Probably ultimately from a prehistoric Germanic base meaning 'rigid' (hence 'taut, stretched'), which is also the ancestor of English *starch*.] —**stretchability** /stréchə bílləti/ *n.* —**stretchable** /stréchəb'l/ *adj.* ◇ **at a stretch 1.** continuously ○ *worked five hours at a stretch* **2.** with great difficulty or effort ○ *could get there by six at a stretch* ◇ **at full stretch** using all the energy or resources available

stretcher /stréchər/ *n.* **1.** MED DEVICE FOR CARRYING SB LYING DOWN a device consisting of a sheet of material such as canvas stretched over a frame, used to carry sb in a lying position who is sick, injured, or dead **2.** *ANZ* CAMPING CAMP BED a camp bed consisting of a folding tubular metal frame and a canvas covering **3.** PAINTING FRAME FOR ARTIST'S CANVAS a wooden frame over which a canvas for an oil painting is stretched **4.** FURNITURE BAR BRACING FURNITURE LEGS a bar that joins and braces the legs of a chair, table, or other piece of furniture **5.** BUILDING STRONG BEAM USED AS BRACE a strong, usually horizontal beam or bar that is used as a brace in the framework of a structure **6.** BUILDING STONE WITH LONG EDGE FACING OUT a brick or stone laid in a wall so that its longer edge forms part of the face of the wall. ◊ **header 7.** ROWING BOARD FOR BRACING ROWER'S FEET a board fixed across the width of a boat, on which a rower's feet can be braced **8.** EXAGGERATED STORY an exaggerated story or a lie based partly on the truth (*slang*) ■ *vt.* (**stretchers, stretchering, stretchered**) CARRY ON STRETCHER to carry a sick, injured, or dead person on a stretcher ○ *Their star player was stretchered off in the first half.*

zh vision In foreign words: kh German Bach; aN French vin; aaN French blanc; ö German schön, French feu; öN French bon; öN French un; ü French rue Stress marks: ´ as in secret \séek rət\; academic \àkə démmik\

stretcher-bearer *n.* sb who helps carry a stretcher, especially a soldier given the task in wartime

stretch knit *n.* knitted fabric that can stretch and return to its original shape afterwards (*hyphenated when used before a noun*)

stretch mark *n.* a mark left on the skin of the abdomen, breasts, buttocks, or thighs after pregnancy or weight loss (*often used in the plural*)

stretchy /stréchi/ (**-ier, -iest**) *adj.* capable of being stretched, usually returning to its original shape afterwards, or tending to stretch —**stretchiness** *n.*

stretto /stréttō/ (*plural* **-tos** *or* **-ti** /-ti/) *n.* **1.** OVERLAPPING PASSAGES IN FUGUE in a fugue or similar work, the successive statements of the theme very close together in time **2.** FAST PASSAGE the speeding up of a piece of music at a climactic moment [Mid-18thC. Via Italian, literally 'narrow, tight', from Latin *strictus* (see STRICT).]

streusel /stroóz'l, stróyz-/ *n. US* a crumbly topping for cakes and pastries. It is made of sugar, flour, butter, cinnamon, and often chopped nuts. [Early 20thC. From German, from *streuen* 'to sprinkle'.]

strew /stroo/ (**strews, strewing, strewed, strewn** /stroon/ *or* **strewed**) *v.* **1.** *vt.* SCATTER STH to scatter sth, especially carelessly or untidily ○ *Clothes were strewn all over the floor.* **2.** *vti.* SPREAD OVER AREA to spread or become spread over a large area ○ *areas strewn with landmines* [Old English *strewian*. Ultimately from an Indo-European word that is also the ancestor of English *straw* and *stratum*.] —**strewer** *n.*

strewth /strooth/, **struth** *interj.* used to express surprise or irritation (*slang*) [Late 19thC. Shortening of *God's truth*, an oath.]

stria /strī ə/ (*plural* **-ae** /-ee/) *n.* **1.** GROOVE OR SCRATCH a thin narrow groove or channel in the surface of sth, e.g. a decorative feature on a column **2.** STRIPE OR BAND a stripe, streak, or narrow band, e.g. a band of nerve fibres or stretch marks seen in pregnancy (**striae gravidarum**) **3.** GEOL = **striation** *n.* 3 [Mid-16thC. From Latin, 'furrow, channel' (originally 'sth grazed'). Ultimately from an Indo-European word that is also the ancestor of English *strike*.]

striate /strī áyt/ *vt.* (**-ates, -ating, -ated**) MARK WITH STRIAE to mark sth with parallel grooves, ridges, stripes, or narrow bands ■ *adj.* = **striated** [Late 17thC. From Latin *striare*, from *stria* (see STRIA).]

striated /strī áytid/ *adj.* marked with parallel grooves, ridges, stripes, or narrow bands

striated muscle *n.* a muscle or muscle tissue, e.g. cardiac muscle or the muscles attached to the skeleton, that shows light and dark bands within the muscle fibres

striation /strī áysh'n/ *n.* **1.** STRIPY PATTERN patterning or marking with parallel grooves or narrow bands **2.** ANAT BANDING OR BAND WITHIN MUSCLE FIBRE the striped pattern of striated muscle, or any of the light and dark bands that make up this effect **3.** GEOL GROOVE OR SCRATCH a narrow groove or scratch on an exposed rock face, caused by abrasion by hard rock fragments embedded in a moving glacier

stricken /stríkən/ past participle of **strike** ■ *adj.* **1.** DEEPLY OR BADLY AFFECTED BY STH deeply or very badly affected by sth such as grief, misfortune, or trouble **2.** AFFECTED BY ILLNESS experiencing severe physical symptoms caused by illness or injury **3.** HIT BY MISSILE injured, struck, or wounded, e.g. by a missile [Originally the past participle of STRIKE] —**strickenly** *adv.*

strickle /strík'l/ *n.* **1.** BOARD FOR LEVELLING OFF EXCESS MATERIAL a board used to level off excess grain or other material in a container or measuring device **2.** TOOL FOR SHAPING MOULD SURFACE a tool used to shape the surface of a mould ■ *vt.* (**-les, -ling, -led**) USE STRICKLE ON STH to level or shape sth with a strickle [Old English *stricel*. Ultimately from a prehistoric Germanic base that is also the ancestor of English *strike*.]

strict /strikt/ *adj.* **1.** SEVERE IN MAINTAINING DISCIPLINE severe in maintaining discipline or rigorous in ensuring that rules are obeyed **2.** ENFORCED RIGOROUSLY needing to be closely obeyed **3.** PRECISE exact, precise, or narrowly interpreted **4.** FAITHFUL closely observing rules, principles, or practices **5.** ABSOLUTE complete, utter, or absolute **6.** BOT GROWING UPRIGHT growing upward at or very close to the vertical [15thC. From Latin *strictus*, past participle of *stringere* 'to draw tight'.] —**strictly** *adv.* —**strictness** *n.*

WORD KEY: ORIGIN

The Latin word Latin *stringere*, from which *strict* is derived, is also the source of English *constrain*, *constrict*, *distress*, *district*, *prestige*, *restrain*, *restrict*, *strain*, *stress*, and *stringent*.

stricture /stríkchər/ *n.* **1.** SEVERE CRITICISM a severe criticism or strongly critical remark (*formal*) **2.** LIMIT OR RESTRICTION a limit or restriction, especially one that seems unfair or too harsh (*formal*) **3.** MED CONSTRICTION OF BODY PASSAGE an abnormal constriction or narrowing of a body passage [14thC. From Latin *strictura*, from, ultimately, *stringere* 'to draw tight'.] —**strictured** *adj.*

striddle /stidd'l/ *v.* walk with the legs apart (*regional*)

stride /strīd/ *v.* (**strides, striding, strode** /strōd/, **stridden** /strídd'n/) **1.** *vi.* WALK WITH LONG REGULAR STEPS to walk with long regular steps, often briskly or energetically **2.** *vti.* TAKE LONG STEP OVER STH to cross or step over sth with a long step **3.** *vti.* STRADDLE to sit or stand astride sth (*archaic or literary*) ■ *n.* **1.** LONG STEP a long step, especially one taken briskly or energetically **2.** DISTANCE COVERED BY LONG STEP the distance covered when sb or sth takes a long step **3.** ADVANCE TOWARDS IMPROVING STH an advance or step towards improving or developing sth **4.** WAY OF WALKING a way of walking or running in long regular steps, often taken briskly or energetically **5.** ZOOL COORDINATED FORWARD MOVEMENT BY ANIMAL an act of forward motion by a four-legged animal consisting of a coordinated cycle of movements that brings the legs back to their original positions **6.** MUSIC = **stride piano** ■ **strides** *npl. Aus* TROUSERS a pair of trousers (*informal*) [Old English *strīdan* 'to straddle', of uncertain origin. Perhaps ultimately from a prehistoric Germanic word meaning 'to diverge', which may also be the ancestor of English *strife* and *strive*.] —**strider** *n.* ◇ **get into your stride** to become familiar and at ease with sth so that you can do it easily and well ◇ **take sth in (your) stride** to accept sth without being unduly upset or worried about it

strident /strīd'nt/ *adj.* **1.** LOUD harsh, loud, grating, or shrill **2.** STRONGLY EXPRESSED loudly, strongly, or urgently expressed [Mid-17thC. From Latin, the present participle stem of *stridere* 'to creak' (source of English *stridulate*).] —**stridence** *n.* —**stridency** *n.* —**stridently** *adv.*

stride piano *n.* a style of jazz piano playing in which the right hand plays the melody while the left hand alternates between playing a single note and playing a related chord [*Stride* in the sense 'to straddle', from the movements of the left hand]

stridor /strī dawr, strīdər/ *n.* **1.** HARSH NOISE a harsh, grating, or creaking noise **2.** PATHOL HARSH HIGH-PITCHED WHEEZE a harsh high-pitched wheezing sound made when breathing in or out, caused by obstruction of the air passages [Mid-17thC. From Latin, from *stridere* (see STRIDENT).]

stridulant *adj.* = **stridulous**

stridulate /stríddyoo layt/ (**-lates, -lating, -lated**) *vi.* to make a chirping or grating sound by rubbing certain parts of the body together, as, e.g., male crickets and grasshoppers do [Mid-19thC. Via French *striduler* from, ultimately, Latin *stridere* (see STRIDENT).] —**stridulation** /stríddyoo láysh'n/ *n.* —**stridulator** /stríddyoo laytər/ *n.* —**stridulatory** /stríddyoo laytəri, -lətəri/ *adj.*

stridulous /stríddyooləss/, **stridulant** /-lənt/ *adj.* **1.** MAKING A GRATING SOUND having or making a shrill, harsh, or grating sound **2.** PATHOL OF OBSTRUCTED BREATHING relating to, affected by, or characteristic of stridor [Early 17thC. Formed from Latin *stridulus* 'creaking', from *stridere* (see STRIDENT).] —**stridulously** *adv.* —**stridulousness** *n.*

strife /strīf/ *n.* **1.** BITTER CONFLICT OR RIVALRY bitter and sometimes violent conflict, struggle, or rivalry **2.** *ANZ* TROUBLE trouble or difficulty (*informal*) **3.** STRIVING hard work to get or achieve sth (*archaic*) [12thC. From Old French *estrif*, of uncertain origin: perhaps ultimately from Old High German *strīt* 'quarrel'.] —**strifeless** *adj.*

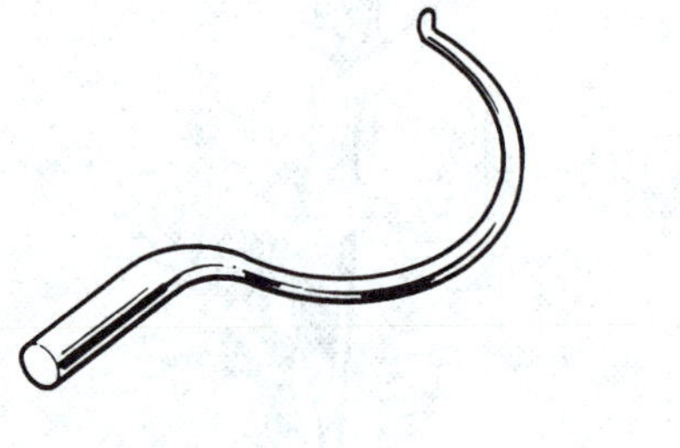

Strigil

strigil /stríjjil/ *n.* an instrument with a curved blade used in ancient Greece and Rome to scrape dirt and sweat from the skin after bathing or exercising [Late 16thC. From Latin *strigilis*.]

strigose /strīgōss, -gōz/ *adj.* **1.** BOT SCALY OR BRISTLY covered with fine scales or short bristles **2.** ZOOL RIDGED with thin, closely spaced grooves or ridges [Late 18thC. From modern Latin *strigosus*, from Latin *striga* 'row'.]

strike /strīk/ *v.* (**strikes, striking, struck** /struk/, **struck**) **1.** *vti.* HIT SB OR STH to hit sb or sth, e.g. with a hand, tool, or weapon ○ *She was struck on the arm by a piece of falling masonry.* **2.** *vti.* DELIVER BLOW to deliver or inflict sth such as a blow or punch **3.** *vti.* COLLIDE WITH SB OR STH to crash into, knock hard against, or collide with sb or sth ○ *The car swerved and struck a tree.* **4.** *vti.* PENETRATE STH to penetrate or seem to go right through sth ○ *The pain struck deep into my shoulder blade.* **5.** *vti.* DAMAGE SB OR STH to hit and damage or injure sth or sb **6.** *vt.* KNOCK AWAY to remove sth with a blow ○ *She struck the wasp from the child's head.* **7.** *vti.* PRODUCE FIRE to produce fire by friction, or be produced by friction **8.** *vti.* LIGHT MATCH to cause a match to light or to be lit by friction ○ *The matches won't strike if they get damp.* **9.** *vt.* OPERATE STH BY PRESSING KEY to operate, produce, or play sth by pressing a key or touching a string, e.g. on a musical instrument or a typewriter **10.** *vti.* INDICATE TIME BY MAKING SOUND to indicate the time by making a sound such as chiming **11.** *vt.* METALL MAKE STH BY STAMPING to make or form sth such as a coin by stamping or punching ○ *Moonbeams struck the placid water on the lake.* **12.** *vti.* SHINE ON STH to fall or shine on sth ○ *Moonbeams struck the placid water on the lake.* **13.** *vt.* BE NOTICED BY SB to catch sb's attention, or be noticed by sb or sth **14.** *vt.* BE PERCEIVED BY SB to be perceived by or become audible to sb **15.** *vt.* MAKE CERTAIN IMPRESSION ON SB to have a certain effect on or make a certain impression on sb **16.** *vt.* ENTER SB'S MIND to enter sb's mind or occur to sb, especially suddenly **17.** *vt.* AFFECT SB WITH EMOTION to affect sb or cause sb to be affected with an emotion in a deep, painful, or sudden way **18.** *vti.* FIND OR DISCOVER STH to come across, find, or discover sth, especially suddenly or unexpectedly **19.** *vti.* MAKE AN ATTACK to make an attack on sb or sth ○ *The enemy struck under cover of darkness.* **20.** *vi.* BITE OR STING SUDDENLY to deliver a sudden, fast bite or sting, typically resulting in injury to the one bitten or stung ○ *Suddenly the snake struck.* **21.** (*past participle* **stricken** *or* **struck**) *vti.* AFFECT SB SUDDENLY to affect sb suddenly or unexpectedly ○ *The illness can strike at any age.* **22.** *vti.* HAPPEN SUDDENLY to happen to sb or sth suddenly or unexpectedly **23.** *vi.* INDUST STOP WORKING AS PROTEST to stop working as a collective form of protest against an employer **24.** *vt. US* INDUST STOP WORKING FOR SB to take part in a strike against an employer ○ *They're striking the auto plant.* **25.** *vt.* CROSS STH OUT to cancel, delete, or cross sth out ○ *The judge ordered that the preceding remark be struck from the record.* **26.** *vt.* AGREE TO TERMS to agree on the terms of sth ○ *struck a deal* **27.** *vt.* ACHIEVE STH BY CAREFUL CONSIDERATION to achieve sth such as a balance or a compromise by careful consideration or calculation **28.** *vt.* ADOPT POSE to adopt or assume sth such as a pose or attitude **29.** *vti.* ANGLING TAKE BAIT to take or attempt to take a bait ○ *The fish are striking today.* **30.** *vti.* BOT GROW ROOTS to send out and establish roots **31.** *vt.* DISMANTLE STH to dismantle sth such as a tent or stage set **32.** *vt.* NAUT LOWER MAST OR SAIL to lower a mast or sail **33.** *vt.* NAUT **LOWER STH IN RESPECT OR SURRENDER** to lower sth such as a flag or sail as a sign of respect or surrender **34.** *vt.* SHIPPING **LOWER STH INTO SHIP'S HOLD** to lower sth into the hold of a ship **35.** *vi. US* NAVY **ATTEMPT TECHNICAL RATING IN US NAVY** to work hard with the aim of achieving a certain technical rating in the US Navy **36.** *vt.* = **strickle** ■ *n.* **1. HIT OR BLOW DELIVERED** a blow delivered by striking **2. SOUND OF HIT** a sound produced by striking sb or sth **3.** INDUST **WORK STOPPAGE** a work stoppage by employees as a protest against an employer **4. REFUSAL TO DO STH AS PROTEST** a refusal to carry out a regular action or activity, e.g. eating or paying rent, as a form of protest **5.** MIL **MILITARY ATTACK USING AIRCRAFT** a military attack, especially one using aircraft **6. SUCCESS IN FINDING STH** a success in finding or discovering sth, especially a valuable mineral source such as gold or oil **7.** BOWLS **KNOCKING DOWN OF BOWLING PINS** the knocking down of all the pins with the first ball in a session of tenpin bowling **8.** COINS **COINS STRUCK AT SAME TIME** the number of coins or medals struck at the same time **9.** GEOL **DIRECTION OF GEOLOGICAL FORMATION** the compass direction of a horizontal line on a sloping rock surface, used to define geological features such as bedding or faults **10.** = **strickle** *n.* 1 **11.** VET **ANIMAL DISEASE CAUSED BY FLIES** an animal disease caused by an infestation of flies or fly eggs in open wounds or moist areas of the skin **12.** ANGLING **PULL ON FISHING LINE BY FISH** a pull on a fishing line indicating that a fish has taken the bait **13.** BOT **SENDING OUT OF PLANT ROOTS** the establishment of roots by a plant cutting or seedling [Old English *strīcan*. Ultimately from a prehistoric Germanic base meaning 'to touch lightly', which is also the ancestor of English *stroke* and *streak*.] ◇ **strike it rich** to be extremely lucky or successful, particularly in money matters

strike down *vt.* **1. CAUSE TO FALL** to cause sb or sth to fall by hitting **2. CAUSE SB TO BECOME VERY ILL** to affect sb or cause sb to become seriously ill, especially suddenly **3. KILL SB** to cause sb to die, especially suddenly

strike off *vt.* **1. PREVENT PROFESSIONAL FROM PRACTISING** to prevent sb, such as a doctor or lawyer, from continuing to practise a particular profession by removing his or her name from the register of authorized practitioners ○ *The surgeon who performed this operation should be struck off.* **2. DELETE STH** to cancel or remove sth from a list, record, or register by crossing it out ○ *A steward struck off the names of the passengers as they boarded the plane.* **3.** PRINTING **PRINT** to print sth

strike out *v.* **1.** *vt.* **DRAW LINE THROUGH STH** to draw a line through sth in order to cancel or delete it **2.** *vt.* **SET OUT ENERGETICALLY** to set out energetically, especially for a particular destination or in a particular direction ○ *We struck out at sunrise, determined to get there by nightfall.* **3.** *vi.* **BEGIN STH** to begin doing sth, especially independently **4.** *vi.* **ATTACK SB OR STH** to attack sb or sth, either physically or verbally **5.** *vi. US, Can* **FAIL** to be unsuccessful (*informal*) ○ *I tried three times to get that job, but struck out completely.*

strike up *v.* **1.** *vti.* **BEGIN TO PLAY** to begin playing or singing sth ○ *struck up the band and played a waltz* **2.** *vt.* **BEGIN STH** to begin sth, or cause sth to begin

strikebound /strīk bownd/ *adj.* closed or unable to operate because people have stopped work as a form of protest

strikebreaker /strīk braykər/ *n.* **1. SB WHO WORKS WHILE OTHERS STRIKE** sb who continues to work for an employer while other employees are on strike **2. SB HIRED TO REPLACE STRIKER** sb hired to do the work of sb who is on strike

strikebreaking /strīk brayking/ *n.* **1. ACTION OF STRIKEBREAKER** the act of working for an employer while other employees are on strike **2. BREAKING UP OF STRIKE** action intended to break up a workers' strike

strike fault *n.* a fault with a strike parallel to the rock strata

strike pay *n.* money paid by a trade union to members who are on strike

striker /strīkər/ *n.* **1.** INDUST **SB ON STRIKE** sb who has stopped working or taken other action as a form of protest **2.** SOCCER **ATTACKING PLAYER IN FOOTBALL TEAM** an attacking player in a football team whose main role is to score goals **3. DEVICE THAT STRIKES TO TELL TIME** a device that strikes to tell the time, e.g. a hammer in a clock or a clapper in a bell **4.** ARMS **MECHANISM THAT DRIVES FIRING PIN FORWARDS** the mechanical part of a firearm that drives the firing pin forwards

strike-slip fault *n.* a geological fault that moves in a direction parallel to its strike

striking /strīking/ *adj.* **1. CONSPICUOUS** conspicuous, marked, or noticeable **2. ATTRACTIVE OR IMPRESSIVE** attracting attention, especially in an impressive or unusual way **3.** INDUST **ON STRIKE** not working as a form of protest —**strikingly** *adv.* —**strikingness** *n.*

striking distance *n.* closeness to sth or to achieving sth

striking price *n.* = **exercise price**

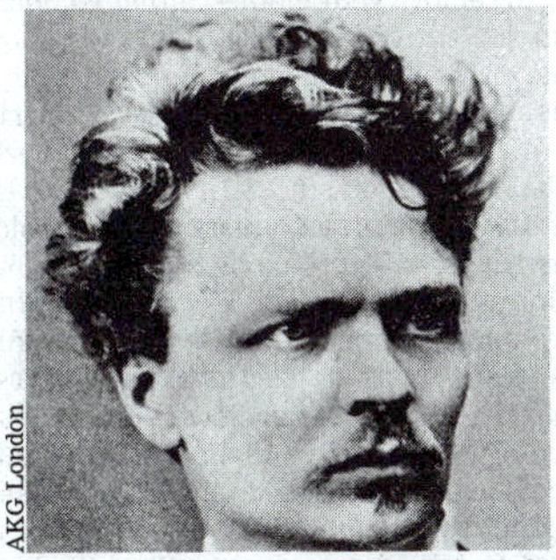

AKG London

August Strindberg

Strindberg /strínd burg/, **August** (1849–1912) Swedish dramatist. Often considered the greatest figure in Swedish literature, he greatly influenced European and US dramatists with his naturalistic novels and plays, notably *The Ghost Sonata* (1908). Full name **Johan August Strindberg** —**Strindbergian** /strind búrgi ən/ *adj.*

Strine /strīn/, **strine** *n.* Australian English, especially a humorous representation in writing of Australian pronunciation, e.g. 'Emma Chisit' for 'How much is it?' (*humorous*) [Mid-20thC. An imitation of the supposed Australian pronunciation of AUSTRALIAN, first used in the books of Alistair Morrison under the pseudonym Afferbeck Lauder, Strine for 'alphabetical order'.]

string /string/ *n.* **1. STRONG THIN CORD** a strong thin cord or twine, usually made of twisted fibres, used for binding, fastening, hanging, or tying **2. STH RESEMBLING STRING** sth that resembles string in form or texture **3. SUCCESSION OF ITEMS** a series of similar or connected acts, events, or things **4. LINE OF THINGS** a series of things forming or arranged in a line, usually one behind another **5. GROUP OF ASSOCIATED THINGS** a group of similar things belonging to, managed by, or connected with a single person or a set of people **6. SEQUENCE OF SIMILAR ELEMENTS** a sequence of elements of the same nature, e.g. letters, numbers, symbols, binary digits, sounds, or words **7. OBJECTS THREADED TOGETHER** a set of objects connected with a single thread **8.** MUSIC **LONG CORD STRETCHED ACROSS MUSICAL INSTRUMENT** a cord made of nylon, wire, or gut that is stretched across a musical instrument and plucked, bowed, or otherwise vibrated in order to produce sound **9.** RACKET GAMES **THIN CORD STRETCHED ACROSS SPORTS RACQUET** any of the thin cords that are tightly stretched across the face of a sports racquet and interwoven to form a mesh **10.** ARCHERY **CORD STRETCHED ACROSS ARCHER'S BOW** the cord stretched between the ends of a bow in archery **11. PLANT FIBRE** a tough chewy fibre in a fruit or vegetable **12. TENDON** a tendon or ligament of an animal (*archaic*) **13.** BUILDING = **stringboard 14.** BUILDING = **string course 15.** SPORTS **PERSON CHOSEN AND RANKED ON ABILITY** a person or group of people chosen, especially for a sports team, and ranked at a specified level on the basis of their ability **16.** CUE GAMES **HIT DETERMINING PLAYING ORDER IN BILLIARDS** an act of hitting the cue ball in billiards towards the head cushion (**lag**) to determine who will play first **17.** CUE GAMES = **baulk line** *n.* 1 **18.** BOWLS **TEN FRAMES OF BOWLING** a game of tenpin bowling consisting of ten frames **19.** PHYS, ASTRON **HYPOTHETICAL ONE-DIMENSIONAL ENTITY** a hypothetical one-dimensional entity that vibrates as it moves through space and is held to be a fundamental component of matter. ◊ **cosmic string, superstring** ■ **strings** *npl.* MUSIC **1. MUSICIANS PLAYING STRINGED INSTRUMENTS** the section of an orchestra consisting of musicians who play stringed instruments **2. STRINGED INSTRUMENTS OF ORCHESTRA** the stringed instruments of an orchestra or other musical ensemble considered as a group ■ *v.* (**strings, stringing, strung** /strung/, **strung**) **1.** *vt.* **THREAD ONTO STRING** to thread things onto a string **2.** *vt.* **HANG STH BETWEEN TWO POINTS** to hang or stretch sth between two points **3.** *vt.* **ARRANGE OR EXTEND STH IN LINE** to arrange or extend sth in a line or series **4.** *vt.* **PROVIDE STH WITH STRING OR STRINGS** to provide sth, e.g. a sports racquet or musical instrument, with a string or strings **5.** *vt.* **FASTEN OR TIE STH WITH STRING** to bind, fasten, hang, or tie sth with a string or strings **6.** *vt.* COOK **REMOVE FIBRES** to remove the stringy fibres from vegetables **7.** *vt.* COOK **REMOVE CURRANTS** to remove currants from their stalks by sliding them off between the prongs of a fork **8.** *vi.* **BECOME STRINGY** to form strings or become stringy **9.** *vti.* CUE GAMES **DETERMINE PLAYING ORDER IN BILLIARDS** to hit the cue ball in billiards towards the head cushion (**lag**) to determine who will play first ■ *adj.* **MADE OF STRING** made of a mesh of string or similar material [Old English *streng*. Ultimately from a prehistoric Germanic base meaning 'stiff' (ancestor also of English *strong*), the underlying idea being of sth twisted until stiff.] —**stringless** *adj.* ◇ **have sb on a string** to be able to control sb easily ◇ **pull strings** to use influence to try to gain an advantage ◇ **pull the strings** to be in control, although not obviously so ◇ **with no strings (attached)** without any conditions or restrictions being made

string along *v.* (*informal*) **1.** *vt.* **DECEIVE OVER A LONG TIME** to deceive or fool sb over an extended period of time, especially by keeping him or her in a state of false hope **2.** *vi.* **ACCOMPANY OR STAY WITH** to accompany or stay with sb, often in a casual manner ○ *She wanted to string along with us when we went to the shops.* **3.** *vi.* **AGREE WITH** to agree or go along with another or another person's idea or suggestion

string band *n.* a group of musicians who play folk or country music on stringed instruments

string bass *n.* = **double bass**

string bean *n.* sb who is tall and thin (*informal*)

stringboard /string bawrd/ *n.* a board that covers the ends of the steps on a staircase [Because the board 'strings' the steps together]

string course /string kawrss/ *n.* a decorative feature on a building in the form of a horizontal band or moulding

stringed instrument, string instrument *n.* a musical instrument in which sound is produced by the vibration of a string or strings tightly stretched across a soundboard. Most stringed instruments, e.g. the violin, cello, guitar, and lute, are played by bowing or plucking the strings.

stringendo /strin jéndō/ *adv.* at an accelerating tempo (*used as a musical direction*) [Mid-19thC. Via Italian, present participle of *stringere* 'to press, squeeze', from Latin, 'to draw tight' (source of English *strict*).] —**stringendo** *adj.*

stringent /strínjənt/ *adj.* strictly controlled or enforced [Early 17thC. From Latin, present participle stem of *stringere* 'to draw tight, bind' (source of English *strict*).] —**stringency** *n.* —**stringently** *adv.*

stringer /stringər/ *n.* **1.** PRESS **FREELANCE OR PART-TIME JOURNALIST** a journalist, often covering a particular geographic area, who works on a freelance or part-time basis for a newspaper or news agency **2.** BUILDING **HORIZONTAL TIMBER** a heavy horizontal timber used for structural purposes **3.** BUILDING = **stringboard 4.** AEROSP **AUXILIARY MEMBER OF WING** a light auxiliary part parallel with the main structural members of a wing or fuselage, used mainly for bracing and stabilizing **5.** SPORTS **PLAYER OF SPECIFIED ABILITY** a member of a team who is ranked according to excellence or skill (*usually used in combination*) **6.** GEOL **NARROW MINERAL VEIN** a narrow or discontinuous linear vein of ore mineral

stringhalt /string hawlt/ *n.* a condition of horses marked by sudden lifting of and lameness in the hind legs, caused by muscle spasms [Early 16thC. From STRING in the sense 'tendon' + HALT 'to limp'.] —**stringhalted** *adj.*

string instrument *n.* = **stringed instrument**

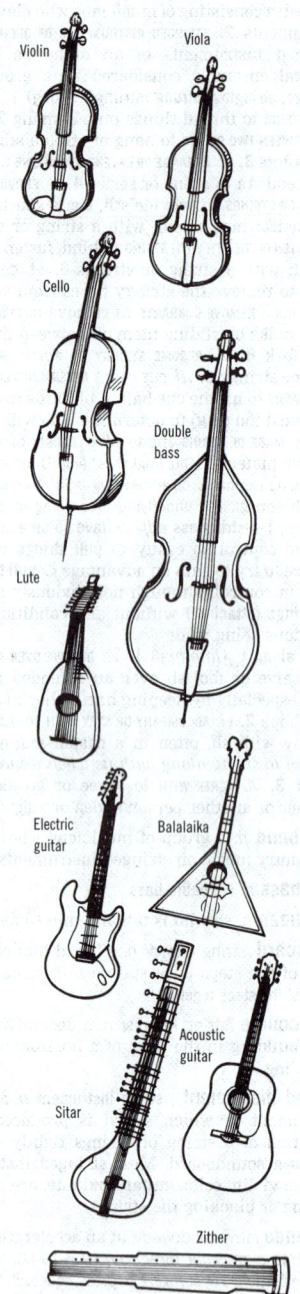

Violin

Viola

Cello

Double bass

Lute

Electric guitar

Balalaika

Sitar

Acoustic guitar

Zither

Stringed instruments

string line *n.* CUE GAMES = **baulk line**

string orchestra *n.* a small orchestra of stringed instruments including violins, violas, cellos, and double basses

stringpiece /stríng peess/ *n.* a beam of wood placed horizontally to support a framework

string quartet *n.* **1.** GROUP OF FOUR STRING PLAYERS a group of four musicians playing stringed instruments, traditionally two violins, a cello, and a viola **2.** MUSIC FOR FOUR STRING PLAYERS a piece of music composed for four stringed instruments, traditionally two violins, a cello, and a viola

string theory *n.* a mathematical theory that provides a unified structure to explain the properties and behaviour of elementary particles and fundamental forces

string tie *n.* **1.** NARROW TIE IN A BOW a narrow tie made of ribbon, tied in a bow, briefly popular in the 1890s **2.** NARROW TIE FASTENED WITH SLIDING CLIP a narrow thong

held by a sliding clip, worn as a tie, especially by cowboys

string vest *n.* a vest knitted or woven with an open mesh

stringy /stríngi/ (**-ier, -iest**) *adj.* **1.** FOOD FIBROUS containing strands of fibre and unpleasant to chew **2.** UNATTRACTIVELY THIN unattractively thin, with bones or muscles showing beneath the skin **3.** RESEMBLING PIECES OF STRING looking like pieces of string or hanging in long thin strands ○ *a stringy beard* **4.** FORMING STRANDS forming long sticky threads

stringy-bark *n. Aus* any of various eucalyptus trees with distinctive thick fibrous grey and brown bark

strip[1] /strip/ *v.* (**strips, stripping, stripped**) **1.** *vi.* GET UNDRESSED to remove your clothes, either completely or to a particular extent **2.** *vt.* UNDRESS SB to remove sb's clothes, either completely or to a particular extent **3.** *vi.* DO STRIPTEASE to do a striptease, or be a striptease artist **4.** *vt.* REMOVE COVERING to take off a covering, or take the covering off sth ○ *strip the wallpaper* **5.** *vt.* REMOVE PAINT OR VARNISH FROM SURFACE to remove old paint or varnish from a surface by scraping or burning it or by using a chemical **6.** *vt.* REMOVE CONTENTS to remove all the contents from a room, building, or similar place **7.** *vt.* GARDENING REMOVE ALL LEAVES OR PLANTS to remove all the leaves or flowers from a plant, or remove all the plants from an area **8.** *vt.* DEPRIVE OF STATUS OR POSSESSIONS to take status or possessions away from sb ○ *stripped him of his rank* **9.** *vt.* TAKE STH APART to take a machine, engine, or weapon to pieces in order to clean or repair it **10.** *vti.* MECH ENG DAMAGE SCREW THREAD OR GEAR TEETH to damage a screw or gearwheel by breaking the thread or teeth, or undergo this damage **11.** *vt.* CHEM REMOVE VOLATILE CONTENT to separate one or more components, especially a volatile one, from a solution or mixture, e.g. by distillation or evaporation **12.** *vt.* PRINTING, PHOTOGRAPHY MAKE INTO PRINTING PLATE to put pieces of photographic film or paper together to make a plate for printing ■ *n.* ACT OF STRIPPING the performance of a striptease [Old English *-strȳpan*, from prehistoric Germanic]

strip off *vi.* to take off all your clothes

strip out *vt.* to take out parts of a machine for cleaning or repair

strip[2] /strip/ *n.* **1.** LONG FLAT PIECE a long flat narrow piece of sth **2.** AIR = **airstrip 3.** PUBL = **comic strip 4.** SPORTS SPORTS CLOTHES the distinctive clothes worn by a particular sports team, e.g. a football team **5.** *US* COMM ROAD LINED WITH BUSINESSES a road lined with stores, shopping centres, restaurants, and other businesses ■ *vt.* (**strips, stripping, stripped**) DIVIDE INTO STRIPS to cut, tear, or divide sth into strips [15thC. Origin uncertain: probably from Low German *strippe* 'strap, thong']. ◇ **tear a strip off sb** to rebuke sb angrily

strip[3] /strip/ (**strips, stripping, stripped**) *vt.* to remove the last remaining milk from the udder of a cow or goat by hand after machine-milking [Early 17thC. Origin uncertain.]

strip cartoon *n.* = **comic strip**

strip club *n.* a club or bar where people can watch striptease acts

strip cropping *n.* the growing of different crops in an arrangement of lines or bands to prevent soil erosion

stripe[1] /strip/ *n.* **1.** LONG NARROW BAND a long narrow band that differs in colour, composition, or texture from the surrounding surface or background **2.** PATTERN a pattern of stripes **3.** TEXTILES FABRIC a fabric with a pattern of stripes **4.** MIL INDICATION OF RANK a narrow band or V-shaped piece of fabric, sewn on to a uniform as a symbol of rank **5.** *US* TYPE OF PERSON a recognizable type of person with a particular character or set of opinions ○ *This is a tyrant of a very different stripe.* **6.** *US* SET OF CHARACTERISTICS a particular set of characteristics ○ '...*portals of all stripes face a challenging future...*' (*Washington Post*; November 1998) ■ *vt.* (**stripes, striping, striped**) MARK WITH STRIPES to put stripes on sth [15thC. Origin uncertain: probably from Middle Dutch or Middle Low German *stripe*.]

stripe[2] /strip/ *n.* a blow from a whip, lash, cane, or belt [15thC. Origin uncertain: probably from Low German or Dutch.]

striped /stript/ *adj.* patterned or marked with stripes

striped bass /-báss/ *n.* a large fish found along the coasts of the United States that travels up rivers to breed, has black stripes, and is a food and game fish. Latin name: *Morone saxatilis.*

striped maple *n.* a maple of the northeastern United States and southeastern Canada with green bark marked with white stripes. Latin name: *Acer pennsylvanicum.*

striped marlin *n.* a large game and food fish of the Pacific with dark blue vertical stripes on the sides. Latin name: *Makaira audax.*

striped muscle *n.* = **striated muscle**

striped skunk *n.* a common North American skunk that has a white cap on its head and white stripes down either side of the spine. Latin name: *Mephitis mephitis.*

striper /stríper/ *n.* **1.** MIL SB WITH STRIPES INDICATING RANK a member of the armed forces whose stripes on the uniform indicate rank or length of service (*slang*) **2.** ZOOL = **striped bass**

strip-grazing *n.* a system in which cattle or other livestock are periodically allocated a fresh strip of pasture to graze by moving an electrified fence across the field

strip joint *n. US* a strip club (*informal*)

striplight /strip līt/ *n.* **1.** FLUORESCENT LAMP a fluorescent lamp in the form of a long tube, especially on a ceiling **2.** THEATRE ROW OF LAMPS a row of shaded lamps used to light a theatre stage

stripling /stríppling/ *n.* a boy in his early teenage years, who has not yet grown to his full size [14thC. Origin uncertain: probably formed from STRIP[2], with the underlying meaning 'thin as a strip'.]

strip mill *n.* an industrial building where steel is rolled into strips

stripped-down *adj.* deprived of all but the most essential or simple features

stripper /strípper/ *n.* **1.** ARTS STRIPTEASE ARTIST sb who performs striptease acts **2.** PAINT OR WALLPAPER REMOVER a tool or substance used for removing paint, varnish, wallpaper, or other substances from a surface **3.** SB WHO STRIPS STH sb whose job is to strip sth

strip poker *n.* a variety of the card game poker in which, at each round, players who lose have to remove an item of their clothing

strippy /stríppi/ *n.* TYPE OF PATCHWORK a type of patchwork in which broad strips of fabric are pieced together in vertical bands, then quilted ■ *adj.* OF STRIPS consisting of strips

strip-search (**strip-searches, strip-searching, strip-searched**) *vti.* to compel sb to undress completely while searching for concealed drugs, weapons, or contraband —**strip search** *n.*

striptease /strip teez, strip teez/ *n.* an entertainment in which the performer slowly undresses in an erotic way, usually with music as an accompaniment —**stripteaser** *n.*

stripy /strípi/ (**-ier, -iest**) *adj.* decorated with, marked with, or in the form of stripes

strive /strīv/ (**strives, striving, strove** /strōv/, **striven** /strívv'n/) *vi.* **1.** TRY HARD to try hard to achieve or get sth **2.** OPPOSE to fight in opposition to sth **3.** COMPETE to compete resolutely against sb or sth [12thC. From Old French *estriver* 'to contend', from *estrif* (see STRIFE).] —**striver** *n.*

strobe /strōb/ *n.* **1.** = **strobe light 2.** = **stroboscope 3.** SHORT ELECTRONIC PULSE an electronic pulse of short duration used to examine the characteristics of a periodic waveform **4.** USE OF A STROBOSCOPE the process of viewing vibrations or rotational motion with a stroboscope [Mid-20thC. Shortening of STROBOSCOPE.]

strobe light, **strobe** *n.* a high intensity flashing beam of light produced by charging a capacitor to a very high voltage then discharging it as a high-intensity flash of light in a tube

strobe lighting *n.* the effect produced by strobe lights or by a perforated disc rotating in front of a high intensity light source, as used in discotheques

strobila /strə bílə/ (*plural* **strobilae** /-lee/) *n.* **1. BODY OF TAPEWORM** the segmented body of a tapeworm, usually excluding the head **(scolex)** and neck **2. EMBRYONIC JELLYFISH** a chain of buds that are attached to the body of certain jellyfish and that later develop into individual offspring [Mid-19thC. Via modern Latin from Greek *strobilē* 'twisted plug of lint', feminine of *strobilos* (see STROBILUS).]

strobilation /stróbbə láysh'n/ *n.* the process of dividing into segments to form repeating units, e.g. buds in jellyfish, as a means of reproduction

strobilus /stróbələss/ (*plural* **-luses** *or* **-li** /-lī/) *n.* **1. CONE OF PLANT** the cone of a coniferous plant, or a similar cone-shaped structure in certain lower plants that consists of closely packed fertile leaves bearing spore-producing organs (*technical*) **2. CONE-SHAPED STRUCTURE IN PLANTS** a cone-shaped structure in flowering plants, e.g. the fruit of the hop [Mid-18thC. Via late Latin from Greek *strobilos* 'twisted object, pine cone', from *strobos* 'whirling'.]

stroboscope /stróbə skōp/ *n.* a flashing lamp of precisely variable periodicity that can be synchronized with the frequency of moving machinery to give the appearance of being stationary. It is often used in conjunction with flash or stop-action photography. [Mid-19thC. Coined from Greek *strobos* 'whirling' + -SCOPE.] —**stroboscopic** /stróbə skóppik, stróbbə-/ *adj.*

strobotron /stróbə tron, -trən/ *n.* the triggered gas-discharge tube used as the pulsed light source in a stroboscope [Mid-20thC. Coined from STROBOSCOPE + -TRON.]

strode past tense of **stride**

stroganoff /stróggə nof/, **Stroganoff** *adj.* **WITH SOUR CREAM** cooked in a wine sauce with sour cream ■ *n.* = **beef stroganoff** [Mid-20thC. From French, named after the Russian diplomat Count Pavel Aleksandrovich *Stroganov* (1772–1817).]

stroke /strōk/ *n.* **1.** MED **STOPPAGE OF THE BLOOD FLOW TO THE BRAIN** a sudden blockage or rupture of a blood vessel in the brain resulting in, e.g. loss of consciousness, partial loss of movement, or loss of speech. Technical name **cerebrovascular accident 2. SUDDEN OCCURRENCE** a sudden instance or occurrence of sth that has a strong or unexpected effect ○ *a stroke of luck* **3. STRIKING OF A CLOCK** a single sound made by a clock that is striking ○ *at the stroke of seven* **4.** SPORTS **HITTING OF A BALL** the hitting of a ball in racket games or golf, or the way in which this is done **5.** SWIMMING **SWIMMING STYLE** a style of swimming, using the arms and legs in a particular way **6.** SWIMMING **SINGLE MOVEMENT IN SWIMMING** a single complete movement of the arms and legs when swimming **7.** ROWING **SINGLE PULL** a single movement of the oars through the water in rowing **8.** ROWING **ROWER WHO KEEPS TIME** a rower in a racing boat who sets the pace for the crew **9.** ROWING **ROWING STYLE** a particular rowing style **10. SINGLE MOVEMENT IN A SERIES** a single movement forming part of a series of movements, e.g. the beat of a wing or the swing of a pendulum ○ *a wing stroke* **11.** ENG **MOVEMENT OF A PISTON** a single movement, up or down, of a piston in an engine or the distance that it travels in a single movement **12. HIT** a hit or blow made by the hand, a cane, or a tool **13.** PRINTING = **slash** *n.* 6 **14.** ARTS **BRUSH OR PEN LINE** a single line or mark made with a pen or brush ○ *a brush stroke* **15.** ARTS **SINGLE MOVEMENT OF A PEN OR BRUSH** a single movement of a pen or brush to make a line or mark **16. CARESSING MOVEMENT** a gentle caressing movement of the hand over fur, hair, or skin **17. ADDITIONAL FEATURE** a small additional feature that has an effect on the style or nature of sth ○ *a stroke of sarcasm* **18. POSITIVE WORD OF ENCOURAGEMENT** a usually positive comment or statement such as a compliment made by one person to another ○ *I need all the positive strokes I can right now.* **19. ELEMENT OF SOCIAL RECOGNITION** in transactional analysis, a unit of social recognition between two or more people that, in its simplest form, can be a one-word greeting such as 'hello' ■ *v.* (**strokes, stroking, stroked**) **1.** *vt.* **CARESS STH** to move the hand gently over sth as if caressing it ○ *stroked the cat gently* **2.** *vt.* SPORTS **HIT A BALL SMOOTHLY** to hit or kick a ball smoothly in various sports **3.** *vt.* **PUSH GENTLY** to push sth somewhere gently with a light movement of the hand **4.** *vt.* **CROSS STH OUT** to draw a line through sth **5.** *vt.* ROWING **SET THE ROWING PACE FOR SB** to be the rower who sets the pace for the crew **6.** *vi.* ROWING **MOVE OARS** to row at a particular speed or rate of the oars **7.** *vt.* **COMPLIMENT SB** to behave encouragingly or solicitously towards sb ■ *adj. US* **PORNOGRAPHIC** pornographic (*slang*) [Old English *strācian*. Ultimately from an Indo-European base meaning 'to rub, press', which is also the ancestor of English *strike, streak*, and *stringent*.] ◇ **different strokes for different folks** used to emphasize that people are all individuals and that what suits one will not necessarily suit another

stroke play *n.* GOLF a way of scoring in golf in which the total number of strokes taken for the round is counted rather than the number of holes won. US term **medal play**

stroll /strōl/ *v.* (**strolls, strolling, strolled**) **1.** *vti.* **WALK UNHURRIEDLY** to walk in a slow unhurried way, especially for enjoyment **2.** *vi.* **DO EFFORTLESSLY** to do, obtain, or achieve sth in a casual effortless way ○ *she strolled through the exam* ■ *n.* **LEISURELY WALK** a slow leisurely walk for pleasure ○ *went for a stroll in the park* [Early 17thC. Origin uncertain: probably from German *strollen* 'to wander', a variant of *strolchen*, from *Strolch* 'vagabond, fortune-teller', perhaps via Italian from, ultimately, Greek *astrologos* 'astronomer'.] ◇ **stroll on** used as an expression of disbelief or frustration (*informal*)

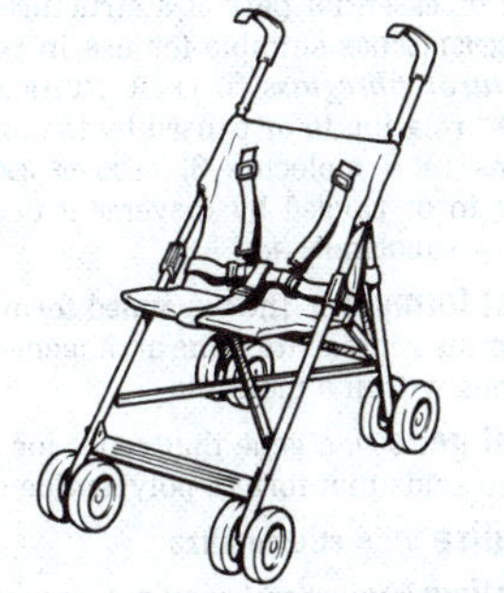

Stroller

stroller /strólər/ *n.* **1. WALKER** sb who is walking in a slow leisurely way for pleasure **2.** *US, Can, Aus* **BABY TRANSPORT** a light chair with wheels in which a young child can be pushed around **3.** THEATRE **TRAVELLING PERFORMER** an actor or performer who travels from place to place (*archaic*) **4. VAGRANT** a man who has no regular home and so wanders from place to place (*archaic*)

strolling /stróling/ *adj.* going from place to place to earn a living, especially by entertaining ○ *strolling minstrels*

stroma /strómə/ (*plural* **-mata** /-mətə/) *n.* **1.** ANAT **CONNECTIVE TISSUE** the connective tissue that provides the framework of an organ or other anatomical structure rather than carrying out its functions **2.** BOT **INTERIOR OF A CHLOROPLAST** the fluid-filled interior of a chloroplast containing enzymes and other components required for photosynthesis, including the light-trapping components [Mid-19thC. Via modern Latin from Greek *strōma* 'bed, cushion'. Ultimately from an Indo-European base meaning 'to spread', which is also the ancestor of English *strew, straw*, and *stratum*.] —**stromatic** /strō máttik/ *adj.*

stromatolite /strō máttə līt/ *n.* a very old fossil formed in sedimentary rock by marine blue-green algae and consisting of a rounded or columnar calcium-containing mass of many layers [Mid-20thC. Coined from late Latin *stromat-*, the stem of *stroma* 'bed-covering' + -LITE.] —**stromatolitic** /strō máttə líttik/ *adj.*

Stromboli /strom bóli/ volcanic island in the Italian Lipari Islands in the Adriatic Sea, north of Sicily. Area: 13 sq. km/5 sq. mi.

strong /strong/ *adj.* **1. PHYSICALLY POWERFUL** having the physical strength needed to exert considerable force, e.g. in lifting, pulling, or pushing sth **2. USING FORCE** using great physical force **3. ROBUST AND STURDY** sturdy, well made, and not easily damaged or broken **4. WITH INNER STRENGTH** having emotional strength that gives the ability to cope with stress, grief, loss, risk, and other difficulties **5. HEALTHY AND WELL** in good health, especially after an illness ○ *getting stronger every day* **6. THRIVING** thriving, developing well, and likely to continue so ○ *a strong economy* **7. LIKELY TO SUCCEED** very likely to succeed, win, or come to be sth ○ *a strong candidate for the post.* **8. CONVINCING** supported by facts or good evidence and likely to be correct or effective ○ *a strong argument* **9. KNOWLEDGEABLE** very skilful or knowledgeable in a particular subject or area **10. EXERTING INFLUENCE** influential or authoritative by virtue of having or holding power **11. EFFECTIVE** having a powerful effect ○ *strong painkillers* **12. FELT OR EXPRESSED POWERFULLY** felt or expressed with a powerful effect ○ *She has strong views on the subject.* **13. DISTINCTIVE** bold, clearly defined, and prominent ○ *strong features* **14. EXTREME** unusually severe of its kind ○ *Strong measures were taken to prevent a riot.* **15. INTENSE IN IMPRESSION** having an intense, powerful, or vivid effect on the senses ○ *a strong smell of garlic* **16. EASY TO DETECT** easy to detect or receive ○ *The signal gets stronger as you get closer.* **17. CONCENTRATED** containing a lot of the main ingredient and not diluted or watery ○ *strong black coffee* **18. ALCOHOLIC** containing much alcohol **19. FAST MOVING** flowing or blowing at high speed ○ *a strong current* **20.** CHEM **FULLY IONIZED** producing ions freely in solution **21.** MIL **WELL DEFENDED** well defended and difficult to defeat ○ *a strong fortress* **22. WITH SPECIFIED NUMBER** having a particular number of members ○ *a force 50,000 strong* **23.** OPTICS **WITH HIGH MAGNIFICATION** having a powerful magnifying or corrective ability ○ *a strong lens* **24.** COMM **WITH HIGH PRICES** characterized by high or rising prices ○ *a strong currency* **25.** GRAM **WITH A CHANGED VOWEL** used to describe an irregular verb that changes the vowel in the stem in its different forms, e.g. 'ring', 'rang', 'rung' [Old English *strang*. Of prehistoric Germanic origin.] —**strongly** *adv.* ◇ **come on strong** to behave or express sth aggressively (*slang*) ◇ **going strong** thriving and doing well

strong-arm *adj.* **USING FORCE** using or prepared to use coercion or physical force (*informal*) ○ *ready to use strong-arm tactics* ■ *vt.* (**strong-arms, strong-arming, strong-armed**) **USE FORCE AGAINST SB** to use coercion against sb to induce cooperation (*informal*)

strongbox /stróng boks/ *n.* a secure metal box or safe where money or valuables can be kept

strong breeze *n.* a wind with a speed between 40 and 50 km/25 and 31 mi. per hour

strong force *n.* PHYS = **strong interaction**

strong gale *n.* a wind with a speed between 76 and 87 km/47 and 54 mi. per hour

stronghold /stróng hōld/ *n.* **1.** MIL **DEFENSIBLE PLACE** a place that is fortified or that can easily be defended **2. CONCENTRATED AREA** a place where a particular group, activity, or set of opinions is concentrated

strong interaction, **strong force** *n.* a fundamental force between elementary particles that is responsible for binding protons and neutrons together in an atomic nucleus and other interactions between elementary particles **(hadrons)**. Mediated by gluons, the interaction is the most powerful force known and is responsible for the particle creation that occurs when high-energy particles collide.

strong language *n.* language that expresses sth in a forceful way, especially with abusive words or swearing

strongman /stróng man/ (*plural* **strongmen** /-men/) *n.* **1. PERFORMER SHOWING STRENGTH** a performer of feats of strength, e.g. at a fair or circus **2. POWERFUL LEADER** a powerful, typically dictatorial, leader who rules by force

strong meat *n.* behaviour or attitudes that generally upset or offend people and that are coped with only by a robust minority

strong-minded *adj.* **1. DETERMINED** determined and persevering in the face of difficulty **2. MENTALLY STRONG** confident, intelligent, and independent in thought —**strong-mindedly** *adv.* —**strong-mindedness** *n.*

strong point, **strong suit** *n.* a particular area for which sb has a talent ○ *Tact was never his strong point.*

strongroom /stróng room, -ro͝om/ *n.* a reinforced room

designed to withstand fire or theft and used for the storage of valuables

strong suit *n.* **1.** = **strong point 2.** CARDS **SUIT WITH MOST CARDS** in various card games, the suit in which a player or team holds the most cards or the most face cards. ◊ **long suit**

strong-willed *adj.* determined to prevail in the face of difficulty or opposition

strongyle /strónjil/, **strongyl** /strónjəl/ *n.* a parasitic nematode worm related to the hookworms that infests the intestinal tract of mammals. Superfamily: Strongyloidea. [Mid-19thC. Anglicization of modern Latin *Strongylus*, genus name, from Greek *stroggulos* 'round, compact', of unknown origin.]

strongyloidiasis /strónji loy dī́ əssiss/ *n.* intestinal infection in mammals by strongyles, producing various severe and sometimes fatal intestinal disorders, especially in individuals with weakened immune systems [Mid-20thC. Formed from modern Latin *Strongyloidea*, superfamily name, from *Strongylus* (see STRONGYLE).]

strongylosis /strónji lṓssiss/ *n.* an illness, usually of horses, caused by infection with strongyles

strontia /strónti ə, -shi ə/ *n.* = **strontium monoxide** [Early 19thC. Back-formation from STRONTIAN.]

strontian /strónti ən, -shi-/ *n.* **1.** MINERALS = **strontianite 2.** CHEM = **strontium monoxide 3.** CHEM = **strontium** [Late 18thC. Shortening of *Strontian earth*; named after the parish of *Strontian* in Scotland, where the mineral was discovered in lead mines.]

strontianite /strónti ə nīt, -shi ə nīt/ *n.* a variously coloured mineral consisting of strontium carbonate, a major source of strontium. Formula: $SrCO_3$. [Late 18thC. Formed from STRONTIAN.]

strontium /strónti əm, -shi-/ *n.* a soft yellow or silvery-white metallic chemical element of the alkaline-earth group, found only in combination with other substances. It is used in fireworks and flares to produce red flames, and in alloys. Symbol **Sr** [Early 19thC. Coined from STRONTIA.]

strontium 90 *n.* a radioactive isotope of strontium with a mass number of 90, present in nuclear fallout and assimilated like calcium in bone formation

strontium monoxide *n.* a white insoluble solid resembling quicklime. It is used in the purification of sugar. Formula: SrO.

strontium unit *n.* a unit of measurement of the amount of strontium 90 in an organic substance such as soil or bone, in relation to the concentration of calcium in the same substance

Stroop effect /stróop-/ *n.* difficulty identifying the colours in which names of colours are written. For example, if the word 'red' is printed in green ink, people are likely to say 'red' when asked the colour of the printed word. [Mid-20thC. Named after J.R. *Stroop*, who first published a study of the effect in English.]

strop /strop/ *n.* **1. LEATHER STRAP FOR SHARPENING** a leather strap used for sharpening a cutthroat razor **2.** NAUT **STRAP FOR CARGO** a strap of leather or rope used for lifting cargo ■ *vt.* **(strops, stropping, stropped) SHARPEN RAZOR** to sharpen a straight razor on a strop [Assumed Old English *strop* 'band, cord', via Latin *stroppus* from Greek *strophos* (see STROPHOID)] ◇ **be in a strop** to be in a bad temper or sulk (*informal*)

strophe /strṓfi/ *n.* ◊ **antistrophe 1.** POETRY **FIRST METRICAL FORM IN A POEM** the first type of metrical form in a poem that alternates two contrasting metrical forms **2.** LITERAT **MOVEMENT IN ANCIENT GREEK DRAMA** the first of two movements made by the chorus in a classical Greek drama, or the part of an ode sung during this [Early 17thC. From Greek *strophē*, literally 'turning' (source of English *catastrophe*). Ultimately from an Indo-European base meaning 'to turn', which is also the ancestor of *strepto-* and *stroboscope*.] —**strophic** /strŏffik, strṓfik/ *adj.*

strophoid /strṓ foyd/ *n.* a plane curve symmetric to the x-axis, generated by a point whose distance from the y-axis along a straight line is equal to the y-intercept [Late 19thC. Formed from Greek *strophos* 'twisted cord'. Ultimately from an Indo-European base meaning 'to turn', which is also the ancestor of English *strophe, stroboscope*, and *strepto-*.]

strophulus /strŏffyŏŏləss/ *n.* a skin eruption seen in children and infants, e.g. hives or heat rash (*dated*) [Early 19thC. From modern Latin, of uncertain origin.]

stroppy /stróppi/ (**-pier, -piest**) *adj.* bad-tempered and uncooperative (*informal*) [Mid-20thC. Origin uncertain: perhaps an alteration of OBSTREPEROUS.]

stroud /strowd/ *n.* a rough woollen fabric [Late 17thC. Origin uncertain.]

Stroud /strowd/ town in Gloucestershire, central England. Population: 38,835 (1991).

strove past tense of **strive**

struck /struk/ past tense, past participle of **strike** ■ *adj. US* **AFFECTED BY STRIKES** closed temporarily or working at reduced output because of a labour dispute

struck measure *n.* a quantity of sth such as grain, measured by levelling the substance with the top of a container

structural /strúkchərəl/ *adj.* **1. RELATING TO STRUCTURE** relating to the way that the parts of sth are put together or how they work together **2. RESULTING FROM STRUCTURE** resulting from the interrelationship of constituent parts, e.g. in a political or economic system **3. BASIC TO A STRUCTURE** constituting an important or essential part of a structure **4.** BUILDING **USED IN CONSTRUCTION** suitable for use in construction ○ *structural fibreglass* **5.** CHEM **CAUSED BY ATOMIC ARRANGEMENT** relating to or caused by the arrangement of atoms in a molecule **6.** GEOG **OF ROCK STRUCTURE** relating to or caused by movement of the earth's surface —**structurally** *adv.*

structural formula *n.* the expanded form of a chemical formula representing the arrangement of atoms and bonds within a molecule

structural gene *n.* a gene that codes for a sequence of amino acids that form a polypeptide or protein

structuralise *vt.* = **structuralize**

structuralism /strúkchərəlizəm/ *n.* **1.** SOC SCI **SOCIOLOGICAL METHOD** a method of sociological analysis based on the notion of human society as a network of interrelated elements whose patterns and significance can be analysed **2.** LING = **structural linguistics 3.** PSYCHOL = **structural psychology** —**structuralist** *n., adj.*

structuralize /strúkchərə līz/ (**-izes, -izing, -ized**), **structuralise** (**-ises, -ising, -ised**) *vt.* to arrange or organize sth so that it has a structure

structural linguistics *n.* a branch of linguistics that emphasizes the significance of the interrelations between the elements that constitute a linguistic system (*takes a singular verb*) —**structural linguist** *n.*

structural psychology *n.* a school of psychology of the early part of the 20th century that sought to organize the components of subjective experience in a hierarchy from simplest to most complex —**structural psychologist** *n.*

structural steel *n.* strong steel shaped and suitable for use in construction

structure /strúkchər/ *n.* **1. STH BUILT OR ERECTED** a building, bridge, framework, or other object that has been put together from many different parts **2. ORDERLY SYSTEM OF PARTS** a system or organization made up of interrelated parts functioning as an orderly whole **3. WAY THAT PARTS LINK OR FUNCTION** the way in which the different parts of sth link or work together, or the fact of being linked together ○ *the structure of local government* ○ *The essay is interesting, but it lacks structure.* **4.** BIOL **ORGANIC FEATURE** a part of a body or organism, e.g. an organ or tissue, identifiable by its shape and other properties **5.** CHEM **ARRANGEMENT OF ATOMS** the specific arrangement of atoms in a molecule **6.** GEOL **COMPONENT PARTS OF ROCKS** the physical disposition of a rock mass, e.g. its folding and faulting, or the disposition of its mineral components, e.g. its texture ■ *vt.* (**-tures, -turing, -tured**) **GIVE STRUCTURE TO** to organize or arrange sth so that it works as a cohesive whole [15thC. Directly or via French from Latin *structura*, from *struct-*, the past participle stem of *struere* 'to build'.]

WORD KEY: ORIGIN

The Latin word *struere*, from which *structure* is derived, is also the source of English *construct, construe, destroy, instruct*, and *obstruct*.

structured /strúkchərd/ *adj.* **1. ORGANIZED** planned, organized, and controlled **2. DEFINED** with a definite shape, form, or pattern ○ *For business wear, suits need a more structured look.*

structured programming *n.* a style of computer programming in which a program consists of a hierarchy of simple subroutines

structured query language *n.* full form of **SQL**

strudel /stróod'l/ *n.* a pastry made with very thin pastry rolled and baked with a filling, usually of chopped apples, raisins, and sugar [Late 19thC. Via German from Middle High German, 'whirlpool'.]

struggle /strúgg'l/ *vi.* (**-gles, -gling, -gled**) **1. TRY TO OVERCOME A PROBLEM** to try very hard to deal with a challenge, problem, or difficulty ○ *he was struggling with his maths homework* **2. MAKE A GREAT PHYSICAL EFFORT** to make a great physical effort to achieve or obtain sth ○ *A rescue party struggled to reach the stranded climbers.* **3. FIGHT BY WRESTLING** to fight with sb by grappling and wrestling **4. WRITHE TO ESCAPE** to move and wriggle forcefully in an attempt to escape **5. MOVE WITH DIFFICULTY** to move with great effort ○ *so weak I just managed to struggle out of bed* ■ *n.* **1. GREAT EFFORT TO OVERCOME DIFFICULTIES** a great effort made over a period of time to overcome difficulties or achieve sth **2. HARD TASK** a strenuous physical or mental effort, or sth requiring this **3. FIGHT** a prolonged fight or conflict [14thC. Origin uncertain.] —**struggler** *n.*

struggle for existence *n.* the ongoing effort to survive and reproduce in an environment of competing organisms

strum /strum/ *v.* (**strums, strumming, strummed**) **1.** *vti.* **PLAY AN INSTRUMENT BY BRUSHING THE STRINGS** to play a guitar or other stringed instrument by brushing the strings with the fingers or a plectrum **2.** *vt.* **PLAY TUNE** to play a tune by strumming an instrument ■ *n.* **SOUND OF STRUMMING** the sound of sb strumming an instrument [Late 18thC. An imitation of the sound.] —**strummer** *n.*

struma /stróomə/ (*plural* **-mae** /-mee/) *n.* **1.** BOT **SWELLING ON MOSS** a swelling at the base of a moss capsule **2.** MED = **goitre 3.** MED **SCROFULA** scrofula (*archaic*) [Mid-16thC. Via modern Latin from Latin, 'scrofulous tumour', of unknown origin.] —**strumatic** /stroo máttik/ *adj.* —**strumose** /-mōss/ *adj.* —**strumous** /stróoməss/ *adj.*

strumpet /strúmpit/ *n.* an offensive term for a prostitute or woman regarded as too sexually active (*archaic insult*) [14thC. Origin uncertain.]

strung past tense, past participle of **string**

strung out *adj.* **1. OVERWROUGHT** tired, tense, or overwrought (*informal*) **2.** DRUGS **DRUGGED** under the influence of a drug, especially a narcotic drug (*slang*) **3.** DRUGS **WEAKENED** debilitated by long-term drug use (*slang*)

strung up *adj.* very tired, tense, and overwrought (*informal*)

strut /strut/ *v.* (**struts, strutting, strutted**) **1.** *vi.* **WALK IN A STIFF ARROGANT WAY** to walk in a conspicuously stiff or proud way, suggesting arrogance or pomposity **2.** *vt.* CONSTR **SUPPORT WITH PLANKS** to prop sth up with supporting planks or boards ■ *n.* **1.** CONSTR **SUPPORTING MEMBER** a long rigid plank, board, or other structural member used as a support in building **2. PROUD WALKING** a stiff, proud, pompous way of walking [Old English *strūtian* 'to protrude stiffly'. Ultimately from Indo-European, meaning 'stiff' (ancestor also of English *starch*). Senses relating to 'support' of uncertain origin: probably from, ultimately, the same Indo-European source.]

struthious /strúthi əss/ *adj.* relating to flightless birds, especially the ostrich [Late 18thC. Formed from late Latin *struthio* 'ostrich', via late Greek *strouthiōn* from Greek *strouthos*.]

strychnine /strík neen, -nin/ *n.* a bitter white poisonous alkaloid obtained from nux vomica and related plants, used as a poison for rodents and medicinally as a stimulant for the central nervous system. Formula: $C_{21}H_{22}N_2O_2$. [Early 19thC. From French, formed from modern Latin *Strychnos*, genus name,

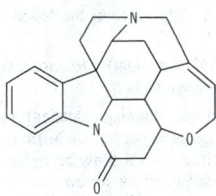

Strychnine

via Latin *strychnon* 'nightshade' from Greek *strukhnos*, of unknown origin.] —**strychnic** *adj.*

Strzelecki Range /strez léki-/ range of hills in southern Victoria, Australia. Highest peak: 500 m/1,640 ft.

Stuart /styóo ərt/, **Charles Edward** (1720–88) British prince and claimant to the British throne. The son of James Francis Edward Stuart, he led the Jacobite uprising in Scotland in 1745 and after its failure lived in exile in Europe. Known as **Bonnie Prince Charlie**, **the Young Pretender**

Stuart, James Francis Edward (1688–1766) British prince and claimant to the British throne. The son of James II, he was supported in his claim to the British throne by France and by the Jacobites in their unsuccessful rising in Scotland (1715). After 1719 he lived in Rome. Known as **the Old Pretender**

Stuart, John McDouall (1815–66) British-born Australian explorer. He made the first south-to-north crossing of Australia (1861–62), from Adelaide to Darwin.

stub /stub/ *n.* **1.** SHORT REMAINING PART a short part of sth that is left after the main part has been removed or used **2.** COMM SMALL SECTION OF A TICKET OR CHEQUE a small detachable section of a ticket, cheque, or voucher, retained as a record of a transaction **3.** STUMP OF A TREE OR PLANT the stump of a tree or plant **4.** SMALL PROJECTION a small projection from a surface ■ *vt.* (**stubs, stubbing, stubbed**) **1.** BANG THE TOE to bang your toe against sth accidentally **2.** GARDENING DIG UP BY THE ROOTS to dig up a plant or tree by the roots **3.** AGRIC CLEAR LAND OF STUMPS to clear land of tree stumps [Old English *stubb* 'tree stump', of prehistoric Germanic origin] **stub out** *vt.* to put out a cigarette or cigar by pushing the burning end against sth

Stubbies /stúbbiz/ *tdmk. Aus* a trademark for short heavy-duty shorts

stubble /stúbb'l/ *n.* **1.** AGRIC SHORT STALKS IN A FIELD short stalks left in the ground after a grain crop has been harvested **2.** SHORT BEARD GROWTH the short spiky growth of beard on a man's face when he has not shaved [13thC. Via Old French *estuble* from Latin *stupula* 'straw', an alteration of *stipula* (see STIPULE).] —**stubbly** *adj.*

stubborn /stúbbərn/ *adj.* **1.** DOGGED carried out in a determined, persistent way ○ *met with stubborn resistance* **2.** UNREASONABLY DETERMINED unreasonably and obstructively determined to persevere or prevail **3.** HARD TO REMOVE difficult to remove or deal with ○ *a stubborn stain* [14thC. Origin uncertain.] —**stubbornly** *adv.* —**stubbornness** *n.*

Stubbs /stubz/, **George** (1724–1806) British painter and engraver. He specialized in painting animals, particularly horses.

stubby /stúbbi/ *adj.* **1.** SHORT AND STOUT short and stout in build **2.** SHORT AND THICK short and thick, broad, or blunt ○ *stubby fingers* **3.** WITH MANY STUBS with projecting stubs or short bristles ■ *n. Aus* BEER BOTTLE a small squat bottle of beer (*informal*)

stub nail *n.* a short thick nail

STUC *abbr.* Scottish Trades Union Congress

stucco /stúkō/ *n.* **1.** WALL PLASTER plaster used for surfacing interior or exterior walls, often used in association with classical mouldings **2.** DECORATIVE PLASTER WORK decorative work moulded from stucco ■ *vt.* (**-coes** *or* **stuccos, -coing, -coed**) COVER WITH STUCCO

to apply a coating of stucco to a wall [Late 16thC. From Italian, of Germanic origin.] —**stuccoer** *n.*

stuccowork /stúkō wurk/ *n.* = stucco *n.* 2

stuck /stuk/ past tense, past participle of **stick**[2] ■ *adj.* **1.** JAMMED OR CAUGHT jammed, caught, or held in a position from which it is impossible to move ○ *the drawer was stuck fast* **2.** UNABLE TO FIND A SOLUTION not able to find a solution or way out of a situation **3.** PIERCED pierced by a sharp object ◇ **stuck on** infatuated with sb or sth (*informal*)

stuckie /stúki/ *n. Scotland* a starling (*nonstandard*)

stuck-up *adj.* snobbish and conceited (*informal*)

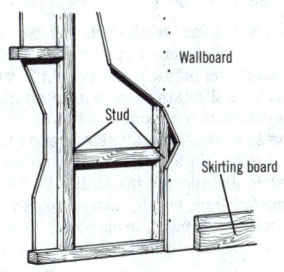

Wallboard

Stud

Skirting board

Stud

stud[1] /stud/ *n.* **1.** METAL KNOB a small metal knob or the head of a nail protruding slightly from a surface, especially for decorative effect **2.** ACCESSORIES EARRING an earring for pierced ears that has a simple rounded head or is set with a single gemstone **3.** ACCESSORIES COLLAR FASTENER a fastener for collars or dress shirts consisting of a small disc attached to a short rod **4.** SPORTS KNOB ON FOOTBALL BOOT one of several knobs fitted to the sole of a football boot or other sports shoe to give a firmer grip on slippery ground. US term **cleat** *n.* 2 **5.** BUILDING VERTICAL SUPPORT a vertical post that is one of the uprights supporting a timber wall or partition **6.** HEADLESS BOLT a headless bolt with threads on both ends separated by a threadless section **7.** ENG PROJECTION ON A MACHINE a short rod or other projection on a machine serving as support for sth else ■ *vt.* (**studs, studding, studded**) **1.** SUPPLY WITH STUDS to fit or decorate sth with studs ○ *a studded leather jacket* **2.** OCCUR THROUGHOUT STH to be present or visible in all parts of sth [Old English *studu*. Ultimately from an Indo-European base meaning 'to stand', which is also the ancestor of English *stand*, *stead*, and *static*.] ◇ **studded with** scattered or dotted with sth

stud[2] /stud/ *n.* **1.** EQU BREEDING STALLION a male animal, especially a stallion, used for breeding **2.** EQU ESTABLISHMENT WITH STALLIONS a stable or farm where male animals, especially stallions, are kept for breeding **3.** EQU GROUP OF STALLIONS a group of male animals, especially stallions, used for breeding **4.** SEXUALLY ACTIVE MAN a man considered to be sexually active or good at sex (*informal*) **5.** CARDS = stud poker [Old English *stōd*, literally 'standing place'] ◇ **at stud** available for breeding with female animals, especially mares

studbook /stúd bòok/ *n.* a book containing a record of the parentage of purebred animals, especially horses or dogs

studdingsail /stúdding sayl, stúnss'l/ *n.* an additional sail on an extra yard and boom at either side of a square sail, for use in light winds [Mid-16thC. *Studding* of uncertain origin: perhaps from Middle Low German or Middle Dutch *stōting* 'thrusting', from *stōten* 'to thrust'.]

student /styóo dnt/ *n.* **1.** PERSON STUDYING sb who is studying at school, college, or university **2.** KNOWLEDGEABLE OR INTERESTED PERSON sb who has studied or takes a great interest in a particular subject ○ *a student of human foibles* ■ *adj.* IN TRAINING FOR A JOB studying as part of the training for a job or profession ○ *student pilots* [15thC. Alteration of Old French *estudiant*, from Latin *student-*, the present participle stem of *studere* (see STUDY).]

student body *n. US* the students of a school collectively

student loan *n.* a loan taken by a student to pay for educational expenses, usually at a favourable rate of interest that is subsidized by the government.

Ex-students may be exempted from repayment in certain financial circumstances.

studentship /styóod-t ship/ *n.* = scholarship *n.* 1

Student's t-test *n.* = t-test [Named after *Student*, the pen name of W. S. Gosset (1876–1937), the British statistician who invented it.]

students' union *n.* **1.** STUDENT ORGANIZATION an organization of students in a college or university that represents students' interests **2.** BUILDING WITH STUDENT FACILITIES a building or area at a college or university with a bar and other facilities for the social or recreational activities of students. US term **student union**

student union *n. US* = students' union

studhorse /stúd hawrss/ *n.* a stallion used for breeding [Old English *stod hors*]

studied /stúddid/ *adj.* thought about or planned in advance rather than being spontaneous ○ *an air of studied nonchalance*

studio /styóodi ō/ *n.* (*plural* **studios**) **1.** ARTS ARTIST'S WORKPLACE a place where an artist, photographer, or musician works **2.** RECORDING RECORDING PRODUCTION ROOM a room or building equipped for making films, television or radio productions, or musical recordings **3.** *US* = studio flat **4.** DANCE DANCE SCHOOL a place where dance is taught or where dancers can practise **5.** CINEMA FILM COMPANY a commercial film production company ■ **studios** *npl.* CINEMA FILM PRODUCTION BUILDINGS all the buildings connected with a film production company, used for shooting and producing films [Early 19thC. Via Italian from Latin *studium* (see STUDY).]

studio couch *n.* a usually backless sofa that can be converted into a double bed by sliding out a frame from underneath

studio flat *n.* a small one-roomed flat, perhaps with a separate kitchen and bathroom. US term **studio** *n.* 2

studio system *n.* the process for making a large number of films economically, efficiently, and simultaneously, as used by the major Hollywood studios from the silent era into the 1950s. Each studio was a self-contained factory with separate departments for each aspect of production and had a number of actors under contract.

studious /styóodi əss/ *adj.* **1.** INCLINED TO STUDY having a thoughtful nature and given to studying **2.** CAREFUL AND PAINSTAKING careful and painstaking, with considerable attention to detail ○ *a studious investigation* [14thC. From Latin *studiosus*, from *studium* (see STUDY).] —**studiously** *adv.* —**studiousness** *n.*

studmuffin /stúd mufin/ *n. US* a man regarded as being physically attractive (*slang*)

stud poker, **stud** *n.* a variety of the card game poker in which all but the first card are dealt face up, allowing players to see one another's hands. A round of betting follows each round of dealing. [Mid-19thC. Probably a shortening of earlier *studhorse poker*, of uncertain origin: perhaps in reference to the exchange of money involved in horse breeding and horseracing.]

studwork /stúd wurk/ *n.* **1.** BUILDING STUD ARRANGEMENT the arrangement of studs in a building framework **2.** STUD DECORATION the decoration of sth with studs

study /stúddi/ *v.* (**-ies, -ying, -ied**) **1.** *vti.* LEARN ABOUT STH to learn about a particular subject by reading and researching **2.** *vti.* TAKE AN EDUCATIONAL COURSE to follow a course at college or university **3.** *vt.* INVESTIGATE to discover facts about sth by doing research or experiments ○ *a team of researchers studying the effects of sleep deprivation* **4.** *vt.* LOOK AT AND CONSIDER to look at or read sth and think about it carefully ○ *He studied the map, frowning.* **5.** *vt.* THEATRE LEARN LINES to learn the lines spoken by a character in a play ■ *n.* (*plural* **-ies**) **1.** PROCESS OF LEARNING the process of learning about a subject by reading, thought, intuition, or research ○ *devoted the afternoons to study* **2.** INVESTIGATION an investigation or research project designed to discover facts about sth **3.** REPORT ON RESEARCH a report or book describing an investigation or piece of research **4.** ROOM FOR STUDYING a room used for work that involves reading, thinking, or writing **5.** ARTS SMALL PREPARATORY WORK OF ART a small drawing or sculpture done as preparation for a larger work **6.** MUSIC INSTRUMENTAL WORK an instrumental work intended for teaching or practice **7.** THEATRE **ACTOR LEARNING LINES** sb who learns a role in a play, considered in terms of the particular amount of time this takes ○ *she's a quick study* ■ **studies** *npl.* EDUC **SUBJECT OF STUDY** a particular subject of study, especially as an educational course or academic specialization ○ *social studies* [12thC. Via Old French *estudier* (verb) and *estudie* (noun) from, ultimately, Latin *studium* 'zeal, care', from *studere* 'to be diligent'.] ◇ **in a brown study** deep in thought (*dated*)

stuff /stuf/ *vt.* **(stuffs, stuffing, stuffed) 1. FILL** to fill sth by pushing things into it ○ *What are you stuffing the cushions with?* **2. PUSH THINGS INTO CONTAINER** to push things into a container, often hurriedly or forcefully **3. PUT HURRIEDLY** to put sth somewhere in a quick careless way ○ *stuffed it under the pillow, out of sight* **4. EAT TOO MUCH** to eat or feed sb a lot of food **5.** COOK **FILL FOOD WITH STUFFING** to put stuffing or filling into food such as pasta, meat, or vegetables **6. RESTORE THE SHAPE OF A DEAD ANIMAL** to fill a dead animal's skin with material to make it look lifelike and suitable for display **7.** *US, Can* POL **SUBMIT INVALID VOTES** to put invalid ballots into a ballot box to rig an election **8.** SPORTS **BEAT OPPONENT THOROUGHLY** to beat an opponent or opposing team easily and thoroughly **9. OFFENSIVE TERM** a highly offensive term used typically by men meaning to have sex with a woman (*slang taboo*) **10.** INDUST **TREAT LEATHER** to treat leather with chemicals that preserve and soften it ■ *n.* **1. THINGS** material things generally, especially when unidentified, worthless, or unwanted ○ *What's all this stuff doing in my office?* **2. WORDS OR ACTION** action, speech, or writing of a particular kind ○ *all that stuff in the news about changing weather patterns* ○ *I really like her stuff.* **3. POSSESSIONS** personal possessions ○ *called by to collect her stuff* **4. PERSONAL QUALITIES** personal qualities of a particular kind ○ *She's got the stuff heroes are made of.* **5. SPECIALITY** sth that sb does uniquely or very well **6. FOOLISH WORDS OR ACTION** foolish or blameworthy action, speech, or writing **7. MONEY** money (*slang*) **8. DRUGS** a drug, especially heroin (*informal*) **9.** TEXTILES **WOOLLEN FABRIC** woollen fabric, especially as distinguished from fabric made from other natural fibres ■ *interj.* **USED TO DISMISS STH** used, often with 'it', to dismiss sth angrily or carelessly (*slang*) [14thC. From Old French *estoffer* 'to equip', of prehistoric Germanic origin.] —**stuffer** *n.* ◇ **do your stuff** to do what is required or expected ◇ **strut your stuff 1.** *US* to do sth impressively, suggesting talent for it or thorough preparation (*slang*) **2.** to dance, especially in an expressive way (*informal*) ◇ **that's the stuff!** used to indicate satisfaction with what has been done or given

WORD KEY: CULTURAL NOTE

The Right Stuff, a book by US writer Tom Wolfe (1979). This imaginative account of the early years of the US space programme contrasts the media's manipulation of the story and the public's hunger for heroes with the real-life experiences of the astronauts. It was made into a film by Philip Kaufman in 1983. Subsequent to the novel, *right stuff* entered the general language, meaning 'the complex of courage, self-worth, technical know-how, emotional stability, and dependability needed for a person to accomplish great things in any profession or field'.

stuff up *vti.* to make a mess of sth (*informal*)

stuffed /stuft/ *adj.* **1.** FOOD **WITH FILLING** filled with stuffing or some other filling **2. COMPLETELY FULL** completely full, especially after eating too much (*informal*) **3.** *Aus* **IN DIFFICULTIES** thwarted, ruined, or broken (*informal*) **4.** *Aus* **EXHAUSTED** completely exhausted (*informal*) ◇ **get stuffed!** used in anger to show contempt and rejection (*slang*)

stuffed shirt *n.* sb who behaves in a formal self-important way (*informal*) [Origin uncertain: perhaps from the image of a puffed-up man in a tight-fitting, starched shirt; perhaps also from the implied absence of ideas]

stuffing /stúffing/ *n.* **1.** FOOD **WELL-FLAVOURED FILLING FOR FOOD** a mixture of well-flavoured or highly seasoned ingredients used to stuff meat or vegetables. Stuffings often have a breadcrumb or rice base and may include herbs, spices, fruit, or vegetables. **2.** INDUST **FILLING FOR CUSHIONS** feathers, fabric, or artificial fibre used to fill cushions or pillows ◇ **knock the stuffing out of sb 1.** to beat or defeat sb severely (*informal*) **2.** to have a sudden or immediate weakening effect on sb (*informal*)

stuffing box *n.* an enclosure containing compressed packing that is used to prevent leakage around a moving part such as a piston rod

stuff-up *n.* *Aus* a blunder (*informal*)

stuffy /stúffi/ **(-ier, -iest)** *adj.* **1. AIRLESS** without any fresh air, and often too warm **2. STRAIT-LACED** too old-fashioned, strict, or conventional **3. BLOCKED WITH MUCUS** blocked up with mucus, making breathing difficult ○ *a stuffy nose* —**stuffily** *adv.* —**stuffiness** *n.*

stull /stul/ *n.* a supporting timber in a mine or mineshaft [Late 18thC. Origin uncertain: perhaps from German *Stollen* 'support, prop' (source of English *stollen*).]

stultify /stúlti fī/ **(-fies, -fying, -fied)** *vt.* **1. DIMINISH INTEREST** to diminish sb's interest and liveliness of mind by being repetitive, tedious, and boring **2. MAKE SB SEEM STUPID** to cause sb or sth to seem unintelligent or silly **3. RENDER USELESS** to render sth useless or ineffectual **4.** LAW **PROVE SB INCAPABLE OF LEGAL RESPONSIBILITY** to show or allege sb to be not legally responsible because of a psychiatric disorder or instability [Mid-18thC. From late Latin *stultificare*, literally 'to make foolish', from Latin *stultus* 'foolish', literally 'immovable'.] —**stultification** /stúltifi káysh'n/ *n.* —**stultifier** /st/ *n.*

stum /stum/ *n.* WINE = **must**[2] ■ *vt.* **(stums, stumming, stummed) ADD STUM** to ferment wine by adding stum to it while it is in a cask or vat [Mid-17thC. From Dutch *stom*, literally 'dumb', a translation of French *muet*.]

stumble /stúmb'l/ *vi.* **(-bles, -bling, -bled) 1. TRIP OVER** to trip when walking or running **2. WALK UNSTEADILY** to walk unsteadily, as if intoxicated **3. SPEAK OR ACT HESITATINGLY** to speak or act hesitatingly, confusedly, or incompetently ○ *spoke the verse without stumbling* **4. FIND BY CHANCE** to find or come across sth by chance ○ *I stumbled across the note while I was cleaning the closet.* ■ *n.* **1. ACT OF TRIPPING** an instance of tripping over sth **2. MISTAKE** a mistake or hesitation [14thC. Origin uncertain: probably from assumed Old Norse *stumla*, a variant of *stumra* 'to walk unsteadily', from a prehistoric Germanic word that is also the ancestor of English *stammer*.] —**stumbler** *n.*

WORD KEY: SYNONYMS

See Synonyms at ***hesitate***.

stumblebum /stúmb'l bum/ *n.* *US* an offensive term for sb who does things in a blundering unskilful way (*slang insult*)

stumbling block *n.* sth that stands in the way of achieving a goal or of understanding sth [Early 16thC. Translation of Greek *proskomma*, literally 'sth you stumble against'.]

stumer /styoōmər/ *n.* sth that is forged or fraudulent (*slang*) [Late 19thC. Origin unknown.]

stump /stump/ *n.* **1. BASE OF A TREE** the base of a tree trunk and its roots after the tree has been felled **2. REMAINING SMALL PART** the part of sth such as a limb that is left after the main part has been cut off or removed **3.** CRICKET **PART OF WICKET** in cricket, each of the three upright posts that form part of the wicket **4.** DRAWING **CYLINDRICAL IMPLEMENT USED IN DRAWING** a short cylindrical piece of rolled paper, cork, rubber, or leather with ends formed into a point, used in drawing especially to soften lines and in representing shade and shadow ■ **stumps** *npl.* **LEGS** sb's legs (*slang*) ■ *v.* **(stumps, stumping, stumped) 1.** *vt.* **BAFFLE SB** to baffle sb by presenting a problem that seems impossible to solve **2.** *vt.* CRICKET **DISMISS BATSMAN BY TOUCHING THE STUMPS** to put a batsman out by knocking a bail off the wicket with the ball while the batsman is out of the crease **3.** *vi.* *US* POL **CAMPAIGN** to campaign for elective office (*informal*) **4.** *vi.* **WALK HEAVILY** to walk heavily and often angrily **5.** *vt.* **LOP** to lop the top off a tree, leaving a stump **6.** *vt.* **REMOVE STUMPS** to clear an area of land of tree stumps [13thC. From Middle Low German, of prehistoric Germanic origin.] —**stumper** *n.* ◇ **on the stump** *US, Can* engaged in making political speeches to win office

stump up *vt.* to pay the amount of money that is asked (*informal*) [Originally, 'to dig up by the roots']

stumpage /stúmpij/ *n.* *US* standing timber, or the amount of money it would bring if felled

stumpwork /stúmp wurk/ *n.* raised embroidery, with small decorative stitches made over pieces of padding [Early 20thC. Because the designs are raised upon stumps of wood.]

stumpy /stúmpi/ **(-ier, -iest)** *adj.* short, thick, and unattractive —**stumpiness** *n.*

stun /stun/ **(stuns, stunning, stunned)** *vt.* **1. MAKE UNCONSCIOUS** to make a person or animal unconscious for a short time with a blow or by using a drug **2. SHOCK** to shock, upset, or amaze sb ○ *a tragedy that left the nation stunned and bewildered* **3. OVERWHELM** to overwhelm one of the senses, e.g. with loud noise or very bright light [14thC. Via Anglo-Norman *estuner* from assumed Vulgar Latin *extonare*, from Latin *tonare* 'to thunder' (source of English *astonish*, *detonate*, and *tornado*).]

stung past tense, past participle of **sting**

stun gun *n.* a gun used for stunning animals or people for a short while without causing injury

stunk past tense, past participle of **stink**

stunner /stúnnər/ *n.* **1. IMPRESSIVE PERSON OR THING** sb who or sth that is extraordinarily impressive or beautiful (*informal*) **2.** ARMS = **stun gun**

stunning /stúnning/ *adj.* strikingly impressive or attractive in appearance ○ *They looked stunning at the reception.* —**stunningly** *adv.*

stunsail /stúnss'l/ *n.* NAUT = **studdingsail** [Mid-18thC. Contraction of STUDDINGSAIL.]

stunt[1] /stunt/ *vt.* **(stunts, stunting, stunted) RESTRICT THE GROWTH OF** to restrict the growth of sth so that it does not develop to its normal size ■ *n.* **1. STH NOT FULLY DEVELOPED** sth that has not grown to its normal size because its growth has been restricted **2.** BOT **PLANT DISEASE** a plant disease resulting in retarded growth [Old English, 'unintelligent, dull', from a prehistoric Germanic base that may also be the ancestor of English *stump*. The meaning was influenced by the related Old Norse *stuttr* 'short, dwarf'.]

stunt[2] /stunt/ *n.* **1. DANGEROUS FEAT** sth dangerous that is done as a challenge or to entertain people **2. STH UNUSUAL DONE FOR ATTENTION** sth silly or unusual that is done to attract attention ○ *a publicity stunt* ■ *vi.* **(stunts, stunting, stunted) PERFORM STUNTS** to perform dangerous feats as a challenge or to entertain people [Late 19thC. Origin unknown. Originally college athletics slang.]

stuntman /stúnt man/ (*plural* **-men** /-men/) *n.* a man whose job is to take the place of an actor in a scene involving danger or requiring acrobatic skill

stuntwoman /stúnt wŏomən/ (*plural* **-en** /-wimin/) *n.* a woman whose job is to take the place of an actor in a scene involving danger or requiring acrobatic skill

stupa /stoōpə/ *n.* a Buddhist shrine, temple, or pagoda that houses a relic or marks the location of an auspicious event [Late 19thC. From Sanskrit *stūpah* (source of English *tope*).]

stupe /styoop/ *n.* a hot, damp, sometimes medicated, cloth or sponge applied in former times to the skin as a compress or a counterirritant to relieve pain [14thC. Via Latin *stuppa* 'tow' from Greek *stuppē*; from the use of tow in making compresses.]

stupefacient /styoōpi fáysh'nt/ *adj.* **STUPEFYING** causing stupor ■ *n.* **STUPEFYING DRUG** a drug or other agent that causes stupor [Mid-17thC. From Latin *stupefacient-*, the present participle stem of *stupefacere* (see STUPEFY).]

stupefaction /styoōpi fáksh'n/ *n.* **1. AMAZEMENT** great amazement or astonishment (*literary*) **2. INABILITY TO THINK CLEARLY** the inability to think clearly because of boredom, tiredness, or amazement [15thC. Via French, from, ultimately, Latin *stupefacere* (see STUPEFY).]

stupefy /styoōpi fī/ **(-fies, -fying, -fied)** *vt.* **1. AMAZE** to amaze or astonish sb **2. MAKE SB UNABLE TO THINK CLEARLY** to make sb unable to think clearly because of boredom, tiredness, or amazement [15thC. Via French *stupéfier* from Latin *stupefacere*, from *stupere* 'to be stunned' (see STUPID) + *facere* 'to make'.] —**stupefier** *n.* —**stupefyingly** *adv.*

stupendous /styoo péndəss/ *adj.* impressively large, excellent, or great in extent or degree ○ *a stupendous achievement* [Mid-17thC. Formed from Latin *stupendus*, the gerundive of *stupere* 'to be stunned', source of English *stupor*.] —**stupendously** *adv.* —**stupendousness** *n.*

stupid /styo͞opid/ *adj.* **1.** UNINTELLIGENT thought to show a lack of intelligence, perception, or common sense ○ *a stupid mistake* **2.** SILLY irritatingly silly or time-wasting ○ *had us playing stupid games* **3.** EXPRESSING IRRITATION used to express anger, annoyance, or frustration (*informal*) ○ *I can't get the stupid thing to work!* **4.** DAZED in a dazed state, e.g. from shock, fatigue, or from the effects of drugs or alcohol ○ *almost stupid with tiredness* [Mid-16thC. From Latin *stupidus*, from *stupere* 'to be stunned'.]

stupidity /styoo píddəti/ (*plural* **-ties**) *n.* **1.** LACK OF INTELLIGENCE lack of intelligence, perception, or common sense **2.** RASHNESS OR THOUGHTLESSNESS extremely rash or thoughtless behaviour

stupidly /styo͞opidli/ *adv.* **1.** IN UNINTELLIGENT WAY in a way that demonstrates lack of intelligence, perception, or common sense ○ *I had stupidly forgotten to note down the date I mailed it.* **2.** IN BEWILDERMENT in a way that suggests diminished ability to perceive or reason ○ *He gazed stupidly after her.*

stupor /styo͞opər/ *n.* **1.** DAZED STATE an acute lack of mental alertness brought on e.g. by shock or lack of sleep **2.** UNCONSCIOUSNESS a state of near-unconsciousness induced by e.g. drugs or alcohol [14thC. From Latin, formed from *stupere* 'to be stunned'.] —**stuporous** *adj.*

sturdy /stúrdi/ (**-dier, -diest**) *adj.* **1.** WELL MADE solidly made and likely to withstand prolonged use **2.** WITH A STRONG BUILD having a well-developed strong-looking body and limbs **3.** RESOLUTE having or displaying decisiveness, resoluteness, or firmness of purpose ○ *sturdy defenders of the right to free speech* [13thC. Via Old French *estourdir* 'dazed' from, ultimately, Latin *turdus* 'thrush', formerly associated with drunkenness. The earliest sense was 'recklessly violent'.] —**sturdily** *adv.* —**sturdiness** *n.*

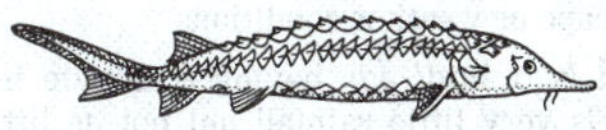

Sturgeon

sturgeon /stúrjən/ (*plural* **-geons** *or* **-geon**) *n.* a large bottom-feeding fish with a long snout and tough bony-plated skin, found in northern rivers and coastal waters. It is important as a source of caviar and isinglass. Family: Acipenseridae. [13thC. From Old French *esturgeon*, of Germanic origin.]

Sturmer /stúrmər/ *n.* a pale-green English variety of eating apple [Mid-19thC. Named after the village on the border of Essex and Suffolk where the variety was developed.]

Sturm und Drang /shto͝om o͝ont dráng/ *n.* **1.** LITERAT GERMAN LITERARY MOVEMENT a movement in late 18th-century German literature whose works typically portray the tortured emotions of a central character who violently rejects society **2.** EMOTIONAL TURMOIL a state of extreme emotional upheaval (*literary*) ○ *films that explore his own personal Sturm und Drang* [Late 18thC. From German, literally 'storm and stress'.]

Sturt /sturt/, **Charles** (1795–1869) Indian-born British explorer and administrator. He explored the river system of south eastern Australia (1829–30) and attempted to reach the centre of the continent (1844–46).

Sturt's desert pea *n.* an Australian plant of the bean family. Its bright-red flower is the emblem of South Australia. Latin name: *Clianthus formosus.* [Mid-19thC. Named after Charles STURT explorer.]

Sturt's desert rose *n.* an Australian shrub whose pink flower is the emblem of the Northern Territory. Latin name: *Gossypium sturtianum.* [Mid-20thC. Named after Charles STURT.]

stushie /sto͞oshi/, **stishie** /stíshi/ *n. Scotland* (*informal*) **1.** RUMPUS a bout or scene of heated discussion or argument **2.** STATE OF NERVOUSNESS a nervous, anxious, or upset state ○ *She was in a right stushie about the exam.* [Early 19thC. From Scots dialect, of unknown origin.]

stutter /stúttər/ *v.* (**-ters, -tering, -tered**) **1.** *vti.* SAY OR SPEAK WITH STAMMER to say sth haltingly, repeating sounds frequently when attempting to pronounce them, either from nervousness or as the result of a speech disorder ○ *managed to stutter an apology* **2.** *vi.* MAKE SHORT NOISES to make repeated short noises that suggest mechanical inefficiency or failure ○ *The motor stuttered briefly and then died again.* ■ *n.* **1.** STAMMERING AS A SPEECH DISORDER a speech disorder that makes the speaker repeat certain speech sounds that are found difficult to pronounce ○ *has a slight stutter* **2.** BURST OF REPEATED SOUNDS a burst of repeated short sounds [Early 16thC. Alteration of obsolete *stut*, of Germanic origin.] —**stutterer** *n.* —**stuttering** *adj.* —**stutteringly** *adv.*

Stuttgart /sto͝ot gaart/ capital of Baden-Württemberg State, in southwestern Germany. Population: 592,000 (1994).

STV *abbr.* **1.** Scottish Television **2.** single transferable vote

sty[1] /stī/ *n.* (*plural* **sties**) AGRIC PIG'S ENCLOSURE an enclosure in which pigs are kept ■ *vt.* (**sties, stying, stied**) AGRIC HOUSE A PIG to put or keep a pig in a sty [Old English *stī* 'pen'. Variant of stig (see STEWARD).]

sty[2] /stī/ (*plural* **sties**), **stye** *n.* MED a temporary swelling on an eyelid at the base of an eyelash [Early 17thC. By folk etymology from obsolete *styanye*, as if 'sty-on-eye'. From Old English *stīgend* 'rising' + *ye* 'eye'.]

Stygian /stíjji ən/ *adj.* **1.** PITCH-BLACK unremittingly dark and frightening, as hell is imagined to be (*literary*) **2.** MYTHOL OF THE STYX relating to the Styx, the river in Greek mythology that the souls of the dead were ferried across into Hades **3.** BINDING eternally binding, as were promises sworn on the banks of the river Styx in Greek mythology (*literary*) [Mid-16thC. Via Latin *Stygius* from Greek *Stugios*, from *Stux* (see STYX).]

styl- *prefix.* = **stylo-** (*used before vowels*)

stylar /stílə/ *adj.* relating to or using a stylus

style /stīl/ *n.* **1.** ARTS DISTINCTIVE FORM a distinctive and identifiable form in an artistic medium such as music, architecture, or literature ○ *a facade in the neoclassical style* ○ *a different style of jazz* **2.** WAY OF DOING STH a way of doing sth, especially a way regarded as expressing a particular attitude or typifying a particular period (*often used in combination*) ○ *a hands-on management style* ○ *old-style politics* ○ *Confrontation just isn't his style.* ○ *Self-catering holidays were not really her style.* **3.** WAY OF WRITING OR PERFORMING the way in which sth is written or performed as distinct from the content of the writing or performance **4.** FLAIR impressive flair in the way sth is done, especially a quality that suggests a self-confident willingness to exhibit skill or good taste ○ *furnished with impeccable style* **5.** FASHIONABLE STATUS fashionable status or quality ○ *a look that has gone out of style* **6.** FASHION an example of cut or shape of garment or way of wearing the hair ○ *dressed in all the latest styles* ○ *That style really suits you.* **7.** LUXURIOUSNESS extravagance or lavishness ○ *dining in style* **8.** PUBL PUBLISHING CONVENTIONS the ways in which written material is presented, usually in a particular publication or by a particular publisher ○ *editing text into the publisher's house style* **9.** BOT FLOWER PART an extension of a flower's ovary, shaped like a stalk, that supports the stigma **10.** ZOOL = **stylet** *n.* 2 **11.** = **stylus** *n.* 3 **12.** TITLE a name or title, especially one that is official or legally correct (*formal*) ■ *vt.* (**styles, styling, styled**) **1.** SHAPE STH to give sth a particular shape or design ○ *hair styled in the most up-to-date fashion* **2.** CAUSE TO CONFORM to bring sth into conformity with a particular style **3.** NAME SB to give sb or sth a name or title (*formal*) [13thC. Via Old French from Latin *stilus* 'writing instrument, style'.] —**styler** *n.* ◇ **cramp sb's style** to limit what sb is able to do, often by limiting the person's capacity to impress others (*informal*)

stylebook /stīl bo͝ok/ *n.* a publishing company's gathered conventions in presenting printed material, used as a guide by writers and editors

stylet /stílət/ *n.* **1.** MED WIRE PREVENTING BLOCKAGE IN A NEEDLE a fine wire inserted into a catheter or hollow needle to prevent it from becoming blocked when not in use **2.** ZOOL PART SHAPED LIKE A BRISTLE a thin long organ or appendage shaped like a bristle, e.g. any of the mouthparts of some insects **3.** LONG POINTED INSTRUMENT any long thin pointed instrument (*formal*) [Late 17thC. Via French from Italian *stiletto* (see STILETTO).]

styli plural of **stylus**

styli- *prefix.* = **stylo-**

styliform /stíli fawrm/ *adj.* long, thin, and pointed, like a bristle (*formal*) [Late 16thC. From modern Latin *stiliformis*, from Latin *stilus* 'style' + *forma* 'form'.]

styling *n.* **1.** SHAPING OF THE HAIR the act or an instance of giving a particular shape or design to sb's hair (*often used before a noun*) ○ *styling mousse* **2.** INSTANCE OF CREATING STH an instance of creating sth, especially sth artistic, in a particular or idiosyncratic way (*informal*) ○ *the zany comedy stylings of the country's favourite stand-up*

stylish /stílish/ *adj.* **1.** SOPHISTICATED AND FASHIONABLE having confident good taste and appreciation of what is fashionable **2.** IMPRESSIVE having or showing impressive skill or accomplishment ○ *the most stylish player in the team* —**stylishly** *adv.* —**stylishness** *n.*

stylist /stílist/ *n.* **1.** HAIR HAIRDRESSER a hairdresser, especially a more senior hairdresser in a salon **2.** ARTS, LITERAT ACCOMPLISHED ARTIST sb whose creative work shows a distinctive and accomplished style **3.** COMM DESIGNER a designer who is consulted on matters of style, especially sb responsible for creating a distinctive visual image for a product or company **4.** PUBL SB WHO PREPARES A SCENE TO BE PHOTOGRAPHED sb employed to set up scenes to be photographed in a magazine, including supplying any accessories or decorative objects required

stylistic /stī lístik/ *adj.* relating to matters of style, especially in literature and the arts ○ *stylistic brilliance compromised by a certain thinness of content* —**stylistically** *adv.*

stylistics /stī lístiks/ *n.* the branch of linguistics that deals with determining which features of written or spoken language characterize particular groups or contexts, especially particular literary genres or works (*takes a singular verb*)

stylite /stí līt/ *n.* a Christian ascetic in ancient times who lived alone on top of a tall pillar [Mid-17thC. From late Greek *stulitēs*, from Greek *stulos* 'pillar'.] —**stylitic** /stī líttik/ *adj.*

stylize /stí līz/ (**-izes, -izing, -ized**), **stylise** (**-ises, -ising, -ised**) *vt.* to give sth a distinctive, often artificial artistic style —**stylization** /stīlī záysh'n/ *n.* —**stylizer** /stí līzər/ *n.*

stylized /stí līzd/, **stylised** *adj.* created or performed according to distinctive established styles, usually in order to achieve a particular artistic effect, often at the expense of naturalness or spontaneity ○ *a highly stylized backhand stroke*

stylo- *prefix.* style, column ○ *stylograph* ○ *styloid* [From Latin *stylus* (see STYLUS)]

stylobate /stílə bayt/ *n.* a continuous raised platform of masonry supporting a row of columns [Mid-16thC. Via Latin *stylobata* from Greek *stulobatēs*, literally 'column step'.]

stylograph /stílō graaf-graf/ *n.* a fountain pen that has a thin hollow tube as its writing point instead of the traditional nib

stylography /stī lóggrəfi/ *n.* the art of drawing or engraving using a stylus —**stylographic** /stílō gráffik/ *adj.* —**stylographically** /-l/ *adv.*

styloid /stí loyd/ *adj.* ANAT used to describe a bony protuberance (**process**) that is long and thin

stylolite /stílə līt/ *n.* a join between two layers of limestone that in cross-section looks like a row of interlocking pegs —**stylolitic** /stílə líttik/ *adj.*

Stylophone /stíləfōn/ *tdmk.* a trademark for a small battery-operated musical instrument with a surface like a keyboard, played using an electronic pen attached by wire

stylopodium /stílō pódi əm/ (*plural* **-a** /-ə/) *n.* the typically broad base of the style of flowers in plants of the carrot family

Stylus

stylus /stíləss/ (*plural* **-li** /-lī/) *n.* **1.** RECORDING **RECORD PLAYER NEEDLE** the jewel-tipped needle of a record player that rests in the grooves of a record as it revolves. It transmits vibrations to the cartridge. **2.** ELECTRON ENG **MACHINE'S TRACING PEN** the tracing pen on an electronic device such as a seismograph or polygraph that converts an electrical signal into a written record **3.** ENGRAVING **TOOL** a pointed instrument used for engraving, especially one used in ancient times for writing on clay or wax tablets [Early 18thC. From Latin, a spelling variant of *stilus*, 'stake, pointed writing instrument', influenced by Greek *stulos*, 'pillar'.]

stymie /stími/, **stymy** *vt.* (**-mies, -mieing, -mied; -mies, -mying, -mied**) **1.** HINDER **THE PROGRESS OF** to prevent sb or sth from making further progress **2.** GOLF **BLOCK AN OPPONENT'S LINE** to obstruct the line between a golf opponent's ball and the hole (*dated*) ■ *n.* (*plural* **-mies**) **1.** PROBLEM **SITUATION** a situation in which obstacles hinder progress **2.** GOLF **OBSTRUCTION OF AN OPPONENT'S BALL** a situation in which one golf player's ball blocks another's. In the modern game, the obstructing ball is lifted and replaced by a marker. (*dated*) [Mid-19thC. Origin unknown.]

stypsis /stípsiss/ *n.* the use of a styptic substance, or its antibleeding effect [Late 19thC. Via late Latin from Greek *stupsis*, from *stuphein* 'to contract'.]

styptic /stíptik/ *adj.* ABLE **TO STOP BLEEDING** slowing down the rate of bleeding or stopping bleeding altogether, whether by causing the blood vessels to contract or by accelerating clotting ■ *n.* STYPTIC **SUBSTANCE** a styptic drug, cream, or lotion [14thC. Via late Latin *stypticus* from Greek *stuptikos*, from *stuphein* 'to contract'.]

styptic pencil *n.* an astringent substance in solid form in a small cylindrical container that is applied to stop bleeding in small cuts, e.g. after shaving

styrax *n.* = **storax** *n.* 3

styrene /stí reen/ *n.* a colourless flammable liquid hydrocarbon used in the manufacture of synthetic rubber and plastic. Formula: C_8H_8. [Late 19thC. Coined from Latin *styrax* (see STORAX) + -ENE.]

Styrofoam /stírə fōm/ *tdmk.* a trademark for a light plastic material used to make disposable items, insulation, and packing materials

Styron /stírən/, **William** (*b.* 1925) US writer. His novel

William Styron

The Confessions of Nat Turner (1967) won a Pulitzer Prize. Full name **William Clark Styron, Jr.**

Styx /stiks/ *n.* in Greek mythology, the river across which the souls of the dead were ferried into the underworld [14thC. Via Latin from Greek *Stux*.]

SU *abbr.* **1.** Soviet Union (*dated*) (*international vehicle registration*) **2.** strontium unit

suable /soo-, syoo əb'l/ *adj.* able or liable to be made the subject of a lawsuit —**suability** /soo ə bílləti, syoo ə bílləti/ *n.*

Suárez González /swaár ez gon zaál eez, swár eth gon thál eth/, **Adolfo** (*b.* 1932) Spanish statesman. As prime minister of Spain (1976–81) after the death of General Franco, he guided the country towards democracy.

suasion /swáyzh'n/ *n.* the art of persuasion or an instance of persuading (*formal*) [14thC. Via Old French or directly from Latin *suasion-*, the stem of *suasio*, from, ultimately, *suadere*, 'to advise'.] —**suasive** /swáyssiv/ *adj.*

suave /swaav/ (**suaver, suavest**) *adj.* **1.** CHARMING polite and charming, especially in a way that seems affected or insincere **2.** PLEASINGLY **DRESSED** well groomed and smartly dressed (*informal*) [Early 16thC. Via French or directly from Latin *suavis* 'sweet, agreeable', from, ultimately, an Indo-European base that is also the ancestor of English *sweet*.] —**suavely** *adv.* —**suaveness** *n.* —**suavity** /swáavity/ *n.*

sub[1] /sub/ *n.* (*informal*) **1.** A **SUBSTITUTE** a substitute, especially a substitute player in a game **2.** PUBL **SUBEDITOR** a subeditor **3.** MIL **SUBALTERN** a subaltern **4.** SMALL **LOAN** a small sum of money borrowed, especially a small advance on wages due ○ *You could ask her for a sub.* **5.** SUBSCRIPTION **FEE** a subscription fee ○ *Have you paid your subs for this season?* **6.** SUBTITLE a subtitle to a document or printed matter ■ *v.* (**subs, subbing, subbed**) (*informal*) **1.** *vi.* REPLACE to take the place of sb temporarily, usually in a work situation **2.** *vti.* SUBCONTRACT to subcontract work, or work as a subcontractor **3.** *vt.* SUBTITLE **STH** to add subtitles to sth **4.** *vti.* SUBEDIT to subedit sth, or work as a subeditor **5.** *vt.* LEND **MONEY** to lend sb a small amount of money, especially as an advance on wages due ○ *He could have subbed me a few quid until payday.* [Late 17thC. Shortening.]

sub[2] /sub/ *n.* (*informal*) **1.** NAVY **SUBMARINE** a submarine **2.** US FOOD **SANDWICH** a sandwich made with a long roll cut horizontally

sub. *abbr.* **1.** subito **2.** suburb **3.** suburban

sub- *prefix.* **1.** under, below, beneath ○ *subcutaneous* ○ *subfloor* **2.** subordinate, secondary ○ *subparagraph* **3.** less than completely ○ *subliterate* **4.** subdivision ○ *subkingdom* ○ *subcontinent* **5.** bordering on ○ *subequatorial* **6.** smaller or younger than ○ *subcompact* ○ *subteen* **7.** nearly, partly, somewhat ○ *subfossil* **8.** containing less than the normal amount of an element ○ *suboxide* [From Latin *sub* 'under']

sub A *n.* S Africa the former term for the first year of schooling in some provinces in South Africa (*dated*) ♦ **grade 1** [*Sub* a shortening of SUB-STANDARD, the second year being *Sub B*, and the third year being *Standard 1*]

subacid /súb ássid/ *adj.* **1.** SLIGHTLY **SOUR** moderately sour in flavour (*archaic*) **2.** SOMEWHAT **CRITICAL** mildly unkind or critical in tone (*literary*) —**subacidity** /súbə síddəti/ *n.* —**subacidly** /súb ássidli/ *adv.*

subacute /súbə kyóot/ *adj.* used to describe a medical condition that develops less rapidly and with less severity than an acute condition —**subacutely** *adv.*

subacute sclerosing panencephalitis /-pán en seffə lítiss/ *n.* a severe, usually fatal, inflammatory disease of the brain, chiefly affecting children and linked to infection from measles

subadar /sóoba daar/, **subahdar** *n.* the chief Indian officer in a company of Indian soldiers in the former British Indian army [Late 17thC. From Urdu and Persian *ṣūbahdār*, literally 'subah holder' (see SUBAH).]

subaerial /súb airi əl/ *adj.* formed or situated on or just below the surface of the soil ○ *a plant with subaerial roots*

subah /sóo baa/ *n.* **1.** HIST **MOGUL PROVINCE** any of the provinces of the Mogul empire **2.** MIL = **subadar** [Mid-18thC. Via Urdu and Persian *ṣūbah* from Arabic, 'heap'.]

subahdar *n.* MIL = **subadar**

subalpine /súb ál pīn/ *adj.* relating to or growing naturally on the lower slopes of mountains, especially the areas below the tree line

subaltern /súbb'ltərn/ *n.* **1.** MIL **JUNIOR OFFICER** a junior officer in some armies, e.g. a commissioned officer below the rank of captain in the British army **2.** SUBORDINATE **PERSON** sb who holds a subordinate or inferior position **3.** LOGIC **IMPLIED PROPOSITION** a particular proposition that is implied by a universal proposition ■ *adj.* **1.** SUBORDINATE in a subordinate or inferior position **2.** LOGIC **IMPLIED** implied as a particular proposition by a universal proposition [Late 16thC. From late Latin *subalternus*, from Latin *alternus* 'alternate' (see ALTERNATE).]

subalternate /sub áwltərnət, -ól-/ *adj.* **1.** BOT **WITH LEAFLETS NOT FULLY ALTERNATE** used to describe a leaf whose leaflets are arranged in semistaggered rows, neither fully alternate nor fully opposite **2.** SUBORDINATE in a subordinate or inferior position —**subalternation** /sub áwltər náysh'n, sub ól-/ *n.*

subantarctic /súb ant aárktik/ *adj.* relating to the area between the Antarctic Circle and the South Pole

subapostolic /súb apə stóllik/ *adj.* belonging to the period in the history of the Christian Church that immediately followed the time of the Apostles

subaqua /súb ákwə/ *adj.* relating to or providing facilities for underwater sports such as scuba diving [Mid-20thC. Coined from SUB- + Latin *aqua* 'water'.]

subaquatic /súbə kwáttik/ *adj.* **1.** BIOL **IN WATER AND ON LAND** existing or able to exist partly in water and partly on land **2.** RELATING **TO UNDERWATER REGIONS** relating or belonging to underwater regions

subaqueous /súb áykwi əss/ *adj.* living, found, or formed under water

subarachnoid /súbə ráknoyd/ *adj.* situated beneath the middle of the three membranes (**arachnoids**) that cover the brain and spinal cord

subarctic /súb aárktik/ *adj.* **1.** SOUTH **OF THE ARCTIC CIRCLE** relating to the area bordering the Arctic Circle to the south **2.** LIKE **THE BORDERS OF THE ARCTIC** similar to the regions that border the Arctic Circle, e.g. in landscape or weather conditions

subarid /súb árrid/ *adj.* having a climate in which there is very little rainfall but not as little as in arid regions

subassembly /súbə sémbli/ (*plural* **-blies**) *n.* a group of pieces assembled separately and incorporated into a larger assembled structure

subatomic /súbə tómmik/ *adj.* **1.** PHYS **PART OF OR SMALLER THAN AN ATOM** occurring as part of an atom, or smaller than an atom **2.** SCI **ON A SMALLER-THAN-ATOM SCALE** on a scale smaller than the atom, or involving phenomena at this level

subaudition /súb awdísh'n/ *n.* **1.** IMPLICATION the act of understanding a word or thought that is implied but not actually expressed in speech or writing **2.** IMPLIED **WORD OR IDEA** a word, idea, or thought understood by a hearer or reader that is implied but not expressed [Mid-17thC. From late Latin *subaudition-*, the stem of *subauditio*, from, ultimately, Latin *audire* 'to hear'.]

subaxillary /súb ak sílləri/ *adj.* **1.** ZOOL, ANAT **BELOW THE ARMPIT** located beneath the armpit **2.** BOT **BELOW THE AXIL** growing beneath the axil in plants

subbase /súb bayss/ *n.* **1.** BUILDING **BOTTOM STRUCTURAL LAYER** a deep layer of large stones that forms the lowest level of a roadbed or of the foundation of a building **2.** BOTTOM **OF A BASE** the lowest section of any base or foundation, e.g. the bottom part of a pedestal

subbasement /súb bayssmənt/ *n.* a storey below the basement in a building

subcalibre /sub kállibər/ *adj.* used to describe ammunition whose calibre is smaller than that of the gun from which it is fired. Smaller ammunition is often used for practice because it is cheaper.

subcartilaginous /súb kaárti lájjinəss/ *adj.* **1.** BENEATH **CARTILAGE** lying beneath cartilage or a body part composed of cartilage **2.** PARTLY **OF CARTILAGE** made up partly of cartilage

subcategory /súb katəgəri/ (*plural* **-ries**) *n.* any one of

Popperfoto

the smaller sections into which a main category is divided

subcelestial /súb sə lésti əl/ *adj.* belonging to the earth, not to the heavens or the stars (*literary*)

subcellular /súb séllyŏŏlər/ *adj.* **1.** BIOL **INSIDE A CELL** existing inside a cell, or relating to the component parts of cells **2.** SCI **ON A SMALLER-THAN-CELL SCALE** on a scale smaller than a cell, or involving phenomena at this level

subclass /súb klaass/ *n.* **1. SUBORDINATE CLASS** any of the smaller groups into which a main class is divided **2.** BIOL **BIOLOGICAL CLASS** a subdivision of a class in the classification of plants and animals **3.** MATH = **subset**

subclavian /sub kláyvi ən/ *adj.* located under the collarbone (**clavicle**) [Mid-17thC. Formed from modern Latin *subclavius*, from Latin *clavis* 'key' (source of English *clavicle*).]

subclinical /sub klínnik'l/ *adj.* used to describe an early stage or mild form of a medical condition, no symptoms of which are detectable —**subclinically** *adv.*

subcommittee /súbkəmiti/ *n.* a committee set up by and consisting of members of an existing committee to deal with a particular issue

subconscious /sub kónshəss/ *adj.* **EXISTING UNKNOWN IN THE MIND** present in your mind without you being aware of it ■ *n.* **UNCONSCIOUS PART OF THE MIND** mental activity not directly perceived by your consciousness, from which memories, feelings, or thoughts can influence your behaviour without you realizing it —**subconsciously** *adv.* —**subconsciousness** *n.*

subcontinent /sub kóntinənt/, **Subcontinent** *n.* a large area that is an identifiably separate part of a continent, especially the area encompassing the countries of India, Pakistan, and Bangladesh regarded as a distinct part of Asia —**subcontinental** /súb kont inént'l/ *adj., n.*

subcontract /súbkən trákt/ *n.* **SECONDARY CONTRACT** a secondary contract in which the person or company originally hired in turn hires sb else to do all or part of the work ■ *v.* (**-tracts, -tracting, -tracted**) **1.** *vt.* **GIVE WORK UNDER A SUBCONTRACT** to pass on work to a second person or company under the terms of a subcontract **2.** *vi.* **TAKE ON WORK FROM A CONTRACTOR** to work on contract with a person or company who is a contractor to sb else —**subcontractor** /súbkən tráktər/ *n.*

subcontrary /sub kóntrəri/ *adj.* **NOT FALSE TOGETHER** used to describe logical propositions that are related to each other in such a way that both cannot be false at the same time, although both may be true ■ *n.* (*plural* **-ies**) **SUBCONTRARY PROPOSITION** a subcontrary logical proposition [Early 17thC. From late Latin *subcontrarius*, a translation of Greek *hupenantios* 'contrary'.]

subcortex /sub káwrteks/ (*plural* **-tices** /-seez/) *n.* the parts of the brain that lie immediately beneath the cerebral cortex —**subcortical** /-káwrtik'l/ *adj.*

subcranial /sub kráyni əl/ *adj.* located beneath the dome of the skull

subculture /súb kulchər/ *n.* **1.** SOCIOL **SEPARATE SOCIAL GROUP** an identifiably separate social group within a larger culture, especially one regarded as existing outside mainstream society **2.** BIOL **SECONDARY BIOLOGICAL CULTURE** a bacterial culture that is grown from another culture —**subcultural** *adj.*

subcutaneous /súbkyoo táyni əss/ *adj.* located, living, or made beneath the skin —**subcutaneously** *adv.*

subdeacon /sub deékən/ *n.* **1. DEACON'S ASSISTANT** a member of the Roman Catholic clergy who acts as a deacon's assistant, e.g. by preparing the vessels that are to be used in celebrating Mass **2. CLERGYMAN ABOVE LECTOR** a clergyman ranking just above a lector in an Eastern Church

subdiaconate /súb dī ákənət, -nayt/ *n.* the position or term of office of a subdeacon —**subdiaconal** /súb dī ákən'l/ *adj.*

subdirectory /súbdi rektəri e, -dī-/ (*plural* **-ries**) *n.* a division of a directory on a magnetic storage device such as a hard disk

subdivide /súbdi vīd/ (**-vides, -viding, -vided**) *v.* **1.** *vt.* **DIVIDE FURTHER** to divide a section, or all the sections of sth into sections that are smaller still **2.** *vi.* **BE DIVIDED FURTHER** to be divided, or be able to be divided, into sections that are smaller still —**subdivider** *n.*

subdivision /súb divizh'n/ *n.* **1. SUBDIVIDING OF STH** the dividing of a divided part into units that are smaller still **2. SUBSIDIARY SECTION** a section of sth that is itself a division of a larger thing —**subdivisional** *adj.*

subdominant /sub dómminənt/ *n.* **1. FOURTH NOTE IN A SCALE** the fourth note in a major or minor scale **2. SUBDOMINANT HARMONY** a key, chord, or harmony based on a subdominant

subduct /səb dúkt/ (**-ducts, -ducting, -ducted**) *vi.* to be carried under the edge of an adjoining continental or oceanic plate, causing tensions in the Earth's crust that can produce earthquakes or volcanic eruptions [Late 16thC. From Latin *subduct-*, the past participle stem of *subducere* 'to draw up', from *ducere* 'to lead'.] —**subduction** /səb dúksh'n/ *n.*

subdue /səb dyoo/ (**-dues, -duing, -dued**) *vt.* **1. BRING UNDER FORCIBLE CONTROL** to bring a person or group of people under control using force **2. SOFTEN** to soften sth or make it less intense ○ *idealism subdued by experience* **3. REPRESS** to repress or control feelings or emotions ○ *worked hard to subdue her irritation* [14thC. Via Old French *souduire* 'to seduce' from Latin *subducere* 'to draw up' (see SUBDUCT).] —**subduable** *adj.* —**subduer** *n.*

subdued /səb dyood/ *adj.* **1. NOT HARSH** not bright, loud, or intense, or made less bright, loud, or intense ○ *subdued lighting* **2. VERY QUIET** sad or in low spirits **3. QUIET** quiet and restrained ○ *speaking in subdued tones*

subdural /sub dyóorəl/ *adj.* beneath the dura mater that covers the brain and spinal cord

subedit /súb éddit/ (**-its, -iting, -ited**) *vt.* to read and correct written material before it is published, particularly for newspapers and magazines, under the general supervision of an editor. US term **copyedit** [Mid-19thC. Back-formation from SUBEDITOR.]

subeditor /súb édditər/ *n.* **1. ASSISTANT EDITOR** an assistant editor helping to prepare material for publication **2. SB CHECKING MATERIAL TO BE PUBLISHED** sb whose job is to read and correct written material before it is published, particularly for newspapers and magazines, under the general supervision of an editor. US term **copyreader**

subequatorial /súbekwə táwri əl/ *adj.* relating to or situated in the regions that lie just north and south of the equator

suberin /syoobərin/ *n.* a fatty substance found in the cell walls of many plants, especially in cork tissue where it provides resistance to water and decay [Early 19thC. From French *subérine*, from Latin *suber* 'cork'.]

suberize /syoobə rīz/ (**-izes, -izing, -ized**), **suberise** (**-ises, -ising, -ised**) *vt.* to deposit suberin in plant cell walls during their conversion to cork tissue [Late 19thC. Coined from Latin *suber* 'cork' + -IZE.]

suberose /syoobə rōss/ *adj.* relating to cork, or similar to cork in appearance or texture [Mid-19thC. From modern Latin *suberosus*, from Latin *suber* 'cork'.]

subfamily /súb famli/ (*plural* **-lies**) *n.* **1.** BIOL **BIOLOGICAL CLASSIFICATION** a subdivision of a family in the classification of plants and animals **2.** LING **LINGUISTIC CATEGORIZATION** a smaller group of related languages within a language family

subfield /súb feeld/ *n.* a mathematical field that is a subset of another field

subfloor /súb flawr/ *n.* an underlying layer of rough or unfinished material supporting a finished floor —**subflooring** *n.*

subfossil /súb foss'l/ *adj.* **PARTLY FOSSILIZED** partially fossilized ■ *n.* **SUBFOSSIL ORGANISM** a partially fossilized organism

subframe /súb fraym/ *n.* the underlying metal frame on which a vehicle's bodywork is built

subfreezing /sub freézing/ *adj.* lower than 0° Celsius or 32° Fahrenheit

subfusc /súb fusk, sub fúsk/ *adj.* dark or drab in colour (*literary*) [Mid-18thC. From Latin *subfuscus* 'darkish', from *fuscus* 'dark'.]

subgenus /súb jeenəss, -jenəss/ (*plural* **-genera** /-jénnərə/) *n.* a category in the classification of plants and animals that is larger than a species but smaller than a genus

subglacial /sub gláysh'l/ *adj.* formed below or at the bottom of a glacier —**subglacially** *adv.*

subgrade /súb grayd/ *n.* the bed of ground on which the foundations of a road, railway, or building are laid

subgroup /súb groop/ *n.* **1. DIVISION OF GROUP** a smaller group distinguished in some way from the larger group of which it is a part **2.** MATH **MATHEMATICAL GROUP** a mathematical group whose members are also members of a larger group

subhead /súb hed/, **subheading** /-heding/ *n.* PRINTING a heading or title subordinate to the main one

subhuman /sub hyoomən/ *adj.* **1. LESS THAN HUMAN** relating to or displaying behaviour that is distastefully inferior in sophistication, moral standards, or intelligence to what is regarded as normal for human beings ○ *a subhuman thug* **2.** BIOL **NEARLY HUMAN** at the level of development that is considered just below humans

sub-imago (*plural* **sub-imagoes** *or* **sub-imagines**) *n.* a mayfly or related insect in a metamorphic stage in which functional wings are present but not all adult features have developed fully

subindex /sub índeks/ (*plural* **-dexes** *or* **-dices** /-índi seez/) *n.* **1. INDEX OF SUBSECTION** an index to a section of a main classification **2.** MATH = **subscript**

subinfeudation /súb infyoo dáysh'n/ *n.* **1. SUBDIVIDING OF FEUDAL LAND** in the feudal system, the leasing of a portion of the land held by a feudal lord's servant (**vassal**) to sb else who became the servant's servant in turn **2. LAND GRANTED** a portion of land granted to a feudal servant under the terms of subinfeudation —**subinfeudate** /súb in fyoo dayt/ *vt.*

subirrigate /sub írri gayt/ (**-gates, -gating, -gated**) *vt.* to irrigate land from below the surface of the ground, e.g. with porous pipes laid underground —**subirrigation** /súb iri gáysh'n/ *n.*

subito /soobitō/ *adv.* suddenly or abruptly (*used as a musical direction*) [Early 18thC. Via Italian from, ultimately, Latin *subire* 'to come over'.]

subj. *abbr.* **1.** GRAM subject **2.** subjective **3.** GRAM subjunctive

subjacent /sub jáyss'nt/ *adj.* (*formal*) **1. UNDERLYING** lying under or just below sth **2. LOWER** next to sth and at a lower level than it ○ *'in the damper tracts of subjacent country and along the river-courses'* (Thomas Hardy, *Jude the Obscure*; 1895) [Late 16thC. From Latin *subjacent-*, the present participle stem of *subjacere* 'to lie under'.] —**subjacency** *n.* —**subjacently** *adv.*

subject /súb jékt/ *n.* **1. TOPIC** a matter that is being discussed, examined, studied, or otherwise dealt with **2.** EDUC **COURSE OF STUDY** a branch of learning that forms a course of study (*often used in the plural*) **3. RULED PERSON** sb who is under the rule of a king, queen, or other authority ○ *British subjects* **4. SB TREATED OR ACTED UPON** sb who undergoes treatment or who is the focus of an activity ○ *not an appropriate subject for hypnosis* **5.** ARTS **THING REPRESENTED BY AN ARTIST** sb who or sth that a painter, sculptor, or photographer represents in a piece of work **6.** LITERAT **SB FEATURED IN A BIOGRAPHY** the main person written about in a biography **7.** GRAM **GRAMMATICAL PERFORMER OF A VERB'S ACTION** the part of a sentence or utterance, a noun, noun phrase, or equivalent, that the rest of the sentence asserts sth about and that agrees with the verb. The subject typically performs the action expressed by the verb. 'She' and 'The dog' are the subjects of 'She gave me the book' and 'The dog was found asleep' respectively. **8.** MUSIC **MUSICAL THEME** the principal theme or melodic phrase that is developed in the course of a musical composition ■ *adj.* **1. PRONE TO** likely to be affected by or with a tendency to be affected by a particular thing ○ *areas subject to flooding* ○ *a child subject to mood swings* **2. RULED** under the control of sb or sth such as a ruler or a law, and obliged to obey ○ *a subject nation* ○ *not* subject to the laws that apply in this country ■ adv. **DEPENDING** depending on or conditional on sb or sth ○ *The plans have been drawn up, subject to your final approval.* ■ vt. (-jects, -jecting, -jected) **1. CAUSE TO HAVE AN UNPLEASANT EXPERIENCE** to cause sb to undergo sth unpleasant ○ *recruits subjected to rigorous physical training* **2. SUBMIT TO TREATMENT** to make sth undergo treatment of a particular kind ○ *proposals subjected to detailed scrutiny* **3. OVERPOWER** to bring a person or group under the power or influence of another person or group ○ *a nation subjected to rule from overseas* [14thC. Via Old French from Latin *subjectus*, from, ultimately, *subicere* 'to place under', from *jacere* 'to throw'.]

——— WORD KEY: SYNONYMS ———
subject, **topic**, **subject matter**, **matter**, **theme**, **burden**
CORE MEANING: what is under discussion

subject a general word that describes what is under discussion or investigation; **topic** an item selected for discussion; **subject matter** a fairly formal term meaning the same as *subject*. It is sometimes used when drawing a distinction with the style or form of a piece of writing; **matter** a formal word used in the same way as *subject matter*; **theme** an important unifying idea in sth such as a piece of writing, a painting, or a film; **burden** a formal or literary word used to mean the main argument or recurrent theme of sth such as a piece of writing.

subjection /səb jéksh'n/ n. **1. DOMINATION** the bringing of a person or people under the control of another, usually by force **2. ACT OF SUBJECTING** the subjecting of sb to sth

subjective /səb jéktiv/ adj. **1. NOT IMPARTIAL** based on sb's opinions or feelings rather than on facts or evidence ○ *Of course, that's only my subjective impression.* **2. PHILOSOPHY EXISTING BY PERCEPTION** existing only in the mind and not independently of it **3. MED OBSERVED ONLY BY THE PATIENT** used to describe a medical condition that is perceived to exist only by the patient and is not recognizable to anyone else **4. GRAM RELATING TO THE SUBJECT OF VERB** relating to or forming the subject of a verb —**subjectively** adv. —**subjectiveness** n.

subjective idealism n. a philosophical theory arguing that the external world only exists because it is perceived to exist, and does not have existence of its own

subjectivism /səb jéktivizəm/ n. **1. PHILOS THEORY OF THE VALIDITY OF KNOWLEDGE** a theory stating that people can only have knowledge of what they experience directly **2. PHILOS THEORY OF THE VALIDITY OF MORAL STANDARDS** a theory stating that the only valid moral standard is the one imposed by sb's own conscience, and therefore that society's moral codes are invalid **3. EMPHASIS ON PERSONAL INTERPRETATION** emphasis on personal feelings or responses as opposed to external facts or evidence —**subjectivist** adj. —**subjectivistic** /səb jékti vístik/ adj. —**subjectivistically** adv.

subjectivity /súb jek tívvəti/ n. **1. PERSONAL INTERPRETATION** interpretation based on personal opinions or feelings rather than on external facts or evidence **2. ARTS PERSONAL VISION** concentration on personal, individual responses in artistic expression

subject matter n. the matter dealt with in a book, film, discussion, or other pursuit ○ *contains subject matter unsuitable for children*

——— WORD KEY: SYNONYMS ———
See Synonyms at **subject**.

subjoin /sub jóyn/ vt. to add sth at the end of what has already been written or said (*formal*)

sub judice /súb joódəssi/ adj. currently under consideration by a judge or a court of law and therefore not to be commented upon publicly [Early 17thC. From Latin, literally 'under a judge'.]

subjugate /súbjoŏ gayt/ (-gates, -gating, -gated) vt. to bring sb, especially a people or nation, under the control of another, e.g. by military conquest [15thC. From Latin *subjugat-*, the past participle stem of *subjugare*, from, ultimately, *jugum* 'yoke'.] —**subjugable** adj. —**subjugator** n.

subjunctive /səb júngktiv/ n. **1. GRAMMATICAL MOOD** a grammatical mood that expresses doubts, wishes,

and possibilities. The verb 'were' is in the subjunctive in the phrase 'if I were you'. **2. SUBJUNCTIVE VERB** a verb or form in the subjunctive ■ adj. **RELATING TO THE SUBJUNCTIVE** in or relating to the subjunctive [Mid-16thC. Via late Latin *subjunctivus* from, ultimately, Latin *subjungere* 'to subordinate', from *jungere* 'to join'.] —**subjunctively** adv.

——— WORD KEY: USAGE ———
Use of the subjunctive in English: Most people associate the *subjunctive* with Latin and Greek, and are sometimes surprised to realize that they are using it themselves as a regular (if now limited) feature of English grammar. The subjunctive is distinguishable from the regular form of verbs (called the *indicative*) only in the third person singular present tense, which omits the final *-s* (as in *make* rather than *makes*), and in the forms *be* and *were* of the verb *to be*. A typical use of the subjunctive is in clauses introduced by *that* expressing a wish or suggestion, of the type *I suggested to her that she drop by for a drink before the concert. They demanded that he answer their questions.* The form *were* is used in clauses introduced by *if*, *as if*, *as though*, or *supposing*, as in: *If you were to go, you might regret it. It's not as though he were an expert. Supposing I were to meet you outside the theatre.* The subjunctive also occurs in fixed expressions such as *as it were*, *be that as it may*, *come what may*, and *far be it from me.*

subkingdom /sub kíngdəm/ n. a category in the classification of plants and animals that is smaller than a kingdom and larger than a phylum

sublease /sub leéss/ n. **LEASE TO RENT FROM A TENANT** an arrangement to rent a property from sb who is already renting it from sb else ■ vt. (-leases, -leasing, -leased) = **sublet** —**sublessee** /súb le seé/ n. —**sublessor** /súb le sáwr/ n.

sublet /sub lét/ vti. (-lets, -letting, -let) **RENT PROPERTY UNDER A SUBLEASE** to rent a property to or as a subsidiary tenant ■ n. **PROPERTY RENTED UNDER A SUBLEASE** a property that is rented from sb who is renting it from sb else

sublimate v. /súbbli mayt/ vt. **PSYCHOL REDIRECT** to channel impulses or energies regarded as unacceptable, especially sexual desires, towards an activity that is more socially acceptable, often a creative activity **2. vti. CHEM = sublime** v. 1 ■ n. /súbbli mayt, -mət/ **CHEM SUBSTANCE FORMED FROM SUBLIMATION** a chemical substance formed as a result of sublimation [15thC. From Latin *sublimat-*, the past participle stem of *sublimare* 'to elevate', from *sublimis* 'elevated'.]

sublimation /súbbli máysh'n/ n. **1. CHEM CHEMICAL CONVERSION** a chemical process in which a solid substance is converted into a gas directly, without passing through an intermediate liquid phase **2. PSYCHOL REDIRECTING OF UNACCEPTABLE IMPULSES** the channelling of impulses or energies regarded as unacceptable, especially sexual desires, towards activities regarded as more socially acceptable, often creative activities

sublime /sə blím/ adj. (-limer, -limest) **1. BEAUTIFUL** so awe-inspiringly beautiful as to seem almost heavenly ○ *Monteverdi at his most sublime* **2. MORALLY WORTHY** of the highest moral or spiritual value **3. EXCELLENT** excellent or particularly impressive (*informal*) ○ *a sublime pasta creation* **4. COMPLETE** complete or utter ○ *in sublime ignorance* ■ n. **STH SUBLIME** sth that is sublime ○ *going from the sublime to the ridiculous* ■ v. (-limes, -liming, -limed) **1. vti. CHEM CONVERT A SOLID SUBSTANCE TO GAS** to convert a solid substance directly into a gas without there being an intermediate liquid phase, or to undergo this process **2. vti. CHEM CONVERT THEN RECONVERT** to convert a solid directly into a gas and then back to a solid again without an intermediate liquid phase, or to undergo this process **3. vt. MAKE PURE** to make sth such as an emotion finer or purer [14thC. From Latin *sublimis* 'elevated'.] —**sublimely** adv. —**sublimeness** n. —**sublimity** /sə blímməti/ n.

Sublime Porte n. HIST = **Porte** [Early 17thC. From French, literally 'High Gate', a translation of Turkish *Babiâli*, referring to the palace gate where justice was administered.]

subliminal /sub límmin'l/ adj. entering, existing in, or affecting the mind without conscious awareness

○ *subliminal messages* [Late 19thC. Coined from SUB- + Latin *limin-*, the stem of *limen* 'threshold'.]

subliminal advertising n. advertising in the form of images flashed onto the screen during a film or television programme that are too brief to be noticed but long enough to be registered subconsciously

sublingual /sub líng gwəl/ adj. **1. ANAT UNDER THE TONGUE** situated under the tongue **2. MED PLACED UNDER THE TONGUE** used to describe medicines that are administered by being placed under the tongue to dissolve —**sublingually** adv.

subliterate /sub líttərət/ adj. having or demonstrating a level of language competence that is below the level regarded as literate

sublittoral /sub líttərəl/ adj. **RELATING TO SHALLOW COASTAL WATERS** relating to, living near, or located in the shallow water near a shoreline ■ n. **COASTAL PART OF A SEA** the area of a sea that lies between the shore and the continental shelf

sublunary /sub loónəri/ adj. **1. ASTRON BETWEEN MOON AND EARTH** relating to or found in the area of space that lies between the Moon and the Earth **2. WORLDLY OR MUNDANE** belonging to the material world rather than to the spiritual or intellectual world (*archaic or literary*)

subluxation /súb luk sáysh'n/ n. a partial dislocation of bones that leaves them misaligned but still in some contact with each other

submachine gun /súbmə sheén-/ n. a lightweight portable machine gun fired from the hip or the shoulder. It can fire either in single rounds or continuous bursts

submandibular /súb man díbbyōolər/ adj. relating to or located under the lower jaw

submarginal /sub maárjinəl/ adj. falling below a necessary minimum, especially the minimum conditions necessary for profitability —**submarginally** adv.

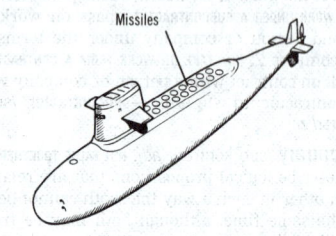
Missiles

Submarine

submarine /súbmə reen, súbmə reén/ n. **1. NAUT UNDERWATER BOAT** a boat built to operate and travel for long periods underwater **2. FOOD LONG SANDWICH** a sandwich made with a long roll cut horizontally ■ adj. **UNDERWATER** taking place or growing underwater, especially in the sea ○ *submarine research* [Mid-17thC. Originally, 'underwater'.]

submarine chaser n. a small manoeuvrable ship designed for pursuing and attacking submarines (*informal*)

submariner /sub márrinər/ n. a crew member on a submarine

submaxillary /súb mak sílləri/ adj. = submandibular

submediant /sub meédi ənt/ n. **1. SIXTH NOTE IN A SCALE** the sixth note in a major or minor scale **2. SUBMEDIANT HARMONY** a key, chord, or harmony based on a submediant

submerge /səb múrj/ (-merges, -merging, -merged) v. **1. vt. PLUNGE IN LIQUID** to put sth into water or some other liquid so that all of it is under the surface **2. vi. GO UNDER WATER** to go under the surface of water or another liquid **3. vt. SUPPRESS** to keep sth such as feelings or a secret hidden from others [Early 17thC. From Latin *submergere*, from *mergere* 'to dip'.] —**submerged** adj. —**submergence** /səb múrjənss/ n.

submerged tenth *n.* the ten per cent of any population that, according to some economic theories, will always remain in poverty

submerse /səb múrss/ (**-merses, -mersing, -mersed**) *vt.* = **submerge** [Early 18thC. From Latin *submers-*, the past participle stem of *submergere* (see SUBMERGE).]

submersible /səb múrssəb'l/ *adj.* **1.** FOR UNDERWATER USE designed for use under water **2.** NOT DAMAGED UNDERWATER capable of being put underwater without being damaged ■ *n.* UNDERWATER BOAT an underwater vessel, especially a small craft designed for use at deep levels

submicroscopic /súb mīkrə skóppik/ *adj.* too small to be seen with an optical microscope —**submicroscopically** *adv.*

subminiature /sub mínnichər/ *adj.* SMALLER THAN MINIATURE smaller in size than miniature ■ *n.* **subminiature, subminiature camera** VERY SMALL CAMERA a camera substantially smaller than a compact camera, using film smaller than the 35mm miniature format

subminiaturize /sub mínnichə rīz/ (**-izes, -izing, -ized**), **subminiaturise** (**-ises, -ising, -ised**) *vt.* to manufacture sth that is very small in scale —**subminiaturization** /sub mínnichə rī záysh'n/ *n.*

submission /səb mísh'n/ *n.* **1.** YIELDING, OR READINESS TO YIELD a willingness to yield or surrender to sb, or the act of doing so ○ *demanded nothing less than total submission to his authority* **2.** IDEA SUBMITTED sth put forward for consideration or approval, e.g. a suggestion, proposal, or plan **3.** ACT OF SUBMITTING STH the act of submitting or handing in sth, e.g. a proposal to be considered or written work to be judged **4.** LAW AGREEMENT TO ARBITRATE an agreement between parties in a dispute to have a contested matter arbitrated **5.** WRESTLING WITHDRAWAL FROM WRESTLING BOUT an acknowledgment by a wrestler that he or she cannot continue a bout because of pain

submissive /səb míssiv/ *adj.* giving in or tending to give in to the demands or the authority of others —**submissively** *adv.* —**submissiveness** *n.*

submit /səb mít/ (**-mits, -mitting, -mitted**) *v.* **1.** *vt.* PROPOSE OR HAND IN STH to hand sth in or put sth forward for consideration, approval, or judgment ○ *Applications must be submitted in triplicate.* **2.** *vi.* YIELD TO SB to give in to sb's authority, control, or demands **3.** *vi.* AGREE TO to agree to undergo sth ○ *had to submit to intensive questioning* **4.** *vi.* DEFER TO to defer to another's knowledge, judgment, or experience **5.** *vt.* ARGUE A POINT to state or argue that sth is the case (*formal*) [14thC. From Latin *submittere*, literally 'to send under', from *mittere* 'to send' (source of English *mission*).] —**submittable** *adj.* —**submittal** *n.* —**submitter** *n.*

WORD KEY: SYNONYMS

See Synonyms at ***yield***.

submolecular /súb mə lékyoolər/ *adj.* relating to, consisting of, or involving a particle smaller than a molecule

submontane /sub món tayn/ *adj.* **1.** ON LOWER PART OF A MOUNTAIN relating to or found in the foothills or on the lower slopes of a mountain **2.** PASSING UNDER A MOUNTAIN passing under or through a mountain —**submontanely** *adv.*

submucosa /súb myoo kṓssə/ *n.* a layer of loosely meshed microscopic fibres and associated cells occurring beneath a mucous membrane, e.g. in the small intestine [Late 19thC. From modern Latin, from Latin *mucosa* 'mucous', the feminine of *mucosus*, from *mucus*.]

submultiple /sub múltip'l/ *n.* EXACTLY DIVISIBLE NUMBER a number that can be divided into another an exact number of times and leave no remainder. For example 7 is a submultiple of 35. ■ *adj.* EXACTLY DIVISIBLE INTO ANOTHER NUMBER able to be divided into another number an exact number of times without leaving a remainder [Late 17thC. From late Latin *submultiplus*, from *multiplus* (see MULTIPLE).]

subnormal /sub náwrm'l/ *adj.* **1.** WITH LOWER INTELLIGENCE THAN NORMAL with a level of intelligence that is lower than the level regarded as normal **2.** LOWER THAN NORMAL lower or less than normal or average —**subnormality** /súb nawr mállə ti/ *n.* —**subnormally** /sub náwrm'li/ *adv.*

suboceanic /súb ōshi ánnik/ *adj.* found, formed, or occurring beneath the sea or the sea bed

suborbital /sub áwrbit'l/ *adj.* **1.** BELOW THE EYE SOCKET relating to the region below the eye socket (**orbit**) **2.** ASTRON NOT MAKING A FULL ORBIT OF A PLANET not designed to make a complete orbit of the Earth or another celestial body

suborder /súb awrdər/ *n.* a taxonomic category that is a subdivision of an order and usually contains several similar families

subordinary /sub áwrd'nəri/ (*plural* **-ies**) *n.* a small shape or design such as a lozenge that can appear on a coat of arms and is smaller than the most prominent shape (**ordinary**)

subordinate (*vt*) /sə báwrdi nayt/ *adj.* /sə báwrdinət/ **1.** LOWER IN RANK lower than sb in rank or status **2.** OF SECONDARY IMPORTANCE secondary in importance **3.** GRAM MODIFYING acting as a modifying noun, adjective, or adverb within a sentence ■ *n.* /sə báwrdinət/ SB IN A JUNIOR POSITION sb who is junior in rank or status ■ *vt.* (**-ates, -ating, -ated**) **1.** MAKE STH SECONDARY to treat sth as less important and allow sth else to dominate or take priority ○ *had increasingly subordinated her research to the demands of her busy work schedule* **2.** PLACE IN A LOWER RANK to give or regard sb as having a more junior rank or status [15thC. From medieval Latin *subordinare*, literally 'to place below', from Latin *ordinare* 'to place' (source of English *ordain*), from, ultimately, *ordo* (see ORDER).] —**subordinately** /sə báwrdinatli/ *adv.* —**subordinateness** /sə báwrdinətnəss/ *n.*

subordinate clause *n.* a clause that cannot stand alone as a separate sentence since its meaning depends on the meaning of the main clause and simply gives additional information. In the sentence 'We had to run because we were late', the clause 'because we were late' is the subordinate clause and 'We had to run' is the main clause.

subordinate conjunction, **subordinating conjunction** *n.* a conjunction that introduces a subordinate clause, either one word such as 'although', 'because', or 'since', or a group of words such as 'in order that' or 'as long as'

subordination /sə báwrdi náysh'n/ *n.* **1.** RELEGATION TO A SECONDARY POSITION the assignment of sb or sth to a position of secondary importance, status, or rank **2.** STATUS OF SUBORDINATE CLAUSE the position of a subordinate clause within a sentence

subordinationism /sə báwrdi náysh'n izəm/ *n.* the theological doctrine that the first person of the Holy Trinity is superior to the second, and the second to the third —**subordinationist** *n.*

subordinator /sə báwrdi naytər/ *n.* GRAM = **subordinate conjunction**

suborn /sə báwrn/ (**-orns, -orning, -orned**) *vt.* to persuade sb to commit a crime or other wrongdoing, e.g. to bribe another party to tell lies in court [Early 16thC. From Latin *subornare*, literally 'to equip secretly', from *ornare* (see ORNATE).] —**subornation** /súbbawr náysh'n/ *n.* —**subornative** /sə báwrnətiv/ *adj.* —**suborner** /-ər, -/ *n.*

suboxide /sub ók sīd/ *n.* an oxide that contains less oxygen than the normal oxide formed by a particular element

subparagraph /súb parə graaf, -graf/ *n.* a section of a paragraph, especially a numbered section of a paragraph in a legal document

subpena *n.*, *vt.* = **subpoena**

subperiosteal /súb peri ósti əl/ *adj.* relating to the region immediately underlying the connective tissue that surrounds bones (**periosteum**)

subphylum /sub fīləm/ (*plural* **-la** /-lə/) *n.* a subcategory of a phylum, used in the classification of animals and containing one or more similar classes. ◊ **subdivision** [Mid-20thC. From modern Latin, from *phylum* 'phylum'.] —**subphylar** *adj.*

subplot /súb plot/ *n.* **1.** STORY SECONDARY TO MAIN STORY a second and less prominent story within a book, play, or film **2.** SMALLER SECTION OF PLOT OF LAND a division of a plot of land, used especially for crop husbandry experiments

subpoena /sə peénə, səb-/ *n.* LEGAL ORDER DEMANDING EVIDENCE a written legal order summoning a witness or requiring evidence to be submitted to a court ■ *vt.* (**-nas, -naing, -naed**) SUMMON TO GIVE EVIDENCE to issue a written legal order summoning a witness or requiring sth to be submitted in evidence to a court [15thC. From Latin *sub poena* 'under penalty' (the first words of the writ), from *sub* 'under' + *poena* 'penalty'.] —**subpoenaed** *adj.*

subpolar /sub pṓlər/ *adj.* **1.** NEAR THE POLAR REGIONS being near the Arctic or the Antarctic polar region **2.** FOUND IN AREAS NEAR POLAR REGIONS relating to, belonging to, or found in the areas that border the Arctic and Antarctic

subpopulation /súb popyoo láysh'n/ *n.* a section of a statistical population that is identifiably separate or distinctive

sub-post office *n.* a small post office offering limited postal services, located inside a larger shop and managed by sb who is an agent but not an employee

subprincipal /sub prínssəp'l/ *n.* an assistant principal or a vice-principal in a school, college, or other place of education

subregion /súb reejən/ *n.* a part of a region, especially an ecological or zoogeographical division —**subregional** /sub reéj'nəl/ *adj.*

subreption /səb répsh'n/ *n.* the deliberate concealment or distortion of the truth in order to gain some benefit, or the benefit gained by doing this (*archaic*) [Early 17thC. Via the Latin stem *subreption-* from, ultimately, *subripere* 'to snatch secretly', from *rapere* (see RAPE[1]).] —**subreptitious** /súb rep tíshəss/ *adj.*

subring /súbring/ *n.* a ring that is a subset of a larger ring

subrogate /súbbrə gayt/ (**-gates, -gating, -gated**) *vt.* to substitute one person for another, especially in transferring a right or claim [15thC. From Latin *subrogare* (see SURROGATE).]

subrogation /súbbrə gáysh'n/ *n.* the substitution of one claim for another, especially the transfer of the right to receive payment of a debt to sb other than the original creditor

sub rosa /-rṓzə/ *adv.* in a secret or private way (*formal*) [Mid-17thC. From Latin, literally 'under the rose', because the rose was an emblem of confidentiality hung above council tables to remind those present of the need for secrecy.]

subroutine /súb roo teen/ *n.* COMPUT a sequence of programming statements that performs a single task and can be used repeatedly

subscapular /sub skáppyoolər/ *adj.* situated underneath, or on the underside of, the shoulder blade (**scapula**)

subscribe /səb skrīb/ (**-scribes, -scribing, -scribed**) *v.* **1.** *vi.* MAKE ADVANCE PAYMENT FOR STH to agree to pay for and receive sth over a particular period of time, e.g. a periodical, series of books, or set of tickets to musical or dramatic performances **2.** *vti.* PROMISE TO GIVE MONEY REGULARLY to pledge to make regular donations to sth, especially a charity **3.** *vti.* GUARANTEE TO INVEST IN STH to promise to pay for sth when it will occur, e.g. the financing of a new business or a new issue of shares **4.** *vi.* SUPPORT VIEW to support or believe in a theory or view **5.** *vt.* LAW SIGN NAME ON LEGAL DOCUMENT to sign a legal document to indicate agreement or approval of its terms (*formal*) [15thC. From Latin *subscribere* 'to write underneath', from *scribere* (see SCRIBE).] —**subscriber** *n.*

subscriber trunk dialling *n.* the facility to make long-distance telephone calls directly, without the help of an operator (*dated*)

subscript /súb skript/ *n.* CHARACTER PRINTED ON LOWER LEVEL a character that is printed on a level lower than the rest of the characters on the line, e.g. the '2' in the chemical formula 'H_2O'. ◊ **superscript** ■ *adj.* PRINTED BELOW CHARACTER printed below a character in a line of type. ◊ **superscript** [Early 18thC. From Latin *subscript*, the past participle stem of *subscribere* (see SUBSCRIBE). Originally, 'writing at the end of a document'.]

subscription /səb skrípsh'n/ *n.* **1.** ADVANCE PAYMENT FOR STH an agreement to pay for and receive sth over a particular period of time, e.g. a periodical, series of books, or set of tickets to musical or dramatic performances ○ *a subscription film channel* **2. MEMBERSHIP FEE** a fee paid for membership in a club or society **3. PLEDGE TO PAY FOR STH** a promise to pay for sth when it will occur, e.g. the financing of a new business or a new issue of shares **4.** LAW **SIGNING OF DOCUMENT OR SIGNATURE** the process of signing, or a signature on, a legal document as an indication of approval of its terms (*formal*) **5. TOTAL AGREEMENT OR APPROVAL** a full agreement with or approval of sth (*literary*) [15thC. Originally in the sense 'writing at the end of a document'.]

subscription library *n.* a library that lends books in return for a regular fee

subsellium /sub sélli əm/ (*plural* **-lia** /-li ə/) *n.* = **misericord** [Early 18thC. From Latin, literally 'low seat', from *sella* 'seat'. Originally used for 'seat in an amphitheatre'.]

subsequence[1] /súbsikwənss/ *n.* sth that happens after sth else, or the occurrence of sth after sth else

subsequence[2] /súb seekwənss/ *n.* a sequence within another mathematical sequence

subsequent /súb ssikwənt/ *adj.* happening or existing after sth [15thC. Directly or via French *subséquent* from Latin *subsequent-*, the present participle stem of *subsequi* 'to follow closely', from *sequi* (see SEQUENCE).]

subsequently /súbs sikwəntli/ *adv.* occurring or happening after sth else

subsere /súb seer/ *n.* a secondary development of natural plant and animal communities after these have been destroyed by fire, flood, or human action [Early 20thC. Coined from SUB- + SERE[2].]

subserve /səb súrv/ (**-serves, -serving, -served**) *vt.* to help to further, promote, or bring sth about [Early 17thC. From Latin *subservire*, literally 'to serve under', from *servire* (see SERVE).]

subservient /səb súrvi ənt/ *adj.* **1. TOO EAGER TO OBEY** too eager to follow the wishes or orders of others **2. SECONDARY IN IMPORTANCE** in a position of secondary importance **3. INSTRUMENTAL IN STH** helping to achieve or bring sth about [Mid-17thC. From Latin *subservire*, literally 'to serve under', from *servire* (see SERVE).] —**subservience** *n.* —**subserviently** *adv.*

subset /súb set/ *n.* MATH a mathematical set whose elements are contained in another set

subshrub /súb shrub/ *n.* a low-growing plant with woody stems and main branches and nonwoody tips that die back each year [Mid-19thC. Translation of modern Latin *suffrutex*, from Latin *frutex* 'shrub'.] —**subshrubby** *adj.*

subside /səb sīd/ (**-sides, -siding, -sided**) *vi.* **1. DIMINISH IN INTENSITY** to become less active or intense **2. DROP TO LOWER LEVEL** to sink to a low or lower level **3. SINK TO BOTTOM OF LIQUID** to sink to the bottom of a liquid **4. GRADUALLY SIT OR LIE DOWN** to sink into a sitting or lying position, e.g. out of exhaustion (*formal*) [Mid-17thC. From Latin *subsidere*, literally 'to settle down', from *sidere* 'to settle'.] —**subsider** *n.*

subsidence /səb sīd'nss, súbz sidənss/ *n.* **1. SINKING OF LAND LEVEL** the sinking down of land resulting from natural shifts or human activity, frequently causing structural damage to buildings **2. DECREASING OF STH** the waning or lessening of sth

subsidiarity /səb síddi árrəti/ *n.* **1. ASSIGNMENT OF POWER TO SMALL UNITS** the principle that political power should be exercised by the smallest possible unit of government **2. QUALITY OF BEING SUBSIDIARY** the fact or quality of being subsidiary [Mid-20thC. Translation of German *Subsidiarität*.]

subsidiary /səb síddi əri/ *adj.* **1. SECONDARY IN IMPORTANCE** having secondary importance or occupying a subordinate position **2. HELPING OR SUPPORTING** serving to aid, supplement, or support ■ *n.* (*plural* **-aries**) **1. SB OR STH AUXILIARY** sb or sth that occupies a secondary or subordinate position **2. COMPANY CONTROLLED BY LARGER ONE** a company controlled or owned by a larger one —**subsidiarily** *adv.* —**subsidiariness** *n.*

subsidiary coin *n.* a coin that has a lower denomination than that of a standard unit of currency

subsidiary company *n.* = **subsidiary** *n.* 2

subsidize /súb si dīz/ (**-dizes, -dizing, -dized**), **subsidise** (**-dises, -dising, -dised**) *vt.* to contribute money to sb or sth, especially in the form of a government grant to a private company, organization, or charity to help it to continue to function —**subsidizable** *adj.* —**subsidization** /súbssi dī záysh'n/ *n.* —**subsidizer** *n.*

subsidy /súbssidi/ (*plural* **-dies**) *n.* **1.** FIN, ECON **MONEY GIVEN BY GOVERNMENT** a grant or gift of money from a government to a private company, organization, or charity to help it to continue to function **2.** FIN **HELP WITH EXPENSES** a monetary gift or contribution to sb or sth, especially to pay expenses **3. FORMER PARLIAMENTARY GRANT TO CROWN** a grant of money given in the past by the English Parliament to the Crown [14thC. Via Anglo-Norman from Latin *subsidium* 'reserve troops', from, ultimately, *sedere* (see SEDENTARY).]

subsist /səb síst/ (**-sists, -sisting, -sisted**) *v.* **1.** *vi.* **MANAGE TO LIVE** to remain alive or viable, especially with the help of sth **2.** *vt.* **MAINTAIN SB OR STH** to support or maintain sb by providing sth that is needed, e.g. by supplying troops with food or businesses with capital (*formal*) **3.** *vi.* **BE ATTRIBUTABLE TO STH** to have sth as its reason or origin (*formal*) **4.** *vi.* **INHERE IN STH** to reside in or consist of sth (*formal*) **5.** *vi.* PHILOS, MATH **HAVE ABSTRACT EXISTENCE** to have a timeless conceptual existence (*refers to numbers or mathematical sets*) [Mid-16thC. Directly or via French *subsister* from Latin *subsistere*, literally 'to stand up to', from *sistere* (see ASSIST).] —**subsistent** *adj.* —**subsister** *n.*

subsistence /səb sístənss/ *n.* **1. CONDITION OF MANAGING TO STAY ALIVE** the condition of being or managing to stay alive, especially when there is only just enough food or money for survival **2. CONTINUING TO EXIST** the condition of continuing to exist **3.** MATH, PHILOS **QUALITY OF ABSTRACT EXISTENCE** the quality that sth possesses of existing independently, timelessly, or by virtue of its essence

subsistence allowance *n.* **1. MONEY COVERING SPECIAL EXPENSES** a sum of money given to an employee to cover special expenses incurred in the performance of his or her work **2. ADVANCE ON SB'S FIRST WAGE** an advance paid to a new employee or soldier to help to meet living costs until wages begin to be paid

subsistence crop *n.* a crop grown by a farmer principally to feed his or her family, with little or nothing left over to sell

subsistence farming *n.* farming that generates only enough produce to feed the farmer's family, with little or nothing left over to sell —**subsistence farmer** *n.*

subsistence level *n.* a poor standard of living, with barely enough food and money on which to survive

subsistence wage *n.* a wage so low that it is barely enough to live on

subsocial /sub sṓsh'l/ *adj.* used to describe insects that associate with others but without any fixed or organized social structure —**subsocially** *adv.*

subsoil /súb soyl/ *n.* **SOIL BENEATH TOPSOIL** the compacted soil beneath the topsoil ■ *vt.* (**-soils, -soiling, -soiled**) **TURN LOWER LAYER OF SOIL** to turn, break, or stir the compacted soil beneath the topsoil

subsoiler /súb soylər/ *n.* **1. PLOUGH FOR BREAKING UP SUBSOIL** a farm implement consisting of a frame with long stout vertical tines. It is drawn through the soil to break up compacted subsoil in order to improve drainage and aeration. **2. SB OPERATING SUBSOILER** sb who operates a subsoiler

subsolar /sub sṓlər/ *adj.* **1. DIRECTLY BENEATH SUN** located directly below the Sun on the Earth's surface when the Sun is at its highest point **2. LOCATED BETWEEN TROPICS** located in the equatorial region that lies between the Tropics of Cancer and Capricorn

subsong /súb song/ *n.* an unstructured birdsong that is quieter and lower-pitched than full birdsong and is often performed by young adult birds

subsonic /sub sónnik/ *adj.* **1. SLOWER THAN SPEED OF SOUND** slower than 1,220 kmph/760 mph, the speed at which sound travels in air **2. FLYING SLOWER THAN SOUND** flying at speeds slower than the speed of sound, especially not designed to fly above the speed of sound **3.** PHON = **infrasonic** —**subsonically** *adv.*

subspecialise *vi.* = **subspecialize**

subspeciality /súb speshi állәti/ (*plural* **-ties**) *n.* a very narrow or specialized field of study, within an existing speciality

subspecialize /sub spéshə līz/ (**-izes, -izing, -ized**), **subspecialise** (**-ises, -ising, -ised**) *vi.* to work in a very narrow field or area of study within an existing speciality

subspecies /súb spee sheez/ (*plural* **-cies**) *n.* a category used to classify plants and animals whose populations are distinct, e.g. in distribution, appearance, or feeding habits, but can still interbreed —**subspecific** /súb spə síffik/ *adj.* —**subspecifically** *adv.*

subst. *abbr.* 1. substantive 2. substitute

substage /súb stayj/ *n.* a component assembly in a microscope that contains the condenser, mirror, or other accessories and is located below the stage

substance /súbstənss/ *n.* **1. MATERIAL** a particular kind of matter or material **2. TANGIBLE PHYSICAL MATTER** physical reality that can be touched and felt **3. PRACTICAL VALUE** real or practical value or importance ○ *There was nothing of substance in the document.* **4. MATERIAL WEALTH** wealth in the form of money and possessions **5. GIST OF MEANING** the actual meaning of sth said or written ○ *the substance of their argument* **6.** PHILOS **UNCHANGING ESSENCE** the unchanging essence of sth **7.** PHILOS **STH INDIVIDUAL AND CAUSED** sth that is individual and caused [13thC. Via French from Latin *substantia* 'essence' (a translation of Greek *hupostasis*), from, ultimately, Latin *substare*, literally 'to stand under', from *stare* (see STAND).]

substance abuse *n.* the excessive consumption or misuse of any substance for the sake of its nontherapeutic effects on the mind or body, especially drugs or alcohol

substance P *n.* a peptide found in body tissues, especially nervous tissue, that is involved in the transmission of pain and in inflammation

substandard /sub stándərd/ *adj.* below the expected or required standard of quality

substantial /səb stánsh'l/ *adj.* **1. CONSIDERABLE** considerable in amount, extent, value, or importance **2. SOLID OR STURDY** solidly built **3. FILLING** providing a lot of nourishment **4. RICH** wealthy and prosperous **5. REAL AND TANGIBLE** actual and real in a palpable way **6.** PHILOS **CONSISTING OF SUBSTANCE** consisting of or involving substance ■ *n.* **IMPORTANT PART** an important or essential part [14thC. Directly or via French *substantiel* from Christian Latin *substantialis* 'having substance' (a translation of Greek *hupostatikos*), from, ultimately, *substare*, literally 'to stand under', formed from *stare* (see STAND).] —**substantiality** /səb stánshi álləti/ *n.* —**substantialness** *n.*

substantialise *vt.* = **substantialize**

substantialism /səb stánshlizəm/ *n.* the philosophical doctrine that beings or entities of substantial reality underlie all phenomena —**substantialist** *n.*

substantialize /səb stánshlīz/ (**-izes, -izing, -ized**), **substantialise** (**-ises, -ising, -ised**) *vti.* to make sth that is imaginary, theoretical, or spiritual become palpable, or to become palpable

substantially /səb stánsh'li/ *adv.* **1. CONSIDERABLY** in an extensive, substantial, or ample way **2. ESSENTIALLY** generally or in essence

substantiate /səb stánshi ayt/ (**-ates, -ating, -ated**) *vt.* **1. PROVE OR SUPPORT STH** to confirm that sth is true or valid **2. MAKE STH ACTUAL** to give sth an actual physical existence [Mid-17thC. From medieval Latin *substantiare*, literally 'to give substance to', from Latin *substantia* 'substance', from, ultimately, *stare* (see STAND).] —**substantiative** *adj.* —**substantiable** *adj.* —**substantiation** /səb stánshi áysh'n/ *n.* —**substantiator** /səb stánshi aytər/ *n.*

substantival /súbstən tív'l/ *adj.* = **substantive** *adj.* 3 —**substantivally** *adv.*

substantive *n.* /súbstəntiv/ GRAM **NOUN** a noun, or a word or group of words used like a noun ■ *adj.* /səb stántiv, súbstəntiv/ **1. WITH PRACTICAL IMPORTANCE** with practical importance, value, or effect ○ *a substantive agreement* **2. ESSENTIAL** relating to the substance of sth **3.** GRAM **USED LIKE NOUN** relating to or used like a noun **4.** GRAM **EXPRESSING EXISTENCE** expressing existence, as e.g. the verb 'to be' **5. INDEPENDENT** continuing independently **6. SUBSTANTIAL** substantial in amount or quantity ○ *a substantive meal* **7.** LAW **RELATING TO LEGAL PRINCIPLES NOT PROCEDURE** relating to the essential principles that a court applies in its work, not to the rules of procedure and practice. ◊ **adjective** **8.** DIRECTLY ATTACHING AS DYE COLOUR attaching as a colour directly to a material being dyed without the use of a fixing substance **9.** MIL PERMANENT used to describe a rank or appointment that is permanent —**substantively** /səb stántivli/ *adv.*

substantive right *n.* a basic human right such as the right to life or liberty that is regarded as existing naturally and indispensably

substantivize /súbstənti vīz/ (**-vizes, -vizing, -vized**), **substantivise** (**-vises, -vising, -vised**) *vt.* to make a word or words function like a noun —**substantivization** /súb stənti vīzáysh'n/ *n.*

substation /súb stayshʼn/ *n.* **1.** ELEC BRANCH OF POWER STATION a branch of a main electrical power station where electrical current is converted, redistributed, or modified in strength **2.** MAIL SUBSIDIARY OFFICE OR STATION any office, building, or installation that is a branch of sth larger, especially one attached to a larger station

substituent /səb stíttyoo ənt/ *n.* an atom or group of atoms that replaces another atom or group in a molecule [Late 19thC. From Latin *substituere*, literally 'to set up under', from *statuere* (see STATUE).]

substitutable /súbsti tyootəb'l/ *adj.* capable of replacing or taking the place of another —**substitutability** /súbsti tyootə bílləti/ *n.*

substitute /súbsti tyoot/ *v.* (**-tutes, -tuting, -tuted**) **1.** *vti.* REPLACE OR TAKE PLACE OF to put sb or sth in place of another, or to take the place of another (*often passive*) **2.** *vt.* CHEM REPLACE ATOM OR ATOMS IN MOLECULE to replace an atom or group of atoms in a molecule with another atom or group **3.** *vt.* MATH REPLACE MATHEMATICAL ELEMENT WITH EQUIVALENT to replace one mathematical element with another of equal value ■ *n.* **1.** SB OR STH REPLACING ANOTHER sb or sth that takes the place of another, e.g. a team member in a game who is ready to replace another on the field **2.** GRAM GRAMMATICALLY REPLACEABLE WORD a word that can take the place of another grammatically, such as 'did' for 'yelled' in the sentence 'I yelled and he did, too' [15thC. From Latin *substitutus*, the past participle of *substituere*, literally 'to set up under', from *statuere* (see STATUE).] —**substituter** *n.*

WORD KEY: USAGE

substitute or **replace**? The constructions used by these two words are different, although the resulting meaning is usually the same. You ***substitute*** item A *for* item B, but ***replace*** item B *with* (or less often *by*) item A.

substitute teacher *n. US* = **supply teacher**

substitution /súbsti tyóo sh'n/ *n.* **1.** ACT OF REPLACING the replacement of sb or sth with another, especially one team member with another **2.** SB OR STH THAT REPLACES sb or sth that replaces another, especially one team member who replaces another **3.** MATH MATHEMATICAL ELEMENT REPLACING EQUIVALENT the replacement of one mathematical element with another of equal value **4.** LOGIC REPLACEMENT OF LOGICAL EXPRESSION the replacement of one logical expression with another, or the expression so replaced —**substitutional** *adj.* —**substitutionally** *adv.*

substitutive /súbsti tyootiv/ *adj.* acting or usable as a substitute [Early 17thC. Partly formed from SUBSTITUTE, partly from Latin *substitutivus*, from the past participle stem of *substituere* (see SUBSTITUTE).] —**substitutively** *adv.* —**substitutivity** /súbsti tyoo tívvəti/ *n.*

substrate /súb strayt/ *n.* **1.** CHEM STH ACTED UPON IN BIOCHEMICAL REACTION a substance that is acted upon, especially by an enzyme, in a biochemical reaction **2.** ELECTRON ENG SEMICONDUCTOR CRYSTAL USED AS BASE a single crystal of a semiconductor used as the basis for an integrated circuit or transistor **3.** BIOL = **substratum** *n.* 6 **4.** SCI = **medium** *n.* 7 [Early 19thC. Anglicization of SUBSTRATUM.]

substratosphere /sub stráttə sfeer/ *n.* the lowest layer of the Earth's atmosphere, at a height of about 20 km/12 mi. above the Earth. ◊ **exosphere, ionosphere, stratosphere**

substratum /-stráatəm, -stráytəm/ (*plural* **-ta** /-tə, -stráytə/) *n.* **1.** UNDERLYING BASE an underlying base, layer, or element **2.** AGRIC = **subsoil 3.** GEOL = **bedrock 4.** PHOTOGRAPHY BASE FOR EMULSION a layer of a substance placed on a film or plate as a foundation for an emulsion **5.** LING SET OF RETAINED INDIGENOUS LINGUISTIC FEATURES a set of linguistic features retained from the speech of an indigenous culture, especially one that influences the language of a colonizer. ◊ **superstratum** **6.** BIOL NON-LIVING FOUNDATION FOR GROWING ORGANISM the non-living material or base on which an organism lives or grows **7.** PHILOS ESSENTIAL SUBSTANCE the essential substance of sth [Mid-17thC. From modern Latin, a noun use of the neuter past participle of Latin *substernere* 'to spread underneath', from *sternere* (see STRATUM).] —**substratal** *adj.* —**substrative** *adj.*

substructure /súb strukchər/ *n.* **1.** BUILDING FOUNDATION OF BUILDING the foundation of an erected structure **2.** UNDERLYING STRUCTURE any underlying structure that supports or gives strength to sth —**substructural** /sub strúkchərl/ *adj.*

subsume /səb syóom/ (**-sumes, -suming, -sumed**) *vt.* **1.** INCLUDE STH to include or incorporate sth into a larger order, category, or classification **2.** MAKE SUBJECT TO RULE to show that a rule applies to sth [Mid-16thC. From medieval Latin *subsumere*, literally 'to take up so as to include', from Latin *sumere* (see SUMPTUOUS). Originally, 'to make one point within another'.] —**subsumable** *adj.*

subsumption /səb súmpsh'n/ *n.* **1.** ACT OF SUBSUMING the act of subsuming or the fact of being subsumed **2.** STH SUBSUMED sth that is subsumed [Mid-17thC. From the medieval Latin stem *subsumption-*, from, ultimately, *subsumere* (see SUBSUME).] —**subsumptive** *adj.*

subsurface /súb surfiss/ *adj.* LOCATED BELOW SURFACE OF STH relating to or located in an area that lies just below the surface of sth, especially of the Earth or a body of water ■ *n.* MATERIAL BELOW SURFACE material that is located just below the surface of sth, especially of the Earth or a body of water

subsystem /súb sistəm/ *n.* a system that forms part of a larger system

subtangent /súb tanjənt/ *n.* the part of the x-axis included by the ordinate of a given point on a curve and the tangent at that point

subteen /súb teen/ *n. US, Can* = **preteen** [Mid-20thC]

subtemperate /sub témpərət/ *adj.* relating to or occurring in the colder areas of the Temperate Zone

subtenant /súb tenənt/ *n.* sb who rents property from a tenant who in turn rents it from the owner —**subtenancy** *n.*

subtend /səb ténd/ (**-tends, -tending, -tended**) *vt.* **1.** GEOM EXTEND OPPOSITE to extend from one side to the other, opposite an angle or side of a geometric figure **2.** BOT ENCLOSE A PART to lie underneath sth so as to surround or enclose it [Late 16thC. From Latin *subtendere* 'to stretch underneath', from *tendere* (see TEND[1]).]

subterfuge /súbtər fyooj/ *n.* a plan, action, or device designed to hide a real objective, or the process of hiding a real objective [Late 16thC. Directly or via French from late Latin *subterfugium*, from Latin *subterfugere* 'to flee secretly', from *fugere* (see FUGITIVE).]

subterminal /sub túrmin'l/ *adj.* positioned very near the end of sth

subterranean /súbtə ráyni ən/, **subterraneous** /-ráyni əss/ *adj.* **1.** UNDERGROUND existing or situated below ground level **2.** SECRET existing or carried on in secret [Early 17thC. Formed from Latin *subterraneus* 'underground', from *terra* (see TERRACE).] —**subterraneanly** *adv.*

subtext /súb tekst/ *n.* an underlying meaning or message —**subtextual** /sub tékschoo əl/ *adj.*

subthreshold /súb thresh hōld, -thresh ōld/ *adj.* used to describe a stimulus that is not strong or large enough to have an effect

subtile /sútt'l/ *adj.* subtle (*archaic*) [14thC. Via French *subtil* from Latin *subtilis* (see SUBTLE).]

subtilise *vt.* = **subtilize**

subtilisin /súbti líssin/ *n.* an enzyme that breaks down proteins and peptides and is derived from a bacterium [Mid-20thC. Formed from modern Latin *subtilis* 'subtle', from Latin (see SUBTLE).]

subtilize /sútt'līz/ (**-izes, -izing, -ized**), **subtilise** (**-ises, -ising, -ised**) *v.* **1.** *vti.* BE SUBTLE IN DISCUSSING to make or use subtle distinctions in discussing sth **2.** *vt.* REFINE STH to make sth increasingly refined —**subtilization** *n.* —**subtilizer** *n.*

subtitle /súb tīt'l/ *n.* **1.** CAPTION FOR FOREIGN-LANGUAGE FILM a printed translation of the dialogue in a foreign-language film, usually appearing at the bottom of the screen. ◊ **supertitle, surtitle 2.** PRINTED WORDS FOR HEARING-IMPAIRED the printed text of what is being said in a television programme, provided for the hearing-impaired and usually at the bottom of the screen **3.** CAPTION IN SILENT FILM a caption for the action or dialogue of a silent film, appearing at intervals as a full-screen panel **4.** LESSER TITLE a second and subsidiary title for sth such as a book ■ *vt.* (**-tles, -tling, -tled**) **1.** PROVIDE SUBTITLES FOR to provide subtitles for a film or television programme **2.** to give a subtitle to sth such as a book —**subtitular** /sub tí chŏŏ lər/ *adj.*

subtle /sútt'l/ *adj.* **1.** SLIGHT slight and not obvious **2.** PLEASANTLY UNDERSTATED pleasantly delicate and understated **3.** ABLE TO MAKE REFINED JUDGMENTS intelligent, experienced, or sensitive enough to make refined judgments and distinctions **4.** INGENIOUS cleverly indirect and ingenious [14thC. Via Old French *sutil* from Latin *subtilis* 'fine, thin', from, ultimately, *sub tela*, literally 'beneath the weaving', from *sub* 'beneath' + *tela* 'weaving'. The underlying idea is 'finely woven'.] —**subtly** *adv.* —**subtleness** *n.*

subtlety /sútt'lti/ (*plural* **-ties**) *n.* **1.** QUALITY OF BEING SUBTLE the quality or state of being subtle **2.** FINE DISTINCTION a distinction that is difficult to make but is important (*often used in the plural*)

subtopia /sub tōpi ə/ *n.* an area of suburban development that is regarded as an ideal area in which to live [Mid-20thC. Blend of SUBURB and UTOPIA. Coined by Ian Nairn, a British architectural critic.] —**subtopian** *adj.*

subtorrid /sub tórrid/ *adj.* = **subtropical**

subtotal /súb tōt'l/ *n.* TOTAL OF PARTIAL SET OF FIGURES a sum or total of part of a set of figures ■ *vt.* (**-tals, -talling, -talled**) CALCULATE SUBTOTAL OF to calculate the total of part of a set of figures

subtract /səb trákt/ (**-tracts, -tracting, -tracted**) *v.* **1.** *vti.* ARITH DEDUCT ARITHMETICALLY to perform the arithmetical calculation of deducting one number or quantity from another **2.** *vt.* REMOVE STH FROM STH LARGER to withdraw or take away sth from a larger unit [Mid-16thC. From Latin *subtract-*, the past participle stem of *subtrahere* 'to pull away', from *trahere* (see TRACTOR).] —**subtracter** *n.*

subtraction /səb tráksh'n/ *n.* **1.** ARITH DEDUCTION OF NUMBER the act or process of deducting one number or quantity from another. Symbol - **2.** REMOVAL FROM STH LARGER a withdrawal or deduction of sth from a larger whole **3.** LAW WITHDRAWAL OF BENEFIT the withdrawal or withholding of a benefit

subtractive /səb tráktiv/ *adj.* **1.** ARITH ABLE TO SUBTRACT with the power to subtract sth **2.** ARITH INDICATING SUBTRACTION indicating or needing subtraction **3.** PHYS REMAINING AFTER ABSORPTION BY TINTED FILTERS used to describe the colour that remains after all other components of the visible spectrum have been absorbed by tinted filters

subtrahend /súbtrə hend/ *n.* ARITH a number that is to be deducted from another number. ◊ **minuend** [Late 17thC. From Latin *subtrahendus*, literally 'to be subracted', a form of *subtrahere* 'to pull away', from *trahere* (see TRACTOR).]

subtribe /súb trīb/ *n.* a subdivision of a tribe

subtropical /sub tróppik'l/ *adj.* relating to or found in areas between tropical and temperate regions, and experiencing tropical conditions at some times of the year or near-tropical conditions all year round

subtype /súb tīp/ *n.* a type that is a subdivision of a larger type —**subtypical** /sub típpik'l/ *adj.*

subulate /súbbyŏŏlət/ *adj.* used to describe a plant part that is long and thin and tapers to a point [Mid-18thC. From modern Latin *subulatus*, from Latin *subula* 'awl'.]

subumbrella /súb um brelə/ *n.* the inwardly curving underside of a jellyfish

subunit /súb yoonit/ *n.* **1.** SUBSIDIARY UNIT a unit that forms part of a larger unit **2.** CHEM SEPARABLE PART OF MOLECULE a part of a large molecule or complex that can be dissociated from the whole without rupture of covalent chemical bonds

subunit vaccine *n.* a vaccine that creates a bodily immunity to a virus or bacterium from whose DNA the vaccine is made

suburb /súbburb/ *n.* a district, especially a residential one, on the edge of a city or large town [14thC. Directly or via French *suburbe* from Latin *suburbium*, literally 'near a city', from *urbs* (see URBAN).]

suburban /sə búrbən/ *adj.* **1. RELATING TO SUBURB** relating to, belonging to, or located in a suburb **2. RESEMBLING SUBURB** resembling a suburb or its residents **3. UNEXCITING AND CONVENTIONAL** typical of the undesirable aspects of a suburb or its residents, especially in being dull, conventional, and materialistic (*disapproving*)

suburbanite /sə búrbə nīt/ *n.* sb who lives in the suburbs

suburbanize /sə búrbə nīz/ (**-izes, -izing, -ized**), **suburbanise** (**-banises, -banising, -banised**) *vt.* to give sth an appearance or character typical of the suburbs —**suburbanization** /sə búrbə nī záysh'n/ *n.*

suburbia /sə búrbi ə/ *n.* suburbs collectively, or the people who live in them

subvene /səb véen/ (**-venes, -vening, -vened**) *vi.* to happen or appear in a helpful way, especially in avoiding or preventing sth (*formal*) [Mid-18thC. From Latin *subvenire*, literally 'to come from below', from *venire* (see VENUE).]

subvention /səb vénsh'n/ *n.* (*formal*) **1. GRANT OR SUBSIDY** a sum of money given by an official body such as a government, especially to an institution of learning, study, or research **2. AID OR SUPPORT** the giving of help or support, especially financial —**subventionary** *adj.*

subversion /səb vúrsh'n/ *n.* **1. ACTIVITY UNDERMINING GOVERNMENT** an action, plan, or activity intended to undermine or overthrow a government or other institution **2. OVERTHROW OF STH** the destruction or ruining of sth [14thC. Directly or via French from the late Latin stem *subversion-*, from, ultimately, *subvertere* (see SUBVERT).]

subversive /səb vúrssiv/ *adj.* **DESIGNED TO OVERTHROW GOVERNMENT** intended or likely to undermine or overthrow a government or other institution ■ *n.* **SB INVOLVED IN SUBVERSIVE ACTIVITIES** sb involved in activities intended to undermine or overthrow a government or other institution —**subversively** *adv.* —**subversiveness** *n.*

subvert /səb vúrt/ (**-verts, -verting, -verted**) *vt.* to undermine or overthrow a government or other institution [14thC. Directly or via Old French *subvertir* from Latin *subvertere*, literally 'to turn from below', from *vertere* (see VERSE).] —**subverter** *n.*

subvirus /súb vīrəss/ *n.* an infective agent such as a prion that is structurally more primitive than a virus —**subviral** /súb vīrəl/ *adj.*

subvocal /sub vōk'l/ *adj.* LING mouthed or mentally pictured but not sounded out loud —**subvocally** *adv.*

subvocalize /sub vōkə līz/ (**-izes, -izing, -ized**), **subvocalise** (**-calises, -calising, -calised**) *vti.* LING to mouth words or other speech sounds without saying them out loud —**subvocalization** /sub vōkə lī záysh'n/ *n.*

subway /súb way/ *n.* **1. UNDERGROUND PASSAGE** a passage under a road or railway for pedestrians to get to the other side **2.** *US, Can* = **underground**

subzero /sub zéerō/ *adj.* being below zero degrees in temperature

succah *n.* = **sukkah**

succeed /sək séed/ (**-ceeds, -ceeding, -ceeded**) *v.* **1.** *vi.* **ACHIEVE INTENTION** to manage to do what is planned or attempted ○ *We succeeded in persuading them to change their decision.* **2.** *vi.* **GAIN FAME, WEALTH, OR POWER** to realize a goal, especially to gain fame, wealth, or power **3.** *vi.* **MAKE SIGNIFICANT PROGRESS** to do well in an activity, making admirable progress or recording impressive achievements ○ *She was one of the first women to succeed in the sciences.* **4.** *vi.* **PROSPER** to thrive or prosper **5.** *vti.* **BE NEXT AFTER SB** to be the next person to occupy a post or position after sb ○ *Mary succeeded him as president over a year ago.* **6.** *vt.* **FOLLOW IN TIME** to come after sth in time (*often passive*) **7.** *vi.* **BE INHERITED BY SB** to pass to sb as an inheritance (*formal*) [14thC. Directly or via French *succéder* from Latin *succedere*, literally 'to go after', from *cedere* (see CEDE).] —**succeedable** *adj.* —**succeeder** *n.*

succentor /sək séntər/ *n.* CHR a deputy to a precentor [Mid-17thC. From late Latin, from Latin *succinere* 'to sing to', from *canere* (see CANT[2]).] —**succentorship** *n.*

succès de scandale /syōōk sáy də skaan dáal/ (*plural* **succès de scandale**) *n.* sth such as a book, film, or play that is successful because it is controversial, or the success that is gained as a result of controversy (*literary*) [From French, literally 'success of scandal']

succès d'estime /syōōk sáy des téem/ (*plural* **succès d'estime**) *n.* sth such as a book, film, or play that is successful with the critics but not with the public, or the success that is gained through critical acclaim (*literary*) [From French, literally 'success of esteem']

succès fou /syōōk sáy fóo/ (*plural* **succès fous** /syōōk say fóo/) *n.* an overwhelming success (*literary*) [From French, literally 'mad success']

success /sək séss/ *n.* **1. ACHIEVEMENT OF DESIRED AIM** the achievement of sth planned or attempted **2. ATTAINMENT OF FAME, WEALTH, OR POWER** impressive achievement, especially the attainment of fame, wealth, or power **3. STH THAT TURNS OUT WELL** sth that turns out as planned or intended **4. SB WHO HAS SIGNIFICANT ACHIEVEMENTS** sb who has a record of achievement, especially in gaining wealth, fame, or power [Mid-16thC. From Latin *successus*, from *success-*, the past participle stem of *succedere* (see SUCCEED). The original English sense was 'result, outcome'.]

successful /sək séssf'l/ *adj.* **1. TURNING OUT WELL** having the intended result **2. POPULAR** popular and making a lot of money **3. WITH RECORD OF SIGNIFICANT ACHIEVEMENTS** having achieved or gained much, especially wealth, fame, or power —**successfully** *adv.* —**successfulness** *n.*

succession /sək sésh'n/ *n.* **1. SERIES IN TIME** a sequence of people or things coming one after the other in time ○ *rented a succession of dingy flats around town* **2. FOLLOWING ON** the following on of one thing after another ○ *three wins in succession.* **3. TAKING UP OF TITLE OR POSITION** the assumption of a position or title, the right to take it up, or the order in which it is taken up **4. DEVELOPMENT OF PLANT AND ANIMAL COMMUNITY** the series of changes that create a full-fledged plant and animal community, e.g. from the colonization of bare rock to the establishment of a forest —**successional** *adj.* —**successionally** *adv.*

succession crop *n.* a crop that follows another crop as a successive planting, or a crop of a variety with a different rate of growth

succession state *n.* a nation created from territory once ruled by another, larger nation

successive /sək séssiv/ *adj.* following in an uninterrupted sequence —**successively** *adv.* —**successiveness** *n.*

successor /sək séssər/ *n.* sb or sth that follows another and takes up the same position —**successoral** *adj.*

success story *n.* sb or sth that is very successful

succinate /súksi nayt/ *n.* a salt or ester of succinic acid [Late 18thC. Formed from SUCCINIC.]

succinct /sək síngkt/ *adj.* **1. BRIEF AND TO THE POINT** showing or expressed with brevity and clarity, with no wasted words **2. ENCLOSED OR RESTRICTED** confined tightly by sth such as a belt or girdle (*archaic*) [15thC. Directly or via French from Latin *succinctus*, the past participle of *succingere*, literally 'to encompass from below', from *cingere* (see PRECINCT).] —**succinctly** *adv.* —**succinctness** *n.*

succinic /sək sínnik/ *adj.* **1. RELATING TO SUCCINIC ACID** relating to or containing succinic acid or succinate **2. RELATING TO AMBER** relating to or obtained from amber [Late 18thC. Formed from Latin *succinum* 'amber', from *succus* (see SUCCUS).]

succinic acid *n.* a colourless odourless acid synthesized or derived from amber and the tissues of plants and animals. It is used in making lacquers, perfumes, and pharmaceuticals. Formula: $C_4H_6O_4$.

succinylcholine /súksi nīl kō leen/ *n.* *US* = **suxamethonium** [Mid-20thC. Coined from SUCCINIC (ACID) + -YL + CHOLINE.]

succor /súkər/ *n., vt.* US = **succour**

succory /súkəri/ *n.* = **chicory** [Mid-16thC. Alteration of obsolete French *cicorée* (see CHICORY) on the model of Middle Low German *suckerie* and Middle Dutch *sūkerie*.]

succotash /súkə tash/ *n.* in the United States, sweetcorn and butter beans cooked together, often with tomatoes [Mid-18thC. From Narragansett *msiquatash*, literally 'boiled corn or maize and beans'.]

Succoth, **Succot** *n.* = **Sukkoth**

succour *n.* (*literary*) **1. HELP FOR SB OR STH** help or relief for sb or sth **2. SB OR STH GIVING HELP** sb or sth that provides help or relief ■ *vt.* (**-cours, -couring, -coured**) **GIVE HELP TO** to provide help or relief to sb or sth (*literary*) [13thC. Via Old French *socorre* from Latin *succurrere*, literally 'to run under', formed from *currere* 'to run' (source of English *current*). The underlying idea is 'running to someone's assistance'.] —**succourable** *adj.* —**succourer** *n.*

succubus /súkyōōbəss/ (*plural* **-bi** /-bī/ *or* **-buses**) *n.* a woman demon that was believed in medieval times to have sexual intercourse with men while they were asleep. ◊ **incubus** [14thC. From medieval Latin, an alteration (modelled on English *incubus*) of late Latin *succuba*, literally 'one who lies under another', from, ultimately, *cubare* 'to lie'.]

succulent /súkyōōlənt/ *adj.* **1. JUICY AND TASTY** juicy and pleasant to the taste **2. WITH FLESHY WATER-STORING PARTS** with thick fleshy leaves and stems that can store water **3. INTERESTING** exciting and interesting (*informal*) ■ *n.* **SUCCULENT PLANT** a plant with thick fleshy leaves and stems that can store water. Succulents such as cacti and aloes typically grow in hot, arid conditions or in salty soils. [Early 17thC. Directly or via French from Latin *succulentus*, from *succus* (see SUCCUS).] —**succulence** *n.* —**succulently** *adv.*

succumb /sə kúm/ (**-cumbs, -cumbing, -cumbed**) *vi.* **1. GIVE IN** to yield to sb or sth powerful **2. DIE FROM STH** to die from an illness or injury [15thC. Directly or via French *succomber* from Latin *succumbere*, literally 'to lie under', from *cumbere* 'to lie' (source of English *incumbent*).] —**succumber** *n.*

WORD KEY: SYNONYMS

See Synonyms at ***yield***.

succus /súkəss/ (*plural* **-ci** /súk sī, -see/) *n.* a fluid, especially a secretion, of plant or animal origin [Late 18thC. From Latin, 'juice, moisture, sap' (source of English *succulent*).]

succuss /sə kúss/ (**-cusses, -cussing, -cussed**) *vt.* MED to shake a patient in order to detect the abnormal presence of air or fluid in a body cavity, especially the space between the lungs and the chest wall [Mid-19thC. Back-formation from *succussion*.] —**succussion** *n.* —**succussive** *adj.*

such /such/ *adj.* **1. OF PARTICULAR KIND** of a particular kind ○ *I've never heard such nonsense.* **2. SO MUCH** to so great an extent or degree ○ *Don't be such a fool.* ■ *adv.* **VERY** extremely or to a great degree ○ *I had never seen such lovely flowers.* ■ *n.* **THIS** this, or sth of this kind ○ *Such was his fate.* [Old English *swilc*, *swelc*, *swylc*. Ultimately from a prehistoric Germanic compound word meaning literally 'so formed', from the ancestors of SO + LIKE.] ◇ **as such** being what has been specified ◇ **such as 1.** for example **2.** resembling sth ◇ **such as it is** being what it is and no more

WORD KEY: USAGE

We are such stuff as dreams are made on (Shakespeare, *The Tempest* Act 4, scene 1, modernized spelling) In sentences of this type ***such*** is followed by *as* and not by a relative pronoun *that, who,* etc.: *the new law affects only such people as (not: that) are eligible for supplementary benefit.* However, the construction *such ... that ...* is used to indicate the consequence of a stated circumstance: *The country faces such hardship that it will need a great deal of foreign aid.*

such and such *adj.* **UNSPECIFIED** not specified or named ■ *pron.* **STH UNSPECIFIED** sth that is not specified or named

suchlike /súch līk/ *pron.* **OTHERS OF THE SAME KIND** others of the same kind as those just mentioned (*informal*)

■ *det.* SIMILAR TO THOSE JUST MENTIONED similar to the kind just mentioned

suchness /súchnəss/ *n.* PHILOS an essential quality or condition [Old English *swilcnes*]

suck /suk/ *v.* (**sucks, sucking, sucked**) **1.** *vti.* DRAW LIQUID OUT WITH MOUTH to draw the liquid out of sth with the mouth ○ *The baby sucked on her bottle.* **2.** *vti.* MAKE PULLING MOUTH MOVEMENTS ON STH to hold sth in the mouth and make movements with the tongue and lips as if drawing liquid out of it ○ *sucked his thumb* **3.** *vti.* MAKE STH DISSOLVE IN MOUTH to consume sth by making it slowly dissolve in the mouth, rolling the tongue around it and making pulling movements with the cheeks and lips ○ *sucking lozenges for a sore throat* **4.** *vt.* EXTRACT STH to draw sth out of a container (*often passive*) ○ *Fuel is sucked into the cylinder.* **5.** *vt.* PULL IRRESISTIBLY to pull or draw sth somewhere with a powerful or irresistible force ○ *The swirling currents suck swimmers under.* **6.** *vi.* US BE VERY BAD to be very bad or inferior (*slang*) ○ *The movie really sucked, so we walked out.* ■ *n.* ACT OF SUCKING STH an act of sucking sth [Old English *sūcan*. Ultimately from an Indo-European base meaning 'to take liquid' that is also the ancestor of Latin *sugere* 'to suck' (source of English *suction*) and of English *soak*.]

suck in *v.* **1.** *vt.* INVOLVE SB IN STH to make sb become more and more involved in sth in a way that he or she is unable to prevent **2.** *vti.* BREATHE IN to breathe in sharply **3.** *vt.* DECEIVE SB to trick or deceive sb (*slang*)

suck off *vt.* an offensive term meaning to perform fellatio or cunnilingus on sb (*offensive taboo*)

suck up *vt.* to try to please or win the favour of sb important by being extremely flattering or helpful (*informal*)

sucker /súkər/ *n.* **1.** SB EASILY FOOLED sb who can be easily fooled or tricked (*informal*) **2.** SB WHO GIVES IN EASILY sb who finds it very hard to resist, or who is easily influenced by, some particular thing (*informal*) ○ *a sucker for a pair of big blue eyes* **3.** US ANY PERSON OR THING used to refer, usually with emphasis or some degree of irritation, to any person or thing sb happens to be dealing with (*slang*) ○ *Let's see if we can get this sucker to work.* **4.** ZOOL ORGAN THAT CLINGS BY SUCTION a muscular organ, found, e.g. on the tentacles of octopuses and similar sea animals, used to cling to or hold things such as prey **5.** ZOOL ORGAN FOR SUCKING IN FOOD the mouth of an animal such as the leech or lamprey that is adapted for sucking in food **6.** BOT SHOOT GROWING FROM ROOT a shoot that grows from the underground root or stem of a plant, and that is often able to produce its own roots and grow into a new plant **7.** STH THAT ADHERES BY SUCTION a round, slightly cupped piece of plastic or rubber that when pressed onto a flat surface sticks to it by suction. US term **suction cup 8.** ZOOL ANIMAL LIVING ON MOTHER'S MILK a young animal such as a young pig or whale that is still taking milk from its mother **9.** SUCTION PUMP PISTON the piston of a suction pump, or the valve of the piston in a suction pump **10.** SUCTION PIPE a pipe that a liquid is drawn through by means of suction **11.** ZOOL FRESHWATER FISH WITH A SUCKING MOUTH a bony bottom-feeding freshwater fish found mostly in North America that has a downward facing sucking mouth without teeth and resembles the carp. Family: Catostomidae. ■ *v.* (**-ers, -ering, -ered**) **1.** *vt.* US TRICK SB to take advantage of sb's ignorance, innocence, or foolishness to trick him or her (*informal*) ○ *got suckered into the scheme* **2.** *vi.* BOT PRODUCE SUCKERS to produce or form suckers **3.** *vt.* BOT REMOVE SUCKERS to remove the suckers from a plant

suckerfish /súkər fish/ (*plural* **-fish** *or* **-fishes**) *n.* = **remora**

sucker punch *n.* US a blow delivered when sb is not expecting it

sucker-punch (**sucker-punches, sucker-punching, sucker-punched**) *vt.* US to hit sb with a sucker punch

sucking /súking/ *adj.* still feeding on its mother's milk and not yet weaned ○ *sucking pig* [Old English *sūcende*]

sucking louse *n.* a wingless primitive parasitic insect with mouth parts specially adapted for sucking body fluids, e.g. the head louse and pubic louse that infest human beings. Suborder: Siphunculata.

suckle /súk'l/ (**-les, -ling, -led**) *v.* **1.** *vti.* FEED FROM BREAST, TEAT, OR UDDER to take milk from a mother's breast, teat, or udder, or to allow a young child or animal to feed on milk from the breast, teat, or udder **2.** *vt.* NOURISH to nourish sb or sth (*literary*) [14thC. Origin uncertain: probably a back-formation from SUCKLING.] — **suckler** *n.*

suckling /súkling/ *n.* a human baby or young animal such as a calf or pig that is still feeding on its mother's milk [13thC. Formed from SUCK, probably on the model of Middle Dutch *sūgeling*.]

sucks /suks/ *interj.* used to express disappointment, contempt, or derision (*informal*) ○ *Sucks to her! Who cares what she thinks?*

sucrase /soō krayz, syoō-/ *n.* = **invertase** [Early 20thC. Formed from SUCROSE + -ASE.]

sucre /soō kray/ *n.* **1.** ECUADOREAN UNIT OF CURRENCY the main unit of currency in Ecuador, worth 100 centavos. See table at **currency 2.** NOTE WORTH ONE SUCRE a note worth one sucre [Late 19thC. Named after Antonio José de SUCRE.]

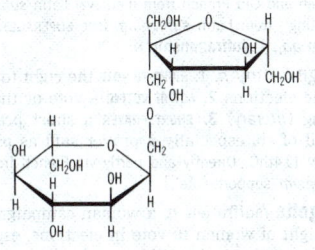

Sucrose

sucrose /soō krōss, syoō-/ *n.* a white water-soluble crystalline carbohydrate, found naturally in many plants and extracted from sugar cane and sugar beets to make common sugar. Formula: $C_{12}H_{22}O_{11}$. [Mid-19thC. Formed from French *sucre* 'sugar', from Old French *sukere* (see SUGAR).]

suction /súksh'n/ *n.* **1.** FORCE CREATED BY PRESSURE DIFFERENCE physical force created by a difference in pressure such as that caused by sucking a liquid through a straw **2.** SUCKING the act or process of sucking [Early 17thC. From the late Latin stem *suction-*, from *suct-*, the past participle stem of *sugere* 'to suck'.] — **suctional** *adj.*

suction cup *n.* US = **sucker**

suction pump *n.* a pump that works by means of the suction created when a piston is moved up and down inside a cylinder. One example of a suction pump is the type of pump used to raise water from an underground source by moving a handle up and down.

suction stop *n.* PHON a click (*technical*)

suctorial /suk táwri əl/ *adj.* **1.** ZOOL USED FOR ADHERING AND SUCKING specially adapted for sucking or for clinging on by suction **2.** WITH SUCKERS having one or more suckers for feeding or for clinging on to sth [Mid-19thC. Formed from modern Latin *suctorius*, from Latin *suct-*, the past participle stem of *sugere* (see SUCTION).]

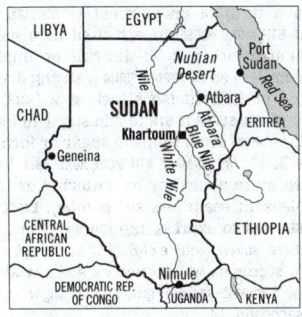

Sudan

Sudan /soō dán/ **1.** republic in northeastern Africa, and the continent's largest country. Language:

Arabic. Currency: dinar. Capital: Khartoum. Population: 31,065,000 (1996). Area: 2,505,813 sq. km/967,500 sq. mi. Official name **Republic of the Sudan 2.** region of savanna and dry grassland in western Africa, between the Sahara and the tropical forest belt — **Sudanese** *n., adj.*

Sudanic /soō dánnik/ *n.* GROUP OF LANGUAGES SPOKEN IN SUDAN a group of languages belonging to the Chari-Nile branch of the Nilo-Saharan family of languages, spoken by peoples in some areas of Sudan ■ *adj.* **1.** RELATING TO SUDANIC LANGUAGES relating to the Sudanic group of languages **2.** RELATING TO SUDAN relating to or typical of Sudan, its people, or culture

sudatorium /soōdə táwri əm, syoōdə táwri əm/ (*plural* **sudatoria** /-əl/) *n.* a room, especially in an ancient Roman bath-house, in which people are made to sweat by hot air or steam [Mid-18thC. From Latin, a noun use of the neuter singular of *sudatorius* (see SUDATORY).]

sudatory /soōdətəri, syoō-/ *n.* (*plural* **sudatories**) **1.** = **sudorific** *n.* **2.** = **sudatorium** ■ *adj.* = **sudorific** *adj.* [Early 17thC. From Latin *sudatorius* 'for sweating', from, ultimately, *sudare* 'to sweat' (source of English *exude*).]

Sudbury /súdbəri, súdbri/ *n.* city north of Georgian Bay in east-central Ontario, Canada. Population: 160,488 (1996).

sudd /sud/ *n.* a floating mass of reeds and weeds that obstructs some tropical rivers, especially the White Nile [Late 19thC. From Arabic, literally 'obstruction', from *sadda* 'to obstruct'.]

sudden /súdd'n/ *adj.* done or happening quickly, unexpectedly, and often without warning [13thC. Via Anglo-Norman *sudein* from, ultimately, Latin *subitaneus*, itself from, ultimately, *subire*, literally 'to go secretly' (hence 'taking by surprise'), from *ire* 'to go'.] — **suddenly** *adv.* — **suddenness** *n.* ◇ **all of a sudden** in a sudden and unexpected way

sudden death *n.* the continuation of play in a tied sports contest until one team or player scores, that team or player being declared the winner

sudden infant death syndrome *n.* cot death (*technical*)

Sudetenland /soō dáyt'n land/ region in the northern Czech Republic, in the Sudetes Mountains Range. It was annexed by Germany in 1938 and returned to Czechoslovakia in 1945.

sudoriferous /soōdə rífferəss, syoōdə-/ *adj.* producing sweat (*formal*) [Late 16thC. Formed from late Latin *sudorifer* 'sudorific' (the original sense in English), from Latin *sudor* 'sweat'.] — **sudoriferousness** *n.*

sudorific /soōdə ríffik, syoōdə-/ *adj.* CAUSING PRODUCTION OF SWEAT causing the production of sweat ■ *n.* DRUG CAUSING SWEATING a drug or other agent that causes sweating [Early 17thC. From modern Latin *sudorificus*, from late Latin *sudorifer* (see SUDORIFEROUS).]

Sudra /soōdrə/ *n.* **1.** LOWEST HINDU CASTE the lowest of the four main Hindu castes, traditionally comprising artisans and labourers and their families. There is a wide range of subgroups within the Sudra caste, however, some being landowners. **2.** MEMBER OF SUDRA a member of the Sudra caste [Mid-17thC. From Sanskrit *śūdra*.]

suds /sudz/ *npl.* BUBBLES a froth of bubbles on the surface of soapy water ■ *n.* US, Can BEER beer (*slang*) [Mid-16thC. Origin uncertain: probably from Middle Dutch *sudse* 'marsh, bog'. Originally used for 'dregs, muck'.] — **sudsy** *adj.*

sue /syoo, soo/ (**sues, suing, sued**) *v.* **1.** *vti.* UNDERTAKE LEGAL PROCEEDINGS to take legal action against sb in order to obtain sth, usually compensation for a wrong **2.** *vi.* BEG FOR STH to make a humble, earnest, or begging request for sth (*formal*) [12thC. Via Anglo-Norman *suer* 'to follow' (the original English sense), from, ultimately, Latin *sequi* (source of English *pursue*). The underlying idea is of 'following up' a matter.] — **suer** *n.*

suede /swayd/ *n.* **1.** LEATHER WITH VELVETY SURFACE leather with the flesh side outward and rubbed up to make a velvety nap **2.** FABRIC LIKE SUEDE a woven fabric that looks like suede ■ *vti.* (**suedes, sueding, sueded**) GIVE LEATHER A VELVETY NAP to give leather a velvety nap [Mid-17thC. From French *gants de Suède* 'gloves of Sweden', from *Suède* 'Sweden', where it originated.]

suet /soo it/ *n.* a hard white fat found on the kidneys and loins of sheep and cattle, used in cooking and as a source of tallow [14thC. Origin uncertain: probably from Anglo-Norman, literally 'small suet', from *sue, seu* 'tallow, suet', from Latin *sebum* (source of English *sebaceous*).] —**suety** *adj.*

Suetonius /swee tṓni əss/, **Gaius Tranquillus** (*b.* 69?–70?AD) Roman biographer and historian. His works include biographies of eleven Roman emperors.

suet pudding *n.* a sweet or savoury pudding made with suet, usually cooked by boiling or steaming

Suez /soo əz/ city and port at the head of the Gulf of Suez and at the southern end of the Suez Canal, northeastern Egypt. Population: 388,000 (1992).

Suez Canal canal in Egypt, connecting the Mediterranean and Red seas. It was opened in 1869. Length: 163 km/101 mi.

suff. *abbr.* **1.** suff. **2.** suffix

Suff. *abbr.* **1.** Suffolk **2.** Suffragan

suffer /súffər/ (**-fers, -fering, -fered**) *v.* **1.** *vti.* FEEL PAIN TO feel pain or great discomfort in body or mind **2.** *vti.* UNDERGO STH UNPLEASANT to experience or undergo sth unpleasant or undesirable **3.** *vti.* ENDURE to endure or put up with sth painful or unpleasant ○ *I do not suffer fools gladly.* **4.** *vi.* HAVE AN ILLNESS to have a disease or a physical or psychological condition **5.** *vi.* HAVE AS WEAKNESS to have as a bad quality, weakness, or flaw ○ *Their whole manifesto suffers from a lack of vision.* **6.** *vi.* APPEAR TO BE LESS GOOD to become or appear to be less good **7.** *vi.* BE ADVERSELY AFFECTED to be adversely affected by sth ○ *The business suffered when the partnership was dissolved.* **8.** *vt.* ALLOW to allow sb to do sth (*archaic or literary*) [12thC. Via Anglo-Norman *suffrir* from, ultimately, Latin *sufferre*, literally 'to carry up from underneath', hence 'to sustain', from *ferre* 'to carry' (source of English *fertile*).] —**sufferer** *n.*

sufferable /súffərəb'l/ *adj.* able to be endured or tolerated

sufferance /súffərənss/ *n.* **1.** TOLERANCE OF STH PROHIBITED tacit permission for or tolerance of sth, because no action is taken to prevent it **2.** ENDURANCE OF DIFFICULTY OR PAIN the capacity to withstand difficulty or pain **3.** PATIENT ENDURANCE the fact of enduring hardship patiently (*archaic*) ◇ **on sufferance** as a result of permission or consent given reluctantly and liable to be withdrawn

suffering /súffəring/ *n.* physical or psychological pain and distress, or an experience of it

suffice /sə físs/ (**-fices, -ficing, -ficed**) *vti.* to be enough for sb or sth (*formal*) [14thC. From Old French *suffic-*, from, ultimately, Latin *sufficere*, literally 'to make up to', hence 'to be enough', which was formed from *facere* 'to make' (source of English *fact*).] ◇ **suffice it to say that** used to indicate that what you are saying is all that needs to be said on a subject

sufficiency /sə físh'nssi/ (*plural* **-cies**) *n.* **1.** SUFFICIENT AMOUNT an amount of sth that is enough for sb or sth **2.** STATE OF BEING SUFFICIENT the fact or state of being enough

sufficient /sə físh'nt/ *adj.* as much as is needed [14thC. Directly or via Old French from Latin *sufficient-*, the present participle stem of *sufficere* (see SUFFICE).] —**sufficiently** *adv.*

suffix *n.* /súffiks/ ELEMENT ADDED AT END OF WORD a letter or group of letters added at the end of a word part to form another word, e.g. '-ly' in 'quickly' or '-ing' in 'talking' ■ *vt.* /súffiks, sə fíks/ (**-fixes, -fixing, -fixed**) ADD AS SUFFIX to add sth as a suffix [Early 17thC. Via modern Latin *suffixum* from, ultimately, Latin *suffigere*, literally 'to fasten underneath', from *figere* (see FIX).] —**suffixal** /súffiks'l/ *adj.* —**suffixation** /súffik sáysh'n/ *n.*

suffocate /súffə kayt/ (**-cates, -cating, -cated**) *vti.* **1.** STOP BREATHING to deprive sb of air or prevent sb from breathing, or to be unable to breathe **2.** DIE FROM LACK OF AIR to die from lack of air or kill sb by stopping him or her from breathing **3.** MAKE OR FEEL TOO WARM to feel uncomfortable or make sb feel uncomfortable through excessive heat and lack of fresh air **4.** NOT ALLOW TO DEVELOP to confine and restrict sb or sth with adverse effects, or be or feel confined and restricted in development or self-expression [15thC. From Latin *suffocat-*, the past participle stem of *suffocare*, literally 'to narrow up', from the stem *fauc-* 'throat, narrow en-

trance'.] —**suffocating** *adj.* —**suffocatingly** *adv.* —**suffocation** /súffə káysh'n/ *n.* —**suffocative** *adj.*

Suffolk[1] /súffək/ county in East Anglia, eastern England. It is largely agricultural. Ipswich is the county town. Population: 648,000 (1992). Area: 3,800 sq. km/1,467 sq. mi.

Suffolk[2] /súffək/ *n.* a large black-faced hornless sheep belonging to a breed originating in England and bred for meat [Mid-19thC. Named after the county of SUFFOLK.]

Suffolk punch *n.* a powerful horse with short legs and a chestnut-brown coat, belonging to a breed originating in England, used for pulling loads such as ploughs or carts [*Punch* from English dialect, 'stocky draught horse' (originally 'short overweight person'), a shortening of PUNCHINELLO.]

Suffr. *abbr.* Suffragan

suffragan /súffrəgən/ *n.* **1.** ASSISTANT BISHOP a bishop appointed to assist the main bishop in a diocese **2.** BISHOP AS ASSISTANT TO ARCHBISHOP the bishop of a diocese who is an assistant to the archbishop of the province to which the diocese belongs [14thC. Via Anglo-Norman and Old French from medieval Latin *suffraganeus* 'assisting', from Latin *suffragium* (see SUFFRAGE).] —**suffragan** *adj.* —**suffraganship** *n.*

suffrage /súffrij/ *n.* **1.** RIGHT TO VOTE the right to vote in public elections **2.** ACT OF VOTING a vote or the act of voting (*literary*) **3.** SHORT PRAYER a short prayer on behalf of sb, especially a prayer said as part of a litany [14thC. Directly and partly via French from Latin *suffragium* 'support, vote'.]

suffragette /súffrə jét/ *n.* a woman campaigning for the right of women to vote in elections, especially one who took part in militant protests in the United Kingdom in the early 20th century. Among the leaders of the suffragette movement in Great Britain were Emmeline Pankhurst and her daughters Christabel and Sylvia. —**suffragettism** *n.*

suffragist /súffrəjist/ *n.* a supporter of the extension of the right to vote to a particular group, especially to women, or to all people above a particular age —**suffragism** *n.*

suffuse /sə fyooz/ (**-fuses, -fusing, -fused**) *vt.* to spread over or through sth (*usually passive*) ○ *A blush suffused his face with colour.* [Late 16thC. From Latin *suffus-*, the past participle stem of *suffundere*, literally 'to pour from below', from *fundere* 'to pour' (source of English *fuse*).] —**suffusion** /sə fyoozh'n/ *n.* —**suffusive** /sə fyoossiv/ *adj.*

Sufi /soofi/ (*plural* **-fis**) *n.* a Muslim mystic [Mid-17thC. From Arabic *sūfī*, literally 'woollen' (because of their woollen garments).] —**Sufi** *adj.* —**Sufic** *adj.* —**Sufism** *n.* —**Sufistic** *adj.*

sugar /shoogger/ *n.* **1.** SWEET-TASTING SUBSTANCE a sweet-tasting substance, usually in the form of tiny hard white or brown grains, obtained commercially from sugar cane and sugar beets, and used to sweeten food and drinks. Different types of sugar, e.g. granulated sugar, brown sugar, or icing sugar, are made at different processing levels. **2.** PORTION OF SUGAR a spoonful, lump, cube, or other portion of sugar ○ *likes his coffee black with two sugars* **3.** SWEET CARBOHYDRATE any of a group of simple carbohydrates found in many plants that are sweet-tasting, crystalline, and soluble in water **4.** TERM OF ENDEARMENT used as a term of endearment (*informal*) **5.** WAY OF MAKING STH MORE AGREEABLE sth used as a means of persuasion or to make a difficult or unpleasant thing seem less so **6.** STRONG DRUG a strong drug such as heroin or LSD (*dated slang*) ■ *v.* (**-ars, -aring, -ared**) **1.** *vt.* ADD SUGAR TO STH to add sugar to food or a drink **2.** *vi.* MAKE SUGAR to make sugar or form sugar crystals **3.** *vt.* TRY TO MAKE STH MORE AGREEABLE to try to make sth more appealing or flattering or to make sth unpleasant seem less so ■ *interj.* EXPRESSION OF ANNOYANCE used to express annoyance [13thC. Via Old French *çukre, sukere* (source of English *sucrose*) from medieval Latin *succarum*, which came via Arabic *sukkar* from, ultimately, Sanskrit *śarkarā* 'grit, ground sugar' (source of English *saccharin*).]

sugar apple *n.* = sweetsop

sugar beans *npl.* S Africa dried beans that are reddish or brown speckled

sugar beet *n.* a variety of beet with a large whitish conical root that is an important commercial source of sugar. Latin name: *Beta vulgaris*.

sugar bird *n.* either of two African nectar-eating birds with dull brownish plumage, a long curved bill, and a very long drooping tail. Genus: *Promerops*.

sugar bush *n.* a wood or group of trees consisting mainly of sugar maples

sugar candy *n.* sugar in the form of large crystals made by suspending a string or stick in a strong sugar solution and allowing crystals to form and grow

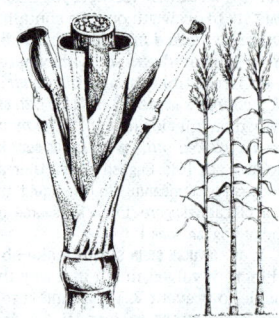

Sugar cane

sugar cane *n.* a tall tough-stemmed species of grass grown in warm regions throughout the world as a source of sugar, which is obtained from its sweet sap. Latin name: *Saccharum officinarum*. (*hyphenated when used before a noun*)

sugarcoat /shoogger kṓt/ (**-coats, -coating, -coated**) *vt.* **1.** COAT WITH SUGAR to enclose sth in a hard sugar shell or coat sth with sugar **2.** MAKE STH SEEM LESS UNPLEASANT to make sth unpleasant seem less so

sugar daddy *n.* a rich man who gives money and gifts to a younger partner in a relationship (*informal*)

sugar diabetes *n.* diabetes mellitus (*informal*)

sugared /shoogger'd/ *adj.* **1.** COATED WITH SUGAR covered or coated in a layer of sugar **2.** SWEETENED sweetened with sugar **3.** MADE MORE APPEALING marked by an attempt to make sb or sth seem more pleasant, appealing, or acceptable

sugar glider *n.* an eastern Australian possum that feeds on flowers, sap, and insects, and has flaps of skin attached to its limbs enabling it to glide from tree to tree. Latin name: *Petaurus norfolcensis*.

sugar gum *n.* a small eucalyptus tree that has smooth bark, barrel-shaped fruit, and sweet-tasting leaves that are often eaten by cattle. Latin name: *Eucalyptus cladocalyx*.

sugar loaf *n.* **1.** CONE-SHAPED MASS OF SUGAR a solid cone-shaped mass of refined sugar **2.** STH SHAPED LIKE SUGAR LOAF sth that has a conical shape like a cone of sugar, e.g. a hill

Sugarloaf Mountain

Sugarloaf Mountain /shoogger lṓf-/ peak on the edge of Rio de Janeiro, Brazil, that provides a panoramic view of the city. Height: 395 m./1,296 ft.

sugar maple *n.* a North American maple that produces a sweet sap from which maple sugar and maple syrup are made. Latin name: *Acer saccharum*.

sugar of lead *n.* = **lead acetate**

sugar pea *n.* a variety of garden pea that has an edible thin flat pod. Latin name: *Pisum sativum.*

sugar pine *n.* a tall pine tree native to the west coast of North America that has a sugary resin and large cones. Latin name: *Pinus lambertiana.*

sugarplum /shŏŏggər plum/ *n.* a small round sweet made of boiled and flavoured sugar

sugar possum *n.* = **sugar glider**

sugar soap *n.* a strong alkaline mixture of soap and washing soda used, e.g. for stripping paint or for cleaning surfaces before they are painted

sugar squirrel *n.* = **sugar glider**

sugary /shŏŏggəri/ *adj.* **1. CONTAINING SUGAR** containing a great deal of sugar **2. LIKE SUGAR** looking or tasting like sugar **3. EXAGGERATEDLY PLEASANT** exaggeratedly and often insincerely pleasant or amiable **4. SENTIMENTAL** excessively sentimental —**sugariness** *n.*

suggest /sə jésst/ (**-gests, -gesting, -gested**) *vt.* **1. PROPOSE FOR CONSIDERATION** to state or refer to sb or sth as a possible choice, plan, or course of action for sb else to consider **2. REMIND SB OF STH** to remind sb of sth or make sb think of sth **3. IMPLY** to imply or hint at sth **4. INDICATE AS LIKELY** to indicate that sth is likely [Early 16thC. Back-formation from SUGGESTION.] —**suggester** *n.*

WORD KEY: SYNONYMS

See Synonyms at ***recommend.***

suggestibility /sə jéstə bílləti/ *n.* **1. SUSCEPTIBILITY TO SUGGESTIONS** the condition of being easily influenced by other people's suggestions **2.** PSYCHOL **MENTAL STATE OF HEIGHTENED ACCEPTANCE** a mental state in which sb accepts without question the ideas, attitudes, or instructions of others, usually occurring under hypnosis

suggestible /sə jésstəb'l/ *adj.* **1. EASILY INFLUENCED** easily influenced by other people **2. ABLE TO BE SUGGESTED** capable of being suggested —**suggestibleness** *n.* —**suggestibly** *adv.*

suggestion /sə jéschən/ *n.* **1. IDEA OR PROPOSAL** an idea or proposal put forward for consideration ○ *If I might make a suggestion, why don't we ask Ed to help us?* **2. SLIGHT TRACE** a slight trace, indication, or hint of sth **3. ACT OF SUGGESTING** the act or process of suggesting sth ○ *He was roused to fury by the mere suggestion of their innocence.* **4. ABILITY TO CONJURE UP ASSOCIATIONS** the ability of words or images to conjure up ideas or feelings, the process by which they do this, or a particular idea or image conjured up by sth **5. PUTTING IDEAS INTO SB'S MIND** the deliberate introduction into sb's mind of an opinion, belief, or instruction, e.g. through hypnosis or advertising, so that it is accepted or acted on as that person's own idea ○ *The power of suggestion is used in TV commercials to make us want a product.* [14thC. Directly or via French from the Latin stem *suggestion-*, from, ultimately, *suggerere*, literally 'to bring up', from *gerere* 'to bring' (source of English *digest*).]

suggestive /sə jéstiv/ *adj.* **1. CONJURING UP IDEAS OR IMAGES** able to conjure up ideas or images in the mind or start a train of thought **2. IMPROPER** implying or hinting at sth rude or improper —**suggestively** *adv.* —**suggestiveness** *n.*

Sui /sway/ *n.* a Chinese dynasty lasting from AD 581 to AD 618 that succeeded the Han dynasty, united all of northern China, and reconquered southern China

suicidal /sŏŏ i sīd'l/ *adj.* **1. WANTING TO COMMIT SUICIDE** intending or wishing to commit suicide **2. RELATING TO SUICIDE** produced by or involving a wish to commit suicide **3. EXTREMELY DANGEROUS** likely to lead to death, destruction, or ruin, or very much against sb's own best interests **4. VERY UNHAPPY** deeply unhappy or frustrated (*informal*) —**suicidally** *adv.*

suicide /sŏŏ i sīd/ *n.* **1. KILLING YOURSELF** the act of deliberately killing yourself. ◊ **parasuicide 2. SB WHO COMMITS SUICIDE** sb who deliberately kills himself or herself. ◊ **parasuicide 3. DOING STH AGAINST OWN BEST INTERESTS** the act of doing sth that seems contrary to your own best interests and likely to lead to a disaster such as financial ruin or loss of position or reputation [Mid-17thC. From modern Latin *suicidium* 'killing of yourself' and *suicida* 'sb who kills himself or herself', both formed from Latin *sui* 'of yourself'.]

suicide bombing *n.* a bomb attack in which the person carrying out the attack deliberately allows himself or herself to be killed in the process of attempting to destroy sth or kill sb —**suicide bomber** *n.*

suicide pact *n.* an agreement between two or more people that they will kill themselves at the same time

suicide watch *n.* the regular checking by prison warders of the cells of prisoners who are thought likely to commit suicide

sui generis /sŏŏ ī jénnəriss/ *adj.* unique, or in a class of its own [From Latin, literally 'of its own kind']

sui juris /sŏŏ ī jŏŏriss/ *adj.* competent to assume legal responsibility for his or her own affairs [From Latin, literally 'of its own right']

suint /swint/ *n.* the grease found in sheep's wool, formed from dried perspiration [Late 18thC. From French, from *suer* 'to sweat', from Latin *sudare* (see SUDATORY).]

suit /soot, syoot/ *n.* **1.** CLOTHES **CLOTHES MADE OF SAME MATERIAL** a set of clothes made from the same material, consisting of a jacket and trousers or a skirt, sometimes together with a waistcoat **2.** CLOTHES **CLOTHES FOR PARTICULAR PURPOSE** a piece of clothing or set of clothes worn for a particular purpose (*often used in combination*) ○ *a diving suit* **3.** CARDS **SET OF PLAYING CARDS** one of the four different sets of playing cards in a pack **4.** LAW **LEGAL PROCEEDINGS** a case brought to a law court **5. PETITION** a petition, especially to sb in authority (*formal*) **6. BUSINESS EXECUTIVE** a business executive, especially when seen as an anonymous bureaucrat (*slang*) **7. SET OF SAILS OR TOOLS** a set of sails or tools **8. WOOING OF A WOMAN** a man's wooing of a woman and attempts to persuade her to marry him (*archaic*) ■ *v.* (**suits, suiting, suited**) **1.** *vti.* **BE RIGHT FOR STH OR SB** to be appropriate to or the right thing for sb or sth **2.** *vti.* **BE CONVENIENT TO SB** to be convenient or acceptable to sb **3.** *vt.* **LOOK GOOD ON SB** to look good on sb or go well with sth ○ *The colour suits you.* **4.** *vt. Scotland* **LOOK GOOD IN STH** to look good in a particular colour or garment ○ *Emma really suits purple.* **5.** *vt.* **BE SATISFYING TO SB** to be sth that a person likes or enjoys **6.** *vt.* **MAKE SUITABLE** to adapt sth in order to meet requirements or circumstances **7.** *vr.* **PLEASE YOURSELF** to do what you prefer [13thC. Via Anglo-Norman *siute* from, ultimately, assumed Vulgar Latin *sequere* 'to follow', alteration of Latin *sequi* (source of English *persecute*). Originally, 'body of followers', later 'set of things generally'.] ◇ **be sb's strong suit** to be sth at which sb is particularly good ◇ **follow suit 1.** to do the same as sb else has done **2.** to play a card of the same suit as a card played before

suitable /sŏŏtəb'l, syŏŏ-/ *adj.* of the right type or quality for a particular purpose or occasion [Late 16thC. Originally in the sense 'matching'.] —**suitability** /sŏŏtə bílləti, syŏŏt-/ *n.* —**suitableness** /syŏŏt-/ *n.*

suitably /sŏŏtəbli, syŏŏt-/ *adv.* **1. APPROPRIATELY** in a way that is right for a particular purpose or occasion **2. TO AN APPROPRIATE DEGREE** to an appropriate or the expected extent

suitcase /sŏŏt kayss, syŏŏt-/ *n.* a rectangular case used for carrying clothes and other belongings during travel

suite /sweet/ *n.* **1. SET OF MATCHING FURNITURE** a set of matching furniture for a room, e.g. a sofa and two armchairs (**a three-piece suite**) for a lounge **2. SET OF ROOMS** a set of rooms, e.g. in a hotel **3.** MUSIC **SET OF INSTRUMENTAL WORKS PERFORMED TOGETHER** a set of instrumental pieces, especially dances, intended to be performed together. This type of composition was especially popular in the Baroque period. **4. PEOPLE WITH SB IMPORTANT** a group of followers, servants, or advisers accompanying sb important **5.** COMPUT **COLLECTION OF INTEGRATED SOFTWARE** a collection of integrated application programs functioning as a single program, each of which can incorporate data from the others, eliminating the need for re-entry or transfer of data. A typical suite includes word processing, spreadsheet, database management, and electronic mail programs, and additionally such functions as presentation graphics, address book, and appointment calendar. [Late 17thC. Via French from, ultimately, assumed Vulgar Latin *sequere* (see SUIT).]

suiting /sŏŏting, syŏŏt-/ *n.* CLOTHES material for making suits

suitor /sŏŏtər, syŏŏtər/ *n.* **1. MAN WOOING WOMAN** a man who is trying to persuade a woman to marry him (*dated*) **2.** LAW **SB WHO BRINGS LAWSUIT** sb on whose behalf a case is brought to a law court **3.** BUSINESS **SB TAKING OVER BUSINESS** sb who wants to buy or tries to take over a business [13thC. Via Anglo-Norman *seutor, suitour* from Latin *secutor* 'follower', from, ultimately, *sequi* (see SUIT).]

Sukarno

Sukarno /soo kaárnō/ (1901–70) Indonesian statesman. He led the fight for Indonesia's independence from the Netherlands and became the country's first president (1949–67), but his autocratic rule eventually led to his forced resignation.

sukiyaki /sŏŏki yaáki/ *n.* a Japanese dish consisting of thin slices of beef or other meat, vegetables, bean curd, and noodles, cooked quickly in a sweet soy sauce, usually at the table [Early 20thC. From Japanese, literally 'slice-grill'.]

sukkah /sŏŏkə/, **succah** *n.* a temporary light shelter with a roof of branches built in Jewish homes, gardens, or temples for the festival of Sukkoth. The shelters are built in memory of the huts or tents the Israelites lived in during the time they were wandering in the desert after leaving Egypt. [Late 19thC. From Hebrew *sukkāh*, literally 'hut'.]

Sukkoth /sŏŏkəss, sŏŏ kōt, sŏŏ kōth, sŏŏ kōss/, **Succoth, Sukkot** *n.* CALENDAR an eight-day Jewish autumn harvest festival beginning on the eve of the 15th day of Tishri [Late 19thC. From Hebrew *sukkōt*, the plural of *sukkāh* (see SUKKAH).]

Sukkur /sŏŏkər/ city and district in Sind Province, Pakistan, on the banks of the Indus. Population: 190,551 (1981).

sulcate /súl kayt/ *adj.* marked with lengthwise parallel grooves [Mid-18thC. From Latin *sulcatus*, the past participle of *sulcare* 'to furrow', from *sulcus* (see SULCUS).] —**sulcation** /sul káysh'n/ *n.*

sulcus /súl kəss/ (*plural* **-ci** /súl sī/) *n.* a shallow groove or depression, especially any of those separating the convolutions of the surface of the brain [Mid-17thC. From Latin, 'furrow, trench'.]

Suleiman I /sŏŏli maán, sŏŏli maán, sŏŏl ay maán/ = **Sulayman I**

sulfur *n.* **1.** US = **sulphur 2.** CHEM **SULPHUR** sulphur (*technical*)

sulk /sulk/ *vi.* (**sulks, sulking, sulked**) **BE ANGRILY SILENT** to refuse to talk to or associate with others as a show of resentment for a real or imagined grievance ■ *n.* **1. BAD-TEMPERED SILENCE** a period, state, or show of resentfulness and refusal to communicate **2. SB WHO SULKS** sb who tends to sulk [Late 18thC. Back-formation from SULKY.] —**sulker** *n.*

sulky /súlki/ *adj.* (**-ier, -iest**) **ANGRILY SILENT** in a bad mood and refusing to communicate because of resentment for a real or imagined grievance ■ *n.* (*plural* **-ies**) **HORSE-DRAWN VEHICLE FOR ONE PERSON** a light open two-wheeled vehicle for one person, pulled by one horse. Sulkies are nowadays used mostly for racing. [Mid-18thC. Origin uncertain: perhaps an alteration of earlier *sulke* 'sluggish', from, perhaps, Old English *āsolcen*, an adjectival use of the past participle of *āseolcan* 'to become sluggish'. In the noun sense, perhaps from its having room for only one person.] —**sulkily** *adv.* —**sulkiness** *n.*

Sulla /súllə, sŏŏllə/, **Lucius Cornelius** (138–78 BC) Roman general. He successfully led the aristocratic party during the civil war of 88–86 BC and then became dictator (82–79 BC).

sullage /súllij/ *n.* **1.** WASTE MATERIAL sewage or any other form of waste or refuse **2.** SILT solid material deposited by flowing water, e.g. by a river [Mid-16thC. Origin uncertain: perhaps from Anglo-Norman *suillage*, from Old French *soill(i)er* 'to soil' (see SOIL).]

sullen /súllən/ *adj.* **1.** HOSTILELY SILENT showing bad temper or hostility by a refusal to talk, behave sociably, or cooperate cheerfully **2.** CLOUDY AND DULL dull and grey because of clouds, fog, or haze (*literary*) **3.** SLOW-MOVING moving slowly (*literary*) ○ *a sullen stream* [14thC. From Anglo-Norman *sulein* 'alone', from *sol* 'sole, single' (the original English sense), from Latin *solus* (see SOLE).] —**sullenly** *adv.* —**sullenness** *n.*

Sullivan /súllivən/, **Sir Arthur** (1842–1900) British composer. He is best known for his 14 popular comic operas, containing much musical parody, to librettos by Sir William S. Gilbert. Full name **Sir Arthur Seymour Sullivan**

Sullom Voe /sŏŏləm vṓ/ inlet on Mainland Island, Shetland Islands, Scotland. It is home to the principal UK oil terminal in the North Sea. Length: 13 km/8 mi.

sully /súlli/ (**-lies, -lying, -lied**) *v.* **1.** *vti.* SPOIL to spoil or detract from sth, especially sb's reputation, that has previously been pure and honourable, or to become spoiled or tarnished **2.** *vt.* MAKE DIRTY to make sth dirty (*literary*) [Late 16thC. Origin uncertain: perhaps from French *souiller* 'to soil', from Old French *soill(i)er* (see SOIL).] —**sullied** *adj.*

sulph- *prefix.* sulphur ○ *sulphite* [From SULPHUR]

sulphadiazine /súllfə dī́ə zeen/ *n.* a sulpha drug used to fight bacterial infections, especially in patients weakened by other conditions. Formula: $C_{10}H_{10}N_4O_2S$. [Mid-20thC. Coined from *sulpha-* (see SULPHA DRUG) + DIAZINE.]

sulphadimidine /súlfə dímmi deen/ *n.* a sulphonamide used together with other sulphonamides or with antibiotics to treat bacterial infections. Formula: $C_{12}H_{14}N_4O_2S$. US term **sulfamethazine** [Mid-20thC. Coined from SULPH- + DI- + *pyrimidine*.]

sulpha drug *n.* a drug synthesized from sulphonamide, once used to treat a range of bacterial infections. Sulpha drugs are now restricted because of their toxicity and increased bacterial resistance to them. [*Sulpha* shortening of SULPHANILAMIDE]

sulphanilamide /súllfə níllə mīd/ *n.* the first of the sulpha drugs, once used to treat bacterial infections, including gonorrhea and urinary tract infections. Formula: $C_6H_8N_2O_2S$. [Mid-20thC. Coined from SULPH- + ANILINE + AMIDE.]

sulphatase /súllfə tayz/ *n.* an enzyme found in animal tissue and some microorganisms that accelerates the decomposition of sulphuric esters

sulphate /súlfayt/ *n.* SULPHURIC ACID SALT OR ESTER a salt or ester of sulphuric acid ■ *v.* (**-phates, -phating, -phated**) **1.** *vti.* MAKE LAYER OF LEAD SULPHATE to make a layer of lead sulphate form on the plates of an accumulator, or become covered with lead sulphate **2.** *vt.* TREAT STH WITH SULPHUR to treat sth with sulphur, sulphuric acid, or a sulphate **3.** *vt.* CONVERT TO SULPHATE to convert sth to a sulphate —**sulphation** /súll fáysh'n/ *n.*

sulphide /súllfīd/ *n.* a chemical compound containing sulphur and one or more other elements

sulphite /súllfīt/ *n.* a salt or ester of sulphurous acid —**sulphitic** /sul fíttik/ *adj.*

sulphon- *prefix.* sulphonic ○ *sulphonyl* [From SULPHONE]

sulphonamide /sul fónnəmīd/ *n.* a substance that is responsible for the antibacterial action of sulpha drugs. Sulphonamides work by depriving bacteria of the ability to synthesize the essential nutrient folic acid. [Late 19thC. From SULPHONE + AMIDE.]

sulphonate /súlfənayt/ *n.* SULPHONIC ACID SALT OR ESTER a salt or ester of sulphonic acid ■ *vt.* TREAT WITH SULPHURIC ACID to treat an organic substance with sulphuric acid [Late 19thC. Formed from SULPHONIC.] —**sulphonation** /súllfə náysh'n/ *n.*

sulphone /súlfōn/ *n.* a compound containing the sulphonyl group in which sulphur is attached to two carbon atoms [Late 19thC. From German *Sulfon*, from *Sulfur* 'sulphur'.]

sulphonic /sulfónnik/ *adj.* relating to, containing, or derived from the acid group SO_2OH [Late 19thC. Formed from German *Sulfon* (see SULPHONE).]

sulphonic acid *n.* an organic acid used in the making of dyes and drugs

sulphonium /sulfṓniəm/ *n.* an ion or radical containing sulphur with a valence of three [Late 19thC. Formed from SULPHUR.]

sulphonmethane /súlfon meéthayn/ *n.* a hypnotic and potentially addictive drug used in medicine. Formula: $C_7H_{16}O_4S_2$.

sulphonyl /súlfənil/ *n.* the bivalent chemical group SO_2 [Early 20thC. Formed from SULPHONIC.]

sulphonylurea /súlfənīl yŏŏ reéə/ *n.* a drug given orally to lower blood sugar in diabetic patients

sulphur /súlfə/ *n.* **1.** YELLOW NON-METALLIC ELEMENT a non-metallic yellow chemical element that occurs alone in nature or combined in sulphide and sulphate minerals and is used to make sulphuric acid, matches, fungicides, and gunpowder. Symbol **S** **2.** YELLOWISH-GREEN COLOUR a yellowish-green colour [14thC. Via Anglo-Norman *sulf(e)re*, from, ultimately, Latin *sulfur, sulphur*.] —**sulphur** *adj.* —**sulphury** *adj.*

sulphurate /súll fyŏŏ rayt/ (**-rates, -rating, -rated**) *vt.* to treat or combine sth with sulphur —**sulphuration** /súllfyŏŏ ráysh'n/ *n.*

sulphur bacterium *n.* a bacterium that is capable of metabolizing sulphur or inorganic sulphur compounds. Genus: *Thiobacillus.*

sulphur butterfly *n.* a butterfly that has yellow or orange wings with black markings. Genus: *Colias.*

sulphur-crested cockatoo *n.* a large white cockatoo found throughout northern and eastern Australia and Tasmania that lives in large noisy flocks and has a distinctive yellow crest. Latin name: *Cacatua galerita.*

sulphur dioxide *n.* a colourless pungent toxic gas used in making sulphuric acid and as a preservative, fumigant, and bleaching agent. It is formed by burning sulphur and constitutes a major component of air pollution in industrial regions. Formula: SO_2.

sulphureous /sul fyŏŏ əriəs/ *adj.* = **sulphurous** *adj.* 1 —**sulphureously** *adv.* —**sulphureousness** *n.*

sulphuric /sul fyŏŏ ərik/ *adj.* relating to or containing sulphur, especially with a higher valence than in sulphurous compounds

sulphuric acid *n.* a strong colourless oily corrosive acid that is used in batteries and in the manufacture of many products such as fertilizers, explosives, detergents, dyes, and chemicals. Formula: H_2SO_4.

sulphurize /súl fyoo rīz/ (**-izes, -izing, -ized**), **sulphurise** (**-ises, -ising, -ised**) *vt.* to treat or combine sth with sulphur or a sulphur compound —**sulphurization** /súll fyoo rī záysh'n/ *n.*

sulphurous /súlfərəs/, **sulphureous** *adj.* **1.** CONTAINING SULPHUR relating to or containing sulphur, especially with a valency of 4 **2.** SIMILAR TO BURNING SULPHUR with the colour or acrid smell of burning sulphur **3.** RELATING TO HELL relating to hell or hellfire (*literary*) **4.** FIERY fiery, especially in having or showing a violent temper or in being emotionally charged and containing many swearwords or blasphemies (*literary*) [15thC. Formed from Latin *sulphurosus*, or from SULPHUR.] —**sulphurously** *adv.* —**sulphurousness** *n.*

sulphurous acid *n.* a weak colourless acid that is a solution of sulphur dioxide in water and is used as a disinfectant, food preservative, and bleaching agent. Formula: H_2SO_3.

sulphur pearl *n.* a very large bacterium, typically between 0.1 and 0.3 mm in size but sometimes larger, found in sediments off the west coast of Namibia. It uses nitrates as its source of oxygen in oxidizing and breaking down sulphur compounds. Latin name: *Thiomargarita nambibiensis.*

sulphur spring *n.* a spring with significant amounts of sulphur compounds in the water

sultan /súltən/ *n.* **1.** MUSLIM RULER the sovereign ruler of a Muslim country, especially in the past and especially the head of the Ottoman Empire. Only three countries now have sultans as their head of state: Brunei, Oman, and Malaysia. **2.** POWERFUL AND DOMINEERING MAN a man who is powerful in some sphere of activity, especially one who behaves in a domineering or tyrannical fashion (*literary*) [Mid-16thC. Directly or via French from medieval Latin *sultanus*, from Arabic *sulṭān* 'ruler, power' from Aramaic *saliṭa* 'to rule'.] —**sultanic** /sul tánnik/ *adj.* —**sultanship** /súltənship/ *n.*

sultana /sul taánə/ *n.* **1.** DRIED GRAPE a small dried seedless white grape **2.** SULTAN'S WOMAN RELATIVE a wife, mother, sister, daughter, or mistress of a sultan [Late 16thC. From Italian, the feminine of *sultano* 'sultan', from, ultimately, Arabic *sulṭān* (see SULTAN).]

sultanate /súltənət/ *n.* **1.** COUNTRY RULED BY SULTAN a country ruled by a sultan **2.** RANK OF SULTAN the rank or position of sultan **3.** SULTAN'S REIGN the period of a particular sultan's reign

sultry /súltri/ *adj.* **1.** HOT AND DAMP oppressively hot and damp **2.** SENSUAL giving a suggestion of underlying passion and sensuality [Late 16thC. Formed from earlier *sulter* 'to swelter', of uncertain origin: perhaps an alteration of SWELTER.] —**sultrily** *adv.* —**sultriness** *n.*

sum /sum/ *n.* **1.** AMOUNT OF MONEY an amount of money **2.** ARITHMETICAL CALCULATION a mathematical problem involving adding, subtracting, multiplying, or dividing numbers, especially one given to students to solve **3.** TOTAL the total amount resulting when two or more numbers or quantities are added together **4.** COMBINED TOTAL the combined total amount of anything **5.** GIST the essential point of sth that sb has said or written (*literary*) **6.** MATH LIMIT OF SUM OF SERIES the limit, as n increases indefinitely, of the sum of the first n terms of an infinite series ■ **sums** *npl.* ARITHMETIC simple arithmetical work, especially for schoolchildren, involving addition, subtraction, multiplication, and division (*informal*) ■ *vt.* (**sums, summing, summed**) ADD UP to add together two or more amounts to find their total (*formal*) [13thC. Via Old French *summe* from Latin *summa* 'sum, substance' (literally 'highest (thing)'), a noun use of the feminine of *summus* 'highest' (source of English *consummate, summary,* and *summit*), from, ultimately, *super* 'above' (source of English *super*) from Latin *summa* 'sum'.] ◇ **in sum** in short or as a summary

WORD KEY: ORIGIN

The semantic development of ***sum*** from 'highest' to 'sum total' resulted from the Roman practice of counting columns of figures from the bottom upwards, the total being written at the top.

sumach /shŏŏ mak, sŏŏ/, **sumac** *n.* **1.** TREE OF CASHEW FAMILY a tree or shrub of the cashew family that has clusters of green flowers, red hairy fruit, and feathery leaves. Genus: *Rhus.* ◊ **poison sumach** **2.** GROUND AND DRIED SUMACH LEAVES the ground dried leaves of one species of sumach, used in tanning and dyeing [14thC. Directly or via French *sumac* from medieval Latin *sumac(h)*, from Arabic *summāķ*.]

Sumatra /sŏŏ maátrə/ island in western Indonesia, in the Indian Ocean, separated from the Malay Peninsula by the Strait of Malacca. It is the westernmost of the Sundra Islands. Population: 36,881 (1990). Area: 425,150 sq. km/164,150 sq. mi. —**Sumatran** *n., adj.*

Sumer /sṓōmər/ ancient country of western Asia in southern Mesopotamia, in present-day Iraq. Archeological discoveries reveal the area to have been first settled in the 5th millennium BC. It became prosperous and powerful from about 3000 BC, and fell into decline from about 1760 BC, when it was absorbed into Babylonia and Assyria.

Sumerian /soo méeri ən/ *n.* **1.** PEOPLES MEMBER OF ANCIENT BABYLONIAN PEOPLE a member of an ancient people that built the flourishing civilization of Sumer **2.** LANG SUMERIAN LANGUAGE the language spoken in ancient Sumer. It is not related to any other known language. Sumerian is the oldest language preserved in writing, its cuneiform tablets dating from about 3000 BC. —**Sumerian** adj.

summa /súmmə, soómə/ (plural **summae** /-mee, -mee/) n. a summary of what is known of a subject, especially a medieval treatise on theology, philosophy, canon law, or alchemy [15thC. From Latin, 'main thing, substance, gist', a noun use of the feminine of summus (see SUM). The original English meaning was 'sum total'.]

summa cum laude /súmmə kum láwdi, soómə koóm lów day/ adv. US achieving the highest academic honours at graduation, usually awarded on the basis of the average of the candidates' marks. ◊ **cum laude, magna cum laude** [From Latin, literally 'with highest praise'] —**summa cum laude** adj.

summae plural of **summa**

summand /súmmand, su mánd/ n. any of the numbers or quantities in a sum [Mid-19thC. From medieval Latin summandus, literally 'for adding', a form of summare 'to add', from summa (see SUM).]

summarily /súmmərəli/ adv. immediately and without discussion or attention to formalities [Early 16thC. Originally in the sense 'briefly'.]

summarize /súmmə rīz/ (**-rizes, -rizing, -rized**), **summarise** (**-rises, -rising, -rised**) vti. to make or give a shortened version of sth that has been said or written, stating its main points —**summarist** n. —**summarizable** adj. —**summarization** /súmmə rī záysh'n/ n. —**summarizer** n.

summary /súmməri/ n. (plural **-ries**) SHORT VERSION CONTAINING GIST OF STH a shortened version of sth that has been said or written, containing only the main points ■ adj. 1. IMMEDIATE done immediately and with little discussion or attention to formalities 2. GIVING ONLY MAIN POINTS shortened and giving only the main points of sth 3. LAW RELATING TO MAGISTRATES' COURTS relating to, dealt with, or given by magistrates' courts operating without the formality of full proceedings [15thC. From Latin summarium, from summa (see SUM).] —**summariness** n.

summate /súmmayt/ (**-mates, -mating, -mated**) vti. to summarize what has been said before, especially to make a final summary of a case in a law court (formal) [Early 20thC. Back-formation from SUMMATION.]

summation /su máysh'n/ n. 1. ADDITION the process of adding sth up to find a total 2. TOTAL a total amount or aggregate 3. SUMMARY OF STH SAID a summary of sth that has been said or written 4. US LAW FINAL ARGUMENT IN COURT the final summing-up of an argument in a court of law [Mid-18thC. From the modern Latin stem summation-, from medieval Latin summare (see SUMMAND).] —**summational** adj. —**summative** /súmmətiv/ adj.

summer[1] /súmmər/ n. 1. WARMEST SEASON the warmest season of the year, falling between spring and autumn, and reckoned astronomically from the summer solstice to the autumn equinox 2. WARM WEATHER the warm weather associated with the summer season 3. PERIOD OF GREAT HAPPINESS a period of greatest happiness, success, or fulfilment in the life of sb or sth 4. YEAR a year, especially of sb's age (literary) ■ v. (**-mers, -mering, -mered**) 1. vi. SPEND SUMMER to spend the summer ○ They summer at the lake. 2. vt. PASTURE FOR SUMMER to keep cattle or other animals on a particular pasture during the summer [Old English sumor, sumer. Ultimately from a prehistoric Germanic word that is also the ancestor of Dutch zomer and German Sommer.] —**summery** adj.

summer[2] /súmmər/ n. 1. PRINCIPAL FLOOR BEAM a principal horizontal beam in a building used to support floor joists 2. STONE SUPPORTING ARCH ON COLUMN a stone that lies on top of a pier, column, or wall and supports one or more arches 3. = **lintel** [13thC. Via Anglo-Norman sumer, Old French som(i)er 'main beam' (originally 'pack horse') from, ultimately, late Latin sagmarius 'pack horse', from sagma 'pack-saddle', from Greek. The semantic development resulted from analogy between a burdened pack horse and a main supporting beam in a structure.]

summer cypress n. = **kochia**

summerhouse /súmmər howss/ (plural **summerhouses** /súmmər howziz/) n. a small building or structure in

a garden or park to give seating and shade during the summer [Old English summerhūs]

summer pudding n. a cold pudding consisting of summer fruits such as blackberries, raspberries, and strawberries, cooked together and placed inside a casing of white bread that absorbs their juice

summersault n., vi. = **somersault**

summer savory n. = **savory**[2]

summer school n. a course of study held during the summer vacation or holiday, in Britain usually a course of university lectures

summer time n. time that is one hour ahead of standard time, used in order to extend the hours of daylight in the evening

summertime /súmmər tīm/ n. the season of summer

summer tree n. = **summer**[2] n. 1

summerwood /súmmər wood/ n. the part of a tree's annual wood growth produced late in the growing season that is harder and less porous than its earlier growth (**springwood**)

summit /súmmit/ n. 1. HIGHEST POINT OF MOUNTAIN the highest point or top of sth, especially a mountain 2. HIGHEST POINT OF STH the highest point, level, or degree of sth such as a career 3. TOP-LEVEL DIPLOMATIC CONFERENCE a meeting between heads of government or other high-ranking officials to discuss a matter of great importance [14thC. From Old French som(m)ete, sumet, literally 'small top', from som, sum 'top', from Latin summum, the neuter of summus (see SUM).] —**summital** adj.

summit conference n. a meeting between heads of government to discuss some important matter such as disarmament

summiteer /súmmi teér/ n. sb who takes part in a summit conference

summitry /súmmitri/ n. US the practice of holding, or deciding matters of international importance through, summit conferences

summon /súmmən/ (**-mons, -moning, -moned**) v. 1. vt. CALL INTO COURT to order sb to attend court by serving a summons 2. vt. SEND FOR SB to send or be a signal for sb to come ○ We were summoned to his presence. 3. vt. CONVENE GROUP to call together a formal or official body ○ They summoned a meeting to debate the issue. 4. vt. CALL UPON SB to request or require sb to do sth ○ She summoned him to help her. 5. vi. MANAGE TO GET STH to gather the resources, especially courage or strength, to cope with or do sth ○ trying to summon up the courage to tell him the news [13thC. Via Old French sumondre from, ultimately, Latin summonere, literally 'to remind secretly', from sub- 'under' + monere 'to warn' (see MONISH).]

summons /súmmənz/ n. 1. COURT ORDER TO DEFENDANT a written order to sb to attend court to answer a complaint 2. COURT ORDER TO WITNESS a written order to a witness to attend court 3. ORDER BY AUTHORITY TO APPEAR an authoritative demand to appear at a particular place for a particular purpose ■ vt. (**-monses, -monsing, -monsed**) SERVE SB WITH SUMMONS to serve sb with a summons to attend court [13thC. From Old French somonse, the feminine past participle of somondre (see SUMMON).]

Sumo

sumo /soómō/ n. traditional Japanese wrestling in which each contestant tries to force the other outside a circle or to touch the ground other than

with the soles of his feet [Late 19thC. From Japanese sumō.]

sump /sump/ n. 1. RESERVOIR FOR LIQUID a low area such as a pit or reservoir into which a liquid drains 2. AUTOMOT LOWEST PART OF CRANKCASE a part located at the bottom of the crankcase of an internal-combustion engine that serves as a lubricating oil reservoir. US term **oil pan** 3. = **cesspool** 4. MINING DRAINAGE RESERVOIR IN MINE an area at the bottom of a mineshaft into which water drains and is then pumped away 5. CIV ENG ADVANCE EXCAVATION an excavation ahead of the main excavation of a mineshaft or tunnel [15thC. From Middle Dutch somp or Middle Low German sump. Ultimately from a prehistoric Germanic word meaning 'spongy' that is also the ancestor of English swamp.]

sumpter /súmptər/ n. a packhorse, mule, or other pack animal (archaic) [Late 16thC. Via Old French sommetier 'pack-horse driver' from assumed Vulgar Latin saumatarius, from Latin sagma 'packsaddle', from Greek, from sattein 'to pack', of unknown origin.]

sumptuary /súmptyoo əri/ adj. 1. REGULATING EXPENDITURE relating to or controlling personal spending 2. REGULATING BEHAVIOUR intended to regulate personal behaviour on moral or religious grounds [Early 17thC. From Latin sumptuarius, from sumptus 'expense', the past participle of sumere 'to spend', literally 'to take up', from emere (see EXAMPLE).]

sumptuous /súmptyoo əss/ adj. 1. SPLENDID magnificent or grand in appearance 2. EXTRAVAGANT entailing great expense [15thC. Via Old French somptueux from Latin sumptuosus, from sumptus 'expense' (see SUMPTUARY).] —**sumptuously** adv. —**sumptuousness** n.

sum total n. 1. EVERYTHING PUT TOGETHER a combined total of separate elements ○ The sum total of his belongings is the clothes on his back. 2. FINAL TOTAL a numerical amount obtained by adding sums

sun /sun/ n. 1. **Sun, sun** ASTRON STAR AROUND WHICH EARTH REVOLVES the star at the centre of our solar system around which the Earth and the eight other planets orbit. It provides us with heat and light. 2. STAR any star or bright celestial body, especially one around which planets orbit 3. ASTRON SUN'S RADIATION the light or heat emitted by the Sun 4. SB LIKE THE SUN sb or sth thought to resemble the Sun in radiance, glory, or warmth, or in being the centre of a society (literary) 5. DAY OR YEAR a day or year (literary) 6. SUNRISE OR SUNSET the rising or setting of the Sun (archaic) ○ working from sun to sun ■ v. (**suns, sunning, sunned**) 1. vt. BASK IN THE SUN to expose the body to the sun's rays for warmth or for a suntan ○ The cat lay sunning herself on the lawn. 2. vt. WARM OR DRY IN THE SUN to expose sth to the sun's rays for warmth or drying [Old English sunne. Ultimately from an Indo-European word that is also the ancestor of English south, solar, and helium.] ◇ **catch the sun** to become a little tanned or sunburnt through exposure to the sun ◇ **take the sun** to go out in the sunshine, especially with the aim of gaining some benefit to your health or wellbeing ◇ **under the sun** in the whole world

Sun. abbr. CALENDAR Sunday

sunbake /sún bayk/ vi. (**-bakes, -baked, -baked**) Aus SUNBATHE to sunbathe ■ n. Aus SUNBATH a sunbath

sunbaked /súnn baykt/ adj. 1. HARDENED BY THE SUN hard and dry from prolonged exposure to the sun 2. BAKED IN THE SUN baked by a process of exposure to the sun

sunbath /sún baath/ n. an act or period of exposing the body to the sun or a sun lamp, especially in order to get a tan

sunbathe /súnn bayth/ (**-bathes, -bathing, -bathed**) vi. to expose the body to sun or a sun lamp, especially in order to get a tan —**sunbather** n.

sunbeam /sún beem/ n. a ray of light emitted by the sun —**sunbeamy** adj.

sun bear n. a small bear of forests of southeastern Asia with sleek black fur, a light-coloured muzzle, and a yellowish breast marking. Latin name: Helarctos malayanus.

sunbed /sún bed/ n. 1. TANNING APPARATUS an apparatus resembling a bed with a special canopy that emits rays of ultraviolet light so that the person lying on it develops a suntan. US term **tanning bed** 2. = **sunlounger**

sunbird /sún burd/ *n.* a small brightly coloured singing bird native to southern and southeastern Asia, Africa, and Australia. It has a long thin curved bill and feeds on insects and nectar. Family: Nectariniidae.

sun bittern *n.* a semiarboreal solitary wading bird of tropical Central and South America that has mottled brownish plumage featuring a chestnut marking like a sunburst when its wings are spread. Latin name: *Eurypyga helius.*

sun blind *n.* a blind or awning that shades a room from bright sunlight

sunblock /sún blok/ *n.* a substance that is applied to the skin as a cream or lotion to protect it from the sun's harmful ultraviolet rays

sunbonnet /sún bonit/ *n.* a bonnet with a wide brim and a flap at the back, worn by babies and, in the past, by women to protect the face and neck from sun

sunbow /sún bō/ *n.* a spectrum of colours similar to a rainbow produced by sunlight refracting through spray, mist, or water vapour, e.g. above a waterfall [Modelled on 'rainbow']

sunburn /sún burn/ *n.* BURNT SKIN FROM OVEREXPOSURE TO SUN an inflammation and sometimes blistering of the skin caused by overexposure to ultraviolet radiation from the sun ■ *vi.* (-burns, -burning, -burned *or* -burnt) BURN SKIN IN SUN to cause the skin to become inflamed and sometimes blistered as a result of overexposure to ultraviolet radiation from the sun

sunburnt /sún burnt/, **sunburned** /-burnd/ *adj.* 1. BURNT BY SUN affected by sunburn 2. TANNED with a suntan

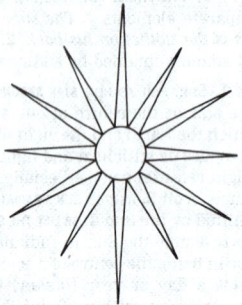
Sunburst

sunburst /sún burst/ *n.* 1. SUDDEN BURST OF SUNSHINE a sudden appearance of the sun from behind clouds 2. SUN-SHAPED DESIGN a design meant to resemble the sun, consisting of a series of rays extending outwards from a central circle 3. SUN-SHAPED BROOCH a brooch or other ornament designed as a sunburst

Sunbury /súnbri/ *town in southern Victoria, Australia, a residential and agricultural centre. Population: 22,126 (1996).

Sunbury-on-Thames /súnbri ən témz/ *town in Surrey, southeastern England. Population: 27,392 (1991).

sun cream *n.* a cosmetic cream used to protect the skin from the sun and usually also to help sb develop a suntan. US term **suntan lotion**

sundae /sún day, -di/ *n.* an ice-cream dessert served with toppings such as whipped cream, fruit, nuts, and flavoured syrup [Late 19thC. Alteration of SUNDAY.]

Sunda Islands /súndə-/ *island group of the Malay Archipelago between the South China Sea and the Indian Ocean. It consists of two groups, the Greater Sunda Islands, which include Sumatra, Java and Borneo, and the Lesser Sunda Islands, which include Bali and Timor.

sun dance *n.* an important ceremonial dance of Native North American peoples living on prairies, held annually in honour of the sun

Sunday /sún day, -di/ *n.* CALENDAR 1. 7TH DAY OF WEEK the day of the week after Saturday and before Monday 2. CHRISTIAN SABBATH DAY in Christian tradition, the day set aside for the Sabbath ■ *adj.* 1. OF SUNDAY relating to or occupying a Sunday 2. FOR SPECIAL OCCASIONS worn or used for special occasions 3. ONLY AT WEEKENDS OR AS HOBBY lacking experience, efficiency, or professional

skill ○ *These Sunday drivers are a menace on the roads.* [Old English *sunnandæg,* literally 'day of the sun', a translation of Latin *dies solis*]

Sunday best *n.* sb's best clothes, traditionally worn on a Sunday to go to church

Sunday punch *n. US* 1. KNOCKOUT PUNCH a boxer's most powerful punch, especially a knockout blow 2. EFFECTIVE WEAPON a means of delivering a devastating blow to an opponent

Sundays /sún dayz, -diz/ *adv.* ON SUNDAYS every Sunday ■ *npl.* SUNDAY NEWSPAPERS special format newspapers published on Sundays ○ *It's in all the Sundays.*

Sunday school *n.* a school or class offering children religious education or activities on Sundays

sun deck *n.* 1. NAUT SHIP'S DECK an open upper deck on a passenger ship 2. *US, ANZ* PLACE TO SUNBATHE a balcony, terrace, or platform attached to a building, used for sunbathing

sunder /súndər/ (-ders, -dering, -dered) *vti.* to separate or make sth separate into parts, especially with force (*archaic or literary*) [Old English *sundrian,* from *sundor* 'apart'. Ultimately from an Indo-European base that is also the ancestor of Latin *sine* 'without'.] —**sunderer** *n.*

Sunderland /súndərlənd/ *city and port in Tyne and Wear County, England. Population: 295,800 (1995).

sundew /sún dyoo/ *n.* a plant that produces a rosette of hairy sticky leaves that are used to trap and digest insects. Sundews occur worldwide, but especially in Australia and New Zealand. Family: Droseraceae. [Translation of Latin *ros solis*; so called because the drops of juice the plant secretes resemble dew]

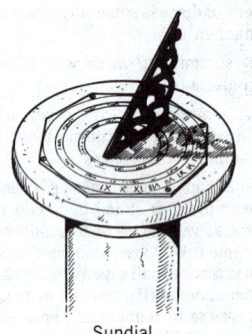
Sundial

sundial /sún dī əl/ *n.* an instrument that shows the time of day by the position of a sun-generated shadow cast by a fixed arm (**gnomon**) onto a graduated plate or surface

sun disc *n.* an ancient Egyptian sun-god symbol, consisting of a disc with wings and two serpents

sundog /sún dog/ *n.* 1. = **parhelion** 2. SMALL RAINBOW NEAR SUN a small spectrum of light occasionally visible in the sky at the same altitude as the sun, either to the left or right of the sun and sometimes on both sides simultaneously

sundown /sún down/ *n.* the time when the sun sets

sundowner /sún downər/ *n. UK, S Africa* an alcoholic drink taken early in the evening, around sunset (*informal*)

sundress /sún dress/ *n.* a light sleeveless summer dress with a low bodice that exposes the shoulders, back, and arms to the sun

sun-dried *adj.* dried out naturally by the sun, not by applying artificial heat

sundries /súndriz/ *npl.* 1. MISCELLANEOUS THINGS small miscellaneous items, often of too little value to be enumerated 2. EXTRA FOOD ITEMS ON MENU items of food, especially breads or other small extras, that can be ordered in a restaurant as an accompaniment to a meal

sundry /súndri/ *adj.* VARIOUS assorted but, perhaps for convenience, being considered as a single category or group ○ *and other sundry items.* ◊ **sundries** ■ *n. Aus* CRICKET EXTRA an extra [Old English *syndrig* 'separate'] ◊ **all and sundry** everyone without exception (*takes a plural verb*)

Sundsvall /sóondz val/ *town and port on the Gulf of Bothnia, Sweden, situated about 400 km/250 mi. north of Stockholm. Population: 94,531 (1995).

sunfish /sún fish/ (*plural* -**fish** *or* -**fishes**) *n.* 1. LARGE OCEAN FISH a large brownish-blue marine fish that is nearly oval and has high dorsal and anal fins that it uses like oars for locomotion. Family: Molidae. US term **ocean sunfish** 2. N AMERICAN FRESHWATER FISH a small to medium sized spiny-finned North American freshwater fish, often with iridescent colours. The family includes several game fish. Examples are the smallmouth bass, the largemouth bass, the black-and-white crappie, the bluegill, and the pumpkinseed.

sunflower /sún flowər/ *n.* 1. TALL PLANT WITH YELLOW-RAYED FLOWERS a tall annual plant with large yellow-rayed flowers and edible seeds that yield an oil. It is grown for ornament and as a farm crop for sunflower oil. Latin name: *Helianthus annus.* 2. PLANT RELATED TO COMMERCIALLY GROWN SUNFLOWER any of several plants related to the seed- and oil-giving sunflower. Genus: *Helianthus.* [Mid-16thC. Translation of modern Latin *flos solis* and Greek *helianthos.* So called from its yellow-rayed flowers and because it turns to follow the sun throughout the day.]

WORD KEY: CULTURAL NOTE

Sunflowers, a series of paintings by Dutch artist Vincent Van Gogh (1888). These simple still lifes constitute one of Van Gogh's most successful attempts to transform everyday objects into powerful poetic symbols. Their intense colours and ragged, writhing forms suggest the life forces inherent in nature as well as the energy of the artist, but also hint at an underlying sense of anxiety and despair.

sung past participle of **sing**

Sung /sóong/, **Song** *n.* a Chinese imperial dynasty lasting from AD 960–1279, under which science, philosophy, and the arts thrived [Late 17thC. From Chinese *Song.*]

sungazer /sún gayzər/ *n.* a lizard of southern Africa that grows to about 355 cm/14 in and is known for its habit of basking in the sun. Latin name: *Cordylus giganteus.*

sunglass /sún glaass/ *n.* LENS TO FOCUS SUN'S RAYS a convex lens used to focus the sun's rays to produce heat, especially in order to start a fire ■ **sunglasses** *npl.* GLASSES THAT SHIELD EYES FROM GLARE glasses with tinted or darkened lenses to protect the eyes from sunlight or its glare

sunglow /sún glō/ *n.* a pale pink or yellow glow seen in the sky just before sunrise or just after sunset

sun-god *n.* 1. SUN AS GOD the sun worshipped as a god 2. GOD OF THE SUN a god that personifies or is seen as controlling the sun

sungrebe /sún greeb/ (*plural* -**grebes**) *n.* a diving bird that lives along rivers and lakes of tropical America, Africa, and Asia. It has brownish plumage and lobed toes and feeds on aquatic invertebrates. Family: Heliornithidae.

sunhat /sún hat/ *n.* a hat with a broad brim that is designed to keep the sun off the face and neck

suni /sóni/ (*plural* -**nis** *or* -**ni**) *n.* a small southern African antelope, growing to only about 355 cm/14 in long, that has small straight horns and a strong musky odour from facial glands. Latin name: *Neotragus moschatus.* [Late 19thC. Of Bantu origin.]

sunk /sungk/ past participle, past tense of **sink** ■ *adj.* DOOMED TO FAILURE without hope of success (*informal*)

—— **WORD KEY: USAGE** ——

See Usage note at *sink.*

sunken /súngkən/ *adj.* 1. SUBMERGED having sunk beneath the surface of sth 2. HOLLOW-LOOKING appearing hollow or concave ○ *sunken cheeks* 3. SUNK LOWER having settled to a lower level 4. AT LOWER ELEVATION at a lower level than sth adjoining

—— **WORD KEY: USAGE** ——

See Usage note at *sink.*

sunk fence *n.* a ditch containing a fence or wall that separates lands without marring the appearance of the landscape

sunlamp /sún lamp/ *n.* **1.** LAMP USED FOR TANNING a lamp that emits ultraviolet light, used to get a suntan or for therapeutic purposes **2.** PHOTOGRAPHER'S LAMP a lamp with parabolic mirrors that are directed to focus light, used in cinema photography

sunless /súnləss/ *adj.* **1.** WITHOUT SUNLIGHT deprived of or lacking sunlight **2.** JOYLESS without joy or happiness

sunlight /sún līt/ *n.* light emitted by the sun —**sunlit** /súnlit/ *adj.*

sun lotion *n.* = **suntan lotion**

sun lounge *n.* a room with large windows designed to receive the maximum sunlight. US term **sunroom**

sunlounger /sún lownjər/ *n.* a light folding chair with an extended section for the legs, used for sunbathing

sunn /sun/ *n.* **1.** PLANTS TROPICAL ASIAN LEGUMINOUS PLANT a plant of the pea family that has thin branches and clusters of yellow flowers and grows in tropical Asia and Australia. Latin name: *Crotalaria juncea.* **2.** INDUST FIBRE FROM SUNN PLANT strong light fibre obtained from the inner bark of the sunn plant, used for such things as rope and sacks [Late 18thC. Via Hindustani *san* from Sanskrit *śāṇa-* 'hempen'.]

Sunna /sŏŏnə, súnnə/ *n.* one of the basic sources of Islamic law based on Muhammad's words and deeds as recorded in the Hadith. The Sunna complements and often explains the Koran. [Early 18thC. From Arabic, 'rule, custom'.]

Sunni /sŏŏni, súnni/ (*plural* **-ni** *or* **-nis**) *n.* **1.** BRANCH OF ISLAM the largest branch of Islam, which believes in the traditions of the Sunna and accepts the first four caliphs as rightful successors to Muhammad **2.** SUNNI MUSLIM a member of the Sunni branch of Islam [Late 16thC. From Arabic, 'lawful', from *sunna* 'rule, custom'.]

sunnies /súnniz/ *npl. ANZ* sunglasses (*informal*)

Sunnite /sŏŏnīt, súnn-/ *n.* = **Sunni** *n.* 2

sunny /súnni/ (**-nier, -niest**) *adj.* **1.** FULL OF SUNSHINE with a lot of sunshine **2.** FULL OF SUNLIGHT bright with or exposed to sunlight **3.** CHEERFUL characterized by or showing happiness or cheerfulness —**sunnily** *adv.* —**sunniness** *n.*

sunny-side up *adj.* used to describe fried eggs that are not turned over in cooking and so have a visible yellow yolk uppermost

sun protection factor *n.* full form of **SPF**

sunrise /sún rīz/ *n.* **1.** COMING UP OF SUN the rising of the sun above the eastern horizon each morning **2.** GLOW FROM RISING SUN an atmospheric glow and colouring near the horizon as the sun rises **3.** TIME SUN RISES the time at which the sun rises above the horizon in the morning

sunrise industry *n.* a new industry showing rapid growth, e.g. the microcomputer industry

sunroof /sún roof/ *n.* a small panel in the roof of a car that can be raised or slid back to let in air and light

sunroom /sún room, -rŏŏm/ *n. US, ANZ* = **sun lounge**

sunscreen /sún skreen/ *n.* a cosmetic cream, lotion, or oil, or an ingredient of one, intended to protect the skin from burning without preventing tanning

sunset /sún set/ *n.* **1.** GOING DOWN OF SUN the setting of the sun below the western horizon in the evening **2.** GLOW FROM SETTING SUN an atmospheric glow and colouring near the horizon as the sun sets **3.** TIME SUN SETS the time at which the sun sets below the horizon in the evening **4.** LAST PART the period during which sth is declining or coming to an end

WORD KEY: CULTURAL NOTE

Sunset Boulevard, a film by US director Billy Wilder (1950). Wilder uses the story of the relationship between an out-of-favour screenwriter and a faded and eccentric silent-movie star to create one of the cinema's most savage satires on the cynicism and ruthlessness of the Hollywood system. The performances, camerawork, and direction all reinforce the powerful atmosphere of corruption and decay.

sunshade /sún shayd/ *n.* sth, e.g. an awning or parasol, under which sb is protected from the sun

sunshine /sún shīn/ *n.* **1.** DIRECT SUNLIGHT direct rays of the sun, producing heat and light ○ *a ray of sunshine* **2.** SUNNY PLACE a place where the sun's rays are falling ○ *Let's sit in the sunshine.* **3.** SOURCE OF GOOD FEELINGS sb or sth producing joy, happiness, or warmth ○ *bringing a little bit of sunshine into people's lives* **4.** FAMILIAR TERM OF ADDRESS used to address sb in a cheerful or familiar way (*informal*) (*often used ironically*) ○ *Listen, sunshine, you just watch what you're saying, okay?* —**sunshiny** *adj.*

Sunshine Coast region in southeastern Queensland, Australia, consisting of the 45 km/28 mi. stretch of coastline between Noosa Heads and Caloundra. It is a popular tourist destination.

sunspecs /sún speks/ *npl.* sunglasses (*informal*)

sunspot /sún spot/ *n.* **1.** DARK PATCH ON THE SUN one of the relatively cool dark patches that appear in cycles on the Sun's surface and possess a powerful magnetic field **2.** WARM PLACE a place that has a warm and sunny climate and is usually popular as a holiday destination (*informal*)

sunstone /súnstōn/ *n.* = **aventurine** [Translation of Latin *gemma solis*]

sunstroke /súnstrōk/ *n.* a condition caused by prolonged and excessive exposure to the sun and characterized by feverishness, faintness, convulsions, and coma. It results when the temperature becomes too extreme to be handled by the body's heat-regulating mechanism. Technical name **insolation**

sunsuit /sún soot, -syoot/ *n.* a child's one-piece garment usually consisting of shorts and a bib top with shoulder straps, worn in hot weather

suntan /sún tan/ *n.* = **tan**[1] *n.* 2 —**suntanned** *adj.*

suntan cream *n.* = **sun cream**

suntan lotion *n.* a cosmetic lotion used to protect the skin from the sun and usually also to help sb develop a suntan

suntrap /sún trap/ *n.* a sheltered area with bright sunlight and little or no wind

sunup /súnnup/ *n. US* = **sunrise** *n.* 3

sunward /súnwərd/ *adj.* FACING THE SUN turned towards or in the direction of the sun ■ *adv.* **sunward, sunwards** = **sunwards**

sup[1] /sup/ *vti.* (**sups, supping, supped**) **1.** SIP LIQUID to drink small amounts of liquid at one time **2.** EAT BY THE SPOONFUL to eat sth that is swallowed directly, e.g. soup or porridge, with a spoon ■ *n.* SIP OF LIQUID a small amount or mouthful of liquid [Old English *sūpan*. Ultimately from a prehistoric Germanic base that is also the ancestor of English *sip, soup,* and *sup*[2].]

sup[2] /sup/ *vi.* (**sups, supping, supped**) HAVE SUPPER to eat the evening meal (*archaic*) ■ *n.* SUPPER the evening meal (*archaic*) [14thC. From Old French *souper*, from *soupe* (see SOUP).]

sup. *abbr.* **1.** supra **2.** GRAM superlative **3.** GRAM supine **4.** supplement **5.** supplementary **6.** supply **7.** superior

supari /sŏŏpaari/ *n. S Asia* areca palm nuts chewed with betel leaves, especially after meals as a digestive [Mid-17thC. From Hindi *supārī*.]

Supdt *abbr.* PUBLIC ADMIN superintendent *n.* 3.

super /sŏŏpər/ *adj.* **1.** EXCELLENT with outstanding or excellent qualities (*informal*) ○ *a super idea* **2.** VERY GREAT exceptionally large or powerful (*informal*) **3.** EXCESSIVE greater than what is normal ■ *adv.* ESPECIALLY to or in a high or extreme degree (*informal*) ○ *Everyone has been super helpful.* ■ *n.* **1.** SUPERINTENDENT a superintendent (*informal*) **2.** SUPERVISOR a supervisor (*informal*) **3.** *US* STH BIGGER OR BETTER sth superior in grade or quality or large in size **4.** *ANZ* SUPERANNUATION superannuation (*informal*) **5.** THEATRE ACTOR EMPLOYED AS WALK-ON a supernumerary, especially an actor with a walk-on part (*informal*) **6.** HIGH-OCTANE PETROL high-octane petrol **7.** *Aus* LEADED PETROL leaded petrol ■ *interj.* GREAT! used to express enthusiasm, approval, or agreement (*informal*) [Mid-19thC. From SUPER-, or a shortening of various words beginning with SUPER-.]

super. *abbr.* **1.** superfine **2.** superior

super- *prefix.* **1.** sth larger, stronger, or faster than others of its kind ○ *superstore* **2.** over, above, on ○ *supernatant* ○ *superstructure* **3.** exceeding the usual or normal limits ○ *superheat* **4.** a more inclusive group or category ○ *superclass* **5.** in addition to, over and above ○ *superfetation* **6.** greater in size, quality, number, or degree, superior ○ *superhuman* [From Latin *super* 'over, above' (source of English *supreme* and *sovereign*). Ultimately from an Indo-European base that is also the ancestor of *over* and *hyper-*.]

superable /sŏŏpərəb'l/ *adj.* capable of being overcome [Early 17thC. From Latin *superabilis*, from *superare* 'to overcome', from *super* (see SUPER-).] —**superability** /sŏŏpərə bíllәti/ *n.* —**superableness** /sŏŏpərəb'l nəss/ *n.* —**superably** /sŏŏpərəbli/ *adv.*

superabound /sŏŏpərə bównd/ (**-bounds, -bounding, -bounded**) *vi.* to be too numerous or abundant [14thC. From late Latin *superabundare*, from *abundare* (see ABOUND).]

superabundant /sŏŏpərə búndənt/ *adj.* present in excess of what is sufficient [15thC. From late Latin *superabundant-*, the present participle stem of *superabundare* (see SUPERABOUND).] —**superabundance** *n.* —**superabundantly** *adv.*

superadd /sŏŏpər ád/ (**-adds, -adding, -added**) *vt.* to add sth onto what has already been added [15thC. From Latin *superaddere*, from *addere* (see ADD).] —**superaddition** /sŏŏpərə dísh'n/ *n.* —**superadditional** *adj.*

superalloy /sŏŏpər álloy/ *n.* a heat-resistant alloy with superior mechanical properties, often having aerospace applications

superannuate /sŏŏpər ánnyoo ayt/ (**-ates, -ating, -ated**) *v.* **1.** *vti.* RETIRE WITH A PENSION to become retired or retire sb with a pension **2.** *vt.* GET RID OF STH to reject sth or cause sth to be rejected because of obsolescence [Mid-17thC. Back-formation from SUPERANNUATED.]

superannuated /sŏŏpər ánnyoo aytid/ *adj.* **1.** RETIRED having been retired with a pension **2.** TOO WORN too much used for more useful service **3.** OUT-OF-DATE no longer in fashion [Mid-17thC. From medieval Latin *superannuatus* 'more than a year old', from *annus* 'year'.]

superannuation /sŏŏpər anyoo áysh'n/ *n.* **1.** DEDUCTION FOR PENSION SCHEME the amount contributed regularly from an employee's pay towards a pension **2.** RETIREMENT PENSION the pension paid on retirement to a contributing employee **3.** RETIREMENT the process of retiring or the state of being retired with a pension

superannuitant /sŏŏpər ə nyŏŏ itənt/ *n.* sb receiving superannuation, especially the age benefit in New Zealand

superb /sŏŏ púrb, syŏŏ/ *adj.* **1.** EXCELLENT of the highest quality **2.** GRAND impressive in size or appearance **3.** SUMPTUOUS rich and sumptuous in appearance or detail [Mid-16thC. Via French from Latin *superbus* 'proud, superior', from *super* (see SUPER-).] —**superbly** *adv.* —**superbness** *n.*

Super Bowl *tdmk.* a trademark for the championship game of the US National Football League played each year between the champions of the National Football Conference and the American Football Conference

superbug /sŏŏpər bug/, **supergerm** /sŏŏpər jurm/ *n.* a bacterium that has become resistant to the antibiotics normally used to treat it

supercalender /sŏŏpər kálləndər/ *n.* MACHINE FOR FINISHING PAPER a machine with an extra large number of rollers to give a glossy finish to paper ■ *vt.* (**-ders, -dering, -dered**) GIVE PAPER A SHEEN to produce a glossy finish on paper using a supercalender

supercargo /sŏŏpər kaargō/ (*plural* **-gos**) *n.* an officer who is in charge of the cargo and commercial matters aboard a merchant ship [Late 17thC. Alteration (influenced by SUPER-) of earlier *supracargo*, an alteration (influenced by SUPRA-) of Spanish *sobrecargo*, from *sobre-* 'over' (from Latin *super-*) + Spanish *cargo* (see CARGO).]

supercharge /sŏŏpər chaarj/ (**-charges, -charging, -charged**) *vt.* **1.** AUTOMOT INCREASE ENGINE'S POWER to increase the power of an internal-combustion engine by means of a supercharger **2.** FILL STH WITH TOO MUCH FEELING to charge sth, e.g. the atmosphere or a remark, with excessive emotion or energy

supercharger /sóopər chaarjər/ *n.* a device that supplies air to an internal-combustion engine at a pressure greater than the ambient atmospheric pressure in order to increase its power. The blower or air pump on an engine's intake system could be a supercharger.

superciliary /sóopər sílli əri/ *adj.* **1.** OF THE EYEBROW relating to or in the region of the eyebrow **2.** ABOVE THE EYE used to describe markings above an animal's eye [Mid-18thC. Formed from Latin *supercilium* 'eyebrow' (see SUPERCILIOUS).]

supercilious /sóopər sílli əss/ *adj.* full of contempt and arrogance [Early 16thC. From Latin *superciliosus*, from *supercilium* 'eyebrow', from *super* 'above' + *cilium* 'eyelid', referring to raised eyebrows as a sign of haughty disdain.]

superclass /sóopər klaass/ *n.* a taxonomic category of related organisms ranking below a phylum and above a class

supercluster /sóopər klustər/ *n.* an association of clusters of galaxies

supercolumnar /sóopər kə lúmnər/ *adj.* ARCHIT with one order of columns above another —**supercolumniation** /sóopər kə lùmni áysh'n/ *n.*

supercomputer /sóopər kəm pyootər/ *n.* a state-of-the-art computer with the highest processing speeds technologically possible at a given time, used for solving complex scientific and engineering problems

superconductivity /sóopər kon duk tívvəti/ *n.* the ability of some metals, alloys, and ceramics to conduct electric current with negligible internal resistance at temperatures near absolute zero and, in some cases, at higher temperatures. Scientists have developed superconductors that function at temperatures up to 100 degrees above absolute zero. —**superconducting** /sóopər kən dúkting/ *adj.* —**superconduction** /-kən dúksh'n/ *n.* —**superconductive** /-kən dúktiv/ *adj.* —**superconductor** /-kən dúktər/ *n.*

supercontinent /sóopər kontinənt/ *n.* one of the large continental masses believed to have broken into several parts that drifted apart to form the present continents. These land masses included Pangaea, Gondwana, and Laurasia.

supercool /sóopər kóol/ *vti.* (**-cools, -cooling, -cooled**) COOL BELOW FREEZING POINT WITHOUT SOLIDIFYING to cool a liquid, or become cooled, to a temperature below freezing point without change to a solid ■ *adj.* TOTALLY MODERN extremely fashionable in attitude or image (*informal*)

super-duper /sóopər dóopər/ *adj.* of the greatest excellence, size, or efficiency (*informal*) (*often used ironically*) [Doubling of SUPER]

superego /sóopər éegō/ (*plural* **-gos**) *n.* according to Freudian theory, the part of the mind that acts as a conscience to the ego, developing moral standards and rules through contact with parents and society [Early 20thC. Translation of German *Über-Ich*, coined by Sigmund Freud.]

superelevation /sóopər eli váysh'n/ *n.* the distance in height between the inside and outside edges of the bed of a banked road or track

supereminent /sóopər émminənt/ *adj.* higher than others in distinction, estimation, or prominence [Mid-16thC. From Latin *supereminent-*, the present participle stem of *supereminere* 'to rise above', from *eminere* (see EMINENT).] —**supereminence** *n.* —**supereminently** *adv.*

supererogate /sóopər érrə gayt/ (**-gates, -gating, -gated**) *vi.* to do or perform sth beyond what is required or expected (*archaic*) [Late 16thC. From late Latin *supererogare* 'to pay over and above', from *erogare* 'to spend', from *rogare* (see ROGATION).] —**supererogator** *n.*

supererogation /sóopər erə gáysh'n/ *n.* the performance of work beyond what is required or expected [Early 16thC. From the medieval Latin stem of *supererogatio*, from *supererogare* (see SUPEREROGATE).]

supererogatory /sóopər i róggətəri/ *adj.* **1.** BEYOND THE CALL OF DUTY performed to an extent beyond what is required or expected **2.** SUPERFLUOUS beyond what is sufficient or necessary, and not wanted —**supererogatorily** *adv.*

superfamily /sóopər famli/ (*plural* **-lies**) *n.* a taxonomic category of related organisms ranking below an order and above a family

superfecundation /sóopər fekən dáysh'n/ *n.* **1.** SEPARATE FERTILIZATION OF OVA the fertilization of two or more ova at different times during one menstrual cycle by sperm from the same or different males **2.** FERTILIZATION OF MANY OVA the fertilization of an unusually large number of ova at the same time

superfetation /sóopər fee táysh'n/ *n.* the fertilization of a second ovum after the start of pregnancy, resulting in the presence of two foetuses at different stages of development in the same uterus. It is a normal occurrence in some animal species. [Early 17thC. Via French from, ultimately, modern Latin *superfetare* 'to conceive a second time', from Latin *foetus* (see FOETUS).]

superficial /sóopər físh'l/ *adj.* **1.** NOT PROFOUND concerned with or understanding only the obvious ○ *a superficial knowledge of the text* **2.** RELATING TO THE SURFACE on, near, relating to, or affecting the surface of sth ○ *a superficial wound* **3.** WITHOUT DEPTH OF CHARACTER shallow in character or attitude ○ *I find her quite superficial.* **4.** CURSORY swift and not thorough ○ *after a superficial examination of the injury* **5.** ONLY APPARENTLY SO only seeming to be real or the case ○ *The picture bears a superficial resemblance, nothing more.* **6.** INSIGNIFICANT with little significance or substance ○ *superficial changes to the policy* [14thC. Formed from Latin *superficies* (see SUPERFICIES).] —**superficiality** /sóopər fishi állәti/ *n.* —**superficially** /sóopər físh'li/ *adv.*

superficies /sóopər físhi eez/ (*plural* **-cies**) *n.* **1.** OUTER SURFACE an outer surface or area of sth **2.** OUTWARD APPEARANCE the outward appearance or form of sth [Mid-16thC. From Latin, from *super* 'above' + *facies* (see FACE).]

superfine /sóopər fīn/ *adj.* **1.** FINEST IN TEXTURE of extremely fine grain or texture **2.** FINEST IN QUALITY of the highest quality or grade **3.** AFFECTEDLY REFINED excessively refined in manner —**superfineness** *n.*

superfluid /sóopər floo id/ *n.* FLUID FLOWING FREELY AT LOW TEMPERATURES a fluid characterized by the absence of viscosity at temperatures near absolute zero. The only known example is liquid helium. ■ *adj.* BEHAVING LIKE SUPERFLUID relating to or exhibiting the properties of a superfluid —**superfluidity** /sóopər floo íddəti/ *n.*

superfluity /sóopər flóo əti/ (*plural* **-ties**) *n.* **1.** EXCESSIVE QUANTITY an excessive or overabundant supply of sth **2.** STH INESSENTIAL sth beyond what is necessary

superfluous /soo púr floo əss/ *adj.* **1.** MORE THAN NECESSARY that is in excess of what is needed ○ *a lot of superfluous detail* **2.** INESSENTIAL not essential ○ *superfluous to the discussion* **3.** EXTRAVAGANT extravagant in living or spending (*archaic*) [14thC. Directly or via Old French *superflueux* from Latin *superfluus*, from *superfluere* 'to overflow', from *fluere* (see FLUENT).] —**superfluously** *adv.* —**superfluousness** *n.*

supergene /sóopər jeen/ *n.* a group of genes that lie close together on a chromosome, function as a unit, and are rarely separated

supergerm *n.* = **superbug**

supergiant /sóopər jī ənt/ *n.* an extremely large brilliant star with a luminosity of thousands of times greater than that of the Sun. The stars Rigel and Betelgeuse are examples.

superglue /sóopər gloo/ *n.* a fast acting glue that forms a strong bond by polymerization

supergrass /sóopər graass/ *n.* an informer who gives information to the police implicating a large number of criminals (*informal*)

supergroup /sóopər groop/ *n.* a rock music group whose performers are already famous from having performed individually or in other groups

superheat /sóopər heet/ *vt.* (**-heats, -heating, -heated**) **1.** HEAT LIQUID WITHOUT VAPORIZATION to heat a liquid above its pressure-related boiling point without causing it to vaporize **2.** HEAT VAPOUR TO SATURATION to heat a vapour not in contact with its liquid to the point at which a lowering of temperature or increase in pressure will not change it to a liquid **3.** GET STH VERY HOT to heat sth to an extremely high temperature ■ *n.* HEAT FOR SUPERHEATING the heat used to superheat a vapour —**superheater** *n.*

superhelix /sóopər heeliks/ (*plural* **-helices** /-heeli seez/) *n.* a molecule with a helical structure formed by another helical molecule, e.g. a nucleosome formed of DNA

superhero /sóopər heerō/ (*plural* **-roes**) *n.* a fictional character, e.g. from a cartoon, who has superhuman powers and uses them to fight crime or evil

superheterodyne /sóopər héttərō dīn/ *adj.* WITH MIXING OF RADIO FREQUENCIES relating to a method of receiving radio signals in which the incoming signal is mixed with a frequency generated by the receiver. The resulting intermediate frequency is amplified then decoded. ■ *n.* SUPERHETERODYNE RECEIVER a radio receiver that operates using the superheterodyne method of receiving signals [Early 20thC. Formed from SUPERSONIC + HETERODYNE, because the incoming signals are outside the range of sound.]

superhigh frequency /sóopərhī-/ *n.* a radio frequency between 3,000 and 30,000 megahertz

superhighway /sóopər hī way/ *n.* **1.** = **information superhighway** **2.** *US* MOTORWAY a motorway in the United States designed for high-speed traffic, with several lanes in each direction

superhuman /sóopər hyóomən/ *adj.* **1.** BEYOND HUMAN CAPABILITY beyond ordinary human capability **2.** SUPERNATURAL with higher or greater powers than those within human experience ○ *a superhuman being* [Early 17thC. From late Latin *superhumanus*, from *humanus* (see HUMAN).] —**superhumanity** /sóopər hyoo mánnəti/ *n.* —**superhumanly** /-hyóomənli/ *adv.* —**superhumanness** /-hyóomən nəss/ *n.*

superimpose /sóopərim pṓz/ (**-poses, -posing, -posed**) *vt.* **1.** LAY STH OVER STH to place sth, e.g. a transparent image, on or over sth else, often with the result that both things appear simultaneously, although one may partially obscure the other **2.** ADD ONTO STH to add a feature or element without incorporating it ○ *superimpose one culture on another* —**superimposition** /sóopər impə zísh'n/ *n.*

superincumbent /sóopərin kúmbənt/ *adj.* lying or resting on or above sth [Mid-17thC. From Latin *superincumbere* 'to lie on top of', from *incumbere* (see INCUMBENT).] —**superincumbence** *n.* —**superincumbency** *n.* —**superincumbently** *adv.*

superinduce /sóopərin dyóoss/ (**-duces, -ducing, -duced**) *vt.* to introduce sb or sth additional [Mid-16thC. From Latin *superinducere*, literally 'to bring in upon', from *inducere* (see INDUCE).] —**superinduction** /sóopərin dúksh'n/ *n.*

superinfection /sóopərin féksh'n/ *n.* an infection that develops during drug treatment for another infection, caused by a different microorganism that is resistant to the treatment used for the first infection —**superinfect** /-fékt/ *vt.*

superintend /sóopərin ténd/ (**-tends, -tending, -tended**) *vt.* to be responsible for and supervise sth, e.g. a project or job [Early 17thC. Back-formation from SUPERINTENDENT.]

superintendence /sóopərin téndənss/ *n.* = **superintendency** *n.* 2

superintendency /sóopərin téndənssi/ (*plural* **-cies**) *n.* **1.** JOB OF SUPERINTENDENT the office, position, authority, or administrative district of a superintendent **2.** MANAGEMENT supervision or administration by a superintendent

superintendent /sóopərin téndənt/ *n.* **1.** SB IN CHARGE an administrator or manager of sth, e.g. an office or organization **2.** HIGH-RANKING POLICE OFFICER a police officer ranking higher than an inspector **3.** *US* = **porter** ■ *adj.* IN CHARGE acting in an administrative or supervisory capacity [Mid-16thC. Formed from ecclesiastical Latin *superintendere* 'to oversee', from *intendere* (see INTEND), as a translation of Greek *episkopos* 'overseer'.]

superior /soo péeri ər/ *adj.* **1.** HIGHER IN QUALITY above average or better than another in quality or grade **2.** BETTER THAN OTHERS surpassing others in sth, e.g. intellect, achievement, or ability **3.** HIGHER IN RANK higher in rank, position, or authority than another **4.** CONDESCENDING adopting or showing an attitude of condescension towards others ○ *He gave a superior smile.* **5.** UNCONCERNED above being affected or influenced by sth ○ *A player has to be superior to such taunts.* **6.** LARGER greater in number or amount ○ *a quantity superior to our needs* **7.** HIGHER upper, or situated higher up **8.** PRINTING = **superscript** *adj.* **9.** BOT ABOVE OTHER FLOWER PARTS used to describe an ovary of a flower whose stamens, petals, and sepals arise either beside or below it **10.** ANAT NEARER THE HEAD nearer the head than another body part ■ *n.* **1.** SB OR STH HIGHER OR BETTER sb or sth higher in rank, position, authority, or quality than another ○ *Don't argue with your superiors.* **2.** PRINTING = **superscript** *n.* **3.** RELIG SB IN CHARGE OF RELIGIOUS ORDER a head of a religious order or institution [14thC. Via Old French from Latin, literally 'higher', from *superus* 'above', from *super* (see SUPER-).] —**superiority** /soo pèeri órrəti/ *n.* —**superiorly** /soo pèeri ərli/ *adv.*

Superior, Lake /-/ lake in North America. The northernmost and westernmost of the Great Lakes, it is also the world's largest freshwater lake. Area: 82,100 sq. km/31,700 sq. mi. Depth: 406 m/1,333 ft. Length: 563 km/350 mi.

superior conjunction *n.* a position of a celestial body in which it is opposite the Earth on the far side of the Sun

superiority complex *n.* an exaggerated sense of being better than other people

superior planet *n.* a planet whose distance from the Sun is greater than that of the Earth. The superior planets are Mars, Jupiter, Saturn, Uranus, Neptune, and Pluto.

superjacent /soòpər jáyss'nt/ *adj.* lying on or above sth [Late 16thC. Formed from Latin *superjacere*, literally 'to lie above', from *jacere* 'to lie, throw' (see JET[2]).]

superjet /soòpər jet/ *n.* a large supersonic jet plane

superlative /soo púrlətiv/ *adj.* **1.** EXCELLENT of the highest quality or degree **2.** GRAM HIGHEST IN DEGREE OF COMPARISON expressing the highest degree of grammatical comparison of an adjective or adverb ○ *The superlative form of an adjective or adverb typically has the ending '-est'.* ■ *n.* **1.** GRAM GRAMMATICAL FORM the grammatical form expressing the highest degree of comparison ○ *Put 'tiny' into the superlative and you get 'tiniest'.* **2.** GRAM SUPERLATIVE ADJECTIVE OR ADVERB a superlative form of an adjective or adverb ○ *the difference between a comparative and a superlative* **3.** SB OR STH SUPERLATIVE sb or sth of the highest quality **4.** EXAGGERATED PRAISE an exaggerated description or way of referring to sb or sth, usually expressing admiration ○ *heaping superlatives on their performance* [14thC. Via Old French from Latin *superlativus*, from *superlat-*, the past participle stem of *superferre*, literally 'to carry above'.] —**superlatively** *adv.* —**superlativeness** *n.*

Super League *n.* an international rugby league competition that was introduced alongside or superseded various national Rugby League competitions. In Australia it is controversial as being a direct rival to the competition of the Australian Rugby League.

superliner /soòpər līnər/ *n.* a large luxurious ocean-going passenger ship

superlunary /soòpər loònəri/, **superlunar** /-loònər/ *adj.* **1.** ASTRON BEYOND THE MOON located beyond the Moon **2.** RELIG CELESTIAL belonging to a higher world or celestial plane [Early 17thC. Modelled on SUBLUNARY.]

superman /soòpər man/ (*plural* **-men** /-men/) *n.* **1.** EXCEPTIONAL MAN a man possessing exceptional or superhuman strength, abilities, or powers **2.** NIETZSCHE'S IDEAL MAN according to the philosophy of Nietzsche, an ideal man who through creativity and integrity is able to transcend good and evil and is the goal of human evolution [Early 20thC. Coined by George Bernard Shaw as a translation of German *Übermensch*, which was coined by Friedrich Nietzsche.]

WORD KEY: CULTURAL NOTE

Superman, a comic strip created by US writer Jerry Siegal and drawn by US artist Joseph Shuster which first appeared in 1938. The alter ego of 'mild-mannered reporter' Clark Kent, Superman is an almost invincible, crime-fighting superhero in a red cape who was originally sent to Earth as a child from the doomed planet Krypton. The story has been made into radio shows, musicals, television series, and feature films.

supermarket /soòpər maarkit/ *n.* a large self-service retail store selling food and household goods

supermax /soòpər maks/ *n.* US protected or made secure by the most extensive and elaborate security arrangements that are available or in current use ○ *a supermax penitentiary*

supermodel /soòpər mod'l/ *n.* one of an elite group of fashion models who are very well paid and in high demand by fashion designers and photographers

supernal /soo púrn'l/ *adj.* (*literary*) **1.** IN THE SKY coming from or located in the heavens **2.** HEAVENLY suited to or characteristic of the heavens [15thC. Via Old French from, ultimately, Latin *supernus* 'heavenly', from *super* (see SUPER-).] —**supernally** *adv.*

supernatant /soòpər náyt'nt/ *n.* LIQUID ON THE SURFACE a usually clear liquid above material deposited by precipitation, centrifugation, or sedimentation ■ *adj.* ON THE SURFACE lying or floating on the surface of a liquid after precipitation, centrifugation, or sedimentation [Mid-17thC. From Latin *supernatant-*, the present participle stem of *supernatare*, literally 'to float above', from *natare* (see NATANT).]

supernational /soòpər násh'nəl/ *adj.* = **supranational**

supernatural /soòpər náchərəl/ *adj.* **1.** NOT OF NATURAL WORLD relating or attributed to phenomena that cannot be explained by natural laws **2.** RELATING TO A DEITY relating or attributed to a deity **3.** MAGICAL relating or attributed to magic or the occult ■ *n.* **1.** SUPERNATURAL THINGS supernatural beings or phenomena **2.** WORLD OF SUPERNATURAL THINGS the realm of supernatural beings or phenomena —**supernaturally** *adv.* —**supernaturalness** *n.*

supernaturalism /soòpər náchərəlizəm/ *n.* **1.** STATE OF BEING SUPERNATURAL the quality or condition of being supernatural **2.** BELIEF IN SUPERNATURAL the belief that supernatural or divine beings and phenomena intervene in human events —**supernaturalist** *n.*, *adj.* —**supernaturalistic** /soòpər náchərə lístik/ *adj.*

supernormal /soòpər náwrm'l/ *adj.* **1.** BEYOND WHAT IS NORMAL exceeding what is normal or usual **2.** = **paranormal** —**supernormality** /soòpər nawr mállәti/ *n.* —**supernormally** /soòpər náwrm'li/ *adv.*

supernova /soòpər nōvə/ (*plural* **-vae** /-vee/ *or* **-vas**) *n.* a catastrophic explosion of a large star in the latter stages of stellar evolution, with a resulting short-lived luminosity from 10 to 100 million times that of the Sun

supernumerary /soòpər nyoòmərəri/ *adj.* **1.** EXTRA exceeding the usual number **2.** HR SUBSTITUTING employed as a substitute or extra worker ■ *n.* (*plural* **-ies**) **1.** SB OR STH EXTRA sb or sth in addition to the usual number **2.** THEATRE WALK-ON ACTOR an actor who appears on stage but has no lines to speak **3.** HR SUBSTITUTE EMPLOYEE sb employed as a substitute or extra worker [Early 17thC. From late Latin *supernumerarius*, from Latin *super* 'above' + *numerus* 'number'.]

superorder /soòpər awrdər/ *n.* a taxonomic category of related organisms ranking below a class and above an order

superordinate /soòpər áwrdinət/ *n.* **1.** LING UMBRELLA TERM a word whose meaning encompasses the meaning of another more specific word. 'Animal' is a superordinate of 'cat'. ◊ **hyponym 2.** SB OR STH SUPERIOR sb or sth of superior rank, status, or class [Early 17thC. Coined from SUPER- + SUBORDINATE.] —**superordinate** *adj.*

superorganism /soòpər áwrgənizəm/ *n.* a group of organisms functioning as a social unit. An insect colony is an example of a superorganism.

superovulation /soòpər ovjoò láysh'n/ *n.* increased frequency of ovulation or production of a large number of ova at one time. It is often caused by the administration of gonadotropin hormones, which are prescribed to induce ovulation in infertility. —**superovulate** /soòpər óvvjoò layt/ *vi.*

superplastic /soòpər plástik/ *adj.* used to describe alloys that are capable of being easily deformed and moulded at high temperatures without fracturing —**superplasticity** /soòpər plas tíssəti/ *n.*

superpose /soòpər pōz/ (**-poses, -posing, -posed**) *vt.* **1.** PLACE ON TOP OF ANOTHER to place or lay one object on top of or above another **2.** GEOM MAKE GEOMETRIC FIGURES COINCIDE to move one geometric figure so that it coincides exactly with another [Early 19thC. Origin uncertain: probably from French *superposer*, a back-formation from *superposition* 'superposition', from, ultimately, Latin *superponere* 'to place over', from *super-* (see SUPER-) + *ponere* 'to place'.] —**superposable** *adj.* —**superposed** *adj.* —**superposition** /soòpər pə zísh'n/ *n.*

superpower /soòpər powər/ *n.* **1.** POL POWERFUL NATION an extremely powerful nation with greater political, economic, or military power than most other nations, or with all three **2.** PHYS EXTREMELY HIGH POWER extremely high electrical or mechanical power —**superpowered** *adj.*

supersaturated /soòpər sáchə raytid/ *adj.* **1.** CONTAINING MORE SOLUTE THAN NORMAL used to describe a chemical solution containing a greater amount of solute than normally possible at a given temperature and pressure, often as a result of cooling **2.** CONTAINING MORE GASEOUS MATERIAL THAN NORMAL used to describe a vapour containing more gaseous material than normally possible at a given temperature and pressure —**supersaturation** /soòpər sachə ráysh'n/ *n.*

supersaver /soòpər sáyvər/ *n.* an airline, coach, or train ticket that is cheaper than the normal price and must usually be bought a certain amount of time before the date of travel [Late 20thC]

superscribe /soòpər skríb/ (**-scribes, -scribing, -scribed**) *vt.* to write or print sth such as a name or address above, outside, or on the surface of sth else

superscript /soòpərskript/ *n.* STH WRITTEN ABOVE ANOTHER CHARACTER a letter, character, or symbol that is written above, or above and to the right or left of, another character ■ *adj.* WRITTEN ABOVE ANOTHER CHARACTER written or printed as a superscript

superscription /soòpər skrípsh'n/ *n.* **1.** STH WRITTEN ABOVE STH ELSE sth that is written, printed, or engraved above, outside, or on the surface of sth else **2.** ACT OF SUPERSCRIBING STH the act of writing or printing sth above, outside, or on the surface of sth else

supersede /soòpər seèd/ (**-sedes, -seding, -seded**) *vt.* **1.** REPLACE STH LESS EFFICIENT to take the place or position of sth that is less efficient, less modern, or less appropriate, or cause sth to do this **2.** SUCCEED SB OR STH to succeed sb or sth in a particular role, office, or function (*formal*) [15thC. Via Old French *superceder* 'to refrain from', from Latin *supersedere* 'to be superior to', from *super-* (see SUPER-) + *sedere* 'to sit'.] —**supersedable** *adj.* —**supersedence** *n.* —**superseder** *n.*

WORD KEY: USAGE

Spelling trap: Note that ***supersede*** is correctly spelt *-sede* and not *-cede*. It is derived not from the Latin verb *cedere* 'to go' (as *intercede* and *precede* are) but from *sedere* 'to sit'.

supersensible /soòpər sénssəb'l/, **supersensory** /-sénssəri/ *adj.* above or beyond the perception of the senses —**supersensibly** *adv.*

supersensitive /soòpər sénssətiv/ *adj.* = **hypersensitive** —**supersensitively** *adv.* —**supersensitivity** /soòpər sénssə tívvəti/ *n.*

supersensory *adj.* = **supersensible**

superserver /soòpər survər/ *n.* an extremely powerful computer that controls a network or networks of other computers

supersonic /soòpər sónnik/ *adj.* produced by, capable of reaching, or relating to a speed that is faster than the speed at which sound travels through the air [Early 20thC. Coined from SUPER- + Latin *sonus* 'sound'.] —**supersonically** *adv.*

supersonics /soòpər sónniks/ *n.* the science or study of supersonic motion or phenomena (*takes a singular verb*)

supersonic transport *n.* a transport aircraft that travels at supersonic speed

superstar /soòpər staar/ *n.* sb who is extremely famous or successful, especially in sports or entertainment, and who has great public appeal —**superstardom** *n.*

superstition /soòpər stísh'n/ *n.* **1.** IRRATIONAL BELIEF an irrational but usually deep-seated belief in the magical effects of a particular action or ritual, especially in the likelihood that good or bad luck will result from performing it **2.** IRRATIONAL BELIEFS irrational and often quasi-religious belief in and reverence for the magical effects of certain actions and rituals or the magical powers of certain objects [15thC. Via Old French from the Latin stem *superstition-*, from *superstes* 'standing over' (in awe), from *stare* 'to stand' (see STATION).]

superstitious /sòopər stíshəss/ *adj.* **1.** BELIEVING IN SUPERSTITIONS convinced that performing or not performing certain actions brings good or bad luck, that certain events or phenomena are omens, and, generally, fearfully believing in a supernatural dimension to events **2.** BASED ON IRRATIONAL BELIEF based on a false or irrational belief in, or fear of, the supernatural

superstore /sòopər stawr/ *n.* **1.** VERY LARGE SUPERMARKET a very large supermarket or store offering a wider and more varied range of consumer goods than other stores of the same type **2.** SPECIALIST RETAILER a retail chain or single store that specializes in a range of related products offered at discount prices ○ *a computer superstore*

superstratum /sòopər straatəm, -straytəm/ (*plural* **-ta** /-tə/) *n.* **1.** OVERLYING LAYER a layer, especially of rock or sedimentation, on top of another one **2.** LING ELEMENTS OF CONQUERING LANGUAGE the language of an invading or colonizing population in relation to the language of an indigenous population that it changes or influences

superstring /sòopər string/ *n.* a hypothetical one-dimensional entity (**string**) of extremely short length held to be a fundamental component of matter in some theories of elementary particles involving supersymmetry

superstructure /sòopər strukchər/ *n.* **1.** NAUT UPPER PART OF SHIP the part of a ship above the main deck **2.** CONSTR VISIBLE PART OF BUILDING the part of a building above its foundations **3.** PART DEVELOPED ON BASE any physical or intellectual structure built on or developed from a fundamental form, base, or concept **4.** POL INSTITUTIONS ASSOCIATED WITH TYPE OF ECONOMY in Marxist theory, the complex of social, legal, and political institutions that are an extension and reflection of the type of economy operating in a given society —**superstructural** /sòopər strúkchərəl/ *adj.*

supersymmetry /sòopər símmətri/ *n.* a theory in physics proposing a type of symmetry that would apply to all elementary particles, both bosons and fermions

supertanker /sòopər tangkər/ *n.* a very large tanker ship, usually with a capacity of 275,000 tonnes/300,000 tons or more

supertax /sòopər taks/ *n.* = **surtax** *n.* 2

supertitle /sòopər tīt'l/ *n.* = **surtitle** [Late 20thC. Modelled on *subtitle*.]

supertonic /sòopər tonik/ *n.* the note one step above the tonic in a major or minor scale, or the harmony built upon this note

supervene /sòopər véen/ (**-venes, -vening, -vened**) *vi.* (*formal*) **1.** FOLLOW UNEXPECTEDLY to follow or come about unexpectedly, usually interrupting or changing what is going on **2.** FOLLOW IMMEDIATELY to follow immediately after sth [Mid-17thC. From Latin *supervenire*, literally 'to come above', from *venire* 'to come' (see VENUE).] —**supervenience** *n.* —**supervenient** *adj.* —**supervention** /-vénsh'n/ *n.*

supervise /sòopər vīz/ (**-vises, -vising, -vised**) *vti.* **1.** OVERSEE ACTIVITY to watch over a particular activity or task being carried out by other people and ensure that it is carried out correctly **2.** OVERSEE PEOPLE to be in charge of a group of people engaged in some activity and to keep order or ensure that they carry out a task adequately [Late 16thC. From medieval Latin *supervis-*, the past participle stem of *supervidere* 'to look over, oversee', from Latin *videre* 'to see' (see VISION).] —**supervision** /sòopər vízh'n/ *n.*

supervision order *n.* an order mandating the personal supervision by a named social worker or probation officer of a child involved in care proceedings

supervisor /sòopər vīzər/ *n.* **1.** BOSS sb whose job is to oversee and guide the work or activities of a group of other people **2.** *US* EDUC MAIN TEACHER OF SUBJECT a teacher or other school official who oversees the teaching and teachers of a single subject area **3.** UNIV TUTOR FOR A GRADUATE in some British universities, a teacher assigned to supervise the work of an individual student, especially research done by a postgraduate student —**supervisorship** *n.* —**supervisory** /sòopər vīzəri, sòopər vīzəri/ *adj.*

superwoman /sòopər wòomən/ (*plural* **-en** /-wimin/) *n.* **1.** HIGH ACHIEVER a woman who succeeds triumphantly in combining several roles, e.g. as worker, wife, mother, and homemaker, and does it all with apparent ease (*informal*) **2.** SUPERHUMAN WOMAN an imaginary or fictional woman with superhuman powers

supinate /sòopi nayt, syòo-/ (**-nates, -nating, -nated**) *v.* **1.** *vti.* TURN PALM UPWARDS to turn the hand so that the palm faces upwards, or be turned in this way **2.** *vti.* TURN SOLE UPWARDS to turn the foot so that the sole is facing upwards, or be turned in this way **3.** *vi.* LIE FACING UPWARDS to turn the face upwards, or lie in a supine position with the face upwards [Mid-19thC. From Latin *supinat-*, the past participle stem of *supinare* 'to turn backwards', from *supinus* 'backwards' (see SUPINE).] —**supination** /sòopi náysh'n, syòo-/ *n.*

supinator /sòopi naytər, syòo-/ *n.* a muscle, especially of the forearm, that brings about supination

supine /sòo pīn, syòo-/ *adj.* **1.** LYING ON THE BACK lying on the back and with the face upwards **2.** PALM UPWARDS with the palm of the hand facing upwards or away from the body **3.** LETHARGIC utterly passive or inactive, especially in a situation where a vigorous reaction is called for ■ *n.* GRAM TYPE OF LATIN NOUN a Latin noun formed from a past participle stem and having only accusative and ablative inflections [15thC. From Latin *supinus* 'lying on the back'. Ultimately from an Indo-European word meaning 'under, up', which is also the ancestor of English *up*, *above*, and *subterfuge*.]

supp. *abbr.* **1.** supplement **2.** supplementary

supper /súppər/ *n.* **1.** EVENING MEAL a light meal eaten in the evening **2.** MAIN EVENING MEAL the main meal of the day when taken in the evening **3.** SOCIAL EVENT an evening social event that includes a meal [13thC. From Old French *soper* 'to eat supper', from *soupe* 'sop, broth' (see SOUP).] ◇ **sing for your supper** to work or do sth in exchange for your food and board, or for sth that you want

WORD KEY: USAGE

See Usage note at ***dinner***.

WORD KEY: CULTURAL NOTE

The Last Supper, a painting by Italian artist Leonardo da Vinci (1495–97). Painted directly onto a wall in the monastery of Santa Maria delle Grazie in Milan, it depicts the moment when Jesus Christ declares that one of his companions will betray him. It is noted for its magnificent composition and powerful depiction of the outrage of the disciples, the serenity of Jesus Christ, and the guilt of Judas.

suppertime /súppər tīm/ *n.* the time at which supper is served or eaten

suppl. *abbr.* **1.** supplement **2.** supplementary

supplant /sə plaánt/ (**-plants, -planting, -planted**) *vt.* **1.** OUST SB to take sb's place or position by force or intrigue **2.** REPLACE to take the place of sth, especially sth much used, inferior, outmoded, or irrelevant [13thC. Directly or via French from Latin *supplantare* 'to trip up, overthrow', from *sub-* 'up from beneath' + *planta* 'sole of the foot' (see PLANT).] —**supplantation** /súpplaan táysh'n/ *n.* —**supplanter** /sə plaántər/ *n.*

supple /súpp'l/ (**-pler, -plest**) *adj.* **1.** FLEXIBLE flexible and elastic **2.** MOVING EASILY capable of bending, stretching, and moving with ease, fluidity, and grace **3.** ADAPTABLE adaptable and responsive in grappling with problems or dealing with new challenges **4.** COMPLIANT excessively compliant and agreeable (*literary*) [13thC. Via French from, ultimately, Latin *supplex* 'submissive', literally 'bending under', from *-plex* 'fold' (source of English *duplex*).] —**supplely** *adv.* —**suppleness** *n.*

supplejack /súpp'l jak/ (*plural* **-jacks** *or* **-jack**) *n.* **1.** WOODY VINE a woody vine of the southeastern United States with tiny white flowers and bluish fruits. Latin name: *Berchemia scandens*. **2.** TROPICAL VINE a tropical American vine whose wood is used for walking sticks. Latin name: *Paullinia curvassica*. [*Supple* from its pliant stem]

supplement *n.* /súpplimənt/ **1.** ADDITION an addition to sth to increase its size or make up for a deficiency ○ *a useful supplement to the family income* **2.** PUBL PUBLICATION a publication that amplifies or corrects one already published **3.** PRESS PERIODICAL PART an additional section included in or sold with a magazine or newspaper, especially an additional section that appears regularly **4.** FOOD FOOD a substance with a particular nutritional value taken to make up for a real or supposed deficiency in diet **5.** COMM EXTRA CHARGE a charge payable in addition to the basic charge for a special service or under certain conditions **6.** MATH ANGLE OR ARC an angle or arc that, when added to another, makes 180° or a semicircle ■ *vt.* /súppli ment/ (**-ments, -menting, -mented**) **1.** MAKE ADDITION TO STH to increase, extend, or improve sth by adding sth to it ○ *supplemented their meagre diet with vitamins* **2.** BE ADDITIONAL PART to be a supplement to sth ○ *Her remarks supplemented the report.* [14thC. From Latin *supplementum*, from *supplere* 'to fill out, complete' (see SUPPLY).] —**supplemental** /súppli mént'l/ *adj.* —**supplementally** *adv.* —**supplementation** /súppli men táysh'n/ *n.* —**supplementer** /súppli mentər/ *n.*

supplementary /súppli méntəri/ *adj.* **1.** ADDITIONAL additional to an existing one, or to the normal number or amount **2.** COMPLETING making up for sth that is lacking ■ *n.* (*plural* **-ries**) STH ADDITIONAL an additional thing, person, or question —**supplementarily** *adv.*

supplementary angle *n.* an angle that when added to another angle makes up 180°

supplementary benefit *n.* an allowance formerly paid weekly by the state to bring a person's or family's income up to what was considered to be a minimum acceptable level

suppletion /sə pléesh'n/ *n.* the use of an unrelated word to fill the gap when some inflected or derived forms of a word are missing, as 'was' forms the past tense of 'to be' —**suppletive** *adj.*

suppliant /súppli ənt/ *adj.* ENTREATING expressing a humble but heart-felt appeal to sb who has the power to grant a request (*formal*) ■ *n.* = **supplicant** *n.* [15thC. From French, present participle of *supplier* 'to supplicate', from Latin *supplicare*, literally 'to bend under', from *supplex* (see SUPPLE).] —**suppliance** *n.* —**suppliantly** *adv.*

supplicant /súpplikənt/ *n.* HUMBLE PETITIONER sb who addresses a humble but heart-felt appeal to sb who has the power to grant his or her request (*formal*) ■ *adj.* = **suppliant** *adj.* [Late 16thC. From Latin *supplicant-*, present participle stem of *supplicare* (see SUPPLIANT).] —**supplicatory** /súpplikətəri, -káytəri/ *adj.*

supplication /súppli káysh'n/ *n.* (*formal*) **1.** APPEAL MADE TO SB IN AUTHORITY a humble appeal to sb who has the power to grant a request **2.** ADDRESSING OF REQUESTS the addressing of humble requests and prayers to sb with the power to grant them —**supplicate** /súppli kayt/ *vti.*

supply /sə plī/ *vt.* (**-plies, -plying, -plied**) **1.** PROVIDE to give, sell, or make available sth that is wanted or needed by sb or sth ○ *supplied equipment for the expedition* **2.** SATISFY A NEED to satisfy a need or requirement (*formal*) **3.** MAKE UP FOR A LACK to make up for a deficiency, loss, or lack **4.** SERVE AS A SUBSTITUTE to act as a substitute for sb, especially in a church or a school (*formal*) ■ *n.* (*plural* **-plies**) **1.** AVAILABLE AMOUNT an amount or quantity of sth available for use ○ *a plentiful supply of food and drink* **2.** PROVISION the act or business of bringing sth needed to the people or things that need it, or the system that brings sth needed ○ *the supply of electric power to villages in the mountains* **3.** ECON QUANTITY AVAILABLE IN A MARKET the quantity of a type of goods or services available in a market at a given time **4.** SUBSTITUTE sb who acts as a substitute, especially for a preacher (*formal*) **5.** EDUC SUPPLY TEACHER a supply teacher (*informal*) ■ **supplies** *npl.* NEEDED THINGS the things, especially food and equipment, that a group of people need to survive and operate, or that are needed to carry out a particular task or activity ○ *Our supplies were running very low.* [14thC. Via Old French *supplier* 'to meet a deficiency' from Latin *supplere*, literally 'to fill up', from *plere* 'to fill' (source of English *complete* and *deplete*).] —**suppliable** *adj.* —**supplier** *n.* ◇ **in short supply** present or available only in small or insufficient quantities

supply and demand *n.* the relationship between the availability of a good or service and the need or desire for it among consumers

supply-side economics *n.* economic policies that promote conditions favouring the producers of goods and services (*takes a singular or plural verb*)

supply teacher *n.* a teacher who takes the place of another temporarily. US term **substitute teacher**

support /sə páwrt/ *vt.* (**-ports, -porting, -ported**) **1.** KEEP FROM FALLING to keep sth or sb upright or in place, or prevent sth or sb from falling ○ *Those pillars support the roof.* **2.** BEAR CERTAIN WEIGHT to be strong enough to hold a particular object or weight in place without breaking or giving way ○ *Are you sure the ice is thick enough to support the weight?* **3.** SUSTAIN FINANCIALLY to provide sb with money and the other necessities of life over a period of time ○ *She succeeds in supporting her family on what she earns in a part-time job.* **4.** GIVE ACTIVE HELP AND ENCOURAGEMENT to give active help, encouragement, or money to sb or sth ○ *We support the charity through voluntary work.* **5.** BE IN FAVOUR OF STH to be in favour of sth such as a cause, policy, organization, or sports team and wish to see it succeed **6.** BE PRESENT AND GIVE ENCOURAGEMENT to give encouragement to sb or sth by being present at an event **7.** GIVE ASSISTANCE OR COMFORT to give assistance or comfort to sb in difficulty or distress ○ *He supported me throughout my crisis.* **8.** PROVIDE TECHNICAL SUPPORT to provide technical support for a computing system or package **9.** CORROBORATE to give sth greater credibility by being consistent with it or providing further evidence for it ○ *There is further evidence that supports the defendant's claim.* **10.** ARTS PLAY SMALL ROLE ALONGSIDE SB to play a subsidiary role in a play or film alongside another actor with a leading part **11.** TOLERATE STH to put up with sth unpleasant (*literary*) ■ *n.* **1.** STH THAT SUPPORTS a means of holding sth upright or in place, or of preventing it from falling ○ *If you remove those supports the plank will fall down.* **2.** REINFORCEMENT TO HOLD THINGS IN PLACE physical force or reinforcement used to hold things steady or in place ○ *Stakes give the plant extra support.* **3.** ACTIVE ASSISTANCE OR ENCOURAGEMENT active assistance and encouragement to, or an approving and encouraging attitude towards, sb or sth ○ *Support for the cause continues to rise.* **4.** HELP IN CRISIS the encouragement and help sb gets from others, e.g. friends, family, and charitable organizations, especially during times of crisis and change. It may be emotional, moral, or practical. **5.** SUPPORTIVE PERSON sb who provides assistance, money, encouragement, or comfort **6.** SUPPORTERS the supporters of an organization such as a political party, or of an individual, considered as a group ○ *His support is drawn mainly from the rural areas.* **7.** ARTS SUPPORTING BANDS OR ENTERTAINERS the other band or bands, or the other entertainers, appearing in a programme along with the main attraction **8.** CLOTHES SUPPORTING GARMENT a garment that supports or protects a part of the body, especially one used by male athletes to protect the genitals. US term **athletic supporter** [14thC. Via French from Latin *supportare*, literally 'to bear up', from *portare* 'to carry' (see PORT[1]).] —**supportability** /sə páwrtə bílləti/ *n.* —**supportable** /sə páwrtəb'l/ *adj.* —**supportably** *adv.* ◇ **in support of** in order to support sb or sth

support area *n.* an area with a supply of military material and personnel standing ready for use

supporter /sə páwrtər/ *n.* **1.** SB WHO SUPPORTS STH sb who supports a cause, person, idea, course of action, political party, or sports team ○ *greeted by a crowd of supporters* **2.** HERALDRY STANDING FIGURE either of a pair of standing figures on either side of a shield in a coat of arms

support group *n.* a group of people with a problem or concern in common who meet regularly to discuss it and support one another

support hose *npl. US* = **support stockings**

supporting /sə páwrting/ *adj.* **1.** SECONDARY accompanying and assisting, but secondary to, the main action or the main participants in sth ○ *a supporting role* **2.** ARTS APPEARING OR SHOWN WITH MAIN ATTRACTION appearing in the same film, play, or programme as the main star or attraction

supportive /sə páwrtiv/ *adj.* giving support, especially moral or emotional support —**supportiveness** *n.*

support level *n.* the price at which a security whose price has been falling begins to attract investors again because of its intrinsic worth

support stockings *npl.* elasticized stockings that support the veins in the lower legs, used by people with varicose veins or bad circulation

support system *n.* the group of friends, colleagues, or professionals available to help a person or organization when required

supposable /sə pṓzəb'l/ *adj.* considered to be possible ○ *a supposable scenario* —**supposably** *adv.*

suppose /sə pṓz/ (**-poses, -posing, -posed**) *v.* **1.** *vti.* BELIEVE TO BE TRUE to believe or imagine sth to be the case ○ *I suppose you haven't heard the news.* **2.** *vi.* IMAGINE AS POSSIBLE to consider or imagine sth to be a possibility ○ *Suppose that he doesn't know about your plan.* **3.** *vt.* TAKE AS PRECONDITION to require sth as a precondition ○ *Your plan supposes that there are enough presents to go around.* **4.** *vt.* BE REQUIRED TO DO STH to be expected to do sth as the result of a previous agreement or arrangement or an obligation (*usually passive*) ○ *You're supposed to leave tomorrow.* **5.** *vt.* BE EXPECTED TO DO STH to be expected to do sth as a consequence of a particular action or set of conditions (*usually passive*) ○ *The light's supposed to come on when the tank is almost empty.* **6.** *vti.* AGREE TO STH RELUCTANTLY used when agreeing to do sth or that sth is the case, reluctantly, uncertainly, or noncommittally ○ *I suppose we'd better get going.* [14thC. Via French from, ultimately, Latin *supponere*, literally 'to place under', from *ponere* 'to place' (see POSITION). The meaning was influenced by Greek *hypothesis* 'supposition'.] —**supposer** *n.*

supposed /sə pṓzd, sə pṓzid/ *adj.* accepted, at least by some, as correct, real, or having a particular quality, but on slender or uncertain evidence ○ *Frankly, I'm very dubious about this supposed brilliant idea of his.*

supposedly /sə pṓzidli/ *adv.* as some people believe, or as people were led to believe ○ *He was supposedly going to pick us up after work.* ○ *a supposedly instant remedy*

supposing /sə pṓzing/ *conj.* imagining or assuming sth to be the case ○ *Supposing she comes, will you let her in?*

supposition /súppə zísh'n/ *n.* **1.** HYPOTHESIS sth that it is suggested might be true, or that is accepted as true, on the basis of some evidence but without proof **2.** MENTAL ACT OF SUPPOSING the mental act of supposing sth to be the case, or ideas that result from supposing, especially as opposed to ideas based on firm evidence ○ *All this is mere supposition.* [Late 16thC. Directly and via French from the Latin stem *supposition-*, from *supposit-*, the past participle stem of *supponere* (see SUPPOSE). Translation of Greek *hupothesis.*] —**suppositional** *adj.* —**suppositionally** *adv.*

suppositious /súppə zíshəss/ *adj.* based on some evidence but without proof (*formal*)

supposititious /sə pózzi tíshəss/ *adj.* substituted for sth else in order to deceive (*formal*) [Early 17thC. From Latin *supposititius*, from *suppositus*, the past participle of *supponere* (see SUPPOSE).] —**supposititiously** *adv.*

suppositive /sə pózzitiv/ *adj.* EXPRESSING SUPPOSITION expressing or relating to supposition, or introducing a clause expressing a supposition ■ *n.* SUPPOSITIVE CONJUNCTION a conjunction such as 'if', 'provided that', or 'supposing' that introduces a clause expressing a supposition

suppository /sə pózzitəri/ (*plural* **-ries**) *n.* a medicated solid preparation, usually in the form of a cylinder or cone, that melts at body temperature and is designed to be inserted into the rectum, vagina, or urethra. The drug or active ingredient is incorporated in an inert base, commonly cocoa butter, glycerinated gelatin, or polyethylene glycol. [14thC. From medieval Latin *suppositorium*, from Latin *supposit-*, the past participle stem of *supponere* 'to place under' (see SUPPOSE).]

suppress /sə préss/ (**-presses, -pressing, -pressed**) *vt.* **1.** PUT AN END TO STH to put an end to sth, especially sth perceived as a threat, by the use of force or a prohibition ○ *suppressed all complaints with a gagging order* **2.** PREVENT STH to prevent sth from happening, operating, or becoming apparent, or restrain sth and limit its effects **3.** STOP SPREAD OR PUBLICATION OF STH to prevent information or evidence from becoming known, or written material from being published ○ *The report was suppressed for political reasons.* **4.** PSYCHOL RESIST STH CONSCIOUSLY to resist particular thoughts or feelings consciously as they arise, and try to banish them from the mind ○ *Try to suppress your anger.* **5.** ELECTRON ENG DIMINISH OSCILLATION to reduce unwanted noise or oscillation in a circuit or unwanted frequencies in a signal **6.** BIOL REDUCE BODILY FUNCTION to cause or undergo the reduction or cessation of a normal bodily function, e.g. menstruation or growth **7.** GENETICS INHIBIT GENE EFFECT to cancel or reverse the effects of a gene [14thC. From Latin *suppress-*, the past participle stem of *supprimere*, literally 'to push down', from *premere* 'to press' (see PRESS).] —**suppresser** *n.* —**suppressibility** /sə préssə bílləti/ *n.* —**suppressible** /sə préssəb'l/ *adj.*

suppressant *n.* a substance, medication, or activity that restrains or limits the effects of sth (*often used in combination*) ○ *an appetite suppressant*

suppression /sə présh'n/ *n.* **1.** FORCEFUL PREVENTION conscious and forceful action to put an end to sth, destroy it, or prevent it from becoming known **2.** STATE OF CONSTRAINT the state of being forcefully restrained or held back **3.** PSYCHOL AVOIDANCE OF THOUGHTS AND FEELINGS conscious avoidance or inhibition of particular memories, desires, or thoughts **4.** ELECTRON ENG DIMINISHING OF OSCILLATION reduction of unwanted noise or oscillation in a circuit or of unwanted frequencies in a signal **5.** BIOL DEVELOPMENTAL FAILURE the failure of an organ, tissue, or part to develop **6.** PHYSIOL CESSATION OF BODILY FUNCTION the reduction or stoppage of a normal bodily function, e.g. secretion or excretion. ◊ **immunosuppression** **7.** MED REMOVAL OF SYMPTOMS the lessening or abolition of a symptom or the outward signs of a disease **8.** GENETICS REVERSAL OF MUTATION the cancellation or reversal of the effect of a gene, especially of one genetic mutation by another

suppressive /sə préssiv/ *adj.* having the effect of suppressing sth —**suppressively** *adv.*

suppressor /sə préssər/ *n.* **1.** GENETICS SUPPRESSING GENE a gene that prevents the expression of another gene **2.** ELECTRON ENG SUPPRESSING DEVICE a device that reduces unwanted interference or current in a circuit

suppressor T cell, **suppressor cell** *n.* a T cell that diminishes or suppresses the immune response to an antigen of B cells and other T cells

suppurate /súppyoo rayt/ (**-rates, -rating, -rated**) *vi.* to produce or discharge pus as a result of an injury or infection [Mid-16thC. From Latin *suppurat-*, the past participle stem of *suppurare*, from *pus* (see PUS).] —**suppuration** /súpyoo ráysh'n/ *n.* —**suppurative** /súppyoorətiv, -raytiv/ *adj.*

supra /sóoprə/ *adv.* used in formal writing to refer the reader back to sth at an earlier point in the same text (*formal*) [Early 16thC. From Latin, 'above'.]

supra- *prefix.* **1.** over, on top of ○ *suprarenal* **2.** transcending ○ *supranational* [From Latin *supra* 'above, beyond' (source of English *soprano*). Related to *super* 'above, over' (see SUPER-).]

supralapsarian /sóoprə lap sáiri ən/ *n.* sb who believes in or expounds the Calvinist view that God preordained the Fall, and had preordained the salvation of some souls in advance of it [Mid-17thC. Coined from SUPRA- + Latin *lapsus* 'sin, fall' (see LAPSE).] —**supralapsarianism** *n.*

supraliminal /sóoprə límmin'l/ *adj.* at or above the threshold of consciousness —**supraliminally** *adv.*

supramolecular /sóoprə mə lékyoolər/ *adj.* **1.** MORE COMPLEX THAN A MOLECULE more complex in form than a molecule **2.** COMPOSED OF MOLECULES composed of more than one molecule

supranational /sóoprə násh'nəl/ *adj.* not limited by the concerns or boundaries of a single nation —**supranationalism** *n.* —**supranationally** *adv.*

supraorbital /soopra áwrbit'l/ *adj.* located above the bony socket (**orbit**) of the eye

suprarenal /soopra reen'l/ *adj.* located above the kidneys

suprasegmental /soopra seg ment'l/ *adj.* connected with features of speech such as pitch and stress that accompany rather than constitute phonemes — **suprasegmentally** *adv.*

supremacist /soo prémmassist, syoo-/ *n.* sb who holds the view that a particular group is innately superior to others and therefore is entitled to dominate them (*usually used in combination*)

supremacy /soo prémmassi, syoo-/ *n.* a position of superiority or authority over all others [Mid-16thC. Formed from SUPREME, on the model of *primacy*.]

suprematism /soo prémmatizam, syoo-/ *n.* a school of cubist painting from early 20th-century Russia [Mid-20thC. From Russian *suprematizm*, from French *suprématie* 'supremacy'.] —**suprematist** *n.*

supreme /soo preem, syoo-/ *adj.* **1.** ABOVE ALL OTHERS above all others in power, authority, rank, status, or skill ○ *holding supreme authority* **2.** HIGHEST IN DEGREE of the greatest or most admirable kind ○ *a supreme example of the architect's skill* **3.** ULTIMATE greater than any that have gone before, or the greatest possible ○ *the supreme sacrifice* **4.** IN THE HIGHEST DEGREE in the highest degree or of the most unmitigated kind ○ *viewed them with supreme contempt* [15thC. From Latin *supremus*, literally 'uppermost', from *superus* 'upper', from *super* 'above' (see SUPER-).] —**supremely** *adv.*

suprême /soo preem, syoo-, -prém/ *n.* **1.** FINEST CUT the finest cut from any piece of meat, especially boneless breast of chicken ■ *adj.* WITH SUPRÊME SAUCE served with a suprême sauce ○ *chicken suprême* [Early 19thC. From French, 'supreme'.]

Supreme Being *n.* God

supreme commander *n.* the highest ranking and controlling military officer in a theatre of war

Supreme Court *n.* **1.** = Supreme Court of Judicature **2.** HIGHEST COURT in the United States, the highest federal court, consisting of nine justices appointed by the president and making decisions solely on constitutional matters **3.** HIGHEST STATE COURT the highest appellate court in many states of the United States **4.** HIGHEST COURT IN COUNTRY the highest court in a country, or in a state or territory of a federation

Supreme Court of Judicature, **Supreme Court** *n.* the highest national court in England and Wales consisting of two divisions, the High Court of Justice and the Court of Appeal

suprême sauce *n.* a rich sauce made of chicken or veal stock with added cream and egg yolks

Supreme Soviet *n.* the two-chamber national legislature of the former Soviet Union, or a similar legislature in any of the former Soviet republics

supremo /soo prée mo, syoo-/ *n.* (*plural* -**mos**) *n.* sb with overriding authority in a particular sphere (*informal*) [Mid-20thC. From Spanish (*generalísimo*) *supremo* 'supreme commander'.]

supt, **Supt** *abbr.* superintendent

suq *n.* = souk

sur- *prefix.* **1.** over, above, on top of ○ *surprint* **2.** additional, extra ○ *surcharge* [Via French from Latin *super* (see SUPER-)]

sura /soora/ *n.* a chapter of the Koran [Early 17thC. From Arabic *sūra*, of uncertain origin: probably from Syriac *šūrtā* 'scripture'.]

Surabaya /soora bí a/ city on northeastern Java Island, Indonesia. Population: 2,473,272 (1990).

surah /soora/ *n.* a twilled silk or rayon fabric, used in making women's clothing [Late 19thC. Anglicization of French *surat* 'Surat', the town in India where it was first produced.]

sural /sooral, syoo-/ *adj.* relating to the calf of the leg (*technical*) [Early 17thC. Formed from Latin *sura* 'calf of the leg', of unknown origin.]

surat /soo rat, soo rát/ *n.* a coarse cotton fabric formerly produced in and around the town of Surat in India

Surat /soo rát, sooraat/ city, port, and administrative headquarters of Surat District, Gujarat State, western India. Population: 1,496,943 (1991).

surbase /súr bayss/ *n.* an architectural moulding at the top of a base such as a pedestal or baseboard — **surbasement** /sur báyssmant/ *n.*

surbased[1] /súr bayst/ *adj.* featuring an architectural moulding at the top of a base

surbased[2] /sur báyst/ *adj.* used to describe an arch with a rise of less than half its span [Mid-18thC. From French *surbaissé*, the past participle of *surbaisser* 'to flatten', from *baisser* 'to lower', ultimately from medieval Latin *bassus* 'low'.]

surburbanise *vt.* = surburbanize

surcease /sur seess/ *vti.* (-**ceases**, -**ceasing**, -**ceased**) STOP DOING STH to cease, or bring sth to an end or stop doing it (*formal*) ■ *n.* STOPPAGE a cessation, especially a temporary one (*literary*) [15thC. Via Anglo-Norman *surseser* (influenced by CEASE) from, ultimately, Latin *supersedere* 'to refrain' (see SUPERSEDE).]

surcharge /súr chaarj/ *v.* (-**charges**, -**charging**, -**charged**) **1.** *vti.* CHARGE EXTRA to add an additional charge to the amount sb has to pay **2.** *vti.* OVERCHARGE to charge sb too much for sth **3.** *vt.* STAMPS RAISE STAMP VALUE BY OVERPRINTING to overprint an existing postage stamp so as to increase its face value **4.** *vt.* OVERBURDEN to overburden sb or sth, or overload sth such as a ship (*literary*) ■ *n.* **1.** EXTRA CHARGE an excess or extra charge **2.** STAMPS MARK ON STAMP a mark on a postage stamp increasing its face value [15thC. From Old French *surcharger*, from *chargier* 'to charge' (see CHARGE).] —**surcharger** *n.*

surcingle /súr sing g'l/ *n.* **1.** EQU STRAP AROUND HORSE a broad band fastened around the body of a horse to hold a rug or pack in place **2.** CLOTHES BELT FOR CASSOCK a belt worn around a priest's cassock (*archaic*) [14thC. From Old French *surcingle*, literally 'belt over', from *cengle* 'belt, girdle', from Latin *cingulum* (see CINGULUM).]

Surcoat

surcoat /súr kōt/ *n.* **1.** TUNIC WORN OVER ARMOUR a short tunic worn over armour in medieval times **2.** SLEEVELESS CEREMONIAL GARMENT a short sleeveless garment worn as part of the ceremonial costume of an order of knighthood [14thC. From Old French *surcote*, literally 'overcoat', from *cote* 'coat' (see COAT).]

surd /surd/ *n.* **1.** MATH IRRATIONAL ROOT OR NUMBER an irrational root or irrational number, or an expression containing one or the other **2.** PHON VOICELESS SOUND a consonant pronounced without vibration of the vocal cords [Mid-16thC. From Latin *surdus* 'unable to hear or speak'.]

sure /shoor, shawr/ *adj.* **1.** DEFINITELY TRUE unquestionably true or real and not in doubt ○ *One thing is sure, we'll never make the same mistake again!* **2.** FIRMLY BELIEVING believing strongly and for a good reason, or knowing for a fact that sth is true or the case ○ *Are you sure that she understood you?* **3.** BOUND TO inevitably going to do sth or to happen, or confidently expected to be going to do sth or to happen ○ *He's sure to notice something's missing.* **4.** CERTAIN TO OBTAIN STH definitely able to or definitely going to obtain or achieve sth ○ *Many people book early in order to be sure of getting the best seats.* **5.** VERY CONFIDENT very confident about sth, especially personal beliefs or abilities ○ *It was her self-confidence that made her so sure of her answer.* **6.** ALWAYS EFFECTIVE effective, accurate, and reliable at all times ○ *His aggressive manner is a sure sign that he is fright-* ened. **7.** FIRM AND SECURE firm, secure, and steady ○ *The fashion had gained a sure hold on every boy.* **8.** UNERRING showing both confidence and competence ○ *a sure grasp of the complexities of the situation* **9.** DEPENDABLE able to be safely relied on ○ *a sure friend in time of trouble* ■ *adv.* US (*informal*) **1.** UNDOUBTEDLY used to give emphasis to sth that sb is saying and to indicate that sb does not expect anyone to disagree with it ○ *This sure tastes good.* **2.** YES used to indicate emphatic or enthusiastic assent ○ *I asked him if he'd like to come and he said, 'Sure!'* [14thC. Via Old French from Latin *securus* (see SECURE).] —**sureness** *n.* ◇ **be sure** and *or* **to do sth** used to tell sb to remember to do sth ○ *Be sure and remember to introduce us.* ◇ **for sure 1.** without a doubt, or inevitably (*informal*) **2.** definitely and precisely ◇ **make sure (that) 1.** to take the necessary action to have sth done or make sth happen **2.** to check that sth is the case, or that sth has been done as instructed or requested ◇ **sure enough** as was expected ◇ **to be sure** used when admitting or agreeing that sth is true, even though it may not agree with most of what you are saying

— WORD KEY: USAGE —
We sure are glad to see you! The use of *sure* as an intensifying adverb is characteristic of informal American usage and has not fully entered British use except as a conscious Americanism. Note that it does not mean the same as *surely*, which is more judgmental in tone: *They surely don't want us to pay for this?*

sure-fire *adj.* always successful or effective (*informal*)

sure-footed *adj.* **1.** UNLIKELY TO STUMBLE OR FALL skilled and confident in moving or climbing, and so unlikely to stumble or fall **2.** CONFIDENT confident and competent, and so unlikely to err —**surefootedly** *adv.* —**sure-footedness** *n.*

surely /shoorli, sháwr-/ *adv.* **1.** USED TO INVITE A RESPONSE used as a means of getting sb to confirm, deny, agree, or disagree with sth being said, by adding in an element of challenging self-assurance or considerable hesitancy ○ *Surely you've met before.* **2.** WITHOUT FAIL definitely or unavoidably ○ *slowly but surely* **3.** US WITHOUT DOUBT without a doubt or without fail ○ *Did he get his message across? He surely did.* **4.** *Southern US* YES used to show ready agreement

sure thing *n.* STH CERTAIN sth that can be relied on to happen or to be successful (*informal*) ■ *adv.* US YES OF COURSE used to express assent, agreement, or willingness to do sth (*informal*)

surety /shoorati, sháwr-/ *n.* (*plural* -**ties**) *n.* **1.** LAW LEGAL INSTRUMENT a pledge, bond, or guarantee against loss or damage **2.** GUARANTOR sb who assumes responsibility for another's obligations in case of default, particularly by giving a guarantee **3.** CERTAINTY the condition or quality of being sure (*formal*) [14thC. Via Old French *surete* from Latin *securitas*, from *securus* 'secure' (see SECURE).] —**suretyship** *n.*

Surf: A surfer rides a wave at La Jolla Beach, California

Popperfoto

surf /surf/ *n.* FOAMY WAVES the lines of foamy waves that break on a seashore or reef ○ *play in the surf* ■ *v.* (**surfs, surfing, surfed**) **1.** *vi.* USE A SURFBOARD to ride waves on a surfboard **2.** *vt.* RIDE WAVES IN A PARTICULAR AREA to go surfing in a particular place ○ *Have you surfed Waikiki?* **3.** *vti.* COMPUT SEARCH MEDIUM FOR ENTERTAINMENT to go on the Internet for recreation, frequently changing the site [Late 17thC. Origin unknown.] —**surfable** *adj.* —**surfer** *n.* —**surfing** *n.* —**surfy** *adj.*

surface /súrfiss/ *n.* (*plural* **-faces**) **1.** OUTER PART the outermost or uppermost part of a thing, the one that is usually presented to the outside world, and can be seen and touched **2.** UPPER PART OF EARTH, SEA, WATER the part of the Earth, the sea, or any water that meets the atmosphere **3.** SOLID FLAT AREA a solid flat area, e.g. on top of a fitment or piece of furniture, especially an area on which it is suitable to work **4.** THIN APPLIED OUTER LAYER a relatively thin outer layer or coating applied to sth, usually to give it a smooth finish ○ *a nonstick surface* **5.** SUPERFICIAL PART the superficial parts or aspects of sth, especially when contrasted with the essence of the thing **6.** GEOM TWO-DIMENSIONAL EXTENT a flat or curved continuous area definable in two dimensions ○ *the surface of a sphere* ■ *adj.* **1.** USED ON SURFACE occurring or used on, or relating to, the surface of sth ○ *surface lubricants* **2.** SUPERFICIAL applying only to the outermost or uppermost part **3.** APPARENT put on for effect and not natural, deep-seated, or deeply felt **4.** ON LAND OR SEA operating or transported over land or sea but not in the air ■ *v.* (**-faces, -facing, -faced**) **1.** *vi.* COME TO THE TOP to come to or appear at the surface, especially of water ○ *She surfaced after a dive of 20 minutes.* **2.** *vi.* APPEAR to reappear after being hidden or out of reach for a time ○ *She surfaced in Berlin after the war.* **3.** *vi.* BECOME KNOWN to become apparent or known ○ *The information surfaced during a routine investigation.* **4.** *vi.* WAKE UP OR GET UP to wake up, or get out of bed (*informal*) ○ *She didn't surface till three o'clock the next afternoon.* **5.** *vt.* GIVE A SURFACE TO STH to provide sth with a surface, especially with a smooth outer layer ○ *surfacing the road* **6.** *vt.* TREAT A SURFACE to treat a surface, especially in order to smooth or perfect it **7.** *vi.* MINING WORK NEAR THE TOP to mine at or near the Earth's surface [Early 17thC. From French, formed from *sur-* 'upon' and *face* (see FACE), on the model of Latin *superficies* 'surface' (see SUPERFICIES).] —**surfaceless** *adj.* —**surfacer** *n.* ◇ **on the surface** to outward appearances or when examined superficially ○ *appears cool and collected on the surface* ◇ **scratch the surface** to deal with only a very small or relatively unimportant part of sth

surface-active *adj.* having the property of reducing the surface tension of a liquid so that the liquid spreads out, rather than collecting in droplets

surface mail *n.* mail that is transported by sea or land, as opposed to by air

surface noise *n.* noise produced as a record player stylus travels over a revolving record, caused by friction, dust, scratches, or static electricity on the record

surface runoff *n.* the flow of water over the surface of the ground occurring when rainfall is not absorbed into the soil or evaporated

surface structure *n.* in certain types of grammar, a representation of the sequence of syntactic elements that constitute an actual phrase or sentence. ◊ **deep structure**

surface tension *n.* the property of liquids that gives their surfaces a slightly elastic quality and enables them to form into separate drops. It is caused by the interaction of molecules at or near the surface that tend to cohere and contract the surface into the smallest possible area. Symbol γ, '

surface-to-air *adj.* launched from a ship or from the ground against a target in the air ○ *surface-to-air missiles*

surface-to-surface *adj.* launched from a ship or from the ground against another ship or a target on the ground ○ *a surface-to-surface missile*

surfactant /sur fáktənt/ *n.* **1.** SUBSTANCE REDUCING SURFACE TENSION OF LIQUIDS an agent, e.g. a detergent or a drug, that reduces the surface tension of liquids so that the liquid spreads out, rather than collecting in droplets **2.** PHYSIOL SUBSTANCE SECRETED IN LUNGS a surface-active lipoprotein substance secreted naturally in the lungs, lack of which causes respiratory problems especially in premature babies [Mid-20thC. Coined from SURFACE + ACTIVE + -ANT.]

surf and turf *n. US, Aus* a meal, menu, or dish including both seafood and meat, especially steak and lobster [*Surf* in reference to the seafood; *turf* in reference to the beef, cattle being land-dwelling animals]

surfbird /súrf burd/ *n.* a winter shorebird of the American Pacific coast that has dark spotted plumage and a black-and-white tail. It breeds in Alaska and the Yukon. Latin name: *Aphriza virgata.* [*Surf* from its being found among wave-washed rocks along the shoreline]

surfboard /súrf bawrd/ *n.* a long narrow board, with a rounded or pointed front end, on which a surfer stands while riding waves —**surfboarder** *n.* —**surfboarding** *n.*

surfboat /súrf bōt/ *n.* a light sturdy boat, often with a raised prow and stern and buoyancy chambers, suitable for use in high surf

surf carnival *n.* an Australian sports festival held at a beach and involving surfing, swimming, canoeing, and running events

surfcasting /súrf kaasting/ *n.* a method of fishing in which a baited line is tossed into the surf from the shore or a boat —**surfcaster** *n.*

surf club *n.* **1.** LIFESAVERS' ORGANIZATION an organization of lifesavers in Australia **2.** LIFESAVERS' CLUBHOUSE in Australia, a clubhouse where lifesavers are based, usually with changing rooms, showers, and other facilities that can be used by members of the public

surf duck *n.* = **surf scoter**

surfeit /súrfit/ *n.* **1.** EXCESSIVE NUMBER an excessive number or quantity of sth, especially so much of it that people become sickened, repelled, or bored by it **2.** OVERINDULGENCE overindulgence, or a bout of overindulgence, in sth, especially food or drink **3.** DISGUST OR REVULSION disgust or revulsion resulting from overindulgence (*literary*) ■ *vt.* (**-feits, -feiting, -feited**) GIVE SB SURFEIT to give sb a surfeit of sth [13thC. From Old French, the past participle of *surfaire*, literally 'to overdo', from *faire* 'to do' (see AFFAIR).] —**surfeiter** *n.*

Surfers Paradise /súrferz párrə dīss/ coastal town in southeastern Queensland, Australia. It is a major tourist resort, and the centre of the Gold Coast region. Population: 24,033 (1996).

surficial /sur físh'l/ *adj.* relating to or occurring on a surface, especially the surface of the Earth [Late 19thC. Blend of SURFACE and SUPERFICIAL.]

surfie /súrfi/ *n. ANZ* sb whose main interest is surfing (*informal*)

surf-lifesaver *n. Aus* sb, usually a volunteer, who patrols a beach and assists swimmers or surfers who get into difficulties in the water

surf-lifesaving *n. Aus* the activities of lifesavers, e.g. rowing canoes and swimming, engaged in as a sport

surfperch /súrf purch/ (*plural* **-perches** *or* **-perch**) *n.* a bony fish living in shallow Pacific waters off North America and resembling a perch. Family: Embiotocidae.

surf scoter *n.* a large marine duck of North America, the male of which is mostly black with white patches on its head. Latin name: *Melanitta perspicillata.*

surg. *abbr.* **1.** surgical **2.** surgery **3.** surgeon

surge /surj/ *vi.* (**surges, surging, surged**) **1.** MOVE LIKE WAVES to move in or like a wave, rising up and subsiding and sweeping forwards or back ○ *The boat surged in the rising swell.* **2.** MAKE CONCERTED RUSH to move in a body with a sudden rush in a particular direction **3.** INCREASE SUDDENLY to increase strongly and suddenly **4.** NAUT SLIP to slip while being turned on a capstan or windlass (*refers to ropes and cables*) ■ *n.* **1.** LARGE MOTION a powerful rising and falling, or forward rushing movement, like that of the sea **2.** SUDDEN INCREASE a sudden increase in sth, especially one that seems to rush through sb or sth like a wave **3.** ELEC POWER INCREASE a sudden and temporary increase in electrical current or voltage **4.** ASTRON ENERGETIC SOLAR PROMINENCE an energetic solar prominence lasting for several minutes, which accompanies a solar flare **5.** NAUT SLIP OF ROPE a sudden slipping or slackening of a rope or cable on a boat or ship [Early 16thC. From French *surgir* 'to rise up' and *sourge-*, the stem of *sourdre* 'to spring up', both ultimately from Latin *surgere*, literally 'to rise up from below'.] —**surger** *n.*

surgeon /súrjən/ *n.* **1.** MED DOCTOR SPECIALIZING IN SURGERY a doctor specializing in operations that involve gaining access to the patient's body, e.g. by making incisions into it, in order to correct defects, repair injuries, or treat diseases **2.** MIL FORCES' MEDICAL OFFICER a medical officer in the armed services or on board a ship [14thC. Via Anglo-Norman from Old French *cirurgien*, from *cirurgie* (see SURGERY).]

surgeoncy /súrjənsi/ *n.* the position, profession, office and duties of a military or naval surgeon

surgeonfish /súrjən fish/ (*plural* **-fish** *or* **-fishes**) *n.* a tropical fish that is often brightly coloured and has spines at the base of its tail that it uses to inflict wounds. Family: Acanthuridae. [*Surgeon* from an imagined resemblance of its spines to a surgeon's needle]

surgeon general (*plural* **surgeons general**) *n.* **1.** MIL MILITARY DOCTOR the chief medical officer in many branches of the military service **2.** POL PUBLIC HEALTH CHIEF the cabinet-level chief public health officer of the United States, or the chief public health officer of some individual states

surgeon's knot *n.* a surgical knot of a type that can be relied on to remain tight

surgery /súrjəri/ (*plural* **-ies**) *n.* **1.** MEDICAL PROCEDURES INVOLVING OPERATIONS medical treatment that involves operations or manipulations on the patient's body and, usually, cutting the body open to perform these **2.** BRANCH OF MEDICINE the branch of medicine that deals with diseases and conditions treated by operation or manipulation, or the range of diseases treated in this way **3.** SURGEON'S ART OR ACTIVITY the art or activity of performing surgery **4.** DOCTOR'S OFFICE a doctor's, dentist's, or veterinary surgeon's office **5.** DOCTOR'S CONSULTATION TIME a time when a doctor, dentist, or veterinary surgeon is available for consultation by patients at a surgery **6.** POLITICIAN'S OR LAWYER'S CONSULTATION TIME a time when a Member of Parliament, a councillor, or a professional such as a lawyer is available for consultation by members of the general public **7.** *US, Can* OPERATING ROOM a hospital or clinic room where surgery is performed [14thC. Via Old French *cirurgerie* from, ultimately, Greek *kheirourgia*, literally 'working with the hands', from *kheir* 'hand' + *ergon* 'work'.]

surgical /súrjik'l/ *adj.* **1.** OF SURGERY relating to or accomplished by surgery **2.** RESULTING FROM SURGERY due to or as a consequence of surgery **3.** PRECISE like surgery in requiring or being characterized by great skill or great precision [Late 18thC. Alteration (under the influence of SURGEON) of French *cirurgical*, from *cirurgien* 'surgeon' (see SURGERY).] —**surgically** *adv.*

surgical boot *n.* a specially fitted shoe that compensates for physical deformity. US term **corrective shoe**

surgical spirit *n.* methylated spirits mixed with castor oil and oil of wintergreen. It is used to prevent bed sores and for hardening the skin of the feet, and was formerly widely used to sterilize the skin before injections and operations.

suricate /syoōri kayt/ *n.* ZOOL = **meerkat** [Late 18thC. Via French from obsolete Dutch *surikat*, of uncertain origin: probably of African origin.]

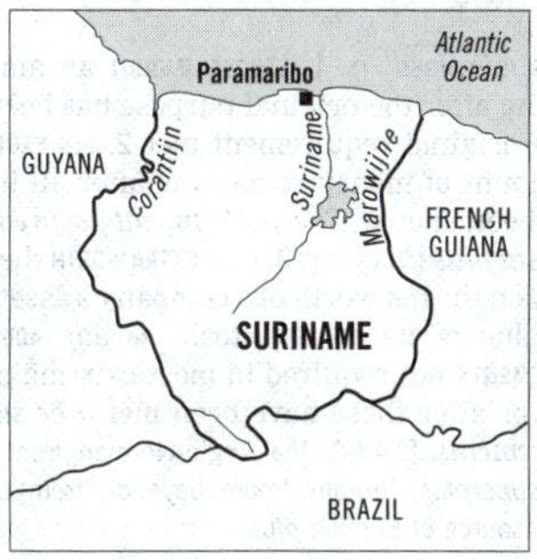

Suriname

Suriname /soōri nám, -náamə/ republic in northeastern South America, north of Brazil, on the Atlantic Ocean. Language: Dutch. Currency: Suriname guilder. Capital: Paramaribo. Population: 436,418 (1996). Area: 163,265 sq. km/63,037 sq. mi. Official name **Republic of Suriname**. Former name **Netherlands Guiana** —**Surinamese** /soōrina méez/ *n., adj.*

Suriname toad *n.* ZOOL = **pipa**

surjection /sur jéksh'n/ *n.* a mathematical function for which each element of a set is the image of at least one element of another set [Mid-20thC. Formed from SUR-, on the model of INJECTION.] —**surjective** *adj.*

surly /súrli/ (**-lier, -liest**) *adj.* bad-tempered, unfriendly, rude, and somewhat threatening ○ *a person with a surly manner* [Late 16thC. Alteration of obsolete *sirly* 'lordly, imperious', from SIR.]

surmise /sur míz/ *vti.* (**-mises, -mising, -mised**) **MAKE GUESS ABOUT STH** to conclude that sth is the case on the basis of only limited evidence or intuitive feeling ■ *n.* **GUESSWORK** a conclusion drawn on only limited evidence or intuitive feeling [Early 16thC. From Anglo-Norman *surmis*, past participle of *surmettre* 'to accuse', literally 'to put over', ultimately from Latin *mittere* 'to send' (source of English *mission*).] —**surmisable** *adj.* —**surmiser** *n.*

surmount /sur mównt/ (**-mounts, -mounting, -mounted**) *vt.* **1. OVERCOME DIFFICULTY** to deal with a difficulty successfully **2. GET TO TOP OF STH** to get over the top of a physical obstacle (*formal*) **3. BE PLACED ON TOP OF STH** to be positioned on top of sth or rise above it (*formal*) ○ *the statues surmounting the parapet* **4. PUT STH ON TOP OF STH** to place sth on top of or above sth (*formal*) ○ *surmount the parapet with a row of statues* [14thC. From French *surmonter*, literally 'to climb over', from *monter* 'to mount' (see MOUNT[1]).] —**surmountability** /sur mówntə bílləti/ *n.* —**surmountable** /sur mówntəb'l/ *adj.* —**surmounter** /-mówntər/ *n.*

surmullet /sur múllit/ (*plural* **-lets** *or* **-let**) *n.* = **red mullet** [Late 17thC. From French *surmulet*, from Old French *sor* 'red, brown' + *mulet* 'mullet' (see MULLET).]

surname /súr naym/ *n.* **1. SB'S FAMILY NAME** the name that identifies sb as belonging to a particular family and that he or she has in common with other members of the family **2. DESCRIPTIVE ADDITION TO NAME** a descriptive addition to sb's name e.g. 'the Great' in 'Catherine the Great' (*archaic*) ■ *vt.* (**-names, -naming, -named**) **GIVE SB A SURNAME** to give or transmit a surname to sb (*usually passive*) [14thC. Translation of Old French *surnom*, literally 'name above', from *nom* 'name'.] —**surnamer** *n.*

surpass /sur pa'ass/ (**-passes, -passing, -passed**) *vt.* **1. EXCEED EXPECTATIONS** to go beyond what was expected or hoped for, usually by being bigger, better, or greater **2. DO BETTER THAN SB OR STH** to be bigger, greater, better, or worse than sb or sth else **3. BE BEYOND SB'S ABILITY** to be beyond sb's ability to deal with or understand (*formal*) [Mid-16thC. From French *surpasser* 'to transgress', literally 'to pass beyond', from *passer* 'to pass' (see PASS).] —**surpassable** *adj.*

surpassing /sur pa'assing/ *adj.* of a quality far superior to others (*literary*) ○ *a view of surpassing beauty* —**surpassingly** *adv.*

surplice /súrpliss/ *n.* a white ecclesiastical outer garment like a smock, with wide, often flared sleeves, and varying in length [13thC. Via Anglo-Norman *surpliz* from medieval Latin *superpellicium*, literally '(vestment worn) over a fur garment', from *pellicium* 'fur coat'.]

surplus /súrpləss/ *n.* **1. EXCESS AMOUNT** an amount remaining after the original purpose has been served or the original requirement met **2.** FIN **EXCESS MONEY** an amount of money remaining after all liabilities have been met ○ *The government is predicting a trade surplus this year.* **3.** ACCT **EXTRA WORTH** the amount by which the net worth of a company's assets exceed the value of its owned stock ■ *adj.* **ADDITIONAL TO REQUIREMENTS** not required to meet existing needs, or left over after these have been met ○ *be surplus to requirements* [14thC. Via Anglo-Norman from medieval Latin *superplus*, literally 'more beyond', from Latin *plus* 'more' (source of English *plus*).]

surplusage /súrpləssij/ *n.* **1.** LAW **IRRELEVANT MATTER** an irrelevant matter introduced into legal proceedings **2. VERBIAGE** redundant words or arguments (*formal*) **3. SURPLUS** an excess of sth (*formal*)

surplus value *n.* in Marxist economic theory, the difference between the price of a product produced by labour and the value of labour itself in terms of the wages paid to workers

surprint /sur prínt/ *vt.* (**-prints, -printing, -printed**) = **overprint** *v.* ■ *n.* = **overprint** *n.* 1

surprise /sər príz/ *vt.* (**-prises, -prising, -prised**) **1. MAKE SB AMAZED** to cause sb to feel sudden wonder or amazement, especially because of sth unexpected **2. TAKE SB OR STH UNAWARES** to attack, come upon, or catch sb or sth unexpectedly **3. GIVE SB STH UNEXPECTEDLY** to make an unexpected gift to sb ○ *surprised me with flowers* **4. TRICK SB** to cause sb to do sth unexpected by trickery or deceit **5. ELICIT STH FROM SB** to cause sb to admit sth unexpectedly by trickery or deceit ■ *n.* **1. AMAZING EVENT** the act or an instance of causing sb to feel unexpected wonder or delight **2. STH UNEXPECTED** an unexpected gift or event **3. AMAZEMENT** a feeling of unexpected amazement or delight [15thC. From French, the feminine past participle of *surprendre*, literally 'to overtake', from *sur-* 'over' + Latin *prehendere* (see PREHENSION).] —**surpriser** *n.* —**surprising** *adj.* —**surprisingly** *adv.* ◇ **take sb by surprise** to happen unexpectedly to sb ○ *Their arrival took everybody by surprise.*

surra /sóorə/ *n.* a tropical disease similar to sleeping sickness that affects camels and horses, and occasionally cattle and dogs. It is caused by a protozoan but transmitted by biting flies. [Late 19thC. From Marathi *sūra*, literally 'air breathed through the nostrils'.]

surreal /sə reé el/ *adj.* **DREAMLIKE** suggesting or having qualities associated with surrealism, e.g. bizarre landscapes and distorted objects ■ *n.* **DREAMLIKE QUALITIES OR CHARACTER** the bizarre or unreal qualities associated with surrealism [Mid-20thC. Back-formation from SURREALISM.]

surrealism /sə reé elizəm/ *n.* **1. ART MOVEMENT** an early 20th-century movement in art and literature that tried to represent the subconscious mind by creating fantastic imagery and juxtaposing elements that seem to contradict each other **2. TYPE OF ART** surreal art or literature [Early 20thC. From French *surréalisme*, literally 'beyond realism'.] —**surrealist** *n., adj.* —**surrealistic** /sə reé ə lístik/ *adj.* —**surrealistically** /-lístikli/ *adv.*

surrebuttal /súrri bútt'l/ *n.* in a civil court action, an act of giving evidence to support the third reply (**surrebutter**) of the person bringing the action (**plaintiff**)

surrebutter /súrri búttər/ *n.* in a civil court action, the third reply of the person bringing the action (**plaintiff**), in response to the defendant's third statement (**rebutter**) [Late 16thC. Formed from RE-BUTTER, on the model of SURREJOINDER.]

surrejoinder /súrri jóyndər/ *n.* in a civil court action, the second reply of the person bringing the action (**plaintiff**), in response to the defendant's second statement (**rejoinder**)

surrender /sə réndər/ *v.* (**-ders, -dering, -dered**) **1.** *vi.* MIL **STOP FIGHTING BECAUSE UNABLE TO WIN** to declare to an opponent that he or she has won and that fighting can cease **2.** *vt.* **GIVE UP POSSESSION OF STH** to relinquish possession or control of sth because of coercion or force **3.** *vt.* **GIVE STH OUT OF COURTESY** to give sb a seat, position, or office as a courtesy or as a gesture of goodwill **4.** *vt.* **GIVE STH UP** to give up or abandon sth such as an idea or intention **5.** *vi.* **GIVE SELF UP TO STH** to yield to a strong emotion, influence, or temptation **6.** *vt.* LAW **ABANDON RIGHTS TO STH** to give up or abandon rights to sth, especially to give up a lease before it has expired ■ *n.* **1.** MIL **GIVING UP A FIGHT** an act of declaring defeat at the hands of an opponent ○ *The French demanded an unconditional surrender.* **2. GIVING UP CONTROL** a relinquishment of control to sb or sth **3. DELIVERY INTO LEGAL CUSTODY** the delivery of a prisoner or fugitive into legal custody **4.** LAW **ABANDONMENT OF LEGAL RIGHTS** the abandonment of legal rights, especially the giving up of a lease or an insurance policy before it has expired **5. GIVING SELF UP TO AUTHORITIES** an act of willing submission to authorities [15thC. From Anglo-Norman, literally 'to give over', from *render* 'to give (back)', a variant of Old French *rendre* (see RENDER).] —**surrenderer** *n.*

WORD KEY: SYNONYMS

See Synonyms at ***yield***.

surreptitious /súrrəp tíshəss/ *adj.* **1. SECRET** done, made, or acquired by secret or sneaky methods **2. STEALTHY** operating with or characterized by stealth [15thC. Via Latin *surreptitius* from, ultimately, *surripere* 'to seize secretly', literally 'to seize from beneath', from *rapere* (see RAPE[1]).] —**surreptitiously** *adv.* —**surreptitiousness** *n.*

WORD KEY: SYNONYMS

See Synonyms at ***secret***.

surrey /súrri/ (*plural* **-reys**) *n.* a late 19th-century horse-drawn four-wheeled carriage with two or four seats, used for short pleasure trips [Late 19thC. Named after *Surrey*, where it was originally manufactured.]

Surrey /súrri/ county in southern England. The administrative centre is Kingston-upon-Thames. Population: 1,044,000 (1995). Area: 1,677 sq. km/648 sq. mi.

surrogacy /súrrəgəssi/ (*plural* **-cies**) *n.* the condition or act of being a substitute, especially a surrogate mother

surrogate *adj.* /súrrəgət, -gayt/ **TAKING PLACE OF SB OR STH** taking the place of sb or sth else ■ *n.* **1. SUBSTITUTE** sb who takes the place or fills the role of sb else **2.** MED **WOMAN WHO GIVES BIRTH FOR ANOTHER** a woman who bears a child for a couple, with the intention of handing it over at birth. She usually either is artificially inseminated by the man or implanted with a fertilized egg from the woman. **3.** PSYCHOL **SUBSTITUTE AUTHORITY FIGURE** a respected person, e.g. a teacher or older sibling, who replaces a lost or nonexistent parent in sb's unconscious ■ *vt.* /súrrə gayt/ (**-gates, -gating, -gated**) **APPOINT AS A STAND-IN** to put sb in sb else's place [Mid-16thC. From Latin *surrogatus*, the past participle of *surrogare*, literally 'to ask for in place of', from *rogare* (see ROGATION).] —**surrogateship** /súrrə gət ship, súrrə gayt ship/ *n.* —**surrogation** /súrrə gáysh'n/ *n.*

surround /sə równd/ *vt.* (**-rounds, -rounding, -rounded**) **1. ENCLOSE** to occupy the space all around sth **2. CLOSE OFF MEANS OF ESCAPE** to encircle sth completely, especially an enemy's military position **3. BE AROUND SB** to associate closely with sb ■ *n.* **1. OUTSIDE BORDER** an area around the edge of sth, especially the space between the edge of a carpet and the walls of the room **2. AREA AROUND** an area or border around a specific thing or place **3. SURROUNDINGS** the immediate environment of sth or sb (*often plural*) [Early 17thC. Via Old French *suronder* 'to overflow' from late Latin *superundare*, from Latin *unda* 'wave' (see UNDULATE).]

WORD KEY: USAGE

Risk of redundancy: ***Surround*** and its synonyms such as *encircle* and *enclose* do not occur by degrees. Thus a spit of land, for example, should not be said to be *partly surrounded* (or *partly encircled* or *partly enclosed*) by water; it is *almost surrounded* (etc). By the same token, *completely surrounded* may be excusable as emphatic, but it is redundant.

surroundings /sə równdingz/ *npl.* the immediate environment of sb or sth, including events, circumstances, scenery, conditions, people, and objects

surround sound *n.* a system of recording and reproducing sound that uses three or more channels and speakers in order to create the effect of the listener being surrounded by sound sources

sursum corda /súr ssəm káwrdə, -sòom-/ *n.* **1.** CHR **PART OF MASS** in the Roman Catholic Church, a short sentence (**versicle**) spoken by a priest during Mass, just before the preface **2. EXHORTATION** a cry or exhortation, especially of hope (*literary*) [From late Latin, literally '(lift) up (your) hearts', the versicle's opening words]

surtax /súr taks/ *n.* **1. ANOTHER TAX** a tax that is charged in addition to other taxes **2. HIGHER TAX** a higher level or levels of tax imposed on individuals and corporations when income or profits exceed a certain amount ■ *vt.* (**-taxes, -taxing, -taxed**) **CHARGE SB SURTAX** to charge sb with an additional or higher tax [Late 19thC. From French *surtaxe*, literally 'over tax', from *taxe* 'tax', from *taxer* (see TAX).]

Surtees /súrt eez/, **John** (*b.* 1934) British motorcyclist and motor racing driver. He was world motorcycling champion at 500 cc (1956, 1958–60) and at 350 cc (1958–60), and Formula One world champion (1964).

surtitle /súr tīt'l/ *n.* a translation of words being spoken in a foreign language during the performance of a play or opera, projected on a screen above the stage (*often used in the plural*) —**surtitled** *adj.*

surveillance /sur váylənss/ *n.* continual observation of a person or group, especially one suspected of doing sth illegal [Early 19thC. From French, formed from *surveiller* 'to watch over', from *veiller* 'to keep watch', from Latin *vigilare* (see VIGILANT).] —**surveillant** *adj., n.*

survey /sur váy, súr vay/ *vt.* (**-veys, -veying, -veyed**) **1.** **CONSIDER STH GENERALLY** to look at or consider sth in a general or very broad way **2.** **LOOK AT STH CAREFULLY** to look at or consider sb or sth closely, especially in order to form an opinion **3.** GEOG **PLOT A MAP OF SOMEWHERE** to make a detailed map of an area of land, including its boundaries, area, and elevation, using geometry and trigonometry to measure angles and distances **4.** BUILDING **INSPECT A BUILDING** to inspect a building in order to determine its structural soundness or assess its value **5.** STATS **QUESTION PEOPLE IN A POLL** to do a statistical study of a sample population by asking questions about age, income, opinions, buying preferences, and other aspects of people's lives **6.** **GAZE AT STH** to look at or over sth in a casual or leisurely way ■ *n.* /súr vay/ (*plural* **-veys**) **1.** STATS **ANALYSIS OF POLL SAMPLE** a statistical analysis of answers to a poll of a sample of a population, e.g. to determine opinions, preferences, or knowledge **2.** BUILDING **INSPECTION OF A BUILDING** an inspection of a building to determine its condition and assess its value **3.** BUILDING **REPORT FROM INSPECTING BUILDING** a report that results from inspecting the condition and assessing the value of a building **4.** **GENERAL VIEW** a very broad or general view of a subject or situation **5.** **CRITICAL INSPECTION** a very detailed, critical examination of sth such as a situation or event **6.** **ACT OF MEASURING LAND** an act of taking detailed measurements of an area of land **7.** **REPORT ON LAND MEASUREMENT** a report that shows the results of a survey undertaken to measure an area of land **8.** **GROUP DOING A SURVEY** a team of surveyors working together **9.** GEOG **AREA SURVEYED** an area of land that is being or has been surveyed [15thC. Via Anglo-Norman *surveier* from medieval Latin *supervidere* 'to oversee' (source of English *supervise*), from Latin *videre* (see VISION).] —**surveyable** /súr vayəb'l, sur váyəb'l/ *adj.*

surveyor /sur váyər/ *n.* **1.** **SB WHO SURVEYS LAND** sb whose occupation is taking accurate measurements of land areas in order to determine boundaries, elevations, and dimensions **2.** **BUILDING INSPECTOR** sb whose occupation is inspecting buildings to determine the soundness of their construction or to assess their value **3.** = **quantity surveyor**

surveyor's chain *n.* = **chain** *n.* 7

surveyor's level *n.* an instrument with a telescope and a spirit level attached, mounted on a tripod and rotating around the vertical axis, used for measuring elevations of land

surveyor's measure *n.* a system of measurement based on the unit the surveyor's chain, 22 yd (about 20 m)

survival /sur vív'l/ *n.* **1.** **STAYING ALIVE** continuation in life or existence **2.** **FACT OF LIVING THROUGH STH** the fact of having managed to live through sth **3.** **STH FROM THE PAST** a custom, idea, or belief that remains when other similar things have been lost or forgotten

survival bag *n.* a protective bag that climbers or hikers get into to protect themselves from exposure

survive /sər vív/ (**-vives, -viving, -vived**) *v.* **1.** *vi.* **REMAIN ALIVE OR IN EXISTENCE** to manage to stay alive or continue to exist, especially in difficult situations **2.** *vt.* **STAY ALIVE LONGER THAN SB** to remain alive after the death of sb else **3.** *vt.* **LIVE THROUGH STH** to remain alive or in existence after sth such as an accident or war that threatens life [15thC. Via Anglo-Norman *survivre* from Latin *supervivere*, literally 'to live beyond', from *vivere* (see VIVID).] —**survivability** /sər vívə bílləti/ *n.* —**survivable** /sər vívəb'l/ *adj.* —**survivor** /sər vívvər/ *n.*

sus[1] /suss/ *n.* **SUSPICION** a state of doubt or misgiving about sb or sth (*slang*) ■ *adj.* **NOT TRUSTWORTHY** acting like sb who has done sth wrong or illegal (*slang*) [Mid-20thC. Shortening of SUSPICION and SUSPICIOUS.]

sus[2] /suss/ *n.* sb who is thought to have done sth wrong or illegal (*slang*) [Mid-20thC. Shortening of SUSPECT.]

Jacqueline Susann

Susann /soo zán/, **Jacqueline** (1926–74) US writer. Her first novel, *Valley of the Dolls* (1968), was a best seller.

Susanna *n.* in the Apocrypha, a woman of Babylon who was saved by the prophet Daniel after being falsely accused of adultery

susceptibility /sə séptə bílləti/ (*plural* **-ties**) *n.* **1.** **LIKELIHOOD OF BEING AFFECTED** the likelihood of being affected by sth **2.** **SENSITIVITY** the ability to be affected by strong feelings and emotions **3.** **FEELINGS** sb's feelings, especially those of sb who easily becomes upset **4.** PHYS = **magnetic susceptibility** **5.** ELEC = **electric susceptibility**

susceptible /sə séptəb'l/ *adj.* **1.** **EASILY AFFECTED** easily influenced or affected by sth **2.** **LIKELY TO BE AFFECTED** liable to being affected by sth ○ *susceptible to hay fever and other allergies* **3.** **EMOTIONAL** easily affected emotionally **4.** **CAPABLE OF STH** capable or permitting of sth [Early 17thC. Directly or via French from, ultimately, Latin *suscipere*, literally 'to take up', from *capere* (see CAPTURE).] —**susceptibleness** *n.* —**susceptibly** *adv.*

susceptive /sə séptiv/ *adj.* **1.** **SUSCEPTIBLE** easily affected by sth **2.** **RECEPTIVE** open to new ideas and suggestions [Mid-15thC. Formed from Latin *suscept-*, the past participle stem of *suscipere* (see SUSCEPTIBLE).] —**susceptiveness** *n.* —**susceptivity** /sússep tívvəti/ *n.*

sushi /sóo shee/ *n.* small cakes of cold boiled rice, shaped by hand or wrapped in seaweed and topped with pieces of raw or cooked fish, vegetables, or egg [Late 19thC. From Japanese.]

Susian /sóozi ən/ *n.* LANG = **Elamite** *n.* 2 [Mid-16thC. Via Latin *Susianus* from, ultimately, Greek *Sousa* 'Susa', where Elamite was spoken.] —**Susian** *adj.*

sus laws *npl.* laws that permit the arrest and prosecution of people suspected of frequenting or loitering in public places for the purpose of committing a crime (*informal*)

suslik /sóoss lik/ (*plural* **-liks** *or* **-lik**), **souslik** (*plural* **-liks** *or* **-lik**) *n.* a ground squirrel of Europe and Asia with large eyes and small ears that lives in dry open areas. Latin name: *Citellus citellus.* [Late 18thC. From Russian.]

suspect *v.* /sə spékt/ *v.* (**-pects, -pecting, -pected**) **1.** *vt.* **BELIEVE SB IS GUILTY** to believe that sb may have committed a crime or wrongdoing without having any proof **2.** *vt.* **DOUBT STH** to doubt the truth or validity of sth **3.** *vt.* **BELIEVE STH TO BE SO** to think that sth is probable or likely **4.** *vti.* **HAVE SUSPICIONS** to be suspicious about sth ■ *n.* /súss pekt/ **SB WHO MIGHT BE GUILTY** sb who is thought to be possibly guilty of wrongdoing or doing sth illegal ■ *adj.* /súss pekt/ **1.** **SUSPICIOUS** thought or likely to be false or untrustworthy ○ *All his claims about the wealth of his family are rather suspect.* **2.** **LIKELY TO CONTAIN STH ILLEGAL** looking likely to contain sth dangerous or illegal [14thC. From Latin *suspect-*, the past participle stem of *suspicere*, literally 'to look up at', from *specere* (see SPECTACLE).] ◇ **the usual suspects** people, businesses, or organizations frequently mentioned in the context of a particular activity

WORD KEY: USAGE

Suspect as it is used in criminal contexts denotes sb who has been or may be charged with a crime, and who is entitled to seek to prove his or her innocence, as opposed to someone who has been already found guilty. But unless the word is referring to a specific individual, its refusal to affirm guilt may be beside the point, as it is in *The day after the burglary the police began searching for suspects.* And when guilt is evident, even though ***suspect*** serves to acknowledge that a legal defence may yet be possible, it may seem foolish: *After the jewels were found in his house and he confessed to the burglary, the suspect was remanded for trial.*

suspend /sə spénd/ (**-pends, -pending, -pended**) *v.* **1.** *vt.* **HANG STH FROM ABOVE** to hang sth from above, especially so that it can swing freely **2.** *vt.* **STOP STH FOR A PERIOD** to stop sth or make sth ineffective, usually for a short time **3.** *vt.* **BAR SB FOR A PERIOD** to bar sb from a privilege, a position, or an organization, usually when under suspicion of wrongdoing **4.** *vt.* **POSTPONE STH** to delay or defer action on a decision or a judgment until more of the facts are known **5.** *vt.* **HANG ABOVE** to hang over or above sth **6.** *vt.* CHEM **DISPERSE STH IN LIQUID** to cause particles to be dispersed in a liquid **7.** *vt.* MUSIC **SUSTAIN A NOTE** to hold a note until the next note or chord is sounded, so that they are heard together **8.** *vi.* FIN **STOP MAKING PAYMENTS** to cease payment on sth, especially because of an inability to meet financial obligations [13thC. Directly or via French *suspendre* from Latin *suspendere*, literally 'to hang up', from *pendere* (see PENDANT).] —**suspendibility** /sə spénndə bílləti/ *n.* —**suspendible** /sə spénndəb'l/ *adj.*

suspended animation *n.* **1.** BIOL **TEMPORARY SLOWING OF LIFE FUNCTIONS** the stopping or slowing of the vital functions of an organism for some period of time, especially by freezing **2.** PHYSIOL **STATE LIKE DEATH** a state, often caused by asphyxia, in which an organism loses consciousness and stops breathing so that it appears to be dead

suspended sentence *n.* a sentence imposed on sb found guilty of a crime that need not be served as long as the individual commits no other crime during the term of the sentence

suspender /sə spéndər/ *n.* **1.** **STRAP FOR WOMAN'S STOCKINGS** an elastic strap, usually attached to a girdle or belt, with a clamp at one end to hold up a woman's stockings. US term **garter** **2.** **STRAP FOR MAN'S SOCK** an elastic strap with a clamp on one end that attaches to and holds up a man's sock **3.** *US* **STRAP FOR HOLDING UP TROUSERS** a strap, usually made of elastic, worn over the shoulders and with a clip at either end to attach to trousers so that they do not fall down (*usually plural*) **4.** **STH THAT LETS STH HANG** sth that allows sth else to hang, e.g. one of the cables on a suspension bridge

suspender belt *n.* a belt with four elastic straps hanging from it, one down the back and front of each leg, with clamps on the ends to hold up a woman's stockings. US term **garter belt**

suspense /sə spénss/ *n.* **1.** **UNCERTAINTY** the state or condition of being unsure or in doubt about sth **2.** **ENJOYABLE TENSION** a feeling of tense excitement about how sth such as a mystery novel or film will end **3.** **ANXIETY** a state of anxiety or intense worry about sth [15thC. Via Anglo-Norman from Latin *suspensus*, the past participle of *suspendere* (see SUSPEND).] —**suspenseful** *adj.*

suspense account *n.* an account in which entries are made temporarily, until it is determined where they belong

suspension /sə spén sh'n/ *n.* **1.** **TEMPORARY STOP OF STH** an interruption of sth for a period of time **2.** LAW **POSTPONEMENT OF A SENTENCE** a delay in the carrying out of a sentence or the making of a decision or judgment **3.** **TEMPORARY REMOVAL OF SB** the temporary removal of sb from a team, position, school, or organization, especially as punishment **4.** FIN **END TO REPAYING DEBTS** an end to the repayment of financial obligations because of a lack of money **5.** TRANSP **SYSTEM REDUCING VEHICLE'S VIBRATION** a system of springs and shock absorbers on a wheeled vehicle that reduces the impact of bumps and uneven running surfaces on the occupants and gives the wheels better contact **6.** CHEM **DISPERSION OF PARTICLES** a dispersion of fine solid particles in a liquid **7.** MUSIC **TECHNIQUE FOR CREATING DISSONANCE** a technique in which a note of the first chord is held into the second chord, the dissonance created being resolved by moving a step lower in the third chord

suspension bridge *n.* a bridge that has the roadway suspended from cables that are anchored by towers at either end and, sometimes, with supporting structures for the cables placed at regular intervals

suspension point *n. US* one of a series of dots, usually three, used in printed and written material to indicate an omission from text being reproduced or an incomplete phrase (*often used in the plural*)

suspensive /sə spénsiv/ *adj.* **1.** STOPPING STH causing or tending to cause sth to stop or be deferred **2.** CAUSING TENSION causing, arousing, or relating to a feeling of doubt or anxious excitement **3.** UNDECIDED ABOUT STH inclined to delay making a decision or judgment — **suspensively** *adv.* —**suspensiveness** *n.*

suspensoid /sə spén soyd/ *n.* a solution made up of solid particles dispersed throughout a liquid [Early 20thC. Formed from SUSPENSION.]

suspensory /sə spénsəri/ *n.* (*plural* **-ries**) **1.** ANAT LIGAMENT OR MUSCLE a ligament or muscle from which a structure or part is suspended **2.** MED BANDAGE OR SLING sth such as a bandage or a sling that holds part of the body in position while it heals ■ *adj.* TEMPORARILY STOPPING STH temporarily interrupting or delaying the completion of sth

suspensory ligament *n.* a ligament that provides support for an organ or another body part, especially a fibrous membrane that holds the lens of the eye in place

suspicion /sə spísh'n/ *n.* **1.** FEELING OF STH WRONG an unsubstantiated belief that sth is the case, especially a belief that sth wrong has happened or that sb may have committed a crime ○ *a sneaking suspicion that she was the one who ate the last biscuit* **2.** MISTRUST a feeling of mistrust or doubt, especially because sth wrong has happened and has not been explained ○ *an atmosphere of suspicion* **3.** CONDITION OF BEING SUSPECTED the condition of being suspected of sth, especially wrongdoing ○ *under suspicion* **4.** SMALL AMOUNT OF STH a tiny amount of sth, e.g. a colour or flavour [13thC. Via Anglo-Norman *suspeciun* from, ultimately, Latin *suspicere* (see SUSPECT).] —**suspicional** *adj.*

suspicious /sə spíshəss/ *adj.* **1.** AROUSING SUSPICION creating or liable to create suspicion **2.** TENDING TO SUSPECT inclined or tending to believe that sth is wrong ○ *a suspicious nature* **3.** SUGGESTING DOUBT indicating suspicion —**suspiciously** *adv.* —**suspiciousness** *n.*

suspire /sə spír/ (**-pires**, **-piring**, **-pired**) *vi.* (*dated literary*) **1.** BREATHE IN to draw in breath **2.** SIGH to give a sigh [15thC. From Latin *suspirare*, literally 'to breathe up', from *spirare* (see SPIRIT).] —**suspiration** /súspi ráysh'n/ *n.*

Susquehanna *n.* = **Susquehannock**

Susquehannock /súskwi hánnək/ (*plural* **-nock** *or* **-nocks**), **Susquehanna** /súskwi hánnə/ (*plural* **-na** *or* **-nas**) *n.* a member of a Native North American people who occupied lands along the Susquehanna River in New York, Pennsylvania, and Maryland. The Susquehannock were extinct by around 1768. [Early 17thC. Of Algonquian origin.]

suss out *vt.* to get to the bottom of sth, or discover what sb is up to (*informal*)

Sussex /sússiks/ former county of southeastern England. Since 1974 it has been divided into the counties of East Sussex and West Sussex.

Sussex Downs hilly region in southeastern England, forming part of the South Downs. It was designated an Area of Outstanding Natural Beauty in 1966. Area: 983 sq. km/379 sq. mi.

Sussex Drive, **24 Sussex Drive** *n.* the address of the official residence of the Prime Minister of Canada

Sussex spaniel *n.* a breed of short-legged spaniel with long ears and a golden-brown silky coat, or a dog of this breed [Mid-19thC. Named after SUSSEX where it was developed.]

sustain /sə stáyn/ *vt.* (**-tains**, **-taining**, **-tained**) **1.** WITHSTAND STH to manage to withstand sth and continue doing it in spite of it **2.** BE AFFECTED BY STH to experience a setback, injury, damage, loss, or defeat ○ *The child who fell sustained no more than several broken bones.* **3.** MAINTAIN to make sth continue to exist **4.** NOURISH to provide sb with nourishment or the necessities of life **5.** SUPPORT FROM BELOW to keep sth in position by holding it from below ○ *The floor will not sustain the weight of a grand piano.* **6.** PROVIDE WITH MORAL SUPPORT to keep sb going with emotional or moral support **7.** LAW VALIDATE STH to decide that a statement or objection is valid or justified **8.** CONFIRM STH to confirm that sth is true or valid **9.** KEEP A PRETENCE GOING to maintain a pretence successfully ■ *n.* MUSIC PROLONGED NOTE a note that is prolonged [13thC. Via Anglo-Norman *sustein-*, the stem of *sustenir*, from Latin *sustinere*, literally 'to hold up', from *tenere* (see TENANT).] —**sustainability** /sə stáynə bílləti/ *n.* —**sustainment** /sə stáynmənt/ *n.*

sustainable /sə stáynəb'l/ *adj.* **1.** ABLE TO BE MAINTAINED able to be maintained **2.** ENVIRON MAINTAINING AN ECOLOGICAL BALANCE exploiting natural resources without destroying the ecological balance of a particular area ○ *'Sustainable development is the principle which should guide politicians in planning the future…'* (*BBC website*; April 1999)

sustainable development *n.* economic development maintained within acceptable levels of global resource depletion and environmental pollution

sustained yield *n.* **1.** CONSISTENT RESOURCE the ongoing supply of a natural resource, e.g. timber, by scheduled harvesting **2.** AMOUNT HARVESTED the amount of a natural resource obtained by scheduled harvesting

sustaining pedal *n.* the right pedal of a piano, which is used to keep the dampers off the strings so that they can vibrate freely

sustenance /sústənənss/ *n.* **1.** NOURISHMENT sth, especially food, that supports life ○ *There isn't much sustenance in a small chocolate bar.* **2.** CONDITION OF BEING SUSTAINED the condition of being supported ○ *'I have hardly a penny in the world – I am staying with my aunt for my bare sustenance'.* (Thomas Hardy, *Far from the Madding Crowd*; 1874) **3.** LIVELIHOOD a means of supporting sb financially [13thC. From Anglo-Norman *sustenaunce*, from *sustenir* (see SUSTAIN).]

sustentacular /súss ten tákyŏŏlər/ *adj.* used to describe cells or fibres that serve as a support and have no other function [Late 19thC. Formed from modern Latin *sustentaculum* 'support', from Latin *sustentare* (see SUSTENTATION).]

sustentation /súss ten táysh'n/ *n.* (*formal*) **1.** SUPPORT sth that supports or sustains sth **2.** MEANS OF SUPPORT a means of support [14thC. Via French from, ultimately, Latin *sustentare*, literally 'to keep holding up', from *sustinere* (see SUSTAIN).] —**sustentative** /sústən táytiv, sə sténtativ/ *adj.*

susu *n.* = **sou-sou**

Susu /sóo soo/ (*plural* **-su** *or* **-sus**) *n.* **1.** PEOPLES W AFRICAN PEOPLE a member of a people who live in West Africa, mainly in Guinea, Sierra Leone, and Sudan **2.** LANG W AFRICAN LANGUAGE the language of the Susu people, belonging to the Mande group of Niger-Congo languages. Susu is spoken by about 700,000 people. [Late 18thC. From Susu.] —**Susu** *adj.*

susurrate /sússə rayt/ (**-rates**, **-rating**, **-rated**) *vi.* to whisper or rustle softly [Early 17thC. Back-formation from *susurration*, from Latin *susurrare*, from *susurrus* 'whisper', ultimately an imitation of the sound.] —**susurrant** *adj.* —**susurration** /sússə ráysh'n/ *n.*

susurrus /sússərəss/ *n.* a whispering or murmuring sound (*literary*) [15thC. From Latin (see SUSURRATE).]

Sutcliffe /sútklif/, **Herbert** (1894–1978) British cricketer. An opening batsman, he played for Yorkshire (1919–45) and for England (1924–35), for whom he formed a highly successful regular opening partnership with Jack Hobbes.

Sutherland /súthərlənd/ former county of northern Scotland. Since 1975 it has been part of Highland council area.

Sutherland, Graham (1903–80) British painter. He is noted for his semi-abstract works, portraits, and the design for the tapestry *Christ in Majesty* (1952–58) for Coventry Cathedral. Full name **Graham Vivian Sutherland**

Dame Joan Sutherland: Performing in *Lucia di Lammermoor*

Sutherland, Dame Joan (b. 1926) Australian singer. In a career stretching from 1947 to 1990, she became an opera singer of international renown, noted especially for her coloratura roles in Italian opera.

Sutherland Falls waterfall on the South Island, New Zealand. It is one of the highest in the world. Height: 580 m/1,904 ft.

Sutlej /sút lij/ river in southern Asia, flowing through Tibet, India, and Pakistan. Length: 933 km/850 mi.

sutler /sútt lər/ *n.* sb who follows an army and sells merchandise to the soldiers (*archaic*) [Late 16thC. From obsolete Dutch *soeteler*, from *soetelen* 'to befoul, do menial work'.] —**sutlership** *n.*

sutra /sóotrə/ *n.* **1.** INDIAN RELIG SUMMARY OF HINDU TEACHING a short aphoristic summary of the teachings of Hinduism, created to be memorized and later incorporated into Hindu literature **2.** sutra, sutta BUDDHISM BUDDHIST TEXT a classic religious text of Buddhism, especially one regarded as a discourse of the Buddha [Early 19thC. From Sanskrit *sūtram* 'aphorism', literally 'thread'. Ultimately from an Indo-European base meaning 'to sew', which is also the ancestor of English *sew*, *seam*, and *suture*.]

suttee /súttee, su teé/, **sati** *n.* **1.** SUICIDE ON HUSBAND'S FUNERAL PYRE in the Indian subcontinent, the practice, now illegal, of a widow throwing herself on her husband's funeral pyre **2.** WIDOW COMMITTING SUICIDE ON FUNERAL PYRE a Hindu widow who throws herself on her husband's funeral pyre [Late 18thC. From Sanskrit *satī*, literally 'good woman', the feminine present participle of *as-* 'to be'. Ultimately from an Indo-European base that is ancestor also of English *is* and *sooth*.] —**sutteeism** *n.*

Sutton /sútt'n/, **Henry** (1856–1912) Australian inventor. He was a pioneer of aviation, telecommunications, and colour photography, and in 1885 designed a prototype television.

Sutton Coldfield /sútt'n kŏld feeld/ town in the West Midlands, in central England, northeast of Birmingham. Population: 90,325 (1991).

suture /sóo chər/ *n.* **1.** SURG MATERIAL FOR SURGICAL STITCHING a piece of material, e.g. catgut, thread, or wire, used to close a wound or connect tissues **2.** SURG SURGICAL SEAM the line formed where a wound has been closed or tissues have been joined **3.** SEAM any seam or line at which two edges have been joined **4.** ANAT IMMOVABLE JOINT a type of joint, found especially in the skull, in which the bones are tightly bound together by fibrous connective tissue, permitting no movement between them **5.** ZOOL LINE AT POINT OF JUNCTURE a distinguishable line at the junction of adjacent structures, e.g. between the chambers of a mollusc shell or between the exoskeletal plates of an insect **6.** BOT LINE ON SEED POD OR FRUIT a line along which a seed pod or fruit will split to release its seeds ■ *vt.* (**-tures, -turing, -tured**) SURG CLOSE A WOUND to close a wound by joining the edges [15thC. From Latin *sutura*, from *sut-*, the past participle stem of *suere* 'to sew'.] —**sutural** *adj.* —**suturally** *adv.*

Suu Kyi /sóo keé/, **Daw Aung San** (b. 1945) Burmese political leader. Cofounder (1988) and leader of the National League for Democracy, she was awarded a Nobel Peace Prize (1991) for her campaign for democracy in Myanmar, in the face of fierce opposition from the military government.

SUV *abbr. US* sport-utility vehicle

Suva /sóovə/ capital and largest city of Fiji. Situated on the southeastern coast of Viti Levu Island, it is Fiji's main port. Population: 69,665 (1986).

Suwannee /sóo wónni/ river in the southeastern United States. It rises in southern Georgia and flows 306 km/190 mi. through Florida into the Gulf of Mexico.

suzerain /sóo zə rayn/ *n.* a nation that controls a dependent nation's international affairs but otherwise allows it to control its internal affairs [Early 19thC. From Old French *suserain*, of uncertain origin: probably formed from *sus* 'up' (from Latin *su(r)sum*) on the model of *souverain* (see SOVEREIGN).] —**suzerainty** /-rənti/ *n.*

Suzhou /sóo jō/ city on the Grand Canal in southern Jiangsu Province, eastern China. Population: 706,459 (1990).

Suzman /sóozmən, sóozmən/, **Helen** (*b.* 1917) South African politician. As an MP and cofounder (1959) of the Progressive Party, she campaigned against apartheid and assisted the transition to majority rule in South Africa.

Sv *symbol.* sievert

SV *abbr.* RELIG **1.** Holy Virgin **2.** Your Holiness

s.v., **sv** *abbr.* **1.** sailing vessel **2.** under the word or term **3.** side valve

SV40 /éss vée fáwrti/ *n.* a virus that causes cancer in monkeys and is widely used in genetic and medical research [SV from *simian virus*]

Svalbard /svál baard/ Norwegian archipelago in the Arctic Ocean. Population: 2,864 (1996). Area: 62,050 sq. km/23,958 sq. mi.

svelte /svelt/ *adj.* graceful and slender in figure or contour [Early 19thC. Via French from Italian *svelto* 'stretched', the past participle of *svellere* 'to pluck out', from assumed Vulgar Latin *exvellere*, from Latin *vellere* 'to pull' (source of English *convulse*).]

Svengali /sven gaáli/ *n.* sb who controls and manipulates sb else, usually for evil purposes [Early 20thC. From the name of a villainous hypnotist in the novel *Trilby* (1894), by George du Maurier.]

Sverdrup Islands /sfáirdrəp-/ island group in Nunavut, Canada, within the Queen Elizabeth Islands, comprising Axel Heiberg, Ellef Ringnes, and Amund Ringnes

SW *abbr.* **1.** COMPASS southwest **2.** COMPASS southwestern **3.** RADIO short wave

Sw. *abbr.* **1.** GEOG Sweden **2.** LANG Swedish

SWA *abbr.* Namibia (*international vehicle registration*)

swab /swob/ *n.* **1.** SURG **SOFT MATERIAL FOR MOPPING UP BLOOD** a small piece of gauze, cotton, or other soft material, used to mop up blood during surgery **2.** MED **SMALL STICK WITH COTTON WOOL** a small stick, wire, or plastic wand with cotton wool attached to one or both ends, often used to clean wounds, apply medicine, or obtain a specimen of sth **3.** MED **SPECIMEN** a specimen of mucus or another secretion obtained by using a swab **4.** ARMS **PIECE OF MATERIAL FOR CLEANING GUN** a small piece of absorbent material that is used to clean the bore of a firearm **5.** **MOP** a mop used to clean decks or floors **6.** **SB WHO MOPS** sb who uses a mop to clean, especially on a ship **7.** **WORTHLESS PERSON** sb who is regarded as uncouth or worthless (*archaic slang*) ■ *vt.* (**swabs, swabbing, swabbed**) **1.** MED **CLEAN WITH A SWAB** to clean out or apply medicine to a wound with a soft piece of material **2.** **MOP STH** to clean sth such as a floor or a deck with a mop **3.** **CLEAN STH UP** to clean up sth such as a spill [Mid-17thC. Back-formation from obsolete *swabber* 'deck mop', from assumed Dutch *zwabber*, from obsolete Dutch *zwabben* 'to mop'.]

swaddle /swódd'l/ (**-dles, -dling, -dled**) *vt.* **1.** **WRAP SB IN STH** to wrap or bandage sb or sth with sth **2.** **WRAP BABY UP TIGHTLY** to wrap a baby tightly in soft material **3.** **SMOTHER** to restrain sb or sth with a complete wrapping [15thC. Origin uncertain: probably a back-formation from Middle English *swadling band*, ultimately from an earlier form of SWATHE.]

swaddling clothes, **swaddling bands** *archaic npl.* **1.** **WRAPPING FOR A BABY** long strips of linen or some other soft material, used in some cultures to wrap babies in order to keep them still and calm **2.** **LIMITATIONS** restrictions or limitations placed on those who are not adults

swaddy /swóddi/ (*plural* **-dies**), **swaddie** *n.* a private soldier (*dated slang*) [Early 19thC. Formed from a dialectal word used as an insult for a country person, of uncertain origin: perhaps from a Scandinavian source.]

Swadeshi /swə dáyshi/ *adj.* *S Asia* **PRODUCED WITHIN INDIA** used in India to describe goods produced within the country of India ■ *n.* *S Asia* HIST **FAVOURING OF INDIAN PRODUCTS** the practice of favouring domestic products and refusing to buy imported goods as part of the struggle for independence in India [Early 20thC. Via Hindi *svadeśī* from, ultimately, Sanskrit *svadeśaḥ* 'your own country'.]

swag /swag/ *n.* **1.** DOMESTIC **CURTAIN** an ornamental drapery or curtain that hangs in a curve between two points **2.** **FESTOON** an ornamental draping of fruit or flowers **3.** **LOOT** stolen property (*slang*) **4.** **PROPERTY** sb's goods or valuables (*slang*) **5.** *Aus* **PACK** a pack or rolled-up blanket containing the personal belongings of a wanderer **6.** **LURCHING MOVEMENT** a lurching or swaying movement ■ *vi.* (**swags, swagging, swagged**) **MOVE WITH LURCH** to move with a lurching or swaying movement [Early 16thC. Origin uncertain: probably from a Scandinavian source.]

swagbelly /swág beli/ *n.* a large overhanging stomach (*informal*) —**swagbellied** /swágbelid/ *adj.*

swage /swayj/ *n.* **1.** **TOOL USED TO SHAPE COLD METAL** a tool or die used to shape cold metal by hammering or applying pressure **2.** = **swage block** ■ *vt.* (**swages, swaging, swaged**) **SHAPE METAL** to bend or shape metal with a swage [14thC. From Old French *souage* 'decorative moulding', of unknown origin.] —**swager** *n.*

swage block *n.* a metal block with holes or grooves used to work cold metal

swagger /swággər/ *vi.* (**-gers, -gering, -gered**) **1.** **STRUT AROUND** to walk in an arrogant or proud way **2.** **BRAG** to talk boastfully about personal accomplishments ■ *n.* **ARROGANT WALK** an arrogant way of walking or behaving [Early 16thC. Origin uncertain: probably formed from SWAG.]

swagger stick *n.* a short stick often carried by army officers

swagman /swág man/ (*plural* **-men** /-men/) *n.* *Aus* a tramp or itinerant worker who carries his belongings in a pack or rolled-up blanket (*informal*)

Swahili /swə heéli, swaa-/ (*plural* **-li** *or* **-lis**) *n.* **1.** PEOPLES **MEMBER OF E AFRICAN PEOPLE** a member of a people who live mainly along the eastern coasts of Central and Southern Africa, and on the islands lying off these regions **2.** LANG **LANGUAGE OF SWAHILI PEOPLE** the national language of Tanzania and Kenya, widely used in Uganda, Congo, and neighbouring countries. Swahili belongs to the Bantu group of Benue-Congo languages, spoken as a native language by around 2 million speakers, but used as a lingua franca by over 20 million people. [Early 19thC. Via Kiswahili from Arabic *sawāḥilīy* 'of the coasts', from *sāḥil* 'coast'.] —**Swahili** *adj.*

swain /swayn/ *n.* (*archaic or literary*) **1.** **YOUNG COUNTRYMAN** a young man who lives in the country **2.** **WOMAN'S ADMIRER** a woman's male admirer or lover [Late 16thC. From Old Norse *sveinn* 'boy, servant', ultimately from a prehistoric Germanic word meaning 'your own'.]

swale /swayl/ *n.* a depression between slopes that provides for drainage [Early 16thC. Origin uncertain.]

Swaledale /swáyl dayl/ (*plural* **-dales** *or* **-dale**) *n.* a breed of hardy sheep originating in northern England and noted for its long fleece. It has long curled horns, a black face, and mottled or grey legs. [Early 20thC. Named after *Swaledale*, an area in North Yorkshire, where it was developed.]

SWALK /swawlk/ *abbr.* sealed with a loving kiss (*sometimes written on the back of an envelope containing a letter to a beloved person*)

swallow[1] /swóllō/ *v.* (**-lows, -lowing, -lowed**) **1.** *vti.* **TAKE IN FOOD** to take in food or liquid through the mouth and pass it down the throat into the stomach **2.** *vi.* **GULP** to perform the act of swallowing, usually as an emotional response to sth ○ *swallowing hard to hold back the tears* **3.** *vt.* **DESTROY STH** to engulf or destroy sth **4.** *vt.* **SUPPRESS FEELINGS** to refrain from expressing thoughts or feelings ○ *Swallow your pride and apologize.* **5.** *vt.* **BELIEVE STH** to accept sth as true without questioning it (*informal*) ○ *They'll never swallow anything so far-fetched.* **6.** *vt.* **ENDURE STH** to put up with sth unpleasant without saying or doing anything to stop it **7.** *vt.* **RETRACT A REMARK** to withdraw a statement or remark as false or unjustified **8.** *vt.* **SPEAK UNCLEARLY** to say words in such a way that you cannot be understood ■ *n.* **1.** **ACT OF TAKING STH DOWN THROAT** the act of taking sth in through the mouth and down the throat **2.** **AMOUNT PASSED DOWN THROAT** an amount taken into the mouth and passed down the throat [Old English *swelgan*; of prehistoric Germanic origin]

Swallow

swallow[2] /swóllō/ *n.* a small graceful swift-flying migratory songbird, with long pointed wings and a notched or forked tail. It eats insects that it catches in flight. Family: Hirundinida. [Old English *swealwe*, of prehistoric Germanic origin]

swallow dive *n.* a dive performed with the back arched, the legs held together straight, and the arms outstretched. US term **swan dive** [From the resemblance of the diving position to the shape of a swallow in flight]

swallow hole *n.* = **sinkhole** [Old English *geswelg* 'deep hole']

swallowtail /swóllō tayl/ (*plural* **-tails** *or* **-tail**) *n.* **1.** ZOOL **BUTTERFLY** a colourful butterfly distinguished by the small tails that extend from the ends of its hind wings. Family: Papilionidae. **2.** BIOL **TAIL OF A SWALLOW** the tail of a swallow or similar bird —**swallow-tailed** *adj.*

swallow-tailed coat *n.* a man's evening tail coat with a split rounded tail

swallowwort /swóllō wurt/ *n.* PLANTS = **greater celandine**

swam past tense of **swim**

swami /swaámi/ *n.* a title of respect for a Hindu saint or religious teacher [Late 18thC. Via Hindi from Sanskrit *svāmin-* 'being your own master'. Ultimately from an Indo-European word meaning 'self', which is also the ancestor of English *suicide*.]

swamp /swomp/ *n.* **WETLAND** an area of land, usually fairly large that is always wet and is overgrown with various shrubs and trees ■ *v.* (**swamps, swamping, swamped**) **1.** *vt.* **INUNDATE AN AREA** to submerge an area in water **2.** *vti.* NAUT **SINK A BOAT** to cause a boat to fill with water and sink, or become full of water and sink **3.** *vt.* **OVERBURDEN SB** to overwhelm sb by being too much or too many to cope with (*usually passive*) [Early 17thC. Origin uncertain.] —**swampy** *adj.*

swamp boat *n.* a flat-bottomed boat used to travel in swamps and shallow water. It is powered by an aeroplane propeller.

swamp cypress *n.* TREES = **bald cypress**

swamper /swómpər/ *n.* *US* **1.** **SWAMP DWELLER OR WORKER** sb who works or lives in a swamp, especially in the southern United States **2.** **SB WHO CLEARS SWAMP** sb who works clearing a swamp of trees and undergrowth or who clears a path through a forest so that logs can be moved **3.** **LORRY DRIVER'S ASSISTANT** an assistant to a lorry driver **4.** **HELPER IN RESTAURANT** a helper in a restaurant

swamp fever *n.* **1.** *US* MED **DISEASE PREVALENT IN SWAMPS** any disease such as malaria or leptospirosis that is liable to be contracted by people in swampy areas **2.** VET **HORSE DISEASE** equine infectious anaemia (*dated*)

swampland /swómp land/ *n.* an area of land that is always moist or that has many swamps in it

swamp pink *n.* an orchid found in the northeastern United States, with rose-coloured flowers marked with purple. Genus: *Arethusa*.

Swan

swan /swon/ *n.* **LARGE LONG-NECKED AQUATIC BIRD** a large graceful aquatic bird with webbed feet and a long slender neck and usually with white plumage. Family: Anatidae. ■ *vi.* (**swans, swanning, swanned**) **WANDER ABOUT IDLY** to wander around in a relaxed way, especially one regarded as irresponsible or selfish (*informal*) [Old English, literally 'singer'. Ultimately from an Indo-European base meaning 'to make a sound', which is also the ancestor of English *sound*.]

───── **WORD KEY: CULTURAL NOTE** ─────

Swan Lake, a ballet by Russian composer Pyotr Ilyich Tchaikovsky (1876). Tchaikovsky's first ballet is the romantic tale of Prince Siegfried, who falls in love with Odette, one of a group of swans he has seen metamorphose into beautiful maidens. When he is tricked into declaring his love for another swan-maiden, Siegfried rushes to Odette and the two drown themselves in the Lake of Tears.

───────────────────────

Swan /swon/ river in southwestern Western Australia, flowing through the city of Perth. Length: 386 km/240 mi.

swan dive *n. US* = **swallow dive**

swank /swangk/ *n.* **SHOW-OFF** an arrogant or conceited person (*informal*) ■ *vi.* (**swanks, swanking, swanked**) **SHOW OFF** to behave or swagger in a pretentious way (*informal*) [Early 19thC; of uncertain origin; originally a dialect word]

swanky /swángki/ *adj.* (*informal*) 1. **HIGH-CLASS** very stylish and expensive 2. **GIVEN TO SHOWING OFF** conceited and boastful —**swankily** *adv.* —**swankiness** *n.*

swannery /swónnəri/ (*plural* -**ies**) *n.* a place where swans are bred and reared

swansdown /swónz down/, **swan's-down** *n.* 1. **SWAN FEATHERS** the soft down feathers of a swan 2. **SOFT FABRIC** a soft woollen fabric often used to make baby clothes 3. = **flannelette**

Swansea /swónzi/ city in southern Wales. It is a major port, at the mouth of the River Tawe, and a university city. Population: 188,200 (1995).

swanskin /swón skin/ *n.* any of several cotton or woollen fabrics that are very soft to the touch

swan song *n.* 1. **FINAL PUBLIC ACT** a final appearance, performance, or work, as a farewell to a career or profession 2. **DYING SONG** a song of legendary beauty said to be sung only once by a swan during its lifetime, when it is dying

swap, **swop** *vti.* (**swaps, swapping, swapped; swops, swopping, swopped**) **EXCHANGE STH** to trade or exchange one thing or person for another (*informal*) ■ *n.* 1. **AN EXCHANGE** the exchanging of one thing or person for another (*informal*) 2. **STH EXCHANGED** sb or sth that is traded or exchanged (*informal*) 3. **FIN CONTRACT** a contract in which the parties exchange liabilities on outstanding debts, often exchanging fixed-rate interest for debts with floating-rate interest, either as a means of managing debt or in the business of trading [14thC. Origin uncertain: probably from an earlier meaning 'to strike' (ultimately an imitation of the sound), from the practice of striking hands together to seal an agreement.]

swaption /swópsh'n/ *n.* an option giving the holder the right to enter into a swap [Contraction of *swap option*]

swaraj /swə ráaj/ *n. S Asia* self-government as a political objective in British India [Early 20thC. Via Hindi

svarāj from Sanskrit *svarājyam*, literally 'own rule'.] —**swarajism** *n.* —**swarajist** *n.*

sward /swawrd/ *n.* **AREA OF GRASS** an area of turf or grass ■ *vti.* (**swards, swarding, swarded**) **COVER OR BECOME COVERED WITH GRASS** to cover or become covered with turf or grass [Old English *sweard* 'hairy skin, rind', of prehistoric Germanic origin]

swarf /swawrf/ *n.* 1. **ORBITING DEBRIS** debris, especially from disintegrating satellites, orbiting the Earth (*informal*) 2. **GRINDINGS** the fine metallic shavings removed by grinding or cutting tools [Mid-16thC. Origin uncertain: possibly from a Scandinavian source.]

swarm[1] /swawrm/ *n.* 1. **GROUP OF INSECTS** a large group of insects, especially bees or gnats, in flight 2. **LARGE MASS** a large crowd or group of people or animals moving in a confused or disorderly way ■ *v.* (**swarms, swarming, swarmed**) 1. *vi.* **FORM A FLYING GROUP** to form a flying group, especially to found a new colony ○ *Do bees swarm often?* 2. *vi.* **MOVE IN A MASS** to move or gather in a large crowd ○ *people swarmed all over the road* 3. *vi.* **BE OVERRUN** to be overrun with a large mass or group ○ *swarming with people* 4. *vt.* **CAUSE STH TO SWARM** to cause sth to swarm, or produce a swarm [Old English *swearm*. Ultimately from a prehistoric Germanic word that was an imitation of the sound of buzzing.]

swarm[2] /swawrm/ (**swarms, swarming, swarmed**) *vi.* to climb up somewhere using the arms and legs [Mid-16thC. Origin unknown.]

swarm cell, **swarm spore** *n.* = **zoospore**

swart /swawrt/ *adj.* swarthy (*archaic or literary*) [Old English *sweart*. Ultimately from an Indo-European base meaning 'dirty, black', which is also the ancestor of English *sordid*.]

swarthy /swáwrthi/ *adj.* (-**ier**, -**iest**) *adj.* with a dark and often weather-beaten complexion [Late 16thC. Alteration of obsolete *swarty*, from SWART.] —**swarthily** *adv.* —**swarthiness** *n.*

swash /swosh/ *n.* 1. **GEOG CHANNEL** a narrow channel through which tides flow 2. **GEOG SANDBAR** a sandbar that is washed over by waves 3. **SPLASH** the motion or sound of the motion of water splashing or washing over sth 4. **ARROGANCE** boastful or arrogant behaviour (*archaic*) 5. = **swashbuckler** ■ *v.* (**swashes, swashing, swashed**) 1. *vi.* **WASH OVER** to strike or move with a splashing sound 2. *vt.* **SPLASH STH** to throw a liquid at or on sth, especially with a splashing sound 3. *vi.* **STRUT** to move in a swaggering, pretentious way (*dated*) [Early 16thC. Origin uncertain: probably an imitation of the sound of splashing liquid or of a blow.]

swashbuckler /swósh buklər/ *n.* 1. **ADVENTURER** a bold and swaggering swordsman or adventurer 2. **LITERAT, CINEMA NOVEL OR FILM ABOUT ADVENTURER** a play, novel, or film about an adventurer [Mid-16thC. From SWASH + BUCKLER, from the sound of swords striking shields.] —**swashbuckling** *adj.*

swash letter /swósh-/ *n.* an ornate italic letter with elaborate flourishes and tails [Origin unknown]

swastika /swósstikə/ *n.* 1. **POL NAZI SYMBOL** a Nazi and fascist symbol formed by a Greek cross with the four ends of the arms bent in a clockwise direction. It became the official symbol of Nazi Germany in 1935. 2. **RELIG RELIGIOUS SYMBOL** an ancient religious symbol formed by a Greek cross, usually with the four ends of the arms bent at right angles in a clockwise or anticlockwise direction [Late 19thC. From Sanskrit *svastikaḥ* 'good-luck sign', from *svasti* 'good luck', literally 'well-being'.]

swat /swot/, **swot** *vti.* (**swats, swatting, swatted; swots, swotting, swotted**) **STRIKE OR SLAP STH** to strike or slap sb or sth sharply ■ *n.* 1. **SHARP BLOW** a sharp blow or slap 2. = **swatter** [Early 17thC. Alteration of SQUAT, in the obsolete meaning 'to crush, flatten'.]

swatch /swoch/ *n.* a piece cut from a material, e.g. fabric or carpeting, used as a sample [Early 16thC. Originally a northern English dialect word meaning 'counterfoil', later 'tally attached to cloth sent for dyeing', of unknown origin.]

swath /swoth/, **swathe** /swayth/ *n.* 1. **WIDTH CUT** the width cut by a single passage of a scythe or mowing machine 2. **PATH CUT** the path through a crop made during a single passage of a scythe or mowing

machine 3. **AMOUNT CUT** the amount of grass or corn left in the path made by a single passage of a scythe or mowing machine [Old English *swæþ* 'track', of prehistoric Germanic origin] ◇ **cut a swath through sth** to destroy or use up a large part of sth

swathe[1] /swayth/ *vt.* (**swathes, swathing, swathed**) 1. **WRAP COMPLETELY** to wrap or cover sb or sth completely with bandages or as if with bandages 2. **ENFOLD** to envelop sb or sth ■ *n.* **WRAPPING** a bandage, wrapping, or other binding [Old English *swapian* 'to wrap up': of uncertain origin]

swathe[2] *n.* = **swath**

swatter /swóttər/, **swotter** *n.* a flat meshed flexible piece of metal or plastic attached to a long handle, used to kill insects, especially flies

sway /sway/ *v.* (**sways, swaying, swayed**) 1. *vti.* **SWING** to swing or cause sth to swing back and forth 2. *vi.* **LEAN OVER** to lean or bend to one side or in different directions in turn 3. *vti.* **WAVER BETWEEN OPINIONS** to go back and forth or cause sb to go back and forth between two or more opinions 4. *vt.* **INFLUENCE** to persuade or influence sb to believe or do sth (*usually passive*) ○ *Don't let yourself be swayed.* 5. *vi.* **MOVE GRACEFULLY** to move back and froth in a graceful way 6. *vi.* **STAGGER** to move from side to side in a clumsy and unsteady way 7. *vt.* **SAILING HOIST STH** to hoist a yard, mast, or other spar (*technical*) ■ *n.* 1. **SWINGING MOTION** the act of swinging back and forth 2. **CONTROL OVER SB** influence or control over a person, groups or country [13thC. Origin uncertain: probably from a Scandinavian source.] —**swayable** *adj.* —**swayer** *n.*

sway-back *n.* an extreme inward or downward curving of the spine in horses and human beings

Swazi /swáazi/ (*plural* -**zi** *or* -**zis**) *n.* 1. **PEOPLES MEMBER OF AFRICAN PEOPLE** a member of an African people who live in Swaziland and parts of Transvaal in South Africa 2. **LANG SWAZI LANGUAGE** an official language of Swaziland, along with English. It belongs to the Benue-Congo family of languages. Swazi is spoken by around two million people. [Late 19thC. Alteration of Nguni *Mswati*, the name of a former Swazi king.] —**swazi** *adj.*

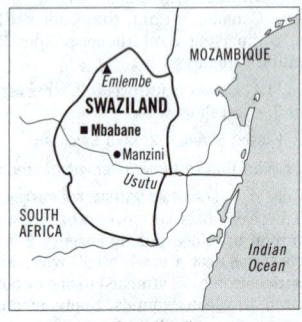

Swaziland

Swaziland /swázi land/ landlocked monarchy in southern Africa. It became independent from Britain in 1968. Language: Swazi, English. Currency: lilangeni. Capital: Mbabane. Population: 934,000 (1996). Area: 17,363 sq. km/6704 sq. mi. Official name **Kingdom of Swaziland**

swbd *abbr.* switchboard

SWbS *abbr.* southwest by south

SWbW *abbr.* southwest by west

swear /swair/ *v.* (**swears, swearing, swore** /swawr/, **sworn** /swawrn/) 1. *vti.* **AFFIRM TRUTH OF STH** to declare solemnly or forcefully that what is said is true, sometimes calling sb or sth thought to be sacred as a witness ○ *She swore on her mother's grave that she had done as she had been asked.* 2. *vti.* **SOLEMNLY PROMISE** to promise sth very solemnly ○ *He swore that he would serve humanity.* 3. *vi.* **SAY STH OFFENSIVE** to use blasphemous or obscene language, usually as an expression of strong feelings or with the intention of giving offence 4. *vti.* **TAKE AN OATH** to make a formal promise in a court of law or when taking up an official position 5. *vti.* **DECLARE STH ON OATH** to make a solemn statement under oath, especially in a court of law, or cause sb to make such a statement 6. *vt.* **MAKE SB PROMISE SOLEMNLY** to cause sb to take an oath or make a promise ■ *n.* **BURST OF OFFENSIVE LANGUAGE** a short spell of using blasphemous or obscene language [Old English *swerian.* Ultimately, from an Indo-European base that is also the ancestor of English *sermon* and *answer.*] —**swearer** *n.*

swear by *vt.* **1. TRUST STH OR SB** to have great faith or complete confidence in the effectiveness of sth or the ability of sb for a particular purpose or task **2. CALL ON SB AS WITNESS** to use the name of a person or thing thought to be sacred to reinforce a solemn declaration or promise

swear in *vt.* to cause sb to make a formal promise in a court of law or when taking up an official position

swear off *vt.* to make a solemn promise to give sth up, especially a bad habit

swearword /swáir wurd/ *n.* a word or phrase that is considered unacceptable in polite language, especially one that is blasphemous or obscene, used to express strong feelings or give offence

sweat /swet/ *n.* **1. MOISTURE ON SKIN** the clear salty liquid that passes to the surface of the skin when sb is hot or as a result of strenuous activity, fear, anxiety, or illness **2. STATE OF HAVING SWEAT ON SKIN** the production or secretion of sweat, e.g. during strenuous activity or illness, or a state of fear or anxiety that causes this **3.** SCI **MOISTURE CONDENSED ON SURFACE** drops of liquid that appear on the surface of sth, usually by condensation of water vapour from the surrounding warmer air **4.** SCI **LIQUID EXUDED TO THE SURFACE** drops of liquid that ooze through and collect on the surface of sth, e.g. sap on a tree **5. HARD OR BORING WORK** hard, unpleasant, or tedious work **6.** HORSERACING **RUN BEFORE RACE** a run that a horse has before a race, as exercise **7. EXPERIENCED PERSON** an experienced person, especially a soldier (*dated informal*) ■ **sweats** *npl. US* CLOTHES **TWO-PIECE SPORTS OUTFIT** a sweatshirt and sweatpants made of matching fabric and worn together for sport or casual activities ■ *v.* **(sweats, sweating, sweated) 1.** *vt.* **MAKE SB SWEAT** to make sb sweat, e.g. as a medical treatment, **2.** *vt.* **WET OR MARK WITH SWEAT** to make sth damp or stained with sweat **3.** *vti.* SCI **FORM OR APPEAR AS MOISTURE** to produce or form as moisture on the surface of sth, usually by condensation of water vapour from the surrounding warmer air **4.** *vti.* SCI **EXUDE LIQUID AT THE SURFACE** to produce or form as liquid beads by oozing through the surface of sth and collecting there **5.** *vti.* AGRIC **REMOVE MOISTURE** to remove moisture, e.g. when fermenting fruits or tobacco or when curing animal hides **6.** *vti.* COOK **COOK STH IN OWN JUICES** to cook sth in a covered pan in its own juices until tender **7.** *vt.* **HEAT SOLDER UNTIL IT MELTS** to heat solder until it melts and runs between surfaces to bond them **8.** *vi.* **WORK HARD** to work very hard or overwork (*informal*) **9.** *vt.* **OVERWORK OR UNDERPAY EMPLOYEES** to make sb work very hard, often in poor conditions or for low wages (*informal*) **10.** *vt. US* **EXTORT INFORMATION FROM SB** to force sb to give up information, especially by relentless interrogation or physical violence (*informal*) **11.** *vi.* **BE UNDER STRESS** to be very anxious, impatient, or afraid (*informal*) ○ *He left them sweating in the corridor while he made up his mind.* **12.** *vi.* **SUFFER FOR WRONGDOING** to suffer physically or mentally, especially as a punishment (*informal*) [Old English *swǣt.* Ultimately from an Indo-European base that is also the ancestor of Latin *sudor* (source of English *exude*).] —**sweatless** *adj.* ◇ **no sweat** used to say that sth can be done with ease and without foreseeable problems (*slang*)

sweat off *vt.* to get rid of excess weight by sweating, e.g. in a sauna or through strenuous activity

sweat out *vt.* **1.** MED **GET RID OF ILLNESS BY SWEATING** to relieve the symptoms of an illness by maintaining a raised body temperature, and hence cause profuse sweating **2. ENDURE STH TO THE END** to carry on doing sth difficult or put up with sth unpleasant until it is over (*informal*) ◇ **sweat your guts out** to work very hard (*informal*)

sweatband /swét band/ *n.* **1.** SPORTS **BAND WORN TO ABSORB SWEAT** a strip of terry cotton or other fabric worn around the head or wrists to stop sweat running into the eyes or onto the hands while playing sport **2.** CLOTHES **BAND PROTECTING HAT FROM SWEAT** a strip of fabric or leather sewn inside a hat to protect it from damage by sweat

sweatbox /swét boks/ *n.* **1. DEVICE FOR REMOVING WATER FROM HIDES** a device in which hides or some fruits are placed to remove water **2. CONFINED PLACE** a very small room, especially a narrow cell where a prisoner is confined for punishment (*informal*) **3. PLACE WHERE SB SWEATS** a place where sb is made to sweat through heat or fear (*informal*)

sweated /swéttid/ *adj.* **1. OVERWORKED AND UNDERPAID** made to work very hard in poor conditions for low wages (*disapproving*) **2. DONE OR MADE BY EXPLOITED WORKERS** performed or produced by employees who are made to work very hard in poor conditions for low wages

sweater /swéttər/ *n.* **1.** CLOTHES **KNITTED GARMENT** a warm knitted piece of clothing, usually with long sleeves, worn on the upper part of the body **2. SB WHO IS SWEATING** sb who is sweating visibly, or who sweats to a specified degree **3.** HR **SB OVERWORKING UNDERPAID EMPLOYEES** an employer who makes people work very hard in poor conditions for low wages [The meaning 'knitted garment' developed from 'clothes worn to produce sweat and reduce weight']

sweat gland *n.* any of numerous small tube-shaped glands in the skin of most parts of the body from which sweat is released

sweatpants /swét pants/ *npl. US* long trousers made of a soft knitted fabric that has fleece on the reverse, often with elastic at the waist and ankles, worn casually or for exercising

sweatshirt /swét shurt/ *n.* a long-sleeved pullover or zipped jacket made of soft knitted fabric with fleece on the inside, worn casually or for sport

sweatshop /swét shop/ *n.* a small factory or other establishment where employees are made to work very hard in poor conditions for low wages

sweat suit *n. US* a sweatshirt and sweatpants made of matching fabric and worn together for sport or casual activities

sweaty /swétti/ **(-ier, -iest)** *adj.* **1. DAMP WITH SWEAT** damp with or smelling of sweat **2. CAUSING SWEAT** making sb sweat **3.** SCI **WITH MOISTURE ON SURFACE** with drops of exuded or condensed liquid on the surface —**sweatily** *adv.* —**sweatiness** *n.*

swede /sweed/ *n.* US term **rutabaga 1.** PLANTS **EUROPEAN TURNIP** a European turnip of the mustard family with a large edible yellowish root. Latin name: *Brassica napus napobrassica.* **2.** FOOD **ROOT EATEN AS VEGETABLE** the large round root of the swede plant, with yellowish flesh that is cooked and eaten as a vegetable [Early 19thC. From SWEDE, from its introduction (into Scotland) from Sweden.]

Swede /sweed/ *n.* sb who was born or brought up in Sweden, or who has Swedish citizenship [Early 17thC. From Middle Low German or Middle Dutch *Swēde,* of uncertain origin: probably, ultimately, from Old Norse *Svíar* (plural) 'Swedes' + *þjóð* 'people'.]

Sweden

Sweden /swéed'n/ kingdom in Scandinavia, in northwestern Europe. Language: Swedish. Currency: krona. Capital: Stockholm. Population: 8,858,000 (1996). Area: 449,964 sq. km/173,732 sq. mi. Official name **Kingdom of Sweden**

Swedenborg /swéed'n bawrg/, **Emanuel** (1688–1772) Swedish scientist and theologian. His theology, deriving from his mystical experiences, led to the formation of the Swedenborgian religious movement. Real name **Emanuel Swedberg** —**Swedenborgian** /swéed'n báwrji ən, -gi ən/ *n., adj.*

Swedish /swéedish/ *n.* **OFFICIAL LANGUAGE OF SWEDEN** the official language of Sweden and one of the two official languages of Finland. Swedish belongs to the North Germanic branch of the Indo-European family of languages. It is spoken by about 8.5 million people. ■ *adj.* **1. OF SWEDEN** relating to Sweden, or its people or culture **2. OF SWEDISH** relating to the Swedish language [Early 17thC. Formed from either SWEDEN or SWEDE.]

Swedish massage *n.* a system of massage employing both active and passive exercising of the muscles and joints [*Swedish* from the system of massage having originated in Sweden]

Swedish mile *n.* a unit of measure used in Sweden equal to 10 km/6.2 mi

sweeny /swéeni/, **sweeney** *n.* atrophy of the shoulder muscles of horses due to harness pressure on nerves going to these muscles [Early 19thC. Origin uncertain: perhaps from German dialect *Schweine* 'emaciation, atrophy'.]

sweep /sweep/ *v.* **(sweeps, sweeping, swept** /swept/, **swept) 1.** *vti.* **CLEAN A PLACE WITH A BROOM** to remove sth such as dust, dirt, debris, or snow from the floor or ground with a broom, brush, or similar implement **2.** *vt.* **CLEAR A CHIMNEY** to remove soot from the inside of a chimney with a long-handled brush **3.** *vt.* **MOVE STH WITH A HORIZONTAL STROKE** to move sth with a long smooth stroke or a quick brushing stroke ○ *I swept the papers off the desk.* **4.** *vti.* **BRUSH AGAINST THE GROUND** to brush against a horizontal surface such as the floor or the ground **5.** *vi.* **MOVE WITH SPEED AND FORCE** to move quickly, smoothly, and forcefully, often in a large body or group ○ *the crowd swept across the bridge* **6.** *vi.* **MOVE WITH DIGNITY** to move quickly and smoothly with a proud, majestic, or self-important air ○ *swept angrily out of the room* **7.** *vti.* **MOVE ACROSS A PLACE** to move quickly and forcefully across an area ○ *the gales that are sweeping the country* **8.** *vti.* **SPREAD THROUGH A PLACE** to pass or spread quickly through a place ○ *the news swept through the city* **9.** *vt.* **CARRY SB OR STH ALONG** to carry sb or sth quickly and forcefully in the same direction ○ *swept along by the current* **10.** *vt.* **GET RID OF STH** to remove, dismiss, or destroy sth quickly, forcefully, and completely ○ *All her illusions were swept away.* **11.** *vt.* **STRONGLY INFLUENCE SB** to strongly influence or overwhelm sb (*often passive*) ○ *We were swept along by their enthusiasm.* **12.** *vti.* **WIN STH OVERWHELMINGLY** to win sth easily and overwhelmingly, or win all the games in a series or set of games for a championship ○ *watched them sweep to victory* **13.** *vi.* **STRETCH OUT IN AN ARC** to extend in a long smooth graceful curve or a wide circle ○ *plains sweeping down to the coast* **14.** *vti.* **EXTEND OVER A WIDE AREA** to be directed over a wide range or the entire area of sth ○ *Her eyes swept around the room.* **15.** *vti.* **SEARCH A PLACE FOR STH** to search a place for sth, e.g. an area of water for mines or a room for hidden recording devices **16.** *vti.* CRICKET **HIT BALL WITH HORIZONTAL BAT** in cricket, to hit a ball from a half-kneeling position by bringing the bat, held almost horizontally, across the body with a long smooth stroke ■ *n.* **1. BOUT OF CLEANING WITH A BRUSH** a cleaning of sth with a brush, broom, or similar implement **2. BRUSHING STROKE** a quick brushing stroke **3. LONG SMOOTH MOVEMENT** a long smooth curved movement ○ *with a sweep of her arm* **4. LONG SMOOTH CURVE** a long smooth graceful curve ○ *the sweep of the coastline* **5. WIDE EXPANSE** a wide expanse or extent ○ *the sweep of the horizon* **6. CURVED RANGE** the range over which sth is directed, usually a wide arc or circle ○ *stay out of the sweep of the searchlights* **7. BROAD RANGE** the broad range or comprehensive nature of sth ○ *the sweep of history* **8. SEARCH** a thorough search ○ *a sweep of the neighbourhood* **9. OVERWHELMING VICTORY** an overwhelming or absolute victory ○ *their sweep to power* **10. SWEEPSTAKE** a sweepstake (*informal*) **11.** = **chimney sweep 12.** CRICKET **SHOT WITH BAT HORIZONTAL** in cricket, a shot in which the ball is hit from a half-kneeling position, bringing the bat, held almost horizontal, across the body with a long smooth stroke **13.** ROWING **OAR FOR PROPELLING A BOAT** a long oar that is used to propel small boats or sometimes act as a rudder **14.** ELECTRON ENG **ELECTRON BEAM MOTION IN CATHODE-RAY TUBE** the steady movement of the electron beam across the fluorescent surface of a cathode-ray tube. The motion may be straight, as with television screens, or circular, as with radar screens. **15. WINDMILL SAIL** a sail of a windmill **16. POLE**

FOR LIFTING A BUCKET IN A WELL a long pole used as a lever to raise or lower a bucket in a well ■ **sweeps** *npl.* *US* TELEVISION RATINGS IN A PARTICULAR PERIOD a periodic survey of television ratings that is used to determine advertising rates, or the period when these ratings are done [13thC. Origin uncertain: probably from the past tense of Old English *swāpan* 'to sweep', from a prehistoric Germanic base meaning 'to swing' (see SWIFT).] —**sweepy** *adj.* ◇ **make a clean sweep (of sth)** 1. to have a complete change by getting rid of everything or everyone unwanted or unnecessary 2. to win everything ◇ **sweep sb off his** *or* **her feet** to attract sb with a sudden and intense romantic passion ○ *I wanted to be swept off my feet by a mysterious lover.*

sweep up *vti.* to remove dust, dirt, or debris from the floor or ground with a brush or similar implement

sweepback /swéep bak/ *n.* an aircraft wing that slants backwards towards the tail assembly, forming an acute angle with the fuselage

sweeper /swéepər/ *n.* 1. SB WHO SWEEPS sb whose job involves sweeping sth, usually floors or roads 2. STH THAT SWEEPS a device or machine, usually fitted with brushes, that sweeps sth such as a floor or a road 3. SOCCER ROVING DEFENSIVE PLAYER in soccer, a defensive player who is not assigned to cover an attacking player but plays across the pitch in the space between other defenders and the goalkeeper

sweep hand *n.* a long hand, mounted concentrically with the minute hand of an analogue watch or clock, that indicates seconds as it sweeps around the same dial as the minute hand

sweeping /swéeping/ *adj.* 1. ON A LARGE SCALE wide-ranging and comprehensive, and usually affecting a large number of things or people ○ *sweeping reforms* 2. TOO GENERAL failing to take specific exceptions or details into consideration ○ *a sweeping condemnation of modern youth* 3. OVERWHELMING complete, overwhelming, or decisive ○ *a sweeping victory* 4. WITH BROAD EXTENT covering a large area, usually a wide arc or circle ○ *included in her sweeping glance* ■ *n.* ACT OF USING A BROOM the action of sb who sweeps with a broom or brush —**sweepingly** *adv.* —**sweepingness** *n.*

sweepings /swéepingz/ *npl.* dirt and refuse swept up

sweep-saw *n.* a thin-bladed saw that is held taut in a frame and used for cutting curves

sweep-second hand *n.* TIME = **sweep hand**

sweepstake *n.* a lottery in which the payout is determined by the amount paid in and the winner determined by the outcome of a horserace, or the prize itself [From the obsolete meaning 'person who takes (sweeps) all the stakes in a game']

sweet /sweet/ *adj.* 1. TASTING OR SMELLING OF SUGAR tasting or smelling of sugar or a similar substance 2. CONTAINING OR RETAINING SUGAR containing a relatively large amount of sugar, or retaining some natural sugars ○ *sweet cider* 3. PHYSIOL NOT SALT, BITTER, OR SOUR associated with the basic taste sensation that is not bitter, salt, or sour 4. FRESH not stale, rancid, or soured ○ *sweet water* 5. NOT SALTY not salty or saline ○ *sweet butter* 6. PLEASING TO THE SENSES pleasing to any of the senses ○ *the sweet strains of the violin* 7. SATISFYING desirable, gratifying, or satisfying ○ *Revenge turned out not to be sweet after all.* 8. KIND kind, thoughtful, or generous ○ *He's so sweet, he never forgets my birthday.* 9. VERY PLEASING TO LOOK AT having an appearance that is charming or endearing ○ *a sweet little cottage by the lake* 10. AGRIC NOT ACIDIC used to describe land that contains no acid or corrosive substances 11. ENERGY CONTAINING LITTLE OR NO SULPHUR used to describe petrol or oil that contains little or no sulphur 12. *Aus* OK satisfactory (*informal*) 13. RESPECTED dear, respected, or beloved (*archaic*) ○ *Indeed, my sweet lord.* ■ *adv.* PLEASANTLY in a pleasant manner ○ *sing sweet* ■ *n.* 1. FOOD SHAPED ITEM OF CONFECTIONERY a small hard, chewy, or soft piece of food made from sugar and other ingredients or flavourings such as chocolate, nuts, fruit, or peppermint. US term **candy** 2. FOOD DESSERT a course or dish of sweet food served at or near the end of a meal ○ *Would you like a sweet?* 3. SWEET FOOD any item of sweet food 4. *US* SWEET POTATO a sweet potato (*informal*) 5. SENSATION OF SWEETNESS a sweet taste or smell 6. STH PLEASANT a pleasant thing or experience (*literary*) ○ *squander the sweets of life* 7. DEAR used as a term of endearment ○ *Come to me, my sweet.* 8. INDUST SULPHUR-FREE NATURAL GAS OR OIL a natural gas or crude oil that is essentially free from acidic or odorous sulphur compounds [Old English *swēte*. Ultimately from an Indo-European word that is also the ancestor of English *assuage* and *suave*.] —**sweetly** *adv.* —**sweetness** *n.* ◇ **be sweet on sb** to be in love with sb (*dated*) ◇ **keep sb sweet** to treat sb with particular kindness or indulgence as a tactic to win favour or secure help or support (*informal*)

sweet alyssum *n.* a perennial European plant widely cultivated for its clusters of low-growing fragrant white, pink, or purple flowers. Latin name: *Lobularia maritima.*

sweet-and-sour *adj.* cooked in or served with a sauce that has sugar and vinegar among the ingredients

sweet basil *n.* a herb with aromatic leaves used for seasoning. Latin name: *Ocimum basilicum.*

sweet bay *n.* 1. = **laurel** *n.* 1 2. N AMERICAN MAGNOLIA a small magnolia bush or tree of the eastern United States that has large fragrant white flowers, yellow-green leaves, and red fruit. Latin name: *Magnolia virginia.*

sweet birch *n.* 1. TREES N AMERICAN BIRCH TREE a birch of the eastern United States with smooth blackish-brown bark, hard dark wood, and aromatic stems that are a source of methyl salicylate. Latin name: *Betula lenta.* 2. INDUST WOOD OF THE SWEET BIRCH the wood from the sweet birch tree

sweetbread /swéet bred/ *n.* the pancreas or thymus of a calf, lamb, or other young animal soaked, fried, and eaten as food [*Bread* probably from Old English *brǣd* 'flesh']

sweetbriar /swéet brīr/ (*plural* **-ars** *or* **-ar**), **sweetbrier** (*plural* **-ers** *or* **-er**) *n.* a rose of Europe and Asia that has a long stem with stout prickles, fragrant leaves, and rosy pink or white single flowers. Latin name: *Rosa rubiginosa.*

sweet cherry *n.* 1. TREES CHERRY TREE a large cherry tree of Europe and Asia that has reddish bark and white flowers and is widely grown for its sweet edible fruit. Latin name: *Prunius avium.* 2. FOOD FRUIT OF THE SWEET CHERRY the fruit of the sweet cherry tree

sweet chestnut *n.* = **chestnut** *n.* 1, **chestnut** *n.* 2

sweet cicely /-síssəli/ (*plural* **sweet cicely**) *n.* 1. HERB WITH AROMATIC ROOTS a herb of the carrot family that is native to America and Asia, with aromatic fleshy roots and clusters of small white flowers. Genus: *Osmorhiza.* 2. EUROPEAN HERB a perennial European herb that has umbels of small white flowers and aromatic compound leaves. Latin name: *Myrrhis odorata.*

sweet clover *n.* = **melilot**

sweetcorn /swéet kawrn/ *n.* 1. PLANTS EDIBLE MAIZE a variety of maize with kernels that contain a high concentration of sugar and are yellowish in colour. Latin name: *Zea mays rugosa.* 2. FOOD MAIZE KERNELS AS FOOD the sweet yellowish kernels of some varieties of maize plant, cooked and eaten as a vegetable

sweeten /swéet'n/ (**-ens, -ening, -ened**) *v.* 1. *vti.* INCREASE IN SWEETNESS to make sth taste sweet or sweeter by adding sugar or some other natural or artificial substance, or to become sweet or sweeter in flavour 2. *vt.* IMPROVE THE TASTE OR SMELL OF STH to make sth taste or smell more pleasant 3. *vt.* MAKE STH MORE DESIRABLE to make sth more attractive, agreeable, or acceptable ○ *sweeten the offer* 4. *vt.* SOFTEN OR PERSUADE SB to make sb kinder, gentler, friendlier, or calmer, or persuade sb by flattery, cajolery, or bribery to accept or agree to sth ○ *might sweeten his temper* 5. *vti.* CHEM ENG IMPROVE THE PROPERTIES OF STH to improve a product by making it less corrosive, its odour less offensive, or its colour more acceptable. Petroleum products are sweetened during refining by the removal of sulphides or the conversion of them into disulphides. 6. *vt.* *US* FIN INCREASE THE VALUE OF COLLATERAL to add securities to collateral so that its value is increased 7. *vt.* CARDS INCREASE VALUE OF A POT in poker, to add stakes to a pot remaining from a previous deal (*informal*)

sweetener /swéet'nər/ *n.* 1. FOOD SUBSTANCE MAKING STH SWEETER a natural or artificial substance that is added to food or drink to make it sweet or sweeter, especially a synthetic substance used in place of sugar 2. EXTRA PAYMENT OR GIFT sth given as a bribe, incentive, or means of persuading sb to accept or agree to sth (*informal*)

sweetening /swéet'ning/ *n.* 1. FOOD SUBSTANCE MAKING STH SWEETER a substance that makes food or drink sweet or sweeter, especially an artificial additive 2. ACT OF MAKING STH SWEET the act of making sth sweet or sweeter

sweet FA /-ef áy/, **sweet Fanny Adams** /-fanni áddəmz/ *n.* nothing at all (*slang*)

sweet fern *n.* an eastern North American shrub of the wax myrtle family that has heads of small brownish flowers and aromatic leaves similar to those of a fern. Latin name: *Comptonia peregrina.*

sweet flag *n.* a perennial marsh herb that has narrow sword-shaped leaves, tiny greenish flowers, and an aromatic rootstock. Latin name: *Acorus calamus.*

sweet gale *n.* a shrub of the bayberry family that is native to marshy regions of Europe, Asia, and North America and has aromatic lance-shaped leaves. Latin name: *Myrica gale.*

sweet gum *n.* 1. N AMERICAN TREE WITH HARD WOOD a North American tree of the witch hazel family that has lobed leaves, hard wood, and round prickly fruit clusters. Latin name: *Liquidambar styraciflua.* 2. AROMATIC RESIN the amber aromatic resin of the sweet gum tree

sweetheart /swéet haart/ *n.* 1. BOYFRIEND OR GIRLFRIEND sb who is a boyfriend, girlfriend, or lover (*dated*) 2. AFFECTIONATE TERM OF ADDRESS used as a term of endearment, usually addressed to a lover or child 3. KIND PERSON a kind or obliging person ○ *Be a sweetheart and make me a cup of coffee, will you?* 4. STH CHERISHED sth cherished for its fine qualities and often considered one of a kind

sweetheart agreement *n.* 1. AGREEMENT SUITING SOME BUT NOT OTHERS an arrangement arrived at secretly to benefit some at the expense of the rest, especially an industrial agreement between union and management representatives that is not in the workers' best interest 2. *Aus* INDUSTRIAL AGREEMENT WITHOUT ARBITRATION in industrial relations, an agreement reached through direct discussions between workers and their employer without recourse to arbitration [*Sweetheart* from the privileged treatment of one party]

sweetheart neckline *n.* on women's clothing, a low-cut neckline with two curves over the bust, making the bodice look heart-shaped

sweetie /swéeti/ *n.* 1. PIECE OF CONFECTIONERY a boiled sweet, toffee, or other piece of confectionery (*informal; except in Scotland, usually used by or to children*) 2. TERM OF ENDEARMENT used as a term of endearment (*informal*) 3. ENDEARING PERSON OR ANIMAL a likeable or lovable person or animal (*informal*) 4. SWEET GRAPEFRUIT a seedless variety of grapefruit with a greenish-coloured rind and sweet juicy flesh

sweetie pie *n.* a lovable or likeable person (*informal*)

sweeting /swéeting/ *n.* loved or cherished person (*archaic*)

sweet marjoram *n.* a Mediterranean herb that has small purple flowers and aromatic leaves used as a seasoning in cookery and salads. Latin name: *Origanum majorana.*

sweetmeal /swéet meel/ *adj.* made with wholemeal flour that has been sweetened, usually by adding sugar

sweetmeat /swéet meet/ *n.* a superior type of sweet or confectionery served at the end of a meal or with tea (*archaic*)

sweetness and light *n.* pleasantness and friendliness or peace and harmony, especially in contrast to normal behaviour or circumstances ○ *He has a vile temper, but when he gets his way, he's all sweetness and light.*

sweet nothings *npl.* romantic words and phrases

sweet oil *n.* any mild-flavoured oil, e.g. sweet almond oil or grapeseed oil

sweet pea *n.* a climbing plant of the legume family, native to Italy and widely cultivated for its sweet-scented butterfly-shaped flowers. Latin name: *Lathyrus odoratus.*

sweet pepper *n.* **1.** PLANTS **PEPPER PLANT** a variety of pepper plant with large bell-shaped fruits. Latin name: *Capsicum frutescens grossum.* **2.** FOOD **PEPPER USED AS A VEGETABLE** the fruit of the sweet pepper plant, eaten raw or cooked as a vegetable

sweet potato *n.* **1.** PLANTS **PLANT PRODUCING FLESHY EDIBLE TUBERS** a tropical American vine with funnel-shaped purplish flowers, cultivated for its fleshy yellow tuberous root. The tuber is similar to that of the yam, but the plants are unrelated. Latin name: *Ipomoea batatas.* **2.** FOOD **SWEET POTATO ROOT USED AS A VEGETABLE** the fleshy orange root of the sweet potato plant, cooked and eaten as a vegetable

sweetshop /swéet shop/ *n.* a shop that sells sweets and sometimes other items, e.g. cigarettes or newspapers. US term **candy store**

sweetsop /swéet sop/ (*plural* **-sops** *or* **-sop**) *n.* **1.** PLANTS **TROPICAL AMERICAN EVERGREEN SHRUB** a tropical evergreen shrub that is native to America and is grown for its edible fruit. Latin name: *Annona squamosa.* **2.** FOOD **FRUIT OF THE SWEETSOP** the fruit of the sweetsop, which has a hard green rind and a sweet edible pulp [From the sweet pulp of its fruit]

sweet sorghum *n.* = **sorgo**

sweet spot *n.* the most effective place to hit the ball on a racket, bat, club, or other piece of sports equipment [*Sweet* in the sense of 'desirable']

sweet sultan (*plural* **sweet sultans** *or* **sweet sultan**) *n.* a shrub native to the countries of the eastern Mediterranean that is noted for its large variously coloured flowers. Latin name: *Centaurea moschata.* [Ultimately from *sultan's flower*]

sweet talk *n.* flattering or pleasing words used to persuade sb (*informal*)

sweet-talk *vti.* to use flattering or pleasing words to persuade sb to do sth (*informal*)

sweet tooth *n.* a particular fondness for sweet food

sweet william /-wíllyəm/ (*plural* **sweet williams** *or* **sweet william**) *n.* a plant of Europe and Asia widely grown for its flat clusters of white, pink, red, or purple flowers with banded or mottled patterns. Latin name: *Dianthus barbatus.* [*William* from the first name *William*]

sweet woodruff *n.* = **woodruff**

swell /swel/ *v.* (**swells, swelling, swelled, swollen** /swṓlən/ *or* **swelled**) **1.** *vti.* **INCREASE IN SIZE** to make sth larger, fuller, or rounder, or to expand in size or shape, usually as a result of pressure from within ○ *the wind swelled the sails* **2.** *vi.* MED **BECOME LARGER THAN NORMAL** to increase in size temporarily, typically as a result of injury, infection, or other medical condition ○ *my ankles had swelled in the heat* **3.** *vti.* **INCREASE IN QUANTITY** to increase sth in number or amount, usually by adding to it, or to increase in this way ○ *new members to swell the ranks of the Party* **4.** *vti.* **INCREASE IN DEGREE** to make sth stronger or more intense, or become stronger or more intense ○ *could feel indignation swelling inside her* **5.** *vti.* MUSIC **INCREASE AND DECREASE IN LOUDNESS** in music, to alternate in growing gradually louder and softer, or alternately increase and decrease in volume **6.** *vti.* **FILL WITH EMOTION** to be filled, or cause sb's heart or soul to be filled, with a strong feeling or emotion ○ *His heart swelled with pride.* **7.** *vi.* **UNDULATE ON A SURFACE** to rise and fall in long large waves ■ *n.* **1.** **UNDULATION OF THE SEA SURFACE** the rising and falling movement of a large area of the sea as a long wave travels through it without breaking ○ *There's quite a swell out there today.* **2.** **ROUND SHAPE** the full, round shape of sth **3.** **BULGE** a bulge or protuberance **4.** **INCREASING OF SIZE** an increase in size, fullness, or roundness **5.** **INCREASING OF NUMBER** an increase in number, amount, or degree **6.** MUSIC **CRESCENDO THEN DIMINUENDO** a gradual increase in the loudness of music followed by a gradual decrease, or the sign indicating this **7.** MUSIC = **swell box** **8.** **GENTLE SLOPE** a low hill or gentle slope **9.** **FASHIONABLE PERSON** a fashionably and expensively dressed person (*dated informal*) **10.** **SB OF HIGH STATUS** a very important person, especially in society or politics (*dated informal*) ■ *adj.* *US* **GOOD** very good (*dated informal*) [Old English *swellan*, from prehistoric Germanic. The meaning 'fashionable person', which gave rise to the adjective, probably evolved from '(showing) swollen, pompous behaviour'.]

swell box *n.* a device on an organ, usually an enclosed box with pipes, that permits crescendo and diminuendo, a characteristic otherwise lacking on this instrument [*Swell* from the part of the organ housed in the box]

swelled head *n.* *US* = **swollen head**

swellfish /swél fish/ (*plural* **-fish** *or* **-fishes**) *n.* ZOOL a puffer fish [*Swell* from its ability to inflate by swallowing air]

swellhead /swél hed/ *n.* *US* sb who is conceited and arrogant (*informal*) —**swellheaded** /-héddid/ *adj.* —**swellheadedness** /-héddidnəss/ *n.*

swelling /swélling/ *n.* **1.** MED **ENLARGEMENT** an increase in size of part of the body, typically as a result of injury, infection, or other medical condition ○ *The swelling should go down in a couple of days.* **2.** **LUMP OR PROTUBERANCE** a bulge or protuberance caused by swelling

swelter /swéltər/ *v.* (**-ters, -tering, -tered**) **1.** *vi.* **BE OPPRESSED BY HEAT** to feel uncomfortably hot ○ *We had been sweltering in a hot car all afternoon.* **2.** *vt.* **EXUDE STH** to exude sth such as venom (*archaic*) ○ *'Toad, that under cold stone Days and nights has thirty-one Swelter'd venom sleeping got, Boil thou first i' the charmed pot.'* (William Shakespeare, *Macbeth*; 1623) ■ *n.* **UNPLEASANT HEAT OR SENSATION OF HOTNESS** excessive or oppressive heat, or the uncomfortable feeling it produces [15thC. Literally 'to faint repeatedly', formed from *swelten* 'to faint', from Old English *sweltan* 'to die', from a prehistoric Germanic base meaning 'to burn'.]

sweltering /swéltəring/ *adj.* **1.** **OPPRESSIVELY HOT** oppressively hot **2.** **FEELING VERY HOT** feeling uncomfortably hot —**swelteringly** *adv.*

swept past tense, past participle of **sweep**

sweptback /swépt bák/ *adj.* used to describe a wing that is angled backwards towards the aircraft's tail

sweptwing /swépt wing/ *adj.* used to describe an aircraft or missile that has sweptback wings

swerve /swurv/ *vti.* (**swerves, swerving, swerved**) **TURN AWAY FROM A DIRECT COURSE** to make a sudden change in direction, often to avoid a collision, or make sth change direction suddenly ○ *had to swerve to avoid a pedestrian* ■ *n.* **ABRUPT CHANGE IN DIRECTION** a sudden change in direction [Old English *sweorfan* 'to file, scour, turn aside'. Ultimately from an Indo-European word meaning 'to turn'.] —**swerver** *n.*

sweven /swévv'n/ *n.* a dream or a vision experienced in sleep (*archaic literary*) [Old English *swef(e)n*. Ultimately from an Indo-European word meaning 'to sleep', which is also the ancestor of English *hypnosis, somnolent,* and *soporific*.]

Sweyn I /swayn/, **King of Denmark** (960?–1014). He first invaded England in 994, and by 1014 established his rule sufficiently for his son Canute II to become king (1016–35). Known as **Sweyn Forkbeard**

SWG *abbr.* standard wire gauge

Swift

swift /swift/ *adj.* **1.** **HAPPENING FAST** happening or done very quickly or suddenly ○ *issued a swift denial* **2.** **ACTING FAST** acting very quickly or promptly ○ *they were swift to respond* **3.** **MOVING FAST** moving or able to move very quickly ■ *adv.* **QUICKLY** very quickly ○ *a swift-flowing river* ■ *n.* **1.** (*plural* **swift** *or* **swifts**) BIRDS **SMALL BIRD RESEMBLING SWALLOW** a small dark bird related to the hummingbirds and resembling a swallow, that has long narrow wings. Swifts are noted for their rapid flight. Family: Apodidae. **2.** ZOOL **SMALL FAST LIZARD** a small fast-running North American lizard. Genera: *Sceloporus* and *Uta.* **3.** TEXTILES **REEL OR CYLINDER ON A MACHINE** the reel on which yarn is placed while it is wound off, or the cylinder on a machine that cards flax [Old English, 'quick, moving along a course', from a prehistoric Germanic base meaning 'to swing, bend', which is also the ancestor of English *sweep, swivel,* and *swoop*] —**swiftly** *adv.* —**swiftness** *n.*

Swift /swift/, **Jonathan, Dean** (1667–1745) Irish author and clergyman. The dean of St Patrick's, Dublin, he was the leading satirist of his age. He wrote *Gulliver's Travels* (1726) and *A Tale of a Tub* (1704). —**Swiftian** *adj.*

Swift Current /swift kúrrənt/ town and railway junction 245 km/152 mi. west of Regina in southwestern Saskatchewan, Canada. Population: 16,437 (1996).

swift fox *n.* a small western North American fox with large ears. Latin name: *Vulpes velox.*

swiftie /swífti/ *n.* *ANZ* a trick or deception (*informal*)

swiftlet /swíftlət/ *n.* a small cave-dwelling Asian swift whose nest is used in making birds' nest soup. Genus: *Collocalia.*

swig /swig/ *vti.* (**swigs, swigging, swigged**) **DRINK IN LARGE GULPS** to drink sth in large gulps (*informal*) ■ *n.* **LARGE GULP OF DRINK** a large gulp of drink (*informal*) [Mid-16thC. Origin unknown.] —**swigger** *n.*

swill /swil/ *v.* (**swills, swilling, swilled**) **1.** *vt.* **WASH STH WITH WATER** to wash or rinse sth by flooding or filling it with water **2.** *vti.* **MOVE LIQUID AROUND IN STH** to make liquid move around or over sth, or move in this way ○ *He swilled the water around in the bucket.* **3.** *vti.* **DRINK A LOT OF STH** to drink large amounts of sth (*disapproving*) **4.** *vt.* AGRIC **FEED PIGS WITH WATERY FEED** to feed animals, especially pigs, with a watery feed typically containing kitchen waste or food by-products ■ *n.* **1.** AGRIC **PIG FEED** a watery feed for livestock, especially pigs, typically containing kitchen waste or food by-products **2.** **KITCHEN WASTE** kitchen waste or general refuse **3.** **WASHING OF STH WITH WATER** a wash or rinse using a large amount of water **4.** **LARGE DRINK** a large drink or mouthful of drink **5.** **INFERIOR FOOD OR DRINK** inferior or unpleasant food or drink **6.** **SLOPPY LIQUID MIXTURE** a sloppy liquid mixture or mess **7.** **NONSENSE** talk or writing that is utter nonsense (*informal*) [Old English *swillan*. Ultimately from an Indo-European base that is also the ancestor of English *swallow*. Originally in the meaning 'to wash, gargle'.] —**swiller** *n.*

swim /swim/ *v.* (**swims, swimming, swam** /swam/, **swum** /swum/) **1.** *vi.* **MOVE THROUGH WATER** to move or propel yourself unsupported through water using natural means of propulsion such as legs, tails, or fins **2.** *vt.* **TRAVEL A DISTANCE BY SWIMMING** to cross a particular stretch of water or travel a particular distance by swimming **3.** *vt.* **COMPETE IN A SWIMMING RACE** to take part as a competitor in a swimming race **4.** *vt.* **SWIM WITH A PARTICULAR STROKE** to swim using a particular stroke **5.** *vi.* **BE DIZZY** to be dizzy or confused ○ *The noise made my head swim.* **6.** *vi.* **SEEM TO MOVE OR SPIN** to appear to move, whirl, or sway ○ *words swimming on the page* **7.** *vi.* **FLOAT ON THE SURFACE** to float on the surface of a liquid ○ *oil swimming on the water* **8.** *vi.* **BE COVERED IN LIQUID** to be surrounded or covered with a large quantity of liquid ○ *mushrooms swimming with garlic butter* **9.** *vi.* **HAVE PLENTY** to have a large amount of sth ○ *not exactly swimming in offers* ■ *n.* **1.** **SPELL OF SWIMMING** a period of time spent swimming, usually for pleasure or exercise ○ *went for her morning swim* **2.** **SMOOTH MOVEMENT** a smooth gliding movement **3.** **DIZZINESS** dizziness or confusion ○ *with my head in a swim* **4.** ANGLING **PLACE WITH MANY FISH** a place where fish are found in abundance [Old English *swimman*, from a prehistoric Germanic base that also produced Old Norse *sund* 'swimming' (source of English *sound* 'channel')] —**swimmable** *adj.* —**swimmer** *n.* ◇ **be in the swim** to be involved with the latest fashions or trends (*informal*)

swim bladder *n.* ZOOL = **air bladder**

swimmeret /swímmə rét, swímmə ret/ *n.* an abdominal appendage of shrimp, lobsters, and some other crustaceans that is adapted for swimming and, in females, for carrying eggs

swimmers /swímmərz/ *npl. Aus* a swimming costume (*informal*)

swimmer's itch *n.* an inflammation of the skin caused by the larvae of some schistosomes that penetrate the skin and cause itching. It often occurs after swimming in infested waters.

swimming /swímming/ *n.* the action or activity of making progress unsupported through water using the arms and legs, usually for pleasure, exercise, or sport

swimming baths, **swimming bath** *n.* a building containing a swimming pool for public use (*dated*) (*takes a singular or plural verb*)

swimming costume *n.* a piece of clothing worn for swimming, especially by women

swimmingly /swímmingli/ *adv.* very smoothly, easily, and successfully ○ *The whole evening went swimmingly.*

swimming pool *n.* a water-filled structure in which people can swim, usually set into the ground outdoors or the floor indoors, or a building that houses such a structure

swimming trunks *npl.* a piece of clothing worn by men and boys for swimming. Swimming trunks may be brief, like close-fitting underpants, or larger and looser, like shorts.

swimsuit /swím soot, -syoot/ *n.* = **swimming costume**

swimwear /swím wair/ *n.* any type of clothing worn for swimming

Swinburne /swín burn/, **Algernon Charles** (1837–1909) British poet. Author of *Poems and Ballads* (*First Series* 1866; *Second Series* 1878) and *Tristam of Lyonesse* (1882). Following an alcoholic breakdown he spent the last 30 years of his life in seclusion.

swindle /swínd'l/ *vt.* (**-dles, -dling, -dled**) CHEAT SB OF STH to obtain sth from sb, especially money, by deception or fraud ○ *I've been swindled!* ■ *n.* FRAUDULENT TRANSACTION a transaction in which one person or organization obtains sth from another by deception or fraud [Late 18thC. Back-formation from *swindler*, from German *Schwindler* 'cheat', from *schwindeln* 'to be dizzy', literally 'to vanish repeatedly', ultimately, from Old High German *swintan* 'to vanish'.] —**swindler** *n.*

swindle sheet *n.* an expense account (*slang disapproving*)

swine /swīn/ (*plural* **swine**) *n.* **1.** (*plural* **swine** *or* **swines**) OFFENSIVE TERM an offensive term that deliberately insults sb's manners or behaviour (*insult*) **2.** AGRIC PIG a pig, boar, or similar animal [Old English *swīn*. Ultimately, from an Indo-European word that is also the ancestor of English *hyena* and *sow* 'female pig'.] —**swinish** *adj.* —**swinishly** *adv.*

swine fever *n.* a very infectious and often fatal viral disease of pigs marked by fever, weakness, lesions, loss of appetite, and diarrhoea. US term **hog cholera**

swineherd /swín hurd/ *n.* sb who looks after pigs (*archaic or literary*)

swinepox /swín poks/ *n.* an infectious viral disease of pigs marked by lesions of the skin

swine vesicular disease *n.* a mild viral disease in pigs that causes lesions on the feet and in the mouth

swing /swing/ *v.* (**swings, swinging, swung** /swung/, **swung**) **1.** *vti.* MOVE TO AND FRO to move freely from side to side or backwards and forwards, usually hanging from a fixed point, or make sth move in this way **2.** *vti.* PIVOT OR ROTATE to move or turn in a circle or an arc, usually pivoting around a fixed point, or make sth move or turn in this way ○ *The door swung open.* **3.** *vti.* SUSPEND OR HANG STH to fix sth so that it can swing, or be fixed in this way **4.** *vti.* MOVE IN A CURVE to move in a smooth curve, or make sth move in this way ○ *The limousine swung into the drive.* **5.** *vi.* WALK WITH A SWAYING MOTION to walk with a swaying motion in a relaxed or easy manner **6.** *vti.* STRIKE WITH A SWEEPING BLOW to hit or attempt to hit sb or sth with a sweeping blow or stroke ○ *swing at the ball wildly* **7.** *vti.* RIDE ON A SWINGING SEAT to move backwards and forwards on a swinging seat, or make sb move in such a way by pushing the person or the seat **8.** *vti.* FLUCTUATE OR VACILLATE to change from one feeling or condition to another, sometimes quickly or suddenly, or make sth or sb change in this way ○ *Their mood swung between elation and gloom.* **9.** *vt.* ARRANGE OR MANIPULATE STH to achieve a desired change or result by using influence, persuasion, or other means (*informal*) ○ *You want the job? I can swing it for you.* **10.** *vi.* BE HANGED FOR STH to be hanged as punishment for sth (*informal*) **11.** *vi.* SWAP SEXUAL PARTNERS to have a number of sexual partners, especially by exchanging them within a group (*slang*) **12.** *vi.* BE LIVELY to be lively or animated (*informal*) ○ *The party was really swinging by the time we arrived.* **13.** *vi.* BE MODERN AND FASHIONABLE to be interested in and involved in modern or fashionable trends (*informal*) **14.** *vti.* MUSIC PLAY JAZZ to play in a style of big-band jazz music suitable for dancing **15.** *vti.* CRICKET BOWL BALL WITH SIDEWAYS CURVE to bowl a ball in such a way that it moves sideways in the air, or move in this way ■ *n.* **1.** HANGING SEAT a seat hung from a frame or branch for sb to sit on and move backwards and forwards, especially one on which children play **2.** SWINGING MOVEMENT the process of swinging, or a swinging movement **3.** RANGE OF MOVEMENT the curve or distance covered by sth as it swings **4.** SWEEPING STROKE OR BLOW a sweeping stroke, blow, or punch ○ *took a swing at the ball* **5.** RELAXED SWINGING MOTION a relaxed or graceful swaying motion **6.** SPORTS WAY SB SWINGS STH the manner of movement used to swing a bat or club or bowl a ball ○ *practising her golf swing* **7.** CRICKET SIDEWAYS MOVEMENT OF BOWLED BALL the sideways movement through the air of a ball bowled **8.** BOXING PUNCH FROM SIDE a wide punch from the side **9.** SHIFT OR FLUCTUATION a sudden or significant change, especially in the way people think or act ○ *frequent mood swings* ○ *a massive swing in popularity towards the younger candidate* **10.** UP-AND-DOWN CYCLICAL CHANGES the up-and-down cycles of sth, e.g. business profits, economic growth, or share prices **11.** STEADY PROGRESSION a steady progression or advance across territory, or through a process, activity, or phase **12.** MUSIC STYLE OF JAZZ MUSIC a style of jazz music suitable for dancing, popular especially in the 1930s and 1940s and generally played by big bands (*often used before a noun*) ○ *swing dance* [Old English *swingan* 'to flog, rush', from a prehistoric Germanic base meaning 'violent circulatory movement', which also produced English *swinge* and *swink*] —**swingy** *adj.* ◇ **be in full swing** to be in vigorous progress ◇ **get into the swing of things** to get back into your normal rhythm or routine ◇ **go with a swing** to be lively and animated ○ *The evening really went with a swing.* ◇ **swings and roundabouts** used to indicate that a situation has both advantages and disadvantages, or is sometimes good and sometimes bad

swing around, **swing round** *vi.* **1.** TURN AROUND QUICKLY to turn around quickly or suddenly **2.** CHANGE DIRECTION QUICKLY to change direction quickly or suddenly

swingboat /swíng bōt/ *n.* a boat-shaped carriage with seats in which people swing backwards and forwards for fun, usually at a fairground or amusement park

swing bridge *n.* a low movable bridge that pivots horizontally on a pier in midstream and is swung parallel to the stream to allow a ship to pass

swing door *n.* a door that can be opened by pushing from either side, especially one that swings shut automatically. US term **swinging door**

swinge /swinj/ (**swinges, swingeing** *or* **swinging, swinged**) *vt.* to punish sb severely, especially by beating or flogging (*archaic*) [Mid-16thC. Ultimately from a prehistoric Germanic base that is also the ancestor of English *swing*.]

swingeing /swínjing/ *adj.* causing great harm or hardship ○ *swingeing cuts in spending*

swinger /swíngər/ *n.* sb who lives a somewhat unconventional and hedonistic life, especially sb who exchanges sexual partners with others (*slang*)

swinging /swínging/ *adj.* **1.** FASHIONABLE lively and fashionable (*dated*) **2.** LIVELY lively and animated **3.** OFTEN CHANGING SEXUAL PARTNERS frequently changing or exchanging sexual partners (*slang*)

swinging door *n. US* = **swing door**

swinging voter *n. ANZ* sb who does not consistently vote for the same political party in elections

swingle /swíng g'l/ *n.* INSTRUMENT FOR BEATING AND SCRAPING FLAX a wooden instrument like a knife or paddle used to beat hemp or flax and scrape woody portions out of the material ■ *vt.* (**-gles, -gling, -gled**) TREAT MATERIAL WITH SWINGLE to beat and scrape hemp or flax with a swingle [15thC. From Middle Dutch *swinghel*.]

swingletree /swíng g'l tree/ *n.* a horizontal crossbar by means of which the harness traces of a draught animal are attached to a vehicle or device. US term **whiffletree**

swingometer /swing ómmitər/ *n.* a device used on television during an election to show the swing of votes from one political party to another [Mid-20thC. Coined on the model of BAROMETER.]

swing voter *n. US* = **floating voter**

swing-wing *adj.* WITH MOVABLE WINGS used to describe an aircraft whose wings are constructed to allow them to move backwards and forwards relative to the fuselage during flight. The rearward configuration improves streamlining at high speeds, while the forward configuration improves lifting qualities during take-off and landing. ■ *n.* AEROPLANE WITH MOVABLE WINGS an aeroplane with variable-sweep wings

swink /swingk/ *vi.* (**swinks, swinking, swinked**) WORK HARD to toil or labour (*archaic*) ■ *n.* HARD WORK hard work or drudgery (*archaic*) [Old English *swincan*. From a prehistoric Germanic base that is also the ancestor of English *swing*.] —**swinker** *n.*

swipe /swīp/ *v.* (**swipes, swiping, swiped**) **1.** *vti.* HIT SB OR STH HARD to strike or attempt to strike sb or sth with a forceful swinging or sweeping blow **2.** *vt.* STEAL STH to steal sth, often with a snatching movement (*informal*) **3.** *vt.* PUT A CARD THROUGH MACHINE to pass a card on which data has been stored magnetically through an electronic reading device, e.g. to gain access to a building or to initiate a banking transaction, or to be read successfully by such a device ○ *the card won't swipe through the machine* ■ *n.* **1.** SWINGING BLOW a forceful swinging or sweeping blow ○ *took a swipe at me but missed* **2.** CRITICAL ATTACK a critical remark or attack (*informal*) **3.** PIVOTED POLE a long pole used as a lever to raise or lower a bucket in a well [Early 19thC. Partly from a Scottish variant of SWEEP and partly from obsolete English *swip* 'stroke, blow', from SWEEP.] —**swiper** *n.*

swipe card *n.* a plastic card such as a credit card on which data have been stored magnetically and that can be passed through and read by an electronic reading device and decoded

swipes /swīps/ *npl.* weak or inferior beer (*dated slang*) [Late 18thC. Origin unknown.]

swirl /swurl/ *v.* (**swirls, swirling, swirled**) **1.** *vti.* TURN WITH A CIRCULAR MOTION to turn around and around with a twisting or spiralling movement, or to make sth move in this way ○ *caught up in a swirling throng of dancers and musicians* **2.** *vi.* BE DIZZY to be dizzy or confused ■ *n.* **1.** CIRCULAR MOTION a turning, twisting, spiralling movement, or sth that moves in this way **2.** SPIRAL a curl, twist, or spiral ○ *the water swirled and eddied around us* ○ *a carpet with black swirls on a red background* **3.** CONFUSION dizziness or confusion [15thC. Originally 'whirlpool', of uncertain origin: perhaps from a Low German or Scandinavian word, thought to be an imitation of the sound of whirling water.] —**swirly** *adj.*

swish /swish/ *v.* (**swishes, swishing, swished**) **1.** *vi.* MAKE OR MOVE WITH A WHISTLING SOUND to make the soft smooth whistling or rustling sound of sth moving quickly through the air, or to move with such a sound **2.** *vt.* MOVE STH WITH A WHISTLING SOUND to cause sth to make or move with a swishing sound ○ *swishing a sword* **3.** *vt.* CUT WITH A SWIFT SHARP BLOW to cut or strike sth or sb with a swift sharp swishing blow ■ *n.* **1.** SWISHING SOUND OR MOVEMENT a soft smooth whistling or rustling sound, or a movement that makes such a sound ○ *the angry swish swish of its tail* **2.** STICK OR STROKE a rod used to beat or flog a person or animal, or a blow from such a rod **3.** *US* OFFENSIVE TERM an offensive term for a homosexual man that deliberately insults his manner or behaviour as being more typical of a woman (*insult*) ■ *adj.* **1.** ELEGANT elegant and fashionable (*informal*) **2.** *US* OFFENSIVE TERM an offensive term that deliberately insults a homosexual man whose manner or behaviour is regarded as more typical of a woman (*insult*) [Mid-18thC. Origin uncertain: probably an imitation of the sound made when moving through or brushing against sth.] —**swishy** *adj.*

Swiss /swiss/ *n.* (*plural* **Swiss**) **1.** SB FROM SWITZERLAND sb who was born or brought up in Switzerland, or who has Swiss citizenship **2.** DIALECT SPOKEN IN SWITZERLAND any of the dialects of German, French, and Italian spoken in Switzerland ■ *adj.* OF SWITZERLAND relating to Switzerland, or its people or culture [Early 16thC. From French *Suisse*, ultimately, from Middle High German *Swīz* 'Switzerland'.]

Swiss army knife *n.* a pocketknife with a number of additional items that fold into the handle, e.g. a corkscrew, nail file, bottle opener, and scissors

Swiss chard, **chard** *n.* a variety of beet with large edible leaves and stems that are similar to spinach, cooked and eaten as a vegetable. Latin name: *Beta vulgaris cicla*.

Swiss cheese plant *n.* a houseplant with large perforated leaves. Latin name: *Monstera deliciosa*.

Swiss Guard *n.* a group of Swiss-born soldiers employed to protect the pope at the Vatican, or a member of this group

swiss muslin *n.* a fine cotton fabric, often with a raised pattern, used to make light clothes or curtains

swiss roll, **Swiss roll** *n.* a thin light sponge spread with jam or cream and rolled up into a cylinder before it cools. US term **jelly roll**

switch /swich/ *n.* **1.** ELEC ENG BUTTON OR LEVER CONTROLLING AN ELECTRICAL CIRCUIT a mechanical or electronic device that opens, closes, or changes the connections in an electrical circuit, e.g. one used to turn a light or machine on or off **2.** SUDDEN CHANGE a quick or sudden change **3.** SUBSTITUTION an exchange or substitution **4.** THIN ROD OR CANE a thin flexible stick, especially one used for punishment, or a blow or beating with such a stick **5.** HAIR PONYTAIL HAIRPIECE a hairpiece in the form of a false ponytail **6.** ZOOL TIP OF AN ANIMAL'S TAIL a tuft of hair at the end of the tail of a cow or other animal **7.** CARDS CARD GAME any card game in which the suit can be changed during play **8.** UTIL ROUTING DEVICE USED WITHIN TELEPHONE EXCHANGES a device used within a telephone exchange to route transmissions between network nodes **9.** COMPUT TECHNIQUE FOR CONTROLLING A PROGRAM'S LOGIC a programmed technique for indicating which alternative path to take at a decision point in a program's logic ■ *v.* (**switches**, **switching**, **switched**) **1.** *vti.* CHANGE, SHIFT, OR TRANSFER to change from one time, activity, or situation to another, often quickly or suddenly, or to cause sb or sth to make such a change ○ *The dancing class has been switched from Friday afternoon to Saturday morning.* **2.** *vti.* MAKE AN EXCHANGE OR SUBSTITUTION to exchange two similar or related things, or put one in the place of the other, sometimes secretly or surreptitiously **3.** *vti.* ELEC CHANGE AN ELECTRICAL FUNCTION to make an electrical device do sth different by operating a switch to cause current to stop or start flowing or change its path ○ *He switched the radio to a different station.* **4.** *vti.* FLICK OR SWING TO AND FRO to move quickly from side to side or backwards and forwards, or make sth move in this way **5.** *vt.* BEAT SB WITH SWITCH to beat sb with a switch, especially as a punishment [Late 16thC. Origin uncertain: probably from Middle Dutch *swijch* 'twig'. The verb originally meant 'to beat with a switch', hence 'to bend like a flexible stick, divert, exchange'.] —**switchable** *adj.* —**switcher** *n.*

switch off *vti.* to stop paying attention, lose interest, or stop thinking about sth, or make sb do this (*informal*)

switch on *v.* **1.** *vti.* ELEC TURN ON ELECTRICAL EQUIPMENT to start the flow of electricity to sth by operating a switch or other device **2.** *vt.* MAKE INSINCERE SHOW OF EMOTION to suddenly and automatically produce sth, e.g. a smile, charm, or tears, for effect and without sincerity

Switch /swich/ *tdmk.* a trademark for a type of debit card

switchback /swich bak/ *n.* **1.** TWISTY ROAD WITH MANY HILLS a road or track with many steep uphill and downhill slopes and sharp bends **2.** SHARP BEND ON A STEEP SLOPE a sharp bend on a road or track going steeply uphill or downhill **3.** LEISURE = roller coaster [Mid-19thC. Originally a zigzag railway track used on steep slopes, where the individual tracks were connected by switches (points) at each of which the train was reversed in direction.]

switchblade /swich blayd/, **switchblade knife** *n. US* = flick knife

switchboard /swich bawrd/ *n.* **1.** UTIL MANUAL DEVICE FOR CONNECTING TELEPHONE LINES a manually operated device for interconnecting telephone lines and routing telephone calls, usually within a telephone exchange or in a workplace, hotel, or other large building **2.** ELEC ENG CONTROL PANEL CONTAINING ELECTRICAL DEVICES one or more insulating panels containing the electrical devices and instruments, e.g. switches, circuit breakers, fuses, and meters, required to operate electrical equipment

switched-on *adj.* **1.** AWARE alert or aware (*informal*) **2.** MODERN modern in outlook or appearance (*dated informal*) **3.** DRUGGED intoxicated by drugs (*dated slang*)

switchgear /swich geer/ *n.* a device used solely to open and close electric circuits, especially one used to control a high-current application, e.g. a power and transforming station or electric motor

swither /swíth ər/ *vi.* (**-ers**, **-ering**, **-ered**) *Scotland* HESITATE to hesitate or be indecisive ■ *n. Scotland* HESITATION a state of hesitation or indecision [Early 16thC. Origin unknown.]

Swithun /swíth n, swíth n/, **St** (d. 862) English bishop. The greatest of the Anglo-Saxon bishops, he was religious adviser to Kings Egbert and Ethelwulf. The weather on his feast day, 15 July, is believed to hold for the next 40 days.

Switz. *abbr.* Switzerland

Switzer /switsər/ *n.* **1.** SWISS PERSON a Swiss person (*archaic*) **2.** SWISS GUARD a member of the Swiss Guard [Mid-16thC. From Middle High German *Switzer*, from *Swiz* 'Switzerland'.]

Switzerland

Switzerland /switsər lənd/ federal republic consisting of 23 cantons in west-central Europe. It has been neutral since 1515. Language: French, German, Italian. Currency: Swiss Franc. Capital: Bern. Population: 7,207,060 (1996). Area: 41,284 sq. km/15,940 sq. mi. Official name **Swiss Confederation**

swive /swīv/ (**swives**, **swiving**, **swived**) *vti.* to have sexual intercourse with sb (*archaic*) [14thC. Via Old English *swīfan* 'to sweep' (source of English *swivel*) from a prehistoric Germanic base that is also the ancestor of English *swift*.]

swivel /swívv'l/ *v.* (**-els**, **-elling**, **-elled**) **1.** *vti.* PIVOT OR ROTATE to turn freely or horizontally in a circle, or make sth turn in this way **2.** *vt.* PROVIDE STH WITH A PIVOTING JOINT to fit, attach, or support sth with a joint that allows complete freedom of movement ■ *n.* **1.** DEVICE ALLOWING PARTS TO TURN a joint or fastening that allows sth attached to it to turn freely **2.** SUPPORT ALLOWING STH TO PIVOT a pivoting support that allows sth such as a gun, chair, or camera to turn from side to side or up and down, sometimes in a full circle **3.** ARMS PIVOTING GUN a gun that can be turned from side to side horizontally because of the pivoting mount supporting it [14thC. From Old English *swīfan* 'to sweep'. Ultimately from a prehistoric Germanic base that is also the ancestor of English *swift*.]

swivel chair *n.* a chair, generally an office chair, mounted on a central support with a device that enables it to turn horizontally in a circle

swivel-hipped *adj.* moving with loosely swinging hips, usually in an exaggerated manner

swivel pin *n.* = kingpin

swiz, **swizz** *n.* (*plural* **swizzes**) (*informal*) **1.** DISAPPOINTMENT a great disappointment, especially sth that makes sb feel cheated **2.** SWINDLE a swindle ■ *vt.* (**swizzes**, **swizzing**, **swizzed**; **swizzs**, **swizzing**, **swizzed**) CHEAT SB to swindle or cheat sb (*informal*) [Early 20thC. Shortening of SWIZZLE.]

swizzle /swízz'l/ *n.* **1.** *US* MIXED ALCOHOLIC DRINK an iced cocktail, usually containing rum, that is stirred to make it frothy or to frost the glass **2.** = swiz *n.* 1, swiz *n.* 2 (*informal*) ■ *v.* (**-zles**, **-zling**, **-zled**) **1.** *vt.* STIR DRINK WITH A SWIZZLE STICK to stir a drink with a swizzle stick to mix the ingredients, make it frothy, or reduce its effervescence **2.** *vti.* = swiz *v.* (*informal*) [Early 19thC. Origin uncertain: perhaps an alteration of earlier American English *switchel* 'drink of molasses and water', of unknown origin.]

swizzle stick *n.* a small thin plastic rod used for stirring a drink to mix the ingredients, make it frothy, or reduce its effervescence

swob /swob/ *n.* SWAB a swab (*archaic*) ■ *vt.* (**swobs**, **swobbing**, **swob**, **swobbed**) SWAB STH to swab sb or sth (*archaic*)

swollen past participle of **swell**

swollen head *n.* a feeling of conceited self-importance, usually stimulated by personal success or by praise received from others. US term **swelled head** —**swollen-headed** *adj.* —**swollen-headedness** *n.*

swoon /swoon/ *vi.* (**swoons**, **swooning**, **swooned**) **1.** FEEL FAINT WITH JOY to be overwhelmed by happiness, excitement, adoration, or infatuation **2.** FALL IN A FAINT to experience a sudden and usually brief loss of consciousness ■ *n.* LOSS OF CONSCIOUSNESS a sudden and usually brief loss of consciousness [13thC. Origin uncertain: probably from Old English *iswowen* 'in a swoon', from *geswōgen*, past participle of assumed *swōgan* 'to suffocate', of unknown origin.]

swoop /swoop/ *v.* (**swoops**, **swooping**, **swooped**) **1.** *vi.* MAKE SWEEPING DESCENT to descend quickly and suddenly with a sweeping movement, usually from the air **2.** *vi.* POUNCE to make a sudden swift attack or raid on sth or sb ○ *The police swooped in on the terrorists.* **3.** *vt.* SEIZE QUICKLY OR SUDDENLY to seize or snatch sth in a sudden swift attack ■ *n.* **1.** SUDDEN DESCENT a quick sudden sweeping descent **2.** SUDDEN ATTACK a sudden swift attack or raid [Mid-16thC. Origin uncertain: probably from a variant of Old English *swāpan*, an earlier form of SWEEP.]

swoosh /swoosh, swoōsh/ *v.* (**swooshes**, **swooshing**, **swooshed**) **1.** *vi.* MAKE OR MOVE WITH RUSHING SOUND to make the rushing or swirling sound of fast-moving water or air, or move with such a sound **2.** *vt.* MOVE STH WITH RUSHING SOUND to cause sth to make or move with a swooshing sound ■ *n.* SWOOSHING SOUND a swooshing sound or movement [Mid-19thC. An imitation of the sound.]

swop *vti.*, *n.* = swap

Sword

sword /sawrd/ *n.* **1.** LONG-BLADED WEAPON a hand-held weapon with a long blade that is sharp on one or both edges and sometimes slightly curved. It is used for cutting and thrusting. **2.** USE OF FORCE the use of force, violence, or military power ○ *The pen is mightier than the sword.* [Old English *sweord*. Ultimately from a prehistoric Germanic word that also produced German *Schwert* 'sword.'] —**swordless** *adj*. ◇ **cross swords (with sb)** to argue or come into conflict with sb ◇ **put sb to the sword** to kill sb violently, especially in war (*literary*)

sword and sorcery *adj*. set in a fantasy place or time with a technology that has not advanced beyond bladed weapons and in which magic is important (*informal*)

sword bayonet *n*. a type of bayonet with a very long blade

swordbearer /sáwrd bairər/ *n*. an official who carries a sword that is a symbol of sb's authority, e.g. a sovereign's sword

swordbill /sáwrd bil/ *n*. a South American hummingbird that has a bill longer than its body. Latin name: *Ensifera ensifera*.

sword cane *n*. = **swordstick**

swordcraft /sáwrd kraaft/ *n*. = **swordsmanship**

sword dance *n*. a dance in which swords are used, especially a traditional Highland dance in which sb dances over swords crossed on the ground

sword fern *n*. a fern with long fronds shaped like swords

Swordfish

swordfish /sáwrd fish/ (*plural* **-fish** *or* **-fishes**) *n*. a large ocean fish with an upper jaw that extends into a long point. It is caught for food and sport. Latin name: *Xiphias gladius*.

sword grass *n*. a type of grass with leaves that have very sharp edges

sword knot *n*. a decorative ribbon or tassel on the hilt of a sword

sword lily *n*. = **gladiolus** [From its sword-shaped leaves]

Sword of Damocles *n*. sth that threatens to bring imminent disaster [(See **DAMOCLES**)]

swordplay /sáwrd play/ *n*. fighting with a sword, especially when done with skill

swordsman /sáwrdzmən/ (*plural* **-men** /-mən/) *n*. sb who fights with a sword with a particular degree of skill

swordsmanship /sáwrdzmən ship/ *n*. the skill of fighting with a sword

swordstick /sáwrd stik/ *n*. a hollow walking stick or cane whose handle is also the handle of a narrow sword hidden inside the stick

sword-swallower /sáwrd swolōwər/ *n*. a performer who passes or creates an illusion of passing a sword down his or her throat to its hilt

swordswoman /sáwrdz woŏmən/ (*plural* **-en** /-wimin/) *n*. a woman who fights with a sword with a particular degree of skill

swordtail /sáwrd tayl/ *n*. a small brightly coloured freshwater fish of Central America that has a long sword-shaped tail and is popular as an aquarium fish. Latin name: *Xiphophorus helleri*.

swore past tense of **swear**

sworn past participle of **swear**

swot[1] /swot/ (**swots, swotting, swotted**), **swat** (**swats, swatting, swatted**) *vi.* **STUDY VERY HARD** to study very hard and intensively, especially for an examination (*informal*) ■ *n*. (*informal*) **1. DILIGENT STUDENT** sb who

studies very hard or excessively **2. PERIOD OF HARD STUDY** a period of time spent studying hard, especially for an examination [Mid-19thC. Originally a Scottish variant of SWEAT.]

swot[2] *vti.* = **swat**

SWOT /swot/ *abbr.* MARKETING strengths, weaknesses, opportunities, and threats

swotter *n*. = **swatter**

swotty /swótti/, **swottier, swottiest** *adj*. given to studying very hard or excessively (*informal disapproving*)

SWPA *abbr*. South-West Pacific Area

swum past participle of **swim**

swung past participle, past tense of **swing**

swung dash *n*. a character (~) used in printing to represent all or part of a word previously spelt out

swy /swī/ *n*. ANZ the gambling game two-up (*informal*) [Early 20thC. From German *zwei*, literally 'two']

SY *abbr*. Seychelles (*international vehicle registration*)

sybarite /síbbə rīt/ *n*. sb devoted to luxury and the gratification of sensual desires [Mid-16thC. Via Latin *Sybarita* from, ultimately, Greek *Subaris* 'Sybaris', an ancient Greek city in southern Italy known as a place of luxury and indulgence.] —**sybaritic** /síbbə ríttik/ *adj*. —**sybaritical** *adj*. —**sybaritically** *adv*. —**sybaritism** /síbbə rītizəm/ *n*.

Sybarite *n*. sb who was born in or was a citizen of Sybaris, an ancient Greek city in southern Italy — **Sybaritic** *adj*.

syboe /sí bō/ *n*. Scotland a spring onion [Late 16thC. Via French *ciboule* from, ultimately, Latin *caepa* 'onion'.]

sycamine /síkə mīn, -meen/ *n*. a tree that is mentioned in the Bible and is thought to be the black mulberry [Early 16thC. Via Greek *sukaminon* from Hebrew *šikmāh*.]

Sycamore

sycamore /síkə mawr/ (*plural* **-mores** *or* **-more**) *n*. **1. TYPE OF MAPLE TREE** a maple tree with five-lobed leaves, hanging clusters of greenish-yellow flowers, and two-winged fruits. Originally grown in central and southern Europe and Asia, it has been naturalized in Britain and North America. Latin name: *Acer pseudoplatanus*. **2.** US **LARGE SPREADING PLANE TREE** a large spreading plane tree that grows in eastern and central North America and has lobed leaves, round spiked fruit clusters, and flaking bark. Latin name: *Platanus occidentalis*. **3. FIG TREE** a fig tree that grows in Africa and southwestern Asia and has edible fruit. Latin name: *Ficus sycomorus*. [14thC. Via Old French *sicamor* from, ultimately, Greek *sukomoros*, literally 'fig-mulberry'.]

syce /sīss/, **saice, sice** *n*. formerly in India a groom, stable hand, or other attendant [Mid-17thC. Via Persian and Urdu *sā'is* from Arabic, formed from *sūs* 'to tend a horse'.]

syconium /sī kốni əm/ (*plural* **-a** /-ni ə/) *n*. a type of fleshy fruit, e.g. a fig, in which numerous seeds are borne inside the enlarged hollow tip of the flower stalk [Mid-19thC. Via modern Latin from Greek *sukon* 'fig'.]

sycophancy /síkəfənssi, -fanssi/ *n*. servility, obsequious flattery, and other fawning behaviour

sycophant /síkəfənt, -fant/ *n*. sb who servilely or obsequiously flatters a powerful person for personal gain [Mid-16thC. Via Latin *sycophanta* from Greek *sukophantēs* 'informer', from *sukon* 'fig, obscene gesture' + *-phantes* 'shower' (formed from *phanein* 'to show').] —

sycophantic /síkə fántik/ *adj*. —**sycophantically** /-fántikli/ *adv*.

sycosis /sī kŏssiss/ *n*. inflammation of hair follicles, especially of the beard, caused by bacterial infection and marked by pustules and encrustations [Late 16thC. Via modern Latin from Greek *sukōsis*, from *sukon* 'fig'. From the pustule's resemblance to a fig.]

Sydenham's chorea /sídd'nəmz-/ *n*. a neurological disease of children and pregnant women, sometimes following rheumatic fever, in which those affected experience involuntary jerking movements of the body [Late 19thC. Named after the English physician Thomas *Sydenham* (1624–89), who first described it.]

Sydney /sídni/ city on the southeastern coast of Australia. Founded in 1788, it is the capital of the state of New South Wales. Population: 3,276,207 (1996).

Sydney Opera House

Sydney Opera House *n*. an arts centre in Sydney Harbour, Australia, that was designed by Jörn Utzon and completed in 1973. Its unusual sail-shaped towers make it Australia's best-known building.

syenite /sí ə nīt/ *n*. a light-coloured coarse-grained igneous rock consisting mainly of feldspar [Late 18thC. From Latin *syenites (lapis)*, literally '(stone of) Syene'. Named after Syene (Aswan), where it was mined.]

SYHA *abbr*. Scottish Youth Hostels Association

syl. *abbr*. **1.** syllable **2.** syllabus

Sylhet /sil hét/ city and administrative headquarters of Sylhet District, Chittagong Division, in northeastern Bangladesh. Population: 114,284 (1991).

syll. *abbr*. **1.** syllable **2.** syllabus

syllabary /sílləbəri/ (*plural* **-ies**) *n*. a list or set of written characters in which each character represents a single syllable e.g. the Japanese kana

syllabi plural of **syllabus**

syllabic /si lábbik/ *adj*. **1. INVOLVING SYLLABLES** relating to, involving, or typical of a syllable or syllables **2. BEING A SYLLABLE WITHOUT A VOWEL** used to describe a consonant that acts as a syllable without a vowel, as does the 'l' in 'bottle' **3. MARKED BY CLEAR ENUNCIATION** clearly enunciated with every syllable distinct **4.** POETRY **BASED ON THE NUMBER OF SYLLABLES** used to describe verse in which the rhythm is set by the number of syllables rather than accents, stresses, or vowel strengths ■ *n*. **SYLLABIC CONSONANT OR SOUND** a syllabic consonant, character, or sound

syllabify /si lábbi fī/ (**-fies, -fying, -fied**), **syllabicate** /si lábbi kayt/ (**-cates, -cating, -cated**) *vt.* to break a word down into syllables in speech or writing [Early 20thC. Back-formation from *syllabification*, from Latin *syllaba* 'syllable'.] —**syllabication** *n*. —**syllabification** /si lábbifi káysh'n/ *n*.

syllabism /sílləbizəm/ *n*. **1. USE OF SYLLABIC CHARACTERS** the use of characters that stand for individual syllables in writing **2. DIVISION INTO SYLLABLES** the breaking down of words into syllables, in speech or writing

syllable /sílĺəb'l/ *n*. **1. UNIT OF SPOKEN LANGUAGE** a unit of spoken language that consists of one or more vowel sounds alone, a syllabic consonant alone, or any of these with one or more consonant sounds **2. LETTERS CORRESPONDING TO SPOKEN SYLLABLE** one or more letters in a word that roughly correspond to a syllable of spoken language **3. MENTION** the slightest mention of sth (*usually used in negative statements*) ■ *vt.* (**-bles, -bling, -bled**) **PRONOUNCE STH CLEARLY** to pronounce sth in distinct or separate syllables [14thC. Via Anglo-Norman *sillable* and Old French *sillabe* from, ultimately, Greek *sullabē*, from *sullambanein* 'to bring together', from *lambanein* 'to take'.]

syllabogram /si lábbō gram/ *n.* a written or printed symbol that stands for a single syllable

syllabub /sílla bub/, **sillabub** *n.* **1.** FOOD DESSERT OF CREAM WHIPPED WITH BRANDY a light soft cold dessert made from cream whipped with brandy, wine or sherry, lemon juice, and a little sugar **2.** BEVERAGES DRINK OF MILK AND WINE a drink made of sweetened milk or cream curdled with wine or cider (*dated*) [Mid-16thC. Origin unknown.]

syllabus /sílləbass/ (*plural* **-bi** /-bī/ *or* **-buses**) *n.* **1.** OUTLINE OF COURSE OF STUDY a summary or list of the main topics of a course of study, text, or lecture **2.** LIST OF SUBJECTS OFFERED the subjects offered for study by a school, college, or university, or a list of these [Mid-17thC. From modern Latin, originally a misprint of Latin *sittybas* 'indexes', from, ultimately, Greek *sittuba* 'index, label'.]

Syllabus, **Syllabus of Errors** *n.* a list of religious doctrines condemned by the Roman Catholic Church as erroneous

syllepsis /si lépsiss/ (*plural* **-ses** /-seez/) *n.* **1.** GRAMMATICAL AGREEMENT WITH ONLY ONE ELEMENT the use of a word that relates to, qualifies, or governs two or more other words but agrees in number, gender, or case with only one of them. 'Neither Fred nor I want to' is an example of syllepsis where 'want' agrees with 'I' but not 'Fred'. **2.** DIFFERENT SEMANTIC RELATIONSHIP the use of a word that relates to, qualifies, or governs two or more other words but has a different meaning in relation to each, as in the example 'He picked up his hat and a taxi' [Late 16thC. Via late Latin and Greek *sullēpsis*, literally 'a taking together', from, ultimately, *lambanein* (see SYLLABLE).]

syllogise *vti.* = **syllogize**

syllogism /sílla jizəm/ *n.* **1.** ARGUMENT INVOLVING THREE PROPOSITIONS a formal deductive argument made up of a major premise, a minor premise, and a conclusion. An example is 'all birds have feathers, penguins are birds, therefore penguins have feathers'. **2.** DEDUCTIVE REASONING reasoning from the general to the specific, or an example of this **3.** SPECIOUS ARGUMENT a subtle piece of reasoning, or one that seems true but is actually false or deceptive [14thC. Via Latin from Greek *sullogismos*, from *sullogizesthai* 'to infer', from, ultimately, *logos* 'reason' (source of English *logic*).]

syllogistic /sílla jístik/ *adj.* relating to, using, or typical of syllogisms [Mid-17thC. Via Latin from Greek *sullogistikos*, from *sullogizesthai* (see SYLLOGISM).] —**syllogistically** *adv.*

syllogize /sílla jīz/ (**-gizes**, **-gizing**, **-gized**), **syllogise** (**-gises**, **-gising**, **-gised**) *vti.* to reason or infer sth by means of syllogisms [15thC. Via late Latin *syllogizare* from Greek *sullogizesthai* (see SYLLOGISM).] —**syllogization** /sílla jī záysh'n/ *n.* —**syllogizer** /sílla jīzər/ *n.*

sylph /silf/ *n.* **1.** SLIM AND GRACEFUL GIRL a woman or girl who is slight and graceful **2.** MYTHOL FEMALE CREATURE THAT INHABITS THE AIR an elemental soulless female being imagined to inhabit the air [Mid-17thC. From modern Latin *sylpha*, of uncertain origin: perhaps a blend of Latin *sylvestris* 'of the forest' and *nympha* 'nymph'.] —**sylphic** *adj.* —**sylphish** *adj.* —**sylphy** *adj.*

sylphlike /sílf līk/ *adj.* slight and graceful as a female figure

sylva *n.* = **silva**

sylvan /sílvən/ *adj.* **1.** OF A FOREST relating to, typical of, or found in a forest (*literary*) **2.** WOODED covered in or full of trees (*literary*) **3.** RURAL typical of the countryside, especially in an idyllic way ■ *n.* INHABITANT OF A FOREST a person, animal, or spirit that lives in a forest

sylvanite /sílvə nīt/ *n.* a mixed telluride mineral containing gold and silver, occurring in long striated crystals. Formula: (Au,Ag)Te₂. [Late 18thC. Named after TRANSYLVANIA, where tellurium, to which the word was originally applied, was first discovered.]

sylvatic /sil váttik/ *adj.* **1.** OF WILD ANIMALS affecting wild animals ○ *sylvatic plague* **2.** WOODED covered in or full of trees

sylviculture *n.* = **silviculture**

sylvite /síl vīt/, **sylvine** /-vīn/ *n.* a colourless transparent mineral form of potassium chloride, used as a source of potassium [Mid-19thC. Formed from modern Latin (*sal digestivus*) *Silvii* '(digestive salt) of Silvius'. Named after François de la Boë *Sylvius* (1614–72), Flemish physician who first discovered its medicinal use.]

sym. *abbr.* **1.** symbol **2.** symptom **3.** symphony **4.** CHEM symmetrical

sym- *prefix.* = **syn-** (*used before b, m, and p*)

symbiont /símbi ont, -bī-/ *n.* an animal or plant living in close and often mutually beneficial association with another of a different species. Formed from Greek *bioun* 'to live', from *bios* (see SYMBIOSIS).] —**symbiontic** /símbi óntik, -bī-/ *adj.* —**symbiontically** /sím bi óntikli, -bī-/ *adv.*

symbiosis /sím bī óssiss, -bi-/ (*plural* **-ses** /-ő seez, -/) *n.* **1.** ZOOL CLOSE ASSOCIATION OF ANIMALS OR PLANTS a close association of animals or plants of different species that is often, but not always, of mutual benefit. The relationship between a small fish and a larger fish on which it eats parasites is an example of symbiosis. **2.** MUTUALLY BENEFICIAL RELATIONSHIP a cooperative, mutually beneficial relationship between two people or groups [Early 17thC. Via modern Latin and Greek *sumbiōsis*, literally 'a living together', from, ultimately, *bios* 'life'.] —**symbiotic** /sím bī óttik, -bi-/ *adj.* —**symbiotical** /-óttik'l, -/ *adj.* —**symbiotically** /-ikli/ *adv.*

●	Intermittent rain	●●	Continuous rain
ꝯ	Intermittent drizzle	ꝯꝯ	Continuous drizzle
★	Intermittent snow	★★	Continuous snow
▽	Rain shower	▽	Snow shower
⌐⌐	Thunderstorm	⌐⌐	Heavy thunderstorm
⌐	Tropical storm	⚫	Hurricane
⧊	Sleet	▲	Hail shower
▽	Squall	⌇	Freezing rain
∿	Smoke	=	Mist
≡	Fog	⌐S	Sand storm or dust storm
∿	Surface warm front	∿	Upper warm front
∿	Surface cold front	∿	Upper cold front
∿	Occluded front	∿	Stationary front
○	Clear sky	◑	Overcast sky
◔	Cloudy sky	◕	Very cloudy sky
⊗	Obscured sky	◗	Slightly covered sky

Symbol: Weather symbols

symbol /símb'l/ *n.* **1.** STH THAT REPRESENTS STH ELSE sth that stands for or represents sth else, especially an object representing an abstraction **2.** SIGN WITH SPECIFIC MEANING a written or printed sign or character that represents sth in a particular context, e.g. an operation or quantity in mathematics or music **3.** PSYCHOANAL OBJECT REPRESENTING STH REPRESSED IN UNCONSCIOUS an object or act that represents an impulse or wish in the unconscious mind that has been repressed [15thC. Via Latin from Greek *sumbolon* 'mark', from *sumballein* 'to compare', from *ballein* 'to throw' (source of English *problem*).]

symbolic /sim bóllik/, **symbolical** /-bóllik'l/ *adj.* **1.** OF SYMBOLS relating to or typical of symbols **2.** USING SYMBOLS using a symbol or symbols to represent sth else **3.** REPRESENTING STH ELSE acting as a symbol ○ *a gesture symbolic of repentance* **4.** INVOLVING USE OF SYMBOLS characterized by or involving the use of symbols or symbolism ○ *symbolic art* —**symbolically** *adv.*

symbolic language *n.* **1.** ARTIFICIAL LANGUAGE USING SYMBOLS EXTENSIVELY an artificially constructed language with many symbols, used for precise formulations, e.g. in symbolic logic or mathematics **2.** COMPUT PROGRAMMING LANGUAGE a computer programming language that expresses memory addresses and operation codes in symbols recognizable to the programmer rather than in machine language

symbolic logic *n.* the branch of formal logic that studies the meaning and relationships of statements through precise mathematical methods and a standardized system of symbols and rules of inference

symbolise /símbə līz/ *vt.* = **symbolize**

symbolism /símbəlizəm/ *n.* **1.** USE OF SYMBOLS the use of symbols to invest things with a representative meaning or to represent sth abstract by sth concrete **2.** SYSTEM OF SYMBOLS a set or system of symbols **3.** SYMBOLIC MEANING symbolic meaning or quality **4.** ARTS ARTISTIC USE OF SYMBOLS the artistic method of revealing ideas or truths through the use of symbols **5.** symbolism, **Symbolism** ARTS 19THC LITERARY AND ARTISTIC MOVEMENT a 19th century literary and artistic movement that sought to evoke, rather than describe, ideas or feelings through the use of symbolic images **6.** CHR BELIEF IN SYMBOLIC NATURE OF EUCHARIST the belief that the bread and wine used in the Eucharist are symbols and not literally the flesh and blood of Jesus Christ

symbolist /símbəlist/ *n.* **1.** SB USING SYMBOLS sb who uses symbols or symbolism **2.** SB SKILLED AT INTERPRETING SYMBOLS sb skilled in the study or interpretation of symbols **3.** symbolist, **Symbolist** ARTS SB INVOLVED IN 19C ARTISTIC SYMBOLISM a writer or artist involved in or associated with the 19th century movement of symbolism **4.** CHR SB BELIEVING EUCHARIST USES SYMBOLS sb who believes that the bread and wine used in the Eucharist are symbols and not literally the flesh and blood of Jesus Christ ■ *adj.* **1.** OF OR USING SYMBOLS relating to, involving, or using symbols **2.** symbolist, **Symbolist** ARTS ASSOCIATED WITH 19C ARTISTIC SYMBOLISM involved in, associated with, or typical of the 19th century movement of symbolism —**symbolistic** /símbə lístik/ *adj.* —**symbolistically** /símbə lístikli/ *adv.*

symbolize /símbə līz/ (**-izes**, **-izing**, **-ized**), **symbolise** (**-ises**, **-ising**, **-ised**) *v.* **1.** *vt.* BE SYMBOL OF STH to serve as or be understood as a symbol of sth **2.** *vt.* REPRESENT STH to represent sth by means of a symbol **3.** *vi.* USE SYMBOLS to use symbols or symbolism —**symbolization** /símbə lī záysh'n/ *n.*

symbology /sim bólləji/ *n.* **1.** STUDY OF SYMBOLS the study or interpretation of symbols **2.** USE OF SYMBOLS the use of symbols to represent things —**symbological** /símbə lój jik'l/ *adj.* —**symbologist** /sim bólləjist/ *n.*

symmetallism /si métt'lizəm/ *n.* a system of coinage in which the unit of currency consists of a combination of two or more metals in fixed relative proportions

symmetrical /si méttrik'l/, **symmetric** /si méttrik/ *adj.* **1.** EXHIBITING SYMMETRY having both sides of a central dividing line correspond or be identical to each other **2.** BALANCED relating to or having balanced proportions, especially in two halves of a whole **3.** MATH WITH PARTICULAR PAIRS OF POINTS used to describe two points that can be joined by a line bisected by a given point or perpendicular, or a shape that has such pairs of points **4.** MATH WITH INTERCHANGEABLE TERMS used to describe an equation or function in which terms or variables may be interchanged without altering its value or form **5.** CHEM WITH SYMMETRICAL MOLECULAR STRUCTURE with atoms or groups that display symmetry about a plane in a chemical structure **6.** ANAT ON OPPOSITE SIDES used to describe body parts that have the same function but are situated on opposite sides, either of the same organ or the same body —**symmetrically** *adv.*

symmetric matrix *n.* a square matrix that is identical

to the matrix formed by transposing its rows and columns

symmetrize /símmə trīz/ (-**trizes**, -**trizing**, -**trized**), sym-**metrise** (-**trises**, -**trising**, -**trised**) vt. to give symmetry to sth —**symmetrization** /símmə trī záysh'n/ n.

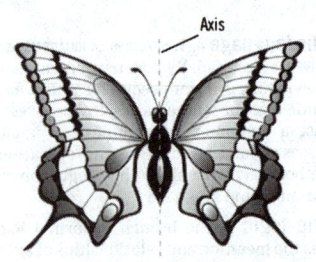

Axis

Symmetry

symmetry /símmə tri/ (plural -**tries**) n. 1. PROPERTY OF SAMENESS the property of being the same or corresponding on both sides of a central dividing line 2. BALANCED PROPORTIONS harmony or beauty of form that results from balanced proportions 3. MATH EXACT CORRESPONDENCE IN POSITION a correspondence in the position of pairs of points of a geometric object that are equally positioned about a point, line, or plane that bisects the object 4. PHYS STATE OF INVARIANCE a state of invariance shown by some phenomena when changes of orientation, charge, or parity are made [Mid-16thC. Via Latin and Greek summetria, literally 'similar measure', from, ultimately, metron 'measure' (source of English meter).]

sympathectomy /símpə théktəmi/ (plural -**mies**) n. the surgical interruption of a pathway in the sympathetic nervous system, e.g. by cutting out a nerve segment. The operation was formerly common, especially to improve the blood supply to a limb, but is now rarely if ever performed. [Early 20thC. Coined from SYMPATHETIC + -ECTOMY.]

sympathetic /símpə théttik/ adj. 1. FEELING OR SHOWING SYMPATHY showing, having, or resulting from shared feelings, pity, or compassion 2. APPROVING showing favour, agreement, or approval 3. PROVOKING SYMPATHY provoking sympathy, interest, or compassion 4. SUITED agreeably suited to sb's tastes or mood 5. ACOUSTICS PRODUCED BY OTHER SOUNDS used to describe vibrations such as musical tones that are produced in sth as a result of similar vibrations at the same frequency from sth else 6. ANAT OF SYMPATHETIC NERVOUS SYSTEM relating or belonging to the sympathetic nervous system or one of its components [Mid-17thC. Formed from SYMPATHY on the model of PATHETIC.] —**sympathetically** adv.

sympathetic magic n. magic based on the belief that sb or sth can be supernaturally affected by sth done to an object representing the person or thing

sympathetic nervous system n. the part of the autonomic nervous system that is active during stress or danger and is involved in regulating pulse and blood pressure, dilating pupils, and changing muscle tone

sympathetic string n. a string on some musical instruments that is not played but is made to vibrate by the vibrations of the bowed or plucked strings

sympathize /símpə thīz/ (-**thizes**, -**thizing**, -**thized**), sym-**pathise** (-**thises**, -**thising**, -**thised**) vi. 1. FEEL OR SHOW SYMPATHY to share the feelings of sb else or show pity or compassion for another ○ I can sympathize; the same thing happened to me. 2. BE OF SAME OPINION to share the ideas or ideals of another person or group —**sympathizer** n.

sympatholytic /símpə thō líttik/ adj. ACTING AGAINST NERVE IMPULSES used to describe a drug that opposes or blocks the effects of the sympathetic nervous system ■ n. SYMPATHOLYTIC DRUG a drug or agent that acts against the sympathetic nervous system [Mid-20thC. Coined from SYMPATHETIC + -LYTE.]

sympathomimetic /símpə thō mi méttik/ adj. STIMU-LATING SYMPATHETIC NERVOUS SYSTEM used to describe a

drug that stimulates the sympathetic nervous system or produces similar effects ■ n. SYM-PATHOMIMETIC DRUG a drug or agent that stimulates or initiates the sympathetic nervous system [Early 20thC. Coined from SYMPATHETIC + MIMETIC.]

sympathy /símpəthi/ (plural -**thies**) n. 1. CAPACITY TO SHARE FEELINGS the ability to enter into, understand, or share sb else's feelings 2. FEELINGS CAUSED BY SYMPATHY the feelings of sb who enters into or shares another's feelings 3. SORROW FOR ANOTHER'S PAIN the feeling or expression of pity or sorrow for the pain or distress of sb else ○ We extended our sympathies to the widow. 4. INCLINATION TO FEEL ALIKE the inclination to think or feel the same as sb else ○ A sympathy exists between them. 5. AGREEMENT agreement or harmony with sth or sb else 6. ALLEGIANCE OR LOYALTY allegiance or loyalty to a group or cause (often used in the plural) ○ nationalist sympathies [Late 16thC. Via Latin from Greek sumpatheia, from sumpathēs, literally 'feeling with', from pathos 'feeling' (source of English pathetic and pathology).] ◇ **come out in sympathy** to go on strike in support of other strikers (informal)

sympathy strike n. a strike by workers demonstrating their support for another group of strikers rather than against their own employer

sympathy vote n. a vote that people give to sb for whom they feel pity or affection

sympatric /sim páttrik/ adj. used to describe species that occupy roughly the same area of land but do not interbreed [Early 20thC. Formed from Greek patra 'fatherland', from patēr 'father'.] —**sympatrically** adv.

symphonic /sim fónnik/ adj. 1. OF OR LIKE MUSICAL SYMPHONY relating to, involving, or typical of a musical symphony, or resembling one in form or content 2. HARMONIOUS harmonious in sound, colour, or composition

symphonic poem n. an extended piece of music for a symphony orchestra that is based on a literary, artistic, or ideological theme, e.g. a folktale or landscape

symphonious /sim fóni əss/ adj. in agreement or harmony, especially in sound (literary) —**symphoniously** adv.

symphonist /símfənist/ n. sb who composes symphonies or other musical works for symphony orchestra

symphony /símfəni/ (plural -**nies**) n. 1. COMPLEX MUSICAL COMPOSITION a major work for an orchestra, including wind, string, and percussion instruments, usually composed in four movements, at least one of which is in sonata form 2. = symphony orchestra 3. CONCERT BY SYMPHONY ORCHESTRA a concert performed by a symphony orchestra 4. HARMONIOUS COMPOSITION OR ARRANGEMENT sth that is harmoniously composed of various elements ○ The colour scheme was a symphony of blues, greens, and yellows. 5. HARMONY OF SOUNDS OR COLOURS harmony or agreement of sounds or colours (archaic) [13thC. Via Latin and Greek sumphōnia 'harmony', literally 'sounding together', from, ultimately, phōnē 'sound'. Originally used for any of several medieval musical instruments.]

symphony orchestra n. a large orchestra that includes wind, string, and percussion instruments and plays symphonies and other works scored for these instruments

symphysis /símfəssiss/ (plural -**ses** /-seez/) n. 1. ANAT GROWING TOGETHER OF BONES OR PARTS the natural merging of two or more separate bones or parts of the body, or a point where this occurs 2. MED ABNORMAL CONDITION an abnormal condition in which two or more separate bones or parts of the body have merged 3. ANAT JOINT WITH LITTLE MOVEMENT a joint in which the bones are connected by tough cartilage (**fibrocartilage**) and there is very little movement between them, e.g. between adjacent vertebrae in the spinal column 4. BOT FUSION OF PLANT PARTS a fusion of two similar organs or parts of a plant, or a line marking such a fusion [Late 16thC. Via modern Latin from Greek sumphusis 'growing together', from phusis 'growth'.] —**symphyseal** /sim fízzi əl/ adj. —**symphystic** /sim fístik/ adj. —**symphytic** /sim fíttik/ adj.

sympodium /sim pódi əm/ (plural -**a** /-di ə/) n. a main plant stem, e.g. the stem of a grapevine, that develops from a series of lateral branches, often in a

zigzag pattern [Mid-19thC. From modern Latin, formed from the Greek stem pod- 'foot'.] —**sympodial** adj. —**sympodially** adv.

symposia plural of **symposium**

symposiarch /sim pózi aark/ n. sb who is in overall charge of a symposium [Early 17thC. From Greek sumposiarkhos, from sumposion (see SYMPOSIUM).]

symposiast /sim pózi ast/ n. sb who takes part in a symposium (formal) [Mid-17thC. Formed from Greek sumposiazein 'to drink together', from sumposion (see SYMPOSIUM).]

symposium /sim pózi əm/ (plural -**ums** or -**a** /-ə/) n. 1. FORMAL MEETING FOR DISCUSSION OF SUBJECT a formal meeting held for the discussion of a particular subject and during which individuals may make presentations 2. PUBL PUBLISHED COLLECTION OF OPINIONS a published collection of opinions or writings on a subject, often in a periodical 3. HIST DRINKING PARTY IN ANCIENT GREECE a drinking party in ancient Greece, usually with music and philosophical conversation [Late 16thC. Via Latin from Greek sumposion 'drinking party', from sumpotēs 'fellow drinker', from potēs 'drinker'.] —**symposiac** adj.

symptom /símptəm/ n. 1. MED INDICATION OF ILLNESS FELT BY PATIENT an indication of some disease or other disorder, especially one experienced by the patient, e.g. pain, dizziness, or itching, as opposed to one observed by the doctor (**sign**) 2. SIGN OF STH ELSE a sign or indication of the existence of sth, especially sth undesirable [Mid-16thC. Via late Latin from Greek sumptōma 'occurrence', from sumpiptein, literally 'to fall together', from piptein 'to fall'.] —**symptomless** adj.

symptomatic /símptə máttik/ adj. 1. MED INDICATING ILLNESS indicating or typical of a specific illness 2. CHARACTERISTIC typical or indicative of sth, especially sth undesirable ○ symptomatic of the breakdown in communication between children and parents 3. MED OF SYMPTOMS relating to, affecting, or based on a symptom or symptoms of bodily disorder ○ Only symptomatic relief is available for the common cold. [Late 17thC. From late Latin symptomaticus, ultimately from Greek sumptoma (see SYMPTOM).] —**symptomatically** adv.

symptomatology /símptəmə tólləji/ (plural -**gies**) n. 1. STUDY OF SYMPTOMS the study of the relationships between symptoms and diseases 2. SET OF SYMPTOMS the set of symptoms that associated with a particular disease or that affect a patient [Late 18thC. Coined from Greek sumptōmat- stem of sumptōma (see SYMPTOM) + -LOGY.]

symptomize /símptəmīz/ (-**izes**, -**izing**, -**ized**), symp-**tomise** (-**ises**, -**ising**, -**ised**) vt. to be an indication of the existence of sth

syn. abbr. 1. synonym 2. synonymous

syn- prefix. together, together with, united ○ syn-carpous [From Greek sun 'together']

synaeresis n. = syneresis

synaesthesia /sínnəss theezhə/ n. 1. PHYSIOL SENSATION FELT ELSEWHERE IN BODY the feeling of sensation in one part of the body when another part is stimulated 2. PSYCHOL STIMULATION OF ONE SENSE ALONGSIDE ANOTHER the evocation of one kind of sense impression when another sense is stimulated, e.g. the sensation of colour when a sound is heard 3. LITERAT RHETORICAL DEVICE in literature, the description of one kind of sense perception using words that describe another kind of sense perception, as in the phrase 'shining metallic words' (literary) [Late 19thC. From modern Latin, which was coined from syn- (see SYN-) + the stem of Greek aisthēsis 'sensation', modelled on anaesthesia.] —**synaesthetic** /-théttik/ adj.

synagogue /sínnə gog/ n. 1. HOUSE OF WORSHIP FOR JEWISH CONGREGATION the place of worship and communal centre of a Jewish congregation 2. JEWISH CONGREGATION a body of followers of Judaism who worship together [12thC. Via French and late Latin from Greek sunagōgē 'assembly', from sunagein 'to bring together', from agein 'to lead'.] —**synagogal** /sínnə góggəl/ adj. —**synagogical** /-gójjik'l/ adj.

synalepha /sínnə leéfə/, **synaloepha** n. the blending of two adjacent vowels into one, e.g. when a word ending in a vowel is immediately followed by a word beginning with a vowel [Mid-16thC. Via late

Latin from Greek *sunaloiphē*, from *sunaleiphein* 'to smear together', from *aleiphein* 'to smear'.]

synapse /sī naps, sínnaps/ *n.* GAP BETWEEN NERVE ENDS a junction between two nerve cells, where the club-shaped tip of a nerve fibre almost touches another cell in order to transmit signals ■ *vi.* **(-apses, -apsing, -apsed)** FORM SYNAPSE to form a synapse between nerve cells [Late 19thC. Anglicization of SYNAPSIS.]

synapsis /si nápsiss/ (*plural* **-ses** /-seez/) *n.* the pairing of homologous chromosomes from each parent during the initial phase (**prophase**) of cell division [Mid-17thC. Via modern Latin and Greek *sunapsis* 'connection' from, ultimately, *haptein* 'to join'.]

synaptic /si náptik/ *adj.* **1.** ANAT OF SYNAPSE relating to or involving a junction between nerve cells **2.** BIOL OF SYNAPSIS relating to, involving, or typical of synapsis [Late 19thC. Formed from SYNAPSIS or SYNAPSE on the model of Greek *sunaptikos* 'connective'.]

synarchy /sínnərki/ (*plural* **-chies**) *n.* joint rule over sth [Mid-18thC. From Greek *sunarkhia.*]

synarthrosis /sín aar thrṓssiss/ (*plural* **-ses** /-seez/) *n.* a rigid joint formed by the union of two bones and connected by fibrous tissue —**synarthrodial** /-thrṓ di əl/ *adj.* —**synarthrodially** *adv.*

sync /singk/, **synch** *n.* (*informal*) **1.** SYNCHRONIZATION the relationship between things that are happening or working at the same time, especially the correspondence of sound and image in a film **2.** HARMONY harmony or agreement ■ *vti.* **synced, synched, syncing, synching, syncs, synchs** SYNCHRONIZE to synchronize sth, or be synchronized (*informal*) [Early 20thC. Shortening.]

syncarpous /sin káarpəss/ *adj.* used to describe the female reproductive parts (**gynoecium**) of a flower in which the carpels are fused —**syncarpy** /síng kərpi/ *n.*

syncategorematic /sín kátəgərə máttik/ *adj.* used to describe an expression that has meaning only in conjunction with another expression [Early 19thC. Via medieval Latin *syncategorematicus* and Greek *sugkatēgorēmatikos*, literally 'predicating jointly', from, ultimately, *katēgorein* 'to predicate' (source of English *category*).]

synch *n., vti.* = **sync** (*informal*)

synchondrosis /síng kon drṓssiss/ (*plural* **-ses** /-seez/) *n.* **1.** JOINT WITH BONES LINKED BY CARTILAGE a type of joint in which there is slight movement between bones that are held together by cartilage, e.g. between the ribs and the breastbone **2.** JOINT WITH CARTILAGE CONVERTING TO BONE a type of joint in which the cartilage linking two bones in childhood is replaced by bone as development progresses [Late 16thC. Via modern Latin from late Greek *sugkhondrōsis*, from *khondros* 'cartilage'.]

synchro /síngkrō/ (*plural* **-chros**) *n.* ELEC ENG = **selsyn** [Mid-20thC. Shortening of *synchronizing* (see SELSYN).]

synchro- *prefix.* synchronous, synchronized ○ *synchroscope* [From SYNCHRONOUS]

synchrocyclotron /síngkrō sīklə tron/ *n.* a particle accelerator that compensates for increases in the relativistic mass of accelerated particles, and so achieves greater energies, by using the synchronizing effects of a frequency-modulated electric field

synchroflash /síngkrō flash/ *n.* a mechanism in a camera that opens the shutter at the moment when the light from the flashbulb or electronic flash is brightest

synchromesh /síngkrō mesh/ *n.* a gear system in which the speeds of the driving and driven parts are synchronized before they engage, making gear changes smoother —**synchromesh** *adj.*

synchronal /síngkrən'l/ *adj.* happening at the same time [Mid-17thC. Formed from late Latin *synchronus* (see SYNCHRONOUS).]

synchronic /sin krónnik/ *adj.* relating to or studying sth, especially a language, as it exists at a certain point in time, without considering its historical development. ◊ **diachronic** [Mid-19thC. Formed from late Latin *synchronus* (see SYNCHRONOUS).] —**synchronically** *adv.*

synchronicity /síngkrə nísəti/ *n.* **1.** COINCIDENCE OF EVENTS THAT SEEM RELATED the coincidence of events that seem related but are not obviously caused one by the other. The term was first used in this sense in the work of the psychologist Carl Jung. **2.** = **synchronism** *n.* 1

synchronise *vti.* = **synchronize**

synchronism /síngkrənizəm/ *n.* **1.** OCCURRENCE AT SAME TIME the simultaneous occurrence of two or more things **2.** ARRANGEMENT OF CONTEMPORARY EVENTS AND PEOPLE an arrangement in chronological order showing historical events that happened or people who were alive around the same time [Late 16thC. From Greek *sugkhronismos*, from *sugkhronos* (see SYNCHRONOUS).] —**synchronistic** /síngkrə nístik/ *adj.* —**synchronistically** /-nístiklee/ *adv.*

synchronize /síngkrə nīz/ (**-nizes, -nizing, -nized**), **synchronise** (**-nises, -nising, -nised**) *v.* **1.** *vi.* HAPPEN TOGETHER to happen at the same time **2.** *vi.* GO TOGETHER to go or work together or in unison **3.** *vt.* MAKE THINGS WORK AT SAME TIME to make sth work at the same time or the same rate as sth else **4.** *vt.* CINEMA ALIGN SOUND AND IMAGE OF FILM to make the soundtrack of a film match up with the action **5.** *vt.* REPRESENT CONTEMPORARY HISTORICAL EVENTS AND PEOPLE to represent historical events or people in an arrangement that shows which of them happened or lived around the same time [Early 17thC. Formed from SYNCHRONISM.] —**synchronization** /síngkrə nī záysh'n/ *n.*

synchronized swimming *n.* a sport in which swimmers perform coordinated movements in time to music in the manner of a dance

synchronoscope *n.* = **synchroscope**

synchronous /síngkrənəss/ *adj.* **1.** OCCURRING SIMULTANEOUSLY happening at the same time **2.** WORKING AT SAME RATE working or moving at the same rate **3.** PHYS WITH SAME PERIOD AND PHASE with the same period and phase of oscillation or cyclical movement [Mid-17thC. Formed from late Latin *synchronus*, from Greek *sugkhronos*, from *khronos* 'time'.] —**synchronously** *adv.* —**synchronousness** *n.*

synchronous motor *n.* a type of electric motor that operates at a speed directly proportional to the frequency of the applied voltage source

synchronous orbit *n.* an orbit that keeps time with the rotation of the orbited object, so that the orbiting body is always directly over the same point on the surface of the orbiting body

synchrony /síngkrəni/ (*plural* **-nies**) *n.* occurrence at the same time or movement at the same rate, or an example of this phenomenon

synchroscope /síngkrə skōp/, **synchronoscope** /sing krónnə skōp/ *n.* **1.** MECH ENG DEVICE FOR DETERMINING SYNCHRONICITY an instrument used to find whether or not two things such as moving machine parts are synchronous **2.** ELEC ENG INSTRUMENT INDICATING FREQUENCY DIFFERENCE an instrument used to indicate the difference in frequency between two alternating current supplies

synchrotron /síngkrə tron/ *n.* a very high-energy circular particle accelerator that operates by using a high-frequency electric field and a magnetic field in synchrony with the movement of the particles. The particles are guided around inside a large hollow ring by strategically placed electromagnets while being accelerated by the electric field.

synchrotron radiation *n.* the electromagnetic radiation emitted by charged particles, usually electrons, moving in curved paths in a magnetic field at speeds approaching that of light. Such radiation is emitted from synchrotrons, supernova remnants, and radio galaxies.

syncline /síng klīn/ *n.* a fold in a rock formation that is shaped like a basin or trough and contains younger rocks in its core —**synclinal** /sing klīn'l/ *adj.*

Syncom /síng kom/ *n.* a communications satellite that is in synchronous orbit over the Earth [Late 20thC. Contraction of *synchronous communications.*]

syncopate /síngkə payt/ (**-pates, -pating, -pated**) *vt.* **1.** MUSIC MODIFY RHYTHM BY ACCENTING WEAK BEAT to modify a musical rhythm by shifting the accent to a weak beat of the bar **2.** PHON SHORTEN WORD BY LOSS OF SOUNDS to shorten a word by the loss of one or more sounds or letters from the middle —**syncopator** *n.*

syncopation /síngkə páysh'n/ *n.* **1.** MUSIC PLACING OF ACCENT ON WEAK BEAT a rhythmic technique in music in which the accent is shifted to a weak beat of the bar **2.** PHON = **syncope** *n.* 2

syncope /síngkəpi/ *n.* **1.** MED FAINTING EPISODE a loss of consciousness due to lack of oxygen to the brain (*technical*) **2.** PHON LOSS OF SOUNDS FROM WORD the shortening of a word by the loss of sounds or letters from its middle [Mid-16thC. Via late Latin from Greek *sugkopē*, from *sugkoptein* 'to cut short', from *koptein* 'to cut'.] —**syncopal** *adj.* —**syncopic** /sing kóppik/ *adj.*

syncretise *vti.* = **syncretize**

syncretism /síngkrətizəm/ *n.* **1.** RELIG, PHILOS COMBINATION OF DIFFERENT BELIEFS the attempted combination of different systems of philosophical or religious belief or practice **2.** GRAM MERGING OF DIFFERENT INFLECTIONAL FORMS the use of a single inflectional form of a word to cover functions previously covered by two separate forms, e.g. 'spun' in English, now used for both the past tense and the past participle although the past tense used to be 'span' [Early 17thC. Via modern Latin *syncretismus* from Greek *sugkrētismos* 'union', from *sugkrētizein* (see SYNCRETIZE).] —**syncretic** /sing kréttik/ *adj.* —**syncretist** /síngkrə tist/ *n.* —**syncretistic** /síngkrə tístik/ *adj.*

syncretize /síngkrə tīz/ (**-tizes, -tizing, -tized**), **syncretise** (**-cretises, -cretising, -cretised**) *vti.* to combine, or try to combine, elements from different systems of philosophical or religious belief or practice [Late 17thC. From Greek *sugkrētizein* 'to unite (against a common enemy)', of unknown origin.] —**syncretization** /síngkrə tī záysh'n/ *n.*

syncytium /sin sítti əm/ (*plural* **-a** /-tti ə/) *n.* a mass of cytoplasm within a cell membrane that contains multiple nuclei and is often the result of cellular fusion, e.g. in certain slime moulds [Late 19thC. Formed from Greek *kutos* (see -CYTE).] —**syncytial** /-sítti əl/ *adj.*

synd /sīnd/, **syne** /sīn/ *vt.* (**synds, synding, synded; synes, syning, syned**) *Scotland* RINSE STH to rinse sth, usually with water ■ *n. Scotland* RINSE an act of rinsing sth [14thC. Origin unknown.]

synd. *abbr.* syndicate

syndactyl /sin dáktil/ *adj.* having two or more fingers or toes joined together. This may be a natural condition, as in certain animals, or a congenital abnormality, as in people with webbed toes. —**syndactyl** *n.* —**syndactylism** *n.* —**syndactyly** *n.*

syndesis /sin deéssiss/ *n.* the use in grammar of constructions in which clauses are joined by conjunctions [Early 20thC. From German, formed from Greek *desis* 'binding', from, ultimately, *dein* (see SYNDETIC).]

syndesmosis /sín dess mṓssiss/ (*plural* **-ses** /-seez/) *n.* a type of immovable joint in which the bones are held firmly by fibrous tissue but are not very close together, e.g. at the lower ends of the tibia and fibula [Late 16thC. Formed from Greek *sundesmos* 'ligament', from *sundein* (see SYNDETIC).] —**syndesmotic** /sín dess móttik/ *adj.*

syndetic /sin déttik/ *adj.* used to describe a construction in grammar in which two clauses are joined by a conjunction [Early 17thC. From Greek *sundetikos*, from *sundein* 'to bind together', from *dein* 'to bind'.] —**syndetically** *adv.*

syndeton /síndə toón, -tən/ *n.* a grammatical construction in which two clauses are joined by a conjunction [Mid-20thC. Back-formation from ASYNDETON and POLYSYNDETON.]

syndic /síndik/ *n.* **1.** BUSINESS BUSINESS AGENT sb appointed to represent an organization, e.g. a corporation or a university, in business transactions **2.** POL EUROPEAN OFFICIAL a government official, especially a civil magistrate, in some European countries [Early 17thC. Via French, 'delegate', from, ultimately, Greek *sundikos* 'defendant's advocate', from *dikē* 'judgment'.] —**syndical** *adj.* —**syndicship** *n.*

syndicalism /síndikəlizəm/ *n.* **1.** REVOLUTIONARY POLITICAL DOCTRINE a revolutionary political doctrine that advocates the seizure of the means of production by workers organized in trade unions **2.** **WORKERS' CONTROL OF MEANS OF PRODUCTION** a system of government in which workers organized in trade unions control the means of production [Early 20thC. Via French *syndicalisme* from, ultimately, *syndic* (see SYNDIC).] —**syndical** *adj.* —**syndicalist** *n.* —**syndicalistic** /sìndikə lístik/ *adj.*

syndicate *n.* /síndi kət/ **1.** BUSINESS **GROUP OF BUSINESSES** an association of businesses jointly contributing capital to a major project **2.** COMMUNICATION **BUSINESS THAT SELLS NEWS MATERIALS** a business or agency that sells news stories or photographs to the media **3.** PRESS **GROUP OF NEWSPAPERS UNDER SAME OWNER** a group of newspapers that have the same owner **4.** **GROUP OF PEOPLE** a group of people who combine to carry out a business, enterprise, or some other common purpose **5.** CRIMINOL **ASSOCIATION OF GANGSTERS** an association of gangsters that controls a particular area of organized crime **6.** POL **COUNCIL OR JURISDICTION OF CIVIL MAGISTRATE** a council or body of syndics, or the office or jurisdiction of a government official, especially a civil magistrate, in some European countries ■ *v.* /síndi kayt/ (**-cates, -cating, -cated**) **1.** *vt.* PUBL **SELL STH FOR MULTIPLE PUBLICATION** to sell sth, e.g. an article or a cartoon strip, for publication in a number of newspapers or magazines simultaneously **2.** *vt.* US TV **SELL TV PROGRAMMES TO INDEPENDENT STATIONS** to sell television or radio programmes directly to independent stations **3.** *vt.* **CONTROL STH AS SYNDICATE** to control or manage sth as a syndicate **4.** *vi.* **COME TOGETHER AS SYNDICATE** to come together to form a syndicate

syndrome /síndrōm/ *n.* **1.** MED **GROUP OF IDENTIFYING SIGNS AND SYMPTOMS** a group of signs and symptoms that together are characteristic or indicative of a specific disease or other disorder **2.** **THINGS THAT FORM PATTERN** a group of things or events that form a recognizable pattern, especially of sth undesirable [Mid-16thC. Via modern Latin and Greek *sundromē*, literally 'running together', from, ultimately, *dramein* 'to run'.]

syne[1] /sīn/ *adv.* *Scotland* **AGO** since then ■ *prep.* *Scotland* **SINCE** from a particular time onward ■ *conj.* *Scotland* **FROM WHEN** from the time that [14thC. Contraction of *sithen* (see SINCE).]

syne[2] *vt., n.* = **synd**

synecdoche /si nékdəki/ *n.* a figure of speech in which the word for part of sth is used to mean the whole, e.g. 'sail' for 'boat', or vice versa [14thC. Via Latin from Greek *sunekdokhē*, from *sunekdekhesthai* 'to take on a share of', from *ekdekhesthai* 'to take'.] —**synecdochic** /sìnnek dókik/ *adj.* —**synecdochical** /-dókik'l/ *adj.* —**synecdochically** /-dókikəlee/ *adv.*

synecology /sìnni kólləji/ *n.* a branch of ecology dealing with the structure and development of entire ecological communities and the interrelationships of the plants and animals within them —**synecologic** /sìnnikə lójjik/ *adj.* —**synecological** /-lójjik'l/ *adj.* —**synecologically** /-lójjikli/ *adv.*

synectics /si néktiks/ *n.* an approach to solving problems based on the creative thinking of a group of people from different areas of experience and knowledge (*takes a singular verb*) [Mid-20thC. Formed from late Latin *synecticus* 'producing an effect immediately', via Greek *sunektikos* from, ultimately, *ekhein* 'to hold'.]

syneresis /si néerəssiss/, **synaeresis** *n.* **1.** **LIQUID SEPARATION IN GEL** the process by which a liquid is separated from a gel owing to further coagulation **2.** **MERGING OF VOWELS INTO DIPHTHONG** the merging of two vowels into a diphthong **3.** **MERGING OF VOWELS INTO ONE SYLLABLE** the merging of two vowels into one syllable without making it into a diphthong [Late 16thC. Via late Latin and Greek *sunairesis*, literally 'contraction', from, ultimately, *hairein* 'to take'.]

synergism /sínnərjìzəm/ *n.* **1.** = **synergy** **2.** CHR **CHRISTIAN THEOLOGICAL DOCTRINE** the doctrine in Christian theology that the human will and the Holy Spirit work together to bring about spiritual regeneration or salvation [Mid-18thC (see SYNERGY)] —**synergistic** /sìnnər jístik/ *adj.* —**synergistically** /-jístikəlee/ *adv.*

synergist /sínnərjist/ *n.* sth that works in combination with sth else to increase its effect, e.g. a drug that increases the effect of another drug

synergy /sínnərji/ (*plural* **-gies**) *n.* **1.** **COMBINED EFFORT BEING GREATER THAN PARTS** the working together of two or more things, people, or organizations, especially when the result is greater than the sum of their individual effects or capabilities **2.** MED **COMBINED ACTION OF DRUGS OR MUSCLES** the phenomenon in which the combined action of two things, e.g. drugs or muscles, is greater than the sum of their effects individually. In the case of drugs, the result may be dangerous to the patient. [Mid-17thC. Via Latin from Greek *sunergia*, from *sunergein* 'to work together', from, ultimately, *ergos* 'work'.] —**synergetic** /sìnnər jéttik/ *adj.* —**synergetically** /-jéttikəlee/ *adv.* —**synergic** /si núrjik/ *adj.*

synesis /sínnəssiss/ *n.* grammatical agreement according to meaning rather than strict syntax, e.g. the use of a plural form of a verb or a plural pronoun with a collective noun. Synesis is shown, e.g., in 'The team are playing badly so we have stopped supporting them', with 'are' and 'them' rather than 'is' and 'it'. [Late 19thC. Via modern Latin from Greek *sunesis* 'union', from *sunienai* 'to bring together', from *hienai* 'to send'.]

synesthesia *n.* US = **synaesthesia**

synfuel /sín fyoo əl/ *n.* a liquid fuel synthesized from a nonpetroleum source such as coal, oil shale, or waste plastics, and used as a substitute for a petroleum product [Late 20thC. A blend of SYNTHETIC and FUEL.]

syngamy /síng gəmi/ *n.* sexual reproduction through the fusion of gametes [Early 20thC. Coined from SYN- + Greek *gamos* 'marriage'.] —**syngamic** /sing gámmik/ *adj.* —**syngamous** /síng gəməss/ *adj.*

J. M. Synge: Portrait by John B. Yeats

Synge /sing/, **J. M.** (1871–1909) Irish dramatist. A dominant figure of the Irish Renaissance, he wrote the controversial masterpiece, *The Playboy of the Western World* (1907). Full name **John Millington Synge**

syngeneic /sínji néeik, -náyik/ *adj.* having an identical or closely similar genetic make-up, especially one that will allow the transplantation of tissue without provoking an immune response [Mid-20thC. Formed from Greek *sungeneia* 'kinship', from *genos* 'kind'.] —**syngeneically** *adv.*

syngenesis /sin jénnəssiss/ *n.* reproduction involving fusion of male and female genetic material —**syngenetic** /sínji néttik/ *adj.*

synkaryon /sin kárri on/ *n.* a cell nucleus formed through the fusion of male and female nuclei [Early 20thC. Formed from Greek *karuon* 'seed'.] —**synkaryonic** /sín kari ónnik/ *adj.*

synkinesis /sínki néessis, -kī-/, **synkinesia** /sínki néezi ə, -kī-/ *n.* the performing of an unintended movement when making a voluntary one —**synkinetic** /-néttik/ *adj.*

synod /sínnəd/ *n.* **1.** **CHURCH COUNCIL** a special council of church members that holds regular meetings to discuss religious issues **2.** **PRESBYTERIAN CHURCH COURT** a Presbyterian church court between the Presbytery and the General Assembly **3.** **ASSEMBLY OR COUNCIL** an assembly or council held for the discussion of issues (*formal*) [14thC. Via late Latin from Greek *sunodos* 'meeting', from *hodos* 'way'.] —**synodal** *adj.*

synodic /si nóddik/, **synodical** /-ik'l/ *adj.* **1.** ASTRON **OF ALIGNMENT OF SAME CELESTIAL BODIES** relating to the alignment of celestial bodies, or the interval between occasions when the same celestial bodies are aligned **2.** CHR **OF CHURCH SYNOD** relating to or having the character of a church synod —**synodically** *adv.*

synodic month *n.* = **lunar month**

synoecious /si néeshəss/ *adj.* with male and female organs on the same flower or other structure [Mid-19thC. Formed from Greek *oikos* 'house'.]

synonym /sínnənim/ *n.* **1.** **WORD MEANING SAME AS ANOTHER** a word that means the same, or almost the same, as another word in the same language, either in all of its uses or in a particular context. Examples of synonyms in this sense are 'environment' and 'surroundings' and the verbs 'tear' and 'rip'. **2.** **ALTERNATIVE NAME** a word or expression that is used as another name for sth in certain styles of speaking or writing or to emphasize a particular aspect or association. Examples of synonyms in this sense are 'Caledonian' and 'Scottish'. **3.** BIOL **REJECTED DUPLICATE TAXONOMIC NAME** a duplicate taxonomic name that has been rejected or replaced [15thC. Via Latin *synonymum* from, ultimately, Greek *sunōnumos* 'synonymous', from *onuma* 'name'.] —**synonymic** /sínnə nímmik/ *adj.* —**synonymity** /-nímməti/ *n.*

synonymize /si nónni mīz/ (**-mizes, -mizing, -mized**), **synonymise** (**-mises, -mising, -mised**) *vt.* to provide an analysis or listing of the synonyms of a word or expression

synonymous /si nónniməss/ *adj.* **1.** **HAVING SAME MEANING** meaning the same, or almost the same, as another word in the same language, or being an alternative name for sb or sth **2.** **HAVING SIMILAR CONNOTATION** having an implication similar to the idea expressed by another word ○ *Andy Warhol is synonymous with pop art.* —**synonymously** *adv.* —**synonymousness** *n.*

synonymy /si nónnimi/ (*plural* **-mies**) *n.* **1.** **EQUIVALENCE OF MEANING** the state or quality of being synonymous **2.** **STUDY OF SYNONYMS** the study, classification, and distinguishing of synonyms **3.** **ANNOTATED LIST OF SYNONYMS** a list or book of synonyms, with emphasis on the discrimination of meanings

synopsis /si nópsiss/ (*plural* **-ses** /-seez/) *n.* **1.** **SUMMARY OF TEXT** a condensed version of a text, e.g. a summary of the plot of a book, film, or television programme **2.** **SUMMARY OF SUBJECT** a concise outline or survey of a subject [Early 17thC. Via late Latin from Greek *sunopsis* 'general view', from *opsis* 'view'.]

synoptic /si nóptik/ *adj.* **1.** **PERTAINING TO SYNOPSIS** constituting a general view of the whole of a subject **2.** METEOROL **DISPLAYING WIDESPREAD WEATHER** pertaining to or showing simultaneous weather conditions over a large area **3.** **Synoptic, synoptic** BIBLE **SHARING VIEWS OF JESUS CHRIST'S LIFE** used to describe the gospels of Matthew, Mark, and Luke that tell the story of Jesus Christ's life and ministry from a similar point of view and are similar in structure ■ *n.* **1.** **Synoptic, synoptic** **SYNOPTIC GOSPEL** any one of the Synoptic gospels of Matthew, Mark, or Luke **2.** **Synoptic** = **synoptist** [Early 17thC. Via modern Latin from Greek *sunoptikos*, from *sunopsis* (see SYNOPSIS).] —**synoptical** *adj.* —**synoptically** *adv.*

synoptist /si nóptist/, **synoptic** *n.* an author of one of the Synoptic gospels

synostosis /sín o stóssiss/ (*plural* **-ses** /-seez/) *n.* the formation of a single bone from the fusion of two adjacent bones —**synostotic** /sí o stóttik/ *adj.*

synovia /sī nóvi ə/ *n.* a clear viscous fluid that lubricates the linings of joints and the sheaths of tendons [Mid-17thC. From modern Latin *sinovia*, of uncertain origin: probably coined by Philippus PARACELSUS.] —**synovial** *adj.*

synovitis /sīnō vítiss/ *n.* inflammation of the sinovial membrane of a joint —**synovitic** /sīnō víttik/ *adj.*

synsepalous /sin séppələss/ *adj.* BOT = **gamosepalous** [Mid-19thC. Coined from SYNTHETIC + SEPAL + -OUS.]

syntactic /sin táktik/, **syntactical** /-ik'l/ *adj.* **1.** **OF SYNTAX** relating to the rules or patterns of syntax **2.** **CONFORMING TO RULES OF SYNTAX** correctly formed according to the rules or accepted structures of syntax [Early 19thC. Via Latin from Greek *suntaktikos*, from *suntassein* (see SYNTAX).] —**syntactically** *adv.*

syntagma /sin tágmə/ (*plural* **-mata** /sin tágmə tə/ *or* **-mas**), **syntagm** /sín tam/ *n.* linguistic units made up of sets of phonemes, words, or phrases that are arranged sequentially [Mid-17thC. Via late Latin from Greek *suntagma*, from *suntassein* (see SYNTAX).] —**syntagmatic** /sín tag máttik/ *adj.*

syntagmatic /sín tag máttik/, **syntagmic** /sin tágmik/ *adj.* relating to syntactic units, or the function and behaviour of a word or phrase within a syntactic unit

syntax /sín taks/ *n.* **1. ORGANIZATION OF WORDS IN SENTENCES** the ordering of and relationship between the words and other structural elements in phrases and sentences. The syntax may be of a whole language, a particular phrase or sentence, or of a particular speaker. **2. BRANCH OF GRAMMAR** the branch of grammar that studies syntax **3. RULES OF SYNTAX** an exposition of or set of rules for producing grammatical structures according to the syntax of a language **4. LOGIC RULES FOR DERIVING LOGICAL FORMULAS** the part of logic that gives the rules that define which combinations of expressions in the logical system yield well-formed formulas **5. COMPUT RULES GOVERNING PROGRAM STRUCTURE** the rules governing which statements and combinations of statements in a programming language will be acceptable to a compiler for that language **6. RULE-BASED ARRANGEMENT** the arrangement of any group of elements in a systematic or rule-based manner [Late 16thC. Via French or late Latin from Greek *suntaxis*, from *suntassein* 'to put in order', from *tassein* 'to arrange'.]

synth /sinth/ *n.* a synthesizer (*informal*)

synthesis /sínthəssiss/ (*plural* **-ses** /-seèz/) *n.* **1. RESULT OF COMBINING DIFFERENT ELEMENTS** a new unified whole resulting from the combination of different ideas, influences, or objects **2. COMBINING OF DIFFERENT ELEMENTS INTO WHOLE** the process of combining different ideas, influences, or objects into a new whole (*formal*) **3. CHEM FORMATION OF CHEMICAL COMPOUNDS** the process of forming a complex compound through a series of one or more chemical reactions involving simpler substances **4. MUSIC PRODUCING OF SOUND WITH SYNTHESIZER** the production of music or speech using an electronic synthesizer **5. LING USE OF INFLECTIONS** the expression of syntactic relationships by means of inflections rather than word order or prepositions and other function words **6. PHILOS IDEA RESOLVING CONTRADICTIONS** in Hegelian philosophy, the new idea that resolves the conflict between the initial proposition (**thesis**) and its negation (**antithesis**) **7. PHILOS DEDUCTIVE REASONING** the process of deductive reasoning from first principles to a conclusion [15thC. Via Latin, literally 'collection', from Greek *sunthesis*, from *suntithenai* 'to put together', from *tithenai* 'to put'.] —**synthesist** *n.*

synthesise *vti.* = **synthesize**

synthesiser *n.* = **synthesizer**

synthesis gas *n.* a mixture of carbon monoxide and hydrogen, derived from the breakdown of carbon- and hydrogen-containing materials, used as a raw material for many chemical products. It is used as a source of hydrogen for the manufacture of ammonia and other products.

synthesize /sínthə sīz/ (**-sizes**, **-sizing**, **-sized**), **synthesise** (**-sises**, **-sising**, **-sised**), **synthetize** (**-tizes**, **-tizing**, **-tized**) *v.* **1. *vti.* COMBINE DIFFERENT ELEMENTS INTO NEW WHOLE** to combine different ideas, influences, or objects into a new whole, or be combined in this way **2. *vt.* SCI PRODUCE SUBSTANCE BY CHEMICAL PROCESS** to produce a substance or material by chemical or biological synthesis —**synthesization** /sínthə sī záysh'n/ *n.*

synthesizer /sínthə sīzər/, **synthesiser** *n.* **1. MUSIC ELECTRONIC MUSICAL INSTRUMENT** an electronic device capable of generating and modifying sounds electronically, often one designed as a musical instrument **2. SCI MANUFACTURER OF SYNTHETIC SUBSTANCES** sb or sth involved in the synthesis of substances or materials **3. SB WHO COMBINES DIFFERENT ELEMENTS** sb who combines different ideas, influences, or objects into a new whole

synthetic /sin théttik/ *adj.* **1. CHEM MADE BY A CHEMICAL PROCESS** made artificially by a chemical process of synthesis, especially so as to resemble a natural product **2. INSINCERE** not genuine, especially expressed but not genuinely felt ○ *synthetic expressions of sympathy* **3. PHILOSOPHY WITH TRUTH DEPENDING ON FACTS** used to describe a proposition whose truth or falsity is a matter of facts and not merely a matter of the meaning of the words in the sentence **4. LING USING INFLECTIONS TO EXPRESS SYNTAX** used to describe a language that expresses syntactic relationships by

means of inflections rather than word order or prepositions and other function words ■ *n.* CHEM **CHEMICALLY PRODUCED SUBSTANCE OR MATERIAL** a substance or material produced by chemical processes rather than occurring naturally [Late 17thC. Via French or modern Latin from Greek *sunthetikos* 'component', from *sunthetos* 'combined', from *suntithenai* (see SYNTHESIS).] —**synthetical** *adj.* —**synthetically** *adv.*

synthetic resin *n.* a resin produced by polymerization of simple molecules rather than obtained directly from plant substances

synthetic rubber *n.* a compound synthesized from unsaturated hydrocarbons that resembles rubber

synthetize /sínthə tīz/ *vti.* = **synthesize** —**synthetization** /sínthə tī záysh'n/ *n.*

syntonic /sin tónnik/ *adj.* **1. EMOTIONALLY RESPONSIVE TO SURROUNDINGS** used to describe sb who is normally attuned to the environment **2. ACCORDING WITH BELIEFS** in ego psychology, used to describe behaviour that does not conflict with sb's basic attitudes and beliefs and, therefore, is not anxiety-provoking (*used in combination*) ○ *ego-syntonic* [Late 19thC. Formed from Greek *suntonos* 'attuned', from *suntenein* 'to draw tight'.] —**syntonically** *adv.*

syphilis /síffəliss/ *n.* a serious sexually transmitted disease caused by the spirally twisted bacterium *Treponema pallidum* that affects many body organs and parts, including the genitals, brain, skin, and nervous tissue [Early 18thC. From modern Latin the name of the person allegedly first affected according to a poem *Syphilis sive morbus Gallicus* (Syphilis or the French Disease) (1530) by Girolamo Fracastoro, 1483–1553, a physician from Verona.]

syphilitic /síffə líttik/ *adj.* **OF SYPHILIS** relating to, caused by, or affected by syphilis ■ *n.* **SB WITH SYPHILIS** sb who has been infected with the spirochaete that causes syphilis (*offensive*) [Late 18thC. From modern Latin *syphiliticus*, from SYPHILIS.] —**syphilitically** *adv.*

syphiloid /síffə lòyd/ *adj.* resembling syphilis or having similar characteristics

syphiloma /síffə lōmə/ (*plural* **-mata** /-mətə/ *or* **-mas**) *n.* = **gumma**

syphon *n.*, *vt.* = **siphon**

SYR *abbr.* Syria (*international vehicle registration*)

Syracuse /sírrə kyooz/ capital city and port of Syracuse Province, Sicily, situated about 56 km/35 mi. south of Catania. Population: 126,800 (1992).

syrah /sírrə/ *n.* **1. BLACK GRAPE GROWN FOR WINE** a black grape grown mainly in the Rhône valley of France but also in California and Australia, and used to make wine **2. SYRAH WINE** a typically strong full-bodied wine made from the syrah grape variety [Early 19thC. Alteration of SHIRAZ, where the grape is supposed to have originated.]

Syria

Syria /sírri ə/ republic in the Middle East, bordered by Turkey, Iraq, Jordan, Israel, Lebanon, and the Mediterranean Sea. Language: Arabic. Currency: Syrian pound. Capital: Damascus. Population: 14,798,000 (1996). Area: 185,050 sq. km/71,498 sq. mi. Official name **Syrian Arab Republic** —**Syrian** *n.*, *adj.*

Syriac /sírri ak/ *n.* a form of Aramaic used in the 3rd to 13th centuries that survives in some Eastern Orthodox churches —**Syriac** *adj.*

syringa /si ríng gə/ *n.* **1.** = **mock orange** *n.* **1 2. LILAC FLOWER OR TREE** a lilac flower or shrub. Genus: *Syringa.* [Mid-

17thC. Modern Latin from Greek *surigx* 'panpipe'. From the former use of lilac stems for making pipes.]

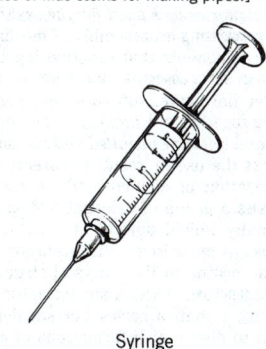

Syringe

syringe /si rínj/ *n.* **1.** MED **INSTRUMENT FOR WITHDRAWING AND EJECTING FLUIDS** an instrument consisting of a piston in a small tube, used in conjunction with a hollow needle or tube for the withdrawal and ejection of fluids and for cleaning wounds. ◊ **hypodermic syringe** **2. DEVICE FOR PUMPING AND SPRAYING LIQUIDS** a device similar to a medical syringe that is used for spraying or extracting fluids by means of pressure or suction ■ *vt.* (**-ringes**, **-ringing**, **-ringed**) **USE SYRINGE ON STH** to clean, spray, or inject sth using a syringe [15thC. Via medieval Latin *syringa* from, ultimately, Greek *surigx* 'panpipe'. From its shape.]

syringes plural of **syrinx**

syringomyelia /si ríng gō mī eéli ə/ *n.* a chronic progressive disease of the spinal cord in which tubular fluid-filled cavities form in the nerve tissue, causing sensory disturbances and, eventually, paralysis [Late 19thC. Coined from SYRINGE + MYEL- + -IA.] —**syringomyelic** *adj.*

syrinx /sírringks/ (*plural* **syrinxes** *or* **syringes** /si rín jeez/) *n.* **1. MUSIC PANPIPE** a panpipe or set of panpipes **2. BIRDS VOCAL ORGAN OF BIRDS** the vocal organ of a bird, usually situated near the junction between the trachea and bronchi **3. ARCHAEOL CORRIDOR IN EGYPTIAN TOMB** a narrow corridor or gallery in an ancient Egyptian tomb **4. MED CAVITY IN SPINAL CORD** one of the tubular fluid-filled cavities formed in the nerve tissue of the spinal cord in cases of syringomyelia [Early 17thC. Via Latin from Greek *surigx* (see SYRINGE).] —**syringeal** /si rínji əl/ *adj.*

syrphid /súrfid/ *n.* a dipteran fly that hovers and darts, feeds on nectar and pollen, and has coloration mimicking that of a bee or wasp. Family: Syrphidae. [Late 19thC. From modern Latin *Syrphidae*, family name, from *Syrphus* (see SYRPHUS FLY).] —**syrphid** *adj.*

Syrtis Major /súrtiss-/ *n.* a highly conspicuous wedge-shaped dark area on the surface of Mars in the equatorial region, first observed in 1659

syrup /sírrəp/, **sirup** *n.* **1. SWEET LIQUID** a liquid made of sugar dissolved in water by heating, widely used in sweet cookery. Syrups vary in density and strength, and can be boiled down to form caramel. **2. FLAVOURED SWEET LIQUID** a flavoured thick sweet liquid **3. PHARM PHARMACEUTICAL LIQUID** a thick sweet liquid used as vehicle for various medicinals **4. GOLDEN SYRUP** golden syrup **5. SENTIMENTALITY** excessive sentimentality (*informal*) [14thC. Via French *sirop* or medieval Latin *siropus* from Arabic *šarāb* 'drink'.]

syrupy /sírrəpi/ (**-ier**, **-iest**) *adj.* **1. RESEMBLING SYRUP** resembling syrup in taste, quality, or consistency **2. MAWKISH** excessively sentimental in a cloying saccharine fashion

sysop /síssop/ *n.* a system operator (*informal*) [Late 20thC. Contraction.]

syst. *abbr.* system

system /sístəm/ *n.* **1. COMPLEX BODY** a combination of related elements organized into a complex whole **2. SET OF PRINCIPLES** a scheme of ideas or principles, e.g. for classification or for forms of government or religion **3. WAY OF PROCEEDING** a method or set of procedures for achieving sth **4. TRANSP TRANSPORT NETWORK** a physical network of roads, railways, and other routes for travel, transport, or communication **5. PHYSIOL GROUP OF RELATED BODY PARTS** a set of organs or structures in the body that have a common function

○ *the nervous system* **6.** PHYSIOL **WHOLE BODY** the human or animal body as a unit ○ *My grandmother used to insist that liquorice was good for the system.* **7.** ENG **ASSEMBLY OF COMPONENTS** an assembly of mechanical or electronic components that function together as a unit **8.** COMPUT **SET OF COMPUTER COMPONENTS** an assembly of computer hardware, software, and peripherals functioning together ○ *A turnkey system has all the hardware and software installed and is ready to run.* **9.** ORDERLINESS the use or result of careful planning and organization of elements **10.** ASTRON **GROUP OF CELESTIAL BODIES** a group of celestial bodies or other gravitationally linked objects **11.** MINERALS **MINERAL CLASSIFICATION** any of various divisions used to classify minerals according to their crystal structures **12.** GEOL **STRATIGRAPHIC UNIT OF ROCK** a stratigraphic division of rocks larger than a series but smaller than a stage, used to distinguish formations of a specific era or period **13.** SCI **ASSEMBLY OF SUBSTANCES IN EQUILIBRIUM** an assembly of substances in chemical or physical equilibrium **14.** MUSIC **GROUP OF MUSICAL STAVES** a number of musical staves that are grouped together by a line or brace in a score and are played simultaneously **15. system, System THE WAY THINGS ARE** the established order, especially regarded as thwarting the individual [Early 17thC. Via French or late Latin from Greek *sustēma*, from *sunistanai* 'to combine', from *histanai* 'to set up'.] —**systemless** *adj.* ◇ **all systems go** used to indicate that everything is functioning and an operation or activity can start

systematic /sístə máttik/, **systematical** /-k'l/ *adj.* **1.** DONE METHODICALLY carried out in a methodical and organized manner **2.** WELL ORGANIZED habitually using a method or system for organization **3.** METHODICAL deliberate and regular in a methodical manner **4.** BASED ON SYSTEM constituting, based on, or resembling a system **5.** BIOL **PERTAINING TO TAXONOMIC CLASSIFICATION** in accordance with a system of taxonomic classification (**systematics**) [Mid-17thC. Via late Latin from Greek *sustēmatikos*, from *sustēma* (see SYSTEM).] —**systematically** *adv.*

——————— **WORD KEY: USAGE** ———————
systematic or **systemic** These two words are distinct. The former means, essentially, 'according to a system or plan'. The latter means 'within or throughout a system', the system in question here often being a biological

one. Thus, *a systematic effort to defraud*; *systemic poison.*

systematic desensitization *n.* a therapy for phobias and other anxiety disorders in which patients are gradually given longer and longer exposures to the object of their fears

systematics /sístə máttiks/ *n.* the study of systems and classification, especially the science of classifying organisms

systematise *vt.* = systematize

systematism /sístəmətizəm/ *n.* **1.** PRACTICE OF CLASSIFYING the practice of classifying information in a systematic manner **2.** SYSTEMATIC APPROACH adherence to a system

systematist /sístəmətist/ *n.* **1.** SB WHO CONSTRUCTS SYSTEMS sb engaged in constructing a system or systems **2.** BIOL SB WHO CLASSIFIES ORGANISMS sb engaged in classifying organisms according to a taxonomic system **3.** SB ADHERING TO SYSTEM sb who conforms to a method or system

systematize /sístə tíz/ (**-tizes, -tizing, -tized**), **systematise** (**-tises, -tising, -tised**), **systemize** (**-izes, -izing, -ized**) *vti.* to arrange sth, or be arranged, according to a system [Mid-18thC. Formed from the Greek stem *sustēmat-* (see SYSTEM).] —**systematization** /sístəmə tī záysh'n/ *n.* —**systematizer** /sístəmə tīzər/ *n.*

system building *n.* building with prefabricated components —**system-built** *adj.*

systemic /si stémmik, si steémik/ *adj.* **1.** OF A SYSTEM affecting or relating to a system as a whole **2.** PHYSIOL **AFFECTING WHOLE BODY** affecting the whole body as distinct from having a local effect ○ *a systemic infection* **3.** AGRIC **AFFECTING WHOLE PLANT** used to describe an herbicide or other chemical that works by spreading through all the tissues of a plant rather than just staying on the surface ▪ *n.* AGRIC **SYSTEMIC CHEMICAL** a systemic herbicide, pesticide, or other chemical —**systemically** *adv.*

——————— **WORD KEY: USAGE** ———————
See Usage note at *systematic*.

systemic circulation *n.* the main part of the blood circulation as distinct from the pulmonary circulation

systemic lupus erythematosus *n.* a chronic inflammatory autoimmune disease of connective tissue that occurs especially in women, marked by fever, muscle pain, arthritis, anaemia, skin eruptions, pleurisy, and kidney disease

systemize /sístə mīz/ *vt.* = systematize —**systemization** /sístə mī záysh'n/ *n.* —**systemizer** /sístə mīzər/ *n.*

system operator *n.* sb who manages an online bulletin board or maintains a small computer network

systems analysis *n.* the determination of the data-processing requirements of a company, project, procedure, or task, and the designing of computer systems to fulfil them —**systems analyst** *n.*

systems engineering *n.* the design and implementation of production systems that require the integration of diverse and complex tasks, e.g. motor car assembly lines —**systems engineer** *n.*

system software *n.* the operating system and utility programs used to operate and maintain a computer system and provide resources for application programs such as word processors and spreadsheets

systole /sístəli/ *n.* the contraction of the heart, during which blood is pumped into the arteries [Mid-16thC. Via late Latin from Greek *sustolē*, from *sustellein* 'to contract', from *stellein* 'to put'.] —**systolic** /si stóllik/ *adj.*

syzygy /sízzəji/ (*plural* **-gies**) *n.* **1.** ASTRON **CONJUNCTION OF THREE CELESTIAL BODIES** the straight-line conjunction or opposition of three celestial bodies, e.g. the Sun, Earth, and Moon **2.** TWO CONNECTED THINGS a pair of related things that are either similar or opposite (*formal*) **3.** POETRY **TWO METRICAL FEET** a metrical unit of two feet in classical Greek and Latin verse [Early 17thC. Via late Latin from Greek *suzugia*, from *suzugos* 'paired', from *zugon* 'yoke'.] —**syzygetic** /sízzə jéttik/ *adj.* —**syzygetically** /-jéttikli/ *adv.* —**syzygial** /si zíjji əl/ *adj.*

Szczecin /shtét shin/ capital city and port of Szczecin Province, in northwestern Poland. Population: 419,300 (1995).

Szechuan pepper /séch waan-/, **Szechwan pepper** *n.* a pepper with a hot aniseed flavour, one of the spices used in Chinese five spice powder [Mid-20thC. Named after Szechuan (now Sichuan).]

Szeged /ségged/ city and river port in southeastern Hungary. Population: 178,878 (1994).

t¹ /tee/ (*plural* **t's**), **T** (*plural* **T's** *or* **Ts**) *n.* **1.** 20TH LETTER OF ENGLISH ALPHABET the 20th letter of the modern English alphabet **2.** SPEECH SOUND CORRESPONDING TO LETTER 'T' the speech sound that corresponds to the letter 'T' **3.** LETTER 'T' WRITTEN a written representation of the letter 'T' **4.** STH 'T'-SHAPED sth shaped like a 'T' ◇ **to a T** exactly

t² *symbol.* **1.** time **2.** troy **3.** Student's t distribution

t³ *abbr.* **1.** tare **2.** teaspoon **3.** teaspoonful **4.** tempo **5.** tempore **6.** tenor **7.** tense **8.** ton **9.** tons **10.** transitive

T¹ *symbol.* **1.** absolute temperature **2.** kinetic energy **3.** PHYS period **4.** surface tension **5.** temperature **6.** tesla **7.** tritium

T² *abbr.* **1.** tera- **2.** tablespoon **3.** tablespoonful **4.** Tuesday **5.** Thailand (*international vehicle registration*)

ta /taa/ *interj.* thank you (*informal*) [Late 18thC. Baby-talk alteration of *thank you*.]

Ta *symbol.* tantalum

TA *n.*, *abbr.* Territorial Army ■ *abbr.* transactional analysis

Taal /taal/ *n.* S Africa LANG the Afrikaans language [Late 19thC. Via Afrikaans from Dutch *taal* 'language'.]

tab¹ /tab/ *n.* **1.** FLAP FOR HOLDING a small strip, loop, or other attachment to sth, used for lifting, moving, hanging, opening, or closing **2.** CLOTHES FLAP ON GARMENT a small strip or square of fabric attached to a garment for decoration **3.** TAG OR LABEL a small piece of paper, cloth, or plastic attached to sth and containing information about the object **4.** AEROSP AUXILIARY AEROFOIL a small auxiliary aerofoil on a control surface such as an aileron or rudder, used to stabilize an aircraft **5.** MIL STAFF OFFICER'S INSIGNIA the insignia on a staff officer's collar **6.** = **ring-pull 7.** US, Can, Aus RESTAURANT BILL the bill for a meal or drinks in a restaurant or bar (*informal*) ■ *vt.* (**tabs, tabbing, tabbed**) ATTACH TAB TO to attach a tab to sth [Early 17thC. Origin unknown.] ◇ **keep tabs on sb** *or* **sth** to watch sb or sth closely (*informal*) ◇ **pick up the tab** US, Can, Aus to pay the bill (*informal*)

tab² /tab/ *n.* a key on a computer keyboard, or a device or key on a typewriter, that advances the next character to a predetermined position, used to align lines or columns. Full form **tabulator** [Early 20thC. Shortening of TABULATOR.]

tab³ /tab/ *n.* a tablet or piece of paper containing a drug, especially one that is illegal [Mid-20thC. Shortening of TABLET.]

tab⁴ /tab/ *n.* = **tableau curtain** [Early 20thC. Shortening.]

TAB *abbr.* **1.** paratyphoid A **2.** paratyphoid B (vaccine) **3.** typhoid ■ *n.* ANZ NEW ZEALAND BETTING AGENCY in New Zealand, the state-run agency that runs legal betting on horseracing, greyhound-racing, and other sporting events, or a branch of this. Abbr of **Totalizator Agency Board**

tab. *abbr.* table

tabanca /tə bángka/ *n.* Carib a state of sadness resulting from unrequited or lost love (*slang*) [Late 19thC. Origin uncertain: probably from a Cariban language, possibly Macusi *tabangke* 'wonder'.]

tabanid /tábbənid/ *n.* a stout-bodied bloodsucking fly such as a horsefly. Family: Tabanidae. [Late 19thC. Formed from Latin *tabanus* 'horsefly'.]

Tabard

tabard /tábbaard/ *n.* **1.** SLEEVELESS OVERGARMENT a sleeveless tunic with slits at the sides, worn by women and girls **2.** HERALD'S COAT an official coat worn by a herald, bearing the sovereign's coat of arms **3.** HIST KNIGHT'S JACKET a sleeveless or short-sleeved garment worn by a knight over his armour [13thC. From Old French *tabart*, of unknown origin.]

tabaret /tábbərit/ *n.* a hard-wearing fabric with alternate satin and watered-silk stripes, used for upholstery [Late 18thC. Origin uncertain: probably from TABBY.]

Tabasco /tə báskō/ *tdmk.* a trademark for a hot-tasting sauce made from peppers, vinegar, and spices

tabbouleh /tə boŏ lay/ *n.* a Middle Eastern salad made with bulgur wheat, tomatoes, mint, olive oil, and parsley, served finely ground with lettuce leaves for scooping it up [Mid-20thC. From Arabic *tabbūla*.]

tabby /tábbi/ *n.* (*plural* -**bies**) **1.** tabby, tabby cat STRIPED CAT a brown or grey cat with a striped or mottled coat **2.** PET FEMALE CAT a domestic cat, especially a female one **3.** OFFENSIVE TERM an offensive term that deliberately insults a woman who is thought to be gossiping, spiteful, and interfering (*informal insult*) **4.** TEXTILES SILK WITH STRIPED PATTERN watered silk or taffeta with a striped or wavy pattern **5.** TEXTILES PLAIN WEAVE FABRIC a plain-woven fabric ■ *adj.* **1.** HAVING STRIPED COAT having a brown or grey coat with a striped or mottled pattern **2.** STRIPED OR BRINDLED having a striped or wavy pattern **3.** TEXTILES RESEMBLING TABBY resembling or made of tabby [Late 17thC. Via French *tabis* from Arabic *'attābī*. Named after al-'Attābiyya, a quarter in Baghdad, Iraq, where the (originally striped) fabric was made.]

--- **WORD KEY: ORIGIN** ---
It was the stripes on the fabric called **tabby** that led to the application of the word to brindled cats. The usage is first recorded in the 1660s.

tabernacle /tábbər nak'l/ *n.* **1.** tabernacle, Tabernacle RELIG TENT FOR CARRYING ARK OF COVENANT a portable tent used as a sanctuary for the Ark of the Covenant by the Israelites during the Exodus **2.** tabernacle, Tabernacle JUDAISM JEWISH TEMPLE the Jewish Temple, regarded as representing the presence of God **3.** JUDAISM = **sukkah 4.** RELIG NONCONFORMIST PLACE OF WORSHIP a place of worship, especially in some nonconformist Christian denominations **5.** CHR CONTAINER FOR HOLY BREAD AND WINE a box or case in which the consecrated elements of Communion are kept **6.** ARCHIT NICHE FOR ICON a canopied recess or niche for an icon **7.** HUMAN BODY the human body considered as a place temporarily housing the soul or principle of life (*literary*) **8.** NAUT SOCKET FOR MAST a support for the foot of a mast [13thC. Directly or via French from Latin *tabernaculum* 'tent', from *taberna* 'hut' (source of English *tavern*).] —**tabernacular** /tábbər nák yŏŏlər/ *adj.*

Tabernacles /tábbər nak'lz/ *n.* CALENDAR = **Sukkoth**

tabes /táy beez/ (*plural* -**bes**) *n.* **1.** PROGRESSIVE EMACIATION progressive wasting of the body, usually as a result of a chronic disease **2.** MED = **tabes dorsalis** [Late 16thC. From Latin, 'wasting away'.] —**tabetic** /tə béttik/ *adj.*

tabes dorsalis /-dawr sáyliss/, **tabes** *n.* a disorder of the nervous system characteristic of late-stage syphilis and marked by degeneration of nerve fibres, wasting, pain, and inability to move the leg muscles. Tabes dorsalis is now rare because syphilis can be effectively treated at a much earlier stage. [From late Latin, literally 'dorsal tabes']

tabi /taábi/ (*plural* -**bis** *or* -**bi**) *n.* a Japanese sock with a thick sole and a separate section for the big toe [Early 17thC. From Japanese.]

tabla /táblə/ *n.* an Indian musical instrument consisting of a pair of small drums played with the hands [Mid-19thC. Via Persian and Hindi from Arabic *ṭabl* 'drum'.]

tablature /tábləchər/ *n.* **1.** MUSIC SPECIAL MUSICAL NOTATION a special kind of musical notation in which the notes themselves are not represented but rather the hand positions required to play them. It is used especially in early lute and modern popular guitar music. **2.** ARTS ENGRAVED TABLET a tablet or other flat surface that has been engraved or painted [Late 16thC. Via French from, ultimately, *tavolare* 'to set to music', from *tavola* 'table'.]

table /táyb'l/ *n.* **1.** ITEM OF FURNITURE WITH FLAT TOP a piece of furniture with a flat top and one or more legs, used for placing things on or doing things at **2.** TABLE FOR FOOD a table at which people sit to eat meals, or a similar structure provided outdoors at which birds may feed **3.** FLAT SURFACE FOR PARTICULAR PURPOSE a raised flat surface with a nondomestic or office use, e.g. one at which a surgeon operates or one on which a piece of machinery rests **4.** FOOD SERVED the food provided in a household or restaurant in terms of its quality or quantity **5.** PEOPLE SITTING AT TABLE a group of people sitting at a table, especially for a meal ○ *The whole table erupted in laughter.* **6.** ARRANGEMENT OF INFORMATION IN COLUMNS an arrangement of information or data into columns and rows or a condensed list **7.** ARITH MULTIPLICATION TABLE a multiplication table (*informal*) **8.** GEOG = **tableland 9.** ARCHIT BAND OR PANEL ON WALL a band of masonry or a rectangular panel on a wall either raised or depressed and with ornamentation or inscriptions **10.** FLAT SURFACE OF GEM the upper horizontal surface of a cut gem **11.** SLAB FOR INSCRIPTION a slab of wood, stone, or metal for inscription **12.** BACKGAMMON PART OF BACKGAMMON BOARD either of the two hinged halves of a backgammon board **13.** MUSIC FRONT PART OF STRINGED INSTRUMENT the part of the body of a stringed instrument that acts as a sounding board **14.** ANAT PLATE OF BONE a flat layer of bone, especially either of the inner or outer surfaces of the skull that are separated by a more spongy bone (**diploë**) **15.** AREA ON PALM an area on the palm defined by four lines, regarded as significant in palmistry ■ **tables** *npl.*

HIST **ANCIENT TABLETS WITH LAWS INSCRIBED** tablets on which certain ancient Greek, Roman, and Hebrew laws were inscribed, or the laws themselves ■ *vt.* **(-bles, -bling, -bled) 1. PROPOSE STH** to put forward a bill or proposal for discussion at a meeting **2.** *US* **POSTPONE DISCUSSION OF STH** to postpone discussion of a bill or motion for a later time **3. ENTER INFORMATION INTO TABLE** to enter information in a tabular form **4. PUT STH ON TABLE** to place or lay sth on a table [Pre-12thC. Directly or via French from Latin *tabula* 'board, slab'.] —**tableful** *n.* ◇ **on the table** put forward for discussion at a meeting ◇ **turn the tables (on sb)** to reverse a situation and gain the advantage from sb who had previously held it

tableau /tábblō/ (*plural* **-leaux** /-lōz/ *or* **-leaus**) *n.* **1. PICTURESQUE DISPLAY** a vivid and wide-ranging description or display **2.** THEATRE = **tableau vivant 3. STRIKING VISUAL SCENE** a visually dramatic scene or situation that suddenly arises [Late 17thC. Via French from Old French *tablel*, literally 'a small table' (see TABLE).]

tableau curtain *n.* either of a pair of stage curtains that are drawn to each side and upwards by a cord

tableau vivant /-vee vaáN/ (*plural* **tableaux vivants**) *n.* a representation of a scene by a group in appropriate costume posing silent and motionless [From French, literally 'living picture']

Table Bay /táyb'l-/ inlet of the Atlantic Ocean, overlooked by Table Mountain, southwestern South Africa. Length: 19 km/12 mi.

tablecloth /táyb'l kloth/ *n.* a cloth for covering a table, especially before it is set for a meal

table d'hôte /taáb'l dōt/ *n.* a restaurant meal or menu offering a series of courses at a fixed price [Early 17thC. From French, literally 'host's table'.]

table football *n. UK* a game based on football that is played on a table with rows of small model players. The models are attached to metal poles that pass through the sides of the table and are spun and moved from side to side in order to hit the ball. US term **foosball**

tableland /táyb'l land/ *n.* an extensive elevated region of flat land

table licence *n.* a licence authorizing a restaurant to serve alcoholic drinks only with meals

table mat *n.* a mat placed under hot dishes to protect the table

table money *n.* an entertainment allowance for members of the armed forces

Table Mountain flat-topped mountain overlooking Cape Town, southwestern South Africa. Height: 1,086 m/3,563 ft.

table salt *n.* fine salt suitable for use at table

table soccer *n. ANZ* table football

tablespoon /táyb'l spoon/ *n.* **1. SERVING SPOON** a large serving spoon a size larger than a dessertspoon **2. tablespoon, tablespoonful** MEASURE **MEASURE BASED ON CAPACITY OF TABLESPOON** a unit of capacity used in recipes, equal to 15 ml/half a fluid ounce or three teaspoons **3. tablespoon, tablespoonful AMOUNT HELD BY TABLESPOON** the amount of food or liquid that a tablespoon can hold

tablet /táblət/ *n.* **1. COMPRESSED POWDERED DRUG FOR SWALLOWING** a small shaped cake of a fixed amount of a compressed powdered drug, usually intended to be swallowed whole **2. SMALL FLAT CAKE OF STH** a small compressed cake of a substance such as soap **3. INSCRIBED STONE OR WOODEN SLAB** a slab of stone, wood, or metal used for inscription or engraving **4. SHEETS OF PAPER FASTENED TOGETHER** a number of sheets of paper for writing or drawing, fastened together along one edge **5. SHEET OF MATERIAL TO WRITE ON** a thin stiff sheet of wood, slate, or ivory on which sb writes **6.** ARCHIT = **table** *n.* 9 **7.** *Scotland* FOOD **SWEET FUDGELIKE CONFECTIONERY** a kind of confectionery made from sugar, butter, and condensed milk, usually made in an oblong tray. It resembles fudge but is less sticky. **8.** *NZ* RAIL **TOKEN USED BY TRAIN DRIVER** a token held by train drivers on single lines, giving them the right of way [14thC. From Old French, literally 'little table', from *table* (see TABLE). Sense 1 evolved via the idea of sth 'flat', hence 'compressed'.]

table talk *n.* **1. INFORMAL CONVERSATION** informal conversation on subjects considered suitable during a meal **2.** BRIDGE **IMPROPER DISCUSSION OF STRATEGY IN BRIDGE** in bridge, the discussion of bidding and strategy across the table with a partner, which is not permitted

table tennis *n.* a game that resembles tennis and is played with small bats and a light hollow ball on a table divided by a net

tabletop /táyb'l top/ *n.* the flat upper surface of a table

tableware /táyb'l wair/ *n.* dishes, plates, glasses, cutlery, and other articles used at meals

table wine *n.* an unfortified wine for drinking with meals

tabloid /tábbloyd/ *n.* **1. tabloid, tabloid newspaper SMALL NEWSPAPER WITH SHORT ARTICLES** a small-format popular newspaper with a simple style, many photographs, and sometimes an emphasis on sensational stories **2. CONDENSED PIECE OF WRITING** a piece of writing, especially a news story, in a condensed form ■ *adj.* **SENSATIONALIST** relating to or characteristic of tabloid newspapers, especially in having a popular sensationalist style [Late 19thC. Originally a proprietary name for tablets of condensed medicine; the underlying idea is of condensed writing.]

WORD KEY: ORIGIN

Tabloid was registered as a proprietary name for a brand of tablet in 1884 by Burroughs, Wellcome, and Company. It was the underlying notion of 'compression' or 'condensation' that led to its application to newspapers of small page size and 'condensed' versions of news stories, which emerged at the beginning of the 20th century.

taboo /tə bo͞o/, **tabu** *adj.* **1. SOCIALLY OR CULTURALLY PROSCRIBED** forbidden to be used, mentioned, or approached because of social or cultural rather than legal prohibitions **2.** RELIG **SACRED AND PROHIBITED** set apart as sacred and at the same time forbidden to be used ■ *n.* **1. PROHIBITION** a prohibition or rejection of particular types of behaviour or language because they are considered socially unacceptable **2. FORBIDDEN BEHAVIOUR** a type of behaviour or a subject that is forbidden or disapproved of because it is considered socially unacceptable **3.** RELIG **PROHIBITION ON GROUNDS OF BEING SACRED** the practice, especially in some Polynesian societies, of regarding particular things, people, or types of behaviour as sacred and therefore forbidden to be used, made contact with, or engaged in ■ *vt.* **(-boos, -booing, -booed; -bus, -buing, -bued) 1. FORBID OR DISCOURAGE STH** to prohibit or disapprove of particular types of behaviour or language because they are considered socially unacceptable **2.** RELIG **PROHIBIT STH BECAUSE SACRED** to regard particular things, people, or types of behaviour as sacred and therefore forbidden to be used, made contact with, or engaged in [Late 18thC. From Tongan *tabu*, allegedly introduced into English by Captain James COOK.]

tabor /táybər/, **tabour** *n.* a small drum played with one hand while the other hand plays a pipe. Tabors were used especially in the Middle Ages. [13thC. From Old French *tabour*, of uncertain origin: probably from Persian *tabīr* 'drum' (source of English *tambourine*).] —**taborer** *n.*

Tabor, Mount /táyb awr/ peak in northern Israel, east of Nazareth. In the Bible, it is the site of the transfiguration of Jesus Christ. Height: 588 m/1,929 ft.

Tabora /ta báwrə/ capital city of Tabora Region, west-central Tanzania, situated about 354 km/220 mi. northwest of Dodoma. Population: 214,000 (1986).

taboret /tábbə rét/, **tabouret** *n.* **1.** FURNITURE **LOW CYLINDRICAL STOOL** a low solid seat without arms or a back **2.** SEW = **tambour** *n.* 1 **3.** MUSIC **SMALL TABOR** a small tabor or tambourine [Mid-17thC. From French, literally 'small tabor' (see TABOR).]

tabour *n.* = **tabor**

tabouret *n.* = **taboret**

tabu *adj., n., vt.* = **taboo**

tabular /tábbyo͝olər/ *adj.* **1. ARRANGED IN TABLE** arranged in a table or in columns and rows **2. HAVING FLAT SURFACE** having a flat surface that resembles a table **3.** CRYSTALS **BROAD AND FLAT** used to describe crystals that are broad and flat **4.** GEOL **SPLITTING INTO THIN PLATES** made up of and splitting into thin horizontal plates **5.** MATH **COMPUTED USING TABLE** calculated with or making use of a table, e.g. of logarithms [Mid-17thC. From Latin *tabularis*, from *tabula* (see TABLE).] —**tabularly** *adv.*

tabula rasa /tábbyo͝olə raázə/ (*plural* **tabulae rasae** /tábbyo͞o lee raá zee/) *n.* **1.** PHILOSOPHY **MIND PRIOR TO EXPERIENCES** the mind at birth, regarded as having no innate conceptions **2. CHANCE TO START AFRESH** an opportunity to make a clean break or a fresh start [Mid-16thC. From Latin, literally 'scraped table'.]

tabularize /tábbyo͝olə rīz/ **(-izes, -izing, -ized), tabularise (-ises, -ising, -ised)** *vt.* = **tabulate** *v.* 1 —**tabularization** /tábbyo͝olə rī záysh'n/ *n.*

tabulate /tábbyo͞o layt/ *vt.* **(-lates, -lating, -lated) 1. ARRANGE INFORMATION IN TABLE** to arrange information systematically in a table or in columns and rows **2. MAKE STH FLAT** to give a flat top or upper surface to sth (*usually passive*) ■ *adj.* **FLAT** with a flat surface that resembles a table [Late 16thC. Via late Latin *tabulatus* from, ultimately, Latin *tabula* (see TABLE).] —**tabulable** /tábbyo͝oləb'l/ *adj.* —**tabulation** /tábbyo͞o láysh'n/ *n.*

tabulator /tábbyo͞o laytər/ *n.* **1. SB OR STH TABULATING DATA** a person or device that tabulates information **2.** COMM, COMPUT full form of **tab**[2] *n.*

tabun /taa bo͞on/ *n.* an organic phosphorus compound used in chemical warfare. Formula: $C_5H_{11}N_2O_2P$. [Mid-20thC. From German, of unknown origin.]

tacamahac /tákəmə hak/, **tacmahack** /tákmə hak/ *n.* **1. STRONG-SMELLING RESINOUS SUBSTANCE** a resinous gum obtained from particular trees and used to make ointments and incense **2. TREE YIELDING TACAMAHAC RESIN** a tree from which tacamahac resin is obtained, especially the balsam poplar [Late 16thC. Via obsolete Spanish *tacamahaca* from Aztec *tecomahiyac*.]

Tacan /ták an/ *n.* an aircraft navigation system using ultrahigh-frequency signals emitted from a transmitting station to determine distance and bearing [Mid-20thC. Acronym formed from TACTICAL + AIR + NAVIGATION.]

tacet /táy set/ *n.* a musical direction instructing a musician not to play or sing a certain passage [Early 18thC. From Latin, literally '(it) is silent', formed from *tacere* (see TACIT).]

tach /tak/ *n. US* a tachometer (*informal*) [Mid-20thC. Shortening.]

tache /tash/, **tash** *n.* a moustache (*informal*) [Late 19thC. Shortening.]

tacheometer /táki ómmitər/ *n.* = **tachymeter**

tacheometry /táki ómmətri/ *n.* = **tachymetry** —**tacheometric** /táki ə méttrik/ *adj.* —**tacheometrical** /-méttrik'l/ *adj.* —**tacheometrically** /-méttrikli/ *adv.*

tachina fly /tákinə-/ *n.* a bristly fly whose larvae live as parasites on other insects. They are sometimes used to control harmful insect species. Family: Tachinidae. [*Tachina* via modern Latin, genus name, from, ultimately, Greek *takhinos* 'swift']

tachinid /tákənid/ *n.* = **tachina fly** ■ *adj.* **RELATING TO TACHINA FLY** relating to the family of insects that the tachina fly belongs to [Late 19thC. From modern Latin *Takhinidae*, family name, from *Takhina* (see TACHINA FLY).]

tachism /táshizəm/, **tachisme** *n.* a type of action painting in which random blotches of colour are used as a method of instinctive expression [Mid-20thC. From French *tachisme*, from *tache* 'spot'.] —**tachist** *n., adj.*

tachistoscope /tə kístə skōp/ *n.* an instrument for displaying visual images very briefly, used to test perception and memory [Late 19thC. Coined from Greek *takhistos* 'swiftest' (formed from *takhus* 'swift') + -SCOPE.] —**tachistoscopic** /tə kístə skóppik/ *adj.* —**tachistoscopically** /-skóppikli/ *adv.*

tachogram /tákə gram/ *n.* a record in graph form produced by a tachograph

tachograph /tákə graaf, -graf/ *n.* an instrument that produces a record of the use and readings of a tachometer, especially one in a commercial vehicle or coach recording speeds and distances travelled. In effect, a tachograph records the hours worked by a driver.

tachometer /ta kómmitər/ n. a device used to determine speed of rotation, typically of a vehicle's crankshaft and usually in revolutions per minute —**tachometric** /tákə méttrik/ adj. —**tachometrically** /-méttrikli/ adv. —**tachometry** /ta kómmətri/ n.

tachy- prefix. accelerated, rapid ○ tachygraphy [From Greek takhus 'swift']

tachyarrhythmia /táki ə ríthmi ə/ n. a medical condition in which the heartbeat is fast and irregular

tachycardia /táki kaàrdi ə/ n. an excessively rapid heartbeat, typically regarded as a heart rate exceeding 100 beats per minute in a resting adult [Late 19thC. Coined from TACHY- + Greek kardia 'heart' (see CARDIA).] —**tachycardiac** adj.

tachygraphy /ta kíggrəfi/ n. 1. ANCIENT SHORTHAND the shorthand system used by the ancient Greeks and Romans 2. ABBREVIATED MEDIEVAL WRITING the abbreviated cursive writing used in medieval times for Latin and Greek —**tachygrapher** n. —**tachygraphic** /táki gráffik/ adj. —**tachygraphically** adv. —**tachygraphist** /ta kíggrəfist/ n.

tachylite /táki līt/, **tachylyte** n. black volcanic glass formed by the chilling of basaltic magma [Mid-19thC. Via German Tachylyt, which was coined from Greek takhu- 'quickly' (see TACHY-), from its rapid decomposition in acids, + lutos 'soluble'.] —**tachylitic** /-litik/ adj.

tachymeter /ta kímmitər/, **tacheometer** /táki ómmitər/ n. an instrument used in surveying to work out distances, elevations, and directions at speed

tachymetry /ta kímmətri/, **tacheometry** n. the measurement of distances, elevations, and directions using a tachymeter —**tachymetric** /táki méttrik/ adj. —**tachymetrically** adv.

tachyon /táki on/ n. a hypothetical elementary particle that always travels faster than the speed of light

tachypnea n. US = tachypnoea

tachypnoea /tákip neè ə/ n. abnormally fast breathing, usually considered to be over 20 breaths per minute in a resting adult [Late 19thC. Coined from TACHY- + Greek pnoiē 'breathing' (formed from pnein 'to breathe').]

tacit /tássit/ adj. 1. IMPLIED BUT NOT EXPRESSED understood or implied without being stated openly 2. SILENT not spoken (archaic) [Early 17thC. From Latin tacitus, the past participle of tacere 'to be silent'.] —**tacitly** adv. —**tacitness** n.

taciturn /tássi turn/ adj. habitually uncommunicative or reserved in speech and manner [Late 18thC. Via French taciturne from Latin taciturnus, from tacitus (see TACIT).] —**taciturnity** /tássi túrnəti/ n. —**taciturnly** /tássi turnli/ adv.

——— **WORD KEY: SYNONYMS** ———
See Synonyms at **silent**.

Tacitus /tássitəss/ (55?–117?) Roman historian. The author of histories of the Roman Empire, he also held various government posts and was famed as an orator. Full name **Gaius Cornelius Tacitus**

tack[1] /tak/ n. 1. JOINERY, DIY SMALL NAIL a small sharp nail with a broad head 2. SEW TEMPORARY STITCH a long loose temporary stitch, often used to align seams in preparation for final sewing 3. SAILING CHANGE IN DIRECTION OF SAILING a change in the direction of movement of a sailing ship or sailing boat made in order to maximize the benefit from the wind 4. SAILING PART OF ZIGZAG SAILING COURSE a stage or series of stages in the zigzag movement of a sailing ship or sailing boat that is changing direction in order to maximize the benefit from the wind 5. COURSE OF ACTION a course of action or method of approach intended to achieve sth, especially one adopted after another has failed 6. SAILING DIRECTION OF SAILING the direction of movement of a sailing ship or sailing boat in relation to the side from which the wind is blowing, effected by the position of its sails 7. SAILING ROPE HOLDING DOWN SAIL a rope holding down the corner of some sails, or the corner that is held down 8. SLIGHT STICKINESS slight stickiness, e.g. of glue or paint that has not yet dried ■ v. (tacks, tacking, tacked) 1. vt. JOINERY, DIY FASTEN STH WITH TACKS to attach sth with small sharp broad-headed nails 2. vt. ATTACH STH WITH DRAWING PIN to attach sth light to a board or wall with

a drawing pin 3. vt. SEW SEW STH TEMPORARILY to sew sth with long loose temporary stitches 4. vt. PUT THINGS TOGETHER ARBITRARILY to bring different things together to form an arbitrary or illusory whole 5. vti. SAILING CHANGE DIRECTION OF SAILING SHIP to change the direction or course of a sailing ship or sailing boat, or to steer it on alternate tacks 6. vi. CHANGE APPROACH to take a different course of action or use a different method [14thC. From Old Northern French taque 'fastening', of Germanic origin.] ◇ **tack on** vt. add sth to sth else either as a supplement or an afterthought

tack[2] /tak/ n. saddles, bridles, and other parts of a horse's harness [Late 18thC. Shortening of TACKLE.]

tack[3] /tak/ n. goods that are tasteless and vulgar or cheap and shoddy (informal) [Late 20thC. Back-formation from TACKY.]

tack[4] /tak/ n. foodstuff, especially of the poor quality fed to a ship's crew in the days of sailing ships (slang) ◊ hardtack [Late 16thC. Origin unknown.]

tackboard /ták bawrd/ n. US a bulletin board (informal)

tacket /tákit/ n. Scotland, N England a nail or hobnail

tackety boots /tákəti-/ npl. Scotland hobnailed boots (informal) ['Tackety' formed from TACKET]

tackle /ták'l/ n. 1. SPORTS ATTEMPT TO STOP OPPONENT'S PROGRESS a physical challenge against an opposing player who has the ball in football, hockey, and some other games. A tackle is made using the foot in football, the stick in hockey, and in rugby and American football by seizing and forcing the opponent to the ground. 2. SPORTS EQUIPMENT the equipment used for a particular activity such as angling, or rock climbing 3. MECH ENG ROPES AND PULLEYS equipment consisting of ropes and pulleys used for lifting heavy weights through increased mechanical advantage 4. NAUT SHIP'S RIGGING the gear and rigging of a ship 5. MAN'S GENITALS a man's genitals (slang; considered offensive by some people) 6. AMERICAN FOOTBALL LINEMAN NEXT TO END in American football, a lineman positioned between a guard and an end, or the position of such a player ■ vt. (-les, -ling, -led) 1. EMBARK ON DOING STH to undertake or deal with sth that requires effort 2. CONFRONT SB to open a conversation or discussion on a difficult issue with sb who would prefer to avoid it 3. SPORTS MAKE TACKLE ON SB to challenge an opposing player 4. HARNESS AN ANIMAL to put a harness on an animal, especially a horse [13thC. Origin uncertain: probably from Low German takel 'ship's rigging', from taken 'to seize'.] —**tackler** n.

tacksman /táksmən/ (plural -men /-mən/) n. Scotland in former times, a leaseholder, especially one who sublet land [Mid-16thC. 'Tack' from Scots and northern English dialect, 'tenure', from Old Norse tak 'hold'.]

tack welding n. the welding of two metals by individual welds at isolated points

tacky[1] /táki/ (-ier, -iest) adj. slightly sticky to the touch [Late 18thC. Formed from TACK[1].] —**tackily** adv. —**tackiness** n.

tacky[2] /táki/ (-ier, -iest) adj. (informal) 1. IN BAD TASTE perceived of as vulgar, lacking in taste, or no longer fashionable 2. SHABBY appearing to be cheaply made or in need of repair [Early 19thC. Origin unknown. Originally in the meaning 'inferior horse'.] —**tackily** adv. —**tackiness** n.

tacmahack n. = tacamahac

taco /tákō/ (plural -cos) n. a crisp fried maize tortilla usually filled with meat, lettuce, tomatoes, cheese, and hot sauce [Mid-20thC. Via American Spanish from Spanish, 'wad'.]

Tacoma /tə kṓmə/ city in western Washington State, a deepwater port on Commencement Bay, an arm of Puget Sound. Population: 183,060 (1994).

taconite /tákə nīt/ n. a banded iron formation consisting of layers of the iron oxides magnetite and haematite that may be extracted from ground-up rock using a magnet [Early 20thC. Named after Taconic, a mountain range in New York State, where it was first found.]

tact /takt/ n. 1. ABILITY TO AVOID GIVING OFFENCE skill in situations in which other people's feelings have to be considered 2. DISCRETION an intuitive sense of what

is right or appropriate [Early 17thC. Via French from Latin tactus 'sense of) touch', from tangere 'to touch'.]

tactful /táktf'l/ adj. having or showing concern about upsetting or offending people —**tactfully** adv. —**tactfulness** n.

tactic /táktik/ n. a method used or a course of action followed in order to achieve an immediate or short-term aim [Mid-17thC. Via modern Latin from Greek taktikos 'of arrangement', from taktos 'arranged', from tassein 'to arrange'.]

tactical /táktik'l/ adj. 1. OF TACTICS relating to or involving tactics 2. AS MEANS TO END done or made for the purpose of trying to achieve an immediate or short-term aim 3. SHOWING SKILFUL PLANNING showing skilful planning in order to accomplish sth 4. MIL WITH LIMITED MILITARY OBJECTIVE used or made to support limited military operations 5. MIL SUPPORTING OTHER MILITARY OBJECTIVE undertaken or for use in support of other military and naval operations —**tactically** adv.

tactical voting n. the act of voting for the second strongest candidate in an election with a view to preventing the strongest candidate from winning

tactician /tak tísh'n/ n. sb who is skilled at using tactics or responsible for tactics, or sb with a particular kind of tactical ability

tactics /táktiks/ n. (takes a singular verb) 1. MIL DIRECTION OF FORCES IN BATTLE the science of organizing and manoeuvring forces in battle to achieve a limited or immediate aim 2. FINDING MEANS TO END the art of finding and implementing means to achieve particular immediate or short-term aims

tactile /ták tīl/ adj. 1. OF TOUCH relating to or used for the sense of touch 2. TANGIBLE capable of perception by the sense of touch 3. ARTS APPARENTLY THREE-DIMENSIONAL giving an illusion of physical solidity and tangibility 4. PLEASANT TO TOUCH pleasing or interesting to the sense of touch 5. HABITUALLY TOUCHING PEOPLE inclined to touch people a lot, e.g. while talking to them [Early 17thC. Directly or via French from Latin tactilis, from tactus (see TACT).] —**tactilely** adv. —**tactility** /tak tílləti/ n.

tactile corpuscle, **tactile bud** n. a tiny egg-shaped touch receptor that responds to light pressure and is found in the skin of the palms, lips, soles, and other hairless sensitive areas

tactless /táktləss/ adj. lacking or showing a lack of concern about upsetting or offending people —**tactlessly** adv. —**tactlessness** n.

tactual /tákchoo əl/ adj. relating to the sense of touch or imparting the sensation of contact [Mid-17thC. Formed from Latin tactus (see TACT).] —**tactually** adv.

tad /tad/ n. a very slight amount or degree of sth (informal) [Late 19thC. Origin uncertain: perhaps a shortening of TADPOLE.]

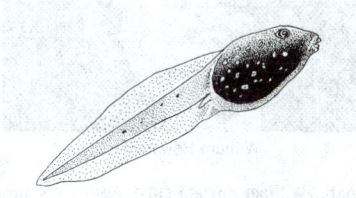
Tadpole

tadpole /tád pōl/ n. the aquatic larva of a frog, toad, or salamander that has a limbless round body, gills, and a tail [15thC. From earlier forms of TOAD + POLL.]

Tadzhik, **Tadzhiki** n. PEOPLES, LANG = Tajik

Tadzhikistan = Tajikistan

taedium vitae /teédi əm veè tī/ n. the feeling of being weary of or disgusted with life (literary) [Mid-18thC. From Latin.]

tae kwon do /tí kwon dṓ/ n. a Korean martial art resembling karate but also employing a wide range of kicking moves [Mid-20thC. From Korean, literally 'art of hand and foot fighting'.]

tael /tayl/ *n.* **1.** MEASURE FAR EASTERN UNIT OF WEIGHT a varying unit of weight used in the Far East, usually around 38 g/1.75 oz **2.** MONEY OLD UNIT OF CHINESE CURRENCY a silver coin that was a unit of currency in China between 1889 and 1912, equivalent to a tael of silver [Late 16thC. Via Portuguese from Malay *tahil*, unit of weight.]

ta'en /tayn/ *v.* taken (*archaic or literary*)

taenia /téeni ə/ (*plural* **-ae** /-ni ee/) *n.* **1.** ANAT PART SHAPED LIKE RIBBON a body part that resembles a ribbon, especially muscle or nervous tissue **2.** ARCHIT HORIZONTAL BAND IN DORIC ARCHITECTURE in the Doric order of ancient Greek architecture, a narrow band (**fillet**) between the main beam (**architrave**) across the top of the columns and the frieze above **3.** ZOOL PARASITIC TAPEWORM a large parasitic tapeworm. Genus: *Taenia*. **4.** CLOTHES, HISTORY NARROW HEADBAND a fillet or headband worn in ancient Greece [Mid-16thC. Via Latin from Greek *tainia* 'band'.]

taeniacide /téeni ə sīd/ *n.* a substance for killing tapeworms

taeniafuge /téeni ə fyōöj/ *n.* a drug or other agent that expels tapeworms from the body

taeniasis /tee nī əssiss/ *n.* infestation with adult tapeworms, usually following the eating of raw or undercooked meat containing tapeworm larvae

TAFE /tayf/ *n.* in Australia, a system of higher education providing instruction in technical subjects. Abbr of **Technical and Further Education**

taffeta /táffitə/ *n.* a stiff lustrous silk or a silky fabric with a slight rib, usually used for women's clothes [14thC. Via medieval Latin or Old French *taffetas* from, ultimately, Persian *tāftah*, from *tāftan* 'to shine'.]

taffrail /táf rayl/ *n.* NAUT **1.** STERN RAIL the rail round the stern of a ship **2.** TOP PART OF STERN the upper flat and often carved part of a ship's stern [Early 19thC. From Dutch *taffereel*, literally 'a small table', from *tafel* (see TABLE).]

taffy /táffi/ (*plural* **-fies**) *n.* **1.** US, Can CHEWY SWEET a chewy confectionery made of sugar or molasses boiled down and pulled until glossy and light in colour **2.** INSINCERE FLATTERY flattery of an insincere kind (*informal dated*) [Early 19thC. Origin uncertain: probably originally a dialect form of TOFFEE.]

Taffy (*plural* **-fies**) *n.* an offensive term for a Welsh person (*slang insult*) [Mid-17thC. From the alleged Welsh pronunciation of the male forename *David*.]

William Howard Taft

Taft /taft/, **William Howard** (1857–1930) US statesman and 27th president of the United States. A Republican, he was president from 1909 to 1913 and chief justice of the Supreme Court from 1921 to 1930.

tag[1] /tag/ *n.* **1.** LABEL a small piece or strip of cloth, paper, plastic, or other material attached to sth, especially by one end, or hung on it as a label or means of identification **2.** CRIMINOL ELECTRONIC DEVICE WORN BY OFFENDER an electronic device worn, usually on the ankle or wrist, by a convicted offender serving a sentence in the community to allow him or her movements to be monitored **3.** COMPUT CLASSIFYING LABEL FOR DATA a label that classifies a piece of data, e.g. by its type, to facilitate later retrieval **4.** TIP AT END OF SHOELACE a plastic or metal tip attached to the end of shoelace or cord to prevent it from fraying **5.** ZOOL TIP OF ANIMAL'S TAIL the tip of an animal's tail, especially if in a contrasting colour with the rest of the tail **6.** SMALL LOOSE OR RAGGED PIECE a small piece of a material hanging loosely or raggedly from the main

piece **7.** AGRIC, ZOOL MATTED LOCK OF WOOL a dirty matted lock of wool or hair in an animal's fleece or coat **8.** ANGLING ATTACHMENT TO ARTIFICIAL FLY a piece of usually brightly coloured material tied around the shank of the hook in the body of an artificial fly **9.** LANG WELL-KNOWN QUOTATION a well-known or hackneyed quotation, often in Latin, usually intended to add dignity or weight to a speech or piece of writing **10.** LANG EPITHET a descriptive word or phrase used, especially frequently, about sb or sth **11.** LANG ENDING FOR PIECE OF WRITING an ending or added endpiece for a piece of writing, e.g. a refrain, the cue line ending an actor's speech, or a final speech addressed to the audience **12.** LING = tag question **13.** GRAFFITI ARTIST'S SIGNATURE a signature or identifying symbol used by a graffiti artist ■ *v.* (**tags, tagging, tagged**) **1.** *vt.* LABEL WITH TAG to attach a tag to sth or label sth with a tag **2.** *vt.* ADD STH AT END to add an additional piece or section to the end of sth, especially a piece of writing ◇ *tagged on a couple of extra lines at the end* **3.** *vt.* LANG ATTACH EPITHET TO to give sb a nickname or assign a verbal label to sb **4.** *vt.* CRIMINOL ATTACH ELECTRONIC TAG TO OFFENDER to make an offender wear an electronic tag **5.** *vt.* US LAW TICKET CAR to attach a ticket to a vehicle to notify the driver that a traffic or parking offence has been committed **6.** *vt.* US LAW CHARGE SB WITH CRIME to charge sb with a crime (*often passive*) ◇ *tagged for theft* **7.** *vt.* LANG ATTACH RHYMES TO STH to put unrhymed verse or prose into rhyme **8.** *vt.* AGRIC REMOVE TAGS FROM WOOL to remove tags from an animal's fleece or hair **9.** *vti.* FOLLOW CLOSELY to follow along close behind sb [From Middle English *tagge* 'dangling section of garment', of unknown origin]

tag along *vi.* to accompany or follow sb, often when your presence is unwanted

tag[2] /tag/ *n.* **1.** GAME CHILDREN'S CHASING AND TOUCHING GAME a children's game in which one player is chosen to chase the others and try to touch one of them. Anyone touched then becomes 'it' and is then the player who does the chasing. **2.** BASEBALL INSTANCE OF TAGGING RUNNER OUT an instance of tagging a runner out in baseball **3.** WRESTLING = tag wrestling **4.** WRESTLING INSTANCE OF TAGGING IN WRESTLING an instance of tagging a partner in wrestling ■ *vt.* (**tags, tagging, tagged**) **1.** CATCH PLAYER IN GAME OF TAG to touch a player in the children's game of tag, making that player 'it' **2.** BASEBALL TOUCH RUNNER WITH BALL to get a runner out in baseball by touching him or her with the ball before he or she reaches the base **3.** WRESTLING TOUCH PARTNER'S HAND IN WRESTLING to touch the hand of a partner in tag-team wrestling in order to switch places **4.** Aus MARK SB in Australian Rules football, to mark an opponent [Mid-18thC. Origin uncertain: perhaps a variant of Scots *tig* 'touch', ultimately from TICK in the obsolete sense 'to touch lightly'.] ◇ **tag up** *vi.* in baseball, to touch a base before running to the next one after a fly ball is caught

Tagalog /tə gaálog, tə gaáləg, tə gálog/ (*plural* **-logs** or **-log**) *n.* **1.** PEOPLES MEMBER OF FILIPINO PEOPLE a member of a people who originally lived in the Manila area of the Philippines **2.** LANG TAGALOG LANGUAGE the Austronesian language of the Tagalog people. Tagalog is the basis of Filipino, the national language of the Philippines. It is spoken by about 17 million people. [Early 19thC. From Tagalog *tagá* 'native' + *ilog* 'river'.] —**Tagalog** *adj.*

tag day *n.* US = flag day

tag end *n.* **1.** US LAST BIT the very last or last remaining part of sth **2.** LOOSE PIECE a loose or detached piece of sth

tagetes /ta jée teez/ *n.* a marigold, especially an African or French marigold. Latin name: *Tagetes*. [Late 18thC. From modern Latin *Tagetes*, genus name, from Latin *Tages*, name of an Etruscan god.]

tagger /tággər/ *n.* a graffiti artist who spray-paints his or her name or symbol on a public structure (*slang*) [Mid-20thC]

taggers /tággərz/ *npl.* iron or steel in thin sheets coated with tin [Mid-19thC. Perhaps because such sheets were used to make shoelace tags.]

tagliatelle /tállyə télli/ *n.* pasta in the form of long narrow ribbons [Late 19thC. From Italian, formed from *tagliare* 'to cut into strips'.]

tagma /tágmə/ (*plural* **-mata** /-mətə/) *n.* a distinct functional region of the body of an arthropod, e.g. the thorax [Early 20thC. From Greek, 'sth arranged', from *tag-*, the stem of *tassein* 'to arrange' (see TAXIS).]

tagmeme /tág meem/ *n.* any of the various positions in the structure of a sentence into which a word or phrase of a particular grammatical type can fit [Mid-20thC. Formed from Greek *tagma* 'sth arranged'.] —**tagmemic** /tag meémik/ *adj.*

tagmemics /tag meémiks/ *n.* a grammatical analysis of language based on the way in which the different elements that make up a sentence are arranged within it (*takes a singular verb*)

Rabindranath Tagore

Tagore /tə gáwr/, **Rabindranath** (1861–1941) Indian writer. A prolific author of poetry, plays, short stories, and novels, he revolutionized Bengali poetry by using colloquial language and new verse forms, and translated his own works into English. He was awarded the Nobel Prize in literature in 1913.

tag question *n.* a short clause added on to a statement to turn it into a question, e.g. 'don't you?' or 'isn't it?', or a statement with a question clause attached. The main function of a tag question is to cue a response from the listener or obtain his or her agreement to the original statement.

tag team *n.* a team of two wrestlers, only one of whom may wrestle at a time. Wrestlers change places only after touching hands.

taguan /tág wan/ *n.* a large nocturnal East Indian flying squirrel that leaps from tree to tree with the help of skin flaps that stretch between its limbs. Latin name: *Petaurista petaurista*. [Early 19thC. Origin uncertain: probably from a local name in the Philippines.]

tague *n.* Ireland = taig (*slang insult*)

Tagus /táygəss/ the longest river of the Iberian Peninsula, in southwestern Europe. It enters the Atlantic Ocean at Lisbon, Portugal. Length: 1,007 km/626 mi.

tag wrestling *n.* a form of wrestling in which wrestlers compete in teams of two or more, taking it in turns to enter the ring, a touch of hands being required for a changeover

tahini /tə heéni, tə heénə/, **tahina** *n.* an oily paste made from crushed sesame seeds, used as seasoning [Mid-20thC. From Arabic *ṭaḥīnā*, from *ṭaḥana* 'to grind'.]

Tahiti /tə heéti/ island of French Polynesia, the largest of the Society Islands, in the southern Pacific Ocean. Population: 115,820 (1998). Area: 1,036 sq. km/400 sq. mi. —**Tahitian** *n., adj.*

tahr /taar/ *n.* a ruminant mammal similar to a goat, with a shaggy coat and curved horns, that is native to mountainous regions in southern Asia. Genus: *Hemitragus*. [Mid-19thC. From Nepalese *thār*.]

tahsil /taa seel/ *n.* an administrative district in some states of India [Mid-19thC. Via Urdu and Persian from *taḥsīl* 'revenue', from Arabic *ḥasala* 'to collect'.]

tahsildar /taa seél daar/ *n.* in India, a government official in charge of collecting taxes and other revenues in a tahsil [Late 18thC. Via Urdu *taḥsīldār* from Persian, literally 'revenue-holder', from *taḥsīl* (see TAHSIL).]

Tai /tī/ (*plural* **Tai** or **Tais**) *n.* LANG a group of tonal languages spoken in Southeast Asia, including Thai and Lao. Tai is sometimes considered to be related to the Sino-Tibetan language family. —**Tai** *adj.*

taiaha /tī ə haa/ *n. NZ* a carved Maori staff, formerly used as a weapon, now carried by speakers at public ceremonies [Mid-19thC. From Maori.]

T'ai Chi /tī chee/, **t'ai chi ch'uan** /-chwáan/, **T'ai Chi Ch'uan, Tai Chi Chuan** *n.* a Chinese form of physical exercise characterized by a series of very slow and deliberate balletic body movements

taig /tayg/, **tague, teigue** *n. Ireland* an offensive term for a Roman Catholic used in Northern Ireland (*slang insult*) [Late 20thC. Variant of *Teague*, an anglicization of the Irish name *Tadhg*.]

taiga /tígə/ *n.* the subarctic coniferous forests of North America, northern Europe, and Asia located south of tundra [Late 19thC. From Russian, of Altaic origin.]

taihoa /tī hō ə/ *interj. NZ* used to tell sb to slow down, wait, or be patient for a short while [Mid-19thC. From Maori.]

tail /tayl/ *n.* **1.** ZOOL **REAR PART OF ANIMAL'S BODY** the flexible rear part, or a movable extension to the rear part, of a vertebrate animal's body, that begins above the anus and often contains the terminal vertebrae **2. REAR PART OF STH** the rear, last, or lowest part of sth ○ *the tail of the procession* **3.** AIR **REAR OF AIRCRAFT** the rear part of an aircraft together with the fin and the tailplane **4.** ARMS **REAR OF MISSILE** the rear part of a missile or bomb, including structures for controlling the angle of the trajectory **5.** ASTRON **STREAM OF GAS FROM COMET** the luminous stream of gas and dust particles driven by the solar wind from a comet as it approaches and then recedes from the Sun **6. PEOPLE IN A QUEUE** a queue of people or things **7.** HAIR **LONG LOCK OR BRAID OF HAIR** a long lock or braid of hair **8.** PRINTING **BOTTOM OF PAGE** the bottom of a printed page, or the margin between the bottom of the page and the lowest line of type **9. SB FOLLOWING ANOTHER** sb who secretly follows or observes another (*informal*) ○ *The police put a round-the-clock tail on the suspect.* **10. TRAIL** sb's trail, especially when he or she is being followed or pursued (*informal*) **11.** HIST = **horsetail** *n.* 2 **12. BUTTOCKS** the buttocks (*informal*) **13. OFFENSIVE TERM** an offensive term used to refer to a woman's genitals (*taboo offensive*) **14.** *US* **OFFENSIVE TERM** an offensive term used by some men to refer to sexual intercourse with a woman (*taboo offensive*) **15. OFFENSIVE TERM** an offensive term used only by some men to refer to a woman perceived only as a potential partner for sexual intercourse (*taboo offensive*) ■ **tails** *npl.* **1.** CLOTHES **MAN'S FORMAL COAT WITH TAILS** a formal, usually black coat for a man, cut short at the front and with two long tails at the back **2.** CLOTHES **MAN'S EVENING CLOTHES** full evening clothes for a man **3. REVERSE OF COIN** the reverse side of a coin ■ *v.* (**tails, tailing, tailed**) **1.** *vt.* **FOLLOW SB SECRETLY** to follow sb secretly in order to keep watch on him or her (*informal*) ○ *Someone must have tailed you back to the house.* **2.** *vi.* **FOLLOW** to follow behind sb or sth ○ *She strode out purposefully, leaving the rest of the party to tail along behind.* **3.** *vi.* **FORM LINE** to form a long line when moving, especially a long spread-out line **4.** *vt.* VET, AGRIC **REMOVE TAIL OF ANIMAL** to remove or cut short the tail of an animal **5.** *vt.* **REMOVE STALK FROM FRUIT** to remove the stalk from sth such as a piece of fruit **6.** *vt.* **JOIN THINGS END TO END** to join two or more things end to end **7.** *vti.* CONSTR **BUILD STH INTO WALL** to build one end of sth such as a joist, beam, or brick, into a wall, or to be fixed into a wall at one end **8.** *vi.* NAUT **LIE WITH STERN IN PARTICULAR DIRECTION** to lie with the stern pointing in a particular direction when moored [Old English *tægel*, from prehistoric Germanic] —**tailless** *adj.* ◇ **turn tail** turn and walk or run away ◇ **with your tail between your legs** in an abject, ashamed manner

WORD KEY: SYNONYMS

See Synonyms at ***follow***.

tail away *vi.* = **tail off**

tail off, tail away *vi.* to grow less, smaller, or fainter, usually gradually

tailback /táyl bak/ *n.* a queue of stationary or slow-moving traffic caused by an obstruction ahead

tail beam *n.* = **tailpiece**

tailboard /táyl bawrd/ *n.* = **tailgate** *n.* 1

tailbone /táyl bōn/ *n.* = **coccyx**

tail coat *n.* a formal, usually black coat for a man, cut short at the front and with two long tails at the back

tail covert *n.* any one of the small feathers on a bird's tail that cover the bases of the tail feathers

tail end *n.* **1. LAST PART** the last or hindmost part of sth **2. BUTTOCKS** the buttocks (*informal*)

tailender /tayl éndər/ *n.* sb or sth that comes at or towards the end of sth or in last place (*informal*)

tail fan *n.* a fan-shaped structure at the rear end of some crustaceans such as the lobster

tailgate /táyl gayt/ *n.* **1. GATE AT BACK OF VEHICLE** a gate at the back of a lorry that can be laid flat or dropped down during loading or unloading **2. tail gate GATE IN WATERWAY** a gate controlling the flow of water at the lower end of a lock in a waterway ■ *vti.* (**-gates, -gating, -gated**) **DRIVE CLOSE BEHIND** to drive very close behind another vehicle —**tailgater** *n.*

tailgate party *n. US* a social gathering before a sports event game held in a parking lot outside the stadium. Spectators park close together and use their vehicles and the adjoining space for picnicking, barbecuing, and other activities.

tailing /táyling/ *n.* **BUILT-IN END** the end of sth such as a beam that is built into a wall during construction ■ **tailings** *npl.* **WASTE LEFT AFTER PROCESSING** the waste left after sth has been processed from rock

taille /tīl, tayl/ *n.* a tax levied by the French monarch on his subjects before the French Revolution [Mid-16thC. From French, 'tax', literally 'a cut'.]

tail light /táyl līt/ *n.* = **rear light**

tailor /táylər/ *n.* **1. CLOTHES MAKER** sb who makes, alters, or repairs clothes, especially men's outer clothes such as suits, jackets, and trousers **2.** *Aus* **FISH WITH SHARP TEETH RESEMBLING SCISSORS** a fast-moving, aggressive Australian fish with a large, strong mouth containing sharp teeth that resemble scissors. Latin name: *Pomatomus saltatrix.* ■ *v.* (**-lors, -loring, -lored**) **1.** *vti.* **MAKE CLOTHES FOR PARTICULAR NEED** to make clothes to meet a particular need or for a particular person **2.** *vt.* **ADAPT STH** to adapt sth to make it suitable for a particular purpose **3.** *vi.* **WORK AS TAILOR** to work as a tailor [13thC. Via Anglo-Norman *taillour* from Old French *tailleur* 'cutter', from *taillier* 'to cut', from late Latin *taliare*, from Latin *talea* 'twig, cutting'.]

tailorbird /táylər burd/ *n.* a tropical Asian warbler that makes a nest by sewing leaves together with plant fibres. Genus: *Orthotomus.*

tailored /táylərd/ *adj.* **1.** CLOTHES **MADE BY TAILOR** made by a tailor **2.** CLOTHES **MADE TO FIT NEATLY** marked by a neat fit with trim lines and a clean and formal or severe look **3. MADE FOR PARTICULAR PURPOSE** made or adapted for a particular purpose

tailor-made *adj.* **1. IDEAL FOR SB OR STH** perfectly suited to sb or for a particular purpose **2. MADE BY TAILOR** made by a tailor rather than in a factory ■ *n.* **1. STH MADE BY TAILOR** a garment made by a tailor **2. MANUFACTURED CIGARETTE** a cigarette bought ready-made rather than rolled by hand (*informal*)

tailor's chalk *n.* a chalk used by tailors to mark out the positions of cuts or alterations on material

tailpiece /táyl peess/ *n.* **1. END** sth that forms an end or is added at the end of sth **2.** PRINTING **DECORATION AT BOTTOM OF PAGE** a decoration at the bottom of a page, e.g. at the end of a chapter **3.** MUSIC **PART OF STRINGED INSTRUMENT** a piece of wood or metal at the lower end of a stringed instrument such as a violin, to which the strings are attached **4. BEAM EMBEDDED IN WALL** a beam that has one end embedded in a wall

tailpipe /táyl pīp/ *n.* = **exhaust pipe**

tailplane /táyl playn/ *n.* the horizontal part of the tail of an aircraft, designed to give stability

tailrace /táyl rayss/ *n.* **1. CHANNEL CARRYING WATER AWAY FROM MILL** a channel that carries away water that has passed through a mill wheel or turbine **2. CHANNEL CARRYING AWAY MINE TAILINGS** a channel that carries away mine tailings in water

tail rotor *n.* a small propeller on the tail of a helicopter that counteracts the main rotor, preventing the body of the helicopter from rotating in the opposite direction to it

tailskid /táyl skid/ *n.* **1. SUPPORT UNDER AIRCRAFT TAIL** a support or runner on the underside of the tail of an aircraft **2. REAR WHEEL SKID** a skidding of the rear wheels of a motor vehicle

tailspin /táyl spin/ *n.* **1. SPIRAL DESCENT** a rapid spiral descent of an aircraft **2. STATE OF PANIC** a state of great confusion or distress (*informal*)

tailstock /táyl stok/ *n.* a movable part of a lathe, used to support the free end of the workpiece and permitting it to rotate freely

tailwind /táyl wind/ *n.* a wind that is blowing in the same direction as a ship or aircraft is travelling

Taino /tī nō/ (*plural* **-nos** *or* **-no**) *n.* PEOPLES a member of a Native Central American people that formerly lived on the Caribbean islands of the Greater Antilles and the Bahamas and died out during the 16th century [Mid-19thC. From Taino.]

taint /taynt/ *v.* (**taints, tainting, tainted**) **1.** *vt.* **POLLUTE STH** to pollute or contaminate sth with sth undesirable or dangerous **2.** *vt.* **CORRUPT SB MORALLY** to corrupt sb morally or detract from sb's reputation by associating him or her with sth reprehensible **3.** *vt.* **FLAVOUR STH** to give a scent or flavour of one thing to another **4.** *vi.* **SPOIL** to spoil or become rotten ■ *n.* **1. IMPERFECTION DETRACTING FROM QUALITY** an imperfection that detracts from the quality of sb or sth ○ *a taint on her reputation* **2. STH DETRACTING FROM PURITY OF STH** sth that detracts from the purity or cleanliness of sth [Late 16thC. Partly via Anglo-Norman *teint*, literally 'coloured, dyed', from Latin *tingere* (see TINGE), and partly from Old French *ataint* 'convicted', the past participle of *ateindre* (see ATTAIN).] —**taintless** *adj.*

taipan[1] /tī pan/ *n.* a foreigner in charge of a business or trading operation in China, especially a powerful business tycoon [Mid-19thC. From Chinese (Cantonese) *daaihbāan*.]

taipan[2] /tī pan/ *n.* a large, rare, highly venomous snake found in northern Australia, brown in colour with a lighter brown belly, that can grow to 3.3 m/11 ft in length. Latin name: *Oxyuranus scutellatus.* [Mid-20thC. Of Australian Aboriginal origin.]

Taipei /tī páy/, **T'aipei** capital city of Taiwan. The largest city in the country, it is officially regarded as its temporary capital. Population: 2,702,678 (1994).

Taiping /tī píng/ *n.* sb who supported or took part in the Taiping rebellion against the Manchu dynasty in China between 1850 and 1864 [Mid-19thC. From Chinese *tài píng*, literally 'great peace'.]

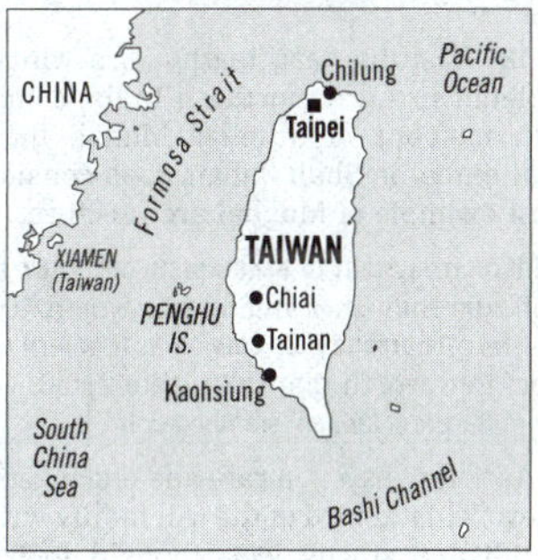

Taiwan

Taiwan /tī wáan/ country occupying the island of Taiwan and neighbouring small islands, administered separately since 1949 by the Chinese Nationalist government after its retreat from mainland China. It is claimed as a province by the People's Republic of China. Language: Mandarin Chinese. Currency: New Taiwan dollar. Capital: Taipei. Population: 21,703,304 (1997). Area: 36,000 sq. km/13,900 sq. mi. Official name **Republic of Taiwan** —**Taiwanese** *n., adj.*

Taiyuan /tī ywán, tī yoo án/ capital city of Shanxi Province in northern China, southwest of Beijing. Population: 1,960,000 (1990).

taj /taaj/ *n.* a tall brimless conical cap, often richly decorated, worn by Muslims as a mark of distinction [Late 19thC. Via Arabic from Persian *tāj* 'crown'. Ultimately from an Indo-European word meaning 'to cover' that is also the ancestor of English *tegument* and *tile*.]

Tajik /taa jéek/ (*plural* **-jiks** *or* **-jik**), **Tadzhik** (*plural* **-dzhiks** *or* **-dzhik**) *n.* **1.** PEOPLES **SB FROM TAJIKISTAN** sb who was born and brought up in Tajikistan, or who has Tajik citizenship **2. Tajik, Tadzhik, Tajiki, Tadzhiki** LANG **OFFICIAL LANGUAGE OF TAJIKISTAN** the official language of Tajikistan. It belongs to the Iranian group of Indo-European languages. Tajik is spoken by about 4.5 million people. [Early 19thC. From Persian.] —**Tajik** *adj.*

Tajiki /taa jéeki/, **Tadzhiki** *n.* LANG = **Tajik** *n.* **2** ■ *adj.* PEOPLES **RELATING TO TAJIKS** relating to the Tajiks or their culture

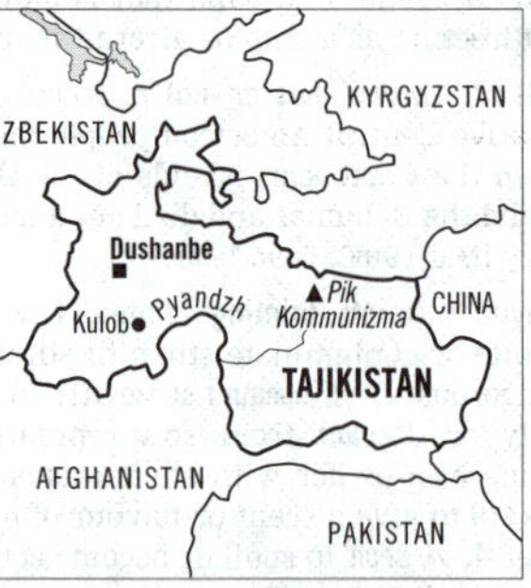

Tajikistan

Tajikistan /tə jéeki staán/, **Tadzhikistan** republic in southeastern Central Asia, bordered by Kyrgyzstan, Uzbekistan, China, and Afghanistan. It was part of the Soviet Union until 1991. Language: Tajik. Currency: Tajik ruble. Capital: Dushanbe. Population: 5,945,903 (1997). Area: 143,100 sq. km/55,250 sq. mi. Official name **Republic of Tajikistan**

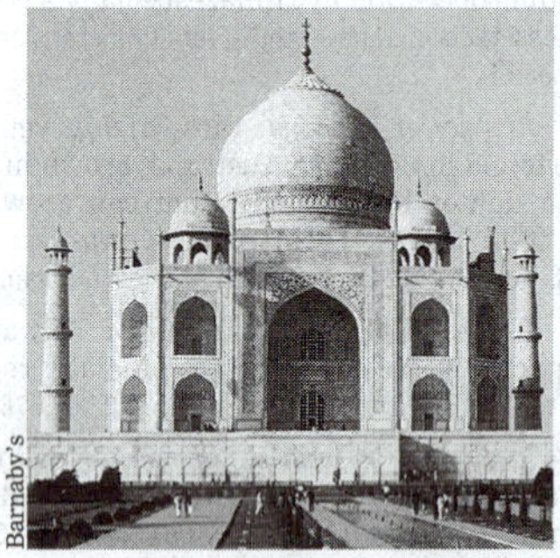

Taj Mahal

Taj Mahal /taáj mə haál, taázh-/ *n.* a white marble mausoleum in Agra, northern India, completed in 1643 in memory of Mumtaz Mahal, the wife of Mughal emperor Shah Jahan. It is considered the greatest example of Mughal architecture.

taka /táakə/ *n.* **1. UNIT OF BANGLADESHI CURRENCY** the main unit of currency in Bangladesh, worth 100 paisas. See table at **currency 2. COIN OR NOTE WORTH ONE TAKA** a coin or note worth one taka [Late 20thC. Via Bengali *ṭākā* from Sanskrit *ṭaṅkaḥ* 'stamped coin'.]

takahe /táakəhi, -hay/ *n.* a rare and endangered flightless New Zealand bird of the rail family with a large stout bill and sturdy legs, thought to be extinct until rediscovered in 1948. It is now confined to a small corner of Fiordland. Latin name: *Notornis mantelli* and *Porphyrio mantelli.* [Mid-19thC. From Maori.]

Takakkaw Falls /tə kák aw-/ Canada's highest waterfall, located in Yoho National Park, British Columbia. Height: 503 m/1,650 ft.

take /tayk/ *v.* (**takes, taking, took** /tŏok/, **taken** /táykən/) **1.** *vt.* **REMOVE STH** to remove or steal sth belonging to sb else ○ *Did you take my gardening gloves?* ○ *I wish you wouldn't take things without asking.* **2.** *vt.* **CARRY STH** to carry, bring, or transport sth or sb from one place to another ○ *I took a notebook with me.* ○ *We decided to take him to the doctor.* **3.** *vt.* **WIN STH** to capture or gain possession of a place, area, or object, or win sth in a contest or competition ○ *took the town after a long siege* ○ *took first prize in the competition* **4.** *vt.* **GET HOLD OF SB** to get hold of sth or sb using a hand, or receive sth into your hand ○ *She took him by the arm and steered him out of the room.* **5.** *vt.* **SELECT STH OR SB** to choose an individual object or person from a number available ○ *Here, take a chocolate.* **6.** *vt.* **GET INTO OR ONTO STH** to place yourself in sth, or start to occupy sth ○ *Please take a seat.* **7.** *vt.* **CLAIM OR ASSUME STH** to obtain sth, especially credit, glory, or blame, or accept or maintain that this is deserved ○ *He doesn't mind taking the credit for the party's recent successes.* **8.** *vt.* **REGULARLY RECEIVE STH** to buy, consume, or perform sth as a regular habit ○ *We take the Sunday papers.* ○ *I've stopped taking lunch breaks.* **9.** *vt.* **LEAD SB SOMEWHERE** to enable sb to go towards a particular place or in a specified direction, or go along sth that leads to a particular place ○ *Will this road take us to the beach?* ○ *Take the first road on the left.* **10.** *vt.* **AGREE TO PERFORM STH** to agree to perform or assume the duties associated with sth ○ *I decided to take the job.* **11.** *vt.* **BE WILLING TO ACCEPT STH** to be prepared to accept sth as valid, true, or satisfactory ○ *The machine refused to take my card.* **12.** *vt.* **BE ABLE TO BEAR STH** to endure, deal with, accept, or put up with sth, especially when it is unpleasant or unavoidable ○ *She cannot take criticism.* **13.** *vt.* **REACT TO STH** to behave, feel, or act in response to being told or finding out about sth ○ *I don't know how they will take the news.* **14.** *vt.* **HAVE STRENGTH TO HOLD UP STH** to be capable of supporting sth physically, without collapsing or breaking ○ *Will the shelf take the weight of all those books?* **15.** *vt.* **TRAVEL BY MEANS OF STH** to use a particular means of transport to make a journey ○ *Let's take a taxi.* **16.** *vt.* **HAVE ROOM FOR STH** to be capable of containing a specified amount or quantity of sth ○ *The tank takes 20 gallons.* **17.** *vt.* **WRITE STH** to record sth in a written form ○ *Do you mind if I take notes?* **18.** *vt.* PHOTOGRAPHY **CAPTURE STH ON CAMERA** to use a camera to make a photograph ○ *Let's take a few photos to record the event.* **19.** *vt.* EDUC **STUDY STH** to study sth, or to teach sb or sth, on a formal basis ○ *We both took French in the sixth form.* ○ *Do you remember that teacher who took the French class?* **20.** *vt.* **START TO DO STH** to start to perform or occupy sth ○ *The new treasurer takes office next month.* **21.** *vt.* **CARRY OUT STH** to perform or carry out sth ○ *I'll take action on this immediately.* **22.** *vt.* **TRAVEL OVER OR ROUND STH** to travel over or round sth, especially in a vehicle or on a motorcycle or horse and in a particular way ○ *He took the bend too fast.* **23.** *vt.* **DERIVE FROM STH OR SB** to copy or derive sth from a particular text or author (*often passive*) ○ *That quote is taken from Shakespeare.* **24.** *vt.* **CONSIDER STH** to use sb or sth as an example or as a subject for consideration or discussion ○ *Let's take your last point first.* **25.** *vt.* **REQUIRE PARTICULAR LENGTH OF TIME** to need a particular amount of time to be completed or performed ○ *The journey usually takes about three hours.* **26.** *vt.* **NEED STH IN ORDER TO FUNCTION** to need a particular thing in order to operate ○ *This cassette recorder takes four size C batteries.* **27.** *vt.* **REQUIRE STH** to require sth, especially a particular quality or characteristic, for sth to be achieved ○ *It took a lot of courage to admit that you were wrong.* **28.** *vt.* **EXPERIENCE EMOTION OR HAVE VIEW** to experience a particular emotion, have a particular reaction, or adopt a particular opinion with regard to sth ○ *They looked so pathetic I took pity on them.* **29.** *vt.* **INTERPRET STH IN PARTICULAR WAY** to interpret, recognize, or understand sth, especially sb's words or actions, in a particular way ○ *I took you to mean that the loan would be approved.* ○ *May we take it that this was a one-off occurrence?* **30.** *vt.* **ASSUME STH** to make an assumption, usually a mistaken one, about sb's identity or about the nature of a thing or a situation ○ *I took you for his daughter.* **31.** *vt.* **CONSUME STH** to swallow or receive sth into the body or system ○ *He refuses to take his medicine.* **32.** *vt.* **EXPOSE BODY TO ELEMENTS** to go or sit out in the sun, or expose the body to other elements ○ *She was lying on the beach, taking the sun.* **33.** *vi.* **WORK OR BE SUCCESSFUL** to work or have an effect in the intended way ○ *The perm didn't take because you rinsed out the solution too soon.* **34.** *vi.* BOT **START TO GROW** to start to grow by producing roots ○ *The cutting has taken nicely.* **35.** *vt.* **MEASURE STH** to measure sth in an accurate way using a special instrument or procedure ○ *His temperature was normal when I took it this morning.* **36.** *vi.* **BECOME ILL** to become noticeably or suddenly unwell or more unwell ○ *The whole family took sick and it turned out to be food poisoning.* **37.** *vt.* MATH **SUBTRACT NUMBER** to subtract a number or quantity from sth ○ *Take 19 from 36 and you get 17.* **38.** *vt.* **ASSUME CHARGE OF STH** to assume control of sth as a person who holds authority or has the attention of others ○ *She took the chair at the meeting.* **39.** *vt.* **HAVE SEX WITH SB** to penetrate sb in an act of sexual intercourse, especially perfunctorily or without the person's consent **40.** *vti.* ANGLING **BITE** to bite the hook or fly at the end of an angler's line or the bait containing the hook ○ *The fish just weren't taking that morning.* **41.** *vt.* US **CHEAT SB** to cheat or swindle sb, especially out of a particular amount of money ■ *n.* **1.** COMM **MONEY OBTAINED IN BUSINESS TRANSACTIONS** the amount of money received from customers or clients during a specified period of time ○ *What was the take last week?* **2.** CINEMA **CAMERA SHOT** a single uninterrupted recording of a piece of the action in a film by a camera ○ *This is the 15th take of this scene.* **3.** MUSIC **SINGLE UNINTERRUPTED SOUND RECORDING** a single uninterrupted session in which a work or section of a work is recorded by audio recording equipment **4.** ANGLING **GRABBING OF BAIT** the action of a fish in picking up or grabbing a bait or lure **5. IMPRESSION** a personal impression or opinion of sth ○ *What's your take on his presentation?* [Pre-12thC. From Old Norse *taka.*] —**takable** *adj.* ◇ **be taken aback** to be startled or disconcerted ◇ **be taken with sb** *or* **sth** to find sb or sth pleasing or attractive ◇ **on the take** taking or willing to take bribes (*informal*) ◇ **take it 1.** to be able to tolerate a situation, usually one involving hardship, punishment, or criticism **2.** to assume that sth is true ○ *I take it that you want some breakfast.* ◇ **take it or leave it 1.** used to indicate that sb can either accept or refuse sth, but cannot alter the conditions **2.** to be able either to accept or do sth, or decline or not do sth ◇ **take part** to be actively involved in sth, usually as a member of a group

take after *vt.* **1. RESEMBLE SB** to look or behave like sb else, especially within the same family **2. BEGIN CHASING SB** to begin to pursue sb

take apart *vt.* **1. DISMANTLE STH** to reduce sth whole to its individual parts or pieces **2. CRITICIZE STH** to criticize sb or sth in a severe and detailed way (*informal*) **3. BEAT SB SEVERELY** to give sb a severe beating or inflict a heavy defeat on sb (*informal*)

take away *vt.* **1. REMOVE STH** to remove or take sth or sb elsewhere **2. SUBTRACT A NUMBER** to subtract a number or quantity

take back *v.* **1.** *vt.* **WITHDRAW STH** to withdraw sth said or written **2.** *vt.* **REGAIN POSSESSION OF STH** to gain possession of sth previously held but lost or given up **3.** *vt.* COMM **RETURN STH BOUGHT AS UNACCEPTABLE** to return an unwanted or unsatisfactory article to the place where it was bought for a refund or exchange **4.** *vt.* COMM **ACCEPT GOODS BACK** to accept an article returned as unwanted or unsatisfactory and offer a refund or exchange **5.** *vt.* **REACCEPT SB** to reaccept sb into a relationship or home **6.** *vt.* **REMIND SB OF PAST** to remind sb of an earlier time **7.** *vti.* PRINTING **MOVE COPY** to move a portion of text back to the previous line

take down *vt.* **1. WRITE STH DOWN** to make a note of sth in writing ○ *take down the names and addresses of the witnesses* **2. DISMANTLE STH** to dismantle or demolish sth **3. HUMILIATE SB** to make sb less arrogant or powerful **4.** WRESTLING **FORCE OPPONENT TO FALL** to force an opponent to the mat during a wrestling match **5. REMOVE ACCUSED FROM DOCK** to remove the accused from the dock to the cells at the end of or during a trial

take for *vt.* to think of sb or sth as being of a particular description, often mistakenly ○ *Do you take me for a fool?*

take in *vt.* **1. UNDERSTAND STH** to understand and remember sth ○ *Children can't be expected to take in so much new information in one lesson.* **2. ACCEPT STH AS REAL** to accept sth as real or true ○ *The news was such a shock that we still haven't taken it in.* **3. INCLUDE STH** to include sth within its scope ○ *The study takes in the whole postwar period.* **4. DECEIVE SB** to deceive or cheat sb by presenting a false appearance ○ *We were all taken in by her plausible manner.* **5. ACCEPT PEOPLE AS PAYING GUESTS** to accept people as paying guests into a home **6. GIVE SB SHELTER** to give sb shelter in your home **7.** BUSINESS **WORK ON STH AT HOME** to do paid work on sth at home ○ *takes in ironing twice a*

a at; aa father; aw all; ay day; air hair; ə about, edible, item, common, circus; e egg; ee eel; hw when; i it, happy; ī ice; ʼl apple; ʼm rhythm; ʼn fashion; o odd; ō open; ŏo good; oo pool; ow owl; oy oil; th thin; th this; u up; ur urge;

week **8.** SEW **MAKE GARMENT NARROWER** to alter a garment to make it narrower **9.** *US* **GO AND SEE** to go and see some kind of entertainment or sport ○ *take in a movie*

take off *v.* **1.** *vt.* **REMOVE A GARMENT** to remove sth you are wearing **2.** *vt.* **HAVE AS A BREAK FROM WORK** to spend a particular amount of time not working ○ *I took a day off for the wedding.* **3.** *vt.* **DEDUCT AN AMOUNT** to deduct an amount from a price or sum **4.** *vt.* **IMITATE SB** to imitate sb or sth, especially for comic effect (*informal*) **5.** *vt.* **STOP STH OPERATING** to end the operation of sth ○ *took off regular flights to the island* **6.** *vi.* **BEGIN FLYING** to leave the ground and begin flying **7.** *vi.* **JUMP** to leave the ground at the beginning of a jump **8.** *vi.* **DEPART** to leave, especially in a hurry or at short notice (*informal*) **9.** *vi.* **SUCCEED** to begin suddenly to be very successful or popular (*informal*)

WORD KEY: SYNONYMS

See Synonyms at ***imitate***.

take on *v.* **1.** *vt.* **UNDERTAKE** to begin doing sth or accept responsibility for sth ○ *I can't take on any more projects at the moment.* **2.** *vt.* **HIRE SB** to hire additional people to do work **3.** *vt.* **ADOPT STH** to acquire or display a different character ○ *Her voice took on a kindlier tone.* **4.** *vt.* **OPPOSE SB OR STH** to oppose sb or sth in a competition or fight ○ *took on the city council* **5.** *vt.* TRANSP **TAKE PEOPLE OR THINGS ON BOARD** to have people or things loaded on board a vessel or vehicle **6.** *vi.* **BE UPSET** to show extreme feelings, especially grief (*dated informal*) **7.** *vti. Carib* **WORRY ABOUT STH** to pay attention to or worry about sb or sth (*slang*)

take out *v.* **1.** *vt.* **BRING STH INTO OPEN** to bring sth into the open from a place where it was contained or concealed **2.** *vt.* **REMOVE STH** to remove or extract sth from another substance **3.** *vt.* **OBTAIN STH** to obtain sth such as a permit, mortgage, or insurance by applying for it **4.** *vt.* **HAVE SB AS COMPANION AT STH** to take sb as a companion or guest to a social event or function **5.** *vt.* **DIRECT ANGER AT SB OR STH** to express or relieve a strong feeling such as anger or frustration by directing it against sb or sth that is not the actual cause of it ○ *Don't take it out on me because you didn't get the job.* **6.** *vt.* **DESTROY STH** to destroy, kill, or neutralize sb or sth (*slang*) ○ *took out enemy artillery* **7.** *vt. Aus* **WIN** to win sth, especially a sporting event (*informal*) ○ *They took out this year's premiership.* **8.** *vi. US* **BEGIN JOURNEY** to start out on a journey ○ *took out for the frontier*

take over *vti.* **1.** **TAKE CONTROL** to obtain or assume control of sth, or gain control of sth from sb else ○ *taken over by a larger company* **2.** **TAKE SB'S PLACE** to begin to do sth or operate sth in place of sb else ○ *She takes over when I finish my shift.* **3.** PRINTING **MOVE COPY FORWARD** to move a portion of text forward to the next line

take to *vt.* **1.** **FORM LIKING FOR SB** to develop a liking for sb or sth, especially quickly **2.** **START DOING OR USING STH** to start doing or using sth as a habit, especially for help or consolation ○ *I've taken to checking that all the windows are locked before I leave the house.* **3.** **ADAPT YOURSELF** to adapt yourself to sth or become comfortable with sth new ○ *quickly took to the new procedure* **4.** **GO TO A PLACE** to go to a place, especially for safety ○ *The slightest cough or sneeze would make him take to his bed.* ○ *took to their cars and fled*

take up *vt.* **1.** **BEGIN DOING STH REGULARLY** to begin doing sth regularly either as an occupation or a hobby **2.** **BEGIN DOING STH AGAIN** to begin doing sth again after a break ○ *take up where you left off* **3.** **ACCEPT** to accept sth offered **4.** **LIFT SB OR STH** to lift or raise sth or sb **5.** SEW **SHORTEN GARMENT** to raise the hem of a garment such as a skirt to make the garment shorter **6.** **USE STH WASTEFULLY** to make use of or occupy sth, especially in a wasteful or unwelcome way **7.** **ABSORB STH** to absorb a liquid **8.** *US* **PAY OFF** to pay off a debt, e.g. a mortgage

take up on *vt.* **1.** **ACCEPT STH FROM SB** to accept sb's offer or wager **2.** **ARGUE** to argue with sb on a point

take up with *vt.* **1.** **RAISE STH FOR DISCUSSION WITH SB** to raise a matter for discussion with sb **2.** **BEGIN ASSOCIATING WITH SB** to begin associating with a particular person or people

takeaway /táykə way/ *adj.* US term **takeout 1.** **FOR EATING ELSEWHERE** bought ready-cooked and taken away to be eaten elsewhere ○ *a takeaway Chinese meal* **2.** **SELLING COOKED FOOD FOR EATING ELSEWHERE** selling ready-cooked food to be eaten elsewhere ○ *an Indian takeaway shop* ■ *n.* US term **takeout 1.** **RESTAURANT SELLING FOOD FOR EATING ELSEWHERE** a restaurant or shop that sells ready-cooked food for eating elsewhere ○ *Let's try the new Vietnamese takeaway.* **2.** **MEAL OR FOOD FOR EATING ELSEWHERE** a meal or food bought ready-cooked for eating elsewhere ○ *It's nice to have a home-cooked meal instead of a takeaway for once.*

take-down *adj.* capable of being disassembled quickly

take-home pay *n.* the amount of pay left to an employee after all deductions, e.g. for tax, have been made

taken past participle of **take**

take-no-prisoners *adj.* persistent in an assertive way

takeoff /táyk of/ *n.* **1.** **BEGINNING OF FLIGHT** the process of leaving the ground and beginning to fly **2.** **BEGINNING OF JUMP** the act or point of leaving the ground at the beginning of a jump **3.** **POINT OF RAPID GROWTH** a point at which substantial success or economic expansion is achieved and the prospect of further success or growth seems assured **4.** **IMITATION** an imitation of sb or sth, especially for comic effect (*informal*)

takeout /táyk owt/ *adj., n. US* = **takeaway**

takeover /táyk ōvər/ *n.* an assumption or seizure of control of sth, especially of a company, political entity, or organization

taker /táykər/ *n.* sb who accepts sth, especially a wager or an offer (*often plural*)

take-up *n.* **1.** **LEVEL OF ACCEPTANCE** the degree to which sth offered or made available is accepted or made use of by people **2.** **WINDING PART OF MECHANISM** a part of a mechanism onto which sth passing through it, e.g. tape, is wound

takin /taá keen/ *n.* a large ruminant mammal of mountainous regions of southern Asia with a heavy build, shaggy coat, and heavy horns that curve back. Latin name: *Budorcas taxicolor*. [Mid-19thC. Origin uncertain: probably from a local Tibeto-Burman name.]

taking /táyking/ *adj.* **1.** **CHARMING** displaying a charming or fascinating appeal **2.** **CATCHING** infectious (*informal*)

takings /táykingz/ *npl.* money received through sales by a business

taki-taki /taáki taaki/ *n.* LANG = **Sranantongo** [Alteration of *talk*]

tala /taálə/ (*plural* **-la** *or* **-las**) *n.* **1.** **UNIT OF SAMOAN CURRENCY** the main unit of currency in Samoa, worth 100 sene. See table at **currency 2.** **COIN OR NOTE WORTH A TALA** a coin or note worth one tala

talapoin /tállə poyn/ *n.* **1.** **GUENON MONKEY** a small olive-green guenon monkey that lives in swampy forests, often near villages, in western equatorial Africa. Latin name: *Cercopithecus talapoin* and *Miopithecus talapoin*. **2.** **BUDDHIST MONK** in Myanmar and Thailand, a Buddhist monk [Late 16thC. Via French and Portuguese from, ultimately, Mon *tala pói*, literally 'lord of merit'. 'Guenon monkey' from the imagined resemblance of its fur to a Buddhist monk's robes.]

talaria /tə láiri ə/ *npl.* winged sandals worn by characters in Greek myth, especially by Hermes [Late 16thC. From Latin, the plural of *talaris* 'of the ankles', from *talus* 'ankle' (source of English *talon*).]

talbot /táwlbət, tól-/ *n.* a dog belonging to an extinct breed of large hound with long ears and a white or pale coat [15thC. Origin uncertain: probably from the English name *Talbot*, because hounds of this type are one of the family's traditional heraldic emblems.]

Talbot /táwlbət, tól-/, **William Henry Fox** (1800–77) British inventor. A pioneer of photography, he invented the calotype (1841). He later worked on the decipherment of the cuneiform script of Nineveh.

talc /talk/ *n.* **1.** **SOFT HYDRATED MINERAL** a soft mineral consisting of hydrated magnesium silicate, found in igneous and metamorphic rocks and used especially in making talcum powder **2.** **TALCUM POWDER** talcum powder (*informal*) ■ *vt.* (**talcs, talcking** *or* **talcing, talcked** *or* **talced**) **APPLY TALC** to put talc onto sth [Late 16thC. Via French *talc* and medieval Latin *talcum* from, ultimately, Persian *ṭalk*.] —**talcose** /tal kŏss/ *adj.* —**talcous** *adj.*

talcum powder /tálkəm-/ *n.* a powder made from purified talc, often scented, that is put onto the skin to perfume it and absorb moisture

tale /tayl/ *n.* **1.** **NARRATIVE** a narrative or account of events **2.** **SHORT PIECE OF FICTION** a short piece of fiction, often one of a connected series **3.** **PIECE OF GOSSIP** an item of gossip or a malicious rumour **4.** **FALSEHOOD** a story or report that is untrue [Old English *talu*, from a prehistoric Germanic base meaning 'to count or recount', which is also the ancestor of English *tell* and *talk*] ◇ **tell tales, tell tales out of school** to report acts of wrongdoing to sb in authority

talebearer /táyl bairər/ *n.* sb who informs against other people or spreads malicious rumours —**talebearing** *n.*

talent /tállənt/ *n.* **1.** **ABILITY** a natural ability to do sth well **2.** **SB WITH AN EXCEPTIONAL ABILITY** a person or people with an exceptional ability **3.** **POSSIBLE ROMANTIC PARTNERS** people considered collectively as possible romantic or sexual partners (*slang*) **4.** **ANCIENT UNIT** any of various ancient units of weight and money [14thC. Via Old French 'mental inclination' (the original sense in English), from Latin *talentum* 'balance, sum of money' (from the idea of desiring things), from Greek *talanton*.]

WORD KEY: SYNONYMS

talent, gift, aptitude, flair, bent, knack, genius

CORE MEANING: the ability to do sth well

talent a great natural ability to do sth that can be developed into an even greater skill; **gift** a more informal word meaning the same as ***talent***. It is used especially to talk about creative or artistic abilities; **aptitude** a natural ability to do sth or to learn sth; **flair** a natural ability to do sth, especially sth creative or artistic; **bent** an inclination towards or liking for doing sth, especially when this is accompanied by ability; **knack** a fairly informal word for an intuitive ability to do sth well; **genius** truly exceptional talent and skill, especially when this is accompanied by original thinking.

talent contest *n.* = **talent show**

talent scout *n.* sb whose job is to search for people who have exceptional abilities in some field, e.g. entertainment or sport, and recruit them for professional work

talent show *n.* a public performance made up of acts by amateur entertainers who compete for a prize and are sometimes given professional opportunities

tales /taylz/, **tales** /táy leez/ *n.* (*plural* **tales**; *plural* **-les**) **SUMMONS TO JURY DUTY** a writ used to summon people to court to fill vacancies on a jury (*takes a singular verb*) ■ *npl.* **PEOPLE FILLING JURY VACANCIES** a group of people summoned to court to fill vacancies on a jury [15thC. From Latin *tales de circumstantibus* 'such of the bystanders', a phrase in the writ.]

talesman /táy leezmən/ (*plural* **-men** /-mən/) *n.* sb selected from a group to fill a vacant seat in a jury

taleteller /táyl tellər/ *n.* **1.** **STORYTELLER** sb who tells stories **2.** **SB WHO INFORMS AGAINST OTHER PEOPLE** sb who informs against other people or spreads malicious rumours —**taletelling** *n.*

tali plural of **talus**[2]

Taliesin /tálli éssin/ (*fl.* 6th century AD) Welsh poet. Possibly mythical, he is claimed as the author of a dozen poems collected in the 13th-century *Book of Taliesin*.

talipes /tállə peez/ *n.* club foot (*technical*) [Mid-19thC. From modern Latin, formed from Latin *talus* 'ankle' + *pes* 'foot'.]

talipot /tálli pot/ *n.* a palm tree of Southeast Asia with large fan-shaped leaves. Latin name: *Corypha umbraculifera*. [Late 17thC. Via Malayalam from, ultimately, Sanskrit *tālī* 'fan palm' + *patra* 'leaf'.]

talisman /tállizmən/ *n.* **1.** **MAGICAL OBJECT** an object, e.g. a stone or jewel, believed to give magical powers to sb who carries or wears it **2.** **STH WITH MAGIC POWER** anything believed to have magical properties [Mid-17thC. Via French or Spanish from, ultimately, Greek *telesma* 'sth consecrated', from *telein* 'to complete, consecrate', from *telos* 'result'.] —**talismanic** /tálliz mánnik/ *adj.*

TALISMAN /tállizmən/ *n.* a computer system used for buying and selling securities on the London Stock Exchange. Abbr of **Transfer Accounting Lodgement for Investors and Stock Management, Transfer Accounting Lodgement for Investors and Stock Management**

talk /tawk/ *v.* (**talks, talking, talked**) **1.** *vti.* EXPRESS STH BY SPEAKING to speak, or to express sth using speech **2.** *vi.* HAVE CONVERSATION ABOUT STH to address spoken words to sb or have a conversation with sb **3.** *vt.* DISCUSS SUBJECT to discuss a particular subject ○ *talk business* **4.** *vi.* COMMUNICATE to communicate in a way other than by speaking ○ *talk in sign language* **5.** *vti.* SPEAK IN SPECIFIED LANGUAGE to use, or be able to use, a particular language to communicate with people ○ *talks Italian with his grandmother* **6.** *vi.* REVEAL INFORMATION to reveal information, especially when being pressured to do so ○ *They interrogated her for hours but she wouldn't talk.* **7.** *vi.* GOSSIP to discuss the affairs of others, or to spread rumours ○ *People are starting to talk.* **8.** *vi.* MAKE SOUNDS LIKE SPEECH to imitate the sounds of speech ○ *The baby is beginning to talk.* **9.** *vi.* BE PERSUASIVE to have the power to influence or persuade people (*informal*) ○ *Money talks!* **10.** *vi.* LECTURE to give a speech or lecture on a subject **11.** *vt.* SPEAK IN TERMS OF STH PARTICULAR to have to do or deal with sth when discussing a particular topic (*informal*) ○ *You're talking big money for a job like that.* **12.** *vi.* BE FRIENDLY WITH SB to be on sufficiently friendly terms with sb to be able to have a conversation (*informal*) ○ *Don't bother asking me how she is, because we're not talking.* ■ *n.* **1.** CONVERSATION a conversation or exchange of ideas or information between two or more people **2.** THINGS SAID the things said by sb or by a group of people in conversation ○ *The talk after dinner was mostly about politics.* **3.** SPEECH ON PARTICULAR SUBJECT a speech or lecture on a particular subject, given before an audience **4.** GOSSIP ABOUT AFFAIRS OF OTHERS idle or malicious conversation about the affairs of others **5.** EMPTY SPEECH speech about sth without any intention of taking action ○ *He's all talk; he won't do anything!* **6.** THING TALKED ABOUT a subject of discussion or gossip among a group of people ○ *the talk of the town* **7.** WAY OF SPEAKING a particular way of speaking ■ **talks** *npl.* NEGOTIATIONS formal discussions among parties to bring about a resolution to a problem ■ *adj.* BROADCAST USING INFORMAL INTERVIEWS made up mainly of informal interviews with guests or telephone calls from viewers or listeners ○ *talk radio* [13thC. Ultimately from a prehistoric Germanic base.] —**talker** *n.*

talk at *vt.* to speak to sb without showing any interest in listening to the person's reply

talk back *vi.* to make an impudent reply

talk down *v.* **1.** *vi.* SPEAK PATRONIZINGLY to speak to sb in a superior or condescending way **2.** *vt.* PREVENT SB FROM SPEAKING to prevent sb from speaking by speaking loudly and ignoring attempts to interrupt **3.** *vt.* TELL SB HOW TO LAND AIRCRAFT to give radio guidance to sb on how to land an aircraft

talk into *vt.* to persuade sb to do sth by talking to him or her ○ *We talked her into staying for dinner.*

talk out *vt.* **1.** RESOLVE STH BY TALKING to settle a difference of opinion through discussion **2.** BLOCK LEGISLATION BY DISCUSSION to prevent the passage of a piece of legislation, especially a bill in Parliament, by prolonging the discussion of it until it is too late to vote on it

talk out of *vt.* to dissuade sb from doing sth by talking to him or her ○ *talked him out of buying a car*

talk over *vt.* **1.** DISCUSS STH to discuss sth at length or thoroughly **2.** PERSUADE SB TO AGREE to persuade sb to agree with an opinion or point of view ○ *talked them over to our side*

talk round *vt.* **1.** PERSUADE SB TO AGREE WITH OPINION to persuade sb to agree with an opinion ○ *She didn't like the idea but we talked her round in the end.* **2.** DISCUSS STH INCONCLUSIVELY to talk about matters relating to a topic without discussing the topic itself or the really central issue and without coming to any conclusions

talk up *vt.* to praise sth in the hope of making it popular or successful

talkathon /táwkə thon/ *n.* *US* a long period of discussion [Mid-20thC. Coined from TALK + MARATHON.]

talkative /táwkətiv/ *adj.* tending to talk readily and at length —**talkatively** *adv.* —**talkativeness** *n.*

WORD KEY: SYNONYMS

talkative, chatty, gossipy, loquacious

CORE MEANING: for sb who talks a lot

talkative a general and fairly neutral word for sb who talks a lot, especially as a matter of disposition; **chatty** a fairly informal word for sb who talks a lot in a friendly way, especially on a particular occasion; **gossipy** a fairly informal word used disapprovingly of sb who talks a lot about other people and their lives; **garrulous** a formal word used disapprovingly of sb who talks too much or at great length, especially as a matter of disposition; **loquacious** a formal word for sb who talks a great deal but who is exceptionally articulate.

talkback /táwk bak/ *n.* a system of communication in a broadcasting studio that enables the staff to speak to each other without the speech being broadcast

talkie /táwki/ *n.* an early film with a soundtrack (*dated*) [Early 20thC. Shortening of *talking picture*, on the model of 'movie'.]

talking book /táwking-/ *n.* a book that has been recorded onto an audio cassette, originally designed for people who cannot see

talking head *n.* sb such as a newsreader who talks at length into a camera in a television broadcast, usually shown only from the shoulders up

talking point *n.* **1.** INTERESTING ITEM FOR DISCUSSION a topic, or aspect of sth, that provokes a lot of discussion **2.** *US* STH SUPPORTING AN ARGUMENT sth that supports an argument, e.g. a particularly convincing point **3.** PUBLICITY POINT a claim made about a product in publicity material that is considered particularly interesting or persuasive to potential customers

talking-to *n.* a scolding given to sb, especially by sb in authority (*informal*)

talk show *n.* = **chat show**

talky /táwki/ (**-ier, -iest**) *adj.* containing too much dialogue and not enough action ○ *a talky and dull film*

tall /tawl/ *adj.* **1.** VERY HIGH reaching or having grown to a considerable or above-average height ○ *tall trees* **2.** CERTAIN HEIGHT having reached a particular height ○ *five foot tall* **3.** LARGE substantial, demanding, or difficult to deal with ○ *a tall order* **4.** INCREDIBLE exaggerating the events of sth beyond the bounds of probability ○ *a tall tale* **5.** POMPOUS having an excessively grand or boastful style **6.** GOOD fine or admirable, especially by being brave and good (*archaic*) ■ *adv.* PROUDLY in a proud or courageous way ○ *There are times when you must stand tall and defend your beliefs.* ■ *n.* CLOTHES SIZE FOR TALL PEOPLE a clothing size for tall people, or a garment in this size [Old English *getæl* 'quick, ready', from a prehistoric Germanic base meaning 'to count', which is also the ancestor of English *tell* and *talk*] —**tallish** *adj.* —**tallness** *n.*

tallage /tállij/ *n.* **1.** ROYAL TAX a tax levied by the Norman and Angevin kings of England on royal lands and towns **2.** TAX LEVIED BY LORD in feudal times, a tax levied by a lord on his vassals or tenants ■ *vt.* (**-lages, -laging, -laged**) LEVY TAX ON SB OR STH to levy a tax, especially a tallage, on sb or sth [13thC. From Old French *taillage*, from *taillier* 'to cut'.]

Tallahassee /tállə hássi/ capital city of Florida, situated in the northern part of the state. Population: 133,718 (1994).

tallboy /táwl boy/ *n.* **1.** CHEST OF DRAWERS a high set of drawers, made up of two chests of drawers set one on top of the other. US term **highboy 2.** PART OF CHIMNEY a narrow fitting at the top of a chimney to prevent smoke being carried back down

Talleyrand /tálli ránd/, **Charles Maurice de** (1754–1838) French statesman. His long career spanned the French Revolution and the Napoleonic period. As foreign minister, he represented France at the Congress of Vienna (1814–15). Full name **Charles Maurice de Talleyrand-Périgord**

Tallinn /tállin, ta lín, -leen/ capital city of Estonia. A major port, it is situated on the Bay of Tallinn, an inlet of the Gulf of Finland, opposite Helsinki, Finland. Population: 490,000 (1994).

tallis *n.* = **tallith**

Tallis /tálliss/, **Thomas** (1510?–85) English composer. He was a major composer of religious choral works.

tallith /tállith, tálliss/ (*plural* **-lithim** /tali theem, -seem/ *or* **-liths**), **tallis** /tálliss/ (*plural* **-lisim**) *n.* a Jewish four-cornered fringed prayer shawl of white material with a black, blue, or purple stripe, worn at morning prayers [Early 17thC. From Rabbinical Hebrew *ṭallīṯ*, from biblical Hebrew *ṭillēl* 'to cover'.]

tall oil *n.* an oily liquid produced as a by-product of a chemical process in the manufacture of wood pulp and used in making soaps and emulsions [Early 20thC. Partial translation of German *Tallöl*, from Swedish *tallolja*, from *tall* 'pine' + *olja* 'oil'.]

tallow /tá lló/ *n.* **1.** FATTY SUBSTANCE USED TO MAKE CANDLES a hard fatty substance extracted from the fat of sheep and cattle and used to make candles and soap **2.** SUBSTANCE MADE FROM VEGETABLE MATTER a substance similar to tallow, made from vegetable matter ■ *vt.* (**-lows, -lowing, -lowed**) COVER STH WITH TALLOW to cover or grease sth with tallow [13thC. From Low German.] —**tallowy** *adj.*

tall poppy (*plural* **tall poppies**) *n.* *Aus* sb who, through achievements or wealth, has become a prominent member of society (*informal*)

tall poppy syndrome *n.* *Aus* a tendency among the media and the public to denigrate the achievements of prominent members of society

tall ship *n.* a square-rigged sailing ship [*Tall* from the lofty masts carried on full-rigged ships]

tally /tálli/ *v.* (**-lies, -lying, -lied**) **1.** *vti.* AGREE OR CAUSE THINGS TO AGREE to agree, correspond, or come to the same amount, or to cause two or more things to agree **2.** *vi.* KEEP SCORE to keep a record of a score or account **3.** *vt.* COUNT STH to count or reckon sth **4.** *vt.* REGISTER STH IN AN ACCOUNT to register sth in an account of items **5.** *vt.* PUT LABEL OR TAG ON STH to put an identifying label or tag on sth ■ *n.* (*plural* **-lies**) **1.** RECORD a record or account of items, e.g. things bought or points scored ○ *keep a tally* **2.** SCORE the total or current number of things achieved by sb, especially sb's score in a game or competition ○ *added to his personal tally of nine goals for the season* **3.** *US* SPORTS, GAME SINGLE SCORE a single score, e.g. a run or a touchdown, in a contest **4.** IDENTIFYING LABEL OR MARK sth, e.g. a label or mark, that identifies sth **5.** COUNTERPART sth that corresponds to or is the counterpart of sth else **6.** NOTCHED STICK a stick with notches cut into it as a record of sth, e.g. loans made or items bought on credit **7.** NOTCH CUT INTO STICK AS RECORD any of the notches cut into a tally as a record **8.** MARK REPRESENTING NUMBER a mark or marks representing a number, especially a set of four short vertical lines crossed by a diagonal fifth line used for numbering things in fives [15thC. Via Anglo-Norman from, ultimately, Latin *talea* 'twig, cutting'.] —**tallier** *n.*

WORD KEY: ORIGIN

The Latin word *talea*, from which ***tally*** is derived, is also the source of English *detail, entail, retail,* and *tailor.*

tally-ho /tálli hó/ *interj.* EXCLAMATION THAT FOX HAS BEEN SIGHTED used by a participant in a fox hunt to let others know that a fox has been sighted ■ *n.* (*plural* **tally-hos**) **1.** FOX HUNTER'S CRY a cry by a participant in a fox hunt to let others know that a fox has been sighted **2.** = **four-in-hand** *n.* 1 ■ *vi.* (**tally-hos, tally-hoing, tally-hoed**) SHOUT 'TALLY-HO' to give a shout of 'tally-ho' [Origin uncertain: probably an alteration of French *taïaut*]

tallyman /tállimən/ (*plural* **-men** /-mən/) *n.* **1.** RECORD KEEPER sb who keeps a record or account of sth, e.g. items bought on credit or points scored **2.** TRAVELLING SALES REPRESENTATIVE a travelling sales representative who sells goods to be paid for in instalments

Talmud /tálmo͝od, -məd/ *n.* the collection of ancient Jewish writings that makes up the basis of Jewish religious law, consisting of the early scriptural interpretations (**Mishnah**) and the later commentaries on them (**Gemara**) [Mid-16thC. From post-biblical Hebrew *talmūḏ*, literally 'instruction', from Hebrew *lāmaḏ* 'to learn'.] —**Talmudic** /tal mo͝odik, -myo͝odik/ *adj.* —**Talmudical** /-mo͝odik'l, -myo͝odik'l/ *adj.* —**Talmudism** /tálmo͝odizəm, -mədizəm/ *n.* —**Talmudist** /tálmo͝odist/ *n.*

talon /tállən/ *n.* **1.** HOOKED CLAW a hooked claw, especially of a bird of prey **2.** STH LIKE A CLAW sth that looks like a claw, e.g. a curled human finger **3.** PART OF A LOCK the part of a lock that the key is pressed against when turned and that causes the bolt to slide out **4.** ARCHIT = **ogee** *n.* 2 **5.** CARDS **UNDEALT CARDS** the remainder of the deck of cards after a deal in particular games, e.g. in piquet or solitaire [14thC. Via French from the assumed Vulgar Latin stem *talon-* 'heel, spur', from Latin *talus* 'ankle'.] —**taloned** *adj.*

taluk /taa lóok/ (*plural* **-luka** /taa lóokə/ *or* **-looka**) *n. S Asia* **1.** **SUBDIVISION OF DISTRICT** a subdivision of a district in India **2.** **PIECE OF HEREDITARY LAND** a piece of hereditary land in India [Late 18thC. Via Urdu and Persian *ta'alluk* 'estate' from, ultimately, Arabic *ta'allaka* 'to be attached'.]

talus[1] /táyləss/ *n.* **1.** MIL **AREA OF RUBBLE** a sloping area of rock rubble **2.** **ROCK RUBBLE** rock rubble, e.g. at the base of a cliff **3.** MIL **BASE OF FORTIFICATION** the sloping base of a fortification [Mid-17thC. Origin unknown.]

talus[2] /táyləss/ (*plural* **-li** /táy lī/) *n.* the bone in the ankle that connects with the lower leg bones to form the ankle joint [Late 16thC. From Latin, 'ankle', of uncertain origin: possibly from Celtic.]

talweg /taal veg/ *n.* = **thalweg**

tam /tam/ *n.* a tam-o'-shanter (*informal*) [Shortening]

TAM /tam/ *abbr.* Television Audience Measurement

tamale /tə maali/ *n.* a Mexican dish made by mixing fried chopped meat with peppers and seasonings, rolling the mixture in cornmeal dough, wrapping it in maize husks, and then steaming it [Late 17thC. Back-formation from American Spanish *tamales*, the plural of *tamal*, from Nahuatl *tamalli*.]

tamandua /támmən dóo ə/, **tamandu** /-dóo/ *n.* a small tree-living toothless anteater of Central and South America with a long prehensile tail. Latin name: *Tamandua tetradactyla* and *Tamandua mexicana*. [Early 17thC. Via Portuguese from Tupi *tamanduá*, literally 'ant hunter'.]

Tamar /táym aar/ **1.** river that rises near the northern coast of Devon, southwestern England, and flows south to the English Channel. The Tamar valley is an Area of Outstanding Natural Beauty. Length: 97 km/60 mi. **2.** river in northern Tasmania, Australia, formed by the confluence of the North and South Esk rivers. Length: 65 km/40 mi.

tamarack /támmə rak/ *n.* **1.** TREES **N AMERICAN LARCH** a deciduous North American larch with bluish-green needles and oval cones. Latin name: *Larix laricina*. **2.** INDUST **WOOD OF TAMARACK** the wood of the tamarack tree [Early 19thC. From Canadian French *tamarac*, of uncertain origin: probably of Algonquian origin.]

tamarau /támmə row/ (*plural* **-raus**), **tamarao** (*plural* **-raos**) *n.* a small rare buffalo that lives in swamps of the island of Mindoro in the Philippines. Latin name: *Bubalus mindorensis*. [Late 19thC. From Tagalog.]

tamari /tə maari/ *n.* a rich Japanese soy sauce [Late 20thC. From Japanese.]

tamarillo /támmə ríll ō/ (*plural* **-los**) *n. US* TREES = **tree tomato** [Mid-20thC. Alteration of TOMATILLO.]

tamarin /támmərin/ *n.* a small South American monkey that has a long tail and is highly vocal. Genus: *Saguinus*. [Late 18thC. Via French from Galibi.]

tamarind /támmərind/ *n.* **1.** TREES **TROPICAL TREE** a tropical evergreen tree that has yellow flowers with red streaks and pods containing an edible acid pulp. Latin name: *Tamarindus indica*. **2.** FOOD **FRUIT OF TAMARIND TREE** the edible acid fruit of the tamarind tree, used in making preserves, drinks, and medicines **3.** INDUST **WOOD FROM TAMARIND** the wood of the tamarind tree [Mid-16thC. Via Old French from Arabic *tamr hindī*, literally 'Indian date'.]

tamarisk /támmərisk/ *n.* a tree or shrub with leaves resembling scales and masses of small flowers that grows in Europe, Asia, and Africa. Genus: *Tamarix*. [14thC. From late Latin *tamariscus*, a variant of Latin *tamarix*, of unknown origin.]

Tamatave /tamatáav/ former name for **Toamasina**

tambac *n.* = **tombac**

tambala /taam baalə/ (*plural* **-la** *or* **-las**) *n.* **1.** **SUBUNIT OF MALAWIAN CURRENCY** a subunit of currency in Malawi, 100 of which are worth one kwacha. See table at **currency 2.** **COIN WORTH A TAMBALA** a coin worth one tambala

Tambo /támb ō/, **Oliver** (1917–93) South African political leader. He was leader of the African National Congress (1967–91) and a prominent opponent of apartheid. He was in exile from 1960 to 1990.

tambour /tám boor, -bawr/ *n.* **1.** SEW **EMBROIDERY FRAME** a round frame on which material is stretched while it is being embroidered **2.** SEW, FURNITURE **EMBROIDERY** embroidery done on a tambour **3.** **FLEXIBLE ROLLING TOP OF DESK** a flexible rolling top of a desk or sliding front of a cabinet made of thin strips of wood attached to canvas **4.** MUSIC, MIL **DRUM** a drum, especially a side drum **5.** ARCHIT **CIRCULAR WALL** a circular wall, especially one supporting a dome ■ *vti.* (**-bours, -bouring, -boured**) SEW **EMBROIDER DESIGN USING TAMBOUR** to embroider using a tambour, or embroider a design onto material using a tambour [15thC. Via Old French from, ultimately, Persian *tabīra* 'drum', perhaps influenced by Arabic *ṭunbūr* 'lute'.]

tamboura /tam bóorə, tam báwrə/ *n.* a fretless stringed Asian instrument resembling a lute, played to produce a harmonic drone [Late 16thC. Via Arabic and Persian from Persian *dunbara*, literally 'lamb's tail'.]

tambourin /támbóorin/ *n.* **1.** DANCE **DANCE** an 18th-century Provençal dance in a two-beat rhythm, usually accompanied by a drum **2.** MUSIC **MUSIC FOR TAMBOURIN** a piece of music composed for or in the rhythm of a tambourin **3.** MUSIC **DRUM** a small Provençal drum [Late 18thC. From French, literally 'small drum', from *tambour* (see TAMBOUR).]

tambourine /támbə réen/ *n.* a shallow single-headed drum with jingling metallic discs in its frame, held in one hand and played by shaking it or striking it with the free hand [Late 16thC. From French, literally 'small drum', from *tambour* (see TAMBOUR).] —**tambourinist** *n.*

tambu-bambu band /támboo bámboo band/ *n. Carib* a small band of musicians using bamboo sticks as instruments and parading through the streets during Carnival, especially in Trinidad. The forerunners of the modern steel bands, they are rarely seen nowadays. (*dated*)

Tamburlaine /támbə layn/ = **Tamerlane**

tame /taym/ *adj.* (**tamer, tamest**) **1.** **NO LONGER WILD** changed from a wild or uncultivated state to one suitable for domestic use or life **2.** **FRIENDLY TOWARDS PEOPLE** unafraid of human contact **3.** **WITHOUT SPIRIT** lacking in spirit or vigour **4.** **BLAND** showing little of the qualities that make sth interesting, e.g. imagination, adventurousness, or inspiration ○ *Considering the controversial nature of his other films, this latest one is very tame.* **5.** **SLOW-MOVING** with very little current ○ *a tame stretch of river* ■ *vt.* (**tames, taming, tamed**) **1.** **DOMESTICATE STH** to make a wild animal or uncultivated land suitable for domestic life or use **2.** **SUBDUE SB** to remove the wildness, spirit, or energy from sb or sth **3.** **MODERATE STH** to make sth much less harsh or extreme **4.** **BRING STH UNDER HUMAN CONTROL** to bring a natural force under human control ○ *a series of dams to tame the raging river* [Old English *tam*. Ultimately from an Indo-European word meaning 'to constrain', which is also the ancestor of English *daunt*, *indomitable*, and *diamond*.] —**tamable** *adj.* —**tameableness** *n.* —**tamely** *adv.* —**tameness** *n.* —**tamer** *n.*

Tamerlane /támmər layn/, **Tamburlaine** /támbər layn/ (1336–1405) Turkic ruler and conqueror. His conquests established an empire that extended from India to the Mediterranean Sea. He died whilst trying to invade China, and was buried in his capital, Samarkand. Born **Timur**

Tamil /támmil/ (*plural* **-ils** *or* **-il**) *n.* **1.** PEOPLES **MEMBER OF S ASIAN PEOPLE** a member of a people who live in southern India and northern Sri Lanka **2.** LANG **TAMIL LANGUAGE** the Dravidian language of the Tamil people. Tamil has an ancient literary tradition and is spoken by over 50 million people. [Mid-18thC. From Tamil *Tamiḻ*.] —**Tamil** *adj.*

Tamil Nadu /támmil naa dóo/ state in southern India. Capital: Chennai. Population: 58,840,000 (1994). Area: 130,058 sq. km/50,215 sq. mi.

tamis /támmi, -miss/ (*plural* **-is**) *n.* = **tammy**[2] [Early 17thC. Via French from medieval Latin *tamisium*, ultimately from prehistoric Germanic.]

Tammany Hall /támməni-/ *n.* a political organization formed as a fraternal society in New York in 1789 but mainly known for political corruption in the early 20th century [Mid-19thC. Named after the headquarters of the *Tammany* Society.] —**Tammanyism** *n.* —**Tammanyite** *n.*

tammar /támmər/ *n.* a rabbit-sized wallaby that lives in the arid scrub of southern Australia and has a reddish-brown coat with whitish underparts. It can live for months without drinking water, consuming only plants. Latin name: *Wallabia eugenii*. [Mid-19thC. From Aborigine.]

Tammuz /taa mooz/ *n.* CALENDAR in the Jewish calendar, the tenth month of the civil year and the fourth month of the religious year. It is 29 days long. [Mid-16thC. Via Hebrew *Tammūz* from Babylonian *Du'uzu*, the name of a deity.]

tammy[1] /támmi/ *n.* a tam-o'-shanter (*informal*) [Late 19thC. Formed from TAM.]

tammy[2] /támmi/ *n.* (*plural* **tammies**) **tammy, tammy cloth** **STRAINING CLOTH** a fine strainer made of woollen cloth ■ *vt.* (**tammies, tammying, tammied**) **STRAIN STH** to strain sth such as a sauce using a tammy [Mid-18thC. Origin uncertain: probably from French *tamis* (source of English *tamis*).]

tam-o'-shanter /támə shántər/ *n.* a brimless Scottish woollen hat, usually with a bobble at the centre of the crown [Mid-19thC. From *Tam O' Shanter*, the eponymous hero of a poem by Robert Burns.]

tamoxifen /tə móksi fen/ *n.* a drug used to treat breast cancer by inhibiting the actions of oestrogen. It is also used in treating some types of infertility. Formula: $C_{26}H_{29}NO$. [Late 20thC. Alteration of form coined from TRANS- + AMINE + OXY- + PHENOL.]

tamp /tamp/ *vt.* (**tamps, tamping, tamped**) **1.** **PACK STH DOWN** to pack or push sth down, especially by tapping it repeatedly **2.** **FILL DRILL HOLE WITH SUBSTANCE** to pack a substance such as sand or earth into a drill hole above an explosive ■ *n.* = **tamper**[2] *n.* 2 [Early 19thC. Origin uncertain: perhaps a back-formation from *tampin*, variant of TAMPION, taken as 'tamping'; perhaps influenced by STAMP.]

Tampa /támpə/ industrial city, seaport, and tourist resort on the western coast of Florida, at the mouth of the Hillsborough River. Population: 285,523 (1994).

Tampax /tám paks/ *tdmk.* a trademark for a tampon for use during menstruation

tamper[1] /támpər/ (**-pers, -pering, -pered**) *vi.* **1.** **INTERFERE WITH AND DAMAGE STH** to interfere with sth in a way that damages it or has harmful results **2.** **INFLUENCE STH CORRUPTLY** to try to corrupt or influence sb or affect the outcome of sth [Mid-16thC. Origin uncertain: probably a variant of TEMPER; the current meaning 'interfere' developed from the earlier 'work in, mix thoroughly', used of clay.] —**tamperer** *n.*

tamper[2] /támpər/ *n.* **1.** **SB OR STH THAT TAMPS STH** sb or sth that packs sth down with repeated blows **2.** **TAMPING DEVICE** a device for pushing tobacco down into the bowl of a pipe. US term **tamp** *n.* **3.** MIL **CASING ON NUCLEAR WEAPON** the casing around the core of a nuclear weapon that reflects neutrons back into the core, slowing the expansion of the nuclear reaction and increasing the weapon's power

Tampere /támpərə, támp e re/ city in Häma Province, southwestern Finland, situated about 169 km/105 mi. northwest of Helsinki. Population: 182,742 (1995).

Tampico /tam péekō/ seaport in eastern Mexico, situated on the Pánuco River close to the Gulf of Mexico. Population: 262,690 (1990).

tampion /támpi ən/, **tompion** /tómpi ən/ *n.* a plug or cover for the muzzle of a gun to keep out moisture and dust when it is not in use [15thC. From French *tampon* (see TAMPON).]

tampon /tám pon/ *n.* **1.** **PLUG OF MATERIAL USED DURING MENSTRUATION** a cylindrical plug of soft material inserted in the vagina during menstruation to absorb blood **2.** **PAD TO CHECK BLEEDING** a pad of cotton or other absorbent fabric that is used for plugging wounds or for controlling blood flow in body cavities, especially during surgery ■ *vt.* (**-pons, -poning, -poned**) **CONTROL BLOOD FLOW** to use a tampon to plug a wound or to control blood flow in a body cavity, especially during surgery [Mid-19thC. From French *tampon* 'plug, bung', variant of *tapon* 'piece of cloth to stop a hole', from assumed Frankish *tappo* 'stopper'.]

tamponade /támpə náyd/ *n.* the insertion of a tampon during surgery to check bleeding

tam-tam /tám tam/ *n.* a large gong [Mid-19thC. Origin uncertain: perhaps from Hindi *ṭam-ṭam* 'tom-tom'.]

Tamworth[1] /tám wurth/ *n.* a reddish-gold pig with a long snout belonging to a hardy breed developed in the Midlands and traditionally reared for pork. It is now regarded as a rare breed in its native region, but herds have been created in North America, Australia, and elsewhere. [Mid-19thC. Named after the town of TAMWORTH, Staffordshire.]

Tamworth[2] /tám wurth, támmwərth/ **1.** market town in Staffordshire, central England. Population: 68,440 (1991). **2.** city in northeastern New South Wales, Australia, an agricultural centre and site of an annual country music festival. Population: 31,865 (1996).

tan[1] /tan/ *n.* **1.** COLOURS **LIGHT BROWN COLOUR** a light brown colour tinged with orange **2. SUNTAN** the brownish colour that the skin takes on after being exposed to ultraviolet light, especially from the Sun or a sunlamp **3.** = **tanbark** *n.* 1 **4.** = **tannin** ■ *v.* **(tans, tanning, tanned) 1.** *vti.* **GET OR GIVE SB A SUNTAN** to give sb's skin a brownish colour, or take on such a colour **2.** *vt.* MANUF **CONVERT HIDE TO LEATHER** to convert an animal skin or hide into leather by treating it with sth such as tannin **3.** *vt.* **BEAT SB** to give a beating to sb (*informal*) ■ *adj.* **(tanner, tannest) 1. OF LIGHT BROWN COLOUR** of a light brown colour tinged with orange **2.** *US* = **tanned 3.** MANUF **OF PROCESS OF TANNING HIDES** relating to or used in the process of tanning animal skins and hides [Pre-12thC. From medieval Latin *tannare* 'to tan, dye a tawny colour', from *tannum* 'tanbark' (source of English *tannin*), of uncertain origin: probably from Celtic.] —**tannable** *adj.* —**tannish** *adj.*

tan[2] /tan/ *abbr.* tangent

tana /taánə/ *n.* **1. SMALL MADAGASCAN LEMUR** a small Madagascan lemur with a grey-brown back, whitish underparts, and a dark stripe that runs along the back and encircles each eye. Latin name: *Phaner furcifer*. **2. ASIAN TREE SHREW** a mainly ground-dwelling tree shrew that is native to Borneo and Sumatra and has a brownish coat with a black stripe along the back. Genus: *Lyongale*. [Early 19thC. Via modern Latin from Malay *tūpai tāna* 'ground-squirrel' (source of English *tupaia*).]

Tana, Lake /taánə/ the largest lake in Ethiopia, situated on the north-central plateau of the Ethiopian highlands. Area: 2,156 sq. km/1,219 sq. mi.

Tanach /taa naákh/, **Tanakh** *n.* the sacred book of Judaism consisting of the Torah, Prophets, and Hagiographa [Mid-20thC. From Hebrew *tᵉnaḵ*, an acronym formed from *tōrāh* 'law' + *nᵉḇī'īm* 'prophets' + *kᵉṯūḇīm* 'hagiographa'.]

tanager /tánnəjər/ *n.* a songbird found in the forests of North and South America that is usually fairly small and brightly coloured in bold patterns with a conical bill. Tanagers feed on insects and fruit, and some are popular as cage birds. Family: Thraupidae. [Early 17thC. From modern Latin *Tanagra*, genus name, ultimately an alteration of Tupi *tangará*.]

Tanakh *n.* = **Tanach**

tanbark /tán baark/ *n.* **1.** MANUF **TREE BARK USED AS TANNIN** the bark of some kinds of tree, especially oak and hemlock, used as a source of tannin **2.** TREES = **tan oak**

T & E *abbr.* tired and emotional (*informal*)

tandem /tándəm/ *n.* **1. BICYCLE FOR TWO RIDERS** a bicycle with two saddles and two sets of handlebars and pedals, one behind the other, so that it can be ridden by two people at the same time. US term **tandem bicycle 2. HORSE-DRAWN CARRIAGE** a two-wheeled carriage drawn by two horses harnessed one behind the other **3. HORSE TEAM HARNESSED IN SINGLE FILE** a team of two horses harnessed one behind the other **4. ARRANGEMENT IN SINGLE FILE** a setup in which two things are arranged one behind the other ■ *adv.* **ONE BEHIND ANOTHER** with one behind the other ○ *We'll ride tandem.* [Late 18thC. From Latin *tandem* 'at length' (from *tam* 'so' + demonstrative suffix *-dem*), humorously interpreted as 'in a straight line'; originally 'carriage drawn by two horses one behind the other'.] ◇ **in tandem 1.** in partnership or cooperation **2.** with one behind the other

tandem bicycle *n. US* = **tandem**

tandoor /tan dóor/ *n.* a clay oven used especially in the cuisine of or derived from the north of the Indian subcontinent for cooking food quickly at high temperature. It is traditionally fuelled by charcoal or wood, which gives the food a distinctive smoky flavour, although it can also now be gas-fired. [Mid-19thC. Via Urdu *tandūr*, Persian *tanūr* from, ultimately, Arabic *tannūr* 'oven, furnace'.]

tandoori /tan dóori/ *adj.* **COOKED IN CLAY OVEN** baked or cooked in a tandoor. In the cuisine of or derived from the north of the Indian subcontinent, meat or seafood is generally cooked in this way after being marinated in a mixture of yoghurt and spices. ■ *n.* **TANDOORI MEAL** a dish or meal of tandoori food (*informal*) ■ *vt.* **COOK STH IN TANDOORI STYLE** to cook sth in a tandoor, or after marinating the food in the mixture of yoghurt and spices traditionally used for such dishes [Mid-20thC. From Persian and Urdu, formed from Urdu *tandūr* and Persian *tanūr* (see TANDOOR).]

tang[1] /tang/ *n.* **1. STRONG TASTE** a distinctively sharp strong taste **2. PUNGENT SMELL** a smell that has a sharp biting quality **3. SUGGESTION** a slight hint or flavour of a particular thing ○ *a cake with a tang of lemon* **4. SHARP END GOING INTO HANDLE** the sharp part at one end of a chisel, knife blade, or other similar tool that secures it to the handle or shaft [14thC. From a Scandinavian word.]

tang[2] /tang/ *n.* **RINGING SOUND** a loud, often harsh, ringing noise ■ *vti.* **(tangs, tanging, tanged) MAKE RINGING SOUND** to make or cause sth to make a loud, often harsh, ringing noise [Early 17thC. An imitation of the sound.]

Tang /tang/, **T'ang** *n.* **CHINESE DYNASTY** a wealthy Chinese dynasty that lasted from AD 618–907 and was renowned for its encouragement and patronage of the arts, especially poetry and ceramics, and the development of printing ■ *adj.* **OF TANG DYNASTY** relating to or characteristic of the Tang dynasty or the literature, pottery, and other arts and crafts that flourished in China during this period [Mid-17thC. From Chinese *táng*.]

tanga /táng gə/ *n.* an undergarment or the lower part of a bikini made of two small triangles of fabric fastened with ties [Early 20thC. Via Portuguese, in which the word denoted a triangular loincloth worn in tropical America, from Bantu.]

Tanga /táng gə/ town in northeastern Tanzania, on the Indian Ocean. Population: 188,000 (1994).

Tanganyika /táng gən yeékə/ former country in East Africa constituting the mainland part of what is now Tanzania —**Tanganyikan** /táng gə nyeékən/ *n., adj.*

Tanganyika, Lake the second largest lake in Africa, located in the east-central part of the continent, with shorelines in Burundi, Tanzania, Zambia, and the Democratic Republic of the Congo. Area: 32,900 sq. km/12,700 sq. mi. Length: 680 km/420 mi.

tangata whenua /tánguttə fénnoo ə/ *npl. NZ* the Maori people of a particular area

Tange Kenzo /táng gay kénnzō/ (*b.* 1913) Japanese architect. He is often considered Japan's greatest modern architect. His works include the Peace Centre at Hiroshima (1955).

tangelo /tánjəlō/ (*plural* **-los**) *n.* **1.** TREES **HYBRID CITRUS TREE** a hybrid citrus tree produced by crossing a tangerine tree with a grapefruit tree **2.** FOOD **FRUIT OF TANGELO TREE** the fruit of the tangelo, bigger than an orange and with smooth easily peeled skin and sharp-tasting orange flesh [Early 20thC. Blend of TANGERINE and POMELO, sometimes used to refer to grapefruit in the United States.]

tangent /tánjənt/ *n.* **1. LINE OR SURFACE THAT TOUCHES ANOTHER** a line, curve, or surface that touches another curve or surface but does not cross or intersect it **2.** MATH **TRIGONOMETRIC FUNCTION** for a given angle in a right-angled triangle, a trigonometric function equal to the length of the side opposite the angle divided by the length of the adjacent side. ◊ **cosine, sine 3. PART OF SURVEY LINE** the part of a survey line that is straight

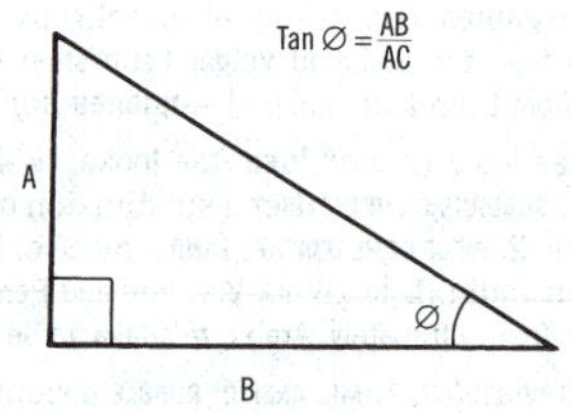

Tangent

4. MUSIC **PART OF CLAVICHORD** a part of the clavichord that resembles a small hammer and strikes the strings ■ *adj.* **1.** = **tangential** *adj.* 1 **2. TOUCHING AT A SINGLE POINT** touching only at a single point **3. TOUCHING BUT NOT CROSSING** in contact, but not crossing or intersecting **4. AWAY FROM THE POINT** not relevant to the subject currently under consideration [Late 16thC. From Latin *tangent-*, present participle stem of *tangere* 'to touch'. Originally 'line touching a circle'.] —**tangency** /tánjənssi/ *n.* ◇ **go off at** *or* **on a tangent** to change quickly and suddenly to a different subject or line of thought

WORD KEY: ORIGIN

The Latin word *tangere*, from which ***tangent*** is derived, is also the source of English *contact, intact, tact, taste,* and *tax*.

---

tangent galvanometer *n.* a device with a compass needle suspended horizontally in a vertical coil through which a direct current is passed, causing deflection of the needle proportional to the current size. It can be used to calculate the strength of the Earth's magnetic field.

tangential /tan jénsh'l/ *adj.* **1. OF TANGENT** relating to or involving a tangent **2. ALMOST IRRELEVANT** with only slight relevance to the current subject —**tangentiality** /tan jénshi álləti/ *n.* —**tangentially** /tan jénsh'li/ *adv.*

tangerine /tánjə reén/ *n.* **1.** FOOD **CITRUS FRUIT** an edible citrus fruit with an orange skin that is easily peeled and sweet-tasting flesh **2.** TREES **WIDELY CULTIVATED CITRUS TREE** a citrus tree native to Southeast Asia but widely cultivated in tropical and warm regions for its fruit. Many varieties and hybrids have been produced, including the clementine, satsuma, and tangelo. Latin name: *Citrus reticulata*. **3.** COLOURS **BRIGHT ORANGE COLOUR** a bright orange colour like that of a tangerine ■ *adj.* COLOURS **OF BRIGHT ORANGE COLOUR** of a bright orange colour like a tangerine [Early 17thC. Origin uncertain: probably modelled on Spanish *Tangerino* 'of or from Tangier', the current senses via *Tangerine orange*.]

Tangerine /tánjə reén/ *adj.* relating to the Moroccan port of Tangier, or its people or culture

tangi /túng ee/ (*plural* **-gis**) *n. NZ* a Maori funeral ceremony and the feast that accompanies it [Mid-19thC. From Maori, 'lament, action of crying'.]

tangible /tánjəb'l/ *adj.* **1. ABLE TO BE TOUCHED** able to be touched or perceived through the sense of touch ○ *a tangible coldness* **2. ACTUAL** capable of being understood and evaluated, and therefore regarded as real ○ *There is no tangible evidence to support this claim.* **3. ABLE TO BE REALIZED** capable of being given a physical existence ○ *some very tangible financial benefits* ■ *n.* **STH TANGIBLE** sth that has a physical form, especially a financial asset (*often used in the plural*) [Late 16thC. Directly or via French from late Latin *tangibilis* 'that may be touched', from Latin *tangere* (see TANGENT).] —**tangibility** /tánjə bílləti/ *n.* —**tangibleness** /tánjəb'lnəss/ *n.* —**tangibly** /tánjəbli/ *adv.*

Tangier /tán jeér/ port city in northern Morocco. Population: 307,000 (1993).

tangle[1] /tángg'l/ *v.* **(-gles, -gling, -gled) 1.** *vti.* **BECOME TWISTED** to become or make sth become twisted together into a jumbled mass **2.** *vt.* **CATCH AND HOLD STH** to catch and entwine sb or sth in sth that is difficult to get out of, e.g. a net or trap ○ *I got my jacket tangled in the branches.* **3.** *vt.* **TRAP SB IN DIFFICULT SITUATION** to trap sb in a complicated, awkward, or dangerous situation ○ *tangled in a web of controversy*

4. *vi.* COME INTO CONFLICT to become involved in a confrontation or disagreement with sb, especially sb powerful or important ○ *You'll regret it if you tangle with them.* ■ *n.* **1.** JUMBLED MASS a mass of fibres, lines, or other things twisted together **2.** DIFFICULTY a complicated situation or problem **3.** STATE OF MENTAL UPSET a state of mental or emotional confusion or upset [14thC. Earlier *tanglen*, variant of *tagilen* 'to involve in an embarrassing situation', of uncertain origin: probably from Scandinavian.] —**tanglement** *n.* —**tangler** *n.* —**tangly** *adj.*

tangle[2] /táng'l/, **tangle weed** *n.* a large brown seaweed, various kinds of which grow on shores at or below the level of low tide [Mid-16thC. Origin uncertain: probably from Norwegian *tångel*, from Old Norse *þongull*, from *þang* 'bladder-wrack'.]

Tango

tango /táng gō/ *n.* (*plural* **tangos**) **1.** DANCE DANCE OF LATIN AMERICAN ORIGIN a highly stylized ballroom dance of Latin American origin in 2/4 time in which the steps are punctuated by glides and sudden pauses **2.** MUSIC MUSIC FOR TANGO a piece of music that is suitable for a tango ■ *vi.* (**tangos, tangoing, tangoed**) DANCE DANCE TANGO to dance a tango [Late 19thC. From Argentine Spanish *tango*, originally a dance to the sound of drums, of uncertain origin: probably from a Niger-Congo language.] —**tangoist** *n.*

Tango *n.* a word used to represent the letter 'T' in radio communications

tangram /tán gram/ *n.* a puzzle of Chinese origin that involves putting together seven pieces, usually a square, a parallelogram, and five triangles, to form different shapes. The seven pieces can also be put together to form a square. [Mid-19thC. Origin uncertain: perhaps coined from Chinese *t'ang* 'Chinese' + -GRAM.]

Tangshan /táng shán/ *city* in Hebei Province, northern China, southeast of Beijing. Population: 1,500,000 (1991).

tangy /tángi/ (**-ier, -iest**) *adj.* with a strong sharp taste or smell

tanist /tánnist/ *n.* the heir apparent to a Celtic chieftain, usually a member of the chieftain's own clan and elected by the tribe during the chieftain's lifetime [Mid-16thC. From Irish Gaelic *tánaiste*, literally 'second in excellence, second in rank'.]

tanistry /tánnistri/ *n.* the process of selecting an heir apparent to a Celtic chieftain while the current chieftain is still alive

taniwha /tún ee faa/ *n.* NZ a Maori water spirit that inspires fear [Mid-19thC. From Maori.]

Tanizaki Junichiro /taán ee zaák ee jóon ee cheér aw/ (1886–1965) Japanese writer. His novels present the conflict between modern Western-influenced realities and traditional values.

tank /tangk/ *n.* **1.** LARGE CONTAINER FOR LIQUIDS OR GASES a large container for storing liquids or gases **2.** AMOUNT HELD BY TANK the amount of liquid or gas that a particular tank holds ○ *We should get there and back on a couple of tanks of petrol.* **3.** MIL ARMOURED VEHICLE a large armoured combat vehicle with Caterpillar™ tracks and a rotating turret **4.** *US* JAIL prison or a prison cell (*informal*) **5.** PHOTOGRAPHY CONTAINER FOR DEVELOPING FILM a lightproof container for developing film, designed so that processing chemicals can be poured in and out without light entering **6.** PHOTOGRAPHY TRAY FOR PROCESSING SHEETS OF FILM a large tray or container for processing a number of sheets of film together **7.** POND OR RESERVOIR a fairly small

Tank

body of water, especially one used for water storage (*regional*) ■ *v.* (**tanks, tanking, tanked**) **1.** *vt.* PUT STH IN A TANK to put or keep sth in a tank **2.** *vi.* GO FAST to move quickly or heavily, often with great purpose or determination ○ *He tanked up the road to the bus stop.* **3.** *vt.* BEAT SB IN COMPETITION to defeat a person or team heavily in a sport or competition (*informal*) [Early 17thC. From Gujarati *tāku* and Marathi *tākē* 'pond, cistern', perhaps with influence from Portuguese *tangue* (from Latin *stagnum* 'pond').]

tank up *v.* **1.** *vti.* FILL UP WITH FUEL to fill the fuel tank of a motor vehicle (*informal*) **2.** *vi.* GET DRUNK to drink enough alcohol to become drunk (*slang*)

tanka /tángkə/ (*plural* **-kas** *or* **-ka**) *n.* **1.** JAPANESE VERSE FORM a five-line Japanese verse form in which the first and third lines have five syllables each and the other lines have seven syllables each. ◊ **haiku 2.** JAPANESE POEM a poem with a tanka verse structure [Late 19thC. From Japanese, from *tan* 'short' + *ka* 'song'.]

tankage /tángkij/ *n.* **1.** TANK CAPACITY the amount that can be held by a tank or tanks **2.** STORAGE IN TANK the storage of sth in a tank, or the cost of this **3.** AGRIC FERTILIZER a by-product of the slaughter of livestock consisting of carcass trimmings cooked to reduce moisture and drained of surplus fat, used as a feed supplement or fertilizer

tankard /tángkərd/ *n.* **1.** BIG BEER MUG a large mug with a handle and sometimes a hinged lid, made of glass, pewter, or silver plate, typically used for drinking beer **2.** AMOUNT HELD IN TANKARD the amount of liquid that a tankard holds

tank car *n.* *US* = tank wagon

tanked /tangkt/, **tanked-up** *adj.* extremely drunk (*slang*)

tank engine, **tank locomotive** *n.* a steam engine that carries its water supply in tanks at the sides of the boiler instead of carrying it in a tender

tanker /tángkər/ *n.* a ship, lorry, or aeroplane designed to carry large quantities of liquid or gas

tank farm *n.* a site with several large storage tanks, especially ones containing oil

tank farming *n.* = hydroponics

tankful /tángkfŏŏl/ *n.* the amount a tank can hold

tank locomotive *n.* = tank engine

tank top *n.* a close-fitting, sleeveless, usually knitted garment with a low U-shaped or V-shaped neck. It first became popular in the 1970s, when it was often worn over a long-sleeved shirt. [Because it resembles either the top half of a tank suit, or a garment worn by the crews of armoured tanks]

tank trap *n.* sth such as a concrete block designed to stop or slow the movement of military tanks

tank wagon *n.* a railway wagon that has a large tank for transporting liquids or gases in bulk. US term **tank car**

tannage /tánnij/ *n.* **1.** HIDE TANNING the tanning of animal hides or skins **2.** TANNED HIDE an animal skin or hide that has been tanned [Mid-17thC. Formed from TAN[1]; perhaps also from French *tannage*.]

tannate /tánnayt/ *n.* a salt or ester of tannic acid [Early 19thC. Formed from TANNIC.]

tanned /tand/ *adj.* with a tan from the Sun or an artificial source of ultraviolet light. US term **tan**[1]

adj. **2** [15thC. The current sense developed via 'that has been made brown' from 'made into leather'.]

tanner[1] /tánnər/ *n.* sb who tans animal skins or hides [Pre-12thC. Both formed from TAN[1] and via Old French *tanere* from medieval Latin *tannator*.]

tanner[2] /tánnər/ *n.* a sixpence, or the sum of sixpence (*dated informal*) [Early 19thC. Origin uncertain; perhaps named after John Sigismund *Tanner* (died 1775), an engraver at the Mint.]

tannery /tánnəri/ (*plural* **-ies**) *n.* a building or factory where animal skins and hides are tanned

tannic /tánnik/ *adj.* relating to, containing, or derived from tannin [Mid-19thC. From French *tannique*, from *tanin* (see TANNIN).]

tannic acid *n.* = tannin

tannin /tánnin/ *n.* a brownish or yellowish substance found in plants and used in tanning, dyeing, and as an astringent [Early 19thC. From French *tanin*, from *tan* 'tanbark', from medieval Latin *tannum* (see TAN[1]).]

tanning /tánning/ *n.* **1.** CONVERSION OF ANIMAL SKIN INTO LEATHER the conversion of animal skins and hides into leather **2.** BROWNING OF SKIN the browning of skin when it is exposed to the sun or some other ultra-violet light source **3.** SOUND BEATING a sound beating or whipping

tanning bed *n.* *US* = sunbed

Tannoy /tánnoy/ *tdmk.* a trademark for a public address system.

Tanoan /tə nó ən/ *n.* a group of languages spoken mainly in New Mexico and Arizona. Tanoan languages are spoken by about 3,000 people. [From Spanish *Tano* 'Tewa']

tanrec *n.* = tenrec

tansy /tánzi/ (*plural* **-sies**) *n.* **1.** PLANT WITH YELLOW FLOWERS an aromatic perennial European and Asian plant of the daisy family with leaves divided into toothed leaflets and flat-topped clusters of yellow flower heads. The leaves were traditionally used as a piquant culinary flavouring, as a rodent repellent, and as a medicine. Latin name: *Tanacetum vulgare*. **2.** PLANT RESEMBLING TANSY any plant similar to the tansy, e.g. the ragwort [13thC. Origin uncertain: perhaps from Old French *tanesie*, ultimately from late Latin *tanacetum* 'wormwood'; or from medieval Latin *athanasia*, from Greek, 'immortality'.]

Tanta /tántə/ *city* in the Nile delta, northeastern Egypt, capital of Gharbiyah Governorate. Population: 380,000 (1992).

tantalic /tan tállik/ *adj.* relating to tantalum, especially when it has a valency of five

tantalise *vt.* = tantalize

tantalite /tántə līt/ *n.* a reddish-black mineral that is an ore of tantalum and also contains iron and manganese. It occurs in granites and pegmatite. Formula: $(Fe,Mn)Ta_2O_6$.

tantalize /tántə līz/ (**-lizes, -lizing, -lized**), **tantalise** (**-lises, -lising, -lised**) *vt.* to tease or torment people by letting them see, but not have, sth they desire [Late 16thC. Formed from Latin *Tantalus* (see TANTALUS).] —**tantalization** /tántə līzáysh'n/ *n.* —**tantalizer** /tántə līzər/ *n.*

tantalizing /tántə līzing/ *adj.* tempting but unavailable or unattainable ○ *a really tantalizing offer* —**tantalizingly** *adv.*

tantalum /tántələm/ *n.* a dense blue-grey metallic chemical element used in making electronic components, alloys, and in plates and pins for orthopaedic surgery. Symbol **Ta** [Early 19thC. Via modern Latin from Latin *Tantalus* (see TANTALUS), because of its inability to absorb acid even when it is immersed in it.]

tantalus /tántələss/ *n.* a lockable stand or case for decanters of alcoholic drinks, especially spirits. The decanters are visible but without the key the contents cannot be reached. [Late 19thC. Ultimately from Latin *Tantalus* (see TANTALUS).]

Tantalus *n.* in Greek mythology, a king who was condemned to stand in water under a fruit tree. Whenever he tried to drink or eat, the water or fruit receded beyond his reach. [Mid-18thC. Via Latin from Greek.]

tantamount /tántə mownt/ *adj.* equivalent to a particular thing in effect, outcome, or value, especially sth unpleasant ○ *an answer that was tantamount to a refusal* [Mid-17thC. Ultimately from Anglo-French *tant amunter* 'to amount to as much', from Old French *tant* 'as much' + *amonter* 'to amount' (source of English *amount*).]

tantara /tántə raá/ *n.* a fanfare or blast on a horn, or a sound that resembles this, especially when used to announce sth important [Mid-16thC. An imitation of the sound.]

tantie /tánti/, **Tantie** *n. Carib* an older aunt, or any older woman [Late 19thC. From French Creole, a blend of French *tante* and AUNTIE.]

tantivy /tan tívvi/ *n.* (*plural* **-ies**), *interj.* **HUNTER'S SHOUT** a hunting cry, especially one given by a hunter riding a horse at full gallop ■ *n.* (*plural* **-ies**) **FAST MOVEMENT** a fast ride, especially on a horse going at full gallop ■ *adj.* **SPEEDY** moving very fast, especially when on a horse going at full gallop ■ *adv.* **SPEEDILY** in a very fast way, especially at full gallop [Mid-17thC. Origin uncertain: probably an imitation of the sound of galloping horses, with influence from TANTARA.]

tant mieux /taáN myő/ *interj.* so much the better [Mid-18thC. From French.]

tant pis /taáN peé/ *interj.* so much the worse [Late 18thC. From French.]

Tantra /tántrə, tún-/ *n.* the sacred books of Tantrism. They were written between the 7th and 17th centuries AD and mostly consist of a dialogue between Shiva and his wife Shakti. [Late 18thC. From Sanskrit, 'loom, warp, groundwork, system, doctrine'.]

Tantrism /tántrizəm, tún-/ *n.* a movement in Hinduism and Buddhism, especially a variety based on yoga and intended to release energy through sexual intercourse in which the orgasm is withheld or delayed —**Tantric** *adj.* —**Tantrist** *n.*

tantrum /tántrəm/ *n.* an outburst of anger, especially a childish display of rage or bad temper [Early 18thC. Origin unknown.]

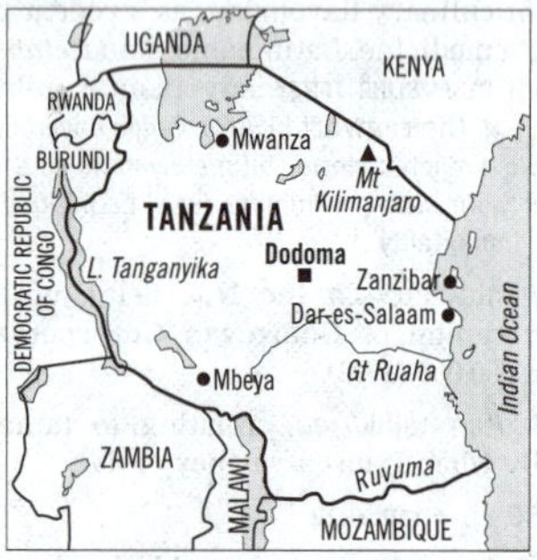

Tanzania

Tanzania /tánzə neé ə/ republic in southeastern Africa, including the islands of Zanzibar and Pemba. Language: Swahili, English. Currency: Tanzanian shilling. Capital: Dodoma. Population: 29,898,774 (1997). Area: 945,100 sq. km/364,900 sq. mi. Official name **United Republic of Tanzania** —**Tanzanian** /tánzə neé ən/ *n., adj.*

Tao /tow, dow/ *n.* **1. ULTIMATE REALITY** in Taoist philosophy, the ultimate reality in which all things are located or happen **2. Tao, tao UNIVERSAL ENERGY** the universal energy that makes and maintains everything that exists **3. RELATIONSHIP BETWEEN INDIVIDUAL AND UNIVERSE** the order and wisdom of individual life, and the way that this harmonizes with the universe as a whole [Mid-18thC. From Chinese *dào* 'way, path, right way (of life), reason'.]

Taoiseach /teéshək/ *n.* the prime minister of the Republic of Ireland [Mid-20thC. From Irish, literally 'chief, leader'.]

Taoism /tówizəm, dów-/ *n.* **1. PHILOSOPHY OF SIMPLICITY AND NONINTERFERENCE** a Chinese philosophy that advocates a simple life and a policy of noninterference with the natural course of things. It was founded in the 6th century BC by the mystic and philosopher Lao-tzu. **2. RELIGION BASED ON TAOISM** a popular Chinese religion that seeks harmony and long life through the philosophy of Taoism combined with pantheism and magical practices —**Taoist** *n., adj.* —**Taoistic** /tow ístik, dow-/ *adj.*

taonga /ta óngə/ *n. NZ* sth that should be cherished and is considered very valuable

Taormina /towr meénə/ winter resort town in Messina Province, eastern Sicily, situated about 45 km/28 mi. north of Catania. Population: 9,979 (1991).

Tao Te Ching /tów tə chíng, dów də jíng/ *n.* the most important Taoist text, a collection of 81 poems by the mystic and philosopher Lao-tzu, the founder of Taoism [Literally, 'the Book of the Way']

tap[1] /tap/ *v.* (**taps, tapping, tapped**) **1.** *vti.* **HIT STH LIGHTLY** to hit sth or sb lightly, especially more than once **2.** *vt.* **HIT OBJECT AGAINST STH ELSE** to hit an object lightly against sth else **3.** *vt.* **MAKE SOUND** to produce sth such as a noise or rhythm by tapping **4.** *vi.* **MOVE MAKING LIGHT SOUNDS** to move making a series of light noises **5.** *vt.* **REINFORCE SHOE** to attach a small piece of leather or metal to the toe or heel of a shoe to cover worn parts or to protect against wear **6.** *vi.* **TAP-DANCE** to tap-dance **7.** *vt. US* **GIVE POST TO SB** to select and appoint sb for a particular role or office (*usually passive*) ○ *'The coal industry was tapped to lead the way for reform'* (*US News & World Report*; December 1998) ■ *n.* **1. LIGHT BLOW** a light blow, especially one that produces a noise **2. SOUND OF BLOW** the sound made by a light blow **3. REINFORCEMENT FOR SHOE** a small piece of leather or metal attached to the toe or heel of a shoe to cover a worn part or to protect against wear **4. METAL PART ON TAP-DANCING SHOE** a metal tip attached to the toe or heel of a tap-dancing shoe so that it can produce a noise **5. TAP-DANCING** tap-dancing (*informal*) **6.** PHON **TOUCH OF TONGUE TO MOUTH TOP** the production of a speech sound made when any flexible speech organ hits any hard part of the mouth, such as when the tongue is brought into contact with the hard palate [12thC. Origin uncertain: perhaps an imitation of the sound, or via French *taper* 'tap, strike', from Gallo-Romance, Germanic, or Scandinavian.] —**tappable** *adj.* —**tapper** *n.*

tap[2] /tap/ *n.* **1. VALVE ON PIPE** a valve on a pipe that is operated by a handle and used to draw off or control the flow of liquid, especially from a water supply. US term **faucet 2. BARREL PLUG** a stopper in a cask or barrel, used to seal in the contents and also to allow liquid to be drawn off at a controlled rate **3. BEER FROM CASK** liquid, especially beer, that has been drawn from a tap in a cask or barrel and is regarded as having particular qualities because of this **4.** = **taproom 5.** TELECOM **LISTENING DEVICE** a device put into a telephone or other telecommunication equipment in order to secretly listen to or record other people's conversations **6.** SURG **SURGICAL FLUID EXTRACTION** a surgical procedure that involves drawing off a body fluid using a hollow needle or tube **7.** TECH **TOOL FOR MAKING INTERNAL SCREW THREADS** a tool used to make an internal screw thread. ◊ **die 8.** *US* ELEC = **tapping 9.** STOCK EXCH **SECURITY ON MARKET AT PREDETERMINED PRICE** a government security made available gradually on the stock market when its price reaches a predetermined level ■ *v.* (**taps, tapping, tapped**) **1.** *vt.* **ATTACH TAP** to attach a tap to sth in order to draw off or control the flow of liquid **2.** *vt.* **DRAW LIQUID FROM BARREL** to draw off liquid, e.g. wine or beer, from a barrel by means of a tap **3.** *vt.* SURG **DRAW FLUID FROM BODY** to surgically draw off fluid from a part of the body **4.** *vt.* FORESTRY **OBTAIN SAP** to cut into a tree in order to draw off sap or resin **5.** *vt.* ELEC ENG **GET INTO POWER SUPPLY** to connect to a power supply and divert energy from it, usually illegally **6.** *vt.* TELECOM **PLACE LISTENING DEVICE ON PHONE LINE** to fit a device into a telephone or other telecommunication equipment in order to secretly listen to or record other people's conversations **7.** *vt.* TELECOM **SECRETLY LISTEN TO PHONE CONVERSATIONS** to secretly listen to and record other people's conversations using a device fitted into a telephone or other telecommunication equipment **8.** *vti.* **PUT RESOURCE TO USE** to make use of a resource or supply of sth (*informal*) ○ *tapping into the reserves of goodwill that exist in the community* **9.** *vt.* **BORROW MONEY** to borrow a sum of money from sb (*informal*) ○ *She tapped me for 20 quid.* **10.** *vt.* TECH **MAKE INTERNAL SCREW THREAD** to cut an internal screw thread into sth [Old English *tæppa* (noun) and *tæppian* (verb), from prehistoric Germanic] —**tappable** *adj.* —**tapper** *n.* ◇ **on tap 1.** available for immediate use (*informal*) **2.** on draught (*informal*)

tapa /taápə/ *n.* **1. TREE BARK** the inner bark of the paper mulberry tree **2. FABRIC MADE FROM TAPA** a strong fabric made from the inner bark of the paper mulberry tree [Early 19thC. From Polynesian.]

tapas /táppəss/ *npl.* small savoury snacks that are often served as an appetizer along with alcoholic drinks, originally in Spain [Mid-20thC. Plural of Spanish *tapa* 'cover, lid'.]

tap dance *n.* a step dance performed by a dancer wearing shoes with metal tips at the toes and heels to make a rhythmic sound as they hit the floor

tap-dance *vi.* to perform a dance or dances wearing shoes with metal tips at the toes and heels to make a rhythmic sound —**tap-dancer** *n.* —**tap-dancing** *n.*

tape /tayp/ *n.* **1. LONG NARROW STRIP OF MATERIAL** a long narrow strip of material such as paper, fabric, or plastic used to secure or tie sth **2. STRIP OF STICKY MATERIAL** a long strip of plastic or cloth with adhesive on one or both sides, usually on a roll **3. MAGNETIC TAPE** magnetic tape used in cassettes and some computers **4.** = **tape recording 5. VIDEO OR AUDIO CASSETTE** a cassette used for audio or video recording or playback ○ *Put the tape in the player.* **6.** SPORTS **FINISHING LINE MARKER** a long strip of material that marks the finishing line in a race **7. TAPE MEASURE** a tape measure **8.** MIL **STRIPE** a stripe (*informal*) ■ *v.* (**tapes, taping, taped**) **1.** *vti.* **RECORD STH** to record sth, especially music or a television programme on magnetic tape **2.** *vt.* **FIX STH USING TAPE** to secure, fasten, or strengthen sth using tape **3.** *vt.* **MEASURE STH USING TAPE MEASURE** to measure sth using a tape measure [Old English *tæppe* 'narrow strip of cloth', of uncertain origin] ◇ **have sb** *or* **sth taped** to have a clear understanding of sb or sth (*informal*)

tape deck *n.* an electrical device that plays and records tapes, especially audio cassettes

tape grass *n.* a perennial grass that grows largely submerged in fresh water, forming tufts of long narrow leaves and bearing inconspicuous pinkish-white flowers. Latin name: *Vallisneria spiralis.*

tapeline /táyp līn/ *n.* = **tape measure**

tape machine *n.* STOCK EXCH an electronic machine that receives and displays or prints current stock quotations. US term **ticker**

tape measure *n.* a long roll or strip of fabric, plastic, paper, or thin metal that is marked off in inches or centimetres and used for measuring

tapenade /táppə naad/ *n.* a paste, originally from Provence in France, made from puréed black olives, capers, and anchovies [From French Provençal *tapeno* 'caper']

taper /táypər/ *vti.* (**-pers, -pering, -pered**) **1. GET OR MAKE NARROWER** to become or make sth narrower at one end, especially gradually **2. REDUCE GRADUALLY** to become or make sth smaller in size or amount, or less important, especially gradually ○ *Sales of the first album are beginning to taper off.* ■ *n.* **1. SLIM CANDLE** a slim candle that is narrower at the top than at the bottom **2. STRIP FOR TRANSFERRING FLAME** a strip of wood or waxed paper used for taking a flame to light sth else **3. NARROWING OF SHAPE** a gradual narrowing in the shape of sth ○ *a spire with a pronounced taper* **4. DIM LIGHT** a faint source of light, e.g. from a small candle [Pre-12thC. Originally 'candle' (hence 'get narrower'); alteration of Latin *papyrus* 'papyrus' (source of English *paper*), whose pith was used for candle wicks.] —**tapering** *adj.* —**taperingly** *adv.*

tape-record (**tape-records, tape-recording, tape-recorded**) *vt.* to record sth, especially sound, on a magnetic tape

tape recorder *n.* a machine that can record and play audio tapes, especially one with its own speaker

tape recording *n.* a recording made on magnetic tape, especially an audio recording

tapestried /táppistrid/ *adj.* **1. COVERED WITH TAPESTRY** covered with tapestry or tapestries **2. SHOWN IN TAPESTRY** depicted in tapestry (*archaic or literary*)

tapestry /táppistri/ (*plural* **-tries**) *n.* **1. FABRIC WITH WOVEN DESIGN** a heavy fabric with a woven pattern or picture, used as a wall hanging or for upholstery

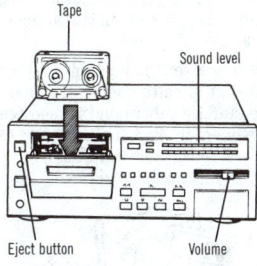

Tape recorder

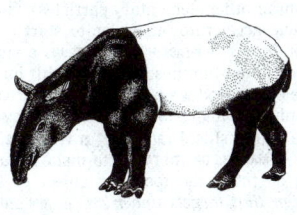

Tapir

2. = needlepoint 3. STH VARIED AND INTRICATE sth that is considered to be rich, varied, or intricately interwoven ○ *the rich tapestry of life* [14thC. Via French *tapisserie* from, ultimately, *tapis* 'carpet', ultimately from Greek *tapēt-*, of uncertain origin: probably from Iranian.]

—— WORD KEY: CULTURAL NOTE ——
The Bayeux Tapestry, a large embroidery found at Bayeux in northern France (1092). A remarkable work of art and an important historical document, it consists of a band of linen measuring 231 ft./70 m by 20 in./50 cm, embroidered with vivid scenes that depict the Norman conquest of England. Its existence was first recorded in 1476 at Bayeux, where it was used to decorate the nave of the cathedral.

tapestry moth *n.* a moth whose caterpillars eat fabrics made from wool and other natural fibres. The adults are brown with white-tipped forewings and prefer damp conditions. Latin name: *Trichophaga tapetzella*.

tapetum /tə peĕtəm/ (*plural* **-ta** /-tə/) *n.* **1.** BIOL LAYER OF CELLS a specialized membrane or layer of cells **2.** ANAT REFLECTIVE LAYER IN EYE a layer of cells in the wall of the eye that reflects light back onto the retina, enhancing visual sensitivity in dim light. It occurs in nocturnal and deep-sea animals. Light reflected by this layer is responsible for the shining eyes of cats seen when they are illuminated at night. [Early 18thC. Via late Latin from Latin *tapete*, and, ultimately, from Greek *tapēt-* (see TAPESTRY).] **—tapetal** *adj.*

tapeworm /táyp wurm/ *n.* a flatworm with a long ribbon-shaped segmented body that exists in many varieties and lives mainly as a parasite in the gut of vertebrate animals. Infestation is common among domestic animals, and humans can also become infested, especially by eating undercooked meat containing tapeworm larvae. Class: Cestoda. Technical name **cestode**

taphole /táp hōl/ *n.* a hole at the bottom of a furnace for drawing off molten metal or slag

taphonomy /tə fónnəmi/ *n.* the scientific study of fossilization [Mid-20thC. Formed from Greek *taphos* 'grave'.] **—taphonomic** /táffə nómmik/ *adj.* **—taphonomist** /tə fónnəmist/ *n.*

taphouse /táp howss/ (*plural* **-houses** /-hówziz/) *n.* an inn, bar, public house, or other place where alcohol is served (*archaic*)

tap-in *n.* **1. = tip-in** *n.* 1 **2.** EASY GOAL in soccer, a goal scored with minimum effort by a player who is very close to the opposition's goal **3.** SHORT PUTT in golf, a short putt to put the ball in the hole

tapioca /táppi ṓkə/ *n.* **1.** STARCH FROM CASSAVA PLANT a starch obtained from the roots of the cassava plant. It comes in the form of small hard beads and is used in making puddings and for thickening sauces. **2.** PUDDING a milk pudding made from tapioca [Mid-17thC. Via Portuguese or Spanish from Tupi *tipioca*, from *tipi* 'residue, dregs' + *ok* 'to squeeze out'.]

tapir /táypər/ (*plural* **-pirs** *or* **-pir**) *n.* a nocturnal hoofed forest-dwelling mammal of Central and South America and Southeast Asia. Tapirs have short limbs and a fleshy snout and feed on fruit and vegetation. They are related to rhinoceroses and horses. Family: Tapiridae. [Late 18thC. Ultimately from Tupi *tapira*.]

tapis /táppi/ (*plural* **-is** /táppi/) *n.* a heavy tapestry used as a wall covering, curtain, carpet, or tablecloth

(*archaic*) [15thC. Via French from, ultimately, Greek *tapēt-* (see TAPESTRY).] ◇ **on the tapis** currently being considered or discussed

tap-off *n.* **= tip-off²** *n.*

tappet /táppit/ *n.* a lever, arm, or other machine part that transfers motion from a cam to a part such as a valve or push rod [Mid-18thC. Formed from TAP¹.]

tapping /tápping/ *n.* ELEC a point in a circuit where a temporary connection may be made. US term **tap²** *n.* 8

taproom /táp room, -room/ *n. UK* a bar in a place such as a hotel or pub

taproot /táp root/ *n.* a prominent and often bulky root that extends downwards below the stem of some plants and has fine lateral roots. It often serves as a food storage organ, e.g. in the carrot. [Early 17thC. *Tap* from TAP².]

taps /taps/ *n.* (*takes a singular verb*) **1.** SIGNAL FOR LIGHTS OUT a bugle call or other signal given at the end of the day, especially in a military camp, as an order that lights should be put out **2.** SIGNAL AT FUNERAL a bugle call or other signal given at a funeral or memorial service, especially a military one **3.** GUIDE SONG a song sung by members of the Guide movement at the close of a meeting or around a campfire at the end of the day [Early 19thC. Origin uncertain: either formed from TAP¹ or an alteration of *taptoo*, variant of TATTOO.]

tapsalteerie /tápss'l teĕri/ *adj., adv. Scotland* in a confused state or manner (*informal*) [Early 16thC. Scottish alteration of TOPSY-TURVY.]

tapster /tápstər/ *n.* sb who serves drinks in a bar or pub (*archaic*) [Old English *tæpestre*, originally feminine of *tapper*, from TAP².]

tapstress /tápstrəss/ *n.* a woman who serves drinks in a bar or pub (*archaic*)

tapu /taă poo/ *adj. NZ* taboo [Mid-19thC. Variant of TABOO.]

tap water *n.* water that comes out of the tap, from a domestic or commercial water supply, as opposed to water from some other source, e.g. mineral water or rainwater

tar¹ /taar/ *n.* **1.** THICK BLACK LIQUID a thick black liquid obtained through the destructive distillation of an organic substance such as wood or coal **2.** RESIDUE FROM TOBACCO SMOKE the residue from tobacco smoke ■ *vt.* (**tars, tarring, tarred**) COVER WITH TAR to coat or cover sth, especially a road surface, with tar [Old English *teoru*. Ultimately from an Indo-European word that is also the ancestor of English *tree*. The original application was probably to trees' tarry resins.]

tar² /taar/ *n.* a sailor (*archaic informal*) [Late 17thC. Origin uncertain: perhaps from TAR¹, or a shortening of TARPAULIN, used to refer to sailors in the mid-17thC.]

Tara, Hill of /taărə/ hill in County Meath, northwest of Dublin, Ireland, which was the seat of the Irish kings until about AD 560. Height: 155 m/507 ft.

taradiddle *n.* **= tarradiddle**

Tarahumara /taărə hoo maărə/ (*plural* **-ra** *or* **-ras**) *n.* **1.** PEOPLES MEMBER OF NATIVE N AMERICAN PEOPLE a member of a Native North American people who live in northern Mexico **2.** LANG TARAHUMARA LANGUAGE the Uto-Aztecan language of the Tarahumara people [Late 19thC. From Spanish, with ultimate origin unknown.]

tarakihi /taárra kee hee/, **terakihi** /térrə-/ *n.* a fish found in New Zealand waters that has a silvery body and

a black saddle behind the head. It is an important food fish in New Zealand. Latin name: *Nemadactylus macropterus*. [From Maori]

taramasalata /tárrəməssə laátə/ *n.* a light creamy pink or beige paste of Greek origin, made from smoked fish roe, olive oil, lemon juice, and garlic. It is usually served in the form of a pâté or dip as an appetizer or snack. [Early 20thC. From modern Greek, from *taramas* 'preserved roe' (from Turkish *tarama* 'preparation of soft roe or red caviar') + *salata* 'salad'.]

Taranaki /tárrə naáki/ administrative region of New Zealand, located in the southwestern part of the North Island and including the city of New Plymouth. Population: 106,570 (1996). Area: 12,640 sq. km/4,880 sq. mi.

Taranaki, Mount dormant volcano near the western coast of the North Island, New Zealand. Height: 2,518 m/8,260 ft.

tarantass /taáran táss/ *n.* a large Russian horse-drawn carriage with four wheels and no springs [Mid-19thC. From Russian *tarantas*.]

tarantella /tárrən téllə/ *n.* **1.** ITALIAN RURAL DANCE a fast whirling dance from southern Italy in 6/8 time **2.** MUSIC FOR TARANTELLA music in 6/8 time that is suitable for a tarantella [Late 18thC. From Italian, from *Taranto*, a town in southern Italy (source of English *tarantism* and *tarantula*).]

Quentin Tarantino

Tarantino /tárrən teĕnō/, **Quentin** (*b.* 1963) US film director and screenwriter. His first film, *Reservoir Dogs* (1992), was followed by *Pulp Fiction* (1994), establishing him as an important but controversial film-maker. He has often been accused of glamorizing violence.

tarantism /tárrəntizəm/ *n.* a nervous condition characterized by uncontrollable body movements, common during the 15th to 17th centuries in southern Italy and believed to be caused by the bite of the tarantula [Mid-17thC. From Italian *tarantismo*, from *Taranto* (see TARANTELLA).]

Taranto /ta rántō/ city, port, and administrative centre of Taranto Province, Apulia Region, southern Italy. Population: 230,207 (1992).

Tarantula

tarantula /tə rántyoŏlə/ (*plural* **-las** *or* **-lae** /-lee/) *n.* **1.** LARGE HAIRY AMERICAN SPIDER a large tropical or subtropical American spider that has a hairy body and legs. Tarantulas are typically nocturnal and feed on invertebrates, toads, small reptiles, and young birds. Some can inflict a painful bite if handled. Family: Theraphosidae. **2.** WOLF SPIDER a European wolf spider formerly believed to cause tarantism with its bite. Latin name: *Lycosa tarantula*. [Mid-

16thC. Via medieval Latin from Italian *tarantola*, from *Taranto* (see TARANTELLA), near where such spiders are found.]

Tararua Range /tárrə rōō ə-/ mountain range in the southern part of the North Island, New Zealand, north of Wellington. Its highest point is Mitre Peak, 1,571 m/5,154 ft.

taraxacum /tə ráksəkəm/ *n.* **1. PLANT SUCH AS THE DANDELION** a plant such as the dandelion that produces flower heads made up of numerous florets and with seeds attached to whitish hairs. Genus: *Taraxacum.* **2. PREPARATION OF DANDELION ROOTS OR LEAVES** a herbal remedy extracted from dandelion roots or leaves, used as a mild laxative, liver tonic, and diuretic [Early 18thC. Via medieval Latin *altaraxacon* from Arabic and Persian *ṭarakšakūn* 'dandelion, wild endive', ultimately from Persian *talḵ* 'bitter' + *čakūk* 'purslane'.]

tarboosh /taar bōōsh/, **tarbush, tarbouche** *n.* a brimless usually red felt hat, similar to a fez, that has a silk tassel and is worn by Muslim men by itself or with a turban [Early 18thC. Via Egyptian Arabic *ṭarbūš* from Ottoman Turkish *terpōš* and Turkish *tarbuş*, from Persian *sarpūš*, from *sar* 'head' + *pūš* 'cover'.]

tardigrade /taárdi grayd/ *n.* **TINY WATER CREATURE** a tiny aquatic invertebrate animal with a short body and four pairs of stubby legs. Phylum: Tardigrada. ■ *adj.* **1. RELATING TO TARDIGRADES** relating or belonging to the tardigrades **2. SLUGGISH** sluggish or slow-moving [Early 17thC. Directly or via French from Latin *tardigradus*, literally 'walking slowly', from *tardus* 'slow' (source of English *tardy*).]

tardive dyskinesia /taárdiv dískí neé zi ə/ *n.* a condition marked by involuntary movements of the tongue and facial muscles, especially after prolonged treatment with phenothiazine tranquillizers and similar drugs [*Tardive* from French *tardif* (see TARDY)]

tardy /taárdi/ (**-dier, -diest**) *adj.* **1. LATE** later than the expected or usual time **2. SLUGGISH** slow to move or react (*archaic or literary*) [Mid-16thC. Alteration of *tardyve*, from French *tardif*, from, ultimately, Latin *tardus* 'slow, sluggish' (source of English *bustard*).] —**tardily** *adv.* —**tardiness** *n.*

tare[1] /tair/ *n.* **1. VETCH PLANT** a trailing or scrambling vetch plant of Europe and North Africa that has compound leaves with paired leaflets and tendrils, and spikes of bluish or purplish flowers. Genus: *Vicia.* **2. VETCH SEED** the seed of a vetch or tare **3. PROBLEMATIC WEED** in the Bible, a weed found growing among crops, usually considered to be the darnel [13thC. Origin uncertain.]

tare[2] /tair/ *n.* **1. WEIGHT OF PACKAGING** the weight of a container or packaging used to wrap goods **2. ALLOWANCE FOR WEIGHT OF PACKAGING** an allowance for the packaging around goods, deducted from the total weight and not included in transportation costs **3. VEHICLE'S UNLADEN WEIGHT** the weight of a motor vehicle without fuel, cargo, passengers, or equipment **4. CONTAINER OF KNOWN WEIGHT** a container of known weight that is used as a counterbalance when calculating the net weight of a cargo ■ *vt.* (**tares, taring, tared**) **WEIGH PACKAGING** to weigh packaging in order to calculate the amount of tare to be deducted from a particular cargo [15thC. Via French *tāre* 'waste in goods, deficiency' from, ultimately, Arabic *ṭarḥ* 'that which is deducted', from *ṭaraḥa* 'to reject, subtract'.]

Taree /ta reé/ town in eastern New South Wales, Australia, a commercial and manufacturing centre. Population: 16,702 (1996).

targe /taarj/ *n.* a round shield, especially used by Scottish Highlanders (*archaic*) [Pre-12thC. Origin uncertain: probably from Old Norse *targa* 'shield'; later reinforced by Old French *targe* 'light shield'.]

target /taárgit/ *n.* **1. OBJECT AIMED AT IN SHOOTING** a round object or surface marked with concentric circles that is aimed at in archery, rifle shooting, and similar sports **2. STH AIMED AT** an area, surface, object, or person aimed at ○ *The bird's bright plumage makes it an easy target.* **3. GOAL** a goal or objective towards which effort is directed ○ *Our target is to raise £20,000 for cancer research.* **4. SB OR STH ON RECEIVING END** sb or sth that is the focus or object of the behaviour or actions of others ○ *the target of her anger* **5.** CIV ENG **MARKER FOR TAKING LEVELS** a sliding weight on a surveyor's levelling rod that is used to help determine proper levels **6.** PHYS **STH HIT BY PARTICLE ACCELERATOR BEAM** a substance that is hit by a beam of electrons or other elementary particles or ions from a particle accelerator in order to start a nuclear reaction **7.** PHYS **SURFACE HIT BY ELECTRONS** a surface or electrode, often luminescent, that is hit by an electron beam to produce an output signal, e.g. in an X-ray tube or a television camera tube **8. SMALL SHIELD** a small round shield (*archaic*) ■ *vt.* (**-gets, -geting, -geted**) **1. MAKE SB OR STH TARGET** to make a particular person or thing the focus or object of sth ○ *A campaign that targets under-35s.* **2. AIM STH** to aim sth at or direct sth towards a particular person, group, or thing ○ *The missiles were targeted on the enemy capital.* [13thC. Formed from TARGE, and originally meaning 'small targe'.]

targetcast /taárgit kaast/ (**-casts, -casting, -cast** *or* **-casted**) *vi.* to advertize a website to a particular group of people who are known to be potentially interested in its contents, rather than to everyone on the Internet [Late 20thC. Blend of TARGET + BROADCAST.]

target date *n.* a date by which it is expected that sth such as a project or piece of work will be completed

target language *n.* **1. TRANSLATION LANGUAGE** the language into which a particular text is to be translated **2. LANGUAGE BEING LEARNED** a foreign language that is being learned **3.** COMPUT **LANGUAGE INTO WHICH SOURCE CODE COMPILED** the computer language into which a source code is to be compiled

target man *n.* a soccer forward whose role is to receive high passes and crosses, especially in front of the goal

Targum /taárgəm/ *n.* a translation of part of the Bible in Aramaic [Late 16thC. Via Hebrew from Aramaic *targūm* 'interpretation', from *targēm* 'to interpret'.] —**Targumic** /taar gōōmik/ *adj.* —**Targumist** /taárgəmist/ *n.*

tariff /tárrif/ *n.* **1. DUTY LEVIED ON GOODS** a duty or duties levied by a government on imported or sometimes exported goods **2. LIST OF TARIFFS** a list or system of tariffs **3. LIST OF COSTS** a list of fees, fares, or other prices charged by a business **4. PRICED MENU** a list of the available dishes at a restaurant together with their prices **5. SYSTEM OF CHARGING FOR UTILITIES** a system of charging for utility services such as gas and electricity, or a list of such charges ■ *vt.* (**-iffs, -iffing, -iffed**) **SET COST** to fix a specified tariff or price on sth [Late 16thC. Via Italian *tariffa* from Arabic *ta'rīf* 'notification, inventory of fees to be paid', from *'arrafa* 'to notify'.]

tariff office *n.* an insurance company that charges premiums according to a schedule established by a group of companies

Tarkington /taárkingtən/, **Booth** (1869–1946) US writer. His novels include the Pulitzer Prize-winning *The Magnificent Ambersons* (1918). Full name **Newton Booth Tarkington**

Tarkovsky /taar kófski/, **Andrey** (1932–86) Russian film director. He is noted for his highly personal and symbolic films such as *Ivan's Childhood* (1962).

tarlatan /taárlətən/ *n.* an open-weave transparent highly starched cotton muslin, used for stiffening collars and other parts of clothes [Early 18thC. From French *tarlatane*, an alteration of *tarnatane*, of uncertain origin: probably of Indian origin.]

Tarmac /taár mak/ *tdmk.* a trademark for a material used for surfacing roads

tarn /taarn/ *n.* a small mountain lake, especially one formed by the action of glaciers [14thC. From Scandinavian.]

tarnation /taar náysh'n/ *interj.* *US* used to express anger and annoyance (*regional*) [Late 18thC. Alteration of *darnation* (formed from DARN) or DAMNATION.]

tarnish /taárnish/ *vti.* (**-nishes, -nishing, -nished**) **1. BECOME DULL AND DISCOLOURED** to lose or make sth lose its shine and become dull because of oxidation or rust **2. DAMAGE SB'S REPUTATION** to damage sb's reputation or good name, or to become damaged ■ *n.* **1. DISCOLORATION** the dullness or discoloration of metal affected by oxidation or rust **2. FILM OF DISCOLORATION ON METAL** the film of discoloration that forms on metal **3. SULLIED CONDITION** the damaged condition of sb's reputation or good name [15thC. From French *terniss-*, stem of *ternir* 'make dull', of uncertain origin: probably formed from *terne* 'dull, dark', ultimately from Frankish.] —**tarnishable** *adj.*

taro /taárō/ (*plural* **-ros**) *n.* a perennial plant of Southeast Asia that is cultivated in tropical regions for its edible starchy tubers and is also widely grown as an ornamental plant. Latin name: *Colocasia esculenta.* [Mid-18thC. From Polynesian.]

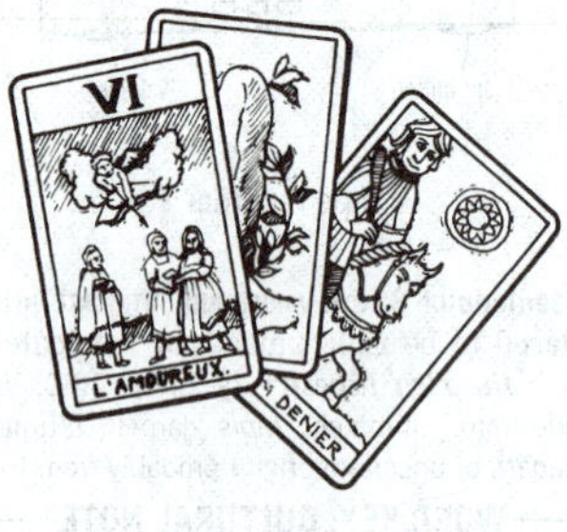

Tarot

tarot /tárrō/ *n.* **1. FORTUNE-TELLING WITH CARDS** a system of fortune-telling using a special pack of 78 cards that consists of 4 suits of 14 cards together with 22 picture cards **2. tarot, tarot card CARD USED FOR FORTUNE-TELLING** any of the cards used in tarot [Late 19thC. From French, from Italian *tarocchi*, plural of *tarocco*, of unknown origin.]

tarp /taarp/ *n.* a tarpaulin (*informal*) [Early 20thC. Shortening.]

tarpan /taár pan/ *n.* a small grey-brown horse with a short thick neck, erect mane, and a stripe along the back. It lived wild in southern Russia and Poland until the mid-19th century. Animals similar to the tarpan have been bred from related horses such as Przewalski's horse and reintroduced to parts of their ancestral habitat. [Mid-19thC. From Turkic.]

tarpaper /taár paypər/ *n.* a heavy paper coated with tar and used in building for waterproofing

tarpaulin /taar páwlin/ *n.* **1. WATERPROOF MATERIAL** a heavy waterproof material, especially treated canvas, used as a covering and to protect things from moisture **2. SHEET OF TARPAULIN** a sheet of tarpaulin [Early 17thC. Origin uncertain: probably from TAR[1] + PALL[2] + -ING[2], from the fact that the canvas is sometimes made waterproof with a coating of tar.]

Tarpeian Rock /taar peé ən-/ *n.* a rock on the Capitoline Hill in ancient Rome, from which traitors were hurled to their deaths [Early 17thC. Named after *Tarpeia*, legendary daughter of the commander of the citadel, which she betrayed to the Sabines; she was reputedly buried at the foot of the rock.]

tar pit *n.* an area where tar or asphalt naturally accumulates, trapping animals and preserving their bones

tarpon /taárpən/ (*plural* **-pon** *or* **-pons**) *n.* a tropical or subtropical marine fish with a streamlined body and thick silvery scales. Genus: *Megalops.* [Late 17thC. Origin uncertain: probably from Dutch *tarpoen*, perhaps ultimately from a Central American language.]

Tarquinius Superbus /taar kwínni əss soo púrbəss/, **Lucius** (*fl.* 6th century BC) King of Rome. According to tradition, he was the last of the Etruscan kings of Rome (534–510 BC), and was dethroned after his son raped Lucretia, a Roman matron.

tarradiddle /tárrədid'l/, **taradiddle** *n.* (*informal*) **1. IDLE TALK** nonsense or idle talk **2. LIE** a small lie [Late 18thC. Origin uncertain: probably thought to suggest unintelligible speech; the second part is perhaps from DIDDLE[1].]

tarragon /tárrəgən/ *n.* an aromatic perennial herb native to temperate Asia that is widely cultivated for its leaves, that are used in cooking. It bears clusters of small greenish-white flowerheads. Latin name: *Artemisia dracunculus.* [Mid-16thC. From medieval Latin *tragonia* and *tarchon*, of uncertain origin: perhaps via Arabic *ṭarḵūn* from, ultimately, Greek *drakont-* 'dragon', associated with *drakontion* 'dragonwort'.]

Tarragona /tárrə gṓnə/ city, port, and administrative centre of Tarragona Province, northeastern Spain.

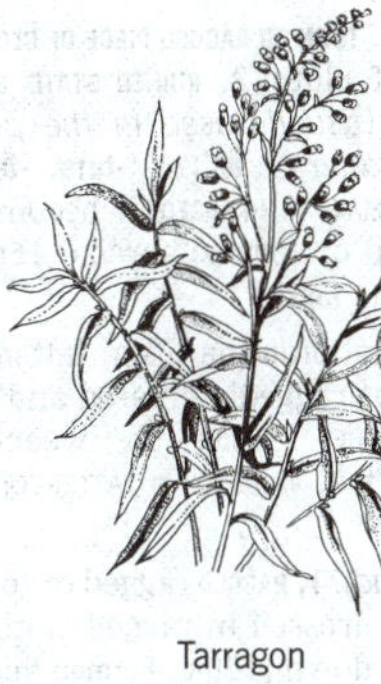
Tarragon

It has extensive Roman remains. Population: 114,931 (1995).

tarriance /tárri ənss/ *n.* a short stay or visit (*archaic*)

tarry[1] /tárri/ *vi.* (**-ries, -rying, -ried**) 1. **REMAIN** to stay temporarily at a place 2. **LINGER** to delay a departure or arrival, especially in an idle way 3. **WAIT** to wait ■ *n.* (*plural* **-ries**) **SHORT STAY** a short stay or visit (*archaic or literary*) [13thC. Origin unknown.] —**tarrier** *n.*

tarry[2] /taári/ (**-rier, -riest**) *adj.* similar to or covered with tar [Mid-16thC] —**tarriness** *n.*

tarsier /taársi ər/ *n.* a small tree-living nocturnal animal that has large eyes and delicate grasping fingers and toes ending in pads. It is found in the Philippines, Indonesia, and neighbouring islands. It is able to swivel its head around almost 360 degrees. Genus: *Tarsius.* [Late 18thC. From French, from *tarse* 'tarsus'; from the animal's long tarsal bones.]

tarsometatarsus /taár sō méttə taársəss/ (*plural* **-si** /-taár sī/) *n.* the bone in the lower leg of birds that connects to the toes [Mid-19thC. Formed from TARSUS + METATARSUS.]

tarsus /taársəss/ (*plural* **-si** /-sī/) *n.* 1. **ANKLE BONES** the group of bones that forms the ankle joint in vertebrates, located between the inner bone of the lower leg (**tibia**) and the main skeleton of the foot (**metatarsus**) 2. **PART OF EYELID** the small section of connective tissue along the edge of the eyelid 3. = **tarsometatarsus** 4. **PART OF ARTHROPOD LEG** the part of the leg of an arthropod that is furthest from the tibia [Late 17thC. Via modern Latin from Greek *tarsos* 'eyelid, flat part of the foot'.]

Tarsus /taársəss/ city in southern Turkey, near the Mediterranean Sea. During Roman rule in the 1st century BC it was one of the most prominent cities of Asia Minor. Population: 146,502 (1985).

tart[1] /taart/ *adj.* 1. **SHARP-TASTING** with a sharp and sour but usually pleasant flavour 2. **SHARPLY CRITICAL** sharp, cutting, or critical [14thC. From Old English *teart* 'painful, severe', of uncertain origin: perhaps literally 'tearing'.] —**tartness** *n.*

tart up *vt.* (*informal*) 1. **TRY TO IMPROVE PLACE'S APPEARANCE** to change the decor of a place in a not very successful attempt to improve its appearance 2. **TRY TO IMPROVE APPEARANCE** to use make-up, accessories, or different clothing in order to try to improve your appearance

tart[2] /taart/ *n.* a pie that has no top crust and is usually filled with sth sweet such as fruit or custard [14thC. From Old French *tarte*, of uncertain origin: perhaps ultimately from late Latin *torta* 'round loaf of bread'.]

tart[3] /taart/ *n.* an offensive term referring to a woman thought to be a prostitute or to behave like one (*slang insult*) [Mid-19thC. Origin uncertain: probably a shortening of SWEETHEART. Originally a term of endearment for a girl or woman.]

tartan[1] /taárt'n/ *n.* 1. **WOOL FABRIC** a Scottish wool or worsted fabric woven in a wide range of checked or plaid patterns, many of which are associated with particular Scottish clans. The association between clans and tartan has no historical basis and arose in the 19th century. 2. **PATTERN OF TARTAN** a particular pattern of tartan, officially registered and associated with a particular clan, regiment, or other organization 3. **FABRIC WITH TARTAN DESIGN** fabric, especially wool fabric, with a tartan design 4. **TARTAN GARMENT** a piece of clothing made of tartan 5. *Scotland* **TRADITIONAL HIGHLAND DRESS** the traditional dress of the Scottish Highlands ○ *wearing the tartan with pride* ■ *adj.* **SCOTTISH** relating to Scotland (*informal*) [15thC. Origin uncertain: perhaps from French *tiretaine* 'linen and wool fabric', from *tiret*, a kind of cloth, ultimately from medieval Latin *tyrius* 'cloth from Tyre', named after *Tyre*, Phoenician capital.]

tartan[2] /taárt'n/ *n.* a Mediterranean sailing ship with a single mast and a lateen sail [Early 17thC. Via French *tartane* from, ultimately, Old Provençal *tartana* 'buzzard', thought to imitate the sound of a buzzard.]

tartar /taártər/ *n.* 1. DENT **HARD DEPOSIT ON TEETH** a hard deposit consisting mostly of organic material that forms on the teeth at the gum line. Failure to remove it regularly contributes to dental decay. 2. BEVERAGES **SUBSTANCE DEPOSITED IN WINE CASKS** a substance found on the inner surface of wine casks and consisting mostly of potassium bitartrate. It is deposited during the fermentation process. [14thC. Via medieval Latin *tartarum* from medieval Greek *tartaron*, of unknown origin.]

Tartar /taártər/ *n.* 1. PEOPLES, LANG = **Tatar** 2. **tartar, Tartar FEARSOME PERSON** a fearsome or ferocious person (*offensive in some contexts*) [14thC. Directly or via French from medieval Latin *Tartarus* (influenced by TARTARUS in Latin), an alteration of a Turkish word.] —**Tartarian** /taar táiri ən/ *adj.* —**Tartaric** /taar tárrik/ *adj.*

tartare sauce, tartar sauce *n.* mayonnaise mixed with capers, chopped pickles, olives, onion, and herbs, often served as an accompaniment to fish [*Tartare* from French (see TARTAR)]

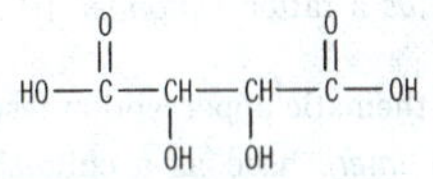
Tartaric acid

tartaric acid /taar tárrik-/ *n.* a white crystalline organic acid obtained from tartar in wine vats and used in the food industry. Formula: $(CHOH)_2(COOH)_2$.

tartarous /taártərəss/ *adj.* containing or resembling tartar

tartar steak *n.* = **steak tartare**

Tartarus /taártərəss/ *n.* MYTHOL 1. **LOWEST PART OF UNDERWORLD** in Greek mythology, the lowest part of the underworld where the worst evildoers were imprisoned 2. **THE UNDERWORLD** in Greek mythology, Hades or the underworld in general [Mid-16thC. Via Latin from Greek *Tartaros.*]

tartlet /taártlət/ *n.* a miniature tart, usually intended to serve one person [15thC. From French *tartelette*, a diminutive of *tarte* (see TART).]

tartly /taártli/ *adv.* in a tone of voice or with words conveying strong but tight-lipped disapproval or annoyance

tartrate /taár trayt/ *n.* a salt or ester of tartaric acid [Late 18thC. From French, from *tartre* (see TARTAR).]

tartrated /taár traytid/ *adj.* in the form of a tartrate

tartrazine /taártrə zeen/ *n.* a dye widely used in processed foods to give a yellow colour [Late 19thC. Coined from French *tartrate* 'tartrate' + AZO- + -INE.]

Tartu /taártoo/ city in eastern Estonia, on the River Emajogi. Population: 101,901 (1997).

Tartuffe /taar toóf, -tyóof/, **Tartufe** *n.* sb who hypocritically affects religious piety —**Tartuffian** *adj.*

tarty /taárti/ (**-ier, -iest**) *adj.* an offensive term that deliberately insults a woman's appearance (*slang insult*) [Old English]

Tarzan /taárz'n/ *n.* a man who is very strong and looks rugged and muscular (*informal*)

TAS *abbr.* true airspeed

Tas. *abbr.* Tasmania

tash /tash/ *n.* a moustache (*informal*)

Tashkent /tásh ként/ capital city of Uzbekistan, situated in the eastern part of the country. Population: 2,100,000 (1994).

task /taask/ *n.* 1. **JOB ASSIGNED** a particular piece of work that is assigned, especially one that is unpleasant or difficult 2. **DIFFICULT JOB** an unpleasant or difficult job or mission 3. **ANY JOB TO BE DONE** a piece of work or assignment, especially one that is important ■ *vt.* (**tasks, tasking, tasked**) 1. **BURDEN SB** to burden sb excessively with work or duties 2. **ASSIGN WORK** to assign a task to sb [13thC. Via Old North French *tasque* 'duty, tax', from medieval Latin *tasca*, from, ultimately, Latin *taxare* 'to censure, assess' (see TAX).] ◇ **take sb to task** to scold or criticize sb

tasker /taáskər/ *n.* 1. **PERSON WHO DOES PIECE-WORK** a person who is paid for work according to the amount of work done 2. **PERSON SETTING TASKS** a person who sets tasks for others to carry out [15thC]

task force *n.* 1. **TEMPORARY GROUP FOR PERFORMING TASK** a group of people and resources temporarily brought together for a particular purpose 2. MIL **TEMPORARY MILITARY GROUP** a formation of military units put together on a temporary basis to accomplish a particular mission

taskmaster /taásk maastər/ *n.* 1. **PERSON WHO SUPERVISES WORK DEMANDINGLY** a person who assigns and supervises work, especially in a demanding way 2. **A DEMANDING RESPONSIBILITY** a responsibility or discipline that is very demanding or requires a lot of hard work

taskwork /taásk wurk/ *n.* unpleasant, hard, or difficult work

Tasman /tázmən/ administrative region of New Zealand, occupying the northwestern corner of the South Island. Population: 40,036 (1996). Area: 14,538 sq. km/5,613 sq. mi.

Tasman, Mount the second highest mountain in New Zealand, located in the Southern Alps in the South Island. Height: 3,498 m/11,476 ft.

Tasman /tázmən/, **Abel Janszoon** (1603?–59) Dutch navigator. Between 1632 and 1655, he made several expeditions to the Indian and Pacific Oceans, reaching Australia and New Zealand (1642–45). Tasmania is named after him.

Tasman Bay bay on the northern coast of the South Island, New Zealand. It extends from Separation Point in the west to Cape Stephens in the east.

Tasman Glacier the largest glacier in New Zealand, situated on the eastern side of the Southern Alps in the South Island. Length: 29 km/18 mi.

Tasmania /taz máyni ə/ 1. island in the Tasman Sea, separated from the southeastern coast of Australia by the Bass Strait. Area: 68,331 sq. km/26,383 sq. mi. 2. state of southeastern Australia, occupying the island of Tasmania. First settled by the British in 1803, it became a separate colony in 1825. Capital: Hobart. Population: 475,000 (1996). Former name **Van Diemen's Land** —**Tasmanian** *n., adj.*

Tasmanian blue gum /taz máyni ən-/ *n.* a large Australian eucalyptus tree, originally native to Tasmania and Victoria, that has a stout trunk and small yellow flowers. It is the floral emblem of Tasmania. Latin name: *Eucalyptus globulus.*

Tasmanian devil *n.* a burrowing carnivorous marsupial characterized by a black coat with white markings and large powerful jaws, once ranging all over Australia but now confined to remote regions of Tasmania. Latin name: *Sarcophilus harrisii.*

Tasmanian tiger *n.* = **thylacine**

Tasmanian wolf *n.* = **thylacine**

Tasman Peninsula peninsula in southeastern Tasmania, Australia. Area: 520 sq. km/200 sq. mi.

Tasman Sea region of the South Pacific Ocean lying between Australia and New Zealand

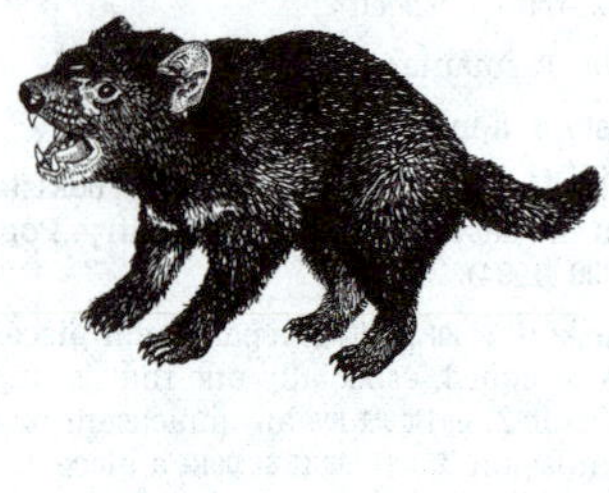

Tasmanian devil

tass /tass/ *n. Scotland or N England* = **tassie** (*literary*)

tasse /tass/ *n.* any of the overlapping metal plates attached to and hanging below an armoured breastplate in a suit of armour to protect the lower part of the trunk and the thighs [Mid-16thC. Origin uncertain: perhaps from Old French, 'purse', via Middle High German *tasche* 'pouch, pocket' from, ultimately, medieval Latin *tasca* 'assessment'.]

tassel /táss'l/ *n.* **1.** DECORATION MADE OF BUNCHED LOOSE THREADS a bunch of loose parallel threads that are tied together at one end and used as a decoration, e.g. on curtains, cushions, or clothes **2.** AGRIC TUFT AT END OF MAIZE sth resembling a tassel, especially the tuft of male flowers at the top of the main stem of a maize plant ■ *v.* (**-sels, -selling, -selled**) **1.** *vt.* DECORATE STH WITH TASSELS to decorate or fringe sth with tassels **2.** *vi.* AGRIC PRODUCE A TUFT ON MAIZE to produce a tuft of stamens at the end of a flower cluster, especially as seen on an ear of maize **3.** *vt.* AGRIC REMOVE TASSEL FROM MAIZE to remove the tassel from an ear of maize [14thC. From Old French 'clasp', of uncertain origin: perhaps from, ultimately, Latin *talus* 'knuckle-bone'.] —**tasselly** *adj.*

tasset /tássit/ *n.* = **tasse** [Mid-19thC. From French *tassette*, from *tasse* 'pouch', of uncertain origin: perhaps ultimately from Latin *tasca* (see TASK).]

tassie /tássi/, **tass** *n. Scotland or N England* a small cup, glass, or goblet (*literary*) [Early 18thC. Formed from TASS, which came via French *tasse* from Arabic *ṭās* 'cup', from Persian *tašt* 'bowl'.]

Tassie /tázzi/, **Tassy** (*plural* **-sies**) *n. Aus* (*informal*) **1.** TASMANIA Tasmania **2.** TASMANIAN PERSON a person who lives in or is from Tasmania

taste /tayst/ *n.* **1.** PHYSIOL SENSE THAT IDENTIFIES FLAVOURS the sense that perceives the particular qualities of sth such as a food by means of the sensory organs in the tongue (**taste buds**) **2.** PHYSIOL SENSATION STIMULATED IN TASTE BUDS the sensation stimulated in the taste buds when food, drink, or other substances are in contact with them. Sweetness, saltiness, bitterness, and sourness are considered the four basic taste sensations, and all flavours combine these in various ways with the sense of smell. **3.** ACT OF TASTING an act of tasting sth **4.** SMALL QUANTITY TASTED a very small quantity of sth eaten, drunk, or tasted ○ *Can I have a taste of that?* **5.** FIRST EXPERIENCE a brief sample, preview, or first experience of sth ○ *a taste of freedom* **6.** LIKING FOR STH a tendency to like or enjoy a particular thing or type of thing ○ *She has a taste for modern art.* **7.** QUALITY the distinctive quality of sth **8.** ABILITY TO JUDGE AESTHETICALLY the faculty of making discerning judgments in aesthetic matters ○ *He has good taste.* **9.** SENSE OF THE SOCIALLY ACCEPTABLE a sense of what is proper or acceptable socially ○ *The remark was in bad taste.* ■ *v.* (**tastes, tasting, tasted**) **1.** *vt.* PHYSIOL DISCERN FLAVOUR to discern the flavour of a substance by means of the taste buds **2.** *vt.* HAVE PARTICULAR FLAVOUR to have a particular flavour ○ *This tastes horrible.* **3.** *vt.* TEST STH FOR FLAVOUR to put a small amount of food or drink into the mouth in order to try it or to test its flavour ○ *Taste this for salt.* **4.** *vti.* EXPERIENCE STH to experience sth, especially for the first time or only briefly ○ *He had tasted success.* **5.** *vt.* ENJOY STH to enjoy sth very much (*archaic*) [13thC. From Old French *taster* 'to touch', of uncertain origin: possibly from, ultimately, Latin *tangere* (see TAX). Originally also in the meaning of 'touch'.] —**tastable** *adj.* ◇ **a taste of your own medicine** unpleasant treatment

taste bud *n.* a sensory receptor on the surface of the tongue or in the mouth that sends signals to the brain when stimulated by certain chemicals, producing the sense of taste. Taste buds are classified according to the type of substance they respond to: sweet, salty, bitter, or sour.

tasteful /táystf'l/ *adj.* **1.** SHOWING GOOD TASTE having or exhibiting good aesthetic taste **2.** NICE TASTING having a pleasant flavour —**tastefully** *adv.* —**tastefulness** *n.*

tasteless /táystləss/ *adj.* **1.** WITHOUT FLAVOUR having little or no flavour **2.** SHOWING LACK OF GOOD TASTE showing a lack of taste or judgment in aesthetic or social matters —**tastelessly** *adv.* —**tastelessness** *n.*

tastemaker /táyst maykər/ *n. US* sb who is influential in deciding what is tasteful, stylish, or worthwhile, e.g. in fashion or the arts

taster /táystər/ *n.* **1.** JUDGE OF FOOD OR DRINK QUALITY a specialist who tastes food or drink to judge its quality **2.** SHORT PREVIEW a sample or short preview of sth **3.** FOOD FREE SAMPLE OF FOOD a small quantity of food or drink given free as a sample **4.** DEVICE USED FOR TASTING a device or container used for tasting, e.g. a small cup for tasting wine **5.** PERSON TESTING FOR POISON sb engaged, especially in the past, to test an important person's food or drink by sampling it first in case it contains poison

tasty /táysti/ (**-ier, -iest**) *adj.* **1.** HAVING PLEASANT FLAVOUR having a pleasant flavour **2.** ATTRACTIVE attractive or interesting (*informal*) —**tastily** *adv.* —**tastiness** *n.*

tat[1] /tat/ *n.* **1.** THINGS IN POOR CONDITION articles in very poor condition (*informal*) **2.** TASTELESS THINGS tasteless or very low quality articles (*informal*) **3.** KNOTTED MASS a knotted mass of sth, especially hair [Mid-19thC. Origin uncertain: perhaps by back-formation from TATTY.]

tat[2] /tat/ (**tats, tatting, tatted**) *vti.* to work at or produce tatting [Late 19thC. Back-formation from TATTING.]

tat[3] /tat/ *n. Aus* a tattoo (*informal*) [Mid-19thC. Shortening.]

TAT *n., abbr.* thematic apperception test

ta-ta /tə táa/ *interj.* used as a childish or familiar way of saying goodbye (*informal*) [Early 19thC. Origin unknown.]

tatami /tə taámi, taa-/ (*plural* **-mi** *or* **-mis**) *n.* a straw mat, used especially in Japanese homes as a floor covering [Early 17thC. From Japanese.]

Tatar /taátər/, **Tartar** /taártər/ *n.* **1.** PEOPLES MEMBER OF HISTORICAL CENTRAL ASIAN PEOPLE a member of a people that originally came from eastern Central Asia and who established a huge empire stretching into Serbia, Russia, and Ukraine. The Tatars joined with the Mongols and their combined empire flourished until the 16th century, when they were defeated by the Russians and the Ottoman Turks. **2.** PEOPLES DESCENDANT OF TATARS a descendant of the Tatar people. Most now live in an area of European Russia between the Volga River and the Ural Mountains, with communities in Crimea and Siberia. **3.** LANG TATAR LANGUAGE The Turkic language of the Tatar people. Tatar is spoken by about 6 million people. ■ *adj.* OF TATAR PEOPLE relating to the Tatar people, their empire, or their culture [Early 17thC. From Turkish.] —**Tatarian** /taa táiri ən/ *adj.* —**Tataric** /taa tárrik/ *adj.*

Tate Gallery /táyt-/ *n.* a museum in London that houses part of the national collection of British and modern art. It was founded in 1897, and has branches in Liverpool and St Ives.

tater /táytər/ *n.* a potato (*regional*) [Mid-18thC. Alteration of POTATO.]

Tati /ta teé/, **Jacques** (1908–82) French actor and film director. He is noted for his wryly humorous films, in several of which he played the lovably bumbling character Monsieur Hulot. Real name **Jacques Tatischeff**

Tatlin /tátlin/, **Vladimir** (1885–1953) Russian sculptor and painter. He founded constructivism in the early 20th century with his abstract sculptures made from different industrial materials.

Tatra Mountains /taátrə-, táttrə-/ the highest range of the Carpathian Mountains of central Europe, extending along the border between Poland and Slovakia. The highest peak is Gerlachovka, 2,655 m/8,711 ft.

tatter /táttər/ *n.* **1.** TORN OR RAGGED PIECE OF CLOTH a torn or ragged piece of cloth **2.** RUINED STATE a ruined or damaged state (*usually used in the plural*) ○ *The policy was in tatters.* ■ *vti.* (**-ters, -tering, -tered**) BECOME RAGGED OR MAKE STH RAGGED to become ragged or make sth ragged or torn to shreds [15thC. From Old Norse *totrar* (plural) 'rags'.]

tatterdemalion /táttərdə máyli ən, táttərdə málli ən/ *adj.* DRESSED IN RAGS raggedly dressed and unkempt ■ *n.* RAGGEDLY CLOTHED PERSON sb wearing ragged clothes [Early 17thC. *Tatter* from TATTERED; *-demalion* of unknown origin.]

tattered /táttərd/ *adj.* **1.** RAGGED ragged or torn to shreds **2.** DRESSED IN RAGS dressed in ragged clothes **3.** SHABBY shabby and run-down [15thC. Formed from TATTER.]

tattersall /táttər sawl/ *n.* **1.** DESIGN PATTERN OF SQUARES OR CHECKS a pattern of squares or checks formed by dark lines on a light or brightly coloured background **2.** TEXTILES TATTERSALL-PATTERNED CLOTH cloth with a tattersall pattern [Late 19thC. Named after *Tattersall's* horse market, London, named after Richard *Tattersall* (1724–95), English auctioneer; referring to the traditional design of horse blankets.]

tattie-bogle /tátti bŏg'l/ *n. Scotland* a scarecrow, or a person who resembles a scarecrow (*informal*)

tatting /tátting/ *n.* **1.** TYPE OF LACE a form of lace made with a shuttle **2.** PROCESS OF MAKING TATTING the process or craft of making tatting [Mid-19thC. Origin unknown.] —**tatter** *n.*

tattle /tátt'l/ *v.* (**-tles, -tling, -tled**) **1.** *vi.* GOSSIP to gossip about the personal secrets or plans of others **2.** *vti.* DISCLOSE SECRET to disclose sb's personal or private information **3.** *vi.* TALK IDLY to talk or chatter idly ■ *n.* **1.** SB WHO GOSSIPS a gossip or informer **2.** IDLE GOSSIP idle talk, chatter, or gossip [15thC. Origin uncertain: probably from Middle Flemish *tatelen*, an imitation of the sound.]

tattler /táttlər/ *n.* **1.** **tattler, tattle-tongue** PERSON WHO TATTLES sb who gossips, reveals secrets, or talks idly **2.** SHOREBIRD WITH LOUD CRY a long-legged shorebird that is related to the sandpipers and is noted for its loud cries. Genus: *Heteroscelus.*

tattletale /tátt'l tayl/ *n. US* = **telltale** (*often used by or to children*) ■ *adj. US* = **telltale**

tattoo[1] /ta toó, tə-/ *n.* (*plural* **-toos**) PERMANENT PICTURE OR DESIGN ON SKIN a permanent picture, design, or other markings made on the skin by pricking it and staining it with an indelible dye ■ *vt.* (**-toos, -tooing, -tooed**) MAKE TATTOO to mark the skin with a tattoo, or to form a tattoo on the skin [Mid-18thC. Of Polynesian origin.] —**tattooer** *n.* —**tattooist** *n.*

tattoo[2] /ta toó, tə-/ *n.* (*plural* **-toos**) **1.** CALL TO RETURN TO QUARTERS a bugle or drum call that tells soldiers to return to their quarters in the evening **2.** MIL EVENING MILITARY DISPLAY FOR ENTERTAINMENT a military display, often with a variety of items, performed as an entertainment, usually in the evening ■ *vti.* (**-toos, -tooing, -tooed**) BEAT ON STH WITH STEADY RHYTHM to beat a steady rhythm, or to beat rhythmically on sth such as a drum [Mid-17thC. From Dutch *taptoe*, literally 'shut the tap (of the beer barrel)', a signal at closing time in the taverns. Originally 'signal for soldiers to return to quarters'.]

tatty /tátti/ (**-tier, -tiest**) *adj.* shabby, rundown, or in poor condition [Mid-20thC. Formed from *tat* 'rag', of uncertain origin.] —**tattily** *adv.* —**tattiness** *n.*

Tatum /táytəm/, **Edward Lawrie** (1909–75) US geneticist. His work with Joshua Lederberg and George W. Beadle on genetic mutations earned them a Nobel Prize in physiology or medicine (1958).

tau /taw, tow/ *n.* the 19th letter of the Greek alphabet, represented in the English alphabet as 't'. See table at **alphabet** [14thC. From Greek.]

tau cross *n.* a cross shaped like a T

taught past tense, past participle of **teach**

tau neutrino *n.* a subatomic particle of the lepton family with no electric charge and a mass less than 69 times that of an electron, created during the decay of a tauon

taunt[1] /tawnt/ *vt.* (**taunts, taunting, taunted**) **1.** PROVOKE OR RIDICULE SB to provoke, ridicule, or tease sb in a hurtful or mocking way **2.** TO TANTALIZE SB to tantalize sb, e.g. by refusing to disclose a secret ■ *n.* **1.**

HURTFUL REMARK a hurtfully mocking or provocative remark **2.** OBJECT OF TAUNTS sb at whom a taunt is directed (*archaic*) [Early 16thC. From French *tant (pour tant)* 'so much (for so much)', from Latin *tantus* 'so great'. In English, anglicized as 'taunt for taunt' and used for 'sarcastic rejoinder'.] —**taunter** *n.* —**taunting** *adj.* —**tauntingly** *adv.*

taunt[2] /tawnt/ *adj.* used to describe a mast that is taller than normal [Early 17thC. Origin unknown.]

Taunton /táwntən/ town and administrative centre of Somerset, southwestern England. Population: 60,300 (1993).

Taunus /táwnəss, tównəss/ mountain range in west-central Germany, extending northeastwards from the eastern bank of the River Rhine. Height: 880 m/2,887 ft.

tauon /tów on/ *n.* an unusually massive subatomic particle of the lepton family with the same charge as an electron but nearly 3,500 times its mass [Late 20thC. Formed from TAU.]

taupe /tōp/ *n.* a dark grey colour tinged with brown ■ *adj.* DARK BROWNISH-GREY of a dark grey colour tinged with brown, like moleskin [Early 20thC. Via French from Latin *talpa* 'mole'.]

Taupo /tówpō/ city in the centre of the North Island, New Zealand, on the northern shore of the lake of the same name. It is a commercial centre and tourist resort. Population: 21,044 (1996).

Taupo, Lake the largest lake in New Zealand, located in the centre of the North Island. It was originally formed by an enormous volcanic explosion. Area: 606 sq. km/234 sq. mi.

Tauranga /tow ráng gə/ city and port in the north of the North Island, New Zealand, situated on the Bay of Plenty. Population: 82,832 (1996).

Taurean /táwri ən, taw rée ən/ *n.* **1.** = **Taurus** *n.* 3 **2.** = **Taurus** —**Taurean** *adj.*

taurine[1] /táw rīn/ *adj.* relating to or resembling a bull [Early 17thC. From Latin *taurinus*, from *taurus* (see TAURUS).]

taurine[2] /táw reen, -rin/ *n.* a crystalline derivative of cysteine found in the bile, nervous tissue, and muscle juices of many animals. Formula: $C_2H_7NO_3S$. [Mid-19thC. Formed from TAUROCHOLIC ACID.]

taurocholic acid /táw rō kolik-/ *n.* a crystalline bile acid that is found as a sodium salt in humans and other carnivores and in certain herbivores. Formula: $C_{26}H_{45}NO_7$. [Mid-19thC. Coined from TAURO- + CHOLE-.]

tauromachy /taw rómmәki/ *n.* the activity or skill of bullfighting —**tauromachian** /táwrə máyki ən/ *adj.*

Taurus /táwrəss/ (*plural* **-ruses** *or* **-ri** /-rī/) *n.* **1.** ASTRON CONSTELLATION IN THE NORTHERN HEMISPHERE a constellation in the northern hemisphere located between Aries and Gemini and containing the bright star Aldebaran, the Pleiades and Hyades, and the Crab Nebula **2.** ZODIAC SIGN OF THE ZODIAC the second sign of the zodiac, represented by a bull and lasting from approximately 20 April to 20 May. Taurus is classified as an earth sign, and its ruling planet is Venus. **3.** ZODIAC SB BORN UNDER TAURUS sb whose birthday falls between 20 April and 20 May [14thC. From Latin *taurus* 'bull'. Ultimately from an Indo-European word meaning 'bull', which is also the ancestor of English *toreador*.] —**Taurus** *adj.*

TAURUS /táwrəss/ *n.* a computerized system used for buying and selling securities on the International Stock Exchange. Abbr of **Transfer of Automated Registration of Uncertified Stock**

Taurus Mountains /táwrəss-/ mountain range in southern Turkey, parallel to the Mediterranean coast. Its highest point is Aladag, 3,734 m/12,251 ft.

taut /tawt/ *adj.* **1.** STRETCHED TIGHTLY pulled or stretched tightly **2.** PHYSIOL FIRM AND FLEXED flexed and working, as opposed to being in a relaxed state ○ *taut muscles* **3.** STRESSED stressed, tense, or anxious **4.** CONCISE concise and efficient in its use of language or reasoning **5.** KEPT IN GOOD ORDER trim, tidy, and well-run ○ *a taut ship* [13thC. Origin uncertain.] —**tautly** *adv.* —**tautness** *n.*

taut- *prefix.* = **tauto-** (*used before vowels*)

tauten /táwt'n/ (**-ens, -ening, -ened**) *vti.* to become tightly stretched, or to pull sth, such as a rope, tight [Early 19thC]

tautog /taw tóg/ *n.* a large dark-coloured edible fish of the wrasse family, found along the Atlantic coast of North America, growing to 1 m/3 ft in length. Latin name: *Tautoga onitis.* [Mid-17thC. From Narragansett *tautauog*.]

tautologize /taw tóllə jīz/ (**-gizes, -gizing, -gized**), **tautologise** (**-gises, -gising, -gised**) *vi.* to use tautology — **tautologist** *n.*

tautology /taw tólləji/ (*plural* **-gies**) *n.* **1.** LING REDUNDANCY a redundant repetition of a meaning in a sentence or idea using different words **2.** INSTANCE OF TAUTOLOGY an instance of redundant repetition **3.** LOGIC LOGICAL TRUE PROPOSITION a proposition or statement that, in itself, is logically true —**tautologize** *vi.* —**tautological** /táwtə lójjik'l/ *adj.* —**tautologically** *adv.*

tautomer /táwtəmər/ *n.* a compound exhibiting tautomerism [Early 20thC. Coined from TAUTO- + ISOMER.]

tautomerism /taw tómmərizəm/ *n.* the property of a compound that permits it to exist as a mixture of two isomers that are interconvertible and thus exist in equilibrium —**tautomeric** /táwtə mérrik/ *adj.*

tautonym /táwtənim/ *n.* a species name in which the epithet for the species is the same as that of the genus, e.g. the name of the filarial worm *Loa loa.* This kind of name is used for animal but not plant species. —**tautonymic** /táwtə nímmik/ *adj.* —**tautonymy** /taw tónnəmi/ *n.*

tav /taav, taaf/ *n.* the 23rd and final letter of the Hebrew alphabet, represented in the English alphabet as 't'. See table at **alphabet** [Mid-17thC. From Hebrew *tāw*.]

Tavel /taa vél/ *n.* a dry rosé wine produced in the Rhône region of France [Late 19thC. Named after the locale in France where the wine is produced.]

Tavener /távvərnər/, **John** (*b.* 1944) British composer. He is particularly noted for his choral works, which are often based on religious or spiritual themes. Full name **John Kenneth Tavener**

tavern /távvərn/ *n.* **1.** PUB a pub or inn (*dated*) **2.** ESTABLISHMENT WHERE ALCOHOL IS SOLD AND DRUNK in the United States and some other countries, a place where alcohol is sold to be consumed on the premises [13thC. Via French *taverne* from Latin *taberna* 'hut, inn'.] —**taverner** *n.*

taverna /tə vúrnə/ *n.* **1.** RESTAURANT IN GREECE a small restaurant or café in Greece **2.** GREEK GUESTHOUSE WITH BAR a guesthouse in Greece that has a bar [Early 20thC. Via modern Greek from Latin *taberna* 'hut, inn'.]

taverner /távvərnər/ *n.* a person who runs a tavern (*archaic*)

Taverner /távvərnər/, **John** (1490?–1545) English composer. His church music, complex and elaborate, is transitional between the late medieval and Renaissance styles.

taw[1] /taw/ (**taws, tawing, tawed**) *vt.* to whiten animal skins by applying alum or other mineral salts [Old English *tawian*, from a prehistoric Germanic base meaning 'to make', which is also the ancestor of English *tool* and *heriot*] —**tawer** *n.*

taw[2] /taw/ *n.* **1.** MARBLE USED AS A SHOOTER a fancy marble used as a shooter **2.** LINE FROM WHICH PLAYER SHOOTS MARBLES in a game of marbles, the line from which a player must shoot **3.** GAME PLAYED WITH MARBLES a game of marbles in which the object is to shoot as many marbles as possible out of a circular area where they have been placed [Early 18thC. Origin unknown.]

tawa /taáwə/ *n.* a tall tree of the laurel family that grows in New Zealand and has edible purple fruit. Latin name: *Beilschmiedia tawa.* [Mid-19thC. From Maori.]

tawdry /táwdri/ *adj.* (**-drier, -driest**) **1.** GAUDY AND POOR QUALITY gaudy, cheap in appearance, and of inferior quality **2.** SHABBY BUT WITH PRETENSIONS shabby and worthless, though possibly with a superficial air of grandeur **3.** MEAN-SPIRITED mean-spirited and lacking in human decency ■ *n.* CHEAP GAUDY FINERY gaudy finery of inferior quality [Early 17thC. Shortening of *tawdry lace*, an alteration of *St Audrey's lace*.] —**tawdrily** *adv.* —**tawdriness** *n.*

WORD KEY: ORIGIN

Anna, Anglo-Saxon king of East Anglia, had a daughter called Etheldreda, who became queen of Northumbria. She had an inordinate fondness in her youth for fine lace neckerchiefs, and when she later developed a fatal tumour of the neck, she regarded it as divine retribution for her former extravagance. After her death in 679 she was canonized and made patron saint of Ely. In the Middle Ages fairs were held in her memory, known as 'St. Audrey's fairs' (*Audrey* is a conflated form of *Etheldreda*) at which lace neckties were sold. These were often made from cheap gaudy material, and by the 17th century the eroded form ***tawdry*** was being used generally for 'cheap and gaudy'.

tawney *n., adj.* = **tawny**

Tawney /táwni/, **R. H.** (1880–1962) Indian-born British economic historian. He is best known for *Religion and the Rise of Capitalism* (1926). Full name **Richard Henry Tawney**

tawny /táwni/, **tawney** (**-nier, -niest**) *adj.* **1.** ORANGEY BROWN of an orange-brown colour tinged with gold **2.** BEVERAGES MATURED FOR TEN YEARS PLUS used to describe port wine that has matured for at least ten years in the barrel before bottling, and is therefore paler than ruby port [14thC. Via Anglo-Norman *tauné* from Old French *tané* 'tan' (see TAN).] —**tawniness** *n.*

tawny frogmouth (*plural* **tawny frogmouths**) *n.* a common nocturnal insectivorous bird found throughout Australia that has a wide mouth resembling that of a frog and brown or grey plumage streaked with black. Latin name: *Podargus strigoides.*

tawny owl *n.* a common round headed owl with brown or grey plumage, black eyes, and tawny markings found in woodlands from Europe to China. Latin name: *Strix aluco.*

Tawny Owl *n.* formerly the official name for an assistant to the woman in charge of a group of Brownies

tawny pipit *n.* a pale sandy-brown bird related to the wagtail, found in open country in Europe and Asia. Latin name: *Anthus campestris.*

tawse, **taws** *n. Scotland* LEATHER STRAP USED FOR PUNISHMENT a leather strap split at the end, formerly used to punish school pupils with a blow to the palm of the hand ■ *vti.* (**tawses, tawsing, tawsed**) *Scotland* HIT WITH TAWSE to hit a pupil on the hand with a tawse [Early 16thC. Plural of TAW[1] in the earlier sense 'lash, whip'.]

tax /taks/ *n.* **1.** ECON MONEY PAID TO A GOVERNMENT an amount of money levied by a government on its citizens and used to run the government and the country or state **2.** FIN CHARGE PAID BY MEMBERS an amount charged to members of a club or organization to be used for expenses **3.** STRAIN a strain or heavy demand ■ *vt.* (**taxes, taxing, taxed**) **1.** ECON CHARGE TAX to charge a tax on sth such as a company's or individual's income **2.** TRANSP PAY TAX FOR CAR to pay the annual tax required in order to drive a motor vehicle **3.** STRAIN OR MAKE HEAVY DEMANDS ON to strain or make heavy demands on sth or sb ○ *You're starting to tax my patience.* **4.** ACCUSE OR CHARGE to accuse or charge sb **5.** LAW DETERMINE COSTS OF LITIGATION to determine the costs of litigation and the total amount of costs payable at the end of a trial [13thC. Via French *taxer* from Latin *taxare* 'to censure, assess', literally 'to touch repeatedly', from *tangere* 'to touch' (source of English *tact* and *attain*).] —**taxer** *n.* —**taxless** *adj.*

tax- *prefix.* = **taxo-** (*used before vowels*)

taxa plural of **taxon**

taxable /táksəb'l/ *adj.* SUBJECT TO A TAX subject to a tax ○ *taxable income* ■ *n.* SB OR STH SUBJECT TO TAX sb or sth that is subject to taxation —**taxability** *n.* —**taxableness** *n.* —**taxably** *adv.*

taxation /tak sáysh'n/ *n.* **1.** SYSTEM OF LEVYING TAXES the system whereby taxes are levied upon certain types of income, earnings, or purchases **2.** MONEY COLLECTED IN TAXES the amount of money raised by collecting taxes **3.** TAX ON STH an amount levied as a tax on sth —**taxational** *adj.*

tax avoidance *n.* the practice of paying as little tax as possible by claiming all allowable deductions from income. ◊ **tax evasion**

tax-deductible *adj.* used to describe an expenditure that can be deducted from taxable income to lower the amount of tax owed by an individual or business

tax-deferred *adj.* not taxable until a later time, often after retirement

tax disc *n.* a small circular official document displayed on a motor vehicle, typically on the inside of the windscreen, showing that the annual road tax has been paid

taxeme /ták seem/ *n.* a small linguistic feature such as selection, order, or phonetic modification [Mid-20thC. Coined from TAXIS + -EME.] —**taxemic** /tak seémik/ *adj.*

tax evasion *n.* an illegal activity in which a taxpayer seeks to hide taxable income or claim unauthorized tax deductions. ◊ **tax avoidance**

tax-exempt *adj.* legally exempt from taxation

tax exile *n.* sb who leaves a country in order to avoid paying taxes there

tax file number *n.* in Australia, a numeric code required by all employers, and obtained when an individual registers with the Tax Office

tax haven *n.* a country with favourable tax rates

tax holiday *n.* a period during which a company is exempt from taxation, e.g. when just starting out in business

taxi /táksi/ *n.* (*plural* **-is** *or* **-ies**) TRANSP CAR TAKING PAYING PASSENGERS a car, usually with a taximeter, whose driver is paid to transport passengers, typically for short distances ■ *vti.* (**-ies**, **-iing** *or* **-ying**, **-ied**) **1.** AIR MOVE AIRCRAFT ON GROUND to make an aircraft move under its own power on the ground, typically before take-off or after landing, or to move on the ground in this way **2.** TRANSP TRAVEL IN TAXI to transport sb or sth in a taxi, or to travel in a taxi **3.** TRANSPORT SB OR BE TRANSPORTED to transport sb or sth or be transported, especially in a car (*informal*) ○ *taxi the children to school* [Early 20thC. Shortening of *taximeter cab* (see TAXIMETER).]

taxi- *prefix.* = taxo-

taxi dancer *n.* sb who is paid, dance by dance, to dance with patrons of a nightclub or dance hall —**taxi dancing** *n.*

taxidermy /táksi durmi/ *n.* the art or skill of preparing, stuffing, and presenting dead animal skins so that they appear lifelike [Early 19thC. Coined from Greek *taxis* 'arrangement' (see TAXIS) + -DERM.] —**taxidermal** /táksi dúrm'l/ *adj.* —**taxidermist** /-durmist/ *n.*

taximeter /táksi meetər/ *n.* a device installed in a taxi that automatically computes the fare, which is usually based on time, distance travelled, or a combination of both [Late 19thC. From French *taximètre*, from *taxe* 'charge, tariff'.]

taximetrics /táksi metriks/ *n.* = **numerical taxonomy**

taxing /táksing/ *adj.* placing numerous or severe demands on sb —**taxingly** *adv.*

taxiplane /táksi playn/ *n.* US an aircraft that is available for hire

taxi rank *n.* an area reserved for parked taxis awaiting customers. US term **taxi stand**

taxis /táksiss/ *n.* **1.** BIOL MOVEMENT OF CELL movement of a cell or microorganism towards or away from the source of a stimulus **2.** SURG REPOSITIONING OF ORGAN the manipulating of a displaced body part to return it to its normal position, such as in a case of hernia [Late 16thC. From Greek, 'arrangement', formed from the stem of *tassein* 'to arrange' (source of English *tactics*).]

-taxis *suffix.* **1.** movement in response to a stimulus ○ *hydrotaxis* **2.** arrangement, order of parts ○ *phyllotaxis* [From Greek *taxis* 'order, arrangement' (see TAXIS).]

taxi stand *n.* US = **taxi rank**

taxi truck *n.* Aus a truck and driver for hire, often used for moving house

taxiway /táksi way/ *n.* a path used by aircraft when taxiing to and from a runway or other ground facility

tax loss *n.* a transaction that results in a reduced tax liability, even though it may not be associated with an actual cash loss, the loss associated with depreciation expenses

taxman /táks man/ (*plural* **-men** /-men/) *n.* **1.** TAXING AUTHORITY the taxing authority (*informal*) **2.** TAX COLLECTOR a person who collects taxes [Mid-19thC]

taxo- *prefix.* order, arrangement ○ *taxonomy* [From Greek *taxis* (see TAXIS)]

taxon /ták son/ (*plural* **taxa** /-sə/) *n.* any of the groups to which organisms are assigned according to the principles of taxonomy, including species, genus, family, order, class, and phylum [Early 20thC. Back-formation from TAXONOMY.]

taxonomy /tak sónnəmi/ (*plural* **-mies**) *n.* **1.** GROUPING OF ORGANISMS the science of classifying plants, animals, and microorganisms into increasingly broader categories based on shared features. Traditionally, organisms were grouped by physical resemblances, but in recent times other criteria such as genetic matching have also been used. **2.** PRINCIPLES OF CLASSIFICATION the practice or principles of classification **3.** STUDY OF CLASSIFICATION the study of the rules and practice of classifying living organisms [Early 19thC. From French *taxonomie*, from Greek *taxis* 'arrangement' (see TAXIS).] —**taxonomic** /táksə nómmik/ *adj.* —**taxonomically** *adv.* —**taxonomist** /tak sónnəmist/ *n.*

taxpayer /táks pay ər/ *n.* sb who pays tax, especially income tax —**taxpaying** *adj.*

tax rate *n.* the percentage of income paid in income tax

tax return *n.* the collection of government forms on which earnings and expenses are recorded in order to calculate the tax liability of an individual or business

tax shelter *n.* an investment activity that tends to reduce income tax liability —**tax-sheltered** *adj.*

-taxy *suffix.* order, arrangement ○ *epitaxy* [From Greek *-taxia*, from *tag-*, the stem of *tassein* (see TAXIS)]

tay /tay/ *n.* Ireland tea [Mid-17thC. Dialect variant of TEA, reflecting Irish and, until the 18thC, English pronunciation.]

Tay /tay/ the longest river in Scotland, flowing eastwards through Loch Tay and emptying into the North Sea through the Firth of Tay estuary. Length: 190 km/118 mi.

Tay, Firth of estuary of the River Tay on the eastern coast of Scotland, an inlet of the North Sea. It is spanned by the Tay Bridge.

tayberry /táybəri, -berri/ (*plural* **-berries**) *n.* **1.** TREES BLACKBERRY RASPBERRY CROSS a berry-bearing shrub that is produced by crossing a blackberry with a raspberry **2.** FOOD BERRY OF TAYBERRY a sweet dark red berry produced by the tayberry [Late 20thC. Named after the *Tay*, a river in Scotland.]

Taylor /táylər/, Dennis James (*b.* 1949) UK snooker player, Irish champion (1982), world champion (1985), and winner of the Rothmans Grand Prix (1984) and B & H Masters (1987).

Elizabeth Taylor

Taylor, Elizabeth (*b.* 1932) British-born US actor. She became a star in her early film *National Velvet* (1944). She continued in the public eye both as an actor and as a celebrity. Full name **Elizabeth Rosemond Taylor**

Taylor, Sir Gordon (1896–1966) Australian aviator. With Charles Kingsford Smith, he completed the first flight from Australia to America in a single-engine aircraft. Full name **Sir Patrick Gordon Taylor**

Zachary Taylor

Taylor, Zachary (1785–1850) US soldier and 12th president of the United States. He was a hero of the Mexican War (1846–47) prior to becoming president (1849–50). Known as **Old Rough and Ready**

Taylor's series /táylərz -/ *n.* a basic theorem of calculus relating an approximation of the value of a continuous function at a point to the successive derivatives of the function evaluated at the point [Early 19thC. Named after the English mathematician Brook *Taylor* (1685–1731).]

Taymyria /tay míri ə/ autonomous region in north-central Siberia, Russia. Area: 862,100 sq. km/332,850 sq. mi.

tayra /tírə/ *n.* an agile South American weasel similar to the marten, with a brown coat and a buff patch on the throat. Latin name: *Eira barbara*. [Mid-19thC. Via Portuguese or Spanish *taira* from Tupi.]

Tay-Sachs disease /táy sáks-/ *n.* a genetic disease that principally affects Jewish people of eastern European ancestry. Marked by accumulation of lipids in the brain and nerves, it results in loss of sight and brain functions. [Early 20thC. Named after Warren *Tay* (1843–1927), an English ophthalmologist, and Bernard *Sachs* (1858–1944), a US neurologist.]

tazza /tátsə/ *n.* an ornamental vessel that has a shallow bowl, usually mounted on a pedestal [Early 19thC. Via Italian from Arabic *ṭasa* (see TASS).]

Tb *symbol.* terbium

TB *abbr.* **1.** torpedo boat **2.** tuberculosis **3.** TB, t.b. ACCT trial balance

t.b.a. *abbr.* **1.** to be announced **2.** to be agreed

T-bar *n.* **1.** METAL BAR T-SHAPED IN CROSS SECTION a metal bar that is T-shaped in cross section **2.** SKIING SKI TOW FOR TWO PEOPLE a ski tow for two people, shaped like an inverted T. Skiers rest against a horizontal bar on either side of a central shaft that pulls them along with their skis on the ground. **3.** ACCESSORIES T-SHAPED STRAP ON SHOE a T-shaped strap cut from the upper part of a shoe

TBD *abbr.* to be discussed (used in e-mail communications)

Tbilisi /tibi léessi/ capital city of Georgia, in the east-central part of the country, on the River Kura. Population: 1,268,000 (1990).

T-bone steak *n.* a large thick sirloin steak containing a T-shaped bone

tbs., tbsp. *abbr.* tablespoon

Tc *symbol.* technetium

TC *abbr.* twin carburettors

TCCB *abbr.* Test and County Cricket Board

TCDD *n.* an extremely toxic by-product of herbicide manufacture. Full form **tetrachlorodibenzodioxin**

T-cell *n.* a type of white blood cell (**lymphocyte**) that matures in the thymus and is essential for various aspects of immunity, especially in combating virus infections and cancers. ◊ **cytotoxic T cell, helper T cell, suppressor T cell** [*T* is a shortening of *thymus-derived*]

Peter Ilich Tchaikovsky

Tchaikovsky /chī kófskī/, **Peter Ilich** (1840–93) Russian composer. A major composer of the romantic era, his works include symphonies, piano concertos, and ballet scores such as *Swan Lake* (1876).

TCP *tdmk.* a trademark for a mild liquid antiseptic trichlorophenylmethyliodisalicyl

TCP/IP *abbr.* transmission control protocol/Internet protocol

TD *abbr.* 1. tank destroyer 2. FOOTBALL touchdown 3. Territorial Decoration 4. technical drawing 5. Member of the Dáil

td. *abbr.* touchdown

t.d.c. *abbr.* top dead-centre

TDD *abbr.* telecommunications device for the deaf

TDM *abbr.* time-division multiplexing

te *n.* a syllable that represents the seventh note in a scale, used for singing solfeggio. In fixed solfeggio it represents the note B, the seventh note in the scale of C, while in solfeggio with movable doh it is used to represent the seventh note of the key being sung. US term **ti**

Te *symbol.* tellurium

Tea

tea /tee/ *n.* 1. PLANTS ASIAN EVERGREEN SHRUB an evergreen shrub of the Theaceae family, native to Asia, with toothed leathery leaves and fragrant cup-shaped flowers. Latin name: *Camellia sinensis*. 2. BEVERAGES PLANT'S DRIED LEAVES FOR MAKING DRINK the dried leaves of the tea plant, often shredded, used to make a drink by adding boiling water 3. TEA DRINK a tea drink, usually served hot but sometimes with ice 4. BEVERAGES DRINK MADE BY INFUSION any drink made by infusion of particular plant leaves, or the dried leaves used as the basis of a drink 5. PLANTS PLANT USED FOR INFUSED DRINK a plant other than the tea plant used to make an infused beverage 6. *UK, Aus, NZ, Scotland* FOOD MAIN MEAL OF DAY the main meal of the day when it is eaten early in the evening 7. FOOD AFTERNOON MEAL OF CAKES AND TEA a light meal taken in the afternoon, usually consisting of cakes, sandwiches, and tea or other nonalcoholic drinks, or an afternoon social event at which this meal is eaten 8. BREAKFAST IN GUYANA in Guyana, the first meal of the day 9. *US, Can* DRUGS MARIJUANA marijuana (*dated slang*) [Mid-17thC. Origin uncertain: probably via earlier Dutch *tee* from, ultimately, Chinese (Amoy dialect) *te*.]

—— WORD KEY: USAGE ——
See Usage note at *dinner*.

—— WORD KEY: REGIONAL NOTE ——
The names used for meals can reveal a lot about the user's social and regional origins. *Tea* is perhaps the most ambiguous term. It can refer to an optional light snack around 4 p.m. or a meal eaten around 6 p.m. In parts of West Africa, it may refer to any hot drink including coffee or cocoa, and in Guyana it is used to refer to the first meal of the day.

tea bag *n.* a small bag made of permeable paper or cloth containing tea leaves that is placed in boiling water to make one serving of tea

tea ball *n.* a small perforated metal ball for holding tea leaves that is placed in boiling water to make tea

teaberry /tee'bəri, -berri/ (*plural* -ries) *n.* = wintergreen [Late 18thC. *Tea* from the fact that its leaves can be used as a substitute for tea.]

teabread /tee' bred/ *n.* a lightly sweetened bread, usually containing dried fruit, that is served sliced and buttered. In some recipes, the dried fruit has been soaked in hot tea before being added to the mixture.

tea break *n.* a break from work in order to have a drink, usually of tea or coffee

tea caddy *n.* a small container, usually with a tight-fitting lid, for holding tea leaves

teacake /tee' kayk/ *n.* a large round flattened yeast bun made with currants and chopped mixed peel or other fruit, sometimes spiced

tea ceremony *n.* a Japanese ritual in which tea is prepared, served, and drunk in a prescribed manner

teach /teech/ (**teaches, teaching, taught** /tawt/, **taught**) *v.* 1. *vt.* IMPART KNOWLEDGE OR SKILL to impart knowledge or skill to sb by instruction or example 2. *vti.* GIVE LESSONS to give lessons in a subject, or to give lessons to a person or animal 3. *vt.* MAKE UNDERSTAND BY EXPERIENCE to bring understanding to sb, especially through an experience ○ *The episode taught me a lesson I'll never forget.* 4. *vt.* TEACH REGULARLY to engage in imparting knowledge or instruction for a period of time in a particular place ○ *teaches college* 5. *vt.* ADVOCATE OR PREACH STH to advocate or preach sth [Old English *tǣcan*. Ultimately from an Indo-European base meaning 'to show', which is also the ancestor of English *token*, *digit*, and *deictic*.]

—— WORD KEY: SYNONYMS ——
teach, educate, train, instruct, coach, tutor, school, drill
CORE MEANING: to cause to acquire knowledge or skill in sth
teach to impart information to sb or show sb how to do sth; **educate** to teach sb generally, e.g. in a school or college, especially when taking into account all that a person learns over a period of time; **train** to teach sb how to do sth by means of instruction, observation, and practice. Used especially in relation to jobs; **instruct** a formal word meaning the same as *teach*; **coach** to teach a specific subject or skill to one person or a very small group of people, especially in preparation for an exam. It is used especially to talk about specialized sports instruction; **tutor** to give sb individual tuition on a particular subject or in a particular skill; **school** a fairly formal word used to talk about teaching sb a particular skill or area of expertise in a thorough and detailed way; **drill** to teach sth by means of repeated exercises and practice. Used especially when this seems rigorous or severe.

teachable /tee'chəb'l/ *adj.* 1. WILLING TO LEARN willing and able to learn 2. ABLE TO BE TAUGHT relating to sth such as a skill or subject that can be taught

teacher /tee'chər/ *n.* 1. SB WHO TEACHES sb who teaches, especially as a profession 2. ANYTHING THAT TEACHES anything from which sth may be learnt ○ *Experience is a great teacher.* —**teacherless** *adj.* —**teacherly** *adj.*

teacher bird *n.* = ovenbird [*Teacher* is an imitation of the sound made by the bird]

teachers' centre *n.* a resource centre where all the teachers in a particular area can go for materials and assistance

teacher's pet *n.* 1. TEACHER'S FAVOURITE STUDENT a student who is specially favoured by a teacher (*insult*) 2. SB

FAVOURED BY AUTHORITY FIGURE sb who is in special favour with a figure in authority

tea chest *n.* a large box made of thin wood lined with metal in which tea is packed for transport after drying

teach-in *n.* an extended period of speeches, lectures, and discussions, usually held at a college or university as part of a political or social protest

teaching /tee'ching/ *n.* 1. PRACTICE OR PROFESSION OF A TEACHER the profession or practice of being a teacher 2. STH TAUGHT sth that is taught, e.g. a point of doctrine (*often used in the plural*) ■ *adj.* 1. USED FOR TEACHING used for or in teaching 2. THAT TEACHES being a person or establishment that teaches

teaching assistant, **teaching fellow** *n.* = teaching fellow —**teaching assistantship** *n.*

teaching fellow *n.* a postgraduate student in a university who teaches, especially undergraduates, in return for tuition and usually a small stipend —**teaching fellowship** *n.*

teaching hospital *n.* a hospital that provides supervised practical training for medical students, student nurses, or other health-care professionals, often in conjunction with a medical school

teaching practice *n.* the part of a student teacher's training that consists of a placement at a school where classroom teaching is undertaken by the student

tea cloth *n.* = tea towel

tea cosy *n.* a soft, padded cover for keeping a teapot warm, usually with slits to fit over the handle and spout

teacup /tee' kup/ *n.* 1. CUP FOR TEA a small to medium-sized cup, usually used with a saucer, especially for serving tea 2. **teacup, teacupful** AMOUNT IN TEACUP the amount a teacup holds

tea dance *n.* an afternoon social event at which tea is often served and people do ballroom or other partner dancing

tea egg *n.* = tea ball

tea garden *n.* 1. GARDEN WHERE TEA IS SERVED a garden or outdoor restaurant where tea and light refreshments are served to the public 2. AGRIC TEA PLANTATION a plantation where tea is grown

tea gown *n.* a loose, usually waistless, dress of light thin fabric trimmed with lace, worn by women in the late 19th century for afternoon social occasions at which men would not be present

teahouse /tee' howss/ (*plural* -**houses** /-howziz/) *n.* a restaurant, especially in China or Japan, that serves tea and light refreshments

teak /teek/ *n.* 1. TREES TALL E INDIAN TREE a tall East Indian tree of the vervain family, valued for its wood. Latin name: *Tectona grandis*. 2. **teak, teakwood** INDUST WOOD OF THE TEAK TREE the wood of the teak tree, used for making furniture and in shipbuilding 3. TREES TREE OR WOOD SIMILAR TO TEAK a tree or wood that is similar to teak 4. COLOURS YELLOWISH-BROWN COLOUR a yellowish-brown colour ■ *adj.* COLOURS YELLOWISH-BROWN of a yellowish-brown colour like teak [Late 17thC. Via Portuguese *teca* from Tamil or Malayalam *tēkku*.]

teakettle /tee' kett'l/ *n.* a kettle used for boiling water for making tea

teal /teel/ *n.* (*plural* **teals** *or* **teal**) 1. BIRDS SMALL DUCK a small freshwater surface-feeding duck with bright iridescent blue or green patches on the wings. Genus: *Anas*. 2. COLOURS GREENISH-BLUE COLOUR a greenish-blue colour ■ *adj.* COLOURS OF A GREENISH-BLUE COLOUR of a greenish-blue colour [13thC. Origin unknown.]

tea lady (*plural* **tea ladies**) *n.* a woman employed to make tea during tea breaks, e.g. in a factory or office

tea leaf *n.* 1. PLANTS DRIED LEAF OF TEA PLANT a dried leaf or shredded part of the dried leaf of the tea plant, used to make tea 2. BEVERAGES TEA LEAF AFTER INFUSION a tea leaf, or part of a leaf, after it has been infused (*often used in the plural*) 3. THIEF a thief (*slang*)

team /teem/ *n.* 1. SPORTS GROUP FORMING SIDE IN SPORTS COMPETITION a group of people forming one side in a sports competition 2. COOPERATIVELY FUNCTIONING GROUP a number of people organized to function cooperatively as a group **3. ANIMALS WORKED TOGETHER** two or more animals worked together, especially to pull a vehicle or agricultural equipment **4. TEAM OF ANIMALS WITH VEHICLE** a team of animals and the vehicle harnessed to them **5. GROUPING OF ANIMALS** a grouping of animals such as a flock, brood, or herd (*regional*) ■ *v.* **(teams, teaming, teamed) 1.** *vti.* **FORM OR FORM INTO A TEAM** to form a team, or to form people or animals into a team **2.** *vt. US, Can* **TRANSPORT BY A TEAM** to transport sth using a team of animals **3.** *vi. US, Can* **DRIVE A TEAM** to drive a team of farm animals or a truck [Old English *tēam*. Ultimately from an Indo-European base meaning 'to lead', which is also the ancestor of English *tug* and *duct*.]

tea-maker *n.* **1. MACHINE TO MAKE TEA** a machine that is designed to make tea automatically, usually with a timer so that it switches itself on at the required time **2.** = **tea ball**

team leader *n.* a senior nurse in charge of a ward and of the other junior nurses working on the ward

team-mate *n.* a player on the same team

team player *n.* sb who is willing to work co-operatively with others and to subordinate personal interests in order to achieve a common goal

team spirit *n.* an enthusiastic attitude towards working productively with a team or work group

teamster /téemstər/ *n.* **1. SB WHO DRIVES A TEAM OF ANIMALS** sb who drives a team of animals used for hauling **2.** *US, Can* **LORRY DRIVER** sb who drives a lorry that is used commercially for hauling loads, especially as an occupation **3.** *US* **MEMBER OF THE TEAMSTERS UNION** a member of the Teamsters Union

Teamsters Union /téemstərz-/ *n.* a labour trade union whose members are mainly lorry drivers. Full form **International Brotherhood of Teamsters, Chauffeurs, Warehousemen, and Helpers of America**

team teaching *n.* an instructional programme involving two or more subjects that are taught in a coordinated way by specialist teachers

teamwork /téem wurk/ *n.* **1. COOPERATIVE WORK BY A GROUP** a cooperative effort by a group or team **2. WORK PRODUCED BY A GROUP** work produced by a group or team

Te Anau /te áan ow/ town in the southwestern part of the South Island, New Zealand, on Lake Te Anau. It is a tourist resort and the gateway to the Fiordland region. Population: 1,782 (1996).

Te Anau, Lake the second largest lake in New Zealand, located in the southwestern part of the South Island. Area: 344 sq. km/133 sq. mi.

tea party *n.* an afternoon social event at which tea is served

teapot /tée pot/ *n.* a covered container with a spout and handle, used for making and serving tea

teapoy /tée poy/ *n.* **1. SMALL TABLE** a small three-legged ornamental table or stand **2. SMALL TABLE USED FOR TEA** a small table used to hold a tea caddy and tea service [Early 19thC. By folk etymology (from TEA) from Hindi *tipāī*, an alteration of Persian *si-pāya*, literally 'three-footed'.]

tear[1] /tair/ *v.* **(tears, tearing, tore** /tawr/, **torn** /tawrn/) **1.** *vti.* **PULL OR COME APART** to pull sth such as paper or cloth into pieces, or to come apart or rip ○ *She tore open the parcel.* **2.** *vt.* **MAKE A HOLE IN STH** to make a hole or opening in sth such as a garment ○ *tore her skirt on a nail* **3.** *vt.* **CUT STH LEAVING JAGGED EDGES** to cut sth, especially flesh, leaving jagged edges **4.** *vt.* MED **SPRAIN** to injure a muscle or ligament so that some of the tissue is pulled apart and separated **5.** *vt.* **SEPARATE STH USING FORCE** to remove or separate sth using force **6.** *vti.* **UPSET OR DISTRESS** to upset or distress sb ○ *the memory tore at his heart* **7.** *vt.* **DIVIDE STH** to divide or fragment sth ○ *an organization torn by internal conflict* **8.** *vi.* **MOVE OR ACT QUICKLY OR CARELESSLY** to move or act with great or careless speed ○ *He went tearing off down the road.* ■ *n.* **1. SPLIT CAUSED BY TEARING** a hole or split caused by tearing **2. ACT OF TEARING** an act of tearing **3. A HURRY** a hurry or rush [Old English *teran*. Ultimately from an Indo-European base meaning 'to split', which is also the ancestor of English *turd* and probably *tart*.] —**tearable** *adj.* —**tearer** *n.* ◇ **that's torn it!** used to indicate that sth unfortunate has happened, often sth that will lead to trouble (*dated informal*)

WORD KEY: SYNONYMS

tear, rend, rip, slit

CORE MEANING: to pull apart forcibly

tear a general word for pulling sth apart forcibly, either by accident or on purpose; **rend** a formal or literary word suggesting tearing with extreme strength or violence, most often now used figuratively; **rip** to tear sth with one rapid uninterrupted movement, either by accident or on purpose; **split** to divide sth into two parts with a single movement usually with the blade of a tool or weapon.

tear apart *vt.* **1. FRAGMENT** to cause division, separation, or conflict in a group or organization ○ *a family torn apart by war* **2. DISTRESS SB** to cause sb distress or emotional conflict ○ *the strain of separation was tearing us apart* **3. SEARCH** to search a place thoroughly, often causing disruptions and mess ○ *The police tore apart the house looking for the weapon.*

tear away *vt.* to force or persuade yourself or sb else to leave a place or object

tear down *vt.* to demolish, destroy, or dismantle sth such as a building

tear into *vt.* to attack sb or sth vigorously, either physically or verbally

tear off /táir of/ *vt.* **1. REMOVE CLOTHES QUICKLY** to remove clothes quickly and carelessly **2. PRODUCE STH QUICKLY** to produce sth quickly and carelessly

tear up *vt.* to tear sth into small pieces, e.g. in order to destroy it

tear[2] /teer/ *n.* **1.** PHYSIOL **SINGLE DROP OF FLUID FROM THE EYE** a single drop of salty fluid secreted by the lacrimal gland of the eye **2. DROP OF LIQUID** a drop of liquid or hardened fluid, especially one with a round base and narrower top ■ **tears** *npl.* **1. CRYING** weeping accompanied by intense emotion **2.** PHYSIOL **LIQUID BATHING THE EYE** the salty liquid secreted by the lacrimal gland that moistens and protects the surface of the eye and its surrounding tissue **3. EXCESS OF LIQUID IN THE EYES** a greater than usual amount of liquid produced by the eye or eyes, often accompanying intense emotions, or caused by irritation of the eye ■ *vi.* **(tears, tearing, teared) PRODUCE TEARS** to produce tears, especially in excessive amounts ○ *My eyes tear a lot during the hayfever season.* [Old English *tēar*. Ultimately from an Indo-European word meaning 'tear', which is also the ancestor of English *lachrymose*.] —**tearless** *adj.*

tearaway /táirə way/ *n.* a reckless, impulsive, and undisciplined person, often a child

teardrop /téer drop/ *n.* **1.** = **tear**[2] *n.* 1 **2. SHAPE RESEMBLING A TEAR** a shape that resembles a tear, or sth having this shape

tear duct /téer-/ *n.* a passage that conveys tears, especially the duct that drains tears from the inner corner of the eye into the nasal cavity

tearful /téerf'l/ *adj.* **1. CRYING** crying, about to cry, or feeling like crying, usually because of an emotion such as great sadness **2. LIKELY TO CAUSE TEARS** sad enough to cause weeping ○ *a tearful occasion* —**tearfully** *adv.* —**tearfulness** *n.*

tear gas /téer-/ *n.* a chemical agent, delivered by a grenade or other means, that incapacitates a person by irritating the eyes

tear-gas /téer gass/ **(teargases, teargassing, teargassed)** *vt.* to spray sb with tear gas

tearing /táiring/ *adj.* violent or frenzied ○ *in a tearing hurry*

tear-jerker *n.* a story or artistic work that is excessively sentimental (*informal*) —**tear-jerking** *adj.*

tear-off *adj.* produced in a block of paper in sheet form, or perforated, so that individual pieces can be removed easily

tearoom /tée room, -ro͝om/ *n.* **1. RESTAURANT SERVING TEA** a restaurant or café serving tea and other beverages, and usually cakes and other light refreshments (*often used in the plural*) **2.** *S Africa* **SMALL SHOP SELLING VARIETY OF GOODS** a small shop in which some staple groceries, newspapers, and small consumer goods are sold

tea rose *n.* any of one several varieties of a bush rose native to China that grows large tea-scented pink or yellow flowers. Latin name: *Rosa odorata.*

tear sheet /táir-/ *n.* a single page taken from a magazine or other periodical, often used to prove to an advertiser that an advertisement has been published

tearstain /téer stayn/ *n.* a mark or track left by tears —**tear-stained** *adj.*

teary /téeri/ (**-ier, -iest**) *adj.* **1. WET WITH TEARS** wet with or full of tears **2. ABOUT TO CRY** seeming to be about to cry **3. CAUSING WEEPING** causing or sad enough to cause weeping **4. LIKE TEARS** resembling tears —**tearily** *adv.* —**teariness** *n.*

teary-eyed *adj.* **1. WITH TEARS IN THE EYES** with tears in the eyes, especially if caused by emotion **2. CHARACTERIZED BY WEEPING** characterized by weeping, especially when caused by sadness

tease /teez/ *v.* **(teases, teasing, teased) 1.** *vti.* **MAKE FUN OF SB** to make fun of sb, either playfully or maliciously **2.** *vti.* **DELIBERATELY ANNOY OR IRRITATE** to deliberately annoy or irritate a person or an animal **3.** *vt.* **PERSUADE BY COAXING** to urge sb, especially to do sth, by continual coaxing **4.** *vt.* **AROUSE PHYSICAL DESIRE WITHOUT GIVING SATISFACTION** to arouse hope, curiosity, or especially physical desire in sb with no intention of giving satisfaction **5.** *vt.* TEXTILES **PULL FIBRES APART** to pull fibres apart by combing or carding **6.** *vt.* TEXTILES **RAISE A NAP BY COMBING** to raise the nap on cloth by combing it with a wire brush **7.** *vt.* BIOL **SEPARATE TISSUE** to separate the parts of a tissue specimen gently with a needle in preparation for examination under a microscope **8.** *vt. US* HAIR = **backcomb** ■ *n.* **1. SB WHO TEASES** a person who has a tendency to tease others **2. PERSON WHO TEASES SEXUALLY** a person who teases sb else sexually **3. PROVOCATIVE OPENING REMARK** an opening remark or action intended to stimulate curiosity or interest **4. ACT OF TEASING** an act of teasing [Old English *tǣsan*. Originally 'to separate the fibres of wool' (with the prickly 'teasel' flower), hence 'irritate', later 'make fun of'.] —**teasing** *adj.* —**teasingly** *adv.*

tease apart = **tease out** *v.* 1

tease out *vt.* **1. tease out, tease apart GRADUALLY SEPARATE STH** to gradually separate things that are tangled up, or gradually separate sth from an object with which it is entangled **2. EXTRACT THE TRUTH** to extract sth gradually, e.g. the truth or information

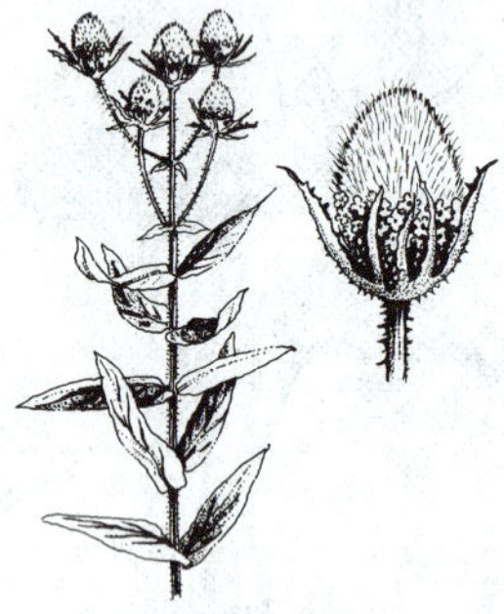

Teasel

teasel /téez'l/, **teazel, teazle** *n.* **1.** PLANTS **PRICKLY PLANT OF EUROPE AND ASIA** a prickly plant native to Europe and Asia with flowers covered with hooked leaves (**bracts**). Genus: *Dipsacus.* **2.** TEXTILES **TEASEL FLOWER HEADS** the flower heads of the teasel, used in the textile industry to raise the nap on fabric **3. IMPLEMENT USED TO RAISE NAP** an industrial implement or device used to raise the nap on fabric [Old English *tǣsel*] —**teaseller** *n.*

teaser /téezər/ *n.* **1. TRICKY PROBLEM** a tricky or difficult problem or question **2.** = **tease** *n.* 1 **3.** MARKETING **ADVERTISEMENT OFFERING A GIFT** an advertisement offering sth for free such as a bonus or gift **4.** TEXTILES **IMPLEMENT FOR TEASING WOOL** an implement for teasing fibres, especially wool

tea service, tea set *n.* a set of matching articles such as cups, saucers, and a teapot, used for serving tea

teashop /tée shop/ *n.* = **tearoom** *n.* 1 [Mid-19thC]

teaspoon /tée spoon/ *n.* **1. SMALL SPOON** a small spoon, used especially for stirring tea and other beverages and for eating desserts **2. teaspoon, teaspoonful AMOUNT HELD BY A TEASPOON** the amount held by a teaspoon **3. ONE THIRD OF A TABLESPOON** a standard household measure equal to one-third of a tablespoon or 5 ml

teat /teet/ *n.* **1.** ANAT, ZOOL **BODY PART FOR PRODUCING MILK** a protuberance on the breast or udder of a female mammal through which milk is excreted for the nourishment of young **2. MOUTHPIECE OF BABY'S FEEDING BOTTLE** a part designed to resemble a nipple or teat on a baby's or baby animal's feeding bottle. US term **nipple** *n.* 2 [12thC. From Old French *tete*, of Germanic origin.] —**teated** *adj.*

tea table *n.* a small table at which tea is served

tea-time *n.* the usual time at which tea is served, typically mid- or late afternoon

tea towel, **tea cloth** *n.* a cloth for drying dishes and other kitchen items. US term **dishtowel**

tea tray *n.* a tray intended for carrying a tea service

tea tree *n.* an Australian and New Zealand tree or shrub whose leaves were formerly used to make tea. It is now used to produce an oil (**tea tree oil**) used in cosmetics and lotions as an antiseptic. Genus: *Leptospermum.*

tea trolley *n.* a small household trolley from which tea can be served. US term **tea wagon**

tea wagon *n. US* = **tea trolley**

teazel, **teazle** *n.* = **teasel**

Tebet /te vét/, **Tevet** *n.* CALENDAR in the Jewish calendar, the fourth month of the civil year and the tenth month of the religious year. It is 29 days long.

TEC /tek/ *abbr.* Training and Enterprise Council

tec. *abbr.* technician

tech /tek/ *n.* (*informal*) **1.** EDUC **TECHNICAL COLLEGE** a technical college or institute **2.** THEATRE **TECHNICAL REHEARSAL** a theatre technical rehearsal [Early 20thC]

tech. *abbr.* **1.** technician **2.** technology **3.** technical

tech city (*plural* **tech cities**) *n.* a town or city where a large number of people are employed in advanced technology industries, especially those connected with computing and electronic engineering

techie /téki/, **tekkie** *n.* sb who is interested in, adept at, or studying a technical discipline, especially one that is based on computing or electronics (*informal*) [Mid-20thC. Formed from TECH.]

technetium /tek néeshi əm/ *n.* a silvery grey radioactive metallic element found only in the fission products of uranium or made artificially by the particle bombardment of molybdenum. Symbol **Tc** [Mid-20thC. From modern Latin, formed from Greek *tekhnētos* 'artificial', from *tekhnē* (see TECHNICAL).]

technetronic /tékni trónnik/ *adj.* associated with or marked by the changes brought about by modern technology and electronics [Mid-20thC. Blend of Greek *tekhnē* 'art, skill' (see TECHNICAL) and ELECTRONIC.]

technic /téknik/ *n.* **1.** INDUST = **technics 2. TECHNIQUE** the way in which the basics of sth are treated or skill in handling a technique (*dated*) [Early 17thC. From Greek *tekhnikos* 'of art' (see TECHNICAL).]

technical /téknik'l/ *adj.* **1. RELATING TO INDUSTRY OR APPLIED SCIENCE** relating to or specializing in industrial techniques or subjects or applied science **2. SKILLED IN PRACTICAL SUBJECTS** skilled in practical or scientific subjects **3. BELONGING TO PARTICULAR SUBJECT OR PROFESSION** belonging to or involving a particular subject, field, or profession ○ *technical glossaries* **4. STRICTLY INTERPRETED** according to a strict interpretation of rules or words **5. EXHIBITING TECHNIQUE** exhibiting or deriving from technique or the use of technique ○ *a high level of technical expertise* **6.** FIN **ANALYSING PRICES AND MARKET INDICATORS** used to describe a type of security analysis based on past prices and volume levels as well as other market indicators **7.** CLOTHES **HIGH-TECH** used to describe outdoor clothing that has been made using state-of-the-art materials and techniques ○ *Our technical fleece jacket has advanced dual construction.* ■ *n.* BASKETBALL = **technical foul** [Early 17thC. Formed from Greek *tekhnikos* 'of art', from *tekhnē* 'art, skill'. Ultimately from an Indo-European base meaning 'to weave', which is also the ancestor of English *text* and *tectonic*.] —**technicalness** *n.*

technical drawing *n.* **1.** EDUC **TECHNIQUE OF DRAUGHTING** the technique or practice of drawing objects and plans in a precise and detailed way, especially as taught in school **2.** ENG **PRECISE DRAWING SHOWING QUANTITIES OR MEASUREMENTS** a precise scale drawing of sth, usually prepared by a draughtsman for architectural, engineering, or industrial purposes, showing dimensions or quantities. Computer-assisted design programs have automated many of the draughting functions and made it possible to reduce significantly the time from concept to finished product.

technical foul *n.* in basketball, a foul against a player or coach for unsporting behaviour or language rather than for physical contact with an opponent

technicality /tékni kálləti/ (*plural* **-ties**) *n.* **1. INFORMATION UNDERSTOOD ONLY BY SPECIALISTS** information such as a detail or a term that is understood by or relevant only to a specialist **2. TRIVIAL POINT FROM STRICTLY APPLYING RULES** a minor point arising from a rigorous interpretation of laws or rules ○ *the case was dismissed on a legal technicality* **3. QUALITY OR STATE OF BEING TECHNICAL** the quality or state of being technical

technical knockout *n.* a decision in boxing that ends a match because one of the participants is too badly injured to continue fighting

technically /téknikli/ *adv.* **STRICTLY INTERPRETED** according to a very strict, even unnecessarily strict interpretation of rules or regulations ■ *adv., adj.* **IN TECHNIQUE** showing particular skill or ability in technique ■ *adv.* **SCIENTIFICALLY OR TECHNOLOGICALLY** relating to or making use of technology

technical rehearsal *n.* a rehearsal of a play or other theatrical presentation for the purpose of making sure that lights, sound, and any other technical effects are cued correctly and in working order

technical sergeant *n.* a noncommissioned rank in the US Air Force higher than staff sergeant and lower than master sergeant

technical support *n.* a repair or advice service offered to customers by some computer hardware and software manufacturers, usually by telephone, fax, or e-mail

technician /tek nísh'n/ *n.* **1. SPECIALIST IN INDUSTRIAL TECHNIQUES** a person who is skilled in specific industrial techniques **2. LABORATORY EMPLOYEE** sb employed to do practical work in a laboratory **3. SB SKILLED RATHER THAN EXPERT** sb who has skills but lacks originality or flair

Technicolor /tékni kulər/ *tdmk.* a trademark for an early colour process for making films that used three-colour separation negatives and a dye transfer process with three matrices made from the negatives

technics /tékniks/, **technic** *n.* the science or rules of a particular field of knowledge, especially a technical one (*takes a singular or plural verb*) [Mid-19thC. Plural of TECHNIC.]

technique /tek néek/ *n.* **1. PROCEDURE OR SKILL USED IN A TASK** the procedure, skill, or art used in a particular task **2. WAY IN WHICH THE BASICS ARE TREATED** the way in which the basics of sth, e.g. an artistic work or a sport, are treated **3. SKILL IN HANDLING THE TECHNIQUE OF STH** skill or expertise in handling the technique of sth ○ *a pianist with superb technique* **4. SPECIAL ABILITY** a special ability or knack [Early 19thC. Via French from Greek *tekhnikos* 'of art' (see TECHNICAL).]

techno- *prefix.* technology, technological ○ *technophobia* [From TECHNOLOGY]

technobabble /téknō bab'l/ *n.* language in which technical jargon or terms are overused, with the effect of making straightforward information difficult or impossible to understand

technocracy /tek nókrəssi/ (*plural* **-cies**) *n.* **1. GOVERNMENT BY TECHNICIANS** a social system in which scientists, engineers, and technicians have high social standing and political power **2. PHILOSOPHY PROMOTING TECHNOCRACY** a philosophy that advocates the enlistment of a bureaucracy of highly trained engineers, scientists, or technicians to run the government and society

technocrat /téknə krat/ *n.* **1. ENGINEER OR ECONOMIST AS BUREAUCRAT** a bureaucrat who is intensively trained in engineering, economics, or some form of technology **2. ADHERENT OF TECHNOCRACY** a proponent of government by technicians —**technocratic** /téknə kráttik/ *adj.*

technofreak /téknō freek/ *n.* sb who is a technical expert in, or obsessively enthusiastic about, information systems (*informal*) [Late 20thC]

technol. *abbr.* technology

technologize /tek nóllə jīz/ (**-gizes, -gizing, -gized**), **technologise** (**-gises, -gising, -gised**) *vti.* to modify or modernize sth by introducing technology —**technologization** /tek nóllə jī záysh'n/ *n.*

technology /tek nólləji/ (*plural* **-gies**) *n.* **1. APPLICATION OF TOOLS AND METHODS** the study, development, and application of devices, machines, and techniques for manufacturing and productive processes ○ *recent developments in seismographic technology* **2. METHOD OF APPLYING TECHNICAL KNOWLEDGE** a method or methodology that applies technical knowledge or tools ○ *a new technology for accelerating incubation* ○ *'...Maryland-based firm uses database and Internet technology to track a company's consumption of printed goods...'* (*Forbes Global Business and Finance*; November 1998) **3.** ANTHROP **SUM OF A SOCIETY'S OR CULTURE'S KNOWLEDGE** the sum of a society's or culture's practical knowledge, especially with reference to its material culture [Early 17thC. From Greek *tekhnologia*, literally 'systematic treatment', literally 'science of craft', from *tekhnē* 'art, craft'.] —**technologic** /téknə lójjik/ *adj.* —**technological** /-lójjik'l/ *adj.* —**technologist** /tek nóllәjjist/ *n.* —**technologically** /téknə lójjikli/ *adv.*

technophile /téknō fīl/ *n.* sb who is comfortable with and adapts readily to new technology or computerization

technophobe /téknə fōb/ *n.* sb who is intimidated and confused by new technology and computerization

technophobia /téknō fōbi ə/ *n.* fear of or resistance to new technology and computerization —**technophobe** /téknō fōb/ *n.*

technostructure /téknō strukchər/ *n.* a network of controlling technocrats in an organization or society

technothriller /téknō thrilər/ *n.* a suspenseful book or film in which the plot turns on seemingly plausible technological wonders

techy *adj.* = **tetchy** —**techily** *adv.* —**techiness** *n.*

tecta plural of **tectum**

tectonic /tek tónnik/ *adj.* **1.** GEOL **OF THE DEFORMATION OF ROCKS** relating to the forces that produce movement and deformation of the Earth's crust **2.** CONSTR **OF CONSTRUCTION** relating to construction and architecture [Mid-17thC. Via late Latin from Greek *tektonikos*, from *tekton* 'builder, carpenter' (source of English *architect*).] —**tectonically** *adv.*

tectonic plate *n.* a segment of the Earth's crust that moves relative to other plates and is characterized by volcanic and seismic activity around its margins

tectonics /tek tónniks/ *n.* **1.** GEOL **STUDY OF THE EARTH'S CRUST** the study of the mechanisms and results of large-scale movement of the Earth's crust, such as that producing mountain ranges and extensive fault systems (*takes a singular verb*) ◊ **plate tectonics 2.** BUILDING **SCIENCE OF BUILDING** the science or practice of building construction

tectrix /téktriks/ (*plural* **-trices** /téktri seez/) *n.* ZOOL = **covert** *n.* 3 [Late 19thC. From modern Latin, from Latin *tect-*, past participle stem of *tegere* (see TECTUM).] —**tectricial** /tek trísh'l/ *adj.*

tectum /téktəm/ (*plural* **-ta** /-tə/) *n.* a part in the body that forms a covering or is arranged like a roof [Early 20thC. From Latin, 'roof', from *tegere* 'to cover' (source of English *detect* and *protect*).] —**tectal** *adj.*

Tecumseh /tə kúmssə/ (1768?–1813) Native North American leader. As leader of the Shawnee people he attempted to form an alliance of Native American tribes to fight against US expansion into the Midwest. He was killed in battle fighting on the British side in the War of 1812.

ted /ted/ *n.* **TEDDY BOY** a teddy boy (*informal*) ■ *vt.* (**teds, tedding, tedded**) **DRY HAY** to spread or shake up mown grass in order to dry it when making hay [15thC. From Old Norse *teðja* 'to spread (manure)'.] —**tedder** *n.*

Tedder /téddər/, **Arthur William, 1st Baron** (1890–1967) British air force commander. He played a major role as an RAF commander and strategist during World War II. He was made marshal of the RAF in 1961.

teddy[1] /téddi/ (*plural* -**dies**) *n.* **1.** = **teddy bear 2.** CLOTHES **WOMAN'S UNDERWEAR** a woman's one-piece undergarment serving as both bra and panties [Early 20thC. Origin of sense 2 uncertain: probably from sense 1, perhaps because the loose-fitting, all-in-one shape was thought to resemble a teddy bear.]

teddy[2] /téddi/ (*plural* -**dies**) *n.* W Country a potato [Early 20thC. Alteration of TATTIE.]

teddy bear, **teddy** *n.* a furry stuffed toy in the shape of a stylized bear cub [Early 20thC. Named after *Theodore* ('Teddy') ROOSEVELT, who was fond of bear-hunting.]

— **WORD KEY: ORIGIN** —
President Theodore Roosevelt was fond of bear-hunting. His nickname 'Teddy', was used in a humorous poem in the *New York Times* about the adventures of two bears. Their names (Teddy B and Teddy G) were then appropriated to two bears in the Bronx Zoo whose popularity caused toy manufacturers to market toy bears as *teddy bears*.

teddy boy *n.* **1.** 50S YOUTH a young man in Britain in the 1950s and early 1960s who followed the fashion of dressing in neo-Edwardian style with tight narrow trousers, pointed shoes, and long sideboards **2.** REBELLIOUS YOUTH any rebellious and tough young man (*dated*) [Mid-20thC. *Teddy* from the pet form of *Edward*, alluding to EDWARD VII.]

teddy girl *n.* a teddy boy's female companion

Te Deum /tay dáy əm, tee deé əm/ (*plural* **Te Deums**) *n.* **1.** CHRISTIAN HYMN an ancient Christian hymn praising God that is sung or recited at matins in the Roman Catholic Church or at morning prayers in the Church of England **2.** CHRISTIAN SERVICE OF THANKSGIVING a Christian service of thanksgiving that uses the Te Deum [Pre-12thC. From Latin *Te Deum laudamus* 'Thee God, we praise', the first words of the hymn.]

tedious /teédi əss/ *adj.* boring because of being long, monotonous, or repetitive —**tediously** *adv.* —**tediousness** *n.*

— **WORD KEY: SYNONYMS** —
See Synonyms at **boring**.

tedium /teédi əm/ *n.* the quality of being boring, monotonous, too long, or repetitive [Mid-17thC. From Latin *taedium* 'weariness, disgust', from *taedere* 'to be wearisome'.]

tee[1] /tee/ *n.* **1.** LETTER T the letter T **2.** US CLOTHES **T-SHIRT** a T-shirt (*informal*) **3.** T-SHAPED THING sth with the shape or form of a capital T, e.g. two pipes joined to form this shape **4.** SPORTS **TARGET** the mark aimed at in curling, quoits, and some other games [15thC. The sense 'target' is of uncertain origin: perhaps from the meaning 'T-shaped thing', from the shape of the marks that were originally used.]

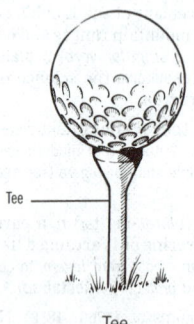
Tee

tee[2] /tee/ *n.* **1.** GOLF **PEG** a small wooden or plastic peg with one pointed and one cupped end, inserted in the ground to hold a golf ball **2.** GOLF **STARTING AREA** an area on a golf course where play for a new hole begins **3.** AMERICAN FOOTBALL, RUGBY **BALL STAND** a plastic device that supports a football or rugby ball on the ground in kicking position ■ *vti.* (**tees, teeing, teed**) GOLF **POSITION THE BALL** to place a ball on a tee ready

for striking [Late 17thC. Originally Scottish dialect, of uncertain origin: perhaps a back-formation from earlier *teaz* (taken as plural), of unknown origin.]

tee off *vi.* **1.** GOLF **START PLAY** to hit the ball from a tee at the start of a hole of golf **2.** START STH NEW to start a new activity (*informal*)

TEE *abbr.* Trans-Europe Express (train)

teed off /teéd-/ *adj.* US angry, especially because of sth that sb has done (*informal*) [Origin uncertain: probably an alteration of *peed* (*pissed*) *off*.]

tee-hee /tee heé/, **te-hee** *interj.* EXPRESSING LAUGHTER used to indicate brief, especially mocking or gloating laughter ■ *vi.* (**tee-hees, tee-heeing, tee-heed; te-hees, te-heeing, te-heed**) LAUGH to laugh or chuckle [14thC. An imitation of the sound.]

tee-joint *n.* = **T-joint**

teem[1] /teem/ (**teems, teeming, teemed**) *vi.* to have an extremely large number of people or animals in a place ○ *streets teeming with people* [Old English *tēman*, from a prehistoric Germanic word, which is also the ancestor of English *team*. The meaning 'abound' evolved from 'give birth' via 'produce offspring prolifically'.]

teem[2] /teem/ (**teems, teeming, teemed**) *v.* **1.** *vi.* RAIN HEAVILY to rain very hard **2.** *vt.* DISCHARGE STH to pour out or empty sth [14thC. From Old Norse *tœma* 'to empty', from *tómr* 'empty'.]

teen[1] /teen/ *adj.* TEENAGE teenage (*informal*) ■ *n.* TEENAGER a teenager (*informal*) [Early 20thC. Shortening.]

teen[2] /teen/ *n.* a feeling of misery or pain (*archaic*) [Old English *tēona*. Ultimately from an Indo-European word meaning 'misfortune, suffering'.]

teenage /teén ayj/, **teenaged** /teén ayjd/ *adj.* **1.** BETWEEN 13 AND 19 aged between 13 and 19 ○ *teenage girls* **2.** OF TEENAGERS relating to teenagers ○ *teenage styles*

teenager /teén ayjər/ *n.* a boy or girl between the ages of 13 and 19

— **WORD KEY: SYNONYMS** —
See Synonyms at **youth**.

teens /teenz/ *npl.* **1.** YEARS BETWEEN 13 AND 19 the years in sb's life between the ages of 13 and 19 **2.** 13 TO 19 the numbers ending in '-teen' [Late 16thC. Formed from -TEEN.]

teensy /teénzi/ (-**sier**, -**siest**) *adj.* = **teeny** (*informal*) [Late 19thC. Origin uncertain: probably formed from TEENY.]

teensy-weensy /teénzi weénzi/ *adj.* = **teeny-weeny** (*informal*) [Modelled on TEENY-WEENY]

teeny /teéni/ (-**nier**, -**niest**) *adj.* very small (*informal*) [Early 19thC. Variant of TINY, modelled on WEENY.]

teenybopper /teéni bopər/ *n.* a young teenager, usually a young girl, who follows the latest fads in fashion and music (*informal insult*) [Mid-20thC. An allusion to the teenager's preoccupation with dancing and pop music.]

teeny-weeny *adj.* very small (*informal*)

teepee *n.* = **tepee**

tee-piece *n.* = **T-piece**

tee-plate *n.* = **T-plate**

Tees /teez/ river of northeastern England, flowing into the North Sea at Teesmouth. Length: 128 km/80 mi.

tee shirt *n.* = **T-shirt**

tee-square *n.* = **T-square**

Teesside /teéz sīd/ industrial region around the mouth of the River Tees in northeastern England. It includes the city of Middlesbrough.

teeter /teétər/ (-**ters**, -**tering**, -**tered**) *vi.* **1.** TOTTER to walk or move unsteadily and as if about to fall ○ *teetering along in her high heels* **2.** BE IN PRECARIOUS POSITION to be in a precarious position in which things could imminently go badly wrong ○ *For 24 hours the country teetered on the brink of war.* [Mid-19thC. Variant of TITTER.]

teeth plural of **tooth**

teethe /teeth/ (**teethes, teething, teethed**) *vi.* to grow baby teeth [15thC. Formed from TEETH.]

teething ring /teéthing-/ *n.* a ring of hard rubber or plastic on which a baby can bite when teething

teething troubles *npl.* temporary difficulties that arise at the outset of a new activity

teetotal /tee tót'l/ *adj.* **1.** RESOLVED TO ABSTAIN completely abstaining from alcoholic beverages **2.** TOTAL complete and absolute [Mid-19thC. Formed from the initial letter of TOTAL + TOTAL. Allegedly coined by the Englishman Richard Turner in a speech calling for abstinence from all alcohol, including beer.] —**teetotalism** *n.* —**teetotaller** *n.* —**teetotally** *adv.*

teetotum /tee tótəm/ *n.* a top spun with the fingers, once used in a game of chance [Early 18thC. Formed from Latin *totum* 'all' + its initial letter 'T', which is inscribed on one side of the toy.]

teff /tef/, **tef** *n.* an annual North African grass cultivated for its seed, which is used as a grain. Latin name: *Eragrostis tef*. [Late 18thC. From Amharic *tēf*.]

tefillin /tə fíllin/ *npl.* the small leather boxes containing Hebrew texts ritually worn by orthodox Jewish men. ◊ **phylactery** [Early 17thC. From Aramaic *təpillīn* 'prayers'.]

TEFL /téff'l/ *abbr.* Teaching (of) English as a Foreign Language

Teflon /téf lon/ *tdmk.* a trademark for a plastic material with non-stick properties that is used as a coating, e.g. for cookware

teg /teg/ *n.* a sheep of either sex between weaning and first shearing [Early 16thC. Origin unknown.]

tegmen /tégmən/ (*plural* -**mina** /-mənə/), **tegmentum** /tegméntəm/ *n.* **1.** BOT INNER LAYER IN A SEED the inner layer of a seed's coat **2.** INSECTS INSECT FOREWING the forewing of a primitive insect such as the cockroach **3.** BIOL COVERING PART a covering part in a plant or animal [Early 19thC. Ultimately from Latin *tegere* (see TECTUM).] —**tegminal** /tégminəl/ *adj.*

tegu /ti góo/ (*plural* -**gus** or -**gu**) *n.* a fast-running lizard of Central and South America that grows up to 4 feet long. Genus: *Tupinambis*. [Mid-20thC. Shortening of *teguexin*, from Aztec *tecoixin* 'lizard'.]

Tegucigalpa /te góossi gálpə/ capital city of Honduras, in the Central District in the south-central section of the country. It is the nation's largest city. Population: 738,500 (1993).

tegular /téggyoölər/, **tegulated** /téggyoö làytid/ *adj.* relating to or resembling tiles [Early 19thC. Ultimately from Latin *tegula* 'tile' (source of English *tile*), from Latin *tegere* (see TECTUM).] —**tegularly** *adv.*

tegument /téggyoömənt/ *n.* an integument [15thC. From Latin *tegumentum* 'covering', from *tegere* (see TECTUM).] —**tegumental** /téggyoö mént'l/ *adj.* —**tegumentary** /-méntəri/ *adj.*

te-hee *interj.*, *vi.* = **tee-hee**

Tehran /te ra'an/, **Tehrān** capital city of Iran, located in the northern part of the country. Population: 6,475,527 (1991).

Teide, Pico de /táythə/ the highest mountain in Spain, on the island of Tenerife. Height: 3,715 m/12,188 ft.

te igitur /táy íggitoor/ *n.* the first prayer of the Roman Catholic mass, beginning 'te igitur clementissime Pater' [Early 19thC. From Latin, 'thee, therefore'.]

teiglach /táyg laakh, tíg-/ *n.* a Jewish or German biscuit made from spiced dough shaped into small balls and simmered in honey, nuts, and spices. When cold, the cooked biscuits can be packed in a syrup made from the remains of cooking honey. (*takes singular or plural verb*) [Early 20thC. From Yiddish *teyglekh*, from *teyg* 'dough', ultimately from Old High German *teic*.]

Teilhard de Chardin /táy jaa də shaárdan/, **Pierre** (1881–1955) French priest, palaeontologist, and theologian. He was one of the discoverers of Peking Man, and in his major work, *The Phenomenon of Man* (1955), he argued that scientific evolutionary theory is compatible with Christian doctrine.

teind /teend/ *n.* Scotland TITHE a tithe ■ *vti.* (**teinds, teinding, teinded**) *Scotland* TO TITHE to tithe [13thC. Alteration of TENTH.]

Te Kanawa /tə ka'anəwə, tay-/, **Dame Kiri** (b. 1944) New Zealand opera singer. She made her debut as a soprano at Covent Garden in 1970 and went on to perform at major opera houses worldwide. Full name **Kiri Janette Te Kanawa**

Tekapo, Lake /tékəpō/ lake in the centre of the South Island, New Zealand. Area: 83 sq. km/32 sq. mi.

tekkie *n.* = **techie** (*informal*)

Te Kooti /te koóti/, **Arikirangi Te Turuki** (1830?–93) New Zealand Maori leader. He was the founder of the Ringatu Church, and conducted a guerrilla campaign against the British authorities.

tektite /ték tīt/ *n.* a small dark-coloured glassy object, possibly resulting from meteoric impact, found in groups at various locations throughout the world [Early 20thC. Formed from Greek *tēktos* 'molten', from *tēkein* 'to melt'.]

tel. *abbr.* 1. telegraphic 2. telegram 3. telegraph 4. telephone

tela /teélə/ (*plural* **-ae** /-lee/) *n.* a delicate part or tissue in the body with a fine or intricate pattern like a web [Early 20thC. From Latin, 'web'.]

telaesthesia /teélliss theézh ə, télliss theézi ə/ *n.* the supposed perception of phenomena or events considered beyond the range of normal senses [Late 19thC. Literally 'perception from afar', formed from Greek *aisthēsis* 'perception'.] —**telaesthetic** /télliss théttik/ *adj.*

telamon /téllə mon, -mən/ (*plural* **telamones** /téllə mṓneez/ *or* **telamons**) *n.* ARCHIT. = **atlas** *n.* 3 [Early 17thC. Ultimately from Greek *Telamon*, the name of a Greek mythical hero.]

telangiectasia /te lánji ek táyzi ə/, **telangiectasis** /-ek táyssiss/ *n.* permanent dilation of the capillaries and small blood vessels, especially in the face and thighs, producing dark red blotches [Mid-19thC. Ultimately from Greek *telos* 'end' + *aggeion* 'vessel' + *ektasis* 'extension'.] —**telangiectatic** /te lánji ek táttik/ *adj.*

Telautograph /tel áwtə graaf, -graf/ *tdmk.* a trademark for a device used to transmit writing or drawings down a telegraph line, using an electromagnetically controlled pen at each end

Tel Aviv /tél ə veév/, **Tel Aviv-Jaffa** /tél ə veév jáffə/ city in Israel on the Mediterranean Sea. It comprises the historical Arab town of Jaffa and modern Tel Aviv. Population: 353,100 (1997).

tele- *prefix.* 1. distant, operating at a distance ○ *telepathy* 2. television ○ *telecourse* 3. telegraph, telephone ○ *teleprinter* [From Greek *tēle* 'far away']

telebanking /télli bangking/ *n.* a system of transacting business with a bank by telephone

telebridge /télli brij/ *n.* a telephone system that enables three or more people to be connected simultaneously ○ *'Group classes are limited to 15 participants and are held on a telebridge.' (The Washington Post; July 1998)*

telecast /télli kaast/ *n.* TV BROADCAST a television broadcast ■ *vti.* (**-casts, -casting, -cast** *or* **-casted**) BROADCAST A TV PROGRAMME to broadcast a programme on television —**telecaster** *n.*

telecom /télli kom/ *n.* telecommunication (*informal*) [Mid-20thC. Shortening.]

telecommunication /télli kə myóoni káysh'n/ *n.* the transmission of encoded sound, pictures, or data over significant distances, using radio signals or electrical or optical lines

telecommunications /télli kə myóoni káysh'nz/ *n.* the science and technology of transmitting information electronically by means of wires or radio signals with integrated encoding and decoding equipment (*takes a singular or plural verb*)

telecommute /télli kə myóot/ (**-commutes, -commuting, -commuted, -commuted**) *vi.* to work from home on a computer linked to the workplace via modem —**telecommuter** *n.*

telecommuting /télli kə myóoting/ *n.* the process of working at home while transmitting data and documents to and from a nominal workplace over telephone lines using a telephone, fax machine, and modem-equipped computer

teleconference /télli kónfərənss/ *n.* MEETING VIA TELECOMMUNICATIONS EQUIPMENT a meeting held among people in different places by means of telecommunications equipment ■ *vi.* (**-ences, -encing, -enced**) TAKE PART IN A TELECONFERENCE to hold a teleconference, or take part in one

teleconferencing /télli kónfərənssing/ *n.* a system of video-conferencing that uses a restricted band of frequencies and allows participants to be connected by telephone lines

Telecopier /télli kopi ər/ *tdmk.* US a trademark for a device used for sending copies of documents electronically over a telephone line

telecottage /télli kotij/ *n.* a place where people can use computers and other electronic equipment, which allows them to work without having to commute to an office. They are often in rural areas. —**telecottaging** *n.*

teledu /télli doo/ (*plural* **-dus** *or* **-du**) *n.* a Southeast Asian carnivorous mammal of the weasel family with a dark coat and a white stripe down its back. It emits a foul-smelling secretion from anal glands when provoked. Latin name: *Mydaus javanensis*. [Early 19thC. From Javanese.]

telefacsimile /télli fak símməli/ *n.* fax (*formal*)

téléférique /téllifə reék/ *n.* = **téléphérique** [Variant of TÉLÉPHÉRIQUE]

teleg. *abbr.* 1. telegraph 2. telegraphic 3. telegraphy 4. telegram

telega /te láygə/ *n.* a primitive four-wheeled Russian cart [Mid-16thC. From Russian.]

telegenic /télli jénnik/ *adj.* pleasant and attractive when viewed on television —**telegenically** *adv.*

telegnosis /téllə nṓssiss, télləg-/ *n.* knowledge of phenomena beyond the range of normal sense perception —**telegnostic** /téllə nóstik, télləg-/ *adj.*

telegony /ti léggəni/ *n.* the now discredited idea that characteristics from the sire of a female's earlier pregnancy can be inherited by offspring from a subsequent sire —**telegonic** /télli gónnik/ *adj.* —**telegonous** /ti léggənəss/ *adj.*

telegram /télli gram/ *n.* a message sent by telegraph [Mid-19thC. Coined on the model of TELEGRAPH.] —**telegrammatic** /télli grə máttik/ *adj.* —**telegrammic** /télli grámmik/ *adj.*

telegraph /télli graaf, -graf/ *n.* 1. LONG-DISTANCE COMMUNICATION METHOD THROUGH WIRES a method of long-distance communicating by coded electric impulses transmitted through wires 2. = **telegram** ■ *v.* (**-graphs, -graphing, -graphed**) 1. *vti.* SEND BY WIRE to send a message to sb by telegraph 2. *vt.* INDICATE to communicate a thought or feeling indirectly or nonverbally 3. *vt.* SHOW INTENTION to give advance notice of intentions, especially unwittingly, to an audience or opponent [Early 18thC. From French *télégraphe*, literally 'sth that writes far', from *-graphe* (see -GRAPH).] —**telegrapher** /ti léggrəfər/ *n.* —**telegraphist** /ti léggrəfist/ *n.*

telegraphese /télli gra feéz/ *n.* language reduced to its essential elements without regard to elegance or grammar, as typically found in telegrams

telegraphic /télli gráffik/ *adj.* 1. RELATING TO TELEGRAMS relating to telegraphy or telegrams 2. CONCISE concise or elliptical in spoken or written expression —**telegraphically** *adv.*

telegraph plant *n.* a tropical Asian shrub of the legume family, with small leaflets that jerk spasmodically under solar radiation. Latin name: *Desmodium gyrans*. [*Telegraph* from the movement of its leaves, suggesting the movement of semaphore signals]

telegraph pole, **telegraph post** *n.* a high wooden pole for supporting telephone wires. US term **telephone pole**

telegraphy /ti léggrəfi/ *n.* the system, study, or operation of telegraph communications

Telegu *n.*, *adj.* = **Telugu**

telekinesis /télli ki neéssiss, -kī-/ *n.* the supposed psychic power to move or deform inanimate objects without the use of physical force —**telekinetic** /télli ki néttik, -kī-/ *adj.* —**telekinetically** /-néttikli/ *adv.*

Telemachus /tə lémməkəss/ *n.* in Greek mythology, the son of Odysseus, who waited with his mother, Penelope, for his father's return after the Trojan War

Telemann /táylə man, téllə-/, **Georg Philipp** (1681–1767) German composer. A prolific composer, he bridged the baroque and early classical periods in works that include 40 operas and numerous orchestral suites and chamber pieces.

telemark /télli maark/ *n.* a turn in cross-country skiing accomplished by putting the outside ski forwards and turning it slowly inwards [Early 20thC. Named after *Telemark*, a region in Norway where it originated.]

telemarketing /télli maarkiting/ *n.* selling or promoting goods and services by telephone —**telemarketer** *n.*

telemedicine /télli medəss'n/ *n.* the use of video links, e-mail, telephone, or another telecommunications system to transmit medical information, e.g. in consultations between a doctor and patient or supervision of medical staff

Telemessage /télli messij/ *tdmk.* a trademark for a message sent by telephone or telex and printed out for the person receiving it. It has taken the place of the telegram in Britain.

telemeter *n.* /ti lémmitər, télli meétər/ 1. REMOTE MEASURING DEVICE a device used to record information about a remote object or event and transmit it to an observer 2. DEVICE FOR MEASURING DISTANCES DIRECTLY a device used for measuring distances directly that does not use rods or chains across the distance to be measured ■ *vt.* /télli meétər/ (**-ters, -tering, -tered**) TRANSMIT DATA to collect and transmit data about a remote object, especially using a satellite —**telemetric** /télli méttrik/ *adj.* —**telemetrical** /-méttrik'l/ *adj.* —**telemetrically** /-méttrikli/ *adv.*

telemetry /ti lémmətri/ *n.* 1. SCIENCE OF REMOTE MEASUREMENT the science or activity of gathering data about remote objects and transmitting the data electronically 2. MEASUREMENT OF DISTANCES measurement of distances using a tellurometer

telencephalon /téll en séffə lon/ *n.* the frontmost part of the brain, consisting of the cerebral hemispheres —**telencephalic** /téll enssə fállik/ *adj.*

teleological /télli ə lŏjjik'l, teéli ə lójjik'l/, **teleologic** *adj.* relating to the study of ultimate causes in nature or of actions in relation to their ends or utility —**teleologically** *adv.*

teleological argument *n.* an argument for God's existence from the existence of order and design in the universe

teleology /teéli ólləji/ *n.* 1. STUDY OF CAUSES the study of ultimate causes in nature 2. APPROACH TO ETHICS an approach to ethics that studies actions in relations to their ends or utility 3. GOAL-DIRECTED ACTIVITY any activity that tends towards the achievement of a goal [Mid-18thC. From modern Latin *teleologia*, literally 'science of ends', from Greek *telos* 'end'.] —**teleologism** /teéli ólləjizəm/ *n.* —**teleologist** /-ólləjist/ *n.*

teleost /télli ost/, **teleostean** /télli ósti ən/ *n.* any bony fish with rayed fins in a suborder that includes most living species, numbering around 20,000, but excluding sturgeons, gars, sharks, rays, and related fish. Subclass: Teleostei. [Mid-19thC. Coined from Greek *telos* 'end' + *osteon* 'bone'.]

telepath /télli path/ *n.* sb who is believed or who claims to communicate by telepathy

telepathize /tə léppə thīz/ (**-thizes, -thizing, -thized**), **telepathise** (**-thises, -thising, -thised**) *vi.* to claim or be believed to communicate by telepathy

telepathy /tə léppəthi/ *n.* supposed communication directly from one person's mind to another's without speech, writing, or other signs or symbols —**telepathic** /télli páthik/ *adj.* —**telepathically** *adv.*

téléphérique /téllifə reék/, **téléférique** *n.* 1. CABLE CAR a cable car 2. CABLEWAY a cableway [Early 20thC. From French, literally 'carrying far', from Greek *pherein* 'to carry'.]

telephone /télli fōn/ *n.* 1. ELECTRONIC COMMUNICATIONS DEVICE an electronic apparatus containing a receiver and transmitter that is connected to a telecommunications system, enabling the user to speak to and hear others with similar equipment 2. COMMUNICATION USING TELEPHONES a system of communications using telephones ○ *a telephone*

Telephone

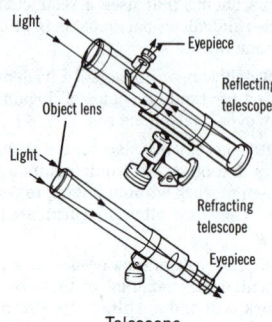

Telescope

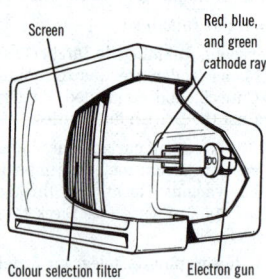

Television set

company ■ *vti.* (**-phones, -phoning, -phoned**) **1.** USE TELEPHONE to contact and speak to sb using the telephone **2.** CONVEY STH BY TELEPHONE to send a message by telephone ○ *Bob couldn't come to the party and telephoned his regrets.* —**telephoner** *n.* —**telephonic** /télli fónnik/ *adj.* —**telephonically** /-fónnikli/ *adv.*

telephone answering machine *n.* an answering machine

telephone book *n.* = telephone directory

telephone booth *n.* US = telephone box

telephone box *n.* an enclosed or partly enclosed space with a pay telephone in it. US term **telephone booth**

telephone directory *n.* an alphabetical listing of individuals or businesses who have telephones, along with their addresses and telephone numbers

telephone exchange *n.* a centre that houses equipment used for interconnecting telephone lines

telephone pole *n.* US = telegraph pole

telephone tag *n.* a situation in which two people repeatedly return each other's telephone calls and leave recorded messages without succeeding in speaking directly to each other (*informal*)

telephonist /tə léffənist/ *n.* a telephone switchboard operator

telephony /tə léffəni/ *n.* the science, technology, or system of communication by telephone

telephoto /télli fótō/ *adj.* MAGNIFYING A DISTANT OBJECT producing a large image of a distant object ■ *n.* (*plural* **-tos**) **1.** = telephoto lens **2.** PHOTO TAKEN WITH TELEPHOTO LENS a photograph taken using a telephoto lens [Early 20thC. Shortening.]

telephotography /télli fə tóggrəfi/ *n.* the photographing of distant objects with the use of special lenses or electronic equipment —**telephotographic** /télli fōtə gráffik/ *adj.*

telephoto lens *n.* a camera lens that integrates a telescope

teleplay /télli play/ *n.* a treatment or script for a play written for presentation on television

teleport /télli pawrt/ (**-ports, -porting, -ported**) *v.* **1.** *vt.* MOVE STH USING MENTAL POWER to move an object supposedly using telekinesis **2.** *vi.* MOVE SOMEWHERE WITHOUT TRAVELLING in science fiction and fantasy, to move instantly from one place to another by some paranormal or magical means [Mid-20thC. Coined from TELE- + Latin *portare* 'to carry'.] —**teleportation** /télli pawr táysh'n/ *n.*

teleprinter /télli printər/ *n.* a piece of equipment for telegraphic communication that uses a device like a typewriter for data input and output. US term **teletypewriter**

teleprocessing /télli prō sessing/ *n.* the use of computer terminals in different locations, connected to a main computer, to process data

Teleran /télla ran/ *tdmk.* trademark for a radar system that gathers information about the airspace surrounding an airport and relays it to local air traffic via television

telerecording /télli ri káwrding/ *n.* the recording of a television programme on tape or film as it is being broadcast

telesales /télli saylz/ *n.* = telemarketing

telescience /télli sī ənss/ *n.* the technology of making observations and performing experiments from a great distance

telescope /télli skōp/ *n.* **1.** DEVICE FOR LOOKING AT DISTANT OBJECTS a device for making distant objects appear nearer and larger by means of compound lenses or concave mirrors **2.** = radio telescope ■ *v.* (**-scopes, -scoping, -scoped**) **1.** *vi.* COLLAPSE NEATLY to slide neatly one inside another like the sections of a telescope **2.** *vt.* CONDENSE STH to make sth shorter in time or length ○ *telescoped his adventure into a one-hour talk* [Mid-17thC. From Italian *telescopio* or modern Latin *telescopium*, both literally 'looking far', from, ultimately, Greek *skopein* 'to look' (source of English *scope* and *bishop*).]

telescopic /télli skóppik/ *adj.* **1.** OF TELESCOPES relating to or visible only by using a telescope **2.** ENLARGING with the ability to make sth distant seem nearer or larger ○ *a telescopic lens* **3.** ABLE TO SEE FAR able to see great distances ○ *telescopic vision* **4.** COLLAPSIBLE consisting of parts that slide one inside another ○ *a tripod with telescopic legs* —**telescopically** *adv.*

telescopic sight *n.* a telescope mounted on a rifle and used for sighting, especially on distant targets

Telescopium /télla skópi əm/ *n.* a constellation in the sky of the southern hemisphere between Sagittarius and Pavo

telescopy /tə léskəpi/ *n.* the science and technology of making and using telescopes

teleshopping /télli shoping/ *n.* the practice or activity of ordering goods advertised on television by phone or computer

telestereoscope /télli stérri ə skōp, -steéri-/ *n.* a binocular telescope or telescopic stereoscope adapted to provide a three-dimensional view of distant objects or landscapes

telesthesia *n.* US = telaesthesia

telestich /ti léstik, télli stik/ *n.* an acrostic or poem in which the last letters in each line spell a word [Mid-17thC. From Greek *telos* 'end' + *stikhos* 'row, line of verse' (see ACROSTIC).]

Telesto /ti léstō/ *n.* a very small natural satellite of Saturn, discovered in 1980. It is irregular in shape with a maximum dimension of 30 km/19 mi., and occupies an intermediate orbit.

teletex /télli teks/ *n.* a trademark for a method of transmitting text between teleprinters [Late 20thC. Origin uncertain: probably a blend of TELEX and TEXT.]

Teletext *tdmk.* a trademark for a system of broadcasting news and other information in written form that can be viewed on specially equipped televisions.

telethon /télla thon/ *n.* a lengthy television broadcast that combines entertainment with appeals to donate to a particular charity [Mid-20thC. Blend of TELE- and MARATHON.]

Teletype /télli tīp/ *tdmk.* a trademark for a teleprinter

teleutospore /ti lóotə spawr/ *n.* BIOL = teliospore [Late 19thC. Formed from Greek *teleutē* 'completion' (from *telos* 'end') + SPORE.] —**teleutosporic** /ti lóotə spáwrik, -spórrik/ *adj.*

televangelist /télli vánjəlist/ *n.* a Christian evangelist whose services and revivals are broadcast on television [Late 20thC. Blend of TELEVISION and EVANGELIST.] —**televangelism** *n.*

televise /télli vīz/ (**-vises, -vising, -vised**) *vt.* to broadcast sth on television [Early 20thC. Back-formation from TELEVISION.]

television /télli vizh'n, -vízh'n/ *n.* **1.** VIDEO BROADCASTING SYSTEM a system of capturing images and sounds, broadcasting these via a combined electronic audio and video signal, and reproducing them to be viewed and listened to **2.** TV SET an electronic device for receiving and reproducing the images and sounds of a television signal **3.** TV INDUSTRY the television industry ○ *works in television* **4.** BROADCAST CONTENT the image, sound, or content of a television broadcast ○ *appearing on television for the first time*

television set *n.* = television *n.* 2

television tube *n.* = tube *n.* 7

televisual /télli vízhyoo əl, télla-, -víz-/ *adj.* relating to television or suitable for appearing on television — **televisually** *adv.*

teleworking /télli wurking/ *n.* = telecommuting

telex /télleks/ *n.* **1.** COMMUNICATIONS SYSTEM a communications system using teleprinters that communicate via telephone lines **2.** MESSAGE a message sent or received by telex ■ *vti.* (**-exes, -exing, -exed**) SEND BY TELEX to send a message to sb by telex [Mid-20thC. Blend of TELEPRINTER and EXCHANGE.]

telfer *n.* = telpher

telferage *n.* = telpherage

Telford /télfərd/ industrial town in Shropshire, England, designated as a new town in 1968. Population: 115,000 (1991).

Telford, Thomas (1757–1834) British civil engineer. He was a pioneer in the building of roads, canals, and bridges, most notably the Menai Suspension Bridge (1826) in Wales.

telia plural of telium

telic /téllik/ *adj.* directed towards a definite end or purpose [Mid-19thC. From Greek *telikos* 'final', from *telos* 'end'.]

Telidon /télli don/ *tdmk.* a trademark for a Canadian system that sends information by computer and telephone, allowing people to buy tickets or shop from home

teliospore /teéli ə spawr/ *n.* a resting spore that develops in rust and smut fungi in the autumn and germinates in the spring [Early 20thC. Formed from TELIUM + SPORE.] —**teliosporic** /teéli ə spáwrik, -spórrik/ *adj.*

telium /teéli əm, télli-/ (*plural* **-a** /-li ə/) *n.* the spore case of a rust or smut fungus that bears teliospores [Early 20thC. Formed from Greek *telos* 'end'.] —**telial** *adj.*

tell /tel/ (**tells, telling, told**) *v.* **1.** *vt.* INFORM SB to inform sb, or inform sb of sth ○ *Who told you?* ○ *Jim told us the news.* **2.** *vt.* RELATE EVENTS OR FACTS to give an account in speech or writing of events or facts ○ *tell a story* **3.** *vti.* EXPRESS IN WORDS to express thoughts or feelings to sb in words **4.** *vt.* EXPRESS STH to speak, expressing a particular thing ○ *tell a lie* **5.** *vt.* ORDER SB to command or order sb to do sth **6.** DISTINGUISH SB to be able to distinguish things ○ *couldn't tell one from the other* **7.** *vt.* REVEAL THE FUTURE to purport to reveal future events ○ *tell your fortune* **8.** *vt.* COUNT THINGS to count things, e.g. votes cast or beads as part of a prayer ○ *tell a rosary* **9.** *vi.* REVEAL A SECRET to reveal secret or damaging information, especially to an authority [Old English *tellan*, from a prehistoric Germanic word meaning 'put in order' (both in narration and counting), which is also the ancestor of English *tale* and *talk*] —**tellable** *adj.* ◇ **all told** altogether, or when everything else is taken into consideration ◇ **tell it like it is** to give a complete and accurate account of sth (*informal*) ◇ **tell me about it! 1.** used to indicate heartfelt agreement (*informal*) **2.** used to indicate that you have experienced what sb is talking about (*informal*) ◇ **you're telling me!** used to indicate agreement with an observation (*informal*)

tell apart *vt.* to distinguish two or more similar things or people

tell off *vt.* to scold or rebuke sb, especially in anger (*informal*)

tell on *vt.* **1. AFFECT ADVERSELY** to have an adverse effect on sb or sth **2. REPORT TO AUTHORITY** to report damaging or incriminating information to an authority

Tell, William /tel/ *n.* in Swiss legend, a patriot who liberated Switzerland from Austrian rule in the 14th century. He was forced by an Austrian governor to shoot an arrow through an apple on his son's head, and later killed the governor.

tell-all *adj.* not withholding any information, even what may be considered secret, private, or unsuitable

teller /téllər/ *n.* **1.** BANKING **BANK EMPLOYEE** an employee in a bank or savings institution who receives and pays out money **2. COUNTER OF VOTES** sb who counts votes in an election or legislature **3. SB WHO TELLS** sb who tells sth ○ *a teller of tales*

tellin /téllin/ (*plural* **-lins** *or* **-lin**) *n.* a marine bivalve mollusc that lives in intertidal sand. Genus: *Tellina*. [Early 18thC. Via Latin from Greek *tellinē* 'type of shellfish'.]

telling /télling/ *adj.* **1. REVEALING** revealing information inadvertently or indirectly ○ *a telling glance* **2. EFFECTIVE** very effective or expressive ○ *a telling indictment* —**tellingly** *adv.*

telling-off *n.* a scolding or admonition for doing sth wrong (*informal*)

telltale /tél tayl/ *adj.* **CLEARLY SHOWING STH** clearly showing or indicating sth that is secret or hidden ○ *telltale signs* ■ *n.* **1. TATTLER** sb who tells people about sb else's secrets or bad behaviour (*informal*) US term **tattletale 2. DEVICE** a device or signal intended to monitor a machine or system **3.** SAILING **WIND STRIPS** strips of ribbon hung aloft on a sailing boat to show apparent wind direction **4.** RACKET GAMES **METAL STRIP** a horizontal metal strip across the front wall of a squash or racquetball court, above which the ball must be bounced

tellurate /téllyoo rayt/ *n.* a salt or ester of telluric acid [Early 19thC. Formed from TELLURIUM.]

tellurian /te lóori ən/ *adj.* **RELATING TO EARTH** relating to the Earth or life on Earth ■ *n.* **EARTHLING** an inhabitant of the Earth, as described in science fiction [Mid-19thC. Formed from Latin *tellus* 'earth'.]

telluric[1] /te lóorik/ *adj.* **1. FROM EARTH** originating or proceeding from the Earth or its atmosphere **2.** = **tellurian** *adj.* [Mid-19thC. Formed from Latin *tellus* 'earth'.]

telluric[2] /te lóorik/ *adj.* containing or relating to tellurium, especially in a high valency [Early 19thC. Formed from TELLURIUM.]

telluric acid *n.* a white crystalline inorganic acid produced by the action of hydrogen peroxide on tellurium. Formula: H_6TeO_6. [From TELLURIC[2]]

telluride /téllyoo rīd/ *n.* a binary compound of tellurium with an electropositive element or group [Mid-19thC. Formed from TELLURIUM.]

tellurion /te lóori on, -lyóori ən, -lyóori on/ *n.* a model that shows how day and night and the seasons result from the Earth's orbit and its tilted axis in relation to the Sun [Mid-19thC. Formed from Latin *tellus* 'earth'.]

tellurise *vt.* = **tellurize**

tellurium /te lóori əm/ *n.* a semimetallic element that occurs naturally, both in a native state and in mineral ores, and is used in alloys and various manufacturing processes. Symbol **Te** [Early 19thC. Formed from Latin *tellus* 'earth', on the model of URANIUM.]

tellurize /téllyoo rīz/ (**-izes, -izing, -ized**), **tellurise** (**-ises, -ising, -ised**) *vt.* to cause sth to combine with tellurium

tellurometer /téllyoo rómmitər/ *n.* a device that measures distances from the travel time of microwaves or radiowaves transmitted across the distance to be measured [Mid-20thC. Formed from Latin *tellus* 'earth'.]

tellurous /téllyoorəss, te lóorəss/ *adj.* containing or relating to tellurium, especially in a low valency [Mid-19thC. Formed from TELLURIUM, on the model of FERROUS.]

Tellus /télləss/ *n.* in Roman mythology, the goddess of the earth and of fertility [From Latin, literally 'earth']

telly /télli/ (*plural* **-lies**) *n.* television, or a television set (*informal*) [Mid-20thC. Shortening.]

TELNET /tél net/, **Telnet** *n.* a terminal emulation program that allows computer users to connect interactively to a server and access remote sites, e.g. on the Internet [Late 20thC. Coined from TELETYPE + NETWORK.]

telo- *prefix.* end, terminal ○ *telophase* [Formed from Greek *telos* 'end']

telocentric /téllə séntrik/ *adj.* used to describe a chromosome whose centromere is located at or near one end. ◊ **acentric, acrocentric**

telolecithal /téllə léssithəl/ *adj.* used to describe reptile, shark, or bird's eggs in which the yolk is concentrated at one end [Late 19thC. Coined from TELO- + Greek *lekithos* 'egg yolk'.]

telomere /téllə meer/ *n.* a region of DNA at the end of a chromosome that protects the start of the genetic coding sequence against shortening during successive replications

telophase /téllə fayz/ *n.* the final stage of cell division, in which daughter cell nuclei form around chromosomes at opposite ends of the dividing mother cell. ◊ **anaphase, metaphase, prophase** —**telophasic** /téllə fáyzik/ *adj.*

telotaxis /téllə táksiss/ *n.* an organism's movement towards or away from a particular stimulus while maintaining a constant angle to that stimulus. This behaviour is seen in some insects.

telpher /télfər/, **telfer** *n.* **CABLE CAR** a car or other carrying unit suspended from a cable in a telpherage ■ *vt.* (**-phers, -phering, -phered; -fers, -fering, -fered**) **TAKE BY TELPHER** to transport sth in a container suspended from cables [Late 19thC. Contraction of *telephore*, from TELE- + -PHORE.] —**telpheric** *adj.*

telpherage /télfərij/, **telferage** *n.* a transport system in which cargoes or passengers are carried in containers suspended from cables

telson /télss'n/ *n.* the terminal segment of an arthropod or arachnid body, e.g. the stinger of a scorpion [Mid-19thC. From Greek, literally 'limit'.] —**telsonic** /tel sónnik/ *adj.*

Telstar /tél staar/ *n.* a communications satellite used for transmitting television programmes and telephone messages. Two of these were launched by the United States in 1962 and 1963. [Mid-20thC. Blend of TELE- and STAR.]

Telugu /téllə goo/ (*plural* **-gu** *or* **-gus**), **Telegu** (*plural* **-gu** *or* **-gus**) *n.* **1.** LANG **INDIAN LANGUAGE** a language spoken in southeastern and central India. Telugu is a member of the Dravidian family of languages. **2.** PEOPLES **SB WHO SPEAKS TELUGU** a member of the Dravidian people who speak Telugu [Late 18thC. From Kannada and Tamil.] —**Telugu** *adj.*

Tema /téemə/ city in southeastern Ghana, on the Gulf of Guinea, near Accra. Population: 180,600 (1990).

TEMA *n., abbr.* Telecommunications Engineering and Manufacturing Association

temblor /témblər, -blawr/ *n.* *US* an earthquake or tremor [Late 19thC. From American Spanish, literally 'trembling', from, ultimately, Vulgar Latin *tremulare* 'to tremble' (source of English *tremble*).]

temerity /tə mérrəti/ *n.* reckless confidence that might be offensive [15thC. From Latin *temeritas* 'rashness', ultimately from assumed *temus* 'darkness'. The underlying idea is of 'acting in the dark'.] —**temerarious** /témmə ráiri əss/ *adj.*

temmoku /témmō koo/ *n.* a Japanese iron glaze that is black in colour but breaks into rust where the glaze coat is thin [Late 19thC. Via Japanese from Chinese *tiān mù* 'eye of heaven'.]

Temne /témni/ (*plural* **-nes** *or* **-ne**) *n.* **1.** PEOPLES **MEMBER OF PEOPLE OF SIERRA LEONE** a member of a people who live in Sierra Leone, where they are one of the dominant ethnic groups **2.** LANG **TEMNE LANGUAGE** the language of the Temne people, belonging to the Niger-Congo family of languages. About one million people speak Temne. [Late 18thC. From Temne.] —**Temne** *adj.*

temp /temp/ *n.* **TEMPORARY WORKER** a temporary worker, especially one hired from an agency ■ *vi.* (**temps, temping, temped**) **WORK TEMPORARILY** to do temporary work, especially through an agency [Early 20thC. Shortening.]

temp. *abbr.* **1.** temperance **2.** temperature **3.** template **4.** temporal **5.** temporary **6.** temperate

tempe *n.* = **tempeh**

tempeh /tém pay/, **tempe** *n.* fermented soya beans popular as a health food and in some Asian cuisines [Mid-20thC. From Indonesian *tempe*.]

temper /témpər/ *n.* **1.** (*plural* **-pers** *or* **-per**) **TENDENCY TO ANGER** a tendency to get angry easily and suddenly ○ *has quite a temper* **2. ANGRY STATE** a state of anger or ill temper ○ *got himself into a terrible temper* **3. EMOTIONAL CONDITION** an emotional condition or predisposition of a particular kind ○ *an even temper* **4. CALM STATE** a state of calm and balance ○ *lost your temper* **5.** METALL **HARDNESS OF METAL** the degree of hardness of a metal **6. ADDITIVE** sth added to improve the consistency or strength of sth ■ *vt.* (**-pers, -pering, -pered**) **1. SOFTEN** to make sth less harsh or unacceptable, especially by adding sth to it ○ *temper criticism with kindness* **2.** METALL **HARDEN METAL** to harden metal by heating it to very high temperatures and then cooling it ○ *temper steel* **3. MAKE SB STRONGER** to make sb stronger through exposure to hardship ○ *tempered by combat duty* **4.** MUSIC **TUNE EARLY KEYBOARD INSTRUMENT** to tune a baroque keyboard instrument so that consistent harmonic intervals are achieved throughout its range [Pre-12thC. From Latin *temperare* 'to mix, restrain yourself', from *tempus* 'time' (see TEMPORAL[1]). Originally 'mixture', which led to 'emotional condition', and finally 'angry state'.] —**temperability** /témpərə bílləti/ *n.* —**temperable** /témpərəb'l/ *adj.* —**temperer** /témpərər/ *n.*

tempera /témpərə/ *n.* **1. PAINTING TECHNIQUE** a technique of painting with colours made from powdered pigments mixed with water and egg yolk, size, or casein **2. TEMPERA PAINTING** a painting done in tempera [Mid-19thC. Via Italian, from, ultimately, Latin *temperare* (see TEMPER).]

temperament /témprəmənt/ *n.* **1. QUALITY OF MIND** a prevailing or dominant quality of mind that characterizes sb **2. MOODINESS** excessive moodiness, irritability, or sensitivity **3.** HIST **MEDIEVAL PHYSIOLOGICAL CLASSIFICATION** in medieval physiology, the quality of mind resulting from various proportions of the four cardinal humours in an individual **4.** MUSIC **NOTE INTERVAL SETTING** the subtle relationship of the pitches of notes of keyboard instruments, and the consequences this has on harmony

temperamental /témprə mént'l/ *adj.* **1. EASILY UPSET** easily upset or irritated **2. UNPREDICTABLE** unpredictable and erratic in behaviour **3. OF TEMPERAMENT** relating to temperament —**temperamentally** *adv.*

temperance /témpərənss/ *n.* **1. ABSTINENCE FROM ALCOHOL** total abstinence from alcoholic drink **2. RESTRAINT** self-restraint in the face of temptation or desire

temperate /témpərət/ *adj.* **1. MILD** mild or restrained in behaviour or attitude **2.** METEOROL **WITHOUT EXTREMES** used to describe a climate that has a range of temperatures within moderate limits **3.** MICROBIOL **NOT SPREADING** used to describe viruses that exist in host cells but do not cause lysis —**temperately** *adv.* —**temperateness** *n.*

Temperate Zone *n.* the parts of the Earth that lie between the tropics and the polar circles and have generally hot summers, cold winters, and intermediate autumns and springs

temperature /témprichər/ *n.* **1.** DEGREE OF HEAT the degree of heat as an inherent quality of objects expressed as hotness or coldness relative to sth else **2.** RELATIVE DEGREE OF HEAT the heat of sth measured on a particular scale such as the Fahrenheit or Celsius scale. Symbol **T, t 3.** BODY HEAT the degree of heat in a living organism **4.** FEVER human body heat in excess of 37.0° C/98.6° F or sb's normal body heat ○ *running a temperature* [15thC. The meaning evolved from 'mixture' via 'mild (well balanced) weather'.]

temperature gradient *n.* the rate of change in air temperature over distance, especially elevation

temperature-humidity index *n.* a measure of ambient humidity relative to heat as it affects human comfort

temperature inversion *n.* METEOROL = **inversion** *n.* 4

tempered /témpərd/ *adj.* **1.** WITH A PARTICULAR TEMPER with a temper or temperament of a particular quality (*usually used in combination*) ○ *even-tempered* **2.** INDUST HARDENED hardened through a tempering process ○ *tempered steel* **3.** WELL PROPORTIONED with elements combined in balanced and suitable proportion **4.** MUSIC TUNED TO A TEMPERAMENT tuned to a particular temperament, especially equal temperament

tempest /témpist/ *n.* **1.** STORM a severe storm with very high winds and often rain, hail, or snow (*literary*) **2.** EMOTIONAL UPHEAVAL a severe commotion or disturbance, especially an emotional upheaval [13thC. Via Old French from, ultimately, Latin *tempestas*, from *tempus* 'time'. The Latin word originally meant 'period of time', which evolved into 'weather' and, finally, 'storm'.]

WORD KEY: CULTURAL NOTE

The Tempest, a play by William Shakespeare (1611). An elaborate blend of comedy, drama, and fantasy, it is set on an enchanted island where Prospero, rightful duke of Milan, has lived since being usurped by his brother Antonio. Using his magical powers, Prospero conjures up a storm that forces Antonio and his companions onto the island, paving the way for an ingenious reconciliation. The word *sea-change*, meaning a change caused by the sea, and figuratively, a major transformation, comes from Act I, scene ii of this play: 'Nothing of him that doth fade,/ But doth suffer a sea-change/ Into sth rich and strange'.

tempestuous /tem péstyoo əss/ *adj.* **1.** WITH STORMS having or affected by frequent or violent storms ○ *tempestuous seas* **2.** EMOTIONALLY TURBULENT frequently turbulent and giving rise to many emotions ○ *a tempestuous relationship* —**tempestuously** *adv.* —**tempestuousness** *n.*

tempi plural of **tempo**

Templar /témplər/ *n.* **1.** = **Knight Templar 2.** LONDON BARRISTER a barrister or law student with offices in the Temple, London [13thC. From the place in Jerusalem (*Temple of Solomon*), where the medieval order had its headquarters.]

template /tém playt, -plət/ *n.* **1.** MASTER sth that serves as a master or pattern from which other similar things can be made **2.** ENG PATTERN a mechanical pattern or mould with one or more shapes used to guide the manufacture or drawing of objects with a similar shape **3.** BUILDING SHORT BEAM a short beam of metal, wood, or stone, used to distribute weight or pressure in a structure **4.** BIOCHEM MASTER MOLECULE a molecule that provides a pattern for the synthesis of other molecules in biochemical reactions **5.** COMPUT MASTER FILE a computer file that is used as a master for creating others similar to it [Late 17thC. Alteration of earlier TEMPLET, on the model of PLATE.]

temple[1] /témp'l/ *n.* **1.** RELIG BUILDING FOR WORSHIP a building used as a place of worship **2.** SPECIAL PLACE an institution or building considered as a guardian of, or reservation for, a particular activity ○ *a temple of learning* **3.** JUDAISM BIBLICAL PLACE OF WORSHIP IN JERUSALEM either of the two places of worship in Jerusalem, Solomon's Temple and Herod's Temple, built in biblical times **4.** MEETING PLACE a building where a fraternal order holds meetings and rites **5.** RELIG HOLY DWELLING a place where sth holy or divine is thought to dwell, e.g. the body of a holy person **6.** *US* JUDAISM SYNAGOGUE a synagogue **7.** CHR MORMON CHURCH a Mormon place of worship where sacred ordinances such as marriage are executed [Pre-12thC. From Latin *templum* 'sacred place, place marked out for worship', of uncertain origin: perhaps ultimately from an Indo-European word meaning 'cut' (source of English *-tomy*).]

temple[2] /témp'l/ *n.* ANAT the part of either side of the head between the eye and the ear [14thC. Via Old French from, ultimately, Latin *tempora*, plural of *tempus* 'temple, time' (see TEMPORAL). The meaning evolved via 'right time' and 'right place (for dealing a fatal blow)'.]

temple[3] /témp'l/ *n.* the part of a loom that keeps the cloth being woven stretched to the proper width [15thC. From French, of uncertain origin: probably from Latin *templum* (see TEMPLE[1]) in its secondary meaning 'plank, raft'.]

Temple[1] *n.* either of two groups of buildings in Paris and London built on sites that once belonged to the Knights Templar. The London site is now the home of two of the Inns of Court.

Temple[2] *n.* either of two successive temples in Jerusalem. The First Temple, built by Solomon in 957 BC, was destroyed by Nebuchadnezzar in 586 BC. The Second Temple was destroyed by the Romans in AD 70.

Shirley Temple

Temple /témp'l/, **Shirley** (*b.* 1928) US actor. She made 25 films from 1934 as an internationally popular child star. She was later US ambassador to the United Nations, under her married name of Shirley Temple Black.

templet /témplət/ *n.* a template (*archaic*) [Formed from TEMPLE[3]]

tempo /témpō/ (*plural* **-pos** /témpee/ *or* **-pi**) *n.* **1.** MUSIC MUSIC'S SPEED the speed at which a musical composition or passage is performed **2.** PACE the pace or rate of sth ○ *the tempo of urban life* [Mid-17thC. Via Italian from Latin *tempus* (see TEMPORAL[1]).]

tempolabile /témpō láy bīl/ *adj.* changing at an uneven rate [Mid-20thC. From Latin *tempus* 'time' + *labilis*, from *labi* 'to slip'.]

temporal[1] /témpərəl/ *adj.* **1.** RELATING TO TIME relating to measured time **2.** CHR RELATING TO LAITY relating to the laity rather than the clergy in the Christian Church **3.** RELIG OF THIS WORLD connected with life in the world, rather than spiritual life **4.** BRIEF lasting only a short time **5.** GRAM RELATING TO TENSES relating to grammatical tenses or the expression of time in a language [14thC. Directly or via French from Latin *temporalis*, from *tempus* 'time', of uncertain origin: perhaps ultimately from an Indo-European word meaning 'stretch' (ancestor of English *thin*).] —**temporally** *adv.*

temporal[2] /témpərəl/ *adj.* relating to or in the region of the temples on the head [Late 16thC. From late Latin *temporalis*, ultimately from Latin *tempus* (see TEMPLE[2]).]

temporal bone *n.* either of a pair of bones that form part of the sides and base of the skull and contain the middle and inner ears

temporality /témpə rálləti/ *n.* BEING TEMPORAL the quality or state of being connected with time or the world ■ **temporalities** *npl.* CHR CHURCH ASSETS the secular property and assets of a church

temporal lobe *n.* either of two lobes of the brain, located on the side of each cerebral hemisphere, that contain the auditory centres responsible for hearing

temporary /témpərəri/ *adj.* HAVING A LIMITED DURATION lasting for or relating to a limited time ■ *n.* (*plural* **-ies**) WORKER HIRED FOR LIMITED TIME sb who is hired to work in an office or other workplace for a limited time only —**temporarily** *adv.* —**temporariness** *n.*

WORD KEY: SYNONYMS

temporary, fleeting, passing, transitory, ephemeral, evanescent

CORE MEANING: lasting only a short time

temporary lasting for a short time, usually because this is what is intended. It is often used to suggest that sth is makeshift or not ideal; **fleeting** very short-lived or brief in duration, especially when it does not seem long enough; **passing** describes sth such as an interest, feeling, or fashion that is not permanent; **transitory** a fairly formal word used to suggest that sth, by its very nature, is bound to come to an end; **ephemeral** a formal or literary word used to describe sth that lasts for only a very short time, especially when it is sth that also seems unimportant; **evanescent** a literary word used to describe sth that lasts for only a very short time or is soon forgotten.

temporomandibular joint /témpərō man díbbyoōlər-/ *n.* either of the joints connecting the lower part of the jaw (**mandible**) with the temporal bone on each side of the head. Both joints act together when the jaw is moved. [*Temporomandibular* formed from TEMPORAL[2] + MANDIBLE]

temporomandibular syndrome *n.* a painful condition involving the temporomandibular joint and the muscles used for chewing, sometimes causing clicking sounds and restricted jaw movement. It is usually associated with a faulty dental bite.

tempt /tempt/ *vt.* **1.** INCITE DESIRE to cause desire or craving to arise in sb ○ *tempted by that chocolate cake* **2.** INCITE TO TRANSGRESSION to persuade or attempt to persuade sb to do sth considered wrong **3.** INVITE to invite or attract sb ○ *The sightseeing tour tempted us.* **4.** RISK to risk the possible destructive powers of sth ○ *tempt the gods* —**temptable** *adj.* —**tempter** *n.*

temptation /temp táyshən/ *n.* **1.** FEELING a craving or desire for sth, especially sth thought wrong ○ *yield to temptation* **2.** ENTICING ACT the enticing of desire or craving in sb **3.** ENTICING THING sth that or sb who tempts sb ○ *too many temptations for me here*

Tempter /témp tər/ *n.* RELIG Satan

tempting /témp ting/ *adj.* causing craving or desire to arise ○ *a tempting offer* —**temptingly** *adv.* —**temptingness** *n.*

temptress /témp triss/ *n.* an offensive term for a woman that deliberately insults her sexuality and public behaviour

tempura /tém pŏŏrə/ *n.* a Japanese dish of vegetables or seafood coated in light batter and deep-fried

tempus fugit /témpŏŏs fyōojit/ time flies

ten /ten/ *n.* **1.** NUMBER 10 the number 10 **2.** STH WITH VALUE OF 10 sth in a numbered series, e.g. a playing card, with a value of ten ○ *the ten of clubs* ○ *to play the ten* **3.** GROUP OF TEN a group of ten objects or people

tenable /ténnəb'l/ *adj.* **1.** WITH REASONABLE ARGUMENTS TO SUPPORT IT justified in a fair or rational way and able to be defended because there is sufficient evidence or reason behind it **2.** ABLE TO BE OCCUPIED capable of being occupied or held, usually by a particular person or for a particular period of time (*formal*) **3.** MIL CAPABLE OF BEING DEFENDED IN BATTLE able to be held successfully against an enemy attack [Late 16thC. From French *tenir* 'to hold'.] —**tenability** /ténnə bílləti/ *n.* —**tenableness** /ténnəb'lnəss/ *n.* —**tenably** /ténnəbli/ *adv.*

tenace /ténn ayss/ *n.* a combination of two high cards in the same suit that do not form a sequence, e.g. a jack and king [Mid-17thC. Via French from Spanish *tenaza*, literally 'pincers, tongs', the underlying idea being 'holding'.]

tenacious /tə náyshəss/ *adj.* **1.** VERY DETERMINED OR STUBBORN tending to stick firmly to any decision, plan, or opinion without changing or doubting it **2.** TIGHTLY HELD difficult to loosen, shake off, or pull away from **3.** ABLE TO REMEMBER MANY THINGS capable of absorbing and retaining a large store of information and of recalling details accurately **4.** STICKY OR CLINGING sticking or clinging to sth else, especially a surface **5.** NOT EASILY DISCONNECTED holding together tightly or fused solidly [Early 17thC. Formed from Latin *tenax* 'holding fast', from *tenere* 'to hold'.] —**tenaciously** *adv.* —**tenaciousness** *n.*

ten-acre block *n. NZ* a block of farmland, usually near a city

tenaculum /tə nákyŏŏləm/ (*plural* **-la** /-lə/ *or* **-lums**) *n.* a long-handled instrument with a slender sharp hook, used especially in surgery to grasp and hold arteries or other bodily parts [Late 17thC. From Latin, 'holder', from *tenere* 'to hold'.]

tenaille /te náyl/ *n.* a low outwork in front of the curtain between two bastions in a fortification ditch [Late 16thC. Via French from Latin *tenacula* 'pincers, forceps'.]

tena koe /tə naá kwáy/ *interj. NZ* a Maori greeting addressed to one person (*formal*) [From Maori, literally 'there you are']

tenancy /ténnənssi/ (*plural* **-cies**) *n.* **1.** OCCUPATION OF PROPERTY FOR RENT exclusive possession of property or land owned by sb else for a fixed period, in return for an agreed rent. This is usually under the terms of a lease or some similar legal entitlement or agreement. **2.** TIME OF SB'S TENANCY a period of time when a piece of property, e.g. a house or farm, is legally occupied and used by sb paying an agreed rent **3.** PLACE LIVED IN BY A TENANT a piece of property that sb is entitled to use or occupy on condition that an agreed rent is paid to the owner [15thC. Formed from TENANT.]

tenant /ténnənt/ *n.* **1.** RENTER OF PROPERTY sb who rents a building, house, set of rooms, plot of land, or some other piece of property for a fixed period of time. This arrangement is usually under the terms of a lease or some similar legal entitlement or agreement. **2.** OCCUPIER OF A PLACE sb living in or on a particular piece of property (*dated literary*) ■ *vti.* (**-ants, -anting, -anted**) PAY RENT TO OCCUPY PROPERTY to live in or on another person's property as a tenant [14thC. Via Anglo-Norman *tenaunt* from Old French *tenant*, from *tenir* 'to hold', from Latin *tenere* 'to hold, keep'.] —**tenantable** *adj.* —**tenanted** *adj.* —**tenantless** *adj.*

WORD KEY: ORIGIN

The Latin word *tenere*, from which ***tenant*** is derived, is also the source of English *abstain, contain, continent, continue, countenance, detain, maintain, obtain, retain, sustain, tenacious, tenement, tenet, tennis, tenon, tenor,* and *tenure.*

tenant farmer *n.* a farmer who rents a farm, smallholding, or agricultural land, and pays the owner in cash or with produce

tenant-in-chief (*plural* **tenants-in-chief**) *n.* a tenant in a feudal society who holds land granted by the sovereign

tenantry /ténnəntri/ *n.* **1.** PEOPLE OCCUPYING RENTED PROPERTY all tenants or tenant farmers, especially all those renting property from a particular landowner (*formal*) **2.** TENANCY tenancy (*dated*)

tenants' association *n.* an official representative body formed by tenants to negotiate with their landlord. A tenants' association usually works to ensure that tenants' rights are protected and represents the tenants in disputes or when they want particular improvements made or changes introduced.

tenants' charter *n.* in the United Kingdom, the legal rights of tenants in new towns, local authorities, and housing associations. These include the right to buy their houses cheaply and to take in lodgers.

tench /tench/ (*plural* **tench** *or* **tenches**) *n.* a European freshwater food and game fish related to the carp, with a heavy greenish body, small scales, and a barbel on each side of its mouth. Latin name: *Tinca tinca.* [14thC. Via Old French *tenche* from late Latin *tinca*.]

Ten Commandments *npl.* the ten laws given by God to Moses, according to the Bible. They summarize human obligations to each other and to God.

tend[1] /tend/ (**tends, tending, tended**) *vi.* **1.** BE GENERALLY INCLINED OR LIKELY to be generally inclined or likely to react or behave in a particular way, or be in the habit of doing sth **2.** MOVE GRADUALLY OR SLIGHTLY TOWARDS STH to make a gentle steady movement in a particular direction **3.** WORK TO ENCOURAGE OR INFLUENCE to have the purpose or effect of helping to produce a particular result, especially a worthwhile result (*archaic literary*) [14thC. Via Old French *tendre* 'to move towards', from Latin *tendere* 'to stretch, extend'.]

WORD KEY: ORIGIN

The Latin word *tendere*, from which ***tend*** is derived, is also the source of English *attend, contend, détente, distend, extend, intend, ostensible, portend, pretend, standard, tense,* and *tent.*

tend[2] /tend/ (**tends, tending, tended**) *v.* **1.** *vt.* LOOK AFTER STH OR SB to do or provide the things that a person, animal, or plant needs, or a group of them need, for their health, comfort, and welfare **2.** *vt.* BE IN CHARGE OF STH to manage sth, especially sth that needs constant supervision **3.** *vti.* SERVE SB to be sb's attendant, waiter, or servant (*archaic*) [12thC. Shortening of ATTEND.]

tendance /téndənss/ *n.* the act of looking after or attending to sth (*archaic or formal*) [Late 16thC. Either a shortening of ATTENDANCE, or formed from TEND[2] 'to look after'.]

tendencious *adj.* = **tendentious** —**tendenciously** *adv.* —**tendenciousness** *n.*

tendency /téndənssi/ (*plural* **-cies**) *n.* **1.** GENERAL INCLINATION OR LIKELIHOOD a way that sb or sth typically behaves or is likely to react or behave **2.** PREDISPOSITION TOWARDS STH a character or quality that makes it likely that sth will happen ○ *My ankle has a tendency to twist.* **3.** MOVEMENT TOWARDS STH a gradual but steady progress, development, or shift of opinion in a particular direction (*dated or formal*) [Early 17thC. From medieval Latin *tendentia*, from, ultimately, Latin *tendere* 'to tend, be inclined to'.]

tendentious /ten dénsshəss/, **tendencious** *adj.* written or spoken by sb who obviously wants to promote a particular cause or who supports a particular viewpoint [Early 20thC. Formed from TENDENCY.] —**tendentiously** *adv.* —**tendentiousness** *n.*

tender[1] /téndər/ *adj.* **1.** PHYSICALLY PAINFUL hurting or unusually sensitive when touched or pressed **2.** WITH GENTLE FEELING showing care, gentleness, and feeling **3.** KIND AND SYMPATHETIC sensitive and caring towards others and often feeling emotions intensely **4.** EMOTIONALLY PAINFUL particularly uncomfortable, hurtful, or upsetting to discuss or think about, and so best avoided **5.** FOOD PLEASANTLY SOFT FOR EATING soft enough for the teeth to go through easily without much chewing **6.** BOT, AGRIC NEEDING PROTECTION FROM HARSH WEATHER easily damaged or killed by unsuitable weather or conditions, especially frost and cold **7.** YOUNG AND DEFENCELESS vulnerably or pitifully young, weak, and inexperienced **8.** FRAGILE so delicate, soft, or weak as to be hurt, crushed, or broken easily (*literary*) [13thC. Via French *tendre* from Latin *tener* 'delicate, tender' (source also of English *tendril*).] —**tenderly** *adv.* —**tenderness** *n.*

WORD KEY: CULTURAL NOTE

Tender is the Night, a novel by US writer F. Scott Fitzgerald (1934). Set on the French Riviera in the 1930s, it focuses on a group of glamorous American expatriates. Psychologist Richard Diver's attempts to nurse his wife and former patient, Nicole, and his involvement with a visiting woman actor lead to his mental collapse. A powerful depiction of human frailty, it is also admired for the elegance of its prose.

tender[2] /téndər/ *v.* (**-ders, -dering, -dered**) **1.** *vt.* OFFER STH FORMALLY IN WRITING to present sth formal or official, in the form of a document ○ *tender a resignation* **2.** *vi.* COMM OFFER TO SUPPLY STH to offer to undertake a job or supply particular goods ○ *tender for a contract* **3.** *vt.* LAW OFFER A SUM IN SETTLEMENT to offer to pay money or goods as a way of settling a debt or claim ■ *n.* **1.** COMM OFFER TO UNDERTAKE A JOB a formal offer to undertake a job or supply particular goods ○ *Their tender was accepted because it was the lowest.* **2.** COMM ACT OF TENDERING the act of tendering for a contract **3.** LAW OFFER MADE TO SETTLE STH a formal offer to settle legal proceedings on payment of an amount of damages [Mid-16thC. Via Old French *tendre* from Latin *tendere* 'to hold out, stretch' (source also of English *tendency*).] —**tenderable** *adj.* —**tenderer** *n.*

tender[3] /téndər/ *n.* **1.** SHIPPING SMALL BOAT FERRYING TO LARGE BOAT a small boat used to go to and from a larger one such as a yacht **2.** RAIL VEHICLE CARRYING STEAM ENGINE'S SUPPLIES the permanently coupled rear part of a large steam locomotive, which carries its coal and water **3.** TRANSP EMERGENCY VEHICLE a road vehicle that carries tools and specialized equipment and personnel to assist in an emergency (*usually used in combination*) [15thC. Either a shortening of *attender* (from ATTEND), or formed from TEND[2].]

tenderfoot /téndər fŏŏt/ (*plural* **-foots** /-feet/ *or* **-feet**) *n.* **1.** BEGINNER AT STH sb just starting to do or try sth, with little or no previous experience of it (*informal*) **2.** BEGINNER IN THE SCOUTS OR GUIDES a new member of a Scout troop or Guide company (*dated*)

tenderhearted /téndər haártid/ *adj.* quick to show compassion and sympathy to other people —**tenderheartedly** *adv.* —**tenderheartedness** *n.*

tenderise *vt.* = **tenderize**

tenderize /téndə rīz/ (**-izes, -izing, -ized**), **tenderise** (**-ises, -ising, -ised**) *vt.* to make meat tender, usually by beating it, soaking it in a marinade, or sprinkling it with a special substance (**tenderizer**) that breaks down the fibres in the meat —**tenderization** /téndə rī záysh'n/ *n.*

tenderizer /téndə rīzər/, **tenderiser** *n.* **1.** SUBSTANCE FOR MAKING MEAT TENDER a commercial preparation containing enzymes that break down fibrous tissue in meat **2.** HAMMER FOR POUNDING MEAT a wooden or metal mallet used to tenderize meat. It has a short handle and a fairly broad head with a hammering surface covered in shallow bumps.

tenderloin /téndər loyn/ *n.* a prime cut of lean tender pork or lamb taken from the curve of the ribs at the backbone

tendinitis /téndə nītiss/, **tendonitis** *n.* inflammation of a tendon. It is often painful, usually occurs after excessive use, as in a sports injury, and is generally cured by rest. [Early 20thC. From modern Latin *tendin-*, the stem of *tendo* 'tendon'.]

tendinous /téndinəss/ *adj.* relating to, consisting of, or resembling a tendon or tendons [Mid-17thC. Via French *tendineux*, from, ultimately, the medieval Latin stem *tendon-* (see TENDON).]

tendon /téndən/ *n.* an inelastic cord or band of tough white fibrous connective tissue that attaches a muscle to a bone or other part [Mid-16thC. Directly and via French from medieval Latin *tendon-*, stem of *tendo*, a translation of Greek *tenōn* 'sinew', from, ultimately, *teinein* 'to stretch'.]

tendon hammer *n.* = **plexor**

tendonitis *n.* = **tendinitis**

tendril /téndrəl/ *n.* **1.** BOT THREADLIKE PLANT PART ATTACHED TO SUPPORT a modified stem, leaf, or other part of a climbing plant, usually in the form of a thread, that coils around and attaches the plant to supporting objects **2.** DELICATE TWIST OR COIL a slim, wispy, curling, or winding piece of sth, especially hair (*literary*) [Mid-16thC. Via Middle French *tendrillon*, literally 'little shoot, little cartilage', from *tendron*, 'shoot, cartilage', from Old French *tendre* (see TENDER[1]).]

Tenebrae /ténnə bray/ *n.* in the Roman Catholic Church, the office of matins and lauds for the last three days of Holy Week (*takes a singular or plural verb*) [Mid-17thC. From Latin, literally 'darkness', because candles are extinguished during the service in memory of the darkness at the crucifixion.]

tenebrionid /tə nébbri ənid/ (*plural* **-nids** *or* **-nid**) *n.* = **darkling beetle** [Early 20thC. From modern Latin.]

tenebrious *adj.* = **tenebrous**

tenebrism /ténnəbrizəm/, **Tenebrism** *n.* a style of painting, popular in 17th-century Naples and Spain and largely associated with Caravaggio, that uses large areas of shadow and dark colours, sometimes with a shaft of light [Mid-20thC. Formed from Italian *tenebroso*, literally 'dark', a term for one of a group of 17thC Italian painters.] —**tenebrist** *n.*

tenebrous /ténnəbrəss/, **tenebrious** /tə nébbri əss/ *adj.* dark, murky, or obscured by shadows (*literary*) [15thC. Via Old French *tenebrus* from, ultimately, Latin *tenebrae* 'darkness'.] —**tenebrosity** /ténnə bróssəti/ *n.* —**tenebrousness** /ténnəbrəssnəss/ *n.*

tenement /ténnəmənt/ *n.* **1. LARGE MULTIPLE-OCCUPANCY RESIDENTIAL BUILDING** a large residential building in a town, usually of three or more storeys, divided into flats for separate householders, or the section of such a building served by one stair. The dwellings may be owner-occupied or rented. This type of building is characteristic of Scottish urban architecture from an early period because Scots law allowed for multiple ownership. **2. RENTED ACCOMMODATION IN MULTISTOREY BUILDING** in England and Wales, a room or flat in a multistorey residential building, especially one used by a tenant (*regional dated*) **3.** LAW **ITEM OF PROPERTY** a piece of property such as land or houses held by sb [14thC. Via Old French, 'tenure', the original sense in English, from, ultimately, Latin *tenere* 'to hold'.]

Tenerife /ténnə réef/, **Teneriffe** the largest of the Canary Islands, in Santa Cruz de Tenerife Province, Spain. Population: 759,388 (1986). Area: 2,059 sq. km/795 sq. mi.

tenesmus /tə nézməss/ *n.* an urgent, painful, and unsuccessful attempt to defecate or urinate [Early 16thC. Via medieval Latin from, ultimately, Greek *tēnesmos*, from *teinein* 'to stretch, strain'.]

tenet /ténnit/ *n.* any of a set of established and fundamental beliefs, especially one relating to religion or politics (*formal*) ○ *a tenet of Christianity* [Late 16thC. From Latin, literally 'he or she holds', the 3rd person present singular form of *tenere* 'to hold'.]

tenfold /tén fōld/ *adj.* **1. WITH TEN PARTS** made up of ten parts **2. TIMES TEN** multiplied by ten ■ *adv.* **TEN TIMES OVER** to ten times the amount or number, or multiplied by or up to that amount or number

ten-four, 10–4 *interj.* *US* used to express affirmation or confirmation [From a code originally used by US police in the sense 'message received']

ten-gallon hat *n.* a cowboy hat with a high round uncreased crown and a wide brim

tenge /téngay/ (*plural* **-ge**) *n.* **1. UNIT OF KAZAKH CURRENCY** the main unit of currency in Kazakhstan. See table at **currency 2. NOTE WORTH ONE TENGE** a note worth one tenge **3. tenge** (*plural* **-ga**) **MINOR UNIT OF TURKMEN CURRENCY** a minor unit of currency in Turkmenistan, 100 of which are worth one manat

Tenn. *abbr.* Tennessee

Tennant /ténnənt/, **Kylie** (1912–88) Australian writer. She is the author of *The Battlers* (1941), a novel about itinerant workers set during the Depression.

Tennant Creek town in north-central Australia, in the interior of the Northern Territory. Population: 3,856 (1996).

tenner /ténnər/ *n.* (*informal*) **1. TEN POUNDS** ten pounds sterling, either as cash or as a sum **2.** *US, ANZ, Can* **TEN DOLLARS** ten dollars, either as cash or as a sum

Tennessee

Tennessee /ténnə sée/ **1.** state in the eastern-central United States, bordered by Kentucky, Virginia, North Carolina, Georgia, Alabama, Mississippi, Arkansas, and Missouri. Capital: Nashville. Population: 5,368,198 (1997). Area: 109,158 sq. km/42,146 sq. mi. **2.** river of the southeastern United States, formed by the confluence of the Holston and French Broad rivers and flowing into the Ohio River. Length: 1,050 km/652 mi. —**Tennessean** *n., adj.*

Tenniel /ténni əl/, **Sir John** (1820–1914) British illustrator. He contributed more than 2,300 cartoons to *Punch* from 1851 to 1901. His illustrations for *Alice's Adventures in Wonderland* (1865) and *Through the Looking-Glass* (1871) fixed the images of Lewis Carroll's characters for generations of children.

tennis /ténniss/ *n.* a game played on a rectangular court by two, or two pairs of, players with rackets who hit a ball back and forth over a net. ◊ **lawn tennis, real tennis, paddle tennis, table tennis** [14thC. Origin uncertain: probably from Old French *tenez* 'hold!', a plural form of *tenir* 'to hold', hence, 'to receive', presumably shouted by the serving player to the opponent.]

tennis ball *n.* a white or yellow fuzzy cloth-surfaced hollow rubber ball about 7.5 cm/3 in in diameter, used in tennis. In lawn tennis the ball is pressurized.

tennis elbow *n.* painful inflammation of the tendon in the outer elbow region caused by excessive and repetitive strain from overuse, e.g. as a result of playing tennis and similar sports. It may be treated with rest, massage, and steroid drugs.

tennis shoe *n.* CLOTHES, SPORTS a rubber-soled white canvas shoe with long laces, worn for playing tennis

tennis skirt *n.* a short skirt, traditionally white, worn by some women tennis players

Tennyson /ténniss'n/, **Alfred, 1st Baron Tennyson of Freshwater and Aldworth** (1809–92) British poet. His many works include *The Lady of Shalott* (1832), *In Memoriam* (1850), and *The Charge of the Light Brigade* (1854). He was poet laureate from 1850. —**Tennysonian** *n., adj.*

tenon /ténnən/ *n.* **PROJECTION ON WOOD FOR MAKING JOINT** a projection made on the end of one piece of wood that fits into a mortise on another piece, making a joint ■ *vt.* **(-ons, -oning, -oned) 1. MAKE A TENON** to make a tenon on a piece of wood **2. JOIN PIECES OF WOOD USING TENON** to join two pieces of wood using a tenon [Early 17thC. From Old French, from *tenir* 'to hold'.] —**tenoner** *n.*

tenon saw *n.* a small thin saw with a strong back, used especially for cutting tenons

tenor /ténnər/ *n.* **1.** MUSIC **HIGH MALE VOICE** the highest natural male singing voice, or an adult whose voice is in this register **2.** MUSIC **HIGH OR FAIRLY HIGH INSTRUMENT** an instrument with a range similar to a tenor voice (*often used before a noun*) **3. WAY STH IS PROGRESSING** the direction in which sth is steadily moving (*formal*) **4. WHAT STH IS MAINLY ABOUT** the overall nature, pattern, or meaning of sth, especially a written or spoken statement (*formal*) **5.** LAW **EXACT WORDS OF DEED** the exact wording of a document, rather than its effect **6.** LAW **EXACT COPY** an exact copy or transcript of a document **7.** FIN **TIME FOR BILL TO BE PAID** the period of time over which cash flows are exchanged with a swap contract [13thC. Via Anglo-Norman *tenur* and Old French *tenour*, from Latin *tenor* 'continuous course', from *tenere* 'to hold', the underlying idea being 'sth that is held to'.]

tenor clef *n.* one of the C clefs, in which middle C is represented by the second highest line on the staff, used in the past to notate the tenor voice

tenorite /ténnə rīt/ *n.* a black mineral form of copper oxide, occurring with copper ores or near volcanoes [Mid-19thC. Named after Michelo *Tenore* (1781–1861), president of the Naples Academy of Sciences.]

tenosynovitis /ténnō sīnə vítiss/ *n.* inflammation of a tendon sheath, usually in the wrist, with swelling and audible creaking on movement. It often results from repetitive movements as in typing or some sports. [Late 19thC. From modern Latin, from Greek *tenōn*, 'tendon', and SYNOVITIS.]

tenotomy /tə nóttəmi/ (*plural* **-mies**) *n.* the surgical cutting of a tendon

tenpenny /ténpəni/ *adj.* costing or worth ten pence (*dated*)

tenpin /tén pin/ *n.* one of the ten skittles used in tenpin bowling

tenpin bowling *n.* an indoor game in which players try to knock down ten skittles at the far end of a special bowling alley by rolling a heavy ball at them

tenrec /tén rek/ (*plural* **-recs** *or* **-rec**), **tanrec** /tán-/ (*plural* **-recs** *or* **-rec**) *n.* a small to medium-sized insect-eating mammal with a long pointed snout, native to Madagascar and the Comoro Islands. Some have spines and some fur. Family: Tenrecidae. [Late 18thC. Via French *tanrec* from Malagasay *tàndraka, tràndraka*.]

TENS /tenz/ *n.* a method of treating chronic pain by applying electrodes to the skin and passing small electric currents through sensory nerves and the spinal cord, thus suppressing the transmission of pain signals. Full form **transcutaneous electrical nerve stimulation**

tense[1] /tenss/ *adj.* **(tenser, tensest) 1. WORRIED AND NERVOUS** affected by anxious feelings or mental strain, so that it is impossible to behave in a natural relaxed way **2. RESTRAINED AND UNNATURAL** making people feel unusually anxious, nervous, and uncertain, so that they do not talk or behave in a natural relaxed way **3. TIGHT AND STIFF** stretched or held tight and stiff **4.** PHON **PRONOUNCED WITH TAUT MUSCLES** used to describe a speech sound that is pronounced with muscular effort, is relatively long in duration, and is accurate in articulation ■ *vti.* **(tenses, tensing, tensed) BECOME OR MAKE TENSE** to become tense or make sth tense [Late 17thC. From Latin *tensus* 'stretched', the past participle of *tendere* 'to stretch' (source also of English *tent*).] —**tensely** *adv.* —**tenseness** *n.*

tense up *vti.* = **tense**[1] *v.*

tense[2] /tenss/ *n.* the facet of a verb that expresses the different times at which action takes place relative to the speaker or writer, e.g. the present, past, or future [14thC. Via Old French *tens*, 'time', from Latin *tempus*.] —**tenseless** *adj.*

tensile /tén sīl/ *adj.* **1. RELATING TO TENSION** relating to or involving tension **2. STRETCHABLE** capable of being stretched or pulled out of shape [Early 17thC. From medieval Latin *tensilis* from, ultimately, Latin *tendere* (see TENSE[1]).] —**tensilely** *adv.* —**tensileness** *n.* —**tensility** /ten síllәti/ *n.*

tensile strength *n.* the maximum stretching force that a material, e.g. wire, can withstand before breaking

tensimeter /ten símmitər/ *n.* an instrument used to measure differences in vapour pressure [Early 20thC. Coined from TENSION + -METER.]

tensiometer /ténssi ómmitər/ *n.* **1. INSTRUMENT FOR MEASURING TENSILE STRESS** an instrument used to measure tensile stress **2. INSTRUMENT FOR MEASURING SURFACE TENSION** an instrument used to measure the surface tension of liquids **3.** GEOL **INSTRUMENT FOR MEASURING SOIL MOISTURE** an instrument used to measure the moisture content of soils [Early 20thC. Coined from TENSION + -METER.]

tension /ténsh'n/ *n.* **1. ANXIOUS FEELINGS** mental worry or emotional strain that makes natural relaxed behaviour impossible **2. UNEASY FEELING IN RELATIONSHIP** a state of wariness, mistrust, controlled hostility, or fear of hostility felt by countries, groups, or individuals in their dealings with one another (*often used in the plural*) **3.** LITERAT **SENSE OF DIFFERENT ELEMENTS CONFLICTING** the way that opposing elements or characters clash or interact interestingly with each other in a literary work **4.** LITERAT **BUILDUP OF SUSPENSE** the buildup of suspense in a fictional work, leading to the dénouement **5. TAUTNESS** how tightly sth such as wire, string, thread, or a muscle is stretched **6.** SEW **DEVICE CONTROLLING TIGHTNESS OF THREAD** a device on a sewing machine or a loom that regulates how tight the thread is **7.** PHYS **PULLING FORCE** a force that pulls or stretches sth **8.** PHYS **STRESS FROM TENSION** the stress resulting from a force of tension, or a measure of it **9.** ELEC **VOLTAGE** voltage or electromotive force (*often used in combination*) [Mid-16thC. Directly or via French from Latin *tension-* 'stretching', from, ultimately, *tendere*, 'to stretch' (source also of English *tent*).] —**tensional** *adj.*

tensity /ténssəti/ *n.* the state or quality of being tense

tensive /ténssiv/ *adj.* causing or relating to tension [Early 18thC. Via French *tensif* from, ultimately, Latin *tendere* (see TENSE[1]).]

tensometer /ten sómmitər/ *n.* = **tensiometer** *n.* 1, **tensiometer** *n.* 2

tensor /ténssər, -sawr/ *n.* **1.** ANAT **STRETCHING MUSCLE** a muscle that tenses or stretches a part of the body **2.** MATH **GENERALIZATION OF A VECTOR** the generalization of a vector, a mathematical entity specified with respect to a given coordinate system and able to undergo transformation to other coordinate systems [Early 18thC. From modern Latin, from Latin *tendere* (see TENSE[1]).] —**tensorial** /ten sáwri əl/ *adj.*

ten-strike *n.* BOWLING = **strike**

tent[1] /tent/ *n.* **1.** COLLAPSIBLE SHELTER a collapsible movable shelter consisting of a tough fabric or plastic cover held up by poles and kept in place by ropes and pegs **2.** TENT-SHAPED OBJECT sth that looks like a tent, is constructed in a similar way, or serves a similar purpose ○ *an oxygen tent* ■ *v.* (**tents, tenting, tented**) **1.** *vt.* COVER STH AS A TENT DOES to form a raised nonrigid cover over sth ○ *Tent the roast with aluminium foil.* **2.** *vi.* CAMP to live or camp in a tent **3.** *vt.* SUPPLY A TENT FOR SB to accommodate a person or group of people in tents, or provide sb or sth with tents [13thC. Via Old French *tente*, from Latin *tenta*, 'tent', from *tendere*, 'to stretch'. Because a tent consists of a cover stretched over a framework.]

tent[2] /tent/ *n.* PLUG FOR WOUND a cone-shaped expandable plug of soft material, e.g. gauze, used to keep a wound or orifice open ■ *vt.* (**tents, tenting, tented**) INSERT A TENT to open or expand a wound or orifice with a tent [14thC. Via French *tente* from, ultimately, Latin *temptare*, 'to feel, try'.]

tentacle /téntək'l/ *n.* **1.** ZOOL LONG FLEXIBLE ORGAN a long flexible organ around the mouth or on the head of some animals, especially invertebrates such as squid, and used in holding, grasping, feeling, or moving **2.** PLANTS HAIR ON A PLANT LEAF a sticky glandular hairy projection from the leaf of an insect-eating plant such as the sundew, whose secretions trap and digest prey **3.** STH FAR-REACHING sth that gradually or unnoticeably insinuates its way into and around things and takes hold of them firmly or has a definite presence or effect (*literary*) [Mid-18thC. Anglicization of modern Latin *tentaculum* from, ultimately, Latin *temptare*, 'to feel, try' (source also of English *tempt*).] —**tentacled** *adj.* —**tentacular** /ten tákyŏŏlər/ *adj.*

tentage /tént ij/ *n.* tents in general or as a group

tentative /téntətiv/ *adj.* **1.** UNCERTAIN said or done in a slow, hesitant, and careful way, revealing a lack of confidence **2.** ROUGH OR PROVISIONAL likely to have many later changes before it becomes final and complete [Late 16thC. From medieval Latin *tentativus*, from, ultimately, Latin *tentare*, a variant of *temptare*, 'to feel, try' (source of English *tempt*).] —**tentatively** *adv.* —**tentativeness** *n.*

tent caterpillar *n.* a destructive caterpillar that builds large tent-shaped communal webs in the branches of trees. Genus: *Malacosoma.*

tent dress *n.* a dress made so that the fabric hangs in a full loose shape from the shoulders

tented /téntid/ *adj.* **1.** WITH TENT SHAPE constructed or shaped like a tent **2.** WITH TENTS covered in tents (*literary*) **3.** CAMPED IN TENTS staying in tents, or supplied with tents as shelter

tenter /téntər/ *n.* FRAME FOR CLOTH a frame on which cloth is held taut during various phases of its manufacture, especially while it dries ■ *vt.* (**-ters, -tering, -tered**) STRETCH ON TENTER to stretch cloth on a tenter [13thC. From medieval Latin *tentorium* from, ultimately, Latin *tendere* 'to stretch'.]

tenterhook /téntər hŏŏk/ *n.* any one of the hooks used to hold cloth taut on a frame during manufacture, especially while it dries ◇ **be on tenterhooks** to be anxious or in suspense

tenth /tenth/ *n.* **1.** ONE OF TEN PARTS OF STH one of ten equal parts of sth **2.** ORDINAL NUMBER CORRESPONDING TO 10 the ordinal number assigned to item number 10 in a series **3.** MUSIC MUSICAL INTERVAL an interval equal to an octave plus a third [Old English *teogoþa*, *tēoþa*, from an earlier form of TEN] —**tenth** *adj., adv.*

tent stitch *n.* a type of short parallel diagonal stitch used to fill in an area in needlepoint or embroidery, or a single stitch of this kind

tenuis /ténnyoo iss/ (*plural* **-es** /-eez/) *n.* LING a voiceless stop consonant in classical Greek grammar [Mid-17thC. Formed from Latin, 'thin, fine', a translation of Greek *psilon* 'bare, smooth'.]

tenuous /ténnyoo əss/ *adj.* **1.** WEAK AND UNCONVINCING not based on anything significant or substantial, and so liable to break down easily when challenged ○ *That's an extremely tenuous argument.* **2.** EXTREMELY

DELICATE AND FINE thin and fine and so easily broken (*literary*) **3.** SCI DILUTED thin or diluted in consistency [Late 16thC. Formed by alteration from Latin *tenuis* (see TENUIS).] —**tenuity** /te nyŏŏ əti/ *n.* —**tenuously** /ténnyoo əssli/ *adv.* —**tenuousness** /ténnyoo əss-nəss/ *n.*

tenure /ténnyər, ténnyoor/ *n.* **1.** APPOINTMENT OR PERIOD OF APPOINTMENT the occupation of an official position, or the length of time a position is occupied (*formal*) ○ *her tenure of the presidency* **2.** PROPERTY-HOLDING the rights of a tenant to hold property, or the holding of property as a tenant **3.** US, Can EDUC, HR PERMANENT STATUS the position of having a formal secure appointment until retirement, especially at an educational institution after working on a temporary or provisional basis [15thC. Via Old French 'tenure, estate', from, ultimately, Latin *tenere* 'to hold'.]

tenured /ténnyərd, ténnyoord/ *adj.* **1.** US, Can HR PERMANENTLY HELD formally granted to sb to possess or occupy until retirement, especially in an educational institution ○ *a tenured position at a good university* **2.** US EDUC HAVING PERMANENT STATUS formally granted the right to hold an academic job until retirement ○ *She's a tenured professor.* **3.** LAW HAVING TENURE subject to a guaranteed period of time during which rights cannot be withdrawn

tenuto /te nyóōtō/ *adv., adj.* indicating that a musical note should be held for its full value (*used as a musical direction*) [Mid-18thC. Via Italian, the past participle of *tenere*, 'to hold', from Latin, 'to hold'.]

Tenzing Norkay /ténssing náwrk ay/ (1914?–86) Nepalese mountaineer. He and Sir Edmund Hillary were the first to reach the summit of Mount Everest (1953).

teocalli /teé ō kálli/ *n.* a temple in ancient Mexico or Central America, or the pyramidal mound on which one was built [Early 17thC. Via American Spanish from Nahuatl *teokalli*, literally 'deity's house'.]

teosinte /táy ō sínti/ *n.* a tall annual grass of Mexico and Central America, related to, and perhaps the ancestor of, maize, and grown as forage. Latin name: *Zea mexicana.* [Late 19thC. Via French *téosinté* from Nahuatl *teocintli*, perhaps literally 'dried maize ear of a deity'.]

tepa /teépə/ *n.* a crystalline compound used in the sterilization of insects, treatment of some cancers, and fireproofing of textiles. Formula: $C_6H_{12}N_3OP$. [Mid-20thC. Acronym formed from TRI- + ETHYLENE + PHOSPH- + AMIDE.]

tepal /teép'l/ *n.* any of the parts that form the outer whorl (**perianth**) of flowers such as in the tulip, in which there is no differentiation into petals and sepals [Mid-19thC. From French, a blend of *sépale* 'sepal', and *pétale* 'petal'.]

Te Papa Tongarewa /te pá pə tongə reé wə/ *n.* a museum in Wellington that contains the New Zealand national collections. It was created in 1998 by combining the collections of the National Museum and National Art Gallery. [Late 20thC. From Maori.]

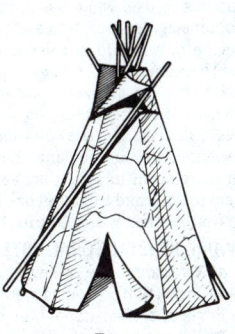

Tepee

tepee /teé pee/, **teepee, tipi** *n.* a conical tent built around several long branches or wooden poles that meet and cross at the top. A tepee is traditionally made of animal hide and used as a dwelling by Plains Indians and some other Native North American people. [Mid-18thC. From Sioux *típi* 'dwelling'.]

tephra /téffrə/ *n.* solid material ejected explosively from a volcano, e.g. ash, dust, and boulders [Mid-20thC. From Greek, 'ashes'.]

tepid /téppid/ *adj.* **1.** LUKEWARM slightly warm **2.** UNENTHUSIASTIC showing little enthusiasm or warmth ○ *tepid applause* [14thC. From Latin *tepidus*, from *tepere*, 'to be warm'.] —**tepidity** /te píddəti/ *n.* —**tepidly** /téppid li/ *adv.* —**tepidness** /téppidnəss/ *n.*

TEPP /tep/ *n.* a crystalline compound used as an insecticide and in medicine as a stimulant of the parasympathetic nervous system. Formula: $C_8H_{20}O_7P_2$. Full form **tetraethyl pyrophosphate**

Te Puea Herangi /te poó ay ə he rángi/ (1884–1952) New Zealand Maori leader. She was prominent in the revival of Maori culture and the provision of social welfare for Maori.

tequila /ti keélə, te-/ *n.* a strong Mexican spirit made by redistilling the fermented juice of the agave plant (**mescal**). It is drunk neat or used as a base for cocktails. [Mid-19thC. From Mexican Spanish, named after *Tequila*, a town in Central Mexico where the drink is produced.]

tequila sunrise *n.* a cocktail based on tequila that also contains orange juice and grenadine

ter. *abbr.* **1.** territory **2.** territorial **3.** terrace

Ter. *abbr.* Terrace (*used in street names and addresses*)

ter- *prefix.* three, threefold ○ *terpolymer* [From Latin *ter* 'three times'. Ultimately from the Indo-European word for 'three'.]

tera- *prefix.* **1.** ONE MILLION MILLION one million million (10^{12}). Symbol **T 2.** a binary trillion ○ *terabyte* [Formed from Greek *teras* 'monster']

terabyte /térrə bīt/ *n.* an information unit of one billion bytes

teraflop /térrə flop/ *n.* one billion floating-point operations per second, a measure of computer speed [Late 20thC. Coined from TERA- and an acronym formed from *floating-point operations per second*.]

terahertz /térrə hurts/ (*plural* **-hertz**) *n.* a unit of frequency equal to one billion hertz

terai /tə rí/, **terai hat** *n.* a wide-brimmed felt hat with a double crown, once widely worn in the subtropics [Late 19thC. Named after the TERAI region, where such a hat would have been worn.]

Terai *n.* in India, an area of marshy land at the foot of mountains, especially one in the foothills of the Himalayas in northern India and southern Nepal [Late 19thC. From Hindi *tarāī* 'marshy lowlands'.]

terakihi *n.* = **tarakihi**

teraph /térrəf/ (*plural* **-aphim** /térrəfim/) *n.* an image or idol worshipped by ancient Semitic peoples [Early 19thC. Back-formation from 14thC *teraphim* via late Latin *theraphim* and Greek *theraphin* from Hebrew *térāpīm*.]

terato- *prefix.* **1.** malformed, grotesque ○ *teratogen* **2.** tumour ○ *teratoma* [From Greek *terat-*, the stem of *teras* 'monster']

teratocarcinoma /térrətō kaárssi nōmə/ (*plural* **-mas** or **-mata** /-mətə/) *n.* a malignant teratoma, most often occurring in the testes

teratogen /tə rá ttəjən/ *n.* an agent, e.g. a chemical, virus, or ionizing radiation, that interrupts or alters the normal development of a foetus, with results that are evident at birth —**teratogenic** /té rə tō jénn ik/ *adj.*

teratogenesis /térrətə jénnəssiss/ *n.* the process of interrupting or altering normal development, especially of a foetus, with results that are evident at birth

teratoid /térrə toyd/ *adj.* affected by a visible condition caused by the interruption or alteration of normal development

teratology /térrə tólləji/ *n.* the scientific study of visible conditions caused by the interruption or alteration of normal development —**teratologic** /térrətə lójjik/ *adj.* —**teratologist** /térrə tólla jist/ *n.*

teratoma /térrə tōmə/ (*plural* **-mata** /-mətə/ *or* **-mas**) *n.* a tumour composed of various tissues, e.g. bone, hair, and teeth, not normally found together at the site of origin, and probably derived from embryonic remnants. They most often occur in the ovary, where they are benign, and in the testis, where they are malignant. —**teratomatous** /térrə tṓmətəss/ *adj.*

Te Rauparaha /te rówpə raahə/ (1768?–1849) New Zealand Maori leader. Under his leadership, the Ngata Toa people conquered much of the southwest of the North Island and the north of the South Island, a territory they held until the arrival of Europeans.

terbium /túrbi əm/ *n.* a silvery-grey metallic chemical element of the rare-earth group that is used in lasers and X-ray and television tubes. Symbol **Tb** [Mid-19thC. Named after *Ytterby*, the village in Sweden where it was discovered.] —**terbic** /túrbik/ *adj.*

terce /turss/ *n.* in the Roman Catholic Church, the third of the seven prayer times (**canonical hours**) when specific prayers are said [14thC. Via Old French, a variant of *tierce* (see TIERCE).]

Terceira /tər sáyrə, -sírə/ the second largest island in the Azores archipelago, in the North Atlantic Ocean. Population: 55,800 (1987). Area: 397 sq. km/153 sq. mi.

tercel /túrss'l/ (*plural* **-cels** *or* **-cel**), **tiercel** /teérss'l/ (*plural* **-cels** *or* **-cel**) *n.* a male falcon or hawk used in falconry [14thC. Via Old French *terçuel* from, ultimately, Latin *tertius* 'third', because it is about a third smaller than the female, or from the belief that the third egg hatched was male.]

tercentenary /túr sen teénəri, -ténnəri/ *n.* (*plural* **-ries**) **300TH ANNIVERSARY** a year, or an exact day, 300 years after a specific thing happened, usually sth of special historic significance ■ *adj.* **MARKING 300 YEARS SINCE STH HAPPENED** coinciding with the 300th anniversary of a particular event, and often celebrating or commemorating this [Mid-19thC. Coined from Latin *ter* 'three times'+ CENTENARY or CENTENNIAL.]

tercet /túrssit, tur sét/ *n.* a group of three lines of verse that rhyme with each other or with another group of three [Late 16thC. Via French from Italian *terzetto*, from, ultimately, Latin *tertius* 'third'.]

terebinth /térr əbinth/ (*plural* **-binths** *or* **-binth**) *n.* a small Mediterranean tree of the cashew family that has clusters of small flowers and yields a turpentine. Latin name: *Pistacia terebinthus.* [14thC. Directly and via Old French *t(h)erebinte* from Latin *terebinthus*, from Greek *terebinthos.*]

terebinthine /térrə bín thīn/ *adj.* **1.** BOT **OF TEREBINTH TREE** relating to the terebinth tree **2.** CHEM **LIKE TURPENTINE** like or consisting of turpentine [Early 16thC. From Latin *terebinthinus*, from *terebinthus* (see TEREBINTH).]

teredo /te reédō/ (*plural* **-dos** *or* **-do**) *n.* MARINE BIOL = **shipworm** [14thC. Via Latin from Greek *terēdōn*, from the base of *teirein* 'to rub hard, wear away, bore'.]

Terence /térrənss/ (185–159 BC) Roman playwright. His six surviving comedies, based on Greek originals, are forerunners of the modern comedy of manners. Full name **Publius Terentius Afer**

Teresa (of Ávila) /tə reézə/, **St** (1515–82) Spanish nun. Famous for the mystical visions she experienced, she was also the founder of the order of the Discalced Carmelites (1562). Real name **Teresa de Cepeda y Ahumada**

Express Newspapers

Mother Teresa

Teresa (of Calcutta) /tə reéssə, -ráyzə-/, **Mother** (1910–97) Albanian-born nun. From 1948 she devoted her life to helping the poor and the sick of Calcutta. She founded the Missionaries of Charity (1950) and opened a shelter for dying people (1952). Real name **Agnes Gonxha Bojaxhiu**

Tereshkova /térrish kṓvə/, **Valentina** (*b.* 1937) Soviet cosmonaut. She was the first woman to fly in space (16–19 June, 1963).

terete /té reet/ *adj.* used to describe a plant part that is smooth, cylindrical, and tapering, e.g. a grass stem [Early 17thC. From Latin *teret-*, the stem of *teres* 'rounded'.]

terga plural of **tergum**

tergiversate /túrjivər sayt/ (**-sates, -sating, -sated**) *vi.* (*formal*) **1.** **CHANGE SIDES** to change sides or opinions **2.** **BE EVASIVE** to use evasions or subterfuges [Mid-17thC. From Latin *tergiversare* 'to turn your back', from *tergum* 'back' + *vertere* 'to turn'.] —**tergiversant** *n.* —**tergiversator** *n.* —**tergiversatory** /túrjivər sáytəri/ *adj.*

tergum /túrgəm/ (*plural* **-ga** /-gə/) *n.* a thick plate covering the dorsal surface of a body segment of an arthropod, or the movable segments of a barnacle's shell [Early 19thC. From Latin, 'back'.] —**tergal** *adj.*

teriyaki /térri yáki/ *n.* a Japanese dish consisting of grilled shellfish or meat brushed with a marinade of soy sauce, sugar, and rice wine [Mid-20thC. From Japanese, literally 'glaze grill'.]

term /turm/ *n.* **1.** **NAME OR WORD FOR STH** a particular word or combination of words, especially one used to mean sth very specific or one used in a specialized area of knowledge or work ○ *The correct legal term is 'easement'.* **2.** **PERIOD OF TIME STH LASTS** the length of time that sth lasts, with a fixed or specified beginning and end, often a period during which sb holds a specific appointment or office (*formal*) **3.** **PERIOD OF TIME BODY CONTINUES MEETING** a length of time over which a political or legal body, e.g. a parliament or court of law, regularly assembles and carries out its formal duties **4.** EDUC **DIVISION OF ACADEMIC YEAR** one of the sections of the academic year during which students attend a school, college, or university and receive regular tuition **5.** GYN **EXPECTED TIME FOR BIRTH OF CHILD** the time at the end of a woman's pregnancy when the baby is expected to be born ○ *came to term* **6.** LOGIC **SUBJECT OR PREDICATE OF PROPOSITION** in traditional Aristotelian logic, the subject or the predicate of a categorical proposition **7.** LOGIC **NAME OR INDIVIDUAL VARIABLE** in modern logic, a name or individual variable **8.** MATH **MATHEMATICAL EXPRESSION** a mathematical expression that forms part of a fraction or proportion, is part of a series, or is associated with another by a plus or minus sign **9.** SCULPTURE **SCULPTURED PILLAR** a sculptured pillar, especially one with an armless bust, or an animal portrait, on top of a square post **10.** LAW **ESTATE RUNNING FOR LIMITED PERIOD** an estate limited to a prescribed period ■ **terms** *npl.* **1.** **WAY PEOPLE GET ON TOGETHER** the treatment given by one person, nation, or power to another, or the opinions or attitudes they have or express towards each other ○ *on good terms with the neighbours* **2.** **PARTS THAT MAKE UP AN AGREEMENT** the particular requirements laid down formally in an agreement or contract, or proposed by one side when negotiating an agreement **3.** **LANGUAGE** the words that sb uses, or specifically chooses to use, when speaking or writing ■ *vt.* (**terms, terming, termed**) **USE A PARTICULAR WORD FOR STH** to describe or refer to sth using a particular name or expression ○ *His followers were termed 'Roundheads'.* [13thC. Via French *terme* 'limit of time or space' (the original sense in English), from Latin *terminus* (see TERMINUS).] ◇ **come to terms (with sth)** to reach a state of acceptance or agreement about sth ◇ **in terms of sth** in relation to sth ◇ **not be on speaking terms (with sb)** to have had a quarrel or disagreement with sb, so that neither will speak to the other

WORD KEY: CULTURAL NOTE

For the Term of His Natural Life, a novel by Australian writer Marcus Clark (1874). An epic work set in early 19th-century England and Australia, it tells the story of a young man transported to Australia. He endures the horrors of various penal settlements before drowning during an escape attempt.

term. *abbr.* terminal

termagant /túrməgənt/ *n.* an offensive term that deliberately insults a woman's temperament and supposed propensity for arguing, criticizing, and quarrelling (*literary or humorous disapproving*) [13thC. Via Old French *Tervagant*, the name of an overbearing non-Christian deity in medieval mystery plays (the original sense in English), from Italian *Trivigante*.] —**termagancy** *n.*

term assurance *n.* = **term insurance**

-termer /túrmər/ *suffix.* sb who is serving a particular term as a political appointee or in a prison ○ *a second-termer*

terminable /túrminəb'l/ *adj.* **1.** **CAPABLE OF TERMINATION** able to be terminated (*formal*) ○ *The contract is terminable at any time.* **2.** INSUR **WITH A FIXED END POINT** ending or capable of being ended after a certain period or on a particular date ○ *a terminable annuity* [15thC. Formed from earlier *termine* 'to terminate', via French *terminer* from Latin *terminare*.] —**terminability** /túrminə bílləti/ *n.* —**terminably** /túrminəbli/ *adv.*

terminal /túrminəl/ *adj.* **1.** **CAUSING DEATH** inevitably, but often gradually, leading to the death of the person affected by the condition ○ *a terminal illness* **2.** **DYING** affected by a fatal illness or condition that is approaching its final stages **3.** **RELATING TO DYING PATIENTS** for or concerned with patients with a terminal condition ○ *terminal care* **4.** **EXTREME** extremely intense or overwhelming (*informal humorous*) ○ *terminal boredom* **5.** **AT THE VERY END** forming or found at the extreme point or limit of sth, or relating to the very end of sth ○ *the terminal moraine of the glacier* **6.** BOT **AT END OF STEM** at the end of a stem, stalk, or branch **7.** EDUC **RELATING TO AN ACADEMIC TERM** taking place during or after an academic term, or every term (*formal*) ■ *n.* **1.** TRANSP **STATION AT END OF TRANSPORT ROUTE** a building or complex containing facilities needed by transport operators and passengers at either end of a travel or shipping route by air, rail, road, or sea **2.** INDUST **ONSHORE INDUSTRIAL SITE FOR OFFSHORE PRODUCTS** an industrial installation where raw material is brought onshore and often also processed, e.g. for the offshore gas or oil industry **3.** ELEC **ELECTRICAL CONDUCTOR** a conductor attached at the point where electricity enters or leaves a circuit, e.g. on a battery **4.** COMPUT **DEVICE LINKED TO COMPUTER** a remote input or output device linked to a computer, or a combination of such devices, e.g. a keyboard and video display **5.** TRANSP = **terminus** *n.* 1 **6.** ARCHIT **ORNAMENTAL CARVING** an ornamental carving or figure at the end of a larger structure [15thC. From Latin *terminalis*, from *terminus* 'end, boundary, limit'.]

WORD KEY: SYNONYMS

See Synonyms at ***deadly.***

terminally /túrminəli/ *adv.* **1.** **INEVITABLY LEADING TO DEATH** in a way that leads inevitably to the death of a sick person ○ *terminally ill* **2.** **EXTREMELY** in a very intense or overwhelming way (*informal humorous*) **3.** SCI **AT THE END** at the tip or end section

terminal platform *n.* an offshore platform from which gas or petroleum is piped ashore

terminal tackle *n.* the hook or lure attached to the end of a fishing line

terminal velocity *n.* the constant speed that a falling object reaches when the downward gravitational force equals the frictional resistance of the medium through which it is falling, usually air. This is the maximum speed that a freely falling body can reach under particular conditions.

terminate /túrmi nayt/ (**-nates, -nating, -nated**) *vti.* to come to an end, or bring sth to an end (*formal*) [Late 16thC. From Latin *terminare*, from *terminus* 'end, boundary, limit'.] —**terminative** /túrminətiv/ *adj.* —**terminatory** /túrm in áyt əri/ *adj.*

terminating decimal *n.* a decimal fraction with a finite number of digits

termination /túrmi náysh'n/ *n.* **1.** **ENDING OF STH** the process of bringing sth to an end or of being brought to an end, or an individual example of this (*formal*) **2.** GYN **ABORTION** an induced abortion **3.** LING **WORD ENDING** a word ending such as a suffix or an inflection **4.** **TIP OR EDGE** sth that forms the end or final limit of sth (*formal*) **5.** **FINAL OUTCOME** sth that happens or is produced as a result of sth else (*formal*) [14thC. Directly or via French from Latin, from *terminare* (see TERMINATE).] —**terminational** *adj.*

terminator /túrmi naytər/ *n.* **1.** SB WHO OR STH THAT TER-MINATES STH sb who or sth that puts an end to sth (*formal*) **2.** ASTRON LINE BETWEEN MOON'S LIGHT AND DARK the boundary between the part of the moon or a planet that is illuminated and that which is dark

terminator gene *n.* a gene inserted into genetically modified plants that makes them unable to produce seed after one season

terminology /túrmi nóləji/ (*plural* **-gies**) *n.* **1.** SPECIALIZED VOCABULARY the expressions and words, or a set of expressions and words, used by people involved in a specialized activity or field of work **2.** LING STUDY OF NAMES AND TERMS the systematic study of names and terms [Early 19thC. Via German *Terminologie*, from medieval Latin *terminus* 'term.'] —**terminological** /túrminə lójjik'l/ *adj.* —**terminologically** /-lójjikli/ *adv.* —**terminologist** /túrm i nóllǝjist/ *n.*

term insurance, **term assurance** *n.* life assurance that pays a sum of money only if the person who is covered has a loss within a particular period of time

terminus /túrminǝss/ (*plural* **-ni** /-nī/ *or* **-nuses**) *n.* **1.** TRANSP PLACE WHERE PUBLIC TRANSPORT ROUTE ENDS a town, city, or location at the end or beginning of a fixed transport route such as a railway line or bus route **2.** VERY LAST POINT a point where sth stops or reaches its end (*literary or formal*) **3.** SCULPTURE = term [Mid-16thC. From Latin 'end, boundary, limit'.]

terminus ad quem /túrminǝss ad kwém/ *n.* the aim or finishing point of sth [From Latin, literally 'end to which']

terminus a quo /túrmǝnǝss aa kwō/ *n.* the starting point of sth [From Latin, literally 'end from which']

Termitarium: Queensland, Australia

termitarium /túrmi táiri ǝm/ (*plural* **-a** /-ri ǝ/ *n.* a nest, sometimes extremely large, made by a group of termites [Mid-19thC. Coined from TERMITE + -ARIUM.]

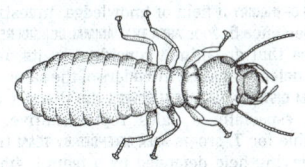

Termite

termite /túr mīt/ *n.* a light-coloured social insect that forms large colonies. Many species live in warm or tropical regions, feed on wood, and are highly destructive to trees and wooden structures. Order: Isoptera. [Late 18thC. From Latin *termit-*, the stem of *termes* 'woodworm', an alteration of *tarmes*, perhaps influenced by *terere* 'to rub'.] —**termitic** /tur míttik/ *adj.*

termless /túrmlǝss/ *adj.* **1.** ENDLESS having no end or limit (*literary*) **2.** UNCONDITIONAL not depending on any particular terms and conditions (*formal*)

termly /túrmli/ *adj.* **1.** HAPPENING EVERY SCHOOL TERM taking place every academic term **2.** FOR EACH TIME-PERIOD for each fixed or agreed time-period (*formal*)

term paper *n.* US a long essay required of a student during an academic term

terms of trade *npl.* ECON the ratio of a nation's export prices to its import prices, used to measure the country's trading position

tern[1] /turn/ (*plural* **terns** *or* **tern**) *n.* a seabird, typically black and white, related to the gulls but with a more slender body and wings, a pointed bill, and a forked tail. Subfamily: Sterninae. [Late 17thC. From Scandinavian.]

tern[2] /turn/ *n.* **1.** GAMBLING GROUP OF THREE a set of three things, especially three numbers that together form a winning combination in a lottery or other gambling game **2.** NAUT THREE-MASTED SCHOONER a schooner with three masts [14thC. Via French *terne* from Latin *terni* 'three each'.]

ternary /túrnǝri/ (*plural* **-ries**) *adj.* **1.** THREEFOLD consisting of three things or parts, or arranged in groups of three (*formal*) ○ *ternary form* **2.** MATH WITH A BASE OF THREE used to describe a number system, or a number belonging to it, that has three as its base ○ *a ternary logarithm* **3.** MATH WITH THREE VARIABLES involving or having three variables **4.** METALL WITH THREE COMPONENTS used to describe an alloy that consists of three components **5.** CHEM WITH THREE ATOMS OR MOLECULES used to describe a chemical compound that consists of three active elements, e.g. three atoms, molecules, or radicals [15thC. From Latin *ternarius*, from *terni*, 'three at a time', from *ter* 'three times'.]

ternary form *n.* in musical composition, a three-part form in which the first section is repeated or slightly varied in the last section, following a second, contrasting section

ternary system, **ternary number system** *n.* the number system that has 3 as its base. Decimal numbers are expressed as sequences of the digits 0, 1, and 2.

ternate /túr nayt/ *adj.* used to describe a compound leaf that is divided into three more or less equal parts [Mid-18thC. From modern Latin *ternatus*, from medieval Latin, the past participle of *ternare* 'to make three-fold'.] —**ternately** *adv.*

terne /turn/ *n.* **1.** METAL ALLOY an alloy of lead and tin with antimony, used as a coating **2.** = terneplate [Mid-19thC. Origin uncertain: probably from French, 'dull, tarnished'.]

terneplate /túrn playt/ *n.* a steel or iron plate coated with terne

Terni /túrni/ capital of Terni Province, Umbria Region, central Italy. Population: 108,150 (1992).

ternion /túrni ǝn/ *n.* PRINTING three sheets of paper folded once to make 12 pages [Late 16thC. From Latin *ternion-*, from, ultimately, *ter* 'thrice'.]

terotechnology /teérō tek nóllǝji/ *n.* a branch of technology that uses managerial and financial expertise as well as engineering skills when installing and running machinery [Late 20thC. Coined from Greek *tērein*, 'to watch over, take care of' + TECHNOLOGY.]

terpene /túr peen/ *n.* any of a class of hydrocarbons obtained from the essential oils of plants such as conifers and used in organic synthesis. Formula: $C_{10}H_{16}$. [Late 19thC. Formed from German *Terpentin* 'turpentine'.] —**terpenic** /túr peénik/ *adj.*

terpineol /tur pínni ol/ *n.* a combustible colourless derivative of pine oil, usually found as one of three isomers with a lilac or hyacinth aroma, used in flavourings and perfumes, and as a solvent. Formula: $C_{10}H_{17}OH$. [Late 19thC. Coined from earlier *terpin*, from TERPENE.]

terpolymer /tur póllimǝr/ *n.* a polymer consisting of three monomers [Mid-20thC. Coined from Latin *ter* 'three times' + POLYMER.]

Terpsichore /turp síkǝri/ *n.* the Muse of choral songs and dance in Greek mythology

terpsichoreal /túrpsikǝ reé ǝl/ *adj.* = terpsichorean *adj.* (*formal humorous*)

terpsichorean /túrpsikǝ reé ǝn/ *adj.* RELATING TO DANCE relating to or like dance (*formal humorous*) ■ *n.* DANCER a dancer (*formal humorous*) [Early 19thC. Formed from Greek *Terpsikhorē*, literally 'delighting in dance', from *terpein* 'delight' + *khoros* 'dance'.]

terr /tur/ *n.* S Africa a term applied in the past by members of the white communities in South Africa and Rhodesia (now Zimbabwe) to those opposed to their minority rule (*dated informal*) [Late 20thC. Shortening of TERRORIST.]

terr. *abbr.* **1.** territory **2.** territorial **3.** terrace

Terr. *abbr.* Terrace (*used in street names and addresses*)

terra /térrǝ/ (*plural* **terrae** /-reǝ/) *n.* any of the light-coloured highland or mountainous areas of the moon or of a planet [Early 17thC. Directly or via Italian from Latin, 'earth, land'.]

terra alba /térrǝ álbǝ/ *n.* a white substance such as kaolin or gypsum, used in the making of paints and paper [From Latin, literally 'white earth']

terrace /térrǝss/ *n.* **1.** ARCHIT PORCH OR WALKWAY WITH PILLARS a promenade or portico, usually with columns or a balustrade along the side or sides **2.** AGRIC STRIP OF AGRICULTURAL LAND ON HILLSIDE a flat, fairly narrow, level strip of ground, bounded by a vertical or steep slope and constructed on a hillside so that the land can be cultivated **3.** GEOG AREA OF NATURAL GROUND ALONG COAST a flat raised strip of beach or ground that has been formed naturally along the coast, beside a river or lake, or along the side of a valley by erosion or the changing sea level **4.** ROW OF IDENTICAL HOUSES JOINED TOGETHER a long row of houses built together in the same style, separated only by shared dividing sidewalls (**party walls**) **5.** CIV ENG CONSTRUCTED BANK OF GROUND a raised bank of ground, artificially constructed **6.** FLAT AREA BESIDE A BUILDING a paved or grassy area immediately outside and on a level with a building, used for sitting or eating outdoors **7.** BUILDINGS SET ON RAISED GROUND a row of houses facing down from a raised position on or along the top of a piece of sloping ground, or built on a raised bank of ground ■ **terraces** *npl.* **1.** STANDING AREAS AROUND FOOTBALL PITCHES the broad shallow open-air steps built around football pitches to provide cheap standing areas for spectators, outlawed at larger football grounds in the United Kingdom in the early 1990s **2.** FOOTBALL SPECTATORS ON THE TERRACES the football spectators standing on the terraces (*informal*) ■ *vt.* (**-races**, **-racing**, **-raced**) FORM TERRACE ON LAND to convert land into a terrace or terraces [Early 16thC. Via Old French, 'rubble, platform' and, ultimately, Latin *terra* (see TERRA).]

Terrace *n.* a street name for a residential terrace

terraced house, **terrace house** *n.* any house in a row of similar houses joined side by side and facing the street. US term **row house** —**terraced housing** *n.*

terracing /térrǝss ing/ *n.* **1.** STRIPS OF AGRICULTURAL LAND IN STEPS a series of level, fairly narrow strips of ground constructed on a hillside that would otherwise be too steep for cultivation **2.** TERRACED AREA OR STRUCTURE sth built in shallow, gradually rising steps or tiers such as the open-air terraces in a football ground or an area of landscaped garden **3.** TERRACED HOUSES a group of buildings designed or built as a terrace or terraces **4.** MAKING OF TERRACES the act or process of creating a terrace or terraces

terracotta /térrǝ kó tǝ/ *n.* **1.** CERAMICS REDDISH-BROWN POTTERY CLAY unglazed reddish-brown hard-baked clay, often used to make pottery objects **2.** CRAFT STH MADE OF TERRACOTTA a work of art or craft modelled in terracotta, or terracotta items generally **3.** COLOURS BROWNISH-RED COLOUR a brownish-red colour, like that of terracotta ■ *adj.* BROWNISH-RED of a brownish-red colour, like terracotta [Early 18thC. From Italian, literally 'baked earth'.]

terrae, **terrae incognitae** plural of **terra**, **terra incognita**

terra firma /-fúrmǝ/ *n.* solid ground, in contrast to water or air (*literary or humorous*) [From Latin, literally 'firm land']

terrain /tǝ ráyn/ (*plural* **-rains** *or* **-rain**) *n.* **1.** GEOG, MIL LAND OR COUNTRYSIDE ground or a piece of land seen in terms of its surface features or general physical character, especially when crossing it or using it for military purposes **2.** GEOL = terrane [Early 18thC. Via French from, ultimately, Latin *terrenum* 'land, ground', from *terrenus* 'of the earth', from *terra* (see TERRA).]

terra incognita /-in kógnitǝ/ (*plural* **terrae incognitae** /térree in kógni tee/) *n.* **1.** UNEXPLORED REGION a country or region that is unknown or has not been explored

2. UNEXPLORED SUBJECT a subject or area of knowledge that has not been explored and about which nothing is known [From Latin, 'unknown land']

Terramycin /térrə mīssin/ *tdmk.* a trademark for oxytetracycline

terrane /térrayn/ *n.* a section of the Earth's crust that is defined by clear fault boundaries, with stratigraphic and structural properties that distinguish it from adjacent rocks [Early 18thC. Via French from, ultimately, Latin *terrenus*, from *terra* 'earth'.]

terra nullius /térrə nŏŏlli əss/ *n.* in Australia, the idea and legal concept that when the first Europeans arrived in Australia the land was owned by no one and therefore open to settlement. It has been judged not to be legally valid.

terrapin /térrəpin/ (*plural* **-pins** *or* **-pin**) *n.* **1.** N AMERICAN TURTLE a moderate-sized turtle found in brackish water in eastern North America. Numbers have been severely reduced by overharvesting. Latin name: *Malaclemys terrapin.* **2.** SMALL FRESHWATER TURTLE a turtle with four webbed feet, a shell like that of a tortoise, and a retractable head. They are usually smaller than tortoises, live in fresh water and on land, and are carnivorous. Family: Emydidae. [Early 17thC. Formed from an alteration of an Algonquian word, perhaps *torope*, + -IN, of unknown origin.]

terraqueous /te ráykwi əss/ *adj.* consisting of areas of water and areas of dry land (*archaic or literary*) [Mid-17thC. Coined from Latin *terra* 'earth' + AQUEOUS.]

terrarium /tə ráiri əm/ (*plural* **-ums** *or* **-a** /-ri ə/) *n.* **1.** ENCLOSURE FOR SMALL ANIMALS an enclosure that is used for keeping or observing small land animals such as lizards in a simulated natural environment **2.** CONTAINER FOR PLANTS a sealed glass container often in the shape of a globe that is used for growing ornamental plants that require a high level of humidity [Late 19thC. From medieval Latin, from Latin *terra* 'earth' (modelled on AQUARIUM), because it was designed for land animals.]

terrazzo /te rátsō/ *n.* a type of mosaic used as a floor or wall covering that is made by laying marble or stone chips in mortar and grinding them to a polished level surface [Early 20thC. From Italian, 'terrace', of uncertain origin: perhaps from Old Provençal *terrassa*.]

terrene /te reén/ *adj.* (*archaic or literary*) **1.** WORLDLY OR EARTHLY worldly or earthly as opposed to heavenly or spiritual **2.** EARTHY consisting of or like earth ■ *n.* LAND a land or territory, or the entire earth (*archaic or literary*) [14thC. Via Anglo-Norman from, ultimately, Latin *terra* 'earth'.] —**terrenely** *adv.*

terreplein /táir playn/ *n.* a raised embankment or platform behind a parapet where heavy guns are positioned [Late 16thC. Via French from, ultimately, Italian *terrapienare* 'to fill with earth', from *terra* 'earth' + *pieno* 'full' (from Latin *plenus*).]

terrestrial /tə réstri əl/ *adj.* **1.** RELATING TO EARTH relating to Earth rather than other planets **2.** BELONGING TO THE LAND belonging to the land rather than the sea or air **3.** BIOL LIVING OR GROWING ON LAND living or growing on land rather than in the sea or the air **4.** BROADCAST BROADCAST BY A LAND-BASED TRANSMITTER broadcast by a land-based transmitter rather than by satellite **5.** WORLDLY OR MUNDANE worldly or mundane as opposed to heavenly ■ *n.* DWELLER ON PLANET EARTH a person or creature who lives on the Earth, especially in science fiction [14thC. Formed from Latin *terrestris*, from *terra* 'earth' (source of English *terrier*).] —**terrestrially** *adv.* —**terrestrialness** *n.*

terrestrial guidance *n.* a missile or rocket guidance system in which the missile is given precise details of its flight path, enabling it to follow a predetermined route. Data given include gravitational field, magnetic field, and atmospheric pressure. ◊ **inertial guidance**

terrestrial planet *n.* any of the four planets, Mars, Venus, Mercury, and Earth, that are nearest the Sun and are similar in density and composition

terrestrial radiation *n.* electromagnetic radiation in the form of heat emitted by the earth as it cools down at night, especially when the air is dry and there are no clouds

terrestrial telescope *n.* a telescope used for viewing objects on Earth rather than in space. It has an objective and a four-lens eyepiece that give an upright image.

terret /térrit/ *n.* **1.** METAL RING ATTACHED TO HARNESS PAD either of two metal rings attached to the driving harness of a horse, through which the reins are passed to prevent them from slipping round the horse's flanks **2.** METAL RING ON DOG'S COLLAR a metal ring on a dog's collar to which a leash can be attached [Late 15thC. From Old French *toret* 'little ring', from *tour* (see TOUR).]

terre verte /táir vúrt/ *n.* a greyish-green pigment of powdered glauconite that is used in paints [From French, 'green earth']

terrible /térrəb'l/ *adj.* **1.** EXTREME very serious or severe ○ *a terrible cold* **2.** VERY UNPLEASANT very unpleasant or harrowing ○ *The past few days have been a terrible time.* **3.** EXTREMELY LOW IN QUALITY of a very low standard or quality ○ *My cooking isn't that great, but it's not terrible.* **4.** ILL OR UNHAPPY unwell, or extremely unhappy ○ *You look terrible. Are you ill?* **5.** TROUBLING causing considerable fear or anxiety ○ *a terrible sight* **6.** FORMIDABLE causing awe or dread ○ *a terrible responsibility* [14thC. Via Old French from Latin *terribilis*, from *terrere* 'to frighten' (source also of English *terror*).] —**terribleness** *n.*

terribly /térrəbli/ *adv.* **1.** EXTREMELY to an extreme degree ○ *I'm terribly pleased that you can come.* **2.** IN PAINFUL WAY in a way that is extremely difficult or painful ○ *affected terribly by the news*

terricolous /te ríkələss/ *adj.* living in or on the soil [Mid-19thC. Formed from Latin *terricola*, literally 'earth-dweller', from *terra* 'earth'.]

Terrier

terrier /térri ər/ *n.* any of several types of small lively dog that were initially bred to hunt animals living in underground burrows, but are now common as pets. They include the Airedale, cairn, fox, Scottish, and West Highland terriers, and the schnauzer. [15thC. From Old French *(chien) terrier* 'terrier (dog)', from, ultimately, Latin *terra* 'earth', because it pursues animals into their burrows.]

Terrier *n.* a member of the British Army's Territorial and Volunteer Reserve (*informal*) [Early 20thC. From TERRITORIAL.]

terrific /tə ríffik/ *adj.* **1.** VERY GOOD exceptionally good in a way that inspires enthusiasm (*informal*) **2.** VERY GREAT very great in size, force, or degree ○ *terrific speed* **3.** VERY FRIGHTENING inspiring a sense of terror (*archaic*) [Mid-17thC. From Latin *terrificus* 'frightening', from *terrere* 'to frighten'. 'Very good' evolved from 'frightening' via 'very great' in a way similar to, for example AWFUL.]

terrifically /tə ríffikli/ *adv.* to a very high degree or very great extent

terrify /térri fī/ (**-fies, -fying, -fied**) *vt.* **1.** MAKE SB VERY FRIGHTENED to make sb feel very frightened or alarmed **2.** INTIMIDATE SB to coerce sb to do sth by using threats ○ *terrified into naming the members* [Late 16thC. From Latin *terrificare*, from *terrificus* (see TERRIFIC).] —**terrifier** *n.* —**terrifying** *adj.* —**terrifyingly** *adv.*

terrigenous /te ríjjinəss/ *adj.* relating to a sediment derived from land erosion that may be formed or deposited on the land or found underwater in shallow ocean areas [Late 17thC. Formed from Latin *terrigenus* 'earth-born', from *terra* 'earth'.]

terrine /te reén/ *n.* **1.** HOUSEHOLD COOKING DISH a small dish with a tight-fitting lid that is used for cooking and serving food, especially cooked pâtés **2.** FOOD FOOD COOKED IN TERRINE the food that is cooked and served in a terrine dish, often a coarse pâté **3.** HOUSEHOLD = **tureen** [Early 18thC. From French, the feminine of Old French *terrin* 'earthen', from Latin *terra* 'earth'.]

territorial /térrə táwri əl/ *adj.* **1.** RELATING TO OWNED LAND relating to land or water owned or claimed by an entity, especially a government **2.** ZOOL ASSERTING OWNERSHIP OF AN AREA having a tendency to appropriate an area or territory and to protect that area or territory against intruders of the same species, particularly other males **3.** MIL RELATING TO RESERVE ARMY relating to a reserve army that has been trained for use in emergencies —**territorially** *adv.*

Territorial *n.* a member of a reserve army that has been trained for use in emergencies, especially the British Army's Territorial and Volunteer Reserve. ◊ **Territorial Army**

Territorial Army *n.* the British Army's Territorial and Volunteer Reserve, a reserve army established between 1907 and 1908 to assist with national defence in emergencies

territorialise *vt.* = **territorialize**

territorialism /térrə táwri əlizəm/ *n.* **1.** SYSTEM WITH LANDOWNERS HOLDING POWER a social system in which the landowners hold or control most of the positions of power and authority **2.** STATE REGULATION OF RELIGIOUS PRACTICES a system of civil government in which the citizens of a territory are penalized unless they adopt the same religion as their civil ruler. Historically it is associated particularly with the Lutheran Church in Germany. —**territorialist** *n.*

territoriality /térrə táwri álləti/ *n.* **1.** POL RANKING OF REGION AS TERRITORY the ranking of a region as a territory **2.** ZOOL ANIMAL DEFENCE OF TERRITORY a pattern of animal behaviour marked by the establishment, demarcation, and defence of an area that can support the growth and activity of an animal or group of animals

territorialize /térrə táwri ə līz/ (**-izes, -izing, -ized**), **territorialise** (**-ises, -ising, -ised**) *vt.* **1.** ORGANIZE INTO TERRITORIES to organize sth on a territorial basis **2.** POL ENLARGE A COUNTRY BY ADDING TERRITORY to enlarge a country by adding more territory or territories to it —**territorialization** /térrə táwri ə lī záysh'n/ *n.*

territorial waters *npl.* the area of sea around a country's coast recognized as being under that country's jurisdiction

Territorian /térrə táwri ən/ *n. Aus* sb who was born in or lives in the Northern Territory of Australia

territory /térrətəri/ (*plural* **-ries**) *n.* **1.** GEOG LAND land, or an area of land **2.** POL GOVERNED GEOGRAPHICAL AREA a geographical area that is owned and controlled by a particular government or country **3. territory, Territory** POL AREA OF COUNTRY WITH SEPARATE GOVERNMENT an area of a country or empire such as the United States, Canada, or Australia that is not a state or province but has a separate organized government **4.** FIELD OF INQUIRY a field of knowledge, investigation, or experience **5.** ZOOL AREA THAT ANIMAL CONSIDERS ITS OWN an area that an animal considers as its own and that it defends against intruders of the same species **6.** COMM DISTRICT THAT AGENT COVERS the district that an agent, especially a sales representative, is responsible for **7.** SPORTS AREA DEFENDED BY TEAM the area of a playing field defended by a team [14thC. From Latin *territorium*, from *terra* 'earth'), modelled on, for example DORMITORY from Latin *dormitorium*.] ◇ **come or go with the territory** to be an inseparable part of or accompaniment to sth else

terror /térrər/ *n.* **1.** INTENSE FEAR intense or overwhelming fear **2.** TERRORISM violence or the threat of violence carried out for political purposes **3.** STH CAUSING FEAR sth such as an event or situation that causes intense fear ○ *Her anger was the terror of the earth.* **4.** ANNOYING PERSON an annoying, difficult, or unpleasant person, particularly a naughty child (*informal*) [14thC. Via Old French from Latin, from *terrere* 'to frighten' (source also of English *deter*).] —**terrorful** *adj.*

Terror *n.* HIST = **Reign of Terror**

terrorise *vt.* = **terrorize**

terrorism /térrərizəm/ *n.* violence or the threat of violence, especially bombing, kidnapping, and assassination, carried out for political purposes

terrorist /térrərist/ *n.* sb who uses violence or the threat of violence, especially bombing, kidnapping, and assassination, to intimidate, often for political purposes —**terroristic** /térrə rístik/ *adj.*

terrorize /térrə rīz/ (**-izes, -izing, -ized**), **terrorise** (**-ises, -ising, -ised**) *vt.* **1.** MOTIVATE SB BY VIOLENCE to intimidate or coerce sb with violence or the threat of violence **2.** MAKE SB VERY FEARFUL to fill sb with feelings of intense fear over a period of time —**terrorization** /térrə rī záysh'n/ *n.* —**terrorizer** /térrə rīzər/ *n.*

terror-stricken, terror-struck *adj.* filled with a feeling of intense fear

terry /térri/ (*plural* **-ries**) *n.* **1.** UNCUT LOOP OF THREAD an uncut loop of thread in the pile of a fabric that consists of such loops **2.** = **terry towelling 3.** TERRY NAPPY a square of terry towelling used as a nondisposable nappy [Late 18thC. Origin uncertain: perhaps an alteration of French *tiré* 'drawn', ultimately from *tirer* 'to draw out'.]

Terry /térri/, **Dame Ellen** (1847–1928) English actor. A noted Shakespearean actor, she maintained a stage partnership with Sir Henry Irving that lasted 24 years. Full name **Dame Ellen Alicia Terry**

terry towelling *n.* a type of fabric used for items such as towels, bath mats, and nappies that has uncut loops of thread on both sides

terse /turss/ (**terser, tersest**) *adj.* **1.** ABRUPT brief and unfriendly, often conveying annoyance **2.** CONCISE concise and economically phrased [Early 17thC. From Latin *tersus* 'wiped off, clean', the past participle of *tergere* 'to wipe'. The modern meanings evolved via the sense 'polished, smooth'.] —**tersely** *adv.* —**terseness** *n.*

tertial /túrsh'l/ *adj., n.* BIRDS = **tertiary** *adj.* 3 [Mid-19thC. Formed from Latin *tertius* (see TERTIARY).]

tertian /túrsh'n/ *adj.* APPEARING EVERY OTHER DAY used to describe a fever, especially a malarial fever, with symptoms that appear every other day ■ *n.* TERTIAN FEVER a tertian fever or set of symptoms [14thC. From Latin *(febris) tertiana* '(fever) of the third (day)', from *tertius* (see TERTIARY).]

tertiary /túrshəri/ *adj.* **1.** THIRD third in degree, order, place, or importance (*formal*) **2.** BIRDS RELATING TO BIRD'S SHORT FLIGHT FEATHERS relating to the short flight feathers nearest the body on the rear edge of a bird's wing, so named because they make up the third row of feathers **3.** FROM EARLY CENOZOIC ERA formed in, occurring in, or relating to the first period of the Cenozoic era, during which mammals became dominant and modern plants evolved **4.** CHEM CHARACTERIZED BY REPLACEMENT IN THIRD DEGREE characterized by replacement in the third degree, particularly replacement of three of the hydrogens present in a methyl group or ammonia by three organic groups ■ *n.* (*plural* **-ies**) **1.** BIRDS BIRD'S SHORT FLIGHT FEATHER a bird's tertiary feather, on the rear edge of its wing **2.** FIRST PERIOD OF CENOZOIC ERA the first period of the Cenozoic era during which mammals became dominant and modern plants evolved, 65 million to 1.6 million years ago. It is divided into the Palaeocene, Eocene, Oligocene, Miocene, and Pliocene epochs. **3. tertiary, Tertiary** CHR MEMBER OF LAY GROUP in the Roman Catholic Church, a member of a group of the laity associated with a religious order [Mid-16thC. From Latin *tertiarius* 'of the third part or rank', from *tertius* 'third'. Ultimately from an Indo-European word that is also the ancestor of English *third*.]

tertiary colour *n.* a colour made by mixing two secondary colours together or by mixing a primary colour with the secondary colour closest to it

tertiary education *n.* education at college or university level

tertiary industry *n.* the field of industry that provides services, e.g. transport or finance, rather than manufacturing or extracting raw materials

tertiary syphilis *n.* the final stage of syphilis in which the disease spreads throughout the body, affecting the brain, spinal cord, heart, skin, bones, and joints

tertium quid /túrshi əm kwíd/ *n.* an unknown or indefinite thing or factor that is related to but cannot be classified as belonging to either of two other areas or categories (*formal*) [From late Latin, literally 'some third thing']

Tertullian /tər túlli ən/ (160?–225?) Roman theologian. The first important theological writer in Latin, his often impassioned works greatly influenced his successors.

tervalent /tur váylənt/ *adj.* = **trivalent** —**tervalency** /tur váylənssi/ *n.*

Terylene /térrə leen/ *tdmk.* trademark for a light polyester fabric used mainly for clothing and bed linen

terza rima /táirtsə réemə/ (*plural* **terze rime** /táirt say rée may/) *n.* a rhyming verse form of Italian origin, consisting of three-line, 11-syllable verses (**tercets**), with the middle line of one verse rhyming with the first and third lines of the next [From Italian, 'third rhyme']

terzetto /tur tséttō/ (*plural* **-tos** *or* **-ti** /tsétti/) *n.* a musical trio for instruments or voices [Early 18thC. From Italian (see TERCET).]

TES *abbr.* Times Educational Supplement

TE score *n.* in Australia, a score awarded on the basis of final secondary school examinations that determines whether or not a student is accepted into some tertiary education institutions. Full form **Tertiary Entrance Score**

TESL /téss'l/ *abbr.* Teaching (of) English as a Second Language

tesla /tésslə/ *n.* the derived unit of magnetic flux density in the SI system, equal to a flux of one weber in an area of one square metre. Symbol **T** [Late 19thC. Named after Nikola TESLA.]

Tesla /tésslə/, **Nikola** (1856–1943) Croatian-born US electrical engineer. He is credited with many inventions, and was a pioneer of alternating-current systems.

tesla coil *n.* an air-core transformer that is used to produce high voltages at high frequencies, e.g. in X-ray tubes [Named after Nikola TESLA, its inventor]

TESOL /tée sol/ *abbr.* **1.** Teaching (of) English to Speakers of Other Languages **2.** Teachers of English to Speakers of Other Languages

TESSA, Tessa *n., abbr.* Tax-Exempt Special Savings Account

tessellate /téssə layt/ (**-lates, -lating, -lated**) *v.* **1.** *vt.* ARCHIT DECORATE STH WITH MOSAIC EFFECT to construct, pave, or decorate sth with small pieces of stone or glass to give a mosaic effect **2.** *vi.* GEOM FIT TOGETHER EXACTLY to fit together without leaving any spaces (*refers to geometric shapes*) [Late 18thC. From Latin *tessellatus* 'made of small square stones', ultimately from *tessera* (see TESSERA).] —**tessellation** /téssə láysh'n/ *n.*

tessera /téssərə/ (*plural* **-ae** /-ree/) *n.* **1.** MOSAIC PIECE a small square of stone, tile, or glass used to make a mosaic **2.** DICE a piece of bone or wood that was used in ancient Greece and Rome as a dice, tally, or ticket [Mid-17thC. Via Latin from, ultimately, Greek *tesseres*, a variant of *tessares* 'four', from the sides of the square.] —**tesseral** *adj.*

tesseract /téssə rakt/ *n.* the four-dimensional extension of a cube [Late 19thC. Formed from Greek *tessera-*, from *tesseres* (see TESSERA) + Greek *aktis* 'ray'.]

tessitura /téssi tóorə/ (*plural* **-turas** *or* **-ture** /-ray/) *n.* the pitch range that predominates in a particular piece of music [Late 19thC. Via Italian from Latin *textura* 'web, structure' (source also of English *texture*).]

test[1] /test/ *n.* **1.** EDUC EXAMINATION a series of questions, problems, or practical tasks to gauge sb's knowledge, ability, or experience **2.** TRIAL RUN-THROUGH OF A PROCESS a trial run-through of a process or on equipment to find out if it works **3.** BASIS FOR EVALUATION a basis for evaluating or judging sth or sb **4.** DIFFICULT SITUATION an often difficult situation or event that will provide information about sb or sth **5.** MED EXAMINATION OF PART OF THE BODY an examination of part of the body or of a bodily fluid or specimen in order to find sth out, e.g. whether it is functioning properly or is infected ○ *an allergy test* **6.** CHEM PROCEDURE TO DETECT PRESENCE OF STH a procedure to ascertain the presence of or the properties of a particular substance ○ *a test for nitrates in drinking water* **7.** CHEM REACTIVE SUBSTANCE a substance or a reagent that reacts in a particular way to show the presence of a particular substance **8.** CHEM RESULT OF A PROCEDURE a result of a procedure to ascertain the presence of a specific substance ○ *Your test hasn't come back yet.* **9.** SPORTS = **test match 10.** OATH a declaration, demonstration, or oath of conformity or loyalty, especially to the Anglican Church (*archaic*) ■ *v.* (**tests, testing, tested**) **1.** *vt.* TRY STH OUT to try sth out, e.g. by touching, operating, or experiencing it, in order to find out what it is like, how well it works, or what it feels like **2.** *vt.* EVALUATE STH to use sth on a trial basis in order to evaluate it **3.** *vt.* ASK SB QUESTIONS to ask sb questions or make sb do a practical activity in order to gauge knowledge, skill, or experience **4.** *vt.* MED CARRY OUT A MEDICAL TEST to carry out a test on part of the body or on a bodily specimen **5.** *vti.* EXAMINE STH TO DETECT A PRESENCE to examine sth in order to ascertain the presence of or the properties of a particular substance ○ *test for bacteria* **6.** *vi.* ACHIEVE PARTICULAR TEST RESULT to achieve a particular result on a test ○ *She tested positive for rubella immunity.* **7.** *vt.* MAKE DEMANDS ON SB to make considerable demands on sb, particularly sb's skills or abilities [14thC. Via Old French, 'pot', from Latin *testum* 'earthenware pot'. The main modern meaning evolved from 'pot in which metals are heated' via 'examination of properties or qualities'.] —**testability** /téstə bílləti/ *n.* —**testable** *adj.*

test[2] /test/ *n.* the hard outer covering or shell of some invertebrates such as molluscs and crustaceans [Mid-16thC. From Latin *testa* 'tile, shell'.]

Test. *abbr.* BIBLE Testament

testa /téstə/ (*plural* **-tae** /-tee/) *n.* the protective covering of a seed from a flowering plant [Late 18thC. From Latin (see TEST[2]).]

testaceous /te stáyshəss/ *adj.* **1.** OF SHELL OR HAVING A SHELL made of shell, or having a shell or other hard covering **2.** BROWNISH-RED of a brownish-red colour like a brick or a terracotta tile (*technical*)

Test Act *n.* an act passed by the English Parliament in 1673 that barred from public office anyone who would not take Anglican Communion or renounce transubstantiation. It was intended to prevent Catholics from occupying civil or military posts, and was repealed in 1828. ['Test' from TEST[1] in the archaic sense of 'oath']

testacy /téstəssi/ *n.* the condition of having made a legally valid will [Mid-19thC. Formed from TESTATE on the model of *intestacy*.]

testae plural of **testa**

testament *n.* **1.** PROOF sth that shows that sth else exists or is true ○ *His remarkable recovery is a testament to the doctor's skill.* **2.** FORMAL STATEMENT OF BELIEFS a formal statement or speech outlining beliefs (*formal*) **3.** LAW A WILL an old word for a legal will, used most often in the phrase 'last will and testament' (*archaic*) **4.** JUD-CHR COVENANT BETWEEN GOD AND HUMANKIND a covenant made between God and humankind (*archaic or formal*) [13thC. From Latin *testamentum* 'will', from, ultimately, *testis* 'witness', the underlying idea being of a 'witnessed' document.] —**testamental** /téstə mént'l/ *adj.*

WORD KEY: ORIGIN

The Latin word *testis*, from which ***testament*** is derived, is also the source of English *attest, contest, detest, intestate, protest, testicle, testify,* and *testimony.*

Testament *n.* **1.** EITHER HALF OF BIBLE either of the two major divisions of the Bible, known as the Old Testament and the New Testament **2.** COPY OF NEW TESTAMENT a printed copy of the New Testament [13thC. Mistranslation of Greek *diathēkē* 'covenant', as well as 'will, testament'. Originally intended to apply to the 'covenant' between God and human beings.]

testamentary /téstə méntəri/ *adj.* **1.** RELATING TO WILLS relating to a will (*formal*) **2.** STATED IN A WILL bequeathed or set out in a will

testate /té stayt/ *adj.* HAVING MADE A WILL having made a legally valid will ■ *n.* SB HAVING MADE A WILL sb who has made a legally valid will [15thC. From Latin *testatus*, the past participle of *testari* 'to bear witness, make your will', from *testis* (see TESTAMENT).]

testator /te stáytər/ *n.* sb, especially a man, who has made a legally valid will [14thC. Via Anglo-Norman from Latin, from *testari* (see TESTATE).]

testatrix /te státriks/ (*plural* **-trices** /-trə seez/) *n.* a woman who has made a legally valid will [Late 16thC. From late Latin, the feminine of *testator* (see TESTATOR).]

test ban *n.* an agreement between nations to suspend testing of some or all nuclear weapons

test bed *n.* a facility designed and equipped to test engines and machinery under circumstances as close to actual operating conditions as possible

test card *n.* TV a geometric pattern usually incorporating areas of different colours, transmitted by a television broadcasting organization to help viewers to tune in their television sets and obtain optimum reception. US term **test pattern**

test case *n.* **1.** GROUND-BREAKING LEGAL CASE an important legal case that establishes a precedent referred to in future cases **2.** TELLING EVENT an event that provides an opportunity to prove or disprove a hypothesis

testcross /tést kross/ *n.* **1.** GENETIC CROSS TECHNIQUE a procedure used especially in plant breeding whereby an individual's genetic constitution is inferred by examining the progeny resulting from crossing it with another individual of known genetic makeup **2.** RESULT OF TESTCROSS an organism produced by a testcross ■ *vt.* (**-crosses, -crossing, -crossed**) SUBJECT ORGANISM TO TESTCROSS to subject an organism to a testcross

test drive *n.* a short drive in a car or other motor vehicle in order to see what it is like, usually with a view to buying it

test-drive *vt.* to drive a car or other motor vehicle for a short period in order to see what it is like, usually with a view to buying it

tester[1] /téstər/ *n.* **1.** SB WHO TESTS NEW PRODUCTS sb whose job it is to try out new products **2.** SAMPLE OF PRODUCT a sample of a product, especially a cosmetic **3.** EQUIPMENT TO CHECK PROPER FUNCTIONING a piece of equipment that tests if a machine or device is working properly **4.** SMALL STICK a small stick inserted into sth that is baking to determine if it is done **5.** SB WHO TESTS sb who administers or carries out tests ○ *a water tester*

tester[2] /téstər/ *n.* a canopy, especially one over a four-poster bed or a pulpit [14thC. Via medieval Latin *testerium* from late Latin *testa* 'head', from Latin, 'tile, shell'.]

testes plural of TESTIS

testicle /téstik'l/ *n.* the male gonad or sperm-producing gland (**testis**) usually with its surrounding membranes, particularly in humans or other higher vertebrates [15thC. From Latin *testiculus*, literally 'small testis', from *testis* (see TESTIS).] —**testicular** /te stíkyoōlər/ *adj.*

testify /tésti fī/ (**-fies, -fying, -fied**) *vi.* **1.** MAKE FACTUAL STATEMENT BASED ON EXPERIENCE to make a factual statement based on personal experience or to declare sth to be true from personal experience **2.** DECLARE STH UNDER OATH IN COURT to declare sth that can be taken as evidence under oath in a court of law **3.** PROVE OR DEMONSTRATE to be clear evidence of sth (*formal*) **4.** CHR TALK ABOUT EXPERIENCE AS A CHRISTIAN to talk to an audience or group of listeners about personal experience as a Christian [14thC. From Latin *testificari*, literally 'to make yourself a witness', from *testis* 'witness' (source also of English *testament*).] —**testification** /téstifi káysh'n/ *n.* —**testifier** *n.*

testimonial /tésti mṓni əl/ *n.* **1.** RECOMMENDATION a favourable report on the qualities and virtues of sb or sth **2.** STATEMENT BACKING UP CLAIM a statement backing up a claim or supporting a fact **3.** TRIBUTE sth given, held, or done in order to honour or thank sb ■ *adj.* RELATING TO TESTIMONY OR TESTIMONIAL relating to or consisting of testimony or a testimonial

testimony /téstiməni/ (*plural* **-nies**) *n.* **1.** EVIDENCE GIVEN BY WITNESS IN COURT evidence that a witness gives to a court of law. It may take the form of a written or oral statement detailing what the witness has seen or knows about a particular case. **2.** PROOF sth that supports a fact or a claim ○ *This win is testimony to the tactical skill of the coach.* **3.** BIBLE TEN COMMANDMENTS the Ten Commandments inscribed on two stone tablets, or the Ark of the Covenant in which the tablets were stored **4.** CHR PUBLIC AVOWAL a public profession of Christian faith or religious experience [14thC. From Latin *testimonium*, from *testis* 'a witness' (source also of English *testament*).]

testing /tésting/ *adj.* subjecting sb or sth to challenging difficulties ○ *A testing time lies ahead for the new administration.*

testis /téstiss/ (*plural* **-tes** /-steez/) *n.* either of the paired male reproductive glands, roundish in shape, that produce sperm and male sex hormones, and hang in a small sac (**scrotum**) [Early 18thC. From Latin, 'a witness', because it 'bears witness' to a man's virility.]

test marketing *n.* the use of a sample of a larger market to try out a particular marketing strategy or product

test match, **test** *n.* one of a series of cricket or rugby matches between two international teams

testosterone /te stóstərōn/ *n.* a male steroid hormone produced in the testicles and responsible for the development of secondary sex characteristics. It can also be made synthetically and used to treat androgen deficiency. Formula: $C_{19}H_{28}O_2$. [Mid-20thC. Coined from TESTIS + *-sterone* (a blend of STEROL and KETONE).]

test paper *n.* **1.** QUESTION OR ANSWER SHEET a sheet of paper with examination questions or the student's answers on it **2.** PAPER FOR TESTS a small piece of paper soaked in a particular chemical or reagent, e.g. litmus, that is used to show the presence or properties of a particular substance

test pattern *n.* US TV = test card

test pilot *n.* a pilot who flies new aircraft in order to assess their performance

test-screening *n.* a screening of a provisional version of a film to test audience reaction

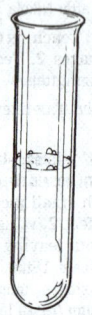

Test tube

test tube *n.* GLASS TUBE a small glass tube-shaped container that is closed and rounded at one end and open at the other, used to mix, heat, and store chemicals in laboratories ■ *adj.* **test-tube** ARTIFICIAL made in a test tube or by other artificial means, rather than occurring or arising naturally

test-tube baby *n.* a baby that has been conceived by fertilizing a woman's egg in a laboratory (**in vitro fertilization**) and then inserting it in her womb to develop normally for the remainder of the pregnancy (*informal*)

testudinal /te styo̅o̅dinəl/, **testudinary** /-əri/ *adj.* resembling a tortoise or the shell of a tortoise

testudo /te styo̅o̅dō/ (*plural* **-dines** /-dineez/) *n.* a type of shelter against missiles from above, used by the ancient Roman army in siege warfare. It was either a single structure that could be carried or was made by soldiers holding their shields above their heads to form a protective roof. [14thC. From Latin, 'tortoiseshell, shelter', from *testa* 'pot, shell'.]

testy /tésti/ (**-tier, -tiest**) *adj.* impatient and easily upset or annoyed (*informal*) [14thC. Via Anglo-Norman *testif*, ultimately from Latin *testa* 'tile, pot', and later used humorously in the sense 'head'. The modern meaning evolved from the sense 'headstrong, impetuous'.] —**testily** *adv.* —**testiness** *n.*

Tet /tet/ *n.* CALENDAR a festival held in Vietnam over three days to celebrate the lunar New Year [Late 19thC. From Vietnamese.]

tetanic /te tánnik/ *adj.* **1.** RELATING TO TETANUS relating to tetanus or to the sustained contraction of the muscles that is characteristic of tetanus **2.** SPASM-PRODUCING capable of producing muscle spasms such as are seen in tetanus [Early 18thC. Via Latin *tetanicus* from, ultimately, Greek *tetanos* (see TETANUS).] —**tetanically** *adv.*

tetanize /téttə nīz/ (**-nizes, -nizing, -nized**), **tetanise** (**-nises, -nising, -nised**) *vt.* to cause tetanic spasms in a muscle —**tetanization** /téttə nī záysh'n/ *n.*

tetanus /téttənəss/ *n.* **1.** INFECTIOUS DISEASE an acute infectious disease, usually contracted through a penetrating wound, that causes severe muscular spasms and contractions, especially around the neck and jaw. The spasms are caused by a toxin released by the bacterium *Clostridium tetani*. **2.** MUSCLE CONTRACTION sustained muscle contraction, as induced by electrical stimulation [14thC. Via Latin from Greek *tetanos* 'muscular spasm', from *teinein* 'to stretch' (source also of English *hypotenuse*).] —**tetanal** /téttənəl/ *adj.* —**tetanoid** /téttənoyd/ *adj.*

tetany /téttəni/ *n.* repeated prolonged contraction of muscles, especially of the face and limbs, caused by low blood calcium arising from, e.g. an underactive parathyroid gland or vitamin D deficiency [Late 19thC. Via French, 'intermittent tetanus', from Latin *tetanus* (see TETANUS).]

tetchy /téchi/ (**-ier, -iest**), **techy** (**-ier, -iest**) *adj.* oversensitive and easily upset or annoyed (*informal*) [Late 16thC. Origin uncertain: probably formed from *tache* in the obsolete sense of 'blemish, defect'.] —**tetchily** *adv.* —**tetchiness** *n.*

tête-à-tête /tát ə tát/ *n.* **1.** INTIMATE CONVERSATION FOR TWO a private conversation between two people **2.** TYPE OF SOFA a two-seater sofa shaped like an S, allowing those seated to face each other ■ *adv.* INTIMATELY in private with only two people present [From French, literally 'head-to-head']

tête-bêche /tát bésh/ *adj.* used to describe a pair of stamps, one of which is printed the right way up and the other upside-down [From French, literally '(sleeping) head to foot']

teth /teth, tess, tet/ *n.* the ninth letter of the Hebrew alphabet [Early 19thC. From Hebrew.]

tether /téthər/ *n.* ROPE ATTACHED TO AN ANIMAL a rope or chain attached to an animal and attached to sth at the other end, thus restricting the animal's movement ■ *vt.* (**-ers, -ering, -ered**) TIE ANIMAL WITH TETHER to tie sth, especially an animal, with a rope or chain in order to restrict its movement [14thC. From Old Norse *tjóðr*, from a prehistoric Germanic base meaning 'to fasten'.] ◇ **at the end of your tether** having reached the limit of your patience, strength, or endurance

Tethys /téethiss, téth-/ *n.* **1.** MYTHOL TITAN a Titan in Greek mythology who was the wife of Oceanus and the mother of thousands of sea and river gods and nymphs **2.** ASTRON SATELLITE OF SATURN the third moon of the planet Saturn to be discovered. It has a diameter of 1,050 km/651 mi. and is Saturn's ninth most distant satellite, orbiting at a distance of 295,000 km/182,900 mi. **3.** GEOL ANCIENT SEA an ancient sea that is thought to have separated Laurasia and Gondwanaland, surviving vestigially today as the Mediterranean [Late 19thC. Via Latin from Greek *Tēthus*.]

Teton[1] /téet'n, tēe ton/ (*plural* **-ton** or **-tons**), **Teton Dakota** *n.* **1.** PEOPLES NATIVE N AMERICAN a member of a group of Native North American peoples that originally occupied western parts of the Great Plains, and whose members now live mainly in North and South Dakota. Included in this group are the Oglala, Hunkpapa, Brulé, and Miniconjou peoples. **2.** LANG TETON LANGUAGE the Siouan language of the Teton people. Teton is spoken by about 6,000 people. [Early 19thC. From Dakota *thíthuwa*, literally 'dwellers on the prairie'.]

Teton[2] /téeton, téet'n/ range of the Rocky Mountains in northwestern Wyoming and southwestern Idaho. The highest peak is Grand Teton, 4,197 m/13,770 ft.

Tétouan /te twaán/, **Tetuán** city in northern Morocco on the Mediterranean Sea, near Tangier. Population: 272,000 (1992).

tetr- *prefix.* = **tetra-** (*used before vowels*)

tetra /téttrə/ (plural **-ras** or **-ra**) n. a brightly-coloured freshwater fish that lives in tropical regions and is a popular aquarium fish. Family: Characidae. [Mid-20thC. Shortening of modern Latin *Tetragonopterus*, the former name of the genus, from late Latin *tetragonum* (see TETRAGON) + Greek *pteron* 'wing'.]

tetra- prefix. four ○ *tetrastich* [From Greek *tetra-*. Ultimately from the Indo-European word for 'four'.]

tetrabasic /téttrə báyssik/ adj. containing four atoms of replaceable hydrogen in a molecule (*refers to acids*) [Mid-19thC. Coined from TETRA- + BASIC.] —**tetrabasicity** /téttrə bay síssəti/ n.

tetrabrach /téttrə brak/ n. a word consisting of four short syllables in Latin or classical Greek literature [From Greek *tetrabrakhus*, literally 'four short', from *brakhus* 'short']

tetrachloride /téttrə kláwr īd/ n. a compound that has four chlorine atoms in each molecule

tetrachloromethane /téttrə kláwrō mee thayn/ n. = **carbon tetrachloride** [Early 20thC. Coined from TETRA- + CHLOROMETHANE.]

tetrachord /téttrə kawrd/ n. a group of four notes, the first and last of which form a perfect fourth, used principally in ancient Greek music [Early 17thC. Coined from TETRA- + CHORD.] —**tetrachordal** adj.

tetracid /te trássid/ n. **1.** BASE NEEDING FOUR MOLECULES TO REACT a base that can react with four molecules of a monobasic acid to form a salt **2.** ALCOHOL WITH FOUR OH GROUPS an alcohol with four OH groups per molecule [Coined from TETRA- + ACID.]

tetracyclic /téttrə síklik/ adj. containing four rings in its molecular structure [Late 19thC. Coined from TETRA- + CYCLIC.]

tetracycline /téttrə sí kleen/ n. a broad-spectrum antibiotic made from chlortetracycline or derived from some microorganisms of the genus *Streptomyces*. Tetracycline is used in the treatment of acne and for treating general infections. Formula: $C_{22}H_{24}N_2O_8$. [Mid-20thC. Coined from TETRACYCLIC + -INE.]

tetrad /té trad/ n. **1.** SERIES OF FOUR a group or series of four things or people **2.** GENETICS GROUP OF FOUR CHROMOSOMES a group of four chromosomes in a diploid cell that is about to undergo the cell division (**meiosis**) that produces sex cells **3.** BIOL GROUP OF FOUR CELLS a group of four cells produced by the division (**meiosis**) of a single parent cell, e.g. as it occurs in the formation of pollen and spores **4.** CHEM ATOM WITH VALENCY OF FOUR an atom or chemical group with a valency of four [Mid-17thC. From Greek *tetrad-*, the stem of *tetras* 'a group of four, the number four'.]

tetradactyl /téttrə dáktil/ adj. with four toes or fingers. US term **tetradactylous** [Mid-19thC. Coined from TETRA- + DACTYL.]

tetradymite /te tráddi mīt/ n. a grey metallic ore of tellurium, found in veins with quartz and gold. Formula: Bi_2Te_2S. [Mid-19thC. Via German from Greek *tetradumos* 'fourfold', from the double twin crystals in which it is usually found.]

tetradynamous /téttrə dínəməss/ adj. with four long stamens and two short stamens, e.g. in flowers of the mustard family [Early 20thC. Coined from TETRA- + Greek *dynamis* 'strength' (see DYNAMIC) + -OUS.]

tetraethyl lead /téttrə eé thīl-/ n. a colourless extremely poisonous oily liquid that used to be added to petrol as an antiknock agent. Use of tetraethyl lead has declined because it poisons the catalysts in catalytic converters. Formula: $Pb(C_2H_5)_4$. [*Tetraethyl* coined from TETRA- + ETHYL.]

tetragon /téttrə gon/ n. a geometric figure with four sides and four angles [Early 17thC. Via late Latin *tetragonum* from, ultimately, Greek *tetragōnos*, literally 'four-angled', from *gōnos* 'angled'.]

tetragonal /te trággən'l/ adj. relating to the crystal system characterized by three axes at right angles to each other of which only the two horizontal axes are usually equal. Zircon crystals are tetragonal. —**tetragonally** adv.

tetragram /téttrə gram/ n. a word that has four letters

Tetragrammaton /téttrə grámmətən/ n. a four-letter Hebrew name for God, usually written YHVH or YHWH, and revealed to Moses (Exodus 3:13–14). Orthodox Jews regard this name as too sacred to

be pronounced. [14thC. From Greek *Tetragrammaton*, the neuter of *tetragrammatos*, literally 'having four letters', from *gramma* 'letter'.]

tetrahedrite /téttrə heé drīt/ n. a grey to black metallic sulphide of copper, iron, and antimony. It is often found as tetrahedral crystals and is an important ore of copper and other metals. [Mid-19thC. Formed either from *tetrahedron* or from Greek *tetraedron* (see TETRAHEDRON).]

tetrahedron /téttrə heédrən/ (plural **-drons** or **-dra** /-drə/) n. a solid figure that has four faces [Late 16thC. From Greek *tetraedron*, the neuter of *tetraedros* 'four-sided', from *hedra* 'face'.] —**tetrahedral** /téttrə heédrəl/ adj. —**tetrahedrally** adv.

tetrahydrocannabinol /téttrə hídrō kə nábbi nol/ n. full form of **THC** [Mid-20thC. Coined from TETRA- + HYDRO- + *cannabinol*.]

tetrahydroxy /téttrə hī dróksi/ adj. with four hydroxyl groups in a molecule

tetralogy /te trálləji/ (plural **-gies**) n. a series of four related literary, dramatic, artistic, or musical works [Mid-17thC. From Greek *tetralogia*, literally 'four dramas', from *-logia* 'discourse'.]

tetramer /téttrəmər/ n. a polymer that is formed from four identical monomers —**tetrameric** /téttrə mérrik/ adj.

tetramerous /te trámmərəss/ adj. with four parts, or with parts arranged in multiples of four —**tetramerism** /-rizəm/ n.

tetrameter /te trámmitər/ n. POETRY **1.** VERSE LINE WITH FOUR FEET a line of verse that has four metrical feet **2.** LINE WITH FOUR PAIRS OF FEET in classical poetry, a line of verse made up of four pairs of feet **3.** VERSE IN TETRAMETER verse written in tetrameters [Early 17thC. Via late Latin from Greek *tetrametron*, a form of *tetrametros*, literally 'having four measures', from *metron* 'measure'.]

tetraploid /téttrə ployd/ adj. WITH FOUR SETS OF CHROMOSOMES possessing four matched sets of chromosomes in the cell nucleus ■ n. TETRAPLOID CELL OR ORGANISM a tetraploid cell, nucleus, or organism —**tetraploidy** /téttrə ploydi/ n.

tetrapod /téttrə pod/ n. **1.** VERTEBRATE WITH FOUR LEGS a vertebrate animal that has four limbs or legs **2.** DEVICE FORMING TRIPOD a device comprising four arms projecting from a central point at 120° to each other, making a tripod with the fourth arm projecting vertically upwards [Early 19thC. Via modern Latin *tetrapodus* from, ultimately, the Greek stem *tetrapod-*, literally 'four-footed', from *pous* 'foot'.]

tetrapody /te tráppədi/ (plural **-dies**) n. a poetic measure of four feet —**tetrapodic** /téttrə póddik/ adj.

tetrapterous /te tráptərəss/ adj. used to describe insects that have four wings

tetrarch /té traark/ n. **1.** RULER OF QUARTER OF COUNTRY the ruler of a quarter of a country or province **2.** JOINT RULER one of four joint rulers **3.** SUBORDINATE PRINCE a ruler of a subordinate principality, especially in the eastern provinces of the Roman Empire **4.** PHALANX COMMANDER the commander of a subdivision of a Macedonian phalanx in ancient Greece [Pre-12thC. Via late Latin *tetrarcha* from, ultimately, Greek *tetrarkhēs*, literally 'four ruling', from *arkhēs* 'ruler'.] —**tetrarchic** /te traárkik/ adj.

tetrarchy /té traarki/ (plural **-chies**), **tetrarchate** /te traárkayt/ n. **1.** GOVERNMENT OF TETRARCHS government by four rulers **2.** DOMAIN OF TETRARCH the rule or domain of one of four joint rulers

tetraspore /téttrə spawr/ n. an asexual spore that occurs after cell division (**meiosis**), usually in groups of four, in red algae —**tetrasporic** /téttrə spórrik/ adj.

tetrastich /téttrə stik/ n. a poem, stanza, or strophe that has four lines [Late 16thC. Via Latin *tetrastichon* from, ultimately, Greek *tetrastikhos*, literally 'containing four rows', from *stikhos* 'row, line of verse'.] —**tetrastichic** /téttrə stíkik/ adj.

tetrasyllable /téttrə sílləb'l/ n. a word with four syllables —**tetrasyllabic** /téttrə si lábbik/ adj.

tetratomic /téttrə tómmik/ adj. **1.** WITH FOUR ATOMS with four atoms per molecule **2.** WITH FOUR REPLACEABLE ATOMS with four replaceable atoms or radicals

tetravalent /téttrə váylənt/ adj. with a valency of four —**tetravalency** /téttrə váylənssi/ n.

tetrode /téttrōd/ n. a four-element electron tube containing an anode, a cathode, a control grid, and an additional electrode or screen grid

tetrodotoxin /te trōdə tóksin/ n. a potent neurotoxin that is found in puffer fish and some newts and causes a general loss of the ability to move in humans who ingest it. Formula: $C_{11}H_{17}N_3O_8$.

tetroxide /te tróksīd/, **tetroxid** /-tróksid/ n. a chemical compound that has four oxygen atoms per molecule [Mid-19thC. Coined from TETRA- + OXIDE.]

tetryl /téttrīl, -tril/ n. a yellow crystalline compound that is used as a detonator in explosives. Formula: $C_7H_5N_5O_8$.

teuchter /tyoókhtər/ n. Scotland a word used by Lowlanders in Scotland to refer to a Highlander in a disrespectful or teasing way (*informal*) [Mid-20thC. Origin unknown.]

Teucrian /tyoókri ən/ n., adj. Trojan (*literary*) [Ultimately from Greek *Teukros* 'Teucer', first king of Troy]

Teut. abbr. Teutonic

Teutoburg Forest /tóytō burg-/, **Teutoburger Wald** /tóytō burgər válj/ ridge of wooded hills in northwestern Germany, scene of a major Roman defeat by Germans in AD 9

Teuton /tyoót'n/ n. **1.** PEOPLES ANCIENT GERMAN a member of an ancient Germanic people that originally came from Jutland. During the second century BC they invaded Gaul but were wiped out by the Romans in 102 BC. **2.** GERMAN SPEAKER sb from a German-speaking culture, especially from Germany, Switzerland, or Austria (*informal or humorous*) [Early 18thC. From Latin *Teutoni* or *Teutones* (plural) 'the Teutons'. Ultimately from an Indo-European word meaning 'tribe', which is also the ancestor of English *Dutch*.]

Teutonic /tyoo tónnik/ adj. **1.** RELATING TO GERMANIC PEOPLES relating to German-speaking cultures or people (*informal or humorous*) **2.** RELATING TO TEUTONS relating to the ancient Teuton people, or their culture —**Teutonically** adv.

Teutonic Knights npl. a German religious and military order that was founded as a charitable order in Palestine in 1190 during the Third Crusade, but became a military organization operating in Eastern Europe. In the 13th century it conquered Prussia where it introduced Christianity through killing many of the native inhabitants and colonizing it with Germans.

Teutonise vti. = **Teutonize**

Teutonism /tyoótənizəm/ n. **1.** STH TYPICALLY GERMAN a German characteristic, custom, or idiom **2.** GERMAN WAY OF LIFE German society or civilization **3.** = Germanism —**Teutonist** n.

Teutonize /tyoótə nīz/ (**-izes, -izing, -ized**), **Teutonise** (**-ises, -ising, -ised**) vti. to become German or to make sth German —**Teutonization** /tyoótə nī záysh'n/ n.

Tevet n. CALENDAR = **Tebet**

Tewa /táywə/ (plural **-was** or **-wa**) n. **1.** PEOPLES MEMBER OF NATIVE N AMERICAN PEOPLE a member of a group of Native North American Pueblo peoples that originally occupied lands in New Mexico, and whose members now live mainly in the north of the state **2.** LANG TEWA LANGUAGE the Tanoan language of the Tewa people [Mid-19thC. From Tewa *téwa* 'moccasins'.]

Te Whiti /te fítti/ (1830–1907) New Zealand Maori leader and prophet. He was the leader of passive resistance to European settlement of the Taranaki region. Full name **Erueti Te Whiti-o-Rongomai**

Tewkesbury /tyoóksbəri/ market town in Gloucestershire, western England, with a medieval abbey church. Population: 87,400 (1991).

Tex. abbr. **1.** Texas **2.** Texan

Texas

Thailand

Texas /téks əss/ state of the southwestern United States, bordered by Oklahoma, Arkansas, Louisiana, the Gulf of Mexico, Mexico, and New Mexico. Capital: Austin. Population: 19,439,337 (1997). Area: 691,201 sq. km/266,873 sq. mi.

Texas fever *n.* an infectious disease of cattle characterized by high fever, anaemia, and severe weight loss, that is transmitted by tick bites and caused by a protozoan [Mid-19thC. Named after TEXAS, because it was first identified there.]

Texel /téks'l/ *n.* a breed of sheep originally from the Netherlands that has a heavy white fleece and a short neck and is bred for meat and milk production [Mid-20thC. Named after an island in the West Frisian group off the north coast of the Netherlands.]

Tex-Mex /téks méks/ *adj.* showing a blend of Texan and Mexican cultures or cuisines [Shortening]

text /tekst/ *n.* **1.** MAIN BODY OF BOOK the main body of a book or other printed material as distinct from the introduction, index, illustrations, and headings **2.** WRITTEN MATERIAL words that have been written down, typed, or printed **3.** WRITTEN VERSION OF STH a complete written, typed, or printed version of sth such as a speech or a statement ○ *the full text of the president's speech* **4.** EDITION one among the extant forms or versions of a written work ○ *compared various texts to arrive at this reading* **5.** EDUC BOOK FOR STUDY a book or piece of writing that is used for academic study or discussion **6.** EDUC = **textbook 7.** BIBLE BIBLE PASSAGE a short passage from the Bible that is read aloud and on which a sermon is based **8.** ORIGINAL WORDING the original wording of a piece of writing, especially the Bible, as opposed to a translation, summary, or revision **9.** PRINTING TYPEFACE FOR TEXT a style of type that is suitable for printing running text **10.** COMPUT WORDS APPEARING ON COMPUTER SCREEN computer data that represents words, numbers, and other typographic characters, typically stored in ASCII format ■ *adj.* COMPUT USING WORDS associated with or designed for use with words in written form [14thC. Via Old French from Latin *textus* 'woven material', hence 'literary composition', from the past participle stem of *texere* 'to weave' (source also of English *tissue*).]

───── **WORD KEY: ORIGIN** ─────

The Latin word *texere*, from which **text** is derived, is also the source of English *context*, *pretext*, *texture*, and *tissue*.

textbook /tékst bŏŏk/ *n.* EDUC BOOK FOR STUDY a book that treats a subject comprehensively and is used by students as a basis for study ■ *adj.* TYPICAL typical overall and in detail, and thus a suitable example for study ○ *a textbook case of superpower aggression*

text editor *n.* COMPUT a software program that permits the creation and editing of stored text

text file *n.* COMPUT a file consisting of alphanumeric characters exclusive of transmission characters

textile /téks tīl/ *n.* **1.** FABRIC cloth or fabric that is woven, knitted, or otherwise manufactured **2.** RAW MATERIAL USED FOR MAKING FABRICS raw material such as fibre or yarn that is used for making fabrics [Early 17thC. From Latin *textilis*, from the past participle stem of *texere* 'to weave' (source also of English *text*).]

text processing *n.* the use of a computer to create, store, edit, and print or display text

textual /tékschoo əl/ *adj.* **1.** CONCERNING THE WAY STH IS WRITTEN relating to the way a book or piece of writing

is written **2.** CONSISTING OF WORDS consisting of words or text [14thC. From medieval Latin *textualis*, from *textus* (see TEXT).] —**textually** *adv.*

textual criticism *n.* **1.** STUDY OF MANUSCRIPTS the study of a group of manuscripts, especially of the Bible or works of literature, in order to determine which is the original or most authentic one **2.** LITERARY ANALYSIS the critical study of a work of literature involving a detailed analysis of the way in which it was written, e.g. its context, use of language, and principal themes —**textual critic** *n.*

textualism /tékschoo əlizəm/ *n.* **1.** STRICT ADHERENCE TO TEXT unswerving adherence to a text, especially a text from the Bible **2.** DETAILED ANALYSIS OF TEXT detailed and critical analysis of a text —**textualist** *n.*

textuary /tékschoo əri/ *adj.* TEXTUAL textual (*formal*) ■ *n.* (*plural* **-ies**) BIBLE STUDENT sb who has studied the Bible extensively and systematically (*archaic*) [Early 17thC. From medieval Latin *textuarius*, from *textus* (see TEXT).]

texture /tékschər/ *n.* **1.** FEEL OF A SURFACE the feel and appearance of a surface, especially how rough or smooth it is **2.** STRUCTURE OF STH the structure of a substance or material such as soil or food, especially how it feels when touched or chewed **3.** ROUGH QUALITY the rough quality of a surface or fabric ○ *a fabric that has plenty of texture* **4.** DISTINCTIVE CHARACTER the typical and distinctive character of sth complex ○ *The book captures the texture of 1950s provincial England.* **5.** WAY AN ARTIST DEPICTS A SURFACE the way in which an artist depicts the quality or appearance of a surface **6.** EFFECT OF DIFFERENT COMPONENTS OF MUSIC the effect of the different components of a piece of music, e.g. melody, harmony, rhythm, or the use of different instruments ■ *vt.* (**-tures, -turing, -tured**) GIVE A SURFACE A PARTICULAR FEEL to give a surface a particular feel, usually one that is rough and grainy [15thC. Via Old French from Latin *textura* 'a weaving', from the past participle stem of *texere* 'to weave' (source also of English *text*).] —**textural** *adj.* —**texturally** *adv.*

textured /tékschərd/ *adj.* with a distinctive texture or surface ○ *textured rice paper*

textured vegetable protein *n.* full form of **TVP**

TG *abbr.* **1.** transformational grammar **2.** Togo (*international vehicle registration*)

TGAT /tee gat/ *n., abbr.* Task Group on Assessment and Testing

TGIF, T.G.I.F. *abbr.* Thank God It's Friday *or* Thank Goodness It's Friday (*informal*)

TGV *n.* in France and some other countries, a very high-speed train [From French, from *t(rain) (à) g(rande) v(itesse)* 'high-speed train']

TGWU *abbr.* Transport and General Workers' Union

Th *symbol.* thorium

Th. *abbr.* **1.** BIBLE Thessalonians **2.** CALENDAR Thursday

Thackeray /tháke ray/, **William Makepeace** (1811–63) British novelist. Serialization of his novel *Vanity Fair* (1847–48) established him as a major literary figure. He is remembered for his humorous and moralizing portraits of middle- and upper-class life in Britain.

Thaddaeus /tháddi əss/ *n.* in the New Testament, one of the 12 apostles. He is traditionally identified with St Jude (Mark 3:16–19) (Matthew 10:2–4).

Thai /tī/ *n.* (*plural* **Thais** *or* **Thai**) **1.** PEOPLES SB FROM THAILAND sb who was born or brought up in Thailand, or who has Thai citizenship **2.** LANG OFFICIAL LANGUAGE OF THAILAND the official language of Thailand. It belongs to the Thai language group. Thai is spoken by about 25 million people. ■ *adj.* PEOPLES RELATING TO THAILAND relating to Thailand, or its people or culture [Early 19thC. From Thai, 'free'.]

Thailand /tī land, tī lənd/ kingdom in Southeast Asia bordered by Myanmar, Laos, Cambodia, the Gulf of Thailand, Malaysia, and the Andaman Sea. Language: Thai. Currency: baht. Capital: Bangkok. Population: 59,450,818 (1997). Area: 513,115 sq. km/198,115 sq. mi. Official name **Kingdom of Thailand**. Former name **Siam**

Thailand, Gulf of wide inlet of the South China Sea separating Vietnam, Cambodia, and eastern Thailand from the Malay Peninsula. Length: 800 km/500 mi. Former name **Gulf of Siam**

Thaïs /tháy iss/ (*fl.* 4th-century BC) Greek courtesan. According to legend, she accompanied Alexander the Great to Asia and persuaded him to raze Persepolis.

thalamus /thálləməss/ (*plural* **-mi** /-mī/) *n.* **1.** BRAIN PART either of a pair of egg-shaped masses of grey matter lying beneath each cerebral hemisphere in the brain. They relay sensory information to the cerebral cortex and are concerned with awareness of all the main senses except for smell. **2.** BOT = **receptacle** *n.* 2 [Late 17thC. Via Latin, 'inner chamber', from Greek *thalamos*.] —**thalamic** /thə lámmik/ *adj.* —**thalamically** /-lámmikli/ *adv.*

Thalassa /thə lássə/ *n.* a small inner natural satellite of Neptune, discovered in 1989 by the space probe Voyager 2. It is approximately 80 km/50 mi. in diameter.

thalassaemia /thállə seémi ə/ *n.* a hereditary form of anaemia, particularly prevalent around the Mediterranean, that is caused by a dysfunction in the synthesis of the red blood pigment haemoglobin [Mid-20thC. Formed from Greek *thalassa* 'sea' (from its discovery in Mediterranean countries) + *haima* 'blood'.] —**thalassaemic** *adj.*

thalassic /thə lássik/ *adj.* **1.** LIVING IN THE SEA living in or growing in the sea **2.** RELATING TO THE SEA relating to a sea or ocean, especially a smaller inland sea [Mid-19thC. From French, from Greek *thalassa* 'sea'.]

thalassocracy /thállə sókrəssi/ (*plural* **-cies**), **thalattocracy** /-tókrəssi/ (*plural* **-cies**) *n.* naval or commercial supremacy over a large area of sea or ocean [Mid-19thC. From Greek *thalassokratia*, literally 'authority over the sea', from *thalassa* 'sea'.] —**thalassocrat** /thə lássəkrat/ *n.*

thalassotherapy /thálləssō thérrəpi/ *n.* a therapeutic treatment that involves bathing in sea water [Late 19thC. Coined from Greek *thalassa* 'sea' + THERAPY.]

thaler /taalər/ (*plural* **-ler** *or* **-lers**), **taler** (*plural* **-ler** *or* **-lers**) *n.* any of several silver coins that were used as currency in Germany, Austria, and Switzerland between the 15th and 19th centuries [Late 18thC. From archaic German (now *Taler*).]

Thales (of Miletus) /ttháy leez əv mī leétəss/ (625?–546? BC) Greek philosopher. One of the Seven Wise Men of Greece, he is traditionally regarded as the founder of Greek philosophy.

Thalia /thə lī ə/ *n.* **1.** MYTHOL GREEK MUSE the muse of comedy in Greek mythology. ◊ **Muse 2.** ONE OF THE THREE GRACES one of the three Graces in Greek mythology who lived on Mount Olympus and tended the goddess Aphrodite. ◊ **Grace**

thalidomide /thə líddə mīd/ *n.* a synthetic sedative and hypnotic drug that has caused physical defects, including limb malformation, in foetuses when taken by women in the first three months of pregnancy [Mid-20thC. Coined from an alteration of phthalic acid (shortening of *naphthalic*, from NAPHTHALENE) + (IM)ID(E) + (IM)IDE, elements of its chemical name.]

thallic /thállik/ *adj.* made of or containing thallium, especially with a valency of three

thallium /thálli əm/ *n.* a soft highly toxic white metallic element that in the past was used in pesticides and insecticides. It is used in the manufacture of low-melting glass, photocells, and infrared detectors, and several of its isotopes are members of the uranium, actinium, neptunium, and thorium radioactive series. Symbol **Tl** [Mid-19thC. Formed from Greek *thallos* 'green shoot' (because its spectrum is marked by a green band).]

thallophyte /thállə fīt/ *n.* a plant that has no stem, roots, or leaves, e.g. algae, lichens, and fungi [Mid-19thC. Formed from modern Latin *Thallophyta*, group name, from Greek *thallos* (see THALLIUM) + *phuton* 'plant'.] —**thallophytic** /thállə fíttik/ *adj.*

thallous /thálləs/ *adj.* made of or containing thallium, especially with a valency of one

thallus /thálləs/ (*plural* **-li** /-lī/ *or* **-luses**) *n.* the body of a plant such as an alga or liverwort that is not differentiated into leaves, stems, and roots [Early 19thC. From Greek *thallos* 'a green shoot', from *thallein* 'to bloom'.] —**thalloid** /thálloyd/ *adj.*

thalweg /taal veg/, **talweg** *n.* GEOG a line connecting the lowest points of successive cross sections through a river channel or valley [Mid-19thC. From German, from obsolete *thal* 'valley' (now *Tal*) + *weg* 'path'.]

Thames /temz/ major river of southern England. It flows through London before empyting into the North Sea. Length: 338 km/210 mi.

than *(stressed)* /than/; *(unstressed)* /thən/ CORE MEANING: used after a comparative adjective or adverb in order to introduce the second element of a comparison ○ (prep) *paying more than £490 a year in fees* ○ (prep) *The hole was no deeper than 12 ft.* ○ (conj) *The risk may be higher than the figures indicate.*

conj. used to introduce a rejected alternative in a contrast between two alternatives, in order to state a preference ○ *more a state of mind than a physical condition* [Old English *þanne, þonne, þænne,* and *þan*; ultimately the same word as English *then*]

WORD KEY: USAGE

older than he or **older than him**? Because ***than*** is a preposition as well as a conjunction, either construction is possible, as is the fuller form *older than he is*. The form *older than him* is generally considered to be more informal, although it is usually more natural in any context.

thanatology /thánnə tólləji/ *n.* the study of the medical, psychological, and sociological aspects of death and the ways in which people deal with it [Mid-19thC. Coined from Greek *thanatos* 'death' + -LOGY.] —**thanatological** /thánnətə lójjik'l/ *adj.* —**thanatologist** /-tólləjist/ *n.*

thanatopsis /thánnə tópsiss/ (*plural* **-ses** /-seez/) *n.* an expression of sb's thoughts about death, e.g. in a poem (*literary*) [Early 19thC. Coined from Greek *thanatos* 'death' + *-opsis* 'sight' (see -OPSY).]

Thanatos /thánnə toss/ *n.* **1.** MYTHOL **PERSONIFICATION OF DEATH** in Greek mythology, the personification of death and the son of Nyx, goddess of the night. Roman equivalent **Mors 2.** PSYCHOL **DEATH INSTINCT** the universal death instinct theorized by Sigmund Freud [Mid-20thC. From Greek, 'death'.]

thane /thayn/ *n.* **1. RETAINER OF ANGLO-SAXON LORD** an Anglo-Saxon nobleman of low rank who held lands in return for military service to a lord **2. FEUDAL BARON IN SCOTLAND** a baron in feudal Scotland, or a hereditary tenant of the Scottish crown [Old English *þegn*. Ultimately from a prehistoric Germanic word meaning 'boy, man'.] —**thanage** *n.* —**thaneship** *n.*

Thanet, Isle of /thánnit/ coastal region in northeastern Kent, southeastern England. It was formerly an island.

thank /thangk/ (**thanks, thanking, thanked**) *vt.* **1. EXPRESS GRATITUDE** express feelings of gratitude to sb **2. BLAME SB FOR STH** to blame sb or hold sb responsible for sth ○ *You have only yourself to thank for this situation.* **3. BE GRATEFUL** to be grateful to sb or sth because of sth that has happened ○ *Thank goodness you got here in time.* [Old English *þancian*. Ultimately from an Indo-European word that is also the ancestor of English *think* and *thought*.] ◇ **I'll thank you (not) to** used in an ironic or angry way to ask sb to do or not do sth ○ *I'll thank you not to bring any more of your friends round.* ◇ **thank you** used to express gratitude to sb

thankful /thángkf'l/ *adj.* **1. FEELING GRATITUDE** feeling or expressing gratitude ○ *We must be thankful for small mercies.* **2. GLAD ABOUT STH** glad or relieved about sth —**thankfulness** *n.*

thankfully /thángkf'li/ *adv.* **1. USED TO EXPRESS RELIEF** used to express approval or relief about a situation (*informal*) ○ *Thankfully, he didn't fall.* **2. WITH GRATITUDE** with feelings or expressions of gratitude ○ *They thankfully accepted her offer of a room for the night.*

WORD KEY: USAGE

Sentence adverb The adverb ***thankfully*** is used in two ways: as a conventional adverb of manner (*They received the good news thankfully*), and as a sentence adverb (*Thankfully, the news was good*). Some people dislike the second use, although the objection is not as strong as that to *hopefully* used in a corresponding way.

thankless /thángkləss/ *adj.* **1. UNAPPRECIATED** not likely to be appreciated or rewarded ○ *a thankless task* **2. UNGRATEFUL** not showing or feeling gratitude — **thanklessly** *adv.* —**thanklessness** *n.*

thank offering *n.* sth offered or given to sb as a sign of gratitude

thanks /thangks/ *interj.* **USED TO EXPRESS GRATITUDE** used to express gratitude to sb (*informal*) ○ *Goodbye, and thanks!* ■ *npl.* **1. EXPRESSION OF GRATITUDE** an expression of gratitude for sth ○ *Many thanks for your help yesterday.* **2. GRATITUDE FOR STH** gratitude or appreciation for sth ◇ **no thanks to sb** *or* **sth** despite sb or sth or without sb's assistance ◇ **thanks a lot** used to express great gratitude, sometimes ironically (*informal*) ○ *Thanks a lot for coming over.* ○ *You took my glass? Thanks a lot!* ◇ **thanks to sb** *or* **sth** because of sb or sth

thanksgiving /thángks giving/ *n.* **1.** RELIG **PRAYER OF THANKS** a prayer that offers thanks to God **2. GIVING OF THANKS** an expression or an act of giving thanks **3.** RELIG **PUBLIC ACKNOWLEDGMENT OF DIVINE GOODNESS** a public acknowledgment or celebration of divine goodness

Thanksgiving Day, Thanksgiving *n.* CALENDAR **1.** *US* **LEGAL HOLIDAY IN UNITED STATES** the fourth Thursday in November, observed as a legal holiday in the United States to commemorate the feast given in thanks for the harvest by the Pilgrim colonists in 1621 **2.** *Can* **LEGAL HOLIDAY IN CANADA** the second Monday in October, observed in Canada as a legal holiday and day of giving thanks for the harvest and other good things received

thank-you *n.* **EXPRESSION OF GRATITUDE** an expression of gratitude to sb ○ *a big thank-you to all our readers* ■ *adj.* **EXPRESSING GRATITUDE** expressing gratitude to sb for sth ○ *Send a thank-you note promptly.*

thar /thaar/ *adv.* there (*regional nonstandard*)

Thar Desert /taar-/ desert in northwestern India, in the state of Rajasthan, extending across the border into Pakistan. Area: 199,429 sq. km/77,000 sq. mi.

Tharsis /thaarsiss/ *n.* an extensive shallow bulge on the surface of Mars in the northern hemisphere about 2000 km/1200 mi. across and 8 km/5 mi. high, supporting several volcanoes

Thásos /táss oss/ island in northeastern Greece, in the Aegean Sea, about 8 km/5 mi. from the mainland. Population: 13,111 (1981). Area: 378 sq. km/146 sq. mi.

that *(stressed)* /that/; *(unstressed)* /thət/ CORE MEANING: a grammatical word used to indicate sb or sth that has already been mentioned or identified, or sth that is understood by both the speaker and hearer ○ (det) *Do you remember that discussion we had?* ○ (det) *Later that week I saw her again.* ○ (pron) *Is that why you're here?* ○ (pron) *Don't touch that!*

1. *det., pron.* **INDICATING DISTANCE FROM THE SPEAKER** indicating sb or sth a distance away from you, or further away from another, referred to as 'this' ○ (det) *You see that girl over there?* ○ (det) *That bag looks more spacious than this one.* ○ (pron) *What's that you're doing?* ○ (pron) *That looks much nicer than this.* **2.** *det., pron.* **INDICATING A FAMILIAR PERSON OR THING** used to refer to sb or sth not described, but familiar to the speaker and hearer and not requiring identification ○ (det) *Did you read that e-mail I sent?* ○ (det) *that woman we met yesterday* ○ (pron) *That was a great year.* **3.** *det.* **INDICATING A TYPE** used to characterize a particular type, person, or thing ○ *I really want a sleep that goes on forever.* **4.** *pron.* **IDENTIFYING SB OR STH** used to introduce a clause giving more information to identify the person or thing mentioned ○ *the committee that deals with such matters* ○ *Take the road that forks to the left.* ○ *on the day that he left* **5.** *conj.* **EXPRESSING A COMMENT OR FACT** used to introduce a noun clause expressing a comment on a situation or a supposed or real fact ○ *It was clear that she wanted to see the concert.* ○ *The report stated that sales were improving.* **6.** *conj.* **EXPRESSING A RESULT** used to introduce a clause expressing result or effect ○ *It made such a noise that we had to cover our ears.* **7.** *conj.* **EXPRESSING A CAUSE** used to introduce a clause expressing the cause of a feeling ○ *I feel hurt that you should think such a thing.* ○ *He's sorry that he told her now.* **8.** *conj.* **EXPRESSING PURPOSE** used to introduce a clause expressing purpose ○ *We continue to give, that others will receive and live.* **9.** *conj.* **EXPRESSING DESIRE OR AMAZEMENT** used after an understood but unspoken statement such as 'I wish' or 'If only' to introduce a clause expressing desire, amazement, or indignation ○ *Oh that I had never set eyes on her!* ○ *That you could think such a thing!* **10.** *adv.* **TO THE STATED DEGREE** used to specify the extent of sth ○ *I came that close to hitting the car in front.* **11.** *adv.* **SO VERY** used before adjectives to emphasize the quality they are describing (*informal*) ○ *I didn't think she'd be that upset.* **12.** *adv. Scotland* **SO** so ○ *I was that angry!* [Old English *þæt*. Ultimately from an Indo-European demonstrative base (see THE).] ◇ **and (all) that** and everything else that is similar or included (*informal*) ○ *I've painted the doors and window frames and all that.* ◇ **at that 1.** in addition ○ *It was a coincidence, and a happy one at that.* **2.** nevertheless, or in spite of sth else ○ *It just might work at that.* **3.** at a specific point or place ○ *I think we'll leave it at that for today.* ◇ **just like that** without great effort, trouble, or inconvenience ○ *I can't move to another country just like that.* ◇ **that is** in other words, or to be specific ○ *You need a further qualification, that is, a PhD.* ◇ **that's that 1.** used to say that sth is finished or dealt with **2.** used to say that sth has been settled and there will be no more discussion on it ◇ **with that** immediately after saying or doing sth specified ○ *With that, she turned to go.*

WORD KEY: USAGE

that or **which**? As relative pronouns the two words are often interchangeable: *The house that/which stands on the corner is up for sale. The school that/which they go to is several miles away.* (When ***that*** or ***which*** is the object of a following verb, it can be omitted altogether, as in *The school they go to ....*) When the relative clause adds incidental information rather than identifying the noun it follows, ***which*** is used and is preceded by a comma: *The house, which stands on the corner, is up for sale.*

WORD KEY: USAGE

That in reference to people For centuries ***that*** has been used to refer to people as well as things. Sometimes this usage can be clumsy: *He's the one that did it.* But it is not incorrect, and occasionally ***that*** is the most artful choice possible of relative pronoun: *Anything or anyone that helps me is my friend.*

thataway /tháttə way/ *adv. US* in that direction, or over there (*regional humorous*) ○ *The masked man went thataway, Sheriff.* [Mid-19thC. Alteration of *that way*.]

thatch /thach/ *n.* **1.** BUILDING **PLANT MATERIAL USED FOR A ROOF**

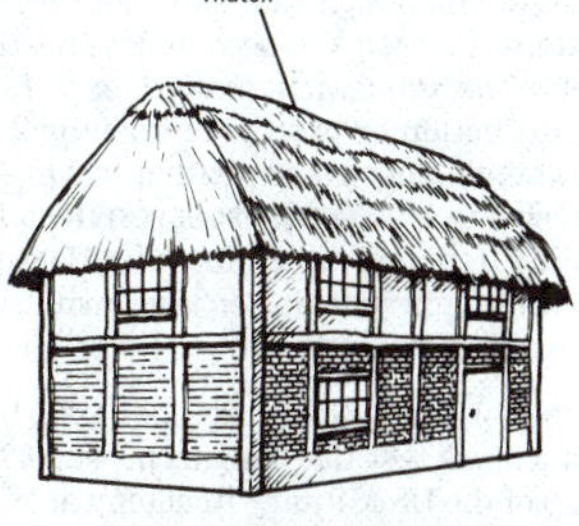

Thatch

a plant material such as straw or rushes used as roofing on a house **2.** BUILDING **ROOF OF THATCH** a roof made of thatch **3. HAIR ON SB'S HEAD** the hair on sb's head, especially when it is thick ○ *The child had an unmistakable thatch of red hair.* **4.** GARDENING **LAYER OF DEAD MATERIAL IN GRASS** a matted layer of dead plant material that builds up next to the soil at the base of lawn grasses ■ *vti.* **(thatches, thatching, thatched)** BUILDING **ROOF BUILDING WITH THATCH** to put a roof of thatch on a building, or to work at doing this [Old English *þeccan*. Ultimately from an Indo-European word meaning 'to cover', which is also the ancestor of English *deck, protect,* and *tile.*] —**thatcher** *n.*

thatched /thacht/ *adj.* made of thatch, or with a roof made of thatch ○ *an old-fashioned thatched cottage*

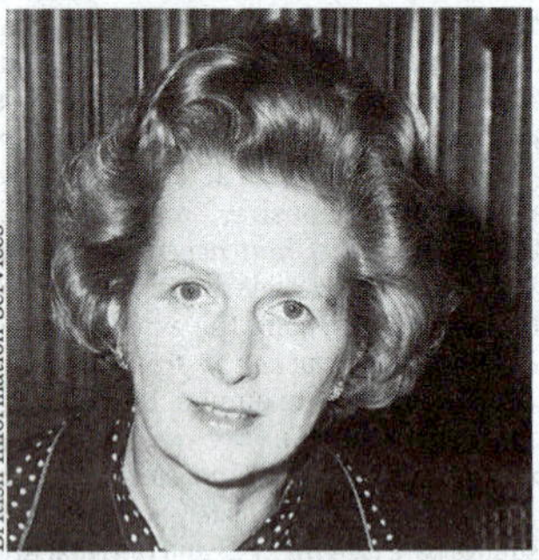

British Information Services

Margaret Thatcher

Thatcher /tháchər/, **Margaret, Baroness Thatcher of Kesteven** (*b.* 1925) British political leader. Leader of the Conservative Party from 1975, and first woman prime minister (1979–90), she pursued policies of privatization and economic deregulation. Born **Margaret Hilda Roberts**

Thatcherism /tháchərizəm/ *n.* the political policies and style of government of Margaret Thatcher, typified by privatization, monetarism, and hostility to trade unions —**Thatcherite** /táchə rīt/ *n., adj.*

thatching /tháching/ *n.* **1. CRAFT OF MAKING THATCHED ROOFS** the craft or process of constructing or repairing thatched roofs **2.** = **thatch** *n.* 1

thaumato- *prefix.* miracle ○ *thaumatology* [From Greek *thaumat-*, the stem of *thauma* 'marvel, wonder', of unknown origin]

thaumatology /tháwmə tólləji/ *n.* the study or description of miracles [Mid-19thC. Coined from Greek *thauma* 'wonder' + -LOGY.]

thaumatrope /tháwmə trōp/ *n.* a card with different pictures on either side so that when the card is rapidly twirled, the images appear to combine [Early 19thC. Coined from Greek *thauma* 'wonder' + *tropos* 'turning'.] —**thaumatropical** /tháwmə tróppik'l/ *adj.*

thaumaturge /tháwmə turj/, **thaumaturgist** /tháwmə turjist/ *n.* sb who performs magic or miracles [Early 18thC. Via medieval Latin from Greek *thaumatourgos*, from *thauma* 'wonder' + *-ergos* 'working'.]

thaumaturgy /tháwmə turji/ *n.* the performance of miracles or magic —**thaumaturgic** *adj.*

thaw /thaw/ *v.* **(thaws, thawing, thawed) 1.** *vti.* **MELT** to melt or make sth melt **2.** *vti.* FOOD **DEFROST** to defrost frozen food or become defrosted ○ *Leave the gateau out to thaw.* **3.** *vi.* **BECOME LESS COLD** to become less cold or numb through exposure to heat ○ *Come and thaw out by the fire.* **4.** *vi.* METEOROL **BE WARM ENOUGH TO MELT ICE** to be warm enough that snow and ice will melt **5.** *vi.* **BECOME LESS HOSTILE** to become less hostile, tense, or aloof ○ *The atmosphere thawed.* ■ *n.* **1. PROCESS OF THAWING** the action or process of thawing **2.** METEOROL **WARMER WEATHER** a period of weather warm enough to melt snow and ice **3. LESSENING OF HOSTILITY** a lessening of hostility, tension, or aloofness [Old English *þawian*. Ultimately from a prehistoric Germanic word that also produced German *tauen* 'to thaw'.]

Thayer /tháy ər, thair/, **Sylvanus** (1785–1872) US soldier and educator. As the long-term superintendent (1817–33) of the US Military Academy at West Point, he is credited with transforming it into a fully effective institution. Known as **Father of West Point**

ThB *abbr.* Bachelor of Theology [Latin, *Theologiae Baccalaureus*]

THC *n.* the main active chemical constituent of cannabis. Full form **tetrahydrocannabinol**

ThD *abbr.* Doctor of Theology [Latin, *Theologiae Doctor*]

the *(stressed/emphatic)* /thee/; *(unstressed; before a vowel)* /thi/; *(unstressed; before a consonant)* /thə/ CORE MEANING: a determiner, the definite article, used before sb or sth that has already been mentioned or identified, or sth that is understood by both the speaker and hearer, as distinct from 'a' or 'an' ○ *The film ended with the hero riding off into the desert.* ○ *The food was excellent but the service was poor.*

1. *det.* **INDICATING ONE AS DISTINCT FROM ANOTHER** used to refer to a particular one of a number of things or people, identified as distinct from all others by the use of some kind of modifier ○ *Put them in the small bag.* ○ *the door on the left* ○ *the girl who answered the phone* ○ *the right to vote* ○ *the points made earlier.* ◊ **a, an 2.** *det.* **INDICATING GENERIC CLASS** used to refer to a person or thing considered generically or universally ○ *Exercise is good for the heart.* ○ *she played the violin* ○ *The dog is a loyal pet.* **3.** *det.* **INDICATING SHARED EXPERIENCE** used to refer to objects and concepts associated with the shared experience of a culture, society, or community ○ *go to the hospital* ○ *thinking about the future* ○ *lying in the sun* **4.** *det.* **ALL PEOPLE OF A PARTICULAR TYPE** used before adjectives to refer generically to people of a particular type or class ○ *new measures to help the unemployed* ○ *They say the good always die young.* **5.** *det.* **TITLES AND NAMES** used before titles and some names, e.g. placenames ○ *the King of Spain* ○ *the Times newspaper* ○ *the President of the United States* **6.** *det.* **QUALIFYING NAMES AND TITLES** used in names and titles before adjectives and nouns that distinguish sb from others of the same name or title ○ *Ivan the Terrible* ○ *Henry the Fifth* **7.** *det.* **INDICATING PARTS OF THE BODY** used instead of 'my', 'your', etc. to refer to a part of sb's body. ○ *patted him on the head* ○ *took her by the hand* **8.** *det.* **INDICATING MOST FAMOUS OR IMPORTANT** the best, only, or most outstanding ○ *It's* THE *place to be.* **9.** *det.* **EXPRESSING RATES AND RATIOS** used to indicate how many units apply to the particular items being measured ○ *ordered in at £60 the ton* **10.** *det.* **INDICATING A FAMILY RELATIONSHIP** used instead of 'your', 'my', etc. to refer to sb having a particular family relationship. *(informal)* ○ *Give my regards to the family.* ○ *How's the wife?* **11.** *det.* **PERIOD OF TIME** used to refer to a specified period of time, especially a decade or an era ○ *living in the sixties* **12.** *det.* **TO THAT EXTENT** used adverbially to emphasize that sb or sth is true to a particular extent *(used before comparatives)* ○ *She looks the better for her holiday.* ○ *the worse for wear* **13.** *det., adv.* **BY HOW MUCH OR BY THAT MUCH** used adverbially to indicate how one amount or quality changes in relation to another *(used before each of two comparative adjectives or adverbs)* ○ *the cheaper the better* ○ *The more you exercise, the fitter you'll feel.* **14.** *det. Scotland* used in various constructions where standard English requires no article, particularly before public institutions like 'the school' and 'the church', and names of diseases, e.g. 'the mumps' *(informal)* **15.** *det. Scotland* used before a surname to indicate the chief of a clan, e.g. 'the MacGregor'; also historical, e.g. 'Hughie the Graham', with surnames other than Highland ones **16.** *det. Scotland* used in various constructions, notably 'the baith' (also, in informal Scottish English, 'the both'), 'the maist' (also, 'the most'); 'the day', 'the morn', 'the nicht', that is today, tomorrow, tonight [Old English *þe*, alteration of earlier *se*. Ultimately from an Indo-European demonstrative base that is also the ancestor of English *that, then, there , they,* and *this.*]

WORD KEY: USAGE

Pronunciation: It is a curious fact that one of the English words used most often, consisting of one syllable and spelt with three letters, has two distinct pronunciations, according to context. Before a word beginning with a consonant sound the vowel in ***the*** is pronounced as a schwa, as in *thuh gray mare, thuh gray mare,* but before a word beginning with a vowel sound it is pronounced with a long *e*, as in *thee old gray mare.*

the- *prefix.* = **theo-** *(used before vowels)*

theanthropism /thi ánthrəpizəm/ *n.* **1. ASSIGNMENT OF HUMAN CHARACTERISTICS TO GOD** the assigning of human characteristics to a god or gods **2. CHRISTIAN DOCTRINE** the Christian doctrine that the human and the divine are united in Jesus Christ [Early 19thC. Formed from Greek *theanthrōpos* 'god-man', from *theos* 'god' + *anthrōpos* 'man'.] —**theanthropic** /thée ən thróppik/ *adj.* —**theanthropist** /thi ánthrəpist/ *n.*

thearchy /thée aarki/ *(plural* **-chies**) *n.* **1. RULE BY GOD** rule by God, by a god, or by priests **2. COMMUNITY UNDER DIVINE RULE** a community that is ruled by God, by a god, or by priests **3. HIERARCHY OF GODS** a hierarchy or system of gods [Mid-17thC. From Greek *thearkhia*, from *theos* 'god'.] —**thearchic** /thi áarkik/ *adj.*

theat. *abbr.* **1.** theatre **2.** theatrical

theater *n.* US = **theatre**

theatre /théertər/ *n.* **1.** THEATRE **PLACE FOR PLAYS** a building, room, or other setting where plays or other dramatic presentations are performed **2.** MED **OPERATING THEATRE** an operating theatre *(informal)* **3. ROOM WITH TIERS OF SEATS** a room with rising tiers of seats, used for lectures, demonstrations, or assemblies **4.** THEATRE **PLAYS** plays or other dramatic literature **5.** THEATRE **DRAMA AS ART OR PROFESSION** dramatic performance as an art, profession, or way of life ○ *She decided to make the theatre her life.* **6.** THEATRE **DRAMATIC QUALITY** dramatic or theatrical quality or effectiveness ○ *As a public speaker he has a great sense of theatre.* **7. PLACE OF SIGNIFICANT EVENTS** the place or realm where significant actions or events take place ○ *the political theatre* ■ *adj.* **FOR USE IN THEATRE OF OPERATIONS** relating to or for use in a military theatre of operations [14thC. Via Old French and Latin from Greek *theatron*, from *theasthai* 'to watch'.]

theatregoer /théertər gō ər/ *n.* sb who often goes to the theatre —**theatregoing** *n., adj.*

theatre-in-the-round *(plural* **theatres-in-the-round**) *n.* **1. THEATRE WITH STAGE IN THE CENTRE** a theatre in which the stage is in the centre with the seats around it on all sides **2. DRAMA FOR THEATRE-IN-THE-ROUND** drama or the style of drama written for performance in a theatre-in-the-round

theatre of cruelty *n.* a form of surrealist drama emphasizing that human beings live in a threatening world with precarious moral values. It was originated by Antonin Artaud in the early 1930s.

theatre of operations *n.* an area where fighting takes place during a war

theatre of the absurd *n.* a form of drama that represents the absurdity of human life in a meaningless universe by deliberately unrealistic means and by ignoring or distorting conventions of plot and characterization

theatre of war *n.* a large area of land, sea, and air in which warfare may take place. ◊ **theatre of operations**

theatrical /thi áttrik'l/ *adj.* **1.** THEATRE **RELATING TO THEATRE** relating to or typical of the theatre or dramatic performance **2. MARKED BY ARTIFICIAL EMOTION** full of exaggerated or false emotion ■ *n.* THEATRE **ACTOR** a professional actor —**theatricalism** *n.* —**theatricality** /thi áttri kálləti/ *n.* —**theatrically** /thi áttrikli/ *adv.* —**theatricalness** /-áttrik'lnəss/ *n.*

theatricals /thee áttrik'lz/, **theatrics** /thi áttriks/ *npl.* **1. PERFORMANCE OF PLAYS** the performance of plays, often by amateurs **2. DRAMATIC BEHAVIOUR** showy dramatic gestures and actions

thebaine /théebə een, thi báy-/ *n.* a poisonous alkaloid component of opium that causes convulsions similar to those caused by strychnine and that was once used medicinally. Formula: $C_{19}H_{21}NO_3$. [Mid-19thC. Formed from Greek *Thēbai* 'Thebes' (in Egypt) because Upper Egypt was an important source of opium.]

thebe /tébbe/ *(plural* **-be**) *n.* **1. SUBUNIT OF BOTSWANAN CURRENCY** a subunit of currency in Botswana, 100 of which are worth one pula. See table at **currency 2. COIN WORTH A THEBE** a coin worth one thebe

Thebe /théebi/ *n.* the fourteenth moon of the planet Jupiter to be discovered, with a diameter of 100 km/60 mi. It is Jupiter's fourth most distant satellite, orbiting at a distance of 222,000 km/138,000

mi. [Mid-18thC. Via Latin, name of the nymph who was daughter of the river god Asopus, from Greek.]

Thebes /theebz/ 1. city of ancient Greece, in Boethia, northwest of present-day Athens. A celebrated city in Greek myth, it was the most important city in Boeotia from the beginning of the 6th century BC, and was destroyed by Alexander the Great in 335 BC. 2. capital city of ancient Egypt, situated on both sides of the River Nile, south of present-day Cairo. It first appeared in Egyptian records in the middle of the 3rd millennium BC, and served as the capital of Egypt until 1085 BC. It is the site of the tombs of the pharaohs in the Valley of the Kings. —**Theban** n., adj.

theca /theéekə/ (plural **-cae** /-see, -kee/) n. an enclosing organ, capsule, or sheath, e.g. the spore case of a moss or the horny covering of the pupa of an insect [Early 17thC. Via Latin from Greek thēkē 'case'.] —**thecal** adj. —**thecate** /theé kayt/ adj.

thecodont /theéka dont/ adj. WITH TEETH IN SOCKETS used to describe animals whose teeth are set in sockets ■ n. 1. EXTINCT PREHISTORIC REPTILE any of an order of extinct reptiles that lived in the Triassic period, had teeth set in sockets, and were the ancestors of the dinosaurs. Order: Thecodontia. 2. THECODONT REPTILE a thecodont reptile [Mid-19thC. Coined from Latin theca (see THECA) + -ODONT.]

thé dansant /táy daaN saáN/ (plural **thés dansants**) n. a tea dance (dated) [From French, literally 'dancing tea']

thee /thee/ pron. 1. OBJECTIVE OF 'THOU' the objective form of 'thou' used as the object of a verb or preposition to mean 'you' (archaic) 2. 'THOU' AS USED BY QUAKERS a subjective form of 'thou' as used by members of the Christian denomination, the Society of Friends ○ See that thee keepest silence. [Old English þē, the objective form of þū (see THOU)]

theft /theft/ n. 1. STEALING OF PROPERTY the stealing of sb else's property 2. STH STOLEN sth that has been stolen (archaic) [Old English þēoft. Ultimately from a prehistoric Germanic word that is also the ancestor of English thief.]

──────── **WORD KEY: SYNONYMS** ────────
theft, robbery, burglary, hold-up, mugging, shoplifting, embezzlement, larceny
CORE MEANING: taking property unlawfully

theft a general word used to talk about the unlawful taking of sb else's property or money; **robbery** theft that involves force or violence, or the threat of it; **burglary** the act of illegally entering a building in order to commit a felony, usually in order to steal; **hold-up** a robbery involving the threat or use of guns; **mugging** an informal word used to describe an attack on sb when the attacker's motive is to steal from that person; **shoplifting** stealing goods from shops; **embezzlement** the unlawful taking of money by sb who has been placed in a position of trust, especially taking money from an employer; **larceny** a formal or legal word meaning the same as theft.

theine /theé een, -in/ n. caffeine, particularly as found in tea [Mid-19thC. Formed from modern Latin Thea, former genus name of the tea plant, from Dutch thee (see TEA).]

their /thair/ det. 1. BELONGING TO THEM belonging to or relating to a particular group of people or things ○ They have sold their house and moved to London. 2. BELONGING TO AN INDIVIDUAL belonging to an individual person ○ Everyone should make their own way home. [12thC. From Old Norse þeirra 'theirs'.]

──────── **WORD KEY: USAGE** ────────
See Usage note at **they.**

theirs /thairz/ pron. 1. BELONGING TO THEM belonging to a particular group of people or things ○ Theirs was the biggest house in the town. 2. BELONGING TO AN INDIVIDUAL belonging to an individual person ○ I have spare copies of the agenda if anyone has forgotten theirs.

theism /theé izəm/ n. 1. BELIEF IN GOD belief that one God created and rules humans and the world, not necessarily accompanied by belief in divine revelation such as through the Bible 2. BELIEF IN GOD OR GODS belief in the existence of a god or gods [Late 17thC. Formed from Greek theos (see THEO-).] —**theist** n. —**theistic** /thee ístik/ adj. —**theistical** —**theistically** /-ístikli/ adv.

them (stressed) /them/; (unstressed) /thəm/ pron. 1. OBJECTIVE FORM OF 'THEY' used to refer to a group of people or things other than the speaker or people addressed ○ I'll put them in a box for you. 2. HIM OR HER used instead of 'him' or 'her' to refer to a person without specifying gender ○ If anyone is looking for me, tell them I'll be back soon. 3. THOSE a dialect form of 'those' (nonstandard) ○ Give me one of them oranges. 4. US THEMSELVES used instead of 'themselves' when the object of a verb refers to the same people or things as the subject of the verb (regional nonstandard) ○ They got them a new car. [12thC. From Old Norse þeim.]

thematic /thi máttik/ adj. 1. RELATING TO THEME relating to or being a theme 2. LING RELATING TO WORD STEM relating to the stem of a word 3. LING LAST BEFORE INFLECTION being the last part of a word stem before the inflectional ending [Late 17thC. From Greek thematikos, from thema (see THEME).] —**thematically** adv.

thematic apperception test n. a test for exploring aspects of personality in which sb is shown pictures of people in various situations and asked to describe what is happening. The presumption is that emotions, prejudices, and other psychological states of the subject will be projected onto the figures in the picture.

theme /theem/ n. 1. SUBJECT OF DISCUSSION OR COMPOSITION a subject of a discourse, discussion, piece of writing, or artistic composition 2. DISTINCT AND UNIFYING IDEA a distinct, recurring, and unifying quality or idea ○ Efficiency will be the theme of this organization. 3. MUSIC REPEATED MELODY a melody that is repeated, often with variations, throughout a piece of music ○ one of the themes of the concerto 4. MUSIC IN FILM a song or tune that is played at the beginning or end of, or during, a film or television programme, and is identified with it ○ the theme from The Magnificent Seven 5. ESSAY OR WRITTEN EXERCISE a short essay or written exercise for a student 6. GRAM = stem[1] n. 6 ■ adj. WITH DISTINCT SUBJECT with one distinct and recurring subject, organizational principle, or idea ○ We ate at a Wild West theme restaurant. ■ vt. (themes, theming, themed) GIVE STH DISTINCT CHARACTER to give sth a single distinct character or subject ○ The local bar has been themed as an Irish pub. [13thC. Via Old French and Latin from Greek thema 'proposition'.] —**themed** adj.

──────── **WORD KEY: SYNONYMS** ────────
See Synonyms at **subject.**

theme park n. an amusement park in which all of the entertainments and facilities are designed around a particular subject or idea

Themistocles /thə místə kleez/ (527?–460? BC) Greek general and statesman. He built up the Athenian navy and led it to victory over the Persians at the battle of Salamis (480 BC), laying the foundations for Athenian domination of Greece.

themselves /thəm sélvz/ pron. 1. REFLEXIVE OF 'THEY' OR 'THEM' used to refer to a group of people or things when the object of a verb is the same as the subject ○ They all made themselves at home. 2. THEIR NORMAL SELVES their real or normal selves (usually used in negative constructions) ○ They haven't been themselves since the accident. 3. EMPHASIZING used to emphasize the people or things being referred to ○ They themselves would rather have gone to a movie. 4. HIMSELF OR HERSELF used to refer to an individual person without using 'himself' or 'herself' (informal) ○ Everyone needs to take care of themselves.

then /then/ CORE MEANING: an adverb used to indicate a particular time in the past or future ○ We were much happier then. ○ Until then, he'll be staying with me.
1. adv. AFTER THAT after that or subsequently in time, order, or position ○ Fry the onions and garlic, then the vegetables. ○ We went for a walk, then came home. 2. adv. THEREFORE that being the case, or in that case ○ Then why don't you go back? 3. adv. ON THE OTHER HAND on the other hand, or at the same time ○ It was a brave thing to do, but then I would have expected no less of her. 4. adv. IN ADDITION in addition to sth else, or besides what has been mentioned ○ I have to pay the money, then a penalty on top of that! 5. adj. BEING AT THAT TIME being at that time, or existing

or belonging to the time mentioned ○ the then governor [Old English þænne. Ultimately from an Indo-European demonstrative base (see THE).] ◇ **but then again** used to introduce a contrasting and additional fact that has to be taken into account ○ It was a brave thing to do, but then again I would have expected no less of her. ◇ **then and there** immediately and in that very place (informal) ○ Did you expect me to hand over the money then and there?

thenar /theé naar/ n. 1. PALM OF HAND the palm of the hand (technical) 2. BASE OF THUMB the fleshy area at the base of the thumb ■ adj. IN PALM OR BALL OF THUMB relating to or in the palm of the hand or the fleshy area at the base of the thumb [Mid-17thC. From Greek, 'palm of the hand'.]

thence /thenss/ adv. (formal or literary) 1. FROM THERE from that place ○ We went by boat to Rotterdam and thence to Amsterdam. 2. THEREFORE from that fact, or therefore 3. THEREAFTER from that time, or thereafter [13thC. Formed from earlier thenne. Ultimately from an Indo-European demonstrative base (see THE).]

thenceforth /thénss fáwrth/ adv. from that time on

thenceforward /thénss fáwrwərd/ adv. from that place or time on or forwards

theo- prefix. god ○ theocentric [From Greek theos. Ultimately from an Indo-European base meaning 'to shine, sky, heaven', which is also the ancestor of English deity, jovial, and Tuesday.]

theobromine /theé ō brṓ meen, -brṓ.min/ n. a white powder derived from the cocoa bean that has effects similar to caffeine and has been used as a diuretic and in treating cardiovascular disorders. Formula: $C_7H_8N_4O_2$. [Mid-19thC. Formed from modern Latin Theobroma, genus name of the cacao tree, literally 'food of the gods', from Greek brōma 'food'.]

theocentric /theé ō séntrik/ adj. with God, a god, or gods as the focal point —**theocentricism** /theé ō séntrissizəm/ n. —**theocentricity** /-sen tríssəti/ n. —**theocentrism** /-séntrizəm/ n.

theocracy /thi ókrəssi/ (plural **-cies**) n. 1. GOVERNMENT BY GOD government by a god or by priests 2. COMMUNITY GOVERNED BY GOD a community governed by a god or priests [Early 17thC. From Greek theokratia, literally 'rule of the gods'.] —**theocrat** /theé ə krat/ n. —**theocratic** /-kráttik/ —**theocratical** /-kráttik'l/ adj. —**theocratically** /-kráttikli/ adv.

Theocritus /thi ókrətəss/ (310?–250? BC) Greek poet. His graceful lyrics were the foundation of European pastoral poetry.

theodicy /thi óddssi/ (plural **-cies**) n. argument in defence of God's goodness despite the existence of evil [Late 18thC. Anglicization of French Théodicée, the title of a book by Gottfried Leibniz, literally 'justice of the gods', from Greek dikē 'justice'.] —**theodicean** /thi ódd seé ən/ adj.

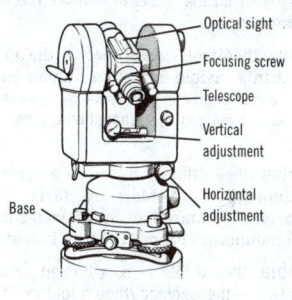

Theodolite

theodolite /thi óddə līt/ n. an optical instrument consisting of a rotating telescopic sight, used by a surveyor to measure horizontal and vertical angles [Late 16thC. From modern Latin theodelitus, of unknown origin.] —**theodolitic** /thi óddə líttik/ adj.

Theodorakis /theé ə daw raákiss/, **Mikis** (b. 1925) Greek composer. His wide-ranging output includes music for the film Zorba the Greek (1965).

Theodore I Lascaris /theé ə dawr láskərəss/ (1174?–1221) Byzantine emperor. During the Crusaders' occupation of Byzantium, he made Nicaea in Asia Minor the centre of a new Byzantine state.

Theodoric /thi ódderik/, **King of the Ostrogoths** (d. 526?). King from 474, he invaded Italy in 488 and became its leader in 493, making Ravenna the capital and bringing a period of peace to Italy. Known as **Theodoric the Great**

Theodosius I /thee̱ ə dṓssi əss/ (346?–395) Spanish-born Roman emperor. As emperor of both the eastern (379–95) and western (392–95) Roman empires, he was the last ruler to unite the empire. He was a champion of Orthodox Christianity. Known as **Theodosius the Great**

Theodosius II (401–450) Roman emperor. He was the grandson of Theodosius I, and ruled the eastern Roman empire from 408 until his death.

theogony /thi óggəni/ (plural **-nies**) n. the origin and descent of the gods, or an account of this [Early 17thC. From Greek theogonia, literally 'birth of the gods'.] — **theogonic** /thee̱ ə gónnik/ adj. — **theogonist** /thi óggənist/ n.

theol. abbr. **1.** theologian **2.** theological **3.** theology

theologian /thee̱ ə lṓjən/ n. sb who is an expert in or a student of theology

theological /thee̱ ə lójjik'l/, **theologic** /-lójjik/ adj. about, using, engaged in, or typical of theology — **theologically** adv.

theological virtues npl. faith, hope, and charity, the three spiritual graces that, according to Christian theology, are given directly by God

theologize /thi óllə jīz/ (**-gizes, -gizing, -gized**), **theologise** (**-gises, -gising, -gised**) v. **1.** vt. TREAT THEOLOGICALLY to give a theological or religious significance to sth **2.** vi. SPECULATE ON RELIGIOUS TOPICS to theorize, speculate, or discourse on religious topics — **theologizer** n.

theology /thi ólləji/ (plural **-gies**) n. **1.** STUDY OF RELIGION the study of religion, especially the Christian faith and God's relation to the world **2.** RELIGIOUS THEORY a religious theory, school of thought, or system of belief **3.** COURSE OF RELIGIOUS TRAINING a course of specialized religious training, especially one intended to lead students to a vocation in the Christian Church [14thC. Via French and Latin from Greek theologia, literally 'study of divine things'.] — **theologist** n.

theomachy /thi ómməki/ (plural **-chies**) n. a battle among gods or against gods [Late 16thC. From Greek theomakhia, literally 'fighting of the gods'.]

theomorphic /thee̱ ə máwrfik/ adj. in the form or likeness of a deity [Late 19thC. Formed from Greek theomorphos, literally 'of divine form'.] — **theomorphism** n.

theonomy /thi ónnəmi/ n. the state of being governed by God, a god, or priests [Late 19thC. Coined from THEO- + -NOMY on the model of German Theonomie.] — **theonomous** adj.

theophany /thi óffəni/ (plural **-nies**) n. the appearance of a god in a visible form to a human being [Mid-17thC. Via medieval Latin from Greek theophaneia, literally 'appearance of the gods'.] — **theophanic** /thee̱ ə fánnik/ adj.

Theophilus /thee̱ óffiləss/ n. ASTRON a crater on the Moon northwest of Mare Nectaris. It is approximately 100 km/60 mi. in diameter and has a central mountain 2200 m/7200 ft in height.

theophobia /thee̱ ə fṓbi ə/ n. a hatred or abnormal fear of God — **theophobiac** /thee̱ ə fṓbi ak/ n.

Theophrastus /thee̱ ə frástəss/ (372?–287BC) Greek philosopher. Succeeding Aristotle as head of the Lyceum in Athens, he is remembered for an influential treatise on botany and his Characters, sketches of personality types.

theophylline /thee̱ ə fílleen, -fíllin, -leen, -lin/ n. an alkaloid substance extracted from tea leaves or made synthetically, used medicinally as a vasodilator, smooth muscle relaxant, and diuretic, and in treating bronchial asthma. Formula: $C_7H_8N_7O_2.H_2O$. [Late 19thC. Coined from modern Latin Thea (see THEINE) + PHYLLO- + -INE.]

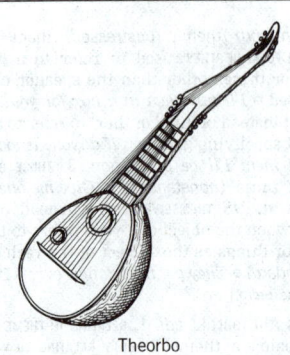
Theorbo

theorbo /thi áwr bō/ n. a stringed instrument from the 17th century similar to the lute except larger and with an extra set of bass strings longer than the main set [Early 17thC. Via Italian tiorba from, ultimately, Turkish torba 'bag'.] — **theorbist** n.

theorem /thee̱ərəm/ n. **1.** LOGIC, MATH PROVABLE PROPOSITION OR FORMULA a proposition or formula in mathematics or logic that is provable from a set of axioms and basic assumptions **2.** IDEA ACCEPTED AS TRUE an idea accepted or proposed as true [Mid-16thC. Via late Latin from Greek theōrēma 'speculation', from theōrein 'to look at', from theōros (see THEORY).] — **theorematic** /thee̱ərə máttik/ adj. — **theorematically** /-máttikli/ adv. — **theoremic** /theer rémmik/ adj.

theoretical /theer réttik'l/, **theoretic** /-réttik/ adj. **1.** BASED ON THEORY about, involving, or based on theory **2.** DEALING WITH THEORY dealing with theory or speculation rather than practical applications **3.** SPECULATIVE inclined to or skilled in speculative contemplation or theorizing **4.** HYPOTHETICAL existing only in theory [Early 17thC. Formed from late Latin theoreticus, from Greek theoretikos, from theōrētos 'observable', from theōrein 'to look at'.]

theoretically /theer réttikli/ adv. **1.** IN THEORY NOT REALITY in theory only, not in reality ○ Time travel is theoretically possible. **2.** IN TERMS OF WHAT IS POSSIBLE in terms of what is possible in theory ○ Theoretically speaking, it could be done. **3.** SUPPOSEDLY supposedly or ideally, but probably not in reality ○ Can we still win the election? Yes, theoretically.

theoretician /theer tish'n/ n. sb who is inclined to or skilled in speculative contemplation or theorizing, or is learned in the theoretical aspect of a subject

theoretics /theer réttiks/ n. the theoretical or speculative aspect of a subject (takes a singular or plural verb)

theorist /thee̱ e rist, thír Tz/ n. sb who holds or expounds a theory

theorize /thee̱ e rīz, thír Tz/ (**-rizes, -rizing, -rized**), **theorise** (**-rises, -rising, -rised**) v. **1.** vi. SPECULATE to speculate or form a theory about sth **2.** vt. CONCEIVE OF THEORETICALLY to conceive of sth in a theoretical way ○ Research scientists were able to theorize the existence of the particle before it was actually discovered. — **theorization** /theer rī záysh'n/ n. — **theorizer** /theer rīzər/ n.

theory /thee̱əri/ (plural **-ries**) n. **1.** RULES AND TECHNIQUES the body of rules, ideas, principles, and techniques that applies to a particular subject, especially when seen as distinct from actual practice ○ economic theories **2.** SPECULATION abstract thought or contemplation **3.** IDEA FORMED BY SPECULATION an idea of or belief about sth arrived at through speculation or conjecture ○ She believed in the theory that you catch more flies with honey than with vinegar. **4.** HYPOTHETICAL CIRCUMSTANCES a set of circumstances or principles that is hypothetical ○ That's the theory, but it may not work out in practice. **5.** SCIENTIFIC PRINCIPLE TO EXPLAIN PHENOMENA a set of facts, propositions, or principles analysed in their relation to one another and used, especially in science, to explain phenomena [Late 16thC. Via late Latin from Greek theōria 'contemplation, theory', from theōros 'spectator'.] ◇ **in theory** under hypothetical or ideal circumstances but perhaps not in reality

theory of games n. = game theory

theos. abbr. **1.** theosophical **2.** theosophy

theosophy /thi óssəfi/ (plural **-phies**) n. any religious philosophy based on intuitive insight into the nature of God [Mid-17thC. Via medieval Latin from late Greek theosophia, literally 'knowledge of the gods'.] — **theosophic** /thee̱ ə sóffik/ adj. — **theosophical** /-sóffik'l/ adj. — **theosophically** /-sóffikli/ adv. — **theosophism** /thi óssə fizəm/ n. — **theosophist** /-óssəfist/ n.

Theosophy n. the teachings of the Theosophical Society, a religious movement founded in New York in 1875, incorporating chiefly Buddhist and Brahmanic theories such as reincarnation and karma — **Theosophical** adj. — **Theosophist** n.

Thera /thee̱rə/ island and tourist centre in the Cyclades group, Greece, north of Crete. Destroyed by a volcanic eruption in 1500 BC, it is sometimes claimed as the origin of the Atlantis legend. Population: 10,000 (1994). Area: 76 sq. km/29 sq. mi.

therap., therapeut. abbr. **1.** therapeutic **2.** therapeutics

therapeutic /thérrə pyóotik/ adj. **1.** USED IN TREATING DISEASE about, involving, or used in the treatment of disease or disorders **2.** RESTORING OR MAINTAINING HEALTH working or done to restore or maintain sb's health [Mid-16thC. Via French therapeutique or late Latin therapeutica from, ultimately, Greek therapeutēs 'one who treats', from therapeuein (see THERAPY).] — **therapeutically** adv.

therapeutic index n. a ratio that indicates the relative efficiency of a drug, calculated by dividing the dose of the drug that causes cell damage by the dose needed to produce results

therapeutics /thérrə pyóotiks/ n. the branch of medicine that deals with methods of treatment and healing, especially the use of drugs to treat diseases (takes a singular verb)

therapist /thérrəpist/ n. **1.** SB TRAINED IN THERAPY sb trained to treat disease, disorders, or injuries, especially sb who uses methods other than drugs and surgery **2.** PSYCHOL PSYCHOTHERAPIST a psychoanalyst or a professional from another school of psychotherapy who is trained to treat mental and emotional problems with psychological methods

therapsid /thə rápsid/ n. any extinct reptile of an order that lived during the Permian and Triassic periods. Many of them are thought to be ancestors of the mammals. Order: Therapsida. [Early 20thC. From modern Latin Therapsida, order name, from Greek thēr 'wild animal' + hapsis 'vault'. From the opening at the base of its skull.]

therapy /thérrəpi/ (plural **-pies**) n. **1.** TREATMENT TO CURE treatment of physical, mental, or behavioural disorders that is meant to cure or rehabilitate sb (often used in combination) ○ radiation therapy **2.** US PSYCHOL PSYCHOTHERAPY psychoanalysis or techniques from another school of psychotherapy, intended to treat mental and emotional problems with psychological methods [Mid-19thC. Via modern Latin from Greek therapeia, from therapeuein 'to treat medically', from theraps 'attendant'.]

Theravada /thérrə vaadə/ n. the doctrines of the Hinayana Buddhists [Late 19thC. From Pali, literally 'doctrine of the elders'.]

there (stressed) /thair/; (unstressed) /thər/ CORE MEANING: an adverb used to indicate a place, either one that has already been mentioned or is understood, or one indicated by pointing or looking ○ I don't know how to get there by car. ○ May I sit there?
1. adv. AT THAT POINT used to refer to a point reached in an activity or process ○ I suggest we pause there and have coffee. ○ And there we end our news bulletin. **2.** adv. ON THAT MATTER on that matter, or with respect to that ○ I can't agree with you there. **3.** adv. AT A SUCCESSFUL POINT used to indicate that sth has reached a final or successful point or stage ○ We're not the best yet, but we're getting there. **4.** USED TO IDENTIFY used to identify sb or sth emphatically ○ They ran into that house there. **5.** pron. INTRODUCING A SENTENCE used to introduce a sentence stating that sth exists, develops, or can be seen ○ There's a stain on this sweater. ○ There remain several important issues to be discussed. **6.** interj. USED TO EXPRESS FEELINGS used to express strong feelings such as anger, satisfaction, relief, finality, or reassurance ○ There! I told you she would make it. [Old English þǣr. Ultimately from an Indo-European demonstrative base (see THE).] ◇ **be there**

for sb to be ready to give your support, sympathy, or friendship to sb ◇ **not all there** not fully conscious, rational, or aware of sth ◇ **so there** used to express defiance, triumph, or finality ◇ **there and then** immediately and in that very place ◇ **there or thereabouts** there or somewhere nearby (*informal*) ◇ **there, there** used to console, soothe, or comfort sb ○ *There, there. Don't cry.* ◇ **there you are 1.** used when giving sb sth **2.** used to express triumph at having been seen to be right **3.** used to express resignation or sorrow at sth that has happened

thereabouts /tháirə bowts, -bówts/, **thereabout** *US* /-bowt/ *adv.* near that place, amount, number, or time ○ *We're expecting twenty guests or thereabouts.*

thereafter /tháir aáftər/ *adv.* after that time or from that time on ○ *She graduated from college, and shortly thereafter found a good job.*

thereat /tháir át/ *adv.* (*archaic*) **1. AT THAT TIME** at that time or place **2. FOR THAT REASON** because of that

thereby /tháir bí, -bī/ *adv.* **1. BY MEANS OF THAT** by means of or because of that ○ *Interest rates may fall, thereby discouraging investment.* **2. IN CONNECTION WITH THAT** in connection with or with reference to that ○ *Thereby hangs a tale.*

therefor /tháir fáwr/ *adv.* for this, that, or it (*archaic*)

therefore /tháir fawr/ *adv.* **1. AND SO** and so, or because of that ○ *This statement is true; therefore that statement must be false.* **2. ACCORDINGLY** accordingly, or to that purpose ○ *We were forbidden to attend and therefore stayed at home.*

therefrom /tháir fróm/ *adv.* from that place or thing (*archaic or formal*)

therein /tháir ín/ *adv.* **1. INSIDE** in or into that place (*formal*) **2. IN THAT MATTER** in that matter, respect, or detail ○ *Therein lies the problem.*

thereinafter /tháirin aáftər/ *adv.* from then on in sth, especially a legal document (*formal*)

thereinto /tháir ín too/ *adv.* into that place or thing (*archaic*)

theremin /thérrə min/ *n.* an early electronic musical instrument producing a tremulous sound whose pitch and volume is controlled by the distance between two antennae and the player's hands [Early 20thC. Named after its inventor, the Russian engineer Leo Theremin (1896–1993).]

thereof /tháir óv/ *adv.* (*formal*) **1. OF THAT** of or about that ○ *a levy of £50 per annum or part thereof* **2. FROM THAT CAUSE** from that as a reason or cause

thereon /tháir ón/ *adv.* **1. ON THAT** on the place or surface just mentioned (*formal*) ○ *a metal plate with an inscription thereon* **2. ON THAT POINT** regarding the point just mentioned (*archaic*) ○ *income and capital expense, including tax thereon*

Theresa of Lisieux /tə réezə əv lee zyő/ (1873–97) French nun. She is the author of *The Story of a Soul* (1898), in which she described the 'little way', the simple path to Christianity. With Joan of Arc, she is a patron saint of France.

thereto /tháir too/ *adv.* to that thing just mentioned (*formal*)

theretofore /tháirtoo fáwr/ *adv.* before or up to that time (*formal*)

thereunder /tháir úndər/ *adv.* **1. BELOW THAT** below that, or after that, especially in a legal document (*formal*) **2. UNDER THAT** under that place or thing mentioned (*archaic*)

thereupon /tháirə pón/ *adv.* **1. AT THAT POINT** at that point in time (*archaic*) ○ *She was found to have leaked information to a rival firm, and he thereupon insisted on her dismissal.* **2. UPON THAT POINT** upon or concerning that point (*formal*)

therewith /tháir wíth, -with/, **therewithal** /tháir with áwl/ *adv.* **1. WITH THAT** with that, or as well as that (*formal*) **2. AT THAT POINT** at that point, or immediately

therianthropic /theeri ən thróppik/ *adj.* MYTHOL used to describe a mythological creature such as a centaur that is partly human and partly animal [Late 19thC. Coined from Greek *thērion* 'small wild animal' + anthrōpos (see ANTHROPO-) + -IC.] **—therianthropism** /theeri ánthrəpizəm/ *n.*

theriomorphic /theeri ō máwrfik/ *adj.* in the form of an animal, or thought of as being in animal form [Late 19thC. Coined from Greek *thērion* (see THERIANTHROPIC) + -MORPHIC.]

therm /thurm/ *n.* a unit of heat equal to 100,000 British thermal units or 1.055×10^8 joules [Early 20thC. From Greek *thermē* 'heat'.]

therm. *abbr.* thermometer

therm- *prefix.* = thermo- (*used before vowels*)

thermae /thúr mee/ *npl.* hot springs or baths, especially the public baths of ancient Rome [Mid-16thC. Via Latin from Greek *thermai*, from *thermē* 'heat'.]

thermaesthesia /thúrməss theézi ə/ *n.* sensitivity to heat and cold, or to changes in temperature [Late 19thC. From modern Latin, formed from Greek *thermē* 'heat' + *aisthēsis* 'perception'.]

thermal /thúrm'l/, **thermic** /thúrmik/ *adj.* **1. INVOLVING HEAT** about, involving, affected by, or producing heat ○ *thermal energy* **2. HOT OR WARM** hot or warm, especially because of the presence of hot springs ○ *thermal baths* **3. MANUF USING HEAT FOR PRODUCTION** using heat to produce sth **4. CLOTHES FOR RETENTION OF BODY HEAT** designed to retain body heat ○ *thermal underwear* ■ *n.* METEOROL **AIR COLUMN** a current of warm air rising through cooler surrounding air ○ *watching hawks ride thermals* ■ **thermals** *npl.* **THERMAL CLOTHING** thermal clothing, especially underwear (*informal*) [Mid-18thC. From French, formed from Greek *thermē* 'heat'.] **—thermally** *adv.*

thermal barrier *n.* the problematic heating effect caused by air friction on an aircraft flying at high speed

thermal conductivity *n.* the rate at which heat flows through a material between points at different temperatures, measured in watts per metre per degree. Symbol λ, k

thermal efficiency *n.* the work done by a heat engine divided by the thermal energy required to operate it

thermal imaging *n.* the use of a device that detects the different levels of infrared energy given off by areas of different temperatures and displays these as a pattern on a screen

thermalize (-izes, -izing, -ized), **thermalise** (-ises, -ising, -ised) *vt.* to slow neutrons in a nuclear reactor to give them thermal energy and thus produce fission **—thermalization** /thúrmə lī záysh'n/ *n.*

thermal neutron *n.* = slow neutron

thermal noise *n.* noise in an electronic circuit, e.g. an amplifier, caused by electrons in conducting elements that are agitated by the absorption of heat

thermal pollution *n.* the discharge into a natural body of water of heated water or other liquid that is hot enough to harm aquatic life

thermal printer *n.* **1. PRINTING DEVICE USING HEAT** a printing device that uses heat to print characters onto specially coated paper **2. COMPUT COMPUTER OUTPUT DEVICE** an output device that produces visible characters by moving heated wires over specially treated heat-sensitive paper

thermal reactor *n.* a nuclear reactor in which the chain reaction, and thus fission, is brought about mainly by thermal neutrons. It contains a moderator to slow down fast neutrons to thermal energies.

thermal shock *n.* stress in a material caused by rapid changes in temperature, often resulting in fractures

thermesthesia *n.* US = thermaesthesia

thermic *adj.* = thermal **—thermically** *adv.*

-thermic *suffix.* having to do with heat ○ *exothermic* [Formed from Greek *thermē* (see THERM)]

thermic lance *n.* a cutting tool that works by heating steel wool held inside a steel tube

Thermidor /thúrmi dawr/ *n.* CALENDAR the 11th month of the year in the French Revolutionary calendar, corresponding to 20 July to 18 August in the Gregorian calendar [Early 19thC. From French, formed from Greek *thermē* 'heat' + *dōron* 'gift'. From the fact that it is the hottest time of year.]

thermion /thúrmi ən, -on/ *n.* a positive ion or electron given off by a very hot material such as a hot cathode **—thermionic** /thúrmi ónnik/ *adj.*

thermionic current *n.* an electric current generated by the flow of electrons leaving a heated cathode and flowing to other electrodes

thermionic emission *n.* the emission of electrons or ions from a solid or liquid as a result of its thermal energy

thermionics /thúrmi ónniks/ *n.* a branch of electronics that deals with the emission of electrons from hot bodies (*takes a singular verb*)

thermionic tube *n.* US = thermionic valve

thermionic valve *n.* an electronic component that consists of an evacuated glass tube containing a heated cathode that emits electrons, an anode that collects the electrons, and other electrodes. US term **thermionic tube**

thermistor /thur místər/ *n.* a semiconductor device with a resistance that is very sensitive to temperature, resistance decreasing as the temperature increases [Mid-20thC. Contraction of *thermal resistor*.]

Thermit /thúrmit/, **Thermite** /-mīt/ *tdmk.* a trademark for a mixture of aluminium powder and metal oxide, usually of iron, that gives off great heat when ignited. It is used in welding and in incendiary bombs.

thermo- *prefix.* **1.** heat ○ *thermochemistry* **2.** thermoelectricity ○ *thermocouple* [Formed from Greek *thermē* 'heat' (see THERM)]

thermobarometer /thúrmō bə rómmitər/ *n.* an instrument that measures both air temperature and pressure

thermocautery /thúrmō káwtəri/ *n.* the use of a heated instrument, e.g. a hot wire, to destroy tissue, especially in cauterizing wounds

thermochemistry /thúrmō kémmistri/ *n.* a branch of chemistry concerned with the relationship between chemical action and heat **—thermochemical** /thúrmō kémmik'l/ *adj.* **—thermochemically** /-kémmikli/ *adv.* **—thermochemist** /-kémmist/ *n.*

thermocline /thúrmō klīn/ *n.* a layer of water, e.g. in a lake, where there is an abrupt change in temperature that separates the warmer surface water from the colder deep water

thermocouple /thúrmō kup'l/ *n.* a device for measuring temperature in which two wires of different metals are joined. The potential difference between the wires is a measure of the temperature of sth they touch.

thermoduric /thúrmō dyooórik/ *adj.* used to describe a microorganism that is capable of surviving high temperatures or pasteurization [Early 20thC. Coined from THERMO- + Latin *durare* 'to endure' + -IC.]

thermodynamic /thúrmō dī námmik/, **thermodynamical** /-námmik'l/ *adj.* **1. OF THERMODYNAMICS** about or involving thermodynamics **2. OBEYING THE LAWS OF THERMODYNAMICS** obeying or affected by the laws of thermodynamics **—thermodynamically** *adv.*

thermodynamics /thúrmō dī námmiks/ *n.* PHYSICS OF ENERGY AND MECHANICAL ACTIONS the branch of physics that deals with the conversions from one to another of various forms of energy and how these affect temperature, pressure, volume, mechanical action, and work (*takes a singular verb*) ■ *npl.* PROCESSES OF THERMODYNAMICS thermodynamic processes or phenomena **—thermodynamicist** *n.*

thermodynamic temperature *n.* = absolute temperature

thermoelectric /thúrmō i léktrik/, **thermoelectrical** /-léktrik'l/ *adj.* involving a direct relationship between temperature of materials and electricity **—thermoelectrically** *adv.*

thermoelectricity /thúrmō ilek tríssəti, -éllek-/ *n.* electricity produced by maintaining a temperature difference at the point where two different materials come into contact, e.g. in a thermocouple

thermoelectron /thérmō i lék tron/ *n.* an electron emitted by a material that is at high temperature

thermogenesis /thúrmō jénnəssiss/ *n.* the production of heat in a person's or animal's body by physiological processes, especially metabolic processes — **thermogenetic** /thúrmō jə néttik/ *adj.*

thermogram /thúrmə gram/ *n.* **1.** MED IMAGE FROM THERMOGRAPHY an image or record of the heat radiating from the body, made by thermography **2.** PHYS TEMPERATURE RECORD a record of temperatures made by a thermograph

thermograph /thúrmə graaf, -graf/ *n.* **1.** RECORDING THERMOMETER an instrument that continuously records temperature readings **2.** MED DEVICE SHOWING BODY HEAT a device that shows patterns of heat radiated from a person's or an animal's body, used in diagnostic thermography

thermography /thər móggrəfi/ (*plural* **-phies**) *n.* **1.** MED RECORDING IMAGE OF BODY HEAT the recording of a visual image of the heat that bodies emit as infrared radiation. The technique is used to diagnose disease and tumours, especially breast tumours. **2.** PRINTING PRINTING PROCESS USING HEAT the process of producing a raised image on a printed surface by using heat to fuse a resinous powder and wet ink to the surface — **thermographer** *n.* — **thermographic** /thúrmə gráffik/ *adj.* — **thermographically** /-gráffikli/ *adv.*

thermojunction /thúrmō júngksh'n/ *n.* a point at which two dissimilar metals of differing temperatures come into contact, producing a thermoelectric current

thermolabile /thúrmō láy bīl/ *adj.* used to describe substances such as some enzymes that are easily destroyed or altered by heat

thermoluminescence /thúrmō loōmi néss'nss/ *n.* phosphorescence released by certain previously irradiated substances when they are heated. The process is used by geologists and archaeologists to date rocks and pottery. — **thermoluminescent** *adj.*

thermolysis /thər mólləssiss/ *n.* **1.** PHYSIOL HEAT LOSS loss of heat from the body, e.g. by sweating **2.** CHEM DECOMPOSITION BY HEAT the breaking down of a substance by heat — **thermolytic** /thurme líttik/ *adj.*

thermomagnetic /thúrmō mag néttik/ *adj.* relating to the relationship between heat and magnetism, and especially the effects of heat upon the magnetic properties of a substance

thermometer /thər mómmitər/ *n.* an instrument for measuring temperature, e.g. an instrument with a graduated glass tube and a bulb containing mercury or alcohol that rises in the tube when the temperature increases [Mid-17thC. From French *thermomètre*, from Greek *thermos* 'warm' (see THERM) + *mètre* '-meter'.]

thermometry /thər mómmətri/ *n.* temperature measurement and the branch of physics concerned with measuring temperature — **thermometric** /thúrmō méttrik/ *adj.* — **thermometrical** /-méttrik'l/ *adj.* — **thermometrically** /-méttrikli/ *adv.*

thermonasty /thúrmə nasti/ *n.* the movement of plant parts, e.g. the opening of flowers, in response to a change in temperature [Mid-20thC. Coined from THERMO- + -NASTY.]

thermonuclear /thúrmō nyoōkli ər/ *adj.* **1.** NUCLEAR PHYS, INDUST OF NUCLEAR FUSION relating to nuclear fusion or making use of nuclear fusion ○ *thermonuclear energy* **2.** ARMS BASED ON FUSION making use of nuclear fusion ○ *thermonuclear war*

thermoperiodism /thúrmō peéri ədizəm/, **thermoperiodicity** /-díssəti/ *n.* the response of a plant to cycles of temperature, e.g. the regular cycles of day and night — **thermoperiodic** /thúrmō peéri óddik/ *adj.*

thermophile /thúrmə fīl/, **thermophil** /-fil/ *n.* an organism that thrives in a warm environment, e.g. a bacterium — **thermophile** *adj.* — **thermophilic** /thúrmə fíllik/ *adj.* — **thermophilous** /thər móffələss/ *adj.*

thermophyllous /thúrmō fílləss/ *adj.* bearing leaves only in the warmer part of the year

thermopile /thúrmə pīl/ *n.* a set of thermocouples, either joined in series for increased voltage or in parallel for increased current, used to measure radiant energy or to convert radiant energy into electric current

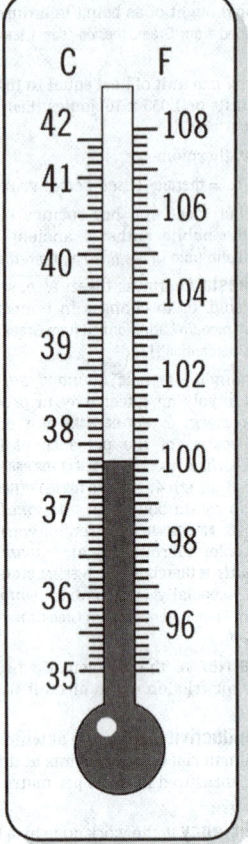

Thermometer

thermoplastic /thúrmō plástik/ *n.* a substance that becomes soft and pliable when heated, without a change in its intrinsic properties. Polystyrene and polythene are thermoplastics. — **thermoplastic** *adj.* — **thermoplasticity** /thúrmō pla stíssəti/ *n.*

Thermopylae /thə móppəli/ pass in ancient Greece, northwest of Athens, that controlled entry to central Greece. It was the site of the battle of 480 BC fought by Leonidas I and thousands of his troops, all of whom were killed by the Persian army, led by Xerxes.

thermoreceptor /thúrmō ri séptər/ *n.* a sensory receptor, usually a nerve ending in the skin, that is stimulated by heat or cold

thermoregulation /thúrmo réggyoō láysh'n/ *n.* the maintenance of a particular body temperature regardless of changes in the environment — **thermoregulate** /thúrmo réggyoō layt/ *vi.* — **thermoregulator** /-laytər/ *n.*

Thermos /thúrməss/ *tdmk.* a trademark for an insulated or vacuum container used to hold a liquid and maintain it at a constant temperature

thermoscope /thúrməskōp/ *n.* an instrument that measures changes in temperature by their effects on a substance, e.g. the change in volume of a gas — **thermoscopic** /thúrmə skóppik/ *adj.* — **thermoscopical** /-skóppik'l/ *adj.* — **thermoscopically** /-skóppikili/ *adv.*

thermosetting /thúrmō seting/ *adj.* used to describe a plastic that sets permanently when heated

thermosphere /thúrmə sfeer/ *n.* the region of the atmosphere above the mesosphere in which temperature steadily increases with height, beginning at about 85 km/53 mi. above the earth's surface

thermostable /thúrmō stáyb'l/ *adj.* used to describe substances such as some toxins that are able to withstand heat without being destroyed or altered — **thermostability** /thúrmō stə billəti/ *n.*

thermostat /thúrmə stat/ *n.* **1.** TEMPERATURE REGULATOR a device that regulates temperature by means of a temperature sensor, e.g. a bimetallic strip. Thermo-

stats are used in vehicle engines and domestic heating systems. **2.** DEVICE TRIGGERED BY TEMPERATURE CHANGE a device that activates a mechanism or system, e.g. a fire alarm or a sprinkler system, in response to a change in temperature [Mid-19thC. Coined from THERMO- + -STAT 'instrument holding constant value', from, ultimately, Greek *statikos* 'causing to stand'.] — **thermostatic** /thúrmə státtik/ *adj.* — **thermostatically** /-státtikli/ *adv.*

thermotaxis /thúrmə táksiss/ *n.* movement of a living organism towards or away from a heat source — **thermotactic** /thúrmə táktik/ *adj.* — **thermotaxic** /-táksik/ *adj.*

thermotherapy /thúrmō thérrəpi/ (*plural* **-pies**) *n.* the use of heat to alleviate pain and stiffness, especially in joints and muscles, and to increase circulation

thermotropism /thúrmō trópizəm/ *n.* the movement of a plant part towards or away from a source of heat — **thermotropic** /thúrmo trópik, -tróppik/ *adj.*

-thermy *suffix.* heat ○ *diathermy* [Via modern Latin -*thermia* from, ultimately, Greek *thermē* 'heat' (see THERM)]

theropod /theérə pod/ *n.* any carnivorous dinosaur with strong hind legs and short front limbs. Tyrannosaurs and megalosaurs are theropods. Suborder: Theropoda. [Early 20thC. From modern Latin *Theropoda*, suborder name, from Greek *thēr* 'wild animal' (see TREACLE) + POD- 'foot'.] — **theropodan** /thi róppədən/ *adj.*

thesaurus /thə sáwrəss/ (*plural* **-ri** /-rī/ *or* **-ruses**) *n.* **1.** BOOK OF WORD GROUPS a book that lists words related to each other in meaning, usually giving synonyms and antonyms **2.** BOOK OF SPECIALIST VOCABULARY a dictionary of words relating to a particular subject **3.** TREASURY a place in which valuable things are stored [Early 19thC. Via Latin, 'treasury', from Greek *thēsauros* 'storehouse' (source also of English *treasure*).]

these /theez/ *pron., det.* the form of 'this' used before a plural noun or with a multiple referent ○ (pron) *These are the people I was telling you about.* ○ (det) *These delays, along with the paperwork demanded by government, can be costly for banks.* [Old English *þæs, þās,* plural of *þes* (see THIS)]

Theseus /theéssi əss, theésyooss/ *n.* in Greek mythology, a great hero who performed many brave deeds, including slaying the Minotaur, defeating the Amazons, and descending into Hades to rescue Persephone

thesis /theésiss/ (*plural* **-ses** /-seez/) *n.* **1.** LENGTHY ACADEMIC PAPER a dissertation based on original research, especially as work towards an academic degree **2.** PROPOSITION a proposition advanced as an argument **3.** STATEMENT an unproved statement, especially one serving as a premise in an argument **4.** ESSAY SUBJECT a subject for an essay **5.** MUSIC DOWNBEAT the downbeat of a bar of music **6.** POETRY STRESSED SYLLABLE a long syllable, on which the stress naturally falls, in classical Greek and Latin poetry. ◊ **arsis** *n.* 1 **7.** POETRY UNSTRESSED SYLLABLE a short unstressed syllable in modern accentual poetry. ◊ **arsis** *n.* 2 **8.** PHILOS FIRST STAGE OF DIALECTIC the first of three stages in Hegelian dialectic [14thC. Via Latin from Greek, 'proposition, stressed beat'. Ultimately from an Indo-European base that is also the ancestor of English *do* and *fact*.]

thespian /théspi ən/ *n.* ACTOR an actor or actress ■ *adj.* **1.** thespian, Thespian OF THE THEATRE relating to the theatre or the profession of acting (*literary*) **2.** OF THESPIS relating to the ancient Greek poet Thespis [Early 19thC. Formed from *Thespis*, the name of the Greek poet (6thC BC) who was the father of Greek tragedy.]

Thess. *abbr.* BIBLE Thessalonians

Thessalonian /théssə lōni ən/ *n.* PEOPLES SB FROM THESSALONIKI sb who was born in or lived in the ancient Greek city of Thessaloniki ■ **Thessalonians** *npl.* BIBLE BOOK OF BIBLE either of two letters written to the Christians of Thessaloniki by the Apostle Paul, included as books of the Christian Bible (*takes a singular verb*) — **Thessalonian** *adj.*

Thessaloníki /théssələ neéki/ capital city of the department of Thessaloníki, northeastern Greece. Population: 377,951 (1991).

Thessaly /théssəli/ region in north central Greece,

consisting mainly of a broad plain. Area: 13,000 sq. km/5,000 sq. mi. —**Thessalian** *n., adj.*

theta /theétə/ *n.* the eighth letter of the Greek alphabet, represented in the English alphabet as 'th'. See table at **alphabet** [Early 17thC. From Greek, of Phoenician origin.]

theta rhythm, theta wave *n.* a pattern of brain waves with a frequency between 4 and 7 Hz seen on an electroencephalogram. The pattern is normal in children under the age of 12 but in adults may be a sign of stress or mental disorder.

Thetford /thétfərd/ town of Saxon origin in Norfolk, eastern England. Population: 20,058 (1991).

thetic /théttik/, **thetical** *adj.* **1. OF STRESS IN POETRY** relating to or having stress in classical poetry **2. ARBITRARY** imposed arbitrarily [Late 17thC. From Greek *thetikos*, from *thetos* 'placed, stressed', from *tithenai* 'to place'.] —**thetically** *adv.*

theurgy /theé urji/ *n.* **1. SUPERNATURAL OR DIVINE INTERVENTION** intervention of supernatural or divine powers in human affairs **2. PERSUADING THE SUPERNATURAL TO INTERVENE** the art of securing the intervention of supernatural or divine powers in human affairs **3. MAGIC PERFORMED FOR GOOD** magic with the help of benevolent spirits, as practised by Neo-Platonists [Mid-16thC. Via late Latin *theurgia* from Greek *theourgia* 'ritual, mystery', from *theos* 'god' + *ergon* 'work'.] —**theurgic** /thi úrjik/ *adj.* —**theurgically** /-úrjikli/ *adv.* —**theurgist** /theé urjist/ *n.*

thew /thyoo/ *n.* muscle or muscular strength (*literary; often used in the plural*) [Old English *þēaw* 'custom, habit', literally 'observance'. Ultimately from an Indo-European base meaning 'to watch', (ancestor also of English *tutor*). The underlying meaning is 'good habit, virtue, strength'.] —**thewy** *adj.*

they /thay/ *pron.* **1. PEOPLE IN GENERAL** used to refer to people in general when making statements about the things people do, think, or say ○ *As people and businesses move out of inner cities, bank branches follow, they say.* **2. HE OR SHE** used instead of 'he' or 'she' to refer to a person without specifying gender (*informal*) ○ *A friend phoned the other day and they told me what you had said.* **3. THOSE** an archaic word for 'those' (*archaic*) [12thC. Old Norse *þeir*. Ultimately from an Indo-European word meaning 'the, that', which is also the ancestor of English *the, this, that,* and *there*.]

WORD KEY: USAGE

Everyone taking the test should do the best they can. Because English is deficient in that it lacks a gender-neutral third person singular pronoun, ***they***, together with associated words such as *their*, is often used in this role and is a revival of an older use that was once well established in English. In more formal contexts, and when the individuality of the subject is significant, it is necessary to use *he or she*, but this phrase is too cumbersome to provide a solution in informal conversational usage such as that given in the example.

they'd /thayd/ *contr.* **1. THEY HAD** a short form of 'they had' **2. THEY WOULD** a short form of 'they would'

they'll /thayl/ *contr.* **1. THEY WILL** a short form of 'they will' **2. THEY SHALL** a short form of 'they shall'

they're /thair/ *contr.* a short form of 'they are'

they've /thayv/ *contr.* a short form of 'they have'

THI *abbr.* temperature-humidity index

thi- *prefix.* = **thio-** (*used before vowels*)

thiabendazole /thī ə béndəzōl/ *n.* a white compound used as a drug to destroy a wide variety of parasitic worms and as an antifungal agent. Formula: $C_{10}H_7N_3S$. [Mid-20thC. Contraction of THIAZOLE + BENZENE + IMIDAZOLE.]

thiamine /thī əmeen, -əmin/, **thiamin** /thī əmin/ *n.* one of the group of B vitamins, found in grains, meat, and yeast. It metabolizes carbohydrates and has been found to prevent beriberi and diseases of the nervous system. Formula: $C_{12}H_{17}ClN_4OS$. [Mid-20thC. Coined from THIO- + AMINE.]

thiazide /thī ə zīd/ *n.* one of a group of compounds used to treat high blood pressure and as a diuretic. These compounds work by inhibiting the reabsorption of sodium and increasing the release of calcium by the kidneys, causing greater excretion of water. [Mid-20thC. Coined from THIO- + AZINE + OXIDE.]

thiazine /thī ə zeen/ *n.* one of a group of organic compounds containing a ring of four carbon atoms, a sulphur atom, and a nitrogen atom. Some are used as dyes and others as tranquillizers. [Early 20thC. Coined from THIO- + AZINE.]

thiazole /thī ə zōl/, **thiazol** /thīəzol/ *n.* **1. LIQUID CHEMICAL COMPOUND** a volatile colourless liquid with a sharp odour. Formula: C_3H_3NS. **2. DERIVATIVE OF THIAZOLE** one of a group of compounds derived from thiazole. Some are used as dyes, others as fungicides or in chemical reactions as accelerators. [Late 19thC. Coined from THIO- + AZOLE.]

thick /thik/ *adj.* **1. DEEP OR BROAD** of relatively large extent from surface to surface or side to side ○ *a thick carpet* ○ *The child wrote her name in thick capital letters.* **2. LARGE IN DIAMETER** having a large diameter ○ *a thick cable* **3. OF STATED DEPTH OR BREADTH** having a specified depth or breadth ○ *a wall two feet thick* **4. VISCOUS** having a liquid consistency that is not free-flowing ○ *thick paint* **5. DENSE** composed of many densely packed objects ○ *a thick forest* ○ *thick hair* **6. OF HEAVY FABRIC** made of thick material ○ *thick socks* **7. FILLED** densely covered or filled ○ *The air was thick with mosquitoes.* **8. HARD TO SEE THROUGH** permitting little or no light to enter ○ *a thick mist* **9. PRONOUNCED** readily noticeable or distinct ○ *a thick country accent* **10. UNINTELLIGENT** slow to learn or understand (*insult*) **11. NOT CLEAR** not articulating words clearly ○ *a voice thick with emotion* **12. FRIENDLY** allied in a close relationship (*informal*) ○ *They seem very thick with each other.* **13. PREVENTING CLEAR THOUGHT** feeling numb and not conducive to clear thought or perception, e.g. because of a cold or a hangover (*informal*) ○ *woke up with a thick head* ■ *adv.* **MAKING DEEP LAYER** in a way that produces sth deep, broad, or dense ■ *n.* **1. MOST ACTIVE PART** the most intense, crowded, or busiest part of sth ○ *in the thick of the battle* **2. DENSEST PART** the part of sth with the greatest depth, density, or breadth ○ *in the thick of the jungle* [Old English *þicce*] —**thickly** *adv.* ◇ **be a bit thick** to go beyond what is fair or reasonable (*informal*) ○ *It's a bit thick, expecting me to look after the baby for nothing.* ◇ **thick and fast** in large numbers and with great frequency ◇ **through thick and thin** no matter what might happen

thicken /thíkən/ (**-ens, -ening, -ened**) *v.* **1.** *vti.* **MAKE OR BECOME THICKER** to become thick or thicker or to make sth thick or thicker **2.** *vi.* **BECOME MORE COMPLEX** to become more complicated or puzzling —**thickener** *n.* —**thickening** *n.*

thicket /thíkit/ *n.* a dense or tangled growth of small trees or bushes [Old English *þiccet*, from *þicce* 'thick']

thickfilm technology /thík film-/ *n.* a method of fabricating electronic circuitry in which a glaze is printed onto a glass or ceramic support. Wiring and components such as microchips are then added. ◊ **thinfilm technology**

thickhead /thík hed/ *n.* an offensive term that deliberately insults sb's intelligence (*offensive insult*) —**thickheaded** /thík héddid/ *adj.* —**thickheadedness** /-héddidnəss/ *n.*

thick-headed fly *n.* a fly with a head broader than its thorax, whose larvae live as parasites on wasps and other insects. Family: Conopidae.

thickie /thíki/, **thicky** (*plural* **-ies**) *n.* an offensive term applied to sb regarded as slow-witted or unintelligent (*offensive insult*)

thick-knee *n.* = **stone curlew** [From its knobby knee joints]

thickness /thíknəss/ *n.* **1. THICK QUALITY** the quality or state of being thick **2. DIMENSION** the dimension between two surfaces of an object, especially the shortest dimension as opposed to the width or the length **3. LAYER** an individual layer **4. THICK PART** a part of sth that is thick

thicko /thíko/ (*plural* **-os**) *n.* an offensive term for sb who is regarded as unintelligent (*offensive insult*) [Late 20thC. Formed from THICK.]

thickset /thík sét/ *adj.* **1. OF STOCKY BUILD** with a stocky physique **2. DENSE** growing closely together

thick-skinned *adj.* **1. UNSYMPATHETIC** insensitive to other people's feelings or circumstances **2. IMPERVIOUS TO CRITICISM** not easily offended by criticism or insults

thick-witted *adj.* lacking intelligence (*insult*) —**thickwittedly** *adv.* —**thick-wittedness** *n.*

thicky *n.* = **thickie**

thief /theef/ (*plural* **thieves** /theevz/) *n.* sb who steals sth, especially with the intention of escaping notice [Old English *þēof*] —**thievish** /theévish/ *adj.* —**thievishly** /-li/ *adv.* —**thievishness** /-nəss/ *n.*

thief ant *n.* any small ant that pillages the colonies of other ants, taking food stores and even the young of the colony

Thiele /teel/, **Colin Milton** (*b.* 1920) Australian writer. His volumes of poetry and books for children include *Storm Boy* (1963).

thieve /theev/ (**thieves, thieving, thieved**) *vti.* to steal things [Old English *þēofian*, from *þēof* 'thief'] —**thievery** (*plural* **-ries**) *n.*

thigh /thī/ *n.* **1. TOP PART OF LEG** the top of the leg between the knee and the hip **2. UPPER PART OF ANIMAL'S LEG** the part of an animal's leg that corresponds to a human thigh [Old English *þēoh*. Ultimately from an Indo-European base meaning 'to swell', which is also the ancestor of English *thumb, tumour,* and *thousand*.]

thighbone /thíbōn/ *n.* = **femur** *n.* 1

thigmotaxis /thígmo táksiss/ *n.* BIOL movement of a cell or organism in response to a touch stimulus from a specific direction, e.g. contact with a surface. US term **stereotaxis** [Early 20thC. Coined from Greek *thigma* 'touch' + -TAXIS.] —**thigmotactic** /-táktik/ *adj.* —**thigmotactically** /-táktikli/ *adv.*

thigmotropism /thig móttrəpizəm/ *n.* a directional growth movement (**tropism**) of a plant part, especially a tendril, in response to physical contact with a surface [Early 20thC. Coined from Greek *thigma* 'touch' + TROPISM.] —**thigmotropic** /-trópik, -tróppik/ *adj.*

thill /thill/ *n.* one of the two shafts of a carriage or cart [15thC. Origin uncertain: perhaps from Old English *þille* 'plank'.]

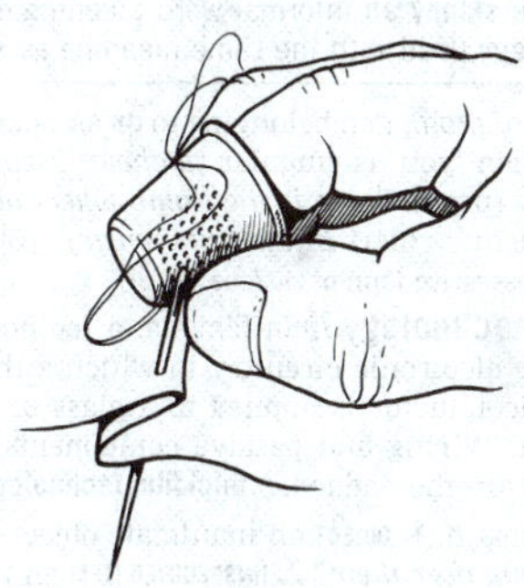

Thimble

thimble /thímb'l/ *n.* **1. COVER FOR FINGER WHEN SEWING** a small protective cap for a finger, used to push a needle through fabric **2.** NAUT **RING PROTECTING LOOP FROM WEAR** a metal ring, concave on the outside, that fits into a loop in a rope or an eye in a sail **3.** MECH ENG **METAL SLEEVE** any small metal tube or sleeve used in machinery [Old English *þȳmel* 'leather thumb protector', from *þūma* (see THUMB)]

thimbleful /thímb'lfŏŏl/ *n.* a very small amount of liquid

thimblerig /thímb'lrig/ *n.* **1. GUESSING GAME USING TRICKERY** a trick in which a participant guesses which of three cups covers an object after sb has moved them about, using sleight of hand to change the object's location **2.** *US* **SB MOVING CUP** sb moving the cup in thimblerig ■ *vt.* (**-rigs, -rigging, -rigged**) **SWINDLE** to cheat or swindle sb [Early 19thC. From THIMBLE + RIG^2.] —**thimblerigger** *n.*

thimerosal /thī mérrə sal/ *n.* a cream-coloured mercury compound used as a local antiseptic. Formula: $C_9H_9HgNaO_2S$. [Mid-20thC. Origin uncertain: probably a contraction of THIO- + MERCURY + SALICYLATE.]

Thimphu /thímfoo/, **Thimbu** capital city of Bhutan, situated in the western part of the country at an altitude of 2,368 m/7,770 ft. Population: 30,340 (1993).

thin /thin/ *adj.* (**thinner, thinnest**) **1. SHALLOW OR NARROW** of relatively small extent from surface to surface or side to side ○ *A thin layer of snow covered the path.*

○ *Draw a thin line.* **2.** OF SMALL DIAMETER having a small diameter ○ *thin wire* **3.** SLIM with little body fat **4.** SPARSE composed of few things widely spaced ○ *thin hair* ○ *a thin forest* **5.** WATERY with a free-flowing consistency similar to that of water ○ *a thin soup* ○ *thin paint* **6.** LIGHTWEIGHT made of light or flimsy material ○ *a thin summer dress* ○ *thin cotton socks* **7.** EASY TO SEE THROUGH permitting light to enter or pass through ○ *thin mist* **8.** QUIET lacking volume or resonance ○ *a thin sound* **9.** *US* WEAK lacking intensity or colour **10.** UNCONVINCING lacking credibility or adequacy ○ *a thin excuse* **11.** PHOTOGRAPHY LACKING CONTRAST of a photographic negative, lacking density or contrast ■ *adv.* MAKING THIN LAYER in a way that produces sth shallow, narrow, or sparse ○ *Spread the paint thin.* ■ *vti.* (**thins, thinning, thinned**) MAKE OR BECOME THINNER to reduce sth in thickness or number or to become reduced in thickness or number ○ *You can thin down the paint before you use it.* ○ *The crowd started to thin out in the evening.* [Old English *þynne*. Ultimately from an Indo-European base meaning 'to stretch', which is also the ancestor of English *tense, tenuous,* and *tone.*] —**thinly** *adv.* —**thinness** *n.*

WORD KEY: SYNONYMS

thin, lean, slim, slender, emaciated, scrawny, skinny, scraggy

CORE MEANING: without much flesh, the opposite of fat

thin a general word used to describe sb with little or no spare flesh on his or her body. It can also be used to describe animals. It can be used fairly neutrally, but is often seen as implying disapproval; **lean** used showing approval to describe a person or animal that is muscular and fit-looking without excess fat; **slim** used showing approval to describe sb who is not at all fat; **slender** used showing approval to describe sb who is not at all fat, especially sb who appears graceful and fragile as a result; **emaciated** a fairly formal word used to describe a person or animal who is unhealthily thin, usually because of illness or starvation; **scrawny** describes a person or animal who is so thin as to appear undernourished; **skinny** an informal word meaning extremely thin; **scraggy** used with the same meaning as ***scrawny.***

thine /thīn/ *pron., det.* belonging to or associated with you, when 'you' is singular (*archaic; used before a vowel*) ○ (pron) *Thine is the womb where our riches have birth.* ○ (det) *Know thine enemy.* [Old English *þīn*, a possessive form of *þū* (see THOU)]

thinfilm technology /thín film-/ *n.* a method of fabricating electronic circuitry in which a thin layer of semiconductor is applied to a glass or ceramic support. Wiring and passive components, e.g. resistors, are then added. ◊ **thickfilm technology**

thing /thing/ *n.* **1.** OBJECT an inanimate object ○ *What's that thing over there?* **2.** UNSPECIFIED ITEM an unnamed or unspecified object ○ *I need a few things in town.* **3.** OCCURRENCE sth that occurs or sth that is done ○ *The fire was a terrible thing.* **4.** WORD OR THOUGHT a thought or an utterance ○ *Don't say another thing!* **5.** DETAIL a piece of information ○ *You forgot one important thing.* **6.** AIM the objective of an action ○ *The thing is to win.* **7.** CONCERN a matter of responsibility or concern ○ *I have several things to do.* **8.** DEED an act or deed ○ *She promises to do great things.* **9.** LIVING CREATURE a person or animal, often spoken of affectionately ○ *The poor thing was soaked to the bone.* **10.** GARMENT an article of clothing ○ *This old thing?* **11.** PREFERRED ACTIVITY a favourite activity or special interest (*informal*) ○ *Golf's not really my thing.* **12.** WHAT CAN BE POSSESSED an object or right that can be possessed or owned **13.** FASHION the fashion (*informal*) ○ *When we were young, we considered it the latest thing.* **14.** STRONG LIKE OR DISLIKE a particularly strong feeling of attraction or repulsion (*informal*) ○ *He's got a thing about spiders.* **15.** IDEAL what is needed or desirable (*informal*) ○ *Iced tea would be just the thing.* ■ **things** *npl.* **1.** BELONGINGS personal items owned or carried ○ *You can leave your things in my room.* **2.** APPARATUS equipment for a particular activity ○ *a drawer for all my writing things* **3.** AFFAIRS general matters or circumstances ○ *How are things today?* [Old English *þing* 'assembly'. From a prehistoric Germanic word meaning 'time' (from the idea of an 'appointed time'). The sense 'unspecified object' evolved via 'matter for discussion' and 'matter'.] ◇ **be on to a good thing** to be in an advantageous or desirable situation ◇ **first thing 1.** very early in the morning **2.** before doing anything else ◇ **it comes to the same thing** it has the same result ◇ **make a (big) thing of sth** to exaggerate the importance of sth and make a fuss about it

WORD KEY: ORIGIN

The long-lost ancestral meaning of ***thing*** is 'time' (the related Gothic *theihs*, for example, meant 'time'). Its prehistoric Germanic precursor evolved semantically via 'appointed time' to 'judicial or legislative assembly'. This was the meaning it originally had in English, and it survives in other Germanic languages (the Icelandic parliament is known as the *Althing*, literally 'general assembly'). In English, however, the word moved on through 'subject for discussion in such an assembly' to 'subject in general, affair, matter' and finally 'entity, object'.

thingamabob *n.* = **thingamajig** (*informal*) [Mid-18thC. Alteration of *thingumbob*, from THING + BOB.]

thingamajig /thíngəməjig/, **thingumajig, thingamabob** /thíngəməbob/, **thingumabob, thingummy** /thíngəmi/ (*plural* **-mies**) *n.* a word used when the proper word for sth is not known or does not come to mind (*informal*) [Early 19thC. Formed from obsolete *thingum* (see THINGUMMY) + JIG.]

thing-in-itself (*plural* **things-in-themselves**) *n.* an object that exists even though we have no experience or perception of it [Translation of German *Ding an sich*]

thingness /thíngnəss/ *n.* status as a material thing, as distinct from sth that is abstract

thingumabob *n.* = **thingamajig** (*informal*)

thingumajig *n.* = **thingamajig** (*informal*)

thingummy *n.* = **thingamajig** (*informal*) [Late 18thC. Alteration of obsolete *thingum*, from THING.]

think *regional* /thingk/ *v.* (**thinks, thinking, thought** *or* **thunk, thought** /thawt/ *or* **thunk** *US*) **1.** *vti.* FORM THOUGHTS to use the mind to consider ideas and make judgments ○ *Think carefully before you start writing.* **2.** *vt.* HAVE AS AN OPINION to believe sth or have sth as an opinion ○ *I don't think it will rain today.* ○ *She seems to think she's a good dancer.* **3.** *vti.* HAVE IN MIND to bring sth to mind ○ *I can't think what the date is today.* ○ *I hadn't thought about him for months.* **4.** *vti.* COMPREHEND STH to imagine or understand sth or the possibility of sth ○ *I can't think of letting you leave so soon.* **5.** *vt.* CONCENTRATE ON to focus the attention on sth ○ *He thinks golf day and night.* **6.** *vi.* HAVE REGARD to regard sb with care or concern ○ *You need to think of your family.* **7.** *vt.* VIEW IN CERTAIN WAY to regard sb or sth in a specified way ○ *Don't think me unkind.* **8.** *vti.* INTEND to have sth as a plan ○ *She thought she'd go out after dinner.* **9.** *vt.* FORESEE to anticipate sth happening ○ *I didn't think he'd actually do it.* **10.** *vt.* BE HEEDFUL OF to be attentive or considerate enough to do sth ○ *Didn't you think to ask about her mother?* **11.** *vi.* CHOOSE to make a mental choice ○ *Think of a card and I'll try to guess what it is.* **12.** *vt.* INFLUENCE WITH THE MIND to bring sth to a particular condition using the mind ○ *Try to think the pain away.* ■ *n.* SPELL OF THINKING an act of thinking or a period of time spent thinking (*informal*) ○ *She sat down to have a think.* [Old English *þencan*] —**thinker** *n.* ◇ **have got another think coming** used to say that sb is mistaken (*informal*) ○ *If he thinks I'm going to help him he's got another think coming.* ◇ **I don't think** used to indicate that the opposite is true (*informal*) ○ *You can rely on him to be generous – I don't think!* ◇ **not think much of sb** *or* **sth** to regard sb or sth as not being very good ◇ **think better of sth** to change an opinion about sth after consideration ○ *She was about to speak her mind, but then thought better of it.* ◇ **think nothing of sth** to regard sth as not being unusual ○ *She thinks nothing of working all night to finish a project.* ◇ **think twice** to consider sth very carefully ○ *You should think twice about lending them so much money.*

think out *vt.* to consider sth carefully, taking account of possible problems or consequences ○ *He hadn't really thought the policy out properly.*

think over *vt.* to reflect on sth ○ *Maybe you'd like to think it over before you sign.*

think through *vt.* to consider or reflect on sth carefully, especially in order to reach a decision ○ *I needed some time to think it through.*

think up *vt.* to invent or devise sth ○ *I've thought up an easy way to do it.*

thinkable /thíngkəb'l/ *adj.* **1.** UNDERSTANDABLE capable of being understood **2.** FEASIBLE capable of happening —**thinkably** *adv.*

thinking /thíngking/ *adj.* RATIONAL capable of using the mind to reason or reflect ○ *the thinking person's choice* ■ *n.* **1.** FORMING OF THOUGHTS use of the mind to form thoughts ○ *There's a lot of thinking to do before we make that decision.* **2.** JUDGMENT opinions or conclusions arrived at ○ *What's your thinking on the political situation?*

thinking cap ◇ **put your thinking cap on** to think carefully about sth, especially to find a solution to a problem

think-tank *n.* a committee of experts that undertakes research or gives advice, especially to a government

thinner /thínnər/ *n.* a liquid used to dilute paint or varnish. Turpentine is a thinner.

thin-skinned *adj.* **1.** SENSITIVE TO CRITICISM easily offended by criticism or insults **2.** WITH THIN PEEL covered in a thin peel or rind

thio- *prefix.* containing sulphur ○ *thiophene* [From Greek *theion* 'sulphur']

thiocarbamide /thí ō kaárbə mīd/ *n.* CHEM = **thiourea**

thiocyanate /thí ō sí ə nayt/ *n.* a salt or ester of thiocyanic acid

thiocyanic acid /thí ō sī ánnik-/ *n.* a colourless liquid used in the form of salts or esters in insecticides. Formula: HSCN.

thiol /thí ol/ *n.* an organic compound similar to an alcohol but in which the oxygen atom has been replaced by a sulphur atom. Thiols are liquids with penetrating unpleasant smells. [Late 19thC. Coined from THIO- + -OL.]

thionic /thī ónnik/ *adj.* relating to, derived from, or containing sulphur [Late 19thC. Formed from Greek *theion* 'sulphur'.]

thionyl /thí ənil/ *n.* containing the chemical group SO [Mid-19thC. Coined from THIO- + -IN + -YL.]

thiopentone sodium /thí ə pén tōn-/, **thiopental sodium** /-t'l-/ *n.* a substance used intravenously as a general anaesthetic and in psychotherapy as a hypnotic. Formula: $C_{11}H_{17}N_2O_2SNa$.

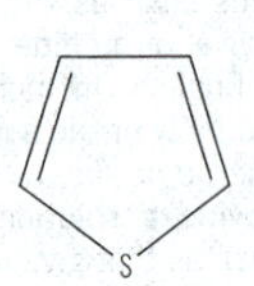

Thiophen

thiophen /thí ə fen/, **thiophene** /-feen/ *n.* a colourless liquid used as a solvent and to make dyes, pharmaceuticals, and resins. Formula: C_4H_4S. [Late 19thC. Coined from THIO- + PHENO-.]

thiosulphate /thí ō súl fayt/ *n.* a salt or ester of thiosulphuric acid

thiosulphuric acid /thí ō sul fyóorik-/ *n.* an acid known in the form of salts or esters or in solution. Formula: $H_2S_2O_3$.

thiotepa /thí ō teépə/ *n.* a compound used in the treatment of malignant tumours. Formula: $C_6H_{12}N_3PS$. [Mid-20thC. Coined from THIO- + tepa, name of a compound, an acronym formed from TRI-, ETHYLENE, PHOSPHORUS and AMIDE.]

thiouracil /thí ō yóorəssil/ *n.* a white bitter-tasting substance used in the treatment of hyperthyroidism. Formula: $C_4H_4N_2OS$.

thiourea /thí ō yoo reé ə, -yóoriə/ *n.* a crystalline substance used to make resins and in photographic fixing. Formula: $CS(NH_2)_2$.

third /thurd/ n. **1.** ONE OF THREE PARTS one of three equal parts of sth **2.** ORDINAL NUMBER CORRESPONDING TO 3 the ordinal number assigned to item number three in a series **3.** ONE AFTER SECOND IN IMPORTANCE sb or sth ranking next after second in authority or precedence **4.** VEHICLE GEAR in a motor vehicle, the forward gear between second and fourth **5.** MUSIC MUSICAL INTERVAL in a standard musical scale, the interval between one note and another that lies two notes above or below it. In the scale of C major, C and E form a third. **6.** MUSIC NOTE A THIRD AWAY FROM ANOTHER in a standard musical scale, a note that is a third away from another note **7.** MUSIC HARMONIC a harmonic of a combination of two tones a third apart **8.** EDUC UNIVERSITY DEGREE the lowest class of honours degree awarded by a British university **9.** BALLET = **third position** [Old English thirdda, thridda. Ultimately from an Indo-European base meaning 'three', which is also the ancestor of English three.] —**third** adj., adv.

— WORD KEY: CULTURAL NOTE —
The Third Man, a film by British director Sir Carol Reed (1949). Set in Vienna immediately after World War II, this stylish and gripping film noir recounts American writer Holly Martins's attempts to discover the truth behind the mysterious death of his old friend Harry Lime. It is made particularly memorable by its dramatic war-ravaged setting, innovative lighting and editing, and haunting zither theme.

third class n. **1.** THIRD IN A CLASSIFICATION SYSTEM the next below second in grade or category **2.** CHEAPEST ACCOMMODATION formerly, the least expensive and least luxurious accommodation on a ship or train **3.** EXAMINATION DIVISION the third highest division in an examination. For British honours degrees, third class is the lowest class. **4.** MAIL CLASS a class of mail in the United States and Canada for unsealed printed matter —**third-class** adj., adv.

third degree n. intensive interrogation, often also implying rough treatment (informal) ○ *The interrogators gave the suspects the third degree.* [From the interrogation required to reach the 'third degree', the highest rank in Freemasonry]

— WORD KEY: SYNONYMS —
See Synonyms at *question*.

third-degree burn n. a burn of the most serious kind, in which the skin and the tissues beneath it are severely damaged

third dimension n. **1.** DEPTH the added dimension of depth that distinguishes a solid object from one that is two-dimensional or planar **2.** ENHANCING QUALITY a quality that makes sth more vivid —**third-dimensional** adj.

third estate n. the third social class, traditionally the commons, in a society divided into estates

third eyelid n. = nictitating membrane

third force n. a group that mediates between two opposing political groups or parties

thirdhand /thúrd hánd/ adj., adv. **1.** TWICE PREVIOUSLY OWNED used by, or after having been used by, two previous owners **2.** TWICE PREVIOUSLY COMMUNICATED from or through two intermediate sources [Mid-16thC. Modelled on SECONDHAND.]

thirdly /thúrdli/ adv. used to introduce the third point in an argument or discussion

third man n. **1.** BOUNDARY FIELDER in cricket, a deep fielder on the off side behind the slips **2.** FIELDING POSITION the position played by a third man

Third Market n. a market on the London Stock Exchange trading in shares of companies not on the main market or the Unlisted Securities Market, e.g. new or small companies

third party n. sb who is involved in a legal matter incidentally, as distinct from the principal parties ○ *The signatures need to be witnessed by a third party.* ○ *third-party motor-vehicle insurance*

third person n. **1.** GRAM VERB OR PRONOUN FORM the form of a verb or a pronoun indicating sb or sth being spoken about. In English, the third-person subject pronouns are 'he', 'she', 'it', 'one', and 'they'. **2.** GRAM SET OF GRAMMATICAL FORMS the grammatical set containing the forms indicating the third person **3.** WRITING IN THIRD-PERSON a style of writing using third-person forms ○ *Write your account in the third person.*

third position n. a position in ballet in which the feet are turned outwards with the heel of the front foot touching the instep of the back foot

third rail n. a rail from which some electrically powered trains pick up current

third-rate adj. of a low or the lowest quality

third reading n. the third presentation of a bill to a legislative assembly. In the UK Parliament, it is to discuss a committee's report. In the US Congress, it is the final presentation before a vote.

Third Reich n. the Nazi regime in Germany between 1933 and 1945

Third Republic n. the French system of government set up after Napoleon III's reign. It lasted until 1940.

thirdstream /thúrd streem/ n. music that draws from both classical music and jazz [Mid-20thC. Modelled on MAINSTREAM.] —**third-stream** adj.

Third World, third world n. the nations outside the capitalist industrial nations of the First World and the industrialized Communist nations of the Second World, generally less economically advanced but with varied economies (hyphenated when used before a noun) [Translation of French tiers monde] —**Third Worlder** n.

thirl[1] /thurl/ (thirls, thirling, thirled) vt. (regional) **1.** PIERCE to pierce or drill sth **2.** THRILL to thrill sb [Old English þyrlian, from þyrel 'hole' (see THRILL)]

thirl[2] /thurl/ (thirls, thirling, thirled) vt. Scotland to bind or subject sb, e.g. to a lease [Mid-16thC. Alteration of earlier thrill, an alteration of THRALL.]

Thirlmere, Lake /thúrl meer/ lake in Cumbria, in northwestern England, that serves as a main reservoir for Manchester. Length: 5 km/3.25 mi.

thirst /thurst/ n. **1.** NEED FOR LIQUID a desire or need to drink a liquid, or the feeling of dryness in the mouth and throat caused by a need for a liquid **2.** CRAVING a strong desire for sth ○ *a thirst for knowledge* ■ vi. (thirsts, thirsting, thirsted) **1.** EXPERIENCE THIRST to feel a thirst for a liquid **2.** TO DESIRE to desire sth strongly ○ *thirsted for news of home* [Old English þurst. Ultimately from an Indo-European base meaning 'to be dry', which is also the ancestor of English terrain and toast.] —**thirster** n.

thirst snake n. a small non-poisonous snake found in southeastern Asia and tropical America. It has long needle-like teeth for preying on slugs and snails. Genus: *Dipsas*.

thirsty /thúrsti/ (-ier, -iest) adj. **1.** NEEDING LIQUID feeling the need to drink a liquid ○ *Gardening always makes me thirsty.* **2.** LACKING WATER having insufficient water, especially in the form of irrigation ○ *The land was thirsty for rain.* **3.** DESIRING having a strong desire or craving ○ *thirsty for companionship* **4.** CAUSING THIRST causing the need to drink a liquid (informal) ○ *thirsty work* —**thirstily** adv. —**thirstiness** n.

thirteen /thúr teén/ n. **1.** NUMBER 13 the number 13 **2.** STH WITH VALUE OF THIRTEEN sth in a numbered series with a value of thirteen **3.** GROUP OF THIRTEEN a group of thirteen objects or people [Old English þrēotīne, from þrēo 'three' (see THREE) + -tīne 'ten']

thirteenth /thúr teénth/ n. **1.** ONE OF 13 PARTS one of thirteen equal parts of sth **2.** ORDINAL NUMBER CORRESPONDING TO 13 the ordinal number corresponding to item number thirteen in a series **3.** MUSIC MUSICAL NOTE the note an octave and a sixth above the principal note in a musical scale —**thirteenth** adj., adv.

thirteenth chord n. a complex musical chord that in addition to a seventh, also contains the interval of a thirteenth

thirtieth /thúrti əth/ n. **1.** ONE OF 30 PARTS OF STH one of thirty equal parts of sth **2.** ORDINAL NUMBER CORRESPONDING TO 30 the ordinal number assigned to item number thirty in a series —**thirtieth** adj., adv.

thirty /thúrti/ n. (plural -ties) **1.** NUMBER 30 the number 30 **2.** GROUP OF 30 a group of thirty objects or people **3.** TENNIS SCORE IN TENNIS in a game of tennis, the score awarded to a player with a score of fifteen on

winning a further point ■ **thirties** npl. **1.** NUMBERS 30 TO 39 the numbers 30 to 39, particularly as a range of temperature ○ *in the low thirties* **2.** YEARS 1930 TO 1939 the years 1930 to 1939 **3.** PERIOD FROM AGE 30 TO 39 the period of sb's life from the age of 30 to 39 [Old English þrītig. Ultimately from the Indo-European word for 'three'.]

thirty-eight n. US a handgun with a .38 calibre.

Thirty-nine Articles n. the basic teachings and beliefs of the Church of England, written in the 16th century and still the Church's doctrinal basis

thirty-second note n. US, Can MUSIC = demisemiquaver

thirty-three n. MUSIC a long-playing record (dated) [From its playing speed of 33⅓ rpm]

thirty-twomo /-toōomō/ (plural thirty-twomos) n. PRINTING **1.** PAPER SIZE a size of page that is formed when a standard printing sheet is cut or folded into 32 leaves or 64 pages **2.** BOOK WITH THIRTY-TWOMO PAGES a book made with thirty-twomo pages [Late 18thC. Pronunciation of the printer's abbreviation 32mo.]

this /thiss/ (plural these) CORE MEANING: a grammatical word used to indicate sb or sth that has already been mentioned or identified or sth that is understood by both the speaker and hearer ○ (det) *This book is brilliant.* ○ (det) *This holiday – how much is it going to cost?* ○ (pron) *Is this why you've been so happy lately?* ○ (pron) *I first encountered this while travelling abroad.*
1. det., pron. CLOSE BY indicating sb or sth present or close by, especially as distinct from sb or sth further away, referred to as 'that' ○ (det) *I much prefer this painting to that one.* ○ (pron) *What's this?* **2.** det., pron. INDICATING WORDS TO FOLLOW used to indicate a phrase or statement about to be said ○ (det) *All I can say is this – he hadn't called by the time I left.* ○ (pron) *Hey, listen to this!* **3.** pron., det. A STATED TIME used to refer to a particular time in the past or present ○ (pron) *I expected him back before this.* ○ (det) *At this particular moment she felt she'd never experience such happiness again.* **4.** det. NOT PREVIOUSLY MENTIONED used to indicate sb or sth not previously mentioned, especially when telling a story to give a sense of immediacy (informal) ○ (det) *Then this woman came running up to me, shouting at the top of her voice.* **5.** adv. TO THIS DEGREE used to emphasize the degree of a feeling or quality ○ *I was this close to walking out.* [Old English þis, þes] ◇ **this and that** miscellaneous unimportant things

Thisbe /thízbi/ n. MYTHOL ♦ Pyramus and Thisbe

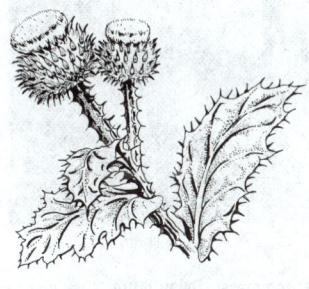
Thistle

thistle /thíss'l/ n. **1.** PRICKLY WEED a prickly composite plant with dense, usually purple, flower heads surrounded by thorny bracts. Genera: *Carduus* and *Cirsium* and *Onopordum*. **2.** SCOTTISH NATIONAL EMBLEM the representation of a thistle that is the national emblem of Scotland [Old English þistel]

Thistle n. **1.** ♦ Order of the Thistle **2.** EMBLEM OF ORDER OF THISTLE the emblem of the Order of the Thistle **3.** MEMBERSHIP OF ORDER OF THISTLE membership of the Order of the Thistle

thistle butterfly n. = painted lady [So called because its larvae live on thistles]

thistledown /thíss'l down/ n. **1.** FLUFFY SEED MASS the fluffy mass of hairs attached to the seeds of the mature flower head of a thistle **2.** LIGHT FINE SILKY SUBSTANCE anything fine and silky that resembles thistledown, e.g. a baby's hair or a delicate fabric

thistly /thíss'li/ (**-lier, -liest**) *adj.* **1.** FULL OF THISTLES full or consisting of thistles **2.** AWKWARD difficult to deal with

thither /thíthər/ *adv.* IN THAT DIRECTION to or in the direction of that place (*archaic formal*) ○ '*I will set thee on thy way to Benares, if thou goest thither, and tell thee what must be known by us*'. (Rudyard Kipling, *Kim*; 1901) ■ *adj.* MORE DISTANT farther or on the more distant side (*archaic formal*) [Old English *þider*, an alteration (under the influence of *hider* 'hither') of *þæder*, literally 'to that place']

thitherto /thíthər tóo/ *adv.* until that time (*archaic formal*) [15thC. Modelled on HITHERTO.]

thitherward /thíthərwərd/ *adv.* = thither

thixotropic /thíksə tróppik/ *adj.* becoming fluid when shaken or stirred and returning to a gel state when allowed to stand [Early 20thC. Coined from Greek *thixis* 'touch' + -TROPIC, literally 'changing at a touch'.] —**thixotropy** /thik sóttrəpi/ *n.*

tho' /tho/ *adv., conj.* though (*informal or literary*)

thole[1] /thōl/ *n.* = tholepin [Old English *þol*. Ultimately from an Indo-European base meaning 'to stick out', which is also the ancestor of English *tumour* and *tuber*.]

thole[2] /thōl/ *vt. Scotland, N England* to experience or bear sth such as pain or grief patiently or uncomplainingly [Old English *þolian*. Ultimately from an Indo-European base meaning 'to support, lift up', which is also the ancestor of English *tolerate* and *extol*.]

tholepin /thōl pin/ *n.* a small upright wooden peg in the side of a rowing boat, usually provided in pairs to support an oar and act as a pivot when the oar is used

tholos /thō loss/ (*plural* **-loi** /thō loy/) *n.* an ancient Greek circular domed building, especially a Mycenaean drystone tomb [Mid-17thC. From Greek.]

Thomas /tómməss/ *n.* in the New Testament, one of the 12 apostles of Jesus Christ. His reluctance to recognize Jesus Christ's resurrection until he had seen and touched his wounds gave rise to the phrase 'doubting Thomas' (John 14:1–7, John 20:19–29).

Thomas (of Erceldoune) /-rímər-úrsəl doon/ (1220?–97?) Scottish poet and seer. He was the reputed author of the romance *Sir Tristram* and various prophecies, among them the Battle of Bannockburn. Known as **Thomas the Rhymer**

Dylan Thomas

Thomas /tómməss/, **Dylan** (1914–53) Welsh poet. His best known work includes the poem 'Fern Hill' and the radio play *Under Milk Wood* (1954).

Thomas á Kempis /-ə kémpiss/ (1379?–1471) German monk and writer. His most famous work is the devotional treatise *The Imitation of Christ*, written from about 1415 to 1424. Born **Thomas Hemerken**

Thomism /tōmizəm/ *n.* the philosophical and theological doctrines of Thomas Aquinas, which formed the basis of medieval scholasticism [Early 18thC. Formed from the name of St. THOMAS.] —**Thomist** *n., adj.* —**Thomistic** /tō místik/ *adj.* —**Thomistical** /-místik'l/ *adj.*

Thompson /tómps'n/ the main tributary of the Fraser River in southern British Columbia, Canada. Length: 489 km/304 mi.

Thompson, Daley (*b.* 1958) British athlete. In the decathlon he was Olympic gold medallist (1980 and 1984) and world champion (1983). Real name **Francis Morgan Thompson**

Thompson, Jack (*b.* 1940) Australian actor. He is noted for his roles in television dramas and films such as *Sunday Too Far Away* (1975). Full name **John Payne Thompson**

Thompson submachine-gun *n.* a relatively lightweight submachine-gun introduced in 1915. It was intended as an infantry weapon. [Early 20thC. Named after US army officer John T. *Thompson* (1860–1940), whose company manufactured it.]

Thomson /tómssən/ river in southwestern Queensland, Australia. Length: 380 km/236 mi.

Thomson, Sir Joseph John (1856–1940) British physicist. A pioneer in nuclear physics, he discovered the electron and demonstrated the existence of stable isotopes.

Thomson, Peter (*b.* 1929) Australian golfer. He was the winner of the British Open championship (1954–56, 1958, 1965). Full name **Peter William Thomson**

Thomson effect *n.* the phenomenon of temperature differences within a conductor or semiconductor causing an electric potential gradient [Late 19thC. Named after William *Thomson* (William KELVIN), who described the phenomenon.]

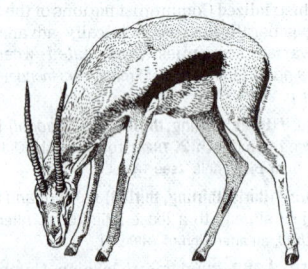

Thomson's gazelle

Thomson's gazelle *n.* a small gazelle that has a broad black stripe on its side and is found in the grasslands and dry woodlands of Africa. Latin name: *Gazella thomsoni*. [Late 19thC. Named after the Scottish explorer Joseph *Thomson* (1858–94).]

-thon *suffix.* a long session devoted to a single activity ○ *talkathon* [From MARATHON]

thong /thong/ *n.* **1.** LONG THIN PIECE OF LEATHER a thin strip of sth, especially leather, used for fastening or supporting things **2.** WHIP a whip made of plaited leather, cord, or some other material **3.** CLOTHES LIGHT SANDAL a light sandal held on by strips of material that join the sole of the sandal at either side of the foot and between the first and second toes **4.** BIKINI OR UNDERWEAR BOTTOM a narrow piece of cloth or leather that goes between the legs and is attached to a band around the hips, worn as a bikini bottom or as underwear [Old English *þwong*]

Thor /thawr/ *n.* in Norse mythology, the god of thunder and eldest son of Odin. Thursday is named after him.

thoracentesis /tháwrə sen téessiss/ (*plural* **-ses** /-téeseez/) *n.* a surgical procedure in which a needle is inserted through the chest wall in order to withdraw fluid, blood, or air [Mid-19thC. Coined from THORACO- + Greek *kentēsis* 'pricking' (from *kentein* 'to prick'; source of English *centre*).]

thoraces plural of **thorax**

thoracic /thaw rássik/ *adj.* involving or located in the chest —**thoracically** *adv.*

thoracic duct *n.* the main duct of the lymphatic system that drains lymph from smaller lymph vessels in the trunk and returns it to the bloodstream by emptying into a major vein. In human beings, it ascends in front of the spinal column and discharges into the left subclavian vein at the base of the neck.

thoraco- *prefix.* chest, thorax ○ *thoracolumbar* [From Greek *thōrak-*, the stem of *thōrax* (see THORAX)]

thoracotomy /tháwrə kóttəmi/ (*plural* **-mies**) *n.* a surgical incision made in the chest wall

thorax /tháw raks/ (*plural* **-raxes** *or* **-races** /tháw rə seez/) *n.* **1.** ANAT UPPER PART OF TORSO the part of the human body between the neck and abdomen, enclosed by the ribs and containing the heart and lungs **2.** ZOOL UPPER PART OF ANIMAL'S BODY the area corresponding to the human thorax in other vertebrates **3.** ZOOL PART BETWEEN HEAD AND ABDOMEN the middle division of the body of an insect, crustacean, or arachnid [14thC. Via Latin from Greek *thōrax* 'chest, breastplate', of unknown origin.]

Thorburn /tháwr burn/, **Archibald** (1860–1935) British artist. He painted most of the plates for *Coloured Figures of the Birds of the British Isles* (1885–97). His other works include *Observer's Book of British Birds* (1937).

Henry David Thoreau

Thoreau /thawr ố, tháwr ō/, **Henry David** (1817–62) US essayist and philosopher. He was a leading transcendentalist and libertarian. His works include 'Civil Disobedience' (1849) and *Walden* (1854), in which he describes a life lived simply and close to nature. Born **David Henry Thoreau**

thoria /tháwri ə/ *n.* CHEM = thorium dioxide [Mid-19thC. Formed from THORIUM, on the model of MAGNESIA.]

thorianite /tháwri ə nīt/ *n.* a rare black radioactive mineral that is an oxide of thorium mixed with rare-earth metals. It is used as a source of thorium and uranium. Formula: $ThO_2U_3O_8$. [Early 20thC. Coined from THORIA + -ITE.]

thorite /tháw rīt/ *n.* a rare brown, black, or yellow radioactive mineral that is a silicate of thorium. It is used as a source of thorium. Formula: $ThSiO_4$. [Mid-19thC. Coined from THOR + -ITE.]

thorium /tháwri əm/ *n.* a soft silvery-white radioactive metallic chemical element that is found in thorite, thorianite, and monazite. It is used in alloys and as a source of nuclear energy. Symbol **Th** [Mid-19thC. Coined from THOR + -IUM.] —**thoric** *adj.*

thorium dioxide *n.* a white powder that is an oxide of thorium, used in incandescent mantles, refractories, ceramics, and optical glass and as a catalyst. Formula: ThO_2.

thorium series *n.* one of the natural radioactive decay series that shows how the unstable isotope thorium-232 changes by stages into the stable isotope lead-208

thorn /thawrn/ *n.* **1.** SHARP POINT ON A PLANT STEM a sharply pointed woody growth projecting from the stem of some trees, shrubs, and woody plants **2.** PLANT WITH THORNS a tree, shrub, or woody plant that has thorns **3.** WOOD OF TREE WITH THORNS the wood of a tree or shrub with thorns **4.** RUNIC LETTER a runic letter used to represent both of the 'th' sounds, as in 'this' and 'thick', in Old English and Middle English. It also represents the voiceless sound, as in 'thick', in Old Norse and Icelandic and was formerly used as a phonetic symbol. [Old English *þorn*. From a prehistoric Germanic word that is also the ancestor of Dutch *doorn* and German *Dorn*.] —**thornless** *adj.* ◊ **be a thorn in sb's flesh or side** to be a source of constant irritation to sb

thorn apple *n.* a tall poisonous weed of the nightshade family, with large trumpet-shaped white or purple flowers, foul-smelling foliage, and spiny capsule fruits. Latin name: *Datura stramonium*. US term **jimsonweed**

thornback /tháwrn bak/ (*plural* **-backs** *or* **-back**) *n.* a ray with one to three rows of large hooked spines on its back. Latin name: *Raja clavata* and *Platy-rhinoidis triseriatis.*

thornbill /tháwrn bil/ (*plural* **-bills** *or* **-bill**) *n.* **1.** AUSTRALIAN WARBLER a small Australian bird of the warbler family that has a short sharp bill. Genus: *Acanthiza.* **2.** S AMERICAN HUMMINGBIRD a South American hummingbird with a bill that resembles a thorn. Latin name: *Ramphomicron microrhynchum.*

Dame Sybil Thorndike

Thorndike /tháwrn dīk/, **Dame Sybil** (1882–1976) British actor. A member of the Old Vic Theatre, she played the title role in George Bernard Shaw's *St Joan* more than 2,000 times after he wrote the part for her in 1924. Full name **Dame Agnes Sybil Thorndike**

Thornhill /tháwrn hil/, **Sir James** (1675–1734) British painter. His work, in the baroque style and executed chiefly for royal and noble patrons, includes decorations for the cupola of St Paul's Cathedral, London.

thorny /tháwrni/ (**-ier, -iest**) *adj.* **1.** PROBLEMATIC complicated and difficult to resolve **2.** PRICKLY WITH THORNS covered in or full of thorns —**thornily** *adv.* —**thorniness** *n.*

thorny devil *n. Aus* ZOOL = **moloch**

thoron /tháw ron/ *n.* a radioactive isotope of radon with a half-life of 55 seconds, formed by the radioactive decay of thorium [Early 20thC. Formed from THORIUM, on the model of RADON.]

thorough /thúrrə/ *adj.* **1.** EXTREMELY CAREFUL extremely careful and accurate in doing sth ○ *She's very thorough in her research methods.* **2.** DONE FULLY complete in every detail and carried out with care ○ *The doctor gave me a thorough examination.* **3.** ABSOLUTE that is so to the fullest extent or in the truest sense of the word ○ *a thorough bore* ■ *prep.* THROUGH through (*archaic*) [Old English *þuruh* 'from end to end', a variant of *þurh* (see THROUGH)] —**thoroughly** *adv.* —**thoroughness** *n.*

―――――― **WORD KEY: SYNONYMS** ――――――
See Synonyms at *careful.*

thoroughbass /thúrrə bayss/ *n.* MUSIC = **continuo** [Mid-17thC. From THOROUGH in the obsolete sense 'all the way through'.]

thorough brace *n. US* a strong leather strap running underneath a carriage from front to back, forming, with several other such straps, the carriage's support and springs [From THOROUGH in the obsolete meaning 'from end to end'] —**thorough-braced** /thúrrə braysst/ *adj.*

thoroughbred /thúrrə bred/ *n.* **1.** PUREBRED ANIMAL a purebred animal, especially a horse **2.** ARISTOCRAT SB descended from ancestors of high social status ■ *adj.* **1.** PUREBRED bred from pure stock **2.** OF AN ARISTOCRATIC FAMILY descended from ancestors of high social status [Early 18thC. From THOROUGH in the obsolete meaning 'all the way through'.]

Thoroughbred *n.* a pure breed of horse descended from English mares and Arab stallions, originally bred in Britain and most often used for racing —**Thoroughbred** *adj.*

thoroughfare /thúrrə fair/ *n.* **1.** PUBLIC ROAD a public highway that passes through a place ○ *a lorry blocking a busy thoroughfare* **2.** MEANS OF ACCESS a way or passage from one place to another **3.** RIGHT OF PASSAGE the right to go from one place to another along a certain route **4.** HEAVILY USED ROUTE a stretch of road or water, or a pathway between two places, that is

used by many people [14thC. From THOROUGH in the obsolete meaning 'from end to end' + obsolete *fare* 'way, journey'.]

thoroughgoing /thúrrə gố ing/ *adj.* **1.** THOROUGHLY DONE carried out in an extremely careful and thorough way ○ *not very thoroughgoing when it comes to housework* **2.** ABSOLUTE that is so to the fullest extent or in the truest sense of the word ○ *a thoroughgoing pragmatist* [Early 19thC. From THOROUGH in the obsolete meaning 'all the way through'.]

thoroughpaced /thúrrə páysst/ *adj.* **1.** TRAINED TO PERFORM ALL PACES thoroughly trained so as to be able to perform all paces well (*refers to horses*) **2.** THOROUGHGOING thoroughgoing (*archaic*)

thoroughpin /thúrrə pin/ *n.* inflammation and swelling above the hock joint on both sides of a horse's leg, affecting the flexor tendon and causing lameness [Late 18thC. From THOROUGH in the obsolete meaning 'all the way through'; from the appearance of the swelling, like a pin passing through the tendon.]

thorp /thawrp/, **thorpe** *n.* a small village (*archaic; often used in placenames*) [Old English *þorp* (related to Dutch *dorp* and German *Dorf*)]

those /thōz/ *pron., det.* the form of 'that' used before a plural noun or with a multiple referent ○ *Those are the ones I prefer.* ○ *Do you remember those outings to the seaside?* [Old English *þās* (see THESE)]

Thoth /thoth/, **Thot** *n.* in ancient Egyptian mythology, the god of the moon, associated with writing and wisdom. He is usually depicted as a man with the head of an ibis, or as a baboon. ♦ **Hermes Trismegistus**

thou¹ /thow/ (*plural* **thous** *or* **thou**) *n.* **1.** THOUSANDTH one thousandth of an inch. A thou is equal to 0.03 mm. **2.** THOUSAND a thousand, especially when referring to money (*informal*) [Mid-19thC. Shortening of THOUSAND.]

thou² /thow/ *pron.* **1.** YOU you (*archaic or regional; used in familiar address*) **2.** thou, Thou YOU, GOD used to address God, e.g. in prayers and hymns ■ *vt.* ADDRESS SB AS 'THOU' to address as 'thou' (*archaic or regional*) [Old English *þū*. Ultimately from an Indo-European word that is also the ancestor of Latin *tu*.]

though /thō/ *conj.* ALTHOUGH in spite of the fact that ○ *He didn't receive any special treatment, even though he is close friends with the chairman.* ○ *Though she served as president of the student union, she was attracted to journalism rather than politics.* ■ *adv.* **1.** AND YET indicating a statement that modifies a statement just made ○ *The weather has improved a lot, though it still doesn't feel like spring.* **2.** NEVERTHELESS follows a statement modifying the statement that preceded it ○ *It rained all the time. We still enjoyed ourselves, though.* [13thC. Partly from Old English *þeah* and partly Old Norse *þó.* Ultimately from an Indo-European base meaning 'that', which is also the ancestor of English *the, this,* and *thus.*] ◇ **as though** as if ○ *It seems as though every week we hear about some incredible new development.*

―――――― **WORD KEY: USAGE** ――――――
See Usage note at *although.*

thought¹ /thawt/ *n.* **1.** THINKING the activity or process of thinking ○ *deep in thought* **2.** IDEA PRODUCED BY MENTAL ACTIVITY an idea, plan, conception, or opinion produced by mental activity ○ *The thought had crossed my mind.* **3.** SET OF IDEAS the intellectual, scientific, and philosophical ideas associated with a particular place, time, or group ○ *medieval religious thought* **4.** REASONING POWER the ability to think and reason ○ *felt incapable of rational thought* **5.** PROCESS OF CONSIDERING the process of applying the mind to thinking about a particular person or subject ○ *I didn't give it another thought.* **6.** INTENTION an intention or desire to do sth ○ *I had no thought of offending anybody.* **7.** EXPECTATION an expectation or hope that sth will happen ○ *entertained no thoughts of failure* **8.** COMPASSIONATE CONSIDERATION a feeling of respect, affection, or consideration for sb or sth ○ *no thought for other people* **9.** SMALL AMOUNT a small amount on a comparative scale ○ *Could you be a thought quieter, please?* [Old English *þōht.* From a prehistoric Germanic base that is also the ancestor of English *think* and *thank.*]

thought² past participle, past tense of **think**

thought disorder *n.* an abnormality in sb's thought processes or the way they are composed or connected, e.g. delusions or an inability to concentrate or think clearly. Thought disorders are a particular feature of schizophrenia and dementia.

thoughtful /tháwtf'l/ *adj.* **1.** CONSIDERATE treating people in a kind and considerate way, especially by anticipating their wants or needs **2.** PENSIVE appearing to be deep in thought **3.** CAREFULLY THOUGHT OUT showing the application of careful thought —**thoughtfully** *adv.* —**thoughtfulness** *n.*

thoughtless /tháwtləss/ *adj.* **1.** INCONSIDERATE showing a lack of consideration for other people or for consequences **2.** DONE WITHOUT THOUGHT showing a lack of planning or forethought **3.** UNABLE TO THINK not having or using the faculty of thought —**thoughtlessly** *adv.* —**thoughtlessness** *n.*

thought police *n.* an oppressive and intrusive police force or similar group that tries to monitor and regulate people's thoughts in order to stamp out any original or potentially subversive ideas [Coined by George Orwell in his novel *Nineteen Eighty-four* (1949)]

thousand /thówz'nd/ *n.* (*plural* **-sand** *or* **-sands**) **1.** NUMBER 1,000 the number 1,000 **2.** FOURTH DIGIT FROM RIGHT the fourth digit to the left of the decimal point in the decimal number system **3.** LARGE NUMBER a very large number or amount (*informal*) ○ *must have told him a thousand times* ■ **thousands** *npl.* VERY MANY a very large but unspecified number ○ *sold thousands of copies* [Old English *þūsend.* From a prehistoric Germanic word meaning 'swollen hundred'; ultimately from an Indo-European base meaning 'to swell', which is also the ancestor of English *thigh, thumb,* and *tumour.*]

Thousand Guineas, 1000 Guineas *n.* a flat horse race for fillies run annually since 1814 at Newmarket, England (*takes a singular verb*)

Thousand Island dressing *n.* a salmon-pink salad dressing containing mayonnaise, tomato sauce, chopped gherkins, onions, and spices [Early 20thC. Origin uncertain: perhaps named after the THOUSAND ISLANDS.]

thousandth /thówz'nth/ *n.* one of a thousand equal parts of sth

thp *abbr.* thrust horsepower

Thrace /thráyss/ region in southeastern Europe, forming part of present-day Greece, Bulgaria, and Turkey. Area: 8578 sq. km/3,312 sq. mi.

Thracian /tháysh'n/ *n.* **1.** PEOPLES SB FROM THRACE a member of an ancient people who inhabited Thrace **2.** LANG ANCIENT THRACIAN LANGUAGE the language of the ancient Thracians, which belonged to the Indo-European family ■ *adj.* PEOPLES OF THRACE relating to Thrace, its ancient people or culture, or their extinct language

Thraco-Phrygian /thráykō fríjiy ən/ *n.* LANG a branch of the Indo-European family of languages of which all members are now extinct with the exception of Armenian

thraldom /thráwldəm/ *n.* = **thrall** n. 3

thrall /thrawl/ *n.* **1.** SB WHOSE LIFE IS CONTROLLED sb whose life is completely controlled by a more powerful person or a moral or intellectual force **2.** SB CONTROLLED BY STH sb who is completely controlled by a particular physical or mental need **3.** DOMINATION a condition of being controlled by a more powerful person or force (*literary*) ■ *vt.* (**thralls, thralling, thralled**) DOMINATE SB to control sb completely (*archaic*) [Old English *þræl,* from Old Norse *þræll.* Ultimately from a prehistoric Germanic word meaning 'to run'.]

thralldom *n. US* = **thraldom**

thrapple /thrápp'l/ *n. Scotland* THROAT the throat or windpipe ■ *vt.* (**-ples, -pling, -pled**) *Scotland* THROTTLE to throttle sb [14thC. Variant of *thropple,* of unknown origin.]

thrash /thrash/ *v.* (**thrashes, thrashing, thrashed**) **1.** *vt.* BEAT PERSON OR ANIMAL to beat a person or animal with a whip or stick **2.** *vt.* SPORTS DEFEAT PERSON OR TEAM DECISIVELY to defeat a person or team decisively, especially in a sporting competition ○ *The home team got thrashed in the final.* **3.** *vti.* TOSS ABOUT to toss or move the body and limbs about in an uncontrolled or restless way ○ *thrashed around unable to sleep* **4.** *vi.* **PADDLE WITH LEGS** to move the legs up and down in the water while performing a swimming stroke **5.** *vti.* = **thresh** *v.* 1 **6.** *vti.* **SAIL BOAT AGAINST TIDE OR WIND** to sail a boat so that it is forcing its way against the direction of the tide or wind ■ *n.* **1. BEATING** a blow or beating with a whip or stick **2. SOCIAL PARTY** a party or celebration (*dated informal*) **3.** MUSIC = **thrash metal** [Late 16thC. Variant of THRESH.]

WORD KEY: SYNONYMS

See Synonyms at ***defeat***.

thrash out *vt.* to discuss and develop all the possibilities of a situation in order to reach a decision about it. US term **hash out**

thrasher /thráshər/ *n.* **1.** BIRDS **BIRD WITH DOWNWARD-CURVED BILL** a long-tailed brownish North American bird that has a downward-curved bill and a speckled breast. It is related to the mockingbird. Genus: *Toxostoma*. **2.** ZOOL = **thresher** *n.* 3 **3.** AGRIC **THRESHER OF CROPS** a person or machine that threshes crops

thrashing /thráshing/ *n.* **1. PHYSICAL BEATING** a physical beating, e.g. with a whip or stick **2. SPORTING DEFEAT** a decisive defeat in a sporting competition

thrash metal *n.* a very fast, often discordant, type of heavy metal music, strongly influenced by punk

thrasonical /thrə sónnik'l/ *adj.* boastful (*literary*) [Mid-16thC. Formed from Greek *Thrasō*, name of an arrogant character in Terence's play *Eunuchus*.] —**thrasonically** *adv.*

thrawn /thrawn/ *adj. Scotland, N England* **1. PERVERSE** stubborn and uncooperative or ill-tempered **2. CROOKED** twisted or crooked (*archaic*) [15thC. From an archaic past participle of THROW.]

thread /thred/ *n.* **1. FINE TWISTED CORD** fine cord made of two or more twisted fibres, used in sewing and weaving **2. PIECE OF THREAD** a length of thread **3. VERY THIN LINE OF STH** a fine strand of solid material, trickle of liquid, or wisp of gas **4.** MECH ENG **RIDGE ON SCREW** the continuous helical ridge on a screw or pipe **5.** ZOOL **FILAMENT OF SPIDER'S WEB** one of the filaments of a spider's web **6. STH CONNECTING ELEMENTS** a continuous unifying element running through a story, argument, discussion, or series of events **7.** COMPUT **ELEMENT OF DISCUSSION ON INTERNET** one of a series of messages in an Internet discussion group (**forum**), commenting on or replying to a previous message **8. HUMAN LIFE** the course of human life, believed by the ancient Greeks to be spun, measured out, and cut by the Fates **9. VEIN OF ORE** a thin seam of ore or coal ■ **threads** *npl. US* CLOTHES **CLOTHING** clothes (*slang*) ■ *v.* (**threads, threading, threaded**) **1.** *vt.* **PASS THROUGH STH** to pass sth such as thread, photographic film, magnetic tape, or ribbon through a hole or gap in sth else **2.** *vt.* **STRING ON THREAD** to string beads or pearls on a thread **3.** *vt.* **INTERSPERSE WITH STH** to distribute sth at intervals in sth else ○ *hair threaded with grey* **4.** *vti.* **GO CAREFULLY** to move along carefully, following a winding route **5.** *vt.* MECH ENG **PRODUCE SCREW THREAD** to produce a thread on a screw or bolt, or within a material into which a bolt or screw may be inserted **6.** *vi.* COOK **FORM THREAD** to form a fine thread when dropped from a spoon (*refers to sugar syrup*) [Old English *þræd* 'twisted cord'. Ultimately from an Indo-European word meaning 'to turn, twist', which is also the ancestor of English *throw*.]

threadbare /thréd bair/ *adj.* **1. WORN AWAY TO REVEAL THREADS** so heavily used that the soft part of the fabric has been worn away to reveal the threads beneath **2. OVERUSED SO NO LONGER CONVINCING** having been used so often as to be no longer convincing ○ *the same old threadbare excuses* **3. MEAGRE** not large, varied, or substantial enough to be satisfactory ○ *eked out a threadbare existence* **4. SHABBILY DRESSED** wearing worn-out shabby clothes —**threadbareness** *n.*

threader /thréddər/ *n.* a device for threading a needle, consisting of a loop of extremely fine wire attached to a flat metal disc that is held between the thumb and forefinger. The loop is passed through the eye of the needle, the thread is passed through the loop, and the loop is withdrawn through the eye, taking the thread with it.

threadfin /thréd fin/ (*plural* **-fins** *or* **-fin**) *n.* a tropical marine fish with long rays resembling threads on the lower part of its pectoral fin and a small mouth on the underside of its head. Family: Polynemidae.

thread mark *n.* a strand of silk fibres put inside a paper bank note during manufacture to make it more difficult to counterfeit

thread snake *n.* a small nonvenomous snake resembling a worm, found in Africa, Asia, and Central and South America. It has no teeth on its upper jaw and feeds on termites and underground insects. Genus: *Leptotyphlops*.

threadworm /thréd wurm/ *n.* a long nematode worm, such as a pinworm

thready /thréddi/ (**-ier, -iest**) *adj.* **1. THREADLIKE** resembling thread **2. HAVING MANY THREADS** consisting of or containing many threads, especially loose or visible ones **3.** COOK **FORMING THREADS** thick and sticky enough to form threads when dropped from a spoon or other utensil **4. SOUNDING WEAK** sounding thin and lacking in power and tone **5.** MED **ONLY JUST PERCEPTIBLE** used to describe a weak and barely perceptible pulse —**threadiness** *n.*

threap /threep/ (**threaps, threaping, threaped**), **threep** (**threeps, threeping, threeped**) *vt. Scotland, N England* **1. SCOLD** to rebuke or criticize sb harshly **2. MAINTAIN AN ASSERTION** to state sth vehemently or persistently, especially sth that sb else has contradicted [Old English *þrēapian*, of unknown origin] —**threaper** *n.*

threat /thret/ *n.* **1. DECLARATION OF INTENT TO CAUSE HARM** the expression of a deliberate intention to cause harm or pain **2. INDICATION OF STH BAD** a sign or danger that sth undesirable is going to happen ○ *a threat of severe thunderstorms* **3. SB OR STH LIKELY TO CAUSE HARM** a person, animal, or thing likely to cause harm or pain ○ *The dog is no threat.* ■ *vt.* (**threats, threating, threated**) **THREATEN** to threaten sb or sth (*archaic*) [Old English *þrēat* 'crowd, menace'. Ultimately from an Indo-European word meaning 'to press in', which is also the ancestor of English *thrust* and *protrude*.]

threaten /thrétt'n/ (**-ens, -ening, -ened**) *v.* **1.** *vti.* **EXPRESS A THREAT TO SB** to express a deliberate intention to harm or hurt sb unless the person does what is demanded **2.** *vti.* **ENDANGER WELLBEING** to be a threat to the wellbeing, safety, or happiness of sb or sth **3.** *vti.* **SIGNIFY STH BAD HAPPENING** to signify that sth bad is going to happen, especially that bad weather is going to arrive **4.** *vt.* **SUGGEST IN A THREAT** to suggest or announce sth by means of a threat [Old English *þrēatnian*, literally 'to press in on', from *þrēat* (see THREAT)] —**threatener** *n.*

threatened /thrétt'nd/ *adj.* used to describe an organism or species that is in danger of becoming extinct

Thredbo /thrédbō/ ski resort in the Australian Alps, New South Wales, Australia. Population: 2,100 (1996).

three /three/ *n.* **1.** MATH **NUMBER 3** the number 3 **2. STH WITH VALUE OF 3** sth in a numbered series, e.g. a playing card, with a value of 3 ○ *the three of clubs* ○ *to throw a three* **3. GROUP OF THREE** a group of three objects or people [Old English *þrēotīne*. Ultimately from the Indo-European word for 'three', which is also the ancestor of English *triple, triad, troika,* and *testament*.]

three-card monte *n.* a game in which three cards are dealt face up and then turned face down and moved round. The player must then guess the new position of a particular card.

three-card trick *n.* a game in which three cards are dealt face up, and then turned face down and moved round. The player must then guess which is the queen.

three-colour *adj.* using, produced by, or relating to a colour printing process in which the print is produced by superimposing separate plates for the colours yellow, magenta, and cyan

three-D, **3-D** *n.* **THREE DIMENSIONS** a three-dimensional effect ■ *adj.* = **three-dimensional** *adj.* 1, **three-dimensional** *adj.* 2 (*informal*)

three-day event *n.* a competition for horses and riders consisting of dressage, cross-country, and showjumping events, held over a three-day period

three-day measles *n.* rubella (*informal*)

three-decker *n.* **1. STH WITH THREE LEVELS** a vehicle, building, or other construction with three levels or floors **2. SHIP WITH THREE DECKS** a warship with three decks set with guns, or any ship with three decks **3. SANDWICH WITH THREE SLICES OF BREAD** a sandwich consisting of two layers of filling between three slices of bread

three-dimensional *adj.* **1. WITH THREE DIMENSIONS** possessing or appearing to possess the dimensions of height, width, and depth **2. APPEARING TO HAVE DEPTH** creating the illusion of depth behind a flat surface **3. BELIEVABLE** represented with sufficient complexity to be convincing

threefold /threé fōld/ *adj.* **1. CONSISTING OF THREE** made up of three parts or elements **2. THREE TIMES AS MANY OR MUCH** being or having three times as many or as much ■ *adv.* **BY THREE TIMES** by three times as many or as much

Three Kings Islands group of uninhabited islands 50 km/31 mi. northwest of the North Island, New Zealand. The islands are a wildlife refuge. Area: 8 sq. km/3 sq. mi.

three-legged race *n.* a race in which pairs of runners compete with their adjacent legs bound together

three-line whip *n.* a notice, underlined three times for emphasis, issued to members of a political party requiring them to attend and vote in a specified way in a specified vote in parliament

three-mile limit *n.* the outer limit of a country's territorial waters, three nautical miles from shore

threep *vt.* = **threap**

threepence /threppənss, thrúp-/, **thruppence** /thrúppənss, thróop-/ *n.* a sum of three pennies, especially old pence (*dated; takes a singular verb*) ○ *a loaf costing threepence*

threepenny /thrépni, thrúp-/, **thruppenny** /thrúpni, thróop-/ *adj.* (*dated*) **1. WORTH THREE PENNIES** worth or costing three pennies, especially old pence **2. OF LITTLE VALUE** worth or costing very little

threepenny bit, **thruppenny bit** *n.* a twelve-sided nickel-brass coin worth three old pennies, used in the UK until 1971

three-phase *adj.* **1. IN THREE PHASES** consisting of three separate phases **2.** ELEC **USING THREE ALTERNATING VOLTAGES** used to describe an electrical system or circuit of three alternating voltages that have the same frequency but are separated by one third of a cycle

three-piece *adj.* **IN THREE MATCHING PIECES** consisting of three matching or coordinated pieces ■ *n.* **SUIT OF THREE MATCHING GARMENTS** a suit consisting of matching trousers or skirt, waistcoat or blouse, and jacket

three-piece suite *n.* a set of living-room furniture consisting of a sofa with two matching armchairs

three-ply *adj.* **1. WITH THREE LAYERS** consisting of three layers or laminations **2. WITH THREE STRANDS** made up of three twisted strands ■ *n.* **THREE-PLY KNITTING YARN** knitting yarn made up of three twisted strands

three-point landing *n.* an aircraft landing in which the two main wheels of the landing gear and the nose or tail wheel touch the ground at the same time

three-point turn *n.* a turn to reverse the direction of travel of a motor vehicle that involves two forward movements and one reverse movement. The turn must be successfully completed without touching the kerb as part of the UK driving test.

three-quarter *adj.* **1. BEING THREE QUARTERS OF STH** being three quarters of sth measurable or countable, e.g. length, an area, or a time interval **2. BEING THREE QUARTERS OF FULL LENGTH** being three quarters of the full or usual length **3.** ARTS **WITH FACE SLIGHTLY TURNED** showing the subject's face turned slightly to one side (*refers to a portrait*) ■ *n.* RUGBY **RUGBY PLAYER** a rugby player in one of the four positions between the forwards and the full back, or this position

three-quarter binding *n.* a type of binding in which the spine and most of the sides of a book are covered in the same material

three-ring circus *n. US* **1. CIRCUS WITH THREE RINGS** a circus in which performances take place sim-

three ... ultaneously in three separate rings **2. HECTIC SITUATION** a situation full of activity and confusion (*informal*)

three Rs /-aárz/, **3 Rs** *npl.* the skills of reading, writing, and arithmetic, considered as the basis of primary education [Presumed to have originated with a toast proposed by Sir William Curtis (1752–1829), illiterate Lord Mayor of London]

threescore /thrée skáwr/ *adj.*, *n.* sixty (*archaic*)
○ *threescore years and ten*

threesome /thréessəm/ *n.* **1.** **GROUP OF THREE** a group of three people **2. ACTIVITY FOR THREE** a game or activity for three people **3. SEXUAL EXPERIENCE** a sexual experience involving three people **4. TYPE OF GOLF GAME** a golf game involving three players, one playing one ball and the other two taking alternate shots to ... ball

three-spine stickleback *n.* ... stickleback ... ... fresh and salt ... spines and is found ... a small stickleback ... hemisphere. Latin name: water that has ... throughout ... shaped like an equilateral triangle *Gasterost* ... in cross section

three-s...kes and you're out *n.* a law that requires ...andatory life sentences for criminals convicted three times for major capital offences

three-toed sloth *n.* a slow tree-dwelling mammal of the sloth family that has three long-clawed toes on each forefoot. Genus: *Bradypus*.

three-way *adj.* **1. WITH THREE PARTICIPANTS** involving three participating people or things **2. WITH THREE ROUTES** providing routes to three different places from one point ○ *a three-way junction*

three-wheeler *n.* a vehicle with three wheels such as a small car or a tricycle

Three Wise Men *n.* = Magi

thremmatology /thrémmə tólləji/ *n.* the science of breeding domesticated plants and animals [Late 19thC. Coined from the Greek stem *thremmat-* 'nursling' + -LOGY.]

threnody /thrénnədi/ (*plural* -dies), **threnode** /thrénnod/ *n.* a song, poem, or speech of lament for the dead [Mid-17thC. From Greek *thrēnōidia*, from *thrēnos* 'lament' + *ōidē* 'song' (see ODE).] —**threnodial** /thri nódi əl/ *adj.* —**threnodic** /-nóddik/ *adj.* —**threnodist** /thrénnədist/ *n.*

$$H_3C-CH_2-CH-C-OH$$
(with O double-bonded above C and NH_2 below CH)

Threonine

threonine /thrée ə nīn/ *n.* a colourless crystalline essential amino acid obtained from the hydrolysis of some proteins. Formula: $C_4H_9NO_3$. [Mid-20thC. Coined from *threose*, a kind of sugar + -INE.]

thresh /thresh/ *v.* (**threshes, threshing, threshed**) **1.** *vti.* **AGRIC SEPARATE SEEDS FROM PLANT** to use a machine, flail, or other implement to separate the seeds of a harvested plant from the straw and chaff, husks, or other residue **2.** *vt.* **BEAT** to beat a person, animal, or object **3.** *vi.* **FLAIL ABOUT** move the body and limbs about in an uncontrolled or restless way **4.** *vt.* **EXAMINE EXHAUSTIVELY** to examine sth such as an issue or a proposal, exhaustively ■ *n.* **AGRIC THRESHING** an act of threshing a harvested crop [Old English *perscan*. Ultimately from an Indo-European base meaning 'to rub', which is also the ancestor of English *attrition* and *threshold*.]

thresher /thréshər/ *n.* **1. SB WHO THRESHES PLANTS** sb who threshes a harvested crop with a machine, flail, or other implement **2.** = **threshing machine 3. thresher, thresher shark SHARK WITH LONG TAIL** a large, widely distributed shark that has a curved elongated upper lobe on the tail with which it agitates or threshes the water. Family: Alopiidae.

Threshing machine

threshing machine *n.* a static power-driven agricultural machine formerly widely used to beat or rub harvested plants in order to separate the seeds from the rest of the plant

threshold /thrésh hōld, -old/ *n.* **1. WOOD OR STONE BELOW DOOR** a piece of stone or hardwood that forms the bottom of a doorway **2. DOORWAY** a doorway or entrance **3. STARTING POINT** the point where a new era or experience begins ○ *on the threshold of maturity* **4. LEVEL AT WHICH AN EFFECT STARTS** the level at which a psychological or physiological effect or state starts ○ *the threshold of consciousness* [Old English *perscold*. Ultimately from a prehistoric Germanic word whose first element (related to English *thresh*) meant 'tread'.]

threshold agreement *n.* an agreement that raises wages in order to compensate for rises in the cost of living that reach a specified level

threw past tense of **throw**

thrice /thrīss/ *adv.* **1. THREE TIMES** three times over (*archaic or literary*) **2. THREEFOLD** by three times as many or as much (*archaic or literary*) **3. GREATLY** to a high degree (*archaic*) [12thC. Alteration of *thries*, from obsolete *thrie* 'three times', from Old English *priga*, from *prī* (see THREE).]

thrift /thrift/ *n.* **1. PRUDENT USE OF MONEY AND GOODS** the sensible and cautious management of money and goods in order to waste as little as possible and obtain maximum value **2. PLANT WITH PINK OR WHITE FLOWERS** a perennial evergreen plant of the plumbago family with pointed leaves and dense round pink or white flower heads. Genus: *Armeria*. **3.** ZOOL **STRONG GROWTH** vigorous and healthy growth of living things such as plants **4.** **PROSPERITY** the enjoyment of wealth and a good standard of living (*archaic*) [13thC. From Old Norse *prift* 'prosperity', from *prífask* (see THRIVE).]

thriftless /thríftləss/ *adj.* showing carelessness and wastefulness in the handling of money and other resources —**thriftlessly** *adv.* —**thriftlessness** *n.*

thrift shop *n.* US a shop that sells used goods, particularly clothing, usually for charity

thrifty /thrífti/ (**-ier, -iest**) *adj.* **1. CAREFUL WITH MONEY AND RESOURCES** managing money and resources in a cautious and sensible way so as to waste as little as possible **2. PROSPEROUS** prosperous and thriving (*archaic*) —**thriftily** *adv.* —**thriftiness** *n.*

thrill /thril/ *vti.* (**thrills, thrilling, thrilled**) **1. BE OR MAKE SB VERY EXCITED** to feel or make sb experience intense excitement ○ *The children were thrilled by the amusement park.* **2. BE PLEASURABLE** to feel or make sb feel great pleasure ○ *It thrilled me to see my old friends.* **3. VIBRATE OR CAUSE TO VIBRATE** to vibrate or make sth or sb quiver or vibrate ■ *n.* **1. CAUSE OF GREAT EXCITEMENT** a source or cause of great excitement, and often pleasure **2. FEELING OF EXCITEMENT** a feeling of great excitement, which may be experienced as a quivering or trembling sensation **3. TREMOR ASSOCIATED WITH HEART-VALVE DEFECTS** a slight vibration of the chest wall often associated with some types of heart-valve defect [Old English *pyrlian* 'to go through', from *pyrel* 'hole' (source of English *nostril*)]

thriller /thríllər/ *n.* **1. STH WITH EXCITING PLOT** a book, play, or film that has an exciting plot involving crime,

mystery, or espionage **2. PROVIDER OF THRILLS** sb or sth that thrills people

thrilling /thrílling/ *adj.* **1. VERY EXCITING** causing intense excitement **2. VIBRATING** characterized by trembling or vibrating —**thrillingly** *adv.*

thrips /thrips/ (*plural* **thrips**) *n.* a tiny sucking insect with four long thin wings fringed with hairs. It feeds on the sap of plants. Order: Thysanoptera. [Late 18thC. Via Latin from Greek, 'woodworm', of unknown origin.]

thrive /thrīv/ (**thrives, thriving, thrived** or **throve** /thrōv/, **thrived** or **thriven** /thrívv'n/) *vi.* **1. GROW WELL** to grow vigorously and healthily **2. DO WELL** to be successful and often profitable [13thC. From Old Norse *prífask*, literally 'to grasp for oneself', from *prífa* 'to seize', of unknown origin.] —**thriver** *n.*

thrive on *vt.* to enjoy and be stimulated by sth generally considered difficult or undesirable

thro' /throo/, **thro** *prep.*, *adv.* through (*informal or literary*) [15thC. From an earlier form of THROUGH.]

throat /thrōt/ *n.* **1. ANAT DIGESTIVE AND BREATHING PASSAGE** the part of the airway and digestive tract between the mouth and both the oesophagus and the windpipe **2. ANAT FRONT OF NECK** the front part of the neck of an animal or human being **3. NARROW PART** a narrow part or passage that resembles a human's or animal's throat in shape or function **4. BOT OPENING OF TUBULAR ORGAN OF FLOWER** the opening of a tubular organ of a flower, e.g. of a corolla **5. SORE THROAT** a throat infection (*informal*) [Old English *prote* (source also of English *throttle*)] ◇ **jump down sb's throat** to speak angrily and impatiently to sb ◇ **ram** or **force sth down sb's throat** to make repeated and emphatic attempts to get sb to listen to or accept a view or belief ◇ **stick in your throat** to be extremely difficult to accept

throatlash /thrōt lash/, **throatlatch** /-lach/ *n.* the strap that passes under a horse's jaw to hold its bridle in place

throat microphone, **throat mike** *informal n.* a microphone that is placed in contact with the throat to pick up the vibrations produced by speech

throaty /thrōti/ (**-ier, -iest**) *adj.* **1. HUSKY-SOUNDING** sounding deep and husky **2. DEEP OR ROUGH IN TONE** deep or rough in tone, as though having been produced in the throat —**throatily** *adv.* —**throatiness** *n.*

throb /throb/ *vi.* (**throbs, throbbing, throbbed**) **1. BEAT RAPIDLY AND FORCEFULLY** to beat or pulsate in a rapid forceful way ○ *My head is throbbing.* **2. BEAT REGULARLY** to have a regular rhythmical beat ■ *n.* **1. SINGLE BEAT** a single beat or pulsation **2. REGULAR BEAT** a regular beat or pulsation ○ *a heart throb* [14thC. Origin uncertain: probably an imitation of pulsating.] —**throbbingly** *adv.*

throe /thrō/ *n.* **PANG** a spasm of pain ■ **throes** *npl.* **1. EFFECTS OF PANGS** the effects of severe physical pain **2. EFFECTS OF UPHEAVAL** the effects of an upheaval or struggle [12thC. Origin uncertain: perhaps an alteration of Old English *prawu*, from *prēah* 'pain', of unknown origin.] ◇ **in the throes of sth** in the process of doing sth, usually sth difficult or unpleasant

thromb- *prefix.* = **thrombo-** (*used before vowels*)

thrombi plural of **thrombus**

thrombin /thrómbin/ *n.* an enzyme in blood that causes clotting by catalysing the conversion of fibrinogen to fibrin [Late 19thC. Coined from THROMBO- + -IN.]

thrombo- *prefix.* blood clot ○ *thromboplastic* [From Greek *thrombos* 'clot', of unknown origin]

thrombocyte /thrómbō sīt/ *n.* = **platelet** —**thrombocytic** /thrómbō sittik/ *adj.*

thrombocytopenia /thrómbō sītō peéni ə/ *n.* the state of having fewer than the normal number of blood platelets per unit volume of blood, often associated with haemorrhaging [Early 20thC. Coined from THROMBOCYTE + Greek *penia* 'poverty'.] —**thrombocytopenic** *adj.*

thromboembolism /thrómbō émbəlizəm/ *n.* the blockage of a blood vessel by a blood clot (**thrombus**) that has broken away from its site of origin —**thromboembolic** /-em bóllik/ *adj.* —**thromboembolitic** /thrómbō émbə líttik/ *adj.*

thrombokinase /-kī́ nay, thrómbokī́nayss/ *n.* = **thromboplastin**

thrombolysis /throm bólləssiss/ *n.* the breaking down of a blood clot by infusion of a specific enzyme into the blood —**thrombolytic** /thrómbō líttik/ *adj.*

thrombophlebitis /thrómbō fli bítiss/ *n.* inflammation of a vein with the formation of a blood clot

thromboplastin /thrómbō plástin/ *n.* an enzyme found in blood platelets that converts prothrombin to thrombin during the process of blood clotting

thrombosis /throm bṓssiss/ (*plural* **-ses**) *n.* the formation or presence of one or more blood clots that may partially or completely block an artery, e.g. flowing to the heart or brain, or a vein [Early 18thC. Via modern Latin from, ultimately, Greek *thrombos* 'clot'.] —**thrombotic** /throm bóttik/ *adj.*

thromboxane /throm bók sayn/ *n.* a substance that is formed in platelets and that causes blood clotting and constriction of blood vessels

thrombus /thrómbəss/ (*plural* **-bi** /thróm bī/) *n.* a blood clot that forms in a blood vessel and remains at the site of formation. ◊ **embolism** [Late 17thC. Via modern Latin from Greek *thrombos* 'clot'.]

throne /thrōn/ *n.* **1.** CHAIR OF MONARCH OR BISHOP an ornate chair, often raised on a platform and covered by a canopy, occupied by a monarch or bishop on ceremonial occasions **2.** POWER OF ROYAL PERSON the power, rank, and privileges of a monarch **3.** TOILET the part of a lavatory on which people sit (*informal humorous*) ■ **Thrones, thrones** *npl.* CHR ORDER OF ANGELS the third group of angels, ranking after the Seraphim and Cherubim, in the first circle of the traditional Christian hierarchy (*literary*) ■ *vti.* (**thrones, throning, throned**) PUT SB ON THRONE to place sb or be placed on a throne [12thC. Via Old French *trone* from, ultimately, Greek *thronos*. Ultimately from an Indo-European word meaning 'to support', which is also the ancestor of English *firm*.]

throng /throng/ *n.* CROWD a large crowd of people or objects (*literary*) ■ *v.* (**throngs, thronging, thronged**) **1.** *vt.* CROWD INTO PLACE to crowd into or fill a place **2.** *vi.* MOVE IN CROWD to move or gather in a throng **3.** *vt.* CROWD AROUND SB to surround and push against sb [Old English *geprang*. Ultimately from a prehistoric Germanic word meaning 'to press, crowd'.]

throstle /thróss'l/ *n.* **1.** SONG THRUSH a thrush, especially a song thrush (*literary*) **2.** OLD SPINNING MACHINE a machine formerly used for the continuous spinning of cotton or wool fibres [Old English *prostle*. Ultimately from an Indo-European word that is also the ancestor of English *thrush*, *ostrich*, and *sturdy*.]

throttle /thrótt'l/ *n.* **1.** MECH ENG VALVE CONTROLLING FLUID FLOW a valve used to control the flow of a fluid, especially the amount of fuel and air entering the cylinders of an internal-combustion engine **2.** MECH ENG CONTROL FOR THROTTLE a pedal or lever for controlling a throttle valve **3.** THROAT a throat, either when regarded as part of the neck or as a digestive or breathing passage (*regional*) ■ *vt.* (**-tles, -tling, -tled**) **1.** MECH ENG REGULATE FUEL FLOW USING THROTTLE to regulate the amount of fuel entering an engine using a throttle **2.** MECH ENG REGULATE ENGINE SPEED to regulate the speed of an engine by using a throttle **3.** KILL PERSON OR ANIMAL BY CHOKING to kill or injure a person or animal by squeezing the throat **4.** SILENCE OR SUPPRESS SB OR STH to prevent sb or sth from expressing an opinion freely or from engaging in an activity [14thC. Formed from THROAT.] —**throttler** *n.*

through /throo/ CORE MEANING: a grammatical word used to indicate movement from one side or end of sth to or past the other side or end

1. *prep., adv.* TRAVELLING ACROSS travelling across or to various places in a town, country, or area ○ *He spent the summer travelling through Europe.* ○ *We're not stopping long; we're just passing through.* **2.** *prep., adv.* AMONG in the midst of, or having things or people all around or on either side of ○ *She wandered through the crowds milling around outside the cathedral.* ○ *Massage the conditioner through to the ends of the hair.* **3.** *prep., adv.* PAST A BARRIER past the limitations or difficulties of sth such as a barrier or a problem ○ *the problems involved in wading through acres of bureaucracy* ○ *The road has been narrowed to prevent larger vehicles getting through.* **4.** *prep., adv.* FROM BEGINNING TO END from the beginning until the end or conclusion of ○ *Martin and Johanson's works will be on view through June.* ○ *I can't come I'm afraid; I'm working through.* **5.** *adv., prep.* TO CONCLUSION to a successful conclusion ○ *We've been trying to get through all morning but the lines are busy.* ○ *The bill will never get through the House of Lords.* **6.** *prep.* VIA by way or means of ○ *How the marketing is done, through a branch or telemarketing or a future service, is up to each bank.* **7.** *prep.* OVER THE EXTENT OF happening or existing over the entire extent of or affecting all of ○ *A flu of epidemic proportions swept through the town.* **8.** *prep.* BECAUSE OF as a result of ○ *Through his mishandling of our affairs, we'll be lucky to be in credit at all this year.* **9.** *adv.* THOROUGHLY completely and in every part **10.** *prep. US* UP TO up to and including that time ○ *Museum hours are 2–4:30 p.m. Tuesdays through Fridays.* **11.** *adj.* GOING DIRECTLY going directly without stopping or requiring a change ○ *The through train leaves on the hour.* [Old English *þurh*. Ultimately from an Indo-European base meaning 'to pass through', which is also the ancestor of English *thrill*, *trans-*, and *nectar*.] ◇ **be through with sb** to want to have nothing else to do with sb (*informal*) ◇ **be through with sth** to have finished with sth (*informal*) ◇ **through and through** completely

through-composed *adj.* used to describe a song with different music for each verse, especially without pauses between the verses, or an opera that is not clearly divided into arias and recitatives

throughly /throoli/ *adv.* thoroughly (*archaic*)

through-other *adj., adv. Scotland, Ireland* IN CONFUSION in a state of confusion or disorder (*informal; not hyphenated when used after a verb*) ■ *adj. Scotland, Ireland* WILD-LOOKING in a dishevelled, disorderly, or agitated state (*informal*)

throughout /throo ówt/ *prep., adv.* **1.** THROUGH THE WHOLE OF through or during the whole of ○ *Societies throughout history believed they had reached the frontiers of human accomplishment.* ○ *Throughout, they maintained their dignity.* **2.** IN ALL PARTS OF happening or existing in all parts of ○ *The group is seeking out experts of any age throughout the area.* ○ *The house is carpeted throughout.*

throughput /throo poot/ *n.* the amount of sth such as data or raw material that is processed over a given period [Modelled on INPUT and OUTPUT]

throughway /throo way/, **thruway** *n. US* = **expressway**

throve past tense of **thrive**

throw /thrō/ *v.* (**throws, throwing, threw** /throo/, **thrown** /thrōn/) **1.** PROPEL STH FROM THE HAND to make sth move relatively quickly from the hand and through the air **2.** DROP STH CARELESSLY to put or drop sth somewhere without paying proper attention to where it is left ○ *throws magazines all over the place* **3.** FORCE SB OR STH SOMEWHERE to move sb or sth forcefully or suddenly into a particular position or in a particular direction **4.** PUT SB OR STH IN DIFFERENT CIRCUMSTANCES to bring sb or sth suddenly or unexpectedly into a particular state, especially an undesirable one ○ *thrown out of a job* **5.** HURL SB TO THE GROUND to make a movement that causes sb, e.g. an opponent in wrestling or judo or a horserider, to fall to the ground **6.** PROJECT LIGHT to send out light to illuminate a particular place, or create a shadow by blocking light **7.** CAST DOUBT OR SUSPICION to cause doubt or suspicion in people's minds by saying or doing sth **8.** DIRECT THE EYES to direct a look or glance quickly or suddenly in a particular direction ○ *She threw me a warning look.* **9.** DISCONCERT SB to take sb by surprise to the extent that he or she does not know how to react (*informal*) ○ *His unexpected arrival threw me.* **10.** MOVE AN OPERATING SWITCH OR LEVER to move sth, usually a switch or lever, to make a machine or system operate or to connect up a system **11.** HAVE AN EXTREME REACTION to be affected by a sudden outburst of strong emotion such as anger or ill-temper ○ *throw a tantrum* **12.** SEND STH ACROSS to make sth that extends from one point to another, especially hastily ○ *The enemy threw a bridge across the moat.* **13.** DELIVER A PUNCH to deliver a punch or blow with a movement of the arm **14.** ARTS MAKE AN OBJECT ON POTTER'S WHEEL to produce a ceramic object by turning clay on a potter's wheel **15.** TURN MATERIAL ON LATHE to turn wood or metal on a lathe **16.** HOST A PARTY to ... and be the host at a party **17.** LOSE STH INTENTIONALLY to lose a fight, race, or contest deliberately, e.g. by not trying or by committing a foul **18.** MAKE MATERIAL INTO YARN to make silk or filaments into thread by twisting or spinning **19.** PROJECT VOICE project a vocal sound so that it seems to be coming from elsewhere **20.** ROLL DICE to tip or roll dice onto a flat surface to obtain a score, or score a particular number in this way **21.** GIVE BIRTH TO YOUNG to give birth to young (refers especially to cows) **22.** *Malaysia, Singapore* THROW AWAY to throw sth away ○ *Once you get your new card you can throw the old one.* ■ *n.* **1.** ACT OF THROWING an act of throwing sth, e.g. a ball or missile, or ... in a game **2.** DISTANCE THROWN the distance that an ... own or can be thrown **3.** WAY OF THROWING opponent ... thrown, or a way of throwing an ... score obtained ... in a game **5.** EA... wrestling or judo **4.** SCORE THROWN the ... throwing sth, e.g. dice or darts, or attempt (*informal*) ○ *I didn't buy any – ... pounds a throw.* **6.** HOUSEHOLD COVER FOR FURNITURE ... cover or rug that covers and protects furniture ... OF MACHINE PART the maximum ... direction of a machine part driven ... or eccentric **8.** PHYS DEFLECTION OF MEASURING ... the distance moved by the tip of the needle ... a single ... measuring instrument **9.** GEOL VERTICAL DISPLACEMENT ALONG GEOLOGICAL FAULT the vertical displacement up or down produced by movement along a geological fault [Old English *þrāwan* 'to twist, hurl'. Ultimately from an Indo-European base meaning 'to twist', which is also the ancestor of English *thread*.] —**thrower** *n.* ◇ **throw yourself into sth** to start doing sth with great energy and commitment

WORD KEY: SYNONYMS

throw, *chuck*, *fling*, *heave*, *hurl*, *toss*, *cast*

CORE MEANING: to send sth through the air

throw to cause sth to go through the air using a physical movement; **chuck** to throw sth with force and often in a reckless or aimless way; **fling** an informal word that means to throw sth in a casual or careless way; **heave** to throw sth with effort, for example because it is large or heavy; **hurl** to throw sth with great force; **toss** to throw sth small or light in a casual or careless way; **cast** a literary word that means to throw sth to a particular place or into a particular thing. It is also used with the meaning to throw a fishing line or net.

throw about *vt.* to spend money in an extravagant, ostentatious way

throw away *vt.* **1.** DISCARD STH to get rid of sth no longer wanted **2.** WASTE STH to fail to take advantage of an opportunity to do sth **3.** SAY STH IN OFFHAND MANNER to say a line in a play in a way that makes it seem unimportant, even though it may be crucial to the plot

throw in *vt.* **1.** ADD STH TO DISCUSSION to contribute a comment to a conversation or discussion **2.** ADD STH AS EXTRA to add sth as an extra, especially another item at no extra cost when selling sth **3.** RETURN BALL INTO PLAY BY HAND to return a football to the pitch by means of an overhead throw after it has gone out of play ◇ **throw in the towel, throw in the sponge** to admit or accept defeat (*informal*) ◇ **throw in your hand 1.** to admit defeat in a card game by laying your cards down **2.** to admit or accept defeat

throw off *v.* **1.** *vt.* FREE YOURSELF FROM STH to get rid of sth troublesome or oppressive **2.** *vt.* TAKE CLOTHES OFF HASTILY to remove an item of clothing in a hurried or careless way **3.** *vt.* GIVE OFF STH to emit a substance into the air **4.** *vt.* ESCAPE FROM SB to elude a pursuer **5.** *vt.* SAY STH IN OFFHAND WAY to say or write sth in a casual manner **6.** *vt.* MAKE SB FLUSTERED to confuse or unsettle sb by doing sth unexpected **7.** *vi. ANZ* BE CRITICAL OF SB to make harsh or negative judgments about sb (*informal*)

throw on *vt.* to put an item of clothing on in a hurried or careless way

throw out *vt.* **1.** DISCARD STH to get rid of sth no longer wanted, especially sth that has been kept for a while **2.** EJECT SB to eject sb forcibly from a place **3.** DISMISS SB to expel sb from membership of an organization **4.** SUGGEST STH to make a suggestion, proposal, or hint, especially in an informal way **5.** REJECT BILL to reject a bill in Parliament **6.** REJECT LAWSUIT to reject a lawsuit so that the defendant does not have to stand trial **7.** DISCONCERT SB to confuse or unsettle sb by doing sth unexpected **8.** BUILD A PROJECTING CONSTRUCTION to build sth in such a way that it sticks out **9.** GIVE OFF STH to emit a substance into the air **10.** CRICKET PUT CRICKET PLAYER OUT in cricket, to cause a batsman to be run out by throwing the ball and hitting the wicket **11.** BASEBALL PUT BASEBALL PLAYER OUT in baseball, to throw the ball to a teammate who puts the runner out

throw over *vt.* to end a romantic or sexual relationship with sb (*informal*)

throw together *vt.* (*informal*) **1.** MAKE STH HASTILY to make sth in a hurry or carelessly **2.** BRING PEOPLE INTO CONTACT to cause people to meet and become acquainted with each other in a casual or unplanned way

throw up *v.* **1.** *vt.* ABANDON STH to give sth up, especially sth important or valuable (*informal*) **2.** *vt.* BUILD STH HASTILY to erect a building or structure quickly **3.** *vt.* BRING STH TO NOTICE to produce or reveal sb or sth, especially unexpectedly or indirectly **4.** *vti.* VOMIT to vomit the contents of the stomach (*informal*)

throwaway /thrṓ ə way/ *adj.* **1.** DISPOSABLE designed to be thrown away after use **2.** WASTEFUL tending to discard things too readily ○ *a throwaway society* **3.** OFFHAND said or written in an apparently offhand manner ■ *n.* STH TO BE DISCARDED an object designed to be thrown away after use

throwback /thrṓ bak/ *n.* **1.** ORGANISM REPRESENTING REVERSION TO EARLIER TYPE an organism with the characteristics of an earlier type **2.** REVERSION TO EARLIER TYPE reversion to an earlier ancestral type **3.** ANIMAL OR PERSON RESEMBLING ANCESTOR an animal or person bearing a striking resemblance to an ancestor **4.** STH BELONGING TO THE PAST sth contemporary that seems to belong to the past

throw-in *n.* **1.** SOCCER RETURN OF FOOTBALL TO PLAY an act of returning a football to play from the sideline by propelling it from behind the head with both hands **2.** BASEBALL, CRICKET RETURN OF BALL FROM OUTFIELD an act of returning a baseball or cricket ball after it has been hit to the outfield **3.** BASKETBALL RETURN OF BASKETBALL TO PLAY an act of returning a basketball to play by passing it onto the court

throwing stick *n.* **1.** DEVICE FOR THROWING A SPEAR a grooved rod used for throwing a spear with greater leverage **2.** STICK USED AS HUNTING WEAPON a stick, often with a handgrip, used by hunters in preliterate societies as a weapon to hurl at birds or small game

thrown past participle of **throw**

throw pillow *n. US, Can* = **scatter cushion**

throw rug *n. US, Can* = **scatter rug**

throwster /thrṓstər/ *n.* sb who twists filaments into thread

throw weight *n.* the total weight of a missile's payload, including the warhead and guidance system but not the rocket

thru /throo/ *prep., adv., adj. US* through (*informal*)

thrum[1] /thrum/ *v.* (**thrums, thrumming, thrummed**) **1.** *vti.* STRUM to strum on a stringed instrument **2.** *vi.* TAP STEADILY to drum on sth, especially with the fingers **3.** *vti.* SAY OR SPEAK MONOTONOUSLY to say sth or talk monotonously ■ *n.* MONOTONOUS BEAT a low monotonous beating sound [Late 16thC. An imitation of the sound.] —**thrummer** *n.*

thrum[2] /thrum/ *n.* **1.** THREAD END LEFT ON LOOM an unwoven end or row of ends from warp threads that are left on a loom after the web has been cut off **2.** FRINGE a short fringe or thread end ■ **thrums** *npl.* YARN PIECES ADDED TO CANVAS short pieces of yarn inserted in canvas in order to create a rough surface and prevent chafing or leaks ■ *vt.* (**thrums, thrumming, thrummed**) **1.** ADD FRINGES TO STH to put fringes on sth **2.** INSERT YARN PIECES IN CANVAS to insert pieces of yarn in canvas in order to create a rough surface and prevent chafing or leaks [Old English]

thruppence *npl.* = **threepence**

thruppenny *adj.* = **threepenny**

Thrush

thrush[1] /thrush/ (*plural* **thrushes** *or* **thrush**) *n.* **1.** SLENDER-BILLED SONGBIRD a small to medium-sized songbird with a slender bill and often melodious song. The song thrush, mistle thrush, or blackbird are thrushes. Family: Turdidae. **2.** BIRD RESEMBLING TRUE THRUSH a bird that resembles a thrush, e.g. the North American water thrush [Old English *þrysce*]

thrush[2] /thrush/ *n.* **1.** FUNGAL DISEASE OF MOUTH a fungal infection of the mouth characterized by white patches **2.** FUNGAL INFECTION OF VAGINA a fungal infection of the vagina characterized by a white discharge and itching **3.** DISEASE OF HORSE'S HOOF infection of the fleshy part of a horse's foot (**frog**), causing softening of the horn and a foul-smelling discharge [Mid-17thC. Origin uncertain.]

thrust /thrust/ *v.* (**thrusts, thrusting, thrust**) **1.** *vt.* PUSH SB OR STH FORCEFULLY to push sb or sth with great force **2.** *vti.* FORCE WAY to force a way **3.** *vti.* STRETCH OR EXTEND to stretch or extend sth, or be stretched or extended ○ *towers thrusting skywards* **4.** *vt.* FORCE SB INTO STH to force sb to accept or deal with sth ○ *He was thrust into the limelight.* **5.** *vti.* ATTACK BY STABBING to attack sb with a piercing or stabbing movement with a weapon **6.** *vt.* INSERT STH to add or insert material, usually inappropriately, into a context ■ *n.* **1.** FORCEFUL PUSH a forceful push or shove **2.** FORWARD MOVEMENT a forward movement or impetus **3.** STABBING ACTION a piercing or stabbing action **4.** MILITARY ATTACK a military assault or offensive **5.** GIST OR AIM OF STH the chief meaning, direction, or purpose of sth **6.** ENG FORCE OF PROPELLER a propulsive force produced by a rotating propeller, e.g. on a ship or aircraft **7.** AIR REACTIVE FORCE OF EXPELLED GASES the reactive force of expelled gases, e.g. those generated by a rocket or jet engine **8.** CIV ENG FORCE EXERTED BY STRUCTURE the continuous force exerted sideways or downwards by one structure on another, e.g. by an arch on an abutment or a rafter against a wall **9.** GEOL FORCE IN EARTH'S CRUST a force in the earth's crust that results in recumbent folding of rock strata **10.** GEOL = **thrust fault** [12thC. From Old Norse.] —**thrustful** *adj.*

thrust bearing *n.* a bearing designed to withstand axial loading and to prevent movement along the axis of a loaded shaft

thruster /thrústər/ *n.* **1.** SPACE TECH ROCKET THAT CONTROLS ALTITUDE a rocket on a spacecraft or high-altitude aircraft that controls an altitude or flight path **2.** INDUST MANOEUVRING DEVICE ON OIL-DRILLING VESSEL a jet or propeller on an oil-drilling ship or offshore rig, used to manoeuvre it into position **3.** SB AGGRESSIVELY AMBITIOUS sb who pursues ambitions aggressively **4.** SPORTS SURFBOARD OR SAILBOARD WITH EXTRA FIN a surfboard or sailboard equipped with one or more extra fins designed to give it greater speed or manoeuvrability **5.** HUNT FOXHUNTER GETTING TOO FAR FORWARDS a foxhunter who gets too close to the pack during a hunt (*slang*)

thrust fault *n.* an inclined fault in which rocks on the lower side of the slope are displaced downwards

thrusting /thrústing/ *adj.* tending to pursue ambitions aggressively

thrust stage *n.* a stage surrounded on three sides by the audience

thruway *n. US* = **throughway**

Thucydides /thyoo síddi deez/ (460?–400? BC) Athenian historian. A major figure in the development of historical writing, he is known for his *History of the Peloponnesian War*, a conflict in which he himself had fought.

thud /thud/ *n.* **1.** DULL HEAVY SOUND a loud dull sound made by a heavy object impacting with a surface **2.** DULL HEAVY BLOW a blow that makes a dull heavy sound ■ *vi.* (**thuds, thudding, thudded**) MAKE A THUD to make a dull heavy sound [Early 16thC. Origin uncertain: probably from Old English *þyddan* 'to thrust'.]

thug /thug/ *n.* **1.** BRUTAL PERSON sb, especially a criminal, who is brutal and violent **2. thug, Thug** HIST INDIAN ROBBER a member of a former secret organization of robbers in India, worshippers of the goddess Kali, who strangled their victims [Early 19thC. Via Hindi *ṭhag*, literally 'swindler, cheat, robber', from, ultimately, Sanskrit *sthagayati* 'covers, conceals'.] —**thuggery** *n.* —**thuggish** *adj.*

thuggee /thu gée/ *n.* the method of robbery and murder by strangulation, characteristic of the former thugs of India [Mid-19thC. From Hindi *ṭhagī*, from *ṭhag* (see THUG).]

thuja /thyóoyə/ (*plural* **-jas** *or* **-ja**), **thuya** (*plural* **-yas** *or* **-ya**) *n.* TREES = **arbor vitae** [Mid-18thC. Via modern Latin *Thuja*, genus name, from medieval Latin *thuia* 'cedar', from Greek.]

thulium /thyóoli əm/ *n.* a very rare soft bright silvery-grey metallic element belonging to the lanthanide series. Symbol **Tm** [Late 19thC. Named after THUL; from the fact that it was first found in Norway.]

thumb /thum/ *n.* **1.** ANAT THICKEST DIGIT ON HUMAN HAND the shortest thickest digit of the human hand, located next to the forefinger. Since it is opposable, it can be moved to face and touch the other fingers so that objects can be grasped. **2.** ZOOL ANIMAL'S DIGIT RESEMBLING HUMAN THUMB a short thick digit in some animals, e.g. many primates, that is adapted for grasping and corresponds to the human thumb **3.** CLOTHES SECTION OF GLOVE FOR THUMB the part of a glove or mitten that covers the thumb **4.** ARCHIT = **ovolo** ■ *v.* (**thumbs, thumbing, thumbed**) **1.** *vti.* HITCH LIFT to obtain or try to obtain a lift by signalling with the thumb to passing drivers **2.** *vt.* MAKE STH DIRTY BY USE to soil or cause wear on sth, especially a book, by repeated handling (*often passive*) ○ *a well-thumbed book* **3.** *vti.* FLIP THROUGH PRINTED MATTER to glance through pages of a book or magazine [Old English *þúma*] —**thumbless** *adj.* ◇ **all thumbs** extremely awkward or clumsy ◇ **stick out like a sore thumb** to be completely obvious, or conspicuously out of place ◇ **thumb your nose at sb** *or* **sth** to express defiance or contempt, especially by putting the thumb to the nose and extending the fingers ◇ **twiddle your thumbs** to be idle or unoccupied, especially involuntarily ◇ **under sb's thumb** under the influence and control of sb

thumbhole /thúm hōl/ *n.* **1.** HOLE TO ALLOW THUMB TO GRIP a hole in sth such as a bowling ball into which a thumb can be inserted in order to provide a grip **2.** HOLE FOR THUMB IN WIND INSTRUMENT a hole in a wind instrument that is covered and uncovered by the thumb to produce notes

thumb index *n.* a series of labelled indentations cut into the pages of a book down the edge opposite the binding to facilitate quick location of divisions or sections —**thumb-index** *vt.*

thumb knot *n.* = **overhand knot**

thumbnail /thúm nayl/ *n.* NAIL OF THUMB the hard growing plate of keratin on the back surface of the tip of the thumb ■ *adj.* CONCISE covering the salient points concisely ○ *a thumbnail sketch*

thumbnut /thúm nut/ *n.* = **wing nut**

thumb piano *n.* a box-shaped African musical instrument consisting of a row of tuned metal or wooden strips that vibrate when plucked by the thumb

thumbprint /thúm print/ *n.* an impression of the fleshy pad near the tip of the thumb, often used to identify people

thumbscrew /thúm skroo/ *n.* **1.** TORTURE DEVICE FOR CRUSHING THUMBS an instrument of torture used to crush the thumbs **2.** FLAT-HEADED SCREW a screw with a flat head to be turned with the thumb and forefinger

thumbs-down /thúmz-/ *n.* an indication of disapproval or rejection (*informal*) [From the custom of pointing the thumbs downwards to signify rejection, perhaps originating in the arenas of ancient Rome, where it indicated that a gladiator should be put to death]

thumbstall /thúm stawl/ *n.* a sheath of rubber, leather, or fabric used to protect the thumb, e.g. by covering a dressing on an injured thumb

thumbs-up *n.* an indication of approval or acceptance (*informal*) [From the custom of pointing the thumbs upwards to signify acceptance, perhaps originating in the arenas of ancient Rome, where it indicated that a gladiator should be permitted to live]

thumbtack /thúm tak/ *n. US, Can* = drawing pin ■ *vt.* (-tacks, -tacking, -tacked) *US, Can* AFFIX STH WITH DRAWING PIN to affix papers or cards with one or more drawing pins

Thummim *n.* ♦ Urim and Thummim [Mid-16thC. From Hebrew *tummīm*, plural of *tōm* 'completeness'.]

thump /thump/ *v.* (thumps, thumping, thumped) 1. *vti.* STRIKE HEAVILY to strike sb or sth heavily with the fist or an object 2. *vi.* PALPITATE OR POUND to beat very fast or loudly because of fear or excitement (*refers to the heart*) 3. *vi.* MAKE DULL HEAVY SOUND to make the loud dull sound that a heavy object makes when it impacts with a surface 4. *vti.* DEFEAT CONVINCINGLY to inflict a humiliating defeat upon sb (*informal; often passive*) ○ *Our team was thumped 9–0.* ■ *n.* 1. HEAVY BLOW a heavy blow struck with the fist or an object 2. DULL HEAVY SOUND the loud dull sound made by a heavy object impacting with a surface ○ *I heard a loud thump from next door.* [Mid-16thC. An imitation of the sound.] —**thumper** *n.*

thumping /thúmping/ *adj.* 1. LARGE huge, resounding, or impressive (*informal*) ○ *won by a thumping majority* 2. PAINFUL very painful and throbbing ■ *adv.* VERY extremely or exceptionally (*informal*) ○ *a thumping good read* —**thumpingly** *adv.*

Thun /toon/ town in the canton of Bern, central Switzerland. Population: 39,253 (1996).

thunbergia /thun búrji ə/ *n.* an African and southern Asian plant of the acanthus family with opposite pairs of simple leaves and five-lobed tubular flowers. It is widely cultivated as an ornamental. Genus: *Thunbergia*. [Late 18thC. From modern Latin *Thunbergia*, genus name, named after C. P. *Thunberg* (1743–1822), a Swedish botanist.]

thunder /thúndər/ *n.* 1. LOUD NOISE FOLLOWING LIGHTNING a loud rumbling noise caused by the rapid expansion of air suddenly heated by lightning 2. NOISE RESEMBLING THUNDER a loud deep rumbling noise resembling thunder 3. THREATENING OR VEHEMENT UTTERANCE a manifestation of sb's anger in an explosion of strong words ■ *v.* (-ders, -dering, -dered) 1. *vi.* MAKE LOUD NOISE FOLLOWING LIGHTNING to make a loud rumbling noise caused by the rapid expansion of air suddenly heated by lightning 2. *vi.* RUMBLE LOUDLY LIKE THUNDER to make a loud deep rumbling noise resembling thunder 3. *vti.* SHOUT VEHEMENTLY to shout sth loudly and angrily [Old English *punor* and *punrian*] ◇ **steal sb's thunder** to prevent sb from receiving acclaim for doing sth by doing it or sth similar first

Thunder Bay city in northwestern Ontario, Canada, on Thunder Bay, an arm of Lake Superior. Population: 125,562 (1996).

The Purcell Team/Corbis

Thunderbird: Totem pole, Stanley Park, Vancouver, Canada

thunderbird /thúndər burd/ *n.* in Native North American mythology, a bird that produces thunder

thunderbolt /thúndər bōlt/ *n.* 1. FLASH OF LIGHTNING WITH THUNDER a flash of lightning accompanied by a crash of thunder 2. STARTLING OCCURRENCE a sudden shocking action, occurrence, pronouncement, or piece of news 3. MYTHOLOGICAL WEAPON WIELDED BY GODS in mythology, a destructive missile hurled to earth by a god in a flash of lightning 4. SB OR STH FORMIDABLE sb who or sth that seems to resemble a thunderbolt, especially in energy and destructive power

thunderbox /thúndər boks/ *n.* a lavatory, especially a primitive or portable one (*dated informal humorous*)

thunderclap /thúndər klap/ *n.* 1. CRASH OF THUNDER a loud crashing noise produced by thunder 2. STARTLING OCCURRENCE a sudden shocking occurrence or piece of news 3. NOISE RESEMBLING THUNDER a sudden loud sound resembling thunder

thundercloud /thúndər klowd/ *n.* a large dark cumulonimbus cloud that produces thunder and lightning

Thunderer /thúndərər/ *n.* in mythology, a god of thunder

thunderhead /thúndər hed/ *n. US, Can* the upper rounded mass of a cumulonimbus cloud associated with the development of a thunderstorm

thundering /thúndəring/ *adj.* GREAT very great (*dated informal*) ■ *adv.* VERY extremely or exceptionally (*dated informal*) —**thunderingly** *adv.*

thunderous /thúndərəss/ *adj.* 1. VERY LOUD resembling thunder in its loudness ○ *thunderous applause* 2. THREATENING angry and threatening —**thunderously** *adv.*

thunder run *n.* formerly, either of two inclined wooden troughs down which iron balls were rolled offstage to simulate thunder as a theatrical sound effect

thunder sheet *n.* a large sheet of metal shaken to simulate thunder as a theatrical sound effect

thundershower /thúndər showər/ *n.* a shower of rain during a thunderstorm

thunderstone /thúndər stōn/ *n.* 1. LONG TAPERING ROCK a naturally occurring long tapering piece of rock, formerly believed to be a thunderbolt 2. THUNDERBOLT a thunderbolt (*archaic*)

thunderstorm /thúndər stawrm/ *n.* a storm with thunder, lightning, heavy rain, and sometimes hail

thunderstricken /thúndər strikən/ *adj.* thunderstruck (*literary*)

thunderstruck /thúndər struk/ *adj.* 1. EXTREMELY SURPRISED OR INCREDULOUS so surprised, incredulous, or startled as to be in a state of shock 2. HIT BY LIGHTNING struck by lightning (*archaic*)

thundery /thúndəri/ *adj.* 1. CAUSING OR HERALDING THUNDER causing or indicating the onset of thunder or a thunderstorm 2. SOUNDING LIKE THUNDER resembling thunder in sound

thunk /thungk/ *n.* THUD a thud (*informal*) ■ *vi.* MAKE A THUD to make a thud (*informal*) [Mid-20thC. An imitation of the sound.]

Thur. *abbr.* CALENDAR Thursday

thurible /thyoóribʻl/ *n.* = censer [15thC. Directly or via French from Latin *t(h)uribulum*, from, ultimately, Greek *thuos* 'sacrifice, incense'.]

thurifer /thyoórifər/ *n.* sb who carries the censer in religious ceremonies [Mid-19thC. Via late Latin from, ultimately, Greek *thuos* 'sacrifice, incense'.]

Thurs. *abbr.* CALENDAR Thursday

Thursday /thúrz day, -di/ *n.* CALENDAR the fourth day of the week, coming after Wednesday and before Friday [Old English *zzu(n)resdæg*, literally 'day of thunder', translation of late Latin *Jovis dies* 'day of Jupiter (the god of thunder)']

Thursday Island island in the Torres Strait, off the northeastern coast of Australia. Area: 3.6 sq. km/1.4 sq. mi.

Thursdays /thúrz dayz, -diz/ *adv.* CALENDAR every Thursday

Thurso /thúrssō/ town and seaport on the northern coast of Scotland. It is the northernmost town on the mainland of Great Britain. Population: 8,488 (1991).

thus /thuss/ *adv.* 1. CONSEQUENTLY as a result (*formal*) 2. LIKE THIS in this way (*formal*) 3. TO THIS DEGREE to this degree or extent [Old English]

thusly /thússli/ *adv. US* thus (*humorous*)

Thutmose III /thoot mōse/ (*d.* 1450 BC) Egyptian pharaoh. He became pharaoh in 1504 BC. Through military conquest, he extended the Egyptian empire eastwards as far as the River Euphrates, and with the vast wealth of his Asian territories erected great temples and other imperial buildings in Egypt.

thuya *n.* = thuja

thwack /thwak/ *vt.* (thwacks, thwacking, thwacked) SMACK SB OR STH to strike sb or sth with a flat object such as the flat of the hand ■ *n.* SHARP BLOW WITH FLAT OBJECT a sharp smacking blow with a flat object [Early 16thC. An imitation of the sound of the blow.] —**thwacker** *n.*

thwaite /thwayt/ *n.* a piece of reclaimed wasteland (*regional archaic; often used in placenames*) [Early 17thC. From Old Norse.]

thwart /thwawrt/ *v.* (thwarts, thwarting, thwarted) 1. *vt.* FRUSTRATE STH to prevent sb or sb's plan from being successful 2. *vti.* CROSS to place one thing across another or be placed across sth (*archaic*) ■ *adj.* EXTENDING ACROSS situated or extending across sth ■ *n.* CROSSWISE SEAT IN BOAT a crosswise seat or transverse member on a rowing boat, canoe or similar small boat ■ *prep.* ATHWART athwart (*archaic*) ■ *adv.* ATHWART athwart (*archaic*) [13thC. From Old Norse.] —**thwartedly** *adv.* —**thwarter** *n.*

thy /thī/ *det.* belonging or relating to you, the second person singular possessive corresponding to 'thou' (*archaic*) [12thC. Shortening of an earlier form of THINE.]

Thyestes /thī ést eez/ *n.* in Greek mythology, the brother of Atreus and king of Mycenae. After usurping the throne from his brother, he was tricked into eating the flesh of his own sons. —**Thyestean** *adj.*

thylacine /thílə seen/ *n.* a large carnivorous marsupial of Tasmania that resembles a dog and has brownish fur and black stripes across the back. It was once widespread through Australia but is thought to be extinct. Latin name: *Thylacinus cynocephalus*. [Mid-19thC. From modern Latin *Thylacinus*, genus name, from Greek *thulakos* 'pouch'.]

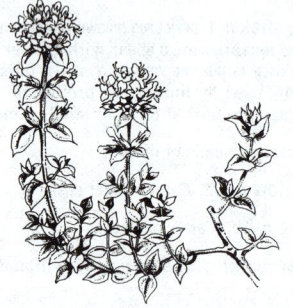

Thyme

thyme /tīm/ *n.* 1. PLANTS AROMATIC SHRUB a small low shrub of the mint family with narrow leaves and white, pink, or red flowers. It also yields an aromatic essential oil containing thymol. Genus: *Thymus*. 2. FOOD CULINARY HERB the tiny leaves of the thyme plant, used fresh or dried as a flavouring in cooking [15thC. Via Old French *thym* from, ultimately, Greek *thumon*, from *thuein* 'to burn, sacrifice', from its use as incense.] —**thymy** *adj.*

thymectomy /thī méktəmi/ (*plural* -mies) *n.* surgical removal of the thymus gland [Early 20thC. Coined from THYMUS + -ECTOMY.]

thymi plural of **thymus**

-thymia *suffix.* condition or state of mind ○ *dysthymia* [Via modern Latin from, ultimately, Greek *thumos* 'mind']

thymic[1] /thī mik/ *adj.* relating to the thymus

thymic[2] /tī mik/ *adj.* relating to thyme

thymidine /thími deen/ *n.* a nucleoside that is one of the principal components of DNA, consisting of one molecule of thymine linked to one molecule of the sugar deoxyribose. Formula: $C_{10}H_{14}N_2O_5$. [Early 20thC. Coined from THYMINE + -IDINE.]

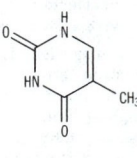

Thymine

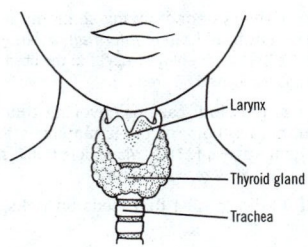

Thyroid gland

Tiara

thymine /thī´ meen/ *n.* a component of nucleic acid that pairs with adenine to carry hereditary information in DNA in cells. Chemically, it is a pyrimidine derivative. Formula: $C_5H_6N_2O_2$. Symbol **T** [Late 19thC. Coined from THYMIC[1] + -INE.]

thymocyte /thī´mə sīt/ *n.* a type of small white blood cell (**lymphocyte**) occurring in the thymus that is a precursor of a T-cell

thymol /thī´ mol/ *n.* a colourless crystalline phenol with an aromatic odour, obtained from thyme oil or made synthetically. It is used as a fungicide and preservative, and in making perfumes. Formula: $C_{10}H_{14}O$. [Mid-19thC. Coined from Greek *thumon* (see THYME) + -OL.]

thymoma /thī mōˊmə/ (*plural* **-mas** *or* **-mata** /-mətə/) *n.* a tumour of the thymus [Early 20thC. Coined from THYMO- + -OMA.]

thymosin /thī´məssin/ *n.* a hormone that influences the development and differentiation of T-cells in the thymus [Mid-20thC. Coined from Greek *thumos* (see THYMUS) + -IN.]

thymus /thī´məss/ (*plural* **-muses** *or* **-mi** /thī´mī/), **thymus gland** *n.* an organ, located at the base of the neck, that is involved in development of cells of the immune system, particularly T-cells. It is prominent in the young but shrinks after puberty. [Late 16thC. Via modern Latin from Greek *thumos* 'warty growth resembling a bunch of thyme'.]

thyratron /thī´rə tron/ *n.* a gas-filled hot-cathode tube that acts as an electronic switch or relay in which a signal applied to the control grid initiates anode current but does not limit it [Early 20thC. Coined from Greek *thura* (see THYROID) + -TRON.]

thyristor /thī rístər/ *n.* a semiconductor device that has two stable switches used for conductive and nonconductive modes [Mid-20thC. Blend of THYRATRON and TRANSISTOR.]

thyro- *prefix.* thyroid ○ *thyrotropin* [From THYROID]

thyrocalcitonin /thī´rō kálssi tōˊnin/ *n.* = **calcitonin**

thyroid /thī´ royd/ *n.* **1.** = thyroid gland **2.** = thyroid cartilage **3.** MEDICINE OBTAINED FROM ANIMAL THYROID GLAND a preparation obtained from the thyroid gland of certain animals that is used in treating conditions of the thyroid gland ■ *adj.* **1.** thyroid, thyroidal OF THYROID GLAND relating to, situated in, supplying, or secreted by the thyroid gland **2.** thyroid, thyroidal OF THYROID CARTILAGE relating to the thyroid cartilage [Early 18thC. Via obsolete French from, ultimately, Greek *thura* 'door', from the oblong shape of the cartilage in front of the throat.]

thyroid cartilage *n.* the largest cartilage of the larynx, forming the projection called the Adam's apple

thyroidectomy /thī´ roy déktəmi, thī´rə-/ (*plural* **-mies**) *n.* surgical removal of the thyroid gland or part of it

thyroid gland *n.* an endocrine gland located in the neck of human beings and other vertebrate animals that secretes the hormones responsible for controlling metabolism and growth. Excessive action of the thyroid gland can cause Graves' disease, whilst underactivity can cause myxoedema.

thyroid hormone *n.* either of the two hormones, thryoxine and triiodothyronine, that are secreted by the thyroid gland and regulate body metabolism and growth

thyroiditis /thī´ roy dítiss/ *n.* inflammation of the thyroid gland. This may be acute, as a result of bacterial infection, or chronic, as a result of an autoimmune response in which lymphocytes invade the gland.

thyroid-stimulating hormone *n.* = **thyrotropin**

thyrotoxicosis /thī´rō tókssi kόssiss/ *n.* = **hyperthyroidism**

thyrotropin /thī´rō trōˊpin/, **thyrotrophin** /-fin/ *n.* a hormone that is secreted by the anterior lobe of the pituitary gland and stimulates release of hormones by the thyroid gland [Mid-20thC. Coined from THYRO- + -TROPIC + -IN.]

thyrotropin-releasing hormone *n.* a peptide hormone that is produced by the hypothalamus and controls the release of thyrotropin by the pituitary gland

thyroxine /thī´ró sseen/, **thyroxin** /-rók sin/ *n.* the principal hormone secreted by the thyroid gland. It stimulates metabolism and is essential for normal growth and development. A synthetic form is used to treat hypothyroidism. [Early 20thC. Coined from THYRO- + OXY- + INDOLE (from a misunderstanding of its chemical structure), altered on the model of -INE.]

thyrse /thurss/ *n.* a flower head, e.g. in lilacs, that consists of numerous branching clusters of individual flowers arising from a single main stem [Early 17thC. Via French from Latin *thyrsus* (see THYRSUS).] —**thyrsoid** /thúr soyd/ *adj.*

thyrsus /thúrssəss/ (*plural* **-si** /thúr sī/) *n.* **1.** MYTHOL STAFF CARRIED BY DIONYSUS in Greek mythology and art, a staff tipped with a pine cone, carried by the Greek god Dionysus and his followers **2.** BOT = **thyrse** [Late 16thC. Via Latin from Greek *thursos* 'stalk of a plant, staff carried by Dionysus', of unknown origin.]

thysanuran /thíssə nyóorən/ *n.* = **bristletail** [Mid-19thC. Formed from modern Latin *Thysanura*, order name, from Greek *thusanos* 'tassel, fringe' + *oura* 'tail'.] —**thysanurous** *adj.*

thyself /thī sélf/ *pron.* (*archaic*) **1.** FORM OF 'THY' the form of 'thy' used to refer to the same individual who is being addressed and is the subject of the verb **2.** USED FOR EMPHASIS used to emphasize that the individual being addressed is also being referred to [Old English. Originally from THEE + SELF (as an adjective), but interpreted as being from THY + SELF (as a noun).]

THz *abbr.* terahertz

ti /tee/ (*plural* **tis**) *n.* a woody Polynesian and Australian plant of the agave family with leaves used for thatching, garments, and fodder, and with roots used as food and for making beverages. Genus: *Cordyline.* [Mid-19thC. From Tahitian and Maori.]

Ti *symbol.* titanium

Tiananmen Square /tyén an mən-/ *n.* a large square in central Beijing, China, that is a traditional site for festivals, rallies, and demonstrations. In 1989 it was the scene of a pro-democracy demonstration led by students in which hundreds were killed when troops were ordered to clear the square.

Tian Shan /tyén shán/ = **Tien Shan**

tiara /ti a´ərə/ *n.* **1.** WOMAN'S JEWELLED CORONET a small jewelled semicircular headdress worn by a woman on formal occasions **2.** POPE'S CROWN a headdress consisting of three coronets with an orb and a cross on top, worn by the pope or carried before him on ceremonial occasions **3.** PERSIAN KING'S CROWN a high headdress worn by an ancient Persian king [Mid-16thC. Directly and via Italian from Latin, from Greek *tiara(s)*, probably from a language of southwestern Asia.] —**tiaraed** /ti a´ərəd/ *adj.*

Tiber /tíbər/ *river of central Italy. Rising in the Apennines, it flows through Rome and empties into the Tyrrhenian Sea. Length: 405 km/252 mi.

Tiberius /tī beėri əss-/ (42 BC–AD 37) Roman emperor. His reign (AD 14–37) was marked by revolts and conspiracies. Full name **Tiberius Julius Caesar Augustus**

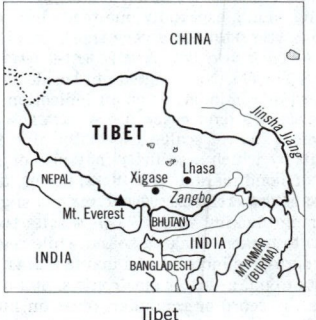

Tibet

Tibet /ti bét/ *country north of the Himalayas, since 1965 a province-level administrative region of China. With an average elevation of more than 4,000 m/12,000 ft, it is the highest region on earth. Capital: Lhasa. Population: 2,196,010 (1990). Area: 1,222,000 sq. km/472,000 sq. mi. Official name **Tibet Autonomous Region**

Tibetan /ti bétt'n/ *n.* **1.** PEOPLES SB FROM TIBET sb who was born or brought up in Tibet, or who is of Tibetan descent **2.** LANG LANGUAGE OF TIBET the language of Tibet, spoken also in neighbouring parts of China, Nepal, and India. It belongs to the Tibeto-Burman branch of the Sino-Tibetan family of languages. Tibetan is spoken by about six million people. —**Tibetan** *adj.*

Tibetan Buddhism *n.* = Lamaism

Tibetan spaniel *n.* a small dog with a long thick coat, a plumed tail curled over the back, and drooping ears, belonging to a breed that originated in Tibet. It was traditionally a sacred breed, confined to monasteries and palaces.

Tibetan terrier *n.* a small terrier with a long shaggy coat that falls over its eyes and a back-curling tail, belonging to a breed that originated in Tibet

Tibeto-Burman /ti béttō-/ *n.* LANG a branch of the Sino-Tibetan family of languages that comprises Tibetan, Burmese, and many other languages of Southern and Southeast Asia [Mid-20thC. Coined from *Tibeto-* (from TIBETAN) + BURMAN.] —**Tibeto-Burman** *adj.*

tibia /tíbbi ə/ (*plural* **-ae** /-bi ee/ *or* **-as**) *n.* **1.** ANAT INNER BONE OF LOWER LEG the inner and larger of the two bones in the lower leg, extending from the knee to the ankle bone alongside the fibula **2.** ZOOL BONE IN ANIMAL'S LEG a bone in the lower leg of vertebrates corresponding to the human tibia **3.** INSECTS **PART OF INSECT'S LEG** the fourth segment of an insect's leg, between the femur and the tarsus **4.** BIRDS **PART OF BIRD'S LEG** the lower feathered segment or drumstick of a bird's leg **5.** MUSIC **ANCIENT WIND INSTRUMENT** an ancient flute, originally made from an animal's tibia [Late 17thC. From Latin, 'shinbone', earlier 'pipe', of unknown origin.] —**tibial** *adj.*

tibiofibular /tíbbi ō fíbbyoolər/ *adj.* relating to the tibia and fibula, the bones of the lower leg

tibiotarsus /tíbbi ō taárssəss/ (*plural* **-si** /-see/) *n.* the main bone of a bird's lower leg, formed by a fusion of the tibia and some of the bones of the tarsus

tic /tik/ *n.* **1. MUSCLE TWITCH** a sudden involuntary spasmodic muscular contraction, especially of facial, neck, or shoulder muscles, which may become more pronounced when sb is stressed **2. QUIRK OF BEHAVIOUR** a distinctive behavioural trait or quirk [Early 19thC. Via French from Italian *ticchio*.]

tical /ti kaál, teék'l, ti káwl/ (*plural* **-als** *or* **-al**) *n.* **1. OLD UNIT OF THAI CURRENCY** a silver coin that was a unit of currency in Thailand between 1909 and 1950 **2. OLD UNIT OF WEIGHT IN THAILAND** a former unit of weight in Thailand, equal to about 14 grams/half an ounce [Mid-17thC. From Portuguese, of uncertain origin: probably from Marathi *ṭakā* or Bengali *ṭākā* 'coin'.]

tic douloureux /-doolə rṓ/ *n.* = **trigeminal neuralgia** [From French, literally 'painful tic']

tichy *adj.* = **titchy**

Ticino /ti cheénō/ river in western Europe, a tributary of the River Po. Length: 248 km/154 mi.

tick[1] /tik/ *n.* **1. RECURRING CLICK** a slight quiet recurring clicking sound, especially one made by a clock or watch **2. VERY SHORT TIME** a very short time (*informal*) ○ *I'll be back in a tick.* **3. MARK NOTING ITEM'S STATUS** a mark (✓) or electronic signal put beside an item as a record or reminder, or as an indication that sth is correct. US term **check** *n.* 7 **4. DEGREE ON SCALE** an increment on a scale, especially the smallest amount by which a security may rise or fall in a stock or bond market ■ *v.* (**ticks, ticking, ticked**) **1.** *vi.* **MAKE RECURRING CLICKING SOUND** to make a slight quiet recurring clicking sound **2.** *vi.* **REGISTER TAXI FARE BY CLICKING** to make a clicking sound while registering the progressive increase of a taxi fare **3.** *vt.* **MARK STH WITH TICK** to put a tick or electronic signal beside an item as a record or reminder, or as an indication that sth is correct **4.** *vi.* **FUNCTION PROPERLY** to function well or in the specified way (*informal*) [13thC. Origin uncertain.] ◇ **what makes sb tick** what causes sb to behave and think in a particular way (*informal*)

tick away, tick by *vi.* to pass or elapse at a steady pace (*refers to time*)

tick off *vt.* **1. MARK STH WITH TICK** to mark sth with a tick, especially an item in a list. US term **check off 2. SCOLD SB** to tell sb off for doing sth wrong (*informal*) **3.** *US* **ANNOY SB** to make sb angry (*informal*)

tick over *vi.* **1. RUN AT SLOW SPEED** to function slowly without causing a vehicle to move (*refers to a motor-vehicle engine*) **2. CONTINUE TO FUNCTION** to keep going or continue to function without any significant progress or achievement

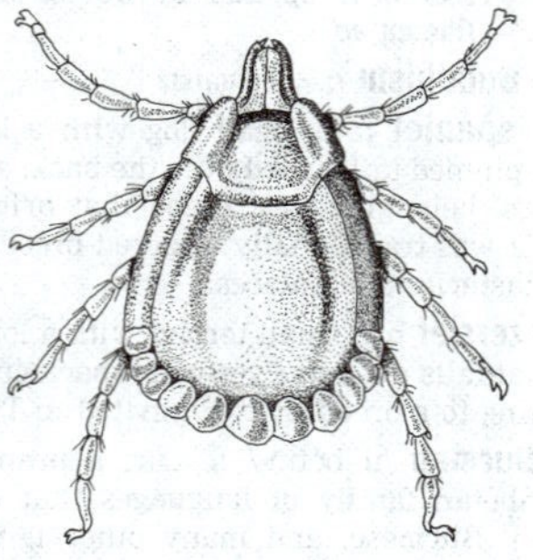

Tick

tick[2] /tik/ *n.* **1. TINY PARASITIC INSECT** a small wingless bloodsucking insect that lives on the skin of humans and warm-blooded animals and may transmit diseases. Families: Argasidae and Ioxidae. **2. BLOODSUCKING FLY** a parasitic fly that lives on the skin of sheep, cattle, horses, and other animals [Old English *ticia*. Ultimately of prehistoric Germanic origin.]

tick[3] /tik/ *n.* the system of owing sb money for goods that are acquired (*dated informal*) ○ *bought it on tick* [Mid-17thC. Shortening of TICKET in the obsolete sense 'note of goods received on credit'.]

tick[4] /tik/ *n.* the cloth case or covering that is filled with cotton, feathers, or other materials to form a pillow or mattress [15thC. Via Middle Dutch *tēke* from, ultimately, Greek *thēkē* 'cover, case'.]

tick-bird /tík-/ *n.* a bird that feeds on ticks, e.g. the oxpecker

tick-borne *adj.* used to describe a disease in which the causative microorganism is transmitted by the bite of a tick, e.g. Lyme disease or many forms of encephalitis

ticker /tíkər/ *n.* **1. HEART** sb's heart (*informal*) **2. WATCH** a wristwatch or pocket watch (*dated informal*) **3.** *US* STOCK EXCH = **tape machine**

ticker tape *n.* formerly, a continuous paper ribbon on which a tape machine automatically printed stock quotations

ticker-tape parade *n.* in the United States, a parade honouring a visiting celebrity who is showered with shredded paper, formerly ticker tape, from buildings while being driven through the streets

ticket /tíkit/ *n.* **1.** TRANSP **TRAVEL PASS** a printed piece of cardboard or paper showing that the holder is entitled to be travelling on a means of transport **2.** LEISURE **PASS FOR ENTERTAINMENT** a printed piece of cardboard or paper showing that the holder is entitled to admission to a place of public entertainment or a sports ground **3.** PUBLIC ADMIN **NOTIFICATION OF TRAFFIC OFFENCE** a printed notice that a traffic or parking offence has been committed and a fine must be paid ○ *a parking ticket* **4.** COMM **LABEL OR TAG** a small piece of card attached to an article, showing the price or other details **5.** TRANSP **QUALIFICATION OF PILOT OR SHIP'S OFFICER** a certificate of qualification as a ship's captain or an aircraft pilot **6.** MIL **ARMY DISCHARGE** a certificate of discharge from the army (*informal*) **7.** *US* POL **GROUP OF CANDIDATES RUNNING TOGETHER** a list of candidates put forward by one party or group in an election **8.** STOCK EXCH **LIST OF STOCK PURCHASERS** a list of investors who have purchased securities during a specified period for the purpose of settling accounts **9. PRECISELY WHAT IS NEEDED** the right, just, desired, or appropriate thing (*informal*) ○ *A week in France would be just the ticket.* ■ *vt.* (**-ets, -eting, -eted**) **1.** COMM **ATTACH A TICKET TO AN ARTICLE** to attach a ticket to an article, showing the price or other details **2.** LEISURE **ISSUE A PASS TO STH** to issue a ticket for admission to sth **3.** PUBLIC ADMIN **GIVE SB A PARKING TICKET** to issue a motor vehicle or its driver with a ticket for a traffic or parking violation **4. CATEGORIZE SB OR STH** to assign sb to a particular category, or designate sth for a particular purpose [Early 16thC. Via obsolete French *étiquet* 'ticket, label' (source of English *etiquette*), from, ultimately, Old French *estiquier* 'to stick', from the idea of sticking on a label.] ◇ **have tickets on yourself** *Aus* to have an inflated opinion of yourself (*informal*)

ticket day *n.* a day on which purchasers of securities during a preceding specified period are listed so that accounts may be settled

ticket of leave *n.* formerly, a permit allowing a convict to leave prison before completion of a sentence, under certain restrictions (*hyphenated when used before a noun*) ○ *a ticket-of-leave man*

ticket tout *n.* sb who buys tickets for a theatrical or sporting event and sells them on at a profit

tickety-boo /tíkəti bóo/ *adj. UK, Can* perfectly fine (*dated informal*) [Origin uncertain: perhaps from Hindi *ṭhīk hai* 'all right']

tickey /tíki/ (*plural* **-eys**) *n. S Africa* a small silver threepenny coin in use in South Africa under British rule, between 1806 and 1961 [Late 19thC. Origin uncertain: perhaps from Malay *tiga* 'three'.]

tick fever *n.* an acute infectious disease transmitted by the bite of a tick, e.g. Rocky Mountain spotted fever or Texas fever

ticking /tíking/ *n.* a strong cotton fabric, often twilled, that is used to cover mattresses and pillows [Mid-17thC. Formed from TICK[4].]

ticking-off (*plural* **tickings-off**) *n.* an act of telling sb off for doing sth wrong (*informal*)

tickle /tík'l/ *v.* (**-les, -ling, -led**) **1.** *vt.* **MAKE SB LAUGH AND TWITCH** to touch, prod, stroke, or caress lightly a sensitive part of sb's body, usually so as to produce involuntary laughter and wriggling **2.** *vti.* **CAUSE ITCHINESS** to cause an itchy or scratchy feeling by lightly touching a sensitive part of the body ○ *This feather boa tickles.* **3.** *vt.* **PLEASE OR AMUSE SB** to make sb pleased, or appeal to sb's sense of humour (*often passive*) **4.** *vt.* **CATCH TROUT WITH HANDS** to catch a trout by stroking it gently so that it moves backwards into the hands ■ *n.* **1. TOUCH THAT MAKES SB LAUGH** a light touch, prod, stroke, or caress applied to a sensitive part of sb's body, usually so as to produce involuntary laughter and wriggling **2. ITCHY FEELING** an itchy or scratchy feeling caused when a sensitive part of the body is touched lightly by sth, especially material [14thC. Origin uncertain: probably formed from TICK[1] in the obsolete sense 'to touch lightly', in which case its original literal sense would have been 'to keep on touching lightly'.] ◇ **tickled pink, tickled silly, tickled to death** extremely pleased (*informal*)

tickler /tík'lər/ *n.* **1.** ELEC ENG = **tickler coil 2. STH DIFFICULT OR PUZZLING** a difficult, delicate, or puzzling problem or situation (*informal*)

tickler coil *n.* a small coil connected in series with a radio vacuum tube's plate circuit and inductively coupled to a coil located in a grid circuit to provide regenerative feedback

tickler file *n. US* a file consisting of reminders of matters that must be dealt with

ticklish /tík'lish/ *adj.* **1. SENSITIVE TO TICKLING** sensitive to being tickled **2. PROBLEMATIC** requiring careful or delicate handling because of its risk or difficulty **3. TOUCHY** easily irritated, angered, or upset —**ticklishly** *adv.* —**ticklishness** *n.*

tickly /tík'li/ (**-lier, -liest**) *adj.* **1. PRODUCING TICKLING SENSATION** producing a tickling or itching sensation on the surface of the skin **2.** *Scotland* **TICKLISH** ticklish

tickseed /tík seed/ *n.* an annual or perennial North American plant with opposite-lobed leaves and flowers resembling daisies. It is sometimes grown as an ornamental. Genus: *Coreopsis.* [Because their seeds resemble the insects]

ticktack /tík tak/, **tictac** *n.* **1. BOOKMAKERS' SIGN SYSTEM** a system of sign language used by bookmakers to convey information at racecourses **2. CLICKING SOUND** a clicking or tapping sound [Mid-16thC. An imitation of the sound.]

tick-tack-toe, tic-tac-toe *n. US* = **noughts and crosses** [Origin uncertain: probably imitative of the sound of an earlier game in which players brought pencils down on slates with their eyes closed]

ticktock /tík tok/ *n.* **TICKING OF TIMEPIECE** the clicking sound made by a clock or watch ■ *vi.* (**-tocks, -tocking, -tocked**) **MAKE TICKING NOISE** to make a quiet recurring clicking sound (*refers to a timepiece*) [Mid-19thC. An imitation of the sound.]

tick trefoil *n.* a leguminous tropical or subtropical plant with trifoliate leaves and jointed seed pods that cling to fur or clothing. Some varieties are cultivated as livestock forage. Genus: *Desmodium.* [Because the joints of the pods stick to things as ticks cling to the fur of animals]

ticky-tacky /tíki táki/, **ticky-tack** *adj. US* **DULL AND SHODDY** dull, unimaginative, and often of uniform quality or design (*informal*) ■ *n. US* **STH DULL AND SHODDY** dull, unimaginative, or inferior materials, or sth made from them (*informal*) [*Ticky*, alteration of TACKY 'shoddy']

tictac *n.* = **ticktack**

tic-tac-toe *n. US* = **tick-tack-toe**

t.i.d. *abbr.* three times a day (*used in doctors' prescriptions*) [Latin *ter in die*]

tidal /tíd'l/ *adj.* **1. OF TIDES** relating to or affected by tides **2. DEPENDENT ON TIDE** having a time of departure dependent on the phase of a tide ○ *a tidal ferry* **3. DEFINED BY TIDE LEVEL** changing in character or accessibility according to the level of the tide **4. FLUC-**

TUATING not constant but fluctuating between periods of intense activity and periods of little activity — **tidally** *adv.*

tidal air *n.* the volume of air that passes in and out of the body during normal breathing [*Tidal* from its obsolete sense 'periodic, intermittent']

tidal basin *n.* an artificial basin cut in rock that fills up at high tide

tidal power, **tidal energy** *n.* the generation of electricity using the force created by the rise and fall of ocean tides

tidal wave *n.* **1.** HUGE OCEAN WAVE an enormous and destructive ocean wave caused by extremely strong winds or seaquakes. ◊ **tsunami 2.** OVERWHELMING SURGE a powerful widespread expression or surge of sth ○ *a tidal wave of public emotion*

tiddle /tídd'l/ *vi.* (**-dles, -dling, -dled**) URINATE to urinate (*babytalk*) ■ *n.* ACT OF URINATION an act of urination (*babytalk*) [Mid-19thC. Alteration of PIDDLE.]

tiddler /tíddlər/ *n.* (*informal*) **1.** TINY FISH a very small fish, especially a minnow or a stickleback **2.** SMALL PERSON OR THING sb or sth that is small compared to most others [Late 19thC. Origin uncertain.]

tiddly[1] /tíddli/ (**-dlier, -dliest**) *adj. UK, Can* slightly intoxicated from having drunk a small amount of alcohol (*informal*) [Mid-19thC. Origin uncertain: perhaps thought to suggest the sensation.]

tiddly[2] /tíddli/ (**-dlier, -dliest**) *adj.* very small (*informal*) [Mid-19thC. Variant of obsolete English *tiddy*, of unknown origin.]

tiddlywink /tíddli wingk/ *n.* a plastic counter used in the game of tiddlywinks [Mid-19thC. Origin uncertain.]

tiddlywinks /tíddli wingks/ *n.* a game in which players try to flip plastic counters into a cup by pressing them on the side with a larger counter

tide /tīd/ *n.* **1.** RISE AND FALL OF SEA the cyclical rise and fall of the sea or another body of water produced by the attraction of the Moon and Sun, occurring about every twelve hours **2.** INFLOW OR OUTFLOW OF WATER the ebb or flow of water at a particular place resulting from the cyclical rise and fall of the sea **3.** = **flood tide 4.** PHYS GRAVITATIONAL STRESS ON STH a stress on sth caused by a gravitational attraction, e.g. in the atmosphere or on a celestial body **5.** GENERAL TREND sth that rises and falls, especially a tendency or trend **6.** CRUCIAL POINT an extreme or critical point or position **7.** PERIOD OF TIME a period of time or a season (*archaic; usually used in combination*) ○ *Yuletide* **8.** APPROPRIATE TIME an appropriate time for sth (*archaic*) ■ *v.* (**tides, tiding, tided**) **1.** *vti.* CARRY ALONG ON TIDE to carry sb or sth along on the tide, or be carried along in this way **2.** *vi.* EBB AND FLOW to ebb and flow like the tide [Old English *tīd* 'time'. Ultimately from an Indo-European base meaning 'to divide', the underlying idea being of a 'portion of time'.] —**tideless** *adj.* ◇ **swim against the tide** to have an opinion or take a stance that is different from or opposite to that taken by others ◇ **swim with the tide** to follow the opinions and attitudes of other people ◇ **turn the tide** to reverse the way things happen

tide over *vt.* to help sb through a difficult time, especially with a loan or gift of money

tide gauge *n.* a gauge used to measure the level of tidal movement

tideland /tīd land/ *n. US* land that is covered by water at high tide

tidemark /tīd maark/ *n.* **1.** MARK LEFT BY TIDE a mark made by the highest or lowest point of a tide **2.** MARKER INDICATING LEVELS OF TIDES a marker indicating the highest or lowest point of a tide **3.** POINT MARKING RISE OR FALL a point that sb or sth has reached, risen above, or fallen below **4.** RING ROUND BATH a usually grimy mark left in a bath showing the level of water it contained (*informal*) **5.** DIRTY MARK ON BODY a dirty mark on the skin showing where sb has stopped washing (*informal*)

tide race *n.* a fast tidal current

tide-rip *n.* = **rip tide**

tide table *n.* a table showing the expected times and levels of tides

tidewaiter /tīd waytər/ *n.* formerly, an officer who boarded incoming ships to enforce customs regulations

tidewater /tīd wawtər/ *n.* **1.** WATER AFFECTED BY TIDES water whose movement or level is affected by tides **2.** WATER COVERING LAND AT HIGH TIDE water at high tide covering land that is dry at low tide **3.** *US* SEACOAST a coastal region, especially that of eastern Virginia

tideway /tīd way/ *n.* **1.** TIDAL CHANNEL a channel in which a tide runs **2.** TIDAL CURRENT a current in a tidal channel

tidings /tīdingz/ *npl.* news or information (*literary*) ○ *I bring you glad tidings.* [Old English *tīdung*, an alteration of Old Norse *tīðendi* 'events']

tidy /tīdi/ *adj.* (**-dier, -diest**) **1.** NEAT IN APPEARANCE having a neat orderly appearance **2.** METHODICAL tending to perform tasks in a systematic way **3.** CONSIDERABLE considerable and significant (*informal*) ○ *cost a tidy sum* **4.** *NZ, US* SATISFACTORY adequate or satisfactory, especially when circumstances are taken into account (*informal*) ○ *negotiated a tidy redundancy package* ■ *vti.* (**-dies, -dying, -died**) MAKE SB OR STH TIDY to make sb or sth neat and orderly ■ *n.* (*plural* **-dies**) **1.** ACT OF MAKING STH TIDY an act of making sth neat and orderly (*informal*) **2.** BOX FOR HOLDING SMALL OBJECTS a box for holding small objects that would otherwise lie around and look untidy ○ *a desk tidy* **3.** SMALL RECEPTACLE FOR WASTE SCRAPS a small receptacle kept beside or in a kitchen sink for the collection of waste scraps ○ *a sink tidy* **4.** *US* HOUSEHOLD COVERING FOR BACK OF CHAIR an ornamental protective covering for the back of a chair or sofa [13thC. Formed from TIDE in the obsolete sense 'time'. The main modern meaning evolved via the senses 'timely, at an appropriate time' and 'good'.] —**tidily** *adv.* —**tidiness** *n.*

tidy-up *n.* = **tidy** *n.* 1 (*informal*)

tie /tī/ *v.* (**ties, tying, tied**) **1.** *vt.* FASTEN THINGS WITH ROPE to fasten things together with a rope, string, or cord ○ *They tied his hands together.* **2.** *vt.* FASTEN STH BY KNOTTING to fasten sth with a knot or bow ○ *Tie your shoelaces.* **3.** *vt.* MAKE A KNOT to make a knot or bow with rope, string, or cord ○ *All Scouts learn how to tie knots.* **4.** *vt.* CONNECT THINGS to make a connection or link between people or things **5.** *vt.* RESTRICT to restrict sb to certain conditions **6.** *vi.* SPORTS, LEISURE HAVE AN EQUAL SCORE to achieve the same score or place as sb else in a game, race, or competition **7.** *vt.* MUSIC SUSTAIN A MUSICAL NOTE to hold a note from one bar to the next, thereby extending its value **8.** *vt.* MUSIC CONNECT NOTES WITH A CURVED LINE in musical notation, to connect two notes with a curved line ■ *n.* (*plural* **ties**) **1.** ACCESSORIES STRIP OF FABRIC WORN ROUND NECK a long tapering piece of fabric worn round the neck, under a shirt collar, and tied at the front so that the ends hang down the front of the shirt. ◊ **bow tie 2.** STH USED FOR ATTACHING a long thin piece of sth such as rope or wire used to fasten or close sth else ○ *ties for bin bags* **3.** STH THAT FORMS A CONNECTION sth that links or unites people or things **4.** STH THAT RESTRICTS sth that restricts or confines sb or sth **5.** SPORTS, LEISURE EQUAL OUTCOME OF A CONTEST an equal score or result in a game, race, or competition **6.** SPORTS MATCH IN KNOCKOUT COMPETITION a match in a knockout competition, especially in football ○ *a cup tie* **7.** CONSTR STRENGTHENING BEAM a connecting, strengthening, or supporting beam or rod **8.** MUSIC CURVED LINE INDICATING EXTENSION OF NOTES a curved line shown above or below two notes of the same pitch, indicating that they are to be sounded without a break for their combined duration **9.** *US, Can* RAIL = **sleeper 10.** CIV ENG SURVEYING MEASUREMENT either of two measurements on a survey line used to fix the position of a reference point ■ *adj. US, Can* SPORTS MADE EQUAL having an equal outcome [Old English *tīgan*. Ultimately from a prehistoric Germanic base meaning 'to pull' (also the ancestor of English *tug*).] ◇ **fit to be tied** extremely angry or exasperated (*informal*)

tie down *vt.* prevent sb from acting freely

tie up *v.* **1.** *vt.* BIND to fasten or bind sth using rope or string **2.** *vti.* NAUT DOCK A BOAT to moor a boat or ship by securing lines, or be moored in this way **3.** *vt.* OCCUPY SB OR STH to keep sb or sth busy **4.** *vt.* COMPLETE STH to complete the work needed for sth **5.** *vti.* STOP to bring sth to a halt, or come to a halt **6.** *vt.* FIN INVEST MONEY WITH RESTRICTIONS to invest money in such a way that it cannot be used for other purposes **7.** *vt.* LAW PLACE RESTRICTIONS ON PROPERTY to place legal restrictions on the selling or alienation of property

tieback /tī bak/ *n.* a length of cord or fabric used to hold a curtain to one side

tie beam *n.* a beam such as the bottom horizontal member of a roof truss that pulls together a structure and stops it spreading outwards

tiebreaker /tī braykər/, **tie-break** /-brayk/ *n.* a means of deciding the winner of a game or competition when there is a tie

tiebreaking /tī brayking/ *adj.* deciding the winner of a game or competition when there is a tie ○ *the tie-breaking question*

tie clip, **tie clasp** *n.* an ornamental clasp that holds a tie in place against a shirt

tied /tīd/ *adj.* **1.** SELLING ONLY OWNER'S PRODUCTS owned by a producer, especially a brewery, and obliged to sell only its products **2.** OWNED BY OCCUPANT'S EMPLOYER owned by the occupant's employer and lived in only for the duration of the employment **3.** LOANED FOR THE PURCHASE OF THE LENDER'S GOODS loaned on condition of being spent only on goods or services supplied by the lender

tie-dye *vt.* DYE DESIGNS USING BUNCHED CLOTH to dye designs on cloth by tightly tying portions of it with waxed thread so that the dye only affects the exposed areas ■ *n.* **1.** FABRIC WITH TIE-DYED DESIGNS a piece of fabric whose designs are made by tie-dyeing (*informal*) **2.** = **tie-dyeing**

tie-dyeing *n.* a method of dyeing textiles to produce patterns by tightly tying waxed thread round sections of the fabric so that they will not become impregnated with the dye

tie-in *n.* **1.** LINK a link or relationship with sth **2.** JOINT PROMOTION OF PRODUCTS an arrangement by which related products are sold, promoted, or marketed together, e.g. a book or toy along with a film **3.** RELATED PRODUCT a product that is sold, promoted, or marketed in close connection with another **4.** *US* SALE REQUIRING DUAL PURCHASES a sale in which items are advertised or sold with the stipulation that they must be purchased together, or a product sold in this way

tie line *n.* a telephone line that connects two private exchanges

tiemannite /teémə nīt/ *n.* a dark grey mineral form of mercury selenide [Mid-19thC. From German *Tiemannit*, named after the German scientist J. C. W. F. *Tiemann* (1848–99).]

Tien Shan /tyén shaán/ mountain range in Central Asia, stretching about 2,400 km/1,500 mi. from Kyrgyzstan in the west through northwestern China to Mongolia in the east. The highest point is Victory Peak, 7,439 m/24,406 ft.

tiepin /tī pin/ *n.* an ornamental pin that holds a tie in place against a shirt. US term **tie tack**

tier /teer/ *n.* **1.** ROW OF SEATS IN RISING SERIES any of a series of rows placed one above and behind another, e.g. seats in a theatre **2.** LAYER any of a series of layers or levels placed one above the other (*often used in combination*) ○ *a three-tier cake* **3.** LEVEL IN HIERARCHY a hierarchical level in an organization (*often used in combination*) ■ *vt.* (**tiers, tiering, tiered**) ARRANGE STH IN RISING ROWS to arrange sth in rows rising one above the other [15thC. From French *tire* 'rank, sequence, order', from *tirer* 'to draw out, elongate'.]

tierce *n.* **1.** CHR = **terce 2.** CARDS THREE CARDS OF THE SAME SUIT a sequence of three cards of the same suit **3.** THIRD PART a third or third part (*archaic*) **4.** FENCING PARRYING POSITION the third of eight positions from which a fencing parry can be made **5.** MEASURE FORMER MEASURE OF CAPACITY a former measure of capacity equal to 42 wine gallons [15thC. Via Old French from Latin *tertia*, a form of *tertius* 'third'.]

tiercel *n.* = **tercel**

tiered /teerd/ *adj.* arranged in layers or levels placed one above the other (*often used in combination*)

tie rod *n.* a metal rod that joins or supports two parts such as one used as a linkage in the steering mechanism of a motor vehicle. Tie rods are also used to keep trusses and arches from spreading.

Tierra del Fuego /ti érrə del fwáygō/ archipelago off the southern tip of South America. Separated from the mainland by the Strait of Magellan, and bounded by the Atlantic, the Antarctic, and the Pacific oceans, the islands belong partly to Argentina and partly to Chile.

tie tack, **tie tac** n. US = **tiepin**

tie-up n. **1. CONNECTION** sth that connects one thing with another **2.** US **DELAY** a temporary delay or obstruction, e.g. in the flow of traffic

tiff /tif/ n. **1. QUARREL** a minor quarrel **2. ILL HUMOUR** a brief period of bad temper ■ vi. (**tiffs, tiffing, tiffed**) **1. ARGUE** to have a minor quarrel with sb **2. BE ILL-HUMOURED** to be in a bad temper [Early 18thC. Origin uncertain: probably originally a dialect word; thought to suggest the sound of a 'burst' of escaping gas.]

TIFF abbr. COMPUT tagged image file format

tiffany /tíffəni/ (plural **-nies**) n. a fine gauzy fabric [Early 17thC. Via Old French tifanie from, ultimately, Greek theophaneia, literally 'vision of God', perhaps because the body is visible through the material.]

TIFF file, **TIF file** n. a graphic file in a format often used for storing bitmapped images

tiffin /tíffin/ n. **1.** S Asia **LIGHT MEAL** a light midday meal or snack of savouries and sweets **2.** = **tiffin-carrier** [Early 19thC. Variant of tiffing, literally 'drinking', from obsolete tiff 'to drink', of unknown origin.]

tiffin-carrier n. S Asia a carrier consisting of several metal containers stacked one on top of another, used to carry prepared food

tig /tig/ n., vt. (**tigs, tigging, tigged**) = **tag** [15thC. The noun came from the verb, a variant of TICK[1], which originally meant 'to touch lightly'.]

Tiger

tiger /tígər/ (plural **-gers** or **-ger**) n. **1. LARGE STRIPED FELINE** a carnivorous Asian cat, the largest member of the cat family, that has a tawny coat and black stripes. Latin name: Panthera tigris. **2.** SB FIERCE sb who is fierce, brave, or forceful [13thC. Via Old French tigre from, ultimately, Greek tigris, of uncertain origin: perhaps from Iranian.] —**tigerish** adj. —**tigerishly** adv. —**tigerishness** n. ◊ **ride a tiger** be in a very difficult, precarious, or dangerous position

Tiger n. = **TIGR**

tiger beetle n. a fast-running predatory beetle that lives in warm regions. It has strong sharp jaws for digging and brightly coloured patterned wing covers. Family: Cicindelidae. [Tiger from its predatory habits]

tiger cat n. **1. SMALL CAT WITH MARKINGS RESEMBLING A TIGER'S** a small striped or spotted cat such as the margay, serval, or ocelot **2. TABBY CAT** a domestic cat with blotched or striped markings resembling those of a tiger **3.** Aus = **spotted-tailed quoll**

tigereye /tígər ī/ n. = **tiger's-eye**

tiger lily n. **1. ASIAN PLANT** an Asian lily that has red or orange flowers with dark purple or brown spots. Latin name: Lilium lancifolium and Lilium tigrinium. **2. LILY RESEMBLING THE ASIAN TIGER LILY** any lily that resembles the Asian tiger lily [Tiger from its colouring]

tiger moth n. a moth that has bold black and yellow or orange markings, especially on its wings. Family: Arctiidae.

tiger's-eye n. a striped yellow-brown rock composed of bands of quartz and fibrous silicate crocidolite, used as a gemstone

tiger shark n. a large striped or spotted shark that lives mainly in tropical seas and has a voracious and indiscriminate appetite. Latin name: Galeocerdo cuvieri.

tiger snake n. a highly venomous brown and yellow snake of southeastern Australia and Tasmania. Genus: Notechis.

tiger swallowtail n. a large North American butterfly with a deeply forked tail and yellow wings with black stripes. Latin name: Palilio glaucus and Palilio rutilus.

tight /tīt/ adj. **1. SNUG** fitting the body very closely ○ a tight sweater **2. TAUT** stretched so that there is no slack ○ pulled the rope tight **3. FIXED** firmly secured or held ○ a tight knot **4. SEALED** sealed against gas or liquid leaks ○ An airlock must have a tight seal. **5. STRICT** strictly controlled or administered ○ security was tight for the conference **6. CRAMPED** lacking sufficient space to move freely ○ It's going to be tight in the back seat. **7. HAVING NO EXTRA TIME** allowing no time beyond what is needed to do sth ○ a tight schedule **8. HAVING NO EXTRA MONEY** allowing no money beyond what is required ○ working to a tight budget **9. MISERLY** excessively frugal with money **10. HARD TO GET OUT OF** difficult or dangerous to handle ○ We're in a tight fix now. **11. WITH CLOSE RIVALS** characterized by well-matched competitors or teams ○ a tight race **12. DRUNK** intoxicated with alcohol (slang) **13. WELL DONE** arranged or performed with style and precision ○ a tight performance by the whole team **14. SUCCINCT** characterized by clear concise expression ○ tight prose **15.** US **INTIMATE** having a very close relationship with sb (informal) ○ He's tight with his boss. **16. HARD TO GET** characterized by conditions in which demand exceeds supply, often with concomitant rising prices ○ a tight economy ■ adv. **FIRMLY** in a firm, close, snug, or secure way ○ hold on tight [14thC. Alteration of obsolete thight 'dense, thick', from Old Norse théttr 'watertight, dense'.] —**tightly** adv. —**tightness** n. ◊ **be in a tight corner** or **spot** be in a difficult or dangerous situation

tighten /tīt'n/ (**-ens, -ening, -ened**) vti. to become or cause sth to become tight or tighter —**tightener** n.

tight end n. in American football, an offensive end who lines up near to the tackle

tightfisted /tīt fístid/ adj. disinclined to spend money

tight head n. in rugby, the prop forward positioned to the right of the hooker in the front row of the scrum

tightknit /tīt nít/ adj. **1. CLOSELY CONNECTED** closely united by love, friendship, or common interests ○ a tight-knit community **2. WELL-ORGANIZED** arranged or functioning as a well-structured whole

tight-lipped /-lípt/ adj. **1. RELUCTANT TO TALK** unwilling to communicate ○ He is remaining tight-lipped in the face of intense press speculation. **2. HAVING THE LIPS TOGETHER** having the lips firmly closed, e.g. in anger or pain

tightrope /tīt rōp/ n. a rope or wire stretched taut and suspended above the ground, on which sb walks or performs a balancing act ◊ **walk a tightrope** to have to deal cautiously with a precarious situation, often one involving a choice or compromise

tights /tīts/ npl. **1. SHEER ONE-PIECE GARMENT** a one-piece close-fitting garment made of sheer nylon, covering the body from waist to feet and worn by women and girls. US term **pantyhose 2. THICK ONE-PIECE GARMENT** a one-piece close-fitting garment made of opaque coloured wool or cotton, covering the body from the waist to the feet and worn by women and girls for warmth and casual wear **3. DANCER'S ONE-PIECE GARMENT** a one-piece close-fitting garment covering the body from the neck or waist to the feet, worn by men and women dancers and acrobats

tightwad /tīt wod/ n. US, Can sb who dislikes spending money (informal insult)

Tiglath-pileser I /tíg lath pī leezər/ (b. 1115?-1077? BC) Assyrian king. He expanded his kingdom by conquering Babylonia and recovering Armenia from invaders.

tiglic acid /tígglik-/ n. a viscous poisonous colourless liquid derived from croton oil, used in the pharmaceutical industry and perfumery. Formula: $C_5H_8O_2$. [Tiglic formed from modern Latin (Croton) tiglium, scientific name of the tree from whose seeds croton oil is obtained, from medieval Latin]

tigon, **tiglon** n. the offspring of a male tiger and a female lion [Mid-20thC. Blend of TIGER and LION.]

TIGR /tígər/ n. a bond linked to US treasury bonds, profits from which are subject to UK tax when the bond is cashed or redeemed. Abbr of **Treasury Investment Growth Receipts**

Tigray /tíg ray/, **Tigre** region in northeastern Ethiopia, bordering Eritrea. Capital: Mekele. Population: 3,136,267 (1994). Area: 65,786 sq. km/25,400 sq. mi.

tigress /tígrəss/ n. **1. FEMALE TIGER** a female tiger **2. FIERCE WOMAN** a fierce, brave, or passionate woman [Late 16thC. Formed from TIGER on the model of French tigresse 'tigress'.]

Tigrinya /ti greényə/ n. LANG a Semitic language of northern Ethiopia that belongs to the Afro-Asiatic family of languages [Mid-19thC. From Tigrinya.]

Tigris /tígriss/ river in southwestern Asia. It rises in southeastern Turkey, flows through Iraq, and joins the Euphrates to form the Shatt Al-Arab, which empties into the Persian Gulf. Length: 1,850 km/1,150 mi.

Tijuana /ti wáanə/ city in northwestern Mexico, just south of the United States border. It is an industrial and tourist centre. Population: 747,381 (1990).

tike n. = **tyke**

tiki /teéki/ n. **1. MAORI AMULET** a small carved human foetal figure, especially in greenstone, representing an ancestor and worn as an amulet by some Maori and Polynesian peoples **2. IMAGE OF A POLYNESIAN GOD** a stone or wooden representation of a Polynesian god [Late 18thC. From Maori.]

tikka /teéka/ adj. an Indian dish of skewered meat that is marinated and then dry-roasted in an oven [Mid-20thC. From Punjabi ṭikkā.]

til /til/ n. PLANTS = **sesame** n. 2 [Mid-19thC. From Sanskrit tila.]

'til /til/, **til**, **'till** contr. until. See Usage note at **till** [Mid-20thC. Shortening.]

Tilak /tíllək/, **B. G.** (1856–1920) Indian journalist and political activist. He was a prominent member of the Indian nationalist movement and founder of the Home Rule League (1916). Full name **Balwantrao Gangadhar Tilak**

tilapia /ti láppi ə, -láy-/ (plural **-as** or **-a**) n. a tropical African freshwater fish of the cichlid family, some species of which are important food fish and have been introduced and cultivated worldwide. Genus: Tilapia. [Mid-19thC. From modern Latin, the genus name.]

Tilburg /tíl burg/ industrial city in North Brabant Province, southern Netherlands. Population: 163,383 (1994).

tilde /tíldə/ n. a mark (~) placed over a letter to show that the pronunciation is nasalized, e.g. over 'n' in Spanish, and over 'a' or 'o' in Portuguese [Mid-19thC. Via Spanish from Latin titulus 'heading', with the sounds in the middle transposed.]

tile /tīl/ n. **1. BUILDING COVERING FOR FLOORS, ROOFS, OR WALLS** a thin flat or curved piece of baked, sometimes glazed, clay or synthetic material used to cover roofs, floors, and walls, or for decoration **2. BUILDING SHORT PIPE IN A DRAIN** a short pipe of baked clay, concrete, or plastic used in making a drain **3. BUILDING TILES COLLECTIVELY** tiles considered collectively **4. GAME PLAYING PIECE** a rectangular playing piece in various games such as mahjong **5. CLOTHES HAT** a hat (dated informal) ■ v. (**tiles, tiling, tiled**) **1.** vt. **LAY TILES ON STH** to cover a surface with tiles **2.** vt. **FIT STH WITH DRAINAGE TILES** to put drainage tiles in sth **3.** vti. COMPUT **ARRANGE WINDOWS** to arrange the windows on a computer screen side by side so that all are visible [Pre-12thC. From Latin tegula. Ultimately from an Indo-European base meaning 'to cover' that is also the ancestor of English thatch.] —**tiler** n. ◊ **on the tiles** in pursuit of drinking and pleasure (informal)

tilefish /tīl fish/ (*plural* **-fish** *or* **-fishes**) *n.* a long blue fish with yellow spots on its upper body, found in deep waters of the Atlantic off the coast of North America. Latin name: *Lopholatilus chamaeleonticeps.* [Late 19thC. *Tile* from the genus Lopholatilus, and perhaps also from the bright colouring resembling ornamental tiles.]

tiling /tīling/ *n.* **1.** LAID TILES tiles that have been laid **2.** LAYING OF TILES the laying of tiles on a wall or floor **3.** TILES tiles collectively

till[1] /til/ *conj., prep.* until [Old English *til* 'up to a particular point', from a prehistoric Germanic word meaning 'aim, goal']

WORD KEY: USAGE

till or **until**? Both words have the same meaning and function (preposition and conjunction), and are largely interchangeable. In practice, however, ***till*** is more informal than ***until*** and is more likely to be heard in speech: *Just wait till we get home!* ***Until*** is more usual at the beginning of a sentence: *Until last week there was no one here that we knew.* The spellings *'til* and *'till* reflect the commonly held belief that ***till*** is a shortened form of ***until***, but ***till*** is in fact the older form.

till[2] /til/ *n.* **1.** CONTAINER FOR MONEY a box, drawer, or tray, e.g. in a cash register, in which money is kept **2.** = **checkout** [15thC. Origin uncertain: perhaps via Anglo-Norman *tylle* from Old French *tille* 'compartment, shelter on a ship', from Scandinavian.]

till[3] /til/ (**tills, tilling, tilled**) *vt.* to prepare land for the growing of crops by ploughing or harrowing [Old English *tilian* 'to cultivate', earlier 'to strive to obtain sth'. Ultimately from a prehistoric Germanic word meaning 'an aim, purpose'.] —**tillable** *adj.* —**tiller** *n.*

till[4] /til/ *n.* GEOG sediment of various particle sizes deposited by the direct action of ice [Late 17thC. Origin unknown.]

tillage /tíllij/ *n.* **1.** TILLING OF LAND the ploughing or harrowing of land in preparation for growing crops **2.** TILLED LAND land that has been tilled

tillandsia /ti lándzi ə/ *n.* an epiphytic plant of the pineapple family such as Spanish moss that grows in tropical or subtropical America. Genus: *Tillandsia.* [Mid-18thC. From modern Latin, the genus name, from the name of Elias *Tillands* (1640–93), a Swedish botanist.]

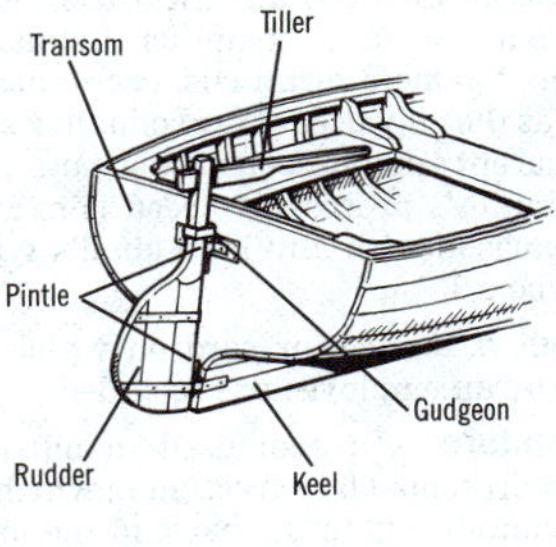
Transom
Tiller
Pintle
Gudgeon
Rudder
Keel

Tiller

tiller[1] /tíllər/ *n.* NAUT the means by which a small boat is steered, consisting of a handle attached to the rudder [14thC. Via Anglo-Norman *telier* 'weaver's beam', from, ultimately, Latin *tela* 'web'. The modern meaning evolved via 'the beam of a crossbow'.]

tiller[2] /tíllər/ *n.* AGRIC a person or machine that ploughs or cultivates the soil

tiller[3] /tíllər/ *n.* BOT a shoot growing from the base of a stem, especially the stem of a grass [Mid-17thC. Origin uncertain: probably from Old English *telgor* 'extended', from *telga* 'branch'.]

tillerman /-mən/ (*plural* **-men** /-mən/) *n.* sb who handles the tiller and steers a boat

Tillich /tíllik/, **Paul** (1886–1965) German-born US philosopher and theologian. He emigrated to the United States in 1933. His scholarly and popular books sought to reconcile existential philosophy and contemporary secular culture with Christian faith, and included *The Courage to Be* (1952) and *Systematic Theology* (1951–63). Full name **Paul Johannes Tillich**

Tilly /tílli/, **Johann Tserclaes, Count** (1559–1632) Flemish soldier. As a commander of the Catholic League, he won many victories in the Thirty Years' War (1618–48), but was eventually defeated and fatally wounded.

tilt[1] /tilt/ *v.* (**tilts, tilting, tilted**) **1.** *vti.* SLOPE to slant or cause sth to slant ○ *She tilted her head as she listened.* **2.** *vi. US* HAVE AS A PREFERENCE to tend towards favouring a particular opinion, course of action, or side in a dispute **3.** *vi.* CRITICIZE to make a spoken or written attack on sb or sth **4.** *vi.* COMBAT to combat or struggle against sb or sth **5.** *vti.* HIST CHARGE WITH A LANCE to attack an opponent using a lance **6.** *vi.* HIST JOUST WITH SB to take part in a joust against sb **7.** *vi.* HIST POINT A LANCE to hold a lance ready for combat in a joust **8.** *vt.* USE A TILT HAMMER ON STH to work on sth using a tilt hammer ■ *n.* **1.** ACT OF TILTING an act of tilting or of causing sth to tilt **2.** INCLINE a slanted surface or position ○ *his hat was at a rakish tilt* **3.** CRITICISM a spoken or written attack on sb or sth **4.** *US* PREFERENCE a tendency to favour a particular opinion, course of action, or side in a dispute **5.** HIST JOUST a jousting contest **6.** HIST LANCE THRUST a thrust made with a lance in a jousting contest **7.** = **tilt hammer** [14thC. Origin uncertain: probably from assumed Old English *tyltan* 'to fall over', from a prehistoric Germanic word meaning 'unsteady'.] —**tilter** *n.* ◇ **(at) full tilt** at full speed

tilt[2] /tilt/ *n.* a canvas cover or canopy used to cover an otherwise open boat, booth, or trailer of a lorry [15thC. From Old English *teld*, perhaps influenced by TENT.]

tilth /tilth/ *n.* **1.** TILLING OF LAND the ploughing of land in preparation for growing crops **2.** TILLED LAND land under cultivation **3.** CONDITION OF LAND the condition of a piece of tilled land, in terms of its cultivation history and suitability for crops **4.** DEGREE OF FINENESS OF SOIL the degree of fineness of soil particles in the topmost soil layer [Old English *tilþ(e)*, from *tilian*, an earlier form of TILL[3]]

tilt hammer *n.* a heavy drop hammer used to forge metal, pivoted by a lever [*Tilt* because it can be tilted]

tiltyard /tílt yaard/ *n.* a place, usually enclosed, where a jousting contest was held

Tim. *abbr.* BIBLE Timothy

Timaru /tímmәroo/ city on the east-central coast of the South Island, New Zealand. Population: 27,521 (1996).

timbal /tímb'l/, **tymbal** *n.* a kettledrum (*archaic*) [Late 17thC. From French *timbal*, alteration (modelled on *cymbale* 'cymbal') of obsolete *tamballe*, from (influenced by *tambour* 'drum') Spanish *atabal*, from Arabic *aṭ -ṭabl*, literally 'the drum'.]

timbale /tam báal/ *n.* **1.** DISH MADE IN A MOULD a dish consisting of a mixture of ingredients, often set with eggs, made in a mould and served hot or cold **2.** COOKING MOULD a small deep or tall mould in which a timbale dish is made [Early 19thC. From French (see TIMBAL), from its shape.]

timber /tímbər/ *n.* **1.** WOOD CONSTRUCTION MATERIAL wood that has been sawn into boards, planks, or other materials for use in building, woodworking, or cabinetmaking. US term **lumber 2.** GROWING TREES standing trees or their wood **3.** WOODED LAND land covered with trees **4.** BUILDING LARGE WOODEN BUILDING SUPPORT a large piece of wood, usually squared, used in a building, e.g. as a beam **5.** PART OF THE FRAMEWORK OF A SHIP a large piece of wood used in the framework of a wooden ship ■ *adj.* WOODEN constructed of wood ■ *interj.* WARNING OF A FALLING TREE used by a lumberjack to warn others that a tree has been cut and is about to fall ■ *vt.* (**-bers, -bering, -bered**) PROVIDE STH WITH TIMBERS to build, cover, or support sth with timbers [Old English, 'a building'. Ultimately from an Indo-European base meaning 'to build' that is also the ancestor of English *domestic*. The modern meaning evolved via the sense 'building material'.]

timbered /tímbərd/ *adj.* **1.** BUILDING CONSTRUCTED OF TIMBER made of timber or having timbers (*often used in combination*) ○ *a half-timbered house* **2.** WOODED covered with growing trees

timberhead /tímbər hed/ *n.* the top of a timber of a ship that projects above the deck and is used as a tall post (**bollard**) for securing the ship to a wharf or dock

timber hitch *n.* a knot used to tie a rope around a spar or log that is to be hoisted or hauled

timbering /tímbəring/ *n.* timber or objects made of timber

timberland /tímbər land/ *n. US* an area of wooded land, especially one with trees that have commercial value as timber

timberline /tímbər līn/ *n. US* = **tree line**

timber rattlesnake *n.* a poisonous rattlesnake of the eastern United States that is yellow-brown with wide dark bands and feeds on small mammals. Latin name: *Crotalus horridus.*

timber wolf *n.* = **grey wolf**

timberwork /tímbər wurk/ *n.* sth constructed of timber, or the timber parts of sth

timberyard /tímbər yaard/ *n.* a place where timber and other building materials are stored and sold. US term **lumberyard**

timbre /támbər, tímbər, táNbrə/ *n.* **1.** PHON SPEECH SOUND QUALITY the quality of a speech sound that comes from its tone rather than its pitch or volume **2.** MUSIC MUSICAL TONE QUALITY the quality or colour of tone of an instrument or voice [Mid-19thC. Via French, originally 'drum, bell hit with a hammer', from, ultimately, Greek *tumpanon* 'drum' (source of English *timpani*).]

timbrel /tímbrəl/ *n.* in the Bible, a tambourine or small hand drum [Early 16thC. Origin uncertain: perhaps literally 'little drum', formed from obsolete *timbre* 'drum', from French (see TIMBRE).]

Timbuktu[1] /tím buk tóo/ *n.* a place that is far away or extremely remote (*informal*)

Timbuktu[2] /tímb uk tóo/, **Timbuctoo** city in central Mali, on the southern edge of the Sahara Desert. Population: 19,165 (1976).

time /tīm/ *n.* **1.** SYSTEM OF DISTINGUISHING EVENTS a dimension that enables two identical events occurring at the same point in space to be distinguished, measured by the interval between the events. Symbol *t* **2.** PERIOD WITH LIMITS a limited period during which an action, process, or condition exists or takes place ○ *elapsed time* **3.** METHOD OF MEASURING INTERVALS a system for measuring intervals of time ○ *sidereal time* ○ *British Summer time* **4.** MINUTE OR HOUR the minute or hour as indicated by a clock ○ *What time is it?* **5.** TIME AS A CAUSATIVE FORCE time conceived as a force capable of acting on people and objects ○ *time's ravages* **6.** MOMENT STH OCCURS a moment or period at which sth takes place ○ *at the time of her 90th birthday* **7.** SUITABLE MOMENT a moment or period chosen as appropriate for sth to be done or to take place ○ *The times for the games will be announced.* **8.** UNALLOCATED PERIOD a period that is not allocated for a particular purpose ○ *I had time on my hands.* **9.** PERIOD NEEDED a period required, allocated, or taken to complete an activity ○ *How much time?* **10.** PERIOD WITH A PARTICULAR QUALITY a period, activity, or occasion that has a particular quality or characteristic (*often used in the plural*) ○ *They've been through some rough times.* ○ *We had an interesting time there.* **11.** APPOINTED MOMENT a designated or customary moment or period at which sth is done or takes place ○ *It's time to get up.* **12.** CLOSING TIME the time at which a pub or bar is legally required to close **13.** CERTAIN INTERVAL a limited but unspecified period ○ *We stayed for a time.* **14.** HISTORICAL PERIOD a period in history, often characterized by a particular event or person (*often used in the plural*) ○ *in Shakespeare's time* ○ *ancient times* **15.** NOW the present as distinguished from the past or future (*often used in the plural*) ○ *technology that is ahead of the times* **16.** GEOL GEOLOGICAL DIVISION a chronological division of geological history **17.** ANTICIPATED MOMENT a moment in which some important event such as a birth or death is expected to happen ○ *He knew his time had come.* **18.** SB'S LIFETIME a period during which sb is alive, especially the most active or productive period in sb's life ○ *She'd been a well-known athlete in her time.* ○ *We didn't worry about such trifles in my time.* **19.** APPRENTICESHIP PERIOD a period during which sb is an apprentice ○ *had served his time* **20.** PRISON TERM a term in prison (*informal*) ○ *serve time for robbery* **21.** MILITARY SERVICE a term of military service **22.** SEASON a period during which particular climatic conditions prevail ○ *the rainy times of the year* **23.** INSTANCE a separate occasion of a recurring event ○ *I told you three times.* **24.** MUSIC TEMPO OF MUSIC the relative speed at which a musical composition is played **25.** MUSIC MUSICAL BEAT the number of beats per bar of a musical composition **26.** PERIOD WORKED the period during a day or week that sb works ○ *working half time* **27.** PAY a rate of pay ○ *paid double time* **28.** SPORTS PLAYING PERIOD a period of play in a game **29.** *US* SPORTS = **timeout** *n.* 1 ■ *v.* **(times, timing, timed) 1.** *vt.* MEASURE HOW LONG STH TAKES to measure or record the duration, speed, or rate of sth **2.** *vt.* SCHEDULE STH to plan the moment or occasion for sth, especially in order to achieve the best result or effect ○ *time an entrance* **3.** *vt.* SET THE TIME OF STH to regulate or set the time of sth such as a clock or a train's schedule **4.** *vi.* STAY IN RHYTHM to keep time to a rhythmical or musical beat [Old English *tīma* 'period of time', from a prehistoric Germanic base meaning 'to extend', which is also the ancestor of English *tide*] ◇ **all in good time** no sooner than is appropriate ◇ **all the time** continuously ◇ **at one time 1.** at a time in the past **2.** simultaneously ◇ **at the same time 1.** simultaneously **2.** nevertheless ◇ **at times** sometimes ◇ **behind the times** out of touch with modern fashions, methods, or attitudes ◇ **for the time being** for a short period of time starting from now ◇ **from time to time** occasionally ◇ **have no time for sb** *or* **sth** to regard sb or sth with dislike or contempt ◇ **have the time of your life** to have a very enjoyable experience ◇ **in good time 1.** early enough ○ *got there in good time so we could find a parking space* **2.** quickly ◇ **in (less than) no time** in a very short period of time ◇ **in time 1.** early enough ○ *We were in time for the concert.* **2.** after some time has passed ○ *He'll understand in time that you were trying to help him.* **3.** in the correct rhythm ○ *clapping in time to the music* ◇ **in your own time 1.** not during working hours **2.** at a speed or pace that feels natural and comfortable ◇ **keep time 1.** to show the time accurately **2.** to do sth in the correct rhythm, or in the same rhythm as sb or sth else ◇ **live on borrowed time** to enjoy an unexpected extension of life ◇ **make time with sb** *US* to pursue sb as a sexual partner (*informal*) ◇ **on time** at the scheduled time ◇ **pass the time of day (with sb)** to engage in casual conversation with sb ◇ **take your time 1.** to take whatever time is necessary **2.** to do sth unacceptably slowly ◇ **time after time, time and (time) again** repeatedly ◇ **time out of mind** for an extremely long time ◇ **time was** there was a time in the past

time and a half *n.* a rate of pay equal to one and a half times the normal rate, usually paid for overtime work

time and motion study *n.* an analysis of the working practices of, e.g. a person, department, or factory, done with the aim of finding ways to increase efficiency

time bomb *n.* **1.** BOMB EXPLODING AT A FIXED TIME a bomb with a timing mechanism that allows it to explode at a specified time **2.** FUTURE DANGER sth that is not dangerous or harmful at the moment but is likely to become so

time capsule *n.* a container of articles representative of the present, placed in a building's foundations or buried for a future generation to find and learn about the period it represents

timecard /tīm kaard/ *n.* a card that an employee has stamped by a time clock when starting and finishing work

time clock *n.* a clock with a mechanism for stamping employees' timecards when they start and finish work

time-consuming *adj.* taking up or wasting a great deal of time

time deposit *n.* a bank deposit from which a withdrawal can be made only after a specified period of time or after giving notice. ◊ **demand deposit**

time dilation, time dilatation *n.* the principle that time elapsed is relative to motion, so that time passes more slowly for a system in motion than for one at rest relative to an outside observer. Further, as predicted by Einstein's Special Theory of Relativity, time passes increasingly slowly as the motion relative to the observer approaches the speed of light.

timed-release, time-release *adj.* formulated with a drug that releases its active ingredient gradually to prolong its effect

time exposure *n.* **1.** RELATIVELY LONG EXPOSURE the exposure of photographic film for an unusually long time to achieve a desired effect **2.** PHOTOGRAPH WITH A RELATIVELY LONG EXPOSURE a photograph taken by time exposure

time frame *n.* a period of time during which sth takes place or is planned to take place ○ *What's the time frame for the project?*

time-honoured *adj.* respected or continued because of having been the custom for a long time

time immemorial *n.* **1.** DISTANT PAST time so distant in the past as to be beyond memory or record **2.** HIST TIME BEFORE 1189 the time prior to the keeping of official legal records in England, fixed at 1189, the beginning of Richard I's reign

timekeeper /tīm keepər/ *n.* **1.** SPORTS SB RECORDING THE TIME ELAPSED sb who keeps a record of the time elapsed during a sporting event **2.** SB RECORDING THE TIME WORKED sb who keeps a record of the time worked by employees **3.** SB CONSIDERED IN TERMS OF PUNCTUALITY an employee considered in terms of his or her punctuality **4.** WATCH OR CLOCK an instrument for recording or showing the time such as a watch or clock **5.** WATCH CONSIDERED IN TERMS OF ACCURACY a watch or clock considered in terms of its accuracy —**timekeeping** *n.*

time lag *n.* an amount of time that passes between two connected events

time-lapse photography *n.* a method of filming a slow process such as the opening of a flower by taking a series of single exposures, then showing them at higher speed to simulate continuous action

timeless /tīmləss/ *adj.* **1.** UNCHANGED remaining invariable throughout time ○ *fiction that has a timeless appeal* **2.** ETERNAL having no beginning or end —**timelessly** *adv.* —**timelessness** *n.*

time limit *n.* a period of time within which sth must be done or is effective

time loan *n.* a loan that has to be repaid by or on a given date. ◊ **call loan**

time lock *n.* a lock on a device such as a safe or bank vault with a timing mechanism that sets it to open only at set times

timely /tīmli/ **(-lier, -liest)** *adj.* **1.** OCCURRING AT A GOOD TIME happening or done at the right time or an appropriate time ○ *a timely invention* **2.** EARLY early (*archaic*) —**timely** *adv.* —**timeliness** *n.*

time machine *n.* a fictional or hypothetical machine that can be used to travel backwards or forwards in time

Time of Troubles *n.* the period between the death of Tsar Ivan IV, when the Boyars attempted to regain control of Russia, and the selection of Michael Romanov as tsar in 1613

time-on *n.* *Aus* in Australian Rules Football, a period of time added on at the end of each quarter to make up for time lost through stoppages

timeous /tīməss/ *adj.* *Scotland* happening or done in good time —**timeously** *adv.*

timeout *n.* **1.** SPORTS TIME DURING WHICH GAME STOPS a break taken to allow players to rest, receive medical treatment, confer, or be substituted **2.** COMPUT LACK OF RESPONSE FROM A COMPUTER DEVICE an interruption in the operation of a computer when a device such as a printer or disk drive does not respond to a command in a predetermined amount of time. A timeout usually results in a message to the user giving the option of retrying or cancelling the command. ■ *interj.* REQUEST FOR A BREAK used to ask for or suggest a break in a game or an activity

time out *n.* *US* a short break or rest from work or other activities ○ *took time out from her studies to travel for a year*

timepiece /tīm peess/ *n.* an instrument for recording or showing the time such as a watch or clock, especially one that does not strike or chime

timer /tīmər/ *n.* **1.** TIME-SETTING DEVICE a device that can be preset to start or stop sth at a given time or that sounds after a set period of time **2.** TIME-RECORDING DEVICE a device for recording, showing, or measuring time such as a stopwatch **3.** SB TRACKING TIME sb who measures or records elapsed time **4.** AUTOMOT DEVICE CONTROLLING IGNITION a device in an internal-combustion engine that controls the timing of the spark in the cylinders

time-release *adj.* = **timed-release**

times /tīmz/ *prep.* used to indicate that a number is to be multiplied by another ○ *Three times two is six.*

timesaving /tīm sayving/ *adj.* designed to reduce the length of time taken to do sth —**timesaver** *n.*

timescale /tīm skayl/ *n.* **1.** PERIOD OF TIME a period of time scheduled for sth to be completed **2.** TIME MEASURED RELATIVE TO MAJOR EVENTS a measurement of time relative to the time in which a typical event occurs, e.g. in geological or cosmic time

time series *n.* a sequence of data gathered at uniformly spaced intervals of time

time-served *adj.* having completed an apprenticeship and therefore fully competent to work as a tradesman

timeserver /tīm survər/ *n.* sb whose opinions and behaviour change to suit the times and circumstances without regard for principle —**timeserving** *n., adj.*

timeshare /tīm shair/ **(-shares, -sharing, -shared)** *n.* **1.** = **time sharing** *n.* 1 **2.** LEISURE JOINTLY OWNED PROPERTY a property, usually an apartment in a resort area, that is jointly owned by people who use it at different times

time-share /tīm shair/ **(time-shares, time-sharing, time-shared)** *vti.* **1.** COMPUT USE A COMPUTER SIMULTANEOUSLY to use a main computer according to a system in which a number of individuals work from remote work stations **2.** JOINTLY OWN PROPERTY to own a property jointly with others who share its use —**time-sharer** *n.*

time sharing *n.* **1.** LEISURE JOINT OWNERSHIP the joint ownership of a property such as an apartment in a resort area in which each owner may occupy the property for a specific time during the year **2.** COMPUT SIMULTANEOUS COMPUTER USE a technique for the concurrent use of a computer by many people working at remote terminals, each apparently operating as the only user of the computer's resources. The apparent simultaneous use is possible because the computer's processing speed is extremely fast in comparison with any individual's typing speed at a keyboard.

time sheet *n.* a sheet or card on which the hours worked by an employee are recorded

time signature *n.* a sign used in music to show metre, represented by a fraction in which the upper figure shows beats to the bar and the lower figure shows each beat's time value

times sign *n.* a multiplication sign (*informal*)

times table *n.* a multiplication table (*informal; often used in combination*)

time study *n.* = **time and motion study**

time switch *n.* an electrical switch that can be set to turn an appliance on or off at a particular time

timetable /tīm tayb'l/ *n.* SCHEDULE a list of the times at which events are to occur, e.g. the arrival and departure times of trains or the times of school classes. US term **schedule** *n.* 4 ■ *vti.* **(-bles, -bling, -bled)** PUT STH IN CHRONOLOGICAL LIST to put sth in its chronological place in a list of events

time-tested *adj.* *US* proven to be effective over a long period

time trial *n.* a race in which competitors compete individually for the fastest time

time warp *n.* a hypothetical distortion in the continuum of space-time, popular in science fiction, allowing time to stand still or people to travel from one time to another

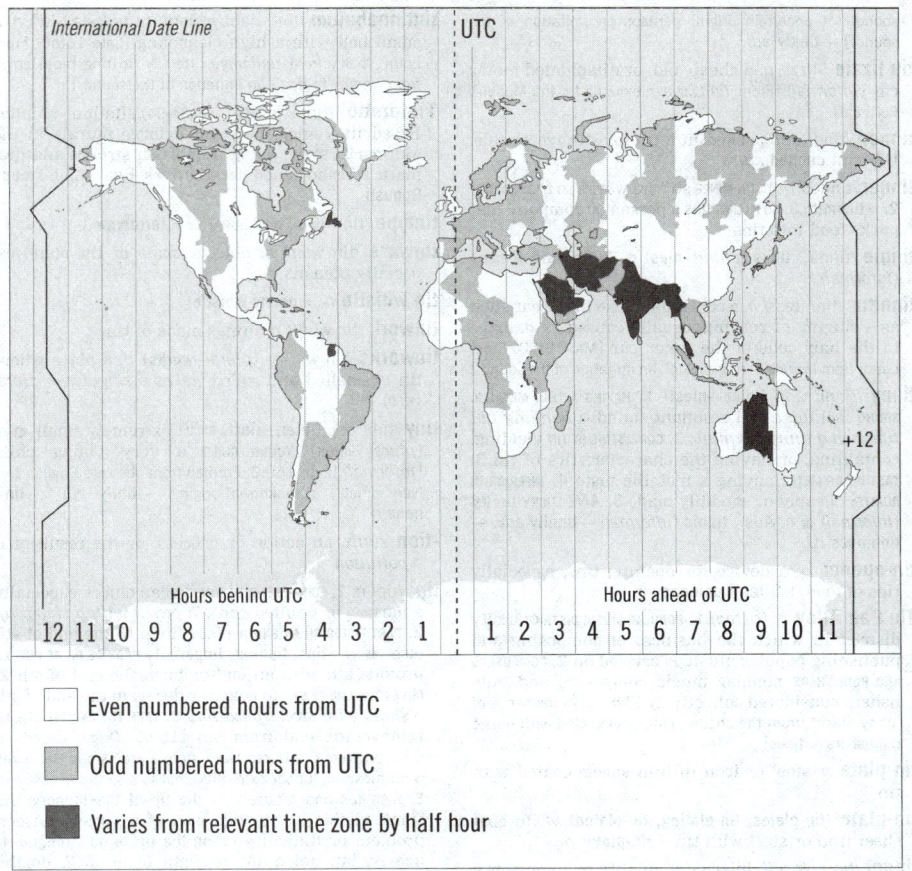

International Date Line   UTC

Hours behind UTC   Hours ahead of UTC

12 11 10 9 8 7 6 5 4 3 2 1   1 2 3 4 5 6 7 8 9 10 11

+12

☐ Even numbered hours from UTC

▨ Odd numbered hours from UTC

■ Varies from relevant time zone by half hour

Time zone

timework /tīm wurk/ *n.* work paid according to the time it takes, especially by the hour or the day — **timeworker** *n.*

timeworn /tīm wawrn/ *adj.* **1.** HAVING DETERIORATED THROUGH LONG USE showing the effects of having been used for a long period of time **2.** HACKNEYED having lost effectiveness through overuse ○ *a timeworn phrase*

time zone *n.* any of the 24 longitudinal areas into which the world is divided and within which the same standard time is used

timid /tímmid/ *adj.* demonstrating a lack of courage or self-assurance [Mid-16thC. Directly or via French from Latin *timidus* 'fearful', from *timere* 'to fear'.] —**timidity** /ti míddəti/ *n.* —**timidly** /tímmidli/ *adv.*

timing /tíming/ *n.* **1.** JUDGMENT OF WHEN TO ACT the ability to choose or the choice of the best moment to do or say sth, e.g. in performing music or comedy or in sport ○ *a comedian with an immaculate sense of timing* ○ *split-second timing* **2.** RECORDING OF TIME the measurement and recording of the time taken to do sth **3.** AUTOMOT ADJUSTMENT OF VALVES OF ENGINE the adjustment of the sequence and relative position of the valves and crankshaft of an automobile engine so that maximum output power is achieved

Timişoara /tímmi swa'arə/ capital city of Timiş County, western Romania. Population: 327,830 (1994).

timocracy /ti mókrəsi/ (*plural* **-cies**) *n.* **1.** GOVERNMENT BY THE PROPERTIED CLASS government in which the possession of property is a qualification for holding office **2.** GOVERNMENT BY PEOPLE OF HONOUR a form of government in which honour is the guiding principle [15thC. Via French *timocratie* from, ultimately, Greek *timokratia*, from *timē* 'honour, value'.] —**timocratic** /tímmə kráttik/ *adj.*

Timor /tée mawr/ island in the Malay Archipelago. It is the largest and easternmost of the Lesser Sunda Islands, bordered on the north by the Savu and Banda seas and on the south by the Timor Sea. Population: 1,382,207 (1980). Area: 30,820 sq. km/11,900 sq. mi.

timorous /tímmərəss/ *adj.* showing fear or hesitancy [15thC. Via Old French *temoreus* from medieval Latin *timorosus*, from, ultimately, Latin *timere* 'to fear' (source of English *timid*).] —**timorously** *adv.* —**timorousness** *n.*

Timor Sea arm of the Indian Ocean separating the island of Timor from northern Australia. Area: 450,000 sq. km/175,000 sq. mi.

timothy /tímməthi/, **timothy grass** *n.* a perennial grass that grows in temperate regions, has a cylindrical flower spike, and is widely cultivated for hay and pasture. Latin name: *Phleum pratense*. [Mid-18thC. Named after *Timothy* Hanson, an American farmer who introduced the grass from New York to the Carolinas around 1720.]

Timothy /tímməthi/ *n.* two books in the Bible, in the form of epistles addressed to Timothy, traditionally believed to be from St Paul. They are concerned with the organization of Christian doctrine and codes of Christian behaviour. See table at **Bible**

Timothy, St *n.* in the Bible, an early Christian missionary, and friend and disciple of St Paul

timpani /tímpəni/, **tympani** *npl.* a set of two or more kettledrums, usually played as part of an orchestra (*takes a singular or plural verb*) [Late 19thC. From Italian, plural of *timpano* 'kettledrum', ultimately from Greek *tumpanon* 'drum' (source of English *timbre*).] —**timpanist** *n.*

timps /timps/ *npl.* timpani (*informal*) [Mid-20thC. Shortening.]

tin /tin/ *n.* **1.** METALLIC ELEMENT a silvery, easily shaped metallic element extracted from its oxide ore. It is used extensively in alloys such as solder, bronze, and pewter and as a protective coating for steel. Symbol **Sn 2.** CONTAINER a sealed container for food or drink, made of thin sheet metal coated with tin or of other thin metal, e.g. aluminium. US term **can 3.** SHEET-METAL CONTAINER a lidded container made of thin sheet metal and often decorated **4.** AMOUNT IN TIN the amount that a tin holds **5.** CORRUGATED IRON corrugated or galvanized iron **6.** MONEY money (*dated informal*) ■ *adj.* **1.** MADE OF TIN made from thin sheet metal

coated with tin **2.** MADE OF CORRUGATED IRON made of corrugated or galvanized iron ■ *vt.* (**tins, tinning, tinned**) **1.** PUT FOOD IN TINS to preserve or seal food in tins. US term **can 2.** COAT STH WITH TIN to coat or plate sth with tin [Old English. Ultimately of prehistoric Germanic origin.]

Tinamou

tinamou /tínni moo/ (*plural* **-mous** or **-mou**) *n.* a short round-bodied ground-dwelling bird of grassy and jungle areas of Central and South America. Family: Tinamidae. [Late 18thC. Via French from Carib *tinamu*.]

Tinbergen /tín burgən/, **Jan** (1903–94) Dutch economist. He was a pioneer of econometrics and economic adviser to the League of Nations Secretariat (1936–38). He shared the first Nobel Prize in economics (1969).

tincal /tíngk'l/ *n.* a sodium borate mineral formed by the weathering of borax [Mid-17thC. Origin uncertain: probably from Portugese *tincal*, from Persian and Urdu *tinkār*, ultimately from Sanskrit *ṭaṅkana*.]

tin can *n.* a container made of tin or aluminium, especially one used for food

tinct /tingkt/ *n.* TINT a tint (*archaic*) ■ *vti.* (**tincts, tincting, tincted**) TINT to tint (*archaic*) ■ *adj.* TINTED tinted or coloured (*literary*) [15thC. From Latin *tinctus* 'a dyeing' (see TINT).]

tinct. *abbr.* tincture

tincture /tíngkchər/ *n.* **1.** ALCOHOL SOLUTION a solution of a plant product or chemical substance in alcohol ○ *tincture of iodine* **2.** TINGE OR COLOUR a tint or slight colouration **3.** TINY AMOUNT OF STH a hint or small amount of sth **4.** HERALDRY HERALDIC COLOUR a colour, metal, or fur used in heraldry **5.** DYE a dye or stain (*archaic*) ■ *vt.* (**-tures, -turing, -tured**) **1.** ADD A TINT TO to give sth a hint of colour **2.** IMBUE WITH to suffuse sth with a quality or property ○ *praise tinctured with criticism* [14thC. From Latin *tinctura* 'dyeing', from the past participle stem of *tingere* 'to dye' (source of English *tinge*).]

Tindal /tínd'l/ = William Tyndale

tinder /tíndər/ *n.* material such as dry sticks that is easily combustible and can be used for lighting a fire [Old English *tynder*, from a prehistoric Germanic base meaning 'to ignite, kindle']

tinderbox /tíndər boks/ *n.* **1.** HIST BOX CONTAINING TINDER a metal box containing tinder, often fitted with a flint and steel, formerly used for lighting fires **2.** SB OR STH POTENTIALLY VIOLENT a person, place, or situation that is likely to become violent

tine /tīn/ *n.* **1.** PRONG a thin pointed projection of a utensil or implement such as a fork or pitchfork **2.** ZOOL ANTLER'S BRANCH a pointed branch of a deer's antler [Old English *tind*] —**tined** *adj.*

tinea /tínni ə/ *n.* an infection of the skin caused by any of several species of fungi that live as parasites on the outer layer of the skin, nails, or hair [14thC. From Latin, 'gnawing worm, moth'.] —**tineal** *adj.*

tinea barbae /-ba'arbi/ *n.* barber's itch (*technical*) [From Latin, literally 'tinea of the beard']

tinea cruris /-kro'oriss/ *n.* dhobi itch (*technical*) [From Latin, literally 'tinea of the leg']

tinea pedis /-péddiss/ *n.* athlete's foot (*technical*) [From Latin, literally 'tinea of the foot']

tin ear *n.* an inability to perceive differences in musical sounds or subtleties in speech (*informal*) [From the idea of metal as incapable of sensation]

tineid /tínni id/ *n.* a very small moth found throughout the world whose larvae either eat fabrics of animal origin or are scavengers. Family: Tineidae. [Mid-19thC. From modern Latin *Tineidae* (plural), family name, ultimately from Latin *tinea* 'moth'.]

tinfoil /tín foyl/ *n.* **1.** THIN ALUMINIUM SHEET aluminium in a very thin sheet, used to wrap food **2.** THIN TIN SHEET tin, or an alloy of tin and lead, in a very thin sheet

ting /ting/ *n.* LIGHT RINGING SOUND a light high-pitched ringing sound, like that of a small bell ■ *vti.* **(tings, tinging, tinged)** RING LIGHTLY to produce or cause sth to produce a light high-pitched ringing sound [Early 17thC. An imitation of the sound.]

ting-a-ling /tíngə ling/ *n.* a tinkling sound resembling that made by a small bell [An imitation of the sound]

tinge /tinj/ *n.* **1.** SLIGHT ADDED COLOUR a slight amount of a colour added to sth **2.** SLIGHT ADDED ELEMENT a slight amount of sth, e.g. an emotion or a flavour ○ *with a tinge of regret in her voice* ■ *vt.* **(tinges, tingeing** *or* **tinging, tinged) 1.** ADD COLOUR TO STH to add a slight amount of colour to sth **2.** MIX IN AN ELEMENT OF STH to mix a slight amount of sth with sth else ○ *celebrations tinged with sadness* [15thC. From Latin *tingere* 'to moisten', hence 'to dye' (via the sense 'to dip into liquid dye') (source of English *taint* and *tint*).]

tingle /tíng g'l/ *vti.* **(-gles, -gling, -gled)** STING OR PRICKLE SB to feel or to cause sb to feel a sensation of stinging, pricking, or vibration, e.g. from cold or a slight electric shock ○ *The frost made our faces tingle.* ■ *n.* STINGING OR PRICKLY FEELING a sensation of stinging, pricking, or vibration [14thC. Variant of an earlier form of TINKLE.] —**tingler** *n.* —**tinglingly** *adv.* —**tingly** *adj.*

tin god *n.* **1.** SB SELF-IMPORTANT sb, often in a position of minor authority, who behaves in a self-important, overbearing way **2.** SB OR STH UNJUSTIFIABLY ESTEEMED sb or sth mistakenly or unjustifiably considered to be worthy of admiration [In reference to tin as a base metal]

tin hat *n.* a steel helmet (*informal*)

tinhorn /tín hawrn/ *n.* *US* sb relatively insignificant who pretends to be wealthy, influential or important, especially a gambler (*informal*) [Late 19thC. From the horn-shaped metal can used to shake the dice in the game of chuck-a-luck, a gambling game.]

tinker /tíngkər/ *n.* **1.** TRAVELLING POT MENDER formerly, sb who travelled from place to place mending metal household items such as pots and pans **2.** UNSKILFUL WORKER sb who works clumsily or unskilfully, especially at repair work **3.** ACT OF FIDDLING WITH STH an act of fiddling with sth in an attempt to repair it **4.** SB GOOD AT MANY TASKS sb able to do many different kinds of work successfully **5.** *Ireland, Scotland* ITINERANT sb who travels from place to place as a way of life **6.** NAUGHTY CHILD a mischievous or badly-behaved child (*informal*) **7.** ZOOL YOUNG MACKEREL a mackerel that is not fully grown ■ *vi.* **(-kers, -kering, -kered) 1.** FIDDLE WITH to fiddle with sth in an attempt to repair it ○ *had been tinkering with the car all morning* **2.** HANDLE STH UNSKILFULLY to handle sth clumsily or unskilfully **3.** BE TRAVELLING POT MENDER to work as a travelling pot mender [13thC. Origin uncertain: perhaps from obsolete English *tink* 'to tinkle', an imitation of the sounds made by tinkers repairing pots.] —**tinkerer** *n.*

tinker's damn, **tinker's cuss** *n.* the slightest possible amount of care, heed, or value (*informal; used in negative statements*) ○ *This car isn't worth a tinker's damn.* [Origin uncertain: probably from the reputation of tinkers for swearing]

Tinkertoy /tíngkər toy/ *tdmk.* *US* a trademark for a construction toy consisting of pieces such as rods and wheels that can be fitted together

tinkle /tíngk'l/ *v.* **(-kles, -kling, -kled) 1.** *vti.* JINGLE to make or cause sth to make light metallic ringing sounds **2.** *vi.* URINATE to urinate (*informal*) ■ *n.* **1.** JINGLING SOUND a series of light metallic ringing sounds **2.** ACT OF URINATING an act of urinating (*informal*) **3.** TELEPHONE CALL a call on the telephone (*informal*) [14thC. Literally 'to keep on making a faint metallic sound', formed from obsolete English *tink* 'to make a faint metallic sound', of uncertain origin: perhaps an imitation of the sound.] —**tinkly** *adj.*

tin lizzie /-lízzi/ *n.* a cheap, old, or dilapidated motor car (*informal*) [From *Tin Lizzie*, nickname for the Model T Ford car]

tinned /tind/ *adj.* packed in a tin for storage or sale. US term **canned** *adj.* 1

tinner /tínnər/ *n.* **1.** TIN MINER sb who works in a tin mine **2.** = **tinsmith 3.** SB FILLING TINS a person or company that packs food into tins

tinnie /tínni/, **tinny** (*plural* **-nies**) *n.* *Aus* a can of beer (*informal*)

tinnitus /tínnitəss/ *n.* a continual noise in the ear such as a ringing or roaring, usually caused by damage to the hair cells of the inner ear [Mid-19thC. From Latin, from *tinnire* 'to ring, tinkle', an imitation of the sound.]

tinny /tínni/ *adj.* **(-nier, -niest) 1.** HAVING A THIN METALLIC SOUND lacking a full resonant sound ○ *banging out tunes on a tinny old piano* **2.** CONSISTING OF TIN yielding, containing, or having the characteristics of tin **3.** TASTING OF METAL having a metallic taste **4.** INFERIOR IN QUALITY cheaply or shoddily made **5.** *ANZ* LUCKY lucky (*informal*) ■ *n.* *Aus* = **tinnie** (*informal*) —**tinnily** *adv.* —**tinniness** *n.*

tin-opener *n.* a device for opening tins, especially tins of food. US term **can opener**

Tin Pan Alley *n.* (*dated*) **1.** POPULAR MUSIC DISTRICT a city district in which the business of composing and publishing popular music is carried on **2.** COMPOSERS AND PUBLISHERS popular music composers and publishers considered collectively [*Tin pan* in the sense of 'tinny piano', from the cheap pianos associated with music publishers' offices]

tin plate *n.* steel or iron in thin sheets coated with tin

tin-plate **(tin-plates, tin-plating, tin-plated)** *vt.* to coat sheet iron or steel with tin —**tin-plater** *n.*

tinpot /tín pot/ *adj.* inferior in quality or importance (*informal insult*) [Late 18thC. In reference to tin as a base metal.]

tinsel /tínss'l/ *n.* **1.** GLITTERING MATERIAL a thin strip of glittering metal foil, paper, or plastic, used for decoration **2.** STH SHOWY sth worthless that appears glamorous ■ *vt.* **(-sels, -selling, -selled) 1.** DECORATE WITH TINSEL to decorate sth with tinsel or other glittering material **2.** MAKE SHOWY to give sth a gaudy, flashy quality ■ *adj.* **1.** MADE OF TINSEL made of or decorated with tinsel **2.** GAUDY appearing glamorous but in fact worthless [15thC. Via French *étincelé* 'sparkling' (particularly used of fabric with metallic thread woven through it), from Old French *estincele* 'spark', from Latin *scintilla* (source of English *scintillate*).] —**tinselly** *adj.*

Tinseltown /tínsəl tōwn/ *n.* a disapproving nickname for Hollywood and the US film industry as a place of substantial glamour (*informal*) [From its perception as superficially glamourous]

tinsmith /tín smith/ *n.* sb who makes or repairs objects made of tin or other easily worked metals

tin snips *npl.* shears used for cutting sheet metal

tinstone /tín stōn/ *n.* MINERALS = **cassiterite**

tint /tint/ *n.* **1.** PALE SHADE a shade of a colour, especially a pale one **2.** COLOUR WITH WHITE ADDED a colour mixed with white to give low saturation and high lightness **3.** TRACE OF COLOUR a slight amount of a colour **4.** HAIR DYE a dye for the hair **5.** HINT OF STH a barely noticeable addition of sth **6.** PRINTING BACKGROUND COLOUR a pale colour printed as a background onto which another colour is printed **7.** ARTS SHADING IN ENGRAVING a shading effect in engraving, produced by a series of parallel lines ■ *vti.* **(tints, tinting, tinted)** GIVE A TINT TO STH to colour or shade sth with a tint, or to acquire a tint [Early 18thC. Variant of TINCT, from the past participle of Latin *tingere* 'to soak', later 'to dye' (source of English *tinge*), from the idea of 'dipping into liquid dye'.] —**tinter** *n.*

Tintagel /tin tájjəl/ coastal village in Cornwall, south-western England, said to be the birthplace of the legendary King Arthur

tintinnabulation /tínti nábbyŏŏ láysh'n/ *n.* the ringing of bells [Mid-19thC. Formed from Latin *tintinnabulum* (see TINTINNABULUM).] —**tintinnabular** /tínti nábbyŏŏlər/ *adj.*

tintinnabulum /tínti nábbyŏŏləm/ (*plural* **-la** /-lə/) *n.* a small bell with a high clear ring [Late 16thC. From Latin, 'bell', from *tintinnare*, literally 'to ring repeatedly', from *tinnire* 'to ring', an imitation of the sound.]

Tintoretto /tíntə réttō/ (1518?–94) Italian painter. Based in Venice, he painted large murals in the Mannerist style, using free brush strokes and dramatic foreshortened perspectives. Real name **Jacopo Robusti**

tintype /tín tīp/ *n.* PHOTOGRAPHY = **ferrotype**

tinware /tín wair/ *n.* objects made of tin plate, especially utensils

tin whistle *n.* = **penny whistle**

tinwork /tín wurk/ *n.* things made of tin

tinworks /tín wurks/ (*plural* **-works**) *n.* a place where tin is smelted and rolled (*takes a singular or plural verb*)

tiny /tíni/ *adj.* **(-nier, -niest)** SMALL extremely small ■ *n.* (*plural* **-nies**) YOUNG CHILD a very young child (*informal*) [Late 16thC. Formed from obsolete English *tine* 'very small', of unknown origin.] —**tinily** *adv.* —**tininess** *n.*

-tion *suffix.* an action or process, or the result of it ○ *pollution*

tip[1] /tip/ *n.* **1.** POINTED END the end of an object, especially a narrow or pointed end ○ *a pencil with a sharp tip* **2.** PART FITTED ON AN END a piece fitted to the end of sth else ■ *vt.* **(tips, tipping, tipped) 1.** PROVIDE OR BE END to provide sth with an end or form the end of sth **2.** COVER THE END OF STH to cover or decorate the end of sth ○ *shoes with steel-tipped toes* **3.** TAKE THE END OFF STH to remove the end from sth [15thC. Origin uncertain: probably from Old Norse *typpi*, from a prehistoric Germanic word meaning 'upper extremity' that is also the ancestor of English *top* and *toupee*.] ◇ **the tip of the iceberg** the small visible or obvious part of a largely unseen problem or difficulty ◇ **on the tip of sb's tongue 1.** nearly, but not quite, brought to mind **2.** on the verge of being said but remaining unsaid

tip[2] /tip/ *v.* **(tips, tipping, tipped) 1.** *vti.* TILT STH to cause sth to slant or to become slanted ○ *sitting with his chair tipped back* **2.** *vti.* KNOCK STH OVER to turn sth on its side or upside down or become turned on the side or upside down ○ *high winds caused the truck to tip over on its side* **3.** *vti.* DUMP RUBBISH to dispose of refuse **4.** *vt.* TAKE OFF YOUR HAT to touch or lift a hat as a greeting ■ *n.* **1.** ACT OF TIPPING an act of tipping sth **2.** TILT an incline from vertical or horizontal **3.** RUBBISH DUMP a place to dump refuse **4.** UNTIDY PLACE an extremely untidy or dirty place (*informal*) [14thC. Origin uncertain: perhaps from Scandinavian.] —**tippable** *adj.*

tip[3] /tip/ *n.* **1.** GRATUITY a gift of money for a service, especially as an amount above what is owed **2.** WARNING OR INFORMATION an item of advance, inside, or confidential information given, e.g. to warn of sth about to occur or to help in solving a crime **3.** HELPFUL HINT a useful suggestion or idea for doing sth ○ *cooking tips* ■ *vti.* **(tips, tipping, tipped) 1.** GIVE A GRATUITY to give sb a gift of money in return for a service, especially in addition to what is owed **2.** INFORM SB to give sb advance, inside, or confidential information [Early 17thC. Origin uncertain: perhaps from TIP[4].] —**tippable** *adj.*

tip off *vt.* to give sb a warning or some useful advance information ○ *The police had been tipped off about their whereabouts.*

tip[4] /tip/ *n.* **1.** LIGHT HIT a light glancing blow **2.** CRICKET DEFLECTED BALL IN CRICKET a stroke in cricket in which the ball glances off the bat ■ *vt.* **(tips, tipping, tipped) 1.** HIT SB LIGHTLY to strike sb or sth with a light glancing blow **2.** CRICKET DEFLECT CRICKET BALL WITH BAT to hit a ball in cricket so that it glances off the bat [15thC. Origin uncertain: perhaps from Low German *tippen*, or from TIP[1], from the idea of touching sth with the 'tip' of sth else.]

tip and run *n.* a variety of cricket in which the batter must run if his or her bat strikes the ball ['Tip' from TIP[4]]

tip-and-run *adj.* striking quickly then withdrawing immediately

tipcart /típ kaart/ *n.* a type of cart whose load is emptied by tilting its body

tipi *n.* = **tepee**

tip-in *n.* **1.** BASKETBALL **BASKETBALL GOAL** in basketball, a goal scored by lightly pushing a rebound into the basket with the fingertips **2.** HOCKEY **HOCKEY GOAL** in hockey, a goal scored at very close range by giving a short stroke with the stick

tip-off[1] *n.* advance information or a warning given in an effort to help (*informal*)

tip-off[2] *n.* BASKETBALL in basketball, the start of a period of play in which two players try to tap a jump ball to one of their teammates

tipper /típpər/ *n.* sb who leaves a tip or gratuity

Tipperary /tìppə ráiri/ former county in Munster Province, southern Republic of Ireland. It now comprises the counties of Tipperary North Riding and Tipperary South Riding.

tipper truck, **tipper lorry** *n.* a lorry built so that the front of the platform carrying the load can be raised to allow the load to slide off. US term **dump truck**

tippet /típpit/ *n.* **1.** CLOTHES **STOLE WITH HANGING ENDS** a stole or cape, often made of fur, with long ends that hang down the front **2.** CHR **STOLE OF ANGLICAN CLERGY** the long stole worn around the shoulders and over the robes of Anglican clergy during services **3.** CLOTHES **HANGING END OF A GARMENT** a long hanging end worn attached to a sleeve, hood, or cape up to the 16th century **4.** BIRDS **BIRD'S RUFF** the ruff of a bird **5.** ANGLING **PART TO WHICH A FLY IS TIED** in angling, the thin end section of a leader to which a fly is tied [14thC. Origin uncertain: probably formed from TIP[1].]

Tippett /típpit/, **Sir Michael** (1905–98) British composer. He is noted for the mystical quality of many of his orchestral, instrumental, and vocal works.

Tipp-Ex /típ eks/ *tdmk.* a trademark for correction fluid.

tipple[1] /típp'l/ *v.* (**-ples, -pling, -pled**) **1.** *vi.* **DRINK ALCOHOL HABITUALLY** to drink alcoholic liquor habitually or excessively **2.** *vti.* **DRINK ALCOHOL REPEATEDLY** to drink alcoholic liquor repeatedly a little at a time ■ *n.* **ALCOHOLIC DRINK** an alcoholic drink (*informal*) [Mid-16thC. Origin uncertain: probably a back-formation from *tippler* 'ale seller', of Scandinavian origin.]

tipple[2] /típp'l/ *n.* **1.** **DEVICE FOR UNLOADING ORE TRUCKS** a device for tipping coal or ore trucks to unload them **2.** **PLACE FOR UNLOADING ORE** a place where ore or coal trucks are unloaded **3.** **PLACE FOR SCREENING COAL** a place where coal is screened and loaded into trucks or railway goods wagons ■ *vti.* (**-ples, -pling, -pled**) *N England* **TO FALL OR TIP** to fall over or tip sth over [Mid-19thC. Literally 'to keep on unloading', formed from TIP[2].]

tippler[1] /típlər/ *n.* sb who is a habitual drinker of alcohol

tippler[2] /típplər/ *n.* a breed of domestic pigeon bred for flight or show [Mid-19thC. Formed from TIPPLE[2], so called because it often turns over backwards in flight.]

tipstaff /típ staaf/ (*plural* **-staves** /-stayvz/ *or* **-staffs**) *n.* **1.** **METAL-TIPPED STAFF** a metal-tipped staff carried as a sign of official authority **2.** LAW **COURT OFFICIAL** a court official who once carried a staff, e.g. a bailiff or constable

tipster /típstər/ *n.* sb who provides or sells information to people who bet on horse races or to speculators in financial markets [Mid-19thC. Formed from TIP[3].]

tipsy /típsi/ (**-sier, -siest**) *adj.* **1.** **DRUNK** slightly drunk **2.** **LIKELY TO TIP** inclined to tilt or tip —**tipsily** *adv.* —**tipsiness** *n.*

tipsy cake *n.* a sponge cake soaked with alcohol or alcohol-laced syrup

tip-tilted *adj.* slightly turned up

tiptoe /típ tō/ *vi.* (**-toes, -toeing, -toed**) **1.** **WALK WITH HEELS RAISED** to walk on the toes and the balls of the feet with the heels off the ground **2.** **MOVE CAUTIOUSLY** to move or proceed quietly or cautiously ■ *n.* **POSITION WITH HEELS RAISED** a standing position in which the heels are raised off the ground and the weight is on the front part of the feet, with the body often also stretched up to gain extra height ○ *walking on tiptoe* ■ *adj.* **1.** **WALKING ON THE TOES** walking or standing on the toes or balls of the feet **2.** **CAUTIOUS** proceeding with caution or stealth ■ *adv.* **ON THE TIPS OF TOES** on the toes or the balls of the feet [14thC. Formed from TIP[1] + TOE.]

tiptop /típ tóp/ *adj.* **TOP QUALITY** of the highest quality or rank (*informal*) ■ *adv.* **WELL** exceptionally well (*informal*) ■ *n.* (*informal*) **1.** **HIGHEST POINT** the highest point **2.** **HIGHEST IN QUALITY** the highest degree of quality or excellence [Early 18thC. Doubling of TOP, under the influence of TIP[1].]

tip truck *n.* = **tipper truck**

tip-up *adj.* designed to tilt upward or fold up

TIR *abbr.* Transports Internationaux Routiers

tirade /tī ráyd, ti-/ *n.* a long angry speech, usually of criticism or denunciation [Early 19thC. From French, 'volley', from *tirer* 'to draw', from assumed Vulgar Latin *tirare*.]

tiramisu /tìrrə mee sóo, -mée soo/ *n.* an Italian dessert made with layers of sponge cake soaked in coffee, especially espresso, Marsala or other alcohol, mascarpone cheese, and chocolate [Late 20thC. From Italian *tira mi sù* 'pick me up'.]

Tirana /ti ráanə/ capital city of Albania, in the central part of the country, situated 27 km/17 mi. from the Adriatic coast. Population: 251,000 (1991).

tire[1] /tīr/ (**tires, tiring, tired**) *vti.* **1.** **GROW OR MAKE SB TIRED** to make sb feel in need of rest or sleep, or to grow weaker and less energetic and feel a need for rest or sleep **2.** **EXHAUST SB'S INTEREST** to lose interest in and become bored and impatient with sb or sth, or to cause sb to do this [Old English *tyrian*, of uncertain origin]

tire[1] /tīr/ *n.* US = **tyre**

tire[2] /tīr/ *vt.* (**tires, tiring, tired**) **CLOTHE SB** to attire or adorn sb or sth (*archaic or literary*) ■ *n.* (*archaic*) **1.** **ATTIRE** clothing or attire **2.** **HEAD COVERING** a woman's head covering or ornament [14thC. Shortening of ATTIRE.]

tired /tīrd/ *adj.* **1.** **NEEDING REST** in need of rest or sleep, or weakened and made less active by exertion **2.** **NO LONGER INTERESTED** having lost patience or interest ○ *grew tired of hearing the same complaints* **3.** **OVERUSED** no longer new or fresh because of overuse ○ *a tired old slogan* —**tiredly** *adv.* —**tiredness** *n.* ◇ **tired and emotional** drunk

tired out *adj.* thoroughly tired

Tiree /tī rée/ island of the Inner Hebrides, western Scotland. Population: 950 (1991). Area: 76 sq. km/29 sq. mi.

tireless /tírləss/ *adj.* never slackening or stopping, and apparently immune to tiredness or fatigue —**tirelessly** *adv.* —**tirelessness** *n.*

Tiresias /tī reési əss/ *n.* in Greek mythology, a seer from Thebes who often delivered prophecies to Oedipus. In the most common version of the myth, Athena struck him sightless after he saw her bathing, but gave him the power of prophecy.

tiresome /tírsəm/ *adj.* causing weariness, annoyance, or boredom —**tiresomely** *adv.* —**tiresomeness** *n.*

Tirgu Mures /túrgoo mŏor esh/ capital city of Mures County in central Romania. Population: 166,315 (1994).

tiring *adj.* causing sb to feel tired, usually because requiring great physical or mental exertion

tiring house *n.* a dressing room for actors in the Renaissance theatre (*archaic*) [15thC. Formed from ATTIRE.]

Tír na n-Óg /teér na nog/ *n.* in Irish legend, a land of eternal youth [Late 19thC. From Irish *tír na n-óg* 'land of the young'.]

Tiros /tī rŏss/ (*plural* **-ros**) *n.* a satellite with infrared and television equipment for transmitting weather data to Earth [Late 20thC. An acronym formed from *television infrared observational satellite*.]

Tirso de Molina /teérss ō day mə léenə/ (1571?–1648) Spanish playwright and theologian. He is the author of several hundred plays, including the comedy *The Trickster of Seville* (1630), which has the first literary presentation of Don Juan. Pseudonym of **Gabriel Téllez**

Tirthankara /teer tàngkərə/ *n.* a traditional holy man of Jainism, belonging to a group who have attained personal immortality through enlightenment and by their teaching have made a path for others to follow [Mid-19thC. From Sanskrit *tīrthaṁkaraḥ*, literally 'ford maker', from *tīrtham* 'ford, passage' + *kr-* 'to make' (source of English *karma*).]

Tiruchchirappalli /tìrrə chirə púlli, ti rŏochi ráapəli/ city in southern India, Tamil Nadu State, capital of the Tiruchchirappalli District. Population: 387,223 (1991). Former name **Trichinopoly**

Tirunelveli /tìrrŏo nélvəli/ town in Tirunelveli District, Tamil Nadu State, southern India. Population: 135,762 (1991).

Tiryns /tírrinz/ ancient city in Argolis Department in the Peloponnesus, southern Greece, situated between Naplion and Mycenae

'tis /tiz/ *contr.* it is (*archaic or literary*)

tisane /ti zán, tee-/, **ptisan** *n.* an infusion of leaves or flowers used as a beverage, e.g. a herbal tea [14thC. Via French from, ultimately, Greek *ptisanē* 'barley water' (see PTISAN).]

Tisha b'Av /ti sháa bə áv/ *n.* in Judaism, a fast on the ninth day of the month of Av to commemorate the destruction of the First and Second Temples [From Hebrew *tišāh bĕāḇ* 'ninth of Av']

Tishri /tíshri/ *n.* in the Jewish calendar, the first month of the religious year and the seventh month of the civil year, 30 days long and falling in September and October [Mid-17thC. From Hebrew *tišrī*, of uncertain origin.]

Tisiphone /tī síffəni/ *n.* in Greek mythology, one of the three Furies. The others were Alecto and Megaera.

Tissot /teéssō/, **Jacques-Joseph** (1836–1902) French painter. He won great success with his scenes of fashionable society in London and Paris.

tissue /tíshoo, tíssyoo/ *n.* **1.** **PIECE OF ABSORBENT PAPER** a piece of soft absorbent paper that can be used as a handkerchief, toilet paper, or a towel **2.** = **tissue paper** **3.** CELL BIOL **GROUP OF CELLS IN AN ORGANISM** organic body material in animals and plants made up of large numbers of cells that are similar in form and function and their related intercellular substances. The four basic types of tissue are nerve, muscle, epidermal, and connective. **4.** **INTRICATE SERIES** an intricate interrelated series of things ○ *a tissue of lies* **5.** TEXTILES **GAUZY FABRIC** a thin, finely woven fabric with a gauzy texture [14thC. From Old French *tissu*, from the past participle of *tistre* 'to weave', from Latin *texere* (see TEXT).]

tissue culture *n.* **1.** **GROWTH OF TISSUE** the growth of tissue outside an organism in a nutrient medium, or the techniques involved in the process **2.** **TISSUE** the tissue grown in a culture medium

tissue paper *n.* a thin soft paper used for wrapping and protecting delicate items

tissue plasminogen activator *n.* an anticlotting enzyme that is produced naturally in blood vessel linings and is genetically engineered for use in treating heart attacks, to dissolve blood clots, and to prevent heart muscle damage

tissue type *n.* the chemical characteristics of the body tissue of an individual that determine whether or not the tissue is immunologically compatible with the tissue of another individual

Tisza /tíss aw/ major tributary of the River Danube in eastern Europe. Length: 970 km/600 mi.

tit[1] /tit/ *n.* **1.** **OFFENSIVE TERM** an offensive term for a woman's breast (*slang offensive*) **2.** **TEAT** a teat **3.** **OFFENSIVE TERM** a highly offensive term referring to sb who is regarded as unintelligent or obnoxious (*slang offensive*) [Old English *titt*; ultimately from prehistoric Germanic]

tit[2] /tit/ *n.* a small active songbird of the northern hemisphere with a short bill and strong feet, e.g. the bluetit, crested tit, or great tit [Early 18thC. Shortening of TITMOUSE.]

Tit. *abbr.* Titus

titan /tít'n/ *n.* sb whose power, achievement, intellect, or physical size is extraordinarily impressive [Early 19thC. Via Latin from Greek, 'Titan'.]

Titan[1] *n.* MYTHOL in Greek mythology, one of the twelve children of Uranus and Gaea, supreme rulers of the

Tit: Great tit

universe until they were overthrown by Zeus [Mid-17thC. Via Latin from Greek.]

Titan[2] *n.* ASTRON the largest natural satellite of Saturn, discovered in 1655. It is 5,150 km/3,198 mi. in diameter and has a significant atmosphere that is composed mainly of nitrogen. [15thC. From Latin, used for the sun god Helios (the original sense in English), from Greek.]

titanate /títə nayt/ *n.* a chemical compound that is a salt or an ester of titanic acid

Titania /ti taáni ə/ *n.* **1.** QUEEN OF FAIRIES in medieval folklore, the wife of Oberon and queen of the fairies **2.** ASTRON **SATELLITE OF URANUS** the largest moon of the planet Uranus, the fourth most distant satellite observable from the Earth, orbiting at a distance of 436,000 km/262,000 mi. with a diameter of 1578 km/947 mi. Although it was one of the first two satellites of Uranus to be discovered in 1787, Oberon being the other, Titania is officially designated as Uranus III.

titanic /tī tánnik/ *adj.* **1.** VERY LARGE OR STRONG having extraordinary physical strength or size **2.** POWERFUL of extraordinary power, scope, or impressiveness **3.** CHEM ELEM OF TITANIUM relating to or containing titanium —**titanically** *adv.*

Titanic *adj.* MYTHOL relating to or like the Titans of mythology

titanic oxide *n.* = titanium dioxide

titaniferous /títənífferəss/ *adj.* yielding or containing titanium [Early 19thC. Coined from TITANIUM + -FEROUS.]

Titanism /títənizəm/ *n.* the spirit of defiance of authority, conventional society, and the established order

titanite /títənīt/ *n.* MINERALS = sphene [Mid-19thC. Formed from TITANIUM.]

titanium /tī táyni əm, ti–/ *n.* a corrosion-resistant silvery metallic chemical element that occurs in rutile and ilmenite and whose strength and light weight make it useful in the manufacture of alloys for the aerospace industry. Symbol Ti [Late 18thC. Formed from TITAN, on the model of URANIUM.]

titanium dioxide *n.* a white crystalline compound that occurs naturally in rutile and other minerals and is used as a pigment in paint for its durability and its ability to cover surfaces. Formula: TiO_2.

titanium white *n.* **1.** = titanium dioxide **2.** WHITE PAINT PIGMENT a brilliant white paint pigment consisting primarily of titanium dioxide

titanosaur /tī tánnə sawr/ *n.* a huge herbivorous sauropod dinosaur of the Cretaceous and Jurassic periods, found especially in South America. Genus: *Titanosaurus*. [Late 19thC. From modern Latin *Titanosaurus*, genus name, from Greek *Titan* 'Titan' + *sauros* 'lizard'.]

titanothere /tī tánnə theer/ *n.* a large mammal similar to a rhinoceros that lived in North America during the Tertiary Period [Mid-20thC. From modern Latin *Titanotherium*, genus name, from Greek *Titan* 'Titan' + *therion* 'wild beast'.]

titanous /títənəss/ *adj.* relating to or containing titanium with a valency of three

titarakura /teé taarə koorə/ (*plural* **-a**) *n.* NZ ZOOL = bully[1] *n.*

titbit /tít bit/ *n.* **1.** SMALL MORSEL a small, usually bite-sized, piece of delicious food **2.** PIECE OF GOSSIP a small

piece of interesting information or gossip [Mid-17thC. *Tid* perhaps from obsolete English dialect, 'tender'.]

titchy /títchi/ (**-ier, -iest**) *adj.* very small (*informal*) [Mid-20thC. Formed from Little *Tich*, the stage name of the English comedian Harry Relph (1868–1928), who was very small.]

——— **WORD KEY: ORIGIN** ———

Relph got his nickname from his supposed resemblance to the so-called 'Tichborne claimant'. This was the title given to Arthur Orton, who, in an English cause célèbre of the 1860s, returned from Australia claiming to be Roger Tichborne, the heir to an English baronetcy who had supposedly been lost at sea.

titer *n.* CHEM US = titre

titfer /títfər/ *n.* a hat (*slang*) [Early 20thC. Shortening of rhyming slang TIT FOR TAT.]

tit for tat *n.* the process or act of repaying a wrong or injury suffered by inflicting equivalent harm on the doer (*hyphenated before a noun*) ○ *tit-for-tat strikes* [Mid-16thC. Origin uncertain: perhaps an alteration of *tip for tap*.]

tithable /títhəb'l/ *adj.* required to pay or subject to the payment of tithes

tithe /tīth/ *n.* **1.** CHR INDIVIDUAL'S FINANCIAL SUPPORT FOR A CHURCH one tenth of sb's income or produce paid voluntarily or as a tax for the support of a church or its clergy **2.** CHR OBLIGATION OF SUPPORTING A CHURCH FINANCIALLY the obligation to pay a tithe to a church or its clergy **3.** ASSESSMENT OR CONTRIBUTION any voluntary contribution or tax payment, especially when it constitutes one tenth of sb's income **4.** SMALL PART OF STH one tenth or a small part of anything ■ *v.* (**tithes, tithing, tithed**) **1.** *vti.* PAY ONE TENTH OF INCOME to contribute or pay one tenth of your income or produce, especially to support a church **2.** *vt.* COLLECT ONE TENTH OF SB'S INCOME to assess or collect the payment of one tenth of sb's income [Old English *tēopa* 'tenth'] —**tither** *n.*

tithe barn *n.* in former times, a barn that served as a store for the produce contributed by the parish to the church as a tithe

tithing /títhing/ *n.* **1.** CHR PAYING OF TITHES the assessing or paying of tithes **2.** HIST TEN HOUSEHOLDERS a small district in medieval England composed of ten householders and their households, each bearing responsibility for the conduct of the others **3.** POL RURAL DIVISION a rural administrative region in medieval England equal to one tenth of the county division known as a hundred **4.** ONE TENTH one tenth part of anything [Old English *tēopung*]

titi[1] /teé teé/ (*plural* **-tis**) *n.* ZOOL a tropical South American arboreal monkey with a round face, thick soft fur, and a long tail. Genus: *Callicebus*. [Mid-18thC. Via Spanish *tití* from Aymara.]

titi[2] /teé teé/ *n.* BOT **1.** EVERGREEN SHRUB WITH FRAGRANT FLOWERS an evergreen shrub or small tree of the southeastern United States that has glossy leathery leaves and fragrant white or pinkish flowers. Latin name: *Cliftonia monophylla*. **2.** EVERGREEN TREE a small American evergreen tree or shrub with leathery leaves and yellow fruit. Latin name: *Cyrilla racemiflora*. [Early 19thC. Origin unknown.]

titian /tísh'n/, **Titian** *adj.* of a bright auburn colour tinged with gold ○ *titian hair* [Late 19thC. Named after TITIAN, who used the colour frequently.]

Titian: Self-portrait (1555)

AKG London

Titian /tísh'n/ (1477?–1576) Italian painter. The foremost Venetian painter of the Renaissance, he painted portraits and religious and mythological scenes that are noted for their rich coloration. Real name **Tiziano Vecellio**

Titicaca, Lake /títti ka'a kaa/ lake in east-central South America, extending from southeastern Peru to western Bolivia. It is the largest lake on the continent and the highest navigable lake in the world, about 3,810 m/12,500 ft above sea level. Area: 8,288 sq. km/3,200 sq. mi.

titillate /títti layt/ (**-lates, -lating, -lated**) *v.* **1.** *vti.* EXCITE SB to excite or stimulate sb pleasurably, usually in a mildly sexual way **2.** *vt.* CAUSE SB TO TINGLE to cause a tingling sensation in sb by touching him or her lightly [Early 17thC. From Latin *titillare* 'to tickle'.] —**titillating** *adj.* —**titillatingly** *adv.* —**titillation** /títti láysh'n/ *n.* —**titillative** /títtilətiv/ *adj.*

titivate /títti vayt/ (**-vates, -vating, -vated**), **tittivate** (**-vates, -vating, -vated**) *vti.* to improve the appearance of sb or sth by tidying, neatening, or adding some decoration [Early 19thC. Alteration of earlier *tidivate*, of uncertain origin: perhaps formed from TIDY.] —**titivation** /títti váysh'n/ *n.* —**titivator** /títti vaytər/ *n.*

titlark /tít laark/ *n.* BIRDS = pipit [Mid-17thC. Formed from TIT[2] + LARK[1].]

title /tít'l/ *n.* **1.** NAME a name that identifies a book, film, play, painting, musical composition, or other literary or artistic work **2.** DESCRIPTIVE HEADING a descriptive heading for sth such as a book chapter, a magazine article, or a speech **3.** PUBL = title page **4.** PUBL PUBLISHED WORK a work published or recorded by a company ○ *this spring's new titles* **5.** DESIGNATION ADDED TO A NAME a word such as 'Mr', 'Ms', 'Dr', or 'Lord' added to and usually preceding sb's name to indicate his or her rank, social status, or profession, or as a courtesy **6.** NAME DESCRIBING A POSITION a name that describes sb's job or position in a company or organization ○ *a job title* **7.** SPORTS CHAMPIONSHIP the status of champion in a sport or competition ○ *a title fight* **8.** LAW RIGHT OR PROOF OF IT any legitimate right or anything providing proof or justification for that claim **9.** CHR REQUIREMENT OF ORDINATION a source of income or office in the church required of a candidate by the Church of England before ordination **10.** LAW CLAIM BASED ON A RIGHT a claim based on a legitimate right **11.** CHR ROMAN CATHOLIC CHURCH IN ROME a Roman Catholic church in or near Rome that has a bishop or cardinal as its nominal head **12.** LAW RIGHT TO POSSESS PROPERTY a legal right to possess and dispose of property **13.** LAW EVIDENCE OF PROPERTY RIGHTS the evidence of legal right to property **14.** LAW DOCUMENT a document giving the legal right to property **15.** LAW DIVISION a division of a law, statute, or law book **16.** LAW LAW HEADING a heading for a lawsuit or legal action, or one that names a document or statute ■ **titles** *npl.* CINEMA, TV CREDITS OR SUBTITLES ON SCREEN the written presentation on the screen of credits, narration, or subtitles in a film or television programme ■ *vt.* (**-tles, -tling, -tled**) **1.** NAME STH to give a name or title to sb or sth **2.** CALL SB BY A TITLE to call sb by a title [14thC. From Old English *titul* and Old French *title*, both from Latin *titulus* 'inscription'.]

titled /tít'ld/ *adj.* having a title, especially of nobility

title deed *n.* LAW a deed or document that is evidence of sb's legal right to property

titleholder /tít'l hōldər/ *n.* **1.** SPORTS HOLDER OF A CHAMPIONSHIP TITLE sb who holds a sports championship title **2.** LAW SB WITH TITLE TO PROPERTY sb who holds legal title to property —**titleholding** *n.*

title page *n.* PUBL a page at the beginning of a book that gives its title and the name of the author and publisher

title role *n.* CINEMA, THEATRE the role in a play or film that gives the work its name

titmouse /tít mowss/ (*plural* **-mice** /tít mīss/) *n.* a small bird widespread in Europe, Asia, Africa, and North America. Genus: *Parus*. [14thC. Alteration (influenced by *mouse*) of *titmose*, from obsolete *tit* 'sth small, runt' (of uncertain origin: probably from Scandinavian) + *mose* 'titmouse' (from Old English *māse*).]

Tito

Tito /teetŌ/ (1892–1980) Yugoslav statesman. After leading partisan forces against the Germans in World War II, as president of Yugoslavia (1942–77) he established a Communist state independent of the Soviet Union. Known as **Marshal Tito**. Real name **Josip Broz**

Titoism /teetŌ izəm/ *n.* the form of Communism associated with Tito and practised by him in Yugoslavia, especially involving the pursuit of national interests independent of the then Soviet Union and its satellites —**Titoist** *n., adj.*

titrant /títrənt/ *n.* a reagent, e.g. a solution of known concentration, that is added in titration [Mid-20thC. Formed from TITRATE.]

titrate /tī tráyt/ (**-trates, -trating, -trated**) *vt.* to measure the concentration of a solution by titration [Late 19thC. From French *titrer*, from *titre* (see TITRE).] —**titratable** *adj.*

titration /tī tráysh'n/ *n.* a method of calculating the concentration of a dissolved substance by adding quantities of a reagent of known concentration to a known volume of test solution until a reaction occurs

titre /títər, teetər/ *n.* **1.** CHEM SUBSTANCE CONCENTRATION the concentration of a substance in solution as determined by titration **2.** BIOCHEM ANTIBODY CONCENTRATION the concentration of an antibody determined by how much it is diluted before it no longer reacts positively to an antigen [Mid-19thC. From French *titre* 'qualification, quality (of gold or silver alloy)', a variant of *title* (see TITLE).]

titrimetric /títri méttrik/ *adj.* using or calculated by titration [Late 19thC. Coined from TITRATION + -METRIC.] —**titrimetrically** *adv.*

titter /títtər/ *vi.* (**-ters, -tering, -tered**) LAUGH NERVOUSLY to laugh in a nervous self-conscious way ■ *n.* NERVOUS GIGGLE a short high-pitched nervous laugh or giggle [Early 17thC. An imitation of the sound.] —**titterer** *n.* —**tittering** *n.* —**titteringly** *adv.*

tittivate *vti.* = titivate

tittle /títt'l/ *n.* **1.** PRINTING MARK USED IN PRINTING a small mark used in printing and writing such as an accent, punctuation, or diacritical mark **2.** TINY BIT the tiniest bit [14thC. From medieval Latin *titulus*, literally 'small superscript mark', from Latin, 'title'.]

tittle-tattle *n.* GOSSIP idle gossip ■ *vi.* (**tittle-tattles, tittle-tattling, tittle-tattled**) TO GOSSIP to gossip or chatter idly [Early 16thC. Doubling of TATTLE.] —**tittle-tattler** *n.*

tittup /títtəp/ *vi.* (**-tups, -tupping, -tupped**) PRANCE to move in a lively prancing way ■ *n.* PRANCING MOVEMENT a sometimes exaggerated lively prancing movement [Late 17thC. Origin uncertain: perhaps an imitation of the sound of horse's hooves.]

titubation /títtyŏŏ báysh'n/ *n.* an unsteady or stumbling gait or a head tremor, often caused by a disorder of the cerebellum [Mid-17thC. From Latin *titubare* 'to stagger', of unknown origin.]

titular /títtyŏŏlər/ *adj.* **1.** IN NAME ONLY having a particular title, rank, or position but not possessing the power or exercising the functions usually associated with it **2.** WITH A TITLE OF RANK holding a title of rank **3.** FROM A TITLE derived from or figuring in the title of a work such as a book or film **4.** CHR FROM AN INACTIVE SEE bearing the title of a see or monastery that is no longer active ■ *n.* **1.** SB WITH A TITLE OF RANK sb who holds a title of rank **2.** HOLDER OF A NOMINAL TITLE sb who

holds a title in name only [Late 16thC. Formed from Latin *titulus* 'title'.] —**titularly** *adv.* —**titulary** *n.*

Titus[1] /títəss/ *n.* in the Bible, an early Christian leader, and a disciple of St Paul

Titus[2] *n.* in the Bible, a letter addressed to Titus, traditionally believed to be from St Paul. It contains advice on the organization of the Christian Church. See table at **Bible**

Titus /títəss/ (39–81) Roman general and emperor. He captured and destroyed Jerusalem in AD 70. As emperor (79–81) he was noted for his leniency and generosity, and he also completed the Colosseum in Rome. Full name **Titus Flavius Sabinus Vespasianus**

Tiv /tiv/ (*plural* **Tivs** or **Tiv**) *n.* **1.** PEOPLES MEMBER OF A W AFRICAN PEOPLE a member of a people living in West Africa, mainly in southern Nigeria and neighbouring Cameroon **2.** LANG TIV LANGUAGE the language of the Tiv people, belonging to the Benne-Congo family of languages. It is spoken by around 1.5 million people. [Mid-20thC. Of Bantu origin.]

Tivoli /tívvəli/ town in central Italy, near Rome, location of the Renaissance-period Tivoli Gardens and the ruined villa of the emperor Hadrian. Population: 54,352 (1990).

Tiwa /teéwə/ (*plural* **-was** or **-wa**) *n.* **1.** PEOPLES MEMBER OF NATIVE N AMERICAN PEOPLE a member of a group of Native North American Pueblo peoples who originally occupied lands in New Mexico, and whose members now live mainly in Texas and northern New Mexico **2.** TIWA LANGUAGE the language of the Tiwa people. It belongs to the Tanoan family of languages and is spoken by fewer than 5,000 people. [Early 18thC. From Tiwa.]

Tizard /tíz aard/, **Dame Cath** (*b.* 1931) New Zealand politician. She was the first woman to become governor-general of New Zealand (1990–96). Full name **Dame Catherine Anne Tizard**

tizzy /tízzi/, **tizz** /tíz/, **tiz-woz** /tíz woz/ *n.* a nervous agitated state (*informal*) [Mid-20thC. Origin unknown.]

T-joint, **tee-joint** *n.* a joint in wood or other material forming the letter T

T-junction *n.* a junction where a road joins another road, especially at a right angle, but does not cross it

tk *abbr.* truck

TKO *abbr.* BOXING technical knockout

tkt *abbr.* ticket

Tl *symbol.* thallium

t.l. *abbr.* INSUR total loss

Tlaxcala /tlass kaʾälə, -kállə/ capital city of Tlaxcala State in east-central Mexico. It is the site of the Church of San Francisco, the oldest church in North America (1521). Population: 50,631 (1990).

TLC *abbr.* tender loving care (*informal*)

Tlemcen /tlem sén/ town in northwestern Algeria. Population: 126,882 (1987).

Tlingit /tlíng git/ (*plural* **-gits** or **-git**) *n.* **1.** PEOPLES MEMBER OF NATIVE N AMERICAN PEOPLE a member of a group of Native North American peoples that originally occupied coastal lands in southeastern Alaska, and whose members continue to live mainly there and in British Columbia **2.** LANG TLINGIT LANGUAGE the Na-Dene language of the Tlingit people. It is spoken by about 2,000 people. [Mid-19thC. From Tlingit, 'person'.]

t.l.o. *abbr.* INSUR total loss only

TLS *abbr.* Times Literary Supplement

T-lymphocyte *n.* = T-cell

Tm *symbol.* thulium

TM *abbr.* **1.** transcendental meditation **2.** trademark

T-man (*plural* **T-men**) *n.* a special investigator of the US Department of the Treasury (*informal*)

tmesis /tmeé siss, tə meé-/ *n.* the separation of the parts of a word by inserting a word or words between them, as in 'pretty un-bloody-likely' [Mid-16thC. From Greek *tmēsis* 'cutting', from *temnein* 'to cut'.]

TMJ syndrome *n., abbr.* temporomandibular joint syndrome

TMOT *abbr.* trust me on this (*used in e-mail messages*)

TN *abbr.* Tennessee

tng *abbr.* training

TNT *n.* a yellow flammable crystalline compound used as an explosive and in making dyestuffs. Formula: $C_7H_5N_3O_6$. Full form **trinitrotoluene**

to (*stressed*) /too/; (*unstressed*) /tŏŏ, tə/ CORE MEANING: a preposition or adverb indicating the direction, destination, or position of sb or sth ○ *I met him on his way to school.* ○ *She climbed all the way to the top.* ○ *You'll see a supermarket to your left.* **1.** INDICATES DIRECTION indicates the direction or destination of sb or sth ○ *He was on his way to the party.* ○ *You hit the space bar and go to the next screen.* **2.** INDICATES POSITION indicates the position of sb or sth ○ *To the right of the door you will see a noticeboard.* **3.** FORMS INFINITIVE used before the base form of a verb to make the infinitive of that verb ○ *I want to leave now.* **4.** INDICATES PURPOSE used with the base form of a verb to indicate the intention or purpose of an action ○ *The news system is used to distribute information to large groups of people.* **5.** INDICATES RECIPIENT indicates the recipient of sth (*used with a noun phrase to form the indirect object*) ○ *Give it to me.* ○ *mail sent to another user on the same computer* **6.** INDICATES DIRECTION OF FEELING OR ACTION indicates who or what a particular feeling or action is directed towards ○ *I was very grateful to her for everything she did for me.* **7.** INDICATES ATTACHMENT indicates that two things are joined together ○ *Each triangle consists of three square faces joined to one another along two edges.* **8.** UNTIL indicates that sth goes on until a certain time or until it reaches a certain amount ○ *He shuts the shop on Mondays and opens from Tuesday to Saturday.* **9.** INDICATES RANGE indicates a range of things or topics ○ *Studies have explored everything from pollution to pesticides to genetics to parental occupations to electromagnetic fields and proven nothing.* **10.** INDICATES RESULT OF CHANGE indicates what sb or sth is changing into or becoming ○ *Their excitement soon turned to gloom when they saw what the climb entailed.* **11.** INDICATES SIMULTANEITY indicates that two things are happening at the same time, especially that a particular sound or music accompanies another action ○ *I woke up to the sound of the telephone ringing.* **12.** INDICATES EQUALITY indicates equality, e.g. of two weights, amounts, or measurements ○ *There are 12 inches to the foot.* **13.** AS COMPARED WITH indicates comparison between two things, e.g. scores in a game ○ *The score was 5 to 3 in favour of our team.* **14.** BEFORE HOUR indicates the number of minutes before the hour ○ *It was five to seven before they arrived home.* **15.** AT at (*regional*) ○ *Where's he to?* ○ *He's over to the doctor's.* ■ *adv.* **1.** SHUT OR ALMOST SHUT indicates that a door is shut or across the opening but not completely or firmly shut ○ *He pulled the door to after him.* **2.** CONSCIOUS AGAIN into a state of lucidity and consciousness ○ *came to in the recovery room* ○ *brought the patient to* **3.** NAUT INTO WIND into the direction from which the wind is blowing ○ *turned the yacht to* [Old English *tō*. From a prehistoric Germanic word that is also the ancestor of English *too* and *tattoo*.]

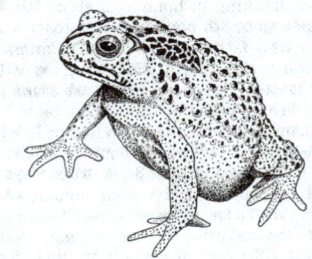

Toad

toad /tōd/ *n.* **1.** TERRESTRIAL AMPHIBIAN SIMILAR TO FROG a small squat tailless amphibian distributed nearly worldwide. It is similar to a frog but has dry warty skin and, except for breeding in water, lives mostly on land. Family: Bufonidae. **2.** SIMILAR AMPHIBIAN an amphibian similar to a toad, for example the midwife toad, but belonging to a different taxonomic family **3. OFFENSIVE TERM** an offensive term used to refer to sb considered loathsome or disgusting (*offensive insult*) [Old English *tādige*, of unknown origin] —**toadish** *adj.*

toadeater /tṓd eetər/ *n.* a toady (*archaic*)

WORD KEY: ORIGIN

The term ***toadeater*** originated in the dubious selling methods of itinerant doctors. They employed an assistant who pretended to eat a toad (toads were thought to be poisonous), so that the doctor could appear to effect a miraculous cure with his medicine.

toadfish /tṓd fish/ (*plural* **-fish** *or* **-fishes**) *n.* a scaleless spiny bottom-feeding fish that lives in tropical and temperate seas and has a broad flattened head and wide mouth. Family: Batrachoididae.

toadflax /tṓd flaks/ (*plural* **-flaxes** *or* **-flax**) *n.* **1. PLANT WITH ORANGE-AND-YELLOW FLOWERS** a plant native to Europe but widespread in North America, with narrow leaves and spurred two-lipped orange-and-yellow flowers similar to those of a snapdragon. Latin name: *Linaria vulgaris.* **2. PLANT RELATED TO COMMON TOADFLAX** a plant related to the common toadflax and similar to it, but usually with lilac-coloured flowers. Genus: *Linaria.*

toad-in-the-hole *n.* a dish consiting of sausages or sausage meat baked in a batter similar to Yorkshire pudding

toad spit, toad spittle *n.* = **cuckoo spit**

toadstone /tṓd stōn/ *n.* **1. BASALT FOUND IN DERBYSHIRE** a dark brownish-grey type of amygdaloidal basalt found in the limestone regions of Derbyshire **2. CHARM AGAINST EVIL AND DISEASE** a stone or similar object believed to have formed in the head or body of a toad, formerly worn around the neck as a charm against evil and disease

toadstool /tṓd stool/ *n.* a poisonous umbrella-shaped fungus with a spore-producing round flat cap on a stalk [14thC. So called because it resembles a small stool and grows in environments where toads are found.]

toady /tṓdi/ *n.* (*plural* **-ies**) **SB SERVILE AND INGRATIATING** a self-serving person who behaves in a servile sycophantic manner, flattering and fawning on people with power or influence ■ *vi.* (**-ies, -ying, -ied**) **BEHAVE INGRATIATINGLY** to behave in an obsequious and ingratiating manner [Early 19thC. Shortening of TOADEATER.] —**toadyish** *adj.* —**toadyism** *n.*

Toamasina /twaàmə seénə/ city and major port on the Indian Ocean, in eastern Madagascar, situated about 209 km/130 mi. northeast of Antananarivo. Population: 127,441 (1993). Former name **Tamatave**

to and fro *adv.* **1. BACK AND FORTH** moving backwards and forwards **2. HERE AND THERE** moving about here and there —**to-and-fro** *adj.* —**to-and-fro** *n.* —**toing and froing** *n.*

toast /tōst/ *n.* **1.** FOOD **BREAD BROWNED WITH HEAT** sliced bread that has been browned on both sides with heat, under a grill, in a toaster, or in front of an open fire **2. CALL TO HONOUR SB OR STH** a call to a gathering to honour sb or sth by raising glasses and drinking **3. RAISING OF GLASSES TO HONOUR SB** an act of raising a glass and drinking in honour of sb or sth **4. SB OR STH HONOURED** sb or sth honoured by a toast **5. ADMIRED PERSON** sb who is the object of much attention or admiration ○ *the toast of Hollywood* ■ *v.* (**toasts, toasting, toasted**) **1.** *vti.* FOOD **HEAT AND BROWN FOOD** to heat and brown bread or other food, or to become browned, on a grill, over an open fire, or in a toaster **2.** *vt.* **WARM BODY** to warm the body or a part of the body near a source of heat **3.** *vti.* **DRINK IN SB'S HONOUR** to drink or propose a drink in honour of sb or sth [14thC. Via Old French *toster* 'to roast' from, ultimately, Latin *tost-*, the past participle stem of *torrere* 'to scorch'.] ◇ **be toast** *US* to be in serious trouble (*informal*) ○ *Do that again and you're toast!*

toaster /tṓstər/ *n.* a small electrical appliance for making toast that works by exposing the bread to heated electrical coils [Late 16thC. Originally used for 'someone that toasts things'.]

toastie *n.* = **toasty** (*informal*)

toastmaster /tṓst maastər/ *n.* sb who proposes toasts and introduces speakers at a banquet or reception

toastmistress /tṓst mistrəss/ *n.* a woman who proposes toasts and introduces speakers at a banquet or reception

toast rack *n.* a stand that holds slices of toast on end and separate from each other

toasty /tṓsti/ *adj.* (**-ier, -iest**) **WARM** pleasantly warm ■ *n.* **toasty, toastie** (*plural* **-ies**) FOOD **TOASTED SANDWICH** a toasted sandwich (*informal*)

Tob. *abbr.* BIBLE Tobit

tobacco /tə bákō/ (*plural* **-cos** *or* **-coes** *or* **-co**) *n.* **1. PLANT WHOSE LEAVES ARE SMOKED** a plant of the nightshade family, native to tropical America and cultivated for its large leaves that are dried and processed primarily for smoking. Genus: *Nicotiana.* **2. DRIED PROCESSED LEAVES** the dried processed leaves of the tobacco plant [Late 16thC. From Spanish *tabaco*, of uncertain origin: possibly from Taino 'roll of tobacco, or pipe, for smoking' or perhaps from Arabic *ṭabbāḳ* 'herbs'.]

tobacco mosaic virus *n.* a retrovirus that causes mosaic disease in tobacco and other plants belonging to the nightshade family

tobacconist /tə bákənist/ *n.* a person or shop that specializes in selling tobacco products and supplies such as cigarettes, tobacco, and pipes [Mid-17thC. Formed from TOBACCO + -IST.]

tobacco road *n. US* a shabby poverty-stricken rural community [Mid-20thC. From the title of a novel by Erskine Caldwell.]

Tobago /tə báygō/ island in the West Indies, a constituent part of Trinidad and Tobago. Population: 50,282 (1990). Area: 300 sq. km/116 sq. mi.

Tobit /tṓbit/ *n.* **1. BIBLICAL CHARACTER** in the Bible, a pious Israelite living in Nineveh at the end of the 8th century BC **2. BOOK IN BIBLE** a book in the Roman Catholic Bible and the Protestant Apocrypha. It tells the story of Tobit. See table at **Bible**

toboggan /tə bóggən/ *n.* **LONG NARROW RUNNERLESS SLEDGE** a long narrow sledge without runners, made of strips of wood running lengthwise and curled up at the front, used for coasting downhill on snow ■ *vi.* (**-gans, -ganing, -ganed**) **RIDE A TOBOGGAN** to ride on a toboggan [Early 19thC. Via Canadian French *tabagane* from Micmac *topağan* 'sled'.] —**tobogganer** *n.* —**tobogganist** *n.*

Tobruk /tə bro͝ok/ city and port in northeastern Libya, on the Mediterranean Sea. British forces were besieged there during World War II. Population: 94,006 (1984).

toby jug, toby (*plural* **-bies**), **Toby** (*plural* **-bies**) *n.* a beer mug or jug in the shape of a stout man wearing a three-cornered hat [Mid-19thC. From *Toby* (nickname for *Tobias*), a common 19th-century name for a man or boy.]

TOC *n.* a train company that has been franchised to provide passenger services over particular routes as part of the arrangements by which the UK national railway system was privatized. Full form **train operating company**

toccata /tə kaátə/ (*plural* **-tas**) *n.* a composition for a keyboard instrument written in a free style that includes full chords and elaborate runs and is intended to show off the player's technique [Early 18thC. From Italian, from the feminine past participle of *toccare* 'to touch', from assumed Vulgar Latin *toccare*.]

Toc H /tók áych/ *n.* an interdenominational association formed in England after World War I to encourage Christian fellowship [Early 20thC. From telegraphic code for *TH*, standing for Talbot House, the name of the recreation centre founded at Poperinghe, Belgium, on which the British association was modelled.]

Tocharian /to kaári ən, tə-/, **Tokharian** *n.* **1.** PEOPLES **MEMBER OF EARLY CHINESE PEOPLE** a member of a people that lived in the Tarim Pendi in western China before being defeated by the Uigurs during the 9th century AD. They are believed to have spread into China from Eastern Europe. **2.** LANG **TOCHARIAN LANGUAGE** the extinct Indo-European language of the Tocharian people. It forms a separate branch of the Indo-European family and shows close resemblances to some western branches of the family. [Early 20thC. Formed from Latin *Tochari*, from Greek *Tokharoi* 'the Tocharians'.] —**Tocharian** *adj.*

tocher /tókhər/ *n. Scotland* **DOWRY** a dowry (*literary*) ■ *vt.* (**-ers, -ering, -ered**) *Scotland* **GIVE STH AS DOWRY** to give sth as a dowry (*literary*) [15thC. From Scottish Gaelic *tochradh*.]

tocopherol /to kóffə rol/ *n.* a fat-soluble oily compound with vitamin-E properties, present in vegetable oils, leafy greens, and milk, and required for normal growth in most vertebrates [Mid-20thC. Coined from Greek *tokos* 'childbirth' + *pherein* 'to bear' + -OL.]

Tocqueville /tók vil/, **Alexis de** (1805–59) French historian and political writer. After visiting the United States, he wrote the influential *Democracy in America* (1833), his most famous work. Full name **Alexis Charles Henri Maurice Clérel de Tocqueville**

tocsin /tóksin/ *n.* **1. ALARM** an alarm sounded by means of a bell **2. BELL** a bell that sounds an alarm **3. WARNING** any warning signal [Late 16thC. Via French from, ultimately, Old Provençal *tocasenh*, from *tocar* 'to strike' (from assumed Vulgar Latin *toccare*) + *senh* 'bell' (from Latin *signum* 'signal').]

tod[1] /tod/ *n.* **1. UNIT OF WEIGHT FOR WOOL** a unit of weight for wool, usually equal to 12.7 kg/28 lb **2. MASS OF FOLIAGE** a mass of foliage, especially ivy **3.** *Scotland, N England* **FOX** a fox [15thC. Origin unknown.]

tod[2] /tod/ [Shortening of *Tod Sloan*, a US jockey (1874–1933); rhyming slang for *alone*] ◇ **on your tod** alone (*informal*)

today /tə dáy/ *n.* **1. THIS DAY** this day, as distinct from yesterday or tomorrow **2. PRESENT AGE** the present time or age ○ *the fashions of today* ■ *adj.* **MODERN** modern or of the present day ○ *a today look* ■ *adv.* **1. ON THIS DAY** on or during this day ○ *She is working today.* **2. IN PRESENT TIME** during the present time or age ○ *Children today have far more sophisticated toys than we ever had.* [Old English *tō dæge*, literally 'to (this) day']

Todd /tod/, **Alexander R., Baron Todd of Trumpington** (1907–97) British chemist. For his work on vitamins B_1 and E, he was awarded a Nobel Prize in chemistry (1957). He was the first chancellor of the University of Strathclyde, Scotland. Full name **Alexander Robertus Todd**

toddle /tódd'l/ *vi.* (**-dles, -dling, -dled**) **1. TAKE SHORT UNSTEADY STEPS** to walk with short unsteady steps, as a child does when learning to walk **2. WALK UNHURRIEDLY** to walk at a leisurely pace (*informal*) ■ *n.* **1. UNHURRIED WALK** a leisurely walk (*informal*) **2. UNSTEADY STEPS** an unsteady, tottering gait [Late 16thC. Origin unknown.]

toddler /tódd'lər/ *n.* a young child who is learning to walk

toddy /tóddi/ (*plural* **-dies**) *n.* **1. HOT ALCOHOLIC DRINK** a drink made with alcoholic liquor, hot water, sugar, and sometimes spices **2. PALM TREE SAP** the sweet sap of a variety of Asian palm tree used as a beverage, either fresh or fermented [Late 18thC. Via Hindi *tāṛī* 'palm sap' from, ultimately, Sanskrit *tālaḥ* 'palm', probably of Dravidian origin.]

to-do /tə do͞o/ *n.* a fuss, especially an angry complaint or protest (*informal*)

tody /tṓdi/ (*plural* **-dies**) *n.* a small Caribbean bird similar to a kingfisher with a short tail and round wings, a bright green back, red throat, and a long straight beak. Family: Todidae. [Late 18thC. Origin uncertain: probably via French *todier* from, ultimately, Latin *todus*, a small bird.]

toe /tō/ *n.* **1.** ANAT **FOOT PART** any one of the digits of the foot, equivalent to the fingers and thumb of the hand **2.** ZOOL **VERTEBRATE'S FOOT PART** a part corresponding to the human toe in other vertebrates **3.** ZOOL **PART OF HOOF** the forepart of an animal's hoof **4.** CLOTHES **PART OF SHOE OR SOCK** the part of a shoe, boot, sock, or stocking that covers the toes and the front part of the foot **5.** GOLF **PART OF GOLF CLUB** the end of the head of a golf club **6. PART RESEMBLING TOE** a part that resembles the front part of a foot in form or position ○ *the toe of Italy* **7.** MECH ENG **LOWER END OF SHAFT** the lower end of a vertical shaft that turns in a bearing **8.** GEOG **BASE OF EMBANKMENT** the base of an embankment, cliff, wall, or dam ■ *v.* (**toes, toeing, toed**) **1.** *vt.* **TOUCH STH WITH TOES** to touch, kick, reach, or mark sth with the toes or the front part of the foot **2.** *vt.* GOLF **STRIKE GOLF BALL** to strike a golf ball with the front part of the head of the club **3.** *vt.* **DRIVE NAIL AT ANGLE** to drive in a nail or spike at an angle **4.** *vt.* **FASTEN STH WITH ANGLED NAIL** to fasten sth with a nail or spike driven in at an angle **5.** *vi.* **STAND WITH TOES POINTED** to stand or move with the toes pointed in a particular direction [Old English *tā*. Ultimately from an Indo-European base meaning 'to point' that is also the ancestor of English *digit* and *index*.] ◇ **on your toes** alert and ready for action ◇ **tread on sb's toes** to offend or upset sb by interfering with sth considered to be that person's own responsibility ◇ **turn up your toes** to die (*informal*)

toea /tố i ə, tố aa/ (*plural* **-a** *or* **-as**) *n.* **1.** **SUBUNIT OF PAPUA NEW GUINEAN CURRENCY** a subunit of currency in Papua New Guinea, 100 of which are worth one kina. See table at **currency 2.** **COIN WORTH A TOEA** a coin worth a toea [Late 20thC. From Motu, literally 'conical shell', used as currency.]

toe and heel *n.* **MOTOR SPORTS** a technique used by racing drivers for operating the brake and accelerator simultaneously with the right foot, using the heel for one pedal and the toe for the other

toecap /tố kap/ *n.* a metal or leather covering reinforcing the toe of a shoe or boot

toed /tōd/ *adj.* **1.** **ANAT, ZOOL HAVING TOES** having toes of a particular kind or number (*usually used in combination*) ○ *three-toed* **2.** **BUILDING DRIVEN IN AT AN ANGLE** used to describe nails driven in at an angle, or sth fastened by nails or spikes driven in at an angle

toe dance *n.* **DANCE ON TOES** a dance performed on the toes ■ *vi.* **DO TOE DANCE** to perform a toe dance —**toe dancer** *n.*

TOEFL /tốf'l/ *n.* a test of English for speakers of other languages that is an entrance requirement for study at a US university. Full form **Test of English as a Foreign Language**

toehold /tố hōld/ *n.* **1.** **CLIMBING SMALL RECESS IN ROCK** a small recess or ledge in a rock giving support for the toes **2.** **SMALL ADVANTAGE** a small advantage or gain in an endeavour **3.** **WRESTLING HOLD ON FOOT** a wrestling hold in which one competitor holds the foot and twists the leg of the other

toe-in *n.* the alignment of a motor vehicle's front wheels so that the front edges are slightly closer together than the rear edges to improve its steering capabilities and reduce tyre wear

toe loop *n.* a jump in which an ice skater, skating backwards, takes off from one skate, makes one rotation in the air, and lands on the outer edge of the same skate

toenadering /toŏ naadərəng/ *n. S Africa* a getting together or rapprochement between political parties (*informal*) [Early 20thC. Via Afrikaans from Dutch, from *toe* 'to' + *nadering* 'approach' (translation of French *rapprochement*).]

toenail /tố nayl/ *n.* **1.** **ANAT, ZOOL NAIL ON TOE** the nail of a toe **2.** **BUILDING NAIL DRIVEN IN AT ANGLE** a nail driven in at an angle, e.g. to join intersecting structural parts **3.** **PRINTING PARENTHESIS** a parenthesis (*slang*) ■ *vt.* (**-nails, -nailing, -nailed**) **BUILDING JOIN WITH ANGLED NAILS** to join parts of a structure with nails driven in at an angle

toerag /tố rag/ *n.* a person considered to be worthless, despicable, or generally no good (*slang insult*) [Late 19thC. The word originally referred to beggars with their feet bound in rags.]

toe ring *n.* a ring worn on the toe, particularly a silver ring worn by married Hindu women

toetoe /tố i tố i, tóy toy/ *n.* = **toitoi**

toey /tố i/ *adj. Aus* easily annoyed or irritated (*informal*) [Mid-20thC. The underlying meaning is 'on one's toes, ready to race'.]

toff /tof/ *n.* sb who is rich or upper-class, especially sb who is also smartly dressed (*informal*) [Mid-19thC. Origin uncertain: probably a variant of *tuft*, a golden plume worn by titled students at Oxford and Cambridge.]

toffee /tóffi/ *n.* a sweet that can be soft and chewy or hard and brittle, made by boiling brown sugar or treacle with butter and sometimes flavourings or nuts [Early 19thC. Variant of TAFFY.] ◇ **sb cannot do sth for toffee** used to emphasize sb's lack of ability or competence (*informal*)

toffee apple *n.* a caramel-coated apple mounted on a stick. US term **candy apple**

toffee-nosed *adj.* behaving in an aloof condescending way (*informal insult*) [Alteration of TOFF]

toft /toft/ *n.* (*archaic*) **1.** **HOUSE AND BUILDINGS** a house with its adjoining buildings and land **2.** **ENTIRE HOLDING** an entire holding including a homestead and all additional land [Old English. From Old Norse *topt*.]

tofu /tố foo/ *n.* a soft food with no particular flavour made from soya milk curd pressed into a cake [Late 18thC. Via Japanese from Chinese *dòufŭ*, literally 'fermented beans'.]

tog /tog/ *vti.* (**togs, togging, togged**) **DRESS UP** to dress up, or dress sb up, usually in smart clothing (*informal*) ■ *n.* **MEASURE OF THERMAL INSULATION** a measure of the thermal insulation properties of fabrics, quilts, and clothes. It is equal to ten times the temperature difference in Celsius between the two surfaces when the flow of heat across the material is one watt per square metre. ■ **togs** *npl.* (*informal*) **1.** **CLOTHES** clothes of any kind **2.** *ANZ, Ireland* **SWIMMING COSTUME** clothes worn for swimming [Late 18thC. Shortening of obsolete slang *togeman*, from obsolete French *togue* 'cloak', from Latin *toga* (see TOGA).]

toga /tốgə/ *n.* **1.** **GARMENT WORN BY ROMAN CITIZENS** an outer garment worn by the citizens of ancient Rome, consisting of a semicircular piece of cloth draped around the body **2.** **ROBE OF OFFICE** a robe of office [Early 17thC. From Latin. Ultimately from an Indo-European base meaning 'to cover' that is also the ancestor of English *deck*, *thatch*, and *tile*.] —**togaed** *adj.*

toga praetexta /-pree tékstə/ (*plural* **togae praetextae** /tố gee pree ték stee/) *n.* a toga with a purple border worn in ancient Rome by some magistrates and priests and by boys before the age of puberty [From Latin, 'bordered toga']

toga virilis /-vi rílliss/ (*plural* **togae viriles** /tố gee viríleez/) *n.* a white toga worn by boys in ancient Rome from the age of 14 or 15 as a sign of manhood and citizenship [From Latin, 'men's toga']

together /tə géthər/ *adv.* CORE MEANING: an adverb indicating that people are with each other, or that sth is done with another person or other people, or by joint effort ○ *My brother and I always walked to school together.*
1. **WITH OTHERS** in company with others in a group or in a place ○ *Spawning cod come together near the seafloor in huge schools.* **2.** **INTERACTING WITH ONE ANOTHER** interacting, communicating, or in a relationship with one another ○ *They spend all their time together talking in low voices.* ○ *They get on well together.* **3.** **BY JOINT EFFORT** cooperating with one another or by joint or combined effort ○ *The only way we'll get anywhere is if we work together on this one.* **4.** **INTO CONTACT** indicates that two or more things are put into contact with one another, or unite to form a single whole ○ *The mummy wore moccasins made of three kinds of animal skin, sewn together with two types of stitching.* ○ *Mix together mustard, lime, salt and pepper, cayenne pepper, and jalapeño.* **5.** **COLLECTIVELY** considered collectively or as a whole ○ *Taken together, these developments add up to a significant change in policy.* ○ *He earns more than all the others together.* **6.** **UNINTERRUPTEDLY** without interruption ○ *It has been raining for all of four days together.* **7.** **IN AGREEMENT** in or into agreement or harmony ○ *They can't seem to get together on anything.* **8.** **IN INTEGRATED COHERENT STRUCTURE** in or into a unified structure or a coherent integrated whole ○ *If you understand how something is put together, you will use it better.* **9.** **INTO ORDERLY CONDITION OR STATE** into an orderly condition or a stable and effective emotional state (*informal*) ○ *"I'm just trying to get my life together," he said quietly.* **10.** **IN A COUPLE** indicates that two people are married, having a sexual relationship, or form an established and recognized couple (*informal*) ○ *got back together again after a trial separation* ■ *adj.* **STABLE AND SELF-CONFIDENT** emotionally stable, self-confident, and well-organized (*informal*) ○ *She's a very together person.* [Old English *tōgædere*, from *to* 'to' + a prehistoric Germanic word meaning 'joined together'] ◇ **get it together** *vr.* to become organized and calm so as to perform efficiently (*slang*) ◇ **together with** as well as or in addition to

—— WORD KEY: USAGE ——
This remark, together with earlier comments of the same kind, was not well received When *together with* forms an addition to the grammatical subject of a verb, the verb agrees with the subject proper, in this case *remark*.

togetherness /tə gétharnəss/ *n.* a feeling of closeness in being with others

toggery /tóggəri/ *n.* (*informal*) **1.** **CLOTHES** clothes **2.** *US* **CLOTHING STORE** a clothes shop [Early 19thC. Formed from TOG.]

toggle /tógg'l/ *n.* **1.** **PEG INSERTED IN LOOP** a peg or rod that is inserted crosswise into a loop at the end of a rope, chain, or strap to hold or fasten sth **2.** **CLOTHES FASTENER ON CLOTHES** a small peg sewn on clothes or on a bag, inserted crosswise into a loop or buttonhole and used as a fastener **3.** **COMPUT KEY FOR SWITCHING BETWEEN OPERATIONS** a key or command that switches back and forth between computer operations each time it is used **4.** **NAUT PIN INSERTED INTO KNOT** a pin inserted into a nautical knot to keep it from coming undone **5.** **STH WITH TOGGLE JOINT** a toggle joint or a device with a toggle joint ■ *v.* (**-gles, -gling, -gled**) **1.** *vti.* **COMPUT SWITCH BETWEEN OPERATIONS WITH ONE KEY** to switch back and forth between two computer operations using the same key or command **2.** *vt.* **SUPPLY OR FASTEN STH WITH TOGGLES** to supply or fasten sth with a toggle or toggles [Late 18thC. Origin unknown.] —**toggler** *n.*

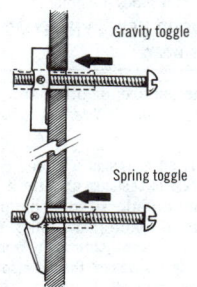

Toggle bolt

toggle bolt *n.* a threaded bolt that has a nut with spring-loaded hinged wings attached and is used especially for securing things to hollow walls. When the bolt is inserted into a hole in the wall, the wings spread open inside, pressing back against the wall's inner surface and allowing the bolt to be tightened.

toggle iron, **toggle harpoon** *n.* a whaling harpoon with a pivoting barb that keeps the whale from freeing itself

toggle joint *n.* a device with two arms hinged together so that pressure applied at the pivot point to straighten the device exerts force along the two arms

toggle switch *n.* **1.** **ENG SWITCH FOR ELECTRICAL CIRCUITS** a small spring-loaded mechanical switch that opens and closes an electric circuit by manual operation **2.** **COMPUT** = **toggle** *n.* 3

Togliatti /to lyátti/ industrial city on the Volga River in southern European Russia. Population: 642,000 (1990).

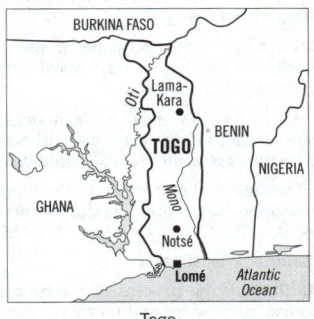

Togo

Togo /tốgō/ republic in West Africa, bordered by Burkina Faso, Benin, the Gulf of Guinea, and

Ghana. Language: French. Currency: franc. Capital: Lomé. Population: 4,735,610 (1997). Area: 56,785 sq. km/21,925 sq. mi. Official name **Togolese Republic** — **Togolese** /tṓgə léez/ n., adj.

Togoland /tṓgō land/ former German protectorate in western Africa, divided between British and French administration in 1922. British Togoland was incorporated into Ghana (1956), and French Togoland became independent as Togo (1960).

Togrul Beg /tṓgril bég/ (993?–1063) Turkish statesman. The founder of the Seljuk dynasty, he conquered most of Iran and Iraq, gaining control of Baghdad in 1055.

toheroa /tṓ ə rṓ ə/ (plural **-a** or **-as**) n. **1.** MARINE BIOL LARGE EDIBLE MOLLUSC OF NEW ZEALAND a large edible mollusc with a hinged shell found along the coasts of New Zealand. Latin name: Amphidesma ventricosum. **2.** TOHEROA SOUP a greenish soup made from the toheroa [Late 19thC. From Maori.]

Tohono O'Odham /tōhṓ nō ṓdəm/ n. PEOPLES, LANGUAGE = **Papago**

toil[1] /toyl/ n. **1.** HARD WORK hard exhausting work or effort **2.** STRIFE strife or struggle (archaic) ■ v. (**toils, toiling, toiled**) **1.** vi. WORK HARD to work long and hard **2.** vi. PROGRESS SLOWLY to progress slowly and with difficulty **3.** vt. ACHIEVE STH BY EFFORT to achieve sth by hard work (archaic) [13thC. Via Anglo-Norman toiler 'to drag around' from, ultimately, Latin tudicula 'machine for bruising olives', from tudes 'hammer'.]

———— **WORD KEY: SYNONYMS** ————
See Synonyms at **work**.

toil[2] /toyl/ n. a net, snare, or other thing that entraps or entangles (archaic or literary; often used in the plural)

toile /twaal/ n. **1.** SHEER FABRIC a sheer cotton or linen fabric **2.** PROTOTYPE OF DESIGNER GARMENT a prototype of a designer garment made up in a cheap fabric so that alterations can be made [Late 18thC. Via French from, ultimately, Latin tela 'web'. Ultimately from an Indo-European base meaning 'to weave' that is also the ancestor of English subtle and text.]

toile de Jouy /-də jweé/ n. a fabric with a white or light-coloured background and a floral or pastoral print usually in one colour only, used for curtains and upholstery [Mid-18thC. From French, named after Jouy-en-Josas, the French town near Paris where the fabric was made.]

toilet /tóylət/ n. **1.** FIXTURE FOR DISPOSING OF BODILY WASTE a bowl-shaped fixture with a waste drain and a flushing device connected to a water supply, used for defecating and urinating **2.** ROOM WITH TOILET a room with a toilet and usually a washbasin **3.** WASHING AND DRESSING the process of attending to your personal appearance and making it presentable, e.g. by washing, dressing, shaving, and tidying your hair (formal) **4.** MED CLEANSING ASSOCIATED WITH A SURGICAL PROCEDURE a cleansing of part of the body after a medical or surgical procedure, often in preparation for applying dressings or bandages **5.** DRESSING TABLE a dressing table (archaic) [Late 17thC. From French toilette 'bag for clothing', from Old French tellette, from teile 'cloth', from Latin tela 'web'.]

toilet paper n. a usually soft absorbent paper, especially in a roll, used for cleaning the body after defecating or urinating

toilet roll n. a length of toilet paper wound around a cardboard cylinder, or the cardboard cylinder on which the paper is wound

toiletry /tóylətri/ (plural **-ries**) n. an article such as shampoo, deodorant, or soap, used in washing or caring for the appearance (usually used in the plural)

toilette /twaa lét/ n. the process of attending to your personal appearance and making it presentable (literary) [Mid-16thC. From French (see TOILET).]

toilet tissue n. = **toilet paper**

toilet training n. the process of teaching a young child to control bladder and bowel movements and to use the toilet

toilet water n. a lightly perfumed liquid used to freshen or scent the skin

toilsome /tóyɪssəm/ adj. requiring long hard work (literary) —**toilsomely** adv. —**toilsomeness** n.

toilworn /tóyl wawrn/ adj. worn, damaged, or exhausted from hard work

toitoi /tóy toy/ (plural **-tois** /tóy toyz/), **toetoe** n. **1.** TALL GRASS OF NEW ZEALAND a tall grass with feathery fronds that grows in New Zealand. Genus: Cortederia. **2.** NZ ZOOL = **bully**[1] [Mid-19thC. From Maori.]

Tokaj /tó káy, to-, -kī/ town in northeastern Hungary. Tokay wines are produced in the surrounding region. Population: 5,371 (1990).

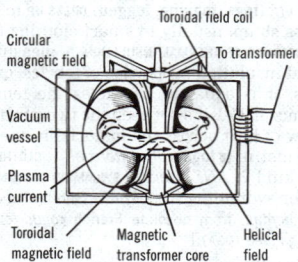

Tokamak

tokamak /tókə mak/ n. an experimental doughnut-shaped nuclear reactor for producing fusion using an electric current and a magnetic field to heat and contain a gaseous plasma [Mid-20thC. From Russian, a contraction of toroidal'naya kamera s aksial'nym magnitnym polem 'toroidal chamber with axial magnetic field'.]

tokay /tó kay/ n. a small lizard of southern and Southeast Asia that has a retractile claw at the tip of each digit. Latin name: Gekko gecko. [Mid-18thC. Via Malay dialect toke' from Javanese tekèk, ultimately an imitation of the animal's call.]

Tokay /tó káy, to-, tō kī/ n. **1.** PLANTS LARGE SWEET GRAPE OF HUNGARY a large sweet variety of grape originally grown near Tokaj, Hungary **2.** WINE SWEET WINE A sweet wine made near Tokaj, Hungary, from the Tokay grape, or a similar sweet wine produced elsewhere [Early 18thC. Named after TOKAJ (Tokay), where the wine is made.]

toke /tók/ n. PUFF OF MARIJUANA a puff on a cigarette or pipe containing marijuana (slang) ■ vti. (**tokes, toking, toked**) PUFF MARIJUANA to puff on a cigarette or pipe containing marijuana (slang) [Mid-20thC. Origin uncertain: perhaps from Spanish toque 'a hit', from tocar 'to touch'.]

token /tókən/ n. **1.** STH REPRESENTING STH ELSE sth that represents, expresses, or is a symbol of sth else ○ Please accept this gift as a token of our appreciation. **2.** DISC USED LIKE MONEY a disc of metal or plastic used instead of money, e.g. in slot machines **3.** KEEPSAKE an object kept in memory of sth **4.** PAPER EXCHANGED FOR GOODS a paper or card certificate that can be exchanged for goods up to the stated value ○ a book token for £10 **5.** LING INSTANCE OF EXPRESSION a particular instance of a word or expression **6.** LING CONCRETE EXAMPLE a written or spoken expression considered as a concrete example ■ adj. EXISTING AS GESTURE ONLY made, given, or existing merely because expected or required, not because sincere or serving a real purpose ○ the token student on the committee [Old English tācen. Ultimately from an Indo-European word meaning 'to point, show' that is also the ancestor of English teach and digit.]

tokenism /tókənizəm/ n. the practice of making only a symbolic effort at sth, especially in order to meet the minimum requirements of the law —**tokenistic** /tókə nístik/ adj.

Tokharian n., adj. PEOPLES, LANG = **Tocharian**

tokoloshe /tóko lósh, -lóshi/ n. a small mischievous evil spirit or water sprite in African folklore that takes on human or animal appearance [Mid-19thC. Of Nguni origin.]

tokonoma /tókə nṓmə/ n. an alcove in the living room of a Japanese house where a decoration such as flowers or an ornament is displayed [Early 18thC. From Japanese.]

Tokoroa /tókō rṓ ə/ town in the northwestern part of the North Island, New Zealand, that services the paper and timber mills at nearby Kinleith. Population: 15,528 (1996).

Tok Pisin /tók píssin/ n. LANG a creole, originating as a Pidgin based on English, that is widely spoken in Papua New Guinea. Tok Pisin is spoken by over 2 million people. [Mid-20thC. From Pidgin English, 'to talk pidgin'.]

Tokyo /tóki ō/ capital city of Japan, located on Tokyo Bay on the eastern coast of Honshu Island. Population: 8,019,938 (1995).

tola /tṓlə/ n. an Indian unit of weight equal to 180 grains troy weight or 11.7 grams [Early 17thC. Via Hindi tolā from Sanskrit tulā 'weight'. Ultimately from an Indo-European base meaning 'to lift up, weigh', which is also the ancestor of English toll[1] and tolerate.]

tolar /tólaar/ n. **1.** UNIT OF SLOVENIAN CURRENCY a unit of currency in Slovenia, worth 100 stotins. See table at **currency 2.** COIN OR NOTE WORTH A TOLAR a coin or note worth one tolar [From Slovene, from German Taler (see THALER)]

tolbooth /tól booth, -booth/ n. **1.** Scotland TOWN HALL OR PRISON a town hall or a prison, or a building that performed both functions (archaic) **2.** = **tollbooth**

tolbutamide /tol byoōtə mīd/ n. a drug used in the treatment of adult-onset diabetes to lower blood-glucose levels by stimulating the islets in the pancreas to produce more insulin. Formula: $C_{12}H_{18}N_2O_3S$. [Mid-20thC. Contraction of TOLUENE + BUTYL + AMIDE.]

told past tense, past participle of **tell**

tole /tōl/ n. lacquered or enamelled metal used to make decorative objects, usually brightly painted or gilded or both, or objects made of this kind of decorated metal [Mid-20thC. Via French tôle 'sheet iron' from, ultimately, Latin tabula 'board' (source of English table).]

Toledo[1] /to láydō/ (plural **-dos**) n. a sword or sword blade of highly tempered steel, made in Toledo, Spain

Toledo[2] /to láydō/ historic city in central Spain, the administrative centre of Toledo Province. Population: 63,561 (1991).

tolerable /tólərəb'l/ adj. **1.** CAPABLE OF BEING TOLERATED not too unpleasant or severe to put up with **2.** FAIRLY GOOD moderately good, but not outstanding —**tolerability** /tóllərə bílləti/ n. —**tolerableness** /tóllərəb'lnəss/ n. —**tolerably** /tóllərəbli/ adv.

tolerance /tóllərənss/ n. **1.** ACCEPTANCE OF DIFFERENT VIEWS the acceptance of the differing views of other people, e.g. in religious or political matters, and fairness towards the people who hold these different views **2.** TOLERATING OF STH the act of putting up with sth or sb irritating or otherwise unpleasant **3.** ABILITY TO ENDURE HARDSHIP the ability to put up with harsh or difficult conditions **4.** ENG ALLOWANCE MADE FOR DEVIATION allowance made for sth to deviate in size from a standard, or the limit within which it is allowed to deviate **5.** MED ABILITY TO REMAIN UNAFFECTED the loss of or reduction in the normal response to a drug or other agent, following use or exposure over a prolonged period **6.** BIOL ABILITY TO WITHSTAND EXTREMES the ability of an organism to survive in extreme conditions

tolerant /tóllərənt/ adj. **1.** ACCEPTING DIFFERENT VIEWS accepting the differing views of others, e.g. different religious or political beliefs **2.** WITHSTANDING HARSH TREATMENT able to put up with harsh conditions or treatment **3.** MED NOT AFFECTED BY A DRUG no longer responding to a drug that has been taken over a prolonged period, or suffering no ill effects from exposure to a harmful substance —**tolerantly** adv.

tolerate /tóllə rayt/ (**-ates, -ating, -ated**) vt. **1.** PERMIT STH to be willing to allow sth to happen or exist **2.** ENDURE STH to withstand the unpleasant effects of sth **3.** ACCEPT EXISTENCE OF DIFFERENT VIEWS to recognize other people's right to have different beliefs or practices without an attempt to suppress them **4.** MED BE UNAFFECTED BY A DRUG to fail to respond to a drug because the body has built up a resistance to it, or suffer no ill effects from being exposed to a harmful substance [Early 16thC. From Latin tolerare. Ultimately from an Indo-European base meaning 'to support', which is also the ancestor of English *toll[1]* and *talent*.] —**tolerative** /tóllərətiv, -raytiv/ *adj.* —**tolerator** /tóllə raytər/ *n.*

toleration /tóllə ráysh'n/ *n.* **1.** OFFICIAL ACCEPTANCE OF DIFFERENT RELIGIONS official acceptance by a government of religious beliefs and practices that are different from those it upholds **2.** TOLERATING OF STH the act of tolerating sth —**tolerationism** *n.* —**tolerationist** *n.*, *adj.*

tolidine /tóllə deen/ *n.* an isomeric derivative of toluene used in making dyes. Formula: $C_{14}H_{16}N_2$. [Late 19thC. Coined from TOLYL + *benzidine*.]

Tolkien /tól keen/, **J. R. R.** (1892–1973) South African-born British scholar and writer. A philologist at Oxford University, he wrote *The Hobbit* (1937) and its large-scale sequel *The Lord of the Rings* (1954–55). Full name **John Ronald Reuel Tolkien**

toll[1] /tól/ *n.* **1.** TRANSP FEE FOR USING A ROAD a fee charged for a privilege, usually crossing a bridge or using a road **2.** TRANSP BOOTH a tollbooth, where tolls are paid (*often used in the plural*) **3.** DAMAGE SUSTAINED the damage done by an accident or disaster in terms of, e.g. people killed, property destroyed, or financial loss ○ *The toll on the environment was significant.* **4.** TELECOM CHARGE FOR A TELEPHONE CALL in the United States, a charge for a long-distance telephone call, or, in New Zealand, for a call made to a place outside a free-dialling area **5.** FIN FEE FOR SERVICES a fee charged for services, e.g. transport ■ *vti.* (**tolls, tolling, tolled**) TRANSP CHARGE A TOLL ON A ROAD to charge a toll for the use of a road or bridge [Old English *toll, toln*. Via medieval Latin *toloneum*, from, ultimately, Greek *telōnion* 'toll house', from *telos* 'tax' (source of English *philately*).]

toll[2] /tól/ *v.* (**tolls, tolling, tolled**) **1.** *vti.* RING SLOWLY AND REPEATEDLY to ring a bell, repeatedly and with long pauses between each ring, especially to announce a death, or be rung in this way ○ *'never send to know for whom the bell tolls; it tolls for thee'* (John Donne, *Devotions*; 1624) **2.** *vt.* ANNOUNCE STH WITH A BELL to announce sth or call sb with the repeated slow ringing of a bell ○ *bells tolling the death of the king* ■ *n.* ACT OR SOUND OF BELL TOLLING the act of ringing a bell slowly and repeatedly, or the sound so made [15thC. Origin uncertain: probably from Old English *-tyllan* 'to pull'; the underlying meaning is 'to pull on a bell rope'.] —**toller** *n.*

tollbooth /tól booth, -booth/, **tolbooth** *n.* a booth on a road or bridge where tolls for use of the road or bridge are collected

toll call *n.* **1.** *US, NZ* LONG-DISTANCE CALL a long-distance telephone call charged at a higher rate than a local call **2.** *NZ* TELEPHONE CALL OUTSIDE FREE-DIALLING AREA a telephone call made to a place outside a free-dialling area, and therefore charged for

Toller /tóllər/, **Ernst** (1893–1939) German playwright. He wrote *Masses and Man* (1920) and other plays of social protest in the tradition of German expressionism.

tollgate /tól gayt/ *n.* a gate barring the way on a road or bridge where a toll must be paid to proceed

tollhouse /tól howss/ (*plural* **-houses** /-howziz/) *n.* a shelter or kiosk for a toll collector at a tollgate

tollhouse cookie *n.* a biscuit made with flour, brown sugar, chocolate chips, and often chopped nuts

tolly /tólli/ (*plural* **-lies**), **tollie** *n.* *S Africa* a calf that has been castrated [19thC. From Xhosa *ithole* 'calf just growing its horns'.]

Tolstoy /tólstoy/, **Count Leo Nikolayevich** (1828–1910)

Count Leo Nikolayevich Tolstoy

AKG London

Russian writer. He wrote the epic novels *War and Peace* (1865–69) and *Anna Karenina* (1875–77). A profound social thinker and moralist, he was excommunicated from the Russian Orthodox Church for his radical views on Church authority.

Toltec /tól tek/ (*plural* **Toltecs** *or* **Toltec**) *n.* PEOPLES a member of a Native Central American people who formerly occupied lands in central Mexico. They dominated the area from around the 10th to the 12th centuries AD, when they were defeated by the Chichimecs and their lands were later taken over by the Aztecs. [Late 18thC. Via Spanish *tolteca* from Nahuatl *toltecatl*, literally 'someone from Tula', an ancient Toltec city.] —**Toltec** *adj.*

tolu /tə loō, tō-, to-/ *n.* an aromatic resin obtained from a South American tree, used in cough medicine [Late 17thC. From Spanish *tolú*, named after the town of Santiago de *Tolú* in Colombia, from which it was exported.]

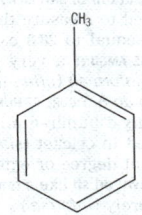

Toluene

toluene /tóllyoo een/ *n.* a colourless liquid aromatic hydrocarbon resembling benzene but less flammable, used in high-octane fuels and organic synthesis. Formula: C_7H_8. [Late 19thC. Formed from TOLU, from which it was originally obtained.]

toluidine /tol yoō i deen/ *n.* any of three isomeric derivatives of toluene used in making dyes. Formula: C_7H_9N.

toluol /tóllyoo ol/ *n.* = toluene

tolyl /tóllil/ *n.* any of three chemical groups derived from toluene. Formula: C_7H_7.

tom /tom/ *n.* the male of various animals, especially the domestic cat [14thC. From the name *Tom*.]

Tom, Dick, and Harry /tóm dík ənd hárri/, **Tom, Dick, or Harry** *n.* anyone at all

Tomahawk

tomahawk /tómmə hawk/ *n.* **1.** NATIVE N AMERICAN WEAPON a small axe, formerly used as a weapon by some Native North American peoples. It could be thrown like a knife and used as a hand weapon in close combat. **2.** *ANZ* SMALL AXE a small short-handled axe ■ *vt.* (**-hawks, -hawking, -hawked**) ATTACK SB WITH TOMAHAWK to attack or kill sb with a tomahawk [Early 17thC. From Virginia Algonquian *tamahaac*.]

tomalley /tóm alli, tə málli/ *n.* a soft green part of the insides of a cooked lobster, often called the liver but technically an organ called the hepatopancreas, eaten as a delicacy [Mid-17thC. Via French *taumalin* from Carib *taumali*.]

toman /tə maän/ *n.* **1.** IRANIAN COIN an Iranian coin worth ten rials **2.** OLD UNIT OF PERSIAN CURRENCY a gold coin that was a unit of currency in Persia between 1600

and 1912 [Mid-16thC. Via Persian *tūmān* from, ultimately, western Tocharian *tmān*, of uncertain origin.]

Tomato

tomatillo /tómə teèyō/ (*plural* **-los**) *n.* **1.** FOOD MEXICAN FRUIT a purplish sticky edible fruit that grows on a Mexican ground cherry **2.** PLANTS PLANT BEARING TOMATILLOS the ground cherry plant that bears tomatillos. Latin name: *Physalis ixocarpa*. [Early 20thC. From Spanish, literally 'small tomato', from *tomate* (see TOMATO).]

tomato /tə maátō/ (*plural* **-toes**) *n.* **1.** FOOD RED VEGETABLE a round vegetable with bright-red, occasionally yellow skin and pulpy seedy flesh. It grows like fruit on climbing plants and is widely eaten cooked or raw. **2.** PLANTS TOMATO PLANT a climbing plant that yields tomatoes and is native to South America but is grown as an annual throughout the world, in regions usually in greenhouses. Genus: *Lycopersicon*. [Early 17thC. Alteration of Spanish *tomate*, from Nahuatl *tomatl*.]

tomb /toom/ *n.* **1.** GRAVE a grave or other place for burying a dead person **2.** BURIAL CHAMBER a cave or chamber used for burial of a dead person **3.** MONUMENT a monument to a dead person, often built over the place where he or she is buried **4.** DEATH death (*literary*) ○ *go to the tomb unrepentant* **5.** REACTOR ENCLOSURE a hardened enclosure for a closed nuclear reactor, designed to contain radioactive emissions [12thC. Via French *tombe* from, ultimately, Greek *tumbos* 'mound, tomb'.] —**tombless** *adj.*

Tomba /tómba/, **Alberto** (b. 1966) Italian skier. In 1988 he won the first of many medals, including Olympic gold medals and World Cups in slalom and giant slalom events.

tombac /tóm bak/, **tambac** /tám-/ *n.* an alloy of copper and zinc, often with tin and arsenic, originally used in eastern countries to make gongs and bells and now used worldwide to make inexpensive jewellery [Early 17thC. Via French from, ultimately, Malay *tembaga* 'copper, brass'.]

tombola /tom bōlə/ *n.* a kind of small-scale lottery, often held at a community event, with tickets drawn from a revolving drum turned by hand [Late 19thC. Via French or Italian from Italian *tombolare* 'to tumble'.]

tombolo /tómbələ/ (*plural* **-los**) *n.* a narrow strip of sand or shingle that links one island to another or to the mainland [Late 19thC. Via Italian, literally 'sand dune', from Latin *tumulus* (see TUMULUS).]

Tombouctou /tómb ok toō/ = Timbuktu

tomboy /tóm boy/ *n.* a girl who dresses or behaves in a way regarded as boyish, especially a girl who enjoys rough boisterous play [Mid-16thC. From the name *Tom* (short for *Thomas*). The word originally referred to a boisterous or cheeky boy.] —**tomboyish** *adj.* —**tomboyishly** *adv.* —**tomboyishness** *n.*

tombstone /toòm stōn/ *n.* an ornamental stone on or at the site of a grave, often with the dead person's name and dates of birth and death engraved on it

Tombstone /toōmstōn/ city in southeastern Arizona. Its history as a lawless mining town has made it a popular tourist centre. Population: 1,414 (1996).

tomcat /tóm kat/ *n.* **1.** MALE CAT a male domestic cat **2.** OFFENSIVE TERM an offensive term for a man who seeks many sexual partners, or who has casual sex with many partners (*offensive insult*) ■ *vi.* OFFENSIVE TERM an offensive term meaning to seek many sexual partners, or have casual sex with many partners (*offensive; refers to a man*)

tomcod /tóm kod/ *n.* either one of two small sea fishes of the cod family, one of North American Atlantic waters and the other of northern Pacific waters. Both are valued as food fish. Latin name: *Microgradus tomcod* and *Microgradus proximus.*

Tom Collins *n.* an alcoholic cocktail consisting of gin, lemon or lime juice, soda water, and sugar [Late 19thC. Origin uncertain: said to have been named after a London barman.]

tome /tōm/ *n.* **1. LARGE BOOK** a book, especially a large heavy book on a serious subject (*formal or humorous*) **2. SINGLE VOLUME** a single volume of a book made up of several volumes [Early 16thC. Via French from, ultimately, Greek *tomos* 'section, volume'. Ultimately from an Indo-European base meaning 'to cut', which is also the ancestor of English *atom* and *anatomy.*]

-tome *suffix.* **1.** segment, part ○ *myotome* **2.** cutting instrument ○ *microtome* [Via modern Latin *-tomus* from, ultimately, Greek *tomos* 'cutting' (see TOME)]

tomentum /tə méntəm/ (*plural* **-ta** /-tə/) *n.* a downy covering of tiny hairs on leaves and other plant parts [Late 17thC. From Latin, literally 'stuffing for a cushion', of unknown origin.] —**tomentose** /tə méntōss, tṓ men-/ *adj.*

tomfool /tóm fóol/ *n.* **FOOL** a very foolish person (*dated informal*) ■ *adj.* **FOOLISH** remarkably foolish (*dated informal*) [14thC. From the name *Tom* (short for *Thomas*).] —**tomfoolish** *adj.* —**tomfoolishness** *n.*

tomfoolery /tom fóoləri/ (*plural* **-ies**) *n.* **1. SILLINESS** silly behaviour (*informal*) **2. STH FOOLISH** a foolish action or statement (*dated informal*)

tommy /tómmi/ (*plural* **-mies**), **Tommy Atkins** /-átkinz/ *n.* a private in the British army (*dated slang*) [Late 19thC. From *Thomas Atkins*, a fictitious name used on specimen forms in the British army.]

tommy bar *n.* a rod used to provide leverage in turning a box spanner [From the name *Tommy* (short for *Thomas*)]

Tommy gun *n.* a hand-held machine gun, especially a Thompson submachine-gun (*informal*)

tommyrot /tómmi rot/ *n.* complete nonsense (*dated informal*) [Late 19thC. *Tommy* from the use of *Tommy* (short for *Thomas*) as a name for sb foolish.]

tommy rough, **tommy ruff** *n.* a fish of southern Australian waters that is green on the top and silver on its undersides and is related to the Australian salmon. Latin name: *Arripis georgianus.* [Early 20thC. *Tommy* (shortening of the name *Thomas*) meaning 'little'; *rough* either from its rough texture, or in the sense 'unrefined' because it is considered inadequate for sport and food.]

tomogram /tṓmə gram/ *n.* an image, especially one of the body, made using tomography

tomography /tō móggrəfi/ *n.* the technique of using ultrasound, gamma rays, or X-rays to produce a focused image of the structures across a certain depth within the body, while blurring details at other depths. A series of such images can be combined, e.g. by computer, to give a high-definition three-dimensional image. [Mid-20thC. Coined from Greek *tomos* (see TOME) + -GRAPH + -Y.]

tomorrow /tə mórrō/ *n.* **1. THE NEXT DAY** the day after today **2. THE FUTURE** a future time, or the future in general ○ *the leaders of tomorrow* ■ *adv.* **1. ON THE NEXT DAY** on the day after today **2. IN FUTURE** in the future, or at some time in the future [Old English *tō morgenne*, literally 'in the morning'] ◇ **like** *or* **as if there was** *or* **were no tomorrow** used to emphasize the degree of speed, intensity, or carelessness with which sb is doing sth (*informal*) ○ *ran from the fire like there was no tomorrow*

tompion *n.* = **tampion**

toms /toms/ *npl.* = **tom-tom** *n.* 2 [Early 20thC. Shortening.]

Tomsk /tomsk/ city and port on the River Tom in southern Siberian Russia. Population: 502,000 (1990).

Tom Thumb *n.* a character in English folklore who was no taller than his father's thumb

tomtit /tómtit/ *n.* a bird of the tit family, especially the blue tit (*informal*) [Early 18thC. *Tom* from the name *Tom* (short for *Thomas*).]

tom-tom *n.* **1. DRUM HIT WITH THE HANDS** a drum hit with the hands, especially a drum with a long narrow shell and a small head, first used by Native North Americans and other peoples as a signalling instrument **2. DEEP-SIDED DRUM IN MODERN DRUM KIT** a deep-sided drum that forms part of a modern drum kit, deeper in tone than a snare drum but not as deep as a bass drum **3. SOUND OF BEATING DRUM** the sound of a drum being repeatedly beaten, especially slowly and monotonously [Late 17thC. From Telugu *ṭamaṭama* or Hindi *ṭam ṭam*, ultimately an imitation of the drum's sound.]

-tomy *suffix.* cutting, incision ○ *lobotomy* [Via modern Latin *-tomia* from, ultimately, Greek *tomos* 'cutting' (see TOME)]

ton[1] /tun/ *n.* **1. US UNIT OF WEIGHT** an imperial unit of weight, equal to 907 kilograms in the United States **2. UK UNIT OF WEIGHT** an imperial unit of weight, equal to 1016 kg/2,240 lb in the United Kingdom **3.** = **metric ton 4.** = **displacement ton 5. UNIT MEASURING SHIP'S INTERNAL CAPACITY** a unit used to measure the capacity of the inside of a ship, equal to 28.3 c. m/100 cu.ft **6.** = **freight ton 7. LARGE AMOUNT** a very great number of things or of sth (*informal*) (*often used in the plural*) ○ *tons of things to do* **8. FIGURE OF HUNDRED** a figure of a hundred, especially a hundred miles per hour or a score of a hundred in cricket (*slang*) ■ *adv.* **tons A GREAT DEAL** to a great degree or extent [13thC. Variant of TUN.] ◇ **come down on sb like a ton of bricks** to scold or punish sb severely (*informal*)

WORD KEY: USAGE

See Usage note at ***tonne***.

ton[2] /toN/ *n.* the current trend in fashion, or the group of people who like to stay at the cutting edge of fashion [Mid-18thC. From French, literally 'tone'.]

tonal /tṓn'l/ *adj.* **1. RELATING TO TONE** relating to tone or tonality **2. RELATING TO HARMONIC MUSIC** relating to music written in a harmonic system in which there is a key. ◊ **atonal** —**tonally** *adv.*

tonality /tō nálləti/ *n.* **1. QUALITY OF TONE** the quality of tone, especially that of an instrument or voice **2.** MUSIC **SYSTEM OF MUSICAL TONES** the relationship between the notes and chords of a passage or work that tends to establish a central note or harmony as its focal point. ◊ **atonality 3.** ARTS **ARRANGEMENT OF COLOURS** the scheme connecting the colour tones in a work of art such as a painting

Tonbridge /túnbrij/ town in western Kent, southeastern England. Population: 34,260 (1991).

tondo /tóndō/ (*plural* **-dos**) *n.* a circular painting or relief carving [Late 19thC. From Italian, a shortening of *rotondo* 'round', from Latin *rotundus* (see ROTUND).]

tone /tōn/ *n.* **1. PARTICULAR KIND OF SOUND** a sound with a particular quality ○ *The first bell has a clearer tone.* **2. WAY OF SPEAKING** the way sb says sth as an indicator of what that person is feeling or thinking ○ *a defiant tone in her voice* **3. GENERAL QUALITY** the general quality or character of sth as an indicator of the attitude or view of the person who produced it ○ *the optimistic tone of the report* **4. MACHINE SOUND** a sound, especially one produced by a machine **5. PREVAILING CHARACTER** the characteristic style that sth has, particularly in relation to elegance or standing ○ *neon signs that lower the tone of the place* **6.** COLOURS **SHADE OF COLOUR** any of the possible shades of a particular colour ○ *a green with a more vibrant tone* **7.** ARTS **COMBINATIONS OF COLOUR AND SHADING** the overall blend of colour and light and shade in a painting or photograph **8.** PHYSIOL **FIRMNESS OF MUSCLES** the natural firmness of muscles when they are not being flexed, or of the body generally **9.** PHON **INTONATION** the way a syllable of a word is spoken in terms of pitch ○ *the rising tone signifying a question* **10.** MUSIC **TIMBRE** the quality of a sound that makes it distinctive to a particular source, e.g. a voice or musical instrument **11.** MUSIC = **whole tone 12.** MUSIC **PLAINSONG** a melody used in singing plainsong, e.g. in singing psalms **13.** *Can, US* MUSIC = **note** *n.* 9 ■ *v.* (**tones, toning, toned**) **1.** *vi.* **BLEND IN WITH STH** to be similar to sth else, especially in colour or brightness, and fit well with it **2.** *vti.* PHOTOGRAPHY **CHANGE COLOUR OF PHOTOGRAPH** to develop the colour image of a silver negative in making a photograph **3.** *vt.* PHON **SAY STH WITH PARTICULAR PITCH** to say a syllable or word with a particular pitch [13thC. Via French *ton* from, ultimately, Greek *tonos* 'tension, tone'. Ultimately from an Indo-European base meaning 'to stretch' that is also the ancestor of English *thin, tenuous,* and *tendon.*]

tone down *vt.* **1. MAKE STH LESS INTENSE** to make sth less intense or extreme, usually in order to make it less offensive or controversial **2. MAKE STH LESS BRIGHT** to make sth less intense, bright, or loud

tone up *vt.* to make muscles, or the body in general, firmer and stronger

Tone /tōn/, **Wolfe** (1763–98) Irish revolutionary. He was the founder of the Society of United Irishmen in 1791. His efforts on behalf of Irish nationalism resulted in a death sentence. Full name **Theobald Wolfe Tone**

tone arm *n.* a record player's pivoting or sometimes sliding arm with a stylus on its end

tone cluster *n.* a group of adjacent notes played together and forming a chord, usually resulting in a dissonant sound

tone colour *n.* = **timbre** *n.* 2

tone control *n.* a control on a radio, record player, or other piece of audio equipment that adjusts the tone it produces, accentuating the higher or lower sound frequencies

tone-deaf *adj.* unable to hear the differences between musical notes —**tone-deafness** *n.*

tone language *n.* a language in which the meaning of a fixed sequence of sounds depends on the pitch in which it is pronounced, different tones identifying different words. Tone languages include the Bantu languages of Africa and Mandarin Chinese.

toneless /tṓnləss/ *adj.* **1. EXPRESSIONLESS** lacking expression in speech **2. LIFELESS** lacking brightness or vitality —**tonelessly** *adv.* —**tonelessness** *n.*

toneme /tṓ neem/ *n.* a phoneme in a tone language in which the distinctive feature is a tone [Early 20thC. Modelled on *phoneme.*] —**tonemic** /tō neémik/ *adj.*

tone poem *n.* MUSIC = **symphonic poem**

toner /tṓnər/ *n.* **1.** COSMETICS **SKIN COSMETIC** a lotion or light astringent used to improve the look or feel of the skin, especially of the face **2.** PRINTING **INK** ink in powder or liquid form for a photocopier or computer printer **3.** PHOTOGRAPHY **PHOTOGRAPHIC CHEMICAL** a chemical solution used in photograph development

tone row, **tone series** *n.* a sequence of notes that is the basis of a piece of serial music, especially a series of 12 notes

tonetic /tō néttik/ *adj.* relating to a language in which changes in pitch distinguish meaning [Early 20thC. Modelled on *phonetic.*] —**tonetically** *adv.*

tong[1] /tong/ (**tongs, tonging, tonged**) *vt.* to lift or move sth with tongs

tong[2] /tong/ *n.* a Chinese secret society thought to be involved in criminal activity [Late 19thC. From Chinese (Cantonese) *t'ōng* 'hall, meeting place'.]

tonga /tóng gə/ *n.* a light horse-drawn carriage in southern and central India [Late 19thC. From Hindi *tāgā.*]

Tonga[1] /tóng gə/ (*plural* **-gas** *or* **-ga**) *n.* **1.** PEOPLES **MEMBER OF CENTRAL AFRICAN PEOPLE** a member of a people living in southern central Africa, mainly in southwestern Zambia and northwestern Zimbabwe **2.** LANG **TONGA LANGUAGE** the language of the Tonga people. It belongs to the Bantu group of Benue-Congo languages. [Mid-19thC. From Tonga.]

Tonga[2] /tóngə, tóng gə/ independent island nation

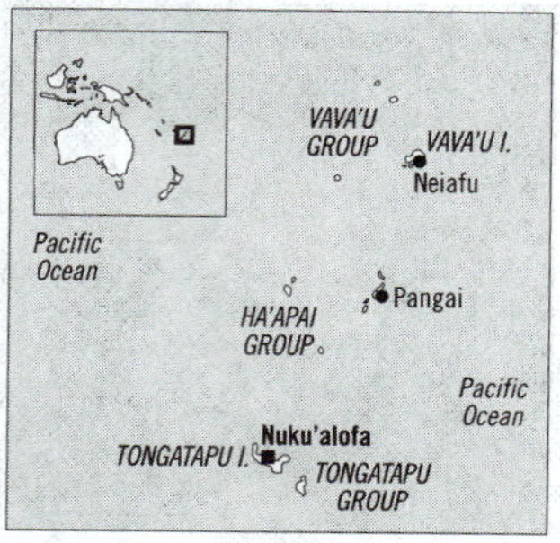

Tonga

consisting of more than 150 islands in the southern Pacific Ocean. Language: English, Tongan. Currency: pa'anga. Capital: Nuku'alofa. Population: 107,335 (1997). Area: 750 sq. km/290 sq. mi. Official name **Kingdom of Tonga** —**Tongan** *n., adj.*

Tongariro, Mount /tóngə réerō/ active volcano in New Zealand, in the central part of the North Island. It last erupted in 1926. Height: 1,967 m/6,453 ft.

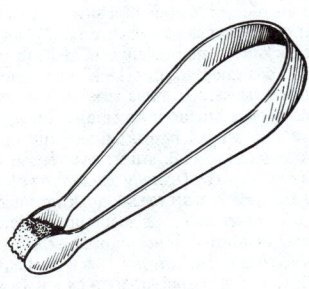

Tongs

tongs /tongz/ *npl.* **1.** UTENSIL WITH TWO ARMS a utensil for handling things that consists of two hinged or sprung arms that press together in a pinching movement around the object to be lifted **2.** CURLING TONGS curling tongs [Old English *tang*. Ultimately from an Indo-European word meaning 'to bite' that is also the ancestor of English *tang*[1] and **tough**.]

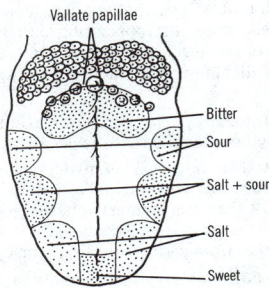

Tongue: Taste-sensitive areas of the human tongue

tongue /tung/ *n.* **1.** FLESHY ORGAN INSIDE MOUTH the movable fleshy organ attached to the bottom of the inside of the mouth of humans and most animals, used for tasting, licking, swallowing, and, in humans, speech. Technical name **glossa 2.** FOOD ANIMAL'S TONGUE USED AS FOOD the tongue of an animal, especially a cow, used as food **3.** LANGUAGE a language or dialect **4.** WAY OF SPEAKING sb's manner of speaking (*formal*) **5.** ABILITY TO SPEAK the power of speech ○ *She found that her tongue had deserted her.* **6.** CLOTHES FLAP IN SHOE the middle flap in the opening of a shoe or boot **7.** PIN IN BUCKLE the pivoting pin in a buckle **8.** CLAPPER IN BELL the small swinging hammer inside a bell that hits against the inside of the bell to make the sound **9.** GEOG STRIP OF LAND a narrow strip of land sticking out into a sea, a lake, or river **10.** MUSIC VIBRATING END OF MUSICAL REED the vibrating end of a reed in a wind instrument **11.** TRANSP POLE ON CARRIAGE the pole at the front of a coach or carriage to which the horses' harnesses are fastened **12.** CONSTR PROJECTING STRIP FITTING INTO GROOVE a strip that sticks out along the edge of a wooden board and is designed to fit into a corresponding groove along the edge of another board **13.** STH LIKE TONGUE sth shaped or moving like a tongue ■ **tongues** *npl.* RELIG SPEECH RESULTING FROM RELIGIOUS ECSTASY speech in no known language that results from religious ecstasy. Also called **gift of tongues, glossolalia, speaking in tongues** ■ *v.* (**tongues, tongueing, tongued**) **1.** *vt.* TOUCH STH WITH TONGUE to touch or lick sth with the tongue **2.** *vt.* KISS SB USING TONGUE to kiss sb with the lips open and the tongue touching the inside of the other person's mouth (*informal*) **3.** *vti.* MUSIC USE TONGUE TO ARTICULATE INSTRUMENT'S NOTES to use the tongue to block the flow of air on a wind or brass instrument, thereby separating one note from another **4.** *vt.* CONSTR CUT TONGUE ALONG BOARD'S EDGE to cut a tongue along the edge of a wooden board, to

make one half of a tongue-and-groove joint [Old English *tunge*. Ultimately from the Indo-European word for 'tongue' that is also the ancestor of English *lingual* and **language**.] —**tongueless** *adj.* ◇ **hold your tongue** to keep silent

― **WORD KEY: SYNONYMS** ―

See Synonyms at **language**.

tongue-and-groove joint *n.* a joint made between two wooden boards consisting of a projecting strip or tongue along the edge of one board and a groove along the edge of the other

tongued /tungd/ *adj.* having a particular kind of tongue, especially a particular way of speaking (*usually used in combination*) ○ *sharp-tongued*

tongue depressor *n. US* = **spatula**

tongue-in-cheek *adj.* spoken with gentle irony and meant as a joke

tongue-lashing *n.* a severe scolding

tongue-tie *vt.* MAKE SB TOO NERVOUS TO SPEAK to make sb unable to speak, especially because of awe, shyness, or embarrassment ■ *n.* MED INABILITY TO MOVE TONGUE FREELY the inability to move the tongue with the normal amount of freedom, because the small membrane (**frenulum**) that attaches the tongue to the floor of the mouth is unusually short

tongue-tied *adj.* **1.** SPEECHLESS THROUGH NERVOUSNESS unable to speak because of awe, shyness, or embarrassment **2.** MED AFFECTED BY TONGUE-TIE unable to move the tongue freely because of tongue-tie

tongue twister *n.* a word, phrase, or sentence that is difficult to say because of its unusual sequence of sounds, especially an invented sentence such as 'She sells seashells on the seashore'

tongue worm *n.* a tongue-shaped parasite with a hooked mouth that infests the lungs or nostrils of mammals, reptiles, and birds. Phylum: Arthropoda.

tonic /tónnik/ *n.* **1.** STH THAT LIFTS THE SPIRITS sth that lifts the spirits or makes sb feel better generally **2.** MED MEDICINE PRODUCING SENSE OF WELL-BEING a medicine that purports to make patients feel stronger, more energetic, and generally healthier **3.** BEVERAGES TONIC WATER tonic water (*informal*) **4.** MUSIC FIRST NOTE OF SCALE the first note in a scale and the harmony built on this note **5.** PHON STRESSED SYLLABLE the syllable that has the main stress in a word ■ *adj.* **1.** LIFTING THE SPIRITS lifting the spirits and generally creating a feeling of well-being **2.** BOOSTING ENERGY designed or serving to boost energy and generally create a feeling of strength and health **3.** PHYSIOL RELATING TO MUSCLE TONE relating to or affecting muscular tone or contraction **4.** MUSIC RELATING TO FIRST NOTE based on the first note of a scale **5.** PHON OF A STRESSED SYLLABLE constituting or relating to the main stressed syllable in a word **6.** LING = **tonetic** [Mid-17thC. Via French *tonique* from Greek *tonikos* 'of stretching', from *tonos*.] —**tonically** *adv.*

tonic accent *n.* **1.** MUSIC MUSICAL ACCENT PRODUCED BY HIGHER PITCH a musical accent produced by higher pitch rather than by stress **2.** PHON SYLLABLE STRESS CREATED BY HIGHER PITCH stress on a syllable created through a change in pitch

tonicity /tō níssəti/ *n.* **1.** BEING TONIC the state or quality of being tonic **2.** PHYSIOL STATE OF SLIGHT MUSCLE CONTRACTION the state or quality of muscles being slightly contracted or ready to contract

tonic sol-fa *n.* a system of using syllables to denote degrees of a musical scale, and in which the syllables are movable depending on the key of the piece

tonic water *n.* a carbonated drink with a bitter taste, originally and still sometimes containing quinine, drunk on its own as a soft drink or used as an ingredient in cocktails. US term **quinine water** [So called because it was originally drunk to stimulate the appetite or digestion]

tonight /tə nít/ *n.* NIGHT OF PRESENT DAY the night or evening of the present day ■ *adv.* ON PRESENT DAY'S NIGHT on or during the night or evening of the present day [Old English *tō niht*, literally 'at night']

tonka bean /tóngkə-/ *n.* **1.** FRAGRANT BLACK SEED USED IN PERFUME the fragrant black almond-shaped seed of a

tropical American tree used to make perfumes and to perfume tobacco and snuff **2.** TROPICAL AMERICAN TREE a tall tropical American tree that produces tonka beans. Latin name: *Dipteryx odorata*. [Origin uncertain: possibly from Tupi or Galibi *tonka*]

Tonkin, Gulf of /tón kin, tóng kin/ northwestern arm of the South China Sea, bounded by Vietnam, mainland China, and the Chinese island of Hainan

Tonle Sap /tón lay sáp/ the largest lake in Southeast Asia, in western Cambodia, linked to the Mekong River by the Tonle Sap River. A shallow lake, it swells from 2,600 sq. km/1,000 sq. mi. in the dry season to 10,400 sq. km/4,020 sq. mi. in the monsoon season.

tonnage /túnnij/, **tunnage** *n.* **1.** MEASURE WEIGHT IN TONS weight measured in imperial or metric tons **2.** SHIP'S SIZE OR CAPACITY the size of a ship measured in tons or cubic feet or metres of seawater displaced, or the capacity of a ship measured in cubic feet or metres **3.** SHIPPING WEIGHT OF SHIP'S CARGO the weight of a ship's cargo, measured in tons **4.** SHIPPING DUTY CHARGED ON SHIP'S CARGO the duty charged at a rate per ton on a ship's cargo **5.** SHIPPING SIZE OF FLEET OF SHIPS the size of a fleet of ships, e.g. a merchant company's fleet or a nation's warships, calculated as the combined weights or carrying capacities of all ships [15thC. Formed from TON[1].]

tonne /tun/ *n.* = **metric ton** [Late 19thC. Via French from medieval Latin *tunna*, of uncertain origin: probably from Celtic.]

― **WORD KEY: USAGE** ―

tonne, ton, or **tun**? All three words are pronounced the same way (tun), although **tonne** is sometimes pronounced *ton* to distinguish it from **ton**. A **ton** is a non-metric unit and differs in value in British and American usage (see **ton**). A **tonne** is a metric unit equal to 1000 kilograms. A **tun** is a large beer cask or a unit of liquid capacity equal to 210 gallons.

tonneau /tónnō/ (*plural* **-neaus** *or* **-neaux** /tónnō, -nōz/) *n.* the back-seat compartment of an open-top vintage car, or a flexible cloth cover protecting it when it is not being used [Late 18thC. From French, literally 'barrel' (so called because of its shape), from *tonne* (see TONNE).]

tonometer /tō nómmitər/ *n.* **1.** PHYS INSTRUMENT MEASURING SOUND'S PITCH an instrument, often one fitted with a range of tuning forks, that measures the exact pitch of a sound **2.** MED INSTRUMENT MEASURING PRESSURE IN BODY PART an instrument that measures pressure in a part of the body such as the blood vessels, or the eyeball as a test for glaucoma [Early 18thC. Coined from Greek *tonos* (see TONE) + -METER.] —**tonometric** /tónnə méttrik, tōnə-/ *adj.* —**tonometry** /tō nómmətri/ *n.*

tonoplast /tónə plast/ *n.* the semipermeable membrane separating a fluid-filled internal cavity (**vacuole**) from the surrounding cytoplasm inside a plant cell [Late 19thC. Coined from Greek *tonos* (see TONE) + -PLAST.]

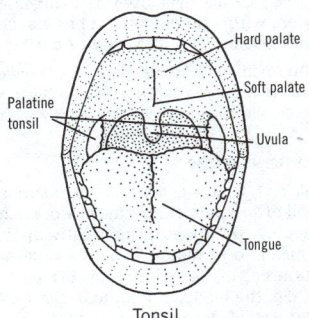

Tonsil

tonsil /tónss'l, -sil/ *n.* **1.** OVAL TISSUE MASS IN THE MOUTH either of two small oval masses of tissue, one on each side of the back of the mouth, that are important for the body's immune system **2.** TONSIL-SHAPED LUMP OF TISSUE ELSEWHERE any of various lumps of tissue shaped like the tonsils of the mouth, e.g. either of two small lumps in the brain (**tonsils of the cerebellum**) [Late 16thC. From Latin *tonsillae* 'tonsils', of uncertain origin.] —**tonsillar** *adj.*

tonsillectomy /tónssi léktəmi/ (*plural* **-mies**) *n.* a surgical procedure to remove the tonsils of the mouth

tonsillitis /tónssi lítiss/ *n.* inflammation of the tonsils of the mouth, caused either by bacteria or a virus, which makes the throat very sore and can lead to fever and earache —**tonsillitic** /tónssi líttik/ *adj.*

tonsorial /ton sáwri əl/ *adj.* relating to barbers or their work (*formal or humorous*) [Early 19thC. Formed from Latin *tonsorius*, from *tonsor* 'barber', from *tondere* 'to clip' (source of English *tonsure*).]

tonsure /tónshər, -syər/ *n.* PARTIALLY SHAVED HEAD a shaved patch on the crown of the heads of priests and monks in some religious orders, or the shaving of the head in this way ■ *vt.* (**-sures, -suring, -sured**) PARTIALLY SHAVE THE HEAD to shave the crown of the head [14thC. Directly or via French from, ultimately, Latin *tondere* 'to clip'.]

tontine /tón tīn, -teen, -teén/ *n.* an investment or insurance scheme in which contributors pay equal amounts into a common fund and receive equal dividends and benefits from it, with the final surviving contributor receiving everything [Mid-18thC. From French, named after a Neapolitan banker, Lorenzo *Tonti* (1630–95), who started such a scheme.]

tonto /tón tō/ *adj.* an offensive term used to describe sb who is thought to be mentally ill (*offensive insult*) [Late 20thC. From Spanish.]

ton-up *adj.* (*dated informal*) **1.** CAPABLE OF OVER 100 MPH used to describe a motorcycle travelling at or capable of travelling at over 100 miles per hour **2.** FOND OF RIDING MOTORCYCLES FAST fond of riding motorcycles at high speeds, especially recklessly ■ *n.* SPEED OVER 100 MPH a speed in excess of 100 miles per hour, or a motorcyclist who frequently rides at these speeds (*dated informal*)

tonus /tónəss/ *n.* the normal state of a healthy muscle when resting in a state of slight contraction [Late 19thC. Via Latin from Greek *tonos* (see TONE).]

tony /tóni/ *adj. Can, US* having an aristocratic, expensive, or stylish presentation (*informal*)

Tony /tóni/ (*plural* **-nys** *or* **-nies**) *n.* an award made annually in the United States for achievement in the theatre [Mid-20thC. From *Tony*, nickname of the US actor and producer Antoinette Perry (1888–1946).]

too /too/ *adv.* **1.** AS WELL used to indicate that a person, thing, or aspect of a situation applies in addition to the one just mentioned ○ *Can cats be affected by it too?* ○ *You ought to see a doctor, and quickly too!* ◊ **also** **2.** MORE THAN IS DESIRABLE more of an amount or degree of sth than is desirable, necessary, or fitting ○ *He's a little too conservative for me.* **3.** EXTREMELY used to emphasize a quality ○ *She's only too aware of how this will affect her career.* **4.** VERY used to modify the force of a negative statement in order to sound polite or cautious ○ *It didn't look too good.* **5.** *Can, US* INDEED used to emphasize the force of a statement or command ○ *'I didn't touch it'. – 'You did too!'* [Old English *tō* (see TO), in the sense 'in addition, furthermore'] ◇ **too right** used to express emphatic agreement with a statement that has just been made ○ *'So you're leaving?' – 'Too right I am!'*

toodle-oo /tood'l óo/, **toodle-pip** *interj.* farewell (*dated informal or humorous*) [Early 20thC. Origin uncertain: possibly an alteration of French *à tout à l'heure* 'see you later'.]

took past tense of **take**

tool /tool/ *n.* **1.** MECH ENG DEVICE FOR DOING WORK an object designed to do a particular kind of work, e.g. cutting or chopping, by directing manually applied force or by means of a motor **2.** MECH ENG CUTTING PART OF MACHINE the cutting or shaping part of a power-driven device, e.g. the blade on a lathe **3.** CRAFT BOOKBINDER'S IMPLEMENT any of the implements that a bookbinder uses to make a design on leather, or the design made by such an implement **4.** MEANS TO AN END sth used as a means of achieving sth **5.** STH USED FOR A JOB an item people use in the course of their everyday work ○ *Words are the poet's tool.* **6.** SB MANIPULATED BY ANOTHER sb who is manipulated by sb else, especially one person who carries out the unsavoury or dishonest tasks the other person does not want to do **7.** GUN a criminal's gun (*slang*) **8.** OFFENSIVE TERM an offensive term for a human penis (*slang offensive*) ■ *v.* (**tools, tooling, tooled**) **1.** *vt.* CRAFT WORK STH USING HAND TOOLS to cut, shape, or form sth, especially to press a design into the leather cover of a book, using hand tools **2.** *vt.* INDUST GIVE SB OR STH TOOLS to equip sb or sth with tools **3.** *vti. US* CARS DRIVE A CAR to drive a car in a particular way, especially at high speeds (*slang*) ○ *tooling along at a cool 65* [Old English *tōl*. Ultimately from a prehistoric Germanic base meaning 'to manufacture'.] —**tooler** *n.*

tool up *vti.* INDUST on a large scale, to provide a factory or an industry with the equipment needed to manufacture many things ○ *tooled up the automotive industry for the war effort*

toolbar /tóol baa/ *n.* a row of icons on a computer screen that are clicked on to perform certain frequently used functions

tooled up *adj.* (*slang*) **1.** EQUIPPED equipped, especially well-enough equipped to do a particular job **2.** HAVING GUN carrying a gun

tooling /tóoling/ *n.* any kind of decorative work done with hand tools, especially the carving of stone or the pressing or stamping of designs onto leather

toolmaker /tóol maykər/ *n.* sb who makes or repairs precision tools, especially the cutting or shaping parts of industrial machines —**toolmaking** *n.*

tool pusher *n.* sb who supervises drilling operations on an oil rig (*informal*)

toolroom /tóol room, -rŏŏm/ *n.* a room in a machine shop where tools are stored, maintained, or made

tool shed *n.* a small outbuilding where tools are kept, especially one in a garden used for storing gardening tools

tool steel *n.* hard steel used to make the cutting or shaping parts of hand tools and power tools

toon[1] /toon/ *n.* **1.** TREES RED-FLOWERED TREE a tree of the mahogany family native to Australia and tropical Asia. It has fragrant hard wood and red flowers that are used to make dye. Latin name: *Cedrela toona.* **2.** INDUST REDDISH HARDWOOD the fragrant reddish wood of the toon tree, whose exceptional hardness makes it a highly prized wood for furniture and top-quality joinery [Early 19thC. Via Hindi *tūn* from Sanskrit *tunnah.*]

toon[2] /toon/ *n.* any kind of cartoon or cartoon character, or the whole of the cartoon-making industry

toonie /tóoni/ *n. Can* a coin worth two Canadian dollars [Blend of TWO and LOONIE (the one-dollar coin)]

toorie /tóori/ *n. Scotland* a soft flat cap, with or without a brim, that has a bobble on its top, or a bobble on such a hat (*informal*) [Early 19thC. Originally in the sense 'little tower', formed from *tour*, a variant of TOWER.]

toot[1] /toot/ *n.* SOUND OF VEHICLE HORN the high-pitched hooting sound that a vehicle's horn makes, or a similar sound ■ *v.* (**toots, tooting, tooted**) **1.** *vti.* MAKE SHORT HOOTING SOUND to make, or cause the horn of a vehicle to make, a short high-pitched hooting sound **2.** *vi.* PASS GAS to pass gas noisily (*slang*) [Early 16thC. An imitation of the sound.] —**tooter** *n.*

toot[2] /toot/ *n.* INHALED ILLEGAL SUBSTANCE a quantity of an illegal drug, especially cocaine, taken by inhaling through the nose (*slang*) ■ *vti.* (**toots, tooting, tooted**) *US* INHALE ILLEGAL SUBSTANCE to inhale an illegal drug, especially cocaine (*slang*) [Late 17thC. Origin unknown.]

toot[3] /toot/ *n. Aus* a lavatory (*dated slang*) [Mid-20thC. Origin uncertain.]

tooth /tooth/ *n.* (*plural* **teeth** /teeth/) **1.** PHYSIOL WHITISH BONY OBJECT IN THE MOUTH any of the hard whitish bony objects arranged in two arched rows inside a human or vertebrate animal's mouth and used for biting and chewing food **2.** ZOOL INVERTEBRATE PART RESEMBLING A TOOTH a sharp part on an invertebrate made of horny, calcareous, or chitinous material and functioning like or resembling a vertebrate tooth **3.** INDENTATION an object resembling the shape of or performing the function of a tooth, e.g. one of the jagged indentations along the edge of a saw or a leaf **4.** MECH ENG PART STICKING OUT ON GEAR WHEEL any of a set of parts that stick out from the edge of a gear wheel or sprocket, designed to interlock with another set **5.** SURFACE ROUGHNESS ALLOWING SUBSTANCE TO ADHERE the roughness of a surface, especially the surface of paper, which allows paints, glues, and other substances to stick to it **6.** STH DESTRUCTIVE sth that has the power to destroy (*usually used in the plural*) ○ *the teeth of the gale* **7.** TASTE FOR STH a liking for the taste of sth ○ *a sweet tooth* ■ **teeth** *npl.* EFFECTIVE POWER the power or ability to accomplish sth ○ *Sanctions without teeth won't do any good.* ■ *v.* (**tooths, toothing, toothed**) **1.** *vt.* MECH ENG PUT TEETH ON STH to give sth teeth, especially to cut teeth into a saw blade or around the edge of a gear wheel or sprocket **2.** *vti.* FIT TOGETHER WITH INTERLOCKING TEETH to interlock by means of teeth that fit one set inside the other [Old English *tōþ*. Ultimately from the Indo-European word for 'tooth', which is also the ancestor of English *tusk, dental,* and *mastodon.*] ◇ **armed to the teeth (with sth)** extremely well armed or equipped with sth (*informal*) ◇ **cut your teeth (on sth)** to learn how to do sth and gain experience from it ◇ **get your teeth into sth** to start doing sth that will be challenging and satisfying ◇ **in the teeth of** against opposition or contradiction from ◇ **set your teeth on edge** to irritate ◇ **show your teeth** to indicate that you have power and intend to use it

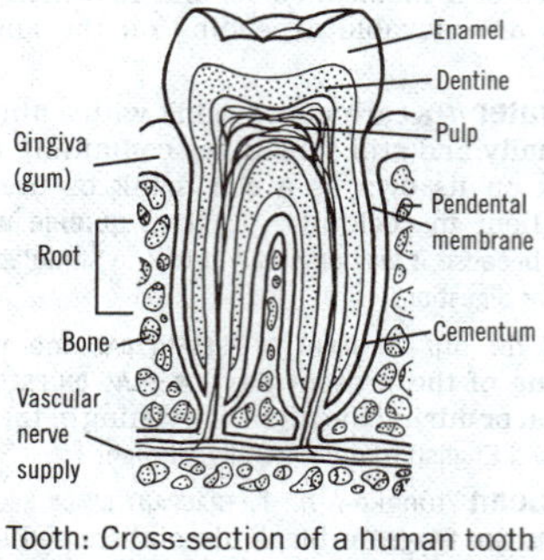
Enamel
Dentine
Pulp
Gingiva (gum)
Root
Pendental membrane
Cementum
Bone
Vascular nerve supply
Tooth: Cross-section of a human tooth

toothache /tóoth ayk/ *n.* pain in or around a tooth, especially because the tooth is decaying

toothache tree *n.* either of two prickly-branched North American varieties of ash that have a fragrant bark that was formerly chewed as a cure for toothache. Latin name: *Zanthoxylum americanum* and *Zanthoxylum clava-herculis.* ◊ **prickly ash**

tooth and nail *adv.* very aggressively or with every available means

toothbrush /tóoth brush/ *n.* a small brush for cleaning the teeth, with a long handle and a comparatively small head —**toothbrushing** *n.*

toothed /tootht/ *adj.* having a particular number or kind of teeth (*often used in combination*)

toothed whale *n.* a smallish whale that has teeth and feeds on fish and molluscs. Suborder: Odontoceti.

tooth fairy *n.* a fairy who, in children's folklore, takes away the milk tooth that a child leaves under the pillow and replaces it with a coin or small gift

toothless /tóothləss/ *adj.* **1.** LACKING TEETH lacking teeth, especially because the teeth have decayed and fallen out **2.** LACKING POWER lacking power, authority, or a forceful manner

toothless whale *n.* a whale without teeth but with thin horny plates hanging from the upper jaw through which it filters plankton. Toothless whales are larger than toothed ones. ◊ **toothed whale**

toothpaste /tóoth payst/ *n.* paste brushed onto the teeth to clean them and protect them from decay

toothpick /tóoth pik/ *n.* a thin pointed stick of wood or plastic used to remove pieces of food from between the teeth

tooth powder *n.* powder that is mixed to a lather with a damp toothbrush and used to clean the teeth and protect them from decay

toothsome /tóothsəm/ *adj.* **1.** DELICIOUS having a pleasing smell, taste, and appearance **2.** ATTRACTIVE attractive, especially sexually (*dated informal; offensive in some contexts*) —**toothsomely** *adv.* —**toothsomeness** *n.*

toothwort /tóoth wurt/ (*plural* **-worts** *or* **-wort**) *n.* **1.** EUROPEAN PLANT WITH SCALY ROOTS a leafless European plant that grows on tree roots and has pinkish flowers and horizontal underground stems (**rhizomes**) that are covered with scales resembling teeth. Latin name: *Lathraea squamaria*. **2.** N AMERICAN PLANT WITH SCALY ROOTS a North American flowering plant with scaly rhizomes and often showy pink or purple flowers. Latin name: *Cardamine bulbifera*.

toothy /tóothi/ (**-ier, -iest**) *adj.* having or showing a lot of teeth, large teeth, or protruding teeth —**toothily** *adv.* —**toothiness** *n.*

tootle /tóot'l/ *v.* (**-tles, -tling, -tled**) (*informal*) **1.** *vi.* DRIVE SLOWLY to proceed slowly or aimlessly, especially in a car **2.** *vti.* MAKE HOOTING SOUND to make or cause sth to make repeated high-pitched tooting sounds ■ *n.* (*informal*) **1.** LEISURELY DRIVE a drive at a leisurely pace **2.** REPEATED SOUND a gentle repeated tooting sound [Early 19thC. Formed from TOOT[1].] —**tootler** *n.*

toots /tóots/ *n. US* an affectionate or patronizing way of addressing sb, especially a woman (*dated informal; offensive in some contexts*) [Mid-20thC. Origin unknown.]

tootsie /tóotsi/ *n.* = **toots** (*dated informal; offensive in some contexts*) [Mid-20thC. Origin unknown.]

tootsy (*plural* **-sies**) *n.* **1.** FOOT OR TOE a child's word for foot or toe (*babytalk or humorous*) **2.** *US* = **toots** (*dated informal; offensive in some contexts*) [Mid-19thC. Alteration of FOOTSIE.]

Toowoomba /tə wóombə/ city in southeastern Queensland, Australia, the commercial centre of the Darling Downs agricultural region. Population: 83,350 (1996).

top[1] /top/ *n.* **1.** HIGHEST PART the highest part or point (*often used in combination*) ○ *snow on the mountain tops* **2.** UPPER SURFACE the upper side or surface ○ *dust on the top of the cupboard* **3.** LID OR COVER the part covering and sealing the open upper side of an object or an opening on the upper side (*often used in combination*) ○ *bottle tops* **4.** CLOTHES GARMENT COVERING UPPER BODY a piece of clothing, especially women's clothing, covering the upper body **5.** MOST IMPORTANT POSITION OR PERSON the most important position or most senior rank, or the person occupying it ○ *at the top of her profession* ○ *He's top of the class.* **6.** BEST PART the best part or section ○ *They only take the top of the group.* **7.** MOST EXCELLENT LEVEL the level of highest excellence ○ *not at the top of his game* **8.** MOST INTENSE LEVEL the level of greatest intensity, power, or force ○ *at the top of her voice* **9.** FARTHEST END the farthest end of sth, e.g. a road or street **10.** BEGINNING OR EARLIEST PART the beginning or the first or earliest section ○ *Take it from the top.* **11.** CROWN OF HEAD the crown of the head ○ *from top to toe* **12.** AUTOMOT CAR ROOF the roof of a car, especially a convertible **13.** AUTOMOT TOP GEAR top gear in a motor vehicle (*informal*) US term **high** *n.* 7 **14.** SPORTS TOPSPIN topspin (*informal*) **15.** SPORTS STROKE HITTING BALL ABOVE CENTRE a stroke that puts topspin on a ball by hitting the ball above its centre **16.** CARDS PLAYER'S BEST CARD OR CARDS the best card or group of cards in a player's hand **17.** ACOUSTICS HIGH-FREQUENCY PART OF SOUND the high-frequency element of any sound **18.** CHEM VOLATILE PART OF A SOLUTION the part of a distilled solution that volatilizes first **19.** SAILING PLATFORM ON A MAST a platform around the head of a lower mast on a sailing ship, used to stand on or to support rigging ■ **tops** *npl.* ROOT VEGETABLE'S VISIBLE PARTS the parts of a root vegetable that are visible above the ground when it is growing (*often used in combination*) ■ *adj.* **1.** UPPERMOST OR HIGHEST situated at the top, or higher than all others ○ *the top shirt on the pile* **2.** LEADING OR MOST SUCCESSFUL most important, senior, successful, or respected ○ *a convention of top academics* **3.** OF BEST QUALITY of the finest quality available ○ *one of the city's top hotels* **4.** MAXIMUM being at the highest level or degree ○ *at top speed* ■ *vt.* (**tops, topping, topped**) **1.** ADD TOPPING TO STH to put a topping on sth (*often passive*) ○ *topped with a layer of melted cheese* **2.** CUT TOP OFF STH to cut the top off sth, especially a vegetable prior to cooking ○ *First top and tail the carrots.* **3.** OUTRANK ALL OTHERS IN STH to be at the head of sth such as a list or hierarchy ○ *They've topped the music charts for the fifth week in a row.* **4.** EXCEED OR BETTER STH to do better than sth, or be greater than sth ○ *profits topping $500 million* **5.** REACH APEX OF STH to reach or go over the top of sth, e.g. a mountain **6.** KILL SB to kill sb or kill yourself (*slang*) **7.** SPORTS PUT TOPSPIN ON BALL to hit a ball above its centre, putting topspin on it **8.** GOLF HIT GOLF BALL ABOVE CENTRE to hit a golf ball too far above its centre, so that it runs along the ground instead of rising into the air **9.** CHEM DISTIL VOLATILE PART OF SOLUTION to take the most volatile part of a solution through distillation [Old English *topp*. Ultimately from a prehistoric Germanic word meaning 'tuft, crest', which is also the ancestor of English *tip*[1], *tuft*, and *toupee*.] ◇ **blow your top** to lose your temper and fly into a rage (*informal*) ◇ **off the top of your head** without thinking deeply, checking, or planning sth

top up *vt.* **1.** FILL CONTAINER to fill or refill a container that is partly empty **2.** FIN INCREASE SUM BY ADDING MONEY to give extra money to augment a sum or fund of money, especially in order to bring it up to a required or desirable level **3.** GIVE SB MORE TO DRINK to refill sb's drink, especially when it is not yet finished (*informal*)

top[2] /top/ *n.* a toy that spins round on a rounded or pointed base, traditionally a conical wooden toy that is set spinning by pulling a string wrapped round it [Pre-12thC. Origin unknown.]

top- *prefix.* = **topo-** (*used before vowels*)

topaz /tő paz/ *n.* **1.** MINERALS TRANSPARENT BROWN GEMSTONE a mineral found in granites and pegmatite that occasionally occurs as well-formed crystals in a variety of colours including brown and pink that are valued as gemstones **2.** MINERALS YELLOWISH GEMSTONE a yellowish gemstone, especially yellow sapphire or a yellow variety of quartz **3.** BIRDS HUMMINGBIRD WITH YELLOWISH THROAT either of two vividly-coloured yellowish-throated hummingbirds of the South American rainforest. Latin name: *Topaza pyra* and *Topaza pella*. **4.** COLOURS YELLOWISH-BROWN COLOUR a light-brown colour tinged with yellow ■ *adj.* COLOURS OF YELLOWISH-BROWN COLOUR of a light brown colour tinged with yellow [13thC. Via Old French *topace* from, ultimately, Greek *topazos*, of unknown origin.]

topazolite /tő pázzə līt/ *n.* a yellowish-green variety of garnet used as a gemstone [Early 19thC. Coined from TOPAZ + -LITE.]

top banana *n. US* the main person in a group (*slang*)

top billing *n.* **1.** ARTS STATUS AS STAR PERFORMER a performer's status as the star attraction in a show with his or her name appearing first in any list of performers or promotional material **2.** PROMINENCE the position of greatest prominence in sth

top boot *n.* a knee-length boot with a band of differently coloured leather around the top

top brass *n.* the highest-ranking officers or officials (*informal*)

topcoat /tópkōt/ *n.* **1.** FINAL COAT OF PAINT a finishing coat of paint, applied over an undercoat **2.** CLOTHES OVERCOAT a coat for outdoor wear (*dated*)

top dead-centre *n.* the position of a piston in an engine or pump when it is at the top of its stroke

top dog *n.* the most important or powerful person, often sb who has beaten all other competitors (*informal*)

top-down *adj.* **1.** CONTROLLED BY THE MOST SENIOR PEOPLE having all control in the hands of the people at the most senior levels **2.** WORKING FROM GENERAL TO SPECIFIC starting at the most general level and working towards details or specifics ○ *a top-down approach*

top drawer *n.* **1.** THE BEST the highest level of excellence, or the people at this level **2.** UPPER CLASS the upper class or highest class in society —**top-drawer** *adj.*

top-dress *vt.* to spread a thin layer of sth on the ground, especially fertilizer on the surface of soil, a growing crop, or a lawn

top dressing *n.* **1.** AGRIC SURFACE FERTILIZER fertilizer spread thinly on the surface of soil, a growing crop, or on a lawn **2.** TRANSP LOOSE GRAVEL AS A ROAD SURFACE loose gravel spread thinly on the surface of a road or path **3.** SUPERFICIAL COVERING a thin or superficial covering, especially a deceptively pleasant facade hiding an unpleasant reality

tope[1] /tōp/ (**topes, toping, toped**) *vti.* to drink alcohol heavily and habitually (*archaic or literary*) [Mid-17thC. Origin uncertain: possibly from TOP[1].]

tope[2] /tōp/ (*plural* **topes** *or* **tope**) *n.* a small grey European shark with a long snout. Its liver is used as a source of vitamin A. Latin name: *Galeorhinus galeus*. [Late 17thC. Origin uncertain: perhaps from Cornish.]

tope[3] /tōp/ *n.* RELIG = **stupa** [Early 19thC. From Hindi *top*, of uncertain origin: probably from Prakrit *thūpo*.]

topee /tő pee/, **topi** *n.* = **pith helmet** [Mid-19thC. From Hindi *ṭopī* 'hat'.]

Topeka /tō peékə/ capital city of Kansas, in the northeastern part of the state, on the Kansas River, east of Manhattan and west of Kansas City. Population: 119,658 (1996).

top end *n.* = **little end**

Top End *n. Aus* the northern part of the Northern Territory in Australia (*informal*) —**Top Ender** *n.*

toper /tőpər/ *n.* sb who drinks alcohol heavily and habitually (*literary or informal*) [From TOPE[1]]

top-flight *adj.* of the highest quality or status

topgallant /top gállənt/ *n.* **1.** **topgallant mast, topgallant** SHIP'S MAST a ship's mast that is taller than a topmast or is an extension of a topmast **2.** **topgallant sail, topgallant** SAIL SET ON TOPGALLANT a sail set on a topgallant mast [Early 16thC. The underlying idea is that the extension of the top mast presents a gallant display above the other masts.]

top gear *n.* **1.** HIGHEST GEAR IN A MOTOR VEHICLE the highest of a motor vehicle's gears, selected for the fastest speed of travel. US term **high gear** **2.** MOST INTENSE STATE the state of greatest intensity, e.g. the fastest working rate or the highest level of enthusiasm (*informal*)

top gun *n. US* sb who is the very best in his or her field (*informal*)

WORD KEY: CULTURAL NOTE

Top Gun, a film by English director Tony Scott (1986). A drama about US Navy fighter pilots in training, it centres on two outstanding pilots in the class competing for the much coveted title of 'Top Gun'. An encounter with enemy aircraft provides them with an opportunity to prove their worth. The film is memorable for its spectacular, high-speed dog-fights. The term 'top gun' promptly moved into the general language, meaning 'sb who is the very best in his or her field'.

top-hamper *n.* the uppermost sails, spars, and other equipment on a sailing ship, especially when regarded as weight to be minimized or monitored because of the destabilizing effect it can have [From HAMPER[1]]

top hat *n.* a man's tall cylindrical hat with a flat top and a narrow brim. It is usually black, is often made of silk, and is worn as part of formal dress.

top-heavy *adj.* **1.** UNBALANCED BECAUSE TOO HEAVY AT TOP unbalanced or unstable owing to excessive weight at the top **2.** BUSINESS OVERBURDENED WITH EXECUTIVES with too many executives or managers in proportion to the numbers of staff at junior levels —**top-heavily** *adv.* —**top-heaviness** *n.*

Tophet /tőfət/, **Topheth** *n.* **1.** BIBLE PLACE OF PUNISHMENT AFTER DEATH according to the Bible, a place of torment and punishment where the wicked are sent after death **2.** TERRIBLE SITUATION an extremely unpleasant situation or condition (*archaic or literary*) [14thC. From Hebrew *Tōpeṯ*, an area near Jerusalem associated first with primitive religious worship and later with the burning of rubbish and, by extension, Hell.]

top-hole *adj. UK* first-rate or excellent (*dated informal*) [Late 19thC. Origin uncertain: probably by analogy with the earlier TOPNOTCH.]

tophus /tőfəss/ (*plural* **-phi** /tőfī/) *n.* a hard deposit of crystalline uric acid and its salts in cartilage, joints, or skin. It is a characteristic of gout. [Mid-16thC. From Latin, 'tufa'.] —**tophaceous** /tō fáyshəss/ *adj.*

topi[1] /tő pee/ (*plural* **-pis** *or* **-pi**) *n.* an African antelope that has curved horns, a long muzzle, and bluish-black and yellow markings. It is said to be the fastest of all the antelopes. Latin name: *Damaliscus lunatus*. [Late 19thC. Origin uncertain.]

topi[2] *n.* = **pith helmet**

topiary /tőpi əri/ (*plural* **-ies**) *n.* **1.** ART OF SHAPING BUSHES the art of trimming bushes, hedges, and trees into decorative shapes **2.** SHAPED BUSH a bush, hedge, or

Topi

tree trimmed into a decorative shape **3. TOPIARY GARDEN** a garden in which topiaries feature prominently [Late 16thC. Via French from Latin *topiarius* from, ultimately, Greek *topos* 'place'.] —**topiarist** *n.*

topic /tóppik/ *n.* **1. SUBJECT** a subject written or spoken about **2. LOGIC ARGUMENTS USED IN REASONING** a class of arguments used as a source of proofs in formal reasoning [15thC. Formed from *Topics*, title of Aristotle's treatise on rhetorical commonplaces, from Latin *Topica*, from, ultimately, Greek *topos* 'place'.]

WORD KEY: SYNONYMS
See Synonyms at **subject**.

TOPIC *n., abbr.* Teletext Output of Price Information by Computer

topical /tóppik'l/ *adj.* **1. OF CURRENT INTEREST** relating to sth that is of particular interest at the moment **2. OF TOPICS** relating to topics or in the form of topics **3. LOCAL** relating to, or situated in, a particular place or part **4. MED APPLIED EXTERNALLY** used to describe drugs or medications that are applied directly to the surface of the part of the body being treated —**topically** *adv.*

topicality /tóppi kálləti/ *n.* relevance to matters that are of interest at the moment

topic sentence *n.* a sentence that states the main idea of a paragraph or larger section of writing, usually placed at or near the beginning

topknot /tóp not/ *n.* **1. HAIR HAIR DECORATION** a decorative arrangement of hair, or of hairbands or bows, worn on top of the head **2. EUROPEAN FLATFISH** a European flatfish, especially a species that has an oval, dark-brown body with darker patches. Latin name: *Zeugopterus*. **3. BIRDS BIRD'S CREST** a small tuft of feathers on the head of some birds, e.g. the quail

topless /tópləss/ *adj.* **1. WITH NOTHING COVERING BREASTS** wearing no covering over the breasts or upper torso **2. WHERE WOMEN SHOW BREASTS** where women can or do expose their breasts in public ○ *a topless beach* **3. WITH NO TOP PART** with no covering for the upper torso **4. MISSING A TOP** without or missing a top **5. ELEVATED** very high, either physically or in rank or importance (*archaic or literary*) —**toplessness** *n.*

top-level *adj.* **1. INVOLVING IMPORTANT PEOPLE** involving the most senior or influential people **2. AT MOST SENIOR LEVEL** at the highest level of influence or authority

toplofty /tóp loftí/ (**-ier, -iest**) *adj. US* haughty, pretentious, or condescending (*informal*) —**toploftily** *adv.* —**toploftiness** *n.*

topmast /tóp maast/ *n.* a mast that is taller than the lowest mast and is usually the tallest mast on a ship whose sails run fore-and-aft. It is the next tallest after the topgallant mast on a ship whose sails are square-rigged.

topminnow /tópminō/ (*plural* **-nows** *or* **-now**) *n.* a small freshwater fish that swims near the surface in warmer waters and has an upturned mouth for catching prey. Guppies and mollies are topminnows. Families: Cyprinodontidae and Poeciliidae and Goodeidae.

topmost /tópmōst/ *adj.* highest or uppermost

topnotch /tòp nóch/ *adj.* meeting the highest standards of excellence and quality (*informal*) —**topnotcher** *n.*

topo /tópō/ (*plural* **-pos**) *n.* a photograph of a mountain

that has possible routes for climbing marked on it [Late 20thC. Shortening of *topographic*.]

topo- *prefix.* place, region ○ *topotype* [From Greek *topos* 'place']

topog. *abbr.* topography

topography /tə pógrəfi/ (*plural* **-phies**) *n.* **1. GEOG MAPPING OF SURFACE FEATURES** the study and mapping of the features on the surface of land, including natural features such as mountains and rivers and constructed features such as roads and railways **2. AREA'S FEATURES** the features on the surface of a particular area of land **3. DESCRIPTION OF STRUCTURE** a study or detailed description of the various features of any object or entity and the relationships between them **4. MAP** a map or chart of an area's topography —**topographer** *n.* —**topographic** /tóppə gráffik/ *adj.* —**topographical** /-gráffik'l/ *adj.* —**topographically** /-gráffikli/ *adv.*

topoi plural of **topos**

topology /tə póllǝji/ *n.* **1. GEOM STUDY OF GEOMETRICAL PROPERTIES** the study of the properties of figures that are independent of size or shape and are not changed by stretching, bending, knotting, or twisting **2. MATH FAMILY OF SUBSETS** the family of all open subsets of a mathematical set, including the set itself and the empty set, which is closed under set union and finite intersection **3. ANAT ANATOMY OF BODY PART** the anatomy of a specific part of the body **4. STUDY LINKING TOPOGRAPHY AND TIME** the study of changes in topography that occur over time and, in particular, of how such changes taking place in a particular area affect the history of that area **5. RELATIONSHIPS BETWEEN LINKED ELEMENTS** the relationships between elements linked together in a system, e.g. a computer network (*formal*) —**topologic** /tóppə lójjik/ *adj.* —**topological** /-lójjik'l/ *adj.* —**topologically** /-lójjikli/ *adv.* —**topologist** /tə póllǝjist/ *n.*

Topolski /tə pólski/, **Feliks** (1907–89) Polish-born British artist. He was a British government war artist during World War II (1940–45), and is noted for his scenes of daily life.

toponym /tóppənim/ *n.* **1. PLACENAME** a name given to a place (*formal*) **2. NAME DERIVED FROM A PLACENAME** a name, e.g. a personal name, that is derived from the name of a place [Late 19thC. Coined from TOPO- on the model of SYNONYM]

toponymy /tə pónnəmi/ *n.* the study of the place names of a particular region or language —**toponymic** /tóppə nímmik/ *adj.* —**toponymical** /-nímmik'l/ *adj.*

topos /tópposs/ (*plural* **-poi** /tóppoy/) *n.* a traditional theme, especially one developed in literature or rhetoric [Mid-20thC. From Greek, 'place, rhetorical commonplace']

topotype /tóppə tīp/ *n.* a biological specimen taken from its typical habitat

topper /tóppər/ *n.* **1. CLOTHES TOP HAT** a top hat (*informal*) **2. SB OR STH DEALING WITH TOPS** a person or machine that removes or adds tops **3. CROWNING COMMENT** a remark or joke that improves on or triumphs over a preceding one (*informal*) **4. PLEASANT PERSON** an outstandingly kind or popular person (*dated informal*) **5. BEST OF ITS KIND** sth that surpasses all others of its kind (*dated informal*)

topping /tópping/ *n.* **1. GARNISH FOR FOOD** sth put on top of food, especially a sauce or garnish **2. FEATHER FOR A FISHING FLY** a feather from the crest of a golden pheasant put at the top of a fishing fly ■ *adj. UK* **FIRST-RATE** excellent (*dated informal*)

topple /tópp'l/ (**-ples, -pling, -pled**) *v.* **1. vti. FALL OR MAKE STH FALL OVER** to fall forward or over, or make sth fall forward or tip over **2. vi. TOTTER** to lean or sway precariously, as if about to fall over **3. vt. OVERTHROW SB OR STH** to overthrow sb or sth from a position of authority [Mid-16thC. Literally in the sense 'to keep on falling over' (as if top-heavy), from TOP[1].]

top-ranking *adj.* of a senior rank or the highest rank

tops /tops/ *n.* **BEST PERSON OR THING** sb or sth ranking highest in quality, importance, or popularity (*dated informal*) ■ *adv.* **AT MOST** at the most (*informal*) ■ *n.* (*plural* **tops**) **BEST PERSON OR THING** the very best person or thing (*informal*) ○ *Thanks, mum, you're the tops.* [Mid-20thC. From plural of TOP[1].]

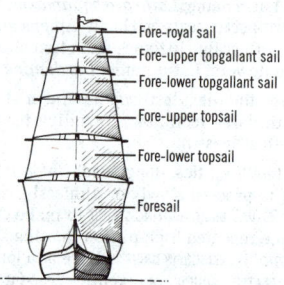

Topsail: Topsails on a square-rigged ship

topsail /tóp sayl, tópss'l/ *n.* a sail set above the lowermost sail on a mast on a square-rigged sailing vessel, or above the gaff on a fore-and-aft-rigged vessel

top-secret *adj.* requiring complete secrecy or containing information that must be kept completely secret, especially because its disclosure would pose the gravest danger to national security

top-shelf *adj.* **1. SEXUALLY EXPLICIT** relating to pornographic magazines that are very sexually explicit and are therefore displayed on the top shelf in a shop, out of direct view **2.** *Aus* **BEST QUALITY** of the finest quality

topside /tóp sīd/ *n.* **1. UPPER SIDE** the uppermost side of sth **2. FOOD CUT OF BEEF** a lean boneless cut of beef from the outer thigh. US term **top round**. **3. NAUT UPPER HULL** the part of a ship's hull that lies above the water ■ *adj. NAUT* **ON THE TOPSIDE OF A SHIP** relating to or situated on the topside of a ship ■ *adv.* topside, topsides *US SAILING* **TO A SHIP'S DECK** up on or to the deck of a ship

topsoil /tóp soyl/ *n.* **SOIL'S TOP LAYER** the upper fertile layer of soil, from which plant roots take nutrients ■ *vt.* (**-soils, -soiling, -soiled**) **1. SPREAD WITH TOPSOIL** to spread topsoil onto farming or gardening land to improve fertility **2. REMOVE TOPSOIL** to remove the top layer of soil from farming or gardening land

topspin /tópspin/ *n.* forward spin given to a ball by hitting it on its upper half, making it arc more sharply in the air or bounce higher on impact

topstitch /tópstich/ *n.* **ROW OF STITCHING ON OUTSIDE** a row of stitching on the outer or upper side of a garment, near the seam ■ *vt.* (**-stitches, -stitching, -stitched**) **SEW TOPSTITCH ON STH** to sew a topstitch on a garment —**topstitching** *n.*

topsy-turvy /tópsi túrvi/ *adj., adv.* **1. UPSIDE DOWN** with the bottom at the top and the top at the bottom **2. IN OR INTO CONFUSION** in or into a confused or chaotic state, especially one in which the natural order or arrangement of things is inverted ■ *n.* **DISORDER OR CONFUSION** a state of complete disorder or confusion [Early 16thC. Origin uncertain: perhaps formed from TOP[1] + obsolete English *terve* 'to turn over'.] —**topsy-turvily** *adv.* —**topsy-turviness** *n.*

top-up *n.* **1. EXTRA SERVING OF A DRINK** a refilling of a glass or cup out of which sb has drunk all or part of the drink **2. ADDITIONAL MONEY** an additional sum of money, especially one that brings a fund up to a required or desirable level (*often used before a noun*) ○ *a top-up loan*

toque /tōk/ *n.* **1. BRIMLESS HAT** a close-fitting, brimless

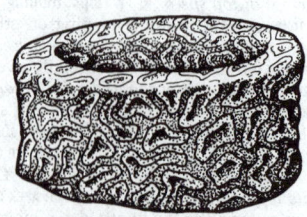

Toque

hat worn by women **2.** CHEF'S HAT a tall white hat worn by chefs **3.** HAT WORN IN THE PAST a velvet hat with a narrow brim and pouched crown, popular in the 16th century with men and women [Early 16thC. From French, of uncertain origin: perhaps from Spanish *toca*, which in turn may be of Arabic origin.]

tor /tawr/ *n.* a rocky peak of a hill or mountain, specifically one exposed by the weathering of surrounding rock (*often used in placenames*) [Old English *torr*. Origin uncertain: perhaps from Celtic.]

Torah /táwrə/ *n.* **1.** FIVE BOOKS OF MOSES the Jewish Pentateuch, or a parchment scroll on which the Pentateuch is written for use in services in synagogues **2.** JEWISH SCRIPTURE the collective body of Jewish teaching embodied in the Hebrew Bible and the Talmud [Late 16thC. From Hebrew *tôrāh* 'law'.]

torbernite /táwrbə nīt/ *n.* a green mineral that is an ore of uranium. It occurs in platelike crystals in places where uranium and copper minerals have been altered. [Mid-19thC. Named after the Swedish chemist *Torbern* Olof Bergman (1735–84).]

torch /tawrch/ *n.* **1.** PORTABLE LIGHT SOURCE a small handheld lamp usually powered by batteries. US term **flashlight 2.** BURNING STICK a stick of wood dipped in wax or with one end wrapped in combustible material, set on fire and carried, especially in the past, as a source of light **3.** DEVICE EMITTING FLAME a portable device that emits an extremely hot flame, e.g. one used in welding or for stripping paint **4.** SOURCE OF ENLIGHTENMENT a source of guidance or enlightenment (*literary*) ■ *vt.* **(torches, torching, torched)** SET ON FIRE to set fire to sth, especially as an act of arson or terrorism (*informal*) [13thC. Via French *torche* from, ultimately, Latin *torques* 'torque', from *torquere* 'to twist'. The French word earlier denoted a twist for burning.] ◇ **carry a torch for sb** to be in love with sb, especially when this feeling is secret or unrequited (*informal*)

torchbearer /táwrch bairər/ *n.* **1.** SB WHO CARRIES A TORCH sb who carries a torch, usually in a procession or ceremony **2.** SB WHO LEADS OR INSPIRES sb who provides leadership or inspiration

torchère *n.* a tall decorated stand for holding a candle or candelabrum [Early 20thC. From French, formed from *torche* 'torch' (see TORCH).]

torchier /táwrchi ər/, **torchiere** *n.* a tall floor lamp that gives indirect upward lighting [Early 20thC. Variant of TORCHÈRE.]

torchlight /táwrch līt/ *n.* **1.** LIGHT OF TORCH the light from a torch or torches **2.** = **torch** *n.* 2

torchon lace /táwrsh'n-/ *n.* lace made from coarse linen or cotton, with a simple open pattern

torch song *n.* a popular sentimental song about unrequited love. Such songs were popular in the 1930s. [From the idea of the torch as a symbol of unrequited love] —**torch singer** *n.*

torchwood /táwrch wŏŏd/ *n.* **1.** TREES RESINOUS FLORIDA TREE a tree found in Florida and the West Indies whose resinous wood was once used to make torches. Genus: *Amyris.* **2.** INDUST RESINOUS WOOD the resinous wood of the torchwood tree

tore[1] past tense of **tear**

tore[2] /tawr/ *n.* ARCHIT = **torus** *n.* 2 [Mid-17thC. Via French from Latin *torus* 'bulge'.]

toreador /tórri ə dawr/ *n.* a bullfighter, especially one on horseback [Early 17thC. From Spanish, formed from *torear* 'to fight bulls', from *toro* 'bull' (see TORERO).]

torero /to ráirō/ (*plural* **-ros**) *n.* a bullfighter, especially one on foot [Early 18thC. From Spanish, formed from *toro* 'bull', from Latin *taurus*.]

toreutics /tə rŏŏtiks/ *n.* the art of making detailed reliefs in metal using the techniques of embossing and engraving (*takes a singular verb*) [Mid-19thC. Via Greek *toreutikos* from, ultimately, *toreus* 'boring tool'.] —**toreutic** *adj.*

tori plural of **torus**

toric /tórrik/ *adj.* ring- or doughnut-shaped like a torus, or relating to tori

toric lens *n.* a spectacles lens used to correct the vision of sb with astigmatism. It is curved in such a way as to have a different focal length along each axis.

torii /táwri ee/ (*plural* **-i**) *n.* a form of gateway to a Japanese Shinto temple that has two posts and two crosspieces [Early 18thC. From Japanese, literally 'bird's perch'.]

torment *vt.* /tawr mént/ **(-ments, -menting, -mented) 1.** INFLICT PAIN ON SB OR STH to inflict torture, pain, or anguish on sb or sth **2.** TEASE SB to tease a person or an animal persistently **3.** TWIST STH to severely distort, twist, or wrench sth (*archaic or literary*) ■ *n.* /táwr ment/ **1.** TORTURE severe mental anguish or physical pain **2.** CAUSE OF ANGUISH a source of severe mental anguish or physical pain **3.** CAUSE OF ANNOYANCE a source of annoyance or anxiety [13thC. Via Old French from Latin *tormentum* 'catapult, torment', from *torquere* 'to twist'.] —**tormented** /tawrméntid/ *adj.* —**tormentedly** /-méntidli/ *adv.* —**tormentingly** /-méntingli/ *adv.*

tormenter *n.* = **tormentor**

tormentil /táwrmәntil/ (*plural* **-tils** *or* **-til**) *n.* a downy plant of the rose family that has yellow flowers and an astringent root used in medicine, tanning, and dyeing. Latin name: *Potentilla erecta.* [14thC. Via French *tormentille* from, ultimately, Latin *tormentum* 'torment' (see TORMENT).]

tormentor /tawr méntər/, **tormenter** *n.* **1.** CAUSE OF TORMENT sb who or sth that causes sb mental anguish, physical pain, annoyance, or anxiety **2.** THEATRE CURTAIN MASKING STAGE WINGS a curtain or screen at either side of a theatre stage that hides the wings from the audience **3.** CINEMA ECHO-REDUCING DEVICE IN FILMING a panel of sound-absorbent material used to eliminate echo on a film set [13thC. Via Anglo-Norman *tormentour* and Old French *tormenteor* from, ultimately, Latin *tormentum* 'to torment' (see TORMENT).]

torn past participle of **tear** ■ *adj.* UNDECIDED favouring or tending towards both options and therefore unable to choose between them ◇ **that's torn it** an expression of annoyance at, or fear of the consequences of, a sudden and unexpected problem (*dated informal*)

tornado /tawr náydō/ (*plural* **-dos** *or* **-does**) *n.* **1.** COLUMN OF SWIRLING WIND an extremely destructive funnel-shaped rotating column of air that passes in a narrow path over land **2.** AFRICAN WIND a short-lived but severe windstorm, especially one that occurs on the West African coast **3.** FRANTIC PERSON OR STATE a state of frenzied activity or intense emotion, or sb in such a state (*informal*) [Mid-16thC. Origin uncertain: probably an alteration of Spanish *tronada* 'thunderstorm' from, ultimately, Latin *tonare* 'to thunder'.] —**tornadic** /tawr náddik/ *adj.*

toroid /táw royd/ *n.* GEOM = **torus** *n.* 1

Toronto /tə róntō/ capital city of Ontario Province, Canada, located on the northwestern shore of Lake Ontario. Population: 4,263,757 (1996). —**Torontonian** /tə ron tŏnee ən/ *n.*

torose /táwrōz/, **torous** /táwrəss/ *adj.* cylindrical and knotted or bulging [Mid-18thC. From Latin *torosus* 'brawny', from *torus* 'bulge'.] —**torosity** /taw róssəti/ *n.*

torpedo /tawr peédō/ *n.* (*plural* **-does**) **1.** NAVY SELF-PROPELLED UNDERWATER WEAPON a cylindrical self-propelled missile that is launched from an aircraft, ship, or submarine and travels underwater to hit its target **2.** NAVY UNDERWATER MINE an underwater explosive mine (*dated*) **3.** *US* FIREWORK a gravel-filled firework that explodes when thrown against a hard surface **4.** *US* RAIL RAILWAY DANGER SIGNAL a detonating device placed on a railway track that acts as a danger signal to the crew of a train that runs over it **5.** *US* INDUST EXPLOSIVE FOR OIL WELLS an explosive device used to release the oil from an oil well **6.** ZOOL = **electric ray** ■ *vt.* **(-does, -doing, -doed) 1.** NAVY HIT WITH TORPEDO to hit or destroy a ship with a torpedo **2.** DESTROY to spoil, thwart, or destroy sth completely (*informal*) [Early 16thC. From Latin, 'numbness', from *torpere* 'to be stiff'.]

torpedo boat *n.* a small light fast boat used to launch torpedoes

torpedo bomber *n.* an aircraft that carries and launches torpedoes

torpedo tube *n.* a tube from which torpedoes are fired from submarines or ships

torpid /táwrpid/ *adj.* **1.** SLUGGISH lacking physical or mental energy **2.** BIOL DORMANT in a dormant state, especially when hibernating **3.** MED NUMB used to describe a part of the body that has lost the ability to move or feel [Early 17thC. From Latin *torpidus*, from *torpere* 'to be stiff'.] —**torpidity** /tawr píddəti/ *n.* —**torpidly** /táwrpidli/ *adv.*

torpor /táwrpər/ *n.* **1.** LACK OF ENERGY lack of mental or physical energy **2.** BIOL DORMANCY dormancy, especially in hibernation **3.** MED NUMBNESS absence of the ability to move or feel [13thC. From Latin, formed from *torpere* 'to be stiff'.] —**torporific** /tàwrpə ríffik/ *adj.*

Torquay /táwr keé/ popular seaside resort in Devon, southwestern England. Population: 59,587 (1991).

torque[1] /tawrk/ *n.* **1.** PHYS ROTATING FORCE force that causes rotation, twisting, or turning, e.g. the force generated by an internal-combustion engine to turn a vehicle's drive shaft **2.** MECH ENG ABILITY TO OVERCOME RESISTANCE the measurement of the ability of a rotating gear or shaft to overcome turning resistance [Late 19thC. Formed from Latin *torquere* 'to twist' (source of English *torture* and *torment*).]

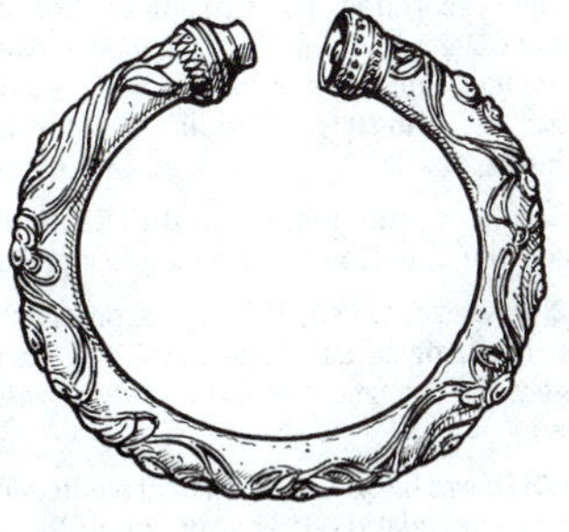

Torque

torque[2] /tawrk/, **torc** *n.* a metal collar or armband worn by the ancient Gauls and Britons [Mid-19thC. Via French from Latin *torques* (see TORCH).]

torque converter *n.* a hydraulic coupling designed to change the mechanical advantage or torque speed between an input and an output shaft

Torquemada /táwrkwi maádə/, **Tomás de** (1420–98) Spanish monk. As grand inquisitor for Spain (1483–98), he was notorious for his cruelty. He was largely responsible for the expulsion of the Jews from Spain (1492).

torques /tawrks/ (*plural* **torques**) *n.* a ring of colour, hair, or feathers around the neck of an animal [Mid-16thC. From Latin *torques* 'torque, collar' (see TORCH).]

torque spanner *n.* a spanner with a gauge attached for regulating the amount of torque applied to a bolt. US term **torque wrench**

torr /tawr/ (*plural* **torr**) *n.* a unit of pressure equal to about 133.3 pascals or one millimetre of mercury supported in a column [Mid-20thC. Named after Evangelista TORRICELLI.]

Torre del Greco /tór ay də grékō/ coastal city near Naples, southern Italy, at the base of Mount Vesuvius. Population: 100,688 (1992).

torrefy /tórri fī/ **(-fies, -fying, -fied)** *vt.* to subject sth to intense heat, especially an ore or a chemical, for the purpose of removing excess water [Early 17thC. Via French *torréfier* from, ultimately, Latin *torrere* 'to scorch'.] —**torrefaction** /tórri fáksh'n/ *n.*

Torremolinos /tórrimə leén oss/ major seaside resort in Malaga Province, Andalusia Autonomous Region, southern Spain

Torrens, Lake /tórrənz/ salt lake in South Australia. The second largest lake in Australia, it is often dry at times at low rainfall. Area: 5,780 sq. km/2,230 sq. mi.

Torrens title /tórrənz-/ *n.* in Australia, a system of registering land ownership in which ownership occurs when the document that transfers the property (**the instrument of transfer**) is lodged at the local land office [Mid-19thC. Named after the British administrator Sir Robert *Torrens* (1814–84).]

torrent /tórrənt/ *n.* **1.** RUSH OF LIQUID a fast and powerful rush of liquid, especially water **2.** TUMULTUOUS OUTPOURING a violent or tumultuous flow [Late 16thC.

Via Latin *torrens* 'hot, rushing' from, ultimately, *torrere* 'to scorch'.]

torrential /tə rénsh'l/ *adj.* **1.** FLOWING POWERFULLY flowing or falling fast and in great quantities ○ *torrential rain* **2.** INTENSE intense or abundant —**torrentially** *adv.*

Torres Strait /tórriss-/ area of sea lying between the northern tip of Cape York, Australia, and the southern coast of Papua New Guinea

Torres Strait Islands group of about 60 Australian islands located in the Torres Strait, with a mixed Melanesian, Polynesian, and Aboriginal population. Population: 8,905 (1996).

Torricelli /tórri chélli/, **Evangelista** (1608–47) Italian mathematician and physicist. He invented the barometer and defined atmospheric pressure. A unit of pressure, the torr, is named after him.

torrid /tórrid/ *adj.* **1.** FULL OF PASSION full of passion, especially sexual passion **2.** SCORCHING HOT used to describe weather that is hot and dry enough to scorch land **3.** SCORCHED used to describe land that has been scorched by extremely hot and dry weather [Late 16thC. Via French *torride* or directly from Latin *torridus*, from *torrere* 'to scorch'.] —**torridity** /tə ríddəti/ *n.* —**torridly** /tórridli/ *adv.* —**torridness** /tórridnəss/ *n.*

Torrid Zone *n.* the region of the Earth that lies between the Tropics of Cancer and Capricorn

torsade /tawr saad, -sáyd/ *n.* a decorative twist of beads, cord, or fabric [Late 19thC. Via French from, ultimately, an alteration of Latin *tortus* 'twisted' (see TORSION).]

Tørshavn /táwrz haav'n/ administrative headquarters of the Faeroe Islands. It is situated on the island of Streymoy. Population: 15,272 (1995).

torsi plural of **torso**

torsibility /táwrsə bílləti/ *n.* the ability to undergo or resist twisting [Mid-19thC. Formed from TORSION + -IBILITY.]

torsion /táwrsh'n/ *n.* **1.** TWISTING OF AN OBJECT the twisting of an object by applying equal and opposite torques to its ends **2.** MECHANICAL STRESS the stress placed on an object that has been twisted **3.** TWISTING the twisting of sth, or a twisted state (*technical*) [15thC. Via French from, ultimately, Latin *tortus*, the past participle of *torquere* 'to twist'.] —**torsional** *adj.* —**torsionally** *adv.*

torsion balance *n.* an instrument that measures small electrical or magnetic forces by the degree of twist they produce in a filament

torsion bar *n.* a metal bar that acts as a spring when subjected to torsion, e.g. in a motor vehicle's suspension system

torsk /tawrsk/ (*plural* **torsks** *or* **torsk**) *n.* ZOOL a soft-finned marine fish of the cod family found in northern coastal waters. Latin name: *Brosmius brosme.* US term **cusk** [Early 18thC. Via Norwegian from Old Norse *þorskr.*]

torso /táwrssō/ (*plural* **-sos** *or* **-si** /táwr see/) *n.* **1.** ANAT UPPER BODY the upper part of the human body, not including the head and arms **2.** SCULPTURE SCULPTURE a sculpture of a torso, or a broken statue of a human figure, with the head, arms, and legs missing **3.** STH WITH PARTS MISSING sth that has parts missing, either because it has been mutilated or because it has not been completed (*literary*) [Late 18thC. Via Italian, 'trunk of a statue', from Latin *thyrsus* (see THYRSUS).]

tort /tawrt/ *n.* in civil law, a wrongful act for which damages can be sought by the injured party [14thC. Via Old French from medieval Latin *tortum* from, ultimately, Latin *torquere* 'to twist'.]

torte /táwrtə, tawrt/ *n.* a very rich cake consisting of layers sandwiched together with a cream filling [Mid-18thC. Via German *Torte* from Italian *torta* 'cake' from late Latin, a type of bread.]

Tortelier /tawr télli ay/, **Paul** (1914–90) French cellist. He had an international career as a solo performer and was also a skilled teacher.

tortellini /táwrtə léeni/ *npl.* small filled pasta that is shaped into rings, boiled, and served in a soup or sauce [Mid-20thC. From Italian, the plural of *tortellino*, literally 'little cake', from *torta* 'cake'.]

tort-feasor /táwrt féezər/ *n.* sb who commits a tort [Mid-17thC. From Old French *tort-fesor*, literally 'wrong-doer'.]

torticollis /táwrti kólliss/ *n.* a twisting of the neck to one side, resulting in the head being tilted. It can be temporary, caused by muscle spasm, or a permanent result of a structural condition, e.g. a short neck muscle. [Early 19thC. From modern Latin, formed from Latin *tortus* 'twisted' (see TORSION) + *collum* 'neck'.] —**torticollar** /-kóllər/ *adj.*

tortilla /tawr tée ə/ (*plural* **-las**) *n.* **1.** FLAT MEXICAN BREAD a thin flat Mexican bread made with either corn meal or wheat flour, cooked on a hot griddle and eaten folded, with a filling of beans, cheese, or shredded meat **2.** SPANISH OMELETTE a thick omelette made with eggs, potatoes, and fried onion. It originated in Spain and is eaten either hot or cold. [Late 17thC. From Spanish, formed from *torta* 'cake', from late Latin, a type of bread.]

tortilla chip *n.* a thin crunchy crisp made of maize meal, often served with dips, e.g. salsa or guacamole

tortillon /tawr tíllyən, táwrti óN/ *n.* DRAWING = **stump** *n.* 4 [Late 19thC. From French, formed from *tortiller* 'to twist', from, ultimately, Latin *torquere.*]

tortious /táwrshəss/ *adj.* involving or constituting a tort in civil law —**tortiously** *adv.*

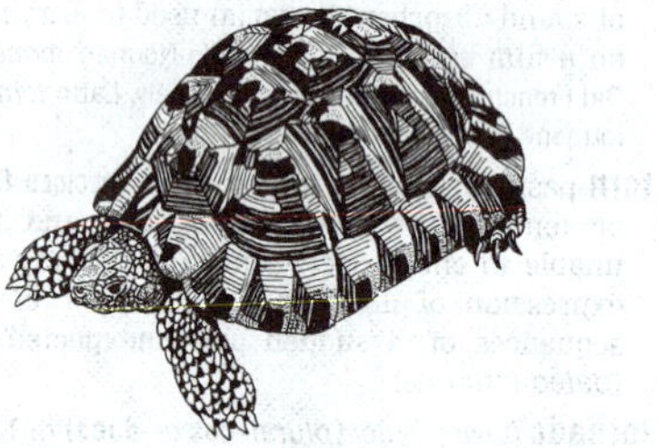

Tortoise

tortoise /táwrtəss/ *n.* **1.** REPTILE WITH SHELL a slow-moving land-dwelling reptile with a large dome-shaped shell into which it can retract its head and limbs. Family: Testudinidae. **2.** MIL, HIST = **testudo 3.** SLOW MOVER sb who moves very slowly [15thC. Alteration of obsolete *tortuce* from medieval Latin *tortuca* from late Latin *tartaruchus* 'of Tarturus' (see TURTLE).]

tortoise beetle *n.* a brightly-coloured beetle that has a flat rounded body and whose larvae eat leaves. Subfamily: Cassidinae.

tortoiseshell /táwrtəss shel/ *n.* **1.** ZOOL OUTER PART OF TURTLE SHELL the hard mottled outer layer of the shell of a hawksbill turtle, used to make combs, ornaments, and jewellery **2.** INDUST SYNTHETIC TORTOISESHELL a synthetic substance made to resemble tortoiseshell **3.** ZOOL TYPE OF CAT a type of domestic cat with black, cream, and brownish markings **4.** INSECTS ORANGE-BROWN BUTTERFLY a butterfly that has jagged orange-brown wings with black markings. Family: Nymphalidae. **5.** ZOOL = **hawksbill** ■ *adj.* COLOURS MOTTLED YELLOW AND BROWN with mottled yellow and brown markings

tortoni /tawr tōni/ *n.* rich Italian ice cream often flavoured with sherry or rum and chopped cherries or almonds [Early 20thC. Origin uncertain: probably named after an Italian café-owner of 18thC Paris.]

tortricid /táwrtrissid/ *n.* any of a family of small moths whose larvae live in coiled leaves and are often destructive to plants. Family: Tortricidae. [Late 19thC. Coined from modern Latin *tortrix*, genus name (from Latin *tortus* 'twisted'; see TORSION) + -ID.]

Tortuga Island /tawr tóogə-/ island in northern Haiti, in the West Indies. Population: 22,880 (1982). Area: 180 sq. km/70 sq. mi.

tortuosity /táwrtyoo óssəti/ (*plural* **-ties**) *n.* **1.** TWISTEDNESS the state of being twisted or crooked **2.** BEND a twist or turn

tortuous /táwrtyoo əss/ *adj.* **1.** TWISTING AND WINDING with many turns or bends **2.** INTRICATE extremely complex or intricate **3.** DEVIOUS devious or deceitful [14thC. Via Anglo-Norman from Latin *tortuosus* from, ultimately, *torquere* 'to twist'.] —**tortuously** *adv.* —**tortuousness** *n.*

WORD KEY: USAGE

tortuous or **torturous**? Even though both words come ultimately from a Latin word meaning 'twist', their meanings diverge in English. A mountain pass is ***tortuous*** ('twisting, winding'), and by figurative extension, a legal argument can be ***tortuous*** ('circuitous, devious') as well. A severe illness is ***torturous*** ('agonizing, painful'), and by figurative extension, a ***torturous*** decision is one that is highly painful, even agonizing, to make.

torture /táwrchər/ *vt.* (**-tures, -turing, -tured**) **1.** INFLICT PAIN ON SB to inflict extreme pain or physical punishment on people **2.** CAUSE SB ANGUISH to cause sb mental or physical anguish ○ *This headache is torturing me.* **3.** DISTORT STH to twist or distort sth into an unnatural form ■ *n.* **1.** INFLICTING OF PAIN the inflicting of severe physical pain on sb, e.g. as punishment or to persuade sb to confess or recant sth **2.** METHODS OF INFLICTING PAIN the methods used to inflict physical pain on people **3.** ANGUISH mental or physical anguish [Mid-16thC. Via French from, ultimately, Latin *tortus* 'twisted' (see TORSION).] —**torturer** *n.* —**torturingly** *adv.*

torturous /táwrchərəss/ *adj.* **1.** INFLICTING PAIN inflicting, or designed to inflict, severe physical pain, e.g. as punishment **2.** CAUSING ANGUISH causing great physical or mental anguish [15thC. Via Anglo-Norman, from *torture* 'torture', from, ultimately, Latin *torquere* 'to twist'.] —**torturously** *adv.*

WORD KEY: USAGE

See Usage note at ***tortuous.***

torula /tórryələ/ (*plural* **-lae** /-lee/ *or* **-las**) *n.* **1. torula, torula yeast** NUTRITIOUS YEAST an edible yeast that is cultivated for use as a medicine and food additive. Latin name: *Candida utilis.* **2.** FUNGUS a yeast fungus that does not have sexual spores. Many of them grow on dead vegetation and fermented sugars. Genus: *Torula.* [Mid-19thC. From modern Latin, genus name, formed from Latin *torus* 'bulge'.]

torus /táwrəss/ (*plural* **-ri** /-rī/) *n.* **1.** GEOM RING-SHAPED SURFACE a doughnut-shaped geometric surface generated by rotating a circle about a line in the same plane as the circle but not intersecting it **2.** ARCHIT MOULDING a large convex moulding, especially at the base of a classical column **3.** ANAT RIDGED BODY PART a body part in the shape of a rounded ridge or bulge, e.g. the bony ridge below an eyebrow **4.** BOT FLOWER PART the receptacle of a flower [Mid-16thC. From Latin, 'bulge'.]

Torvill /táwrvil/, **Jayne** (*b.* 1957) British ice skater. Her skating partnership with Christopher Dean dominated British, European, and world ice dancing competitions in the early 1980s. Their most famous performance, to Maurice Ravel's *Boléro*, was awarded perfect marks in the 1984 Olympics.

Tory /táwri/ *n.* (*plural* **-ries**) **1.** UK CONSERVATIVE in the UK, a member of the Conservative and Unionist Party **2.** CANADIAN CONSERVATIVE in Canada, a member of the Progressive Conservative Party **3.** ENGLISH ROYALIST a member of an English political party, active from the late 17th century until the 1830s, that supported the social order represented by the monarchy and the Church of England **4. Tory, tory** SUPPORTER OF CONSERVATIVE PRINCIPLES sb who holds politically conservative or reactionary views **5.** AMERICAN SUPPORTER OF BRITAIN a resident of the American colonies of Great Britain who supported the British Crown during the War of Independence in the 18th century **6.** 17C IRISH OUTLAW in 17th century Ireland, any of the Irish people who became outlaws harrying the English settlers who had displaced and dispossessed them ■ *adj.* **1.** CONSERVATIVE relating to, belonging to, or supporting any Conservative Party **2. Tory, tory** VERY CONSERVATIVE politically conservative or reactionary [Mid-17thC. Via Irish *tóraidhe* 'highwayman', from Old Irish *tóir* 'chase'.] —**Toryism** *n.*

WORD KEY: ORIGIN

In English ***Tory*** originally denoted an Irish guerrilla, one of a group of Irishmen who in the 1640s were thrown off their property by the British and took to a life of harrying and plundering the British occupiers. In the 1670s it was applied as a term of abuse to Irish Catholic royalists, and then more generally to supporters of the

Catholic James II, and after 1689 it came to be used for the members of the British political party that had at first opposed the removal of James and his replacement with the Protestants William and Mary.

Toscanini /tóskə néeni/, **Arturo** (1867–1953) Italian-born conductor. He was conductor at La Scala opera house, Milan, and the Metropolitan Opera, New York, and also conducted the NBC Symphony Orchestra (1937–57).

tosh /tosh/ n. nonsense or foolishness (dated informal) [Mid-19thC. Origin unknown.]

toss /toss/ v. (**tosses, tossing, tossed**) **1.** vt. LIGHTLY THROW STH to throw sth lightly, especially with the palm of the hand upwards ○ tossed the letter on the table **2.** vti. THROW OR BE THROWN UP AND DOWN to be thrown, or throw sth, repeatedly up and down or to and fro ○ tossed by the waves **3.** vti. THROW COIN to throw a coin upwards, usually spinning it with the thumb on the way, the side it falls on being a way of deciding between two options **4.** vt. MIX STH to mix sth, especially a salad with its dressing, by lifting and turning its parts rather than by stirring **5.** vt. EQU THROW RIDER to throw the rider of a horse or other animal off its back **6.** vt. HURL UPWARDS to hurl sb or sth upwards with apparent ease **7.** vt. JERK HEAD UPWARDS to jerk the head upwards, e.g. in a gesture of anger or impatience **8.** vi. MOVE RESTLESSLY to move about restlessly, especially in sleep **9.** vi. MOVE QUICKLY to move abruptly, e.g. in anger ■ n. **1.** THROWING an act of throwing sb or sth **2.** HEAD JERK an abrupt jerk of the head **3.** DECIDING THROW OF COIN a spinning of a coin in the air as a method of deciding between two options [Early 16thC. Origin unknown.] ◇ **argue the toss** to take part in a prolonged argument, especially in disputing a decision ◇ **not give a toss** not to care in the least (informal)

— WORD KEY: SYNONYMS —
See Synonyms at **throw**.

toss off v. **1.** vti. MASTURBATE to masturbate (slang offensive) **2.** vt. DO STH QUICKLY to do sth quickly and easily **3.** vt. DRINK STH QUICKLY to drink sth quickly, often in one gulp

tosser /tóssər/ n. an offensive term for an unintelligent or contemptible person, especially a man (slang insult)

tosspot /tósspot/ n. **1.** DRUNKARD a drunken person (archaic or literary) **2.** OFFENSIVE TERM an offensive term used to refer to sb regarded as inferior or unintelligent (slang insult)

toss-up n. **1.** DECIDING THROW OF A COIN a throw of a coin into the air that decides, by which side it falls on, between two options **2.** EVEN CHANCE an even risk or chance

tostada /to staádə/, **tostado** /to staádō/ n. a crisply fried Mexican-style tortilla, usually served with several meat and vegetable toppings [Mid-20thC. From Spanish, formed from the past participle of tostar 'to toast'.]

tot /tot/ n. **1.** LITTLE CHILD a small child (informal) **2.** SMALL AMOUNT a small amount of sth, especially alcoholic spirit [Early 18thC. Origin unknown.]

total /tótl/ n. SUM the sum of several amounts added or considered together ■ adj. **1.** USED FOR EMPHASIS used to emphasize how good, bad, or complete sth is ○ a total success **2.** OVERALL with all elements added or considered together ○ the total price ■ vt. (-tals, -talling, -talled) **1.** ADD TOGETHER to add several amounts together to arrive at a total **2.** AMOUNT TO TOTAL to amount to a total when added or considered together ○ The numbers totalled in the hundreds. **3.** US KILL OR DESTROY to kill, destroy, wreck, or demolish sb or sth (slang) [14thC. Via Old French from medieval Latin totalis, from Latin totus 'entire'.]

total eclipse n. an eclipse in which the entire surface of a celestial body, e.g. the Sun or the Moon, is obscured

total football n. a style of football in which players' positions are interchangeable as part of a general method of attack. This playing style was developed by the Dutch national team of the 1970s.

total heat n. PHYS = enthalpy

total internal reflection n. the complete reflection of a light ray at the boundary of the medium in which it is travelling, when the angle of incidence exceeds the critical angle

totalise vt. = totalize

totalitarian /tō tálli táiri ən/ adj. CENTRALIZED AND DICTATORIAL relating to or operating a centralized government system in which a single party without opposition rules over political, economic, social, and cultural life ■ n. SUPPORTER OF A TOTALITARIAN SYSTEM sb who advocates or operates a totalitarian system [Early 20thC. Formed from TOTALITY on the model of AUTHORITARIAN.] —**totalitarianism** n.

totality /tō tálləti/ (plural -ties) n. **1.** COMPLETENESS the state of being complete or total **2.** TOTAL AMOUNT the sum or total amount of sth **3.** ASTRON FULLNESS OF ECLIPSE the stage of an eclipse at which light is completely obscured

totalizator /tótə lT zaytər/, **totalisator** n. **1.** BETTING SYSTEM a system of betting on horse races using an electronic machine that totals all bets, deducts management charges and taxes, and determines the final odds and payouts **2.** BETTING MACHINE a machine that records bets, odds, and totals, and calculates winnings in the tote betting system [Late 19thC. Formed from TOTALIZE + -ATOR, modelled on French totalisateur.]

totalize /tótə lTz/ (-izes, -izing, -ized), **totalise** (-ises, -ising, -ised) vt. to add several amounts to make a total —**totalization** /tótə lT záysh'n/ n.

totalizer, **totaliser** n. = totalizer

totally /tótli/ adv. **1.** COMPLETELY in a complete or utter way **2.** USED FOR EMPHASIS used to emphasize how good, bad, or complete sth is (informal) ○ I totally hate this!

total recall n. the ability to remember accurately in every detail

total reflection n. = total internal reflection

totara /tótərə/ n. a tall coniferous tree native to New Zealand that produces lightweight, dark-red, durable wood. Latin name: Podocarpus totara. [Mid-19thC. From Maori tótara.]

tote[1] /tōt/ vt. (**totes, toting, toted**) (informal) **1.** CARRY to carry or haul sth, especially sth heavy **2.** HAVE ON YOUR PERSON to carry sth, especially a gun, on your person ■ n. HEAVY LOAD a heavy load that is hauled or carried [Late 17thC. Origin uncertain: perhaps originally a dialect form of Gullah tot 'to carry', probably from a West African language.] —**toter** n.

tote[2] /tōt/ n. a system of betting on horse races using an electronic machine that totals all bets, deducts management charges and taxes, and determines the final odds and payouts (informal) US term **parimutuel** [Late 19thC. Shortening of TOTALIZATOR.]

tote bag n. a soft open bag with handles, often made of canvas, leather, plastic, or straw

totem /tótəm/ n. **1.** IMPORTANT TRIBAL OBJECT an object, animal, plant, or other natural phenomenon revered as a symbol of a tribe and often used in rituals among some tribal or other traditional groups of people **2.** CARVING a carving or other representation of a totem **3.** SYMBOLIC THING sth regarded as a symbol, especially sth treated with the kind of respect normally reserved for religious icons [Mid-18thC. From Ojibwa nindoodem 'my totem'.] —**totemic** /tō témmik/ adj.

totemism /tótəmizzəm/ n. **1.** USE OF TOTEMS the use of totems as symbols of kinship **2.** SOCIAL ORGANIZATION the organizing of societies into groups whose members share a common totem —**totemist** n. —**totemistic** /tótə místik/ adj.

totem pole n. **1.** CARVED POLE among some Native North American peoples, a tall wooden pole carved with totems that symbolize family and historical relationships **2.** US HIERARCHY a hierarchy, e.g. in a company or organization (informal)

tother /túthər/, **t'other** adj., pron. the other or that other (regional humorous) [14thC. Contraction of the other.]

totipalmate /tóti pál mayt/ adj. used to describe birds that have all four toes webbed, e.g. pelicans and

Totem pole

gannets [Late 19thC. Coined from Latin totus 'whole' + PALMATE.] —**totipalmation** /tóti pal máysh'n/ n.

totipotent /tō típpətənt/ adj. used to describe a cell, e.g. a fertilized ovum, that is capable of generating new tissue, organs, or individuals [Early 20thC. Coined from Latin totus 'whole' + POTENT.] —**totipotency** n.

tot lot n. Can, US a playground for young children (informal)

totsiens /tót séens/ interj. S Africa used as a friendly farewell greeting (informal) [Mid-20thC. From Afrikaans, literally 'till seeing'.]

totter /tóttər/ vi. (-ters, -tering, -tered) **1.** WALK UNSTEADILY to move or walk unsteadily **2.** WOBBLE to sway or wobble as if about to fall **3.** BE UNSTABLE to be unstable or on the point of collapse ○ an economic system tottering on the brink of collapse ■ n. WOBBLING GAIT a wavering or wobbling gait [13thC. Origin uncertain; perhaps from Scandinavian.] —**totterer** n. —**tottering** adj. —**totteringly** adv. —**tottery** adj.

tottie /tótti/, **totty** n. (plural -ties) OFFENSIVE TERM an offensive term used by men to refer to a woman or women they regard only as objects for sexual pleasure (slang insult) ■ adj. TINY very small (regional informal) [Early 19thC. From TOT.]

totting /tótting/ n. the salvaging of items from rubbish for re-use or sale [Late 19thC. Formed from obsolete tot 'bone, rubbish', of unknown origin.]

totty adj., n. (plural -ties) = tottie

tot up (**tots up, totting up, totted up**) v. **1.** vi. MOUNT UP to grow larger in amount or amount to a large total **2.** vt. ADD AMOUNTS TOGETHER to add several amounts together to arrive at a total [Mid-18thC. From tot, a shortening of TOTAL or verbal use of Latin tot, 'this number, so many'.]

Toucan

toucan /tookən/ (plural -cans or -can) n. a fruit-eating bird with bright plumage and a very large curved beak. It is native to the tropics of Central and South America. Family: Ramphastidae. [Mid-16thC. Via French from Portuguese tucano, from, ultimately, Tupi tucan, of uncertain origin: probably an imitation of the bird's call.]

touch /tuch/ n. **1.** FEELING SENSE the sense by which the texture, shape, and other qualities of objects are felt through contact with parts of the body, especially the fingertips ○ the sense of touch **2.** FELT QUALITIES the quality or combination of qualities experienced through the sensation of touch **3.** CONTACT MADE a coming into contact with sth ○ felt the touch of her hand on my face **4.** LIGHT STROKE a light pushing or pressing stroke **5.** SMALL AMOUNT a small but noticeable amount ○ *a touch of malice in her voice* **6. DISTINCTIVE STYLE** a distinctive style or general facility in doing sth ○ *a sure touch* **7. DETAIL** a detail that adds to or completes sth **8. ATTACK OF ILLNESS** a mild attack of an illness or disease ○ *a touch of bronchitis* **9. COMMUNICATION** the fact of getting into communication, or the state of being in communication ○ *I completely lost touch with my brother.* ○ *Keep in touch.* **10. LENDER OF MONEY** sb considered in terms of his or her willingness to lend money (*informal*) ○ *He's always been a soft touch.* **11. REQUEST FOR MONEY** an act of asking for money or a sum of money given (*informal*) **12.** SPORTS **AREA OUT OF PLAY** in some team sports, the area beyond the touchlines in which the ball is out of play **13.** FENCING **FENCING SCORE** in competitive fencing, a scoring hit delivered to a specified part of an opponent's body ■ *v.* **(touches, touching, touched) 1.** *vti.* **PUT THE BODY IN CONTACT WITH STH** to put a part of the body, especially the fingertips, in contact with sth so as to feel it **2.** *vti.* **BE OR PUT IN CONTACT** to be in, or bring sth into, physical contact with an object ○ *so that the ends are just touching* **3.** *vt.* **PRESS STH LIGHTLY** to apply the slightest pressure to sth ○ *You only have to touch the brake.* **4.** *vt.* **INTERFERE WITH STH** to interfere with or disturb sth by handling it ○ *told the kids not to touch anything on my desk* **5.** *vt.* **HAVE AN EFFECT ON** to have an effect or influence on sb or sth ○ *events that touched all our lives* **6.** *vt.* **AFFECT SB EMOTIONALLY** to affect sb emotionally, usually arousing gratitude, affection, pity, or compassion ○ *Your concern for my welfare touches me greatly.* **7.** *vt.* **CONSUME STH** to consume sth, especially food or drink, or otherwise make use of sth ○ *You've hardly touched your meal.* **8.** *vt.* **HAVE DEALINGS WITH STH** to have dealings or become involved with sth ○ *Don't touch that issue; it's very controversial.* **9.** *vt.* **MATCH SB OR STH** to come close to sb or sth in level of excellence ○ *Others may have more technique, but nobody can touch her style.* **10.** *vt.* **APPROACH A LEVEL** to approach or reach a level ○ *profits touching 2 billion* **11.** *vt.* **APPROACH SB FOR MONEY** to ask sb for a loan or gift of money (*informal*) [13thC. Via Old French *to(u)chier* from assumed Vulgar Latin *toccare* 'to strike', originally 'to make a sound by striking' (the probable source of English *toccata*), perhaps of imitative origin.] —**touchability** /túchə bíllətí/ *n.* —**touchable** /túchəb'l/ *adj.* —**touchableness** /túchəb'lnəss/ *n.* —**toucher** /túchər/ *n.*

touch down *v.* **1.** *vi.* **LAND** to land in an aircraft or spacecraft **2.** *vt.* RUGBY **TOUCH THE BALL TO THE GROUND** to touch the ball to the ground, either in scoring a try or when behind your own goal line as a way of forcing a restarting of play

touch off *vt.* **1. MAKE STH EXPLODE** to make sth explode, especially by touching it with a flame or smouldering match **2. INITIATE STH** to make sth begin, especially sth that is difficult to control ○ *touched off a bitter disagreement between them*

touch on, touch upon *vt.* **1. MENTION BRIEFLY** to write or talk about sth briefly during the course of a discussion ○ *The report only touches on the financial implications.* **2. VERGE ON** to come close to a particular quality, state, or condition ○ *a sympathetic attitude touching on pity*

touch up *vt.* **1. IMPROVE STH** to make slight improvements to sth, e.g. with paint **2. FALSIFY STH** to make changes to sth, especially a photograph, so that it is no longer an accurate representation (*disapproving*) **3. CARESS SB** to fondle sb sexually (*slang*)

touch-and-go *adj.* highly uncertain or unpredictable (*not hyphenated when used after a verb*) ○ *a touch-and-go situation*

touchback /túchbak/ *n.* a play in American football in which the defence recovers and downs a ball that has been kicked or passed into its end zone

touchdown /túch down/ *n.* **1.** AEROSP **LANDING** a landing made by an aircraft or spacecraft, or the precise moment when it lands **2.** RUGBY **TOUCHING THE BALL ON THE GROUND** in rugby, a touching of the ball on the ground that scores a try **3.** AMERICAN FOOTBALL **SCORING PLAY** in American football, a scoring of six points achieved by being in possession of the ball behind an opponent's goal line

touché /tŏŏ shay/ *interj.* **1. ACKNOWLEDGMENT OF A TELLING REMARK** a word used to acknowledge that sb has made an especially witty, penetrating, or cogent remark, usually in retaliation **2.** FENCING **ACKNOWLEDGMENT OF A SCORING HIT** a word used to acknowledge that an opponent has made a scoring hit [Early 20thC. From French *touché*, past participle of *toucher* 'to touch', from Old French *touchier* (see TOUCH).]

touched /tucht/ *adj.* **1. AFFECTED EMOTIONALLY** affected emotionally, usually with gratitude, affection, pity, or compassion **2. MODIFIED BY STH** slightly marked or modified by sth (*literary*) ○ *blonde hair touched with grey* **3. OFFENSIVE TERM** an offensive term used to describe sb who appears unable to behave in a reasonable or conventional way (*informal offensive*)

touch football *n.* an informal noncompetitive version of American football in which touching replaces tackling

touchhole /túch hōl/ *n.* the opening in the breech of an early cannon or gun where a flame or smouldering material was applied to set off the gunpowder

touching /túching/ *adj.* **CAUSING EMOTIONS** giving rise to feelings of sympathy, tenderness, or tearfulness ■ *prep.* **ABOUT** concerning or relating to sth (*archaic or literary*) —**touchingly** *adv.* —**touchingness** *n.*

touch-in-goal *n.* the area at each end of a rugby pitch, behind the goal line and bounded by the dead-ball line, where the ball may be touched down to score a try

touch judge *n.* either of the two assistant referees in rugby, whose main task is to decide when and where the ball has gone into touch

touchline /túch līn/ *n.* either of the lines that mark the side boundaries of a playing area, especially in rugby or football

touchmark /túch maark/ *n.* a mark stamped on sth made of pewter that identifies the maker

touch-me-not *n.* **1. PLANT WITH BURSTING SEED PODS** a flowering plant with seed pods that burst open if touched when they are ripe. Genus: *Impatiens.* **2.** *US* = **sensitive plant** *n.* 1 [Late 16thC. Translated from Latin *noli me tangere.*]

touch pad *n.* an electronic device, e.g. an input device in a computer system or a control panel on a microwave oven, on which sb can choose options by touching the display

touchpaper /túch paypər/ *n.* paper soaked in saltpetre that is lit to set off gunpowder, especially used for the part of a firework that is lit

touch screen *n.* a computer screen that displays options that a user can choose by touching it with a finger

touchstone /túch stōn/ *n.* **1. EXCELLENT EXAMPLE** a standard by which sth is judged **2.** METALL **STONE USED TO TEST GOLD** a hard black stone formerly used to test the purity of gold and silver according to the colour of the streak left when the metal was rubbed against it [Translation of Old French *touchepierre*]

touch-tone *adj.* used to describe a type of telephone with keys that produce tones when pressed, each of which is decoded as a number at the telephone exchange

touch-type **(touch-types, touch-typing, touch-typed)** *vi.* to type without having to look at the keyboard —**touch-typist** *n.*

touch-up *n.* **1. IMPROVEMENT** an improvement to sth such as makeup or paintwork **2. ALTERATION** an alteration, especially one made to cover up or repair a flaw

touchwood /túch wŏŏd/ *n.* dry decayed wood that can be used as tinder

touchy /túchi/ **(-ier, -iest)** *adj.* **1. EASILY UPSET** liable to become, or make sb, angry or upset ○ *a touchy subject* **2. TRICKY** needing care or tact to prevent an undesirable outcome **3. FLAMMABLE** easily catching fire —**touchily** *adv.* —**touchiness** *n.*

touchy-feely /-feeli/ *adj.* (*informal*) **1. DEMONSTRATIVE** physically and emotionally demonstrative, e.g. in hugging other people or crying openly, often in a way that is considered excessive **2. ENCOURAGING DEMONSTRATIVENESS** encouraging demonstrativeness, especially in losing inhibitions about touching other people and the free expression of emotions

tough /tuf/ *adj.* **1. DURABLE** able to withstand much use, strain, or wear without breaking, tearing, or other damage ○ *boots made of tough leather* **2.** FOOD **HARD TO CHEW OR CUT** not easily chewed or cut ○ *This steak is pretty tough.* **3. VERY STRONG** physically or mentally strong and possessing great endurance ○ *Is he tough enough to make the climb?* **4. THREATENING** characterized by antisocial behaviour, crime, and social deprivation ○ *a tough neighbourhood* **5. RESOLUTE** having or showing firm resolve ○ *She's a tough person to negotiate with.* **6. DIFFICULT** difficult to do or deal with, or needing great effort to do ○ *That's a tough question.* **7. SEVERE** involving or inflicting severe punishment or strict rules ○ *the police policy of being tough on drink-driving* **8. HARD TO ENDURE** unfortunate or hard to bear (*informal*) ○ *a tough break* ■ *n.* **THUG** an aggressive or antisocial person ■ *adv.* **AGGRESSIVELY** in an aggressive way that makes the person appear to be strong, forceful, and unafraid (*informal*) ○ *act tough* ■ *interj.* **BAD LUCK!** used to comment that sth is unfortunate but cannot be helped, and often that the speaker does not really care that this is so [Old English *tōh*, of prehistoric Germanic origin] —**toughly** *adv.* ◇ **tough it out** to be strong and hold out during a time of difficulty (*informal*)

WORD KEY: SYNONYMS

See Synonyms at ***hard***.

toughen /túff'n/ **(-ens, -ening, -ened)** *vti.* **1. MAKE OR BECOME TOUGHER** to become, or make sth, less easy to cut or chew or less liable to wear or damage **2. MAKE OR BECOME STRONGER** to become, or make sb, more resolute, hardier, or physically or emotionally stronger **3. MAKE OR BECOME MORE SEVERE** to become, or make sb or sth, stricter or more severe —**toughener** *n.*

toughie /túffi/ *n.* (*informal*) **1. STH DIFFICULT** sth that is difficult to deal with **2. TOUGH PERSON** a tough person, especially a child, regarded with some affection or amusement because he or she is rather self-assertive and resilient

tough love *n.* a caring but strict attitude adopted towards a friend or loved one with a problem, as distinct from an attitude of indulgence

tough-minded *adj.* able to face hardship and misfortunes in a realistic, determined, and unsentimental way —**tough-mindedly** *adv.* —**tough-mindedness** *n.*

toughness /túffnəss/ *n.* **1. STATE OF BEING TOUGH** the fact or quality of being tough **2.** METALL **RESISTANCE OF A METAL TO STRESS** the resistance of a metal to breaking under repeated twisting and bending forces, measured in kilojoules

Toulon /too lóN/ city, port, and naval base in southeastern France, on the Mediterranean Sea. Population: 170,167 (1990).

Toulouse /too lóoz/ capital city of Haute-Garonne Department, Languedoc-Roussillon Region, southern France. Population: 365,933 (1990).

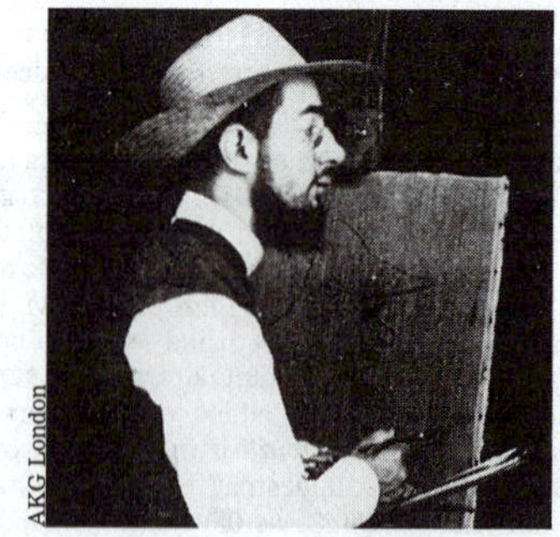

Henri de Toulouse-Lautrec

Toulouse-Lautrec /too lóoz lō trék/, **Henri de** (1864–1901) French artist. He is noted especially for his portraits, paintings of Paris nightlife, and posters advertising Parisian artists. Full name **Henri Marie Raymond de Toulouse-Lautrec-Monta**

toun /toon/ *n.* **1. toun, toon TOWN** a town (*regional*) **2.** *Scotland* **FARM** a farm, including all of its buildings and land [Old English *tūn* (see TOWN)]

toupee /tóo pay/ *n.* **1.** WIG a wig or partial wig worn to cover a bald area **2.** TUFT ON A WIG a prominent lock or tuft on a wig (*archaic*) [Early 18thC. Alteration of French *toupet* 'tuft of hair', from, ultimately, a prehistoric Germanic word meaning 'topknot'.]

tour /toor, tawr/ *n.* **1.** LEISURE **PLEASURE TRIP** a journey visiting several places, usually taken for pleasure, e.g. on holiday **2.** ARTS **PERFORMING TRIP** a long series of performances in different places, e.g. by a rock band or a theatre company **3.** SPORTS **PLAYING TRIP** a series of games or tournaments played by the same team in different places, often overseas **4.** BRIEF TRIP TO SEE STH a short trip, especially for the purpose of viewing or inspecting different items **5.** PERIOD OF DUTY a period of duty, especially in a particular place or for a specific length of time ■ *vti.* **(tours, touring, toured)** TAKE PART IN A TOUR to take part in a tour, for some purpose or of a specified place [14thC. Via Old French from Latin *tornus* 'lathe'; the underlying meaning is 'circular movement'.]

touraco /tóorə kō/ (*plural* **-cos**), **turaco** (*plural* **-cos**) *n.* an African bird resembling the cuckoo that has brightly coloured feathers and a long tail. Touracos are found in dense forest. They are weak flyers and hop around branches. Family: Musophagidae. [Mid-18thC. Via French from a West African language.]

tour de force /tóor də fáwrss, táwr-/ (*plural* **tours de force**) *n.* sth done with supreme skill or brilliance [Early 19thC. From French, 'feat of strength'.]

Touré /tóor ay/, **Sékou** (1922–84) Guinean statesman. He campaigned for Guinea's independence from French rule and was first president of Guinea (1958–84). Full name **Ahmed Sékou Touré**

tourer /tóorər, táw-/ *n.* a convertible car designed for long-distance leisure driving

Tourette syndrome /toor rét-/, **Tourette's syndrome** /toor réts-/ *n.* a condition in which sb experiences multiple tics and twitches, and utters involuntary vocal grunts and obscene speech [Late 19thC. Named after Gilles de la *Tourette* (1857–1904), the French neurologist who identified the condition.]

touring company *n.* a theatre company that takes part in performing tours rather than performing solely in one venue

tourism /tóorizəm, táw-/ *n.* **1.** LEISURE **TRAVEL FOR PLEASURE** the visiting of places away from home for pleasure **2.** BUSINESS **TRAVEL BUSINESS** the business of organizing travel and services for people travelling for pleasure

tourist /tóorist, táw-/ *n.* **1.** SB WHO TRAVELS FOR PLEASURE sb who visits places away from home for pleasure **2.** SPORTS **MEMBER OF A TOURING TEAM** a member of a team that is making a playing tour **3.** TRANSP = **tourist class** ■ *adj.* LEISURE **FOR OR RELATING TO TOURISTS** typical of or involving tourists, or suitable or intended for tourists, e.g. in terms of cheapness or exploitative prices ■ *adv.* TRANSP **TOURIST CLASS** in tourist class —**touristic** /toor rístik, taw-/ *adj.*

tourist class, **tourist** *n.* the cheapest class of accommodation on an aircraft or ship

tourist trap *n.* a place that is popular with tourists but where, as a result, the prices of goods and services are higher than average

touristy /tóoristi, táw-/ *adj.* relating to, appealing to, or full of tourists, especially when this is looked down upon (*informal*)

tourmaline /tóormə leen, túr-/ *n.* a hard crystalline borosilicate mineral with a range of compositions, used in electrical and optical devices and, in green, pink, blue, and black varieties, as semiprecious gemstones [Mid-18thC. From, ultimately, Sinhalese *toramalli* 'cornelian'.] —**tourmalinic** /tóormə línnik, túr-/ *adj.*

Tournai /toor náy/ city in Hainault Province, southwestern Belgium. Population: 67,939 (1996).

tournament /tóornəmənt, táwr-/ *n.* **1.** SPORTS **SERIES OF GAMES** a sports event made up of a series of games, rounds, or contests **2.** HIST **MOCK FIGHTING** a sporting contest popular in the Middle Ages in which knights took part in jousting or combat, generally with blunted weapons **3.** MIL **MILITARY SHOW** a military show with competitions [12thC. From Old French *torneiement*, literally 'act of jousting', from *torneier* (see TOURNEY). The sense 'series of games' came into use in the mid-18thC.]

tournedos /tóornə dō/ (*plural* **-dos**) *n.* a small round cut of fillet steak [Late 19thC. From French, from *tourner* 'to turn' + *dos* 'back'.]

tourney /tóorni, túr-, táwr-/ *n.* (*plural* **-neys**) = **tournament** ■ *vi.* **(-neys, -neying, -neyed)** COMPETE IN A TOURNAMENT to take part in a tournament [13thC. Via Old French *torneier* 'to joust, tilt', from, ultimately, Latin *tornare* 'to turn'.] —**tourneyer** *n.*

tourniquet /tóorni kay, táwr-/ *n.* a tight encircling band applied around an arm or leg in an emergency to stop severe arterial bleeding that cannot be controlled in any other way [Late 17thC. From French, of uncertain origin: possibly from Old French *tournicle* 'coat of mail', literally 'small tunic', ultimately from Latin *tunica* 'tunic'; influenced by *tourner* 'to turn'.]

tour of duty *n.* = **tour** *n.* 5

tour operator *n.* a person or company that organizes package holidays

Tours /toor, toorz/ capital city of Indre-et-Loire Department, Centre Region, west-central France. Population: 133,403 (1990).

tousle /tówz'l/ *vt.* **(-sles, -sling, -sled)** TANGLE HAIR to make hair or fur tangled or ruffled ■ *n.* TANGLED MASS a tangled mass of sth, especially hair or fur [15thC. Literally 'to pull repeatedly', formed from *touse* 'to pull, handle roughly', ultimately from a prehistoric Germanic base that is also the ancestor of English *tease*.] —**tousled** *adj.*

tout /towt/ *v.* **(touts, touting, touted) 1.** *vi.* ATTRACT CUSTOMERS to try to attract customers or support, especially in an aggressive or persistent way ○ *street traders touting for business* **2.** *vt.* OFFER OR ADVERTISE STH to claim to have sth available or to hand, or offer sth for sale **3.** *vt.* PRAISE SB OR STH to praise or recommend sb or sth enthusiastically (*usually passive*) ○ *was touted as the next champion* **4.** *vi.* SPY ON RACEHORSES to spy on racehorses in training to gain information useful to people who bet on horse races **5.** *vti.* SELL INFORMATION ABOUT RACEHORSES to sell information about racehorses to potential gamblers ■ *n.* **1.** SB WHO SELLS INFORMATION ABOUT RACEHORSES sb who spies on racehorses in training to obtain information and then sells it to people who bet on horse races **2.** AGGRESSIVE SELLER sb who tries to attract customers or sell things aggressively **3.** = **ticket tout** [14thC. Ultimately from a prehistoric Germanic base meaning 'to poke out, project'. The original English meaning was 'to peek', which became 'to spy on' and, later, 'to look for business'.] —**touter** *n.*

tout à fait /tóot aa fáy/ *adv.* in a complete or thorough manner [From French]

tout court /tóo káwr/ *adv.* in a brief or simple manner [From French, literally 'very short']

tout de suite /tóot swéet/ *adv.* as quickly as possible [From French, literally 'completely in succession']

tout ensemble /tóot on sómb'l/ *adv.* ALL TOGETHER all together at the same time or all in all ■ *n.* TOTAL EFFECT the total appearance or effect of sth [Early 18thC. From French, 'all together'.]

tout le monde /tóo lə móNd/ *n.* everyone everywhere [From French, literally 'all the world']

tovarish /tə váarish/ (*plural* **-rishes**), **tovarich** /tə váarich/ (*plural* **-riches**), **tovarisch** /tə váarish/ (*plural* **-risches**) *n.* a friend or comrade, often used as a term of address, especially in the former Soviet Union [Early 20thC. From Russian *tovarishch*, of uncertain origin: possibly from a Tatar word.]

tow[1] /tō/ *vt.* **(tows, towing, towed)** PULL STH to pull sth such as a barge or a broken-down car along by a rope or chain attached to it ■ *n.* **1.** ACT OF PULLING STH ALONG the act of pulling sth along by a rope or chain attached to it **2.** STATE OF BEING PULLED ALONG the state of being towed by a rope or chain **3.** ROPE a rope or chain used for towing sth **4.** STH THAT PULLS sth that tows sth else **5.** STH TOWED sth that is towed [Old English *togian*. Ultimately from an Indo-European word meaning 'to lead', which is also the ancestor of English *education* and *team*.] —**towable** *adj.* —**tower** *n.* ◇ **have** *or* **take sb in tow 1.** to be followed or accompanied by sb **2.** *US* to act as a protector or guide for sb

WORD KEY: SYNONYMS

See Synonyms at ***pull***.

tow[2] /tō/ *n.* fibres of flax, hemp, or jute, or of a synthetic material such as rayon [Old English *tow-*, from prehistoric Germanic] —**towy** *adj.*

towage /tō ij/ *n.* **1.** ACT OF TOWING OR BEING TOWED the act or process of towing sb or sth, or the state of being towed **2.** CHARGE FOR TOWING a charge made for towing sth

towards /tə wáwrdz/, **toward** *prep.* **1.** IN A PARTICULAR DIRECTION used to indicate that some person or thing is moving or facing in the direction of another person or thing ○ *They headed off towards town.* **2.** SHORTLY BEFORE shortly before a particular time ○ *towards midnight* **3.** WITH SPECIFIC AUDIENCE INTENDED with a particular target group in mind ○ *remarks slanted towards those sitting in the front row* **4.** REGARDING concerning or with regard to ○ *his attitude towards her* **5.** CONTRIBUTING TO as a contribution to or means of achieving sth ○ *a grant towards the cost of refurbishment* [Old English *tōweardes*, from TOWARD + *-es*, adverbial ending]

towbar /tō baar/ *n.* a rigid metal bar or frame attached to the back of a vehicle and used for towing other vehicles

towboat /tō bōt/ *n.* **1.** = **tug 2.** *US* BARGE-PUSHING BOAT a powerful boat with a broad bow, designed for pushing barges on rivers or canals

tow-coloured *adj.* having a pale yellow colour like hemp or flax

towel /tówəl/ *n.* **1.** ABSORBENT CLOTH a usually rectangular piece of absorbent cloth or paper, used to dry the body **2.** DISHTOWEL a towel used in the kitchen to dry dishes **3.** = **sanitary towel** ■ *vti.* **(-els, -elling, -elled)** DRY SB WITH TOWEL to use a towel to dry sb or sth [13thC. Via Old French *toaille*, from a prehistoric Germanic base meaning 'to wash'.] ◇ **throw in the towel** to give up doing sth that is proving difficult, or give in to sb (*informal*)

towelette /tówə lét/ *n.* *US* a small moistened piece of paper or cloth used for cleaning the hands and face

towelling /tówəling/ *n.* a soft absorbent, usually looped cotton fabric, used to make towels and bathrobes

tower[1] /tówər/ *n.* **1.** ARCHIT **TALL BUILDING** a tall structure, sometimes the upper part or a tall part of a building or structure and sometimes a separate building **2.** MIL **FORTRESS** a building designed to withstand attack **3.** HOUSEHOLD **CD STAND** a tall wooden, plastic, or metal case in which to store CDs or videos ■ *vi.* **(-ers, -ering, -ered) 1.** BE TALL to be very high or tall, or much higher or taller than sb or sth else **2.** BE SUPERIOR to be considerably superior to sb or sth [12thC. Via Latin *turris* from Greek.] ◇ **a tower of strength** sb who is reliable and supportive (*informal*)

tower[2] /tō ər/ *n.* sb or sth, e.g. a vehicle, that tows sth by a rope or chain. ◊ **tow**

tower block *n.* a tall building, especially a residential one

tower crane *n.* a crane mounted on top of a very high steel frame, used on building sites

tower house *n.* a tall fortified house, especially one built in Scotland in the 14th to 16th centuries

towering /tówəring/ *adj.* **1.** HIGH OR TALL rising very high or standing very tall **2.** OUTSTANDING being of the highest quality or importance **3.** INTENSE characterized by extreme or intense emotion or pain ○ *a towering rage* —**toweringly** *adv.*

Tower of Babel *n.* according to the Book of Genesis, the overambitious tower that the people on earth started to build, causing God to show his anger by making them speak different languages, which led to the collapse of the project and ultimately to the scattering of people across the world

tower of silence *n.* in Zoroastrianism, an open tower in which the dead are exposed to be eaten by vultures, the bones then being deposited in the centre of the tower

tow-haired *adj.* having blond or tousled hair [From TOW[2]]

towhead /tṓ hed/ *n.* HAIR **1.** SB WITH BLOND HAIR sb with fair or tousled hair **2.** HEAD OF WHITE-BLOND HAIR a head that is covered with light blond hair [From TOW²] —**towheaded** *adj.*

towhee /tów hi, tṓ-/ *n.* a large long-tailed North American sparrow, typically a ground feeder. Genera: *Pipilo* and *Chlorura*. [Mid-18thC. An imitation of the call of the bird.]

towkay /tów káy/ *n.* a term of address meaning 'sir' or 'master' [Mid-19thC. From Malay *tauke.*]

towline /tṓ līn/ *n.* = **towrope**

town /town/ *n.* **1.** LARGE AREA OF BUILDINGS a densely populated area with many buildings, larger than a village and smaller than a city **2.** URBAN AREA a large urban area, either a town, a city, or a borough **3.** *US, Can* POL UNIT OF LOCAL GOVERNMENT in certain parts of the United States, a unit of local government that is smaller than a county or city **4.** LOCAL TOWN the nearest large town or city, or the town or city in which sb lives ○ *moving into town* **5.** CENTRE OF SETTLED AREA the centre of a town or city **6.** POPULATION OF SETTLED AREA the people who live in a town ○ *The whole town's talking about it.* **7.** NONACADEMIC POPULATION the permanent residents of a town that has a university, as opposed to the staff and students of the university ○ *town and gown* **8.** ZOOL PRAIRIE DOG BURROWS a group of prairie dog burrows [Old English *tūn* 'yard, buildings within an enclosure'. The term came to mean 'cluster of dwellings' and, by the 12thC, its main present meaning was in use.] —**townish** *adj.* ◇ **go to town (on sb or sth)** to do sth with great enthusiasm or thoroughness (*informal*) ◇ **on the town** spending time enjoying the entertainment available in a town or city, especially if a lot of money is spent (*informal*) ◇ **paint the town red** to go out and celebrate, especially by spending a lot of money for entertainment (*informal*)

WORD KEY: SYNONYMS

See Synonyms at *city*.

town-and-gown *adj.* relating to a town that has a large population of students in higher education, especially Oxford or Cambridge

town clerk *n.* **1.** ADMINISTRATIVE OFFICER the secretary and chief administrative officer of a town in the United Kingdom before the reorganization of local government in 1974 **2.** *US* RECORDKEEPER a public official responsible for such things as keeping the records of a town and issuing licences

town council *n.* the people elected or appointed to govern a town

town crier *n.* sb employed by a town, especially formerly, to make public announcements in the streets

townee *n.* = **townie**

town gas *n.* gas manufactured from coal, for domestic and industrial use

town hall *n.* a building that houses the offices of the local administration and often has a public hall that can be used for meetings

townhall clock /tówn hawl-/ *n.* = **moschatel** [From the plant's flowerhead of five green flowers, one on top, and four below that face different directions]

town house *n.* **1.** HOUSE IN TOWN a house in a town or city, especially one that belongs to sb who also has a house in the country **2.** ARCHIT TERRACED HOUSE a terraced house in a town or city, especially one in a fashionable area **3.** *US* ARCHIT = **row house 4.** *ANZ* ARCHIT MODERN TOWN DWELLING in New Zealand, a modern, usually two-storey town dwelling of superior quality, semidetached or in a block of three or four and with limited garden space

townie /tówni/, **towny** (*plural* **-ies**), **townee** /tow néé/ *n.* **1.** TOWN DWELLER sb who lives permanently in a town, as opposed to sb who lives in the country (*informal*) **2.** NONACADEMIC RESIDENT a nonacademic town resident as opposed to a student or member of staff at a university in the town

townland /tównlənd/ *n. Ireland* **1.** SUBDIVISION OF PARISH an area of land that is a subdivision of a parish, or an area of land consisting of a town and the region around it **2.** POSTAL LAND DIVISION a land division, used in postal addresses, averaging about 350 acres

town manager *n. US* an official in charge of the administrative activities of a town

town meeting *n.* **1.** MEETING OF INHABITANTS a public meeting involving all of the inhabitants of a town **2.** *New England* MEETING OF VOTERS a public meeting involving all of the voters of a town, with the authority to make legislative decisions **3.** POL, TV TELEVISED GATHERING a television programme centring on an issue of national interest, in which people from a particular area ask questions of debaters or speakers ○ *a televised national town meeting on the role of the military in global peacekeeping*

town planning *n.* the organized planning and control of the construction or extension of a town. US term **urban planning** —**town planner** *n.*

townscape /tówn skayp/ *n.* **1.** VISIBLE AREA OF TOWN the part of a town within the sight of sb looking at it **2.** PICTURE OF TOWN a painting or photograph of an urban scene

townsfolk /tównz fōk/ *npl.* = **townspeople**

township /tówn ship/ *n.* **1.** SMALL TOWN a small town **2.** *US, Can* POL SUBDIVISION OF A COUNTY a subdivision of a county, often serving as a unit of local government **3.** *US* POL AREA GOVERNED BY TOWN MEETING in some parts of the United States, an area governed by a town meeting **4.** *US* MEASURE 36 SQUARE MILES an area of surveyed public land equal to 36 sections or 36 square miles **5.** *Scotland* CROFTING COMMUNITY a small community of crofts in the Highlands and Islands **6.** *S Africa* HIST URBAN SETTLEMENT FOR BLACK PEOPLE an urban settlement planned for Black people only, usually implying inferior facilities and services **7.** PARISH a former term for an English parish or subdivision of a parish **8.** *ANZ* VILLAGE a small town or village [Old English. The meaning 'subdivision of a parish' is found in the mid-16thC.]

townsman /tównzmən/ (*plural* **-men** /-mən/) *n.* **1.** TOWN-DWELLER a man who lives in a town **2.** MAN LIVING IN SAME TOWN a man who lives in the same town as sb else

townspeople /tównz peep'l/ *npl.* the people who live in a town or who have lived in a town and are used to the ways of town life

Townsville /tównzvil/ city on the eastern coast of Queensland, Australia. It is a commercial and industrial centre. Population: 101,398 (1996).

townswoman /tównz wŏŏmən/ (*plural* **-en** /-wimin/) *n.* **1.** TOWN-DWELLER a woman who lives in a town **2.** WOMAN LIVING IN SAME TOWN a woman who lives in the same town as sb else

towny *n.* = **townie**

towpath /tṓ paath/ (*plural* **-paths** /-paathz/) *n.* a path beside a canal or river for people or animals to walk along, originally as they pulled a barge or boat

towrope /tṓ rōp/, **towline** *n.* a rope used to tow sth, e.g. a boat or a broken-down car

tox. *abbr.* toxicology

tox- *prefix.* = **toxi-** (*used before vowels*)

toxaemia /tok séémi ə/ *n.* a condition produced by the presence of bacterial toxins in the blood, usually with tissue or organ damage, fever, and severe intestinal upset [Mid-19thC. Coined from TOX- + Greek *haima* 'blood' + -IA.] —**toxaemic** *adj.*

toxalbumin /toks álbyŏŏmin, -al byŏŏmin/ *n.* a toxic albumin protein found in some plants such as toadstools and in bacteria and snake venom

toxaphene /tóksə feen/ *n.* a waxy amber-coloured poisonous compound that smells of pine and is used as an insecticide. Formula: $C_{10}H_{10}Cl_8$. [Mid-20thC. Coined from TOXI- + a shortening of *chlorinated camphene.*]

toxemia *n.* US = **toxaemia**

toxi- *prefix.* poison, poisonous ○ *toxigenic* [From TOXIC]

toxic /tóksik/ *adj.* **1.** INVOLVING STH POISONOUS relating to or containing a poison or toxin **2.** DEADLY causing serious harm or death ■ *n.* POISONOUS SUBSTANCE a toxic substance [Mid-17thC. Via medieval Latin *toxicus* 'poisoned' from, ultimately, Greek *toxikos* 'of the bow' (Greek *toxikon pharmakon* meant 'poison for smearing arrows').] —**toxically** *adv.*

toxicant /tóksikənt/ *n.* a toxic substance, especially one used as a pesticide

toxicity /tok síssəti/ (*plural* **-ties**) *n.* **1.** DEGREE OF POISONOUSNESS the degree to which sth is poisonous **2.** CAPABILITY TO POISON SB the state of being poisonous to sb or sth

toxico- *prefix.* poison ○ *toxicogenic* [From Latin *toxicum* (see TOXIC)]

toxicogenic /tóksi kō jénnik/ *adj.* = **toxigenic**

toxicology /tóksi kólləji/ *n.* the scientific study of poisons, especially their effects on the body and their antidotes —**toxicologic** /tóksikə lójjik/ *adj.* —**toxicologically** /-lójjikli/ *adv.* —**toxocologist** /-kólləjist/ *n.*

toxicosis /tóksi kṓssiss/ (*plural* **-ses** /-seez/) *n.* the harmful effects of a poison, including any disease caused by toxins

toxic shock syndrome *n.* acute, potentially fatal circulatory failure, commonly associated with the use of vaginal tampons, which can create conditions promoting the growth of a toxin-producing staphylococcal bacterium

toxigenic /tóksi jénnik/ *adj.* **1.** POISON-PRODUCING producing poisonous substances **2.** PRODUCED BY TOXIN caused or produced by a toxin —**toxigenicity** /tóksijə níssəti/ *n.*

toxin /tóksin/ *n.* **1.** POISON FROM A LIVING CREATURE a poison produced by a living organism, especially bacteria, capable of causing disease and also of stimulating the production within the body of antibodies to counter their effects **2.** any substance said to accumulate in the body that is considered to be harmful or poisonous to the system ○ *drinking plenty of water to eliminate toxins* [Late 19thC. Coined from TOXIC + -IN.]

toxin-antitoxin *n.* a mixture of a toxin and its antitoxin in which the toxin is in slight excess, formerly used as a vaccine, e.g. for diphtheria

toxocariasis /tóksōkə rī́ əsiss/ *n.* an infestation of the larvae of a kind of roundworm in human beings, from worm eggs picked up from contaminated soil or domestic pets [Mid-20thC. Coined from TOX- + Greek *kara* 'head' + -IASIS.]

toxoid /tók soyd/ *n.* a preparation of a toxin produced by infectious agents, largely rendered harmless by chemical treatment but still capable of stimulating antibodies and used as a vaccine [Early 20thC. Coined from shortening of TOXIN + -OID.]

toxophilite /tok sóffi līt/ *n.* an archer or archery enthusiast (*literary or humorous*) [Late 18thC. Formed from *Toxophilus*, 'lover of the bow', which was coined by Roger ASCHAM (1545) (from TOXO- + Greek *philos* 'friend').] —**toxophily** /tok sóffəli/ *n.*

toxoplasma /tóksō plázmə/ *n.* a microscopic protozoan organism that lives as a parasite in the organs of vertebrates, especially birds and mammals, and can cause disease. Genus: *Toxoplasma*. [Early 20thC. From modern Latin, coined from toxo-, a variant of TOXI- + PLASMA.] —**toxoplasmic** *adj.*

toxoplasmosis /tóksō plaz mṓssiss/ (*plural* **-ses** /-seez/) *n.* a disease of mammals caused by a toxoplasma transmitted to humans via undercooked meat or through contact with infectious animals, especially cats

toy /toy/ *n.* **1.** THING TO PLAY WITH sth meant to be played with, especially by children **2.** REPLICA a replica of a real object, meant to be played with or used as an ornament **3.** MINIATURE BREED an animal, especially a dog, that is a miniature version of another animal ○ *a toy poodle* **4.** STH UNIMPORTANT sth of little value or importance ■ *adj.* EASILY DISMISSED used pejoratively to belittle sb or sth or make sb or sth deemed irrelevant or of inferior quality appear insignificant (*insult*) [14thC. Origin unknown. Its original meaning was 'amorous dalliance', and the sense 'plaything' came into use in late 16thC.] —**toyer** *n.*

toy with *vt.* **1.** PLAY WITH STH to play or fiddle with sth, especially because of a lack of real interest in it or preoccupation with sth else **2.** THINK ABOUT STH to consider doing sth **3.** TREAT SB OR STH CRUELLY to behave in a cruelly insincere or offhand way towards sb or sth **4.** TREAT SB INSINCERELY to treat sb in an insincere or flirtatious way, merely for amusement

toy boy *n.* an offensive term for a young man who is the lover of sb who is older (*slang insult*)

toyi-toyi /tóy toy/ *n.* *S Africa* a militant dance performed by a circular group of protesters, with high steps, accompanied by chanting of slogans and singing [Late 20thC. From an African language, perhaps Xhosa.]

Toynbee /tóyn bee/, **Arnold** (1889–1975) British historian. His masterwork, the 12-volume *Study of History* (1934–61), treated history as a succession of civilizations rather than of nations. Full name **Arnold Joseph Toynbee**

toyon /tóy on/ *n.* an evergreen Californian shrub with white flowers and red berry-like fruit. Latin name: *Heteromeles arbutifolia*. [Mid-19thC. From Mexican Spanish *tollón*.]

tp, Tp *abbr.* troop

t.p. *abbr.* PUBL title page

TPA *abbr.* tissue plasminogen activator

TPC *abbr.* Trade Practices Commission

TPI *abbr.* tax and price index

T-plate, tee-plate *n.* a metal plate, shaped like a letter T, used to strengthen a right-angled joint, e.g. between two beams

TPN *abbr.* triphosphopyridine nucleotide

Tpr *abbr.* Trooper

TQM *abbr.* BUSINESS total quality management

TR *abbr.* **1.** TELECOM transmit-receive **2.** Turkey (*international vehicle registration*)

tr. *abbr.* **1.** GRAM transitive **2.** LANG, BUSINESS translator **3.** PRINTING transpose **4.** PRINTING transposition **5.** FIN treasurer **6.** MUSIC trill **7.** troop **8.** FIN trust **9.** FIN trustee

trabeated /tráybi aytid/, **trabeate** /tráybi ət, -ayt/ *adj.* ARCHIT built using horizontal beams rather than arches [Mid-16thC. Formed from the Latin stem *trab-* 'beam'.] —**trabeation** /tráybi áysh'n/ *n.*

trabecula /trə békyoōlə/ (*plural* **-lae** /-lee/) *n.* **1.** ANAT **ROD-SHAPED SUPPORT IN AN ORGAN** a rod-shaped body part that forms an internal support of an organ and divides it into separate chambers **2.** ANAT **BAR OF BONY TISSUE** any of the thin bars of bony tissue in spongy bone that form a meshwork with interconnecting spaces that contain bone marrow **3.** BOT **ROD-SHAPED CELL** a rod-shaped cell or structure that bridges a cavity, e.g. between cells [Mid-19thC. From Latin, literally 'small beam', from the stem *trab-* 'beam'.] —**trabecular** *adj.* —**trabeculate** *adj.*

trace[1] /trayss/ *n.* **1.** **REMAINING SIGN** a sign that remains to show the former presence of a person or thing no longer there **2.** **TINY QUANTITY** a tiny amount or the slightest amount **3.** CHEM **JUST DETECTABLE AMOUNT** an amount of sth that is detectable but too small to be quantified **4.** **FOOTPRINT** a footprint or physical sign of the passage of a person or animal **5.** *US* **PATH** a path or track left by people or animals regularly passing **6.** **LINE MARKING STH** a line made by a recording instrument, e.g. one drawn by a seismograph or one formed on the screen of a cathode ray tube, or the record made in this way **7.** **DRAWING** a drawing, especially one made using tracing paper **8.** **ATTEMPT TO FIND ANOTHER** an attempt to find or follow sb or sth **9.** PSYCHOL = **engram** **10.** GEOM **INTERSECTION** the point of intersection of a line or plane with the surface of a coordinate plane **11.** MATH **SUM OF DIAGONAL ENTRIES** the sum of the diagonal entries of a square matrix **12.** METEOROL **AMOUNT OF PRECIPITATION** an amount of precipitation that is too small to be recorded by instruments, or the record of such an amount ■ *v.* (**traces, tracing, traced**) **1.** *vt.* **FIND SB OR STH** to find out where sb or sth is or who or what sb or sth was **2.** *vti.* **FOLLOW OR BE FOLLOWED** to follow or show a course or series of developments, or be able to be followed back in time or to a source **3.** *vti.* **COPY STH** to copy writing, a design, or drawing by putting translucent paper on top of it and drawing the visible outlines on this paper **4.** *vt.* **DRAW STH CAREFULLY** to draw or write sth with great care **5.** *vt.* **OUTLINE STH** to give an outline or brief description of sth **6.** *vt.* ARCHIT **DECORATE STH** to decorate sth with tracery **7.** *vi.* **SEARCH STH** to search through sth [13thC. Via Old French *tracier* 'to make one's way' from, ultimately, Latin *trahere* 'to pull'.] —**traceability** *n.* —**traceable** *adj.* —**traceableness** *n.* —**traceably** *adv.* —**traceless** *adj.* —**tracelessly** *adv.*

WORD KEY: ORIGIN

See Origin note at ***trace***[2].

trace[2] /trayss/ *n.* **1.** EQU **HORSE'S PULLING STRAPS** either of the two straps or chains connected to a horse's harness by means of which it pulls sth such as a cart (*often used in the plural*) **2.** MECH ENG **BAR TRANSFERRING MOTION** a hinged bar that enables motion to be transferred from one part of a machine to another **3.** ANGLING **FLY-TYING THREAD** in angling, thread or wire for attaching a fly to a line [14thC. From Old French *trais*, plural of *trait* 'strap for harnessing', from Latin *tractus* 'drawing' (see TRACTOR).] ◇ **kick over the traces** to reject restrictions and controls and do sth unconventional (*informal*)

WORD KEY: ORIGIN

The Latin word *tractus*, from which ***trace*** is derived, passed into Old French as *trait* 'pulling, draught', hence 'harness-strap' (source of English *trait*). Its plural *trais* was borrowed into English in the 14th century as ***trace*** 'harness-strap'. It also formed the basis of a Vulgar Latin verb that evolved into Old French *tracier*, from which English in the 14th century got the verb ***trace***. A noun ***trace*** was also derived from *tracier*, and this too was acquired by English as ***trace***, in the 13th century. At first it denoted a 'path' or 'track'; the modern sense 'visible sign' did not develop until the 17th century.

trace element *n.* **1.** CHEM **ELEMENT PRESENT IN TINY AMOUNT** a chemical element present in minute but detectable amounts, much less than one percent, in sth such as a metal or ore **2.** BIOL **ELEMENT ESSENTIAL FOR HEALTH** an element such as zinc, iodine, or manganese that is required in minute amounts for normal growth and development and the functioning of vital enzyme systems **3.** **MINUSCULE AMOUNT** a very tiny amount ○ *only a trace element of truth to that statement*

trace fossil *n.* a feature in sedimentary rocks that resulted from the activity of an animal, e.g. a worm cast or footprint

tracer /tráyssər/ *n.* **1.** = **tracer bullet** **2.** **AMMUNITION ACTING AS TRACERS** ammunition that has been treated to act as tracers ○ *a gun loaded with tracer* **3.** MED = **tracer element** **4.** **INVESTIGATION OR INVESTIGATOR** an investigation into the whereabouts of sth missing, e.g. an item of mail or a cargo shipment, or sb who carries out such an investigation **5.** **SB OR STH THAT MAKES TRACINGS** sb or sth that makes tracings **6.** a device that gives out a signal that can be tracked and followed when attached to a vehicle or person

tracer bullet, tracer *n.* a bullet that has been treated with chemicals to make it leave a glowing or smoky trail as it flies

tracer element, tracer *n.* MED a radioactive element used in experiments so that its movements can be monitored

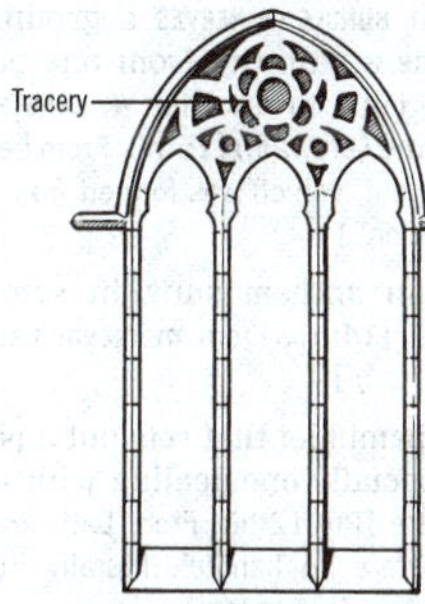

Tracery

tracery /tráyssəri/ (*plural* **-ies**) *n.* **1.** ARCHIT **WINDOW ORNAMENTATION** decorative ribs in windows, especially medieval church windows, and screens **2.** DRAWING **INTERLACED PATTERN** a decorative pattern of interlaced lines, especially one that resembles the form or patterns found in church windows —**traceried** *adj.*

trachea /trə kée ə/ (*plural* **-ae** /-kée ee/ *or* **-as**) *n.* **1.** ANAT **WINDPIPE** the tube in air-breathing vertebrates that conducts air from the throat to the bronchi, strengthened by incomplete rings of cartilage **2.** ZOOL **BREATHING TUBE** a tube in insects and related air-breathing animals through which air is drawn into the body by the pumping action of the abdominal muscles **3.** BOT **TUBE OF PLANT CELLS** a tubular part of water-conducting plant tissue that provides mechanical support and transport of water and nutrients [14thC. From medieval Latin, ultimately from Greek (*artēria*) *trakheia* 'rough (artery)'. From its rings of cartilage.] —**tracheal** *adj.* —**tracheate** /trə kée ət/ *adj.*

tracheid /tráyki id/, **tracheide** *n.* BOT a cell in the trachea of conifers and other gymnosperm plants, with bands of lignin thickening the cell walls and adding structural support [Late 19thC. From German *Tracheïde*, literally 'sth belonging to the trachea'.] —**tracheidal** /trə kée id'l, tráyki íd'l/ *adj.*

tracheitis /tráyki ítiss/ *n.* inflammation of the trachea

tracheo- *prefix.* trachea ○ *tracheostomy*

tracheobronchial /tráyki ō bróngki əl/ *adj.* relating to or in both the trachea and the bronchi

tracheole /tráyki ōl/ *n.* any of the fine channels that branch off from an insect's trachea and carry oxygen to its tissues [Early 20thC. Literally 'small trachea'.]

tracheo-oesophogeal *adj.* relating to or in both the trachea and the oesophagus

tracheophyte /tráyki ō fīt/ *n.* a plant that has a system of vascular tissues for conducting water and nutrients through it [Mid-20thC. Coined from TRACHEA- + Greek *phuton* 'plant'.]

tracheoscopy /tráki óskəpi/ (*plural* **-pies**) *n.* the examination of the inside of the trachea, e.g. using a laryngoscope —**tracheoscopic** *adj.*

tracheostomy /tráki óstəmi/ (*plural* **-mies**) *n.* **1.** **HOLE IN THE TRACHEA** a hole cut in the trachea, e.g. to ensure the airway is unblocked and to suck out secretions **2.** **CUTTING INTO THE TRACHEA** an operation to cut a hole in the trachea

tracheotomy /tráki óttəmi/ (*plural* **-mies**) *n.* the making of an incision through the neck into the trachea to assist breathing when the upper airways are blocked

trachoma /trə kṓmə/ *n.* a contagious bacterial eye disease in which scar tissue forms inside the eyelid, eventually causing it to curve inwards and the eyelashes to scrape the eye, often leading to infection [Late 17thC. From Greek *trakhōma* 'roughness'.] —**trachomatous** *adj.*

trachyte /tráy kīt, trák-/ *n.* fine-grained volcanic rock, characterized by the presence of alkaline feldspar minerals [Early 19thC. Formed from Greek *trakhus* 'rough' + -ITE.] —**trachytoid** /tráki toyd, tráyki-/ *adj.*

trachytic /trə kíttik/ *adj.* used to describe igneous rocks in which the crystals are arranged in parallel and show the flow of the molten lava from which they were formed

tracing /tráyssing/ *n.* **1.** **TRACED COPY** a copy of sth made by tracing it onto a sheet of translucent paper laid on top of it **2.** **INSTRUMENT RECORD** a graphic record made by an instrument such as a seismograph

tracing paper *n.* a type of paper through which it is possible to see what is underneath, and on which it is possible to draw a copy of sth underneath

track /trak/ *n.* **1.** **MARK LEFT** a mark left by a moving person, animal, or thing, e.g. a footprint, an animal's paw print, or the mark of a wheel **2.** **PATH** a path or road, especially one made by the continual passing of people or animals or one specially created for some purpose **3.** RAIL **RAIL STRUCTURE** a rail or pair of parallel rails on which a vehicle, especially a train, runs, along with the supporting structures such as sleepers **4.** **COURSE OF TRAVEL** the path taken by sb or sth while travelling **5.** **LINE OF ACTION OR THOUGHT** a line of thought or investigation, or course of action ○ *realized our research was on the wrong track* **6.** SPORTS **RACE COURSE** a course laid out for racing **7.** *US, Can* SPORTS **SPORTS TAKING PLACE ON SPORTS TRACK** a collective term for all sports that take place on a sports track **8.** *US, Can* SPORTS = **track and field** **9.** RECORDING **SEPARATE RECORDING OF MUSIC** a separate piece of music or song on a disc, tape, or record **10.** RECORDING **PATH FOR RECORDING** a separate section of a magnetic tape where the input of a single channel is recorded **11.** RECORDING **RECORDED INPUT** a recording on separate tracks of a magnetic tape that are combined to give a final version, e.g. of a piece of recorded music or a film **12.** RECORDING = **soundtrack** *n.* 1 **13.** COMPUT **SECTION OF COMPUTER DISK** a path on the surface of a storage medium such as a diskette or CD-ROM on which information is recorded and from which recorded information is read. The path is a series of concentric rings on floppy disks and hard files and a spiral on videodisks and CD-ROMs. **14.** CINEMA = **tracking shot** **15.** AUTOMOT **TREADS OF A TANK OR BULLDOZER** a continuous loop of rubber or metal plates driven by wheels, giving great traction over soft or rough ground, used especially on bulldozers and heavy military vehicles such as tanks **16.** *US* EDUC **COURSE OF STUDY** a course of study that is tailored to the relative abilities or needs of students **17.** BUSINESS **CAREER PATH** the course or projected course of a career **18.** INDUST **MOVING ASSEMBLY LINE** a moving belt carrying things along a factory assembly line **19.** HOUSEHOLD **SUPPORTING RAIL** a usually grooved rail along which sth moves, e.g. a lighting fitment or the supporting hooks of a curtain **20.** PHYS **PATH OF A PARTICLE** the path taken by a particle of ionizing radiation in a cloud chamber, bubble chamber, or photographic emulsion **21.** ENG **DISTANCE BETWEEN WHEELS** the distance between a pair of wheels, e.g. the front wheels of a motor vehicle ■ **tracks** *npl.* **NEEDLE MARKS** marks or scars on the body of a drug user caused by frequent injections (*slang*) ■ *v.* **(tracks, tracking, tracked) 1.** *vti.* **FOLLOW A TRAIL** to follow a trail made by sb or sth, or to try to find sb or sth by following a trail left behind **2.** *vt.* ELEC ENG **FOLLOW THE FLIGHT PATH** to follow the flight path of a vehicle such as a spacecraft using electronic equipment or radar **3.** *vt.* **FOLLOW PROGRESS** to follow the progress or development of sth **4.** *vti.* **FOLLOW A PATH** to follow a path through a place **5.** *vti.* CINEMA **FOLLOW A MOVING OBJECT** to film a moving person or object with a mobile camera **6.** *vi.* ENG **ALIGN** to be in alignment or the correct distance apart, especially wheels on a motor vehicle **7.** *vi.* RECORDING **FOLLOW THE GROOVE ON A RECORD** to follow the groove on a gramophone record **8.** *vi.* *US* **TRAVEL** to travel, especially on a long or laborious journey (*informal*) **9.** *vt.* *US* **BRING AND LEAVE DIRT** to carry sth, especially mud, on the shoes or feet and leave some of it on a floor **10.** *vt.* *US* EDUC **ASSIGN SB TO A TRACK** to assign a student to an educational track [15thC. From French *trac* 'footprint, mark', of uncertain origin: perhaps from Middle Dutch *trek* 'pulling' (source of English *trek*).] —**trackable** *adj.* ◇ **cover your tracks** remove all signs of having been somewhere or done sth (*informal*) ◇ **from the wrong side of the tracks** from the less affluent and socially advantaged part of a town or area (*informal insult*) ◇ **in your tracks** suddenly and immediately, just where sb or sth is or in the middle of what sb or sth is doing (*informal*) ◇ **keep track (of)** to follow, pay attention to, or keep a check on the position or progress of ◇ **lose track (of)** to fail to follow or pay attention, or fail to keep an adequate check on the position or progress of ◇ **make tracks** to leave (*informal*) ◇ **off the beaten track** away from main roads and busy populated areas, and perhaps difficult to find or gain access to as a result (*informal*) ○ *The cottage is lovely but it's a bit off the beaten track.* ◇ **on track** on the correct or desired path or schedule

track down *vt.* to find a person, animal, or object by searching or following a trail

trackage /trákij/ *n.* *US* railway tracks collectively

track and field *n.* *US, Can* = **athletics**

trackball /trák bawl/ *n.* a freely rotating ball moved by the fingers to control a cursor on a computer screen

tracked /trakt/ *adj.* moving on tracks, as a military tank or bulldozer does, or along a fixed track, as a dockside crane does

tracked vehicle *n.* a vehicle such as a military tank or a bulldozer that is propelled by tracks instead of wheels

tracker /trákər/ *n.* sb who follows another person's or an animal's trail, especially sb who is particularly skilled at doing this in order to guide others, e.g. police, soldiers, or hunters

tracker dog *n.* a dog trained to find people, e.g. fugitives or people who are lost, by following the trail of their scent

track event *n.* a sports competition that takes place on a running track

tracking /tráking/ *n.* **1. FOLLOWING OF A TRAIL** the act or process of following the trail of a person or animal **2.** VIDEO **FINDING BEST PICTURE** the finding by a video player of the best quality picture **3.** ELEC ENG **LEAKING OF CURRENT** the leaking of current between two insulated points, e.g. caused by damp or dirt

tracking radar *n.* a radar system that emits a beam that oscillates about an object being tracked, allowing it to detect sudden changes of direction

tracking shot *n.* a camera shot filmed from a moving dolly, following the movement of sb or sth

tracking station *n.* a place from which the movement of sth such as a launched missile or a space vehicle can be followed using radar or radio signals

trackless /trákləss/ *adj.* **1. LACKING PATHS** so isolated that there are no trails or paths **2. LEAVING NO TRAIL** leaving no track or trail **3.** RAIL **RUNNING WITHOUT RAILS** not needing rails on which to run —**tracklessly** *adv.* —**tracklessness** *n.*

track light *n.* an electric light that can be moved and repositioned anywhere along the length of an electrified track mounted on a wall or ceiling —**track lighting** *n.*

trackman /trákmən/ (*plural* **-men** /-mən/) *n.* *US* = **platelayer**

track meet *n.* *US* an athletic competition in which teams from several places participate in track events

track record *n.* **1. PAST PERFORMANCE** a record of the past performance of a person, organization, or thing (*informal*) **2.** SPORTS **SPORTS ARENA RECORD** a record for a particular sports arena, as opposed to a national or international record

track rod *n.* the rod that connects the two front wheels of a motor vehicle

track shoe *n.* either of a pair of lightweight spiked running shoes

trackside /trák sīd/ *n.* the area immediately beside a running track or racetrack

tracksuit /trák soot, -syoot/ *n.* a loose-fitting long-sleeved top and matching trousers in knitted nylon or cotton, worn by athletes over their sports clothes and by other people as casual wear

trackwalker /trák wawkər/ *n.* sb employed to inspect railway track

tract[1] /trakt/ *n.* **1. AREA OF LAND OR WATER** an unmeasured expanse of land or water, or a measured area, especially of land **2.** ANAT **GROUP OF ORGANS** a system of organs or body parts that work together to provide for the passage of sth such as food or bodily waste products **3.** ANAT **BUNDLE OF NERVES** a group of nerve fibres that forms a pathway from one part of the brain or spinal cord to another **4. LENGTH OF TIME** a long period of time (*archaic*) [15thC. From Latin *tractus*, literally 'a drawing out' (which was formed from *trahere* 'to pull'), hence 'duration'.]

tract[2] /trakt/ *n.* an anthem sung in some Roman Catholic masses [14thC. From medieval Latin *tractus*, from Latin (see TRACT[1]).]

tract[3] /trakt/ *n.* a pamphlet that sets out a position or an analysis, especially one dealing with a political or religious issue [Pre-12thC. From Latin *tractatus*, ultimately from *tractare* 'to handle', literally 'to draw repeatedly', from *trahere* (see TRACT[1]).]

tractable /tráktəb'l/ *adj.* **1. DOCILE** very easy to control or persuade **2. MALLEABLE** very easy to bend or work with [15thC. From Latin *tractabilis*, from *tractare* (see TRACT[3]).] —**tractability** /tráktə bílləti/ *n.* —**tractably** /tráktəbli/ *adv.*

Tractarianism /trak táiri ənizəm/ *n.* CHR = **Oxford Movement** [Mid-19thC. So called because of the tracts distributed.] —**Tractarian** *n., adj.*

tractate /trák tayt/ *n.* a short essay on a particular subject (*formal*) [15thC. From Latin *tractatus* (see TRACT[3]).]

tract house *n.* *US* one of many similar houses built on a tract of land —**tract housing** *n.*

tractile /trák tīl/ *adj.* able to be stretched into another shape without breaking [Mid-19thC. Formed from Latin *tract-*, past participle stem of *trahere* (see TRACT[1]).] —**tractility** /trak tílləti/ *n.*

traction /tráksh'n/ *n.* **1.** MED **APPLICATION OF WEIGHTS** application of a pulling force for surgical purposes, e.g. to reduce a fracture, maintain bone alignment, relieve pain, or prevent spinal injury **2.** MECH ENG **FRICTION ALLOWING MOVEMENT** the adhesive friction between a moving object and the surface on which it is moving, e.g. between a tyre and the ground, without which the object cannot move **3.** ENG **PULLING** the act or process of pulling sth, especially by means of a motor, or the fact or state of being pulled along **4.** AUTOMOT **WAY TO MOVE VEHICLES** a means of moving vehicles **5. WAY TO ACHIEVE PROGRESS** a means by which, or the degree to which, progress can be made ○ *could not get any traction in trying to push through the legislation* [Early 17thC. From either French *traction* or medieval Latin *traction-*, formed from Latin *tract-*, past participle stem of *trahere* (see TRACT[1]).] —**tractional** *adj.*

traction engine *n.* a steam-powered road locomotive used for hauling heavy loads by road, as a source of power in fairgrounds, and for ploughing

traction load *n.* the coarse grained fraction of a river's sedimentary load, carried along the river bed by sliding and rolling

tractive force /tráktiv-/ *n.* the force exerted by a tractor or locomotive through a drawbar as it pulls a load

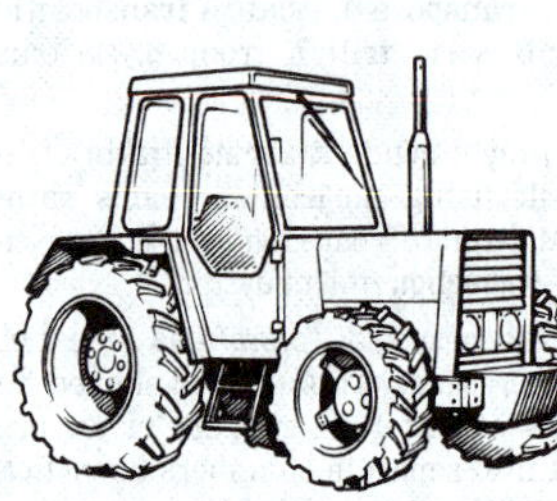

Tractor

tractor /tráktər/ *n.* **1.** AGRIC **FARM VEHICLE** a motor vehicle used for pulling heavy loads, especially on farms, where its typically large deep-treaded rear wheels enable it to move in fields **2.** TRANSP **FRONT PART OF ARTICULATED LORRY** the powered, self-contained front section of an articulated lorry, with driving cab, engine, and coupling for trailers **3.** AIR **AIRCRAFT WITH THE PROPELLER IN FRONT** an aircraft that has its propeller in front of the engine, exerting a pull through the air rather than a pushing force **4.** AIR **PROPELLER** a propeller at the front of an aircraft engine **5.** PRINTING = **tractor feed** [Late 18thC. Formed from Latin *tract-*, past participle stem of *trahere* 'to draw' (see TRACT[1]).]

WORD KEY: ORIGIN

The Latin word *trahere*, from which ***tractor*** is derived, is also the source of English *abstract, attract, contract, detract, distract, extract, retract, retreat, subtract, trace, train, trait, treat, treatise,* and *treaty.*

tractor feed, tractor *n.* a mechanism for feeding paper into a printer, using toothed wheels to mesh with the perforations in continuous stationery

tractor-trailer *n.* *US* a truck for pulling heavy loads, consisting of a tractor attached to a trailer or semi-trailer

Tracy /tráyssi/, **Spencer** (1900–67) US actor. He won Academy Awards for his films *Captains Courageous* (1937) and *Boy's Town* (1938).

trad /trad/ *n.* **TRADITIONAL JAZZ** traditional jazz (*informal*) ■ *abbr.* traditional [Mid-20thC. Shortening.]

trade /trayd/ *n.* **1. AREA OF BUSINESS OR INDUSTRY** a particular area of business or industry ○ *the book trade* **2. OCCUPATION** sb's particular occupation, especially one that involves a skill ○ *learn a trade* **3. PEOPLE IN BUSINESS** the people who work in a particular area

Spencer Tracy

of business or industry ○ *You'll never convince the trade that this tax is fair.* **4. BUYING AND SELLING** the activity of buying and selling, or sometimes bartering, goods ○ *a suspension of trade between the two countries* **5. WORK IN COMMERCE** work in commerce as opposed to a profession ○ *graduates going into trade* **6. CUSTOMERS** customers or business generated by customers ○ *losing trade to their competitors* **7. COMMERCIAL CUSTOMERS** customers in business and industry, as opposed to the general public, who purchase products related to their business or industry ○ *This counter is for trade only.* **8. US, Can EXCHANGE** an exchange of sb or sth for another ○ *If neither of you likes your room, why don't you do a trade?* **9. METEOROL TRADE WIND** a trade wind ○ *the southern trades* **10. BUSINESS PUBLICATION** a publication meant for people in a particular line of business ○ *advertising in all the trades* ■ *v.* (**trades, trading, traded**) **1.** *vi.* **BUY AND SELL GOODS** to take part in buying and selling goods for trade **2.** *vt.* **EXCHANGE STH** to give and receive sth alternately with sb else ○ *trading punches* **3.** *vt.* **DEAL IN STH** to buy and sell a particular commodity **4.** *vti.* **MAKE AN EXCHANGE** to make an exchange, or exchange sb or sth for another ○ *Each had something the other wanted and they were happy to trade.* **5.** *vi. US* **SHOP OR BUY REGULARLY FROM BUSINESS** to shop or buy sth regularly at a particular place of business [14thC. From Middle Low German, 'track', which became used to denote 'regular path (of business) pursued by someone' and hence, in the 16thC, 'buying and selling'.] —**tradable** *adj.* —**tradeless** *adj.*

trade down *vi.* to sell sth large or expensive and buy sth smaller or less expensive

trade in *vt.* to give an old or used item, especially a car, in part payment for a new one

trade on *vt.* to take advantage of a personal quality or situation, often unfairly or excessively

trade up *vi.* to sell sth small or inexpensive and buy sth larger and more expensive

trade acceptance *n.* a bill of exchange for the amount of a purchase drawn by the seller on the buyer, signed by the buyer and often specifying the place and date of payment

trade agreement *n.* a treaty between two or more countries to regulate trade between them

trade association *n.* an organization formed to represent the collective interests of a number of businesses in the same trade

trade book, **trade edition** *n.* a standard edition of a book, meant for sale to the general public, as opposed to a deluxe or book-club edition

trade cycle *n.* the recurrent fluctuation between depression and prosperity in a capitalist economy. US term **business cycle**

trade discount *n.* a reduction in the standard price of sth, offered by one business to another, e.g. by a manufacturer to a retailer, especially within the same trade

traded option *n.* a stock option that is marketable

trade edition *n.* = trade book

trade gap *n.* the difference, measured in monetary value, between a nation's imports and its exports when the exports exceed the imports

trade-in *n.* **1. ITEM USED IN PARTIAL PAYMENT** a used item such as a car that is used as partial payment for sth new **2. ACT OF TRADING STH IN** a transaction in which an old or used item serves as partial payment for sth new

trade journal *n.* a periodical devoted to news and features relating to a particular trade or profession

trade language *n.* a language used between native speakers of different languages to allow them to communicate so that they can trade with each other

trade-last *n. US* an exchange in which sb repeats an overheard compliment to the complimented person if that person will first offer an overheard compliment about the other (*informal*)

trademark /tráyd maark/ *n.* **1. COMM COMPANY SYMBOL** a name or symbol used to show that a product is made by a particular company and legally registered so that no other manufacturer can use it **2. DISTINCTIVE CHARACTERISTIC** a distinctive characteristic associated with a particular person ○ *Quick exits are her trademark.* ■ *vt.* (**-marks, -marking, -marked**) **1. REGISTER STH AS A TRADEMARK** to register a name or symbol as a trademark **2. LABEL PRODUCT WITH A TRADEMARK** to place a trademark on a product

trade name *n.* **1. PRODUCT NAME** a name given by a manufacturer to a product or service **2. NAME USED IN A TRADE** a name for sth that is usually only known to or used by people working in a particular trade **3. COMPANY NAME** a name under which a company or business operates

trade-off, **tradeoff** *n.* a situation in which sb is prepared to compromise by giving up all or part of one thing in exchange for another ○ *a trade-off between quality and price*

trade paperback *n.* a paperback edition of a book that is superior in production quality to a mass-market paperback edition and is similar to a hardback in size

trade plate *n.* a temporary number plate given to a vehicle before it is registered. US term **dealer's plates**

trader /tráydər/ *n.* **1. SB TRADING IN GOODS** sb who buys and sells retail goods **2. STOCK EXCH SB TRADING IN STOCKS** sb who deals in stocks and shares, especially a person who tries to profit by making frequent deals, each netting a small profit **3. SHIPPING SHIP** a merchant ship

trade reference *n.* a person or company that furnishes a report concerning sb's credit standing in response to an inquiry by sb else in the same trade, especially a supplier

trade route *n.* a route used by merchant ships or trading vehicles

Tradescant /trə déskənt/, **John** (1570–1638?) English naturalist. Head gardener to Charles I, he introduced many foreign plants into England, and opened an early public museum.

tradescantia /tráddi skánti ə/ (*plural* **-tias** *or* **-tia**) *n.* a plant grown for its striped leaves and blue, white, or pink flowers. Genus: *Tradescantia.* ◊ **spiderwort** [Early 18thC. From modern Latin, named after John TRADESCANT or his son.]

trade school *n.* a school that gives instruction in a particular trade or that offers vocational courses in general

trade secret *n.* **1. COMPANY'S SECRET** a secret formula or technique that is used to make a product, known only to the company that manufactures it **2. SECRET** any secret (*informal*) ○ *Which shampoo do you use – or is it a trade secret?*

trades holiday /tráydz-/ *n. Scotland* an annual two-week summer holiday taken by industries in a particular town

tradesman /tráydzmən/ (*plural* **-men** /-mən/) *n.* **1. SKILLED WORKER** a man who works in a skilled trade, especially a job related to the building trade such as plumbing and carpentry **2. SHOPKEEPER** a man involved in trade, especially a shopkeeper (*dated*)

tradespeople /tráydz peep'l/ *npl.* people employed in trade, especially shopkeepers (*dated*)

trades union *n.* = labour union

Trades Union Congress *n.* an association of trade unions in Britain, to which most of the largest unions belong

tradeswoman (*plural* **-en**) *n. US* a woman who works in a skilled trade, especially a job related to the construction industry such as plumbing and carpentry

trade union, **trades union** *n.* an organized association of people who work in a particular trade or profession, formed to represent their interests and help them improve their working conditions —**trade unionism** *n.* —**trade unionist** *n.*

trade wind *n.* a prevailing tropical wind blowing towards the equator from the northeast in the northern hemisphere or from the southeast in the southern hemisphere. The trade winds are major components of the global weather system. [From *blow trade* 'to blow in a constant direction', which was based on obsolete *trade* 'course']

trading card *n.* a card with a picture or information on it that is one of a set designed to be collected. Trading cards often feature pictures of popular sports figures.

trading estate *n.* = industrial estate

trading post *n.* **1. SHOP IN REMOTE AREA** especially formerly, a shop in a remote area, where local products can be bartered for supplies **2. STOCK EXCH LOCATION IN STOCK EXCHANGE** a location where a particular security is traded on the floor of a stock exchange

trading stamp *n.* a stamp that can be exchanged for goods, given by a shop to customers each time they spend a certain amount of money

tradition /trə dísh'n/ *n.* **1. CUSTOM OR BELIEF** a long-established custom or belief, often one that has been handed down from generation to generation **2. BODY OF CUSTOMS** a body of long-established customs and beliefs viewed as a set of precedents **3. HANDING DOWN OF CUSTOMS** the handing down of customs, practices, and beliefs that are valued by a particular culture **4. tradition, Tradition** CHR **ACCEPTED UNWRITTEN CHRISTIAN DOCTRINES** the body of Christian doctrines that are accepted as the teachings of Jesus Christ and the apostles without written evidence **5. tradition, Tradition** ISLAM **TEACHINGS SUPPLEMENTING KORAN** the body of Islamic beliefs and customs that are not written in the Koran, e.g. the words of Muhammad **6.** LAW **TRANSFER OF OWNERSHIP** especially in Roman and Scots law, the formal transfer of ownership of movable property [14thC. Via Old French from, ultimately, Latin *tradere* 'to hand over, betray' (source also of English *traitor*), from *trans-* 'across, over' + *dare* 'to give'.] —**traditionless** *adj.*

------ **WORD KEY: SYNONYMS** ------
See Synonyms at *habit*.

traditional /trə dísh'nəl/ *adj.* **1. OF TRADITION** based on or relating to tradition **2. MUSIC IN OLDER JAZZ STYLE** used to describe older styles of jazz, usually played by small ensembles featuring clarinet, trumpet, trombone, and rhythm sections. Traditional jazz flourished in New Orleans, Chicago, and Kansas City in the early 20th century. —**traditionality** /trə dísh'n álləti/ *n.* —**traditionalize** /trə dísh'nə līz/ *vt.* —**traditionally** *adv.*

traditionalism /trə dísh'nəlizəm/ *n.* **1. RESPECT FOR TRADITION** deep respect for tradition, especially cultural or religious practices **2. RELIG BELIEF IN TRANSMISSION OF DIVINE REVELATION** the idea that all knowledge comes from divine revelation and is passed on by tradition —**traditionalist** *n.* —**traditionalistic** /trə dísh'nə lístik/ *adj.*

traditional option *n.* on the Stock Exchange, an option that cannot be resold after it has been bought

traditional policy *n.* a type of life assurance policy in which premiums are paid into a general fund and benefits are based on actuarial statistics

traditor /tráddi tər/ (*plural* **-tores** /-táw reez/) *n.* an early Christian who betrayed other Christians during the Roman persecutions [14thC. From Latin (See TRAITOR).]

traduce /trə dyóoss/ (**-duces, -ducing, -duced**) *vt.* to say very critical or disparaging things about sb [Late 16thC. From Latin *traducere* 'to convert, transfer', also 'to scorn, disgrace', from *trans-* 'across, over' + *ducere* 'to lead'.] —**traducement** *n.* —**traducer** *n.* —**traducible** *adj.*

traducianism /trə dyóosh'nizəm/ *n.* the belief that a child inherits a soul as well as its bodily characteristics from its parents [Mid-18thC. Formed from late Latin *traducianus* 'believer in traducianism', from Latin *tradux* 'inheritance, transmission', from *traducere* (see TRADUCE).] —**traducian** *n., adj.* —**traducianist** *n., adj.* —**traducianistic** /trə doo͝sh'n ístik/ *adj.*

Trafalgar, Cape /trə fálgər/ cape in southwestern Spain between Cadiz and the Strait of Gibraltar

traffic /tráffik/ *n.* **1.** TRANSP **MOVEMENT OF VEHICLES** the movement of vehicles along the roads in a particular area **2.** TRANSP **SEA OR AIR TRANSPORT** the movement of ships, trains, or aircraft between two places, or the volume of passengers or goods transported by sea, rail, or air **3.** COMM **BUSINESS OF TRANSPORTATION** the business of transporting goods or people **4.** CRIMINOL **TRADE** illegal trade in goods such as drugs or weapons **5.** COMMUNICATION **FLOW OF COMMUNICATIONS** the volume or flow of messages carried by a communications system in a particular period **6.** **NEGOTIATIONS** dealings or negotiations between people (*formal*) ■ *v.* **(-fics, -ficking, -ficked) 1.** *vi.* CRIMINOL **TRADE ILLEGALLY** to engage in illegal trading **2.** *vi.* **HAVE DEALINGS** to have dealings with sb or sth **3.** *vt.* **TRADE STH** to trade or exchange anything ○ *We spent the afternoon trafficking gossip.* [Early 16thC. Via obsolete French *trafique* from Old Italian *traffico*, from *trafficare* 'to carry on trade', of uncertain origin.]

trafficator /tráffi kaytər/ *n.* an illuminated signal on either side of an old motor vehicle, raised by the driver to signal a turn [Mid-20thC. A blend of TRAFFIC and INDICATOR.]

traffic calming *n.* the use of obstructions such as speed bumps to force drivers to slow down, especially in residential areas (*hyphenated when used before a noun*)

traffic circle *n. US, Can* = **roundabout**

traffic cone *n.* a marker in the shape of a cone, usually made of orange plastic, used to separate lines of traffic during road repairs or to prevent vehicles from entering an area

traffic cop *n.* (*informal*) **1.** **POLICE OFFICER DIRECTING TRAFFIC** a police officer who supervises traffic **2.** *NZ* **TRAFFIC OFFICER** a traffic officer

traffic court *n.* a court that deals with people who have committed traffic offences

traffic engineering *n.* the design and planning of roads and walkways, considering such factors as pedestrian and vehicular capacity and means for controlling traffic

traffic island *n.* a raised area in the centre of a road to separate lanes of traffic and allow pedestrians to wait safely until they can cross

traffic jam *n.* a line of traffic that cannot move or moves very slowly or spasmodically because of overcrowding or an obstruction —**traffic-jammed** *adj.*

traffic light *n.* a signal that uses red, green, and amber lights to control traffic, especially at a junction

traffic officer *n. NZ* a member of an official force responsible for enforcing traffic regulations and controlling the flow of traffic

traffic pattern *n.* the pattern of routes to which an aircraft is restricted when approaching or circling an airport

traffic signal *n.* = **traffic light**

traffic warden *n. UK* a uniformed public official who enforces parking restrictions on the highway and may also direct traffic

tragacanth /trággə kanth/ *n.* **1.** **NATURAL GUM** a gum used in the manufacture of pills and adhesives, in textile printing, and as a stabilizer and thickener in sauces **2.** **PLANT YIELDING TRAGACANTH** a plant from which tragacanth gum is obtained, especially a spiny Asian plant with white, yellow, or purple flowers. Genus: *Astragalus.* [Late 16thC. Via French *tragacanthe* from, ultimately, Greek *tragakantha*, literally 'goat's thorn', from *tragos* 'goat' + *akantha* 'thorn' (see ACANTHUS).]

tragedian /trə jeédi ən/ *n.* **1.** **SB WHO WRITES TRAGEDIES** a playwright who specializes in tragedies **2.** **ACTOR IN TRAGEDIES** an actor who plays tragic roles

tragedienne /trə jeédi én/ *n.* a woman actor who performs tragic roles (*dated*) [Mid-19thC. From French, formed from *tragédie* (see TRAGEDY).]

tragedy /trájjədi/ (*plural* **-dies**) *n.* **1.** **VERY SAD EVENT** an event in life that evokes feelings of sorrow or grief **2.** **DISASTROUS EVENT** a disastrous circumstance or event such as serious illness, financial ruin, or fatality **3.** THEATRE, LITERAT **TRAGIC PLAY** a serious play with a tragic theme, often involving a heroic struggle and the downfall of the main character **4.** LITERAT **TRAGIC PIECE OF LITERATURE** a literary work that deals with a tragic theme **5.** THEATRE, LITERAT **TRAGEDIES AS A GENRE** the genre of plays or other literary works that deal with tragic themes [14thC. Via French *tragédie* from, ultimately, Greek *tragōidia*, literally 'goat's song', from *tragos* 'goat' + *aeidein* 'to sing' (source of English *ode*).]

tragi plural of **tragus**

tragic /trájjik/, **tragical** /-ik'l/ *adj.* **1.** **DEEPLY SAD** provoking deep sadness, distress, or grief **2.** THEATRE, LITERAT **OF TRAGEDY** relating to tragedies as a dramatic genre [Mid-16thC. Via Latin from Greek *tragikos* 'of tragedy', from *tragos* 'goat' (see TRAGEDY).] —**tragically** *adv.*

tragic flaw *n.* a character flaw that causes the downfall of the protagonist in a tragedy

tragic irony *n.* the revealing to an audience of a tragic event or consequence that remains unknown to the character concerned. It is a kind of dramatic irony.

tragicomedy /trájji kómmədi/ (*plural* **-dies**) *n.* **1.** THEATRE, LITERAT **WORK COMBINING TRAGEDY AND COMEDY** a play or other literary work that combines elements of tragedy and comedy **2.** THEATRE, LITERAT **TRAGICOMIC PLAYS AS A GENRE** tragicomic plays or literary works considered as a genre **3.** **EVENT MIXING TRAGEDY AND COMEDY** an event or situation that has both tragic and comical aspects [Late 16thC. Via French *tragicomédie* from late Latin *tragicomoedia*, a shortening of *tragicocomoedia*, from *tragicus* 'tragic' (see TRAGIC) + *comoedia* 'comedy' (see COMEDY).] —**tragicomic** /trájji kómmik/ *adj.* —**tragicomical** /-kómmik'l/ *adj.* —**tragicomically** /-kómmikli/ *adv.*

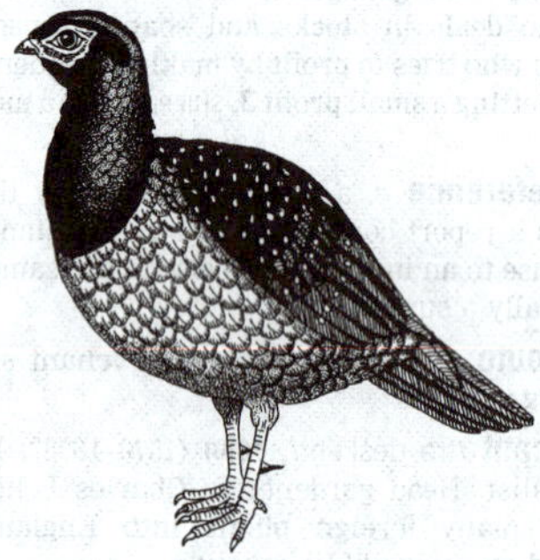

Tragopan

tragopan /trággə pan/ *n.* a brightly coloured pheasant native to Asia. The male has a bright blue bare throat and fleshy appendages on its head that look like horns. Latin name: *Tragopan temminckii.* [Early 17thC. Via Latin from Greek, type of hornbill, from *tragos* 'goat' + *pan* 'Pan', the horned god of flocks and fields.]

tragus /tráygəss/ (*plural* **-gi** /-jī, -gī/) *n.* the pointed flap of cartilage that lies above the earlobe and partly covers the entrance to the ear passage [Late 17thC. Via modern Latin from Greek *tragos* 'goat', also 'hairy part of the ear'.] —**tragal** *adj.*

trail /trayl/ *v.* **(trails, trailing, trailed) 1.** *vti.* **DRAG STH OR BE DRAGGED** to be pulled or dragged along, or pull or drag sth along **2.** *vi.* **DRAPE** to hang, grow, or float loosely ○ *Her curly hair trailed along her shoulders and down her back.* **3.** *vi.* **LAG** to walk slowly, usually from tiredness or boredom **4.** *vt.* **FOLLOW SB SECRETLY** to follow a person or animal either by staying close but out of sight or by looking for signs of movement left behind, e.g. footprints or scent **5.** *vti.* SPORTS **FALL BEHIND IN ATHLETIC COMPETITION** to be losing in a race, match, or competition **6.** *vt.* CINEMA, TV **SHOW EXCERPT OF IN ADVANCE** to advertise an upcoming film or programme by showing a clip from it **7.** *vt.* CERAMICS **DECORATE STH BY DRIZZLING LIQUID CLAY** to decorate ceramics with liquid clay (**slip**) that is drizzled or sprayed on **8.** *vt.* **TOW STH** to tow sth such as a caravan behind a vehicle **9.** *vt.* **CARRY WEAPON IN LOW POSITION** to carry a weapon horizontally or with the butt near to the ground **10.** *vti.* **MAKE TRACK** to make a track through a place ■ *n.* **1.** **ROUTE THROUGH COUNTRYSIDE** a route through the countryside that links paths and points of interest ○ *a nature trail* **2.** **MARKS WHERE SB OR STH MOVED** a sequence of marks left by sb or sth moving along a surface **3.** HUNT **SCENT FOLLOWED** a scent or track that is followed in a hunt **4.** **PATH** a path or track, especially one that has been beaten through a wild area **5.** ARMS **BOTTOM OF GUN CARRIAGE** the part of a gun carriage that rests on the ground **6.** ENG **DISTANCE FROM STEERING WHEEL** the distance between the centre of a steering wheel and a line intersecting the steering axis and the ground [14thC. Via Old French *trailler* 'to tow' from, ultimately, Latin *tragula* 'dragnet, sledge', which was probably formed from *trahere* 'to pull'.]

WORD KEY: SYNONYMS

See Synonyms at ***follow.***

trail away, trail off *vi.* to become quieter or fainter in sound and gradually fade away

trail bike *n.* a lightweight motorcycle for use on rough terrain

trailblazer /tráyl blayzər/ *n.* **1.** **PIONEER** a pioneer or innovator in a particular field **2.** **CREATOR OF ROUTE** sb who makes a new path through a wilderness —**trailblazing** *adj., n.*

trailer /tráylər/ *n.* **1.** **TOWED VEHICLE** a vehicle that is towed by another vehicle, e.g. a small open cart or a platform used for transporting a boat **2.** **PART OF LORRY** the rear part of an articulated lorry **3.** *Can, US* = **caravan** *n.* 1 **4.** CINEMA, TV **ADVERTISEMENT FOR FILM** an advertisement for a film consisting of extracts from it, shown on television or in a cinema **5.** PHOTOGRAPHY **END OF REEL OF FILM** a blank piece of film at the end of a reel **6.** **SB OR STH THAT TRAILS** sb who or sth that trails, especially sb who lags behind others **7.** BOT **PLANT** a trailing plant ■ *vt.* **(-ers, -ering, -ered) 1.** TRANSP **MOVE STH BY TRAILER** to transport sth using a trailer **2.** CINEMA, TV **ADVERTISE WITH TRAILER** to advertise a film with extracts from it

trailer park *n. US* a caravan site

trailer tent *n.* a large tent that packs into a trailer. When erected, the trailer's base becomes a raised sleeping or living area.

trailing arbutus *n.* a trailing evergreen shrub with leathery leaves and clusters of fragrant pink-and-white flowers. It is native to eastern North America. Latin name: *Epigaea repens.*

trailing edge *n.* **1.** **REAR EDGE OF WING** the rear edge of a wing, aerofoil, or propeller blade **2.** PHYS **PART OF PULSED SIGNAL** the part of a pulsed signal during which its amplitude decreases

trail mix *n.* a snack containing nuts, dried fruit, and seeds [From its use by walkers]

trail rope *n.* **1.** AEROSP **BALLOON ANCHOR** a rope that hangs from a balloon or airship and is used for mooring or as a brake **2.** ARMS **ROPE TO GUN CARRIAGE** a long rope attached to the trail of a gun carriage

train /trayn/ *n.* **1.** RAIL **LINKED RAILWAY CARRIAGES** a number of railway carriages or trucks pulled by a locomotive (*often used before a noun*) **2.** CLOTHES **TRAILING PART OF GOWN** a long part at the back of a gown or robe that trails on the ground **3.** **LONG MOVING LINE** a long moving line of people or animals **4.** MIL **ARMY FOLLOWERS** the people and military vehicles supporting or supplying an army unit **5.** **SEQUENCE OF EVENTS** a series or sequence of events, actions, or things **6.** MECH ENG **MECHANICAL SERIES** a series of connected wheels or other mechanical parts **7.** **LINE OF GUNPOWDER** a line of gunpowder or other combustible material **8.** **ENTOURAGE** a retinue or group of followers **9.** **STH DRAGGED BEHIND** sth that is pulled or dragged along or that follows sth else ■ *v.* **(trains, training, trained) 1.** *vti.* **LEARN OR TEACH SKILLS** to learn or teach sb the skills necessary to do a particular job, especially through practical experience **2.** *vt.* **DOMESTICATE ANIMAL** to teach an animal to behave in ways acceptable to people, especially by repetition or practice **3.** *vti.* SPORTS **PREPARE FOR SPORTING COMPETITION** to prepare or prepare sb for a sporting competition, usually with a planned programme of appropriate physical exercises **4.** *vt.* GARDENING **MAKE PLANT GROW AS WANTED** to make a plant, bush, or tree grow in a particular way, e.g. by pruning or tying it **5.** *vt.* HAIR **SHAPE HAIR TO ENCOURAGE PARTICULAR GROWTH** to comb or otherwise arrange hair to encourage it to grow in a particular direction **6.** *vt.* AIM STH to aim sth such as a weapon or a camera at sb or sth **7.** *vt.* **PRODUCE IMPROVEMENT** to improve sth, especially the mind, with discipline **8.** *vi.* RAIL **TRAVEL BY TRAIN** to make a journey by train (*informal*) [Mid-15thC. From Old French *train* 'sth that drags or trails behind', from *traîner* 'to draw, pull', of uncertain origin: perhaps via assumed Vulgar Latin *traginare* from Latin *trahere* 'to pull, draw'.]

—— **WORD KEY: SYNONYMS** ——
See Synonyms at **teach.**

trainband /tráyn band/ *n.* a company of trained civilian militia operating in England and North America from the 16th to the 18th centuries [Mid-17thC. Contraction of *trained band*.]

trainbearer /tráyn bairər/ *n.* an attendant who holds up the train of sb walking in a procession or other ceremony

trainee /tráy neé/ *n.* sb who is being trained to do a job (*often used before a noun*) ○ *a trainee hairdresser*

—— **WORD KEY: SYNONYMS** ——
See Synonyms at **beginner.**

trainer /tráynər/ *n.* **1.** SB WHO TRAINS ANIMALS OR PEOPLE sb who trains animals or people, especially racehorses or athletes **2.** TRAINING APPARATUS an apparatus or device used in training, especially a simulation cockpit in which pilots train **3.** FASHION **SPORTS SHOE** a sports shoe with a thick cushioned sole, often worn as leisure wear. US term **sneaker**

training /tráyning/ *n.* **1.** ACQUIRING OF SKILL the process of teaching or learning a skill or job (*often used before a noun*) ○ *a training programme* **2.** IMPROVING OF FITNESS the process of improving physical fitness by exercise and diet

Training Agency *n.* an organization that provides training and retraining for adults and school-leavers

training college *n.* a college that trains people for a particular profession, especially the teaching profession

training shoe *n.* either of a pair of trainers

training wheels *npl. US* = **stabilizers**

trainload /tráyn lōd/ *n.* the number of people or the amount of cargo that a train can carry ○ *a trainload of tourists*

trainman /tráynmən/ *n.* (*plural* **-men** /-mən/) *n.* a man who is a member of a train crew, especially a brakeman, who works to assist the conductor

train oil *n.* oil from the blubber of a whale or other marine animal. It is used, e.g. in the manufacture of soap and margarine, as a lubricant, and to dress leather. [*Train* from Low German *trān* or Middle Dutch *traen* 'train oil']

train operating company *n.* full form of **TOC**

trainspotter /tráyn spotər/ *n.* **1.** COLLECTOR OF LOCOMOTIVE NUMBERS sb whose hobby is collecting the numbers of locomotives **2.** BORING PERSON sb who is dismissed as boring because of his or her staid outlook, conventional lifestyle, or unfashionable appearance (*slang*)

trainspotting /tráyn spoting/ *n.* **1.** LEISURE HOBBY OF COLLECTING RAILWAY LOCOMOTIVE NUMBERS a hobby that consists of collecting the numbers of railway locomotives **2.** DRUGS LOOKING FOR A VEIN the search for a vein that is prominent enough to inject drugs into (*slang*)

traipse /trayps/, **trapes** *vi.* (**traipses, traipsing, traipsed; trapeses, trapesing, trapesed**) WALK PLODDINGLY to trudge in a weary way (*informal*) ■ *n.* TIRING WALK a tiring or wearisome walk [Late 16thC. Origin uncertain: perhaps from Old French *trapasser* 'to pass over, beyond' (source of English *trespass*).]

trait /trayt, tray/ *n.* **1.** INDIVIDUAL CHARACTERISTIC a particular characteristic or quality that distinguishes sb **2.** GENETICS INHERITED CHARACTERISTIC a quality or characteristic that is genetically determined **3.** INDICATION a hint or trace of sth (*literary*) [Late 16thC. Via French, literally 'act of pulling or drawing', hence 'line drawn, feature', from Latin *tractus*.]

traitor /tráytər/ *n.* sb who behaves in a disloyal or treacherous manner [13thC. Via Old French from Latin *traditor* 'betrayer', from *tradere* (see TRADITION).]

traitorous /tráytərəss/ *adj.* **1.** TREACHEROUS behaving in a disloyal or treacherous way **2.** TREASONABLE constituting treason —**traitorously** *adv.* —**traitorousness** *n.*

Trajan /tráyjən/ (AD 53?–117) Roman emperor. Becoming emperor in AD 97, he conducted several military campaigns, notably that in Dacia (modern Romania), commemorated by the carvings on Trajan's Column in Rome.

traject /trə jékt/ (**-jects, -jecting, -jected**) *vt.* to transmit or convey sth, especially sth abstract such as a quality (*literary*) [Mid-17thC. From Latin *traject-*, the past participle stem of *trajicere* 'to throw across, pass through', from *trans-* 'across, over' + *jacere* 'to throw' (source of English *jet* and *adjacent*).] —**trajection** /trə jéksh'n/ *n.*

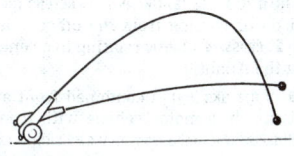

Trajectory

trajectory /trə jéktəri/ (*plural* **-ries**) *n.* **1.** AEROSP **PATH OF FLYING OBJECT** the path a projectile makes through space under the action of given forces such as thrust, wind, and gravity **2.** GEOM **CURVE INTERSECTING AT CONSTANT ANGLE** a curve or surface that intersects all of a family of curves or surfaces at a constant angle [Late 17thC. From medieval Latin *trajectorius* 'relating to throwing across', from Latin *traject-* (see TRAJECT).]

Tralee /trə leé/ town and administrative centre of County Kerry, in the southwestern Republic of Ireland. Population: 17,206 (1991).

Tralee Bay /trə leé-/ inlet of the Atlantic Ocean on the southwestern coast of the Republic of Ireland

tram¹ /tram/ *n.* **1.** TRANSP **PASSENGER VEHICLE ON RAILS** a passenger vehicle that runs along rails on a road. It has an overhead wire from which it draws electricity. US term **streetcar 2.** MINING **VEHICLE IN COAL MINE** a small vehicle on rails used to carry coal and other materials in a coal mine [Early 16thC. Originally a Scottish dialect word meaning '(shaft of) wheelbarrow', of uncertain origin: perhaps from Middle Flemish *tram* 'beam'.]

tram² /tram/ *n.* ADJUSTMENT TO KEEP MACHINE RUNNING a fine adjustment that keeps a machine functioning correctly ■ *vt.* (**trams, tramming, trammed**) ADJUST MECHANICAL PARTS ACCURATELY to adjust or align mechanical parts accurately [Late 19thC. From *tram-staff* 'straight edge used by millwrights to adjust the millstone spindle', from *tram* 'instrument for drawing ellipses', shortening of TRAMMEL.]

tram³ /tram/ *n.* heavy silk thread used for the horizontal weave in velvet or silk [Late 17thC. Via French *trame* from Latin *trama* 'woof of a web'.]

tramcar /trám kaar/ *n.* = **tram¹** *n.* 1

tramline /trám līn/ *n.* **1.** TRANSP **TRAM TRACK** a track for a tram **2.** TRANSP **TRAM ROUTE** the route driven by a tram **3.** RACKET GAMES **MARKINGS ON COURT** either of a pair of parallel lines at the sides of a tennis court or at the side and back of a badminton court that delimit the singles and doubles court (*informal; usually used in the plural*)

trammel /trámm'l/ *n.* **1.** LIMITATION TO FREEDOM sth that limits a person's freedom **2.** ZOOL **FISHING NET** a fishing net consisting of a fine net between two layers of coarse mesh **3.** DRAWING INSTRUMENT an instrument used to draw ellipses **4.** MECH ENG = **tram²** *n.* **5.** HOUSEHOLD **FIREPLACE HOOK** a hook in a fireplace on which a kettle or pot can be hung and raised or lowered ■ *vt.* (**-mels, -melling, -melled**) **1.** CONFINE SB to restrain sb or sth **2.** ENSNARE STH to catch or entangle sb or sth

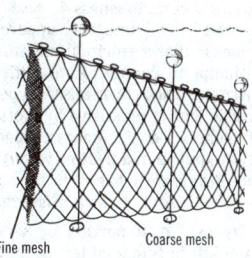

Fine mesh   Coarse mesh

Trammel

3. MECH ENG = **tram²** *v.* [14thC. Via Old French *tramail* from late Latin *tremaculum*, from Latin *tres* 'three' + *macula* 'mesh'.]

tramontana /trámmon táanə/ *n.* a cold dry wind that blows down from mountains, especially a north wind that blows into Italy from the Alps [Late 18thC. Via Italian, 'north wind', from, ultimately, Latin *transmontanus* 'beyond the mountains', which was coined from *trans-* 'trans-' + *mont-*, the stem of *mons* (see MOUNTAIN).]

tramontane /trə món tayn/ *adj.* **1.** BEYOND MOUNTAINS living or situated on the far side of the mountains, especially the Alps as seen from Italy **2.** FOREIGN foreign and uncivilized, originally from an Italian point of view ■ *n.* **1.** METEOROL = **tramontana 2.** FOREIGNER sb who lives or comes from beyond the mountains, especially from beyond the Alps as seen from Italy [Late 16thC. Via Italian *tramontano* from Latin *transmontanus* (see TRANSMONTANE.]

tramp /tramp/ *n.* **1.** VAGRANT sb who has no home and travels on foot, often begging for a living **2.** *UK* LONG JOURNEY ON FOOT a long journey on foot, e.g. as part of a walking tour **3.** SOUND OF FEET the sound of heavy footsteps or horses' hooves **4.** HEAVY STEP a heavy step or tread **5.** OFFENSIVE TERM an offensive term that deliberately insults a woman who is considered sexually promiscuous or who works as a prostitute (*slang insult*) **6.** METAL PLATE ON BOOT a metal plate that protects the sole of a boot when the wearer is digging **7.** GARDENING PART OF SPADE FOR FOOT the part of a spade on which the digger's foot presses ■ *v.* (**tramps, tramping, tramped**) **1.** *vi.* TREAD HEAVILY to tread heavily or noisily **2.** *vi.* WALK to walk, especially a long way **3.** *vi.* LIVE AS VAGRANT to live or wander about as a vagrant **4.** *vt.* COVER DISTANCE ON FOOT to traverse an area, especially wearily, or cover a distance in a steady weary way **5.** *vt.* CRUSH STH UNDERFOOT to crush sth by treading on it **6.** *vi.* *NZ* HIKE IN BUSH to go hiking in the countryside for recreation [14thC. From Middle Low German *trampen* 'to stamp'. Ultimately from a prehistoric Germanic word that is also the ancestor of English *trap*. The noun is first recorded in the mid-17thC.] —**tramper** *n.* —**tramping** *n.* —**trampish** *adj.*

tramping club *n. NZ* an organization of people who go walking in the bush

tramping hut *n. NZ* a hut for the use of people walking in the bush

trample /trámp'l/ (**-ples, -pling, -pled**) *vti.* **1.** TREAD ON STH to tread heavily, or to tread heavily on sth or sb so as to cause damage or injury **2.** TREAT SB ARROGANTLY to behave in an insulting contemptuous way or to treat sb in a hurtful insulting way [14thC. Formed from TRAMP.] —**trampler** *n.*

trampoline /trámpə leen/ *n.* a strong sheet, usually of canvas, that is stretched tightly on a horizontal frame to which it is connected by springs. It is used for jumping and tumbling. [Late 18thC. From Italian *trampolino* 'springboard', from *trampoli* 'stilts'.] —**trampoline** *vi.* —**trampoliner** *n.* —**trampolinist** *n.*

tramp steamer *n.* a merchant ship that carries cargo but does not follow a fixed route

tramway /trám way/ *n.* **1.** = **tramline. 2.** SYSTEM USING TRAMS a light-rail system that uses trams, or a company that operates such a system

trance /traanss/ *n.* **1.** DAZED STATE a state in which sb is dazed or stunned or in some other way unaware of the environment and unable to respond to stimuli **2.** HYPNOTIC STATE a hypnotic or cataleptic state **3.**

RAPTUROUS STATE a state of rapture or exaltation in which sb loses consciousness **4.** PARANORMAL **SPIRITUAL MEDIUM'S STATE** the state of apparent semi-unconsciousness that a spiritual medium enters into in an attempt to communicate with the dead **5.** MUSIC **HYPNOTIC ELECTRONIC DANCE MUSIC** a type of electronic dance music with a repetitive hypnotic beat. It is a kind of techno. ■ *vt.* **(trances, trancing, tranced) ENTRANCE SB** to put sb in a trance (*literary*) [14thC. From Old French *transe*, from *transir* 'to be numb with fear', originally 'to die', from Latin *transire* (see TRANSIENT).]

tranche /traansh/ *n.* a portion or section, often a division of sth in financial terms, such as a single repayment of a loan or an individual class of securities [Mid-20thC. From French, literally 'slice', from Old French *trenchier* 'to cut' (source of English *trench*).]

trannie /tránni/, **tranny** (*plural* **-nies**) *n.* **1.** RADIO a transistor radio (*informal*) **2.** TRANSSEXUAL a transsexual (*slang*) **3.** TRANSVESTITE a transvestite (*slang*) [Mid-20thC. Shortening.]

tranquil /trángkwil/ *adj.* **1.** FREE FROM COMMOTION free of any disturbance or commotion ○ *a tranquil morning* **2.** COMPOSED free from or showing no signs of anxiety or agitation [Mid-15thC. Via French *tranquille* from Latin *tranquillus*, which may have been formed from the same base as *quies* 'quiet' (source of English *coy* and *quiet*).] —**tranquilly** *adv.* —**tranquilness** *n.*

——— WORD KEY: SYNONYMS ———
See Synonyms at **calm**.

tranquilize *vti.* US = tranquillize

tranquillise *vt.* = tranquillize

tranquilliser *n.* = tranquillizer

tranquillity /trang kwílləti/ *n.* a state of peace and calm [14thC. Via Old French *tranquillité* from Latin *tranquillitas* 'quietness', from, ultimately, *quies* 'quiet' (source of English *coy* and *quiet*).]

tranquillize (**-quillizes, -quillizing, -quillized**), **tranquillise** (**-lises, -lising, -lised**) *v.* **1.** *vt.* MAKE SB CALM to induce calmness in a person or an animal, usually with medication **2.** *vi.* BECOME CALM to become calm or calmer **3.** *vi.* HAVE CALMING EFFECT to have a calming effect —**tranquilization** /trángkwi ı̄ záysh'n/ *n.*

tranquillizer, tranquilliser *n.* **1.** CALMING DRUG a medication that reduces anxiety and tension. Major tranquillizers are used to treat such psychoses as schizophrenia, while minor tranquillizers such as diazepam treat anxiety and other lesser conditions. **2.** STH MAKING PERSON OR ANIMAL CALM anything that renders a person or animal calm

trans. *abbr.* **1.** transaction **2.** transferred **3.** GRAM transitive **4.** translated **5.** translation **6.** transport **7.** transpose **8.** transverse

trans- *prefix.* **1.** across, on the other side of, beyond ○ *transcontinental* ○ *transfinite* **2.** through ○ *transdermal* **3.** indicating change, transfer, or conversion ○ *transliterate* [From Latin *trans* 'across, over, through']

transact /tran zákt, -sákt/ (**-acts, -acting, -acted**) *vti.* to conduct or carry out sth such as business [Late 16thC. Back-formation from TRANSACTION.] —**transactor** *n.*

transactinide /transs ákti nī́d/ *n.* an element with an atomic number greater than 103 (*often used before a noun*) [Late 20thC. Coined from TRANS- + ACTINIDE by Dr Glenn T. Seaborg, modelled on transuranium, which he discovered.]

transaction /tran záksh'n, -sák-/ *n.* **1.** BUSINESS **BUSINESS** a business deal that is being negotiated or has been settled **2.** BUSINESS **ACT OF NEGOTIATING** the act of negotiating sth or carrying out a business deal **3.** INTERACTION a communication or activity between two or more people that influences and affects all of them (*formal*) **4.** COMPUT **ADDITION TO DATABASE** an action that adds, removes, or changes data in a database or other computer program ■ **transactions** *npl.* PROCEEDINGS the published records of a learned society [Mid-15thC. Via French from, ultimately, Latin *transigere* 'to drive through, accomplish', from *agere* 'to drive, do' (see AGENT).] —**transactional** *adj.* —**transactionally** *adv.*

transactional analysis *n.* a form of psychotherapy that emphasizes the interactions within and between individuals and classifies these interactions as 'adult', 'parent', or 'child'

transactivation /tránss akti váysh'n, tránz-/ *n.* the process whereby an infecting virus activates another virus's genes that are already integrated into the chromosome of the host bacterium, inducing the host cell to replicate the initial virus

transalpine /tranz ál pīn/ *adj.* **1.** BEYOND THE ALPS relating to or found in the area beyond the Alps, especially as seen from Italy **2.** CROSSING ALPS relating to or engaged in crossing the Alps ■ *n.* SB FROM BEYOND THE ALPS sb who comes from or lives beyond the Alps, especially as seen from Italy [Late 16thC. From Latin *transalpinus*, from *alpes* 'the Alps'.]

transaminase /tranz ámmi nayz, -nayss/ *n.* an enzyme that catalyses the transfer of an amino group in the process of transamination

transamination /tranz ámmi náysh'n/ *n.* a process in the metabolism of amino acids and in the synthesis of proteins in the body in which one amino acid is formed from another

transatlantic /tránzət lántik/ *adj.* **1.** BEYOND THE ATLANTIC situated on or coming from the other side of the Atlantic **2.** CROSSING ATLANTIC relating to or engaged in crossing the Atlantic

transaxle /tránz aks'l/ *n.* a combined front axle and transmission in a motor vehicle with front-wheel drive [Mid-20thC. Coined from TRANSMISSION + AXLE.]

transboundary /tránz bówndəri/ *adj.* crossing or existing across national boundaries

Transcaucasia /tránz kaw káyzhə, -káyzi ə/ region in southeastern Europe, south of the Caucasus Mountains, between the Black and Caspian seas, forming the southern part of Caucasia. It consists of the republics of Georgia, Armenia, and Azerbaijan. —**Transcaucasian** *adj.*

transceiver /tran seévər/ *n.* **1.** RADIO COMBINED RADIO TRANSMITTER AND RECEIVER a radio transmitter and receiver combined in a single, often portable unit **2.** COMPUT DATA TRANSMITTER AND RECEIVER a device that can receive and transmit data, e.g. a modem [Mid-20thC. A blend of TRANSMITTER and RECEIVER.]

transcend /tran sénd/ (**-scends, -scending, -scended**) *vt.* **1.** GO BEYOND LIMIT to go beyond a limit or range, e.g. of thought or belief **2.** SURPASS STH to go beyond sth in quality or achievement **3.** BE INDEPENDENT OF WORLD to exist above and apart from the material world [14thC. Via Old French from Latin *transcendere* 'to climb over, beyond', from *scandere* 'to climb, mount'.]

transcendence /tran séndənss/, **transcendency** /-séndənssi/ *n.* **1.** INDEPENDENCE FROM WORLD existence above and apart from the material world **2.** GREATER STATUS the quality or state of exceeding or surpassing sth

transcendent /tran séndənt/ *adj.* **1.** BETTER superior in quality or achievement **2.** PHILOS BEYOND LIMITS OF EXPERIENCE in Kant's philosophical system, exceeding the limits of experience and therefore unknowable except hypothetically **3.** PHILOS BEYOND CATEGORIES above or outside all known categories **4.** RELIG INDEPENDENT OF THE WORLD existing outside the material universe and so not limited by it ■ *n.* STH OR SB TRANSCENDENT sth that or sb who is or appears to be transcendent —**transcendently** *adv.* —**transcendentness** *n.*

transcendental /trán sen dént'l/ *adj.* **1.** = transcendent *adj.* 1 **2.** PHILOS NOT EXPERIENCED BUT KNOWABLE independent of human experience of phenomena but within the range of knowledge **3.** RELIG MYSTICAL relating to mystical or supernatural experience and therefore beyond the material world **4.** MATH NOT ALGEBRAIC used to describe a number or function that is not algebraic and is not the root of an algebraic equation ■ *n.* MATH NUMBER IMPOSSIBLE TO EXPRESS AS INTEGER a number that cannot be expressed as an integer, e.g. a nonrepeating decimal such as pi [Early 17thC. From late Latin *transcendentalis* 'transcending the bounds of all categories', from *transcendere* (see TRANSCEND).] —**transcendentality** /trán sen den tálləti/ *n.* —**transcendentally** *adv.*

transcendentalism /trán sen dént'lizəm/ *n.* **1.** PHILOS PHILOSOPHY EMPHASIZING REASONING a system of philosophy, especially that of Kant, that regards the processes of reasoning as the key to knowledge of reality **2.** PHILOS PHILOSOPHY EMPHASIZING DIVINE a system of philosophy, especially that associated with Ralph Waldo Emerson and other New England writers, that emphasizes intuition or the divine **3.** TRANSCENDENTAL THOUGHT transcendental thought or language **4.** TRANSCENDENTAL NATURE the state or quality of being transcendental —**transcendentalist** *n., adj.*

transcendental meditation *n.* a form of meditation in which a mantra is repeated silently. It is based on Hindu traditions.

transcontinental /tránz konti nént'l/ *adj.* **1.** ACROSS CONTINENT extending across a continent **2.** BEYOND CONTINENT situated on or coming from the other side of a continent ■ *n.* TRANSP TRAIN CROSSING CONTINENT a train or railway that crosses a continent —**transcontinentally** *adv.*

transcribe /tran skríb/ (**-scribes, -scribing, -scribed**) *vt.* **1.** COPY OUT STH to write out an exact copy of sth **2.** EXPAND STH IN WRITING to write sth out in full from notes or shorthand **3.** PHON WRITE SOUNDS PHONETICALLY to write speech sounds phonetically **4.** TRANSLATE STH to translate or transliterate sth **5.** MUSIC REARRANGE MUSIC to arrange a piece of music for a different instrument, voice, or combination **6.** BROADCAST RECORD STH FOR LATER BROADCASTING to record sth so that it can be broadcast at a later time **7.** BROADCAST BROADCAST STH TRANSCRIBED to broadcast sth that has been transcribed earlier **8.** COMPUT TRANSFER STH TO OTHER STORAGE FORMAT to transfer information from one way of storing it on computer to another, or from a computer to an external storage device **9.** GENETICS CONVERT CODE FOR TRANSMISSION TO RNA to convert the genetic code carried by DNA into an equivalent form carried by a molecule of messenger RNA **10.** GENETICS CONVERT GENETIC CODE INTO DNA MOLECULE to convert the genetic code carried by the RNA of a retrovirus into a molecule of DNA [Mid-16thC. From Latin *transcribere* 'to copy, convey', literally 'to write across', from *scribere* 'to write'.] —**transcribable** *adj.* —**transcriber** *n.*

transcript /trán skript/ *n.* **1.** WRITTEN RECORD a written record of sth, e.g. a copy of the script of a broadcast programme or a record of court proceedings **2.** US EDUC STUDENT'S ACADEMIC HISTORY an official document showing the educational work of a student in a North American school or college **3.** COPY any copy or record **4.** GENETICS RNA WITH TRANSCRIBED CODE a molecule of messenger RNA that carries coded genetic information converted from the genetic code held by the DNA during the process of transcription in living cells **5.** GENETICS DNA CARRYING CODED RETROVIRUS the DNA that carries the coded information of a retrovirus, converted from the genetic code held by the virus's RNA during transcription following the infection of a living cell [Mid-15thC. From Latin *transcriptum*, from the past participle of *transcribere* (see TRANSCRIBE).]

transcriptase /tran skríp tayz, -tayss/ *n.* an enzyme that catalyses the synthesis of messenger RNA from a DNA template during transcription

transcription /tran skrípsh'n/ *n.* **1.** TRANSCRIBING the act or process of transcribing sth **2.** TRANSCRIPT sth that has been transcribed **3.** PHON PHONETIC REPRESENTATION a phonetic representation of speech using special symbols **4.** GENETICS TRANSFER OF GENETIC CODE the first step in carrying out genetic instructions in living cells, in which the genetic code is transferred from DNA to molecules of messenger RNA, which subsequently direct protein manufacture **5.** GENETICS TRANSFER OF GENETIC INFORMATION the first step in the replication of a retrovirus following its infection of a living cell, in which its genetic code is transferred from RNA to a molecule of RNA

transcriptional /tran skrípsh'nəl/ *adj.* relating to transcripts, or to the transcribing of things —**transcriptionally** *adv.*

transcriptive /tran skríptiv/ *adj.* used for transcribing or in the form of a transcript —**transcriptively** *adv.*

transcultural /tranz kúlchərəl/ *adj.* extending across cultures or involving more than one culture

transculturation /tránz kulchə ráysh'n/ *n.* the change in a culture brought about by the diffusion within it of elements from other cultures

transcurrent /tranz kúrrənt/ *adj.* running across sth, especially perpendicular to an expected direction or flow [Early 17thC. From Latin, from the present participle stem of *transcurrere* 'to run across, traverse', from *currere* 'to run' (see CURRENT).]

transcutaneous /tránz kyŏŏ táyni əss/ *adj.* = **transdermal**

transcutaneous electrical nerve stimulation /tránz kyoo tàynee əss-/ *n.* MED full form of **TENS**

transdermal /tranz dúrm'l/ *adj.* used to describe sth, especially a drug, that is introduced into the body through the skin

transdermal patch *n.* a patch applied to the skin as a way of releasing a preset dose of medication into the body in a controlled manner

transduce /tranz dyóoss/ (**-duces, -ducing, -duced**) *vt.* **1.** PHYS CONVERT INTO DIFFERENT ENERGY to change one type of energy into another type **2.** GENETICS TRANSFER GENETIC MATERIAL to effect the transfer of genetic material from one bacterium to another using a bacteriophage [Mid-20thC. Back-formation from TRANSDUCER.]

transducer /tranz dyóossər/ *n.* **1.** PHYS DEVICE THAT CONVERTS ENERGY a device that transforms one type of energy into another, e.g. a microphone, a photoelectric cell, or a car horn **2.** BIOL BIOLOGICAL CONVERTER OF ENERGY a biological entity that converts energy in one form to another, e.g. the rods and cones of the eye or the hair cells of the ear [Early 20thC. Formed from Latin *transducere* 'to lead across, transfer' (see TRADUCE).]

transduction /tranz dúksh'n/ *n.* **1.** GENETICS TRANSFER OF GENETIC MATERIAL the transfer of genetic material from one bacterium to another using a bacteriophage **2.** PHYSIOL TRANSPORTATION OF STIMULI TO NERVOUS SYSTEM the conversion of stimuli detected in receptor cells to electrical impulses that are then transported by the nervous system, as occurs when the ear converts sound waves into nerve impulses —**transductional** *adj.*

transect /tran sékt/ *vt.* (**-sects, -secting, -sected**) CUT ACROSS STH to divide sth by running or cutting across it ■ *n.* ECOL LINE FOR ECOLOGICAL MEASUREMENTS a strip of ground along which ecological measurements, e.g. the number of organisms, are made at regular intervals [Mid-17thC. Coined from TRANS- + INTERSECT.] —**transection** /tran séksh'n/ *n.*

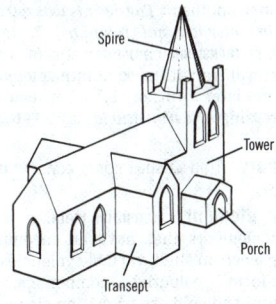

Transept

transept /trán sept/ *n.* **1.** WINGS OF CHURCH the part of a cross-shaped church that runs at right angles to the long central part (**nave**) **2.** ARM OF TRANSEPT either of the two arms of a transept [Mid-16thC. From modern Latin *transeptum*, literally 'across enclosure', from Latin *saeptum* 'enclosure, wall, fence'.] —**transeptal** /tran sépt'l/ *adj.*

transeunt /tránzi ənt/, **transient** *adj.* that produces effects outside the mind

transf. *abbr.* transferred

trans-fatty acid /tránss fátti-/, **trans-fat** /tránss fat/ *n.* a potentially harmful unsaturated fat produced when a liquid vegetable oil is solidified by the process of hydrogenation, especially in the manufacture of low-fat spreads. Trans-fatty acids are viewed as a health risk because they raise cholesterol levels.

transfect /transs fékt/ (**-fects, -fecting, -fected**) *vt.* to infect a cell with viral nucleic acid or DNA from a source other than the cell itself [Mid-20thC. Backformation from TRANSFECTION.]

transfection /transs féksh'n/ *n.* the infection of a cell with viral genetic material leading to the subsequent production of the virus in the cell [Mid-20thC. Coined from TRANS- + INFECTION.]

transfer *v.* /transs fúr/ (**-fers, -ferring, -ferred**) **1.** *vti.* MOVE FROM ONE PLACE TO ANOTHER to move from one place to another, or cause sb or sth to do so **2.** *vti.* PASS FROM ONE PERSON TO ANOTHER to pass from one person, group, or organization to another, or cause sth to be passed from one person, group, or organization to another ○ *not clear when power will transfer to the new government* **3.** *vti.* BUSINESS START WORKING ELSEWHERE to employ sb, or to begin employment, at a different job or in a different place while working for the same company ○ *transfer to Chicago* **4.** *vti.* SPORTS START PLAYING FOR DIFFERENT CLUB to sign, or sign sb, for a different sports club, especially in professional football **5.** *vti.* TRANSP CHANGE VEHICLES to change from one vehicle or method of transport to another, or cause sb to do this **6.** *vt.* LAW GIVE OWNERSHIP OF to pass ownership rights in sth to sb else ○ *transfer a deed* **7.** *vt.* PUT IMAGE ON ANOTHER SURFACE to copy a design or image from a piece of paper onto a different material **8.** *vti.* EDUC CHANGE SCHOOLS OR SUBJECTS to move from one school or university to another, or change from one course to another ■ *n.* /tránss fur/ **1.** CHANGE OF PLACE the conveying of sb or sth from one place, e.g. one department of an organization, to another **2.** DESIGN APPLIED TO SURFACE an image on a piece of film or paper that is specially designed to be lifted off by heat or pressure and applied permanently to the surface of a material **3.** SB TRANSFERRED sb who is transferred, e.g. a football player moving from one team to another **4.** LAW CONVEYANCE the passing of rights or property from one person to another, or a document that conveys rights or property between persons **5.** FIN RECORDING OF SALE the recording of a change of ownership of shares or bonds in the books of the issuer **6.** US TRANSP TICKET ALLOWING PASSENGER TO TRANSFER a ticket that allows a passenger to change from one vehicle to another on a journey, or the place where this is done [14thC. From Latin *transferre* 'to carry across', from *ferre* 'to carry' (see FERTILE).]

transferable /transs fúrəb'l/, **transferrable** *adj.* able to be transferred, especially to sb else's ownership —**transferability** /transs fúrə bílləti/ *n.*

transferable vote *n.* a vote that will be given to a voter's second choice if his or her first choice candidate is eliminated from the ballot

transferase /tránssfə rayz, -rayss/ *n.* any enzyme that catalyses the transfer of a chemical group from one molecule to another

transfer characteristic *n.* a graphic illustration of the relationship between the input and output of an electronic system

transferee /tránss fur reé/ *n.* **1.** LAW SB TO WHOM STH IS TRANSFERRED sb to whom a right or property is transferred by law **2.** SB TRANSFERRED sb who has been transferred, e.g. to a new department or organization

transference /tránssfərənss/ *n.* **1.** ACT OF TRANSFERRING the transferring of sth from one place or person to another **2.** PROCESS OF BEING TRANSFERRED the change from one person or place to another that happens when sth is transferred **3.** PSYCHOL REDIRECTION OF FEELING the process in psychoanalysis or other psychotherapy whereby sb unconsciously redirects feelings, fears, or emotions onto a new object, often the analyst or therapist —**transferential** /tránssfə rénsh'l/ *adj.*

transfer factor *n.* a polypeptide that is produced by white blood cells and can transfer immunity from one cell to another or from one person to another

transfer fee *n.* a fee that is paid for a professional footballer or rugby player who is transferred from one club to another before his contract has expired

transfer list *n.* a list of footballers who are available to be transferred

transferor /transs fúrər/, **transferrer** *n.* sb who transfers a title, right, or property to another person

transfer payment *n.* an item of personal income that comes from the state or a financial institution and is not included in calculating the national income

transferrable *adj.* = transferable

transferral /transs fúrəl/ *n.* = transference *n.* 1

transferral *n.* = transferal

transferrer *n.* = transferor

transferrin /transs férrin/ *n.* a protein in blood serum that binds to iron and transports it to the bone marrow where it is used in the production of red blood cells [Mid-20thC. Coined from TRANS- + Latin *ferrum* 'iron' + -IN.]

transfer RNA *n.* a type of RNA that attaches amino acids to a ribosome to allow protein to be produced in living cells

transfiguration /transs fíggəráysh'n/ *n.* **1.** CHANGE IN APPEARANCE a dramatic change in appearance, especially one that glorifies or exalts sb **2.** TRANSFIGURED STATE the transfiguring of sb or sth, or the changed state that results

Transfiguration *n.* **1.** RADIANT APPEARANCE OF JESUS CHRIST the radiant appearance of Jesus Christ on the mountaintop before three of his disciples, as recorded in the Bible **2.** FESTIVAL OF THE TRANSFIGURATION the Christian festival that commemorates the Transfiguration, held on 6 August or, in the Eastern Orthodox Church, on 19 August

transfigure /transs fíggər/ (**-ures, -uring, -ured**) *vt.* to transform the appearance of sb or sth, revealing great beauty, spirituality, or magnificence [14thC. From Latin *transfigurare* 'to change the shape of', literally 'to (put) across the shape', from *figura* 'shape' (see FIGURE).] —**transfigurement** *n.*

transfinite /transs fí nīt/ *adj.* used to describe a mathematical entity such as a number, group, or quantity that extends beyond infinity [Early 20thC. From German *transfinit*, from Latin *trans-* 'across, over' + *finitus* 'finite, limited'.]

transfinite number *n.* a system of cardinal and ordinal numbers, used in the comparison of infinite sets, to which several types of infinity can be assigned concurrently

transfix /transs fíks/ (**-fixes, -fixing, -fixed**) *vt.* **1.** PIERCE THROUGH SB to pierce sb or sth through with a weapon or other sharp object **2.** MAKE SB IMMOBILE WITH SHOCK to shock or terrify sb so much as to induce a momentary inability to move **3.** MED CUT COMPLETELY THROUGH LIMB to cut through a part of the body completely, e.g. when amputating a limb [Late 16thC. Directly or via Old French *transfixer* from Latin *transfix-*, the past participle stem of *transfigere* 'to pierce, run through', literally 'to fix through', from *figere* 'to fix' (see FIX).] —**transfixion** *n.*

transform[1] /transs fáwrm/ (**-forms, -forming, -formed**) *v.* **1.** *vt.* CHANGE STH DRAMATICALLY to change people or things completely, especially improving their appearance or usefulness **2.** *vi.* UNDERGO TOTAL CHANGE to change completely for the better **3.** *vt.* PHYS CONVERT STH TO DIFFERENT ENERGY to convert one form of energy to another **4.** *vt.* ELEC ENG CHANGE ELECTRICAL CURRENT BY TRANSFORMER to increase or decrease current or voltage by means of a transformer **5.** *vt.* MATH CHANGE MATHEMATICAL EXPRESSION BY OPERATOR to change the form of a mathematical expression in keeping with a mathematical rule, especially by the substitution of variables or the change of coordinates **6.** *vt.* LING CHANGE CONSTRUCTION BY LINGUISTIC TRANSFORMATION to apply transformational rules to a linguistic construction [14thC. Directly or via French *transformer* from Latin *transformare*, literally 'to form across', from *formare* 'to form' (see FORM).] —**transformable** *adj.* —**transformative** *adj.*

——— **WORD KEY: SYNONYMS** ———
See Synonyms at *change*.

transform[2] /tránss fawrm/ *n.* **1.** LING = transformation *n.* 7 **2.** MATH RESULT OF MATHEMATICAL TRANSFORMATION a process or rule by which one mathematical entity such as a line or expression can be derived from another

transformation /tránsfər máysh'n/ *n.* **1.** COMPLETE CHANGE a complete change, usually into sth with an improved appearance or usefulness **2.** TRANSFORMING the act or process of transforming sb or sth **3.** MATH SUBSTITUTION OF VARIABLES the mathematical conversion of an expression, equation, or function into another equivalent entity, e.g. by the substitution of one set of variables with another **4.** BIOL **CELL MODIFICATION** the conversion of a normal cell into a malignant cell brought about by the action of a carcinogen or virus **5.** MATH **CHANGE IN POSITION OF AXIS** a change in the position or direction of the axes of a mathematical coordinate system without changing their relative angles **6.** PHYS **CHANGE IN ATOMIC NUCLEUS** the change of one type of atom to another, resulting from a nuclear reaction **7.** LING **CHANGE OF GRAMMATICAL STRUCTURE** in transformational grammar, the process of converting one linguistic construction or structure to another, following the rules that convert deep structure to surface structure **8.** LING **STAGE IN TRANSFORMATIONAL PROCESS** in transformational grammar, a construction or structure generated by using the rules that convert deep structure into surface structure **9.** THEATRE **SUDDEN SET CHANGE** a sudden changing of a stage set that takes place in sight of the audience **10.** GENETICS **GENETIC CHANGE** a permanent change in the genetic make-up of a cell when it acquires foreign DNA

transformational grammar /tránsfər máysh'nəl-/ *n.* a kind of grammar that is based on the theory that language has a deep structure and that there are rules that transform the deep structure into the surface structure. It uses transformational rules to describe a language.

transformational rule /tránsfər máysh'nəl-/ *n.* **1.** LING **RULE CHANGING UNDERLYING GRAMMATICAL STRUCTURE** in transformational grammar, a rule that generates one stage from another in the conversion of deep structure into surface structure **2.** LOGIC **RULE FOR DERIVING THEOREMS** in logic, a rule for deriving theorems from axioms

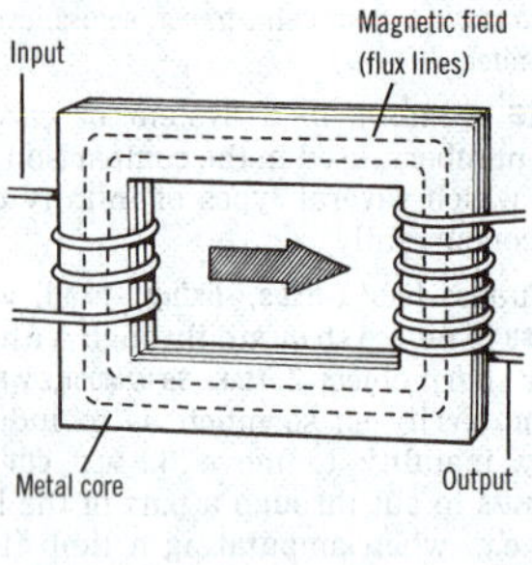

Transformer

transformer /transs fáwrmər/ *n.* **1.** ELEC ENG, ELEC **DEVICE FOR CHANGING ELECTRICAL ENERGY** a device that transfers electrical energy from one alternating circuit to another with a change in voltage, current, phase, or impedance **2.** **SB OR STH THAT TRANSFORMS** sb who or sth that effects a transformation

transformism /transs fáwrmizəm/ *n.* the theory of evolution —**transformist** *n.*

transfuse /transs fyóoz/ (**-fuses, -fusing, -fused**) *vt.* **1.** **SPREAD THROUGHOUT STH** to spread throughout sth and affect every part of it **2.** **TRANSFER STH BY POURING** to pour sth from one container into another (*formal or technical*) **3.** MED **GIVE BLOOD TO SB** to administer blood obtained from one person into the bloodstream of another person **4.** MED **PUT FLUID INTO BLOODSTREAM OF** to administer a fluid such as saline or plasma into sb's bloodstream [Early 15thC. From Latin *transfus-*, the past participle stem of *transfundere* 'to decant, transfer', literally 'to pour across (into another vessel)', from *fundere* 'to pour' (see FUSE).] —**transfusable** *adj.* —**transfuser** *n.* —**transfusive** /-fyóossiv, -fyóoziv/ *adj.*

transfusion /transs fyóozh'n/ *n.* **1.** **TRANSFUSING** the act or process of transfusing sth **2.** MED **GIVING OF BLOOD** the transfer of whole blood, blood components, or bone marrow from a healthy donor into the bloodstream of sb who has lost blood or who has a blood disorder

transgenic /tranz jénnik/ *adj.* GENETICS **1.** **WITH GENES FROM DIFFERENT SPECIES** used to describe an animal or plant that contains genes from a different species, transferred using genetic engineering techniques. Using such techniques can, e.g. induce disease resistance in plants and modify animals so that their organs can be used in human transplants. **2.** **INVOLVING TRANSFER OF GENETIC MATERIAL** used to describe the technique of transferring genetic material from one organism into the DNA of another —**transgenically** *adv.*

transgress /tranz gréss/ (**-gresses, -gressing, -gressed**) *v.* **1.** *vi.* **DO WRONG** to commit a crime or do wrong by disobeying a law, command, or moral code ○ *He transgressed against the organization's code of conduct.* **2.** *vt.* **BREAK LAW** to break a law, rule, or moral code ○ *transgress the law* **3.** *vt.* **OVERSTEP PROPER LIMIT** to go beyond a limit, usually in a blameworthy way ○ *She'd transgressed the bounds of civil behaviour.* [15thC. Directly or via French *transgresser* from Latin *transgress-*, the past participle stem of *transgredi* 'to step across, go over', from *gradi* 'to step, go'.] —**transgressive** *adj.* —**transgressively** *adv.* —**transgressor** *n.*

transgression /tranz grésh'n/ *n.* **1.** **ACTION VIOLATING LAW OR CODE** a crime or any act that violates a law, command, or moral code **2.** **COMMISSION OF WRONGS** the committing of acts that violate a law, command, or moral code **3.** **OVERSTEPPING A LIMIT** an act or the process of overstepping a limit

tranship *vti.* = **transship**

transhumance /transs hyóomənss/ *n.* the practice of moving livestock between different grazing lands according to season, especially up to mountain pastures in summer and back down into the valleys in winter [Early 20thC. From French, from *transhumer*, literally 'to go across ground', ultimately from Latin *humus* 'ground'.] —**transhumant** /-hyóomənt/ *adj.*

transient /tránzi ənt/ *adj.* **1.** **SHORT IN DURATION** lasting for only a short time and quickly coming to an end, disappearing, or changing ○ *a transient emotion* ○ *transient sunlight on an otherwise cloudy day* **2.** **NOT PERMANENTLY SETTLED IN PLACE** staying in a place for only a short period of time ○ *transient workers* **3.** PHILOS = **transeunt** ■ *n.* **1.** **SB STAYING BRIEFLY** sb who stays in a place for only a short time, e.g. a migrant labourer or hotel guest **2.** ELEC ENG **BRIEF DISTURBANCE IN ELECTRICAL CIRCUIT** an oscillation or brief disturbance in a system, e.g. a sudden pulse of current or voltage in an electrical circuit [Late 16thC. Alteration of Latin *transiens* (stem *transeunt-*), the present participle of *transire* 'to pass away, go across', from *ire* 'to go'.] —**transience** *n.* —**transiency** *n.* —**transiently** *adv.*

transilluminate /tránzi lóomi nayt/ (**-nates, -nating, -nated**) *vt.* to shine a bright light through a body organ or cavity to detect disease or other abnormality —**transillumination** /tránzi loomi náysh'n/ *n.* —**transilluminator** /tránzi lóomi naytər/ *n.*

transistor /tran zístər/ *n.* **1.** ELECTRON ENG **SOLID-STATE ELECTRONIC DEVICE** a small low-powered solid-state electronic device consisting of a semiconductor and at least three electrodes, used as an amplifier and rectifier and frequently incorporated into integrated circuit chips **2.** **RADIO** a transistor radio [Mid-20thC. Blend of TRANSFER and RESISTOR (from its transference of electrical current across a resistor).]

transistorize /tran zístə rīz/ (**-izes, -izing, -ized**), **transistorise** (**-ises, -ising, -ised**) *vt.* to equip a device or circuit with transistors

transistor radio *n.* a small portable radio using transistors in its circuits

transit /tránzit/ *n.* **1.** **ACT OF TRAVELLING ACROSS STH** the act of travelling or being transported through or across an area, over a distance, or from one place to another ○ *a transit permit* **2.** **ROUTE** a particular route or method used in travelling through or across an area ○ *overland transit* **3.** *US* TRANSP **PUBLIC TRANSPORT** the transportation of passengers by means of a local public transport system ○ *travelled by rapid transit* **4.** ASTRON **PLANET'S CROSSING OF SUN** the movement of Venus or Mercury across the face of the Sun, or of a moon or its shadow across the face of a planet, as seen from Earth **5.** ASTRON **PASSAGE OF STAR ACROSS MERIDIAN** the apparent movement of a star or planet across the meridian from which it is being observed, caused by the Earth's rotation **6.** ZODIAC **PLANET'S CROSSING OF ZODIAC** the passing of a planet across a particular point on the zodiac **7.** **TRANSITION** a transition or passing, e.g. from life to a supposed spiritual existence after death ■ *v.* (**-sits, -siting, -sited**) **1.** *vti.* **PASS THROUGH** to pass through or over sth ○ *They transited the area on foot.* **2.** *vti.* ASTRON **MAKE A TRANSIT** to make a transit across the face of the Sun or a planet, or across a meridian **3.** *vt.* CIV ENG **REVERSE DIRECTION OF SURVEYING TELESCOPE** to rotate the telescope of a surveying instrument horizontally through 180 degrees, thus reversing its direction [15thC. From Latin *transitus* 'passage', from *transire* 'to go across', from *ire* 'to go'.] —**transitable** *adj.* ◇ **in transit** in the process of travelling or being transported from one place to another

WORD KEY: CULTURAL NOTE

The Transit of Venus, a novel by Australian writer Shirley Hazzard (1980). Set in post-war England and the United States, it tells of the long-term relationship between an English astronomer and an Australian woman.

transit camp *n.* a camp set up to accommodate people such as refugees, soldiers, or prisoners of war temporarily, until they can be sent on to a final destination

transit circle *n.* an astronomical telescope that moves in a north-south plane enabling it to be used to determine the exact time a star, planet, or other celestial object passes most nearly overhead

transit instrument *n.* a telescopic instrument that can move only in the plane of a meridian, used to determine the exact time a star, planet, or other celestial object crosses that meridian

transition /tran zísh'n/ *n.* **1.** **PROCESS OF CHANGE** a process or period in which sth undergoes a change and passes from one state, stage, form, or activity to another **2.** MUSIC **MUSICAL PASSAGE** a passage connecting two sections of a musical composition **3.** MUSIC **CHANGE OF KEY** a progression from one key to another in a piece of music **4.** GRAM **LINKING WORD OR PHRASE** a word, phrase, or passage that links one subject or idea to another in speech or writing **5.** PHYS, CHEM **CHANGE BETWEEN PHASES** a change between phases such as solid to liquid or liquid to gas **6.** ARCHIT **ACHITECTURAL STYLE BETWEEN ROMANESQUE AND GOTHIC** a style of architecture in many buildings dating from the 12th century in western Europe, in which elements of the Romanesque and Gothic styles are combined **7.** NUCLEAR PHYS **CHANGE IN AN ATOMIC NUCLEUS** a change in the energy level or state of an atomic nucleus in which a single quantum of electromagnetic radiation is either lost or gained [15thC. From the Latin stem *transition-*, from *transire* (see TRANSIT).]

transitional /tran zísh'nəl/ *adj.* **1.** **DURING TRANSITION** marked by or during a transition from one state or condition to another ○ *The détente was a transitional period in international relations.* **2.** ARCHIT **CHARACTERISTIC OF TRANSITION** characteristic of a period of architectural transition, combining elements of the earlier and later forms or styles between which sth is progressing ○ *a transitional style* —**transitionally** *adv.*

transitionary /tran zíshə nəri/ *adj.* = **transitional** (*literary*)

transition element, **transition metal** *n.* any of the metallic elements that have an incomplete penultimate electron shell, variable valencies, and typically form coloured compounds. Copper, chromium, and gold are transition elements.

transition point *n.* **1.** **POINT OF CHANGE IN FLOW** the point at which laminar flow in a moving fluid changes to turbulent flow **2.** = **transition temperature**

transition temperature *n.* the temperature at which a substance loses or gains a particular property, especially superconductivity

transitive /tránssətiv/ *adj.* **1.** GRAM **REQUIRING DIRECT OBJECT** needing or usually taking a direct object ○ *a transitive verb* **2.** LOGIC, MATH **INVOLVING SAME RELATION BETWEEN TERMS** used to describe a given relation such that if it exists between 'a' and 'b' and between 'b' and 'c' then it also exists between 'a' and 'c'. Typical transitive relationships include 'is greater than', 'is equal to', and 'is similar to'. —**transitively** *adv.* —**transitiveness** *n.* —**transitivity** /tránsə tívvəti/ *n.*

transit lane *n. Aus* a traffic lane reserved, usually during peak hours, for the exclusive use of some types of vehicles and private cars carrying a minimum number of passengers

transit lounge *n.* a waiting room at an international airport used mainly by passengers transferring from one flight to another without presenting themselves to customs or immigration officials

transitory /tránssətəri/ *adj.* not permanent or lasting, but existing only for a short time ○ *a transitory infatuation* —**transitorily** *adv.* —**transitoriness** *n.*

transit theodolite *n.* a surveying instrument equipped with a rotating telescope, used to measure vertical and horizontal angles

Transkei /tránss kī/ former homeland in South Africa, now part of Eastern Cape Province

transl. *abbr.* **1.** translator **2.** translation **3.** translated

translate /transs láyt/ (**-lates, -lating, -lated**) *v.* **1.** *vti.* **TURN WORDS INTO DIFFERENT LANGUAGE** to give an equivalent in another language for a particular word or phrase, or reproduce a written or spoken text in a different language while retaining the original meaning ○ *Can you translate that phrase?* **2.** *vi.* **BE CAPABLE OF BEING TRANSLATED** to be capable of being translated, or have an equivalent in another language ○ *The idiom doesn't translate well.* **3.** *vt.* COMPUT **CONVERT CODE** to convert data to a different form following an algorithm ○ *translate the program into machine code* **4.** *vt.* **SAY STH IN UNDERSTANDABLE TERMS** to say or explain sth in terms that are easier to understand ○ *What he really means is 'We don't know what happened to your car'.* **5.** *vt.* **INTERPRET MEANING** to explain the meaning of sth not expressed in words, e.g. an action, gesture, or look ○ *I translated his silence as approval.* **6.** *vti.* **CHANGE FORM OF STH** to change sth, or be changed, from one form or effect into another ○ *'Microchips controlled by software now translate the flick of a pilot's wrist into the movement of a wing flap'* (Evan I. Schwartz, *Trust Me, I'm Your Software, Discover Magazine; May 1996*) **7.** *vt.* **MOVE SB OR STH** to move or carry sb or sth from one place to another, usually involving a complete change of condition or scene ○ *She was translated from her small country home to a high-rise city apartment* **8.** *vt.* CHR **TRANSFER CLERGY** to transfer a member of the clergy to another office, especially to transfer a bishop to another see **9.** *vt.* CHR **MOVE SAINT'S REMAINS** to move the remains or relics of a saint from one place to another **10.** *vt.* RELIG **CONVEY SB TO HEAVEN** to convey sb to heaven, especially in a way that is believed not to involve death **11.** *vt.* GENETICS **DECIPHER GENETIC INSTRUCTIONS FOR MAKING PROTEIN** to decipher the genetic message carried by a molecule of messenger RNA and assemble the amino acids of a protein chain according to the instructions **12.** *vt.* PHYS **MOVE BODY SIDEWAYS IN STRAIGHT LINE** to move a body sideways through space in a direct straight line without rotation [14thC. From Latin *translatus* (source of English *elation*), used as the past participle of *transferre* 'to carry across', from *ferre* 'to carry' (source of English *transfer*).] —**translatability** /tráns laytə bílləti/ *n.* —**translatable** /transs láytəb'l/ *adj.*

translation /transs láysh'n/ *n.* **1.** **VERSION IN ANOTHER LANGUAGE** a word, phrase, or version in another language that has a meaning equivalent to that of the original **2.** **EXPRESSING OF STH IN A DIFFERENT LANGUAGE** the rendering of sth written or spoken in one language in words of a different language ○ *She read the novel in translation.* **3.** **CHANGE OR TRANSFERENCE** a change in form or state, or transference to a different place, office, or sphere **4.** GENETICS **PROCESS DETERMINING AMINO ACID SEQUENCE** the process by which information in messenger RNA directs the sequence of amino acids assembled by a ribosome during protein synthesis **5.** PHYS **MOTION IN STRAIGHT LINE** the movement of a body in a straight line so that every point on the body follows a parallel path and no rotation takes place —**translational** /transs láysh'nəl/ *adj.*

translator /transs láytər/ *n.* **1.** **SB WHO TRANSLATES** sb or sth that translates, in writing or speech, from one language into another **2.** RADIO **TRANSMITTER THAT ALTERS SIGNAL FREQUENCY** a radio transmitter that receives a signal on one frequency and retransmits it on another **3.** COMPUT **CONVERTING COMPUTER PROGRAM** a computer program that converts other programs from one computer language into another —**translatorial** /tránslə táwri əl/ *adj.*

transliterate /transs líttə rayt, tranz-/ (**-ates, -ating, -ated**) *vt.* to represent a letter or word written in one alphabet using the corresponding letter or letters of another, so that the sound of the letter or word remains approximately the same [Mid-19thC. Formed from TRANS- + Latin *litera* 'letter' (see LETTER) + -ATE.] —**transliteration** /transs líttə ráysh'n, trans-/ *n.* —**transliterator** /trans líttə raytər, tranz-/ *n.*

translocate /tráns lō káyt/ (**-cates, -cating, -cated**) *vt.* to move sb or sth from one place or position to another

translocation /tráns lō káysh'n/ *n.* **1.** **MOVEMENT FROM ONE PLACE TO ANOTHER** movement, or the act of moving sth or sb, from one place or position to another **2.** BOT **MOVEMENT OF FOOD IN PLANTS** the movement of soluble materials within a plant. Common examples are the movement of food materials from the leaves to storage organs, and the movement of dissolved minerals upwards from the roots. **3.** GENETICS **TRANSFER OF PART OF CHROMOSOME** the transfer of part of a chromosome to a new position on the same or on a different chromosome with resultant rearrangement of the genes

translucent /transs lóoss'nt/ *adj.* **1.** **LETTING LIGHT THROUGH DIFFUSELY** allowing light to pass through, but only diffusely, so that objects on the other side cannot be clearly distinguished ○ *a translucent membrane* **2.** **GLOWING** having a glowing appearance, as if light were coming through ○ *translucent skin* [15thC. From Latin *translucent-*, the present participle stem of *translucere* 'to shine through', from *lucere* 'to shine' (see LUCID).] —**translucence** /trans lóos'ns/ *n.* —**translucency** *n.* —**translucently** *adv.*

translunar /transs lóonər/, **translunary** /-lóonəri/ *adj.* situated or coming from beyond the Moon or its orbit around the Earth

transmarine /tránzmə réen/ *adj.* **1.** **CROSSING THE SEA** involving crossing a sea or ocean **2.** **FROM ACROSS THE SEA** situated or coming from across a sea or ocean [Late 16thC. From Latin *transmarinus*, from *marinus* 'relating to the sea' (see MARINE).]

transmigrant /tranz mígrənt/ *n.* **SB PASSING THROUGH** sb passing through a country on the way to another country in which he or she intends to settle ■ *adj.* **BEING IN TRANSIT** passing through a country or place on the way to somewhere else, or through a transitional stage in a process of development [Mid-17thC. From Latin *transmigrant-*, the present participle stem of *transmigrare* 'to transmigrate', from *migrare* 'to migrate' (see MIGRATE).]

transmigrate /tránz mī gráyt/ (**-grates, -grating, -grated**) *vi.* **1.** **MOVE FROM ONE PLACE TO ANOTHER** to move from one place or country to another **2.** INDIAN RELIG **PASS TO ANOTHER BODY** in some religions, to pass into another body at or after death (*refers to the soul*) [15thC. From Latin *transmigrat-*, the past participle stem of *transmigrare*, from *migrare* 'to migrate' (see MIGRATE).] —**transmigration** /-gráysh'n/ *n.* —**transmigrational** /-gráysh'nəl/ *adj.* —**transmigrative** /-mígrətiv/ *adj.* —**transmigrator** /tránz mī gráytər/ *n.* —**transmigratory** /tranz mígrətəri/ *adj.*

transmissible spongiform encephalopathy *n.* full form of **TSE**

transmission /tranz mísh'n/ *n.* **1.** **ACT OF TRANSMITTING** the act or process of transmitting sth, especially radio signals, radio or television broadcasts, data, or a disease **2.** **STH TRANSMITTED** sth transmitted, e.g. a radio or signal **3.** BROADCAST **RADIO OR TV BROADCAST** a radio or television broadcast **4.** AUTOMOT **MECHANISM TRANSFERRING POWER TO WHEELS** the mechanical system, including gears and shafts, by which power is transmitted from the engine of a motor vehicle to the drive wheels **5.** *US* AUTOMOT = **gearbox** **6.** PHYS **ABILITY TO LET RADIATION THROUGH** the ability of a material to let incoming radiation pass completely through it [Early 17thC. Directly or via French from the Latin stem *transmission-*, from *missio* 'a letting go, release' (see MISSION).] —**transmissibility** /tranz míssə bílləti/ *n.* —**transmissible** /tranz míssəbl'l/ *adj.* —**transmissive** /-míssiv/ *adj.* —**transmissively** /-míssivli/ *adv.* —**transmissiveness** /-míssivnəss/ *n.*

transmission line *n.* a conductor such as a coaxial cable that carries electricity or other electromagnetic waves, usually over long distances

transmit /tranz mít/ (**-mits, -mitting, -mitted**) *v.* **1.** *vt.* **SEND STH** to send sth, pass sth on, or cause sth to spread from one person, thing, or place to another ○ *The disease is transmitted by droplet infection.* **2.** *vt.* **COMMUNICATE INFORMATION** to communicate a message, information, or news ○ *Data was quickly transmitted.* **3.** *vti.* TELECOM, RADIO **SEND A SIGNAL** to send a signal by radio waves, satellite, or wire **4.** *vti.* BROADCAST **BROADCAST A PROGRAMME** to broadcast a radio or television programme **5.** *vt.* PHYS **MAKE RADIATION PASS THROUGH STH** to make heat, sound, light, or other radiation pass or spread through space or a medium **6.** *vt.* PHYS **ALLOW RADIATION THROUGH** to allow heat, sound, or light or other radiation to pass through **7.** *vt.* MECH ENG **TRANSFER POWER** to transfer power, force, or movement from one part of a mechanism to another [14thC. From Latin *transmittere*, literally 'to send across', from *mittere* 'to send'.] —**transmittable** *adj.* —**transmittal** *n.* —**transmittible** *adj.*

transmittance /tranz mítt'nss/ *n.* **1.** **ACT OF TRANSMITTING STH** the act or process of transmitting sth **2.** PHYS **ABILITY TO LET RADIATION THROUGH** the ability of a material to let incoming radiation pass completely through it, measured as the ratio of incident radiation to transmitted radiation

transmitter /tranz míttər/ *n.* **1.** **AGENT OR MEANS OF TRANSMISSION** sb or sth that transmits sth **2.** BROADCAST **PART OF BROADCASTING EQUIPMENT** a piece of broadcasting equipment that generates a radio-frequency wave, modulates it so that it carries a meaningful signal, and sends it out from an antenna **3.** TELECOM **TELEPHONE PART** the part of a telephone that converts sound waves to electrical impulses

transmogrify /tranz móggri fī/ (**-fies, -fying, -fied**) *vt.* to change the appearance or form of sth, especially in a grotesque or bizarre way [Mid-17thC. Origin uncertain: perhaps an alteration of TRANSMIGRATE modelled on verbs ending in -FY.] —**transmogrification** /tranz móggrifi káysh'n/ *n.*

transmontane *adj.*, *n.* = **tramontane** *adj.* 1, **tramontane** *adj.* 2, **tramontane** *n.* 2

transmundane /tranz mún dayn/ *adj.* not belonging to this material world and its concerns, or extending beyond them (*literary*)

transmutation /tránzmyoo táysh'n/ *n.* **1.** **CHANGE** a change, or the process of changing, from one form, substance, nature, or state to another **2.** PHYS **CHANGE OF ONE ELEMENT INTO ANOTHER** the transformation of the atom of one chemical element into the atom of another by disintegration or nuclear bombardment **3.** HIST **CONVERSION TO GOLD** the supposed conversion of base metals into gold or silver by alchemy —**transmutational** *adj.*

transmute /tranz myóot/ (**-mutes, -muting, -muted**) *vti.* **1.** **CHANGE** to change sth, or be changed, from one form, nature, substance, or state to another **2.** PHYS **CHANGE FROM ONE ELEMENT TO ANOTHER** to change one element into another through disintegration or nuclear bombardment, or undergo a change of this kind **3.** HIST **CONVERT BASE METAL TO GOLD** to convert a base metal into gold or silver by alchemy, or be converted in this way [14thC. From Latin *transmutare*, literally 'to change thoroughly', from *mutare* 'to change'. Perhaps also partly a back-formation from TRANSMUTATION.] —**transmutability** *n.* —**transmutable** /tranz myóotəb'l/ *adj.* —**transmutably** /-myóotəbli/ *adv.* —**transmutative** *adj.* —**transmuter** *n.*

WORD KEY: SYNONYMS

See Synonyms at ***change***.

transnational /tranz násh'nəl/ *adj.* not confined to a single nation or state, but including, extending over, or operating within several of them

transoceanic /tránz ōshi ánnik/ *adj.* **1.** **CROSSING AN OCEAN** involving crossing an ocean **2.** **FROM ACROSS AN OCEAN** situated or coming from across an ocean

transom /tránssəm/ *n.* **1.** BUILDING **STRUCTURAL BEAM ABOVE A WINDOW** a horizontal beam or stone above a window that supports the structure above **2.** BUILDING **CROSSPIECE ABOVE DOOR** a crosspiece over a door or between the top of a door and a window above **3.** *US* BUILDING = **fanlight** **4.** BUILDING **CROSSBAR THAT DIVIDES WINDOW** a crossbar of wood or stone that divides a window horizontally **5.** NAUT **BEAM FOR STRENGTHENING STERN** any of several transverse beams for strengthening the stern of a ship **6.** NAUT **PLANKING AT SHIP'S STERN** the planking forming a flat surface across the stern of a ship **7.** **HORIZONTAL BEAM OF CROSS OR GALLOWS** the horizontal beam of a cross or gallows [14thC. Origin uncertain: probably an alteration of Latin *transtrum* 'cross-

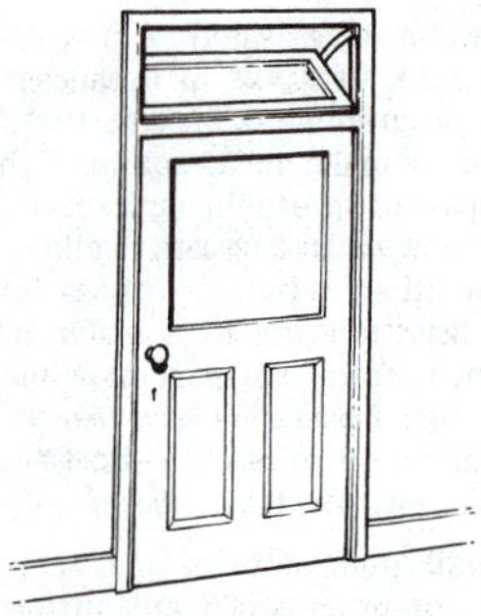

Transom

beam' (source of English *trestle*), from *trans* 'across'.] —**transomed** *adj.*

transonic /tran sónnik/ *adj.* relating to speeds close to the speed of sound or conditions encountered when travelling at those speeds [Mid-20thC. Formed from TRANS- + SONIC on the model of SUPERSONIC and ULTRASONIC.]

transonic barrier *n.* the sound barrier (*technical*)

transp. *abbr.* 1. transport 2. transportation

transpacific /tránzpə síffik/ *adj.* **1.** CROSSING THE PACIFIC involving crossing the Pacific Ocean **2.** FROM ACROSS THE PACIFIC situated or coming from across the Pacific Ocean

transpadane /tránzpə dayn/ *adj.* from or on the north side of the River Po in northern Italy [Early 17thC. From Latin *transpadanus*, from *padanus* 'of the Padus (River Po)'.]

transparency /transs párrənsi/ (*plural* **-cies**) *n.* **1.** STATE OF BEING TRANSPARENT the quality or state of being transparent **2.** PHOTOGRAPHY SEE-THROUGH PHOTOGRAPH OR PICTURE a positive photographic image on a transparent material, especially film or a slide, that can be viewed when light is shone through it. Transparencies are generally viewed using a projector, a light table, or a hand-held viewer. [Late 16thC. From medieval Latin *transparentia*, from the stem *transparent-* (see TRANSPARENT).]

transparent /transs párrənt/ *adj.* **1.** EASILY SEEN THROUGH allowing light to pass through with little or no interruption or distortion so that objects on the other side can be clearly seen ○ *transparent plastic* **2.** FINE ENOUGH TO SEE THROUGH thin or fine enough in texture to see through ○ *transparent fabric* **3.** OBVIOUS AND EASY TO RECOGNIZE clearly recognizable as what it, he, or she really is ○ *a transparent motive* **4.** FRANK completely open and frank about things ○ *was grateful for the transparent honesty of the reply* **5.** PHYS LETTING RADIATION THROUGH allowing electromagnetic radiation of specified wavelengths to pass through [15thC. Directly or via French from medieval Latin *transparent-*, the present participle stem of *transparere* 'to shine through', from Latin *parere* 'to appear'.] —**transparently** *adv.* —**transparentness** *n.*

transparent context *n.* in logic, an expression in which the truth-value is not changed when any term is replaced by another with the same reference

transpicuous /tran spíkyoo əss/ *adj.* easily understood or seen through (*literary*) [Mid-17thC. Formed from modern Latin *transpicuus*, from Latin *transpicere* 'to look through', from *specere* 'to look'.] —**transpicuously** *adv.*

transpierce /transs péerss/ (**-pierces, -piercing, -pierced**) *vt.* to pierce through sth (*literary*)

transpire /tran spír/ (**-spires, -spiring, -spired**) *v.* **1.** *vt.* COME TO LIGHT to become known or be disclosed ○ *It later transpired that they had been furious at what had happened* **2.** *vi.* HAPPEN to take place ○ *What transpired after they left remains a secret.* **3.** *vti.* PHYSIOL GIVE OFF VAPOUR THROUGH SKIN to give off water vapour through the pores of the skin. ◊ **sweat 4.** *vti.* BOT LOSE WATER VAPOUR to lose water vapour from a plant's surface, especially through minute surface pores (**stomata**) [15thC. Directly or via French *transpirer* from medieval Latin *transpirare*, literally 'to breathe through', from Latin *spirare* 'to breathe'.] —**transpirable** *adj.* —**transpiration** /tránsspi ráysh'n/ *n.* —**transpiratory** /tran spírətəri/ *adj.*

WORD KEY: USAGE

Tell me what transpired at the meeting. This use of ***transpire*** to mean 'to happen' is sometimes objected to, although it has been in common use for several centuries and conveys sth of the sense inherent in its other (uncontroversial) meaning 'to become known, come to light': *It transpired that the President had known about the plan all along.*

transplant *v.* /transs pláant/ (**-plants, -planting, -planted**) **1.** *vt.* GARDENING RELOCATE PLANT to remove a plant from the place where it is growing and replant it somewhere else **2.** *vt.* MOVE SB TO ANOTHER PLACE to move sb or sth to another place or position **3.** *vt.* SURG TRANSFER BODY ORGAN to transfer an organ or tissue from one body to another, or from one place in sb's body to another **4.** *vi.* BE CAPABLE OF BEING MOVED to be capable of being transplanted ○ *Poppies do not transplant well.* ■ *n.* /tráns plaant/ **1.** SURG SURGICAL PROCEDURE a surgical operation or procedure to transplant an organ or tissue **2.** SURG TRANSPLANTED ORGAN OR TISSUE an organ or tissue that has been transplanted **3.** GARDENING TRANSPLANTED PLANT a plant that has been transplanted [15thC. Directly or via French *transplanter* from late Latin *transplantare*, literally 'to plant across', from Latin *plantare* 'to plant' (see PLANT).] —**transplantable** /transs pláantəb'l/ *adj.* —**transplantation** /tránss plaan táysh'n/ *n.* —**transplanter** /transs pláantər/ *n.*

transpolar /tranz pólər/ *adj.* crossing or extending across either of the polar regions

transponder /tran spóndər/, **transpondor** *n.* **1.** RADIO RADIO OR RADAR TRANSCEIVER a radio or radar transceiver that automatically transmits a signal of its own when it receives a predetermined signal from elsewhere, used especially for locating and identifying objects **2.** TELECOM SATELLITE RECEIVER AND TRANSMITTER a receiving and transmitting device in a communication or broadcast satellite that relays the signals it receives back to Earth [Mid-20thC. Formed from TRANSMIT + RESPOND + -ER.]

transpontine /tranz pón tīn/ *adj.* **1.** ON OTHER SIDE OF BRIDGE on or from the other side of a bridge (*formal*) **2.** SOUTH OF THE THAMES on or from the south side of the River Thames in London (*archaic*) [Mid-19thC. Formed from Latin *pont-*, the stem of *pons* 'bridge' (see PONS).]

transport *vt.* /transs páwrt/ (**-ports, -porting, -ported**) **1.** TRANSP CARRY SB OR STH to carry people or goods from one place to another, usually in a vehicle **2.** MAKE SB IMAGINE BEING ELSEWHERE to take sb on a mental or imaginative journey to another place or time ○ *The sounds of the game transported him back to his youth.* **3.** AFFECT SB WITH STRONG EMOTION to put sb in a state of intense or uncontrollable emotion, especially joy ○ *She was transported with joy.* **4.** HIST SEND SB TO PENAL COLONY to exile sb to a penal colony ■ *n.* /tráns pawrt/ **1.** TRANSP CONVEYANCE OF SB OR STH the act or business of carrying people or goods from one place to another, especially in vehicles **2.** TRANSP MEANS OF TRAVELLING a means of travelling, or of carrying people or goods, from one place to another ○ *public transport.* US term **transportation 3.** MIL A CRAFT CARRYING PEOPLE OR FREIGHT a ship or aircraft for carrying passengers, especially military personnel, or freight **4.** EXPERIENCE OR DISPLAY OF INTENSE EMOTION an experience or display of intense and uncontrollable emotion, especially joy (*often used in the plural*) ○ *in transports of delight* **5.** HIST SB SENT TO PENAL COLONY sb exiled to a penal colony [14thC. Directly or via French *transporter* from Latin *transportare* 'to carry across', from *portare* 'to carry'.] —**transportability** /tránss pawrtə bílləti/ *n.* —**transportable** /-páwrtəb'l/ *adj.* —**transportive** /-páwrtiv/ *adj.*

transportation /tránsspawr táysh'n/ *n.* **1.** = **transport 2.** *US* CHARGE the fare paid or charge made for travelling in a bus, train, or other public vehicle **3.** HIST PENAL EXILE exile to a penal colony

transport café *n.* a roadside café that offers plain and inexpensive meals, used mainly by long-distance lorry drivers. US term **truck stop**

transporter /transs páwrtər/ *n.* **1.** SB OR STH THAT TRANSPORTS sb or sth that transports sth **2.** AUTOMOT LARGE VEHICLE a large vehicle used to carry heavy loads, often other vehicles

transporter bridge *n.* a bridge consisting of a high overarching framework from which a moving platform is suspended on cables. The platform goes back and forth carrying vehicles across a body of water.

transpose /trans póz/ *v.* (**-poses, -posing, -posed**) **1.** *vt.* REVERSE ORDER to make two things change places or reverse their normal order, e.g. to reverse the order of two letters in a word **2.** *vt.* MOVE STH TO DIFFERENT POSITION to move sth to a different position, especially in a sequence ○ *transposed that section to the end of the essay* **3.** *vt.* CHANGE SETTING OF STH to take sth such as a story, incident, or play out of its usual setting or time and relocate it in another ○ *transposing the action from Shakespeare's time to the present* **4.** *vti.* MUSIC CHANGE MUSIC TO A DIFFERENT KEY to rewrite or play a musical composition in a key or at a pitch other than the one in which it was originally written or in which it is usually performed **5.** *vt.* MATH MOVE TERM IN EQUATION to transfer a term from one side of an equation to the other, reversing its sign ■ *n.* MATH TYPE OF MATRIX a matrix created by interchanging the rows and columns of a previously given matrix [14thC. From French *transposer*, an alteration (by association with *poser* 'to place') of Latin *transponere*, literally 'to place across', from *ponere* 'to place' (see POSITION).] —**transposability** /transs pózə bílləti/ *n.* —**transposable** /transs pózəb'l/ *adj.* —**transposal** *n.* —**transposer** /transs pózər/ *n.* —**transpositive** /trans pózzətiv/ *adj.*

transposing instrument *n.* a musical instrument such as a horn or clarinet that plays in a key other than C major, and whose part must therefore be written transposed to be in tune with other instruments

transposition /tránsspə zísh'n/ *n.* **1.** REVERSAL OF ORDER a reversal or alteration of the positions or order in which things stand **2.** RECASTING a placing of sth in a different setting, or its recasting in a different language, style, or medium **3.** MUSIC PUTTING IN DIFFERENT KEY a rewriting or playing of a piece of music in a key or at a pitch other than the original or usual one **4.** MATH TRANSFER OF TERM IN EQUATION a transfer of a term from one side of an equation to another, reversing the sign —**transpositional** *adj.*

transposon /transs pó zon/ *n.* a segment of DNA that can move to a new position on the same or another chromosome, often modifying the action of neighbouring genes [Late 20thC. Formed from TRANSPOSITION + -ON.]

transputer /tranz pyóotər/ *n.* a powerful microchip with the functions of a microprocessor, having its own memory and the ability to carry out parallel processing

transsexual /tranz sékshoo əl/ *n.* **1.** SB WHOSE SEX IS SURGICALLY CHANGED sb who has undergone surgical and hormonal treatment to change his or her anatomical sex **2.** SB WHO IDENTIFIES WITH OPPOSITE SEX sb who identifies himself or herself as and wants to become a member of the opposite sex —**transsexual** *adj.* —**transsexualism** *n.*

transship /transs shíp/ (**-ships, -shipping, -shipped**), **tranship** (**-ships, -shipping, -shipped**) *vti.* to transfer goods, or be transferred, from one means of transportation to another —**transshipment** *n.*

transubstantiate /tránssəb stánshi ayt/ (**-ates, -ating, -ated**) *v.* **1.** *vi.* CHR CHANGE SUBSTANCE in the belief of some Christian churches, to undergo a change in substance, from bread and wine to the body and blood of Jesus Christ during Communion **2.** *vti.* CHANGE SUBSTANCE to change, or change sth, from one substance into another (*formal*) [15thC. From medieval Latin *transubstantiat-*, the past participle stem of *transubstantiare*, literally 'to change the substance of thoroughly', from Latin *substantia* (see SUBSTANCE).] —**transubstantial** *adj.* —**transubstantially** *adv.*

transubstantiation /tránssəb stanshi áysh'n/ *n.* **1.** CHR CHRISTIAN DOCTRINE the Roman Catholic and Eastern Orthodox doctrine that the bread and wine of Communion become, in substance but not appearance, the body and blood of Jesus Christ at consecration. ◊ **consubstantiation 2.** CHANGE OF SUBSTANCE a process whereby one substance changes into another (*formal*) —**transubstantiationalist** *n.*

transudate /tránss yoo dayt/ *n.* a fluid that passes through the pores or interstices of a membrane

transude /tran syoód/ (**-sudes, -suding, -suded**) *vi.* to pass through pores, interstices, or a membrane, as a fluid such as sweat does [Early 17thC. Via French *transsuder*, literally 'to sweat through' from, ultimately, Latin *sudare* 'to sweat'.] —**transudation** /tránss yoo dáysh'n/ *n.* —**transudatory** /tran syoódətəri/ *adj.*

transuranic /tránzyoo ránnik/, **transuranian** /-ráyni ən/, **transuranium** /-ráyni əm/ *adj.* having a higher atomic number than uranium

Transvaal /tránz vaal/ former province of South Africa, situated in the northeastern part of the country

transvalue /tranz vállyoo/ (**-ues, -uing, -ued**) *vt.* to re-evaluate sth using a different standard, especially one that differs from conventional or accepted standards and results in a very different assessment of the worth of sth —**transvaluation** /tránz valyoo áysh'n/ *n.* —**transvaluer** /tranz vállyoo ər/ *n.*

transversal /tranz vúrss'l/ *n.* LINE INTERSECTING OTHER LINES a line that intersects two or more other lines ■ *adj.* = **transverse** *adj.* 1, **transverse** *adj.* 2 —**transversally** *adv.*

transverse /tranz vúrss/ *adj.* **1.** CROSSWISE lying or going crosswise or at right angles to sth **2.** GEOM PASSING THROUGH THE FOCI OF A HYPERBOLA passing through a hyperbola's foci ■ *n.* CROSSWISE THING sth lying or extending crosswise [14thC. From Latin *transversus*, the past participle of *transvertere* 'to turn across', from *vertere* 'to turn'.] —**transversely** *adv.* —**transverseness** *n.*

transverse colon *n.* the part of the colon that passes from right to left across the upper abdominal cavity just beneath the liver and stomach

transverse flute *n.* a flute with the mouth hole on top of the barrel near one end, so that the player blows across the hole while holding the flute in a sideways-on position. The modern flute used to be known as the transverse flute in order to distinguish it from an end-blown flute such as a recorder.

transverse process *n.* ANAT either of the two bony projections on the sides of a vertebra

transverse wave *n.* PHYS a wave that makes the medium through which it travels vibrate in a direction at right angles to the direction of its travel

transvestite /tranz vés tīt/ *n.* sb who habitually or frequently adopts the dress and often the behaviour of the opposite sex [Early 20thC. From German *Transvestit*, literally 'cross-dresser', from Latin *vestire* 'to clothe, dress' (see VEST).] —**transvestism** *n.* —**transvestitism** *n.*

Transylvania /tránssil váyni ə/ historic region in eastern Europe that now forms the central and northwestern parts of Romania. Area: 62,000 sq. km/24,000 sq. mi. —**Transylvanian** *adj.*

Transylvanian Alps /tránssil váyni ən-/ mountain range in the Carpathian Mountains, running east to west through south-central Romania

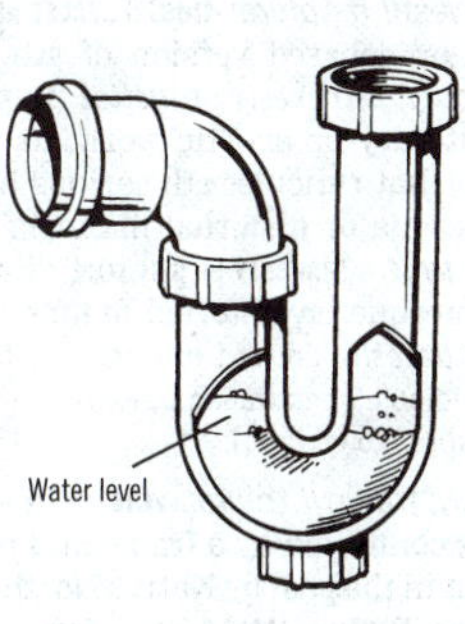

Trap

trap[1] /trap/ *n.* **1.** STH DESIGNED TO CATCH ANIMALS a device designed to catch an animal and kill it or prevent it escaping, e.g. a concealed pit or a mechanical device that springs shut **2.** SCHEME TO CATCH SB OUT an ambush, scheme, or trick intended to catch sb unawares and put the person at a disadvantage or in sb else's power **3.** CONFINING SITUATION a situation from which it is difficult to escape and in which sb feels confined, restricted, or in another person's power ○ *wanted to avoid the trap of being typecast in the same roles* **4.** CONSTR SECTION OF DRAINPIPE BLOCKING GAS a curved section of a drainpipe that holds a quantity of water to act as a barrier to prevent sewer gas from rising up the pipe **5.** CONSTR DEVICE PREVENTING THE PASSAGE OF GAS any device designed to prevent gas, vapour, or other substances passing through or escaping from sth **6.** = **trap door 7.** MOUTH the mouth (*informal*) ○ *If the cops ask questions, keep your trap shut.* **8.** SPORTS DEVICE USED IN TRAPSHOOTING a device that throws clay pigeons into the air for trapshooting **9.** GOLF GOLF BUNKER a hazard, especially a bunker, on a golf course **10.** SPORTS STARTING STALL FOR A GREYHOUND one of the set of stalls from which greyhounds are released at the start of a race **11.** TRANSP CARRIAGE a light horse-drawn carriage with two wheels ■ **traps** *npl.* MUSIC PERCUSSION INSTRUMENT a set of percussion instruments, especially the drum set used in a dance orchestra or jazz band (*informal*) ■ *v.* (**traps, trapping, trapped**) **1.** *vt.* CATCH IN TRAP to catch an animal in a trap so that it is killed or unable to escape **2.** *vi.* HUNT SET TRAPS FOR ANIMALS to set traps for animals or make a living by catching animals in traps **3.** *vt.* HOLD STH IN A TIGHT GRIP to catch or hold sth in a tight grip or narrow space so that it cannot be moved or is painfully squeezed ○ *I trapped my finger in the door.* **4.** *vt.* PLACE SB IN A CONFINING SITUATION to put sb in a situation from which it is difficult or impossible to escape ○ *They were trapped inside the burning building.* ○ *felt trapped in a dead-end job* **5.** *vt.* TAKE SB BY SURPRISE to put sb at a disadvantage by means of an ambush, surprise, clever plan, or trick ○ *She was trapped into admitting the truth.* **6.** *vt.* SOCCER CONTROL A BALL to bring a moving ball quickly under control using a part of the body **7.** *vt.* CRIMINOL CATCH AN OFFENDER to identify or catch an offender by means of a speed trap or a security device **8.** *vt.* PREVENT AIR FROM ESCAPING to prevent air, gas, heat, or a fluid from escaping **9.** *vt.* CONSTR EQUIP STH WITH A TRAP to put a trap into a drainpipe [Old English *træppe* (in *coltetræppe*, a plant name) and *treppe* 'trap, snare', from a prehistoric Germanic base. The etymological sense is perhaps 'sth that is trodden on'.] ◇ **have been around the traps** *Aus* to have wide experience of sth (*informal*)

trap[2] /trap/ *n.* MINERALS any of various types of dark fine-grained igneous rock, e.g. basalt. US term **traprock** [Late 18thC. From Swedish *trapp*, from *trappa* 'stair' (from the rock's common appearance).]

trap[3] /trap/ *n.* TRAPPINGS trappings (*archaic*) ■ **traps** *npl.* BELONGINGS sb's personal belongings (*informal*) ■ *vt.* (**traps, trapping, trapped**) PROVIDE STH WITH TRAPPINGS to provide sb or sth with trappings or adornments ○ *they were all trapped out in the gaudiest of clothes* [14thC. Alteration of French *drap* 'cloth' (source of English *drape*), from late Latin *drappus*, of uncertain origin: perhaps from a Celtic source.]

Trapani /tra paáni/ seaport and capital city of Trapani Province, northwestern Sicily. Population: 69,497 (1996).

trap door *n.* a hatch covering a horizontal or sloping opening in a floor, ceiling, or roof

trapdoor spider *n.* a spider found in warm regions that constructs a tubular silk-lined burrow with a hinged lid like a trap door. Family: Ctenizidae.

trapes *vi., n.* = **traipse**

trapeze /trə peéz/ *n.* a horizontal bar attached to the ends of two ropes hanging parallel to each other, used for gymnastics or for acrobatics, especially in a circus [Mid-19thC. Via French *trapèze* from late Latin *trapezium* (see TRAPEZIUM), from the quadrilateral shape formed by the trapeze's crossbar and ropes and the roof.]

trapeze artist *n.* sb who performs acrobatics on a trapeze, especially in a circus

trapezia plural of **trapezium**

trapeziform /trə peézi fawrm/ *adj.* shaped like a trapezium

trapezii plural of **trapezius**

trapezium /trə peézi əm/ (*plural* **-ums** *or* **-a** /-zi ə/) *n.* **1.** GEOM QUADRILATERAL WITH TWO PARALLEL SIDES a quadrilateral that has two parallel sides. US term **trapezoid** *n.* 1 **2.** *US* GEOM = **trapezoid 3.** ANAT WRIST BONE a small bone in the wrist at the base of the thumb [Late 16thC. Via late Latin (source of English *trapeze*) from Greek *trapezion*, literally 'small table', from *trapeza* 'table', literally 'with four feet', from *peza* 'foot'.] —**trapezial** *adj.*

trapezius /trə peézi əss/ (*plural* **-uses** *or* **-i**) *n.* either of the two large flat triangular muscles that run from the back of the neck and cover each shoulder. They help to move the shoulder blades and draw the head backwards. [Early 18thC. From modern Latin, from late Latin *trapezium* (see TRAPEZIUM), from the pair together forming a trapezium.]

trapezohedron /trə peézō heédrən/ (*plural* **-drons** *or* **-dra** /-drə/) *n.* a form of crystal with faces that are all trapeziums in shape [Early 19thC. Coined from TRAPEZIUM + -HEDRON on the model of, for example, TETRAHEDRON.] —**trapezohedral** *adj.*

trapezoid /tráppi zoyd/ *n.* **1.** *US* GEOM = **trapezium** *n.* 2 **2.** GEOM QUADRILATERAL WITH NO PARALLEL SIDES a quadrilateral that has no parallel sides. US term **trapezium** *n.* 2 **3.** ANAT WRIST BONE a small bone in the wrist near the metatarsal bone that connects with the index finger —**trapezoidal** *adj.*

trapper /tráppər/ *n.* sb who makes a living by trapping animals for their fur or hides

trappings /tráppingz/ *npl.* **1.** ACCESSORIES AND OUTWARD SIGNS the dress, accessories, insignia, and other outward signs associated with an office, position, or status ○ *the trappings of power* **2.** EQU ORNAMENTAL HARNESS FOR A HORSE an ornamental or ceremonial rig for a horse, including a decorated harness, saddle, and cloth covering

Trappist /tráppist/ *n.* a member of the main reformed branch of the Cistercian order of Christian monks, established in 1664 at La Trappe monastery in Normandy and noted for its vow of silence [Early 19thC. From French *trappiste*, from *La Trappe*, name of the monastery in Normandy.]

traprock /tráp rok/ *n.* = **trap**[2]

trapshooting /tráp shooting/ *n.* the sport of shooting at clay pigeons thrown by a trap —**trapshooter** *n.*

trapunto /trə poóntō/ *n.* quilting in which only the design, which is outlined with parallel lines of stitches, is padded to give it a raised look [Early 20thC. From Italian, past participle of *trapungere* 'to embroider' (literally 'to prick across'), from Latin *pungere* 'to prick' (see PUNGENT).]

Traralgon /trə rálgən/ mining town in southeastern Victoria, Australia. Population: 18,993 (1996).

trash /trash/ *n.* **1.** NONSENSE sth spoken or written that is viewed as meaningless or absurd ○ *You're talking trash!* **2.** POOR QUALITY LITERATURE OR ART literature or art considered worthless or offensive ○ *How can you read such trash?* **3.** *US* DISCARDED MATERIAL discarded, unwanted, or worthless material or objects **4.** *US* OFFENSIVE TERM an offensive term that deliberately insults sb's social position or morals **5.** AGRIC TRIMMINGS FROM PLANTS twigs, branches, or leaves that have fallen or been trimmed from trees and plants **6.** INDUST SUGAR CANE REFUSE the dry refuse of sugar cane after it has been crushed for the juice, often used as fuel ■ *vt.* (**trashes, trashing, trashed**) **1.** DESTROY STH to destroy, severely damage, or vandalize sth deliberately (*informal*) ○ *wondered whether rock stars still trashed their hotel rooms* ○ *'The storm trashed bridges in Honduras and Central America'.* (*US News & World Report*; December 1998) **2.** *US* DISCARD STH to throw away or discard sth (*informal*) **3.** *US* CRITICIZE SB SAVAGELY to criticize sth or sb savagely, or condemn sth or sb as worthless (*informal*) **4.** AGRIC REMOVE TWIGS AND BRANCHES to remove twigs, branches, or leaves from plants **5.** INDUST STRIP LEAVES FROM SUGAR CANE to strip the outer leaves from sugar cane [14thC. Origin uncertain: probably from a Scandinavian source (compare Norwegian dialect *trask* 'rubbish' and Old Norse *tros* 'fallen leaves and twigs, rubbish').] ◇ **talk trash** *US* to try to intimidate sb, especially a rival or an opponent in a sporting contest, by being boastful or insulting (*slang*)

trash fish *n. US* a fish such as skate or monkfish formerly thought of as unfit for human consumption but now valued for its quality

trashy /tráshi/ (**-ier, -iest**) *adj.* cheap or of very little worth or merit ○ *a trashy novel* —**trashily** *adv.* —**trashiness** *n.*

Trasimeno, Lake /trázzi meénō/ lake in central Italy, and the largest lake in the Italian peninsula. Area: 128 sq. km/49 sq. mi.

trass /trass/ *n.* a light-coloured volcanic rock (**tuff**) used in making hydraulic cement [Late 18thC. Via Dutch *tras* or German *Trass* from, ultimately, Latin *terra* 'earth'.]

trattoria /tráttə reé ə/ (*plural* **-as** *or* **-e** /-reé ay/) *n.* an Italian restaurant, especially one that is simple in style [Early 19thC. From Italian, from *trattore* 'restaurateur', from, ultimately, Latin *tractare* 'to drag, manage', from *trahere* 'to pull' (source of English *tractor*).]

trauchled /traákh'ld/ *adj. Scotland* exhausted or overburdened with physical or mental work or with responsibilities and cares [Early 20thC. Past participle of *trauchle* 'to tire out, trudge', of uncertain origin.]

trauma /tráwmə/ (*plural* **-mas** *or* **-mata** /-mətə/) *n.* **1.** PSYCHOL **EMOTIONAL SHOCK** an extremely distressing experience that causes severe emotional shock and may have long-lasting psychological effects **2.** MED **BODILY INJURY** a physical injury or wound to the body [Late 17thC. From Greek, 'wound'.]

traumatic /traw máttik/ *adj.* **1. EXTREMELY DISTRESSING** extremely distressing, frightening, or shocking, and sometimes having long-term psychological effects **2.** PSYCHOL **RELATING TO TRAUMA** relating to or caused by psychological trauma **3.** MED **RELATING TO INJURIES** relating to wounds or injuries [Mid-17thC. Via late Latin *traumaticus* from Greek *traumatikos*, from *traumat-*, the stem of *trauma* 'wound'.] —**traumatically** *adv.*

traumatism /tráwmətizəm/ *n.* the condition resulting from a physical injury or wound or from an emotional shock [Mid-19thC. Formed from Greek *traumat-* (see TRAUMATIC).]

traumatize /tráwmə tīz/ (**-tizes, -tizing, -tized**), **traumatise** (**-tises, -tising, -tised**) *vt.* **1.** PSYCHOL **CAUSE EMOTIONAL SHOCK TO** to cause sb to experience severe emotional shock or distress, often resulting in long-lasting psychological damage **2.** MED **INJURE** to cause physical injury to sb or sth [Early 20thC. Formed from Greek *traumat-* (see TRAUMATIC).] —**traumatization** *n.*

traumatology /tráwmə tólləji/ *n.* the branch of medicine that deals with serious injuries and wounds and their long-term consequences [Late 19thC. Coined from Greek *traumat-* (see TRAUMATIC + -LOGY).] —**traumatologist** *n.*

travail /trávvayl/ *n.* **1. HARD WORK** work, especially work that involves hard physical effort over a long period **2.** CHILDBIRTH labour pains (*archaic*) ■ *vi.* (**-vails, -vailing, -vailed**) **1. WORK LONG AND HARD** to work long and hard (*literary*) **2. BE IN LABOUR** to be in labour (*archaic; refers to a woman*) [13thC. From French, 'pain', and its source *travailler* 'to toil', ultimately from assumed Vulgar Latin *tripalium* 'instrument of torture', from Latin *tripalis* 'having three stakes', from *palus* 'stake'.]

trave /trayv/ *n.* **1.** BUILDING = **crossbeam 2.** BUILDING **STH FORMED BY CROSSBEAMS** a section of a building, e.g. in a ceiling, formed by crossbeams **3.** EQU **FRAME FOR A DIFFICULT HORSE** a frame to restrain a difficult horse while it is being shod [14thC. Via Old French, 'beam', from Latin *trab-*, the stem of *trabs* (source of English *architrave* and *trabeated*).]

travel /trávv'l/ *v.* (**travels, travelling, travelled, travelled**) **1.** *vi.* **GO ON A JOURNEY** to go on a journey to a particular place, usually using some form of transport **2.** *vi.* **GO FROM PLACE TO PLACE** to go from place to place or visit various places and countries for business or pleasure ○ *We hope to travel more when we retire.* **3.** *vt.* **JOURNEY THROUGH AN AREA** to go on journeys through, around, or within a particular area ○ *They travelled the world.* **4.** *vt.* **COVER A PARTICULAR DISTANCE** to go or cover a particular distance ○ *travel 10 miles* **5.** *vi.* **GO AT A PARTICULAR SPEED** to move at a particular speed or in a particular way ○ *The train was travelling at 90 mph when it had to stop.* **6.** *vi.* **MOVE FAST** to move swiftly (*informal*) ○ *With the new engine this car can really travel.* **7.** *vi.* COMMUNICATION **GO TO DIFFERENT PLACES TO DO BUSINESS** to go from place to place as a salesperson or as part of a business ○ *After five years travelling, she wanted an office job.* **8.** *vi.* **TOLERATE BEING TRANSPORTED** to retain its quality or freshness while being transported ○ *Some products do not travel well.* **9.** *vi.* **BE TRANSMITTED** to be transmitted or communicated ○ *News travelled fast.* **10.** *vi.* **SCAN** to scan an object or scene in the process of observing or filming it **11.** *vi.* MECH ENG **MOVE IN A FIXED PATH** to move in a fixed path while operating (*refers to a machine part*) **12.** *vi. US* **ASSOCIATE WITH A SPECIFIC GROUP** to associate with a particular person or group ○ *They've been travelling with a new crowd.* **13.** *vi.* BASKETBALL **TAKE AN ILLEGAL NUMBER OF STEPS** to take more steps while holding the ball than the rules of basketball allow ■ *n.* **1. ACTIVITY OF TRAVELLING** the activity of going on journeys, often using a particular form of transport, or visiting different places ○ *air travel* **2.** MECH ENG **TOTAL DISTANCE A MECHANICAL PART MOVES** the total distance that a mechanical part such as a piston inside a cylinder moves **3.** *US* **TRAFFIC** the amount of traffic at a given place along a route ■ **travels** *npl.* **1. SERIES OF JOURNEYS** a series of journeys undertaken by a particular person or group ○ *She's off on her travels again.* **2.** LITERAT **ACCOUNT OF SB'S JOURNEYS** an account of the journeys undertaken by a particular person or group ■ *adj.* **FOR TRAVELLERS** designed for use by travellers, especially by being lightweight and smaller than usual ○ *a travel kettle* [14thC. Variant of TRAVAIL (the underlying notion perhaps being 'wearisome journey').]

travel agency *n.* a business that arranges transport, accommodation, and tours for travellers —**travel agent** *n.*

travelator *n.* = **travolator**

travel bureau *n.* = **travel agency**

travelcard /trávv'l kaard/ *n.* a ticket entitling the user to an unlimited number of journeys on a specified public transport system within a certain area and over a specific period of time

traveled *adj.* US = **travelled**

traveler *n.* US = **traveller**

travelled *adj.* **1. EXPERIENCED IN TRAVEL** having been on many journeys, or being experienced as a traveller **2. MUCH USED** used by many travellers ○ *Keep to the travelled roads.*

traveller *n.* **1. SB ON A JOURNEY** sb who is on a journey to a particular place or who uses a particular form of transport **2. SB WHO HAS TRAVELLED** sb who has travelled or travels extensively ○ *an experienced traveller* **3.** = **travelling salesman 4. MEMBER OF TRAVELLING FOLK** a Gypsy or other person living an itinerant lifestyle **5.** MECH ENG **MOVING PART** a part of a mechanism that is designed to move in a fixed path **6.** NAUT **RING ON A ROPE** a metal ring that moves freely on a rope, spar, or rod **7.** NAUT **ROPE** a rope, spar, or rod on which a metal ring moves

traveller's cheque *n.* an internationally accepted cheque for a sum in a particular currency that can be exchanged elsewhere for local currency or for goods and is usually guaranteed against loss or theft

traveller's joy *n.* a European climbing plant of the buttercup family that has white flowers and feathery fruits. Latin name: *Clematis vitalba.*

traveller's tale *n.* a fantastic, unlikely, or obviously untrue account of sth, as given by a traveller to people who do not travel

travelling folk, **travelling people** *npl.* a term for Romany and other itinerant people, most often used by themselves

travelling salesman *n.* a salesperson whose work consists of travelling around calling on potential customers within a territory

travelling saleswoman *n.* a woman salesperson whose work consists of travelling around calling on potential customers within a territory

travelling wave *n.* PHYS a wave that continuously carries energy away from its source

travelogue /trávvə log/ *n.* a film, video tape, or piece of writing, or a lecture accompanied by pictures, video or film, about travel, especially to interesting or remote places, or about sb's travels in particular

travel sickness *n.* a feeling of nausea caused by movement, especially by the movement of the vehicle, train, ship, or aircraft in which sb is travelling. US term **motion sickness** —**travel-sick** *adj.*

Travers, Mount /trávvərz/ mountain in the north of the South Island, New Zealand, situated in the northern part of the Southern Alps. Height: 2,338 m/7,671 ft.

Travers, Ben (1886–1980) British playwright, noted for his farces. Full name **Benjamin Travers**

traverse /trávvurss, trə vúrss/ *v.* (**-verses, -versing, -versed**) **1.** *vt.* **MOVE ACROSS AN AREA** to travel or move across, over, or through an area or a place ○ *traverse the countryside* **2.** *vti.* **MOVE BACK AND FORTH** to move backwards and forwards across sth ○ *volunteers traversed the field looking for clues* **3.** *vt.* **REACH ACROSS STH** to extend or reach across sth ○ *traverse the river* **4.** *vti.* MOUNTAINEERING **MOVE AT AN ANGLE** to move at an angle across a rock face while ascending or descending it **5.** *vti.* SKIING **FOLLOW A ZIGZAG COURSE** to ski in diagonal runs following a zigzag course down a slope **6.** *vti.* **SWIVEL A GUN** to swivel sth, especially a gun, from side to side on a pivot **7.** *vi.* FENCING **SLIDE A BLADE TOWARDS AN OPPONENT'S HILT** to slide the blade of a sword towards an opponent's hilt while at the same time applying pressure to his or her blade **8.** *vt.* **THWART SB** to thwart sb or sth (*literary*) **9.** *vt.* LAW **DENY ALLEGATIONS** to deny the opposing party's allegations as set out in the pleading in a lawsuit, formally and, usually, in their entirety ■ *n.* **1. JOURNEY** a movement or journey across, over, or through sth **2. ROUTE** a route or way across or over sth **3.** MOUNTAINEERING **MOVEMENT ACROSS A ROCK FACE** a horizontal or oblique movement across a rock face in climbing **4.** SKIING **DIAGONAL RUN** a diagonal zigzag skiing run down a ski slope **5.** BUILDING **CROSSBEAM** sth that is fixed across a gap or lies crosswise such as a structural member of a building **6.** BUILDING **GALLERY** a gallery or loft that crosses from side to side inside a building **7.** BUILDING **BARRIER WITHIN A BUILDING** a railing, curtain, screen, or partition forming a barrier **8.** MIL **BARRIER ACROSS A TRENCH** a defensive barrier of earth across a trench **9. OBSTRUCTION** sth that thwarts or obstructs (*literary*) **10.** GEOM = **transversal** *n.* **11.** NAUT **ZIGZAG COURSE** the zigzag course of a sailing vessel in contrary winds **12.** MECH ENG **LATERAL MOVEMENT** the horizontal movement of a machine part such as a lathe or grinding tool as it moves across the work piece **13.** LAW **DENIAL OF ALLEGATIONS** a formal denial of the opposing party's allegations as set out in their pleading in a lawsuit **14.** CIV ENG **TYPE OF SURVEY** a survey made using a series of intersecting straight lines of known length whose angles of intersection are measured for recording on a map or in a table of data ■ *adj.* **CROSSWISE** lying across sth [14thC. Via French *traverser* from late Latin *tra(ns)versare*, from Latin *transversus*, the past participle of *transvertere* 'to turn across', from *vertere* 'to turn' (see VERTICAL).] —**traversable** *adj.* —**traversal** *n.* —**traverser** *n.*

travertine /trávvərtin/, **travertin** *n.* a hard semicrystalline white or light-coloured limestone precipitated in hot springs and caves and used as a facing material in building [Late 18thC. Via Italian *travertino* from, ultimately, Latin *(lapis) tiburtinus* '(stone) of Tibur (Tivoli, a town in Italy)'.]

travesty /trávvəsti/ *n.* (*plural* **-ties**) **1. FALSE REPRESENTATION** a distorted or debased version of sth ○ *it was a kangaroo court, a travesty of justice* **2.** ARTS **GROTESQUE IMITATION** a literary or artistic work, usually meant as a parody, that ridicules sth serious by imitating it in a grotesque or distorted manner ■ *vt.* (**-ties, -tying, -tied**) **MAKE A TRAVESTY OF STH** to imitate or mock sth in a grotesque or distorted manner [Mid-17thC. From French *travesti*, 'dressed in disguise', from *travestir*, 'to disguise, ridicule', and Italian *travestire*, from Latin *tra-*, 'trans-', + *vestire*, 'to clothe'.]

travois /trə vóy, trávvoy/ (*plural* **-vois**) *n.* a sledge made of two poles connected by a frame and pulled by an animal, used in the past by Native North Americans of the Great Plains [Mid-19thC. From French, from *travail*, from Latin *trabs*, 'beam'.]

travolator /trávvə laytər/, **travelator** *n.* a moving walkway for pedestrians, e.g. in an airport or shopping precinct [Mid-20thC. Formed from TRAVEL, modelled on ESCALATOR.]

trawl /trawl/ *n.* **1. FISHING NET** a large net that is dragged along the sea bottom behind a commercial fishing boat **2. SUSPENDED FISHING LINE** a long fishing line suspended between buoys that has several shorter lines with baited hooks attached **3.** SEARCH a search for sth, especially information ■ *vti.* **(trawls, trawling, trawled) 1.** FISH WITH A TRAWL to use or put out a trawl to catch fish **2.** SEARCH THROUGH LARGE AMOUNT OF INFORMATION to search for sth through a large amount of information or many possibilities [Mid-16thC. From Middle Dutch *traghelen*, 'to drag', from *traghel*, 'trawl net', from Latin *tragula*, from *trahere*, 'to pull' (source of English *tractor*).]

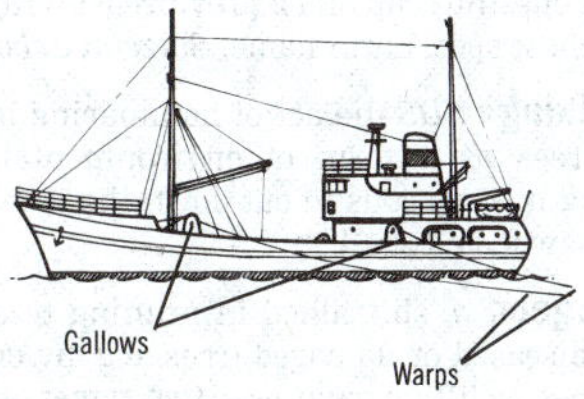

Trawler

trawler /tráwlər/ *n.* **1.** FISHING BOAT a boat that is used in trawling for fish **2.** SB WHO TRAWLS sb who fishes by trawling

trawlerman /tráwlərmən/ (*plural* **-men** /-mən/) *n.* a fisherman who works on a trawler

trawl line *n.* = **trawl** *n.* 2

trawl net *n.* = **trawl** *n.* 1

tray /tray/ *n.* **1.** FLAT CARRIER FOR SMALL OBJECTS a flat piece of plastic, wood, or metal with a raised edge, used for carrying or displaying light objects **2.** TRAY AND THINGS IT CARRIES a tray and the objects on it ○ *dropped a tray of dishes* **3.** CONTAINER IN WHICH TO ORGANIZE THINGS a shallow container, sometimes part of a desk drawer or cabinet, in which to keep items such as stationery or jewellery [Old English *trīg*. Ultimately from an Indo-European word that is also the ancestor of English *tree* and *trough*.]

tray-bake *n.* a cake made in a baking tray and cut up into squares (*regional*)

tray table *n.* a small table that folds down from the back of the seat in front of you in a plane or train

treacherous /tréchərəss/ *adj.* **1.** TRAITOROUS betraying or ready to betray sb's trust, confidence, or faith **2.** PERILOUS involving hidden dangers or hazards ○ *treacherous seas* [14thC. From Old French *trecheros* 'deceitfulness', from *trechier* (see TREACHERY).] —**treacherously** *adv.* —**treacherousness** *n.*

treachery /tréchəri/ (*plural* **-ies**) *n.* **1.** BETRAYAL betrayal or deceit **2.** ACT OF BETRAYAL an act or instance of betrayal or deceit [12thC. From Old French *trecherie*, from *trechier*, *trichier* (see TRICK).]

treacle /treék'l/ *n.* **1.** SYRUP FROM SUGAR REFINING a thick brown sticky sweet liquid, produced during the process of refining raw sugar, that is used to make cakes, sweets, and puddings (*often used before a noun*) ○ *treacle toffee.* US term **molasses 2.** STH CLOYING sth cloying or excessively sentimental **3.** FORMER ANTIDOTE TO POISON a preparation used in the past as an antidote to poison [14thC. Via Old French *triacle* and Latin *theriaca* from Greek *thēriakē (antidotos)*, '(antidote to) poisonous animals', from *thērion*, 'wild or poisonous animal', from *thēr*, 'wild'.]

WORD KEY: ORIGIN

Treacle retained its original meaning of 'antidote' when it came into English, but it later gradually broadened out into 'medicine', and the practice of disguising the unpleasant taste of medicine with sugar syrup led in the 17th century to its application to 'syrup'.

treacly /treékli/ *adj.* **1.** RESEMBLING TREACLE sticky and sweet like treacle **2.** MAWKISH cloying or excessively sentimental —**treacliness** *n.*

tread /tred/ *v.* **(treads, treading, trod** /trod/, **trodden** /tródd'n/ *or* **trod) 1.** *vi.* TRAMPLE STH to step or put a foot on sth, especially so as to crush or damage it ○ *She trod on his toe.* **2.** *vti.* WALK OR STEP ON STH to take a step or steps, or walk or step on, across, or along sth ○ *Don't tread on the wet concrete.* **3.** *vt.* SPREAD STH DIRTY BY WALKING to spread sth unwanted from the feet or footwear by walking, often grinding it in ○ *food trodden into the carpet* **4.** *vt.* FORM A PATH to form sth such as a path by trampling or walking **5.** *vt.* DANCE STEPS to perform the steps of a dance (*dated*) **6.** *vi.* ACT IN STATED WAY to proceed or behave in a particular way ○ *tread carefully* **7.** *vi.* CRUSH to repress or treat sb or sth harshly ■ *n.* **1.** WAY OF TREADING a way or sound of walking or stepping ○ *heard the heavy tread of marching feet* **2.** ACT OF TREADING an act of walking or of trampling sth **3.** HORIZONTAL PART OF A STEP the horizontal part of a step in a staircase **4.** WIDTH OF A STEP the width of the horizontal part of a step, measured from front to back **5.** AUTOMOT OUTER SURFACE OF A TYRE the part of the surface of a tyre or wheel that comes in contact with a road or rail **6.** DEPTH OF GROOVES ON A TYRE SURFACE the depth of grooves on the surface of a tyre **7.** CLOTHES PART OF SHOE THAT TOUCHES THE GROUND the part of the sole of a shoe that touches the ground [Old English *tredan*, from a prehistoric Germanic word that is also the ancestor of English *trade* and *trot*] —**treader** *n.*

treadle /trédd'l/ *n.* FOOT-OPERATED PEDAL a lever pushed repeatedly by the foot to provide drive for a machine such as a sewing machine or potter's wheel ■ *vti.* **(-les, -ling, -led)** POWER MACHINE WITH A TREADLE to operate a treadle, or operate a machine by using a treadle [Old English *tredel*, from *tredan* (see TREAD). The modern meaning, 'foot lever', evolved from 'step, stair'.] —**treadler** *n.*

treadmill /trédmil/ *n.* **1.** MECH ENG CYLINDER PROVIDING POWER a continuous belt or series of steps kept moving by people or animals walking on it that is used to provide power to a machine, e.g. to grind grain or raise water from a well **2.** FITNESS EXERCISE MACHINE a machine with an endless belt on which sb can walk, jog, or run, used for exercise and stress testing **3.** NEVER-ENDING ROUTINE a monotonous and seemingly endless task, job, or routine

treas. *abbr.* 1. treasurer 2. treasury

treason /treéz'n/ *n.* **1.** BETRAYAL OF COUNTRY violation of the allegiance owed by a person to his or her own country, e.g. by aiding an enemy. ◊ **high treason 2.** TREACHERY betrayal or disloyalty **3.** ACT OF BETRAYAL an act of betrayal or disloyalty [12thC. Via Anglo-Norman *treisoun*, 'treacherous handing over, betrayal', from the Latin stem *tradition-*, from *tradere*, 'to hand over' (source of English *traitor*, *betrayal*, and *tradition*).]

treasonable /treéz'nəb'l/, **treasonous** /treéz'nəss/ *adj.* involving, being, or punishable as treason —**treasonableness** *n.* —**treasonably** *adv.*

treasure /trézhər/ *n.* **1.** JEWELS AND PRECIOUS OBJECTS AS WEALTH wealth, especially in the form of jewels and precious objects, often accumulated or hoarded **2.** STH VALUABLE sth of great value or worth **3.** SB HIGHLY VALUED sb who is highly valued or loved ○ *an actor considered as one of our national treasures* ■ *vt.* **(-ures, -uring, -ured) 1.** REGARD AS VERY VALUABLE to prize sb or sth as being of great value or worth ○ *treasured the memory of that day* **2.** ACCUMULATE AND STORE STH VALUABLE to accumulate and store sth regarded as valuable [12thC. Via French *trésor* from Latin *thesaurus*, from Greek *thēsauros*, 'treasure'.] —**treasurable** *adj.*

WORD KEY: CULTURAL NOTE

Treasure Island, a novel by Scottish writer Robert Louis Stevenson (1883). This classic romance recounts young Jim Hawkins' adventures with a treacherous band of pirates searching for lost treasure on a distant island. The book's most memorable character is one-legged pirate Long John Silver, who carries a pet parrot given to shrieking 'Pieces of eight!'.

treasure house *n.* **1.** STORE OF VALUABLE THINGS a place or collection in which many valuable things are located **2.** TREASURY a building in which treasure is kept

treasure hunt *n.* a game in which competitors attempt to solve a series of clues, sometimes leading to a hidden prize

treasurer /trézhərər/ *n.* a manager of the finances of an organization, e.g. a club, society, government, or corporation —**treasurership** *n.*

Treasurer *n.* in Australia, the finance minister in the federal government and in each of the state governments

treasure-trove /-trōv/ *n.* **1.** DISCOVERED UNCLAIMED WEALTH silver or gold coins or bullion found buried in the earth and for which there is no known owner. In the United Kingdom such finds become Crown property. **2.** STH FOUND OF VALUE sth discovered that is valuable or the source of sth valuable ○ *The new shop is a treasure-trove of antiques.* [Mid-16thC. *Trove* from Anglo-Norman *tresor trove*, from Old French *tresor* 'treasure' + *trove*, the past participle of *trover* 'to find'.]

treasury /trézhəri/ (*plural* **-ies**) *n.* **1.** PLACE FOR THINGS OF VALUE a place in which treasure or other valuable items are stored and preserved **2.** BUSINESS STORE OF MONEY the funds or revenues of a government, organization, or corporation, or the place in which they are deposited and disbursed **3.** COLLECTION OF VALUABLE THINGS a source or collection of valuable things, e.g. literary or artistic works [13thC. Via Old French *tresorie* from *trésor* (see TREASURE).]

Treasury (*plural* **Treasuries**) *n.* in many countries, the government department in charge of collecting and managing public revenue

Treasury Bench *n.* the front bench of the row to the Speaker's right in the House of Commons, where members of the government sit

Treasury bill *n.* a financial security issued by the Treasury payable to the bearer after a fixed period, usually three months

Treasury bond *n.* an interest-bearing debt security issued by the US government, with an initial life of between ten and thirty years

Treasury note *n.* **1.** MEDIUM-TERM OBLIGATION an intermediate-term, interest-paying debt instrument issued by the US government, with an initial life of between one and ten years **2.** BRITISH CURRENCY NOTE a currency note issued by the British Treasury in 1914 and valid until 1928

treasury tag *n.* a short length of cord with metal ends that is passed through punched holes in sheets of paper to hold them together

treat /treet/ *v.* **(treats, treating, treated) 1.** *vt.* REGARD SB IN A PARTICULAR WAY to behave towards or think of sb or sth in a particular way ○ *They treated us practically like family.* **2.** *vt.* MED UNDERTAKE TO CURE SB to give medical aid to sb or apply medical techniques to a disease or symptom in order to provide a cure **3.** *vt.* TECH SUBJECT TO A PROCESS OR AGENT to subject sth to a physical, chemical, or biological process or agent such as a chemical reaction or the application of a coating **4.** *vt.* PAY FOR SB ELSE to pay for sb else's food, drink, entertainment, or gifts ○ *I'll treat you to lunch at the hotel.* **5.** *vt.* PROVIDE SB WITH STH PLEASURABLE to give sb or yourself sth enjoyable ○ *They treated their mother to breakfast in bed.* **6.** *vt.* DEAL WITH STH IN A PARTICULAR WAY to present or handle a subject, especially in art or literature, in a particular way ○ *treat a delicate subject with great sensitivity* **7.** *vi.* DISCUSS A TOPIC to discuss or deal with a topic in writing or speech ○ *a play that treats of greed and revenge* **8.** *vi.* NEGOTIATE TERMS to negotiate, especially in order to reach a settlement (*formal*) ○ *refusing to treat with the enemy* ■ *n.* **1.** ENTERTAINMENT PAID FOR BY SB ELSE sth such as food, entertainment, or a gift that is given to sb and paid for by sb else **2.** ACT OF PAYING FOR SB ELSE an act of paying for sth such as food, entertainment, or a gift, for sb else **3.** STH ENJOYABLE sth enjoyable, especially when a surprise ○ *It's a treat to see a smile on his face again.* [13thC. Via Old French *traitier*, 'to bargain with, negotiate', from Latin *tractare*, 'to handle', literally 'to drag about', from *trahere*, 'to pull' (source of English *contract*).] —**treatable** *adj.* —**treater** *n.* ◇ **a treat** in a pleasing or successful way (*informal*) ○ *The woodwork's come up a treat.*

treatise /treétiss, -iz/ *n.* a formal written work that deals with a subject systematically and usually extensively [14thC. Via Anglo-Norman *tretiz* from Old French *traitier* (see TREAT).]

treatment /treétmənt/ *n.* **1.** MED PROVISION OF MEDICAL CARE the application of medical care to cure disease, heal injuries, or ease symptoms **2.** MED MEDICAL CARE a particular remedy, procedure, or technique for curing or alleviating a disease, injury, or condition ○ *a new treatment for asthma* **3.** WAY OF HANDLING SB OR

STH the particular way in which sb or sth is dealt with or handled ○ *had pretty rough treatment* **4.** ARTS **PRESENTATION OF A SUBJECT** the way of presenting or handling a subject, especially in art or literature **5.** CINEMA **SCHEMATIC VERSION OF A FILM** a schematic version of a film script, generally without dialogue and individual shots, indicating how the story is to be dealt with in a screenplay **6.** TECH **TREATING STH WITH AGENT** an act of subjecting sth to a physical, chemical, or biological process or agent **7. USUAL ACTIONS TAKEN** the usual way of dealing with sb or sth in a particular situation (*informal*) ○ *As guests of the government we got the full VIP treatment.*

treaty /treéti/ (*plural* **-ties**) *n.* **1.** POL **AGREEMENT BETWEEN STATES** a formal contract or agreement negotiated between countries or other political entities **2. PACT** an agreement or contract between two or more parties [14thC. Via Old French *traité*, 'assembly, agreement, treaty', from Latin *tractatus*, from *tractare* (see TREAT).]

treaty Indian *n. Can* = **Status Indian**

treaty port *n.* in the past, a port where foreign trade was allowed by a treaty, especially in China, Japan, and Korea

treble /trébb'l/ *adj.* **1. TRIPLE** three times as many or much **2.** MUSIC **OF OR FOR THE HIGHEST MUSICAL RANGE** relating to or intended for a soprano voice or a high-pitched instrument **3. HIGH-PITCHED** high-pitched or shrill ■ *n.* **1.** MUSIC **HIGH-PITCHED INSTRUMENT OR VOICE** a treble voice, singer, instrument, or part **2. HIGH-PITCHED SOUND** a high-pitched or shrill sound **3.** RECORDING **AUDIO FREQUENCY RANGE** the higher audio frequencies electronically reproduced by a radio, recording, or sound system **4.** RECORDING **CONTROL FOR HIGH-FREQUENCY AUDIO RESPONSE** a control for increasing or decreasing the high-frequency response on a radio or audio amplifier **5. STH TRIPLED** sth three times as many or as much **6.** DARTS **RING ON DARTBOARD** the narrow inner ring on a dartboard, or a hit landing within this ring, which scores three times the stated value **7.** SPORTS **SET OF THREE WINS** the winning of three major competitions in one season, especially in football **8.** BETTING **BET ON THREE RACES** a bet on three races in which the winnings and stake from each race are placed on the next ■ *vti.* (**-les, -ling, -led**) **TRIPLE STH** to become or make sth become three times as many or as much ○ *output has trebled over the past year* [13thC. Via Old French from Latin *triplus*, 'triple'. In the sense 'high-pitched', from early contrapuntal music, in which the highest voice part was the third part (after tenor and alto).] — **trebleness** *n.* —**trebly** *adv.*

treble chance *n.* a way of betting on football pools. in which the person betting chooses a number of games as being likely to result in a draw, home win, or away win.

treble clef *n.* a clef that puts G above middle C on the second line of the staff, used for soprano and alto voices, high-pitched instruments, and the right hand of keyboard instruments

Treblinka /tre blíngkə/ site of two Nazi concentration camps in eastern Poland, situated near Malkinia, about 97 km/60 mi. northeast of Warsaw

trebuchet /trébbyoo̅ shet/, **trebucket** /treé bukit/ *n.* a medieval siege engine with a sling attached to a wooden arm for hurling large stones [14thC. From French *trébuchet*, from *trébucher*, 'to overturn', of uncertain origin: perhaps ultimately from Latin *trans-* 'across' + Old French *buc* 'trunk (of the body)', from prehistoric Germanic.]

trecento /tray chéntō/ *n.* the 14th century, used especially in referring to Italian art and literature [Mid-19thC. From Italian, shortening of *mil trecento* 'one thousand three hundred'.] —**trecentist** *n.*

tree /tree/ *n.* **1.** PLANTS **LARGE PERENNIAL WOODY PLANT** a woody perennial plant that grows to a height of several metres and typically has a single erect main stem with side branches **2.** PLANTS **PLANT RESEMBLING A TREE** a large shrub or nonwoody plant that resembles a tree such as a palm tree or tree fern **3. STH BRANCHED LIKE A TREE** sth that has branches or pegs on which to hang things ○ *a mug tree* **4.** CONSTR **WOODEN SUPPORT** a wooden beam, bar, or post that supports or is part of a structure **5. DIAGRAM OF A HIERARCHICAL STRUCTURE** a diagram of a hierarchical structure that shows the relationships between components as branches **6.** COMPUT **HIERARCHICAL DATA STRUCTURE** a hierarchical data structure in which each element contains data and may be linked by branches to two or more other elements. Every element has only a single predecessor, except for the first, which is called the root and has no predecessor. **7.** CRYSTALS **CRYSTALLINE GROWTH** a branching growth of crystals, particularly of a metal **8. GALLOWS** a gallows (*archaic*) **9.** CHR **CROSS JESUS CHRIST DIED ON** in Christianity, the cross on which Jesus Christ was crucified (*archaic*) ■ *vt.* (**trees, treeing, treed**) **1. FORCE UP A TREE** to chase or force an animal or person to climb a tree **2.** *US, Can* **PUT IN A DIFFICULT SITUATION** to force sb into a position of difficulty or disadvantage (*informal*) **3. STRETCH ON A SHOETREE** to stretch or shape a shoe or a boot on a shoetree [Old English *trēo(w)*. Ultimately from an Indo-European word meaning 'oak tree', which is also the ancestor of English *druid, tray,* and *trough*.] —**treeless** *adj.* — **treelessness** *n.* ◇ **be barking up the wrong tree** to be mistaken, especially as regards the best way to achieve sth ◇ **out of your tree** behaving irrationally (*slang*) ◇ **up a tree** *US* in a position of difficulty or disadvantage (*informal*)

WORD KEY: CULTURAL NOTE

The Tree of Man, a novel by Australian writer Patrick White (1955). The story of a pioneer couple who settle in New South Wales, Australia, it charts the establishment of their farm, the birth of their children, and their gradual estrangement as they search for greater fulfilment in their respective lives.

tree creeper *n.* a small inconspicuous forest bird with large claws for climbing tree trunks in search of insects. Family: Certhidae.

tree diagram *n.* = **tree** *n.* 5

tree farm *n.* an area where trees are grown commercially for their wood products

tree fern *n.* a tropical fern that grows to the height of a tree and has a crown of fronds. Family: Cyatheaceae and Marattiaceae.

tree frog *n.* a small frog, found mainly in Asia, Australia, and America, that has long digits with adhesive discs that allow it to climb trees. Family: Hylidae.

treehopper /treé hopər/ *n.* a small tree-dwelling insect that feeds on the sap of trees. Many species have grotesque projections on their backs. Family: Membracidae.

tree house *n.* a platform, often with a roof and walls, built among the branches of a tree, especially for children to play in

tree kangaroo *n.* a kangaroo, found in New Guinea and northern Australia, that has sharp claws and grasping forepaws that allow it to climb trees. Genus: *Dendrolagus.*

tree line *n.* **1. BOUNDARY OF TREE GROWTH** the limit of altitude, or northern or southern latitude, beyond which no trees can grow. US term **timberline 2. FOREST EDGE** the edge of a wood or forest

treen /treen/ *n.* **WOODEN UTENSILS** tableware and other household utensils made of wood ■ *adj.* **WOODEN** made of wood (*archaic*) [Old English *trēowen*, 'made of wood', from TREE. 'Wooden tableware' dates from the early 20thC.]

treenail /treé nayl, trénn'l/, **trenail, trunnel** /trúnn'l/ *n.* a large cylindrical peg made of dry wood that expands to give a tight fit when it is wet and is used to fasten timbers together, e.g. in ships

treenware /treén wair/ *n.* = **treen** *n.*

tree of heaven *n.* a deciduous tree, originally Chinese but now cultivated elsewhere, that grows rapidly and has foul-smelling flowers. Latin name: *Ailanthus altissima* and *Ailanthus glandulosa.*

tree of knowledge *n.* in the Bible, the tree that grew in the Garden of Eden and produced the fruit that was forbidden to Adam and Eve (Genesis 2:9, 3)

tree of life *n.* in the Bible, the tree that grew in the Garden of Eden and produced a fruit that gave eternal life to sb who ate it (Genesis 3:22–24)

tree ring *n.* BOT = **growth ring**

tree shrew *n.* a small mammal resembling a squirrel with a long snout that lives in the forests of Southeast Asia and eats insects. Family: Tupaiidae.

tree snake *n.* a slender tree-living snake of the East Indies, some of which are reputed to launch themselves from tree to tree

tree sparrow *n.* **1. SMALL EURASIAN SPARROW** a small sparrow of Europe and Asia that differs from the house sparrow in having a black spot near its ear and a chestnut crown. It does not normally nest in towns. Latin name: *Passer montanus.* **2. LARGE N AMERICAN SPARROW** a large North American sparrow with a chestnut cap and a grey breast with a single dark chest spot. Latin name: *Spizella arborea.*

tree spiking *n. US* the act of hammering long nails into trees as a form of environmental protest, making it dangerous to cut down the trees using a chainsaw [Late 20thC]

tree surgeon *n.* sb trained in pruning trees or treating diseased or damaged trees, e.g. by cutting off branches or filling cavities —**tree surgery** *n.*

tree tomato *n.* US term **tamarillo 1. S AMERICAN SHRUB** a cultivated shrub of the nightshade family, originally from South America, with edible red fruit. Latin name: *Cyphomandra betacea* and *Cyphomandra crassifolia.* **2. FRUIT OF TREE TOMATO SHRUB** the edible red fruit of the tree tomato shrub

treetop /treé top/ *n.* the highest branches of a tree

trefoil /tréffoyl/ *n.* **1.** PLANTS **PLANT WITH THREE-LOBED LEAVES** a plant of the pea family that has three-lobed leaves, especially clover **2.** BOT **THREE-LOBED LEAF OR PART** a leaf or other plant part with three lobes **3. THREE-LOBED SHAPE OR OBJECT** an object or design with three lobes or connected parts, such as an emblem used in heraldry **4.** ARCHIT **ORNAMENT IN THE SHAPE OF A CLOVER LEAF** an architectural ornament or form resembling a clover leaf [14thC. Via Anglo-Norman *trifoil* from Latin *trifolium*, literally 'with three leaves', from *folium* 'leaf' (source of English *foil*).]

trehala /tri haálə/ *n.* an edible sugary substance that comes from the pupal case of an Asian beetle [Mid-19thC. Via Turkish *tigale* from Persian *tīgāl*.]

trehalase /tri haá layss, -layz/ *n.* an enzyme found in yeast and moulds that catalyses the breakdown of the sugar trehalose [Late 19thC. Coined from TREHALA + -ASE.]

trehalose /tri haá lōss, -lōz/ *n.* a sugar found in yeast, some fungi, bacteria, and the blood of many insects. Formula: $C_{12}H_{22}O_{11}$. [Mid-19thC. Coined from TREHALA + -OSE.]

treillage /tráylij/ *n.* a trellis or latticework [Late 17thC. From French, from *treille*, from Latin *trichila* 'bower, arbour'.]

trek /trek/ *vi.* (**treks, trekking, trekked**) **1. MAKE A LONG DIFFICULT JOURNEY** to make a long difficult journey, especially on foot and often over rough or mountainous terrain **2. GO SLOWLY OR LABORIOUSLY** to go somewhere slowly or with difficulty ○ *I had to trek across town to the other bookshop* **3.** *S Africa* **GO BY OX WAGON** to travel in a wagon pulled by an ox ■ *n.* **1. LONG DIFFICULT JOURNEY** a long difficult journey, especially on foot and often over rough or mountainous terrain **2.** *S Africa* **OX WAGON JOURNEY** a journey or migration by ox wagon [Mid-19thC. Via Afrikaans from Dutch, 'to draw, pull, travel'. The modern meaning 'to travel cross-country by foot' evolved from 'to travel by ox wagon'.] — **trekker** *n.*

WORD KEY: CULTURAL NOTE

Star Trek, a television series created in 1966 by US writer and producer Gene Roddenberry (1921–91). The adventures of the Starship Enterprise, a 23rd-century spacecraft on a mission 'to boldly go where no man has gone before', initially ran for 79 episodes. The popularity of the series later gave rise to numerous film spinoffs, the follow-up television series *Star Trek: The Next Generation*, *Star Trek: Voyager* and *Star Trek: Deep Space Nine*, and a worldwide network of dedicated fans known as Trekkies.

Trekkie /tréki/ *n.* a fan of the science-fiction television series 'Star Trek' (*informal*)

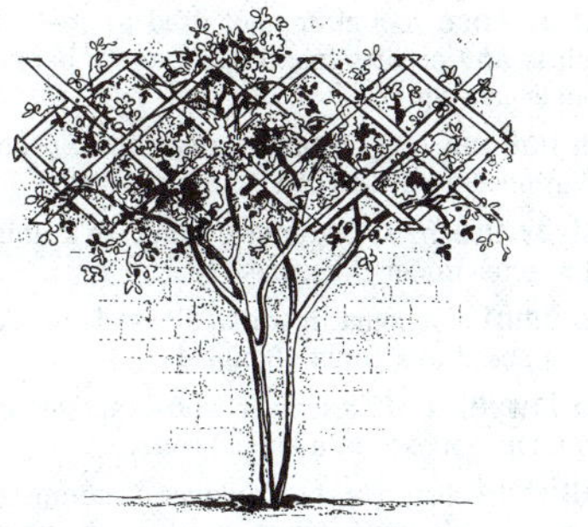

Trellis

trellis /trélliss/ *n.* **1. LATTICE FOR SUPPORTING A PLANT** a lattice of wood, metal, or plastic used to support plants, usually fixed to a wall **2. LATTICEWORK STRUCTURE** a structure made of latticework, especially an arch ■ *vt.* **(-lises, -lising, -lised) 1. TRAIN A PLANT ON A LATTICE** to support or train a plant such as a vine on a trellis **2. MAKE STH INTO A TRELLIS** to interweave pieces of wood, metal, or plastic to make a trellis [14thC. Via Old French *trelis* from Latin *trilix*, literally 'three threads', from *licium* 'thread of a warp'.]

trelliswork /trélliss wurk/ *n.* latticework, usually for supporting plants

trematode /trémmətōd, trée-/ *n.* a flatworm that lives as a parasite in the liver, gut, lungs, or blood vessels of vertebrates, attaching itself by suckers or hooks and sometimes causing serious disease. Class: Trematoda. [Mid-19thC. Via modern Latin *Trematoda* from Greek *trēmatōdēs* 'perforated' (because many worms of this class have perforated skins), from *trēma* 'hole, orifice'.]

tremble /trémb'l/ *vi.* **(-bles, -bling, -bled) 1. SHAKE SLIGHTLY BUT UNCONTROLLABLY** to shake with slight movements, continuously and uncontrollably, e.g. from fear, cold, or anger **2. VIBRATE** to shake or vibrate as a result of an external force ○ *We felt the house tremble as the train passed.* **3. BE AFRAID** to be afraid or anxious about sth ■ *n.* **QUIVERING** a shaking, vibration, or quivering [14thC. Via Old French *trembler* from medieval Latin *tremulare* 'to shake', from *tremulus* 'shaking', from *tremere* 'to shake' (source of English *tremulous*).] —**tremblingly** *adv.* —**trembly** *adj.*

trembles /trémb'lz/ *n.* poisoning in sheep and cattle that have fed on white snakeroot. Affected animals tremble and become weak. (*takes a singular verb*)

trembling poplar *n.* = **aspen**

tremendous /trə méndəss/ *adj.* **1. VERY GREAT** extremely large, powerful, or great ○ *There was a tremendous clap of thunder.* **2. VERY GOOD** extremely good, successful, or impressive ○ *a tremendous improvement* **3. FRIGHTENING** causing fear or horror (*archaic*) [Mid-17thC. Formed from Latin *tremendus* 'fearful', literally 'to be trembled at', from *tremere* (see TREMBLE).] —**tremendously** *adv.* —**tremendousness** *n.*

tremie /trémmi/ *n.* a device consisting of a funnel-shaped hopper at the top connected to a large metal pipe with a valve at the bottom, used to spread concrete underwater [Early 20thC. Via French, and Old French *tremuie* '(mill-)hopper', from Latin *trimodia* 'three-peck measure', from *modius* 'peck'.]

tremolite /trémmə līt/ *n.* a white, grey, or pale green mineral silicate of calcium and magnesium with traces of iron, found in metamorphic rocks and used as a substitute for asbestos [Late 18thC. Named after *Tremola*, a valley in Switzerland where it was discovered.]

tremolo /trémməlō/ (*plural* **-los**) *n.* **1. TREMULOUS SOUND IN MUSIC** the rapid repetition of a tone or the rapid alternation between two tones in singing or playing a musical instrument, which produces a quavering effect **2. DEVICE FOR PRODUCING A TREMOLO** a device in an organ for producing tremolo [Mid-18thC. Via Italian from Latin *tremulus* (see TREMBLE).]

tremolo arm *n.* a lever fixed to the bridge of an electric guitar and used to move the bridge slightly, so as to stretch the strings to alter the pitch of a note

tremor /trémmər/ *n.* **1.** SEISMOL **MINOR EARTHQUAKE** a quivering or vibration caused by slippage of the Earth's crust at a fault, especially before or after a major earthquake **2.** MED **TREMBLING** a slight shaking or trembling movement **3. SHUDDER** a quiver or shudder, e.g. from fear, illness, or nervousness **4. SUDDEN SENSATION** a sudden and usually brief feeling of excitement, nervousness, or anticipation **5. WAVERING SOUND OR LIGHT** a fluctuation in a sound or light [14thC. Directly or via Old French *tremour* from Latin *tremor* 'trembling, terror', from *tremere* 'to shake'.] —**tremorous** *adj.*

tremulant /trémmyŏŏlənt/ *adj.* **TREMULOUS** shaking or trembling ■ *n.* = **tremolo** [15thC. Coined from TREMULOUS + -ANT.]

tremulous /trémmyŏŏləss/ *adj.* **1. TREMBLING** shaking, trembling, or quavering, e.g. from fear or nervousness ○ *in a tremulous voice* **2. FEARFUL** showing fear or nervousness about sth [Early 17thC. Formed from Latin *tremulus*, from *tremere* (see TREMBLE).] —**tremulously** *adv.* —**tremulousness** *n.*

trenail *n.* = **treenail**

trench /trench/ *n.* **1. DITCH WITH STEEP SIDES** a long deep hole dug in the ground, usually with steep or vertical sides **2.** MIL **PROTECTION AGAINST ENEMY FIRE** a long excavation, often with the excavated earth banked up in front, used as a defence against enemy fire ○ *warfare conducted in the trenches* **3.** OCEANOG **VALLEY ON THE OCEAN FLOOR** a long narrow valley on an ocean or sea floor ■ *v.* **(trenches, trenching, trenched) 1.** *vti.* **DIG A TRENCH IN STH** to dig a long deep hole in or through sth **2.** *vt.* MIL **FORTIFY STH WITH TRENCHES** to fortify a position with trenches as a defence against enemy fire **3.** *vt.* **PUT STH IN A TRENCH** to place sth such as a pipe in a trench [14thC. From Old French *trenche* 'ditch, cutting, slice', from *trenchier* 'to cut', from Latin *truncare* 'to cut (off)', from *truncus* 'tree trunk'.]

trenchant /trénchənt/ *adj.* **1. INCISIVE** direct, incisive, and deliberately hurtful ○ *trenchant criticism* **2. ENERGETIC** effective and relevant in the pursuit or achievement of a goal ○ *trenchant opinions* [14thC. From Old French, 'cutting', formed from *trenchier* (see TRENCH).] —**trenchancy** *n.* —**trenchantly** *adv.*

Trenchard /trénch aard, trénchərd/, **Hugh Montague, 1st Viscount** (1873–1956) British air force commander. In World War I he played a central role in the formation of the RAF (1918), and became its first marshal.

trench coat *n.* a belted double-breasted raincoat, originally modelled on a military coat of World War I

trencher[1] /trénchər/ *n.* in the past, a wooden platter used to serve or cut food (*archaic*) [14thC. Via Anglo-Norman *trenchour* from Old French *trenchoir*, from *trenchier* (see TRENCH).]

trencher[2] /trénchər/ *n.* sb or sth that digs trenches, especially a machine that cuts a furrow or ditch in which to lay cables or pipes

trencherman /trénchərmən/ (*plural* **-men** /-mən/) *n.* sb who eats heartily and enjoys food

trench fever *n.* a contagious illness whose symptoms include fever, headaches, and muscle aches, common among soldiers fighting in trenches in World War I and caused by the bacterium *Rochalimaea quintana*

trench foot *n.* a painful condition of the feet caused by prolonged exposure of the feet to cold and wet. It results in loss of sensation, tissue damage, and sometimes gangrene.

trench mortar *n.* a small cannon capable of firing shells at high trajectories over short distances, often used in trench warfare

trench mouth *n.* MED = **Vincent's angina**

trench warfare *n.* **1.** MIL **WARFARE BETWEEN ENTRENCHED ARMIES** a form of warfare in which armies conduct attacks on each other from opposing positions in fortified trenches **2. LONG-STANDING DISAGREEMENT** long-standing and bitter conflict in which opposing parties continually attack each other

trend /trend/ *n.* **1. TENDENCY** a general tendency, movement, or direction ○ *a report documenting recent such trends* **2. PREVAILING STYLE** a current fashion or mode ○ *the latest trends in designer kitchens* ■ *vi.* **(trends, trending, trended) TEND OR MOVE** to show a tendency or movement towards sth or in a particular direction ○ *public opinion trending towards reunification* [Late 16thC. From Old English *trendan* 'to revolve' (hence 'to turn', 'to turn in a particular direction'), from a prehistoric Germanic word meaning 'roundness'.]

trendoid /trénd oyd/ *n.* **SLAVISH FOLLOWER OF FASHIONS** sb who follows the latest trends or fashions slavishly (*informal*) ■ *adj.* **FOLLOWING FASHION SLAVISHLY** following trends or fashions slavishly (*informal*) [Late 20thC. Coined from TRENDY + -OID.]

trendsetter /trénd setər/ *n.* sb or sth that starts or popularizes a new trend or fashion —**trendsetting** *adj.*

trendy /tréndi/ *adj.* **(trendier, trendiest)** (*informal*) **1. CURRENTLY FASHIONABLE** relating to or exemplifying the latest fashion ○ *a trendy restaurant* **2. REFLECTING THE LATEST FAD** deliberately reflecting or adopting fashionable, often faddish, ideas or tastes ■ *n.* (*plural* **trendies**) **SB FOLLOWING CURRENT FASHION** sb who follows the latest trends or fashions, often slavishly (*informal*) —**trendily** *adv.* —**trendiness** *n.*

Trent /trent/ the third longest river in England. It rises at Biddulph Moor, Staffordshire, and flows into the North Sea via Humber Estuary. Length: 270 km/170 mi.

trente et quarante /tróNt ay ka róNt/ *n.* GAMBLING = **rouge et noir** [Late 17thC. From French, literally 'thirty-and-forty'; because thirty and forty are respectively winning and losing numbers.]

Trenton /tréntən/ capital city of New Jersey, in the west-central part of the state, 45 km/28 mi. northeast of Philadelphia. Population: 88,675 (1990).

trepan[1] /tri pán/ *n.* **1.** SURG **EARLY TYPE OF TREPHINE** an early cylindrical surgical instrument (**trephine**) used especially to cut a hole in the skull **2.** MECH ENG **TOOL FOR CUTTING DISC OR CYLINDER** a machine tool used to remove a circular disc from a metal sheet or a shallow cylindrical core from a metal ingot or block. The hole is made by removing a concentric ring of material as opposed to disintegrating the material originally within the hole, as with drilling and boring. **3.** MINING **ROCK-BORING TOOL** a tool for boring holes in rock ■ *vt.* **(trepans, trepanning, trepanned) 1.** SURG = **trephine 2.** MECH ENG **CUT STH OUT USING A TREPAN** to cut a disc or cylindrical core from sth using a trepan **3.** MINING **BORE HOLE IN ROCK WITH TREPAN** to bore a hole in rock using a trepan [14thC. Via medieval Latin *trepanum* 'rotary saw', from Greek *trupanon* 'borer', from *trupan* 'to pierce', from *trupē* 'hole'.] —**trepanation** /tréppə náysh'n/ *n.* —**trepanner** /tri pánnər/ *n.*

trepan[2] /tri pán/, **trapan** *vt.* **(-pans, -panning, -panned) LURE SB OR STH** to trap or ensnare sb or sth (*archaic*) ■ *n.* **SB OR STH THAT LURES OTHERS** sb or sth that entraps or ensnares others (*archaic*) [Mid-17thC. From earlier *trapan*. Probably a variant of TRAP.]

trepang /tri páng/ *n.* a large sea cucumber that lives in the southern Pacific and Indian oceans. It is eaten in soups, especially in China and Indonesia. Genera: *Holothuria* and *Actinopyga*. [Late 18thC. From Malay *teripang*.]

trephine /tri féen, -fīn/ *n.* **SURGICAL INSTRUMENT** a cylindrical sharp or sawtooth-edged surgical instrument used especially to cut a hole in the skull. It is also used in corneal grafting to remove an opaque disc from a cornea so that it can be replaced with a clear disc. ■ *vt.* **(-phines, -phining, -phined) REMOVE A CIRCLE OF BONE OR TISSUE** to remove a circular section from a bone, especially the skull, or from corneal tissue with a trephine [Early 17thC. From Latin *tres fines* 'three ends', partly modelled on TREPAN.] —**trephination** /tréffi náysh'n/ *n.*

trepidation /tréppi dáysh'n/ *n.* **1. APPREHENSION** fear or uneasiness about the future or a future event **2. TREMBLING** an involuntary trembling (*archaic*) [15thC. From the Latin stem *trepidation-*, from *trepidare* 'to startle, be agitated'.]

treponema /tréppə néemə/ (*plural* **-mas** *or* **-mata** /-mətə/), **treponeme** /tréppə neem/ *n.* a spirochaete bacterium that lives as a parasite in warm-blooded animals. One species causes syphilis in humans. Genus: *Treponema*. [Early 20thC. From modern Latin, from Greek *trepein* 'to turn', + *nēma* 'thread'.] —**treponemal** *adj.*

trespass /tréspəss/ *vi.* (-passes, -passing, -passed) **1.** LAW ENTER SB ELSE'S LAND UNLAWFULLY to go onto sb else's land or enter sb else's property without permission **2.** LAW CAUSE INJURY TO to cause injury to the person, property, or rights of another **3.** ENCROACH ON SB to intrude on sb's privacy or time **4.** BREAK A MORAL OR SOCIAL LAW to commit a sin or break a social law (*archaic*) ■ *n.* **1.** UNLAWFUL ENTRY ONTO SB ELSE'S LAND the act or an instance of going onto sb else's land or entering sb else's property without permission **2.** ENCROACHMENT an intrusion into sb's privacy or time **3.** SIN a sin or act of wrongdoing (*archaic*) [14thC. From Old French *trespas* 'transgression', from *trespasser* 'to pass beyond or across', from medieval Latin *transpassare*.] —**trespasser** *n.*

tress /tress/ *n.* **1.** LOCK OF HAIR a lock of long hair, especially a woman's hair **2.** PLAIT OF WOMAN'S HAIR a plait of hair, especially a woman's hair (*archaic*) ■ **tresses** *npl.* HAIR sb's hair, especially a woman's long hair ■ *vt.* (**tresses, tressing, tressed**) STYLE HAIR IN TRESSES to arrange or style hair in tresses [13thC. From Old French *tresse*, of uncertain origin: perhaps ultimately from Greek *trikhia* 'rope', from *thrix* 'hair'.]

tressure /tréshər, tréss yoor/ *n.* an inner border with ornamental fleurs-de-lis on a heraldic shield [14thC. From Old French *tressour*, from *tresse* (see TRESS); originally in the meaning of 'ribbon worn to secure the hair'.] —**tressured** *adj.*

trestle /tréss'l/ *n.* **1.** SUPPORTING FRAMEWORK a supporting framework consisting of a horizontal beam held up by a pair of splayed legs at each end **2.** CONSTR TOWER FOR SUPPORTING A BRIDGE any of a series of timber, steel, or reinforced concrete towers that supports a bridge **3.** CONSTR BRIDGE SUPPORTED BY TOWERS a bridge consisting of multiple short spans supported by braced towers [14thC. From Old French *trestel*, literally 'small beam', from Latin *transtrum* 'beam, crossbar'.]

Trestle table

trestle table *n.* a table whose top is supported on trestles

trestletree /tréss'l tree/ *n.* either of two horizontal timbers fixed to the masthead to support the crosstrees

trestlework /tréss'l wurk/ *n.* a system of supporting trestles, e.g. one that supports a bridge

tretinoin /trə tínnō in, trétti noyn/ *n.* a drug related chemically to vitamin A and applied to the skin to treat acne and other skin disorders [Late 20thC. Coined from TRANS- + *retinoic (acid)* (coined from RETINO- + -IC) + -IN.]

trevally /tri válli/ (*plural* **-lies**) *n.* an Australian marine food fish with a slender body and sharply forked tail. Family: Carangidae. [Late 19thC. Alteration of *cavally* (see CAVALLA).]

Trevelyan /trə vélliyən/, **G. M.** (1876–1962) British historian. An influential historian, he wrote for both scholarly and popular audiences. His work includes much British history and biographical studies of Giuseppe Garibaldi. Full name **George Macaulay Trevelyan**

Treviso /tre veéssō/ capital city of Treviso Province, Veneto Region, northeastern Italy. Population: 84,100 (1990).

Trevithick /trə víthik/, **Richard** (1771–1833) British engineer and inventor. His steam locomotives, using the high-pressure steam engines that he developed, were the first regularly to carry passengers or freight.

trews /trooz/ *npl.* close-fitting trousers, usually made of tartan cloth, worn by some Scottish army regiments [Mid-16thC. From Irish *triús* or Gaelic *triubhas* 'close-fitting shorts' (also the sources of English *trousers*).]

trey /tray/ (*plural* **treys**) *n.* a card, or the face of a dice or domino, with three spots [14thC. Via Old French *trei(s)* from Latin *tres* 'three'.]

TRH *abbr.* **1.** Their Royal Highnesses **2.** thyrotropin-releasing hormone

tri- *prefix.* three, third ◊ *trilateral* [From Latin and Greek. Ultimately from the Indo-European word for 'three', which is also the ancestor of English *three*.]

triable /trí əb'l/ *adj.* **1.** LAW SUBJECT TO COURT TRIAL subject to or fit for trial in a court of law **2.** CAPABLE OF BEING TESTED able to be tested or tried [15thC. From Anglo-Norman, from TRY + -ABLE.] —**triableness** *n.*

triacid /trī ássid/ *adj.* **1.** REACTING WITH 3 HYDROGEN ATOMS used to describe a base capable of reacting with three hydrogen atoms per molecule, so that one molecule of the base can react with three molecules of a monobasic acid **2.** CONTAINING 3 REPLACEABLE HYDROGEN ATOMS used to describe an acid or a salt that contains three replaceable hydrogen atoms [Mid-19thC. Coined from TRI- + ACID.]

triad /trí ad, -əd/ *n.* **1.** SET OF 3 a group of three people or things **2.** MUSIC MUSICAL CHORD a musical chord consisting of three notes, especially a chord made up of a tonic, a third, and a fifth **3.** CHEM ATOM WITH VALENCY OF 3 an atom or chemical group with a valency of three **4.** MIL US STRATEGIC MISSILE FORCE a US strategic missile force made up of bombers, land-based ballistic missiles, and submarine-launched ballistic missiles **5.** LITERAT WELSH LITERARY FORM a form of composition in ancient Welsh literature in which subjects or statements are arranged in groups of three [Mid-16thC. Via French *triade* or the late Latin stem *triad-* from Greek *triados* 'of three'.] —**triadic** /trī áddik/ *adj.*

Triad *n.* a Chinese secret society, especially one involved in organized crime [Mid-20thC. Said to be from the early rituals of such societies, using a triangle as a symbol, where the *Triad* refers to a trinity of heaven, earth, and man.]

triage /treé aazh, trí ij/ *n.* the process of prioritizing sick or injured people for treatment according to the seriousness of the condition or injury [Early 18thC. From French, from *trier* (see TRY).]

trial /trí əl/ *n.* **1.** LAW FORMAL LEGAL PROCESS a formal examination of the facts and law in a civil or criminal action before a court of law in order to determine an issue **2.** LAW USE OF A COURT TRIAL the use of a court trial to determine an issue or sb's guilt or innocence ◊ *standing trial for fraud* **3.** TEST a test or experiment to determine the quality, safety, performance, usefulness, or public acceptance of sth **4.** PAINFUL EXPERIENCE an instance of trouble or hardship, especially one that tests sb's ability to endure **5.** SB OR STH TROUBLESOME sb or sth that causes trouble or annoyance to sb ◊ *He's such a trial!* **6.** EFFORT an earnest attempt to do sth (*formal*) ◊ *a trial to circle the globe in a hot-air balloon* **7.** SPORTS PRELIMINARY COMPETITION a sports competition or preliminary test to select candidates for a later competition ■ **trials** *npl.* COMPETITION FOR ANIMALS a competition to test the skills of a working animal or one used in sport ◊ *sheepdog trials* ■ *adj.* **1.** EXPERIMENTAL done as a test or experiment ◊ *a trial separation* **2.** LAW OF A COURT TRIAL relating to or used in a court trial ◊ *a trial judge* ■ *vt.* (**-als, -alling, -alled**) TEST STH to test sth, especially under the conditions in which it is intended to be used [Mid-15thC. Via Anglo-Norman, or medieval Latin *triallum*, from Old French *trier* (see TRY).]

WORD KEY: CULTURAL NOTE
The Trial, a novel (1925) by Austrian writer Franz Kafka. It is the story of Josef K, a young bank clerk who is abruptly arrested for an unspecified misdemeanour. After a long, unsuccessful attempt to discover the nature of his crime, Josef is executed. This enigmatic work is seen as a disturbing allegory of the human condition.

trial and error *n.* a method of finding a satisfactory solution or means of doing sth by experimenting with alternatives and eliminating failures

trial balance *n.* a statement used to check that the debits and credits in a double-entry book-keeping ledger are equal

trial balloon *n.* a tentative suggestion, proposal, or plan put forward to test opinion or reaction

trial by fire *n.* a thorough test of sb's abilities or character under pressure

trial court *n.* a court in which a case is first decided, as opposed to a court of appeal

trial lawyer *n. US* a lawyer who practises in a trial court as opposed to a appeal court

triallist /trí əlist/ *n.* a sports player or competitor who is given a chance to prove worthy of being included in a team for a major competition

trial of strength *n.* a contest between two individuals or sides to decide which is the stronger

trial run *n.* a test of sth new or untried, especially to assess its performance

triamcinolone /trí am sínnəlōn/ *n.* a synthetic drug (**corticosteroid**) used to treat inflammation of the mouth, gums, skin, and joints. Formula: $C_{21}H_{27}FO_6$. [Mid-20thC. Coined from TRI- + *amyl* + *cinene* + *prednisolone*.]

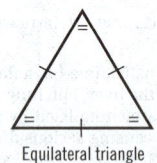

Equilateral triangle
(3 sides =, 3 angles =)

Isoceles triangle
(2 sides =, 2 angles =)

Acute triangle
(a, b, c < 90°)

Obtuse triangle

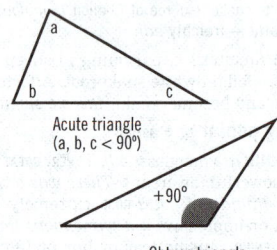

Right triangle

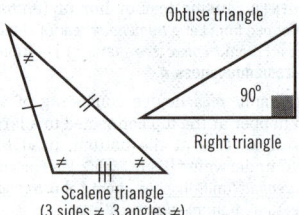

Scalene triangle
(3 sides ≠, 3 angles ≠)

Triangle

triangle /trí ang g'l/ *n.* **1.** 3-SIDED PLANE POLYGON a plane figure that has three sides and three angles. The triangle is a fundamental figure of plane geometry, since it is the polygon with the fewest sides and any other polygon can be subdivided into triangles. **2.** OBJECT WITH 3 SIDES sth shaped like a triangle **3.** *US =* set square **4.** MUSIC PERCUSSION INSTRUMENT a metal bar bent into the shape of a triangle with one angle open, used as a percussion instrument **5.** 3-PERSON RELATIONSHIP an emotional relationship involving three people. ◊ **eternal triangle** [14thC. Via Old French or directly from Latin *triangulum*, from *triangulus* 'three-cornered' (source of English *angle*).]

triangular /trí áng gyŏolər/ *adj.* **1.** OF A TRIANGLE relating to or in the shape of a triangle **2.** WITH A TRIANGULAR BASE having a base in the shape of a triangle **3.** HAVING 3 ELEMENTS consisting of or involving three parts or people [14thC. From late Latin *triangularis*, from *triangulum* (see TRIANGLE).] —**triangularity** /trī áng gyŏŏ lárrəti/ *n.* —**triangularly** /trī áng gyŏŏlərli/ *adv.*

triangulate *vt.* /trī áng gyŏŏ layt/ (**-lates, -lating, -lated**) **1.** MEASURE STH USING TRIGONOMETRIC RELATIONSHIPS to measure sth using the trigonometric relationships between pairs of the sides and angles of triangles **2.** SURVEY OR MAP STH BY TRIANGULATION to survey or map an area by the process of triangulation **3.** SPLIT STH INTO TRIANGLES to divide a surface into triangles **4.** MAKE STH TRIANGULAR to make sth into the shape of a triangle ■ *adj.* /trī áng gyŏŏlit, -layt/ MADE UP OF TRIANGLES shaped like a triangle or made up of triangles [15thC. Formed from Latin *triangulum* (see TRIANGLE). The adjective came via medieval Latin *triangulatus*.] —**triangulately** *adv.*

triangulation /trī áng gyŏŏ láysh'n/ *n.* **1.** NAVIG METHOD FOR DETERMINING LOCATION TRIGONOMETRICALLY a navigation technique that uses the trigonometric properties of triangles to determine a location or course by means of compass bearings from two points a known distance apart. Space-age global positioning systems enable people to triangulate their location relative to the known positions of Earth-orbiting satellites. **2.** DIVIDING OF AN AREA INTO TRIANGLES FOR SURVEYING the division of a large area into adjacent triangles for survey purposes using trigonometric relationships to calculate the dimensions of an area bounded by each triangle. One side (**baseline**) and the angles to the third point of each adjacent triangle are measured, enabling the lengths of the other sides to be calculated. **3.** NAVIG SYSTEM OF TRIANGLES USED IN TRIANGULATION the system of triangles laid out in triangulation [Early 19thC. Coined from the verb TRIANGULATE and -ATION.]

Triangulum /trī áng gyŏŏləm/ *n.* a small constellation in the northern hemisphere near Aries and Perseus

Triangulum Australe /-o strάyli/ *n.* a small constellation in the southern hemisphere near the Southern Cross

triarchy /trī aarki/ (*plural* **-chies**) *n.* **1.** RULE BY 3 LEADERS a system in which a country is ruled by three leaders **2.** COUNTRY WITH 3 RULERS a country ruled by three leaders [Early 17thC. Either from Greek *triarkhia* 'triumvirate', or coined from TRI- + -ARCH.]

Triassic /trī ássik/ *n.* the period of geological time when reptiles flourished and dinosaurs, modern corals, and coniferous forests first appeared, 245 to 208 million years ago [Mid-19thC. Coined from German *Trias*, from Latin, 'three, triad', from Greek, + -IC. From there being three subdivisions to this period.] —**Triassic** *adj.*

triathlete /trī áth leet/ *n.* sb who competes in a triathlon

triathlon /trī áthlən, -lon/ *n.* an athletic contest in which the contestants take part in three events, usually swimming, cycling, and running [Late 20thC. Coined from TRI- + Greek *athlon* 'contest' (source of English *athletics*). Modelled on such words as DECATHLON.]

triatomic /trī ə tómmik/ *adj.* **1.** CONTAINING 3 ATOMS containing three atoms in each molecule **2.** HAVING THREE REPLACEABLE ATOMS having three replaceable atoms or chemical groups [Mid-19thC. Coined from TRI- + ATOMIC.] —**triatomically** *adv.*

triaxial /trī áksi əl/ *adj.* MATH having or involving three axes [Late 19thC. Coined from TRI- + AXIAL.] —**triaxiality** /trī áksi álləti/ *n.*

triazine /trī ə zeen, trī áy zeen/ *n.* **1.** COMPOUND WITH A 6-MEMBERED RING any of three organic compounds with a six-membered ring containing three carbon atoms and three nitrogen atoms. Formula: $C_3H_3N_3$. **2.** SUBSTITUTED DERIVATIVE OF TRIAZINE ISOMER any substituted derivative of a triazine isomer, several of which are used as herbicides and pesticides and others as dyes [Late 19thC]

triazole /trī ə zol, -zōl, trī ázzol, -zōl/ *n.* **1.** COMPOUND WITH A 5-MEMBERED RING any organic compound with a five-membered ring containing two carbon atoms and three nitrogen atoms. Formula: $C_2H_3N_3$. **2.** CHEMICAL DERIVED FROM TRIAZOLE any chemical derivative of triazole, several of which are used in photocopying systems [Late 19thC]

tribade /tríbbəd/ *n.* a lesbian, especially one who takes part in tribadism [Early 17thC. Via French or Latin from Greek *tribas*, from *tribein* 'to rub'.]

tribadism /tríbbədizəm/ *n.* a lesbian practice in which one partner rubs her genitals against the other's [Early 19thC. Formed from TRIBADE.]

tribalism /tríbəlizəm/ *n.* **1.** TRIBAL LIFE the customs, beliefs, and social organization of a tribe **2.** ALLEGIANCE TO A GROUP loyalty to a tribe or social group [Late 19thC. Coined from TRIBAL + -ISM (see TRIBE).] —**tribalist** *n., adj.* —**tribalistic** /tríbə lístik/ *adj.*

tribasic /trī báyssik/ *adj.* **1.** REACTING WITH 3 HYDROXYL IONS used to describe an acid that contains three replaceable hydrogen atoms and is capable of reacting with three hydroxyl ions per molecule **2.** CONTAINING 3 UNIVALENT METAL ATOMS used to describe a compound that contains three univalent metal atoms or groups in each molecule [Mid-19thC. Coined from TRI- + BASIC.]

tribe /trīb/ *n.* **1.** SOCIAL DIVISION OF PEOPLE a society or division of a society whose members have ancestry, customs, beliefs, and leadership in common **2.** FAMILY a large family (*informal humorous*) **3.** GROUP WITH STH IN COMMON a group of people who have sth in common such as an occupation, social background, or political viewpoint (*disapproving*) ○ *rebelled against the whole tribe of earnest policy works* **4.** BIOL TAXONOMIC DIVISION a division in the scientific classification of animals and plants, between a subfamily and a genus **5.** HIST ANCIENT ROMAN SOCIAL GROUP any of the three groups, Latins, Sabines, and Etruscans, into which ancient Roman society was divided [13thC. Via Old French *tribu* from Latin *tribus* 'one of three ethnic divisions of the Roman people', from *tri-* 'three' (source of English *tribune* and *contribution*).] —**tribal** *adj.* —**tribally** *adv.*

tribesman /tríbzmən/ (*plural* **-men** /-mən/) *n.* a man who is a member of a tribe

tribespeople /tríbz peep'l/ *npl.* people who belong to a tribe

tribeswoman /tríbz wŏŏmən/ (*plural* **-en** /-wimin/) *n.* a woman who belongs to a tribe

triblet /tríbblət/ *n.* a cylindrical or tapered rod used for making annular and cylindrical items such as rings or nuts or in drawing tubes [Early 17thC. From French *triboulet*, of ultimately unknown origin.]

tribo- *prefix.* friction ○ *triboelectricity* [From Greek *tribos* 'rubbing', from *tribein* 'to rub' (source also of English *diatribe*)]

triboelectricity /tríbō i lek tríssəti, tríbō éllek tríssəti/ *n.* an electric charge generated by friction, e.g. by rubbing materials together —**triboelectric** /tríbō i léktrik/ *adj.*

tribology /trī bólləji/ *n.* the science and technology of interacting surfaces in relative motion, including the study of friction, lubrication, and wear [Mid-20thC. Coined from TRIBO- + -LOGY.] —**tribological** /tríbə lójjik'l/ *adj.* —**tribologist** /trī bólləjist/ *n.*

triboluminescence /tríbō loomi néss'nss/ *n.* luminescence caused by friction [Late 19thC. Coined from TRIBO- + LUMINESCENCE.] —**triboluminescent** *adj.*

tribrach /tríbrak, trī brak/ (*plural* **-brachs**) *n.* a metrical foot made up of three short syllables [Late 16thC. Via Latin *tribrachys* from Greek *tribrakhus*, from *tri-* 'three' + *brakhus* 'short'.] —**tribrachic** *adj.*

tribromoethanol /trī brōmō éthə nol/ *n.* a white crystalline organic compound used as a general anaesthetic. Formula: CBr_3CH_2OH. [Early 20thC. Coined from TRI- + BROMO- + ETHANOL.]

tribulation /tríbbyŏŏ láysh'n/ *n.* **1.** HARDSHIP great difficulty, affliction, or distress **2.** CAUSE OF SUFFERING sth such as an ordeal that causes difficulty, affliction, or distress ○ *the trials and tribulations of the struggling author* [13thC. Via Old French *tribulation* from, ultimately, Latin *tribulare* 'to afflict, press', from *tribulum* 'threshing tool' (board with sharp points), from *terere* 'to rub' (source of English *attrition*).]

tribunal /trī byŏŏn'l, tri-/ *n.* **1.** LAW COURT a court of justice **2.** JUDGING BODY a body that is appointed to make a judgment or inquiry ○ *an industrial tribunal* **3.** COURT CONVENED BY GOVERNMENT a court convened, under English law, by the British government to judge or investigate a particular matter **4.** RAISED SEAT a bench or seat on a platform where a judge or magistrate sits [15thC. Directly and via Old French from Latin *tribunal* 'platform for magistrates', from *tribunus* (see TRIBUNE[1]).]

tribunate /tríbbyŏŏnət/ *n.* the office, rank, or authority of a tribune in ancient Rome [Mid-16thC. From Latin *tribunatus*, from *tribunus* (see TRIBUNE[1]).]

tribune[1] /tríbyoon/ *n.* **1.** HIST REPRESENTATIVE ELECTED BY THE ROMAN COMMON PEOPLE a representative of the common people in the ancient Roman republic, elected annually **2.** DEFENDER OF PUBLIC RIGHTS a person or institution that defends the rights of the people [14thC. Via Old French *tribun* from Latin *tribunus* 'magistrate', literally 'head of a tribe', from *tribus* (see TRIBE).] —**tribunary** *adj.* —**tribuneship** *n.*

tribune[2] /tríbyoon/ *n.* **1.** ARCHIT BISHOP'S THRONE OR SITE OF IT a bishop's throne, or an apse of a Christian basilica containing the throne **2.** ARCHIT CHURCH GALLERY a gallery in a Christian church **3.** PLATFORM a raised platform for a speaker [Mid-18thC. From French and Italian *tribuna* 'raised platform', alteration of Latin *tribunal*, from *tribunus* (see TRIBUNE[1]).]

Tribune Group *n.* a left-wing group of Labour Members of Parliament, founded in 1966 (*takes a singular or plural verb*) —**Tribunite** /tríbbyŏŏ nīt/ *n., adj.*

tributary /tríbbyŏŏtəri/ *n.* (*plural* **-ies**) **1.** STREAM FEEDING A LARGER BODY OF WATER a stream, river, or glacier that joins a larger stream, river, or glacier, or a lake **2.** HIST PAYER OF TRIBUTE a person or nation that pays a monetary tribute to another ■ *adj.* **1.** FLOWING INTO A LARGER BODY OF WATER joining a larger stream, river, or glacier, or a lake **2.** HIST PAID AS TRIBUTE paid or owed as a tribute **3.** PAYING TRIBUTE paying tribute in praise, money, or goods [14thC. From Latin *tributarius* 'liable to tax or tribute', from *tributum* (see TRIBUTE).] —**tributarily** *adv.*

tribute /tríbyoot/ *n.* **1.** EXPRESSION OF GRATITUDE OR PRAISE sth said or given to show gratitude, praise, or admiration **2.** EVIDENCE OF GOOD sth that is indicative of a value, benefit, or good quality in sb or sth ○ *The result is a tribute to her powers of persuasion.* **3.** HIST PAYMENT BY ONE RULER TO ANOTHER a payment made by one ruler or state to another as a sign of submission **4.** HIST PAYMENT TO A FEUDAL LORD in medieval society, a payment made by a vassal to a lord, or an obligation for such payment [14thC. Via Old French *tribut*, or directly from Latin *tributum*, from *tribuere* 'to give out among the tribes', from *tribus* (see TRIBE).]

tricarboxylic acid cycle /trī kaar bok síllik-/ *n.* = **Krebs cycle**

tricarpellary /trī kaarp'ləri/ *adj.* used to describe a flower that has three carpels

trice[1] /trīss/ *n.* a very short period of time [15thC. From TRICE[2]. The meaning evolved from 'resulting from a single pull or tug', via 'taking a short time'.]

trice[2] /trīss/ (**trices, tricing, triced**) *vt.* to haul up or fasten sth, especially with a rope [14thC. From middle Dutch *trīsen* 'to pull', from *trīse* 'pulley'.]

tricentenary /trī sen teénəri, -tén-/ *adj., n.* = **tercentenary**

tricentennial *adj., n.* = **tercentenary**

triceps /trī seps/ (*plural* **-cepses** *or* **-ceps**) *n.* a muscle that has three points of anchorage, especially the large muscle running along the back of the upper arm that straightens the elbow [Late 16thC. From Latin *triceps* 'three-headed', from *caput* 'head'.]

triceratops /trī sérrə tops/ *n.* a plant-eating dinosaur of the Cretaceous Period, somewhat similar in appearance to a rhinoceros, with a bony crest on the back of its neck and three horns. Genus: *Triceratops*. [Late 19thC. From modern Latin, formed from Greek *trikeratos* 'three-horned' + *ōps* 'face'.]

trich- *prefix.* = **tricho-** (*used before vowels*)

trichiasis /tri kī ə siss/ *n.* the inward growth of hair around a body opening, especially inward growth of the eyelashes, causing irritation of the eyeball [Mid-17thC. Via late Latin from, ultimately, Greek *trikhian* 'to be hairy'.]

trichina /tri kīnə/ (*plural* **-nae** /-nee/) *n.* a small slender nematode worm that infests the intestines of meat-eating mammals, and whose larvae form cysts in skeletal muscle. Infection may derive from undercooked meat. Symptoms include diarrhoea, nausea, and fever. Latin name: *Trichinella spiralis*. [Mid-19thC. Via modern Latin from, ultimately, Greek *trikhinos* 'hairy', from *thrix* 'hair'.] —**trichinal** *adj.* —**trichinous** *adj.*

Trichinopoly /trínchin óppəli/ former name for **Tiruchchirappalli**

trichinosis /tríki nṓsiss/ *n.* a disease caused by infestation with trichinae and marked by fever, muscle pain, and diarrhoea, often resulting from eating undercooked pork infected with the larvae

trichite /trík īt/ *n.* a dark needle-shaped crystal found in volcanic rock —**trichitic** /tri kíttik/ *adj.*

trichlorethylene *n.* = **trichloroethylene**

trichlorfon, trichlorphon *n.* an organophosphorus insecticide used typically in agricultural sheep dips and in household ant killer. Formula: $C_4H_8Cl_3O_4P$. [Mid-20thC. Coined from TRI- + CHLORO- + *-fon*, a shortening of *phosphonate*.]

trichloride /trī kláw rīd/, **trichlorid** /-rid/ *n.* any compound with three chloride atoms per molecule

trichloroacetic acid /trī klawrō ə sséetik-/ *n.* a corrosive toxic acid used in weed control and as an astringent and antiseptic. Formula: $C_2Cl_3HO_2$. [Late 19thC]

trichloroethane /trī klawrō ée thayn/ *n.* a volatile colourless nonflammable liquid used in industry as a solvent, especially for cleaning electrical equipment. Formula: $C_2H_3Cl_3$. [Early 20thC. Coined from TRI- + CHLORO- + ETHANE.]

trichloroethylene /trī klawrō éthə leen/, **trichlorethylene** /trī klawr éthə leen/ *n.* a volatile colourless nonflammable liquid used as a solvent and degreaser, and as an anaesthetic. Formula: C_2HCl_3.

trichlorphon *n.* CHEM = **trichlorfon**

tricho- *prefix.* hair, filament, thread ○ *trichoid* [From Greek *trikh-*, the stem of *thrix* 'hair' (source of English *tress* and *trichina*)]

trichocyst /tríkə sist/ *n.* a stinging or grasping organ resembling a thread that protrudes from minute cavities on the surface of some protozoans, especially ciliates, ejected from minute cavities —**trichocystic** /tríkə sístik/ *adj.*

trichogyne /tríkə jīn, -jin/ *n.* a projection resembling a hair on the female sex organ of some fungi, lichens, and algae that attracts and receives the male sex cell prior to fertilization —**trichogynial** /tríkə jíni əl, -jínni əl/ *adj.* —**trichogynic** /-jínik, -jínnik/ *adj.*

trichoid /tríkoyd/ *adj.* resembling hair or a hair

trichology /tri kóllə ji/ *n.* the study and treatment of hair and its diseases —**trichological** /tríkə lójjik'l/ *adj.* —**trichologist** /tri kóllə jist/ *n.*

trichome /tríkōm, tríkōm/ *n.* **1.** PLANT OUTGROWTH an outgrowth of a plant's outer cell layer (**epidermis**). Trichomes have various shapes and functions, and include root hairs. **2.** SLENDER CHAIN OF CELLS a filamentous chain of bacterial or cyanobacterial cells [Late 19thC. Formed from Greek *trikhōma* 'growth of hair', from, ultimately, *thrix* 'hair'.] —**trichomic** /tri kómmik/ *adj.*

trichomonad /tríkō mónnad/ *n.* a flagellated protozoan that lives as a parasite in the digestive and reproductive tracts of humans and animals. Genus: *Trichomonas.* —**trichomonadal** /-mónnə dəl/ *adj.* —**trichomonal** /-mónn'l, -mṓn'l, tri kómmən'l/ *adj.*

trichomoniasis /tríkō mō nī́ əssiss/ *n.* **1.** MED SEXUALLY TRANSMITTED DISEASE a sexually transmitted infection, especially of the vagina, marked by persistent discharge and intense itching. It is caused by a protozoan parasite *Trichomonas vaginalis.* **2.** VET INFECTION OF ANIMALS an infection of animals caused by parasitic protozoans (**trichomonads**). In cattle, this condition can lead to spontaneous abortion or sterility. [Early 20thC. Coined from TRICHOMONAD + -IASIS.]

trichopteran /trī kóptərən/ *n.* = **caddis fly** [Mid-19thC. From modern Latin *Trichoptera*, order name, from Greek *trikho-* (see TRICHO-) + *ptera*, plural of *pteron* 'wing'.]

trichotomy /trī kóttə mi/ (*plural* **-mies**) *n.* **1.** DIVISION INTO 3 SECTIONS the division of sth into three categories, classes, elements, or parts (*formal*) **2.** TRIPARTITE DIVISION OF HUMAN NATURE the division of human nature into body, soul, and spirit [Early 17thC. From modern Latin *trichotomia*, from Greek *trikha* 'in three parts' + -TOMY.] —**trichotomic** /tríkə tómmik/ *adj.* —**trichotomous** /trī kóttə məss/ *adj.* —**trichotomously** *adv.*

trichroism /trī krō izəm/ *n.* the property possessed by some crystals of showing three different colours when viewed along each of their three axes [Mid-19thC. Formed from Greek *trikhroos*, literally 'three-coloured'.] —**trichroic** /trī krṓ ik/ *adj.*

trichromat /tríkrō mat, tríkrə-/ *n.* sb who has normal colour vision and is able to perceive red, green, and blue [Early 20thC. Back-formation from TRICHROMATIC.]

trichromatic /trī krō máttik/, **trichrome** /trī krōm/, **trichromic** /trī-/ *adj.* **1.** 3-COLOUR relating to, involving, or using three colours **2.** COMBINING PRIMARY COLOURS involving the combination of the three primary colours to produce the other colours **3.** RELATING TO NORMAL COLOUR VISION relating to normal colour vision, which is able to perceive red, green, and blue —**trichromatism** /trī krṓmətizəm/ *n.*

trichuriasis /tríkyoo rī́ ə siss/ *n.* intestinal infection with nematodes of the genus *Trichuris*. It usually produces no symptoms, but may cause diarrhoea and bleeding in severely infected children. [Early 20thC. Formed from modern Latin *Trichuris*, genus name, from TRICH- + Greek *oura* 'tail'.]

trick /trik/ *n.* **1.** CUNNING DECEPTION a cunning action or plan that is intended to cheat or deceive **2.** PRANK a prank, joke, or mischievous action or plan ○ *played a trick on his sister* **3.** SPECIAL SKILL a special, effective, or ingenious knack, skill, or technique ○ *taught me the tricks of the trade* **4.** SKILFUL ACT DESIGNED TO AMUSE a skilful act or feat, designed to amuse or entertain ○ *taught the dog to do tricks* **5.** ACT OF MAGIC an act of magic or illusion, especially one involving sleight of hand, designed to puzzle or entertain ○ *a conjuring trick* **6.** DECEPTIVE EFFECT OF LIGHT an illusion, especially one caused by the light **7.** PECULIAR HABIT a peculiar characteristic, habit, mannerism, or way of behaving ○ *He has this trick of scratching his ear when he's being evasive.* **8.** UNFORESEEN EVENT a strange event or development that was not anticipated or that seems unfair or sad ○ *a cruel trick of fate* **9.** CHILDISH ACT a childish, disgraceful, or unacceptable action (*informal*) ○ *Up to your usual tricks, are you?* **10.** CARDS CARDS FROM EACH PLAYER IN A ROUND the cards played by all the players participating in one round of a card game and won by an individual player **11.** CARDS GOOD CARD a card likely to win a trick, especially in bridge **12.** PERIOD OF DUTY a period of duty, e.g. at the helm of a ship **13.** *US* PROSTITUTE'S CUSTOMER sb who pays for sex with a prostitute (*slang*) **14.** *US* SEX WITH SB FOR MONEY an individual engagement between a prostitute and a client (*slang*) ■ *vti.* (**tricks, tricking, tricked**) CHEAT to cheat or deceive sb ○ *Hundreds of readers were tricked into sending them money.* ■ *adj.* **1.** OF TRICKS involving or intended to be used for tricks or trickery ○ *trick photography* **2.** MADE AS AN IMITATION FOR A JOKE made as an imitation of sth so that it can be used to play a joke on sb **3.** *US, Can* MED OCCASIONALLY SYMPTOMATIC displaying symptoms of injury from time to time (*informal*) ○ *a trick ankle* [15thC. From Old North French *trique*, of uncertain origin: probably from, ultimately, Latin *tricae* 'complications, trifles'.] —**tricker** *n.* —**trickless** *adj.* ◇ **can't take a trick** *Aus* to have a run of back luck (*informal*) ◇ **do the trick** to be effective and do what is needed (*informal*) ◇ **how's tricks?** used as a greeting (*informal*) ◇ **never** *or* **not miss a trick** to notice everything that is happening, or any opportunity that is advantageous (*informal*) ◇ **show sb a trick or two** to demonstrate more skill than sb who is watching

trick out, trick up *vt.* to decorate or dress sb or sth up, especially in a fancy or garish way (*literary*) [15thC. Origin uncertain: probably from the underlying sense of 'deception' in the verb, easily extended to denote 'adornment'. Perhaps influenced by the obsolete French *s'estriquer* 'to deck oneself, adorn'.]

trick cyclist *n.* **1.** PERFORMER DOING TRICKS ON CYCLE sb who performs tricks on a bicycle or monocycle, especially in a circus **2.** PSYCHIATRIST a psychiatrist (*dated humorous informal*)

trickery /tríkəri/ (*plural* **-ies**) *n.* a trick, or the use of tricks, especially in order to cheat or deceive

trickle /trík'l/ *v.* (**-les, -ling, -led**) **1.** *vti.* FLOW SLOWLY IN A THIN STREAM to flow or cause sth to flow in a thin stream or in drops ○ *sweat trickled down his face* **2.** *vi.* MOVE SLOWLY OR GRADUALLY to move, come, or go slowly or gradually ○ *The crowd trickled slowly away and the park emptied.* ■ *n.* **1.** THIN SLOW FLOW a thin slow flow, movement, or stream ○ *a trickle of blood* **2.** ACT OF FLOWING IN THIN STREAM an act of flowing or of causing a liquid to flow in a thin stream [14thC. Origin uncertain: perhaps an imitation of the sound.] —**trickling** *adj.* —**tricklingly** *adv.* —**trickly** *adj.*

trickle charger *n.* a small low-current device used to recharge batteries slowly and maintain them in a fully charged state —**trickle charge** *n.*

trickle-down theory *n.* the economic theory that financial and other benefits received by big businesses gradually spread to benefit the rest of society

trick or treat *n.* CHILDREN'S HALLOWE'EN CUSTOM a Hallowe'en custom in which children call at neighbours' houses and threaten to play a trick on the householder unless they are given a treat such as sweets ■ *interj.* GREETING WHEN TRICK-OR-TREATING used as a greeting by children when they call on a house in order to ask for sweets at Hallowe'en

trick-or-treat (**trick-or-treats, trick-or-treating, trick-or-treated**) *vi.* to go to neighbours' houses and ask for sweets at Hallowe'en

trickster /tríks tər/ *n.* sb who deceives, swindles, or plays tricks

tricksy /tríksi/ *adj.* **1.** MISCHIEVOUS mischievous, playful, or inclined to play tricks **2.** NOT STRAIGHTFORWARD intricate, complicated, or over-elaborate **3.** GIMMICKY new and ingenious **4.** DECEITFUL employing craft, cunning, or deceit (*archaic*) **5.** DAPPER sprucely or smartly dressed (*archaic*) —**tricksiness** *n.*

tricky /tríki/ (**-ier, -iest**) *adj.* **1.** PROBLEMATIC difficult to do or deal with and requiring skill, caution, or tact ○ *a tricky manoeuvre* ○ *a tricky situation* **2.** CRAFTY OR SLY likely to cheat or outwit sb —**trickily** *adv.* —**trickiness** *n.*

triclad /trī klad/ *n.* a flatworm with an intestine that is divided into three sections. Order: Tricladida. [Late 19thC. Shortening of modern Latin *Tricladida*, from Greek *tri-* 'three' + *klados* 'branch'.]

triclinic /trī klínnik/ *adj.* used to describe a crystal that has three unequal axes, none of which is perpendicular to another [Mid-19thC. From -CLINIC.]

triclinium /tri klíni əm, trī klínni əm, tri klī́n-/ (*plural* **-a** /-ni ə/) *n.* **1.** COUCH a couch arranged around three sides of a table and used by ancient Romans to recline on at meals **2.** ROMAN DINING ROOM an ancient Roman dining room, especially one containing a triclinium [Mid-17thC. Via Latin from Greek *triklinion*, from *triklinos* 'room with three couches', from *klinē* 'couch'.]

tricolour /tríkələr, trī kulər/ *n.* **1.** 3-COLOURED FLAG a flag with three colours **2.** **tricolour, Tricolour** FRENCH NATIONAL FLAG the French national flag, consisting of three equal vertical bands of blue, white, and red **3.** ZOOL 3-COLOURED DOG a black, tan, and white dog ■ *adj.* **tricolour, tricoloured 1.** 3-COLOURED with, involving, or using three colours **2.** ZOOL PIEBALD having a coat of black, tan, and white

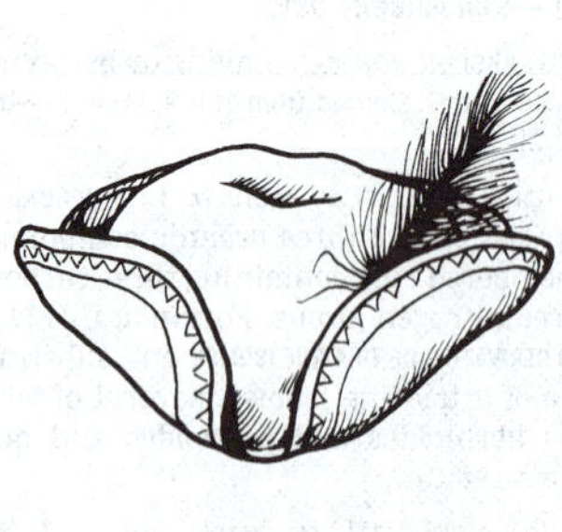

Tricorn

tricorn /trī kawrn/, **tricorne** *n.* **1.** CLOTHES COCKED HAT a hat with its brim turned up on three sides that was worn by men in the 18th century **2.** MYTHOL MYTHICAL ANIMAL an imaginary animal with three horns ■ *adj.* 3-HORNED having three horns or corners [Mid-18thC. Via French *tricorne* or directly from Latin *tricornis* 'three-horned', which was formed from *cornu* 'horn'.]

tricornered /trī́ kawrnərd/ *adj.* having three corners

tricot /trīkō, treékō/ *n.* **1. CLOSE-KNIT FABRIC** a plain close-knit fabric of natural or artificial fibre, used particularly for underwear **2. RIBBED DRESS FABRIC** a soft ribbed dress fabric made of wool or a wool and cotton mix [Late 18thC. From French *tricoter* 'to knit', of Germanic origin.]

tricotine /trīkə teén, treé-/ *n.* a strong woollen fabric woven with a double twill [Early 20thC]

tricuspid /trī́ kúss pid/ *adj.* **tricuspid, tricuspidal, tricuspidate 3-POINTED** having three cusps or points ■ *n.* **PART WITH THREE CUSPS** sth such as a tooth, valve, or leaf that has three cusps

tricuspid valve *n.* a heart valve consisting of three flaps that prevents blood from flowing back into the right atrium when the right ventricle contracts

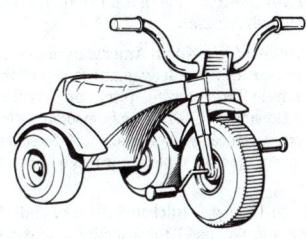

Tricycle

tricycle /trī́ssik'l/ *n.* **1. PEDAL-DRIVEN 3-WHEELED VEHICLE** a pedal-driven vehicle with two wheels at the back and one at the front, ridden now especially by young children **2. MOTOR-DRIVEN THREE-WHEELED VEHICLE** a motor-driven vehicle with three wheels ■ *vi.* **(-cles, -cling, -cled) RIDE A TRICYCLE** to ride a tricycle —**tricyclist** *n.*

tricyclic /trī sīklik/ *adj.* **CHEM WITH 3 RINGS** having a molecular structure containing three rings ■ *n.* **PHARM ANTIDEPRESSANT DRUG** a tricyclic drug used to treat depression

tridactyl /trī dáktil/, **tridactylous** /trī dáktiləss/ *adj.* **ZOOL** having three claws, fingers, or toes on each limb

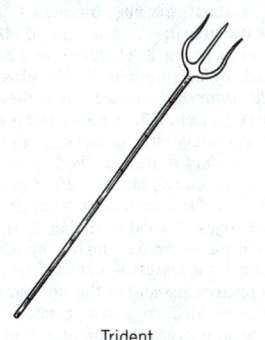

Trident

trident /trī́d'nt/ *n.* **1. 3-PRONGED SPEAR** an instrument, spear, or weapon with three prongs **2. MYTHOL 3-PRONGED SPEAR OF POSEIDON OR NEPTUNE** in classical mythology, the three-pronged spear carried by the Greek sea god, Poseidon, or his Roman equivalent, Neptune ■ *adj.* **trident, tridental, tridentate 3-PRONGED** having three prongs, points, or teeth [15thC. From Latin *trident-*, the stem of *tridens*, from *dens* 'tooth'.]

Trident /trī́d'nt/ *n.* a US-manufactured ballistic missile system fired from nuclear submarines and in service with the US Navy and the British Royal Navy

Tridentine /trī dén tīn, tri-/ *adj.* **OF THE COUNCIL OF TRENT** relating to the Council of Trent or its decrees, in which the traditional doctrines of Roman Catholicism were reasserted and the Counter Reformation were begun ■ *n.* **TRADITIONALIST ROMAN CATHOLIC** a Roman Catholic who adheres to doctrines laid down by the Council of Trent, especially in opposition to the reforms of the Second Vatican Council [Mid-16thC. Via medieval Latin *Tridentinus* from, ultimately, Latin *Tridentum* 'Trent'.]

tridimensional /trī dī ménsh'nəl, -di-/ *adj.* **SCI** having three dimensions —**tridimensionality** /trī́ dī ménsh'n álleti, -di-/ *n.* —**tridimensionally** /trī́ dī ménsh'nǝli/ *adv.*

triduum /tríddoo əm, trī-/ *n.* a period of three days of prayer before a Roman Catholic feast [Early 18thC. From Latin, formed *dies* 'day'.]

tried /trīd/ past tense, past participle of **try** ■ *adj.* (often used in combination) **1. PROVED TO BE GOOD** proved through experience or testing to be good, effective, or reliable ○ *using this tried and tested method* ○ *a tried and tested formula for successful game shows* **2. HARRIED** subjected to considerable strain, stress, or worry ○ *the sorely tried teacher of a class of noisy pupils*

triene /trī́ een/ *n.* any chemical compound that has three double bonds

triennial /trī énni əl/ *adj.* **1. HAPPENING EVERY 3 YEARS** taking place once every three years **2. LASTING 3 YEARS** lasting for a period of three years ■ *n.* **1. THIRD ANNIVERSARY** a third anniversary of an event **2. THREE-YEARLY EVENT** an event that takes place every three years **3. 3-YEAR PERIOD** a period of three years [Mid-16thC. From Latin *triennis*, from *triennium* (see TRIENNIUM).] —**triennially** *adv.*

triennium /trī énni əm/ (*plural* **-ums** *or* **-a** /trī énni ə/) *n.* a period of three years [Mid-19thC. From Latin, formed from *annus* 'year'.]

trier /trī́ ər/ *n.* **1. SB WHO TRIES** sb or sth that tries, e.g. a tester of new things **2. SB WHO PERSEVERES** sb who perseveres or makes an effort despite limited ability or lack of success **3. TECH TOOL FOR TESTING MATERIALS** a tool or implement designed and used for testing materials, particularly food products, during manufacture

Trier /treer/ city in Rhineland-Palatinate State, southwestern Germany, in the centre of a wine-growing region. Population: 98,900 (1992).

trierarch /trī́ ə raark/ (*plural* **-archs**) *n.* **1. TRIREME CAPTAIN** the captain of a trireme in ancient Greece **2. OUTFITTER OF A TRIREME** in ancient Greece, a citizen commissioned to fit out a trireme for the use of a city-state [Mid-17thC. Via Latin *trierarchus* or directly from Greek *triērarkhos*, literally 'trireme commander'.]

trierarchy /trī́ ə raarki/ (*plural* **-chies**) *n.* **1. SYSTEM FOR SUPPORTING THE ANCIENT GREEK NAVY** in ancient Greece, the system that required citizens to subsidize triremes **2. OFFICE OF TRIERARCH** the authority, office, or position of a trierarch **3. TRIERARCHS** trierarchs as a group [Mid-19thC. From Greek *triērarkhia*, from *triērarkhos* (see TRIERARCH).]

Trieste /tri ést/ seaport and capital city of Friuli-Venezia Region, northeastern Italy. Population: 228,398 (1992).

Trieste, Gulf of inlet of the northern Adriatic Sea, bordered by Italy, Slovenia, and Croatia

trifecta /trī féktə/ *n. Australia, US* a bet, especially on a horse race, that involves selecting the competitors that will come in the first three places in the correct order [Late 20 century. Blend of TRI- + PERFECTA.]

triffid /trī́ffid/ *n.* a very large fictional plant capable of moving about and killing people, or any large plant thought to resemble a triffid [Mid-20thC. Coined by John Wyndham, author of *The Day of the Triffids* (1951).]

trifid /trī́fid/ *adj.* **BIOL** used to describe a tail or organ that is deeply divided into three parts [Mid-18thC. Via Latin *trifidus* 'having three clefts' from, ultimately, *findere* 'to split'.]

trifle /trī́f'l/ *n.* **1. STH TRIVIAL** sth that has little or no importance, significance, or value ○ *dismissed the complaint as a mere trifle* **2. SMALL QUANTITY** a small amount of sth ○ *What he'd earned seemed a trifle beside his mountain of debts.* **3. COOK COLD DESSERT** a cold dessert typically consisting of sponge cake soaked in sherry or fruit juice, spread with jam, jelly, or fruit, and topped with custard or whipped cream or sometimes both **4. METALL MEDIUM-HARD PEWTER** pewter of medium hardness ■ **trifles** *npl.* **HOUSEHOLD PEWTER UTENSILS** objects or utensils made of trifle [13thC. From Old French *trufle*, a variant of *truffe*, 'deception', of unknown origin.] —**trifler** *n.* ◇ **a trifle** slightly or somewhat (*formal or humorous*)

trifle with *vt.* to treat or take advantage of sb or sth

thoughtlessly or without due respect or consideration ○ *had trifled with her affections*

trifling /trī́fling/ *adj.* **1. INSIGNIFICANT** insignificant, trivial, or of little value **2. FRIVOLOUS** concerned with matters of little importance ○ *'He is not a trifling, silly young man'* (Jane Austen, *Emma*; 1816) —**triflingly** *adv.*

trifocal /trī́ fṓk'l/ *adj.* **WITH THREE FOCAL POINTS** used to describe a lens that has three different sections, each with a different focal point ■ **trifocals** *npl.* **SPECTACLES WITH TRIFOCAL LENSES** spectacles with trifocal lenses whose three sections correct separately for near, medium, and distant vision

trifold /trī́ fṓld/ *adj.* consisting of three parts

trifoliate /trī́ fṓli ət, -ayt/, **trifoliated** /trī́ fṓli aytid/ *adj.* **1. trifolilate, trifoliated** /-ə layt/ **BOT WITH 3 LEAFLETS** used to describe a compound leaf consisting of three leaflets that arise from the same point, e.g. a clover leaf **2. WITH OR SHAPED LIKE 3-PART LEAVES** with leaves composed of three leaflets or shaped like such a leaf

triforium /trī́ fáwri əm/ (*plural* **-a** /-ri ə/) *n.* an arcaded storey in a church between the nave arches and the clerestory [13thC. From Anglo-Latin, of uncertain origin: perhaps an alteration of TRIFOLIUM.] —**triforial** *adj.*

triform /trī́ fawrm/, **triformed** /trī́ fawrmd/ *adj.* having or consisting of three different forms or parts

trifurcate *adj.* **trifurcate, trifurcated THREE-BRANCHED** divided into three branches or forks ■ *vi.* **(-cates, -cating, -cated) DIVIDE INTO THREE** to divide into three branches or forks [Early 18thC. From Latin *trifurcus*, from *furca* 'fork'.] —**trifurcation** /trī́ fur káysh'n/ *n.*

trig[1] /trig/ *n.* trigonometry, especially as a school subject (*informal*) [Mid-19thC. Shortening.]

trig[2] /trig/ *n.* **CHOCK** a brake or supporting block used to stop sth from rolling (*regional*) ■ *vt.* **(trigs, trigging, trigged) HOLD IN POSITION WITH A BLOCK** to support sth or stop sth from moving with a block or wedge (*regional*) [Late 16thC. Origin uncertain: perhaps from Old Norse *tryggja* 'to secure'.]

trig[3] /trig/ *adj.* **1. TIDY** neat, smart, tidy, or trim (*regional archaic or regional*) **2. FIRM** steady or firm (*regional archaic*) ■ *vt.* **(trigs, trigging, trigged) TO MAKE STH NEAT** to make sb or sth neat, smart, tidy, or trim (*regional archaic or regional*) [13thC. From Old Norse *tryggr* 'true'.] —**trigly** *adv.* —**trigness** *n.*

trig. *abbr.* **1.** trigonometrical **2.** trigonometry

trigeminal /trī́ jémmin'l/ *adj.* relating to or involving the trigeminal nerve [Mid-19thC. Formed from modern Latin *trigeminus*, literally 'three twins', from Latin *geminus* 'twin'.]

trigeminal nerve, **trigeminal** *n.* either of the fifth pair of cranial nerves that provide the jaw, face, and nasal cavity with motor and sensory functions

trigeminal neuralgia *n.* a condition involving recurring sudden sharp pain in the face along the branches of the trigeminal nerve

trigger /trī́ggər/ *n.* **1. ARMS SMALL LEVER THAT FIRES A GUN** a small lever that is pressed with a finger to fire a gun **2. MECH ENG LEVER THAT OPERATES A MECHANISM** a small lever or device that is pressed or squeezed to operate a mechanism, e.g. by releasing a spring **3. STIMULUS FOR STH** a stimulus that sets off an action, process, or series of events **4. ENG SIGNAL FOR STARTING AN OPERATION** an automatic or manual pulse or signal for an operation to start ■ *vt.* **(-gers, -gering, -gered) 1. MAKE STH HAPPEN** to set sth off, bring sth about, or make sth happen ○ *memories triggered by the sight of old photos* **2. ARMS FIRE A WEAPON BY PULLING A TRIGGER** to fire a weapon or initiate an explosion by operating a trigger **3. ENG SET STH IN MOTION** to initiate electrical or mechanical activity that will then allow a device to function for a time under its own control [Early 17thC. From Dutch *trekker*, formed from *trekken* 'to pull'.]

trigger finger *n.* **1. FOREFINGER** the finger used to pull the trigger on a gun, usually the right-hand forefinger **2. MED BENT-FINGER DISORDER** a disorder, caused by inflammation of the fibrous sheath around a tendon, in which one or more fingers are locked in a bent position and click if forcibly straightened

triggerfish /trī́ggər fish/ (*plural* **-fish** *or* **-fishes**) *n.* a tropical marine fish found on coral reefs with a thin body and a dorsal fin spine that locks in an erect position as a protection against predators. Family: Balistidae.

trigger-happy *adj.* (*informal*) **1. OVEREAGER TO SHOOT** likely or overeager to shoot a firearm without considering the consequences **2. RASH** liable to act in a rash or violent way without considering the consequences

triggerman /trígger man/ (*plural* **-men**) *n. US* sb who shoots sb else, usually as part of a gang committing a crime (*informal*) [Mid-20thC. Coined during the height of Prohibition in the United States, an era of violent criminal activity, especially shootings.]

triglyceride /trī glíssə rīd/ *n.* a chemical compound (**ester**) formed from a molecule of the alcohol glycerol and three molecules of fatty acids. Triglycerides constitute many of the fats and oils of animal and vegetable tissues and, like cholesterol, may have an adverse effect on human health in excessive amounts.

triglyph /trí glif/ *n.* in classical architecture, a block carved with three vertical groves that separates the square panels (**metopes**) in a Doric frieze [Mid-16thC. Via Latin from Greek *trigluphos*, from tri- 'three' + *glupe* 'carving'.] —**triglyphic** /trī glíffik/ *adj.*

trigon /trī gon/ *n.* **1. MUSIC ANCIENT TRIANGULAR HARP OR LYRE** a triangular harp or lyre of ancient Greece and Rome **2. ZODIAC = triplicity** *n.* 3 [Mid-16thC. Via Latin *trigonum* from Greek *trigōnon* 'triangle', from, ultimately, *gōnia* 'angle'.]

trigonal /tríggən'l/ *adj.* **1. TRIANGULAR** in the shape of a triangle **2. CRYSTALS WITH THREEFOLD SYMMETRY** used to describe a crystal that has threefold symmetry [Late 16thC.] —**trigonally** *adv.*

trigonometric function /tríggənə méttrik-/ *n.* any of a group of functions of an angle or arc expressed as a ratio of the two sides of a right triangle containing the angle. The trigonometric functions are sine, cosine, tangent, cotangent, secant, and cosecant.

trigonometry /tríggə nómmə tri/ *n.* a branch of mathematics dealing with properties of trigonometric functions and their applications, e.g. in surveying —**trigonometric** /tríggənə méttrik/ *adj.* —**trigonometrical** /-méttrik'l/ *adj.* —**trigonometrically** /-méttrikli/ *adv.*

trigonous /tríggənəss/ *adj.* BOT used to describe a stem or other plant part that is triangular in cross section

trig point *n. Aus* a land surveyor's reference point on high ground, usually marked by a stone pillar set into the ground [Mid-19thC. Shortening of trigonometrical point.]

Yang	Yin		
Ch'ien (heaven) NW	K'un (earth) SW	Chen (thunder) E	Sun (wind) SE
K'an (moon) N	Li (sun) S	Ken (mountain) NE	Tui (lake) W

Trigram

trigram /trí gram/ *n.* **1. GROUP OF 3 LETTERS** a group of any three alphabet letters **2. DESIGN OF 3 LINES** one of the eight combinations of three solid or broken lines that are joined in pairs to form the hexagrams of the I Ching, the Chinese system of divination —**trigrammatic** /trígrə máttik/ *adj.* —**trigrammatically** /-máttikli/ *adv.*

trigraph /trí graaf, -graf/ *n.* a group of three successive letters, especially one representing a single sound such as 'igh' in 'might' —**trigraphic** /trī gráffik/ *adj.* —**trigraphically** /-gráffikli/ *adv.*

trihalomethane /trī háylō meé thayn/ *n.* a chemical compound, such as chloroform, derived from methane, that contains three halogen atoms and is formed especially during the chlorination of drin-

---

king water [Mid-20thC. Coined from TRI- + HALO- + METHANE.]

trihedral /trī heédrəl/ *adj.* **3-FACED** having three plane faces ■ *n.* = trihedron

trihedron /trī heédrən/ (*plural* **-drons** or **-dra** /-drə/), **trihedral** /trī heédrəl/ *n.* GEOM a figure formed by the intersection of three planes

triiodothyronine /trí ī ōdō thīrə neen/ *n.* an iodine-containing amino acid with activity similar to thyroxine but more potent, used to treat hypothyroidism. Formula: $C_{15}H_{12}I_3NO_4$. [Mid-20thC. Coined from TRI- + IODO- + THYRONINE.]

trijet /trí jet/ *n.* an aeroplane propelled by three jet engines

trike /trīk/ *n.* a child's tricycle (*informal*) [Late 19thC. Shortening and alteration of TRICYCLE.]

trilateral /trī láttərəl/ *adj.* **1. 3-SIDED** used to describe a geometric figure that has three sides **2. TRIPARTITE** involving three countries or parties ■ *n.* **3-SIDED FIGURE** a geometric figure with three sides —**trilaterally** *adv.*

trilateralism /trī láttərəlizəm/ *n.* three-sided relations or discussions between nations, areas, or groups —**trilateralist** *n.*

trilby /trílbi/ (*plural* **-bies**) *n.* a soft felt hat with a deep crease in the crown and a narrow brim [Late 19thC. Named after *Trilby*, a novel by George Du Maurier.]

— WORD KEY: ORIGIN —
In the novel, *Trilby* was an artist's model who fell under the spell of the hypnotist Svengali. In the stage version of the book, the character *Trilby* wore a soft felt hat with an indented top, and the style soon became fashionable. The novel also dwells on the erotic qualities of *Trilby's* feet, and for a while in the early 20th century *trilbies* was a slang term for 'feet'.

trilinear /trī línni ər/ *adj.* consisting of, contained by, or involving three lines

trilingual /trī líng gwəl/ *adj.* **1. KNOWING 3 LANGUAGES** able to speak or use three languages, especially fluently **2. IN 3 LANGUAGES** relating to or expressed in three languages. ◊ **bilingual, monolingual** ■ *n.* **TRILINGUAL PERSON** sb who speaks three languages well or to an equal extent —**trilingualism** *n.* —**trilingually** *adv.*

triliteral /trī líttərəl/ *adj.* **1. 3-LETTERED** consisting of three alphabetic letters **2. WITH 3 CONSONANTS** consisting of three consonants ■ *n.* **TRILITERAL WORD OR ROOT** a root or word consisting of three alphabetic letters or consonants. Roots in Semitic languages are triliterals.

AKG London

Trilithon

trilithon /trī li thon, trīli-/, **trilith** /trī lith/ *n.* a prehistoric structure consisting of two large vertical stones supporting a horizontal stone laid on top of them [Mid-18thC. Via Greek, from, ultimately, *lithos* 'stone'.] —**trilithic** /trī líthik/ *adj.*

trill¹ /tril/ *n.* **1. WARBLING SOUND** a high-pitched warbling sound, especially one made by a bird **2. MUSIC MELODIC ORNAMENT** a musical ornament consisting of rapid alternation between two adjacent notes. The interval between the notes of a trill can vary but is usually a semitone or major second. **3. PHON SOUND MADE BY VIBRATING VOCAL ORGANS** a sound or consonant made by two vocal organs vibrating rapidly against each other, e.g. the tip of the tongue vibrating against the ridge behind the front teeth ■ *vti.* (**trills, trilling, trilled**) **UTTER STH WITH A TRILL** to play,

---

sing, pronounce, or utter sth with a trill or sound resembling a trill [Mid-17thC. From Italian *trillare*, of uncertain origin: perhaps an imitation of the sound.]

trill² /tril/ (**trills, trilling, trilled**) *vi.* **1. TRICKLE** to trickle (*archaic or literary*) **2. SPIN** to spin or twirl around [14thC. Of uncertain origin.]

trillion /tríllyən/ (*plural* **-lion** or **-lions**) *n.* **1. 1 FOLLOWED BY 12 ZEROS** the number equal to 10^{12}, written as 1 followed by 12 zeros **2. 1 FOLLOWED BY 18 ZEROS** the number equal to 10^{18}, written as 1 followed by 18 zeros (*dated*) **3. LARGE NUMBER OF STH** an exceptionally large but unspecified number or amount of sth (*informal; often used in the plural*) ◊ *had trillions of fans wanting to meet her* [Late 17thC. From French, modelled on *million*.] —**trillion** *adj.*

— WORD KEY: USAGE —
See Usage note at *billion*.

trillionth /tríllyənth/ *n.* one of a trillion equal parts of sth —**trillionth** *adj.*, *adv.*

trillium /trílli əm/ *n.* a North American or Asian plant with a cluster of three leaves at the top of the stem and a single large white, pink, or purple three-petalled flower [Mid-19thC. From modern Latin, of uncertain origin: probably an alteration of Swedish *trilling* 'triplet', referring to the triplets of leaves and petals in the plant.]

trilobate /trī lō bayt/, **trilobated** /trílə baytid/, **trilobed** /trī lōbd/ *adj.* BOT used to describe a leaf that has three lobes

trilobite /trílə bīt/ *n.* an extinct Palaeozoic marine arthropod with a flat oval body and a dorsal exoskeleton divided into three vertical sections. Class: Trilobita. [Mid-19thC. Via modern Latin *Trilobites* from, ultimately, Greek *lobos* 'lobe'.] —**trilobitic** /trílə bíttik/ *adj.*

trilocular /trī lókyōōlər/ *adj.* having or consisting of three cavities, cells, or chambers [Mid-19thC. Coined from TRI- + Latin *loculus* 'a little place', from *locus* 'place'.]

trilogy /tríllə ji/ (*plural* **-gies**) *n.* **1. SET OF 3 RELATED WORKS** a group or series of three related works, especially of literature or music **2. SET OF THREE** a set of three related things [Mid-17thC. From Greek *trilogia*, from *logos* 'word' (see -LOGY).]

trim /trim/ *v.* (**trims, trimming, trimmed**) **1.** *vt.* **MAKE STH TIDY BY CUTTING** to make sth neat and tidy by clipping, cutting, or pruning **2.** *vt.* **CUT TO THE REQUIRED SIZE** to reduce sth by cutting it to the required shape or size ◊ *The editor said I needed to trim the manuscript down to 40,000 words.* **3.** *vt.* **REMOVE EXCESS BY CUTTING** to reduce or remove sth, especially sth excess, by cutting ◊ *We had to trim the budget.* **4.** *vt.* **DECORATE** to decorate or embellish sth ◊ *He trimmed the hat with fur.* **5.** *vt.* **WOODWORK SHAPE TIMBER** to shape and finish the edges of wood or timber **6.** *vt.* **CINEMA EDIT A FILM** to cut pieces from a film during editing **7.** *vti.* **SAILING CHANGE THE ARRANGEMENT OF SAILS** to change the position or arrangement of the sails so that a ship is ready to set sail **8.** *vti.* **SHIPPING CHANGE THE DISTRIBUTION OF CARGO** to improve, alter, or maintain a vessel's balance by changing the way the ballast or cargo is distributed **9.** *vi.* **NAUT BE BALANCED IN THE WATER** to be or become well-balanced in the water (*refers to a vessel*) **10.** *vt.* **AIR MAKE ADJUSTMENTS TO IMPROVE AIRCRAFT STABILITY** to improve the stability of an aircraft, e.g. by redistributing the load before takeoff or by transferring fuel during flight **11.** *vti.* **ALTER AN OPINION TO SUIT CIRCUMSTANCES** to alter opinions or behaviour to suit the circumstances of a particular time as an expedient means of gaining an advantage **12.** *vi.* **ADOPT A NEUTRAL POSITION** to adopt a neutral position between two parties that are in dispute **13.** *vt.* **BEAT THOROUGHLY** to beat or overwhelm sb completely (*informal*) ◊ *got trimmed regularly at tennis by her partner* **14.** *vt.* **SCOLD** to reprimand or scold sb (*informal*) **15.** *vt.* **DEFEAT** to inflict a heavy defeat on sb or sth (*informal*) **16.** *vt.* **CHEAT** to cheat or deceive sb (*informal*) ■ *adj.* (**trimmer, trimmest**) **1.** **FIT** fit, healthy, slim, or in good physical condition ◊ *had a trim figure* **2.** **NEAT AND TIDY** neat and tidy, compact, or in good order **3.** **READY FOR USE** fitted out or made ready for use (*archaic*) ■ *n.* **1.** **ACT OF CUTTING** the cutting of sth in order to make it neater or tidier ◊ *gave the hedge a trim* **2.** **HAIR HAIRCUT** a haircut that tidies rather than changes a hairstyle **3.** STH USED AS DECORATION sth used for decoration such as contrasting material attached to a piece of clothing **4.** CARS DECORATIVE PARTS OF A VEHICLE the accessories and decorative parts added to the interior or exterior of a vehicle **5.** CONSTR DECORATIVE ADDITIONS TO A BUILDING the nonstructural decorative additions to a building, especially mouldings around doorways, windows, and walls **6.** STH TRIMMED OFF a piece of sth removed by trimming **7.** CINEMA FILM CUT DURING EDITING a piece of film eliminated from a shot during editing **8.** AIR ADJUSTMENT OF AN AIRCRAFT FOR STABILITY adjustment of the controls of an aircraft to give stability **9.** AIR FLIGHT POSITION the position of an aircraft in flight relative to the horizon **10.** NAUT APPEARANCE OF A VESSEL the way a vessel appears when it is fitted out and prepared for sailing **11.** NAUT RELATION BETWEEN A SAIL AND A DIRECTION the relation between the plane of a sail and the direction in which the vessel is pointing **12.** NAUT POSITION OF A VESSEL the position of a ship or boat, especially with reference to the horizontal and to the difference between the depth in water at the front and back of the vessel **13.** NAUT BUOYANCY the relative buoyancy of a submarine [Old English *trymman* 'to strengthen'. Ultimately from an Indo-European base meaning 'to be solid' that is also the ancestor of English *tree*.] —**trim** *adv.* —**trimly** *adv.* —**trimness** *n.*

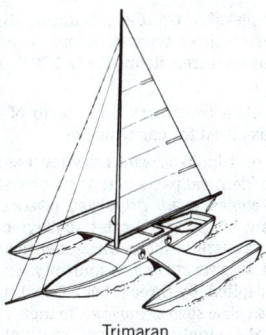

Trimaran

trimaran /trímə ran, trímə rán/ *n.* a sailing boat with three hulls arranged side by side [Mid-20thC. Blend of TRI- and CATAMARAN.]

Trimble /trímb'l/, **David** (*b.* 1944) British politician. He became leader of the Ulster Unionist party (1995), and shared the Nobel Peace Prize (1998) for his role in the peace negotiations that led to the Good Friday peace agreement in Northern Ireland (1998). Full name **William David Trimble**

trimer /trímər/ *n.* a polymer formed by combining three identical molecules [Mid-20thC. Coined from TRI- + -MER.] —**trimeric** /trí mérrik/ *adj.*

trimerous /trímmərəss/ *adj.* **1.** WITH 3 PARTS having or consisting of three similar parts or segments **2.** BOT WITH PARTS IN THREES used to describe a flower with parts arranged in groups of three [Early 19thC. Formed from Greek *trimerēs*, from *meros* 'part'.]

trimester /trí méstər/ *n.* **1.** PERIOD OF 3 MONTHS a period of three months, especially one of the three three-month periods into which human pregnancy is divided for medical purposes **2.** US EDUC 1 OF 3 COLLEGE TERMS one of the three terms into which the academic year is divided by some US colleges, schools, and universities [Early 19thC. Via French *trimestre* from Latin *trimestris* 'of three months', from *mensis* 'month'.] —**trimestral** *adj.* —**trimestrial** *adj.*

trimeter /trímmitər/ *n.* a line of verse made up of three metrical feet [Mid-16thC]

trimethadione /trí methə dí on/ *n.* a bitter white crystalline compound with an odour similar to camphor, used as an anticonvulsant in the treatment of epilepsy. Formula: $C_6H_9NO_3$. [Contraction of TRI- + METHYL + DI- + -ONE]

trimethoprim /trí méthə prim/ *n.* a synthetic drug used as an antibacterial and in the treatment of malaria [Mid-20thC. Contraction of TRI- + METHYL + OXY- + PYRIMIDINE.]

trimetric /trí méttrik/, **trimetrical** /trí méttrik'l/ *adj.* **1.** POETRY IN TRIMETERS consisting of one or more trimeters **2.** CRYSTALS = **orthorhombic**

trimetric projection *n.* a geometric projection in which the three axes are measured on different scales and are at arbitrary angles

trimetrogon /trí méttrə gon/ *n.* a technique in which three aerial photographs are taken at the same time, one vertical and two at oblique angles, in order to obtain more topographical detail [Mid-20thC. Coined from TRI- + *Metrogon*, the name of a commercial lens.]

trimmer /trímmər/ *n.* **1.** SB OR STH THAT TRIMS sb or sth that trims such as a machine for trimming hedges, lawns, or timber **2.** SB ALTERING AN OPINION ACCORDING TO CIRCUMSTANCES sb whose opinions or behaviour change to suit the circumstances of a particular time in order to gain an advantage (*disapproving*) **3.** ELECTRON ENG VARIABLE CAPACITOR a small variable capacitor used, usually in parallel with a larger capacitor, to adjust the overall capacitance of the combination **4.** CONSTR CROSSWISE JOIST a joist or beam that is set crosswise and has the ends of the joists running lengthwise fitted into it **5.** SHIPPING SB WHO STOWS CARGO sb who stows the cargo on a ship to ensure good stability **6.** AEROSP = **trim tab**

trimming /trímming/ *n.* **1.** STH ATTACHED AS DECORATION a piece of material used as a decoration on clothing or furnishings, e.g. a strip of lace, fur, or braid along the edge of a piece of clothing **2.** ACT OF STH THAT TRIMS the act of sb or sth that trims **3.** BEATING a vigorous beating or thrashing (*dated informal*) ■ **trimmings** *npl.* **1.** COOK FOOD ACCOMPANYING A MAIN DISH the items of food traditionally served as accompaniments to a main dish **2.** EXTRAS things added to sth as accessories or extras **3.** PIECES CUT OFF DURING TRIMMING the parts or pieces cut off when sth is trimmed **4.** *NZ* CHRISTMAS DECORATIONS Christmas decorations

trimming capacitor *n.* ELECTRON ENG = **trimmer** *n.* 3

trimming tab *n.* = **trim tab**

trimolecular /trímə lékyŏolər/ *adj.* relating to or consisting of three molecules

trimonthly /trí múnthli/ *adj.* occurring or done every three months —**trimonthly** *adv.*

trimorph /trí mawrf/ *n.* **1.** MULTIFORM MINERAL a substance, especially a mineral, that occurs in three distinct crystalline forms **2.** FORM OF TRIMORPH one of the crystalline forms in which a trimorph exists

trimorphism /trí máwrfizəm/ *n.* **1.** CRYSTALS CONDITION OF HAVING 3 CRYSTAL FORMS the property of existing in three different crystalline forms **2.** BIOL ADOPTION OF 3 FORMS the adoption of three successive forms during a life cycle, e.g. the forms of larva, pupa, and adult in some insects [Mid-19thC. Formed from Greek *trimorphos*, from *morphē* 'form'.] —**trimorphic** *adj.* —**trimorphous** *adj.* —**trimorphically** *adv.*

trimotor /trí mōtər/ *n.* a vehicle, typically an aeroplane, with three engines

trim tab *n.* a flight control surface that can be adjusted in flight by the pilot, for trimming out control forces

Trimurti /tri moòrti/ *n.* the Hindu gods Brahma, Vishnu, and Shiva, the creator, preserver, and destroyer respectively, who represent the three forms of the supreme being [Mid-19thC. From Sanskrit, formed from *murti* 'form'.]

trinal /trín'l/ *adj.* consisting of three parts

trinary /trínəri/ *adj.* **1.** TRIPLE consisting of three parts **2.** BY THREES progressing in threes

Trincomalee /tríngkōmə leé/ town and port in north-eastern Sri Lanka. Population: 52,000 (1986).

trine /trín/ *adj.* **1.** TRIPLE consisting of three parts **2.** ZODIAC 120° APART AS SEEN FROM EARTH used in astrology to describe two planets or celestial bodies separated by an angle of 120° as seen from the Earth ■ *n.* **1.** GROUP OF 3 a group of three, or sth consisting of three parts **2.** ZODIAC ASPECT OF 120° BETWEEN TWO PLANETS in astrology, an aspect of 120° between two planets or celestial bodies as seen from the Earth [14thC. Via Old French from Latin *trinus*, the singular of *trini* 'in threes'.]

Trinidad /trínni dad/ island in the West Indies, a constituent part of Trinidad and Tobago. Population: 1,184,106 (1990). Area: 4,828 sq. km/1,864 sq. mi. —**Trinidadian** *n.*, *adj.*

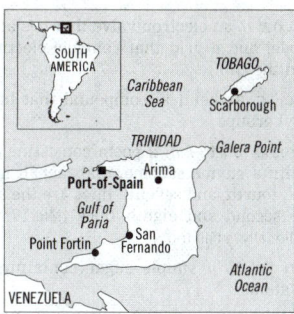

Trinidad and Tobago

Trinidad and Tobago republic comprising the two southernmost of the Caribbean Islands, situated off the northeastern coast of Venezuela. Language: English. Currency: Trinidad and Tobago dollar. Capital: Port-of-Spain. Population: 1,130,337 (1997). Area: 5,128 sq. km/1,980 sq. mi. Official name **Republic of Trinidad and Tobago**

Trinitarian /trínnitáiriən/ *n.* sb who believes in the Christian doctrine of the Trinity —**Trinitarian** *adj.* —**Trinitarianism** *n.*

trinitrobenzene /trí nītrō bén zeen/ *n.* an explosive yellow crystalline compound. Formula: $C_6H_3(N_3O_2)_3$.

trinitroglycerin /trí nītrō glíssərin/ *n.* = **nitroglycerine**

trinitrotoluene /trí nītrō tóllyoo een/, **trinitrotoluol** /trí nītrō tóllyoo ol/ *n.* full form of **TNT**

trinity /trínnə ti/ (*plural* **-ties**) *n.* **1.** THREE a group of three **2.** THREENESS the condition of existing as three persons or things [13thC. Via Old French *trinité*, from Latin *trinitas*, from *trinus* 'threefold' (see TRINE).]

Trinity *n.* **1.** CHR FATHER, SON, AND HOLY SPIRIT the union of the three persons of the Christian God, the Father, Jesus Christ, the Son, and the Holy Spirit, in a single Godhead **2.** CHR = **Trinity Sunday 3.** EDUC = **Trinity term**

Trinity Brethren *npl.* the members of Trinity House

Trinity House *n.* an association that licenses maritime pilots and maintains lighthouses and buoys around the coasts of England, Wales, the Channel Islands, and Gibraltar

Trinity Sunday, **Trinity** *n.* the Sunday eight weeks after Easter when Christians celebrate the doctrine of the Trinity. It marks an important division in the Christian liturgical calendar.

Trinity term, **Trinity** (*plural* **Trinities**) *n.* **1.** EDUC SUMMER TERM the term at some universities that begins after Easter **2.** LAW SUMMER TERM IN ENGLISH LAW COURTS one of the English court terms, beginning in the early summer after Trinity Sunday

Trinitytide /trínnə ti tíd/ *n.* the season from Trinity Sunday to Advent [Early 16thC. From TIDE.]

trinket /tríngkit/ *n.* **1.** SMALL ITEM OF LITTLE VALUE a small article of little value such as an ornament or piece of jewellery **2.** STH TRIVIAL sth trivial or unimportant [Mid-16thC. Origin uncertain.] —**trinketry** *n.*

trinomial /trí nómi əl/ *adj.* **1.** MATH HAVING 3 MATHEMATICAL EXPRESSIONS consisting of three mathematical terms or expressions **2.** BIOL HAVING 3 NAMES relating to or consisting of three taxonomic names, denoting the genus, species, and subspecies or variety of an organism ■ *n.* MATH POLYNOMIAL WITH 3 TERMS a polynomial made up of three terms linked by plus or minus signs [Late 17thC. A blend of TRI- and BINOMIAL.] —**trinomially** *adv.*

trinucleotide /trí nyoókli ə tíd/ *n.* a chemical compound consisting of three linked mononucleotides

trio /treé ō/ (*plural* **-os**) *n.* **1.** GROUP OF 3 a group or set of three **2.** MUSIC GROUP OF 3 MUSICIANS a group of three musicians who perform together **3.** MUSIC MUSIC FOR 3 MUSICIANS a piece of music composed for a group of three musicians **4.** MUSIC MIDDLE SECTION OF A MUSICAL PIECE the middle section of a minuet, march, or other piece of music, composed in a contrasting style and originally written for three instruments **5.** CARDS SET OF 3 PIQUET CARDS a set of three equal-ranking cards in piquet [Early 18thC. From Italian, formed from *tri-* on the model of *duo* 'duet'.]

---

triode /trī ōd/ *n.* an electron valve that has an anode, a cathode, and a grid that controls electron flow between the two

triol /trī ol/ *n.* a chemical compound that has three hydroxyl groups

triolet /trée ə let, trī-/ *n.* a poem consisting of eight lines with a rhyme scheme of abaaabab in which the first, fourth, and seventh lines are the same, as are the second and eighth lines [Mid-17thC. From French, literally 'small trio'.]

triose /trī ōz/ *n.* a simple sugar containing three carbon atoms

trio sonata *n.* a baroque sonata composed for three instruments, usually two violins and one cello or bass viol, with keyboard continuo accompaniment

trioxide /trī ók sīd/ *n.* an oxide containing three oxygen atoms per molecule

trip /trip/ *n.* **1. JOURNEY** a journey of relatively short duration, especially to a place and back again, usually for a specific purpose such as a holiday or business meeting **2. FALL CAUSED BY CATCHING THE FOOT** a fall or stumble caused by catching the foot on sth **3. ACTION THAT CAUSES A FALL** an action that causes sb to fall or stumble **4. LIGHT STEP** a light or nimble skip, step, or tread **5. ERROR** a blunder, error, or mistake **6.** TECH **STH ACTING AS A SWITCH** a catch or switch that activates a mechanism **7.** DRUGS **DRUG-INDUCED HALLUCINATION** the experience produced by taking a hallucinogenic drug (*informal*) **8. STIMULATING EXPERIENCE** an intense, emotional, or stimulating experience (*informal*) ○ *a nostalgia trip* **9. INTENSE INTEREST** an obsessive and often shortlived interest in sth (*informal*) ■ *v.* **(trips, tripping, tripped) 1.** *vti.* **STUMBLE OR CAUSE SB TO STUMBLE** to stumble or fall as a result of catching the foot on sth, or to cause sb to stumble or fall by making the person's foot catch on sth ○ *I tripped and fell.* **2.** *vt.* **CATCH SB IN A MISTAKE** to detect or catch sb out through a mistake **3.** *vti.* **MAKE A MISTAKE** to make or cause sb to make a mistake **4.** *vi.* **MOVE WITH RAPID LIGHT STEPS** to move, run, walk, or dance with rapid light steps ○ *went tripping off down the road* **5.** *vt.* TECH **CAUSE A DEVICE TO OPERATE** to operate or to cause a device or system to operate **6.** *vi.* DRUGS **EXPERIENCE DRUG EFFECTS** to experience the effects of a hallucinogenic drug (*informal*) **7.** *vi.* **GO ON A JOURNEY** to go on a journey, tour, or excursion **8.** *vt.* NAUT **FREE AN ANCHOR** to free an anchor from the sea bed so that it hangs loose on the end of its rope or chain **9.** *vt.* SAILING **TIP UP A YARD** to tilt or tip up a yard or mast so that it can be lowered **10.** *vt.* SAILING **RAISE AN UPPER MAST** to raise one of the upper masts of a sailing ship to remove the bar (**fid**) that supports it so that it can be lowered [14thC. From Old French *tripper*, of Germanic origin.] —**trippingly** *adv.* ◇ **trip off the tongue** to be easy or pleasant to say

tripalmitin /trī pálmitin/ *n.* = **palmitin**

tripartite /trī pa̋ar tīt/ *adj.* **1. INVOLVING 3 PARTIES** involving, made between, or ratified by three parties, groups, or nations ○ *a tripartite agreement* **2. IN 3 PARTS** divided into or made up of three parts **3.** BOT **WITH 3 LOBES** used to describe a leaf that has three deeply divided lobes [15thC] —**tripartitely** *adv.*

tripartition /trī paar tísh'n/ *n.* a division of sth into three parts or among three parties

tripe /trīp/ *n.* **1. STOMACH LINING OF A COW OR SHEEP** the stomach lining of a ruminant such as a cow or sheep, used as food **2. RUBBISH** sth absurd, untrue, or worthless (*informal*) [14thC. From Old French, of unknown origin.]

trip hammer, triphammer /tríp hamər/ *n.* a power hammer with a massive head raised by a cam

triphenylmethane /trī fée nīl mée thayn, trī fénnīl mée thayn/ *n.* a colourless crystalline hydrocarbon used in the preparation of dyes. Formula: $CH(C_6H_5)_3$.

triphibian /trī fíbbi ən/ *n.* **1.** TRANSP **ALL-PURPOSE CRAFT** a craft that can operate on water, on land, and in the air **2.** SPORTS **TRIATHLETE** a competitor in a triathlon ■ *adj.* = **triphibious** [Mid-20thC. A blend of TRI- and AMPHIBIAN.]

triphibious /trī fíbbi əss/, **triphibian** *adj.* operating or occurring in the water, on the land, and in the air [Mid-20thC. A blend of TRI- and AMPHIBIOUS.]

trip hop *n.* a rhythmic dance music developed from hip-hop in the 1990s and using electronic sampling to create a psychedelic effect

triphosphate /trī fóss fayt/ *n.* a salt or ester with three phosphate groups

triphosphopyridine nucleotide /trī fosfō pírri deen-/ *n.* = **NADP**

triphthong /tríf thong, tríp thong/ *n.* **1. VOWEL SOUND WITH 3 ELEMENTS** a vowel sound that combines three elements in one syllable. ◊ **diphthong 2.** = **trigraph** [Mid-16thC. Via French *triphtongue* from, ultimately, medieval Greek *triphthongos*, from Greek *phthongos* 'sound'.] —**triphthongal** /trif thóng g'l, trip-/ *adj.*

tripinnate /trī pínnət, -pínnayt/ *adj.* used to describe a leaf in which the main stalk bears opposite pairs of leaflets that themselves have a similar arrangement of secondary leaflets that are also similarly subdivided —**tripinnately** *adv.*

Tripitaka /tríppi ta̋akə/ *n.* the three long canonical texts of Buddhism, the 'Vinayapitaka', the 'Suttapitaka', and the 'Abhidhammapitaka' [Late 19thC. From Sanskrit, formed from *piṭaka* 'basket'.]

tripl. *abbr.* triplicate

triplane /trī playn/ *n.* an aeroplane with three main wings positioned one above the other

triple /trípp'l/ *adj.* **1. HAVING 3 PARTS** consisting of three parts, members, or units **2. 3 TIMES AS MUCH** three times as great, as much, or as many **3. DONE 3 TIMES** done or occurring three times **4.** POETRY **WITH 3 SIMILAR SYLLABLES** having three similar or corresponding syllables in a verse **5.** MUSIC **WITH 3 BEATS** having three musical beats in a bar ■ *vti.* **(-ples, -pling, -pled) MAKE 3 TIMES AS MUCH** to become or cause sth to become three times as great, as much, or as many ■ *n.* **1. STH 3 TIMES GREATER** a number or amount that is three times greater than another or than usual **2.** BEVERAGES **TREBLE MEASURE** a measure, usually of spirits, containing three times the amount of a single measure **3. SET OF 3** a group, series, or set of three things **4.** *US* HORSERACING = **trifecta** [14thC. Via French or directly from Latin *triplus*, from Greek *triplous*.]

triple bond *n.* a chemical bond having three covalent bonds between two atoms

triple crown, Triple Crown *n.* **1.** SPORTS **VICTORY IN SPORTS EVENTS** victory in all three of a set of major events in certain sports **2.** HORSERACING **HORSERACING VICTORY** in horseracing, victory in the Derby, St Leger, and 2000 Guineas in the same season **3.** RUGBY **VICTORY OVER THREE TEAMS** in rugby, victory in the home championships contested between England, Ireland, Scotland, and Wales by one team over the other three in the same season **4.** CHR **POPE'S TIARA** the tiara that the Pope wears as a symbol of the papacy

triple-decker /-dékər/ *n.* sth such as a structure or sandwich with three levels or layers

Triple Entente *n.* the understanding that developed between the United Kingdom, France, and Russia, initially on an informal basis, for dealing with their various colonial differences, but later more formally, as a military pact in 1914

triple jump *n.* an event requiring an athlete to perform a short run and three consecutive jumps, landing first on one foot, then the opposite foot, and finally both feet, in continuous motion

triple measure *n.* US = **triple time**

triple-nerved /-núrvd/ *adj.* used to describe a leaf that has three main veins

triple point *n.* CHEM the temperature and pressure at which the solid, liquid, and gaseous phases of a substance exist in equilibrium

triple rhyme *n.* a rhyme in which three syllables rhyme with another three, e.g. 'snobbery' and 'robbery'

triple sec /-sék/ *n.* a sweet colourless liqueur that is orange-flavoured

triplet /trípplət/ *n.* **1. GROUP OF 3** three things that are connected or related to each other in some way **2. ONE OF 3 OFFSPRING** one of three children or animals that are delivered by the same mother during one birth **3.** MUSIC **GROUP OF 3 NOTES** a group of three notes played in the time usually taken by two notes of the same value **4.** POETRY **VERSE OF 3 LINES** a poetic stanza of three lines, usually with a single rhyme and sometimes sharing the same metrical pattern **5.** CHEM **CHEMICAL UNIT WITH 2 UNPAIRED ELECTRONS** an atom, molecule, or radical with two unpaired electrons **6.** PHYS **GROUP OF 3 ELEMENTARY PARTICLES** a group of three elementary particles with similar characteristics that differ only in their charge **7.** GENETICS = **codon** [Mid-17thC. Formed from TRIPLE, on the model of *doublet*.]

tripletail /trípp'l tayl/ *n.* a large bony marine fish found mainly in tropical waters whose long dorsal, anal, and caudal fins together resemble a three-lobed tail. Latin name: *Lobotes surinamensis*. [Early 19thC]

triple time *n.* a musical metre or time signature with three beats to the bar ○ *a waltz in triple time*

triple-tongue *vti.* to produce a rapid series of articulated notes in a wind instrument such as a trumpet by repeating articulated syllables with the tongue. ◊ **single-tongue, double-tongue**

triple witching hour *n.* a time when stock options, stock index futures, and options on such futures all mature at once. Triple witching hours occur quarterly and are usually marked by highly volatile trading.

triplex /trípplеks/ *n.* *US, Can* a building divided into three flats on three separate floors, or a single flat that occupies three floors [Early 17thC. From Latin, 'threefold'.]

Triplex *tdmk.* a trademark for a form of laminated safety glass used for car windows

triplicate *n.* /trípplikət/ **WITH 3 IDENTICAL PARTS** sth that has three identical parts to it or that exists in three identical copies ■ *adj.* /trípplikət/ **THREEFOLD** triple or tripled ■ *v.* /trípli kayt/ **(-cates, -cating, -cated) 1.** *vt.* **MAKE 3 COPIES OF STH** to make three identical copies of sth **2.** *vti.* **MULTIPLY STH BY 3** to multiply, or cause sth to be multiplied, by three [15thC. From Latin *triplicat-*, the past participle stem of *triplicare* 'to triple', from *triplex* (see TRIPLEX).] —**triplication** /trípli káysh'n/ *n.*

triplicity /tri plíssəti, trī-/ (*plural* **-ties**) *n.* **1. EXISTENCE OF 3 IDENTICAL COPIES** the condition of existing in three identical copies **2. GROUP OF 3** a group or combination of three **3.** ZODIAC **ZODIACAL DIVISION** one of the four groups that the zodiac is traditionally divided into, each separated from the other by 120° and consisting of three astrological signs [14thC. From late Latin *triplicitas*, from Latin *triplex* (see TRIPLEX). Originally only in the meaning 'group of three star signs'.]

triploblastic /trípplō blástik/ *adj.* used to describe a multicellular animal that has three primary germ layers (**ectoderm, endoderm, mesoderm**) during embryonic development. This is typical of all multicellular animals except coelenterates. ◊ **diploblastic** [Late 19thC. Coined from Greek *triploos* 'threefold' + *-blastic* (see -BLAST).]

triploid /tríp ployd/ *adj.* **WITH 3 OF EACH CHROMOSOME** possessing three representatives of each chromosome ■ *n.* **TRIPLOID CELL OR ORGANISM** a triploid cell, nucleus, or organism —**triploidy** *n.*

triply /tríppli/ *adv.* threefold or in a triple number, measure, or degree

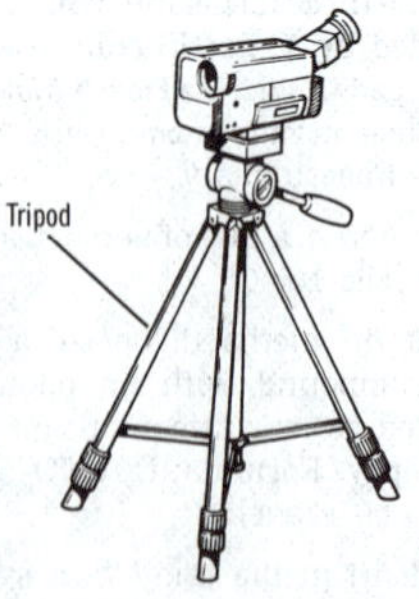

Tripod

tripod /trī pod/ *n.* **1. 3-LEGGED SUPPORT** a frame or stand with three legs that are usually collapsible, used for supporting sth such as a camera, compass, theodolite, or other piece of equipment **2. 3-LEGGED HOUSE-**

HOLD OBJECT a piece of furniture such as a pot, cauldron, stool, or table with three legs [Early 17thC. From Latin *tripod-*, the stem of *tripus*, from Greek *tripous*, literally 'three-footed', from *pous* 'foot'.] —**tripodal** /tríppəd'l/ *adj.*

tripoli /tríppəli/ *n.* a light porous siliceous sedimentary rock containing schist or shells of diatoms and used in powdered form for polishing [Early 17thC. From French; named after Tripoli, either the city in Lebanon or that in Libya.]

Tripoli /tríppəli/ **1.** capital city of Libya, situated on the Mediterranean Sea, in the northwestern part of the country. Population: 1,500,000 (1994). **2.** city in northwestern Lebanon, on the Mediterranean Sea. Population: 500,000 (1985).

Tripolitania /tríppəli táyni ə/ ancient region surrounding Tripoli in northwestern Libya. Founded as a Phoenician colony in the 7th century BC, it was captured by the Turks in the 16th century, and occupied by Italy between 1912 and 1941. —**Tripolitanian** /tríppəli táyni ən/ *n., adj.*

tripos /trī́ poss/ (*plural* **-poses**) *n.* a final honours examination for the BA degree at Cambridge University [Late 16thC. Alteration of Latin *tripus* 'tripod' (see TRIPOD). From the stool occupied by the speaker at commencement, and later his humorous speech, on the reverse of which was printed the honours list.]

tripper /tríppər/ *n.* **1. SB ON A TRIP** sb who is on a journey or outing, especially one taken for pleasure (*informal*) **2.** *US* DRUGS **SB TAKING LSD** sb who takes, or is taking, a hallucinogenic drug such as LSD (*slang*) **3.** ELEC ENG = **trip**

trippet /tríppit/ *n.* a mechanism that strikes another part at regular intervals or is struck by it [15thC. Formed from TRIP.]

trippingly /tríppingli/ *adv.* in a manner that is nimble, lively, or fluent

trippy /tríppi/ (**-pier, -piest**) *adj.* accompanied by or producing distorted visual or sound effects similar to those associated with psychedelic drugs, especially LSD (*slang*)

trip switch *n.* an electric switch designed to interrupt a circuit, or the power to a machine, quickly

triptane /tríp tayn/ *n.* a colourless liquid alkane used for its antiknock properties in aviation fuel. Formula: C_7H_{17}. [Mid-20thC. Contraction of *trimethylbutane*.]

triptych /tríptik/ *n.* **1. WORK OF ART IN 3 PIECES** a painting or carving consisting of three panels, often made as an altarpiece hinged together so that when the smaller outer panels are folded the middle part is entirely covered **2. 3 CONNECTED WRITING TABLETS** in ancient times, a set of three writing tablets hinged or tied together [Mid-18thC. From Greek *triptukhos* 'threefold', from *ptux* 'fold'.]

tripwire /tríp wīr/ *n.* **1. WIRE THAT ACTIVATES EQUIPMENT** a wire that is attached to a trap, mine, weapon, alarm, camera, or other device in such a way that it will set the device off if disturbed **2. HIDDEN WIRE FOR TRIPPING PEOPLE** a concealed length of wire or rope stretched across a piece of land at ground level in such a way that an enemy or intruder will likely trip over it

triquetral bone /trī kwéetrəl-, -kwéttrəl-/, **triquetral** *n.* a pyramid-shaped bone in the wrist that connects with the inner bone of the forearm (**ulna**) on the side of the little finger [Mid-17thC. Formed from Latin *triquetrus* 'three-cornered'.]

triquetrous /trī kwéetrəss, -kwét-/ *adj.* triangular, especially in a cross section of sth [Mid-17thC. Formed from Latin *triquetrus* 'three-cornered'.]

triradiate /trī ráydi ət, -ayt/ *adj.* having three rays or radiating branches —**triradiately** *adv.*

Triratna /tree rátnə/ *n.* the three principal components of Buddhism, namely the Buddha or teacher, the teaching, and the priesthood [From Sanskrit, 'three jewels', formed from *ratna* 'jewel']

trireme /trī́ reem/ *n.* a galley, originally used by the ancient Greeks as a warship and later adopted by the Romans, that had three rows of oars on each side, arranged one above the other [Early 17thC. Directly or via French *trirème* from Latin *triremis*, literally 'having three banks of oars', from *remus* 'oar'.]

trisaccharide /trī sákə rīd/ *n.* a sugar that has three linked monosaccharide units

trisect /trī sékt/ (**-sects, -secting, -sected**) *vt.* to divide sth into three parts, especially equal parts —**trisection** /trī séksh'n/ *n.* —**trisector** /trī séktər/ *n.*

trisepalous /trī séppələss/ *adj.* used to describe the outer whorl (**calyx**) of a flower with three sepals

trishaw /trī́ shaw/ *n.* = **rickshaw**

triskaidekaphobia /tríss kī dékə fṓbi ə/ *n.* an irrational or obsessive fear of the number 13 [Early 20thC. Coined from Greek *triskaideka* 'thirteen' + -PHOBIA.] —**triskaidekaphobe** /-dékə fōb/ *n.* —**triskaidekaphobic** /tríss kī dékə fṓbik/ *adj.*

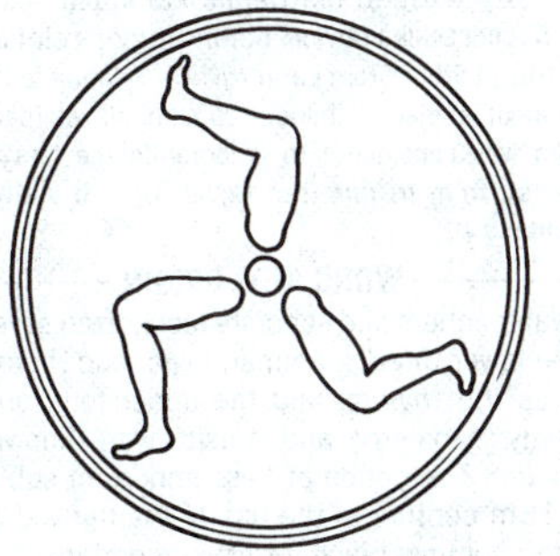

Triskelion

triskelion /tri skélli on, trī-/ (*plural* **-a** /-li ə/), **triskele** /trī́ skeel, tríss-/ *n.* a symbol in the form of three bent or curved lines or limbs radiating from a common centre. It is sometimes a representation of three human limbs, as in the emblem of the Isle of Man. [Mid-19thC. Via modern Latin from Greek *triskelēs* 'three-legged', from *skelos* 'leg'.]

trismus /trízməss/ *n.* a sustained spasm of the jaw muscles, characteristic of the early stages of tetanus [Late 17thC. Via modern Latin from Greek *trismos* 'grinding'.] —**trismic** *adj.*

trisoctahedron /triss óktə héedrən/ (*plural* **-drons** *or* **-dra** /-drə/) *n.* a solid with 24 identical triangular faces, each triplet of which rests on a face of an underlying octahedron [Mid-19thC. Coined from Greek *tris* 'thrice' + OCTAHEDRON.] —**trisoctahedral** *adj.*

trisodium /trī sṓdi əm/ *adj.* containing three sodium atoms in a molecule

trisomy /trī́ sōmi/ *n.* the genetic condition of having one or more sets of three chromosomes instead of the usual two chromosomes. Trisomy is usually followed by the number of the affected chromosome pair. For example, Down's syndrome is trisomy 21. —**trisomic** /trī sṓmik/ *adj.*

Tristan and Iseult, Tristram and Isolde *n.* a pair of lovers in medieval legend. Tristan was a knight who fell in love with Iseult, his uncle's bride, after drinking a love potion.

Tristan da Cunha /trístən də kóonə/ group of volcanic islands in the South Atlantic Ocean, part of the British dependency of St Helena. Population: 313 (1988). Area: 202 sq. km/78 sq. mi.

tristate /trī́ stayt/ *adj.* *US* GEOG relating to three adjacent states of the United States or the adjoining parts of them

triste /treest/, **tristful** /trístfòol/ *adj.* with a sad, melancholy, or mournful quality (*literary*) [15thC. Via French from Latin *tristis* 'sad'.] —**tristfully** /trístfəli/ *adv.* —**tristfulness** /-fəlnəss/ *n.*

tristearin /trī stéerin/ *n.* = **stearin**

tristesse /tree stéss/ *n.* sadness, sorrow, or melancholy (*archaic or literary*) [14thC. Via French from Latin *tristitia*, from *tristis* 'sad'.]

tristich /trístik/ *n.* a poem, stanza, refrain, or other division of poetry that consists of three lines [Early 19thC. Modelled on *distich*.] —**tristichic** /tri stíkik/ *adj.*

tristichous /trístikəss/ *adj.* used to describe an arrangement of leaves in which successive leaves arise one-third of the way around the stem from the previous leaf, thus forming three rows up the stem [Mid-19thC]

tristimulus values /trī stímyòoləss-/ *npl.* the three values representing the amounts of red, green, and blue light that in combination match a particular colour

Tristram *n.* ♦ **Tristan and Iseult**

trisyllable /trī sílləb'l/ *n.* a word of three syllables, e.g. 'enormous' —**trisyllabic** /trī́ si lábbik/ *adj.* —**trisyllabically** /-lábbikli/ *adv.*

tritanopia /trītə nṓpi ə, trít-/ *n.* a rare condition in which perception of blue and green becomes confused. It is due to the absence of blue-sensitive pigment in the cone cells of the retina. [Early 20thC. Coined from Greek *tritos* 'third' + *anōpia* 'blindness'. From not seeing a third of the colour spectrum.] —**tritanopic** /-nóppik/ *adj.*

trite /trīt/ *adj.* overused and consequently lacking in interest or originality [Mid-16thC. From Latin *tritus*, the past participle of *terere* 'to wear out' (source of English *attrition* and *contrite*).] —**tritely** *adv.* —**triteness** *n.*

tritheism /trī́ thi izzəm/ *n.* belief in three gods, especially the belief or doctrine that the Christian Trinity of Father, Son, and Holy Spirit consists of three distinct divinities —**tritheist** /trī́ thi ist/ *n.* —**tritheistic** /-ístik/ *adj.*

tritiate /trítti ayt/ (**-ates, -ating, -ated**) *vt.* to replace normal hydrogen atoms, or chemically combine sth, with tritium —**tritiation** /trítti áysh'n/ *n.*

triticale /trítti kaáli, -káyli/ *n.* a high-protein high-yielding cereal plant that is a hybrid of wheat and rye [Mid-20thC. A blend of the modern Latin genus names *Triticum* 'wheat' and *Secale* 'rye'.]

tritium /trítti əm/ *n.* a radioactive isotope of hydrogen occurring naturally in trace amounts and having atomic mass 3 and a half-life of 12.3 years. Although rare in nature it can be produced artificially and is used in tracers and hydrogen bombs. Symbol **T** [Mid-20thC. Via modern Latin from Greek *tritos* 'third'. So named from its atomic weight of 3.]

triton[1] /trī́t'n/ *n.* a large tropical marine gastropod mollusc with a heavy multicoloured spiral shell. Family: Cymatiidae. [Late 18thC. Via the modern Latin genus name *Triton*, from Latin *Triton* (see TRITON). From representations of the sea god holding a conch shell.]

triton[2] /trī́ ton/ *n.* the nucleus of a tritium atom, consisting of one proton and two neutrons [Mid-20thC. Formed from TRITIUM.]

Triton[1] /trī́t'n/ *n.* a god of the sea in Greek mythology, the son of Poseidon and Amphitrite, represented as having the tail of a fish and the upper body of a man [Late 16thC. Via Latin from Greek *Tritōn*.]

Triton[2] *n.* the largest moon of the planet Neptune, about 2,700 km/1,680 mi. in diameter, and revolving in a direction counter to that of the planet [From its dependence on the planet Neptune, in allusion to the demigod Triton's dependence on the sea god Neptune]

tritone /trī́tōn/ *n.* a dissonant musical interval composed of three whole tones

triturate *vt.* /tríttyòo rayt/ (**-rates, -rating, -rated**) **MAKE STH INTO POWDER** to grind or rub a substance into a fine powder ■ *n.* /tríttyòorət/ **FINELY GROUND POWDER** a finely ground powder, especially a drug [Mid-18thC. From late Latin *triturat-*, the past participle stem of *triturare* 'to thresh', from, ultimately, Latin *terere* 'to rub'.] —**triturable** /tríttyòorəb'l/ *adj.* —**triturator** /tríttyòo raytər/ *n.*

trituration /tríttyòo ráysh'n/ *n.* **1. PROCESS OF GRINDING STH INTO POWDER** the process of grinding or rubbing a substance into a fine powder **2. BEING A FINE POWDER** the condition of having been ground or rubbed into a fine powder **3.** PHARM **POWDERED DRUG MIXTURE** a mixture of powdered drugs prepared pharmaceutically, especially one containing lactose **4.** DENT **MIXING OF AMALGAM** the mixing of an amalgam, usually of silver and mercury, for use in filling cavities in teeth

triumph /trī́ umf/ *n.* **1. SUCCESS** an act or occasion of winning, being victorious, or overcoming sth **2. JOY ABOUT SUCCESS** the happiness, pride, or feeling of elation that comes from winning, being victorious, or overcoming sth **3. OUTSTANDING SUCCESS** sth that is notable for its exceptional quality or for being a great achievement ○ *The reviews hailed the company's new production of Hamlet as a triumph.* **4. ROMAN VICTORY PARADE** in ancient Rome, a procession through the streets of Rome to the Capitoline Hill to mark a general's victory over a foreign army **5.** CELEBRATORY SPECTACLE a public display or parade, especially one held as a festival or celebration (*archaic*) ■ *vi.* (**-umphs, -umphing, -umphed**) **1.** WIN OR ACHIEVE SUCCESS to be successful, especially against an adversary or in combating the odds against success **2.** BECOME EXULTED to experience the happiness, pride, or feeling of elation that comes from winning, being victorious, or overcoming sth [14thC. Via Old French *triumphe* from Latin *triumphus*, of uncertain origin: probably via Etruscan from Greek *thriambos* 'hymn to Dionysus'.]

triumphal /trī úmf'l/ *adj.* celebrating or commemorating a victory ○ *a triumphal procession*

WORD KEY: USAGE

triumphal or **triumphant**? ***Triumphal*** is a neutral word that classifies sth as being connected with a success or victory, usually of a military kind: *There is a triumphal arch in the centre of the city. The band will play a triumphal march.* ***Triumphant*** is a more judgmental word describing the feelings that follow a success: *The winning team returned home triumphant. She told us of her win with a triumphant look on her face.*

triumphal arch *n.* a monument, usually in the form of an ornamental free-standing arch spanning a street, built to commemorate sth, especially an outstanding military victory

triumphalism /trī úmf'lizzəm/ *n.* **1.** PLEASURE IN HAVING WON a display or feeling of often excessive pride in having achieved a victory or been proved right **2.** BELIEF IN SUPERIORITY OF VIEW the conviction that one belief or set of beliefs, especially religious or political ones, is victorious and far superior to any others —**triumphalist** *n.*

triumphant /trī úmfənt/ *adj.* **1.** FULL OF PRIDE AT VICTORY displaying or feeling great pride in having achieved a victory **2.** SUCCESSFUL OR VICTORIOUS successful or victorious **3.** VERY IMPRESSIVE outstandingly successful ○ *made a triumphant reappearance in the role he made famous* **4.** TRIUMPHAL triumphal (*archaic*) [15thC] —**triumphantly** *adv.*

WORD KEY: USAGE

See Usage note at ***triumphal***.

triumvir /trī úmvər/ (*plural* **-virs** *or* **-viri** /-vi ree/) *n.* **1.** MEMBER OF A TRIUMVIRATE one of the three people who made up a triumvirate, especially in ancient Rome **2.** SB SHARING POWER WITH 2 OTHERS sb who has an equal share in a position of authority with two other people (*formal*) [Late 16thC. From Latin, a back-formation from *triumviri* 'board of three men', from *trium virum* 'of three men'.] —**triumviral** *adj.*

triumvirate /trī úmvərət/ *n.* **1.** ROMAN COMMITTEE OF 3 RULERS a group of three men who together were responsible for public administration or civil authority in the government system of ancient Rome **2.** 3 SHARING AUTHORITY a group of three people who jointly share some responsibility, authority, or power **3.** POSITION OF SHARING POWER the position of being one of three who exercise power or authority **4.** TERM OF OFFICE OF SHARED POWER the duration of the term of office for sb who shares power or authority with two others **5.** RULE BY A GROUP OF 3 government or rule by a group of three [Late 16thC. From Latin *triumviratus*, from *triumviri* (see TRIUMVIR).]

triune /trī yoon/, **Triune** *adj.* THREE IN ONE consisting of or being three in one, e.g. in the Christian Trinity ■ *n.* GROUP OF THREE a group consisting of three members, especially the Christian Trinity [Early 17thC. Coined from TRI- + Latin *unus* 'one'.]

triunity /trī yoonəti/ (*plural* **-ties**) *n.* = **trinity**

trivalent /trī váylənt/, **turváylənt** /tur váylənt/ *adj.* **1.** WITH VALENCY OF 3 having a chemical valency of three **2.** WITH 3 VALENCES with three chemical valences —**trivalency** *n.*

Trivandrum /tri vándrəm/ port and capital city of Kerala State, southern India. Population: 523,723 (1991).

trivet /trívvit/ *n.* **1.** 3-LEGGED STAND a stand or support, usually metal with three legs, for hot pans and dishes **2.** 3-LEGGED SUPPORT FOR PAN a device, usually metal with three legs, that fits over the grate of a fire to support a pan or kettle [15thC. Origin uncertain: probably an alteration of the Latin *triped-*, the stem of *tripes* 'three-footed', from *pes* 'foot'.]

trivia[1] /trívvi ə/ *npl.* a collection of insignificant or obscure items, details, or information (*takes a singular or plural verb*) [Early 20thC. Latinized back-formation from TRIVIAL.]

trivia[2] plural of **trivium**

trivial /trívvi əl/ *adj.* **1.** HAVING LITTLE VALUE lacking in seriousness, importance, significance, or value **2.** COMMONPLACE lacking any qualities that are unique or interesting **3.** CONCERNED WITH TRIVIA relating to or concerned with trivia **4.** MATH WITH ZERO VALUES used to describe the simplest possible case mathematically, especially with all mathematical variables equal to zero **5.** CONCERNING TRIVIUM belonging or relating to the trivium [15thC. From Latin *trivialis* 'relating to the trivium division of subjects', hence 'commonplace' (because the trivium was considered to incorporate the less important subjects), from *trivium* (see TRIVIUM).] —**trivially** *adv.* —**trivialness** *n.*

WORD KEY: ORIGIN

Medieval teachers and scholars recognized seven liberal arts: the lower three, grammar, logic, and rhetoric, were known as the *trivium*, and the upper four, arithmetic, astronomy, geometry, and music, were known as the *quadrivium*. The notion of 'less important subjects' led in the 16th century to the use of the derived adjective ***trivial*** for 'commonplace, of little importance'.

triviality /trívvi álləti/, **trivialism** /trívvi əlizzəm/ *n.* **1.** UNIMPORTANCE the condition or quality of having little importance or seriousness **2.** STH UNIMPORTANT sth that is considered to lack importance or seriousness

trivialize /trívvi ə līz/ (**-izes, -izing, -ized**), **trivialise** (**-ises, -ising, -ised**) *vt.* to treat sth as, or make it appear, less important, significant, or valuable than it really is —**trivialization** /trívvi ə lī záysh'n/ *n.*

trivial name *n.* **1.** CHEM POPULAR NAME FOR A SUBSTANCE a common or popular name for a substance that does not describe its exact chemical composition **2.** BIOL PART OF SCIENTIFIC NAME the noun or adjective that follows the genus name in a taxonomic binomial. US term **specific epithet**

trivium /trívvi əm/ (*plural* **-a** /-vi ə/) *n.* grammar, rhetoric, and logic, three of the seven liberal arts that formed the basis of medieval university study, traditionally considered to be less important than the other four. ◊ **quadrivium** [Early 19thC. From medieval Latin, a variant sense of Latin *trivium* 'place where three roads cross' (see TRIVIAL.]

triweekly /trī weékli/ *adj.* **1.** APPEARING OR DONE EVERY 3 WEEKS occurring, published, or performed once every three weeks **2.** APPEARING OR DONE 3 TIMES WEEKLY occurring, published, or performed three times each week ■ *adv.* **1.** EVERY 3 WEEKS once every three weeks **2.** 3 TIMES A WEEK three times each week ■ *n.* (*plural* **-lies**) **1.** 3-WEEKLY PUBLICATION a publication that comes out every three weeks **2.** PUBLICATION 3 TIMES A WEEK a publication that comes out three times each week

-trix *suffix.* **1.** a woman who performs a particular function ○ *administratrix* **2.** a geometric element that performs a particular function ○ *directrix* [From Latin, the feminine form of *-tor*]

t-RNA *abbr.* transfer RNA

Trobriand Islands /trō bri ənd-/ island group of Papua New Guinea in the Solomon Sea, east of New Guinea. Area: 440 sq. km/170 sq. mi.

trocar /trō kaar/ *n.* a sharply pointed steel rod sheathed with a tight-fitting cylindrical tube (**cannula**), used together to drain or extract fluid from a body cavity. The whole instrument is inserted then the trocar is removed, leaving the cannula in place. [Early 18thC. From French *trocart*, from carre 'side of an instrument', from, ultimately, Latin *quadrum* 'square'.]

trochaic /trō káy ik/ *adj.* OF TROCHEES relating to, belonging to, or consisting of trochees ■ *n.* **1.** = **trochee** **2.** POEM WRITTEN IN TROCHEES a poem, or part of a poem, written in trochees —**trochaically** *adv.*

trochal /trōk'l/ *adj.* ZOOL shaped like a wheel [Mid-19thC. Formed from Greek *trokhos* 'wheel' (see TROCHOID).]

trochanter /trō kántər/ *n.* **1.** PART OF FEMUR one of two rough knobs on the upper thigh bone (**femur**), where the muscles between the thigh and pelvis are attached in humans and other vertebrates **2.** PART OF AN INSECT'S LEG the second segment from the base of an insect's leg [Early 17thC. Via French from Greek *trokhantēr* 'ball on which the hip bone turns in its socket', from *trekhein* 'to run'.]

troche /trōsh/ *n.* a medicinal lozenge [Late 16thC. Alteration of earlier *trochisk*, from, ultimately, Greek *trokhiskos* 'small wheel', from *trokhos* 'wheel' (see TROCHOID).]

trochee /trṓki/ *n.* a metrical foot that consists of one stressed syllable followed by an unstressed syllable, e.g. the word 'human'. ◊ **iamb** [Late 16thC. Via Latin *trochaeus* from Greek *trokhaios* 'running', from, ultimately, *trekhein* 'to run'. From the rhythmic pattern that resembles a gallop.]

trochlea /trókli ə/ *n.* an anatomical part or structure with a grooved surface that resembles a pulley, especially the surface of a bone over which a tendon passes [Late 17thC. Via Latin from Greek *trokhileia* 'pulley'.]

trochlear /trókli ər/ *adj.* relating to, situated near, or resembling a trochlea or trochlear nerve [Late 17thC]

trochlear nerve *n.* either of the fourth pair of cranial nerves serving the muscle that is used to rotate the eyeball outward and downward

trochoid /trṓ koyd/ *n.* GEOM CURVE FORMED BY POINT ON RADIUS a curve formed by a point on the radius of a circle, or on the extended radius, as the circle rolls along a straight line ■ *adj.* **trochoid, trochoidal 1.** MATH ROTATING ABOUT CENTRAL AXIS rotating, showing rotation, or able to rotate about a central axis **2.** ANAT RESEMBLING PIVOT resembling or functioning in the body like a pivot or pulley [Early 18thC. From Greek *trokhoeidēs* 'wheel-like', from *trokhos* 'wheel', from *trekhein* 'to run'.] —**trochoidally** /trō kóyd'li/ *adv.*

trochophore /trókə fawr/, **trochosphere** /trókə sfeer/ *n.* a free-swimming ciliated larval form of certain invertebrates such as molluscs and rotifers [Late 19thC. Coined from Greek *trokhos* 'wheel' + -PHORE.]

trockenbeerenauslese /trókən bairən óws layzə/ *n.* the highest grade of German table wine, made from individually selected shrivelled grapes and typically very sweet [Mid-20C. From German *Trockenbeerenauslese*, literally 'picking out dry grapes'.]

trod past tense, past participle of **tread**

trodden past participle of **tread**

trode past tense of **tread** (*archaic*)

trog /trog/ (**trogs, trogging, trogged**) *vi.* to walk slowly and heavily (*informal*) [Late 20thC. Origin uncertain: perhaps a blend of TRUDGE or TREK and SLOG or JOG.]

troglodyte /tróggla dīt/ *n.* **1.** CAVE DWELLER sb who lives in a cave, especially sb who belonged to a prehistoric cave-dwelling community **2.** SB LIVING IN SECLUSION sb who lives alone and has little to do with other people, especially sb considered to be antisocial or unconventional [Late 15thC. Via Latin *Troglodyta* from, ultimately, Greek *Trōglodutai*, literally 'ones who enter a hole', an alteration of *Trōgodutai*, an Ethiopian people.] —**troglodytic** /tróggla díttik/ *adj.*

trogon /trṓ gon/ *n.* a tropical or subtropical tree-dwelling bird with a short hooked bill, long tail, and brightly coloured plumage. Family: Trogonidae. ◊ **quetzal** [Late 18thC. Via modern Latin from, ultimately, Greek *trōgein* 'to gnaw'.]

troika /tróykə/ *n.* **1.** TRANSP HORSE-DRAWN RUSSIAN VEHICLE a carriage of Russian origin drawn by three horses harnessed abreast of each other **2.** TRANSP 3 HORSES HARNESSED TOGETHER a team of three horses harnessed abreast of each other **3.** = **triumvirate** *n.* **2** [Mid-19thC. From Russian, formed from *troe* 'group of three'.]

troilism /tróylizəm/ *n.* sexual activity involving three people [Mid-20thC. Origin uncertain: perhaps formed from French *trois* 'three'.] —**troilist** *n.*

troilite /tróy līt/ *n.* a variety of iron sulphide that is found in some meteorites [Mid-19thC. Named after Domenico *Troili*, the 18th-century Italian who described a meteorite containing this mineral.]

Troilus /tróyləss/ *n.* in Greek mythology, the son of the Trojan king Priam. He was killed during the Trojan War by the Greek warrior Achilles. In medieval legend he is depicted as the betrayed lover of Cressida.

Trois-Rivières /twaá rívvi áir/ city on the St Lawrence River between Quebec City and Montreal, in southern Quebec Province, Canada. Population: 48,419 (1996).

Trojan /trṓjən/ *n.* **1.** PEOPLES **CITIZEN OF ANCIENT TROY** sb who was born in or was a citizen of ancient Troy **2. DEDICATED WORKER** sb who does sth with great dedication, determination, stamina, or courage —**Trojan** *adj.*

Trojan Horse *n.* **1.** MYTHOL **HOLLOW HORSE CONCEALING GREEKS** in Greek legends, a hollow wooden horse that hid Greek soldiers, left at the gates of Troy. The Trojans were convinced it was a gift to Athena and dragged it inside. **2. CONCEALED STRATAGEM** sb or sth that is meant to disrupt, undermine, subvert, or destroy an enemy or rival, especially sb or sth that operates while concealed within an organization **3.** COMPUT **DESTRUCTIVE COMPUTER PROGRAM** a computer program that appears to be useful but that actually does damage. ◊ **virus**

troll[1] /trōl/ *v.* (**trolls, trolling, trolled**) **1.** *vti.* ANGLING **DRAG BAITED LINE THROUGH WATER** to drag a baited line through water, often from the back of a boat moving slowly **2.** *vti.* ANGLING **TROLL IN ONE AREA** to troll a particular area **3.** *vti.* ANGLING **TROLL FOR PARTICULAR FISH** to try to catch a particular kind of fish by trolling **4.** *vi.* **AMBLE ABOUT** to walk casually about **5.** *vti.* **WANDER AROUND SEARCHING FOR SB** to wander round a particular area or place, especially in search of a sexual partner (*slang*) **6.** *vti.* MUSIC **SING LOUDLY OR ENTHUSIASTICALLY** to sing or be sung loudly and with vigour, especially in a round, refrain, or chorus (*archaic*) **7.** *vti.* **ROLL OR CAUSE STH TO ROLL** to roll or rotate, or cause sth to roll or rotate ■ *n.* ANGLING **ACTIVITY OF DRAGGING BAITED FISHING LINE** the act or process of fishing by trolling [14thC. Origin uncertain: perhaps from Old French *troller* 'to wander', probably of Germanic origin.] —**troller** *n.*

troll[2] /trōl, trol/ *n.* a supernatural being in Scandinavian legends depicted as either a dwarf or giant and living in caves or under bridges [Early 17thC. Via Swedish or Norwegian from Old Norse, 'demon'.]

trolley /trólli/ *n.* (*plural* **-leys**) **1.** *UK Canada* **WHEELED CART PUSHED BY HAND** a wheeled cart that is pushed by hand, and used for transporting things, especially luggage at an airport or railway station or goods in a supermarket **2.** MED **WHEELED HOSPITAL BED** a wheeled bed used for taking patients from one part of a hospital to another, e.g. from the ward to the operating theatre. US term **gurney 3.** *UK Canada* FOOD **WHEELED TABLE** a small wheeled table used for serving or moving food and drinks **4.** TRANSP = **trolleybus 5.** ELEC **DEVICE COLLECTING POWER FROM AN OVERHEAD WIRE** a device such as a wheel or pulley carried at the end of a pole that collects current from an overhead electric wire in order to power a vehicle **6.** TRANSP **WAGON ON RAILS FOR MOVING THINGS** a small open cart that runs on rails and carries materials, especially goods in a factory or coal or other minerals in a mine or quarry **7.** TRANSP **SUSPENDED TRUCK** a small cart or basket suspended from an overhead rail and used, especially in factories and mines, for transporting loads ■ *vti.* (**-leys, -leying, -leyed**) **MOVE BY TROLLEY** to travel by or transport sth using a wheeled cart on a track or a vehicle powered by electrical current from overhead wires [Early 19thC. Origin uncertain: probably from TROLL[1], in the sense of 'to roll'.] ◇ **be off your trolley** to be mentally ill (*slang*)

trolleybus /trólli buss/ (*plural* **-buses**), **trolley** *n.* an electric bus that takes its power from overhead wires by means of a trolley pole

trolley car *n. US, Can* a streetcar

trollop /tróllәp/ *n.* **1. OFFENSIVE TERM** an offensive term referring to a woman who is a prostitute or who is reputed to be too active sexually (*offensive*) **2. OFFENSIVE TERM** an offensive term that deliberately insults a girl's or a woman's appearance or her indifference to household chores (*informal insult*) [Early 17thC. Origin uncertain: perhaps from TROLL[1].] —**trollopy** *adj.*

Trollope /tróllәp/, **Anthony** (1815–82) British novelist. He is best known for two sequences of novels, the Barsetshire novels (1855–67), which have a clerical setting, and the political Palliser novels (1865–80). —**Trollopian** *adj.*

trombiculiasis /trom bíkyoo lī́ әssiss/, **trombidiasis** /trómbi dī́ әssiss/ *n.* infestation with mite larvae (**chiggers**) that often causes severe rickettsial disease or viral disease [Early 20thC. Coined from modern Latin *Trombicula* (a genus of mites) + -IASIS.]

trombone /trom bṓn/ *n.* **1. BRASS MUSICAL INSTRUMENT** a brass wind instrument of varying size with valves resembling those of a trumpet or a U-shaped slide that is moved to produce different pitches **2. TROMBONE PLAYER** sb who plays the trombone in an orchestra or brass band [Early 18thC. Directly or via French from Italian, literally 'big trumpet', from *tromba* 'trumpet', of Germanic origin.]

trommel /trómm'l/ *n.* a rotating sieve for sizing or screening crushed rock or ore [Late 19thC. From German *Trommel*, 'drum'.]

trompe /tromp/ *n.* a device formerly used for supplying air in a forge by means of a thin column of falling water [From French, 'trumpet']

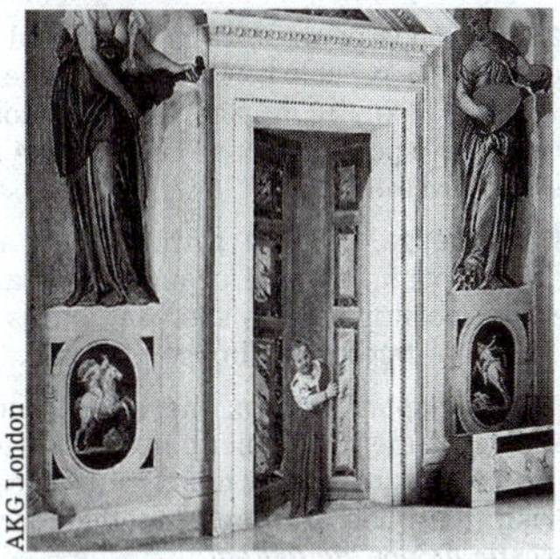

Trompe l'oeil: Fresco (1561?) by Paolo Veronese at the Villa Barbaro, Maser, Italy

trompe l'oeil /trómp lṓyә/ (*plural* **trompe l'oeils** /trómp lṓyә/) *n.* **1. 3-D PAINTING TECHNIQUE** a technique used in realistic paintings to trick the eye, especially through the use of perspective to create an illusion of three-dimensionality **2. ARTISTIC WORK THAT TRICKS THE EYE** a painting or other artistic object that uses trompe l'oeil [Late 19thC. From French, literally 'deceives the eye'.]

Tromsø /trómssö/ town and fishing port in northern Norway, located on the offshore island of Tromsøy. Population: 51,218 (1990).

tron /tron/ *n. Scotland* formerly, a public weighing machine set up in the marketplace of a burgh for weighing merchandise, now the place or building where the tron stood, particularly in Edinburgh and Glasgow [13thC. Via Old French *trone* from Latin *trutina* from Greek *trutanē* 'balance'.]

-tron *suffix.* **1.** a device for manipulating atoms or subatomic particles, accelerator ○ *cyclotron* **2.** a vacuum tube ○ *klystron*

trona /trṓnә/ *n.* a greyish-white or yellowish mineral consisting of a hydrated sodium carbonate found in salt deposits [Late 18thC. From Swedish, of uncertain origin: probably from a dialect variant of Arabic *naṭrūn* (see NATRON).]

Trondheim /trónd hīm/ city and port in central Norway. It is situated on Trondheim Fjord, which opens onto the Norwegian Sea. Population: 140,718 (1993).

Troon /troon/ coastal resort on the Firth of Clyde, southwestern Scotland, known for its golf course. Population: 15,231 (1991).

troop /troop/ *n.* **1. BIG GROUP** a large group of similar people, animals, or things **2.** MIL **MILITARY UNIT** a unit of soldiers that forms a subdivision of a cavalry or armoured cavalry squadron or artillery battery and is about the size of a platoon (*often used before a noun*) ○ *troop movements in the area* **3.** SCOUTING **SCOUTING UNIT** a unit of Boy Scouts or Guides under an adult leader and usually subdivided into several patrols. ◊ **company 4.** ZOOL **COLLECTIVE NAME FOR SOME ANIMALS** a collective name for some animals, especially monkeys and kangaroos ■ **troops** *npl.* **1.** MIL **MILITARY GROUP** a body of soldiers ○ *Order was restored by flooding the area with troops.* **2. LARGE NUMBER OF PEOPLE OR THINGS** a large number of people or things ■ *vi.* (**troops, trooping, trooped**) **1. GO AS A LARGE ORDERLY GROUP** to move or gather together as a large orderly group **2. GO AS IF MARCHING** to walk somewhere in a deliberate or heavy-footed way, as if marching ○ *After breakfast the family trooped off to church.* **3. CONSORT WITH SB** to associate with sb (*archaic*) [Mid-16thC. From French *troupe*, of uncertain origin: probably from Germanic.] ◇ **troop the colour** to parade a military flag ceremonially along ranks of soldiers

trooper /tróopәr/ *n.* **1. MEMBER OF A CAVALRY UNIT** a member of a cavalry unit **2. CAVALRY HORSE** a cavalry horse **3. TROOPSHIP** a troopship (*informal*) **4.** *US* **MOUNTED POLICE OFFICER** a member of a mounted police unit **5.** *US* **STATE TROOPER** a state trooper

troopship /tróop ship/ *n.* a ship, sometimes one originally in the merchant navy, used for transporting military personnel

troostite /tróost īt/ *n.* a greyish or reddish form of the mineral willemite in which zinc is partly replaced by manganese [Mid-19thC. Named after the US geologist Gerard *Troost* (1776–1850), who discovered it.]

trop. *abbr.* **1.** tropical **2.** tropic

trop- *prefix.* = **tropo-** (*used before vowels*)

troparion /trō párri on, -pári-/ *n.* a short hymn or stanza sung in Greek Orthodox services [Mid-19thC. From Greek, 'little trope', from *tropos* (see TROPE).]

trope /trōp/ *n.* **1.** LANG **FIGURE OF SPEECH** a word, phrase, expression, or image that is used in a figurative way, usually for rhetorical effect **2.** CHR **MEDIEVAL RELIGIOUS TEXT** in the medieval Christian church, a phrase or text interpolated into the service of the Mass [Mid-16thC. Via Latin *tropus* from Greek *tropos* 'turn'. Ultimately from an Indo-European base meaning 'to turn' which is also the ancestor of English *contrive*.]

troph- *prefix.* = **tropho-** (*used before vowels*)

trophallaxis /tróffә láksiss/ (*plural* **-es** /-lák seez/) *n.* an exchange of food between organisms, especially the liquid secretions exchanged by social insects such as the adults or larvae of termites and ants [Early 20thC. Coined from TROPH- + Greek *allaxis* 'exchange'.] —**trophallactic** /tróffә láktik/ *adj.*

trophic /tróffik/ *adj.* relating to the nutritive value of food [Late 19thC] —**trophically** *adv.*

-trophic *suffix.* **1.** needing or pertaining to a particular kind of food or nutrition ○ *autotrophic* **2.** = **-tropic** [Formed from Greek *trophē* (see TROPHO-)]

trophic level *n.* a stage in a food chain that reflects the number of times energy has been transferred through feeding, e.g. when plants are eaten by animals that are in turn eaten by predators. Plants and plant-eating animals occupy the first two levels, followed by carnivores, usually to a maximum of six levels.

tropho- *prefix.* nutrition, feeding ○ *trophoblast* [From Greek *trophē* 'food, nutrition', from *trephein* 'to nourish']

trophoblast /tróffә blast/ *n.* a thin outer layer (**ectoderm**) that encloses the embryo of mammals, attaches the fertilized ovum to the wall of the womb, and absorbs nutrients —**trophoblastic** /tróffә blástik/ *adj.*

trophoderm /tróffә durm/ *n.* a trophoblast and its underlying layer (**mesoderm**)

trophozoite /tróffә zṓ īt/ *n.* the active or feeding form of a protozoan, especially a parasite, as opposed to the resting or reproductive form

trophy /trṓfi/ *n.* (*plural* **-phies**) **1. TOKEN OF VICTORY** a cup, shield, plaque, medal, or other award given in acknowledgment of a victory, success, or some other achievement, especially in a sporting contest **2. HUNTING OR WAR SOUVENIR** a memento that symbolizes victory or success, e.g. the head of an animal killed during a hunting expedition or sth taken from an enemy killed in battle **3. MEMENTO OF SUCCESS** sth that symbolizes a personal victory or achievement **4.** HIST **GREEK OR ROMAN VICTORY MEMORIAL** in ancient Greece or Rome, a victory memorial in a public place or near a battlefield, originally a display of enemy weapons **5.** HIST **GREEK OR ROMAN BATTLE COMMEMORATION** a representation of a Greek or Roman battle trophy, e.g. on a commemorative medal, plaque, or monument **6.** ARCHIT **DECORATIVE CARVING OF WEAPONS** a decorative casting or carving showing weapons or armour on a square or circular base ■ *adj.* **ENHANCING SB'S STATUS** used to describe a romantic or sexual partner apparently chosen by sb to impress others and enhance his or her status (*disapproving*) ○ *a trophy wife* [Early 16thC. Via French *trophée* from Latin *tropaeum* 'monument to victory' from Greek *tropaion* from, ultimately, *tropē* 'a turning'.]

-trophy *suffix.* **1.** nutrition, food ○ *dystrophy* **2.** growth ○ *hypertrophy* [From Greek *-trophia*, from *trophē* (see TROPHO-)]

tropic[1] /tróppik/ *n.* **1. LINE OF LATITUDE** a line of latitude on the Earth's globe either 23° 26′ north of the equator (**tropic of Cancer**) or 23° 26′ south (**tropic of Capricorn**) **2.** ASTRON **CIRCLE ON THE CELESTIAL SPHERE** either of two circles on the celestial sphere that have the same latitudes and mark the limits of the apparent north-and-south movement of the Sun. The tropics lie in the same planes as the tropic of Cancer and the tropic of Capricorn. ■ **tropics, Tropics** *npl.* **AREA BETWEEN THE TROPICS** the area between or near the tropic of Cancer and the tropic of Capricorn ■ *adj.* **TROPICAL** tropical [Early 16thC. Via Old French *tropique* from Latin *tropicus* from, ultimately, Greek *tropē* 'a turning', from the ancient belief that the sun 'turned back' at the tropics of Cancer and Capricorn.]

WORD KEY: CULTURAL NOTE

Tropic of Cancer, a novel (1934) by US writer Henry Miller. It is an autobiographical account of a struggling American writer's sojourn in 1930s Paris. Its focus on the protagonist's erotic encounters gained it notoriety and led to it being banned in both the United States and Britain until the 1960s, but its openness was an inspiration for many contemporary writers.

tropic[2] /trṓ pik/ *adj.* BIOL relating to or showing tropism

-tropic *suffix.* **1.** turning, changing, or reacting in a particular way ○ *dexiotropic* **2.** attracted to, having an affinity for, or moving towards a particular thing ○ *neurotropic* **3.** acting on sth in a particular way ○ *vagotropic* [Formed from Greek *tropē* 'turning' (see TROPIC)]

tropical /tróppik'l/ *adj.* **1. TYPICAL OF THE TROPICS** relating to or characteristic of the tropics **2. HOT AND SULTRY** very hot and often combined with a high degree of humidity —**tropicality** /tróppi kálləti/ *n.* —**tropically** *adv.*

tropical cyclone *n.* a cyclone that develops over tropical oceans and has winds up to hurricane force

tropical fish *n.* a fish, usually small, that is native to warm waters and is frequently kept in aquariums because of its often brightly coloured appearance

tropicalize /tróppikə līz/ (**-izes, -izing, -ized**), **tropicalise** (**-ises, -ising, -ised**) *vt.* to make or adapt sth so that it becomes tropical in character or appearance or can be used under tropical conditions —**tropicalization** *n.*

tropical storm *n.* a severe storm that develops offshore over tropical seas with less than hurricane force winds but with the ability to develop into a hurricane

tropical year *n.* = **solar year** [From calculating the time from solstice to solstice]

tropicbird /tróppik burd/ *n.* a tropical aquatic web-footed bird, found in the tropics and related to the pelicans, that has long slender tail feathers, small legs, and white plumage with black markings. Family: Phaethontidae.

tropic of Cancer *n.* a line of latitude that is about 23.5 ° north of the equator [From the constellation that its celestial projection intersects]

tropic of Capricorn *n.* a line of latitude that is about 23.5° south of the equator [From the constellation that its celestial projection intersects]

tropine /trṓ peen, -pin/ *n.* a colourless crystalline alkaloid formed by heating atropine with barium hydroxide. Formula: $C_8H_{15}NO$. [Mid-19thC. Shortening of ATROPINE.]

tropism /trṓpizəm/ *n.* BIOL the involuntary response of an organism or one of its parts towards or away from a stimulus such as heat or light [Late 19thC. From -TROPISM.] —**tropismatic** /trṓpiz máttik/ *adj.* —**tropistic** /trō pístik/ *adj.* —**tropistically** /-pístikli/ *adv.*

tropo- *prefix.* **1.** turning, change ○ *tropopause* **2.** tropism ○ *tropotactic* [From Greek *tropē*]

tropology /tro póllәji/ (*plural* **-gies**) *n.* **1. USE OF FIGURATIVE LANGUAGE** the use of figurative language in speaking or writing **2. TREATISE ON FIGURATIVE LANGUAGE** a piece of discursive writing on the use of figurative language **3.** CHR **METHOD OF INTERPRETING THE BIBLE** a method of interpreting the moral teaching of the Bible through its use of figurative language [Early 16thC. From TROPE.] —**tropologic** /tróppə lójjik/ *adj.* —**tropologically** /-lójjikli/ *adv.*

tropomyosin /tróppə mī́ əssin/ *n.* a protein in muscle that acts with troponin to regulate the interaction of actin and myosin in muscle contraction

troponin /tróppənin/ *n.* a muscle protein that binds with calcium ions to bring about muscular contraction and acts with tropomyosin to control the interaction of actin and myosin [Mid-20thC. Coined from TROPOMYOSIN + -IN, with arbitrary insertion of *n*.]

tropopause /tróppə pawz/ *n.* the transitional region of the atmosphere between the troposphere and stratosphere, 16 km/10 mi. above the equator and 9 km/6 mi. above polar regions [Early 20thC. A blend of TROPOSPHERE and PAUSE.]

tropophyte /tróppə fīt/ *n.* a plant that is adapted to living through seasonal changes in heat, cold, dryness, or moisture, e.g. by shedding leaves during a dry season —**tropophytic** /tróppə fíttik/ *adj.*

troposphere /tróppə sfeer/ *n.* the lowest and most dense layer of the atmosphere, extending 10 to 20 km/6 to 12 mi., in which temperature decreases with rising altitude and most weather occurs —**tropospheric** /tróppə sférrik/ *adj.*

tropotaxis /tróppə táksiss/ *n.* the movement of an organism towards or away from a stimulus as a result of comparing sensory input received from paired receptors on both sides of the body —**tropotactic** /tróppə táktik/ *adj.* —**tropotactically** /-táktikli/ *adv.*

-tropous *suffix.* turning or growing in a particular way ○ *anatropous* ○ *orthotropous* [Formed from Greek *tropos* 'turning, changing', from *trepein* 'to turn']

troppo[1] /tróppō/ *adv.* excessively or too much (*used in musical directions*) ◊ **non troppo** [From Italian, 'too much']

troppo[2] /tróppō/ *adj. Aus* mentally disturbed or ill (*slang*) ○ *He's been acting very strange – gone a bit troppo, I think.* [Mid-20thC. Formed from TROPIC.]

-tropy *suffix.* the condition of taking a particular molecular form ○ *allotropy* [From Greek *-tropia*, from *tropos* (see -TROPOUS)]

trot /trot/ *v.* (**trots, trotting, trotted**) **1.** *vti.* RIDING **MOVE AT PACE SLOWER THAN CANTERING** to move or cause a four-legged animal such as a horse to move at a rate that is faster than walking but slower than cantering, and in which diagonal pairs of feet are off the ground alternately. ◊ **pace 2.** *vi.* **MOVE AT A JOGGING PACE** to move at a jogging pace that is faster than walking but not as fast as running ○ *The team trotted onto the field.* ■ *n.* **1. PACE FASTER THAN A WALK** the forward movement of a four-legged animal, especially a horse, in which it trots **2.** RIDING **RIDE AT A TROTTING PACE** a ride on a horse in which it trots **3. JOGGING PACE** a jogging pace that is faster than a walk but slower than a run **4.** HORSERACING **TROTTERS' RACE** a race for horses who run in harness **5.** ANGLING = **trotline** ■ **trots** *npl.* (*informal*) **1.** MED **DIARRHOEA** a prolonged bout of diarrhoea **2.** *ANZ* HORSERACING **TROTTER RACES** races for trotters in harness [13thC. Via Old French *troter* from, ultimately, a prehistoric Germanic base that is also the ancestor of English *tread*.] ◇ **on the trot 1.** one after the other in succession. US term **in a row 2.** *UK, Can* busy, especially doing sth that involves walking about a lot

trot out *vt.* to bring sth out or display sth repeatedly, especially in the expectation of gaining admiration or approval (*informal*) ○ *He trots out the same old excuses every time he's late.*

Trot /trot/ *n.* a Trotskyite (*dated insult*) [Mid-20thC. Shortening of TROTSKYIST or TROTSKYITE.]

troth /trōth/ *n.* **1. SOLEMN VOW** a solemn pledge, especially the promise to remain faithful exchanged by a bride and groom or an engaged couple (*formal*) **2. BETROTHAL** a betrothal (*archaic*) [13thC. Variant of TRUTH.]

trotline /trót līn/ *n.* a long fishing line with shorter baited lines attached, used in streams or near the shore [Mid-19thC. Origin uncertain: perhaps from TROT.]

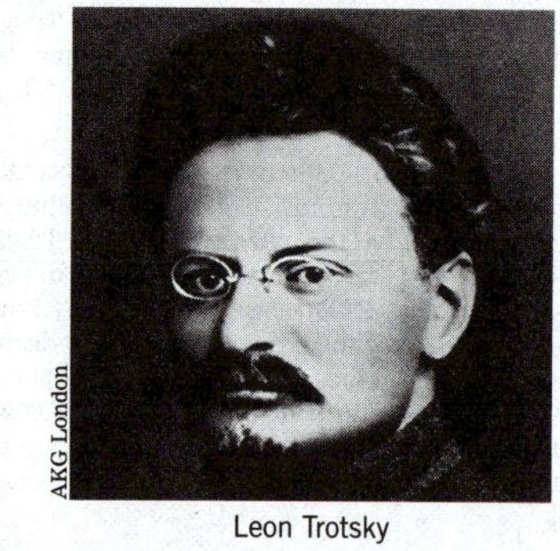

Leon Trotsky

Trotsky /trótski/, **Leon** (1879–1940) Russian revolutionary leader. With Lenin he played a major part in the Bolshevik Revolution of 1917 in Russia. He is credited with creating and directing the Red Army, but failed to take power on Lenin's death and was murdered in exile by one of Stalin's agents. Born **Lev Davidovich Bronstein**

Trotskyism /trótski izəm/ *n.* an interpretation of socialism advanced by Leon Trotsky, asserting that fully developed Marxist principles and practices would culminate in a world revolution by the proletariat. ◊ **Leninism, Stalinism** —**Trotskyist** *n., adj.* —**Trotskyite** *n., adj.*

trotter /tróttər/ *n.* **1.** FOOD **PIG OR SHEEP FOOT** the foot of an animal, especially that of a pig or sheep, when used as food **2.** HORSERACING **TROTTING PERSON OR ANIMAL** sb who or sth that trots, especially a horse that has been specially trained to trot in harness. ◊ **pacer**

trotting race *n. ANZ* a harness race

trotyl /trṓtil, -tīl/ *n.* TNT [Early 20thC. Coined from TRINITROTOLUENE + -YL.]

troubadour /tróobə dawr, -door/ *n.* **1. MEDIEVAL POET OR SINGER** a writer or singer of lyric verses about courtly love, especially in parts of Europe during the 11th to the 13th centuries **2. LOVE POET OR SINGER** a writer or singer of love poems or songs **3.** *US* **SINGER** sb who sings while strolling around an area such as a restaurant [Early 18thC. Via French from Old Provençal *trobador*, from *trobar* 'to compose', of uncertain origin: perhaps from, ultimately, Latin *tropus* 'trope' (see TROPE).]

trouble /trúbb'l/ *n.* **1. CONDITION OF DISTRESS** a condition of distress, anxiety, or danger ○ *When the bills started to come in they realized they were in serious trouble.* **2. SB OR STH UPSETTING** a source or cause of worry, distress, or concern ○ *This car has been nothing but trouble.* **3. SOURCE OF DIFFICULTY** sth that is extremely difficult or presents a problem ○ *Sorry I'm late – I had trouble getting the car to start.* **4. REAL OR APPARENT WEAKNESS** an actual or perceived failing or drawback ○ *Your trouble is that you give up too easily.* **5.** MED **MEDICAL PROBLEMS** an illness or physical condition involving a particular body part that is not functioning as it should ○ *off work with back trouble* **6. EFFORT** the effort or exertion involved in doing sth ○ *I hope you like your CD – I went to a lot of trouble to find it.* **7. DISORDER OR UNREST** disorder or unruly behaviour in a public place **8. MALFUNCTIONING** a condition in which sth mechanical or electronic is not functioning or operating as it should ○ *My car has engine trouble.* ■ *v.* (**-bles, -bling, -bled**) **1.** *vt.* **WORRY OR UPSET SB** to cause worry, distress, or concern to sb or sth ○ *I'm troubled by the fact that she hasn't been in touch.* **2.** *vt.* **PHYSICALLY AFFECT SB** to cause pain or discomfort to sb or sth ○ *My arthritis troubles me from time to time.* **3.** *vt.* **IMPOSE ON SB** to put sb to the inconvenience of doing sth ○ *Could I trouble you to open the window?* **4.** *vti.* **TO MAKE AN EFFORT** to make an effort to do sth or take pains in doing it ○ *He hadn't troubled to check the figures.* **5.** *vt.* **MAKE WATER ROUGH** to agitate or disturb sth, especially the surface of water (*often passive*) [13thC.

Via Old French *troubler* from, ultimately, late Latin *turbidare*, from Latin *turbidus* 'confused, muddy' (source of English *turbid*).] —**troubler** *n.* —**troubling** *adj.* —**troublingly** *adv.* ◇ **in trouble 1.** discovered in wrongdoing and liable to be punished **2.** pregnant and unmarried (*dated informal; used euphemistically*)

——— **WORD KEY: SYNONYMS** ———
See Synonyms at **bother**.

troubled /trúbb'ld/ *adj.* **1.** ANXIOUS OR UPSET experiencing worry or distress **2.** MARKED BY PROBLEMS characterized by difficulties or adversity ○ *The bill has had a troubled passage through Parliament.* **3.** LACKING INNER CALM experiencing or prone to emotional conflict or psychological difficulties

troublemaker /trúbb'l maykər/ *n.* sb who deliberately and frequently tries to make difficulties

Troubles /trúbb'lz/ *npl.* the political and civil unrest in Northern Ireland during the period from 1919 to 1923 and after 1969

troubleshoot /trúbb'l shoot/ (-**shoots**, -**shooting**, -**shot** /trúbb'l shot/, -**shot**) *vti.* to act or operate as sb who finds and eliminates problems [Mid-20thC. Back-formation from TROUBLESHOOTER.]

troubleshooter /trúbb'l shootər/ *n.* **1.** SB WHO FINDS AND SOLVES PROBLEMS sb who has the task of finding problems, difficulties, or faults and then eliminating them **2.** MEDIATOR sb who is called upon to settle political, industrial, or diplomatic disagreements

troubleshooting /trúbb'l shooting/ *n.* **1.** FINDING AND ELIMINATING OF PROBLEMS the act or process of identifying and eliminating problems, difficulties, or faults, especially in electronic or computer equipment **2.** MEDIATION the act or process of mediating in political, industrial, or diplomatic disagreements **3.** OCCUPATION OF FINDING AND SOLVING PROBLEMS the occupation of finding and eliminating problems, e.g. in an organization

troublesome /trúbb'lssəm/ *adj.* **1.** DIFFICULT TO DO OR WORK OUT causing difficulties or taking a great deal of time ○ *Fixing the bug in the program proved more troublesome than I thought.* **2.** WORRYING OR IRRITATING producing annoyance, discomfort, or anxiety, especially in a recurrent way ○ *a troublesome knee injury* —**troublesomely** *adv.* —**troublesomeness** *n.*

trouble spot *n.* a place where trouble occurs, especially a place that is notorious for disruption to civil order or a lack of political control

troublous /trúbbləss/ *adj.* **1.** VERY DIFFICULT fraught with difficulty or many problems (*archaic or literary*) **2.** UNEASY full of uneasiness or anxiety (*archaic or literary*) **3.** TROUBLESOME troublesome (*archaic*) [15thC] —**troublously** *adv.* —**troublousness** *n.*

trough /trof/ *n.* **1.** AGRIC CONTAINER FOR ANIMAL FOOD OR WATER a long low narrow open container that holds feed or water for animals **2.** INDUST INDUSTRIAL CONTAINER a long, low, narrow, open container used in industry, e.g. in washing, kneading, or mixing substances **3.** CHANNEL FOR LIQUID a narrow channel, gully, or gutter in which liquid passes, especially one under the eaves of a roof for catching rainwater **4.** METEOROL AREA OF LOW PRESSURE an elongated area of low atmospheric pressure that may be associated with a front. ◊ **ridge 5.** SUNKEN AREA a long hollow area in the surface of the ground or the sea bed, or between waves **6.** LOW POINT any low or negative point, especially a temporary one **7.** ECON LOWEST POINT OF AN ECONOMIC CYCLE the lowest point or period of an economic cycle. ◊ **peak 8.** PHYS LOW PART OF A WAVE OR SIGNAL the low or negative half of the amplitude in the cycle of a periodic wave or alternating signal [Old English *trog*. Ultimately from an Indo-European base meaning 'wood, tree', which is also the ancestor of English *tree*.]

trounce /trownss/ (**trounces**, **trouncing**, **trounced**) *vt.* **1.** BEAT SB OR STH DECISIVELY to defeat an opponent or team convincingly **2.** BEAT UP SB OR STH to beat sb or sth severely (*dated*) [Mid-16thC. Origin unknown.]

——— **WORD KEY: SYNONYMS** ———
See Synonyms at **defeat**.

troupe /troop/ *n.* GROUP OF TRAVELLING PERFORMERS a group of actors, circus people, or other entertainers, especially one that travels around ■ *vi.* (**troupes**, **trouping**, **trouped**) TRAVEL OR PERFORM WITH A TROUPE to travel as or perform in a troupe of actors or entertainers [Early 19thC. From French (see TROOP).]

trouper /troopər/ *n.* **1.** MEMBER OF A TROUPE sb who is a member of a group of travelling entertainers **2.** SB RELIABLE AND DEDICATED sb who is conscientious, dependable, and selfless **3.** VETERAN THEATRICAL PERFORMER sb who has been involved in the theatre for many years, especially an actor or entertainer

troupial /troopi əl/ *n.* **1.** LARGE S AMERICAN ORIOLE a large oriole of South America with bright black-and-orange plumage. Latin name: *Icterus icterus.* **2.** GREGARIOUS BIRD a member of a family of gregarious birds in the Americas that includes the bobolinks, blackbirds, and orioles. Family: Icteridae. [Early 19thC. From French *troupiale*, an alteration (influenced by *troupe* 'flock') of American Spanish *turpial*, of Caribbean origin.]

trouser /trówzər/ *adj.* ASSOCIATED WITH TROUSERS belonging to, concerning, suitable for, or part of trousers ○ *a trouser pocket* ■ *n.* TROUSERS a pair of trousers, especially one suitable for a smart or formal occasion [Mid-19thC. Back-formation from TROUSERS.] —**trousered** *adj.*

trousers /trówzərz/ *npl.* a garment for the lower body that covers the area from the waist to the ankles and has separate tube-shaped sections for each leg [Early 17thC. From, ultimately, Gaelic *triubhas*, of uncertain origin.] ◇ **be caught with your trousers down** UK to be caught in an unprepared or embarrassing position ◇ **wear the trousers** UK be the member of a household who makes the important decisions (*dated informal*)

trouser suit *n.* a woman's suit of matching or coordinating trousers and jacket or top. US term **pantsuit**

trousseau /troossō/ (*plural* -**seaus** *or* -**seaux** /troossōz/) *n.* a bride's clothes and linen, especially items such as nightdresses, underwear, and bedclothes, that she has collected during the period of her engagement [Early 19thC. From French, literally 'little bundle', from, ultimately, *trousser* 'to truss' (source of English *truss*).]

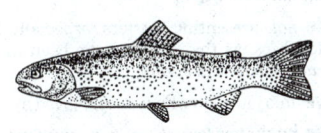

Trout

trout /trowt/ (*plural* **trouts** *or* **trout**) *n.* **1.** ZOOL FRESHWATER FISH SIMILAR TO A SALMON a freshwater fish that is typically smaller than the related salmon and has a speckled body, small scales, and soft fins. Genus: *Salmo.* **2.** ZOOL GAME FISH OF THE SALMON FAMILY a game fish of the salmon family such as the sea trout. Genus: *Salvelinus.* **3.** ZOOL FISH UNRELATED TO THE TROUT a fish similar to but unrelated to, the trout such as the troutperch **4.** OFFENSIVE TERM an offensive term that deliberately insults a woman's age, appearance, or behaviour (*insult*) [Pre-12thC. From late Latin *tructa*, of uncertain origin: perhaps from Greek *trōktēs*, a type of sea fish, from *trōgein* 'to nibble'.]

troutperch /trówt purch/ (*plural* -**perch**) *n.* a small North American freshwater fish that has a spotted body, an adipose fin, and rough scales. Family: Percopsidae.

trouvaille /troo ví/ *n.* sth interesting, amusing, or beneficial discovered by chance ○ *The anecdote was one of her many literary trouvailles.* [From French, 'a find']

trouvère /troo váir/ *n.* a poet-musician of northern France during the 12th and 13th centuries who wrote poems and songs of courtly love, as well as narrative and satirical works [Late 18thC. Via French

from Old French *trovere* from, ultimately, *trover* 'to compose' (see TROVER).]

trove /trōv/ *n.* **1.** COLLECTION OF VALUABLES a collection of discovered valuable items **2.** VALUABLE DISCOVERY a discovery of great importance or monetary value [Late 19thC. Shortening.]

trover /trōvər/ *n.* a common law action to recover goods that have been wrongly appropriated by sb else (*archaic*) [Late 16thC. Via Anglo-Norman from Old French, 'to find', of uncertain origin.]

trow /trō/ (**trows**, **trowing**, **trowed**) *vti.* to think, believe, or suppose that sth is the case (*archaic*) [Old English *trēowian*. From a prehistoric Germanic base that is also the ancestor of English *true*, *betroth*, and *truce*.]

Trowbridge /trō brij/ town and administrative centre of Wiltshire, western England. Population: 29,334 (1991).

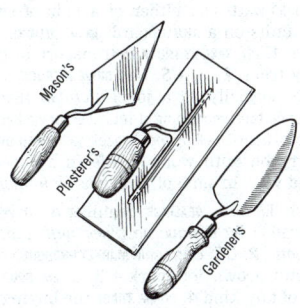

Trowel

trowel /trówəl/ *n.* **1.** FLAT-BLADED HAND TOOL a small hand tool with a short handle and a flat, usually pointed, blade used for spreading, shaping, and smoothing plaster, cement, or mortar **2.** GARDENING GARDENER'S SHORT-HANDLED TOOL a hand tool with a short handle and a curved tapering blade, used for making holes to put plants and seedlings in and for other light digging work ■ *vt.* (**trowels**, **trowelling**, **trowelled**) WORK MATERIAL WITH A TROWEL to dig, spread, or level sth such as earth or mortar using a trowel [14thC. Via Old French *troele* from late Latin *truella* 'dipper', from Latin *trua* 'ladle'.] —**troweller** *n.* ◇ **lay it on with a trowel** to exaggerate, especially in order to flatter sb (*informal*)

troy /troy/ *adj.* measured in or using the troy weight system [14thC. Origin uncertain: probably from *Troyes*, a city in France with a fair at which this weight was used.]

Troy /troy/ city of ancient Greece on the Aegean sea coast, in present-day Turkey. Site of the ten-year Trojan War described in the epic poems of Homer, the city, also called Ilium, was thought to be purely legendary until ruins were discovered by the archaeologist Heinrich Schliemann in 1870. It is now believed to have been founded during the Bronze Age in 3000 BC.

Troyes /trwa/ capital of Aube Department, in Champagne, northeastern France. Population: 60,755 (1990).

troy weight *n.* a system of weights used for precious metals and gemstones, based on a 12-ounce pound, a 20-pennyweight ounce, and a 24-grain pennyweight

trp. *abbr.* troop

trs. *abbr.* PRINTING transpose

truancy /troo ənssi/ (*plural* -**cies**) *n.* **1.** ABSENTEEISM absence from school without permission **2.** OCCASION OF BEING ABSENT a single occasion on which a pupil is absent from school without permission

truant /troo ənt/ *n.* **1.** SB ABSENT FROM SCHOOL sb who is absent without permission or good reason, especially from school **2.** SHIRKER sb who avoids work or shirks responsibilities (*dated*) ■ *adj.* ABSENT absent without permission ■ *vi.* (-**ants**, -**anting**, -**anted**) BE ABSENT to be absent without permission, especially from school [14thC. From Old French, 'beggar, vagabond', of Celtic origin.]

truce /trooss/ *n.* **1.** MIL AGREED BREAK IN FIGHTING a cessation of military hostilities that both sides agree to hold to, usually for a fixed period ○ *Both sides called a truce.* **2.** MIL AGREEMENT TO STOP FIGHTING an agreement to suspend military hostilities **3.** AGREED BREAK IN ARGUING an agreed break in any kind of dispute or feud, or the agreement to stop arguing [14thC. Variant of earlier *trewes*, the plural of *trewe* 'treaty, pledge', from Old English *trēow*.]

Trucial States /trōosh'l-/ former name for **United Arab Emirates** (until 1971)

truck[1] /truk/ *n.* **1.** LARGE GOODS VEHICLE a large vehicle for transporting goods by road **2.** TRANSP = **lorry 3.** CART PUSHED BY HAND any kind of cart or barrow with two or more wheels that is pushed by hand and is used for moving heavy objects **4.** RAIL RAILWAY GOODS WAGON an open railway wagon that carries freight **5.** RAIL TRAIN'S WHEEL UNIT a swivelling frame that the wheels and springs are mounted on at either end of a railway vehicle **6.** SAILING ROPE GUIDE ON A SHIP'S MAST a guide for a ship's ropes, in the form of a disc with holes, fitted horizontally to the top of the mast **7.** SKATEBOARD WHEEL UNIT either of a pair of swivelling wheel units on a skateboard ■ *v.* (**trucks, trucking, trucked**) **1.** *vti.* TAKE BY TRUCK to transport, or transport sth, by truck **2.** *vi.* US, Can DRIVE A TRUCK to drive a truck, especially as a job (*informal*) [Early 17thC. Origin uncertain: shortening of TRUCKLE[2], or via Latin *trochus* 'iron hoop' from Greek *trokhos* 'wheel'.] ◇ **keep on trucking** to carry on with work or life in a cheerful and relaxed way, in spite of problems (*informal*)

truck[2] /truk/ *n.* **1.** DEALINGS dealings or involvement (*informal*) ○ *We'll have no truck with that kind of behaviour.* **2.** US, Can AGRIC MARKET PRODUCE vegetables and fruit grown for market **3.** COMM GOODS traded goods of any kind **4.** COMM TRADE the buying, selling, or bartering of goods **5.** STUFF miscellaneous items (*informal*) ○ *'Now I wanted thirty dollars' worth of artist truck, for I was always sketching in the woods'.* (Robert Louis Stevenson, *The Wrecker*; 1896) **6.** PAYMENT IN KIND payment in goods rather than with money (*archaic*) ■ *vti.* (**trucks, trucking, trucked**) (*dated*) **1.** EXCHANGE STH to exchange or barter sth, or take part in the business of bartering **2.** BE INVOLVED WITH SB to have dealings with sb, especially secret or dishonest dealings [12thC. From Old French dialect *troquer* 'to barter', of unknown origin.]

trucker[1] /trúkər/ *n.* sb who drives a truck, especially sb whose job is transporting goods by truck

trucker[2] /trúkər/ *n.* US, Can sb who barters

trucking /trúking/ *n.* the carrying of freight on roads in trucks

truckle[1] /trúk'l/ (**-les, -ling, -led**) *vi.* to behave in a weak or servile way [Early 17thC. Shortening of TRUCKLE BED, from the use of such beds by servants.] —**truckler** *n.*

truckle[2] /trúk'l/ *n.* **1.** CASTER a small wheel on which sth runs **2.** FOOD SMALL CHEESE a small cylindrical cheese [14thC. Via Anglo-Norman *trocle* from, ultimately, Greek *trokhileia* 'system of pulleys', from *trokhos* 'wheel'.]

truckle bed *n.* a low bed on casters that can be stowed away under another bed

truckload /trúk lōd/ *n.* the quantity carried by a truck, or a quantity large enough to fill a truck

truculence /trúkyōōlənss/, **truculency** /trúkyōōlənssi/ *n.* **1.** AGGRESSIVE DEFIANCE aggressive or sullen uncooperativeness **2.** FEROCITY extreme anger or aggression (*archaic*)

truculent /trúkyōōlənt/ *adj.* **1.** AGGRESSIVELY DEFIANT aggressively or sullenly refusing to accept sth or do what is asked **2.** FIERCE displaying great anger or aggression (*archaic*) [Mid-16thC. From Latin *truculentus*, from *trux* 'fierce'.] —**truculently** *adv.*

trudge /truj/ *vti.* (**trudges, trudging, trudged**) WALK WEARILY to walk, or walk a particular path or distance, with slow heavy weary steps ■ *n.* LONG WALK a long and exhausting walk [Mid-16thC. Origin unknown.] —**trudger** *n.*

true /trōō/ *adj.* (**truer, truest**) **1.** REAL OR CORRECT conforming with reality or fact **2.** GENUINE genuine, not pretended, insincere, or artificial **3.** PERSONALLY FAITHFUL showing loyalty to another person ○ *a true friend* **4.** COMMITTED faithful to a cause, purpose, or religious belief ○ *a true believer* **5.** CONFORMING TO A STANDARD OR MEASURE conforming to a standard, measure, or pattern ○ *a true fit* **6.** RIGHTFUL conforming to the way things should be by right ○ *returned to the true owners* **7.** GEOG IN RELATION TO EARTH'S POLES measured in relation to geographical points on the earth's surface, rather than to points of magnetic attraction ○ *true north* **8.** CONFORMING TO INCLUSION CRITERIA meeting the criteria for inclusion in a particular category, in contrast to being given the same name because of superficial resemblance to members of that category ○ *A shooting star is not a true star.* **9.** PHYS NOT RELATIVE not relative as a value and corrected for all error factors, e.g. the difference between true time and mean time **10.** MUSIC IN TUNE perfectly in tune ○ *The orchestra maintained true pitch throughout.* ■ *adv.* **1.** SO AS TO CORRESPOND WITH REALITY in a way that corresponds with reality or fact ○ *His explanations just didn't ring true.* **2.** ACCURATELY so as to arrive at the precise position aimed for ○ *The arrow flew straight and true.* **3.** HONESTLY in a frank and open way that seeks to hide nothing ○ *Tell me true.* **4.** CERTAINLY used to admit the validity or accuracy of a statement, often in a discussion or when considering the advantages and disadvantages of sth ○ *True, it does rain a lot here.* **5.** AGRIC WITHOUT LOSS OF ANCESTRAL FEATURES without variation from the ancestral form, or producing offspring with the same hereditary characteristics ○ *breed true* ■ *vt.* (**trues, truing, trued**) ADJUST POSITION OF STH to adjust sth to make it straight or level or put it in any other required position ■ *n.* **1.** ALIGNMENT a correct position, especially a position in relation to the horizontal or vertical **2.** REALITY the absolute truth [Old English *trēowe* 'trustworthy'. Ultimately from an Indo-European word meaning 'to be solid', which is also the source of English *tree* and *durable*.] —**trueness** *n.* ◇ **come true** to happen as hoped or expected ◇ **not true** impossible to believe or accept (*informal*)

true bill *n.* US a legal document requesting a criminal trial (**bill of indictment**), formally endorsed by a grand jury and certifying that sb can be brought to trial

true blue *n.* sb with staunchly loyalist, royalist, or conservative views (*informal*) [From the adoption by 17th-century Scottish Presbyterians of the colour blue, in opposition to the Royalists' red]

true-born *adj.* having your true social position or nationality beyond doubt, because it was established at birth ○ *a true-born Londoner*

true bug *n.* ZOOL = **bug** *n.* 1

true-life *adj.* presenting matters, especially human relationships, as they are or have been in reality ○ *a true-life adventure story*

truelove /trōō luv/ *n.* sb who is deeply loved by another

truelove knot, **true lovers' knot** *n.* a complicated bow-knot that is difficult to untie, symbolizing lovers' faithfulness

Trueman /trōōmən/, **Fred** (*b.* 1931) British cricketer. A skilled fast bowler, he took 307 test wickets in his career, then a record. Full name **Frederick Sewards Trueman**

true rib *n.* a rib that is attached to the breastbone (**sternum**) by cartilage. The seven uppermost ribs in the human body are true ribs.

François Truffaut

Truffaut /trōōfō/, **François** (1932–84) French film director and critic. His first film, the semi-autobiographical *The 400 Blows* (1959), was one of the first films of the French New Wave movement. Other films include *Shoot the Piano Player* (1960) and *Jules et Jim* (1961).

truffle /trúff'l/ *n.* **1.** FLESHY FUNGUS EATEN AS DELICACY an underground fungus whose fleshy edible fruiting body is highly valued as a delicacy. Pigs and dogs are often used to sniff out truffles. Genus: *Tuber*. **2.** CHOCOLATE CANDY a rich ball-shaped chocolate with a centre of soft chocolate [Late 16thC. Alteration of French *trufe*, via Provençal *trufa* from, ultimately, Latin *tuber* (see TUBER).]

trug /trug/ *n.* a shallow rectangular basket made from curved strips of wood, used especially for carrying garden produce [14thC. Origin uncertain: perhaps a dialectal variant of TROUGH.]

Truganini (1812?–76) Australian Aboriginal. He is said to have been the last full-blooded Aboriginal in Tasmania.

truism /trōō izəm/ *n.* a statement that is so obviously true and so often repeated that people find it trite or meaningless —**truistic** /troo ístik/ *adj.*

trull /trul/ *n.* a prostitute (*archaic*) [Early 16thC. From Middle High German *trulle*.]

truly /trōōli/ *adv.* **1.** SINCERELY honestly, without affectation or pretence ○ *feel truly sorry* **2.** USED FOR EMPHASIS used to emphasize the extent or degree of sth ○ *a truly remarkable achievement* **3.** COMPLETELY to the fullest extent or in the fullest degree ○ *Only she can truly appreciate how happy I feel.* ◇ **yours truly 1.** used as a rather formal way of signing off in a letter **2.** used to refer to yourself (*humorous*) ○ *Doubtless they're expecting yours truly to pick them up from the airport.*

Truman /trōōmən/, **Bess** (1885–1982) US first lady. She married Harry S. Truman, a childhood sweetheart, in 1919, and during his presidency (1945–53) was one of his most trusted advisers. Born **Elizabeth Virginia Wallace**

Harry S. Truman

Truman, Harry S. (1884–1972) US statesman and 33rd president of the United States. A Democrat, he became president on the death of F. D. Roosevelt (1945), serving until 1953. He actively opposed Communism overseas, notably in Korea (1950–53).

Trumbull /trúmbəl/, **John** (1750–1831) US lawyer and poet. One of the 'Connecticut Wits', he is known for the comic epic *'M'Fingal'* (1776–82), satirizing British Loyalists during the American War of Independence.

trumeau /trōō mō/ (*plural* **-meaux** /trōō mōz/) *n.* a pillar or a section of wall that separates two doors or two sections of a door [Late 19thC. From French, literally 'calf of the leg'.]

trump[1] /trump/ *n.* **1.** CARDS CARD FROM HIGHEST SUIT in card games, a card from a suit declared to be higher in value than any other suit, or the suit itself **2.** KEY RESOURCE a highly valuable resource or advantage, especially one held in reserve for future use **3.** FINE PERSON an admirable or reliable person (*informal*) ■ *vt.* (**trumps, trumping, trumped**) **1.** CARDS DEFEAT BY PLAYING A TRUMP in card games, to beat an opponent or an opponent's card by playing a trump **2.** OUTDO to defeat or outdo a competitor by bringing a valuable resource or advantage into play [Early 16thC. Alteration of TRIUMPH.] ◇ **turn up trumps** to prove unexpectedly to be a valuable asset, especially one that plays a decisive role in the success of sth

trump up *vt.* to invent false accusations or false evidence in order to incriminate sb wrongly

trump[2] /trump/ *n.* a trumpet, or the sound of a trumpet (*literary*) [13thC. From Old French *trompe* (see TRUMPET).]

trump card *n.* = trump[1] *n.* 1, trump[1] *n.* 2 ◇ **play your trump card** to make use of a highly valuable resource or advantage that has been held in reserve

trumped-up *adj.* false and deliberately invented, usually in order to incriminate sb wrongly ○ *trumped-up charges* [*Trumped* formed from TRUMP[1] in the obsolete sense 'to fabricate, invent', the underlying idea being 'to deceive']

trumpery /trúmpəri/ (*plural* **-ies**) *n.* (*archaic or literary*) **1.** WORTHLESS THING sth worthless or useless, often sth showy that seems appealing at first glance **2.** NONSENSE empty or ridiculous talk **3.** DECEPTION the deceiving of sb, or schemes conceived for the purpose of deceiving [15thC. From French *tromperie* 'trickery', from *tromper* 'to deceive', of unknown origin.]

trumpet /trúmpit/ *n.* **1.** MUSIC BRASS INSTRUMENT a brass musical instrument, either straight or coiled, with three valves and a flared bell. It has a brilliant tone and a middle to high register. **2.** STH SHAPED LIKE A TRUMPET sth shaped like the flared bell of a trumpet **3.** SOUND LIKE TRUMPET'S a loud high sound made by a trumpet, or a similarly strident sound such as the call of an elephant **4.** EAR TRUMPET an ear trumpet **5.** MUSIC ORGAN STOP a solo organ stop that imitates the sound of a trumpet ■ *v.* (**-pets, -peting, -peted**) **1.** *vti.* ANNOUNCE STH to announce sth loudly, proudly, or with great ceremony **2.** *vt.* SPEAK PROUDLY OF SB OR STH to speak of sb or sth with ostentatious admiration or pride **3.** *vi.* MAKE ELEPHANT'S CALL to make an elephant's characteristically high-pitched, penetrating call **4.** *vt.* EXPRESS BY TRUMPETING to convey sth with a trumpeting call ○ *The elephant trumpeted a warning.* [14thC. From Old French *trompette*, literally 'small horn', from *trompe* 'horn', of prehistoric Germanic origin; probably ultimately an imitation of the sound of a horn.] ◇ **blow your own trumpet** to speak confidently, proudly, or boastfully about your own achievements, qualities, or possessions (*informal*)

trumpet creeper, **trumpet vine** *n.* a woody deciduous North American vine with compound leaves and large red trumpet-shaped flowers. Latin name: *Campsis radicans.*

trumpeter /trúmpitər/ *n.* **1.** MUSIC TRUMPET PLAYER a musician who plays the trumpet **2.** BIRDS TROPICAL BIRD WITH A LOUD CALL a medium-sized South American bird that rarely flies and has long legs, a short stout bill, dark glossy plumage, and a loud call. Family: Psophidae. **3.** BIRDS PIGEON a domestic pigeon that has a long ruff, heavily feathered feet, and a loud call

trumpeter swan *n.* a large white swan with a black bill and a loud call, found in western Canada and Alaska. Latin name: *Cygnus buccinator.*

trumpetfish /trúmpit fish/ (*plural* **-fishes** *or* **-fish**) *n.* a name given to various tropical reef fish with long bodies and tubular snouts. Family: Aulostomidae.

trumpet flower *n.* **1.** PLANT WITH TRUMPET-SHAPED FLOWERS a plant with trumpet-shaped flowers, e.g. the trumpet creeper **2.** FLOWER the flower of a trumpet flower

trumpet honeysuckle *n.* a North American variety of honeysuckle plant with scarlet or orange trumpet-shaped flowers. Latin name: *Lonicera sempervirens.*

trumpet vine *n.* = **trumpet creeper**

trumps *npl.* in card games, the suit that is chosen at the outset to be the highest in value (*takes a singular or plural verb*) ○ *Diamonds are trumps.*

truncate *vt.* /trung káyt/ (**-cates, -cating, -cated**) **1.** SHORTEN STH BY REMOVING PART to shorten sth by cutting off or removing a part **2.** MATH SHORTEN DECIMAL NUMBER to restrict the precision of a decimal number by limiting the digits to the right of the decimal point without rounding ■ *adj.* **1.** = **truncated** *adj.* 1 **2.** BOT NOT POINTED used to describe a leaf that has a blunt end, giving the impression that a part has been cut off [15thC. From Latin *truncare* 'to cut short, mutilate', from *truncus* (see TRUNK).] —**truncately** *adv.* —**truncation** /trung káysh'n/ *n.*

truncated /trung káytid/ *adj.* **1.** WITH END REMOVED shortened by having a part cut off or removed **2.** GEOM WITH END REPLACED BY PLANE used to describe a geometric figure that has the apex or an end removed and replaced with a plane section, often parallel to the base **3.** CRYSTALS HAVING INCOMPLETE CORNERS used to describe a crystal lacking the fully formed corners or faces that would be present in a simple form of the crystal **4.** POETRY WITH ONE SYLLABLE FEWER used to describe a line of poetry that has one syllable fewer in one of its feet than in others in the line

truncheon /trúnchən/ *n.* **1.** ARMS POLICE OFFICER'S CLUB a short heavy stick carried by a police officer **2.** SYMBOLIC STICK a baton carried as a symbol of rank or authority **3.** ARMS SPEAR'S SHAFT the shaft of a spear **4.** ARMS CLUB any short heavy stick used as a weapon of attack (*archaic*) ■ *vt.* (**-cheons, -cheoning, -cheoned**) HIT SB WITH A TRUNCHEON to hit sb or sth with a truncheon [13thC. Via Old Northern French *tronchon* from, ultimately, Latin *truncus* (see TRUNK).]

trundle /trúnd'l/ *v.* (**-dles, -dling, -dled**) **1.** *vti.* MOVE HEAVILY ON WHEELS to move, or move sth, slowly and heavily, especially on wheels or rollers **2.** *vt.* ROTATE STH to turn sth round and round repeatedly (*archaic*) ■ *n.* **1.** WHEEL a small wheel or roller by which sth is moved along **2.** ROLLING MOVEMENT a slow heavy movement, especially a rolling movement **3.** CART WITH WHEELS a trolley or cart with small wheels [Mid-16thC. Variant of *trendle* 'wheel', from Old English *trendel* 'circle'.]

trundle bed, **trundle** *n.* = **truckle bed**

trundler /trúndlər/ *n. NZ* **1.** GOLF CART a cart for pulling a golf bag along by hand **2.** TROLLEY a shopping trolley **3.** PUSHCHAIR a child's pushchair

trunk /trungk/ *n.* **1.** TREES TREE'S MAIN STEM the main stem of a tree, excluding branches and roots **2.** LARGE TRAVELLING CASE a large strong travelling case or box with a hinged lid that is bigger, more rigid, and less portable than a suitcase **3.** ANAT, ZOOL UPPER BODY the main part of the body of a human being or an animal, excluding the head, neck, and limbs **4.** ZOOL ELEPHANT'S NOSE the long muscular proboscis of an elephant, used for grasping, feeding, and drinking **5.** MAIN PART the main part of sth that has branches or subsidiary parts leading off it, e.g. a transport network or an electrical or communications network **6.** *US* CARS = **boot 7.** ANAT STEM OF BLOOD VESSEL the main stem of a blood vessel or nerve, with branches leading off it **8.** NAUT PART OF CABIN ABOVE DECK the part of a boat's cabin that sits above the deck **9.** BUILDING DUCT any kind of duct in a building, e.g. a ventilation duct or a duct carrying electrical wires **10.** ARCHIT PART OF COLUMN the shaft of an architectural column, excluding the base and the capital ■ **trunks** *npl.* CLOTHES MEN'S SWIMWEAR men's shorts worn for sports, especially swimming [15thC. Via French *tronc* 'tree trunk, alms box' from Latin *truncus*, literally 'sth cut off' (source of English *truncate* and *trench*).]

trunk call *n.* formerly, a long-distance telephone call (*dated*)

trunkfish /trúngk fish/ (*plural* **-fishes** *or* **-fish**) *n.* a brightly coloured tropical fish that has a body covered in bony plates. Family: Ostraciidae.

trunk hose *n.* short puffed-out breeches worn by men in the late 16th and early 17th centuries. They extended from the waist to the upper or mid thigh.

trunking /trúngking/ *n.* **1.** CABLE CASING casing used to anchor, conceal, and protect cables and small pipes **2.** TRANSP FREIGHT TRANSPORT SYSTEM a freight transport system in which bulk deliveries are made to local distribution centres. Individual stores or customers order or collect items from these centres as required.

trunk road *n.* a designated major long-distance A road used by high volumes of traffic

trunnion /trúnni ən/ *n.* either of a pair of pivots, especially the cylindrical knobs on the side of a cannon's barrel that allow it to pivot on the gun carriage [Early 17thC. From French *trognon* 'fruit core, tree stump', of uncertain origin.] —**trunnioned** *adj.*

Truro /tróoró/ **1.** city and administrative centre of Cornwall, southwestern England. Population: 18,966 (1991). **2.** town on Cobequid Bay in central Nova Scotia, Canada. Population: 11,938 (1996).

truss /truss/ *vt.* (**trusses, trussing, trussed**) **1.** BIND STH to tie sth or sb tightly **2.** COOK TIE STH FOR COOKING to prepare meat for roasting by tying it into a neat shape. Birds such as chickens and turkeys are trussed to keep wings and legs close to the body. **3.** CIV ENG SUPPORT STH WITH LOAD-BEARING MEMBERS to support or strengthen a roof, bridge, or other elevated structure with a network of beams and bars **4.** MED SUPPORT A HERNIA to support a hernia with a specially designed device ■ *n.* **1.** ARCHIT CORBEL a corbel **2.** MED SUPPORT FOR A HERNIA a device designed to apply pressure to a hernia to stop it enlarging or protruding **3.** BOT FRUIT CLUSTER a cluster of flowers or fruit on a single branching stem, e.g. on a tomato plant **4.** SAILING MAST FITTING a metal fitting used to attach a ship's beam (**yard**) to a mast **5.** BUNDLE a bundle, especially a bundle of hay of varying weight [12thC. From Old French *trousse*, from *trousser* 'to truss', of uncertain origin: perhaps via assumed Vulgar Latin *torsare* from, ultimately, Latin *torquere* 'to twist' (see TORQUE[1]).] —**trusser** *n.*

truss bridge *n.* a bridge whose supporting structure consists of a network of beams in a series of triangular sections

trussing /trússing/ *n.* a framework of beams arranged in triangular sections and supporting a roof, bridge, or other structure, or the beams themselves

trust /trust/ *n.* **1.** RELIANCE confidence in and reliance on good qualities, especially fairness, truth, honour, or ability **2.** CARE responsibility for taking good care of sb or sth ○ *We put our children in the trust of a good child-minder.* **3.** POSITION OF OBLIGATION the position of sb who is expected by others to behave responsibly or honourably ○ *breached the public trust* **4.** STH IN WHICH CONFIDENCE IS PLACED sb who or sth that people place confidence or faith in (*archaic or literary*) **5.** HOPE FOR THE FUTURE hopeful reliance on what will happen in the future **6.** LAW HOLDING OF ANOTHER'S PROPERTY the legal holding and managing of money or property belonging to sb else, e.g. that of a minor **7.** LAW ARRANGEMENT TO MANAGE ANOTHER'S PROPERTY a legal arrangement by which one person (**trustee**) holds and manages money or property belonging to sb else **8.** COMM CREDIT credit given to sb on purchases made ○ *let me have it on trust* ■ *v.* (**trusts, trusting, trusted**) **1.** *vti.* RELY ON STH to place confidence in sb's good qualities, especially fairness, truth, honour, or ability **2.** *vt.* CONFIDENTLY ALLOW SB TO HAVE STH to allow sb to do or use sth in confidence that the person will behave responsibly or properly ○ *I trust you to do the right thing.* **3.** *vt.* PLACE STH IN SB'S CARE to place sb or sth in the care of another person ○ *You could certainly trust him with such an important job.* **4.** *vt.* SUPPOSE to hope or suppose sth ○ *I trust you had a good holiday.* **5.** *vt. Carib* GIVE CREDIT TO SB to give sb credit on a purchase ○ *wouldn't even trust me a carton of milk* [12thC. From Old Norse *traust* 'confidence' and *treysta* 'to trust'. Ultimately from an Indo-European base meaning 'to be solid', which is also the ancestor of English *true, tryst,* and *tree*.] —**trustability** /trústə bílləti/ *n.* —**trustable** /trústəb'l/ *adj.* —**truster** *n.* ◇ **take sth on trust** to accept sth as true or honest without checking that this is the case

trustafarian /trústə fáiri ən/ *n.* a young person from an affluent background who is temporarily living in circumstances less comfortable than he or she can expect to enjoy in the future, typically in a bohemian or socially disadvantaged area (*humorous informal*) [Late 20thC. Blend of TRUST and RASTAFARIAN.]

trust company *n.* a bank or other commercial organization that sets up and operates trusts for private individuals and businesses

trustee /tru stée/ *n.* **1.** LAW MANAGER OF ANOTHER'S PROPERTY sb who is given the legal authority to manage money or property on behalf of sb else **2.** FIN FINANCE MANAGER a member of a group of people responsible for managing the financial affairs of an institution or organization **3.** POL COUNTRY SUPERVISING TRUST TERRITORY a country responsible for administering a trust territory

trusteeship /tru stée ship/ *n.* **1.** LAW, FIN TRUSTEE'S POSITION the status or responsibilities of a trustee, or the period of time for which a trustee holds office **2.** POL GOVERNMENT UNDER UNITED NATIONS' TERMS the administration of a country that is not self-governing by a foreign country under terms laid down by the United Nations

trustful /trústf'l/ *adj.* = **trusting** —**trustfully** *adv.* —**trustfulness** *n.*

trust fund *n.* an investment fund managed on behalf

of sb, particularly a minor, by one or more people given legal authority to do so

trust hotel *n. NZ* a hotel operated by elected members of a local community, with profits going to finance community projects

trusting /trústing/, **trustful** /trústf'l/ *adj.* willing or tending to trust people —**trustingly** *adv.* —**trustingness** *n.*

trustless /trústləss/ *adj.* (*archaic or literary*) **1.** SUSPICIOUS tending not to trust others **2.** UNTRUSTWORTHY not worthy of being trusted —**trustlessly** *adv.* —**trustlessness** *n.*

trust tavern *n. NZ* a bar operated by elected members of a local community, with profits going to finance community projects

trust territory *n.* a country that does not have its own government but is run by a foreign country under terms laid down by the United Nations

trustworthy /trúst wurthi/ *adj.* deserving trust, or able to be trusted —**trustworthily** *adv.* —**trustworthiness** *n.*

trusty /trústi/ *adj.* (**-ier, -iest**) RELIABLE able to be relied on (*dated or humorous*) ■ *n.* (*plural* **-ies**) **1.** TRUSTED PERSON sb who is trusted by others **2.** TRUSTED PRISONER a prisoner regarded by the prison authorities as trustworthy and given special privileges —**trustily** *adv.* —**trustiness** *n.*

truth /trooth/ *n.* **1.** TRUE QUALITY correspondence to fact or reality **2.** STH FACTUAL sth that corresponds to fact or reality ○ *spoke the truth* **3.** TRUE STATEMENT a statement that corresponds to fact or reality **4.** OBVIOUS FACT sth that is so clearly true that it hardly needs to be stated **5.** STH GENERALLY BELIEVED a statement that is generally believed to be true ○ *a religious truth* **6.** HONESTY honesty, sincerity, or integrity **7.** DESCRIPTIVE ACCURACY accuracy in description or portrayal ○ *a criticism that had an element of truth in it* **8.** CONFORMITY adherence to a standard or law **9.** LOYALTY faithfulness to a person or a cause (*dated*) **10.** ACCURACY accuracy of alignment, setting, position, or shape (*dated*) [Old English *trēowth* 'faithfulness' (source also of TROTH)] ◇ **be economical with the truth** to tell lies (*ironic*)

Truth *n.* in Christian Science, the word used to refer to God

truth-condition *n.* the condition that must apply if a given philosophical proposition is to be true

truth drug *n.* a drug that is supposed to make the person taking it tell the truth, usually by reducing inhibitions or causing hypnosis. Thiopental sodium is held by some to induce truth-telling.

truthful /troothf'l/ *adj.* **1.** HONEST telling the truth, or tending to tell the truth **2.** ACCURATE corresponding to fact or reality —**truthfulness** *n.*

truthfully /troothf'li/ *adv.* **1.** SO AS TO EXPRESS TRUTH in a way that corresponds to fact or reality or that expresses the truth **2.** EMPHASIZING TRUTH used to reinforce the truth of what has just been said or is about to be said ○ *Truthfully, I did not know she was there.*

truth serum *n.* = truth drug

truth set *n.* a set of all the values that make a given mathematical or logic statement true when substituted in the statement

truth table *n.* **1.** LOGIC TABLE USED IN LOGIC a table used to work out the truth or falsity of a compound statement in logic **2.** ELECTRON ENG TABLE USED IN TRANSISTOR TECHNOLOGY in electronics and computing, a table used to indicate the value of the output signal from a logic circuit or device for every possible input

truth-value *n.* in logic, the truth or falsity of a proposition or of a compound statement consisting of two or more propositions

try /trī/ *v.* (**tries, trying, tried**) **1.** *vti.* MAKE AN EFFORT to make an effort or an attempt to do or achieve sth **2.** *vt.* TEST STH FOR PURPOSE OF ASSESSMENT to test, sample, or experiment with sth in order to assess its usefulness, worth, or quality ○ *You get to try the software out at home.* **3.** *vt.* STRAIN OR VEX SB to subject sb or sth to great strain ○ *The long wait tried her patience.* **4.** *vt.* LAW SUBJECT SB TO LEGAL TRIAL to carry out the trial in court of sb accused of a crime or offence **5.** *vt.* LAW CONDUCT A CASE IN COURT to conduct a legal

case in court ○ *asked when the case would be tried* **6.** *vt.* FOOD = **render** *v.* 8 ■ *n.* (*plural* **tries**) **1.** EFFORT an attempt made to do or achieve sth **2.** RUGBY SCORE IN RUGBY a score achieved by touching the ball on the ground behind the line of the opponent's posts (**goal line**). In Rugby Union, five points are scored, while the score is three points in Rugby League. [13thC. Via Old French *trier* 'to sift out' from assumed Vulgar Latin *triare*, of unknown origin.] ◇ **try it on** to behave in an unacceptable way, or make an unjustified claim or request, in order to find out whether this will be allowed or accepted (*informal*)

—————— **WORD KEY: USAGE** ——————

try and or **try to**? The two expressions are often interchangeable (*We'll try and come* or *We'll try to come*), although **try and** is somewhat more informal. In the past tense and in negative and continuous constructions, however, **try to** is needed: *They tried to deliver the package on Friday. We are not trying to be funny. Are you trying to tell me sth?*

—————— **WORD KEY: SYNONYMS** ——————

try, attempt, endeavour, strive
CORE MEANING: to make an effort to do sth
try to make an effort to do or achieve sth; **attempt** used in a similar way to *try*, but often used to suggest that the task is difficult and so the chances of success are not high; **endeavour** a fairly formal word meaning to try to do or achieve sth that involves great exertion or effort; **strive** like *endeavour*, but often with the implication of persistence.

try on *vt.* to put on an item of clothing to test its fit or suitability

try out *vi. US, Can* to undergo a competitive test of suitability, especially for a place on a sports team or for a part as an actor ○ *plans to try out for the play*

trying /trī ing/ *adj.* placing great strain on sb's patience, composure, or good nature, and often physically exhausting as a result —**tryingly** *adv.*

trying plane *n.* a woodworking plane with a long body, used for planing long surfaces [From the phrase *to try up* 'to smooth rough-planed wood']

try-on (*plural* **try-ons**) *n.* a test of a person's gullibility or patience (*informal*)

tryout /trī owt/ *n. US, Can* a trial to test sb's suitability, especially to play on a sports team or play a specific role as an actor

trypan blue /tríppən-/ *n.* a blue dye used to distinguish live cells from dead cells. Only dead cells turn blue in the presence of trypan blue. [Shortening of TRYPANOSOME]

trypanosome /tríppənə sōm/ *n.* a simple microscopic organism (**protozoan**) that lives as a parasite in the blood of certain vertebrates, including human beings. It is transmitted by insect bites and causes serious diseases. Genus: *Trypanosoma.* [Early 20thC. From modern Latin, genus name, from Greek *trupanon* 'borer' + *sōma* 'body'.] —**trypanosomal** /tríppənə sōm'l/ *adj.*

trypanosomiasis /tríppənō sō mí əssiss/ *n.* a disorder caused by infestation with a microscopic organism that lives as a parasite in the blood, especially sleeping sickness

trypsin /trípsin/ *n.* an enzyme in pancreatic juice that acts as a catalyst for breaking proteins down into peptides [Late 19thC. Origin uncertain: probably formed from Greek *tripsis* 'rubbing', because it was first obtained by rubbing a pancreas with glycerine.] —**tryptic** *adj.*

trypsinogen /trip sínnəjən/ *n.* the inactive substance secreted in the juices of the pancreas and converted into trypsin

tryptamine /tríptə meen/ *n.* a crystalline amine found in plant and animal tissue, formed synthetically or by the decomposition of the amino acid tryptophan. Formula: $C_{10}H_{12}N_2$. [Early 20thC. Coined from TRYPTOPHAN + -AMINE.]

tryptophan /tríptō fan/ *n.* an essential amino acid found in proteins such as casein and fibrin. Formula: $C_{11}H_{12}O_2N_2$. [Late 19thC. Coined from *tryptic* 'of trypsin' + -PHANE.]

trysail /trī sayl/ *n.* a strong sail used in stormy weather that is either square or triangular and is set to run

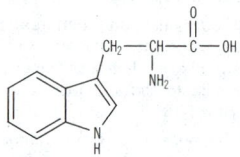

Tryptophan

parallel to the length of the ship (**fore-and-aft**) [Mid-18thC. From *a-try* 'hove to'.]

try square *n.* a woodworking tool used to test and mark out right angles, consisting of a rectangular handle with a thin flat rectangular metal blade fitted perpendicular to it

tryst /trist/ *n.* (*old or literary*) **1.** ARRANGEMENT TO MEET an arrangement to meet, especially one made privately or secretly by lovers **2.** SECRET MEETING a secret meeting, or place of meeting, especially between lovers ■ *vi.* (**trysts, trysting, trysted**) MEET OR ARRANGE TO MEET to arrange a meeting with sb or keep an arrangement to meet, especially secretly with a lover (*old or literary*) [14thC. From Old French *triste* 'place to lie in wait', of prehistoric Germanic origin.] —**tryster** *n.*

tsaddik *n.* = tzaddik

tsar /zaar/, **tzar, czar** *n.* **1.** RUSSIAN EMPEROR an emperor of Russia, before 1917 **2.** TYRANT sb who behaves in an autocrat way **3.** PERSON IN AUTHORITY an official or a person in a position of authority (*informal*) —**tsardom** *n.*

tsarevitch /zaʹərə vich/, **czarevitch** *n.* a son of a Russian emperor, especially the eldest son [Early 18thC. From Russian *tsarevich*, from *tsar'* (see TSAR).]

tsarevna /zaa révnə/, **czarevna** *n.* **1.** TSAREVITCH'S WIFE the wife of a tsarevitch **2.** TSAR'S DAUGHTER the daughter of a tsar [Late 19thC. From Russian *tsarevna*, from *tsar'* (see TSAR).]

tsarina /zaa reénə/, **tsaritsa** /zaa reétsə/, **czarina, czaritza** *n.* **1.** RUSSIAN EMPRESS an empress of Russia, before 1917 **2.** TSAR'S WIFE OR WIDOW the wife or widow of a tsar [Early 18thC. From Italian or Spanish *zarina*, feminine of *zar*, from Russian *tsar'* (see TSAR).]

tsarism /zaaʹr izzəm/ *n.* **1.** RULE BY TSAR government by an emperor who has absolute power **2.** DICTATORSHIP absolute rule of any kind, especially the cruel abuse of absolute power by a despot —**tsarist** *adj., n.*

tsaritsa *n.* HIST = tsarina [Late 17thC. From Russian.]

Tsavo National Park /tsaʹávō-/ national park and game reserve in Kenya, established in 1948. Area: 20,700 sq. km/8,000 sq. mi.

TSE *n.* a disease that affects the nervous system and can be transmitted from one species to another. Full form **transmissible spongiform encephalopathy**

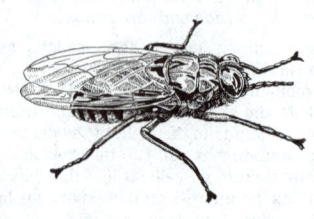

Tsetse fly

tsetse fly /tétsi-, tsétsi-/, **tzetze fly** *n.* a two-winged biting fly found in central Africa that feeds on the blood of humans and animals and is responsible for transmitting several diseases, including sleeping sickness. Genus: *Glossina*. [Mid-19thC. Via Afrikaans from Setswana.]

TSH *abbr.* thyroid-stimulating hormone

T-shirt, **tee-shirt** *n.* **1.** COLLARLESS SHORT-SLEEVED SHIRT a collarless buttonless, often short-sleeved, knit shirt, usually made of cotton and worn for leisure and sports. T-shirts are often printed with designs and slogans. **2.** *US* VEST a man's short-sleeved vest [Early 20thC. From its T-shape when spread out.]

Tshombe /chómbi/, **Moise** (1919–69) Congolese statesman. He was president of the secessionist state of Katanga (1960–63) and prime minister of the Democratic Republic of the Congo (1964–65). Full name **Moise Kapenda Tshombe**

tshwala /chwáalə/ *n.* *S Africa* thick home-brewed beer made from sorghum millet, maize, or other grain that is a traditional drink in South Africa [From Zulu *utshwala*]

tsimmes *n.* = **tzimmes**

Tsimshian /chímshi ən/ (*plural* **-an** *or* **-ans**) *n.* **1.** PEOPLES MEMBER OF NATIVE N AMERICAN PEOPLE a member of a Native North American people who originally occupied coastal lands in southeastern Alaska and British Columbia, and whose members mainly continue to live in the same area **2.** LANG **TSIMSHIAN LANGUAGE** the language of the Tsimshian and other Native North American peoples. It is spoken by about 1,500 people. [Mid-19thC. From Tsimshian *čamsián*, literally 'inside the Skeena River'.] —**Tsimshian** *adj.*

Tsonga /tsóng gə/ (*plural* **-ga** *or* **-gas**) *n.* **1.** PEOPLES MEMBER OF SOUTHERN AFRICAN PEOPLE a member of a people who live in southern Africa, mainly in Mozambique, Swaziland, and South Africa **2.** LANG **TSONGA LANGUAGE** the language of the Tsonga people. It belongs to the Bantu group of Benue-Congo languages. Tsonga is spoken by about 4 million people. [Early 20thC. Of Bantu origin.] —**Tsonga** *adj.*

tsotsi /tsótsi/ *n.* *S Africa* a young Black man who belongs to a gang involved in criminal activities of various kinds, especially one that operates in townships (*informal*) [Mid-20thC. Origin uncertain: perhaps from Nguni *-tsotsa* 'to dress in exaggerated clothing', from the type of clothing such members wear.]

tsp. *abbr.* teaspoon

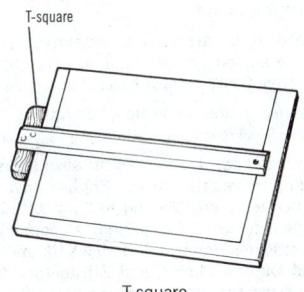

T-square

T-square, **tee-square** *n.* a drawing-board ruler consisting of a rectangular handle with a straight-sided wooden or plastic blade attached perpendicular to it, to form a T shape. The handle sits against the board's edge.

TSS *abbr.* toxic shock syndrome

T-strap *n.* a style of shoe, usually worn by women or children, with a T-shaped strap cut from the upper part of the shoe

tsunami /tsoo náami/ (*plural* **-mis**) *n.* a large destructive ocean wave caused by an underwater earthquake or some other movement of the earth's surface [Late 19thC. From Japanese, literally 'harbour wave'.] —**tsunamic** *adj.*

tsuris /tsoórriss/, **tzuris** *n.* problems or difficulties (*informal*) [Early 20thC. Via Yiddish *tsores* 'troubles' from, ultimately, Hebrew *ṣārāh* 'trouble'.]

Tsushima /tsoo sheémə/ island group in the Korea Strait, southwestern Japan. Population: 48,875 (1985). Area: 702 sq. km/271 sq. mi.

tsutsugamushi disease /tsoótsəgə moóshi-/ *n.* = **scrub typhus** [Early 20thC. From Japanese, literally 'disease tick'.]

Tswana /tswáanə/ (*plural* **-na** *or* **-nas**) *n.* **1.** PEOPLES MEMBER OF SOUTHERN AFRICAN PEOPLE a member of a people living in southern Africa, mainly in Botswana, where they form the largest ethnic group **2.** LANG **TSWANA LANGUAGE** the language of the Tswana people belonging to the Sotho group of Benue-Congo languages [Mid-20thC. Of Bantu origin.]

TT *abbr.* **1.** teetotal **2.** BANKING telegraphic transfer ■ *n.* MOTORCYCLE RACES IN ISLE OF MAN a series of motorcycle races held every year in the Isle of Man. Full form **Tourist Trophy** ■ *abbr.* tuberculin-tested

t-test *n.* a test of whether a sample of observations comes from a larger sample with a normal distribution of statistical properties

TTL[1] *n.* a method of constructing electronic logic circuits. Full form **transistor transistor logic**

TTL[2] *abbr.* through-the-lens

TTYTT *abbr.* to tell you the truth (*used in e-mail messages*)

TU *abbr.* trade union

Tu. *abbr.* CALENDAR Tuesday

tuan /toó aan/ *n.* in Malay-speaking countries, a respectful form of address for a man [Early 18thC. From Malay.]

Tuareg /twaá reg/ (*plural* **-reg** *or* **-regs**) *n.* **1.** PEOPLES AFRICAN PEOPLE a member of a nomadic people who live in northwestern Africa, mainly in the Sahara and Sahel regions **2.** LANG **TUAREG LANGUAGE** the Berber language of the Tuareg people. It belongs to the Afro-Asiatic family of languages. [Early 19thC. From Berber.]

tuart /toó aart/ *n.* a variety of eucalyptus tree grown for its very pale durable wood [Mid-19thC. Of Australian aboriginal origin.]

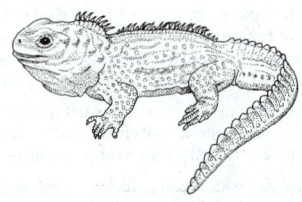

Tuatara

tuatara /toó ə taárə/ *n.* a large spiny greenish-grey reptile that looks like an iguana but does not belong to the iguana family. It is found only on islands off New Zealand. Latin name: *Sphenodon punctatum*. [Late 19thC. From Maori, literally 'with spines on its back'.]

tub /tub/ *n.* **1.** LOW OPEN CONTAINER a low open, often round, container of any size that is used for purposes such as storage and washing **2.** ROUND CONTAINER FOR LIQUIDS a small, often round, plastic or cardboard container for liquid, semi-liquid, or soft substances such as ice cream or margarine **3.** AMOUNT HELD BY TUB the contents of a tub **4.** BATH a bath (*informal*) **5.** NAUT POOR QUALITY BOAT a slow unreliable boat (*informal*) **6.** MINING MINE VEHICLE an open-top vehicle on rails used to transport coal and other excavated minerals in a mine ■ *v.* (**tubs**, **tubbing**, **tubbed**) **1.** *vt.* STORE STH IN TUB to store or package sth in a tub **2.** *vti.* BATHE to wash, or wash sth or yourself, in a bath (*informal*) [14thC. From Middle Low German or Middle Dutch.]

tuba /tyóobə/ *n.* a low-pitched brass musical instrument held vertically with the bell pointing upwards and the mouthpiece set horizontally. It has three to five valves. [Mid-19thC. Via French or Italian from Latin, 'large war trumpet'.]

tubal /tyóob'l/ *adj.* **1.** OF TUBES relating to or in the form of a tube or tubes **2.** ANAT OF FALLOPIAN TUBE relating to or developing in a fallopian tube

tubal ligation *n.* a sterilization technique in which a woman's fallopian tubes are tied to prevent ova entering the uterus. It is usually performed using endoscopic surgery.

tubate /tyoó bayt/ *adj.* tubular in shape

tubby /túbbi/ (**-bier**, **-biest**) *adj.* **1.** OFFENSIVE TERM an offensive term referring to sb regarded as being overweight (*informal insult*) **2.** TUB-SHAPED like a tub in shape **3.** MUSIC LACKING RESONANCE used to describe a violin or other string instrument that lacks resonance —**tubbiness** *n.*

tube /tyoob/ *n.* **1.** CYLINDER FOR TRANSPORTING OR STORING LIQUIDS any long hollow cylinder used to transport or store liquids **2.** ANAT CYLINDRICAL BODY ORGAN any hollow cylindrical organ that transports liquids or gases around the body **3.** COLLAPSIBLE CONTAINER WITH CAP a collapsible, generally cylindrical, container sealed at one end and closed with a cap at the other. It is used for packaging semi-liquid substances such as toothpaste. **4.** RAIL UNDERGROUND RAILWAY the underground railway system in London (*informal*) **5.** *UK* RAIL UNDERGROUND TRAIN a train on an underground railway system **6.** INNER TUBE an inner tube of a pneumatic tyre **7.** TV CATHODE RAY TUBE IN TV a cathode ray tube used to reproduce television images **8.** *Aus* CAN OF BEER a can of beer (*informal*) **9.** *Scotland* OFFENSIVE TERM a foolish or unintelligent person (*informal*) **10.** BOT CHANNEL IN PLANT any narrow enclosed channel in a plant such as the organ in a germinating pollen grain that conveys the male gametes to the ovule **11.** BOT FLOWER PART a roughly cylindrical fusion of the petals of a flower such as a daffodil **12.** ELECTRON ENG VALVE a valve (*informal*) **13.** MUSIC BODY OF WIND INSTRUMENT the hollow cylinder that forms the main body of a wind instrument, through which the player's breath passes **14.** PART OF A WAVE the tunnel formed when a large rolling wave prepares to break ■ *vt.* (**tubes**, **tubing**, **tubed**) **1.** FIT WITH TUBE to supply or fit sth with a tube **2.** ENCLOSE IN TUBE to put sth in a tube [Early 17thC. Via French from Latin *tubus*, of uncertain origin.]

tubectomy /tyoo béktəmi/ (*plural* **-mies**) *n.* the surgical removal of a fallopian tube (*informal*)

tube foot *n.* an outgrowth of the body wall of marine invertebrates of the sea urchin family (**echinoderms**), used for feeding, moving around, or performing other functions depending on the species

tubeless tyre /tyóobləss-/ *n.* a pneumatic tyre that does not require an inner tube because the casing and wheel rim form an airtight seal

tuber /tyóobər/ *n.* **1.** BOT FLESHY UNDERGROUND PLANT PART a fleshy swollen part of a root, e.g. a dahlia root, or of an underground stem, e.g. a potato, that stores food over winter and produces new growth in spring. A stem tuber has buds, popularly called eyes, unlike a root tuber. **2.** ANAT SMALL BULGE ON BODY a small raised area or swelling on the body [Mid-17thC. From Latin, 'swelling' (source of English *truffle*). Ultimately from an Indo-European base meaning 'to swell' that is also the ancestor of *thumb* and *tumour*.]

tubercle /tyóobərk'l/ *n.* **1.** BOT, ZOOL NODULE a small raised area on a plant or animal part **2.** MED SMALL LESION a small rounded swelling on the skin or on a mucous membrane, caused by a disease, especially a nodule in the lungs that is the characteristic symptom of tuberculosis [Late 16thC. From Latin *tuberculum*, literally 'small swelling', from *tuber* (see TUBER).]

tubercle bacillus *n.* a rod-shaped bacterium that causes tuberculosis. Latin name: *Mycobacterium tuberculosis*.

tubercular /tyoo búrkyoolər/, **tuberculous** *adj.* **1.** OF TUBERCULOSIS relating to, characteristic of, or affected by tuberculosis **2.** CAUSED BY TUBERCLE BACILLUS caused by the tubercle bacillus ○ *tubercular meningitis* **3.** NODULE-SHAPED taking the form of a small rounded swelling or nodule [Late 18thC. Formed from Latin *tuberculum* (see TUBERCLE).]

tuberculate /tyoo búrkyoolət/ *adj.* covered with small rounded swellings or nodules (**tubercles**) [Late 18thC. Formed from Latin *tuberculum* (see TUBERCLE).] —**tuberculately** *adv.* —**tuberculation** /tyoo búrkyoo láysh'n/ *n.*

tuberculin /tyoͦo búrkyoͦolin/ *n.* a sterile liquid obtained from cultures of the tubercle bacillus and used in a scratch test to establish whether sb has or has had tuberculosis [Late 19thC. Formed from Latin *tuberculum* (see TUBERCLE).]

tuberculin-tested *adj.* used to describe a dairy herd that has been certified as not having tuberculosis, or to describe milk from such a herd (*dated*)

tuberculoid /tyoͦo búrkyoͦo loyd/ *adj.* producing symptoms that resemble those produced by tuberculosis ○ *tuberculoid leprosy* [Late 19thC. Formed from Latin *tuberculum* (see TUBERCLE).]

tuberculosis /tyoͦo búrkyoͦo lóssiss/ *n.* an infectious disease that causes small rounded swellings (**tubercles**) to form on mucous membranes, especially a disease (**pulmonary tuberculosis**) that affects the lungs [Mid-19thC. Formed from Latin *tuberculum* (see TUBERCLE).]

tuberculous *adj.* = **tubercular** [Mid-18thC. Formed from Latin *tuberculum* (see TUBERCLE).]

Tuberose

tuberose[1] *n.* a perennial Mexican plant with blade-shaped leaves and spikes of fragrant white flowers. It is a kind of agave. Latin name: *Polianthes tuberosa.* [Mid-17thC. From modern Latin *tuberosa,* species name, from Latin *tuberosus,* from *tuber* (see TUBER).]

tuberose[2] /tyoͦobə róss/ *adj.* = **tuberous**

tuberosity /tyoͦobə róssəti/ (*plural* **-ties**) *n.* a rounded protuberance, especially at a point on a bone where muscles or ligaments are attached

tuberous /tyoͦobərəss/, **tuberose** /tyoͦobəróss/ *adj.* **1.** OF TUBERS relating to tubers or in the form of tubers **2.** HAVING WARTS producing or covered with knobbly growths [Mid-17thC. From Latin *tuberosus* (see TUBEROSE[1]).]

tube top *n.* US = **boob tube**

tube worm *n.* a worm that builds itself a tube-shaped shelter that sticks out of the soil

tubifex /tyoͦobi feks/ *n.* a thin reddish freshwater worm that builds a tube-shaped shelter in the sand of riverbeds. Such worms are often used as food for aquarium fish. Genus: *Tubifex.* [Mid-20thC. From modern Latin, genus name, from *tubus* 'tube' + *-fex* 'maker'.]

tubing /tyoͦobing/ *n.* **1.** SYSTEM OF TUBES a system or series of tubes **2.** MATERIAL USED FOR TUBES the hollow, cylindrical material that tubes are made of **3.** = **piping**

Tübingen /toͦobingən/ city in Baden-Württemberg State; southwestern Germany. Population: 82,900 (1992).

Tubman /túbmən/, **Harriet** (1830–1913) US abolitionist.

Library of Congress/Corbis
Harriet Tubman

Escaping from slavery (1849), she helped other enslaved labourers escape to freedom along the clandestine route known as the Underground Railroad.

Tubman, William (1895–1971) Liberian statesman. He was president of Liberia from 1943 to 1971. Full name **William Vacanarat Shadrach Tubman**

tubocurarine /tyoͦobō kyoͦo raˊarin/ *n.* **1.** ACTIVE CONSTITUENT OF CURARE a toxic substance that is an alkaloid and the active constituent of curare, used as a muscle relaxant **2.** HYDROCHLORIDE SALT OF TUBOCURARINE the hydrochloride salt of tubocurarine [Late 19thC. Coined from TUBE (from the fact that it is shipped in bamboo tubes) + CURARE + -INE.]

tuboplasty /tyoͦobō plasti/ (*plural* **-ties**) *n.* the surgical repair of one or both fallopian tubes, especially when these have been cut and tied for contraceptive reasons

tub-thumper *n.* a passionate or aggressive public speaker (*informal*) —**tub-thumping** *adj., n.*

tubular /tyoͦobyoͦolər/, **tubulate, tubulous** *adj.* **1.** TUBE-SHAPED shaped like a tube **2.** HAVING TUBES having a tube or tubes [Late 17thC. Formed from Latin *tubulus* (see TUBULE).]

tubular bells *npl.* a set of tuned metal tubes, usually arranged in a scale and hung from a frame, that are struck with a mallet

tubulate *adj.* /tyoͦobyoͦolət/ = **tubular** [Mid-18thC. From Latin *tubulatus,* from *tubulus* (see TUBULE).]

tubule /tyoͦob yool/ *n.* a very small tubular part in a plant or animal organism [Late 17thC. From Latin *tubulus,* literally 'small tube', from *tubus* (see TUBE).]

tubulin /tyoͦobyoͦolin/ *n.* a globular protein found in cells, the molecules of which assemble into microscopic filamentous tubes (**microtubules**) that help maintain cell shape and participate in cell movement

tubulous /tyoͦobyoͦoləss/ *adj.* = **tubular**

TUC *abbr.* Trades Union Congress

Tucana /too kaˊanə/ *n.* a small faint constellation in the polar region of the southern hemisphere, near the constellations of Eridanus and Hydrus and containing much of the Small Magellanic Cloud

tuchun /too chóon, dóo jóon/ *n.* formerly, the military leader of a Chinese province [Early 20thC. From Chinese *dūjūn,* from *dū* 'to govern' + *jūn* 'military'.]

tuck[1] /tuk/ *v.* (**tucks, tucking, tucked**) **1.** *vt.* FOLD STH INTO POSITION to push, fold, or bend sth such as a flap of material into a particular place or position **2.** *vti.* DRAW STH TOGETHER to pull or draw sth together, or be pulled or drawn together **3.** *vt.* SEW SEW FOLD INTO FABRIC to sew a fold into fabric, e.g. to reduce its length or for decoration **4.** *vt.* SURG TIGHTEN SKIN WITH SURGERY to perform a surgical operation to remove loose or wrinkled skin, usually for cosmetic reasons ■ *n.* **1.** TUCKED PART any part that is tucked safely or neatly into position **2.** SEW PLEAT a fold sewn into a piece of fabric, e.g. to reduce its length or for decoration **3.** FOOD FOOD food, especially sweets and cakes (*often used before a noun*) **4.** SURG SURGICAL REMOVAL OF LOOSE SKIN a surgical operation to remove loose or wrinkled skin, especially one performed for cosmetic reasons **5.** SPORTS BODY POSITION a compact body position with the knees drawn up to the chest, the hands round the shins, and the chin held on the chest. It is adopted in various sports such as diving and gymnastics. **6.** PART OF SHIP'S STERN the part of a ship's hull where the side planks or plates join the spar or spars forming the stern [15thC. Origin uncertain: probably from Middle Dutch *tucken* 'to draw up'. Ultimately from a prehistoric Germanic word that is also the source of English *tug.*]

tuck away *vt.* **1.** PUT STH SOMEWHERE SAFE OR CONCEALED to put sth in a safe or secluded place **2.** EAT STH IN LARGE QUANTITIES to eat large quantities of food heartily or hungrily (*informal*)

tuck in *v.* **1.** *vt.* MAKE SB COMFORTABLE IN BED to make sb, especially a child, comfortable in bed by tucking the bedclothes snugly around the body **2. tuck in, tuck into** *vti.* EAT HUNGRILY to eat, or eat sth, hungrily (*informal*)

tuck up *vt.* = **tuck in** *v.* 1

tuck[2] /tuk/ *n.* a beating of a drum or a blast on a trumpet or a flourish [15thC. Via Old North French *toquer* 'to strike' from assumed Vulgar Latin *toccare* (see TOUCH).]

tuck[3] /tuk/ *n.* a rapier (*archaic*) [Early 16thC. Origin uncertain: probably via a dialect form of Old French *estoc,* of prehistoric Germanic origin.]

tuckahoe /túkəhō/ *n.* **1.** PLANT WITH EDIBLE ROOT any of various North American plants with arrow-shaped leaves and edible rootstocks. They are species of arum and were traditionally used as food by Native North Americans. **2.** EDIBLE FUNGUS the large edible food storage body of a fungus that grows underground on the roots of trees. It is found in the southern United States. Latin name: *Poria cocos.* [Early 17thC. From Virginia Algonquian *tockawhoughe.*]

tucker[1] /túkər/ *n.* **1.** ANZ FOOD food (*informal; often used before a noun*) **2.** SEW SEWING-MACHINE ATTACHMENT an attachment for a sewing machine, used to sew tucks **3.** CLOTHES DETACHABLE PART OF DRESS a detachable lace or linen cover for the neck and chest, formerly worn by women under a low-cut dress [13thC. Formed from TUCK[1].]

tucker[2] /túkər/ (**-ers, -ering, -ered**) *vt.* US, Can to tire a person or animal out completely (*informal*) [Mid-19thC. Origin uncertain: perhaps from TUCK[1].]

Tucker /túkər/, **Albert** (*b.* 1914) Australian painter. He was a pioneer of expressionism and surrealism in Australia.

tucket /túkit/ *n.* a fanfare played on a trumpet (*archaic*) [Late 16thC. Formed from TUCK[2].]

tuck-in *n.* a large and delicious meal (*dated*)

tuck shop *n.* a small shop, especially one in or near a school, selling sweets, drinks, and snacks

tucotuco /toͦokō toͦokō/ (*plural* **-cos**) *n.* a South American rodent that closely resembles the North American gopher. It uses its sharp claws to dig complex systems of burrows in sandy soils. Latin name: *Ctenomys talarum.* [Mid-19thC. An imitation of the animal's call.]

Tucson /toͦo son/ city in southern Arizona, on the Santa Cruz River. Population: 449,002 (1996).

Tucuman /toͦokoo man, toͦokoo mán/ province in northern Argentina. Its capital is San Miguel de Tucuman. Population: 1,142,105 (1991). Area: 22,524 sq. km/8,694 sq. mi.

'tude /tood/ *n.* an arrogant or assertive manner or stance assumed as a challenge or for effect (*slang*) [Late 20thC. From *attitude.*]

-tude *suffix.* state, condition, or quality ○ *decrepitude* [Via French from Latin *-tudo*]

Tudor /toͦodər/ *adj.* **1.** HIST OF ENGLISH ROYAL FAMILY OR REIGN belonging or relating to the English royal family that ruled between 1485 and 1603, or to this period of English history. The period is spanned by the reigns of Kings Henry VII, Henry VIII, and Edward VI, and Queens Mary I and Elizabeth I. **2.** ARCHIT RELATING TO TUDOR ARCHITECTURAL STYLE relating to or being a style of architecture popular throughout the Tudor period. Its buildings typically have a timber framework, visible from the outside, filled in with plaster or brick. ■ *n.* HIST MEMBER OF TUDOR FAMILY a member of the Tudor royal family [Mid-18thC. Named after the Welsh squire Owen *Tudor* (d.1461), the father of Henry VII.]

Tue., Tues. *abbr.* CALENDAR Tuesday

Tuesday /tyoͦoz day, -di/ *n.* CALENDAR the second day of the week, coming after Monday and before Wednesday [Old English *Tiwesdæg* 'Tiu's day', from *Tiw,* the Germanic god of war (a translation of Latin *Martis dies* 'Mars' day')]

Tuesdays /tyoͦoz dayz, -diz/ *adv.* CALENDAR every Tuesday

tufa /tyoͦofə/ *n.* porous rock that has a spongy appearance and is often used as a medium in which to grow alpine plants. It is a calcium carbonate deposit that is found naturally in areas near salty springs. [Late 18thC. Via obsolete Italian from Late Latin *tofus* 'porous rock', of unknown origin.] —**tufaceous** /tyoͦo fáyshəss/ *adj.*

tuff /tuf/ *n.* rock made up of very small volcanic fragments compacted together [Mid-16thC. Via French from, ultimately, Latin *tofus* (source of English *tufa*).] —**tuffaceous** /tu fáyshəss/ *adj.*

tuffet /túffit/ *n.* **1.** GRASSY MOUND a small mound or clump of grass **2.** SEAT a low seat or stool [Mid-16thC. Alteration of TUFT.]

tuft /tuft/ *n.* **1.** BUNCH OF FIBRES OR GRASS a small bunch of hair, grass, feathers, or fibres held or growing together at the base **2.** CLUMP OF PLANTS a small clump of plants or trees **3.** BUNCH OF THREADS DRAWN THROUGH UPHOLSTERY a group of threads drawn through fabric and tied to secure it to material beneath ■ *v.* **(tufts, tufting, tufted) 1.** *vti.* FORM INTO TUFTS to grow in tufts, or form sth into tufts **2.** *vt.* SEW SEW TUFTS IN STH to sew tufts in fabric, either for decoration or to secure one surface to another [14thC. Alteration of Old French *toffe*, of uncertain origin: possibly from late Latin *tufa* 'helmet crest', or from Germanic.] —**tufted** *adj.* —**tufty** *adj.*

tufted duck *n.* a common diving duck found in Europe and Asia. Males are black with white flanks and bellies and have feathery crests dangling over the back of the neck. Latin name: *Aythya fuligula.*

tug /tug/ *v.* **(tugs, tugging, tugged) 1.** *vti.* PULL AT OR MOVE STH to pull at or haul sth with a sharp forceful movement **2.** *vt.* SHIPPING TOW SHIP to tow a ship with a tugboat **3.** *vi.* MAKE LABORIOUS EFFORT to work hard or struggle to do sth ■ *n.* **1.** STRONG PULL a quick sharp or forceful pull ○ *gave it a tug* **2.** STRUGGLE OR CONTEST a struggle or strenuous contest between opposing forces or individuals **3.** SHIPPING BOAT USED FOR TOWING SHIPS a small powerful boat used to tow ships and barges. US term **tugboat 4.** TRANSP VEHICLE THAT PULLS ANOTHER any type of vehicle, whether land, sea, air, or space, that is used to pull another **5.** CHAIN OR STRAP FOR HAULING a chain, rope, or strap that is used for hauling or pulling sth [13thC. Ultimately from an Indo-European word meaning 'to pull' that is also the ancestor of English *tie* and *tow*.] —**tugger** *n.*

WORD KEY: SYNONYMS

See Synonyms at ***pull***.

tugboat /túg bōt/ *n.* = **tug** *n.* 3

Tugela /too gáylə/ river in eastern South Africa, flowing into the Indian Ocean. Length: 502 km/312 mi.

Tugela Falls /too gáylə-/ series of waterfalls on the River Tugela, KwaZulu-Natal Province, South Africa. Height: 948 m/3,110 ft.

tughrik *n.* = **tugrik**

tug of love *n.* a struggle between divorced parents or between natural and foster or adoptive parents over custody of a child

tug of war *n.* **1.** SPORTS CONTEST OF STRENGTH an athletic contest in which two teams pull at opposite ends of a rope, the winner being the one who drags the other across a specified line **2.** STRUGGLE any struggle between two evenly-matched people, parties, or influences

tugrik /toóg reek/ (*plural* **-grik** *or* **-griks**), **tughrik** (*plural* **-ghrik** *or* **-ghriks**) *n.* **1.** UNIT OF MONGOLIAN CURRENCY the main unit of currency in Mongolia, worth 100 mongo. See table at **currency 2.** COIN WORTH ONE TUGRIK a coin worth one tugrik [Mid-20thC. From Mongolian *dughurik*, literally 'round thing'.]

tui /toó i/ *n.* a common New Zealand bird that has iridescent dark blue-green plumage, white tufts at the throat, and white spots on the wings. It feeds on nectar, insects, and fruit. Latin name: *Prosthemadera novaeseelandiae.* [Mid-19thC. From Maori.]

Tuileries Gardens /twéeləri-/ formal gardens beside the River Seine, central Paris, formely belonging to a royal palace. Area: 25 hectares/63 acres.

tuition /tyoo ísh'n/ *n.* **1.** EDUC TEACHING instruction or teaching, especially instruction given individually or in a small group **2.** FIN FEE FOR INSTRUCTION a sum charged for instruction at a school or university [15thC. Via Old French from Latin *tuitio* 'support', from *tueri* 'to protect'.] —**tuitional** *adj.*

tularaemia /toólə réemi ə/ *n.* an acute infectious disease of rabbits and rodents caused by the bacterium *Francisella tularensis* that can be spread to other animals and humans by insect bites, animal contact, or water. Symptoms include enlarged lymph nodes, headaches, muscular pain, and weight loss. [Early 20thC. Coined from *Francisella tularensis*, species name of the causative bacterium (named after *Tulare* County, California) + -AEMIA.] —**tularaemic** *adj.*

tularemia *n.* US = **tularaemia**

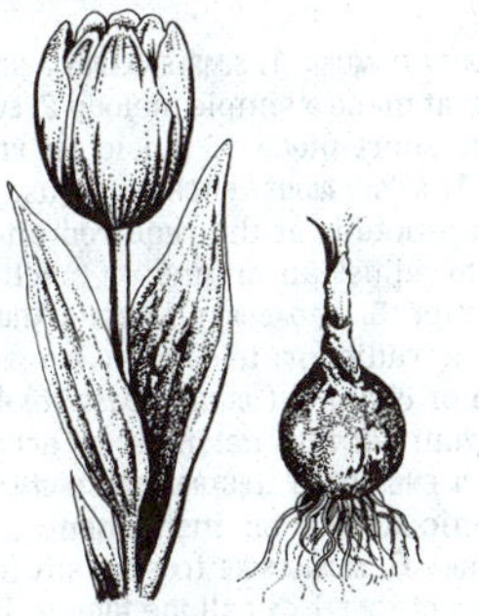

Tulip

tulip /tyoólip/ *n.* **1.** PLANT WITH CUP-SHAPED FLOWERS a plant that has lance-shaped leaves and a large, usually single, variously coloured flower shaped like a bell or cup. Growing from bulbs, they are originally native to western Asia. Genus: *Tulipa.* **2.** TULIP FLOWER OR BULB the flower or bulb of a tulip plant [Late 16thC. Via French *tulipe* from Turkish *tülbend* (see TURBAN); from the shape of the expanded flower.]

tulip tree *n.* a tall deciduous North American tree of the magnolia family that has large tulip-shaped greenish-yellow flowers, and soft light wood. The tulip tree is the US state tree of Indiana, Kentucky, and Tennessee. Latin name: *Liriodendron tulipifera.*

tulipwood /tyoólip wood/ *n.* the light soft wood of the tulip tree, or the striped wood of similar trees, used in making wooden objects or in cabinetmaking

tulle /tyool/ *n.* a thin netted, often stiffened, silk, nylon, or rayon fabric, used to trim hats and on ballet costumes and evening dresses and for veils [Early 19thC. Named after the French city *Tulle* where it was originally made.]

tullibee /túlli bee/ (*plural* **-bees** *or* **-bee**) *n.* ZOOL a cisco that lives in the Great Lakes in Canada [Late 18thC. Via Canadian French *toulibi* from Ojibwa *too-nie-bie*.]

Tulsa /túlssə/ city in northeastern Oklahoma, on the Arkansas River, northeast of Oklahoma City. Population: 367,302 (1990).

tulu /toó loo/ *n.* a camel that is a hybrid between a dromedary and a bactrian, found in some areas of western Asia where their ranges overlap

tum[1] /tum/ *n.* sb's stomach (*informal*) [Mid-19thC. Shortening of TUMMY.]

tum[2] /tum/ *adj. Scotland, N England* empty [Old English]

tumatakuru /too maátə kóorroo/ (*plural* **-rus** *or* **-ru**) *n.* *NZ* PLANTS = **matagouri** [Mid-19thC. From Maori.]

tumble /túmb'l/ *v.* **(-bles, -bling, -bled) 1.** *vti.* FALL OR MAKE FALL OVER to fall suddenly and awkwardly, especially rolling over and over, or cause sth to fall in this way **2.** *vi.* MOVE HASTILY to move heedlessly or hastily ○ *The puppies tumbled from the room.* **3.** *vi.* ROLL ABOUT to roll about, especially in play **4.** *vi.* DROP STEEPLY to fall quickly and by a significant amount ○ *Prices have tumbled on the stock market.* **5.** *vi.* CASCADE OVER STH to flow, fall, or spill out over sth **6.** *vi.* REALIZE STH to realize the full significance of sth, or see through a deceit (*informal*) ○ *She finally tumbled to it.* **7.** *vi.* GYMNASTICS LEAP OR ROLL to perform athletic or gymnastic leaps, rolls, or somersaults **8.** *vt.* ROTATE IN TUMBLER to roll or spin sth in a drum or tumbler ■ *n.* **1.** BAD FALL an awkward or sudden fall ○ *He had a nasty tumble.* **2.** DISORDERLY HEAP a disorderly or disorganized heap or arrangement **3.** GYMNASTICS ATHLETIC MOVEMENT an athletic or gymnastic leap, roll, or somersault [13thC. From obsolete Low German *tummelen*.]

tumbledown /túmbl down/ *adj.* ruined or dilapidated and falling down

tumble-dry **(tumble-dries, tumble-drying, tumble-dried)** *vt.* to dry washing in a tumble dryer —**tumble-dryer** *n.*

tumble dryer, **tumble drier** *n.* a machine that dries wet laundry by revolving it through heated air in the rotating metal drum of a dryer

tumbler /túmblər/ *n.* **1.** HOUSEHOLD DRINKING GLASS a drinking glass with a thick flat bottom and no stem or handle **2.** HOUSEHOLD ROUND-BOTTOMED GLASS a drinking glass, used in the past, that had a rounded or pointed bottom and so could not be put down until it was empty **3.** AMOUNT IN TUMBLER the amount of liquid that a tumbler holds **4.** GYMNASTICS ACROBAT sb who performs athletic or gymnastic leaps, rolls, and somersaults **5.** PART OF LOCK the part of a lock that must be engaged by a key in order to move the bolt **6.** HOUSEHOLD = **tumble dryer 7.** ROTATING CONTAINER a box, drum, or barrel that pivots or rotates, e.g. one used to polish gemstones. US term **tumbling barrel 8.** MECH ENG MACHINE PART a part of a machine that moves or engages a gear **9.** ARMS PART OF GUNLOCK a lever in a gunlock that forces the hammer forward when a trigger is pressed **10.** BIRDS PIGEON THAT DOES SOMERSAULTS IN FLIGHT a domestic pigeon that can perform backward somersaults in flight

tumbler dryer *n.* = **tumble dryer**

tumbleweed /túmb'l weed/ (*plural* **-weeds** *or* **-weed**) *n.* any densely branched plant such as the Russian thistle that grows in arid regions and in late summer withers and breaks from its roots to be blown about by the wind

tumbling /túmbling/ *n.* the art, practice, or act of performing leaps, rolls, and somersaults

tumbling barrel, **tumbling box** *n.* *US* = **tumbler** *n.* 7

tumbling flower beetle *n.* a tiny black beetle that preys on the larvae of other beetles or small moths. Family: Mordellidae.

tumbrel /túmbrəl/, **tumbril** /-bril/ *n.* **1.** HIST CART CARRYING PRISONERS TO BE GUILLOTINED a cart used during the French Revolution to carry condemned prisoners to be executed by guillotine **2.** AGRIC FARM CART a tiltable farm cart used to carry manure **3.** ARMY MILITARY CART a covered cart formerly used to carry ammunition and equipment for the artillery [14thC. From Old French *tumberel*, from *tomber* 'to fall'.]

tume /tyoom/ **(tumes, tuming, tumed)** *vti. Scotland* to empty or empty sth [Old English. Variant of TOOM.]

tumefacient /tyoómi fáyshi ənt/ *adj.* causing or tending to cause swelling [Late 19thC. From Latin, the present participle stem of *tumefacere* (see TUMEFY).]

tumefaction /tyoómi fáksh'n/ *n.* **1.** SWELLING OF TISSUE the swelling of tissue as a result of a build-up of fluid within it **2.** SWOLLEN PART a swollen part or area [15thC. From French *tuméfaction*, from Latin *tumefacere* (see TUMEFY).]

tumefy /tyoómi fī/ **(-fies, -fying, -fied)** *vti.* to swell, or cause tissue to swell [Late 16thC. Via French *tuméfier* from Latin *tumefacere* 'to make swollen', from *tumere* (see TUMOUR) + *facere* 'to make'.]

tumescent /tyoo méss'nt/ *adj.* swollen or showing signs of swelling, usually as a result of a build-up of blood or water within body tissues [Mid-19thC. From Latin, the present participle stem of *tumescere* 'to become swollen', from *tumere* (see TUMOUR).] —**tumescence** *n.*

tumid /tyoómid/ *adj.* **1.** MED SWOLLEN used to describe a body part or organ that is swollen **2.** BULGING bulging or sticking out **3.** POMPOUS IN STYLE having language or a style that is bombastic or inflated [Mid-16thC. From Latin *tumidus*, from *tumere* (see TUMOUR).] —**tumidity** /tyoo míddəti/ *n.* —**tumidness** /tyoómidnəss/ *n.*

tummy /túmmi/ (*plural* **-mies**) *n.* sb's stomach (*informal*) [Mid-19thC. Babytalk alteration of STOMACH.]

tummy button *n.* the human navel (*informal*)

tummy tuck *n.* a cosmetic surgical operation to remove excess fat, skin, and tissue from the abdomen (*informal*)

tumor *n.* US = **tumour**

tumorigenic /tyoómәri jénnik/ *adj.* used to describe a drug or other agent that may initiate or promote the growth of tumours —**tumorigenesis** /tyoómәri jénnəssiss/ *n.* —**tumorigenicity** /tyoómərijə nísseti/ *n.*

tumour /tyóomər/ *n.* **1.** ABNORMAL MASS OF TISSUE an abnormal uncontrolled growth or mass of body cells, which may be malignant or benign and has no physiological function **2.** SWOLLEN PART any abnormal swelling in or on the body [15thC. From Latin, formed from *tumere* 'to swell'.] —**tumorous** *adj.*

tumour necrosis factor *n.* a protein that can cause the destruction of tumours. The gene encoding this factor has been used in gene therapy trials for cancer.

tump /tump/ *n.* a small mound, hill, or clump, especially of vegetation (*regional*) [Late 16thC. Origin unknown.]

tumpline /túmp līn/ *n.* US, Can a band or strap strung across the forehead or chest to support a backpack [Late 18thC. *Tump* from Algonquian *mattump*.]

tumular /tyóomyŏolər/ *adj.* resembling or in the form of a mound or tumulus

tumuli plural of **tumulus**

tumulose /tyóomyŏolōss/, **tumulous** /-ləss/ *adj.* **1.** HAVING MOUNDS having many mounds or small hills **2.** LIKE A MOUND forming or resembling a mound —**tumulosity** /tyóomyŏo lóssəti/ *n.*

tumult /tyóomult/ *n.* **1.** NOISY COMMOTION a violent or noisy commotion **2.** EMOTIONAL UPHEAVAL a psychological or emotional upheaval or agitation [14thC. Directly or via French *tumulte* from Latin *tumultus* 'commotion', from *tumere* (see TUMOUR).]

tumultuary /tyoo múlchoo əri/ *adj.* marked by tumult or turbulence (*archaic*)

tumultuous /tyoo múlchoo əss/ *adj.* **1.** NOISY AND UNRESTRAINED noisy and unrestrained in a way that shows excitement or great happiness **2.** CONFUSED AND AGITATED involving great excitement, confusion, and emotional agitation —**tumultuously** *adv.* —**tumultuousness** *n.*

tumulus /tyóomyŏoləss/ (*plural* -**li** /-lī/) *n.* ARCHAEOL = **barrow**[2] *n.* [15thC. From Latin, 'mound', formed from *tumere* (see TUMOUR).]

tun /tun/ *n.* **1.** CASK a large cask for beer or wine **2.** MEASURE OF VOLUME a measure of liquid volume, especially one for wine equal to 955 litres/210 gallons [Pre-12thC. From medieval Latin *tunna* (see TUNNEL).]

Tun. *abbr.* **1.** Tunisia **2.** Tunisian

Tuna

tuna[1] /tyóonə/ (*plural* -**na** or -**nas**) *n.* **1.** ZOOL LARGE EDIBLE FISH a large fast-swimming, widely distributed marine fish with a tapering body, large forked tail, and pointed head, found in warm and temperate waters. Genus: *Thunnus*. **2.** FOOD TUNA FLESH the firm meaty flesh of the tuna, used for food [Late 19thC. From American Spanish, of uncertain origin: probably via Spanish *atún* and Arabic *at-tún* from Latin *thunnus* (see TUNNY).]

tuna[2] /tyóonə/ *n.* **1.** PLANTS PRICKLY PEAR CACTUS a tropical prickly pear cactus that has coloured flowers and sweet edible fruit. Latin name: *Opuntia tuna*. **2.** FOOD TUNA CACTUS FRUIT the edible fruit of the tuna cactus [Mid-16thC. Via Spanish from Taino.]

tunable /tyóonəb'l/, **tuneable** *adj.* capable of being tuned

tuna fish *n.* = **tuna**[1] *n.*[2]

Tunbridge Wells /túnbrij wélz/ spa town in Kent, southeastern England. Population: 102,700 (1994). Official name **Royal Tunbridge Wells**

tundish /túndish/ *n.* **1.** METALL TROUGH FOR MOLTEN METAL a trough at the top of a mould into which molten metal is poured **2.** N Ireland FUNNEL a funnel

tundra /túndrə/ *n.* the level or nearly level treeless plain between the ice cap and the timber line of North America and Eurasia that has permanently frozen subsoil [Late 16thC. Via Russian from Lappish *tundar*.]

tune /tyoon/ *n.* MUSIC **1.** SIMPLE MELODY a series of musical notes that make a simple melody **2.** SONG a melodious song or short piece of music ■ *vt.* (**tunes**, **tuning**, **tuned**) **1.** MUSIC ADJUST PITCH to adjust an instrument so that a note is at the required pitch **2.** ENG ADJUST ENGINE to adjust an engine or machine to make it run better **3.** BROADCAST ADJUST STATION OR CHANNEL to adjust a radio or television set to a particular station or channel (*usually passive*) **4.** ADAPT TO STH to bring yourself into harmony or accord with sth **5.** ELECTRON ENG ADJUST ELECTRONIC INSTRUMENT to adjust an electronic device or instrument to the required frequency **6.** MUSIC SING to sing sth (*archaic*) [14thC. Alteration of TONE.] ◇ **call the tune** to be in charge ◇ **change your tune** to change your attitude or opinion ◇ **in tune 1.** MUSIC played or sung at the appropriate pitch **2.** in accord or agreement with sb or sth **3.** ELECTRON ENG adjusted to the correct frequency ◇ **out of tune 1.** MUSIC played or sung at the wrong pitch **2.** out of harmony or in disagreement with sb or sth **3.** ELECTRON ENG not adjusted to the correct frequency ◇ **to the tune of sth** to the stated exact or approximate amount

tune in *v.* **1.** *vti.* BROADCAST ADJUST RECEPTION OF BROADCAST to adjust a radio or television to receive a signal, programme, or channel **2.** *vi.* PAY ATTENTION to be attentive or receptive to sb or sth (*informal*)

tune out *v.* **1.** *vt.* BROADCAST RID RECEPTION OF INTERFERENCE to adjust a radio or television set to eliminate the reception of sth undesired such as interference **2.** *vi.* IGNORE STH to ignore or be unreceptive to sb or sth (*informal*) ○ '*The country was tuning out all things when suddenly there was focus on scandal*'. (*US News & World Report*; December 1998)

tune up *vti.* **1.** MUSIC ADJUST TO CORRECT PITCH to adjust one or more musical instruments to an accurate or common pitch **2.** PREPARE FOR STH to test and improve sth as a preparation, e.g. for a competition or meeting

tuneable *adj.* = **tunable**

tuneful /tyóonf'l/ *adj.* having a pleasant melody —**tunefully** *adv.* —**tunefulness** *n.*

tuneless /tyóonləss/ *adj.* unmusical, lacking a tune, or not producing a tune —**tunelessly** *adv.* —**tunelessness** *n.*

tuner /tyóonər/ *n.* **1.** MUSIC SB WHO TUNES INSTRUMENTS sb who tunes musical instruments, especially pianos **2.** ELECTRON ENG DEVICE THAT ACCEPTS SIGNALS a device, e.g. in a radio or television set containing one or more resonant circuits, used for accepting a desired signal from a mixture of signals

tunesmith /tyóon smith/ *n.* US a composer of popular songs or music (*informal*)

tune-up *n.* a set of adjustments to an engine to make it run better

tung oil /túng-/ *n.* a quick-drying yellow oil extracted from the seeds of the tung tree, used in paints and varnishes to speed up drying, and also as a waterproofing agent [*Tung* from Chinese *tóng*, the name of the tree]

tung-oil tree *n.* = **tung tree**

tungstate /túng stayt/ *n.* a salt or ester of tungstic acid. Many tungstates are found in the ores from which tungsten is extracted.

tungsten /túngstən/ *n.* a hard lustrous grey metallic chemical element with a very high melting point that is used in various high-temperature alloys, lamp filaments, and high-speed cutting tools. Symbol **W** [Late 18thC. From Swedish, literally 'heavy stone'. Coined by its discoverer, the Swedish chemist Karl Wilhelm Scheele.]

tungsten carbide *n.* a fine, very hard, grey crystalline powder made by heating tungsten and carbon together, used in making dies, drill bits,

cutting and abrasion tools, and wear-resistant machine parts

tungsten lamp *n.* an incandescent electric lamp with a filament made of tungsten

tungsten steel *n.* a hard heat-resistant steel containing between 1% and 20% tungsten, used in tools and high-temperature engineering equipment

tungstic /túngstik/ *adj.* relating to or containing tungsten in its highest oxidation state. ◊ **tungstous**

tungstic acid *n.* a yellow powder that is a weak acid, used in making textiles and plastics. Formula: H_2WO_4.

tungstite /túng stīt/ *n.* a rare yellow-green oxide of tungsten that is found associated with ores of tungsten such as wolframite. Formula: WO_3.

tungstous /túngstəss/ *adj.* relating to or containing tungsten in its low oxidation state. ◊ **tungstic**

tung tree /túng-/ *n.* a tree of eastern Asia whose large round fruit contain hard seeds that yield tung oil. Genus: *Aleurites*. [See TUNG OIL]

Tungus /tŏong gŏoss, tŏongéss/ (*plural* -**gus** or -**guses**) *n.* PEOPLES = **Evenki** [Early 17thC. From Yakut.]

Tungusic /tŏong gŏossik/ *n.* LANG a group of languages spoken in northern parts of the People's Republic of China and eastern parts of Asiatic Russia. It forms a branch of the Altaic family of languages. Tungusic languages are spoken by about 50,000 people. —**Tungusic** *adj.*

tunic /tyóonik/ *n.* **1.** CLOTHES LOOSE GARMENT a loose wide-necked garment that extends to the hip or knee and is usually worn with a belt or gathered at the waist **2.** CLOTHES SHIRTLIKE GARMENT WORN IN PAST a shirtlike knee-length garment worn by men in ancient Rome, or a similar garment worn during the Middle Ages **3.** CLOTHES, MIL POLICE OR MILITARY JACKET a close-fitting high-collared jacket worn as part of a police or military uniform **4.** CLOTHES SPORTS DRESS a short belted dress worn when playing sports **5.** ANAT ENVELOPING MEMBRANE a covering or membrane that envelops an organ or part **6.** ZOOL = **tunica 7.** BOT PAPERY COVERING ON BULB a dry, often brown and papery, covering around a bulb or corm such as of an onion **8.** RELIG = **tunicle** [Pre-12thC. Directly or via French *tunique* from Latin *tunica*.]

tunica /tyóonikə/ (*plural* -**cae** /-see/) *n.* a layer of tissue that covers or lines a body part or organ, especially tubular parts such as the blood vessels [Late 17thC. From Latin, 'tunic'.]

tunicate /tyóonikət/ *n.* MARINE BIOL MARINE ANIMAL a sac-shaped marine chordate animal such as a sea squirt or ascidian that has a tough leathery or rubbery outer coat. Subphylum: Urochordata. ■ *adj.* **1.** MARINE BIOL RELATING TO TUNICATES relating to or classified as a tunicate **2.** **tunicate, tunicated** BOT WITH DRY PAPERY COVERING used to describe a bulb or corm that has a dry, often brown and papery, covering **3.** **tunicate, tunicated** ANAT WITH COVERING OF TISSUE used to describe an organ or body part that is covered or lined with a layer of tissue [Mid-18thC. Via Latin *tunicatus* 'covered with a tunic', from, ultimately, *tunica* (see TUNIC).]

tunicle /tyóonik'l/ *n.* in Christian worship, a short vestment worn over the alb by a subdeacon at a Mass, or under the dalmatic by a bishop or cardinal at other ceremonies [14thC. Directly or via Old French from Latin *tunicula*, literally 'small tunic', from *tunica* (see TUNIC).]

tuning /tyóoning/ *n.* **1.** SET OF PITCHES the standard range of pitches to which a musical instrument is tuned **2.** MUSICAL INTONATION the degree to which musical instruments or the voices of a choir are adjusted to a standard norm

tuning fork *n.* an instrument consisting of a stem and two prongs that produces a constant pitch when struck, used to tune musical instruments and in acoustics

Tunis /tyóoniss/ capital city of Tunisia, situated on a shallow lake near the Gulf of Tunis. Population: 674,100 (1994).

Tunis, Gulf of arm of the Mediterranean Sea in northeastern Tunisia

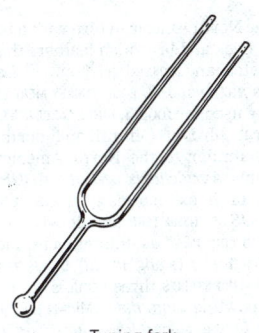

Tuning fork

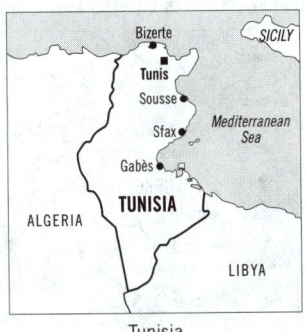

Tunisia

Tunisia /tyoo nízzi ə/ republic in North Africa, bordered by the Mediterranean Sea, Libya, and Algeria. Language: Arabic. Currency: Tunisian dinar. Capital: Tunis. Population: 9,245,284 (1997). Area: 164,418 sq. km/63,482 sq. mi. Official name **Republic of Tunisia** —**Tunisian** *n.*, *adj.*

tunnage *n.* = tonnage

tunnel /túnn'l/ *n.* **1.** TRANSP PASSAGEWAY UNDER OBSTRUCTION a long passage that allows pedestrians or vehicles to proceed under or through an obstruction such as a river, mountain, or congested area **2.** ZOOL ANIMAL'S UNDERGROUND PASSAGE an underground passage or system of passages dug by a burrowing animal **3.** MINING PART OF MINE a corridor or working area in a mine **4.** PASSAGE any passage, channel, or route through or under sth ■ *v.* (**-nels, -elling, -elled**) **1.** *vti.* MAKE TUNNEL to make, burrow, or excavate a tunnel under or through sth **2.** *vt.* MAKE STH LIKE TUNNEL to produce or dig sth that resembles or is shaped like a tunnel [15thC. Via Old French *tonel*, literally 'small barrel', from, ultimately, medieval Latin *tunna* 'cask' (source of English *ton*), of uncertain origin: probably from Gaulish.] —**tunneller** *n.*

tunnel disease *n.* = ancylostomiasis [*Tunnel* because it is caused by tunnel worms]

tunnel effect *n.* a quantum mechanical effect in which elementary particles can pass through an energy barrier such as a thin layer even if they do not have enough energy to do so

tunnelling /túnn'ling/ *n.* = tunnel effect

tunnel vault *n.* = barrel vault

tunnel vision *n.* **1.** OPHTHALMOL RESTRICTED FIELD OF VISION a condition in which peripheral vision is lost or severely limited, so that only objects directly in line with the eyes can be seen **2.** CLOSE-MINDED THINKING a very limited viewpoint or conception of things

tunny /túnni/ (*plural* **-ny** *or* **-nies**) *n.* = tuna¹ n. 1 [Mid-16thC. Via French *thon* and Latin *thunnus* from Greek *thunnos*.]

tup /tup/ *vt.* (**tups, tupping, tupped**) AGRIC MATE WITH A EWE to copulate with a ewe ■ *n.* **1.** Scotland, N England AGRIC RAM a male sheep used for breeding **2.** MECH ENG HEAD OF HAMMER the head of a power hammer or a mechanism resembling a hammer [14thC. Origin unknown.]

tupek /toópək/, **tupik** /-pik/ *n.* a tent made of animal skins, used in the summer by the Inuit in the Arctic [Mid-19thC. From Inuit *tupiq*.]

tupelo /tyoópəlō/ (*plural* **-los**) *n.* **1.** TREE WITH SOFT PALE WOOD a North American or Asian deciduous tree

that grows in swamps and on river banks and has soft pale wood. Genus: *Nyssa*. **2.** TUPELO WOOD the soft pale wood of the tupelo [Mid-18thC. From Creek *ito opilwa*, literally 'swamp tree'.]

Tupi /toó pee/ (*plural* **-pi** *or* **-pis**) *n.* **1.** PEOPLES MEMBER OF NATIVE S AMERICAN PEOPLE a member of a group of Native South American peoples who live in the Amazon valley **2.** LANG TUPI LANGUAGE the language of the Tupi people. It belongs to the Tupi-Guarani language family. Tupi was once an important lingua franca in Brazil but is now only spoken by a few thousand people in the Amazon valley. [Mid-19thC. From Tupi, literally 'comrade'.] —**Tupi** *adj.*

tupik *n.* = tupek

tuppence *n.* = twopence

tuppenny *adj.* = twopenny

tupuna /toó poónə/ (*plural* **-na**), **tipuna** /ti-/ (*plural* **-na**) *n.* NZ an ancestor or grandparent [From Maori]

tuque /took/ *n.* Can a cylindrical stocking cap of double-thickness wool or synthetic yarn, worn in winter [Late 19thC. Via Canadian French from French *toque* (see TOQUE).]

tu quoque /toó kwô k way/ *interj.* used when accused of a crime to accuse the accuser of the same crime [Late 17thC. From Latin, literally 'you too'.]

Tur. *abbr.* **1.** Turkey **2.** Turkish

Turanian /tyoo ráyni ən/ *n.* **1.** PEOPLES URAL-ALTAIC SPEAKER a member of any of the peoples who speak a Ural-Altaic language **2.** LANG OLD LANGUAGE GROUPING a formerly accepted grouping of Asian languages roughly corresponding to the modern Altaic family with the addition of others (*dated*) ■ *adj.* PEOPLES RELATING TO ANCIENT TURKESTAN relating to ancient Turkestan, or its people or culture [Late 18thC. Formed from Persian *Turān* 'Turkestan'.]

turban /túrbən/ *n.* **1.** HEADDRESS a man's headdress that consists of a long piece of fabric wrapped around the head or around a small cap, completely covering the hair, worn especially by Sikhs and Muslims **2.** WOMAN'S HAT a woman's hat that is similar in shape to a man's turban [Mid-16thC. Via obsolete French *turbant*, Italian *turbante*, and Turkish *tülbend* from Persian *dulband* (source also of English *tulip*).] —**turbaned** *adj.*

turbary /túrbəri/ *n.* an area of land where turf or peat may be cut or dug [14thC. Via Anglo-Norman *turberie* from, ultimately, French *tourbe* 'turf', of Germanic origin.]

turbellarian /túrbi láiri ən/ *n.* a free-living flatworm such as a planarian that inhabits wet soil, freshwater, and marine environments. Turbellarians glide over stones and weeds by means of cilia on their undersurface and swim by undulating their bodies. Class: Turbellaria. [Late 19thC. From modern Latin *Turbellaria*, class name, from Latin *turbella*, literally 'small commotion'. From the little eddies created by its movement.] —**turbellarian** *adj.*

turbid /túrbid/ *adj.* **1.** MUDDY opaque and muddy as when particles and sediment are stirred up **2.** FOGGY dense and cloudy or dark **3.** CONFUSED confused and muddled ○ *turbid thought processes* [Early 17thC. From Latin *turbidus* 'troubled', from *turba* 'disorder'.] —**turbidity** /tur bíddəti/ *n.* —**turbidly** /túrbidli/ *adv.* —**turbidness** /túrbidnəss/ *n.*

──────── **WORD KEY: USAGE** ────────

turbid or **turgid**? The two words are unrelated in form but curiously both describe water in their literal meanings (either 'opaque and cloudy' in the case of **turbid** or 'swollen and overflowing' in the case of **turgid**), and both describe literary styles in their figurative meanings. *Turgid* is the more common and means 'pompous, bombastic' (as in *turgid prose*), whereas **turbid** means 'confused, muddled'.

turbidimeter /túrbi dímmitər/ *n.* an instrument that determines the amount of material in suspension in a liquid or gas by measuring the decrease in light transmittance through the fluid —**turbidimetric** /túrbidi méttrik/ *adj.* —**turbidimetrically** /-métrikli/ *adv.* —**turbidimetry** /túrbi dímmətri/ *n.*

turbidite /túrbi dīt/ *n.* a sedimentary deposit laid down by a turbidity current, e.g. on the ocean floor at the bottom of the continental shelf

turbidity current *n.* a rapidly moving current containing dispersed sediments, sometimes started off by seismic shocks or slumping. The current arises from density differences created by the presence of the dispersed sediments.

turbinate /túrbinət, -nayt/ *adj.* **1.** ANAT OF BONE IN NASAL PASSAGE used to describe any of the three scroll-shaped bones found on the walls of the nasal passages of mammals **2.** SPIRAL IN SHAPE having a shape like a spiral or scroll **3.** ZOOL SHAPED LIKE INVERTED CONE used to describe a shell that spirals and is shaped like an inverted cone ■ *n.* **1.** ANAT TURBINATE BONE a turbinate bone in the nasal passage of mammals **2.** ZOOL MOLLUSC SHELL a turbinate mollusc shell [Mid-17thC. From Latin *turbinatus*, from the Latin stem *turbin-* (see TURBINE).] —**turbination** /túrbi náysh'n/ *n.*

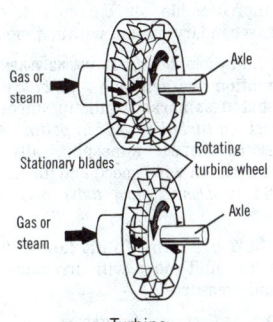

Turbine

turbine /túrb īn, -bin/ *n.* a machine in which a moving fluid such as steam acts upon the blades of a rotor to produce rotational motion that can be transformed to electrical or mechanical power. Electrical power is frequently produced from steam turbines. [Mid-19thC. From French, formed from the Latin stem *turbin-* 'spiral, spinning-top'.]

turbit /túrbit/ *n.* a domestic pigeon of a breed with a ruffed neck and breast [Late 17thC. Origin uncertain: perhaps formed from Latin *turbo* (see TURBO²), from its shape.]

turbo¹ /túrbō/ (*plural* **-bos**) *n.* **1.** = turbine **2.** = turbocharger

turbo² /túrbō/ (*plural* **-bos**) *n.* a gastropod mollusc that has a whorled spiral shell. Genus: *Turbo*. [Mid-17thC. From Latin, 'spiral, spinning-top'.]

turbo- *prefix* **1.** using the principle of a turbine, or driven by a turbine ○ *turbocharger* **2.** turbojet ○ *turboprop* [From TURBINE]

turbocharger /túrbō chaarjər/ *n.* a specialized turbine driven by the exhaust gases of an engine that supplies air under pressure to the engine for combustion [Mid-20thC. Contraction of TURBOSUPERCHARGER.] —**turbocharged** *adj.*

turbo-electric *adj.* using or relating to an electric generator driven by a turbine

turbofan /túrbō fan/ *n.* **1.** JET ENGINE AUGMENTED BY FANS a jet engine in which fans driven by a turbine force air into the exhaust gases, thereby increasing the propelling thrust of the engine **2.** AIRCRAFT WITH TURBOFAN ENGINES a jet aircraft that has turbofan engines

turbogenerator /túrbō jénnə raytər/ *n.* a machine used to generate electricity in which steam from coal, oil, or gas, is used to drive the turbine

turbojet /túrbō jet/ *n.* **1.** JET AIRCRAFT WITH ENGINES USING TURBINE an aircraft powered by jet engine with a gas turbine that uses exhaust gases to provide the propulsive thrust **2.** JET ENGINE USING TURBINE a jet engine with a gas turbine that uses exhaust gases to provide the propulsive thrust for an aircraft

turboprop /túrbō prop/ *n.* **1.** AIRCRAFT USING TURBINE TO DRIVE PROPELLER an aircraft whose propellers are driven by a gas turbine **2.** TURBOJET ENGINE WITH PROPELLER a turbojet engine that powers a propeller

turboramjet /túrbō rám jet/ *n.* **1.** TURBOJET ENGINE USING FUEL COMPRESSION a turbojet engine in which forward motion is achieved by compression of the fuel, used, e.g., in guided missiles **2.** TURBORAMJET-POWERED AIRCRAFT an aircraft powered by a turboramjet

turbosupercharger /túrbō soŏpər chaarjər/ *n.* = **turbocharger**

turbot /túrbət/ *n.* (*plural* **-bot** *or* **-bots**) *n.* **1.** EUROPEAN FLATFISH a European flatfish that is almost circular with bony tubercles on its body and both eyes on the left side. It is a prized food fish. Latin name: *Scophthalmus maximus*. **2.** FLATFISH a flatfish in the same family as the European turbot, e.g. the spotted turbot of the Pacific. Family: Pleuronectidae. [13thC. Via Old French from Old Swedish *törnbut*, literally 'thornflatfish', from the spines on its back.]

turbulence /túrbyoŏlənss/, **turbulency** /-lənssi/ *n.* **1.** UNREST a state of confusion characterized by unpredictability and uncontrolled change **2.** METEOROL INSTABILITY IN ATMOSPHERE an instability in the atmosphere that disrupts the flow of the wind, causing gusty, unpredictable air currents **3.** PHYS EDDIES eddies or secondary motion within a moving fluid

turbulent /túrbyoŏlənt/ *adj.* **1.** MOVING VIOLENTLY full of violent motion and agitation ○ *turbulent rapids* **2.** CHAOTIC AND RESTLESS marked by disturbances, changes, and unrest ○ *a turbulent year in politics* **3.** METEOR ATMOSPHERICALLY UNSTABLE atmospherically unstable, with variations in wind speed and direction [15thC. From Latin *turbulentus*, from *turba* 'disorder'.] —**turbulently** *adv.*

turbulent flow *n.* a form of fluid flow in which particles of the fluid move with irregular local velocities and pressures

Turcoman *n., adj.* PEOPLES = **Turkmen**

turd /turd/ *n.* (*taboo offensive*) **1.** OFFENSIVE TERM an offensive term used to refer to a piece of excrement or dung **2.** OFFENSIVE TERM a highly offensive term used to refer to sb who is seen as contemptible [Old English. Ultimately from an Indo-European word that is also the ancestor of English *tear* (verb). The underlying idea is of sth which is separated from the body.]

tureen /tyoŏ reén/ *n.* a wide deep bowl with a lid that is used especially to serve soups, stews, and casseroles [Mid-18thC. Alteration of TERRINE (perhaps partly through some association with TURIN).]

turf /turf/ *n.* (*plural* **turfs** *or* **turves** /turvz/) **1.** DENSE LAYER OF GRASS a dense thick even cover of grass and roots in the top layer of soil **2.** ARTIFICIAL GRASS artificial grass, used, e.g., on a playing field **3.** GARDENING PIECE OF SOIL WITH GRASS a piece of soil with grass growing in it put down to form lawns and new grassed surfaces **4.** PEAT FOR FUEL peat, especially when sold for fuel **5.** HORSERACING HORSERACING horseracing as a sport or industry **6.** HORSERACING HORSERACING TRACK a track where horses are raced **7.** AREA OF EXPERTISE an area in which sb feels confident or has authority or expertise (*informal*) **8.** TERRITORY a territory or geographical area (*informal*) **9.** GANG TERRITORY an area or territory that a gang claims to be its own (*informal*) ■ *vt.* (**turfs, turfing, turfed**) COVER WITH TURF to cover an area with pieces of turf (*informal*) [Old English. Ultimately from an Indo-European word that also produced German *Torf* 'peat'.] —**turfy** *adj.*

turf out *vt.* to eject sb from a place or organization (*informal*)

turf accountant *n.* GAMBLING a bookmaker (*formal*)

Ivan Turgenev

Turgenev /tur gáy nyef/, **Ivan** (1818–83) Russian writer. His best known works include the novel *Fathers and Sons* (1862) and the play *A Month in the Country* (1855). Full name **Ivan Sergeyevich Turgenev**

turgescent /tur jéss'nt/ *adj.* swollen or becoming swollen, usually as a result of an accumulation of blood or other fluids [Early 18thC. From Latin, the present participle stem of *turgescere* 'to begin to swell', from *turgere* (see TURGID).] —**turgescence** *n.* —**turgescency** *n.*

turgid /túrjid/ *adj.* **1.** POMPOUS AND OVERCOMPLICATED pompous, boring, and overcomplicated ○ *a turgid speech* **2.** MED SWOLLEN swollen or distended by a build-up of fluid [Early 17thC. From Latin *turgidus*, from *turgere* 'to swell'.] —**turgidity** /tur jíddəti/ *n.* —**turgidly** /túrjidli/ *adv.* —**turgidness** /túrjidnəss/ *n.*

―――― **WORD KEY: USAGE** ――――
See Usage note at **turbid**.

turgor /túrgər/ *n.* the normal rigid state of plant cells, caused by outward pressure of the water content of each cell on its membrane. The rigidity of plants relies on the turgor of the cells, a decrease in which leads to wilting. [Late 19thC. From late Latin, formed from *turgere* (see TURGID).]

Turin /tyoor rín/ capital city of Turin Province, Piedmont Region, northwestern Italy. Population: 952,736 (1992).

Turing /tyoŏring/, **Alan** (1912–54) British mathematician. He was a major figure in the theoretical development of the computer. During World War II (1939–45) he worked as a British government cryptographer, and helped to break the German Enigma machine's code. Full name **Alan Mathison Turing**

Turing machine /tyoŏring-/ *n.* a mathematical model of a device that can modify its instructions and read from, write on, or erase a potentially infinite tape. It was instrumental in the evolution of computer theory. [Named after its inventor, Alan TURING]

turion /toŏri ən/ *n.* **1.** WINTERING BUD OF WATER PLANT a bud that breaks off from an aquatic plant and lies submerged and dormant until the following spring when it produces a new plantlet that floats to the surface **2.** SHOOT FROM UNDERGROUND PART a shoot from an underground root or stem, e.g. in asparagus [Early 18thC. Via French from Latin *turio* 'young sprig'.]

Turk /turk/ *n.* **1.** PEOPLES SB FROM TURKEY sb who was born or brought up in Turkey, or who has Turkish citizenship **2.** PEOPLES MEMBER OF TURKISH ETHNIC GROUP a member of the dominant, Turkish-speaking ethnic group in Turkey, or, in former times, in the Ottoman Empire **3.** LANG TURKIC SPEAKER a member of a people speaking a Turkic language **4.** RELIG OFFENSIVE TERM an offensive term used to refer to a Muslim (*archaic offensive*) **5.** OFFENSIVE TERM an offensive term used to refer to a cruel or tyrannical person (*archaic offensive*) [14thC. Via French *Turc* and medieval Latin *Turcus* from, ultimately, Turkish *Türk*.]

Turk. *abbr.* **1.** Turkey **2.** Turkish

Turkana, Lake /tur káanə/ lake in northwestern Kenya, extending into Ethiopia at its northern end. Area: 7,100 sq. km/2,700 sq. mi. Former name **Rudolf, Lake**

Turkestan /túrki stán, -staán/, **Turkistan** a mountainous region of central Asia that stretches from the Caspian Sea to the Gobi Desert. It is divided into three sections, Russian or Western Turkestan, which includes Kazakhstan, Kyrgyzstan, and Uzbekistan, Chinese or Eastern Turkestan, made up of the Xinjiang Uygur Autonomous Region of China, and Afghan Turkestan, consisting of the northeastern part of Afghanistan.

turkey /túrki/ *n.* (*plural* **-keys**) *n.* **1.** BIRDS LARGE N AMERICAN BIRD a large North American bird with a bare wattled head and neck and brownish feathers that is widely domesticated and raised as poultry. Latin name: *Meleagris gallopavo*. **2.** FOOD TURKEY MEAT the meat of the turkey used for food **3.** BIRDS LARGE CENTRAL AMERICAN BIRD a large bird of Central and northern South America, similar to the North American turkey. Latin name: *Agriocharis ocellata*. **4.** US FAILURE sth that fails or flops, especially a bad play or film (*slang*) **5.** US OFFENSIVE TERM an offensive term used to describe sb regarded as unintelligent, incompetent, or socially inept (*slang insult*) **6.** SPORTS THREE CONSECUTIVE BOWLING STRIKES three strikes in a row in the sport of bowling (*informal*) [Mid-16thC. From its resemblance to the guinea fowl, which was named after TURKEY because it was imported through Turkish territory.]
◇ **talk turkey** US to talk honestly and bluntly

Turkey

Turkey /túrki/ republic in southeastern Europe and southwestern Asia, bordered by Bulgaria, Greece, the Black Sea, Georgia, Armenia, Iran, Iraq, Syria, the Mediterranean Sea, and the Aegean Sea. Language: Turkish. Currency: Turkish lira. Capital: Ankara. Population: 63,528,225 (1997). Area: 779,452 sq. km/300,948 sq. mi. Official name **Republic of Turkey**

turkey buzzard *n.* = **turkey vulture**

Turkey carpet *n.* a handwoven woollen carpet with rich colours and a deep pile

turkey cock *n.* **1.** BIRDS MALE TURKEY a male turkey, especially when fully grown **2.** ARROGANT INDIVIDUAL sb who is arrogant or conceited (*insult*)

Turkey red *adj.* of the vibrant bright red colour produced using alizarin as a dye [Late 18thC. From the colour used in cotton fabrics made in the Ottoman Empire.] —**Turkey red** *n.*

turkey trot *n.* a round dance to ragtime music in which dancers walk springily and make birdlike movements with their shoulders and upper body

turkey vulture *n.* a blackish-brown vulture of the Americas that has a bare wrinkled red head and neck and feeds on carrion. Latin name: *Cathartes aura*.

Turkic /túrkik/ *n.* LANG a group of languages spoken in western and central Asia, constituting a subfamily of the Altaic family of languages. As well as Turkish, it includes Azerbaijani, Kazakh, Kyrgyz, Tatar, Uighur, and Uzbek. —**Turkic** *adj.*

Turkish /túrkish/ *adj.* **1.** OF TURKEY relating to Turkey, or its people, or culture **2.** LANG OF TURKISH relating to the Turkish language ■ *n.* LANG OFFICIAL LANGUAGE OF TURKEY the official language of Turkey, also spoken in Cyprus and several European countries. It belongs to the Turkic branch of Altaic languages. Turkish is spoken by about 50 million people. Before 1928, when the Roman alphabet was adopted, it was written in Arabic script. —**Turkishness** *n.*

Turkish bath *n.* **1.** STEAM BATH a bath in which the bather sweats freely in hot air or steam, followed by a shower and often a massage **2.** ESTABLISHMENT OFFERING TURKISH BATH a commercial establishment where sb can have a Turkish bath **3.** HOT PLACE a place that is very hot

Turkish coffee *n.* a strong coffee, usually sweetened, made by simmering finely ground coffee and serving the liquid with the grounds

Turkish delight *n.* a sweet made with flavoured gelatin, cut into cubes and dusted with icing sugar

Turkey

Turkish tobacco *n.* an aromatic dark tobacco grown in southeastern Europe and Turkey

Turkish towel *n.* a large coarse-fibred cotton towel

Turkism /túrkizəm/ *n.* the culture and traditions of the Turks, or an example of these

Turkmen /túrk men/ (*plural* **-men** *or* **-mens**), **Turkoman** /túrkəmən/ (*plural* **-mans**), **Turcoman** (*plural* **-mans**) *n.* **1.** PEOPLES **MEMBER OF CENTRAL ASIAN PEOPLE** a member of an originally nomadic Turkic-speaking people who now live mainly in Turkmenistan and Afghanistan **2.** LANG **TURKMEN LANGUAGE** the language spoken by the Turkmen people and the official language of Turkmenistan, belonging to the Turkic group of Altaic languages. Turkmen is spoken by about 4 million people. [Early 20thC. Via Persian *turkmān* from Turkish *türkmen*. The form *Turkoman* dates from the early 17thC, and a rare *Turkman* from the 15thC.] —**Turkmen** *adj.*

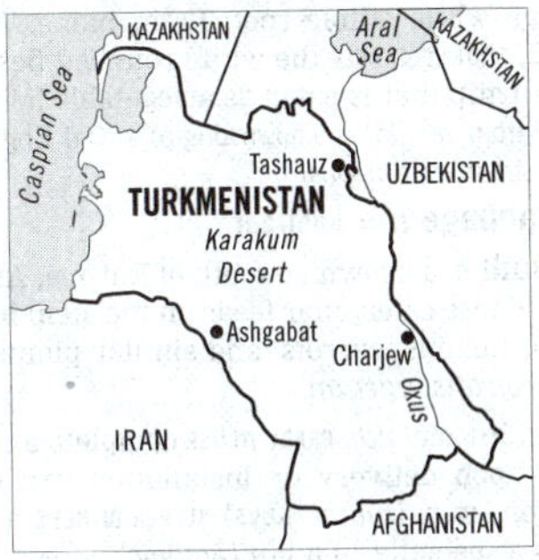

Turkmenistan

Turkmenistan /turk mènni staán/ republic in the southwestern portion of Central Asia, bordered by Kazakhstan, Uzbekistan, Afghanistan, Iran, and the Caspian Sea. Language: Turkmen. Currency: manat. Capital: Ashgabat. Population: 4,229,249 (1997). Area: 488,100 sq. km/188,500. Official name **Republic of Turkmenistan**

Turkoman *n., adj.* PEOPLES, LANG = **Turkmen**

Turks and Caicos Islands /túrks ənd káykoss īləndz/ British dependency consisting of two island groups in the West Indies, southeast of the Bahamas. Capital: Cockburn Town. Population: 14,302 (1996). Area: 430 sq. km/166 sq. mi.

Turk's-cap lily /túrks kap-/ *n.* either of two lilies that have bright nodding flowers with petals that bend sharply backwards. Latin name: *Lilium martagon* and *Lilium superbum*.

Turk's-head *n.* a knot shaped like a turban, made by weaving a smaller rope around a larger rope or spar

turmeric /túrmərik/ *n.* **1.** **BRIGHT YELLOW SPICE** a yellow spice made from the dried rhizomes of an Asian plant and used as a condiment and as a yellow dye **2.** **PLANT WITH YELLOW FLOWERS AND RHIZOMES** a tropical Asian plant of the ginger family with yellow flowers and rhizomes that are dried to produce turmeric. Latin name: *Curcuma longa*. [Mid-16thC. From French *terre-mérite*, literally 'worthy earth' (perhaps an alteration of Arabic *kurkum* 'saffron').]

turmeric paper *n.* a paper impregnated with turmeric that turns brown in the presence of alkalis and red-brown in the presence of boric acid

turmoil /túr moyl/ *n.* **1.** **CONFUSED DISTURBANCE** a state of great confusion, commotion, or disturbance **2.** **EVENT CAUSING CONFUSION** a disruptive event that causes confusion, commotion, or disturbance ○ *a leader untroubled by the nation's turmoils* [Early 16thC. Origin unknown.]

turn /turn/ *v.* (**turns, turning, turned**) **1.** *vti.* **MOVE TO FACE DIFFERENT DIRECTION** to move to face in a particular direction or towards a particular location, or move sth so that it does this ○ *She turned to see what was happening.* ○ *turning his eyes skywards* **2.** *vti.* **MOVE ROUND AN AXIS** to move around an axis or point in a particular direction, or move sth in this way ○ *Turn the handle to the left.* **3.** *vt.* **USE CONTROL TO OPERATE STH** to control sth such as a machine or an appliance or some aspect of its performance by moving a knob, switch, or slider to a particular setting ○ *Turn the heat to high.* **4.** *vti.* **TRAVEL IN NEW DIRECTION** to go in a different direction when moving or travelling, or make a vehicle change direction ○ *Turn left at the crossroads.* **5.** *vt.* **GO AROUND STH** to change direction and go round sth ○ *to turn a corner* **6.** *vi.* **FOLLOW DIFFERENT COURSE** to change direction and follow a different course ○ *The path turns uphill.* **7.** *vti.* **MOVE PAGE OVER** to move a page so that the other side, or another page, can be read or looked at ○ *He turned the pages slowly.* **8.** *vti.* **CHANGE** to change or be transformed, or change or transform sb or sth, into sb or sth different **9.** *vti.* **CHANGE COLOUR** to change colour, or cause sth to change colour **10.** *vti.* **ALTER FOCUS OF STH** to direct the focus of sth towards sth else, or be focused on sth ○ *Her thoughts turned to the past.* **11.** *vi.* **START DOING STH DIFFERENT** to start doing sth new or different, especially as a way of solving a problem or improving a situation **12.** *vi.* **APPEAL** to seek or appeal for help from sb ○ *He turned to his mother for advice.* **13.** *vi.* **CHANGE IN WEATHER** to change to become a different temperature or type of weather ○ *It's turned cold again.* **14.** *vti.* **MAKE SB FEEL SLIGHTLY SICK** to be sufficiently unpleasant or upsetting to make sb feel nauseated, or respond with feelings of nausea ○ *The scenes of carnage turned his stomach.* **15.** *vt.* GYMNASTICS **PERFORM CARTWHEEL** to rotate the body to perform a physical action such as a cartwheel or somersault **16.** *vt.* MED **TWIST ANKLE** to injure the ankle or wrist by twisting or spraining it ○ *She turned her ankle getting off the bus.* **17.** *vt.* **SEARCH EXTENSIVELY** to search a place extremely thoroughly ○ *They turned the house upside down looking for the ticket.* **18.** *vt.* **PASS TIME OR AGE** to pass a particular age, time, or speed ○ *She's just turned sixty.* **19.** *vi.* **BECOME SOUR** to become sour (*refers to milk*) ○ *The milk has turned.* **20.** *vi.* OCEANOG **START TO EBB OR FLOW** to reach high tide and ebb, or reach low tide and start to rise ○ *The tide has turned.* **21.** *vt.* WOODWORK, METALL **SHAPE STH ON LATHE** to shape or cut sth on a lathe **22.** *vt.* **FORM STH INTO ROUND SHAPE** to shape clay or a pot into a rounded form with the hands or with tools **23.** *vt.* BUSINESS **EARN MONEY** to earn or achieve a monetary gain ○ *The business should turn a profit in this financial year.* **24.** *vti.* **CHANGE SB'S ALLEGIANCE** to cause a change in sb's allegiance, or undergo a change of allegiance ○ *a diplomat who turned spy* **25.** *vt.* **SAY OR WRITE STH WELL** to give a distinctive or pleasing form to sth said or written **26.** *vt.* GARDENING, AGRIC **DIG UP LOWER LEVELS OF SOIL** to dig soil so as to bring lower layers up to the surface **27.** *vt.* MIL **PASS ROUND ENEMY** to pass round an enemy in order to attack from the flank or rear **28.** *vt.* CRICKET **SPIN A BALL** to make a cricket ball spin **29.** *vt.* **BLUNT A WEAPON** to blunt the edge of a weapon (*archaic*) **30.** *vt.* **COMPLIMENT SB** to pay a compliment to sb (*archaic*) ■ *n.* **1.** **CHANCE OR RIGHT TO DO STH** a time when sb gets an opportunity to do sth or sb is asked to do sth, especially when this is rotated among other people ○ *It's your turn to do the washing up.* **2.** **CHANGE OF DIRECTION** a change of direction in sth such as a road or the plot of a book ○ *Slow down for the turn in the road ahead.* **3.** = **turning 4.** **MOVEMENT OF ROTATION** a full or partial rotation ○ *Give the screw a few more turns.* **5.** **PARTICULAR INCLINATION** a particular inclination or tendency ○ *She has an academic turn of mind.* **6.** **SUDDEN SCARE** a sudden shock or scare ○ *It gave me quite a turn.* **7.** **SPELL OF ILLNESS** a short period of feeling unwell or faint ○ *She had a nasty turn but she's OK now.* **8.** **SHORT OUTING** a short walk, excursion, or dance (*dated*) ○ *They took a turn around the park.* **9.** **END OF TIME PERIOD** the point at which one period of time ends and another begins **10.** **GOOD OR BAD DEED** a deed that helps or harms another person ○ *a good turn* **11.** MUSIC **MELODIC EMBELLISHMENT** a melodic embellishment that is played around a given note, using one note above and one note below the principal note **12.** THEATRE **INDIVIDUAL THEATRICAL PERFORMANCE** a short theatrical solo performance, e.g. in a cabaret or variety show **13.** STOCK EXCH **STOCK MARKET TRANSACTION** a stock market transaction that includes both a sale and a purchase **14.** MIL **ADVANCE PASSING ROUND ENEMY** a military advance that passes around an enemy in order to attack from the flank or rear [Pre-12thC. Via Latin *tornare* 'to turn on a lathe' from, ultimately, Greek *tornos* 'lathe'.] —**turnable** *adj.* ◇ **at every turn** everywhere, or at every significant moment ◇ **be on the turn 1.** to be on the point of going sour **2.** to be on the point of changing **3.** to be at high or low tide and just about to ebb or return ◇ **by turns** one after the other, alternately ◇ **in turn** in a regular order, one after the other ◇ **out of turn 1.** not in a regular or correct order **2.** in an inappropriate way, or at an inappropriate time ◇ **to a turn** perfectly ○ *meat done to a turn*

turn against *vti.* to stop approving of sth or being friendly towards sb and show definite disapproval or unfriendliness instead, or make sb change attitude in this way

turn away *v.* **1.** *vti.* **TURN TO FACE SOMEWHERE ELSE** to change position so as to face away from sb or sth, or move sb or sth so as to face in another direction **2.** *vt.* **REFUSE ADMISSION TO SB** to send sb away, refusing to see, entertain, or accommodate him or her **3.** *vt.* **REFUSE TO ACCEPT STH** to refuse to listen to sb or to what sb wants to say or offer **4.** *vi.* **REJECT** to reject sth as unworthy or undesirable ○ *to turn away from a life of sin*

turn back *v.* **1.** *vti.* **STOP GOING FORWARD AND RETURN** to stop and return in the direction you have come from, or stop people or vehicles and make them return in the direction they have come from **2.** *vt.* **FOLD BACK** to fold sth over and down ○ *turned back the top sheet on the bed*

turn down *vt.* **1.** **REJECT** to reject or refuse sth such as an offer or application **2.** **REDUCE VOLUME OR INTENSITY** to make sth less powerful, bright, loud, or hot, especially by moving a knob, switch, or slider **3.** **FOLD STH DOWNWARDS** to fold sth or the top part of sth towards the bottom, so that a double layer is formed

turn in *v.* **1.** *vt.* **RETURN STH AFTER USE** to hand sth over or give sth back to its owner or to whoever is responsible for it ○ *turn in your key at reception before leaving* **2.** *vt.* **SUBMIT STH** to hand in or send in sth such as work assigned in school **3.** *vt.* **TAKE SB TO THE POLICE** to hand over sb or sth to the police or other authorities **4.** *vi.* **GO TO BED** to go to bed at the end of the day (*informal*) **5.** *vt.* **PRODUCE RESULT** to achieve a particular outcome ○ *turned in a creditable performance* **6.** *vti.* **FOLD INWARDS** to arrange sth so that it bends or points inwards, or be arranged in this way

turn off *v.* **1.** *vt.* **OPERATE SWITCH TO STOP STH** to make a machine or appliance stop working, or sth stop flowing, by operating a control **2.** *vt.* **SET TO OFF POSITION** to move a device such as a button, knob, or lever so that a machine stops working or sth stops flowing **3.** *vti.* **DIMINISH ENTHUSIASM** to diminish or destroy sb's interest, enthusiasm, or sexual arousal, or lose interest or become unresponsive (*informal*) **4.** *vti.* **GO IN A NEW DIRECTION** to split off from a road or path and head a different way, or take a road or path that goes in a new direction **5.** *vt.* **DISMISS** to dismiss sb from work (*archaic*)

turn on *v.* **1.** *vt.* **OPERATE SWITCH TO START STH** to make a machine or appliance operate, or make sth start flowing, by operating a control **2.** *vt.* **SET TO ON POSITION** to move a device such as a button, knob, or lever so that a machine starts working or sth starts flowing **3.** *vt.* **BEHAVE IN CALCULATED WAY** to display a particular behaviour or emotion in a way that people find calculated, irritating, or insincere ○ *He'll really turn on the charm if he thinks he's losing the sale.* **4.** *vt.* **REACT AGGRESSIVELY OR VIOLENTLY** to react aggressively or violently to sb **5.** *vt.* **MAKE SB EXCITED** to interest sb greatly or fill sb with pleasure, energy, or excitement (*informal*) **6.** *vt.* **AROUSE** to make sb feel sexually excited (*informal*) **7.** *vti.* DRUGS **TAKE ILLEGAL DRUGS** to take drugs, especially a hallucinogenic drug, or cause sb to take a hallucinogen or similar drug (*informal*)

turn out *v.* **1.** *vt.* **SWITCH OFF** to make an electric light go out by operating its power switch **2.** *vi.* **COME TO EVENT** to assemble in a particular place, especially for a special event or public occasion ○ *Hardly anybody turned out for the reunion.* **3.** *vt.* **MAKE SB LEAVE** to force sb to leave a room, building, or residence **4.** *vi.* **HAPPEN IN PARTICULAR WAY** to happen in a particular way, often in a way that was not expected **5.** *vi.* **END UP** to have a particular result ○ *The birthday party turned out OK, despite our fears.* **6.** *vt.* **MAKE STH** to create or produce sth, especially in a consistent way or by mass production ○ *a factory that turns out tennis rackets* **7.** *vt.* **DRESS SB UP** to clothe yourself or sb else in a particular way **8.** *vti.* MIL **SIGNAL GROUP TO ASSEMBLE** to call an organized group of people, usually soldiers, to assemble for duty or for a military parade **9.** *vt.* EMPTY CONTENTS to take out the contents of a pocket or bag, usually to check or reorganize what is there **10.** *vti.* FOLD OUTWARDS to be arranged so as to bend or point outwards, or arrange sth in this way **11.** *vi.* GET UP to get out of bed (*informal*)

turn over *v.* **1.** *vt.* TURN STH THE OTHER WAY UP to alter the position of the body or of an object, bringing the underside uppermost, or move so that the underside is uppermost **2.** *vt.* THINK ABOUT to give sth slow and careful thought, considering different aspects or possibilities **3.** *vt.* GIVE TO SB ELSE to hand sth over to the police or other authorities, especially when required to do so **4.** *vt.* DELEGATE to give the responsibility for sth to sb else ○ *turned over some duties to her assistant* **5.** *vt.* PUT UNDER SB'S RESPONSIBILITY to transfer the responsibility for sb to another person or authority ○ *The principal turned him over to his parents.* **6.** *vt.* ROB to break into a building or premises and steal anything thought to be valuable (*slang*) (*often used in the passive*) **7.** *vti.* AUTOMOT START to start an engine or motor, or be started ○ *couldn't get it to turn over* **8.** *vt.* FIN HAVE SALES OF to have sales or other business transactions totalling a specified amount ○ *The firm turns over several million a month.* **9.** *vti.* COMM SELL AND RESTOCK GOODS to sell and restock all items for sale ○ *The produce usually turns over in 10 days.*

turn round, turn around *vt.* **1.** COMPLETE ALL NECESSARY PROCEDURES to carry out all the necessary procedures between receiving an order or task and shipping the order or completing the task ○ *How long will it take you to turn this work round?* **2.** PREPARE VEHICLE BETWEEN JOURNEYS to prepare an aircraft for its next flight or a ship for its next sailing **3.** IMPROVE SIGNIFICANTLY to cause a significant improvement in sth, especially in the profits made by a company or organization ○ *moves to turn the debt round*

turn to *vi.* to set to work, especially vigorously (*dated*)

turn up *v.* **1.** *vt.* INCREASE STH to make sth louder, brighter, hotter, or more powerful, especially by operating its control **2.** *vti.* UNFOLD UPWARDS to unfold sth so that it stands up instead of lying in a flat double layer, or be capable of unfolding in this way **3.** *vt.* SEW SHORTEN GARMENT to fold and sew the bottom edge of a garment or piece of fabric, so as to shorten it **4.** *vi.* BE FOUND to reappear or be rediscovered after being lost or in an unknown place, often in a surprising or unexpected way ○ *It'll turn up sooner or later.* **5.** *vt.* FIND STH BY SEARCHING to uncover sth that was hidden or previously unknown by investigating, hunting, or digging ○ *He didn't expect to turn up such an interesting story.* **6.** *vi.* ARRIVE to come or appear somewhere, especially in a casual or unplanned way ○ *She just turned up yesterday morning.* **7.** *vi.* HAPPEN to take place luckily or unexpectedly to settle matters or put things right ○ *They manage to get along somehow … something always seems to turn up.* ◇ **a turn-up for the book** *or* **books** sth fortunate that happens unexpectedly (*informal*)

turnabout /túrn ə bowt/ *n.* **1.** TOTAL CHANGE IN OUTLOOK OR BEHAVIOUR a shift from one situation, opinion, policy, or attitude to another that is the complete opposite **2.** ACT OF TURNING COMPLETELY AROUND the act of turning to face in the opposite direction

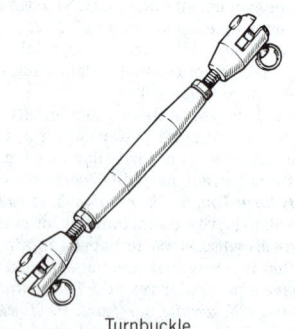
Turnbuckle

turnbuckle /túrn buk'l/ *n.* a device to tighten or loosen rope or wire, consisting of a sleeve through which the rope or wire is threaded and held so that the tension can be adjusted

turncoat /túrnkōt/ *n.* sb who abandons or betrays a group or cause and joins the opposing side

turndown /túrn down/ *adj.* FOLDED DOWN folded down or over from the top ■ *n.* **1.** = downturn **2.** *US* REJECTION a rejection of sth such as an offer or application

turned-on *adj.* **1.** SEXUALLY EXCITED sexually aroused or excited (*informal*) **2.** UP-TO-DATE aware of or involved in the most modern trends in culture and fashion (*dated informal*) **3.** HIGH ON DRUGS under the influence of a drug such as cannabis or LSD, or familiar with its effects as a result of having taken it (*dated informal*)

turner /túrnər/ *n.* **1.** SB OR STH THAT TURNS sb or sth that turns or that is used for turning sth else, e.g. a device for turning food while it is cooking ○ *a pancake turner* **2.** LATHE OPERATOR sb whose job involves operating a lathe

Turner /túrnər/, **J.M.W.** (1775–1851) English painter and watercolourist. His powerful landscape and seascape paintings used colour to explore the effects of light, and influenced the French impressionists. His works include *Hannibal and his Army Crossing the Alps* (1812) and *Rain, Steam, and Speed* (1844). Full name **Joseph Mallord William Turner**

Turner, Lana (1920–95) US actor. She is known for her roles in such Hollywood films as *The Postman Always Rings Twice* (1946) and *The Bad and the Beautiful* (1952). Real name **Julia Jean Mildred Frances Turner**

Ted Turner

Turner, Ted (b. 1938) US business executive and philanthropist. He built Turner Broadcasting System into an international media empire. Full name **Robert Edward Turner III**

Turner's syndrome *n.* an inherited disorder affecting women, caused by an absence or abnormality of one of the two X chromosomes and resulting in an underdeveloped womb, vagina, and breasts, and infertility. It may also cause short stature, webbed neck skin, and irregularly shaped ears. [Mid-20thC. Named after Henry Hubert *Turner* (1892–1970), the US physician who described the syndrome.]

turnery /túrnəri/ (*plural* **-ies**) *n.* **1.** WORK ON LATHE the technique, art, or skill of forming and contouring using a lathe **2.** ARTICLES TURNED ON LATHE articles that have been made or turned on a lathe **3.** WORKSHOP a room or building where lathes are used

turning /túrning/ *n.* **1.** JUNCTION a road or path that joins the main road or the road that is being travelled. US term **turn** *n.* 3 **2.** DEVIATION a deviation from a straight or planned course **3.** = turnery *n.* 1 **4.** SEW FABRIC THAT FORMS HEM the amount of fabric that will be turned back to form a hem at the edge of a piece of sewing ■ **turnings** *npl.* WOODWORK, METALL WASTE MATERIAL FROM LATHE the waste material produced when sth is turned on a lathe

turning circle *n.* the smallest circle in which a vehicle can complete a 360-degree turn. US term **turning radius**

turning point *n.* **1.** IMPORTANT MOMENT OF CHANGE a particular time or incident that marks the beginning of a completely new, and usually better, stage in sb's life or in the development of sth **2.** MATH POINT ON CURVE a minimum or maximum point on a plane curve

turning radius *n.* US = **turning circle**

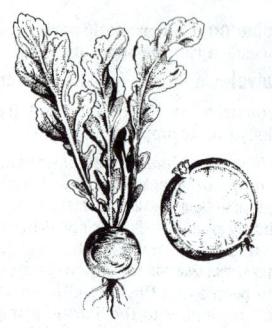
Turnip

turnip /túrnip/ *n.* **1.** PLANT WITH EDIBLE ROOT a plant belonging to the cabbage family, widely cultivated for its large white edible root. Latin name: *Brassica rapa.* **2.** ROOT VEGETABLE the white rounded fleshy root of the turnip that is eaten as a vegetable [Mid-16thC. Formed from *tur-* (of unknown origin) + Old English *nǣp* 'turnip' (from Latin *napus*).]

turnip cabbage *n.* = **kohlrabi**

turnip moth *n.* a brownish moth of Europe, Asia, and Africa whose caterpillar feeds on the stem base and roots of turnips, carrots, and similar plants. Latin name: *Agrotis segetum.*

turnkey /túrn kee/ *adj.* READY TO USE complete and ready to use upon delivery or installation ○ *a turnkey operation* ■ *n.* (*plural* **-keys**) KEEPER OF KEYS a keeper of keys, especially in a jail (*archaic*)

turn-off *n.* **1.** ROAD BRANCHING OFF MAIN ROAD a road that branches off a main road **2.** ROAD JUNCTION a junction formed by two roads, especially a larger and smaller one **3.** STH DISGUSTING OR OFF-PUTTING sb or sth that causes a complete loss of interest, enthusiasm, or sexual arousal (*informal*)

turn-on *n.* sb or sth that causes sexual arousal (*informal*)

turnout /túrn owt/ *n.* **1.** ATTENDANCE the number of people who attend or take part in a particular event ○ *expecting a huge turnout for the carnival this weekend* **2.** POL NUMBER OF VOTERS the number or proportion of voters who register their vote in an election **3.** BUSINESS AMOUNT OF WORK PRODUCED the total quantity or amount produced, e.g. by a particular company or manufacturing process **4.** CLOTHES OUTFIT the clothes or equipment sb is wearing ○ *a smart turnout* **5.** BALLET OUTWARD ROTATION OF DANCER'S LEGS the outward rotating movement from the hip sockets of a classical ballet dancer's legs

turnover /túrnōvər/ *n.* **1.** FIN AMOUNT OF BUSINESS the amount of business transacted over a given period of time, especially when expressed as gross revenue **2.** COMM THROUGHPUT OF STOCK the rate at which business stock is sold and replaced **3.** HR CHANGE IN EMPLOYEES the number of employees in an organization who leave and are replaced over a given period ○ *job dissatisfaction that results in high turnover* **4.** COOK FILLED PASTRY a filled pastry, made by folding a square or circle of pastry in half over a filling to form a semicircle or triangle ■ *adj.* ABLE TO BE FOLDED OVER designed to be turned or folded over

turnpike /túrn pīk/ *n.* **1.** TRANSP TOLL ROAD in the United States, a motorway on which a toll is charged. Drivers usually receive a ticket when they start their journey and pay a fee at the end that depends on the length of journey. **2.** HIST ROAD BARRIER a gate formerly used to bar the way onto a section of road or a bridge until a toll had been paid **3.** HIST ROAD WITH TURNPIKE in former times, a road that travellers were only allowed to use after paying a toll at the turnpike **4.** TURNSTILE a turnstile (*archaic*) [14thC. From TURN + PIKE[5].]

turnround /túrn rownd/, **turnaround** /túrn ə rownd/ *n.* **1.** BUSINESS TIME TAKEN TO DO ENTIRE JOB the time it takes to carry out all the necessary procedures between receiving an order or task and the shipment of the order or completion of the task **2.** TRANSP PREPARATION OF VEHICLE BETWEEN JOURNEYS the process of unloading and reloading, refuelling, and checking an aircraft, ship, or vehicle between journeys **3.** BIG IMPROVEMENT a dramatic improvement in a bad or unsatisfactory situation **4.** *US* TRANSP **PLACE FOR TURNING CAR ROUND** a circular or curved driveway or section of road where vehicles can turn round

turnsole /túrnsōl/ *n.* **1.** PLANTS **MEDITERRANEAN PLANT YIELDING PURPLE DYE** a Mediterranean annual plant that yields a purple dye. Latin name: *Chrozophora tinctoria.* **2.** INDUST **PURPLE DYE** the purple dye obtained from the turnsole plant [14thC. Via Old French *tournesole* from Old Italian *tornasole*, from *tornare* 'to turn' + *sol* 'sun'.]

turnstile /túrn stīl/ *n.* a mechanical barrier designed to let people pass through a narrow opening one at a time between bars that revolve around a central post

turnstone /túrn stōn/ *n.* a wading bird with mottled black or tortoiseshell markings that breeds along Arctic coasts and migrates south for the winter. Genus: *Arenaria.* [Late 17thC. From the way the bird turns over stones to expose the small creatures it feeds on.]

turntable /túrn tayb'l/ *n.* **1.** REVOLVING PLATFORM ON RECORD PLAYER the flat round revolving plate on which the record rests on a record player **2.** RECORD PLAYER DECK a record player deck, especially without the amplifier and speakers, and as distinct from a separate tape player, compact disc player, or tuner **3.** TRANSP ROTATING PLATFORM a rotating platform for turning round a vehicle such as a railway locomotive, so that it is facing the opposite way

turntable ladder *n.* an extending ladder mounted on a rotating platform on the back of a fire engine. US term **aerial ladder**

turn-up *n.* **1.** *UK* CLOTHES **FOLD AT BOTTOM OF TROUSER LEG** a fold of material that is turned up at the bottom of a trouser leg **2.** STH SURPRISING an unexpected, unlikely, or unusual event (*informal*) ○ *That's a turn-up for the book!* ■ *adj.* **FOR TURNING UP** designed to be folded or turned up

turpentine /túrpən tīn/ *n.* **1.** SUBSTANCE FROM PINE TREES a viscous substance obtained from coniferous trees and used to manufacture a paint solvent **2.** STICKY SUBSTANCE FROM TEREBINTH TREE a brownish-yellow sticky mixture of essential oil and resin that comes from the terebinth tree **3.** LIQUID FROM TURPENTINE a colourless, flammable, strong-smelling essential oil distilled from turpentine. It is used as a paint solvent and in medicine. **4.** PAINT THINNER a colourless petroleum-based liquid used as a thinner for paint and varnish ■ *vt.* (**-tines, -tining, -tined**) **1.** TREAT STH WITH TURPENTINE to treat or thin sth with turpentine **2.** EXTRACT TURPENTINE FROM to extract turpentine from trees [14thC. Via Old French *terbentine* 'terebinth resin' from, ultimately, Greek *terebinthos* 'terebinth tree'.]

turpentine tree *n.* **1.** TREE YIELDING TURPENTINE a tree such as the terebinth that yields turpentine **2.** AUSTRALIAN TREE an Australian tree belonging to the eucalyptus family that yields a viscous resin and is often planted as a shade tree. Family: Myrtaceae.

turpeth /túrpith/ *n.* (*plural* **-peths** *or* **-peth**) **1.** MEDICINAL PLANT an Asian plant, belonging to the bindweed family, that has a medicinal root. Latin name: *Operculina turpethum.* **2.** ROOT the root of the turpeth, formerly used as a purgative [14thC. Via medieval Latin *turbithum* and Persian *turbid* from Sanskrit *triputin* 'castor-oil plant'.]

Turpin /túrpin/, **Dick** (1706–39) British bandit. His exploits, including an alleged swift ride from London to York on his horse, Black Bess, were later romanticized. Full name **Richard Turpin**. Known as **the King of the Road**

turpitude /túrpi tyood/ *n.* extreme immorality or wickedness (*formal or literary*) [15thC. Directly or via French from Latin *turpitudo*, from *turpis* 'repulsive', of unknown origin.]

turps /turps/ *n.* (*informal*) **1.** TURPENTINE turpentine **2.** *Aus* BEVERAGES **ALCOHOL** beer or other alcoholic drink [Early 19thC. Shortening.]

turquoise /túrkwoyz, -kaaz/ *n.* **1.** SEMIPRECIOUS STONE a greenish-blue mineral form of aluminium and copper phosphate that occurs in igneous rocks and is used as a gemstone **2.** GREENISH-BLUE COLOUR a bright greenish-blue colour ■ *adj.* GREENISH-BLUE of a greenish-blue colour [15thC. From Old French (*pierre*) *turqueise* 'Turkish (stone)'; so called because the stone was first found in Turkestan.]

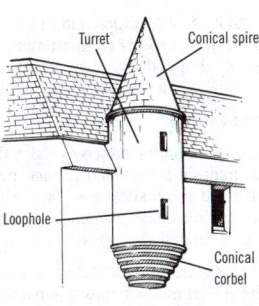

Turret

turret /túrrit/ *n.* **1.** SMALL TOWER a small rounded tower that projects from a wall or corner of a large building such as a castle **2.** INDUST **DOME CONTAINING GUN** a rotating armoured structure on a ship or tank, or a Perspex™ dome projecting from the fuselage of an aircraft, containing one or more guns and a gun crew **3.** MECH ENG **PART OF LATHE** a device on a lathe, used for holding a range of tools [14thC. From Old French *tourete*, literally 'small tower', from *tour* (see TOWER).]

turreted /túritid/ *adj.* **1.** HAVING TURRETS constructed or designed to include turrets **2.** ZOOL WITH SPIRAL SHAPE shaped like a long pointed spiral

turret lathe *n.* = **capstan lathe**

Turtle

turtle[1] /túrt'l/ *n.* **1.** ZOOL **WATER REPTILE WITH SHELL** a water-dwelling reptile with a body that is protected by a bony, often rounded shell, and limbs that are shaped like flippers. Order: Chelonia. US term **sea turtle 2.** *US* ZOOL **REPTILE WITH SHELL** a water- or land-dwelling reptile such as a tortoise or terrapin with a body protected by a bony shell **3.** FOOD TURTLE MEAT the flesh of any edible type of turtle, tortoise, or terrapin [Mid-16thC. Origin uncertain: perhaps via French *tortue* 'tortoise' from medieval Latin *tortuca*, of uncertain origin.] ◇ **turn turtle** to turn upside down

turtle[2] /túrt'l/ *n.* a turtledove (*archaic*) [Old English *turtla*. From Latin *turtur*, an imitation of the bird's voice.]

turtleback /túrt'l bak/ *n.* an arched cover for protecting the deck of a ship in heavy seas

turtledove /túrt'l duv/ *n.* **1.** DOVE WITH PURRING COO a slender dove with black-and-chestnut upper parts, a pink breast, and a black-and-white neck, noted for its purring call. It breeds in northern Europe and winters in Africa. Latin name: *Streptopelia turtur.* **2.** DEAR PERSON a tender, faithful, and affectionate person or an affectionate address for sb the speaker is very fond of (*archaic or literary*) [13thC. Formed from TURTLE[2].]

turtleneck /túrt'l nek/ *n.* **1.** *US* = **polo neck 2.** HIGH ROUND COLLAR a high tight-fitting round collar on a garment such as a sweater **3.** SWEATER WITH A TURTLENECK a sweater with a turtleneck

turves plural of **turf**

Tuscan /túskən/ *adj.* **1.** OF TUSCANY relating to the Italian region of Tuscany, or its people or culture **2.** ARCHIT OF STYLE OF ARCHITECTURE relating to a classical order of architecture characterized by plain bases and capitals and unfluted columns ■ *n.* **1.** PEOPLES SB FROM TUSCANY sb who was born or lives in the Italian region of Tuscany **2.** LANG STANDARD ITALIAN the standard and literary form of Italian, principally based on

the dialect of Florence [14thC. Via Old French from, ultimately, Latin *Tuscus* 'Etruscan'.]

Tuscany /túskəni/ region in northern Italy, a centre of culture during the Renaissance period. Capital: Florence. Population: 3,526,031 (1995). Area: 22,993 sq. km/8,878 sq. mi.

Tuscarora /túskə ráwrə/ (*plural* **-ras** *or* **-ra**) *n.* PEOPLES a member of a Native North American people who originally occupied lands in North Carolina, and whose members now live mainly in New York State and Ontario. In 1722 the Tuscarora joined the Iroquois Confederacy, which then became known as the Six Nations. [Mid-17thC. From Iroquois, literally 'hemp gatherer'.]

tusche /toosh/ *n.* a thick black liquid that is used as a drawing medium in lithography and as a resist in silk-screen printing and etching [Late 19thC. From German, a back-formation from *tuschen* 'to draw in ink', via French *toucher* from Old French *touchier* (see TOUCH).]

tush[1] /toosh/ *n.* *US* sb's buttocks or bottom (*slang*) [Mid-20thC. Alteration of Yiddish *tokhes* (see TOKHES).]

tush[2] /tush/ *interj.* an expression of mild disapproval or disdain (*archaic*) [Mid-16thC. An imitation of a spontaneous exclamation.]

tushery /túshəri/ *n.* an affected style of writing full of artificial and archaic-sounding expressions, such as 'Tush!' (*literary*) [Late 19thC. Coined from TUSH[2] by Robert Louis STEVENSON.]

tusk /tusk/ *n.* **1.** ZOOL **ENLARGED TOOTH** an enlarged pointed front tooth that projects from the mouth in animals such as the elephant, walrus, and wild boar and is often used for fighting **2.** JOINERY **TENON JOINT** in joinery, a form of tenon that has a short projecting part to make it stronger ■ *vti.* (**tusks, tusking, tusked**) JAB **TUSK INTO SB OR STH** to use a tusk or tusks to attack, dig at, or stab sb or sth [Old English *tūsc, tux.* Ultimately from an Indo-European word meaning 'tooth' that is also the ancestor of English *tooth* and *dental*.] —**tusked** *adj.*

tusker /túskər/ *n.* a wild boar, elephant, or other animal with large tusks (*informal*)

tusk shell *n.* a marine mollusc with a slender, tapering, and often curved shell that is open at both ends. It lives partly buried in sand. Order: Scaphopoda. US term **tooth shell**

tussah /tússə/ (*plural* **-sahs** *or* **-sah**) *n.* = **tussore**

Tussaud /tooss ō/, **Madame** (1760–1850) Swiss wax-modeller. She made death masks in Paris of victims of the French Revolution, which she exhibited in Great Britain, and founded Madame Tussaud's Exhibition in London (1835). Born **Marie Grosholtz**

tussis /tússiss/ *n.* a cough or coughing (*technical*) [From Latin] —**tussal** *adj.* —**tussive** *adj.*

tussle /túss'l/ *vi.* (**-sles, -sling, -sled**) HAVE VIGOROUS FIGHT to have a vigorous physical or verbal struggle with sb ■ *n.* VIGOROUS FIGHT a vigorous physical or verbal struggle [15thC. Origin uncertain: probably formed from a northern English dialect word meaning 'to pull about'.]

tussock /tússək/ *n.* **1.** TUFT OF GRASS a small thick clump of growing vegetation, usually coarse grass **2.** *ANZ* = **tussock grass** [Mid-16thC. Origin uncertain.] —**tussocky** *adj.*

tussock grass *n.* any of various grasses, native to New Zealand and Australia, that grow in clumps

tussock moth *n.* a moth whose caterpillars are covered in tufts of brightly coloured hairs. They often cause skin irritation if handled, and some are pests of crops and shade trees. Family: Lymantriidae.

tussore /tússər/ (*plural* **-sores** *or* **-sore**) *n.* **1.** SILKWORM the silkworm of an Asian moth, from which a coarse silk is obtained. Latin name: *Antheraea paphia.* US term **tussah 2.** SILK THREAD the silk thread produced by the tussore silkworm **3.** SILK FABRIC the silk fabric woven from tussore. It is a coarse brownish or yellowish fabric with an attractive uneven surface. [Early 17thC. From Hindi *tasar* (see TUSSAH).]

tut /tut/, **tut-tut** *interj.* EXPRESSION OF IRRITATION OR DISAPPROVAL a clicking sound made with the tongue, or a spoken imitation of this sound, used as an expression of annoyance or disapproval, sometimes ironically ■ *vi.* (**tuts, tutting, tutted; tut-tuts, tut-tutting, tut-tutted**)

EXPRESS DISAPPROVAL to make a clicking sound with the tongue to express annoyance or dissatisfaction, or to express these feelings in some other way [Early 16thC. An imitation of a spontaneous exclamation.]

Tutankhamen

Tutankhamen /tooʹtən kaaʹmən/, **Tutankhamun** /tooʹtən kaa mooʹn/ (1343–1325 BC) Egyptian pharaoh. His sumptuously decorated tomb was discovered virtually intact in 1922.

tutee /tyoo teeʹ/ *n.* the student of a particular tutor, or sb being tutored [Early 20thC. Formed from TUTOR + -EE.]

tutelage /tyooʹtəlij/ *n.* **1.** TEACHING instruction and guidance provided by sb such as a tutor ○ *Under her tutelage, he became a first-rate marksman.* **2.** BEING A TUTOR the condition of being a tutor or guardian **3.** SUPERVISION BY A TUTOR the condition of being supervised or protected by a tutor or guardian ○ *continued my studies under private tutelage* [Early 17thC. Formed from Latin *tutela* 'guardianship', from *tut-*, the past participle stem of *tueri* 'to watch over' (source of English *tutor*).]

tutelary /tyooʹtələri/, **tutelar** /tyooʹtələr/ *adj.* (*formal or literary*) **1.** ACTING AS PROTECTOR acting in the role of a protector or guardian ○ *tutelary saints* **2.** OF GUARDIAN relating to or belonging to a guardian ■ *n.* (*plural* -ies) GUARDING PRESENCE a tutelary being or person, especially a saint or deity (*literary*) [Early 17thC. From Latin *tutelarius*, from *tutela* (see TUTELAGE).]

tutor /tyooʹtər/ *n.* **1.** TEACHER a teacher who instructs an individual pupil or a small group of pupils **2.** BRITISH UNIVERSITY TEACHER an academic who is responsible for teaching and advising an allocated group of students **3.** US LOW-RANKING US UNIVERSITY TEACHER in some US universities, a teacher ranking below an instructor **4.** GUARDIAN OF PUPIL in Scottish law, sb who is the guardian of a pupil (*formal*) ■ *v.* (-tors, -toring, -tored) **1.** *vti.* ACT AS TUTOR to act as a tutor to sb or in a particular discipline **2.** *vi.* US RECEIVE PRIVATE TUITION to study under a tutor [14thC. Via Anglo-Norman from Latin *tutor* 'guardian', from *tut-*, the past participle stem of *tueri* 'to watch over'.] —**tutorage** *n.* —**tutorship** *n.*

——— **WORD KEY: SYNONYMS** ———
See Synonyms at **teach.**

tutorial /tyoo tawʹri əl/ *n.* **1.** LESSON WITH TUTOR a teaching session spent individually or in a small group under the direction of a tutor **2.** LESSON FROM BOOK a chapter of a book or manual, or a section of a computer program, designed to provide instruction or training using exercises and assignments ■ *adj.* RELATING TO TUTOR relating to or belonging to a tutor, or to the role and responsibilities of a tutor

tutsan /tútsʹn/ (*plural* -sans *or* -san) *n.* a woodland shrub, native to Europe and Asia, with large stalkless leaves, yellow flowers, and small round red fruits that turn black when ripe. The leaves have antiseptic properties and were traditionally used in treating wounds. Latin name: *Hypericum androsaemum.* [14thC. From French *toute-saine*, from *toute* 'all' + *saine* 'healthy'.]

Tutsi /tooʹtsi/ (*plural* -si *or* -sis) *n.* PEOPLES a member of a people living in Rwanda and Burundi, where they are one of the minority ethnic groups. ◊ **Hutu** [Mid-20thC. Of Bantu origin.]

tutti /tooʹtti/ *n.* the part of a concerto or other orchestral composition in which all the musicians play, as opposed to a solo section [Early 18thC. Via Italian from, ultimately, Latin *totus* (see TOTAL).]

tutti-frutti /tooʹti fooʹti/ (*plural* **tutti-fruttis**) *n.* an ice cream, dessert, or type of confectionery containing a variety of chopped, usually dried or candied, fruit [Mid-19thC. From Italian, literally 'all fruits'.]

tut-tut *interj., vi.* = **tut**

tutu[1] /tooʹtoo/ *n.* a ballet dancer's skirt that is very short and made of layers of stiffened net so that it stands out from the body [Early 20thC. From French, a baby-talk alteration of *cucu*, from *cul* 'buttocks', from Latin *culus* (source of English *culottes* and *recoil*).]

tutu[2] /tooʹtoo/ (*plural* -tus *or* -tu) *n.* a tree native to New Zealand that has poisonous sap and seeds. The Maoris are said to have prepared an intoxicating beverage from the deseeded berries. Latin name: *Coriaria arborea.* [Mid-19thC. From Maori.]

Desmond Tutu

Tutu /tooʹtoo/, **Desmond** (*b.* 1931) South African clergyman and political activist. A leader of the anti-apartheid movement, he became bishop of Johannesburg in 1984, and was archbishop of Cape Town (1986–96). In 1995 he was appointed chair of the Truth and Reconciliation Committee set up to investigate political and human rights crimes of the apartheid era. Full name **Desmond Mpilo Tutu**

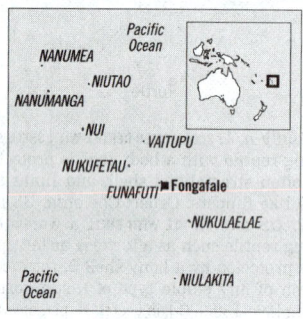
Tuvalu

Tuvalu /too vaaʹloo/ small country consisting of coral islands in the western Pacific Ocean. Fiji and Samoa, each about 1,050 km/650 mi. away, are the islands' nearest neighbours. Language: English, Tuvaluan. Currency: Australian dollar. Capital: Fongafale. Population: 10,297 (1997). Area: 26 sq. km/10 sq. mi. Former name **Ellice Islands** —**Tuvaluan** *n., adj.*

Tuwhare, Honi (*b.* 1922) New Zealand poet. He is the author of *No Ordinary Sun* (1964).

tu-whit tu-whoo /tə wít tə wooʹ/ *interj.* used to represent the sound of an owl hooting (*informal*) [Late 16thC. An imitation of the sound.]

tux /tuks/ *n.* US a tuxedo (*informal*) [Early 20thC. Shortening.]

tuxedo /tuk seeʹdō/ (*plural* -dos) *n.* US **1.** = dinner jacket **2.** MEN'S FORMAL CLOTHING a formal set of clothing for a man including a tuxedo jacket and matching trousers, usually with a band of silk down each leg, dress shirt, bow tie, and cummerbund [Late 19thC. Named after the town of *Tuxedo* Park, New York, in the US, where the garment was first worn at a country club.]

tuyère /twee air/, **twyer** /twíʹ ər/ *n.* an opening in the refractory lining and shell of a furnace through which air is forced to promote combustion [Late 18thC. From French, formed from *tuyau* 'pipe', of uncertain origin; probably from Germanic.]

TV[1] *n.* television or a television set (*informal*)

TV[2] *abbr.* transvestite (*informal*)

TVEI *abbr.* technical and vocational initiative

Tver /tvair/ city at the confluence of the Volga and Tvertsa rivers in western Russia. Population: 454,000 (1990). Former name **Kalinin** (1933–90)

TVP *n.* a high-protein product made from processed soya beans that are formed into chunks or minced and flavoured to taste like meat. Full form **textured vegetable protein**

TVR *abbr.* television rating

TVRO *n.* a type of antenna used for receiving television signals from a broadcasting satellite. Full form **television receive only**

twa /twaw/ *n. Scotland* two [Scots dialect variant of TWO]

twaddle /twódd'l/ *n.* NONSENSE nonsensical or pretentious speech or writing (*informal*) ■ *vi.* (-dles, -dling, -dled) TALK TWADDLE to speak or write twaddle (*dated informal*) [Late 18thC. Origin uncertain.] —**twaddler** *n.*

twain /twayn/ *npl.* two (*archaic or literary*) ○ *'Oh, East is East, and West is West, and never the twain shall meet'.* (Rudyard Kipling, *The Ballad of East and West*) [Old English *twēgen*]

Mark Twain

Twain /twayn/, **Mark** (1835–1910) US writer. He wrote humorous travel books and the classic stories *The Adventures of Tom Sawyer* (1876) and *The Adventures of Huckleberry Finn* (1884). Pseudonym of **Samuel Langhorne Clemens**

twang /twang/ *n.* **1.** SOUND OF TIGHT STRING VIBRATING the sharp resonating noise made when sth such as a tight string on an instrument is plucked or released **2.** LANG SOUND IN CERTAIN ACCENTS a nasal quality of voice associated with various accents ○ *a Texas twang* ■ *vti.* (twangs, twanging, twanged) **1.** VIBRATE WITH A TWANG to make a twang or cause sth to make a twang **2.** MUSIC STRUM STH CARELESSLY to play a stringed instrument, or a tune on a stringed instrument, in a rough amateur style **3.** MOVE WITH A TWANG to move, spring, or be released suddenly with a twang ○ *The lid of the box twanged shut.* **4.** LANG SPEAK WITH A TWANG to speak or say sth with a twang [Mid-16thC. An imitation of the sound.] —**twangy** *adj.*

'twas /twoz/ *contr.* it was (*archaic or literary*)

twat /twot/ *n.* (*taboo offensive*) **1.** OFFENSIVE TERM a highly offensive term used to refer to a woman's vagina or genital area **2.** OFFENSIVE TERM a highly offensive term used to refer to sb regarded as unintelligent, worthless, or detestable [Mid-17thC. Origin unknown.]

twayblade /twáy blayd/ *n.* an orchid that has only two leaves, arranged opposite each other, at the base. Genera: *Listera* and *Liparis* and *Ophrys.* [Late 16thC. Formed from an obsolete variant of TWAIN + BLADE.]

tweak /tweek/ *vt.* (tweaks, tweaking, tweaked) **1.** TWIST STH QUICKLY to take hold of sth between the finger and thumb and twist it sharply **2.** ADJUST STH SLIGHTLY to make a slight adjustment or change in sth, especially in order to improve it or fix it (*informal*) ○ *tweaked the engine to refine its performance* ■ *n.* **1.** SHARP PINCH a sharp pinch or twist **2.** SLIGHT ADJUSTMENT a slight adjustment or change in sth, especially in order to improve it or fix it (*informal*) [Early 17thC. Origin uncertain: probably a variant of obsolete *twick*, from Old English *twiccian.*] —**tweaky** *adj.*

twee /twee/ adj. dainty or pretty in an overdone and affected way ○ *Those frilly curtains are a bit twee for my taste.* [Early 20thC. Baby-talk alteration of SWEET.] —**tweely** adv. —**tweeness** n.

tweed /tweed/ n. **WOOLLEN CLOTH** a fairly rough, thick woollen fabric used for warm clothing and often made with several different shades of wool to give it a distinctive flecked appearance ■ **tweeds** npl. **CLOTHES MADE OF TWEED** a tweed suit, an outfit, or clothes made of tweed [Mid-19thC. Alteration of *tweel*, a Scottish variant of TWILL, under the influence of the name of the river *Tweed*.]

──── **WORD KEY: ORIGIN** ────

Early accounts date the coinage of **tweed** to 1831, and ascribe it to the London cloth merchant James Locke (although Locke himself in his book *Tweed and Don* (1860) does not make any such claim). The term was in general use by 1850, and it was registered as a trademark.

Tweed /tweed/ river of southern Scotland and north-eastern England, flowing into the North Sea at Berwick-upon-Tweed. Its lower course runs along the Scottish-English border. Length: 160 km/97 mi.

tweedy /tweedi/ (-ier, -iest) adj. 1. **TEXTILES OF TWEED** made of tweed or resembling tweed in appearance or texture 2. **UPPER-CLASS AND COUNTRY-DWELLING** belonging to or showing a liking for the attitudes and outdoor lifestyle traditionally associated with the upper classes, especially activities such as hunting and shooting (*informal*) —**tweediness** n.

'tween /tween/ contr. between (*archaic or literary*) [13thC. Shortening.]

tweet /tweet/ n. **SOUND MADE BY BIRD** a light high-pitched note, especially one sung by a small bird ■ vi. (**tweets, tweeting, tweeted**) **MAKE SOUND OF SMALL BIRD** to make the light high-pitched sound of a small bird [Mid-19thC. An imitation of the sound.]

tweeter /tweetər/ n. a loudspeaker used to reproduce high-frequency sounds, e.g. in a hi-fi system. ◊ **woofer**

tweeze /tweez/ (**tweezes, tweezing, tweezed**) vt. *US* to pull out or manipulate sth using tweezers [Mid-20thC. Back-formation from TWEEZERS.]

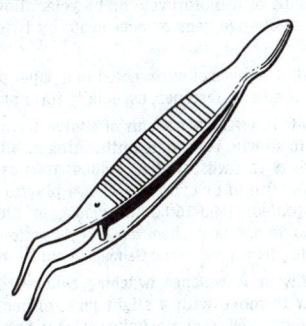

Tweezers

tweezers /tweezərz/ npl. a metal tool consisting of two narrow slightly curved arms joined at one end, typically used for extracting or holding small objects [Mid-17thC. Alteration of obsolete *tweeze* 'tweezer case', from French *étuis*, plural of *étui* (see ÉTUI).]

twelfth /twelfth/ n. one of twelve equal parts of sth [Old English *twelfta*. Ultimately from the prehistoric Germanic base of English *twelve*.] —**twelfth** adj., adv.

Twelfth Day n. = Epiphany

twelfth man (*plural* **twelfth men**) n. a reserve player in a cricket team

Twelfth Night n. 1. **EVENING OF 6 JANUARY** the evening of 6 January or the Christian feast of the Epiphany. This is traditionally the time by which all Christmas decorations should be taken down, and was formerly a night of celebration and feasting. 2. **CALENDAR 5 JANUARY** 5 January, the day before Epiphany in the Christian calendar, or the evening of that day. It was formerly a time of special celebration at the end of the Christmas season.

twelve /twelv/ n. 1. **NUMBER 12** the number 12 2. **STH WITH VALUE OF 12** sth in a numbered series with a value of

twelve 3. **GROUP OF TWELVE** a group of twelve objects or people [Old English *twelf*. Ultimately from a prehistoric Germanic compound meaning literally 'two left', that is 'two left beyond ten'.] —**twelve** adj., pron.

Twelve Apostles, the Twelve n. eleven of the twelve followers originally chosen by Jesus Christ, according to the Bible, together with Matthias who was chosen to replace Judas

twelve-inch n. a record that is 30.5 cm/12 in in diameter and played at 45 rpm, usually containing a single, often extended, track (*informal*)

twelve-mile limit n. an offshore boundary 12 miles from a country's coast, claimed by some countries as marking the territorial limit of their jurisdiction in order to safeguard fishing rights and limit the approach of foreign vessels. ◊ **three-mile limit**

twelvemo /twelvmō/ (*plural* -mos) n. = duodecimo [Early 18thC. Spelling of the abbreviation *12mo*.]

twelvemonth /twelvmunth/ n. a year (*archaic*) [Old English *twelf monaþ*]

twelve-step programme n. a programme for recovery from addiction, based on the methods of Alcoholics Anonymous and involving gradual self-improvement techniques

Twelve Tables n. the earliest code of Roman law on civil, criminal, and religious matters, dating back to 451–450 BC

twelve-tone adj. **MUSIC** relating to or using compositional techniques based on strict sequences of notes selected from the 12 notes of the chromatic scale

twelve-tone row n. **MUSIC** = tone row

twentieth /twenti əth/ n. one of twenty equal parts of sth [Old English *twentigoþa*] —**twentieth** adj., adv.

twentieth man n. *Aus* in Australian Rules football, the second of two substitutes that can be used during a regular match

twenty /twenti/ n. (*plural* -ties) 1. **NUMBER 20** the number 20 2. **GROUP OF 20** a group of twenty objects or people 3. **MONEY £20 NOTE** a banknote worth twenty pounds (*informal*) ■ **twenties** npl. 1. **NUMBERS 20 TO 29** the numbers 20 to 29, particularly as a range of temperature ○ *in the low twenties* 2. **YEARS 1920 TO 1929** the years 1920 to 1929 ○ *in the late twenties* 3. **PERIOD FROM AGE 20 TO 29** the period of sb's life from the age of 20 to 29 ○ *when I was in my twenties* [Old English *twēntig*, ultimately from a prehistoric Germanic compound meaning literally 'twice ten'] —**twentieth** adj., pron.

twenty-first n. sb's 21st birthday, formerly marking the person's legal coming of age

twenty-one n. = pontoon

twenty questions n. a game in which one player imagines an object and others try to work out what it is by asking questions that can be answered only with 'yes' or 'no'

twenty-six counties npl. the counties of the Irish Republic

twenty-twenty, **20/20** adj. used to describe normal vision or eyesight [From the figures denoting normal eyesight at a distance of 20 feet]

.22 n. a gun or rifle that uses a bullet with a diameter of .22 in., typically used for killing small game.

'twere /twur/ contr. it were (*archaic or literary*) [Early 17thC. Contraction.]

twerp /twurp/, **twirp** n. an offensive term used to refer to sb who is seen as silly or insignificant (*informal insult*) [Late 19thC. Origin unknown.]

Twi /twee/ (*plural* **Twi** or **Twis**) n. 1. **PEOPLES MEMBER OF GHANAIAN PEOPLE** a member of a people who live in southern Ghana 2. **LANG TWI LANGUAGE** the language of the Twi people, belonging to the Kwa group of Niger-Congo languages, and now generally recognized as a dialect of Akan [Late 19thC. From Kwa.] —**Twi** adj.

twibill /twibil/ n. 1. **DOUBLE-EDGED TOOL** a large pick (**mattock**) with one blade shaped like an axe and one blade like an adze 2. **DOUBLE-EDGED WEAPON** a double-edged battle-axe, formerly used as a weapon [Old English *twibil*. Formed from *twi-* 'two' (ultimately) + *bill* 'bladed weapon'.]

twice /twīss/ adv. 1. **TWO TIMES** on two occasions, or in two instances 2. **DOUBLE** double in amount or degree [Old English *twige*. Ultimately from an Indo-European word that is also the ancestor of English *twilight*, *twine*, *bis*, and *di-*.]

twice-laid adj. used to describe ropes or cables that are made from previously used rope

twice-told adj. familiar or hackneyed through frequent repetition (*archaic or literary*) ○ *'Life is as tedious as a twice-told tale'* (William Shakespeare, *King John*; 1623)

Twickenham /twikənəm/ residential district in western London, location of a rugby football stadium used for international matches

twiddle /twidd'l/ vti. (-dles, -dling, -dled) 1. **TURN STH BACK AND FORTH** to turn sth round or back and forth repeatedly ○ *twiddling the dial on the radio to get a better reception* 2. **TWIST OR TURN STH ABSENT-MINDEDLY** to keep twisting sth or turning it round in a bored or absent-minded way ○ *sitting at a desk twiddling his pencil and staring out of the window* ■ n. 1. **TWISTING ACTION** a to-and-fro turning or twisting action 2. **LITTLE PIECE OF EXTRA DECORATION** a small extra twist or curve added to sth for ornamentation, e.g. a small flourish on a letter of script, or a musical ornament such as a mordent or trill [Mid-16thC. Origin uncertain: perhaps a blend of TWIST and FIDDLE.] —**twiddler** n. —**twiddly** adj.

twig[1] /twig/ n. 1. **SMALL BRANCH** a small branch or shoot, especially one from a tree or shrub 2. **STRUCTURE RESEMBLING A BRANCH** a structure that resembles a branch, e.g. a minute offshoot of a nerve or blood vessel [Old English *twigge*, literally 'forked branch'. Ultimately from a prehistoric Germanic word.]

twig[2] /twig/ (**twigs, twigging, twigged, twigged**) vti. to understand or realize sth (*informal*) ○ *finally twigged what was going on* [Mid-18thC. Origin uncertain: perhaps from Irish Gaelic *tuigim* 'I understand'.]

twiggy /twiggi/ (-gier, -giest) adj. 1. **COVERED IN TWIGS** covered in twigs rather than branches or leaves ○ *a twiggy shrub* 2. **THIN** very thin or fragile ○ *twiggy legs*

twilight /twī līt/ n. 1. **TIME AFTER SUNSET** the time of day just after sunset or before dawn, when the Sun is below the horizon 2. **HALF-LIGHT** the faint diffuse light that occurs at twilight. It is caused by the light from the Sun being refracted through the Earth's atmosphere. 3. **PERIOD OF OFFICIAL TWILIGHT** the period during which the sun is at a specified angle below the horizon. The angle is 6° for civil twilight, 12° for nautical twilight, and 18° for astronomical twilight. 4. **FINAL PERIOD** the time when sth is declining or approaching its end, especially in a gentle or peaceful way ○ *the twilight of the empire* ■ adj. **OUTSIDE NORMAL SOCIETY** existing or operating beyond the laws and morals of normal society ○ *the twilight world of prostitution* [15thC. Formed from *twi-* 'two, half' (from Old English; ultimately) + LIGHT.]

Twilight of the Gods n. = Götterdämmerung, Ragnarök [Translation of German *Götterdämmerung*]

twilight sleep n. a state of partial consciousness in which awareness of pain is diminished or abolished. It was formerly induced during childbirth by injecting morphine and scopolamine but is no longer part of medical practice. (*dated*)

twilight zone n. 1. **UNCERTAIN STATE** an ambiguous or unsettled state or condition, especially between two opposing conditions 2. **RUN-DOWN AREA** a neglected or run-down area, especially one on the edge of a city or town between the business centre and residential areas 3. **OCEANOG LOWEST PART OF THE SEA WITH LIGHT** the lowest layer of the sea that natural light can reach

──── **WORD KEY: CULTURAL NOTE** ────

The Twilight Zone, a television series (1959–65) created by US writer Rod Serling. These dramatized fictional tales were the first adult television programmes to present paranormal events in a serious and believable way. Staple topics included time travel, accidental journeys, premonitions, and encounters with the dead and with aliens. The series inspired a film, *Twilight Zone – The Movie* (1983), and was revived sporadically from 1985–87, and run in syndication 1987–88. The expression *twilight zone* has long had the meaning 'the lowest layer of the sea's photic zone'. The show, however, popularized another preexisting meaning, 'an ambiguous area, or grey area, between two opposing conditions, such as life and death, good and evil, or real and unreal'.

twilit /twī́lit/ *adj.* lit by twilight or a similar kind of half-light, especially when this creates a feeling of mystery [Mid-19thC. Past participle of TWILIGHT, used as a verb.]

twill /twil/ *n.* **1.** STRONG FABRIC a strong woven material with diagonal ridges or ribs across its surface **2.** TEXTILE WEAVE the weave used to produce twill ■ *vt.* **(twills, twilling, twilled)** WEAVE TWILL to weave fabric with diagonal ridges or ribs across its surface [14thC. From a northern English dialect variant of Old English *twilic*, literally 'having two threads'. Ultimately from a prehistoric Germanic word.]

'twill /twil/ *contr.* it will (*archaic or literary*) [Mid-17thC. Contraction.]

twin /twin/ *n.* **1.** EITHER OF TWO OFFSPRING BORN TOGETHER either of two people or animals born to the same mother at the same time. Fraternal twins arise from different egg cells and are equivalent to ordinary siblings, while identical twins are derived from the same egg cell and are genetically identical. (*often used before a noun*) ○ *twin boys* **2.** ONE OF TWO SIMILAR THINGS sb or sth similar or identical to another, or unusually closely associated with another **3.** TOWN LINKED WITH ANOTHER either of a pair of towns in two different countries with cultural and administrative links (*often used before a noun*) ○ *twin towns* **4.** CHEM COMPOUND CRYSTAL a compound crystal consisting of two mirror-image crystals that share a common plane ■ *adj.* DOUBLE used to describe two identical things that operate together ○ *the streamlined twin hulls of a racing catamaran* ■ *v.* **(twins, twinning, twinned) 1.** *vti.* PAIR PEOPLE OR THINGS to group people or things in pairs, or to link them very closely **2.** *vt.* LINK UP WITH ANOTHER TOWN to create a cultural and administrative link in one town or city with another town or city in a different country **3.** *vi.* HAVE TWINS to give birth to twins [Old English *twinn*. Ultimately from an Indo-European word meaning 'two by two' that is also the ancestor of English *binary*.]

twin bed *n.* either of a pair of matching single beds

twinberry /twínbəri/ (*plural* **-ries**) *n.* **1.** = **partridgeberry 2.** N AMERICAN SHRUB WITH PURPLE FLOWERS a North American shrub of the honeysuckle family with purple flowers. Latin name: *Lonicera involucrata*.

twine /twīn/ *n.* **1.** STRING string or cord made from threads or strands that have been twisted together **2.** STH MADE BY TWISTING sth that is formed by twisting or coiling separate strands together **3.** TWISTING ACTION a twisting or weaving action ■ *v.* **(twines, twining, twined) 1.** *vti.* TWIST AROUND STH to grow, wind, or twist around or together, or make sth grow, wind, or twist around sth else ○ *the ivy twining around the old oak tree* **2.** *vi.* HAVE WINDING COURSE to take or follow a winding route (*literary*) **3.** *vt.* WEAVE STH to make sth by weaving or twisting separate strands together [Old English *twīn* 'double thread'. Ultimately from a prehistoric Germanic base that is also the ancestor of English *twice* and *twist*.] —**twiner** *n.*

twinflower /twín flow ər/ *n.* a creeping semi-woody North American plant of the honeysuckle family with opposite oval leaves and pairs of pinkish-white bell-shaped flowers. Latin name: *Linnaea borealis*.

twinge /twinj/ *n.* **1.** BRIEF PAIN a sudden brief stab of pain **2.** BRIEF UNCOMFORTABLE EMOTION a brief uncomfortable pang of an emotion such as guilt or fear ■ *vti.* **(twinges, twingeing, twinged)** FEEL A TWINGE to feel a twinge, or make sb feel a twinge, either physical or emotional [Old English *twengan* 'to pinch'. Ultimately from prehistoric Germanic.]

twinkle /twíngk'l/ *vi.* **(-kles, -kling, -kled) 1.** SHINE WITH FLICKER to give out or reflect a bright but unsteady light, especially from a small or distant source **2.** SHINE WITH AMUSEMENT to be bright because of a feeling such as amusement, delight, or mischief (*refers to people's eyes*) ■ *n.* **1.** FLICKERING SHINE a bright unsteady light, especially one that is small or seen from a distance **2.** BRIGHTNESS IN SB'S EYES a brightness in sb's eyes, caused by a feeling such as amusement, delight, or mischief **3.** = **twinkling** [Old English *twinclian*, literally 'to keep blinking', from *twincan* 'to blink', ultimately from prehistoric Germanic] —**twinkler** *n.* —**twinkly** *adj.*

twinkling /twíngkling/ *n.* MOMENT an instant of time ■ *adj.* FLICKERING giving out or reflecting light brightly but unsteadily, especially from a small or distant source ◇ **in the twinkling of an eye** very quickly or very soon

twin-lens reflex *n.* a camera that has two forward-facing lenses, one for focusing through and one for taking pictures

twinned /twind/ *adj.* **1.** EXISTING AS MATCHING PAIR linked together as or like a couple **2.** SHARING CULTURAL LINK used to describe towns or cities in different countries that share cultural and administrative links **3.** CRYSTALS SYMMETRICAL used to describe a compound crystal consisting of two mirror-image crystals that share a common plane

Twins /twinz/ *n.* the constellation or zodiac sign Gemini

twin-screw *adj.* used to describe a ship that has two propellers

twinset /twín set/ *n.* a woman's matching short-sleeved jumper and cardigan designed to be worn together

twin town *n.* a town or city that has special cultural and administrative links with another town or city in a different country. Towns that are twinned often display the names of their counterparts on boundary signs.

twin-tub *n.* a washing machine with two separate compartments, one for washing and the other for spin-drying

twirl /twurl/ *v.* **(twirls, twirling, twirled) 1.** *vti.* SPIN ROUND QUICKLY to turn lightly and rapidly round in a circle, or spin sth so that it turns rapidly round and round ○ *twirled his partner around the dance floor* **2.** *vt.* TURN STH ROUND to fiddle with sth by turning or spinning it between the fingers **3.** *vi.* TURN AND FACE OTHER WAY to turn round suddenly to face sb or face the other way ○ *She twirled round, her eyes blazing.* ■ *n.* **1.** QUICK SPINNING MOVEMENT a quick turning or spinning movement, e.g. when sb is dancing or modelling clothes **2.** SPIRAL a twisting or spiral shape, pattern, or line, especially sth used for decoration [Late 16thC. Origin uncertain: probably influenced by *whirl*.] —**twirly** *adj.* —**twirler** *n.*

twirp *n.* = **twerp**

twist /twist/ *v.* **(twists, twisting, twisted) 1.** *vti.* MAKE ENDS TURN IN OPPOSITE DIRECTIONS to make one part or end of sth turn in the opposite direction to the other, or to turn in this way ○ *I twisted my handkerchief into a knot.* **2.** *vti.* DISTORT STH to distort the shape or position of sth, or become distorted ○ *His face was twisted in a grimace of disgust.* **3.** *vti.* WIND STH to wind sth, make sth wind, or wind things together ○ *constantly twisting her hair round her fingers* **4.** *vt.* INJURE PART OF BODY to injure part of the body by turning or moving it out of position ○ *I've twisted my ankle.* **5.** *vti.* ROTATE STH to rotate, or turn sth so that it rotates ○ *The lid just twists and comes off.* **6.** *vt.* DISTORT MEANING to distort the meaning of sth ○ *keeps twisting what I'm saying to make it sound as if I agree* **7.** *vt.* HAVE BAD EFFECT to distort sb's mind or outlook **8.** *vi.* CONSTANTLY CHANGE DIRECTION to change direction constantly instead of continuing in a direct or straight line **9.** *vi.* SQUIRM to squirm or wriggle ○ *a child twisting restlessly in her chair* **10.** *vi.* DANCE to dance the twist **11.** *vt.* CHEAT SB to cheat sb (*informal*) ■ *n.* **1.** TWISTING MOVEMENT the action or movement performed when sb twists sth ○ *a twist of the screw* **2.** STH SHAPED BY BEING TWISTED sth that has been shaped, split, or gathered together by being twisted ○ *a twist of paper* **3.** UNEXPECTED DEVELOPMENT an unexpected development in a narrative or a sequence of events ○ *The story had a strange twist.* **4.** BEND a bend in sth such as a road or river ○ *a road full of twists and turns* **5.** DANCE 1960S DANCE a popular 1960s dance that involved twisting the hips **6.** BEVERAGES SLICE OF LEMON a thin slice of lemon, lime, or some other peel that is cut and twisted and added to a drink **7.** FOOD BREAD OR ROLL a roll or loaf of bread made by twisting pieces of dough **8.** PAINFUL WRENCH a painful wrench or pull in a wrist, ankle, or some other body part **9.** LENGTH OF YARN OR THREAD a length of yarn or thread whose strands have been twisted together **10.** PHYS FORCE a force that causes stress or strain by twisting **11.** SPORTS SPIN GIVEN TO BALL spin imparted to a hit or thrown ball **12.** SPORTS ROTATION OF THE BODY a complete turn of the body around a vertical axis, e.g. in gymnastics or diving **13.** DISTORTION a contortion or distortion in the shape of sth **14.** QUIRK OF CHARACTER an eccentricity or strange personal characteristic **15.** CIGAR OR TOBACCO a cigar made from three cigars twisted together, or chewing tobacco twisted into a roll [Mid-16thC. From Old English, 'sth split in two, twisted yarn'. Ultimately from a prehistoric Germanic base that is also the ancestor of English *twine* and *twice*.] —**twistability** /twìstə bíllәti/ *n.* —**twistable** /twístəb'l/ *adj.* —**twisting** /twísting/ *adj.* —**twistingly** *adv.* —**twisty** *adj.* ◇ **be** *or* **go round the twist** to be or become mentally ill (*slang*)

WORD KEY: CULTURAL NOTE

Oliver Twist, a novel (1837–39) by the English writer Charles Dickens. It tells the tale of an abandoned child who runs away from his workhouse home to London, where he falls in with a band of criminals led by Fagin and his young assistant, a streetwise pickpocket called the Artful Dodger. The novel inspired a musical, *Oliver!* (1960) and several films, most notably David Lean's 1948 adaptation.

twist drill *n.* a drill bit with one or more helical grooves along its axis to expel cuttings or swarf

twisted /twístid/ *adj.* **1.** AFTER TWISTING having undergone twisting ○ *twisted strands of fibre* **2.** DISTORTED IN SHAPE severely distorted in shape or form ○ *The force of the blast reduced the car to a twisted heap of metal.* **3.** BADLY AFFECTED BY EXPERIENCES badly affected by unpleasant experiences or constant disappointment (*informal*) ○ *The experience left her bitter and twisted.* **4.** CORRUPT morally unacceptable ○ *What kind of twisted mind could think up a thing like that?*

twister /twístər/ *n.* **1.** US TORNADO a tornado, cyclone, or whirlwind (*informal*) **2.** SB OR STH THAT TWISTS a person or device that twists **3.** CHEAT sb who cheats or misleads others (*dated informal insult*) **4.** SPORTS BALL WITH TWIST a ball that has been thrown or hit with a twist

twist grip *n.* a control mounted in one of the handlebar grips of a motorcycle or bicycle, allowing the rider to change gear or accelerate by twisting the grip

twist-tie *n.* a piece of wire sealed in a paper or plastic strip, used as a fastener, especially for a plastic bag

twit /twit/ *n.* OFFENSIVE TERM an offensive term used to refer to sb who is seen as unthinking or silly (*slang insult*) ■ *vt.* **(twits, twitting, twitted)** TEASE SB PLAYFULLY to make fun of or criticize sb in a playful friendly way (*dated*) [Mid-16thC. Shortening of Old English *ætwītan* 'to find fault', from *æt-* AT + *wītan* 'to reproach', ultimately from a prehistoric Germanic word.] —**twitter** *n.*

twitch /twich/ *v.* **(twitches, twitching, twitched) 1.** *vi.* JERK SLIGHTLY to move with a slight jerk, either once or repeatedly ○ *His eyebrow twitches when he's nervous.* **2.** *vt.* PULL STH LIGHTLY AND QUICKLY to give sth a sudden light tug or jerk **3.** *vi.* HURT SHARPLY to hurt with a sharp or sudden pain ■ *n.* **1.** JERKY MOVEMENT a very quick jerky movement **2.** PHYSIOL MUSCLE CONTRACTION a brief, rapid contraction of a muscle. ◊ **tic 3.** VET HORSE RESTRAINT a restraint used on a horse during a veterinary procedure, consisting of a cord loop that can be pulled tight around the animal's upper lip [12thC. Origin uncertain: possibly from Low German.]

twitcher /twíchər/ *n.* **1.** SB OR STH THAT TWITCHES sth that twitches or sb who twitches **2.** OBSESSIVE BIRDWATCHER a birdwatcher who will go to excessive lengths to spot rare birds (*informal*)

twitch grass *n.* = **couch grass** [Alteration of *quitch (grass)*]

twitchy /twíchi/ (**-ier, -iest**) *adj.* **1.** NERVOUS nervous and jittery (*informal*) **2.** TWITCHING twitching frequently

twite /twīt/ *n.* a northern European finch with streaked brown plumage, the male of which has a pink rump. Latin name: *Acanthis flavirostris*. [Mid-16thC. An imitation of the bird's call.]

twitter /twíttər/ *v.* **(-ters, -tering, -tered) 1.** *vi.* CHIRP to sing in a succession of light high-pitched chirping sounds (*refers to birds*) **2.** *vi.* CHATTER to chatter or giggle in an overexcited or nervous way **3.** *vti.* USE

SMALL HIGH VOICE to sing or say sth in a light shaky high-pitched voice **4.** *vi.* **TREMBLE** to quiver or move about nervously and quickly ■ *n.* **1. REPETITIVE HIGH-PITCHED SONG** a continuous light string of high sounds made by a small bird or other small animal **2. EXCITEMENT** a state of great agitation or excitement ○ *all of a twitter* [14thC. Originally an imitation of birds chirping.] —**twitterer** *n.* —**twittery** *adj.*

'twixt /twikst/ *prep.* betwixt (*archaic*)

twizzle /twízz'l/ *vt.* (**-zles, -zling, -zled**) **TWIRL STH** to twirl or twist sth vigorously (*informal*) ■ *n.* **TWIRLING MOVEMENT** a vigorous twirl or twist (*informal*) [Late 18thC. Origin uncertain: probably an alteration of TWIST or TWIRL.]

two /too/ (*plural* **twos**) *n.* **1. NUMBER 2** the number 2 **2. STH WITH VALUE OF 2** sth in a numbered series, e.g. a playing card, with a value of 2 ○ *the two of clubs* **3. GROUP OF TWO** a group of two objects or people ○ *arrived in twos and threes* [Old English *twā.* Ultimately from the Indo-European word for 'two'that is also the ancestor of English *dual, dyad,* and *binary.*] —**two** *adj., pron.* ◇ **it takes two to tango** used to indicate that both of the people involved in an awkward or unpleasant situation, not just one, are responsible or to blame ◇ **put two and two together** to work sth out from the available evidence ◇ **that makes two of us** used to indicate agreement with sth expressed, or acknowledgment of sth shared

two-bit *adj. US* **1. CHEAP** of very low quality or importance (*informal*) **2. 25-CENT** costing or worth 25 cents (*archaic*)

two-by-four , 2 x 4 *n.* **1. TIMBER** wood in lengths that are 10 cm wide and 5 cm thick/4 in wide and 2 in thick. It is the standard material for buildings of wood-frame construction. **2. LENGTH OF WOOD** a length of two-by-four

twoc /twok/ , **twock** *vt.* (**twocs, twoccing, twocced; twocks, twocking, twocked**) **STEAL CAR** to steal a car, often only temporarily for the purpose of joyriding (*slang*) ■ *n.* **CAR THEFT** a theft of a car (*slang*) [Late 20thC. An acronym formed from *taken without owner's consent.*] —**twoccer** *n.*

two cents worth *n. US* an opinion, when expressed assertively as one of many ○ *just had to add her two cents worth*

twock /twok/ *vt., n.* = **twoc** (*slang*)

two-cycle *adj. US* = **two-stroke**

two-dimensional *adj.* **1. MATH HAVING TWO DIMENSIONS** used to describe a figure that has length and width but no depth, e.g. a geometric figure on a single plane **2. ARTS DONE ON A FLAT SURFACE** used to describe works of art such as paintings and drawings that exist on a flat surface, as opposed to art forms such as sculpture that also have depth **3. HAVING NO DEPTH OF CHARACTER** lacking the emotional or psychological depth that creates the impression of realism ○ *a two-dimensional character* —**two-dimensionality** *n.* —**two-dimensionally** *adv.*

two-edged *adj.* **1. CUTTING TWO WAYS** having two sharp edges for cutting in opposite directions **2. WORKING TWO WAYS** having two effects, one positive and one negative, especially two possible and opposite interpretations or meanings

two-faced *adj.* **1. HYPOCRITICAL** insincere in dealings with people, especially by being outwardly friendly but secretly disloyal **2. HAVING TWO FACES** having two faces or surfaces —**two-facedly** *adv.* —**two-facedness** *n.*

twofer /tóofər/ *n. US* an offer of two items for the price of one, or a coupon giving entitlement to such a discount (*informal*) [Late 19thC. Alteration of *two for (one).*]

twofold /tóofōld/ *adj.* **1. HAVING TWO ELEMENTS** consisting of two parts or elements **2. DOUBLE** twice as much or as many ■ *adv.* **DOUBLY** by the same amount over again

2,4-D *n.* a white crystalline compound used as a weedkiller. Formula: $C_8H_6Cl_2O_3$. [Mid-20thC. *D* from DI-.]

2,4,5-T *n.* a chemical weedkiller and plant hormone in a solid, crystalline, insoluble form. Formula: $C_8H_5Cl_3O_3$. [Mid-20thC. *T* from TRI-.]

two-four time *n.* a rhythm with two crotchet beats to the bar

two-handed *adj.* **1. USING TWO HANDS** using, or requiring the use of, two hands **2. DESIGNED FOR TWO** designed for two people, especially for two players or operators **3. AMBIDEXTROUS** able to use either the left or right hand with equal skill —**two-handedly** *adv.* —**two-handedness** *n.*

two-hander *n.* a play written for and performed by two actors

two-master *n.* a sailing ship with two masts

two-pack *n.* a set of two identical products packaged together and sold as one

twopence /túppəns/ , **tuppence** *n.* **1. SUM OF TWO PENCE** the value of two pence, especially two pennies in the predecimal British monetary system **2. ANYTHING AT ALL** the least amount (*used in negative sentences*) ○ *I don't care twopence what they think.*

twopenny /túppəni/ , **tuppenny** *adj.* **1. COSTING TWOPENCE** costing or worth twopence **2. CHEAP** cheap and of the poorest quality

two-phase *adj.* used to describe an electrical system in which there are two alternating voltages of the same frequency, with a phase difference of 90° between them

two-piece *adj.* **BEING IN TWO PARTS** consisting of two parts or pieces, especially pieces of clothing ■ *n.* **CLOTHES SUIT IN TWO PARTS** a suit consisting of two garments such as a bikini

two-ply *adj.* consisting of two layers or strands

two-pot screamer *n. Aus* sb who becomes drunk very easily (*informal*) [Late 20thC. *Pot* in the Australian sense of 'glass of beer', from the idea of having an extreme reaction to a small amount of alcohol.]

two-seater *n.* **1. AUTOMOT VEHICLE WITH TWO SEATS** a vehicle with seats for two people, especially a sports car **2. FURNITURE SEAT FOR TWO** a seat for two people, especially a sofa

two-shot *n.* a film or television shot in which two people more or less fill the screen

two-sided *adj.* **1. HAVING TWO SURFACES** having two sides or surfaces **2. USING TWO SIDES** using both sides of a page **3. HAVING TWO CONTESTING SIDES** consisting of two contesting sides, e.g. two groups opposing each other, or two equally valid opinions

twosome /tóossəm/ *n.* **1. PAIR** a pair of people, especially two golfers paired to play together, a couple on a date together, or a team consisting of two players **2. GOLF** = **single** *n.* 6

two-spot *n.* **1. GAME PIECE** a game piece such as a playing card or a domino with two marks on it **2. US MONEY TWO-DOLLAR BILL** a two-dollar bill (*informal*)

two-step *n.* **1. DANCE BALLROOM DANCE** a ballroom dance in two-four time with sliding steps **2. MUSIC DANCE MUSIC** a piece of music written for the two-step ■ *vi.* (**two-steps, two-stepping, two-stepped**) **DANCE DANCE TWO-STEP** to dance the two-step

two-stroke *adj.* used to describe an internal-combustion engine in which the piston makes two movements, usually one upwards and one downwards, in each power cycle. US term **two-cycle**

two-tailed pasha *n.* a southern European butterfly that has brownish wings with an orange border. Latin name: *Charaxes jasius.*

two-tier *adj.* having two levels, especially two levels of administration or two standards of treatment or privilege

two-time (**two-times, two-timing, two-timed**) *vt.* (*informal*) **1. BE UNFAITHFUL TO SB** to be unfaithful to a romantic or sexual partner **2. DOUBLE-CROSS SB** to deceive or betray a partner in an undertaking —**two-timer** *n.*

two-toed sloth *n.* a mainly nocturnal Central and South American sloth with two digits on either forefoot. Latin name: *Choloepus didactylus.*

two-tone *adj.* **1. COLOURS HAVING TWO COLOURS** consisting of two colours or two shades of the same colour ○ *toe-tone shoes* **2. ACOUSTICS CONSISTING OF TWO SOUNDS** consisting of two sounds with different frequencies ○ *a two-tone siren*

'twould /twood/ *contr.* it would (*archaic or literary*)

two-up *n. Aus* an Australian gambling game in which bets are placed on how two tossed coins will land

two-way *adj.* **1. MOVING IN BOTH DIRECTIONS** moving in opposite directions or allowing for movement in opposite directions **2. SPORTS INVOLVING TWO CONTESTANTS** involving two people or teams ○ *a two-way race* **3. RADIO ABLE TO TRANSMIT AND RECEIVE** able both to transmit and receive radio signals ○ *two-way radio* **4. RECIPROCAL** requiring cooperation between two people or groups

two-way mirror *n.* a sheet of glass that is a mirror on one side and can be seen through from the other. Such mirrors are installed, e.g. in police stations to allow witnesses to identify suspects without themselves being seen. US term **one-way mirror**

two-wheeler *n.* a vehicle with two wheels, especially a bicycle

twyer /twí ər/ *n.* = **tuyère**

TX *abbr.* Texas

Tycho /tíkō/ *n.* a crater on the south of the Moon that is the centre of the Moon's most extensive ray system. It is 84 km/52 mi. in diameter, 4500 m/14,750 ft high, and is surrounded by terraced walls.

tycoon /tī koon/ *n.* **1. SB POWERFUL** sb who has amassed great wealth and power, especially in business **2. SHOGUN** a shogun (*archaic*) [Mid-19thC. From Japanese *taikun* 'great lord, shogun', from Chinese *dà* 'great' + *jūn* 'prince'.]

tyiyn /ti yeén/ (*plural* **-iyn** or **-iyns**) *n.* **1. SUBUNIT OF KYRGYZ CURRENCY** a subunit of currency in Kyrgyzstan, 100 of which are worth one som. See table at **currency** **2. COIN WORTH ONE TYIYN** a coin worth one tyiyn

tyke /tike/ , **tike** *n.* **1. NAUGHTY CHILD** a little child, especially one who is naughty or mischievous (*informal*) **2. MONGREL** a dog of mixed breed **3. BOOR** a man with coarse manners (*dated informal*) **4. YORKSHIREMAN** a Yorkshireman (*regional slang*) [14thC. From Old Norse *tík* 'bitch'.]

tylectomy /tī léktəmi/ (*plural* **-mies**) *n.* = **lumpectomy** [Late 20thC. Coined from Greek *tulos* 'lump' + -ECTOMY.]

Tyler /tílər/ , **Anne** (*b.* 1941) US writer. Her novels include *Dinner at the Homesick Restaurant* (1982) and *The Accidental Tourist* (1985).

John Tyler

Tyler, John (1790–1862) US statesman and 10th president of the United States. He was William Henry Taft's vice president, and set a controversial historical precedent by assuming the presidency after Taft's death. As president (1841–45), his greatest achievement was the annexation of Texas (1844).

Tyler, Wat (*d.* 1381) English revolutionary leader. The leader of the Peasants' Revolt of 1381, he secured concessions from Richard II but was killed during negotiations.

tylosis[1] /tī lōssiss/ , **tylose** /tílōs/ (*plural* **tyloses** /-seez/) *n.* a sac that grows into the water-conducting vessels of the older wood of a tree, often formed in response to drought or disease. Tyloses may cause blockage, and often fill with resins, gums, or pigments that may help to preserve, strengthen, or colour the wood, or provide a source of dyes. [Late 19thC. Formed from Greek *tulos* 'lump'.]

---

zh vision   In foreign words: kh German Bach; aN French vin; aaN French blanc; ö German schön, French feu; oN French bon; öN French un; ü French rue   Stress marks: ´ as in secret \séek rət\; academic \ákə demmik\

tylosis² /tī lṓssis/ *n.* a callus or thickening, especially of the eyelids [Late 19thC. Via modern Latin from Greek *tulōsis* 'formation of a callus', from *tulē* 'callus'.]

tymbal *n.* = timbal

tympan /tímpən/ *n.* **1.** PRINTING PART OF PRINTING PRESS a padding device that fits between the impression cylinder of a printing press and the paper to be printed so as to ensure a uniform image **2.** ARCHIT = **tympanum** *n.* **1 3.** ACOUSTICS VIBRATING MEMBRANE a membrane or diaphragm that vibrates to produce or transmit sound, e.g. the skin on a drum or the diaphragm in a telephone receiver [Pre-12thC. From Latin *tympanum* 'drum' (see TYMPANUM).]

tympani = timpani

tympanic /tim pánnik/ *adj.* relating to a tympanum

tympanic membrane *n.* the eardrum (*technical*)

tympanites /tímpə nī́ teez/ *n.* swelling of the abdominal wall caused by gas trapped in the intestines or peritoneal cavity [14thC. Via late Latin from Greek *tumpanitēs*, from *tumpanon* 'drum' (see TYMPANUM).] — **tympanitic** /tímpə níttik/ *adj.*

tympanitis /tímpə nī́tis/ *n.* inflammation of the eardrum [Mid-19thC. Formed from TYMPANUM.]

tympanoplasty /tímpə nō plasti/ (*plural* **-ties**) *n.* the surgical repair or reconstruction of the eardrum, usually in order to close a perforation [Mid-20thC. Formed from TYMPANUM.]

Tympanum

tympanum /tímpənəm/ (*plural* **-nums** *or* **-na** /-nə/) *n.* **1.** ARCHIT RECESSED SPACE a recess, especially the recessed space between the top of a door or window and the arch above it, or between the cornices forming a classical triangular gable (**pediment**) **2.** ANAT **EAR PART** the eardrum or the cavity of the middle ear (*technical*) **3.** INSECTS **INSECT ORGAN** a vibrating membrane in some insects that serves as a hearing organ **4.** = **tympan** *n.* 3 [Early 16thC. Via Latin from Greek *tumpanon* 'drum'. Ultimately from an Indo-European word denoting 'sth struck' that is also the ancestor of English *type*.]

tympany /tímpəni/ *n.* = **tympanites** [Early 16thC. From Greek *tumpanias*, from *tumpanon* (see TYMPANUM).]

Tyndale /tínd'l/, **Tindal, William** (1492?–1536) English religious reformer. His translation of the Bible into English laid the foundations of the Authorized Version (1611), but he was condemned for heresy and murdered by the Church authorities.

Tyndall effect /tínd'l-/ *n.* the scattering of light by minute particles in its path, such as dust in the air [Early 20thC. Named after John *Tyndall* (1820–93), a British physicist who described the phenomenon.]

tyndallimetry /tínd'l ímmətri/ *n.* the measurement of the concentration of particles suspended in a liquid by gauging the amount of light scattered by them [Formed from TYNDALL EFFECT.]

Tyne /tín/ river in northeastern England, formed by the union of the North Tyne and South Tyne rivers. It flows through Newcastle upon Tyne shortly before reaching the North Sea. Length: 48 km/30 mi.

Tynemouth /tín mowth, tínməth/ town at the mouth of the River Tyne, northeastern England. Population: 17,422 (1991).

Tyneside /tín sīd/ industrial and shipbuilding region along both banks of the lower River Tyne, northeastern England

typ. *abbr.* **1.** typographer **2.** typographic **3.** typographical **4.** typography

typal /típ'l/ *adj.* relating to a type or types

type /tīp/ *n.* **1.** KIND OR SORT a category of things or people whose members share some qualities **2.** PERSON OR THING sb or sth regarded as belonging to a group or category by virtue of having the main qualities associated with it ○ *the paraffin type of burner* **3.** KIND OF PERSON a person regarded as having the stated characteristics or temperament (*informal*) ○ *a gathering of sporty types* **4.** SB WHO APPEALS sb with the qualities that appeal to sb else (*informal*) ○ *He's really not my type.* **5.** TEMPLATE sth used as a pattern or template for making other things of the same kind **6.** PRINTING PRINTING BLOCK a small metal block with, on one of its sides, a raised figure that is the mirror image of a number or letter, used with others for printing **7.** PRINTING SET OF PRINTING BLOCKS printing blocks collectively **8.** PRINTING PRINTED LETTERS printed words, letters, or symbols on a page **9.** BIOL REPRESENTATIVE GENUS OR SPECIES a genus or species of plant or animal whose characteristics best represent the next higher category of taxonomic classification **10.** BIOL REPRESENTATIVE ORGANISM a plant or animal that represents its genus by having the main qualities that define it **11.** LING LINGUISTIC UNIT a letter, word, or other linguistic unit regarded as representing all units that are forms of it, as distinct from an individual form (**token**) **12.** PHILOS GENERAL EXPRESSION an expression regarded not as a physical object but as an abstract pattern that individual expressions can conform to **13.** CHR SIGN OF STH TO COME an event, figure, or sign taken as foreshadowing sth in the future ■ *v.* (**types, typing, typed**) **1.** *vti.* KEY WORDS ON KEYBOARD to key words using a computer keyboard, word processor, or typewriter **2.** *vt.* CLASSIFY STH to classify sth, especially blood, according to its type **3.** *vt.* TYPECAST SB to characterize sb as being a person who plays a particular kind of role **4.** *vt.* CHR FORESHADOW STH to foreshadow a future event or fact [15thC. Via Latin from Greek *tupos* 'blow, impression'. Ultimately from an Indo-European base meaning 'to strike'. The sense 'form, kind' evolved from 'impression made by striking'.]

— **WORD KEY: USAGE** —

See Usage note at *kind*.

— **WORD KEY: SYNONYMS** —

type, kind, sort, category, class, species, genre
CORE MEANING: a group having a common quality or qualities

type a group of people or things with strongly marked and readily defined similarities; **kind** a general word for a group of people or things that has been loosely defined according to their similarities; **sort** a general word used in the same way as *kind*; **category** a deliberately defined group, usually used to help sort or classify a larger group; **class** used in the same way as *category*; **species** used in the classification of living things to describe a specific group of animals, plants, insects, or other organisms; **genre** a formal word for a particular type of painting, writing, dance, or other art form.

type A *n.* a type of person who is anxious and hard-working, who has a strong drive to succeed, who over-works, and finds it hard to delegate or share tasks with colleagues

type B *n.* a personality type inclined toward patience and friendliness

typebar /típ baar/ *n.* a lever operated by a typewriter key. Each lever has one or more printing blocks on the end that print characters on the paper.

typecase /típ kayss/ *n.* a tray or box for storing printer's type

typecast /típ kaast/ (**typecasts, typecasting, typecast**) *vt.* **1.** CAST SB REPEATEDLY IN SIMILAR ROLES to give an actor a series of parts of the same type, to the extent that the performer becomes associated with that kind of role and is overlooked for others **2.** CAST ACTOR SUITABLY to give an actor a part that suits his or her physical or emotional type — **typecaster** *n.*

typeface /típ fayss/ *n.* **1.** STYLE OF PRINTED CHARACTERS a particular style of printed character such as Helvetica or bold **2.** PRINTING BLOCK SURFACE the side of a printing block that has the shape of the printed character on it

type founder *n.* a manufacturer of metal printing type — **type foundry** *n.*

type genus *n.* the genus of a family or other higher taxonomic category that is most typical of it and usually bears the same name

type-high *adj.* as high as the standard height of a block of printer's type, 23.3 mm/0.9186 in

type I error *n.* in statistics, the error of rejection of a null hypothesis when it is true

type II error *n.* in statistics, the failure to reject a false null hypothesis

type locality *n.* a place where a rock formation or other geological feature was first found and described, and after which it is named

type metal *n.* the alloy from which printing type is made, consisting mostly of lead, antimony, and tin

typescript /típ skript/ *n.* a typewritten document or other text [Late 19thC. Formed from TYPE + MANUSCRIPT.]

typeset /típ set/ (**typesets, typesetting, typeset**) *vt.* to prepare text for printing, either by the use of computers or by arranging blocks of type manually

typesetter /típ setər/ *n.* **1.** PRINTER sb who prepares text for printing **2.** TYPESETTING MACHINE a mechanical or electronic device that prepares text for printing

type-site *n.* an archaeological site that is thought to typify a culture and that gives the culture its name

type species *n.* a species of plant or animal that is most typical of its genus and bears the same name or a related name

type specimen *n.* an individual plant or animal that serves as the basis for the description of its species. Its name is usually taken as the name of the species.

type style *n.* = **typeface** *n.* 1

typewrite /típ rīt/ (**typewrites, typewriting, typewrote** /-rōt/, **typewritten** /-rit'n/) *vti.* to type (*dated*) [Late 19thC. Back-formation from TYPEWRITER.]

Typewriter

typewriter /típ rītər/ *n.* **1.** WRITING MACHINE an electrical or mechanical device for printing words on individual sheets of paper **2.** TYPEFACE a printing typeface that looks like characters produced by a typewriter

typhlitis /ti flítisz/ *n.* inflammation of the entrance to the large intestine (**caecum**) [Mid-19thC. Formed from Greek *tuphlon* 'caecum', from *tuphlos* 'sightless'.] — **typhlitic** /ti flíttik/ *adj.*

typhlology /ti flólləji/ *n.* the scientific study of sightlessness [Late 19thC. Formed from Greek *tuphlos* 'blind'.]

Typhoeus /tī fée əss/ *n.* in Greek mythology, a monster with a hundred dragon heads who fought with Zeus and was thrown down into the ground under Mount Etna — **Typhoean** *adj.*

typhoid /tí foyd/ *n.* INFECTIOUS DISEASE OF DIGESTIVE SYSTEM a serious and sometimes fatal bacterial infection of the digestive system, caused by ingesting food or water contaminated with the bacillus *Salmonella typhi*. It causes fever, severe abdominal pain, and sometimes intestinal bleeding. ■ *adj.* OF TYPHOID OR TYPHUS relating to typhoid or typhus — **typhoidal** /tī fóyd'l/ *adj.*

typhoid fever *n.* = **typhoid**

Typhoid Mary /tī́ fóyd máirri/ *n.* **1.** OFFENSIVE TERM an offensive term used to refer to sb who spreads a disease or is held to be responsible for spreading it (*insult*) **2.** OFFENSIVE TERM an offensive term used to refer to sb who spreads sth undesirable such as pessimism or bad news, and is generally avoided (*informal*) [Early 20thC. Nickname of *Mary* Mallon (died 1938), an Irish-born cook in the US who was found to be a typhoid carrier.]

typhoon /tī foón/ *n.* a violent tropical storm in the western Pacific and Indian oceans. ◊ **hurricane** [Late 16thC. Partly from Chinese (Cantonese) *toi fung*, literally 'big wind', and partly via Portuguese *tufão*, Urdu *ṭūfān*, and Arabic from Greek *tuphōn*.] —**typhonic** /tī fónnik/ *adj.*

typhus /tī́fəss/, **typhus fever** *n.* an infectious disease that causes fever, severe headaches, a rash, and often delirium. It is spread by ticks and fleas carried by rodents. [Late 18thC. From Greek *tuphos* 'smoke, stupor', from *tuphein* 'to smoke'. Ultimately from an Indo-European base that is also the ancestor of English *fume*, *dizzy*, and *deaf*.] —**typhous** *adj.*

typical /típpik'l/ *adj.* **1.** REPRESENTATIVE having all or most of the characteristics shared by others of a type and therefore suitable as an example of the type **2.** CONFORMING TO EXPECTATION conforming to what is expected **3.** BIOL RESEMBLING OTHERS IN TAXONOMIC GROUP used to describe an organism, species, or genus that has most of the characteristics that identify the larger taxonomic group to which it belongs [Early 17thC. Via French from, ultimately, Greek *tupikos*, from *tupos* (see TYPE).] —**typicality** /típpi kálləti/ *n.* —**typicalness** *n.*

typically /típpikli/ *adv.* **1.** IN THE USUAL WAY with all or many of the usual or expected characteristics **2.** IN MOST CASES in most cases or on most occasions **3.** PREDICTABLY as is to be expected ○ *not her typically cheerful self today*

typify /típpi fī/ (**typifies, typifying, typified**) *vt.* **1.** BE TYPICAL OF STH to have all or most of the characteristics of others of a type and therefore be a suitable example of the type **2.** EPITOMIZE STH to be a typical representation of sth [Mid-17thC. Formed from Latin *typus* (see TYPE).] —**typification** /típpifi káysh'n/ *n.* —**typifier** /típpi fīər/ *n.*

typist /tī́pist/ *n.* sb who uses a typewriter, especially sb whose job is producing documents using a typewriter or word processor

typo /tī́pō/ (*plural* -**pos**) *n.* a typographical error (*informal*) [Early 19thC. Shortening.]

typo., **typog.** *abbr.* **1.** typographer **2.** typographic **3.** typographical **4.** typography

typographer /tī póggrəfər/ *n.* a person or business engaged in preparing text for printing

typographical /tī́pə gráffik'l/, **typographic** /tī́pə gráffik/ *adj.* **1.** OF TEXT PREPARATION relating to the activity of preparing texts for printing **2.** OF PRINTED CHARACTERS relating to the appearance of printed characters on the page

typographical error *n.* a printing error such as a misspelled word that results from striking the wrong key or keys on a keyboard

typography /tī póggrəfi/ *n.* **1.** PREPARATION OF TEXTS the activity or business of preparing texts for printing **2.** LOOK OF PRINTED MATTER the appearance of printed characters on the page [Early 17thC. Via French from modern Latin *typographia*, from Greek *tupos* (see TYPE) + -*graphia* (see -GRAPHY).]

typology /tī póləji/ *n.* **1.** CLASSIFICATION OF TYPES the study or systematic classification of types **2.** LING LANGUAGE STUDY the study of syntactic and morphological similarities in languages without regard to their history **3.** CHR STUDY OF RELIGIOUS TEXTS the study of religious texts for the purpose of identifying episodes in them that appear to prophesy later events [Mid-19thC. Coined from Greek *typos* (see TYPE) + -LOGY.] —**typologic** /tī́pə lójjik/ *adj.* —**typological** /-lójji-k'l/ *adj.* —**typologically** /-lójjikli/ *adv.* —**typologist** /tī póləjist/ *n.*

typw. *abbr.* **1.** typewriter **2.** typewritten

tyramine /tī́rəmin/ *n.* an amine found in cheese, rotting meat, and mistletoe that results from the breakdown of the amino acid tyrosine, and has the effect of simulating sympathetic nervous system action. Formula: $C_8H_{11}NO$. [Early 20thC. Blend of TYROSINE and AMINE.]

tyrannical /ti ránnik'l/, **tyrannic** /ti ránnik/ *adj.* **1.** POL RULING UNJUSTLY ruling with absolute power over a population cruelly kept submissive and fearful **2.** AUTHORITARIAN cruelly or irrationally insisting on complete obedience and giving harsh punishment to those who disobey [Mid-16thC. Via French *tyrannique* from, ultimately, Greek *turannikos*, from *turannos* (see TYRANT).] —**tyrannically** *adv.* —**tyrannicalness** *n.*

tyrannicide /ti ránni sīd/ *n.* **1.** ASSASSINATION OF TYRANT the killing of a tyrant **2.** ASSASSIN OF TYRANT the killer of a tyrant [Mid-17thC. From Latin *tyrannicidium* 'tyrant-killing' and Latin *tyrannicida* 'tyrant-killer', both from *tyrannus* (see TYRANT) + *caedere* 'to kill' (see -CIDE).] —**tyrannicidal** *adj.*

tyrannize (-**nizes, -nizing, -nized**), **tyrannise** (-**nises, -nising, -nised**) *vti.* **1.** POL GOVERN CRUELLY to govern with extreme cruelty and harshness **2.** TREAT HARSHLY to treat sb in a cruelly unfair way [15thC. Via French *tyranniser* from Old French *tyrant* (see TYRANT).] —**tyrannizer** *n.*

tyrannosaur /ti ránnə sawr/, **tyrannosaurus** /-əss/, **tyrannosaurus rex** /-réks/ *n.* a large fierce flesh-eating dinosaur that walked on powerful hind legs and had small front legs. It lived during the Jurassic and Cretaceous Periods and was the largest carnivore. [Early 20thC. From modern Latin *Tyrannosaurus*, genus name, from Greek *turannos* (see TYRANT) + *sauros* (see -SAUR).]

tyrannous /tírrənəss/ *adj.* **1.** POL RULING CRUELLY ruling cruelly and with absolute power **2.** TREATING OTHERS CRUELLY cruelly demanding complete obedience and punishing disobedience severely

tyranny /tírrəni/ (*plural* **tyrannies**) *n.* **1.** CRUEL USE OF POWER cruelty and injustice in the exercising of power or authority over others **2.** POL OPPRESSIVE GOVERNMENT oppressive government by one or more people who exercise absolute power cruelly and unjustly **3.** POL STATE RULED BY TYRANT a country or state under the power of an oppressive ruler **4.** CRUEL ACT an act of cruelty committed by sb with great power **5.** OPPRESSIVE FORCE a harsh or oppressive force [14thC. Via French from, ultimately, Greek *turannos* (see TYRANT).]

— **WORD KEY: CULTURAL NOTE** —
The Tyranny of Distance, a book by Australian writer Geoffrey Blainey (1966). A historical account of the way in which distance both within Australia and between Australia and the United Kingdom influenced the formation of the nation. The phrase is now part of the Australian English language.

tyrant /tī́rənt/ *n.* **1.** POL ABSOLUTE RULER an absolute ruler who exercises power cruelly and unjustly **2.** AUTHORITARIAN PERSON sb who exercises authority unjustly and oppressively **3.** STH THAT OPPRESSES sth that oppresses harshly or cruelly **4.** HIST ANCIENT GREEK RULER in ancient Greece, a ruler who took control of a state without legal sanction and governed with absolute power [13thC. Via Old French and Latin from Greek *turannos*, of uncertain origin; perhaps from Phrygian or Lydian.]

tyrant flycatcher *n.* BIRDS = **flycatcher** *n.* 2 [Translation of modern Latin *Tyrannidae*, family name]

tyre /tīr/ *n.* **1.** HOLLOW RUBBER EDGING a circular hollow band of rubber fitted around the edge of a vehicle's wheel to ease movement and help absorb bumps in road surfaces. It is filled with compressed air. **2.** SOLID RUBBER EDGING a circular solid band of rubber fitted to a wheel's edge, e.g. on prams and children's bicycles **3.** METAL EDGING a band of metal fitted for reinforcement to the rims of wheels on various vehicles, e.g. handcarts and railway carriages

Tyre /tīr/ town in southern Lebanon, on the Mediterranean Sea. It was the most important city of ancient Phoenicia. Population: 14,000 (1988).

Tyree, Mount /tī rée/ peak in the Ellsworth Mountains, the second highest mountain in Antarctica, first climbed in 1966. Height: 4,965 m/16,290 ft.

Tyrian /tírri ən/ *adj.* relating to the ancient Mediterranean port of Tyre, or its people or culture [Early 16thC. Coined from Latin *Tyrius*, from *Tyre*, an ancient Phoenician city, + -AN.]

Tyrian purple *n.* **1.** DEEP PURPLE DYE a deep purple dye extracted from molluscs **2.** COLOURS RICH PURPLE COLOUR a deep rich purple colour tinged with crimson ■ *adj.* COLOURS RICH PURPLE of a deep rich purple colour tinged with crimson [Named after the city of TYRE, where the dye was made]

tyro /tī́rō, tiro/ (*plural* -**ros** /tiros/) *n.* sb who is beginning to learn sth [Early 17thC. Via medieval Latin, 'squire', from Latin *tiro* 'young soldier, recruit', of unknown origin.] —**tyronic** /tī rónnik/ *adj.*

— **WORD KEY: SYNONYMS** —
See Synonyms at *beginner*.

tyrocidine /tī́rō sī́deen/, **tyrocidin** /tī́rō sī́din/ *n.* an antibiotic polypeptide extracted from a soil bacillus that is the main constituent of the antibiotic drug tyrothricin [Mid-20thC. Contraction of TYROTHRICIN + GRAMICIDIN + -INE.]

Tyrol /tirṓl/ province in western Austria, lying within the Alps. Capital: Innsbruck. Population: 660,000 (1996). Area: 12,648 sq. km/4,883 sq. mi. —**Tyrolean** *n.*, *adj.* —**Tyrolese** *n.*, *adj.*

Tyrolienne /ti rṓli én/ *n.* **1.** DANCE FOLK DANCE a lively folk dance that originated in the Tyrol **2.** MUSIC DANCE MUSIC a piece of music composed for a Tyrolienne, typically with yodelling [Late 19thC. From French *tyrolienne*, feminine of *tyrolien* 'Tyrolean'.]

tyropitta /ti róppitə/ *n.* a Greek cheese pie [Late 20thC. From modern Greek *turopēta* 'cheese pie'.]

tyrosinase /tī róssə nayz/ *n.* a copper-containing enzyme that is important in the production of the skin pigment melanin. The absence of the enzyme results in albinism. [Late 19thC. Formed from TYROSINE.]

Tyrosine

tyrosine /tī́rō seen/ *n.* an amino acid that is the precursor of epinephrine, thyroxine, and other hormones and of melanin. Formula: $C_9H_{11}NO_3$. [Mid-19thC. Formed from Greek *turos* 'cheese' (source of English *butter*). Ultimately from an Indo-European word meaning 'to swell' that is also the ancestor of *tumour* and *tuber*.]

tyrothricin /tī́rō thríssin/ *n.* an antibiotic drug made from tyrocidine and gramicidin that is effective against gram-positive bacteria in local infections [Mid-20thC. Formed from modern Latin *Tyrothric-*, the stem of *Tyrothrix*, former genus name of a gram-positive bacterium, from Greek *turos* 'cheese' + *thrix* 'hair'.]

Tyrrhenian Sea /ti reéni ən-/ arm of the Mediterranean Sea, partially enclosed by the Italian Peninsula and the islands of Corsica, Sardinia, and Sicily. Area: 155,000 sq. km/60,000 sq. mi.

Tyson /tī́ss'n/, **Mike** (b. 1966) US boxer. He is the youngest heavyweight fighter to win a world title (1986). Real name **Michael Gerald Tyson**

tzaddik /tsaʹdik/ (*plural* -**dikim** /tsaʹdi keém/), **tsaddik** (*plural* -**dikim**), **zaddik** (*plural* -**dikim**) *n.* **1.** RIGHTEOUS MAN in Judaism, a righteous man **2.** = **rebbe** [Late 19thC. From Hebrew *ṣaddīq* 'righteous'.]

tzar /zaar, tsaar/ *n.* = **tsar**

tzatziki /sat seéki, tsat/ *n.* a dip of Greek origin made from yogurt, chopped cucumber, mint, and garlic [Mid-20thC. Via modern Greek *tsatsiki* from Turkish *cacik*.]

tzetze fly *n.* = tsetse fly

tzigane /tsi gaán, si/ *n.* PEOPLES a member of a Romany people, especially one from Hungary [Mid-18thC. Via French from Hungarian *czigany*.] —**tzigane** *adj.*

tzimmes /tsímməss/ (*plural* -mes), **tsimmes** (*plural* -mes) *n.* **1.** CASSEROLE a stew of meat, vegetables, and dried fruits, baked in a casserole **2.** *US* CONFUSION a confused, muddled, or agitated state (*slang*) [Late 19thC. From Yiddish *tsimes*, of uncertain origin: perhaps from Middle High German *ze* 'to, as' + *imbiz* 'light meal'.]

tzitzith /tsítsiss/, **tzitzit, tzitzes, tsitses** *n.* the fringes on the corners of a Jewish prayer shawl (**tallis**) to remind Jews of God's commandments (Num. 15:38). [Late 17thC. From Hebrew *ṣīṣīt*.]

tzuris *n.* = tsuris

u /yoo/ (*plural* **u's**), **U** (*plural* **U's** *or* **Us**) *n.* **1.** 21ST LETTER OF ENGLISH ALPHABET the 21st letter of the modern English alphabet **2.** PHON SPEECH SOUND CORRESPONDING TO LETTER 'U' any of the speech sounds that correspond to the letter 'U' **3.** LETTER 'U' WRITTEN a written representation of the letter 'U' **4.** SHAPE LIKE 'U' the shape of the letter 'U'

U[1] *pron.* a written form of 'you' (*informal*) [Because the letter *U* and *you* are pronounced the same]

U[2] *symbol.* **1.** CHEM ELEM uranium **2.** potential difference **3.** PHYS internal energy **4.** U, Ⓤ kosher certification

U[3] *abbr.* **1.** EDUC unsatisfactory **2.** U, U. university **3.** U, U. united ■ **4.** a British film classification for films that can be seen by everybody, regardless of age. Abbr of **universal 5.** typical of the upper class. Abbr of **upper-class, upper class** ■ *abbr.* **6.** you (*informal*)

U[4] /oo/ *n.* a title of respect for a man used in Myanmar (Burma), equivalent to 'Mr' [Mid-20thC. From Burmese.]

u., U. *abbr.* **1.** upper **2.** unit **3.** uncle

UAE *abbr.* United Arab Emirates

uakari /wə káari/ (*plural* **-ri**) *n.* a South American short-tailed monkey that lives high in the forest canopy, seldom coming down onto the ground. Genus: *Cacajao.* [Mid-19thC. From Tupi.]

UAM *abbr.* underwater-to-air missile

UART /yoó aart/ *abbr.* COMPUT universal asynchronous receiver/transmitter

Ubangi /yoo báng gi/ river in central Africa. The chief tributary of the River Congo, it is formed by the confluence of the Bomu and Uele rivers. Length: 1,062 km/660 mi.

Ubangi-Shari /yoo báng gi shaári/ former name for **Central African Republic**

U-bend *n.* a U-shaped section of water pipe fitted in a waste system, e.g. beneath a basin, to trap water and so prevent the backflow of noxious vapours

Übermensch /oóbər mensh, yoóbər-/ (*plural* **-menschen** /-mensh'n/) *n.* a superior kind of human being, especially in Nietzschean philosophy or Nazi ideology (*literary*) [Late 19thC. From German, a back-formation from *übermenschlich* 'superhuman'.]

ubiety /yoo bí əti/ *n.* the condition of existing in a particular place (*literary*) [Late 17thC. From medieval Latin *ubietas*, from *ubi* 'where' (source of English *ubiquitous*).]

ubiquinone /yoo bíkwinōn/ *n.* a derivative of the compound quinone that acts as an electron carrier in reactions that occur in mitochondria during cellular respiration [Mid-20thC. Blend of UBIQUITOUS and QUINONE.]

ubiquitarianism /yoo bíkwi táiri ənizəm/ *n.* the Christian belief, held particularly by the Lutheran Church, that Jesus Christ is present in all places and at all times, not just in the Eucharist —**ubiquitarian** *n.*, *adj.*

ubiquitous /yoo bíkwitəss/ *adj.* present everywhere at once, or seeming to be [Mid-19thC. Formed from modern Latin *ubiquitas* 'presence everywhere', from Latin *ubique* 'everywhere', from *ubi* 'where'.] —**ubiquitously** *adv.* —**ubiquitousness** *n.* —**ubiquity** *n.*

U-boat *n.* a German submarine, especially one used during World Wars I and II [Early 20thC. Partial translation of German *U-Boot*, a shortening of *Unterseeboot*, literally 'undersea boat'.]

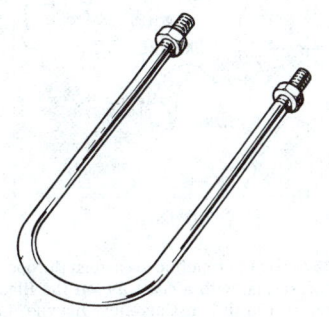

U-bolt

U-bolt *n.* a U-shaped bolt, threaded at the two ends

ubuntu /oo boón too/ *n.* S Africa humanity, compassion, and goodness, regarded as fundamental to the way Africans approach life [Late 20thC. From Xhosa.]

u.c. *abbr.* upper case

UCAS /yoó kass/ *abbr.* Universities and Colleges Admissions Service

UCATT /úkat/ *abbr.* Union of Construction, Allied Trades, and Technicians

Ucayali /oó kaa yaáli/ river in eastern Peru, formed by the confluence of the Apurímac and Urubamba rivers. It is one of the headwaters of the River Amazon. Length: 1,900 km/1,200 mi.

UCCA /úkə/ *abbr.* Universities Central Council on Admissions. Now called **UCAS**

UCLA *abbr.* University of California at Los Angeles

UCW *abbr.* Union of Communication Workers

UDA *abbr.* Ulster Defence Association

Udaipur /yoo díʼpoor, yoó díʼpoor/ city and administrative headquarters of Udaipur District, Rajasthan State, northwestern India. Population: 309,000 (1991).

UDC *abbr.* Urban District Council

udder /úddər/ *n.* a bag-shaped structure containing two or more milk-secreting glands, each with its own teat, found in mammals such as cows, sheep, and goats [Old English *ūder.* Ultimately from an Indo-European word meaning 'udder', which is also the ancestor of English *exuberant*.]

UDI *abbr.* unilateral declaration of independence

UDM *abbr.* Union of Democratic Mineworkers

Udmurt /óod moort/ *n.* **1.** PEOPLES MEMBER OF CENTRAL RUSSIAN PEOPLE a member of a people who live mainly in Udmurtia in central Russia **2.** LANG UDMURT LANGUAGE the language spoken by the Udmurt people. It belongs to the Finno-Ugric family of languages and is spoken by about 500,000 people.

Udmurtia /óod moórti ə/ republic in eastern European Russia between Tatarstan and Bashkortostan. Area: 42,100 sq. km/16,300 sq. mi.

udo /oódō/ (*plural* **udos**) *n.* a perennial Asian plant of the ginseng family whose tender shoots are cooked and eaten as a vegetable. Latin name: *Aralia cordata.* [Late 20thC. From Japanese.]

udometer /yoo dómmitə/ *n.* a rain gauge (*technical*) [Early 19thC. From French *udomètre*, from Latin *udus* 'wet' + *mètre* 'meter'.]

UDR *abbr.* Ulster Defence Regiment

UEFA /yoo áyfə/ *abbr.* Union of European Football Associations

Ufa /oo fáa/ industrial city in southeastern European Russia, situated at the confluence of the Ufa and Belaya rivers, on the western slopes of the Ural Mountains. Population: 1,097,200 (1992).

Uffington /úffingtən/ village in Oxfordshire, England. A large figure of a white horse cut in the chalk hill nearby is believed to date from the Iron Age.

Uffizi /yoo fítsi/ *n.* a museum in Florence that contains one of the world's finest collections of Italian paintings. It is located in 16th-century buildings first used to house the Medici family's art collection, the nucleus of the museum's present holdings. [Mid-19thC. From Italian, literally 'offices', because it was built to house the administrative centre of the Florentine State, by order of Cosimo I MEDICI.]

UFO /yoó ef ō, yoofṓ/ (*plural* **UFOs**) *n.* a flying object that cannot be identified and is thought by some to be an alien spacecraft [Mid-20thC. Acronym formed from *unidentified flying object*.]

ufology /yoó fólləji/ *n.* the study of UFOs, especially the investigation of recorded sightings of them

Uganda

Uganda /yoo gándə/ republic in East Africa. It gained independence from Britain in 1962. Language: English. Currency: Uganda shilling. Capital: Kampala. Population: 19,136,000 (1996). Area: 236,036 sq. km/91,134 sq. mi. Official name **Republic of Uganda** —**Ugandan** *n.*, *adj.*

Ugaritic /oógə ríttik/ *n.* LANG an ancient and extinct Semitic language once spoken in the region that is now northern Syria. It is closely related to Hebrew and Phoenician. [Mid-20thC. Formed from *Ugarit*, the name of an ancient city in northern Syria.] —**Ugaritic** *adj.*

UGC *abbr.* University Grants Committee

ugh /ug, oôkh, u/ *interj.* used as the written form of a grunting exclamation of disgust, strain, or horror [Mid-19thC. An imitation of an involuntary utterance.]

ugh boot /úg-/ *tdmk.* Aus a trademark for a sheepskin boot with a fleecy lining

Ugli /úggli/ *tdmk.* a trademark for a juicy West Indian citrus fruit that is a cross between a grapefruit and a tangerine

uglify /úggli fī/ (uglifies, uglifying, uglified) *vt.* to make sb or sth physically unappealing —**uglification** /úgglifi káysh'n/ *n.* —**uglifier** /úggli fī ər/ *n.*

ugly /úggli/ (uglier, ugliest) *adj.* 1. UNATTRACTIVE lacking appealing physical features, especially facial ones 2. ANGRY characterized by anger or hostility ○ *an ugly mood* 3. POTENTIALLY VIOLENT threatening or involving violence ○ *Things were turning ugly.* 4. UNPLEASANT generally unpleasant ○ *a dull ugly afternoon* [13thC. From Old Norse *uggligr* 'frightful', from *uggr* 'fear', of unknown origin.] —**uglily** *adv.* —**ugliness** *n.*

ugly duckling *n.* 1. UNATTRACTIVE PERSON OR THING sb or sth regarded as physically unappealing in comparison to others 2. UNDERVALUED PERSON OR THING sb or sth whose true beauty or value is yet to be revealed or appreciated [From *The Ugly Duckling*, a children's story by Hans Christian Andersen in which a cygnet raised by a duck is considered ugly until it grows into a beautiful swan]

Ugrian /yoógri ən/ *n.* PEOPLES a member of a group of peoples, including the Magyars and Voguls, who live in Hungary and parts of Siberia [Mid-19thC. Formed from Russian *Ugry* 'Hungarians', of Turkic origin.] —**Ugrian** *adj.*

Ugric /yoógrik/ *n.* LANG one of the two branches of the Finno-Ugric family of languages. It includes the Hungarian language. [Mid-19thC. Formed from Russian *Ugry* 'Hungarians' (see UGRIAN).] —**Ugric** *adj.*

uh /u/ *interj.* used as the written form of a grunting exclamation made to express surprise or request sth to be said again [Early 17thC. An imitation of an inarticulate sound.]

UHF *n.* any or all radio frequencies between 300 and 3000 megahertz, typically used for television transmission. Full form **ultrahigh frequency**

uh-huh /u hú/ *interj.* used as the written form of a grunting exclamation made to express agreement or to answer affirmatively [An imitation of an inarticulate sound]

uh-oh /ú ō/ *interj.* used as the written form of a grunting exclamation made to express apprehension [An imitation of an articulate sound]

UHT *adj.* sterilized and having a long shelf-life as a result of being heated to a very high temperature. Full form **ultra heat treated**

uh-uh /u ú, ú u/ *interj.* used as the written form of a grunting exclamation made to express disagreement or to answer in the negative [An imitation of an inarticulate sound]

uhuru /oo hoóroo/ *n.* freedom or national independence, especially for the people of East Africa [Mid-20thC. From Kiswahili.]

UI *abbr.* COMPUT user interface

U-ie /yoó i/ (*plural* **U-ies**) *n.* a U-turn (*informal*) [Late 20thC. Shortening and alteration of U-TURN.]

Uigur /weégər, -goor/ (*plural* **Uigur** *or* **Uigurs**), **Uighur** *n.* 1. PEOPLES MEMBER OF CHINESE PEOPLE a member of a people who live in parts of western China, mainly in Xinjiang Uygur Autonomous Region in the far northwest, where they are the dominant ethnic group 2. LANG LANGUAGE OF UIGURS the language spoken by the Uigurs people, belonging to the Turkic branch of the Altaic family of languages. Uigur is spoken by about 7 million people. [Mid-18thC. From Eastern Turkic.] —**Uigurian** *adj.* —**Uiguric** *adj.*

uilleann pipes /óoli ən-/ *npl.* a type of Irish bagpipes played by squeezing the bellows under the arm [Early 20thC. From Irish *píob uilleann* 'elbow pipe', from *uille* 'elbow', from Old Irish *uilind.*]

uintaite /yoo ínta īt/ *n.* a bitumen mined in the Uinta mountains in Utah in the United States, used in manufacturing

uitlander /áyt landər/, **Uitlander** *n.* S Africa a foreigner, especially a British person resident in the former Transvaal or Orange Free State [Late 19thC. Via Afrikaans from, ultimately, Middle Dutch *uteland* 'foreign country'.]

UK *abbr.* United Kingdom

UKAEA *abbr.* United Kingdom Atomic Energy Authority

ukase /yoo káyz/ *n.* 1. TSAR'S ORDER in pre-Revolutionary Russia, an order from the tsar that had the force of law 2. RULING any order or ruling, especially one handed down by a self-styled expert or guru [Early 18thC. From Russian *ukaz* 'edict', from *ukazat* 'to show'.]

uke /yook/ *n.* a ukulele (*informal*) [Early 20thC. Shortening.]

ukelele *n.* = ukulele

ukiyo-e /oó kee yō yáy/, **ukiyo-ye** *n.* a movement in Japanese painting in which scenes and objects from ordinary life were depicted. It flourished from the 17th to 19th centuries. [Late 19thC. From Japanese, literally 'transitory-world picture'.]

Ukraine

Ukraine /yoo kráyn/ republic in eastern Europe, southwest of Russia, with a coastline on the Black Sea. Language: Ukrainian. Currency: hryvna. Capital: Kiev. Population: 51,639,000 (1995). Area: 603,700 sq. km/233,090 sq. mi.

Ukrainian /yoo kráyni ən/ *n.* 1. PEOPLES SB FROM UKRAINE sb who was born or brought up in the Ukraine, or who has Ukrainian citizenship 2. LANG OFFICIAL LANGUAGE OF UKRAINE the official language of the Ukraine, also spoken by some people in Poland and the Czech Republic. It belongs to the Balto-Slavic branch of the Indo-European family of languages. Ukrainian is spoken by about 45 million people. —**Ukrainian** *adj.*

ukulele /yoókə láyli/, **ukelele** *n.* an instrument like a small guitar with four strings [Late 19thC. From Hawaiian *'ukulele*, literally 'jumping flea', of uncertain origin: perhaps from the Hawaiian nickname of Edward Purvis, a British army officer who popularized the instrument.]

Ulaanbaatar = Ulan Bator

ulama /óolimə/, **ulema** *npl.* a body of Islamic scholars who have jurisdiction over religious and social matters for the people of Islam [Late 17thC. Via Turkish *'ulemā* from Arabic *'ulamā* 'learned men'.]

Ulan Bator /oó laan baátər/, **Ulaanbaatar** capital city of the Republic of Mongolia, situated in the north-central part of the country, on the River Tuul. Population: 600,900 (1992).

Ulan-Ude /oó laán oo dáy/ port city in southern Siberian Russia, located at the confluence of the Uda and Selenge rivers. Population: 366,000 (1992).

Ulbricht /óol brikht/, **Walter** (1893–1973) German statesman. He was the co-founder and secretary of the Socialist Unity Party (1950–71) and president of the German Democratic Republic (1960–73).

ulcer /úlssər/ *n.* 1. INTERNAL SORE a slow-healing sore on the surface of a mucous membrane, especially the membrane lining the stomach or other part of the digestive tract 2. EXTERNAL SORE a suppurating sore on the skin that does not heal and results in the destruction of tissue 3. BAD INFLUENCE a corrupting or debilitating influence [14thC. From Latin *ulcer-*, the stem of *ulcus* 'a sore'.]

ulcerate /úlssə rayt/ (ulcerates, ulcerating, ulcerated) *vti.* to cause or undergo the formation of an ulcer or ulcers —**ulcerative** /úlssərətiv/ *adj.*

ulceration /úlssə ráysh'n/ *n.* 1. FORMING OF ULCER the formation of an ulcer 2. ULCER an ulcer or collection of ulcers

ulcerative colitis *n.* inflammation of the walls of the bowel accompanied by the formation of ulcers. The condition can result in permanent bowel damage.

ulcerous /úlssərəss/ *adj.* affected with, causing, consisting of, or resembling ulcers

-ule *suffix.* small one, miniature ○ *lobule* [Via French from Latin *-ulus*]

ulema *npl.* = ulama

-ulent *suffix.* having a great deal of sth ○ *flocculent* [From Latin *-ulentus*]

ullage /úllij/ *n.* (*formal*) 1. VACANT CONTAINER SPACE the amount or volume by which a container, especially one for liquids, is short of being full 2. LOST LIQUID the amount of liquid lost from a container through evaporation or leakage [15thC. Via Anglo-Norman *ulliage* from Old French *ouillier* 'to fill a barrel to the bunghole', from *oeil* 'eye, bunghole', from Latin *oculus* 'eye'.]

Ullswater /úlz wawtər/ the second largest lake in England, in the Lake District, northwestern England. Area: 8 sq. km/3 sq. mi.

Ulm /oólm/, **Charles** (1898–1934) Australian aviator. He flew as co-pilot with Charles Kingsford-Smith on several flights including the first crossing of the Pacific in 1928. Full name **Charles Thomas Philippe Ulm**

ulmaceous /ul máysh əss/ *adj.* belonging or relating to the family of temperate and tropical deciduous trees that includes the elms [Mid-19thC. Formed from modern Latin *Ulmaceae*, family name, from Latin *ulmus* 'elm'.]

ulna /úlnə/ (*plural* **-nae** /úlnee/ *or* **-nas**) *n.* 1. BONE OF HUMAN FOREARM the longer of the two bones in the human forearm, situated on the inner side 2. BONE OF LOWER FORELIMB OF ANIMAL a bone in the lower forelimb of vertebrate animals, roughly corresponding to the human ulna [Mid-16thC. From Latin, 'elbow, forearm'. Ultimately from an Indo-European word that is also the ancestor of English *elbow*.] —**ulnar** *adj.*

ulnar nerve *n.* a major nerve of the arm that runs down the inner side of the upper arm and is situated just under the skin at the elbow

ulotrichous /yoo lóttrikəss/ *adj.* with hair that is naturally tightly curled, especially belonging to a group of people with this kind of hair [Mid-19thC. Coined from Greek *oulos* 'crisp, curly' + *trikh-*, the stem of *thrix* 'hair'.]

ulster /úlstər/ *n.* a man's long heavy double-breasted overcoat [Mid-19thC. Named after ULSTER, where the original fabric (Irish frieze) for the coats was manufactured.]

Ulster /úlstər/ 1. historic province in the north of Ireland comprising nine counties, including the six that make up Northern Ireland 2. an informal name for Northern Ireland

Ulsterman /úlstərmən/ (*plural* **-men** /-mən/) *n.* a man who was born or brought up in Ulster

Ulsterwoman /úlstər woommən/ (*plural* **-en** /-wimin/) *n.* a woman who was born or brought up in Ulster

ult. *abbr.* 1. ultimate 2. ultimo

ulterior /ul teéri ər/ *adj.* 1. UNDERLYING existing in addition to or being other than what is apparent or assumed 2. LYING OUTSIDE lying beyond or outside a point or area 3. HAPPENING IN THE FUTURE happening or expected in the future [Mid-17thC. From Latin, 'further', formed from assumed *ulter* 'beyond'.] —**ulteriorly** *adv.*

ulterior motive *n.* a second and underlying motive, usually a selfish or dishonourable one

ultima /últimə/ *n.* the final syllable of a word [Early 20thC. From Latin, a form of *ultimus* (see ULTIMATE).]

ultimata plural of ultimatum

ultimate /últimət/ *adj.* 1. FINAL coming or expected as the very last ○ *our ultimate destination* 2. FUNDAMENTAL existing as an underlying reality, when all other things are disregarded ○ *the ultimate truth* 3. GREATEST greatest, most nearly perfect, or highest in quality (*informal*) ○ *the ultimate home entertainment system* 4. FARTHEST AWAY outermost or most remote ■ *n.* GREATEST THING the greatest or most nearly perfect thing (*informal*) ○ *seats that were the ultimate in passenger comfort* [Mid-17thC. Via late Latin *ultimatus*, past participle of *ultimare* 'to be at an end', from Latin *ultimus* 'last, final', from assumed *ulter* 'beyond'.] —**ultimacy** *n.* —**ultimateness** *n.*

ultimately /últimətli/ *adv.* **1.** FUNDAMENTALLY most importantly, when all things are considered **2.** EVENTUALLY in the end, as the culmination of a process or event

ultima Thule /-thyóoli/ *n.* (*literary*) **1.** REMOTE PLACE a distant or very remote place **2.** FINAL GOAL an ultimate or distant goal [Late 18thC. From Latin, 'farthest Thule', the northernmost part of the inhabited world.]

ultimatum /últi máytəm/ (*plural* **ultimatums** *or* **ultimata** /-tə/) *n.* a demand accompanied by a threat to inflict some penalty if the demand is not met [Mid-18thC. From modern Latin, formed from Latin *ultimatus* (see ULTIMATE).]

ultimo /últimō/ *adj.* used, especially in the past, in formal correspondence to refer to the previous month (*formal*) ○ *your letter of the 20th ultimo* [Late 16thC. From Latin *ultimo (mense)* 'in the last (month)', from *ultimus* (see ULTIMATE).]

ultimogeniture /últimō jénnichə/ *n.* the principle of inheritance or succession by the youngest son [Late 19thC. Formed from Latin *ultimus* 'last', on the model of *primogeniture*.]

ultra /últrə/ *adj.* **1.** EXTREME going beyond all else **2.** HOLDING EXTREMIST VIEWS holding extremist views, especially in religious or political matters **3.** EXCELLENT excellent or superior (*slang*) ■ *n.* EXTREMIST sb with extremist views, especially in religious or political matters [Late 19thC. Via French from Latin, 'beyond' (see ULTRA-).]

ultra- *prefix.* **1.** more than normal, excessively, completely ○ *ultrasophisticated* **2.** outside the range of ○ *ultrasound* [From Latin *ultra*, 'beyond'. Ultimately from an Indo-European base meaning 'beyond', which is also the ancestor of English *alter, other, alias,* and *else*.]

ultrabasic /últrə báyssik/ *adj.* WITH HIGH IRON CONTENT used to describe igneous rock that is high in iron and magnesium and contains no free quartz. ◊ **ultramafic** ■ *n.* ULTRABASIC ROCK a rock of ultrabasic composition. ◊ **ultramafic**

ultracentrifuge /últrə séntri fyooj/ *n.* FAST CENTRIFUGE a centrifuge for separating microscopic or submicroscopic particles by using a force many times greater than gravity ■ *vt.* (**ultracentrifuges, ultracentrifuging, ultracentrifuged**) SPIN FAST to subject sth to the action of an ultracentrifuge —**ultracentrifugal** /últrə séntri fyoóg'l/ *adj.* —**ultracentrifugally** *adv.* —**ultracentrifugation** /últrə séntrifyoo gáysh'n/ *n.*

ultraconservative /últrəkən súrvətiv/ *adj.* EXTREMELY CONSERVATIVE extremely conservative in religious or political views ■ *n.* SB ULTRACONSERVATIVE sb who holds ultraconservative views

ultrafiche /últrə feesh/ *n.* **1.** SMALL MICROFICHE a sheet of microfilm of similar size to a microfiche but with a much greater number of much smaller microcopied documents on it **2.** VIEWING DEVICE a device for viewing ultrafiches that has much greater magnification than a microfiche

ultrafilter /últrə fíltər/ *n.* a filter for separating extremely small particles from a solution or colloid [Early 20thC. Back-formation from ULTRAFILTRATION.]

ultrafiltrate /últrə fíl trayt/ *n.* the material that is not filtered out and remains in the liquid phase after ultrafiltration

ultrafiltration /últrə fil tráysh'n/ *n.* a filtration process that uses a porous membrane to isolate and remove particles such as bacteria and viruses. The process is used for water purification and in the pharmaceutical industry.

ultra heat treated *adj.* full form of **UHT**

ultrahigh frequency /últrə hīT-/ *n.* full form of **UHF**

ultraism /últrə izəm/ *n.* religious or political extremism —**ultraist** *n.* —**ultraistic** /-ístik/ *adj.*

ultralarge crude carrier /últrəlaarj-/ *n.* a very large oil tanker, even larger than a supertanker, that has a capacity greater than 400,000 tons

ultramafic /últrə máffik/ *adj.* WITH HIGH FERROMAGNESIUM CONTENT used to describe a dark igneous rock, over 90% of whose content consists of ferromagnesian minerals, including olivine and pyroxenes. ◊ **ul-**

trabasic ■ *n.* ULTRAMAFIC ROCK a rock of ultramafic composition. ◊ **ultrabasic**

ultramarine /últrəmə reén/ *n.* **1.** BLUE PIGMENT a deep blue pigment or dye, especially one made from the blue mineral lapis lazuli **2.** COLOURS DEEP BLUE COLOUR a brilliant deep blue colour ■ *adj.* **1.** COLOURS OF A DEEP BLUE of a brilliant deep blue colour **2.** BEYOND THE SEA coming from or lying beyond the sea (*literary*) [Late 16thC. From medieval Latin *ultramarinus*, literally 'beyond the sea'.]

ultramicrometer /últrə mī krómmitər/ *n.* a measuring device designed to measure spaces and thicknesses more minute than those measurable using a standard micrometer

ultramicroscope /últrə míkrəskōp/ *n.* a microscope that uses scattered light to make submicroscopic objects visible

ultramicroscopic /últrə míkrə skóppik/ *adj.* **1.** = submicroscopic **2.** USING AN ULTRAMICROSCOPE involving the use of an ultramicroscope

ultramodern /últrə móddərn/ *adj.* more modern than anything comparable, especially in using the very latest designs or making use of the most advanced technology —**ultramodernism** *n.* —**ultramodernist** *n.*

ultramontane /últrə món tayn/ *adj.* **1.** BEYOND MOUNTAINS coming from or lying beyond mountains, especially beyond the Alps as viewed from ancient Rome **2.** CHR SUPPORTING THE POPE supporting the power and authority of the pope within the Roman Catholic Church ■ *n.* **1.** DWELLER BEYOND MOUNTAINS sb who lives beyond mountains, especially beyond the Alps as viewed from ancient Rome **2.** CHR PAPAL SUPPORTER sb who supports the power and authority of the pope in the Roman Catholic Church [Late 16thC. From medieval Latin *ultramontanus* 'beyond the mountains'.]

ultramontanism /últrə móntənizəm/ *n.* in the Roman Catholic Church, the policy of investing all power and authority in the pope

ultramundane /últrə mun dáyn/ *adj.* (*literary*) **1.** EXTRATERRESTRIAL coming from or lying beyond the Earth or its solar system **2.** SPIRITUAL belonging or relating to heaven or to the realm of the spirit, and not to the physical world [Mid-16thC. From Latin *ultramundanus*, literally 'beyond the world', from *ultra* 'beyond' + *mundus* 'world'.]

ultranationalism /últrə násh'nəlizəm/ *n.* nationalism that is so extreme as to be detrimental to international interests or cooperation —**ultranationalist** /últrə násh'nəlist/ *n.* —**ultranationalistic** /-ístik/ *adj.*

ultra-Orthodox *adj.* supporting or practising very strict observance of Orthodox Judaism —**ultra-Orthodoxy** *n.*

ultrared /últrə réd/ *n., adj.* infrared (*dated*)

ultrareligious /últrə ri líjjəss/ *adj.* showing great devotion to religious rites and rituals

ultrashort /últrə sháwrt/ *adj.* **1.** RADIO SHORTER THAN 10 M used to describe wavelengths that are shorter than 10 m **2.** EXTREMELY SHORT extremely short in length or duration

ultrasonic /últrə sónnik/ *adj.* used to describe sound waves that have frequencies above the upper limit of the normal range of human hearing, which is about 20 kilohertz —**ultrasonically** *adv.*

ultrasonics /últrə sónniks/ *n.* the study of sound waves that have frequencies above the upper limit of the normal range of human hearing, which is about 20 kilohertz (*takes a singular verb*)

ultrasonic testing *n.* the scanning of surfaces with

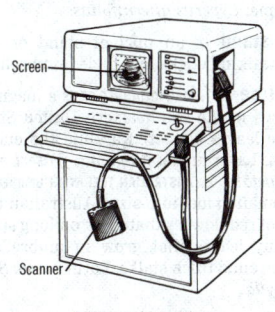

Screen

Scanner

Ultrasonic testing

high-frequency sound waves in order to gauge their integrity and check for defects or to measure the thickness of materials

ultrasonic welding *n.* the bonding of two components by bombarding them with ultrasonic waves to cause vibrations between them

ultrasonogram /últrə sónə gram/ *n.* a picture made with ultrasound for the purpose of medical examination or diagnosis

ultrasonography /últrə sə nóggrəfi/ *n.* the use of ultrasound to make pictures for the purpose of medical examination or diagnosis [Mid-20thC. Modelled on *sonography*.] —**ultrasonographic** /últrə sónə gráffik/ *adj.*

ultrasound /últrə sownd/ *n.* **1.** ACOUSTICS HIGH-FREQUENCY SOUND sound of a frequency above the upper limit of the normal range of human hearing, which is about 20 kilohertz **2.** MED SOUND-WAVE TECHNOLOGY FOR MEDICAL EXAMINATIONS an imaging technique that uses high-frequency sound waves reflecting off internal body parts to create images, especially of the foetus in the womb, for medical examination. Ultrasound vibrations can also be used to treat deep tissue disorders in physiotherapy, and can break up kidney stones. **3.** MED = ultrasound scan (*informal*)

ultrasound scan *n.* a medical examination of an internal body part, especially a foetus in the womb, using ultrasound technology

ultrastructure /últrə strúkchər/ *n.* the minute structure of an organic substance or object that becomes evident only under electron microscopy —**ultrastructural** *adj.*

Ultrasuede /últrə swáyd/ *tdmk.* a trademark for a synthetic fabric that resembles suede

ultraviolet /últrə vī′ əlet/ *adj.* RELATING TO INVISIBLE LIGHT relating to or producing electromagnetic radiation of wavelengths from about 5 to about 400 nanometers, beyond the violet end of the visible light spectrum ■ *n.* ULTRAVIOLET RADIATION radiation with ultraviolet wavelengths. Radiation of this kind is a component of sunlight and is the light that makes exposed skin become darker.

ultra vires /últrə vī′ reez/ *adj., adv.* beyond the legal capacity of a person, company, or other legal entity [From Latin, 'beyond the powers']

ultravirus /últrə vírəss/ *n.* a virus small enough to pass through an ultrafilter —**ultraviral** /-vírəl/ *adj.*

ulu /oo loó/ *adj. Malaysia, Singapore* not economically or technologically advanced (*informal*)

ululate /yóolyoo layt/ (**-lates, -lating, -lated**) *vi.* to howl or wail, in grief or in jubilation (*literary*) [Early 17thC. From Latin *ululare*, ultimately an imitation of the sound.] —**ululation** /yóolyoo láysh'n/ *n.*

Uluru /oólə roó/ the largest individual rock mass in the world, located in the south of the Northern Territory, Australia. Height: 335 m/1,100 ft. Former name **Ayers Rock**

Ulverstone /úlvərstōn/ town situated on the northern coast of Tasmania, Australia, at the mouth of the River Leven. Population: 9,792 (1996).

Ulyssean /yoo líssi ən/ *adj.* **1.** RELATING TO ULYSSES relating to the mythological character Ulysses, called Odysseus by the Greeks **2.** LIKE ULYSSES OR HIS STORY like Ulysses, especially in being courageous or cunning, or like the life story of Ulysses, especially in involving a long journey full of adventure

Ulysses /yoo lísseez, yoóli seez/ *n.* the name used by the Romans for the Greek hero Odysseus [Early 17thC. From Latin.]

um /um/ *interj.* a word used in writing to represent the kind of grunting sound that people make when they hesitate in speaking [Early 17thC. An imitation of an inarticulate sound.]

Umayyad /oo mí yad/, **Omayyad** *n.* the family that dominated the politics and commercial economy of Mecca and later established a dynasty as rulers (**caliphs**) of Islam [Mid-18thC. From *Umayya*, the name of a cousin of Muhammad's grandfather.] —**Umayyad** *adj.* —**Ommiad** *adj.* —**Omayad** *adj.*

umbel /úmb'l/ *n.* an umbrella-shaped flower head in which the individual flowers are borne on short stems arising from the top of a main stem. It is typical of plants such as parsley, carrot, dill, and fennel. [Late 16thC. Directly or via Old French *umbelle*, from Latin *umbella* 'parasol', from *umbra* 'shade'.] —**umbellar** /um béllər/ *adj.* —**umbellate** /úmbələt, -layt/ *adj.* —**umbellated** /úmbə laytid/ *adj.*

umbelliferous /úmbə líffərəss/ *adj.* with flower heads shaped like an opened umbrella [Mid-17thC. Coined from Latin *umbella* 'parasol' (see UMBEL) + -FEROUS.]

umbellule /um béllyool/ *n.* a small umbel that is part of, and has a similar arrangement to, a larger umbel [Late 18thC. From modern Latin *umbellula* 'little umbel', from *umbella* (see UMBEL).]

umber /úmbər/ *n.* **1.** SOIL USED FOR PIGMENTS AND DYES a kind of soil that contains oxides of iron and manganese and is used to make pigments and dyes. It is dark yellowish-brown in its natural state (**raw umber**), and dark reddish-brown when roasted (**burnt umber**). **2.** PIGMENT pigment or dye made from umber **3.** ZOOL = **umber moth** ■ *adj.* COLOURS OF BROWN PRODUCED BY UMBER PIGMENT of any of the shades of brown that are produced by umber pigment ■ *vt.* (**-bers, -bering, -bered**) PAINT STH WITH UMBER to paint or dye sth with umber, or generally to colour sth dark brown [Mid-16thC. Via French *terre d'ombre* or Italian *terra di ombre*, from Latin *umbra* 'shadow'.]

umber moth *n.* a dark brown moth whose markings make it difficult to pick out when it is resting on tree bark. Family: Geometridae.

Umberto I /óom búrtō/, **King of Italy** (1844–1900). Reigning from 1878, he sought to consolidate Italy as a unified country.

Umberto II, King of Italy (1904–83). He abdicated in 1946, a month after becoming king, when Italy became a republic as a result of a referendum.

umbilical /um bíllik'l/ *adj.* **1.** ANAT OF THE UMBILICAL CORD relating to or situated in the umbilical cord, the navel, or the area of the abdomen that surrounds the navel **2.** RESEMBLING A NAVEL resembling a navel (**umbilicus**) in appearance **3.** PROVIDING A LIFELINE providing a link to sth essential, e.g. supplies or services in wartime, or connecting an astronaut to a spacecraft while outside of it ■ *n.* = **umbilical cord** [Mid-16thC. Via French from Latin *umbilicus* (see UMBILICUS).]

umbilical cord *n.* **1.** TUBE CONNECTING FOETUS TO PLACENTA the flexible, often spirally twisted tube that connects the abdomen of a foetus to the mother's placenta in the womb, and through which nutrients are delivered and waste expelled. It contains two arteries, which carry oxygen-depleted blood to the placenta, and one vein, which returns oxygen-rich blood to the foetus. **2.** CABLE OR PIPE PROVIDING ESSENTIAL LINK a cable, tube, or pipe attaching sb or sth to an essential supply, e.g. the tube that connects a deep-sea diver to an oxygen supply on a ship

umbilicate /um bíllikət/, **umbilicated** /um bílli kaytid/ *adj.* **1.** ZOOL, BOT WITH STH LIKE A NAVEL with a mark, depression, or perforation that resembles a navel **2.** BIOL NAVEL-SHAPED shaped like a navel [Late 17thC. Formed from UMBILICUS.] —**umbilication** /um bílli káysh'n/ *n.*

umbilicus /um bíllikəss/ (*plural* **-ci** /-li síí/) *n.* **1.** ANAT NAVEL a navel (*technical*) **2.** BIOL HOLLOW RESEMBLING A NAVEL a dip or hollow, e.g. the hollow at each end of the shaft of a feather, that resembles a navel [Late 17thC. From Latin. Ultimately from the Indo-European word for 'navel', which is also the ancestor of English *navel* and *nave*.]

umbo /úmbō/ (*plural* **-bones** /um bṓ neez/ *or* **-bos**) *n.* **1.** BIOL BUMP ON PLANT OR ANIMAL PART a small protuberance on a plant or animal part, e.g. the hump on the caps of some mushrooms, or the bump just above the hinge of a bivalve shell **2.** ANAT SMALL HOLLOW IN THE EARDRUM a small hollow in the centre of the outer surface of the eardrum, at the point where the malleus joins it on the inside **3.** ARMS KNOB ON SHIELD a knob at the centre of a round shield, especially a Saxon shield [Early 18thC. From Latin, 'shield boss', related to *umbilicus* 'navel' (see UMBILICUS).] —**umbonal** /um bṓnal/ *adj.* —**umbonate** /úmbənət/ *adj.*

umbra /úmbrə/ (*plural* **-brae** /úm bree/ *or* **-bras**) *n.* **1.** PHYS COMPLETE SHADOW an area of complete shadow caused by light from all points of a source being prevented from reaching the area, usually by an opaque object **2.** ASTRON DARKEST PART OF MOON'S SHADOW the darkest portion of the shadow cast by a celestial body during an eclipse, especially that cast on the Earth during a solar eclipse **3.** ASTRON DARK PART OF SUNSPOT the inner, darker area of a sunspot [Late 16thC. From Latin, 'shadow'.] —**umbral** *adj.*

umbrage /úmbrij/ *n.* **1.** OFFENCE resentment or annoyance arising from some offence ○ *took umbrage* **2.** GIVER OF SHADE sth that gives shade, e.g. a tree (*literary*) **3.** VAGUE SHAPE a vague or shadowy shape, or simply an outline (*archaic*) [15thC. Via Old French, from, ultimately, Latin *umbra* 'shadow'.]

WORD KEY: ORIGIN

The Latin word *umbra*, from which **umbrage** is derived, is also the source of English *adumbrate*, *penumbra*, *sombre*, *sombrero*, and *umbrella*.

---

umbrageous /um bráyjəss/ *adj.* **1.** SHADY providing shade and coolness (*literary*) **2.** IRRITABLE easily offended or likely to become irritated —**umbrageously** *adv.* —**umbrageousness** *n.*

umbrella /um bréllə/ *n.* **1.** COLLAPSIBLE CANOPY THAT PROTECTS FROM RAIN a round collapsible canopy of plastic or waterproof material on a frame at the top of a handle, held in the hand to protect sb from rain or sun **2.** OBJECT LIKE AN UMBRELLA an object that looks like an open umbrella, or that collapses like an umbrella, e.g. the folding paper decoration sometimes served in cocktails **3.** ZOOL JELLYFISH'S BODY the rounded body of a jellyfish **4.** MIL AIRCRAFT FLYING OVERHEAD FOR PROTECTION a group of aircraft patrolling the sky above a place where troops are carrying out operations, to give them protection **5.** MIL SHIELD OF GUNFIRE gunfire used to suppress enemy fire and thus shield friendly forces making a movement or attack **6.** *US* MIL PARACHUTE a parachute (*slang*) **7.** SUPPORT OR AUTHORITY sth that gives support, protection, or authority ○ *under the umbrella of the United Nations* ■ *adj.* **1.** UNIFYING MEMBER ORGANIZATIONS acting to coordinate or protect a number of member organizations or bodies **2.** INCLUDING SEVERAL THINGS including or containing a number of things ○ *an umbrella term for a variety of plants* [Early 17thC. Via Italian *ombrella* from late Latin *umbrella*, an alteration of Latin *umbella* 'parasol'(see UMBEL) under the influence of *umbra* 'shadow'.]

Umbrella bird

umbrella bird *n.* a bird of Central and South America with a large feathered crest that resembles an umbrella. Genus: *Cephalopterus*.

umbrella pine *n.* = **stone pine**

umbrella plant *n.* a plant of the sedge family, native to Africa, that has thin leaves radiating from the top of long stems. It is widely grown as a houseplant. Latin name: *Cyperus alternifolius*.

umbrella stand *n.* an upright stand or rack for holding walking sticks and folded umbrellas

umbrella tree *n.* **1.** MAGNOLIA TREE OF US a magnolia tree that grows in the southeastern United States and has large leaves clustered around the ends of the branches. Latin name: *Magnolia fraseri* and *Magnolia tripetala*. **2.** AUSTRALIAN TREE WITH UMBRELLA-SHAPED LEAVES a small to medium-sized Australian tree with clusters of red flowers that grow on long spikes and long shiny leaves that grow in umbrella-shaped clusters around thick stalks. Latin name: *Schefflera actinophylla*.

Umbria /úmbri ə/ agricultural region in central Italy, west of the Apennines. Population: 822,972 (1991). Area: 8,456 sq. km/3,265 sq. mi.

Umbrian /úmbri ən/ *n.* **1.** PEOPLES SB FROM UMBRIA sb who was born or brought up in the Italian region of Umbria **2.** LANG LANGUAGE OF ANCIENT UMBRIA an extinct language spoken in ancient southern Italy. It belongs to the Italic branch of Indo-European languages. —**Umbrian** *adj.*

Umbriel /úmbri əl/ *n.* one of the five major moons circling the planet Uranus [Named after a sprite in the poem 'The Rape of the Lock' by Alexander Pope]

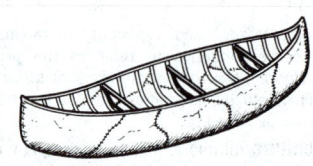

Umiak

umiak /óomi ak/ *n.* a large Inuit boat made of animal skins stretched across a wooden frame, larger and more open than a kayak and traditionally paddled by women [Mid-18thC. From Inuit (Eskimo) *umiaq*.]

UMIST /yóomist/ *n., abbr.* University of Manchester Institute of Science and Technology

umlaut /óom lowt/ *n.* **1.** CHANGE IN A VOWEL SOUND in Germanic languages, a change in the way a vowel is pronounced, caused by the influence of another vowel in a syllable immediately after it **2.** TWO DOTS ABOVE A VOWEL the mark (¨) that is placed above a vowel in Germanic languages to show that it is pronounced differently from the way the vowel is usually pronounced ■ *v.* (**-lauts, -lauting, -lauted**) **1.** *vti.* CHANGE A VOWEL SOUND to change a sound, or make a vowel change its sound, because of other vowel sounds next to it **2.** *vt.* MARK A VOWEL WITH TWO DOTS to write or print a vowel with an umlaut above it [Mid-19thC. From German, from *um-* 'about, change' + *Laut* 'sound'.]

umma /óomə/, **ummah** *n.* within Islam, the community of the faithful that transcended long established tribal boundaries to create a degree of political unity [Late 19thC. From Arabic, 'people, community'.]

umpire /úm pīr/ *n.* **1.** SPORTS OFFICIAL ENFORCING A SPORT'S RULES an official who supervises play and enforces the rules of the game in some sports such as cricket and baseball **2.** SB SETTLING A DISPUTE sb called in to settle a dispute ■ *vti.* (**-pires, -piring, -pired**) **1.** SPORTS ACT AS AN UMPIRE IN SPORT to supervise play in a game or sport and enforce the rules **2.** SETTLE A DISPUTE to give a ruling on a dispute as an impartial arbitrator [Late 16thC. By false division from earlier *noumper*, from Old French *nonper*, from *non* 'not' + *per* 'pair', literally 'not one of a pair'.]

umpteen /úmp téen/ *det.* a large but unspecified number of (*informal*) [Early 20thC. Formed from *umpty*, a humorous formation after cardinal numbers; modelled on *thirteen*, *fourteen*, etc.] —**umpteenth** *det.*

Umtata /um taátə/ town in Eastern Cape Province, South Africa. Population: 67,000 (1995).

un /ən, 'n/, **'un** *pron.* a spelling of the pronoun 'one' designed to reflect the way it is sometimes pronounced in informal speech (*informal*) [Early 19thC. Representing a pronunciation of ONE.]

UN *abbr.* United Nations

un-[1] *prefix.* **1.** not ○ *unavoidable* **2.** opposite of, lack of ○ *unrest* [Old English]

WORD KEY: USAGE

un- or **non-**: Many adjectives formed with *un-* have special (usually unfavourable) meanings, for example *unprofessional* and *unscientific*. In these cases neutral equivalents that mean simply 'not . . .' are formed by means of *non-*, for example *nonprofessional*, *nonscientific*.

---

un-[2] *prefix.* **1.** to do the opposite of, reverse ○ *unclose* **2.** to deprive of, remove sth from ○ *unfrock* **3.** to release from ○ *unchain* **4.** completely ○ *unloose* [Old English *on-*, an alteration of *ond- and-* 'against', under the influence of *un-*[1] 'un-']

unabashed /únnə básht/ *adj.* not ashamed or embarrassed by sth

unabated /únnə báytid/ *adj.* still as forceful or intense as before —**unabatedly** *adv.*

unable /un áyb'l/ *adj.* not able to do sth

unaccommodated /únnə kómmə daytid/ *adj.* (*formal*) **1.** NOT ADAPTED not adapted to or for sth ○ *unaccommodated to the dryness of the desert* **2.** WITHOUT ACCOMMODATION OR PROVISIONS lacking accommodation, equipment, or supplies

unaccompanied /únnə kúmpənid/ *adj., adv.* **1.** ALONE alone, especially when a companion would be expected **2.** MUSIC WITHOUT OTHER INSTRUMENTS OR VOICES playing or singing alone, without any other instruments or voices

unaccomplished /únnə kúmplisht/ *adj.* **1.** NOT COMPLETED not carried out or completed **2.** LACKING SOCIAL OR INTELLECTUAL SKILLS lacking talents or abilities, especially those abilities educated people may be expected to have

unaccountable /únnə kówntəb'l/ *adj.* **1.** INEXPLICABLE impossible to explain or give a reason for **2.** NOT ANSWERABLE not answerable or responsible to anyone —**unaccountability** /únnə kówntə bílləti/ *n.*

unaccountably /únnə kówntəbli/ *adv.* for some unknown and usually puzzling reason

unaccounted-for *adj.* **1.** MISSING missing or absent, for unknown reasons **2.** UNEXPLAINED not explained or understood

unaccredited /únnə krédditid/ *adj.* **1.** WITH NO SOURCE GIVEN with the source or origin not given **2.** NOT OFFICIALLY APPROVED not officially declared to be of the required standard, or with no official status

unaccustomed /únnə kústəmd/ *adj.* **1.** NOT ACCUSTOMED not used or accustomed to sth **2.** UNFAMILIAR not usual or known before —**unaccustomedness** *n.*

una corda /óonə káwrdə/ *adj., adv.* in piano music, using only one string per pitch. This is achieved by depressing the soft pedal, causing the hammers to strike only one string and thus reducing the volume and changing the quality of the tone. [From Italian, literally 'one string']

unadopted /únnə dóptid/ *adj.* **1.** NOT ADOPTED not adopted by new parents **2.** NOT MAINTAINED BY LOCAL GOVERNMENT used to describe a road that is not maintained or repaired by a local authority

unadulterated /únnə dúltə raytid/ *adj.* **1.** PURE not mixed or diluted with sth else **2.** ABSOLUTE free from any element that would spoil or detract from it —**unadulteratedly** *adv.*

unadvised /únnəd vízd/ *adj.* **1.** WITHOUT CAREFUL CONSIDERATION done without being carefully considered **2.** WITHOUT ASKING ADVICE without asking the advice of others —**unadvisedly** /-vízidli/ *adv.* —**unadvisedness** /-vízidnəss/ *n.*

unaffected /únnə féktid/ *adj.* **1.** GENUINE sincere and genuine, with no intention to mislead or deceive **2.** NOT AFFECTED BY STH not influenced or affected by sth —**unaffectedly** *adv.* —**unaffectedness** *n.*

Unaipon /yoo níp on/, **David** (1873–1967) Australian writer and inventor. He was the author of *Native Legends* (1929), the first book by an Aboriginal writer to be published in Australia. He also designed agricultural machinery.

Unalaska /únnə láskə/ island in southwestern Alaska, between the Bering Sea and the Pacific Ocean. It is the most important and second largest of the Aleutian Islands. Area: 1,287 sq. km/800 sq. mi.

unalienable /un áyli ənəb'l/ *adj.* not alienable

unalloyed /únnə lóyd/ *adj.* **1.** METALL IN A PURE STATE containing no impurities, and not mixed or alloyed with other metals **2.** ABSOLUTE not mixed with anything else, especially anything that would dilute it or any other feeling that would diminish it ○ *unalloyed pleasure*

un-American *adj.* **1.** NOT AMERICAN at odds with the customs, traditions, or ways of the people of the United States ○ *It's practically un-American not to like apple pie.* **2.** NOT LOYAL TO UNITED STATES unpatriotic or disloyal to the United States

unaneled /únnə neéld/ *adj.* in the Roman Catholic Church, not having received the last rites given to people who are dying or very ill (*archaic*) [Early 17thC. Formed from UN- + *aneled*, past participle of obsolete *anele* 'to anoint', literally 'to put oil on', from Old English *ele* 'oil', from Latin *oleum*.]

unanimous /yoo nánniməss/ *adj.* **1.** AGREED ON BY EVERYONE shared or taken as a view by all of the people concerned, with nobody disagreeing **2.** IN COMPLETE AGREEMENT with all members in agreement with each other ○ *Board members were unanimous in their rejection of the proposed merger.* [Early 17thC. Formed from Latin *unanimus*, from *unus* 'one' + *animus* 'mind'.] —**unanimity** /yóonə nímməti/ *n.* —**unanimously** /yoo nánniməssli/ *adv.*

unanswerable /un aánssərəb'l/ *adj.* **1.** IMPOSSIBLE TO RESOLVE impossible to answer or solve **2.** IMPOSSIBLE TO CONTRADICT so clearly true that nobody could contradict or deny it —**unanswerableness** *n.* —**unanswerably** *adv.*

unanticipated /ún an tíssi paytid/ *adj.* **1.** UNFORESEEN not foreseen or prepared for in advance **2.** UNEXPECTED not expected or scheduled in advance

unappealable /únnə peéləb'l/ *adj.* used to describe a case or judgment that is not open to appeal —**unappealably** *adv.*

unappealing /únnə peéling/ *adj.* not attractive or likely to be enjoyable —**unappealingly** *adv.*

unapproachable /únnə próchəb'l/ *adj.* **1.** TOO UNFRIENDLY TO APPROACH OR CONTACT characterized by a formal, unfriendly, or hostile manner that discourages communication **2.** INACCESSIBLE difficult to get to **3.** UNRIVALLED so excellent that nothing or nobody else is nearly as good —**unapproachability** /únnə próchə bílləti/ *n.* —**unapproachableness** *n.* —**unapproachably** /únnə póchəbli/ *adv.*

unappropriated /únnə própri aytid/ *adj.* **1.** NOT YET MARKED FOR A PURPOSE not yet set aside for a specific purpose and therefore still available or free **2.** WITH OWNERSHIP OR CONTROL NOT DECIDED not yet brought under the ownership or control of a particular person or organization

unapt /un ápt/ *adj.* **1.** NOT APPROPRIATE lacking the qualities suitable or appropriate to a particular context **2.** NOT LIKELY TO DO STH not likely or liable to do sth (*formal*) ○ *unapt to cause any problems* —**unaptly** *adv.* —**unaptness** *n.*

unarguable /un aárgyoo əb'l/ *adj.* **1.** UNDENIABLY TRUE OR CORRECT so clearly true or correct that nobody can argue with it or deny it **2.** NOT FIT TO USE AS ARGUMENT not sound or convincing enough to be put forward as an argument

unarm /un aárm/ (**-arms, -arming, -armed**) *vt.* to take arms away from a country, armed force, or person

unarmed /un aármd/ *adj.* **1.** ARMS WITHOUT WEAPONS not carrying or using weapons **2.** BIOL WITH NO OBVIOUS MEANS OF SELF-DEFENCE with no horns, claws, shells, thorns, prickles, or other means of self-protection **3.** MIL UNABLE TO FIRE used to describe a missile or projectile whose fuse or firing mechanism has been disabled

unary /yóonəri/ *adj.* used to describe a mathematical operation that is applied to only one member of a set at a time, e.g. squaring a number [Early 20thC. Formed from Latin *unus* 'one'.]

unashamed /únnə sháymd/ *adj.* **1.** NOT ASHAMED OR APOLOGETIC not ashamed or embarrassed, and not feeling the need to apologize to others **2.** UNRESTRAINED not limited, restrained, or avoided out of a feeling of shame or embarrassment —**unashamedly** /-sháymidli/ *adv.* —**unashamedness** /-sháymidnəss/ *n.*

unasked /un aáskt/ *adj.* **1.** NOT ASKED not having been asked **2.** NOT INVITED coming to a gathering without an invitation **3.** NOT ASKED FOR providing sth, e.g. assistance, that has not been asked for

unassailable /únnə sáyləb'l/ *adj.* **1.** IMPOSSIBLE TO CHALLENGE so sound or well established that it cannot be challenged or overtaken ○ *an unassailable lead* **2.** IMPOSSIBLE TO ATTACK so strong or impregnable that it cannot be successfully attacked —**unassailability** /únnə sáylə bílləti/ *n.* —**unassailably** /únnə sáyləbli/ *adv.*

unassuming /únnə syóoming/ *adj.* acting in a way that does not assume superiority —**unassumingly** *adv.* —**unassumingness** *n.*

unattached /únnə tácht/ *adj.* **1.** WITHOUT A SPOUSE OR PARTNER not married and not in a long-term romantic or sexual relationship **2.** NOT JOINED not joined or attached, especially to other or larger organizations or bodies **3.** LAW NOT SEIZED FOR SECURITY used to describe property that is not taken away from its owner for security under the orders of a court of law

unattended /únnə téndid/ *adj.* **1.** WITH NO ONE THERE with no one present to listen, watch, or participate **2.** NOT CARED FOR not looked after or seen to **3.** NOT ESCORTED not accompanied or escorted (*formal*) **4.** NOT HEEDED not listened to or heeded (*formal*) **5.** NOT HAVING STH AS CONSEQUENCE not accompanied by sth, or not having sth as a result or consequence (*formal*)

unau /yóo now/ (*plural* **unaus** *or* **unau**) *n.* = **two-toed sloth** [Late 18thC. Via French from Tupi *unáu*.]

unavailing /únnə váyling/ *adj.* done but failing to achieve the desired result —**unavailingly** *adv.*

unavoidable /únnə vóydəb'l/ *adj.* that cannot be avoided —**unavoidability** /únnə vóydə bílləti/ *n.* —**unavoidably** /únnə vóydəbli/ *adv.*

unaware /únnə wáir/ *adj.* **1.** NOT AWARE not conscious or aware of sth **2.** NOT KNOWLEDGEABLE lacking important information or analysis ○ *a politically unaware generation* ■ *adv.* = **unawares** —**unawarely** *adv.* —**unawareness** *n.*

WORD KEY: USAGE

unaware or **unawares**? ***Unaware*** is normally used as an adjective, *They were unaware of the danger*, whereas ***unawares*** is an adverb, used especially in the idiom *to catch (or take) sb unawares*, but also in other ways: *They crept up on us unawares.*

unawares /únnə wáirz/ *adv.* **1.** UNEXPECTEDLY without any warning or anticipation ○ *His question caught me unawares.* **2.** WITHOUT INTENDING TO without planning or intending to do sth ○ *He took the wrong coat, unawares.* [Mid-16thC. Coined from UNAWARE + *-s*, an adverbial ending originally meaning 'of'.]

WORD KEY: USAGE

See Usage note at ***unaware***.

unb. *abbr.* PUBL unbound

unbacked /un bákt/ *adj.* **1.** NOT SUPPORTED OR BACKED with no support or backing, especially financial backing **2.** FURNITURE WITHOUT A BACK used to describe a chair that has been made without a back **3.** RIDING NEVER RIDDEN used to describe a horse that has never been ridden ○ *an unbacked mare* **4.** GAMBLING NOT BET ON used to describe a horse that has had no bets placed on its performance

unbalance /un bállənss/ *vt.* (**-ances, -ancing, -anced**) **1.** KNOCK STH OFF BALANCE to make sth lose its balance or equilibrium **2.** MAKE SB PSYCHOLOGICALLY UNSTABLE to make sb psychologically or emotionally unstable ■ *n.* STATE OF INSTABILITY the state of being unstable and out of balance —**unbalanceable** *adj.*

unbalanced /un bállənst/ *adj.* **1.** WITHOUT EQUILIBRIUM lacking the proper distribution of weight or forces that would provide balance **2.** PSYCHOLOGICALLY UNSTABLE unable to make sound judgments **3.** ONE-SIDED done or provided from only one perspective ○ *unbalanced reporting* **4.** ACCT WITH UNEQUAL DEBITS AND CREDITS in which the totalled debits and credits are not equal

unbar /un baár/ (**-bars, -barring, -barred**) *vt.* **1.** UNLOCK A DOOR to unlock or open a door or gate **2.** REMOVE BARS to remove the bars or obstructions from sth

unbated /un báytid/ *adj.* lacking a protective button or guard on its point (*archaic*) ○ *an unbated sword* [Late 16thC. Formed from UN- + *bated*, the past participle of *bate* 'to abate, blunt', a shortening of ABATE.]

unbd *abbr.* PUBL unbound

unbearable /un báirəb'l/ *adj.* difficult, unpleasant, or impossible to bear or tolerate —**unbearableness** *n.* —**unbearably** *adv.*

unbeatable /un beétəb'l/ *adj.* too good or favourable to be beaten or surpassed —**unbeatably** *adv.*

unbeaten /un beét'n/ *adj.* **1. UNDEFEATED** never having been defeated or outdone **2. COOK NOT WHIPPED OR POUNDED** not subjected to pounding, whipping, or beating as part of the preparation for cooking or eating **3. TRANSP NOT TRAVELLED** not made smooth from pedestrian or vehicular traffic **4. CRICKET NOT OUT** without being got out

unbecoming /ún bi kúmming/ *adj.* **1. CLOTHES NOT FLATTERING** unsuitable or unattractive on the wearer **2. NOT RIGHT OR PROPER** not suitable, especially as not conforming with accepted attitudes or behaviour —**unbecomingly** *adv.* —**unbecomingness** *n.*

unbeknown /únbi nó̃n/, **unbeknownst** /únbi nó̃nst/ *adj.* **1. WITHOUT SB KNOWING** happening without a particular person knowing about it **2. NOT KNOWN TO SB** not known or familiar to sb ■ *adv.* **unbeknownst WITHOUT BEING SEEN** without being noticed or seen by anybody ○ *slipped away unbeknownst* [Mid-17thC. Formed from UN- + *beknow*, the past participle of obsolete *beknow*, literally 'to know thoroughly', from KNOW.]

unbelief /únbi leéf/ *n.* lack of religious or political belief

unbelievable /únbi leévəb'l/ *adj.* **1. IMPLAUSIBLE** too unrealistic or improbable to be believed **2. EXTRAORDINARY** used to emphasize that sth is very great, or very good, bad, or impressive ○ *reacted with unbelievable agility* —**unbelievably** *adv.*

unbeliever /únbi leévər/ *n.* sb who does not believe in a particular religious faith or subscribe to conventional beliefs

unbelieving /únbi leéving/ *adj.* **1. SCEPTICAL** lacking belief or expressing disbelief about sth **2. WITHOUT BELIEFS** with no religious faith or doctrinal beliefs —**unbelievingly** *adv.*

unbelt /un bélt/ (**-belts, -belting, -belted**) *vt.* **1. UNDO GARMENT'S BELT** to unfasten the belt on a garment **2. REMOVE SB OR STH FROM BELT** to remove sb or sth from a supporting or restraining belt

unbend /un bénd/ (**-bends, -bending, -bent, -bent** /-bént/) *v.* **1.** *vti.* **MAKE OR BECOME RELAXED** to become, or make sb become, more informal, relaxed, or friendly **2.** *vti.* **MAKE OR BECOME STRAIGHT** to become, or make sth become, straight after being bent, twisted, or flexed **3.** *vt.* **NAUT UNFASTEN SAIL OR ROPE** to free a sail, rope, or mooring line that was fastened —**unbendable** *adj.*

unbending /un bénding/ *adj.* **1. RESOLUTE** not willing to change opinions, beliefs, or attitudes **2. STRICTLY OBSERVED** strictly applied or observed **3. ALOOF** formal or unfriendly in manner or behaviour —**unbendingly** *adv.*

unbent[1] /un bént/ *adj.* **1. NOT FORCED INTO SUBMISSION** not forced into submitting or giving in **2. STRAIGHT** not bent or twisted

unbent[2] past tense, past participle of **unbend**

unbiased /un bí̇ əst/, **unbiassed** *adj.* **1. NOT BIASED** fair and impartial rather than biased or prejudiced **2. STATS WITH ZERO BIAS** with an expected value that is equal to the parameter being estimated —**unbiasedly** *adv.* —**unbiasedness** *n.*

unbiblical /un bíbblik'l/ *adj.* opposed or in contrast to the teachings of the Bible, or not present or approved in biblical teaching

unbidden /un bídd'n/ *adj., adv.* (*literary*) **1. SPONTANEOUS** not wished for or willed **2. UNSOLICITED** not asked for or invited [Old English *unbeden*, formed from *beden*, the past participle of *biddan* 'to ask for', an earlier form of BID]

unbind /un bí̇nd/ (**-binds, -binding, -bound, -bound** /-bó̃wnd/) *vt.* (*literary*) **1. FREE SB FROM RESTRICTIONS** to free sb from sth restraining or restricting, e.g. a duty or obligation **2. UNTIE** to untie a person or animal

unbleached /un bleécht/ *adj.* not treated with a bleach or whitener

unblessed /un blést/ *adj.* **1. WITHOUT A BLESSING** not given a blessing **2. UNFORTUNATE** unfortunate or wretched (*literary*) **3. REGARDED AS EVIL** in particular religions, regarded as behaving in unrighteous ways (*literary*) —**unblessedness** /un bléssidnəss/ *n.*

unblinking /un blíngking/ *adj.* **1. WITHOUT HESITATION** showing no emotion, reluctance, or hesitation **2. WITHOUT BLINKING** failing or unable to close and open the eyes in quick succession —**unblinkingly** *adv.*

unblushing /un blúshing/ *adj.* feeling or showing no shame or embarrassment —**unblushingly** *adv.* —**unblushingness** *n.*

unbolt /un bó̃lt/ (**-bolts, -bolting, -bolted**) *vt.* to pull back the bolt or bolts on a door or gate, so that it can be opened

unbolted /un bó̃ltid/ *adj.* **1. NOT FASTENED WITH BOLTS** not fitted with bolts, or with bolts not fastened **2. UNSIFTED** not having had the coarse particles sifted from the fine ones (*refers to flour or grain*)

unborn /ún báwrn/ *adj.* **1. NOT BORN YET** not yet born, but usually already conceived and gestating ○ *behaviour that could benefit the unborn child* **2. NOT THOUGHT OF YET** not thought of or begun yet (*literary*)

unbosom /un boózzəm/ (**-oms, -oming, -omed**) *v.* (*literary*) **1.** *vti.* **EXPRESS STH PREVIOUSLY HIDDEN** to express sth previously suppressed or hidden **2.** *vr.* **SAY WHAT IS ON YOUR MIND** to reveal the thoughts, feelings, or secrets you have been keeping inside yourself

unbound[1] /ún bó̃wnd/ *adj.* **1. WITHOUT A COVER** not fastened inside a permanent cover **2. UNRESTRICTED** having had restraints or fetters removed **3. SCI NOT IN CHEMICAL COMBINATION** free from chemical or physical combination **4.** **LING CONSTITUTING A WORD** used to describe a morpheme that can form a word on its own without any added elements

unbound[2] past tense, past participle of **unbind**

unbounded /un bó̃wndid/ *adj.* **1. NOT RESTRAINED** not controlled or restrained in any way **2. WITHOUT RESTRICTIONS** not subject to limits, boundaries, or restrictions —**unboundedly** *adv.* —**unboundedness** *n.*

unbowed /un bó̃wd/ *adj.* **1. UNDEFEATED** having refused to submit or admit defeat **2. NOT BENT** remaining in an erect position, not bent or bowed

unbrace /un bráyss/ (**-braces, -bracing, -braced**) *vt.* to make sth less tense or strained (*literary*)

unbred /un bréd/ *adj.* **1. NOT TRAINED** not given training or instruction (*literary*) **2. NOT WELL BRED** lacking refinement or breeding (*literary*) **3. AGRIC NOT YET MATED** not yet mated with another animal

unbridle /un brí̇d'l/ (**-dles, -dling, -dled**) *vt.* **1. EQU REMOVE BRIDLE** to take the bridle from a horse **2. FREE STH FROM RESTRAINTS** to take away the limits, controls, or restraints that apply to sth

unbridled /un brí̇d'ld/ *adj.* **1. OPENLY EXPRESSED** freely and openly expressed **2. EQU WITHOUT BRIDLE** not fitted with a bridle —**unbridledly** *adv.* —**unbridledness** *n.*

unbroken /un bró̃kən/ *adj.* **1. WITHOUT GAPS OR PAUSES** with no gaps or pauses **2. ONGOING** continued without interruption **3. UNDEFEATED** not beaten or subdued **4. UNTAMED** not yet having submitted to human control ○ *an unbroken horse* **5. NOT FRAGMENTED** remaining intact or in one piece **6. NOT VIOLATED** having remained viable or in force —**unbrokenly** *adv.* —**unbrokenness** *n.*

unbundle /un búnd'l/ (**-dles, -dling, -dled**) *vt.* to sell or charge for related products and services separately, rather than as a unit

unburden /ún búrd'n/ (**-dens, -dening, -dened**) *v.* **1.** *vr.* **GET STH OFF YOUR MIND** to relieve yourself of sth that has been worrying you by telling sb about it (*formal*) **2.** *vt.* **REMOVE PERSON'S OR ANIMAL'S LOAD** to take off a load that a person or animal has been carrying (*literary*)

unbutton /un bútt'n/ (**-tons, -toning, -toned**) *v.* **1.** *vt.* **UNDO CLOTHES WITH BUTTONS** to undo a garment by unfastening the buttons **2.** *vi.* **RELAX** to relax and become more talkative (*informal*)

uncaged /un káyjd/ *adj.* **1. RELEASED FROM A CAGE** no longer restrained in a cage **2. NOT LIMITED TO A CAGE** allowed to fly or roam freely

uncalled-for /un káwld-/ *adj.* beyond what is necessary or expected, especially in being unjustifiably unkind or impolite

uncanny /un kánni/ (**-nier, -niest**) *adj.* **1. EERIE** too strange or unlikely to seem merely natural or human **2. KEEN** unexpectedly accurate or precise ○ *an*

uncanny resemblance to the president —**uncannily** *adv.* —**uncanniness** *n.*

uncap /un káp/ (**-caps, -capping, -capped**) *vt.* to remove an upper limit or restriction from sth

uncared-for *adj.* neglected and allowed to deteriorate

unceasing /un seéssing/ *adj.* continuing without stopping, pausing, or diminishing —**unceasingly** *adv.* —**unceasingness** *n.*

unceremonious /ún serri mó̃ni əss/ *adj.* **1. ABRUPT** sudden and rather rude, with no concern for politeness or good manners **2. INFORMAL** done without formality or ceremony —**unceremoniously** *adv.* —**unceremoniousness** *n.*

uncertain /un súrt'n/ *adj.* **1. WITHOUT KNOWLEDGE** lacking clear knowledge or a definite opinion **2. NOT KNOWN OR SETTLED** not yet known, or remaining undecided **3. CHANGEABLE** likely to change, and therefore not reliable or stable **4. LACKING SELF-ASSURANCE** lacking self-assurance or confidence —**uncertainly** *adv.* —**uncertainness** *n.*

—— **WORD KEY: SYNONYMS** ——
See Synonyms at ***doubtful***.

uncertainty /un súrt'nti/ (*plural* **-ties**) *n.* **1. FACT OF BEING UNCERTAIN** the quality or state of being uncertain **2. UNPREDICTABLE THING** sth that nobody can predict or guarantee (*often plural*)

uncertainty principle *n.* a principle in quantum mechanics holding that it is impossible to determine both the position and momentum of a particle at the same time

unchain /un cháyn/ (**-chains, -chaining, -chained**) *vt.* **1. REMOVE CHAINS FROM SB** to take off the chain or chains holding a person or animal **2. FREE STH OR SB FROM RESTRAINTS** to take away the limits, controls, or restraints that apply to sth or sb

uncharged /un cháarjd/ *adj.* with no electric charge

uncharitable /un chárritəb'l/ *adj.* lacking in kindness or mercy —**uncharitably** *adv.*

uncharted /un cháartid/ *adj.* **1. NOT MAPPED** not surveyed or recorded on a map **2. UNKNOWN** not previously encountered, experienced, or investigated

unchartered /un cháartərd/ *adj.* not officially authorized or permitted

unchecked /ún chékt/ *adj.* **1. NOT CURBED** not limited or controlled, especially when restraint or control is required **2. NOT TESTED** remaining unverified or untested, especially for problems or imperfections

unchristian /ún krístyən/ *adj.* **1. UNCHARITABLE** unkind or selfish, and therefore against Christian principles and teachings **2. RELIG NON-CHRISTIAN** not belonging to the Christian church

unchurch /ún chúrch/ (**-churches, -churching, -churched**) *vt.* **1. EXCOMMUNICATE** to expel sb from a church **2. DECLARE TO BE NO LONGER A CHURCH** to remove the status of being a church from a building

Uncial

uncial /únssi əl/ *n.* **1. STYLE OF LETTER USED IN MANUSCRIPTS** a letter of the kind used in Greek and Latin manuscripts written between the third and ninth centuries that resembles a modern capital letter but is more rounded **2. MANUSCRIPT IN UNCIALS** a manuscript written in uncials ■ *adj.* **WRITTEN IN UNCIALS** relating to or written in uncials [Mid-17thC. From late Latin *unciales* (*litterae*), literally 'inch-high (letters)', from *uncia* 'twelfth part, inch'.] —**uncially** *adv.*

unciform /únssi fawrm/ *adj.* BIOL **HOOK-SHAPED** shaped like a hook ■ *n.* ANAT **BONE IN THE WRIST** a small hook-shaped bone in the wrist, at the base of the third and little fingers [Mid-18thC. Formed from Latin *uncus* 'hook'.]

uncinariasis /únssinə rī́ əssiss/ *n.* infestation of the intestines with hookworms [Early 20thC. From modern Latin *Uncinaria*, name of a genus of hookworms, from Latin *uncus* 'hook'.]

uncinate /únssinət/ *adj.* shaped like a hook at the end [Mid-18thC. From Latin *uncinatus*, from *uncus* 'hook'.]

uncinus /un sī́nəss/ (*plural* **-ni** /-sī́nī/) *n.* **1.** ZOOL **HOOKED PART OF AN ANIMAL'S BODY** a small hooked body part, e.g. the hook-shaped tooth of a gastropod or a chitinous hook on the body of an annelid **2.** METEOROL **CIRRUS CLOUD** a cirrus cloud that is curled in a hook shape at one of its elongated ends [Mid-19thC. From Latin, from *uncus* 'hook'.]

uncircumcised /ún súrkəm sīzd/ *adj.* not having had the prepuce of the penis or clitoris removed — **uncircumcision** /ún surkəm sízh'n/ *n.*

uncivil /un sívv'l/ *adj.* **1. RUDE** behaving in a way that is seen as hostile or indifferent **2. UNCIVILIZED** lacking features thought to reflect a civilized society or individual (*archaic*) —**uncivility** /únssi vílləti/ *n.* — **uncivilly** /un sívv'li/ *adv.* —**uncivilness** /-sívv'lnəss/ *n.*

uncivilized /un sívvəlīzd/, **uncivilised** *adj.* **1. NOT CULTURALLY ADVANCED** existing in a condition or behaving in ways that are thought to be socially or culturally primitive **2. REMOTE** far from civilized or settled areas **3. NOT POLITE, REFINED, OR COMFORTABLE** unacceptable or unbecoming to educated, cultured people used to refinement and comfort (*humorous*) —**uncivilizedly** /un sívvə līzidli/ *adv.* —**uncivilizedness** *n.*

unclad /un klád/ *adj.* not wearing any clothes

unclasp /un klaásp/ (**-clasps, -clasping, -clasped**) *vt.* **1. SEPARATE HANDS** to separate hands previously held together **2. UNDO THE CLASP ON STH** to unfasten the clasp holding sth closed

unclassified /un klássi fīd/ *adj.* **1. NOT ARRANGED SYSTEMATICALLY** not arranged or grouped systematically **2. NOT SECRET** remaining open for examination by anyone who wishes access **3.** TRANSP **NOT FOR MAIN TRAFFIC** not classed as a motorway, an A-road, or a B-road

uncle /úngk'l/ *n.* **1. PARENT'S BROTHER OR BROTHER-IN-LAW** the brother of sb's mother or father, or the husband of sb's aunt (*capitalized before a name*) **2. PAWNBROKER** a pawnbroker (*dated slang*) [13thC. Via Old French *oncle* from, ultimately, Latin *avunculus* 'maternal uncle'.]

Uncle *n.* a name some children are encouraged to call a man friend of one or both of their parents

unclean /ún kleén/ *adj.* **1. DIRTY** dirty or unsanitary **2. UNCHASTE** sinful, especially involving or guilty of committing a sexual sin **3.** RELIG **RELIGIOUSLY OR RITUALLY IMPURE** not pure according to religious rules or rituals [Old English *unclæne*] —**uncleanness** *n.*

WORD KEY: SYNONYMS

See Synonyms at ***dirty***.

uncleanly /un klénnli/ *adj.* = **unclean** (*formal or literary*) ■ *adv.* **IN UNCLEAN WAY** in a way that is not clean [Old English *unclænic, unclænice*] —**uncleanliness** *n.*

unclear /ún kleér/ *adj.* **1. NOT OBVIOUS** not obvious or easy to understand **2. NOT SURE** not sure or not free from doubt

unclench /ún klénch/ (**-clenches, -clenching, -clenched**) *vti.* to release the muscles in a part of your body that were being held tightly, or to relax from a tightened state

Uncle Sam *n.* **1. PERSONIFICATION OF THE UNITED STATES** a personification of the government of the United States, shown in a tall thin man with a white beard, wearing red and white striped trousers, a blue tail coat, and a stovepipe hat with a band of stars **2. UNITED STATES** the United States or the American people [19thC. Invented from *US*, abbreviation of *United States*.]

Uncle Tom /-tóm/ *n.* a highly offensive term used to describe a Black man who is thought to be too solicitous of or subservient to whites (*insult*) [Mid-19thC. After a character in Harriet Beecher Stowe's novel *Uncle Tom's Cabin*.] —**Uncle Tomism** *n.*

unclog /un klóg/ (**-clogs, -clogging, -clogged**) *vt.* to remove a blockage from sth such as a pipe

unclose /un klṓz/ (**-closes, -closing, -closed**) *vti.* **1. MAKE OR BE OPEN** to make or become open rather than closed **2. DISCLOSE** to reveal sth, or to be revealed

unclosed /un klṓzd/ *adj.* not in a closed condition

unclothe /un klṓth/ (**-clothes, -clothing, -clothed**) *vt.* to remove the clothes or covering from sb or sth — **unclothed** *adj.*

unco[1] /úngkō/ *adv. Scotland* **VERY** very or extremely ■ *adj. Scotland* **UNUSUAL** unusual or unfamiliar [15thC. Variant of UNCOUTH.]

unco[2] /úngkō/ *adj. Aus* a common term of abuse used particularly by children to tease someone who is clumsy or inept at sports and games (*informal*) [Late 20thC. Shortening.]

uncoil /ún kóyl/ (**-coils, -coiling, -coiled**) *vti.* to release sth, or be released, from a coiled or wound position

uncomfortable /un kúmftəb'l/ *adj.* **1. NOT PHYSICALLY COMFORTABLE** feeling a lack of or not providing physical comfort **2. AWKWARD OR UNEASY** feeling or making others feel awkward and ill-at-ease —**uncomfortableness** *n.* —**uncomfortably** *adv.*

uncommercial /únkə múrsh'l/ *adj.* **1. NOT CONCERNED WITH COMMERCE OR BUSINESS** not involved in commerce, especially not operated or organized for profit **2. AGAINST BUSINESS PRINCIPLES OR PRACTICES** contrary to the way things are usually done in commerce or business **3. UNPROFITABLE** unappealing to consumers and so not likely to turn a profit

uncommitted /únkə míttid/ *adj.* **1. WITH NO SENSE OF COMMITMENT** not dedicated to a particular principle, cause, or organization **2. NOT PLEDGED** not pledged to a particular cause, purpose, or course of action ○ *uncommitted funds*

uncommon /un kómmən/ *adj.* **1. RARE** appearing or happening infrequently **2. VERY GREAT** used to emphasize the great extent of sth —**uncommonness** *n.*

uncommonly /un kómmənli/ *adv.* **1. SELDOM** not frequently **2. UNUSUALLY** to a degree or extent that is unusual or rare

uncommunicative /únkə myóonikətiv/ *adj.* not willing to say much or tending not to say much —**uncommunicatively** *adv.* —**uncommunicativeness** *n.*

WORD KEY: SYNONYMS

See Synonyms at ***silent***.

uncompromising /un kómprə mīzing/ *adj.* feeling or showing no willingness to compromise or back down —**uncompromisingly** *adv.* —**uncompromisingness** *n.*

unconcern /únkən súrn/ *n.* lack of concern or interest, especially where concern would be expected or thought appropriate

unconcerned /únkən súrnd/ *adj.* **1. NOT ANXIOUS** not worried or anxious, especially when this seems unexpected or unnatural **2. INDIFFERENT** lacking concern or interest or unwilling to become involved in sth —**unconcernedly** /-súrnidli/ *adv.* —**unconcernedness** /-súrnidnəss/ *n.*

unconditional /únkən dísh'nəl/ *adj.* complete or guaranteed, with no conditions, limitations, or provisos attached ○ *unconditional love* —**unconditionality** /únkən dishə nálləti/ *n.* —**unconditionally** /únkən dísh'nəli/ *adv.*

unconditioned /únkən dísh'nd/ *adj.* **1. WITHOUT CONDITIONS** without any conditions or limits restricting or affecting it **2.** PSYCHOL **NATURAL** arising spontaneously and not as a result of learning or conditioning ○ *an unconditioned reflex* —**unconditionedness** *n.*

unconditioned stimulus *n.* a stimulus that evokes a reflexive response without prior conditioning or learning

unconformable /únkən fáwrməb'l/ *adj.* **1. UNWILLING TO CONFORM** unwilling or unable to follow conventional social customs **2.** GEOL **SHOWING GEOLOGICAL UNCONFORMITY** used to describe a layer of rock that lies directly on a much older stratum, indicating a period of erosion —**unconformability** /únkən fáwrmə bílləti/ *n.* — **unconformably** /únkən fáwrməbli/ *adv.*

unconformity /únkən fáwrməti/ (*plural* **-formities**) *n.* **1. LACK OF CONFORMITY** behaviour or thinking that refuses to follow conventional social prescriptions **2.** GEOL **BREAK IN CONTINUITY IN SEDIMENTARY ROCKS** a break in the continuity of sedimentary rocks resulting from erosion or cessation of deposition **3.** GEOL **SURFACE BETWEEN MISMATCHED STRATA** the contact surface between two unconformable strata, often marked by angular discordance

unconnected /únkə néktid/ *adj.* not related or connected to sth else or each other ○ *The two incidents are entirely unconnected.* —**unconnectedly** *adv.* —**unconnectedness** *n.*

unconscionable /un kónsh'nəb'l/ *adj.* **1. MORALLY UNACCEPTABLE** shocking and morally unacceptable **2. UNREASONABLE** far beyond what is considered reasonable —**unconscionableness** *n.* —**unconscionably** *adv.*

unconscious /un kónshəss/ *adj.* **1.** MED **EXPERIENCING LOSS OF SENSES** unable to see, hear, or otherwise sense what is going on, usually temporarily and often as a result of an accident or injury **2. UNAWARE** not aware of sth **3. UNINTENTIONAL** not intended, or not realized or recognized ○ *unconscious irony* ■ *n.* PSYCHOL **MIND'S HIDDEN PART** the part of the mind containing memories, thoughts, feelings, and ideas that the person is not generally aware of but that manifest themselves in dreams and dissociated acts — **unconsciously** *adv.* —**unconsciousness** *n.*

unconsidered /únkən síddərd/ *adj.* done without being properly thought about beforehand

unconstitutional /ún konsti tyóosh'nəl/ *adj.* not allowed by or against the principles set down in a constitution, especially a nation's written constitution —**unconstitutionality** /ún konsti tyóosh'n álləti/ *n.* —**unconstitutionally** /-tyóosh'nəli/ *adv.*

uncontrollable /únkən trṓləb'l/ *adj.* **1. TOO STRONG TO SUPPRESS** too strongly felt to be suppressed **2. TOO UNRULY TO CONTROL** too unruly or wild to discipline or control —**uncontrollability** /únkən trōlə bílləti/ *n.* — **uncontrollably** /únkən trṓləbli/ *adv.*

unconventional /únkən vénsh'nəl/ *adj.* different from what is regarded as normal or standard —**unconventionality** /únkən vénshə nálləti/ *n.* —**unconventionally** /únkən vénsh'nəli/ *adv.*

uncool /ún kóol/ *adj.* **1. UNDESIRABLE** unfashionable, undesirable, or unacceptable, especially in the opinion of young people (*slang*) **2. UNRELAXED** not suitably relaxed, casual, or self-assured, especially in the opinion of young people (*informal*)

uncoordinated /ún kō áwrdi naytid/ *adj.* **1. CLUMSY IN MOVEMENT OR ACTION** awkward when moving or doing sth, as if different parts of the body were not acting in harmony **2. NOT ORGANIZED** with no organization or proper cooperation between individuals or groups

uncork /un káwrk/ (**-corks, -corking, -corked**) *vt.* **1. REMOVE THE CORK FROM** to open a bottle of sth, especially wine, by taking out its cork **2. UNLEASH** to release sth that has been restrained or repressed such as a strong emotion

uncountable /un kówntəb'l/ *adj.* **1. NOT ABLE TO BE COUNTED** too various or great in number to be counted **2.** GRAM **NOT REFERRING TO AN INDIVIDUAL** used to describe a noun that does not refer to a single object

uncounted /un kówntid/ *adj.* **1. INNUMERABLE** too numerous to be counted **2. NOT COUNTED** not, or not yet, subjected to a count

uncouple /un kúpp'l/ (**-ples, -pling, -pled**) *v.* **1.** *vti.* **UNFASTEN** to separate two things or one thing from another by undoing a fastening that connects them **2.** *vt.* **RELEASE FROM RESTRAINT** to let loose sth that has been restrained

uncouth /un kóoth/ *adj.* **1. ILL-MANNERED** behaving in an ill-mannered or unrefined way **2. AWKWARD** clumsy and ungraceful [Old English *uncūþ* 'unknown', from *cūþ* 'known', past participle of *cunnan* 'to know', an earlier form of CAN] —**uncouthly** *adv.* —**uncouthness** *n.*

uncovenanted /un kúvvənəntid/ *adj.* not bound, sanctioned, or guaranteed by a covenant

uncover /un kúvvər/ (**-ers, -ering, -ered**) *v.* **1.** *vti.* **TAKE THE COVER OFF** to remove a covering from sth **2.** *vt.* **EXPOSE** to find, find out about, or reveal sth secret or previously hidden ○ *uncover the truth about somebody* **3.** *vti.* **TAKE OFF YOUR HAT** to take off a hat or other head covering (*dated*)

uncovered /un kúvvərd/ *adj.* **1. WITH NO COVERING** without any covering or protection **2.** INSUR **NOT INSURED** not protected by insurance or guaranteed by some security **3. WITH THE HEAD BARE** with a hat or other head covering removed, usually as a sign of respect (*dated*)

uncritical /un kríttik'l/ *adj.* accepting or approving sth without analysing or questioning it or discriminating between good and bad —**uncritically** *adv.*

uncross /un króss/ (**-crosses, -crossing, -crossed**) *vt.* to straighten out from a crossed position ○ *She sat crossing and uncrossing her arms impatiently.*

uncrowned /ún krównd/ *adj.* **1. WITH POWER BUT NO TITLE** possessing power, status, or wide respect but without an official title or recognition **2. ROYAL BUT NOT YET CROWNED** with royal rank but not yet crowned

unction /úngksh'n/ *n.* **1. ANOINTING WITH OIL** the rubbing or sprinkling of oil on sb as part of a religious ceremony **2. SUBSTANCE USED IN A RITE** an oil, ointment, or salve used in religious rites **3. REAL OR PRETENDED EARNESTNESS** real or pretended earnestness or fervour, especially with regard to spiritual matters and especially when expressed in suitably solemn language **4. FLATTERING EFFORTS TO CHARM** excessively ingratiating efforts to charm or convince sb **5. STH SOOTHING** sth that soothes or comforts sb [14thC. From Latin *unction-*, from *unguere* 'to smear, anoint' (source of English *ointment* and *anoint*).]

unctuous /úngkchoo əss/ *adj.* **1. EXCESSIVELY INGRATIATING** attempting to charm or convince sb in an unpleasantly suave, smug, or smooth way **2. OILY, FATTY, OR GREASY** resembling or containing oil, fat, or grease [14thC. From medieval Latin *unctuosus*, from Latin *unctus* 'anointing', from *unguere* (see UNCTION).] —**unctuosity** /úngkchoo óssəti/ *n.* —**unctuously** /-əssli/ *adv.* —**unctuousness** /-əssnəss/ *n.*

uncurl /un kúrl/ (**-curls, -curling, -curled**) *vti.* to straighten sth that was previously wound in a curl, coil, or spiral, or to become unwound or straight

uncus /úngkəss/ (*plural* **-ci** /ún sī/) *n.* ANAT a body part shaped like a hook [Early 19thC. Via modern Latin from Latin, 'hook'.]

uncut /ún kút/ *adj.* **1. NOT CUT** with no part removed or divided by cutting **2. COMPLETE** not abridged, shortened, or censored **3. NOT FACETED** used to describe a gemstone in its original shape, before facets have been cut **4.** PUBL **WITH UNSEPARATED PAGES** with the edges of the pages not yet trimmed to separate them **5.** DRUGS **NOT ADULTERATED** in a pure and unadulterated form (*informal*)

undamped /un dámpt/ *adj.* **1. NOT DIMINISHED** not subdued or discouraged **2.** PHYS **ABLE TO OSCILLATE** used to describe a scientific instrument or system that is allowed to oscillate unchecked

undaunted /un dáwntid/ *adj.* not afraid or deterred by the prospect of defeat, loss, or failure —**undauntedly** *adv.* —**undauntedness** *n.*

undead *npl.* in fiction, especially vampire stories, people or other beings who are technically dead but still exist, move, and interact with the living in a physical form —**undead** *adj.*

undecagon /un dékəgən/ *n.* a plane figure with eleven sides and eleven angles [Early 18thC. Formed from Latin *undecim* 'eleven' + -GON, on the model of DECAGON.]

undeceive /úndi seév/ (**-ceives, -ceiving, -ceived**) *vt.* to tell the truth to sb who has been misled (*often passive*) —**undeceiver** *n.*

undecided /úndi sídid/ *adj.* **1. NOT HAVING DECIDED** not yet having made a choice or decision **2. NOT FINALIZED** not yet settled or resolved ■ *n.* **SB WITHOUT MIND MADE UP** sb who has not yet made a decision or choice about sth ○ *She was counted among the undecideds.* —**undecidedly** *adv.* —**undecidedness** *n.*

undefined /úndi fínd/ *adj.* **1. WITHOUT FIXED LIMITS** for which no definite limits have been decided **2. NOT EXPLAINED** not given a definition, meaning, or value

undelete /úndi léet/ (**-letes, -leting, -leted**) *vt.* COMPUT to reinstate text or a file that has been deleted on a computer

undemocratic /ún demmə kráttik/ *adj.* not in accordance with or not practising democracy —**undemocratically** *adv.*

undemonstrative /úndi mónstrətiv/ *adj.* tending not to show emotions openly —**undemonstratively** *adv.* —**undemonstrativeness** *n.*

undeniable /úndi nī əb'l/ *adj.* **1. BEYOND QUESTION** unquestionably true or real and beyond dispute **2. UNABLE TO BE REFUSED** not able to be refused because of its importance or impact **3. INDISPUTABLY WORTHY** with worth, merit, or quality that cannot be doubted ○ *a person of undeniable character* —**undeniableness** *n.* —**undeniably** *adv.*

under /úndər/ CORE MEANING: a grammatical word used to express the concept of being beneath or below sth, e.g. in location, size, age, or price ○ (prep) *Johnny had the book hidden under his tunic.* ○ (prep) *The machine is under a foot high and will fit on to any work surface.* ○ (prep) *The toy should not be given to children under three years old.* ○ (prep) *It's the best meal you can get for under £5.* ○ (adv) *For one week only, kids five and under eat free.*

1. *prep.* **BELOW** directly below or underneath the base of sth ○ *They were sheltering under a huge umbrella.* **2.** *prep.* **BENEATH** beneath a layer of sth ○ *He had two sweaters on under his jacket.* **3.** *prep.* **LESS THAN** fewer in number than or less than sth, e.g. in age, quantity, size, or price ○ *By the age of sixteen she was still under five feet tall.* **4.** *prep.* **SUBORDINATE TO** lower in rank or status than sb ○ *I was under him in the company hierarchy.* **5.** *prep.* **SUBJECT TO** subject to the control or authority of sb or sth ○ *under existing legislation* ○ *working under a new boss* **6.** *prep.* **DURING THE RULE OF** during the rule of a person or government ○ *The crime rate had in fact gone down under the new mayor.* **7.** *prep.* **IN VIEW OF** in view of sth or while sth, especially conditions or circumstances, prevails ○ *Serious work is impossible under these conditions.* **8.** *prep.* **UNDERGOING A PROCESS** used to indicate that sb or sth is going through a particular process or experience ○ *The proposals have come under attack.* **9.** *prep.* **USING THE NAME OF** using a particular name, especially an assumed name ○ *travelling under a false name* **10.** *prep.* **CLASSIFIED WITHIN** classified as or in sth ○ *You should find it in the filing cabinet under 'Miscellaneous'.* **11.** *prep.* **PLANTED WITH** planted with a particular crop ○ *That field will be under rye next year.* **12.** *prep.* **POWERED BY** powered or driven by sth ○ *under sail* **13.** *prep.* **IN A SIGN OF THE ZODIAC** during a period in which the sun is in a particular position in the zodiac ○ *I was born under Sagittarius.* **14.** *adv.* **BELOW A SURFACE OR POINT** at or to a point or place at a lower level, especially one below a surface ○ *lifted the wire and crawled under* **15.** *adv.* **FEWER OR LESS** fewer or less than a previously given figure ○ *Employers with 50 employees or under are exempt.* **16.** *adv., adj.* **SUBSERVIENT** in or into a position of submissiveness or subservience (*informal*) ○ *policies designed to keep the masses under* **17.** *adv., adj.* **UNCONSCIOUS** in or into a state of unconsciousness or hypnosis (*informal*) ○ *could feel myself going under* [Old English *under*. Ultimately from an Indo-European word that is also the ancestor of English *inferior* and *inferno*.]

underachieve /úndər ə cheév/ (**-chieves, -chieving, -chieved**) *vi.* to fail to fulfil your potential or sb's expectations —**underachievement** *n.*

underachiever /úndər ə cheévər/ *n.* **1. SB WHO UNDERPERFORMS ACADEMICALLY** sb who does less well in academic work than might have been expected, given the evidence of the person's intelligence and aptitude **2. UNDERPERFORMER** sb or sth that performs below expectations

underact /úndər ákt/ (**-acts, -acting, -acted**) *v.* **1.** *vti.* **ACT A ROLE POORLY** to fail to play a role with enough power or conviction **2.** *vt.* **PLAY DOWN EFFECTIVELY** to play a role in an understated way deliberately, for dramatic effect

underage /úndər áyj/ *adj.* **1. BELOW AGE** below the legal or required age for sth **2. DONE BY PEOPLE UNDER THE LEGAL AGE** carried on by people who are below the age at which sth is legally permitted

underarm /úndər aarm/ *adj.* **1.** SPORTS **DONE WITH ARM BELOW SHOULDER** with the arm kept below shoulder height and usually close to the body when performing the action, e.g. throwing, serving, or bowling a ball. US term **underhand** **2. BELOW THE ARM** below the arm or for use under the arm, especially the armpit **3. FROM WRIST TO ARMPIT** relating to the area along the underside of the arm from armpit to wrist ■ *adv.* SPORTS **WITH ARM LOW** with the arm kept below shoulder height. US term **underhand** ■ *n.* **AREA JUST BELOW THE ARM** the area below the arm on the body or on a garment, especially the armpit

underbelly /úndər belli/ (*plural* **-lies**) *n.* **1.** ZOOL **LOWEST PART OF AN ANIMAL'S BELLY** the underside of an animal, normally the part of the belly that is closest to the ground **2. WEAK POINT** a weak or vulnerable part of sth ○ *the soft underbelly of the regime* **3. LOWER SURFACE** the underside of an object, especially an aircraft

underbid /úndər bíd/ *v.* (**-bids, -bidding, -bid**) **1.** *vti.* **OFFER LESS** to offer a lower price than sb else in competitive bidding **2.** *vi.* **MAKE TOO LOW A BID** to make a very low bid or too low a bid to obtain sth **3.** *vti.* CARDS **BID LESS THAN THE VALUE OF YOUR CARDS** to bid less than the full value of a hand in cards ■ *n.* **VERY LOW BID** a bid that is lower than sb else's, or too low to obtain sth —**underbidder** *n.*

underbite /úndər bīt/ *n.* DENT a dental condition in which the lower incisor teeth overlap the upper. ◊ **overbite** [Late 20thC. Modelled on OVERBITE.]

underbody /úndər boddi/ (*plural* **-ies**) *n.* the underside of the body of a motor vehicle or of an animal

underbred /úndər bréd/ *adj.* **1. NOT PUREBRED** not bred from pure stock **2. NOT WELL-BRED** not brought up well or well-mannered —**underbreeding** /úndər breéding/ *n.*

undercapitalize /úndər káppit'l īz/ (**-izes, -izing, -ized**), **undercapitalise** (**-ises, -ising, -ised**) *vti.* to fail to supply an organization, especially a business, with enough capital to operate efficiently (*often passive*) —**undercapitalization** /úndər káppit'l ī záysh'n/ *n.*

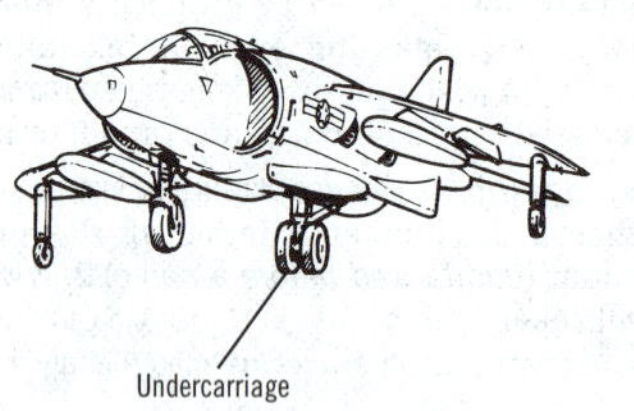

Undercarriage

undercarriage /úndər karrij/ *n.* **1. WHEEL STRUCTURE FOR AN AIRCRAFT** the framework of struts and wheels on which an aircraft runs when it moves on the ground **2. SUPPORTING STRUCTURE UNDERNEATH A VEHICLE** the supporting framework underneath a vehicle, to which wheels, tracks, or other means of locomotion are attached

undercharge *v.* /úndər chaárj/ (**-charges, -charging, -charged**) **1.** *vti.* **NOT CHARGE SB ENOUGH** to charge sb too low a price for sth **2.** *vt.* ARMS **INSERT TOO WEAK A CHARGE IN** to put an inadequate charge in a firearm ■ *n.* /úndər chaarj/ **EXCESSIVELY LOW PRICE** a price charged that is too low

underclass /úndər klaass/ *n.* a social class consisting of people so underprivileged that they are seen as being excluded from mainstream society

underclay /úndər klay/ *n.* a layer of fine-grained sedimentary clay found beneath a coal seam, containing the fossilized roots of the plants that became the coal

underclothes /úndər klōthz/ *npl.* = **underwear**

underclothing /úndər klōthing/ *n.* = **underwear**

undercoat /úndər kōt/ *n.* **1. COAT BENEATH THE FINAL PAINT COAT** a coat of paint or emulsion applied to a surface before a top coat is applied **2. PAINT TO BE COVERED** paint or emulsion designed to be used as an undercoat **3.** ZOOL **SHORT HAIRS UNDER AN ANIMAL'S COAT** a dense layer of short hairs, fur, or wool beneath the longer growth of an animal's outer coat ■ *vt.* (**-coats, -coating,**

-coated) 1. PAINT WITH AN UNDERCOAT to apply an undercoat to a surface 2. *US* CARS = **underseal**

undercoating /úndər kōting/ *n. US* = **underseal**

undercool /úndər kóol/ (**-cools, -cooling, -cooled**) *vt.* CHEM = **supercool**

undercover /úndər kúvvər/ *adj.* engaged in or involving the secret gathering of information, especially by sb who disguises himself or herself as a member of the group whose activities are being investigated ○ *an undercover police officer* —**undercover** *adv.*

undercroft /úndər kroft/ *n.* an underground room, especially the crypt of a church

undercurrent /úndər kurrənt/ *n.* 1. UNDERLYING CURRENT a current in a body of water or air that flows beneath another current or the surface 2. HIDDEN FEELING OR FORCE a feeling, opinion, force, or tendency that is felt to be present in sb, but that is not openly shown or expressed and often differs markedly from the person's outward reaction ○ *an undercurrent of resentment*

undercut *v.* /úndər kút/ (**-cuts, -cutting, -cut**) 1. *vt.* BUSINESS CHARGE A LOWER AMOUNT THAN to charge less for sth than sb else 2. *vt.* REDUCE STH'S FORCE to undermine sth or detract from its force (*often passive*) 3. *vt.* CUT THE LOWER PART OF to cut away or cut into the lower part of sth, especially so as to leave a portion overhanging 4. *vti.* SPORTS HIT A BALL WITH BACKSPIN to hit a ball with a downward oblique stroke, e.g. in golf or tennis, so that it has backspin ■ *n.* /úndər kut/ 1. CUT MADE IN A LOWER PART a cut made below another or into the lower part of sth 2. STH CUT AWAY a piece of material that has been cut away from the lower part of sth 3. *US* FORESTRY NOTCH IN A TREE TRUNK a notch cut in a tree that is being felled that helps it make a clean break and directs its fall 4. SPORTS STROKE WITH BACKSPIN a stroke that gives backspin to a ball

underdaks /úndər daks/ *npl. Aus* underpants, especially men's underpants (*informal*)

underdeveloped /úndər di véllәpt/ *adj.* 1. NOT FULLY GROWN not grown to a full or normal extent 2. ECON WITHOUT MEANS FOR ECONOMIC GROWTH lacking the technology and capital to make efficient use of available resources 3. PHOTOGRAPHY NOT DEVELOPED ENOUGH used to describe a photograph, negative, or film that was inadequately developed during processing, usually through being taken out of the developer too soon, and that lacks contrast as a result —**underdevelopment** *n.*

underdog /úndər dog/ *n.* 1. EXPECTED LOSER sb who is expected to lose a fight or contest 2. SB AT A DISADVANTAGE sb who tends to be unsuccessful in life

underdone /úndər dún/ *adj.* 1. INADEQUATELY COOKED not cooked as thoroughly as intended or required 2. RARE cooked only lightly or partially to achieve a desired flavour or texture

underdrain *vt.* /úndər dráyn/ (**-drains, -draining, -drained**) PROVIDE WITH UNDERGROUND DRAINS to equip an area, especially of cultivated land, with a system of underground drains ■ *n.* /úndər drayn/ UNDERGROUND DRAIN an underground drain or system of drains on agricultural land —**underdrainage** /úndər draynij/ *n.*

underdress *(vi)* /úndər dréss/ *vi.* (**-dresses, -dressing, -dressed**) DRESS INADEQUATELY FOR AN OCCASION to dress less fully or formally than an occasion or circumstance demands, e.g. in cold weather or for a social event (*often passive*) ◊ **dress down** ■ *n.* /úndər dréss/ GARMENT WORN BENEATH OTHERS a garment or set of garments worn beneath others, especially if designed to be seen when worn

underemphasize /úndər émfə sīz/ (**-sizes, -sizing, -sized**), **underemphasise** (**-sises, -sising, -sised**) *vt.* to fail to give sth the emphasis or importance it deserves —**underemphasis** *n.*

underemployed /úndər im plóyd/ *adj.* 1. NOT USED FULLY not being used to full capacity in a job 2. NOT WORKING FULL-TIME working part-time but preferring full-time employment —**underemployment** *n.*

underestimate *v.* /úndər ésti mayt/ (**-mates, -mating, -mated**) 1. *vti.* MAKE TOO LOW AN ESTIMATE to make an estimate of sth that is too low ○ *We underestimated the time it would take.* 2. *vt.* MISJUDGE THE WORTH OF to judge people or things as being inferior to their real value or ability ○ *Don't underestimate her – she's tougher than she looks.* ■ *n.* /úndər éstimət/ TOO LOW AN ESTIMATE an estimate that is too low, or a judgment that is too unfavourable to sb or sth —**underestimation** /úndər ésti máysh'n/ *n.*

underexpose /úndər ik spṓz/ (**-poses, -posing, -posed**) *vt.* 1. PHOTOGRAPHY EXPOSE FILM INADEQUATELY to expose film to light for too short a time or to inadequate light 2. PUBLICIZE INADEQUATELY to fail to give sb or sth enough publicity —**underexposure** *n.*

underfeed (**-feeds, -feeding, -fed** /-féd/) *vt.* 1. /úndər féed/ FEED INADEQUATELY to fail to give a person or animal enough to eat 2. /úndər feed/ FUEL FROM UNDERNEATH to fuel sth, e.g. an engine or a furnace, from underneath

underfelt /úndər felt/ *n.* a layer of felt or other material put down on a floor before a carpet is laid to give better insulation and wear

underfinanced /úndər fi nánst, úndər fī nanst/ *adj.* not provided with sufficient capital or funds to be able to run efficiently

underfloor /úndər fláwr/ *adj.* locating beneath the flooring of a room or building ○ *underfloor heating*

underflow /úndərflō/ *n.* the inability of a location in computer memory to handle data of an excessively small magnitude, or an instance of this. ◊ **overflow**

underfoot /úndər fóot/ *adv.* 1. BENEATH THE FEET under the feet of a person or animal, on the ground, or between the feet and the ground ○ *It was muddy underfoot.* 2. IN THE WAY creating an obstacle or obstruction 3. WITH ARROGANT DISREGARD OR DESTRUCTIVE INTENT in a way that shows an arrogant or callous disregard or an intention to destroy ○ *trampled underfoot the feelings of everyone who worked for them*

underfund /úndər fúnd/ *vt.* to fail to provide adequate funding for sth such as a project or scheme (*often passive*) ○ *It was an ambitious plan, hopelessly underfunded from the start.*

underfunding /úndər fúnding/ *n.* failure to make enough funds available for sth ○ *The programme eventually foundered after years of underfunding.*

underfur /úndər fur/ *n.* a soft layer of short fur beneath the outer, coarser fur of some animals such as the beaver

undergarment /úndər gaarmənt/ *n.* a piece of clothing worn beneath outer clothes, especially next to the skin, and not normally seen in public

undergird /úndər gúrd/ (**-girds, -girding, -girded** *or* **-girt** /-gúrt/, **-girded** *or* **-girt**) *vt.* 1. SUPPORT FROM BELOW to support or secure sth from below, e.g. with ropes passed underneath 2. SUPPORT to provide sth with support or reinforcement of any kind

underglaze /úndər glayz/ *adj.* APPLIED PRIOR TO GLAZING used to describe decoration or pigment applied to a piece of pottery before the glaze is put on ○ *an underglaze pigment* ■ *n.* STH APPLIED BEFORE GLAZING sth, especially a decoration or pigment, that is applied to a piece of pottery before the glaze is put on

undergo /úndər gṓ/ (**-goes, -going, -went** /-wént/, **-gone** /-gón/) *vt.* to experience or endure sth, or have sth happen to you ○ *You'll be obliged to undergo a thorough medical examination.* ○ *The city underwent a period of great change.*

undergrad /úndər grad/ *n.* an undergraduate (*informal; often used before a noun*) ○ *undergrad humour* [Early 19thC. Shortening.]

undergraduate /úndər grájjoo ət/ *n.* a student at university or college who is studying for a first degree (*often used before a noun*) ○ *undergraduate courses*

underground *adj.* /úndər grownd/ 1. BENEATH THE EARTH'S SURFACE located, happening, or operating beneath the surface of the Earth 2. COVERT concealed and done in secret 3. CONTRARY TO THE PREVAILING CULTURE separate from a prevailing social or artistic environment, and often exercising a subversive influence ○ *The story had been circulating in the underground press for years.* ■ *n.* /úndər grownd/ 1. RAILWAY RUNNING BELOW GROUND a railway system that runs below ground (*often used before a noun*) US term **subway** 2. RESISTANCE MOVEMENT a secret movement that aims to overthrow a government or fight against an occupying enemy 3. MOVEMENT CONTRARY TO THE PREVAILING CULTURE a movement or group that is separate from the prevailing social or artistic environment and often exerts a subversive influence ■ *adv.* /úndər grównd/ 1. BELOW GROUND below the surface of the ground 2. SECRETLY in secret or in hiding

Underground Railroad *n.* a secret organization that helped enslaved labourers flee from the southern United States to Canada or other places of safety prior to the abolition of slavery

undergrown /úndər grōn, úndər grṓn/ *adj.* 1. NOT FULLY GROWN not grown to the expected size 2. WITH UNDERGROWTH having or covered with undergrowth

undergrowth /úndər grōth/ *n.* 1. VEGETATION UNDER TREES shrubs, small trees, or other vegetation growing beneath the trees in a forest 2. STUNTED GROWTH growth that is less than expected 3. ZOOL = **undercoat, underfur**

underhand /úndər hánd, úndər hand/ *adj.* 1. SECRET AND DISHONEST done secretively and dishonestly or with the intention to deceive or cheat sb 2. *US* SPORTS = **underarm** ■ *adv.* 1. SECRETLY AND DISHONESTLY in a secretive and dishonest way 2. *US* = **underarm** [Late 16thC. Origin uncertain: possibly from a sleight of hand in gambling as in Old French *par sous main*, literally 'by under hand'.]

underhanded /úndər hándid/ *adj., adv.* = **underhand** *adj.* 1, **underhand** *adv.* 1 —**underhandedly** *adv.* —**underhandedness** *n.*

underhung /úndər húng/ *adj.* 1. MED JUTTING BEYOND THE UPPER JAW used to describe a lower jaw that projects beyond the upper jaw 2. CONSTR RUNNING ON A RAIL UNDERNEATH running on a rail or track situated underneath ○ *underhung sliding doors*

underinsure /úndərin shóor/ (**-sures, -suring, -sured**) *vt.* to take out insufficient insurance to cover the value of the article that is being insured

underlain past participle of **underlie**

underlay[1] *vt.* /úndər láy/ (**-lays, -laying, -laid** /-láyd/) PROVIDE WITH STH UNDERNEATH to lay sth underneath sth else (*often passive*) ■ *n.* /úndər lay/ 1. LAYER BENEATH CARPET a layer of cushioning and insulating material put down on a floor before a carpet is laid 2. SUPPORT FOR STH sth laid beneath sth else as a base, support, or foundation [Old English *underleegan*] —**underlaid** /úndər láyd/ *adj.*

WORD KEY: USAGE

underlay or **underlie**? Unlike the root words *lay* and *lie*, both verbs are transitive (i.e. take an object). The more common word is ***underlie***, and this has a wider range of meanings including the nonphysical meaning 'to form the basis of': *This trend underlies all the social changes of recent times.* The primary meaning of ***underlay*** is 'to cover the bottommost part of' (*We underlaid the carpet with felt*) and in this meaning it also acts as a noun (with the stress on the first syllable).

underlay[2] past tense of **underlie**

underlet /úndər lét/ (**-lets, -letting, -let**) *v.* 1. *vt.* LET CHEAPLY to let a property for less than its full value 2. *vti.* = **sublet**

underlie /úndər lí/ (**-lies, -lying, -lay** /-láy/, **-lain** /-láyn/) *vt.* 1. LIE BENEATH to lie or be put under sth else 2. BE THE FOUNDATION OF STH to be the basis or cause of sth ○ *the assumptions that underlie this argument* 3. FIN HAVE FINANCIAL PRIORITY OVER to take priority over other financial rights or securities ○ *This claim underlies yours.* [Old English *underliegan*]

WORD KEY: USAGE

See Usage note at ***underlay***[1].

underline *vt.* /úndər lín/ (**-lines, -lining, -lined**) 1. PUT LINE BELOW to draw or type a line under sth 2. EMPHASIZE to give emphasis or extra force to sth ■ *n.* /úndər līn/ 1. LINE BENEATH STH a line drawn or typed under sth 2. PRINTING CAPTION UNDER AN ILLUSTRATION a caption placed below an illustration

underlinen /úndər linnin/ *n.* underwear, especially when made of linen (*archaic*)

underliner /úndər līnər/ *n.* a marker pen

underling /úndərling/ *n.* 1. SUBORDINATE PERSON a servant or subordinate of sb else, especially one regarded as of little worth or importance 2. PIGLET a young or baby pig (*regional*)

WORD KEY: REGIONAL NOTE

As well as its standard meaning, the noun *underling* is one of the many words used in rural dialects for a weak piglet or for the weakest of the litter. Others include *cad, crit, dack, dawl, dwindler, harry, joey, little dawling, nestle-draf, nisgal, nuzzle-tripe, piggy-whidden, rackling, runt, tiddling,* and *whidden.*

underlip /úndər lip/ *n.* the lower lip of a person or animal

underlying /úndər lī ing/ *adj.* **1.** LYING UNDERNEATH positioned beneath sth else ○ *the underlying rock strata* **2.** HIDDEN AND SIGNIFICANT present and important but not immediately obvious ○ *the underlying reasons for his odd behaviour* **3.** ESSENTIAL basic or fundamental to sth ○ *at odds with the underlying ideology of the party* **4.** FIN FINANCIALLY MOST IMPORTANT used to describe financial obligations or assets that take priority over others

undermentioned /úndər mensh'nd/ *adj.* named or listed below, or later in a document (*formal*)

undermine /úndər mīn/ (**-mines, -mining, -mined**) *vt.* **1.** ERODE to weaken sth by removing or wearing away material from its base or from beneath it ○ *The chalk cliffs are being gradually undermined by the waves.* **2.** WEAKEN GRADUALLY to diminish or weaken sth gradually ○ *Successive failures at job interviews began to undermine my confidence.* **3.** WEAKEN INSIDIOUSLY to demoralize sb or sth by covert and malicious action

undermost /úndər mōst/ *adj.* LOWEST OF ALL lowest or last in position, status, or level ■ *adv.* IN THE LOWEST PLACE in the lowest or last place

underneath /úndər nēeth/ CORE MEANING: a grammatical word indicating that sth is below or beneath another thing, and may be covered by it ○ (adv) *Underneath, on the floor, was what appeared to be a heap of black clothes.* ○ (prep) *I left the key underneath the doormat.*

1. *prep., adv.* UNDERLYING STH underlying sth that is shown on the surface or openly expressed ○ (prep) *Underneath her confident exterior she was a very shy person.* ○ (adv) *There must be deeper problems underneath.* **2.** *adv., adj.* ON THE LOWER PART OF STH on the bottom of sth or the part that faces towards the ground ○ (adv) *brown with white feathers underneath* ○ (adj) *The underneath part is hard to reach.* **3.** *n.* THE LOWER PART OF STH the bottom part of sth or the part that faces towards the ground [Old English *underneoþan*, from UNDER + *neoþan* 'beneath' (source of English *beneath*)]

undernourish /úndər núrrish/ (**-ishes, -ishing, -ished**) *vt.* to fail to supply sb with enough food or other resources to provide for proper development (*often passive*) —**undernourishment** *n.*

underpants /úndər pants/ *npl.* briefs or shorts worn as underclothes (*takes a plural verb*)

underpass /úndər paass/ *n.* **1.** ROAD UNDER ANOTHER ROAD a part of a road that crosses under another road or a railway line **2.** TUNNEL UNDER A ROAD a tunnel for pedestrians beneath a road or railway

underpay /úndər páy/ (**-pays, -paying, -paid**) *vt.* to pay sb less than he or she deserves or than is usual, or to fail to pay the full amount of sth —**underpayment** *n.*

underperform /úndər pər fáwrm/ (**-forms, -forming, -formed**) *vi.* to do less well than expected or than sth or sb else ○ *underperforming investments* —**underperformance** *n.* —**underperformer** *n.*

underpin /úndər pín/ (**-pins, -pinning, -pinned**) *vt.* **1.** CONSTR SUPPORT FROM BELOW to support a weakened wall or structure by propping it up from below **2.** ACT AS SUPPORT FOR to act as a support or foundation for sth (*often passive*) ○ *the hard facts that underpin these assumptions*

underpinning /úndər pinning/ *n.* **1.** CONSTR SUPPORTING STRUCTURE a structure built to support a weakened wall or building **2.** FOUNDATION FOR STH sth that supports or acts as a foundation for sth (*usually plural*)

underplay /úndər pláy/ (**-plays, -playing, -played**) *v.* **1.** *vti.* ARTS ACT A ROLE SUBTLY to act a role in a deliberately restrained or subtle way **2.** *vt.* DO SUBTLY to present or deal with sth in a deliberately restrained or subtle way **3.** *vi.* CARDS PLAY A LOWER CARD to play a lower card while holding a higher one

underplot /úndər plot/ *n.* a secondary plot in a play, novel, or other work of fiction

underprice /úndər príss/ (**-prices, -pricing, -priced**) *vt.* to put a price on sth for sale that is less than its actual value

underprivileged /úndər prívvəlijd/ *adj.* DENIED SOCIAL PRIVILEGES AND RIGHTS deprived of many of the rights and privileges enjoyed by most people in society, usually as a result of poverty (*used euphemistically*) ■ *n.* UNDERPRIVILEGED PEOPLE underprivileged people considered as a social group (*used euphemistically*)

underproof /úndər proof/ *adj.* used to describe an alcoholic drink that contains less alcohol than is standard or than is legally required

underprop /úndər próp/ (**-props, -propping, -propped**) *vt.* to prop sth up from underneath —**underpropper** *n.*

underquote /úndər kwṓt/ (**-quotes, -quoting, -quoted**) *v.* **1.** *vti.* SELL BELOW ITS ACTUAL VALUE to offer sth for sale at a lower price than the market value **2.** *vt.* QUOTE A LOWER PRICE THAN to quote a price for sth that is lower than that quoted by sb else

underrate /úndər ráyt/ (**-rates, -rating, -rated**) *vt.* to judge the value, degree, or worth of sb or sth to be less than it really is ○ *a greatly underrated writer*

underreport /úndər ri páwrt/ (**-ports, -porting, -ported**) *vt.* to declare or report a number or amount to be smaller than is actually the case

underrepresent /úndər réppri zént/ (**-sents, -senting, -sented**) *vt.* **1.** REPRESENT INADEQUATELY to contain a disproportionately small number of representatives of a particular population group or a particular type of thing (*often passive*) ○ *addressing the problem of women being underrepresented in government.* **2.** PRESENT STH AS LESS to present sth as smaller, less widespread, or less important than it actually is —**underrepresentation** /úndər réppri zen táysh'n/ *n.*

underrun *v.* /úndər rún/ (**-runs, -running, -ran** /-rán/, **-run** /únder run/) **1.** *vt.* MOVE UNDER to run, pass, or go under sth **2.** *vti.* NAUT PASS STH OVER A BOAT FOR INSPECTION to pass sth such as a net or cable over the deck of a boat, hauling it in on one side and putting it back into the water on the other, so that it can be inspected or repaired ■ *n.* **1.** FIN LOWER-THAN-ESTIMATED COST a cost or expense that is less than anticipated **2.** INDUST LOWER-THAN-REQUIRED PRODUCTION RUN a production run of a manufactured or printed item that is less than the quantity ordered

undersaturated /úndər sáchə raytid/ *adj.* GEOL used to describe igneous rock that contains low levels of combined silica and no free silica

underscore *vt.* /úndər skáwr/ (**-scores, -scoring, -scored**) **1.** DRAW A LINE UNDER to draw a line underneath sth **2.** EMPHASIZE to give emphasis or extra force to sth ■ *n.* /úndər skawr/ **1.** LINE UNDER STH a line drawn underneath sth **2.** BACKGROUND MUSIC a piece of background music accompanying action or dialogue in a film

undersea /úndər see/ *adj.* RELATING TO THE AREA BELOW THE SEA existing, carried out, or designed for use below the surface of the sea ■ *adv.* **undersea, underseas** TO THE AREA BELOW THE SEA in or into the area below the surface of the sea

underseal *n.* /úndər seel/ PROTECTIVE COATING FOR VEHICLE'S UNDERSIDE a coating applied to the underside of a motor vehicle to retard rust and corrosion. US term **undercoating** ■ *vt.* /úndər seel/ (**-seals, -sealing, -sealed**) APPLY UNDERSEAL TO to apply an underseal to the underside of a motor vehicle. US term **undercoat**

undersecretary /úndər sékrətri/ (*plural* **-ies**) *n.* **1.** ASSISTANT SECRETARY sb who is immediately subordinate to a principal secretary in a government or bureaucratic organization **2.** SUBORDINATE OF A SECRETARY OF STATE a government minister who is subordinate to the secretary of state for a government department —**undersecretariat** /úndər sékrə táiri ət/ *n.* —**undersecretaryship** /úndər sékrətri ship/ *n.*

undersell /úndər sél/ (**-sells, -selling, -sold**) *vt.* **1.** SELL BELOW ITS PROPER VALUE to sell sth at a price below its full or usual value **2.** SELL MORE CHEAPLY THAN to sell sth more cheaply than a competitor **3.** ADVERTISE WITH TOO LITTLE ENTHUSIASM to present the merits of sth or sb with too little enthusiasm or conviction or in too restrained or understated a way —**underseller** *n.*

underset *n.* /úndər set/ **1.** OCEAN UNDERCURRENT an ocean undercurrent that runs in a direction contrary to the direction of the surface waves **2.** MINING UNDERLYING ORE a vein of ore lying beneath another layer ■ *vt.* /úndər sét/ (**-sets, -setting, -set**) PROVIDE A PROP FOR to support sth from below

undersexed /úndər sékst/ *adj.* having less sex drive or less interest in sex than some other people

undershirt /úndər shurt/ *n.* US = **vest**

undershoot /úndər shoot/ (**-shoots, -shooting, -shot, -shot** /-shót/) *vti.* **1.** AIR LAND TOO SHORT to land an aircraft short of a landing area ○ *The pilot undershot the runway.* **2.** FIRE SHORT to shoot sth, e.g. an arrow, so that it lands short of the target

undershot /úndər shot/ *adj.* **1.** = **underhung** *adj.* 1 **2.** DRIVEN BY WATER PASSING BENEATH used to describe a device, especially a waterwheel, that is driven by water flowing beneath it

undershrub /úndər shrub/ *n.* = **subshrub**

underside /úndər sīd/ *n.* **1.** LOWER SIDE the lower side or bottom of sth **2.** UNDESIRABLE SIDE an aspect of sth that is undesirable or unpleasant and usually hidden

undersigned /úndər sīnd/ *n.* (*plural* **-signed**) PERSON SIGNING BELOW the person who has signed a document below ■ *adj.* SUPPLYING SIGNATURES with their signatures appearing below

undersized /úndər sīzd/ *adj.* smaller than the prevailing or preferred size

underskirt /úndər skurt/ *n.* a skirt worn under another skirt

underslung /úndər slúng/ *adj.* suspended or supported from above, like a motor vehicle chassis that is suspended from the axles

undersoil /úndər soyl/ *n.* = **subsoil**

undersold past tense, past participle of **undersell**

underspend /úndər spénd/ (**-spends, -spending, -spent** /-spént/) *vi.* to spend less money than is required or expected —**underspend** *n.*

understaff /úndər staaf/ (**-staffs, -staffing, -staffed**) *vt.* to provide a workplace or an organization with inadequate or insufficient staff

understand /úndər stánd/ (**-stands, -standing, -stood** /-stood/) *v.* **1.** *vti.* GRASP THE MEANING OF STH to know or be able to explain to yourself the nature of sb or sth, or the meaning or cause of sth ○ *I can't understand what all the fuss is about.* **2.** *vti.* COME TO KNOW STH to realize or become aware of sth ○ *Only then did she understand the urgency of the situation.* **3.** *vt.* BE ABLE TO HANDLE to know and be able to use sth such as a foreign language ○ *She thoroughly understood the workings of the system.* **4.** *vti.* KNOW AND SYMPATHIZE to recognize sb's character or sb's situation, especially in a sympathetic, tolerant, or empathetic way ○ *It's such a relief to find someone who understands.* **5.** *vt.* TAKE AS MEANT to interpret sth in a particular way, or to infer or deduce a particular meaning from sth ○ *I understood it as a peacemaking gesture.* ○ *Am I to understand from this that you are refusing our offer?* **6.** *vt.* TAKE AS SETTLED to believe sth to be agreed, settled, or firmly communicated ○ *The bank was given to understand that you would repay the loan in six months.* **7.** *vt.* KNOW BY LEARNING OR HEARING to gather or assume sth on the basis of having heard or been told it ○ *They're not due back, so I understand, until next Tuesday.* [Old English *understandan*, from UNDER + *standan*, an earlier form of STAND. The underlying idea is 'to be close to'.]

understandable /úndər stándəb'l/ *adj.* **1.** ABLE TO BE UNDERSTOOD having a meaning or nature that can be understood ○ *Try to make it understandable to a nonspecialist.* **2.** REASONABLE able to be accepted as normal, reasonable, or forgivable ○ *Under the circumstances it was a perfectly understandable reaction.* —**understandability** /úndər stándə bíllati/ *n.* —**understandably** /úndər stándəbli/ *adv.*

understanding /úndər stánding/ *n.* **1.** ABILITY TO GRASP A MEANING the ability to perceive and explain the meaning or the nature of sb or sth ○ *Surely even* *someone with a very limited understanding could see the logic in that.* **2.** INTERPRETATION OF STH sb's interpretation of sth, or a belief or opinion based on an interpretation of or inference from sth ○ *It was my understanding that the costs would be shared equally.* **3.** MUTUAL COMPREHENSION an agreement, often an unofficial or unspoken one ○ *I'm sure we can come to an understanding about this.* **4.** KNOWLEDGE OF ANOTHER'S NATURE a sympathetic, empathetic, or tolerant recognition of sb else's nature or situation ○ *I thought you of all people would show a little understanding.* ■ *adj.* **1.** SYMPATHETICALLY AWARE sympathetic, empathetic, or tolerant in recognizing sb's or sth's character and situation ○ *fortunate in having understanding parents* **2.** ABLE TO KNOW STH able to comprehend the sense or meaning of sth (*archaic*) —**understandingly** *adv.*

understate /úndər stáyt/ (**-states, -stating, -stated**) *vt.* **1.** EXPRESS WITH RESTRAINT to express sth in a deliberately less dramatic, emphatic, or emotional way than it seems to warrant, often in order to increase its actual effect or for the sake of irony **2.** STATE STH AS BELOW ITS TRUE AMOUNT to describe sth as being smaller in quantity or number than it really is ○ *The official account understates the true costs of the delay.*

understated /úndər stáytid/ *adj.* achieving its effect through restraint, subtlety, and good taste ○ *understated elegance* —**understatedness** *n.*

understatement /úndər staytmənt, úndər stáytmənt/ *n.* **1.** RESTRAINED OR MUTED STATEMENT a statement, or a way of expressing yourself, that is deliberately less forceful or dramatic than the subject would seem to justify or require **2.** INCOMPLETE STATEMENT a statement that underrepresents or underreports sth

understeer *vi.* /úndər stéer/ (**-steers, -steering, -steered**) TURN TOO WIDE to turn less sharply than the turning of a steering wheel would lead the driver to expect ■ *n.* /úndər steer/ TENDENCY TO TURN TOO WIDE a motor vehicle's tendency to turn less sharply than expected

understood[1] /úndər stóod/ past tense, past participle of **understand**

understood[2] /úndər stóod/ *adj.* agreed, assumed, or implied, especially without being openly or officially expressed

understorey /úndər stawri/ (*plural* **-reys**) *n.* a layer of small trees and shrubs below the level of the taller trees in a forest

understrapper /úndər strapər/ *n.* an underling or subordinate [Early 18thC. Formed from *strapper* in the sense of 'person who straps or harnesses horses'.]

understrength /úndər stréngth/ *adj.* having inadequate strength, especially less than usual or desirable number of personnel

understudy /úndər studi/ *n.* (*plural* **-ies**) **1.** SUBSTITUTE ACTOR an actor who learns the role of another actor so as to be able to act as a replacement if necessary **2.** TRAINED SUBSTITUTE sb who is trained to do the work of sb else so as to be able to act as a replacement if necessary ■ *vti.* (**-ies, -ying, -ied**) BE A SUBSTITUTE ACTOR to learn the role of another actor so as to be able to replace him or her if necessary

undersubscribed /úndər səb skríbd/ *adj.* with fewer than the expected number of people subscribing or showing an interest, often not enough people to make sth viable ○ *We couldn't offer the course as it was undersubscribed.*

undertake /úndər táyk/ (**-takes, -taking, -took** /-tóok/, **-taken** /-táykən/) *v.* **1.** *vti.* MAKE A PLEDGE TO DO STH to make a commitment to do sth ○ *Jo undertook to find out the cost of flights.* **2.** *vt.* SET ABOUT DOING to begin to do sth or to set out on sth ○ *They were prepared to undertake the work at the formerly agreed price.*

undertaker *n.* **1.** SB WHO ARRANGES FUNERALS sb whose profession is to prepare the dead for burial or cremation and to arrange funerals. US term **funeral director 2.** SB WHO SETS ABOUT STH sb who attempts or agrees to attempt a task

undertaking *n.* **1.** TASK a task or project ○ *It was a colossal undertaking.* **2.** PLEDGE TO DO STH a promise or agreement to do sth **3.** FUNERAL BUSINESS the business of preparing the dead for burial or cremation and arranging funerals

under-the-counter *adj.* sold or obtained clandestinely or illegally (*not hyphenated after a verb*)

under-the-table *adj.* done or organized clandestinely and often illegally (*not hyphenated after a verb*)

underthings /úndər thingz/ *npl.* underwear, especially women's underwear

underthrust /úndər thrust/ *n.* GEOL a reverse fault in which a lower layer of rock is driven underneath a higher, relatively passive layer

undertint /úndər tint/ *n.* a slight or subtle tint

undertone /úndər tōn/ *n.* **1.** LOW TONE a quiet, subdued, or background tone, especially of the voice ○ *He spoke in an undertone.* **2.** UNDERLYING QUALITY OR ELEMENT sth that is suggested or implied rather than stated openly ○ *undertones of menace* **3.** COLOURS MUTED COLOUR a pale, subdued, or unobtrusive colour

undertow /úndər tō/ *n.* **1.** SEAWARD PULL OF WATER the seaward pull of water away from a shore after a wave has broken **2.** OPPOSING UNDERCURRENT an underlying tendency or force that runs in the opposite direction to the apparent one ○ *An undertow of dissatisfaction made it difficult to carry everyone with us.*

undertrick /úndər trik/ *n.* CARDS in bridge, a trick short of the number declared by a player

undertrump /úndər trúmp/ (**-trumps, -trumping, -trumped**) *vi.* in cards, to play a trump that is lower than a trump that has already been played in a hand

undervalue /úndər vállyoo/ (**-ues, -uing, -ued**) *vt.* **1.** APPLY TOO LOW A VALUE TO to judge the value of sth or sb as being lower than it really is ○ *buy up stock that is undervalued* **2.** HOLD IN LOW ESTEEM to hold too low an opinion of sth or sb —**undervaluation** /úndər vállyoo áysh'n/ *n.*

underwater *adj.* /úndər wawtər/ **1.** BELOW THE WATER SURFACE existing, carried out, or designed for use below the surface of water **2.** UNDER A SHIP'S WATERLINE below the waterline in a ship ■ *adv.* /úndər wáwtər/ BELOW THE WATER SURFACE in or to a place below the surface of a body of water ■ *n.* /úndər wawtər/ WATER UNDERNEATH THE SURFACE the water beneath the surface of a river, lake, or sea

under way /úndər wáy/, **underway** *adj.* **1.** PROCEEDING in motion or progress ○ *not long before the project was underway* **2. underway, under weigh** NAUT DONE WHILE MOVING carried out while a ship is in motion, not in port or at anchor

WORD KEY: USAGE

under way or **underway**? Although the form ***underway*** is often seen, and has long been in use, ***under way*** is still widely preferred. The only exception to this is the rare adjectival use that precedes the noun: *The submarine received underway servicing.*

underwear /úndər wair/ *n.* clothes worn beneath outer clothes, usually next to the skin and not normally seen in public

underweight /úndər wáyt/ *adj.* weighing less than is normal or required

underwent past tense of **undergo**

underwhelm /úndər wélm/ (**-whelms, -whelming, -whelmed**) *vt.* to fail notably to impress or excite sb (*humorous*) [Mid-20thC. Modelled on OVERWHELM.] —**underwhelming** *adj.*

underwing /úndər wing/ *n.* **1.** INSECTS HIND WING OF AN INSECT a hind wing of an insect such as a beetle, especially when covered by a forewing while the insect is not in flight **2.** ZOOL MOTH WITH BRIGHT WINGS a moth that has brightly coloured hind wings that become visible only in flight. Genus: *Catocala.* **3.** BIRDS LOWER SIDE OF A BIRD'S WING the underside of a bird's wing

underwire /úndər wīr/ *n.* a wire sewn into the lining under each cup of a brassiere to provide support —**underwired** *adj.*

underwood /úndər wood/ *n.* = **undergrowth** *n.* 1

underworld /úndər wurld/ *n.* **1.** CRIMINAL SOCIETY the part of society that lives by crime (*often used before a noun*) ○ *an underworld shooting* **2.** MYTHOL ABODE OF THE DEAD in classical mythology, the place beneath the earth where the souls of the dead go

underwrite /úndər rít, úndər rīt/ (**-writes, -writing, -wrote** /úndər rṓt, úndər rōt/, **-written** /úndər rítt'n, úndər ritt'n/) *v.* **1.** *vti.* INSUR ISSUE INSURANCE to insure sb or sth by accepting liability for specified losses, or to be in the business of doing this **2.** *vti.* STOCK EXCH AGREE TO BUY UNSOLD SECURITIES to guarantee the sale of an issue of securities at a fixed price **3.** *vti.* SUBSIDIZE STH to agree to provide funds for sth and to cover any losses ○ *The tour was underwritten by an electronics company.* **4.** *vt.* LEND SUPPORT TO to give support to sb or sth, especially by signing a document **5.** *vt.* WRITE BENEATH OTHER WRITING to write sth, or add a signature, underneath other written matter [15thC. Modelled on Latin *subscribere* 'to write underneath, sign'.]

underwriter /úndər rītər/ *n.* **1.** INSUR INSURER COVERING LIABILITIES a person, firm, or organization that issues insurance and accepts liability for specified risks **2.** INSUR SB ASSESSING RISKS ON INSURANCE sb employed by an insurance company to assess risks and fix premiums **3.** STOCK EXCH GUARANTOR OF A SECURITIES ISSUE a person or organization that agrees to buy at a fixed price any unsold part of an issue of securities

undescended /úndi séndid/ *adj.* used to describe a testicle that has remained in the inguinal canal and has not descended into the scrotum

undeserved /úndi zúrvd/ *adj.* unfairly awarded or endured, or not merited on the basis of the facts —**undeservedly** /úndi zúrvidli/ *adv.*

undesigning /úndi zíning/ *adj.* not trying to deceive or manipulate

undesirable /úndi zírəb'l/ *adj.* NOT WANTED not wanted, liked, or approved of ■ *n.* SB UNDESIRABLE sb or sth regarded as undesirable —**undesirability** /úndi zírə bílləti/ *n.* —**undesirably** /-zírəbli/ *adv.*

undetermined /úndi túrmind/ *adj.* **1.** NOT SETTLED not resolved, decided, or fixed **2.** NOT KNOWN unknown or undiscovered

undeviating /un déevi ayting/ *adj.* remaining loyal or constant —**undeviatingly** *adv.*

undid past tense of **undo**

undies /ún diz/ *npl.* underclothes, especially women's underclothes (*informal*) [Late 19thC. Formed from a shortening of UNDERCLOTHES, probably on the model of *frillies* 'frilled underwear'.]

undine /ún deen/ *n.* a female spirit that lives in water, especially one that could become human by bearing the child of a human male [Early 19thC. From modern Latin *undina* (coined by Paracelsus), from Latin *unda* 'wave' (see UNDULATE).]

undiplomatic /ún diplə máttik/ *adj.* lacking in tact and diplomacy —**undiplomatically** *adv.*

undirected /úndi réktid, ún dī-/ *adj.* **1.** PURPOSELESS without a purpose or object **2.** WITHOUT ADDRESS not marked with an address in the proper way

undisguised /úndiss gízd/ *adj.* expressed fully and openly —**undisguisedly** /úndiss gízidli/ *adv.*

undisposed /úndi spṓzd/ *adj.* **1.** NOT DEALT WITH not resolved or dealt with **2.** NOT FAVOURABLY INCLINED not prepared or inclined to do sth

undissociated /úndi sṓshi aytid, -sṓssi-/ *adj.* CHEM used to describe a molecule that has not been broken down into simpler molecules, atoms, or ions

undistinguished /úndi stíng gwisht/ *adj.* **1.** MEDIOCRE not very good or ever rising above the ordinary ○ *an undistinguished career* **2.** COMMONPLACE not at all striking or likely to stand out from others ○ *undistinguished appearance* **3.** NOT MADE SEPARATE not differentiated from others **4.** NOT ATTRACTING NOTICE not noticeable or noticed

undistributed /úndi stríbbyootid/ *adj.* **1.** BUSINESS NOT PAID TO SHAREHOLDERS not paid out as a dividend to shareholders, but invested back into the business ○ *undistributed profits* **2.** LOGIC NOT REFERRING TO ENTIRE CLASS used to describe a term that does not refer to all members of the class it designates. The term 'dogs' is undistributed in the statement 'Some dogs are unfriendly'.

undo /un dóo/ (**-does** /-dúz/, **-doing, -did** /-díd/, **-done** /-dún/) *v.* **1.** *vti.* UNFASTEN to open, unfasten, untie, or unwrap sth ○ *I can't undo this button.* **2.** *vt.* NULLIFY to cancel or reverse the effect of an action ○ *What's done can't be undone.* **3.** *vt.* COMPUT REVERSE AN ACTION to cancel the effect of the last command or action done on a computer, restoring the material being worked on to its previous condition **4.** *vt.* RUIN SB to bring sb or sth to ruin or disaster

undock /un dók/ (**-docks, -docking, -docked**) *vi.* SPACE TECH to become detached from each other, a space station, or another spacecraft, in space

undoing *n.* **1.** ACT OF BRINGING TO RUIN the ruin, downfall, or destruction of sb or sth, or sth that causes this ○ *Pride was our undoing.* **2.** ACT OF UNFASTENING the opening, unfastening, untying, or unwrapping of sth **3.** ACT OF NULLIFYING STH'S EFFECT the cancelling or reversing of the effect of an action

undone *adj.* **1.** UNCOMPLETED not yet done or completed **2.** UNFASTENED not tied or fastened **3.** BROUGHT TO RUIN ruined, destroyed, or brought to the brink of collapse

undoubted /un dówtid/ *adj.* not subject to doubt or dispute

undoubtedly /un dówtidli/ *adv.* without any doubt or question

undreamed-of /un dreémd ov/, **undreamt-of** /un drémt ov/ *adj.* impossible to imagine in advance, usually through being so wonderful and so unlikely

undress *v.* /un dréss/ (**-dresses, -dressing, -dressed**) **1.** *vti.* TAKE CLOTHES OFF to remove the clothes from sb's body **2.** *vt.* TAKE DRESSING OFF to remove a dressing from a wound **3.** *vt.* REMOVE ORNAMENTATION to strip sth of its decoration ■ *n.* **1.** CONDITION OF HAVING NO CLOTHES ON a condition of nakedness or of being scantily clothed **2.** INFORMAL CLOTHING informal attire or an everyday uniform. ◊ **dress** ■ *adj.* /ún dress/ INFORMAL not full or formal in dress, or for which informal clothing can be worn ○ *an undress uniform*

undressed /un drést/ *adj.* **1.** WITHOUT CLOTHES naked or scantily clothed **2.** UNTREATED not processed or treated in some way ○ *undressed leather* **3.** NOT READY FOR TABLE not fully prepared for cooking or eating **4.** WITHOUT DRESSING not covered with a dressing or sauce **5.** INFORMALLY DRESSED appropriately but not formally dressed for an event or occasion **6.** WITHOUT A BANDAGE without a dressing or bandage ○ *an undressed wound*

WORD KEY: SYNONYMS

See Synonyms at ***naked***.

undue /un dyoó/ *adj.* **1.** EXCESSIVE OR VERY INAPPROPRIATE going beyond the limits of what is proper, normal, justified, or permitted ○ *using undue force to disperse the crowd* **2.** NOT PAYABLE NOW not owed or payable at present

undulant /úndyoólənt/ *adj.* resembling waves in motion or form (*literary*) [Early 19thC. Formed from UNDULATE.]

undulant fever *n.* = **brucellosis**

undulate *v.* /úndyoo layt/ (**-lates, -lating, -lated**) **1.** *vti.* MOVE SINUOUSLY LIKE WAVES to move, or cause sth to move, in waves or in a movement resembling waves **2.** *vi.* GO UP AND DOWN GRACEFULLY to rise and fall gracefully in volume or pitch ■ *adj.* /úndyoolət, -layt/ **undulate, undulated** WAVY IN APPEARANCE with a wavy appearance, edge, or markings [Mid-17thC. From Latin *undulatus* 'wavy', from *unda* 'wave'. Ultimately from an Indo-European word that is also the ancestor of English *water*.] —**undulatory** /úndyoolətəri/ *adj.*

WORD KEY: ORIGIN

The Latin word *unda*, from which ***undulate*** is derived, is also the source of English *abound, inundate, redundant, sound,* and *surround*.

undulation /úndyoo láysh'n/ *n.* **1.** WAVY MOVEMENT a sinuous or wavy motion **2.** CURVE a curving form or outline, especially one in a series such as a wave

unduly /un dyoóli/ *adv.* to a very great extent, or to an excessive, improper, or unjustifiable degree ○ *We were not unduly concerned.*

undutiful /un dyoótif'l/ *adj.* **1.** LACKING SENSE OF OBLIGATION lacking a sense of moral or legal obligation **2.** UNWILLING TO FULFIL OBLIGATIONS unwilling to fulfil moral or legal obligations —**undutifully** *adv.* —**undutifulness** *n.*

undying /un dí ing/ *adj.* continuing forever

unearned /un úrnd/ *adj.* **1.** NOT GAINED BY WORK not acquired by labour or service ○ *unearned income* **2.** UNDESERVED not deserved ○ *unearned criticism*

unearned increment *n.* an increase in property value resulting from factors other than labour or improvements made by the owner

unearth /un úrth/ (**-earths, -earthing, -earthed**) *vt.* **1.** DIG STH UP to bring sth up out of the ground **2.** DISCLOSE STH to discover or disclose sth, especially after an investigation **3.** FIND STH LOST to find sth that has been lost or hidden

unearthly /un úrthli/ *adj.* **1.** NOT FROM THIS WORLD not being or seeming to be from this world **2.** EERIE looking or sounding so strange as to be frightening **3.** COMPLETELY UNREASONABLE completely inappropriate or unreasonable ○ *at this unearthly hour* **4.** PERFECT embodying perfection —**unearthliness** *n.*

uneasy /un eézi/ (**-ier, -iest**) *adj.* **1.** ANXIOUS anxious or afraid **2.** UNCERTAIN not certain enough to let people relax completely ○ *an uneasy truce* **3.** ILL AT EASE awkward or lacking confidence **4.** RESTLESS not allowing sb to rest properly —**unease** *n.* —**uneasily** *adv.* —**uneasiness** *n.*

uneconomic /ún eekə nómmik, -ekə-/ *adj.* **1.** NOT MAKING PROFIT not making or not likely to make a profit **2.** **uneconomic, uneconomical** NOT EFFICIENT not efficient or worth the expense

unedited /un édditid/ *adj.* **1.** NOT CORRECTED not corrected or revised **2.** NOT ADAPTED not adapted to a particular audience, purpose, or medium

uneducated /un éddyoo kaytid/ *adj.* lacking the learning that is usually acquired in schools

unelectable /únni léktəb'l/ *adj.* certain to be defeated as a candidate for public office, e.g. because of extreme positions on controversial issues

unemotional /únni mósh'nəl/ *adj.* **1.** SHOWING NO FEELING showing little or no feeling **2.** REASONED AND OBJECTIVE involving reason or intellect rather than feelings —**unemotionally** *adv.*

unemployable /únnim plóy əb'l/ *adj.* lacking the skills, education, or ability to get a job

unemployed /únnim plóyd/ *adj.* **1.** JOBLESS not in paid employment **2.** NOT IN USE not being used ■ *npl.* JOBLESS PEOPLE people who are out of work

unemployment /únnim plóymənt/ *n.* **1.** JOBLESSNESS the condition of having no job **2.** NUMBER OF UNEMPLOYED the number of people who are unemployed in an area, often given as a percentage of the total labour force

unemployment benefit *n.* a regular payment made by the government to sb who is out of work

unending /un énding/ *adj.* continuing or seeming to continue forever

un-English /un íng glish/ *adj.* **1.** NOT LIKE THE ENGLISH not characteristic of the English **2.** NOT STANDARD ENGLISH USAGE not considered standard English usage

unequal /un eékwəl/ *adj.* **1.** NOT MEASURABLY THE SAME not measurably the same, e.g. in size or number **2.** NOT OF SAME SOCIAL POSITION not of the same status, rank, or position in society **3.** NOT EVENLY MATCHED not evenly matched in competition **4.** VARIABLE uneven or variable in quality or character **5.** ASYMMETRICAL not evenly balanced **6.** UNABLE TO DO STH having less than the required ability to do sth ○ *unequal to the task* **7.** UNFAIR not fair or just (*archaic*) ■ *n.* SB NOT EQUAL TO ANOTHER sb or sth not equal to another —**unequally** *adv.*

unequalled /un eékwəld/ *adj.* without equal or parallel among things of its kind

unequivocal /únni kwívvək'l/ *adj.* allowing for no doubt or misinterpretation —**unequivocally** *adv.*

unerring /un úr ing/ *adj.* **1.** ACCURATE striking the mark or target without fail **2.** WITHOUT MISTAKES free of any mistakes —**unerringly** *adv.*

UNESCO /yoo néskō/, **Unesco** *abbr.* United Nations Educational, Scientific, and Cultural Organization

unessential /únni sénsh'l/ *adj.* DISPENSABLE not absolutely needed ■ *n.* STH UNNECESSARY sth that is not necessary or important

uneven /un eév'n/ *adj.* **1.** NOT LEVEL without a level or smooth surface **2.** VARYING varying and inconsistent, e.g. in quality, thoroughness, or duration **3.** NOT PARALLEL not straight or parallel **4.** NOT FAIRLY MATCHED not fairly matched in competition **5.** ODD not divisible by two **6.** NOT THE SAME SIZE unequal in number or measurement to another **7.** UNFAIR not just (*archaic*) [Old English *unefen*] —**unevenly** *adv.* —**unevenness** *n.*

uneventful /únni véntf'l/ *adj.* not marked by any unusual or momentous occurrence —**uneventfully** *adv.* —**uneventfulness** *n.*

unexampled /únnig zaámp'ld/ *adj.* without a similar case or occurrence

unexceptionable /únnik sépsh'nəb'l/ *adj.* good enough to provide no reason for criticism or objection —**unexceptionability** /únnik sépsh'nə bílləti/ *n.* —**unexceptionableness** /únnik sépsh'nəb'lnəss/ *n.* —**unexceptionably** /-sépsh'nəbli/ *adv.*

WORD KEY: USAGE

See Usage note at ***unexceptional***.

unexceptional /únnik sépsh'nəl/ *adj.* **1.** NOT SPECIAL not special or unusual **2.** WITH NO EXCEPTIONS allowing no exception —**unexceptionally** *adv.*

WORD KEY: USAGE

unexceptional or **unexceptionable**? The distinction in meaning corresponds to that between the positive forms *exceptional* and *exceptionable*. Something is described as ***unexceptional*** when it is ordinary or commonplace, and perhaps a little dull: *Her performance got a good review, but I thought it was unexceptional.* ***Unexceptionable*** comes close to this in meaning, but its strict meaning is 'not open to criticism' and therefore 'satisfactory, acceptable': *Their behaviour has been unexceptionable so far.*

unexcited /únnik sítid/ *adj.* **1.** NOT AROUSED not emotionally aroused **2.** PHYS AT LOWEST ENERGY LEVEL used to describe particles that remain at the lowest energy level

unexpected /únnik spéktid/ *adj.* coming as a surprise —**unexpectedly** *adv.* —**unexpectedness** *n.*

unexperienced /únnik speéri ənst/ *adj.* **1.** NOT UNDERGONE BEFORE not having been known or undergone before **2.** INEXPERIENCED lacking experience

unexpressed /únnik sprést/ *adj.* **1.** NOT MADE KNOWN not spoken or made known **2.** UNDERSTOOD WITHOUT SAYING ANYTHING understood without anything being said **3.** GENETICS WITH NO EFFECT ON ORGANISM used to describe a gene that does not have an observable effect on the organism that carries it

unfailing /un fáyling/ *adj.* **1.** LIMITLESS never used up or exhausted **2.** ALWAYS RELIABLE able to be relied on at all times **3.** ALWAYS ACCURATE totally accurate and reliable —**unfailingly** *adv.* —**unfailingness** *n.*

unfair /un fáir/ *adj.* **1.** NOT JUST not equal or just **2.** UNETHICAL IN BUSINESS not ethical in business dealings —**unfairly** *adv.* —**unfairness** *n.*

unfaithful /un fáythf'l/ *adj.* **1.** UNTRUE TO COMMITMENTS untrue to commitments, duties, beliefs, or ideals **2.** ADULTEROUS engaging in sexual relations with sb other than one to whom monogamy has been pledged **3.** NOT LIKE ORIGINAL not true to the original **4.** WITH NO RELIGIOUS FAITH not having religious faith (*archaic*) —**unfaithfully** *adv.* —**unfaithfulness** *n.*

unfaltering /un fáwltering, -fólte-/ *adj.* strong, steady, and not becoming weaker —**unfalteringly** *adv.*

unfamiliar /únfə mílli ər/ *adj.* **1.** NOT PREVIOUSLY KNOWN not previously known or recognized **2.** NOT ACQUAINTED with no previous knowledge or experience ○ *unfamiliar with the software.* —**unfamiliarity** /únfə mílli árrəti/ *n.* —**unfamiliarly** /únfə mílli ərli/ *adv.*

unfashionable /un fásh'nəb'l/ *adj.* **1.** NOT POPULAR NOW not in the current style **2.** UNFAVOURED SOCIALLY not socially approved of ○ *an unfashionable suburb* —**unfashionably** *adv.*

unfasten /un faáss'n/ (**-tens, -tening, -tened**) *vt.* undo sth that holds things together, e.g. the buttons of a garment

unfathomable /un fáthəməb'l/ *adj.* **1.** IMPOSSIBLE TO MEASURE too deep to be measured **2.** IMPOSSIBLE TO

UNDERSTAND so mysterious or complicated that understanding is impossible —**unfathomableness** *n.* —**unfathomably** *adv.*

unfavourable /un fáyvərəb'l/ *adj.* 1. DISAPPROVING expressing disapproval or opposition 2. NOT GOOD unlikely to be beneficial —**unfavourableness** *n.* —**unfavourably** *adv.*

unfeeling /un féeling/ *adj.* 1. NOT SYMPATHETIC without caring or sympathy for sb else's feelings 2. NUMB unable to experience physical sensation [Old English *unfēlend*] —**unfeelingly** *adv.* —**unfeelingness** *n.*

unfetter /un féttər/ (**-ters, -tering, -tered**) *vt.* 1. RELEASE SB OR STH to release sb or sth from fetters 2. FREE SB FROM CONSTRAINTS to allow sb to act without restraint

unfettered /un féttərd/ *adj.* not subject to limits or restrictions

unfinished /un fínnisht/ *adj.* 1. NOT COMPLETED not completed satisfactorily 2. NOT FINALLY TREATED not finally processed or treated with dye, varnish, paint, or bleach 3. TEXTILES WITH SLIGHT NAP woven with a slight nap

unfit /un fít/ (**-fits, unfitting, unfitted**) *adj.* 1. UNSUITABLE unsuitable for a specific purpose 2. UNQUALIFIED lacking the necessary skills or qualifications to perform a specific task adequately 3. NOT HEALTHY not physically or mentally healthy —**unfitly** *adv.* —**unfitness** *n.* —**unfittingly** *adv.*

unfitted /un fíttid/ *adj.* 1. NOT SUITED not suited or adapted for a specific purpose 2. NOT FITTED used to describe furniture that is not fitted

unfitting /un fítting/ *adj.* not suitable or appropriate for sb or sth

unfix /un fíks/ (**-fixes, -fixing, -fixed**) *vt.* 1. DETACH STH to loosen or detach sth 2. MAKE STH UNSTABLE to upset the certainty or stability of sth

unflagging /un flágging/ *adj.* remaining strong and unchanging —**unflaggingly** *adv.*

unflappable /un fláppəb'l/ *adj.* able to maintain composure under all circumstances —**unflappability** /un fláppə bílləti/ *n.* —**unflappably** /un fláppəbli/ *adv.*

unfledged /un fléjd/ *adj.* 1. BIRDS NOT HAVING FEATHERS FOR FLYING not having developed the feathers required for flight 2. INEXPERIENCED young and inexperienced

unflinching /un flínching/ *adj.* strong and unhesitating —**unflinchingly** *adv.*

unfocused /un fókəst/, **unfocussed** *adj.* 1. NOT ADJUSTED not adjusted for a clear image 2. WITH NO CLEAR PURPOSE lacking a clear purpose or objective

unfold /un fóld/ (**-folds, -folding, -folded**) *v.* 1. *vti.* OPEN OUT to open sth and spread it out, or to open and spread out 2. *vti.* MAKE STH UNDERSTOOD to make sth clear and understood by gradual exposure, or to become clear in this way 3. *vi.* DEVELOP to develop or expand over time ○ *His talent unfolded as he grew older.* [Old English *unfealdan*]

unforeseen /ún fawr séen/ *adj.* not expected beforehand

unforgettable /únfər géttəb'l/ *adj.* remarkable in a way that cannot be forgotten —**unforgettably** *adv.*

unforgivable /únfər gívvəb'l/ *adj.* so bad that it can never be forgiven —**unforgivably** *adv.*

unforgiving /únfər gívving/ *adj.* 1. UNWILLING TO FORGIVE unwilling or unable to forgive 2. PROVIDING NO MARGIN FOR MISTAKES providing little or no margin for mistakes or weakness —**unforgivingly** *adv.*

unformed /un fáwrmd/ *adj.* 1. WITH NO REAL SHAPE without coherent shape or structure ○ *the unformed restless desire in her mind* 2. UNDEVELOPED not yet fully developed 3. NOT CREATED not yet created

unfortunate /un fáwrchənət/ *adj.* 1. UNLUCKY never experiencing good luck 2. WITH BAD LUCK accompanied by or bringing bad luck 3. INAPPROPRIATE not appropriate to a given situation ○ *The unfortunate comment was an example of his lack of social polish.* ■ *n.* POOR PERSON sb who is pitied by others for having bad luck or inadequate resources —**unfortunateness** *n.*

unfortunately /un fáwrchənətli/ *adv.* 1. USED TO EXPRESS REGRET used when sb wishes sth were not true ○ *I didn't get there before he left, unfortunately.* 2. INAPPROPRIATELY in a way that is inappropriate to a given situation ○ *an unfortunately worded critique*

unfounded /un fówndid/ *adj.* 1. NOT SUPPORTED BY EVIDENCE not supported by evidence or facts 2. NOT ESTABLISHED not yet established

unfreeze /un fréez/ (**-freezes, -freezing, unfroze** /-fróz/, **unfrozen** /-fróz'n/) *vt.* to remove controls or restrictions fixing wages, hiring, prices, or rents

unfrequented /únfri kwéntid/ *adj.* not often visited, especially by tourists or travellers

unfriendly /un fréndli/ *adj.* 1. HOSTILE behaving in an obviously cold or hostile way 2. UNFAVOURABLE not beneficial or advantageous —**unfriendliness** *n.*

unfrock /un frók/ (**-frocks, -frocking, -frocked**) *vt.* 1. RELIG REMOVE ORDAINED PERSON FROM OFFICE to remove an ordained person from office and duties as a punishment for doing sth considered immoral or heretical 2. TAKE AWAY SB'S RIGHT to take away sb's right to practise a profession 3. REMOVE SB FROM POSITION to remove sb from an honorary or privileged position

unfruitful /un fróotf'l/ *adj.* 1. NOT FERTILE not bearing fruit or offspring (*literary*) 2. UNSUCCESSFUL not having a successful outcome —**unfruitfully** *adv.* —**unfruitfulness** *n.*

unfurl /un fúrl/ (**-furls, -furling, -furled**) *vti.* to unroll or spread out sth, or to become extended in this way

ungainly /un gáynli/ *adj.* 1. LACKING GRACE lacking grace while moving 2. AWKWARD awkward to handle 3. GANGLING having an awkward long-limbed appearance ■ *adv.* CLUMSILY in a clumsy or graceless way (*archaic*) [Early 17thC. Formed from obsolete *gain* 'straight, convenient', from Old Norse *gegn*. Ultimately from a prehistoric Germanic word meaning 'against', which is also the ancestor of English *against* and *again*.]

Ungava /óong gáavə/ region in northeastern Canada, situated east of Hudson Bay and north of the Eastmain River

Ungava Bay /óong gáyvə báy, -gáavə báy/ bay in northeastern Quebec, Canada, opening into Hudson Strait

ungenerous /un jénnərəss/ *adj.* 1. STINGY slow to give, forgive, or share things 2. MEAN-SPIRITED mean-spirited and ignoble —**ungenerously** *adv.*

ungodly /un góddli/ *adj.* 1. RELIG NOT REVERING GOD not devoted to or obeying God 2. WICKED behaving in a way thought to violate moral strictures 3. UNREASONABLE not meeting standards for reasonableness (*informal*) ○ *at this ungodly hour* —**ungodliness** *n.*

ungovernable /un gúvvərnəb'l/ *adj.* incapable of being governed or restrained —**ungovernableness** *n.* —**ungovernably** *adv.*

ungracious /un gráyshəss/ *adj.* 1. ILL-MANNERED inconsistent with good manners 2. NOT PLEASANT extremely unpleasant or difficult 3. EVIL behaving in a way perceived as immoral or inappropriate (*archaic*) [13thC. The original underlying meaning was 'lacking the grace of God'.] —**ungraciously** *adv.* —**ungraciousness** *n.*

ungrateful /un gráytf'l/ *adj.* 1. NOT APPRECIATIVE not thankful or appreciative 2. UNREWARDING unpleasant or unrewarding —**ungratefully** *adv.* —**ungratefulness** *n.*

ungrudging /un grújjing/ *adj.* without reluctance or reservation —**ungrudgingly** *adv.*

ungual /úng gwəl/ *adj.* 1. ANAT OF FINGERNAILS OR TOENAILS relating to or affecting the fingernails or toenails 2. ZOOL OF NAIL, CLAW, OR HOOF relating to, occurring in, or supporting a nail, claw, or hoof [Mid-19thC. Formed from Latin *unguis* 'nail, claw' (see UNGUIS).]

unguarded /un gáardid/ *adj.* 1. WITH NO PROTECTION lacking a guard or protection 2. NATURAL free from pretence or guile 3. NOT WARY showing a lack of thought or care —**unguardedly** *adv.* —**unguardedness** *n.*

unguent /úng gwənt/ *n.* a healing or soothing ointment [15thC. From Latin *unguentum*, from *unguere* 'to anoint' (source of English *ointment, anoint*, and *unctuous*).]

unguis /úng gwiss/ (*plural* **ungues** /-gweez/) *n.* 1. ZOOL NAIL, CLAW, OR HOOF a nail, claw, hook, or hoof on a digit or foot of an animal 2. BOT CLAW-SHAPED BASE OF PETAL the claw-shaped base of some petals [Early 18thC. From Latin, 'nail, claw' (source of English *ungulate*). Ultimately from an Indo-European word that is also the ancestor of English *nail* and *onyx*.]

ungulate /úng gyoo layt, -lət/ *adj.* 1. WITH HOOFS having hoofs 2. SHAPED LIKE HOOF resembling a hoof in shape or function ■ *n.* HOOFED MAMMAL a mammal with hoofs, e.g. the horse, rhinoceros, pig, giraffe, deer, or camel [Early 19thC. From late Latin *ungulatus*, from Latin *ungula* 'hoof, claw', literally 'small claw', from *unguis* 'nail' (see UNGUIS).]

unguligrade /úng gyóoli grayd/ *adj.* used to describe a mammal that walks on hoofs [Mid-19thC. Coined from Latin *ungula* 'hoof' (see UNGULATE) + GRADE.]

unhair /un háir/ (**-hairs, -hairing, -haired**) *vt.* to remove hair from sth, especially a hide (*archaic*)

unhallowed /un hállōd/ *adj.* 1. NOT CONSECRATED not consecrated or blessed 2. IRREVERENT lacking religious reverence 3. IMMORAL not conforming to the standards of a religion [Old English *unhālgod*]

unhand /un hánd/ (**-hands, -handing, -handed**) *vt.* to let sb go by releasing a grasp

unhandy /un hándi/ (**-ier, -iest**) *adj.* 1. NOT SKILLED WITH HANDS not skilled at working with the hands or with tools 2. INCONVENIENTLY LOCATED in an inconvenient location 3. DIFFICULT TO USE not easy to use or handle

unhappily /un háppili/ *adv.* 1. IN UNHAPPY WAY in an way that expresses or is characterized by unhappiness 2. UNFORTUNATELY used to express a wish that sth were not true (*dated*)

unhappy /un háppi/ (**-pier, -piest**) *adj.* 1. SAD not cheerful or joyful 2. UNFORTUNATE not bringing good luck 3. INAPPROPRIATE done without proper thought or inappropriate in a specific context 4. DISPLEASED not pleased or satisfied with sb or sth 5. UNFAVOURABLE not advantageous (*archaic*) —**unhappiness** *n.*

unharness /un háarnəss/ (**-nesses, -nessing, -nessed**) *vt.* 1. REMOVE HARNESS FROM HORSE to remove the harness from a horse 2. RELEASE ENERGY OR PASSIONS to release energy or passions from restraints 3. REMOVE ARMOUR to remove the armour from sb (*archaic*)

UNHCR *abbr.* United Nations High Commission for Refugees

unhealthy /un hélthi/ (**-ier, -iest**) *adj.* 1. SICK affected by ill health 2. BAD FOR HEALTH not good for the health 3. SYMPTOMATIC OF ILL HEALTH showing the symptoms of or resulting from ill health 4. HARMING CHARACTER harmful to the character 5. CORRUPT morally corrupt or unwholesome 6. RISKY taking unnecessary risks (*informal*) —**unhealthily** *adv.* —**unhealthiness** *n.*

unheard /un húrd/ *adj.* 1. NOT HEARD not perceived by the ear 2. NOT GIVEN A HEARING not listened to or given a hearing 3. UNKNOWN unknown or obscure (*archaic*)

unheard-of *adj.* 1. UNKNOWN not previously known 2. UNPRECEDENTED never having happened before 3. OFFENSIVE extremely offensive or rude

unhesitating /un hézzi tayting/ *adj.* 1. PROMPT without pause or indecision 2. UNCHANGING without change or deviation —**unhesitatingly** *adv.*

unhinge /un hínj/ (**-hinges, -hinging, -hinged**) *vt.* 1. REMOVE STH FROM HINGES to remove sth from its hinges 2. REMOVE HINGES to remove the hinges of sth 3. DISLOCATE STH to dislodge or detach sth 4. DISRUPT to throw sth into confusion 5. MAKE PSYCHOLOGICALLY UNSTABLE to cause sb to become emotionally or mentally unstable

unhip /un híp/ *adj.* not in keeping with popular fashions or ideas (*dated informal*)

unhitch /un hích/ (**-hitches, -hitching, -hitched**) *vt.* to unfasten sth that is tied up

unholy /un hóli/ (**-lier, -liest**) *adj.* 1. NOT BLESSED not blessed or consecrated by a church ritual 2. DEFYING RELIGIOUS PRECEPTS deliberately defiant of specific religious precepts 3. OUTRAGEOUS extremely annoying or disturbing ○ *This place is an unholy mess!* [Old English *unhālig*] —**unholiness** *n.*

unhook /un hóok/ (**-hooks, -hooking, -hooked**) *vt.* 1. REMOVE STH FROM HOOK to remove sth from a hook 2. UNDO HOOKS OF STH to unfasten the hooks of sth

unhoped-for /un hópt-/ *adj.* not expected or anticipated ○ *an unhoped-for victory* [14thC.]

unhorse /un háwrss/ (**-horses, -horsing, -horsed**) *vt.* 1. KNOCK SB FROM HORSE to knock or throw sb from a horse

2. BRING SB DOWN FROM OFFICE to bring sb down from a high office or position

unhurried /un húrrid/ *adj.* done in a relaxed and deliberate way —**unhurriedly** *adv.*

uni /yóoni/ *n.* a university (*informal*) [Late 19thC. Shortening.]

uni- *prefix.* one, single ○ *unicellular* [From Latin, formed from *unus* 'one'. Ultimately from the Indo-European word for 'one', which is also the ancestor of English *one*, *alone*, and *inch*.]

Uniat /yóoni ət, -ayt, yóoni at/, **Uniate** *n.* MEMBER OF EASTERN CHRISTIAN CHURCH a member of any of the Eastern Christian Churches that recognize papal supremacy but keep their own liturgy, language, and canon law ■ *adj.* OF UNIAT CHURCHES relating to or typical of the Uniat Churches [Mid-19thC. From Russian *uniyat* and Polish *uniat*, from *unia* 'union' (of the Roman Catholic and Greek Churches), ultimately from Latin *unio* (see UNION).]

uniaxial /yóoni áksi əl/ *adj.* **1.** CRYSTALS WITH SINGLE REFRACTION IN ONE DIRECTION used to describe a crystal or mineral that has one direction, parallel to the principal axis, along which single refraction occurs **2.** BOT WITH AN UNBRANCHED MAIN STEM used to describe a plant with an unbranched main stem —**uniaxially** *adv.*

unicameral /yóoni kámmərəl/ *adj.* having only one legislative chamber [Mid-19thC. Formed from Latin *camera* 'chamber' (see CAMERA).] —**unicameralism** *n.* —**unicameralist** *n.* —**unicamerally** *adv.*

UNICEF /yóoni sef/, **Unicef** *n.*, *abbr.* United Nations Children's Fund

unicellular /yóoni séllyoŏlər/ *adj.* consisting of a single cell —**unicellularity** /yóoni séllyoŏ lárrəti/ *n.*

unicolour /yóoni kúllər/ *adj.* composed of or containing only one colour

Unicorn

unicorn /yóoni kawrn/ *n.* **1.** MYTHICAL ONE-HORNED HORSE a mythical animal usually depicted as a white horse with a single straight spiralled horn growing from its forehead **2.** BIBLE BIBLICAL HORNED ANIMAL a horned animal mentioned in the Bible, now believed to be a rhinoceros or aurochs [13thC. Via Old French from Latin *unicornis*, literally 'one-horned', from *cornu* 'horn' (see CORN). Translation of Greek *monokerōs*.]

unicostate /yóoni kóst ayt/ *adj.* BOT used to describe a leaf with one main rib

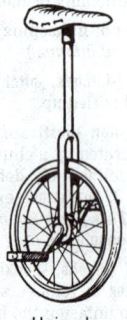

Unicycle

unicycle /yóoni sík'l/ *n.* a vehicle having a single wheel with a seat mounted on a frame above it. It is steered and kept upright by balance and propelled

by pedals. [Mid-19thC. Modelled on BICYCLE.] —**unicyclist** *n.*

unidentified /ún ī dénti fīd/ *adj.* **1.** UNABLE TO BE NAMED unable to be recognized or given a name **2.** WANTING TO REMAIN ANONYMOUS wishing not to be associated with or held responsible for sth

unidirectional /yóoni di réksh'nəl, -dī-/ *adj.* thinking, moving, or operating in only one direction

UNIDO /yoo néedō/, **Unido** *n.*, *abbr.* United Nations Industrial Development Organization

unifactorial /yóoni fak táwri əl/ *adj.* used to describe an inherited characteristic dependent on a single gene

unification /yóonifi káysh'n/ *n.* **1.** ACT OF UNITING the act or process of uniting or joining together **2.** RESULT OF UNITING a result of uniting or joining

Unification Church *n.* a religious denomination founded in 1954 by the South Korean industrialist Sun Myung Moon

unified field theory *n.* a single theory capable of defining the nature of the interrelationships among nuclear, electromagnetic, and gravitational forces

unifoliate /yóoni fóli ət/ *adj.* with a single leaf or leaf-shaped part

uniform /yóoni fawrm/ *n.* **1.** DISTINCTIVE CLOTHES a distinctive set of clothes worn to identify sb's occupation, affiliation, or status **2.** COMPLETE OUTFIT a single outfit of identifying clothes **3.** PARTICULAR IDENTIFYING LOOK a particular style or other feature that identifies sb as a member of a certain group ■ *adj.* **1.** UNCHANGING always the same in quality, degree, character, or manner **2.** CONSISTENT conforming to one standard or rule **3.** LIKE ANOTHER being the same as another or others **4.** UNVARYING IN DESIGN unvarying in colour, texture, or design ■ *vt.* **(-forms, -forming, -formed) 1.** PROVIDE PEOPLE WITH UNIFORMS to provide people or a group with uniforms **2.** MAKE STH THE SAME to make sth homogeneous, unvarying, or consistent [Mid-16thC. Directly or via French from Latin *uniformis*, literally 'having one form', from *forma* 'shape' (source of English *form* and *formal*).] —**uniformed** *adj.* —**uniformity** /yóoni fáwrməti/ *n.* —**uniformly** /yóoni fawrmli/ *adv.*

Uniform /yóoni fawrm/ *n.* COMMUNICATION the NATO phonetic alphabet code word for the letter 'U', used in international radio communications

uniformitarianism /yóoni fáwrmi táiri ənizəm/ *n.* the theory that the same geological processes occurred in the past as occur today, and that geological formations and structures can be interpreted by observing present-day actions —**uniformitarian** *adj.*, *n.*

Uniform Resource Locator *n.* full form of URL

unify /yóoni fī/ *vt.* **(-fies, -fying, -fied)** to bring people or things together to form a single unit or entity [Early 16thC. Via French *unifier* from Latin *unificare*, literally 'to make one'.] —**unifiable** /yóoni fī əb'l/ *adj.* —**unified** *adj.* —**unifier** *n.* —**unifying** *adj.*

unijugate /yóoni jóogət, -gayt/ *adj.* used to describe a compound leaf with a single pair of leaflets [Mid-19thC. Formed from JUGUM.]

unilateral /yóoni láttərəl/ *adj.* **1.** DECIDED BY ONE PARTY decided or acted on by only one involved party or nation irrespective of what the others do **2.** ACCOUNTING FOR ONE SIDE ONLY taking into account only one side of a subject **3.** BINDING ONLY ONE PARTY binding or at the insistence of only one party to a contract, obligation, or agreement **4.** MED AFFECTING ONLY ONE SIDE affecting or involving only one side of the body, only one of a pair of organs, or only one side of an organ **5.** BOT WITH PARTS ON ONLY ONE SIDE having parts that are arranged on only one side of a stem or other axis **6.** WITH ONE SIDE having only one side **7.** THROUGH ONE PARENT ONLY tracing lineage through one parent only —**unilaterally** *adv.*

unilateralism /yóoni láttərəlizəm/ *n.* the implementation of a foreign policy with little or no regard for the views of allies —**unilateralist** *n.*

unilineal /yóoni línni əl/ *adj.* = **unilateral** *adj.* 7

unilinear /yóoni línni ər/ *adj.* developing or evolving progressively through defined stages from primi-

tive to advanced and excluding any variation on this course

unilingual /yóoni líng gwəl/ *adj.* using or knowing only one language

uniliteral /yóoni líttərəl/ *adj.* having only a single letter

unilocular /yóoni lókyŏolər/ *adj.* with a single loculus, cell, or cavity

unimaginable /únni májjinəb'l/ *adj.* beyond anything that could be imagined or described —**unimaginably** *adv.*

unimaginative /únni májjinətiv/ *adj.* **1.** UNABLE TO THINK OF NEW IDEAS unable to think of new or interesting ideas, plans, or situations **2.** BORING AND WITHOUT NEW IDEAS boring and ordinary, without any new ideas

unimpaired /únnim páird/ *adj.* not damaged by sth unpleasant, dangerous, or different that happens

unimpassioned /únnim pásh'nd/ *adj.* unlikely to appeal to the emotions

unimpeachable /únnim peéchəb'l/ *adj.* **1.** IMPOSSIBLE TO DISCREDIT impossible to discredit or challenge **2.** FAULTLESS so good that it is beyond reproach —**unimpeachably** *adv.*

unimportant /únnim páwrt'nt/ *adj.* of little or no significance —**unimportance** *n.*

unimproved /únnim proóvd/ *adj.* **1.** NOT MADE BETTER not made better from an original condition **2.** NOT PUT TO GOOD USE not used to advantage **3.** NOT GETTING HEALTHIER not showing improvement in health **4.** WITHOUT IMPROVEMENTS not modified in a way that would increase value, e.g. by the addition of buildings, landscaping, or services ○ *an unimproved lot*

unincorporated /únnin káwrpə raytid/ *adj.* **1.** NOT ORGANIZED AS ENTITY not organized into a corporation or municipality **2.** NOT INCLUDED not included or a part of sth

uninformative /únnin fáwrmətiv/ *adj.* not providing adequate information —**uninformatively** *adv.*

uninformed /únnin fáwrmd/ *adj.* lacking facts or knowledge of a particular situation or subject

uninhabitable /únnin hábbitəb'l/ *adj.* unfit as a habitation, especially for human beings —**uninhabitability** /únnin hábbitə bílləti/ *n.*

uninhabited /únnin hábbitid/ *adj.* without human habitation

uninhibited /únnin híbbitid/ *adj.* **1.** UNRESTRAINED expressing feelings or views without restraint **2.** UNCONSTRAINED not subject to social or other constraints —**uninhibitedly** *adv.* —**uninhibitedness** *n.*

uninitiate /únni níshi ət/ *adj.* without experience

uninitiated /únni níshi aytid/ *adj.* WITHOUT KNOWLEDGE OF SUBJECT having no knowledge or experience of a particular subject ■ *npl.* PEOPLE UNKNOWLEDGEABLE IN SUBJECT people who have no knowledge or experience of a particular subject (*takes a plural verb*)

uninspired /únnin spírd/ *adj.* lacking originality or distinction

uninspiring *adj.* not arousing interest or excitement

uninstall /únnin stáwl/ *vt.* **(-stalls, -stalling, -stalled)** to remove software from a computer

uninstructed /únnin strúktid/ *adj.* **1.** NOT EDUCATED not educated or informed **2.** NOT TOLD WHAT TO DO not informed how to proceed or vote

uninsurable /únnin shoórəb'l, -sháwr-/ *adj.* considered too great a risk to cover by insurance —**uninsurability** /únnin shoórə bílləti/ *n.*

uninsured /únnin shoórd, -sháwrd/ *adj.* NOT COVERED BY INSURANCE not covered against some hazard by insurance ■ *npl.* SB NOT INSURED a person or group not covered by insurance (*takes a plural verb*)

unintelligent /únnin téllijənt/ *adj.* **1.** LACKING INTELLIGENCE lacking or showing a lack of intelligence **2.** NOT HAVING ABILITY TO THINK not having a mind or the ability to think and reason —**unintelligently** *adv.*

unintelligible /únnin téllijəb'l/ *adj.* difficult or impossible to understand —**unintelligibility** /únnin téllijə bílləti/ *n.* —**unintelligibly** /-téllijəbli/ *adv.*

unintended /únnin téndid/ *adj.* neither planned nor wanted

unintentional /únnin ténsh'nəl/ *adj.* not on purpose or by plan —**unintentionally** *adv.*

uninterest /un íntrəst/ *n.* a lack of interest or concern

uninterested /un íntrəstid/ *adj.* lacking interest or concern [Mid-17thC. The earliest meaning was 'impartial, disinterested'.] —**uninterestedly** *adv.* —**uninterestedness** *n.*

uninteresting /un íntrəsting/ *adj.* without interesting qualities —**uninterestingly** *adv.*

WORD KEY: SYNONYMS

See Synonyms at ***boring***.

uninterrupted /únnintə rúptid/ *adj.* **1.** WITH NO BREAK without interruption or break **2.** WITHOUT OBSTRUCTIONS free from obstructions ○ *an uninterrupted view* —**uninterruptedly** *adv.*

uninucleate /yo͝oni nyo͝okli ət/ *adj.* having a single nucleus

uninvited /únnin vítid/ *adj.* not invited or welcome

uninviting /únnin víting/ *adj.* not appealing or pleasant —**uninvitingly** *adv.*

uninvolved /únnin vólvd/ *adj.* not participating in sth

union /yo͝onyən/ *n.* **1.** ACT OF JOINING TOGETHER the act of joining together people or things to form a whole **2.** RESULT OF BRINGING PEOPLE TOGETHER a result of bringing or joining together people or things **3.** AGREEMENT agreement or unity of interests or opinions **4.** MARRIAGE the state of being married **5.** SEX sexual intercourse **6.** POLITICAL ALLIANCE an alliance formed by the joining of people or organizations for a common political purpose **7.** EMBLEM OF UNION an emblem of union used on a flag (*archaic*) **8.** = **trade union 9.** PARISHES UNITED TO AID THE POOR a number of parishes in 19th-century Britain united to administer relief to the poor **10.** WORKHOUSE a 19th-century workhouse supported by parishes united to aid the poor **11.** MATH SMALL SET OF ELEMENTS the smallest set that consists of all the elements of any or all of two or more given sets and no other elements. An element is counted only once even if it occurs in more than one of the given sets. **12. union, Union** EDUC ORGANIZATION PROVIDING RECREATIONAL FACILITIES an organization that provides recreational facilities for students at a college or university **13. union, Union** EDUC BUILDING FOR RECREATION a building that houses recreational facilities for students at a college or university **14.** CONSTR COUPLING a coupling for parts such as pipes and pipe fittings **15.** TEXTILES FABRIC OF DIFFERENT YARNS a fabric made of two or more different yarns, e.g. cotton and linen **16. union, Union** *Aus* RUGBY UNION Rugby Union, as distinct from Rugby League (*informal*) [15thC. Directly or via French from the Latin stem *union-*, 'oneness', from *unus* 'one'. Ultimately from an Indo-European word meaning 'one', the ancestor of English *one, any, inch,* and *ounce*.]

Union *n.* **1.** NORTHERN SIDE IN US CIVIL WAR the side of the northern states in the US Civil War, or its armed forces. The northern states favoured preservation of the nation as a union of states whereas the southern states declared their secession from that union. **2.** UNION OF BRITAIN AND NORTHERN IRELAND the union of Great Britain and Northern Ireland since 1920 **3.** UNITED STATES OF AMERICA the United States of America

union card *n.* a card signifying membership in a trade union

union catalogue *n.* a library catalogue combining the materials in more than one library or in branches of the same library

Union City 1. residential and industrial city in western California, on Alameda Creek, near San Francisco Bay. Population: 53,762 (1990). **2.** city in northeastern New Jersey, on the Hudson River, adjoining Jersey City and opposite New York City. Population: 58,012 (1990).

Union flag *n.* = **Union Jack**

unionise *vti.* = **unionize**

unionism /yo͝onyə nizəm/ *n.* **1.** PRINCIPLES OF UNIONS the principles or policies of trade unions **2.** ADVOCACY OF UNIONS the advocacy of forming and joining trade unions —**unionist** *n.*

Unionism /yo͝onyə nizəm/ *n.* **1.** SUPPORT FOR UNION WITH NORTHERN IRELAND support or advocacy since 1920 for the union between Northern Ireland and Britain **2.** HIST SUPPORT FOR IRELAND'S UNION WITH BRITAIN support or advocacy before 1920 for the union of all Ireland and Great Britain **3.** LOYALTY TO FEDERAL UNION loyalty to the federal union during the Civil War in the United States —**Unionist** *n.*

unionize /yo͝onyə nīz/ (**-izes, -izing, -ized**), **unionise** (**-ises, -ising, -ised**) *vti.* to organize workers into a trade union, or to join a trade union —**unionization** /yo͝onyə nī záysh'n/ *n.* —**unionizer** /yo͝onyə nīzər/ *n.*

Union Jack, Union flag *n.* the flag of the United Kingdom, which united by superposition the flags of England, Scotland, and Ireland [*Union* because it represents the UNITED KINGDOM + *jack*[1] in the sense 'ship's flag']

union shop *n.* a place of employment where a contract between the employer and a trade union requires employees to be or become members of the union within a specified time. ◊ **open shop**

uniparous /yoo níppərəss/ *adj.* **1.** HAVING ONE CHILD having given birth to only one child **2.** PRODUCING ONE OFFSPRING PER BIRTH producing a single offspring at each birth

unipersonal /yo͝oni púrss'nəl/ *adj.* **1.** EXISTING AS ONE PERSON existing or manifested in the form of only one person **2.** GRAM USED IN ONE PERSON existing as an inflected form in only one person, especially the third person singular

uniplanar /yo͝oni pláynər/ *adj.* occurring or located in a single plane

unipod /yo͝oni pod/ *n.* a one-legged stand, e.g. for a camera [Mid-20thC. Modelled on TRIPOD.]

unipolar /yo͝oni pṓlər/ *adj.* **1.** PHYS HAVING SINGLE POLE operating by means of, having, or produced by a single electric or magnetic pole **2.** BIOL BRANCHING OUT AT ONLY ONE END used to describe a neurone that branches out at only one end **3.** PHYS WITH ONE POLARITY used to describe a transistor that has carriers with only one polarity —**unipolarity** /yo͝onipō lárrəti/ *n.*

unipotent /yo͝oni pṓt'nt/ *adj.* capable of developing into only one type of cell or tissue

unique /yoo néek/ *adj.* **1.** UNUSUAL different from others in a way that makes sth worthy of note ○ *a unique marketing opportunity* **2.** ONLY ONE being the only one of its kind **3.** BETTER THAN OTHERS superior to all others **4.** LIMITED TO SB OR STH limited to a specific place, situation, group, person, or thing ○ *concerns that are unique to resettled refugees* [Early 17thC. Via French from Latin *unicus*, from *unus* 'one' (see UNION).] —**uniquely** *adv.* —**uniqueness** *n.*

WORD KEY: USAGE

Meaning trap: The use of ***unique*** in its weakened sense 'remarkable, outstanding' is common in marketing and advertising (*Don't miss this unique offer*), and these uses have somewhat discredited what is arguably a routine development in meaning. Many dictionaries and usage guides argue that ***unique*** is an absolute concept, thereby rejecting the use of qualifying words such as *very* and *rather*, but in many cases this stricture seems a pedantic objection to what is a linguistic rather than a philosophical convention.

unique selling proposition *n.* full form of **USP**

uniramous /yo͝oni ráyməss/ *adj.* used to describe an appendage without multiple branches [Late 19thC. Formed from Latin *ramus* 'branch'.]

uniseptate /yo͝oni sép tayt/ *adj.* with a single separating wall or membrane [Mid-19thC. Formed from SEPTUM.]

uniserial /yo͝oni séeri əl/, **uniseriate** /-ayt/ *adj.* arranged in or consisting of a single row or series

unisex /yo͝oni seks/ *adj.* **1.** SUITABLE FOR EITHER SEX designed or suitable for people of either sex ○ *unisex fashions* **2.** BIOL NOT DISTINCTLY MALE OR FEMALE not distinctly of either the male or the female sex

unisexual /yo͝oni sékshoo əl, -séksyoo-/ *adj.* **1.** RELATED TO ONE SEX related to or limited to one sex **2.** WITH MALE OR FEMALE REPRODUCTIVE ORGANS having either only male or only female reproductive organs —**unisexuality** /yo͝oni sékshoo álləti/ *n.* —**unisexually** /-əli/ *adv.*

unison /yo͝oniss'n/ *n.* **1.** NOTES AT SAME PITCH two or more notes sharing the same pitch **2.** PERFORMANCE OF PARTS the performance of two or more parts at the same pitch or an octave apart [Late 16thC. Via Old French from, ultimately, late Latin *unisonus*, literally 'having the same sound', from *sonus* 'sound' (see SOUND).] ◇ **in unison 1.** in perfect agreement or harmony **2.** at the same time as sb or sth else

UNISON /yo͝oniss'n/ *n.* the largest trade union for public service employees

unit /yo͝onit/ *n.* **1.** ONE PERSON, THING, OR GROUP a single person, thing, or group, usually regarded as a whole part of sth larger **2.** DISCRETE PART any of the individuals or discrete parts or elements into which sth can be divided, especially for analysis **3.** GROUP WITH SPECIFIC FUNCTION a group of people with a specific function who are part of a larger organization ○ *the cancer research unit* **4.** GROUP OF MILITARY PERSONNEL a group of military personnel with a particular function organized as a subdivision of a larger body **5.** COMPONENT OR ASSEMBLY OF COMPONENTS a component or assembly of components that performs a specific function ○ *a kitchen unit* **6.** *US, Can, Aus, NZ* RESIDENCE one of a number of similar residences within a building or development **7.** EDUC PART OF ACADEMIC COURSE a part of an academic course that focuses on a particular theme **8.** MEASURE MEASUREMENT a standard measurement, e.g. an inch, degree, calorie, volt, or hour, whose multiples are used in determining quantity **9.** MED DRUG AMOUNT an amount of an enzyme, hormone, drug, or other agent that produces a given effect, often as specified by an internationally agreed standard **10.** MED MEASURE OF ALCOHOL INTAKE a measure of alcohol intake used in monitoring the effects of alcohol on the body. One unit is roughly equivalent to the alcohol in half a pint of beer, one glass of wine, or a single measure of spirits. **11.** MATH NATURAL NUMBER the lowest positive natural number **12.** MATH NUMBER LESS THAN TEN the first digit to the left of the decimal point in decimal notation, representing a whole number less than ten. Broadly, the first place in a place-value number system, representing a whole number less than the base (**radix**) multiplied by the base raised to the zero power. **13.** MATH SET WITH SINGLE NUMBER a set having a single number [Late 16thC. Formed from Latin *unus* 'one' (see UNION), on the model of *digit*.]

unitard /yo͝oni taard/ *n.* a one-piece stretchable garment with or without sleeves that covers the body from the neck to the feet [Mid-20thC. Coined from UNI- and LEOTARD.]

unitarian /yo͝oni táiri ən/ *n.* **1.** SUPPORTER OF UNITY a supporter of unity or a unitary system **2.** RELIG SB BELIEVING GOD IS ONE sb who believes that God is one being —**unitarianism** *n.*

Unitarian /yo͝oni táiri ən/ *n.* CHR **1.** MEMBER OF CHRISTIAN CHURCH a member of the Christian Church that upholds the doctrine of Unitarianism **2.** NONBELIEVER IN TRINITY a Christian who does not believe in the Trinity —**Unitarian** *adj.*

Unitarianism *n.* a religious doctrine that rejects the Christian doctrine of the Trinity, the divinity of Jesus Christ, and formal dogma but stresses reason and individual conscience in belief and practice

unitary /yo͝onitəri/ *adj.* **1.** RELATING TO UNIT relating to or consisting of a unit **2.** CHARACTERIZED BY UNITY based on or characterized by unity **3.** EXISTING AS UNIT undivided and existing as a unit **4.** OF CENTRALIZED GOVERNMENT of or based on a system of government in which authority is centralized —**unitarily** *adv.*

unit cell *n.* the smallest structural unit of a crystal that has all its symmetry and by repetition in three dimensions makes up its full lattice

unit cost *n.* the cost of producing a single item

unite /yoo nīt/ (**unites, uniting, united**) *v.* **1.** *vti.* BRING THINGS TOGETHER to bring things together or to come together to form or act as a unit **2.** *vti.* UNIFY PEOPLE to unify people or to become unified by a common interest or concern **3.** *vti.* MARRY to join a couple in marriage **4.** *vti.* ADHERE to adhere or cause things to adhere **5.** *vt.* COMBINE QUALITIES to combine qualities or traits [15thC. From Latin *unit-*, the past participle stem of *unire*, literally 'to make one', from *unus* 'one' (see UNION).] —**uniter** *n.*

united /yoo nītid/ *adj.* **1.** COMBINED INTO ONE combined into or made one **2.** BY OR FROM UNION formed by or resulting from the union of two or more persons or things **3.**

IN HARMONY in agreement or harmony —**unitedness** n.

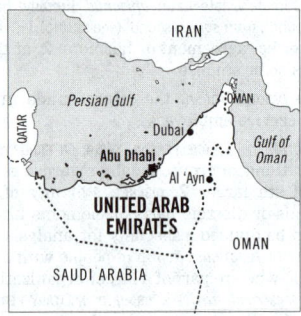

United Arab Emirates

United Arab Emirates /yoŏ nītid árrəb émmərəts/ federation of seven independent states located along the southern coast of the Persian Gulf. Language: Arabic. Currency: dirham. Capital: Abu Dhabi. Population: 2,500,000 (1996). Area: 77,700 sq. km/30,000 sq. mi. Former name **Trucial States**

United Arab Republic former independent union between Egypt and Syria, founded in 1958. It was disbanded when Syria left the union in 1961, although Egypt retained the name until 1971.

United Kingdom

United Kingdom /yoŏ nītid kíngdəm/ constitutional monarchy in northwestern Europe, occupying the British Isles with the exception of most of the island of Ireland. It comprises the historic kingdoms of England and Scotland, the principality of Wales, and the province of Northern Ireland. Language: English. Currency: pound sterling. Capital: London. Population: 58,784,000 (1996). Area: 241,752 sq. km/93,341 sq. mi. Official name **United Kingdom of Great Britain and Northern Ireland**

United Nations n. (takes a singular or plural verb) **1.** ORGANIZATION OF NATIONS an organization of nations that was formed in 1945 to promote peace, security, and international cooperation **2.** HIST ALLIANCE OF NATIONS an

alliance of nations that pledged in January 1942 to defeat the Axis powers in World War II

United States POL federal republic in the continent of North America, consisting of 50 states. Language: English. Currency: dollar. Capital: Washington, D.C. Population: 270,311,758 (1998). Area: 9,629,047 sq. km/3,717,796 sq. mi. Official name **United States of America**

unitise vt. = unitize

unitive /yoŏnitiv/ adj. **1.** ABLE TO UNITE having the ability to unite or promoting unity **2.** CHARACTERIZED BY UNION characterized by union or unity [Early 16thC. From late Latin unitivus, from Latin unit- (see UNITE).]

unitize /yoŏni tīz/ (-izes, -izing, -ized), **unitise** (-ises, -ising, -ised) v. **1.** vti. MAKE ONE to form or to make sth into a single unit **2.** vt. DIVIDE INTO UNITS to separate sth into units **3.** vt. FIN CONVERT TRUST to convert an investment trust into a unit trust —**unitization** /yoŏni tī záysh'n/ n.

unit of account n. **1.** FUNCTION OF MONEY IN ACCOUNTING the way money is used to keep financial accounts **2.** CURRENCY FOR FINANCIAL RECORDS the currency used to record and track financial transactions. It does not have to correspond to a denomination of real currency. US term **money of account 3.** NATION'S OFFICIAL CURRENCY the official currency of a nation

unit operation n. an operation, e.g. mixing, filtration, chemical reaction, or distillation, that is common to the chemical process industries. The study of unit operations is the basis of chemical engineering.

unit price n. the price of goods per item or measure, e.g. per pound or dozen

unit trust n. a trust company that manages investments for investors with holdings in the form of units representing a fraction of the value of the investments that are issued by and bought back by the managers. US term **mutual fund**

unity /yoŏnəti/ (plural -ties) n. **1.** BEING ONE the state of being one **2.** COMBINING INTO ONE the combining or joining of separate things to form one **3.**

STH WHOLE sth whole or complete formed by combining or joining separate things or entities **4.** HARMONY harmony of opinion, interest, or feeling **5.** SINGLENESS AMONG INDIVIDUALS singleness or constancy among individuals or groups **6.** ARTS ARRANGING OF ARTISTIC ELEMENTS AESTHETICALLY the arranging of separate elements in a literary or artistic work to create an overall aesthetic impression **7.** ARTS AESTHETIC IMPRESSION the overall aesthetic impression produced by the arrangement of elements in an artistic or literary work **8.** THEATRE PRINCIPLE OF DRAMATIC STRUCTURE any one of the three principles of dramatic structure derived from Aristotle's *Poetics*. These state that the action of a play should be limited to one plot (**unity of action**), one day (**unity of time**), and one location (**unity of place**). **9.** MATH NUMBER ONE a number by which a given element of a mathematical system can be multiplied with the result being equal to the value of the given element **10.** MATH = **identity element** [13thC. Via Old French unite from Latin unitas, literally 'oneness', from unus 'one' (see UNION).]

univ. abbr. university

univalent /yoŏni váylənt, yoo nívvələnt/ adj. **1.** = **monovalent 2.** REMAINING UNPAIRED DURING CELL DIVISION used to describe a chromosome that remains unpaired during the cell division (**meiosis**) that precedes sex cell formation —**univalency** /yoŏni váylənssi/ n.

univalve /yoŏni valv/ adj. **1.** WITH SINGLE-PIECE SHELL having a shell that is a single piece or valve ○ an univalve gastropod **2.** MADE OF SINGLE PIECE used to describe a shell that is made of a single piece ■ n. MOLLUSC a mollusc or shell that is univalve

universal /yoŏni vúrss'l/ adj. **1.** AFFECTING THE WORLD affecting, relating to, or including the whole world or everyone in the world **2.** RELATING TO UNIVERSE relating to the universe or everything **3.** AFFECTING THOSE IN PARTICULAR GROUP affecting, relating to, or including everyone in a particular group or situation **4.** USED BY EVERYONE used or understood by everyone **5.** APPLICABLE TO ALL applicable to all situations or purposes ○ a universal solution **6.** PRESENT EVERYWHERE present or prevalent everywhere **7.** KNOWLEDGEABLE knowledgeable about or encompassing extensive skills, interests, activities, or subjects **8.** ADAPTABLE TO DIFFERENT SIZES adaptable to many uses or sizes **9.** LOGIC AFFIRMING OR DENYING EVERY MEMBER relating to a proposition that is true or false of every member of a class or group ■ n. **1.** COMMON CHARACTERISTIC a characteristic or behaviour pattern common to everyone or all the people in a particular group or situation **2.** LOGIC TRUE OR FALSE PROPOSITION FOR ALL a proposition that is true or false for all members of a class or group **3.** PHILOSOPHY GENERAL TERM OR CONCEPT a general term or concept or that which it denotes **4.** PHILOSOPHY UNCHANGING METAPHYSICAL ENTITY a metaphysical entity that remains unchanged in character through a series of changing relations **5.** PHILOSOPHY PLATONIC IDEA OR ARISTOTELIAN FORM a Platonic idea or Aristotelian form **6.** LING GRAMMATICAL CHARACTERISTIC COMMON TO ALL LANGUAGES an actual or possible characteristic common to the grammatical description of all human languages —**universality** /yoŏni vur sálləti/ n. —**universally** /-vúrss'li/ adv.

──── **WORD KEY: SYNONYMS** ────
See Synonyms at **widespread**.

universal beam n. a strong steel beam suitable as a support, used either vertically or horizontally

universal class n. = universal set

universal coupling n. = universal joint

universal donor n. sb with group O blood who can potentially donate blood to anyone, regardless of the recipient's blood group. ◊ **universal recipient**

universal grammar n. the set of actual or possible rules that form the grammatical description of all human languages

universalise vt. = universalize

universalism /yoŏni vúrss'lizəm/ n. **1.** COMPREHENSIVE RANGE a comprehensive range of knowledge, interests, or activities **2.** UNIVERSAL FEATURE a universal characteristic or feature **3.** SOC WELFARE PRINCIPLE OF WELFARE SERVICES the principle that welfare services should be publicly funded and available to all

United States

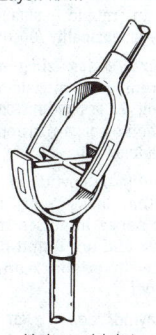

Universal joint

strictly on the basis of need —**universalist** *n.* — **universalistic** /yoóni vurssə lístik/ *adj.*

Universalism /yoóni vúrss'lizəm/ *n.* the doctrine of salvation for all souls —**Universalist** *n.*

universalizability /yoóni vúrssə līzə bílləti/ *n.* **1.** UNIVERSAL APPLICATION OF MORAL JUDGMENT the thesis that any moral judgment must apply equally to all relevantly identical situations **2.** KANTIAN PRINCIPLE OF MORALITY the Kantian principle that any course of action that cannot be universally adopted must be morally impermissible

universalize /yoóni vúrssə līz/ (**-izes, -izing, -ized**), **universalise** (**-ises, -ising, -ised**) *vt.* **1.** MAKE WIDESPREAD to make sth universal in use or distribution, often within a certain field **2.** MAKE GENERAL to generalize a theory, proposition, or idea so that it applies to all people, instances, or situations —**universalization** /yoóni vurssə līt záysh'n/ *n.*

universal quantifier *n.* a word such as 'all' and 'every' in English and the logical operator or constant that performs the same function in symbolic, mathematical, or predicate logic

universal recipient *n.* sb who belongs to the AB blood group and, as a result, can receive transfusions of blood of any ABO group. ◊ **universal donor**

universal set, **universal class** *n.* a mathematical set that contains all of the possible elements and all of the subsets relevant to the solution of a particular problem

universal time *n.* **1.** = Greenwich Mean Time **2.** universal time, universal time coordinated INTERNATIONALLY ACCEPTED STANDARD FOR TIME an internationally accepted standard for calculating time based on International Atomic Time

universe /yoónivurss/ *n.* **1.** ALL MATTER AND ENERGY IN SPACE the totality of all matter and energy that exists in the vastness of space, whether known to human beings or not **2.** HUMANITY AND ITS HISTORY the human race or the totality of human experience **3.** SPHERE OF PERSON OR THING a sphere of activity or field that is centred on and includes everything associated with a person, place, or thing **4.** = **universe of discourse 5.** = **population** *n.* 5 [14thC. Directly or via French from Latin *universum* 'the whole world', from *universus* 'whole', literally 'turned into one', from *versus*, past participle of *vertere* 'to turn' (source of English *versatile*).]

universe of discourse *n.* in logic, all of a set of objects implied by a specific discussion

university /yoóni vúrssəti/ (*plural* **-ties**) *n.* **1.** UNDERGRADUATE AND POSTGRADUATE EDUCATIONAL INSTITUTION faculties comprising departments offering courses of undergraduate and postgraduate study in many subjects **2.** BUILDINGS HOUSING A UNIVERSITY the buildings, other facilities, and grounds of a university **3.** STUDENTS AND FACULTY the students, teachers, and administrative and other staff of a university [14thC. Via French *université* from Latin *universitas* 'the whole, society, guild', from *universus* (see UNIVERSE).]

universal joint, **universal coupling** *n.* a coupling device between two rotating shafts in line with each other that permits rotation in three planes. It is commonly used in vehicle construction.

universal motor *n.* an electric motor that runs with a relatively constant output speed on either alternating or direct current

univocal /yoóni vók'l/ *adj.* UNAMBIGUOUS having only one meaning ■ *n.* **UNIVOCAL WORD** a word or term with only one meaning [Mid-16thC. Formed from Late Latin *univocus*, literally 'having one voice', from *vox* 'voice' (see VOICE).] —**univocally** *adv.*

UNIX /yoóniks/, **Unix** *tdmk.* a trademark for a widely used computer operating system, developed in 1969 at AT&T Bell Laboratories, that can support multitasking in a multiuser environment

unjust /un júst/ *adj.* **1.** NOT JUST OR FAIR contrary to what is right, just, or fair, or lacking fairness or justice **2.** FAITHLESS unfaithful or dishonest (*archaic*) —**unjustly** *adv.* —**unjustness** *n.*

unkempt /un kémpt/ *adj.* **1.** NEEDING GROOMING tangled, matted, or messy, and needing combing or grooming **2.** UNTIDY AND NEGLECTED untidy or disorderly as a result of neglect or a lack of care **3.** UNPOLISHED lacking in polish or elegance [14thC. Formed from *kempt*, past participle of *kemb* 'to comb', from Old English *cemban*, from a prehistoric Germanic word that is also the ancestor of English *comb*.]

unkind /un kínd/ *adj.* **1.** LACKING KINDNESS lacking or resulting from a lack of kindness, sympathy, or consideration **2.** HARSH severe, harsh, or inclement —**unkindness** *n.* —**unkindly** *adj.*

unknowable /un nó əb'l/ *adj.* NOT KNOWABLE impossible to know, often because of lying outside human experience or being inaccessible to human understanding ■ *n.* STH NOT KNOWABLE sth that cannot be known —**unknowability** /un nó ə bílləti/ *n.* —**unknowableness** /-əb'lnəss/ *n.* —**unknowably** *adv.*

unknowing /un nó ing/ *adj.* **1.** UNAWARE unwitting or lacking awareness **2.** UNINTENTIONAL not intended —**unknowingly** *adv.*

unknown /ún nón/ *adj.* **1.** NOT KNOWN not forming part of sb's knowledge or of knowledge in general **2.** NOT IDENTIFIED undetermined or undiscovered **3.** NOT WIDELY KNOWN not known to, or recognized by, many people ■ *n.* **1.** SB OR STH NOT KNOWN sb or sth that is not part of sb's knowledge or of knowledge in general **2.** SB OR STH NOT WIDELY KNOWN sb or sth that is not known or recognized by many people **3.** MATH VARIABLE TO BE DETERMINED a variable in an equation whose values are solutions of the equation

Unknown Soldier *n.* an unidentified soldier killed in battle and selected for burial with national honours to represent all those who died fighting for their country but could not be identified

unlabored *adj.* US = unlaboured

unlaboured /un láybərd/ *adj.* **1.** DONE WITHOUT EFFORT done or produced without toil, effort, or difficulty **2.** NATURAL AND UNSTUDIED exhibiting a naturalness and ease of accomplishment **3.** UNCULTIVATED not subject to tilling or cultivation

unlace /un láyss/ (**-laces, -lacing, -laced**) *vt.* **1.** UNDO LACES OF to loosen or untie the laces of a shoe, piece of clothing, or other item **2.** UNDRESS SB BY UNDOING LACES to loosen or untie laced shoes or clothing on sb

unlade /un láyd/ (**-lades, -lading, -laded, -laded** *or* **-laden** /-láyd'n/) *vt.* **1.** EMPTY SHIP OR VEHICLE to empty a ship or vehicle by removing its cargo or load **2.** REMOVE CARGO to remove a cargo or load from a ship or vehicle

unlash /un lásh/ (**-lashes, -lashing, -lashed**) *vt.* to loosen or untie the ropes or other lashing holding or restraining sth

unlatch /un lách/ (**-latches, -latching, -latched**) *vti.* to unfasten or open by lifting or releasing a latch, or become unfastened or open in this way

unlawful /un láwf'l/ *adj.* **1.** ILLEGAL not permitted by the law **2.** IMMORAL OR UNETHICAL contrary to religious precepts, ethical standards, or the conventions of society **3.** BORN OUT OF WEDLOCK born to parents who are not legally married (*archaic*) —**unlawfully** *adv.* —**unlawfulness** *n.*

unlawful assembly *n.* an assembly of people that is not sanctioned by law and is therefore illegal, e.g. a march or picket that is not in compliance with the Public Order Acts

unlay /un láy/ (**-lays, -laying, -laid** /-láyd/, **-laid**) *vti.* to separate the strands of a rope by untwisting them, or become separated in this way [Early 18thC. From LAY[1].]

unleaded /un léddid/ *adj.* 1. FREE OF TETRAETHYL LEAD not containing tetraethyl lead as an antiknock additive and consequently less harmful to the environment ○ *unleaded gas* 2. PRINTING NOT SEPARATED BY LEADS not separated by spaces created by inserting leads between the lines of type ■ *n.* UNLEADED PETROL petrol that does not contain tetraethyl lead as an antiknock additive

unlearn /un lúrn/ (**-learns, -learning, -learnt** *or* **-learned** /-lúrnt/, **-learnt** *or* **-learned**) *vt.* 1. RID MIND OF to rid the mind of the knowledge or memory of sth 2. END PRACTICE OF to break the habit of sth or end the practice of sth

unlearned /un lúrnid/ *adj.* 1. LACKING EDUCATION not having received an education or schooling 2. DISPLAYING LACK OF EDUCATION showing or resulting from a lack of education 3. UNSKILLED OR UNFAMILIAR lacking a knowledge of, skills in, or familiarity with, a specified field 4. **unlearned, unlearnt** NATURAL OR UNSTUDIED possessed or known without having been practised, studied, or taught [15thC. Formed from LEARN.] —**unlearnedly** /un lúrnidli/ *adv.*

unleash /un léesh/ (**-leashes, -leashing, -leashed**) *vt.* 1. FREE FROM LEASH to set a person or animal free from a leash or other form of restraint or confinement 2. ALLOW STH TO HAVE FULL EFFECT to allow sth, especially sth previously held in check, to have its full effect

unleavened /un lévv'nd/ *adj.* made without yeast or other raising agent

unless /un léss/ *conj.* except under the circumstances that ○ *I won't go unless the weather improves.* [15thC. Formed from *on lesse than* 'on a lower condition, except', of unknown origin.]

unlettered /un léttərd/ *adj.* 1. NOT WELL-EDUCATED lacking a good education or the knowledge and understanding that such an education can provide 2. ILLITERATE unable to read and write 3. NOT HAVING ANY LETTERING not containing or inscribed with any lettering [14thC]

unlicensed /un líss'nst/ *adj.* 1. HAVING NO LICENCE lacking a required official licence, especially an official licence to sell alcohol 2. UNSANCTIONED done without authorization or permission 3. WITHOUT ETHICAL INHIBITIONS lacking ethical or religious constraints

unlike /un lík/ *prep.* 1. DISSIMILAR having qualities and characteristics dissimilar to or different from sb or sth ○ *They were completely unlike each other in appearance.* 2. INDICATES CONTRAST used to indicate a contrast between two things, people, or situations ○ *Unlike the previous government, we intend to fulfil our manifesto promises.* 3. NOT TYPICAL OF used to indicate that sb's words or actions are not typical or characteristic of him or her ○ *It was so unlike her to speak like that.* [Old English] —**unlikeness** *n.*

unlikely /un líkli/ (**-lier, -liest**) *adj.* 1. IMPROBABLE not likely to occur 2. NOT BELIEVABLE not likely to be true or be believed 3. INCONGRUOUS not suitable or appropriate 4. PROBABLY NOT SUCCESSFUL not likely to meet with success —**unlikeliness** *n.* —**unlikelihood** *n.*

unlimber /un límbər/ (**-bers, -bering, -bered**) *vti.* 1. GET STH READY FOR ACTION to prepare sth for action or use 2. REMOVE AND SET UP CANNON to remove a piece of field artillery from its gun carriage and prepare it for use [Early 19thC. Literally 'to withdraw the limber (from a gun before bringing it into use)'.]

unlimited /un límmitid/ *adj.* 1. NOT RESTRICTED without limits, restrictions, or controls 2. INFINITE lacking or appearing to lack a boundary or end 3. COMPLETE OR TOTAL not subject to qualification or exception 4. COMM NOT LIMITED IN MONEY PAYABLE used to describe a financial liability that is not limited in the amount of money that the members of a company are required to pay out if the company ceases to trade 5. COMM NOT HAVING MEMBERS WITH LIMITED LIABILITY used to describe a company in which each of the members is financially liable for his or her full share of the company's debts if the company ceases to trade —**unlimitedly** *adv.* —**unlimitedness** *n.*

unlink /un língk/ (**-links, -linking, -linked**) *vti.* 1. UNFASTEN OR BECOME UNFASTENED to undo one or more links of sth, or to become undone at one or more links 2. SEPARATE OR DISCONNECT to separate or disconnect, or to become separated or disconnected

unlisted /un lístid/ *adj.* 1. NOT ON LIST not included on a list 2. NOT LISTED ON STOCK EXCHANGE not registered on a physical stock exchange and consequently not available for trading on that exchange 3. *US, Can, ANZ* NOT PUBLICLY AVAILABLE not included in a telephone directory available to the public

unlisted securities market *n.* the London market trading in shares that are not included on the official Stock Exchange list

unlive /un lív/ (**-lives, -living, -lived**) *vt.* to reverse or undo the effects of an experience, action, or period of life

unload /un lód/ (**-loads, -loading, -loaded**) *vti.* 1. REMOVE CARGO OR LOAD FROM CARRIER to take off or remove a cargo or load from a ship, lorry, or pack animal 2. DISCHARGE to discharge passengers or cargo 3. REMOVE CHARGE FROM GUN to remove a charge or cartridge from a gun 4. TAKE FILM OUT OF CAMERA to remove a roll of film from a camera 5. SELL ON STH UNWANTED to get rid of sth, especially by selling a large quantity of it 6. TRANSFER STH UNWANTED to pass work, responsibility, or a problem on to sb else 7. SHARE TROUBLES to find an outlet for worries or negative feelings by sharing them with sb else

unlock /un lók/ (**-locks, -locking, -locked**) *v.* 1. *vti.* OPEN OR BECOME OPEN AFTER LOCKING to open a lock or sth locked, or to become open after being locked 2. *vt.* GIVE ACCESS TO STH to provide access to sth previously unavailable 3. *vti.* RELEASE EMOTION to release or unleash a pent-up feeling or emotion, or to be released or unleashed 4. *vti.* REVEAL OR BE REVEALED to expose or explain sth, or to be exposed or explained 5. *vti.* LOOSEN to unclench sth, or to be unclenched

unlooked-for /un lóokt-/ *adj.* not hoped for or expected

unloose /un lóoss/ (**-looses, -loosing, -loosed**), **unloosen** /-lóoss'n/ (**-ens, -ening, -ened**) *vt.* 1. UNFASTEN to untie or undo sth, especially a knot 2. SET FREE BY UNTYING to set a person or animal free by untying restraints 3. RELEASE FROM RESTRAINT OR CONFINEMENT to restore freedom to sb held under restraint or in confinement 4. MAKE LOOSER to relax the tightness of sth 5. MAKE STH LESS INTENSE to reduce the intensity of sth

unlovely /un lúvvli/ (**-lier, -liest**) *adj.* 1. NOT BEAUTIFUL not beautiful or pleasing to look at 2. NOT PLEASURABLE not producing pleasure or delight —**unloveliness** *n.*

unlucky /un lúki/ (**-ier, -iest**) *adj.* 1. HAVING BAD LUCK not experiencing good luck or good fortune 2. FULL OF MISFORTUNE OR FAILURE full of bad luck, misfortune, or failure 3. BRINGING MISFORTUNE causing or heralding misfortune 4. DISAPPOINTING producing disappointment or regret —**unluckily** *adv.* —**unluckiness** *n.*

unmade past tense, past participle of **unmake** ■ *adj.* 1. NOT MADE NEAT AND TIDY not restored to a neat and tidy state after being slept in ○ *an unmade bed* 2. = **unmetalled**

unmake /un máyk/ (**-makes, -making, -made** /-máyd/, **-made**) *vt.* 1. UNDO to undo the effects of sth 2. CHANGE COMPLETELY to make a fundamental change or changes in sth 3. REMOVE FROM POWER to remove sb from office or a position of authority

unman /un mán/ (**-mans, -manning, -manned**) *vt.* 1. STRIP OF COURAGE to cause sb to lose a quality or qualities traditionally attributed to men, especially courage 2. EMASCULATE to deprive a man or boy of the ability to have intercourse or father children

unmanly /un mánnli/ (**-lier, -liest**) *adj.* 1. WEAK AND COWARDLY not strong and brave in the way that a man is traditionally supposed to be 2. UNSUITABLE FOR A MAN not appropriate for or typical of a man, according to traditional perceptions of masculinity —**unmanliness** *n.*

unmanned /ún mánd/ *adj.* not having any personnel, especially not having a pilot or crew [Mid-16thC. Formed from MAN.]

unmannered /un mánnərd/ *adj.* 1. NOT HAVING GOOD MANNERS lacking or displaying a lack of good manners 2. WITHOUT AFFECTATION having an easy, unaffected manner —**unmanneredly** *adv.*

unmannerly /un mánnərli/ *adj.* LACKING GOOD MANNERS lacking or displaying a lack of good manners ■ *adv.* RUDELY in a rude or discourteous manner (*old*) —**unmannerliness** *n.*

unmarked /un maárkt/ *adj.* 1. WITHOUT MARK not bearing any mark 2. LACKING IDENTIFYING MARKINGS lacking identifying letters, numbers, or symbols ○ *an unmarked police car* 3. UNSEEN not seen or spotted 4. LACKING DISTINGUISHING QUALITY having no particular distinguishing quality or character

unmarried /un márrid/ *adj.* not joined to another person by marriage

unmask /un maásk/ (**-masks, -masking, -masked**) *v.* 1. *vti.* TAKE MASK OFF to remove a mask from sb or sb's face 2. *vt.* EXPOSE TRUE NATURE OF to expose the true nature or identity of sb or sth 3. *vi.* LET TRUE NATURE BECOME KNOWN to allow sb's or sth's true nature or identity to become known

unmeaning /un méening/ *adj.* 1. MEANINGLESS lacking meaning or significance 2. UNINTENTIONAL not intended or deliberate 3. UNINTELLIGENT devoid of intelligence —**unmeaningly** *adv.*

unmeant *adj.* not intended

unmeasured /un mézhərd/ *adj.* 1. NOT DETERMINED BY MEASURING not found out by measurement 2. NOT RESTRAINED unrestrained, incautious, or ill-considered 3. MUSIC NOT DIVIDED INTO BARS not marked with bar lines and therefore with no set rhythm

unmentionable /un ménsh'nəb'l/ *adj.* NOT TO BE MENTIONED not to be mentioned or discussed, especially in polite conversation ■ *n.* THING NOT TO BE MENTIONED sth that should not be mentioned or discussed, especially in polite conversation ■ **unmentionables** *npl.* UNDERWEAR undergarments (*dated or humorous*) —**unmentionableness** *n.* —**unmentionably** *adv.*

unmerciful /un múrssif'l/ *adj.* 1. NOT MERCIFUL displaying no mercy or characterized by a lack of mercy 2. EXCESSIVE going beyond what is reasonable —**unmercifully** *adv.* —**unmercifulness** *n.*

unmetalled /un métt'ld/ *adj.* not covered with durable road surfacing material

unmindful /un míndf'l/ *adj.* not aware, attentive, careful, or heedful of sb or sth —**unmindfully** *adv.* —**unmindfulness** *n.*

unmistakable /únmi stáykəb'l/, **unmistakeable** *adj.* easily recognized or understood —**unmistakably** *adv.*

unmitigated /un mítti gaytid/ *adj.* 1. NOT LESSENED not lessened or eased in any way 2. COMPLETE AND UTTER absolute and unqualified —**unmitigatedly** *adv.* —**unmitigatedness** *n.*

unmoor /un móor, un máwr/ (**-moors, -mooring, -moored**) *v.* 1. *vti.* FREE OR BE FREED FROM MOORINGS to free a ship or boat from its moorings, or to be freed from moorings 2. *vt.* LEAVE MOORED BY ONLY ONE ANCHOR to leave a ship or boat moored by only one of its anchors

unmoral /un mórrəl/ *adj.* 1. AMORAL lacking or displaying a lack of a moral sense 2. NONMORAL not subject to morality or ethics —**unmorality** /únmə rálləti/ *n.* —**unmorally** *adv.*

unmusical /un myóozik'l/ *adj.* 1. UNMELODIC lacking melodic qualities and consequently unpleasant to hear 2. HAVING NO EAR FOR MUSIC having no ability for, or no interest in, music —**unmusically** *adv.* —**unmusicalness** *n.* —**unmusicality** /un myóozi kálləti/ *n.*

unmuzzle /un múzz'l/ (**-zles, -zling, -zled**) *vt.* 1. FREE DOG FROM MUZZLE to remove a muzzle from an animal, especially a dog 2. RESTORE FREEDOM OF SPEECH TO to restore to a person or organization the right to say, publish, or broadcast sth

unmyelinated /un mí əli naytid/ *adj.* used to describe a nerve fibre that lacks a myelin sheath. Such fibres transmit nerve impulses more slowly than myelinated ones, and are found mainly in worms, insects, and other invertebrate animals. [Mid-20thC. Coined from MYELIN.]

unnamed /ún náymd/ *adj.* 1. NOT MENTIONED BY NAME having a name but not specified by it 2. HAVING NO NAME not yet assigned a name

unnatural /un náchərəl/ *adj.* 1. CONTRARY TO LAWS OF NATURE contrary to the physical laws of nature 2. NOT CONFORMING TO THE AVERAGE behaving in ways that contradict conventional assumptions about what constitutes normal or acceptable human behaviour 3. CONTRARY TO EXPECTED BEHAVIOUR contrary to a particular habit, custom, or practice 4. ARTIFICIAL affected, artificial, contrived, or strained —**unnaturally** *adv.* —**unnaturalness** *n.*

unnecessary /un néssəssəri/ *adj.* **1.** NOT NECESSARY not essential, needed, or required **2.** GRATUITOUS gratuitous, unjustified, and hurtful —**unnecessarily** *adv.*

unnerve /un núrv/ (**-nerves, -nerving, -nerved**) *vt.* **1.** CAUSE SB TO LOSE NERVE to deprive sb of courage, resolve, or self-confidence **2.** MAKE SB NERVOUS cause sb to feel nervous —**unnerving** *adj.* —**unnervingly** *adv.*

unnumbered /un númbərd/ *adj.* **1.** NOT COUNTABLE too many to be counted **2.** LACKING IDENTIFYING NUMBER not assigned or having an identifying number

UNO *abbr.* United Nations Organization

unobtrusive /únnəb tróossiv/ *adj.* not conspicuous, blatant, or assertive —**unobtrusively** *adv.* —**unobtrusiveness** *n.*

unoccupied /un ókyoo pīd/ *adj.* **1.** NOT IN USE not being used by anybody **2.** NOT DOING ANYTHING not doing anything or anything important **3.** NOT INHABITED not lived in by anybody **4.** NOT UNDER FOREIGN MILITARY RULE not under the control or military rule of a foreign country

WORD KEY: SYNONYMS

See Synonyms at ***vacant***.

unofficial /únnə físh'l/ *adj.* **1.** UNAUTHORIZED not authorized or sanctioned by the proper official or other authority **2.** NOT ACTING OFFICIALLY not acting or employed in an official capacity or position **3.** NOT DONE OR MADE OFFICIALLY not done or made by sb acting in an official capacity **4.** LACKING UNION APPROVAL not ratified by the trade union to which the strikers belong ○ *an unofficial strike* **5.** NOT ON LIST OF APPROVED DRUGS not included on an official list of medicinal drugs —**unofficially** *adv.*

unorganized /un áwrgə nīzd/, **unorganised** *adj.* **1.** NOT DONE IN ORGANIZED WAY not arranged or done in an orderly or systematic way **2.** NOT ACTING IN ORGANIZED WAY not acting, thinking, or working in an orderly or systematic manner **3.** NOT UNIONIZED not organized in a trade union or unions **4.** NOT LIVING lacking the characteristics of a living organism

unorthodox /un áwrthə doks/ *adj.* **1.** UNCONVENTIONAL not following, or resulting from a failure to follow, conventional or traditional beliefs or practices **2.** NOT RELIGIOUSLY ORTHODOX not practising or conforming to the accepted traditional form of a particular religion —**unorthodoxly** *adv.* —**unorthodoxy** *n.*

unpack /un pák/ (**-packs, -packing, -packed**) *v.* **1.** *vt.* TAKE CONTENTS FROM STH to take the contents out of sth **2.** *vti.* TAKE OUT PACKED THINGS to remove sth that has been packed from its container or packaging **3.** *vt.* TAKE PACK OFF to take a pack or other burden from a person or animal that has been carrying it **4.** *vt.* REVEAL WHAT IS HIDDEN IN to reveal what is hidden, buried, or encoded within sth

unpaged /un páyjd/, **unpaginated** /un pájji naytid/ *adj.* not marked with page numbers

unpaid /ún páyd/ *adj.* **1.** NOT YET SETTLED awaiting payment or settlement **2.** HAVING NOT YET RECEIVED PAYMENT not yet in receipt of payment for work done **3.** WORKING FOR NO PAY working without wages or a salary **4.** NOT PAYING MONEY not paying wages or a salary

unpaired /ún páird/ *adj.* **1.** NOT BELONGING TO PAIR not being one of a pair **2.** CHEM CONSISTING OF NO PAIRS characterized by a lack of pairs

unpalatable /un pállətəb'l/ *adj.* **1.** NOT TASTING GOOD having an unpleasant taste **2.** HARD TO ACCEPT not pleasant, agreeable, or acceptable —**unpalatability** /un pálləti bílləti/ *n.* —**unpalatably** /un pállətəbli/ *adv.*

unparalleled /un párrə leld/ *adj.* not equalled, matched, or paralleled in kind or quality

unparliamentary /ún paarlə méntəri/ *adj.* not acceptable according to the practice of a parliament

unpeg /un pég/ (**-pegs, -pegging, -pegged**) *vt.* **1.** TAKE PEG FROM to take a peg or pegs from sth **2.** RELEASE BY REMOVING PEG to release sth by removing a peg or pegs **3.** STOP FIXING PRICES OR WAGES to allow sth, especially prices or wages, to fluctuate freely by removing the restrictions holding them at a fixed level

unpeople /un péep'l/ (**-ples, -pling, -pled**) *vt.* = **depopulate** —**unpeopled** *adj.*

unperson /ún purss'n/ *n.* sb whose existence is not acknowledged officially, especially a public figure whose existence is, for political or ideological reasons, unrecognized by a totalitarian government and the news media it controls

unpick /un pík/ (**-picks, -picking, -picked**) *vt.* to undo sth by pulling out a thread or threads

unpin /un pín/ (**-pins, -pinning, -pinned**) *vt.* **1.** TAKE PIN FROM to take a pin or pins from sth **2.** RELEASE BY REMOVING PIN to release or unfasten sth by removing a pin or pins

unplaced /un pláyst/ *adj.* **1.** NOT AMONG FIRST THREE IN RACE failing to finish first, second, or third in a race **2.** NOT HAVING PARTICULAR POSITION not assigned a particular place or position

unplanned /un plánd/ *adj.* **1.** NOT INTENDED not happening according to a plan **2.** LACKING AN OVERALL PLAN not following or structured according to an overall plan or programme **3.** DONE SPONTANEOUSLY accomplished without advance planning

unpleasant /un plézz'nt/ *adj.* **1.** NOT PLEASING not pleasing, enjoyable, or agreeable **2.** UNFRIENDLY unfriendly and nasty to sb —**unpleasantly** *adv.*

unpleasantness /un plézz'ntnəss/ *n.* **1.** UNPLEASANT STATE OR QUALITY the state or quality of being unpleasant **2.** UNPLEASANT EXPERIENCES OR EVENTS experiences or events that are not pleasing or enjoyable **3.** UNFRIENDLINESS an unfriendly and nasty attitude or behaviour **4.** UNPLEASANT SITUATION a situation that is not pleasing or enjoyable **5.** DISAGREEMENT an argument or disagreement

unplug /un plúg/ (**-plugs, -plugging, -plugged**) *vt.* **1.** TAKE STOPPER FROM to remove a stopper, cork, or other plug from sth **2.** REMOVE BLOCKAGE FROM to remove a blockage, clog, or other obstruction from sth **3.** PULL OUT OF ELECTRIC SOCKET to pull an electric plug out of a socket **4.** DISCONNECT ELECTRICAL APPLIANCE to disconnect an electrical appliance by pulling its plug out of a socket

unplumbed /un plúmd/ *adj.* **1.** NOT FULLY EXAMINED not thoroughly understood or investigated **2.** NOT CHECKED FOR VERTICALITY not checked for verticality with a plumb line **3.** NOT MEASURED FOR DEPTH not measured with a plumb line to determine depth **4.** LACKING PLUMBING having no plumbing or sanitation installed

unpolled /un póld/ *adj.* **1.** NOT INVITED TO PARTICIPATE IN POLL not invited to participate in a survey of public opinion **2.** NOT VOTING not having cast a vote at an election **3.** *US* NOT ON ELECTORAL ROLL not included in a list of electors

unpopular /un póppyoolər/ *adj.* not liked by, approved of, or acceptable to a person, a group of people, or the general public —**unpopularity** /ún poppyoo lárrəti/ *n.* —**unpopularly** /un póppyoolərli/ *adv.*

unpractised /un práktist/ *adj.* **1.** UNTRAINED OR INEXPERIENCED lacking in training or experience **2.** NOT DONE FREQUENTLY not done or not commonly done **3.** NOT REHEARSED not prepared and tried out beforehand

unprecedented /un préssi dentid/ *adj.* having no earlier parallel or equivalent

unpredictable /únpri díktəb'l/ *adj.* not easily foreseen or predicted —**unpredictability** /únpri díktə bílləti/ *n.* —**unpredictably** /-díktəbli/ *adv.*

unpremeditated /ún pree méddi taytid/ *adj.* done without advance planning or thought —**unpremeditatedly** *adv.*

unprepared /únpri páird/ *adj.* **1.** UNREADY not ready for sth or not expecting sth to happen **2.** NOT MADE READY not having been prepared as required or expected **3.** IMPROVISED done without any preparation —**unpreparedly** /únpri páiridli/ *adv.* —**unpreparedness** /-páiridnəss/ *n.*

unprepossessing /ún preepə zéssing/ *adj.* not producing a favourable impression —**unprepossessingly** *adv.*

unpretentious /únpri ténshəss/ *adj.* not putting on a false or showy display of importance, wealth, or knowledge —**unpretentiously** *adv.* —**unpretentiousness** *n.*

unprincipled /un prínssip'ld/ *adj.* lacking, or resulting from a lack of, moral or ethical principles —**unprincipledness** *n.*

unprintable /un príntəb'l/ *adj.* not fit for publication, usually because obscene, libellous, or otherwise illegal or offensive

unproductive /únprə dúktiv/ *adj.* **1.** FRUITLESS not producing useful results, decisions, or achievements **2.** PRODUCING LITTLE not producing very much in terms of work or output —**unproductively** *adv.* —**unproductiveness** *n.*

unprofessional /únprə fésh'nəl/ *adj.* **1.** CONTRARY TO PROFESSIONAL STANDARDS being or behaving contrary to the expected standards of a profession **2.** AMATEURISH unworthy of a professional **3.** NOT BELONGING TO PROFESSION not having membership of a profession —**unprofessionalism** *n.* —**unprofessionally** *adv.*

unprofitable /un próffitəb'l/ *adj.* **1.** MAKING NO PROFIT not producing a profit **2.** NOT HELPFUL OR USEFUL not producing a desirable result or having a useful purpose —**unprofitability** /un próffitə bílləti/ *n.* —**unprofitableness** /-próffitəb'lnəss/ *n.* —**unprofitably** *adv.*

UNPROFOR /un prō fawr/ *abbr.* United Nations Protection Force

unpromising /un prómmissing/ *adj.* **1.** UNLIKELY TO SUCCEED not likely to prove successful **2.** UNFAVOURABLE not favourable —**unpromisingly** *adv.*

unpronounceable /únprə nównssəb'l/ *adj.* very difficult or impossible to pronounce

unpronounced /únprə nównst/ *adj.* **1.** NOT VERY NOTICEABLE not clear or easy to notice **2.** MUTE OR SILENT not sounded or pronounced

unpublishable /un púbblishəb'l/ *adj.* not fit or feasible to publish, usually because of poor quality or expected poor sales

unputdownable /ún poot dównəb'l/ *adj.* so interesting, entertaining, or exciting that the reader cannot stop reading (*informal*) [Mid-20thC. Coined by the US writer Raymond Chandler.]

unqualified /un kwólli fīd/ *adj.* **1.** LACKING REQUIRED QUALIFICATIONS having no academic, professional, or vocational qualifications **2.** GIVEN WITHOUT RESERVATION not limited or modified by any condition or reservation **3.** TOTAL complete and absolute —**unqualifiedly** *adv.* —**unqualifiedness** *n.*

unquestionable /un kwéschənəb'l/ *adj.* **1.** IMPOSSIBLE TO DOUBT impossible to doubt, question, or dispute **2.** UNIVERSALLY RECOGNIZED AND ACKNOWLEDGED acknowledged as not subject to doubt or open to question —**unquestionability** /un kwéschənə bílləti/ *n.* —**unquestionableness** /-kwéschənəb'lnəss/ *n.* —**unquestionably** *adv.*

unquestioned /un kwéschənd/ *adj.* **1.** UNDISPUTED not open to questioning, doubt, or dispute **2.** NOT ASKED QUESTIONS not asked a question or questions

unquestioning /un kwéschəning/ *adj.* not asking questions, expressing doubt, or hesitating because of questions or doubts —**unquestioningly** *adv.*

unquiet /un kwí ət/ *adj.* **1.** NOISY OR TURBULENT full of noise or unrest **2.** ANXIOUS unsettled or restless, especially in thought or feeling ■ *n.* **1.** NOISE OR UNREST a state of noisiness or unrest **2.** ANXIETY restlessness or uneasiness —**unquietly** *adv.* —**unquietness** *n.*

unquote /un kwốt/ *adv.* used when speaking to indicate where the end of a quotation falls ○ *He said, quote, You're fired, unquote.* ◊ **quote**

unquoted /un kwốtid/ *adj.* not listed or quoted on a stock exchange [Early 19thC]

unravel /un rávv'l/ (**-els, -elling, -elled**) *v.* **1.** *vti.* UNDO STRANDS OF STH to undo the knitted or woven yarn, thread, or other strands of sth, or to become undone by having the strands come apart **2.** *vti.* DISENTANGLE OR BECOME DISENTANGLED to separate sth out from a tangle or other mass, or to become disentangled or separated out **3.** *vti.* MAKE OR BECOME UNDERSTANDABLE to make clear or understandable all the complex, baffling, or intricate elements or aspects of sth, or to become clear or understandable **4.** *vi.* START TO FAIL to begin to fail or come to an end

unread /un réd/ *adj.* **1.** NOT READ not read, especially by a usual or intended reader **2.** NOT WELL READ having read very little and consequently lacking knowledge acquired from reading **3. LACKING KNOWLEDGE OF SUBJECT** not acquainted with a specific subject through reading

unreadable /un reedab'l/ adj. **1. ILLEGIBLE** consisting of letters, words, or symbols that are difficult to identify **2. NOT ENJOYABLE TO READ** impossible to read because boring, badly written, or intellectually difficult **3. IMPOSSIBLE TO INTERPRET** impossible to interpret or make sense of ○ his unreadable face —**unreadability** /ún reedə bílləti/ n. —**unreadableness** /un reedəb'lnəss/ n. —**unreadably** /un reedəbli/ adv.

unready /un réddi/ adj. **1. UNAVAILABLE** not available or prepared for use **2. NOT PREPARED TO DO STH** not prepared or available to do sth or to act **3. LACKING MENTAL ALERTNESS OR QUICKNESS** lacking or displaying a lack of mental alertness or quickness —**unreadily** adv. —**unreadiness** n.

unreal /un réel, un reé əl/ adj. **1. NOT EXISTING** having no substance, reality, or existence **2. FALSE** not true or genuine **3. IMAGINARY** imaginary or dream-like **4. EXCELLENT** excellent or extremely good (informal) **5. INCREDIBLE** difficult to believe (informal) —**unreally** adv.

unrealistic /un reé ə lístik/ adj. not taking into account or based on the way the world actually is and how things are likely to happen —**unrealistically** adv.

unreality /únri álləti/ (plural -ties) n. **1. UNREAL QUALITY** an unreal or seemingly unreal state or quality **2. UNREAL THING** sth that is not real, genuine, or true, or lacks substance **3. INABILITY TO FACE REALITY** an inability to accept reality

unreason /un reéz'n/ n. lack of reason or rationality

unreasonable /un reéz'nəb'l/ adj. **1. NOT SUBJECT TO REASON** not acting with or subject to reason **2. EXCESSIVE** being or going beyond accepted or reasonable limits —**unreasonableness** n. —**unreasonably** adv.

unreasonable behaviour n. behaviour that is considered unacceptable in a marital relationship and constitutes grounds for divorce

unreasoning /un reéz'ning/ adj. lacking, or resulting from a lack of, sound judgment or reasoning —**unreasoningly** adv.

unreckonable /un rékənəb'l/ adj. impossible to calculate

unreconstructed /ún reekən strúktid/ adj. **1. CLINGING TO OUTDATED BELIEFS** retaining beliefs, views, or practices that are outdated or associated with a particular place or group **2. NOT REBUILT** not rebuilt, restored, or recreated [Mid-19thC. Originally in the meaning of 'not willing to accept the Reconstruction after the American Civil War'.]

unreeve /un reév/ (-reeves, -reeving, -reeved or -rove, -reeved or -rove /-róv/) vti. to pull out a rope or cable from a block or thimble on a ship, or be pulled out from a block or thimble

unrefined /únri fínd/ adj. **1. NOT PROCESSED** not processed to remove impurities **2. VULGAR** not in accord with socially approved tastes

unreflecting /únri flékting/ adj. not engaging in or resulting from deep or serious thinking —**unreflectingly** adv.

unreflective /únri fléktiv/ adj. not tending to think or reflect, or not resulting from thinking or reflection —**unreflectively** adv.

unregenerate /únri jénnərət/ adj. **1. NOT REFORMED** not reborn spiritually and not repentant **2. VIOLATING SOCIAL OR MORAL STRUCTURES** behaving in a way regarded as violating particular social or moral structures **3. CLINGING TO OUTDATED BELIEFS** retaining beliefs, views, or practices that are outdated or associated with a particular place or group **4. STUBBORN** unyielding or stubborn —**unregenerable** adj. —**unregeneracy** n. —**unregenerately** adv.

unrelenting /únri lénting/ adj. **1. DETERMINED AND UNYIELDING** unyielding or unswerving in determination or resolve **2. NOT WEAKENING OR EASING UP** not weakening, easing up, or otherwise diminishing in strength, speed, or effort —**unrelentingly** adv.

unreliable /únri lí əb'l/ adj. not able to be relied on or trusted —**unreliability** /únri lī ə bílləti/ n. —

unreliableness /únri lí əb'lnəss/ n. —**unreliably** /únri lí əbli/ adv.

Unreliable Memoirs, an autobiography by Australian writer Clive James (1980). A comic memoir recounting the author's childhood in Kogarah, a suburb of Sydney in Australia, and his subsequent departure for London.

unremarked /únri maárkt/ adj. not noticed or observed

unremitting /únri mítting/ adj. continuing, persisting, or recurring without diminishing or ceasing —**unremittingly** adv. —**unremittingness** n.

unrequited /únri kwítid/ adj. **1. NOT RECIPROCATED** not felt in response, or not returned in the same way or to the same degree **2. UNAVENGED** not avenged —**unrequitedly** adv.

unreserved /únri zúrvd/ adj. **1. NOT RESERVED FOR PARTICULAR USE** not set aside or retained for a particular person or group of people to use **2. GIVEN WITHOUT QUALIFICATION** not limited or modified by any condition or reservation **3. FRANK OR OPEN** not cautious, restrained, or reticent —**unreservedly** adv. —**unreservedness** /-zúrvidnəss/ n.

unrest /un rést/ n. **1. VIOLENT SOCIAL OR POLITICAL DISCONTENT** strong social or political discontent or protest that disrupts the established order and is often violent but falls short of true rebellion **2. ANXIOUSNESS** a disturbed, unsettled, or uneasy mental or emotional state

unrestrained /únri stráynd/ adj. **1. NOT CONTROLLED OR RESTRICTED** not subject to control, restriction, or restraint **2. SPONTANEOUS** natural and uninhibited —**unrestrainedly** adv. —**unrestrainedness** /-stráynidnəss/ n.

unrifled /un ríf'ld/ adj. having no spiral grooves (**rifling**) cut on the inside of the barrel

unrig /un ríg/ (-rigs, -rigging, -rigged) vt. to remove the rigging from a ship

unrighteous /un ríchəss/ adj. **1. SINFUL** sinful, wicked, or evil **2. UNJUST** not just, fair, or right —**unrighteously** adv. —**unrighteousness** n.

unripe /un ríp/ (-riper, -ripest) adj. **1. NOT RIPE** not yet ripe or mature **2. NOT FULLY READY** not yet complete or fully developed **3. PREMATURE** occurring too soon or too early (archaic) —**unripeness** n.

unrivalled /un rív'ld/ adj. having no rival or equal

unroll /un ról/ (-rolls, -rolling, -rolled) vti. **1. UNWIND OR BECOME UNWOUND** to unwind, uncoil, or open up sth that is rolled up, or become unwound, uncoiled, or opened up **2. DISCLOSE OR BECOME DISCLOSED** to disclose sth gradually and smoothly, or to become disclosed in this way

unrove past tense, past participle of **unreeve**

UNRRA, **Unrra** abbr. United Nations Relief and Rehabilitation Administration

unruffled /un rúff'ld/ adj. **1. CALM AND POISED** calm and poised, especially in a crisis **2. SMOOTH** having a smooth surface, especially in having no ripples

See Synonyms at **calm**.

unruly /un roóli/ (-lier, -liest) adj. difficult to control, manage, discipline, or govern [15C. Formed from archaic *ruly* 'disciplined, observing rules', from RULE.] —**unruliness** n.

unruly, intractable, recalcitrant, obstreperous, wilful, wild, wayward
CORE MEANING: not submitting to control
unruly boisterous and disruptive and showing a mild resistance to discipline. Often used to describe children; **intractable** a formal word used for sb who stubbornly refuses to be controlled or to submit to discipline; **recalcitrant** a formal word for sb who is obstinate and defiant in refusing to submit to discipline or control; **obstreperous** noisy, difficult to control, and uncooperative; **wilful** used for sb who is stubbornly disobedient or who seems determined to do as he or she pleases; **wild** a fairly informal word used for sb whose behaviour shows a general lack of control or restraint. It can also be used to describe behaviour or an event such as a party; **wayward** used for sb who demonstrates an

obstinate and unpredictable tendency to do what he or she wants or thinks is best, instead of following instructions or doing what everyone else is doing.

UNRWA, **Unrwa** abbr. United Nations Relief and Works Agency

unsaddle /un sádd'l/ (-dles, -dling, -dled) v. **1.** vti. **TAKE SADDLE FROM HORSE** to take a saddle from a horse **2.** vt. **UNHORSE SB** to throw a rider from a saddle (refers to a horse)

unsaddling enclosure n. an enclosure at a racecourse where the horses are brought after a race to have their saddles removed. Prizes are sometimes presented there.

unsaid /un séd/ past tense, past participle of **unsay** ■ adj. **NOT MENTIONED** not spoken of or discussed, although thought about [Old English]

unsatisfactory /ún satiss fáktəri/ adj. not adequate, acceptable, or satisfying —**unsatisfactorily** adv. —**unsatisfactoriness** n.

unsaturate /un sáchərət/ n. an unsaturated chemical compound

unsaturated /un sáchə raytid/ adj. **1. ABLE TO CONTINUE TO DISSOLVE** able to dissolve more of a substance **2. ABLE TO FORM MORE CARBON BONDS** having or able to form double and triple carbon bonds

unsavoury /un sáyvəri/ adj. **1. DISTASTEFUL** not pleasant or agreeable **2. IMMORAL** morally unacceptable **3. UNAPPETIZING** tasting or smelling unappetizing —**unsavourily** adv. —**unsavouriness** n.

unsay /un sáy/ (-says /-séz/, -saying, -said /-séd/) vt. to take back sth said so that it is as if it has never been said

unsayable /un sáy əb'l/ adj. difficult or impossible to say or speak about

unscathed /un skáythd/ adj. not hurt, damaged, or harmed in any way

unschooled /un skoóld/ adj. **1. NOT EDUCATED** not educated or trained **2. NOT ACQUIRED BY EDUCATION** innate and not acquired by education or training

unscientific /únsī ən tíffik/ adj. **1. NOT SCIENTIFIC IN METHOD OR PRINCIPLE** not following, or compatible with, the methods and principles of science **2. NOT INFORMED ABOUT SCIENCE** not possessing knowledge about science and its methods and principles —**unscientifically** adv.

unscramble /un skrámb'l/ (-bles, -bling, -bled) vt. **1. SORT OUT OF ORDER** to restore order to sth jumbled or confused **2. MAKE UNDERSTANDABLE BY REVERSING SCRAMBLING** to make a message understandable by undoing the effects of scrambling, especially electronic scrambling —**unscrambler** n.

unscrew /un skroó/ (-screws, -screwing, -screwed) vti. **1. REMOVE OR LOOSEN SCREWS OF** to remove or loosen a screw or screws holding sth in place, or to have a screw or screws removed or loosened **2. TURN TO REMOVE OR ADJUST** to remove or adjust sth by rotating, or to be removed or adjusted by rotating **3. OPEN BY REMOVING THREADED LID** to open sth by turning and removing a threaded lid or cap, or to be opened in this way

unscripted /un skríptid/ adj. **1. WITHOUT A SCRIPT** without a script that was written or agreed on in advance **2. UNPLANNED** not planned or expected

unscrupulous /un skroópyoóləss/ adj. not restrained by moral or ethical principles —**unscrupulously** adv. —**unscrupulousness** n.

unseal /un seél/ (-seals, -sealing, -sealed) vt. **1. BREAK OR REMOVE SEAL OF** to break or remove the seal of sth, or to open sth by breaking a seal or closure **2. FREE FROM RESTRICTION** to free sth from constraint or restriction [Old English] —**unsealable** adj.

unsealed road n. ANZ a dirt road that has no tar or bitumen surface

unsearchable /un súrchəb'l/ adj. not capable of being searched or investigated —**unsearchableness** n. —**unsearchably** adv.

unseasonable /un seéz'nəb'l/ adj. **1. UNUSUAL FOR TIME OF YEAR** not usual or appropriate for the time of year **2. NOT TIMELY** not occurring at the right time or at a good time —**unseasonableness** n. —**unseasonably** adv.

unseasoned /un seéz'nd/ *adj.* **1. NOT DRIED OUT** not dried, aged, or matured **2. NOT EXPERIENCED** lacking the skills or knowledge that experience provides **3. PREPARED WITHOUT SALT AND PEPPER** lacking salt and pepper, or other herbs or spices

unseat /un seét/ (-seats, -seating, -seated) *vt.* **1. EJECT FROM SADDLE** to eject sb from a seat, especially a saddle **2. REMOVE FROM OFFICE** to remove sb from office or a position, especially by means of an election

unsecured /únssi kyoórd, -kyáwrd/ *adj.* **1. NOT MADE SECURE** not fastened, held in place, or otherwise made secure **2. MADE WITHOUT SECURITY** not protected against financial loss **3. UNPROTECTED FROM BUGGING** not protected against electronic eavesdropping

unseeded /un seédid/ *adj.* SPORTS not assigned a position in a draw so that the best players or teams can, in theory, avoid meeting until the later rounds

unseemly /un seémli/ *adj.* **1. NOT IN GOOD TASTE** contrary to accepted standards of good taste or appropriate behaviour **2. INCONVENIENT** occurring at an inconvenient time or place ■ *adv.* **IN AN UNSEEMLY MANNER** in an improper or inappropriate manner —**unseemliness** *n.*

unseen /ún seén/ *adj.* **1. NOT SEEN** not observed, noticed, watched, or seen **2. DONE WITHOUT PRACTICE** done or comprehended without previous study or practice **3. TRANSLATED AT SIGHT** translated without preparation, especially in a test or examination ■ *n.* **UNSEEN TRANSLATION** a text for translation without preparation, especially in a test or examination

unselective /únssi léktiv/ *adj.* choosing or chosen without regard for quality or value

unselfish /un sélfish/ *adj.* putting the general good or the needs or interests of others first —**unselfishly** *adv.* —**unselfishness** *n.*

unset /un sét/ *adj.* **1. NOT HARDENED** not hardened or firm **2. NOT READY** not prepared or made ready **3. NOT MOUNTED** not mounted in a jewellery setting

unsettle /un sétt'l/ (-tles, -tling, -tled) *vt.* **1. DISRUPT** to disrupt the orderly, fixed, or established state of sth **2. UPSET SB** to make sb ill at ease or insecure —**unsettlement** *n.*

unsettled /un sétt'ld/ *adj.* **1. LACKING ORDER OR STABILITY** characterized by a lack of order or stability ○ *an unsettled political climate* **2. CHANGEABLE** changing frequently within a given period of time ○ *unsettled weather* **3. BEING IN MOTION** not being in a state or position of rest ○ *unsettled sediment in the water* **4. NOT DECIDED** not resolved, determined, or decided ○ *an unsettled issue* **5. UNCERTAIN** not sure, or full of doubt ○ *He was unsettled about his future at the firm.* **6. UNINHABITED** not inhabited or colonized ○ *unsettled territory* **7. UNPAID** not paid or fulfilled ○ *an unsettled debt* **8. MOVING ABOUT** not regular or fixed ○ *an unsettled lifestyle* **9. NOT LEGALLY RESOLVED** not resolved as required by law ○ *an unsettled lawsuit*

unsettling /un séttling/ *adj.* producing a feeling of unease or insecurity

unsex /un séks/ (-sexes, -sexing, -sexed) *vt.* **1. MAKE LESS FEMININE OR MASCULINE** to strip away from sb the qualities stereotypically associated with his or her sex ○ *'Come, you spirits / That tend on mortal thoughts, unsex me here'* (William Shakespeare, *Macbeth*; c. 1605) **2. CASTRATE** to deprive sb of the ability to have sex [Early 17thC. Coined by William Shakespeare.]

UNSF *abbr.* United Nations Special Fund for Economic Development

unshackle /un shák'l/ (-les, -ling, -led) *vt.* **1. FREE FROM SHACKLES** to release sb from shackles **2. FREE FROM RESTRICTIONS** to release sb from restrictions or constraints

unshakable /un sháykəb'l/, **unshakeable** *adj.* not subject to doubt or uncertainty —**unshakably** *adv.*

unshaped /un sháypt/, **unshapen** /-sháp'n/ *adj.* **1. NOT YET GIVEN SHAPE** not yet shaped, formed, or finished **2. NOT PROPERLY FORMED** imperfect in its final or finished form or state

unsheathe /un sheéth/ (-sheathes, -sheathing, -sheathed) *vt.* to remove a sword from a sheath

unship /un ship/ (-ships, -shipping, -shipped) *vti.* **1. SHIPPING UNLOAD OR BE UNLOADED** to unload sth from a ship, or to be unloaded **2. NAUT MOVE OR BE REMOVED FROM POSITION** to move sth, or to be moved, out of its normal position on a ship

unshod /un shód/ *adj.* not wearing shoes or horseshoes

unsighted /un sítid/ *adj.* **1. NOT FITTED WITH SIGHT FOR AIMING** not fitted with a sight or sights to help with aiming **2. OBSTRUCTED FROM SEEING** unable to see sb or sth because the view is obstructed

unsightly /un sítli/ *adj.* not pleasant to look at —**unsightliness** *n.*

unskilful /un skílf'l/ *adj.* lacking or done without skill or expertise —**unskilfully** *adv.* —**unskilfulness** *n.*

unskilled /ún skíld/ *adj.* **1. LACKING SKILL** lacking skill or the basic or proper skills **2. LACKING EDUCATION OR TECHNICAL TRAINING** lacking the skills acquired through technical training or higher education **3. NOT REQUIRING SPECIAL SKILLS** not requiring special training, education, or skill **4. DONE WITHOUT SKILL** done without skill, or displaying a lack of the basic or proper skills

unslakable /un sláykəb'l/, **unslakeable** *adj.* impossible to satisfy or quench [Early 19thC. Formed from SLAKE.]

unslaked lime *n.* = calcium hydroxide

unsling /un slíng/ (-slings, -slinging, -slung /-slúng/, -slung) *vt.* **1. REMOVE STH SLUNG** to remove sth that has been slung, especially over the shoulder or shoulders **2. TAKE OUT OF SLING** to take sth out of a sling **3. NAUT REMOVE SUPPORTING ROPES FROM** to remove the supporting ropes or chains (**slings**) from sth

unsnap /un snáp/ (-snaps, -snapping, -snapped) *vt.* to release or open sth by unfastening a press stud or press studs

unsnarl /un snaárl/ (-snarls, -snarling, -snarled) *vt.* to free sth from a snarl or snarls

unsociable /un sṓshəb'l/ *adj.* **1. PREFERRING OWN COMPANY** not liking or seeking the company of other people **2. NOT ENCOURAGING SOCIAL INTERACTION** not favouring or encouraging social interaction —**unsociability** /ún sōshə bílləti/ *n.* —**unsociableness** /un sṓshəb'lnəss/ *n.* —**unsociably** /un sṓshəbli/ *adv.*

—— **WORD KEY: USAGE** ——
unsociable or **unsocial**? See Usage note at **sociable**. Note that **unsociable** is less strong in force than *antisocial*, which denotes behaviour or attitudes that are harmful to social order.

unsocial /un sṓsh'l/ *adj.* **1. PREFERRING OWN COMPANY** not liking or seeking the company of other people **2. OF UNSOCIAL PERSON** characterized or caused by a dislike of the company of other people **3. ANTISOCIAL** annoying, inconsiderate, or indifferent to the needs of others **4. OUTSIDE NORMAL WORKING HOURS** relating to or done at a time outside normal working hours —**unsocially** *adv.*

—— **WORD KEY: USAGE** ——
See Usage note at **sociable**.

unsolicited /únssə líssitid/ *adj.* given, sent, or received without being requested

unsophisticated /únssə físti kaytid/ *adj.* **1. NOT WORLDLY OR SOPHISTICATED** naive, inexperienced, and not wise in the ways of the world **2. CRUDE** simple and lacking in refinements, especially those required to solve a particular problem —**unsophisticatedly** *adv.* —**unsophisticatedness** *n.* —**unsophistication** /únssə físti káysh'n/ *n.*

—— **WORD KEY: SYNONYMS** ——
See Synonyms at **naive**.

unsought /un sáwt/ *adj.* not looked for or asked for

unsound /un sównd/ *adj.* **1. UNHEALTHY** not in a healthy physical or psychological state **2. NOT SOLID OR FIRM** in a structurally poor or dangerous state ○ *unsound foundations* **3. NOT RELIABLE** not based on reliable facts, information, or reasoning ○ *an unsound conclusion* **4. FINANCIALLY INSECURE** not safe or secure financially ○ *an unsound investment* **5. DISTURBED AND NOT RESTFUL** characterized by periods of restlessness ○ *unsound sleep* —**unsoundly** *adv.* —**unsoundness** *n.*

unsparing /un spáiring/ *adj.* **1. MERCILESS** harsh or without mercy **2. GENEROUS** not frugal or stingy with sth —**unsparingly** *n.* —**unsparingly** *adv.*

unspeakable /un speékəb'l/ *adj.* **1. NOT DESCRIBABLE IN WORDS** incapable of being described in words **2. EXTREMELY BAD OR AWFUL** so bad or awful as to be impossible to describe in words **3. NOT TO BE SPOKEN OF** not allowed to be spoken of, mentioned, or talked about —**unspeakableness** *n.* —**unspeakably** *adv.*

unspoiled /ún spóyld/, **unspoilt** *adj.* **1. UNCHANGED BY DEVELOPMENT** not changed for the worse by modern civilization, industry, or tourism **2. NOT DAMAGED** not damaged or physically harmed **3. UNFLAWED** not lessened or diminished by flaws or imperfections **4. NOT RUINED IN CHARACTER** not ruined in character as a result of success, wealth, or being overindulged

unspoken /un spṓkən/ *adj.* not uttered or talked about, although thought about

unsportsmanlike /un spáwrtsmən līk/ *adj.* = not sporting in behaviour or attitude

unspotted /un spóttid/ *adj.* **1. NOT SPOTTED OR STAINED** not soiled with spots or stains **2. MORALLY UNBLEMISHED** not marred by moral or ethical lapses or failures **3. UNOBSERVED** not seen or observed —**unspottedness** *n.*

unsprung /un sprúng/ *adj.* having no springs or having the springs removed

unstable /un stáyb'l/ *adj.* **1. NOT FIXED** not firm, solid, or fixed ○ *unstable ground* **2. LIKELY TO FALL OR COLLAPSE** likely to fall, collapse, or sway ○ *unstable scaffolding* **3. CHANGEABLE** apt to change ○ *unstable weather* **4. IRREGULAR IN MOVEMENT OR RHYTHM** having a movement or rhythm that changes irregularly ○ *an unstable heartbeat* **5. UNSTEADY IN PURPOSE OR INTENT** unsteady or unsure in purpose or intent ○ *political support that is unstable* **6. LACKING EMOTIONAL OR PSYCHOLOGICAL STABILITY** lacking, or resulting from a lack of, emotional control or psychological stability ○ *unstable behaviour* **7. CHEM APT TO DECOMPOSE** able or likely to change chemical or biological composition readily **8. PHYS HAVING SHORT HALF-LIFE** having a brief existence or half-life **9. PHYS SUBJECT TO SPONTANEOUS CHANGE** used to describe a particle that is subject to spontaneous change, such as radioactive decay —**unstableness** *n.* —**unstably** *adv.*

unsteady /un stéddi/ *adj.* **1. NOT FIXED** not firm, solid, or fixed **2. TOTTERING** staggering or tottering in walking **3. LIKELY TO MOVE** likely to move or shift position ○ *an unsteady ladder* **4. CHANGEABLE** subject to large and frequent changes ○ *unsteady financial markets* **5. IRREGULAR IN RHYTHM** irregular in movement, rhythm, or pitch ○ *a voice that is unsteady* **6. NOT CONSTANT OR RELIABLE** not constant in purpose or actions ■ *vt.* (-ies, -ying, -ied) **MAKE UNSTEADY** to cause sth to become unsteady —**unsteadily** *adv.* —**unsteadiness** *n.*

unstep /un stép/ (-steps, -stepping, -stepped) *vt.* NAUT to take a mast out of its step or socket

unstick /un stík/ *v.* (-sticks, -sticking, -stuck, -stuck /-stúk/) **1.** *vt.* **MAKE STH STOP STICKING** to cause sth to stop sticking **2.** *vti.* to cause an aircraft to take off, or to take off in an aircraft (*informal*) ■ *n.* TAKE-OFF a take-off in an aircraft (*informal*)

unstinting /un stínting/ *adj.* given or giving generously [14thC. The word in its original sense of 'unceasing' disappeared from the language; it was revived in its modern sense in the mid-19thC.] —**unstintingly** *adv.*

unstop /un stóp/ (-stops, -stopping, -stopped) *vt.* **1. REMOVE STOPPER FROM** to remove a stopper from sth **2. UNBLOCK STH** to remove a blockage from sth **3. MUSIC PULL OUT STOPS** to pull out the stops of an organ

unstoppable /un stóppəb'l/ *adj.* not capable of being halted, or not easily halted —**unstoppably** *adv.*

unstopped /un stópt/ *adj.* **1. NOT HALTED** able to continue without being halted **2. NOT BLOCKED OR STOPPERED** not blocked, closed, or stoppered **3. PHON ARTICULATED WITH VOCAL ORGANS PARTLY OPEN** articulated without a complete closure of the vocal organs

unstrained /un stráynd/ *adj.* **1. NOT PUT THROUGH STRAINER** not put through a strainer to remove lumps **2. FREE FROM STRAIN** not subjected to strain

unstrap /un stráp/ (-straps, -strapping, -strapped) *vt.* to remove sth by undoing a strap or straps

unstratified /un strátti fīd/ *adj.* **1.** NOT FORMING LAYERS OR STRATA not arranged in or forming layers or strata **2.** NOT FORMING CLASSES OR RANKS not arranged in or forming social classes, grades, or ranks

unstreamed /un steémd/ *adj.* not split into groups on the basis of ability or educational achievement [Mid-20thC. Formed from STREAM (verb).]

unstressed /un strést/ *adj.* **1.** NOT UNDER PHYSICAL OR MENTAL PRESSURE not subjected to physical, psychological, or emotional pressure **2.** LING NOT ACCENTED not accented or emphasized in pronunciation

unstriated /un strī aytid/ *adj.* lacking transverse striations

unstring /un stríng/ (**-strings, -stringing, -strung, -strung** /-strúng/) *vt.* **1.** REMOVE OR LOOSEN STRINGS OF to remove or loosen a string or strings of sth **2.** REMOVE FROM STRING to remove sth from a string or wire **3.** UPSET SB to make sb upset or nervous

unstructured /un strúkchərd/ *adj.* **1.** NOT ORGANIZED INTO HIERARCHY not organized into a hierarchy or similar system **2.** NOT ORDERED OR CONVENTIONALLY ARRANGED not forced to conform to a particular order or arrangement, especially a conventional one **3.** CLOTHES LOOSE AND FLOWING not tailored to fit tightly, but flowing freely

unstrung past tense, past participle of **unstring** ■ *adj.* **1.** UPSET emotionally upset or nervous **2.** LACKING STRINGS with a string or strings missing, removed, or loosened **3.** NOT ON STRING not threaded on a string or wire

unstuck past tense, past participle of **unstick** ■ *adj.* FREED FROM BEING STUCK freed from being stuck or adhering to sth ◇ **come unstuck** to fail (*informal*)

unstudied /un stúddid/ *adj.* **1.** NATURAL natural or casual in manner **2.** NOT LEARNED THROUGH STUDYING not acquired through studying or training **3.** NOT KNOWLEDGEABLE lacking the knowledge and understanding of a particular field that is acquired through studying or training

unsubstantial /únssəb stánsh'l/ *adj.* **1.** IMMATERIAL not having physical substance **2.** FLIMSY not strong or firm **3.** NOT TRUE OR BASED ON FACT having no basis in truth or fact —**unsubstantiality** /únssəb stánshi álləti/ *n.* —**unsubstantially** /-stánsh'li/ *adv.*

unsubstantiated /únssəb stánshi aytid/ *adj.* not proven factually [Late 18thC. Formed from *substantiated*, the past participle of SUBSTANTIATE.]

unsuccessful /únssək sésf'l/ *adj.* **1.** NOT RESULTING IN SUCCESS not resulting in success or turning out favourably **2.** NOT ACHIEVING SUCCESS not achieving an intended aim or goal —**unsuccessfully** *adv.* —**unsuccessfulness** *n.*

unsuitable /un sóotəb'l/ *adj.* not appropriate or becoming —**unsuitability** /ún sootə bílləti/ *n.* —**unsuitableness** /un sóotəb'lnəss/ *n.* —**unsuitably** /un sóotəbli/ *adv.*

unsung *adj.* **1.** NOT SUNG not sung or not to be sung **2.** NOT PRAISED OR HONOURED not given the praise or honour that is due

unsupportable /únssə páwrtəb'l/ *adj.* **1.** INDEFENSIBLE impossible to defend or excuse **2.** INTOLERABLE impossible to tolerate or endure **3.** IMPOSSIBLE TO SUPPORT PHYSICALLY impossible to support physically in order to prevent collapse

unsure /un shóor, -sháwr/ *adj.* **1.** UNCERTAIN doubtful or uncertain about sb or sth **2.** NOT CONFIDENT lacking in confidence **3.** NOT FIXED OR SECURE not firm or secure **4.** UNRELIABLE not trustworthy or reliable

WORD KEY: SYNONYMS

See Synonyms at ***doubtful***.

unsurprising /únssər prízing/ *adj.* not causing surprise, usually because not unexpected —**unsurprisingly** *adv.*

unsuspected /únssə spéktid/ *adj.* **1.** NOT SUSPECTED not under suspicion of doing sth **2.** UNKNOWN not known or believed to exist —**unsuspectedly** *adv.*

unsuspecting /únssə spékting/ *adj.* not suspicious of sb or sth —**unsuspectingly** *adv.*

unswerving /un swúrving/ *adj.* **1.** STEADY AND UNCHANGING firm and unchanging in intent or purpose **2.** NOT TURNING TO THE SIDE not turning to the side or otherwise altering the direction of movement —**unswervingly** *adv.*

unsworn *adj.* **1.** NOT STATED UNDER OATH not stated under an oath to tell the truth **2.** NOT HAVING TAKEN OATH not having taken an oath to tell the truth [Early 16thC. Formed from *sworn*, the past participle of SWEAR.]

unsymmetrical /únssi méttrik'l/ *adj.* lacking symmetry —**unsymmetrically** *adv.*

untangle /un táng g'l/ (**-gles, -gling, -gled**) *vt.* **1.** FREE STH FROM TANGLES to undo the tangles in sth such as yarn or hair **2.** STRAIGHTEN OUT STH COMPLEX to clarify or resolve sth that is intricate or puzzling **3.** FREE SB FROM BAD SITUATION to remove sb from a difficult or complicated situation

untapped /ún tápt/ *adj.* **1.** POTENTIALLY USABLE not yet in use, but available ○ *untapped talents* **2.** UNOPENED not yet opened or tapped

untaught *adj.* **1.** UNEDUCATED ignorant or not having had a formal education **2.** NATURAL OR INNATE arising from innate or natural talent or ability rather than from instruction [14thC]

untenable /un ténnəb'l/ *adj.* **1.** NOT DEFENDABLE lacking the qualities, e.g. sound reasoning or high ground, that make defence possible ○ *an untenable position* **2.** UNINHABITABLE so shabby, filthy, or poorly built as to be unfit for human occupation (*archaic*) —**untenability** /un ténnə bílləti/ *n.* —**untenableness** *n.* —**untenably** /un ténnəbli/ *adv.*

untether /un téthər/ (**-ers, -ering, -ered**) *vt.* **1.** UNTIE STH to free sth from a restraining rope or other tie **2.** EXPRESS EMOTION FULLY to sth such as an emotion after suppressing it

unthink /un thíngk/ (**-thinks, -thinking, -thought** /un tháwt/) *vt.* **1.** STOP THINKING ABOUT STH to stop thinking about sth **2.** REVERSE OPINION ABOUT to change a view or opinion about sth

unthinkable /un thíngkəb'l/ *adj.* **1.** OUT OF THE QUESTION too strange or extreme even to be considered **2.** INCONCEIVABLE impossible even to conceive of **3.** UNLIKELY TO HAPPEN highly unlikely to happen or succeed [15thC] —**unthinkability** /un thíngkə bílləti/ *n.* —**unthinkableness** *n.* —**unthinkably** *adv.*

unthinking /un thíngking/ *adj.* **1.** INCONSIDERATE not thoughtful or considerate of other people **2.** HEEDLESS without proper attention to the effects of what is said or done **3.** UNAWARE unable or unwilling to think deeply about things —**unthinkingly** *adv.* —**unthinkingness** *n.*

unthought past tense, past participle of **unthink**

unthread /un thréd/ (**-threads, -threading, -threaded**) *vt.* to remove the thread or threads from sth

unthrone /un thrṓn/ (**-thrones, -throning, -throned**) *vt.* to dethrone sb (*archaic*)

untidy /un tīdi/ *adj.* (**-dier, -diest**) **1.** NOT NEAT not neat or tidy **2.** DISORDERED not properly organized or ordered ■ *vt.* (**-dies, -dying, -died**) MESS STH UP to mess up sth that was tidy —**untidily** *adv.* —**untidiness** *n.*

untie /un tī/ (**-ties, -tying, -tied**) *v.* **1.** *vti.* UNDO KNOT IN STH to loosen or unfasten a knot or similar fastening in sth such as a string, ribbon, or rope, or to be loosened or unfastened **2.** *vt.* FREE STH FROM RESTRAINT to release or free sb or sth that is tied up [Old English *untīgan*]

until /ən tíl, un tíl/ *conj., prep.* **1.** UP TO A TIME up to a time or event but not afterwards ○ (conj) *I lived with my grandparents until I was ten.* ○ (prep) *from the late 1980s until 1994* **2.** BEFORE before a time or event (*used with a negative*) ○ (conj) *She agreed not to write about the case until a verdict was reached.* ○ (prep) *He did not open his mail until Monday.* [12thC. From assumed Old Norse *und* 'till' + TILL (the sense 'till' thereby being duplicated).]

WORD KEY: USAGE

See Usage note at ***till***.

untimely /un tīmli/ *adj.* **1.** OCCURRING AT A BAD TIME happening or done at a bad or inconvenient time ○ *an untimely decision* **2.** PREMATURE TIME happening before the expected time ○ *his untimely death* ■ *adv.* (*formal*) **1.** AT AN INAPPROPRIATE TIME at a bad or inappropriate time **2.** PREMATURELY earlier than wanted or expected —**untimeliness** *n.*

untiring /un tīring/ *adj.* **1.** NOT BECOMING TIRED not becoming weary or exhausted **2.** GOING ON continuing in spite of difficulty or frustration ○ *her untiring efforts* —**untiringly** *adv.*

untitled /un tīt'ld/ *adj.* **1.** UNNAMED not having a name or title **2.** NOT BELONGING TO NOBILITY possessing no aristocratic title **3.** WITHOUT PROPER CLAIM having no legitimate right or claim

unto (*stressed*) /ún too/; (*unstressed*) /úntŏŏ/ *prep.* (*archaic*) **1.** TO used to indicate that sth is said, given, or done to sb ○ *the elders of Gilead said unto Jephthah* **2.** UNTIL used to indicate that sth continues until a particular time ○ *faithful unto death* [13thC. Formed from UNTIL, with TO replacing TILL (the original, and still dialectal, sense of which was 'to').]

untold /ún tṓld/ *adj.* **1.** NOT REVEALED not having been revealed or related **2.** INDESCRIBABLE OR UNCOUNTABLE too great or numerous to be properly described or counted [Old English *unteald*. Originally in the sense 'uncounted, not enumerated'.]

untouchable /un túchəb'l/ *adj.* **1.** NOT TO BE TOUCHED not able or allowed to be touched **2.** OUT OF REACH completely out of reach **3.** ABOVE CRITICISM too well known or important to be investigated or criticized **4.** DISAGREEABLE TO TOUCH unpleasant or disagreeable to touch ■ *n.* **untouchable, Untouchable** INDIAN RELIG OFFENSIVE TERM an offensive term for a member of the hereditary Hindu class that was formerly segregated and regarded as ritually unclean by the four castes, and who performed tasks that were considered polluting. The term is regarded as offensive and Gandhi's alternative (**harijan**) meaning 'children of God' has also been rejected by many in favour of a term (**dalit**) meaning 'the oppressed'. (*offensive*) —**untouchability** /un túchə bílləti/ *n.* —**untouchably** /un túchəbli/ *adv.*

untouched /un túcht/ *adj.* **1.** NOT TOUCHED not touched or handled **2.** UNEATEN not eaten or consumed **3.** UNINJURED not injured, damaged, or harmed **4.** UNALTERED not changed or altered **5.** EMOTIONALLY UNAFFECTED emotionally unaffected by sth **6.** NOT MENTIONED omitted from mention or discussion [14thC]

untoward /úntə wáwrd/ *adj.* **1.** INAPPROPRIATE not appropriate or fitting ○ *untoward rudeness* **2.** UNEXPECTED beyond the ordinary or the expected ○ *an untoward piece of luck* **3.** CAUSING MISFORTUNE causing misfortune or disadvantage ○ *several untoward events* [14thC. Originally in the sense 'stubborn, disinclined'.] —**untowardly** *adv.* —**untowardness** *n.*

untrammelled *adj.* not restricted or restrained

untravelled /un trávv'ld/ *adj.* **1.** INEXPERIENCED not having wide knowledge or experience of the world **2.** NOT OFTEN TRAVELLED ON never or rarely travelled along

untried /ún trīd/ *adj.* **1.** NOT TESTED not tried, tested, or proved **2.** LAW NOT TRIED IN COURT not tried in a court of law

untroubled /un trúbb'ld/ *adj.* **1.** NOT ANXIOUS OR DISTURBED not bothered, uneasy, or distracted by sth **2.** CALM tranquil and without disturbances ○ *untroubled sleep* —**untroubledness** *n.*

untrue /un tróo/ *adj.* **1.** WRONG OR FALSE not in accordance with the facts or what is known **2.** NOT PRECISE not precise or accurate according to some standard or measure **3.** UNFAITHFUL not faithful or loyal to sb [Old English *untrēowe* 'unfaithful'] —**untruly** *adv.*

untruth /un tróoth/ *n.* **1.** LIE sth that is presented as being true but is actually false ○ *accused of telling untruths* **2.** FALSENESS a lack of truth, especially as a result of lying [Old English *untrēowþ* 'disloyalty']

WORD KEY: SYNONYMS

See Synonyms at ***lie***.

untruthful /un tróothf'l/ *adj.* **1.** UNTRUE not in accordance with the facts or what is known **2.** NOT TELLING THE TRUTH lying or failing to tell the truth —**untruthfully** *adv.* —**untruthfulness** *n.*

untutored /un tyóotərd/ *adj.* **1.** UNTAUGHT not formally educated or trained **2.** UNSOPHISTICATED without any awareness of or interest in what is socially acceptable behaviour

ununquadium /ún un kwáydi əm/ *n.* the heaviest chemical element currently thought to exist. The first evidence for it was obtained in 1998 after bombarding plutonium atoms with calcium ions in a cyclotron. Symbol **Uuq**

unused /un yóozd/ *adj.* **1. NOT USED** never having been used ○ *unused matches* **2. NOT IN USE** not being put to use ○ *unused land* **3.** /un yóost/ **UNFAMILIAR** not familiar with or accustomed to sth ○ *Our dog is unused to city traffic.* [13thC]

unusual /un yóozhoo əl/ *adj.* **1. RARE** not common or familiar **2. REMARKABLE** remarkable or out of the ordinary —**unusualness** *n.*

unusually /un yóozhoo əli/ *adv.* **1. UNCOMMONLY** to a remarkable or exceptional degree or extent ○ *unusually cold for the time of year* **2. UNLIKE WHAT USUALLY HAPPENS** in contrast with usual practice or events ○ *Unusually, he had taken a taxi to work.* [Early 17thC]

unutterable /un úttərəb'l/ *adj.* impossible to express or describe because of emotional intensity —**unutterableness** *n.* —**unutterably** *adv.*

unvalued /un vállyood/ *adj.* **1. NOT VALUED** not regarded as valuable, especially when true value is being overlooked **2. NOT APPRAISED** not having had a value attached **3. PRICELESS** so valuable as to have no price in monetary terms (*archaic*)

unvarnished /un vaárnisht/ *adj.* **1. NOT VARNISHED** having no protective or decorative coat of varnish **2. STRAIGHTFORWARD** said or presented without any attempt to disguise the truth ○ *the unvarnished facts*

unveil /un váyl/ (**-veils, -veiling, -veiled**) *v.* **1.** *vti.* **REMOVE COVERING FROM** to take off a veil or other covering, especially from sb's face or from a plaque, monument, or work of art during a formal ceremony of inauguration **2.** *vt.* **EXPOSE STH SECRET** to reveal sth that has been hidden or kept secret

unveiling /un váyling/ *n.* **1. INAUGURATION CEREMONY** the formal removal of a covering that has hidden a plaque, monument, or work of art in an inauguration ceremony **2. REVELATION** the revelation of sth for the first time, especially sth kept secret

unvoice /un vóyss/ (**-voices, -voicing, -voiced**) *vt.* = **devoice**

unvoiced /un vóyst/ *adj.* **1. UNSPOKEN** not spoken or explicitly stated **2.** PHON **SPOKEN WITHOUT VOICING** pronounced without vibration of the vocal chords

unwaged /un wáyjd/ *adj.* not in formal paid employment

unwarrantable /un wórrəntəb'l/ *adj.* unable to be justified or condoned —**unwarrantably** *adv.*

unwarranted /un wórrəntid/ *adj.* **1. UNAUTHORIZED** not authorized **2. UNJUSTIFIED** not justified or deserved

unwary /un wáiri/ *adj.* failing to be alert and cautious —**unwarily** *adv.* —**unwariness** *n.*

unwashed /ún wósht/ *adj.* not having been washed [14thC] ◇ **the great unwashed** an offensive term used to refer to the mass of ordinary people (*offensive*)

unwatchable /un wóchəb'l/ *adj.* too bad to be worth watching, or too unpleasant and distressing to watch

unwavering /un wáyvəring/ *adj.* firm in your view or purpose and unable to be swayed or diverted from it —**unwaveringly** *adv.*

unwearied /un wéerid/ *adj.* **1. NEVER TIRING** performing a task or promoting a cause without ceasing **2. NOT TIRED** not tired, e.g. from working or playing —**unweariedly** *adv.*

unwelcome /un wélkəm/ *adj.* **1. NOT WELCOME** unwanted in a particular place or at a particular event **2. CAUSING DISTRESS** causing hurt or unpleasantness [14thC] —**unwelcomely** *adv.* —**unwelcomeness** *n.*

unwell /un wél/ *adj.* not in good health

unwholesome /un hṓlssəm/ *adj.* **1. UNHEALTHY** harmful to health ○ *unwholesome eating habits* **2. REGARDED AS HARMFUL TO MORALS** regarded as being harmful to character or morals **3. LOOKING UNHEALTHY** unhealthy in appearance ○ *an unwholesome pallor* —**unwholesomely** *adv.* —**unwholesomeness** *n.*

unwieldy /un wéeldi/ *adj.* **1. NOT EASY TO HANDLE** hard to handle because of being large, heavy, or awkward **2. DIFFICULT TO MANAGE** too complex or extensive to be manageable [14thC. Originally in the sense 'weak, lacking strength'.] —**unwieldily** *adv.* —**unwieldiness** *n.*

WORD KEY: USAGE

Spelling trap: This word is often incorrectly spelled and pronounced *unwieldly*, as if it were formed with the common adjective ending *-ly*.

unwilled /un wíld/ *adj.* involuntary rather than chosen or planned

unwilling /un wílling/ *adj.* **1. NOT WILLING** not willing to do sth ○ *unwilling to participate* **2. RELUCTANT** given reluctantly or grudgingly ○ *unwilling assistance* [Old English *unwillende*] —**unwillingly** *adv.* —**unwillingness** *n.*

WORD KEY: SYNONYMS

unwilling, reluctant, disinclined, averse, hesitant, loath

CORE MEANING: lacking the desire to do sth

unwilling used to describe sb who states firmly that he or she is not prepared to do sth; **reluctant** used to describe sb who really does not want to do sth, and will only do it if he or she has to; **disinclined** used to suggest that sb has a lack of enthusiasm for sth rather than a strong objection to it; **averse** a fairly formal word used to suggest that sb has a mild dislike or distaste for sth; **hesitant** used to describe sb who is not keen to do sth because he or she is uncertain about it; **loath** a fairly formal word used to suggest that sb has strong objections to or reservations about doing sth.

unwind /un wínd/ (**-winds, -winding, -wound** /un wównd/, **-wound**) *v.* **1.** *vti.* **UNCOIL** to undo sth such as tape or cable by winding, or to come undone in this way **2.** *vt.* **UNTANGLE** to remove or undo the tangles in sth **3.** *vti.* **RELAX** to relieve sb of, or obtain relief from, tension or worry ○ *It's sometimes hard to unwind at the end of a busy day.*

unwinking /un wíngking/ *adj.* never closing the eyes or becoming distracted

unwisdom /un wízdəm/ *n.* lack of wisdom or thought [Old English *unwīsdōm*]

unwise /un wíz/ (**-wiser, -wisest**) *adj.* lacking wisdom, judgment, or good sense [Old English *unwīs*] —**unwisely** *adv.*

unwish /un wísh/ (**-wishes, -wishing, -wished**) *vt.* **1. REVOKE A WISH** to undo or take back a wish **2. DESIRE STH NOT BE** to want sth not to be or not to happen

unwitting /un wítting/ *adj.* **1. UNKNOWING** unaware of what is happening in a particular situation **2. UNINTENTIONAL** said or done unintentionally [Old English *unwitende*, from the present participle of *witan* 'to become aware of, learn', related to English *wit*] —**unwittingly** *adv.*

unwonted /un wṓntid/ *adj.* **1. UNUSUAL** not what is expected or usual **2. UNUSED TO** not used to or in the habit of doing sth (*archaic*) —**unwontedly** *adv.* —**unwontedness** *n.*

unworkable /un wúrkəb'l/ *adj.* **1. NOT PRACTICAL** too complicated or ambitious to be accomplished or established **2.** INDUST **NOT ABLE TO BE WORKED** unable to be cut, shaped, or otherwise fashioned **3.** AGRIC **IMPOSSIBLE TO FARM** so hard or rocky that it is impossible to farm —**unworkability** /un wúrkə bílləti/ *n.* —**unworkableness** *n.* —**unworkably** *adv.*

unworldly /un wúrldli/ *adj.* **1. NOT MATERIALISTIC** not interested in money or material goods **2. INEXPERIENCED** lacking experience of the world **3. NOT OF THIS WORLD** not concerned with or part of the material world —**unworldliness** *n.*

unworn *adj.* **1. NOT WORN** not previously or recently worn ○ *an unworn shirt* **2. LIKE NEW** in good condition, rather than worn out or ruined ○ *unworn tyres*

unworthy /un wúrthi/ *adj.* **1. UNDESERVING** not deserving a particular benefit, privilege, or compliment ○ *They proved themselves unworthy of our trust.* **2. BENEATH SB** not typical of sb's usual standards of behaviour ○ *Such conduct is unworthy of you.* **3. WITHOUT VALUE** lacking value or merit **4. VILE** bad or unpleasant and wholly undeserved [13thC] —**unworthily** *adv.* —**unworthiness** *n.*

unwound past tense, past participle of **unwind**

unwrap /un ráp/ (**-wraps, -wrapping, -wrapped**) *vti.* to take off the wrapping from sth, or to have the wrapping removed [14thC]

unwritten /un rítt'n/ *adj.* **1. NOT WRITTEN DOWN** remaining unprinted or not written down **2. ACCEPTED THROUGH TRADITION** generally accepted and understood even though not formally recorded in writing ○ *unwritten law*

unyielding /un yéelding/ *adj.* **1. STUBBORN** not giving in to persuasion, pressure, or force **2. INFLEXIBLE** hard or rigid rather than flexible —**unyieldingly** *adv.* —**unyieldingness** *n.*

unyoke /un yṓk/ (**-yokes, -yoking, -yoked**) *vt.* **1. UNTIE STH** to release an animal such as a horse from a yoke **2. DISCONNECT STH** to separate two or more connected things **3. FREE** to set sb free (*archaic or literary*) [Old English *ungeocian*]

unzip /un zíp/ (**-zips, -zipping, -zipped**) *v.* **1.** *vti.* **UNDO ZIP OF** to open or unfasten sth such as clothing or luggage by means of a zip, or to become open or unfastened by this means **2.** *vt.* COMPUT **DECOMPRESS FILE** to decompress a computer file that has been compressed

up /up/ *adv., prep.* **AT A HIGHER LEVEL** in, at, or to a higher level or position ○ (adv) *Put your hand up if you know the answer.* ○ (prep) *We climbed up the hill.* ○ (adv) *Prices are going up all the time.* ○ (prep) *I went up the ladder as far as the first-floor window.* ■ *prep., adv.* **ALONG** along ○ (prep) *Go up the road until you come to a school.* ○ (adv) *You'll find her house up at the top of the road* ■ *adv.* **1. INDICATING COMPLETION** used to indicate thoroughness or the completion of an action ○ *I tore up all the photographs.* **2. UPRIGHT** in or to an upright position from a lower or prone position ○ *sitting up in bed* **3. COMING OUT** coming through or out of some medium ○ *The whales came up for air.* **4. OUT** in a way that detaches or removes ○ *Pulling up weeds isn't easy.* ○ *We drew up water from the well.* **5. RISING ABOVE** rising, or seeming to rise, above or over sth ○ *When does the moon come up?* **6. INTO CONSIDERATION** so as to be discussed or mentioned ○ *The subject just didn't come up.* **7. IN NORTHERLY POSITION** towards or in a northerly position relative to the speaker ○ *Our cousins live up in Scotland.* **8. TO A HIGHER VALUE** to or at a higher amount or price ○ *The interest rate is going up again.* **9. TO A GREATER INTENSITY** with or to more intensity or higher pitch or volume ○ *His voice goes up when he's nervous.* ○ *Let's turn up the volume.* **10. NEAR** so as to move towards or closer to the speaker ○ *She ran up to me and gave me a big hug.* ○ *They came up to the door and knocked.* ■ *adv., n.* **AHEAD** to the better or ahead ○ (adv) *Our team is up by two.* ○ (n) *Sales are on the up this month.* ■ *adj.* **1. INCREASED** more than before ○ *Your grades are up this term.* **2. OUT OF BED** awake and out of bed ○ *She was already up when I called.* **3. FACING UPWARDS** having the face or top side upward **4. RAISED UPWARDS** in a raised or lifted position ○ *The switch is in the up position.* **5. GOING HIGHER OR NORTH** located in or moving towards a higher or northern direction ○ *The train is waiting at the up platform.* ○ *Take the up escalator.* **6. CHEERFUL** happy and feeling good ○ *We've been so up since hearing the news.* **7. HAPPENING** going on at a particular time (*informal*) ○ *What's up with you these days?* **8. BEING CONSIDERED** approaching a deadline for an action ○ *The contract is up for renewal.* **9. NOMINATED FOR STH** in the running for an office or professional achievement ○ *I hear she's up for a promotion.* **10. ON TRIAL** charged with an offence or called into a court of law ○ *The accused is up for first-degree murder.* **11. OVER** over or finished ○ *Your time is up.* **12. HAVING KNOWLEDGE** possessing up-to-date or accurate information ○ *I'm not up on the latest gossip.* **13. FUNCTIONING** able to operate or function ○ *Is the computer up?* **14.** BASEBALL **BATTING** taking a turn at bat in baseball ○ *Who's up first in this inning?* ■ *n.* **1. UPWARD SLOPE** sth that gradually rises from a base point ○ *Let's try to avoid the ups on our hike today.* **2. SOURCE OF GOOD FEELING** sth that causes excitement or a feeling of euphoria (*informal*) ○ *The news was a real up for her.* ■ *v.* (**ups, upping, upped**) **1.** *vt.* **RAISE** to raise or increase sth ○ *The insurance company has upped our premiums again.* **2.** *vt.* **PROMOTE** to promote or raise sb or sth to a higher level or position (*usually passive*) ○ *He was upped to manager last week.* **3.** *vi.* **ACT SUDDENLY** to act suddenly or impulsively ○ *She just upped and left.* ○ *He upped and bought a new car without shopping around.* [Old English *up* 'upward' and *uppe* 'on high'. Ultimately from an Indo-European word that is also the ancestor of English *above, eaves,* and *open.*] ◇ **up and about** active and on your feet again after an illness ◇ **be up to sb** to be the duty, responsibility, or job of sb ◇ **it is all up with sb** *or* **sth** used to indicate that sb or sth is bound to fail, be destroyed, or get into trouble or danger (*informal*) ◇ **on the up and up 1.** making very good progress **2.** in an honest or legitimate way (*dated*) ◇ **up against it** facing difficulty or danger ◇ **ups and downs** changes of fortune or alternating spells of good and bad experiences ◇ **up to 1.** occupied with or involved in sth, often in a way that arouses suspicion ○ *I knew what he was up to, but I couldn't do anything about it.* **2.** able to undertake or endure ○ *I don't think I'm up to the journey.* **3.** as many as, or as long as ◇ **up to your ears** *or* **elbows** *or* **eyes in sth** deeply involved in or preoccupied with sth ◇ **up yours** an offensive term used to show anger or resentment (*offensive*) ◇ **what's up** what's the matter?

WORD KEY: USAGE

See Usage note at ***back***.

UP *abbr.* Uttar Pradesh

up. *abbr.* upper

up-and-coming *adj.* successful or improving, and showing signs of continuing to do so

Upanishad /oo púnnishəd, oo pánnə shad/ *n.* any of the sacred texts written in Sanskrit that form the basis for Hindu philosophy and doctrine. They date from 400 BC and represent the last stage in the tradition of the Vedas, the most ancient of Hindu scriptures. [Early 19thC. From Sanskrit *upaniṣad*, literally 'a sitting down near (sth)', from *upa* 'near' + *ni-ṣad* 'to sit down'.] —**Upanishadic** /oo púnni sháddik, -pánnə-/ *adj.*

upas /yóopəss/ (*plural* **upases** *or* **upas**) *n.* **1. TROPICAL TREE** a tropical and subtropical tree found in Southeast Asia with white bark and poisonous sap. Latin name: *Antiaris toxicaria.* **2. POISON FROM UPAS TREE** a poison made from the sap of the upas and used on arrows [Late 18thC. From Malay *(pohun) upas* 'poison (tree)'.]

upbeat /úp beet/ *n.* **1.** MUSIC **UNACCENTED BEAT** an unaccented beat in music, especially one that ends a bar **2.** MUSIC **GESTURE OF BATON** the upward movement of a conductor's baton that indicates an upbeat **3. IMPROVEMENT** an increase in happiness, prosperity, or favourable activity ■ *adj.* **OPTIMISTIC** full of optimism or cheerfulness (*informal*)

upbow /úp bō/ *n.* the movement of the bow across the strings of an instrument in which the tip of the bow moves away from the instrument

upbraid /up bráyd/ (**-braids, -braiding, -braided**) *vt.* to correct or criticize sb in a harsh manner [Old English *upbrēdan*, of uncertain origin: probably literally 'to throw sth up (against someone as a fault)', formed from *bregdan* 'to move quickly, throw'] —**upbraider** *n.* —**upbraidingly** *adv.*

upbringing /úp bringing/ *n.* the way sb has been brought up, or trained and educated early in life [15thC. Originally in the sense of 'building'.]

upbuild /up bíld/ (**-builds, -building, -built** /-bílt/, **-built**) *vt.* to build up, develop, or enlarge sth —**upbuilder** *n.*

upcast /up kaást/ *adj.* **CAST UPWARDS** thrown, propelled, or looking upwards ■ *n.* **1. STH THROWN UP** material that has been thrown up **2.** MINING **VENTILATION SHAFT** a ventilation shaft in a mine that brings air up

upchuck /úp chuk/ (**-chucks, -chucking, -chucked**) *vti.* US to vomit (*slang*)

upcoming /úp kumming/ *adj.* US about to happen or coming soon

upcountry *adj.* /úp kuntri/ **COMING FROM THE INTERIOR** coming from, associated with, or located in an inland region of a country ■ *n.* /úp kuntri/ **INLAND REGION** an inland area of a country ■ *adv.* /up kúntri/ **TOWARDS THE INTERIOR** in, to, or towards the inland region of a country

update *vt.* /up dáyt/ (**-dates, -dating, -dated**) **PROVIDE NEW INFORMATION** to provide sb or sth with the most recent information, or with more recent information than was previously available ○ *The website is updated once a month.* ■ *n.* /úp dayt/ **LATEST INFORMATION** the latest available information or more recent information [Mid-20thC]

Popperfoto

John Updike

Updike /úp dīk/, **John** (*b.* 1932) US writer. He is best known for his novel *Rabbit, Run* (1960), and its sequels, two of which won Pulitzer Prizes. Full name **John Hoyer Updike**

updraught /úp draaft/ *n.* a current of air that is moving upwards

upend /up énd/ (**-ends, -ending, -ended**) *vti.* to place, stand, or turn sth up so that it is standing or resting on one end, or be turned over onto one end

up-front, -upfront, -up front *adj.* (*informal*) **1. STRAIGHTFORWARD** honest, frank, or straightforward **2. IN ADVANCE** paid in advance —**up front** *adv.* —**up-frontness** *n.*

upgrade *v.* /up gráyd/ (**-grades, -grading, -graded**) **1.** *vt.* **PROMOTE** to promote sb or increase the status of sb's job or position **2.** *vti.* **IMPROVE QUALITY** to improve the quality, standard, or performance of sth, especially by incorporating new advances ○ *upgrade a computer* **3.** *vti.* **TRADE UP** to exchange sth for another of better quality ○ *upgrade a seat on a flight* **4.** *vt.* AGRIC **IMPROVE LIVESTOCK** to improve the quality of livestock by breeding with superior animals to introduce desirable traits into the offspring ■ *n.* /úp grayd/ **1. IMPROVEMENT OF STH** an improvement in the quality or performance of sth, e.g. computer hardware or software **2. STH THAT IMPROVES** sth that improves the performance or quality of sth else, or sth that has better performance or qualities **3.** *US, Can* **UPWARD SLOPE** an upward slope or incline

upgrowth /úp grōth/ *n.* the process of growing upwards, or the result of such a process

Upham /úppəm/, **Charles Hazlitt** (1908–94) New Zealand soldier. He fought in World War II, becoming the only combat soldier ever to win the Victoria Cross and Bar.

upheaval /up heév'l/ *n.* **1. DISTURBANCE** a strong or sudden change in political, social, or living conditions **2.** GEOL **UPWARD MOVEMENT** a sudden raising of part of the earth's crust

upheave /up heév/ (**-heaves, -heaving, -heaved** *or* **-hove** /-hṓv/, **-heaved**) *vti.* to lift sth forcefully from underneath, or rise or be thrust upward

uphill *adv.* /up híl/ **1. UP A SLOPE** up a slope or towards the top of a hill **2. WITH DIFFICULTY** against great resistance or in spite of difficulty ■ *adj.* /úp hil/ **1. SLOPING UP** going up a slope or a hill **2. ON HIGHER GROUND** located farther up a slope or hill **3. DIFFICULT** requiring a lot of effort ○ *an uphill struggle*

uphold /up hṓld/ (**-holds, -holding, -held** /up héld/, **-held**) *vt.* **1. MAINTAIN OR SUPPORT** to maintain or defend sth, especially laws or principles, in the face of hostility **2. GIVE SB SUPPORT** to provide sb with moral support, or inspire sb with confidence —**upholder** *n.*

upholster /up hṓlstər/ (**-sters, -stering, -stered**) *vt.* to fit chairs, couches, and similar items of furniture with stuffing, springs, and covering [Mid-19thC. Back-formation from UPHOLSTERY.] —**upholsterer** *n.*

upholstery /up hṓlstəri/ *n.* **1. MATERIALS USED FOR UPHOLSTERING** the stuffing, cushions, fabric, and other materials used to upholster chairs and couches ○ *upholstery fabric* **2. WORK OF UPHOLSTERING** the craft, trade, or business of upholstering furniture [Mid-17thC. Formed from obsolete *upholster* 'upholsterer'.]

UPI *abbr.* United Press International

upkeep /úp keep/ *n.* **1. MAINTENANCE** the maintenance of sb or sth in proper condition or operation **2. COST** the financial cost of providing maintenance for sb or sth

upland /úpplənd, úp land/ *n.* **1. HIGH LAND** land that has a high elevation, or a region of such land **2. INLAND REGION** a region that lies in the interior of a country ■ *adj.* **HIGH OR INLAND** relating to, located in, or native to a region that is at a high elevation or lies in the interior of a country

upland cotton *n.* **1.** PLANTS **COTTON PLANT** a cotton plant that probably originated in Central America and is now grown widely for the woolly fibre that surrounds its seeds. Latin name: *Gossypium hirsutum.* **2.** TEXTILES **COTTON FIBRE OR FABRIC** the woolly fibre of the upland cotton plant, or fabric made from it

uplift *vt.* /up líft/ (**-lifts, -lifting, -lifted**) **1. PHYSICALLY LIFT STH** to raise or lift sb or sth **2. SPIRITUALLY LIFT SB** to help sb attain a higher intellectual or spiritual level, or improve sb's living conditions **3.** *NZ, S Africa, Scotland* **COLLECT** to pick up passengers or baggage ■ *n.* /úp lift/ **1. STH IMPROVING** sth that elevates sb morally or spiritually, or improves sb's living conditions **2. LIFTING UP** the lifting up of sth, or the result of doing so **3.** GEOL **UPWARD MOVEMENT OF EARTH'S CRUST** the slow upward movement of large parts of stable areas of the earth's crust —**uplifter** *n.*

WORD KEY: SYNONYMS

See Synonyms at ***raise***.

uplifting /up lífting/ *adj.* raising people's moral or spiritual level or emotions [Early 19thC]

uplighter /úp līter/ *n.* a lamp or lampshade that directs the light upwards [Mid-20thC]

uplink /úp lingk/ *n.* a transmitter on the ground that sends radio or other signals to an aircraft or communications satellite

upload /úp lōd/ (**-loads, -loading, -loaded**) *vti.* to transfer data or programs, usually from a peripheral computer to a central, often remote computer

upmarket /up maárkit/ *adj.* **EXPENSIVE AND SUPERIOR** intended or designed for wealthy discriminating consumers ■ *adv.* **TOWARDS MORE EXPENSIVE TASTES** towards a higher and more expensive standard that appeals to wealthy, discriminating consumers ○ *The hotel seems to have gone upmarket.*

upmost /úp mōst/ *adj.* = **uppermost**

upon /ə pón/ CORE MEANING: means the same as 'on' but is more formal ○ *He stretched out his legs upon the sofa.* ○ *She climbed upon her father's knee.*

prep. **1. ON SURFACE** on or onto the surface of sth (*formal*) ○ *The great beast bounced to a halt upon the parapet.* **2. ONE AFTER ANOTHER** used to indicate two occurrences of the same noun, referring to a large number ○ *They claimed that the report contained 'innuendo upon innuendo'.* **3. FOLLOWED BY** used to indicate that one event is followed immediately by another event ○ *Upon finding the relevant text, they store it in their own electronic files.* **4. ABOUT TO HAPPEN** used to indicate that an event is imminent ○ *The holidays are upon us again.* [12thC. From UP + ON; modelled on Old Norse *upp á*.]

upper /úppər/ *adj.* **1. HIGHER** located above another part of sth ○ *the upper deck* ○ *a muscle in the upper arm* **2. MORE IMPORTANT** higher in social position or importance ○ *upper management* **3. MORE DISTANT** lying farther inland, upstream, or to the north ○ *the upper reaches of the river* **4.** GEOL **LATER** later in a named geological formation, period, or system **5.** MATH **INDICATING A MATHEMATICAL LIMIT** indicating a limit or bound of a set of numbers equal to or greater than every member of the set ■ *n.* **1. THE ONE ABOVE** the higher of two people or objects **2.** CLOTHES **PART OF SHOE** the part of a boot or shoe that covers the upper surface of the foot **3.** DRUGS **STIMULANT** a drug such as an amphetamine that has a stimulating effect (*slang*) ■ **uppers** *npl.* **UPPER TEETH** the teeth of the upper jaw or of a top set of dentures (*informal*) [13thC. Formed from UP + -ER^2, being originally the comparative of UP.] ◇ **be on your uppers** to be very short of money (*informal*)

upper atmosphere *n.* the part of the Earth's atmosphere above the troposphere, especially at heights unreachable by balloon

upper bound *n.* a number that is greater than or equal to all the members of a set

Upper Canada /úppər kánnədə/ former British province in Canada, corresponding to present-day southern Ontario

uppercase /úppər kayss, úppər káyss/ *n.* CAPITAL LETTERS capital letters used in writing, typing, typesetting, or printing ○ *printed in uppercase* ■ *adj.* IN CAPITAL LETTERS belonging to, written, or printed in capital letters ■ *vt.* (-**cases**, -**casing**, -**cased**) CAPITALIZE STH to write, type, typeset, or print sth in capital letters [Mid-18thC. From typesetters having kept capital letters in the upper of a pair of type cases.]

upper chamber *n.* = upper house

upper circle *n.* the gallery of seats at the top of a theatre, above the dress circle

upper class *n.* the highest social class, or the people in it, e.g. the aristocracy and the very wealthy — **upper-class** *adj.*

upper crust *n.* the upper class (*informal*)

uppercut /úppər kut/ *n.* BLOW a swinging upward blow in which the fist is aimed at an opponent's chin ■ *vt.* (-**cuts**, -**cutting**, -**cut**) STRIKE SB to hit or attempt to hit an opponent with an uppercut

upper hand *n.* the controlling position in a situation

upper house *n.* in a political system, the house in a two-house legislature that is smaller and less representative of the general population, e.g. the House of Lords

Upper Hutt /úppər hút/ city in the south of the North Island, New Zealand, 32 km/20 mi. north of Wellington. Population: 19,686 (1996).

uppermost /úppər mōst/ *adj.* HIGHEST highest in position, rank, or level ■ *adv.* AT THE TOP in, at, or towards the highest point, position, or rank

Upper Palaeolithic *n.* the latest of the three periods of the Palaeolithic era, about 40,000 to 14,000 years ago, when modern human beings first appeared — **Upper Palaeolithic** *adj.*

upper respiratory *adj.* relating to or affecting any of the air passages or associated structures that connect the lungs with the exterior, including the nasal passages, trachea, and bronchi

upper school *n.* the senior students in a secondary school, particularly those in Year 10 and above

Upper Volta /úppər vóltə/ former name for **Burkina Faso**

upper works *npl.* the parts of a boat or ship above the waterline when it is fully loaded

uppity /úppəti/ *adj.* **1.** PRESUMPTUOUS behaving in a way that other people consider presumptuous and more suited to sb belonging a higher social class or position (*informal*) **2.** STUBBORN having a stubborn inflexible personality (*dated informal*) [Late 19thC. Formed fancifully from UP.] —**uppityness** *n.*

Uppsala /úp saalə/ city in eastern central Sweden, location of the country's oldest university. Population: 184,507 (1996).

upraise /up ráyz/ (-**raises**, -**raising**, -**raised**) *vt.* to raise sth or cause sth to rise, e.g. hands, prayers, or voices (*literary*)

uprate /up ráyt/ (-**rates**, -**rating**, -**rated**) *vt.* to increase the value, price, rank, or size of sth

uprear /up reér/ (-**rears**, -**rearing**, -**reared**) *vti.* to rise, or to cause sth to rise (*archaic or literary*) [13thC]

upright /úp rīt/ *adj.* **1.** ERECT standing vertically or straight upwards **2.** RIGHTEOUS behaving in a moral or honourable manner ■ *adv.* VERTICALLY straight upwards rather than at an angle ■ *n.* **1.** VERTICAL SUPPORT sth that stands upright, e.g. a stake or post **2.** MUSIC = upright piano —**uprightly** *adv.* —**uprightness** *n.*

Upright piano

upright piano, **upright** *n.* a piano with a rectangular upright case in which the strings are mounted vertically, and a keyboard at right angles to the case

uprise *vi.* /up rīz/ (-**rises**, -**rising**, -**rose** /-rōz/, -**risen** /-rízz'n/) (*literary or archaic*) **1.** RISE UP to stand or get up **2.** MOVE UPWARDS to stand, go, or move in an upward direction ■ *n.* /úp rīz/ UPWARD SLOPE an upward slope or incline

uprising /úp rīzing/ *n.* an act of rebellion or revolt against an authority

upriver /up rívvər/ *adv., adj.* towards or closer to the source of a river

uproar /úp rawr/ *n.* a loud or noisy disturbance [Early 16thC. By folk etymology from Middle Low German *uprōr* or Dutch *oproer*, literally 'stirring up', formed, respectively, from Middle Low German *rōr* 'stirring, motion' and Dutch *roer*. Originally 'insurrection'.]

uproarious /up ráwri əss/ *adj.* **1.** TUMULTUOUS characterized by noisy confusion **2.** HILARIOUS extremely funny and causing people to laugh loudly **3.** VERY LOUD loud and boisterous —**uproariously** *adv.* —**uproariousness** *n.*

uproot /up róot/ (-**roots**, -**rooting**, -**rooted**) *vt.* **1.** PULL PLANT FROM SOIL to pull a plant and its roots from the soil **2.** REMOVE OR DESTROY to remove or destroy sth completely **3.** DISPLACE to displace sb or sth from a home or habitual environment ○ *I don't want to uproot the children and move to the other end of the country.* —**uprootedness** *n.* —**uprooter** *n.*

uprose past tense of uprise

uprush /úp rush/ *n.* a sudden upwards rush of sth

upsadaisy /úpsə dáyzi/ *interj.* = upsy-daisy

upscale /úp skáyl/ *adj., adv. US* = upmarket

upset *adj.* /up sét/ **1.** DISTURBED OR SAD unhappy, disappointed, or emotionally distressed because of sth that has happened **2.** OVERTURNED overturned or spilled **3.** DISORDERED thrown into disorder or confusion ■ *v.* /up sét/ (-**sets**, -**setting**, -**set**) **1.** *vt.* MAKE SB UNHAPPY to cause sb emotional or mental distress **2.** *vt.* MAKE SB FEEL SICK to make sb feel sick, or cause a disorder of the digestive system ○ *Spicy foods upset my stomach.* **3.** *vti.* TURN STH OVER to turn or tip over, or knock or tip sth over accidentally, usually scattering its contents **4.** *vt.* DISTURB ORDER to disrupt the usual order or course of sth **5.** *vt.* SPORTS DEFEAT UNEXPECTEDLY to defeat a competitor or a team unexpectedly in a sports contest **6.** *vt.* METALL THICKEN RIVET END to make a heated bolt, rivet, or bar shorter and thicker by hammering one end ■ *n.* /úp set/ **1.** DRAMATIC CHANGE an unexpected problem that disturbs people or causes them to change their plans **2.** UNEXPECTED RESULT an unexpected result, e.g. in a sporting contest or an election **3.** EMOTIONAL OR PHYSICAL DISTURBANCE a mild illness of the stomach, or an unhappy experience **4.** METALL TOOL a tool used to make a rivet, bar, or other piece of heated metal shorter and thicker at one end **5.** METALL RIVET a rivet, bar, or other piece of metal that has been hammered and made shorter and thicker at one end —**upsetter** *n.*

upset price *n. US, Can, Scotland* the lowest sale price at which sth can be sold or auctioned. ◊ reserve price

upsetting /up sétting/ *adj.* emotionally distressing or disturbing —**upsettingly** *adv.*

upshift /úp shift/ (-**shifts**, -**shifting**, -**shifted**) *vi. US* to move a vehicle into a higher gear

upshot /úp shot/ *n.* the end result or outcome of sth [Mid-16thC. Originally in the sense 'final shot (in archery)'.]

upside /úp sīd/ *n.* **1.** UPPER SIDE the upper side or part of sth **2.** POSITIVE SIDE the most favourable or positive aspect of a particular situation or event **3.** *US* FIN INCREASE IN VALUE an increase in business profits or stock prices

upside down *adv.* **1.** IN AN INVERTED WAY turned so that the part that should be higher is lower or the side that should be underneath is on top **2.** IN DISORDER in total confusion or great disorder ○ *We turned the house upside down looking for the keys.* —**upside-down** *adj.*

upside-down cake *n.* a sponge cake baked with a layer of fruit at the bottom, then inverted before it is served so that the caramelized fruit is on top

upsilon /up sílən, úpsi lon/ *n.* the 20th letter of the Greek alphabet, represented in the English alphabet as 'y' or 'u' [Mid-17thC. From Greek *u psilon* 'simple u' (named to distinguish it from the diphthong *oi*, which in late Greek had the same pronunciation), from *psilon*, a form of *psilos* 'simple'.]

upspring /up spríng/ (-**springs**, -**springing**, -**sprang** /-spráng/, -**sprung** /-sprúng/) *vi.* to come suddenly into existence or become visible (*archaic or literary*)

upstage /up stáyj/ *vt.* (-**stages**, -**staging**, -**staged**) **1.** OUTDO SB ELSE to divert, or attempt to divert, attention away from sb else **2.** THEATRE TURN ACTOR AWAY FROM AUDIENCE to move towards the back of the stage in order to force another actor to turn his or her back to the audience ■ *adv.* THEATRE TOWARDS REAR in, at, or towards the rear part of a stage ■ *adj.* THEATRE LOCATED AT REAR located in or relating to the rear part of a stage ■ *n.* THEATRE BACK OF STAGE the rear part of the stage —**upstager** *n.*

upstairs /úp stáirz/ *adv.* **1.** UP THE STAIRS to, towards, or on an upper level or floor **2.** MENTALLY in the mind or brain (*humorous*) ○ *not a lot happening upstairs* **3.** TO A HIGHER JOB to a higher level or job in an organization or hierarchy (*informal*) ■ *n.* **1.** UPPER FLOOR an upper floor or the part of a building above the ground floor (*often used before a noun*) ○ *an upstairs bathroom* **2.** OWNERS OF WEALTHY HOUSEHOLD used to refer collectively to wealthy householders, as opposed to the servants who lived downstairs (*archaic informal*) ◊ **downstairs** *n.* **2** ◊ **kick sb upstairs** to promote sb to a rank or position that is officially superior but in fact carries less power and opportunity for influence (*informal*)

upstanding /up stánding/ *adj.* **1.** VIRTUOUS honest and socially responsible **2.** VERTICAL in an erect position (*archaic*) —**upstandingness** *n.* ◊ **be upstanding** to stand in response to a formal request, particularly for a toast or prayer or in a court of law (*formal*)

upstart *n.* /úp staart/ SB WITH NEWLY ACQUIRED STATUS sb who has suddenly acquired wealth, power, or status but is thought not to deserve it ■ *vi.* /up stáart/ (-**starts**, -**starting**, -**started**) RISE SUDDENLY to rise or jump up suddenly or unexpectedly (*archaic*)

upstate /úp stayt/ *adj. US* relating to or living in the northern part of a state

upstream /up streém, úp streem/ *adv.* **1.** AGAINST THE CURRENT in or towards the source of a river or stream **2.** GENETICS IN OPPOSITE DIRECTION TO TRANSCRIPTION in a direction along a strand of a DNA molecule counter to that in which transcription takes place. ◊ **downstream** ■ *adj.* NEARER THE SOURCE located farther towards the source of a stream or river

upstretched /úp strécht/ *adj.* stretched or raised upwards

upstroke /úp strōk/ *n.* **1.** UPWARD STROKE an upward or rising movement of a pen or brush, or the mark it makes **2.** MECH ENG PISTON MOVEMENT the upward movement of a piston in a reciprocating engine

upsurge *n.* /úp surj/ INCREASE a rapid increase in sth ■ *vi.* /up súrj/ (-**surges**, -**surging**, -**surged**) SUDDENLY RISE to rise or increase rapidly (*archaic or literary*)

upswept /úp swépt/ *adj.* curved or brushed upwards

upswing /úp swing/ *n.* an increase or improvement, e.g. in business profits

upsy-daisy /úpsi-/, **upsadaisy** *interj.* a reassuring expression usually addressed to a child being lifted or who has fallen or stumbled (*babytalk*) [Mid-19thC. Alteration of earlier *up-a-daisy*, from UP + *a-day*, expressing surprise, literally '(to) the day' (see LACKADAISICAL).]

uptake /úp tayk/ *n.* **1.** VENT a passage such as a pipe or chimney, that draws up smoke or air **2.** = upcast **3.** BIOL PHYSICAL ABSORPTION the process of physically absorbing sth into a living organism ◇ **be quick** or **slow on the uptake** to be quick or slow to understand things or realize what is happening (*informal*)

up-tempo *n.* MUSIC FAST TEMPO a fast or lively musical tempo ■ *adj.* US EXCITING fast-paced and exciting

upthrow /úp thrō/ *n.* the upward movement of one block of rock over another in a low-angle fault

upthrust /úp thrust/ *n.* **1.** UPWARD PUSH an upward push or thrust **2.** GEOL FAULTED ROCK a block of rock that has moved upwards in a low-angle fault ■ *adj.* RAISED UP raised or lifted up

uptight /úp tít/ *adj.* (*informal*) **1.** TENSE tense as a result of anger, fear, or annoyance in a way that is difficult to control **2.** REPRESSED unable or unwilling to show emotion —**uptightness** *n.*

uptime /úp tīm/ *n.* the time during which a computer or other machine is operating or ready for use

up-to-date *adj.* (*not hyphenated when used after a verb*) **1.** WITH LATEST KNOWLEDGE including or possessing knowledge of the latest information **2.** CURRENT extending up to or reflecting the current time **3.** FASHIONABLE familiar with or knowledgeable about current fashions, styles, or ideas

up-to-the-minute *adj.* including or relating to the most recent events or things

uptown *adv.* /up tówn/ US to, towards, or in the upper part of a city

uptrend /úp trend/ *n.* an upward improving trend, especially in business or an economy

upturn *v.* /up túrn/ (**-turns, -turning, -turned**) **1.** *vti.* TURN OVER to turn over or cause sth to turn over, up, or upside down **2.** *vt.* TURN UPWARDS to turn sth upwards, e.g. a face or gaze (*usually passive*) ■ *n.* /úp turn/ IMPROVEMENT an improvement in the economy or in business conditions [14thC. Originally in the sense 'to overthrow'.]

upward /úpwərd/ *adv.* US = **upwards** ■ *adj.* **1.** GOING TOWARDS going or directed towards a higher level or position ◇ *a steep upward climb* **2.** RISING used to indicate that sth is rising or becoming better ◇ *an upward trend* —**upwardly** *adv.*

upwardly mobile *adj.* ASPIRING TO HIGHER CLASS desiring and attempting to move to a higher social class or to obtain greater social or financial status ■ *npl.* AMBITIOUS PEOPLE those who are becoming richer or more powerful and moving up from a lower class

upward mobility *n.* the ability or opportunity to move to a higher social class and acquire greater wealth, power, or status

upwards /úppwərdz/, **upward** /-werd/ *adv.* **1.** TOWARDS A HIGHER LEVEL in, to, or towards a higher place, level, or position ◇ *She's working her way upwards through the company hierarchy.* ◇ *Keep going upwards and you'll soon see the house.* **2.** TOWARDS INTERIOR OR SOURCE towards the interior of a place, or towards an origin or source ◇ *The hikers left the path and headed upwards along the river.* **3.** TOWARDS A GREATER AMOUNT towards a larger amount, degree, or position ◇ *Sales have gone steadily upwards during the last quarter.* ◇ **upwards of** more than

upwelling /up wélling/ *n.* **1.** EMERGENCE a rising from or as if from lower depths **2.** OCEANOG RISING OF WATER TO SURFACE a process in which cold nutrient-rich water rises to the surface from the ocean depths

upwind /úp wínd/ *adv., adj.* **1.** AGAINST WIND against or into the wind **2.** WINDWARD on the side towards which the wind is blowing

Ur /ur/ ancient city of Mesopotamia, in the southeastern part of present-day Iraq. It was a major city-state of the Sumerian civilization by 2800 BC.

ur-[1] *prefix.* = uro-[1] (*used before vowels*)

ur-[2] *prefix.* = uro-[2] (*used before vowels*)

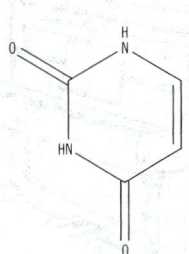
Uracil

uracil /yóórə sil/ *n.* a component of RNA that carries hereditary information in cells. Chemically, it is a pyrimidine derivative. Symbol **U** [Late 19thC. Origin uncertain: perhaps coined from UREA + ACETIC + *-il*, variant of -ILE.]

uraemia /yóó reémi ə/ *n.* a form of blood poisoning caused by the accumulation in the blood of products that are normally eliminated in the urine [Mid-19thC. From modern Latin, from Greek *ouron* 'urine' (see URINE) + *aima* 'blood'.]

Uraeus

uraeus /yóó reé əss/ *n.* the sacred serpent found on the headdresses of Egyptian rulers and divinities, representing sovereignty [Mid-19thC. Via modern Latin from Greek *ouraios* 'cobra', of uncertain origin: perhaps an alteration (modelled on *ouraios* 'of the tail') of an Egyptian word for 'cobra'.]

Ural /yóórəl/ river of southern Russia and northwestern Kazakhstan, rising in the southern Ural Mountains, and flowing southwards into the Caspian Sea. Length: 2,428 km/1,509 mi.

Ural-Altaic *n.* LANG a hypothetical language group that was once proposed by scholars as containing the Uralic and Altaic language families —**Ural-Altaic** *adj.*

Uralic /yóó rállik/ *n.* LANG a family of languages spoken in northern and central Europe and western Siberia. There are two branches of the family, Finno-Ugric and Samoyed. —**Uralic** *adj.*

uralite /yóórə līt/ *n.* a fibrous blue-green mixture of amphibole minerals, with no distinct composition. Uralite is produced by hydrothermal or low-grade metamorphic alteration of pyroxenes. [Mid-19thC. From German *Uralit*, from *Ural* 'Ural Mountains' (where it was first found).]

Ural Mountains /yóórəl mówntinz/ mountain system running from northern Russia southwards to the Kirgiz Steppe in Kazakhstan. It is the traditional dividing line between Asia and Europe. Its highest point is Mount Narodnaya, 1,894 m/6,214 ft. Length: 2,400 km/1,500 mi.

uran- *prefix.* uranium ◇ *uranous* [From URANIUM]

uranalysis /yóórə nálləssiss/ (*plural* **-ses** /-seez/) *n.* = **urinalysis** [Late 19thC. Blend of URINE and ANALYSIS.]

Urania /yóó ráyni ə/ *n.* in Greek mythology, the Muse of astronomy. ◊ **Muse**

uranic /yóó ránnik/ *adj.* derived from or containing uranium, especially in a higher valence state [Mid-19thC. Formed from Latin *uranus*, from Greek *ouranos* 'the heavens'.]

uraninite /yóó ránni nīt/ *n.* a black mineral form of uranium oxide that contains thorium, radium, and lead and is a major ore of uranium [Late 19thC. Coined from German *Uranin* (from modern Latin *uranium* (see URANIUM) + -ITE.]

uranite /yóórə nīt/ *n.* any mineral that contains uranium [Late 19thC. Coined from URANIUM + -ITE[1].] —**uranitic** /yóórə níttik/ *adj.*

uranium /yóó ráyni əm/ *n.* a heavy silvery-white radioactive metallic element that occurs in uraninite and pitchblende in three isotopes, one of which is used as a fuel in nuclear reactors and weapons. Symbol **U** [Late 18thC. From modern Latin, from *Uranus*, the name of the planet (discovered eight years before the element was identified).]

uranium 235 /-tóó thurti fív/ *n.* an isotope of uranium that has a mass number of 235 and is used as a source of nuclear energy because it readily undergoes fission when bombarded with neutrons

uranium 238 /-tóó thurti áyt/ *n.* a stable isotope of uranium that has a mass number of 238 and is the most abundant isotope

uranium-lead dating *n.* the determination of the age of a uranium-containing mineral by measuring the level of lead isotope produced by the radioactive decay of uranium, which occurs at a known rate

uranography /yóórə nóggrəfi/ *n.* the branch of astronomy that deals with making maps of the constellations [Mid-17thC. Formed from Greek *ouranographia*, literally 'science of the skies'.] —**uranographer** *n.* —**uranographic** /yóórənə gráffik/ *adj.* —**uranographist** /yóórə nóggrəfist/ *n.*

uranous /yóórənəss/ *adj.* derived from or containing uranium, especially in a lower valence state

Uranus /yóórənəss, yóó ráynəss/ *n.* **1.** MYTHOL GREEK GOD in Greek mythology, the ruler of the heavens, husband of Gaia, and father of the Titans. He was dethroned by his son Cronus. **2.** ASTRON 7TH PLANET FROM SUN the seventh smallest planet in the solar system and the seventh planet from the Sun. Uranus is blue-green in color and has 17 satellites, all of which are named after characters in the plays of William Shakespeare. [Via Latin from Greek *Ouranos*, the name of the god]

uranyl /yóórənil/ *n.* a compound containing the chemical group UO_2

urase /yóó rayss/ *n.* = urease

urate /yóór ayt, yáwr-/ *n.* a salt of uric acid —**uratic** /yóó ráttik/ *adj.*

urban /úrbən/ *adj.* relating or belonging to a city [Early 17thC. From Latin *urbanus*, from *urbs* 'city' (source of English *suburb*).]

Urban VIII /úrbən/, **Pope** (1568–1644). His reign (1623–44) was marked by diplomatic activity, reform of Church affairs, and lavish artistic and architectural patronage. Real name **Maffeo Barberini**

urban blues *n.* blues music that has a stronger beat than country blues, often played with electric instruments and featuring songs about life in the city (*takes a singular verb*)

urbane /ur báyn/ (**-baner, -banest**) *adj.* showing sophistication, refinement, or courtesy [Mid-16thC. Directly or via Old French *urbaine* 'urban', from Latin *urbanus* (see URBAN). The modern meaning evolved from 'urban' because city life was associated with sophistication.] —**urbanely** *adv.* —**urbaneness** *n.*

urban guerrilla *n.* sb who lives in a city and carries out violent acts there to further a political cause

urbanise *vt.* = urbanize

urbanism /úrbənizzəm/ *n.* **1.** CITY LIFE the typical way of life of people who live in a city or town **2.** STUDY OF CITIES the study of life in cities and towns

urbanite /úrbə nīt/ *n.* sb who lives in a city or town

urbanity /ur bánnəti/ *n.* SOPHISTICATION the quality of being sophisticated, refined, or courteous ■ **urbanities** *npl.* COURTESY polite or courteous actions [Mid-16thC. Directly or via French *urbanité* from Latin *urbanitas*, from *urbanus* (see URBAN).]

urbanize /úrbə nīz/ (**-izes, -izing, -ized**), **urbanise** (**-ises, -ising, -ised**) *vt.* **1.** MAKE AREA INTO TOWN to make an area of countryside or villages into a town or part of one

2. CAUSE COUNTRY PEOPLE TO BECOME URBAN to cause people who live in the countryside to migrate to a town or city **3. MAKE SB URBAN** to accustom sb to living in a town or city rather than in the country —**urbanization** /úrbə nī záysh'n/ n.

urban myth n. a bizarre and untrue story that circulates in a society through being presented to people as sth that actually happened, usually to a friend or relative of sb the speaker knows

urban planning n. US = **town planning** —**urban planner** n.

urban renewal n. the redevelopment of urban areas that have become run down or impoverished, by demolishing or renovating old buildings or building new ones

urban sprawl n. the expansion of an urban area into areas of countryside that surround it

urbi et orbi /úrbi et áwrbi/ adv. a phrase used in a papal blessing, meaning 'to the city of Rome and to the world' [From Latin]

URC n., abbr. United Reformed Church

urceolate /úrssi ələt, -layt/ adj. shaped like an urn or pitcher, with a swollen middle and narrowing top [Mid-18thC. Formed from Latin *urceolus*, literally 'little pitcher', from *urceus* 'pitcher'.]

urchin /úrchin/ n. **1. MISCHIEVOUS CHILD** a mischievous child, especially a young one who is unkempt in appearance **2. SEA URCHIN** a sea urchin **3.** *UKdial* **ZOOL HEDGEHOG** a hedgehog [13thC. Via Old Northern French *herichon* from, ultimately, Latin *(h)ericius* 'hedgehog', from *er*.]

Urdu /óor doo, úr doo/ n. **LANG** the official language of Pakistan, spoken also in Bangladesh and in parts of India. It belongs to the Indic group of Indo-European languages and is closely related to Hindi. Urdu is spoken by about 40 million people. [Late 18thC. Via Persian and Urdu (*zabān i*) *urdū* '(language of the) camp', from, ultimately, Turkish *ordū* 'camp' (source of English *horde*).] —**Urdu** adj.

-ure suffix. **1.** process or condition, or sth resulting from an action ○ *licensure* ○ *erasure* **2.** office or function, or a body performing a particular function ○ *prefecture* ○ *legislature* [Via Old French from Latin *-ura*]

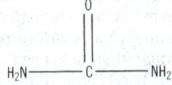

Urea

urea /yoo reé ə, yoóri ə/ n. a nitrogenous compound found in the urine of mammals and produced through protein decomposition. It is also produced synthetically and used in fertilizer, feeds, and in resin manufacturing. Formula: $CO(NH_2)_2$. [Early 19thC. From modern Latin, an alteration of French *urée*, from Old French *urine* (see URINE).] —**ureal** adj.

urea-formaldehyde resin n. a resin made from urea and formaldehyde, used in making electrical fittings and in cavity insulation

urease /yoóri ayss, -ayz/ n. an enzyme occurring in some bacteria and seeds, e.g. soya beans, that aids in the breakdown of urea to produce carbon dioxide and ammonia [Late 19thC. Coined from UREA + -ASE.]

urediniospore n. = **uredospore** [Early 20thC. Coined from UREDINIUM + SPORE.]

uredinium /yoóri dínni əm/ (plural **-a** /-ni ə/), **uredium** /yoóri di əm/ (plural **-a**), **uredosorus** /yoo reédō sáwrəss/ (plural **-i** /-rī/) n. a reddish or black mass of spores produced on a plant by a rust fungus [Early 20thC. Coined from Latin *uredin-*, stem of *uredo* (see UREDO), + -IUM.]

uredo /yoo reédō/ (plural **-dines** /-di neez/) n. = **urticaria** [Early 18thC. From Latin, from *urere* 'to burn'.]

uredosorus n. = **uredinium** [Early 20thC. Formed from UREDO.]

uredospore /yoo reédō spawr/, **urediniospore** /yoóri dínni ə spawr/ n. a reddish unicellular spore that develops in the uredinia of rust fungi

ureide /yoóri īd/ n. an acyl derivative of urea

uremia n. US = **uraemia**

ureotelic /yoóri ə téllik/ adj. producing nitrogen-containing waste in the form of urea [Early 20thC. Coined from UREA + TELIC.] —**ureotelism** n.

ureter /yoóritər/ n. either of a pair of ducts that carry urine from the kidneys to the bladder in mammals or to the common cavity for wastes (**cloaca**) in lower vertebrate animals [Late 16thC. Via modern Latin from Greek *ourētēr*, from *ourein* 'to urinate', from *ouron* 'urine' (see URINE).] —**ureteral** /yoo reétərəl/ adj. —**ureteric** /yoóri térrik/ adj.

urethane /yoóri thayn/, **urethan** /yoóri thán/ n. **1. COLOURLESS CRYSTALLINE COMPOUND** a colourless odourless crystalline compound, the ethyl ester of carbamic ester, used in solvents, pesticides, and pharmaceuticals. Formula: $C_3H_7NO_2$. **2. ESTER OF CARBAMIC ACID** any ester of carbamic acid other than the ethyl ester **3.** = **polyurethane** [Mid-19thC. Coined from modern Latin *urea* + English ETHANE.]

urethra /yoo reéthrə/ (plural **-thras** or **-thrae** /-ree/) n. the tube in mammals that carries urine from the bladder out of the body and in the male also carries semen during ejaculation [Mid-17thC. Via late Latin from Greek *ourēthra*, from Greek *ourein* 'to urinate', from *ouron* 'urine' (see URINE).] —**urethral** adj.

urethritis /yoóri thrítiss/ n. inflammation of the urethra, usually caused by infection [Early 19thC. Coined from URETHRA + -ITIS.] —**urethritic** /yoóri thríttik/ adj.

urethroscope /yoo reéthrə skōp/ n. a medical instrument for examining the inside of the urethra, consisting of a fine flexible tube fitted with lenses and a light [Mid-19thC. Coined from URETHRA+ -SCOPE.] —**urethroscopic** /-skóppik/ adj. —**urethroscopy** /yoóri thróskəpi/ n.

uretic /yoo réttik/ adj. relating to, involving, or in urine [Mid-19thC. Via late Latin *ureticus* from Greek *ourētikos* from *ourein* 'to urinate', from *ouron* 'urine' (see URINE).]

urge /urj/ vt. (**urges, urging, urged**) **1. ADVISE SB STRONGLY** to advise sb strongly to do sth ○ *urged his firm to reconsider* **2. ADVOCATE STH EARNESTLY** to recommend or advise sth earnestly and with persistence ○ *urging restraint* **3. ENCOURAGE SB OR STH** to encourage, drive, or force sb or sth to do sth ○ *could hear the crowd urging her on* **4. EXCITE SB** to excite or stimulate sb (*archaic literary*) ■ n. **STRONG NEED** a strong need, wish, or impulse to do sth ○ *the urge to travel* [Mid-16thC. From Latin *urgere* 'to push, press, compel'.] —**urger** n.

urgency /úrjənssi/ (plural **-cies**) n. **1. IMMEDIATE NEED FOR ACTION** the fact or state of requiring immediate action ○ *a matter of urgency* **2. IMMEDIATE ATTENTION** immediate attention or speed **3. EARNESTNESS** a quality that conveys earnestness or the need for doing sth quickly **4. PRESSING NEED** a pressing and immediate need [Mid-16thC. Formed from French *urgent* (see URGENT).]

urgent /úrjənt/ adj. **1. REQUIRING IMMEDIATE ACTION** calling for immediate action or attention **2. SHOWING EARNESTNESS** showing earnestness or the desire for sth to be done quickly [15thC. Via French from the present participle stem of Latin *urgere* (see URGE).] —**urgently** adv.

-urgy suffix. technique or art of working with sth ○ *metallurgy* [Via modern Latin *-urgia* from, ultimately, Greek *-ourgos* 'working', from *ergon* 'work' (see ERG)]

-uria suffix. **1.** the condition of having a particular substance in the urine ○ *aciduria* **2.** the condition of having a particular kind of urine ○ *polyuria* [Via modern Latin from, ultimately, Greek *ouron* 'urine']

Uriah /yoo rí ə/ n. in the Bible, a Hittite officer purposely killed in battle to allow King David to marry his wife, Bathsheba (2 Samuel 11:2–16)

uric /yoórik/ adj. relating to, involving, or found in urine [Late 18thC. Formed from Old French *urine* 'urine' (see URINE).]

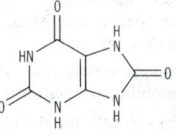

Uric acid

uric acid n. a slightly soluble acid present in urine and blood, produced by the body's breakdown of waste nitrogenous substances. Crystals of uric acid accumulate in the joints of people affected by gout. Formula: $C_5H_4N_4O_3$.

uridine /yoóri deen/ n. a basic compound, pyrimidine nucleoside, that plays an important role in the metabolism of carbohydrates and consists of ribose and uracil. Formula: $C_9H_{12}N_2O_6$. [Early 20thC. Coined from URACIL + -IDINE.]

Urim and Thummim /yoórim ənd thúmmim/ npl. oracles on the breastplate of the high priest of ancient Israel [*Urim* is an Anglicization of Hebrew *'ūrīm*; *Thummim* is an Anglicization of Hebrew *tummīm*]

urin- prefix. = **urino-** (used before vowels)

urinal /yoó rín'l, yoórin'l/ n. **1. RECEPTACLE FOR MEN TO URINATE INTO** a receptacle that is fixed to a wall and plumbed in, used for men to urinate into **2. PLACE WITH URINALS** a room or building in which there are urinals **3. PORTABLE CONTAINER FOR URINE** a container used to transport urine [13thC. Via French from late Latin *urinalis* 'urinary', from Latin *urina* (see URINE).]

urinalysis /yoóri nálləssiss/ (plural **-ses** /-seez/), **uranalysis** /yoórə nálləssiss/ n. analysis of the physical, chemical, and microbiological properties of urine, carried out to help diagnose disease, monitor treatment, or detect the presence of a specific substance [Late 19thC. Blend of URINE and ANALYSIS.]

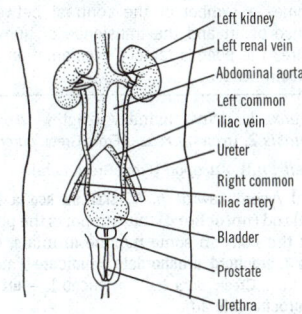

Urinary: Human male urinary system

urinary /yoórinəri/ adj. relating to, involving, or affecting urine or the organs that form and discharge urine [Late 16thC. Formed from Latin *urina* (see URINE).]

urinary bladder n. an expanding muscular sac in mammals and some other vertebrates in which urine collects before it is discharged from the body through the urethra

urinate /yoóri nayt/ (**-nates, -nating, -nated**) vi. to discharge urine from the body [Late 16thC. From the past participle stem of medieval Latin *urinare*, from Latin *urina* (see URINE).] —**urination** /yoóri náysh'n/ n. —**urinative** /yoórinətiv/ adj. —**urinator** n.

urine /yoórin/ n. the yellowish liquid containing waste products that is excreted by the kidneys and discharged through the urethra. In birds and reptiles it is semisolid. [14thC. Directly and via Old French from Latin *urina*.]

uriniferous /yoóri nífferəss/ adj. used to describe a

tube that carries urine, especially the tubules of the kidneys [Mid-18thC. Coined from URINE + -FEROUS.]

urino- *prefix.* urine, urinary ○ *urinometer* [From Latin *urina* (see URINE)]

urinogenital *adj.* = urogenital

urinometer /yoŏri nómmitǝr/ *n.* a hydrometer for measuring the specific gravity of urine [Mid-20thC. Coined from URINO- + -METER.]

urinous /yoŏrinǝss/, **urinose** /yoŏrinōz, -nōss/ *adj.* relating to, resembling, or containing urine

URL *n.* an address identifying the location of a file on the Internet, consisting of the protocol, the computer on which the file is located, and the file's location on that computer. Full form **Uniform Resource Locator**

Urmia, Lake /úrmi ǝ/ large salt lake in northwestern Iran, west of Tabriz. Area: 4,700 sq. km/1,815 sq. mi.

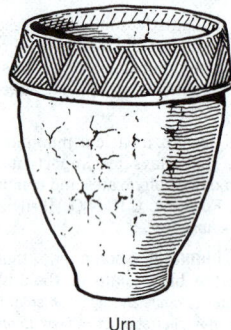

Urn

urn /urn/ *n.* **1. ORNAMENTAL VASE WITH PEDESTAL** an ornamental vase that usually has a foot or a pedestal **2. VASE FOR SB'S ASHES** a sealed vase in which the ashes of sb who has died and been cremated are kept **3. VESSEL FOR HOT DRINKS** a closed vessel in which a hot drink, especially tea or coffee, is made in a large quantity and poured out through a tap **4. SPORE-PRODUCING PART OF MOSS CAPSULE** the part of a moss capsule where spores are produced [14thC. From Latin *urna*.]

---------- **WORD KEY: CULTURAL NOTE** ----------
Ode on a Grecian Urn, a poem by English writer John Keats (1819). It describes the poet's reaction to a Greek vase decorated with reliefs of joyful rural scenes. The urn becomes a symbol of the contrast between the permanence of art and the transience of human life, and inspires the poem's famous proclamation 'Beauty is truth, truth beauty'.

---

uro-[1] *prefix.* **1.** urine, urinary tract ○ *uroscopy* ○ *urolithiasis* **2.** urea ○ *urease* [From Greek *ouron* 'urine']

uro-[2] *prefix.* tail ○ *uropod* [From Greek *oura*]

urochord /yoŏrō kawrd/ *n.* **1. SKELETAL ROD** a flexible skeletal rod (**notochord**) that supports the posterior part of the body in some marine animals, e.g. sea squirts **2. urochord, urochordate** = tunicate [Late 19thC. Coined from Greek *oura* 'tail' + CHORD.] —**urochordal** *adj.* —**urochordate** *adj.*

urochrome /yoŏrō krōm/ *n.* a yellow pigment that gives urine its normal colour [Mid-19thC. Coined from URO- + CHROME.]

urodele /yoŏrō deel/ *n.* an amphibian that has a tail throughout its adult life, a long body, and short limbs, e.g. the salamander or newt. Order: Caudata and Urodela. [Mid-19thC. Directly or formed via French *urodèle* from modern Latin *Urodela,* the order name, from Greek *oura* 'tail' + *dēlos* 'visible'.] —**urodele** *adj.*

urogenital /yoŏrō jénnit'l/, **urinogenital** /yoŏrinō jénnit'l/ *adj.* relating to or involving the organs of the urinary tract and the reproductive organs when considered together [Mid-19thC. Coined from URO- + GENITAL.]

urogenous /yoŏ rójjǝnǝss/ *adj.* producing, obtained from, or formed in urine

urogram /yoŏrō gram/ *n.* an X-ray picture of the urinary tract or some part of it

urography /yoŏ róggrǝfi/ *n.* X-ray photography of all or part of the urinary tract. It is performed after a

patient has been given an opaque substance that highlights the various structures, in order to locate and diagnose urinary disorders. —**urographic** /yoŏrō gráffik/ *adj.*

urokinase /yoŏrō kĭ nays, -nayss/ *n.* an enzyme in blood and urine, produced by the kidneys, that catalyses the conversion of plasminogen to plasmin and is used medicinally to dissolve blood clots [Mid-20thC. Coined from URO- + KINASE.]

urol. *abbr.* **1.** urological **2.** urology

urolith /yoŏrōlith/ *n.* a stony mass (**calculus**) in the urinary tract —**urolithic** /yoŏrō líthik/ *adj.*

urolithiasis /yoŏrōli thí ǝssiss/ *n.* the formation or presence of stony masses in the urinary tract, or the medical condition resulting from this [Mid-19thC. Coined from URO- + LITHIASIS.]

urology /yoŏ rólläji/ *n.* a branch of medicine that deals with the study and treatment of disorders of the urinary tract in women and the urogenital system in men —**urologic** /yoŏrō lójjik/ *adj.* —**urologist** /yoŏ rólläjist/ *n.*

uropod /yoŏrō pod/ *n.* either of a pair of flat appendages on the last abdominal segment of a crustacean, e.g. a lobster or shrimp [Late 19thC. Coined from Greek *oura* 'tail' + -POD.] —**uropodal** /yoŏ róppǝd'l/ *adj.*

uropygial gland /yoŏrō píjji ǝl-/ *n.* a gland in the skin at the base of the tail of most birds that secretes an oil used while preening to condition and waterproof their feathers [*Uropygial* formed from UROPYGIUM.]

uropygium /yoŏrō píjji ǝm/ *n.* the fleshy hindmost part of a bird's body from which the tail feathers grow [Late 18thC. Via medieval Latin from Greek *ouropugion.*] —**uropygial** *adj.*

uroscopy /yoŏ róskǝpi/ *n.* (*plural* **-pies**) the medical examination of urine in order to make a diagnosis —**uroscopic** /yoŏrō skóppik/ *adj.* —**uroscopist** /yoŏ róskǝpist/ *n.*

urostyle /yoŏrō stĭl/ *n.* a fused flexible structure at the end of the spinal column of a toad, frog, or similar amphibian [Late 19thC. Coined from Greek *oura* 'tail' + Greek *stylos* 'pillar'.]

-urous *suffix.* having a particular kind of tail ○ *anurous* [Formed from Greek *oura* 'tail']

Urquhart /úrkǝt/, **Sir Thomas** (1611?–60) Scottish writer and soldier. A fighter for the royalist cause in the Civil War, he also wrote on a wide range of subjects and translated Rabelais.

Ursa Major /úrssǝ-/ *n.* a conspicuous constellation in the sky of the northern hemisphere, near the North Pole, that contains the seven stars forming the Plough

Ursa Minor *n.* a small constellation in the sky of the northern hemisphere that contains the North Star

ursine /úr sĭn/ *adj.* **1. TYPICAL OF BEARS** relating to or typical of bears, or belonging to the bear family **2. HAVING CHARACTERISTICS OF BEARS** having the characteristics usually associated with bears [Mid-16thC. From Latin *ursinus,* from *ursus* 'a bear'.]

Ursuline /úrssyoŏ lĭn/ *n.* a member of a Roman Catholic order of nuns founded by St Angela Merici in Brescia, Italy, in the 16th century and dedicated to teaching [Late 17thC. Formed from *Ursula,* the name of the patron saint of the order's founder.] —**Ursuline** *adj.*

urticaceous /úrti káyshǝss/ *adj.* used to describe a plant that belongs to the nettle family [Mid-19thC. Formed from Latin *urtica* 'a nettle', from *urere* 'to burn'.]

urticant /úrtikǝnt/ *adj.* **STINGING** stinging or causing itching ■ *n.* **AGENT CAUSING ITCHING** sth that stings or causes itching [Late 19thC. From the present participle stem of medieval Latin *urticare* (see URTICATE).]

urticaria /úrti káiri ǝ/ *n.* a skin rash, usually occurring as an allergic reaction, that is marked by itching and small pale or red swellings and often lasts for a few days (*technical*) [Late 18thC. From modern Latin, from *urtica* 'a nettle'.] —**urticarial** *adj.* —**urticarious** *adj.*

urticate /úrti kayt/ *vi.* (**-cates, -cating, -cated**) **HAVE OR CAUSE URTICARIA** to be affected by or cause urticaria ■ *adj.* **CAUSING SMALL SWELLINGS AND ITCHING** producing weals and itching [Mid-19thC. From the past participle stem

of medieval Latin *urticare* 'to sting', from Latin *urtica* 'a nettle'.]

urtication /úrti káysh'n/ *n.* **1. DEVELOPMENT OF URTICARIA** the process by which sb develops the condition urticaria **2. ITCHY SENSATION** an intensely itchy or burning sensation

Uru. *abbr.* Uruguay

Uruguay

Uruguay[1] /yoŏrǝ gwĭ/ republic in southeastern South America, south of Brazil, bordering the Atlantic Ocean. Language: Spanish. Currency: Uruguayan peso. Capital: Montevideo. Population: 3,238,952 (1996). Area: 176,215 sq. km/68,037 sq. mi. Official name **Oriental Republic of Uruguay** —**Uruguayan** *n., adj.*

Uruguay[2] river in southeastern South America, rising in southern Brazil and entering the Atlantic Ocean through the Río de la Plata. Length: 1,600 km/990 mi.

Urumqi /oŏ roŏmchi/ capital city of Xinjiang Uygur Autonomous Region, northwestern China. Population: 1,046,898 (1991).

urus /yoŏrǝss/ *n.* = **aurochs** [Early 17thC. Via Latin from Greek *ouros.*]

urushiol /oŏ roŏshi ol, oo roŏshi ol/ *n.* an oily poisonous irritant found in the resin and on the leaves and stems of poison ivy, the lacquer tree, and some related plants [Early 20thC. Coined from Japanese *urushi* 'lacquer' + English -OL.]

us /uss, ǝss/ *pron.* **1. SELF AND OTHER OR OTHERS** a pronoun used to refer to both yourself and another person or other people (*used after a verb or preposition*) ○ *He told us to go away.* ○ *This problem affects all of us.* **2. ROYAL US** used by a king or queen, or the editor of a newspaper, to mean 'me' (*formal*) ○ *It gives us great pleasure to declare this building open.* **3. OURSELVES** ourselves (*regional informal*) (*used after a verb as the indirect object*) ○ *We'd better find us a place to sleep.* ■ *det.* **OUR** our (*regional nonstandard*) [Old English *ūs,* from, ultimately, prehistoric German]

---------- **WORD KEY: REGIONAL NOTE** ----------
In parts of northern England, **us** is used as both a pronoun (*They like us.*) and as a possessive adjective (*We sat down to have us tea when the phone rang.*). This parallels the widespread use of *me* as an adjective, as in *Where's me book?,* although this is normally regarded as a mispronunciation of *my.*

US, U.S. *abbr.* United States

u.s. *abbr.* **1.** ubi supra **2.** ut supra

U/S *abbr.* unserviceable

USA, U.S.A. *abbr.* United States of America

usable /yoŏzǝb'l/, **useable** *adj.* capable of being used —**usability** /yoŏzǝ bílläti/ *n.* —**usableness** /yoŏzǝb'lnǝss/ *n.* —**usably** *adv.*

USAF, U.S.A.F. *abbr.* United States Air Force

usage /yoŏssij, yoŏz-/ *n.* **1. ACT OR WAY OF USING STH** the act of using sth, the way sth is used, or how much sth is used **2. ACCEPTED PRACTICE** a customary and generally accepted practice or procedure **3. WAY LANGUAGE IS ACTUALLY USED** the way in which words and phrases are actually used in speech or writing **4. EXAMPLE OF LANGUAGE USE** an example of a particular use of language **5. TREATMENT OF STH** the handling or treatment of sth [13thC. Via Old French from, ultimately, Latin *usus* (see USE).]

usance /yōoz'nss/ *n.* the customary length of time allowed for payment of a bill of exchange in foreign commerce [14thC. Via Old French from, ultimately, assumed Vulgar Latin *usare* 'to keep on using', from Latin *uti* (see USE).]

USDAW /úz daw/ *n., abbr.* Union of Shop, Distributive, and Allied Workers

use[1] *v.* /yōoz/ (**uses, using, used**) **1.** *vt.* EMPLOY STH FOR SOME PURPOSE to employ sth for some purpose or to put sth into action or service ○ *use a hammer* **2.** *vt.* DO STH HABITUALLY to do sth habitually ○ *use common sense* **3.** *vt.* CONSUME STH to expend or consume sth, often until none is left ○ *All of the space on the disk has been used.* **4.** *vt.* MANIPULATE OR EXPLOIT SB to exploit or manipulate sb as a means to an end ○ *the type of person who uses others* **5.** *vti.* CONSUME DRUGS OR ALCOHOL REGULARLY to consume sth regularly, especially drugs or alcohol **6.** *vt.* BEHAVE TOWARDS SB OR STH to behave towards sb or sth in a particular way ○ *used his employees poorly* **7.** *vt.* BENEFIT FROM STH to benefit or get satisfaction from sth ○ *I could use a good night's sleep.* ■ *n.* /yōoss/ **1.** ACT OF USING STH the act of using sth for a particular purpose ○ *skilled in the use of computers* **2.** STATE OF BEING EMPLOYED FOR STH the state or fact of being employed for a particular purpose ○ *no longer in use* **3.** WAY OF EMPLOYING STH a way of employing sth ○ *We admired the artist's use of colour.* **4.** HABITUAL OR CUSTOMARY USAGE sth done habitually or customarily **5.** RIGHT TO USE STH the right to use sth or the benefit of using sth **6.** ABILITY TO USE STH the power or ability to use sth **7.** PURPOSE the purpose of sth ○ *Put your education to good use.* **8.** USEFULNESS the quality of being useful **9.** THE NEED TO USE STH the occasion or need to use sth **10.** LAW BENEFIT OF PROPERTY the benefit or profit of property held by one person for another **11.** LAW LEGAL ENJOYMENT OF PROPERTY the legal enjoyment of property in its employment, occupation, or practice **12.** RELIG MODIFIED LOCAL LITURGY a modified liturgical form or observance practised in a particular church or religious order [13thC. Via Old French *user* 'to use', from, ultimately, Latin *usus*, the past participle of *uti* (source of English *utensil*).] ◇ **have no use for sb** *or* **sth 1.** to have no need or purpose for sb or sth **2.** to have no liking or respect for sb or sth (*informal*) ◇ **make use of** to exploit or manipulate sb as a means to an end ◇ **what's the use?** used to suggest that doing sth is pointless (*informal*)

WORD KEY: USAGE

See Usage note at *utilize*.

WORD KEY: SYNONYMS
---

use, employ, make use of, utilize

CORE MEANING: to put sth to use

use a general and widely used word, appropriate in most contexts to talk about the function or purpose sth serves; **employ** a more formal word meaning to use sth such as a tool or a resource in a particular way; **make use of** to use what is readily available, especially in a sensible or economical way; **utilize** a formal word meaning the same as *use*, often used to talk about using sth particularly effectively and practically.

use up *vt.* to expend or consume sth, often until none is left

use[2] /yōoss/ *vi.* used to say that sb or sth habitually or usually did sth ○ *We used to eat out more often.* ○ *He used not to be so grumpy.* ○ *Did you use to make your own bread?*

useable *adj.* = usable

used /yōozd/ *adj.* **1.** PREVIOUSLY OWNED having been owned by sb else **2.** EXPENDED having been put to a purpose or expended

used to *adj.* accustomed to or familiar with sth ○ *We're not used to this weather.*

useful /yōosf'l/ *adj.* **1.** SERVING A PURPOSE capable of being put to use or serving some purpose **2.** HAVING VALUE having value or benefit, or bringing some advantage —**usefully** *adv.* —**usefulness** *n.*

useless /yōossless/ *adj.* **1.** UNUSABLE not able to be used **2.** UNSUCCESSFUL unsuccessful, or unlikely to be worthwhile **3.** INEPT not able to do sth properly (*informal*) —**uselessly** *adv.* —**uselessness** *n.*

Usenet /yōoz net/ *n.* a worldwide system that uses the Internet and other networks to distribute articles of news or information

user /yōozer/ *n.* **1.** PERSON OR THING THAT USES a person or thing that uses sth ○ *computer users* **2.** DRUG TAKER sb who takes illegal drugs (*informal*) **3.** LAW EXERCISE OF RIGHT the exercise of a right to do or use sth

user-friendly (**user-friendlier, user-friendliest**) *adj.* easy to operate, understand, or deal with —**user-friendliness** *n.*

user group *n.* a group of people with common interests in some aspect of computer hardware or software who share information among themselves and with the hardware manufacturer or software developer

user interface *n.* the part of the design of a computer or other device or program that accepts commands from and returns information to the user

usher /úsher/ *n.* **1.** SB WHO SEATS PEOPLE sb who escorts people to their seats in a place such as a theatre or church **2.** DOORKEEPER sb who is in charge of the door of a court, hall, or chamber **3.** COURT OFFICIAL an official in an English law court whose duty is to keep order **4.** OFFICER WALKING BEFORE SB OF RANK an officer who walks in front of people of rank in a procession or who introduces strangers at formal events ■ *v.* (**-ers, -ering, -ered**) **1.** *vt.* ESCORT OR SEAT SB to escort or conduct sb to a place or from a place **2.** *vi.* ACT AS USHER to act as an usher [14thC. Via Anglo-Norman *usser* from, ultimately, Latin *ostarius* 'door-keeper', from *ostium* 'door'.] **usher in** *vt.* to introduce or lead up to sth

usherette /úshə rét/ *n.* a woman or girl who escorts people to their seats in a theatre, cinema, or church (*dated*)

Usk /usk/ river in southeastern Wales. It rises in Brecon Beacons National Park and flows to the Severn Estuary at Newport. Length: 97 km/60 mi.

USM *abbr.* **1.** STOCK EXCH unlisted securities market **2.** underwater-to-surface missile

USN *abbr.* United States Navy

usnea /ússni ə, úzni ə/ (*plural* **-ae** /-ni ee/ *or* **-as**) *n.* a common lichen with a hanging body in which the root, stem, and leaf are not distinguished. Genus: *Usnea*. [Late 16thC. Via modern and medieval Latin from Arabic and Persian *ušna* 'moss, lichen'.]

USO *abbr.* United Services Organization

USP *n.* a characteristic of a product that makes it different from all similar products (*used in advertising and marketing*) Full form **unique selling proposition**

usquebaugh /úskwi baw/ *n.* Scotland, Ireland Scotch or Irish whisky (*archaic or literary*) [Late 16thC. From Gaelic *uisge beatha*, literally 'water of life'.]

USS *abbr.* **1.** United States Senate **2.** United States Ship

USSR *abbr.* Union of Soviet Socialist Republics

AKG London

Sir Peter Ustinov

Ustinov /yōosti nof/, **Sir Peter** (b. 1921) British writer, director and actor. A noted raconteur, he wrote or directed many plays and films.

usu. *abbr.* usually

usual /yōozhoo əl/ *adj.* NORMAL OR TYPICAL normal, customary, or typical of sb or sth ■ *n.* **1.** ORDINARY WAY the ordinary, normal, or customary way of things **2.** WHAT SB CUSTOMARILY HAS what sb customarily has, especially a drink in a bar (*informal*) [14thC. Directly or via Old French *usuel* from late Latin *usualis*, from *usus* (see USE).] —**usually** *adv.* —**usualness** *n.* ◇ **as usual** in a normal or customary way

---
WORD KEY: SYNONYMS
---

usual, customary, habitual, routine, wonted

CORE MEANING: often done, used, bought or consumed

usual a general word used to describe sth that is very commonly done, used, bought, or consumed (and therefore predictable); **customary** a more formal word meaning the same as *usual*; **habitual** used to suggest that sth has been done so often or repeatedly that the behaviour or practice has become difficult to vary, change, or stop; **routine** used to describe sth that is done commonly or often, especially to suggest that it has become tedious or monotonous; **wonted** a very formal or literary word used in the same way as *usual* or *habitual*.

usufruct /yōozyōo frukt, yōoss-/ *n.* the legal right to use and enjoy the advantages or profits of another's property [Early 17thC. From Latin *usufructus*, a variant of *ususfructus*, literally 'use (and) enjoyment', from *usus* (see USE) + *fructus* 'enjoyment' (source also of English *fruit*).]

usufructuary /yōozyōo frúktyoo əri, yōoss-/ (*plural* **-ies**) *n.* sb who is entitled by usufruct to the use of another's property —**usufructuary** *adj.*

usurer /yōozherər/ *n.* sb who loans money to other people and charges them exorbitant or unlawful interest on it [13thC. Via Anglo-Norman from, ultimately, late Latin *usurarius*, from Latin 'that pays interest', from *usura* (see USURY).]

usurp /yōo zúrp/ (**usurps, usurping, usurped**) *vti.* use sth without the right to do so [14thC. Via Old French *usurper* from Latin *usurpare* 'to seize for use', from, perhaps, *usus* 'use' (see USE) + *rapere* 'to seize' (source of English *rape*).] —**usurpation** /yōo zur páysh'n/ *n.* —**usurpative** /yōo zúrpətiv/ *adj.* —**usurper** /-ər/ *n.* —**usurpingly** *adv.*

usury /yōozhəri/ (*plural* **-ries**) *n.* **1.** LENDING AT EXORBITANT INTEREST the lending of money at an exorbitant rate of interest **2.** EXORBITANT INTEREST an exorbitant rate of interest [14thC. Via medieval Anglo-Norman *usurie* from, ultimately, Latin *usura* 'use of money lent', hence 'interest', from *usus* 'use' (source also of English *use*).] —**usurious** /yōo zhóori əss/ *adj.* —**usuriously** *adv.* —**usuriousness** *n.*

USW *abbr.* RADIO ultrashort wave

ut /ut, oot/ *n.* MUSIC the note C, equivalent to 'doh' in the solmization system. It is the first note of the hexachord system devised by Guido d'Arezzo. [14thC. From Latin, the syllable sung to this note in a hymn to Saint John the Baptist.]

UT, **Ut.** *abbr.* **1.** universal time **2.** Utah

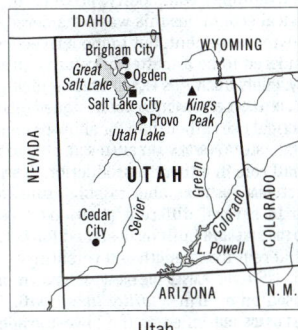

Utah

Utah /yōot aa, -aw/ state in the western United States, bordered by Idaho, Wyoming, Colorado, Arizona, and Nevada. Capital: Salt Lake City. Population: 2,059,148 (1997). Area: 219,902 sq. km/84,904 sq. mi. —**Utahan** *n., adj.*

Utamaro /ōotə maárō/ (1753–1806) Japanese artist. He was noted for his delicate portraits of women in teahouses, shops, and brothels. Full name **Kitagawa Utamaro**

UTC *abbr.* universal time coordinated

ut dict. /út díkt/ *abbr.* as directed (*used on prescriptions*) [Latin *ut dictum*]

ute /yōot/ *n.* ANZ a pick-up truck (*informal*) [Mid-20thC. Shortening of *utility*.]

Ute /yōot, yōoti/ (*plural* **Ute** *or* **Utes**) *n.* **1.** PEOPLES MEMBER OF NATIVE N AMERICAN PEOPLE a member of a Native North American people who originally lived in Colorado, Utah, and New Mexico **2.** LANG UTE LANGUAGE the Uto-

Aztecan language of the Ute people. About 2,500 people speak Ute. [Early 19thC. Shortening of Spanish *Yuta*, an Indian language.]

utensil /yoo ténss'l/ *n.* a tool or container, especially one used in a kitchen [14thC. Via Old French *utensile* from, ultimately, Latin *utensilis* 'usable', from *uti* 'to use' (source also of English *use*).]

uteri plural of **uterus**

uterine /yóotə rīn/ *adj.* **1. OF UTERUS** relating to, in, or affecting the womb **2. HAVING SAME MOTHER** having the same mother but a different father ○ *a uterine brother* [15thC. From late Latin *uterinus*, literally 'from the same womb', from Latin *uterus* 'womb' (see UTERUS).]

uterus /yóotərəss/ (*plural* **-uses** *or* **-i** /-rī/) *n.* **1. WOMB** a hollow muscular organ in the pelvic cavity of female mammals, in which the embryo is nourished and develops before birth (*technical*) **2. ORGAN SIMILAR TO MAMMALIAN WOMB** a structure in some animals that is similar to the mammalian womb, in which eggs or young develop [17thC. From Latin, 'belly, womb'. Ultimately from an Indo-European word that is possibly the ancestor of Greek *hustera* (source of English *hysteria*).]

Utica /yóotikə/ city in eastern New York State, on the Mohawk River, east of Syracuse. Population: 61,368 (1996).

util. *abbr.* utility

utilise *vt.* = **utilize**

utilitarian /yoo tílli táiri ən/ *adj.* **1. BELIEVING VALUE LIES IN USEFULNESS** relating to, typical of, or advocating the doctrine that value is measured in terms of usefulness **2. PRACTICAL** designed primarily for practical use rather than beauty ■ *n.* **BELIEVER IN UTILITARIANISM** sb who believes in the doctrine of utilitarianism

utilitarianism /yoo tílli táiri ənizəm/ *n.* **1. ETHICAL DOCTRINE** the ethical doctrine that the greatest happiness of the greatest number should be the criterion of the virtue of action **2. UTILITARIAN QUALITY** the quality of being designed primarily for practical use rather than beauty

utility /yoo tílləti/ *n.* (*plural* **-ties**) **1. USEFULNESS** the quality or state of being useful for sth **2. STH USEFUL** sth that serves a useful purpose **3.** = **public utility 4. SERVICE PROVIDED BY PUBLIC UTILITY** a service such as electricity, gas, or water that is provided by a public utility **5. SATISFACTION DERIVED FROM CONSUMPTION** the amount of satisfaction or pleasure that sb gains from consuming a commodity, product, or service. In classical economics this was considered to be an absolute measurement, but in modern economics it is considered to be a matter of relative preference. **6. utility, utility truck** *Aus* **PICK-UP TRUCK** a pick-up truck ■ *adj.* **1. INTENDED FOR PRACTICAL USE** designed or intended for practical use rather than for show or appearance **2.** THEATRE **ABLE TO PERFORM ANY SMALL ROLE** able to perform any small role in a theatre production **3.** SPORTS **ABLE TO PLAY SEVERAL POSITIONS** able to substitute for other players in several different positions **4.** *US, ANZ* **DESIGNED FOR STRENGTH** built or designed for performing tasks that require strength and versatility ○ *a utility truck* **5.** *US* AGRIC **RAISED FOR FARM USE** grown or raised to be used on a farm ○ *utility livestock* **6.** *US* AGRIC **OF LOWEST GRADE** classified as the lowest grade of beef by the US Government [14thC. Via French *utilité* from, ultimately, Latin *utilis* 'usable', from *uti* 'to use' (source also of English *use*).]

utility program *n.* a computer program that carries out routine tasks and supports the operation of the computer or another device, as compared to an application program

utility room *n.* a room in a house where there are large domestic appliances, e.g. a washing machine or boiler, and where many household tasks are done

utility truck *n. Aus* = **utility** *n.* 6

utility vehicle *n.* **1.** *US* **SPORT-UTILITY VEHICLE** a sport-utility vehicle **2.** *NZ* **PICK-UP TRUCK** a pick-up truck

utilize /yóoti līz/ (**-izes, -izing, -ized**), **utilise** (**-ises, -ising, -ised**) *vt.* to make use of or find a practical use for sth [Early 19thC. Via French *utiliser* from, ultimately, Latin *utilis* (see UTILITY).] —**utilizable** *adj.* —**utilization** /yóoti lī záysh'n/ *n.* —**utilizer** /yóoti līzər/ *n.*

WORD KEY: USAGE

utilize or **use**? **Utilize** means 'to use in a practical or effective way' and so it means sth more than **use**, which is the general all-purpose word. **Utilize** is common in technical applications: *The device utilizes a special solderless plug-in connection.* It can also refer to using things in unusual or unintended ways, as a more formal equivalent of 'make use of' : *When the fan belt broke we utilized an old pair of tights.* In business jargon and in other contexts **utilize** is often written when **use** is all that is intended, and this should be avoided: *Successful applicants will be able to utilize their skills and experience in this field.*

WORD KEY: SYNONYMS

See Synonyms at ***use***.

uti possidetis /yóo tī póssi deétiss/ *n.* INTERNAT LAW the principle in international law that land and property captured by belligerent parties in war remain their property unless a treaty rules otherwise (*formal*) [From late Latin, literally 'as you possess']

utmost /útmōst/, **uttermost** /úttərmōst/ *adj.* **1. AT THE EXTREMITY** at the most distant point or extremity **2. OF THE GREATEST DEGREE** of the greatest degree, number, or amount ■ *n.* **GREATEST DEGREE OR AMOUNT** the greatest degree, number, or amount of sth, especially the greatest effort that sb is capable of ○ *I did my utmost to persuade her.* [Old English *ūt(e)mest*, from an earlier form of English OUT + an earlier form of -MOST]

Uto-Aztecan /yóotō áz tekən/ *n.* **1.** LANG **N AND CENTRAL AMERICAN LANGUAGE FAMILY** a family of languages, including Ute and Nahuatl, spoken in the western United States and in Mexico **2.** PEOPLES **MEMBER OF AN UTO-AZTECAN PEOPLE** a member of one of the peoples who speak a language classified as Uto-Aztecan [*Uto* formed from UTE] —**Uto-Aztecan** *adj.*

utopia /yoo tōpi ə/, **Utopia** *n.* an ideal and perfect place or state, where everyone lives in harmony and everything is for the best [Mid-16thC. From modern Latin, 'imaginary island', first used in Sir Thomas More's *Utopia* (1516); literally, 'noplace', formed from Greek *ou* 'not' + *topos* 'place'.]

WORD KEY: CULTURAL NOTE

Utopia, a philosophical treatise by English writer and statesman Sir Thomas More (1516). It contrasts the moral decadence and disunity of contemporary Christian Europe with the tolerance and prosperity of More's imaginary ideal state of Utopia, which is run on secular, communist principles. More coined the state's name from the Greek words *ou* 'not' and *topos* 'place', literally meaning 'the land of nowhere'. The term itself has spawned a number of derivatives, such as *utopian*, *utopianism*, and *utopianist*.

utopian, **Utopian** *adj.* **1. IDEAL** belonging to or typical of an ideal perfect state or place **2. ADMIRABLE BUT IMPRACTICABLE** admirable but impracticable in real life **3. IMPRACTICALLY IDEALISTIC** tending to deal in admirable but impracticable ideas ■ *n.* **PROPOSER OF UTOPIAN REFORMS** sb who proposes or advocates visionary but impractical social or political reforms

utopianism /yoo tōpi ənizəm/, **Utopianism** *n.* **1. UTOPIAN IDEAS OR THEORIES** the principles, views, or aims of a utopian **2. BELIEF IN IDEAL SOCIETY** the belief that an ideal society can be achieved —**utopianist** *n.*

utopian socialism *n.* a form of socialism based on the belief that a socialist society can be brought about by peacefully persuading those in power to accept it

Utrecht /yóot rekt, -rekht, yoo trékt, -trékht/ historic university city in the central Netherlands. Population: 234,254 (1996).

utricle /yóotrik'l/, **utriculus** /yoo trí kyóoləss/ (*plural* **-li** /-lī/) *n.* **1.** ANAT **PART OF INNER EAR** the larger of two fluid-filled sacs in the labyrinth of the inner ear and into which the semicircular canals open **2.** BOT **BLADDER-SHAPED FRUIT** the bladder-shaped fruit of some plants [Mid-18thC. Directly or via French *utricule* from Latin *utriculus*, literally 'little leather bottle', from *uter* 'leather bottle'.] —**utricular** /yoo tríkyóolər/ *adj.* —**utriculate** /-layt/ *adj.*

Uttar Pradesh /óottər prə désh/ the most populous state in India, located in the northern part of the country, south of Nepal. Capital: Lucknow. Population: 139,112,287 (1991). Area: 294,413 sq. km/113,673 sq. mi.

utter[1] /úttər/ (**-ters, -tering, -tered**) *vt.* **1. SAY STH** to say or pronounce sth **2. EMIT STH AS VOCAL SOUND** to emit sth as a sound made by the voice **3. PUBLISH STH** to publish sth, e.g. in a book or newspaper ○ *You would not dare to utter this nonsense in print.* **4.** LAW **TO PUT STH INTO CIRCULATION** to put sth into circulation, especially counterfeit money or a forgery, in the pretence that it is genuine (*formal*) [14thC. From Middle Dutch *ūteren* 'to drive out, announce, speak', from Old Low German *ūt* 'out'.] —**utterable** *adj.* —**utterer** *n.*

utter[2] /úttər/ *adj.* at the most extreme point or of the highest degree [Old English *ūtera*, literally 'further out', from *ūt*, an earlier form of OUT]

utterance /úttərənss/ *n.* **1. STH SAID** sth said or emitted as a vocal sound **2. EXPRESSION OF STH** the expression of sth, especially in speech or vocal sound **3. WAY OF SPEAKING** a style, power, or way of speaking **4. ACT OF SAYING** the act of saying sth ◇ **give utterance** to express sth, especially in speech

utterly /úttərli/ *adv.* in an extreme or complete way

uttermost /úttərmōst/ *adj., n.* = **utmost**

utu /óo too/ *n. NZ* recompense or revenge in the Maori culture [Early 19thC. From Maori.]

U-turn *n.* **1. TURN MADE TO FACE OPPOSITE DIRECTION** a turn in the shape of a U made by a vehicle to reverse direction **2. REVERSAL OF ACTIONS OR POLICY** a complete reversal in opinion, actions, or policy

Utzon /óot zon/, **Jørn** (*b.* 1918) Danish architect. He is best known for designing the Sydney Opera House.

UU *abbr.* Ulster Unionist

UV *abbr.* ultraviolet

uvarovite /oo vaárə vīt/ *n.* a bright emerald-green mineral composed of calcium chromium silicate. It is a variety of garnet and is used as a gemstone. [Mid-19thC. Formed from the name of Count Sergei Semenovich *Uvarov* (1785–1855), a Russian statesman.]

uvea /yóovi ə/ *n.* the middle of the three layers of the eyeball, made up of the choroid, ciliary body, and iris surrounding the lens. It contains blood vessels and its pigmentation is responsible for eye colour. [Early 16thC. Via medieval Latin from Latin *uva* (see UVULA).] —**uveal** *adj.* —**uveous** *adj.*

uveitis /yóovi ítiss/ *n.* inflammation of the uvea of the eye

UVF *abbr.* Ulster Volunteer Force

UV Index *n.* a scale used to indicate the intensity of the sun's ultraviolet rays

uvula /yóovyóolə/ (*plural* **-las** *or* **-lae**) *n.* a small fleshy V-shaped extension of the soft palate that hangs above the tongue at the entrance to the throat [14thC. From late Latin, literally 'little grape', from Latin *uva* 'grape', from its shape.]

uvular /yóovyóolər/ *adj.* **1. INVOLVING UVULA** relating to or involving the uvula **2. PRONOUNCED VIBRATING THE UVULA** pronounced with vibration of the uvula ■ *n.* **UVULAR SOUND** a uvular consonant —**uvularly** *adv.*

uvulitis /yóovyóo lítiss/ *n.* inflammation of the uvula

UW *abbr.* **1.** underwriter **2.** underwritten

UWIST /yóo wist/ *abbr.* University of Wales Institute of Science and Technology

ux. *abbr.* uxor [From Latin]

Uzbekistan

UXB *abbr.* unexploded bomb

uxorial /uk sáwri əl/ *adj.* relating to, involving, or typical of a wife [Early 19thC. Formed from Latin *uxor* 'wife'.] —**uxorially** *adv.*

uxoricide /uk sáwri sīd/ *n.* **1.** MURDER OF WIFE murder of a wife by her husband **2.** MAN WHO MURDERS WIFE a man who murders his wife [Mid-19thC. Coined from Latin *uxor* 'wife' + English -CIDE.] —**uxoricidal** /uk sáwri sīd'l/ *adj.*

uxorious /uk sáwri əss/ *adj.* excessively devoted or submissive to your wife [Late 16thC. Formed from Latin *uxoriosus*, from *uxor* 'wife'.] —**uxoriously** *adv.* —**uxoriousness** *n.*

Uzbek /ŏŏz bek, úz-/ (*plural* **-bek** *or* **-beks**) *n.* **1.** PEOPLES MEMBER OF PEOPLE LIVING IN UZBEKISTAN a member of a people that live mainly in Uzbekistan, where they are the dominant ethnic group, and in parts of neighbouring regions. The Uzbek people are made up mainly of descendents of Turkic-speaking nomads who settled in the region in the 15th century and Farsi-speaking inhabitants of the area. **2.** LANG UZBEK LANGUAGE a language spoken in Uzbekistan and central Asia, belonging to the Turkic branch of Altaic languages. About 16 million people speak Uzbek. [Early 17thC. Directly or via Persian or Russian *uzbek* from Turkish and Uzbek *özbek*.]

Uzbekistan /ŏŏz béki staán, uz-/ republic in Central Asia. It was part of the Soviet Union from 1924 to 1991. Language: Uzbek. Currency: soum. Capital: Tashkent. Population: 23,467,724 (1997). Area: 447,400 sq. km/172,700 sq. mi. Official name **Republic of Uzbekistan**

Vv

v¹ /vee/ (*plural* **v's**), **V** (*plural* **V's** *or* **Vs**) *n.* **1. 22ND LETTER OF THE ENGLISH ALPHABET** the 22nd letter of the modern English alphabet **2. SPEECH SOUND CORRESPONDING TO THE LETTER 'V'** the speech sound that corresponds to the letter 'V' **3. LETTER 'V' WRITTEN** a written representation of the letter 'V'

v² (*plural* **v's**), **V** (*plural* **V's** *or* **Vs**) *symbol.* **1.** SCI image distance **2.** PHYS instantaneous potential difference **3.** PHYS instantaneous voltage **4.** PHYS specific volume

v³ (*plural* **v's**), **V** (*plural* **V's** *or* **Vs**) *abbr.* **1.** PHYS vacuum **2.** vagrant **3.** vale **4.** MATH vector **5.** MED vein **6.** PHYS velocity component **7.** velocity speed **8.** MED ventilator **9.** ANAT, BOT ventral **10.** GRAM verb **11.** verbal **12.** verse **13.** versed **14.** verso **15.** versus **16.** vertical **17.** via **18.** CHEM vibrational quantum number **19.** CHR vicarage **20.** victory **21.** vide **22.** MUSIC violin **23.** MED virus **24.** METEOROL (abnormally good) visibility **25.** MED vision **26.** vocative **27.** voice **28.** GEOG volcano **29.** MEASURE voltage **30.** vowel

V¹ /vee/, **v** *n.* the Roman numeral for five

V² *symbol.* **1.** PHYS electric potential **2.** PHYS electromotive force **3.** PHYS luminous efficiency **4.** PHYS potential **5.** PHYS potential efficiency **6.** PHYS potential energy **7.** vanadium

V³ *abbr.* **1.** valine **2.** vanadium **3.** variable region **4.** MONEY vatu **5.** Venerable **6.** Very (*used in titles*) **7.** version **8.** vespers **9.** vicar **10.** vice **11.** victory **12.** village **13.** Viscount **14.** Viscountess **15.** volt **16.** voltmeter **17.** Volunteer **18.** Volunteers

V-1 /vee wún/ (*plural* **V-1's**) *n.* a German robot bomb used in World War II, mainly against England [Abbreviation of German *Vergeltungswaffe eins*, literally 'reprisal weapon one']

V-2 /vee too/ (*plural* **V-2's**) *n.* a German liquid-fuelled ballistic missile used in the latter part of World War II, chiefly against London [Abbreviation of German *Vergeltungswaffe zwei*, literally 'reprisal weapon two']

V6 /vee síks/ (*plural* **V6's**) *n.* an internal-combustion engine with six cylinders arranged in a V shape

V8 /vee áyt/ (*plural* **V8's**) *n.* an internal-combustion engine with eight cylinders arranged in a V shape

va *abbr.* **1.** GRAM verbal adjective **2.** GRAM verb active **3.** MUSIC viola

VA *abbr.* **1.** ECON value-added **2.** value analysis **3.** MED ventricular arrhythmia **4.** CHR Vicar Apostolic **5.** NAVY Vice-Admiral **6.** visual acuity **7.** visual aid **8.** MEASURE volt-ampere **9.** MIL Volunteer Artillery **10.** (Royal Order of) Victoria and Albert **11.** CARS Peterborough

Va. *abbr.* Virginia

V/A *abbr.* voucher attached

Vaal /vaal/ river in northeastern South Africa, a tributary of the River Orange. Length: 1,160 km/720 mi.

Vaasa /vaass aa/ capital city and port of Vaasa Province, in western Finland. Population: 55,502 (1995).

vac /vak/ *abbr.* **1.** vacancy **2.** vacant **3.** vacation **4.** vacuum **5.** vacuum cleaner

vacancy /váykənsi/ (*plural* **-cies**) *n.* **1. VACANT OFFICE OR POSITION** an office, position, or tenancy that is unfilled or unoccupied **2. MENTAL INACTIVITY** mental inactivity or lack of thought or intelligence **3. VACANT STATE** the state of being vacant **4. LEISURE** a period of leisure (*archaic*) **5. PHYS EMPTY SITE IN A CRYSTAL** an empty site, normally containing an atom or ion, in a

crystal [Late 16thC. Formed from VACANT or from late Latin *vacantia*, from the present participle stem of Latin *vacare* (see VACATE).]

vacant /váykənt/ *adj.* **1. WITHOUT AN OCCUPANT** having no occupant or contents ○ *There were several vacant seats on the bus.* **2. UNOCCUPIED BY AN INCUMBENT OR OFFICIAL** not occupied by an incumbent, official, or possessor **3. LACKING EXPRESSION** showing no signs of thought, intelligence, or expression ○ *a vacant stare* **4. FREE FROM ACTIVITY** free from activity, business, or work ○ *a vacant afternoon* [13thC. Via Old French from the present participle stem of Latin *vacare* (see VACATE). It almost disappeared by 1400 but was reintroduced from Latin in the 16thC.] —**vacantly** *adv.* —**vacantness** *n.*

──── WORD KEY: SYNONYMS ────

vacant, unoccupied, empty, unfilled, void
CORE MEANING: lacking contents or occupants
vacant describes a house or room that has no occupants, often temporarily; **unoccupied** describes a building that has no one in it, especially when this has been the case for quite some time; **empty** describes sth such as a container that has no contents or sth such as a room that has no occupants; **unfilled** used to describe sth such as a seat on an aeroplane or in a theatre that has no one sitting in it because no one has bought a ticket for it; **void** a formal or literary word that emphasizes that sth is completely empty.

vacant possession *n.* ownership of a house whose previous occupants have already moved out

vacate /və káyt, vay-/ (**-cates, -cating, -cated**) *vt.* **1. EMPTY OF OCCUPANTS** to empty sth of incumbents or occupants **2. GIVE UP OCCUPANCY OF** to relinquish the possession, or occupancy of sth ○ *vacate the premises* **3. RESIGN FROM** to withdraw from or surrender possession of an office or post ○ *vacate a legislative seat* **4. LAW MAKE INVALID** to make sth legally void [Mid-17thC. From the past participle stem of Latin *vacare* 'to be empty' (source also of English *void*).] —**vacatable** *adj.*

vacation /və káysh'n/ *n.* **1. FIXED HOLIDAY PERIOD** a scheduled period during which the activities of law courts, universities, or other regular businesses are suspended **2. BREAK FROM WORK** a period of time devoted to rest, travel, or recreation **3. ACT OR INSTANCE OF VACATING** an act or an instance or vacating sth ■ *vi.* (**-tions, -tioning, -tioned**) US TAKE A HOLIDAY to take or spend a holiday [14thC. Via Old French from, ultimately, the past participle of Latin *vacare* (see VACATE).]

vacationer /və káysh'nər/, **vacationist** /və káysh'nist/ *n.* US, Can = **holidaymaker**

vaccinal /váksin'l/ *adj.* relating to a vaccine or vaccination

vaccinate /váksi nayt/ (**-nates, -nating, -nated**) *vt.* to inoculate a person or animal with a vaccine to produce immunity —**vaccinator** *n.* —**vaccinatory** /váksinə təri/ *adj.*

vaccination /váksi náysh'n/ *n.* inoculation with a vaccine to produce immunity [Early 19thC. Formed from VACCINE or from VACCINATE.]

vaccine /vák seen/ *n.* **1.** MED INOCULATION a preparation containing weakened or dead microbes of the kind that cause a particular disease, administered to stimulate the immune system to produce antibodies against that disease **2.** COMPUT PROTECTIVE SOFTWARE a program that protects a system against a computer virus [Late 18thC. From Latin *vaccinus* 'of a cow, from

vacca 'cow', because it was originally applied to the cowpox virus and its use to prevent smallpox.]

──── WORD KEY: ORIGIN ────

Vaccine was used by the British physician Edward Jenner at the end of the 18th century in the terms *vaccine disease*, meaning 'cowpox', and hence *vaccine inoculation*, meaning the technique he developed of preventing smallpox by injecting people with cowpox virus. There is no evidence of the use of **vaccine** as a noun to denote the inoculated material until the 1840s.

vaccinee /váksi neé/ *n.* sb who receives or has received a vaccination [Late 19thC. Formed from VACCINATE.]

vaccinia /vak sínni ə/ *n.* a skin eruption in reaction to inoculation with the weakened cowpox virus that was once used to vaccinate people against smallpox [Early 19thC. Via modern Latin from Latin *vaccinus* (see VACCINE).] —**vaccinial** *adj.*

vacherin /vásh raN, vash ráN/ *n.* a soft cow's-milk cheese from France or Switzerland [Mid-20thC. From French.]

vacillant /vássilənt/ *adj.* wavering indecisively [Early 16thC. From the present participle stem of Latin *vaccillare* (see VACILLATE).]

vacillate /vássi layt/ (**-lates, -lating, -lated**) *vi.* **1.** to be indecisive or irresolute **2.** to sway from side to side [Late 16thC. From the past participle stem of Latin *vaccillare* 'to sway, totter'.] —**vacillation** /vássi láysh'n/ *n.* —**vacillator** /-laytər/ *n.*

──── WORD KEY: SYNONYMS ────

See Synonyms at **hesitate**.

vacua plural of **vacuum**

vacuity /va kyoó əti/ (*plural* **-ties**) *n.* (*formal*) **1. EMPTINESS** the condition, state, or quality of being empty of all contents **2. EMPTY SPACE** an empty area or space **3. MEANINGLESS STATE OR THING** a thing or condition that is inane or devoid of any meaningful content ○ *legislative vacuity* [Mid-16thC. Directly or via French *vacuité* from, ultimately, Latin *vacuus* 'empty' (source of English *vacuum*).]

vacuolar membrane /vákyoo ōlər-/ *n.* a membrane containing fluid in the cytoplasm of a cell

vacuolate /vákyoo ələt, -layt/, **vacuolated** /-laytid/ *adj.* having small holes —**vacuolation** /vákyoo ə láysh'n/ *n.* —**vacuolization** /-lī záysh'n/ *n.*

vacuole /vákyoo ōl/ *n.* **1. CAVITY IN TISSUE** a small cavity in tissue **2. COMPARTMENT IN THE CYTOPLASM OF CELL** a membrane-bound compartment containing fluid that is found in the cytoplasm of a cell [Mid-19thC. From French, literally 'little empty (space)', from Latin *vacuus* 'empty' (source of English *vacuum*) + French *-ole* 'little'.] —**vacuolar** /vákyoo ōlər/ *adj.*

vacuous /vákyoo əss/ *adj.* **1. LACKING CONTENT** having no content **2. EMPTY OF MEANING** lacking ideas or intelligence **3. IDLE** lacking serious occupation **4.** MATH, LOGIC NULL null [Mid-17thC. Formed from Latin *vacuus* 'empty' (see VACUUM).] —**vacuously** *adv.* —**vacuousness** *n.*

vacuum /vákyoo əm, vákyoom/ (*plural* **-ums** *or* **-a** /vákyoo á/) *n.* **1. PHYS SPACE EMPTY OF MATTER** a space completely empty of matter but not achievable in practice on Earth **2. PHYS SPACE WITH ALL THE GAS REMOVED** a space from which all air or gas has been extracted **3. EMPTINESS CAUSED BY ABSENCE** an emptiness caused by sb or sth's absence or removal ○ *Her death left a vacuum in his life.* **4.** ISOLATION FROM THE OUTSIDE WORLD isolation from external influences ○ *You can't live in a vacuum.* **5.** = **vacuum cleaner** ■ *vti.* (**-ums, -uming, -umed**) CLEAN STH USING A VACUUM CLEANER to clean an area or object using a vacuum cleaner [Mid-16thC. From the neuter of Latin *vacuus* 'empty'.]

vacuum activity *n.* innate behaviour manifested in the absence of the usual stimulus

vacuum bottle *n.* US = **vacuum flask**

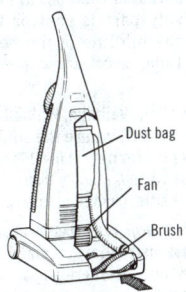

Vacuum cleaner

vacuum cleaner *n.* an electrical appliance that cleans surfaces such as floors, upholstery, and window coverings by sucking dirt and other material into a bag

vacuum drying *n.* the removal of liquid from a solution or mixture at reduced air pressure so that it dries at a lower temperature than it would at full pressure

vacuum flask *n.* a flask with double walls, usually of silvered glass, separated by an airless space, used to hold liquids and maintain them at constant high or low temperatures. US term **vacuum bottle**

vacuum gauge *n.* an instrument that measures pressures below atmospheric pressure

vacuum-packed *adj.* packed in an airtight container or package under low pressure in order to prevent the contents from spoiling or corroding

vacuum pump *n.* **1.** DEVICE FOR REMOVING AIR a device that creates a partial vacuum **2.** = **pulsometer**

vacuum tube *n.* US = **valve**

vada *n.* S Asia = **wada**

vade mecum /vaàdi máykəm/ *n.* **1.** USEFUL BOOK a guidebook, handbook, or manual, especially one carried around or designed to be carried around constantly and referred to often **2.** USEFUL OBJECT an object that a person carries constantly because it is useful [Early 17thC. From Latin, literally 'go with me'.]

Vadodara /wə dódərə/ industrial city in Gujarat State, western India. Population: 1,115,265 (1991).

vadose /váy dōss/ *adj.* used to describe or relating to water in the unsaturated zone of the Earth's crust that is above the level of ground water [Late 19thC. From Latin *vadosus*, from *vadum* 'shallow piece of water'.]

Vaduz /fa dóots/ town and capital of the principality of Liechtenstein, central Europe. Population: 5,085 (1995).

vag- *prefix.* = **vago-** (*used before vowels*)

vagabond /vággə bond/ *n.* **1.** HOMELESS WANDERER sb who has no permanent place to live and wanders from place to place **2.** BEGGAR sb who survives by asking for food or money ■ *adj.* OF VAGABONDS relating to or characteristic of a vagabond ■ *vi.* (**-bonds, -bonding, -bonded**) BE A VAGABOND to wander from place to place [15thC. Via French from Latin *vagabundus*, from *vagari* 'to wander' (source of English *vagrant*).] —**vagabondage** *n.* —**vagabondism** *n.*

vagal /váyg'l/ *adj.* relating to the tenth pair of cranial nerves (**vagus nerves**) —**vagally** *adv.*

vagary /váygəri/ (*plural* **-ries**) *n.* an unpredictable or eccentric change, action, or idea ○ *the vagaries of the weather* [Late 16thC. From Latin *vagari* (see VAGABOND).] —**vagarious** /və gáiri əss/ *adj.*

vagi *plural* of **vagus**

vagile /vájjīl/ *adj.* able to move around within a specific environment [Early 20thC. Formed from VAGUS.] —**vagility** /və jílləti/ *n.*

vagina /və jínə/ (*plural* **-nas** *or* **-nae** /-nee/) *n.* **1.** PART OF THE FEMALE REPRODUCTIVE TRACT in female mammals, a lubricated muscular tube connecting the cervix of the womb to the vulva. It receives the penis during copulation and expands to expel the foetus during birth. **2.** PLANT OR ANIMAL SHEATH a plant or animal part that forms a sheath, e.g. that formed by a leaf around a stem [Late 17thC. From Latin, 'sheath, scabbard' (source of English *vanilla*).] —**vaginal** *adj.* —**vaginally** /və jínəli/ *adv.*

vaginate /vájji nət, -nayt/, **vaginated** /-naytid/ *adj.* having, forming, or resembling a sheath

vaginectomy /vájji néktəmi/ (*plural* **-mies**) *n.* **1.** REMOVAL OF THE VAGINA the removal of all or part of the vagina by surgery **2.** REMOVAL OF THE TESTIS MEMBRANE the removal by surgery of all or part of the smooth moist membrane that encloses the testis and epididymis

vaginismus /vájji nízməss/ *n.* a painful and often prolonged contraction of the vagina in response to the vulva or vagina being touched. It may have a psychological cause, or be due to physical factors such as injury, ulceration, or inflammation

vaginitis /vájji nítiss/ *n.* inflammation of the vagina caused by infection, an ill-fitting contraceptive device, or hormonal deficiency. Its typical symptoms include irritation, vaginal discharge, and painful urination

vago- *prefix.* vagus ○ *vagotomy* [From VAGUS]

vagotomy /və góttəmi/ (*plural* **-mies**) *n.* the surgical cutting of the tenth pair of cranial nerves (**vagus nerves**) or any of their branches, performed to control duodenal ulcers by decreasing acid secretion of the stomach

vagotonia /váygə tóni ə/ *n.* a pathological condition in which overactivity of the tenth pair of cranial nerves (**vagus nerves**) affects bodily functions controlled by these nerves, such as those in blood vessels and the gut. Symptoms may include sweating, constipation, and slowed heartbeat. [Early 20thC. Coined from VAGO- + Greek *tonos* 'stretching, tension' (source of English *tone*).] —**vagotonic** /váygə tónnik/ *adj.*

vagotropic /váygə tróppik, -trópik/ *adj.* used to describe a drug that has an effect on the tenth pair of cranial nerves (**vagus nerves**)

vagrancy /váygrənssi/ (*plural* **-cies**) *n.* **1.** HOMELESSNESS the state of wandering and having no permanent place to live **2.** LAW VAGRANCY AS A LEGAL OFFENCE the legal offence of living on the street without money or a place to live and, in some jurisdictions, begging **3.** LAPSE IN THINKING a lapse in thinking

vagrant /váygrənt/ *n.* **1.** HOMELESS WANDERER sb who wanders from one place to another and has no permanent place to live **2.** WANDERER sb who never stays in one place for long **3.** LAW SB GUILTY OF THE OFFENCE OF VAGRANCY sb guilty of the legal offence of vagrancy **4.** BIRDS BIRD OFF THE NORMAL MIGRATION ROUTE a migratory bird or insect that deviates from its normal migration route ■ *adj.* **1.** HOMELESS wandering from one place to another and having no permanent place to live **2.** WANDERING never staying in one place for long **3.** WAYWARD wayward or capricious in nature **4.** RANDOM acting or done in a random way **5.** BOT GROWING IN AN UNCONTROLLED WAY used to describe plants that grow in a lush uncontrolled way [15thC. From Anglo-Norman *varagarant*, of uncertain origin: ultimately, perhaps from (influenced by French *vaguer* 'to wander') Old French *walcrer* 'to walk', from Germanic.] —**vagrantly** *adv.* —**vagrantness** *n.*

vague /vayg/ (**vaguer, vaguest**) *adj.* **1.** NOT EXPLICIT not clear in meaning or intention ○ *a vague proposal* **2.** NOT DISTINCTLY SEEN not having a clear or perceptible form ○ *a vague form in the shadows* **3.** UNVERIFIED not properly validated or having no clear or identifiable source **4.** UNCLEAR IN THINKING unclear or incoherent in thinking or expression **5.** NOT CLEARLY PERCEIVED IN THE MIND not clearly felt, understood, or recalled ○ *I have a vague recollection of it.* [Mid-16thC. Directly or via French from Latin *vagus* 'wandering, inconstant' (source of English *vagus*).] —**vaguely** *adv.* —**vagueness** *n.*

vagus /váygəss/ (*plural* **-gi** /váy jī, váy gī/), **vagus nerve** *n.* either of the tenth pair of cranial nerves that carry sensory and motor neurons serving the heart, lungs, stomach, intestines, and various other organs [Mid-19thC. From Latin *vagus* (see VAGUE).]

vaidya /vídi ə/ *n.* S Asia an Ayurvedic Hindu physician [Mid-20thC. From Hindi, from *vaidy* 'export of Ayurvedic medicine'.]

vain /vayn/ *adj.* **1.** EXCESSIVELY PROUD excessively proud, especially of your appearance **2.** UNSUCCESSFUL failing to have or unlikely to have the intended or desired result ○ *a vain attempt at persuading them* **3.** EMPTY OF SUBSTANCE devoid of substance or meaning [14thC. Via Old French from Latin *vanus* 'empty, without substance' (source of English *evanescent* and *vanish*).] —**vainly** *adv.* —**vainness** *n.* ◇ **in vain** fruitlessly, pointlessly, or unsuccessfully ○ *We searched in vain for a solution.*

— WORD KEY: SYNONYMS —

vain, empty, hollow, idle

CORE MEANING: without value or worth

vain emphasizes that sth such as a hope or ambition is unlikely to be fulfilled; **empty** describes sth such as a threat or a promise that seems to lack substance and is therefore unlikely to be carried through; **hollow** a more literary word meaning *empty*; **idle** emphasizes that sth such as a threat lacks purpose or seems unlikely to be effective.

vainglorious /vayn gláwri əss/ *adj.* excessively proud or boastful (*literary*) —**vaingloriously** *adv.* —**vaingloriousness** *n.*

vainglory /vayn gláwri/ (*plural* **-ries**) *n.* (*literary*) **1.** EXCESSIVE PRIDE excessive pride in or boastfulness about yourself, your achievements, or your abilities **2.** VAIN DISPLAY an excessive display of sth in order to draw attention to it [12thC. Via Old French from Latin *vana gloria*, literally 'empty glory'.]

vair /vair/ *n.* **1.** FUR TRIMMING FOR ROBES fur used as a trimming on medieval robes **2.** HERALDRY FUR USED ON HERALDIC SHIELDS a blue-and-white fur used on heraldic shields. ◊ **ermine** [14thC. Via Old French from Latin *varius* 'speckled, changeable' (source of English *various*).]

vairy /váiri/ *n.* SW England a weasel (*regional*)

Vaisakha /víss aakə/ *n.* in the Hindu calendar, the second month of the year, made up of 29 or 30 days and falling in approximately April to May

Vaishnava /víshnəvə/ *n.* a member of a group devoted to the worship of the Hindu god Vishnu or one of his incarnations [Late 18thC. From Sanskrit *vaiṣnava*, literally 'relating to Vishnu'.] —**Vaishnavism** *n.*

Vaisya /víssyə, vísh-/ *n.* **1.** HINDU MERCHANT CASTE the third of the four Hindu castes, the members of which were merchants and farmers **2.** MEMBER OF THE HINDU MERCHANT CASTE a member of the Vaisya caste [Mid-17thC. From Sanskrit *vaiśya* 'farm labourer, tradesman'.]

vakil /vaa keél/, **vakeel, wakil** *n.* S Asia a lawyer or legal representative in a court of law in the Indian subcontinent [Early 17thC. Via Persian and Urdu *wakīl* and Turkish *vakīl* from Arabic *wakīl*.]

val. *abbr.* **1.** GEOL valley **2.** FIN valuation **3.** COMM value

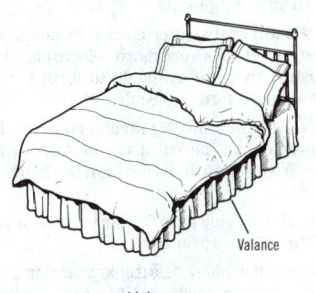

Valance

Valance

valance /vállənss/, **valence** *n.* **1.** FABRIC COVER FOR A BED BASE a plain, pleated, or gathered fabric cover that hangs from a shelf or is used to cover up the base of a bed from mattress to floor **2.** US COVER FOR A CURTAIN ROD a short decorative piece of drapery or wood hung across a window to cover the rod from which curtains hang [15thC. Origin uncertain: perhaps ultimately from Old French (a)valer 'go down'.] —**valanced** adj.

Valdez /val deéz/ city in southeastern Alaska, on the shore of an inlet of Prince William Sound. Population: 4,309 (1996).

vale[1] /vayl/ n. a valley or dale, often one that has a stream running through it (*literary; often used in placenames*) [14thC. Via French from Latin *valles* (see VALLEY).]

vale[2] /vaà lay/ interj. FAREWELL a Latin expression of farewell ■ n. SAYING FAREWELL an act of saying farewell or adieu [Mid-16thC. From Latin, literally 'be well', a form of *valere* 'to be strong or well'.]

valediction /válli díksh'n/ n. (*formal*) **1.** SAYING GOODBYE the act of saying goodbye or an instance of leave-taking **2.** FAREWELL SPEECH a statement, speech, or letter of farewell [Mid-17thC. Formed from Latin *valedicere* 'to say goodbye', on the model of BENEDICTION.]

valedictorian /válli dik táwri ən/ n. US the student who delivers the valedictory address at graduation

valedictory /válli díktəri/ n. (*plural* **-ries**) **1.** FAREWELL SPEECH a statement or speech of farewell (*formal*) **2.** US = **valedictory address** ■ adj. SAYING GOODBYE performing the function of saying farewell (*formal*)

valedictory address n. US a speech delivered at graduation by the student with the best academic record

valence[1] /váylənss/ n. = **valency** [Late 19thC. Variant of VALENCY.]

valence[2] n. = **valance**

Valencia /və lénshi ə, və lénssi ə, ba lénthyə/ **1.** capital city of Valencia Province and the autonomous region of Valencia, in eastern Spain. The city was founded in Roman times. Population: 763,308 (1995). **2.** city in northern Venezuela, on the River Cabriales. Population: 1,034,033 (1992).

Valenciennes[1] /vállənssi én/ n. a fine lace made with bobbins that is usually floral in design and is now made of cotton instead of the original linen [Early 18thC. Named after VALENCIENNES, where the lace was originally produced.]

Valenciennes[2] /vállənssi én, va laaNss yen/ city in the Nord-Pas-de-Calais Region, northern France, and administrative centre of the Nord Department. Population: 39,276 (1990).

valency /váylənss/ n. (*plural* **-cies** /váylənssi/) **1.** valence, valency CHEM COMBINING POWER OF ATOMS the chemical combining power of atoms or groups measured by the number of electrons the atom or group will receive, give up, or share in forming a compound **2.** valence, valency IMMUNOL COMBINING ANTIGENIC DETERMINANTS the number of different antigenic determinants with which a single antibody molecule can combine **3.** GRAM COMBINING POWER OF A VERB the ability of a verb to combine grammatically with noun phrases in a given clause [Mid-19thC. From Latin *valentia* 'power, competence', from *valere* 'to be powerful'.]

valency electron n. an electron in an outer shell of an atom that can be lost to or shared with another atom to form a molecule

valency shell n. the outer electron shell of an atom consisting of one or more electrons (**valency electrons**) that are available to form bonds with other atoms to form molecules

Valens /váyl enz/ (328?–378) Roman emperor. Brother of Valentinian I, he ruled the eastern half of the empire from 364 until his death in the battle against Visigoths.

-valent suffix. having a particular valence or valences ○ *divalent* [Formed from VALENCE.]

valentine /vállən tīn/ n. **1.** VALENTINE'S DAY CARD a greeting card or gift sent, traditionally anonymously, to sb on Valentine's Day as a token of love **2.** RECIPIENT OF A VALENTINE the person to whom sb sends a card or gift on Valentine's Day as a token of love [15thC. Named after St VALENTINE.]

Valentine's Day n. 14 February, the Christian feast day of St Valentine and the traditional day for sending a romantic card or gift, especially anonymously, to sb you love

Valentinian I /vállən tínni ən/ (321–375) Roman emperor. As emperor of the western half of the empire from 364, he was militarily successful and promoted education and medical care.

Valentinian II (371?–392) Roman emperor. After periods of regency and exile he gained power over the western empire in 388, but was murdered four years later.

Valentinian III (419–455) Roman emperor. He ruled the western empire at a time when much of it was overrun by invaders.

Rudolph Valentino

Valentino /vállən teénō/, **Rudolph** (1895–1926) Italian-born US actor. His passionate roles in silent films made him a romantic screen idol. Real name **Rodolpho Guglielmi di Valentina d'Antonguolla**

valerian /və leéri ən/ (*plural* **-ans** or **-an**) n. **1.** PLANTS EURASIAN PLANT WITH MEDICINAL ROOT a plant of Europe and Asia with small sweet-smelling white or pinkish flowers and a root that is used medicinally. Genus: *Valeriana*. **2.** MED SEDATIVE MADE FROM VALERIAN a sedative made from the dried roots of valerian plants [15thC. Via Old French from medieval Latin *valeriana*, named after *Valeria*, a Roman province.]

Valerian /və leéri ən/ (d. 260?) Roman emperor. Reigning from 253, he had to contend with repeated invasions and died in captivity after defeat by the Persians.

valeric acid /və leérik-/ n. a pungent colourless liquid used in flavourings and manufacturing. Formula: C₅H₁₀O₂. [*Valeric* formed from VALERIAN.]

Valéry /válle ree/, **Paul** (1871–1945) French poet and critic. He was considered to be one of France's greatest 20th-century poets and his prolific early output was followed by a 20-year silence, during which he worked mainly on mathematics and philosophical meditations. His later work was heavily influenced by the symbolists. Full name **Paul Ambroise Valéry**

valet /vállit, vállay/ n. **1.** MAN SERVANT a male personal servant of a man, whose duties include looking after his employer's clothes and providing his meals **2.** MALE HOTEL OR PASSENGER SHIP EMPLOYEE a man employee whose duties include cleaning the clothes of hotel guests or passengers on ships **3.** SB PERFORMING CAR PARKING SERVICE sb employed to park the cars of people arriving at a hotel, restaurant, or airport and bring the cars back for them on departure ■ v. (**-ets**, **-eting**, **-eted**) **1.** vti. WORK AS A VALET to work as a valet or provide valet services to sb **2.** vt. CLEAN A CAR to clean sb's car in return for payment [15thC. Via French from, ultimately, assumed medieval Latin *vassus* 'servant to a knight' (source of English *vassal*).]

valeta n. DANCE = **veleta**

valet de chambre /vállay də shaàNbrə/ (*plural* **valets de chambre**) n. = **valet** n. 1 [French, literally 'valet of the room']

valet parking n. a service provided by some hotels, restaurants, and airports whereby an employee parks people's cars for them on arrival and brings the cars back for them on departure

valetudinarian /válli tyoodi náiri ən/, **valetudinary** /válli tyoódinəri/ n. (*plural* **-ies**) **1.** SB WITH POOR HEALTH sb who has persistent ill health **2.** SB OBSESSED WITH HEALTH sb who is excessively concerned with his or her own health **3.** HEALTHY OLD PERSON sb who enjoys good health in spite of old age ■ adj. **1.** OF A VALETUDINARIAN relating to or being a valetudinarian **2.** OF POOR HEALTH relating

to, characterized by, or arising from poor health **3.** TRYING TO BE HEALTHIER trying to recover or improve health —**valetudinarianism** n.

valetudinary n., adj. = **valetudinarian** [Late 16thC. From Latin *valetudinarius* 'in ill health', from *valetudo* 'state of health', from *valere* 'to be well'.]

valgus /válgəss/ adj. MED TWISTED OUTWARDS used to describe a deformity in which a body part such as the knee or foot is bent or twisted outwards away from the midline of the body. ◊ **varus** ■ n. MED STATE OF BEING TWISTED OUTWARDS the position or state in which a bone or body part is bent or twisted outwards away from the midline of the body. ◊ **varus** [Early 19thC. From Latin, 'knock-kneed'.] —**valgoid** /vál goyd/ adj.

Valhalla /val hállə/, **Walhalla, Walhall** n. in Norse mythology, the great hall where the souls of heroes killed in battle spend eternity [Late 17thC. Via modern Latin from Old Norse *valhall*, literally 'hall of the slain', from *valr* 'those slain in battle' (source of English *Valkyrie*).]

valiant /válli ənt/ adj. **1.** COURAGEOUS brave and steadfast **2.** DONE COURAGEOUSLY characterized by or performed with bravery but often ending in failure ○ *despite a valiant attempt at rescue* ■ n. SB COURAGEOUS a brave and steadfast person [14thC. Via Old French from Latin *valent-*, the present participle stem of *valere* 'to be strong'.] —**valiance** n. —**valiancy** /válly ənsi/ n. —**valiantly** /válli əntli/ adv. —**valiantness** n.

valid /vállid/ adj. **1.** JUSTIFIABLE having a solid foundation or justification ○ *It's a perfectly valid argument.* **2.** EFFECTIVE bringing about the results or ends intended **3.** LAW LEGALLY BINDING having binding force in law **4.** LAW LEGALLY ACCEPTABLE acceptable under law **5.** UNEXPIRED usable or acceptable until a specified expiry date or under specified conditions of use ○ *a valid passport* **6.** LOGICAL having premises from which the conclusion follows logically **7.** HEALTHY having good health (*archaic*) [Late 16thC. Directly or via French from Latin *validus* 'strong', from *valere* 'to be strong'.] —**validity** /və líddəti/ n. —**validly** /vállidli/ adv. —**validness** /vállidnəss/ n.

WORD KEY: SYNONYMS

valid, cogent, convincing, reasonable, sound
CORE MEANING: being worthy of acceptance or credence
valid describes sth such as an argument or an excuse that is acceptable on the strength of the evidence it supplies; **cogent** a fairly formal word describing an argument that is forceful and weighty; **convincing** describes sth such as an argument or an excuse that seems likely to overcome the doubts and win the support of those who hear it; **reasonable** describes an argument or excuse that seems worthy of consideration but not necessarily ultimately convincing; **sound** emphasizes that sth such as an argument is based on truth and contains no errors or falsehoods.

validate /válli dayt/ (**-dates, -dating, -dated**) vt. **1.** CONFIRM THE TRUTHFULNESS OF to confirm or establish the truthfulness or soundness of sth **2.** LAW MAKE LEGAL to declare or render sth legal or binding ○ *validate a passport* **3.** REGISTER STH FORMALLY to register sth formally and have its use officially sanctioned [Mid-17thC. From Latin *validare* 'render legally valid', from *validus* (see VALID).] —**validation** /válli dáysh'n/ n. —**validatory** /vállidətəri/ adj.

$$H_3C-CH-CH-\overset{\overset{\textstyle O}{\|}}{C}-OH$$
$$\underset{CH_3}{|}\ \underset{NH_2}{|}$$

Valine

valine /váy leen, vál-/ n. an amino acid essential to normal animal growth, produced from pyruvic acid or during the hydrolysis of some proteins. Formula:

C₅H₁₁NO₂. [Early 20thC. Coined from VALERIC ACID + -INE.]

valise /və leez/ *n.* a small piece of luggage (*dated*) [Early 20thC. Via French from Italian *valigia*, of unknown origin.]

Valium /válli əm/ *tdmk.* a trademark for diazepam, a tranquillizer

Valkyrie /valkəri, vál keeri/, **Walkyrie, Valkyr** /vál keer/ *n.* in Norse mythology, one of the 12 handmaids of Odin who ride their horses over the field of battle and escort the souls of slain heroes to Valhalla [Mid-18thC. From Old Norse *Valkyrja*, literally 'chooser of the slain', from *valr* 'those slain in battle'.] —**Valkyrian** /val keeri ən/ *adj.*

valla plural of **vallum**

Valladolid /vállə do líd, bál a tho líth/ capital city of Valladolid Province, northern Spain. It was the capital of Spain before Madrid. Population: 334,820 (1995).

vallation /va láysh'n/ *n.* **1.** DEFENSIVE EARTHWORK a defensive fortification or embankment made of earth **2.** CONSTRUCTION OF DEFENSIVE EARTHWORKS the planning or building of defensive fortifications or embankments made of earth [Mid-17thC. Via Latin *vallatio* from, ultimately, *vallare* 'to protect', from *vallum* 'rampart' (source of English *wall* and *circumvallate*).]

vallecula /və lékyoōlə/ (*plural* -**lae** /-lee/) *n.* a shallow groove, depression, or furrow in an animal or plant body such as that between the hemispheres of the cerebellum in the brain [Mid-19thC. From Latin *vallicula*, from *valles* (see VALLEY).] —**vallecular** *adj.* —**valleculate** /və lékyoō layt/ *adj.*

Valle d'Aosta /vállay daa óstə/ region in northern Italy on the border with France and Switzerland. It contains the Alpine peaks of the Matterhorn and Mont Blanc. Population: 117,208 (1991). Area: 3,262 sq. km/1,260 sq. mi.

Valles Marineris /válless márri náiriss/ *n.* a system of valleys and canyons in the equatorial region of Mars 4,000 km/2,500 mi. long, up to 240km/150 mi. wide, and 6.5 km/4 mi. deep

Valletta /və léttə/ capital city of Malta, and the country's chief port. Population: 7,172 (1996).

valley /válli/ (*plural* -**leys**) *n.* **1.** GEOG LOW-LYING AREA a long low area of land, often with a river or stream running through it, that is surrounded by higher ground **2.** GEOG LOW-LYING LAND AROUND A RIVER a large area of low-lying land around a river and its tributaries **3.** GEOG VALLEY-SHAPED HOLLOW a long sunken area or groove shaped like a valley **4.** BUILDING ANGLE BETWEEN ROOF SLOPES the angle formed where two slopes of a roof intersect [13thC. Via Old French *valee* from, ultimately, Latin *valles* 'valley' (source of English *vale*).] —**valleyed** *adj.*

valley fever *n.* = **coccidioidomycosis** [Named after the San Joaquin Valley in California]

Valley Forge /válli fawrj/ historic site in Pennsylvania, northwest of Philadelphia on the Schuylkill River, where George Washington kept his winter quarters during the US War of Independence

Valley of the Kings gorge on the western bank of the River Nile, southern Egypt. It was the burial site of pharaohs of the New Kingdom (1570–1070 BC).

Vallis Alpes /válliss al pez/ *n.* a valley on the Moon northeast of Mare Imbrium, orientated approximately from west to east and cutting across Montes Alpes

vallum /válləm/ (*plural* -**lums** *or* -**la** /-ə/) *n.* an ancient Roman fortification or embankment, built for military defence [Early 17thC. From Latin, from *vallus* 'palisade, stake'.]

Valois /vállwaa/, **Dame Ninette de** (*b.* 1898) Irish-born British dancer and choreographer. She was a co-founder in 1931 of the Royal Ballet and Royal Ballet School in London. Real name **Edris Stannus**

valonia /və lóni ə/ *n.* the dried acorn cups and unripe acorns of a Eurasian oak, used in the tanning industry and in the manufacture of inks and dyes [Early 18thC. Via Italian from, ultimately, Greek *balanos* 'acorn'.]

valor *n.* US = **valour**

valorize /vállə rīz/ (-**izes**, -**izing**, -**ized**), **valorise** (-**ises**, -**ising**, -**ised**) *vt.* to set and maintain the price of a

Dame Ninette de Valois
Hulton-Deutsch Collection/Corbis

commodity at an artificially high level through government action [Early 20thC. Via Portuguese *valorizar*, from *valor* 'value', from late Latin (see VALOUR).] —**valorization** *n.*

valorous /vállərəss/ *adj.* having or showing courage, especially in war or battle —**valorously** *adv.* —**valorousness** *n.*

valour /vállər/ *n.* courage, especially that shown in war or battle [Late 16thC. Via Italian *valore* from Latin *valor*, from *valere* 'to be strong'.]

Valparaiso /válpə ráyzō, -rízō/ city and port in central Chile. It is the capital city of Valparaiso Region. Population: 274,228 (1992).

Valpolicella /vál polli chéllə/ *n.* a light red Italian wine from the northern province of Verona [Early 20thC. Named after the district of *Valpolicella* in northwestern Italy, where it is made.]

valproate /válprō ayt/, **valproic acid** /val prō ik-/ *n.* a drug used to help control epileptic convulsions [Late 20thC. Coined from *valproic acid* (from VALERIC ACID + PROPYL) + -ATE.]

Valsalva manoeuvre /val sálvə-/ *n.* MED **1.** FORCING OF AIR INTO THE MIDDLE EAR the action of attempting to breathe out when the mouth is closed and the nostrils are held shut, thereby forcing air into the middle ear via the Eustachian tubes. It can be used to test if the Eustachian tubes are blocked and to counteract increased external pressure on the eardrum. **2.** INCREASING OF PRESSURE IN THE THORACIC CAVITY the action of attempting to breathe out against a closed glottis, which increases pressure in the thoracic cavity and hinders the return of venous blood to the heart. When the breath is released the trapped blood flows rapidly through the heart, causing a brief increase followed by a brief decrease in heart rate. [Named after Antonio Maria Valsalva (1666–1723), an Italian anatomist.]

valse /valss/ *n.* a waltz, especially one written by a French composer or given a French title [Late 18thC. Via French from German *Walzer* (see WALTZ).]

valuable /vállyoōb'l, -yoo əb'l/ *adj.* **1.** WORTH A GREAT DEAL OF MONEY having significant monetary value **2.** USEFUL having great importance or usefulness ○ *a valuable insight* **3.** HELD DEAR cherished or esteemed because of personal qualities **4.** RARE highly prized because of being in short or limited supply **5.** ABLE TO BE VALUED capable of being assigned a value ■ *n.* VALUABLE ITEM a possession, especially a piece of jewellery, that has significant monetary value —**valuableness** *n.* —**valuably** *adv.*

valuable consideration *n.* in English contract law, sth given or undertaken as part of an agreement between two parties that has some objective value and so makes the agreement a valid contract. For example, to form a valid contract for the sale of a car, valuable consideration is the money paid to the person selling the car

valuate /vállyoo ayt/ (-**ates**, -**ating**, -**ated**) *vt.* to value sth

valuation /vállyoo áysh'n/ *n.* **1.** APPRAISAL OF COST the act of determining the value or price of sth, especially property **2.** PRICE the price of sth established by appraisal of its quality, condition, and desirability, or of the cost of replacement **3.** ESTIMATE OF IMPORTANCE an estimate of the importance or usefulness of sth —**valuational** *adj.* —**valuationally** *adv.*

valuator /vállyoo aytər/ *n.* sb who assesses the value of objects such as jewellery or works of art

value /váll yoo/ *n.* **1.** MONETARY WORTH an amount expressed in money or another medium of exchange that is thought to be a fair exchange for sth **2.** FULL RECOVERED WORTH the adequate or satisfactory return on or recompense for sth ○ *it's value for money* **3.** WORTH OR IMPORTANCE the worth, importance, or usefulness of sth to sb ○ *a ring with great sentimental value* **4.** LING MEANING the exact meaning or significance of a word **5.** MATH NUMERICAL QUANTITY a numerical quantity assigned to a mathematical symbol **6.** MUSIC LENGTH OF A NOTE the length of time that a note or pause is held **7.** ARTS SHADE OF A COLOUR in painting and drawing, the lightness or darkness of a colour **8.** PHON SOUND REPRESENTED the quality or tone of a speech sound that a letter or written character represents, especially in a particular context when in isolation it can represent more than one sound ■ **values** *npl.* PRINCIPLES OR STANDARDS the accepted principles or standards of an individual or a group ■ *vt.* (-**ues**, -**uing**, -**ued**) **1.** ESTIMATE THE VALUE OF STH to estimate or determine the value of sth **2.** RATE STH to rate sth according to its perceived worth, importance, or usefulness **3.** REGARD HIGHLY to regard sb or sth as important or useful ○ *I value her as a friend.* [14thC. From Old French, from *valoir* 'to be worth', from Latin *valere* 'to be powerful'.]

value added *n.* **1.** DIFFERENCE BETWEEN OUTCOME AND COSTS the difference between the gross profit of a commercial enterprise, such as a firm or industry, and its costs paid to other businesses **2.** INCREASE IN PRODUCT VALUE the amount by which the value of a product increases as it proceeds through the various stages of its manufacture and distribution —**value-added** *adj.*

value-added tax *n.* full form of **VAT**

value date *n.* in the calculation of exchange rates, the date on which a transaction is judged to have occurred

valued policy *n.* an insurance policy in which the amount payable for a valid claim is established when the policy is issued and is independent of the value of a loss subsequently incurred

value-free *adj.* not affected by or based on value judgments

value judgment *n.* a judgment of the worth, appropriateness, or importance of sb or sth made on the basis of personal beliefs, opinions, or prejudices rather than facts

valueless /vállyoōləss/ *adj.* having no value —**valuelessness** *n.*

valuer /vállyoo ər/ *n.* sb who estimates or determines the value of objects such as property, jewellery, or works of art

value system *n.* a set of personal principles and standards

valuta /və loōtə/ *n.* the value of one nation's currency in terms of its exchange rate with another currency [Late 19thC. From Italian, 'value'.]

valval /válvəl/, **valvar** /válvər/ *adj.* = **valvular**

valvate /vál vayt/ *adj.* **1.** WITH VALVES having valves or parts similar to valves **2.** BOT NOT OVERLAPPING IN BUD used to describe sepals or petals that touch but do not overlap in the bud. ◊ **imbricate 3.** BOT TAKING PLACE BY MEANS OF VALVES used to describe the splitting open of the seed capsules of the iris or lily that takes place by means of valves [Early 19thC. From Latin *valvatus* 'having folding doors', from *valva* (see VALVE).]

valve /valv/ *n.* **1.** ENG DEVICE THAT CONTROLS LIQUID FLOW a device that controls the movement of liquids or gases through piping or other passages by opening or closing ports and channels **2.** MUSIC PART ON A BRASS INSTRUMENT a device in some brass instruments that diverts air down tubes of varying length, thereby altering the pitch **3.** ELECTRON ENG ELECTRON TUBE PRODUCING AMPLIFICATION an electron tube that is either evacuated or filled with low pressure gas and in which electrons are pulled from the cathode by an applied anode voltage. Used to produce amplification, oscillation, or other effects. US term **vacuum tube**. ◊ **thermionic valve 4.** ANAT CLOSABLE FLAP IN AN ORGAN a membranous structure in a hollow organ

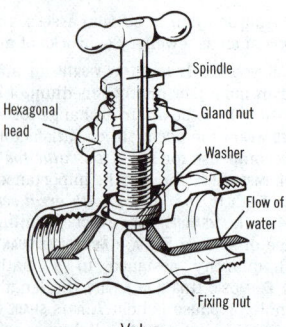

Valve

or vessel such as the heart or a vein that prevents the return flow of fluid passing through it by folding or closing **5.** BOT **PART OF A SEED POD** any of the segments of the wall of a seed pod or other fruit that split apart to reveal the contents **6.** BOT **ANTHER FLAP** a flap that acts like a lid in some types of anther **7.** BOT **PART OF THE CELL WALL** either of the two parts of the silica-impregnated cell wall of a type of alga (**diatom**) that fit together like the lid and base of a box **8.** ZOOL **SEPARABLE PART OF A SHELL** a hinged part of the shell of a brachiopod or some molluscs **9.** ZOOL **SINGLE-UNIT SHELL** the single-unit shell of a snail and some other molluscs **10.** DOOR LEAF a leaf of a double or folding door (*archaic*) [15thC. From Latin *valva* 'leaf of a folding door', of uncertain origin.] —**valveless** *adj.*

valve-in-head engine *n.* US = **overhead-valve engine**

valvelet /válvlət/ *n.* = **valvule**

valvula /válvyŏŏlə/ (*plural* **-lae** /-lee/) *n.* ANAT = **valvule** *n.* **1** [Early 17thC. From modern Latin, from Latin *valva* (see VALVE).]

valvular /válvyŏŏlər/ *adj.* **1.** RELATING TO VALVES relating to, having, or acting like a valve or set of valves **2.** AFFECTING VALVES involving or affecting a valve or set of valves

valvule /vál vyool/ *n.* **1.** ANAT SMALL VALVE a small valve or a part that functions or looks like one **2.** BOT = **palea** [Mid-18thC. Variant of VALVULA.]

valvulitis /válvyŏŏ lítiss/ *n.* inflammation of a valve in the body, especially one in the heart, often caused by rheumatic fever

valvuloplasty /válvyŏŏlō plasti/ (*plural* **-plasties**) *n.* plastic surgery performed to repair a valve in the body, especially one in the heart [Mid-20thC. Coined from VALVULE + -PLASTY.]

vambrace /vám brayss/ *n.* a piece of armour worn over the forearm as protection [14thC. Via Anglo-Norman *vauntbras* from Old French *avantbras*, from *avant* 'before' + *bras* 'arm' (source of English *brace*).]

vamp¹ /vamp/ *n.* SEDUCTIVE WOMAN a woman who is believed to use her sexual attractiveness for the seduction and manipulation of others ■ *v.* (**vamps, vamping, vamped**) **1.** *vti.* SEDUCE SB to seduce and manipulate sb by appearing to offer sexual intercourse **2.** *vi.* ACT LIKE VAMP to act like or play the role of a vamp [Early 20thC. Shortening of VAMPIRE.] —**vampish** *adj.* —**vampishly** *adv.* —**vampy** *adj.*

vamp² /vamp/ *n.* **1.** CLOTHES UPPER PART OF A SHOE the upper part of a shoe that covers the front part of the foot **2.** STH PATCHED UP sth repaired so as to appear new **3.** REHASHING OF STH a reworking of sth already used or available, especially a book or article **4.** MUSIC IMPROVISED MUSICAL INTRODUCTION an improvised musical introduction or accompaniment that is repeated as necessary until the entry of the solo line ■ *v.* (**vamps, vamping, vamped**) **1.** *vt.* CLOTHES PUT A VAMP ON A SHOE to put a vamp on a shoe **2.** *vti.* MUSIC IMPROVISE A MUSICAL INTRODUCTION OR ACCOMPANIMENT to improvise a musical introduction or accompaniment for a solo line [14thC. Shortening of Old French *avantpié*, from *avant* 'before' + *pié* 'foot'.] —**vamper** *n.*

vamp up *vt.* **1.** REPAIR to rework or renovate sth **2.** FABRICATE to make sth up or improvise sth

vampire /vám pīr/ *n.* **1.** MYTHOL BLOODSUCKING EVIL SPIRIT in European folklore, a dead person believed to rise each night from the grave and suck blood from the living for sustenance **2.** SB PREDATORY sb who preys on other people for financial or emotional gain **3.**

ZOOL = **vampire bat 4.** THEATRE TRAP DOOR a trapdoor on the floor of a stage (*technical*) [Mid-18thC. Via French or German from Serbo-Croat *vampir*, of uncertain origin: perhaps via Russian from Kazan Tatar *ubyr* 'witch'.] —**vampiric** /vam pírrik/ *adj.* —**vampirical** /-pírrik'l/ *adj.* —**vampirish** /vám pīrish/ *adj.*

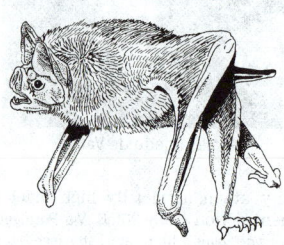

Vampire bat

vampire bat *n.* a bat found in tropical and subtropical Central and South America that bites the skin of birds or other mammals and laps the blood. It takes relatively little blood from its victims but can transmit serious diseases such as rabies. Family: Desmodontidae.

vampirism /vám pīrizzəm/ *n.* **1.** BELIEF IN VAMPIRES the belief that corpses can leave their graves at night and suck the blood of living people **2.** STATE OF BEING A VAMPIRE the supposed state or practices of a vampire **3.** FINANCIAL OR EMOTIONAL EXPLOITATION the act of preying on other people for financial or emotional gain

van¹ /van/ *n.* **1.** AUTOMOT ENCLOSED MOTOR VEHICLE a motor vehicle that has rear or side doors or sliding side panels and is used for transporting goods or people **2.** RAIL RAILWAY WAGON a closed railway wagon for goods, or the section of the carriage for the guard, luggage, parcels, or mail **3.** TRANSP CARAVAN a caravan [Early 19thC. Shortening of CARAVAN.]

van² /van/ *n.* **1.** FRONT the leading position **2.** MIL = **vanguard** *n.* **1** [Early 17thC. Variant of VANGUARD.]

van³ /van/ *n.* in tennis, a score of advantage (*informal*) [Early 20thC. Shortening of ADVANTAGE.] ◊ **van in** in tennis, the score of advantage in favour of the server (*informal*) ◊ **van out** in tennis, the score of advantage against the server (*informal*)

van⁴ /van/ *n.* **1.** AGRIC WINNOWING DEVICE a device used for winnowing grain (*archaic*) **2.** BIRDS WING a bird's wing (*archaic or literary*) [15thC. Originally a dialect form of FAN.]

van⁵ *abbr.* vanilla

Van /van/ city in eastern Turkey, the capital of Van Province. It lies on the eastern shore of Lake Van, about 80 km/50 mi. west of the Turkish-Iranian border. Population: 153,111 (1990).

Van, Lake saltwater lake in eastern Turkey, between the sources of the Euphrates and Tigris rivers, at an altitude of 1,720 m/5,643 ft. Area: 3,763 sq. km/1,453 sq. mi.

vanadate /vánnə dayt/ *n.* a salt or ester of vanadium [Mid-19thC. Formed from VANADIUM.]

vanadic /və náddik, -náyd-/ *adj.* consisting of or containing high-valency vanadium. ◊ **vanadous** [Mid-19thC. Formed from VANADIUM.]

vanadinite /və náddi nīt/ *n.* a rare lead and vanadium mineral, brown, red, or yellow in colour, that is found with other lead minerals and is a source of vanadium. Formula: $Pb_5(VO_4)_3Cl$. [Mid-19thC. Formed from VANADIUM.]

vanadium /və náydi əm/ *n.* a poisonous silvery-white metallic chemical element used in making tough steel alloys and as a catalyst. Symbol **V** [Mid-19thC. Via modern Latin from Old Norse *Vanadis*, a Scandinavian goddess.]

vanadium steel *n.* a low-alloy steel containing the element vanadium for added strength

vanadous /vánnədəss/ *adj.* consisting of or containing low-valency vanadium. ◊ **vanadic** [Mid-19thC. Formed from VANADIUM.]

Van Allen /van állən/, **James** (*b.* 1914) US physicist. A pioneer in high altitude and space research, he discovered (1958) two radiation belts that encircle the Earth. Full name **James Alfred Van Allen**

Van Allen belt /van állən-/, **Van Allen radiation belt** *n.* either of two belts surrounding the Earth and containing charged particles held there by the Earth's magnetic field [Mid-20thC. Named after James Van ALLEN.]

vanaspati /və náspəti/ *n.* a hydrogenated vegetable oil commonly used in Indian cooking instead of butter [Mid-20thC. From Sanskrit *vanas-pati*, literally 'lord of the plants'.]

Vanbrugh /vánbrə/, **Sir John** (1664–1726) English playwright and architect. After achieving great popular success with his comedies *The Relapse* (1696) and *The Provok'd Wife* (1697), he became equally renowned as an architect, designing Castle Howard in Yorkshire (1699–1726) and Blenheim Palace, near Oxford (1705–20).

Vancouver /van kóovə/ city and port in southwestern British Columbia, Canada, opposite Vancouver Island. Population: 514,008 (1996).

Vancouver, Mount /van kóovə mownt/ peak of St Elias Range in southwestern Yukon Territory, Canada. Height: 4,828 m/15,840 ft.

Vancouver Island island off the southwestern coast of British Columbia, Canada. It is the largest island off western North America. Area: 31,284 sq. km/12,079 sq. mi.

vanda /vándə/ (*plural* **-das** *or* **-da**) *n.* an orchid native to East Asia and Australia with strap-shaped leaves and flowers that are typically flattened with a spur on the lip. There are many cultivated varieties and hybrids. Genus: *Vanda*. [Early 19thC. Via modern Latin from Sanskrit *vandā*.]

V and A, **V & A** *abbr.* Victoria and Albert Museum

vandal /vánd'l/ *n.* sb who maliciously and deliberately defaces or destroys sb else's property [Mid-16thC. From Latin *Vandalus*, of Germanic origin (see VANDAL).] —**vandalish** *adj.*

Vandal *n.* a member of an ancient Germanic people who originated in Jutland, now in Denmark. They swept through Roman Europe during the 3rd and 4th centuries AD, conquering Gaul, Spain, Rome, and parts of North Africa, before being defeated at Carthage in 533. [Old English *Wendlas* (plural) 'Vandals', from prehistoric Germanic] —**Vandalic** /van dállik/ *adj.*

vandalism /vánd'lizəm/ *n.* the malicious and deliberate defacement or destruction of sb else's property —**vandalistic** /vándə lístik/ *adj.*

vandalize /vándəlīz/ (**-izes, -izing, -ized**), **vandalise** (**-ises, -ising, -ised**) *vt.* to deface, destroy, or otherwise damage private or public property maliciously and deliberately —**vandalization** *n.*

vanda orchid *n.* = **vanda**

van de Graaff generator /van də graáf-/ *n.* an electrostatic machine that produces electrical discharges at extremely high voltages, used in particle accelerators and for testing electrical insulators. The electric charge from a source of direct current accumulates on a high-speed belt inside an insulated metal sphere filled with Freon™ or nitrogen gas under high pressure. [Named after R. J. *van de Graaff* (1901–67), US physicist.]

Van der Hum /van dər hóom/ *n.* S *Africa* a tangerine-flavoured liqueur [Mid-19thC. Origin uncertain: probably from a personal name.]

van der Waals' equation /van dər waálz-/ *n.* a modified equation of state describing the physical behaviour of gases that takes into account the volumes of molecules and the interactions between them. It explains the difference in behaviour between a real gas and an ideal gas that obeys the gas laws. [Named after Johannes *van der Waals* (1837–1923), Dutch physicist]

van der Waals' force *n.* a weak attractive force between atoms or molecules resulting from the positioning of electrons within the interacting particles [See VAN DER WAALS' EQUATION]

Van Diemen's Land /van deemonz-/ former name for **Tasmania**

van Dyck /van dík/, **Sir Anthony** (1599–1641) Flemish painter. Active in Belgium, Italy, and England, he is noted for his sumptuous, large-scale portraits of English royalty and aristocracy.

Vandyke /van dík/ n. **1.** = **Vandyke beard 2.** CLOTHES = **Vandyke collar 3.** V-SHAPE a V-shape forming part of a decorative border on material or clothing **4.** DECORATIVE BORDER a decorative border on material or clothing made up of V-shaped points [Mid-18thC. Named after Sir Anthony *Van Dyck* (1599–1641), Flemish painter, in reference to various characteristic features of his paintings.] —**vandyked** adj.

Vandyke beard n. a short, neatly trimmed, pointed beard

Vandyke brown adj. DARK BROWN of a deep rich brown colour (*hyphenated before a noun*) ■ n. BROWN COLOUR OR PIGMENT a deep rich brown colour or pigment

Vandyke collar n. a large white collar of linen or lace that has a deeply indented edge

Vandyke stitch n. a V-shaped variation of cross stitch, used as a filling stitch to form a solid decoration

vane /vayn/ n. **1.** ROTATING BLADE a flat blade mounted as part of a set in a circle so as to rotate under the action of wind or liquid. Windmill sails and turbine blades are examples. **2.** METEOROL WEATHER VANE a weathervane **3.** ARMS STABILIZER ON A MISSILE a stabilizing or guiding blade on a missile **4.** BIRDS BLADE OF A FEATHER the flat part of a feather, consisting of interlocking rows of barbs. Each feather has two vanes, one on each side. **5.** PART OF A LEVELLING ROD the moving part on a levelling rod **6.** COMPASS COMPASS OR QUADRANT SIGHT a sight on a compass or quadrant [15thC. Originally a dialect form of FANE.] —**vaned** adj.

Vänern, Lake /vénnərn, váynərn/ the largest lake in Sweden, situated in the southwest of the country. Area: 5,584 sq. km/2,156 sq. mi.

van Eyck /van ík/, **Jan** (1390?–1441) Flemish painter. His religious paintings and portraits, meticulously painted in vivid colours, marked the beginning of the northern European Renaissance.

vang /vang/ n. a guy rope forming part of a pair that extend from a gaff to the deck [Mid-18thC. Variant of FANG.]

van Gogh /van gókh, -góf/, **Vincent** (1853–90) Dutch painter. His highly expressive canvases are characterized by their bright colours and vigorous brushstrokes. Full name **Vincent Willem van Gogh**

vanguard /ván gaard/ n. **1.** MIL ADVANCE TROOPS the military divisions of an army or navy that lead the advance into battle **2.** LEADING POSITION OR PEOPLE the leading position of a movement, field, or cultural trend, or the people who are foremost in a movement, field, or cultural trend [15thC. Shortening of French *avant-garde*, from *avant* 'before' + *garde* 'guard'.] —**vanguardism** n. —**vanguardist** n.

Vanilla

vanilla /və níllə/ n. **1.** PLANTS VINE WITH SEED PODS USED AS FLAVOURING a tropical American vine of the orchid family cultivated for its seed pods, from which a popular flavouring is produced. Genus: *Vanilla*. **2.** PLANTS VANILLA POD the long, narrow, fleshy seed pod of the vanilla vine **3.** COOK VANILLA FLAVOURING a flavouring extracted from the seed pods of the vanilla vine and used in cooking ■ adj. **1.** COOK FLAVOURED WITH VANILLA

flavoured with vanilla, or having a flavour of vanilla **2.** PLAIN OR DULL lacking outstanding or interesting characteristics (*slang*) ○ *vanilla software* [Mid-17thC. From Spanish *vainilla*, literally 'small sheath', from *vaina* 'sheath', from Latin *vagina*. From the shape of the vanilla seed pod.]

vanillic /və níllik/ adj. resembling, containing, or derived from vanilla or vanillin

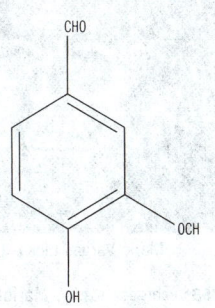
Vanillin

vanillin /və níllin/ n. a white aldehyde obtained from vanilla or prepared synthetically and used as a flavouring and in perfumes. Formula: $C_8H_8O_3$.

Vanir /váan eer/ npl. in Norse mythology, a race of peace-loving gods [From Old Norse, of uncertain origin: probably ultimately from an Indo-European word meaning 'to desire', which is also the ancestor of English *win* and *venerate*]

vanish /vánnish/ (-ishes, -ishing, -ished) vi. **1.** DISAPPEAR SUDDENLY to disappear suddenly or inexplicably ○ *It can't just have vanished!* **2.** STOP EXISTING to cease to exist **3.** MATH BECOME ZERO to assume or be given the value of zero (*refers to a function or variable*) [14thC. From the Old French stem *evaniss-*, from *esvanir*, from Latin *evanescere* 'to die out, pass away', from, ultimately, *vanus* 'empty' (see VAIN).] —**vanisher** n. —**vanishingly** adv. —**vanishment** n.

vanishing point n. **1.** APPARENT MEETING POINT OF PARALLEL LINES a point in a drawing or painting at which parallel lines seem to meet as represented in perspective **2.** POINT WHERE STH DISAPPEARS a point at which sth disappears or ceases being

Vanitory /vánnitəri/ tdmk. a trademark for a type of vanity unit

vanity /vánnəti/ n. (*plural* -**ties**). **1.** EXCESSIVE PRIDE excessive pride, especially in your appearance ○ *She is entirely free of personal vanity.* **2.** STH SB IS VAIN ABOUT an instance or source of excessive pride **3.** FUTILITY the state or fact of being futile, worthless, or empty of significance **4.** STH FUTILE sth that is considered futile, worthless, or empty of significance **5.** US = **vanity case 6.** US = **dressing table 7.** US, NZ = **vanity unit** [13thC. Via Old French from Latin *vanitas*, from *vanus* 'empty' (see VAIN).]

vanity bag n. = **vanity case** (*dated*)

vanity case, **vanity** n. a small case or bag in which sb carries cosmetics

Vanity Fair, **vanity fair** n. a place, especially a very large city or the world in general, considered to be frivolous and full of idle worthless amusements (*literary*) [Coined by John BUNYAN in his *Pilgrim's Progress* (1678)]

vanity publisher, **vanity press** n. a publishing house that publishes an author's work in return for payment from the author. Vanity publishers do not typically market or distribute their publications. —**vanity publishing** n.

vanity table n. US = **dressing table**

vanity unit n. a cabinet that holds a hand basin and its plumbing, usually with drawers or shelves under the sink for storage. US term **dressing table**

vanload /ván lōd/ n. the amount of goods or passengers that a van can transport at one time

vanquish /vángkwish/ (-quishes, -quishing, -quished) vt. **1.** DEFEAT IN BATTLE to defeat an opponent or opposing army in a battle or fight **2.** DEFEAT IN COMPETITION to prove convincingly superior to sb in a contest, competition, or argument **3.** OVERCOME EMOTION to over-

come, suppress, or subdue an emotion, feeling, or idea [14thC. Formed from Old French *venquis*, from *veintre*, from Latin *vincere* 'conquer' (source of English *convince*, *victory*, and *evict*).] —**vanquishable** adj. —**vanquisher** n. —**vanquishment** n.

— WORD KEY: SYNONYMS —
See Synonyms at **defeat**.

vantage /váantij/ n. **1.** ADVANTAGEOUS POSITION a position that provides an advantage **2.** SUPERIORITY IN A CONTEST superiority in a contest or competition **3.** = **vantage point** [14thC. From Old French *avantage* (see ADVANTAGE).] —**vantageless** adj.

vantage ground n. a position of superiority over sb

vantage point n. **1.** vantage point, vantage POSITION GIVING A GOOD VIEW a position or location that provides a broad view or perspective of sth **2.** PERSONAL STANDPOINT a personal point of view

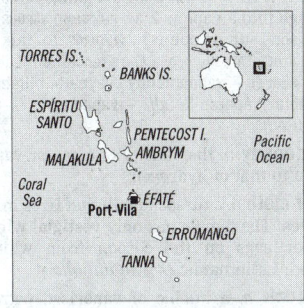
Vanuatu

Vanuatu /vánnoo áa too/ republic in the southwestern Pacific Ocean, comprising approximately 80 islands. Language: English, French. Currency: vatu. Capital: Port-Vila. Population: 172,000. Area: 12,190 sq. km/4,707 sq. mi. Official name **Republic of Vanuatu**. Former name **New Hebrides**

vanward /vánnward/ adj. AT THE FRONT in or at the front or edge of sth ■ adv. MOVING TOWARDS THE FRONT moving towards the front or edge of sth

vapid /váppid/ adj. **1.** DULL lacking interest or liveliness **2.** INSIPID lacking strength, taste, or flavour [Mid-17thC. From Latin *vapidus* 'insipid'.] —**vapidity** /və píddəti/ n. —**vapidly** /váppidli/ adv. —**vapidness** /váppidnəss/ n.

vapor n., vti. US = **vapour**

vaporescence /váypə réss'nss/ n. the formation or creation of vapour —**vaporescent** adj.

vaporetto /váppə réttō/ (*plural* -**ti** /váppə rétti/ or -**tos**) n. a motorboat for transporting passengers along the canals in Venice [Early 20thC. From Italian, literally 'small steamboat', from *vapore*, from Latin *vapor* (see VAPOUR).]

vaporific /váypə ríffik/ adj. **1.** PRODUCING VAPOUR producing, causing, or becoming vapour **2.** BEING VAPOUR being, containing, or resembling vapour **3.** VOLATILE capable of changing easily from a liquid or solid state into vapour

vaporize /váypə rīz/ (-izes, -izing, -ized), **vaporise** (-ises, -ising, -ised) vti. **1.** CHANGE INTO VAPOUR to change into or cause sth to change into vapour **2.** VANISH OR MAKE VANISH to vanish or cause sb or sth to vanish **3.** ANNIHILATE OR BE ANNIHILATED to destroy sb or sth so completely that the person or object is turned into a gas or vapour, or to be destroyed in this way —**vaporizable** adj. —**vaporization** /váypə rī záysh'n/ n.

vaporizer /váypə rīzər/, **vaporiser** n. sth used to produce a vapour, especially a device used to vaporize a medication so that it can be inhaled

vaporous /váypərəss/ adj. **1.** BEING VAPOUR being, containing, or resembling vapour **2.** PRODUCING VAPOUR producing, causing, or becoming vapour **3.** VOLATILE capable of changing easily from a liquid or solid state into vapour **4.** UNSUBSTANTIAL lacking material existence or permanence **5.** FANCIFUL of a fanciful, ridiculous, or implausible nature **6.** OBSCURED BY VAPOUR made hard to see because of being obscured by mist or vapour —**vaporosity** /váypə róssəti/ n. —

vaporously /váypərəssli/ *adv.* **—vaporousness** /-rəssnəss/ *n.*

vapour /váypər/ *n.* **1.** PHYS **GASEOUS SUBSTANCE** a gaseous substance at a temperature lower than that at which it can be liquefied or solidified by an appropriate increase in pressure alone **2.** PHYS **MOISTURE PARTICLES** moisture or some other matter visible in the air as mist, clouds, fumes, or smoke **3.** PHYS **GASEOUS STATE OF A SUBSTANCE** the gaseous state of a liquid or solid at a temperature below its boiling point **4.** CHEM **VAPORIZED SUBSTANCE** a substance prepared for military, industrial, or medical use in vaporized form **5.** ENG **GAS AND AIR MIXTURE** a combination of air with a gaseous substance such as that of air and petrol in an internal-combustion engine **6. STH UNSUBSTANTIAL AND IMPERMANENT** sth without material existence or permanence (*archaic*) **7. FANCIFUL IDEA** a fanciful idea (*archaic*) ■ **vapours** *npl.* **LOW SPIRITS** a bout of low spirits or sadness (*archaic*) ■ *v.* (**vapours, vapouring, vapoured**) **1.** *vti.* PHYS **EVAPORATE** to change or cause sth to change into a vapour **2.** *vi.* PHYS **EMIT VAPOUR** to give off or send up vapour **3.** *vi.* **BRAG** to talk boastfully [14thC. Directly or via Old French from Latin *vapor* 'steam, heat'.] **—vapourability** /váypərə bíllәti/ *n.* **—vapourable** /váypərəb'l/ *adj.* **—vapourer** *n.* **—vapoury** /váypəri/ *adj.*

vapour density *n.* the density of a gas or vapour in relation to that of hydrogen

vapourer moth *n.* a tussock moth that lives in hedges and trees. The female has only vestigial wings and lays her eggs on the cocoon from which she emerged. Latin name: *Orgyia antiqua.*

vapour lock *n.* a bubble of vaporized petrol that blocks the normal flow of fuel in the line that supplies the carburettor of an internal-combustion engine

vapour pressure, **vapour tension** *n.* the pressure exerted by a vapour, particularly a vapour in contact with its liquid form

vapour trail *n.* a visible trail of condensed vapour left by an aircraft flying at high altitude

vapourware /váypər wair/ *n.* new software that has been announced or advertised but has not yet been, and may never be, produced [Late 20thC. Formed from VAPOUR, on the model of SOFTWARE.]

vaquero /va káirō/ (*plural* **-ros**) *n. Southwest US* a cowboy [Early 19thC. From Spanish, from *vaca* 'cow'.]

var *abbr.* volt-ampere reactive

VAR[1] /vaar/ *n.* a retail seller of computers who adds products to computers produced by manufacturers or performs services such as product integration or customization before selling the computers to customers. Abbr of **value-added reseller**

VAR[2] *abbr.* **1.** visual aural range **2.** volt-ampere reactive

var. *abbr.* **1.** variable **2.** variant **3.** variation

vara /vaárə/ *n.* a unit of length used in Spain, Portugal, and Latin America that can be from 80 cm/32 in to 108 cm/43 in in length [Late 17thC. Via Spanish, 'rod, yardstick', from Latin, 'forked pole, trestle', from *varus* 'bent'.]

varactor /váir aktər/ *n.* a semiconductor diode with a capacitance that varies according to the voltage applied to it, used to regulate the frequency of electronic circuits in amplifiers [Mid-20thC. Contraction of VARIABLE + REACTOR.]

Varanasi /və raánəssi/, **Vārānasi** city in Uttar Pradesh State, northern India, on the River Ganges. It is an important place of pilgrimage for Hindus. Population: 925,962 (1991). Former name **Benares**

Varangian /və ránji ən/ *n.* a member of any of the Scandinavian peoples who invaded and settled in Russia between the 8th and the 11th centuries [Late 18thC. Via medieval Latin *Varangus* and medieval Greek *baraggos* from, ultimately, Old Norse *Væringi*, from *vár* 'pledge'.] **—Varangian** *adj.*

Varangian Guard *n.* **1. SCANDINAVIAN FORCE GUARDING A BYZANTINE EMPEROR** the body of Scandinavian soldiers who were the Byzantine emperor's bodyguard in the 10th and 11th centuries **2. MEMBER OF THE VARANGIAN GUARD** a Scandinavian soldier in the Varangian Guard

Vardon /vaárd'n/, **Harry** (1870–1937) British golfer. He won the the British Open championship six times between 1896 and 1914, and the US Open in 1900.

varec /várrek/ *n.* kelp [Late 17thC. From French.]

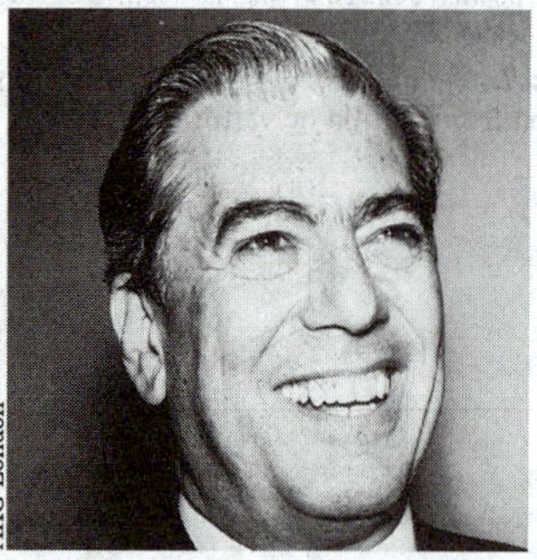

AKG London

Mario Vargas Llosa

Vargas Llosa /vaárgəss lóssə/, **Mario** (*b.* 1936) Peruvian writer and critic. Many of his works deal with issues of social change and political corruption. Full name **Jorge Mario Pedro Varga Llosa**

vari- *prefix.* = **vario-** (*used before vowels*)

variable /váiri əb'l/ *adj.* **1. ABLE TO CHANGE** able or liable to change, especially suddenly and unpredictably **2. INCONSISTENT** inconsistent or uneven in quality or performance ○ *a variable performance* **3. FICKLE** inconstant and capricious in nature or character **4.** METEOROL **LIKELY TO BLOW DIFFERENTLY** used to describe a wind that is likely to change direction or intensity **5.** ELECTRON ENG **WITH RESISTANCE THAT VARIES** used to describe an electrical device that has a resistance that varies **6.** BIOL **DIFFERING FROM THE SPECIES NORM** used to describe a species that tends to differ in some characteristic from a recognized or known type **7.** MATH **WITH NO FIXED NUMERICAL VALUE** not having a fixed numerical value ■ *n.* **1. STH THAT CAN VARY** sth capable of changing or varying **2.** MATH **SYMBOL FOR AN UNSPECIFIED QUANTITY** a symbol that represents an unspecified or unknown quantity, such as 'a', 'b', or 'x' **3.** MATH **RANGE OF VALUES** a range of values, any one of which is a solution to an algebraic expression **4.** LOGIC **LOGIC SYMBOL** a symbol, especially 'x', 'y', or 'z', that is used usually in connection with quantifiers to represent individuals in a universe of discourse **5.** ASTRON = **variable star 6.** METEOROL **VARIABLE WIND** a wind that is likely to change in direction or intensity ■ **variables** *npl.* METEOROL **REGION OF VARIABLE WINDS** a region where variable winds are likely to be encountered [14thC. Via Old French from Latin *variabilis*, from *variare* (see VARY).] **—variability** /váiri ə bíllәti/ *n.* **—variableness** /váiri əb'lnəss/ *n.* **—variably** /-əbli/ *adv.*

variable cost *n.* a cost that varies directly in relation to output

variable-geometry *adj.* used to describe an aircraft with wings that are hinged so that in flight they can move backwards or forwards. The wings are swept back to give low drag in supersonic flight and are moved forwards for takeoff and landing.

variable-rate mortgage *n.* a mortgage on which interest is payable at a rate that changes, usually in accordance with market interest rates. US term **adjustable-rate mortgage**

variable star *n.* a star whose brightness changes at regular or irregular intervals

variable-sweep *adj.* AEROSP = **variable-geometry**

variance /váiri ənss/ *n.* **1. CHANGE IN STH** a change that occurs in sth **2. DIFFERENCE BETWEEN THINGS** a difference between two or more things **3. DISAGREEMENT** a difference of opinion or attitude ○ *The project failed because of variances of opinion about the next step.* **4.** LAW **DISCREPANCY IN STH** a discrepancy between two statements, documents, or steps in a legal proceeding **5.** ACCT **DIFFERENCE IN COST** a difference between actual costs and the usual costs of production **6.** STATS **SQUARE OF STANDARD DEVIATION** a statistical measure of the spread or variation of a group of numbers in a sample, equal to the square of the standard deviation. Other measures of the spread are the ratio of the squared standard deviation to the sample size (**population variance**), and the ratio of the squared standard deviation to the sample size minus one (**sample variance**). **7.** *US* LAW **LEGAL DISPENSATION** a dispensation to ignore a rule or law [14thC. Via Old French from Latin *variantia*, from *variare* (see VARY).]

variant /váiri ənt/ *adj.* **1. DIFFERING SLIGHTLY** having or showing a difference from the norm ○ *variant pronunciations of common words* **2. CHANGEABLE** tending or likely to change ■ *n.* **1. SLIGHTLY DIFFERENT FORM** sth that differs slightly from the norm **2.** LING **DIFFERENT FORM OR SPELLING OF WORD** a different form or spelling of a word or phrase from the standard one **3.** STATS = **random variable** [14thC. Via French, from *varier* 'to vary', from Latin *variare* (see VARY).]

variate /váiri ət, -ayt/ *n.* = **random variable** [Late 19thC. From Latin *variatus*, the past participle stem of *variare* (see VARY).]

variation /váiri áysh'n/ *n.* **1. ACT OF VARYING** the act or a result of varying **2. STATE OF DIFFERING** the state or fact of differing, e.g. from a former state or value, from others of the same type, or from a standard **3. DEGREE OF DIFFERENCE** the degree to which sth differs, e.g. from a former state or value, from others of the same type, or from a standard ○ *There is a variation of several marks in the exam results.* **4. STH DIFFERING SLIGHTLY** sth that differs slightly from the norm **5.** BIOL **BIOLOGICAL DEVIATION** a significant deviation from the normal biological form, function, or structure **6.** BIOL **LIVING ORGANISM THAT DIFFERS** a living organism that differs from the normal form for its kind **7.** MATH **MATHEMATICAL FUNCTION** a mathematical function that relates the values of one variable to those of other variables **8.** MUSIC **REPETITION OF A MUSICAL THEME** the repetition of a musical theme with modifications of melody, rhythm, or harmony **9.** MUSIC **ALTERED VERSION OF A MUSICAL THEME** an altered version of an original musical theme or melody, such that the rhythm or harmony is varied or melodic embellishment is added. Variations are often found in sets, where a theme is followed by several variations. **10.** BALLET **SOLO DANCE** a dance performed by a single dancer **11.** ASTRON **CHANGE IN ORBIT** a change in or deviation from the average motion or orbit of a celestial body **12.** ASTRON **TERM IN EQUATION DESCRIBING THE MOON'S MOTION** a term representing the gravitational attraction of the Sun on the Earth-Moon system in the mathematical equation for the Moon's motion **13.** PHYS = **magnetic declination** [14thC. Via French or directly from the Latin stem *variation-*, ultimately from *variare* (see VARY).] **—variational** *adj.* **—variationally** *adv.*

varic- *prefix.* = **varico-** (*used before vowels*)

variceal /várri seé əl/ *adj.* relating to or caused by a dilated blood vessel (**varix**) or blood vessels [Mid-20thC. Coined from VARICO- on the model of such words as CORNEAL and LARYNGEAL.]

varicella /várri séllə/ *n.* chickenpox (*technical*) [Late 18thC. From modern Latin, literally 'lesser smallpox', from *variola* (see VARIOLA).] **—varicellar** *adj.* **—varicellous** *adj.*

varicellate /várri séllət, -ayt/ *adj.* used to describe a gastropod's shell that has small longitudinal ridges on its surface [Mid-20thC. Formed from modern Latin *varicella*, literally 'little pustule', from medieval Latin *variola* (see VARIOLA), from the ridged surface.]

varicella-zoster virus *n.* a herpes virus that is responsible for chickenpox and shingles

varices plural of **varix**

varico- *prefix.* varix, varicose vein ○ *varicotomy* [From Latin *varic-*, the stem of *varix*]

varicocele /várrikō seel/ *n.* a swelling of the veins in the spermatic cord of the scrotum. It may cause only slight discomfort but can affect fertility, so that surgical correction is required.

varicolored *adj.* US = **varicoloured**

varicoloured *adj.* consisting of or having many colours

varicose /várrikōss/, **varicosed** /várrikōst/ *adj.* **1. SWOLLEN** swollen, knotted, or distended to a greater extent than normal **2.** MED **WITH VARICOSE VEINS** affected with or having varicose veins **3. PRODUCING SWELLING** relating to or producing swelling **4.** ZOOL **RIDGED LIKE A GASTROPOD SHELL** resembling a small longitudinal ridge on the shell of some gastropods [15thC. From Latin *varicosus*, from *varix* 'varix'.]

varicoses plural of **varicosis**

varicose vein *n.* SWOLLEN VEIN a vein that has become abnormally swollen and knotted as a result of defective valves ■ **varicose veins** *npl.* CONDITION WITH SWOLLEN VEINS a condition in which the surface veins, especially of the legs, become knotted and swollen, as a result of defects in the valves of the affected veins. The tendency to develop the condition may be inherited, while other causes include injury, inflammation, or thrombosis.

varicosis /várri kṓssiss/ (*plural* **-ses** /-seez/) *n.* **1.** MED CONDITION WITH SWOLLEN VEINS a condition in which a vein or veins become swollen or knotted **2.** ZOOL FORMATION OF RIDGES ON A GASTROPOD SHELL the formation of small longitudinal ridges on the surface of a gastropod shell

varicosity /várri kóssəti/ (*plural* **-ties**) *n.* **1.** SWOLLEN STATE the state of being abnormally swollen or knotted (**varicose**) **2.** VARICOSE VEIN a varicose vein (*technical*) **3.** HAVING SWOLLEN VEINS the condition of suffering from or having abnormally swollen or enlarged veins

varicotomy /várri kóttəmi/ (*plural* **-mies**) *n.* a surgical incision into a swollen vein, usually performed to treat varicose veins

varied /váirid/ *adj.* **1.** DIVERSE showing or characterized by many different forms or kinds **2.** CHANGED having undergone change or alteration **3.** WITH MANY COLOURS consisting of or having many colours —**variedly** *adv.* —**variedness** *n.*

variegate /váiri gayt/ (**-gates, -gating, -gated**) *vt.* **1.** CHANGE LOOK OF STH to change the way sth looks, especially by adding different colours **2.** ADD VARIETY to add variety to sth [Mid-17thC. From Latin *variegare* 'to make varied', from *varius* 'diverse' (source of English *various*).] —**variegation** /váiri gáysh'n/ *n.* —**variegator** /-gaytər/ *n.*

variegated /váiri gaytid/ *adj.* **1.** WITH PATCHES OF DIFFERENT COLOURS marked with or containing patches of different colours **2.** BOT WITH PATCHES OF LIGHTER COLOUR marked with or containing patches of lighter colour **3.** DIVERSE showing or characterized by many different forms or kinds

varietal /və rī́ ət'l/ *adj.* **1.** BIOL TYPICAL OF BIOLOGICAL VARIETY relating to, typical of, or being a variety of sth, especially a biological variety **2.** WINE MADE FROM SINGLE GRAPE VARIETY made entirely or principally from a single variety of grape ■ *n.* WINE WINE MADE FROM SINGLE GRAPE VARIETY a wine that is made entirely or principally from a single variety of grape, and is usually known by the name of the grape variety —**varietally** *adv.*

variety /və rī́ əti/ (*plural* **-ties**) *n.* **1.** QUALITY OF BEING VARIED the quality of being varied or diversified ○ *It's easy to get bored if there's no variety in your work.* **2.** PARTICULAR TYPE a particular type or kind within a general group ○ *a new variety* **3.** COLLECTION OF VARIED THINGS a collection of varied things, often belonging to the same general group **4.** THEATRE ENTERTAINMENT MADE UP OF DIFFERENT ACTS entertainment made up of a number of different kinds of acts **5.** BOT SUBDIVISION OF SPECIES a rank used in classifying living things, especially plants, that is subordinate to species but superior to form. Varieties of a species generally have certain distinguishing characteristics, such as a particular flower colour, and may arise naturally or through deliberate plant breeding. [Mid-16thC. Via Old French from the Latin stem *varietat-*, from *varius*. See VARIOUS.]

variety show *n.* a theatrical show made up of a number of short performances of different kinds, such as singing, comic sketches, dancing, and magic acts

varifocal /váiri fṓk'l/ *adj.* WITH MANY FOCUSING DISTANCES used to describe composite spectacle lenses with varying focal length that allow different focusing distances for near, far, and intermediate vision ■ **varifocals** *npl.* VARIFOCAL SPECTACLES spectacles with composite lenses for distant, intermediate, and near vision

variform /váiri fawrm/ *adj.* existing in different shapes or forms [Mid-17thC. Coined from VARIOUS + -FORM.] —**variformly** *adv.*

vario- *prefix.* variation, variance, difference ○ *variolite* [From Latin *varius* 'speckled, variegated']

variola /və rī́ ələ/ *n.* smallpox (*technical*) [Early 19thC. From late Latin, literally 'pustule', from Latin *varius* (see VARIOUS).]

variolate *vt.* /váiri ə layt/ (**-lates, -lating, -lated**) INOCULATE WITH SMALLPOX VIRUS to inoculate sb with the smallpox virus (*dated*) ■ *adj.* /váiri ələt/ PITTED OR SCARRED with a pitted or scarred appearance, like the skin of sb who has had smallpox —**variolation** /váiri ə láysh'n/ *n.*

variole /váiri ōl/ *n.* any of the small rounded masses that cause the pock-marked surface in the rock variolite [Early 19thC. From late Latin *variola* (see VARIOLA).]

variolite /váiri ə līt/ *n.* a rock that has a pock-marked surface caused by rounded fibrous crystalline masses that are embedded in it [Late 18thC. Coined from VARIOLA + -ITE.] —**variolitic** /váiri ə líttik/ *adj.*

varioloid /váiri ə loyd/ *adj.* LIKE SMALLPOX having the characteristics of smallpox ■ *n.* MILD FORM OF SMALLPOX a mild form of smallpox that affects people who are partially immune because of having been inoculated or having had smallpox already

variolous /və rī́ ələss/ *adj.* relating to, like, or affected by smallpox

variometer /váiri ómmitər/ *n.* **1.** PHYS MAGNETIC FIELD INSTRUMENT an instrument used to measure magnetic fields, especially variations in Earth's magnetic field **2.** AIR RATE-OF-CLIMB INDICATOR an instrument used to measure the rate of climb of an aircraft such as a glider

variorum /váiri áwrəm/ *adj.* **1.** WITH VARIOUS ANNOTATIONS with commentary or notes written by various editors or scholars **2.** WITH DIFFERENT VERSIONS OF TEXT containing different versions or readings of a text ■ *n.* VARIORUM EDITION an edition of a text with commentary or notes written by various editors or scholars, or with various different versions or readings [Early 18thC. From Latin *editio cum notis variorum*, 'edition with notes of various (commentators)'; *variorum*, genitive plural of *varius* (see VARIOUS).]

various /váiri əss/ *det.* ASSORTED many different ■ *pron.* DIFFERENT EXAMPLES many different examples of sth (*nonstandard*) ■ *adj.* **1.** OF DIFFERENT KINDS of different kinds or categories **2.** INDIVIDUAL individual or separate **3.** BEING AN ASSORTMENT being an assortment or variety **4.** CHANGING changing rather than constant (*archaic*) [Mid-16thC. Formed from Latin *varius*, 'variegated, diverse'.] —**variously** *adv.* —**variousness** *n.*

varisized /váiri sīzd/ *adj.* US being or consisting of different sizes

varistor /və rístər/ *n.* a two-element semiconductor with nonlinear resistance in which the resistance drops as the applied voltage increases. Varistors are often used as a safety device to short circuit transient high voltages in electronic circuits. [Mid-20thC. From VARIABLE + RESISTOR.]

varix /váiriks/ (*plural* **-ices** /váiri seez/) *n.* **1.** MED SWOLLEN OR KNOTTED VEIN an abnormally swollen or knotted vessel, especially a vein **2.** ZOOL RIDGE ON GASTROPOD SHELL a ridge along the length of the shell of a gastropod mollusc [14thC. From Latin, literally 'dilated vein, varicose vein'.]

varlet /vaárlət/ *n.* (*archaic*) **1.** RASCAL a rogue or rascal **2.** SERVANT a servant or attendant **3.** PAGE a knight's page [15thC. From Old French *vaslet* (see VALET).]

varmint /vaármint/ *n.* a troublesome, unpleasant, or despicable person or animal (*regional*) [Mid-16thC. Dialectal variant of VERMIN.]

varna /vaárnə/ *n.* a caste group in Hindu society. The four Aryan social castes or varnas are the priests (**brahmans**), warriors, merchants, and peasants, with, beneath these, the untouchables. [Mid-19thC. From Sanskrit, literally 'colour, cover; class, sort'.]

Varna /vaárnə/ city, port, and tourist centre in eastern Bulgaria, on the Black Sea. Population: 301,421 (1996).

varnish /vaárnish/ *n.* **1.** INDUST TRANSPARENT RESIN SOLUTION a solution of a resin in oil or spirits, applied to a surface to give it a protective gloss **2.** INDUST SMOOTH COATING OF VARNISH a coating of varnish, applied to sth to give it a protective gloss **3.** SUPERFICIALLY ATTRACTIVE MANNER OR APPEARANCE a superficially or deceptively attractive manner or appearance ■ *vt.* (**-nishes, -nishing, -nished**) **1.** INDUST APPLY VARNISH to coat sth with varnish **2.** GIVE STH SMOOTH SURFACE to give sth a smooth and usually glossy surface **3.** MAKE STH SUPERFICIALLY ATTRACTIVE to make sth superficially or deceptively attractive [14thC. Via Old French *vernis* from medieval Latin *vernicium*, 'sandarac', from Greek *Bereníkē*, 'Berenice', a city in Cyrenaica, where varnish was first used.] —**varnisher** *n.*

varnish tree *n.* a tree such as the lacquer tree that when tapped yields a juice that may be used as a varnish or lacquer

Varro /várrō/, **Marcus Terentius** (116–27 BC) Roman scholar. He was one of the most learned Romans of his day, and the author of more than 70 known works on a variety of subjects from farming to the Latin language. Little of his work survives.

varsity /vaárssəti/ (*plural* **-ties**) *n.* a university (*dated*) [Mid-19thC. Dialectal variant of 'versity', shortening of UNIVERSITY.]

Varuna /várrōonə/ *n.* the all-seeing creator god of Hindu tradition, who uses the sun as his eye and acts as a life-sustaining force, ever-present in all he has created [From Sanskrit, literally 'wise one, seer']

varus /váirəss/ *adj.* used to describe an abnormality in which a body part such as the foot is turned or displaced inwards towards the midline of the body or limb [Late 18thC. From Latin, literally 'bent, crooked'.]

varve /vaarv/ *n.* a layer or series of layers of sediment deposited annually in a still body of water, e.g. by a glacier. Varves can be counted back to date a particular layer. [Early 20thC. From Swedish *varv*, 'layer, turn'.]

vary /váiri/ (**-ies, -ying, -ied**) *v.* **1.** *vti.* UNDERGO OR MAKE STH UNDERGO CHANGE to undergo or make sth undergo a change in appearance or characteristics **2.** *vi.* BE DIFFERENT to be different **3.** *vt.* GIVE VARIETY TO STH to give variety or diversity to sth [14thC. Via Old French *varier* from Latin *variare*, derived from *varius* (see VARIOUS).] —**varying** *adj.* —**varyingly** *adv.*

WORD KEY: SYNONYMS

See Synonyms at ***change***.

vas /vass, vaass/ (*plural* **vasa** /váyzə, vaázə/) *n.* a vessel or duct in the body of a human or animal [Mid-17thC. From Latin, literally 'vessel'.] —**vasal** /váyss'l, váyz'l/ *adj.*

vas- *prefix.* = **vaso-** (*used before vowels*)

vasa plural of **vas**

vascular /váskyōolər/ *adj.* relating to, involving, typical of, or having fluid-carrying vessels, e.g. blood vessels in animals or the sap-carrying vessels in plants [Mid-17thC. From modern Latin *vascularis*, formed from VASCULUM.] —**vascularity** /váskyōo lárrəti/ *n.* —**vascularly** *adv.*

vascular bundle *n.* any of the many strands of tissue that contain the xylem and phloem vessels, responsible for conducting sap through the stems and branches of a plant. They are most prominent in annual and young plants, and in perennial and woody plants they become part of an inner cylinder of vascular tissue.

vascular cylinder *n.* = **stele**

vascularization /váskyōolə rī záysh'n/, **vascularisation** *n.* the development of vessels, especially blood vessels, in an organism or tissue

vascular tissue *n.* plant tissue that is specialized for conducting sap. It comprises phloem, which conveys chiefly dissolved sugars, and xylem, which conveys water and dissolved minerals.

vasculature /váskyōoləchər/ *n.* the arrangement of blood vessels in the body or in a particular organ or tissue

vasculitis /váskyōo lítiss/ *n.* inflammation of a blood vessel or lymph vessel

vasculum /váskyōoləm/ (*plural* **-la** /-lə/ *or* **-lums**) *n.* a small box or case used by botanists in the field for storing collected plants or other specimens [Mid-19thC. From Latin, literally 'little vessel', from VAS.]

vas deferens /váss déffə renz, vaáss-/ (*plural* **vasa deferentia** /váyzə defə rénshə, vaázə-/) *n.* either of a pair of ducts that carry sperm from the testes to the urethra during ejaculation. Contraction of its thick muscular wall propels sperm rapidly through the duct, which forms part of the spermatic cord. [Late 19thC. From Latin, literally 'carrying-away vessel'.]

vase /vaaz/ *n.* an open container, usually tall and rounded, used for displaying cut flowers or as an ornament [Mid-16thC. Via French from Latin *vas*, 'vessel'.]

vasectomize /və sёktə mīz/ (-**mizes, -mizing, -mized**), **vasectomise** (-**mises, -mising, -mised**) *vt.* to perform a vasectomy on sb

vasectomy /və sёktəmi/ (*plural* -**mies**) *n.* a surgical operation in which the vas deferens from each testis is cut and tied to prevent transfer of sperm during ejaculation [Late 19thC. Coined from VAS DEFERENS + -ECTOMY.]

Vaseline /vássə leen/ *tdmk.* a trademark for medical petroleum jelly and other products such as lip balm and hand lotion

vaso- *prefix.* **1.** blood vessels, vascular ∘ *vasodilation* **2.** vas deferens ∘ *vasectomy* [From Latin *vas* 'vessel']

vasoactive /váyzō áktiv/ *adj.* making blood vessels contract or dilate —**vasoactivity** /váyzō aktívvəti/ *n.*

vasoconstriction /váyzō kən stríksh'n/ *n.* narrowing of the blood vessels with consequent reduction in blood flow or increased blood pressure

vasoconstrictor /váyzō kən stríktər/ *n.* AGENT THAT NARROWS BLOOD VESSELS any agent such as a nerve or hormone that narrows the blood vessels, which in turn increases resistance to blood flow and raises blood pressure. Vasoconstrictors such as the hormone adrenaline and various drugs are used medically to maintain or raise blood pressure in circulatory disorders or during surgery, or to counteract shock. ■ *adj.* NARROWING BLOOD VESSELS causing narrowing of the blood vessels —**vasoconstrictive** *adj.*

vasodilation /váyzō dīla táysh'n/, **vasodilatation** *n.* widening of the blood vessels, especially the arteries, leading to increased blood flow or reduced blood pressure

vasodilator /váyzō dī láytər/ *n.* AGENT THAT WIDENS BLOOD VESSELS an agent, such as a nerve or hormone that widens the blood vessels, which in turn decreases resistance to blood flow and lowers blood pressure. Drugs that act as vasodilators are used medically to treat high blood pressure and various other circulatory disorders. ■ *adj.* WIDENING BLOOD VESSELS causing widening of the blood vessels —**vasodilatory** *adj.*

vasoinhibitor /váyzō in híbbitər/ *n.* sth that depresses or stops the activity of the nerves that control widening or narrowing of the blood vessels —**vasoinhibitory** *adj.*

vasomotor /váyzō mótər/ *adj.* causing or influencing changes in the diameter of blood vessels

vasopressin /váyzō préssin/ *n.* a hormone produced by the pituitary gland that causes narrowing of the arteries and raises blood pressure. It also reduces the volume of urine excreted by the kidneys. [Early 20thC. Originally a trademark.]

vasopressor /váyzō préssər/ *adj.* RAISING BLOOD PRESSURE causing or promoting the narrowing of blood vessels, which in turn raises blood pressure ■ *n.* STH THAT RAISES BLOOD PRESSURE sth that has the effect of raising blood pressure

vasospasm /váyzō spázzəm/ *n.* sustained contraction of the muscular walls of the blood vessels with a resultant reduction in blood flow. In Raynaud's disease there is vasospasm of the arteries of the fingers, which causes cold or numb fingers. —**vasospastic** /-spástik/ *adj.*

vasovagal /váyzō váyg'l/ *adj.* relating to, or involving the influence of the vagus nerve on circulation. Stimulation of the vagus reduces heart rate and, consequently, the amount of blood being pumped by the heart. [Early 20thC. Coined from VASO- + VAGAL.]

vassal /váss'l/ *n.* **1.** DEPENDENT LANDHOLDER IN FEUDAL SOCIETY sb who was obliged to show loyalty and homage to a feudal lord in return for being allowed to occupy land belonging to the lord and receiving his protection **2.** PERSON OR NATION DEPENDENT ON ANOTHER a person, nation, or group that is dependent on or subordinate to another ■ *adj.* BEING A VASSAL being, or typical of, a vassal [14thC. Via Old French from medieval Latin *vassallus*, from *vassus*, 'servant', from the assumed Celtic stem *wass-*, 'young man, squire'.] —**vassal** *adj.*

vassalage /váss'lij/ *n.* **1.** CONDITION OF BEING VASSAL the dependent condition of being sb's vassal **2.** DEPENDENT CONDITION any condition of being dependent on or subordinate to sb or sth else (*literary*)

vast /vaast/ *adj.* VERY GREAT IN SIZE OR AMOUNT very great in number, size, amount, extent, or degree ■ *n.* IMMENSE SPACE the immense expanse of space (*literary*) [Late 16thC. From Latin *vastus*, 'immense, empty'.] —**vastidity** /va stíddəti/ *n.* —**vastitude** /váasti tyood/ *n.* —**vastity** /váastiti/ *n.*

vastly /váastli/ *adv.* to a very great extent or degree

vastness /váastnəss/ *n.* **1.** STATE OF BEING VAST the state or quality of being vast **2.** IMMENSE EXPANSE an immense expanse or area of space (*literary*)

vasty /váasti/ (-**ier, -iest**) *adj.* vast (*archaic or literary*)

vat /vat/ *n.* **1.** LARGE CONTAINER FOR LIQUID a large container used to hold or store liquid **2.** PREPARATION OF DYE a preparation of weakly coloured soluble dye (**vat dye**) ■ *vt.* (**vats, vatting, vatted**) TREAT OR PUT STH IN VAT to treat, store, or put sth in a vat [12thC. Alteration of *fat*, from Old English *fæt* 'vessel'.]

VAT *n.* a tax added to the estimated value of a product or material at each stage of its manufacture or distribution, in the end paid by the consumer. Full form **value-added tax**

Vat. *abbr.* Vatican

vat dye *n.* any of a class of dyes that are made insoluble and fixed by oxidation after being taken up by fibres —**vat-dyed** *adj.*

vatic /váttik/ *adj.* relating to, involving, or typical of a prophet [Early 17thC. Formed from Latin *vates*, 'prophet, seer'.]

Vatican /váttikən/ *n.* **1.** POPE'S RESIDENCE the palace in the Vatican City that is used as the official residence of the pope and the administrative centre of the papacy **2.** POPE'S AUTHORITY the authority and jurisdiction of the pope [Mid-16thC. From Latin (*mons*) *Vaticanus*, 'Vatican (hill)'.]

Vatican City

Vatican City /váttikən-/ the world's smallest independent nation and headquarters of the Roman Catholic Church. Language: Italian, Latin. Currency: lira. Population: 850 (1996). Area: 44 hectares/110 acres. Official name **State of Vatican City**

Vaticanism /váttikənizəm/ *n.* the policies and authority of the pope, especially the idea of absolute papal authority

vaticinate /va tíssi nayt/ (-**nates, -nating, -nated**) *vti.* to prophesy sth [Early 17thC. From Latin *vaticinari*, derived from *vates*, 'prophet, seer' + *canere*, 'to sing'.] —**vaticinal** /və tíssin'l/ *adj.* —**vaticination** /váttissi náysh'n/ *n.* —**vaticinator** /və tíssi naytər/ *n.*

vatu /vaá too/ (*plural* -**tu**) *n.* a unit of currency in Vanuatu. See table at **currency**

Vauban /vō baáN/, **Sebastien le Prestre de** (1633–1707) French marshal of France. He was a specialist in siegecraft and fortifications during the reign of Louis XIV. He directed the sieges of Mons (1691) and Namur (1692).

vaudeville /váwdəvil/ *n.* **1.** US THEATRE = music hall **2.** US VAUDEVILLE SHOW a vaudeville show **3.** COMIC PLAY WITH SONGS a comic play with songs and dances **4.** MUSIC SATIRICAL POPULAR SONG a satirical popular song of the type performed in cabarets in the 19th and 20th centuries **5.** MUSIC OPERATIC SONG a song used as a finale in an opera. Each verse is sung by a different character, then all join in a refrain. [Mid-18thC. From Old French *vaudevire*, a shortening of *chanson du Vau de Vire*, 'song of the Valley of Vire', a region of Calvados, Normandy, noted for satirical folksongs.]

─── **WORD KEY: ORIGIN** ───

In 15th-century France there was a fashion for songs from the valley of the Vire, in the Calvados region of Normandy (particularly popular, apparently, were the satirical songs composed by a local fuller, Olivier Basselin). The geographical connection had been lost by the time English acquired the word, and the element *-vire* had been replaced with *-ville* 'town'. The semantic transition from 'popular song' to 'light theatrical entertainment' is not recorded until the early 19th century.

vaudevillian /váwdə vílli ən/ *n.* VAUDEVILLE COMPOSER OR PERFORMER sb who performs in or composes for vaudeville shows ■ *adj.* TYPICAL OF VAUDEVILLE typical of, suitable for, or used in vaudeville

Vaudreuil /vō drō i kavvə nyaár/, **Philippe de Rigaud de Vaudreuil de Cavagnal, marquis de** (1698–1778) French soldier and colonial administrator. He was governor of New France (now Canada) from 1755 to 1760, when he was forced to surrender to British forces during the Seven Years' War.

Sarah Vaughan

Vaughan /vawn/, **Sarah** (1924–90) US jazz singer. Performing with Earl Hines, Billy Eckstine, Count Basie, and other leading jazz musicians, she was a major international star known for her complex harmonization and vocal improvisation. Full name **Sarah Lois Vaughan**

Ralph Vaughan Williams

Vaughan Williams /vawn wíllyəmz/, **Ralph** (1872–1958) British composer. He developed a British national style of music from choral tradition and folk song. His works include nine symphonies and many choral pieces.

vault[1] /vawlt, volt/ *n.* **1.** ARCHIT ARCHED CEILING an arched structure of stone, brick, wood, or plaster that forms a ceiling or roof **2.** ARCHIT ROOM WITH ARCHED CEILING a room, especially an underground room, with an arched ceiling **3.** BURIAL CHAMBER a burial chamber, usually underground **4.** STH ARCHING OVERHEAD sth that arches overhead, especially the sky (*literary*) **5.** ANAT ARCHED PART OF BODY a part of the body with an arched shape ■ *v.* (**vaults, vaulting, vaulted**) **1.** *vt.* ARCHIT PUT

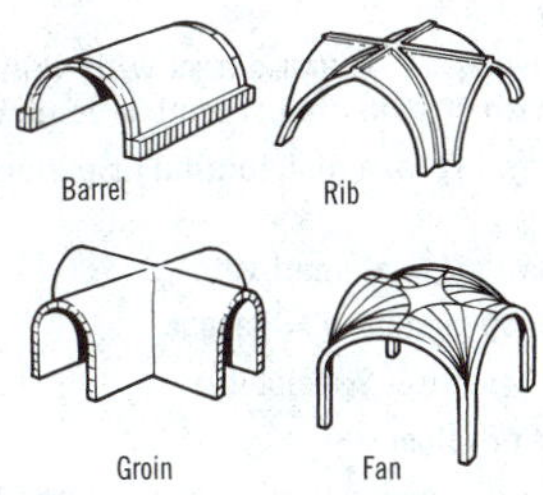
Barrel
Rib
Groin
Fan

Vault

ARCHED STRUCTURE OVER STH to cover a building with an arched ceiling or roof **2.** *vt.* ARCHIT BUILD STH AS VAULT to build sth in the shape of a vault **3.** *vi.* FORM VAULT to arch or curve like a vault [14thC. From Old French *vaute*, from assumed Vulgar Latin *volvita*, 'turn, vault', from Latin *voluta*, feminine past participle of *volvere*, 'to turn'.]

vault[2] /vawlt, volt/ *v.* (**vaults, vaulting, vaulted**) **1.** *vti.* SPRING OVER OBJECT to leap or spring over sth, especially by pushing on it with the hands or using a pole **2.** *vi.* MOVE WITH A BOUND to move with a leap or bound **3.** *vi.* RISE SUDDENLY TO PROMINENCE to arrive somewhere or achieve sth suddenly ○ *She vaulted to fame with the publication of her first novel.* **4.** *vti.* DRESSAGE PERFORM CURVET to perform a curvet in dressage or to make a horse perform a curvet ■ *n.* **1.** ACT OF VAULTING an act of vaulting **2.** DRESSAGE = **curvet** [Mid-16thC. Via Old French *volter*, ultimately from assumed Vulgar Latin *volvitare*, literally 'to roll repeatedly', from Latin *volvere*, 'to roll'.] —**vaulter** *n.*

vaulted /váwltid, vóltid/ *adj.* built with one or more vaults

vaulting[1] /váwlting, vólt-/ *n.* ARCHIT the structural use of brick, stone, or reinforced concrete to form a ceiling or roof over a space

vaulting[2] /váwlting, vólt-/ *adj.* aspiring or confident, especially in an excessive way (*literary*) ○ *vaulting ambition*

vaulting horse *n.* a piece of gymnastic equipment with four legs and a solid leather-covered oblong body, used for exercises and especially for vaulting over

vaunt /vawnt/ *v.* (**vaunts, vaunting, vaunted**) **1.** *vt.* BE BOASTFUL ABOUT STH to boast or act boastfully about sth such as achievements or possessions **2.** *vi.* BOAST to boast or brag (*literary*) ■ *n.* A BOAST a boast, or display of boasting [14thC. Via Old French *vanter* from late Latin *vanitare*, 'to be vain', from *vanus*, 'empty', (see VAIN).] —**vaunter** *n.* —**vauntingly** *adv.*

vaunt-courier *n.* a person or thing sent in advance of another (*archaic or literary*) [Mid-16thC. From French *avant*'before' + COURIER, modelled on French *avant-coureur*.]

vaunted /váwntid/ *adj.* boasted about or praised in an ostentatious way

vav /vawv/, **waw** /waw/ *n.* the sixth letter in the Hebrew alphabet, usually transliterated as 'v' or 'w' [Early 19thC. From Hebrew *wāw*, 'hook'.]

vavasor /vávvə sawr/, **vavasour** *n.* a feudal lord or knight who has power over vassals but is himself a vassal of a more powerful lord [14thC. Via Old French from medieval Latin *vavassor*, of uncertain origin: perhaps a contraction of *vassus vassorum*, 'vassal of vassals'. See VASSAL.]

vb *abbr.* **1.** verb **2.** verbal

VC *abbr.* **1.** vice-chairman **2.** vice chancellor **3.** vice consul **4.** Victoria Cross **5.** Vietcong

VCR *n., abbr.* video cassette recorder ■ *abbr.* visual control room (*on an airfield*)

vd *abbr.* **1.** vapour density **2.** various dates **3.** void

VD *abbr.* venereal disease

V-Day *n.* Victory Day

VDC *abbr.* Volunteer Defence Corps

VDR *abbr.* **1.** video disc recorder **2.** video disc recording

VDRL *abbr.* venereal disease research laboratory

VDT *abbr.* video display terminal

VDU *abbr.* visual display unit

've *contr.* have

veal /vee'l/ *n.* meat from a young calf, light in colour and texture with a delicate flavour [14thC. Via Old French from Latin *vitellus*, a diminutive of *vitulus*, 'calf'.]

veal calf *n.* a calf reared for veal

vealer /veélər/ *n. ANZ, Can, US* a veal calf

vector /véktər/ *n.* **1.** MATH QUANTITY WITH DIRECTION AND MAGNITUDE a quantity, e.g. force or velocity, made up of components of both direction and magnitude **2.** MATH ELEMENT OF VECTOR SPACE an element of a vector space **3.** AIR COURSE OF AIRCRAFT the course taken by an aircraft or a missile **4.** MED, VET DISEASE-TRANSMITTING ORGANISM an organism such as a mosquito or tick that transmits disease-causing microorganisms from infected individuals to other persons, or from infected animals to human beings **5.** GENETICS GENE TRANSFER AGENT an agent such as a plasmid or bacteriophage that is used in genetic engineering to transfer a segment of foreign DNA into a bacterium or other cell. The foreign DNA is spliced into the vector's DNA, which contains the genes necessary for switching on replication and transcription of the foreign DNA in its new setting. **6.** COMPUT COMPUTER ARRAY in computing, an array of any length but only one dimension ■ *vt.* (**-tors, -toring, -tored**) AIR **1.** DIRECT AIRCRAFT BY RADIO to direct an aircraft in flight, or its pilot, by radio, often from the ground **2.** CHANGE THRUST DIRECTION OF AIRCRAFT ENGINE to change the direction of the thrust of an aircraft engine as a means of steering the aircraft [Early 18thC. From Latin, literally 'carrier', from *vectus*, past participle of *vehere*, 'to carry'.] —**vectorial** /vek táwri əl/ *adj.* —**vectorially** *adv.*

vector product *n.* the result of multiplying two vectors. It is perpendicular to the vectors and its magnitude equals the product of their magnitudes multiplied by the sine of the included angle.

vector space *n.* a mathematical set of vectors associated with a field of scalars comprising a commutative group under addition and in which multiplication of a vector and a scalar is a vector

vector sum *n.* the result of adding two vectors, obtained graphically as the directed diagonal of the parallelogram whose sides are the given vectors

Veda /váydə, veédə/ *n.* any or all of the collections of Aryan hymns, originally transmitted orally but written down in sacred books from the 6th century BC [Mid-18thC. From Sanskrit, literally 'knowledge'. Ultimately from an Indo-European word meaning 'to see', which is also the ancestor of English *wise*, *vision*, and *idea*.] —**Vedaic** /vi dáy ik/ *adj.*

Vedaism /váydə izəm/ *n.* = **Vedism**

Vedanta /vi daántə/ *n.* one of the six philosophical schools of Hinduism [Late 18thC. From Sanskrit, literally 'Veda-end', from VEDA + *anta*, 'end'.] —**Vedantic** *adj.* —**Vedantism** *n.* —**Vedantist** *n.*

V-E Day *n.* 8 May, 1945, designated by the Allies to mark their victory in Europe in World War II after the German surrender of the day before

Vedda /véddə/ (*plural* **-da** *or* **-das**), **Veddah** (*plural* **-dah** *or* **-dahs**) *n.* PEOPLES a member of a forest people that is known to have lived in Sri Lanka since Stone Age times, and whose members are now mainly integrated with the Sinhalese [Late 17thC. From Sinhalese *vaddā* 'hunter'.] —**Veddoid** *adj.*

vedette /vi dét/ *n.* **1.** **vedette, vidette** FORWARD SCOUT a mounted soldier posted forwards of a larger force to serve as a scout **2.** **vedette, vedette boat** SMALL FAST SCOUTING VESSEL a small fast boat posted forwards of a larger seaborne force to serve as a scout [Late 17thC. Via French from Italian *vedetta*, alteration (influenced by *vedere*, 'to see') of *veletta*, from Spanish *vela*, 'watch', from Latin *vigilare*, 'to watch', from *vigil*, 'awake'. See VIGIL.]

Vedic /váydik, veédik/ *adj.* **1.** INDIAN RELIG IN THE VEDAS contained in or referring to the Vedas **2.** INDIAN RELIG BELONGING TO CULTURE THAT PRODUCED VEDAS belonging to or typical of the Hindu culture that produced the Vedas **3.** LANG IN ANCIENT SANSKRIT relating to, in, or typical of the ancient form of Sanskrit in which the Vedas are written ■ *n.* LANG ANCIENT SANSKRIT the ancient form of Sanskrit in which the Vedas are written

Vedism /váydizəm, veédizəm/ *n.* the Hindu religious theory and practice contained in, or based on, the Vedas

vee /vee/ *n.* the letter 'V', or sth with a similar shape [Late 19thC. From the pronunciation of the letter's name.]

vee-jay /vee jáy/ *n.* a video jockey (*informal*)

veep /veep/ *n. US* a vice president (*slang*) [Mid-20thC. Formed from VP.]

veer[1] /veer/ *v.* (**veers, veering, veered**) **1.** *vti.* CHANGE DIRECTION SUDDENLY to change direction, especially suddenly, or to make sth do this **2.** *vi.* CHANGE FROM ONE OPINION TO ANOTHER to change from one opinion or state of mind to another, especially when this is sudden or extreme **3.** *vi.* METEOROL SHIFT IN CLOCKWISE DIRECTION to shift in a clockwise direction (*refers to a wind*) **4.** *vti.* NAUT SAIL AWAY FROM WIND to change course in a sailing vessel away from the wind, or to make a vessel do this ■ *n.* CHANGE IN DIRECTION a change in direction or course [Late 16thC. From French *virer*, 'to turn', of uncertain origin: perhaps ultimately from Latin *gyrare* 'to turn round', influenced by Latin *viriae* (plural) 'bracelets'.]

veer[2] /veer/ (**veers, veering, veered**) *vt.* to let out a cable or chain or to make it go slack [15thC. From Middle Dutch *vieren*, 'to let out'.]

veery /veéri/ (*plural* **-ries**) *n.* a thrush that lives in the woodland and dense brush of the eastern United States, with tawny upper parts and a spotted breast. Latin name: *Catharus fuscescens*. [Mid-19thC. Origin uncertain: perhaps an imitation of its call.]

veg[1] /vej/ *n.* (*plural* **veg**) VEGETABLES vegetables or a vegetable (*informal*) ■ *vi.* DO NOTHING to rest and relax in an inactive manner (*informal*) [Mid-20thC. Shortening.]

veg[2] /vej/ *vi.* = **veg out**

Vega /veégə/ *n.* the brightest star in the constellation Lyra, and one of the brightest in the northern hemisphere

Vega /váygə/, **Lope de** (1562–1635) Spanish playwright and poet. He is considered the founder of Spanish national drama. More than 400 of his 2,000 plays survive. Full name **Lope Félix de Vega Carpio**

vegan /veégən/ *n.* PERSON WHO NEVER EATS ANIMAL PRODUCTS sb who does not eat meat, dairy produce, or eggs ■ *adj.* WITHOUT MEAT, DAIRY PRODUCE, OR EGGS not eating or including meat, dairy produce, or eggs [Mid-20thC. Contraction of VEGETARIAN.] —**vegan** *adj.* —**veganism** *n.*

Vegeburger *tdmk.* a trademark for a veggieburger

Vegemite /véjjə mīt/ *tdmk. ANZ* a trademark for a savoury yeast extract that is eaten as a spread

vegetable /véjtəb'l/ *n.* **1.** FOOD EDIBLE PLANT any plant with edible parts, especially leafy or fleshy parts that are used mainly for soups and salads and to accompany main courses **2.** FOOD FRUIT EATEN AS VEGETABLE any of various plant products that are strictly fruits, e.g. tomatoes, but are eaten as, and popularly thought of as, vegetables **3.** PLANTS ANY PLANT any member of the plant kingdom, as opposed to the animal or mineral kingdoms **4.** OFFENSIVE TERM a highly offensive term referring to sb in whom normal functions are severely reduced or absent, often due to injury to the brain (*slang offensive*) **5.** INACTIVE PERSON a term that deliberately insults sb's personality or level of activity (*slang insult*) ■ *adj.* CONSISTING OF VEGETABLES consisting of, made from, using, or like vegetables [14thC. Via Old French from medieval Latin *vegetabilis*, 'animating, able to grow', from Latin *vegetare* (see VEGETATE).]

vegetable ivory (*plural* **vegetable ivories**) *n.* **1.** HARD SUBSTANCE SIMILAR TO IVORY a hard pale material like ivory, used to make decorative items and accessories. It comes from the endosperm of a South American palm nut (**ivory nut**). **2.** = **ivory nut**

vegetable marrow *n.* **1.** PLANTS = **marrow** *n.* 2 **2.** FOOD = **marrow** *n.* 1

vegetable oil *n.* oil that has been extracted from a plant or the seeds of a plant, e.g. olive oil, sunflower oil, sesame oil, and rapeseed oil

vegetable oyster *n.* = **salsify**

vegetable sheep (*plural* **vegetable sheep**) *n. NZ* any of several plants of the daisy family that grow in uplands in New Zealand. Their dense foliage and white flowers make them resemble sheep from a distance. Genus: *Raoulia.*

vegetable wax *n.* a waxy material that forms part of the thin film covering the surfaces of most plants and helps reduce their loss of water through evaporation. It is obtained commercially from certain palms, such as the carnauba.

vegetal /véjjit'l/ *adj.* **1.** TYPICAL OF VEGETABLES relating to, involving, or typical of vegetables or other plants **2.** INVOLVING GROWTH, NOT SEXUAL REPRODUCTION used to describe processes concerned with the maintenance or growth and development of an organism, rather than sexual reproduction [14thC. Via Old French *vegeter,* 'to grow', from Latin *vegetare* (see VEGETATE).]

vegetal pole *n.* the end of an animal egg that contains the greatest concentration of yolk, lying opposite to the animal pole

vegetarian /véjjə táiri ən/ *n.* SB NOT EATING MEAT OR FISH sb who does not eat meat or fish but instead eats vegetables, fruits, grains, seeds, and sometimes eggs and dairy products ■ *adj.* EXCLUDING MEAT AND FISH not eating or including meat and fish, but sometimes eating or including dairy products and eggs [Mid-19thC. Formed from VEGETABLE + *-arian.*] —**vegetarianism** *n.*

vegetate /véjjə tayt/ (**-tates, -tating, -tated**) *vi.* **1.** BEHAVE IN DULL OR INACTIVE WAY to live or behave in a dull, inactive, or undemanding way **2.** BOT GROW OR SPROUT LIKE PLANT to grow or sprout like a plant **3.** MED PRODUCE FLESHY OUTGROWTHS to grow or spread, especially by producing fleshy outgrowths [Early 17thC. From late Latin *vegetare* 'to grow', from Latin *vegere,* 'to quicken'.]

vegetation /véjjə táysh'n/ *n.* **1.** PLANTS IN GENERAL plants in general or the mass of plants growing in a particular place **2.** PROCESS OF VEGETATING the process of vegetating **3.** MED ABNORMAL OUTGROWTH an abnormal outgrowth from a body part such as on the membranes surrounding the heart —**vegetational** *adj.*

vegetative /véjjətətiv/ *adj.* **1.** CONCERNED WITH PLANTS relating to, involving, typical of, or like vegetation, plants, or plant growth **2.** INVOLVING GROWTH, NOT SEXUAL REPRODUCTION relating to, involving, or typical of processes in the maintenance or growth and development of an organism, rather than sexual reproduction **3.** REPRODUCING FROM BODY CELLS OF PARENT used to describe a method of reproduction, especially in plants, in which new individuals originate from the body cells of the parent rather than from specialized sex cells. Organs of vegetative reproduction in plants include bulbs, corms, tubers, and rhizomes. **4.** DULL OR INACTIVE dull, inactive, and undemanding in lifestyle **5.** OFFENSIVE TERM an offensive term referring to sb in whom normal functions are reduced or absent due to injury to the brain —**vegetatively** *adv.* —**vegetativeness** *n.*

vegetative nervous system *n.* the part of the body's nervous system that controls involuntary functions, such as the beating of the heart

veggie /véjji/ *n.* sb who is a vegetarian (*informal*) [Mid-20thC. Shortening.] —**veggie** *adj.*

veggieburger /véjji burgər/, **vegeburger** *n.* a flat cake made from vegetables and legumes, fried or grilled, and often served in the same way as a hamburger

veg out, veg *vi.* to relax, be idle, or loaf, e.g. while watching television (*informal*) [Late 20thC. 'Veg' from VEGETATE.]

vehement /vée əmənt/ *adj.* **1.** WITH CONVICTION expressed with, or showing conviction or intense feeling **2.** DONE FORCEFULLY done with vigour or force [15thC. Via Old French from the Latin stem *vehement-*, 'forceful, violent', of unknown origin.] —**vehemence** *n.* —**vehemently** *adv.*

vehicle /vée ik'l/ *n.* **1.** TRANSP MEANS OF LAND TRANSPORT a usually wheeled conveyance used on land for carrying people or goods, most often by road or rail **2.** SPACE TECH STRUCTURE FOR TRANSPORT IN SPACE a powered structure, device, or rocket used to transport a payload or another craft through space **3.** COMMUNICATION MEDIUM a medium for communicating, expressing, or accomplishing sth **4.** ARTS PERFORMANCE FOR PARTICULAR PERFORMER a film, play, show, or other performance designed or used to show off the talents of a particular performer **5.** PAINTING MIXTURE FOR PAINT PIGMENT a substance or mixture such as linseed oil or an acrylic vinyl polymer in which a pigment is mixed for painting **6.** PHARM SUBSTANCE BLENDED WITH DRUG an inactive substance with which a drug is blended to make it easier to apply, administer, or take [Early 17thC. Via French *véhicule* from Latin *vehiculum,* from *vehere* 'to carry'.]

Vehicle Registration Document *n.* = **registration document**

vehicular /vi hík yoolər/ *adj.* relating to, involving, or for use by vehicles, especially motor vehicles [Early 17thC. From late Latin *vehicularis,* from Latin *vehiculum* (see VEHICLE).]

veil /vayl/ *n.* **1.** CLOTHES FACE COVERING WORN BY WOMEN a length of fabric, usually sheer, worn by women over the head and face as a concealment or for protection **2.** CLOTHES NETTING ATTACHED TO WOMAN'S HAT a piece of netting or other sheer fabric attached to a woman's hat and covering the eyes. This was especially popular as a millinery style in the 1950s. **3.** CHR NUN'S HEADDRESS a part of a nun's headdress covering the sides and back of the head **4.** CHR NUN'S VOWS OR LIFE the vows that a nun takes or the life that she leads **5.** STH LIKE CURTAIN sth that acts like a curtain in hiding, disguising, or obscuring sth else, or separating one thing from another **6.** BOT COVERING MEMBRANE OF YOUNG MUSHROOM a thin membrane that covers the stalk and cap of an immature mushroom. It ruptures as the mushroom matures, leaving remnants at the base of the stalk, and some tissue flecks at the crown of the cap. **7.** ANAT = **caul 8.** CHR = **humeral veil** ■ *v.* (**veils, veiling, veiled**) **1.** *vt.* COVER STH WITH A VEIL to cover sth such as a person's face with a veil **2.** *vt.* HIDE OR DISGUISE to hide or disguise sth, or separate sth from sth else **3.** *vi.* WEAR A VEIL to put on or wear a veil [12thC. Via Old French *veile* from Latin *vela,* 'covering', the plural of *velum,* 'sail'.] —**veiler** *n.* ◇ **draw a veil over sth** to ignore sth deliberately or refrain from mentioning it, in order to be discreet ◇ **take the veil** to become a nun

Veil /vīl/, **Simone** (*b.* 1927) French government official and politician. A lawyer and campaigner for women's rights, she was French minister of health (1974–79) and president of the European Parliament (1979–81).

veiled /vayld/ *adj.* **1.** DISGUISED not open or direct but disguised or suggested **2.** WEARING A VEIL covered with or wearing a veil —**veiledly** /váylidli/ *adv.*

veiling /váyling/ *n.* **1.** FABRIC FOR VEILS fabric used for veils **2.** VEIL a veil

vein /vayn/ *n.* **1.** ANAT VESSEL CARRYING BLOOD TO HEART any of the blood vessels that carry blood to the heart. All carry oxygen-depleted blood, except the pulmonary vein, which carries oxygenated blood from the lungs. **2.** ANY BLOOD VESSEL any of the vessels that carry blood around the body (*not used technically*) **3.** BOT SAP-CONDUCTING LEAF STRAND a distinct strand in a leaf that contains the sap-conducting vessels. It comprises one of several bundles of vessels and associated tissues (**vascular bundles**), and forms part of a network, arranged in a characteristic pattern. **4.** GEOL LAYER OF MINERAL a layer of a mineral in rock, especially an ore or a metal **5.** PARTICULAR QUALITY a particular recurrent quality or characteristic **6.** STREAK OF DIFFERENT COLOUR a streak of different colour or material within a substance such as marble, wood, or cheese **7.** INSECTS SUPPORTING STRUCTURE IN INSECT WING any of a network of hollow supporting structures in the wing of an insect that carry inside them blood vessels, nerves, and air tubes supplying the wing. The pattern of veins is characteristic for particular types of insect, and is useful in identifying and classifying new species. **8.** GEOL FISSURE FILLED WITH MATERIAL a fissure, crack, or channel in rock or ice that has been filled with a crystallized mixture of minerals **9.** DISPOSITION a disposition, tone, or mood ■ *vt.* (**veins, veining, veined**) **1.** STREAK STH to streak or suffuse sth of one colour or material with another **2.** FORM VEINS IN STH to form veins or things like veins in sth [13thC. Via Old French *veine* from Latin *vena,* 'blood vessel, vein of metal, mine'.] —**veinal** *adj.* —**veiny** *adj.*

veined /vaynd/ *adj.* **1.** HAVING VEINS with veins **2.** HAVING STREAKS with streaks that resemble veins in it

veining /váyning/ *n.* a distribution or pattern of veins or streaks

veinlet /váynlət/ *n.* a small vein

veinstone /váyn stōn/ *n.* = **gangue**

vel. *abbr.* **1.** vellum **2.** velocity

vela plural of **velum**

Vela /véelə/ *n.* a constellation in the sky of the southern hemisphere lying across the Milky Way, located between Centaurus and Puppis [Mid-19thC. Latin, literally 'sails', from the shape of the constellation (see VEIL).]

velamen /və láy men/ (*plural* **-mina** /və lámminə/) *n.* PLANTS the spongy layer that covers the aerial roots of some plants such as tree-dwelling orchids. It helps to protect the plant and assists in absorbing moisture from the air. [Late 19thC. From Latin, literally 'covering', from *velare,* 'to cover', from *velum,* 'sail'.]

velar /véelər/ *adj.* **1.** PHON WITH TONGUE NEAR SOFT PALATE spoken with the back of the tongue close to, or in contact with, the soft palate (**velum**) **2.** OF A VELUM relating to, involving, or typical of a velum ■ *n.* PHON VELAR CONSONANT a velar consonant [Early 18thC. From modern Latin *velaris,* from Latin *velum* 'sail'.]

velarium /vi láiri əm/ (*plural* **-a**) *n.* a large awning used in an amphitheatre, e.g. the one used at the Coliseum in Rome, to shade an audience [Mid-19thC. From Latin, 'awning' or 'curtain', from *velum* 'sail'.]

velarize /véelə rīz/ (**-izes, -izing, -ized**), **velarise** (**-ises, -ising, -ised**) *vt.* to pronounce a speech sound by bringing the back of the tongue close to or against the soft palate (**velum**) —**velarization** *n.*

velate /véelət, -layt/ *adj.* with or covered by a velum [Mid-19thC. Coined from VELUM + -ATE.]

Velcro /vélkrō/ *tdmk.* a trademark for a fastener consisting of two strips, one with a dense layer of hooks and the other of loops, used especially on outerwear, athletic shoes, and luggage

veld /velt/, **veldt** *n.* a broad high grassland, especially in southern Africa [Early 19thC. Via Afrikaans from Dutch *veld* 'field'.]

veldskoen /vélt skoon/ *n. S Africa* a shoe or boot made of rough hide [Early 19thC. From Afrikaans, by folk etymology (from *veld* 'veld') from earlier *velskoen,* 'skin shoe', from *vel* 'skin'.]

veleta /və léetə/, **valeta** *n.* a ballroom dance in triple time in which partners sometimes dance side by side and sometimes do a quick waltz

veliger /véllijər/ *n.* a larva of some molluscs, e.g. limpets and mussels, that has a protective shell and a ciliated flap-shaped foot used for swimming and feeding [Late 19thC. Formed from VELUM + Latin *gerere,* 'to carry, bear'.]

velites /véeli teez/ *npl.* lightly-armed footsoldiers of ancient Rome [Early 17thC. From Latin, plural of *veles* 'light-armed soldier, skirmisher'.]

velleity /ve lée əti/ (*plural* **-ties**) *n.* **1.** THE WEAKEST LEVEL OF WILL volition or desire at its weakest level (*literary*) **2.** SLIGHT WISH a vague wish or desire [Early 17thC. Via the medieval Latin stem *velleitat-* from Latin *velle,* 'to wish'.]

vellum /véllәm/ *n.* **1.** HIGH QUALITY PARCHMENT OF ANIMAL SKIN high quality parchment made from calfskin, kidskin, or lambskin **2.** MANUSCRIPT ON VELLUM a manuscript written or printed on vellum **3.** PAPER RESEMBLING VELLUM an off-white heavy paper resembling vellum [15thC. From French *vélin,* literally 'of a calf', from *veel* 'calf' (see VEAL).] —**vellum** *adj.*

veloce /ve lóchi/ *adv.* to be played or performed rapidly (*used as a musical direction*) [Early 19thC. Via Italian from the Latin stem *veloc-* (see VELOCITY).]

velocimeter /vèllə símmitər, véelō-/ *n.* an instrument used to measure the speed of a fluid or sound

velocipede /və lóssi peed/ *n.* any of various early forms of bicycle or tricycle, including some that had pedals attached to the front wheel or were propelled by pushing the feet along the ground [Early 19thC. From French *vélocipède,* 'bicycle', from the Latin

velocipedist n.

velocity /və lóssəti/ (plural -ties) n. 1. SPEED the speed at which sth moves, happens, or is done 2. RATE OF CHANGE IN POSITION a measure of the rate of change in position of sth with respect to time, involving speed and direction 3. = speed n. 2 (not used technically) [Mid-16thC. From Latin velocitat-, from the stem veloc-, 'quick, swift'.]

velocity of circulation n. the rate at which money circulates throughout an economy during a particular period, usually a year

velodrome /véllədrōm/ n. a stadium that has a banked track for bicycle races [Late 19thC. From French, formed from VELOCIPEDE + -DROME.]

velours /və loŏr/ (plural -lours), **velour** n. a fabric with a thick pile, similar to velvet, often used in upholstery and clothing [Early 18thC. Via Old French velous, from Latin villosus, 'shaggy', from villus, 'shaggy hair, wool'.]

velouté /və loŏ tay/ n. a white sauce made from chicken, veal, or fish stock that has been thickened with a butter and flour roux and cream. Velouté sauce is often used on poultry or vegetables. [Mid-19thC. From French, literally 'velvety', from Old French vellute, from velous (see VELVET).]

velum /vēeləm/ (plural -la /-lə/) n. ANAT a layer of tissue or other part that covers sth like a veil, such as the muscular soft palate in the roof of the mouth [Late 18thC. From Latin, literally 'sail, covering' (source of English veil).]

velure /və loŏr/ n. velvet, or a fabric with a similar thick soft pile (archaic) [Late 16thC. From Old French velour, variant of velous (see VELOURS).]

velutinous /və loŏtinəss/ adj. densely covered with short soft hairs [Early 19thC. From modern Latin velutinus, 'velvety', from medieval Latin velutum 'velvet', from assumed Vulgar Latin villutus. See VELVET.]

velvet /vélvit/ n. 1. TEXTILES FABRIC WITH SOFT LUSTROUS PILE a cotton, silk, or nylon fabric with a dense soft usually lustrous pile and a plain underside 2. STH LIKE VELVET sth that is smooth and soft like velvet 3. ZOOL FURRY COVERING ON DEER ANTLERS the furry layer that covers the growing antlers of deer and is sloughed off when the antlers stop growing and harden ■ adj. 1. TEXTILES MADE OF VELVET made of or covered with velvet 2. LIKE VELVET like velvet, especially in being or looking soft, smooth, or lustrous [14thC. From Old French veluotte, from velu, literally 'shaggy (cloth)', from medieval Latin villutus, from villus, 'shaggy hair, wool'.]

velvet ant n. any one of various wasps with bodies covered in soft hair. The females are generally wingless and have a potent sting. Family: Mutillidae.

velveteen /vélvə teen/ n. a brushed fabric with a soft pile like velvet [Late 18thC. Formed from VELVET + '-een', a variant of -INE.]

velvet glove n. kind, careful, or gentle treatment, especially when this disguises strength or determination

velvet scoter n. a large European duck, the males of which are black with white patches, and the females dark brown. It breeds in Arctic regions and winters on northern Eurasian coasts. Latin name: Melanitta fusca.

velvet shank n. an edible mushroom that grows in Europe and North Africa in clusters on hardwood trees, has a yellow cap, and a velvety dark brown stalk. It has a mild flavour and is sometimes cultivated. Latin name: Flammulina velutipes.

velvety /vélvəti/ adj. 1. FEELING LIKE VELVET soft and smooth in a way that suggests the feel of velvet 2. SMOOTH smooth and mellow —**velvetiness** n.

Ven. abbr. 1. CHR Venerable 2. Venezuela

ven- prefix. = veno- (used before vowels)

vena /vēenə/ (plural -nae /veén ee/) n. a vein (technical) [14thC. From Latin.]

vena cava /-káyvə/ (plural **venae cavae** /veé nee káy vee/) n. one of two major veins that carry circulating blood into the right atrium of the heart. One carries blood returning from the upper body and head (**superior vena cava**) and the other brings that from below the chest (**inferior vena cava**). [Late 16thC. From Latin, literally 'hollow vein.'] —**vena-caval** adj.

venal /veén'l/ adj. 1. OPEN TO BRIBERY open to persuasion by corrupt means, especially bribery 2. CORRUPT characterized by corruption 3. ABLE TO BE BOUGHT able to be bought, especially in an illegal or unfair way [Mid-17thC. From Latin venalis, from venum 'sth for sale'.] —**venality** /vee nálləti/ n. —**venally** adv.

— **WORD KEY: USAGE** —

venal or **venial**? The two words are derived from entirely different Latin roots: **venal** comes from venum meaning 'thing for sale' and **venial** from vena meaning 'forgiveness'. **Venial**, meaning 'forgivable', is used in connection with minor faults or transgressions: He was inclined to be thoughtless but that was a venial fault in one so young. In Roman Catholic theology, a venial sin is one that does not deprive the soul of divine grace, as opposed to a mortal sin, which does. **Venal**, meaning 'liable to corruption', describes people as well as processes and organizations: The political system is so venal that bribery is commonplace.

venatic /vee náttik/, **venatical** /-náttik'l/ adj. involving, connected with, or taking part in hunting (formal) [Mid-17thC. From Latin venaticus, from venari, 'to hunt.'] —**venatically** adv.

venation /vee náysh'n/ n. 1. PATTERN OF VEINS the pattern formed by the network of veins in an insect's wing or in a leaf. It is often useful in identifying or classifying specimens. 2. NETWORK OF VEINS all the veins making up a network —**venational** adj.

vend /vend/ (**vends, vending, vended**) v. 1. vt. SELL STH FROM VENDING MACHINE to sell sth from a vending machine 2. vti. SELL IN STREET to sell sth, especially in the street, or make a living doing this [Early 17thC. From Latin vendere, 'to sell'.]

Venda[1] /véndə/ (plural **-da** or **-das**) n. 1. PEOPLES MEMBER OF SOUTHERN AFRICAN PEOPLE a member of a people who live in southern Africa, mainly in northern parts of Transvaal in South Africa 2. LANG VENDA LANGUAGE a language spoken mainly in Transvaal in South Africa. It belongs to the Bantu group of Benue-Congo languages. About 750,000 people speak Venda. [Early 20thC. From Bantu.] —**Venda** adj.

Venda[2] /véndə/ former homeland in South Africa. Abolished in 1994, it is now part of Northern Province.

vendace /vén dayss/ (plural **-daces** or **-dace**) n. a whitefish of northwest Europe and Russia, found mainly in freshwater lakes, with a streamlined body and leading lower jaw. It is dark greenish-blue above and silvery below. Genus: Coregonus. [Late 17thC. Origin uncertain: probably from Old French vendoise, of Celtic origin.]

vendee /vén deé/ n. sb who buys sth

Vendémiaire /váN daym yáir/ n. the first month of the year in the French Revolutionary calendar, corresponding to 23 September to 22 October in the Gregorian calendar [Late 18thC. From French, from vendémi, from Latin vindemia, 'vintage' (see VINTAGE).]

vender n. = vendor

vendetta /ven déttə/ n. 1. BLOOD FEUD BETWEEN FAMILIES a feud between families started by the killing of a member of one family that is then avenged by a killing of a member of the other family 2. PROLONGED FEUD a prolonged bitter feud or quarrel [Mid-19thC. From Italian, from Latin vindicta, 'vengeance'. See VINDICTIVE.]

vendible /véndəb'l/ adj. FIT TO BE SOLD suitable or fit to be sold ■ n. STH THAT CAN BE SOLD sth that can be sold or is available for sale —**vendibility** /véndə bílləti/ n. —**vendibleness** /véndəb'lnəss/ n.

vending machine n. a machine from which people can buy such items as packaged food or drinks by inserting money

Vendôme /vaN dōm/, **Louis Joseph, duc de** (1654–1712) French soldier. He commanded forces in a number of battles during the War of the Spanish Succession (1701–14).

vendor /véndər/, **vender** n. 1. SELLER sb who sells sth 2. VENDING MACHINE a vending machine

veneer /və neér/ n. 1. INDUST THIN LAYER AS SURFACE a thin layer of a material fixed to the surface of another material that is of inferior quality or less attractive 2. DECEPTIVE APPEARANCE an outward appearance that is meant to please or impress others but that is false or only superficial 3. INDUST, BUILDING OUTER LAYER an outer layer fixed to sth for decoration or protection, e.g. a facing of stone on a brick building 4. INDUST LAYER OF PLYWOOD any of the layers of wood that are glued together to make plywood ■ vt. (**-neers, -neering, -neered**) 1. INDUST FIX VENEER TO STH to fix a veneer to a surface 2. HIDE STH BEHIND DECEPTIVELY PLEASANT APPEARANCE to hide or disguise sth behind a deceptively pleasant or impressive appearance 3. INDUST, WOODWORK GLUE LAYERS TO MAKE PLYWOOD to glue layers of wood together to make plywood [Early 18thC. Earlier 'fineering, faneering', from German Fournierung, 'inlay, veneer', from French fournir (see FURNISH).] —**veneerer** n.

venepuncture n. MED = venipuncture

venerable /vénnərəb'l/ adj. 1. WORTHY OF RESPECT worthy of respect as a result of great age, wisdom, remarkable achievements, or similar qualities 2. RELIG REVERED revered for qualities such as great age or holiness 3. ANCIENT extremely old 4. CHR USED AS TITLE BEFORE CANONIZATION used by the Roman Catholic Church to describe sb who has died and attained the first of the three degrees of canonization 5. CHR USED AS ARCHDEACON'S TITLE used as a title to describe an archdeacon in the Church of England [15thC. Directly or via French from Latin venerabilis, from venerari (see VENERATE).] —**venerability** /vénnərə bílləti/ n. —**venerably** /vénnərəbli/ adv.

venerate /vénnə rayt/ (**-ates, -ating, -ated**) vt. 1. RESPECT SB to respect sb with profound respect 2. HONOUR STH OR SB to honour sth or sb as sacred or special [Early 17thC. From Latin venerat-, past participle stem of venerari, from vener-, stem of venus 'love, desire' (source of English venerate).] —**venerator** n.

veneration /vénnə ráysh'n/ n. 1. FEELING OF RESPECT a feeling of great respect or reverence for sb or sth 2. EXPRESSING OF RESPECT the expression of respect or reverence for sb or sth in words or actions 3. BEING RESPECTED the condition of being respected or revered —**venerational** adj.

— **WORD KEY: SYNONYMS** —

See Synonyms at **regard**.

venereal /və neéri əl/ adj. 1. PASSED ON THROUGH SEX used to describe an infection or disease that is caught or transmitted through sexual intercourse 2. ASSOCIATED WITH SEXUALLY TRANSMITTED DISEASE associated with, symptomatic of, or infected with a sexually transmitted disease 3. GENITAL affecting or originating in the genitals 4. ABOUT SEX relating to sex acts or sexual desire (archaic or literary) [15thC. Formed from Latin venereus, from vener-, the stem of venus 'love' (see VENERATE).]

venereal disease n. a disease that is caught or transmitted through sex acts, e.g. syphilis or gonorrhoea (dated)

venereology /və neéri ólləji/ n. the branch of medicine involving the study and treatment of sexually transmitted diseases [Late 19thC. Coined from VENEREAL + -LOGY.] —**venereological** /və neéri ə lójjik'l/ adj. —**venereologist** /və neéri ólləjist/ n.

venery[1] /vénnəri, veén-/ n. the pursuit of or indulgence in sexual pleasure (archaic) [15thC. From medieval Latin veneria, from Latin vener-, the stem of venus 'love, desire' (see VENERATE).]

venery[2] /vénnəri, veén-/ n. GAME the sport or practice of hunting, or the animals hunted (archaic) [14thC. Via French from, ultimately, Latin venari 'to hunt' (source of English venison).]

venesection /vénni seksh'n/ n. = phlebotomy [Mid-17thC. From medieval Latin venae sectio, literally 'cutting of a vein'.]

Veneti /ve nétti/ npl. an ancient people that inhabited northeastern Italy and neighbouring areas from around the 10th century BC [Early 17thC. From Latin.]

Venetian /və neésh'n/ adj. PEOPLES OF VENICE relating to the Italian city of Venice, or its people or culture

verapamil /vi ráppəmil/ *n.* a drug used to treat heart and circulatory disorders, including angina pectoris, hypertension, and irregular heartbeat. It works by inhibiting the movement of calcium ions across membranes, especially in muscle cells. [Mid-20thC. From *v(al)er(ic)* + *am(ino-)* + *(nitr)il(e)* (with inserted 'p'), its chemical name.]

veratridine /vi rátri deen/ *n.* a poisonous yellowish-white substance obtained from sabadilla seeds and used in insecticides and formerly in medicine. Formula: $C_{36}H_{51}NO_{11}$. [Early 20thC. Formed from VERATRUM.]

veratrine /vérrə treen, -trin/, **veratrin** *n.* a poisonous mixture of alkaloids including veratridine, formerly used in medicine to relieve inflammation [Early 19thC. Formed from VERATRUM.]

verb /vurb/ *n.* **1.** WORD INDICATING ACTION OR STATE a word used to show that an action is taking place, or to indicate the existence of a state or condition, or the part of speech to which such a word belongs **2.** PREDICATE OF SENTENCE the part of a clause or sentence that includes the verb but excludes the subject of the verb [14thC. Via Old French from Latin *verbum* 'word'. Ultimately from an Indo-European base meaning 'to speak', which is also the ancestor of English *word* and *irony*.]

verbal /vúrb'l/ *adj.* **1.** USING WORDS RATHER THAN PICTURES expressed in or using words or language, especially as opposed to pictorial representation ○ *a verbal picture of the scene outside* **2.** USING WORDS RATHER THAN ACTION relating to or consisting of words rather than physical action or confrontation ○ *verbal protest* **3.** ORAL RATHER THAN WRITTEN relating to or consisting of spoken rather than written words ○ *They made a verbal agreement.* **4.** USING WORDS WITHOUT MEANING using words without conveying meaning or making any meaningful distinctions ○ *a purely verbal distinction rather than anything more fundamental* **5.** INVOLVING SKILL WITH WORDS involving skill in the use and understanding of words and language ○ *verbal dexterity* **6.** GRAM RELATING TO VERBS derived from or relating to a verb, or to verbs in general **7.** GRAM FORMING VERBS used to form verbs **8.** VERBATIM corresponding word for word (*archaic*) ■ *n.* **1.** GRAM WORD FORMED FROM VERB a word formed from a verb, especially one used as a noun or an adjective, such as a gerund or participle **2.** ADMISSION OF GUILT an admission of guilt upon being arrested for a crime (*slang*) ■ *vt.* **(-bals, -balling, -balled)** MAKE SB SOUND GUILTY to make sb sound guilty during police testimony in court by referring to an admission of guilt allegedly given earlier (*slang*) [15thC. Via Old French from, ultimately, Latin *verbum* (see VERB).] —**verbally** *adv.*

WORD KEY: SYNONYMS

verbal, spoken, oral

CORE MEANING: expressed in words

verbal indicates that sth such as an apology or request is expressed in words, usually spoken words, but sometimes in writing; **spoken** indicates that communication is expressed by means of speech rather than writing; **oral** a more formal word meaning the same as *spoken*.

verbal adjective *n.* a verb participle ending in -ing or -ed that is used as an adjective

verbalism /vúrbəlizəm/ *n.* **1.** VERBAL EXPRESSION sth expressed in words **2.** LONG-WINDED EXPRESSION a wordy expression that has little meaning or relevance **3.** USE OF TOO MANY WORDS the uncritical or undisciplined use of words, especially without any attempt to analyse their meaning or value **4.** *US* WAY STH IS EXPRESSED the manner in which sth is expressed or communicated

verbalist /vúrbəlist/ *n.* **1.** SB SKILLED WITH WORDS sb who is skilled in the use of words and language **2.** SB WHO CONCENTRATES ON WORDS sb who tends to concentrate on words or language rather than on things such as facts, feelings, or ideas —**verbalistic** /vúrbə lístik/ *adj.*

verbalize /vúrbə līz/ **(-izes, -izing, -ized)**, **verbalise (-balises, -balising, -balised)** *v.* **1.** *vt.* EXPRESS STH IN WORDS to express feelings, thoughts, or ideas in words **2.** *vt.* GRAM MAKE WORD INTO VERB to make a word that is another part of speech, e.g. a noun or adjective, into a verb **3.** *vi.* BE VERBOSE to speak or write in a way that uses too many words —**verbalization** *n.* —**verbalizer** *n.*

verbal noun *n.* a form of a verb ending in '-ing' used as a noun, e.g. 'dancing' in 'he teaches dancing'

verbatim /vur báytim/ *adj.* USING IDENTICAL WORDS corresponding word for word with sth else ■ *adv.* IN IDENTICAL WORDS repeated, written down, or copied word for word [15thC. From medieval Latin, from Latin *verbum* 'word'.]

verbena /vur beénə/ *n.* a common plant or shrub, native mainly to North and South America, that bears clusters of small tubular five-lobed flowers and is widely grown for ornament. Genus: *Verbena.* [Mid-16thC. From Latin. Ultimately from an Indo-European base meaning 'to bend', which is also the ancestor of English *warp*, *reverberate*, and *rhombus*.]

verbiage /vúrbi ij/ *n.* **1.** EXCESS OF WORDS an excess of words, especially in writing or speech with little or no meaning **2.** WORDING the style of language in which sth is expressed ○ *bureaucratic verbiage explaining the regulations* [Early 18thC. Via French from, ultimately, Latin *verbum* 'word'.]

verbid /vúrbid/ *n.* LING = **verbal** *n.* 1

verbify /vúrbi fī/ **(-fies, -fying, -fied)** *vt.* = **verbalize** *v.* 2 (*archaic or formal*) —**verbification** /vúrbifi káysh'n/ *n.*

verbigerate /vur bíjji rayt/ **(-ates, -ating, -ated)** *vi.* to repeat the same words or phrases obsessively as a symptom of a psychiatric disorder [Late 19thC. From Latin *verbigerat-*, the past participle stem of *verbigerare* 'to chat', from *verbum* 'word' + *gerare* 'to keep carrying on'.] —**verbigeration** /vur bíjjə ráysh'n/ *n.*

verbose /vur bóss/ *adj.* expressed in or using language that is too long-winded or complicated [Late 17thC. From Latin *verbosus*, from *verbum* 'word'.] —**verbosely** *adv.* —**verboseness** *n.*

WORD KEY: SYNONYMS

See Synonyms at ***wordy***.

verboten /fər bṓt'n, vər-/ *adj.* forbidden or prohibited [Early 20thC. From German.]

verb phrase *n.* a grammatical construction consisting of a verb and any direct and indirect objects and modifiers linked to it, but not including the subject of the verb

Vercingetorix /vúrssin jéttəriks/ (*d.* 46 BC) Gaulish leader. He led a revolt of Gallic tribes against Roman rule, but was eventually captured by Julius Caesar in 52 BC.

verdant /vúrd'nt/ *adj.* **1.** WITH LUSH GREEN GROWTH green with vegetation or foliage **2.** COLOURS GREEN green in colour **3.** NAIVE lacking experience or sophistication (*literary*) [Late 16thC. Via Old French *verdeant*, literally 'becoming green', from, ultimately, Latin *viridis* 'green' (source of English *vireo*).] —**verdancy** *n.* —**verdantly** *adv.*

verd antique /vúrd an teék/, **verde antique** *n.* **1.** GREEN VEINED MARBLE a dark-green mottled or veined variety of serpentine marble that is used in decoration **2.** GREEN STONE a green marble or stone that resembles verd antique **3.** = **verdigris** *n.* 1 [From obsolete French, literally 'antique green']

Verde, Cape /vurd/ **1.** peninsula in western central Senegal. Its tip is the westernmost point of the African mainland. **2.** ➧ **Cape Verde**

verderer /vúrdərər/ *n.* a judicial official in charge of maintaining the royal forests in medieval England [Mid-16thC. Via Anglo-Norman from, ultimately, Latin *viridis* 'green' (source of English *verdant*).]

Verdi /váirdi/, **Giuseppe** (1813–1901) Italian composer. He was one of the greatest operatic composers of all time. His works include *Rigoletto* (1851), *La Traviata* (1853), *Aida* (1871), *Otello* (1887), and *Falstaff* (1893). Full name **Guiseppe Fortunino Francesco Verdi**

verdict /vúrdikt/ *n.* **1.** LAW JURY DECISION the finding of a jury on the matter that has been submitted to it in a trial **2.** DECISION OR OPINION ABOUT STH a judgment, opinion, or conclusion that is expressed about sth [13thC. From Anglo-Norman *verdit*, literally 'true speech', from *ver* 'true' + *dit* 'speech, saying'.]

verdigris /vúrdi gree, -greess/ *n.* **1.** GREEN DEPOSIT ON COPPER a green or greenish-blue deposit (**patina**) on copper, brass, and bronze that is caused by atmospheric corrosion and consists of copper carbonates **2.** GREENISH COPPER POWDER a green or greenish-blue poisonous powder that is used as a paint pigment and fungicide. It is formed by the action of acetic acid on copper and consists of one or more basic copper acetates. [14thC. From Old French *vert de Grece*, literally 'green of Greece'.]

verdin /vúrdin/ *n.* a small bird of the southwestern United States and Mexico, with grey plumage, a white breast, and a yellow head and throat. Latin name: *Auriparus flaviceps.* [Late 19thC. Via French from, ultimately, Latin *viridis* 'green'.]

verditer /vúrditər/ *n.* a basic copper carbonate that is used as a blue or green pigment. The blue variety contains azurite, the green variety contains malachite. [Early 16thC. From Old French *verd de terre*, literally 'green of the earth'.]

Verdun /vur dún/ town in northeastern France. One of the longest and bloodiest battles of World War I was fought around the town during 1916. Population: 23,427 (1990).

verdure /vúrjər/ *n.* **1.** VIVID GREEN OF PLANTS the green colour associated with lush vegetation **2.** VEGETATION extremely lush vegetation **3.** FRESHNESS a fresh, healthy, or flourishing condition [14thC. Via French from, ultimately, Latin *viridis* 'green'.] —**verdured** *adj.* —**verdureless** *adj.* —**verdurous** *adj.* —**verdurousness** *n.*

verecund /vérri kund/ *adj.* shy or modest (*archaic*) [Mid-16thC. From Latin *verecundus*, from *vereri* 'to respect' (source of English *revere*).]

Vereeniging /fə reéniking/ industrial city in Gauteng Province, South Africa. Population: 71,255 (1991).

verge[1] /vurj/ *n.* **1.** POINT BEYOND WHICH STH HAPPENS the point beyond which sth happens or begins ○ *He was on the verge of tears.* **2.** BOUNDARY a line, belt, or strip that acts as a boundary or edge **3.** EDGE the edge, rim, or margin of sth **4.** TRANSP ROADSIDE BORDER a narrow border that runs alongside a road **5.** ARCHIT ROOF EDGE the edge of a sloping roof where it extends beyond the gable **6.** CLOCK SPINDLE the spindle of a balance wheel in early clock and watch mechanisms **7.** HIST AREA AROUND ROYAL COURT an area around the English royal court that was under the jurisdiction of the Lord High Steward **8.** HIST ROD HELD BY TENANT a rod held by a feudal tenant when swearing an oath of loyalty to his or her lord **9.** ROD AS SYMBOL OF OFFICE a rod or staff carried as a symbol of authority or an emblem of office ■ *vi.* **(verges, verging, verged) 1.** APPROACH A STATE OR QUALITY to approach or come close to a particular quality, state, or condition ○ *verging on brilliance* **2.** BORDER ON AN AREA to border on or be on the edge of a particular place or area [14thC. Via French, 'rod' (symbolizing the office of Lord High Steward and the limits of his jurisdiction), from Latin *virga* (source of English *virgule*).]

verge[2] /vurj/ **(verges, verging, verged)** *vi.* **1.** MOVE IN PARTICULAR DIRECTION to move or lean in a particular direction or towards a certain condition **2.** CHANGE GRADUALLY to change gradually from one thing to another (*literary*) **3.** SINK FROM VIEW to descend towards the horizon (*literary*) [Early 17thC. From Latin *vergere* 'to bend, incline' (source of English *converge* and *diverge*). Ultimately from an Indo-European word meaning 'to turn', which is also the ancestor of English *wrench* and *wrinkle*.]

vergence /vúrjənss/ *n.* the inward or outward turning of both eyes when focusing on a near or distant object [Early 20thC. Back-formation from CONVERGENCE and DIVERGENCE.]

verger /vúrjər/ *n.* **1.** CHURCH OFFICIAL a church official who acts as a caretaker and attendant and looks after the inside of a church, usually including the furnishings and the vestments **2.** OFFICIAL WHO CARRIES STAFF a church official in the Church of England who carries the staff of office (**verge**) in front of sb such as a bishop or dean during ceremonies and processions [15thC. Via Anglo-Norman from Old French *verge* 'rod of office' (see VERGE[1]).]

Vergil = **Virgil**

verglas /váir glaa/ *n.* a thin coating of ice found on rock or exposed ground [Early 19thC. From French, from *verre* 'glass' + *glas* 'ice'.]

veridical /və ríddik'l/ *adj.* (*formal*) **1.** TRUTHFUL telling the truth **2.** REAL corresponding to facts or to reality, and therefore genuine or real [Mid-17thC. Formed from Latin *veridicus*, literally 'truth-speaking', from *verus* stem *veloc-*, 'swift', + the stem *ped-*, 'foot'.] —**velocipedist** *n.*

velocity /və lóssəti/ (*plural* **-ties**) *n.* **1.** SPEED the speed at which sth moves, happens, or is done **2.** RATE OF CHANGE IN POSITION a measure of the rate of change in position of sth with respect to time, involving speed and direction **3.** = **speed** *n.* 2 (*not used technically*) [Mid-16thC. From Latin *velocitat-*, from the stem *veloc-*, 'quick, swift'.]

velocity of circulation *n.* the rate at which money circulates throughout an economy during a particular period, usually a year

velodrome /véllədrōm/ *n.* a stadium that has a banked track for bicycle races [Late 19thC. From French, formed from VELOCIPEDE + -DROME.]

velours /və lo͝or/ (*plural* **-lours**), **velour** *n.* a fabric with a thick pile, similar to velvet, often used in upholstery and clothing [Early 18thC. Via Old French *velous*, from Latin *villosus*, 'shaggy', from *villus*, 'shaggy hair, wool'.]

velouté /və lo͞o tay/ *n.* a white sauce made from chicken, veal, or fish stock that has been thickened with a butter and flour roux and cream. Velouté sauce is often used on poultry or vegetables. [Mid-19thC. From French, literally 'velvety', from Old French *vellute*, from *velous* (see VELVET).]

velum /veélәm/ (*plural* **-la** /-lə/) *n.* ANAT a layer of tissue or other part that covers sth like a veil, such as the muscular soft palate in the roof of the mouth [Late 18thC. From Latin, literally 'sail, covering' (source of English *veil*).]

velure /və lóor/ *n.* velvet, or a fabric with a similar thick soft pile (*archaic*) [Late 16thC. From Old French *velour*, variant of *velous* (see VELOURS).]

velutinous /və lo͞otinəss/ *adj.* densely covered with short soft hairs [Early 19thC. From modern Latin *velutinus*, 'velvety', from medieval Latin *velutum* 'velvet', from assumed Vulgar Latin *villutus*. See VELVET.]

velvet /vélvit/ *n.* **1.** TEXTILES FABRIC WITH SOFT LUSTROUS PILE a cotton, silk, or nylon fabric with a dense soft usually lustrous pile and a plain underside **2.** STH LIKE VELVET sth that is smooth and soft like velvet **3.** ZOOL FURRY COVERING ON DEER ANTLERS the furry layer that covers the growing antlers of deer and is sloughed off when the antlers stop growing and harden ■ *adj.* **1.** TEXTILES MADE OF VELVET made of or covered with velvet **2.** LIKE VELVET like velvet, especially in being or looking soft, smooth, or lustrous [14thC. From Old French *veluotte*, from *velu*, literally 'shaggy (cloth)', from medieval Latin *villutus*, from Latin *villus*, 'shaggy hair, wool'.]

velvet ant *n.* any one of various wasps with bodies covered in soft hair. The females are generally wingless and have a potent sting. Family: Mutillidae.

velveteen /vélvə teén/ *n.* a brushed fabric with a soft pile like velvet [Late 18thC. Formed from VELVET + '-een', a variant of -INE.]

velvet glove *n.* kind, careful, or gentle treatment, especially when this disguises strength or determination

velvet scoter *n.* a large European duck, the males of which are black with white patches, and the females dark brown. It breeds in Arctic regions and winters on northern Eurasian coasts. Latin name: *Melanitta fusca*.

velvet shank *n.* an edible mushroom that grows in Europe and North Africa in clusters on hardwood trees, has a yellow cap, and a velvety dark brown stalk. It has a mild flavour and is sometimes cultivated. Latin name: *Flammulina velutipes*.

velvety /vélvəti/ *adj.* **1.** FEELING LIKE VELVET soft and smooth in a way that suggests the feel of velvet **2.** SMOOTH smooth and mellow —**velvetiness** *n.*

Ven. *abbr.* **1.** CHR Venerable **2.** Venezuela

ven- *prefix.* = **veno-** (*used before vowels*)

vena /veénə/ (*plural* **-nae** /veén ee/) *n.* a vein (*technical*) [14thC. From Latin.]

vena cava /-káyvə/ (*plural* **venae cavae** /veé nee káy vee/) *n.* one of two major veins that carry circulating blood into the right atrium of the heart. One carries blood returning from the upper body and head (**superior vena cava**) and the other brings that from below the chest (**inferior vena cava**). [Late 16thC. From Latin, literally 'hollow vein'.] —**vena-caval** *adj.*

venal /veén'l/ *adj.* **1.** OPEN TO BRIBERY open to persuasion by corrupt means, especially bribery **2.** CORRUPT characterized by corruption **3.** ABLE TO BE BOUGHT able to be bought, especially in an illegal or unfair way [Mid-17thC. From Latin *venalis*, from *venum* 'sth for sale'.] —**venality** /vee nálləti/ *n.* —**venally** *adv.*

WORD KEY: USAGE

venal or **venial**? The two words are derived from entirely different Latin roots: ***venal*** comes from *venum* meaning 'thing for sale' and ***venial*** from *vena* meaning 'forgiveness'. ***Venial***, meaning 'forgivable', is used in connection with minor faults or transgressions: *He was inclined to be thoughtless but that was a venial fault in one so young.* In Roman Catholic theology, a *venial sin* is one that does not deprive the soul of divine grace, as opposed to a *mortal sin*, which does. ***Venal***, meaning 'liable to corruption', describes people as well as processes and organizations: *The political system is so venal that bribery is commonplace.*

venatic /vee náttik/, **venatical** /-náttik'l/ *adj.* involving, connected with, or taking part in hunting (*formal*) [Mid-17thC. From Latin *venaticus*, from *venari*, 'to hunt'.] —**venatically** *adv.*

venation /vee náysh'n/ *n.* **1.** PATTERN OF VEINS the pattern formed by the network of veins in an insect's wing or in a leaf. It is often useful in identifying or classifying specimens. **2.** NETWORK OF VEINS all the veins making up a network —**venational** *adj.*

vend /vend/ (**vends, vending, vended**) *v.* **1.** *vt.* SELL STH FROM VENDING MACHINE to sell sth from a vending machine **2.** *vti.* SELL IN STREET to sell sth, especially in the street, or make a living doing this [Early 17thC. From Latin *vendere*, 'to sell'.]

Venda[1] /véndə/ (*plural* **-da** *or* **-das**) *n.* **1.** PEOPLES MEMBER OF SOUTHERN AFRICAN PEOPLE a member of a people who live in southern Africa, mainly in northern parts of Transvaal in South Africa **2.** LANG VENDA LANGUAGE a language spoken mainly in Transvaal in South Africa. It belongs to the Bantu group of Benue-Congo languages. About 750,000 people speak Venda. [Early 20thC. From Bantu.] —**Venda** *adj.*

Venda[2] /véndə/ former homeland in South Africa. Abolished in 1994, it is now part of Northern Province.

vendace /vén dayss/ (*plural* **-daces** *or* **-dace**) *n.* a whitefish of northwest Europe and Russia, found mainly in freshwater lakes, with a streamlined body and leading lower jaw. It is dark greenish-blue above and silvery below. Genus: *Coregonus*. [Late 17thC. Origin uncertain: probably from Old French *vendoise*, of Celtic origin.]

vendee /vén deé/ *n.* sb who buys sth

Vendémiaire /váN daym yáir/ *n.* the first month of the year in the French Revolutionary calendar, corresponding to 23 September to 22 October in the Gregorian calendar [Late 18thC. From French, from *vendémi*, from Latin *vindemia*, 'vintage' (see VINTAGE).]

vender *n.* = **vendor**

vendetta /ven déttə/ *n.* **1.** BLOOD FEUD BETWEEN FAMILIES a feud between families started by the killing of a member of one family that is then avenged by a killing of a member of the other family **2.** PROLONGED FEUD a prolonged bitter feud or quarrel [Mid-19thC. From Italian, from Latin *vindicta*, 'vengeance'. See VINDICTIVE.]

vendible /véndəb'l/ *adj.* FIT TO BE SOLD suitable or fit to be sold ■ *n.* STH THAT CAN BE SOLD sth that can be sold or is available for sale —**vendibility** /véndə bílləti/ *n.* —**vendibleness** /véndəb'lnəss/ *n.*

vending machine *n.* a machine from which people can buy such items as packaged food or drinks by inserting money

Vendôme /vaN dóm/, **Louis Joseph, duc de** (1654–1712) French soldier. He commanded forces in a number of battles during the War of the Spanish Succession (1701–14).

vendor /véndər/, **vender** *n.* **1.** SELLER sb who sells sth **2.** VENDING MACHINE a vending machine

veneer /və neér/ *n.* **1.** INDUST THIN LAYER AS SURFACE a thin layer of a material fixed to the surface of another material that is of inferior quality or less attractive **2.** DECEPTIVE APPEARANCE an outward appearance that is meant to please or impress others but that is false or only superficial **3.** INDUST, BUILDING OUTER LAYER an outer layer fixed to sth for decoration or protection, e.g. a facing of stone on a brick building **4.** INDUST LAYER OF PLYWOOD any of the layers of wood that are glued together to make plywood ■ *vt.* (**-neers, -neering, -neered**) **1.** INDUST FIX VENEER TO STH to fix a veneer to a surface **2.** HIDE STH BEHIND DECEPTIVELY PLEASANT APPEARANCE to hide or disguise sth behind a deceptively pleasant or impressive appearance **3.** INDUST, WOODWORK GLUE LAYERS TO MAKE PLYWOOD to glue layers of wood together to make plywood [Early 18thC. Earlier 'fineering, faneering', from German *Fournierung*, 'inlay, veneer', from French *fournir* (see FURNISH).] —**veneerer** *n.*

venepuncture *n.* MED = **venipuncture**

venerable /vénnərəb'l/ *adj.* **1.** WORTHY OF RESPECT worthy of respect as a result of great age, wisdom, remarkable achievements, or similar qualities **2.** RELIG REVERED revered for qualities such as great age or holiness **3.** ANCIENT extremely old **4.** CHR USED AS TITLE BEFORE CANONIZATION used by the Roman Catholic Church to describe sb who has died and attained the first of the three degrees of canonization **5.** CHR USED AS ARCHDEACON'S TITLE used as a title to describe an archdeacon in the Church of England [15thC. Directly or via French from Latin *venerabilis*, from *venerari* (see VENERATE).] —**venerability** /vénnərə bílləti/ *n.* —**venerably** /vénnərəbli/ *adv.*

venerate /vénnə rayt/ (**-ates, -ating, -ated**) *vt.* **1.** RESPECT SB to regard sb with profound respect **2.** HONOUR STH OR SB to honour sth or sb as sacred or special [Early 17thC. From Latin *venerat-*, past participle stem of *venerari*, from *vener-*, stem of *venus* 'love, desire' (source of English *venereal*).] —**venerator** *n.*

veneration /vénnə ráysh'n/ *n.* **1.** FEELING OF RESPECT a feeling of great respect or reverence for sb or sth **2.** EXPRESSING OF RESPECT the expression of respect or reverence for sb or sth in words or actions **3.** BEING RESPECTED the condition of being respected or revered —**venerational** *adj.*

WORD KEY: SYNONYMS

See Synonyms at ***regard***.

venereal /və neéri əl/ *adj.* **1.** PASSED ON THROUGH SEX used to describe an infection or disease that is caught or transmitted through sexual intercourse **2.** ASSOCIATED WITH SEXUALLY TRANSMITTED DISEASE associated with, symptomatic of, or infected with a sexually transmitted disease **3.** GENITAL affecting or originating in the genitals **4.** ABOUT SEX relating to sex acts or sexual desire (*archaic or literary*) [15thC. Formed from Latin *venereus*, from *vener-*, the stem of *venus* 'love' (see VENERATE).]

venereal disease *n.* a disease that is caught or transmitted through sex acts, e.g. syphilis or gonorrhoea (*dated*)

venereology /və neéri ólləji/ *n.* the branch of medicine involving the study and treatment of sexually transmitted diseases [Late 19thC. Coined from VENEREAL + -LOGY.] —**venereological** /və neéri ə lójjik'l/ *adj.* —**venereologist** /və neéri óllәjist/ *n.*

venery[1] /vénnəri, veén-/ *n.* the pursuit of or indulgence in sexual pleasure (*archaic*) [15thC. From medieval Latin *veneria*, from Latin *vener-*, the stem of *venus* 'love, desire' (see VENERATE).]

venery[2] /vénnəri, veén-/ *n.* GAME the sport or practice of hunting, or the animals hunted (*archaic*) [14thC. Via French from, ultimately, Latin *venari* 'to hunt' (source of English *venison*).]

venesection /vénni seksh'n/ *n.* = **phlebotomy** [Mid-17thC. From medieval Latin *venae sectio*, literally 'cutting of a vein'.]

Veneti /ve nétti/ *npl.* an ancient people that inhabited northeastern Italy and neighbouring areas from around the 10th century BC [Early 17thC. From Latin.]

Venetian /və neésh'n/ *adj.* PEOPLES OF VENICE relating to the Italian city of Venice, or its people or culture

■ *n.* PEOPLES **SB FROM VENICE** sb who lives in or was born or brought up in the city of Venice, Italy [15thC. From Old French, from Latin *Venetia* 'Venice'.]

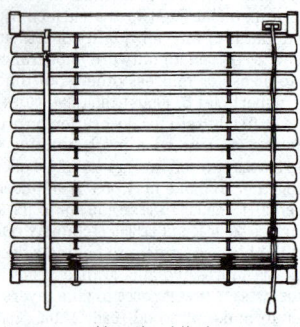

Venetian blind

Venetian blind, **venetian blind** *n.* a window blind consisting of narrow horizontal slats whose angle can be adjusted to let in more or less light

Venetian glass *n.* delicate glassware, often with colourful ornamentation, made in or around Venice, especially at Murano

Venetian red *n.* **1.** RED PIGMENT a dark red pigment made from a natural or synthetic iron oxide **2.** REDDISH-BROWN COLOUR a strong reddish-brown colour ■ *adj.* REDDISH-BROWN of a strong reddish-brown colour

Venetic /və néttik/ *n.* a language once spoken in northwestern Italy by the Veneti people

Venez. *abbr.* Venezuela

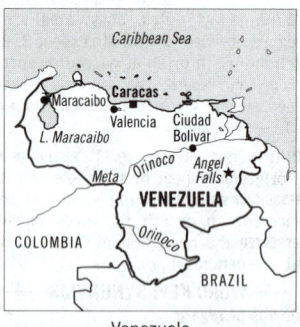

Venezuela

Venezuela /vénnə zwáylə/ republic in northeastern South America, north of Brazil, on the Caribbean Sea and the Atlantic Ocean. Language: Spanish. Currency: bolívar. Capital: Caracas. Population: 22,311,000 (1996). Area: 912,050 sq. km/352,144 sq. mi. Official name **Republic of Venezuela** —**Venezuelan** *n., adj.*

venge /venj/ (**venges, venging, venged**) *vt.* to avenge sb or sth (*archaic*) [13thC. Via Old French *vengier* from Latin *vendicare* (see VINDICATE).]

vengeance /vénjənss/ *n.* punishment that is inflicted in return for a wrong [13thC. Via Old French from, ultimately, Latin *vendicare* 'to avenge' (see VINDICATE).] ◇ **with a vengeance** in an extreme or intense manner

vengeful /vénjf'l/ *adj.* **1.** WANTING REVENGE having or showing a strong desire for revenge **2.** AVENGING serving the purpose of revenge or resulting from sb's desire for revenge —**vengefully** *adv.* —**vengefulness** *n.*

V-engine *n.* an internal-combustion engine with cylinders arranged in two rows to form a V-shaped angle

veni- *prefix.* = veno-

venial /veeni əl/ *adj.* easily forgiven or excused [13thC. Via Old French from, ultimately, Latin *venia* 'forgiveness'.] —**veniality** /veeni álləti/ *n.* —**venially** /veeni əli/ *adv.*

——— **WORD KEY: USAGE** ———
See Usage note at *venal*.

venial sin *n.* in the Roman Catholic Church, a sin that does not deprive the soul of divine grace, either because it was not serious or because it was

committed without intent or without understanding its seriousness. ◇ **mortal sin**

Venice /vénniss/ historic city and seaport in northeastern Italy, built on islands in a lagoon on the coast of the Adriatic Sea. Population: 298,915 (1995).

venipuncture /vénni pungckchər, veeni-/, **venepuncture** *n.* the puncturing of a vein for any medical purpose, e.g. to take blood, to feed sb intravenously, or to administer a drug

venire /vi nîri/, **venire facias** /-fáyshi ass/ *n.* in the United States, and formerly in the UK, a judicial writ ordering the summoning of jurors [Mid-17thC. From medieval Latin *venire facias* 'you should cause to come'.]

venireman /vi nîrimən/ (*plural* **-men** /-mən/) *n.* a citizen summoned for jury duty under a venire

venison /vénniss'n, -z'n/ *n.* **1.** DEER MEAT the meat of a deer used as food, especially for stewing or roasting. Venison is dark in colour and rich in flavour. **2.** GAME MEAT the meat of any animal hunted as game (*archaic*) [13thC. Via Old French from the Latin stem *venation-* 'hunting', from *venari* 'to hunt' (source of English *venery*[2]).]

Venite /vi nîti/ *n.* **1.** CHR **95TH PSALM AS INVITATION TO PRAYER** the 95th Psalm from the Bible sung as an invitation to morning prayer **2.** MUSIC **MUSICAL SETTING OF 95TH PSALM** a musical setting of the 95th Psalm [13thC. From Latin, 'come ye', the first word of the psalm.]

Venlo /vénnlō/ city in Limburg Province, in the southeastern Netherlands. Population: 64,781 (1996).

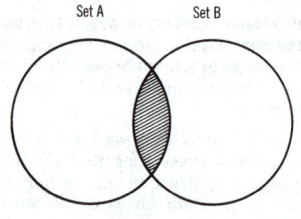

Venn diagram

Venn diagram /vén-/ *n.* a mathematical diagram representing sets as circles, with their relationships to each other expressed through their overlapping positions, so that all possible relationships between the sets are shown [Early 20thC. Named after the British logician John Venn (1834–1923).]

vennel /vénn'l/ *n.* Scotland an alley or narrow lane between buildings [15thC. Via Old French from medieval Latin *venella*, literally 'little vein', from Latin *vena* 'vein' (source of English *vein*).]

veno- *prefix.* vein, venous ○ *venogram* [From Latin *vena* 'vein' (source of English *vein*)]

venogram /veenə gram/ *n.* an X-ray photograph of a vein or network of veins, taken after injecting a substance that absorbs X-rays and so makes the veins visible

venography /vi nóggrəfi/ *n.* the examination of sb's veins by taking an X-ray photograph (**venogram**) after injecting a substance that absorbs X-rays

venom /vénnəm/ *n.* **1.** BIOL **POISONOUS FLUID INJECTED BY ANIMAL** a poisonous fluid produced by an animal and injected by a bite or sting in order to immobilize prey or defend itself. Venoms are produced by a wide range of animals, including snakes, scorpions, spiders, and fish. **2.** MALICE sth that is full of malice, spite, or vicious hostility **3.** POISON any kind of poison (*archaic*) [13thC. Via Old French *venim* from, ultimately, Latin *venenum* 'poison'.]

venomous /vénnəməss/ *adj.* **1.** BIOL **PRODUCING VENOM** producing venom and capable of inflicting a poisonous bite or sting **2.** MALICIOUS full of malice, spite, or extreme hostility **3.** POISONOUS full of or containing poison —**venomously** *adv.* —**venomousness** *n.*

venose /veenōss/ *adj.* with veins, especially many branched veins e.g. an insect's wing or the leaf of a plant [Mid-17thC. From Latin *venosus*, from *vena* 'vein'.]

venosity /vi nóssəti/ *n.* **1.** EXCESSIVE AMOUNT OF BLOOD an excessive amount of blood in the veins, or in an organ or other body part **2.** HIGH NUMBER OF VEINS an unusually large number of veins in an organ or other body part **3.** QUALITY OF VENOUS BLOOD the deoxygenated state of venous blood **4.** VEINED CONDITION the presence or possession of veins, especially many branched veins

venous /veenəss/ *adj.* **1.** OF VEINS relating to or involving the veins **2.** RELATING TO BLOOD IN VEINS used to describe blood in the veins, which is returning to the heart, as opposed to blood in the arteries, which is leaving the heart **3.** WITH VEINS containing or full of veins [Early 17thC. Formed from Latin *vena* 'vein' (source of English *vein*).] —**venously** *adv.* —**venousness** *n.*

vent[1] /vent/ *n.* **1.** OPENING FOR AIR a small opening that allows fresh air to enter or stale air, gas, smoke, or steam to escape **2.** ZOOL OPENING IN ANIMAL'S BODY the external opening through which all waste material and eggs pass in fish, amphibians, reptiles, birds, and primitive mammals **3.** GEOL OPENING IN EARTH'S CRUST an opening in the Earth's crust from which gases or volcanic material escape **4.** ARMS OPENING IN GUN BREECH a small opening in the breech of an old muzzle-loading gun through which the charge is ignited **5.** WAY OF RELEASING STRONG FEELINGS a way of releasing or expressing strong feelings, or a chance to do so ○ *a vent for his anger* ■ *vt.* (**vents, venting, vented**) **1.** RELEASE EMOTIONS to release or forcefully express strong feelings or emotions **2.** LET OUT AIR to let out smoke, gases, steam, or stale air through a vent **3.** MAKE VENT to provide a vent for sth [14thC. Via Old French *esventer* 'to let out air' from assumed Vulgar Latin *exventare*, from Latin *ventus* 'wind' (source of English *ventilate*).] —**ventless** *adj.* ◇ **give vent to sth** to express a strong feeling or emotion freely

vent[2] /vent/ *n.* SEW VERTICAL SLIT IN SEAM OF JACKET a vertical slit at the bottom of a seam in a jacket or other garment, that provides room for movement ■ *vt.* (**vents, venting, vented**) SEW ADD VENT TO JACKET to put a vent in a jacket or other garment [15thC. Alteration of earlier *fent*, via Old French *fente* 'slit' from, ultimately, Latin *findere* 'to split' (source of English *fission*).] —**vented** *adj.* —**ventless** *adj.*

ventage /véntij/ *n.* **1.** MUSIC FINGER HOLE IN WIND INSTRUMENT a finger hole in a recorder or other wind instrument **2.** SMALL VENT a small opening or vent [Early 17thC. Formed from VENT[1].]

ventail /vént ayl/ *n.* a movable covering for the neck or lower face on a medieval helmet [14thC. Via Old French from, ultimately, Latin *ventus* 'wind' (source of English *vent*[1]).]

venter /véntər/ *n.* **1.** ANAT, ZOOL BELLY OF ANIMAL WITH BACKBONE the abdomen of a vertebrate **2.** ZOOL BODY PART RESEMBLING ABDOMEN the part of the body in invertebrates that corresponds to the abdomen in vertebrates **3.** ANAT SOFT PART OF MUSCLE the soft fleshy area that forms the main part of a muscle **4.** ANAT HOLLOW OR CAVITY a hollow or cavity, e.g. on a bone **5.** BOT FEMALE PLANT PART in plants such as mosses and ferns, the swollen lower part of the female sex organ (**archegonium**) where the ovum develops **6.** LAW WOMB in law, a woman's womb. The term is used, e.g. with reference to an unborn child. (*technical*) [Mid-16thC. Directly or via law French and French *ventre* from Latin *venter* 'belly'.]

ventifact /vénti fakt/ *n.* a rock, stone, or pebble that has been shaped, cut, or polished by wind-blown sand [Early 20thC. Formed from Latin *ventus* 'wind', on the model of 'artifact'.]

ventilate /vénti layt/ (**-lates, -lating, -lated**) *vt.* **1.** PROVIDE FRESH AIR to provide a room or other enclosed space with fresh air or a current of air **2.** PROVIDE VENT to provide an enclosed space with a vent or other means of letting fresh air in and stale air out **3.** EXPOSE STH TO MOVING AIR to expose sth to moving fresh air, e.g. in order to dry, cool, or preserve it **4.** PUBLICLY EXAMINE QUESTIONS to examine freely and publicly or discuss grievances, opinions, or questions **5.** PHYSIOL SUPPLY OXYGEN TO BLOOD to oxygenate or aerate the blood through the blood vessels of the lungs [15thC. From Latin *ventilat-*, the past participle stem of *ventilare* 'to fan', from *ventilus* 'fan', from *ventus* 'wind'.]

ventilation /vénti láysh'n/ n. **1.** CIRCULATION OF AIR the movement or circulation of fresh air **2.** MEANS OF SUPPLYING FRESH AIR the means of supplying fresh air to an enclosed space, e.g. an opening or equipment installed in a building **3.** PUBLIC DISCUSSION the public discussion or examination of a particular issue

ventilator /vénti laytər/ n. **1.** DEVICE FOR CIRCULATING FRESH AIR a device that circulates fresh air in an enclosed space **2.** MED MACHINE THAT HELPS SB BREATHE a machine that keeps air moving in and out of the lungs of a patient who cannot breathe normally

ventilatory /véntilətəri, -laytəri/ adj. relating to or used for breathing or for oxygenating the blood

Ventôse /vaaN tôz/ n. the sixth month of the year in the French Revolutionary calendar, corresponding to February 20 to March 21 in the Gregorian calendar [Early 19thC. From French, literally 'windy'.]

ventr- prefix. = ventro- (used before vowels)

ventrad /vén trad/ adv. towards the ventral surface or side

ventral /véntrəl/ adj. **1.** ZOOL OF LOWER BODY AT FRONT located on or affecting the lower surface of an animal's body, or the front of the human body **2.** ANAT OF OR CLOSE TO ABDOMEN relating to or situated in, on, or near the abdomen **3.** BOT FACING AXIS used to describe the upper side of a leaf or other surface that faces towards the stem ■ n. ZOOL = **ventral fin** [Mid-18thC. Formed from the Latin stem ventr- 'belly, abdomen' (source of English ventriloquism).] —**ventrally** adv.

ventral fin, **ventral** n. a fin on the underside of a fish, especially a pelvic fin or anal fin. ◊ **dorsal fin**

ventricle /véntrik'l/ n. **1.** PHYSIOL HEART CHAMBER either of the two lower chambers of the heart that receives blood from the upper chambers (**atria**) and pumps it into the arteries by contraction of its thick muscular walls **2.** PHYSIOL BRAIN CAVITY any of the four interconnected cavities in the brain that are enlargements of the central canal of the spinal cord and contain cerebrospinal fluid **3.** HOLLOW IN BODY PART a small cavity or chamber in the body or in an organ [14thC. From Latin ventriculus, literally 'little belly' (see VENTRICULUS).]

ventricose /véntrikōss/ adj. **1.** MED SWOLLEN ON ONE SIDE used to describe a body part or plant part that is swollen, distended, or protruding on one side **2.** CORPULENT carrying a lot of weight, especially around the midsection (formal) [Mid-18thC. From modern Latin ventricosus, from Latin venter 'belly' (source of English ventriloquism).] —**ventricosity** /véntri kósseti/ n.

ventricular /ven tríkyoolar/ adj. involving, affecting, or relating to a ventricle or a ventriculus

ventricular fibrillation n. an often fatal heartbeat irregularity in which the muscle fibres of the ventricles work without coordination, resulting in loss of effective pumping action of the heart

ventriculus /ven tríkyoolass/ (plural -li /-lī/) n. **1.** INSECTS INSECT GUT the part of an insect's gut where digestion takes place **2.** BIRDS GIZZARD OF BIRD the part of a bird's stomach where digestion takes place [Early 18thC. From Latin, literally 'little belly', from venter 'belly' (source of English ventriloquism).]

ventriloquism /ven tríllekwizem/, **ventriloquy** /-tríll-əkwi/ n. the art or skill of producing vocal sounds that seem to come from sth other than the speaker [Late 18thC. Formed from ventriloquy, from modern Latin ventriloquium, literally 'speaking from the stomach', from Latin venter 'stomach' + loqui 'to speak' (source of English locution).] —**ventriloquial** /véntri lôkwi əl/ adj. —**ventriloquially** /-lôkwi əli/ adv.

ventriloquist /ven tríllekwist/ n. sb who is an expert in ventriloquism, especially a performer who makes a puppet or doll appear to speak —**ventriloquistic** /ven tríllə kwístik/ adj. —**ventriloquistically** /-kwístikli/ adv.

ventriloquize /ven tríllə kwīz/ (-quizes, -quizing, -quized), **ventriloquise** (-quises, -quising, -quised) vi. to produce vocal sounds that seem to come from sth other than the speaker

ventriloquy n. = ventriloquism [Late 16thC. See VENTRILOQUISM.]

Ventris /véntriss/, **Michael** (1922–56) British linguist. He is known for his decipherment of the Linear B script of ancient Crete, revealing it to be a form of Greek. Full name **Michael George Francis Ventris**

ventro- prefix. ventral, having to do with the belly ○ ventromedial [From Latin venter 'belly' (source of English ventral, ventricle, and ventriloquism)]

ventrodorsal /véntrō dáwrss'l/ adj. = dorsoventral adj. 2 —**ventrodorsally** adv.

ventrolateral /véntrō láttərəl/ adj. relating to or extending between the ventral and lateral surfaces of sth such as an animal or organ —**ventrolaterally** adv.

ventromedial /véntrō meédi əl/ adj. located near or facing the middle of a ventral surface on sth such as an animal or organ —**ventromedially** adv.

venture /vénchər/ n. **1.** RISKY PROJECT a risky or daring undertaking that has no guarantee of success **2.** NEW BUSINESS ENTERPRISE a business enterprise that involves risk but could lead to profit **3.** MONEY RISKED the money or property risked in a business venture ■ v. (-tures, -turing, -tured) **1.** vi. MAKE DANGEROUS TRIP to make a trip that is unpleasant or dangerous ○ I ventured out into the storm to close the barn doors. **2.** vt. RISK DANGERS to undertake the risks or dangers of a particular task or project **3.** vt. MAKE SUGGESTION to offer or express sth tentatively at the risk of being contradicted, embarrassed, or ignored **4.** vi. DARE TO DO STH to presume or dare to do sth **5.** vt. FIN PUT MONEY AT RISK to expose money or property to risk by committing it to a particular project [15thC. Shortening of ADVENTURE.] —**venturer** n.

venture capital n. money used for investment in projects that involve a high risk but offer the possibility of large profits —**venture capitalist** n.

Venture Scout, **Venturer** n. a young person aged between 16 and 20 who is a member of the senior branch of the Scouts. US term **Explorer**

venturesome /vénchərssəm/ adj. (formal) **1.** ADVENTUROUS willing to take risks or have new experiences **2.** RISKY involving risk or danger —**venturesomely** adv. —**venturesomeness** n.

venturi /ven tyoori/ n. **1.** CONSTRICTION IN TUBE a constriction in a tube designed to cause a pressure drop when a liquid or gas flows through it **2.** CARBURETTOR AIR INLET a restricted air inlet in a carburettor that produces a drop in pressure, causing fuel vapour to be drawn out of the carburettor bowl [Late 19thC. Named after the Italian physicist Giovanni Battista Venturi (1746–1822), who described the relationship between velocity and pressure in moving fluids.]

Venturi /ven tyoori/, **Robert** (b. 1925) US architect. He led a reaction as both theorist and practitioner against modernist architecture, and is regarded as the founder of postmodernism. He won the Pritzker Prize in 1991. He worked in partnership with his wife, Denise Scott Brown (b. 1931). Full name **Robert Charles Venturi**

venturi tube, **Venturi tube** n. a tube containing a venturi, that is placed in a fluid to measure its rate of flow. The measurement is based on the pressure drop in the fluid as it travels from one end of the tube to the other.

venturous /vénchərəss/ adj. = venturesome adj. 1 —**venturously** adv. —**venturousness** n.

venue /vénnyool/ n. **1.** SCENE a scene or setting in which sth takes place **2.** PLACE WHERE EVENT IS HELD a place where an event such as a sports competition or a concert is held, especially one where events are often held **3.** LAW SCENE OF CRIME the place in which a crime takes place or a cause of action arises **4.** LAW PLACE OF TRIAL a county or other area from which a jury is selected and in which a trial is held **5.** LAW STATEMENT a statement that a case is being brought to the proper court or authority [Mid-16thC. From Old French, past participle of venir 'to come', from Latin venire. Ultimately from an Indo-European word that is also the ancestor of English come, basis, and juggernaut.]

venule /vénnyool/ n. **1.** SMALL BLOOD VESSEL a small blood vessel, especially one that transfers blood from the capillaries to the veins **2.** BRANCHING VEIN a small branching vein in a leaf or an insect's wing [Mid-19thC. From Latin venula, literally 'small vein', from vena 'vein' (source of English vein).] —**venular** /vénnyoolər/ adj.

Venus /veenəss/ n. **1.** MYTHOL ROMAN GODDESS OF LOVE in Roman mythology, the goddess of love and beauty. She was the mother of Aeneas and Cupid. Greek equivalent **Aphrodite 2.** ASTRON PLANET 2ND FROM THE SUN the fourth smallest planet in the solar system and the second planet from the Sun. Seen from the Earth as a bright morning or evening star, Venus has a high surface temperature and is covered with clouds of carbon dioxide gas. [Pre-12thC. From Latin, from venus 'love, desire'.]

Venus flytrap n. = Venus's flytrap

Venushair n. = Venus's-hair

Venusian /və nyoozi ən/ adj. OF PLANET VENUS relating or belonging to the planet Venus ■ n. INHABITANT OF VENUS an inhabitant of the planet Venus, as portrayed in science fiction

Venus's flower basket n. a deep-sea sponge of the western Pacific and Indian oceans with a skeleton of glassy slender pointed structures (**spicules**) that intersect to form a geometrically patterned surface. Genus: Euplectella.

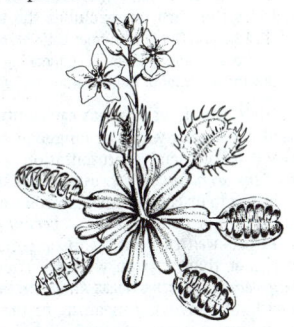

Venus's flytrap

Venus's flytrap, **Venus flytrap** n. an insect-eating plant native to North and South Carolina that has leaves ending in hinged lobes that spring shut, entrapping the insect. Latin name: Dionaea muscipula.

Venus's girdle n. a marine animal (**ctenophore**) that lives in warm seas and has a long virtually transparent belt-shaped body with rows of cilia along the top and bottom edges. Latin name: Cestum veneris.

Venus's-hair /veenəss hair/, **Venushair** n. a delicate fan-shaped fern, a type of maidenhair fern, that is native to wet limestone areas of tropical America and is widely grown as an ornamental plant. Latin name: Adiantium capillus-veneris.

Venus shell n. a common marine mollusc that has a hinged shell with rounded ribbed patterning on it. Family: Veneridae.

Venus's-looking-glass n. an annual plant that has hairy oval leaves and purple flowers. It grows on cultivated and bare land in parts of Eurasia and North Africa. Latin name: Legousia hybrida.

ver. abbr. **1.** verse **2.** version

veracious /və ráyshəss/ adj. **1.** HONEST honest or truthful **2.** TRUE true or accurate (formal or literary) [Late 17thC. Formed from Latin verac-, the stem of verax, from verus 'true' (source of English verify, verdict, and aver.] —**veraciously** adv. —**veraciousness** n.

veracity /və rássəti/ (plural -ties) n. **1.** TRUTH the truth, accuracy, or precision of sth ○ They questioned the veracity of our claims. **2.** TRUTHFULNESS the truthfulness or honesty of a person **3.** TRUE STATEMENT a truth or true statement [Early 17thC. Directly or via French from medieval Latin veracitas, from verax 'truthful' (see VERACIOUS).]

Veracruz /veérə krooz, vérrə-/ city and port in eastern Mexico, located on the Gulf of Mexico. Population: 328,607 (1990).

veranda /və rándə/, **verandah** n. **1.** PORCH a porch, usually roofed and sometimes partly enclosed, that extends along an outside wall of a building **2.** NZ CANOPY a canopy sheltering a walkway along a shopping street [Early 18thC. Via Hindi varaṇḍā from Portuguese varanda 'railing, balcony', of unknown origin.] —**verandaed** adj.

verapamil /vi ráppəmil/ n. a drug used to treat heart and circulatory disorders, including angina pectoris, hypertension, and irregular heartbeat. It works by inhibiting the movement of calcium ions across membranes, especially in muscle cells. [Mid-20thC. From v(al)er(ic) + am(ino-) + (nitr)il(e) (with inserted 'p'), its chemical name.]

veratridine /vi ráttri deen/ n. a poisonous yellowish-white substance obtained from sabadilla seeds and used in insecticides and formerly in medicine. Formula: C₃₆H₅₁NO₁₁. [Early 20thC. Formed from VERATRUM.]

veratrine /vérrə treen, -trin/, **veratrin** n. a poisonous mixture of alkaloids including veratridine, formerly used in medicine to relieve inflammation [Early 19thC. Formed from VERATRUM.]

verb /vurb/ n. 1. WORD INDICATING ACTION OR STATE a word used to show that an action is taking place, or to indicate the existence of a state or condition, or the part of speech to which such a word belongs 2. PREDICATE OF SENTENCE the part of a clause or sentence that includes the verb but excludes the subject of the verb [14thC. Via Old French from Latin verbum 'word'. Ultimately from an Indo-European base meaning 'to speak', which is also the ancestor of English word and irony.]

verbal /vúrb'l/ adj. 1. USING WORDS RATHER THAN PICTURES expressed in or using words or language, especially as opposed to pictorial representation ○ a verbal picture of the scene outside 2. USING WORDS RATHER THAN ACTION relating to or consisting of words rather than physical action or confrontation ○ verbal protest 3. ORAL RATHER THAN WRITTEN relating to or consisting of spoken rather than written words ○ They made a verbal agreement. 4. USING WORDS WITHOUT MEANING using words without conveying meaning or making any meaningful distinctions ○ a purely verbal distinction rather than anything more fundamental 5. INVOLVING SKILL WITH WORDS involving skill in the use and understanding of words and language ○ verbal dexterity 6. GRAM RELATING TO VERBS derived from or relating to a verb, or to verbs in general 7. GRAM FORMING VERBS used to form verbs 8. VERBATIM corresponding word for word (archaic) ■ n. 1. GRAM WORD FORMED FROM VERB a word formed from a verb, especially one used as a noun or an adjective, such as a gerund or participle 2. ADMISSION OF GUILT an admission of guilt upon being arrested for a crime (slang) ■ vt. (-bals, -balling, -balled) MAKE SB SOUND GUILTY to make sb sound guilty during police testimony in court by referring to an admission of guilt allegedly given earlier (slang) [15thC. Via Old French from, ultimately, Latin verbum (see VERB).] —**verbally** adv.

WORD KEY: SYNONYMS

verbal, spoken, oral

CORE MEANING: expressed in words

verbal indicates that sth such as an apology or request is expressed in words, usually spoken words, but sometimes in writing; **spoken** indicates that communication is expressed by means of speech rather than writing; **oral** a more formal word meaning the same as *spoken*.

verbal adjective n. a verb participle ending in -ing or -ed that is used as an adjective

verbalism /vúrbəlizəm/ n. 1. VERBAL EXPRESSION sth expressed in words 2. LONG-WINDED EXPRESSION a wordy expression that has little meaning or relevance 3. USE OF TOO MANY WORDS the uncritical or undisciplined use of words, especially without any attempt to analyse their meaning or value 4. US WAY STH IS EXPRESSED the manner in which sth is expressed or communicated

verbalist /vúrbəlist/ n. 1. SB SKILLED WITH WORDS sb who is skilled in the use of words and language 2. SB WHO CONCENTRATES ON WORDS sb who tends to concentrate on words or language rather than on things such as facts, feelings, or ideas —**verbalistic** /vúrbə lístik/ adj.

verbalize /vúrbə līz/ (-izes, -izing, -ized) (-balises, -balising, -balised) v. 1. vt. EXPRESS STH IN WORDS to express feelings, thoughts, or ideas in words 2. vt. GRAM MAKE WORD INTO VERB to make a word into another part of speech, e.g. a noun or adjective, into a verb 3. vi. BE VERBOSE to speak or write in a way that uses too many words —**verbalization** n. —**verbalizer** n.

verbal noun n. a form of a verb ending in '-ing' used as a noun, e.g. 'dancing' in 'he teaches dancing'

verbatim /vur báytim/ adj. USING IDENTICAL WORDS corresponding word for word with sth else ■ adv. IN IDENTICAL WORDS repeated, written down, or copied word for word [15thC. From medieval Latin, from Latin verbum 'word'.]

verbena /vur beènə/ n. a common plant or shrub, native mainly to North and South America, that bears clusters of small tubular five-lobed flowers and is widely grown for ornament. Genus: *Verbena*. [Mid-16thC. From Latin. Ultimately from an Indo-European base meaning 'to verb', which is also the ancestor of English warp, reverberate, and rhombus.]

verbiage /vúrbi ij/ n. 1. EXCESS OF WORDS an excess of words, especially in writing or speech with little or no meaning 2. WORDING the style of language in which sth is expressed ○ bureaucratic verbiage explaining the regulations [Early 18thC. Via French from, ultimately, Latin verbum 'word'.]

verbid /vúrbid/ n. LING = verbal n. 1

verbify /vúrbi fī/ (-fies, -fying, -fied) vt. = verbalize v. 2 (archaic or formal) —**verbification** /vúrbifi káysh'n/ n.

verbigerate /vur bíji rayt/ (-ates, -ating, -ated) vi. to repeat the same words or phrases obsessively as a symptom of a psychiatric disorder [Late 19thC. From Latin verbigerat-, the past participle stem of verbigerare 'to chat', from verbum 'word' + gerare 'to keep carrying on'.] —**verbigeration** /vur bíjjə ráysh'n/ n.

verbose /vur bṓss/ adj. expressed in or using language that is too long-winded or complicated [Late 17thC. From Latin verbosus, from verbum 'word'.] —**verbosely** adv. —**verboseness** n.

WORD KEY: SYNONYMS

See Synonyms at **wordy**.

verboten /fər bṓt'n, vər-/ adj. forbidden or prohibited [Early 20thC. From German.]

verb phrase n. a grammatical construction consisting of a verb and any direct and indirect objects and modifiers linked to it, but not including the subject of the verb

Vercingetorix /vúrssin jéttəriks/ (d. 46 BC) Gaulish leader. He led a revolt of Gallic tribes against Roman rule, but was eventually captured by Julius Caesar in 52 BC.

verdant /vúrd'nt/ adj. 1. WITH LUSH GREEN GROWTH green with vegetation or foliage 2. COLOURS GREEN green in colour 3. NAIVE lacking experience or sophistication (literary) [Late 16thC. From Old French verdeant, literally 'becoming green', from, ultimately, Latin viridis 'green' (source of English vireo).] —**verdancy** n. —**verdantly** adv.

verd antique /vúrd an teèk/, **verde antique** n. 1. GREEN VEINED MARBLE a dark-green mottled or veined variety of serpentine marble that is used in decoration 2. GREEN STONE a green marble or stone that resembles verd antique 3. = verdigris n. 1 [From obsolete French, literally 'antique green'.]

Verde, Cape /vúrd/ 1. peninsula in western central Senegal. Its tip is the westernmost point of the African mainland. 2. ♦ Cape Verde

verderer /vúrdərər/ n. a judicial official in charge of maintaining the royal forests in medieval England [Mid-16thC. Via Anglo-Norman from, ultimately, Latin viridis 'green' (source of English verdant).]

Verdi /váirdi/, **Giuseppe** (1813–1901) Italian composer. He was one of the greatest operatic composers of all time. His works include *Rigoletto* (1851), *La Traviata* (1853), *Aida* (1871), *Otello* (1887), and *Falstaff* (1893). Full name **Giuseppe Fortunino Francesco Verdi**

verdict /vúrdikt/ n. 1. LAW JURY DECISION the finding of a jury on the matter that has been submitted to it in a trial 2. DECISION OR OPINION ABOUT STH a judgment, opinion, or conclusion that is expressed about sth [13thC. From Anglo-Norman verdit, literally 'true speech', from ver 'true' + dit 'speech, saying'.]

verdigris /vúrdi gree, -greess/ n. 1. GREEN DEPOSIT ON COPPER a green or greenish-blue deposit (patina) on copper, brass, and bronze that is caused by atmospheric corrosion and consists of copper carbonates 2. GREENISH COPPER POWDER a green or greenish-blue poisonous powder that is used as a paint pigment and fungicide. It is formed by the action of acetic acid on copper and consists of one or more basic copper acetates. [14thC. From Old French vert de Grece, literally 'green of Greece'.]

verdin /vúrdin/ n. a small bird of the southwestern United States and Mexico, with grey plumage, a white breast, and a yellow head and throat. Latin name: *Auriparus flaviceps*. [Late 19thC. Via French from, ultimately, Latin viridis 'green'.]

verditer /vúrditər/ n. a basic copper carbonate that is used as a blue or green pigment. The blue variety contains azurite, the green variety contains malachite. [Early 16thC. From Old French verd de terre, literally 'green of the earth'.]

Verdun /vur dún/ town in northeastern France. One of the longest and bloodiest battles of World War I was fought around the town during 1916. Population: 23,427 (1990).

verdure /vúrjər/ n. 1. VIVID GREEN OF PLANTS the green colour associated with lush vegetation 2. VEGETATION extremely lush vegetation 3. FRESHNESS a fresh, healthy, or flourishing condition [14thC. Via French from, ultimately, Latin viridis 'green'.] —**verdured** adj. —**verdureless** adj. —**verdurous** adj. —**verdurousness** n.

verecund /vérri kund/ adj. shy or modest (archaic) [Mid-16thC. From Latin verecundus, from vereri 'to respect' (source of English revere).]

Vereeniging /fə reèniking/ industrial city in Gauteng Province, South Africa. Population: 71,255 (1991).

verge¹ /vurj/ n. 1. POINT BEYOND WHICH STH HAPPENS the point beyond which sth happens or begins ○ He was on the verge of tears. 2. BOUNDARY a line, belt, or strip that acts as a boundary or edge 3. EDGE the edge, rim, or margin of sth 4. TRANSP ROADSIDE BORDER a narrow border that runs alongside a road 5. ARCHIT ROOF EDGE the edge of a sloping roof where it extends beyond the gable 6. CLOCK SPINDLE the spindle of a balance wheel in early clock and watch mechanisms 7. HIST AREA AROUND ROYAL COURT an area around the English royal court that was under the jurisdiction of the Lord High Steward 8. HIST ROD HELD BY TENANT a rod held by a feudal tenant when swearing an oath of loyalty to his or her lord 9. ROD AS SYMBOL OF OFFICE a rod or staff carried as a symbol of authority or an emblem of office ■ vi. (verges, verging, verged) 1. APPROACH A STATE OR QUALITY to approach or come close to a particular quality, state, or condition ○ verging on brilliance 2. BORDER ON AN AREA to border on or be on the edge of a particular place or area [14thC. Via French, 'rod' (symbolizing the office of Lord High Steward and the limits of his jurisdiction), from Latin virga (source of English virgule).]

verge² /vurj/ (verges, verging, verged) vi. 1. MOVE IN PARTICULAR DIRECTION to move or lean in a particular direction or towards a certain condition 2. CHANGE GRADUALLY to change gradually from one thing to another (literary) 3. SINK FROM VIEW to descend towards the horizon (literary) [Early 17thC. From Latin vergere 'to bend, incline' (source of English converge and diverge). Ultimately from an Indo-European word meaning 'to turn', which is also the ancestor of English wrench and wrinkle.]

vergence /vúrjənss/ n. the inward or outward turning of both eyes when focusing on a near or distant object [Early 20thC. Back-formation from CONVERGENCE and DIVERGENCE.]

verger /vúrjər/ n. 1. CHURCH OFFICIAL a church official who acts as a caretaker and attendant and looks after the inside of a church, usually including the furnishings and the vestments 2. OFFICIAL WHO CARRIES STAFF a church official in the Church of England who carries the staff of office (verge) in front of sb such as a bishop or dean during ceremonies and processions [15thC. Via Anglo-Norman from Old French verge 'rod of office' (see VERGE¹).]

Vergil = Virgil

verglas /váir glaa/ n. a thin coating of ice found on rock or exposed ground [Early 19thC. From French, from verre 'glass' + glas 'ice'.]

veridical /və ríddik'l/ adj. (formal) 1. TRUTHFUL telling the truth 2. REAL corresponding to facts or reality, and therefore genuine or real [Mid-17thC. Formed from Latin veridicus, literally 'truth-speaking', from verus 'true' + *dicere* 'to say'.] —**veridicality** /və ríddi kálləti/ *n.* —**veridically** /və ríddikli/ *adv.*

verification /vérrifi káysh'n/ *n.* **1.** ESTABLISHMENT OF TRUTH the establishment of the truth or correctness of sth by investigation or evidence **2.** EVIDENCE the evidence that proves sth true or correct **3.** INTERNAT LAW CONFIRMATION OF PROCEDURES in international law, the process of confirming that procedures laid down in an agreement such as a weapons limitation treaty are being followed **4.** LAW AFFIDAVIT in law, an affidavit swearing to the accuracy of a pleading **5.** LAW CONFIRMATORY EVIDENCE evidence or testimony that confirms sth —**verificative** /vérrifi kaytiv/ *adj.*

verificationism /vérrifi káysh'nizəm/ *n.* the view that every meaningful proposition is capable of being shown to be true or false

verification principle *n.* the principle that a proposition or sentence is meaningful only if it is possible to establish whether it is true or false by experience or observation

verify /vérri fī/ (-**fies**, -**fying**, -**fied**) *vt.* **1.** PROVE STH to prove that sth is true **2.** CHECK WHETHER STH IS TRUE to check whether or not sth is true by examination, investigation, or comparison **3.** LAW SWEAR STH UNDER OATH in law, to swear or affirm under oath that sth is true **4.** LAW ATTEST TO TRUTH BY AFFIDAVIT in law, to support the truth of a pleading by affidavit [14thC. Via French *verifier* from medieval Latin *verificare*, literally 'to make true', from *verus* 'true' (source of English *very*) + *facere* 'to make'.] —**verifiability** /vérri fī ə bílləti/ *n.* —**verifiable** /vérri fī əb'l/ *adj.* —**verifiably** /vérri fī əbli/ *adv.* —**verifier** /vérri fī ər/ *n.*

verily /vérrili/ *adv.* in truth (*archaic*) ○ *Verily, he has admitted it.* [13thC. Formed from VERY, in the sense 'true'.]

verisimilar /vérri símmilər/ *adj.* appearing to be true or real (*literary*) [Late 17thC. Formed from Latin *verisimilis*, literally 'like the truth', from *verus* 'true' and *similis* 'like'.] —**verisimilarly** *adv.*

verisimilitude /vérrissi mílli tyood/ *n.* (*formal*) **1.** APPEARANCE OF BEING TRUE the appearance of being true or real **2.** STH THAT ONLY SEEMS TRUE sth that only appears to be true or real, e.g. a statement that is not supported by evidence [Early 17thC. From Latin *verisimilitudo*, from *verisimilis* (see VERISIMILAR).] —**verisimilitudinous** /vérrissi mílli tyoodinəss/ *adj.*

verism /veérizəm/ *n.* strict realism or naturalism in art and literature [Late 19thC. Formed from Latin *verus* or Italian *vero* 'true'.] —**verist** *n.* —**veristic** /veer rístik/ *adj.*

verismo /ve rízmō/ *n.* a late 19th-century movement in Italian opera that advocated the use of themes drawn from real life and naturalistic portrayal of characters and events. Puccini was one of the principal members of this movement. [Early 20thC. From Italian, 'verism'.]

veritable /vérritəb'l/ *adj.* **1.** ABSOLUTE indicating that sth being referred to figuratively is as good as true **2.** TRUE true as a declaration or statement (*archaic*) [15thC. Via French from, ultimately, Latin *veritas* 'truth' (see VERITY).] —**veritableness** *n.* —**veritably** *adv.*

verity /vérrəti/ (*plural* -**ties**) *n.* (*formal*) **1.** TRUTH OR REALITY the quality of being true or real **2.** STH TRUE sth that is true, especially a statement or principle that is accepted as a fact [14thC. Via French from Latin *veritas*, from *verus* 'true' (source of English *very*, *verify*, and *verdict*).]

verjuice /vúr jooss/ *n.* **1.** LIQUID FROM SOUR FRUIT an acid liquid made from crab apples or other sour or unripe fruit, formerly used in cooking instead of vinegar **2.** UNPLEASANTNESS sourness of temper, attitude, or expression [14thC. From Old French *vertjus*, from *verd* 'green' + *jus* 'juice'.]

verkrampte /fər krámptə/ *n. S Africa* an offensive term for sb who is considered to be bigoted, narrow-minded, or reactionary (*insult*) ◊ **verligte** [Mid-20thC. From Afrikaans, literally 'cramped, narrow'.]

Verlaine /vair lén/, **Paul** (1844–96) French poet. He wrote *Songs Without Words* (1874) while in prison for shooting his friend Arthur Rimbaud. His later symbolist verse influenced the development of French poetry. Full name **Paul Marie Verlaine**

verligte /fər líkhtə/ *n. S Africa* sb who is liberal, enlightened, or progressive. ◊ **verkrampte** [Mid-20thC. From Afrikaans, literally 'enlightened'.]

Vermeer /vər meér, -máir/, **Jan** (1632–75) Dutch artist. A major painter of the Dutch Golden Age, he painted domestic interiors of great serenity. Only 35 of his paintings survive.

vermeil /vúr mayl/ *n.* **1.** GILDED METAL gilded silver, bronze, or copper **2.** VERMILION the colour vermilion (*literary*) [14thC. Via Old French from late Latin *vermiculus*, kermes insect from which red dye was made, literally 'little worm', from Latin *vermis* 'worm' (see VERMI-).]

vermi- *prefix.* worm ○ *vermivorous* [From Latin *vermis* 'worm' (source of English *vermicelli* and *vermin*). Ultimately from an Indo-European word that is also the ancestor of English *worm*.]

vermicelli /vúrmi chélli/ *n.* **1.** PASTA a kind of pasta in long fine threads, often used in soups **2.** SMALL CHOCOLATE STRANDS short thin strands of chocolate that are used to decorate cakes [Mid-17thC. From Italian, literally 'little worms', from, ultimately, Latin *vermis* 'worm'.]

vermicide /vúrmi sīd/ *n.* **1.** CHEM CHEMICAL WORM KILLER a substance used to kill worms **2.** MED REMEDY FOR PARASITIC WORMS a chemical substance that expels parasitic worms from the small intestines —**vermicidal** /vúrmi sīd'l/ *adj.*

vermicomposter /vúrmi kompostər/ *n.* a container in which specially bred worms are used to convert organic matter into compost [Late 20thC. Coined from VERMI- + COMPOSTER.]

vermicomposting *n.* = **vermiculture**

vermicular /vur míkyŏŏlər/ *adj.* **1.** WAVY in wavy lines like the movements, shape, or tracks of worms **2.** OF WORMS relating to worms [Late 17thC. From medieval Latin *vermicularis*, from Latin *vermiculis*, literally 'little worm', from *vermis* 'worm'.] —**vermicularly** *adv.*

vermiculate /vur míkyŏŏ layt/ *vt.* (-**lates**, -**lating**, -**lated**) DECORATE STH WITH WAVY LINES to decorate sth with wavy lines or patterns (*formal*) ■ *adj.* **1.** WITH WAVY LINES with wavy lines like the movements, shape, or tracks of a worm **2.** SINUOUS with many twists and turns (*formal*) **3.** LOOKING WORM-EATEN with a worm-eaten appearance (*literary*) [Early 17thC. From Latin *vermiculat-*, the past participle stem of *vermiculari* 'to be full of worms', from *vermiculus* (see VERMICULAR).]

vermiculation /vur míkyŏŏ láysh'n/ *n.* **1.** MOVEMENT IN WAVES movement in waves, e.g. the muscular contractions of the intestines (**peristalsis**) **2.** WAVY DECORATION decorative wavy lines, patterns, or carvings **3.** WORM INFESTATION infestation by worms, or the resulting worm-eaten condition

vermiculite /vur míkyŏŏ līt/ *n.* a hydrous silicate of aluminium, magnesium, or iron, resulting from the alteration of the mineral constituents of basic rocks. It is used for insulation, as a lubricant, and as a medium for starting or growing plants. [Early 19thC. Formed from Latin *vermiculus* 'little worm' (see VERMICULAR), because of the way flakes of it expand and writhe in long shapes when heated.]

vermiculture /vúrmi kulchər/ *n.* the use of specially bred worms to convert organic matter into compost [Late 20thC. Coined from VERMI- + CULTURE.]

vermiform /vúrmi fawrm/ *adj.* resembling a worm in shape

vermiform appendix, **vermiform process** *n.* ANAT = **appendix** *n.* 1

vermifuge /vúrmi fyooj/ *n.* a drug or other substance that causes worms or other parasites to be expelled from the intestines —**vermifugal** /vúrmi fyoog'l/ *adj.*

vermilion /vər mílli ən/, **vermillion** *n.* **1.** RED PIGMENT a bright red pigment made from mercuric sulphide or created artificially **2.** COLOURS BRIGHT RED COLOUR a bright red colour, sometimes tinged with orange ■ *adj.* OF A BRILLIANT RED of a bright red colour [13thC. From Old French *vermeillon*, from *vermeil* (see VERMEIL).]

vermin /vúrmin/ (*plural* -**min**) *n.* **1.** DESTRUCTIVE ANIMALS OR INSECTS small animals or insects that harm people, livestock, property, or crops and are difficult to control, e.g. rats, weasels, fleas, or cockroaches **2.** OFFENSIVE TERM an offensive term for a person or group considered to be extremely unpleasant or undesirable (*slang insult*) [13thC. Via Old French from assumed Vulgar Latin *verminum* 'noxious life forms', from Latin *vermis* 'worm'.]

vermination /vúrmi náysh'n/ *n.* the spreading of or infestation with vermin, especially parasites

verminous /vúrminəss/ *adj.* **1.** OF OR WITH VERMIN relating to or infested with vermin **2.** CAUSED BY VERMIN OR WORMS caused by vermin or parasitic worms **3.** DISGUSTING extremely unpleasant or offensive —**verminously** *adv.* —**verminousness** *n.*

vermis /vúrmiss/ *n.* the middle lobe of the brain that connects the two hemispheres of the cerebellum [Late 19thC. From Latin, 'worm'.]

vermivorous /vur mívvərəss/ *adj.* used to describe birds or other animals that feed on worms

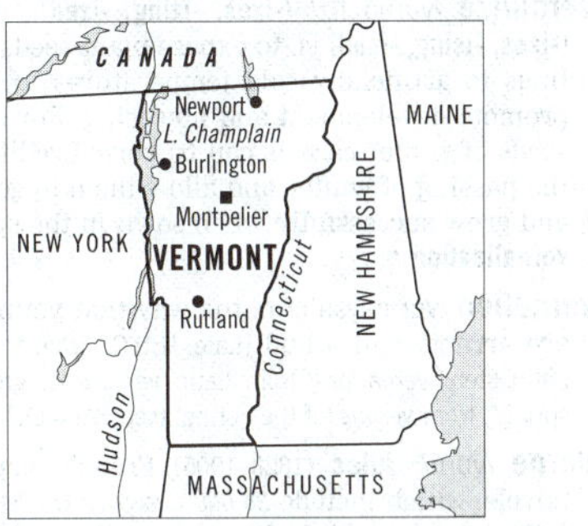

Vermont

Vermont /və mónt/ state in the northeastern United States, bordered by Canada, New Hampshire, Massachusetts, and New York State. Capital: Montpelier. Population: 588,978 (1997). Area: 24,903 sq. km/9,615 sq. mi. —**Vermonter** *n.*

vermouth /vúrməth, vər mooth/ *n.* a wine flavoured with aromatic herbs [Early 19thC. Via French from German *Wermut* 'wormwood', with which it was originally flavoured.]

vernacle /vúrnək'l/ *n.* = **veronica**[2] *n.* 1 [Variant of VERNICLE]

vernacular /vər nákyŏŏlər/ *n.* **1.** LANG ORDINARY LANGUAGE the everyday language of the people in a particular country or region, as opposed to official or formal language **2.** LANG SPOKEN LANGUAGE the common spoken language of a people as opposed to formal written or literary language **3.** LANG LANGUAGE OF PARTICULAR GROUP the distinctive vocabulary or language of a particular profession, group, or class **4.** BIOL COMMON NAME a common name of a plant, animal, or other organism as opposed to its scientific name **5.** ARCHIT ORDINARY BUILDING STYLE the architecture of a particular place or people, especially the architectural style that is used for ordinary houses as opposed to large official or commercial buildings ■ *adj.* **1.** LANG USING ORDINARY LANGUAGE belonging to, relating to, or using the everyday language of the people in a particular country or region, as opposed to official or formal language **2.** LANG IN ORDINARY SPOKEN LANGUAGE belonging to, relating to, or using the common spoken language of a people as opposed to formal written or literary language **3.** BIOL RELATING TO COMMON NAME used to describe the common name of a plant, animal, or other organism as opposed to its scientific name **4.** ARCHIT BUILT IN COMMON STYLE built in the style of architecture used for the ordinary houses of a particular place or people, as opposed to the style used for large official or commercial buildings [Early 17thC. Formed from Latin *vernaculus* 'native', from *verna* 'native-born slave', of uncertain origin: possibly from Etruscan.] —**vernacularly** *adv.*

vernacularism /vər nákyŏŏlərizəm/ *n.* **1.** ORDINARY WORD OR PHRASE a word or phrase from the everyday language of the people in a particular country or region, as opposed to official or formal language **2.** USE OF ORDINARY LANGUAGE the use of everyday language, as opposed to official or formal language

vernacularize /vər nákyŏŏlə rīz/ (-**izes**, -**izing**, -**ized**), **vernacularise** (-**ises**, -**ising**, -**ised**) *vt.* to make a word or phrase a part of ordinary everyday language

vernal /vúrn'l/ *adj.* **1.** IN THE SPRING appearing or happening in the season of spring **2.** YOUTHFUL having the freshness or energy associated with being young (*literary*) [Mid-16thC. From Latin *vernalis*, from *vernus* 'of the spring', from *ver* 'spring'.]

vernal equinox *n.* **1.** TIME **BEGINNING OF SPRING** the time when the sun crosses the celestial equator and day and night are of equal length, marking the beginning of spring. In the northern hemisphere this is around 21 March, in the southern hemisphere around 23 September. **2.** ASTRON **INTERSECTION OF CELESTIAL EQUATOR AND ECLIPTIC** the point on the celestial sphere where the path of the sun (**ecliptic**) crosses the celestial equator, in the constellation of Pisces

vernal grass *n.* an early-blooming grass native to Europe and Asia that smells like new-mown hay when crushed. Genus: *Anthoxanthum.*

vernalize /vúrnə līz/ (**-izes, -izing, -ized**), **vernalise** (**-ises, -ising, -ised**) *vt.* to expose plant seeds or seedlings to artificially cold temperatures in order to promote development and flowering. For example, seeds of winter cereals can be vernalized to mimic the passing of winter and allow them to germinate and grow successfully when sown in the spring. —**vernalization** *n.*

vernation /vur náysh'n/ *n.* the way that young leaves are arranged in a bud [Late 18thC. From the modern Latin stem *vernation-*, from Latin *vernare* 'to grow in the spring', from *vernus* 'of the spring' (see VERNAL).]

Verne /vurn/, **Jules** (1828–1905) French writer. His novels, which include *20,000 Leagues Under the Sea* (1870) and *Around the World in 80 Days* (1873), were pioneering works of science fiction.

vernicle /vúrnik'l/ *n.* CHR = **veronica**[2] *n.* 1 [14thC. From Old French *veronicle,* variant of *veronique* (see VERONICA).]

vernier /vúrni ər/ *n.* **1.** **SMALL SCALE FOR PRECISE READINGS** a small movable graduated scale parallel to a larger graduated scale, used to obtain smaller or more precise readings from the main scale **2.** **DEVICE FOR MAKING FINE ADJUSTMENTS** an auxiliary device used to make fine adjustments to a precision instrument ■ *adj.* **WITH A VERNIER** relating to or fitted with a vernier [Mid-18thC. Named after the French mathematician Pierre *Vernier* (1580–1637).]

vernier rocket *n.* = **thruster** *n.* 1 [Mid-20thC. See VERNIER.]

vernissage /vúrni saazh/ *n.* a private showing or preview before the public opening of an art exhibition [Early 20thC. From French, literally 'varnishing', because it was originally the day before a public exhibition, when exhibitors varnished paintings after they were in place.]

Vernon /vúrnən/ city in southern British Columbia, Canada. Population: 55,359 (1996).

Verona /və rṓnə/ capital city of Verona Province, Veneto Region, northern Italy. Population: 254,145 (1995). —**Veronese** /vérrō néez, vérrō náyzi/ *n., adj.*

Veronal /vérrən'l/ *tdmk.* a trademark for barbitone

Veronese /vérrō náyzi/, **Paolo** (1528–88) Italian artist. A painter of the Venetian school, his large-scale religious and secular compositions make dramatic use of colour and perspective. Real name **Paolo Caliari**

veronica[1] /və rónnikə/ *n.* a perennial or annual plant or shrub of the figwort family, e.g. the speedwell, that bears clusters of small, typically blue flowers. Genus: *Veronica.* [Early 16thC. From modern Latin, genus name, of uncertain origin: possibly an alteration of Greek *berenikion.*]

veronica[2] /və rónnikə/ *n.* **1.** **IMPRESSION OF JESUS CHRIST'S FACE** the impression of Jesus Christ's face believed by some to have been miraculously left on the cloth with which Saint Veronica wiped it on his way to his crucifixion **2.** **CLOTH THAT WIPED JESUS CHRIST'S FACE** the cloth with which Saint Veronica is said to have wiped Jesus Christ's face on his way to his crucifixion **3.** **CLOTH WITH JESUS CHRIST'S FACE** a cloth bearing a representation of Jesus Christ's face, sometimes worn by pilgrims [Late 17thC. Origin uncertain: possibly an alteration (influenced by the name of Saint Veronica) of medieval Latin *vera iconica,* literally 'true image'.]

veronica[3] /və rónnikə/ *n.* a move in bullfighting in which the bullfighter stands in place and slowly swings the cape away from the bull as it charges [Mid-19thC. From Spanish *verónica,* named after Saint *Veronica,* from the gesture involved in wiping Jesus Christ's face.]

verruca /və róokə/ (*plural* **-cas** *or* **-cae** /və róosee, -róokee/) *n.* **1.** **WART ON FOOT** a wart that grows on the foot, usually on the sole **2.** **GROWTH RESEMBLING A WART** a wart-shaped growth or projection on a plant or the skin of an animal [Mid-16thC. From Latin, 'wart'. Ultimately from an Indo-European word meaning 'bump', which is also the ancestor of English *wart* and *varicose.*]

verrucose /vérrookōss/, **verrucous** /vérrookəss, ve róokəss/ *adj.* covered with warts or similar growths or projections [Late 17thC. From Latin *verrucosus,* from *verruca* 'wart' (see VERRUCA).] —**verrucosity** /vérroo kóssəti/ *n.*

vers *abbr.* versed sine

Versailles /vair sī/ *n.* a large and elaborately decorated palace near Paris, built for Louis XIV in the mid-17th century. It is now a museum. The Treaty of Versailles was signed there in 1919, ending World War I.

versant /vúrss'nt/ *n.* **1.** **MOUNTAIN SLOPE** the slope of a mountain or mountain range **2.** **AREA SLOPE** the slope of a particular region [Mid-19thC. From French, the present participle of *verser* 'to turn over', from Latin *versare* (see VERSATILE).]

versatile /vúrssə tīl/ *adj.* **1.** **WITH MANY USES** able or meant to be used in many different ways **2.** **MOVING EASILY BETWEEN TASKS** able to move easily from one subject, task, or skill to another **3.** **CHANGEABLE** subject to rapid or unpredictable change **4.** ZOOL **FREE-MOVING** used to describe a body part or joint that can turn or move freely in more than one direction, e.g. an insect's antenna **5.** BOT **ATTACHED LOOSELY** used to describe an anther that is attached to the filament by a small area, allowing it to move more freely [Early 17thC. From Latin *versatilis,* from *versat-,* the past participle stem of *versare,* literally 'to keep turning or changing', from *vertere* (see VERSE[1]).] —**versatilely** *adv.* —**versatility** /vúrssə tílləti/ *n.*

vers de société /váir də sóssyə táy/ *n.* verse or poetry written in a light witty sophisticated style [From French, literally 'society verse']

verse[1] /vurss/ *n.* **1.** MUSIC, POETRY **GROUP OF SONG OR POEM LINES** a section of a poem or song consisting of a number of lines arranged together to form a single unit **2.** JUD-CHR **NUMBERED DIVISION OF BIBLE CHAPTER** any of the numbered subdivisions into which the chapters of the Bible are divided **3.** POETRY **POETRY** poetry as opposed to prose **4.** POETRY **BODY OF POETRY** a body of poetry, e.g. by a single author or from a particular country or period ○ *an anthology of 19th-century verse* **5.** POETRY **KIND OF POETRY** a particular form of poetry **6.** POETRY **BAD POETRY** poetry that is trivial in content or inferior in quality ○ *It's not poetry at all, it's just verse.* **7.** POETRY **SHORT POEM** a poem, especially a short one **8.** POETRY **LINE OF A POEM** a single line of a poem, arranged rhythmically in metrical feet ■ *vt.* (**verses, versing, versed**) **VERSIFY PROSE CONTENT** to turn sth from prose into poetry (*archaic*) [Pre-12thC. Directly and via Old French *vers* from Latin *versus* 'turning (of a plow), furrow, line', from *vertere* 'to turn'.]

WORD KEY: ORIGIN

The Latin word *vertere,* from which ***verse*** is derived, is also the source of English *adverse, advertise, controversy, conversation, convert, diverse, invert, obverse, pervert, prose, reverse, subvert, universe, versatile, version, versus, vertebra, vertical,* and *vertigo.*

verse[2] /vurss/ (**verses, versing, versed**) *vt.* to instruct sb in sth (*archaic or literary*) [Back-formation from VERSED]

versed /vurst/ *adj.* very knowledgeable about or skilled in sth [Early 17thC. Directly or via French *versé* from Latin *versatus,* the past participle of *versari* 'to occupy oneself with', from *versare* 'to keep turning' (see VERSATILE).]

versed cosine *n.* a trigonometric function equal to one minus the sine of the specified angle [Modelled on VERSED SINE]

versed sine *n.* a trigonometric function equal to one minus the cosine of the specified angle [Translation of modern Latin *sinus versus,* literally 'turned sine']

verset /vúrssit/ *n.* a short verse, especially one from a sacred book [Early 17thC. From French, literally 'short verse', from *vers* 'line' (see VERSE[1]).]

versicle /vúrssik'l/ *n.* **1.** CHR **SHORT SENTENCE IN LITURGY** a short sentence spoken or chanted by the minister during a liturgical service and responded to by the congregation or choir **2.** POETRY **VERSE** a short verse (*literary or archaic*) [14thC. From Latin *versiculus,* literally 'short verse', from *versus* 'line' (see VERSE[1]).] —**versicular** /vur síkyōōlər/ *adj.*

versicolor *adj.* US = **versicolour**

versicolour /vúrssi kull-ər/, **versicoloured** /vúrssi kull ərd/ *adj.* **1.** **MULTICOLOURED** having various colours **2.** **OF CHANGEABLE COLOUR** varying or changing in colour [Early 17thC. From Latin *versicolor,* from *versus,* the past participle of *vertere* 'to turn, change' (see VERSE[1]), + *color* 'colour'.]

versification /vúrssifi káysh'n/ *n.* **1.** **ART OF VERSE-WRITING** the art or practice of writing verse **2.** **METRICAL FORM** the metrical form or structure of a poem **3.** **TURNING PROSE INTO VERSE** the conversion of prose into verse, or the recounting of sth in verse **4.** **VERSION IN POETRY** a poetic or metrical version of a prose work

versify /vúrssi fī/ (**-fies, -fying, -fied**) *v.* **1.** *vt.* **CHANGE PROSE INTO POETRY** to turn prose into verse **2.** *vt.* **TELL STORY IN POETRY** to recount sth in verse **3.** *vi.* **WRITE POETRY** to compose verse [14thC. Via French from Latin *versificare,* literally 'to make verses', from *versus* 'line' (see VERSE[1]).] —**versifier** *n.*

versine /vúrsīn/ *n.* MATH = **versed sine**

version /vúrsh'n, vúrzh'n/ *n.* **1.** **ACCOUNT OF STH** an account of sth, given from a particular point of view **2.** **PARTICULAR FORM OF STH** a particular form or variety of sth that is different from others or from the original **3.** **ADAPTATION OF STH** an adaptation of sth for another medium, e.g. a book made into a play or film **4.** **TRANSLATION OF STH** a translation of sth into another language **5.** **version, Version** **BIBLE TRANSLATION** a particular translation of the Bible **6.** MED **MANIPULATION OF FOETUS** the manipulation of a foetus to change its position in the womb, e.g. so it can be delivered safely **7.** MED **TILTED CONDITION OF ORGAN** a condition in which an internal organ, especially the womb, is abnormally tilted or turned [Late 16thC. Via French from the Latin stem *version-,* from *vers-,* the past participle stem of *vertere* 'to turn' (see VERSE[1]).] —**versional** *adj.*

vers libre /váir léebrə/ *n.* = **free verse** [From French]

verso /vúrssō/ (*plural* **-sos**) *n.* **1.** PUBL **BACK OF PRINTED PAGE** the back of a page or other printed sheet. ◊ **recto 2.** PUBL **LEFT-HAND PAGE** any of the left-hand pages of a book, usually printed with an even page number. ◊ **recto 3.** COINS = **reverse** *n.* 3 [Mid-19thC. From Latin *verso (folio)* '(with the page) turned', from *versus,* the past participle of *vertere* 'to turn' (see VERSE[1]).]

verst /vurst/ *n.* a Russian measure of length equal to 1.07 km/0.66 mi [Mid-16thC. Via French *verste* or German *Werst* from Russian *versta* 'line'.]

versus /vúrssəss/ *prep.* **1.** **AGAINST** against, especially in a competition or court case ○ *The United States versus Canada* **2.** **ALTERNATIVE TO** as opposed to or contrasted with ○ *such considerations as money versus job satisfaction* [15thC. From medieval Latin, 'against', from the past participle of Latin *vertere* 'to turn' (see VERSE[1]).]

vert /vurt/ *n.* **1.** HERALDRY **GREEN COLOUR** in heraldry, the colour green **2.** LAW **RIGHT TO CUT WOOD OR VEGETATION** in former times, the right to cut living wood or green vegetation in a forest **3.** HIST **WOOD OR VEGETATION** in former times, living wood or green vegetation in a forest ■ *adj.* HERALDRY **GREEN** in heraldry, green in colour [15thC. Via Old French, literally 'green', from Latin *viridis* (source of English *verdant* and *vireo*).]

vert. *abbr.* vertical

vertebra /vúrtibrə/ (*plural* **-brae** /-bray, -bree/ *or* **-bras**) *n.* a bone of the spinal column, typically consisting of a stout body, a bony arch enclosing a hole for the spinal cord, and stubby projections that connect with adjacent bones. In humans the spinal column contains 33 vertebrae, including the fused lower vertebrae that form the sacrum and coccyx. [Early 17thC. From Latin, formed from *vertere* 'to turn' (see VERSE[1]).] —**vertebral** *adj.* —**vertebrally** *adv.*

vertebral canal *n.* = **spinal canal**

vertebral column *n.* = **spinal column**

vertebrate /vúrtibrət/ *n.* an animal with a segmented spinal column and a well-developed brain such as a mammal, bird, reptile, amphibian, or fish [Early

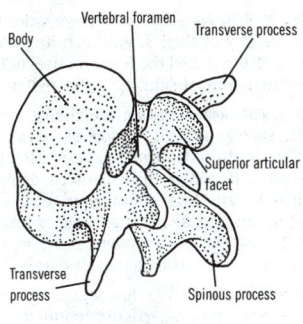

Body · Vertebral foramen · Transverse process · Superior articular facet · Transverse process · Spinous process

Vertebra

19thC. From Latin *vertebratus* 'having joints', from *vertebra* (see VERTEBRA).] —**vertebrate** *adj.*

vertebration /vúrti bráysh'n/ *n.* the formation of or division into vertebral segments, or segments resembling vertebrae, during the development of an embryo

vertex /vúrt eks/ (*plural* -texes *or* -tices /-ti seez/) *n.* **1.** APEX the highest point of sth **2.** ANAT TOP OF THE HEAD the highest point of a body part, especially the top or crown of the head **3.** GEOM POINT OPPOSITE THE BASE the point opposite the base of a figure **4.** GEOM POINT WHERE SIDES OF ANGLE MEET the point where two sides of a plane figure or an angle intersect **5.** GEOM POINT WHERE PLANES OF SOLID MEET the point where three or more planes of a solid figure intersect **6.** ASTRON POINT TOWARDS WHICH STARS MOVE a point on the celestial sphere towards which or from which a group of stars appears to move [Late 16thC. From Latin, 'whirl, spiral of hair at the top of the head', from *vertere* 'to turn' (see VERSE[1]).]

vertical /vúrtik'l/ *adj.* **1.** AT RIGHT ANGLE TO HORIZON at a right angle to the horizon **2.** UPRIGHT extending or standing in an upright position, or running straight up or down sth such as a piece of paper **3.** OVERHEAD at the vertex or directly overhead **4.** ECON INVOLVING ALL STAGES OF PRODUCTION relating to or involving all the consecutive stages in the production of goods, from design to sale **5.** ANAT AT THE TOP OF THE HEAD at or relating to the highest point of a body part, especially the top or crown of the head **6.** MADE UP OF MANY LEVELS involving or made up of successive or many levels ○ *a vertical management structure* ■ *n.* **1.** STH VERTICAL a vertical structure, line, surface, or part **2.** VERTICAL POSITION a position that is upright or at a right angle to the horizon [Mid-16thC. Directly or via French from late Latin *verticalis* 'overhead', from Latin *vertex* (see VERTEX).] —**verticality** /vúrti kálləti/ *n.* —**vertically** /vúrtikli/ *adv.*

vertical angle *n.* either of the pair of equal angles formed on opposite sides of the point at which two lines intersect. The sides of either of the pair of vertical angles are the extensions of those of the other angle.

vertical circle *n.* a great circle on the celestial sphere whose plane is perpendicular to the horizon and passes through the zenith and the nadir

vertical mobility *n.* the movement of people or groups in society either upwards or downwards in terms of class or status

vertices plural of **vertex**

verticil /vúrtissil/ *n.* a circular arrangement of similar

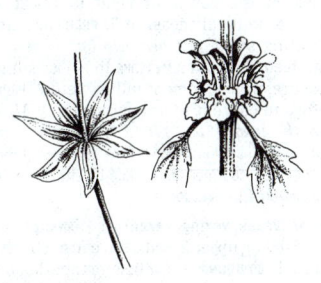

Verticil: Two verticil plants

parts around a central point [Early 18thC. From Latin *verticillus* 'whorl of a spindle'.]

verticillaster /vúrtissi lástər/ *n.* a flower cluster that looks like a whorl of flowers but actually consists of two crowded clusters (**cymes**) arising opposite each other, as in dead nettles and many mints [Mid-19thC. Formed from Latin *verticullus* 'whorl of a spindle' + -ASTER.] —**verticillastrate** /vúrtissi lástrət/ *adj.*

verticillate /vur tíssilət/ *adj.* arranged in whorls, or forming a whorl —**verticillately** *adv.* —**verticillation** /vur tíssi láysh'n/ *n.*

vertiginous /vur tíjjinəss/ *adj.* **1.** DIZZYING causing dizziness, especially because of being very high or exposed ○ *the mountain's vertiginous summit* **2.** SUFFERING FROM VERTIGO relating to or suffering from the whirling or tilting sensation of vertigo **3.** ROTARY whirling or spinning on an axis **4.** FICKLE tending to change frequently or suddenly —**vertiginously** *adv.* —**vertiginousness** *n.*

vertigo /vúrtigō/ (*plural* -tigoes *or* -tigos *or* -tigines /vur tíjji neez/) *n.* **1.** CONDITION MARKED BY WHIRLING SENSATIONS a condition in which sb feels a sensation of whirling or tilting that causes a loss of balance. It is most often caused by disease of the inner ear or of the parts of the brain concerned with balance, or it may precede an epileptic episode. **2.** INSTANCE OF VERTIGO an instance or episode of vertigo [15thC. From Latin (stem *vertigin-*), 'whirling about, giddiness', from *vertere* 'turn'.]

── **WORD KEY: CULTURAL NOTE** ──
Vertigo, a film by English director Alfred Hitchcock (1958). One of Hitchcock's most highly regarded films, it is both a typically suspenseful thriller and a powerful study of obsession. When former policeman Scottie Fergusson is asked to shadow a friend's wife, he first falls in love with her and then, after her suicide, becomes infatuated with a woman who appears to be her double.

vertu *n.* = virtu

Vertumnus /vur túmnəss/ *n.* the Roman god of gardens

vervain /vúr vayn/ *n.* a herbaceous plant with small blue, white, or purple flowers and square stems, especially one with lilac flowers that grows wild in temperate regions. Genus: *Verbena*. [14thC. Via French *verveine* from Latin *verbena* (see VERBENA).]

verve /vurv/ *n.* **1.** CREATIVE ENTHUSIASM enthusiasm, energy, or spirit, especially in the expression of artistic ideas **2.** VITALITY lively vigorous spirit [Late 17thC. Via French, 'vigour, fanciful expression', from Latin *verba* 'whimsical words', literally 'words', plural of *verbum* 'word' (source of English *verb* and *verbal*).]

Vervet

vervet /vúrvit/, **vervet monkey** *n.* an African monkey that lives in large groups in savannah woodlands and has a long tail and black face, hands, and feet. Latin name: *Cercopithecus aethiops*. [Late 19thC. From French, of unknown origin.]

Verwoerd /fər voórt/, **Hendrik** (1901–66) Dutch-born South African statesman. As prime minister of South Africa (1958–66), he was responsible for much apartheid legislation and outlawed the African National Congress. Full name **Hendrik Frensch Verwoerd**

very /vérri/ CORE MEANING: an adverb that is used in front of adjectives and adverbs to emphasize their meaning ○ *That is a very, very strong argument.* ○ *Let me very briefly give you some examples.*
  1. *adv.* GIVES EMPHASIS used to give emphasis to adjectives or adverbs that can be graded ○ *I think*

buying a dog is something we want to be very careful about. ○ *Someone had copied her style very accurately.* **2.** *adj.* EXTREME indicates an extreme position or extreme point in time ○ *They moved to the very back of the set, smiling at the technicians.* **3.** *adj.* RIGHT exactly the right or appropriate person or thing, or exactly the same person or thing ○ *Hello! The very person I wanted to see!* ○ *He died this very day in 1986.* **4.** *adj.* EMPHASIZES IMPORTANCE used before nouns to emphasize seriousness or importance ○ *An event like this can't help but shake the boxing world to its very foundation.* [13thC. Via Old French, ultimately, Latin *verax* 'truthful', from *verus* 'true' (source of English *verdict*, *verisimilitude*, and *verify*).] ◇ **very much so** an emphatic way of saying yes to sth or indicating that it is true or correct ○ *'He was a good man, brave and honest'. 'Yes, very much so'.* ◇ **very well** indicates that sb agrees to do sth or accepts what sb has said

very high frequency *n.* the radio frequency band between 30 and 300 megahertz, reserved for the transmission of television and FM radio signals

Very light /véeri-/ *n.* a coloured flare fired from a pistol, used as a signal [Early 20thC. Named after the US naval officer Edward W. *Very* (1847–1910).]

very low frequency *n.* the radio frequency band between 3 and 30 kilohertz

Very pistol /véeri-/ *n.* a pistol used for firing coloured flares [Early 20thC. See VERY LIGHT.]

Very Reverend *n.* the title of a dean and some other religious officials

vesica /véssikə/ (*plural* -cae /véssi see/) *n.* **1.** ANAT BLADDER a bladder, especially the urinary bladder (*technical*) **2.** ARTS OVAL a pointed oval shape used in medieval art and sculpture, especially to enclose a figure of Jesus Christ or the Virgin Mary [Mid-17thC. From Latin, 'bladder, blister'.]

vesical /véssik'l/ *adj.* occurring in or relating to a bladder, especially the urinary bladder ○ *vesical veins* [Late 18thC]

vesicant /véssikənt/, **vesicatory** /véssi kaytəri/ *n.* (*plural* -ries) BLISTERING SUBSTANCE a substance that causes blisters, especially a substance such as mustard gas used in chemical warfare ■ *adj.* CAUSING BLISTERING causing blisters to form [Mid-17thC]

vesicate /véssi kayt/ (-cates, -cating, -cated) *vti.* to cause or be affected by blisters [Mid-17thC. Formed from VESICA.] —**vesication** /véssi káysh'n/ *n.*

vesicle /véssik'l/ *n.* **1.** MED FLUID-FILLED CYST a small sac or hollow organ in the body, especially one containing fluid **2.** MED FLUID-FILLED BLISTER a very small blister filled with clear fluid (**serum**) **3.** GEOL SPHERICAL CAVITY WITHIN A ROCK a bubble-shaped cavity in an igneous rock, formed by the expansion of gases trapped in lava and often later filled with minerals deposited from percolating solutions **4.** BOT CAVITY IN AN AQUATIC PLANT a cavity filled with air in a seaweed or aquatic plant [Late 16thC. Directly or via French *vésicule* from Latin *vesicula* 'small vesica', from *vesica* 'bladder, blister'.]

vesicular /və síkyŏŏlər/ *adj.* resembling, having, or made up of vesicles —**vesicularly** *adv.*

vesiculate *vti.* /və síkyŏŏ layt/ (-lates, -lating, -lated) FORM OR BECOME A VESICLE to form blisters or vesicles in sth, or to become like a vesicle ■ *adj.* /və síkyŏŏlət/ HAVING VESICLES having or resembling blisters or vesicles —**vesiculation** /və síkyŏŏ láysh'n/ *n.*

Vespasian /ve spáyzh'n/ (AD 9–79) Roman emperor. His reign (69–79) saw the destruction of Jerusalem and the construction of the Colosseum. Born **Titus Flavius Sabinus Vespasianus**

vesper /véspər/ *n.* **1.** vesper, vesper bell BELL RUNG IN THE EVENING a bell rung in the evening, e.g. to summon worshippers to vespers **2.** EVENING evening (*archaic or literary*) ■ *adj.* RELATING TO VESPERS relating to the evening or vespers [14thC. From Latin, 'evening, evening star'.]

Vesper *n.* Venus when seen as a bright star in the evening sky

vesperal /véspərəl/ *n.* **1.** BOOK OF PRAYERS AND HYMNS a book that contains the prayers and hymns used at vespers **2.** ALTAR CLOTH COVERING a covering for an altar cloth

vespers /véspərz/, **Vespers** *n.* **EVENING WORSHIP** an evening church service, particularly evensong (*takes a singular or plural verb*) ■ *npl.* **SIXTH CANONICAL HOUR** the sixth of the seven canonical hours or a service held on Sundays and holy days at this time, especially in the Roman Catholic Church (*takes a singular or plural verb*) [14thC. Via Old French *vespres* (plural) from, ultimately, Latin *vespera* (singular) 'evening', from *vesper* 'evening star'.]

vespertilionid /véspər tílli ənid/ *n.* a common, insect-eating, long-tailed bat. Family: Vespertilionidae. [Late 19thC. From modern Latin *Vespertillionidae*, family name, ultimately from Latin *vespertilio* 'bat', from *vesper* 'evening'.]

vespertine /véspər tīn/ *adj.* **1.** BOT **OPENING IN THE EVENING** used to describe a flower that opens in the evening **2.** ZOOL **ACTIVE IN THE EVENING** tending to be most active in the evening **3.** ASTRON **APPEARING IN THE EVENING** appearing or setting in the evening [Early 16thC]

vespiary /véspi əri/ (*plural* **-ies**) *n.* a nest or colony of social wasps or hornets [Early 19thC. Formed from Latin *vespa* 'wasp' on the model of APIARY.]

vespid /véspid/ *n.* **INSECT OF THE WASP AND HORNET FAMILY** an insect of the family that includes wasps and hornets. Family: Vespidae. ■ *adj.* **BELONGING TO THE WASP AND HORNET FAMILY** belonging or related to the family of insects that includes wasps and hornets [Early 20thC. Formed from Latin *vespa* 'wasp'.]

vespine /vés pīn/ *adj.* relating to or resembling wasps [Mid-19thC. Formed from Latin *vespa* 'wasp'.]

vessel /véss'l/ *n.* **1.** **RECEPTACLE** a hollow receptacle, especially one that is used as a container for liquids **2.** NAUT **LARGE WATERCRAFT** a ship or large boat **3.** AIR **AIRSHIP** a flying craft, especially an airship **4.** ANAT **TUBULAR STRUCTURE CONDUCTING BODY FLUID** a duct that carries fluid, especially blood or lymph, around the body **5.** BOT **TUBE CONDUCTING WATER IN A PLANT** a tube that carries water and dissolved minerals through a plant, forming part of the sap-conducting tissue (**xylem**). Vessels consist of a longitudinal series of fused cylindrical cells whose end walls have broken down, and are found in most flowering plants and some ferns. **6.** **SB WHO EMBODIES A QUALITY** sb seen as the recipient or embodiment of a quality [14thC. Via Anglo-Norman from Latin *vascellum* 'small dish or vase, ship', from *vas* 'dish, vase' (source of English *vase*).]

vest /vest/ *n.* CLOTHES **1.** *US, Can, Aus* **SLEEVELESS GARMENT** a man's or woman's sleeveless and collarless waist-length garment, usually with buttons down the front, worn over a shirt and traditionally worn by men under a suit jacket **2.** *UK, NZ* **SLEEVELESS UNDERGARMENT** a sleeveless garment worn on the upper part of the body, under the clothes. US term **undershirt** ■ *v.* (**vests, vesting, vested**) **1.** *vt.* **CONFER POWER ON** to bestow a power on sb or sth (*usually passive*) ○ *The governor was vested with certain powers.* **2.** *vti.* **CONFER RIGHTS ON** to settle or confer property, power, or rights on sb, or to be a part of sb's property, power, or rights ○ *Sovereignty vests in the state.* ○ *by the authority vested in me* **3.** *vti.* **CLOTHE OR PUT ON CLOTHES** to clothe sb or to put on clothes, especially vestments [15thC. From Old French *vestu*, past participle of *vestir* 'to clothe', from Latin *vestire*, from *vestis* 'clothing, garment' (source of English *invest, travesty,* and *vestry*).]

WORD KEY: REGIONAL NOTE

People commenting on differences between American and British English often point out that a ***vest*** is underwear in Britain. In fact, ***vest*** is only one of the many words used for this garment. Others include *body-flannen, body-sark, flannel, simmit, singlet,* and *undersark.*

Vesta /véstə/ *n.* **1.** MYTHOL **ROMAN GODDESS** the Roman goddess of the hearth. Greek equivalent **Hestia** **2.** ASTRON **LARGE BRIGHT ASTEROID** the brightest and third largest of the asteroids that orbit the Sun [From Latin]

vestal /vést'l/ *adj.* **1.** **CHASTE** chaste, or not having experienced sexual intercourse **2.** MYTHOL **OF VESTA** relating to the Roman goddess Vesta ■ *n.* **1.** **VIRGIN** a woman who is a virgin (*literary*) **2.** **NUN** a nun (*literary*) **3.** = **vestal virgin** [15thC]

vestal virgin *n.* a celibate woman who tended the sacred fire in the temple of Vesta in ancient Rome. There were originally four, and later six vestal virgins, who were vowed to 30 years of service.

vested /véstid/ *adj.* **1.** **HAVING RIGHTS TO STH** having an unquestionable right to the possession of property or a privilege **2.** **CLOTHED** wearing clothes, especially religious vestments

vested interest *n.* **1.** **RIGHT TO POSSESS STH** a right to the present or future possession of property **2.** **SPECIAL INTEREST** a person's particular concern in maintaining or promoting an issue or situation for reasons of private gain **3.** **INDIVIDUAL OR GROUP HAVING A VESTED INTEREST** an individual or group with a vested interest in maintaining or promoting sth (*often plural*)

vestiary /vésti əri/ *n.* (*plural* **-ies**) **DRESSING ROOM** a dressing room or storeroom for clothes ■ *adj.* **OF CLOTHES** relating to clothes (*formal*) [13thC. Via Old French *vestiarie* from Latin *vestiarium* 'clothes chest, wardrobe', later 'vestry', from, ultimately, *vestis* (see VEST).]

vestibular /ve stíbbyoōlər/ *adj.* relating to a vestibule

vestibular nerve *n.* a branch of the acoustic nerve that carries nerve impulses from the semicircular canals and other organs in the inner ear, conveying information about posture and balance

vestibule /vésti byool/ *n.* **1.** ARCHIT **ENTRANCE HALL** a small room or hall between an outer door and the main part of a building **2.** ANAT **BODY CAVITY** a cavity or space in the body that serves as the entrance to another cavity or canal, e.g. the part of the mouth between the teeth and lips **3.** ANAT **MIDDLE CAVITY OF THE INNER EAR** the middle cavity of the inner ear between the cochlea and the semicircular canals [Early 17thC. Directly or via French from Latin *vestibulum*.]

vestibulocochlear nerve /ve stíbbyoō lō kókli ər-/ *n.* either of the eighth pair of cranial nerves, critical to the sense of hearing [*Vestibulocochlear* formed from Latin *vestibulum* 'entrance' + *cochlear* (see COCHLEA)]

vestige /véstij/ *n.* **1.** **TRACE OF STH GONE** a trace or sign of sth that is no longer present **2.** **SLIGHTEST AMOUNT** the slightest amount ○ *There wasn't a vestige of truth in what she wrote.* **3.** BIOL **RUDIMENTARY BODY PART** an organ or part of the body that is now rudimentary and no longer functions, but that was fully developed and useful in the past [Early 17thC. Via French from Latin *vestigium* 'sole of the foot, footprint, trace'.]

vestigial /ve stíji əl/ *adj.* **1.** **BEING A TRACE** remaining after nearly all the rest has disappeared or dwindled ○ *a vestigial stirring of passion* **2.** BIOL **NO LONGER FUNCTIONAL** having become degenerate or functionless in the course of time ○ *the vestigial muscles of the ear* —**vestigially** *adv.*

vestment /véstmənt/ *n.* **1.** **ROBE** a garment, especially a robe worn to show rank or office **2.** **RELIGIOUS ROBE** a ceremonial robe worn by members of the clergy during a religious ceremony [13thC. Via Old French *vestiment* from Latin *vestimentum*, from *vestire* (see VEST).] —**vestmental** /vest mént'l/ *adj.* —**vestmented** /véstməntid/ *adj.*

vestry /véstri/ (*plural* **-tries**) *n.* **1.** **ROOM FOR VESTMENTS** a room attached to a church, where vestments or sacred objects are kept **2.** **MEETING ROOM** a room in a church where meetings or classes are held **3.** **MEETING OF CHURCH MEMBERS** in the Anglican church, a meeting of church members or their representatives [14thC. From an Anglo-Norman form of Old French *vestiarie* (see VESTIARY).] —**vestral** *adj.*

vestryman /véstrimən/ (*plural* **-men** /-mən/) *n.* a member of a church vestry [Early 17thC]

vesture /véschər/ *n.* **CLOTHING** clothing, or sth that covers like clothing (*archaic*) ■ *vt.* (**-tures, -turing, -tured**) **CLOTHE SB OR STH** to clothe or cover sb or sth (*archaic*) [14thC. From Old French, from, ultimately, Latin *vestire* (see VEST).] —**vestural** *adj.*

vesuvian /və soōvi ən/ *n.* = **vesuvianite** [Late 17thC. Named after Mount VESUVIUS in Sicily.]

vesuvianite /və soōvi ə nīt/ *n.* a green, brown, or yellow crystalline mineral that is a complex silicate of calcium and aluminium with magnesium and iron. It occurs in some marbles and is used as a gemstone. [Late 19thC. Named after Mount VESUVIUS in Sicily.]

Vesuvius, Mount /və soōvi əss/ active volcano overlooking the Bay of Naples, southern Italy. An eruption in AD 79 destroyed the Roman cities of Pompeii and Herculaneum. Height: 1,277 m/4,190 ft.

vet[1] /vet/ *n.* **VETERINARY SURGEON** a veterinary surgeon ■ *vt.* (**vets, vetting, vetted**) **1.** **CHECK UP ON SB OR STH** to subject sb or sth to a careful examination or scrutiny, especially when this involves determining suitability for sth **2.** VET **EXAMINE AN ANIMAL** to examine or treat an animal **3.** **STERILIZE ANIMAL** to sterilize an animal by castrating or spaying (*informal*) [Mid-19thC. Shortening of VETERINARY or VETERINARIAN.]

vet[2] /vet/ *n.* *US, Can* sb who has served in the armed forces, especially in a particular conflict (*informal*) ○ *Vietnam vets* [Mid-19thC]

vet. *abbr.* **1.** veteran **2.** veterinarian **3.** veterinary

vetch /vech/ *n.* **1.** **PLANT WITH SMALL FLOWERS** a leguminous plant with small flowers that is often used for silage or fodder. Genus: *Vicia.* **2.** **PLANT LIKE VETCH** a plant related to or similar to vetch, e.g. the kidney vetch [14thC. Via Old Northern French *veche* from Latin *vicia.*]

vetchling /véchling/ *n.* a plant with yellow flowers that is related to vetch. Latin name: *Lathyrus pratensis.* [Late 16thC. Formed from VETCH.]

veteran /véttərən/ *n.* **1.** **SB WITH EXPERIENCE** sb who has had considerable experience of a particular activity **2.** MIL **EXPERIENCED SOLDIER** sb who has been a member of one of the armed forces for many years and has seen a great deal of active service ○ *a veteran of three foreign wars* **3.** *US, Can* MIL **SB WHO HAS SERVED IN THE ARMED FORCES** sb who has served in the armed forces ■ *adj.* MIL **1.** **EXPERIENCED** having a great deal of experience in a particular endeavour or skill, often built up over the whole of the working life **2.** **OF VETERANS** relating to a veteran or veterans [Early 16thC. Directly or via French *vétéran* from Latin *veteranus*, from *vetus* 'old' (source of English *inveterate*).]

veteran car *n.* a car made before 1919 or, strictly, one made before 1905. ◊ **vintage car**

Veterans Day *n.* a United States legal holiday celebrated on 11 November to honour former members of the armed forces

veterinarian /vèttəri náiri ən/ *n.* *US, Can* = **veterinary surgeon** [Mid-17thC. From Latin *veterinarius* (see VETERINARY).]

veterinary /véttərinəri/ *adj.* relating to diseases of animals and their treatment [Late 18thC. From Latin *veterinarius*, from *veterinus*, 'concerning cattle (literally at least one year old)', from *veter-*, stem of *vetus* 'old'.]

veterinary medicine, **veterinary science** *n.* the branch of medicine dealing with the health of animals and the diagnosis and treatment of their diseases and injuries

veterinary surgeon *n.* *UK, Aus* sb who is trained and qualified in the medical treatment of animals. US term **veterinarian**

vetiver /véttivər/ *n.* **1.** **TALL INDIAN GRASS** a tall grass that grows in India, the leaves of which are used to make screens and fans. Latin name: *Vetiveria zizanioides.* **2.** **ROOTS OF VETIVER** the roots of the vetiver, which produce an oil that is used to make perfume [Mid-19thC. Via French *vétiver* from Tamil *veṭṭivēr*, from *vēr* 'root'.]

veto /véetō/ *n.* (*plural* **-toes**) **1.** **RIGHT TO REJECT** the power to reject sth, e.g. a piece of legislation proposed by sb else **2.** **EXERCISE OF THE RIGHT TO REJECT MEASURES** the exercise of the power or right to reject sth, especially a political measure **3.** **PROHIBITION** an order prohibiting sth ○ *put her veto on it* ■ *vt.* (**-toes, -toing, -toed**) **1.** **REJECT A MEASURE** to reject sth such as a measure or government bill by veto **2.** **PROHIBIT STH** to refuse to consent to or approve sth ○ *My teacher vetoed the idea.* [Early 17thC. From Latin, 'I forbid', a formula used in ancient Rome by the Tribunes of the People when they opposed measures taken by either the Senate or the magistrates.] —**vetoer** *n.*

vex /veks/ (**vexes, vexing, vexed**) *vt.* **1.** **ANNOY SB** to make sb annoyed or upset **2.** **AGITATE** to cause sb anxiety or distress **3.** **CONFOUND** to confuse or puzzle sb [15thC. Via French *vexer* from Latin *vexare* 'to shake, disturb'.] —**vexingly** *adv.*

── **WORD KEY: SYNONYMS** ──
See Synonyms at *annoy*.

vexation /vek sáysh'n/ *n.* **1.** STATE OF BEING VEXED the state of being provoked to irritability or anxiety **2.** ACT OF VEXING the act of provoking sb to irritability or anxiety **3.** STH THAT VEXES sth that provokes irritability or anxiety

vexatious /vek sáyshəss/ *adj.* **1.** CAUSING TROUBLE provoking irritation or anxiety by causing trouble **2.** LAW BROUGHT WITH THE INTENTION OF ANNOYING put forward on insufficient grounds and with the intention of causing annoyance to the defendant —**vexatiously** *adv.* —**vexatiousness** *n.*

vexed /vekst/ *adj.* **1.** IRRITATED provoked to irritability or anxiety **2.** DEBATED being the subject of much debate —**vexedly** /véksidli/ *adv.* —**vexedness** /véksidnəss/ *n.*

vexillology /véksi lólləji/ *n.* the study of flags —**vexillologic** /véksíllə lójjik/ *adj.* —**vexillological** /-lójjik'l/ *adj.* —**vexillologist** /véksi lólləjist/ *n.*

VF *abbr.* **1.** TELECOM voice frequency **2.** RELIG Vicar Forane **3.** TV video frequency

VFR *abbr.* AEROSPACE visual flight rules

VFT *abbr.* very fast train

vg *abbr.* very good

VG *abbr.* Vicar General

VGA *n.* a widely used specification for video display controllers used in personal computers. Abbr of **video graphics array**

VHF, **vhf** *abbr.* TV very high frequency

VHS *n.* a system for recording television programmes in the home

vi *abbr.* vide infra

VI, **V.I.** *abbr.* **1.** Vancouver Island **2.** Virgin Islands

via /ví ə, vée ə/ *prep.* **1.** THROUGH by way of or through ○ *Can you come home via the post office?* **2.** BY MEANS OF using the means or agency of ○ *removed the obstruction via surgery* [Early 17thC. From Latin, literally 'by way of', a form of *via* 'way, road'.]

viable /ví əb'l/ *adj.* **1.** PRACTICABLE OR WORTHWHILE able to be done or worth doing ○ *a viable proposition* **2.** BIOL ABLE TO GROW able to germinate or develop normally **3.** MED ABLE TO SURVIVE OUTSIDE THE WOMB used to describe a foetus that can survive outside the womb. This now generally applies to a foetus after about 24 weeks of gestation. [Early 19thC. Via French *vie* from Latin *vita* 'life' (source of English *vitamin, vivid,* and *vital*).] —**viability** /ví ə bílləti/ *n.* —**viably** /ví əbli/ *adv.*

Via Dolorosa /vée ə dóllə róssə/ *n.* **1.** CHR JESUS CHRIST'S ROUTE TO CALVARY the route taken by Jesus Christ to Calvary to be crucified **2.** Via Dolorosa, via dolorosa DIFFICULT EXPERIENCE a difficult or distressing course or experience [From Latin, literally 'sorrowful way']

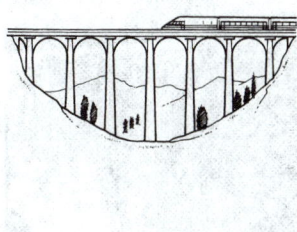

Viaduct

viaduct /ví ə dukt/ *n.* a bridge that consists of a series of short masonry or concrete arched spans supported on towers. Viaducts usually take a road or railway over a wide valley. [Early 19thC. Formed from Latin *via* 'way, road' on the model of AQUEDUCT.]

Viagra /ví ággrə/ *tdmk.* a trademark for an enzyme-inhibiting drug, sildenafil citrate, that is used to treat impotence in men

vial /ví əl/ *n.* a small glass bottle, especially one for medicines [14thC. Alteration of PHIAL.]

via media /ví ə meédi ə/ *n.* a middle course or choice between extreme possibilities (*literary*) [From Latin]

viand /ví ənd, vee-/ *n.* (*formal*) **1.** ARTICLE OF FOOD an article of food **2.** PROVISIONS a store or collection of food, especially the food that makes up a meal or a feast (*often used in the plural*) [14thC. Via French *viande* 'food' (now 'meat') from, ultimately, Latin *vivenda* 'things for living', from *vivere* 'to live'.]

viaticum /ví áttikəm, vi-/ (*plural* -**ca** /-kə, -*/ or* -**cums**) *n.* **1.** CHR HOLY COMMUNION GIVEN TO SB DYING Holy Communion given to sb who is dying or in danger of dying **2.** PROVISIONS FOR A JOURNEY provisions or money for a journey (*literary*) [Mid-16thC. From Latin 'provision for a journey', from *via* 'way, road'.]

vibe /víb/ *n.* a particular kind of atmosphere, feeling, or ambience (*slang*) ○ *The new decor has a kind of 50s vibe to it.* [Mid-20thC. Shortening.]

vibes /víbz/ *npl.* (*slang*) **1.** STH SENSED the atmosphere, feeling, or ambience that sb senses from a person or thing ○ *I'm picking up really negative vibes from this idea.* **2.** MUSIC VIBRAPHONE a vibraphone [Mid-20thC. Shortening.]

vibist /víbist/ *n.* sb who plays the vibraphone (*slang*)

Viborg /vée bawrg/ capital city of Viborg County, north-central Jutland, Denmark. Population: 39,395 (1990).

Vibram /víbrəm/ *tdmk.* a trademark for a brand of hard-wearing moulded rubber sole with a deep tread, used in footwear such as walking boots

vibrant /víbrənt/ *adj.* **1.** PULSATING WITH ENERGY seeming to quiver or pulsate with energy or activity **2.** RESONANT having a full rich sound that tends to continue for some time **3.** BRIGHT dazzling or radiantly bright **4.** VIBRATING vibrating very rapidly [Mid-16thC. From Latin *vibrant-*, past participle stem of *vibrare* (see VIBRATE).] —**vibrancy** *n.* —**vibrantly** *adv.*

vibraphone /víbrə fōn/ *n.* a percussion instrument with electrically driven resonators beneath a set of metal bars that are struck with small mallets or sometimes played with a bow, causing vibration [Early 20thC. Formed from the stem of VIBRATE + PHONE.] —**vibraphonist** *n.*

vibrate /ví bráyt/ (-**brates**, -**brating**, -**brated**) *v.* **1.** *vti.* MAKE SMALL MOVEMENTS RAPIDLY to shake or move to and fro rapidly, or make sth move in this way ○ *The traffic made the whole room vibrate.* **2.** *vti.* PHYS OSCILLATE to oscillate or to make sth oscillate with a continuing periodic change relative to a fixed reference point **3.** *vi.* RESONATE to make a full rich tone that tends to continue for some time **4.** *vi.* THRILL to experience a rush of emotion in response to sth [Early 17thC. From Latin *vibrat-*, past participle stem of *vibrare* 'to shake'. Ultimately from an Indo-European word that is also the ancestor of English *whip* and *weave*.]

vibratile /víbrə tíl/ *adj.* **1.** VIBRATING showing rapid shaking back and forth movements **2.** CAPABLE OF VIBRATING capable of vibrating, or operating by means of vibration [Early 19thC. Alteration of VIBRATORY on the model of PULSATILE.] —**vibratility** /víbrə tílləti/ *n.*

vibration /ví bráysh'n/ *n.* **1.** INSTANCE OF VIBRATING an instance of shaking or moving to and fro very rapidly **2.** PROCESS OF VIBRATING the process of moving or being moved to and fro very rapidly **3.** PHYS REPETITIVE PERIODIC OSCILLATION a continuing periodic oscillation relative to a fixed reference point, or a single complete oscillation **4.** ATMOSPHERE OF A PLACE the atmosphere or aura given off by a place or situation (*informal; often used in the plural*) **5.** FEELINGS COMMUNICATED SUBCONSCIOUSLY feelings communicated from one person to another (*informal; often used in the plural*) —**vibrational** *adj.*

vibrato /vi braátō/ (*plural* -**tos**) *n.* **1.** THROBBING EFFECT IN A MUSICAL INSTRUMENT a throbbing effect in the playing of a stringed or wind instrument made by rapidly varying the pitch **2.** THROBBING EFFECT IN SINGING a throbbing effect in singing produced by rapidly varying the breath pressure or the pitch [Mid-19thC. From Italian, literally 'vibrated'.]

vibrator /ví bráytər/ *n.* **1.** STH THAT VIBRATES sth that vibrates or makes sth vibrate **2.** VIBRATING DEVICE an electric device that vibrates, e.g. one used to give a massage or as a sexual aid **3.** ELEC ENG DEVICE CONVERTING DIRECT TO ALTERNATING CURRENT an electromechanical device, often used in bells and buzzers, that interrupts a direct current to convert it into an alternating current

vibratory /ví bráytəri, víbrətəri/ *adj.* **1.** VIBRATING shaking or moving to and fro very rapidly **2.** CAUSING VIBRATION making sth shake or move to and fro rapidly

vibrio /víbbri ō/ (*plural* -**os** *or* -**ones**) *n.* a bacterium shaped like a comma or like the letter S. Genus: *Vibrio.* [Mid-19thC. Via modern Latin from Latin *vibrare* (see VIBRATE).] —**vibrioid** /víbbri oyd/ *adj.*

vibrissa /ví bríssə/ (*plural* -**sae** /-see/) *n.* **1.** SENSITIVE HAIR ON A MAMMAL a mammal's hair or whisker, usually on the face or limbs, that vibrates when touched, stimulating nervous tissue in the animal's skin **2.** BIRDS FEATHER NEAR THE BEAK a feather that is like a bristle, near the beak of an insect-eating bird [Late 17thC. From Latin, formed from *vibrare* (see VIBRATE).] —**vibrissal** *adj.*

vibronic /ví brónnik/ *adj.* relating to the electronic and vibrational energy states of elementary particles and atoms [Mid-20thC. Coined from VIBRATIONAL + ELECTRONIC.]

vibrotron /víbrə tron/ *n.* a triode valve in which the anode can be vibrated by an external force

viburnum /ví búrnəm/ *n.* a shrub or small tree with flat or rounded clusters of white flowers sometimes tinged with pink. The guelder rose, blackhaw, and nannyberry are all types of viburnum. Genus: *Viburnum.* [Mid-18thC. From modern Latin, from Latin, 'wayfaring tree'.]

vic. *abbr.* RELIG vicar

Vic. *abbr.* Victoria

vicar /víkər/ *n.* **1.** ANGLICAN PRIEST a priest in the Anglican Church who is in charge of a parish and receives a salary but not the tithes **2.** MEMBER OF THE ANGLICAN CLERGY a member of the Anglican clergy who acts in place of a rector or bishop at Communion **3.** ROMAN CATHOLIC PRIEST a Roman Catholic priest who represents or deputizes for a bishop **4.** US EPISCOPAL CHURCH CLERIC a cleric in the Episcopal Church who is in charge of a chapel **5.** CHOIR MEMBER a cleric or member of a choir who sings certain parts of a cathedral service in the Church of England **6.** SUBSTITUTE sb who acts as a substitute for sb else (*archaic*) [14thC. Via Anglo-Norman *vicare* from, ultimately, Latin *vicarius* 'substitute', from the stem *vic-* 'change, place' (source of English *vicissitude*); because the vicar acted as a substitute for the rector.] —**vicarly** *adj.* —**vicarship** *n.*

vicarage /víkərij/ *n.* **1.** VICAR'S RESIDENCE the residence of a vicar **2.** VICAR'S POSITION the office or duties of a vicar

vicar apostolic (*plural* **vicars apostolic**) *n.* a titular bishop or missionary in the Roman Catholic Church

vicarate *n.* = vicariate

vicar general (*plural* **vicars general**) *n.* **1.** ROMAN CATHOLIC BISHOP'S ASSISTANT a priest acting as an assistant to a Roman Catholic bishop **2.** ANGLICAN CHURCH BISHOP'S ASSISTANT a lay official assisting an Anglican bishop with administrative or judicial duties

vicarial /vi káiri əl, ví-/ *adj.* **1.** BEING VICAR being or acting as a vicar **2.** OF VICAR relating to a vicar **3.** = vicarious *adj.* 3

vicariate /vi káiri ət, ví-/, **vicarate** /víkərət/ *n.* **1.** OFFICE OF VICAR the office or authority of a vicar **2.** DISTRICT OF A VICAR the district that falls under the care of a vicar

vicarious /vi káiri əss, ví-/ *adj.* **1.** EXPERIENCED THROUGH ANOTHER BY IMAGINING experienced through another person rather than at first hand, by using sympathy or the power of the imagination **2.** ENDURED FOR SB ELSE done or endured by sb as a substitute for sb else **3.** DELEGATED delegated to sb else or performing a function that has been delegated **4.** MED OCCURRING IN AN UNEXPECTED PART OF BODY occurring in or performed by an unexpected part of the body, e.g. menstrual bleeding in the breasts, nose, or sweat glands [Mid-17thC. Formed from Latin *vicarius* (see VICAR).] —**vicariously** *adv.* —**vicariousness** *n.*

Vicar of Christ *n.* the Roman Catholic pope

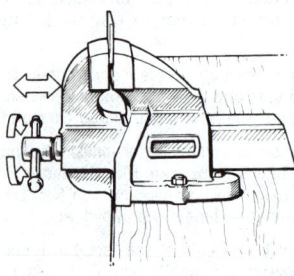

Vice

vice¹ /vīss/ *n.* **TOOL FOR KEEPING THINGS IMMOBILE** a tool with two jaws that close by a lever or screw that is used to hold an object immobile so that it can be worked on ◾ *vt.* (**vices, vicing, viced**) **HOLD IN VICE** to hold sth tightly in a vice [13thC. Via Old French *vis* 'screw' from Latin *vitis* 'vine'. Ultimately from an Indo-European word meaning 'wind' that is also the ancestor of English *wire*.] — **vice-like** *adj.*

vice¹ /vīss/ *n.* **1. IMMORAL HABIT** an immoral or wicked habit or characteristic **2. DEPRAVITY** immoral conduct **3. PROSTITUTION** a form of immoral conduct, especially prostitution **4. MILD DEFECT IN CHARACTER** a mild failing or defect in sb's behaviour or character **5. FAULT IN AN ANIMAL** a fault or undesirable habit in a horse or other domestic animal [13thC. Via French from Latin *vitium* (source of English *vitiate* and *vituperate*).]

vice² /vīssi/ *prep.* in place of or instead of sb or sth [Late 18thC. From Latin *vice* 'in place of', from the stem *vic-* (see VICAR).]

vice admiral *n.* a naval officer ranking below admiral and above rear admiral —**vice-admiralty** *n.*

vice chairperson *n.* sb who takes the place of a chairperson in his or her absence

vice chancellor *n.* **1. UNIV ASSISTANT CHANCELLOR OF A UNIVERSITY** a deputy or assistant chancellor in a university, often the person in charge of administration **2. POL DEPUTY CHANCELLOR** a deputy for the chancellor of a state **3. LAW JUDGE** a US judge ranking below a chancellor, or an English judge who runs the Chancery Division of the High Court —**vice-chancellorship** *n.*

vicegerent /vīss jérrənt, -jeér-/ *n.* a deputy appointed to act on the authority of a ruler or magistrate, especially in administrative duties [Mid-16thC. From medieval Latin, 'deputy', literally 'one carrying on in place of', from *gerent-*, present participle stem of *gerere* 'to carry on'.] —**vicegeral** *adj.* —**vicegerency** *n.*

vicenary /vīssinəri/ *adj.* **1. RELATING TO 20** being based on, or relating to the number 20 **2. NUMBER SYSTEM BASED ON 20** relating or belonging to a number system that has 20 as its base [Early 17thC. From Latin *vicenarius*, from, ultimately, *viginti* 'twenty'.]

vicennial /vi sénni əl/ *adj.* lasting for or occurring every 20 years [Mid-18thC. From Latin *vicennium* 'period of twenty years', from *vic-*, stem of *vicies* 'twenty times'.]

Vicenza /vi chéntsə/ capital of Vicenza Province, Veneto Region, northern Italy. Population: 107,786 (1995).

vice president *n.* an official who ranks immediately below a president and who can take the president's place if necessary —**vice-presidency** *n.* —**vice-presidential** *adj.*

viceregal /vīss reég'l/ *adj.* **1. OF VICEROYS** relating to viceroy **2.** *Aus, NZ* **RELATING TO GOVERNOR** relating to a governor or a governor general —**viceregally** *adv.*

viceregent /vīss reéjənt/ *n.* a deputy for the regent of a country —**viceregency** *n.*

vicereine /vīss ráyn/ *n.* a viceroy who is a woman, or the wife of a viceroy [Early 19thC. From French, literally 'vice-queen']

viceroy /vīss roy/ *n.* **1. POL GOVERNOR REPRESENTING A SOVEREIGN IN A COLONY** a governor who represents a sovereign in a province, colony, or country **2.** *US* **ZOOL ORANGE-AND-BLACK BUTTERFLY** a brightly coloured orange-and-black butterfly of North America that re-

sembles the monarch butterfly. Latin name: *Limenitis archippus*. [Early 16thC. From French, literally 'vice-king'.] —**viceroyship** *n.*

viceroyalty /vīss róy əlti/ (*plural* **-ties**) *n.* **1. OFFICE OF VICEROY** the office, term of office, or authority of a viceroy **2. DISTRICT GOVERNED BY A VICEROY** a district that is governed by a viceroy

vice squad *n.* a police division in charge of enforcing laws relating to prostitution, gambling, and drug abuse

vice versa /vīss vúrssə, víssi-/ *adv.* the other way round [From Latin, literally 'the position being reversed']

Vichy /veéshi/ city in central France, the site of important mineral springs. It was the seat of a French government that collaborated with the Germans during World War II. Population: 28,048 (1990).

vichyssoise /veéshi swaáz, víshi-/ *n.* a creamy soup made from leeks, potatoes, and onions, often served chilled [Mid-20thC. Shortening of French *crème vichyssoise glacée*, literally 'iced cream soup from Vichy'.]

Vichy water, Vichy *n.* a natural sparkling mineral water from Vichy, France, or a similar sparkling water

vicinage /víssinij/ *n.* **1. NEIGHBOURHOOD** a neighbourhood, or the people living in it (*archaic*) **2.** *US* **VICINITY** the area immediately surrounding a place [14thC. Via Old French *vis(e)nage* from, ultimately, Latin *vicinus* (see VICINITY).]

vicinal /víssin'l/ *adj.* **1. NEIGHBOURING** adjacent or neighbouring **2. LOCAL** relating to or restricted to a local area **3. CHEM BEING CONSECUTIVE POSITIONS ON A CARBON CHAIN** relating to two or more adjacent positions on a carbon ring or chain [Early 17thC. Directly or via French from Latin *vicinalis*, from *vicinus* (see VICINITY).]

vicinity /vi sínnəti/ (*plural* **-ties**) *n.* **1. SURROUNDING REGION** a neighbourhood, or the surrounding region of a place ○ *Homes in the vicinity of the fire were evacuated.* **2. PROXIMITY** an area near sth else **3. APPROXIMATION** an approximate amount ○ *something in the vicinity of 1,000 jobs* [Mid-16thC. From Latin *vicinitas*, from *vicinus* 'neighbour', from *vicus* 'village, homestead'.]

vicious /víshəss/ *adj.* **1. FEROCIOUS** showing fierce violence **2. DANGEROUS AND AGGRESSIVE** dangerous because of being aggressive ○ *a vicious dog* **3. MALICIOUS** intended to do harm **4. WICKED AND IMMORAL** displaying or tending to immoral behaviour **5. UNSOUND** incorrect or showing faulty logic [14thC. Formed from VICE¹.] —**viciously** *adv.* —**viciousness** *n.*

——— **WORD KEY: USAGE** ———
vicious circle or **vicious cycle**? Until quite recently the invariable choice was **vicious circle**. Perhaps influenced by such phrases as *the cycle of welfare dependency*, however, the variant **vicious cycle** has been gaining ground, and it is now quite often seen as an alternative to **vicious circle**, in virtually indistinguishable contexts.

vicious circle *n.* **1. SITUATION WORSENED BY ATTEMPTS TO SOLVE IT** a situation in which attempts to solve one problem lead to further problems that only make the original position worse **2. LOGIC REASONING BASED ON AN UNPROVEN ASSUMPTION** a form of reasoning that bases a conclusion on a statement assumed to be true but not proven independently **3. MED LINKING OF TWO DISEASES** a situation in which two diseases or conditions are linked so that each leads to or aggravates the other

vicissitude /vī síssə tyood, vi-/ *n.* **VARIABILITY** the fact of being variable (*literary*) ■ **vicissitudes** *npl.* **UNEXPECTED CHANGES** unexpected changes, especially in a person's fortunes [Mid-16thC. Directly or via French from Latin *vicissitudo*, from *vicissim* 'by turns', from the stem *vic-* (see VICAR).] —**vicissitudinary** /vī síssə tyoódinəri, vi-/ *adj.* —**vicissitudinous** /-tyoódinəss, -/ *adj.*

vicomte /vee koNt/ *n.* a French nobleman who is equal in rank to a British viscount [Mid-19thC. From French, from Old French *vi(s)conte* (see VISCOUNT).]

vicomtesse /vee koN téss/ *n.* a French noblewoman who is equal in rank to a British viscountess [Late 18thC. From French, from *vicomte*.]

victim /víktim/ *n.* **1. SB HURT OR KILLED** sb who is hurt or killed by sb or sth **2. SB OR STH HARMED** sb or sth harmed by an act or circumstance ○ *a victim of her own success* **3. SB DUPED** sb who is tricked or taken advantage of **4. CREATURE USED FOR SACRIFICE** a living crea-

ture used as a sacrifice or in a religious rite **5. HELPLESS PERSON** sb who experiences misfortune and feels helpless to do anything about it [15thC. From Latin *victima* 'animal offered as a sacrifice'. Later meanings did not develop until the 17thC and 18thC.] ◇ **fall victim to** to be affected, harmed, or deceived by sb or sth

victimize /víkti mīz/ (**-izes, -izing, -ized**), **victimise** (**-timises, -timising, -timised, -timised**) *vt.* **1. TREAT UNFAIRLY** to single sb out unfairly for punishment or ill treatment **2. MAKE INTO A VICTIM** to cause sb to become a victim —**victimization** /víkti mī záysh'n/ *n.* —**victimizer** /víkti mīzər/ *n.*

victimless crime *n.* an illegal act such as loitering in which there is no obvious injured party

victor /víktər/ *n.* **1. WINNER** a winner in a contest or battle **2. COMMUNICATION CODE WORD FOR V** the NATO phonetic alphabet code word for the letter 'V', used in international radio communications [14thC. Directly, or via Anglo-Norman, from Latin, from *vic-*, past participle stem of *vincere* 'to conquer'.]

Victor Emmanuel III /víktər i mánnyoo əl/, **King of Italy** (1869–1947). Reigning from 1900, he accepted fascist rule in Italy from 1922. After defeat in World War II he abdicated (1946).

victoria /vik táwri ə/ *n.* **1. PLANTS RED-AND-YELLOW PLUM** a large red-and-yellow variety of plum **2. HORSE-DRAWN CARRIAGE WITH A FOLDING HOOD** a horse-drawn carriage with four wheels and a folding hood, accommodating two passengers **3. PLANTS GIANT WATER LILY** a giant South American water lily with fragrant red or white flowers. Genus: *Victoria*. [Mid-19thC. Named after Queen VICTORIA.]

Victoria /vik táwri ə/ **1.** river in the northwestern part of the Northern Territory, Australia. Length: 640 km/398 mi. **2.** state in southeastern Australia. Capital: Melbourne. Population: 4,561,000 (1996). Area: 227,620 sq. km/87,884 sq. mi. **3.** capital city of British Columbia, Canada, on the southern tip of Vancouver Island. Population: 71,228 (1991). **4.** capital city of the Republic of Seychelles, situated on the northeastern coast of Mahé island. Population: 25,000 (1993).

Victoria, Queen of the United Kingdom (1819–1901). She reigned longer than any other British monarch (1837–1901), and was empress of India (1876–1901). As queen she exhibited an alert and informed understanding of government affairs, and set a national example of domestic harmony and morality in her marriage to Prince Albert (1840–61).

Victoria, Lake the largest lake in Africa, shared between Tanzania, Uganda, and Kenya. Area: 69,482 sq. km/26,828 sq. mi.

Victoria Cross *n.* a decoration in the form of a bronze cross, given to members of British and Commonwealth armed forces for conspicuous bravery. It was instituted by Queen Victoria in 1856.

Victoria Day *n.* a Canadian statutory holiday held on the Monday of or preceding 24 May to commemorate the birthday of Queen Victoria

Victoria Falls

Victoria Falls waterfall on the River Zambezi in south-central Africa, on the border between Zambia and Zimbabwe. Height: 108 m/355 ft.

Victoria Land region of Antarctica, west of Ross Sea and east of Wilkes Land

Victorian /vik táwri ən/ *adj.* **1. CHARACTERISTIC OF THE TIME OF QUEEN VICTORIA** relating to, belonging to, or typical of the reign of Queen Victoria **2. CONVENTIONAL, HYPO-CRITICAL, OR PRUDISH** showing or typical of attitudes commonly associated with the Victorian era, especially prudery or conventionalism **3. ARCHIT ARCHITECTURALLY ELABORATE** in or typical of the elaborate style of architecture popular in Victorian Britain **4. FROM VICTORIA** relating to or from the state of Victoria in Australia, or the cities of Victoria in Canada or the Seychelles ■ *n.* **1. HIST SB LIVING IN VICTORIA'S REIGN** sb who lived in the reign of Queen Victoria **2. SB FROM VICTORIA** sb who lives in or comes from the state of Victoria in Australia, or the cities of Victoria in Canada or the Seychelles —**Victorianism** *n.*

Victoriana /vik táwri aánə/ *npl.* collectible objects dating from the time of Queen Victoria

Victoria Nile section of the upper River Nile in Uganda, between lakes Victoria and Albert

Victoria Peak mountain on Hong Kong Island, overlooking Hong Kong Harbour. Height: 554 m/1,818 ft.

victoria plum *n.* = victoria

victorious /vik táwri əss/ *adj.* **1. HAVING WON** having won sth such as a contest or a battle **2. CHARACTERIZED BY VICTORY** typical of or showing a sense of victory —**victoriously** *adv.* —**victoriousness** *n.*

victory /víktəri/ (*plural* **-ries**) *n.* **1. DEFEAT OF OPPONENT** defeat of an enemy or opponent **2. SUCCESS** success attained over a difficult situation or opponent [14thC. Via Anglo-Norman *victorie* from Latin *victoria*, from *victor* (see VICTOR).]

victory roll *n.* an airborne rolling manoeuvre of an aircraft carried out by a pilot as a sign of victory or celebration

victual /vítt'l/ *n.* **PROVISIONS** provisions of food (*archaic or formal*) ■ ■ **victuals** *npl.* **FOOD** food or other provisions (*often used humorously*) ■ *v.* (**-uals, -ualling, -ualled**) (*archaic or formal*) **1. vt. FEED SB OR STH** to give food to people or animals **2. vi. ASSEMBLE PROVISIONS** to collect a store of food [14thC. Via Old French *vitaille* from Latin *victualia* (which later influenced the spelling of the English word), from *victus* 'livelihood, food' from *vivere* 'to live'.]

victualler *n.* **1. SUPPLIER OF PROVISIONS** sb who supplies food or other provisions (*archaic or formal*) **2. INNKEEPER** an innkeeper, especially one licensed to sell spirits (*archaic or formal*) **3. SHIP CARRYING STORES** a ship carrying food or other provisions

Vicuña

vicuña /vi kyóonə, -kóonyə/, **vicuna** *n.* **1. ZOOL S AMERICAN MAMMAL** a tawny-coloured South American mammal with a silky fleece. It is related to the llama and lives high in the Andes mountains. Latin name: *Vicugna vicugna*. **2. CLOTHES CLOTH MADE FROM VICUÑA WOOL** cloth made from the wool of the vicuña, or an imitation of it [Early 17thC. Via Spanish from Quechua *wikúña*.]

vid *n.* a video cassette (*informal*)

vide /víːdi, véé day/ *vt.* a word used to refer a reader to another place in a text, or tell a musician to skip to a place further ahead in the score (*formal*) [Mid-16thC. From Latin, literally 'see!', a form of *videre* 'to see'.]

vide infra *vt.* a term used to refer a reader to a place further on in a text [From Latin, 'see below']

videlicet /vi deéli set/ *adv.* full form of **viz** (*formal*) [15thC. From Latin, from *vide*, stem of *videre* 'to see' + *licet* 'it is permissible'.]

video /víddi ō/ *n.* (*plural* **-os**) **1. VISUAL PART OF TELEVISION** the visual part of a television broadcast **2. VIDEO RECORDER** a video recorder (*informal*) **3. VIDEO CASSETTE**

video tape, or a video cassette (*informal*) ○ *now available to rent or buy on video* **4. STH RECORDED ONTO VIDEOTAPE** sth, especially a film, that has been recorded onto video tape ■ *adj.* **1. RELATING TO TELEVISION** relating to television, especially the reproduction or broadcasting of televised images **2. RELATING TO VIDEO FREQUENCIES** relating to or using video frequencies ■ *vt.* (**-os, -oing, -oed**) **RECORD STH ON VIDEO** to record sth on video tape [Mid-20thC. Formed from Latin *videre* 'to see' on the model of AUDIO.]

video arcade *n.* a place where people pay to play video games

video camera *n.* a camera that records onto video tape

video cassette *n.* a flat rectangular plastic cassette containing two tape reels and a magnetic video tape

video cassette recorder *n.* = video recorder

video conferencing *n.* the holding of a meeting in which participants are in different places, connected by audio and video links —**video conference** *n.*

videodisk /víddi ō disk/, **videodisc** *n.* = optical disk

video display terminal *n. US, ANZ* a device used to display data from and enter data into a computer, consisting of a visual display such as a cathode-ray tube and a keyboard, mouse, or touch-screen

video frequency *n.* a frequency in the range of signals used to carry the image and synchronizing pulses in a television broadcasting system. Frequencies range from the very high to the ultra high in the United States and are found in two ultra high bands in Europe.

video game *n.* an electronic or computerized game, usually controlled by a microprocessor, played by making images move on a computer or television screen or, for hand-held games, on a liquid-crystal display

video jockey *n.* sb who plays videos, especially music videos, especially on television

video nasty *n.* a film on video tape that contains explicitly violent or pornographic scenes (*informal*)

videophone /víddi ō fōn/ *n.* a communications device that can transmit and receive both video and audio signals, allowing people having a telephone conversation to see as well as hear each other [Mid-20thC]

video recorder *n.* a tape recorder that can record and play video cassettes through a standard television receiver. It can capture live television programmes for later replay and also play back prerecorded cassettes.

video tape *n.* = video cassette

video-tape (**video-tapes, video-taping, video-taped**) *vt.* to make a recording of sth on video tape

video tape recorder *n.* a tape recorder that can record and play back visual images and sound using magnetic tape

videotext /víddi ō tekst/ *n.* a communications service linked to an adapted television receiver or video display terminal by telephone or cable television lines to allow access to pages of information. Systems can be one-way, allowing only for the display of selected information, or on-line or interactive, allowing for two-way communication. [Late 20thC]

vide supra *vt.* a term used to refer a reader to an earlier place in a text [From Latin, 'see above']

vidette *n.* = vedette *n.* 1

vie /vī/ (**vies, vying, vied**) *vi.* to strive for superiority or compete with sb or sth for sth [Mid-16thC. Shortening of Middle English *envien*, from Old French *envier* 'to raise the bid (at cards), challenge', from Latin *invitare* 'to entertain, feast' (source of English *invite*).] —**vier** *n.*

Vienna /vi énnə/ capital city of Austria, located in the east of the country, on the River Danube. Population: 1,539,848 (1991). —**Viennese** /veé ə neéz/ *n., adj.*

Vienna circle *n.* the leading school of logical positivists of the 1920s and 1930s [Because the group was based at Vienna University]

Vientiane /vyén tyaán/ capital city of Laos, in the central part of the country, on the Mekong River. Population: 178,203 (1985).

Viet. *abbr.* **1.** Vietnam **2.** Vietnamese

Vietcong /vyét kóng/ (*plural* **-cong**), **Viet Cong** (*plural* **Viet Cong**) *n.* a member or supporter of the Communist-led armed forces of the National Liberation Front of South Vietnam that fought to unite the country with North Vietnam between 1954 and 1976 [Mid-20thC. From Vietnamese *Việt-công*, a shortening of *Việt-Nam Công Sam* 'Vietnamese Communist'.]

Vietminh /vyét mín/ (*plural* **-minh**), **Viet Minh** (*plural* **Viet Minh**) *n.* **1. COMMUNIST-DOMINATED VIETNAMESE NATIONALIST MOVEMENT** the Vietnamese armed forces led by Ho Chi Minh that resisted and defeated first the Japanese and then the French between 1941 and 1954. The Vietminh operated from a base in southern China during World War II and employed guerrilla tactics similar to the Maoists in China. **2. VIETNAMESE SOLDIER FIGHTING FOR INDEPENDENCE** a member or supporter of the Vietnamese armed forces led by Ho Chi Minh that resisted and defeated first the Japanese and then the French between 1941 and 1954 [Mid-20thC. From Vietnamese *Việt Minh*, a shortening of *Việt-Nam Độc-Lập Dông-Minh* 'Vietnam Independence Federation'.]

Vietnam

Vietnam /vyet nám/ country in Southeast Asia, on the South China Sea, south of China and east of Cambodia and Laos. Language: Vietnamese. Currency: new dồng. Capital: Hanoi. Population: 75,123,880 (1997). Area: 331,690 sq. km/128,066 sq. mi. Official name **Socialist Republic of Vietnam**

Vietnamese /vyétnə meéz/ *adj.* **PEOPLES OF VIETNAM** relating to or typical of Vietnam, or its people or culture ■ *n.* (*plural* **-ese**) **1. PEOPLES SB FROM VIETNAM** sb who was born or brought up in Vietnam, or who has Vietnamese citizenship **2. LANG OFFICIAL LANGUAGE OF VIETNAM** the official language of Vietnam, belonging to the Austro-Asiatic language family. Vietnamese is spoken by the majority of people living in Vietnam.

Vietnamese potbellied pig *n.* a small domesticated pig with a rounded shape and a dark skin with a lighter band running around its middle. It is sometimes kept as a pet.

Vietnam War *n.* a conflict in which the Communist forces of North Vietnam and guerrillas in South Vietnam fought against the non-Communist forces of South Vietnam and the United States. It began in 1954 and ended in 1975 in a Communist victory.

vieux jeu /vyúr zhúr, vyö zhö/ *adj.* no longer fashionable [From French, literally 'old game']

view /vyoo/ *n.* **1. ACT OF LOOKING AT STH** an act of looking at or inspecting sth **2. RANGE OF VISION** the range or extent of sb's ability to see sth **3. SCENE** a scene or an area that can be seen from a particular place, especially one that is pleasing or impressive **4. PICTORIAL REPRESENTATION** a painting, drawing, or photograph of a particular scene or building **5. PERSPECTIVE** a particular position or angle from which sb can look at sth **6. OPINION** sb's opinion on or interpretation of sth such as politics or religion **7. SURVEY** a general survey of a particular subject ■ *v.* (**views, viewing, viewed**) **1. vt. OBSERVE STH** to see or look at sth, especially with interest **2. vt. INSPECT STH** to make an inspection or examination of sth **3. vt. CONSIDER STH** to think over or consider sth, especially a range of things **4. vt. THINK OF SB OR STH** to regard or assess sb or sth, especially in a particular way **5.** *vti.* **WATCH TELEVISION** to watch television, or watch sth on television [15thC. From Old French *vëue*, past participle of *vëoir* 'to see', from Latin *videre* 'to see' (source of English *vision* and *voyeur*).] —**viewless** *adj.* ◇ **in view of sth** because of sth, or bearing sth in mind ◇ **on view** put somewhere so as to be seen ◇ **with a view to sth** with the aim, intention, or hope of doing or achieving sth

WORD KEY: CULTURAL NOTE

A Room with a View, a novel by E.M. Forster (1908). It describes how a young Englishwoman's visit to Italy and her encounter there with a young, unconventional expatriate encourages her to rebel against the emotionally stifling conventions of her upper-class background. It was made into a film by Ismail Merchant and James Ivory in 1985.

viewable /vyoó əb'l/ *adj.* **1. ABLE TO BE SEEN** able to be seen or inspected **2. FIT TO BE WATCHED** of a good enough standard, or in a good enough condition, to be watched

viewdata /vyoó daytə/ *n.* an interactive information system in which text and graphic data stored in a central computer are transmitted over telephone lines to be displayed on a modified home television receiver. Typical applications include airline and theatre reservations, financial transactions, and access to news reports of current events.

viewer /vyoó ər/ *n.* **1. SB WHO WATCHES** sb who watches sth such as television, a film, or an event **2. OPTICAL DEVICE** any optical device for illuminating and magnifying a photographic transparency, video tape, or motion picture film **3. SB WHO MAKES A FORMAL INSPECTION** sb appointed, especially by a court, to inspect sth such as property —**viewership** *n.*

viewfinder /vyoó fīndər/ *n.* a device on a camera that lets the user see what is being photographed

view halloo *interj.* **USED TO SHOW FOX IS SIGHTED** used during a fox hunt as a shout to signal that the fox has been seen breaking cover ■ *n.* **HUNTER'S CRY** a shout of 'view halloo!'

viewing /vyoó ing/ *n.* **1. ACT OF WATCHING** an act or the practice of watching, seeing, or inspecting sth **2. TV SHOWS COLLECTIVELY** television programmes as a body or type

viewpoint /vyoó poynt/ *n.* **1. POINT OF VIEW** a personal perspective from which sb considers sth **2. VIEWING LOCATION** a place or position from which people can look at sth

VIF *abbr.* variable import fee

vigesimal /vī jéssim'l/ *adj.* based on or reckoned in units of the number twenty [Mid-17thC. Formed from Latin *vigesimus*, variant of *vicesimus* 'twentieth', from *viginti* 'twenty'.]

vigia /vi jeé ə/ *n.* NAUT sth marked on a chart as a hazard to navigation, although its existence, position, and nature are unconfirmed [Mid-19thC. From Portuguese, 'lookout', ultimately from Latin *vigilia* (see VIGIL).]

vigil /víjjil/ *n.* **1. NIGHT WATCH** a period spent in doing sth through the night, e.g. watching, guarding, or praying **2. FESTIVAL EVE** the eve of some festivals and holy days, spent in prayer ■ **vigils** *npl.* **RELIGIOUS SERVICES AT NIGHT** religious services or prayers at night, especially on the eve of a festival or holy day [13thC. Via Old French *vigile* from medieval Latin *vigilia*, 'eve of a holy day', from Latin, 'watchfulness', from *vigil* 'awake, alert'.]

vigilance /víjjilənss/ *n.* the condition of being watchful and alert, especially to danger

vigilance committee *n.* US a group of people who pursue and punish suspected or alleged criminals without having the legal authority to do so

vigilant /víjjilənt/ *adj.* watchful and alert, especially to danger or to sth that is wrong —**vigilantly** *adv.*

WORD KEY: SYNONYMS

See Synonyms at ***cautious***.

vigilante /víjji lánti/ *n.* **1. LAW-ENFORCING CITIZEN** sb who punishes lawbreakers personally and illegally rather than relying on the legal authorities **2.** *US* **VIGILANCE COMMITTEE MEMBER** a member of a vigilance committee [Mid-19thC. From Spanish, 'watchman', ultimately from Latin *vigilant-*, the present participle of *vigilare* 'to watch', from *vigil* (see VIGIL).]

vigneron /veénya ron, -roN/ *n.* sb who grows grapes for use in making wine [15thC. From French, from *vigne* (see VINE).]

vignette /vin yét/ *n.* **1.** PRINTING **DESIGN ON A BOOK PAGE** a small decorative design printed at the beginning or end of a book or chapter of a book, or in the margin of a page **2.** LITERAT **SHORT ESSAY** a short descriptive piece of literary writing **3.** ARTS **UNBORDERED PICTURE** a painting, drawing, or photograph that has no border but is gradually faded into its background at the edges **4.** CINEMA **BRIEF SCENE** a brief scene from a film or play **5.** ARCHIT **ARCHITECTURAL ORNAMENTATION** a carved architectural decoration in the form of tendrils and leaves ■ *vt.* (**-gnettes, -gnetting, -gnetted**) **1.** ARTS **FINISH PICTURE OFF BY SOFTENING EDGES** to finish a painting, drawing, or photograph by gradually fading it into its background at the edges rather than giving it a border **2.** LITERAT **DESCRIBE STH BRIEFLY** to describe sth in a brief but elegant way [Mid-18thC. From French, literally 'small vine' (from such decorations on the margins of pages in early books), from *vigne* (see VINE).] —**vignetter** *n.* —**vignettist** *n.*

Vignola /vin yṓlə/, **Giacomo da** (1507–73) Italian architect. His work and writings influenced the development of the baroque style in architecture. Born **Giacomo Barozzi**

Vigo /veégō/ city and port in the autonomous region of Galicia, northwestern Spain, on the Atlantic Ocean. Population: 290,582 (1995).

vigor *n.* US = **vigour**

vigorish /víggərish/ *n.* US (*slang*) **1. BETTING CHARGE** a sum of money that a bookmaker or gambling establishment charges a customer for accepting a bet **2. ADDITIONAL PAYMENT** any additional payment that sb is forced to make, e.g. a bribe or interest paid to a usurer [Early 20thC. Earlier 'viggresh', of uncertain origin: perhaps via Yiddish from Russian *vyigrysh* or Ukrainian *vygrash* 'winnings, profit'.]

vigoroso /víggə róssō/ *adv.* to be played with intensity and liveliness (*used as a musical direction*) [Early 18thC. From Italian, literally 'vigorous', from medieval Latin *vigorosus*, from Latin *vigor* (see VIGOUR).] —**vigoroso** *adj.*

vigorous /víggərəss/ *adj.* **1. VERY HEALTHY** extremely strong and active, physically and mentally **2. ENERGETIC** displaying or using great energy —**vigorously** *adv.* —**vigorousness** *n.*

vigour /víggər/ *n.* **1. VITALITY** great physical or mental strength and energy **2. INTENSITY** intensity or forcefulness in the way sth is done **3. ABILITY TO GROW** the ability of plants or animals to survive, grow, and thrive **4.** *US* **LEGAL VALIDITY** legal validity or force [14thC. Via Old French *vigour* from Latin *vigor* 'liveliness, energy', from *vigere* 'to be lively'.]

Vijayawada /veéj ī ə waádə/ town in Krishna District, Andhra Pradesh State, southern India. Population: 701,351 (1991).

Viking /víking/ *n.* **1.** PEOPLES **MEMBER OF ANCIENT SCANDINAVIAN PEOPLE** a member of any of the Scandinavian peoples who carried out seaborne raids and invasions of various parts of northwestern Europe from the 8th to 11th centuries AD. They usually came by sea in longships, raiding mainly coastal regions, and often settled in the areas they invaded, as in Britain. **2. SPACE PROBE TO MARS** either of two identical, highly instrumented, uncrewed US space probes to Mars, launched in 1975. The probes' orbiters photographed the surface of Mars and its satellites and mapped water vapour and surface temperature variations while the landers transmitted colour pictures and meteorological and soil data. [Early 19thC. From Old Norse *víkingr*, either from *vík* 'creek, inlet' (literally 'person coming from inlets of the sea') or Old English *wīc* 'camp' (from their temporary encampments on raids).]

vil. *abbr.* village

vile /vīl/ (**viler, vilest**) *adj.* **1. DISGUSTING** causing disgust or abhorrence **2. WICKED** very evil or shameful **3. VERY UNPLEASANT** extremely unpleasant to experience **4. DEGRADING** so despicable or undesirable as to be degrading **5. WORTHLESS** of little or no worth (*archaic*) [13thC. Via Old French from Latin *vilis* 'of little value, cheap, base'.] —**vilely** *adv.* —**vileness** *n.*

WORD KEY: SYNONYMS

See Synonyms at ***mean***.

vilify /vílli fī/ (**-fies, -fying, -fied**) *vt.* to make malicious and abusive statements about sb [15thC. From late Latin *vilificare* 'to hold cheap', from Latin *vilis* 'worthless'.] —**vilification** /víllifi káysh'n/ *n.* —**vilifier** /vílli fī ər/ *n.*

WORD KEY: SYNONYMS

See Synonyms at ***malign***.

vilipend /víllə pend/ (**-pends, -pending, -pended**) *vt.* (*literary*) **1. TREAT SB WITH CONTEMPT** to treat or view sb with contempt **2. MALIGN SB** to make malicious or contemptuous statements about sb [15thC. Via Old French *vilipender* from Latin *vilipendere*, literally 'to consider base', from *vilis* 'base, cheap'.]

villa /víllə/ *n.* **1. EXPENSIVE HOUSE** a large, luxurious house in the country **2. HOUSE IN RESIDENTIAL AREA** a detached or semi-detached house in a residential area **3. HOLIDAY HOME** a house rented for a holiday **4.** *NZ* **SUBURBAN HOME** a suburban house with its own land **5.** *Aus* = **villa home 6. ROMAN HOUSE** a country house in ancient Rome or one of its colonies, with living quarters, farm buildings, and a courtyard [Early 17thC. Via Italian from Latin, 'country home, farm'.]

village /víllij/ *n.* **1. RURAL COMMUNITY** a group of houses and other buildings in a rural area, smaller than a town but larger than a hamlet **2. INHABITANTS OF VILLAGE** all of the people who live in a village **3. TEMPORARY COMMUNITY** a place where people live temporarily as a community, e.g. an apartment complex for the use of athletes taking part in Olympic games **4. ANIMAL DWELLINGS** a group of bird or animal dwellings [14thC. Via Old French from Latin *villaticum* 'farmstead', from *villa* (see VILLA).]

village college *n.* an educational and recreational centre for a group of villages

villager /víllijər/ *n.* sb who lives in a village

Villahermosa /veé ə hair mṓssə/ city and capital of Tabasco State, northeastern Mexico. Population: 261,231 (1990).

villa home *n.* *Aus* a type of modern suburban home built on a small allotment and usually separated from a neighbouring home by its garage

villain /víllən/ *n.* **1. EVIL CHARACTER** an evil character in a novel, film, play, or other story, especially one who is the main enemy of the hero **2. CONTEMPTIBLE PERSON** any person regarded as evil or otherwise contemptible **3. CAUSE OF PROBLEM** sb who or sth that is seen as the cause of a particular evil or problem **4. MISCHIEVOUS PERSON** sb who behaves in a mischievous or troublesome way (*humorous*) **5. CRIMINAL** a criminal (*slang*) **6.** = **villein** [14thC. Via Old French *vilein* 'feudal serf', from late Latin *villanus* 'farmhand', from Latin *villa* (see VILLA).]

villainage *n.* = **villeinage**

villainess /víllə ness/ *n.* **1. EVIL WOMAN CHARACTER** an evil woman character in a novel, film, play, or other story, especially one who is the main enemy of the hero **2. CONTEMPTIBLE WOMAN** any woman regarded as evil or otherwise contemptible

villainous /víllənəss/ *adj.* **1. WICKED** typical of an evil or contemptible person **2. UNDESIRABLE** obnoxious or unpleasant —**villainously** *adv.* —**villainousness** *n.*

villainy /vílləni/ *n.* **1. EVIL CONDUCT** behaviour typical of an evil or contemptible person **2. STATE OF BEING EVIL** the state of being evil or contemptible **3.** (*plural* **-ies**) **EVIL ACT** an evil, immoral, or criminal act

villanelle /víllə nél/ *n.* a 19-line poem, originally French, that uses only two rhymes and consists of five three-line stanzas and a final quatrain. The first and third lines of the first stanza are alternately repeated as a refrain that closes the following stanzas, and joined as a final couplet of the quatrain. [Late 16thC. Via French from Italian *villanella* 'old rustic (Italian) song', ultimately from *villano* 'peasant', from medieval Latin *villanus* (see VILLAIN).]

Villanovan /víllə nṓv'n/ *adj.* **BELONGING TO IRON AGE CULTURE** belonging to or typical of an early Iron Age culture that existed near Bologna, Italy, in which bronze was used and also, in a primitive way, iron ■ *n.* **MEMBER OF VILLANOVAN CULTURE** a member of the Villanovan culture [Early 20thC. Named after *Villanova*, a town in northeastern Italy near Bologna, where archaeological finds were made.]

villein /víllən, víllayn/, **villain** *n.* a feudal serf who had the status of a freeman except in relation to his lord, to whom he owed dues and services in exchange for land [14thC. Variant of VILLAIN.]

villeinage /víllənij/, **villainage** *n.* **1. STATUS OF VILLEIN** the status of being a villein in feudal society **2. LAND TENURE OF VILLEIN** the form of feudal tenure by which a villein held land

villi plural of **villus**

villiform /vílli fawrm/ *adj.* in the form of or resembling a minute projection (**villus**) [Mid-19thC. Formed from VILLUS.]

Villon /vee yóN/, **François** (1431?–63?) French poet. He wrote lyric poetry notable for its fresh interpretation of medieval verse forms and its frank expression of feeling. He was repeatedly arrested for criminal acts, and nothing is known of him after he was banished from Paris in 1463. Real name **François de Montcorbier** or **François des Loges**

villose *adj.* = **villous** [Early 18thC. From Latin *villosus* (see VILLOUS).]

villosity /vi lóssəti/ (*plural* **-ties**) *n.* **1. HAIRINESS** the condition of being covered in long shaggy hairs **2. BEING COVERED WITH MINUTE PROJECTIONS** the condition of being covered with minute projections **3. COATING OF FINE PROJECTIONS** a surface or coating of very fine projections resembling hairs **4. PART RESEMBLING HAIR** a fine projection that resembles a hair

villous /vílləss/, **villose** /víllōss/ *adj.* **1. HAIRY** covered with long shaggy hairs **2. WITH MINUTE PROTUBERANCES** relating to, resembling, or covered with minute protuberances [14thC. From Latin *villosus* 'shaggy', from *villus* 'shaggy hair'.] —**villously** *adv.*

villus /vílləss/ (*plural* **-li** /víl lī/) *n.* **1. MINUTE PROTUBERANCE** any of many vascular protuberances growing out from some mucous membranes, e.g. from that of the small intestine of some vertebrates or from the chorion that surrounds an embryo **2. OUTGROWTH ON PLANT** a fine part resembling a hair, growing from the surface of a plant [Early 18thC. From Latin, literally 'shaggy hair'.]

Vilnius /vílni əss/ capital city of Lithuania, situated in the southeast of the country, near the border with Belarus. Population: 580,100 (1997).

vim /vim/ *n.* exuberant vitality and energy (*informal*) [Mid-19thC. Origin uncertain: probably from Latin, a form of *vis* 'power, strength' (source of English *violent*).]

vin- *prefix.* = **vini-**

vina /veénə/ *n.* a stringed instrument used in the Indian subcontinent, similar to the sitar. It has a long fretted fingerboard with resonating gourds at both ends and is played by plucking. [Late 18thC. From Sanskrit *vīṇā*.]

vinaceous /vī náyshəss/ *adj.* **1. LIKE WINE** of the nature of or containing wine **2. REDDISH** of the colour of red wine [Late 17thC. Formed from Latin *vinaceus*, from *vinum* 'wine'.]

vinaigrette /vìnay grét, vìnni-/ *n.* **1. SALAD DRESSING** a salad dressing made with vinegar, oil, salt, pepper, and sometimes other seasonings **2. SMALL CONTAINER** a small bottle or box with a perforated cap, used to hold aromatic substances such as smelling salts or vinegar [Late 17thC. From French, literally 'little vinegar', from *vinaigre* (see VINEGAR).]

vinasse /vi náss/ *n.* the residue left in a still after the distillation of an alcoholic beverage, especially brandy. It is used as a fertilizer and is a source of potassium salts. [Via French from Provençal *vinassa*, ultimately from Latin *vinaceus* (see VINACEOUS)]

vinblastine /vin blás teen/ *n.* an alkaloid drug extracted from the Madagascar periwinkle, used in the treatment of some cancers. It works by blocking cell division (**mitosis**) and is highly toxic. Formula: $C_{46}H_{58}N_4O_9$. [Mid-20thC. Formed from modern Latin *Vinca*, genus name (see VINCA), + LEUKOBLAST + -INE.]

vinca /víngkə/ *n.* = **periwinkle**[2] *n.* [Mid-19thC. From modern Latin, genus name, from late Latin *pervinca* (see PERIWINKLE).]

Vincennes /vin sénz/ town in north-central France, near Paris. It is the site of a medieval castle that was used as a royal residence until 1740. Population: 42,651 (1990).

Vincent de Paul /vínssənt də páwl, vaN saN də páwl/, **St** (1581–1660) French priest. He was the founder of the Congregation of the Mission (1625), also called the Vincentians.

Vincent's angina, **Vincent's infection** *n.* a painful mouth inflammation with ulcers and gum damage. Two organisms that are normally present cause the condition only when sb has a vitamin B deficiency or an immune deficiency. [Early 20thC. Named after Jean Hyacinthe *Vincent* (1862–1950), French physician who discovered the disease.]

vincible /vínssəb'l/ *adj.* able to be defeated or conquered (*archaic*) [Mid-16thC. From Latin *vincibilis*, from *vincere* 'to conquer'.] —**vincibility** /vìnssə bílləti/ *n.* —**vincibleness** *n.*

vincristine /vin krís teen/ *n.* an alkaloid drug produced from the Madagascar periwinkle, used to treat acute leukaemia and lymphomas. It works by blocking cell division (**mitosis**) and is highly toxic. Formula: $C_{46}H_{56}N_4O_{10}$. [Mid-20thC. Formed from modern Latin *Vinca*, genus name (see VINCA), + Latin *crista* 'crest' + -INE.]

vinculum /víngkyōōləm/ (*plural* **-la** /-lə/) *n.* **1. MATH RAISED LINE CONNECTING MATHEMATICAL TERMS** a horizontal line above two or more members of a compound mathematical expression, used like parentheses to show that the expression is to be treated as a single term. Parentheses, brackets, and braces are used more frequently for this purpose than is the vinculum. **2. ANAT BAND OF TISSUE** a band of tissue, especially a ligament [Mid-17thC. From Latin, literally 'fetter, bond', from *vincire* 'to tie, fasten'.]

vindaloo /víndə lōō/ (*plural* **-loos**) *n.* a very hot curry sauce made with coriander, red chilli, ginger, and other spices, or a dish cooked in this [Late 19thC. From Konkani *vindalu*, ultimately from Portuguese *vinho de alho*, a wine and garlic sauce, literally 'wine of garlic'.]

vin de pays /ván də páy ee/ (*plural* **vins de pays**) *n.* a French wine with the third highest grade of classification, which guarantees that the wine comes from a specified area [From French, literally 'wine of (the) region']

vindicable /víndikəb'l/ *adj.* able to be vindicated or justified [Mid-17thC. From medieval Latin *vindicabilis*, from Latin *vindicare* (see VINDICATE).] —**vindicability** /víndikə bílləti/ *n.*

vindicate /víndi kayt/ (**-cates, -cating, -cated**) *vt.* **1. SHOW SB OR STH IS BLAMELESS** to clear sb or sth of blame, guilt, suspicion, or doubt **2. JUSTIFY SB OR STH** to show that sb or sth is justified or correct **3. UPHOLD STH** to defend or maintain sth such as a cause or rights [Mid-16thC. From Latin *vindicatus*, perfect participle of *vindicare* 'to claim, set free, avenge', from the stem *vindic-* 'avenger'.] —**vindicator** *n.*

vindication /víndi káysh'n/ *n.* **1. BEING VINDICATED** the act of vindicating sb or sth, or the condition of being vindicated **2. REASON FOR VINDICATING SB OR STH** evidence or an argument used to vindicate sb or sth

vindicatory /víndikətəri, -kaytəri/ *adj.* providing sth such as facts or an argument that justifies a belief, conclusion, or action

vindictive /vin díktiv/ *adj.* **1. VENGEFUL** looking for revenge or done through a desire for revenge **2. SPITEFUL** feeling, showing, or done through a desire to hurt sb **3. LAW MEANT TO PUNISH** used to describe damages awarded by a court that are set higher than the amount necessary to compensate the victim, in order to punish the defendant [Early 17thC. Formed from Latin *vindicta* 'revenge'.]

vin du pays /ván dyoo páy ee/ (*plural* **vins du pays**) *n.* a locally produced French wine [From French, literally 'wine of the region']

vine /vīn/ *n.* **1. CLIMBING PLANT** a plant that supports itself by climbing, twining, or creeping along a surface **2. STEM** the weak flexible stem of a vine **3.** = **grapevine** *n.* 1 **4. GRAPEVINES COLLECTIVELY** grapevines considered collectively [13thC. Via Old French *vigne* from Latin *vinea* 'vine, vineyard', from *vinum* 'wine' (source of English *wine* and *vinegar*).] —**viny** *adj.*

vinedresser /vín dressər/ *n.* sb who tends and prunes grapevines

vinegar /vínnigər/ *n.* **1. SOUR-TASTING LIQUID** a sour-tasting liquid used to flavour and preserve foods. It is a dilute acetic acid made by fermenting beer, wine, or cider. **2. ILL TEMPER** sourness or ill-tempered behaviour or speech **3.** *US* **VITALITY** exuberant energy and enthusiasm [13thC. From Old French *vyn egre* 'sour wine', from Latin *vinum acre*.] —**vinegarish** *adj.*

vinegar eel, **vinegar worm** *n.* a very small nematode worm that feeds on bacteria that cause fermentation, especially in vinegar. Latin name: *Anguillula aceti.*

vinegarette /vìnnigə rét/ *n.* = **vinaigrette** *n.* 2

vinegar worm *n.* = **vinegar eel**

vinegary /vínnigəri/ *adj.* **1. SOUR-TASTING** with a sour taste or smell like vinegar **2. IRRITABLE** showing an unpleasant, irritable disposition —**vinegariness** *n.*

vinery /vínəri/ (*plural* **-ies**) *n.* an area or building, especially a greenhouse, in which grapevines are grown

vineyard /vínnyərd, -yaard/ *n.* a piece of land where grapevines are grown

vingt-et-un /vánt ay úN/ *n.* CARDS the game of pontoon [Late 18thC. From French, literally 'twenty-one'.]

vinho verde /vínnyō vúrdi/ *n.* a light, dry, acidic, white or red wine from northern Portugal [Mid-20thC. From Portuguese, literally 'green wine' (referring to the youthfulness of the wine).]

vini- *prefix.* wine, grapes ○ *viniculture* [From Latin *vinum*]

viniculture *n.* = **viticulture** —**vinicultural** /vìnni kúlchrəl/ *adj.* —**viniculturist** /-kúlchrist/ *n.*

vinify /vínni fī/ (**-fies, -fying, -fied**) *vt.* to ferment grape juice, or another liquid, into wine

Vinland /vínlənd/ part of North America, now northern Newfoundland, first seen by the Norse voyager Bjarni Herjólfsson during a voyage from Iceland to Greenland in about AD 986. The Icelandic explorer Leif Ericson explored the Newfoundland and Labrador coasts several years later.

vino /veénō/ *n.* wine, especially cheap wine (*informal*) [Late 19thC. From Italian, 'wine'.]

vin ordinaire /ván awrdi náir/ (*plural* **vins ordinaires** /vánz awrdi náir/) *n.* cheap table wine, especially from France [Early 19thC. From French, literally 'ordinary wine'.]

vinosity /vī nóssəti/ *n.* the distinctive and essential character of wine, including qualities such as body, colour, and taste

vinous /vínəss/ *adj.* **1. OF WINE** relating to, typical of, or containing wine **2. WINE-DRINKING** tending to drink a lot of wine, or caused by wine-drinking [Mid-17thC. Formed from Latin *vinum* 'wine'.] —**vinously** *adv.* —**vinousness** *n.*

Vinson Massif /vínssən máss eef/ the highest mountain in Antarctica, in the central Ellsworth Mountains. Height: 5,140 m/16,864 ft.

vintage /víntij/ *n.* **1. WINE PRODUCTION YEAR** the year in which the grapes used in making a particular wine were harvested **2. WINE FROM A PARTICULAR YEAR** wine made from a particular harvest of grapes **3. GRAPE HARVESTING** the harvesting of grapes for wine **4. PERIOD** the period of time when sth appeared or began, or when sb was born or flourished **5. GROUP SHARING CHARACTERISTICS** a group of people or things that are similar or belong to the same period of time (*informal*) ■ *adj.* **1. GOOD FOR WINE** produced from or characterized by a good harvest of grapes for winemaking, so that the wine does not have to be improved by blending with wine from another harvest **2. OF THE BEST** representing what is best or most typical of sb or sth **3. CLASSIC** recognized as being of high quality and lasting appeal **4. OUT OF DATE** no longer fashionable or modern ■ *vt.* (**-tages, -taging, -taged**) **1. GATHER GRAPES** to harvest grapes to make wine **2. MAKE WINE** to make wine from harvested grapes [14thC. Alteration (influenced by *viniter* 'vintner') of *vendage*, from Old French *vendange*, from Latin *vindemia* 'grape-gathering', from *vinum* 'wine' + *demere* 'to take away'.]

vintage car *n.* an old car, especially one built between 1919 and 1930. ◊ **veteran car**

vintager /víntijər/ *n.* sb who takes part in harvesting grapes and making wine

vintner /víntnər/ *n.* sb who sells wine [15thC. Via Old French *vinetier* from medieval Latin *vinetarius*, from Latin *vinetum* 'vineyard', from *vinum* 'wine'.]

vinyl /vín'l/ *n.* **1. CHEMICAL GROUP** a univalent unsaturated chemical group or radical that is formed when one hydrogen atom is removed from ethylene. Formula: CH₂CH. (*often used before a noun*) **2. COMPOUND USED IN PLASTICS** a reactive compound that contains the vinyl radical, usually in polymerized form, used in making plastics (*often used before a noun*) **3. PLASTIC MATERIAL** a plastic material, made from a vinyl polymer **4. PLASTIC RECORDS** gramophone records made of a vinyl polymer, as opposed to compact discs ■ *adj.* **MADE OF VINYL** made of or containing a vinyl polymer [Mid-19thC. Formed from VIN- + -YL.] —**vinylic** /vī níllik/ *adj.*

vinyl chloride *n.* a colourless, carcinogenic, explosive, flammable gas used in organic synthesis, particularly in making polyvinyl chloride, and in adhesives. Formula: CH₂:CHCl.

vinylidene /vī nílli deen/ *n.* a bivalent chemical group or radical, made when two hydrogen atoms are removed from one carbon atom of ethylene. Formula: CH₂:C.

vinyl polymer, **vinyl resin** *n.* any odourless and tasteless thermoplastic material made by polymerizing compounds containing vinyl groups. PVC is a typical example.

viol /ví əl/ *n.* **1. STRINGED INSTRUMENT** a stringed instrument popular during the 16th and 17th centuries with a fretted fingerboard, a flat-backed body, and six strings, played with a curved bow. It is a member of a family of stringed instruments that preceded the violin family. **2.** = **viola da gamba** [15thC. Via Old French *viole* from Old Provençal *viola*, of uncertain origin: perhaps from medieval Latin *vitula* (see VIOLA¹).]

viola¹ /vi ólə/ *n.* **1. STRINGED INSTRUMENT** a stringed instrument slightly larger than a violin held under the chin and played with a long slender bow. It is tuned an octave above the cello and is the alto of the violin family. **2.** = **viola da gamba** [Late 18thC. Via Italian from Old Provençal *viola*, from medieval Latin *vitula* 'stringed instrument' (source of English *fiddle*).]

viola² /ví ələ/ *n.* a plant related to the violets and pansies, especially one with small white, yellow, or purple flowers. Genus: *Viola*. [15thC. From Latin, 'violet' (source of English *violet*).]

violable /ví ələb'l/ *adj.* capable of being disregarded or treated with disrespect —**violability** /ví ələ billəti/ *n.* —**violableness** *n.* —**violably** /ví ələbli/ *adv.*

violaceous /ví ə láyshəss/ *adj.* relating to, belonging to, or typical of the family of plants that includes violets and pansies [Mid-17thC. Formed from Latin *violaceus* 'violet-coloured', from *viola* 'violet'.]

viola da braccio /-də bráchō/ (*plural* **violas da braccio**) *n.* an old stringed instrument of the viol family, held against the shoulder when played [Mid-19thC. From Italian, literally 'viol for (the) arm'.]

viola da gamba /-də gámbə/ (*plural* **violas da gamba**) *n.* an old stringed bass instrument of the viol family, with a range similar to a cello [Late 16thC. From Italian, literally 'viol for (the) leg'.]

viola d'amore /-da máwri/ (*plural* **violas d'amore**) *n.* a fretless stringed instrument of the viol family with six or seven strings and a second set of strings that are not played but are made to vibrate by the first set (**sympathetic strings**) [Late 17thC. From Italian, literally 'viol of love'.]

violate /ví ə layt/ (**-lates**, **-lating**, **-lated**) *vt.* **1. DISREGARD STH** to act contrary to sth such as a law, contract, or agreement, especially in a way that produces significant effects **2. RAPE SB** to rape or sexually assault sb **3. DISTURB STH** to disturb or interrupt sth in a rude or violent way **4. DEFILE STH** to treat sth sacred with a lack of respect [15thC. From Latin *violatus*, perfect participle of *violare* 'to treat with violence,

injure', of uncertain origin.] —**violative** /vī ələtiv, -laytiv/ *adj.* —**violator** /-laytər/ *n.*

violation /vī ə láysh'n/ *n.* **1. ACT OF VIOLATING** the act or an example of violating sb or sth **2. CRIME OR INFRINGEMENT OF RULE** a crime or infringement of a law

violence /ví ələnss/ *n.* **1. PHYSICAL FORCE** the use of physical force to injure sb or damage sth ○ *threats of violence* **2. ILLEGAL FORCE** the illegal use of unjustified force, or the effect created by the threat of this ○ *robbery with violence* **3. DESTRUCTIVE FORCE** extreme, destructive, or uncontrollable force, especially of natural events ○ *the violence of the storm* **4. FERVOUR** intensity of feeling or expression ○ *the violence of her response to our suggestion* ◇ **do violence to sth** to violate, harm, or damage sth

violent /ví ələnt/ *adj.* **1. USING PHYSICAL FORCE** using physical force to hurt sb or damage sth ○ *violent crime* **2. EMOTIONALLY INTENSE** showing emotional intensity or strong feeling ○ *his violent objections to the plan* **3. SHOWING DESTRUCTIVE FORCE** showing extreme, destructive, or uncontrollable force ○ *a violent thunderstorm* **4. INTENSE** very intense or strong ○ *a violent headache* **5. CAUSED BY FORCE** caused by force rather than natural causes ○ *met a violent death* **6. DISTORTING** distorting or misinterpreting the meaning of sth ○ *a violent interpretation of the poem* [14thC. From Latin *violentus* 'forcible, vehement', of uncertain origin.] —**violently** *adv.*

violent storm *n.* a storm that causes widespread damage with winds of force 11 on the Beaufort scale, reaching speeds of 103–117 kph/64–72 mph

Violet

violet /ví ələt/ *n.* **1. FLOWERING PLANT** a low-growing, perennial plant with irregular flowers that are usually but not always a purplish blue. Genus: *Viola*. **2. PLANT RESEMBLING A VIOLET** any of several plants such as the African violet that are like the violet but are not necessarily related to it **3. PURPLISH-BLUE COLOUR** a deep purplish-blue colour like that of a violet flower ■ *adj.* **PURPLISH-BLUE** of a deep purplish-blue colour like a violet flower [14thC. From Old French *violete*, a diminutive of *viole*, from Latin *viola* 'violet'.]

violin /ví ə lín/ *n.* **1. STRINGED INSTRUMENT PLAYED WITH BOW** a wooden musical instrument with four strings and an unfretted fingerboard, held under the player's chin and played with a bow. The violin has the highest range in the family of stringed instruments to which it gives its name. **2. VIOLINIST** a musician who plays a violin, especially in an orchestra [Late 16thC. From Italian *violino*, a diminutive of *viola* (see VIOLA¹).]

violinist /ví ə línnist/ *n.* sb who plays the violin

violin sonata *n.* a sonata for solo violin, usually with piano accompaniment

violist¹ /vi ólist/ *n.* US sb who plays the viola

violist² /ví əlist/ *n.* sb who plays the viol

violoncello /ví ələn chéllō/ (*plural* **-los**) *n.* a cello (*formal*) [Early 18thC. From Italian, a diminutive of *violone* (see VIOLONE).]

violone /ví əlōn/ *n.* the double-bass viol, larger and with a deeper range than the viola da gamba [Early 18thC. From Italian, literally 'large viola', from *viola* (see VIOLA¹).]

VIP *abbr.* **1.** very important person **2.** vasoactive intestinal peptide

vipassana /vi pássənə/, **Vipassana** *n.* Theravada Bud-

dhist meditation that aims at concentrating the mind on the body

Viper

viper /vípər/ *n.* **1. POISONOUS SNAKE** a snake with hollow fangs that it uses to inject venom into its victim when it bites. Vipers are found in Europe, Asia, and Africa. Family: Viperidae. **2.** = **adder²** *n.* **3. POISONOUS SNAKE NOT OF VIPER FAMILY** a poisonous snake such as the horned viper belonging to a family other than the vipers proper **4. PIT VIPER** a pit viper **5. OFFENSIVE TERM** an offensive term used to refer to sb who is considered to be malicious, treacherous, or ungrateful (*offensive*) [Early 16thC. Via Old French *vipere* from Latin *vipera* 'snake', a contraction of assumed *vivipera* 'live-bearing' (from the ancient belief that snakes bore live young), from *vivus* 'alive'.]

viperine *adj.* = **viperous**

viperish /vípərish/ *adj.* **1. MALICIOUS** malicious or spiteful **2.** = **viperous** —**viperishly** *adv.*

viperous /vípərəss/, **viperine** /vípə rīn/ *adj.* typical of or like a viper —**viperously** *adv.*

viper's bugloss *n.* a weed that is native to Europe and Asia and is naturalized in other areas. It has spikes of blue tubular flowers and rough foliage. Latin name: *Echium vulgare*.

VIR *abbr.* Victoria Imperatrix Regina

vir- *prefix.* = **viro-** (*used before vowels*)

viraemia /vī reémi ə/ *n.* the presence of viruses in the bloodstream [Mid-20thC. From modern Latin, from VIRUS + -AEMIA.] —**viraemic** *adj.*

virago /vi ráagō/ (*plural* **-goes** *or* **-gos**) *n.* **1. OFFENSIVE TERM** an offensive term that deliberately insults a woman's temperament or behaviour (*insult offensive*) **2. COURAGEOUS WOMAN** a woman who is strong and brave (*archaic*) [Pre-12thC. From Latin, from *vir* 'man, husband' (source of English *virile*).] —**viraginous** /vi rájjənəss/ *adj.*

viral /vírəl/ *adj.* relating to, typical of, or caused by a virus —**virally** *adv.*

Virchow /vúrkō/, **Rudolf** (1821–1902) German pathologist and anthropologist. His textbook on cellular pathology (1850) was the foundation text of the field. He also published significant works in anthropology and archaeology. Full name **Rudolf Carl Virchow**

virelay /vírrə lay/ *n.* an old French verse form consisting of short lines arranged in stanzas with two rhymes. The end rhyme is repeated as the first line of the next stanza. [14thC. From French *virelai*, an alteration (influenced by *lai* 'lay, song') of obsolete *vireli*, of uncertain origin: perhaps a nonsense word used in the refrain of a song.]

virement /veer moN/ *n.* an authorized transfer of funds from one use to another [Early 20thC. From French, literally 'turning, transfer', from *virer* 'to turn, veer' (source of English *veer*).]

viremia *n.* US = **viraemia**

Viren /veerən/, **Lasse** (*b.* 1949) Finnish athlete. An Olympic gold medallist in the 5,000 and 10,000 metres (1972 and 1976), he set several world records in both events. Full name **Lasse Artturi Viren**

vireo /vírri ō/ (*plural* **-os**) *n.* a small insect-eating songbird that lives in the Americas and has greyish or greenish plumage. Genus: *Vireo*. [Mid-19thC. From modern Latin, genus name, from Latin, a bird (probably the greenfinch), from *virere* 'to be green'.]

virescent /vī réss'nt/ *adj.* **1.** GREENISH having or developing a green or greenish colour **2.** ABNORMALLY GREEN used to describe plant parts that are not normally green but are turned green by disease [Early 19thC. From Latin *virescent-*, present participle stem of *virescere* 'to become green'.] —**virescence** *n.*

virga /vúrgə/ (*plural* **-ga**) *n.* vertical trails of rain, snow, or ice from the underside of a cloud that evaporate before reaching the ground [Mid-20thC. From Latin, literally 'rod, staff, twig'.]

virgate[1] /vúrgət/ *adj.* long and thin like a rod [Early 19thC. From Latin *virgatus*, from *virga* 'rod, staff'.]

virgate[2] /vúrgət/ *n.* an old English land measure thought to be the equivalent of about 12 hectares/30 acres [Mid-17thC. From medieval Latin *virgata*, from Latin *virga* 'rod' (translating Old English *gierdland* 'yard(-measure) of) land'.]

Virgil /vúrjil/, **Vergil** (70–19 BC) Roman poet. Regarded as the finest Latin poet of his age, he wrote pastoral verse before composing his great mythological epic *Aeneid*, which tells the story of the seven-year wanderings of Aeneas after the fall of Troy. Full name **Publius Vergilius Maro** —**Virgilian** /vur jílli ən/ *adj.*

virgin /vúrjin/ *n.* **1.** SB WHO HAS NOT HAD SEX sb, especially a woman, who has never had sexual intercourse **2.** RELIG RELIGIOUS WOMAN COMMITTED TO CHASTITY a woman who has taken a vow of chastity for religious reasons **3.** ZOOL FEMALE ANIMAL a female animal that has never copulated **4.** INSECTS FEMALE INSECT a female insect that produces fertile eggs without the help of a male ■ *adj.* **1.** OF A VIRGIN relating to, typical of, or being a virgin **2.** PURE in a pure, natural, or clean state **3.** ENVIRON NOT TOUCHED BY HUMANS never having been explored or exploited by humans **4.** FIRST first or happening for the first time **5.** FOOD FROM FIRST PRESSING used to describe vegetable oils that come from the first pressing of fruit, leaves, or seeds without the use of heat **6.** METALL PRODUCED DIRECTLY FROM ORE used to describe metals produced directly from an ore, not from scrap metal **7.** MINERALS UNALLOYED found in a pure, unmixed state **8.** PHYS NEVER HAVING COLLIDED used to describe a neutron that has never been in a collision and therefore retains the energy with which it started [12thC. Via Old French *virgine* from Latin *virgin-*, the stem of *virgo* 'maiden'.]

Virgin *n.* **1.** CHR = **Virgin Mary 2.** ZODIAC = **Virgo**

virginal[1] /vúrjin'l/ *adj.* **1.** CHASTE relating to, typical of, or appropriate for sb, especially a woman, who has never had sexual intercourse **2.** LIVING CHASTELY living in a state of virginity **3.** PURE not corrupted or spoiled in any way

virginal[2] /vúrjin'l/ *n.* a smaller, often legless, oblong version of the harpsichord, popular in the 16th and 17th centuries [Early 16thC. Directly or via French from Latin *virginalis* (see VIRGIN), perhaps because the instrument was played by young girls.] —**virginalist** *n.*

Virgin Birth *n.* the Christian doctrine that Jesus Christ was born as the son of God rather than of a human father and that his mother was a virgin

Virginia[1] /vər jínni ə/, **virginia** *n.* a type of tobacco originally grown in the state of Virginia

Virginia

Virginia[2] /və jínni ə/ state of the eastern United States, bordered by Maryland, the Atlantic Ocean, North Carolina, Tennessee, Kentucky, and West Virginia. Capital: Richmond. Population: 6,733,996 (1997). Area: 109,624 sq. km/42,326 sq. mi. Official name **Commonwealth of Virginia** —**Virginian** *n.*, *adj.*

Virginia Beach the largest city in Virginia, situated in the southeastern part of the state, on the Atlantic Ocean and Chesapeake Bay, near the border with North Carolina. Population: 430,295 (1994).

Virginia creeper *n.* a climbing plant with leaves made up of five leaflets and bluish-black berries. Latin name: *Parthenocissus quinquefolia.*

Virginia deer *n.* = **white-tailed deer**

Virginia reel *n.* a U.S. country dance in which a caller instructs couples facing each other in long lines to perform various steps

Virginia stock *n.* a Mediterranean plant with sweet-scented, white and pink four-petalled flowers. Latin name: *Malcomia maritima.*

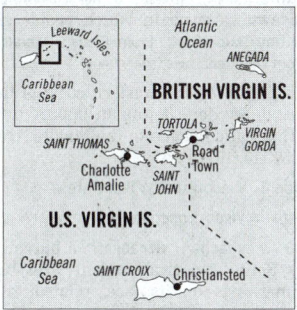

British Virgin Islands and US Virgin Islands

Virgin Islands, British /vúrjin-/ dependent territory of the United Kingdom consisting of 36 islands in the West Indies, east of Puerto Rico. Capital: Road Town. Population: 13,195 (1996). Area: 153 sq. km/59 sq. mi.

Virgin Islands of the United States unincorporated external territory of the United States in the eastern Caribbean Sea, consisting of three main islands and over 60 smaller islands and islets. Capital: Charlotte Amalie. Population: 97,120 (1996). Area: 349 sq. km/135 sq. mi.

virginity /vər jínnəti/ *n.* **1.** VIRGIN STATE the state of being a virgin **2.** UNSPOILT STATE the state of being untouched, unexplored, or unspoilt

Virgin Mary *n.* in Christian tradition, the mother of Jesus Christ

Virgin Queen *n.* a name used for Elizabeth I, Queen of England

virgin's bower *n.* a clematis of eastern North America that has clusters of small white flowers. Latin name: *Clematis virginiana.*

virgin wool *n.* wool that has not already been used to make sth

Virgo /vúrgō/ (*plural* **-gos**) *n.* **1.** ASTRON LARGE CONSTELLATION a constellation located on the celestial equator between Leo and Libra that contains the binary star Spica. The Virgo cluster, which lies near the North Galactic Pole about 16 billion light-years from the Earth, contains about 3,000 galaxies. **2.** ZODIAC ASTROLOGICAL SIGN the sixth sign of the zodiac, represented by a virgin and lasting from approximately 23 August to 22 September. Virgo is classified as an earth sign and its ruling planet is Mercury. **3.** Virgo, Virgoan SB BORN UNDER VIRGO sb whose birthday falls between 23 August and 22 September **4.** PERSON BORN UNDER VIRGO a person born under the sign of Virgo [Pre-12thC. From Latin (see VIRGIN).] —**Virgo** *adj.*

virgo intacta /vúrgō intáktə/ *n.* a girl or woman whose hymen remains unbroken [From Latin, literally 'intact virgin']

virgulate /vúrgyoŏlət/ *adj.* shaped like a rod [Mid-19thC. From Latin *virgula*, a diminutive of *virga* 'rod, staff, twig'.]

virgule /vúr gyool/ *n.* = **solidus** *n.* 1 [Mid-19thC. Via French, 'comma, little rod', from Latin *virgula*, a diminutive of *virga* 'rod, staff'.]

viricide /vírə sīd/, **virucide** *n.* a drug or other agent that neutralizes or destroys a virus or viruses [Mid-20thC. Formed from VIRUS.] —**viricidal** /vírə sīd'l/ *adj.*

virid /vírrid/ *adj.* bright green, or covered with green vegetation (*literary*) [Late 16thC. From Latin *viridis* 'green', a derivative of *virere* 'to be green'.]

viridescent /vírri déss'nt/ *adj.* developing or having a green or greenish colour [Mid-19thC. From late Latin *viridescent-*, present participle stem of *viridescere* 'to become green', from *viridis* (see VIRID).] —**viridescence** *n.*

viridian /vi ríddi ən/ *n.* **1.** GREEN PIGMENT a green pigment made of a form of chromic oxide **2.** BLUISH-GREEN COLOUR a bluish-green colour —**viridian** *adj.*

viridity /vi ríddəti/ *n.* (*literary*) **1.** GREENNESS the state of being green **2.** INNOCENCE the state of being inexperienced

virile /vírrīl/ *adj.* **1.** MASCULINE relating to or having the characteristics of an adult male **2.** POTENT able to carry out the male sexual function **3.** STRONG showing strength and forcefulness [15thC. From Latin *virilis*, from *vir* 'man, husband' (source of English *virtue*).]

virilism /vírrəlizəm/ *n.* the development of male secondary sex characteristics culturally considered to be unusual in a woman, e.g. body hair or a deep voice

virility /və rílləti/ *n.* the state of being male, having male characteristics, or male sexual potency

virion /vírri ən/ *n.* the form taken by a virus when it is outside living cells and capable of causing infection. It consists of a core of DNA or RNA surrounded by a protein coat, sometimes covered by an outer envelope. [Mid-20thC. From French, formed from *virien* 'viral' + -ON.]

viro- *prefix.* virus, viral ○ *virology* [From VIRUS]

viroid /vír oyd/ *n.* an infectious RNA particle that is like a virus but smaller. It causes diseases in plants. [Mid-20thC. Coined from VIRUS + -OID.]

virology /vī rólləji/ *n.* the scientific study of viruses and the diseases caused by them [Mid-20thC. Formed from VIRUS.] —**virologic** /vírə lójjik/ *adj.* —**virological** *adj.* —**virologically** *adv.* —**virologist** /vī rólləjist/ *n.*

virtu /vur toŏ/, **vertu** *n.* **1.** LOVE OF FINE OBJECTS a love of or taste for fine art objects or curios **2.** ART OBJECTS fine art objects or curios [Early 18thC. From Italian, literally 'virtue'.]

virtual /vúrchoo əl/ *adj.* **1.** BEING STH IN PRACTICE being sth in effect even if not in reality or not conforming to the generally accepted definition of the term **2.** PHYS HYPOTHETICAL used to describe a particle whose existence is suggested to explain observed phenomena but is not proved or directly observable **3.** COMPUT GENERATED BY COMPUTER simulated by a computer for reasons of economics, convenience, or performance [14thC. From medieval Latin *virtualis*, from Latin *virtus* (see VIRTUE). The meaning of 'so in effect' developed from 'having power'.] —**virtuality** /vurchoo álliti/ *n.*

virtual assistant *n.* sb who uses computer and phone connections to work from a distance as a personal assistant to sb else, instead of working in the same office or building ○ *'There are many reasons why home-based business owners are hiring virtual assistants.'* (*Washington Post*; December 1998)

virtual community *n.* a group of people communicating with each other via the Internet ○ *'...an interactive virtual community where local residents can do anything from look for local work to book seats at the local cinema.'* (*BBC website*; April 1999)

virtual focus *n.* the point from which divergent reflected or refracted light rays seem to originate

virtual image *n.* an image from which reflected or refracted light rays appear to diverge. It cannot be projected onto a screen or photographic emulsion.

virtually /vúrchoo əli/ *adv.* **1.** PRACTICALLY in effect even if not in fact **2.** NEARLY almost but not quite

virtual machine *n.* a program running on a computer that creates a self-contained operating environment and presents the appearance to the user of a different computer. A virtual machine simulates at a minimum the instruction set of the computer it emulates.

virtual memory, **virtual storage** *n.* a technique for creating the illusion that a computer has more memory than it really has by swapping blocks or pages of data between memory and external storage

virtual reality *n.* **1.** COMPUTER SIMULATION a technique by which a computer simulates a three-dimensional physical environment using visual and auditory stimuli with and within which people can interact to affect what happens in the simulation **2.** SIMULATED REALITY a computer-generated environment that simulates three-dimensional reality

Virtual Reality Modelling Language *n.* full form of **VRML**

virtue /vúrchoo/ *n.* **1.** GOODNESS the quality of being morally good or righteous ○ *a paragon of virtue* **2.** GOOD QUALITY a particular quality that is morally good ○ *Patience is a virtue.* **3.** ADMIRABLE QUALITY a particular quality that is good or admirable, but not necessarily in terms of morality **4.** CHASTITY the moral quality of being chaste, especially in a woman **5.** WORTH the worth, advantage, or beneficial quality of sth ○ *knew the virtue of thrift* **6.** EFFECTIVE FORCE the power or efficacy that sth contains to do sth (*archaic*) ■ **virtues** *npl.* CHR ORDER OF ANGELS the fifth of the nine traditional orders in the hierarchy of angels [12thC. Via Old French *vertu* from the Latin stem *virtut-* 'manliness, excellence, worth', from *vir* 'man, husband'.] —**virtueless** *adj.* ◇ **by** *or* **in virtue of** because of, through the power of, or by the authority of sth ◇ **make a virtue of necessity** to do sth with good grace, when you are obliged to do it anyway

virtuosi plural of **virtuoso**

virtuosity /vúrchoo óssəti/ *n.* **1.** OUTSTANDING SKILL great skill or technique shown by sb who excels at doing sth, especially performing music **2.** ENJOYMENT OF ART OBJECTS interest in, or knowledge and appreciation of, fine art objects

virtuoso /vúrchoo óssō/ (*plural* **-sos** *or* **-si** /-óssi/) *n.* **1.** EXCEPTIONAL PERFORMER a musician who shows exceptional ability, technique, or artistry **2.** TALENTED PERSON sb who shows exceptional technique or ability in sth **3.** CONNOISSEUR sb who cultivates an interest in, or knowledge and appreciation of, fine art objects [Early 17thC. From Italian, literally 'skillful, versed', from late Latin *virtuosus* 'good', from Latin *virtus* (see VIRTUE).] —**virtuosic** /-óssik/ *adj.* —**virtuosically** /-óssikli/ *adv.*

virtuous /vúrchoo əss/ *adj.* **1.** WITH MORAL INTEGRITY having or showing moral goodness or righteousness **2.** CHASTE not having sexual intercourse with anyone except a partner in marriage, especially a husband —**virtuously** *adv.* —**virtuousness** *n.*

virucide *n.* = **viricide**

virulent /vírrōōlənt, vírryōō-/ *adj.* **1.** VERY POISONOUS extremely poisonous, infectious, or damaging to organisms **2.** MALICIOUS showing great bitterness, malice, or hostility ○ *virulent criticism* [14thC. From Latin *virulentus* 'poisonous', from *virus* 'poison, venom' (source of English *virus*).] —**virulence** *n.* —**virulently** *adv.*

viruliferous /vírrōō líffərəss, vírryōō-/ *adj.* used to describe an organism that contains or carries a virus [Mid-20thC. Formed from VIRULENT + -IFEROUS.]

virus /vírəss/ *n.* **1.** BIOCHEM SUBMICROSCOPIC ENTITY a minute particle that lives as a parasite in plants, animals, and bacteria and consists of a nucleic acid core within a protein sheath. Viruses can only replicate within living cells and are not considered to be independent living organisms. **2.** MED VIRAL DISEASE a disease caused by a virus **3.** COMPUT DISRUPTIVE COMPUTER PROGRAM a short computer program, usually hidden within another, that makes copies of itself and spreads them, disrupting the operation of a computer that receives one. A virus may be transmitted on diskettes and through networks, on-line services, and the Internet. ◊ **Trojan horse, worm 4.** STH THAT CORRUPTS anything that has a corrupting or poisonous effect, especially on people's minds [Late 16thC. From Latin, literally 'poison, venom, medicinal liquid'.]

Vis. *abbr.* **1.** Viscount **2.** Viscountess

visa /veézə/ *n.* **1.** PASSPORT INSERTION an official endorsement in a passport authorizing the bearer to enter or leave, and travel in or through, a particular country or region **2.** AUTHORIZATION any mark of official authorization ■ *vt.* (**-sas, -saing, -saed**) **1.** SUPPLY DOCUMENT WITH VISA to insert a visa in a passport or other document **2.** GIVE SB A VISA to provide sb with a visa [Mid-19thC. Via French from Latin *visa*, 'things seen', the perfect participle of *videre* 'to see'.]

visage /vízzij/ *n.* **1.** FACE sb's face or facial expression (*literary*) **2.** APPEARANCE the appearance or look of sth [13thC. From Old French, from *vis* 'face, appearance', from Latin *visus*, perfect participle of *videre* 'to see'.]

visagiste /vézə zhéest/ *n.* sb who specializes in applying facial makeup [Mid-20thC. From French, from *visage* (see VISAGE).]

vis-à-vis /veézə veé/ *prep.* **1.** REGARDING in relation to **2.** OPPOSITE opposite to or face to face with ■ *adv.* FACE TO FACE face to face, or opposite each other ■ *n.* (*plural* **vis-à-vis**) **1.** SB OR STH FACING sb or sth that is face to face with another **2.** COUNTERPART sb who is the counterpart of sb else **3.** HORSE-DRAWN CARRIAGE a horse-drawn carriage in which people sit facing each other [Mid-18thC. From French, literally 'face to face', from Old French *vis* (see VISAGE).]

Visby /vízbi/ port on the western coast of the island of Gotland, Sweden. It was an important member of the Hanseatic League in the Middle Ages. Population: 57,110 (1990).

Visc. *abbr.* **1.** Viscount **2.** Viscountess

visc- *prefix.* = **visco-** (*used before vowels*)

viscacha /vi skaáchə/, **vizcacha** *n.* a burrowing, gregarious South American rodent with black and white markings on its face, related to and resembling the chinchilla. Latin name: *Lagostomus maximus.* [Early 17thC. Via Spanish from Quechua *(h)uiscacha.*]

viscera /víssərə/ *npl.* the internal organs of the body, especially those of the abdomen such as the intestines [Early 18thC. From Latin, 'internal organs, entrails', of uncertain origin: perhaps originally 'coil'.]

visceral /víssərəl/ *adj.* **1.** INSTINCTUAL proceeding from instinct rather than from reasoned thinking **2.** EMOTIONAL characterized by or showing basic emotions **3.** ANAT OF INTERNAL ORGANS relating to or affecting one or more internal organs of the body [Late 18thC] —**viscerally** *adv.*

visceromotor /víssərō mōtər/ *adj.* relating to the nervous control of gut movements, especially to disorders of bowel movement

viscid /víssid/ *adj.* **1.** THICK AND STICKY thick and sticky in consistency **2.** BOT COVERED WITH STICKY SUBSTANCE used to describe a leaf or other plant part that is covered with a sticky substance [Mid-17thC. From late Latin *viscidus*, from Latin *viscum* (see VISCOUS).] —**viscidity** /vi síddəti/ *n.* —**viscidness** /víssidnəss/ *n.* —**viscidly** *adv.*

visco- *prefix.* viscosity ○ *viscoelastic* [From VISCOUS]

viscoelastic /vískō i lástik/ *adj.* used to describe asphalt and many polymers that exhibit both viscous and elastic properties when deformed —**viscoelasticity** /vískō ee la stíssəti/ *n.*

viscometer /vi skómmitər/, **viscosimeter** /vískō símmitər/ *n.* an instrument used to measure the viscosity of a substance [Late 19thC. Coined from late Latin *viscosus* (see VISCOUS) + -METER.] —**viscometric** /vískō méttrik/ *adj.* —**viscometrical** *adj.* —**viscometry** /vi skómmətri/ *n.*

Visconti /vi skónti/, **Luchino** (1906–76) Italian film and theatre director. He is noted for his neo-realist films and literary adaptations. He also directed plays, ballets, and operas. Full name **Count Don Luchino Visconti di Modrone**

viscose /vískōss/ *n.* **1.** CELLULOSE USED IN MAKING RAYON a cellulose solution of thick consistency used in making rayon **2.** RAYON MADE FROM VISCOSE a type of rayon with a soft silky feel made from a viscose solution [Late 19thC. Coined from late Latin *viscosus* (see VISCOUS) + -OSE.]

viscosimeter *n.* = **viscometer**

viscosity /vi skóssəti/ (*plural* **-ties**) *n.* **1.** THICKNESS AND STICKINESS a thick and sticky consistency or quality **2.** PHYS PROPERTY OF FLUID THAT RESISTS FLOWING the property of a fluid or semifluid that causes it to resist flowing **3.** PHYS MEASURE OF SUBSTANCE'S RESISTANCE TO MOTION a measure of the resistance of a substance to motion under an applied force

viscosity index *n.* an arbitrary scale for lubricating oils that is used to indicate how much the viscosity of the oil varies according to its temperature

viscount /ví kownt/ *n.* **1.** BRITISH NOBLEMAN a British nobleman below an earl and above a baron in rank **2.** COUNT'S SON OR YOUNGER BROTHER in European countries other than the United Kingdom, especially France, sb whose father or elder brother is a count **3.** COUNT'S REPRESENTATIVE in medieval Europe, sb acting for or representing a count [14thC. From Anglo-Norman *viscounte*, ultimately from the medieval Latin *vicecomes*, from late Latin *vice-* (see VICE-) + *comes* 'count' (see COUNT).] —**viscountcy** *n.* —**viscounty** *n.*

viscountess /ví kowntəss/ *n.* **1.** WOMAN WITH RANK OF VISCOUNT a woman who holds a rank equivalent to viscount **2.** VISCOUNT'S WIFE OR WIDOW a woman who is or was married to a viscount

viscous /vískəss/ *adj.* **1.** THICK AND STICKY thick and sticky, reluctant to flow, and difficult to stir **2.** PHYS HAVING RELATIVELY HIGH VISCOSITY used to describe a fluid that has a relatively high resistance to flow [14thC. From late Latin *viscosus* 'sticky', from Latin *viscum* 'mistletoe, birdlime made from mistletoe berries', of uncertain origin.] —**viscously** *adv.* —**viscousness** *n.*

Viscount. *abbr.* **1.** Viscount **2.** Viscountess

viscus /vískəss/ *n.* singular of **viscera**

vise /vīss/ *n.* US = **vice**[1] *n.* 1

Vishakhapatnam /vi shaákə pútnəm/ city and port on the Bay of Bengal, in Andhra Pradesh State, southeastern India. Population: 750,024 (1991).

Vishnu /vish noo/ *n.* a Hindu god called the Preserver, the second member of the triad that includes Brahma the Creator and Shiva the Destroyer [Mid-17thC. From Sanskrit *Viṣṇu.*]

visibility /vízzə bílləti/ *n.* **1.** ABILITY TO BE SEEN the fact of being able to be seen **2.** DISTANCE IT IS POSSIBLE TO SEE the distance it is possible to see under the prevailing atmospheric or weather conditions **3.** CLEAR VIEW the ability to provide sb, especially the driver of a vehicle, with a good view of what is around him or her, or the view obtained from a particular position **4.** PUBLIC PROMINENCE the degree to which sb or sth is easily noticed by and catches the attention of the public or a particular group of people ○ *the comparatively low visibility of the board of directors*

visible /vízzəb'l/ *adj.* **1.** ABLE TO BE SEEN capable of being seen by, or perceptible to, the human eye ○ *the visible spectrum* **2.** IN SIGHT in sb's sight at a particular time ○ *The building became visible again as soon as she turned the corner.* **3.** OBVIOUS easily noticeable ○ *the very visible results of the recent floods* **4.** DETECTABLE capable of being discovered by means of the mental faculties ○ *no visible prospect of a solution to the problem* **5.** OFTEN SEEN PUBLICLY frequently in the public eye ○ *the company's very visible head of public relations* **6.** DESIGNED TO KEEP STH IN VIEW designed to keep information or an item in view or able to be readily brought to view ○ *a visible index* **7.** ECON CONSISTING OF ACTUAL GOODS in the form of, or relating to, actual goods imported or exported, as opposed to other types of transaction affecting a country's balance of trade ○ *visible exports* [14thC. From, ultimately, Latin *visibilis*, from *vis-*, past participle stem of *videre* 'to see' (source of *evident* and *survey*).] —**visibleness** *n.* —**visibly** *adv.*

visible radiation *n.* radiation such as sunlight that falls within the range of wavelengths that can be detected by the human eye

visible speech *n.* **1.** SYMBOLS REPRESENTING MOUTH POSITION IN SPEECH a set of phonetic symbols intended to represent the position of the lips, tongue, and other speech organs in creating sounds **2.** VISUAL RECORD OF SPEECH a visual representation of speech using a spectrograph that disperses radiation into a spectrum and photographs it

Visigoth /vízzi goth/ *n.* PEOPLES a member of an ancient Germanic people who invaded and conquered parts of the Roman Empire during the 5th century AD. They destroyed Rome in 410 and took over parts of Spain and southern France, where they established a powerful kingdom that lasted until the beginning of the 8th century. ◊ **Ostrogoth** [Mid-16thC. From late Latin *Visigothi* 'Visigoths', of uncertain origin: perhaps literally 'West Goths'.] —**Visigothic** /vízzi góthik/ *adj.*

vision /vízh'n/ *n.* **1.** EYESIGHT the ability to see **2.** MENTAL PICTURE an image or concept in the imagination ○ *visions of power and wealth* **3.** STH SEEN IN DREAM OR TRANCE an image or series of images seen in a dream or trance, often interpreted as having religious, revelatory, or prophetic significance **4.** FAR-SIGHTEDNESS the ability to anticipate possible future events and developments **5.** TELEVISION PICTURE the picture on a television screen **6.** SB OR STH BEAUTIFUL a beautiful or pleasing sight [13thC. From, ultimately, the Latin stem *vision-*, from *vis-* (see VISIBLE).] —**visional** *adj.* —**visionally** *adv.*

visionary /vízh'nəri/ *adj.* **1.** FULL OF FORESIGHT characterized by unusually acute foresight and imagination **2.** IMAGINARY produced by, resulting from, or originating in the imagination **3.** INCAPABLE OF BEING REALIZED so idealistic or unrealistic as to be unrealizable in practice **4.** GIVEN TO DREAMINESS tending by nature to be dreamy or to have impractical schemes and ideas **5.** RELATING TO MYSTICAL VISIONS relating to or seen in a mystical vision **6.** HAVING VISIONS given to seeing mystical visions ■ *n.* (*plural* **-ies**) **1.** SB WITH MUCH FORESIGHT sb of unusually acute foresight and imagination **2.** SB WHO HAS VISIONS sb who has mystical visions **3.** DREAMER sb who tends by nature to be dreamy or who is given to impractical schemes and ideas —**visionariness** *n.*

vision mixer *n.* **1.** SB COMBINING DIFFERENT CAMERA SHOTS a technician who mixes and combines the different camera shots during the production of a television programme or film **2.** EQUIPMENT USED BY A VISION MIXER a piece of equipment used by a vision mixer in television or film production

vision quest *n.* a personal spiritual search undertaken by an adolescent Native North American boy in order to learn by means of a trance or vision the identity of his guardian spirit

visit /vízzit/ *v.* (**-its, -iting, -ited**) **1.** *vti.* GO TO SEE SB to go to see and spend time with sb, especially as an act of affection or friendship ○ *Nobody visited him in hospital.* **2.** *vt.* STAY WITH SB to go to stay with sb for a time as a guest in his or her home ○ *I'm going to visit my family during the holidays.* **3.** *vti.* GO TO SEE PLACE to go to see or stay at a place for a time, e.g. as a tourist **4.** *vt.* GO TO INSPECT PLACE to go to a place as an official inspector **5.** *vt.* INFLICT STH ON SB to inflict sth unpleasant such as punishment or vengeance on sb (*archaic*) ○ *visited them with plagues* **6.** *vi.* *US* CHAT WITH SB to engage in amiable or casual conversation with sb ■ *n.* **1.** SOCIAL CALL a trip to see sb and a period of time spent in his or her company **2.** STAY IN A PLACE an extended temporary stay in a place, e.g. as sb's guest or as a tourist **3.** OFFICIAL INSPECTION an official call paid for the purpose of inspection **4.** LAW BOARDING OF SHIP the boarding of a ship on the high seas to carry out a search for contraband **5.** *US* CHAT an amiable or casual conversation [12thC. Directly or via French from Latin *visitare* 'to go to see', literally 'to view repeatedly', from *visare* 'to view', from *vis-* (see VISIBLE).] —**visitable** *adj.*

visitant /vízzitənt/ *n.* **1.** BIRDS = **visitor** *n.* **2** **2.** VISITOR a visitor (*archaic*) **3.** PARANORMAL VISITING SPIRIT a being thought to visit from the spirit world ■ *adj.* MAKING VISIT paying a visit to sb or sth

visitation /vìzzi táysh'n/ *n.* **1.** OFFICIAL VISIT an official visit for inspection or examination **2.** SOCIAL VISIT a social visit to sb's home, especially if it is unwelcome or lasts too long (*humorous*) **3.** RELIG PUNISHMENT FROM GOD a punishment or, sometimes, a benefit received, especially one believed to be sent by God **4.** PARANORMAL APPEARANCE FROM SPIRIT WORLD a supposed appearance made by a supernatural being **5.** *US* LAW VISIT WITH CHILD GRANTED TO PARENT the right of a divorced parent to have access to a child for a specified period of time, or a period of time with the child granted by this right —**visitational** *adj.*

Visitation *n.* **1.** VIRGIN MARY'S VISIT TO ELIZABETH the visit made by the Virgin Mary after the Annunciation to her cousin Elizabeth **2.** CHRISTIAN FESTIVAL a Christian festival held on 2 July to celebrate the Visitation of the Virgin Mary to Elizabeth [15thC. Shortening of *the Visitation of Our Lady*.]

visiting card *n.* a small card bearing the name and sometimes the address of a person, presented, especially in former times, when visiting or left behind when calling and finding sb out. US term **calling card**

visiting fireman *n.* *US* an important visitor who is entertained lavishly and impressively

visiting hours *npl.* the period of time during which patients in a hospital may have visitors

visiting professor *n.* a professor from one university who teaches at another for a term or academic year

visitor /vízzitər/ *n.* **1.** SB VISITING sb who visits a person or place **2.** BIRDS MIGRATORY BIRD APPEARING TEMPORARILY a migratory bird that regularly spends a short time in a place

visitor centre *n.* a building offering information and services to visitors in a city or at a historical or archaeological site, a park, or a nature reserve

visitorship /vízzitər ship/ *n.* the total number of tourists visiting a particular place [Late 20thC. Coined from VISITOR + -SHIP.]

visitor's passport *n.* a type of one-year British passport, phased out in 1995, that permitted the holder to visit certain countries for periods of up to three months (*dated*)

visive /vízziv/ *adj.* relating to vision (*archaic*)

visna /víssnə/ *n.* a chronic progressive pneumonia of sheep and goats [Mid-20thC. From Old Norse 'to wither'.]

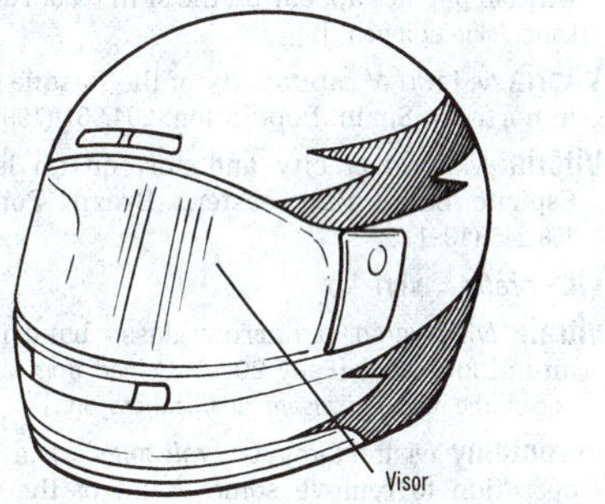

Visor

visor /vízər/, **vizor** *n.* **1.** TRANSPARENT FRONT OF HELMET a hinged front part of a helmet, made of transparent or tinted plastic and designed to protect the face or eyes, especially on helmets worn by motorcyclists or welders **2.** HIST FRONT OF MEDIEVAL HELMET a hinged metal front part of a medieval helmet in a suit of armour designed to protect the face and having slits for the eyes to see through **3.** EYESHADE a shade for the eyes attached to a band worn around the head **4.** *US* CLOTHES CAP PEAK the peak of a cap **5.** CARS FLAP OVER A WINDSCREEN FOR GLARE a flap mounted above the windscreen inside a car used to shield the eyes from glare [13thC. From Anglo-Norman *viser*, from French *vis* (see VISAGE).] —**visored** *adj.*

vista /vístə/ *n.* **1.** SCENIC VIEW a scenic or panoramic view **2.** VIEW THROUGH NARROW OPENING a view seen through a long narrow opening, e.g. between rows of trees or buildings **3.** MENTAL PICTURE a mental picture covering a wide range of objects or a long succession of events in the past or future ○ *open up vistas of expansion into hitherto untapped markets* [Mid-17thC. From Italian, 'view', from the past participle of *vedere* 'to see', from Latin *videre* (see VISIBLE).]

Vistula /vístyŏŏlə/ the longest river of Poland, flowing northwards from the Carpathian Mountains in the southwest of the country, through Cracow, Warsaw, and Torun, before emptying into the Baltic Sea at the Gulf of Gdansk. Length: 1,090 km/675 mi.

visual /vízhoo əl, vízzyoo-/ *adj.* **1.** OF VISION relating to vision or sight **2.** VISIBLE able or intended to be seen by the eyes, especially as opposed to being registered by one of the other senses or by a machine ○ *visual humour* **3.** OPTICAL of or relating to sight **4.** PERCEPTIBLE BY THE MIND'S EYE able to be perceived as a picture in the mind rather than as an abstract idea ○ *a visual memory* **5.** DONE BY SIGHT ONLY done by sight only and without the use of scientific instruments or equipment ○ *visual navigation* ■ *n.* PIECE OF ILLUSTRATIVE MATERIAL a photograph, picture, chart, or graph that displays information or promotional material in a way that appeals to the eye [15thC. From late Latin *visualis*, from Latin *visus* 'sight', from the past participle of *videre* (see VISIBLE).] —**visually** *adv.* —**visualness** *n.*

visual acuity *n.* acuteness of vision as determined by a comparison with the normal ability to identify letters at a distance of 6 m/20 ft

visual aid *n.* sth such as a model, chart, or film that is looked at as a complement to a lesson or presentation

visual arts *npl.* arts such as painting or sculpture that are perceived by sight

visual binary *n.* a star that can be seen to be a double star either with the naked eye or when viewed through a telescope

visual field *n.* = **field of vision**

visualization /vìzhoo ə lī záysh'n, vìzzyoo-/, **visualisation** *n.* **1.** CREATION OF MENTAL PICTURE the creation of a clear picture of sth in the mind **2.** MENTAL PICTURE a clear picture of sth created in the mind **3.** PSYCHOL CREATION OF POSITIVE MENTAL PICTURE a technique whereby sb creates a vivid positive mental picture of sth such as a desired outcome to a problem, in order to promote a sense of well-being **4.** MED PRODUCTION OF IMAGE OF INTERNAL ORGAN a technique used to produce an image of an internal organ or other part of the body by using X-rays or other means such as magnetic resonance imaging

visualize /vízhoo ə līz, vízzyoo-/ (**-izes, -izing, -ized**), **visualise** (**-ises, -ising, -ised**) *v.* **1.** *vti.* IMAGINE to form a visual image of sth in the mind **2.** *vti.* PSYCHOL CREATE POSITIVE MENTAL PICTURE to create a vivid positive mental picture of sth such as a desired outcome to a problem, in order to promote a sense of well-being **3.** *vt.* MED MAKE IMAGE OF INTERNAL ORGANS to produce an image of an internal organ or other part of the body by using X-rays or other means such as magnetic resonance imaging —**visualizer** *n.*

visually impaired *adj.* having reduced vision, especially having eyesight so poor that it interferes with the ability to perform day-to-day activities effectively

visual-motor coordination *n.* the coordination of the body's visual and motor systems, as shown, e.g. in reaching for sth being looked at

visual purple *n.* = **rhodopsin**

visuomotor /vízhoo ō mṓtər, vízzyoo-/ *adj.* relating to or involving motor processes that are linked to vision, e.g. the coordination of movements

vital /vít'l/ *adj.* **1.** CRUCIAL extremely important and necessary, or indispensable to the survival or continuing effectiveness of sth **2.** LIVELY full of animation or vigour **3.** OF LIFE relating to life **4.** NEEDED FOR LIFE required for the continuation of life [14thC. From, ultimately, Latin *vitalis*, from *vita* 'life'.] —**vitalness** *n.*

WORD KEY: SYNONYMS

See Synonyms at ***necessary***.

vital capacity *n.* a measure of the air that can be exhaled from the lungs after maximum inhalation

vitalise *vt.* = **vitalize**

vitalism /vítəlìzəm/ *n.* a doctrine that maintains that life and the functions of a living organism depend on a nonmaterial force or principle separate from physical and chemical processes. ◊ **dynamism, mechanism** —**vitalistic** /vítə lístik/ *adj.* —**vitalistically** *adv.*

vitality /vī tálləti/ *n.* **1.** LIVELINESS abundant physical and mental energy usually combined with a wholehearted and joyous approach to situations and activities **2.** DURABILITY the ability of sth to live and grow or to continue in existence **3.** VITAL PRINCIPLE the nonmaterial force that, according to vitalism, distinguishes the living from the nonliving

vitalize /vítə līz/ (**-izes, -izing, -ized**), **vitalise** (**-talises, -talising, -talised**) *vt.* **1.** GIVE SB OR STH LIFE to cause sb or sth to live **2.** ENERGIZE SB OR STH to make sb or sth lively —**vitalization** /vítə lī záysh'n/ *n.* —**vitalizer** /vítə līzər/ *n.*

vitally /vítəli/ *adv.* extremely or indispensably [Late 17thC]

vitals /vít'lz/ *npl.* **1.** ORGANS ESSENTIAL TO LIFE the internal organs of the body that are essential to life, especially the stomach and intestines **2.** **GENITALS** the genitals, especially those of a man (*humorous*) **3.** **ESSENTIALS** the essential parts of sth [Early 17thC. From Latin *vitalia*, literally 'vital things', from a form of *vitalis* (see VITAL).]

vital signs *npl.* the signs that indicate life, namely pulse, body temperature, breathing, and blood pressure

vital staining *n.* the process of using a substance that colours only live cells in order to study the fate of certain cells in embryonic development

vital statistics *npl.* **1.** **STATISTICS ABOUT HUMAN LIFE** statistics of human births, deaths, marriages, and health **2.** **BODY MEASUREMENTS** the measurements of a woman's bust, waist, and hips (*dated informal; considered offensive by many people*)

vitamin /víttəmin, vítə-/ *n.* **1.** **ORGANIC SUBSTANCE ESSENTIAL TO NUTRITION** any of various organic substances essential in small quantities to the nutrition and normal metabolism of most animals. Vitamins are found in minute quantities in food, in some cases are produced by the body, and are also produced synthetically. **2.** **VITAMIN PILL** a vitamin in a pill or capsule form [Early 20thC. From German *Vitamine*, from Latin *vita* 'life' + AMINE. From the former belief that vitamins contained amino acids.] —**vitaminic** /víttə mínnik, vítə-/ *adj.*

vitamin A *n.* a fat-soluble vitamin found in green and yellow vegetables and animal products such as egg yolk and milk. Vitamin A is important to the health of the outer layer of cells in the skin and organs. A deficiency leads to roughening of the skin and night blindness.

vitamin A_2 *n.* a type of vitamin A obtained from fish liver

vitamin B *n.* **1.** = **vitamin B complex** **2.** = **thiamine**

vitamin B_1 *n.* = **thiamine**

vitamin B_2 *n.* = **riboflavin**

vitamin B_6 *n.* = **pyridoxine**

vitamin B_{12} *n.* a complex water-soluble vitamin obtained from liver, milk, eggs, fish, oysters, and clams that is important to growth, normal blood formation, and neural function. A deficiency of it causes pernicious anaemia.

vitamin B complex *n.* a group of water-soluble vitamins found in yeast, seed germs, eggs, liver, and vegetables

vitamin C *n.* a water-soluble vitamin found in fruits and leafy vegetables or made synthetically and used as an antioxidant. Lack of this vitamin causes scurvy.

vitamin D *n.* any of several fat-soluble vitamins that occur in fish-liver oils and are often added to milk. They are essential for the formation of bones and teeth. Lack of vitamin D causes rickets.

vitamin D_2 *n.* a dietary supplement used in the treatment of rickets, prepared by the ultraviolet irradiation of ergosterol. Formula: $C_{28}H_{43}OH$.

vitamin D_3 *n.* a form of vitamin D that occurs in fish-liver oils and has a slightly different molecular structure from vitamin D_2

vitamin E *n.* a pale yellow viscous fluid occurring in vegetable oils, butter, eggs, and cereal grains that is important for fertility in humans and as an antioxidant

vitamin G *n.* US = **riboflavin**

vitamin H *n.* *US* = **biotin**

vitamin K *n.* any of three fat-soluble vitamins essential for the clotting of blood

vitamin K_1 *n.* a yellowish oily liquid that is found in leafy vegetables, rice, bran, and pork liver and is essential for the clotting of blood

vitamin K_2 *n.* a form of vitamin K that is found in fish meal

vitamin P *n.* = **bioflavonoid**

vitellarium /vítə láiri əm/ *n.* (*plural* **-a** /-ri ə/ *or* **-ums**) *n.* the part of the ovary in some invertebrates that produces yolk-filled cells providing nourishment to the developing eggs

vitellin /vi téllin/ *n.* a protein found in the yolk of eggs

vitelline /vi tél īn, -téllin/ *adj.* **1.** **OF EGG YOLK** relating to egg yolk **2.** **YELLOW** of a yellow colour, like an egg yolk [From medieval Latin *vitellinus*, from Latin *vitellus* (see VITELLUS)]

vitelline membrane *n.* the membrane that encloses a fertilized egg

vitellus /vi télləss/ (*plural* **-luses** *or* **-li** /-lī/) *n.* the yolk of an egg [Early 18thC. From Latin, 'yolk of an egg', of uncertain origin: probably literally 'small calf', from *vitulus* 'calf' (source of English *veal*).]

vitiate /víshi ayt/ (**-ates, -ating, -ated**) *vt.* **1.** **MAKE STH INEFFECTIVE** to destroy or drastically reduce the effectiveness of sth, or make it invalid **2.** **MAKE STH DEFECTIVE** to cause sth to become defective **3.** **DEBASE STH** to degrade sth morally [Mid-16thC. From, ultimately, Latin *vitiare*, from *vitium* 'fault' (see VICE[1]).] —**vitiable** *adj.* —**vitiation** /víshi áysh'n/ *n.* —**vitiator** /víshi aytər/ *n.*

viticulture /vítti kulchər/, **viniculture** /vínni kulchər/ *n.* the science or practice of growing grapevines, especially for wine making [Late 19thC. Coined from Latin *vitis* (see VICE[1]) + CULTURE.] —**viticultural** /vítti kúlchərəl/ *adj.* —**viticulturally** *adv.* —**viticulturist** *n.*

vitiligo /vítti lígō/ *n.* a skin disorder in which smooth whitish patches appear on the skin [Late 16thC. From Latin, 'skin eruption'.]

Vitoria /vi táwri ə/ capital city of the Basque Country in northern Spain. Population: 204,961 (1991).

Vitória /vi táwri ə/ city and port on an island in Espírito Santo Bay, eastern Brazil. Population: 258,245 (1991).

vitr- *prefix.* = **vitri-**

vitrain /vít trayn/ *n.* a narrow glassy band found in bituminous coal [Early 20thC. Coined from VITREOUS + *-ain* on the model of *fusain* 'charcoal crayon'.]

vitrectomy /vi tréktəmi/ (*plural* **-mies**) *n.* a surgical operation to remove some or all of the vitreous humour of the eye

vitreous /víttri əss/ *adj.* **1.** **SIMILAR TO GLASS** having the characteristics or appearance of glass **2.** **OF GLASS** relating to, consisting of, or derived from glass **3.** **OF VITREOUS HUMOUR** relating to the vitreous humour of the eye [Mid-17thC. From Latin *vitreus*, from *vitrum* 'glass', of uncertain origin: perhaps related to *vitrum* 'woad', from the bluish-green colour of glass.] —**vitreosity** /víttri óssəti/ *n.* —**vitreousness** /víttri əsnəss/ *n.*

vitreous body *n.* the transparent gel that fills the main cavity of the eyeball, between the lens and the retina

vitreous enamel *n.* an opaque glassy coating applied to steel or other metals through firing

vitreous humour *n.* the fluid component of the gel (**vitreous body**) that fills the main cavity of the eye between the lens and retina

vitreous silica *n.* a type of glass made solely from silica

vitrescent /vi tréss'nt/ *adj.* capable of being made into glass [Mid-18thC. Coined from Latin *vitrum* (see VITREOUS) + -ESCENT.]

vitri- *prefix.* glass ○ *vitrify* [From Latin *vitrum*]

vitric /víttrik/ *adj.* having the characteristics or appearance of glass [Early 20thC. Coined from Latin *vitrum* (see VITREOUS) + -IC.]

vitrification /víttrifi káysh'n/ *n.* **1.** **CONVERSION INTO GLASS** the process of converting materials to glass **2.** CERAMICS **POINT WHERE FIRED POT LOSES POROSITY** the point at which a pot loses its porosity during a firing

vitriform /víttri fawrm/ *adj.* having the form or appearance of glass [Late 18thC. Coined from Latin *vitrum* (see VITREOUS) + -FORM.]

vitrify /víttri fī/ (**-fies, -fying, -fied**) *vti.* to become changed into glass, or to change materials into glass [Late 16thC. From French *vitrifier* or directly from Latin *vitrum* (see VITREOUS).] —**vitrifiability** /víttri fī ə bílləti/ *n.* —**vitrifiable** *adj.*

vitrine /víttreen/ *n.* a cabinet or case with glass walls for displaying specimens or art objects [Late 19thC. From French, from *vitre* 'glass', from Latin *vitrum* (see VITREOUS).]

vitriol /víttri əl/ *n.* **1.** **BITTER HATRED** extreme bitterness and hatred towards sb or sth, or an expression of this feeling in speech or writing **2.** CHEM **GLASSY METALLIC SULPHATE** a glassy metallic sulphate such as copper sulphate or iron sulphate **3.** CHEM **SULPHURIC ACID** sulphuric acid (*archaic*) [14thC. From, ultimately, medieval Latin *vitriolum*, from Latin *vitrum* 'glass' (see VITREOUS). From its glassy appearance.]

vitriolic /víttri óllik/ *adj.* **1.** **EXPRESSING BITTER HATRED** filled with or expressing violent and bitter hatred towards sb or sth **2.** **LIKE METALLIC SULPHATE** resembling a glassy metallic sulphate —**vitriolically** *adv.*

Vitruvius /vi troóvi əss/ (*fl.* 1st century BC) Roman architect and engineer. His book *De Architectura* provides valuable information about architecture and engineering in classical times. Full name **Marcus Vitruvius Pollio**

vitta /víttə/ (*plural* **-tae** /-tee/) *n.* **1.** BOT **OIL-CONTAINING TUBE IN PLANT** a tube or cavity containing oil in the carpels of the family of plants that includes carrot, parsley, and celery **2.** ZOOL **COLOURED STRIPE ON ANIMAL'S BODY** a stripe or band of colour on the body of an animal [Late 17thC. From Latin, 'headband', originally 'sth that twists'.] —**vittate** /víttayt/ *adj.*

vittles /vítt'lz/ *npl.* food or other provisions (*archaic or humorous*) [Variant of VICTUAL]

vituline /víttyoo līn, -lin/ *adj.* relating to or resembling a calf or veal [Mid-17thC. From Latin *vitulinus*, from *vitulus* 'calf' (source of English *veal*).]

vituperate /vī tyóopə rayt, vi-/ (**-ates, -ating, -ated**) *vti.* to attack sb in harshly abusive or critical language [Mid-16thC. From, ultimately, Latin *vituperare*, from *vitium* (see VICE[1]) + *parare* (see PREPARE).] —**vituperator** *n.* —**vituperatory** /vī tyóopərətəri, vi-/ *adj.*

vituperation /vī tyóopə ráysh'n, vi-/ *n.* **1.** **OUTBURST OF ABUSE** an outburst of violently abusive or harshly critical language **2.** **ACT OF VITUPERATING** the use of violent abuse or extremely harsh criticism —**vituperative** /vī tyóopərətiv, vi-/ *adj.*

viva[1] /veévə/ *interj.* used to express support for sb whose success or life is hoped will continue ○ *Viva the president!* [Mid-17thC. From Italian, 'may he, she, or it live', a present subjunctive form of *vivere* 'to live', from Latin (see VIVID).]

viva[2] /vívə/ *n.* **ORAL EXAMINATION** an examination, especially one taken as part of a university degree, in which a student is asked and answers questions in a spoken interview rather than on paper ■ *vt.* (**-vas, -vaing, -vaed**) **EXAMINE SB ORALLY** to examine a student orally [Late 19thC. Shortening of VIVA VOCE.]

vivace /vi vaáchi/ *adv.* **IN A LIVELY WAY** in a lively and spirited manner (*used as a musical direction*) ■ *n.* **VIVACE PIECE OF MUSIC** a piece of music, or a section of a piece, played vivace [Late 17thC. From Italian, 'lively', from the Latin stem *vivac-* (see VIVACIOUS).] —**vivace** *adj.*

vivacious /vi váyshəss/ *adj.* exhibiting or characterized by liveliness and high-spiritedness [Mid-17thC. From the Latin stem *vivac-* 'lively, long-lived', from *vivus* (see VIVID).] —**vivaciously** *adv.* —**vivaciousness** *n.*

vivacity /vi vássəti/ *n.* liveliness and high-spiritedness

Vivaldi /vi váldi/, **Antonio** (1678–1741) Italian composer. His music epitomizes the Italian baroque style, his concertos being particularly influential on later composers. Full name **Antonio Lucio Vivaldi**

vivandière /vé voN dyáir/ *n.* in former times, a woman who followed an army and sold food and drink to the soldiers [Late 16thC. From French, feminine of *vivandier*, from, ultimately, late Latin *vivenda* (see VIAND).]

vivarium /vī vάiri əm/ (*plural* **-a** /-ri ə/ *or* **-ums**) *n.* a transparent enclosure in which small animals are kept so that their behaviour can be studied [Early 17thC. From Latin, 'game preserve, fish-pond', from a form of *vivarius* 'of living things', from *vivus* (see VIVID).]

viva voce /vívə vóchi/ *n.* = **viva**[2] *n.* ■ *adv.* **ORALLY** by word of mouth [Mid-16thC. From medieval Latin, literally 'with the living voice'.]

vivax malaria /ví vaks-/, **vivax** *n.* a form of malaria marked by convulsions that occur every 48 hours and that is caused by the parasite *Plasmodium vivax*

viverrid /vɪˈvérrid/ *n.* a civet, mongoose, or other similar small carnivorous mammal with a long slender body. Family: Viverridae. [Early 20thC. From modern Latin *Viverridae* (plural), from the genus name *Viverra* (singular), from Latin, 'ferret'.] —**viverrid** *adj.*

vivid /vívvid/ *adj.* **1.** VERY BRIGHT strikingly bright or intense in colour **2.** EXTREMELY CLEAR AND FRESH characterized by striking clarity, distinctness, or truth to life when perceived either by the eye or the mind ○ *a vivid image* **3.** GRAPHIC producing strong and distinct mental images **4.** INVENTIVE active and inventive ○ *a vivid imagination* **5.** LIVELY characterized by spirit and animation [Mid-17thC. From Latin *vividus*, from *vivere* 'to live'.] —**vividly** *adv.* —**vividness** *n.*

vivify /vívvi fī/ (**-fies, -fying, -fied**) *vt.* **1.** GIVE LIFE TO SB OR STH to cause sb or sth to come to life **2.** GIVE LIVELINESS TO to give liveliness or vividness to sth [14thC. Via French *vivifier* from late Latin *vivificare*, literally 'to make alive', from *vivus* (see VIVID).] —**vivification** /vívvifi káysh'n/ *n.* —**vivifier** /vívvi fī ər/ *n.*

viviparous /vi víppərəss/ *adj.* **1.** ZOOL BEARING LIVE YOUNG bearing live young rather than eggs **2.** BOT PRODUCING PLANTLETS used to describe a plant, e.g. the spider plant, that produces plantlets or bulbils from the flower stem **3.** BOT PRODUCING SEEDLINGS ON PLANT used to describe a plant, e.g. a mangrove, with seeds that germinate and develop into seedlings before being shed from the parent plant [Mid-17thC. Formed from Latin *viviparus*, literally 'bringing forth alive', from *vivus* (see VIVID).] —**viviparously** *adv.* —**viviparousness** *n.*

vivisect /vívvi sekt/ (**-sects, -secting, -sected**) *vti.* to perform operations on living animals that involve cutting into their bodies in order to gain knowledge of pathological or physiological processes [Mid-19thC. Back-formation from VIVISECTION.] —**vivesective** /vívvi sektiv, -séktiv/ *adj.* —**vivisector** /-sektər/ *n.*

vivisection /vívvi séksh'n/ *n.* the practice of operating on living animals in order to gain knowledge of pathological or physiological processes [Early 18thC. From Latin *vivus* (see VIVID) + SECTION on the model of DISSECTION.] —**vivisectional** *adj.* —**vivisectionally** *adv.* —**vivisectionist** *n.*

vivisectorium /vívvi sek táwri əm/ *n.* (*plural* **-ums** *or* **-a** /-táwri ə/) *n.* an establishment where vivisection is practised [Late 20thC. Coined from VIVISECTION + Latin *-orium*, neuter of *-orius* '-ory', on the model of EMPORIUM.]

vivo /véevō/ *adv.* in a lively and energetic manner (*used as a musical direction*) [Mid-18thC. Via Italian from Latin *vivus* 'alive'.]

vixen /víks'n/ *n.* **1.** ZOOL FEMALE FOX a female fox **2.** OFFENSIVE TERM an offensive term that deliberately insults a woman regarded as vindictive and bad-tempered (*dated informal offensive*) [15thC. Dialect variant of earlier *fixen*, from Old English *fyxe*, feminine of *fox* (see FOX).] —**vixenish** *adj.* —**vixenishly** *adv.* —**vixenishness** *n.* —**vixenly** *adj., adv.*

Viyella /vī éllə/ *tdmk.* a trademark for a lightweight woollen fabric, typically used for making blouses and shirts

viz /viz/ *adv.* namely. Abbr of **vide licet** [From Latin *videlicet*, literally 'it is permitted to see' (because it is used to introduce lists), from *vide-*, the stem of *videre* 'to see' + *licet* 'it is permitted']

vizard /vízzərd/ *n.* a mask or other form of disguise for the face (*archaic*) [Mid-16thC. Variant of VISOR by folk etymology from words ending in -ARD.] —**vizarded** *adj.*

vizcacha *n.* = viscacha

vizier /vi zéer/ *n.* a high-ranking government officer in various Islamic countries and especially in the former Ottoman empire [Mid-16thC. Via French or Spanish *visir* from Turkish *vezir*, from Arabic *wazīr* 'vizier', earlier 'helper, assistant'.] —**vizierate** *n.* —**vizierial** *adj.* —**viziership** *n.*

vizor *n.* = visor

vizsla /vízhlə/ *n.* a medium-sized hunting dog of a Hungarian breed with a short, smooth, reddish coat [Mid-20thC. Origin uncertain: perhaps named after *Vizsla*, town in Hungary, from the breed's Hungarian origin.]

VJ *abbr.* video jockey

V-J day *n.* 15 August 1945, the day of the Japanese surrender in World War II

Vizsla

vl *abbr.* a variant reading [From Latin *varia lectio*]

VL *abbr.* Vulgar Latin

Vlach /vlaak/ *n.* **1.** PEOPLES MEMBER OF BALKAN PEOPLE a member of a people of southeastern Europe who in the 13th century established the principalities of Wallachia and later Moldavia. These later merged to become Romania. Vlachs now live mainly in the mountainous regions of the Balkans, e.g. in northern Greece, Macedonia, or Albania. **2.** LANG ROMANCE DIALECT any of the languages of the Romance family that are spoken in southeastern Europe, particularly those of the traditionally nomadic Vlachs of northern Greece and Albania [Mid-19thC. From Bulgarian and Serbo-Croat, from, ultimately, a prehistoric Germanic word meaning 'foreign'.] —**Vlach** *adj.*

Vladimir /vláddi meer, vlə deé meer/ city and capital of Vladimir Oblast in western Russia. Population: 353,000 (1990).

Vladivostok /vláddi vóstok/ city and major port in southeastern Russia, on Golden Horn Bay, an inlet of the Sea of Japan. It is the eastern terminus of the Trans-Siberian Railway. Population: 648,000 (1991).

VLCC *abbr.* INDUST very large crude carrier

vlei /flay, vlay/ (*plural* **vleis**) *n.* S Africa a stretch of low-lying ground that is either permanently marshy or is flooded in the rainy season to form a shallow lake [Late 18thC. Via Afrikaans from Dutch *wallei* 'valley'.]

VLF, **vlf** *abbr.* RADIO very low frequency

VN *abbr.* Vietnam (*international vehicle registration*)

V neck *n.* **1.** V-SHAPED NECKLINE a neckline shaped like a letter 'V' (*hyphenated when used before a noun*) **2.** GARMENT WITH V-SHAPED NECKLINE a garment, especially a sweater or T-shirt, with a v-shaped neckline —**V-necked** *adj.*

VO *abbr.* **1.** verbal order **2.** Royal Victorian Order **3.** very old (*used on labels for bottles of brandy, whisky, or port*) **4.** voice-over

vo. *abbr.* verso

VOC *abbr.* volatile organic compound

voc. *abbr.* vocative

vocab /vô kab/ *n.* vocabulary (*informal*) [Early 20thC. Shortening.]

vocable /vôkəb'l/ *n.* WORD AS MERELY SOUNDS OR LETTERS a single word considered only as a grouping of sounds or letters, not in terms of its meaning (*dated formal*) ■ *adj.* CAPABLE OF BEING SPOKEN capable of being pronounced or spoken (*formal*) [Mid-16thC. Directly or via French from Latin *vocabulum* 'name', from *vocare* 'to call, name' (source of English *vouch*, *advocate*, and *provoke*).] —**vocably** *adv.*

vocabular /vô kábbyooˈlər/ *adj.* relating to words [Early 17thC. Formed from Latin *vocabulum* (see VOCABLE).]

vocabulary /vô kábbyooˈləri/ (*plural* **-ies**) *n.* **1.** LANG WORDS KNOWN all the words used by or known to a particular person or group, or contained in a language as a whole **2.** LANG LIST OF WORDS an alphabetical list of words and phrases supplied with definitions or translations **3.** ARTS RANGE OF EXPRESSIVE TECHNIQUES a repertoire of expressive forms or techniques used by an artist or in a particular art form [Mid-16thC. From medieval Latin *vocabularium*, literally 'of words', from Latin *vocabulum* (see VOCABLE).]

vocal /vôk'l/ *adj.* **1.** UTTERED uttered with the voice **2.** OF THE VOICE relating to the voice **3.** HAVING VOICE having a voice or using a voice to produce speech or sound **4.** OUTSPOKEN using frank, forthright, or insistent speech **5.** MUSIC OF OR FOR SINGING composed or arranged for singing, or relating to the art or techniques of singing **6.** NOISY WITH VOICES full of the sound of voices **7.** PHON = vocalic ■ *n.* MUSIC **1.** SUNG PART the sung part of a piece of pop music or jazz **2.** POP OR JAZZ SONG a song in the pop or jazz style [14thC. From Latin *vocalis*, from the stem of *vox* 'voice' (source of English *voice*, *vowel*, and *equivocal*).] —**vocality** /vō kálləti/ *n.* —**vocally** /vôk'li/ *adv.* —**vocalness** /vôk'lnəss/ *n.*

vocal cords, **vocal chords** *npl.* a pair of fibrous sheets of tissue that span the cavity of the voice box (**larynx**) and produce sounds by vibrating. Muscles tighten the cords, narrowing the gap between them, and as air is expelled from the lungs they vibrate.

vocal folds *npl.* a pair of folds in the wall of the voice box (**larynx**) situated just above the vocal cords. They are not involved in producing sound.

vocalic /vō kállik/, **vocal** *adj.* PHON **1.** RELATING TO VOWELS relating to or containing vowels **2.** ACTING AS VOWEL used or acting as a vowel —**vocalically** *adv.*

vocalise[1] *vti.* = vocalize

vocalise[2] /vôkə lees/ *n.* **1.** SINGING EXERCISE a voice training exercise in which a singer sings using only vowel sounds, especially one single vowel sound **2.** VOCAL COMPOSITION USING ONLY VOWEL SOUNDS a passage or composition for performance in which a singer sings only vowel sounds, especially one single vowel sound [Late 19thC. From French, from *vocaliser* 'to vocalize'.]

vocalism /vôkəlizəm/ *n.* **1.** USE OF VOICE the use of the voice in producing speech, singing, or other sounds **2.** MUSIC ART OF SINGING the art or technique of singing **3.** PHON VOWELS OF A LANGUAGE the range of vowels used in a specific language **4.** PHON VOWEL a vowel sound

vocalist /vôkəlist/ *n.* a singer, especially of pop music or jazz —**vocalistic** /vôkə lístik/ *adj.*

vocalize /vôkə līz/ (**-izes, -izing, -ized**), **vocalise** (**-ises, -ising, -ised**) *v.* **1.** *vti.* EXPRESS to use the voice to express sth **2.** *vti.* PHON TRANSFORM INTO A VOWEL to transform a consonant into a vowel sound in speaking, or to be transformed into a vowel. *vt.* PHON = voice *v.* **3** **4.** *vt.* = vowelize **5.** *vi.* MUSIC SING WITHOUT WORDS to sing without words, using only one or more vowel sounds, especially as a vocal exercise to warm up the voice —**vocalization** /vôkə līˈzáysh'n/ *n.* —**vocalizer** /-līzər/ *n.*

vocal score *n.* the score of a vocal work, especially an opera, that gives the vocal parts in full with the orchestral parts transcribed for piano

vocal tic *n.* a sudden noise or shout produced involuntarily, especially as a symptom of Tourette's syndrome or a similar neurological condition

vocat. *abbr.* vocative

vocation /vō káysh'n/ *n.* **1.** SB'S JOB sb's work, job, or profession, especially a type of work demanding special commitment **2.** URGE TO FOLLOW A PARTICULAR CAREER a strong feeling of being destined or called to undertake a particular type of work, especially a sense of being chosen by God for religious work or a religious life [15thC. From, ultimately, the Latin stem *vocation-*, from *vocat-*, the past participle stem of *vocare* (see VOCABLE).]

vocational /vō káysh'nəl/ *adj.* **1.** RELATING TO JOB OR CAREER SKILLS relating to education designed to provide the necessary skills for a particular job or career **2.** OF SB'S VOCATION relating to sb's vocation —**vocationally** *adv.*

vocational guidance *n.* guidance in the form of interviews and tests to see which job or career would best suit sb's individual abilities and personality

vocative /vókətiv/ *adj.* **INDICATING SB OR STH ADDRESSED** used to describe a grammatical case or a form of a word that indicates that sb or sth is being directly addressed by the speaker. In Julius Caesar's dying words 'et tu, Brute', 'Brute' is the vocative form of the name 'Brutus'. ■ *n.* **1. VOCATIVE CASE** the vocative case (*informal*) **2. WORD IN THE VOCATIVE** a word or form in the vocative case [15thC. From, ultimately, Latin *vocativus*, from the stem *vocat-* (see VOCATION).] —**vocatively** *adv.*

vociferate /vō síffə rayt/ (**-ates, -ating, -ated**) *vti.* to shout sth out loudly [Late 16thC. From, ultimately, Latin *vociferari*, literally 'to carry voice', from the stem *voc-* (see VOCAL) + *ferre* (see -FER).] —**vociferation** /vō síffə ráysh'n/ *n.* —**vociferator** /-raytər/ *n.* —**vociferant** *adj.*

vociferous /vō síffərəss/ *adj.* **1. SHOUTING NOISILY** shouting in a noisy and determined way **2. FULL OF NOISY SHOUTING** characterized by noisy and determined shouting [Early 17thC. Coined from Latin *vociferari* (see VOCIFERATE) + -OUS.] —**vociferously** *adv.* —**vociferousness** *n.*

vocoder /vō kṓdər/ *n.* an electronic device or computer program that converts speech into digital form and resynthesizes it at a later time or after transmission as artificial speech. Originally developed to encode speech signals for more efficient electronic transmission, vocoders are now used in audio response units and voice recognition systems. [Mid-20thC. Coined from VOICE + CODE + -ER.]

Vodafone /vṓdəfōn/ *tdmk.* a trademark for a type of cellular telephone

vodka /vódkə/ *n.* a colourless distilled spirit originally from Russia that is made from a grain such as rye or wheat or from potatoes [Early 19thC. From Russian, literally 'small water', from *voda* 'water'. From the belief that vodka is as essential to life as water.]

vodoun /vō do͞on/, **vodun** *n.* = **voodoo** *n.* **1** [Late 19thC. From Fon *vodū* (see VOODOO).]

voe /vō/ *n.* in Orkney or Shetland, a small bay (*regional*) [Late 17thC. From Norwegian *våg* and Icelandic *vogur* 'bay, inlet'.]

voetsak /fo͝ot sak, vo͝ot-/ *interj. S Africa* used to tell sb to go away or to express disbelief (*slang*) [Mid-19thC. From Afrikaans *voertsek*, from Dutch *voort zeg ik* 'be off, I say'.]

voetstoots /fo͝ot stoots, vo͝ot-/ *adv. S Africa* with the seller having no responsibility for any defects in the item sold or for any other problems arising from the sale [Late 20thC. From Afrikaans.] —**voetstoots** *adj.*

Vogel /vṓg'l/, **Sir Julius** (1835–99) British-born New Zealand statesman and journalist. Twice prime minister of New Zealand (1873–75 and 1876), he also founded New Zealand's first daily newspaper, the *Otago Daily Times* (1861).

vogue[1] /vōg/ *n.* **1. PREVAILING FASHION** the prevailing fashion at a particular time **2. POPULARITY** the state of being widely popular and fashionable at a particular time ○ *in vogue* ■ *adj.* **FASHIONABLE** currently popular or fashionable [Late 16thC. From French, literally 'rowing', hence 'smooth, fashionable course', from *voguer* 'to row', of uncertain origin: probably from assumed Old Low German *wogon* 'to float'.]

vogue[2] /vōg/ (**vogues, voguing** *or* **vogueing, vogued**) *vi.* DANCE to dance to music imitating the poses struck by fashion models [Late 20thC. Named after *Vogue*, a fashion magazine.] —**voguing** *n.*

voguish /vṓgish/ *adj.* **1. STYLISH** elegantly fashionable and stylish in appearance **2. BRIEFLY POPULAR** enjoying brief or sudden popularity —**voguishly** *adv.* —**voguishness** *n.*

Vogul /vṓgo͝ol/ (*plural* **-gul** *or* **-guls**) *n.* PEOPLES a member of a people from the regions around the western tributaries of the River Ob and the central and northern Ural mountains in Russia [Late 18thC. From Russian *vogul.*]

voice /voyss/ *n.* **1. SOUND MADE USING VOCAL ORGANS** the sound produced by using the vocal organs, especially the sound used in speech **2.** MUSIC **SOUND OF SINGING** the musical sound produced in singing **3. ABILITY TO USE VOICE** the ability to produce vocal sounds for speaking or singing ○ *have a good voice* **4. SOUND LIKE HUMAN VOICE** a sound similar to a human voice ○ *listen to the voice of the wind* **5. RIGHT TO STATE OPINION** a right to express an opinion ○ *sections of society that feel they have no voice* **6. EXPRESSED OPINION** an expressed opinion or desire ○ *hear the voice of the people* **7. REPRESENTATIVE EXPRESSION** a medium of communication or expression for sb or sth ○ *the voice of reason* **8.** MUSIC **SINGER** a singer taking a part in a musical composition **9.** MUSIC **SINGING PART** a sung part in a musical composition **10.** PHON **VIBRATION OF VOCAL CORDS IN SPEAKING** the passing of air across the vocal cords so as to create audible vibrations **11.** GRAM **FORM OF VERBS** the form of a verb that indicates the relation of the subject to the verb. In the active voice, the subject performs the action, as in 'I hit him', while in the passive voice the subject suffers the effect of the action, as in 'he was hit'. ■ *vt.* (**voices, voicing, voiced**) **1. UTTER STH** to express a sentiment or opinion verbally ○ *voice an opinion* **2.** MUSIC **REGULATE THE TONE OF AN ORGAN** to regulate the tone of an organ pipe in order to produce the desired sound **3.** PHON **PRONOUNCE STH USING THE VOCAL CORDS** to pronounce a consonant or vowel by passing air across the vocal cords so as to create audible vibrations [13thC. Via Old French *vois* from Latin *vox* (see VOCAL).] ◇ **be in (good) voice** to be singing well or speaking well ◇ **with one voice** simultaneously or unanimously

voice box *n.* = **larynx**

voiced /voyst/ *adj.* PHON used to describe a consonant or vowel pronounced by passing air across the vocal cords to create audible vibrations, as for the 's' sound in the word 'his' —**voicedness** *n.*

voiceful /vóysf'l/ *adj.* having a loud or ringing voice (*literary*) —**voicefulness** *n.*

voiceless /vóyssləss/ *adj.* **1. SAYING NOTHING** maintaining a silence **2. HAVING NO SAY** having no vote or influence **3. HAVING NO VOICE** not endowed with a voice **4.** PHON **PRONOUNCED WITHOUT VIBRATION OF VOCAL CORDS** used to describe a consonant or vowel pronounced without passing air across the vocal cords and creating audible vibrations, as in the 's' sound in the word 'hiss' —**voicelessly** *adv.* —**voicelessness** *n.*

voice mail *n.* an electronic communications system that stores digitized recordings of telephone messages for later playback (*hyphenated when used before a noun*)

voiceover /vóyss ōvər/ *n.* the voice of, or the words spoken by, an unseen narrator, commentator, or character in a film or television programme

voiceprint /vóyss print/ *n.* a representation in graph form of the frequencies that make up sb's voice. Each person's voiceprint is unique, and can be used to identify an individual. [Mid-20thC. From VOICE + FINGERPRINT.]

voicer /vóyssər/ *n.* **1. SB WHO VOICES** sb who voices sth such as an opinion or objection **2. SB WHO REGULATES TONE OF ORGAN** sb whose job is to regulate the tone of an organ pipe in order to produce the desired sound

voice recognition *n.* **1.** = **speech recognition 2. DETERMINING SPEAKER BY COMPUTER** a computer function that enables the machine to recognize a particular voice or voices speaking into a microphone attached to it. Like password verification, it is a means for determining the identity of sb trying to use a computer and controlling access to it.

voice vote *n.* a vote taken in a parliament or other legislative body in which voters cry out 'aye' or 'no', or 'yea' and 'nay', with the louder cry winning the vote

void /voyd/ *adj.* **1.** LAW **NOT LEGALLY VALID** having no legal force ○ *declared the will null and void* **2. POINTLESS** ineffective or useless **3. DEVOID** totally lacking in sth (*formal*) ○ *a personality void of all compassion* **4. NOT CONTAINING ANYTHING** having no contents **5. VACANT** having no incumbent, occupant, or holder **6.** CARDS **HAVING NO CARDS IN A SUIT** lacking any cards in a particular suit ■ *n.* **1. VACUUM** an empty space, especially a large empty space **2. PRIVATION** a state of loss or privation, or a feeling of loneliness and emptiness **3. GAP** a gap or opening **4.** CARDS **LACK OF CARDS IN A SUIT** a complete lack of cards in a particular suit ○ *a void in spades* ■ *v.* (**voids, voiding, voided**) **1.** *vt.* LAW **MAKE STH LEGALLY INVALID** to deprive sth of legal force **2.** *vt.* **EMPTY CONTENTS OF STH** to empty out the contents of sth or empty sth of its contents **3.** *vti.* **EMPTY BOWELS OR BLADDER** to empty the bowels or bladder [13thC. From Old French *voide* 'empty', ultimately from assumed Vulgar Latin *vocitus*, alteration of Latin *vocivus*.] —**voider** *n.* —**voidness** *n.*

WORD KEY: SYNONYMS

See Synonyms at ***vacant***.

voidable /vóydəb'l/ *adj.* capable of being deprived of legal force —**voidableness** *n.*

voidance /vóyd'nss/ *n.* **1.** LAW **INVALIDATION OF CONTRACT** the act of depriving a contract of legal force **2. ACT OF EMPTYING** the act of voiding or emptying sth **3. VACANCY** the situation of having no incumbent or occupant, e.g. no bishop in a diocese

void deck *n.* in Malaysia and Singapore, the empty ground floor of a block of flats, used for social events by people living in the block

voided /vóydid/ *adj.* in heraldry, having the centre and a narrow surrounding area removed or left empty

voilà /vwa láa/ *interj.* used to bring sb's attention to sth, especially in order to elicit appreciation or approval [Mid-18thC. From French, from *voi*, imperative of *voir* 'to see' + *là* 'there'.]

voile /voyl/ *n.* a crisp lightweight translucent fabric made from cotton, synthetic fibres, or wool [Late 19thC. From French, 'veil', from Latin *vela*, plural of *velum* (see VEIL).]

voir dire /vwaa déer/ *n.* the preliminary examination of a witness or juror to determine his or her competence to give or hear evidence [Late 17thC. From Law French, from Old French *voir* 'truth' + *dire* 'to speak'.]

voix céleste /vwaa sə lést/ *n.* an organ stop that gives a light wavering otherworldly quality to the notes played [Late 19thC. From French, from *voix* 'voice' + *céleste* 'heavenly'. From the belief that the tone produced resembled heavenly voices.]

vol. *abbr.* **1.** volcano **2.** volume **3.** volunteer

Volans /vṓ lanz/ *n.* a small constellation in the sky of the southern hemisphere between Carina and Hydrus, east of the Large Magellanic Cloud

volant /vṓlənt/ *adj.* **1.** HERALDRY **HAVING WINGS SPREAD** in heraldry, having the wings outspread as in flight **2. ABLE TO FLY** flying or having the power of flight **3. NIMBLE** moving quickly, lightly, and easily (*literary*) [Early 16thC. From French, present participle of *voler* 'to fly', from Latin *volare* (see VOLATILE).]

Volapük /vóllə pook, vṓlə-/ *n.* a language based on English and German, invented by Johann Martin Schleyer in 1880 [Late 19thC. From *vol*, alteration of WORLD, + *pük* 'speech', alteration of SPEAK.]

volar /vṓlər/ *adj.* relating to the palm of the hand or the sole of the foot [Early 19thC. Formed from *vola* 'hollow of the hand or foot', from Latin, 'sole, palm'.]

volatile /vóllə tīl/ *adj.* **1. CHANGING SUDDENLY** characterized by or prone to sudden change **2. UNSTABLE AND POTENTIALLY DANGEROUS** apt to become suddenly violent or dangerous **3. UNPREDICTABLE OR FICKLE** changeable in mood, temper, or desire **4.** CHEM **PRONE TO EVAPORATION** changing into a vapour at a relatively low temperature **5. SHORT-LIVED** continuing for only a short time **6.** COMPUT **LOSING DATA WHEN POWER IS OFF** used to describe a computer memory that does not store data when the power is turned off. Random access memory (**RAM**) is volatile, while read-only memory (**ROM**) is not. ■ *n.* CHEM **VOLATILE SUBSTANCE** a substance that changes into a vapour at a relatively low temperature [Late 16thC. From, ultimately, Latin *volatilis*, from *volat-*, past participle stem of *volare* 'to fly'.] —**volatileness** *n.* —**volatility** /vóllə tíllәti/ *n.*

volatile organic compound *n.* an organic compound, e.g. ethylene, propylene, benzene, or styrene, that changes into a vapour at a relatively low temperature and contributes to air pollution and ozone formation

volatilize /və látti līz/ (**-izes, -izing, -ized**), **volatilise** (**-ises, -ising, -ised**) *vti.* to change into a vapour or to cause a solid or liquid to be changed into a vapour —**volatilizable** *adj.* —**volatilization** /və látti ĺt záysh'n/ *n.* —**volatilizer** /və látti ĺĺzər/ *n.*

vol-au-vent /vólō voN/ *n.* a small light pastry shell filled with meat, fish, game, or fowl in a sauce and baked [From French, literally 'flight in the wind', probably from the lightness of the pastry]

volcanic /vol kánnik/ *adj.* **1.** OF VOLCANOES relating to or originating from a volcano **2.** GEOL CONSISTING OF VOLCANOES made up of or coming from volcanoes **3.** SUDDEN AND VIOLENT characterized by sudden violent outbursts —**volcanically** *adv.*

volcanic arc *n.* = island arc

volcanic bomb *n.* a lump of lava ejected from a volcano that has acquired a characteristic form as a result of its solidification while travelling through the air

volcanic cone *n.* a cone-shaped mass of material that has built up around the crater of a volcano

volcanic dust *n.* fine particles of ash that are suspended in the atmosphere after a volcanic eruption

volcanic glass *n.* natural glass formed when molten lava from a volcano cools too quickly to crystallize

volcanicity /vólkə níssəti/, **vulcanicity** /vúlkə níssəti/ *n.* the tendency or likelihood of a volcano or group of volcanoes to erupt [Mid-19thC. From French *volcanicité*, from *volcan* (see VOLCANO).]

volcanic plug, **volcanic neck** *n.* a massive cylindrical formation of solidified lava that once blocked the vent of a volcano, now exposed after erosion of softer surrounding material

volcanise *vt.* = volcanize

volcanism /vólkənizəm/, **vulcanism** /vúlkənizəm/ *n.* the processes involved in the formation of volcanoes, and in the transfer of magma and volatile material from the interior of the earth to its surface

volcanize /vólkə nīz/ (-**nizes**, -**nizing**, -**nized**), **volcanise** (-**nises**, -**nising**, -**nised**) *vt.* to cause sth to change as a result of volcanic activity —**volcanization** /vólkə nī záysh'n/ *n.*

volcano /vol káynō/ (*plural* -**noes** *or* -**nos**) *n.* **1.** OPENING

MAJOR VOLCANOES OF THE WORLD

Cotopaxi *Ecuador*
Elevation [19,347 ft / 5,897 m]
World's highest active volcano

Mauna Loa *Hawaii*
Elevation [13,680 ft / 4,170 m]
Major eruption 1984

Erebus *Antarctica*
Elevation [12,448 ft / 3,794 m]
Major eruptions 1970s

Cameroon *Cameroon*
Elevation [13,435 ft / 4,095 m]
Major eruption 1982

Etna *Italy*
Elevation [10,902 ft / 3,323 m]
Over 90 recorded eruptions

Ruapehu *New Zealand*
Elevation [9,177 ft / 2,797 m]
Major eruptions 1995, 1996

Saint Helens *United States*
Elevation [8,365 ft / 2,550 m]
Major eruption 1980

Vesuvius *Italy*
Elevation [4,190 ft / 1,277 m]
Major eruption 79 AD —
destroying Roman Pompeii

Soufriere Hills *Montserrat*
Elevation [3,002 ft / 915 m]
Major eruption 1997 —
much of island left uninhabitable

Krakatau *Indonesia*
Elevation [2,667 ft / 813 m]
Major eruption 1883 —
tidal waves from eruption estimated
to have caused over 30,000 deaths

IN EARTH'S CRUST a naturally occurring opening in the surface of the Earth through which molten, gaseous, and solid material is ejected **2.** MOUNTAIN a mountain created by the deposition and accumulation of materials ejected from a vent in a central crater [Early 17thC. Via Italian from Latin *Volcanus, Vulcanus* VULCAN, the Roman god of fire.] —**volcanian** *adj.*

—————— **WORD KEY: CULTURAL NOTE** ——————
Under the Volcano, a novel by English writer Malcolm Lowry (1947). Set in Mexico on the annual Day of the Dead, it describes the last hours of British consul Geoffrey Firman, who, depressed by the failure of his marriage and the onset of war, slowly drinks himself to death. A harrowing psychological study, it can also be read as an allegory of the disintegration of Western values.
————————————————————————

volcanology /vólkə nólləji/, **vulcanology** /vúlkə nólləji/ *n.* the scientific study of volcanoes, including their formation, signs of an eruption, and other aspects of volcanic activity —**volcanologic** /vólkənə lójjik/ *adj.* —**volcanological** *adj.* —**volcanologist** /vólkə nólləjist/ *n.*

Vole

vole[1] /vōl/ (*plural* **voles** *or* **vole**) *n.* a small rodent found mostly in North America and Eurasia, similar to mice and rats but with a shorter tail and legs and a stocky body. Genus: *Microtus*. [Early 19thC. Originally 'vole mouse', from Norwegian *voll mus* 'field mouse'.]

vole[2] /vōl/ *n.* a taking of all the tricks in a single hand in a card game such as bridge [Late 17thC. From French, probably from *voler* 'to fly', from Latin *volare* (source of English *volatile* and *volley*).]

Volga /vólgə/ the longest river in Europe, in western Russia. It rises northwest of Moscow and flows southeast and south and empties into the Caspian Sea. Length: 3,531 km/2,194 mi.

Volgograd /vólgə grad/ industrial and port city in southwestern Russia on the River Volga. It is an important rail junction and inland port. In World War II the city was subjected to a long siege by German forces that proved to be one of the turning points of the war. Population: 1,006,100 (1992). Former name **Stalingrad** (1925–61)

volitant /vóllitənt/ *adj.* **1.** ZOOL ABLE TO FLY flying or capable of flight **2.** MOVING QUICKLY moving about rapidly or constantly [Early 17thC. From Latin *volitare* 'to keep on flying', from *volare* 'to fly'.]

volitation /vólli táysh'n/ *n.* the act of flying or the ability to fly (*formal*) [Mid-17thC. From medieval Latin *volitation-*, the stem of *volitatio*, from *volitare*, literally 'to keep on flying', from *volare* 'to fly'.] —**volitational** *adj.*

volition /vō lísh'n/ *n.* **1.** CHOOSING the act of exercising the will **2.** ABILITY TO CHOOSE the ability to make conscious choices or decisions **3.** CHOICE MADE the result of exercising the will **4.** PHILOS ACT OF WILL an act of will distinguished from the intended physical movement it causes [Early 17thC. Directly or via French from Latin *volitio*, from *vol-* (see VOLUNTARY).] —**volitional** *adj.* —**volitionally** *adv.* —**volitionary** *adj.*

volitive /vóllitiv/ *adj.* **1.** OF THE WILL relating to or beginning in the will **2.** GRAM = desiderative [15thC. From medieval Latin *volitivus*, from the Latin stem *volition-* (see VOLITION).]

volk /folk/ *n.* S Africa a people or nation, especially the nation of Afrikaners [Late 19thC. Via Afrikaans from Dutch, 'nation, people'.]

Völkerwanderung /fólkər vaándərōong, fólkər-/ *n.* a movement of peoples, especially the migration of Germanic and Slavic peoples into southern and western Europe from the 2nd to 11th centuries [Mid-20thC. From German, literally 'migration of nations'.]

Volkslied /fólks leed/ (*plural* -**lieder** /-leedər/) *n.* a traditional German folk song [Mid-19thC. From German, literally 'people's song'.]

volley /vólli/ *n.* **1.** ARMS FIRING OF WEAPONS a simultaneous discharge of several weapons, especially firearms **2.** ARMS MISSILES FIRED a discharge of missiles or other projectiles fired simultaneously **3.** SIMULTANEOUS EXPRESSION OF STH a simultaneous rapid expression of sth, e.g. curses or protests **4.** SPORTS SWING AT A BALL a swing, kick, or hit at a ball, e.g. in tennis or football, before it touches the ground or court **5.** CRICKET BALL the flight of a ball or the ball itself **6.** MINING ROCK BLASTING a simultaneous explosion of several blastings of rock ■ *v.* (-**leys**, -**leying**, -**leyed**) **1.** *vti.* SPORTS STRIKE A BALL BEFORE IT LANDS to hit or kick a ball before it reaches the ground, e.g. in tennis or football **2.** *vti.* ARMS FIRE SIMULTANEOUSLY to fire weapons simultaneously **3.** *vti.* SAY RAPIDLY to say sth forcefully or loudly and rapidly, or to be spoken forcefully and rapidly **4.** *vi.* MOVE RAPIDLY to move or rush rapidly or loudly [Late 16thC. Via French *volée* from, ultimately, Latin *volare* 'to fly'.] —**volleyer** *n.*

Volleyball: Players jump to block a smash

volleyball /vólli bawl/ *n.* **1.** TEAM SPORT a sport played on a rectangular court, in which two teams can each use up to three hits to pass a large ball over a high net **2.** LARGE INFLATED BALL a large, usually white inflated ball used to play volleyball —**volleyballer** *n.*

volost /vó lost/ *n.* **1.** RURAL SOVIET a rural elected council in the former Soviet Union **2.** FORMER PEASANT COMMUNITY IN RUSSIA in tsarist Russia, a peasant community made up of several villages [Late 19thC. From Russian.]

volplane /vól playn/ *vi.* (**volplanes, volplaning, volplaned**) AIR **1.** GLIDE TO THE GROUND to glide towards the ground in an aeroplane with the engine turned off **2.** MOVE BY GLIDING to travel or move by gliding ■ *n.* AIR ACT OF GLIDING a glide towards the ground in an aircraft with the engine turned off [Early 20thC. From French *vol plané*, literally 'planed flight'.]

vols. *abbr.* volumes

Volsci /vólski/ *npl.* an ancient people who occupied lands in Latium, a region of central Italy. Their territory was progressively taken over by the Romans during the 5th and 4th centuries BC.

volt[1] /vōlt/ *n.* the unit of electromotive force and electric potential difference equal to the difference between two points in a circuit carrying one ampere of current and dissipating one watt of power. Symbol **V** [Late 19thC. Named after Alessandro VOLTA.]

volt[2] /vōlt/, **volte** *n.* **1.** DRESSAGE CIRCULAR MOTION BY HORSE a circular movement executed by a horse in dressage **2.** FENCING SUDDEN MOVE a sudden leap made in fencing to elude an opponent's thrust [Late 16thC. Via French *volte* from Italian *volta* (see VOLTA).]

volta /vólta/ (*plural* -**te** /-tay/) *n.* **1.** DANCE ITALIAN DANCE a very fast dance popular in Italy during the 16th and 17th centuries **2.** MUSIC VOLTA MUSIC a piece of music written for the volta or in the triple-time rhythm of the dance **3.** MUSIC ONE PLAYING OF A MUSICAL PASSAGE a single playing of a passage of music that may then be repeated [Late 16thC. From Italian, 'a turn', from *volgere* 'to turn', from Latin *volvere* 'to roll' (source of English *volume*).]

Volta /vóltə/ river in Ghana, formed by the confluence of the Black Volta and White Volta rivers in the central part of the country. Length: 1,500 km/930 mi.

Volta, Alessandro, Count (1745–1827) Italian physicist. He developed the first electric battery (1800).

voltage /vóltij/ *n.* electric potential expressed in volts

voltage divider *n.* a series of resistors or a single resistor used to provide various voltages that are fractions of the source voltage

voltaic /vol táy ik/ *adj.* relating to or denoting direct electric current produced by chemical action [Early19thC. Formed from the name of Alessandro *Volta* (see VOLT[1]).]

Voltaic /vol táy ik/ *adj.* **1.** PEOPLES OF BURKINA-FASO relating to Burkina-Faso, formerly called Upper Volta, or its people or culture **2.** LANG OF GUR LANGUAGES relating to the Gur group of languages, spoken chiefly in Burkina-Faso and Ghana [Mid-20thC. From the name of the River VOLTA.]

voltaic battery *n.* an electric battery made up of one or more primary cells

voltaic cell *n.* = primary cell

voltaic couple *n.* two different metals immersed in an electrolyte that produce a potential difference due to chemical action

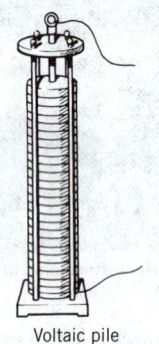

Voltaic pile

voltaic pile *n.* a stack of dissimilar metal discs separated by a porous material soaked in electrolyte that acts as a battery

Voltaire /vol táir/ (1694–1778) French writer and philosopher. A leading figure in the Enlightenment, he produced a range of literary works embodying his radical spirit and religious ideas. They include *Philosophical Letters* (1734), *Candide* (1759), and the *Dictionnaire Philosophique* (1764). Real name **Francois Marie Arouet**

voltaism /vóltə izəm/ *n.* = galvanism *n.* 1

volte *n.* = volt[2]

volte-face /vólt fáass/ *n.* **1.** ABOUT-FACE a sudden reversal in opinion or policy **2.** POSITION CHANGE a change in position so as to be facing the opposite direction [Early 19thC. Via French from Italian *voltafaccia*, literally 'a turn of the face'.]

voltmeter /vólt meetər/ *n.* an instrument calibrated in volts that measures the electromotive force or potential difference between two points in a circuit

voluble /vóllyōob'l/ *adj.* **1.** TALKING A GREAT DEAL talking or spoken easily and at length **2.** BOT TWINING twining or twisting [14thC. Directly or via French from Latin *volubilis*, from, ultimately, *volvere* 'to roll'.] —**volubility** /vóllyōo bílləti/ *n.* —**volubleness** /vóllyōob'lnəss/ *n.* —**volubly** *adv.*

volume /vóllyoom/ *n.* **1.** PHYS SPACE INSIDE AN OBJECT the size of a three-dimensional space enclosed within or occupied by an object. Volume is measured in cubic units. Symbol **V 2.** AMOUNT the total amount of sth **3.** ACOUSTICS LOUDNESS the loudness of a sound **4.** ACOUSTICS SOUND CONTROL the knob or button on a radio, television, or audio player that controls loudness **5.** THICKNESS the thick quality or appearance of sb's hair ○ *Apply to roots for added volume.* **6.** PUBL BOOK a bound collection of printed or written pages **7.** PUBL BOOK OF A SET a single book that belongs to a set of

books **8.** PUBL CONSECUTIVE MAGAZINE ISSUES a set of issues of a periodical spanning one calendar year **9.** HIST SCROLL a roll of parchment or papyrus ■ *adj.* INVOLVING LARGE QUANTITIES using or involving large amounts or quantities ○ *The factory is offering volume discounts on carpet sales.* [14thC. Via Old French *volum* from Latin *volumen* 'roll, scroll, book', from *volvere* 'to roll'. The sense 'loudness' evolved from 'certain size of book' via 'size', hence 'size of sound'.] ◇ **speak volumes** to be highly expressive or significant

volumed /vóllyoomd/ *adj.* **1.** PUBL IN A SET OF BOOKS published in a series or set of a specified number of books (*usually used in combination*) ○ *three-volumed set* **2.** IN A ROUND MASS forming or rolling in a rounded mass (*literary*)

volumeter /vo lyoomitər/ *n.* an instrument used to measure the volume of a solid, liquid, or gas

volumetric /vóllyoo méttrik/ *adj.* of, relating to, or using measurement by volume —**volumetrically** *adv.*

volumetric analysis *n.* CHEM **1.** CHEMICAL ANALYSIS OF LIQUIDS an analysis of liquids using measured volumes of standard chemical reagents **2.** ANALYSIS OF GAS an analysis of gas by volume

voluminous /və loominəss/ *adj.* **1.** LARGE having great size, capacity, or fullness **2.** EXTREMELY LONG very lengthy and taking up many pages or books ○ *a voluminous report* **3.** PROLIFIC producing a large amount of creative work ○ *a voluminous novelist* **4.** WINDING winding or coiling (*archaic*) [Early 17thC. Directly or via late Latin *voluminosus* 'with many coils', from Latin *volumen* (see VOLUME).] —**voluminosity** /və loomi nóssəti/ *n.* —**voluminously** /və loominəssli/ *adv.* —**voluminousness** *n.*

voluntarism /vólləntərizəm/ *n.* **1.** PHILOS PHILOSOPHICAL THEORY the theory that regards the will rather than the intellect as the essential principle of the individual or cosmos **2.** PUBLIC ADMIN RELIANCE ON VOLUNTARY CONTRIBUTIONS the use of or dependence on voluntary contributions rather than government funds to keep an institution such as a school or church in existence **3.** POL NO INTERFERENCE the belief that no level of government or law should interfere in the process of collective bargaining or the organization of trade unions —**voluntarist** *n.* —**voluntaristic** /vólləntə rístik/ *adj.*

voluntary /vólləntəri/ *adj.* **1.** OF FREE WILL arising, acting, or resulting from sb's own choice or decision rather than because of external pressure or force **2.** WITHOUT PAY performing, working, or done without financial reward **3.** USING VOLUNTEERS composed of, functioning, or requiring volunteers **4.** NOT PART OF GOVERNMENT not part of statutory provision, e.g. of social services, and usually maintained at least in part by private charitable donations rather than by government or other official support ○ *Many organizations in the UK voluntary sector receive state funding* **5.** HAVING WILL having the capacity required to make conscious choices or decisions **6.** LAW WITHOUT LEGAL OBLIGATION not involving legal obligation, coercion, or persuasion **7.** LAW DONE ON PURPOSE performed or carried out with intention rather than by accident **8.** LAW GIVEN WITHOUT PAYMENT IN RETURN done or given freely with no promise of money or other recompense ■ *n.* (*plural* **-ies**) **1.** MUSIC SHORT COMPOSITION a short musical composition, often played on a solo instrument, that introduces a longer work **2.** MUSIC CHURCH MUSIC a piece of music or improvisation for the organ, played before, during, or at the end of a church service **3.** VOLUNTEER a volunteer, particularly sb who joins the army (*archaic*) [14thC. From Latin *voluntarius*, from *voluntas* 'will, choice', from *vol-*, stem of *velle* 'to wish'.] —**voluntarily** /vólləntərəli, -térrəli/ *adv.* —**voluntariness** /vólləntərinəss/ *n.*

voluntary arrangement *n.* a procedure in which a failing business can make arrangements with its creditors to resolve its financial problems, often after a court order

voluntaryism /vólləntəri izəm/ *n.* = voluntarism *n.* 2 —**voluntaryist** *n.*

volunteer /vóllən teér/ *n.* **1.** SB WHO WORKS FOR FREE sb who works without being paid **2.** SB WHO DOES STH VOLUNTARILY sb who does sth, especially sth undesirable, without being forced to do it **3.** MIL VOLUNTARY RECRUIT TO ARMED FORCES sb who has offered to serve in one of the

armed services rather than being required to join by law **4.** BOT CULTIVATED PLANT GROWING NATURALLY a cultivated plant, especially a crop plant, that grows without having been intentionally sown or planted **5.** LAW SB ACTING WITHOUT LEGAL OBLIGATION sb who performs an act or participates in a transaction without being legally bound to do so and without expecting to be paid **6.** LAW SB GIVEN PROPERTY sb who receives property without having to pay for it or give anything in return ■ *v.* (**-teers, -teering, -teered**) **1.** *vti.* OFFER FREE HELP to do charitable or helpful work without receiving pay for it ○ *volunteers his time* **2.** *vti.* DO STH BY CHOICE to perform or offer to perform work of your own free will ○ *volunteered to work the night shift* **3.** *vt.* TELL STH WITHOUT BEING ASKED to tell sb sth or give information without being asked ○ *to volunteer information* **4.** *vt.* OFFER SB ELSE'S HELP to suggest sb else as a helper ○ *volunteered her secretary for a few days* **5.** *vi.* MIL OFFER TO DO MILITARY SERVICE to offer to serve in one of the armed services without being required to join by law [Late 16thC. Via French *volontaire* from Latin *voluntarius* (see VOLUNTARY).]

volunteer army *n.* an army that relies on recruiting people who enlist voluntarily rather than conscripting recruits by law

volunteerism /vóllən teérizəm/ *n.* US the practice of using volunteer workers in community service organizations and programs

volunteer vacation *n.* US a holiday during which sb does volunteer work such as cleaning up the environment or housing construction and repair

voluptuary /və lúpchoo əri/ (*plural* **-ies**) *n.* sb whose life is devoted to enjoying luxury and the pleasures of the senses [Early 17thC. From Latin *voluptuarius*, from *voluptas* 'pleasure'.]

voluptuous /və lúpchoo əss/ *adj.* **1.** SENSUAL sensual in appearance **2.** SENSUAL providing sensual pleasure **3.** INDULGENT inclined or devoted to a luxurious sensual life [14thC. Directly or via French *voluptueux* from Latin *voluptuosus*, from *voluptas* 'pleasure'.] —**voluptuously** *adv.* —**voluptuousness** *n.*

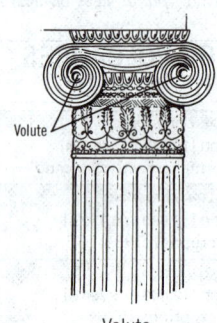

Volute

Volute

volute /və loot, vóllyoot/ *n.* **1.** SPIRAL SHAPE a spiral form or structure, e.g. the whorl in the shell of a snail **2.** ARCHIT DECORATIVE SCROLL a carved spiral decoration, usually on an Ionic capital **3.** MARINE BIOL TROPICAL MOLLUSC a gastropod mollusc that lives in tropical waters and has a spiral shell with colourful markings. Family: Volutidae. ■ *adj.* SPIRALLING moving in or following a spiral path [Mid-16thC. Directly or via French from Latin *voluta*, feminine past participle of *volvere* 'to roll'.]

─── **WORD KEY: ORIGIN** ───
The Latin word *volvere*, from which *volute* is derived, is also the source of English *convolution, convolvulus, devolution, evolution, involve, revolt, revolution, revolve, vault, voluble,* and *volume.*

volutin /vóllyōotin/ *n.* an easily stained substance found in the cytoplasm of some bacterial and fungal cells that serves to store phosphates for the energy needs of the cell [Early 20thC. From modern Latin *Spirillum volutans*, 'rolling spirillum', the species of bacterium in which it was first found, from Latin *volutare* 'to keep rolling around', from *volvere* (see VOLUTE).]

volution /və loosh'n/ *n.* **1.** SPIRAL a shape that coils, twists, or turns around a centre **2.** ZOOL WHORL any of the spiral segments of a gastropod's shell [15thC. From late Latin *volutio*, from *volvere* 'to roll'.]

volva /vólvə/ (*plural* **-vae** /-vee/ *or* **-vas**) *n.* a cup-shaped structure that encircles the base of the stalk of some mushrooms [Mid-18thC. From modern Latin, from Latin *volvere* 'to roll'.] —**volvate** /vólvət, -vayt/ *adj.*

volvox /vól voks/ *n.* freshwater green algae that form communities made up of hollow multicellular spheres. Genus: *Volvox.* [Late 18thC. From modern Latin, from Latin *volvere* 'to roll'.]

volvulus /vólvyŏŏləss/ (*plural* **volvuli** /-lī, -lee/) *n.* an abnormal twisting of the digestive tract that leads to partial or complete obstruction and a reduction in blood supply. Gangrene is a possible consequence. [Late 17thC. From medieval Latin, from Latin *volvere* 'to roll'.]

vomer /vṓmər/ *n.* a thin plate of bone that forms part of the septum dividing the nasal passages inside the nose [Early 18thC. From Latin, literally 'ploughshare'; so called because of its shape.] —**vomerine** /vṓmə rīn/ *adj.*

vomit /vómmit/ *vti.* (**-its, -iting, -ited**) **1.** THROW UP STOMACH CONTENTS to expel the contents of the stomach through the mouth as a result of a series of involuntary spasms of the stomach muscles **2.** GUSH FORTH to send sth out in a forceful stream, or to be ejected forcefully ○ *to vomit curses* ■ *n.* **1.** EXPELLED STOMACH CONTENTS the stomach contents expelled through the mouth. Technical name **vomitus 2.** ACT OF VOMITING the act of expelling the stomach contents through the mouth [15thC. Directly or via Anglo-French from Latin *vomitus*, past participle of *vomere* 'to eject or vomit'.] —**vomiter** *n.*

vomitory /vómmitəri/ *adj.* **vomitory, vomitive** MED CAUSING VOMITING causing the vomiting of stomach contents (*dated*) ■ *n.* (*plural* **-ries**) **1.** OPENING an opening through which matter is ejected **2.** ARCHIT, HIST ANCIENT ROMAN PASSAGEWAY a passageway, usually in an amphitheatre or stadium, connecting a tier of seats with an outside entrance [Early 17thC. From Latin *vomitorius*, from *vomitus* (see VOMIT).]

vomiturition /vómmichŏŏ rísh'n/ *n.* failure to bring up the contents of the stomach in spite of forceful attempts to do so (*dated*) [Mid-19thC. Coined from VOMIT and *micturition* 'urination', from MICTURATE.]

vomitus /vómmitəss/ *n.* vomited contents of the stomach (*technical*) [Early 20thC. From Latin (see VOMIT).]

Von Stroheim /von strṓ hīm/, **Erich** (1885–1957) Austrian-born US actor and film director. In Hollywood after 1914, he directed films of unparalleled realism and psychological intensity, including his masterpiece, *Greed* (1925). His budget overruns ended his directing career after only eight films, and his later years were devoted to acting. Full name **Erich Oswald Stroheim**

voodoo /vóodoo/ *n.* (*plural* **voodoos**) **1.** CARIBBEAN RELIGION a religion practised throughout Caribbean countries, especially Haiti, that is a combination of Roman Catholic rituals and the animistic beliefs of Dahomean enslaved labourers, involving magic and communication with ancestors **2.** PRACTITIONER OF VOODOO sb who practises voodoo **3.** STH MAGIC a charm, spell, or fetish regarded by those who practise voodoo as having magical powers ■ *vt.* (**voodoos, voodooing, voodooed**) CAST A SPELL ON SB to cast a voodoo spell on sb [Early 19thC. Via Louisiana French *voudou* from Fon *vodũ* 'fetish'.]

voodooism /vóo doo izəm/ *n.* **1.** VOODOO AS RELIGION the practises and beliefs of voodoo **2.** MAGIC an attempt to control or affect the world by using magic or sorcery —**voodooist** *n.* —**voodooistic** /-ístik/ *adj.*

voop /voop/ *n. Carib* WILD SWING AT CRICKET BALL in cricket, a wild uncontrolled swing at the ball by a batsman ■ *vi.* (**voops, vooping, vooped**) *Carib* MAKE WILD SWING AT BALL in cricket, to make a wild uncontrolled swing at the ball when batting

voorkamer /fóor kaamər/ *n. S Africa* the front room of a house, especially of a Cape Dutch house or farmhouse [Late 18thC. Via Afrikaans from Dutch, literally 'front room'.]

Voortrekker /fóor trekər/ *n. S Africa* a member of a band of Afrikaner pioneers who, in the early 19th century, left the British-ruled Cape for the eastern Cape and the interior of South Africa [Late 19thC. Via Afrikaans from Dutch, literally 'before-trekker'.]

VOR *abbr.* very-high-frequency omnidirectional radio range

voracious /və ráyshəss/ *adj.* **1.** VERY HUNGRY desiring or consuming food in great quantities ○ *a voracious appetite* **2.** ESPECIALLY EAGER unusually eager or enthusiastic about an activity ○ *a voracious reader* [Mid-17thC. From the Latin stem *vorac-*, from *vorare* 'to devour'.] —**voraciously** *adv.* —**voraciousness** *n.* —**voracity** /və rássəti/ *n.*

Vorlage, **vorlage** *n.* a skiing position in which a skier leans forward from the ankle but keeps his or her heels on the skis [Mid-20thC. From German, literally 'forward position'.]

Voronezh /və rónnezh/ city and capital of Voronezh Oblast in western Russia. Population: 895,000 (1990).

-vorous *suffix.* eating, having a particular kind of food ○ *herbivorous* [Formed from Latin *-vorus*, from *vorare* 'to swallow' (source of English *devour*)]

Vorster /fáwrstər/, **John** (1915–83) South African statesman. He was prime minister (1966–78) and president (1978–79) of South Africa. His career ended after he was implicated in a financial scandal. Real name **Balthazar Johannes Vorster**

vortex /váwr teks/ (*plural* **vortexes** *or* **vortices** /váwrti seez/) *n.* **1.** WHIRLING MASS a whirling mass of sth, especially water or air, that draws everything near it towards its centre **2.** STH OVERWHELMING a situation or feeling that seems to swamp or engulf everything else [Mid-17thC. From Latin, a variant of *vertex* (see VERTEX).]

vortical /váwrtik'l/ *adj.* relating to or moving in a vortex [Mid-17thC. From Latin *vortic-*, stem of *vortex* (see VORTEX).] —**vortically** *adv.*

vorticella /váwrti séllə/ (*plural* **-lae** /-lee/) *n.* an underwater protozoan with a bell-shaped body. It is usually attached to sth such as a plant by a slender stalk. Genus: *Vorticella.* [Late 18thC. From modern Latin, literally 'little vortex', from Latin *vortic-* (see VORTICAL).]

vorticism /váwrtissizəm/ *n.* a short-lived early 20th-century British movement in art and literature that was both abstract and concerned about the future and the machine age [Early 20thC. Formed from Latin *vortic-* (see VORTICAL). So called from Ezra Pound's idea of an image as a whirling centre 'from which ideas are constantly rushing'.] —**vorticist** *n.*

vorticity /vawr tíssəti/ *n.* the state of a fluid moving in a vortex [Late 19thC. From Latin *vortic-* (see VORTICAL).]

vorticose /váwrti kōss/ *adj.* = **vortical** *adj.*

vortiginous /vawr tíjjinəss/ *adj.* vortical (*formal*) [Late 17thC. From Latin *vortigin-*, stem of *vortigo*, variant of *vertigo* (see VERTIGO).]

Vosges /vōzh/ mountain range in northeastern France that extends 190 km/120 mi. from south to north, parallel to the River Rhine. The highest summits in the southern portion rise to about 1,424 m/4,672 ft above sea level, and the northern peaks average about 910 m/3,000 ft.

Vostok /vóstok/ *n.* any of seven numbered spacecraft launched by the former Soviet Union, beginning in April 1961 [Mid-20thC. From Russian.]

votary /vṓtəri/ (*plural* **-ries**), **votarist** /-rist/ *n.* **1.** MONK OR NUN sb who has taken a vow to dedicate his or her life to religious worship or service **2.** DEVOTEE sb who has devoted himself or herself to sth such as a religion or cause [Mid-16thC. From Latin *vot-*, past participle stem of *vovere* 'to vow'.]

vote /vōt/ *n.* **1.** FORMAL CHOICE FOR OR AGAINST STH a formal indication of sb's choice or opinion, especially in an election or referendum **2.** ACT OF CHOOSING the act of making a choice or stating a preference to determine the outcome of sth **3.** BALLOTS CAST the total number of ballots cast by eligible voters ○ *They got 83 per cent of the vote.* **4.** SUFFRAGE the right to express opinions and preferences by casting a ballot ○ *Women struggled for many years to get the vote.* **5.** MEANS OF EXPRESSING A VOTE the ticket, ballot, or other method by which sb expresses a vote **6.** RESULT OF BALLOTING the outcome of an election or referendum ○ *Yesterday's vote indicates that people are tired of being lied to.* **7.** OPINION EXPRESSED the preference of a group of people as indicated by a ballot ○ *Politicians can no longer ignore the youth vote.* **8.** PROPOSAL a proposal to be voted for or against, usually by a committee ■ *v.* (**votes, voting, voted**) **1.** *vti.* INDICATE FORMAL PREFERENCE to express an opinion or preference in an election or referendum ○ *How did you vote in the last election?* **2.** *vt.* VOTE FOR OR AGAINST SB to decide the outcome of an election by voting for or against sb ○ *It's difficult to vote an incumbent out of office.* **3.** *vt.* VOTE TO MAKE STH AVAILABLE to create sth or make sth available by casting a vote ○ *The city council refused to vote additional funds for the new building.* **4.** *vt.* VOTE FOR SB TO WIN to vote for a candidate to win a competition or title ○ *He was voted 'Waiter of the Year'.* **5.** *vt.* SHOW OPINION ON STH to agree on how successful or enjoyable sth is (*informal*) ○ *The meal was voted a great success.* **6.** *vt.* SUGGEST STH to make a suggestion ○ *I vote that we eat out.* [13thC. From Latin *votum* 'a vow', from *vovere* 'to vow', later 'to desire' (source of English *vow*). The underlying sense is of expressing a desire.] —**votable** *adj.* —**voter** *n.*

vote down *vt.* to defeat a proposal or candidate in a vote

vote-catcher *n.* = **vote-winner**

vote of no confidence (*plural* **votes of no confidence**) *n.* a vote originating with an opposition party that censures an act or policy of the government in power and, if passed, requires that the government resign (*formal*)

vote-winner, **vote-catcher** *n.* a policy or strategy that will attract a high proportion of votes

voting booth *n. US* = **polling booth**

votive /vṓtiv/ *adj.* **1.** SYMBOLIZING WISH showing or symbolizing a wish or desire ○ *a votive prayer* **2.** FULFILLING A VOW given, done, or offered in fulfilment of an oath or vow ○ *a votive offering* [Late 16thC. From Latin *votivus*, from *votum* (see VOTE).] —**votively** *adv.* —**votiveness** *n.*

Votyak /vót yak/ (*plural* **-yak** *or* **-yaks**) *n.* **1.** PEOPLES MEMBER OF FINNISH PEOPLE IN RUSSIA a member of a Finnish people living in eastern central European Russia, especially in the Udmurt Autonomous Region **2.** LANG = **Udmurt** [Mid-19thC. From Russian.] —**Votyak** *adj.*

vou. *abbr.* voucher

vouch /vowch/ (**vouches, vouching, vouched**) *vt.* in English law, to summon sb to court to prove ownership of land (*archaic*) [14thC. Via French *voucher* 'to summon' from, ultimately, Latin *vocare* 'to call'. The meaning developed from 'to summon someone as a witness or an authority'.]

vouch for *vt.* **1.** GUARANTEE SB'S BEHAVIOUR to give an assurance that sb will behave well or appropriately **2.** GUARANTEE AUTHENTICITY OF STH to guarantee that sth is accurate or genuine

vouchee /vów chée/ *n.* sb for whom another person vouches

voucher /vówchər/ *n.* **1.** SUBSTITUTE FOR MONEY WHEN BUYING STH a card, token, or other document that can be exchanged for goods and services in place of money **2.** DOCUMENTARY EVIDENCE a document that provides supporting evidence for a claim, e.g. a receipt proving that a purchase was made **3.** GUARANTOR sb or sth that guarantees or provides proof of sth **4.** LAW CREDENTIALS FOR UK RESIDENCE a document that entitles a British national born outside the United Kingdom to live in Britain

vouchsafe /vowch sáyf/ (**-safes, -safing, -safed**) *vt.* **1.** CONDESCEND TO GIVE STH to undertake or deign to grant or give sth, especially a reply **2.** PROMISE STH to promise, agree, or allow sth (*formal*) [14thC (originally as two words)]

voussoir /voo swaár/ *n.* a wedge-shaped brick or stone used to form the curved parts of an arch or vault [14thC. Via French from, ultimately, Latin *volvere* 'to roll'.]

Vouvray /vóo vray/ *n.* a dry white wine produced in the Loire Valley of France [Late 19thC. Named after the village of *Vouvray* in Inde-de-Loire, France.]

vow /vow/ *n.* SOLEMN PLEDGE a solemn promise to perform a certain act, carry out an activity, or behave in a given way ■ **vows** *npl.* RELIGIOUS PROMISE a solemn promise to join a religious order and live in accordance with its rules ■ *v.* (**vows, vowing, vowed**) **1.**

vt. **PLEDGE STH** to promise sth solemnly and seriously **2.** *vti.* **DEDICATE SB** to promise sb to a pledge, task, or to sb such as a deity **3.** *vt.* **ASSERT STH** to assert or declare sth [13thC. Via Old French *vou* from Latin *votum* (see VOTE).] —**vower** *n.*

vowel /vówəl/ *n.* a speech sound produced by the passage of air through the vocal tract, with relatively little obstruction, or the corresponding letter of the alphabet [14thC. Via Old French *vouel* from, ultimately, Latin *vocalis* (see VOCAL).]

vowel gradation *n.* = ablaut

vowelize /vówə līz/ (**-izes, -izing, -ized**), **vowelise** (**-ises, -ising, -ised**) *vt.* to mark the vowel points in a Hebrew or Arabic text —**vowelization** /vów ə līz áysh'n/ *n.*

vowel mutation *n.* = umlaut

vowel point *n.* a diacritical mark placed above or below a consonant to show a preceding or following vowel, used especially in languages such as Arabic and Hebrew that lack symbols for vowel sounds

vox angelica /vóks ən jéllikə/ *n.* a quiet organ stop, usually with vibrato, that enriches the tone of other quiet stops [From Latin, literally 'angelic voice']

vox humana /vóks hyoo máanə/ *n.* an organ reed stop that produces a tone resembling the human voice [From Latin, literally 'human voice']

vox pop /vóks póp/ *n.* the impromptu opinions of ordinary members of the public as gathered by a radio or television interviewer (*hyphenated when used before a noun*) [Shortening of VOX POPULI]

vox populi /vóks póppyoo lī/ *n.* popular public opinion ○ *Let's see if we can detect the vox populi.* [From Latin, literally 'voice of the people']

voyage /vóy ij/ *n.* **1.** **LONG TRIP** a journey by sea or air, especially one to a distant place **2.** **AEROSP SPACE JOURNEY** a journey into space **3.** **JOURNEY EVENTS** the events of an exploratory trip regarded as a story ■ (*literary*) **4.** **NARRATIVE** a story of an exploratory trip ■ *vti.* (**-ages, -aging, -aged**) **TRAVEL** to make a long journey to, through, or over a place [13thC. Via Old French *voiage* from, ultimately, Latin *viaticus* 'of a road or journey', from *via* 'road'.] —**voyager** *n.*

Voyager /vóy ijər/ *n.* the name of two US spacecraft, Voyager 1 and Voyager 2, designed for exploring the outer planets of the solar system without a crew and launched in 1977

voyageur /vóy ə júr/ *n.* *Can.* a boatman, woodsman, trapper, or explorer hired by fur companies to carry furs and supplies from one remote station to another, especially in Canada and the northwestern United States [Late 18thC. From French, literally 'voyager'.]

voyeur /vwee aar/ *n.* **1.** **SB WHO WATCHES FOR SEXUAL PLEASURE** sb who is sexually excited by looking, especially secretly, at other people's naked bodies or the sexual acts in which they participate **2.** **PERSISTENT OBSERVER OF MISERY OR SCANDAL** sb who is fascinated with, or persistently observes, distressing, sordid, or scandalous topics or events [Early 20thC. From French, literally 'one who sees', from *voir* 'to see', from Latin *videre*.] —**voyeurism** *n.* —**voyeuristic** /vwí yur ristik/ *adj.* —**voyeuristically** *adv.*

VP *abbr.* **1.** verb phrase **2.** Vice President

vr *abbr.* verb reflexive

VR *abbr.* **1.** variant reading **2.** virtual reality **3.** Volunteer Reserve **4.** Victoria Regina

vraisemblance /vray soN blóNss/ *n.* the quality of seeming to be true or likely [Early 19thC. From French, literally 'true appearance'.]

VRML *n.* a computer-graphics programming language used to create images of three-dimensional scenes. Abbr of **Virtual Reality Modelling Language**

vroom /vroom/ *n.* **LOUD ENGINE NOISE** the loud noise of an engine when it is being revved up or is running at high speed (*informal*) ■ *vi.* (**vrooms, vrooming, vroomed**) **MOVE NOISILY** to move noisily at high speed [Mid-20thC. An imitation of the sound.]

VS, v. *abbr.* versus

v.S. *abbr.* vide supra

V-shaped *adj.* having the shape of a 'V'

V-sign *n.* **1.** **VICTORY SIGN** a hand sign that indicates victory, approval, or solidarity, made by holding up the index and middle fingers so that their form a 'V' with the palm facing outwards **2.** **RUDE HAND SIGN** a hand sign that indicates contempt, anger, or abuse, made by holding up the index and middle fingers so that they form a V with the palm facing inwards

VSO *n.* **ORGANIZATION FOR VOLUNTEERS WORKING ABROAD** an organization that sends volunteers to work and teach in developing countries. Abbr of **Voluntary Service Overseas** ■ *adj.* **LABEL FOR OLD BRANDY OR PORT** used to indicate that brandy or port is between 12 and 17 years old. Abbr of **very superior old**

VSOP *adj.* used to indicate that brandy or port is between 20 and 25 years old. Abbr of **very special old pale, very superior old pale**

vss. *abbr.* **1.** verses **2.** versions

V/STOL /veé stol/ *abbr.* vertical and short takeoff and landing

vt *abbr.* verb transitive

Vt *abbr.* Vermont

VT *abbr.* **1.** vacuum tube **2.** variable time **3.** Vermont

VTOL /veé tol/ (*plural* **VTOLs**) *n.* **1.** **AIRCRAFT VERTICAL TAKEOFF SYSTEM** a system used by some aircraft that enables them to take off and land vertically. Abbr of **vertical takeoff and landing** **2.** **AIRCRAFT CAPABLE OF VERTICAL TAKEOFF** an aircraft capable of vertical takeoff and landing

VTR *n.* (*plural* **VTRs**), *abbr.* video-tape recorder

vug /vug/ *n.* a small hole in a rock or vein that often contains a mineral lining that differs from that of the surrounding matrix [Early 19thC. From Cornish *vooga*.] —**vuggy** *adj.*

Vuillard /vwee aarl/, **Édouard** (1868–1940) French painter. He designed theatre sets and textiles in addition to the intricately patterned paintings of domestic interiors for which he is best known. Full name **Jean Édouard Vuillard**

Vul. *abbr.* Vulgate

Vulcan /vúlkən/ *n.* in Roman mythology, the god of fire. Greek equivalent **Hephaestus** —**Vulcanian** /vul káyni ən/ *adj.*

vulcanian /vul káyni ən/ *adj.* **GEOL RELATING TO VOLCANIC ERUPTION** relating to or caused by a type of explosive volcanic eruption resulting when the pressure of gases trapped in viscous magma is sufficient to blow off overlying solidified material **2.** **OF METALWORKING** relating to or consisting of metalworking or metal craft

vulcanicity *n.* = volcanicity [Late 18thC. From French *vulcanicité*, variant of *volcanicité* (see VOLCANICITY).]

vulcanise *vt.* = vulcanize

vulcanism *n.* = volcanism

vulcanite /vúlkə nīt/ *n.* a hard rubber produced by vulcanizing natural rubber with large amounts of sulphur [Mid-19thC. Named after VULCAN.]

vulcanize /vúlkə nīz/ (**-nizes, -nizing, -nized**), **vulcanise** (**-nises, -nising, -nised**) *vt.* to strengthen a material such as rubber by combining it with sulphur and other additives and then applying heat and pressure —**vulcanizable** *adj.* —**vulcanizer** *n.*

vulcanology *n.* = volcanology

vulg. *abbr.* **1.** vulgar **2.** vulgarly

Vulg. *abbr.* vulgate

vulgar /vúlgər/ *adj.* **1.** **CRUDE AND INDECENT** crude or obscene, particularly about sex or bodily functions **2.** **TASTELESSLY OSTENTATIOUS** showing a lack of taste or reasonable moderation **3.** **LACKING REFINEMENT** lacking courtesy and manners **4.** **LANG OF ORDINARY PEOPLE'S LANGUAGE** relating to a form of a language spoken by ordinary people **5.** **OF ORDINARY PEOPLE** characteristic of or associated with the majority of ordinary people (*archaic*) ■ *npl.* **ORDINARY PEOPLE** ordinary people regarded or spoken of as a group ○ *She believes that fine food and wine are beyond the taste of the vulgar.* [14thC. From Latin *vulgaris*, from *vulgus* 'the common people'.] —**vulgarly** *adv.*

vulgar fraction *n.* = simple fraction

vulgarian /vul gáiri ən/ *n.* sb who is wealthy but tasteless or overly ostentatious

vulgarise *vt.* = vulgarize

vulgarism /vúlgərizəm/ *n.* **1.** **CRUDE TERM** a crude or indecent word or phrase **2.** **TERM IN ORDINARY PEOPLE'S LANGUAGE** a word or phrase from the language spoken by ordinary people, as contrasted with a more formal or refined usage **3.** = vulgarity

vulgarity /vul gárrəti/ (*plural* **-ties**) *n.* **1.** **BEING VULGAR** a vulgar state or way of behaving **2.** **STH CRUDE OR INDECENT** a crude or tasteless joke, remark, or act

vulgarize /vúlgə rīz/ (**-izes, -izing, -ized**), **vulgarise** (**-ises, -ising, -ised**) *vt.* **1.** **DEBASE STH** to make sth less refined or reduce the quality of sth **2.** **MAKE STH ACCESSIBLE** to present or treat sth in a way that makes it accessible to ordinary people —**vulgarization** /-rī záysh'n/ *n.* —**vulgarizer** *n.*

Vulgar Latin *n.* **LANG** the form of Latin that was the common spoken language of the western Roman Empire

vulgate /vúl gayt/ *n.* **1.** **LING ORDINARY SPEECH** the everyday informal use of a language **2.** **LITERAT ACCEPTED VERSION** a text generally accepted among experts as being the best or most accurate version [Early 16thC. From Latin *vulgatus*, past participle of *vulgare* 'to make public or common', from *vulgus* (see VULGAR).]

Vulgate *n.* a Latin version of the Bible produced by Saint Jerome in the 4th century [From Latin *vulgata editio* 'edition made public, edition for ordinary people', from *vulgatus* (see VULGATE).]

vulnerable /vúlnərəb'l/ *adj.* **1.** **WITHOUT ADEQUATE PROTECTION** open to emotional or physical danger or harm **2.** **MIL OPEN TO ATTACK** exposed to an attack or possible damage **3.** **EXTREMELY SUSCEPTIBLE** easily persuadable or liable to give in to temptation **4.** **PHYSICALLY OR PSYCHOLOGICALLY WEAK** unable to resist illness, debility, or failure **5.** **BRIDGE LIABLE TO INCREASED STAKES** liable to higher penalties as well as bonuses, having won one game of a rubber [Late Latin *vulnerabilis*, from *vulnerare* 'to wound', from *vulnus* 'wound, injury'.] —**vulnerability** /vúlnərə b'lnass/ *n.* —**vulnerableness** /'l/ *n.* —**vulnerably** *adv.*

vulnerary /vúlnərəri/ *adj.* **MED HEALING** capable of or used for healing wounds (*archaic*) ■ *n.* (*plural* **-ies**) **PHARM HEALING AGENT** a drug or other agent used in treating and healing wounds (*archaic*) [Late 16thC. From Latin *vulnerarius*, from *vulnus* 'wound, injury'.]

Vulpecula /vul pékyoólə/ *n.* a constellation in the sky of the northern hemisphere between Cygnus and Sagitta [From Latin, diminutive of *vulpes* 'fox'.]

vulpine /vúl pīn/ *adj.* **1.** **TYPICAL OF A FOX** typical of or resembling a fox **2.** **HAVING A TRAIT ATTRIBUTED TO FOXES** having or displaying a trait such as cunning that is commonly associated with foxes [Early 17thC. From Latin *vulpes* 'fox'.]

Vulture

vulture /vúlchər/ *n.* **1.** **BIRD OF PREY** a large bird of prey found in Africa, Eurasia, and the Americas. It has dark plumage and broad wings and feeds on carrion. Family: Accipitridae and Cathartidae. **2.** **PREDATOR** sb who waits or looks eagerly for opportunities to take advantage of sb else, especially sb weak or harmless [14thC. Via Anglo-Norman *vultur* or Old French *voltour* from, ultimately, Latin *vultur*.]

vulturine /vúlchə rīn/ *adj.* **1.** **TYPICAL OF VULTURE** typical of or resembling a vulture **2.** **vulturine, vulturous** **GREEDY**

a at; aa father; aw all; ay day; air hair; ə about, edible, item, common, circus; e egg; ee eel; hw whet; i it, happy; ī ice; 'l apple; 'm rhythm; 'n button; o pot; ō go; oi oil; oo pool; ōō book; ow owl; oy oil; th thin; th this; u up; ur urge;

having a trait commonly associated with vultures, e.g. opportunism or greed

vulva /vúlvə/ (*plural* **-vae** /-vee/ *or* **-vas**) *n.* the external female genitals. These include two pairs of fleshy folds, the labia majora and labia minora, that surround the opening of the vagina, and the clitoris. [14thC. From Latin, variant of *volva* 'womb', from *volvere* 'to roll'.] —**vulval** *adj.* —**vulvar** *adj.* —**vulviform** *adj.*

vulvectomy /vul véktəmi/ (*plural* **-mies**) *n.* the surgical removal of all or part of a woman's external genitals

vulvitis /vul vítiss/ *n.* painful swelling and redness of the vulva

vulvovaginitis /vúlvō vaji nítiss/ *n.* painful swelling and redness of the vulva and vagina

vv *abbr.* vice versa

vv. *abbr.* **1.** verses **2.** MUSIC (first and second) violins **3.** volumes

VW[1] (*plural* **VWs**) *n.* any car manufactured by Volkswagen

VW[2] *abbr.* very worshipful

VX *n.* an oily, liquid, highly lethal, nerve gas

vying present participle of **vie**

Ww

W /dúbb'l yoo/ (*plural* **w's**), **W** (*plural* **W's** *or* **Ws**) *n.* **1. 23RD LETTER OF ENGLISH ALPHABET** the 23rd letter of the modern English alphabet **2. SPEECH SOUND CORRESPONDING TO LETTER 'W'** the speech sound that corresponds to the letter 'W' **3. LETTER 'W' WRITTEN** a written representation of the letter 'W' **4. STH SHAPED LIKE 'W'** sth that has the shape of the letter 'W'

W[1] *symbol.* **1.** tungsten **2.** ELEC watt **3.** PHYS weight **4.** PHYS work

W[2] *abbr.* **1.** West **2.** women's (*used of clothing sizes*)

w. *abbr.* **1.** MEASURE width **2.** TIME week **3.** wife **4.** with **5.** CRICKET wicket(s) **6.** CRICKET wide(s)

W. *abbr.* **1.** Wales **2.** Warden **3.** CALENDAR Wednesday **4.** Welsh **5.** West **6.** Western

w/ *abbr.* with

W3 *abbr.* World Wide Web

WA *abbr.* **1.** Western Australia **2.** Washington (State) **3.** INSUR with average

WAAAF /waf/ *abbr. Aus* Women's Auxiliary Australian Air Force

WAAC /wak/ *abbr.* Women's Army Auxiliary Corps ■ *n.* (*plural* **WAACs**) **WAAC, Waac MEMBER OF WAAC** a member of the Women's Army Auxiliary Corps (*dated*) [Early 20thC. Acronym.]

WAAF /waf/ *abbr.* Women's Auxiliary Air Force (*dated*) ■ *n.* (*plural* **WAAFs**) **WAAF, Waaf MEMBER OF WAAF OR WAAAF** a member of the Women's Auxiliary Air Force or the Women's Auxiliary Australian Air Force (*dated*) [Mid-20thC. Acronym.]

Waal /waal/ the largest and southernmost of the three branches of the River Rhine in the Netherlands. Length: 84 km/52 mi.

wabbit /wábbit/ *adj. Scotland* weary or exhausted [Late 19thC. Origin unknown.]

WACA /wáka/ *n. Aus* a cricket ground in Perth, Western Australia (*informal*) Full form **West Australian Cricket Association**

wack /wak/, **wacker** /wákar/ *n.* used to address a friend (*regional*) [Origin unknown]

wacky /wáki/ (**-ier, -iest**), **whacky** (**-ier, -iest**) *adj.* **1. OFFENSIVE TERM** an offensive term used to describe sb regarded as unconventional or unpredictable (*slang insult*) **2. SILLY** entertainingly silly (*informal*) [Mid-19thC. Origin uncertain: probably from the phrase *out of whack* 'out of order' (see WHACK).] —**wackily** *adv.* —**wackiness** *n.*

Waco /wáykō/ city on the Brazos River in central Texas. In 1993, 84 people were killed when federal agents stormed the compound of a religious group just outside the city. Population: 105,892 (1994).

wad /wod/ *n.* **1. SOFT MATERIAL** a small rounded mass of soft material, usually used to pack or stuff sth ○ *The vase was carefully packed in wads of cotton.* **2. BUNDLE** a roll or small bundle of paper money ○ *a wad of notes* **3. COMPRESSED MATERIAL** a rounded compressed lump of sth soft, especially tobacco or gum for chewing **4.** ARMS **POWDER PLUG** a plug of material such as paper or cloth used to hold the powder charge in a muzzle-loading gun or cannon **5.** ARMS **DISC IN SHOTGUN CARTRIDGE** a disc made of felt or paper, used to hold the powder or shot in a shotgun cartridge **6.** US, Can FIN **A LOT OF MONEY** a large amount of money (*informal*) **7.** US MANY a large quantity of sth (*informal*) ○ *She has wads of friends.* **8.** MINERALS

MINERAL MIXTURE IN BOGGY GROUND a fine-grained mixture of hydrated barium manganese oxide and other hydrated oxide minerals precipitated from water and poorly drained boggy ground **9.** AGRIC **BIT OF HAY OR STRAW** a segment of a bale of hay or straw **10.** MIL **BUN** a small bread roll (*slang*) ■ *v.* (**wads, wadding, wadded**) **1.** *vti.* **COMPRESS** to form or compress sth into a small mass ○ *He wadded up the speeding ticket and threw it away.* **2.** *vt.* **PUT WADDING INTO STH** to stuff or plug sth with wadding ○ *She wadded her ears so she wouldn't hear the noise.* **3.** *vt.* ARMS **KEEP CHARGE IN PLACE** to hold a charge of powder or shot in place **4.** *vt.* ARMS **INSERT WADDING INTO GUN** to insert a piece of wadding into a gun [Mid-16thC. Origin unknown.] —**wadder** *n.*

wada /vúdda/, **vada** *n. S Asia* a fried lentil ball eaten as a popular snack, particularly in South India [From Hindi *vaḍā*]

wadding /wódding/ *n.* **1. SOFT PROTECTIVE MATERIAL** soft material used to protect sth, especially in packaging **2.** ARMS **GUN WADS** material used to hold powder or shot in a gun or cartridge **3.** TEXTILES **PADDING MATERIAL USED IN SEWING** a bonded fibre material produced in different thicknesses and used as padding for patchwork quilts, or as interlining where bulk is required. US term **batting**[2] *n.*

Waddington /wóddingtən/, **C.H.** (1905–75) British embryologist and geneticist. He was the author of *Principles of Embryology* (1956) and popular books on biology, and contributed to evolutionary theory. Full name **Conrad Hal Waddington**

waddle /wódd'l/ *vi.* (**-dles, -dling, -dled**) **WALK WITH SIDE-TO-SIDE GAIT** to walk with short steps, causing the body to tilt slightly from one side to the other ■ *n.* **DUCK-LIKE GAIT** a way of walking, taking short steps with the body tilting slightly from one side to the other with each step [Late 16thC. From WADE.] —**waddler** *n.* —**waddly** *adj.*

wade /wayd/ *v.* (**wades, wading, waded**) **1.** *vti.* **WALK IN WATER** to walk against the pressure of water or mud **2.** *vi.* **GO THROUGH STH WITH DIFFICULTY** to read through sth with difficulty, especially because it is very long or boring ■ *n.* **WALK TAKEN IN SHALLOW WATER** an act or instance of walking in shallow water [Old English *wadan*. Ultimately from an Indo-European word meaning 'to go' that is also the ancestor of English *invade* and *vamoose*.] —**wadable** *adj.*

wade in *vti.* **1. wade in, wade into INTERRUPT** to interrupt sb forcefully or with determination **2. INTERVENE** to intervene in a situation in an attempt to help or restore order

Wade /wayd/, **Virginia** (*b.* 1945) British tennis player. She won the US Open (1968), Italian Open (1971), French Open (1972), Australian Open (1972), and Wimbledon (1977). Full name **Sarah Virginia Wade**

wader /wáydər/ *n.* **1. SB WHO WADES** sb who or sth that wades through water **2.** = **wading bird 3.** = **shore bird** ■ **waders** *npl.* **WATERPROOF BOOTS OR TROUSERS** waterproof boots or combined boots and trousers that reach to the hips or chest, worn as protection while fishing

wadi /wóddi/ (*plural* **wadis** *or* **wadies**), **wady** (*plural* **wadies**) *n.* **1. MAINLY DRY WATER COURSE** a steep-sided water course in arid regions of North Africa and southern Asia through which water flows only after heavy rainfall **2.** OASIS an oasis, especially in North Africa [Early 17thC. From Arabic *wādī* 'valley, river bed'.]

wading bird *n.* a long-legged bird such as a crane, heron, or stork that stands in water and hunts for its food that includes fish, frogs, invertebrates, carrion, and algae

wadmal /wódməl/ *n.* a dense coarse woollen fabric once made in Orkney and Shetland and used for outer garments [14thC. From Old Norse *vaðmál* 'cloth measure'.]

Wad Medani /waád mi daáni/ capital city of El Gezira Province, central Sudan. Population: 218,714 (1993).

Wafd /woft/ *n.* an Egyptian nationalist party that emerged after an Egyptian delegation was refused a hearing at the Versailles Treaty negotiations following World War I. Negotiations eventually led to limited Egyptian independence beginning in 1922.

wafer /wáyfər/ *n.* **1. THIN CRISP BISCUIT** a thin, crisp, and sometimes sweetened biscuit, usually in a rectangular, fan, or cone shape, often eaten with ice cream **2.** CHR **BREAD IN CHRISTIAN COMMUNION SERVICE** a very thin disc of unleavened bread used to represent the body of Jesus Christ in the Christian Communion **3.** ELECTRON ENG = **chip** *n.* **6 4. ADHESIVE MATERIAL** a small thin disc of adhesive material, used to seal letters and formal documents **5.** PHARM **MEDICINE CASING** a piece of rice paper or dried flour paste formerly used to encase a powdered medicine (*archaic*) ■ *vt.* (**-fers, -fering, -fered**) **1. FASTEN WITH WAFER** to fasten sth such as a letter or formal document with a wafer **2.** PHARM **ENCASE MEDICINE** to encase a powdered medicine in rice paper or dried flour paste (*archaic*) [14thC. Via Anglo-Norman *wafre*, variant of French *gaufre*, from Middle Low German *wāfel*, from a prehistoric Germanic word that is also the ancestor of English *waffle*[2].]

wafer-thin *adj.* extremely thin or narrow

waffle[1] /wóff'l/ *vi.* (**-fles, -fling, -fled**) **SPEAK IRRELEVANTLY AT LENGTH** to speak or write at length without saying anything important or interesting (*informal*) ■ *n.* **POINTLESS VERBIAGE** speech or writing that is lengthy and irrelevant (*informal*) [Late 17thC. From *waff* 'to yelp or bark', an imitation of the sound; literally 'to keep on waffing'.] —**waffly** *adj.*

waffle[2] /wóff'l/ *n.* a thick light pancake, crisp on the outside, that is baked in a waffle iron to give a pattern of indentations on both sides [Mid-18thC. From Dutch *wafel* (see WAFER).]

waffle iron *n.* an appliance used to bake waffles that has hinged indented plates that press a grid design into both sides of the waffle as it cooks

waft /woft, waaft/ *vti.* (**wafts, wafting, wafted**) **FLOAT GENTLY** to float gently through the air, or move sth gently through the air ■ *n.* **1. STH CARRIED THROUGH AIR** sth such as a scent carried on the air or by a breeze **2. WAVING MOTION** a gentle waving or fluttering motion **3. LIGHT BREEZE** a brief gentle gust of air **4.** NAUT **SIGNALLING FLAG** a hoisted flag formerly used for signalling at sea (*archaic*) **5.** NAUT **SIGNAL USING FLAGS** a signal formerly sent at sea using flags (*archaic*) [Early 16thC. Back-formation from *wafter* 'an armed ship used to guard a convoy', from Dutch *wachter*, from *wachten* 'to guard'. The meaning developed via 'to sail'.]

wag[1] /wag/ *v.* (**wags, wagging, wagged**) **1.** *vti.* **MOVE STH RAPIDLY TO AND FRO** to move part of the body to and fro, or move to and fro ○ *The dog wagged its tail.* **2.** *vi.* **GOSSIP** to gossip about sb or other people, especially disapprovingly ○ *tongues are wagging* ■ *n.* **MOTION GOING TO AND FRO** a motion that goes to and fro [Old

English. From or related to *wagian* 'to move backwards and forwards'. Ultimately from a prehistoric Germanic word.]

wag[2] /wag/ *vti.* (**wags, wagging, wagged**) PLAY TRUANT to be absent from school without permission (*slang*) ■ *n.* SB WITTY a humorous or witty individual (*dated*) [Mid-16thC. Originally used as an affectionate term for a mischievous boy. Origin uncertain: probably a shortening of *waghalter* 'sb who swings in a noose', that is, sb likely to be hanged.] —**waggery** *n.* —**waggish** *adj.* —**waggishly** *adv.* —**waggishness** *n.*

WAG *abbr.* (West Africa) Gambia (*international vehicle registration*)

wage /wayj/ *n.* PAYMENT FOR WORK a sum of money paid to a worker in exchange for services, especially for work performed on an hourly, daily, weekly, or piece-rate basis (*often used in the plural*) ■ *vt.* (**wages, waging, waged**) ENGAGE IN FIGHT to engage in war or in a serious fight to achieve an end ○ *wage war* [14thC. From Anglo-Norman or Old Norman French. Ultimately from a prehistoric Germanic word meaning 'pledge' (the original sense in English), which is also the ancestor of English *gage* and *wed*.] —**wageless** *adj.* —**wagelessness** *n.*

────── WORD KEY: SYNONYMS ──────
wage, salary, pay, fee, remuneration, emolument, honorarium, stipend
CORE MEANING: money given for work done
wage a fixed regular payment made on a weekly or daily basis, especially to manual workers; **salary** a fixed regular payment, usually made on a monthly basis, especially when made to white-collar or professional workers. It is usually expressed in terms of the amount earned per year; **pay** an informal general word for 'wage' or 'salary'; **fee** the payment made to a professional person by a client; **remuneration** a more formal word for 'pay', that may also include fringe benefits; **emolument** a formal word for any profit made from a job or office; **honorarium** a formal word for money given in exchange for services for which there is normally no charge; **stipend** a regular payment or allowance to a clergyman.

wage differential *n.* any difference in wages between workers with different skills working in the same industry or workers with similar skills working in different industries or regions

wage earner *n.* **1.** HOUSEHOLD SUPPORTER sb in a family or household who is earning a wage or salary **2.** PERSON PAID WAGES sb who works by the hour, day, or week for wages contrasted with sb who is paid a fixed salary regardless of the hours worked

wage incentive *n.* additional money paid to a worker in order to improve that person's productivity

wage packet *n.* a wage or salary that sb earns

wager /wayjər/ *n.* **1.** GAMBLING BET ON OUTCOME an agreement between two people that whoever loses a bet on an uncertain outcome will pay the other a particular amount or some other form of compensation **2.** GAMBLING AMOUNT BET a sum of money, property, or other compensation to be paid to the person who wins a bet **3.** HIST PLEDGE a pledge to engage in combat, especially in order to establish guilt or innocence by single combat ■ *vt.* (**-gers, -gering, -gered**) GAMBLING BET MONEY to risk or bet money or property on the outcome of a game, event, or uncertain situation [14thC. From Anglo-Norman *wageure*, from *wagier* 'to pledge', from *wage* (see WAGE).] —**wagerer** *n.*

wages /wayjiz/ *n.* a just reward or recompense for sth (*literary; takes a singular verb*) ○ *the wages of sin*

wage slave *n.* sb who relies on earning money in order to live (*informal*)

Wagga Wagga /wóggə wóggə/ city in southern New South Wales, Australia. Population: 42,848 (1996).

waggle /wágg'l/ *vti.* (**-gles, -gling, -gled**) MOVE BACK AND FORTH to move rapidly back and forth, or make sth move rapidly back and forth ■ *n.* WOBBLING MOTION a quick shaking or wobbling motion [Late 16thC. From WAG[1], literally 'to keep on wagging'.] —**waggly** *adj.*

waggon *n.* = wagon

AKG London
Richard Wagner

Wagner /vaagnər/, **Richard** (1813–83) German composer. He developed both the form and content of opera, notably in his opera cycle *The Ring of the Nibelungs* (1852–74), and was a major influence on orchestral composers of the late romantic period.

Wagner /wágnər/, **Robert F.** (1877–1953) German-born US statesman. He took the lead in passing progressive legislation while representing New York in the US Senate (1927–49). Full name **Robert Ferdinand Wagner**

Wagnerian /vaag néeri ən/ *adj.* **1.** MUSIC RELATING TO RICHARD WAGNER resembling or relating to the dramatic musical compositions of Richard Wagner **2.** MUSIC POWERFUL having a voice powerful enough to perform in one of Wagner's musical compositions, with their heavy orchestration **3.** JUNOESQUE used to describe a woman with an imposing statuesque figure or a domineering manner ■ *n.* **Wagnerian, Wagnerite** MUSIC RICHARD WAGNER FOLLOWER sb who believes in and follows the musical theories of Richard Wagner, or who loves his music

wagon /wággən/, **waggon** *n.* **1.** WHEELED VEHICLE a rectangular vehicle that is used to carry heavy loads and is pulled by an animal or tractor or is motor-powered **2.** US DELIVERY VEHICLE a van used to sell or deliver sth **3.** US, Can POLICE PATROL WAGON a van used by the police to transport suspects or criminals **4.** US, Can CHILD'S FOUR-WHEELED CART a low four-wheeled cart with a long handle that a child can use to pull the cart or to control the direction of the front wheels **5.** US SERVING CART a four-wheeled rectangular cart used to display or serve food or drink **6.** FREIGHT TRUCK a railway truck for goods, particularly an open one [15thC. From Dutch *wagen*. Ultimately from a prehistoric Germanic word that is also the ancestor of English *wain*.] —**wagoner** *n.* ◇ **be off the wagon** to resume drinking alcohol after a period of abstinence ◇ **be on the wagon** to abstain from drinking alcohol

wagonette /wággə nét/, **waggonette** *n.* a light four-wheeled horse-drawn vehicle with two lengthwise seats facing each other behind a crosswise driver's seat

wagon-lit /vággon leé/ (*plural* **wagon-lits** *or* **wagons-lits**) *n.* **1.** SLEEPING CAR a sleeping car on a European railway **2.** COMPARTMENT an individual compartment in a railway sleeping car [From French, formed from *wagon* 'railway coach' + *lit* 'bed']

wagonload /wággən lōd/, **waggonload** *n.* the amount that a wagon does or can hold

wagon train *n.* a line of two or more animal-drawn wagons travelling cross-country and carrying people, food supplies, or goods

wagon vault *n.* ARCHIT = barrel vault

Wagram /vaag ram/ village in northeastern Austria. It was the site of the Battle of Wagram in which Napoleon defeated the Austrians in July 1809.

wagtail /wág tayl/ *n.* a songbird, found in Europe, Asia, and Africa, with a long tail that bobs up and down when it walks and especially when it lands. Family: Motacillidae.

Wag the Dog syndrome *n.* US a situation in which a US president uses military attacks on other nations as a diversionary tactic to deflect intense public and media scrutiny from a personal scandal (*slang*) ○ '*Was the bombing of Iraq really a result of Wag the Dog syndrome?*' (*Vanity Fair*; March 1999) [Late 20thC. *Wag the Dog* from a film.]

────── WORD KEY: CULTURAL NOTE ──────
Wag the Dog, a film by Tribeca Productions and screenplay by Hilary Henkin and David Mamet (1997). Based on a novel by Larry Beinhart titled *American Hero*, the film depicts a fictional US president's advisors starting a phony war in order to deflect media attention from a scandal. The film's premiere in early 1998 coincided with a grand jury investigation of US President Bill Clinton, a sex scandal involving him and a former White House intern, and an impeachment trial (which later ended in acquittal). During this period the President responded to military aggression and terrorist acts affecting the United States by launching cruise missiles against Iraq, Sudan, and Afghanistan. The US media and the pop culture soon drew a figurative connection between the film and the Presidential scandal, leading to such expressions as 'Is it Wag the Dog?', 'Was it a Wag the Dog scenario?', and the phrase *Wag the Dog syndrome*.

Wahhabi /wə haábi/ (*plural* **-bis**), **Wahabi** (*plural* **Wahabis**) *n.* a member of a very conservative Islamic group that rejects any innovation that occurred after the 3rd century of Islam. It flourishes primarily in Arabia. [Early 19thC. From Arabic *wahhābī*, named after Muhammad ibn bd-al-*Wahhāb* (1703–92), who founded the sect.] —**Wahhabism** *n.*

wahine /waa héeni/ *n.* **1.** *Hawaii, NZ* HAWAIIAN OR MAORI WOMAN a Hawaiian or Maori woman or wife **2.** *Hawaii* WOMAN SURFER a young woman surfer (*informal*) [Late 18thC. From Hawaiian or Maori.]

wahoo /waá hoo, waa hoó/ (*plural* **-hoos**) *n.* a large fast-swimming fish of the mackerel family that lives in tropical seas worldwide and weighs up to 120 pounds. Latin name: *Acanthocybium solanderi.* [Early 20thC. Origin unknown.]

wah-wah /waá waa/, **wa-wa** *n.* **1.** WAVERING SOUND OF WIND INSTRUMENT the wavering sound made by alternately covering and uncovering the bell of a trumpet or trombone **2.** ELECTRONIC SOUND a sound similar to the wah-wah of a trumpet or trombone created electronically for guitars, keyboards, and other electronic instruments **3.** ELECTRONIC DEVICE an electronic device attached to a musical instrument for producing a wavering wah-wah sound [Early 20thC. An imitation of the sound.]

wah-wah pedal *n.* a foot pedal attached to an electronic musical instrument such as an electric guitar, used to create a wavering wah-wah sound

waiata /wí aatə/ *n.* NZ a Maori song

waif /wayf/ *n.* **1.** ABANDONED CHILD a homeless or friendless person, especially an abandoned child **2.** STRAY ANIMAL a stray animal whose owner is unknown **3.** THIN YOUNG PERSON sb, usually a young person, with a thin fragile appearance who looks in need of care **4.** UNCLAIMED ITEM any item found whose owner is unknown (*literary*) **5.** UNCLAIMED PROPERTY any property that, if found ownerless and unclaimed, becomes the property of the Crown or lord of the manor **6.** NAUT = **waft** *n.* 5 [14thC. From Anglo-Norman *weyf*, earlier *gwayf* 'lost property', from Scandinavian. The sense of 'abandoned child' evolved from 'unclaimed property' through 'lost thing' and 'lost child'.]

Waiheke Island /wī héeki-/ island in the Hauraki Gulf off the northeastern coast of the North Island, New Zealand. Population: 6,286 (1996). Area: 93 sq. km/36 sq. mi.

Waikaremoana /wī kórrəmō aanə/ lake in the eastern part of the North Island, New Zealand. Area: 54 sq. km/21 sq. mi.

Waikato /wík aatō/ the longest river in New Zealand. It rises in Lake Taupo in the centre of the North Island and empties into the Tasman Sea south of Waiuku. Length: 434 km/270 mi.

Waikiki /wí kee kee/ beach resort northeast of Honolulu, Oahu Island, Hawaii

wail /wayl/ *v.* (**wails, wailing, wailed**) **1.** *vti.* MAKE MOURNFUL CRY to express pain, grief, or misery in a long mournful high-pitched cry or in words uttered in a mournful way ○ *He could only wail when he heard the news.* **2.** *vi.* MAKE LONG HIGH-PITCHED NOISE to make a long loud high-pitched sound ○ *The sirens wailed.* **3.** *vt.* LAMENT to express grief over sb or sth (*archaic*) ■ *n.* **1.** LONG HIGH-PITCHED SOUND a long loud high-pitched sound or cry **2.** PROTEST a loud plaintive expression of protest, resentment, or disappointment [13thC. From an Old Norse word that was formed from *vei*, 'woe'.] —**wailful** *adj.* —**wailfully** *adv.*

Wailing Wall *n.* = **Western Wall**

wain /wayn/ *n.* a farm wagon or cart (*archaic or literary*) [Old English *wæ(g)n*, of prehistoric Germanic origin]

wainscot /wáynskət, wáyn skot/ *n.* **1.** WOODEN PANELS LINING ROOM a lining for the walls of a room, especially one made of wood panelling **2.** LOWER PART OF WALL OF ROOM the lower part of the wall of a room, especially when it is panelled in wood or finished differently from the upper part **3.** OAK PANELLING a fine grade of oak used as wall panelling ■ *vt.* (**-scots, -scotting, -scotted**) COVER WALL WITH PANELLING to cover a wall, especially with wood panelling [14thC. From Middle Dutch *waghenscote* or Middle Low German *wagenschot*, literally 'wagon-boarding'.]

wainscoting /wáynskəting, wáyn skotting/, **wainscotting** *n.* **1.** = **wainscot** *n.* 1 **2.** WOOD FOR COVERING WALL the material, especially wood, used to cover a wall

wainwright /wáyn rīt/ *n.* sb who makes and repairs wagons

Wairarapa, Lake /wī́ raa ráapə-/ lake in the southern part of the North Island, New Zealand. Area: 80 sq. km/50 sq. mi.

Wairau /wī́r ow/ river in the northern part of the South Island, New Zealand. It rises in the Southern Alps and empties into the Cook Strait near Blenheim. Length: 169 km/105 mi.

waist /wayst/ *n.* **1.** ANAT BODY AREA BETWEEN RIBS AND HIPS the part of the human trunk between the ribcage and the hips, usually narrower than the rest of the trunk **2.** CLOTHES PART OF CLOTHING the part of a garment that fits around the waist of the body **3.** NARROW PART the narrow middle part of sth, such as the middle of a violin **4.** SHIPPING MIDDLE OF DECK the middle part of a ship or a ship's deck between the raised sections at the bow and stern **5.** AIR MIDDLE OF AEROPLANE the middle section of an aircraft's fuselage **6.** INSECTS MIDDLE OF INSECT the narrow part of an insect's body between the thorax and the abdomen [14thC. Origin uncertain: perhaps from an Old English word meaning 'girth to which sb has grown', from a prehistoric Germanic word meaning 'to grow' (ancestor of English *wax*).] —**waistless** *adj.*

waistband /wáyst band/ *n.* a band of fabric in a piece of clothing, e.g. at the top of a skirt or pair of trousers, that circles the waist

waistcloth /wáyst kloth/ *n.* a loincloth (*archaic*)

waistcoat /wáyss kōt, wáyst-/ *n.* **1.** SLEEVELESS UPPER GARMENT WORN OVER SHIRT a man's or woman's sleeveless and collarless waist-length garment, usually with buttons down the front, worn over a shirt and traditionally worn by men under a suit jacket **2.** HIST GARMENT WORN UNDER DOUBLET a man's sleeveless garment reaching to the hips or knees, worn under a doublet in the 16th century —**waistcoated** *adj.*

waisted /wáystid/ *adj.* made with a waist or a part that resembles a waist

waistline /wáyst līn/ *n.* **1.** MEASUREMENT OF WAIST the measurement round the narrowest part of the waist **2.** CLOTHES MEETING OF BODICE AND WAIST the level, usually near the waist, where the bodice and skirt of a dress meet ○ *a low waistline*

wait /wayt/ *v.* (**waits, waiting, waited**) **1.** *vi.* DO NOTHING EXPECTING STH TO HAPPEN to stay in one place or do nothing for a period of time until sth happens or in the expectation or hope that sth will happen ○ *I'll wait for you here until noon.* **2.** *vi.* STOP SO SB CAN CATCH UP to stop or slow down in order to allow sb else to catch up ○ *Wait for me!* **3.** *vi.* BE HOPING FOR STH to be hoping for sth or on the lookout for sth ○ *He is waiting for a job opportunity.* **4.** *vi.* BE DELAYED OR IGNORED FOR NOW to be postponed or put off until later ○ *Fame would just have to wait.* **5.** *vi.* BE READY OR AVAILABLE to be ready or available for sb to take or use ○ *Your mail is waiting for you.* **6.** *vt.* DELAY STH to delay sth, especially a meal, because sb is expected to arrive soon ○ *We waited dinner for you.* **7.** *vti.* BE A WAITER to work as a waiter ○ *She waits at the local restaurant.* ■ *n.* TIME SPENT WAITING a period of time spent while expecting sth to happen ○ *The wait seemed like forever.* ■ **waits** *npl.* MUSIC BAND OF MUSICIANS a band of musicians who play and sing Christmas carols in the streets (*archaic*) [12thC. Via Old Northern French *waitier*, 'to spy, prepare to ambush', from Frankish.] ◇ **lie in wait for** be waiting to catch or attack sb *or* sth

wait on *vt.* **1.** SERVE SB BY BRINGING REQUESTED ITEMS to go and get the things that sb asks for, usually continuously for a period of time ○ *It's nice to be waited on for a change.* **2.** SERVE SB AT TABLE to bring food and drink to people sitting at a table, usually in a restaurant **3.** SERVE RETAIL CUSTOMER to attend to a customer's purchasing needs **4.** WAIT FOR SB to wait for sb or sth (*informal*) **5.** VISIT SB to pay a formal visit to sb (*archaic*) ■ *interj.* ANZ HOLD ON used to tell sb to wait a while

wait out *vt.* to stay in one place or do nothing until sth ends ○ *We decided to wait out the storm.*

wait up *vi.* to delay going to bed to await an event or sb's arrival ○ *I'll be home late; don't wait up.*

wait upon *vt.* = **wait on** *v.* 1, **wait on** *v.* 2, **wait on** *v.* 3, **wait on** *v.* 5

Waitaki /wī táki/ river in the southeastern part of the South Island, New Zealand. It rises in Lake Benmore and empties into the Pacific Ocean near the town of Waitaki. Length: 209 km/130 mi.

Waitangi /wī túngi/ historic site in the northern part of the North Island, New Zealand. A treaty between the Maori people and the British government was signed there in February 1840.

Waitangi Day /wī tángi-/ *n.* a national day and public holiday in New Zealand on 6 February, commemorating the signing of the Treaty of Waitangi in 1840 by Maori chiefs and representatives of the British government

Waitemata Harbour /wītə máta haárbər/ arm of the Pacific Ocean on the northeastern coast of the North Island, New Zealand. Auckland is situated on part of it.

waiter /wáytər/ *n.* **1.** SB WHO SERVES AT TABLES sb employed to bring food and drink to people, usually in a restaurant **2.** TRAY a tray for carrying dishes or serving food **3.** STOCK EXCH MESSENGER a messenger at the London Stock Exchange or Lloyd's [14thC. Via Anglo-Norman, 'attendant, watchman', from Old Northern French, or directly formed from WAIT.]

waiting game *n.* a tactic whereby sb delays taking any action or making a move in a contest or negotiation, hoping that his or her position will improve with the passage of time

waiting list *n.* a list of people waiting for sth that is not immediately available, e.g. a hospital bed, a table in a restaurant, a place in a school, or an out-of-stock product

waiting room *n.* a room in which people may wait, e.g. for a doctor's appointment or a train

Waitomo Caves /wī tómō-/ limestone cave system in the western part of the North Island, New Zealand, noted for its large colonies of glowworms

waitperson /wáyt purss'n/ (*plural* **waitpeople** *or* **waitpersons**) *n.* US a man or woman employed to serve at tables, usually in a restaurant

waitress /wáytrəss/ *n.* a woman who serves food or drink at tables, usually in a restaurant

waitstaff /wáyt staaf/ *n.* US the group of waiters and waitresses in a café or restaurant

wait state *n.* a period of time during which a central processing unit in a computer sits idle while a slower computer component such as a memory or a bus performs its function

waive /wayv/ (**waives, waiving, waived**) *vt.* **1.** SURRENDER CLAIM to give sth up voluntarily, especially a right or claim ○ *She waived her right to remain silent.* **2.** NOT ENFORCE STH to refrain from enforcing or applying sth in a particular instance ○ *They decided to waive the restrictions.* **3.** TEMPORARILY DELAY STH to put off sth for a time [13thC. From Anglo-Norman *weyver*, 'to make a waif of, abandon', from *weyf*. See WAIF.]

waiver /wáyvər/ *n.* **1.** RELINQUISHMENT OF RIGHT a voluntary giving up of a right or claim **2.** DOCUMENT CONTAINING WAIVER a document or formal statement relinquishing a right or claim, or an action indicating an intention to waive sth

Wajda /vájdə/, **Andrzej** (*b.* 1926) Polish film director. Much of his work focuses on Poland during and after World War II and on Polish nationalism of the 1970s and 1980s.

wakame /waa kaámi/ (*plural* **-mes** *or* **-me**) *n.* a brown seaweed native to the coasts of Japan, China, and Korea, often dried and used in Japanese and Chinese cooking. Latin name: *Undaria pinnatifida.* [Mid-20thC. From Japanese.]

Wakashan /waa káshən/ *n.* a family of languages spoken by Native North American peoples in British Columbia and Washington State. About 3,000 people speak one of the Wakashan languages. [Late 19thC. From Nootka *waukash*, 'good'. Said to have been applied to these peoples by CAPTAIN COOK.] —**Wakashan** *adj.*

Wakatipu /waákə típpoo/ lake in the southwestern part of the South Island, New Zealand. The town of Queenstown is located on its northern shore. Area: 293 sq. km/113 sq. mi.

Wakayama /wákə yaámə/ port and capital city of Wakayama Prefecture, southwest of Osaka, Japan. Population: 396,553 (1990).

wake[1] /wayk/ *v.* (**wakes, waking, woke** /wōk/, **woken** /wṓkən/) **1.** *vti.* END SB'S OR YOUR OWN SLEEP to come back, or bring sb back, to a conscious state after sleeping ○ *I woke suddenly at dawn.* **2.** *vti.* END INACTIVITY to become alert and active, or make sb alert and active, after being inactive, in a daydream, or preoccupied **3.** *vti.* MAKE SB REALIZE STH to make sb aware of sth ○ *Their pleas woke us to the situation.* **4.** *vi.* WATCH OVER CORPSE to hold a vigil over the body of sb who has died **5.** *vi.* STAY AWAKE to be or to remain awake ○ *'Fled is that music — Do I wake or sleep?'* (John Keats, *Ode to a Nightingale*; 1819) **6.** *vti.* KEEP WATCH to keep watch over sb or sth (*archaic*) ■ *n.* **1.** WATCH KEPT OVER CORPSE a watch or vigil held over a corpse before burial or cremation **2.** FESTIVE GATHERING ROUND FUNERAL a social gathering held after a funeral or, in Ireland, often after the death but before the funeral. Traditionally people drink and talk about the dead person, and there is a happy jovial atmosphere. **3.** CHR CHURCH FESTIVAL the festival for the patron saint of a parish church or one held to commemorate its dedication (*regional*) **4.** **wakes** ANNUAL HOLIDAY an annual one- or two-week holiday, originally to celebrate a parish church festival in the industrial areas of northern England, when the local factories shut down (*regional; takes a singular or plural verb*) [Old English *wacan*, 'to become awake'. Ultimately from the same Indo-European word meaning 'be active or lively' as English *vigilance, wait, vigour,* and *watch*.] —**waker** *n.*

WORD KEY: USAGE

See Usage note at ***awake***.

WORD KEY: CULTURAL NOTE

Finnegans Wake, a novel by Irish author James Joyce (1939). Joyce's last novel recounts a single night in the life of a Dublin publican, Humphrey Chimpden Earwicker, and his family. An extraordinary multilayered work consisting chiefly of extended interior monologues, it is crammed with multilingual puns, poetry, and literary and historical allusions that emphasize the universal and cyclical nature of human experience.

wake up *vti.* = **wake**[1] *v.* 1, **wake**[1] *v.* 2, **wake**[1] *v.* 3 ◇ **wake up and smell the coffee** US used to tell sb that he or she is wrong about a particular situation and that it is time to acknowledge the reality (*informal*)

wake[2] /wayk/ *n.* **1.** NAUT TRACK IN WATER the track left in water by a vessel or any other body moving through it **2.** DISTURBED AIR BEHIND VEHICLE the stream of turbulence in the air left by an aircraft or land vehicle passing through it **3.** POSITION BEHIND SB a position or the area behind sb or sth that is moving ahead fast ○ *left the rest of the field trailing in her wake* **4.** AFTEREFFECTS the aftermath or aftereffects of a dramatic event or powerful thing ○ *The bomb left destruction in its wake.* [15thC. Via Middle Low German from Old Norse *vok* 'hole in ice (made by a boat)'.] ◇ **in the wake of sth** immediately after and usually as a result of sth

wakeboarding *n.* a water sport in which sb riding a single board is pulled behind a motor boat and performs jumps while crisscrossing the wake of the boat [Late 20thC. Modelled on SKATEBOARDING.]

Wakefield /wáyk feeld/ city in Yorkshire, northern England, on the River Calder. Population: 73,675 (1991).

Wakefield /wáyk feeld/, **Edward Gibbon** (1796–1862) English-born New Zealand social theorist and statesman. He formulated the programme of selling crown lands in the British colonies to encourage colonization, which became known as 'Wakefield Settlements'.

wakeful /wáykf'l/ *adj.* **1.** NOT SLEEPING unable to sleep **2.** SLEEPLESS passed without sleep ○ *a wakeful night* **3.** ALERT awake, especially while watching or guarding sth ○ *promised to remain wakeful* —**wakefully** *adv.* —**wakefulness** *n.*

wakeless /wáykləss/ *adj.* uninterrupted by waking, or spent in uninterrupted sleep

waken /wáykən/ (**-ens, -ening, -ened**) *vti.* to become, or make sb, conscious after sleeping, active after being inactive, or aware after being unaware (*formal*) —**wakener** *n.*

WORD KEY: USAGE

See Usage note at ***awake***.

wake-robin (*plural* **wake-robins** *or* **wake-robin**) *n.* **1.** *US* = **trillium 2.** = **cuckoopint 3.** ARUM PLANT a member of a group of early-blooming North American arums, e.g. the arrow arum

wake-up call *n.* **1.** CALL TO AWAKEN GUEST a telephone call or a personal visit made to awaken sb, especially a telephone call from or arranged by hotel staff made at an agreed time to awaken a guest **2.** FRIGHTENING EXPERIENCE a frightening experience that is interpreted as a sign that a major change is needed in the way sb lives or conducts business

wakil = **vakil**

Wal. *abbr.* Walloon

Walachia former region in southeastern Europe, in present-day southern Romania. Founded as a principality towards the end of the 13th century, it was ruled by Turkey from 1387 until it joined Moldavia to form Romania in 1861. —**Walachian** *n., adj.*

Waldemar I /vaáldə maár/, **King of Denmark** (1131–82). Having gained sole control of the Danish throne (1157–82), he established a dynastic rule in Denmark. Known as **Waldemar the Great**

Waldemar II, King of Denmark (1170–1241). He was the son of Waldemar I. As king (1202–41), he extended Danish territory and instituted legal and administrative reforms. Known as **Waldemar the Conqueror**

Waldenses /wawl dénseez, wol-/ *npl.* the members of a small Christian denomination, originating in southern France, that broke with the Roman Catholic Church in the 12th century and experienced much persecution. In the 16th century the Waldenses joined the Reformation and adopted Calvinist doctrines. [Mid-16thC. From medieval Latin, from *Waldensis*, a variant of Peter *Valdes* (d. 1205), who founded the movement.] —**Waldensian** /wawl dénssi ən, wol-/ *adj.*

waldgrave /wáwld grayv, wóld-/ *n.* an officer in medieval Germany with jurisdiction over a royal forest [From German *Waldgraf*, 'forest count']

Waldheim /wáwld hīm, vaált-/, **Kurt** (*b.* 1918) Austrian statesman. He was secretary general of the United Nations (1972–81) and president of Austria (1986–91). During his presidency it was alleged he had been complicit in Nazi war crimes.

waldo /wáwldō, wóldō/ (*plural* **-dos** *or* **-does**) *n.* a remote-controlled device for manipulating objects (*dated informal*) [Mid-20thC. From *Waldo F. Jones*, the hero of *Waldo*, a 1940 story by Robert Heinlein. In the story, these devices have been named after their inventor, Waldo Jones.]

Waldorf salad /wáwld awrf-, wóld-/ *n.* a salad made of diced raw apples, celery, and walnuts with a mayonnaise dressing [Early 20thC. Named after the *Waldorf*-Astoria Hotel in New York, USA, where this salad was first served.]

waldsterben /wáwld sturbən/ *n.* widespread disease and death of trees, thought to be the result of atmospheric pollution. It was first identified in central Europe in the 1970s. [Late 20thC. From German, literally 'forest dying'.]

wale /wayl/ *n.* **1.** SKIN WELT a raised mark on the skin made by a blow, particularly with a whip **2.** TEXTILES RIDGE ON FABRIC a ridge on the surface of a woven fabric such as corduroy **3.** TEXTILES WEAVE OF FABRIC the weave or texture of a fabric with ribs **4.** KNITTING VERTICAL ROW OF KNITTING a vertical row of stitches in knitting **5.** NAUT WOOD FORMING SIDES OF SHIP any of the strong horizontal planks forming the sides of a wooden ship ■ *vt.* (**wales, waling, waled**) **1.** RAISE WELT ON SKIN to raise a red swollen mark on the skin by striking a blow, particularly with a whip **2.** TEXTILES WEAVE RIDGED FABRIC to weave fabric with ridges [Old English *walu*, 'ridge', from prehistoric Germanic]

Wales /waylz/ principality in Great Britain, part of the United Kingdom of Great Britain and Northern Ireland. Once a separate kingdom, it was united with England in 1536. It voted in 1997 to have its own assembly, giving it a degree of self-government. Capital: Cardiff. Population: 2,921,000 (1996). Area: 20,766 sq. km/8,018 sq. mi.

Walhalla *n.* = **Valhalla**

walk /wawk/ *v.* (**walks, walking, walked**) **1.** *vi.* MOVE ON FOOT to move or travel on legs and feet, alternately putting one foot a comfortable distance in front of, or sometimes behind, the other and usually proceeding at a moderate pace. When walking, as opposed to running, one of the feet is always in contact with the ground, the one being put down as or before the other is lifted. ○ *a toddler just learning to walk* **2.** *vt.* TRAVEL THROUGH PLACE ON FOOT to travel along or through sth on foot ○ *walking the coastal path* **3.** *vt.* TAKE ANIMAL FOR EXERCISE BY WALKING to lead or exercise an animal, usually a dog on a leash ○ *walked the dog* **4.** *vt.* WALK WITH SB TO STH to accompany sb on foot as far as a particular place such as a home or car ○ *walking a friend home* **5.** *vt.* CAUSE SB TO WALK to help or force sb to walk by holding and pushing from behind ○ *We kept walking him till he was able to stand on his own.* **6.** *vti.* MOVE LARGE OBJECT BY ROCKING to move, or move sth, in a way that suggests walking, e.g. by pivoting a large heavy object alternately on its corners and swinging the other side forwards ○ *The wardrobe's too heavy to lift; we'll have to walk it into the bedroom.* **7.** *vt.* MEASURE STH BY WALKING to measure or inspect sth by walking over or along it, especially the boundaries of an area or piece of property ○ *walk the west property line* **8.** *vt.* PUT STH INTO CONDITION to put sth or sb into a particular condition by walking ○ *They walked us till our feet were sore.* **9.** *vi.* LIVE IN PARTICULAR WAY to conduct your life in a particular way **10.** *vti.* COME BACK AS A GHOST to return to earth after death as a ghost ○ *She walks the tower.* **11.** *vi.* BE STOLEN to disappear or be stolen (*informal*) ○ *The petty cash seems to have walked.* **12.** *vi.* *US* GO ON STRIKE to go out on strike (*slang*) ○ *threatened to walk* **13.** *vi.* *US* LEAVE IN PROTEST to leave a job, event, or meeting to express disagreement (*slang*) ○ *I'd better get an apology or I'm walking!* **14.** *vi.* *US* BE FREED FROM JAIL OR ACQUITTED to be released from prison or found innocent of a crime (*slang*) ○ *I couldn't believe they walked after what they did!* **15.** *vi.* CRICKET ACKNOWLEDGE BEING OUT BY LEAVING WICKET to leave the wicket without waiting to be given out by the umpire **16.** *vi.* BASEBALL GO TO FIRST BASE to proceed, or allow the batter to proceed, to first base after four deliveries from the pitcher, none of which was in the strike zone or swung at **17.** *vi.* BASKETBALL TAKE STEPS ILLEGALLY to take more than two steps in basketball without dribbling while holding the ball ■ *n.* **1.** ROUTE a regular route of a street vendor or delivery person **2.** MARCH a procession **3.** JOURNEY ON FOOT a journey made on foot, especially for pleasure or exercise ○ *a walk in the woods* **4.** DISTANCE OR TIME OF FOOT JOURNEY the distance travelled or the time it takes to go somewhere on foot ○ *a four-mile walk* ○ *a ten-minute walk from home* **5.** EQU HORSE'S SLOWER GAIT a relatively slow-paced way of moving for a horse or other four-legged animal, in which two feet are always on the ground ○ *The mare started at a walk, then broke into a trot.* **6.** WAY OF WALKING sb's characteristic way of walking ○ *She's got a graceful walk.* **7.** PLACE FOR PEDESTRIANS a place designed or set aside for the use of people on foot **8.** ROUTE FOR PEOPLE WALKING a route or path for travellers on foot ○ *The miners' trail is an easy scenic walk.* **9.** ATHLETICS TRACK RACE a track race in which the competitors walk a specified distance **10.** AREA FOR ANIMALS an enclosed area for exercising or pasturing domestic animals such as horses **11.** ROWS OF TREES a plantation of widely spaced trees or shrubs **12.** SPACE BETWEEN ROWS the space between rows of widely spaced trees or shrubs **13.** BASKETBALL ILLEGAL HOLDING INSTEAD OF DRIBBLING in basketball, an illegal taking of steps while holding the ball **14.** *US* STH VERY EASY sth that is very easy to do (*informal*) ○ *We'll certainly beat them. It'll be a walk.* **15.** FOREST a section of a forest controlled by a single keeper (*archaic*) [Old English *wealcan* 'to roll, toss' and *wealcian* 'to roll up', from a prehistoric Germanic word (ancestor of English *gauche*). The meaning developed via 'move about', 'go on a journey'.] —**walkable** *adj.* ◇ **walk it** to gain victory or success easily (*informal*) ◇ **walk all over sb** to ignore sb's rights or feelings ◇ **walk tall** to feel and display self-confidence and pride in your achievements

walk away *vi.* **1.** ABANDON PROBLEM to refrain from becoming, or refuse to become, involved in a situation or problem **2.** HAVE MINOR INJURIES to survive an accident uninjured or with few and minor injuries and be able to walk from the scene **3.** DEFEAT SB to defeat or outdo another person or team easily **4.** WIN STH to win or achieve sth ○ *She walked away with the first prize.*

walk off *v.* **1.** *vi.* LEAVE ABRUPTLY to leave a place abruptly ○ *She walked off without a word.* **2.** *vt.* CURE STH BY WALKING to get rid of sth such as an injury or feeling of sickness by walking

walk off with *vt.* **1.** STEAL STH to steal sth ○ *walked off with all the jewels* **2.** WIN EASILY to win sth effortlessly

walk out *vi.* **1.** LEAVE WITHOUT EXPLANATION to leave, especially in anger or protest, without explanation **2.** GO ON STRIKE to go on strike **3.** LEAVE SB PERMANENTLY to leave a spouse, partner, or family permanently

walk out on *vt.* to leave or abandon sb (*informal*) ○ *My wife walked out on me last summer.*

walk over *vt.* to win or defeat an opponent easily (*informal*) ○ *That horse will walk over the rest.*

walk through *vt.* **1.** ARTS REHEARSE OR PERFORM A PLAY SKETCHILY to rehearse sth in a simple, unelaborate way, mainly practising basic moves and positions, or perform sth in a perfunctory, uncommitted way, as if still in rehearsal **2.** TV REHEARSE WITHOUT CAMERAS to rehearse a television programme without cameras

walkabout /wáwkə bowt/ *n.* **1.** *Aus* JOURNEY THROUGH BUSH an extended journey through a remote area made by an Australian Aboriginal wishing to experience or return to a traditional way of life and to traditional beliefs **2.** PUBLIC WALK an informal walk among the people by royalty or a celebrity **3.** WALK a walking trip ◇ **go walkabout** (*informal*) **1.** *Aus* go for an extended journey on foot in remote country, traditionally alone and living off the land **2.** *Aus* leave your normal surroundings (*informal*) **3.** be stolen

WORD KEY: CULTURAL NOTE

Walkabout, a film by English director Nicholas Roeg (1970). Set in 1960s Australia, it tells the story of two English children who are left to fend for themselves in the outback when their father commits suicide. They are befriended by a young Aboriginal boy who teaches them to cope with and appreciate the seemingly harsh environment.

walker /wáwkər/ *n.* **1.** SB WHO WALKS sb who walks, especially regularly for exercise or in competition **2.** = **baby walker 3.** WALKING SUPPORT a lightweight waist-high framework, usually with four legs and rubber feet, used to help sb who cannot walk without support

Walker /wáwkər/, **Alice** (*b.* 1944) US writer. Her novels, including the Pulitzer Prize-winning *The Color Purple* (1982), are concerned largely with the experience of African American women. Full name **Alice Malsenior Walker**

walkie-talkie /wáwki táwki/, **walky-talky** (*plural* **walky-talkies**) *n.* a hand-held battery-operated radio transmitter and receiver often used by emergency personnel to communicate with one another [Mid-20thC. A playful variant of WALK and TALK.]

Alice Walker

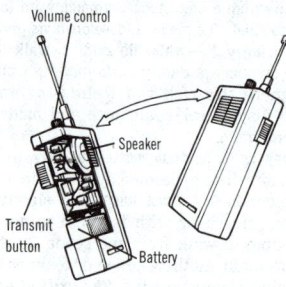

Walkie-talkie

Volume control

Speaker

Transmit button

Battery

walk-in *adj.* large and spacious enough to enter

walking /wáwking/ *adj.* **1. ABLE TO WALK** capable of walking **2. FOR WALKING** used or designed for the purpose of walking ○ *walking shoes* **3. OF WALKING** that involves travelling on foot ○ *a walking tour* ◇ **a walking dictionary** *or* **encyclopaedia** sb who is very knowledgeable

walking bass *n.* a bass accompaniment, usually consisting of small steps or intervals up and down the scale in 4/4 time

walking catfish *n.* a freshwater catfish native to tropical Asia with special organs that enable it to breathe on land for short periods while it moves to another body of water. Latin name: *Clarius batrachus.*

walking delegate *n.* **1.** *US* **LABOUR UNION REPRESENTATIVE** a labour union representative appointed to visit local unions and their employers to ensure compliance with contracts and sometimes to represent the local union in negotiations **2.** *NZ* **TRADE UNION OFFICIAL** a trade union official in a dock area

walking fern, **walking leaf** (*plural* **walking leaves** *or* **walking leaf**) *n.* a fern of eastern North America whose long arching fronds take root at the tip, sprouting new plants. Latin name: *Camptosorus rhizophyllus.*

walking papers *npl. US* official notification that sb has been fired from a job or dismissed from military service (*informal*)

walking stick *n.* a cane or stick used to assist in walking

Walkman /wáwkmən/ *tdmk.* a trademark for a small portable cassette player with earphones

walk of life *n.* sb's occupation or social or economic class ○ *people from all walks of life*

walk-on *n.* **1. SMALL PART IN PLAY OR MOVIE** a small part, usually a nonspeaking one, in a stage or film production **2. SB WITH BRIEF PART** sb who has a small part, usually a nonspeaking one, in a stage or film production

walkout /wáwk owt/ *n.* **1. EMPLOYEE STRIKE** an organized strike by employees in which workers walk out of the building or off the premises **2. ACT OF LEAVING AS PROTEST** a departure in protest or anger about sth

walkover /wáwkōvər/ *n.* **1. EASY VICTORY** an easy victory or one that is obtained without a contest, e.g. because the opposing side did not turn up (*informal*) **2. RACE WITH ONE HORSE** a horserace in which only one horse is entered

walk-through *n.* an early play rehearsal without props or costumes, or a television rehearsal without cameras, usually to practise basic moves and positions

walk-up *n. US* **1. BUILDING WITHOUT LIFT** a building of several stories without a lift (*informal*) **2. FLAT REACHED BY STAIRS** a flat in a building without a lift

walkway /wáwk way/ *n.* **1. SPECIALLY BUILT PATH FOR WALKERS** a specially constructed path for pedestrians **2. PASSAGE ABOVE GROUND LEVEL** a passage above ground level designed for pedestrian use, e.g. one connecting buildings or passing over a roadway

Walkyrie *n.* = **Valkyrie**

walky-talky *n.* = **walkie-talkie**

wall /wawl/ *n.* **1. FLAT SIDE OF BUILDING OR ROOM** a vertical structure forming an inside partition or an outside surface of a building **2. STANDING STRUCTURE THAT SURROUNDS OR BLOCKS** a narrow upright structure, usually built of stone, wood, plaster, or brick, that acts as a boundary or keeps sth in or out ○ *a garden wall* **3. STH IMPENETRABLE** sth similar to a wall in appearance or impenetrability ○ *met with a wall of reporters* **4. STH THAT PREVENTS COMMUNICATION** an obstacle to understanding or communication between people **5.** SOCCER **LINE OF DEFENSIVE PLAYERS** in soccer, a line of defensive players who must stand at least ten yards from a free kick and who try to block a shot on goal **6.** ANAT **BODY MEMBRANE OR LINING** a membrane or lining enclosing or bounding an organ, blood vessel, or cavity of the body ○ *the uterine wall* **7.** BIOL **RIGID COVERING FOR CELLS** a rigid covering over the outer membranes of plant cells and of some prokaryotic animal cells **8.** MOUNTAINEERING **ROCK FACE** a vertical or nearly vertical rock face ○ *a sheer wall of granite* **9.** BUILDING **DEFENSIVE STRUCTURE** a structure of earth or stone built for defensive purposes **10.** CIV ENG **BARRIER TO FLOODING** a structure built as a barrier to flooding ■ *vt.* (**walls**, **walling**, **walled**) **1. SURROUND STH WITH WALLS** to fortify or surround sth or sb with a wall ○ *They walled in the back garden.* **2. SEPARATE STH WITH WALLS** to put up a wall to separate one area from another **3. CLOSE STH WITH WALL** to close an opening with a wall ○ *wall up the passage* **4. TRAP OR BURY BEHIND WALLS** to seal sb or sth in a space with a wall [Pre-12thC. From Latin *vallum*, 'rampart', from *vallus*, 'stake' (source also of English *interval*).] —**walled** *adj.* ◇ **be climbing the wall** *or* **walls** to be extremely bored or frustrated (*informal*) ◇ **drive sb up the wall** to annoy or irritate sb extremely (*informal*) ◇ **go to the wall** to be destroyed or ruined, especially financially

walla *n.* = **wallah**

Wallaby

wallaby /wólləbi/ (*plural* **-bies**) *n.* **1. AUSTRALIAN MARSUPIAL LIKE SMALL KANGAROO** any of various marsupials of Australia and New Guinea that resemble small kangaroos. Family: Macropodidae. **2. Wallabies** RUGBY **AUSTRALIAN RUGBY TEAM** the Australian Rugby Union team (*informal*) [Early 19thC. From Dharuk *walabi* and *waliba*.]

Wallace /wólliss/, **Alfred Russel** (1823–1913) British naturalist. He formulated a theory of natural selection independently of Charles Darwin. The term 'Wallace line' refers to his recognition of the distinctions between the fauna of Asia and Australia.

Wallace, Edgar (1875–1932) British writer. He wrote more than 170 popular crime novels and thrillers, beginning with *The Four Just Men* (1905). Full name **Richard Horatio Edgar Wallace**

Edgar Wallace

Sir William Wallace: Commemorative statue near Melrose, Scotland

Wallace, Sir William (1272?–1305) Scottish patriot. He led a rebellion against the English (1297), but was defeated by Edward I (1298). He was later captured and executed.

Wallace's line /wóllissiz-/ *n.* a hypothetical boundary in the southwestern Pacific separating the Oriental and Australian biogeographic regions and their distinctive types of wildlife. The line runs between Bali and Lombok in the Indonesian island chain and north through the Makassar Strait, passing south of the Philippines. [Mid-19thC. Named after Alfred Russel *Wallace* (1823–1913), the English naturalist who defined this boundary.]

wallah /wóllə/, **walla** *n.* sb in charge of a particular thing or associated with a particular service or occupation (*dated informal*) ○ *a legal wallah* [Late 18thC. Via Hindi *-vālā*, '(sb) responsible for sth or some duty', from Sanskrit *pālaka*, 'keeper'.]

wallaroo /wóllə roó/ (*plural* **-roos** *or* **-roo**) *n.* either of two species of large and sturdy kangaroo found throughout rocky upland areas of mainland Australia. Latin name: *Macropus robustus* and *Macropus bernardus.* [Early 19thC. From Dharuk *walāru.*]

Wallasey /wólləssi/ town on the Wirral Peninsula, northwestern England. Population: 60,895 (1991).

wall bars *npl.* a series of horizontal bars attached to a wall and used for exercises

wallboard /wáwl bawrd/ *n.* = **plasterboard**

wall creeper *n.* a songbird of rocky mountainous regions of Europe and Asia that has a long slender beak and black wings with scarlet markings. It is related to the nuthatch. Latin name: *Tichodroma muraria.*

Wallenberg /vaálən berg, waálən búrg/, **Raoul** (1912–47?) Swedish diplomat. While based as a diplomat in Budapest during World War II, he worked to protect persecuted Jews in Hungary. He was captured by the Soviets, and his fate remains unknown.

wallet /wóllit/ *n.* **1. POCKET-SIZED FOLDED CASE FOR MONEY** a small flat folding case usually made of leather or plastic that holds paper money and credit cards and is usually carried in a pocket or handbag **2.** COMPUT **SOFTWARE FOR ONLINE PURCHASES** a software program that is used to carry out transactions for online purchases made on the Internet **3.** a folder for holding items such as papers, photographs, or maps **4. KNAPSACK** a bag or knapsack for carrying articles on a trip (*archaic*) [14thC. Origin uncertain: probably via an Anglo-Norman word for 'travelling pack', from a Germanic word for 'roll'.]

walleye /wáwl ī/ (plural **walleye** or **walleyes**) n. **1.** OPHTHALMOL EYE THAT APPEARS WHITE an eye with a white or streaked iris, giving the appearance of a pale ring round the pupil **2.** OPHTHALMOL WHITE IN CORNEA an eye with an opaque white cornea, or the condition that causes this opacity **3.** OPHTHALMOL OUTWARDS TURNING EYES a form of squint (**strabismus**) in which one or both eyes turn outwards **4.** ZOOL FRESHWATER FISH OF N AMERICA a large predatory freshwater fish of northeastern North America that has large eyes and is related to the perch. Latin name: *Stizostedion vitreum*. [Early 16thC. Back-formation from WALLEYED.]

walleyed /wáwl īd/ adj. **1.** OPHTHALMOL HAVING WALLEYE having any of the medical conditions known as walleye **2.** WITH BULGING EYES having bulging or staring eyes [14thC. From a Scandinavian word meaning 'speckle-eyed'.]

walleyed pike n. ZOOL = **walleye** n. 4

walleyed pollack n. an important northern Pacific food fish of the cod family that resembles the pollack. Latin name: *Theragra chalcogramma*.

wallflower /wáwl flow ər/ n. **1.** PLANTS SPRING-FLOWERING GARDEN PLANT a common garden plant with rather woody erect stems and fragrant yellow, orange, or brownish flowers clustered at the top of the stem, that blooms in early spring. Genera: *Cheiranthus* and *Erysimum*. **2.** PLANTS PLANT WITH FRAGRANT COLOURFUL FLOWERS a plant originally from southern Europe with fragrant colourful flowers, often found growing on walls, rocks, and cliffs. Latin name: *Cheiranthus cheiri*. **3.** SB UNNOTICED AT SOCIAL EVENT a shy or retiring person who remains unnoticed at social events, especially a woman without a dance partner (*informal*)

wall fruit (plural **wall fruits** or **wall fruit**) n. **1.** FRUIT GROWING AGAINST WALL a fruit of a tree or bush that has been trained to grow against a wall **2.** TREE GROWING AGAINST A WALL a fruit-bearing tree or bush that has been trained to grow against a wall

wall game n. a variant on association football unique to Eton College in which a ball is moved along a wall in a muddied field by two teams using hands and feet

wall hanging n. a tapestry or other large flat object hung on a wall as a decoration

wallies /wálliz/ npl. Scotland false teeth (*informal humorous*) [Plural of WALLY² in the sense of 'made of china']

Wallis /wóliss/, **Sir Barnes Neville** (1887–1979) British aeronautical engineer. He designed the Wellington bomber and the 'bouncing bombs' that destroyed two dams in a raid on Germany during World War II.

Wallis and Futuna Islands /wólliss ənd fə tyóonə-/ island group situated in the southwestern Pacific Ocean, northeast of Fiji. It is an overseas territory of France. Capital: Mata Utu. Population: 13,705 (1988). Area: 200 sq. km/77 sq. mi.

wall knot n. a bulky knot made at the end of a rope by unwinding the strands and tying them together

wall lizard n. a lizard that can be found on walls and rocks. Family: Lacertidae.

wall mustard n. = **wall rocket**

wall of death n. an attraction at a fairground in which a motorcyclist rides round the inside wall of a large cylinder

wall of sound n. a type of recorded sound on pop records achieved by overdubbing or layering many different instruments around a pop tune

Walloon /wo loón/ n. **1.** PEOPLES FRENCH-SPEAKING BELGIAN a member of a French-speaking people living in southern Belgium, mainly in the autonomous region of Wallonia, and in neighbouring parts of France. ◊ **Fleming 2.** LANG BELGIAN DIALECT OF FRENCH the dialect of French spoken in southern Belgium and nearby areas of France [Mid-16thC. Via French *Wallon* from the medieval Latin stem *wallo(n)-*, 'foreigner', ultimately from the same prehistoric Germanic word as English *Welsh*.] —**Walloon** adj.

wallop /wóllap/ vt. (**-lops, -loping, -loped**) (*informal*) **1.** BEAT SB to give sb a sound physical beating **2.** HIT SB VERY HARD to strike sb or sb with great force ○ *She can really wallop the ball.* **3.** DEFEAT SB DECISIVELY to defeat a person or team decisively ■ n. **1.** HARD HIT a powerful blow (*informal*) **2.** ABILITY TO HIT HARD the ability to strike a powerful blow (*informal*) ○ *He's got a wallop that could make him heavyweight champion.* **3.** ABILITY TO IMPRESS the ability to create a powerful impression on others (*informal*) **4.** BEVERAGES = beer (*dated slang*) [14thC. From Old French *waloper*, variant of *galoper*, 'to gallop' (source of English *gallop*), literally 'to run well', from the prehistoric Germanic ancestors of English *well* and *leap*.]

walloping /wólləping/ n. (*informal*) **1.** BEATING a sound physical beating **2.** DECISIVE DEFEAT a decisive defeat or victory ■ adj. BIG very large or impressive (*informal*) ○ *The angler came back with a walloping catch.* ■ adv. VERY to an extreme degree (*informal*) ○ *a walloping big lie*

wallow /wóllō/ vi. (**-lows, -lowing, -lowed**) **1.** ROLL IN STH to lie down and roll around in sth ○ *pigs wallowing in mud* **2.** HEAVILY INDULGE IN STH to immerse yourself in sth, e.g. an emotion or material wealth, in a self-indulgent way **3.** HAVE HUGE AMOUNT OF STH to be amply or overly supplied with sth ○ *We suddenly found ourselves wallowing in kittens.* **4.** WALK WITH DIFFICULTY to move clumsily, as if in mud ■ n. **1.** ACT OF WALLOWING an instance of wallowing in sth such as mud, emotion, or material luxury **2.** ZOOL PLACE WHERE ANIMALS ROLL a muddy, wet, or dusty place which animals use to roll around in **3.** ZOOL DEPRESSION FORMED BY ANIMAL a sunken area in the ground made by a rolling animal [Old English *wealwian*, 'to roll'. Ultimately from the same Indo-European ancestor as English *revolve*, *waltz*, *helix*, and *wallet*.] —**wallower** n.

wallpaper /wáwl paypər/ n. **1.** PAPER TO DECORATE WALLS paper, usually printed with a pattern, that is pasted on walls and sometimes ceilings **2.** COMPUT BACKGROUND PATTERN FOR SCREEN the background pattern for a computer screen, composed of graphics **3.** STH BLAND AND DULL sth that is so bland and unexciting that it serves as a hardly noticed background (*informal*) ■ vti. (**-pers, -pering, -pered**) PUT UP WALLPAPER to cover a surface with wallpaper

wall pass n. a movement in football in which one player passes the ball to another and runs forward to receive the return

wall pepper n. a stonecrop of Europe and Asia with creeping stems, yellow flowers, and leaves with a peppery taste. Latin name: *Sedum acre*.

wall plate n. a horizontal structural member placed along the top of a wall to support the ends of beams, joists, or trusses

wall plug n. a receptacle in the wall connected to an electric circuit, into which appliances can be plugged

wall rock n. the rock that surrounds a vein, mineral deposit, or fault

wall rocket n. either of two cruciferous plants bearing yellow flowers that are native to Europe and grow on walls and waste ground. Latin name: *Diplotaxis muralis* and *Diplotaxis tenuifolia*.

wall rue n. a small delicate fern that grows in fan-shaped clusters on walls or in rocky crevices. Latin name: *Asplenium ruta-muraria*.

Wallsend /wáwlz end/ town in northeastern England, near Newcastle upon Tyne. It marks one end of Hadrian's Wall. Population: 45,280 (1991).

Wall Street /wáwl-/ n. **1.** NEW YORK STREET OF STOCK EXCHANGE the street in Manhattan, New York City, where the New York Stock Exchange and many major financial institutions of the United States are located **2.** US FINANCIAL MARKET the US financial market, especially as represented by the publicly owned companies comprising the stock markets

wall-to-wall adj. **1.** FROM ONE WALL TO ANOTHER completely covering a floor or floors ○ *wall-to-wall carpeting* **2.** CROWDED WITH STH completely filling, covering, or pervading sth, or occurring nonstop (*informal*) ○ *fed up with wall-to-wall pop music*

wally¹ /wólli/ (plural **-lies**) n. an offensive term that deliberately insults sb's intelligence or common sense (*slang*) [Mid-20thC. Origin uncertain: perhaps from the name *Wally*, from *Walter*.]

wally² /wálli/ adj. Scotland **1.** SPLENDID splendid **2.** CHINA made of china **3.** TILED lined with ceramic tiles [15thC. Origin uncertain.]

walnut /wáwl nut/ n. **1.** TREES TREE VALUED FOR NUTS AND WOOD a large deciduous tree with fragrant compound leaves and drooping catkins, grown worldwide for its shade, wood, and nuts. Genus: *Juglans*. **2.** FOOD NUT OF WALNUT TREE the edible nut of a walnut tree, which has a deeply wrinkled surface and is enclosed in a hard shell and a thick leathery husk **3.** INDUST WALNUT WOOD the wood of a walnut tree used in cabinetwork, for panelling, and veneer (*often used before a noun*) **4.** COLOURS LIGHT-BROWN COLOUR a light yellowish-brown colour like that of the wood of the walnut tree ■ adj. COLOURS OF LIGHT-BROWN COLOUR of a light yellowish-brown colour [14thC. From Old English *wealhnutu*, literally 'foreign nut', from *wealh*, 'foreign, Welsh, Celtic'.]

WORD KEY: ORIGIN

The prehistoric Germanic peoples regarded the *walnut* as the 'foreign nut' because it did not originally grow in northern Europe but was introduced from Gaul and Italy, the lands of the Celts and the Romans (the Germans' own native nut was the hazel).

Walpole /wáwlpōl/, **Horace** (1717–97) British writer. The son of Sir Robert Walpole, he was a noted book collector. He wrote the Gothic novel *The Castle of Otranto* (1764) and engaged in an extensive and celebrated literary correspondence.

Walpole, Sir Robert, 1st Earl of Orford (1676–1745) British statesman. He became a Whig MP in 1701. From 1721 to 1742 he wielded considerable political power as chief minister to George I and George II. Although he himself repudiated the title, which did not become official until much later, he is regarded as Britain's first prime minister.

Walpurgis night /val poórgiss-/, **Walpurgis Night** n. **1.** WITCHES' FESTIVAL the eve of May Day, believed in German folklore to be the witches' feast night on the Brocken in the Harz mountains **2.** WILD OR SCARY EVENT a wild celebration or a nightmarish situation [Early 19thC. Translation of German *Walpurgisnacht*, named after *Walpurga*, an 8thC Anglo-Saxon saint, venerated by Christians on this date (the night before her remains were buried at Eichstätt in Germany).]

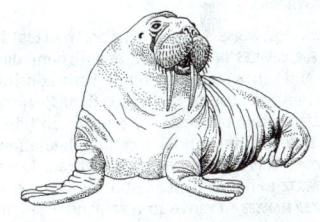

Walrus

walrus /wáwlrəss, wóll-/ (plural **-ruses** or **-rus**) n. a large Arctic sea mammal related to seals and sea lions, with tough wrinkled skin, large tusks, and bristly whiskers. Latin name: *Odobenus rosmarus*. [Early 18thC. From Dutch *walrus*, *walros*, literally 'whale-horse', from *walvis(ch)*, 'whale'.]

walrus moustache n. a thick drooping moustache resembling a walrus's whiskers

Wałęsa /və wénssə/, **Lech** (b. 1943) Polish trade unionist and statesman. At the head of Solidarity after 1980, he led Poland's independent trade union movement and was instrumental in ending Communist rule there. He won the Nobel Peace Prize in 1983. He was the president of Poland from 1990 to 1995.

Walsall /wáwl sawl, wól-/ industrial town in central England, near Birmingham. Population: 174,739 (1991).

Walsingham /wáwlzingəm, wólz-/ village in Norfolk, eastern England. For hundreds of years the Shrine of Our Lady of Walsingham has been a pilgrimage centre.

Walter /wáwltər/, **John** (1739–1812) British newspaper publisher. He founded the London-based *Daily Universal Register* (1785), which in 1788 was retitled *The Times*. It is the oldest newspaper still in publication.

Walter Mitty /wáwltər mítti, wóltər-/ (*plural* **Walter Mitties**) *n.* an unremarkable person who daydreams about great personal adventure and success [Mid-20thC. Named after the hero of 'The Secret Life of Walter Mitty', a 1939 short story by James Thurber, about such a daydreamer.] —**Walter Mittyish** *adj.*

Barbara Walters

Walters /wáwltərz/, **Barbara** (*b.* 1931) US television journalist and presenter. As a reporter and host of television news magazines and celebrity interview shows, she established a reputation for eliciting candid answers to difficult questions from public figures.

Waltham Forest /wáwltəm, wólt-/ residential borough in northeastern London, England. Population: 221,100 (1996).

Walton /wáwlt'n/, **Ernest T. S.** (1903–95) Irish physicist. He helped develop a particle accelerator, which led to the first artificial nuclear reaction. He shared a Nobel Prize in physics (1951). Full name **Ernest Thomas Sinton Walton**

Walton, Izaak (1593–1683) English writer. He is remembered for his contemplation on fishing and the charms of pastoral life, *The Compleat Angler* (1653).

Walton, Sir William (1902–83) British composer. He wrote orchestral works, an opera, and film scores including the music for Laurence Olivier's adaptations of Shakespeare's plays. Full name **Sir William Turner Walton**

waltz /wawlss, wolss, wawlts/ *n.* (*plural* **waltzes**) **1.** DANCE DANCE FOR COUPLES IN TRIPLE TIME a ballroom dance in triple time in which the couple turn continuously while moving around the dance floor **2.** MUSIC MUSIC FOR WALTZ a piece of music for a waltz, in triple time **3.** STH EASY sth that can be accomplished effortlessly (*informal*) ■ *v.* (**waltzes, waltzing, waltzed**) **1.** *vti.* DANCE DANCE WALTZ to dance or lead sb in a waltz **2.** *vi.* MOVE IN RELAXED MANNER to move in a relaxed and confident manner (*informal*) ○ *She just waltzed right in and demanded more money.* **3.** *vi.* GO THROUGH STH EASILY to accomplish sth effortlessly [Late 18thC. From German *Walzer*, from *walzen*, 'to waltz, roll, revolve'. Ultimately from the same Indo-European ancestor as English *wallow* and *revolve*.] ◇ **waltz Matilda** *vt. Aus* to wander around looking for work carrying one's belongings in a swag (*dated slang*)

—— WORD KEY: CULTURAL NOTE ——

Waltzing Matilda, a song with lyrics by Australian writer A.B. Paterson (1895). Set in late nineteenth-century Australia, it is a ballad about an itinerant worker who is arrested for stealing sheep. Rather than go to jail, he drowns himself in a waterhole. A song that evokes the rugged, antiauthoritarian spirit of early Australia, it is now regarded as an unofficial national anthem.

waltz Matilda /-mə tíldə/ *v. Aus* to wander around looking for work carrying one's belongings in a pack (*dated slang*)

Waltzing Matilda /wáwlssing-/ *n.* a traditional Australian song that tells the story of a vagrant worker (**swagman**) who commits suicide at a waterhole to avoid being arrested for sheep-stealing (*informal*) [Because of the dancing motion of a pack carried on sb's shoulder; *Matilda* 'personal pack, bundle', from the name]

Walvis Bay /wáwlviss-/ town and port in western Namibia, on the Atlantic coast. It was a former enclave of South Africa until 1994. Population: 16,652 (1985).

wambenger /wom béngə/ *n.* = **tuan** [Early 20thC. From an Australian Aboriginal language.]

wame /waym/ *n. Scotland* the belly, abdomen, or womb [15thC. Variant of WOMB.]

Wampanoag /wómpə nố ag/ (*plural* **-ag** *or* **-ags**) *n.* a member of a Native North American people who once occupied lands in Rhode Island and Massachusetts [Late 17thC. From Narragansett, literally 'easterners'.] —**Wampanoag** *adj.*

wampum /wómpəm/ *n.* small polished beads made from shells, threaded on string, used by some Native North Americans as decoration, for ceremonial purposes, or formerly for money [Mid-17thC. Shortening of *wampumpeag*, from Algonquian, literally 'white strings', from *wap*, 'white' + *umpe*, 'string'.]

wan /won/ *adj.* (**wanner, wannest**) **1.** PALE unhealthily pale, especially from illness or grief **2.** INDICATIVE OF LOW SPIRITS suggesting ill health or unhappiness ○ *He gave me a wan look.* **3.** FAINT lacking brightness ○ *a wan star* ■ *vti.* (**wans, wanning, wanned**) MAKE OR BECOME PALE OR ILL to make sth pale, or become pale or unhealthy (*literary*) [Old English *wann*, 'dark, dusky, grey', of unknown origin] —**wanly** *adv.* —**wanness** *n.*

WAN /wan/ **1.** international vehicle registration. Abbr of **West Africa Nigeria** ■ *abbr.* **2.** wide area network

Wanaka /wə naákə/ town in the southern part of the South Island, New Zealand, situated at the southern end of Lake Wanaka. It is a tourist resort. Population: 2,133 (1996).

Wanaka, Lake lake in the southern part of the South Island, New Zealand. Area: 194 sq. km/75 sq. mi.

wand /wond/ *n.* **1.** ROD WITH MAGICAL POWERS a thin rod believed to possess magical powers, used by supposed magicians, wizards, and supernatural beings **2.** STAFF SHOWING AUTHORITY a thin staff carried as a symbol of office **3.** HOUSEHOLD VACUUM CLEANER PART an attachment between the hose and cleaning tool of a vacuum cleaner that resembles a pipe **4.** COMPUT BARCODE SCANNER a hand-held optical scanning device used to read and enter bar-code information into a computer **5.** MUSIC BATON a conductor's baton **6.** BOT SLENDER PLANT SHOOT a slender bendable shoot of a shrub or tree (*archaic*) [12thC. Via Old Norse *vondr*, 'straight flexible stick', from a prehistoric Germanic word meaning 'turn' (ancestor of English *wander* and *went*).]

wander /wóndər/ *v.* (**-ders, -dering, -dered**) **1.** *vti.* TRAVEL WITHOUT A DESTINATION to move from place to place, either without a purpose or without a known destination ○ *They wander the countryside looking for work.* **2.** *vi.* TAKE A BENDY PATH to follow a winding course ○ *The river wandered through the meadows.* **3.** *vi.* STROLL SOMEWHERE to go somewhere at a leisurely pace **4.** *vi.* LEAVE A FIXED PATH to stray from a particular course ○ *Don't wander far from the path.* **5.** *vi.* DAYDREAM to lose the ability to concentrate on or listen to a particular thing ○ *My mind was wandering.* **6.** *vi.* FAIL TO THINK OR SPEAK CLEARLY to lose the ability to think, speak, or write in an organized and coherent way ■ *n.* AIMLESS STROLL an aimless or leisurely moving from place to place [Old English *wandrian*, from a prehistoric Germanic word meaning 'turn', which also produced English *wand*.] —**wanderer** *n.* —**wandering** *adj.* —**wanderingly** *adv.*

wandering albatross *n.* a large albatross of southern seas with a white body and black wings and tail that spends most of its life in flight at sea. Latin name: *Diomedea exulans*.

wandering Jew *n.* any of three tropical American trailing plants widely grown as houseplants for their variegated foliage and white or rose-red flowers. Latin names: *Tradescantia fluminensis* and *Tradescantia albiflora* and *Zebrina pendula*.

Wandering Jew *n.* in medieval legend, a Jewish man, sometimes named as Ahasuerus, condemned to remain alive wandering the earth until Judgment Day for having mocked Jesus Christ on the day of the Crucifixion

wanderlust /wóndər lust/ *n.* a strong desire to

travel [Early 20thC. From German, literally 'desire to travel'.]

wane /wayn/ *vi.* (**wanes, waning, waned**) **1.** SHOW LESS LIGHTED AREA to show a decreasing illuminated surface between a full Moon and new Moon (*refers to the moon or a planet*) **2.** GET SMALLER OR LESS to decrease gradually in intensity or power ○ *His interest was waning.* **3.** FINISH to draw to a close ○ *Winter is waning at last.* ■ *n.* **1.** DECREASE IN INTENSITY a gradual lessening of power or intensity **2.** TIME DURING MOON'S WANE the period during which the Moon's visible illuminated surface is decreasing in size **3.** PERIOD OF LESSENING a period of gradual decrease **4.** END OF PERIOD the conclusion of a time or season ○ *the wane of summer* **5.** WOODWORK IRREGULARITY ON PLANK'S EDGE a defective edge left on a rough-sawn plank [Old English *wanian*, 'to lessen', from a prehistoric Germanic word meaning 'lacking'] ◇ **be on the wane** to decrease or pass out of fashion

Wanganui /wóngə noó i/ **1.** river in the southwestern part of the North Island, New Zealand. It rises on Mount Tongariro and flows southwards through the city of Wanganui to the Cook Strait. Length: 290 km/180 mi. **2.** city and port in the southwestern part of the North Island, New Zealand, situated on the Wanganui River. Population: 41,097 (1996).

Wangaratta /wóngə ráttə/ city in northern Victoria, Australia. It is a centre for agriculture and textile production. Population: 15,527 (1996).

wangle /wáng g'l/ *vt.* (**-gles, -gling, -gled**) **1.** GET STH DEVIOUSLY to get sth using indirect and sometimes deceitful methods (*informal*) ○ *I'm trying to wangle some time off work.* **2.** FALSIFY ACCOUNTS to manipulate accounts or records, usually deceitfully ■ *n.* DISHONEST METHOD a devious means of accomplishing sth [Late 19thC. Origin uncertain: perhaps a variant of WAGGLE. The meaning 'to get sth deviously' evolved from printer's slang, 'to manipulate type to achieve a desired appearance'.] —**wangler** *n.*

wank /wangk/ *vi.* (**wanks, wanking, wanked**) OFFENSIVE TERM to masturbate (*taboo offensive*) ■ *n.* (*slang offensive*) **1.** MASTURBATION an instance of masturbation **2.** PRETENTIOUS BEHAVIOUR an instance of self-indulgent, pretentious, or arrogant behaviour [Mid-20thC. Origin unknown.]

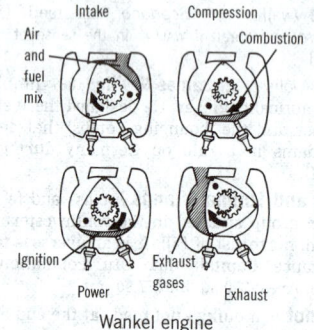

Wankel engine

Wankel engine /wángk'l-, váng-/ *n.* an internal-combustion engine in which an approximately triangular rotor inside an elliptical combustion chamber replaces the pistons of a conventional engine, thus reducing the number of moving parts [Mid-20thC. Named after Felix *Wankel* (1902–88), the German engineer who invented it.]

wanker /wángkər/ *n.* **1.** MASTURBATOR sb who masturbates (*slang offensive*) **2.** UNPLEASANT OR PRETENTIOUS PERSON an unpleasant, self-indulgent, pretentious, or arrogant person (*slang insult*) [Mid-20thC]

wanna /wónnə/ *vt.* want to (*nonstandard*) ○ *I wanna go!* [Late 19thC. Alteration of *want to*.]

wannabe /wónnə bee/ *n.* sb who is trying to be like another person or to belong to a particular group (*informal disapproving*) [Late 20thC. Alteration of *want to be.*]

want /wont/ *vt.* (**wants, wanting, wanted**) **1.** DESIRE STH to feel a need or desire for sth ○ *We want a new car.* **2.** WISH STH DONE to desire to do sth or that sth be done ○ *I don't want you being late.* ○ *He wants his steak well done.* **3.** MISS STH to feel the lack of sth ○ *After a* *week on the road, I want my own bed.* **4.** WISH SB'S PRESENCE to wish to see or speak to sb ○ *He's wanted on the phone.* ○ *Someone wants you at the door.* **5.** SEEK SB AS CRIME SUSPECT to seek sb in connection with a crime (*usually passive*) ○ *wanted for two felonies* **6.** SHOULD used to indicate that sth is desirable or advisable (*informal*) ○ *You want to see a doctor about that.* **7.** NEED STH to have a need for sth (*informal*) ○ *What that kid wants is some discipline!* ○ *The cupboards want cleaning.* **8.** DESIRE SB SEXUALLY to feel sexual desire for sb (*informal*) ■ *n.* **1.** NEED sth that sb desires or needs (*usually used in the plural*) ○ *All your wants can be easily supplied.* **2.** LACK OF STH an absence or shortage of sth ○ *There's been no want of snow for the skiers this winter.* **3.** POVERTY the state of being poor ○ *Freedom from want is a fundamental human right.* [12thC. Via Old Norse *vanta*, 'to be lacking', from a prehistoric Germanic word meaning 'lacking' (ancestor of English *wane* and *wanton*).] —**wanter** *n.* ◇ **for want of** through the lack of sth ○ *No one should be left behind for want of opportunity.*

WORD KEY: SYNONYMS

want, desire, wish, long, yearn, covet, crave

CORE MEANING: to seek to have, do, or achieve sth

want a fairly informal and general word meaning to seek to have, do, or achieve sth; **desire** a more formal and often stronger alternative to 'want'. It can be used specifically to talk about sexual attraction; **wish** a more formal alternative to 'want', often suggesting that the thing wanted will be very difficult or impossible to attain; **long** emphasizes that sb wants sth very much; **yearn** to want sth very much, especially when it seems unlikely that it can ever be obtained; **covet** often used for wanting sth that belongs to another person. It can also be used to indicate that sb wants sth very much; **crave** to desire sth very much, especially when this desire is physical.

want for *vt.* to experience the lack of sth ○ *The family wants for nothing.*

want in *vi.* to wish to be included in sth, especially to want to invest in a business deal (*informal*) ○ *Do you want in?*

want out *vi.* to wish to be excluded from or to leave sth, especially a business deal (*informal*) ○ *We want out before we get into trouble.*

want ad *n. US* a classified advertisement in a newspaper or magazine (*informal*)

wanting /wónting/ *adj.* UNSATISFACTORY not meeting expectations or requirements ○ *found wanting in the area of security* ■ *prep.* missing sth necessary ○ *a chair wanting one leg*

wanton /wóntən/ *adj.* **1.** SEXUALLY INDISCRIMINATE without restraint or inhibition, especially in sexual behaviour **2.** RANDOM without reason or provocation ○ *wanton violence and destruction* **3.** DESIRING TO DO HARM done out of a desire to cause harm **4.** EXCESSIVE unrestrained, heedless of reasonable limits, or characterized by greed and extravagance ○ *wanton indulgence* **5.** UNRULY lacking discipline **6.** LUSH growing luxuriantly (*archaic*) **7.** PLAYFUL engaged in play that is carefree (*archaic*) ■ *n.* **1.** SB WITHOUT SEXUAL RESTRAINT sb who is lascivious or sexually uninhibited **2.** SB PLAYFUL a playful person (*archaic*) **3.** SB GROWING UNRULY an undisciplined person (*archaic*) ■ *vi.* (**-tons, -toning, -toned**) BE WANTON to behave in a wanton manner (*archaic*) [14thC. From Old English *wan-*, 'un-' + *togen*, 'disciplined', from *tēon*, 'to train, discipline, pull'.] —**wantonly** *adv.* —**wantonness** *n.*

wapentake /wóppən tayk, wáppən-/ *n.* a subdivision of certain counties in northern and midland England corresponding to the hundred in other counties [Pre-12thC. From Old Norse *vápnatak*, literally 'weapon-taking'. Said to be from the weapons brought to the assembly of such a district, to be brandished when voting by show of hands.]

wapiti /wóppiti/ (*plural* **-tis** *or* **-ti**) *n.* a large North American deer, found especially in the mountainous west, that has tall branched antlers and lives in herds. Latin name: *Cervus elaphus.* [Early 19thC. From Shawnee *wapiti*, literally 'white rump'.]

war /wawr/ *n.* **1.** ARMED FIGHTING BETWEEN GROUPS an armed conflict between countries or groups that involves killing and destruction ○ *The two countries are at war.* **2.** PERIOD DURING WAR a period of armed conflict ○ *during the Vietnam War* **3.** METHODS OF WARFARE the techniques or the study of the techniques of armed conflict **4.** CONFLICT any serious struggle, argument, or conflict between people ○ *The candidates are at war.* **5.** SERIOUS EFFORT TO END STH an effort to eradicate sth harmful ○ *a war against drugs* ■ *vi.* (**wars, warring, warred**) **1.** MAKE WAR to engage in an armed conflict with sb **2.** BE IN A STRUGGLE to be involved in a serious disagreement with sb or a struggle to combat or eradicate sth [12thC. Via Old Northern French *werre*, from Old French *guerre*, ultimately from a prehistoric Germanic word meaning 'strife, confusion'.]

WORD KEY: SYNONYMS

See Synonyms at ***fight***.

WORD KEY: CULTURAL NOTE

War and Peace, a novel by Russian writer Leo Tolstoy (1865–69). This monumental work is set in Russia during and after the Napoleonic Wars (1805–14). Though it focuses on five fictional families, the story incorporates historical accounts and philosophical essays to create an extraordinarily comprehensive portrait of Russian society that touches on almost every aspect of human experience from love and happiness to grief and war.

war. *abbr.* warrant

War. *abbr.* Warwickshire

waragi /wárrəgi, -ji/ (*plural* **-gis** *or* **-gi**) *n.* a Ugandan alcoholic drink made from bananas [Early 20thC. From Kiswahili *wargi*.]

waratah /wórrə táa, -taa/ (*plural* **-tahs** *or* **-tah**) *n.* a plant with large globular flower heads and dark red flowers that grows on sandy soils in New South Wales, Australia, and is the state's floral emblem. Latin name: *Telopea speciosissima.* [Late 18thC. From Dharuk *warrada*.]

war baby *n.* a baby born or conceived during a war

Warbeck /wáwr bek/, **Perkin** (1474?–99) Flemish royal pretender. Posing as Richard, Duke of York, the murdered son of Edward IV, he challenged Henry VII's right to the English throne, but was captured and hanged.

War Between the States *n.* = **Civil War** *n.* 1

warble[1] /wáwrb'l/ *vti.* (**-bles, -bling, -bled**) **1.** SING NOTES WITH TRILLS to sing a song or note with trills or other vocal modulations ○ *a songbird warbling outside my window* **2.** SING STH to sing, or express sth in song ○ *warble a tune* ■ *n.* **1.** MODULATED SINGING singing with trills or other vocal modulations **2.** MODULATED SOUND a sound with trills or quavers [14thC. Via Old Northern French *werbler*, 'to sing with trills', from a Frankish word for 'whirl, trill'.]

warble[2] /wáwrb'l/ *n.* **1.** VET SWELLING IN HORSES AND CATTLE a swelling under the skin that forms usually on the back in horses and cattle, caused by the warble fly maggot **2.** INSECTS WARBLE FLY OR ITS LARVAE the warble fly, or the maggot of the warble fly **3.** VET LUMP ON HORSE'S BACK FROM SADDLE a hard tumorous lump of tissue on the back of a riding horse caused by the rubbing of the saddle [Late 16thC. Origin uncertain: perhaps from Scandinavian.]

warble fly *n.* a large hairy fly, the larvae of which form painful swellings under the skin of cattle and horses. Family: Oestridae.

warbler /wáwrblər/ *n.* **1.** BIRDS THRUSH RELATIVE a songbird of Europe and Asia that is related to the thrush. Family: Sylviidae. **2.** BIRDS SMALL SINGING BIRD a small American songbird that eats insects and is often brightly coloured. Family: Parulidae. **3.** SB WHO WARBLES sb who warbles or sings

war bride *n.* a woman who meets and marries a serviceman during wartime, especially one from another country

war chest *n. US* funds collected to pay for a war or a campaign of any sort

war clouds *npl.* signs of impending war

war correspondent *n.* a journalist reporting from a war

war crime *n.* a crime committed during wartime that is in violation of international agreements concerning the conventions of war, e.g. the mistreatment of prisoners or genocide (*often used in the plural*) —**war criminal** *n.*

war cry *n.* = **battle cry** *n.* 1

ward /wawrd/ *n.* **1.** POL CITY DIVISION an administrative or electoral division of an area such as a city, town, or county **2.** MED ROOM IN HOSPITAL a room in a hospital, especially one for several patients being given similar treatment **3.** PRISON DIVISION a division in a prison **4.** LAW SB UNDER OFFICIAL CARE sb, especially a child or young person, who is under the care of a guardian or a court **5.** BUILDING AREA IN CASTLE an open area within the walls of a castle **6.** LAW CUSTODY a state of official custody or protection **7.** DEFENCE MOVEMENT a movement or stance used as a means of protection, e.g. in fencing **8.** LOCK OR KEY FEATURE a ridge or groove in a key or a lock that makes one fit the other ■ *vt.* (**wards, warding, warded**) GUARD to guard or protect sb or sth (*archaic*) [Old English *weard*, from a prehistoric Germanic word meaning 'to be on guard', which is also the ancestor of English *guard, aware,* and *wary*]

ward off *vt.* **1.** REPEL to parry or repel a blow or attack **2.** AVERT STH BAD to keep away or avert sth bad

Ward /wawrd/, **Frederick** (1835–70) Australian bushranger. As an outlaw, he was renowned for his nonviolent, chivalrous attitude. Known as **Captain Thunderbolt**

Ward, Sir Joseph George (1856–1930) Australian-born New Zealand statesman. He was prime minister of a Liberal government (1906–12) and a United Party government (1928–30).

Ward, Russel Braddock (*b.* 1914) Australian historian. He wrote *The Australian Legend* (1958), a study of the Australian ideals of freedom, egalitarianism, and comradeship.

-ward *suffix.* **1.** in a particular direction, or towards a particular place ○ *earthward* **2.** lying or occurring in a particular direction ○ *rightward* ○ *windward* [Old English *-weard*. Ultimately from an Indo-European base meaning 'to turn', which is also the ancestor of English *avert*.]

war dance *n.* a dance performed as a ceremony before a battle or to celebrate victory, e.g. by Native North Americans

warded /wáwrdid/ *adj.* used to describe locks or keys that have grooves or ridges

warden[1] /wáwrd'n/ *n.* **1.** SB IN CHARGE OF BUILDING sb who is in charge of a building **2.** SB IN CHARGE OF INSTITUTION sb who is in charge of an institution such as a college or school **3.** *US* PRINCIPAL PRISON OFFICER the principal officer in charge of a prison. = **governor 4.** OFFICIAL CONCERNED WITH REGULATIONS an official, e.g. a traffic warden or air-raid warden, who makes sure that regulations are enforced **5.** CHR = **churchwarden** *n.* 1 [12thC. From Anglo-Norman *wardein*, from a prehistoric Germanic word meaning 'to be on guard' (see WARD).] —**wardenry** *n.* —**wardenship** *n.*

warden[2] /wáwrd'n/ *n.* a kind of pear that is used especially in cooking [14thC. Origin uncertain: perhaps from assumed Anglo-Norman *wardon*, from *warder* 'to keep'.]

warder /wáwrdər/ *n.* **1.** PRISON OFFICER a prison officer **2.** GUARD a guard [14thC. From Anglo-Norman *wardere*, from Old Northern French *warder* 'to guard', variant of French *garder* (see GUARD).]

ward heeler *n. US* sb who carries out minor tasks for a powerful local or city politician (*informal*)

ward manager *n.* a nurse in charge of a ward

wardmote /wáwrdmōt/ *n.* a meeting of the people who live in a ward [14thC. Formed from WARD + MOOT.]

ward of court *n.* sb, especially a minor, who is under the protection of a guardian or court

wardrobe /wáwrdrōb/ *n.* **1.** CLOTHES PLACE FOR CLOTHES a large cupboard with a rail or shelves for clothes and shoes **2.** CLOTHES CLOTHES COLLECTION all the clothes that belong to a particular person **3.** CLOTHES CLOTHES FOR A PURPOSE a collection of clothes for a particular season or purpose **4.** THEATRE THEATRE COSTUMES the costumes used by a theatrical company **5.** THEATRE PLACE FOR COSTUMES a place in a theatre where costumes are kept **6.** ROYAL DEPARTMENT the department in a royal or noble household in charge of robes and jewels [14thC. From Old Northern French *warderobe*, variant of French *garderobe* (source of English *garderobe*), from French *garder* 'to guard' + *robe* 'robe'.]

wardrobe mistress *n.* a woman in charge of the costumes in a theatre or on a film set

wardrobe trunk *n.* a large upright trunk with a rail on which clothes can be hung

wardroom /wáwrd room, -rŏŏm/ *n.* **1.** SHIP'S OFFICERS' ROOM a room on a warship used by all the officers except the captain **2.** WARSHIP'S OFFICERS the officers on a ship who can use the wardroom

-wards *suffix.* = **-ward**

wardship /wáwrdship/ *n.* **1.** GUARDIANSHIP the state of being in the care of a guardian appointed by parents or a court **2.** BEING A WARD the state of being a ward

ward sister *n.* MED = **sister** *n.* 4

ware[1] /wair/ *n.* **1.** SIMILAR THINGS similar things, or things that are made of the same material (*usually used in combination*) **2.** CERAMICS ceramic articles of a particular kind or made by a particular manufacturer ○ *delftware* ■ **wares** *npl.* **1.** THINGS FOR SALE articles offered for sale **2.** MARKETABLE SKILLS skills or talents offered as a service or a commodity [Old English *waru*, of uncertain origin: probably from the same word as WARD, with the underlying idea 'sth taken care of']

ware[2] /wair/ *vti.* (**wares, wared, waring**) BEWARE to beware (*archaic*) ■ *adj.* WARY wary or prudent (*archaic*) [Old English *warian*, from a prehistoric Germanic word meaning 'to be on guard' (see WARD)]

warehouse /wáir howss/ *n.* (*plural* **-houses** /-howziz/) **1.** STORAGE BUILDING a large building in which goods, raw materials, or commodities are stored **2.** BIG SHOP a large store or shop, especially one where goods are sold wholesale ■ *vt.* (**-houses** /-howziz/, **-housing** /-howzing/, **-housed**) STORE IN A WAREHOUSE to store materials, goods, or commodities in a warehouse

warehouseman /wáir howssmən/ *n.* (*plural* **-men** /-mən/) *n.* sb who works in or owns a warehouse

warehousing /wáir howzing/ *n.* the accumulation of a particular security in the hope that demand will push the price up as the result of the reduced supply on the open market

warfare /wáwr fair/ *n.* **1.** WAGING OF WAR the act or fact of engaging in a war **2.** CONFLICT conflict or struggle ○ *economic warfare*

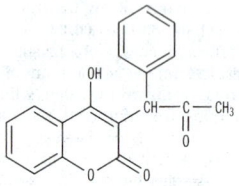

Warfarin

warfarin /wáwrfərin/ *n.* a colourless crystalline compound that is used as a rat poison and, usually in the form of its sodium salt, medicinally as an anticoagulant. Formula: $C_{19}H_{16}O_4$. [Mid-20thC. Formed from the initial letters of *Wisconsin Alumni Research Foundation* and the ending of COUMARIN.]

war game *n.* **1.** MIL MILITARY EXERCISE a military exercise that simulates battle conditions **2.** PLAYING AT WAR a game in which models of soldiers, battlefields, and equipment are used to refight historical battles — **war gaming** *n.*

warhead /wáwr hed/ *n.* the part of a bomb, ballistic or guided missile, rocket, or torpedo that contains the biological, chemical, explosive, incendiary, or nuclear material intended to damage the enemy

Warhol /wáwrhōl/, **Andy** (1928–87) US artist. His stylized multiple depictions of mass-produced objects and celebrities made him a leader of the pop art movement. He also produced a series of films that reproduced the banalities of life. Born **Andrew Wahola**

warhorse /wáwr hawrss/ *n.* **1.** MIL HORSE IN BATTLE a horse ridden in battle **2.** SURVIVOR OF A CONFLICT sb who has taken part in and survived many conflicts (*informal*)

Andy Warhol

3. ARTS STANDARD WORK a play or a piece of music that is familiar and hackneyed because of too frequent performance (*informal*)

Waring /wáiring, wérr-/, **Marilyn Joy** (*b.* 1952) New Zealand politician and writer. She was a National Party MP from 1975 to 1984, and wrote *If Women Counted* (1990).

Warks /wórriks/ *abbr.* Warwickshire

warlike /wáwr līk/ *adj.* **1.** HOSTILE hostile and inclined to fight **2.** RELATING TO WAR relating to war or warfare **3.** MARTIAL martial or military

warlock /wáwr lok/ *n.* a male sorcerer or wizard [Old English *wærloga* 'oath-breaker', from *wær* 'oath, pledge' + *-loga* 'liar']

Warlock /wáwr lok/, **Peter** (1894–1930) British composer and musicologist. He is noted for his songs and choral works, editions of Elizabethan and Jacobean music, and a biography of Frederick Delius. Pseudonym of **Philip Arnold Heseltine**

warlord /wáwr lawrd/ *n.* a military leader, especially a powerful one, operating outside the control of government — **warlordism** *n.*

warm /wawrm/ *adj.* **1.** QUITE HOT moderately or comfortably hot **2.** PROVIDING WARMTH providing warmth or protection against cold **3.** WITH TOO MUCH HEAT having or feeling an undesirable amount of heat, from exertion or ambient temperature **4.** FRIENDLY showing or feeling kindness and friendliness ○ *a warm person.* **5.** PASSIONATE showing passion or liveliness **6.** ENTHUSIASTIC OR ARDENT showing or feeling great enthusiasm **7.** QUICK TO ANGER excitable or easily angered **8.** COLOURS SUGGESTING WARMTH with a colour that suggests warmth, especially yellow or red **9.** PHYSIOL HEATED BY METABOLISM giving off the heat that arises normally in warm-blooded creatures **10.** HUNT FRESH used to describe a scent in hunting that is fresh and strong **11.** CLOSE close to the hidden object in a game or to guessing a secret (*informal*) ○ *You're getting warm.* **12.** UNCOMFORTABLE uncomfortable because of danger (*informal*) ■ *v.* (**warms, warming, warmed**) **1.** *vti.* MAKE WARM to increase the temperature of sth to a desirable or comfortable level, or become warm **2.** *vt.* MAKE SB HAPPY to make sb or sth cheerful or happy ○ *warmed by the presence of all their children* **3.** *vi.* BECOME ENTHUSIASTIC to become enthusiastic about sth ○ *warmed to the idea of buying a new car* **4.** *vi.* BECOME FRIENDLY to become fond of sb ○ *She warmed to him.* **5.** *vt.* BEAT to beat or cane a part of sb's body (*regional*) ■ *n.* (*informal*) **1.** WARM PLACE a warm environment **2.** GETTING WARM an act of making sth warm or becoming warm ○ *Have a warm by the fire.* [Old English *wearm.* Ultimately from an Indo-European word that is also the ancestor of English *furnace*, *fornication*, and *thermometer.*] — **warmness** *n.*

warm down *vi.* to get back to a normal level of activity after strenuous physical exertion in a way that avoids cramp, usually by gentle exercising (*informal*)

warm over *vt.* US, Can **1.** REHEAT to reheat food **2.** SUGGEST STH NOT NEW to suggest sth again, without having greatly altered it

warm up *v.* **1.** *vi.* PREPARE FOR EXERCISE to prepare for physical exercise by stretching or practising **2.** *vi.* PREPARE FOR STH to prepare for sth that is going to happen **3.** *vti.* GET WARM to become, or make sth become, warm or warmer **4.** *vti.* GET TO OPERATING TEMPERATURE to run sth such as an engine to bring it to a temperature at which it works efficiently, or reach

this condition **5.** *vti.* GET ANIMATED to become, or make sb, enthusiastic, animated, or eager

war machine *n.* the combined military resources with which a country can fight a war

warm-blooded *adj.* **1.** PASSIONATE passionate, impetuous, and enthusiastic **2.** ZOOL WITH CONSTANT BODY TEMPERATURE maintaining a nearly constant body temperature, usually higher than, and independent of, the environment — **warm-bloodedness** *n.*

warmboot /wáwrm boot/ (**-boots, -booting, -booted**) *vt.* to restart a computer without switching it off, e.g. by pressing the control, alt, and delete keys together. ◊ **coldboot**

warmer /wáwrmər/ *n.* sth that makes or keeps sth warm

warm front *n.* the gently sloping advancing edge of a warm air mass that displaces colder air, bringing a temperature increase and heavy rain where the front makes contact with the ground

warm-hearted *adj.* having or showing a kind and sympathetic nature — **warm-heartedly** *adv.* — **warm-heartedness** *n.*

warming pan *n.* a long-handled metal pan that in the past was filled with hot coals and placed in a bed to warm it

warmly /wáwrmli/ *adv.* **1.** ENTHUSIASTICALLY with enthusiasm, fondness, or passion **2.** WITH WARM CLOTHES in a way that will keep sb warm ○ *dressed warmly*

warmonger /wáwr mung gər/ *n.* sb who is eager for war or tries to start a war — **warmongering** *n.*

warm sector *n.* a wedge of warm air within the low-pressure region between the cold front and warm front of a storm

warmth /wawrmth/ *n.* **1.** WARM STATE the feeling, quality, or state of being warm **2.** AFFECTION affection and kindness **3.** AMOUNT OF HEAT a moderate amount of heat present in sth **4.** EXCITEMENT strong emotion, especially anger or zeal **5.** EFFECT OF COLOUR the effect gained from using colours such as red and yellow

warm-up, **warmup** *n.* an exercise, or period spent exercising, before a contest or event

warn /wawrn/ (**warns, warning, warned**) *v.* **1.** *vti.* TELL OF RISK to tell sb about sth that might cause injury or harm **2.** *vt.* TELL SB IN ADVANCE to tell sb about sth in advance **3.** *vt.* SCOLD SB to admonish sb **4.** *vt.* KEEP SB FROM DOING STH to tell sb to desist from doing sth or going somewhere ○ *warned us off driving over the pass in the storm* [Old English *war(e)nian*, from a prehistoric Germanic word meaning 'to be cautious'] — **warner** *n.*

warning /wáwrning/ *n.* **1.** SIGN OF STH BAD COMING a threat or a sign that sth bad is going to happen **2.** ADVICE TO BE CAREFUL advice to be careful or to stop doing sth ○ *If you're late again, you'll get a written warning.* **3.** NOTICE a notice (*archaic*) ■ *adj.* MEANT TO WARN intended to warn sb — **warningly** *adv.*

warning coloration *n.* markings on an animal warning predators that it is poisonous or dangerous. Many insects and amphibians have warning coloration.

warning shot *n.* a shot fired deliberately off target as a warning to sb to stop doing sth

war of nerves *n.* a conflict in which psychological tactics are used against an opponent

warp /wawrp/ *v.* (**warps, warping, warped**) **1.** *vti.* GET TWISTED to become or make sth twisted out of shape **2.** *vti.* CHANGE FOR WORSE to change sth so that it no longer follows its usual course, or become distorted or strange **3.** *vti.* SHIPPING MOVE SHIP BY PULLING ON ROPES to move a ship by pulling on ropes fastened to a dock or fixed buoy, or move in this way **4.** *vt.* TEXTILES ARRANGE THREADS to arrange threads to form the warp in a loom ■ *n.* **1.** DISTORTION a twist or distortion in sth, e.g. in wood that curls when dried **2.** PERVERSION a deviation or perversion of mind or character **3.** TEXTILES THREADS RUNNING LENGTHWISE the threads that run lengthwise on a loom or in a piece of fabric. ◊ **weft** *n.* 1 **4.** NAUT ROPE FOR TOWING a rope used to warp a vessel [Old English *weorpan*, from a prehistoric Germanic word meaning 'to throw', of uncertain origin: probably ultimately from an Indo-European word meaning 'to turn'] — **warpage** *n.* — **warper** *n.*

war paint *n.* **1. PAINT FOR DECORATING WARRIORS** paint used to decorate the body before a battle, e.g. that formerly used by some Native North American peoples **2. MAKE-UP** face make-up (*informal*)

warpath /wáwr paath/ *n.* in the past, a route taken by Native North Americans on the way to war ◊ **on the warpath** angry and in the mood for a confrontation (*informal*)

warplane /wáwr playn/ *n.* an aircraft used in war

warrant /wórrənt/ *n.* **1. AUTHORIZATION** sth that authorizes sb to do sth **2. WRITTEN AUTHORIZATION** a written authorization or certifying document **3. LAW DOCUMENT AUTHORIZING POLICE TO DO STH** a document that gives police particular rights or powers, e.g. the right to search or arrest sb **4. FIN OPTION TO BUY STOCK** a document authorizing a stockholder to buy shares from a company at a later date and at a given price **5. MIL WARRANT OFFICER'S CERTIFICATE** a warrant officer's certificate of appointment ■ *vt.* (-rants, -ranting, -ranted) **1. SERVE AS A REASON** to serve as a justifiable reason to do, believe, or think sth **2. GUARANTEE** to guarantee sth such as the truth or dependability of sth or sb **3. AUTHORIZE** to give authority to sb **4. LAW GUARANTEE TITLE** to guarantee the title to property **5. STATE CONFIDENTLY** to state sth with the confidence that it is true or will happen (*archaic*) [12thC. From Old Northern French *warant*, variant of Old French *guarant* (source of English *guarantee*), from, ultimately, a prehistoric Germanic word meaning 'to be on guard' (see WARD).] —**warranter** /wórrəntər/ *n.*

warrantable /wórrəntəb'l/ *adj.* able to be justified or permitted —**warrantability** /wórrəntə bílləti/ *n.* —**warrantably** /wórrəntəbli/ *adv.*

warrantee /wórrən teé/ *n.* sb to whom a warrant is given or a warranty is made

warrant officer *n.* an officer in the armed services ranking between a commissioned and a non-commissioned officer

warrantor /wórrən tawr/ *n.* sb who gives a warranty to sb

warrant sale *n. Scotland* the enforced sale of a debtor's belongings in order to raise money to pay off the debts

warranty /wórrənti/ (*plural* **-ties**) *n.* **1. COMM GUARANTEE** a guarantee on purchased goods that they are of the quality represented and will be replaced or repaired if found defective **2. LAW INSURED PERSON'S UNDERTAKING** a condition in an insurance contract in which the insured person guarantees that sth is the case **3. LAW GUARANTEE OF TITLE** a covenant guaranteeing the security of the title to property being sold **4. JUSTIFICATION** a justification or authorization for an action

warren /wórrən/ *n.* **1. RABBIT HABITAT** a group of connected burrows where rabbits live and breed **2. RABBIT COLONY** a colony of rabbits **3. CROWDED BUILDING OR AREA** an area or building that is crowded or has a complicated layout **4. AREA FOR GAME ANIMALS** a piece of ground where game animals are kept and bred [14thC. From Anglo-Norman *warenne* 'enclosed area for breeding game', of uncertain origin: perhaps, ultimately, from assumed Gaulish *warenna* 'fenced-off area' from assumed *warros* 'post'.]

warrener /wórrənər/ *n.* a gamekeeper or keeper of a rabbit warren

Warrington /wórringtən/ town in Cheshire, northwestern England. Population: 154,900 (1994).

warrior /wórri ər/ *n.* sb who fights or is experienced in warfare [13thC. From Old Northern French *werreior*, ultimately from *werre* 'war' (see WAR).]

Warrnambool /wáwrnəm bool/ city in southwestern Victoria, Australia. It is a commercial and industrial centre. Population: 26,052 (1996).

Warrumbungle Range /wórrəm búng g'l-/ range of volcanic peaks in northern New South Wales, Australia. Highest peak: 1,228 m./4,028 ft.

Warsaw /wáwr sawr/ capital city of Poland, located in the centre of the country, on the River Vistula. Population: 1,638,300 (1995).

warship /wáwr ship/ *n.* an armoured ship that is equipped with weapons and is used in war

wart /wawrt/ *n.* **1. MED SMALL LUMP ON SKIN** a small benign rough lump that grows usually on the hands, feet, or genitals, caused by a virus. ◊ **verruca 2. BOT GROWTH ON PLANT** any abnormal growth that looks like a wart and is found on a plant [Old English *wearte*. Ultimately from an Indo-European word meaning 'raised spot'.] —**warted** *adj.* —**warty** *adj.* ◊ **warts and all** including any flaws, faults, or disadvantages (*hyphenated when used before a noun*)

Wart hog

wart hog *n.* a wild pig that lives in Africa south of the Sahara. It has tusks, a coarse mane, and wartlike growths on its face. Latin name: *Phacochoerus aethiopicus.*

wartime /wáwr tīm/ *n.* a period during which a war is being fought

war-torn *adj.* disrupted by war, especially war between different groups from one country

Warwick /wórrik, wáwr wik/ **1.** town and administrative centre of Warwickshire, central England. Warwick Castle, a large medieval fortification, is located there. Population: 22,588 (1991). **2.** town in southeastern Queensland, Australia. It is an agricultural centre. Population: 10,947 (1996).

Warwickshire /wórrikshər/ county in central England. It is largely agricultural with some light industry. Warwick is the administrative centre. Population: 498,700 (1995). Area: 1,981 sq. km/ 765 sq. mi.

wary /wáiri/ (**-ier, -iest**) *adj.* **1. CAUTIOUS** cautious and watchful ○ *wary of hidden rocks in the water* **2. SHOWING CAUTION** showing caution or watchfulness ○ *a wary approach* [15thC. Formed from WARE[2].] —**warily** *n.* —**wariness** *n.*

—— **WORD KEY: SYNONYMS** ——
See Synonyms at ***cautious***.

was (*stressed*) /woz/; (*unstressed*) /wəz/ past tense of **be** (*used with I, he, she, it, and singular nouns*) [Old English *wæs*, a form of *wesan* 'to be'. Ultimately from an Indo-European word meaning 'to stay, dwell', which is also the ancestor of English *wassail*.]

wash /wosh/ *v.* (**washes, washing, washed**) **1.** *vt.* **CLEAN STH** to clean sth with water, usually with added soap or detergent **2.** *vti.* **REMOVE STH BY WASHING** to remove sth with water and usually with soap, or come off in this way ○ *couldn't get the stain to wash out* **3.** *vr.* **CLEAN YOURSELF** to clean yourself, especially your hands or face, with soap and water **4.** *vi.* **BE WASHABLE** to be capable of being washed without fading or being damaged (*refers to garments or fabrics*) ○ *curtains that wash well* **5.** *vti.* **LICK TO CLEAN** to clean sth by licking ○ *The cat washed her kittens.* **6.** *vi.* **WASH CLOTHES** to clean clothes in soap and water or in a washing machine ○ *spent the morning washing* **7.** *vt.* **MOISTEN** to wet or moisten sth (*literary*) ○ *lashes washed with tears* **8.** *vt.* **FLOW OVER STH** to flow over the surface of sth ○ *washed by the tides* **9.** *vt.* **ERODE STH WITH WATER** to erode sth by the action of water **10.** *vt.* **MOVE STH ON WATER** to carry sth along or away on water, or as if on water **11.** *vt.* **PURIFY** to remove sth corrupting ○ *the power to wash away sins* **12.** *vt.* **MINING SEPARATE STH BY WASHING** to separate sth such as precious stones or valuable minerals by sifting earth or gravel through water **13.** *vt.* **APPLY THIN COATING TO STH** to brush a thin coating or layer over sth **14.** *vi.* **BE CONVINCING** to be convincing or believable (*informal*) ○ *That story won't wash with her.* **15.** *vt.* **CHEM PUT GAS THROUGH LIQUID** to pass a gas or vapour through a liquid to remove contaminants ■ *n.* **1. ACT OF WASHING** the act or process of washing sth or sb **2. QUANTITY OF CLOTHES** a quantity of clothes that have been or are to be washed **3. INDUST THIN LIQUID COATING** a thin or weak liquid, especially one used to rinse or coat sth **4. SKIN TREATMENT** a lotion, antiseptic, or cosmetic that is applied to the skin **5. FLOW OF WATER** the flow of water against a surface, or the sound made by this **6.** *Southwest US* **DRY STREAM BED** the dry bed of a stream that flows only after heavy rains, often found at the bottom of a canyon **7. PAINTING LAYER OF COLOUR** a thin layer of colour applied with a brush **8. PAINTING PAINTING TECHNIQUE** the technique of using washes in painting **9. PAINTING** = **wash drawing 10. SURGE OF DISTURBED WATER OR AIR** the surge of disturbed water, air, or other fluid caused by sth such as an oar, propeller, or jet engine moving through the fluid **11. AGRIC REMOVAL OF SOIL** removal of soil by the action of flowing water **12. GEOL SEDIMENT** alluvial material carried and left by the movement of water. When washed down the side of a mountain, the sediment forms fans and cone-shaped deposits. **13. GEOG LAND PERIODICALLY COVERED BY WATER** land that is periodically covered by a sea or river, e.g. by a tide **14. MINING ORE** material such as gravel from which precious stones and valuable minerals can be extracted by washing **15.** = **swill** *n.* ◊ **16. BEVERAGES FERMENTED MALT** the liquor from fermented malt before it is distilled [Old English *wæscan*, from a prehistoric Germanic word that is also the ancestor of English *water*]

wash down *vt.* **1. WASH STH COMPLETELY** to wash sth thoroughly and completely ○ *had to wash down the kitchen walls afterwards* **2. DRINK AFTER DRINKING OR EATING STH** to follow sth drunk or eaten with another drink ○ *washed down the cake with a glass of milk*

wash out *v.* **1.** *vt.* **CLEAN INSIDE OF STH** to clean sth by washing the inside of it **2.** *vti.* **REMOVE BY WASHING** to come out or get sth out by washing **3.** *vt.* **CANCEL** to cancel sth because of rain **4.** *vti.* **MOVE AWAY ON WATER** to carry away sth, or be carried away, on water ○ *washed out to sea* **5.** *vti.* **WEAR AWAY** to wear sth away, or be worn away, by water

wash over *vt.* **1. FLOW OVER** to cover sth in a flowing or overflowing manner, as a liquid does **2. FILL SB WITH EMOTION** to well up in sb (*refers to feelings*) ○ *A wave of homesickness washed over him.*

wash up *v.* **1.** *vti.* **WASH DISHES** to wash the dishes after a meal **2.** *vi. US* **WASH FACE AND HANDS** to wash your face and hands **3.** *vti.* **ARRIVE BY WATER** to deposit sth on the shore, or land on the shore from tidal or wave action ○ *Look what the tide washed up!*

Wash /wosh thə/ shallow inlet of the North Sea, on the eastern coast of England, between Lincolnshire and Norfolk. Area: 855 sq. km/330 sq. mi.

Wash. *abbr.* Washington

washable /wóshəb'l/ *adj.* capable of being washed without being damaged —**washability** /wóshə bílləti/ *n.*

wash-and-wear *adj.* easily washed and dried and needing little or no ironing

washbasin /wósh bayss'n/ *n.* a bowl or basin for washing the face and hands or small articles

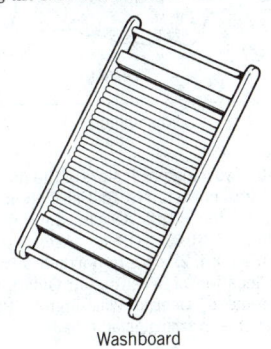

Washboard

washboard /wósh bawrd/ *n.* **1. RIDGED BOARD** a board with a corrugated surface on which clothes that are being washed can be rubbed to help get them clean **2. MUSIC MUSICAL INSTRUMENT** a board similar to a washboard used as a musical instrument to produce a scratching sound **3. NAUT PROTECTIVE FEATURE ON A BOAT** a thin plank on the gunwale of a boat to stop water from splashing over the side ■ *adj.* **MUSCULAR** used to describe a man's stomach that has well-defined muscles

washbowl /wósh bowl/ *n.* = **washbasin**

washcloth /wósh kloth/ *n.* *US, Can* = **facecloth**

washday /wósh day/ *n.* a day when clothes are washed, usually the same day each week

wash drawing *n.* a drawing made in ink to which a wash of colour is applied, or a painting made using washes

washed-out, **washed out** *adj.* **1.** **FADED** faded or without colour **2.** **EXHAUSTED** exhausted or lacking vitality and strength

washed-up, **washed up** *adj.* no longer likely to continue or succeed (*informal*)

washer /wóshər/ *n.* **1.** **SMALL RING** a small disc or ring used to keep a screw or bolt secure or prevent leakage at a joint **2.** **HOUSEHOLD WASHING APPLIANCE** an appliance used for washing, especially a washing machine **3.** **SB WHO WASHES** sb who washes sth **4.** *Aus* **FACECLOTH** a facecloth (*informal*)

washer-dryer *n.* a machine that both washes and dries clothes

washer-up (*plural* **washers-up**) *n.* sb who is employed to wash dishes (*informal*)

washerwoman /wóshər woomən/ (*plural* **-en** /-wimin/), **washwoman** /wósh woomən/ (*plural* **-en** /-wimin/) *n.* a woman who is employed to wash clothes (*dated*)

wash house *n.* a building where laundry or other washing is done

washing /wóshing/ *n.* **1.** **CLOTHES FOR WASHING** clothes to be washed, being washed, or just washed **2.** **DOING LAUNDRY** the act or process of washing clothes **3.** **INDUST THIN COAT** a thin coat of sth ○ *a washing of silver* **4.** **LIQUID USED FOR WASHING** the liquid that has been used to wash sth (*often used in the plural*)

washing machine *n.* a machine for washing clothes, usually an electric one

washing powder *n.* detergent in powder form, used for washing clothes

washing soda *n.* a crystalline form of sodium carbonate used for washing and cleaning

Washington

Washington /wóshingtən/ **1.** state of the northwestern United States, bordered by British Columbia, Idaho, Oregon, and the Pacific Ocean. Capital: Olympia. Population: 5,610,362 (1997). Area: 182,949 sq. km/70,637 sq. mi. **2.** town in northeastern England. It is the location of Washington Old Hall, the ancestral home of George Washington. Population: 61,500 (1996). —**Washingtonian** *n.*, *adj.*

Washington, D.C. capital city of the United States. The city of Washington has the same boundaries as the District of Columbia, a federal territory established in 1790 as the site of the new nation's permanent capital. Located at the confluence of the Potomac and Anacostia rivers, it is bordered by Maryland and Virginia. Population: 543,000 (1996).

George Washington

Washington /wóshingtən/, **George** (1732–99) US statesman and 1st president of the United States. Commander in chief of the American forces during the American War of Independence (1775–83), and president of the second Constitutional Convention, he was the first president of the newly independent United States (1789–97).

washing-up *n.* **1.** **WASHING OF DISHES** the cleaning of dishes, cutlery, and other items used for cooking and eating **2.** **ITEMS NEEDING WASHING** the items that need to be washed after a meal

washing-up liquid *n.* detergent in liquid form, used for washing dishes. US term **dishwashing liquid**

washout /wósh owt/ *n.* **1.** **FAILURE** a complete failure or fiasco (*informal*) **2.** **OFFENSIVE TERM** an offensive term that deliberately insults sb's competence or achievements (*informal insult*) **3.** **GEOL EROSION CAUSED BY RUNNING WATER** erosion caused by running water, e.g. during a flash flood **4.** **GEOL CHANNEL WASHED OUT** a hole or channel made by floodwater

washroom /wósh room, -room/ *n.* **1.** **PUBLIC WASHING FACILITY** a room, especially in a public place, with toilet and washing facilities **2.** *US* **PUBLIC TOILET** a euphemism for a public toilet

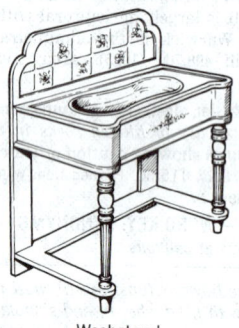
Washstand

washstand /wósh stand/ *n.* a stand on which a basin and jug can be placed for washing the face and hands

washtub /wósh tub/ *n.* a large container in which clothes can be washed

wash-up *n.* **1.** *Aus* **FINAL PHASE** the final phase or summing up of a process (*informal*) **2.** *Aus* **OUTCOME** the outcome of a process or series of events **3.** *Wales* **KITCHEN SINK** a kitchen sink (*informal*)

washwoman /wósh woomən/ (*plural* **-en** /-wimin/) *n.* = **washerwoman**

washy /wóshi/ (**-ier, -iest**) *adj.* **1.** **WEAK** watery or weak **2.** **PALE** faint or faded **3.** **NOT FORCEFUL** without intensity or vitality —**washily** *adv.* —**washiness** *n.*

wasn't /wózz'nt/ *contr.* was not

wasp /wosp/ *n.* **INSECTS** a slender black-and-yellow striped social stinging insect that typically has well-developed wings, biting mouthparts, and a narrow stalk connecting the abdomen and thorax. Family: Vespidae and Sphecidae. [Old English *wæsp*, from an Indo-European word meaning 'to weave', which is also the ancestor of English *web* and *weave*. The name probably refers to the fact that wasps build nests.]

Wasp /wosp/, **WASP** *n.* *US* an offensive term used to refer to a white, who has a Protestant Anglo-Saxon background, and is viewed as belonging to the dom-

Wasp

inant and most powerful level of US society (*informal insult*) [Mid-20thC. Acronym formed from *White Anglo-Saxon Protestant*.]

waspish /wóspish/, **waspy** /wóspi/ (**-ier, -iest**) *adj.* **1.** **OF WASPS** like a wasp, or relating to wasps **2.** **EASILY IRRITATED** easily irritated or annoyed **3.** **SPITEFUL** showing spite —**waspishly** *adv.* —**waspishness** *n.*

wasp waist *n.* a very slender waist, or one that is corseted to make it appear slender —**wasp waisted** *adj.*

waspy *adj.* = **waspish**

wassail /wóssayl/ *n.* (*archaic*) **1.** **FESTIVE SALUTATION** a salutation or drinking toast made during festivities **2.** **FESTIVE OCCASION** a festive occasion at which people drink a great deal **3.** **BEVERAGES** **ALCOHOLIC DRINK** an alcoholic drink, usually mulled wine or ale, drunk on a festive occasion **4.** **MUSIC** **DRINKING OR CHRISTMAS SONG** a drinking song or a song sung at Christmas ■ *v.* (**-sails, -sailing, -sailed**) **1.** *vi.* **DRINK IN CELEBRATION** to celebrate by drinking (*archaic*) **2.** *vi.* **SING CHRISTMAS SONGS** to go from house to house at Christmas, singing carols and greeting people (*regional archaic*) **3.** *vt.* **TOAST SB** to drink to sb's health (*archaic*) [12thC. From Old Norse *ves heill*, literally 'be healthy', *heill* from a prehistoric Germanic word that is also the ancestor of English *hale* and *health*.] —**wassailer** *n.*

Wassermann test /wássərmən-, vássər-/, **Wassermann reaction** *n.* a test for syphilis infection, based on determining the presence in a blood sample of antibodies to the syphilis bacterium [Named after the German bacteriologist August Paul *Wassermann* (1866–1925)]

wast /wost, wəst/ 2nd person past singular of **be** (*archaic*)

wastage /wáystij/ *n.* **1.** **AMOUNT WASTED** an amount that is lost or wasted **2.** **LOSS** loss caused when sth is used, is worn, decays, or leaks **3.** **REDUCTION IN NUMBERS** the reduction in numbers of people working in a place because of deaths and resignations, rather than from redundancies

waste /wayst/ *v.* (**wastes, wasting, wasted**) **1.** *vt.* **USE STH CARELESSLY** to use sth or use sth up carelessly, extravagantly, or without effect **2.** *vt.* **FAIL TO USE STH** to fail to make use of sth such as an opportunity **3.** *vti.* **GET WEAK OR ILL** to become weak, ill, or very thin, or make sb become weak, ill, or very thin **4.** *vt.* **EXHAUST SB** to make sb exhausted **5.** *vt.* **DESTROY STH** to ravage or devastate sth **6.** *vt.* **KILL SB** to kill or murder sb (*slang*) ■ *n.* **1.** **ACT OF WASTING** a failure to use sth wisely, properly, fully, or to good effect **2.** **UNWANTED MATERIAL** unwanted or unusable by-products ○ *chemical waste* **3.** **PHYSIOL FOOD REMAINDER** the undigested remainder of food expelled from the body as excrement **4.** **WILD AREA** an uncultivated, desolate, or wild area (*often used in the plural*) **5.** **DESTROYED AREA** a place or region that has been destroyed or ruined **6.** **RUBBISH** rubbish or refuse ○ *household waste* **7.** **LAW PROPERTY DEPRECIATION** loss of value in a property or estate caused by damage done by the tenant **8.** **ENG USED OR CONTAMINATED WATER** used or contaminated water from domestic, industrial, or mining applications **9.** **MINING ROCK ASSOCIATED WITH A MINERAL** enclosing rock mined with a mineral, or ore with insufficient mineral content to justify further processing ■ *adj.* **1.** **NOT NEEDED** superfluous, useless, or not needed **2.** **UNPRODUCTIVE** unproductive, uninhabited, or uncultivated ○ *waste ground* **3.** **PHYSIOL REJECTED FROM BODY** expelled from the body as unwanted and indigestible ○ *waste matter* **4.** **FOR WASTE** used to carry off or store waste [12thC. Via Old Northern French from, ultimately, Latin *vastus* 'empty' (source of English *devastate* and *vast*).] —**wastable** *adj.* ◇ **lay sth (to) waste** to destroy or devastate sth

wastebasket /wáyst baaskit/ *n. US* = **wastepaper basket**

wasted /wáystid/ *adj.* **1.** **NOT USED** not used or exploited **2.** **USELESS** useless because it achieves nothing **3.** **WITHERED** shrunken or ravaged **4.** **EXHAUSTED** exhausted from exertion (*slang*) **5.** **INTOXICATED** under the influence of drink or drugs (*slang*)

waste disposal, **waste disposal unit** *n.* an electrical device, fitted in a kitchen sink, that grinds up food so that it can go into the waste pipe. US term **garbage disposal**

wasteful /wáystf'l/ *adj.* **1.** **EXTRAVAGANT** using resources unwisely **2.** **CAUSING WASTE** causing waste or devastation —**wastefully** *adv.* —**wastefulness** *n.*

wasteland /wáyst land, wáystlənd/ *n.* **1.** **DESOLATE LAND** an area of land that is desolate or barren and not used **2.** **BARREN PLACE OR TIME** an environment that is thought to be spiritually or intellectually barren ○ *the wasteland of daytime TV*

WORD KEY: CULTURAL NOTE

The Waste Land, a poem by US-born British poet T. S. Eliot (1922). One of the 20th century's major poetic works, it portrays the disintegration of western values, the soullessness of modern society, and humankind's desperate search for salvation. It consists of five seemingly disconnected sections made up of fragmented verses written in a variety of styles but linked by imagery, symbols, and diverse literary and historical references.

wastelot /wáyst lot/ *n. Can* an area of wasteland in a city

wastepaper /wáyst páypər/ *n.* paper that is not needed and has been thrown away

wastepaper basket, **wastepaper bin** *n.* a small container for rubbish, especially paper. US term **wastebasket**

waste pipe *n.* a pipe that carries excess or used fluids from a container such as a sink or bathtub

waste product *n.* a useless or unwanted by-product of a process

waster /wáystər/ *n.* **1.** **ONE WHO WASTES** sb who wastes sth **2.** **STH THAT WASTES** sth that destroys or wastes sth **3.** **LAZY PERSON** sb who is lazy or worthless (*informal insult*) **4.** **RUINED ARTICLE** an article that has been spoiled during manufacture, especially a ceramic piece

wasteweir /wáyst weer/ *n.* = **spillway**

wasting /wáysting/ *adj.* taking away strength and energy —**wastingly** *adv.*

wasting asset *n.* an asset, especially a natural resource such as a mine, that cannot be renewed and that loses its value over time

wastrel /wáystrəl/ *n.* **1.** **OFFENSIVE TERM** an offensive term that deliberately insults sb for being wasteful or spendthrift **2.** **OFFENSIVE TERM** an offensive term that deliberately insults sb for being lazy [Late 16thC. Formed from WASTE + *-rel* an ending indicating 'little' or derogatory sense.]

Wastwater /wóst wawtər/ lake in the Lake District, northwestern England. With a maximum depth of 79 m/258 ft, it is the deepest lake in England. Area: 9 sq. km/1.5 sq. mi.

wat /wot/ *n.* a Buddhist monastery or temple in Thailand, Cambodia, or Laos [Mid-19thC. Via Thai from Sanskrit *vāṭa* 'enclosure'.]

watch /woch/ *n.* **1.** **PERSONAL CLOCK** a small clock worn on the wrist or carried in a pocket **2.** **TIME SPENT OBSERVING** a period of time spent observing sth closely **3.** NAUT **DUTY ON SHIP** a fixed period of a day spent on duty on board a ship **4.** NAUT **CREW ON DUTY** the members of a ship's crew who are on duty at a particular time **5.** TIME **DIVISION OF NIGHT** one of the periods of time into which the night was divided in the past **6.** **GUARD'S DUTY** the period during which a guard is on duty **7.** **PEOPLE WATCHING** a person or group that guards or observes sth, especially at night ○ *posted a watch around the house, day and night* ■ *v.* (**watches, watching, watched**) **1.** *vti.* **LOOK CAREFULLY** to look at sth carefully or closely **2.** *vi.* **BE ALERT** to be vigilant or alert **3.** *vi.* **KEEP LOOKOUT** to keep a lookout for sth that might appear or happen **4.** *vti.* **GUARD STH** to guard or keep sth or sb under observation **5.** *vi.* **KEEP VIGIL** to stay awake and keep a vigil [Assumed Old English *wæccan* 'to keep watch, be awake', from a prehistoric Germanic word that is also the ancestor of English *wake*] ◇ **be on the watch for sb *or* sth** to look out for sb or sth ◇ **watch it** to be careful

watch out *vi.* **1.** **BE CAREFUL** to be careful, alert, or wary **2.** **LOOK** to look and wait for sth or sb

watch over *vt.* to look after, supervise, or guard sb or sth

watchable /wóchəb'l/ *adj.* **1.** **OBSERVABLE** apparent or capable of being observed **2.** **ENJOYABLE** interesting and enjoyable to watch ○ *a very watchable detective series* —**watchability** /wóchə bíllәti/ *n.*

watchband /wóch band/ *n. US, Can, Aus* a strap for a wristwatch

watch cap *n.* a dark-blue close-fitting knitted woollen cap worn in cold weather, especially by sailors

watchcase /wóch kayss/ *n.* the protective casing for a watch mechanism

watchdog /wóch dog/ *n.* **1.** DOMESTIC **DOG FOR GUARDING** a dog used for guarding property or people **2.** PUBLIC ADMIN **GUARD AGAINST UNDESIRABLE PRACTICES** a person or organization guarding against illegal practices, unacceptable standards, or inefficiency ○ *a government watchdog* ■ *vti.* (**-dogs, -dogging, -dogged**) **BE A WATCHDOG** to act as a watchdog on sth

watcher /wóchər/ *n.* **1.** **SB WHO WATCHES OR LOOKS** a person who watches or observes sb or sth or who looks for sb or sth's appearance or occurrence **2.** **SB WHO GUARDS** sb who acts as a guard or guardian **3.** **SB KEEPING VIGIL** sb who keeps a vigil, especially at the bed of an ill person

watch fire *n.* a fire kept burning at night either as a signal or for the comfort of sb keeping watch

watchful /wóchf'l/ *adj.* **1.** **OBSERVING CLOSELY** carefully observant or alert ○ *watchful for signs of recovery* **2.** **AWAKE** not asleep (*archaic*) —**watchfully** *adv.* —**watchfulness** *n.*

watch-glass *n.* **1.** **GLASS PROTECTING WATCH FACE** a piece of glass or plastic fitted to a watch to cover and protect its face. US term **crystal** *n.* **8** **2.** SCI **SHALLOW DISH** a shallow round glass dish used to evaporate liquids or to cover sth

watchmaker /wóch maykər/ *n.* sb who makes or repairs watches

watchman /wóchmən/ (*plural* **-men** /-mən/) *n.* sb employed to patrol or guard buildings or an area

watch night *n.* **1.** **31 DECEMBER** the night of 31 December, celebrated in some Protestant churches with a special night time service that takes in the midnight transition from the old year to the new **2.** **24 DECEMBER** the night of 24 December, celebrated in some Protestant churches with a special night time service to welcome Jesus Christ to the world, and the arrival of Christmas, at midnight

watch pocket *n.* a small pocket for a watch in a waistcoat or trousers

watchstrap /wóch strap/ *n. UK, NZ* a strap for a wristwatch. ◊ **watchband**

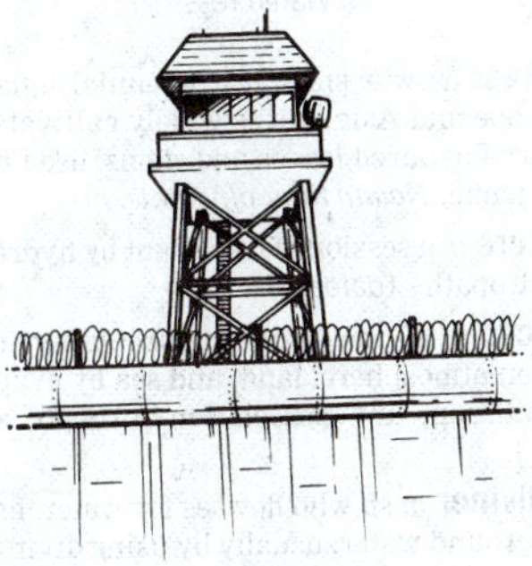

Watchtower

watchtower /wóch tow ər/ *n.* a high tower in which sentries keep watch for the approach of an enemy

watchword /wóch wurd/ *n.* **1.** **SLOGAN** a word or slogan that encapsulates a mode of action, a set of beliefs, or membership of a group **2.** **PASSWORD** a word or phrase that sb has to say to prove a right to be in a particular place

water /wáwtər/ *n.* **1.** **LIQUID OF RAIN AND RIVERS** the clear liquid, essential for all plant and animal life, that occurs as rain, snow, and ice, and forms rivers, lakes, and seas. Pure water is odourless, colourless, and tasteless. Naturally occurring water picks up colour and taste from substances in its environment. Formula: H_2O. **2.** GEOG **AREA OF WATER** an area or body of water, e.g. a river, stream, lake, or sea **3.** **SURFACE OF WATER** the surface of a body of water ○ *swim under water* **4.** PHILOS **ELEMENT** in ancient and medieval philosophy, one of the four elements **5.** TRANSP **TRANSPORT OVER WATER** a means of transport over or through water, especially a boat ○ *can only get there by water* **6.** UTIL **WATER SUPPLY** a supply of water to a house, town, or region **7.** GARDENING **A WATERING** the action of giving water to a plant **8.** **SOLUTION OF SUBSTANCE IN WATER** a solution of a particular chemical or substance in water ○ *lavender water* **9.** PHYSIOL **BODY FLUID** any watery fluid present in or secreted by the body, e.g. urine, sweat, saliva, or tears **10.** TEXTILES **WAVY PATTERN** a lustrous wavy pattern on the surface of some fabrics such as silk **11.** **BRIGHTNESS** the quality of brightness of a gem. ◊ **first water** ■ **waters** *npl.* **1.** **FLUID SURROUNDING FOETUS** the amniotic fluid that surrounds the foetus in the womb (*sometimes singular*) ○ *Her waters have broken.* **2.** **PARTICULAR AREA OF SEA** a particular region of sea, e.g. that belonging to a specific nation ○ *territorial waters* **3.** **WATER CONTAINING MINERALS** naturally occurring water containing minerals, e.g. that found at a spa and used for health reasons ■ *v.* (**-ters, -tering, -tered**) **1.** *vt.* **SPRINKLE OR SOAK STH WITH WATER** to sprinkle, wet, or soak sth with water **2.** *vt.* AGRIC **IRRIGATE LAND** to take water to crops or fields **3.** *vti.* **GIVE OR GET WATER** to give drinking water to an animal, or get or take water as an animal does **4.** *vi.* **FILL WITH TEARS WHEN IRRITATED** to fill with tears, especially because of irritation (*refers to eyes*) **5.** *vi.* **PRODUCE SALIVA** to produce saliva, particularly in pleasant anticipation of food (*refers to the mouth*) **6.** *vi.* NAUT **TAKE ON WATER SUPPLY** to take on a supply of water **7.** *vt.* TEXTILES **GIVE WAVY SHEEN** to give a lustrous wavy pattern to material, especially silk [Old English *wæter*. Ultimately from the Indo-European word meaning 'water' that is also the ancestor of English *hydro-*, *whisky*, and *vodka*.] —**waterer** *n.* ◇ **be dead in the water** to have no chance of success or survival ◇ **be water under the bridge** to be sth that is in the past and that cannot be altered ◇ **clear (blue) water** POL a marked difference or differentiation between two political parties ◇ **hold water** to be well-founded, or stand up under scrutiny ◇ **in deep water** in severe difficulties ◇ **in hot water** in trouble because of having done sth wrong ◇ **muddy the waters** to cause confusion or trouble ◇ **pour *or* throw cold water on *or* onto *or* over sth** to discourage a plan or idea by showing a lack of interest in it or rejecting it as impractical ◇ **tread water 1.** to keep afloat without moving forwards, by moving the legs and arms **2.** to make no progress but manage to keep a situation the same for a period of time ◇ **water off a duck's back** sth said that has absolutely no effect on the attitude or behaviour of the person to whom it is said

WORD KEY: CULTURAL NOTE

Water Music, an orchestral suite by German-born British composer George Frederic Handel (1717). It consists of three separate suites for strings and wind instruments. The exact circumstances of its composition are not known, but it was first performed to accompany a royal barge trip along the Thames from Whitehall to Chelsea on 17 July, 1717.

water down *vt.* **1.** **DILUTE** to weaken or dilute sth by adding water to it **2.** **REDUCE DIFFICULTY OR OFFENSIVENESS OF STH** to moderate or attenuate sth in order to make it less difficult, offensive, or controversial ○ *The producers want to water down her original script.* —**watered-down** *adj.*

waterage /wáwtərij/ *n.* **1.** **CARRIAGE BY WATER** the carrying of passengers or cargo by water **2.** **COST OF CARRIAGE BY WATER** money paid for the carrying of passengers or cargo by water

water arum *n.* an aquatic plant native to cool northern temperate regions and cultivated for its glossy heart-shaped leaves and large white funnel-shaped cone surrounding the flower spike. Latin name: *Calla palustris.*

water ash *n.* TREES = **stinking ash**

water bag *n.* **1.** BAG FOR CARRYING WATER a bag made of leather, canvas, or similar material used for carrying water **2.** ANAT FLUID-FILLED SAC SURROUNDING FOETUS the thin protective sac (**amnion**) around the growing foetus, and the watery fluid (**amniotic fluid**) it contains that is expelled just before or during childbirth

water ballet *n.* the performance of dance movements in water

water bear *n.* = **tardigrade**

Water Bearer *n.* ASTRON = **Aquarius**

water bed *n.* a bed with a special mattress filled with water

Water beetle

water beetle *n.* a member of a group of beetles that live mainly in water. Some have broad hind legs for swimming; others crawl over aquatic vegetation. Family: Hydrophilidae.

water bird *n.* a bird that lives mainly near, and wades in or swims on, water, especially fresh water

water biscuit *n.* a thin plain biscuit made from flour and water, often served with cheese

water blister *n.* a blister that contains clear watery fluid without blood or pus

water bloom *n.* a growth of algae on a body of water such as a lake

water boatman (*plural* **water boatmen**) *n.* **1.** POND BUG any of various insects that live mainly at the bottom of ponds and have oar-like flattened hind legs that they use for swimming. Most water boatmen are good fliers. Family: Corixidae. **2.** = **backswimmer**

waterborne /wáwtər bawrn/ *adj.* **1.** TRANSP CARRIED BY WATER travelling on or transported by water ∘ *a waterborne vessel* **2.** MED TRANSMITTED BY WATER transmitted or transported by water, as certain infectious agents are

water brash *n.* the sudden filling of the mouth with acidic juices from the stomach, usually accompanied by heartburn and often resulting from indigestion. It is common in pregnancy, but may also be an indication of a disorder of the digestive tract.

waterbuck /wáwtər buk/ (*plural* **-bucks** *or* **-buck**) *n.* a large antelope of southern Africa with a shaggy dark-grey or reddish coat, found in grassland and woodland near open water. Latin name: *Kobus ellipsiprymnus.*

water buffalo *n.* a large buffalo native to swamplands of Southeast Asia but widely domesticated, with a grey-black coat and long backward-curving horns. Domestic breeds are more docile, have shorter horns, and are used as draught animals and for milk. Latin name: *Bubalus bubalis.*

water bug *n.* an aquatic insect, e.g. the water boatman or water strider

waterbus /wáwtər buss/ *n.* a boat carrying passengers in a regular service across a river or lake

water butt *n.* a large barrel for collecting rainwater, usually from a drainpipe. US term **rain barrel**

water caltrop *n.* = **water chestnut**

water cannon *n.* an apparatus usually mounted on a lorry that produces a jet of high-pressure water and is used to disperse crowds

Water Carrier *n.* ASTRON = **Aquarius**

water chestnut *n.* **1.** PLANTS AQUATIC PLANT an annual aquatic plant that forms rosettes of diamond-shaped floating leaves, has feathery submerged leaves, and bears hard spiny dark-grey fruit containing edible seeds. It is native to Europe and Asia. Latin name: *Trapa natans.* **2.** PLANTS CHINESE PLANT WITH AN EDIBLE STEM a Chinese sedge that produces edible stems (**corms**). Latin name: *Eleocharis tuberosa.* **3.** FOOD CRUNCHY NUT-LIKE CORM IN ASIAN COOKING the round white crunchy stem (**corm**) of the Chinese water chestnut plant. Water chestnuts are common in Asian cooking, and are used in food manufacture to add crunchiness to processed foods.

water chinquapin *n.* US an American aquatic plant that resembles a water lily and has fragrant cup-shaped pale-yellow flowers. Latin name: *Nelumbo lutea.*

water clock *n.* = **clepsydra**

water closet *n.* **1.** SMALL ROOM CONTAINING TOILET a small room fitted with a toilet and, often, a washbasin **2.** TOILET a flush toilet (*archaic*)

watercolor *n.* US = **watercolour**

watercolour /wáwtər kullər/ *n.* **1.** PAINTING a painting created with pigments mixed with water rather than oil **2.** PIGMENT MIXED WITH WATER painting pigments, or a pigment, mixed with water rather than oil (*often used in the plural*) **3.** METHOD OF PAINTING the method of painting with pigments mixed with water rather than oil —**watercolourist** *n.*

water-cool (**water-cools**, **water-cooling**, **water-cooled**) *vt.* to cool an engine or machine by means of water, typically by circulating water in a water jacket or by pipes —**water-cooled** *adj.*

water cooler *n.* a device that dispenses cooled drinking water

watercourse /wáwtər kawrss/ *n.* **1.** CHANNEL FOR FLOWING WATER a river or stream channel, or an artificial channel, through which water flows **2.** STREAM the water of a river or stream that flows along a watercourse

watercraft /wáwtər kraaft/ *n.* **1.** BOAT OR SHIP a vessel used for travelling on water (*formal*) **2.** SKILL IN WATER-RELATED ACTIVITIES skill in swimming, handling boats, or other water-related activities

Watercress

watercress /wáwtər kress/ *n.* a perennial aquatic plant of Europe and Asia that is widely cultivated for its peppery-flavoured leaves and stems, used in salads. Latin name: *Nasturtium officinale.*

water cure *n.* a session of treatment by hydrotherapy or hydropathy (*dated*)

water cycle *n.* the constant circulation of water between atmosphere, land, and sea by evaporation, precipitation, and percolation through soils and rocks

water diviner *n.* sb who dowses for water, especially underground water, usually by using divining rods. US term **dowser**

water dog *n.* **1.** ZOOL DOG AT HOME IN WATER a dog that likes water, especially one trained to hunt or retrieve game in water **2.** SB WHO LIKES THE WATER sb who

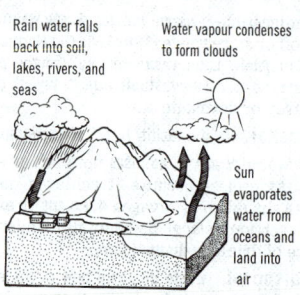

Rain water falls back into soil, lakes, rivers, and seas

Water vapour condenses to form clouds

Sun evaporates water from oceans and land into air

Water cycle

likes being in, on, or near water, e.g. a keen sailor or swimmer (*informal*)

water dropwort *n.* **1.** PLANT OF CARROT FAMILY a perennial plant of the carrot family found alongside watercourses and having a hollow grooved stem, compound leaves, and flat-topped clusters of small white flowers. Latin name: *Oenanthe fistulosa.* **2.** PLANT RELATED TO THE WATER DROPWORT any of several plants related to the water dropwort

WORLD'S HIGHEST WATERFALLS

1	Angel Falls	
Height	[3,212 ft / 979 m*] (also single largest leap, [2,647 ft / 807 m*])	
Location	*Venezuela*	
2	Tugela Waterfall	
Height	[3,110 ft / 948 m*]	
Location	*South Africa*	
3	Mtarazi Waterfall	
Height	[2,500 ft / 762 m*]	
Location	*Zimbabwe*	
4	Yosemite Falls	
Height	[2,425 ft / 739 m*]	
Location	*United States*	
5	Cuquenán Waterfall	
Height	[2,000 ft / 610 m*]	
Location	*Venezuela*	
6	Sutherland Falls	
Height	[1,904 ft / 580 m*]	
Location	*New Zealand*	
7	Kile Waterfall	
Height	[1,840 ft / 561 m*]	
Location	*Norway*	
8	Kahiwa Waterfall	
Height	[1,748 ft / 533 m*]	
Location	*United States*	
9	Mardal Waterfall	
Height	[1,696 ft / 517 m*]	
Location	*Norway*	
10	Takakkaw Falls	
Height	[1,650 ft / 503 m*]	
Location	*Canada*	

* Total height may include more than one leap

waterfall /wáwtər fawl/ *n.* a vertical stream of water that occurs where a river or stream falls over the edge of a steep place

water fern *n.* = **mosquito fern**

water filter *n.* an appliance or fitting for removing unwanted matter from water, especially bacteria or harmful chemicals from drinking water

water flea *n.* a tiny crustacean that swims with rapid jerky movements, using its large forked antennae. Suborder: Cladocera.

Waterford /wáwtərfərd/ *n.* county in Munster Province, in the southern part of the Republic of Ireland. Population: 52,140 (1996). Area: 1,838 sq. km/710 sq. mi. ∎ city and administrative centre of County Waterford, in the Republic of Ireland. Population: 44,155 (1996).

waterfowl /wáwtər fowl/ n. (plural **-fowl** or **-fowls**) AQUATIC BIRD any of various birds that swim on water ■ npl. SWIMMING GAME BIRDS swimming game birds such as ducks, considered collectively

waterfront /wáwtər frunt/ n. **1.** PART OF TOWN ALONGSIDE WATER the part of a town that lies alongside a body of water **2.** SHORE land beside an area of water

water gap n. a deep valley through a mountain ridge, in which water flows

water gas n. a toxic mixture of carbon monoxide and methane generated by the passage of steam through an incandescent bed of coal. It is used for industrial heating, as an illuminant, and as a gas-engine fuel.

water gate n. **1.** = floodgate **2.** GATE INTO AREA OF WATER a gate that gives access to an area of water

Watergate /wáwtər gayt/ n. **1.** HIST **1972 US POLITICAL SCANDAL** a political scandal stemming from a break-in by Republican operatives at the 1972 US Democratic National Committee headquarters, which were in the Watergate complex in Washington, D.C. The scandal led to the resignation of President Nixon and the conviction and imprisonment of a number of his closest aides. **2.** PUBLIC SCANDAL a public scandal involving politicians or officials abusing power, especially if a cover-up is also attempted

water gauge n. a device that indicates the quantity or level of water in a tank, boiler feed, reservoir, or stream

water glass n. **1.** HOUSEHOLD DRINKING GLASS a drinking glass, especially for water **2.** CHEM THICK CHEMICAL SOLUTION an extremely viscous solution of sodium silicate used as a waterproof coating, a cement, a fireproofing agent, and for preserving eggs **3.** GLASS GAUGE a water gauge consisting of a glass tube **4.** DEVICE FOR EXAMINING UNDERWATER OBJECTS an instrument such as an open box or tube with a glass bottom, used for looking at objects under the water's surface

water gum n. any of various Australian trees that grow near water

water gun n. US a toy gun that squirts water

water hammer n. a hammering or stuttering sound in a pipeline that sometimes accompanies a sudden and significant change in the flow rate of the fluid through the pipeline

water hemlock n. any of various poisonous, highly scented plants found in marshy areas of the northern hemisphere that have compound leaves and dense flat-topped clusters of small white flowers. All parts of the plants, especially the tuberous roots, contain a toxic chemical. Genus: *Cicuta*.

water hen n. a bird that lives near water, e.g. a rail or a coot. Family: Rallidae.

water hole n. a natural hollow in the ground containing water, especially one where animals drink

Waterhouse /wáwtər howss, wóttər-/, **Alfred** (1830–1905) British architect. He was a leader in the Gothic Revival. Among his major works is the Natural History Museum, London (1881).

Waterhouse, George Marsden (1824–1906) English-born New Zealand statesman. He was premier of New Zealand (1872–73).

water hyacinth n. a perennial aquatic plant, native to the subtropical Americas but also found elsewhere that has glossy rounded leaves with bulbous stalks, and lilac-blue flowers. Widely cultivated as an ornamental, it has become a troublesome weed of waterways in many subtropical regions, including Australia, Africa, and Southeast Asia. Latin name: *Eichhornia crassipes*.

water ice n. a frozen dessert of sweet-flavoured ice

watering can n. a container with a handle and a spout, often with a perforated nozzle, used for watering plants

watering hole n. **1.** = water hole **2.** PUB SERVING DRINKS a place such as a pub where people meet socially to drink (informal)

watering place n. **1.** = water hole **2.** = watering hole n. **1 3.** SPA a place where people go to drink or bathe in the local water for health reasons **4.** LEISURE SEASIDE RESORT a place by the sea to which people go for swimming and other leisure activities (dated)

waterish /wáwtərish/ adj. a bit watery

water jump n. a place in a race where the runners or horses have to jump over an obstacle that includes a stream, ditch, or pool

waterleaf /wáwtər leef/ n. any of various woodland plants of western North America with deeply toothed leaves and bell-shaped flowers. Genus: *Hydrophyllum*.

waterless /wáwtərləss/ adj. **1.** WITHOUT WATER lacking water **2.** NOT NEEDING WATER not needing water in the making or use of sth

water level n. **1.** GEOG HEIGHT OF WATER SURFACE the level of the surface of a body of water **2.** SHIPPING = water line n. **1 3.** GEOL = water table n. **1**

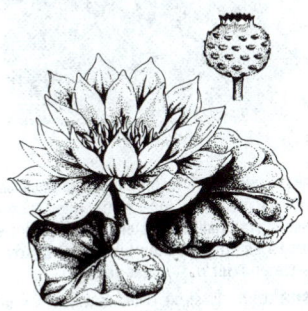

Water lily

water lily n. a perennial aquatic plant with roundish leaves that float on the water and showy cup-shaped often fragrant flowers. Family: Nymphaeaceae.

─── **WORD KEY: CULTURAL NOTE** ───

Water Lilies, the title of a number of paintings by French artist Claude Monet (1899–1925). In his later years, Monet retired to his house at Giverny near Paris, where he painted numerous studies of the water lilies in his garden pond. While tending towards abstraction, many of these works, for example the enormous panels now in the Orangerie in Paris, succeed brilliantly in capturing the evanescent quality of natural phenomena.

water line n. **1.** SHIPPING LINE ON HULL a line on a ship's hull indicating the level to which the ship can sink into the water under various conditions **2.** LINE OF EDGE OF WATER the line to which a body of water rises or reaches

waterlogged /wáwtər logd/ adj. **1.** SOAKED WITH WATER saturated with water ○ a waterlogged pitch **2.** NAUT HARD TO STEER BECAUSE OF WATER filled with water and therefore hard to steer —**waterlog** vt.

Waterloo[1] /wáwtər loó/ town in central Belgium, about 16 km/10 mi. south of Brussels. It was the site of the Battle of Waterloo on 18 June, 1815, where Napoleon was decisively defeated by British and Prussian forces. Population: 27,860 (1991).

Waterloo[2] /wáwtər loó/ (plural **-loos**), **waterloo** (plural **-loos**) ◇ **meet your Waterloo** to be decisively defeated or overcome

water louse n. any of various freshwater crustaceans related to the woodlouse, found in weed-infested ponds and streams. Genus: *Asellu*.

water main n. a large underground pipe supplying water

waterman /wáwtərmən/ n. (plural **-men** /-mən/) sb who works on or hires out boats

watermark /wáwtər maark/ n. **1.** PAPER HIDDEN MARK IN PAPER a design or mark in paper that can be seen when the paper is held up to the light, or the metal tool used to make such a design **2.** SHIPPING = water line n. **2 3.** LINE LEFT BY WATER a line showing where the edge or surface of water has been ■ vt. (**-marks, -marking, -marked**) PAPER PUT WATERMARK OR PATTERN IN PAPER to put a watermark into paper while it is being made, or impress a particular pattern as a watermark

water meadow n. a meadow that is often flooded by a stream or river

water measurer n. INSECTS = marsh treader

watermelon /wáwtər melən/ n. **1.** FOOD LARGE FRUIT WITH SWEET JUICY FLESH a large oval or round fruit with a hard green skin and sweet and very juicy pink, red, or yellow flesh usually with many black seeds **2.** PLANTS AFRICAN PLANT PRODUCING WATERMELON FRUIT an annual climbing plant native to Africa but widely cultivated that has deeply lobed hairy leaves, yellow flowers, and bears the watermelon fruit. Latin name: *Citrullus lanatus*.

water meter n. a device that records the amount of water that passes through a pipe, usually for billing purposes

water milfoil n. any of various perennial aquatic plants that have submerged leaves made up of many feathery segments and bear slender spikes of tiny flowers above the water surface. Genus: *Myriophyllum*.

water mill n. a mill that has machinery powered by moving water

water mint n. a perennial plant of swampy areas with toothed hairy leaves, a hairy stem, and whorls of lilac-pink flowers. It emits a strong scent when crushed. Latin name: *Mentha aquatica*.

water moccasin n. **1.** POISONOUS N AMERICAN SNAKE a venomous semiaquatic snake belonging to the pit viper family and inhabiting wetlands of the southern United States that has an olive to brownish back and indistinct black bars. It feeds on water birds, fish, and other reptiles, and shows the white insides of its mouth when threatened. Latin name: *Agkistrodon piscivorus*. **2.** HARMLESS WATER SNAKE a snake that resembles a venomous water moccasin but is harmless. Genus: *Nerodia*.

water mould n. any of various fungi that inhabit fresh or brackish water and feed mainly on dead organic material but are sometimes parasitic on fish, plants, and other living organisms. Order: Saprolegniales.

water nymph n. **1.** MYTHOL NYMPH LIVING IN WATER in folklore and classical mythology, a nymph that lives in water **2.** PLANTS WATER PLANT a water plant, such as a water lily

water of crystallization, water of crystallisation n. molecules of water incorporated in a crystalline substance and responsible for its properties and structure

water of hydration n. molecules of water chemically incorporated in a substance but removable without affecting the essential composition of the substance

water on the brain n. MED = hydrocephalus

water on the knee n. the accumulation of watery fluid in or around the knee indicating disease or injury of the knee joint

water opossum n. = yapok

water ouzel n. BIRDS = dipper n. **2**

water penny n. any of various circular beetle larvae that cling like tiny suction cups to rocks in swift streams. Family: Psephenidae.

water pennywort n. a creeping plant that grows in water or moist places. Genus: *Hydrocotyle*.

water pepper n. an annual plant widely distributed in damp places that has lance-shaped leaves, a hot peppery taste, and slender spikes of inconspicuous pink or greenish flowers. Latin name: *Polygonum hydropiper*.

water pipe n. **1.** CONSTR PIPE FOR CONVEYING WATER a pipe for transporting water from one place to another **2.** DRUGS WATER-FILLED SMOKING PIPE a pipe for smoking sth, especially marijuana, that is filled with water in order to cool the smoke by drawing it through the water

water pistol n. a toy pistol that squirts out water

water plantain n. a perennial plant found in water or wet places, with a rosette of pointed oval leaves and branching heads of pinkish or white flowers. Genus: *Alisma*.

water polo n. a game played in a swimming pool by two teams of seven players whose object is to score by sending a large ball into the opposing team's goal

water power *n.* **1.** POWER GENERATED BY FORCE OF WATER power, usually generated from an elevated water supply, that is converted to electricity through the use of hydraulic turbines **2.** FALL OF WATER THAT GENERATES POWER the descent of a watercourse capable of providing water power

waterproof /wáwtər proof/ *adj.* IMPERVIOUS TO WATER treated or constructed so as to be impenetrable or unaffected by water ■ *n.* **1.** ITEM OF WATERPROOF CLOTHING an item of waterproof clothing, such as a plastic cape **2.** TEXTILES TEXTILE IMPERVIOUS TO WATER a textile that has been made or treated so as to be impenetrable or unaffected by water ■ *vt.* (-proofs, -proofing, -proofed) MAKE STH WATERPROOF to make sth such as a house or an item of clothing impenetrable by water

water purslane *n.* a creeping annual plant growing in moist places with fleshy rounded leaves and small purplish flowers at the leaf base. Latin name: *Lythrum portula.*

water rail *n.* a Eurasian bird of marshes and other wet places with a long red bill, grey underparts with black-striped flanks, and mottled brown back and wings. Latin name: *Rallus aquaticus.*

water rat *n.* **1.** = water vole **2.** *US* = muskrat **3.** RAT WITH FEET ADAPTED FOR SWIMMING any of various large amphibious rats, native to Australia, New Guinea, and the Philippines, that have broad paddle-shaped hind feet for swimming. Subfamily: Hydromyinae. **4.** *US* WATERFRONT THUG a criminal, loafer, or hooligan who often frequents waterfront areas (*slang*)

water-repellent, water-resistant *adj.* treated or constructed so as to prevent water being absorbed into it or passing through it

water right *n.* **1.** AGRIC RIGHT TO USE A WATER SOURCE the right to use a water source, especially for irrigation (*often plural*) **2.** NAUT RIGHT TO SAIL SOMEWHERE the right to sail on particular rivers, lakes, or seas

Waters /wáwtərz/, **Muddy** (1915–83) US musician. He was a country blues singer who originated the Chicago blues style in the 1950s, and was a leading figure in the revival of folk-blues music in the 1960s. Real name **McKinley Morganfield**

water sapphire *n.* a blue form of the mineral cordierite, found in river gravel and used as a gemstone

waterscape /wáwtər skayp/ *n.* a view or picture of an expanse of water

water scavenger beetle *n.* any of various smooth dark aquatic beetles that are found worldwide in marshes and ponds and eat algae and decaying organic matter. Family: Hydrophilidae.

water scorpion *n.* an aquatic insect that lies submerged in water breathing through a long tubular siphon, and that catches prey by using the front pair of legs. Family: Nepidae.

water seal *n.* water that lies in a waste pipe and forms a seal that prevents the escape of unpleasant smells

watershed /wáwtər shed/ *n.* **1.** GEOG LINE BETWEEN CATCHMENT AREAS the boundary separating the catchment basins of different rivers. US term **divide**. n.2 **2.** GEOG REGION DRAINING INTO RIVER OR OCEAN the land area that drains into a particular lake, river, or ocean **3.** TURNING POINT an important period, time, event, or factor that marks a change or division [Early 19thC. Anglicization of German *Wasserscheide*, literally 'water divide'.]

water shield *n.* **1.** AQUATIC PLANT WITH PURPLE FLOWERS a widely distributed perennial aquatic plant with purple flowers and floating leaves that are purple underneath and covered in a layer of clear jelly. Latin name: *Brasenia schreberi.* **2.** AQUATIC PLANT WITH DISTINCTIVE LEAVES any of various aquatic plants with roundish floating leaves or finely divided needle-shaped submerged leaves. Genus: *Cabomba.* [Because the leaves are shaped like shields]

water shrew *n.* any of various shrews that live in or near water

water-sick *adj.* used to describe land that has been made unproductive by excessive irrigation

waterside /wáwtər sīd/ *n.* LAND BY WATER land alongside an area of water ■ *adj.* LIVING OR WORKING BESIDE WATER living or working beside an area of water

watersider /wáwtər sīdər/ *n.* ANZ a worker on the wharves who loads and unloads ships

water sign *n.* any one of the three signs of the zodiac, Pisces, Cancer, or Scorpio, that are associated with emotional sensitivity

water skater *n.* = pond-skater

Water-ski

water-ski *n.* **water-ski, water ski** SKI FOR SKIING ON WATER a type of ski designed for skiing over water ■ *vi.* (**water-skis, water-skiing, water-skied** *or* **water-ski'd**) SKI ON WATER to ski over water while being towed by a boat —**water-skier** *n.* —**water-skiing** *n.*

water snake *n.* **1.** SNAKE LIVING IN WATER a snake that lives in or near water **2.** NONPOISONOUS MARSH SNAKE a nonvenomous snake found in North America, Europe, and Asia, especially Southeast Asia, that lives in marshes and other wet places. Genus: *Natrix.*

water softener *n.* **1.** APPARATUS FOR REMOVING HARDNESS FROM WATER a device that removes or reduces hardness in water, usually by means of ion-exchange resins **2.** CHEMICAL FOR REDUCING HARDNESS OF WATER a substance used to reduce hardness of water, e.g. by precipitating out the minerals causing the hardness

water soldier *n.* an aquatic European perennial plant that produces a semi-submerged rosette of toothed lance-shaped leaves and bears prominent white flowers. Latin name: *Stratiotes aloides.*

water-soluble *adj.* capable of being dissolved completely by water

water spaniel *n.* any of several breeds of dog that have thick curly water-resistant coats, and that were developed for retrieving from water

water spider *n.* a Eurasian spider that lives underwater in a bell-shaped web, which it spins amongst vegetation and fills with air bubbles transported from the surface in its body hairs. Latin name: *Argyroneta aquatica.*

water splash *n.* a section of road where a stream flows across it

water sports *npl.* SPORTS ASSOCIATED WITH WATER sports carried out on or in water ■ *n.* TABOO OFFENSIVE TERM a euphemism used to describe sexual activity in which urine or the act of urination provides gratification (*taboo offensive*)

waterspout /wáwtər spowt/ *n.* **1.** METEOROL TORNADO OVER WATER a funnel-shaped tornado, sometimes hundreds of feet wide, extending from the surface of the sea or a lake to the cloud base and caused by violent circulation of air **2.** BUILDING SPOUT FROM ROOF GUTTER a hole or spout through which water flows, e.g. from the gutter of a building

water sprite *n.* in folklore and classical mythology, a sprite that lives in water

water starwort *n.* an aquatic plant that can form rosettes of rounded floating leaves at the base of which develop tiny male or female flowers. The underwater leaves are less rounded and the form of the plant can vary markedly depending on its location. Genus: *Callitriche.*

water stick insect *n.* an aquatic bug with a long slender body and a long siphon used for breathing underwater that catches prey by using its front legs. Although winged, it has poorly developed flight muscles and cannot fly. Latin name: *Ranatra linearis.*

water strider *n.* *US* = pond-skater

water supply *n.* **1.** WATER DISTRIBUTED TO PLACE the water distributed to a town, community, or region **2.** WATER SOURCE OR DELIVERY SYSTEM the source or delivery system supplying water to an area, e.g. reservoirs, pipes, or purification plants

water system *n.* **1.** GEOG RIVER AND TRIBUTARIES a river with all its tributaries **2.** UTIL SYSTEM FOR DELIVERING WATER a system for delivering water to a group of users or a town or region

water table *n.* **1.** GEOL GROUNDWATER LEVEL the upper surface of groundwater, below which pores in the rocks are filled with water **2.** ARCHIT BAND DIVERTING RAINWATER a moulding or band that projects from a wall and is intended to divert rainwater

water taxi *n.* a motorboat used to ferry passengers between destinations separated by water for a fare

watertight /wáwtər tīt/ *adj.* **1.** KEEPING WATER IN OR OUT not allowing water to pass in, out, or through **2.** STANDING UP TO SCRUTINY without loopholes or flaws ○ *a watertight argument* —**watertightness** *n.*

water torture *n.* a form of torture in which water is used, especially one in which water is dripped steadily onto sb's forehead

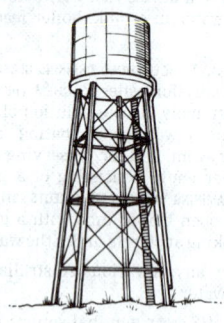
Water tower

water tower *n.* **1.** WATER STORAGE TOWER a tower for water storage where the prevailing water pressure is not sufficient for either firefighting or general distribution **2.** FIREFIGHTING APPARATUS FOR RAISING WATER a firefighting apparatus for lifting hoses to high levels

water vapour *n.* water in the form of a vapour but usually below boiling point

water-vascular system *n.* a system of water-filled vessels connecting the tube feet of echinoderms such as starfish

water vole *n.* any of several amphibious voles of Europe and Asia that live near rivers and streams, often burrowing into the banks. Genus: *Arvicola.*

waterway /wáwtər way/ *n.* **1.** GEOG RIVER OR CANAL a navigable channel such as a river or canal used by boats or ships **2.** SHIPPING DRAIN ON DECK a drain for water at the edge of the deck of a boat

waterweed /wáwtər weed/ *n.* = pondweed n. 2

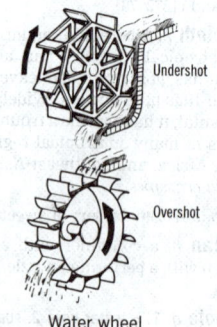
Undershot

Overshot

Water wheel

water wheel *n.* **1.** WATER-DRIVEN WHEEL POWERING MACHINERY a simple wheel driven by water flowing or falling onto vanes or into buckets on the edges of the wheel, used to power machinery **2.** WHEEL FOR LIFTING

WATER a wheel with buckets fixed to its rim, used for lifting water

water wings *npl.* a pair of air-filled supports that fit closely around the upper arms of a swimmer, especially a child learning to swim

water witch *n.* = **water diviner**

waterworks /wáwtər wurks/ *n.* (plural **-works**) **1.** SYSTEM FOR SUPPLYING WATER the entire system of treating, storing, supplying, and managing the distribution networks of pumps and pipes that provide water to a community or region (*takes a singular or plural verb*) **2.** COMPONENT OF WATER SYSTEM a single component of a waterworks system such as a pumping station **3.** DISPLAY OF MOVING WATER a display of water that has been made to move artificially such as a fountain **4.** ANAT URINARY SYSTEM the bodily system involved in excreting urine (*informal; takes a plural verb*) ■ *npl.* TEARS a display of crying (*informal*)

waterworn /wáwtər wawrn/ *adj.* smoothed or eroded by the action of water

watery /wáwtəri/ *adj.* **1.** RELATING TO OR CONTAINING WATER relating to, containing, soaked with, or like water **2.** HAVING EXCESSIVE WATER containing too much water ○ *watery coffee* **3.** FILLED WITH TEARS filled with tears, from either emotion or physical irritation ○ *watery eyes* **4.** LACKING FORCE lacking the usual full force and appearing thin or weak ○ *A watery sun hung in the autumn sky.* **5.** WEAK lacking strength or sincerity ○ *a watery smile* **6.** FULL OF FLUID discharging, secreting, or filled with a watery fluid ○ *watery blister* — **wateriness** *n.*

Watford /wótfərd/ town in Hertfordshire, south-central England. Population: 77,200 (1995).

Watson /wóts'n/, **Chris** (1867–1941) Chilean-born Australian statesman. The leader of the Labor Party, he was prime minister of Australia in 1904. Full name **John Christian Watson**

Watson, James D. (b. 1928) US biochemist. His work with Francis Crick and Maurice Wilkins in exploring the structure of the DNA molecule won them a shared Nobel Prize in physiology or medicine (1962). Full name **James Dewey Watson**

Watson-Crick model *n.* the three-dimensional double-helix model of the DNA molecule proposed by James Watson and Francis Crick in 1953 [Mid-20thC. Named after J. D. WATSON and F. H. C. *Crick*, a British biochemist (born 1916).]

watt /wot/ *n.* the international (**SI**) unit of power equal to the power produced by a current of one ampere acting across a potential difference of one volt. Symbol **W** [Late 19thC. Named after James WATT.]

Watt /wot/, **James** (1736–1819) British inventor. He improved the steam engine and, in partnership with Matthew Boulton, developed a pumping engine and rotative engine. The metric unit of power is named after him.

wattage /wóttij/ *n.* electrical power measured in watts

Watteau /wótt ō/, **Antoine** (1684–1721) French painter. His festive rural scenes and figures from the commedia dell'arte epitomize French rococo painting. Full name **Jean-Antoine Watteau**

watt-hour *n.* a unit of electrical energy equal to that of one watt operating for one hour

wattle /wótt'l/ *n.* **1.** BUILDING STAKES INTERWOVEN WITH BRANCHES stakes or poles interwoven with branches and twigs, used for walls, fences, and roofs **2.** INDUST MATERIAL FOR WATTLE material such as branches or stakes used to make wattle **3.** ZOOL SKIN HANGING FROM ANIMAL'S THROAT a loose, often highly coloured fold of bare skin hanging from the throat or cheek of birds and lizards. It is used in courtship and other displays. **4.** TREES AUSTRALIAN ACACIA TREE any of various Australian trees and shrubs that put out leaves with many leaflets, bear heads of tiny flowers, and produce useful timber. Now used mainly as shade and ornamental trees, wattles were originally used to make fences, while the bark was used for tanning. Genus: *Acacia.* ■ *vt.* (**-tles, -tling, -tled**) BUILDING **1.** MAKE FROM WATTLE to construct sth from wattle **2.** WEAVE BRANCHES INTO WATTLE to weave branches or twigs into wattle [Old English *watul*, of uncertain origin] —**wattled** *adj.*

wattle and daub *n.* building material consisting of wattle covered with mud or clay, often containing lime, dung, or straw (*hyphenated when used before a noun*)

wattlebird /wótt'l burd/ *n.* a slender-bodied grey-brown or olive-brown Australian bird with a long bill, a brush-tipped tongue for lapping nectar, and wattles on the cheeks. Genus: *Anthochaera.*

wattmeter /wót meetər/ *n.* an instrument designed to measure the magnitude of the power in an electric circuit. It may be scaled in watts, kilowatts, or megawatts.

Watts /wots/, **George Frederick** (1817–1904) British painter and sculptor. He painted portraits of well-known contemporary figures and grandly allegorical paintings.

Popperfoto

Evelyn Waugh

Waugh /waw/, **Evelyn** (1903–66) British novelist. His early novels satirizing high society gave way to the more serious later work such as *Brideshead Revisited* (1945) that reflected his preoccupation with Roman Catholicism. Full name **Evelyn Arthur St John Waugh**

waul /wawl/, **wawl** *vi.* (**wauls, wauling, wauled; wawls, wawling, wawled**) CRY SHRILLY to cry out shrilly like a cat or baby ■ *n.* CRY a shrill cry, like that of a cat or baby [Early 16thC. An imitation of the sound.]

waulk /wawk/ *n.* (**waulks, waulking, waulked**) *vt. Scotland* to make cloth, such as tweed, thicker and more felted by soaking and beating it [15thC. From Dutch or Low German *walken*.]

waulking song /wáwking-/ *n. Scotland* a Gaelic work-song traditionally sung while fulling cloth

waur /wawr/ *adj., adv. Scotland* worse [Late 18thC. Scots dialect variant of WAR.]

wave¹ /wayv/ (**waves, waving, waved**) *v.* **1.** *vti.* MOVE HAND REPEATEDLY AS SIGNAL to move the hand or arm from side to side or up and down as a greeting, farewell, or signal **2.** *vti.* MOVE STH REPEATEDLY IN AIR to move or cause sth such as a flag to move from side to side or up and down ○ *The flag waved in the wind.* **3.** *vt.* DIRECT SB OR STH BY WAVING to direct sb or sth by waving a hand, arm, or object ○ *The police waved the traffic around the procession.* **4.** *vti.* MAKE INTO OR BE IN UNDULATIONS to make sth into or be in the form of swells, ridges, or swirls ○ *a field of grain waving in the wind* **5.** *vti.* HAIR BE OR MAKE SLIGHTLY CURLED to be slightly or gently curled, or make hair slightly curled **6.** *vt.* TEXTILES GIVE IMPRESSION A RIPPLED PATTERN to create a rippled pattern in a fabric such as silk [Old English *wafian.* From a prehistoric Germanic base meaning 'to move back and forth', which is also the ancestor of English *waver* and *wobble.*]

wave aside *vt.* to dismiss sth or sb as trivial or inconsequential

wave down *vt.* to stop a vehicle by waving to the driver to halt

wave off *vt.* to watch and wave to sb who is leaving

wave² /wayv/ *n.* **1.** MOVING RIPPLE ON LIQUID OR OCEAN any of a series of ripples moving across the surface of a liquid, especially a large raised ridge of water moving across the surface of the sea **2.** ACT OF WAVING THE HAND an instance of moving the hand or arm as a signal or greeting **3.** LINE CURVING IN ALTERNATING DIRECTIONS a line, shape, surface, or pattern that curves in one direction and then another, especially one with repeated curves **4.** UNDULATING MOTION a movement on a surface or edge that is similar to a wave ○ *The*

wind made waves across the field of grain. **5.** SUDDEN REPETITION OF EVENTS a sudden occurrence of repeated activity ○ *a crime wave* **6.** OVERWHELMING FEELING a sudden overwhelming feeling ○ *a wave of sorrow* **7.** INCOMING GROUP an advancing or incoming group of people ○ *a wave of immigrants* **8.** HAIR LOOSE CURVE IN HAIR a soft, usually large, curve or ripple in the hair where the lie of the hair changes direction, either naturally or after setting **9.** PHYS OSCILLATION OF ENERGY an oscillation that travels through a medium by transferring energy from one particle or point to another without causing any permanent displacement of the medium ○ *sound waves* **10.** TEXTILES RIPPLED PATTERN a rippled pattern in material such as silk **11.** *US* SPORTS = **Mexican wave** ■ **waves** *npl.* SEA the waves of the ocean, or the ocean itself [15thC. Alteration of obsolete *waw* under the influence of the verb WAVE¹.] ◇ **make waves** to cause a disturbance or trouble, e.g. by suggesting or introducing changes or making criticisms

Wave *n.* a member of the WAVES

waveband /wáyv band/ *n.* a range of radio frequencies within which transmissions occur

wave energy *n.* energy produced for domestic or industrial use by harnessing and converting the energy of sea waves

wave equation *n.* an equation, usually a partial differential equation, that defines the propagation of a wave through a medium. The form of the equation is determined by the medium, the method by which the wave is transmitted, and the circumstance of its propagation.

waveform /wáyv fawrm/ *n.* the profile or shape of a wave, especially the graphic representation of one of its characteristics, e.g. frequency or amplitude, relative to time

wavefront /wáyv frunt/ *n.* a line or surface that joins points of the same phase in a wave travelling through a medium

wave function *n.* an equation that shows how a wave's amplitude varies in space and time

waveguide /wáyv gīd/ *n.* a transmission line consisting of a hollow metal conductor used as a path to convey microwave energy along its length. It is used in radar systems to convey transmitted microwave energy from the transmitter to the aerial and received energy from the aerial back to the receiver.

wavelength /wáyv length/ *n.* **1.** PHYS LENGTH OF WAVE CYCLE the distance between two points on adjacent waves that have the same phase, e.g. the distance between two consecutive peaks or troughs. Symbol λ **2.** BROADCAST BROADCASTING WAVELENGTH the wavelength of the fundamental radio wave used by a broadcasting station ◇ **be on the same wavelength** to have the same opinions, attitudes, or tastes

wavelet /wáyvlət/ *n.* a small wave, e.g. a ripple

wavellite /wáyvəlīt/ *n.* a soft light grey, yellow, or brown mineral form of hydrated aluminium phosphate, usually in the form of clusters of radiating crystals in slates and shales [Early 19thC. Named after William *Wavell* (d. 1829), the English physician who discovered the substance.]

wave mechanics *n.* a form of quantum theory in which happenings on the atomic scale are explained in terms of interactions between systems of waves, represented by wave functions (*takes a singular verb*)

wavemeter /wáyv meetər/ *n.* an instrument for measuring wavelengths

wave number *n.* the number of waves in a given unit distance. Wave number is the reciprocal of wavelength. Symbol ν, σ

waveoff /wáyv of/ *n.* a signal or instruction to an aircraft that it is not to land

wave-particle duality *n.* a fundamental concept of quantum theory holding that energy sometimes behaves like particles and sometimes behaves like waves, so that descriptions of energy as one or the other are inadequate

wave pool *n.* a public swimming pool equipped with a device to produce waves

wave power n. = wave energy

waver /wáyvər/ vi. (**-vers, -vering, -vered**) **1. FLUCTUATE BETWEEN POSSIBILITIES** to go back and forth between possibilities, or be indecisive in making a choice **2. BEGIN TO CHANGE OPINION** to become unsure or begin to change from a previous opinion **3. MOVE IN DIFFERENT DIRECTIONS** to move one way and then another in an irregular pattern **4. FLUCTUATE, ESPECIALLY IN TONE** to vary or fluctuate, as, e.g. the voice does from emotion **5. FLICKER** to go on and off, especially due to burning unsteadily (refers to a light or a flame) ■ n. **ACT OF WAVERING** an instance or act of wavering [14thC. From Old Norse vafra.] —**waverer** n. —**waveringly** adv.

— **WORD KEY: SYNONYMS** —
See Synonyms at **hesitate**.

WAVES /wayvz/ n. NAVY the women's branch of the US Naval Reserve that was organized in World War II. It no longer exists as a separate entity. Full form **Women Accepted for Volunteer Emergency Service**

wave theory n. the theory that the behaviour of light or any other electromagnetic radiation can be explained by assuming that it travels in waves. ◊ **corpuscular theory**

wave train n. a series of similar waves produced at equal intervals and travelling in the same direction

wavey /wáyvi/ (plural **-eys**) n. Can a snow goose or other wild goose

wavy /wáyvi/ (**-ier, -iest**) adj. **1. REPEATEDLY CURVING** forming a series of smooth curves that go in one direction and then another **2. HAIR HAVING SOFT CURVES** having loose open waves ○ wavy hair **3. CONTAINING WAVES** full of waves or having a surface covered by waves **4. MOVING LIKE A WAVE** moving with an up-and-down or side-to-side motion **5. WAVERING** wavering or changeable —**wavily** adv. —**waviness** n.

waw n. = vav [Mid-19thC. Variant of VAV.]

wa-wa n. = wah-wah

wa-wa pedal n. = wah-wah pedal

wawl vi., n. = waul

wax[1] /waks/ n. **1. INDUST NATURALLY-OCCURRING GREASY SUBSTANCE** any of various hard or soft and mouldable substances of animal, plant, or mineral origin that feel slightly greasy or oily to the touch **2. DOMESTIC PREPARATION FOR POLISHING** a preparation containing wax used for polishing floors, cars, and other surfaces **3. INDUST** = beeswax **4. PHYSIOL** = earwax **5. MED** = bone wax **6. INDUST RESINOUS MIXTURE USED IN SHOEMAKING** a resinous mixture rubbed onto thread used in shoemaking **7. STH EASILY MOULDED** sb who or sth that is readily moulded, shaped, or manipulated **8. RECORDING RECORD** a gramophone record (dated informal) ■ vt. (**waxes, waxing, waxed, waxed** or **waxen** /wáks'n/ archaic) **1. POLISH STH WITH WAX** to coat or polish sth such as a floor or car with wax **2. COSMETICS REMOVE HAIR WITH WAX** to remove unwanted hair from the skin using heated wax that is left to dry and then removed [Old English wæx from prehistoric Germanic] —**waxer** n.

wax[2] /waks/ (**waxes, waxing, waxed**) vi. **1. ASTRON APPEAR LARGER EACH NIGHT** to show a gradually increasing illuminated surface, as does the Moon between its new and full phases (refers to the Moon or a planet) **2. INCREASE** to increase in size, power, or intensity (literary) **3. BECOME STH STATED** to get into a particular emotional or behavioural state (literary) ○ waxed philosophical [Old English weaxan. Ultimately from an Indo-European base meaning 'to increase', which is also the ancestor of English augment and eke.]

wax[3] /waks/ n. a fit of temper or anger (dated informal) [Mid-19thC. Origin uncertain: perhaps from WAX[2] as used in phrases such as 'to wax angry'.]

wax bean n. US a variety of string bean that is yellow

waxbill /wáks bil/ n. small brightly-coloured African finch with a red conical bill. Waxbills feed on seeds and insects and build roofed nests of grass. Family: Estrildidae.

wax cap n. a mushroom with a cap that has waxy gills. Family: Hygrophoraceae.

waxcloth /wáks kloth/ n. TEXTILES = oilcloth

waxed jacket n. a jacket for outdoor use made from fabric that has been coated with wax to repel moisture

waxed paper n. US = greaseproof paper

waxen[1] /wáks'n/ adj. **1. LIKE WAX** resembling wax in texture and colour **2. MADE OF WAX** covered with, permeated with, or made of wax **3. PALE AND UNHEALTHY-LOOKING** lacking the rosy glow of life or health ○ a waxen face **4. EASY TO SHAPE** easily shaped, changed, or manipulated

waxen[2] past participle of wax (archaic)

wax flower n. a plant that has pink or white flowers with a waxy appearance

waxhead /wáks hed/, **waxie** /wáksi/ n. Aus sb who is keen on surfing (informal)

wax insect n. any of various scale insects that secrete a wax. Superfamily: Coccoidea.

wax light n. a candle or taper made of wax

wax moth n. a small brownish moth whose larvae develop inside beehives, feeding on the wax of the honeycombs and often damaging the honey and the honey bee larvae. Latin name: Galleria mellonella.

wax myrtle n. = bayberry n. 1

wax palm n. = carnauba n. 1

waxplant /wáks plaant/ n. ANZ an Asian and Australian evergreen climbing plant or shrub that is related to milkweed and bears waxy white flowers. Genus: Hoya.

wax tree n. a Southeast Asian tree that was formerly cultivated especially in Japan for its fruits, used as a source of candle wax, and for its resin, used for lacquer. Latin name: Rhus succedanea.

waxwing /wáks wing/ n. a bird of northern regions that is marked by a crest, buff-brown plumage, and waxy-looking red tips on the upper flight feathers. Genus: Bombycilla.

waxwork /wáks wurk/ n. **1. WAX MODEL** a realistic model, usually of a famous person, made from wax **2. WAX OBJECT** an object made of wax, especially an ornament **3. ART OF USING WAX FOR MODELLING** the art of using wax as a modelling or expressive medium

waxy[1] /wáksi/ (**-ier, -iest**) adj. **1. LIKE WAX** resembling wax in appearance, colour, texture, or pliability **2. COVERED WITH WAX** covered with, having a lot of, or made of wax **3. MED HAVING HARD DEPOSITS LIKE WAX** containing deposits of a hard substance resembling wax (**amyloid**) resulting from tissue degeneration —**waxiness** n.

waxy[2] /wáksi/ (**-ier, -iest**) adj. bad-tempered or angry (dated slang) [Mid-19thC. Formed from WAX[3].]

way /way/ n. **1. MANNER OR METHOD** a means, manner, or method of doing or achieving sth ○ You do it your way, I'll do it mine. **2. EXAMPLE** a feature, aspect, or example of sth ○ In some ways, my sisters are very similar. **3. CONDITION** the state or condition of sb or sth, especially with regard to health or finances ○ He was in a bad way after the accident. **4. PREFERENCE** sth sb wants to happen or to do ○ You can't always get your own way. **5. CHARACTERISTIC ASPECT OF BEHAVIOUR** a usual, characteristic, or distinctive activity or style of behaviour ○ How do you put up with those irritating ways of theirs? **6. TRADITION OR CUSTOM** the customary style or practices of sb's life ○ the way of the Sufi **7. TYPICAL HAPPENING** the usual occurrence or pattern of events ○ Isn't it usually the way that all the cabs are taken when you're late? **8. PATH** a path or physical means of getting from one place to another ○ The way out is through here. **9. DOOR OR OPENING** a door or opening leading or providing access to or from somewhere ○ Come in the front way. **10. JOURNEY OR ROUTE** a particular journey or the route followed or to be followed ○ on my way to the office **11. PROGRESS THROUGH LIFE** progress or a path through life and its experiences or difficulties **12. DIRECTION** a direction such as left, right, up, or down **13. MANNER OF PLACING** the manner in which sth is placed, packed, or arranged, or the direction it faces **14. SPACE FOR ACTION** path, room, territory, or space allowing movement, progress, or action ○ Excuse me, you're in my way. **15. AREA** an area or district, e.g. around sb's home (informal) ○ out our way **16. DISTANCE** a distance away in space or time ○ Graduation is still a long

way off. **17. AMOUNT** the extent or amount to which sb does sth ○ He's fallen for her in a big way. **18. way, Way STREET** a street, usually a small or narrow one (often used in placenames) **19. SUBPART** each of a particular number of parts into which sth divides or is split ○ They're going to split the prize four ways. **20. MECH ENG GUIDE OR SUPPORT** a surface used to guide or provide support to moving parts of a machine tool such as a lathe (often used in the plural) **21. SHIPPING MOVEMENT THROUGH WATER** movement or speed of a ship through water ○ The vessel now had some way on. ■ adv. **1. VERY MUCH** to a considerable extent or at a considerable distance (informal) ○ That's way out of our price range. **2. VERY** to a great extent (slang) [Old English weg. Ultimately from an Indo-European base meaning 'to go', which is also the ancestor of English wagon and vehicle.] ◇ **be under way** to be in progress ◇ **by the way** used to introduce sth that is not strictly part of the subject at hand ◇ **by way of sth 1.** as a means of or for the purpose of sth **2.** via ◇ **every which way 1.** US in all directions **2.** US in every way possible (informal) ◇ **get into the way of doing sth** to get into or out of the habit of doing sth ◇ **give way 1.** to give in or give precedence to sb else **2.** to collapse or break under pressure ◇ **give way to** to be overcome by an emotion that you have been trying to resist ◇ **go out of your way to do sth** to do more than is usual or necessary ◇ **have a way with sb** or **sth** to be good at dealing with sb or sth ◇ **have it both ways** to have the benefits of opposing situations or actions ◇ **in a way** from a certain point of view ◇ **make way (for sb** or **sth)** to move aside to make room for sb or sth ◇ **make your way 1.** to go somewhere, especially when getting there requires overcoming some obstacle, e.g. finding the route or some transport **2.** to become successful ◇ **no way** used as an emphatic negative ◇ **there are no two ways about it** there is no room for dispute ◇ **way to go** Can, US used to congratulate sb on sth that he or she has done (informal)

waybill /wáy bil/ n. a document that gives information about goods being shipped or carried

wayfarer /wáy fairər/ n. a traveller, especially sb who makes a journey on foot (literary) —**wayfaring** n., adj.

wayfaring tree n. a shrub that is found in Europe and western Asia and has white flowers and red berries that turn black. Latin name: Viburnum lantana. [Probably because it can provide the traveller with shade]

Wayland /wáylənd/, **Wayland Smith, Wayland the Smith** n. in northern European folklore, a magical smith who was the king of the elves [From Old Norse Völundr. First mentioned in the 13thC Poetic Edda.]

waylay /way láy/ (**-lays, -laying, -laid** /-láyd/, **-laid**) vt. **1. LIE IN WAIT FOR SB** to lie in wait for sb, especially as part of an attack or ambush **2. STOP SB** to stop or accost sb, e.g. in order to talk —**waylayer** n.

wayleave /wáy leev/ n. the right of way over sb else's property, for which payment is usually made

waymark /wáy maark/ n. **waymark, waymarker SIGNPOST** a signpost or other marker used to guide travellers, especially walkers ■ vt. (**-marks, -marking, -marked**) **MARK ROUTE WITH WAYMARK** to mark out a path with a waymark

John Wayne

Wayne /wayn/, **John** (1907–79) US actor. He starred as the rugged hero in numerous westerns, including the Academy Award-winning True Grit (1969). Real name **Marion Michael Morrison**. Known as **the Duke**

Way of the Cross *n.* a series of pictures representing Jesus Christ's progress on the road to Calvary

way-out *adj.* 1. UNUSUAL OR PECULIAR unusual, peculiar, or unconventional (*informal*) 2. WONDERFUL excellent or exciting (*dated informal*)

waypoint /wáy poynt/ *n.* a point on a journey or route where a traveller can stop or change course

ways /wayz/ *n.* 1. US DISTANCE a distance travelled or to be travelled (*informal; takes a singular verb*) ○ *The next gas station is quite a ways from here.* 2. SHIPPING LAUNCH TRACKS FOR SHIP the tracks a ship slides down to be launched (*takes a singular or plural verb*)

-ways *suffix.* in a particular direction or position ○ *edgeways* [Old English *weges*, a form of *weg* 'way', literally 'of (such a) way']

ways and means *npl.* 1. METHODS OF GETTING OR ACCOMPLISHING STH methods of accomplishing or achieving sth, especially finding a way of paying for sth 2. METHODS OF RAISING MONEY FOR GOVERNMENT methods, e.g. legislation, used by a government to raise money

Ways and Means *npl.* in the United States, a legislative committee in charge of methods of raising money for government

wayside /wáy sīd/ *n.* SIDE OF ROAD the side of a road or path ■ *adj.* SITUATED AT SIDE OF ROAD situated at the side of a road or path ◇ **fall by the wayside** 1. to fail to continue or complete sth ○ *Several students fell by the wayside after the first few weeks.* 2. **fall** *or* **go by the wayside** to be abandoned because of other commitments or interests

wayward /wáywərd/ *adj.* 1. WILFUL characterized by wilfulness or disobedience 2. ERRATIC OR UNPREDICTABLE behaving in an erratic, apparently perverse, or unpredictable manner [14thC. Alteration of earlier *awayward*.] —**waywardly** *adv.* —**waywardness** *n.*

WORD KEY: SYNONYMS

See Synonyms at ***unruly***.

wayworn /wáy wawrn/ *adj.* worn out or weary from travelling

wayzgoose /wáyz gooss/ *n.* formerly, an annual outing for people working at a printing house (*archaic*) [Mid-18thC. Alteration of earlier *waygoose*, of unknown origin.]

wazzock /wázzək/ *n.* an offensive term that deliberately insults sb's intelligence or common sense (*informal*) [Late 20thC. Origin unknown.]

wb *abbr.* 1. water ballast 2. **wb, WB, W/B** waybill 3. westbound

Wb *symbol.* weber

WBA *abbr.* World Boxing Association

WBC *abbr.* 1. BIOL white blood cell 2. BOXING World Boxing Council

WbN *abbr.* west by north

W boson *n.* PHYS = **W particle**

WbS *abbr.* west by south

WC *abbr.* 1. water closet 2. GEOG West Central (London)

w.c. *abbr.* without charge

WCC *abbr.* World Council of Churches

wd *abbr.* 1. HEALTH ward 2. word 3. wood 4. **wd, w/d** COMM warranted

WD *abbr.* MIL War Department

WDA *abbr.* ACCT writing-down allowance ■ *n., abbr.* POL Welsh Development Agency

WDM, wdm *abbr.* wavelength division multiplex

wdth *abbr.* width

WDV *abbr.* written-down value

we (*stressed*) /wee/; (*unstressed*) /wi/ *pron.* 1. REFERS TO SPEAKER AND OTHERS refers to the speaker or writer and at least one other person (*first person plural personal pronoun, used as the subject of a verb*) ○ *We are going on holiday.* ○ *We grown-ups should protect our children's rights.* ○ *We all want our children to have a better future.* 2. REFERS TO PEOPLE IN GENERAL refers to all people or to people in general ○ *We are getting closer to the election.* 3. USED INSTEAD OF 'I' used by a writer or speaker to include the listener or speaker in what is being said, used especially to talk about how a book or talk is organized or by a monarch as the people's symbolic head ○ *We will now consider the causes of World War I.* 4. USED INSTEAD OF 'YOU' used sarcastically or condescendingly by a speaker ○ *How are we today? Are we getting better?* [Old English *wē*. Ultimately from an Indo-European word of the same meaning that is also the ancestor of German *wir* and, in a variant form, English *us*.]

WEA *abbr.* Workers' Educational Association

weak /week/ *adj.* 1. NOT STRONG OR FIT not physically or mentally strong 2. EASILY DEFEATED easily overcome or defeated 3. LACKING STRENGTH OF CHARACTER not having strength of character 4. NOT INTENSE not powerful or intense ○ *weak winter sunshine* 5. LACKING SKILLS OR ABILITIES not having particular skills or abilities 6. WATERY OR TASTELESS watery or lacking flavour ○ *weak tea* 7. NOT WORKING TO FULL CAPACITY not working as well as normal 8. UNCONVINCING not persuasive or convincing ○ *a weak argument* 9. NOT STRONG POLITICALLY not politically strong or powerful 10. POETRY UNSTRESSED used to describe a syllable or word that is not stressed or accented 11. POETRY HAVING ACCENT ON NORMALLY UNSTRESSED SYLLABLE used to describe verse that has the accent on a syllable that is normally unstressed 12. GRAM CHARACTERIZED BY REGULAR INFLECTIONAL ENDINGS used to describe a verb whose forms are characterized by regular inflectional endings, not by vowel changes 13. FIN CHARACTERIZED BY FALLING PRICES falling in price, or characterized by falling prices ○ *a weak market* 14. PHOTOGRAPHY LACKING IN CONTRAST not having much contrast between tones [13thC. From Old Norse *veikr* 'pliant'. Ultimately from a prehistoric Germanic word that is also the ancestor of German *weich* and Dutch *week* 'soft'.]

WORD KEY: SYNONYMS

weak, feeble, frail, infirm, debilitated, enervated, decrepit

CORE MEANING: lacking physical strength or energy

weak lacking strength or energy, either temporarily, or as part of the person's constitution; **feeble** describes sb who is very weak, either temporarily or as part of his or her constitution; **frail** used to suggest physical delicacy or weakness, either as part of sb's physical constitution or as a result of illness or advancing years; **infirm** lacking strength as a result of advanced years or illness, especially when it seems unlikely that this condition will improve; **debilitated** made weak by sth such as illness or physical exertion, especially when this condition is likely to be temporary; **enervated** made weak and tired by sth such as extreme heat or physical exertion; **decrepit** a formal or literary word used to describe sb who has been made very weak by advancing years. It is sometimes used humorously.

weaken /wéekən/ (**-ens, -ening, -ened**) *vti.* to make sb or sth weak or weaker, or become weak or weaker —**weakener** *n.*

weaker sex *n.* a highly offensive term used by men to refer to women as a group (*dated offensive*)

weakfish /wéek fish/ (*plural* **-fish** *or* **-fishes**) *n.* = **sea trout** *n.* 2 [Late 18thC. From obsolete Dutch *weekvisch*, literally 'soft fish', from *week* 'soft' + *visch* 'fish'.]

weak force *n.* = **weak interaction**

weak interaction *n.* the fundamental interaction between elementary particles that is mediated by the W and Z particles. It is involved in radioactive decay, which occurs by electron production, and particle decay. One of the four fundamental interactions, it is only effective at distances of less than 10^{-15} metres and is a million million times weaker than the strong interaction.

weak-kneed /-néed/ *adj.* easily persuaded or intimidated (*informal*) —**weak-kneedly** *adv.* —**weak-kneedness** *n.*

weakling /wéekling/ *n.* sb who lacks physical strength or strength of character

weakly /wéekli/ *adj.* (**-lier, -liest**) SICKLY sickly or delicate ■ *adv.* WITHOUT STRENGTH OR FORCE with little strength or force ○ *She nodded weakly.* —**weakliness** *n.*

weak-minded *adj.* 1. EASILY PERSUADED easily persuaded or convinced (*disapproving*) 2. OFFENSIVE TERM an offensive term used to refer to sb considered to be of low intelligence (*offensive*) —**weak-mindedly** *adv.* —**weak-mindedness** *n.*

weakness /wéeknəss/ *n.* 1. LACK OF STRENGTH OR DETERMINATION lack of strength, power, or determination 2. WEAK POINT a weak point or flaw in sth ○ *Unfortunately, the escape plan had a serious weakness.* 3. CHARACTER FLAW a failing or defect in sb's character 4. FONDNESS a strong liking for sth ○ *a weakness for chocolate* 5. OBJECT OF DESIRE an irresistible object of desire ○ *My weakness is adventure stories.*

weak sister *n.* US (*informal insult*) 1. OFFENSIVE TERM an offensive term for a weak or unreliable member or component of a group 2. OFFENSIVE TERM an offensive term for sb timid or cowardly

weak-willed *adj.* not having a strong will

weal[1] /weel/ *n.* US term **wheal** 1. REDDENED AREA ON SKIN FROM BLOW a raised or reddened area on the skin, caused by being hit with sth 2. ITCHY SWELLING ON SKIN a short-lived raised area on the skin, often red and itchy, caused by sth such as a nettle or insect sting or by exposure to an allergen [Early 19thC. Alteration of WALE under the influence of WHEAL.]

weal[2] /weel/ *n.* 1. STATE OF WELL-BEING a general state of well-being, prosperity, and happiness (*literary*) 2. PROSPERITY fortune or prosperity (*archaic*) 3. BODY POLITIC the state or the body politic (*archaic*) [Old English *wela*. Ultimately from an Indo-European base meaning 'to wish', which is also the ancestor of English *will* and *well*.]

weald /weeld/ *n.* open or wooded country (*archaic*) [Old English. Variant of *wald* (see WOLD).]

Weald /weeld/ wooded region in Kent and East Sussex, southeastern England. It was the centre of England's iron industry in medieval times. Area: 1,300 sq. km/500 sq. mi.

wealth /welth/ *n.* 1. LARGE AMOUNT OF MONEY a large amount of money or possessions 2. STATE OF HAVING MUCH MONEY the state of having plenty of money or possessions ○ *came from a background of great wealth* 3. ABUNDANCE OF STH an abundance or great quantity of sth ○ *quoted a wealth of statistics to prove the point* 4. ECON VALUE OF ASSETS the value of assets owned by an individual or a community ○ *need to determine the college's wealth* 5. WELL-BEING well-being or prosperity (*archaic*) [13thC. Formed from WEAL[2].]

WORD KEY: CULTURAL NOTE

The Wealth of Nations, a philosophical treatise by Scottish economist and philosopher Adam Smith (1776). One of the earliest and most comprehensive analyses of economic systems, it began as a study of the relationship between human nature and social evolution. Smith's assertion that the natural outcome of this evolution is an economy based on open markets and driven by competition inspired many modern-day laissez-faire capitalist philosophies.

wealth tax *n.* now called **capital gains tax**

wealthy /wélthi/ (**-ier, -iest**) *adj.* 1. RICH having a large amount of money or possessions 2. CHARACTERIZED BY ABUNDANCE enjoying an abundance or great quantity of sth —**wealthily** *adv.* —**wealthiness** *n.*

wean[1] /ween/ (**weans, weaning, weaned**) *v.* 1. *vti.* GIVE FOOD OTHER THAN MOTHER'S MILK to start feeding a baby or young animal food other than its mother's milk 2. *vt.* STOP SB HAVING STH to cause sb to go without sth that has become a habit or that is much liked ○ *She had weaned herself away from watching all the soaps on TV.* 3. *vt.* ACCUSTOM SB TO STH FROM CHILDHOOD to accustom sb to sth from an early age ○ *children weaned on computer games and videos* [Old English *wenian* 'to accustom'. Ultimately from a prehistoric Germanic base that is also the ancestor of German *gewöhnen* 'to accustom' and English *wont* 'accustomed'.] —**weanedness** /wéenədnəss, wéend-/ *n.*

wean[2] /wayn, ween/ *n.* a child, especially a young one (*regional*) [Late 17thC. Contraction of *wee ane*; *ane* a dialect form of ONE.]

weaner /wéenər/ *n.* 1. WEANED ANIMAL a young animal that has recently been weaned, especially a pig 2. MEANS OF WEANING AN ANIMAL sb who weans animals, or sth used in weaning animals

weanling /wéenling/ *n.* RECENTLY WEANED CHILD OR ANIMAL a child or young animal that has just been weaned ■ *adj.* JUST WEANED newly weaned ○ *a weanling lamb*

weapon /wéppən/ n. **1.** DEVICE DESIGNED TO INJURE OR KILL a device designed to inflict injury or death on an opponent **2.** STH USED TO GAIN ADVANTAGE sth used as a way of getting an advantage in a situation ○ *A teacher's best weapon can be humour.* **3.** ZOOL ANIMAL'S PROTECTIVE PART an animal part, e.g. claws, used for defence or attack ■ vt. (-ons, -oning, -oned) ARM SB to provide sb with weapons [Old English *wæpen*. Ultimately from prehistoric Germanic.] —**weaponed** adj. —**weaponless** adj.

weaponeer /wéppə neér/ n. **1.** SB WHO HELPS DETONATE NUCLEAR WEAPON sb who prepares a nuclear weapon for detonation **2.** DESIGNER OF NUCLEAR WEAPONS sb who designs nuclear weapons

weaponry /wéppənri/ n. **1.** WEAPONS all the weapons possessed by an individual, group, or nation **2.** PRODUCTION OF WEAPONS techniques for producing weapons

weapons system, **weapon system** n. a weapon consisting of two or more major components, e.g. a missile and its ground-based radar guidance

wear[1] /wair/ v. (wears, wearing, wore /wawr/, worn /wawrn/) **1.** vt. USE TO COVER OR ADORN BODY to have sth on all or part of the body as clothing, jewellery, protection, or for another purpose, e.g. to aid sight or hearing, either temporarily or habitually **2.** vt. *Malaysia, Singapore* PUT ON to put on a piece of clothing **3.** vt. DISPLAY ON FACE to display, show, or present an expression or physical manifestation of an emotion on the face ○ *wear a smile* **4.** vti. DAMAGE BY USING OR RUBBING to damage or alter sth by using or rubbing it, or be damaged or altered in this way **5.** vti. PRODUCE BY USING OR RUBBING to produce sth, especially a hole, through continued use, pressure, or friction, or be produced in this way ○ *had worn a hole in his sweater* **6.** vti. RUB OFF to rub sth off or away, or be rubbed off or away **7.** vti. TIRE OUT to tire sb out, or become exhausted **8.** vti. LAST IN SAME CONDITION to last in the same, especially good, condition with much use ○ *That fabric doesn't look as if it would wear well.* **9.** vti. PASS SLOWLY to pass time slowly, or be passed slowly ○ *We wore the evening away worrying about him.* **10.** vt. ACCEPT OR TOLERATE STH to accept or put up with sth (*informal*) ○ *She'll never wear that idea.* **11.** vt. SHIPPING FLY FLAG to fly a particular flag or colours as a ship's identification ■ n. **1.** ACT OF WEARING the act of wearing sth, or the condition of being worn **2.** DAMAGE FROM BEING USED damage or deterioration from sth being used **3.** ABILITY TO LAST the ability to last without deteriorating **4.** CLOTHES CLOTHING OF PARTICULAR KIND clothing, especially clothing of a particular kind (*often used in combination*) ○ *beachwear* [Old English *werian*. Ultimately from a Germanic word that is also the ancestor of Icelandic *varinn* 'clad'.] —**wearer** n. ◇ **the worse for wear 1.** in a poor condition because of much use **2.** looking unwell, especially because of being tired ◇ **wear thin 1.** to weaken or fail ○ *My patience is wearing rather thin.* **2.** to become unacceptable or implausible because of excessive use ○ *That excuse is beginning to wear a bit thin.*

wear down vti. to overcome or weaken sb or sth by a gradual process, or be overcome or weakened in this way

wear off vi. to lose effectiveness or strength gradually

wear out v. **1.** vti. USE STH HEAVILY to use sth heavily or for a long time until it is no longer useful, or to become useless through long use **2.** vt. EXHAUST to tire sb out

wear[2] /wair/ (wears, wearing, wore /wawr/, worn /wawrn/) vti. to bring a ship about by turning the stern to windward, or come about in this way [Early 17thC. Origin unknown.]

Wear /weer/ river in County Durham, northern England. It flows past the city of Durham and empties into the North Sea at Sunderland. Length: 107 km/67 mi.

wearable /wáirəb'l/ adj. SUITABLE FOR WEAR suitable and in a condition to be worn ■ n. WEARABLE ITEM OF CLOTHING an item of clothing that can be worn —**wearability** /wáirə bílləti/ n.

wear and tear /-táir/ n. damage caused by using sth over a period of time

weariful /weéreef'l/ adj. **1.** TEDIOUS AND ANNOYING tedious and causing annoyance or fatigue **2.** TIRED tired and weary —**wearifully** adv. —**wearifulness** n.

weariless /weéreeləss/ adj. not feeling or showing tiredness —**wearilessly** adv.

wearing /wáiring/ adj. **1.** TIRING tiring or tedious ○ *found the long journey very wearing* **2.** MADE TO BE WORN made or designed to be worn ○ *wearing apparel* —**wearingly** adv.

wearing course n. the upper layer of an asphalt or bitumen carriageway

wearisome /weéreessəm/ adj. physically or mentally tiring and tedious ○ *a wearisome task* —**wearisomely** adv. —**wearisomeness** n.

wearproof /wáir proof/ adj. able to withstand normal wear or use

weary /weéri/ adj. (wearier, weariest) **1.** TIRED tired, especially in having run out of strength, patience, or endurance **2.** TIRING tiring or exhausting **3.** SHOWING TIREDNESS showing or characterized by tiredness ■ vti. (wearies, wearying, wearied) BECOME OR MAKE TIRED OR IMPATIENT to become or cause sb to become tired or impatient [Old English *wērig*. Ultimately from a prehistoric Germanic base that also produced Old English *wōrian* 'to wander'.] —**wearily** adv. —**weariness** n. —**wearying** adj. —**wearyingly** adv.

weasand /weéz'nd/ n. the throat, especially the windpipe or the gullet (*archaic*) [Old English *wāsend*. Ultimately from prehistoric West Germanic.]

Weasel

weasel /weéz'l/ n. (*plural* -**sels** *or* -**sel**) **1.** ZOOL SMALL MAMMAL WITH LONG BODY a small carnivorous mammal with a long body and tail, short legs, and brown fur that in northern species may turn white in winter. Genus: *Mustela*. **2.** SB SLY sb who is regarded as sly or underhand (*insult*) ■ vi. (-**sels**, -**selling**, -**selled**) *US, Can* BE EVASIVE to be evasive or try to mislead others [Old English *wesule*. Ultimately from prehistoric Germanic.] —**weaselly** adj.

weasel out vi. to try to get out of an obligation or commitment, especially in a cowardly way (*informal*)

weasel words npl. deliberately misleading or ambiguous language (*informal*) —**weasel-worded** adj.

weather /wéthər/ n. METEOROL **1.** STATE OF THE ATMOSPHERE the state of the atmosphere with regard to temperature, cloudiness, rainfall, wind, and other meteorological conditions **2.** BAD WEATHER adverse weather such as a storm, or the effects of this ○ *protection from the weather* ■ adj. **1.** METEOROL USED IN WEATHER FORECASTING used in or relating to weather forecasting **2.** NAUT WINDWARD towards the wind ■ v. (-**ers**, -**ering**, -**ered**) **1.** vti. EXPOSE STH TO THE WEATHER to expose sth to the weather, or be exposed to it **2.** vti. CHANGE BECAUSE OF EXPOSURE TO WEATHER to change colour or become worn because of prolonged exposure to the weather, or cause such a change **3.** vi. ENDURE THE EFFECTS OF THE WEATHER to endure the damaging effects of the weather **4.** vt. COME SAFELY THROUGH A CRISIS to come safely through a crisis or difficult time **5.** vt. NAUT SAIL WINDWARD OF STH to sail on the windward side of sth **6.** vt. CONSTR SLANT STH TO KEEP OFF RAIN to give a slope to sth such as a roof to keep off rain [Old English *weder*. Ultimately from an Indo-European base meaning 'to blow', which is also the ancestor of English *wind* and *vent*.] —**weatherability** /wéthərə bílləti/ n. —**weatherer** /wéthərər/ n. ◇ **be** *or* **feel under the weather** to feel slightly unwell ◇ **make heavy weather of sth** to

make a task that is quite easy to do seem more difficult than it is

weather balloon n. a balloon used to carry meteorological instruments

weather-beaten adj. damaged, worn, or marked by exposure to the weather ○ *a weather-beaten face*

weatherboard /wéthər bawrd/ n. **1.** BUILDING BOARD ON BOTTOM OF DOOR a sloping piece of wood fitted to the bottom of a door to allow rain to run off **2.** BUILDING GROOVED BOARD FOR CLADDING a grooved piece of timber used as part of a series of overlapping horizontal pieces forming cladding for walls or roofs **3.** NAUT WINDWARD SIDE the windward side of a ship **4.** ANZ ARCHIT = **weatherboard house** ■ vt. (-**boards**, -**boarding**, -**boarded**) BUILDING COVER WITH WEATHERBOARDS to fit a building with weatherboards

weatherboard house n. ANZ a house clad with weatherboarding in horizontal overlapping planks of wood

weatherboarding /wéthər bawrding/ n. weatherboards collectively

weather-bound adj. delayed or kept from functioning by bad weather ○ *a weather-bound plane*

weathercast /wéthər kaast/ n. US = **weather forecast** [Mid-19thC. Contraction of WEATHER FORECAST.]

weather centre n. an agency that collects meteorological information and provides weather forecasts

weather chart n. = **weather map**

weathercock /wéthər kòk/ n. **1.** WEATHER VANE a weather vane shaped like a farmyard cock **2.** SB FICKLE sb who changes opinion or allegiance frequently ■ vi. (-**cocks**, -**cocking**, -**cocked**) AIR TURN IN THE DIRECTION OF THE WIND to tend to turn in the direction of the wind (*refers to aircraft*)

weather deck n. US an open deck on a ship

weathered /wéthərd/ adj. **1.** WORN BY EXPOSURE TO WEATHER worn, damaged, or seasoned by exposure to the weather **2.** GIVEN A WEATHERED APPEARANCE given an artificial appearance of having been exposed to weather **3.** GEOL ERODED BY WEATHER used to describe rocks that have been eroded or changed by the action of the weather **4.** CONSTR WITH A SLOPING SURFACE having a sloping surface so that rain can run off ○ *a weathered roof*

weather eye n. **1.** EYE TRAINED TO WATCH THE WEATHER the eye of sb trained to watch for changes in the weather **2.** ALERTNESS TO CHANGE alertness or watchfulness, especially an alertness to change (*informal*) ◇ **keep a weather eye open, keep a weather eye on** to be alert and watchful for any change or development in sth

weather forecast n. a radio or television broadcast announcing weather conditions —**weather forecaster** n.

weatherglass /wéthər glaass/ n. an instrument such as a barometer used to indicate changes in atmospheric conditions

weathering /wéthəring/ n. GEOL **1.** EFFECT OF THE WEATHER the effect of prolonged exposure to the weather on, e.g. a building **2.** EFFECT OF WEATHER ON ROCKS the disintegration and decomposition of rocks and minerals by natural processes such as the action of frost or percolating groundwater. Weathering makes rock susceptible to erosion.

weatherly /wéthərli/ adj. capable of sailing close to the wind

weatherman /wéthər man/ (*plural* -**men** /-men/) n. a man who works as a weather forecaster

weather map n. a map or chart showing the meteorological conditions over a large area

weatherperson /wéthər purss'n/ n. sb who works as a weather forecaster

weatherproof /wéthər proof/ adj. ABLE TO WITHSTAND BAD WEATHER able to withstand exposure to rain or bad weather ■ vt. (-**proofs**, -**proofing**, -**proofed**) MAKE WEATHERPROOF to make sth able to withstand exposure to rain or bad weather —**weatherproofness** n.

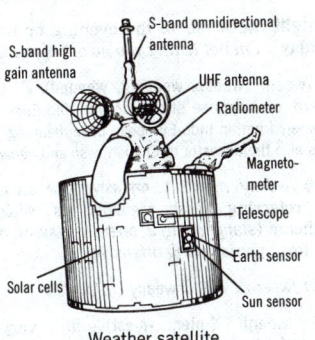

Weather satellite

weather satellite *n.* a satellite that records cloud distribution and temperature to help in predicting weather patterns

weather ship *n.* a ship that collects meteorological information

weather station *n.* an observation post where meteorological conditions are observed and recorded

weather strip *n.* a thin piece of material fitted around a door or window to stop wind, rain, and cold from coming through. US term **weather stripping**

weatherstrip /wéthər strip/ (**weatherstrips, weather-stripping, weatherstripped**) *vt.* to put a weather strip around a door or window

weather stripping *n.* = weather strip

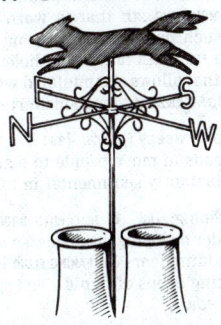

Weather vane

weather vane *n.* a device, usually mounted on a roof, that turns to point in the direction the wind is blowing

weather window *n.* a period of time in which weather conditions are suitable for a particular activity

weather-wise *adj.* **1.** METEOROL GOOD AT PREDICTING THE WEATHER good at predicting what the weather will be **2.** GOOD AT PREDICTING PUBLIC OPINION good at predicting what public opinion will be

weatherworn /wéthər wawrn/ *adj.* worn or damaged by exposure to the weather

weave[1] /weev/ *v.* (**weaves, weaving, wove** /wōv/ *or* **weaved, woven** /wōv'n/ *or* **weaved**) **1.** *vti.* MAKE CLOTH to make cloth by interlacing threads vertically and horizontally, especially on a loom **2.** *vt.* MAKE STH BY INTERLACING STRANDS to make sth by interlacing strands or strips of any material **3.** *vti.* ZOOL SPIN A WEB to spin sth such as a spider's web **4.** *vt.* CONSTRUCT A STORY to construct sth such as a story by combining separate elements **5.** *vt.* INTRODUCE ELEMENTS INTO STH LARGER to introduce separate elements into sth larger ○ *weaving new elements into the plot* ■ *n.* WAY IN WHICH STH IS WOVEN the way in which sth is woven and the pattern formed by it ○ *a fabric with an open weave* [Old English *wefan*. Ultimately from a prehistoric Germanic word that is also the ancestor of German *weven*.] ◇ **get weaving** to hurry and start doing sth (*dated informal*)

weave[2] /weev/ (**weaves, weaving, weaved**) *vi.* to move forwards on a zigzag course [Late 16thC. Origin uncertain: perhaps from Old Norse *veifa*. Ultimately from an Indo-European base meaning 'to move quickly' that is also the ancestor of English *whip* and *vibrate*.]

weaver /weevər/ *n.* sb who weaves, especially as a livelihood

weaverbird /weevər burd/, **weaver, weaver finch** *n.* a gregarious finch of Africa and Asia, known for its communal woven nest. Family: Ploceidae.

web /web/ *n.* **1.** CRAFT WOVEN FABRIC a piece of fabric created by weaving **2.** ZOOL SPIDER'S CONSTRUCTION a delicate structure of threads woven by a spider or other arachnid to catch prey **3.** ZOOL MEMBRANE BETWEEN ANIMAL TOES a membrane of skin joining the digits of an animal's foot, especially the foot of a bird or amphibian **4.** COMPLEX NETWORK a complex structure, network, or design ○ *a web of interconnecting wires* ○ *a web of deceit* **5.** TECH THIN METAL PLATE a thin plate or strip of metal such as the blade of a saw **6.** BIRDS BARBS ON THE SHAFT OF A FEATHER the barbs on either side of the shaft of a feather **7.** ARCHIT RIBBED SURFACE IN A VAULT a ribbed surface within a vaulted structure **8.** PRINTING PRINTING PAPER a roll of paper that is used on a rotary printing press ■ *vi.* (**webs, webbing, webbed**) FORM A WEB to form or produce a web [Old English. Ultimately from an Indo-European base meaning 'to weave' that is also the ancestor of English *weave* and *weft*.]

Web /web/ *n.* the World Wide Web (*informal*)

Webb /web/, **Sir Aston** (1849–1930) British architect. He was the designer of Admiralty Arch and the eastern façade of Buckingham Palace in London.

webbed /webd/ *adj.* joined by a membrane or membranes of skin ○ *webbed feet* [Mid-17thC]

webbing /wébbing/ *n.* **1.** TEXTILES STRONG COARSE FABRIC strong coarse fabric used in belts and harnesses and for supporting upholstery **2.** ZOOL SKIN OF THE FOOT the membrane of skin joining the digits of an animal's foot, especially the foot of a bird or amphibian **3.** STH FORMING A WEB sth that forms a web

Web browser, web browser *n.* a program used for displaying and viewing pages on the World Wide Web

Webcam /wéb kam/, **webcam** *n.* a video camera recording pictures that are broadcast live on the Internet [Late 20thC. Blend of WORLD WIDE WEB + CAMERA.]

Webcast /wéb kaast/, **webcast** *n.* a broadcast made on the World Wide Web ○ '...*they spent $5 million promoting the live Webcast of their Spring Fashion Show* ...' (*The New York Times*; April 1999) [Late 20thC. Blend of WORLD WIDE WEB + BROADCAST.]

Webcasting /wéb kaasting/, **webcasting** *n.* the use of the World Wide Web as a medium to broadcast information [Late 20thC. Blend of WORLD WIDE WEB + BROADCASTING.]

Web crawler, web crawler *n.* a program used to search through pages on the World Wide Web in order to locate documents containing a particular set of words, a phrase, or a topic

weber /váybər/ *n.* the SI unit of magnetic flux, equal to 1 joule per ampere or 1 volt-second. Symbol **Wb** [Late 19thC. Named after Wilhelm Eduard *Weber* (1804–91), a German physicist known for his work on magnetism.]

Weber /váybər/, **Carl Maria von** (1786–1826) German composer. His orchestral works and operas are important in the growth of early romanticism.

Weber, Max (1864–1920) German economist and sociologist. He was a major influence in modern sociological theory, and the author of *The Protestant Ethic and the Spirit of Capitalism* (1904–05).

webfoot /wéb fŏŏt/ (*plural* **webfeet** /-feet/) *n.* ZOOL **1.** FOOT WITH TOES JOINED BY WEBBING a foot that has the toes joined by a membrane of skin **2.** ANIMAL WITH WEBBED FEET an animal with webbed feet —**web-footed** /wéb fŏŏttid/ *adj.*

Webhead /wéb hed/, **webhead** *n.* a frequent user of the World Wide Web (*slang*) [Late 20thC. Blend of WORLD WIDE WEB + HEAD.]

Webisode /wébbi sōd/, **webisode** *n.* an episode, preview, or promotion of a film, television programme, or music video on a World Wide website (*slang*) [Late 20thC. Blend of WORLD WIDE WEB + EPISODE.]

Webliography /wébbli óggrəfi/ (*plural* **-phy**), **web-liography** (*plural* **-phy**) *n.* a list of particular docu-

ments available on the Web [Late 20thC. Blend of WORLD WIDE WEB + BIBLIOGRAPHY.]

Webmaster /wéb maastər/, **webmaster** *n.* sb who creates, organizes, or updates the information content of a World Wide website

web member *n.* a brace that links the top and bottom flanges of a lattice girder or truss

web offset *n.* offset printing carried out on a web press

Web page, web page *n.* a computer file, encoded in HyperText Markup Language (**HTML**) and containing text, graphics files, and sound files, that is accessible through the World Wide Web. Every web page has a unique Uniform Resource Locator (**URL**), or address.

web press *n.* a printing press that is fed paper from a large roll [Late 19C. See WEB.]

Web ring, web ring *n.* a series of interlinked World Wide websites that are visited in sequential order, eventually returning to the original site

Web server, web server *n.* a program such as a Web browser that serves up web pages when requested by a client

Web site, website /wéb sīt/ *n.* a group of related Web pages. Approximately 85 per cent of all websites are in English.

web spinner *n.* an insect that spins a web, especially one with glands that produce a kind of silk used to construct a web. Order: Embioptera.

webster /wébstər/ *n.* a weaver (*archaic*) [Old English *webbestre*]

Webster /wébstər/, **John** (1580?–1623?) English playwright. His plays *The White Devil* (1612) and *The Duchess of Malfi* (1614?) are outstanding examples of the revenge tragedies of their time.

web-toed /-tŏd/ *adj.* having a membrane of skin tissue between the toes

webwheel /wéb weel/ *n.* a wheel with no spokes but a web or plate instead, or a wheel with the centre formed from one piece

webworm /wéb wurm/ (*plural* **-worms** *or* **-worm**) *n.* US a caterpillar, especially a tiger moth caterpillar, that spins a web in which it feeds or rests

wed /wed/ (**weds, wedding, wedded** *or* **wed**) *v.* **1.** *vt.* MARRY to marry sb (*formal or literary*) **2.** *vi.* GET MARRIED to become married to sb **3.** *vt.* JOIN A COUPLE IN MARRIAGE to join two people in marriage **4.** *vt.* UNITE THINGS to bring two things together or regard them as linked ○ *The two concepts had become wedded in his mind.* [Old English *weddian*. Ultimately from an Indo-European base meaning 'pledge' that is also the ancestor of English *engage* and *wager*.]

we'd /weed/ *contr.* **1.** we had **2.** we would

Wed. *abbr.* Wednesday

wedded /wéddid/ *adj.* **1.** MARRIED united in marriage **2.** OF MARRIAGE relating to marriage ○ *wedded bliss* **3.** COMMITTED TO STH strongly attached or committed to sth ○ *wedded to the idea of reform* [Old English]

Weddell Sea /wédd'l-/ arm of the South Atlantic Ocean, south of Cape Horn and the Falkland Islands

wedder *n.* = wether

wedding /wédding/ *n.* **1.** MARRIAGE CEREMONY a marriage ceremony, or the act of marrying (*often used before a noun*) ○ *a wedding veil* **2.** WEDDING ANNIVERSARY the anniversary of a marriage (*used in combination*) ○ *a silver wedding* **3.** UNITING OF TWO THINGS the bringing together of two things ○ *the wedding of form and function* [Old English *weddung*]

wedding band *n.* US = wedding ring

wedding breakfast *n.* a celebratory meal served after a wedding ceremony

wedding cake *n.* a cake, often a fruit cake, decorated with icing, usually white, and arranged in tiers, served at a wedding reception

wedding-cake *adj.* characterized by an extremely ornate style of architecture

wedding dress *n.* a dress worn by a bride at her wedding

wedding march *n.* a piece of music in march time played during a marriage ceremony, usually when the bride enters the church

wedding ring *n.* a ring, usually a gold band, worn on the third finger of the left hand by sb who is married

Wedekind /váydə kínt/, **Frank** (1864–1918) German playwright. His work, often dealing with sexual themes, anticipates expressionism and the theatre of the absurd. Full name **Benjamin Franklin Wedekind**

Wedge

wedge /wej/ *n.* **1.** TAPERING BLOCK a solid block that is thick at one end and thin at the other, used to secure or separate two objects **2.** WEDGE-SHAPED OBJECT an object that has a wedge shape ○ *a wedge of cake* **3.** STH THAT ACTS AS A WEDGE sth that acts as a wedge, e.g. by causing division ○ *drove a wedge between the two families* **4.** CLOTHES = **wedge heel 5.** GOLF GOLF CLUB a golf club with a markedly slanted head, used to hit the ball along a high arcing trajectory **6.** STROKE IN CUNEIFORM WRITING a wedge-shaped stroke used in cuneiform writing ■ *v.* (**wedges, wedging, wedged**) **1.** *vt.* FORCE APART WITH A WEDGE to force sth apart or open with a wedge **2.** *vt.* SECURE WITH A WEDGE to secure or tighten sth with a wedge **3.** *vti.* SQUEEZE to squeeze or pack sth into a small space, or to be squeezed or packed in this way ○ *Hundreds of people were wedged into the room.* [Old English *wecg*. Ultimately from a prehistoric Germanic base, which probably came from an Indo-European word meaning 'ploughshare, wedge' that is also the probable ancestor of English *vomer*.] —**wedgy** *adj.* ◇ **the thin end of the wedge** sth bad or disadvantageous that seems quite minor but may well lead to sth worse

wedge heel *n.* **1.** SHOE HEEL a shoe heel shaped like a wedge, forming a solid extension of the sole so that there is no gap under the instep **2.** SHOE a shoe with a wedge heel

wedge-tailed eagle *n.* a large Australian eagle that has dark brown or black plumage and tail feathers in the form of a wedge. Latin name: *Aquila audax.*

wedgie /wéjji/ *n.* = **wedge heel** (*informal*)

Wedgwood /wéj wŏod/, **Josiah** (1730–95) British potter. He developed a distinctive pottery inspired by ancient Greek ware, and established a highly successful pottery business.

Wedgwood blue *adj.* pale grey-blue in colour [Early 20thC. Named after Josiah WEDGWOOD.] —**Wedgwood blue** *n.*

wedlock /wéd lok/ *n.* the state of being married [12thC. By folk etymology from earlier *wedlac*, literally 'action of pledging', from *wed* 'pledge', by association with LOCK.] ◇ **born out of wedlock, conceived out of wedlock** born to or or conceived by parents who are not married (*dated*)

Wednesday /wénz day, -di/ *n.* the third day of the week, coming after Tuesday and before Thursday [Old English *wōdnesdæg*, literally 'Odin's day', from *Woden* 'Odin' (chief deity of the Germanic peoples) + *dæg* 'day', a translation of Latin *Mercurii dies* 'Mercury's day']

Wednesdays /wénz dayz, -diz/ *adv.* every Wednesday ○ *Wednesdays I leave a little early.*

wee[1] /wee/ *adj.* TINY very small ■ *n. Scotland* SHORT TIME a brief period of time ○ *bide a wee* [Old English *wēg* 'weight'. The modern meaning evolved via its use in phrases such as *little wee* 'small weight'.]

wee[2] /wee/ *n.* (*informal or babytalk*) **1.** URINE urine **2.** ACT OF URINATING an act or instance of urinating ■ *vi.* (**wees, weeing, weed**) URINATE to urinate [Mid-20thC. An imitation of the sound of urinating.]

weed[1] /weed/ *n.* **1.** UNWANTED PLANT a plant, especially a wild plant, growing where it is not wanted **2.** UNWANTED PLANTS weeds in general (*often used before a noun*) ○ *weed control* **3.** PLANT GROWING IN WATER a plant that grows in water, especially seaweed **4.** TOBACCO tobacco or cigarettes (*slang*) **5.** MARIJUANA marijuana for smoking as a drug (*slang*) **6.** WEAK PERSON sb who is regarded as weak, or who is strikingly thin (*informal*) **7.** INFERIOR ANIMAL an inferior animal, especially a horse that cannot be bred ■ *v.* (**weeds, weeding, weeded**) **1.** *vt.* REMOVE WEEDS FROM THE GROUND to clear an area of weeds ○ *to weed the garden* **2.** *vi.* PULL UP WEEDS to pull up and remove weeds ○ *spent several hours weeding* [Old English *wēod*. Ultimately from a prehistoric Germanic plant name.] —**weeder** *n.*

weed out *vt.* to separate out or remove sb or sth undesirable or unwanted ○ *a test to weed out unsuitable candidates*

weed[2] /weed/ *n.* STH WORN AS A SIGN OF MOURNING sth worn as a sign of mourning, especially a black band around a sleeve or hat ■ **weeds** *npl.* **1.** WIDOW'S CLOTHES the black clothes once traditionally worn by widows (*archaic or literary*) **2.** CLOTHES clothes in general (*archaic*) [Old English *wǣd*. Ultimately from a prehistoric Germanic base meaning 'garment'.]

weedkiller /wéed killər/ *n.* a chemical that kills plants by attacking the root, leaf, or vascular system

weedy /wéedi/ (**-ier, -iest**) *adj.* **1.** FULL OF WEEDS filled with or containing many weeds ○ *a weedy patch of ground* **2.** BOT LIKE A WEED resembling or having the characteristics of a weed ○ *weedy plants* **3.** THIN strikingly thin and weak-looking (*insult*) **4.** WEAK physically or morally weak (*informal*) —**weedily** *adv.* —**weediness** *n.*

Wee Free *n. Scotland* a member of the Free Kirk, a body that broke away from the Free Church of Scotland in 1900 (*informal insult*) [Early 20thC. Because it was a minority body of the Free Church of Scotland.]

wee hours *npl.* = **wee small hours**

week /week/ *n.* **1.** 7-DAY PERIOD a period of seven consecutive days **2.** CALENDAR WEEK a period of seven days beginning from a particular day, usually Sunday ○ *the middle of the week* **3.** WORKING WEEK the days of the week on which sb works, or the time that is spent working ○ *goes to bed early during the week* **4.** SPECIAL WEEK a week containing a particular holiday, or dedicated to a particular cause ○ *Easter week* ■ *adv.* ONE WEEK AFTER A PARTICULAR DAY one week after or before a particular day ○ *arranged to meet on Thursday week* [Old English *wice*. Ultimately from a prehistoric Germanic word meaning 'series, succession', which is also the ancestor of German *Woche*.]

weekday /wéek day/ *n.* a day of the week other than Sunday, or, sometimes, other than Saturday or Sunday ○ *only open on weekdays* [Old English *wicdæg*]

weekend /wéek énd/ *n.* FRIDAY EVENING UNTIL SUNDAY EVENING the end of the week, from Friday evening until Sunday evening ■ *vi.* (**-ends, -ending, -ended**) SPEND THE WEEKEND SOMEWHERE to spend a weekend or weekends in a particular place

weekend bag *n.* a bag or small suitcase used to carry clothes and other items needed for a short trip or holiday

weekender /wéek éndər/ *n.* **1.** SB SPENDING A WEEKEND SOMEWHERE sb spending a weekend somewhere, especially on a regular basis **2.** *Aus* HOLIDAY HOME a holiday house (*informal*)

weekends /wéek éndz/ *adv.* at or during the weekend (*informal*)

weeklong /wéek lóng/ *adj.* lasting for a whole week

weekly /wéekli/ *adj.* **1.** HAPPENING ONCE A WEEK happening, produced, or done once a week or every week **2.** CALCULATED BY THE WEEK worked out by the week ○ *weekly pay* ■ *adv.* **1.** ONCE A WEEK once each week ○ *does the shopping weekly* **2.** EVERY WEEK every single week **3.** BY THE WEEK by the week ○ *gets paid weekly* ■ *n.* (*plural* **-lies**) STH PUBLISHED ONCE A WEEK a newspaper or magazine published once a week

weeknight /wéek nīt/ *n.* the evening or night of a weekday ○ *I'm not letting you go out on a weeknight.*

ween /ween/ (**weens, weening, weened**) *vt.* to think, believe, or suppose sth (*archaic*) [Old English *wēnan*. Ultimately from an Indo-European base meaning 'to desire' that is also the ancestor of English *wish* and *venereal*.]

weenie /wéeni/ *n. US* **1.** OFFENSIVE TERM an offensive term referring to sb regarded as weak or insignificant (*slang insult*) **2.** OFFENSIVE TERM an offensive term for a penis (*slang offensive*)

weensy /wéenzi/ *adj.* = **weeny** (*informal*)

weeny /wéeni/ (**-nier, -niest**) *adj.* very small (*informal*) [Late 18thC. Formed from WEE on the model of *tiny.*]

weeny-bopper *n.* a child, especially a young girl, who is keen on pop music and the latest fashions (*informal*) ◊ **teenybopper**

weep /weep/ *v.* (**weeps, weeping, wept** /wept/, **wept**) **1.** *vi.* CRY to shed tears ○ *They walked behind the coffin, weeping silently.* **2.** *vt.* EXPRESS STH WHILE CRYING TEARS to express sth while crying or by crying tears **3.** *vti.* MOURN SB to lament or cry tears for sb or sth (*literary*) **4.** *vti.* LEAK FLUID to leak, drip, or ooze drops of liquid ○ *The eye was inflamed and weeping* ■ *n.* SPELL OF CRYING a period of time spent crying [Old English *wēpan*. Ultimately from a prehistoric Germanic word of uncertain origin: perhaps an imitation of the sound of weeping.]

weeper /wéepər/ *n.* **1.** SB WHO WEEPS sb who weeps, especially sb hired to weep at a funeral **2.** STH WORN AS A SIGN OF MOURNING sth that is worn as a sign of mourning such as a black armband or a veil **3.** BUILDING HOLE FOR WATER TO ESCAPE a hole in a wall or foundation that allows accumulated water to escape ■ **weepers** *npl.* SIDEBURNS long sideburns (*informal*)

weepie /wéepi/, **weepy** (*plural* **-ies**) *n.* a film, play, or book that tends to move people to tears, especially one that is blatantly sentimental in tone (*informal*)

weeping /wéeping/ *adj.* **1.** BOT WITH DROOPING BRANCHES having slender drooping branches ○ *a weeping birch* **2.** CRYING shedding tears **3.** LEAKING FLUID leaking, dripping, or oozing drops of liquid [Old English *wepende*] —**weepingly** *adv.*

weeping fig, **weeping ivy** (*plural* **weeping ivies**) *n.* a small tree of the mulberry family that has glossy leaves and is often grown as a houseplant. Latin name: *Ficus benjamina.*

Weeping willow

weeping willow *n.* an ornamental willow tree, originally from China with long drooping branches and narrow leaves. Latin name: *Salix babylonica.*

weepy /wéepi/ *adj.* (**weepier, weepiest**) **1.** TEARFUL inclined to weep (*informal*) **2.** MOVING PEOPLE TO TEARS tending to make people cry ■ *n.* (*plural* **weepies**) CINEMA, THEATRE = **weepie** (*informal*) —**weepily** *adv.* —**weepiness** *n.*

wee small hours *npl.* the early hours of the morning, especially those just after midnight

weever /wéevər/, **weeverfish** /wéevər fish/ *n.* (*plural* **-fishes** or **-fish**) *n.* a small marine fish with a single long spine on each gill cover and several on its back. Family: Trachinidae. [Early 17thC. Origin uncertain: probably from Old North French *wivre* (see WYVERN).]

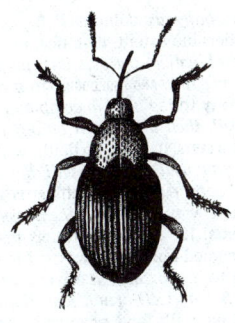

Weevil

weevil /weev'l/ *n.* **1.** DESTRUCTIVE BEETLE WITH A SNOUT a beetle with a long head that forms a snout or rostrum. Many are pests, destroying plants and grain. Family: Curculionidae. **2.** PEA OR BEAN PEST a beetle whose larvae live in the seeds of peas and beans. Family: Bruchidae and Lariidae. **3.** BEETLE LIKE A WEEVIL any beetle similar to a weevil including many that are pests. Family: Rhynchophora. [Old English *wifel* 'beetle'. Ultimately from an Indo-European base meaning 'to move quickly' that is also the ancestor of English *weave*[2] and *whip*.] —**weevily** *adj.*

wee-wee *n.* (*informal babytalk*) **1.** ACT OF URINATING an act or instance of urinating **2.** URINE urine (*offensive in some contexts*) ■ *vi.* (**wee-wees, wee-weeing, wee-weed**) URINATE to urinate (*babytalk; offensive in some contexts*) [Repetition of WEE[2]]

weft /weft/ *n.* **1.** HORIZONTAL THREADS the horizontal threads of a woven fabric or a tapestry. ◊ **warp** *n.* 3 **2.** YARN FOR THE WEFT yarn used for the weft **3.** STH WOVEN an article or piece of woven fabric [Old English. Ultimately from an Indo-European base meaning 'to weave' that is also the ancestor of English *weave* and *web*.]

Wegener /váygənər/, **Alfred** (1880–1930) German meteorologist. His *The Origin of Continents and Oceans* (1915) introduced the theory of continental drift.

Wehrmacht /váir maakht, -maakt/ *n.* the German armed forces, especially the army between 1935 and 1945 [Mid-20thC. From German, literally 'defence force'.]

weigela /wī jeélə, wi geélə/ *n.* a shrub native to Asia with bell-shaped pink, white, or red flowers. Genus: *Weigela*. [Mid-19thC. From modern Latin *Weigela*, the name of the genus, named after Christian E. *Weigel* (1748–1831), German physician.]

weigh[1] /way/ (**weighs, weighing, weighed**) *v.* **1.** *vt.* FIND THE WEIGHT OF STH to find out the weight of sb or sth ○ *He weighed himself regularly.* **2.** *vi.* BE A PARTICULAR WEIGHT to be of a particular weight **3.** *vt.* MEASURE BY WEIGHT to measure or distribute sth by weight ○ *weighed out a kilo of onions* **4.** *vt.* EVALUATE to consider or evaluate sth, especially so as to be able to come to a decision or choice ○ *had to weigh all possible options* **5.** *vi.* HAVE IMPORTANCE to have importance or be influential **6.** *vt.* GUESS THE WEIGHT OF to hold sth in the hand in order to assess its weight **7.** *vi.* BE BURDENSOME to be burdensome, oppressive, or worrying to sb ○ *The problem weighed heavily on my mind.* **8.** *vti.* SHIPPING RAISE ANCHOR to raise the anchor of a vessel [Old English *wegan* 'to weigh, carry'. Ultimately from an Indo-European base meaning 'to carry' that is also the ancestor of English *wagon*.] —**weighable** *adj.* —**weigher** *n.*

weigh down *vt.* **1.** OPPRESS SB to be oppressive or burdensome to sb ○ *weighed down by grief* ○ *weighed down with extra paperwork* **2.** PRESS STH DOWN to press sb or sth down by exerting weight ○ *trees weighed down with fruit*

weigh in *vi.* **1.** SPORTS BE WEIGHED FOR A RACE OR CONTEST to be weighed before or after a race or contest such as a boxing match or horse race **2.** HAVE BAGGAGE WEIGHED to have baggage weighed before a flight **3.** CONTRIBUTE A COMMENT to contribute or produce sth such as an argument or comment, especially in an assertive way (*informal*)

weigh up *vt.* **1.** CONSIDER STH CAREFULLY to consider sth carefully, especially so as to come to a decision or choice ○ *weighing up the pros and cons* **2.** JUDGE SB OR STH to judge the qualities or character of sb or sth (*informal*) ○ *The two boys weighed each other up.*

weigh[2] /way/ [Late 18thC. By folk etymology from WAY by association with WEIGH[1] in *weigh anchor*.] ◊ **under weigh** while a ship is in motion, not in port or at anchor

weighbridge /wáy brij/ *n.* a weighing machine for vehicles, consisting of a metal plate set into a road

weigh-in /wáy in/ *n.* the weighing of a competitor before or after a race or contest

weight /wayt/ *n.* **1.** HEAVINESS the heaviness of sb or sth ○ *Just feel the weight of it!* **2.** MEASURE OF SB'S HEAVINESS the specific amount that a person or animal weighs ○ *I had lost 10 pounds in weight.* **3.** SYSTEM FOR MEASURING HEAVINESS a system of standard measures of weight **4.** PHYS FORCE CAUSED BY GRAVITY the vertical force experienced by a mass because of gravity. Symbol *W* **5.** MEASURE UNIT OF WEIGHT a unit used as a measure of weight **6.** HEAVY OBJECT a heavy object used to hold sth down **7.** MENTAL BURDEN a mental or moral burden or load **8.** HEAVY LOAD a heavy load to carry ○ *had to put him down since he was a heavy weight* **9.** IMPORTANCE importance or significance ○ *a motion that did not carry much weight with the judge* **10.** GREATER PART the preponderance or greater part of sth **11.** PRINTING HEAVINESS OF TYPEFACE the heaviness or thickness of a typeface **12.** SPORTS, GYM OBJECT USED IN WEIGHTLIFTING a heavy object used in weightlifting or for exercise (*often used in the plural*) **13.** TEXTILES THICKNESS OF CLOTH the heaviness or thickness of cloth (*often used in combination*) ■ *vt.* (**weights, weighting, weighted**) **1.** ADD WEIGHT TO to add weight or weights to sth **2.** OPPRESS OR BURDEN to oppress or burden sb, e.g. with problems or cares ○ *The responsibility weighed on him.* **3.** BIAS to slant sth in sb's favour ○ *The choice of candidate was heavily weighted in her favour.* **4.** TEXTILES INCREASE DENSITY OF FABRIC to treat fabric so as to increase its density **5.** SPORTS ASSIGN A HORSE A HANDICAP WEIGHT to assign a handicap weight to a horse [Old English *wiht*. Ultimately from an Indo-European base that is also the ancestor of English *weigh*[1].] —**weighter** *n.* ◊ **be worth its or your weight in gold** to be extremely valuable ◊ **to gain** *or* **lose weight** to become heavier or lighter in body weight ◊ **pull your weight** to do your fair share of work or take your fair share of responsibility ◊ **throw your weight around** *or* **about** to be domineering

weighted /wáytid/ *adj.* adjusted by the addition of a statistical value

weighting /wáyting/ *n.* additional pay given in particular cases, e.g. to sb who has to live in a place where the cost of living is higher ○ *The job carries an inner London weighting.*

weightless /wáytləss/ *adj.* having no weight, especially by virtue of being in an atmosphere in which there is no gravitational pull —**weightlessly** *adv.* —**weightlessness** *n.*

weightlifter /wáyt liftər/ *n.* sb who lifts heavy weights as a sport

weightlifting /wáyt lifting/ *n.* the sport of lifting heavy weights, either for exercise or in competition

weight training *n.* physical training using weights to strengthen the muscles

Weightwatchers /wáyt wochərz/ *tdmk.* a trademark for an organization that helps people who want to lose weight

weighty /wáyti/ (**-ier, -iest**) *adj.* **1.** HEAVY weighing a great deal **2.** IMPORTANT of an important or serious nature ○ *discussing weighty matters* **3.** INFLUENTIAL able to exert influence **4.** OPPRESSIVE oppressive or burdensome ○ *a weighty responsibility* —**weightily** *adv.* —**weightiness** *n.*

Weil /víl/, **Simone** (1909–43) French philosopher and mystic. Her major writings, reflecting her Christian mysticism, were published posthumously and include *Waiting for God* (1950).

Weil's disease /vílz/ *n.* a severe form of leptospirosis, usually resulting from contact with the urine of infected animals such as rats. Symptoms include jaundice, anaemia, haemorrhaging, fever, and meningitis. [Late 19thC. Named after H. Adolf *Weil* (1848–1916), the German physician who described the disease.]

Weimar /vím aar/ city in Thuringia State, east-central Germany, southwest of Leipzig. It was a major cultural centre in the 18th and 19th centuries. Population: 61,583 (1990).

Weimaraner

Weimaraner /vímə raanər, wímə-, -raánər/ *n.* a large hunting dog of a breed with a short-haired silver-grey coat, originally bred in Germany [Mid-20thC. Named after WEIMAR, where the dog was first bred.]

Weimar Republic /vím aar-/ *n.* the government of Germany between 1919 and 1933, so named because the National Assembly met in Weimar in 1919 to establish a new republic and draw up a constitution

weir /weer/ *n.* **1.** DAM a dam built across a river to regulate the flow of water, divert it, or change its level **2.** ANGLING BARRICADE FOR FISH a fence placed in a stream to catch fish [Old English *wer*. Ultimately from an Indo-European base meaning 'to cover' that is also the ancestor of English *garage* and *warn*.]

Weir /weer/, **Peter** (*b.* 1944) Australian film director. After achieving international success with the Australian-made *Picnic at Hanging Rock* (1975), he established himself as a leading Hollywood director. Full name **Peter Lindsay Weir**

weird /weerd/ *adj.* **1.** ODD strange or unusual **2.** SUPERNATURAL belonging to or suggesting the supernatural **3.** OF FATE relating to or influenced by fate (*archaic*) ■ *n. Scotland* FATE fate or destiny (*archaic*) ○ *to dree your weird* [Old English *wyrd* 'fate'. Ultimately from an Indo-European base meaning 'to turn' that is also the ancestor of English *verse*, the underlying idea being 'that which comes about'.] —**weirdly** *adv.* —**weirdness** *n.*

weirdie /weérdi/, **weirdy** (*plural* **-ies**) *n.* sb who behaves in a way regarded as strange or unconventional (*informal*)

weirdo /weérdō/ *n.* an offensive term referring to sb who behaves in a way regarded as strange or unconventional, especially sb whose sexual tastes or habits are regarded as unusual (*informal*)

weird sisters, Weird Sisters *npl.* **1.** MYTHOL FATES the Fates **2.** MYTHOL = the Norns **3.** THEATRE WITCHES IN MACBETH the three witches in Shakespeare's play *Macbeth* [*Weird* in the meaning of 'having the power to control fates']

Weismannism /víssmənizəm/ *n.* the principle that the inherited characteristics of any organism are determined solely by material (**germ plasm**) contained in the male and female sex cells from which the organism develops. This theory excludes any role for the body cells in inheritance and rules out the inheritance of characteristics acquired during an organism's lifetime. It remains a fundamental tenet of modern genetics. [Late 19thC. Named after August F. L. *Weismann* (1834–1914), the German biologist who propounded this principle.]

weka /wáykə/ *n.* a flightless fast-running bird with mainly brown and black plumage, found in the scrubland and forest margins of New Zealand. Latin name: *Gallirallus australis*. [Mid-19thC. From Maori, an imitation of the sound of the bird's call.]

welch *vi.* = welsh

welcome /wélkəm/ *adj.* **1.** RECEIVED GLADLY received or entertained gladly and generously ○ *a welcome gift* **2.** EAGERLY AND DELIGHTEDLY ACCEPTED accepted or anticipated with delight and eagerness, often because it answers a need ○ *It was a welcome break after two solid weeks of writing.* **3.** FREELY INVITED OR PERMITTED freely and willingly invited or permitted ○ *You're welcome to stay for dinner.* **4.** WITH NOTHING EXPECTED IN RETURN with no obligation incurred by a courtesy, favour, gift, or sth else given ○ *You're very welcome, it was no trouble.* ■ *n.* **1.** ACKNOWLEDGMENT OF SB'S ARRIVAL a greeting or reception given to sb upon arrival or being met ○ *a warm welcome to their guests* **2.** REACTION TO STH a particular response or reaction to sth ○ *Local authorities have extended a cautious welcome to the new proposals.* ■ *vt.* **(-comes, -coming, -comed) 1.** RECEIVE IN A PARTICULAR WAY to greet, receive, or entertain sb in a particular way **2.** ACCEPT IN A PARTICULAR WAY to accept or receive sth in a particular way ○ *We welcome any feedback from our customers.* ■ *interj.* USED TO GREET SB used to express a friendly or courteous greeting to sb who has just arrived or is a stranger [Old English *wilcuma*, originally a noun meaning 'welcome guest' (influenced by WELL[2] and either Old Norse *velkominn* or Old French *bien venu*), from *willa* (see WILL[2]) + *cuma* 'comer'] —**welcomely** *adv.* —**welcomeness** *n.* —**welcomer** *n.* ◇ **be welcome to sth** used to indicate that the speaker is happy for sb to have sth (*often used ironically*) ◇ **wear out** *or* **outstay** *or* **overstay your welcome** to stay longer than is polite or accept sb's hospitality for too long

welcome page *n.* ONLINE = **home page**

welcome swallow *n.* a swallow found in southern and eastern Australia, especially in urban areas. It has a long forked tail, glossy dark-blue back and wings, grey underparts, and a reddish throat. Latin name: *Hirundo neoxena.*

weld[1] /weld/ *v.* **(welds, welding, welded) 1.** *vti.* FUSE MATERIAL BY HEATING to join together pieces or parts of some material by heating, hammering, or using other pressure, or to be joined in this way ○ *to weld two pieces of iron together* **2.** *vt.* REPAIR OR CONSTRUCT STH BY FUSING to repair or construct sth by heating its pieces or parts so that they fuse together ○ *to weld a metal sculpture* **3.** *vti.* ASSOCIATE OR BECOME ASSOCIATED to join or become joined in a union or a close association ■ *n.* **1.** FUSION OF PARTS the union or fusion of parts or pieces **2.** JOINT FORMED BY FUSION a joint where pieces or parts have been fused together [Late 16thC. Alteration of WELL[1] (verb) in the obsolete meaning of 'to liquefy by heating'; influenced by its past participle *welled.*] —**weldability** /wéldə bíllәti/ *n.* —**weldable** /wéldəb'l/ *adj.*

weld[2] /weld/ *n.* **1.** BOT = **dyer's rocket 2.** YELLOW DYE a yellow dye extracted from the dyer's rocket plant, widely used from ancient times until the modern era to colour wool and other fabrics [Origin uncertain: perhaps from obsolete Low German *walde, wolde*; or perhaps from assumed Old English *w(e)ald*]

Weld /weld/, **Frederick Aloysius** (1823–91) English-born New Zealand statesman. He was prime minister of New Zealand from 1864 to 1865.

welder /wéldər/ *n.* **1.** SB WHO WELDS STH sb who welds, especially sb who earns a living by welding metal **2.** STH THAT WELDS a device, machine, or other apparatus that is used to make metal welds

welfare /wél fair/ *n.* **1.** PHYSICAL, SOCIAL, AND FINANCIAL WELL-BEING the physical, social, and financial conditions under which sb may live satisfactorily **2.** *US, Can* AID TO PEOPLE IN NEED financial aid and other benefits for people who are unemployed, below a specified income level, or otherwise requiring assistance, especially when provided by a government agency or programme ■ *adj.* **1.** AIDING PEOPLE IN NEED concerning or designed to aid people who are poor, unemployed, or in need of assistance in some other way ○ *a welfare agency* **2.** *US, Can* RECEIVING GOVERNMENT AID OWING TO NEED receiving government financial aid or benefits because of income level, unemployment, or other conditions that create a need for assistance ○ *welfare clients* [14thC. Contraction of *well fare* 'fare well'.]

welfare state *n.* **1.** GOVERNMENT RESPONSIBILITY FOR SOCIAL WELFARE a political system in which a government assumes the primary responsibility for assuring the basic health and financial well-being of all its citizens through programmes and direct assistance **2.** NATION FULLY ASSUMING CITIZENS' WELFARE a nation whose government assumes primary responsibility for the social welfare of its citizens

welfarism /wél fair izzəm/ *n.* the policies, practices, and beliefs that characterize the welfare state (*disapproving*) [Mid-20thC] —**welfarist** *n.*

welkin /wélkin/ *n.* the sky, heaven, or the upper air (*archaic or literary*) [Old English *weolcen, wolc(e)n* 'cloud, firmament'. From a prehistoric Germanic word that is also the ancestor of Dutch *wolk* and German *Wolke* 'cloud'.]

Welkom /wélkəm, vélk-/ town in Free State, central South Africa. It is the centre of a gold-mining region. Population: 185,500 (1985).

Well

well[1] /wel/ *n.* **1.** HOLE MADE TO DRAW UP FLUIDS a hole or shaft that is dug or drilled into the ground in order to obtain water, brine, petroleum, or natural gas ○ *an oil well* **2.** SPRING OF WATER a place where water comes out of the ground as a natural source ○ *get their water from a well* **3.** SOURCE OF STH a source of a freely and abundantly available supply of sth ○ *a well of information* **4.** CONTAINER FOR LIQUID a container or sunken area for holding ink or another liquid ○ *a well on a cutting board* **5.** VERTICAL PASSAGE IN A BUILDING a vertical space within or enclosed by a building, often used as a passageway for stairs or lifts or for air and light **6.** SPACE IN CENTRE OF COURTROOM the open space in the centre of a courtroom **7.** ENCLOSURE FOR A SHIP'S PUMPS an enclosed area in the hold of a ship in which the pumps are located **8.** SHIPBOARD CONTAINER FOR FISH a compartment in a fishing boat in which freshly caught fish are held **9.** ENCLOSING COMPARTMENT a compartment that encloses or is used to store sth temporarily such as the retracted wheels of an aircraft in flight ■ *v.* **(wells, welling, welled) 1.** *vti.* RISE OR BRING TO THE SURFACE to rise or flow to the surface from inside the earth or the body, or to cause sth to do this ○ *Tears welled up in his eyes.* ○ *The fountain welled a stream of clear water into the basin below.* **2.** *vi.* GROW STRONGER to surge from within or grow stronger so as to threaten to burst forth ○ *Fear welled up inside me.* **3.** *vi.* BECOME FILLED WITH LIQUID to become filled with a pool of water, tears, or another liquid ○ *My eyes welled with tears.* [Old English *wella* 'spring of water' and *wellan* 'to boil'. Ultimately from an Indo-European word meaning 'to turn', which also produced English *walk, wallet, waltz,* and *welter.*]

WORD KEY: REGIONAL NOTE

In the standard language, 'very' modifies adjectives such as 'happy', 'kind', and 'thoughtful', whereas ***well*** modifies adjectives formed from verbs. Thus we have *very happy* but *well dressed, very kind* but *well mannered.* There is a growing tendency, thought to have started in Liverpool, for ***well*** to be used in phrases where 'very' is traditional, for example *well happy* and *well rich.*

well[2] /wel/ **(better** /béttər/, **best** /best/) CORE MEANING: a grammatical word indicating that sth is satisfactory or is performed in a satisfactory way ○ *She did very well in her test.*

1. *adv.* PLEASINGLY OR DESIRABLY in an efficient, satisfying, or otherwise desirable way (*often used in combination*) ○ *I thought the party went very well.* **2.** *adv.* ETHICALLY OR PROPERLY in an ethical, proper, or courteous way ○ *He always treated the children very well.* **3.** *adv.* SKILFULLY OR EXPERTLY with proficiency, skill, or expertise (*often used in combination*) ○ *She plays tennis really well.* **4.** *adv.* JUSTLY AND APPROPRIATELY with justice and good reason ○ *I could not very well refuse her request.* **5.** *adv.* COMFORTABLY in ease and comfort (*often used in combination*) ○ *I just want to be rich enough to live well.* **6.** *adv.* ADVANTAGEOUSLY in a way that promotes sb's advantage and well-being (*often used in combination*) ○ *She married well – her husband is a wealthy pig-farmer.* **7.** *adv.* CONDUCIVE TO GOOD HEALTH in a way that promotes health and physical well-being (*often used in combination*) ○ *Both mother and baby are doing well.* **8.** *adv.* CONSIDERABLY to a considerable extent, distance, or degree (*often used in combination*) ○ *I was well prepared for the exams.* **9.** *adv.* FULLY AND THOROUGHLY in a complete and thorough way (*often used in combination*) ○ *Stir the mixture well, then turn it out onto a baking sheet.* **10.** *adv.* WITH CERTAINTY with no doubt whatever about sth ○ *As you well know, I will not tolerate any laziness* **11.** *adv.* FAMILIARLY AND INTIMATELY in a familiar and intimate way ○ *I knew them well when they were students.* **12.** *adv.* GOOD-NATUREDLY taking sth in a tolerant or good-humoured way ○ *I teased him but he took it well.* **13.** *adv.* VERY very or completely (*slang*) ○ *He was well drunk last night.* **14.** *adj.* IN GOOD HEALTH mentally and physically healthy ○ *I'm feeling much better.* ○ *There's a well baby clinic every Wednesday.* **15.** *adj.* PROPER OR APPROPRIATE suitable, proper, or appropriate in the circumstances ○ *It is as well that you apologized to her.* **16.** *adj.* HIGHLY SATISFACTORY in a good, pleasing, or satisfying condition ○ *Is everything well with you?* **17.** *interj.* USED TO EXPRESS EMOTION used to express surprise, agreement, indignation, disapproval, or some other emotion ○ *Well! You've finally come back!* **18.** *interj.* USED TO INTRODUCE OR RESUME STH used to introduce a comment or statement, or to resume a conversation ○ *Well, it looks as if we'll be waiting a while.* [Old English *wel(l).* Ultimately from an Indo-European base meaning 'to wish', which is also the ancestor of Latin *velle* (source of English *benevolent* and *voluntary*) and English *wealth.*] ◇ **as well** in addition to sth ○ *The members were mostly young couples, but there were several grandparents as well.* ◇ **as well as** to an equal degree or extent ○ *Banking, as well as other businesses, will take the demographics into consideration.* ◇ **be as well to do sth** to be advisable or sensible to do sth ○ *It would be as well to look at all the building societies before investing your savings.* ◇ **be well out of sth** to be fortunate in having escaped from a difficult or unhappy situation ○ *You're well out of it – they weren't treating you very well in that job.* ◇ **that's** *or* **it's just as well** used to indicate that sth is fortunate ○ *It's just as well that she's going to be a bit late, because we're not quite ready.* ◇ **well and good** indicating qualified approval ○ *If he wants to come with us, well and good, but he'll have to pay his share.*

we'll /weel, wil/ *contr.* **1.** we will **2.** we shall

well-adjusted *adj.* (*not hyphenated after a verb*) **1.** ALTERED ACCORDINGLY successfully adapted to prevailing conditions **2.** EMOTIONALLY STABLE content with your own self and life and therefore emotionally and psychologically stable

well-advised *adj.* acting with good sense (*not hyphenated after a verb*) ○ *You would be well advised to leave before the storm hits.*

Welland Canal /wélland-/, **Welland Ship Canal** canal system in Ontario, Canada, linking Lake Ontario and Lake Erie. It is part of the St Lawrence Seaway, and bypasses the Niagara Falls. Length: 44 km/28 mi.

well-appointed *adj.* equipped, furnished, or arranged with whatever is necessary or desired (*not hyphenated after a verb*)

wellaway /wéllə wáy/, **welladay** /-dáy/ *interj.* used as a cry of sorrow, distress, or regret (*archaic*) [Old English *wei lā wei*, an alteration (influenced by WELL[2] and Old Norse *vei* 'woe') of *wā lā wā*, literally 'woe lo woe']

well-balanced *adj.* (*not hyphenated after a verb*) **1.** SENSIBLE AND RATIONAL psychologically or emotionally stable **2.** ORGANIZED WITH THE PARTS IN PROPORTION organized, conducted, or constructed so that all the parts are appropriately and sensibly proportioned or coordinated

well-behaved *adj.* behaving, operating, or occurring properly and as expected (*not hyphenated after a verb*)

wellbeing /wél bee ing/ *n.* a good, healthy, or comfortable state

well-beloved *adj.* (*not hyphenated after a verb*) **1.** DEARLY LOVED truly and dearly loved **2.** RESPECTED highly respected or honoured ■ *n.* (*plural* **well-beloved**) DEARLY LOVED PERSON sb who is truly and dearly loved

wellborn /wél báwrn/ *adj.* BELONGING TO A RESPECTED FAMILY born into an aristocratic, highly respected, or wealthy family ■ *n.* PEOPLE FROM ESTEEMED FAMILIES people who were born in aristocratic, highly respected, or wealthy families (*takes a plural verb*) [Old English *welboren*]

well-bred *adj.* (*not hyphenated after a verb*) 1. WITH GOOD MANNERS possessing or displaying good manners or other marks of a good upbringing 2. ZOOL WITH A DESIRABLE PEDIGREE born as an animal from a good breed or of good stock

well-built *adj.* (*not hyphenated after a verb*) 1. PHYSICALLY BIG AND STRONG having a sturdy and strong physique 2. PROPERLY CONSTRUCTED of strong or sound construction

well-chosen *adj.* selected carefully so as to be suitable or appropriate (*not hyphenated after a verb*)

well-connected *adj.* having relatives, friends, or acquaintances in important or influential positions who can provide help when necessary (*not hyphenated after a verb*)

well-defined *adj.* (*not hyphenated after a verb*) 1. STATED PRECISELY AND CLEARLY stated or described with clarity and without ambiguity 2. WITH A DISTINCT OUTLINE OR FORM having a clearly observable outline or form

well-disposed *adj.* feeling or inclined to be approving, friendly, kindly, or sympathetic and potentially helpful (*not hyphenated after a verb*) ○ *She seemed well disposed towards us.*

well-done *adj.* (*not hyphenated after a verb*) 1. PERFORMED CORRECTLY AND WELL carried out or performed correctly, properly, or skilfully 2. COOKED THROUGH cooked right through to the centre

well dressing *n.* in the United Kingdom, the practice of decorating a well with flowers at Whitsuntide in a traditional ancient ceremony

well-earned *adj.* fully deserved, especially as a result of hard work or effort (*not hyphenated after a verb*) ○ *sat down for a well-earned rest*

well-endowed *adj.* (*not hyphenated after a verb*) 1. OFFENSIVE TERM an offensive term meaning having a large penis or large breasts (*informal*) 2. AFFLUENT provided with substantial property, a sizable income, or a good source of income 3. NATURALLY EXCELLENT talented or capable as a result of a natural gift

Orson Welles

Welles /welz/, **Orson** (1915–85) US actor and director. Although *Citizen Kane* (1941) garnered enormous critical respect, Hollywood's mistrust of his maverick talents prevented him from producing more than a handful of films. Full name **George Orson Welles**

Wellesley /wélzli/, **Arthur, 1st Duke of Wellington** (1769–1852) British general and statesman. He led the British forces that helped defeat Napoleon at the Battle of Waterloo (1815) and was prime minister (1828–30).

well-favoured *adj.* good-looking (*dated or formal; not hyphenated after a verb*)

well-fed *adj.* (*not hyphenated after a verb*) 1. WITH A GOOD DIET having a diet that provides proper nourishment 2. OVERWEIGHT overweight, especially as a result of having eaten a great deal of good or rich food

well-formed *adj.* fully conforming to the rules of grammar and syntax in a language (*not hyphenated after a verb*) —**well-formedness** *n.*

well-found *adj.* properly and fully fitted out or equipped (*not hyphenated after a verb*)

well-founded *adj.* based on sound reasons, information, or evidence or on undisputable facts (*not hyphenated after a verb*)

well-groomed *adj.* (*not hyphenated after a verb*) 1. TAKING CARE WITH YOUR APPEARANCE clean, neat, and well-dressed 2. CAREFULLY TENDED carefully cleaned, brushed, or tended

well-grounded *adj.* (*not hyphenated after a verb*) 1. FAMILIAR WITH ESSENTIAL KNOWLEDGE encompassing or thoroughly familiar with the essential details or knowledge of a subject 2. = well-founded

wellhead /wél hed/ *n.* 1. SOURCE OF A SPRING OR STREAM the place where a spring emerges from the earth or a stream begins 2. SOURCE OF STH a principal or primary source of sth 3. STRUCTURE ON TOP OF A WELL a structure or enclosure at the upper end of a water, oil, or natural-gas well, e.g. one containing pipes and pumping equipment [14thC]

well-heeled *adj.* having a large income or substantial property (*informal; not hyphenated after a verb*)

well-hung *adj.* (*not hyphenated after a verb*) 1. OFFENSIVE TERM an offensive term meaning having a large penis or a large penis and testicles (*slang offensive*) 2. HANGING AS DESIRED OR REQUIRED suspended or attached so as to hang in a way that is desired or required 3. HUNG FOR THE PROPER TIME hung up long enough to mature and be good to eat ○ *He liked his venison well hung.*

wellie /wélli/, **wellie boot, welly** (*plural* -ies), **welly boot** *n.* a Wellington boot (*informal*) [Mid-20thC. Shortening and alteration.] ◇ **give it some wellie** or **welly** to put some effort into doing sth (*informal; usually used as a command*)

well-informed *adj.* having a broad and detailed knowledge of sth, especially of the world and current events or of a particular subject (*not hyphenated after a verb*)

Wellingborough /wéllingbərə, -brə/ town in Northamptonshire, central England. Population: 68,200 (1995).

Wellington /wéllingtən/ 1. capital city of New Zealand, built around a deep harbour at the southern end of the North Island. Population: 335,051 (1996). 2. administrative region of New Zealand, occupying the southern tip of the North Island and including the city of Wellington. Population: 416,019 (1996). Area: 15,821 sq. km/6,109 sq. mi.

Wellington, Mount mountain near Hobart in southern Tasmania, Australia. Height: 1,270 m/4,167 ft.

wellington boot, **wellington** *n.* 1. LOOSE RUBBER BOOT FOR WET CONDITIONS a loose waterproof rubber boot extending to the knee or just below it and worn in wet weather or muddy conditions 2. BOOT CUT LOWER AT THE BACK a leather boot that reaches to the top of or above the knee in the front but is cut lower in the back [Early 19thC. Named after Arthur WELLESLEY, the first Duke of *Wellington*.]

wellingtonia /wélling tṓni ə/ (*plural* -as or -a) *n.* = giant sequoia [Mid-19thC. From modern Latin, named in honour of Arthur WELLESLEY, the first Duke of *Wellington*.]

well-intentioned *adj.* intended to be helpful or useful in some way but producing a negative effect or result (*not hyphenated after a verb*)

well-kept *adj.* (*not hyphenated after a verb*) 1. CAREFULLY LOOKED AFTER carefully maintained or looked after 2. CAREFULLY PRESERVED AND CONFIDENTIAL not revealed to anyone or to only a few people

well-knit *adj.* (*not hyphenated after a verb*) 1. BOUND BY CLOSE TIES bound together by close relationships or ties 2. FIRMLY CONSTRUCTED constructed or produced in such a way that the parts are firmly joined together or are integrated well 3. COMPACT IN PHYSIQUE with a compact and strong physique

well-known *adj.* (*not hyphenated after a verb*) 1. WIDELY KNOWN known to many people 2. FULLY UNDERSTOOD fully known or understood

well-man *adj.* monitoring men's health and advising men on ways to prevent illness. ◇ **well-woman**

well-mannered *adj.* behaving with politeness and courtesy (*not hyphenated after a verb*)

well-meaning *adj.* trying to be helpful or useful in some way, but often producing a negative effect or result (*not hyphenated after a verb*)

well-meant *adj.* arising from a desire to be helpful or useful, but often producing a negative effect (*not hyphenated after a verb*)

wellness /wélnəss/ *n.* US physical well-being, especially when maintained or achieved through good diet and regular exercise

well-nigh *adv.* nearly or almost ○ *well-nigh impossible*

well-off *adj.* 1. FAIRLY WEALTHY having a good income or enough money to live comfortably (*not hyphenated after a verb*) 2. FAVOURABLY PLACED in a good or favourable situation or circumstances ○ *It's not a good idea to change jobs, you're better off where you are.* 3. WITH PLENTY having a good supply of sth ○ *well off for fuel right now*

well-oiled *adj.* (*not hyphenated after a verb*) 1. FUNCTIONING SMOOTHLY functioning, operating, or carried out efficiently 2. DRUNK having drunk too much alcohol (*informal*)

well-ordered *adj.* (*not hyphenated after a verb*) 1. PROPERLY ORGANIZED arranged or organized so that things are in the proper place or run smoothly 2. MATH WITH FIRST NUMERICAL ELEMENT having the property that every subset with members has an element that precedes all other elements in that subset

well-padded *adj.* having a greater body weight than is desirable or advisable (*informal; not hyphenated after a verb*)

well-preserved *adj.* in good condition or maintaining a good appearance or good health in spite of advanced age (*not hyphenated after a verb*)

well-read /-réd/ *adj.* knowing much about many things or a particular field from having read widely and thoroughly (*not hyphenated after a verb*)

well-rounded *adj.* (*not hyphenated after a verb*) 1. WITH EXPERIENCE IN MANY AREAS having abilities, experience, or achievements in a wide and balanced variety of fields 2. COMPREHENSIVE AND VARIED encompassing or including a wide, desirable, and balanced variety of subjects or activities 3. SHAPELY having a rounded or otherwise pleasingly shaped body

Wells /welz/ city in Somerset, southwestern England. It is known for its medieval cathedral. Population: 10,000 (1993).

Wells, H. G. (1866–1946) British writer. A prolific writer of history and science books, he is remembered for his science fiction novels, including *The Time Machine* (1895) and *The Shape of Things to Come* (1933). Full name **Herbert George Wells**

well-set *adj.* (*not hyphenated after a verb*) 1. WITH A POWERFUL PHYSIQUE strong and solid in physique 2. FIRMLY SET solidly established or fixed

well-spoken *adj.* (*not hyphenated after a verb*) 1. REFINED speaking clearly, articulately, and in a refined accent, and with an accent that is regarded as the product of a good education 2. EXPRESSED APPROPRIATELY selected or expressed appropriately

wellspring /wél spring/ *n.* 1. SPRING OR STREAM SOURCE a source of a spring or stream 2. PLENTIFUL SOURCE OF STH a plentiful source or supply of sth ○ *a wellspring of artistic talent* [Old English *welspryng, wylspryng*]

well-stacked *adj.* an offensive term meaning having large breasts (*slang offensive*)

well-taken *adj.* (*not hyphenated after a verb*) 1. SPORTS CARRIED OUT EFFECTIVELY performed or executed skilfully or effectively 2. AMPLY JUSTIFIED based on sound reasons, information, or evidence or on indisputable facts

well-tempered *adj.* tuned so as to permit playing in any key (*not hyphenated after a verb*)

well-thought-of *adj.* regarded with respect or esteem or having a good reputation (*not hyphenated after a verb*)

well-thought-out *adj.* carefully and skilfully planned (*not hyphenated after a verb*)

well-thumbed *adj.* with pages that show signs of having been turned many times (*not hyphenated after a verb*)

well-timed *adj.* done or occurring at an appropriate or opportune moment (*not hyphenated after a verb*)

well-to-do *adj.* having a good income or enough money to live comfortably

well-turned *adj.* (*not hyphenated after a verb*) **1. GRACEFULLY OR ATTRACTIVELY SHAPED** having a graceful or attractive shape ◊ *a well-turned ankle* **2. SKILFULLY STATED** skilfully expressed or worded ◊ *a well-turned phrase* **3. MANUFACTURED WITH A GRACEFUL SHAPE** turned on a lathe or formed so as to have a pleasing, graceful shape

well-wisher *n.* sb who expresses good wishes for another's success or who shows good will towards sb or sth —**well-wishing** *adj., n.*

well-woman *adj.* monitoring women's health and advising women on ways to prevent illness. ◊ **well-man**

well-worn *adj.* (*not hyphenated after a verb*) **1. SHOWING WEAR** showing signs of wear as a result of much use **2. OVERUSED** trite or hackneyed as result of being used too often in speech or writing

welly, **welly boot** *n.* = **wellie** (*informal*)

wels /velss/ (*plural* **wels**) *n.* a large Central and Eastern European freshwater catfish. Latin name: *Silurus glanis.* [Late 19thC. From German.]

Welsbach burner /wélz bak-/ *tdmk.* a trademark for a gas burner consisting of a Bunsen burner equipped with a gauze mantle impregnated with cerium oxide and thorium oxide that emits a greenish light when ignited

welsh /welsh/ (**welshes, welshing, welshed**), **welch** (**welches, welching, welched**) *vi.* **1. FAIL TO REPAY A DEBT** to fail to pay money owed as a debt or lost in a wager (*informal*) **2. OFFENSIVE TERM** an offensive term meaning to fail to fulfil or honour an obligation entered into or incurred (*informal offensive*) [Mid-19thC. Origin uncertain: probably from WELSH.] —**welsher** *n.*

Welsh /welsh/ *npl.* PEOPLES **PEOPLE OF WALES** the people of Wales ■ *n.* LANG **CELTIC LANGUAGE** a language spoken in Wales belonging to the Celtic group of Indo-European languages. About 500,000 people speak Welsh. ■ *adj.* **1.** PEOPLES **OF WALES** relating to Wales or its people or culture **2.** LANG **OF WELSH** relating to the Welsh language [Old English *Wēlisc, Wǣlisc,* from *W(e)alh* 'Briton, Celt, Welshman' (literally 'foreigner'), via a prehistoric Germanic word meaning 'foreign' (ancestor of English *walnut*) from Latin *Volcae* 'Celtic people of southern Gaul']

Welsh cob *n.* a horse with a strong neck, powerful shoulders, and compact body, used as a saddle and harness horse. It is descended from the Welsh mountain pony.

Welsh corgi *n.* = **corgi** [*Welsh* from the fact that it originated in Wales]

Welsh dresser *n.* a sideboard with cupboards and drawers in the lower part and open shelves in the top part

Welsh English *n.* the variety of English spoken in Wales

WORD KEY: WORLD ENGLISH

Welsh English is the English language as used in Wales, where it is the majority language, coexisting with Welsh, the surviving Celtic language with the largest number of speakers but a minority language in its homeland. It can be categorized in three overlapping ways. *Welsh English* has three main influences: the Welsh language (mainly in the northern counties, often referred to as 'Welsh Wales'); dialects in neighbouring counties of England; and school and the media. The Welsh are often said to have a 'singsong' accent, perhaps because of their use of a rise-fall tone at the end of sentences (rather than a simple fall), and because of their full vowels and stress on usually weak syllables such as the 'den' in *garden*. *Welsh English* is generally non-rhotic (i.e., 'r' is not pronounced in words such as *art, door,* and *worker*). Two sounds from Welsh are common, especially in names: the 'll' of *Llangollen*, pronounced as /hl/, and the 'ch' in *bach* (dear), pronounced as /kh/.

South Walians, like some dialect speakers in England, generally do not pronounce an initial 'h' (as in *hat* and *home*), whereas North Walians do because it occurs in Welsh. A general influence from Welsh is notable in such usages as 'Coming back soon she is' for 'She's coming back soon' and *there* in exclamations such as 'There's kind he is!' for 'How kind he is!' The catch-all question tag *isn't it?* has long been common, as in 'They'll be here soon, isn't it?' (as opposed to standard *won't they?*). Words from Welsh include: eisteddfod 'cultural festival' (plural eisteddfodau); and iechyd da ('good health', often rendered as 'yachy da').

Welsh harp *n.* a harp with three rows of strings that allow the production of a chromatic scale

Welshman /wélshmən/ (*plural* **-men** /-mən/) *n.* PEOPLES a man who was born or brought up in Wales, or who has Welsh ancestry [Old English]

Welshman's button /wélshmənz-/ *n.* a caddis fly used by anglers as bait. Latin name: *Sericostoma personatum.*

Welsh Mountain, **Welsh Mountain sheep** *n.* a hardy small-bodied sheep, native to Wales, with a grey-white face and legs, and a fleece that often contains red fibres [Late 19thC. From its having originated in high areas of Wales.]

Welsh mountain pony *n.* a pony of a breed native to the Welsh hills that has tiny pointed ears and a compact body. It is popular for harness work and as a child's pony.

Welsh Mountain sheep *n.* = **Welsh Mountain**

Welsh pony *n.* a pony descended from crosses between Welsh cobs and Welsh mountain ponies, slightly larger than the latter. It is used for jumping and riding.

Welsh poppy *n.* a poppy of western Europe that forms branching tufts of deeply divided compound leaves and has yellow flowers borne singly on long slender stems. Latin name: *Meconopsis cambrica.*

Welsh rarebit /-ráir bit/, **Welsh rabbit** *n.* a dish made of hard cheese melted with seasoning, mustard, and a little beer or milk, then spread on toast and grilled until bubbling and golden [Late 18thC. Alteration of WELSH RABBIT, perhaps from a popular association of Wales with cheese, or in the former meaning 'inferior'; *rabbit* perhaps because cheese was commonly substituted for meat.]

Welsh springer spaniel *n.* a spaniel of a breed with a thick silky coat that is chiefly white with large reddish patches. It is very similar to but smaller than the English springer spaniel. [*Welsh* from the fact that it originated in Wales]

Welsh terrier *n.* a wire-haired terrier of a breed originally developed for hunting. It resembles an Airedale and has a long thick, typically black-and-tan coat. [*Welsh* from the fact that it originated in Wales]

Welshwoman /wélsh woŏmən/ (*plural* **-en** /-wímin/) *n.* a woman who was born or brought up in Wales, or who has Welsh ancestry [15thC]

welt /welt/ *n.* **1. RIDGE ON THE SKIN** a raised ridge or bump on the skin caused by a lash from a whip, a scratch, or a similar blow **2. LASH FROM A WHIP CAUSING A RIDGE** a lash from a whip or a similar blow that causes a raised ridge or bump on the skin **3.** CLOTHES **STRIP SEWN INTO A SHOE** a strip of leather or other material that is sewn into a shoe or boot between the upper and the sole in order to strengthen the seam **4.** SEW **REINFORCEMENT FOR A SEAM** a folded strip of cloth, sometimes wrapped around a cord, that is sewn into a seam in a garment or pillow as a reinforcement or decoration ■ *vt.* (**welts, welting, welted**) **1. BEAT SB SEVERELY** to beat or hit sb severely, especially with a whip or switch **2. RAISE SMALL RIDGES ON THE SKIN** to cause raised ridges or bumps on the skin as a result of a lash from a whip or switch **3. STITCH STH REINFORCING OR DECORATIVE** to stitch or supply sth with a strip of material as a reinforcement or decoration [15thC. Origin uncertain: perhaps from assumed Old English *wealt, wǣlt,* of unknown origin.]

Weltanschauung /vélt an show oŏng/ (*plural* **-ungen** /-oŏngən/) *n.* a comprehensive and usually personal conception or view of humanity, the world, or

---

life [Mid-19thC. From German, literally 'world view', from *Welt* 'world' + *Anschauung* 'view'.]

welter /wéltər/ *n.* **1. CONFUSED MASS** a confused or jumbled mass of sth **2. CONFUSED CONDITION** a state of confusion or chaos or a disorderly or chaotic situation **3. SURGING MOTION OF WATER** a surging, rolling, or heaving motion made by the sea or waves **4.** SPORTS **WELTERWEIGHT** a welterweight ■ *vi.* (**-ters, -tering, -tered**) **1. WALLOW IN STH** to wallow or roll around in sth **2. LIE DRENCHED WITH LIQUID** to lie soaked or bathed in water, blood, or some other liquid **3. BE COMPLETELY IMMERSED IN STH** to be completely or deeply involved, absorbed, or entangled in sth **4. SURGE OR ROLL IN WATER** to surge, roll, or heave in the sea or waves [14thC. From Middle Dutch or Middle Low German *welteren* 'to roll'.]

welterweight /wéltər wayt/ *n.* a sports contestant ranked by body weight between a lightweight and a middleweight, especially a professional boxer weighing between 61 kg/135 lb and 66.5 kg/147 lb [Early 19thC. *Welter-* came from *welter* 'heavyweight rider or boxer', of uncertain origin: perhaps formed from the verb WELT.]

Weltschmerz /vélt shmairts/, **weltschmerz** *n.* sadness felt at the imperfect state of the world, especially at the behaviour of human beings [Late 19thC. From German, from *Welt* 'world' + *Schmerz* 'pain'.]

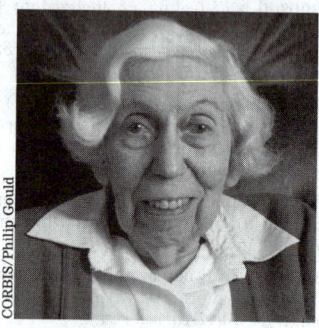
CORBIS/Philip Gould

Eudora Welty

Welty /wéltee/, **Eudora** (b. 1909) US writer. Her novels, set in her native Mississippi, include the Pulitzer Prize-winning *The Optimist's Daughter* (1969).

welwitschia /wel wíchi ə/ (*plural* **-as** *or* **-a**) *n.* a desert plant of South Africa and Namibia that produces two large strap-shaped leaves from the base of a short trunk and scarlet cones in which flowers develop. Latin name: *Welwitschia mirabilis.* [Mid-19thC. From modern Latin, named after Friedrich *Welwitsch* (1806–72), Austrian botanist.]

Welwyn Garden City /wéllin-/ town in Hertfordshire, southeastern England, founded in 1920 as part of the garden city movement, and designated as a new town in 1948. Population: 42,000 (1994).

Wembley /wémbli/ residential area in northwestern London. Wembley Stadium, used for important sporting events, is located there.

wen[1] /wen/ *n.* **1. SKIN CYST** a cyst containing material secreted by a sebaceous gland of the skin, usually on the scalp or genitals. It may grow to an appreciable size and become infected. **2. OVERCROWDED BIG CITY** a very large overpopulated city [Old English *wen(n)*. Origin uncertain.]

wen[2] /wen/ *n.* = **wynn**

Wenceslas IV /wénsəss láwss, -laáss/, **King of Bohemia and Holy Roman Emperor** (1361–1419). Anarchy and unrest marked his reign as Holy Roman Emperor (1378–1400) and he was deposed in 1400, though he remained King of Bohemia until his death.

Wenceslaus /wénsəsləss/, **St, Duke of Bohemia** (907?–929). The patron saint of Czechoslovakia, he encouraged Bohemia's conversion to Christianity. He was murdered by his pagan brother. Known as **Good King Wenceslas**

wench /wench/ *n.* **1. SERVANT GIRL** a girl or young woman who works at a paid job, usually as a servant or on a farm (*archaic*) **2. COUNTRY GIRL** a girl or young woman who lives in a rural area (*archaic*) **3. OFFENSIVE TERM** an offensive term for a prostitute or a woman who is regarded as sexually promiscuous (*offensive*) **4.**

OFFENSIVE TERM an offensive term referring to a young woman (*offensive*) ■ *vi.* (**wenches, wenching, wenched**) **HAVE SEX WITH PROSTITUTES** to engage in sex with prostitutes or with women considered to be promiscuous (*archaic or offensive*) [13thC. Shortening of obsolete *wenchel* 'child, enslaved labourer, prostitute', from Old English *wencel* 'child', of uncertain origin: perhaps ultimately from a prehistoric Germanic base meaning 'to falter'.] —**wencher** *n.*

wend /wend/ (**wends, wending, wended**) *vti.* to proceed along a course or route ○ *The boat wended its way through the reefs.* [Old English *wendan* 'to turn, proceed', from a prehistoric Germanic base meaning 'to turn', which is also the ancestor of English *wand* and *wander*]

Wend *n.* a member of a Slavic people that occupied large parts of northeastern Germany in medieval times. A group descended from the Wends survive today and are known as Sorbs. [Late 18thC. From German *Wende*. The related Old English word was *Winedas* 'Wends'. Both of unknown origin.]

wendigo /wéndi gō/ (*plural* **-gos** or **-goes**), **windigo** /wíndi gō/ (*plural* **-gos** or **-goes**) *n.* Can a demonic creature who according to Cree and Algonquian folklore eats people or possesses them and turns them into cannibals [Early 18thC. From Ojibwa *wintiko*.]

Wendish /wéndish/ *n.* LANG a language spoken in some districts of eastern Germany belonging to the Slavic group of Indo-European languages. About 100,000 people speak Wendish. —**Wendish** *adj.*

Wendy house /wéndi-/ *n.* a model house that is large enough for small children to go inside and play in. US term **playhouse** [Mid-20thC. Named after the house built around the character *Wendy* in the play *Peter Pan* (1904) by J. M. Barrie.]

wenge /wéng gay/ *n.* the dark brown wood of an African tree, often used as a veneer for furniture. Latin name: *Millettia laurentii.* [Mid-20thC]

Wensleydale /wénzli dayl/ *n.* **1. ENGLISH HARD CHEESE** a white crumbly English hard cheese with a slightly tangy flavour **2. SHEEP WITH MOTTLED LEGS** one of a breed of sheep, native to northern England, that has a blue-grey head and ears and dark mottled legs and is raised for its long fleece [Late 19thC. Named after *Wensleydale*, a valley in North Yorkshire, where the sheep originated and where the cheese is chiefly made.]

went past tense of **go**

wentletrap /wént'l trap/ *n.* a marine gastropod mollusc with a spiral prominently ribbed shell that is typically white but is sometimes tinged with brown. Family: Epitoniidae. [Mid-18thC. From Dutch *wenteltrap*, literally 'winding stair', from the appearance of the shells.]

Wentworth /wént wúrth/, **W. C.** (1793–1872) Australian explorer and politician. He was a leader, with Gregory Blaxland and William Lawson, of the first crossing of the Blue Mountains in New South Wales (1813). He established the newspaper *The Australian* (1824–48) to promote self-government. Full name **William Charles Wentworth**

wept past tense, past participle of **weep**

were (*stressed*) /wur/; (*unstressed*) /wər/ past tense of **be** [Old English *wæron* (plural past indicative), *wæren* (plural past subjunctive), and *wære* (2nd person singular past indicative and singular past subjunctive), forms of *wesan* 'to be' (see **WAS**)]

——— **WORD KEY: REGIONAL NOTE** ———
In the north of England, *I were sat* is the usual equivalent of the standard language's *I was sitting*. **Were** regularly follows 'I', 'he', and 'she', whereas *was* tends to be used with 'you', 'we', and 'they', as in *You was stood where?* This usage is still strong, even in urban areas.

we're /weer/ *contr.* we are

weregild *n.* = **wergild**

weren't /wurnt/ *contr.* were not

werewolf /wáir woolf, wéer-/ (*plural* **-wolves** /-woolvz/), **werwolf** (*plural* **-wolves**) *n.* sb who is believed to have been transformed into a wolf, or who is believed to be able to change into a wolf and then back into a human being [Old English *werewulf*, from *were*- 'man' + *wulf* 'wolf'. Ultimately from an Indo-European word meaning 'man', which is also the ancestor of English *virile* and *world*.]

wergild /wúr gild/, **weregild, wergeld** /-geld/ *n.* in Anglo-Saxon and Germanic law, the amount of compensation paid to the relatives of sb slain, calculated on the basis of the person's rank in society [Old English *wergeld*, from *wer* 'man' (see **WEREWOLF**) + *gield* 'payment', an earlier form of **YIELD** (noun)]

wernerite /wúrnə rīt/ *n.* MINERALS = **scapolite** [Early 19thC. Named in honour of Abraham Gottlob *Werner* (1750–1817), a German mineralogist.]

Wernicke-Korsakoff syndrome /váirnikə káwrssə kof-/ *n.* a form of brain damage occurring in long-term alcoholics that results from severe nutritional deficiencies [Mid-20thC. Named after Karl *Wernicke* (1848–1905), German neurologist, and Sergei Sergeevich *Korsakov* (1854–1900), Russian psychiatrist, who independently described it.]

wersh /wursh/ *adj.* Scotland **1. BITTER TO TASTE** bitter in taste or flavour **2. TASTELESS OR INSIPID** having little or no taste or flavour [Origin uncertain: probably a contraction of obsolete (except for dialect) *wearish*, of unknown origin]

wert past tense of **be** (*archaic*)

werwolf *n.* = **werewolf**

Weser /váyzər/ river in northwestern Germany. Formed by the confluence of the Werr and Fulda rivers, it flows northwestwards through Lower Saxony and empties into the North Sea near Bremerhaven. Length: 400 km/300 mi.

weskit /wéskit/ *n.* a waistcoat (*regional*) [Mid-19thC. Alteration of **WAISTCOAT**.]

Wesley /wézli/, **John** (1703–91) British religious leader. He founded Methodism in 1739, and thereafter preached tirelessly to huge crowds and published hymns and other religious works for mass distribution.

Wesleyan /wézzli ən/ *adj.* **BASED ON WESLEY'S TEACHING** based on, consisting of, or resembling the teachings, practices, and beliefs of the Christian preacher John Wesley and his brother Charles, or of Methodism. ◊ **Methodist** ■ *n.* **FOLLOWER OF WESLEY** a follower of the Christian preacher John Wesley and his brother Charles, or a believer in their teachings or those of Methodism —**Wesleyanism** *n.*

Wessex /wéssiks/ former Anglo-Saxon kingdom in southern England

west /west/ *n.* **1. DIRECTION IN WHICH THE SUN SETS** the direction that lies directly ahead of sb facing the setting Sun or that is located towards the left-hand side of a conventional map of the world **2. COMPASS POINT OPPOSITE EAST** the compass point that lies directly opposite east **3. west, West AREA IN THE WEST** the part of an area, region, or country that is situated in or towards the west **4. west, West POSITION EQUIVALENT TO WEST** the position equivalent to west in any diagram consisting of four points at 90-degree intervals ■ *adj.* **1. IN THE WEST** situated in, facing, or coming from the west of a place, region, or country **2. BLOWING FROM WEST** blowing from the west ○ *a west wind* ■ *adv.* **TOWARDS THE WEST** in or towards the west [Old English. Ultimately from an Indo-European word meaning 'evening, night', which also produced Greek *hesperos* 'evening' (source of English *Hesperian*) and Latin *vesper* (source of English *vespers*).] ◊ **go west** to die, disappear, or be destroyed (*informal*)

West, **west** *n.* **1. EUROPE AND THE AMERICAS** the countries of Europe and North and South America. ◊ **western hemisphere 2. COUNTRIES WITH GRAECO-ROMAN AND CHRISTIAN TRADITIONS** those countries of the world, especially in Europe and North and South America, whose culture and society are most influenced by traditions rooted in Greek and Roman culture and in Christianity **3. NON-COMMUNIST COUNTRIES IN THE COLD WAR** the non-Communist countries of Europe and North and South America during the Cold War **4. WESTERN UNITED STATES** the part of the United States west of the Mississippi River or west of the Allegheny Mountains during early phases of the country's history

West /west/, **Mae** (1892–1980) US actor and comedian. She was known for her irreverent wit and disdain for conventional morals. Her films include *She Done Him Wrong* (1933), *I'm No Angel* (1933), and *Klondike Annie* (1936).

Mae West

West, Morris (*b.* 1916) Australian novelist. He is author of *The Shoes of the Fisherman* (1963). Full name **Morris Langlo West**

West, Dame Rebecca (1892–1983) British writer. She wrote noted studies of the Nuremberg war crimes trials and novels including *The Thinking Reed* (1936). Pseudonym of **Cicily Isabel Andrews**. Born **Cicily Isabel Fairfield**

West Bank

West Bank territory in the Middle East on the western bank of the River Jordan, bordered by Israel and Jordan. Once part of Palestine, it was annexed by Jordan in 1950 and occupied by Israel in 1967. As a result of peace agreements between 1993 and 1997 much of it was transferred to Palestinian administration. Population: 1,600,000 (1996). Area: 5,860 sq. km/2,263 sq.mi.

West Bengal state in northeastern India. Capital: Calcutta. Population: 73,600,000 (1994). Area: 87,853 sq. km/33,920 sq. mi.

West Berlin western part of the city of Berlin. It was officially part of West Germany between 1945 and 1990, when the rest of the city was designated East German territory. —**West Berliner** *n.*

westbound /wést bownd/ *adj.* leading, going, or travelling towards the west

West Bromwich /-brómmij, -brómmich/ industrial town in west-central England, near Birmingham. Population: 146,386 (1991).

west by north *n.* the direction or compass point midway between west and west-northwest —**west by north** *adj., adv.*

west by south *n.* the direction or compass point midway between west and west-southwest —**west by south** *adj., adv.*

West Coast 1. administrative region of New Zealand, occupying the western coast of the South Island. Population: 35,671 (1996). Area: 36,116 sq. km/13,944 sq. mi. **2.** region comprising the coastal areas of California, Oregon, and Washington on the Pacific coast of the United States

West Country southwestern part of England, comprising the counties of Cornwall, Devon, and Somerset

West Dunbartonshire /-dun báartənshər/ council area in west-central Scotland, on Loch Lomond and the Clyde estuary. Population: 96,290 (1996). Area: 162 sq. km/63 sq. mi.

wester /wéstər/ *n.* WEST WIND a wind blowing from the west, especially one blowing ahead of or with a storm ■ *vi.* (**-ers, -ering, -ered**) MOVE WEST to move or appear to move across the sky to the west (*refers to the Sun, Moon, or other celestial bodies*) [Late 16thC]

westerly /wéstərli/ *adj.* **1.** IN THE WEST situated in or towards the west **2.** METEOROL COMING FROM THE WEST blowing from the west ■ *n.* (*plural* **-lies**) WIND FROM THE WEST a wind blowing from the west ■ *adv.* **1.** FROM THE WEST coming from the west **2.** TOWARDS THE WEST moving towards the west [15thC] —**westerliness** *n.*

western /wéstərn/ *adj.* **1.** IN THE WEST situated in the west of a region or country **2.** FACING WEST situated in or facing the west ○ *The house has a western aspect.* **3. western, Western** OF THE WEST typical of or native to the west of a region or country **4.** COMING FROM THE WEST blowing from the west ○ *a western wind* **5.** WEST OF THE PRIME MERIDIAN lying west of the prime meridian [Old English *westerne*, from WEST + a suffix denoting direction] —**westernness** *n.*

Western, western *adj.* **1.** INFLUENCED BY GRAECO-ROMAN AND CHRISTIAN TRADITIONS found in or typical of countries, especially in Europe and North and South America, whose culture and society are greatly influenced by traditions rooted in Greek and Roman culture and in Christianity **2.** OF NON-COMMUNIST COUNTRIES IN THE COLD WAR found in or belonging to the non-Communist countries of Europe and North and South America during the Cold War **3.** TYPICAL OF THE AMERICAN WEST found in or relating to the part of the United States west of the Mississippi River or west of the Allegheny Mountains during early phases of the country's history **4.** FOUND IN EUROPE AND AMERICAS located in or relating to Europe and North and South America **5.** CATHOLIC AND PROTESTANT based on, consisting of, or resembling the teachings, practices, and beliefs of Roman Catholicism and Protestantism, as opposed to those of the Eastern churches ■ *n.* FILM OR BOOK ON THE AMERICAN WEST a film, radio or television programme, novel, or story set in the western part of the United States, usually during the second half of the 19th century —**Westernness** *n.*

Western Australia /wéstərn-/ state occupying the western part of Australia. Founded as a British colony in 1829, it is the largest state in Australia. Capital: Perth. Population: 1,766,000 (1996). Area: 2,525,500 sq. km/975,100 sq. mi.

Western blotting, Western blot *n.* a technique in which a mixture of proteins is separated in a gel by electrophoresis, then absorbed by a nylon membrane blotted onto its surface to identify its constituents [Modelled on *Southern blot*]

Western Cape province in southwestern South Africa, formerly part of Cape Province. Capital: Cape Town. Population: 4,055,000 (1996). Area: 129,386 sq. km/49,943 sq. mi.

Western Church *n.* the Christian Church as found in or influenced by that of Europe, especially the Roman Catholic Church

westerner /wéstərnər/ *n.* sb who lives in or comes from the western part of a country or region

Western European Time *n.* the standard time in the time zone centred on 0° longitude (**the prime meridian**), which includes the United Kingdom. It is the same time as Universal Coordinated Time.

Western European Union *n.* an association of European countries, inaugurated in 1955, whose main function is to coordinate defence, economic, and social policy

Western Front *n.* the battle line between the French and British armies and the German armies in western Europe during World War I. It extended from Belgium to the Swiss border.

Western Ghats mountain range in southern India, forming the western edge of the Deccan plateau. The highest peak is Doda Betta, 2,637 m/8,652 ft.

western grey kangaroo *n.* a large grey kangaroo found in the scrubland of southern and western Australia. Latin name: *Macropus fuliginosus.*

western hemisphere *n.* the half of the Earth that is to the west of the Greenwich meridian, including North and South America and portions of western Europe and Africa

western hemlock *n.* a coniferous tree that is native to western North America but widely grown as an ornamental for its attractive drooping foliage, and for timber. Latin name: *Tsuga heterophylla.*

westernise *vti.* = **westernize**

Western Isles ♦ Hebrides

westernism /wéstərnizəm/, **Westernism** *n.* **1.** EUROPEAN OR AMERICAN CUSTOM a custom or practice typical of the countries of Europe and North and South America **2.** TERM USED IN THE WEST a word or idiom chiefly used in the western part of a country or region, especially the western United States

westernize /wéstər nīz/ (**-izes, -izing, -ized**), **westernise** (**-ises, -ising, -ised**) *v.* **1.** *vti.* ADOPT WESTERN CUSTOMS to adopt or cause a person, country, or culture to adopt the customs, practices, or beliefs of the people of Europe or North and South America **2.** *vt.* CHANGE STH TO RESEMBLE WESTERN PRACTICE to change a law, custom, practice, or belief so that it resembles or is replaced by its European or North American counterpart —**westernization** /wéstər nī záysh'n/ *n.*

western larch *n.* a tall coniferous tree, native to western North America, that has purplish-grey, deeply-fissured bark. Latin name: *Larix occidentalis.*

westernmost /wéstərn mōst/ *adj.* situated farthest west

western red cedar *n.* **1.** CONIFER OF WESTERN N AMERICA a coniferous tree native to the Pacific coast of North America but widely grown for timber It has a narrow conical crown with an erect tip. Latin name: *Thuja plicata.* = **red cedar 2.** WESTERN RED CEDAR WOOD the wood of the western red cedar tree

western roll *n.* a high jump in which the body is half-turned over the bar

western saddle, Western saddle *n.* a large and heavy saddle for a horse with a raised pommel. It was originally used on ranches in the western and southwestern United States. US term **stock saddle**

Western Sahara region in northwestern Africa formerly ruled by Spain. It was partitioned between Morocco and Mauritania in 1976 and fully occupied by Morocco in 1979. Area: 267,000 sq. km/103,000 sq. mi. Former name **Spanish Sahara**

Western Samoa former name for **Samoa** (until 1997)

Western Standard Time *n.* a time zone lying west of the 120th meridian and including the whole of Western Australia. It is seven to nine hours ahead of GMT.

western swing *n.* a type of country and western music played on guitars, steel guitars, fiddles, and other instruments that incorporates elements of swing music

Western Wall *n.* a wall in Jerusalem believed to be part of the Second Temple, destroyed in AD 70 by the Romans. It is used by some Jewish people as a place for prayer and lamentation.

West Germanic *n.* a subgroup within the Germanic languages that consists of English, German, Yiddish, Dutch, Flemish, Afrikaans, and Frisian

West Germany republic of western Europe from 1945 to 1990, formed from the territories of Germany occupied by the British, French, and US forces at the end of World War II. In 1990 it was reunited with East Germany. Area: 248,577 sq. km/95,976 sq. mi. Official name **Federal Republic of Germany** —**West German** *n., adj.*

West Goth *n.* PEOPLES = **Visigoth**

West Highland terrier, West Highland white terrier *n.* a small terrier of a hardy long-haired breed with a pure white coat, originally bred for hunting small mammals but now kept as a pet [From its having originated in the West Highlands of Scotland]

West Indian *n.* sb who was born or brought up in the West Indies, who has citizenship of one of the islands of the West Indies, or whose ancestors lived in or came from the West Indies —**West Indian** *adj.*

West Indies chain of islands that separate the Caribbean Sea from the Atlantic Ocean. They consist of three main island groups, the Greater Antilles, the Lesser Antilles, and the Bahamas, that extend from

the southeastern tip of Florida to the coast of Venezuela.

westing /wésting/ *n.* **1.** DISTANCE WEST the distance due west between two points on a course heading in a westwards direction **2.** TRAVEL WESTWARDS travel or progress in a westwards direction

West Lothian /-lóthi ən/ council area and historic county in central Scotland, on the Firth of Forth. Population: 147,870 (1996). Area: 425 sq. km/164 sq. mi.

Westm. *abbr.* Westminster

Westmeath /wést meeth/ county in Leinster Province, in the central part of the Republic of Ireland. The administrative centre is Mullingar. Population: 63,314 (1996). Area: 1,764 sq. km/681 sq. mi.

Westminster /wéstminstər/ borough in central London, England. Many notable buildings including the Houses of Parliament, Buckingham Palace, and Westminster Abbey are located there. Population: 195,300 (1995).

Westminster Abbey *n.* a large Gothic church in London, originally a Benedictine abbey, in which British monarchs are traditionally crowned

west-northwest *n.* COMPASS POINT BETWEEN W AND NW the direction or compass point midway between west and northwest ■ *adj., adv.* IN THE WEST-NORTHWEST in, from, facing, or towards the west-northwest —**west-northwesterly** *adj., adv.*

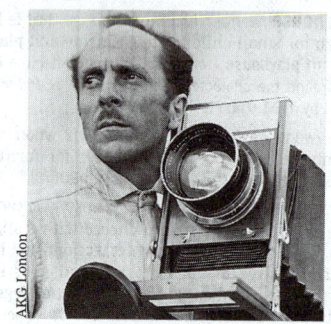

Edward Weston: Photographed in 1923 by Tina Modotti

Weston /wést'n/, **Edward** (1886–1958) US photographer. His sharp, semiabstract photographs often magnify details of natural objects.

Weston-super-Mare /wéstən soŏpər máir/ resort town on the coast of Somerset, southwestern England. Population: 65,000 (1991).

West Pakistan /west paáki staán/ western area of Pakistan from 1947 to 1971, when the nation was geographically divided. West Pakistan comprised the provinces of Baluchistan, North-West Frontier Province, Punjab, and Sind, and it became the state of Pakistan in 1971 after East Pakistan seceded to become independent Bangladesh.

Westphalia /west fáyli ə/ former province in northeastern Germany, in the present-day state of North-Rhine Westphalia. The Peace of Westphalia, signed at Münster and Osnabrück in 1648, marked the end of the Thirty Years' War.

Westphalian /west fáyli ən/ *n.* sb who lives in or was born or brought up in Westphalia [Early 17thC] —**Westphalian** *adj.*

Westphalian ham *n.* German ham that is cured and eaten raw, very thinly sliced

West Point *n.* the site of the United States Military Academy, on the Hudson River in New York State, or the Academy itself

Westport /wést pawrt/ town on the northwestern coast of the South Island, New Zealand. It is the commercial centre of a coal-mining region. Population: 4,236 (1996).

West Riding /west ríding/ historic county in Yorkshire, northern England, abolished in 1974

West Saxon *n.* **1.** LANG WESSEX DIALECT OF OLD ENGLISH the dialect of Old English in use in Wessex during Anglo-Saxon times and the main literary dialect of the language. ◊ **Anglian, Kentish 2.** PEOPLES SB FROM

ANGLO-SAXON WESSEX sb who was born in or lived in Wessex during Anglo-Saxon times —**West Saxon** adj.

west-southwest n. **COMPASS POINT BETWEEN W AND SW** the direction or compass point midway between west and southwest ■ adj., adv. **IN THE WEST-SOUTHWEST** in, from, facing, or towards the west-southwest —**west-southwesterly** adj., adv.

West Sussex /west sússiks/ county in southeastern England, formed in 1974 from the former county of Sussex. Chichester is the administrative centre. Population: 731,500 (1995). Area: 1,989 sq. km/768 sq. mi.

West Virginia

West Virginia /wést vər jínni ə/ state of the eastern United States bordered by Ohio, Pennsylvania, Maryland, Virginia, and Kentucky. Capital: Charleston. Population: 1,815,787 (1997). Area: 62,761 sq. km/24,232 sq. mi. —**West Virginian** n., adj.

westward /wéstwərd/ adj. **TOWARDS OR IN THE WEST** ■ adv. **TOWARDS THE WEST** in a westerly direction ■ n. **POINT IN THE WEST** a direction towards or a point in the west [Old English westweard] —**westwardly** adv., adj. —**westwards** adv.

WORD KEY: USAGE
---

westward or **westwards**? **Westward** is the only form available for the adjective: In a westward direction, but **westwards** is commonly used as well as **westward** for the adverb: The ship was moving slowly westward/westwards.

Vivienne Westwood

Westwood /wést wŏŏd/, **Vivienne** (b. 1941) British fashion designer. She was a pioneer of punk fashion in the late 1970s and is known for her unconventional costumes.

wet /wet/ adj. **1. SOAKED WITH WATER** covered, soaked, or dampened with water or some other liquid **2. NOT YET DRY** not completely dry **3. NOT YET SET** not yet firm or solidified ○ wet cement **4. RAINY, SHOWERY, MISTY, OR FOGGY** characterized by rain, showers, mist, or fog ○ Come in out of the wet. **5. WITH RAINY WEATHER** subject to frequent heavy rain, showers, mist, or fog ○ a wet climate **6. USING OR DONE WITH LIQUID** using or done in water or another liquid **7. UNASSERTIVE** regarded as weak and lacking resolution or decisiveness (insult) **8. US, Can ALLOWING SALES OF ALCOHOL** allowing the legal manufacture, storage, transportation, and sale of alcoholic beverages (informal) ○ a wet town **9. US FAVOURING SALES OF ALCOHOL** favouring the legal manufacture, storage, transportation, and sale of alcoholic beverages (informal) ○ a wet representative ■ n. **1. LIQUID OR MOISTURE** water or another liquid, or moisture from it **2. RAINY OR DAMP WEATHER** rainy, showery, misty, or foggy weather ○ Come in out of

the wet. **3. Aus NORTHERN AUSTRALIAN WET SEASON** the wet season in northern Australia that lasts from December to March **4. WET GROUND** a wet area or surface **5. UNASSERTIVE PERSON** sb who is regarded as weak and lacking in resolution or decisiveness (insult) **6. LIBERAL CONSERVATIVE** a Conservative politician whose policies some other Conservatives consider not to be sufficiently pure or doctrinaire (informal) **7. US SUPPORTER OF LEGAL SALES OF ALCOHOL** sb who supports the legal manufacture, storage, transportation, and sale of alcoholic beverages (informal) ■ v. (wets, wetting, wet or wetted) **1.** vti. **MAKE OR BECOME WET** to become or cause sth to become damp or soaked with water or some other liquid **2.** vt. **MAKE WET BY URINATING** to cause sth to be damp or soaked with urine **3.** vt. **MAKE TEA** to make tea with boiling water (regional) [Old English wǣt, wǣta (noun), wǣt (adjective), and wǣtan (verb). Ultimately from an Indo-European base meaning 'water, wet', which is also the ancestor of English hydro-, undulate, vodka, and winter.] —**wetly** adv. —**wetness** n. —**wetter** n. ◇ **all wet** US, Can completely mistaken or wrong

---
WORD KEY: SYNONYMS
---

wet, damp, moist, dank, humid, sodden, soaked, soaking, sopping

CORE MEANING: not dry

wet a general word used to cover everything from paint that is not yet quite dry to sth that is completely covered in water; **damp** slightly wet, especially undesirably so; **moist** slightly wet, especially desirably so; **dank** describes a place that is unpleasantly damp and cold and that usually also has a bad smell; **humid** describes air that has a high water content, often also suggesting accompanying heat; **sodden** extremely wet; **soaked** an informal word meaning extremely wet; **soaking** an informal word meaning extremely and undesirably wet; **sopping** an informal word emphasizing that sth is extremely and undesirably wet.

weta /wéttə/ n. a heavy-bodied wingless New Zealand insect that resembles a locust. Genus: Deinacrida. [Mid-19thC. From Maori.]

wetback /wét bak/ n. US a highly offensive term referring to a Mexican person recently arrived in the United States, especially sb who has entered the country illegally to work as a labourer (taboo insult) [Early 20thC. From Mexican immigrants having waded or swum across the Rio Grande river to enter the United States.]

wet bar n. US, Can a small bar equipped with a sink in a house or hotel room, used for mixing alcoholic drinks

wet blanket n. sb who spoils or reduces other people's enthusiasm or enjoyment (informal) [From the use of wet blankets to smother small fires]

wet-bulb thermometer n. a thermometer that records the temperature at which pure water must be evaporated to saturate a given volume of air

wet cell n. a primary cell that contains a free-flowing electrolyte. ◊ **dry cell**

wet dream n. a dream that has sexual content and leads to the ejaculation of semen (offensive in some contexts)

wet fish n. fresh fish for sale, as distinguished from frozen or cooked fish

wet fly n. a fishing lure resembling a fly that slips beneath the surface of the water after it is cast. ◊ **dry fly**

wether /wéthər/ n. a male sheep or goat that has been castrated before becoming sexually mature [Old English weper, from prehistoric Germanic]

wetland /wétlənd/ n. a marsh, swamp, or other area of land where the soil near the surface is saturated or covered with water, especially one that forms a habitat for wildlife (often used in the plural)

wet look n. **1. GLOSSY FINISH ON MATERIAL** a glossy finish on a material that gives an appearance of wetness **2. GLOSSY SHEEN ON THE HAIR** a glossy sheen given to the hair by the use of a special hair gel that gives an appearance of wetness —**wet-look** adj.

wet nurse n. a woman who breast-feeds and takes care of another woman's baby

wet-nurse (wet-nurses, wet-nursing, wet-nursed) vt. **1. BREAST-FEED ANOTHER'S BABY** to breast-feed and take care

of another woman's baby **2. GIVE SB EXCESSIVE CARE** to bestow excessive care or attention on sb (informal disapproving)

wet pack n. a piece or pieces of material dampened with hot or cold water and wrapped around a patient's body for therapeutic purposes

wet rot n. a type of rot that affects moist or wet timber, caused by fungi and characterized by brown discoloration of the wood. ◊ **dry rot**

wet steam n. steam that is under low pressure and contains water droplets. ◊ **dry steam**

wet suit n. a tight-fitting garment worn by a diver, made of foam neoprene rubber or a similar material. It traps a thin insulating layer of water near the skin.

wetting agent n. a chemical agent that makes the surface of a substance less repellent to a liquid and allows the liquid to spread across it more easily

WEU abbr. Western European Union

Wexford /wéksfərd/ **1.** county in Leinster Province, in the southeastern part of the Republic of Ireland. Population: 104,371 (1996). Area: 2,353 sq. km/908 sq. mi. **2.** town, port, and administrative centre of County Wexford, in the Republic of Ireland. Population: 9,544 (1991).

Weymouth /wáyməth/ **1.** resort town and ferry port on the coast of Dorset, England. Population: 46,065 (1991). **2.** town in eastern Massachusetts, south of Boston. Population: 54,013 (1990).

wf, w.f. abbr. PRINTING wrong font

wff abbr. LOGIC well-formed formula

WFTU abbr. World Federation of Trade Unions

wg, WG abbr. **1.** water gauge **2.** wire gauge **3. WG** (Windward Islands) Grenada (international vehicle registration)

Wg Cdr abbr. Wing Commander

W. Glam. abbr. West Glamorgan

Wh abbr. watt-hour

wh. abbr. white

whack /wak/ v. (whacks, whacking, whacked) **1.** vti. **HIT WITH A LOUD SHARP BLOW** to hit sb or sth with a swift sharp blow that produces a loud noise **2.** vt. **PLACE STH CASUALLY AND QUICKLY** to put or place sth somewhere casually and quickly (informal) **3.** vti. **CUT OR CHOP STH** to cut or chop sth with a swift sharp blow ■ n. **1. SHARP BLOW** a swift sharp blow **2. SOUND OF A SHARP BLOW** the sound made by a swift sharp blow **3. ATTEMPT AT STH** an attempt at doing sth (informal) ○ That looks like fun – can I take a whack at it? **4. SHARE OF STH** a share or portion of sth, especially one deserved or due (informal) **5. COST** the amount that sth costs (informal) [Early 18thC. Origin uncertain: probably an imitation of the sound, but perhaps an alteration of THWACK.] —**whacker** n.

whack off vti. an offensive term meaning to masturbate (taboo offensive) (refers to men)

whacked /wakt/ adj. **1. UK, Can EXTREMELY TIRED** very tired or exhausted (informal) **2. US UNDER THE INFLUENCE OF DRUGS** relaxed, excited, or euphoric as a result of taking drugs, especially marijuana (slang)

whacking /wáking/ adj. HUGE very large or impressive (informal) ■ adv. UK, Can EXTREMELY to an extreme degree (informal)

whacko /wákō/ n., adj. = wacko

whacky /wáki/ adj. = wacky

whakapapa /fúkə puppə/ (plural -pa) n. NZ in Maori culture, the genealogy of an individual or family

Whakatane /fúkə taá này/ coastal town in the northeastern part of the North Island, New Zealand. It is a commercial centre for an agricultural and timber region. Population: 17,493 (1996).

whale[1] /wayl/ n. **1. BIG MARINE MAMMAL** a large marine mammal that breathes through a blowhole on the top of its head and has front flippers, no hind limbs, and a flat horizontal tail. Its body is insulated by a thick layer of fatty blubber beneath the skin, and many species live in social groups, communicating by sound. Order: Cetacea. **2. IMPRESSIVE EXAMPLE OF STH** an impressive, very large, or very enjoyable example of sth (informal) ■ vi. (whales, whaling,

whaled) HUNT WHALES to hunt for and kill whales [Old English *hwæl*. Related to German *Wal*.]

whale² /wayl/ (**whales, whaling, whaled**) *vt.* **1.** THRASH SB to beat sb severely as a punishment **2.** *US* DEFEAT SB CONVINCINGLY to defeat sb soundly or completely [Late 18thC. Origin uncertain: perhaps a variant of WALE.]

whaleback /wáyl bak/ *n.* **1.** LARGE AND ROUNDED OBJECT sth large and rounded like the back of a whale, e.g. an ocean wave or a small hill **2.** NAUT SHIP WITH A ROUNDED DECK a cargo vessel with a rounded bow and arched upper deck designed to allow the water from waves breaking on it to run off more easily

whaleboat /wáyl bōt/ *n.* a long, narrow, easily manoeuvred boat with a pointed bow and stern, originally rowed in pursuit of whales but now often powered and used as a lifeboat

whalebone /wáyl bōn/ *n.* **1.** = **baleen 2.** PIECE OF MATERIAL FROM WHALES a piece or strip of a hard elastic material found in some whales, formerly used in making corset stays and whips [13thC. Originally in the sense 'ivory from an animal confused with a whale such as a walrus'.]

whalebone whale *n.* = **baleen whale**

whale catcher *n.* a boat with a harpoon launcher mounted in its bow, used for pursuing and catching whales

Whale Island /wayl-/ uninhabited volcanic island in the Bay of Plenty off the northeastern coast of the North Island, New Zealand. Area: 4 sq. km/2 sq. mi.

whale oil *n.* a yellowish oil manufactured by rendering the blubber of whales, formerly used as a lamp fuel and in making soap and candles

whaler /wáylər/ *n.* **1.** SB ENGAGED IN WHALING INDUSTRY sb who hunts or harpoons whales or who processes killed whales **2.** SHIP FOR HUNTING OR PROCESSING WHALES a ship used for hunting whales or processing killed whales **3.** = **whaleboat**

whale shark *n.* the largest of all sharks, found in warm oceanic waters worldwide, with a white-spotted dark body up to 15 m/50 ft in length. It feeds near the surface on small fish and invertebrates and is not aggressive. Latin name: *Rhincodon typus.*

whaling /wáyling/ *n.* the activity or industry of hunting and processing whales

wham /wam/ *n.* (*informal*) **1.** FORCEFUL BLOW a solid forceful blow or impact **2.** SOUND OF FORCEFUL BLOW the loud noise produced by a solid forceful blow ■ *vti.* (**whams, whamming, whammed**) HIT STH WITH LOUD NOISE to hit or crash into sb or sth with a loud noise (*informal*) ○ *The car whammed into the brick wall.* ■ *interj.* USED TO INDICATE THE SOUND OF BLOW used to imitate the sound of a forceful blow or impact (*informal*) ■ *adv.* SUDDENLY AND FORCEFULLY with a startling or jarring suddenness (*informal*) ○ *I ran wham right into my ex-husband.* [Early 20thC. An imitation of the sound.]

whammy /wámmi/ (*plural* **-mies**) *n.* (*informal*) **1.** JINX a jinx or hex **2.** SEVERE SETBACK sth with unpleasant or damaging consequences [Mid-20thC. Origin uncertain.]

whang¹ /wang/ *n.* **1.** THONG a thong, especially a thong made from leather **2.** UNTANNED ANIMAL HIDE untanned hide from cattle or other animals **3.** *US* OFFENSIVE TERM an offensive term for a penis (*slang offensive*) ■ *vt.* (**whangs, whanging, whanged**) HIT SB SEVERELY to beat, whip, or thrash sb [Early 16thC. Alteration of *thwang*, a variant of THONG.]

whang² /wang/ *n.* **1.** RESOUNDING BLOW a blow that resounds when it hits sth **2.** SOUND OF RESOUNDING BLOW the sound produced by a heavy blow when it hits sth ■ *vti.* (**whangs, whanging, whanged**) HIT WITH RESOUNDING SOUND to hit sth and produce a loud resounding sound [Early 19thC. An imitation of the sound.]

Whangarei /wàangə ráy/ coastal town in the northern part of the North Island, New Zealand. It is a commercial and tourist centre. Population: 45,892 (1996).

whangee /wang ée/ *n.* **1.** PLANTS CHINESE BAMBOO PLANT a bamboo plant, native to China, whose stems are used to make canes and walking sticks. Genus: *Phyllostachys.* **2.** BAMBOO WALKING STICK a walking stick or cane made from a piece of whangee bamboo [Late 18thC. From Chinese (Beijing) *huang* 'bamboo sprouts too old for eating, bamboo'.]

whap *n., vt.* = **whop**

wharf /wawrf/ *n.* (*plural* **wharves** /wawrvz/ *or* **wharfs**) **1.** LANDING PLACE FOR SHIPS a structure built alongside or out into the water as a landing place for boats and ships, sometimes with a protective covering or enclosure **2.** SHORE a riverbank or seashore (*archaic*) ■ *v.* (**wharfs, wharfing, wharfed**) **1.** *vti.* MOOR A BOAT AT A WHARF to moor a vessel at a wharf, or to be moored there **2.** *vt.* UNLOAD OR STORE CARGO ON A WHARF to unload cargo onto or store it on a wharf **3.** *vt.* EQUIP A PLACE WITH A WHARF to provide a place with a wharf or wharves [Old English *hwearf* 'embankment, wharf', via a prehistoric Germanic word (source also of German *Werft* 'shipyard') from a base meaning 'to turn', which also produced English *warp*]

wharfage /wáwrfij/ *n.* **1.** USE OF A WHARF the use of a wharf or wharves **2.** FEE TO USE A WHARF a fee that is paid for the use of a wharf or wharves **3.** WHARVES wharves collectively, especially the wharves in a particular location [15thC]

wharfie /wáwrfi/ *n.* *Aus* a worker at a dock or wharf (*informal*)

wharfinger /wáwrfinjər/ *n.* sb who owns or supervises the running of a wharf or group of wharves [Mid-16thC. Alteration of obsolete *wharfager* (perhaps on the model of *harbinger, messenger,* or *passenger*), from WHARFAGE.]

AKG London

Edith Wharton

Wharton /wáwrt'n/, **Edith** (1862–1937) US writer. She wrote on everything from interior decorating to the art of writing but is best known for her novels, particularly the Pulitzer Prize-winning *The Age of Innocence* (1920). Born **Edith Newbold Jones**

wharve /wawrv/ *n.* a wheel or similar part on a spindle, used as a pulley on a spinning machine or as a flywheel on a spinning wheel [Old English *hweorfa*, from *hweorfan* 'to turn'. Ultimately from a prehistoric Germanic base that is also the ancestor of English *whirl*.]

wharves plural of **wharf**

what /wot/ CORE MEANING: a grammatical word used in direct and indirect questions to request further information, e.g. about the identity or nature of sb, or about the purpose of sth ○ (det) *What time do you make it?* ○ (det) *I'm not sure what kind of sauce goes best with this dish.* ○ (pron) *What are they doing?* ○ (pron) *Do you know what she does for a living?*

1. *det., pron.* THAT WHICH the person or persons that, or the thing or things that ○ (det) *We spent what money we did have.* ○ (pron) *picking their way through what remained of the house* **2.** *det.* EMPHASIZING A REACTION used in exclamations to emphasize a reaction or opinion ○ *What fantastic news!* ○ *What a miserable day it's been.* **3.** *adv.* HOW in what respect or to what degree ○ *What does it matter now that they've gone?* **4.** *adv.* AT A GUESS used to indicate a guess or approximation of an amount or value ○ *It must be, what, ten years since we first met.* **5.** *interj.* EXCLAMATION used as an exclamation when expressing an emotion such as surprise, anger, or disappointment ○ *The plane will be delayed by two hours. – What?* [Old English *hwæt*. Ultimately from an Indo-European word that also produced Latin *quot* 'how many' (source of English *quote*) and English *how*.] ◇ **give sb what for** to scold or punish sb severely (*informal*) ◇ **what about ... 1.** used to suggest that sb or sth be taken into consideration ○ *What about all the money we've already paid then?* **2.** used to suggest that sb might like to do sth ○ *What about going on a fishing trip?* ◇ **what for** asking the reason for or the purpose of sth ◇ **what have you** other things similar to those just mentioned ◇ **what if 1.** used to make a suggestion about a possible course of action **2.** used to ask what might or would happen in a given situation ◇ **what of it?** used to suggest that sth is not important ◇ **what's what** the true facts or actual situation (*informal*) ◇ **what with** used to introduce the reason or reasons for sth ○ *I didn't get there until ten, what with all the traffic and setting out late.*

whatchamacallit /wóchəmə kawlit/ (*plural* **-its** *or* **-um** /wóchəmə kawləm/) *n.* sth whose name is forgotten or is not known [Early 20thC. From a pronunciation of *what you may call it*.]

whatever /wot évvər/ CORE MEANING: a grammatical word used to refer to everything of a particular type, without limitation ○ (pron) *Feel free to say whatever you like.* ○ (det) *He lost whatever interest he may have had in it.*

1. *pron., adj.* NO MATTER WHAT being the case in all circumstances ○ (pron) *She always seems to succeed, whatever she does.* ○ (adj) *Whatever problem you come up with they'll deal with.* **2.** *pron.* EMPHATIC 'WHAT' an emphatic form of 'what' used to express an emotion such as surprise or perplexity ○ *Whatever is the matter now?* **3.** *adv.* OF ANY KIND used for emphasis ○ *I can see no reason whatever why you shouldn't go.* **4.** *adv.* EXPRESSING MILD DISAGREEMENT used to indicate that the speaker disagrees with what has just been said but is not prepared to argue (*informal*) ○ *OK, if that's what you think, whatever.* [14thC] ◇ **or whatever** used to refer generally to sth else of the same kind ○ *any tool such as a hoe, fork, or spade, or whatever*

WORD KEY: USAGE

whatever or **what ever**? ***Whatever***, written as one word, is a relative pronoun used in statements or commands: *I'll have whatever you're having. Take whatever things you need. I don't want it, whatever it is.* It is also spelled as one word as an adverb used to reinforce negative statements: *I've no idea whatever about that.* ***What ever*** is sometimes written as two words when each word retains its separate meaning and the expression is equivalent to *what on earth*, usually in questions: *What ever are they doing?*

whatnot /wót not/ *n.* **1.** SB THE SAME OR SIMILAR sth of the same or a similar kind **2.** FURNITURE SET OF SHELVES a set of light shelves for displaying small ornamental items **3.** STH UNIMPORTANT sth nondescript, trivial, or unimportant [Late 16thC. From *what not?* Originally in the sense 'everything'.]

what's /wots/ *contr.* **1.** what is **2.** what has **3.** what does

whatshername /wótsər naym/ *pron.* a woman or girl whose name you have forgotten or do not know (*informal*)

whatshisname /wótsiz naym/ *pron.* a man or boy whose name has been forgotten or is not known (*informal*)

whatsit /wótsit/ *n.* sth whose name you have forgotten or do not know (*informal*) [Contraction of *what-is-it*]

whatsitsname /wótsits naym/ *pron.* sth whose name you have forgotten or do not know (*informal*)

whatsoever /wót sō évvər/ *adv.* AT ALL used to emphasize a negative statement, after words such as 'none', 'no one', and 'anyone' ○ *Did you have any doubts? – None whatsoever.* ■ *pron., det.* WHATEVER whatever (*archaic*) [13thC]

whaup /wawp/ *n.* *Scotland* = **curlew** [Mid-16thC. An imitation of the sound of its cry.]

wheal /weel/ *n.* = **weal**

wheat /weet/ *n.* **1.** GRASS WITH EDIBLE GRAIN an annual grass, native to southwestern Asia and the Mediterranean, some types of which are widely cultivated in temperate regions for their edible grains. The numerous varieties of cultivated wheat are based on three main species: bread wheat, durum or hard wheat, and emmer. Genus: *Triticum.* **2.** GRAIN HARVESTED FROM THE WHEAT PLANT the grain harvested from the wheat plant, which is ground into flour and used to make bread, pasta, and other foods **3.** PALE YELLOW COLOUR a pale yellow or light yellow colour ■ *adj.* PALE YELLOW pale or light yellow in colour [Old

English *hwǣte*, literally 'that which is white'. Ultimately from an Indo-European word meaning 'white', which also produced English *white*; from the 'white' flour produced from the grain.]

wheatear /weé eer/ *n.* a small thrush found in Europe, Asia, Africa, and North America, typically having a white rump and black face. Genus: *Oenanthe*. [Late 16thC. Back-formation from *wheatears*, probably (by folk etymology from WHEAT + EAR) from assumed *whiteeres*, literally '(bird with a) white arse' (with white feathers on its rump).]

wheaten /weé t'n/ *adj.* **1.** FOOD **MADE FROM WHEAT** made from or with wheat or milled wheat flour **2.** COLOURS **PALE YELLOW** pale or light yellow in colour ■ *n.* COLOURS **PALE YELLOW COLOUR** a pale yellow or light yellow colour [Old English *hwǣten*]

wheat germ *n.* the embryonic centre of the wheat grain, rich in B vitamins, that is sold milled finely and sometimes toasted for sprinkling over cereals or used in cooking

wheatgrass /weé t graass/ *n.* wheat grains sprouted to a height of around 17 cm/7 in, cut, and pulped to produce a highly nutritious juice that is drunk in very small quantities

wheatmeal /weé t meel/ *n.* wheat flour that has had some of the bran and germ removed. Wholemeal retains all the bran and germ; white flour has all of it removed. [Old English *hwǣtemelu*]

wheat rust *n.* **1.** FUNGAL DISEASE OF WHEAT a disease of wheat caused by various fungi and marked by blackish, brownish, or yellowish streaks on the leaves and stems **2.** FUNGUS CAUSING WHEAT DISEASE a fungus that causes rust in wheat

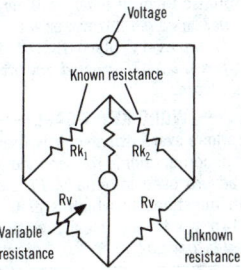

Wheatstone bridge

Wheatstone bridge /weé t stǝn-/ *n.* a device consisting of an electrical circuit, three known resistances, and a galvanometer that is used for measuring an unknown resistance [Late 19thC. Named after its inventor, Sir Charles *Wheatstone* (1802–75), an English physicist.]

wheatworm /weé t wurm/ (*plural* **-worms** *or* **-worm**) *n.* a small nematode worm that lives as a parasite on and is destructive to wheat. Latin name: *Anguina tritici*.

whee /wee/ *interj.* used to express exhilarating or unrestrained joy, pleasure, or excitement [Early 20thC. Natural exclamation.]

wheech /hweekh/ (**wheeches, wheeching, wheeched**) *vt.* *Scotland* to take sth or put sth somewhere with a swift and energetic movement

wheedle /weéd'l/ (**-dles, -dling, -dled**) *v.* **1.** *vti.* COAX SB to coax or try to persuade sb to do sth using flattery, guile, or other indirect means **2.** *vt.* OBTAIN STH BY WHEEDLING to obtain sth from sb by coaxing, flattery, guile, or other indirect means of persuasion [Mid-17thC. Origin uncertain: perhaps from German *wedeln* 'to fawn, cringe, wag the tail', from *Wedel* 'tail, fan', or from Old English *wǣdlian* 'to beg'.] —**wheedler** *n.* —**wheedlingly** *adv.*

wheel /weel/ *n.* **1.** ROTATING ROUND PART a ring or disc that revolves or is turned by a central shaft or pin, sometimes having a central hub with radiating spokes attached to a circular rim (*often used in combination*) ○ *a wagon wheel* **2.** MECH ENG ROUND MACHINE PART THAT TURNS ANOTHER a rotating circular part of a mechanism, often with projections on the outer edge, used to turn another part **3.** STEERING WHEEL a steering wheel (*informal*) **4.** SPINNING WHEEL a spinning

wheel (*informal*) **5.** CASTOR a small rotating or swivelling circular part fitted to the base of sth such as a piece of furniture or luggage to make it easier to move **6.** POTTER'S WHEEL a potter's wheel (*informal*) **7.** MEDIEVAL TORTURE DEVICE a medieval instrument of torture in the form of a large wheel to which the victim was tied. The outstretched arms and legs of the victim were usually broken with a metal bar. **8.** ROTATING FIREWORK a flat round or coiled firework that spins as it burns (*often used in combination*) **9.** WHEEL OF FORTUNE an imaginary wheel said to be spun by fate **10.** GAMBLING ROUND FRAME SPUN IN GAMBLING a circular device that is spun in games of chance such as roulette in order to determine who wins in a random way **11.** STH RESEMBLING A WHEEL sth that resembles a wheel in shape, form, or function **12.** TURN a turn or revolution **13.** MOVEMENT IN A CIRCLE a turning, spinning, pivoting, or circular movement **14.** MIL MILITARY FORMATION a military formation in which the inner unit remains in one place, as a pivot, while the outer units change direction and make an arc around it. It is used in marching performances by a troop of soldiers and displays by a fleet of ships. **15.** POETRY SET OF RHYMING LINES a group of rhyming lines that end a stanza of verse. They are usually shorter than the other lines and often occur in a group of four. ■ **wheels** *npl.* **1.** CAR a car, especially for personal use (*slang*) **2.** DRIVING FORCE OR WORKINGS the system or influences controlling the way sth functions or operates ○ *the wheels of government* ■ *v.* (**wheels, wheeling, wheeled**) **1.** MOVE ON WHEELS to push sth that has wheels or to roll along ○ *wheeled her bicycle up the steep hill* **2.** *vt.* TRANSPORT SB IN A WHEELED OBJECT to move or carry sb or sth in a conveyance with wheels such as a trolley or wheelchair ○ *wheeled the patient out of the room* **3.** *vt.* PROVIDE STH WITH WHEELS to fit sth with a wheel or wheels **4.** *vi.* TURN QUICKLY to move quickly in a circle **5.** *vi.* MAKE A CIRCULAR MOVEMENT to do sth with a circular or curving movement ○ *Her arms wheeled frantically in the air as she tried to signal for help.* **6.** *vi.* MOVE SMOOTHLY to move smoothly and easily ○ *He wheeled through the gathering, making all his appointed stops.* [Old English *hwēol*. Ultimately from an Indo-European word meaning 'to go round', which is also the ancestor of English *cycle* and *encyclopedia*.] —**wheelless** *adj.* ◇ **wheel and deal** to use complex and skilful, sometimes slightly dishonest, negotiating techniques in order to secure sth

wheel about *vi.* **1.** TURN ROUND QUICKLY to turn round quickly or suddenly **2.** REVERSE FORMERLY FIRM OPINION to reverse or radically change an opinion, position, practice, or belief

wheel in *vi.* to approach or enter a place quickly and confidently (*informal*)

wheel out *v.* **1.** *vt.* BRING SB OR STH FORWARD to present sb or use sth readily or repeatedly **2.** *vi.* LEAVE QUICKLY to leave a place quickly (*informal*)

wheel round, wheel around *vi.* = wheel about

wheel and axle *n.* a simple machine, often used to raise or lower loads, typically consisting of a cylindrical drum and wheel mounted on the same axle with ropes wound about each. Depending on the relative diameters of the drum and wheel, various levels of mechanical advantage can be achieved.

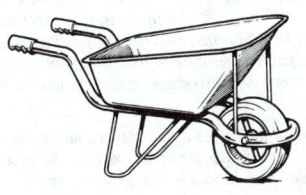

Wheelbarrow

wheelbarrow /weel barō/ *n.* CONTAINER WITH A WHEEL AND HANDLES a small cart used to transport things, usually in the form of an open container with a single wheel at the front and two handles at the back ■ *vt.* (**-rows,**

-rowing, -rowed) MOVE STH IN A WHEELBARROW to move or transport sth in a wheelbarrow

wheelbase /weel bayss/ *n.* the distance between the front axle and the rear axle of a motor vehicle, usually measured in inches. It determines how sharply the vehicle can turn in a given direction.

wheel bug *n.* a large and powerful insect belonging to the assassin bug family that preys on other insects and has an outgrowth on its back resembling a gear. Latin name: *Arilus cristatus*.

wheelchair /weel chair/ *n.* a chair with two small wheels at the front and two large wheels at the sides, used as a way of moving around by sb who cannot walk. Wheelchairs may be propelled by turning the large wheels, by sb pushing from behind, or by a small motor.

wheelchair housing *n.* houses and flats designed or adapted for people who use wheelchairs to enable them to move around easily

wheel clamp *n.* a metal device fitted over the wheel of an illegally parked car to immobilize it until a fine is paid. US term **Denver boot**

wheeled /weel'd/ *adj.* equipped with wheels or a particular number of wheels (*often used in combination*) ○ *a three wheeled vehicle*

wheeler /weélǝr/ *n.* **1.** AUTOMOT WHEELED VEHICLE a vehicle that has a particular number of wheels (*used in combination*) ○ *an eighteen-wheeler* **2.** SB WHO WHEELS sb or sth that wheels or pushes sth with wheels **3.** WHEEL MAKER OR REPAIRER sb who makes or repairs wheels, especially the wheels of carriages or wagons used in former times

Wheeler /weélǝr/, **Sir Mortimer** (1890–1976) British archaeologist. He was noted for his excavations in the Indus Valley and for his scientific approach to archaeological investigation. Full name **Robert Eric Mortimer Wheeler**

wheeler-dealer *n.* sb who uses complex and skilful and perhaps slightly dishonest negotiating techniques to obtain what he or she wants, especially in business or politics (*informal*)

wheel horse *n.* US, Can a steady, diligent, and reliable worker, especially in a political organization

wheelhouse /weel howss/ (*plural* **-houses** /-howziz/) *n.* NAUT = **pilot house**

wheelie /weéli/ *n.* a manoeuvre performed on a moving or stationary bicycle or motorcycle in which the rider raises the front wheel off the ground and balances on the back wheel

wheelie bin *n.* a large rubbish bin that has two wheels at either side of its base so that it can be manoeuvred easily

wheel lock *n.* in some old firearms, a firing mechanism in which a steel spring-wound wheel strikes sparks from a piece of iron pyrites

wheelman /weélmǝn/ (*plural* **-men** /-mǝn/), **wheel man** (*plural* **wheel men** /-mǝn/) *n.* US NAUT = **helmsman** [Mid-19thC]

wheel of fortune, Wheel of Fortune *n.* a revolving wheel said to determine random changes in the course of sb's life, used as a symbol of the inconstancy of fortune

wheel-thrown *adj.* made by being turned on a potter's wheel

wheelwork /weel wurk/ *n.* an arrangement of interlocking wheels or gears within a machine or other device, e.g. the gear train in a mechanical timepiece

wheelwright /weel rīt/ *n.* sb who makes or repairs wheels, especially the wheels of carriages and wagons

wheen /ween/ *n.* Scotland a considerable amount or number (*nonstandard*) [14thC. Representing Old English *hwēne* 'somewhat', a form of *hwōn* 'a few'.]

wheesh /hweesh/, **wheesht** /hweesht/ *interj.* Scotland CALL FOR SILENCE used to command a person or a group to be silent (*informal*) ■ *vti.* (**wheeshes, wheeshing, wheeshed; wheeshts, wheeshting, wheeshted**) Scotland BE SILENT to silence sb or sth, or become or remain silent ■ *n.* Scotland SILENCE the state or condition of making no noise (*informal*) [Imitative of the sound of hushing sb]

wheeze /weez/ *v.* (**wheezes, wheezing, wheezed**) **1.** *vi.* **BREATHE WITH A HOARSE WHISTLING SOUND** to breathe with an audible whistling sound and with difficulty, usually because of a respiratory disorder such as asthma **2.** *vt.* **SAY STH WITH A NOISY WHISTLING SOUND** to say or express sth while breathing noisily and with difficulty **3.** *vi.* **MAKE A WHISTLING OR PUFFING SOUND** to make a noisy whistling or puffing sound that resembles wheezing ○ *The old locomotive wheezed and puffed up the steep slope.* ■ *n.* **1. NOISY BREATHING SOUND** noisy and difficult breathing, or the hoarse whistling sound of this **2. CLEVER IDEA** a good idea or clever plan (*dated informal*) **3. OFTEN REPEATED JOKE** a hackneyed story, joke, or saying (*informal*) [15thC. Origin uncertain: perhaps from Old Norse *hvæsa* 'to hiss'. Ultimately an imitation of the sound.] —**wheezer** *n.* —**wheezily** *adv.* —**wheeziness** *n.* —**wheezy** *adj.*

whelk[1] /welk/ (*plural* **whelk** *or* **whelks**) *n.* a predatory marine gastropod mollusc with a conical spiralling shell. Some kinds of whelk are edible. Family: Buccinidae. [Old English *weoloc*, altered perhaps by association with WHELK[2]]

whelk[2] /welk/ *n.* a raised spot or mark on the skin such as a pimple, boil, or weal [Old English *hwylca* 'pustule, tumour'] —**whelky** *adj.*

whelm /welm/ (**whelms, whelming, whelmed**) *vt.* (*literary*) **1. COVER WITH WATER** to engulf or submerge sth in water **2. OVERWHELM** to overpower or overburden sb or sth [14thC. Origin uncertain: probably an alteration of Old English *āhwylfan* 'to cover over, submerge', influenced by *helmian* 'to cover'.]

whelp /welp/ *n.* **1. YOUNG ANIMAL** a young animal, especially the young of carnivorous mammals such as wolves, lions, bears, and dogs **2. RUDE YOUNG MAN** a boy or young man regarded as showing inappropriate boldness or lack of deference (*insult*) **3. CHILD** a child or young person (*dated humorous*) **4.** NAUT **RIDGE ON CAPSTAN OR WINDLASS** a projection on the barrel of a capstan or windlass **5.** MECH ENG **TOOTH ON A WHEEL** a tooth on a sprocket wheel ■ *vti.* (**whelps, whelping, whelped**) **1. BEAR YOUNG** to give birth to young (*refers to animals, especially carnivores*) **2. GIVE BIRTH** to give birth to a child (*dated disapproving*) [Old English *hwelp*, of prehistoric Germanic origin]

when /wen/ CORE MEANING: an adverb used to ask at what time or at what point things happen ○ *When can we expect you?* ○ *When should you use your rearview mirror?*

1. *conj.* **WHILE** at or during the time that ○ *When I was a child, I lived in the country.* **2.** *conj.* **AS SOON AS** as soon as sb does sth or sth happens ○ *Call me when you get home.* **3.** *conj.* **AT SOME POINT** at some point during an activity, event, or circumstance ○ *We got him when he was still a pup.* **4.** *conj.* **EACH TIME** each time sth happens ○ *When it thunders the whole house shakes.* **5.** *conj.* **IF** considering the fact that ○ *Why walk when you can ride?* **6.** *conj.* **ALTHOUGH** in spite of the fact that ○ *They think I'm really easygoing, when in fact I'm not.* **7.** *adv.* **AT OR DURING WHICH TIME** used to indicate a time at or during which sth happens ○ *He remembered a time when he could run a mile without any difficulty.* **8.** *n.* **UNSPECIFIED TIME PERIOD** used to refer to the time that sth happened or will happen (*often used in the plural*) ○ *We're having trouble determining the whens and hows of the thing.* [Old English *hwonne, hwænne*. Ultimately from an Indo-European base that is also the ancestor of Latin *quando* (source of English *quandary*).]

WORD KEY: USAGE

See Usage note at *if*.

whenas /wen áz/ *conj.* (*archaic*) **1. WHENEVER** at such time as **2. WHILE** at or during the time that **3. ALTHOUGH** in spite of the fact that

whence /wenss/ *adv.* **FROM WHERE** from what place or source (*formal*) ○ *Can we know whence comes this good luck?* ■ *pron.* **WHICH PLACE** the place or thing previously referred to (*formal*) ○ *that envy whence comes hate* ■ *conj.* **AS A RESULT** from which cause or origin (*formal*) ○ *You have treated her badly, whence her anger.* [13thC. From earlier *whennes*, literally 'of or from when'.]

WORD KEY: USAGE

whence or **from whence**? Both uses now sound old-fashioned or literary in tone, but ***from whence***, as an attempt to bring it up to date, fits rather better in the structures of modern English. In everyday English, however, the word can normally be avoided altogether: *They did not know from whence they came* can easily be recast as *They did not know where they came from.*

whencesoever /wénssō évvər/ *adv., conj.* from whatever cause, origin, or source (*archaic*) ○ *accept the gifts whencesoever they come*

whene'er /wen áir/ *adv., conj.* whenever (*literary*)

whenever /wen évvər/ *conj.* **1. AT ANY TIME** at whatever time ○ *Whenever you need me I'll be there.* **2. EACH AND EVERY TIME** at every time or occurrence ○ *Whenever you're around, the dog growls.* ■ *adv.* **whenever, when ever WHEN** used as an intensive form of 'when' (*informal*) ○ *When ever will you learn?*

WORD KEY: USAGE

whenever or **when ever**? ***Whenever*** is written as one word when it is a conjunction, *Come whenever you can*, or an adverb used informally, *I'll do it at the weekend or whenever.* In questions in which *ever* is a reinforcing word, the two words are usually written separately: *When ever did I say that?*

whensoever /wenssō évvər/ *adv., conj.* used as an intensive form of 'whenever'

whenua /fen ŏŏ ə/ *n.* *NZ* land [From Maori]

when-we *n.* *S Africa* a South African who emigrated from another colonial territory (*informal insult*) [Because such an immigrant stereotypically uses phrases beginning with 'When we', for example 'When we were in Kenya']

where /wair/ CORE MEANING: an adverb used to ask a question about the place sb or sth is in, at, coming from, or going to ○ *Where are my keys?* ○ *Where are you going?* ○ *Guess where I've been. – Where?*

1. *adv., rel adv.* **IN OR TO A PLACE** used to indicate the place in which sth is located or happens ○ *I want to live where it's warm.* ○ *Nobody really knew where she had gone.* ○ *They went to the beach, where they spent the afternoon.* **2.** *adv.* **WHAT PURPOSE** used to ask questions about the purpose or goal of sth ○ *Where will all your hard work get you?* **3.** *rel adv.* **IN ANY SITUATION** in any situation in which ○ *Where there's life, there's hope.* ○ *They're at a stage where they can now talk about their problems.* **4.** *n.* **UNKNOWN PLACE** used to refer to an unspecified place or event (*usually used in the plural*) ○ *Let us know the wheres and whens of your itinerary.* [Old English *hwær, hwar*. Ultimately from an Indo-European base that is also the ancestor of English *who, when,* and *why*.]

whereabouts /wáir ə bowts/ *adv.* **IN WHAT PLACE** in, at, or near what location ○ *Do you know whereabouts the hotel is?* ○ *I've forgotten whereabouts I parked the car.* ■ *n.* **LOCATION OF SB OR STH** the approximate place where sb or sth is ○ *Could you give us any information regarding the whereabouts of your brother?*

whereafter /wair aáftər/ *rel adv.* after which time or event (*formal*) ○ *She left, whereafter he also departed.*

whereas /wair áz/ *conj.* **1. WHILE IN CONTRAST** while on the other hand ○ *She was saving money, whereas you were living in the fast lane.* **2. BECAUSE** for the reason that (*formal*) ○ *Whereas you've proven your worth, you're welcome to join the team.* **3. CONNECTING SERIES** used to introduce each clause in a series (*formal*)

whereat /wair át/ *rel adv.* **TO OR AT WHICH PLACE** towards or at which place (*archaic*) ■ *conj.* **BECAUSE OF WHICH** because or as a consequence of which (*archaic*)

whereby /wair bī/ *rel adv.* by means of or through which ○ *the invention whereby he made his millions*

where'er /wair áir/ *adv., rel adv.* wherever (*literary*)

wherefore /wáir fawr/ *n.* **REASON** a reason or purpose for sth ○ *I don't want to know the whys or the wherefores of your decision.* ■ *adv.* (*archaic*) **1. THEREFORE** for the foregoing reason **2. FOR WHAT REASON** for what reason or purpose

wherefrom /wair fróm/ *adv.* from what place or origin (*archaic*) ○ *Do we know wherefrom this stranger comes?*

wherein /wair ín/ *adv.* **HOW** in what particular way or respect (*archaic*) ○ *Wherein did I misspeak myself?* ■ *rel adv.* (*archaic*) **1. WHERE** in which particular place ○ *the country wherein they dwelled* **2. DURING WHICH** during the time which ○ *the years wherein we were ignorant and happy*

whereinto /wair ín too/ *rel adv.* into which place or thing (*archaic*)

whereof /wair óv/ *rel adv.* of or about what thing or person (*formal or archaic*) ○ *Do you know whereof you speak?*

whereon /wair ón/ *adv.* on which thing or place (*archaic or formal*) ○ *the couch whereon she lay*

wheresoever /wáirssō évvər/ *adv., conj.* used as an emphatic form of 'wherever' (*archaic*)

whereto /wair tóo/, **whereunto** /wair ún too/ *adv.* where or to which (*archaic formal*) ○ *the place whereto you've brought me*

whereupon /wáirə pón/ *conj.* **AT WHICH POINT** at which time or as a result of (*formal*) ○ *The rain began to come down hard, whereupon we ran for the house.* ■ *adv.* **ON WHICH** on or upon which (*archaic or formal*) ○ *the pillow whereupon she laid her head*

wherever /wair évvər/ *rel adv.* **TO ANY PLACE** in, at, or to any place ○ *I'll go wherever you go.* ■ *adv.* **1. NO MATTER WHERE** at or in an indefinite place ○ *I'll sleep on the couch, the floor, wherever.* **2. AT AN UNKNOWN PLACE** to, in, or at an unknown or unidentified place or position **3. wherever, where ever WHERE INDEED** used as an emphatic form of *where* ○ *Wherever have my glasses gone?* ■ *conj.* **EVERY TIME OR PLACE THAT** on every occasion or in every place that ○ *Take exercise wherever possible.* ○ *I crossed the fields wherever there was a gate.*

WORD KEY: USAGE

wherever or **where ever**? ***Wherever*** is written as one word when it is a conjunction, *You can go wherever you like*, or an adverb used informally, *I'll stop in Paris or wherever.* In questions in which *ever* is a reinforcing word, the two words are usually written separately: *Where ever did they go?*

wherewith /wair wíth/ *rel adv.* with or by means of which (*archaic*) ○ *the tool wherewith the deed was done*

wherewithal /wáirwith awl/ *n.* the money or resources required for a purpose

wherry /wérri/ (*plural* **-ries**) *n.* **1. LIGHT ROWING BOAT** a small light rowing boat used in inland waters **2. ENGLISH COMMERCIAL BARGE** a small barge, once used for commercial purposes in parts of England, now used largely for pleasure cruises [15thC. Origin unknown.] —**wherryman** /wérrimən/ *n.*

whet /wet/ *vt.* (**whets, whetting, whetted**) **1. SHARPEN A TOOL OR WEAPON** to sharpen the cutting edge or blade of a tool or weapon, usually by rubbing it on a stone **2. STIMULATE STH** to make a feeling, sense, or desire more keen or intense ○ *The thought of easy money whetted my enthusiasm for the undertaking.* ■ *n.* **1. SHARPENING OR INTENSIFYING** an act of sharpening, intensifying, or stimulating sth **2. SHARPENING BLOCK** sth that sharpens a cutting edge **3. STH THAT WHETS THE SENSES** sth that stimulates a feeling, sense, or desire, especially a small amount that makes sb want more (*informal*) [Old English *hwettan* 'to sharpen'. Ultimately from a prehistoric Germanic word meaning 'sharp'.] —**whetter** *n.*

whether /wéthər/ *conj.* **1. INTRODUCES ALTERNATIVES** used to indicate alternatives in an indirect question or a clause following a verb that expresses or implies doubt or the possibility of choice ○ *We should try to meet them whether it's raining or not.* **2. INTRODUCES AN INDIRECT QUESTION** used to introduce an indirect question ○ *I wonder whether it's worth the effort.* **3. EITHER** used to introduce doubt regarding two equal possibilities ○ *She said she'd get here whether by car or by train.* [Old English *hwæþer, hweþer*. Ultimately from an Indo-European word that is also the ancestor of English *where* and *other*.] ◇ **whether or no** whatever the circumstances might be

whetstone /wét stōn/ *n.* **1.** STONE FOR SHARPENING A TOOL OR WEAPON a stone used to sharpen the cutting edge or blade of a tool or weapon by rubbing **2.** STH THAT STIMULATES SENSES sth that makes a feeling, sense, or desire more keen or intense [Old English *hwetstān*]

whew /fyoo, hyoo/ *interj.* used to express great relief, surprise, or discomfort [15thC. An imitation of the sound.]

whey /way/ *n.* the watery liquid that separates from the solid part of milk when it turns sour or when enzymes are added in cheesemaking [Old English *hwæg, hweg*, of prehistoric Germanic origin] —**wheyey** *adj.*

wheyface /wáy fayss/ *n.* **1.** PALE FACE a very pale face (*informal*) **2.** SB WITH VERY PALE FACE sb whose face is regarded as too pale (*insult*) —**wheyfaced** *adj.*

whf *abbr.* wharf

which /wich/ CORE MEANING: used to ask for sth to be identified from a known larger group or range of possibilities ○ (det) *Which part of it don't you understand?* ○ (pron) *Which would you like?* ○ (pron) *Which of the colours do you prefer?* ○ (pron) *At which stage do we start to cut our losses?*

1. *pron.* INTRODUCES A RELATIVE CLAUSE used to introduce a clause that provides additional information about sth previously mentioned ○ *The cabin, which we bought last spring, sits high on the dunes.* ○ *A success for which she is to be congratulated.* **2.** *pron.* THAT used to introduce a relative clause that provides necessary information about its antecedent ○ *Please return the money which I loaned to you.* **3.** *pron.* REFERS BACK TO A PHRASE OR SENTENCE used to refer back to an entire verb phrase or sentence ○ *Swimming after eating, which I've told you not to do, can be very dangerous.* **4.** *det., pron.* ONE FROM KNOWN SET one of a range of things or possibilities specified or implied by the immediate context ○ (det) *I can't decide which activity would be the most fun.* ○ (pron) *He decided which to buy and paid the money.* **5.** *det., pron.* INDICATES CHOICE used to indicate one or any number of things ○ (det) *Use which method best suits you.* ○ (pron) *Take which you prefer.* [Old English *hwilc*, literally 'of what form, like what'. Ultimately from a prehistoric Germanic word that is also the ancestor of English *like* and *such*.]

WORD KEY: USAGE

See Usage note at *that*.

whichever /wich évvər/ *det., pron.* used to refer to any one or any number of items in a class ○ (det) *Whichever job you take, starting out will be hard.* ○ (pron) *I'll buy whichever you think best.*

whichsoever /wíchssō évvər/ *pron., det.* whichever (*archaic*)

whicker /wíkər/ (**-ers, -ering, -ered**) *vi.* to neigh softly [Mid-17thC. An imitiation of the sound.] —**whicker** *n.*

whidah *n.* BIRDS = **whydah**

whiff /wif/ *n.* **1.** SLIGHT OR BRIEF ODOUR a faint smell of sth, pleasant or unpleasant, often perceived briefly ○ *a whiff of disinfectant* **2.** TRACE OF STH a slight sign or trace of sth ○ *a whiff of corruption* **3.** GENTLE GUST OR PUFF a short light gust, puff, or breath of wind **4.** SNIFF OF STH a sniff, smell, or brief inhalation of sth ○ *took one whiff of the concoction and started coughing* **5.** NAUT SMALL SKIFF a narrow skiff for one rower **6.** GOLF COMPLETE MISS a swing that completely misses the golf ball ■ *v.* (**whiffs, whiffing, whiffed**) **1.** *vti.* WAFT OR PUFF to come or send sth in short light gusts or puffs ○ *The smoke whiffed and curled around the room.* **2.** *vt.* SNIFF STH to sniff, smell, or inhale sth ○ *The hyena whiffed the night air for predators.* **3.** *vi.* SMELL BAD to have an unpleasant smell (*informal*) **4.** *vi.* GOLF FAIL TO HIT A BALL to swing at and miss a ball completely [Late 16thC. Thought to suggest a light puff of wind that carries a smell.] —**whiffer** *n.*

whiffle /wíff'l/ (**-fles, -fling, -fled**) *v.* **1.** *vi.* BEHAVE ERRATICALLY to be indecisive or unpredictable in thought or action **2.** *vti.* BLOW GENTLY to blow or move in short light variable gusts or puffs, or to blow or move sth in this way **3.** *vi.* WHISTLE to whistle softly [Late 17thC. Formed from WHIFF.]

whiffler /wífflər/ *n.* sb who vacillates or is evasive

whiffletree /wíff'l tree/ *n.* *Northeast US* = **swingletree** [Mid-19thC. Variant of WHIPPLETREE.]

whiffy /wíffi/ (**-ier, -iest**) *adj.* having an unpleasant smell (*informal*)

Whig /wig/ *n.* **1.** MEMBER OF A FORMER BRITISH POLITICAL PARTY a member of a reforming English political party that supported the aristocracy and later the business community, finally becoming the core of the Liberal Party **2.** *US* SUPPORTER OF THE REVOLUTION AGAINST BRITISH CONTROL sb who supported the American side against the British in the War of American Independence **3.** *US* MEMBER OF 19C US POLITICAL PARTY a member of a 19th-century US political party that favoured loose interpretation of the Constitution and opposed the Democratic Party **4.** CONSERVATIVE IN THE BRITISH LIBERAL PARTY a conservative member of the Liberal Party in the United Kingdom **5.** SUPPORTER OF FREE ENTERPRISE sb who opposes government regulation of commerce and the economy **6.** *Scotland* SCOTTISH PRESBYTERIAN a 17th-century Presbyterian in Scotland [Mid-17thC. Shortening of obsolete Scots dialect *whiggamaire*, literally 'horse driver'.] —**Whiggery** *n.* —**Whiggish** *adj.* —**Whiggism** *n.* —**Whiggishly** *adv.* —**Whiggishness** *n.*

WORD KEY: ORIGIN

The Scots word ***Whig*** seems originally to have been used as a contemptuous term for a country dweller, but by the middle of the 17th century it was being applied to Presbyterian supporters in Scotland. It was later adopted as a name for those who opposed the succession of the Catholic King James II, and by 1689 it had established itself as the title of one of the two main British political parties, opposed to the Tories.

whigmaleerie /wígmə leéri/ *n.* *Scotland* a fanciful ornament or trinket [Mid-18thC. Origin unknown.]

while /wīl/ *conj.* **1.** while, whilst AT OR DURING SAME TIME at or during the same time that ○ *We can talk while I fix supper.* **2.** EVEN THOUGH in spite of the fact that ○ *While I admire your tenacity, I cannot support your aims.* **3.** BUT IN CONTRAST and on the contrary ○ *An older car would be cheaper to buy while a newer one might be more reliable.* **4.** *Scotland* UNTIL until ■ *n.* PERIOD OF TIME a period of time or some interval ○ *It's been a while since I saw her.* [Old English *hwīl* 'period of time'. Ultimately from an Indo-European word meaning 'rest, period of rest', which is also the ancestor of English *tranquil* and *quiet*.] ◇ **once in a while** very occasionally ◇ **worth (sb's) while 1.** deserving sb's time, money, or support **2.** rewarding in terms of money or advantage

WORD KEY: USAGE

while or **whilst**? In both the main meanings ('during the time that' and 'whereas'), ***while*** and ***whilst*** are interchangeable, but ***whilst*** is used more in the north of Britain than in the south. Some people (notably Eric Partridge in *Usage and Abusage*) dislike the use of ***while*** to mean 'whereas, although', as in *While we agree with some of what you say, we do not accept your conclusions.* The example that Partridge cited, *The curate read the First Lesson while the Rector read the Second*, is amusingly ambiguous but wilfully contrived, and in practice there is little difficulty in establishing meaning, especially in speech in which intonation clarifies the intended meaning. Indeed ***while*** and ***whilst*** are a good deal more common than *whereas* in this meaning.

while away *vt.* to pass time in an idle, leisurely, and usually pleasant way

whiles /wīlz/ *adv.* SOMETIMES at some times (*archaic*) ■ *conj.* WHILE while (*archaic*)

whilk /wilk/ *pron.* which (*regional or archaic*) [Early 18thC]

whilom /wíləm/ *adv.* FORMERLY at or during some past time (*archaic*) ■ *adj.* FORMER having been at an earlier time (*archaic*) [Old English *hwīlom*, a form of *whīl* (see WHILE)]

whilst /wīlst/ *conj.* = **while** [15thC. Formed from WHILES.]

WORD KEY: USAGE

See Usage note at *while*.

whim /wim/ *n.* **1.** PASSING IMPULSE a sudden thought, idea, or desire, especially one based on impulse rather than reason or necessity **2.** MINING HORSE-DRAWN WINCH a winch used to lift ore or water from a mine, drawn by a horse [Mid-17thC. Origin uncertain: perhaps a shortening of WHIMSY or WHIM-WHAM. The main modern meaning evolved from 'pun' via 'quaint idea'.]

whimberry /wímbəri/ (*plural* **-ries**) *n.* *Wales* a bilberry (*informal*) [Old English *wīnberge*]

whimbrel /wímbrəl/ (*plural* **-brel** *or* **-brels**) *n.* a large shore bird that has a long downward curving bill and breeds in the Arctic. It is related to but smaller than the curlew. Latin name: *Numenius phaeopus.* [Mid-16thC. Origin uncertain: formed from obsolete dialect *whimp* 'to whimper' (with reference to the bird's cry), or from WHIMPER.]

whimper /wímpər/ *v.* (**-pers, -pering, -pered**) **1.** *vi.* SOB SOFTLY to make repeated weak plaintive crying or whining sounds of pain, distress, or fear **2.** *vi.* COMPLAIN PEEVISHLY to complain in a weak, whining, or irritated manner **3.** *vt.* SAY STH PLAINTIVELY to say sth in a plaintive or whining voice ■ *n.* **1.** WHINE a weak plaintive cry or whine **2.** COMPLAINT a feeble or peevish complaint [Early 16thC. Formed from earlier *whimp* 'to whimper', of imitative origin.] —**whimperingly** *adv.*

whimsical /wímzik'l/ *adj.* **1.** FANCIFUL imaginative and impulsive **2.** AMUSING slightly odd, old-fashioned, or playful, especially in an endearing way ○ *He gave me that whimsical smile of his.* **3.** ERRATIC OR UNPREDICTABLE behaving in such a way as to be impossible to predict ○ *She distrusted his whimsical nature.* [Mid-17thC. Formed from WHIMSY.] —**whimsicality** /wìmzi kálləti/ *n.* —**whimsically** /wímzikli/ *adv.* —**whimsicalness** *n.*

whimsy /wímzi/, **whimsey** *n.* (*plural* **-sies;** *plural* **-seys**) **1.** ENDEARING QUAINTNESS OR ODDITY the quality of being quaint, odd, or playfully humorous, especially in an endearing way ○ *There's a touch of whimsy about the old cottage.* **2.** IMPULSIVE NOTION an idea that has no immediately obvious reason to exist ○ *We can't always be catering to their whimsies.* ■ *adj.* (**-sier, -siest**) ENDEARINGLY DIFFERENT having the quality of quaintness or oddness (*archaic*) [Early 17thC. Origin uncertain: probably based on WHIM-WHAM, perhaps modelled on words like *dropsy*.]

whim-wham *n.* a quaint, odd, or fanciful object such as an ornament, toy, or device (*archaic*) ○ *some whim-wham he bought somewhere* [Origin uncertain: perhaps thought to suggest sth frivolous]

whin[1] /win/ (*plural* **whin** *or* **whins**) *n.* = **gorse** [15thC. Origin uncertain: probably from a Scandinavian word related to Old Danish *hvinegræs*, literally 'rough grass'.]

whin[2] /win/ *n.* = **whinstone**

whinchat /wín chat/ (*plural* **-chat** *or* **-chats**) *n.* a small songbird of the thrush family, native to Asia and Europe, that has mottled brown and white plumage and a streaky reddish-brown breast. It is found in meadows. Latin name: *Saxicola rubetra.* [Late 17thC. From WHIN[2] + CHAT 'warbler'.]

whine /wīn/ *v.* (**whines, whining, whined**) **1.** *vi.* MAKE A HIGH SORROWFUL SOUND to cry, moan, or plead with a long, plaintive, high-pitched sound **2.** *vi.* GRUMBLE PEEVISHLY to complain or protest about sth, often in an annoyingly plaintive voice **3.** *vt.* UTTER STH IN A WHINING VOICE to say sth in a plaintive high-pitched voice **4.** *vi.* MAKE A HIGH-PITCHED SOUND to make a continuous high-pitched sound ○ *The wind whined and moaned through the trees.* ■ *n.* **1.** HIGH-PITCHED CRY a long, plaintive, high-pitched cry **2.** PEEVISH COMPLAINT a complaint or protest, especially one made repeatedly in a whining voice **3.** CONTINUOUS HIGH-PITCHED SOUND a long or continuous high-pitched sound ○ *The whine of the jet engines woke me up.* [Old English *hwīnan* '(of an arrow) to whistle through the air'. Ultimately of imitative origin.] —**whiner** *n.* —**whiningly** *adv.* —**whiny** *adj.*

WORD KEY: SYNONYMS

See Synonyms at ***complain***.

whinge /winj/ *vi.* (**whinges, whingeing, whinged**) (*informal*) **1.** GRUMBLE PEEVISHLY to complain annoyingly or continuously about sth perceived as relatively unimportant **2.** MAKE IRRITATING SORROWFUL SOUND to cry or whimper annoyingly or continuously ■ *n.* PEEVISH COMPLAINT an irritable, peevish complaint about sth (*informal*) [Old English *hwinsian* 'to whine'. Ultimately an imitation of the sound of a whining dog.] —**whinger** *n.*

whingeing Pom *n. Aus* an English person, especially one perceived as constantly complaining, particularly about life in Australia (*insult*)

whinny /wínni/ *v.* (**-nies, -nying, -nied**) **1.** *vi.* NEIGH to neigh softly **2.** *vi.* MAKE A NEIGHING SOUND to make a neighing sound, especially when laughing **3.** *vt.* UTTER WITH A NEIGHING SOUND to say or express sth with a neighing sound ■ *n.* (*plural* **-nies**) NEIGHING SOUND a soft neigh or neighing sound [Mid-16thC. An imitation of the sound.]

whinstone /wín stōn/ *n.* a hard, dark, fine-grained rock such as basalt or chert [Early 16thC. From WHIN² + STONE.]

whip /wip/ *v.* (**whips, whipping, whipped**) **1.** *vt.* LASH SB OR STH to strike a person or animal repeatedly with a flexible rod, length of rope, thin strip of leather attached to a handle, or sth similar, especially as a punishment **2.** *vti.* STRIKE AGAINST STH SHARPLY to strike sth or sb very hard, sharply, or repeatedly ○ *The icy rain whipped our faces.* **3.** *vt.* CRITICIZE SB SEVERELY to criticize or reproach sb very strongly or severely **4.** *vti.* MOVE RAPIDLY to move very quickly, forcefully, or suddenly, or to make sth move in this way ○ *She whipped around guiltily as I came in.* **5.** *vt.* MOVE STH WITH RAPID ACTION to move, remove, or produce sth very quickly, suddenly, or forcefully **6.** *vt.* DEFEAT SB to defeat, overcome, or outdo sb (*informal*) **7.** *vt.* COOK BEAT LIQUID UNTIL STIFF to make a food substance such as batter or whipping cream stiff and creamy by adding air to it with short quick movements using a fork, whisk, or electric beater **8.** *vt.* BIND THE END OF A ROPE to wind thread, cord, or twine around the end of a rope or cable to keep it from fraying or ravelling **9.** *vt.* NAUT LIFT STH BY A ROPE AND PULLEY to lift sth by means of a device consisting of a rope passed through a single pulley **10.** *vt.* SEW SEW STH IN WHIPSTITCH to sew the edge of a piece of fabric using whipstitch **11.** *vt.* SPIN TOP to make a top start to spin **12.** *vt.* STEAL to steal sth or remove sth (*informal*) ■ *n.* **1.** INSTRUMENT FOR INFLICTING PAIN a flexible rod, a length of rope, or a thin strip of leather attached to a handle, used to strike people or animals **2.** LASHING STROKE OR BLOW a stroke or blow with a whip or sth similar ○ *a whip across the face* **3.** STH RESEMBLING A WHIP sth that resembles a whip in form, motion, or flexibility **4.** SB WHO USES A WHIP sb who is experienced or skilled in the use of a whip, e.g. the driver of a horse-drawn carriage **5.** POL SB IN CHARGE OF PARTY DISCIPLINE an elected representative in a legislative body such as Parliament or the US Congress who has special responsibility for ensuring discipline and attendance among his or her party's representatives **6.** POL CALL FOR PARTY SOLIDARITY a call issued to a party's elected legislators to ensure they attend for an important vote and vote the party line **7.** POL WEEKLY LEGISLATIVE AGENDA in Parliament, a weekly agenda sent to a party's members that indicates which items are routine, important, or urgent **8.** FOOD SWEET DISH a light creamy dessert made from whipped cream with added sweetening and flavouring **9.** NAUT HOISTING APPARATUS a device that consists of a rope, a pulley, and a snatch block, used to raise heavy cargo **10.** MUSIC FLEXIBLE PERCUSSION INSTRUMENT a percussion instrument with two flexible strips of wood attached in the shape of a V that make a loud clapping sound when they are waved in the air **11.** HUNT = **whipper-in** *n.* **12.** WINDMILL VANE a sail or arm of a windmill **13.** FAIRGROUND AMUSEMENT a ride at an amusement park with small cars that travel with sudden rapid jerking movements round a track **14.** WRESTLING WRESTLING THROW in wrestling, a throw in which an opponent is seized by an outstretched arm and thrown to the floor **15.** *US* LONG FLEXIBLE BRANCH a long, slender, flexible branch of some trees such as some willows ○ *furniture made of willow whips* [13thC. Origin uncertain: probably from Middle Low German or Middle Dutch *wippen* 'to swing', from, ultimately, a prehistoric Germanic base meaning 'to move quickly' (ancestor also of English *wipe*).] ◇ **crack the whip** a children's game in which they join hands in a line and pull each other around sharply

whip in *v.* **1.** *vi.* HUNT CONTROL A PACK OF HOUNDS to keep a pack of hounds under control **2.** *vt.* POL MAKE PARTY MEMBERS CONFORM to keep the members of a political party in line with the party's aims

whip through *vt.* to do sth very quickly (*informal*)

whip up *vt.* **1.** EXCITE STH OR SB to arouse or provoke a strong feeling or reaction in a group of people **2.** MAKE STH RISE UP to stir or disturb sth with force so that it rises or flies up **3.** PREPARE STH RAPIDLY to make sth quickly, especially an impromptu meal (*informal*)

whip bird *n. Aus* **1.** BIRD WITH LOUD WHISTLING CALL in Australia, a bird with a long tail and prominent crest that emits a loud whistling sound that ends with a whipcrack note. Latin name: *Psophodes olivaceus* and *Psophodes nigrogularis.* **2.** BIRD LIKE WHIP BIRD a bird with a call that that resembles that of a whip bird

whipcord /wíp kawrd/ *n.* **1.** STRONG FABRIC a strong cotton or woollen fabric woven with diagonal ribs **2.** CORD USED TO MAKE A WHIP a tough twisted cord used for the flexible part of a whip

whip graft *n.* a way of grafting two plants by inserting the cut end of a scion into a similar cut in a rootstock and tying them securely together until they join

whip hand *n.* **1.** MOST POWERFUL POSITION the most powerful or advantageous position in a particular situation ○ *She has the whip hand.* **2.** HAND HOLDING A WHIP a hand that holds a whip, especially one used to drive horses

whiplash /wíp lash/ *n.* **1.** FLEXIBLE PART OF A WHIP the flexible part of a whip **2.** LASHING STROKE OR BLOW a stroke or blow from a whip, or sth that resembles this in motion, speed, or force **3.** MED INJURY TO THE NECK an injury to the muscles, ligaments, vertebrae, or nerves of the neck caused when the head is suddenly thrown forward and then sharply back

whipper-in /wíppər-/ (*plural* **whippers-in**) *n.* sb who assists a foxhunter in controlling a pack of hounds

whippersnapper /wíppər snapər/ *n.* sb who is impudent and unimportant, especially a young person (*dated*) [Late 17thC. Origin uncertain: perhaps from WHIP + SNAPPER, modelled on earlier *snipper-snapper* 'sb who cracks whips'.]

whipper snipper /wíppər snipər/ *n. Aus* a machine for trimming the edges of lawns

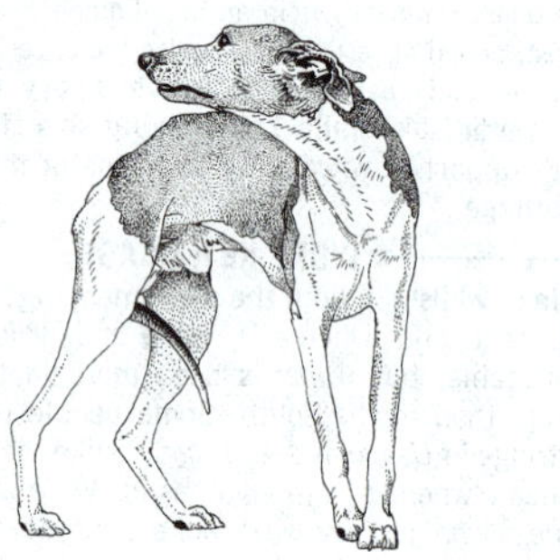

Whippet

whippet /wíppit/ *n.* a fast slender short-haired dog of a breed that resembles but is smaller than a greyhound [Mid-16thC. Formed from WHIP in the sense 'to move quickly'.]

whipping /wípping/ *n.* **1.** PUNISHMENT a beating, spanking, or flogging with a whip or sth similar **2.** CORD BINDING thread, cord, or twine wound round the end of a rope or cable to keep it from fraying or ravelling **3.** SPORTS DEFEAT a convincing defeat (*informal*) ○ *Didn't they give us a whipping in that last game?*

whipping boy *n.* sb who takes the blame or punishment for the mistakes or wrongdoings of more important people [Originally, this referred to a boy raised and educated with a prince. If the prince misbehaved, the whipping boy would be punished in his place (typically by whipping).]

whipping cream *n.* a heavy cream containing a high proportion of butterfat, which causes it to stiffen when whipped

whippoorwill /wíppərwil/ *n.* a common North American nocturnal bird of the nightjar family, with spotted dark plumage and a distinctive song from which its name is derived. Latin name: *Caprimulgus vociferus.*

whipray /wíp ray/ *n.* a marine fish of the ray family that has a flat body, long whip-shaped tail, and venomous spines

whip-round *n.* an informal and often impromptu collection of money from a group of people for a particular purpose, often buying a present for sb (*informal*)

whipsaw /wíp saw/ *n.* SAW WITH FLEXIBLE BLADE any kind of saw that has a flexible blade, e.g. a bandsaw ■ *vt.* (**-saws, -sawing, -sawed, -sawed** *or* **-sawn**) CUT WITH WHIPSAW to saw sth with a whipsaw

whip scorpion *n.* a terrestrial invertebrate related to the scorpion but having a whip-shaped appendage at the end of its abdomen. Order: Uropygi.

whip snake *n.* a fast-moving nonpoisonous snake that pursues its prey, found in North America, Asia, Europe, and Africa. Genus: *Coluber.*

whipstall /wíp stawl/ *n.* a manoeuvre in a small aircraft in which it goes into a vertical climb, pauses briefly, then drops towards the earth nose first

whipstitch /wíp stich/ *n.* OVERSEWING STITCH a small stitch that passes over the edge of a piece of fabric, used to finish the edge or baste two pieces of fabric together ■ *vt.* (**-stitches, -stitching, -stitched**) SEW IN WHIPSTITCH to sew the edge of a piece of fabric using a whipstitch

whipstock /wíp stok/ *n.* the handle of a whip

whiptail /wíp tayl/ *n.* a lizard with a long thin tail found in South America and Mexico. Genus: *Cnemidophorus.*

whipworm /wíp wurm/ *n.* a nematode worm found in human intestines. Its presence usually produces no symptoms but a severe infection with this parasite can cause diarrhoea. Latin name: *Trichuris trichiura.*

whirl /wurl/ *v.* (**whirls, whirling, whirled**) **1.** *vti.* TURN OR SPIN RAPIDLY to turn or spin very quickly, or to make sth revolve in this way **2.** *vti.* MOVE WHILE TURNING QUICKLY to move along while turning or spinning very quickly, or to make sth move along in this way ○ *The dancers whirled round the floor.* **3.** *vi.* FEEL DIZZY OR CONFUSED to seem to spin with dizziness, confusion, or excitement ○ *So much information at one time made my head whirl.* **4.** *vti.* MOVE VERY FAST to move very quickly or make sth move very quickly on a straight or curved course ○ *Cars whirled past on the highway.* ■ *n.* **1.** SPINNING MOTION a rapid turning or spinning movement ○ *gave the prayer wheel a whirl* **2.** STH THAT WHIRLS sth that moves or is moved with a rapid circular or spiral motion ○ *Whirls of dust filled the air.* **3.** SENSATION OF SPINNING a spinning sensation caused, e.g. by confusion, excitement, or dizziness ○ *So much good luck had my head in a whirl.* **4.** THINGS HAPPENING IN QUICK SUCCESSION the bustling activity of an endless series of events or engagements ○ *the whirl and bustle of a large city* **5.** BRIEF TRIP OR GO a short trip, ride, or dance (*informal*) ○ *Let's go for a whirl in my new car.* [13thC. Origin uncertain: probably from Old Norse *hvirfla.* Ultimately from an Indo-European base meaning 'to turn around'.] —**whirler** *n.* —**whirly** *adj.* ◇ **give it** *or* **sth a whirl** to have a try at sth (*informal*)

whirlabout /wúrl ə bowt/ *n.* a turn, spin, or revolution

whirligig /wúrligig/ *n.* **1.** SPINNING TOY any toy that spins or turns very quickly **2.** MERRY-GO-ROUND a merry-go-round or carousel **3.** STH THAT WHIRLS sth that revolves rapidly or changes continuously ○ *Her life's a whirligig since she took over the business.* **4.** INSECTS = **whirligig beetle** [15thC. From *whirling* or *whirly* (see WHIRL) + GIG 'spinning top'.]

whirligig beetle *n.* an aquatic insect with a smooth, oval, flattened body, usually seen spinning around on the surface of calm freshwater in groups. Family: Gyrinidae.

whirling dervish *n.* sb who busily does many things in quick succession ○ *Once we sent out the invitations, he became a whirling dervish, cleaning, shopping, and cooking.* ◊ **dervish**

whirlpool /wúrl pool/ *n.* **1.** SPIRALLING CURRENT OF WATER a spiralling current of water in a stream or river **2.**

STH RESEMBLING A WHIRLPOOL sth that has or seems to have the action, motion, or power of a whirlpool ○ *a whirlpool of despair* **3.** *US* = **whirlpool bath**

whirlpool bath *n.* a bath or outdoor pool with powerful underwater jets that keep the water constantly moving or swirling around your body. It is sometimes used in physical therapy. US term **whirlpool**

whirlwind /wúrl wind/ *n.* **1.** METEOROL **SPINNING COLUMN OF AIR** a column of air rotating rapidly round a core of low pressure **2. STH HAPPENING OR CHANGING SWIFTLY** sth that happens very quickly, or a rapid succession of events (*often used before a noun*) ○ *a whirlwind romance* ○ *a whirlwind visit* **3. STH VERY DESTRUCTIVE** sth having a terrible destructive force ○ *swept up in the whirlwind of war* [14thC. From Old Norse *hvirfilwindr.*]

whirlybird /wúrli burd/ *n.* a helicopter (*informal*)

whirr /wur/, **whir** *vti.* (**whirrs, whirring, whirred; whirs, whirring, whirred**) **MAKE A WHIRLING OR VIBRATING SOUND** to make a continuous soft buzzing or humming sound, usually by vibrating or turning very quickly, or to cause sth to make such a sound ■ *n.* **WHIRLING OR VIBRATING SOUND** a continuous soft buzzing or humming sound like that of sth vibrating or turning very quickly [14thC. Origin uncertain: probably from a Scandinavian source.]

whish /wish/ *v.* (**whishes, whishing, whished**) **1.** *vi.* **MAKE OR MOVE WITH A RUSHING SOUND** to make the soft smooth rushing sound of sth moving quickly through the air, or to move with such a sound ○ *Water whished along the boat as we rowed upstream.* **2.** *vt.* **MOVE STH QUICKLY WITH RUSHING SOUND** to cause sth to make or move with a whishing sound ○ *the dog whished its tail* ■ *n.* **WHISHING SOUND OR MOVEMENT** a soft whistling or rushing sound, or a movement that makes such a sound ○ *the whish of the windscreen wipers* ■ *adv.* **WITH A WHISHING SOUND** moving or falling with a whishing sound ○ *Whish, the branch came down.* [Early 16thC. An imitation of the sound.]

whisht /hwisht/, **whist** /hwist/ *interj., vti.* (**whishts, whishting, whishted; whists, whisting, whisted**), *n. Scotland* = **wheesh** [Mid-16thC. An imitation of the sound made by someone calling for silence.]

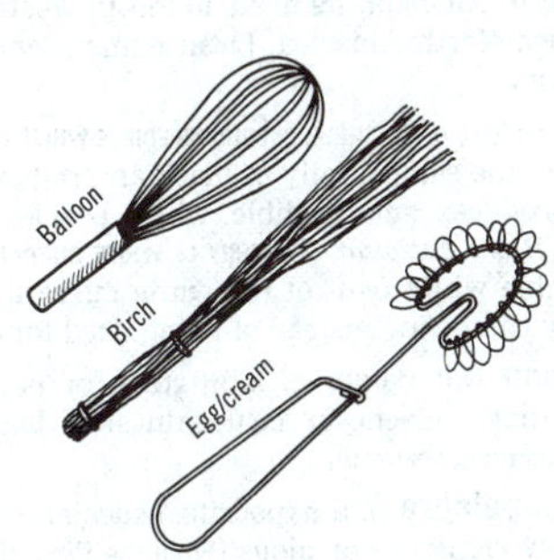
Balloon
Birch
Egg/cream
Whisk

whisk /wisk/ *n.* **1.** COOK **UTENSIL FOR WHIPPING STH** a kitchen tool, usually with curved or coiled wires attached to a handle, used with short quick movements to aerate a soft or liquid substance and make it thick and frothy **2. BRUSHING MOVEMENT** a quick light brushing or sweeping movement ○ *He wiped the table with a whisk of his hand.* **3. STH USED TO SWEEP THINGS AWAY** a small brush or similar implement made of a bundle of twigs, straw, or grass, used to sweep or stir things ■ *v.* (**whisks, whisking, whisked**) **1.** *vt.* **MAKE THICK AND SMOOTH** to make a soft or liquid substance thick and smooth by beating it with a fork, whisk, or other device to create air bubbles in the mixture **2.** *vt.* **BRUSH AWAY LIGHTLY** to remove sth with a quick light sweeping movement ○ *He whisked the crumbs from the table.* **3.** *vt.* **PLACE WITH A SWEEPING MOTION** to move or place sth somewhere with a quick light sweeping motion **4.** *vti.* **MOVE QUICKLY** to move or take sb or sth somewhere very quickly or suddenly ○ *They whisked her off to hospital.* [14thC. Of Scandinavian origin.]

whisker /wískər/ *n.* **1. HAIR NEAR ANIMAL'S MOUTH** a long stiff hair growing near the mouth of some mammals, e.g. cats, mice, and rabbits **2. HAIR ON SB'S FACE** a short stiff hair growing on sb's face, especially on the cheeks, chin, or upper lip **3. SMALL MARGIN** a very small amount or margin ○ *We came within a whisker of losing everything.* **4. whisker, whisker boom** NAUT **LIGHT POLE** a light pole used for extending the corners of a sail **5.** CHEM **THIN CRYSTAL** a strong thin hair-shaped crystal of a metal or mineral, used to strengthen composite material ■ **whiskers** *npl.* **SB'S FACIAL HAIR** a short growth of hair growing on sb's cheeks, chin, or upper lip [15thC. Formed from WHISK. Originally used for 'sth that whisks or sweeps', the main modern meaning evolved because of the supposed resemblance to a small brush.] —**whiskered** *adj.* —**whiskery** *adj.*

whiskey (*plural* **-keys**) *n. US, Ireland* whisky. ◊ **Irish whiskey**

whisky (*plural* **-kies**) *n.* **1. ALCOHOLIC SPIRIT** an alcoholic beverage made from a fermented grain, such as corn, rye, or barley, that is sometimes aged or blended **2. DRINK OF WHISKY** a drink or measure of whisky [Early 18thC. From Scottish Gaelic *usquebea, usque beatha*, literally 'water of life', from *usque* 'water' and *bethu* 'life'.]

Whisky /wíski/ *n.* a code word for the letter 'W', used in international radio communications

whisky mac *n.* a drink made of whisky and ginger wine

whisky sour, **whiskey sour** *n.* a mixed drink containing whisky, often an American whiskey such as bourbon, lemon juice, and sugar

whisper /wíspər/ *v.* (**-pers, -pering, -pered**) **1.** *vti.* **BREATHE WORDS VOICELESSLY** to speak or say sth very softly, without using the vocal cords **2.** *vti.* **SPEAK OR SUGGEST STH SECRETLY** to speak or say sth in a confidential or furtive manner, often to spread gossip, reveal a secret, or conspire with sb ○ *Whisper so that no one else hears.* **3.** *vi.* **RUSTLE SOFTLY** to make a soft rustling sound ■ *n.* **1. VERY LOW VOICE** a soft speaking sound that uses the breath but not the vocal cords ○ *She spoke in a whisper.* **2. STH SAID IN SOFT VOICE** sth said in a whisper **3. RUSTLING SOUND** a soft rustling sound **4. FAINT HINT** a hint or trace of sth ○ *a whisper of perfume* **5. RUMOUR** a rumour expressed confidentially or furtively ○ *Ignore the whispers of the crowd.* [Old English *hwisprian*. Ultimately from a prehistoric Germanic base, imitative of a hissing sound, which is also the ancestor of English *whistle.*] —**whisperer** *n.*

whispering campaign /wíspəring-/ *n.* the spreading of scandalous rumours in order to damage or destroy the reputation of a person or group

whispering gallery *n.* a space or gallery beneath a dome or vault in which whispers can be heard clearly in other parts of the building

whist[1] /wist/ *n.* a card game in which two pairs of people try to take a majority of the tricks and the trump suit is determined by the last card dealt. Whist is a forerunner of bridge. [Mid-17thC. Origin uncertain: perhaps a variant of WHISK (because your cards are 'whisked' away after your turn), or perhaps from WHIST[2] 'be quiet!' (because silence was expected during play).]

whist[2] *interj., vti., n.* = **wheesh**

whist drive *n.* a card party at which the winning players of each hand of whist move to different tables and play the losers of the preceding hand

whistle /wíss'l/ *v.* (**-tles, -tling, -tled**) **1.** *vi.* **MAKE A SHRILL SOUND THROUGH PURSED LIPS** to make a shrill or musical sound by forcing the breath through a small gap between the lips or the teeth **2.** *vi.* **PRODUCE A SHRILL SOUND** to produce a shrill sound or signal by forcing steam or air through a narrow opening (*refers to trains, kettles, etc.*) ○ *heard the train whistle as it came round the bend* **3.** *vi.* **MOVE WITH A SHRILL SOUND** to move at great speed through the air, making a shrill sound ○ *bullets whistling by overhead* **4.** *vt.* **MAKE A MUSICAL SOUND BY WHISTLING** to produce music or give a signal by whistling ○ *whistling a tune* **5.** *vti.* **ISSUE A CALL OR ORDER BY WHISTLING** to express a summons or order to a person or animal by whistling **6.** *vi.* **EMIT A SHRILL CHARACTERISTIC CALL** to make a characteristically shrill sound, using the mouth or throat or by other means (*refers to birds or animals*) ■ *n.* **1. DEVICE PRODUCING A SHRILL SOUND** a device or instrument that produces a shrill or musical sound when air or breath is forced through it **2. WHISTLING SOUND** a sound or signal made by a person, animal, or object whistling ○ *He let out a low whistle.* **3. ACT OF WHISTLING** an act of whistling [Old English *hwistlian*, from a prehistoric Germanic word meaning 'to whistle, hiss' that is also the ancestor of English *whisper* and *whine*] ◇ **blow the whistle (on sb** *or* **sth)** to report sb for doing sth wrong or illegal, especially within an organization ◇ **wet your whistle** to have a drink, especially of alcohol (*dated informal*) ◇ **whistle in the dark** to attempt to or pretend to keep up your courage when afraid

whistle for *vt.* to expect sth that is not going to happen or be given (*dated informal*)

whistle up *vt.* to summon a person or animal by making a whistling call

whistle-blower *n.* sb who exposes wrongdoing, especially within an organization [From the idea of a police officer sounding the alarm when witnessing a crime] —**whistle-blowing** *n.*

whistler /wísslər/ *n.* **1. WHISTLING PERSON OR OBJECT** sb or sth that whistles **2.** RADIO **RADIO DISTURBANCE** an interference signal in a radio receiver, resembling a whistling sound of decreasing pitch and caused by lightning or other electromagnetic disturbance **3.** BIRDS **WHISTLING AUSTRALIAN FLYCATCHER** an often brightly coloured Australian flycatcher with a particularly melodious whistling call. Genus: *Pachycephala.* **4.** ZOOL = **hoary marmot 5.** VET **HORSE WITH A RESPIRATORY PROBLEM** a horse with a breathing defect that causes it to make a whistling noise when it breathes in [Old English *hwistlere*]

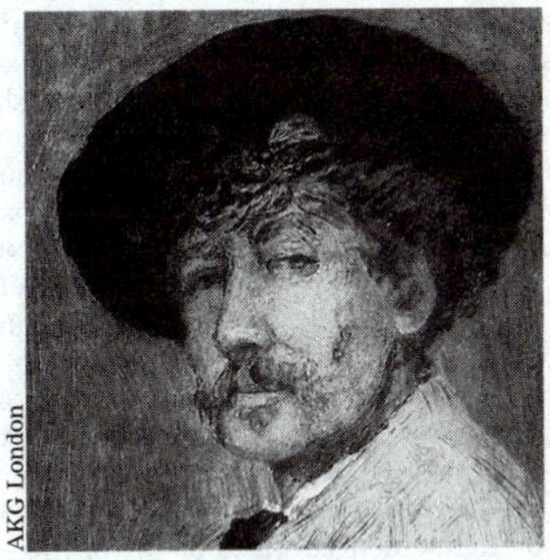
AKG London
James Abbott McNeill Whistler

Whistler /wísslər/, **James Abbott McNeill** (1834–1903) US artist. Influenced by both European and Japanese art, he was renowned for his etchings, subtle landscapes, and portraits such as the one popularly known as *Whistler's Mother* (1871).

whistle stop *n.* **1. SHORT STOP** a short stop to make a brief public appearance, especially one made by a political candidate during an election campaign **2.** *US* **SMALL RAILWAY STATION** a town or railway station where trains stop only when signalled to do so **3.** *US* **SMALL TOWN** a small town or community (*slang*)

whistle-stop *adj.* **HAVING FREQUENT STOPS** conducted very rapidly with frequent brief stops or visits, especially in order to make public appearances or deliver election speeches ○ *a whistle-stop tour of the state* ■ *vi.* (**whistle-stops, whistle-stopping, whistle-stopped**) **1. TOUR SMALL TOWNS** to make a rapid tour that features many stops in small towns **2. MAKE A BRIEF STOP** to make a short stop in a place as part of a rapid tour, especially as a political candidate

whistling duck *n.* a long-legged upright duck found in tropical waters. Genus: *Dendrocygna.* [From the whistling calls made by most of the ducks]

whit /wit/ *n.* used with verbs in the negative to refer to the smallest imaginable degree or amount (*dated informal*) ○ *I don't care a whit whether they succeed or fail.* [15thC. Alteration of WIGHT[1].]

Whit /wit/ *n.* = **Whitsuntide** ■ *adj.* **OF WHITSUNTIDE** occurring at or relating to Whitsuntide [Mid-16thC. Shortening of *Whitsun* or *Whit Sunday.*]

Whitaker /wíttəkər/, **Sir Frederick** (1812–91) British-born New Zealand statesman. He was twice prime minister of New Zealand (1863–64, 1882–83).

Whitby /wítbi/ fishing port and tourist resort in Yorkshire, northeastern England. Population: 14,000 (1994).

white /wīt/ *adj.* (**whiter, whitest**) **1. SNOW-COLOURED** having the colour of fresh snow or milk, which results from the reflection of nearly all light from all visible wavelengths **2. LACKING COLOUR** lacking any colour or hue **3. white, White** CAUCASIAN belonging to a people with naturally pale skin **4. white, White OF CAUCASIAN PEOPLE** of, for, or relating to a pale-skinned people ○ *a white problem* **5.** COMPARATIVELY LIGHT light in colour in comparison with others of the same kind ○ *white cabbage* **6.** WINE MADE FROM WHITE GRAPES made from pale-skinned grapes **7.** LACKING PIGMENT used to describe hair that has lost most or all of its pigment, usually as a result of aging **8.** HAVING A VERY PALE COMPLEXION unusually pale in the face, e.g. from fright or shock **9.** ZOOL HAVING WHITE PARTS OR COLOURINGS used with the names of plants or animals to indicate the presence of light or white parts or colourings ○ *white bass* **10.** FOOD, TECH WITHOUT BRAN OR GERM used to describe flour that has had the bran and wheatgerm removed **11.** COOK MADE FROM WHITE FLOUR made using white flour **12.** BEVERAGES SERVED WITH MILK served with milk added **13.** UNMARKED BY WRITING not written on or printed on **14.** PURE unblemished, especially in character **15.** WEARING WHITE dressed in white or characterized by the wearing of white ○ *a white wedding* **16. white, White** HIST, POL POLITICALLY CONSERVATIVE conservative or royalist in political outlook. ◊ **red 17.** INCANDESCENT heated to such a high degree that the substance turns white in colour **18.** HAVING SNOW accompanied or characterized by the presence of snow ○ *a white Christmas* **19.** MUSIC LACKING TONAL WARMTH relating to a pure musical tone that lacks warmth, colour, and resonance ■ *n.* **1.** COLOURS COLOUR OF SNOW the colour of fresh snow or milk **2.** PAINTING WHITE PAINT a paint or dye that is or is near to the colour of fresh snow **3.** WHITE OBJECT a white object, substance, or fabric, or the part of sth that is white, e.g. an unprinted area on a page **4.** WHITE CLOTHING clothing that is white (*usually used in the plural*) **5. white, White** CAUCASIAN PERSON a member of a people with pale skin **6.** FOOD PART OF EGG the transparent liquid that surrounds the yolk of an egg and turns white when the egg is cooked **7.** ANAT PART OF EYE the part of the eyeball surrounding the iris **8.** ARCHERY PART OF TARGET the white outermost ring of an archery target or a shot that lands in it **9.** BOARD GAMES GAME PIECE OR PLAYER a white or light-coloured piece or set of pieces in a game such as in chess or draughts, or the player using them **10.** INSECTS BUTTERFLY a butterfly that is predominantly white in colour. Family: Pieridae. ■ *v.* (**whites, whiting, whited**) **1.** *vt.* LEAVE BLANK SPACES IN to make or leave blank spaces in sth, especially sth printed **2.** *vti.* WHITEN to become or cause sth to become white (*archaic*) [Old English *hwīt*. Ultimately from an Indo-European base meaning 'to shine', which is also the ancestor of English *wheat* and *Whitsunday*.] — **whiteness** *n.* —**whitish** *adj.*

white out *v.* **1.** *vt.* COVER MISTAKE WITH WHITE CORRECTION FLUID to cover a mistake in written, printed, or typed material using white correction fluid **2.** *vi.* LOSE VISIBILITY to lose visibility in daylight because of snow or fog

Patrick White

White /wīt/, **Patrick** (1912–90) British-born Australian writer. His works, mainly set in Australia, include plays, poems, short stories, and novels. He won a Nobel Prize in literature in 1973. Full name **Patrick Victor Martindale White**

white admiral *n.* **1.** BROWN BUTTERFLY WITH WHITE MARKS a butterfly of Europe and Asia that has brown wings with white marks. Latin name: *Limenitis camilla.* **2.** BLUISH BUTTERFLY WITH WHITE BAND a North American butterfly that has bluish-black wings with a large white band on them. Latin name: *Limenitis arthemis.*

white alkali *n.* a whitish deposit of mineral salts that is sometimes seen on the surface of very alkaline soils

white ant *n.* = termite

white area *n.* an area of land not yet subject to planning proposals or limitations [From the idea of its not being coded in any particular colour on planning maps]

white ash *n.* **1.** N AMERICAN ASH TREE a North American ash tree that has leaves with a paler silvery underside. Latin name: *Fraxinus americana.* **2.** WOOD OF THE WHITE ASH TREE the wood of the white ash tree, used especially for making oars [From the pale colour of the undersides of its leaves]

White Australia Policy *n.* the policy of limiting the number of non white people migrating to Australia, enshrined in the Immigration Restriction Act of 1901 and officially abandoned in 1945. Certain restrictions remained in place for some time afterwards.

whitebait /wīt bayt/ (*plural* -**bait**) *n.* **1.** YOUNG FISH any small young fish fried and eaten whole, especially a young herring **2.** AUSTRALIAN FISH a small marine fish native to Australia and New Zealand that swims into brackish and fresh water to spawn. Latin name: *Galaxias attenuatus.* [Mid-18thC. *White* from the silvery colour of most of the fish.]

whitebark pine /wīt baark-/ *n.* a pine tree with small purplish cones that is native to the Pacific Northwest. Latin name: *Pinus albicaulis.* [*Whitebark* from its whitish-grey bark]

white bass *n.* an edible silvery freshwater fish of the bass family, native to the Great Lakes and the Mississippi valley. Latin name: *Morone chrysops.*

whitebeam /wīt beem/ *n.* a deciduous tree native to Europe and Asia related to the rowan and the service trees that has leaves with pale and hairy undersides. Latin name: *Sorbus aria.* [Early 18thC. From the white undersides of its leaves.]

white bear *n.* = polar bear

white belt *n.* MARTIAL ARTS **1.** BEGINNER'S BELT the belt worn by a beginner in a martial art such as karate or judo **2.** BEGINNER AT MARTIAL ART a martial arts novice

white birch *n.* a birch tree with whitish or greyish bark such as the European silver birch or the North American paper birch. Genus: *Betula.*

white blood cell *n.* a common large blood cell that has no pigmentation. It helps protect the body against infection in the immune response, and also plays a role in inflammation and allergic reactions.

whiteboard /wīt bawrd/ *n.* a board for writing on, similar to a blackboard but with a white plastic surface that is written on with erasable marker pens, used in teaching and in giving presentations [Mid-20thC. Formed from WHITE, on the model of *blackboard*.]

white book *n.* in some countries, an official government report published in a white binding

Whiteboy /wīt boy/ *n.* in the mid-18th century, a member of a secret organization of Irish farmers fighting for agrarian reform [Mid-18thC. *White* from the white shirts they wore. It was also used earlier as a name for various rebellious or illegal groups, ironically from the original sense 'favourite, darling'.]

white bread *n.* bread made from flour that has had the bran and wheat germ removed

white-bread *adj.* (*informal*) **1.** BLAND bland, conventional, and unimaginative **2.** *US* WHITE AND MIDDLE-CLASS relating to, belonging to, or considered typical of white, middle-class North America [From the idea that white bread symbolizes sth overrefined, soulless, and unexciting]

white-breasted sea eagle *n.* a large grey-and-white fish-eating eagle found around the coasts and nearby waterways of Australia and parts of Southeast Asia. Latin name: *Haliaeetus leucogaster.*

white bryony *n.* a climbing plant with lobed leaves and reddish-black berries, belonging to the gourd family and native to Europe, Asia, and North Africa. Genus: *Bryonia.* [From its greenish-white flowers]

whitecap /wīt kap/ *n.* the white crest of a breaking wave

white cedar *n.* **1.** N AMERICAN CONIFER either of two coniferous trees of eastern North America with leaves resembling scales and light-coloured durable wood. Latin name: *Chamaecyparis thyoides* and *Thuja occidentalis.* **2.** WOOD OF WHITE CEDAR TREES the wood from either white cedar, the one used in boatbuilding and the other for telegraph poles [From the light colour of their wood]

white cell *n.* = white blood cell

white chip *n.* **1.** GAMBLING BETTING TOKEN a betting chip with the lowest possible value **2.** STH WORTHLESS a thing of little value

white chocolate *n.* a cream-coloured confection containing the same ingredients as chocolate but lacking cocoa powder

white Christmas *n.* a Christmas when there is snow, especially a Christmas day

white cloud, white cloud mountain fish *n.* a small brightly coloured Asian freshwater fish that belongs to the minnow family and is a popular aquarium fish. Latin name: *Tanichthys albonubes.* [Mid-20thC. Named after *White Cloud*, the English name of a mountain northeast of Guangzhou (Canton), China, where the fish was discovered.]

white clover *n.* a perennial Eurasian plant naturalized in North America, grown with grass as pasture for livestock. It has small white flowers that attract honey bees. Latin name: *Trifolium repens.*

white coal *n.* flowing water considered as a source of hydroelectric power

white-collar *adj.* relating to jobs that are usually salaried and do not involve manual labour. ◊ blue-collar, pink-collar [From the white shirts traditionally worn by people in such jobs]

white-collar crime *n.* crime committed in the workplace by white-collar workers, e.g. embezzlement and fraudulent accounting practices

white corpuscle *n.* = white blood cell

white crab *n.* = ghost crab

white-crowned sparrow *n.* a sparrow with black-and-white bands on its head, found in western and northern North America. Latin name: *Zonotrichia leucophrys.*

white currant *n.* **1.** SHRUB PRODUCING EDIBLE WHITE BERRIES a shrub of the same family as black and red currants that produces small edible white berries. Latin name: *Ribes sativum.* **2.** BERRY OF WHITE CURRANT SHRUB the edible white fruit of the white currant shrub, usually eaten raw instead of being used for jams

whitedamp /wīt damp/ *n.* a mixture of poisonous gases that collects in coal mines. ◊ blackdamp [Modelled on BLACKDAMP]

whited sepulchre *n.* a hypocrite, especially sb who is falsely righteous or pious [From the Bible (Matthew 23:27), which compares such people to whitewashed tombs, appearing '... beautiful outward, but ... within full of dead men's bones ...']

white dwarf *n.* a small, dim, extremely dense star that has collapsed on itself and is in the final stages of its evolution [From its colour]

white elephant *n.* **1.** STH COSTLY TO MAINTAIN an expensive and often rare or valuable possession whose upkeep is a considerable financial burden **2.** POSSESSION OF QUESTIONABLE VALUE sth with a questionable or at least very limited value **3.** CONSPICUOUS FAILED VENTURE a much publicized or keenly anticipated venture that proves to be a spectacular flop **4.** DISCARDED OBJECT an unwanted object of possible use to sb else (*dated; hyphenated before a noun*) **5.** ALBINO ELEPHANT a rare albino Indian elephant regarded as sacred in India and in neighbouring parts of Southeast Asia [Said to derive from the practice of the King of Siam of giving a white elephant to troublesome courtiers, who would be ruined by the cost of keeping the animal]

White Ensign *n.* the flag of the Royal Navy, showing a red cross on a white background with the Union Jack in the upper corner nearest the hoist

white-eye *n.* a small green or greenish-brown songbird with a ring of white feathers round the eye that is found in tropical and subtropical regions. Family: Zosteropidae.

whiteface /wı̄t fayss/ *n.* white makeup for the face, used, e.g. by clowns

white-faced *adj.* **1.** HAVING AN UNUSUALLY PALE FACE having a face that has turned pale through fear, anger, or some other strong emotion **2.** ZOOL HAVING WHITE MARKINGS having white markings on the face, especially when this distinguishes one species from other similar species

white-faced heron *n.* a medium-sized heron common throughout Australia that has grey plumage, yellow legs, and a white face. Latin name: *Ardea novaehollandiae*.

white fish *n.* any or all edible marine fish with whitish flesh, including cod, hake, and whiting, as distinct from flat fish such as plaice and oily fish such as mackerel

white flag *n.* a white cloth or improvised flag waved as an international sign of truce or surrender

white flight *n.* the exodus of white people from neighbourhoods where nonwhites are settling

white flour *n.* flour from which most of the bran and wheatgerm has been removed. It is whitish and much lighter in texture than wholemeal flour.

whitefly /wı̄t flı̄/ (*plural* **-flies** *or* **-fly**) *n.* a minute insect with a white waxy coating on the body. Many species suck the sap from garden and house plants. Family: Aleyrodidae.

white-footed mouse *n.* a mouse with small white feet and undersides, native to North and Central America. Latin name: *Peromyscus leucopus*. ◊ **deer mouse**

white fox *n.* the Arctic fox in its white winter coat. Its coat is dark grey in summer.

white friar, **White Friar** *n.* a member of the Carmelite order of monks [From the white habits of the monks]

white frost *n.* = **hoar frost**

white gold *n.* a silvery-looking gold alloy that contains gold mixed with palladium, nickel, or sometimes zinc and is typically used in jewellery

white goods *npl.* **1.** HOUSEHOLD APPLIANCES large household appliances such as refrigerators, cookers, and dishwashers, typically finished with white enamel **2.** HOUSEHOLD LINEN household goods made of fabric, e.g. bedlinens, towels, and tablecloths

white gum *n.* any Australian eucalyptus tree with a whitish bark. Genus: *Eucalyptus*.

white-haired *adj.* having hair that has become white with advanced age

Whitehall /wı̄t hawl/ *n.* **1.** CENTRAL LONDON STREET a street in central London, between Trafalgar Square and the Houses of Parliament, containing the main offices of the British civil service **2.** BRITISH GOVERNMENT a collective term for the administration and civil service departments of the British government, many of which are located in Whitehall **3.** TRINIDADIAN PRIME MINISTER'S RESIDENCE the official residence of the prime minister of Trinidad

Whitehaven /wı̄t hayv'n/ town and fishing port in Cumbria, northwestern England. Population: 25,721 (1994).

whitehead /wı̄t hed/ *n.* a small pimple with a whitish top formed when a sebaceous gland becomes blocked. Technical name **milium** [Mid-20thC. Modelled on *blackhead*.]

Whitehead /wı̄t hed/, **Alfred North** (1861–1947) British mathematician and philosopher. He wrote *Principia Mathematica* (1910–13) with Bertrand Russell.

white-headed *adj.* **1.** WITH WHITE MARKINGS having white markings on the feathers, hair, or fur of the head, especially when this distinguishes one species from other similar species **2.** FAVOURED AND LUCKIER favoured over others and considered blessed by luck

white heat *n.* **1.** VERY HIGH TEMPERATURE an extremely high degree of heat characterized by the emission of white light **2.** INTENSE EXCITEMENT a state of intense excitement or activity

white hole *n.* a hypothetical region in space from which stars, light, and other forms of energy explosively emerge [Modelled on *black hole*]

white hope *n.* = **great white hope** (*dated*)

white horse *n.* **1.** = **whitecap 2.** HORSE FIGURE the outline of a horse carved in prehistoric times in exposed chalk on a hillside. There are many examples in southern England. [In the sense of 'whitecap', from its imagined resemblance to a horse's head and flowing mane]

Whitehorse /wı̄t hawrss/ capital city of the Yukon Territory, Canada, located on the Yukon River, just off the Alaska Highway. Population: 21,808 (1996).

white-hot *adj.* **1.** EXTREMELY HOT so hot that white light is emitted **2.** EXTREMELY EXCITED characterized by intense excitement or activity

White House, Washington, D.C.

White House *n.* **1.** OFFICIAL RESIDENCE OF US PRESIDENT the large white mansion in Washington, D.C. that is the official residence of the president of the United States. It was built between 1792 and 1800 in the classical Palladian style. **2.** EXECUTIVE BRANCH OF THE US GOVERNMENT the executive branch of the US government **3.** RUSSIAN PARLIAMENT BUILDING the Russian parliament building in central Moscow

white hunter *n.* a white man hunting big game professionally or working as a safari guide, especially in Africa in former times

White Island /wı̄t-/ uninhabited volcanic island in the Bay of Plenty, off the northeastern coast of the North Island, New Zealand. Area: 3.2 sq. km/1.2 sq. mi.

white knight *n.* **1.** RESCUING HERO sb who rescues a person or situation from disaster **2.** FIN FINANCIAL SAVIOUR a person or organization that rescues a business company, especially from an undesirable takeover

white-knuckle *adj.* causing or characterized by fear, apprehension, nervousness, or uncertainty [From the appearance of nervously clenched fists]

white-knuckle ride *n.* **1.** TERRIFYING TIME OR EXPERIENCE a situation, experience, or encounter that causes fear, anxiety, or uncertainty **2.** FAST FAIRGROUND RIDE a frightening or exhilarating fairground ride, especially a rollercoaster

white lady *n.* a cocktail made with gin, Cointreau™, and lemon juice

white lead *n.* **1.** POISONOUS LEAD COMPOUND lead carbonate in the form of a poisonous heavy white powder, used as a pigment in paints and in putty. Formula: $2PbCO_3.Pb(OH)_2$. **2.** PUTTY putty made from white lead suspended in boiled linseed oil

white leather *n.* soft leather treated with salt and alum for a white finish

Whiteley /wı̄tli/, **Brett** (1939–92) Australian artist. His works include sculpture, prints, and photography, but he is best known for expressionistic landscape paintings and portraits.

white lie *n.* a lie perceived or intended not to harm, but told in order to avoid distress or embarrassment [From WHITE in the sense 'benign']

—— **WORD KEY: SYNONYMS** ——

See Synonyms at *lie*.

white light *n.* light such as sunlight that contains all the wavelengths from red to violet at approximately equal intensity

white lightning *n.* US strong, illegally distilled alcohol, usually whisky (*regional*) [*White* because it is usually colourless]

white line *n.* a white line along the middle or edge of a road, used to mark the edge of a road or to separate lanes of traffic, especially ones moving in opposite directions

white list *n.* a list of people, organizations, or items deemed acceptable. ◊ **blacklist** [Modelled on *blacklist*] —**white-listed** *adj.*

white-livered *adj.* = **lily-livered** (*literary*)

whitely /wı̄tli/ *adv.* showing a face pale with anger, fear, or shock

white magic *n.* supposed magic practised for good purposes or as an antidote to evil [Modelled on *black magic*]

white man's burden *n.* the supposed responsibility of Europeans and their descendants to impose their allegedly advanced civilization on the nonwhite original inhabitants of the territories they colonized

white marlin *n.* a large marine fish with a light-coloured belly, found in the western Atlantic. It is one of the smaller species of marlin. Latin name: *Tetrapturus albidus*.

white matter *n.* the whitish nerve tissue of the brain and spinal cord, consisting mostly of myelinated nerve fibres. ◊ **grey matter**

white meat *n.* a light-coloured meat, especially chicken, turkey, or pork, that is usually lower in fat than red meat, more tender, more delicate in flavour, and requires a shorter cooking time

white metal *n.* a light-coloured alloy, especially one with a high tin or lead content such as pewter or babbitt

white mica *n.* = **muscovite**

white mulberry *n.* **1.** CHINESE TREE a mulberry tree of Chinese origin with edible whitish berries. Its leaves are used as food for silkworms. Latin name: *Morus alba*. **2.** FRUIT OF WHITE MULBERRY TREE the edible berry of the white mulberry tree

white mustard *n.* a Eurasian mustard plant with yellow flowers. Its seeds are used to make mustard and mustard oil. Latin name: *Brassica hirta*.

whiten /wı̄t'n/ (**-ens**, **-ening**, **-ened**) *vti.* to become or cause sth to become white or lighter in colour

whitener /wı̄t'nər/ *n.* **1.** WHITE COLOURING SUBSTANCE any substance used to colour sth white or enhance its whiteness, e.g. a dye for sports shoes or bleach **2.** MILK SUBSTITUTE a substance added to tea or coffee as a substitute for milk, usually in powder form and lower in calories or with a longer shelf life than milk

White Nile /wı̄t nı̄l/ the section of the river Nile from near the Sudan-Uganda border to its junction with the Blue Nile at Khartoum. Length: 805 km/500 mi.

white noise *n.* low-volume electrical or radio noise of equal intensity over a wide range of frequencies [By analogy with white light, which contains light from the whole range of visible frequencies]

white oak *n.* **1.** OAK WITH PALE WOOD a variety of oak tree with evenly lobed, hairless leaves and pale-coloured wood. It is native to eastern North America. Latin name: *Quercus alba*. **2.** = **roble 3.** WOOD OF WHITE OAK TREE the wood of the white oak tree (*hyphenated when used before a noun*)

whiteout /wı̄t owt/ *n.* **1.** LOSS OF VISIBILITY an atmospheric condition in which low clouds merge with a snow-covered landscape, greatly restricting visibility, and only darker objects are discernible **2.** BLIZZARD a blizzard that is so severe it reduces visibility to virtually zero [Mid-20thC. Modelled on BLACKOUT.]

white paper *n.* **1.** OFFICIAL GOVERNMENT REPORT in many countries, an official report setting out government policy on a particular issue to be voted on by the country's parliament or congress. ◊ **green paper 2.** AUTHORITATIVE REPORT an official, authoritative, or heavily researched report on a topic, e.g. a report produced by a group of journalists [From the fact that such reports are customarily printed as white pamphlets]

white pepper *n.* light-coloured pepper made from peppercorns that have had their dark husk removed

white perch *n.* a silver-coloured edible fish that is a variety of sea bass. It is found in the western Atlantic and in freshwater streams of eastern North America. Latin name: *Morone americana.*

white pine *n.* **1.** N AMERICAN PINE a fast-growing pine tree native to eastern North America that is grown for its soft durable wood. Latin name: *Pinus strobus.* **2.** WOOD OF WHITE PINE TREE the wood of the white pine tree (*hyphenated when used before a noun*) **3.** SIMILAR PINE TREE any of a number of other pines resembling the white pine, particularly in having five-needle clusters [*White* from its light-coloured wood]

white poplar *n.* **1.** POPLAR WITH WHITE WOOLLY LEAVES a Eurasian poplar tree with white woolly leaves. Latin name: *Populus alba.* **2.** WOOD OF WHITE POPLAR TREE the straight-grained wood of the white poplar tree (*hyphenated when used before a noun*)

white potato *n.* the edible tuber of a potato with whitish flesh, or the plant that it grows on

white pudding *n.* a sausage made from light-coloured offal, e.g. brain and sweetbreads, and bound with oatmeal or a similar starchy ingredient, but not mixed with blood

white rat *n.* an albino variety of the brown rat, used widely in scientific research. Latin name: *Rattus norvegicus.*

white rice *n.* rice that has had both the outer husk and the bran layer removed. ◊ **brown rice**

white room *n.* = **clean room**

White Russian *n.* **1.** = **Belarusian 2.** BOLSHEVIK OPPONENT an opponent of the Bolsheviks during the Civil War (1918–21) that followed the 1917 Russian Revolution **3.** VODKA COCKTAIL a cocktail made from vodka, coffee liqueur, and cream

whites /wīts/ *npl.* **1.** WHITE LAUNDRY white or light-coloured laundry, usually washed separately from coloured laundry items **2.** SPORTS CLOTHES white or off-white clothing of a particular kind, especially as worn by sportspeople such as tennis players or cricketers **3.** US WHITE DRESS MILITARY UNIFORM the white dress uniform of a military service such as that of the US Navy or Coast Guard **4.** MED LEUCORRHOEA leucorrhoea (*informal*)

white sale *n.* a sale of household linen

white sapphire *n.* a colourless variety of the mineral corundum, used as a gemstone

white sauce *n.* a pale milk sauce, thickened with butter and flour or cornflour and variously seasoned or flavoured

White Sea /wīt-/ arm of the Barents Sea, forming an indentation in the coast of northwestern Russia and partly enclosed on the north by the Kola Peninsula. Area: 794,500 sq. km/36,700 sq. mi.

white shark *n.* = **great white shark**

white slave *n.* a white girl or woman sold into prostitution against her will —**white slaver** *n.* —**white slavery** *n.*

whitesmith /wīt smith/ *n.* **1.** WORKER WITH METAL sb who makes or repairs objects made of metal, especially tin and other white metals **2.** METAL POLISHER sb whose job is smoothing and polishing metal articles that have been forged [14thC. Modelled on BLACKSMITH.]

white snakeroot *n.* a poisonous plant native to eastern North America with heart-shaped leaves and clusters of small white flowers. Latin name: *Eupatorium rugosum.*

white space *n.* an area of a page or other printed surface where no text or pictures appear

white spirit *n.* a colourless liquid derived from petroleum and used like turpentine, e.g. to clean paintbrushes and thin paint

white spruce *n.* **1.** N AMERICAN SPRUCE a North American spruce tree with short blue-green needles and non-drooping branches. Latin name: *Picea glauca.* **2.** WOOD OF WHITE SPRUCE TREE the soft wood of the white spruce tree [*White* from its silvery-brown bark]

white squall *n.* a violent tropical or subtropical storm that stirs up the surface of the sea into whitecaps, but is limited to a very localized area, often with no storm clouds present

white stick *n.* a white-coloured walking stick used by a vision-impaired person to detect obstacles in his or her path

white stork *n.* a Eurasian stork with black-and-white plumage, reddish feet, and a reddish bill. Latin name: *Ciconia ciconia.*

white sturgeon *n.* a sturgeon of the North American Pacific coast that is fished commercially and for sport. It is the largest freshwater fish in the United States. Latin name: *Acipenser transmontanus.* [*White* from its greyish-white colour]

white supremacy *n.* the view that white people are supposedly genetically and culturally superior to all other people or races and should therefore rule over them —**white supremacist** *n.*

white-tailed deer /wīt tayl/, **whitetail** *n.* a North American deer with a greyish or reddish-brown coat and a tail that is white on the underside. Latin name: *Odocoileus virginianus.*

whitethorn /wīt thawrn/ *n.* = **hawthorn** [13thC. *White* from the fact that its bark is lighter in colour than the blackthorn's.]

whitethroat /wīt thrōt/ *n.* **1.** SMALL SONGBIRD WITH WHITE THROAT a small songbird with a white throat, native to Europe, Asia, and North Africa. Genus: *Sylvia.* **2.** = **white-throated sparrow**

white-throated sparrow *n.* a North American sparrow with a prominent white throat and black-and-white bands on its head. Latin name: *Zonotrichia albicollis.*

white tie *n.* **1.** WHITE BOW TIE a white bow tie worn as part of a man's formal evening dress. ◊ **black tie 2.** MAN'S EVENING CLOTHES a man's full formal evening clothes, consisting of a black suit with a tail coat and a white bow tie

white-tie *adj.* requiring evening dress for women and full formal evening clothes for men, with tail coats and white bow ties. ◊ **black-tie**

white trash *n.* US an offensive term used to refer to a white person or group of white people considered as possessing the stereotypical characteristics of a member or members of a lower-income group in society (*slang offensive; takes a singular or plural verb*)

white vitriol *n.* = **zinc sulphate**

whitewall /wīt wawl/, **whitewall tyre** *n.* a vehicle tyre with a band of white on the outside sidewall

white walnut *n.* = **butternut** [*White* from the fact that its wood is lighter in colour than that of the black walnut]

whitewash /wīt wosh/ *n.* **1.** WHITE PAINTING SOLUTION lime suspended in water, often with glue or sizing, and used like paint for whitening walls **2.** COVERUP a coordinated attempt to hide unpleasant facts, especially in a political context (*informal*) **3.** THOROUGH DEFEAT a resounding defeat, especially one in which the losing player or team does not score at all (*informal*) ■ *v.* (**-washes, -washing, -washed**) **1.** *vt.* PAINT STH WITH WHITEWASH to paint sth, usually a wall, with whitewash **2.** *vti.* HIDE TRUTH ABOUT to conceal the unpleasant facts about sth **3.** *vt.* DEFEAT SB DECISIVELY to defeat an opposing player or team resoundingly, especially by preventing the player or team from scoring at all —**whitewasher** *n.*

white water *n.* **1.** FAST-FLOWING WATER fast-flowing water with a foamy, choppy surface (*hyphenated when used before a noun*) **2.** SHALLOW WATER lighter-coloured sea water visible in shallow areas

white wedding *n.* a wedding that takes place in a Christian church, with the bride wearing a traditional white dress

white whale *n.* a small white fish-eating whale with a bulbous head that lives mainly in Arctic waters. Latin name: *Delphinapterus leucas.*

white-winged dove *n.* a dove with white patches on its wings, native to the southern United States and Mexico. Latin name: *Zenaida asiatica.*

white-winged scoter *n.* a North American sea duck that is mostly black with a white patch on each wing. Latin name: *Melanitta fusca.*

white witch *n.* a witch whose supposed magic is designed to do good or to counter evil magic [*White* because such a witch practises white magic]

whitewood /wīt wŏŏd/ *n.* **1.** TREE WITH LIGHT WOOD a deciduous tree such as the tulip tree, the cottonwood, or the basswood, with pale-coloured wood **2.** WOOD OF WHITEWOOD TREE the wood of a whitewood tree

whitey /wīti/ (*plural* **-eys**), **whity** (*plural* **-ies**) *n.* an offensive term used to refer contemptuously to a white person (*slang offensive*)

whither /wĭthər/ *adv., rel adv.* TO WHAT PLACE to what place (*archaic or literary*) ■ *adv.* INTO WHAT STATE to what state, condition, outcome, or degree (*literary or humorous*) ○ *a debate entitled 'Whither capitalism?'* [Old English *hwider*, from a prehistoric Germanic base that is also the ancestor of English *who, when,* and *where* (see WHO)]

whithersoever /wĭthərssō évvər/ *adv., rel adv.* to whatever place, or to any place whatsoever (*archaic*)

whitherward /wĭthərwərd/, **whitherwards** /-wərdz/ *adv.* to what place or in what direction (*archaic*)

Whiting

whiting[1] /wīting/ (*plural* **-ing**) *n.* **1.** EUROPEAN FISH a small edible European sea fish related to the cod, with a silvery underside and white flesh. It is an important commercial food fish throughout Europe. Latin name: *Merlangus merlangus.* **2.** PACIFIC AND ATLANTIC FISH a commercially important Pacific and Atlantic fish such as the American silver hake or corbina similar to the European whiting. Genera: *Merluccius* and *Menticirrhus.* [15thC. From Dutch *wijting,* from *wijt* 'white'.]

whiting[2] /wīting/ *n.* pure powdered chalk used as an ingredient in various commercial preparations such as putty and whitewash [15thC. Formed from WHITE.]

Whitlam /wĭt ləm/, **Gough** (*b.* 1916) Australian statesman. While he was the Labor prime minister of Australia (1972–75), his government was controversially dismissed by the governor-general, Sir John Kerr. Full name **Edward Gough Whitlam**

Whitley Council /wĭtli-/ *n.* a consultative committee or organization consisting of representatives from the management and staff of a company or industry, set up to discuss industrial relations, working conditions, and other work-related issues [Early 20thC. Named after J. H. Whitley (1866–1935), the chairman of a committee that recommended such bodies in 1916.]

whitlow /wĭtlō/ *n.* a pus-filled infection on the skin at the side of a fingernail or toenail [14thC. Alteration of earlier *whitflawe,* from WHITE (of uncertain origin: possibly from Middle Dutch *vijt* 'abscess') + FLAW.]

Whitman /wĭt mən/, **Walt** (1819–92) US poet and es-

Walt Whitman

sayist. He is known for his free verse, best exemplified in the stylistically revolutionary collection *Leaves of Grass* (1855–89). Real name **Walter Whitman**

Whit Monday *n.* the Monday after Whit Sunday, an official holiday in England, Ireland and Wales [Modelled on WHIT SUNDAY]

Whitney /wítnee/, **Eli** (1765–1825) US inventor. His cotton gin, a machine for separating the seeds from the fibre of the cotton plant, revolutionized the cotton industry.

Whitstable /wít stəb'l/ town and fishing port in Kent, England. It is famous for its oysters. Population: 28,907 (1991).

Whitsun /wíts'n/ *n.* = **Whitsuntide** ■ *adj.* OF WHITSUNTIDE relating to or happening on Whitsuntide or Whit Sunday [13thC. Back-formation from WHIT SUNDAY, understood as 'Whitsun day'.]

Whit Sunday *n.* a Christian feast day on the seventh Sunday after Easter, commemorating the gift of the Holy Spirit to the Apostles. It is a Scottish quarter day. US term **Pentecost** [Old English *hwīta sunnandæg* 'white Sunday', because of the white robes the priests wear on this day]

Whitsunday Islands /wit súndi-/ group of approximately 70 islands in the Coral Sea, off the coast of southeastern Queensland, Australia. Area: 98 sq. km/38 sq. mi.

Whitsuntide /wíts'n tīd/ *n.* the days around and including Whit Sunday [13thC. From WHITSUN + TIDE in the obsolete sense of 'period of time'.]

whittle /wítt'l/ (**-tles, -tling, -tled**) *vti.* to carve sth out of wood, usually sth small enough to hold in the hand, by cutting away small pieces of wood [Mid-16thC. From *whyttel* 'knife', a variant of *thwitel*, literally 'tool for paring', ultimately from Old English *þwītan* 'to pare, cut'.] —**whittler** *n.*

whittle away *vt.* to deplete sth by using or spending a little of it at a time

whittle down *vt.* to reduce or diminish sth gradually by taking away a little of it at a time

Whittle /wítt'l/, **Sir Frank** (1907–96) British engineer. He invented and developed the turbojet engine (1936), first used to power British fighter aircraft during World War II.

whittlings /wíttlingz/ *npl.* pieces of wood that have been whittled off a larger piece and discarded

Whitworth screw thread /wít wurth-/ *n.* the thread form for all UK screws, produced in a series of standard sizes. It has a 55° flank angle, and a rounded top and foot. [Late 19thC. Named after the English inventor Sir Joseph Whitworth (d. 1887).]

whity (*plural* **-ies**) *n.* = **whitey**

whiz /wiz/, **whizz** *v.* (**whizzes, whizzing, whizzed**) **1.** *vi.* HUM to make a humming, hissing, or buzzing noise **2.** *vti.* MOVE WITH A HUMMING NOISE to move swiftly with a humming, hissing, or buzzing noise, or to cause sth to move in this way ○ *bullets whizzing past* **3.** *vi.* MOVE QUICKLY to move or travel somewhere rapidly ○ *whizz down to the shops* **4.** *vt.* PROCESS STH IN FOOD MIXER to blend or liquidize sth using a food mixer or food processor (*informal*) **5.** *vi. US* OFFENSIVE TERM an offensive term meaning to urinate (*slang offensive*) ■ *n.* (*plural* **whizzes**) **1.** HUMMING SOUND a humming, hissing, or buzzing sound **2.** FAST MOVEMENT a fast movement, often accompanied by a humming, hissing, or buzzing sound **3. whiz, whizz, wiz** (*plural* **wizzes**) EXPERT sb who is very skilled in a particular field (*informal*) ○ *a computer whiz* **4.** AMPHETAMINES amphetamine drugs taken recreationally (*slang*) **5.** *US* OFFENSIVE TERM an offensive term used to refer to an act of urinating (*slang offensive*) [Mid-16thC. An imitation of the sound.]

whiz-bang, **whizz-bang** *n.* (*informal*) **1.** ARMS ARTILLERY SHELL a lightweight artillery shell used in World War I **2.** SB OR STH EXCELLENT sb or sth that is outstandingly successful or effective, loud, or fast ■ *adj.* EXCELLENT, FAST, OR LOUD outstandingly successful or effective, loud, or fast (*informal*) ○ *a whiz-bang presentation*

whiz kid, **whizz kid, wiz kid** *n.* a young and exceptionally talented and successful person in a given field (*informal*) [Possibly an alteration of Quiz Kid, a contestant on an early radio quiz programme]

who /hoo/ *pron.* **1.** INTRODUCES A QUESTION used to introduce a question asking about the name or identity of a person or people ○ *Who's that at the door?* ○ *Who did you see there?* **2.** INTRODUCES A RELATIVE CLAUSE used to introduce a relative clause giving information about a person or people ○ *meals for people who are too busy to cook* [Old English *hwā*. Ultimately from an Indo-European base meaning 'who, what' that is also the ancestor of English *what, how, quote,* and *quantity*.]

WORD KEY: USAGE

See Usage note at ***whom***.

WHO *abbr.* World Health Organization

whoa /wō/ *interj.* used to order an animal, or humorously, a person, to stop [Mid-19thC. Variant of HO.]

who'd /hood/ *contr.* **1.** who had **2.** who would [Mid-17thC]

whodunit /hoo dúnnit/, **whodunnit** *n.* a novel, film, or play centring on the solving of a crime, usually a murder [Mid-20thC. Alteration of 'who done it?'.]

whoever /hoo évvər/ *pron.* **1.** INTRODUCES AN EMPHATIC QUESTION used to introduce an emphatic question indicating surprise or disbelief ○ *Whoever would do such a thing?* **2.** ANY PERSON WHO used to indicate a person or people whose identity is not known ○ *Whoever takes over from her will have difficult decisions to make.* ■ *conj.* NO MATTER WHO used to indicate a person or people whose identity is not important ○ *You can bring whoever you like to the party.*

WORD KEY: USAGE

whoever or **whomever**? ***Whoever*** is a relative pronoun used in statements or commands: *Whoever made this has done a good job. Ask whoever you like.* The objective case ***whomever***, though strictly correct in the last example, is falling out of use just as ***whom*** is, and ***whoever*** is generally considered acceptable.

whole /hōl/ *adj.* **1.** ENTIRE complete, including all parts or aspects, with nothing left out **2.** UNDIVIDED not divided into parts or not regarded as consisting of separate elements **3.** RELATING TO DURATION OR EXTENT relating to or representing the full duration or extent of sth ○ *stayed up the whole night* **4.** UNBROKEN not damaged or broken ○ *not a single item of furniture left whole* **5.** UNIMPAIRED not wounded, impaired, or incapacitated ○ *no longer a whole man* **6.** HEALED OR HEALTHY healed or restored to health physically or psychologically ○ *made him whole again* **7.** HAVING COMMON PARENTS having both parents in common with your siblings ○ *a whole sister* **8.** NOT FRACTIONAL containing no vulgar or decimal fractions ■ *adv.* **1.** AS A SINGLE PIECE in a single piece rather than in several pieces ○ *Many snakes swallow their food whole.* **2.** COMPLETELY completely and in every way (*informal*) ○ *a whole different approach* ■ *n.* **1.** STH COMPLETE sth that is complete and has no parts missing **2.** SINGLE ENTITY OR UNIT sth regarded as a single and complete unit or entity, as opposed to a set of components [Old English *hāl* (source of English *hale*). Ultimately from an Indo-European word meaning 'sound, propitious'.] ◇ **as a whole** as a single and complete entity ◇ **a whole lot** very much or a great deal (*informal*) ◇ **on the whole 1.** as a rule or in general **2.** taking all relevant factors into account

WORD KEY: ORIGIN

The prehistoric Germanic precursor of ***whole*** is also the source of English *hail, hallow, heal, health,* and *holy.*

wholefood /hōl food/ *n.* food that has undergone very little processing and has been grown or produced without the use of synthetic pesticides or fertilizers

whole gale *n.* a wind of force 10 on the Beaufort scale, travelling at 87 to 102 km/55 to 63 mi. per hour and capable of causing considerable structural damage

wholehearted /hōl haártid/ *adj.* characterized by enthusiasm, passion, or commitment —**wholeheartedly** *adv.* —**wholeheartedness** *n.*

wholemeal /hōl meel/ *adj.* US term **whole-wheat 1.** NOT HAVING HAD BRAN REMOVED not having had the bran and wheatgerm taken out **2.** MADE FROM WHOLEMEAL FLOUR made using wholemeal flour [Early 17thC]

whole milk *n.* cow's milk from which no fat has been removed

whole note *n. US* = **semibreve** [*Whole* from the fact that it lasts for one full measure]

whole number *n.* a positive or negative number, including zero, that does not contain a vulgar or decimal fraction

wholesale /hōl sayl/ *n.* TRADE IN QUANTITY the business of buying and selling goods in quantity at discounted prices, usually direct from manufacturers or distributors, in order to sell them on to the consumer ■ *adj.* **1.** OF TRADE IN QUANTITY relating to the buying and selling of goods in quantity at discounted prices **2.** DONE ON LARGE SCALE done on a large scale and indiscriminately ■ *adv.* **1.** IN BULK on a large scale and at a discounted price **2.** INDISCRIMINATELY as a whole, without exercising any judgment or taking individual cases into account ■ *vti.* (**-sales, -saling, -saled**) BUY OR SELL GOODS WHOLESALE to buy or sell goods in large quantities at a discounted price, especially selling to retailers, instead of direct to the consumer, or to be bought or sold in this way [15thC. From the phrase 'by whole sale', that is, sold in a single lot for redistribution at retail.] —**wholesaler** *n.*

wholesome /hṓlssəm/ *adj.* **1.** HEALTH-GIVING beneficial to physical health, usually by virtue of being fresh and naturally produced **2.** MORALLY BENEFICIAL leading to or promoting improved moral wellbeing **3.** SENSIBLE based on openness, honesty, and common sense **4.** HEALTHY AND FIT having a fit, healthy appearance that suggests clean living [Assumed Old English *hālsum*] —**wholesomely** *adv.* —**wholesomeness** *n.*

whole tone *n.* a musical interval consisting of two semitones, such as exists between the notes D and E or A and B. US term **whole step**

whole-tone scale *n.* a musical scale that begins on any of two notes that are a semitone apart and goes up or down in whole notes for one octave

whole-wheat *adj. US* = **wholemeal**

who'll /hool/ *contr.* **1.** who shall **2.** who will

wholly /hōl li/ *adv.* **1.** COMPLETELY AND ENTIRELY totally and in every way or to the fullest extent **2.** SOLELY AND EXCLUSIVELY solely and to the exclusion of all other things

whom /hoom/ *pron.* (*formal*) **1.** INTRODUCES A QUESTION used to introduce a question asking about the name or identity of a person or people ○ *Whom did you expect to see?* **2.** INTRODUCES A RELATIVE CLAUSE used to introduce a relative clause giving information about a person or people ○ *Birch and her colleagues studied 162 infants, none of whom were born prematurely.* [Old English *hwǣm*, from a prehistoric Germanic word that is also the ancestor of English *who*]

WORD KEY: USAGE

who or **whom**? Although ***whom*** is the correct form when it is the object of a verb or preposition, it has fallen into disuse in many contexts, and constructions with ***who*** are taking its place. A sentence of the type *Do you remember whom you saw?* would be expressed as *Do you remember who you saw?*, and *The man to whom I was talking* as *The man I was talking to* (often with ellipsis of the relative pronoun, as in the last example). Note that ***whom*** is incorrectly used in sentences of the type *The woman whom we thought was dead is still alive*, since the relative pronoun is the subject of *was* (not *is*) and not the object of *thought*.

whomever /hoom évvər/ *pron.* a formal word for 'whoever' when used as the object of a verb or preposition (*formal*)

WORD KEY: USAGE

See Usage note at ***whoever***.

whomp /womp/ *v.* (**whomps, whomping, whomped**) *US* **1.** *vti.* STRIKE to hit sb or sth with great force, especially noisily **2.** *vt.* DEFEAT SB to subject sb to a crushing defeat (*informal*) ■ *n. US* BLOW OR NOISE OF A BLOW a heavy blow or the loud deep sound it makes [Early 20thC. An imitation of the sound.]

whomp up *vt. US* to arouse, incite, or stir up interest or enthusiasm (*archaic*)

whomsoever /hoom sō évvər/ *pron.* an emphatic form of whomever (*formal*)

whoop /woop, hoop/ *v.* (**whoops, whooping, whooped**) **1.** *vi.* **CRY OUT** to make a loud howling cry of excitement or joy **2.** *vt.* **EXCLAIM STH** to exclaim sth loudly and with great excitement **3.** *vt.* **URGE OR DRIVE SB FORWARD** to urge sb on, chase after sb, or drive a person or animal forward with a whooping call **4.** *vi.* **MED WHEEZE** to breathe in with the sharp wheezing sound associated with whooping cough ■ *n.* **1.** **LOUD CRY** a loud howling cry of excitement or joy **2.** **BATTLE CRY** a cry uttered before a battle or hunt, by a warrior, soldier, or hunter **3.** **CALL MADE BY BIRD OR ANIMAL** a loud call or hoot, e.g. from a bird or animal **4.** **MED WHEEZING SOUND** a sharply wheezing inhalation associated with whooping cough [14thC. Ultimately an imitation of the sound.] ◇ **whoop it up 1.** to have fun or celebrate in an extravagant or noisy way (*informal*) **2.** *US* to express and try to arouse enthusiasm for sb or sth (*informal*)

whoop-de-do /woop di doo/, **whoop-de-doo** *n.* *US* (*informal*) **1.** **PARTY** a large-scale party or celebration that is lively or noisy **2.** **PUBLICITY** noisy activity meant to attract attention ○ *the whoop-de-do surrounding the film's release* **3.** **FUSS** a noisy public commotion or outcry ■ *interj.* *US* **EXPRESSING EXCITEMENT** used to express excitement (*informal; often used ironically*) [Mid-20thC. Expressive alteration of WHOOP, perhaps under the influence of TO-DO.]

whoopee /woo pee/ *interj.* used to express great and sudden excitement (*informal; often used ironically*) [Mid-19thC. Alteration of WHOOP.] ◇ **make whoopee** /wooppi/ **1.** to celebrate noisily and exuberantly (*dated informal*) **2.** to engage in sexual activity (*dated informal*)

whoopee cushion /wooppi-/ *n.* a practical joker's toy in the form of an inflatable cushion with a small opening, designed to make a noise resembling flatulence when sb sits on it

whooper /hooper, woo-/ *n.* **1.** = whooping crane **2.** = whooper swan

whooper swan *n.* a large white Eurasian swan with a yellow and black bill, straight neck, and loud whooping cry in flight. Latin name: *Cygnus cygnus*.

whooping cough /hooping-/ *n.* an infectious bacterial disease that causes violent coughing spasms followed by sharp, shrill inhalation. It affects children in particular. Latin name: *Bordetella pertussis*. Technical name **pertussis**

whooping crane /hooping-/ *n.* a large white North American crane with black wingtips that makes a loud whooping cry in flight and is now an endangered species. Latin name: *Grus americana*.

whoops /woops/ *interj.* used to express surprise, concern, or embarrassment at making a mistake or having a slight accident [Mid-20thC. Origin uncertain: possibly a variant of OOPS.]

whoosh /woosh/, **woosh** *n.* **1.** **NOISE OF RUSHING AIR OR WATER** the sound made by rushing air or water **2.** **SWIFT MOTION OR RUSH** a swift motion, spurt, or rush ■ *vi.* (**whooshes, whooshing, whooshed; wooshes, wooshing, wooshed**) **1.** **MAKE RUSHING SOUND** to make the sound of rushing air or rushing water **2.** **MOVE FAST** to move rapidly, with a whooshing sound ○ *whooshed into the room* [Mid-19thC. An imitation of the sound.]

whop /wop/, **whap** /wap/ *vt.* (**whops, whopping, whopped; whaps, whapping, whapped**) (*informal*) **1.** **HIT SB OR STH** to strike sb or sth forcefully **2.** **DEFEAT SB DECISIVELY** to subject an opponent to a crushing defeat ■ *n.* **BLOW OR NOISE OF BLOW** a heavy blow or the loud dull sound it makes [14thC. Variant of *wap* 'to strike, slap', also 'a blow', of unknown origin.]

whopper /wopper/ *n.* (*informal*) **1.** **STH BIG** sth that is much bigger than others of its kind **2.** **BIG LIE** a blatant and outrageous lie [Late 18thC. Formed from WHOPPING.]

whopping /wopping/ *adj.* **BIG** very big or great (*informal*) ■ *adv.* **VERY** extremely (*informal*) [Early 18thC. Formed from WHOP.]

whore /hawr/ *n.* **1.** **OFFENSIVE TERM** an offensive term used to refer to a prostitute (*offensive*) **2.** **OFFENSIVE TERM** an offensive term used to refer to sb regarded as being sexually indiscriminate (*taboo insult offensive*) **3.** **OFFENSIVE TERM** an offensive term used to refer to sb who is regarded as willingly setting aside principles

or personal integrity in order to obtain sth, usually for selfish motives (*insult offensive*) ■ *vi.* (**whores, whoring, whored**) (*offensive*) **1.** **OFFENSIVE TERM** an offensive term meaning to work as a prostitute **2.** **OFFENSIVE TERM** an offensive term meaning to be a regular customer of prostitutes [Old English *hōre*. Ultimately from an Indo-European base meaning 'to desire' that is also the ancestor of English *cherish, caress,* and *Kama Sutra*.]

whore after *vt.* an offensive term meaning to pursue sth desperately, making whatever sacrifices of principles or personal integrity are necessary (*offensive*)

whoredom /hawrdəm/ *n.* **1.** **OFFENSIVE TERM** an offensive term used to refer to the state, status, or job of a prostitute (*literary offensive*) **2.** **BIBLE IDOLATRY** the worship of idols (*literary*) [12thC. Origin uncertain: either formed from WHORE, or from Old Norse *hórdómr*.]

whorehouse /hawr howss/ (*plural* **-houses** /-howziz/) *n.* an offensive term used to refer to a brothel or other place of prostitution (*informal offensive*)

whoremonger /hawr mung gər/ *n.* an offensive term used to refer to a sexually indiscriminate man, especially one who frequents prostitutes (*archaic insult offensive*) —**whoremongery** /hawr mung gəri/ *n.*

whoreson /hawrss'n/ *n.* (*archaic insult offensive*) **1.** **OFFENSIVE TERM** an offensive term used to refer to a boy or man whose paternity is unknown or has not been established **2.** **OFFENSIVE TERM** an offensive term used to refer to a man regarded as dishonest, treacherous, or otherwise disreputable ■ *adj.* **OFFENSIVE TERM** an offensive term meaning contemptible or loathsome (*archaic offensive*) [14thC. Translation of Anglo-Norman *fiz a putain*.]

Whorf hypothesis /wáwrf-/ *n.* = **Sapir-Whorf hypothesis**

whorish /háwrish/ *adj.* (*offensive*) **1.** **OFFENSIVE TERM** an offensive term used to refer to traits of character or behaviour stereotypically ascribed to prostitutes **2.** **OFFENSIVE TERM** an offensive term meaning relating to prostitutes or prostitution —**whorishly** *adv.* —**whorishness** *n.*

Whorl

whorl /wurl/ *n.* **1.** **STH SPIRAL-SHAPED** sth in the shape of a spiral, coil, or curl **2.** **ANAT, CRIMINOL PATTERN ON FINGER OR IN FINGERPRINT** a series of concentric circular or elliptical ridges in the pattern of lines on the gripping surface of a finger or thumb, or this shape seen in a fingerprint **3.** **BOT CIRCLE OF PLANT PARTS** a circular arrangement of three or more leaves, petals, or other plant parts arising at the same level on a stem or other axis, like spokes on a wheel **4.** **ZOOL SPIRAL IN SHELL** any of the turns or coils of a mollusc's shell [15thC. Alteration of WHIRL under the influence of *wharve* 'spindle-whorl' (from the same prehistoric Germanic base as *whirl*).]

whorled /wurld/ *adj.* in the shape of a whorl or having a pattern of whorls

whortleberry /wúrt'lbəri/ (*plural* **-ries**) *n.* **1.** **PLANT WITH EDIBLE BERRIES** a low-growing European plant of the heather family, found in heathland and mountainous areas. It has greenish-pink flowers and tiny sweet blue-black edible fruit. Latin name: *Vaccinium myrtillus*. **2.** **PLANT RELATED TO THE WHORTLEBERRY** any of several plants related to the whortleberry that have edible berries, e.g. the blueberry **3.** **FOOD BERRY OF WHORTLEBERRY PLANT** the edible blue-black fruit of any whortleberry plant [Late 16thC. Dialect variant of *hurtleberry*.]

who's /hooz/ *contr.* **1.** who is **2.** who has

whose /hooz/ *pron., det.* a grammatical word used to talk or ask about the person or thing sth belongs to ○ *Whose are these boots?* ○ *'It wasn't my idea'. – 'Well, whose was it then?'* ○ *a theatre whose doors will always be open to such a talented performer* ○ *Whose car shall we use?* ○ *He wanted to know whose the scarf was.* [Old English *hwæs*, the genitive of the pronouns *hwa* (masculine) 'who' (see WHO) and *hwæt* (neuter) 'what' (see WHAT). Influenced in Middle English by *who* and *whom*.]

whose or **who's?** *Whose* means 'of whom' or 'of which' and denotes possession or association: *These are the children whose father we saw yesterday. There was a church whose steeple had been struck by lightning.* (Some people dislike the use of *whose* to mean 'of which', but it is a well established use and the alternatives are usually awkward.) *Who's* is a contraction of *who is* or *who has*: *She's the one who's coming to dinner next week. Who's got my pen?*

whosoever /hoóssō évvər/ *det.* whoever (*literary or archaic*) [12thC]

who's who *n.* a list of or guide to the most important people in a place or field of activity ○ *The guest list to her party reads like a who's who in the publishing world.*

Who's Who *tdmk.* a trademark for a reference work giving brief biographical sketches for notable people in Great Britain. It was first published in 1848.

WH question *n.* a question that starts with *who, what, where, when, why,* or *how*. It cannot be answered by 'yes' or 'no'.

whs. *abbr.* warehouse

whsle *abbr.* wholesale

whump /wump/ *n.* **MUFFLED SOUND** the sound of a dull thump or muffled explosion ■ *vti.* (**whumps, whumping, whumped**) **THUMP** to make the sound of a dull thump or muffled explosion, or to hit sb or sth with such a sound [Late 19thC. An imitation of the sound.]

whup /wup, woop/ (**whups, whupping, whupped**) *vt.* **1.** *US* **DEFEAT SB** to subject an opponent to a crushing defeat (*informal*) **2.** *Southern US* **WHIP SB** to beat sb with a whip [Late 19thC. Dialect variant of WHIP; from Scots dialect.]

why /wī/ **CORE MEANING:** an adverb used to ask or talk about the reason, purpose, or cause of sth ○ *Why didn't you call?* ○ *I wish you'd tell me why you're so unhappy.* ○ *He could not say why he'd done it.* ○ *It seems clear to me why.*

1. *rel adv.* **BECAUSE OF** for or on account of which ○ *There's no reason why you shouldn't go.* **2.** *interj.* **EXCLAMATION** an exclamation used to express surprise, shock, or indignation ○ *Why, John, how could you!* [Old English *hwy*, the instrumental case form of *hwæt* 'what' (see WHAT).] ◇ **why not** used to express agreement with a suggestion or proposed course of action ○ *'Would you like another coffee?' – 'Why not?'*

Whyalla /wī állə/ city and port on the Spencer Gulf in South Australia. It is a centre of iron and steel production. Population: 23,382 (1996).

whydah /wíddə/ (*plural* **-ah** or **-ahs**), **whidah** (*plural* **-ah** or **-ahs**) *n.* an African weaverbird the male of which has long black tail feathers during the breeding season. Genus: *Vidua*. [Late 18thC. Named after *Ouidah*, a West African town where the bird is found. Perhaps influenced by WIDOW, because of the black coloration of the males.]

whys and wherefores *n.* all the reasons and explanations for sth ○ *Without going into all the whys and wherefores, let's just say the wedding's off.*

WI *abbr.* **1.** West Indian **2.** West Indies **3.** Women's Institute **4.** Wisconsin

Wicca /wíkə/ *n.* religious practice involving nature-worship and witchcraft [Mid-20thC. A deliberate revival of Old English *wicca* (see WITCH).]

Wiccan /wíkən/ *n.* sb who practises Wicca —**Wiccan** *adj.*

Wichita[1] /wíchi taw/ (*plural* **-ta** *or* **-tas**) *n.* PEOPLES a member of a Native North American people that originally lived in lands that are now in Kansas, Oklahoma, and Texas. Its members now live mainly in Oklahoma. [Mid-19thC. From Caddo.]

Wichita[2] /wíchi taw/ city in south-central Kansas, on the Arkansas River, southwest of Emporia. Population: 320,395 (1996).

wick /wik/ *n.* **1.** **MATERIAL HOLDING FUEL THAT BURNS** a string or piece of fabric that uses capillary action to draw the fuel to the flame in a candle, oil lamp, or cigarette lighter **2.** MED **MATERIAL THAT DRAWS UP LIQUID** any piece of material that draws liquid up by capillary action, e.g. a strip of gauze put into a wound to drain it ■ *vti.* (**wicks, wicking, wicked**) **MOVE LIQUID BY CAPILLARY ACTION** to take in or transfer liquid by capillary action, or to be taken in or transferred in this way ○ *synthetic materials that wick moisture away from the skin* [Old English *wēoc*. The word has relatives in Dutch and German, but is of unknown origin.] ◇ **get on sb's wick** to annoy or irritate sb greatly (*slang*)

Wick /wik/ town and port near the northeastern tip of Scotland. Population: 7,681 (1991).

wicked /wíkid/ *adj.* **1.** **VERY BAD** very wrong or very bad **2.** **DANGEROUS** capable of causing harm to sb ○ *a knife with a wicked blade* **3.** **DISTRESSING** causing discomfort, distress, or disappointment (*informal*) ○ *I've got a wicked headache.* **4.** **DISGUSTING** tasting or smelling disgusting and repulsive **5.** **MISCHIEVOUS** liking to tease people playfully or cause them slight trouble, but without upsetting them seriously ○ *a wicked sense of humour* **6.** **MEAN** liking to say very unpleasant things to people ○ *She has a really wicked tongue sometimes!* **7.** **VERY GOOD** very impressive or very skilful (*slang*) ○ *What do you think of the car, then? Pretty wicked, eh?* ■ *adv.* *US* **VERY** extremely (*slang*) ○ *It was wicked good!* ■ *npl.* **BAD PEOPLE** people who do very bad things [13thC] —**wickedly** *adv.* —**wickedness** *n.*

wicker /wíkər/ *n.* **1.** = **wickerwork** *n.* 1 **2.** **TWIG, CANE, OR REED** any one of the twigs, canes, or reeds woven together to make such things as baskets or chairs **3.** **STH MADE OF WICKER** sth such as a basket made of twigs, canes, or reeds [14thC. From Scandinavian. Ultimately from an Indo-European base meaning 'to bend' that is also the ancestor of English *weak* and *vicar*.]

wickerwork /wíkər wurk/ *n.* **1.** **WOVEN TWIGS, CANES, OR REEDS** thin twigs, canes, or reeds woven together to make objects such as baskets and chairs **2.** **THINGS MADE OF WICKER** objects such as baskets and chairs made by weaving together thin twigs, canes, or reeds

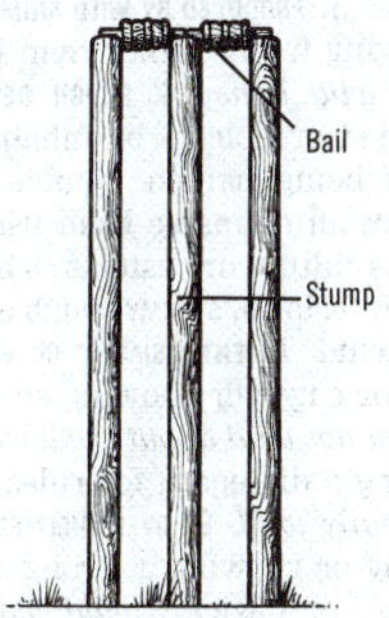

Wicket

wicket /wíkit/ *n.* **1.** **SMALL DOOR OR GATE** a small door or gate, especially one close to or forming part of a larger one **2.** *US* **SMALL OPENING FOR COMMUNICATION** a small opening or window in a wall or door through which people can communicate. Wickets are often fitted with glass, a grating, or a sliding panel. **3.** ENG **GATE CONTROLLING WATER FLOW** a gate used to control the flow of water at a lock or water wheel **4.** CRICKET **UPRIGHT STICKS DEFENDED BY CRICKET BATSMAN** in cricket, either of two sets of three upright sticks (**stumps**) on which are balanced two shorter sticks (**bails**) and in front of which the batsman or batswoman stands **5.** CRICKET **PART OF CRICKET PITCH** the part of a cricket pitch between the two sets of stumps, which are placed 20 m/22 yd apart **6.** CRICKET **TURN OF BATTING** in cricket, a batsman's or batswoman's turn of batting, or that of a pair of batsmen or batswomen ○ *a fifth-wicket partnership between Crawley and Hussein* **7.** CRICKET **ENDING OF TURN OF BATTING** in cricket, the ending of sb's turn of batting, e.g. by knocking down the stumps or catching the ball **8.** SPORTS **CROQUET HOOP** any of the hoops through which the ball is hit in croquet [13thC. Via Old Northern French *wiket*, from prehistoric German. Ultimately from an Indo-European word meaning 'to bend' (see WICKER).]

wicketkeeper /wíkit keepər/ *n.* in cricket, the player positioned behind the wicket to catch the ball or knock the bails off the stumps

wicket maiden *n.* in cricket, an over in which no runs are conceded by the bowler, and at least one wicket falls

wicking /wíking/ *n.* INDUST material used to make wicks

wickiup /wíki up/, **wikiup** *n.* a hut made by Native North Americans of the southwestern United States by covering a framework of arched poles with mats of bark, grass, or branches [Mid-19thC. From Fox *wikiapi*. Ultimately from the same prehistoric Algonquian base as WIGWAM.]

Wicklow /wíklō/ **1.** county in Leinster Province in the southeastern part of the Republic of Ireland. Population: 102,683 (1996). Area: 2,025 sq. km/782 sq. mi. **2.** town and administrative centre of County Wicklow in the Republic of Ireland. Population: 5,850 (1991).

Wicklow Mountains mountain range in County Wicklow, on the eastern coast of the Republic of Ireland. The highest point is Lugnaquill, 926 m/3,039 ft.

widdershins /wíddərshinz/ *adv.* *Scotland* = **withershins**

widdle /wídd'l/ *vi.* (**-dles, -dling, -dled**) **URINATE** to pass urine out of the body (*informal; usually used by or to children*) ■ *n.* **ACT OF URINATION** an act of passing urine out of the body (*informal; usually used by or to children*) () [Mid-20thC. Alteration of PIDDLE.]

wide /wīd/ *adj.* (**wider, widest**) **1.** **WITH SIDES OR EDGES FAR APART** having a relatively large distance or space between one side or edge and the other **2.** **BEING A SPECIFIED DISTANCE APART** having a specified distance between one side or edge and the other ○ *three inches wide* **3.** **OPENED TO GREAT EXTENT** opened to a great extent or as far as possible ○ *staring at him with wide eyes* **4.** **WITH MANY TYPES OR CHOICES** including many varieties, offering many choices, or having a large range ○ *a wide selection of cheeses* **5.** **INVOLVING MANY PEOPLE** from, involving, or given to many people ○ *wide support for the plan* **6.** **LARGE IN SCOPE** with a large scope ○ *a very wide gap between living standards here and in developing countries* **7.** **NOT HITTING TARGET** going some distance away from the intended, expected, or correct place **8.** **GOING BEYOND DETAILS** looking beyond the particular issue involved toward the more general aspects of sth rather than the details ○ *We need to look at the wider implications of these proposals.* **9.** **FITTING LOOSELY** not fitting tightly round the body **10.** **CLEVER AND UNSCRUPULOUS** shrewd and slightly dishonest or unscrupulous (*slang*) ○ *There's some pretty wide characters in this game.* **11.** PHON = **lax** *adj.* 4 ■ *adv.* (**wider, widest**) **1.** **TO GREAT EXTENT** to a great extent or as much as possible ○ *Stand with your legs wide apart.* **2.** **OVER LARGE AREA** over an extensive area ○ *scattered far and wide* **3.** **TO SIDE OF TARGET** to one side of the intended target ○ *A few shots were fired but they all went wide.* ■ *n.* CRICKET **BALL BOWLED BEYOND BATMAN'S REACH** in cricket, a ball bowled beyond the reach of the batsman or batswoman, for which one run is awarded to the batting side [Old English *wīd*. Ultimately from an Indo-European base meaning 'apart' that is also the ancestor of English *with*.] —**wideness** *n.* —**widish** *adj.*

-wide *suffix.* effective throughout a particular place ○ *statewide* ○ *storewide* [From WIDE]

wide-angle *adj.* PHOTOGRAPHY **1.** **GIVING WIDE ANGLE OF VIEW** used to describe a camera lens that gives an unusually wide field of view by making things appear smaller or further away than they really are **2.** **USING WIDE-ANGLE LENS** relating to or using a camera lens with an unusually wide field of view ○ *a wide-angle shot*

wide area network *n.* a network of computers and peripheral devices linked by cable over a broad geographic area

wide-awake *adj.* **1.** **FULLY AWAKE** completely awake and alert (*not hyphenated when used after a verb*) **2.** **ALERT** very aware of surroundings and watching for advantageous possibilities (*informal*) ○ *a wide-awake young go-getter* ■ *n.* **wide-awake, wide-awake hat** CLOTHES **FELT HAT** a soft felt hat with a wide brim and a low crown —**wide-awakeness** *n.*

wide ball *n.* = **wide** *n.*

wide boy *n.* a shrewd and rather unscrupulous man who makes his money in dishonest ways (*informal*) ○ *He's a bit of a wide boy, your mate.*

wide-eyed *adj.* **1.** **WITH EYES WIDE OPEN** with eyes that are wide open, e.g. in amazement or fear **2.** **EASILY FOOLED** lacking experience, wisdom, or common sense and therefore easily fooled by other people

widely /wídli/ *adv.* **1.** **WITH SPACE BETWEEN** with a relatively large distance between ○ *Plant them fairly widely apart.* **2.** **MAKING STH SPREAD OR OPEN WIDE** in such a way as to make sth open or spread as much as possible or to a great extent ○ *smiling a little too widely* **3.** **OVER LARGE AREA** over an extensive area ○ *She is very widely travelled.* **4.** **OVER LARGE RANGE** so as to cover an extensive range ○ *The conversation ranged widely, from politics to bee-keeping.* **5.** **BY MANY PEOPLE** by a large number of people ○ *It is not widely known that he was once an acrobat.* **6.** **GREATLY** to a great degree ○ *widely different examples of this phenomenon*

wide-mouthed /wíd mówthd, -mówtht/ *adj.* **1.** **WITH WIDE MOUTH** with a mouth that is notably wider than average **2.** **WITH MOUTH OPEN WIDE** with the mouth open wide, e.g. in surprise

widen /wíd'n/ (**-ens, -ening, -ened**) *vti.* to become wider or to make sth wider —**widener** *n.*

wide-open *adj.* (*not hyphenated when used after a verb*) **1.** **OPEN TO GREAT EXTENT** open to a great extent, or as much as possible ○ *The door was wide open.* **2.** **UNPREDICTABLE** not as yet decided or even predictable in outcome ○ *The match is still wide open.* **3.** **VULNERABLE TO ATTACK** unprotected and therefore able to be attacked easily **4.** *US* **WITHOUT LAWS OR LAW-ENFORCEMENT** with few laws regulating such things as prostitution, gambling, or the sale of alcohol, or not stringently enforcing the laws that do exist (*informal*)

wide-ranging *adj.* **1.** **DEALING WITH DIFFERENT THINGS** dealing with a great variety of matters **2.** **AFFECTING MANY PEOPLE OR THINGS** affecting a large number of people or things ○ *a decision that has wide-ranging implications*

wide receiver *n.* in American football, a player who positions himself to the side of the offensive formation, and whose role is to catch long passes from the quarterback

wide-screen *adj.* **1.** CINEMA **VERY WIDE** used to describe a type of film projection in which the image is substantially wider than it is tall **2.** **VERY LARGE** used to describe a television whose screen is noticeably larger than average

widespread /wíd spred/ *adj.* **1.** **COMMON** existing or happening in many places, or affecting many people **2.** **SPREAD FAR APART** spread or extending far apart ○ *with arms widespread*

WORD KEY: SYNONYMS

widespread, prevalent, rife, epidemic, universal

CORE MEANING: occurring over a wide area

widespread a general word that describes both concrete and abstract things that occur over a wide area; **prevalent** a more formal word than ***widespread***, often used to suggest that sth occurring over a wide area is also dominant in that area. It can be used to describe both concrete and abstract things; **rife** describes sth undesirable that occurs frequently or in great numbers over a wide area, especially when it appears to be uncontrollable; **epidemic** indicates the widespread occurrence of sth, especially disease, in an area at a particular time; **universal** describes sth that occurs worldwide. It is also used to mean extremely widespread.

widget /wíjit/ n. **1.** UNNAMED DEVICE any little device or mechanism, especially one whose name is unknown or forgotten (*humorous*) **2.** OBJECT a hypothetical manufactured object, considered to represent the typical product of a manufacturer [Early 20thC. Origin uncertain: perhaps an alteration of GADGET.]

Widnes /wídniss/ town near Liverpool, northwestern England, on the River Mersey. Population: 57,162 (1991).

widow /wíddō/ n. **1.** WOMAN WHOSE HUSBAND HAS DIED a woman whose husband has died, especially when she has not remarried **2.** WOMAN LEFT BEHIND a woman whose partner regularly goes away from her to take part in a particular activity (*only used in combination*) ◊ *a golf widow.* ◊ **grass widow 3.** PRINTING SHORT FINAL LINE OF PARAGRAPH a short line at the end of a paragraph, especially when occurring as the top line of a page or column of text. The text is usually altered so that this is removed. ◊ **orphan 4.** CARDS EXTRA HAND OF CARDS an extra hand of cards dealt out in some card games ■ vt. (**-ows, -owing, -owed**) MAKE SB WIDOW OR WIDOWER to cause sb to become a widow or widower (*usually passive*) ◊ *She was widowed a year ago.* [Old English *widuwe*. Ultimately from an Indo-European base meaning 'to separate' that is also the ancestor of English *divide*.] —**widowhood** n.

widow bird (*plural* **widow birds** *or* **widow bird**) n. = **whydah**

widower /wíddō ər/ n. a man whose wife has died, especially when he has not remarried —**widower-hood** n.

widowmaker /wíddō maykər/ n. sth that is so dangerous that it might kill anyone who uses it or tries it

widow's benefit n. a sum of money paid weekly to a widow under the National Insurance scheme in the United Kingdom

widow's cruse n. a source that provides an unending supply of sth [From the miracle of the widow's cruse of oil that supplies Elijah during a famine in the *Bible* (I Kings 17:8–16)]

widow's mite n. a contribution that, although small, is generous because it comes from sb who has very little to give [From the poor widow's contribution of two copper coins to the treasury in the *Bible* (Mark 12:42)]

widow's peak n. a V-shaped line across the top of a person's forehead behind which the hair grows [From the superstition that this feature portends early widowhood]

widow's walk n. a walkway with a rail around it on the rooftop of a house, especially one that was used in the past to keep watch for incoming ships [Said to be so named because, while pacing along it, anxious wives commonly looked in vain for signs of their husbands returning from sea]

widow's weeds npl. the black clothes once traditionally worn by widows (*archaic or literary*)

widow woman n. a widow (*archaic*)

width /width, witth/ n. **1.** DISTANCE ACROSS the distance from one side or edge of sth to the other **2.** STATE OF BEING WIDE the fact of being wide or how wide sth is **3.** SWIMMING SIDE TO SIDE DISTANCE OF POOL the distance from one side of a swimming pool to the other ◊ *Learners begin by swimming widths rather than lengths.* **4.** SEW MATERIAL OF FULL WIDTH a piece of material of its full width

widthwise /width wīz, witth-/, **widthways** /width wayz/ adv. from one side or edge to the other [Late 19thC (WIDTHWAYS: late 18thC)]

Wieland /vée laànt/, **Christoph Martin** (1733–1813) German writer. He wrote both the first German play in blank verse and the first psychological novel.

wield /weeld/ (**wields, wielding, wielded**) vt. **1.** HAVE AND EXERCISE STH to have and be able to use sth, especially power or authority ◊ *the immense economic power wielded by large companies* **2.** USE WEAPON OR TOOL to hold and use a weapon or tool [Old English *wielden* 'to rule', a variant of *wealden*. Ultimately from an Indo-European base meaning 'to be strong' that is also the ancestor of English *valiant* and *valid*.] —**wieldable** adj. —**wielder** n.

Wiener schnitzel /véenər shníts'l/ n. a thin slice of veal coated in egg and breadcrumbs and fried

Wiesbaden /véess baad'n/ industrial city and spa resort in west-central Germany. It is the capital city of Hesse State. Population: 266,400 (1995).

Wiesel /weéz'l/, **Elie** (b. 1928) Romanian-born US writer. He survived the Holocaust, and after settling in the United States in 1956, devoted himself to writing and speaking about it. He won a Nobel Peace Prize in 1986. Full name **Eliezer Wiesel**.

Wiesenthal /véez'n taàl/, **Simon** (b. 1908) Polish-born Austrian war-crimes investigator. He founded (1947) the Jewish Documentation Centre, Vienna, and is thought to have tracked down about 1,000 Nazi war criminals.

wife /wīf/ (*plural* **wives** /wīvz/) n. **1.** SPOUSE the woman to whom a particular man is married **2.** MARRIED WOMAN a woman, especially a married one (*archaic*) **3.** MATURE WOMAN a woman, especially a mature woman (*regional*) [Old English *wīf* 'woman, wife', of unknown origin, but with related forms in other Germanic languages] —**wifehood** n.

wifely /wífli/ (**-lier, -liest**) adj. showing the attitudes or behaviour stereotypically expected of a wife [Old English *wīflic*] —**wifeliness** n.

wig[1] /wig/ (**wigs, wigging, wigged**) n. **1.** FALSE HAIR a covering of hair or sth resembling hair worn on the head for adornment, ceremony, or to cover baldness **2.** TOUPEE a toupee (*informal*) [Late 17thC. Shortening of PERIWIG.] —**wigged** adj.

wig[2] /wig/ (**wigs, wigging, wigged**) vt. UK to speak sternly to sb who has done sth wrong (*dated informal*) [Early 19thC. From WIG[1].]

wigan /wíggən/ n. a tough fabric used for stiffening clothes [Mid-19thC. Named after the town in Lancashire where the material was first made.]

Wigan /wíggən/ industrial town near Manchester, northwestern England. Population: 77,000 (1994).

wigeon /wíjjən/ (*plural* **-geons** *or* **-geon**), **widgeon** (*plural* **-geons** *or* **-geon**) n. a North American duck the male of which has a white crown. Latin name: *Anas americana*.

wigged-out /wígd ówt/ adj. US experiencing an extreme emotional or psychological state such as nervousness or anxiety (*slang*) ◊ *wigged-out from staying up all night*

wigging /wígging/ n. a severely critical scolding (*dated informal*)

wiggle /wígg'l/ vti. (**-gles, -gling, -gled**) MAKE SMALL BACK AND FORTH MOVEMENTS to move from side to side in small quick movements, or to make sth move in this way ■ n. **1.** INSTANCE OF WIGGLING a small quick side-to-side movement **2.** WAVY LINE a line with irregular curves in it [13thC. From Low German or Dutch *wiggelen*, from a prehistoric Germanic base.] —**wiggler** n.

wiggly /wígg'li/ (**-glier, -gliest**) adj. **1.** MAKING WIGGLING MOVEMENTS moving from side to side with small quick movements, or able to be moved in this way (*informal*) **2.** WAVY with many irregular curves ◊ *a wiggly line*

wight[1] /wīt/ n. a living being, especially a human being (*archaic*) [Old English *wiht* (source of English *naught* and *whit*), from a prehistoric Germanic word of unknown origin]

wight[2] /wīt/ adj. brave and strong (*archaic*) [13thC. From Old Norse *vígt*, a form of *vígr* 'skilled in arms'.]

Wight, Isle of /wīt/ the largest offshore island in England, off the southern coast, in the English Channel. Population: 125,100 (1995). Area: 381 sq. km/147 sq. mi.

wiglet /wígglət/ n. a small hairpiece for a woman, worn as an addition to a hairstyle rather than covering the head

wigmaker /wíg maykər/ n. sb who makes wigs for a living

wigwag /wíg wag/ vti. (**-wags, -wagging, -wagged**) **1.** MOVE FROM SIDE TO SIDE to wave or swing from side to side in an arc about a fixed point, or to make sth such as a flag move in this way **2.** NAUT SIGNAL BY WAVING STH to send a message by waving sth such as an arm or a flag ■ n. NAUT **1.** PROCESS OF WIGWAGGING the method of communicating by waving an arm or a flag **2.** MESSAGE SENT BY WIGWAGGING a message

communicated by the moving of arms or flags [Late 16thC. Reduplication of WAG.] —**wigwagger** n.

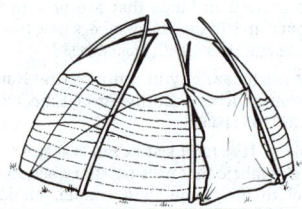

Wigwam

wigwam /wíg wam/ n. **1.** NATIVE N AMERICAN HUT a Native North American hut made by covering a conical or dome-shaped framework of poles with woven rush mats or sheets of bark. Wigwams were used by the Algonquian-speaking Native North Americans of the northeastern United States. **2.** CHILD'S TOY a light tent in the shape of a wigwam for a child to play in [Early 17thC. From Abenaki *wikewam*. Ultimately from the same prehistoric Algonquian base as WICKIUP.]

Wik /wik/ n. a judgment passed by the High Court of Australia in 1996, ruling that the granting of a pastoral lease did not necessarily extinguish all native title rights to land

wikiup n. = **wickiup**

wikiwiki /wíki wiki/ adv. *Hawaii* quickly

Wilberforce /wílbər fáwrss/, **William** (1759–1833) British politician and political reformer. His campaign to end the slave trade resulted in its abolition in the West Indies in 1807, and in the Slave Abolition Act of 1833.

wilco /wílkō/ interj. used to indicate that you understand what has just been said in a radio message and will do what is necessary [Mid-20thC. Blend and shortening of *will comply*.]

Wilcoxon test /wil kóks'n-/ n. a statistical test of the equality of similar or matched groups of data to determine whether they differ significantly from one another, without any assumptions about the underlying distribution patterns [Mid-20thC. Named after Frank *Wilcoxon* (1892–1965), the Irish statistician who developed the test.]

wild /wīld/ adj. **1.** NOT TAME OR DOMESTICATED not kept as a pet or used for display, work, or experimentation, but living freely in a natural habitat **2.** NOT CULTIVATED growing in a natural state rather than being cultivated in fields, parks, or gardens ◊ *picking wild strawberries* **3.** PRODUCED BY WILD ANIMALS produced by animals living freely rather than by domesticated animals ◊ *wild honey* **4.** ROUGH, DESOLATE, OR BARREN not inhabited or able to be inhabited by humans because of being barren, remote, or desolate **5.** OFFENSIVE TERM an offensive term used to describe a people or its culture or customs as being supposedly culturally inferior **6.** STORMY rough and stormy, with a strong wind **7.** ENTHUSIASTIC OR EAGER feeling enthusiastic or eager or showing enthusiasm or eagerness ◊ *I'm not wild about the idea.* **8.** UNRULY lively and showing a disregard for rules ◊ *The kids next door are really wild.* **9.** OVERWHELMED BY EMOTION overwhelmed by or showing a strong emotion such as anger, grief, or desire ◊ *wild with grief.* **10.** UNRESTRAINED marked by a lack of restraint or prudence, especially in things considered to be vices ◊ *a really wild party* **11.** UNTIDY not neat or well-groomed ◊ *His hair was wild.* **12.** NOT CAREFULLY THOUGHT OUT not based on rational thought, evidence, or probability ◊ *I just made a wild guess.* **13.** SPORTS POORLY AIMED not carefully aimed ◊ *throwing wild punches* **14.** UNCONVENTIONAL unconventional, exciting, and slightly irrational (*informal*) ◊ *a wild idea* **15.** EXCELLENT excellent (*dated slang*) ◊ *Hey, man, that's really wild!* **16.** CARDS WITH VALUE ASSIGNED BY PLAYER used to describe a playing card that has any value that the player using it wishes to give it ◊ *Jokers are wild.* ■ adv. **1.** IN UNCULTIVATED WAY in a natural state rather than being cultivated in fields, parks, or gardens

○ *flowers that grow wild in the fields* **2. IN UNCONTROLLED WAY** in an uncontrolled, unpredictable, or unplanned way ○ *She just lets her kids run wild.* **3.** *Ireland* **EXTREMELY** to an extreme degree (*informal*) ○ *That was wild stupid.* ■ *n.* **UNDOMESTICATED STATE** the natural, free state of an undomesticated animal ○ *Most people have never actually seen a panda in the wild.* ■ *n.* **wild, wilds** *npl.* **UNINHABITED AREA** an area that is completely uninhabited or only very sparsely populated because it is remote or rugged ○ *They live somewhere out in the wilds.* [Old English *wilde*. Ultimately from an Indo-European word meaning 'wild, woods' that is also the ancestor of English *wold* and *vole*.] —**wildish** *adj.* —**wildness** *n.*

——— WORD KEY: SYNONYMS ———
See Synonyms at *unruly*.

Wild /wīld/, **Jonathan** (1682?–1725) English criminal. He gained widespread notoriety in England as the organizer of a gang that both stole and sold goods. He was eventually hanged.

wild boar *n.* a wild pig of Europe and Asia that has a coat ranging from pale grey to black, dense bristles, a thin body, and small tusks. Latin name: *Sus scrofa.*

wild brier *n.* = wild rose

wild card *n.* **1. SB OR STH UNPREDICTABLE** sb or sth that is important to a plan or course of action, but whose behaviour cannot be predicted (*informal*) **2.** SPORTS **EXTRA PLAYER OR TEAM IN COMPETITION** an extra player or team selected to take part in a competition although not technically qualified to do so **3.** COMPUT **COMPUTER SYMBOL REPRESENTING ANY CHARACTER** a symbol, usually *, that can be used to represent any character that may appear in the same position in a computer search argument **4.** CARDS **CARD OF NO FIXED VALUE** in card games, a card that can have whatever value its player assigns it

wild carrot *n.* = Queen Anne's lace

Wildcat

wildcat /wīld kat/ *n.* (*plural* **-cats** *or* **-cat**) **1. WILD EUROPEAN OR ASIAN CAT** a cat of Europe, Asia, and Africa that resembles the domestic tabby but is heavier and has a bushy tail. It is regarded as the ancestor of the domestic cat. Latin name: *Felis sylvestris.* **2.** *US, Can* **MEDIUM-SIZED WILD FELINE** any of several medium-sized wild felines such as the bobcat, caracal, lynx, and ocelot **3. QUICK-TEMPERED PERSON** sb who tends to get angry quickly **4.** INDUST, UTIL **SPECULATIVE OIL OR GAS WELL** an exploratory or speculative well drilled in an area not yet known to be productive of oil or gas **5.** *Can, US* COMM **FINANCIALLY UNSOUND BUSINESS** a financially unsound business ■ *adj. US, Can* **NOT FINANCIALLY SAFE** practising unethical or financially risky business methods, or characteristic of such methods ○ *wildcat stocks* ■ *vti.* (**-cats, -catting, -catted**) INDUST, UTIL **DRILL EXPLORATORY WELL** to drill an exploratory well or take samples in an area not yet known to have any reserves of what is being sought, especially oil or gas —**wildcatting** *n., adj.*

wildcat strike *n.* a sudden strike not authorized by the trade union that the strikers belong to

wildcatter /wīld katər/ *n. US, Can* **1.** INDUST, UTIL **PROSPECTOR** sb who prospects for oil in areas not yet known to be productive (*informal*) **2.** COMM **UNETHICAL BUSINESSPERSON** sb who develops or promotes risky or fraudulent business ventures **3. WILDCAT STRIKE PARTICIPANT** sb who participates in a sudden strike not authorized by the trade union he or she belongs to

wild cherry *n.* = gean

wild dog *n.* any wild member of the dog family, especially the dingo, the African hunting dog, or the dhole

Oscar Wilde

Wilde /wīld/, **Oscar** (1854–1900) Irish writer. His works include the plays *Lady Windermere's Fan* (1892) and *The Importance of Being Earnest* (1895) and the novel *The Picture of Dorian Gray* (1891). His flamboyance and legendary wit made him a leading figure in society, but he was convicted of sodomy and sentenced to two years' hard labour in 1895. Full name **Oscar Fingal O'Flahertie Wills Wilde**

wildebeest /vīldə beest, wīldə-/ (*plural* **-beests** *or* **-beest**) *n.* = gnu [Early 19thC. From Afrikaans, literally 'wild beast'.]

wilder /wīldər/ (**-ders, -dering, -dered**) *vti.* (*archaic*) **1. GO OR LEAD ASTRAY** to go astray or lead sb or sth astray **2. BEWILDER** to become confused by a number of complex options, or to confuse sb in this way [Early 17thC. Origin uncertain: perhaps a back formation from WILDERNESS.] —**wilderment** *n.*

Wilder /wīldər/, **Billy** (b. 1906) Austrian-born US film director. At home in a wide variety of film genres, he made several Hollywood classics, including *Sunset Boulevard* (1950) and *Some Like It Hot* (1959). Real name **Samuel Wilder**

wilderness /wīldərnəss/ *n.* **1. NATURAL UNCULTIVATED LAND** a mostly uninhabited area of land such as a forest or mountainous region in its natural uncultivated state, sometimes deliberately preserved like this **2. BARREN AREA** an area that is empty or barren ○ *in the vast wilderness of outer space* **3. DELIBERATELY UNCULTIVATED LAND IN GARDEN** a piece of land, e.g. in a garden, that is deliberately not cultivated but is left to grow wild **4. LOSS OF INFLUENCE** the state of being without power or influence for a time after having been in a position of leadership or authority, especially in politics, **5. UNCOMFORTABLE SITUATION** a place, situation, or multitude of people or things that makes sb feel confused, overwhelmed, or desolate ○ *the wilderness of the big city* [Old English *wilddēornes*, formed from *wilddēor* 'wild beast', from *wilde* 'wild' + *dēor* 'animal' (see DEER)] ◊ **be (a voice) crying in the wilderness** to be giving advice or suggestions that are very unlikely to be followed

wilderness area *n. US* a protected area set aside for preservation in as natural a state as possible, with restrictions on most human activity, except for nonmotorized forms of outdoor recreation ○ *backpacking in the wilderness areas*

wild-eyed *adj.* **1. WITH EYES WIDE WITH EMOTION** with eyes that are wide and glaring because of fear, anger, or a psychological disorder **2. EXTREME** marked by or advocating ideas that are so extreme and far-fetched as to be completely impractical

wildfire /wīld fīr/ *n.* **1. RAPIDLY SPREADING FIRE** a fierce fire that spreads rapidly, especially in an area of wilderness **2. = will-o'-the-wisp 3. LIGHTNING WITHOUT THUNDER** lightning that occurs without audible thunder **4.** HIST, MIL **INFLAMMABLE MATERIAL AS WEAPON** any of various inflammable materials used in warfare in the past, e.g. against enemy ships [Old English] ◊ **like wildfire** very rapidly

wild flower *n.* a flowering plant growing in a natural, uncultivated state, or the flower of such a plant

wildfowl /wīld fowl/ (*plural* **-fowl**) *n.* a bird that is

hunted for food or sport, e.g. a duck or a goose [Old English] —**wildfowler** *n.* —**wildfowling** *n.*

Wild Geese *n.* Irish Jacobites who left Ireland for Europe after the fall of James II at the end of the 17th century, especially those who joined the French army [Mid-19thC. These Irishmen were so called because of their flight to the European continent.]

wild-goose chase *n.* a futile search for sth that there is no chance of finding, especially because it does not exist [Originally the expression referred to following sb or sth along an irregular course, as wild geese follow one another in their patterned flight]

wild hyacinth *n.* = bluebell *n.* 1

wild indigo *n.* a North American plant of the legume family that has three-lobed leaves and bright yellow flowers. Genus: *Baptisia.*

wilding /wīlding/ *n.* **1. WILD PLANT OR TREE** a plant that grows wild or one that has escaped from cultivation, especially a wild crab-apple tree **2. FRUIT** the fruit of a plant that grows wild or that has escaped from cultivation, especially a wild crab apple **3. WILD ANIMAL** a wild animal ■ *adj.* **UNCULTIVATED** uncultivated or undomesticated

wild Irishman *n. NZ* PLANTS = matagouri

wildlife /wīld līf/ *n.* wild animals, birds, and other living things, sometimes including vegetation, living in a natural undomesticated state

wildlife park *n.* = safari park

wildling /wīldling/ *n.* = wilding

wildly /wīldli/ *adv.* **1. WITH ENTHUSIASM** in a very enthusiastic way ○ *cheering wildly* **2. WITHOUT CAREFUL THOUGHT** not considering sth carefully **3. VERY** to a great extent (*informal*) ○ *not wildly enthusiastic about the idea* **4. IN WAY THAT SHOWS FEAR** in an uncontrolled way that betrays fear or anxiety, and often with eyes that are wide and staring ○ *looking wildly in all directions* **5. STRONGLY** in a fierce and rough way ○ *The wind blew wildly through the trees.*

wild man *n.* **1. SB WITH RADICAL IDEAS** a man who has extreme or radical opinions, especially in politics **2. OFFENSIVE TERM** an offensive term used to refer to a man regarded as supposedly being culturally inferior (*archaic offensive*)

wild mustard *n.* = charlock

wild oat *n.* a weedy annual grass of temperate regions that resembles cultivated oats. Latin name: *Avena fatua.* ◊ **sow your wild oats** to behave in an uncontrolled way, especially sexually, while young

wild olive *n.* a tree that resembles the olive tree and bears fruit that resemble olives

wild pansy *n.* a European and Asian plant of the violet family with blue, violet, and yellow flowers. Latin name: *Viola tricolor.*

wild pink *n.* a perennial plant of the eastern United States that has pink or whitish flowers. Latin name: *Silene caroliniana.*

wild pitch *n.* a baseball pitch that a catcher could not have caught and that results in a runner advancing to the next base. ◊ **passed ball**

wild rice *n.* **1. TALL N AMERICAN GRASS** a tall perennial aquatic grass of North America that yields an edible grain. Latin name: *Zizania aquatica.* **2.** FOOD **GRAIN OF WILD RICE** the dark grain of the wild rice plant, used as food

wild rose *n.* any wild-growing rose such as the dog rose and sweetbrier

wild rubber *n.* rubber obtained from uncultivated rubber trees

wild rye *n.* a perennial grass of temperate regions that has flat leaves, paired ears, and resembles cultivated rye. Genus: *Elymus.*

wild silk *n.* **1. SILK FROM WILD SILKWORMS** silk fibre obtained from wild silkworms **2.** TEXTILES **FABRIC MADE OF WILD SILK** fabric woven from the silk of wild silkworms, or an imitation of this made with short silk fibres

wild type *n.* the form of an organism, strain, or gene that results from natural breeding, as opposed to mutant forms or those resulting from selective breeding

wild water *n.* = **white water** (*hyphenated when used before a noun*)

Wild West show *n.* a North American form of entertainment involving the demonstration of skills associated with the Wild West, e.g. shooting, riding, and roping cattle, especially performed by people dressed as cowboys

wildwood /wíld wŏŏd/ *n.* natural uncultivated woodland (*archaic or literary*) [Old English]

wile /wīl/ *n.* **TRICK** a trick or cunning ruse ■ **wiles** *npl.* **TRICKERY MEANT TO PERSUADE** trickery intended to persuade sb to do sth, especially in the form of insincere charm or flattery ■ *vt.* (**wiles, wiling, wiled**) **PERSUADE SB BY WILES** to trick or entice sb into doing or not doing sth (*dated*) [12thC. Origin uncertain: perhaps from or related to Old Norse *vél* 'artifice'.]

Wilfrid /wílfrid/, **Wilfrith, St** (634–709?) British prelate. At the Synod of Whitby (664), he successfully argued for the replacement of Celtic forms of worship with Roman ones in the English Church. Also known as **St Wilfrith**

wilful /wílf'l/ *adj.* **1.** **DELIBERATE** done deliberately, especially with the intention of harming sb or in spite of knowing that it will harm sb **2.** **STUBBORN** always determined to act on a desire, regardless of the opinions or advice of others (*disapproving*) —**wilfully** *adv.* —**wilfulness** *n.*

─── **WORD KEY: SYNONYMS** ───
See Synonyms at **unruly**.

Wilhelmshaven /víl helmz háavən, víl helms háafən/ city and port in northwestern Germany. It was formerly an important naval base. Population: 89,900 (1989).

Wilkes /wilks/, **John** (1725–97) British political leader and reformer. An MP from 1757, he was imprisoned for libel after publishing an attack on a speech by George III. On his release he campaigned for political reforms and supported the patriots during the American War of Independence.

Wilkins /wílkinz/, **Maurice** (*b.* 1916) UK biophysicist. For his study of the structure of DNA, he shared a Nobel Prize (1962) with James Watson and Bernard Crick. Full name **Maurice Hugh Frederick Wilkins**

will[1] /wil/ **CORE MEANING:** a modal verb used to indicate future time ○ *Delegates from all over Europe will attend the forum.* ○ *Will you ever be able to forgive him?* ○ *Your suit will be ready for collection tomorrow.*
v. **1.** *vi.* **RESOLUTION** indicating intent, purpose, or determination ○ *I will be staying with Jean when I come to England.* ○ *I will study harder for these exams.* **2.** *vi.* **POLITE QUESTIONS** used in questions to make polite invitations or offers ○ *Will you sit down please?* ○ *Will you have more coffee?* **3.** *vi.* **REQUESTS** used in questions to make requests ○ *Will you take the washing out for me please?* ○ *Phone the garage, will you?* **4.** *vi.* **COMMANDS** used when ordering sb to do sth ○ *You will do exactly as I say.* ○ *Examination candidates will not start writing until told to do so.* **5.** *vi.* **CUSTOMARY BEHAVIOUR** used to indicate the way that sth usually happens or the way that sb usually does sth ○ *The wetter the road conditions, the harder it will be for a vehicle to stop.* ○ *When they're out together they will shop till they drop!* **6.** *vi.* **WILLINGNESS** used to indicate that sb is willing to do sth ○ *I will mail your letters for you.* ○ *I will not tolerate this kind of behaviour.* **7.** *vi.* **ABILITY** used to indicate the ability or capacity of sth ○ *That wardrobe will not fit in your bedroom.* ○ *The truck will carry loads of up to 10 tons.* **8.** *vi.* **EXPECTATION** used to express surmise or likelihood ○ *That will be them at the door now.* ○ *He will have left the country by now.* **9.** *vi.* **INCLINATION** used to indicate the inevitability of sth happening or being true ○ *She will stay up till all hours in front of the TV.* **10.** *Scotland* **POLITE WAY OF ASKING STH** used in statements to avoid the impoliteness of a question (*informal*) ○ *This will be your brother.* [Old English *wyllan*. Ultimately from an Indo-European base that is also the ancestor of German *wollen* and Latin *velle*.]

─── **WORD KEY: USAGE** ───
See Usage note at **shall**.

will[2] /wil/ *n.* **1.** **PART OF MIND THAT MAKES DECISIONS** the part of the mind with which sb consciously decides things **2.** **POWER TO DECIDE** the power to make decisions ○ *This lawnmower seems to have a will of its own!* **3.** **PROCESS OF MAKING DECISIONS** the use of the mind to make decisions about things **4.** **DETERMINATION** the determination to do sth ○ *She has lots of ability but she lacks the will to succeed.* **5.** **DESIRE OR INCLINATION** a desire or inclination to do sth **6.** **ATTITUDE TOWARD SB ELSE** the attitude or feelings sb has toward sb or sth **7.** **STH DESIRED BY SB TO HAPPEN** what a person or group, especially one in authority, wants to happen (*formal*) ○ *It was her will that he should never be told the truth.* **8.** **LAW DETERMINING DISTRIBUTION OF DECEASED'S PROPERTY** a statement of what sb wants to happen to his or her property after he or she dies, or a legal document containing this statement. ◊ **living will** ■ *vt.* (**wills, willing, willed**) **1.** **TRY TO CAUSE STH BY THOUGHTS** to make or try to make sth happen or sb do sth by the power of the mind ○ *He willed himself to stay awake.* ○ *Her parents were watching her run, willing her on.* **2.** **LAW LEAVE SB STH IN WILL** to give sth officially to sb by declaring it in a will **3.** **WANT OR DECIDE STH** to want sth to happen or to decide that sth will happen (*archaic or formal*) ○ *It shall be as God wills.* [Old English *willa* (noun), *wyllan* (verb), and *willian* (verb from the base of the noun). Ultimately from an Indo-European base meaning 'to will, wish'.] —**willer** *n.* ◊ **at will** when sb wishes (*formal*) ○ *They are free to come and go at will.* ◊ **with a will** with energy and enthusiasm (*formal*) ○ *He set about the task with a will.* ◊ **with the best will in the world** used to indicate that sb cannot do sth however much he or she wishes or tries to do it ○ *With the best will in the world we won't be able to supervise her all the time.*

willable /wíllǝb'l/ *adj.* able to be done or decided by the force of willpower (*old*) [15thC. Formed from WILL[2].]

willemite /wíllǝ mīt/ *n.* a colourless brown, green, or red mineral form of zinc sulphate that occurs with some zinc ores and fluoresces in ultraviolet light [Mid-19thC. Named after the king of the Netherlands, *Willem* I (1772–1843).]

willet /wíllit/ *n.* a large grey North American shore bird that has a long straight moderately stout bill, long legs, and a distinctive black-and-white wing pattern. Latin name *Catoptrophorus semipalmatus.* [Mid-19thC. An imitation of the sound made by the bird.]

willful *adj.* US = **wilful**

William /wíllyǝm/, **Prince of the United Kingdom** (*b.* 1982). The first child of Prince Charles and Diana, Princess of Wales, he is second in line to the British throne.

William I, King of England (1028?–87). A Norman, he invaded England and defeated Harold II at the Battle of Hastings (1066), subsequently imposing a new ruling aristocracy on England. The *Domesday Book* was compiled during his reign. Known as **William the Conqueror**

William II, King of England (1056?–1100). The son and successor of William I, he seized territory in Normandy and Scotland. He was killed, probably accidentally, while hunting in the New Forest. Known as **William Rufus**

William III, King of England, Scotland, and Ireland (1650–1702) Dutch-born English monarch. He was the grandson of Charles I and the husband of James II's daughter Mary. He and Mary replaced James II on the English throne after the Revolution of 1689. Known as **William of Orange**

William IV, King of the United Kingdom (1765–1837). He succeeded his brother George IV on the throne after a 50-year naval career, and during his reign (1830–37) was the last monarch to exercise the royal prerogative. Known as **the Sailor King**

William (of Malmesbury) (1090?–1143?) English monk and chronicler. He wrote histories of the kings of England from Saxon times to 1142 and of the bishops of England to 1123.

Williams /wíllyǝmz/, **Emlyn** (1905–87) UK playwright, novelist, and actor. He is the author of *Night Must Fall* (1935) and of autobiographical works. He acted in his own plays and appeared in films.

Williams, Fred (1927–82) Australian painter. He is noted for his semiabstract paintings of the Australian landscape. Full name **Frederick Ronald Williams**

Williams, Hank (1923–53) US musician. He developed a wide audience for country music through his recordings and performances on radio and at the Grand Ole Opry. His songs include 'Your Cheatin' Heart'. Real name **Hiram Williams**

Williams, John (*b.* 1941) Australian-born British classical guitarist. His solo and orchestral work contributed much to the popularization of the classical guitar. Full name **John Christopher Williams**

Williams, J. P. R. (*b.* 1949) UK Rugby Union footballer. He is known for his skill as a full-back. He was also an accomplished tennis player. He later became a medical registrar. Full name **John Peter Rhys Williams**

Williams, Ted (*b.* 1918) US baseball player. A Boston Red Sox outfielder (1939–60), he was one of the game's greatest hitters, batting .406 in 1941 and compiling a lifetime average of .344. Full name **Theodore Samuel Williams**

Tennessee Williams

Williams, Tennessee (1911–83) US playwright. His plays are largely set in the American South, and he won Pulitzer Prizes for *A Streetcar Named Desire* (1947) and *Cat on a Hot Tin Roof* (1955). Real name **Thomas Lanier Williams**

Williamson /wíllyǝmsǝn/, **David Keith** (*b.* 1942) Australian playwright. He wrote *The Removalists* (1972). His screenplays include *Gallipoli* (1982).

Williamson, Henry (1895–1977) British novelist. He wrote nature stories and novels, including *Tarka the Otter* (1927).

Williams pear /wíllyǝmz-/ *n.* a variety of pear tree [Early 19thC. Named after *William's* Nursery of Middlesex, where the pear was developed.]

willie *n.* = **willy**

willies /wílliz/ *npl.* an uncomfortable, anxious, or fearful feeling (*informal*) [Late 19thC. Origin unknown.]

willing /wílling/ *adj.* **1.** **READY TO DO STH VOLUNTARILY** ready to do sth without being forced to **2.** **HELPFUL** cooperative and enthusiastic **3.** **OFFERED VOLUNTARILY** offered or given by sb readily and enthusiastically [Old English] —**willingly** *adv.* —**willingness** *n.*

willing horse *n.* sb who is willing to work hard whenever necessary (*dated*)

Willis /wílliss/, **Norman** (*b.* 1933) British trade union leader. As secretary general of the Trades Union Congress (1984–93), he was noted for his moderation in negotiating industrial disputes. Full name **Norman David Willis**

williwaw /wílli waw/ *n.* *US, Can* a violent gust of cold wind blowing down from a mountainous region to the coast and out to sea, especially in the Straits of Magellan and in Alaska [Mid-19thC. Origin unknown.]

will-o'-the-wisp /wíll ǝ thǝ wísp/ *n.* **1.** **LIGHT FROM BURNING MARSH GAS** a phosphorescent light sometimes seen at night over marshy ground, caused by the spontaneous combustion of gases given off by rotting organic matter **2.** **SB OR STH ELUSIVE** sb or sth that is misleading or elusive, e.g. a false hope [From *Will*, a shortening of the forename *William*, + OF + THE + WISP] — **will-o'-the-wispish** *adj.*

willow /wíllō/ *n.* **1.** TREES **TREE WITH LONG FLEXIBLE BRANCHES** a tree or shrub with long flexible branches, narrow leaves, and catkins containing small flowers without petals. Some species are valued for their wood, twigs, and tanbark. Genus: *Salix.* **2.** INDUST **WILLOW WOOD** the wood of the willow tree **3.** CRICKET BAT a cricket bat (*informal*) **4.** INDUST **MACHINE FOR CLEANING FIBROUS MATERIALS** a machine with a revolving spiked cylinder inside a box that is also fitted with spikes, used to clean or loosen fibrous materials such as cotton, wool, or rags [Old English *welig.* Perhaps ultimately from an Indo-European base meaning 'to turn' that is the ancestor of English *well* and *helix.*] —**willowish** *adj.*

── WORD KEY: CULTURAL NOTE ──

The Wind in the Willows, a children's story by the British writer Kenneth Grahame (1908). Originally written as a bed-time story for Grahame's son, it recounts the mishaps that befall four animals – Mole, Water Rat, Toad, and Badger – when they venture outside their natural habitats. Much-loved by children, the tales are also enjoyed by adults as entertaining allegories of human behaviour.

willow grouse *n.* a plump ground bird of the grouse family found in northern Europe, Asia, and North America that turns from mottled brown to white in the winter. Latin name: *Lagopus lagopus.* US term **willow ptarmigan**

willowherb /wíllō hurb/ *n.* = **rosebay willowherb**

willow pattern *n.* a pattern used to decorate china, usually blue on a white background, featuring a Chinese landscape with a willow tree, pagoda-style buildings, a bridge, and two swallows. The willow pattern was created for Thomas Turner in about 1799 by Thomas Minton, who later founded his own pottery firm at Stoke-on-Trent. (*hyphenated when used before a noun*)

willow tit *n.* a black-capped member of the tit family found in forest and scrub in northern Europe and Asia. Latin name: *Parus montanus.*

willow warbler *n.* a small bird of the leaf warbler family that lives in woodlands in Europe and Asia and is distinguishable from a chiffchaff by its song. Latin name: *Phylloscopus trochilus.*

Willowware

willowware /wíllō wair/ *n.* china decorated with the willow pattern

willowy /wíllō .i/ (**-ier, -iest**) *adj.* **1.** GRACEFUL used to describe sb who is slim, graceful, and elegant, partly because of being tall **2.** FLEXIBLE able to be bent easily, and springing back into place **3.** COVERED BY WILLOWS covered or shaded by willow trees

willpower /wíl pow ər/ *n.* a combination of determination and self-discipline that enables sb to do sth despite the difficulties involved

Wills /wilz/, **William John** (1834–61) British-born Australian surveyor and explorer. He was second in command to Robert Burke on an ill-fated expedition to northern Australia (1860–61), during which both died.

willy /wílli/ (*plural* **-lies**), **willie** *n.* an offensive term for a penis (*informal offensive*) [Early 20thC. Formed from a shortening of the proper name *William.*]

willy-nilly /wílli nílli/ *adv.* **1.** NOT CONTROLLABLY whether or not sb wants it to happen ○ *He won't be rushed willy-nilly into a quick decision.* **2.** HAPHAZARDLY in a disorganized or unplanned way ○ *Totally confused by now, I handed out the invitations willy-nilly.* ■

adj. **1.** HAPPENING WITHOUT CHOICE happening or existing without plan or choice **2.** HAPHAZARD lacking direction or organization [Early 17thC. From the phrase *will I, nill I* 'whether I wish it or do not wish it'.]

willy wagtail *n.* ANZ a small insect-eating Australian bird that is black with white underparts, frequently wags its wide tail, and is common throughout the continent, particularly in urban areas. Latin name: *Rhipidura leucophrys.* [A form of *William*]

willy-willy *n.* Aus a dust storm or whirlwind [Late 19thC. From Aboriginal Australian.]

Wilson /wílss'n/, **Alexander** (1766–1813) British-born US ornithologist. He conducted the first major studies of North American birds, and wrote and illustrated *American Ornithology* (1808–13).

Wilson, Sir Angus (1913–91) British writer. He wrote short stories and novels including *Anglo-Saxon Attitudes* (1956) and *The Old Men at the Zoo* (1961). Full name **Sir Angus Frank Johnstone Wilson**

AKG London

Harold Wilson

Wilson, Harold, Baron Wilson of Rievaulx (1916–95) British statesman. He served two terms as Labour prime minister (1964–70, 1974–76). He sought to bolster Britain's economy and introduced the first antiracist legislation.

Library of Congress

Woodrow Wilson

Wilson, Woodrow (1856–1924) US statesman and 28th president of the United States. A Democratic president (1913–21), he brought the United States into World War I in 1917 and negotiated the peace treaty in 1918, making the League of Nations a part of the treaty. He was awarded the Nobel Peace Prize in 1919. Full name **Thomas Woodrow Wilson** —**Wilsonian** *adj.*

Wilson's disease *n.* a rare hereditary disease resulting from an inability to metabolize copper and marked by cirrhosis of the liver, damage to other organs, and psychiatric disorder [Early 20thC. Named after S. A. Kinnier *Wilson* (1878–1937), English neurologist.]

Wilson's petrel (*plural* **Wilson's petrels** *or* **Wilson's petrel**) *n.* = **Wilson's storm petrel**

Wilson's Promontory peninsula in southeastern Victoria, Australia. It is the most southerly point on the Australian mainland.

Wilson's storm petrel, **Wilson's petrel** *n.* a small dark seabird of southern oceans that breeds in Antarctica but sometimes wanders to the northern Atlantic. Latin name: *Oceanites oceanicus.*

wilt[1] /wilt/ *v.* (**wilts, wilting, wilted**) **1.** *vti.* BOT **DROOP OR SHRIVEL** to droop or shrivel, or make a plant droop or shrivel through lack of water, too much heat, or

disease **2.** *vi.* **BECOME WEAK** to become weak and tired, e.g. because of heat **3.** *vti.* **LOSE CONFIDENCE** to lose confidence, composure, or enthusiasm, or to make sb do this ■ *n.* **1.** BOT **DROOPING OR SHRIVELLING** the drooping of plants or shrivelling of leaves because of a lack of water, too much heat, or disease **2.** BOT **PLANT DISEASE** a plant disease caused by fungi, bacteria, or viruses that make plants droop and leaves shrivel **3.** **ACT OF WILTING** an instance of wilting or the condition of having wilted [Late 17thC. Origin uncertain: perhaps a dialect variant of obsolete *welk*, probably of Low Dutch origin.]

wilt[2] *vti.* 2nd person present singular of **will** (*archaic*)

Wilton /wíltən/ *n.* carpet with a thick velvety pile [Late 18thC. Named after a town in the county of Wiltshire, known for its carpet industry.]

Wilts /wilts/ *abbr.* Wiltshire

Wiltshire /wíltshər/ county in southwestern England. Trowbridge is the administrative centre. Population: 594,000 (1995). Area: 3,486 sq. km/1,344 sq. mi.

wily /wíli/ (**-lier, -liest**) *adj.* skilled at using clever tricks to deceive people —**wilily** *adv.* —**wiliness** *n.*

wimble /wímb'l/ *n.* **BORING TOOL** a hand-held tool used for boring holes ■ *vt.* (**-bles, -bling, -bled**) **MAKE HOLE WITH WIMBLE** to bore a hole with a wimble [13thC. From Anglo-Norman, probably from Middle Dutch *wimmel* 'augur'.]

Wimbledon /wímb'ldən/ southern suburb of London. It is the home of the All England Lawn Tennis Club, the site of annual international tennis championships.

wimp /wimp/ *n.* an offensive term used to refer to sb who is regarded as weak, timid, unassertive, or ineffectual (*insult offensive*) [Early 20thC. Origin uncertain: perhaps a shortening of WHIMPER.] —**wimpish** *adj.* —**wimpy** *adj.*

wimp out *vi.* to fail to do or finish doing sth because of fear or a weakness of character (*slang*)

WIMP[1] /wimp/ *n.* a graphical user interface for computers designed to make them more user-friendly that includes windows, icons, mice, and pull-down menus. Full form **windows, icons, mice, and pull-down menus**

WIMP[2] /wimp/ *n.* a hypothetical nonbaryonic subatomic particle that has been proposed as a possible form of dark matter. Full form **weakly interacting massive particle**

wimple /wímp'l/ *n.* **1.** CLOTHES, HIST **WOMAN'S HEAD COVERING** a cloth covering for a woman's head and neck. The wimple was common in medieval Europe and it is still worn by some orders of nuns. **2.** **FOLD IN CLOTH** a fold or pleat in a piece of cloth ■ *v.* (**-ples, -pling, -pled**) **1.** *vi.* RIPPLE to form small undulating waves **2.** *vt.* CLOTHES **DRESS SB IN WIMPLE** to put a wimple on sb (*archaic*) [Old English *wimpel.* Perhaps from the Indo-European base meaning 'to turn' that is the ancestor of English *wipe* and *vibrate.*]

Wimpy /wímpi/ *tdmk.* a trademark for a type of hamburger served in a bread roll

win /win/ *v.* (**wins, winning, won** /wun/, **won**) **1.** *vti.* ACHIEVE **VICTORY** to beat any or every opponent or enemy in a competition or fight **2.** *vt.* **GET STH FOR DEFEATING OTHERS** to get sth as a prize by beating other competitors using skill, effort, or luck ○ *proud of the cups he had won for swimming* **3.** *vt.* **MAKE SB SUCCEED IN GETTING STH** to be the reason why sb is first in sth or receives sth as a prize ○ *Their attacking play won them the game.* ○ *That photo is sure to win you a prize.* **4.** *vt.* **GAIN STH** to gain sth such as respect or friendship, e.g. because of sth done or said or an ability shown, or to make sb do this ○ *His attitude won him few friends in the company.* **5.** *vt.* **GET STH** to obtain sth by hard work (*literary*) ○ *winning his livelihood by the sweat of his brow* **6.** *vt.* **REACH PLACE WITH EFFORT** to arrive somewhere by great effort or with difficulty (*literary*) **7.** *vt.* **CAPTURE STH USING FORCE** to capture sth such as a city using force (*formal*) **8.** *vt.* **GAIN SUPPORT** to persuade sb to do sth or agree to sth, or to gain sb's sympathy or support **9.** *vt.* **EARN THE LOVE OF SB** to persuade sb to love or marry you **10.** *vt.* MINING **GET STH BY MINING** to mine coal, oil, or ore from a source **11.** *vt.* MINING **PREPARE LODE FOR MINING** to discover a source of coal, oil, or ore and prepare it for mining **12.** *vt.* MINING **EXTRACT STH FROM ORE** to extract a metal or mineral from its ore ■ *n.* **1.** VICTORY success in a competition, game or bet ○ *The team has had six wins in a row.* **2.** AMOUNT OF MONEY WON the amount of money won, e.g. in a bet [Old English *winnan*. Ultimately from an Indo-European base meaning 'to desire' that is also the ancestor of English *wish* and *Venus*.] —**winnable** *adj.* ◇ **some you win, some you lose** used to indicate philosophically or humorously that in life everyone has some successes and some failures

win out, win through *vi.* to be successful or dominant after a struggle

win over *vt.* to persuade sb to agree with you, support you, or give you permission

wince /winss/ *vi.* (**winces, wincing, winced**) **1.** MOVE BODY BACK SLIGHTLY to make an involuntary movement away from sth because of pain or fear **2.** MAKE PAINED EXPRESSION to make an expression of pain with the face because of seeing or thinking of sth unpleasant or embarrassing ■ *n.* **1.** EXPRESSION OF PAIN a facial expression to pain **2.** SLIGHT MOVEMENT AWAY a slight movement away from sth because of pain or fear **3.** EXPRESSION OF DISPLEASURE OR EMBARRASSMENT a facial reaction to seeing or thinking of sth unpleasant or embarrassing [13thC. From Anglo-Norman, a variant of Old French *guencir* 'to turn aside', from Germanic.] —**wincer** *n.*

──── **WORD KEY: SYNONYMS** ────
See Synonyms at *recoil.*

wincey /winssi/ *n.* a cloth made of linen and wool [Early 19thC. Origin uncertain: probably a variant of *woolsey* in LINSEY-WOOLSEY.]

winceyette /winssi ét/ *n.* cloth made of cotton that has a raised surface. It is used especially for night-clothes. [Early 20thC. From WINCEY.]

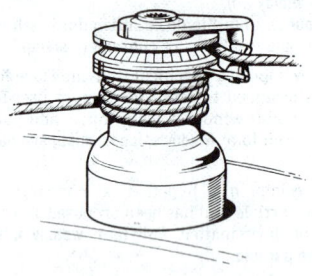

Winch

winch /winch/ *n.* **1.** LIFTING MACHINE a machine for lifting loads by means of a rope or chain that is wound round a cylinder turned by an engine or by hand **2.** CRANK OR HANDLE the handle used to turn a machine ■ *vt.* (**winches, winching, winched**) MOVE STH WITH WINCH to lift or pull sth by means of a winch [Old English *wince*. Ultimately from the prehistoric Germanic base that is the ancestor of English *wink*.] —**wincher** *n.*

winchester /winchistər/ *n.* a large bottle with a short narrow neck, used for carrying or storing liquid chemicals [Early 18thC. Named after the English city of WINCHESTER, where the standards for liquid and dry measures were once kept.]

Winchester /winchistər/ city in Hampshire, southern England. It was the capital of the Anglo-Saxon kingdom of Wessex. Population: 34,700 (1994).

Winchester rifle *tdmk.* a trademark for a rifle first produced in the late 19th century that can fire several shots before it has to be reloaded

winchman /winchmən/ (*plural* **-men** /-mən/) *n.* sb who operates a winch

wind[1] /wind/ *n.* **1.** METEOROL MOVING AIR air moving across the surface of the planet or through the atmosphere at a speed fast enough to be noticed **2.** AIR MOVED ARTIFICIALLY air that is being made to move by a device such as a fan **3.** ASTRON FLOW OF PARTICLES INTO SPACE a flow of particles ejected into space from the surface of the Sun or a star **4.** SOCIAL OR ECONOMIC FORCE a force or movement bringing sth such as change or destruction (*formal*) ○ *'The wind of change is blowing through the continent'.* (Harold Macmillan, *speech*

to South African parliament; 3 Feb 1960) **5.** BREATH the breath of normal breathing and talking **6.** POWER TO BREATHE the power to breathe, especially when making an effort such as running **7.** MUSIC **MUSICAL INSTRUMENTS** the group of musical instruments that require a flow of air to produce a sound. These include both woodwind and brass instruments. ○ *the wind section of the orchestra* **8.** PHYSIOL STOMACH GAS gas that builds up in the stomach and intestines while food is being digested **9.** IDLE TALK talk that is empty and meaningless **10.** INFORMATION HINTING AT STH news that brings information of sth intended to be secret ○ *If wind of this gets out, we've had it.* **11.** HUNT AIR CARRYING A SCENT the air on which a scent, e.g. that of a hunter, is carried **12.** DIRECTION OF WIND the direction from which the wind blows (*literary*) ■ **winds** *npl.* MUSIC **PLAYERS OF WIND INSTRUMENTS** the musicians in an ensemble, especially an orchestra, who play wind instruments ■ *v.* (**winds, winding, winded**) **1.** *vt.* MAKE SB SHORT OF BREATH to make sb unable to breathe in enough air, e.g. because of too much exertion or by a blow to the abdomen **2.** *vt.* MAKE BABY RELEASE STOMACH GAS to help a baby bring up gas from its stomach, e.g. by patting and rubbing its back **3.** *vt.* LET HORSE REST to allow a horse to rest after exertion **4.** *vti.* HUNT SMELL SB OR STH to get a scent of sb or sth in the air **5.** *vt.* HUNT PURSUE ANIMAL BY SCENT to pursue an animal in a hunt by following its scent **6.** *vt.* EXPOSE STH TO WIND to expose sth to the wind, e.g. in order to dry it [Old English. Ultimately from an Indo-European base meaning 'to blow' that is also the ancestor of English *weather* and *vent*.] ◇ **be in the wind** to be about to happen or be likely to happen ◇ **get the wind up** to become nervous or fearful (*informal*) ◇ **get wind of sth** to hear indirectly about sth ◇ **get your second wind** to recover your natural breathing pattern, and your usual energy levels, after a period of breathlessness and great effort ◇ **piss in the wind** to do sth of little or no consequence that is likely to have little or no effect (*slang offensive*) ◇ **put the wind up sb** to make sb nervous or fearful (*informal*) ◇ **sail close to the wind** to come very close to breaking the law or a rule ◇ **see which way** *or* **how the wind is blowing** to wait and find out the nature of a situation before making a decision ◇ **swing** *or* **twist in the wind** to be left in a difficult or unpleasant situation without any help or support from other people (*informal*) ◇ **take the wind out of sb's sails** to make sb feel deflated, silly, or embarrassed, or put sb at a disadvantage

──── **WORD KEY: CULTURAL NOTE** ────
Gone With the Wind, a film (1939) by US director Victor Fleming and producer David O. Selznick. Based on Margaret Mitchell's popular novel (1936), this idealized portrait of the antebellum American South focuses on the relationship between dashing rake Rhett Butler (Clark Gable) and resourceful, prewar plantation belle and postwar 'Iron Magnolia' Scarlett O'Hara (Vivien Leigh).

wind[2] /wīnd/ *v.* (**winds, winding, wound** /wownd/, **wound**) **1.** *vti.* GO ALONG PATH WITH BENDS to move along a course with many bends and twists in it, or to make a route with many bends and twists in it ○ *The river winds lazily through the valley.* ○ *The procession wound its way slowly up the hill.* **2.** *vi.* FOLLOW SPIRAL PATH to go in a spiral path ○ *smoke winding slowly up into the air* **3.** *vti.* GO OR PUT ROUND to go round sth in a coil or coils, or to wrap sth round sth else in a coil or coils ○ *winding the thread onto the bobbin* **4.** *vt.* WRAP STH WITH COILS to cover or decorate sth by wrapping sth else round it in coils ○ *She wound the injured arm with a scarf.* **5.** *vt.* MOVE STH UP OR DOWN to move or lift sth by turning a handle or pressing a button ○ *I wound the car window down.* **6.** *vti.* MOVE STH BACKWARD OR FORWARD to move sth such as a film forwards or backwards by turning a handle or pressing a button, or to be moved in this way ○ *Let's wind the tape back and see that part again.* **7.** *vt.* MAKE STH REVOLVE to turn sth such as a crank with a circular motion **8.** *vt.* MAKE A CLOCKWORK MECHANISM WORK to turn a key or handle in a clock or clockwork device in order to make the mechanism operate, usually by means of a spring that tightens on being wound ■ *n.* **1.** CURVE OR BEND a bend or twist in sth such as a river or a path **2.** ACT OF WINDING STH the act of winding sth such as a clock or motor, or a single

turn in this process [Old English *windan*. Ultimately from a prehistoric Germanic base that is also the ancestor of English *wander* and *wend*.]

wind down *v.* **1.** *vi.* RELAX to relax after a period of feeling stressed or tense **2.** *vti.* STEADILY REDUCE WORK to reduce gradually the amount of work done before stopping completely **3.** *vi.* GO MORE SLOWLY to operate more and more slowly and then stop because the spring by which a mechanism works is losing or has lost its tension

wind up /wīnd-/ *v.* **1.** *vt.* CLOSE BUSINESS DOWN to close down a business, bringing trading to an end **2.** *vt.* FINISH ACTIVITY to conclude sth or to bring an activity to an end **3.** *vi.* END UP to come to be in a particular place or situation as a result of, or at the end of, a series of earlier events (*informal*) **4.** *vt.* LIE TO SB AS A JOKE to tease or trick sb by telling him or her things that are not true (*informal*) ○ *You're winding me up, aren't you?* **5.** *vt.* MAKE SB TENSE to make sb nervous or irritated, usually deliberately (*informal; often passive*)

wind[3] /wīnd/ (**winds, winding, winded** *or* **wound**) *v.* **1.** *vti.* BLOW STH to blow a horn or bugle to create a sound **2.** *vt.* MAKE SIGNAL BY BLOWING to make a signal by blowing a horn [14thC. From WIND[1]. Originally in the meaning of 'to follow by scent'.]

windage /windij/ *n.* **1.** DEFLECTION CAUSED BY WIND the amount of deflection the wind will produce in a projectile **2.** ALLOWANCE MADE FOR WIND DEFLECTION the amount needed to adjust the aim of a projectile to counter wind deflection **3.** DIFFERENCE BETWEEN BORE AND PROJECTILE the amount by which the bore of a gun is larger than the bullet or shell it fires, so that gases can escape **4.** SAILING PART OF SHIP ABOVE WATER the part of a ship's body that is above the water and consequently causes wind resistance **5.** MECH ENG FRICTION BETWEEN AIR AND MOVING PARTS the friction between air and the moving parts of a machine, which tends to slow the machine. For example, in an electric generator, the windage is the friction between the rotating element, the rotor, and the surrounding air.

windbag /wind bag/ *n.* **1.** BORING TALKER sb who talks a great deal but has very little of interest or value to say (*informal*) **2.** MUSIC BAG IN MUSICAL INSTRUMENT the bag in a set of bagpipes into which air is forced by the player's lungs or a set of bellows and from which it flows to produce sound

windball cricket /wind bawl-/ *n.* a form of cricket played with a wooden bat and a tennis ball. It is popular especially in Trinidad, in the Caribbean.

wind-bell /wind-/ *n.* a light bell that rings when the wind moves it

windblast /wind blaast/ *n.* the harmful effect of air friction on a pilot who has ejected from an aircraft travelling at high speed

windblown /wind blōn/ *adj.* **1.** BLOWN BY THE WIND blown about by the wind ○ *They came back from their walk looking a bit windblown.* **2.** GROWING IN SHAPE CAUSED BY WIND growing in a shape caused by the action of the prevailing winds **3.** NZ BLOWN DOWN blown down by the wind

wind-borne /wind-/ *adj.* carried or dispersed by the wind

windbound /wind bownd/ *adj.* unable to sail because the wind is blowing in the wrong direction

windbreak /wind brayk/ *n.* **1.** STH LESSENING FORCE OF THE WIND sth such as a wall or hedge that breaks the force of the prevailing wind **2.** DEVICE TO REDUCE FORCE OF WIND an object consisting of a wide piece of cloth with several sticks along it that can be pushed into the ground to provide shelter from the wind

Windbreaker /wind braykər/ *tdmk.* US a trademark for a jacket of nylon or other wind-resistant fabric, usually gathered at the waist and wrist, and sometimes with a hood

wind-broken /wind-/ *adj.* used to describe a horse that has impaired breathing, e.g. because of heaves

windburn /wind burn/ *n.* redness and inflammation of the skin caused by exposure to harsh wind — **windburnt** /-burnt/ *adj.*

windcheater /wínd cheetər/ *n.* a warm windproof outer jacket with tight-fitting neck, cuffs, and waistband, and sometimes with a hood

wind chest /wínd-/ *n.* MUSIC a compartment in an organ that stores wind from the bellows under pressure before it goes to the pipes

wind-chill factor /wínd-/, **wind-chill** *n.* a temperature in calm conditions that has the equivalent effect on exposed skin as the combination of a given temperature and wind speed

wind chime /wínd-/ *n.* a musical decoration consisting of objects such as beads or metal tubes suspended on strings so that they will make a pleasant noise when moved by the wind

wind cone /wínd kōn/ *n.* = windsock

winded /wíndid/ *adj.* unable to breathe easily because of exertion or a blow to the abdomen

winder /wíndər/ *n.* **1.** MECH ENG STH THAT WINDS UP a key, knob, or other device that is used to wind up a spring-powered mechanism such as a clock **2.** MINING HOISTING MECHANISM OR OPERATOR a mechanism for hoisting or lowering a cage in a mineshaft, or sb who operates such a mechanism **3.** SB OR STH THAT WINDS STH a person or device that winds thread or textiles around a spool, cone, or tube **4.** OBJECT FOR WINDING STH AROUND a spool or bobbin around which sth such as thread is wound **5.** BUILDING STEP IN SPIRAL STAIRCASE a step in a spiral staircase or at the turn of a staircase that is narrower at the inside of the curve

Windermere, Lake /wíndər meer/ the largest lake in England, located in the Lake District, northwestern England. Area: 16 sq. km/6 sq. mi.

windfall /wínd fawl/ *n.* **1.** MONEY OBTAINED UNEXPECTEDLY sth good that is received unexpectedly, especially a sum of money **2.** STH BLOWN DOWN BY WIND sth that the wind has blown down, especially a piece of ripe fruit blown off a tree

wind farm /wínd-/ *n.* an area of land with a large number of electricity-generating windmills or wind turbines

windflaw /wínd flaw/ *n.* = flaw¹ *n.* 1 [Early 20thC. Formed from WIND + FLAW.]

windflower /wínd flowər/ *n.* an anemone plant such as the wood anemone

windgall /wínd gawl/ *n.* a fluid-filled swelling around the fetlock joint of a horse, usually not associated with loss of function or lameness

wind gap /wínd-/ *n.* a shallow pass or gap in a mountain ridge, often originally a water gap

wind gauge /wínd-/ *n.* **1.** METEOROL = anemometer **2.** ARMS GUN-SIGHT ATTACHMENT SHOWING ALLOWANCE FOR WIND an attachment to the sight on a musket or rifle showing how much the aim should be adjusted to allow for the effect of the wind on the bullet

wind harp /wínd-/ *n.* = aeolian harp

Windhoek /wínd hook, wínt-, vínt-/ capital city of Namibia, located in the centre of the country. Population: 125,000 (1990).

windhover /wínd hovər/ *n.* a kestrel (*regional*) [Late 17thC. From its habit of hovering in the air.]

windigo *n.* = wendigo [Early 18thC. From Ojibwa *wintiko*.]

winding /wíndíng/ *adj.* **1.** TWISTING AND CURVING made up of many consecutive curves or twists **2.** SPIRALLING arranged or moving in a spiral ■ *n.* **1.** STH WOUND sth wound or coiled round an object, or a single turn of it **2.** ACT OF COILING the act or process of coiling sth **3.** CURVING COURSE the bending or curving course that sth follows **4.** ELEC ENG WIRE COIL CARRYING ELECTRICITY a wire coil designed to have an electric current passing through it, forming part of numerous electrical devices such as electric motors and transformers [Old English *windung*] —**windingly** *adv.*

winding drum *n.* a revolving drum with a wire rope coiled round it that acts as the lifting mechanism of a hoist or winch

winding sheet, **winding-sheet** *n.* a sheet that a corpse is wrapped in before it is buried

wind instrument /wínd-/ *n.* a musical instrument such as a trumpet or flute played by causing the air in the instrument to vibrate by blowing into or across the air tube

windjammer /wínd jammər/ *n.* **1.** LARGE SAILING SHIP a large sailing ship, especially a large and fast merchant ship **2.** = windcheater (*dated*) [Late 19thC. So called because of its huge sail area.]

windlass /wíndləss/ *n.* REVOLVING LIFTING DEVICE a device that uses a rope or cable wound round a revolving drum to pull and lift things, especially the mechanism on a ship to raise and lower the anchor ■ *vt.* (**-lasses, -lassing, -lassed**) LIFT STH WITH WINDLASS to raise or pull sth using a windlass [14thC. Alteration of Old Norse *vindáss*, from *vinda* 'to wind' + *áss* 'pole'.]

windlestraw /wínd'l straw/ *n.* **1.** DRY GRASS STALK a thin dry stalk of grass (*regional*) **2.** THIN PERSON sb who is regarded as unhealthily thin (*regional archaic or literary*) **3.** WEAK-WILLED PERSON sb who is regarded as lacking in strength of character (*regional archaic or literary*) [Old English *windelstrēaw*, from *windan* 'to wind' + *strēaw* 'straw']

wind machine /wínd-/ *n.* **1.** THEATRE THEATRICAL DEVICE SIMULATING WIND a device used backstage in a theatre to simulate the sound of wind blowing, or a large fan that simulates windy weather on a film set **2.** AGRIC MACHINE PRODUCING STRONG CURRENT OF AIR a machine that creates a strong current of air, e.g. a device that produces warm air to protect crops from frost

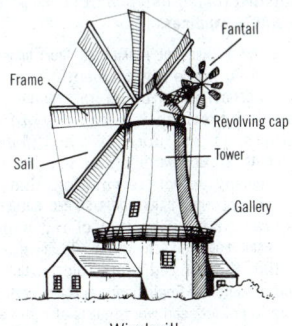

Frame   Fantail   Revolving cap   Sail   Tower   Gallery

Windmill

windmill /wínd mil/ *n.* **1.** BUILDING WITH REVOLVING BLADES a building with a set of wind-driven revolving sails or blades fitted to the site of its roof that drive a grinding machine inside **2.** REVOLVING BLADES OR GRINDING MECHANISM the set of revolving sails or blades on a windmill, or the grinding mechanism inside the building **3.** DEVICE HARNESSING WIND POWER a building or device fitted with a set of revolving blades designed to harness the power of the wind, e.g. to pump water or generate electricity **4.** CHILD'S TOY WITH SPINNING BLADES a child's toy consisting of a stick with a set of plastic or paper blades fitted to it, which spin round when the wind blows them. US term **pinwheel** ■ *v.* (**-mills, -milling, -milled**) **1.** *vti.* SPIN LIKE WINDMILL to spin or turn like the sails of a windmill, or to be spun or turned in this way **2.** *vi.* ROTATE UNPOWERED to rotate solely by wind force and with no engine power ◇ **tilt at windmills** to struggle against imagined enemies or opponents

window /wíndō/ *n.* **1.** GLASS-COVERED OPENING IN BUILDING an opening in a wall of a building, usually with an inner frame of wood or metal with glass fitted to it, to let in light or, when opened, air **2.** GLASS-COVERED OPENING LETTING LIGHT IN any glass-covered opening designed to let in light or, when opened, air, e.g. in a vehicle **3.** = windowpane **4.** DISPLAY IN SHOP WINDOW the area immediately behind a large window in the wall of a shop, where goods are put on display **5.** OPENING WHERE STH IS DISPENSED an opening above a counter where sb provides information, goods, or services to customers **6.** OPENING SIMILAR TO WINDOW an opening that makes it possible to see sth behind or underneath, e.g. the opening on some envelopes **7.** PERIOD OF AVAILABLE TIME a period of free time in a schedule available for use, or a limited time during which conditions are right for sth to take place **8.** OPPORTUNITY TO EXPERIENCE STH an opportunity to see or experience sth **9.** COMPUT SECTION ON COMPUTER SCREEN any of the rectangular frames into which a computer display can be divided and in which images output by application programs can be displayed, moved around the screen, or resized **10.** PHYS PART OF ELECTROMAGNETIC SPECTRUM the range of the electromagnetic spectrum that a given medium will allow to pass through it **11.** AIR FORCE = chaff¹ *n.* 3 [Pre-12thC. From Old Norse *vindauga*, from *vindr* 'wind' + *auga* 'eye'.] ◇ **go out of the window** to be lost for good (*informal*)

window box *n.* **1.** GARDENING PLANTER ON WINDOW LEDGE a soil-filled box on a window ledge with plants growing in it, or a box made to be used in this way **2.** JOINERY SPACE IN SASH WINDOW'S FRAME either of the spaces in the sides of the frame of a sash window that conceal the weights, ropes, and pulleys that raise and lower the window's separate sections

window dressing *n.* **1.** DISPLAY IN SHOP WINDOWS a display of goods for sale in a shop window **2.** DECEPTIVELY APPEALING PRESENTATION deceptively appealing presentation of sth, intended to conceal flaws

window envelope *n.* an envelope with a transparent panel at the front that makes it possible to see the address to which the letter is being sent on the letter inside

windowpane /wíndō payn/ *n.* a sheet of glass that forms part of a window

window seat *n.* **1.** ARCHIT INDOOR SEAT UNDER WINDOW an indoor seat fixed to a wall under a window, especially a window that is set into a recess **2.** TRANSP SEAT BY WINDOW a seat by a window in a plane, train, or bus

window-shop (**window-shops, window-shopping, window-shopped**) *vi.* to look at goods displayed in shop windows without a serious intention of buying anything —**window-shopper** *n.*

windowsill /wíndō sil/ *n.* the shelf on the bottom edge of a window, either a projecting part of the window frame or the bottom of the wall recess that the window fits into

window tax *n.* a tax on windows that was levied between 1691 and 1851, the evasion of which accounts for the blocked-up windows in old houses

windpipe /wínd pīp/ *n.* = trachea

wind-pollinated *adj.* pollinated by pollen that is carried to the plant by the wind

wind power *n.* the force of the wind harnessed by windmills and wind turbines that convert it into electricity, or the electricity produced in this way

windproof /wínd proof/ *adj.* resisting the force of the wind

wind rose *n.* a circular diagram indicating the range of wind speeds and directions for a particular place over a given time period

windrow /wíndrō/ *n.* **1.** ROW OF DRYING HAY a long thin pile of cut hay or grain designed to catch the wind and dry quickly **2.** PILE BLOWN TOGETHER BY WIND a long thin pile of things, especially leaves or snow, heaped up by the wind ■ *vt.* (**-rows, -rowing, -rowed**) GATHER HAY INTO WINDROWS to gather cut grass, hay, or other crop material into windrows for a drying —**windrower** *n.*

windsail /wínd sayl/; *nautical* /wíndss'l, wínss'l/ *n.* **1.** SAILING VENTILATION TUBE a tube or funnel of sailcloth rigged over a companionway or hatch to catch breezes and provide ventilation for a ship **2.** WINDMILL SAIL a sail on a windmill

wind scale *n.* a scale for measuring the strength of a wind, e.g. the Beaufort Scale

windscreen /wínd skreen/ *n.* the piece of glass or plastic that forms the front window of a motor vehicle. US term **windshield**

windscreen wiper *n.* a motorized device consisting of a rubber blade attached to a metal arm that is fixed just below a vehicle's windscreen, used for wiping rain and snow off the windscreen. = **windscreen wiper**

wind shake /wínd-/ *n.* a crack between the growth rings of a tree, thought to be caused when the tree bends violently in the wind

wind shear /wínd-/ *n.* the amount by which the speed of the wind varies at different altitudes, often causing difficulties for aircraft

windshield /wínd sheeld/ *n.* **1.** US = windscreen **2.** SCREEN PROTECTING FROM WIND a screen used to protect sb or sth from the wind, e.g. sunbathers on a beach or plants in a garden. US term **windscreen**

windsock /wínd sok/ n. a fabric tube or cone attached at one end to the top of a pole, so that it blows like a flag to show which way the wind is blowing

Windsor /wínzər/ **1.** town in southern England, on the River Thames. Windsor Castle, located in the town, has been a royal residence for over 900 years. Population: 27,400 (1995). **2.** town in southeastern New South Wales, Australia. Founded in 1810, it is one of Australia's oldest settlements. Population: 21,317 (1996).

AKG London

Duke and Duchess of Windsor

Windsor, Duke of the title granted to Edward VIII after his abdication from the British throne in 1936 and subsequent marriage to Wallis Simpson in June 1937. ♦ **Edward VIII**

Windsor chair n. a wooden chair that traditionally has a back formed of spindles, a saddle-shaped seat, and splayed legs [Mid-18thC. Named after the town of WINDSOR in southern England, where it originated.]

Windsor knot n. a large triangular knot in a man's tie, made by putting an extra turn on each side of the loop that lies beneath the knot [Mid-20thC. Origin uncertain: probably named after the Duke of Windsor.]

windstorm /wínd stawrm/ n. a storm consisting of very strong winds and little or no rain or other precipitation

wind-sucking /wínd-/ n. the habit some horses have of biting the edge of a stall or fence while gulping air or sucking in air by making certain head and neck movements —**wind-sucker** n.

windsurf /wínd surf/ (**-surfs, -surfing, -surfed**) vi. to ride and steer a sailboard fitted with a movable sail —**windsurfer** n.

Popperfoto

Windsurfing

windsurfing /wínd surfing/ n. the sport of riding and steering a sailboard

windswept /wínd swept/ adj. **1.** EXPOSED TO WIND exposed to the wind and usually very windy **2.** DISHEVELLED dishevelled in appearance as a result of exposure to the wind **3.** FASHIONED TO LOOK WINDBLOWN fashioned so as to look blown by the wind ○ a windswept hairstyle

wind tee /wínd-/ n. a T-shaped weather vane at an airfield that shows which way the wind is blowing

wind tunnel /wínd-/ n. a tunnel-shaped chamber through which air can be passed at a known speed in order to test the aerodynamic properties of an object such as an aircraft or automobile placed inside it

wind-up /wínd up/ n. **1.** TEASE a tease, especially a lie told in order to get a reaction (informal) **2.** ENDING OF STH the bringing to a close of sth such as the closing down of a business ■ adj. OPERATED BY TURNING HANDLE made to work by turning a handle or key that winds an internal spring

windward /wíndwərd/ adj. FACING THE WIND facing the wind, or on the side of sth, especially a boat, that is facing the wind ■ adv. INTO THE WIND towards where the wind is coming from ■ n. SIDE FACING WIND the side facing the wind, or the direction that the wind is blowing from

Windward Islands /wíndwərd-/ group of islands in the eastern Caribbean Sea, at the southern end of the Lesser Antilles. It includes Martinique and the independent island states of Dominica, St Lucia, Grenada, and St Vincent and the Grenadines. Area: 3,657 sq. km/1,412 sq. mi.

windway /wínd way/ n. an opening or passage allowing air through, e.g. a ventilation shaft in a mine

windy /wíndi/ (**-ier, -iest**) adj. **1.** WITH WIND BLOWING with strong winds blowing **2.** WHERE WINDS BLOW where strong winds tend to blow ○ a high and windy hill **3.** FULL OF EMPTY WORDS full of long and important-sounding though largely meaningless words designed to impress people (informal) **4.** FLATULENT suffering from flatulence (informal) **5.** NERVOUS nervous or frightened (dated informal) [Old English windig] —**windily** adv. —**windiness** n.

wine /wín/ n. **1.** ALCOHOL FERMENTED FROM GRAPES an alcoholic drink made by fermenting the juice of grapes **2.** ALCOHOL FERMENTED FROM OTHER FRUIT an alcoholic drink made by fermenting the juice of fruit other than grapes, or the juice of other plants **3.** STH STIMULATING OR INTOXICATING sth that has a stimulating or intoxicating effect resembling that of wine (literary) **4.** COLOURS DARK PURPLISH-RED COLOUR a dark purplish-red colour, like that of red wine ■ adj. COLOURS DARK PURPLISH-RED dark purplish-red colour, like that of red wine [Old English wín, from Latin vinum (source of English vine and vinegar). Ultimately from a pre-Indo-European word that is also the ancestor of Greek oinos (source of oenophile).] ◇ **wine and dine** to enjoy, be treated, or treat sb to an expensive meal out

wine bar n. a bar that specializes in serving wine, although beer and spirits may also be served

wine cellar n. **1.** CELLAR FOR STORING WINE a cellar where wine is stored, or any dark cool room used for storing wine **2.** WINE SUPPLY a stock of wine

wine cooler n. **1.** HOUSEHOLD CONTAINER FOR KEEPING WINE COOL a container filled with ice or a refrigerant and used to keep one or more bottles of wine cool **2.** BEVERAGES BOTTLED WINE COCKTAIL a mixture of wine and fruit juice, sometimes with carbonated water, sold in bottles

wine gallon n. an obsolete British unit of capacity equal to 231 cubic inches or 3.79 litres, which is smaller than the imperial gallon but exactly equal to the standard US gallon

wineglass /wín glaass/ n. **1.** GLASS WITH STEM a glass suitable for drinking wine, with a bowl mounted on a stem and usually a rounded base **2.** MEASURE AMOUNT OF LIQUID WINEGLASS HOLDS the amount of liquid that the average wineglass will hold, around four fluid ounces or 0.11 litres, for mixing cocktails or for cooking purposes

wine grower n. sb who grows grapes for making wine, especially the owner or manager of a vineyard who also oversees the winemaking

wine palm n. a palm tree whose fermented sap is used to make palm wine

winepress /wín press/ n. a piece of winemaking equipment that squeezes the juice from grapes

wineskin /wín skin/ n. a container for wine made from the skin of a sheep or goat sewn into a bag

wine tasting n. **1.** SAMPLING OF WINE the sampling of a variety of wines, either as a preliminary to buying wine or as instruction in the appreciation of wine **2.** GATHERING TO SAMPLE WINES a gathering to sample, learn about, and enjoy drinking a variety of wines

Winfrey /wínfri/, **Oprah** (b. 1954) US talk show host and actor. Hosting The Oprah Winfrey Show from 1986, she pioneered television programmes in which people publicly discuss their intimate problems. Full name **Oprah Gail Winfrey**

wing /wíng/ n. **1.** BIRD'S LIMB FOR FLYING BIRD'S LIMB FOR FLYING either of a bird's feather-covered limbs that are typically used for flying **2.** ZOOL INSECT'S OR BAT'S LIMB FOR FLYING any of the large membrane-covered limbs on an insect or a bat that it uses for flying. Many insects have two pairs of wings. **3.** AIR FLAT SURFACE PROJECTING FROM AIRCRAFT'S SIDE either of the large flat surfaces sticking out from the sides of an aircraft's body that provide the aircraft's main source of lift. Although most modern aircraft have only one pair of wings, it was not unusual for earlier aircraft to have two pairs set one above the other. **4.** FLAT PROJECTING PART either of a pair of flat parts that stick out from the main body of sth, e.g. the outgrowths of a wind-dispersed seedcase or the ends of an old-fashioned collar **5.** FLIGHT a means or manner of flying **6.** ARCHIT PART OF BUILDING PROJECTING FROM MIDDLE one of the parts of a building that project from the main part **7.** SPORTS LONGER SIDE OF SPORTS FIELD either of the longer sides of the field of play in some sports, at right angles to the sides where the goals are **8.** SPORTS ATTACKING PLAYER ON SIDE OF FIELD an attacking player who plays down one side of the field in some team sports such as soccer and hockey, or the position the person plays **9.** FOOTBALL = **wingman** n. 2 **10.** POL SUBDIVISION OF POLITICAL GROUP a faction within a political party or movement, especially either of two broad factions, one more conservative, the other more liberal **11.** SUBSIDIARY GROUP a group attached and subordinate to a parent organization **12.** AUTOMOT CORNER OF CAR any of the corner parts of the body of a motor vehicle that surround each wheel. US term **fender 13.** AIR FORCE AIR FORCE UNIT an air force unit that is larger than a group but smaller than a division **14.** MIL PART OF MILITARY FORMATION the left or right part of a large military formation such as a field army or a fleet **15.** THEATRE SCENERY PIECE AT SIDE OF STAGE a piece of scenery at the side of the stage ■ **wings** npl. **1.** THEATRE SIDE OF THEATRE STAGE the areas of a theatre to the sides of the stage, unseen by the audience **2.** AIR QUALIFIED PILOT'S BADGE a badge with a design in the shape of wings, worn by a trained and qualified pilot ■ v. (**wings, winging, winged**) **1.** vti. MOVE SWIFTLY to move or travel somewhere swiftly, or send sth with great speed **2.** vt. WOUND BIRD BY HITTING WING to wound a bird superficially by hitting it on its wing **3.** vt. WOUND SB, OR DAMAGE STH, SUPERFICIALLY to wound sb superficially, especially in the arm or leg, or cause only superficial damage to sth **4.** vt. THEATRE PREPARE PERFORMANCE AT LAST MINUTE to prepare a performance as a last-minute replacement actor, learning the lines in the wings immediately before going on, or perform a part without having thoroughly learned or prepared it [12thC. Of Scandinavian origin. Ultimately from an Indo-European base meaning 'to blow' that is also the ancestor of English wind, weather, ventilate, and nirvana.] ◇ **be (waiting) in the wings** to be ready and prepared to do sth, or available for use when needed ◇ **take sb under your wing** to look after or protect sb ◇ **with wings** to be taken away rather than consumed on the premises (informal) ○ one cappuccino with wings ◇ **wing it** to improvise (informal)

wing and wing adv. NAUT with sails extended on each side

wing bar n. a short white band on the wing of a bird, visible when the wing is folded

wing-case n. INSECTS = **elytron**

wing chair n. an armchair with a high back and large side panels

wing collar n. a high stiff collar on a man's shirt, worn with the points at the upper corner turned down over the tie as part of formal dress

wing commander n. an officer of middle rank in some air forces, or the rank itself. In the Royal Air Force, it is the rank above squadron leader and below group captain, equivalent to the rank of lieutenant-colonel in the US Air Force.

wing covert n. a small feather on a bird's wing, covering the base of the wing quills

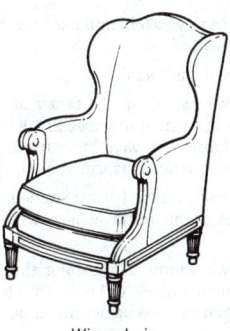

Wing chair

winged /wingd, wíngid/ *adj.* **1.** CAPABLE OF FLIGHT able to fly because having wings **2.** MOVING SWIFTLY moving swiftly in a manner resembling flying (*literary*)

winged bean *n.* = asparagus pea

winger /wíngər/ *n.* SPORTS = wing *n.* 8

wing-footed *adj.* moving swiftly in a manner resembling flying (*archaic or literary*)

wingless /wíngləss/ *adj.* without wings or having only very small wings that are not used for flying. Certain parasitic flies and other primitive insects such as springtails and bristletails are described as wingless. —**winglessness** *n.*

wingman /wíng man/ (*plural* **-men** /-men/) *n.* **1.** AIR PILOT FLYING BEHIND LEADER a pilot who flies in a position behind, and to the side of, the leader of a flying formation **2.** FOOTBALL WINGER IN AUSTRALIAN RULES FOOTBALL in Australian Rules football, either of two players playing in positions on either side of the centre circle

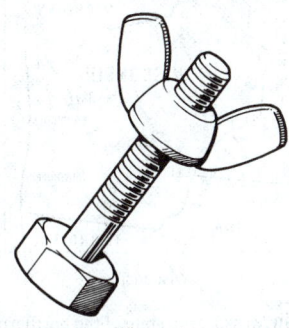

Wing nut

wing nut *n.* a nut that has flat projections on its sides for the fingers to grip

wingover /wíng ōvər/ *n.* a flying manoeuvre to turn an aircraft in which the pilot puts the aircraft into a steep banking climb to a near stall and then allows the nose to fall

wingspan /wíng span/, **wingspread** *n.* the distance from tip to tip of an aircraft's wings, or of the outstretched wings of a bird or insect

wing tip *n.* **1.** AIR, ZOOL POINT OF WING FURTHEST FROM BODY the tip of the wing of a bird, insect, or aircraft that is the point furthest away from the centre of its body **2.** *US* CLOTHES = brogue

wink /wingk/ *v.* (**winks, winking, winked**) **1.** *vti.* GESTURE BY CLOSING ONE EYE BRIEFLY to close one eye briefly, usually either as a friendly greeting or to show that sth just done or said is a joke or a secret **2.** *vi.* SHINE INTERMITTENTLY to shine intermittently or faintly ■ *n.* **1.** BRIEF CLOSING OF ONE EYE a brief closing of one eye as a greeting or signal **2.** TWINKLING LIGHT a twinkling or faintly flashing light **3.** SHORT TIME the briefest period of time **4.** SHORT NAP a brief nap or very short period of being asleep (*informal*) [Old English *wincian* 'to close one's eyes'] ◊ **tip sb the wink** to give sb information privately or confidentially (*informal*)
  wink at *vt.* to pretend not to notice an offence or wrongdoing (*informal*)

winker /wíngkər/ *n.* **1.** SB WHO WINKS sb or sth that winks **2.** FLASHING LIGHT a light that winks or flashes, especially an indicator on a motor vehicle **3.** *US* EYE OR PART OF EYE an eye, or a part of the eye such as an

eyelid or eyelash (*informal*) ■ **winkers** *npl.* BLINKERS a racehorse's blinkers

winkle /wíngk'l/ (**-kles, -kling, -kled**) *n.* a small edible mollusc with a spirally coiled shell that lives in coastal waters. Genus: *Littorina*. [Late 16thC. Shortening of PERIWINKLE[1].]
  winkle out *vt.* to extract sth such as information with difficulty [From the practice of extracting molluscs from their shells]

winkle-pickers *npl.* shoes with narrow pointed toes, popular in the 1950s (*informal*) [So-called because the shoe's pointed toe resembles a pin used for removing winkles from their shells]

Winnebago[1] /wínni báy gō/ (*plural* **-go** *or* **-gos** *or* **-goes**) *n.* **1.** PEOPLES NATIVE N AMERICAN a member of a Native North American people who formerly inhabited areas around Wisconsin and Illinois, and whose members now live principally in Wisconsin and Nebraska **2.** LANG WINNEBAGO LANGUAGE the Siouan language spoken by the Winnebago people [Mid-18thC. From Algonquian *wi:nepye:ko:ha*, literally 'person of the dirty water'.]

Winnebago[2] (*plural* **-gos** *or* **-goes**) *tdmk.* a trademark for a large motor vehicle with cooking and sleeping facilities

Winnebago, Lake /wínni báy gō/ the largest lake in Wisconsin, in the eastern part of the state. It forms part of the course of the Fox River. Area: 557 sq. km/215 sq. mi.

winner /wínnər/ *n.* **1.** SB OR STH WINNING COMPETITION sb or sth that wins a competition or contest **2.** SB OR STH SUCCESSFUL a very successful or popular person or thing, or one that seems likely to become successful or popular

winner's enclosure, **winner's circle** *n.* an enclosure at a racecourse where the winning horses are unsaddled and prizes awarded to owners, trainers, and jockeys

winning /wínning/ *adj.* **1.** VICTORIOUS victorious or bringing victory **2.** CHARMING very charming, to the extent that people are won over ■ **winnings** *npl.* MONEY WON money or other valuables that are won, especially from gambling —**winningly** *adv.* —**winningness** *n.*

winning gallery *n.* an opening in a side wall of a real tennis court into which the ball is hit from the other side of the net in order to win a point

winning post *n.* the post that marks the finish line on a racecourse

Winnipeg /wínni peg/ capital city of Manitoba, Canada, located in the southern part of the province. Population: 666,700 (1996).

Winnipeg, Lake freshwater lake in central Manitoba, Canada. Its greatest depth is 18m/60 ft. Area: 24,390 sq. km/9,417 sq. mi.

winnow /wínnō/ *v.* (**-nows, -nowing, -nowed**) **1.** *vti.* AGRIC USE AIR TO REMOVE CHAFF to separate grain from its husks (**chaff**) by tossing it in the air or blowing air through it **2.** *vt.* EXAMINE STH TO REMOVE BAD PARTS to examine sth in order to remove the bad, unusable, or undesirable parts ■ *n.* PROCESS OF WINNOWING the process of separating grain from chaff, or a device used to do this [Old English *windwian*, from *wind* 'wind'] —**winnower** *n.*

wino /wínō/ (*plural* **-os**) *n.* an offensive term used to refer to sb who is addicted to alcohol, especially wine, and is usually homeless (*informal insult offensive*)

winsome /wínssəm/ *adj.* charming, especially because of a naive, innocent quality [Old English *wynsum* 'pleasant', formed from *wynn* 'joy'. Ultimately from an Indo-European base meaning 'to desire' that is also the ancestor of English *win*, *wish*, and *venerate*.] —**winsomely** *adv.* —**winsomeness** *n.*

winter /wíntər/ *n.* **1.** YEAR'S COLDEST SEASON the coldest season of the year, which comes between autumn and spring and runs in the northern hemisphere from around November or December to February or March and in the southern hemisphere from June to August **2.** CLOSING PERIOD OR PERIOD OF INACTIVITY the closing part or period of sth, or a period of decline or inactivity **3.** A YEAR one of a number of

years, especially a great number (*literary*) ■ *v.* (**-ters, -tering, -tered**) **1.** *vi.* SPEND WINTER SOMEWHERE to spend the winter in a particular place, especially away from home **2.** *vt.* KEEP STH SOMEWHERE IN WINTER to keep sth, especially farm animals, in a particular place during the winter [Old English. Ultimately from an Indo-European base meaning 'wet' that is also the ancestor of English *water*, *hydro-*, *inundate*, and *vodka*.]

winter aconite *n.* a low-growing plant of the buttercup family that is native to Europe and Asia and has a single yellow flower that blooms in winter or early spring. Latin name: *Eranthis hyemalis*.

winterberry /wíntərbəri/ (*plural* **-ries** *or* **-ry**) *n.* a North American shrub of the holly family that has bright red berries and deciduous leaves that turn black in autumn. Latin name: *Ilex verticillata*.

winterbourne /wíntər bawrn/ *n.* a stream that flows only or mostly in winter, after heavy rains [Old English *winterburna*]

winter cherry *n.* **1.** = Chinese lantern **2.** POT PLANT WITH RED FRUIT a small plant with small, round, red fruit, often grown as a pot plant. Latin name: *Solanum capsicastrum*. **3.** BERRY OF WINTER CHERRY PLANT the fruit of the winter cherry

wintercress /wíntər kress/ *n.* a yellow-flowered plant of the mustard family, formerly used as a winter salad. Genus: *Barbarea*.

winterfeed /wíntər feed/ (**-feeds, -feeding, -fed, -fed** /-fəd/) *vt.* to feed livestock in winter, e.g. on hay or silage, when there is little or no grazing

winter garden *n.* **1.** GARDEN CONTAINING EVERGREEN PLANTS a garden planted with evergreen plants, to give growth even in winter **2.** GREENHOUSE CONTAINING WINTER PLANTS a greenhouse or conservatory that contains winter plants

wintergreen /wíntər green/ (*plural* **-greens** *or* **-green**) *n.* **1.** LOW-GROWING EVERGREEN FLOWERING PLANT a low-growing evergreen flowering plant with small leaves. Latin name: *Gaultheria procumbens*. **2.** = oil of wintergreen [Mid-16thC. Translation of Dutch *wintergroen*.]

winter heliotrope *n.* a creeping winter-flowering perennial plant whose lilac-coloured flowers smell of vanilla. Latin name: *Petasites fragrans*.

winterize /wíntə rīz/ (**-izes, -izing, -ized**), **winterise** (**winterises, winterising, winterised**) *vt.* *US, Can* to prepare sth, especially a house or a car, to withstand cold winter conditions —**winterization** /wíntə rī záysh'n/ *n.*

winter jasmine *n.* a variety of jasmine that has yellow flowers in winter. Latin name: *Jasminum nudiflorum*.

winterkill /wíntər kil/ *vti.* (**-kills, -killing, -killed**) *US, Can* KILL PLANT BY EXPOSURE TO WINTER to die, or cause a plant to die, from lack of adequate protection from winter weather conditions ■ *n.* *US, Can* EXPOSURE TO LETHAL WINTER WEATHER exposure to harsh winter weather that kills unprotected plants

winter melon *n.* a variety of fragrant melon similar to the honeydew and cantaloupe that keeps well when stored and has unusually smooth skin. Latin name: *Cucumis melo inodorus*.

winter moth *n.* a brown moth with no wings in the female and whose larvae crawl with a series of looping movements. Latin name: *Operophtera brumata*.

Winter Olympics, **Winter Olympic Games** *npl.* an international gathering of athletes competing in a variety of winter sports, held every four years

winter sports *npl.* sports such as skiing and ice skating performed on snow and ice

wintertide /wíntər tīd/ *n.* wintertime (*archaic or literary*)

wintertime /wíntər tīm/ *n.* the season of winter

winterweight /wíntər wayt/ *adj.* made of thick heavy fabric and designed to protect sb or sth from cold weather

winter wheat *n.* a variety of wheat planted in autumn, left in the ground over winter, and harvested the following spring or early summer

Winthrop /wín throp/, **John** (1588–1649) English-born American colonial governor. For most of the years between 1629 and 1649, he presided over the Massachusetts Bay Colony, exerting a decisive influence in shaping it as a Puritan commonwealth.

wintry /wíntri/ (**-trier, -triest**), **wintery** (**-terier, -teriest**) *adj.* **1. RELATING TO WINTER** relating to or typical of winter, especially in being cold **2. BLEAK** cheerless or unfriendly ○ *She gave him a wintry smile.* —**wintrily** *adv.* —**wintriness** *n.*

win-win *adj.* used to describe a situation in which all parties benefit in some way ○ *a win-win scenario*

winy /wíni/ (**-ier, -iest**) *adj.* like wine in taste or appearance

winze /winz/ *n.* a steeply inclined or vertical shaft between levels in a mine [Mid-18thC. Alteration of obsolete *winds*, of uncertain origin: probably formed from WIND[2].]

wipe /wīp/ *v.* (**wipes, wiping, wiped**) **1.** *vt.* **RUB STH WITH LIGHT STROKES** to rub sth with long light strokes with a soft material, or rub sth lightly on a soft material ○ *wiped their hands on the towel* **2.** *vti.* **REMOVE OR BE REMOVED BY RUBBING** to remove sth such as dirt with long light rubbing strokes, usually with a soft material, or be removed in this way ○ *The mark wiped off easily.* **3.** *vt.* **REMOVE RECORDING FROM TAPE** to remove recorded material from an audiotape or video tape **4.** *vt.* **REMOVE STH** to remove sth or get rid of it as if by wiping ○ *wiped from my memory* **5.** *vt.* **APPLY STH WITH LIGHT RUBBING** to apply sth, especially a liquid or cream, by rubbing it on lightly, e.g. with a cloth or the hand ■ *n.* **1. LIGHT RUBBING STROKE** one or more long light rubbing strokes **2. DISPOSABLE CLEANING CLOTH** a soft disposable cloth or tissue soaked with a cleansing liquid, used for cleaning sth such as the skin ○ *'Remember trash bags, wipes, and napkins. It's no fun sitting next to banana peel for five hours'.* (*Washington Post*; July 1998) **3.** CINEMA, TV **ONE PICTURE PUSHING OTHER OFF SCREEN** an effect in which one picture on the screen appears to be pushed off the side of the screen by another, often used to move from scene to scene [Old English *wīpian.* Ultimately from an Indo-European base meaning 'to move back and forth', which is also the ancestor of English *whip* and *vibrate.*]

wipe out *v.* **1.** *vt.* **DESTROY STH IN LARGE NUMBERS** to destroy large numbers of things or kill large numbers of people, especially suddenly and violently (*informal*) **2.** *vt.* **MURDER SB** to murder or assassinate sb (*slang*) **3.** *vi.* SPORTS **FALL FROM SURFBOARD** to fall from a surfboard, either because of losing control or because of being knocked off by a wave, or fall or crash in some other sport (*informal*)

wiped out *adj.* thoroughly exhausted (*slang*)

wipeout /wíp owt/ *n.* (*informal*) **1.** SPORTS **FALL IN SURFING** a fall from a surfboard, or a fall or crash in other sports, e.g. skiing and cycling **2. FAILURE OR DEFEAT** a total failure or a crushing defeat **3.** RADIO **RECEIVING OF RADIO SIGNAL MASKING OTHERS** the receiving of a radio signal that is so strong it makes receiving other signals impossible

wiper /wípər/ *n.* **1.** AUTOMOT = **windscreen wiper 2.** MECH ENG **CAM PROJECTING FROM SHAFT** a cam that projects from a rotating shaft and is designed to move, dislodge, or lift another component **3.** ELEC ENG **ELECTRICAL DEVICE MOVING CONDUCTING ARM** an electrical device in which a conducting arm may be rotated or moved over a row of contacts, e.g. a rheostat

WIPO /wípō/, **Wipo** *abbr.* World Intellectual Property Organization

wire /wīr/ *n.* **1. STRAND OF METAL** metal in the form of thin flexible strands, or a single strand of it **2.** ELEC **METAL STRAND CARRYING ELECTRIC CURRENT** a strand of metal, usually copper, that is encased in plastic or another insulating material and is used to carry an electric current **3.** TELECOM **CABLE PROVIDING TELECOMMUNICATIONS LINK** a cable that provides a telecommunications link **4.** **MESH STRUCTURE** a mesh made of strands of metal, or a structure such as a fence made of the mesh **5.** US **ANY END OR FINISH** the end of anything, or the time when sth ends (*informal*) ○ *writing in their exam books right down to the wire* **6.** US **ELECTRONIC LISTENING DEVICE** a slimline electronic listening device concealed in sb's clothes (*slang*) **7.** TELECOM **TELEGRAM OR TELEGRAPH** a telegram or the telegraph system ■ *vt.* (**wires, wiring, wired**) **1. FASTEN STH WITH WIRE** to use wire to fasten or secure sth **2. CONNECT ELECTRICAL EQUIPMENT** to connect a piece of electrical equipment to a power source or

to another piece of equipment **3. PROVIDE A PLACE WITH NECESSARY EQUIPMENT** to provide a place with the equipment, especially electrical or electronic equipment, needed to give it a particular facility or capability (*informal*) **4.** US **FIT SB WITH A LISTENING DEVICE** to fit sb or a place with a concealed electronic listening device (*slang*) **5. SEND A TELEGRAM** to send a telegram to sb, or send sth to sb by means of a telegram [Old English *wīr* 'metal thread'. Ultimately from an Indo-European base meaning 'to twist', which is also the ancestor of English *withy* and *garland.*] ◇ **go to the wire** to risk your reputation, job, or life in order to help sb (*informal*) ◇ **have** *or* **get your wires crossed** have a misunderstanding

wire brush *n.* a brush with short stiff wires instead of bristles

wire cloth *n.* a flexible mesh of soft fine wires woven closely together, used to make strainers and some types of screening

wired /wīrd/ *adj.* **1. SUPPORTED BY WIRE** supported or strengthened by wire **2.** COMPUT **EQUIPPED FOR INTERNET** having computer equipment that allows use of the Internet (*informal*) ○ *'Ireland has seen Dublin go wired'.* (*Newsweek*; November 1998) **3.** US **FITTED WITH LISTENING DEVICES** fitted with one or more concealed electronic listening devices (*slang*) **4. NERVOUS** full of nervous energy, especially because under the influence of drugs (*slang*)

wiredraw /wír draw/ (**-draws, -drawing, -drew** /-droo/, **-drawn** /-drawn/) *vt.* **1.** METALL **MAKE WIRE FINER** to reduce the diameter of a wire by pulling it through successively smaller dies **2. SPIN STH OUT** to spin sth out to great lengths, overrefining it and treating it with excessive subtlety [Late 16thC. Back-formation from earlier *wiredrawer* 'sb skilled in drawing metal into threads'.]

wire entanglement *n.* a barrier of barbed wire used to keep enemy troops back

wirefree /wír free/ *adj.* used to describe telephone systems that do not use electrical wires in order to operate ○ *'Today, more than 1.7 million people subscribe to our wirefree services'.* (*Marketing Week*; December 1998)

wire gauge *n.* **1. GAUGE MEASURING WIRE THICKNESS** a gauge used to measure the thickness of wire or sheet metal **2. SYSTEM OF MEASURING WIRE** a standard system of sizes for measuring wire

wire gauze *n.* a fine mesh of thin wires woven closely together

wire glass *n.* glass reinforced with a sheet of wire mesh embedded in it

wire grass *n.* a coarse grass with tough wiry roots

wirehaired /wír háird/ *adj.* having a coat of coarse stiff hair

wireless /wírləss/ *n.* **1.** RADIO a radio or a radio set (*dated*) **2.** TELECOM = **wireless telegraphy**

wireless telegraphy *n.* a system that sends telegrams using radio signals, as opposed to a system connected by wires

wire netting *n.* mesh made of medium to thick wire that is stronger, less flexible, and has larger spaces than wire gauze

wirer /wírər/ *n.* sb who uses snares to catch animals (*informal*)

wire recorder *n.* an early type of magnetic recorder that used stainless steel wire instead of magnetic tape to record sound

wire rope *n.* strong thick rope made of plaited strands of wire

wire service *n.* US a news agency that sends out syndicated news items to various media by means of wire or satellite

wiretap /wír tap/ *vti.* (**-taps, -tapping, -tapped**) **TAP A TELEPHONE LINE** to make a wire connection to a telephone line in order to listen in secret to sb's conversations ■ *n.* **SECRET CONNECTION TO A TELEPHONE LINE** a connection made to a telephone line in order to listen secretly to sb's conversations —**wiretapper** *n.*

wire wheel *n.* **1.** AUTOMOT **VEHICLE WHEEL WITH WIRE SPOKES** a motor vehicle wheel that has wire spokes connecting the hub to the rim **2.** INDUST **WIRE POLISHING DISC ON POWER TOOL** a disc of coarse wires designed to be

attached to a power tool and used for rubbing down metal

wire wool *n.* = **steel wool**

wirework /wír wurk/ *n.* **1. LAYOUT OF WIRES** an arrangement or system of wires **2. STH MADE OF WIRE** sth made by shaping or weaving wire **3.** ARTS **TIGHTROPE ACROBATICS** acrobatics performed on a tightrope

wireworks /wír wurks/ (*plural* **-works**) *n.* a factory where wire is made, or where wire articles are made

wireworm /wír wurm/ *n.* the long thin hard-bodied larva of various kinds of beetle that feeds on plant roots and is a serious agricultural pest

wiring /wíring/ *n.* a network of electrical wires

wirra /wírrə/ *interj.* Ireland used to express concern, sorrow, confusion, or annoyance [Early 19thC. From Irish *a Mhuira* 'oh, Mary!'.]

Wirral /wírrəl/ peninsula in Cheshire, northwestern England, between the rivers Dee and Mersey. Population: 331,500 (1995). Area: 218 sq. km/84 sq. mi.

wiry /wíri/ (**-ier, -iest**) *adj.* **1. SLIM BUT STRONG** slim but muscular and strong **2. COARSE** stiff and coarse like wire **3. PRODUCED BY VIBRATING WIRES** produced by or sounding as though produced by vibrating wires —**wirily** *adv.* —**wiriness** *n.*

wis /wiss/ (**wisses, wissing, wissed** *or* **wist** /wist/, **wissed** *or* **wist**) *vti.* to know, think, or suppose sth (*archaic*) [Old English *wissian*]

Wis. *abbr.* Wisconsin

Wisbech /wíz beech/ town in Cambridgeshire, eastern England. Population: 24,981 (1991).

Wisconsin

Wisconsin /wi skónssin/ state of the northern-central United States, bordered by Lake Superior, Michigan, Lake Michigan, Illinois, Iowa, and Minnesota. Capital: Madison. Population: 4,891,769 (1990). Area: 169,644 sq. km/65,500 sq. mi. —**Wisconsinite** *n.*

Wisd. *abbr.* Wisdom of Solomon

Wisden /wízdən/, **John** (1826–84) British cricketer. A notable player himself, in 1864 he founded *Wisden's Cricketer's Almanack*, an annual review of cricket.

wisdom /wízdəm/ *n.* **1. GOOD SENSE** the knowledge and experience needed to make sensible decisions and judgments, or the good sense shown by the decisions and judgments made **2. ACCUMULATED LEARNING** accumulated knowledge of life or of a particular sphere of activity that has been gained through experience **3. OPINION WIDELY HELD** an opinion that almost everyone seems to share or express **4. SAYINGS** ancient teachings or sayings [Old English *wīsdōm*, formed from *wīs* (see WISE)]

Wisdom literature *n.* a speculative or didactic form of religious writing, exemplified in the Bible by the books of Job, Proverbs, and Ecclesiastes, and the Apocryphal books the Wisdom of Solomon and Ecclesiasticus

Wisdom of Jesus, the Son of Sirach *n.* BIBLE = **Ecclesiasticus**

Wisdom of Solomon *n.* an Apochryphal book of the Bible expounding Jewish doctrines in the terminology of Greek philosophy. It was probably written in the 1st century BC.

wisdom tooth *n.* one of the four teeth at the back of each side of the upper and lower jaw of human beings. They are the last teeth to come through.

[Translation of Latin *dens sapientiae*; so called because the wisdom teeth usually appear in young adulthood]

Wisdom writings *n.* = Wisdom literature

wise[1] /wīz/ (**wiser, wisest**) *adj.* **1. KNOWING MUCH FROM EXPERIENCE** able to make sensible decisions and judgments on the basis of knowledge and experience **2. SENSIBLE** showing good sense or good judgment **3. LEARNED** knowledgeable about many subjects **4. SHREWD** capable of achieving some purpose or goal by cunning **5. SKILLED IN OCCULT PRACTICES** skilled in magic or fortune-telling (*archaic*) [Old English *wīs*. Ultimately from an Indo-European base meaning 'to see, know', which is also the ancestor of English *wit*, *vision*, and *idea*.] ◇ **be** *or* **get wise (to sth)** to be or become aware of sth, usually sth dishonest or secret (*informal*) ◇ **put sb wise (to sth)** to let sb know about sth, or give sb information about sth (*informal*)
wise up *vti.* to become, or make sb, aware or informed (*informal*) —**wisely** *adv.*

wise[2] /wīz/ *n.* a way or manner (*archaic*) [Old English *wīse*. From a prehistoric Germanic word meaning 'shape, form', literally 'sth seen'.]

-wise *suffix.* in a particular manner or direction ○ *crabwise* ○ *coastwise* [Old English *-wīsan*, formed from *wīse* 'manner' (see WISE[2])]

——— **WORD KEY: USAGE** ———
Weatherwise, it's a lovely day. The use of *-wise* in fanciful formations such as *careerwise* and *taxwise* is increasingly found but is best restricted to informal contexts.

wiseacre /wīz aykər/ *n.* sb who speaks with an authority or self-assurance that people find irritating, especially sb who is not genuinely knowledgeable (*dated informal*) [Late 16thC. Alteration of Middle Dutch *wijssegger* 'soothsayer'.]

wisecrack /wīz krak/ *n.* **FLIPPANT REMARK** a flippant or sarcastic remark (*informal*) ■ *vi.* (**-cracks, -cracking, -cracked**) **MAKE WISECRACKS** to make flippant or sarcastic remarks (*informal*) —**wisecracker** *n.*

wise guy *n. US, Can* sb inclined to make impudent or sarcastic remarks (*informal*)

wise man *n.* **1. LEARNED MAN** a scholar or a very learned man **2. ANCIENT PRACTITIONER OF OCCULT ARTS** a man who, in ancient times, practised any of the occult arts such as magic or astrology (*archaic*) **3. SPECIAL ADVISOR** a man chosen as a special senior advisor to a government or other authority (*informal*) **4. BIBLE ONE OF MAGI** one of the three Magi who came to pay homage to the infant Jesus Christ

wisent /weez'nt/ *n.* the bison that is native to Europe. Its head is smaller and higher than that of the North American bison. Latin name: *Bison bonasus*. [Mid-19thC. Via German from, ultimately, Old High German *wisunt*. Ultimately from an Indo-European word that is also the ancestor of English *bison*.]

wisewoman /wīz woomən/ (*plural* **-en** /-wimin/) *n.* a woman who is skilled in the art of using herbs to heal people and ease the pains of childbirth

wish /wish/ *v.* (**wishes, wishing, wished**) **1.** *vt.* **DESIRE STH** to have a strong desire for sth **2.** *vt.* **DEMAND STH** to want or demand sth ○ *I wish you to leave him alone.* **3.** *vti.* **EXPRESS DESIRE** to express or feel a desire that sth is true or will come to pass ○ *They wished me a safe journey.* ○ *We only wish for peace.* **4.** *vt.* **WANT STH TO BE OTHERWISE** to desire sb or sth to be in a particular state ○ *We all wish it were different.* **5.** *vt.* **GREET SB** to greet sb in a particular way ○ *She wished me good afternoon as I left.* ■ *n.* **1. YEARNING** a desire or strong yearning for sth ○ *I certainly had no wish to speak to him.* **2. EXPRESSION OF DESIRE** an expression of a desire or longing for sth **3. STH WISHED** sth that is desired **4. HOPE** a hope for sb's welfare or health (*usually plural*) ○ *Give him our best wishes.* **5. POLITE REQUEST** a polite request (*formal; often plural*) [Old English *wȳscan*. Ultimately from an Indo-European base meaning 'to desire', which is also the ancestor of English *win* and *venerate*.] —**wisher** *n.*

——— **WORD KEY: SYNONYMS** ———
See Synonyms at *want*.

wish on *vt.* to wish that sth, usually sth unpleasant, would happen to sb ○ *I wouldn't wish that on my worst enemy.*

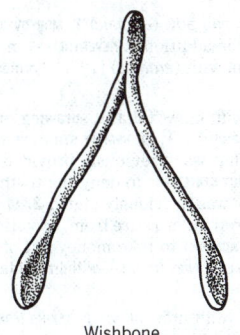
Wishbone

wishbone /wish bōn/ *n.* the V-shaped bone, actually two fused collarbones, found between the breasts of a chicken or other bird. Traditionally two people pull the bones apart and the person left holding the larger piece has a wish granted. Technical name **furcula**

wishbone boom *n.* the boom on a sailboard that a windsurfer holds on to. It has two curving arms, one on either side of the sail, joined at the ends.

wishful /wishf'l/ *adj.* wishing for sth, or expressing a wish or longing —**wishfully** *adv.* —**wishfulness** *n.*

wish fulfilment *n.* in psychoanalytic theory, the process by which unconscious desires are realized in the imagination, mainly through dreams and fantasies

wishful thinking *n.* the unrealistic belief that sth that is wished for is actually true or will be realized

wish list *n. US* an often informal list of things sb would like to have or would like to happen

wish-wash *n.* (*archaic*) **1. WEAK DRINK** an unpleasantly weak or tasteless drink **2. DULL TALK OR WRITING** uninteresting and uninspiring talk or writing [Late 18thC. Doubling of WASH, in the sense 'thin, weak'.]

wishy-washy /wīshi woshi, wīshi wōshi/ *adj.* (*informal*) **1. INCAPABLE OF MAKING FIRM DECISIONS** changeable or fluctuating in character, especially unable to make firm decisions or develop clear opinions **2. LACKING STRENGTH OR COLOUR** weak, lacking taste, or unattractively pale [Late 17thC. Doubling of *washy* 'thin, watery', from WASH.] —**wishy-washily** *adv.* —**wishy-washiness** *n.*

wisp /wisp/ *n.* **1. STH RESEMBLING THREAD** sth that is thin and delicate like thread, especially a lock of hair, a piece of straw, or a streak of smoke **2. SB SLENDER AND DELICATE** sb or sth that is slender and delicate ○ *a wisp of a child* **3. STH INSUBSTANTIAL** sth that is vague and fleeting ○ *a wisp of a memory* **4. BUNDLE** a bundle of sth, especially a bundle of hay or straw ■ *v.* (**wisps, wisping, wisped**) **1.** *vt.* **BUNDLE STRAW OR HAY** to make a handful of straw or hay into a bundle **2.** *vi.* **MOVE LIKE WISP** to float like sth delicate or faint [14thC. Origin unknown.] —**wispily** *adv.* —**wispiness** *n.* —**wispy** *adj.*

wist (*archaic*) **1.** past participle, past tense of **wis 2.** past participle, past tense of **wit**

Wisteria

wisteria /wi steeri ə/ (*plural* **-as** *or* **-a**) *n.* a deciduous climbing shrub native to North America and Asia, with blue, pink, or white flowers that hang down in clusters. Genus: *Wisteria*. [Early 19thC. From modern

Latin, genus name, from the name of the US anatomist Caspar *Wistar* (1761–1818).]

wistful /wistf'l/ *adj.* deep in sad thoughts, especially thoughts of sth yearned for or lost, or expressing this sad yearning [Early 17thC. Formed from obsolete *wistly* 'intently', of uncertain origin.] —**wistfully** *adv.* —**wistfulness** *n.*

wit[1] /wit/ *n.* **1. INGENIOUS HUMOUR** apt, clever, and often humorous association of words or ideas, or a capacity for this **2. SPEECH OR WRITING SHOWING WIT** speech or writing that shows an apt, clever, and often humorous association of words **3. WITTY PERSON** sb known for using wit **4. INTELLIGENCE** mental acumen, intelligence, or reasoning power **5. COMMON SENSE** knowledge, information, or common sense (*regional*) ■ **wits** *npl.* **SHREWDNESS** mental acumen, shrewdness, or reasoning power [Old English *wit* 'mind, understanding'. Ultimately from an Indo-European base meaning 'to see, know', which is also the ancestor of English *wisdom*, *vision*, and *idea*.] ◇ **be at your wits' end** to be in despair as to how to cope with sth ◇ **live by your wits** to use cunning and ingenuity in order to survive

wit[2] /wit/ (**wot** /wot/, **wits** *or* **wot, witting, wist** /wist/, **wist**) *vti.* to know or become aware of sth (*archaic*) [Old English *witan*; ultimately related to WIT[1]] ◇ **to wit** that is to say

witan /witt'n/ *n.* an assembly of the king's counsellors in Anglo-Saxon England [Early 19thC. Revival of Old English, 'counsellors', from *wita* 'counsellor', literally 'one who knows'; ultimately related to WIT[1].]

Witbank /wit bank/ town in Mpumalanga Province, northeastern South Africa. Population: 83,400 (1998).

witblits /vitblits/ *n. S Africa* illegally distilled alcoholic liquor, usually made from grapes [Mid-20thC. From Afrikaans, literally 'white lightning'.]

witch /wich/ *n.* **1. SB WITH MAGIC POWERS** sb, especially a woman, who is supposed to have magical or wonder-working powers that are most often used malevolently **2. FOLLOWER OF NATURE RELIGION** a follower of Wicca, a pre-Christian natural religion **3. OFFENSIVE TERM** an offensive term that deliberately insults a woman regarded as ugly, vicious, or malicious (*insult*) **4. SEDUCTIVE WOMAN** an alluring or seductive woman (*informal; offensive in some contexts*) ■ *vt.* (**witches, witching, witched**) **EXERCISE WITCHCRAFT** to cause or change sth by witchcraft [Old English *wicce* 'witch' and *wicca* 'wizard', both ultimately related to WAKE[1] and WATCH]

witchcraft /wich kraaft/ *n.* **1. EXERCISE OF MAGICAL POWERS** the art or exercise of magical powers **2. EFFECT OF MAGICAL POWERS** the effect or influence of magical powers **3. SEDUCTIVE CHARM** alluring or seductive charm or influence

witch doctor *n.* **1. TRIBAL HEALER OR MAGICIAN** in tribal societies, sb who practices healing, divining, or other magical powers **2. HUNTER OF WITCHES** in some African cultures, sb who detects or identifies supposed witches

witch elm *n.* = wych elm

witchery /wichəri/ *n.* **1. PRACTICE OF MAGIC** the practice of witchcraft or magic (*dated or literary*) **2. BEWITCHING CHARM** charm or influence that has a bewitching quality or effect

witches' brew *n.* **1. DIABOLICAL MIXTURE** a malevolent or diabolical mixture of different things ○ *an article that was a witches' brew of spite and innuendo* **2. POTION** a potion concocted by a witch or witches

witches' broom *n.* an abnormal tufted growth of shoots on a tree or woody plant, usually caused by parasitic fungi. The fungi usually responsible are of the genus *Taphrina*.

witches' butter *n.* = jelly fungus

witches' Sabbath *n.* a midnight assembly for devil-worship or other rites

witchetty grub /wichiti-/ *n.* the wood-eating larva of a number of species of Australian moth, used as food by Aboriginal people and people who live in the bush [Mid-19thC. Origin uncertain: probably from Australian Aboriginal words meaning 'to climb' or 'hooked stick' and 'grub'.]

witch grass *n.* **1. GRASS WITH CREEPING ROOTS** a North American grass with creeping roots. Latin name:

Panicum capillare. 2. = **couch grass** [Origin uncertain: probably an alteration of QUITCH GRASS]

witch hazel, **wych hazel** *n.* 1. TREES **SHRUB WITH YELLOW FLOWERS** a tree or shrub with toothed, egg-shaped leaves and small yellow flowers. There are several species, the best-known being *Hamamelis virginiana* of eastern North America, which blooms in late autumn. 2. PHARM **SOOTHING LOTION** a mixture of alcohol, water, and extract from the bark and dried leaves of the witch hazel tree, used as an astringent and in the treatment of sprains and bruises [Alteration of earlier *wych*]

witch-hunt, **witch hunt** *n.* 1. **CAMPAIGN AGAINST DISSENTERS** an intensive systematic campaign directed against those who have done sth wrong or who hold different views 2. HIST **PERSECUTION OF WITCHES** a persecution of people believed to be witches —**witch-hunter** *n.*

witching /wíching/ *adj.* 1. **SUITABLE FOR WITCHCRAFT** suitable for or resembling witchcraft (*archaic*) 2. **BEWITCHING** bewitching (*literary*) ■ *n.* **WITCHCRAFT** witchcraft or sorcery (*archaic*)

witching hour *n.* midnight, said to be the time when witches appear

witchweed /wích weed/ *n.* a parasitic plant with small red flowers, native to South Africa and introduced into the southern United States. Genus: *Striga.*

witenagemot /wíttənəgi mṓt/ *n.* = **witan** [Old English *witena gemōt* 'assembly of wise men', from *wita* (see WITAN) + *gemōt* 'assembly' (source of English *moot*)]

Wite-Out /wīt-/ *tdmk.* a trademark for a white fluid used to cover up mistakes in writing, typing, or printing

with /wi*th*/ *prep.* 1. **IN THE COMPANY OF** used to indicate that sb is accompanying or is in the company of another person or people, or that sth is accompanying sth else ○ *at the theme park with their children* ○ *Do you still want me to go with you?* 2. **USED TOGETHER** used together or at the same time ○ *He made Yorkshire pudding to go with the roast beef.* 3. **INVOLVING** involving that person or people ○ *He organized the meeting together with the head of his department.* 4. **AGAINST** in opposition to ○ *students competing with each other for a limited number of spaces* 5. **BY MEANS OF** by the means of or using a particular object, substance, or system ○ *After 18 months, all the rats treated with the altered virus were healthy.* 6. **CARRYING** carrying or having in one's possession ○ *He came into the office with a box full of files.* 7. **HAVING** having as a possession, attribute, or feature ○ *The film is in French with English subtitles.* 8. **BECAUSE OF** in a particular condition as a result of sth ○ *I felt heartsick and faint with anxiety.* 9. **ON OR IN** used to indicate that sth has a substance or things on or in it ○ *brightly painted walls covered with photographs of Italy* 10. **CONCERNING** used to indicate the person or thing that a state, quality, or action relates to or affects ○ *not happy with the service provided* 11. **IN THIS WAY** used to indicate the way sth is done, or the degree to which it is done ○ *sitting with her head on his shoulder* 12. **ACCOMPANIED BY** used to indicate the feeling, gesture, sound, or facial expression that accompanies or causes an action ○ *walks with a limp* 13. **IN THE LIGHT OF** in the light of or given the situation mentioned ○ *With all the problems you have, the last thing you need is a lawsuit.* 14. **IN SPITE OF** in spite of the situation mentioned ○ *With all his charm and good breeding, he's not a man to be trusted.* 15. **AT TIME OF** at the same time as ○ *He woke with the alarm and hurriedly dressed.* 16. **FOLLOWING THE DIRECTION OF** in the same direction as ○ *They were to sail with the tide the next day.* 17. **ACCORDING TO** used to indicate that sth happens or is true according to sth else ○ *how much the risk of death increases with age* 18. **AFTER** following on from ○ *With a final wave goodbye she turned the corner.* [Old English *wiþ* 'with, against'. Ultimately from an Indo-European word meaning 'apart', which is also the ancestor of English *wide.*] ◇ **be with it** 1. to be fashionable or up to date with fashion (*informal*) 2. to be able to understand what is going on in a situation (*informal*) ◇ **be with sb** 1. to understand sb 2. to approve of or support sb ○ *Are you with us or not?*

withal /wi*th* áwl/ *adv.* (*archaic*) 1. **MOREOVER** along with the rest or in addition 2. **NEVERTHELESS** in spite of that ■ *prep.* **WITH** with (*archaic*) [12thC. Formed from WITH + ALL.]

withdraw /wi*th* dráw/ (**-draws, -drawing, -drew** /-dróo/, **-drawn** /-dráwn/) *v.* 1. *vt.* **REMOVE STH** to remove or take back sth that was previously provided or in place 2. *vt.* **RETRACT STATEMENT** to deny the truth or validity of sth that was previously stated 3. *vi.* **RETREAT FROM POSITION** to retreat or retire from a position 4. *vt.* **TAKE MONEY FROM ACCOUNT** to take money out of an account [Literally 'to pull away from'] —**withdrawable** *adj.* —**withdrawer** *n.*

withdrawal /wi*th* dráw əl/ *n.* 1. **TAKING MONEY FROM BANK** the act of taking money from a bank or building society account, or the amount of money taken out 2. **PERIOD OF FIGHTING ADDICTION** a period during which sb addicted to a drug or other addictive substance stops taking it, causing the person to experience painful or uncomfortable symptoms 3. **TAKING STH AWAY** the act or condition of taking sth away or no longer taking part in sth 4. **RETREAT OF ARMY** retreat or retirement of an army or other military force from an area in which it was fighting

withdrawing room *n.* a drawing room (*archaic*)

withdrawn /wi*th* dráwn/ *adj.* 1. **INTROVERTED** not friendly or sociable but quiet and thoughtful, especially to an unusual or worrying degree 2. **REMOVED FROM MARKET** removed from circulation, competition, or activity ■ past participle of **withdraw** —**withdrawnness** *n.*

withdrew past tense of **withdraw**

withe /with, wi*th*/ *n.* 1. **FLEXIBLE STEM** a strong flexible twig or stem used to bind sth 2. **FLEXIBLE TOOL HANDLE** a shock-absorbing flexible handle for a tool ■ *vt.* (**withes, withing, withed**) **BIND STH WITH WITHES** to bind sth with withes [Old English *wiþe*. Ultimately from an Indo-European base meaning 'to twist, bend', which is also the ancestor of English *withy* and *wire.*]

wither /wí*th*ər/ (**-ers, -ering, -ered**) *v.* 1. *vti.* **SHRIVEL** to shrivel or dry up as part of the process of dying, or make sth, especially a plant or part of a plant, shrivel in this way 2. *vi.* **FADE AWAY** to fade or lose freshness or vitality 3. *vti.* **MAKE SB LOSE CONFIDENCE** to make sb feel embarrassed, foolish, or incapable of activity as the object of scorn or contempt, or lose confidence in the face of sb's scorn [14thC. Origin uncertain: probably a variant of WEATHER in the sense 'to expose to the elements'.] —**withered** *adj.* —**witherer** *n.*

withering /wí*th*əring/ *adj.* expressing scorn or contempt with the intention of causing sb to feel embarrassed or foolish ○ *'When he assumed this attitude in the courtroom, ears were always pricked up, as it usually foretold a flood of withering sarcasm.'* (Willa Cather, *The Troll Garden*; 1905) —**witheringly** *adv.*

witherite /wí*th*ə rīt/ *n.* a rare greyish-white barium carbonate mineral found in veins associated with lead ore, used as a barium ore [Late 18thC. Named after the English scientist William *Withering* (1741–99), who first described the mineral.]

withe rod /wíth-/ *n.* a viburnum that has tough flexible shoots. Latin name: *Viburnum cassinoides* and *Viburnum nudum.*

withers /wí*th*ərz/ *npl.* the ridge between the shoulder bones of a horse, sheep, ox, or similar four-legged animal, forming the highest part of its back [Early 16thC. Origin uncertain: probably ultimately from Old English *wiþer* 'against'.]

withershins /wí*th*ər shinz/, **widdershins** /wíddər-/ *adv.* (*literary*) 1. *Scotland* **IN THE WRONG DIRECTION** in the direction that is contrary to the natural course 2. **ANTICLOCKWISE** anticlockwise or in the direction that is contrary to the course of the sun [Early 16thC. Alteration of Middle Low German *weddersinnes*, from Middle High German *widersinnes*, from *wider* 'against, opposite' + *sin* 'sense, direction'.]

withhold /wi*th* hṓld/ (**-holds, -holding, -held** /wi*th* héld/, **-held**) *v.* 1. *vti.* **HOLD STH BACK** to refuse to do or give sth until sth else is done 2. *vt.* **DEDUCT TAX** to collect or deduct tax from a salary [Literally 'to hold against or away'] —**withholder** *n.*

withholding tax *n.* 1. **TAX PAID BY NONRESIDENTS** tax deducted at source from dividends paid to non-residents of a country 2. *US* **TAX LIABILITY WITHHELD FROM WAGES** part of an employee's wage or salary withheld and remitted to the government by an employer in payment of taxes

within /wi*th* ín/ *prep., adv.* 1. **INSIDE** used to indicate that sb or sth is inside or enclosed by a place, area, or object ○ (prep) *goods manufactured within a country* ○ (prep) *A natural pool lay within a copse of young trees.* ○ (adv) *The door was locked from within.* 2. **HAPPENING INSIDE** happening inside an organization, system, or society ○ (prep) *keeping companies within a given industry technologically competitive* ○ (adv) *A lot of our Internet development activity is coming from within.* 3. **INSIDE YOURSELF** inside the body or mind ○ (adv) *Her new-found happiness was from within.* ○ (prep) *He needed to find the strength within him to carry on.* ■ *prep.* **INSIDE LIMITS OF** inside the limits or rules of ○ *Try to keep within your budget and avoid overspending.* ■ *adv.* **INDOORS** indoors (*literary*) ■ *prep.* **NOT BEYOND** not beyond the scope, experience, range, time, or distance of ○ *regulations requiring that all accidents be reported within 48 hours* [Old English *wiþinnan* 'on the inside', from WITH + *innan* 'from within']

withindoors /wi*th* in dáwrz/ *adv.* indoors (*archaic*)

with-it *adj.* fashionable and modern in dress and behaviour (*dated informal*)

without /wi*th* ówt/ *prep.* 1. **NOT HAVING** used to indicate that sb or sth does not have the thing mentioned ○ *left without proper tools to finish the job* 2. **NOT ACCOMPANIED BY** not with sb, or not having the involvement of sb ○ *We can't really make any decisions without him.* 3. **BEYOND** beyond (*archaic*) 4. **NOT HAPPENING** used to indicate that sth does not happen or occur ○ *The bill was passed without a dissenting voice.* ■ *prep., adv.* **OUTSIDE** on, at, or to the outside of somewhere (*regional or archaic*) ○ (prep) *Without the town the air was fresher.* ○ (adv) *She knocked and waited without.* ■ *prep.* **LACKING** lacking a feeling of ○ *The accused engaged in physical abuse without remorse or intent to change.* ■ *conj.* **UNLESS** unless (*nonstandard*) [Old English *wiþūtan* 'on the outside of', from WITH + *ūtan* 'from the outside'] ◇ **be** *or* **do without** to manage in spite of not having sth considered necessary or desirable ○ *a form of power he could not buy or do without*

withoutdoors /wi*th* ówt dáwrz/ *adv.* outdoors (*archaic*)

withstand /wi*th* stánd/ (**-stands, -standing, -stood** /-stóod/, **-stood**) *vti.* to be strong enough to stand up to sb or remain unchanged by sth such as extremes of heat or pressure [Literally 'to stand against'] —**withstander** *n.*

withy /wí*th*i/ *n.* (*plural* **-ies**) 1. = **withe** 2. **WILLOW TREE** a willow tree, especially an osier ■ *adj.* **TOUGH AND PLIABLE** tough and pliable, like withes (*dated*) [Old English *wīþig* 'willow'. Ultimately from an Indo-European base meaning 'to twist, bend', which is also the ancestor of English *withe* and *wire.*]

witless /wíttləss/ *adj.* lacking intelligence or common sense —**witlessly** *adv.* —**witlessness** *n.*

witling /wíttling/ *n.* sb who aspires to be witty (*literary insult*)

witness /wítnəss/ *n.* 1. **SB WHO SEES STH** sb who saw or heard sth that happened and gives evidence about it 2. LAW **SIGNATORY OF A DOCUMENT** sb who signs a document to show that it, or a signature on it, is genuine 3. *US* CHR **SB WHO TESTIFIES TO CHRISTIAN BELIEFS** sb who publicly testifies to strong personal Christian beliefs 4. *US* CHR **PUBLIC STATEMENT OF CHRISTIAN BELIEFS** a public statement of strong personal Christian beliefs ■ *v.* (**-nesses, -nessing, -nessed**) 1. *vt.* LAW **SEE STH HAPPEN** to see sth happen, especially a crime or an accident 2. *vt.* LAW **COUNTERSIGN A DOCUMENT** to affirm the authenticity of a document or a signature on a document by signing it 3. *vt.* **EXPERIENCE IMPORTANT EVENTS** to experience important events or changes, or be the time in which they occur 4. *vt.* **BE SIGN OF STH** to be a sign or proof of sth that is happening 5. *vi.* *US* CHR **SPEAK PUBLICLY ABOUT RELIGIOUS BELIEFS** to talk in public about strong personal Christian beliefs [Old English *witnes*, formed from *wit* (see WIT[1])] —**witnessable** *adj.* —**witnesser** *n.* ◇ **bear witness, bear witness to sth** to be evidence or prove that sth is true or that sth happened

witness box *n.* the enclosed place in a courtroom where witnesses give evidence. US term **witness stand**

witness stand *n. US* = **witness box**

Witt /wit/, **Jan De** (1625–72) Dutch statesman. The chief minister of the Netherlands (1653–72) and a leading republican, he secured the Dutch victory in the Second Anglo-Dutch War (1664–67). He resigned when William III assumed Dutch political leadership in 1672 and was murdered by the king's supporters.

witter /wíttər/ (**-ters**, **-tering**, **-tered**) *vi.* to chatter or babble at undue length (*informal*) [Early 19thC. Origin uncertain.]

wittering /wíttəring/ *n.* continuous pointless chatter (*informal*)

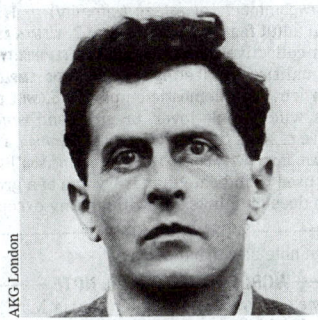
Ludwig Wittgenstein
AKG London

Wittgenstein /vítgən stīn/, **Ludwig** (1889–1951) Austrian-born British philosopher. He is considered one of the most important thinkers of the 20th century. His *Tractatus Logico-philosophicus* (1921) and *Philosophical Investigations* (1953) represent distinct phases in his work in analytic and linguistic philosophy. Full name **Ludwig Josef Johann Wittgenstein**

witticism /wíttissizəm/ *n.* a witty or clever remark [Late 17thC. Coined by the poet John Dryden; a blend of WITTY and CRITICISM.]

witting /wítting/ *adj.* **1.** DELIBERATE done deliberately or intentionally **2.** RESPONSIBLE responsible and fully aware —**wittingly** *adv.*

witty /wítti/ (**-tier**, **-tiest**) *adj.* **1.** USING WORDS CLEVERLY using words in an apt, clever, and amusing way **2.** CLEVERLY DONE strikingly clever, stylish, or original in design or execution —**wittily** *adv.* —**wittiness** *n.*

—— **WORD KEY: SYNONYMS** ——
See Synonyms at *funny*.

Witwatersrand /wit wáwtərz rand/ rocky ridge in northeastern South Africa. Commonly known as the Rand, it is the most productive gold-mining area in the world. Johannesburg is located near its centre. Length: 100 km/60 mi.

wive /wīv/ (**wives**, **wiving**, **wived**) *v.* (*archaic*) **1.** *vti.* MARRY WOMAN to marry a woman **2.** *vt.* GIVE SB WIFE to supply sb with a wife [Old English wīfian, formed from wīf (see WIFE)]

wivern *n.* = **wyvern**

wives plural of **wife**

wiz[1] /wiz/ (*plural* **wizzes**) *n.* a wizard (*informal*) [Shortening]

wiz[2] *n.* = **whiz** *v.* **3** (*informal*)

wizard /wízzərd/ *n.* **1.** MALE WITCH a man who is supposed to have magical or wonder-working powers **2.** SB WHO IS EXCELLENT AT STH sb who is extremely clever at or knowledgeable about sth (*informal*) ■ *adj. UK* VERY GOOD AT STH extremely proficient or adept at sth (*dated*) [15thC. Variant of earlier *wisard*, from *wise*.] —**wizardly** *adj.*

—— **WORD KEY: CULTURAL NOTE** ——
The Wizard of Oz, a film by US producer David O. Selznick and director Victor Fleming (1939). This enchanting musical, based on a novel by L. Frank Baum (1900), tells the story of Dorothy, a young Kansas girl who dreams she is transported to the magical world of Oz, a utopian place without disease, poverty, or political

discussion 'except in the outlying districts'. Evading the Wicked Witch of the West, she sets off along the yellow brick road in search of the mysterious Wizard. The words *Oz* (a magical, unreal, even bizarre place or situation), *Wicked Witch of the West* (evil person) and *munchkin* (from the elflike Munchkins in the movie, now meaning also an elflike person, a young child, or a minor government official) have established a place in the English language.

wizardry /wízzərdri/ *n.* **1.** ART OF WIZARDS the art, activities, or accomplishments of a wizard **2.** SKILL extreme skill or accomplishment

wizen[1] /wízz'n/ (**-ens**, **-ening**, **-ened**) *vti.* to wither or dry up, or make sth wither or dry up [Old English wisnian]

wizen[2] /wízz'n/ *adj.* withered or dried up [Late 18thC. Alteration of WIZENED.]

wizened /wízz'nd/ *adj.* looking wrinkled, shrivelled, or dried up

wk *abbr.* **1.** week **2.** work **3.** weak

wkly *abbr.* weekly

wkt *abbr.* wicket

WL *abbr.* **1.** WL, w.l. INSUR water line **2.** ELEC wavelength **3.** CARS (Windward Islands) St Lucia (*international vehicle registration*)

Wm. *abbr.* William

wmk. *abbr.* watermark

WMO *abbr.* World Meteorological Organization

WNW *abbr.* west-northwest

WO, W.O. *abbr.* **1.** MIL warrant officer **2.** MIL wireless operator **3.** HIST War Office

w/o *abbr.* without

woad /wōd/ *n.* **1.** PLANT THAT YIELDS BLUE DYE a European plant that was formerly cultivated for the blue dye extracted from its leaves. Latin name: *Isatis tinctoria*. **2.** BLUE DYE the blue dye obtained from the woad plant and used in ancient times as a body paint [Old English wād. From a prehistoric Germanic word of unknown origin.]

woadwaxen /wōd waks'n/ (*plural* **-ens** *or* **-en**) *n.* = **dyer's-greenweed** [14thC. Alteration (influenced by *woad*) of *woodwaxen*, from Old English *wuduweaxe*, from *wudu* 'wood' + *weaxan* 'to grow'.]

w.o.b. *abbr.* INSUR washed overboard

wobble /wóbb'l/ *v.* (**-bles**, **-bling**, **-bled**) **1.** *vti.* MOVE FROM SIDE TO SIDE to move or cause sth to move in a swaying, shaking, or trembling way **2.** *vi.* QUAVER to vary uncertainly in pitch or volume **3.** *vi.* BE UNABLE TO DECIDE to be unable or unwilling to reach a decision ■ *n.* WOBBLING EFFECT a wobbling movement or sound [Mid-17thC. Origin uncertain: probably from Low German *wabbeln*; ultimately from a prehistoric Germanic word that is also the ancestor of English *wave* and *waver*.] —**wobbler** *n.* —**wobblingly** *adv.*

wobbler syndrome *n.* a condition in horses and dogs characterized by an unsteady gait and sometimes falling, due to a misalignment of vertebrae in the neck, which impinges on the spinal cord

wobbly /wóbbli/ (**-blier**, **-bliest**) *adj.* **1.** UNSTEADY moving unsteadily from side to side **2.** FEELING WEAK feeling weak and unable to keep balanced (*informal*) —**wobbliness** *n.* ◇ **throw a wobbly, chuck a wobbly** *Aus* suddenly to become very angry or frightened (*informal*)

Wodehouse /wood howss/, **P. G.** (1881–1975) British

writer. He wrote over 100 novels, many of which feature the fictional characters Bertie Wooster and his 'gentleman's gentleman', Jeeves. He became a US citizen in 1955. Full name **Sir Pelham Grenville Wodehouse**

Woden /wōd'n/ *n.* an Anglo-Saxon god, the equivalent of the Norse Odin

wodge /woj/ *n.* a large lump or chunk of sth (*informal*) ○ *They caught him stuffing wodges of banknotes into his pockets.* [Mid-19thC. Blend of WAD and WEDGE.]

woe /wō/ *n.* **1.** UNFORTUNATE HAPPENING a serious affliction or misfortune **2.** GRIEF grief or distress resulting from a serious affliction or misfortune ■ *interj.* EXPRESSING GRIEF used to express grief or distress (*archaic or literary*) [Old English wā, from a prehistoric Germanic base that is also the ancestor of English *wail*; ultimately from an Indo-European exclamation] ◇ **woe betide sb** used as a threat to indicate that sb is going to regret sth or be punished in some way ○ *Woe betide him if he turns up late for work again.* ◇ **woe is me** used to indicate that the speaker is in distress or feels unhappy or unfortunate (*literary or humorous*)

woebegone /wō bi gon/ *adj.* feeling or looking distressed or sorrowful [13thC. Formed from WOE + *begon* 'beset' (ultimately from Old English *gān*; see GO).]

woeful /wōf'l/ *adj.* **1.** UNHAPPY feeling or expressing great distress or sorrow **2.** CAUSING GRIEF bringing or causing great distress or sorrow **3.** PATHETICALLY BAD pitifully or regrettably bad —**woefully** *adv.* —**woefulness** *n.*

wog[1] /wog/ *n.* a highly offensive term referring to a member of any race of people who have dark skin (*taboo offensive*) [Early 20thC. Origin uncertain: probably a shortening of GOLLIWOG.]

wog[2] /wog/ *n. Aus* influenza or a similar illness (*informal*) [Mid-20thC. Origin unknown.]

woggle /wógg'l/ *n.* the thin ring of leather through which a Scout's neckerchief is drawn and secured [Mid-20thC. Origin unknown.]

Wöhler /vö lər/, **Friedrich** (1800–82) German chemist. His work on urea (1828) proved that organic processes can be synthesized in the laboratory. He also isolated aluminium and beryllium.

Wok

wok /wok/ *n.* a large thin metal pan with a curved base, used for stir-frying, steaming, and braising food, especially in Chinese and other Far Eastern cookery [Mid-20thC. From Chinese (Cantonese).]

woke past tense of **wake**

woken past participle of **wake**

Woking /wōking/ town in Surrey, southeastern England. Population: 90,300 (1995).

Wokingham /wōkingəm/ town in southern England, west of London. Population: 38,063 (1991).

wold /wōld/ *n.* upland or rolling country, especially when treeless (*literary*) [Old English *wald*, *weald* 'forest'. Ultimately from an Indo-European word meaning 'wild', which is also the ancestor of English *wild* and *wilderness*.]

Wolds /wōldz/ range of chalk hills in eastern England. It is divided by the Humber Estuary into the Yorkshire Wolds and the Lincolnshire Wolds.

P. G. Wodehouse
Express Newspapers

Wolf

wolf /woolf/ *n.* (*plural* **wolves** /woolvz/) **1.** CARNIVORE THAT HUNTS IN PACKS any one of several predatory animals of North America and Eurasia that are related to the dog and hunt in packs, especially the grey wolf. Genus: *Canis*. **2.** ANIMAL RESEMBLING WOLF an animal that resembles a wolf but is not of the dog family, e.g. the Tasmanian wolf **3.** FUR OF WOLF the fur of the wolf **4.** GREEDY AND CRUEL PERSON sb who is greedy and cruel **5.** MAN WHO PURSUES WOMEN a sexually aggressive or predatory man (*informal*) **6.** INSECTS DESTRUCTIVE LARVA the destructive larva of several moths and beetles that sometimes infests granaries **7.** MUSIC DISCORD an unpleasant discord produced on a string or keyboard instrument (*often used before a noun*) ■ *vt.* (**wolfs, wolfing, wolfed**) EAT STH QUICKLY AND GREEDILY to eat food quickly and greedily or in gulps [Old English *wulf*. Ultimately from an Indo-European word that is also the ancestor of English *lupus*, *lycanthropy*, and *alyssum*.] ◇ **a wolf in sheep's clothing** sb who looks harmless or pleasant but is in fact dangerous or unpleasant ◇ **cry wolf** to give a false alarm or cry for help too many times, so that when help is really needed, no one will give it ◇ **keep the wolf from the door** to be enough to prevent hunger or starvation ◇ **throw sb to the wolves** to abandon sb to be destroyed by enemies in order to save yourself

Wolf /woolf/ *n.* ASTRON = **Lupus**

Wolf /voolf/, **Hugo** (1860–1903) Austrian composer. He is noted especially for several hundred songs exploring a wide range of themes and moods. Full name **Hugo Philipp Jakob Wolf**

wolfberry /woolf berri/ *n.* (*plural* **-ries**) a North American shrub that has grey leaves, pinkish flowers, and white berries. Latin name: *Symphoricarpos occidentalis*.

Wolf Cub *n.* now called **Cub Scout** (*dated*)

wolf dog *n.* **1.** DOG TO HUNT WOLVES a dog used to hunt wolves **2.** OFFSPRING OF WOLF AND DOG an offspring of a wolf and a dog

James Wolfe

Wolfe /woolf/, **James** (1727–59) British general. The second in command of British troops in North America, he is most famous for his capture of Quebec (1759) from the French in the Seven Years' War (1756–63). He was fatally wounded in the attack.

wolf eel *n.* a large long fish with a pointed tail found in Pacific coastal waters of North America. Latin name: *Anarrhichthys ocellatus*. [So called because it is a species of wolffish]

wolfer *n.* = **wolver**

Wolffian body /volfi ən-/ *n.* ANAT, ZOOL = **mesonephros** [Mid-19thC. Named after the German embryologist K. F. *Wolff* (1733–94), who first described the structure.]

wolffish /woolf fish/ (*plural* **-fish** *or* **-fishes**) *n.* a large northern Atlantic fish that has large sharp teeth and no pelvic fins. Genus: *Anarhichas*. [*Wolf* from the fish's voracious appetite]

wolfhound /woolf hownd/ *n.* a large dog of a breed that was originally bred to hunt wolves

wolfish /woolfish/ *adj.* resembling or characteristic of a wolf —**wolfishly** *adv.*

Wolfit /wool fit/, **Sir Donald** (1902–68) British actor and manager. He is noted for his interpretation of Shakespearean characters and, with his own company, his production of Shakespearean plays.

wolf pack *n.* **1.** GROUP OF WOLVES a group of wolves that hunt together **2.** MIL GROUP OF SUBMARINES a group of submarines engaged in hunting and attacking enemy convoys during World War II

wolfram /woolfrəm/ *n.* tungsten (*archaic*) [Mid-18thC. From German, 'wolframite', from *Wolf* 'wolf' + German dialect *Rahm* 'soot, dirt'.]

wolframite /woolfrə mīt/ *n.* a brownish-black crystalline mineral consisting of a tungstate of iron and manganese. It is the chief ore of tungsten. [Mid-19thC. From German (see WOLFRAM).]

wolfsbane /woolfs bayn/ *n.* (*plural* **-banes** *or* **-bane**) any of several wild or cultivated poisonous plants with yellow or purplish-blue flowers, sometimes used for medicinal purposes. Genus: *Aconitum*. [Mid-16thC. Translation of Greek *lukoktonon*, literally 'wolf-killer', from the poison found in the plants.]

Wolfsburg /woolfs burg/ /vólfs boork/ industrial city in Lower Saxony State, north-central Germany. Population: 126,800 (1995).

wolf spider *n.* a ground spider that hunts its prey instead of using a web. Family: Lycosidae.

wolf whistle *n.* a whistle given to signal sexual interest in or admiration of sb (*considered offensive by some people*)

wolf-whistle *vti.* to make a wolf whistle at sb, especially a woman passer-by

wollastonite /woolləstə nīt/ *n.* a grey-white calcium silicate mineral that occurs as fibrous masses in metamorphosed limestones [Early 19thC. Named after the English physicist William Hyde *Wollaston* (1766–1828).]

Wollongong /woolləng gong/ coastal city in eastern New South Wales, Australia. It is an industrial centre and the site of a university. Population: 219,761 (1996).

Mary Wollstonecraft: Portrait (1790) by John Opie

Wollstonecraft /woolstən kráft/, **Mary** (1759–97) British feminist. Her *Vindication of the Rights of Woman* (1792), advocating the equality of the sexes, is an important early document of modern feminism.

Wolof /wól of/ (*plural* **-lof** *or* **-lofs**) *n.* **1.** PEOPLES MEMBER OF W AFRICAN PEOPLE a member of a people who live in West Africa, mainly in Senegal, but also with sizeable communities in the Gambia and Mauritania **2.** LANG NIGER-CONGO LANGUAGE a language spoken in Senegal and the Gambia, belonging to the Niger-Congo language family. About two million people speak Wolof. [Early 19thC. From *Wolof*.] —**Wolof** *adj.*

Wolsey /woolzi/, **Thomas** (1475–1530) English clergyman and statesman. As Henry VIII's Lord Chancellor (1515–29), he exercised great power both in England and abroad. He was impeached for failing to secure Henry's divorce from Catherine of Aragon. Known as **Cardinal Wolsey**

wolver /woolvər/, **wolfer** *n.* sb who hunts wolves

Wolverhampton /woolvər hámptən/ industrial town in the West Midlands of England. Population: 244,300 (1995).

wolverine /woolvə rin/ (*plural* **-ines** *or* **-ine**) *n.* a strong dark-furred usually solitary carnivore of the weasel family, chiefly found in northern Eurasian and North American forests. Latin name: *Gulo gulo*. [Late 16thC. Origin uncertain: probably from WOLF.]

wolves plural of **wolf**

woman /woommən/ (*plural* **-en** /wímmin/) *n.* **1.** FEMALE ADULT an adult female human being **2.** WOMEN AS GROUP women collectively or in general **3.** FEMININITY feminine qualities or feelings **4.** DOMESTIC EMPLOYEE a woman who is a domestic employee **5.** WIFE OR GIRLFRIEND a wife, female lover, or girlfriend (*informal; offensive to some people*) [Old English *wimman*, a variant of *wifman*, from *wif* 'woman, wife' + *man* 'person'] ◇ **to a woman** used to indicate that every one of a group of women does or thinks sth, without any exceptions

──── **WORD KEY: USAGE** ────
See Usage note at **girl** and **person**.

──── **WORD KEY: CULTURAL NOTE** ────
Little Women, a novel by US writer Louisa May Alcott (1868–69). An abidingly popular family saga set in 1860s New England, it recounts the emotional and intellectual development of four sisters – Meg, Jo, Beth, and Amy – as they progress through adolescence to adulthood. It was followed by two sequels, *Little Men* (1871) and *Jo's Boys* (1886).

womanfully /woommənfəli/ *adv.* in a way that shows or is characteristic of womanly spirit or energy [Early 19thC. Modelled on MANFULLY.]

womanhood /woommən hood/ *n.* **1.** CONDITION OF BEING WOMAN the state or condition of being a woman **2.** WOMEN women in general, or as a group

womanise *vti.* = **womanize**

womanish /woommənish/ *adj.* an offensive term for a man perceived to have qualities stereotypically attributed to women, e.g. weakness or fussiness (*insult*) —**womanishly** *adv.* —**womanishness** *n.*

womanist /woommənist/ *adj.* having a respect for and a belief in the abilities and talents of women [Late 20thC. Modelled on *humanist*.]

womanize /woommə nīz/ (**-izes, -izing, -ized**), **womanise** (**-ises, -ising, -ised**) *vi.* to be constantly in search of casual sex with women (*disapproving; refers to men*) —**womanizer** *n.*

womankind /woommən kīnd/, **womenkind** /wímmən-/ *n.* women collectively or in general

womanly /woommənli/ *adj.* having positive characteristics or qualities, especially warmth, calmness, and competence, attributed to mature women —**womanliness** *n.*

woman of the house *n.* a woman who is in charge of or who is the primary woman of a household

woman of the world (*plural* **women of the world**) *n.* a socially experienced and sophisticated woman

womanpower /woommən powər/ *n.* **1.** WOMEN IN WORKFORCE women as part of the workforce in society **2.** INFLUENCE OF WOMEN the influence and impact of women in society [Early 20thC. Modelled on MANPOWER.]

woman suffrage *n.* = **women's suffrage**

woman-to-woman *adj.* **1.** BETWEEN WOMEN marked by directness and candour between women **2.** SPORTS PLAYER PAIRING in sports such as women's football, hockey, or basketball, having each defender of one team mark a corresponding attacker of the other team —**woman-to-woman** *adv.*

womb /woom/ *n.* **1.** UTERUS OF WOMAN the uterus, especially that of a human woman (*not used technically*) **2.** PLACE OF ORIGIN a place where sth is conceived and nurtured **3.** PLACE OF SECURITY a place that offers protection and shelter, or a state of mind that provides comfort [Old English *wamb*, from a prehistoric Germanic word of unknown origin]

Wombat

wombat /wóm bat/ *n.* any of several Australian burrowing marsupials that are short, robust, covered in dense wiry hair, and have a stumpy tail and wide blunt snout. Latin name: *Vombatus ursinus* and *Lasiorhinus latifrons*. [Late 18thC. From Dharuk (an Australian Aboriginal language) *wambaty*.]

womblike /wooóm līk/ *adj.* resembling a womb, especially in being reassuring, all-enclosing, and giving a feeling of security

women plural of **woman**

womenfolk /wímmin fōk/ *n.* women collectively, or a particular group of women, especially those belonging to the same family or society (*dated*)

womenkind /wímmin kīnd/ *n.* = **womankind**

Women's Institute *n.* an organization of affiliated groups of women, especially in rural areas, who hold regular meetings for social and cultural activities, or a group belonging to this

women's lib *n.* women's liberation (*informal disapproving*) —**women's libber** *n.*

women's liberation *n.* a political movement intended to free women from oppression, or the act of a woman's freeing herself

women's movement *n.* a movement seeking to promote and improve the position of women in society

women's refuge *n.* a place where women and children can stay after leaving home to escape domestic violence. US term **women's shelter**

Women's Royal Voluntary Service *n.* a British service run by women that provides support for people in need

women's shelter *n.* US = **women's refuge**

women's studies *npl.* a course of study examining the historical, economic, and cultural roles and achievements of women (*takes a singular or plural verb*)

women's suffrage *n.* the right of women to vote in elections

womenswear /wímminz wair/ *n.* clothing and accessories for women

womera *n.* = **woomera**

won[1] /won/ (*plural* **won**) *n.* **1.** UNIT OF KOREAN CURRENCY the main unit of currency in North and South Korea, worth 100 chon. See table at **currency 2.** ONE WON a note worth one won [Mid-20thC. From Korean *wăn*.]

won[2] past participle, past tense of **win**

wonder /wúndər/ *n.* **1.** AMAZED ADMIRATION amazed admiration or awe, especially at sth very beautiful or new **2.** STH MARVELLOUS a miracle or other cause of intense admiration or awe ■ *adj.* EXTRAORDINARILY GOOD exciting admiration or amazement by virtue of being outstandingly good, effective, or unusual ■ *v.* (-ders, -dering, -dered) **1.** *vti.* SPECULATE ABOUT STH to speculate or be curious to know about sth **2.** *vi.* BE AMAZED to be in a state of amazed admiration or awe [Old English *wundor*, from a prehistoric Germanic word of unknown origin] —**wonderer** *n.* ◇ **for a wonder** as a matter of astonishment or surprise ◇ **no wonder, small wonder, little wonder** used to indicate that sth is not surprising ◇ **work wonders, perform wonders,**

do wonders to achieve remarkable results or be very effective in solving a problem

wonder drug = **miracle drug**

wonderful /wúndərf'l/ *adj.* **1.** OUTSTANDING of a quality that excites admiration or amazement **2.** EXCEEDINGLY PLEASING suiting sb perfectly —**wonderfully** *adv.* —**wonderfulness** *n.*

wonderland /wúndər land/ *n.* a land where wonderful things happen or exist

————— WORD KEY: CULTURAL NOTE —————
Alice's Adventures in Wonderland, a children's story by Lewis Carroll (1865). This extraordinarily inventive and immensely popular tale was based on stories that the author made up to entertain his friends' children. A girl called Alice dreams that she falls down a rabbit hole into a surreal world inhabited by eccentric characters including the Mad Hatter, the March Hare, and the King and Queen of Hearts. The expressions 'Curiouser and curiouser!' and 'Oh my fur and whiskers!' are direct quotations from this book. The oft-used expressions 'grin like a Cheshire cat', 'wild as a March hare', and 'mad as a hatter' have associations with characters in the book.

wonderment /wúndərmənt/ *n.* **1.** AMAZED ADMIRATION amazed admiration or awe **2.** PUZZLEMENT puzzled surprise

wonderwork /wúndər wurk/ *n.* sth made or done that arouses amazed admiration or awe —**wonderworker** *n.*

wondrous /wúndrəss/ *adj.* EXCITING WONDER so good or admirable as to inspire wonder or awe (*literary*) ■ *adv.* AMAZINGLY wondrously or extraordinarily (*literary*) [15thC. Alteration (influenced by MARVELLOUS) of obsolete *wonders*, from WONDER.] —**wondrously** *adv.* —**wondrousness** *n.*

wonk /wongk/ *n.* US sb who is regarded as boringly, narrowly, or obliviously preoccupied with sth, especially work (*informal*) [Early 20thC. Origin unknown.]

wonky /wóngki/ *adj.* (-kier, -kiest), *adv.* (*informal*) **1.** UNRELIABLE IN USE not to be relied on to be steady or secure or to function correctly **2.** ASKEW not straight or level [Early 20thC. Origin uncertain: perhaps ultimately from Old English *wancol* 'unsteady'.]

wont /wŏnt/ *adj.* ACCUSTOMED TO STH accustomed or likely to do sth (*formal*) ○ *He is wont to be rather quick of temper when tired.* ■ *n.* SB'S CUSTOM a habit or custom followed by a particular person or group of people (*formal*) ■ *vti.* (wonts, wonting, wont *or* wonted) BE ACCUSTOMED to have or give sb the habit of doing sth (*archaic*) [12thC. From the past participle of Old English *wunian* 'to be accustomed'. Ultimately from an Indo-European base meaning 'to desire', which is also the ancestor of English *win* and *wean*.]

————— WORD KEY: SYNONYMS —————
See Synonyms at **habit**.

won't /wŏnt/ *contr.* will not

wonted /wŏntid/ *adj.* usual or typical (*formal*) —**wontedly** *adv.* —**wontedness** *n.*

————— WORD KEY: SYNONYMS —————
See Synonyms at **usual**.

won ton /wón tón/ *n.* **1.** CHINESE DUMPLING in Chinese cookery, a small dumpling made from a square of noodle dough with a little filling in the middle, boiled in soup or deep-fried **2.** won ton soup, won ton soup SOUP WITH DUMPLINGS Chinese soup with boiled small dumplings in it [Mid-20thC. From Chinese (Cantonese) *wăn t'ăn*.]

woo /woo/ (woos, wooing, wooed) *v.* **1.** *vti.* SEEK WOMAN'S LOVE to seek the affection or love of a woman in order to marry her (*dated or literary*) **2.** *vti.* SEEK STH to try to please in order to gain sth, especially acceptance, fame, or approval **3.** *vt.* CAUSE STH UNPLEASANT to bring about sth unpleasant as a result of action taken (*formal*) ○ *wooing their own destruction* [Old English *wōgian*, of unknown origin] —**wooingly** *adv.*

wood /wood/ *n.* **1.** SUBSTANCE OF TREES a hard fibrous substance that chiefly composes shrubs and trees and is found beneath their bark **2.** FUEL OR BUILDING MATERIAL wood from trees, cut and dried then used

as a fuel or a building material or in other areas of craft and manufacture **3.** AREA WITH TREES an area of land covered by shrubs or trees. The area of a wood is usually smaller than that of a forest. ◊ **woods 4.** GOLF GOLF CLUB a golf club with a head formerly made of wood, but now usually made of stainless steel or titanium **5.** BOWLS WOODEN BALL USED IN BOWLS a wooden ball, used in the game of bowls, which has slightly flattened sides in order to make it roll in a curve ■ *adj.* **1.** OF WOOD made of or used for wood **2.** AMONG TREES located or living in a forested area ■ *v.* (woods, wooding, wooded) **1.** *vt.* COVER AREA WITH TREES to cover an area of land with trees **2.** *vti.* FUEL STH WITH WOOD to supply sb or sth or be supplied with wood as fuel [Old English *wudu*] ◇ **be out of the woods** to be out of danger or difficulty (*informal*) ◇ **cannot see the wood for the trees** used to indicate that sb is too concerned with the details to appreciate the general nature of a situation or problem ◇ **touch wood** used, whether you are actually touching wood or not, to try to avoid the bad luck that is supposed to come from being too confident or hopeful

————— WORD KEY: ORIGIN —————
The ancestral meaning of *wood* is probably 'collection of trees, forest'. The meanings 'tree' (now obsolete) and 'substance from which trees are made' are secondary developments. It has been suggested that the word *wood* may go back to an Indo-European source meaning 'separate', in which case it would originally have denoted a 'separated' or 'remote' piece of territory, near the outer edge or borders of known land. Since such remote, uninhabited areas were usually wooded, the word came to denote 'forest'.

Wood /wood/, **Sir Henry** (1869–1944) British conductor. In 1895 he initiated what are now known as the Henry Wood Promenade Concerts. He was a noted champion of contemporary music. Full name **Henry Joseph Wood**

Wood (the Elder), John (1704?–54) British architect and town planner. His most notable work is his early Georgian terraces in central Bath, England.

Wood (the Younger), John (1728–81) British architect and town planner. The son of John Wood the Elder, he designed the classical Georgian Assembly Rooms (1771) and Royal Crescent (1775) in Bath, England.

wood alcohol *n.* = **methanol**

wood anemone *n.* any of several anemones in North America and Europe with divided leaves and a single showy flower that can be white to crimson. Latin name: *Anemone quinquefolia.* Latin name: *Anemone nemorosa.*

wood ant *n.* a large reddish European ant that builds huge domed colonies of wood chips. Latin name: *Formica rufa.*

wood avens *n.* = **herb bennet**

wood betony *n.* an eastern North American lousewort that has yellow or reddish flowers. Latin name: *Pedicularis canadensis.*

woodbine /wood bīn/ *n.* (*plural* -bines *or* -bine) *n.* a honeysuckle of Eurasia and North Africa that has fragrant yellow flowers. Latin name: *Lonicera periclymenum.* [Old English *wudubinde*, from *wudu* 'wood' + *bindan* 'to bind'; so called because the plant grows around trees]

woodblock /wood blok/ *n.* **1.** = **woodcut** *n.* **1. 2.** MUSIC PERCUSSION INSTRUMENT a hollow block of wood used as a percussion instrument in an orchestra or band **3.** BUILDING FLOOR TILE a small flat piece of wood laid in a pattern with others to make a floor surface

woodborer /wood bawrər/ *n.* a medium sized moth with a stocky body that, as a large fleshy larva, bores into wood, causing considerable damage. Family: Cossidae.

Wood Buffalo National Park /wood búffələ-/ national park and nature reserve in central Canada, on the Alberta-Northwest Territories border, established in 1922. Area: 44,802 sq. km/17,298 sq. mi.

woodcarving /wood kaarving/ *n.* **1.** CARVING WOOD the art of carving wood **2.** STH CARVED FROM WOOD a decorative article carved from wood

woodchat /wood chat/ (*plural* -chats *or* -chat), **woodchat shrike** *n.* a European and North African songbird of the shrike family that has black-and-white plumage and a reddish-brown crown. Latin name: *Lanius senator*.

woodchop /wŏŏd chop/ *n.* a wood-chopping competition held at country fairs in Australia

woodchopper /wŏŏd choper/ *n.* sb who chops wood, especially sb who chops down trees

woodchuck /wŏŏd chuk/ (*plural* **-chucks** *or* **-chuck**) *n.* a heavy-set short-legged marmot common to northern North America, with brownish fur streaked with grey. Latin name: *Marmota monax*. [Late 17thC. By folk etymology from an Algonquian word.]

wood coal *n.* **1.** = **lignite 2.** = **charcoal**

woodcock /wŏŏd kok/ (*plural* **-cocks** *or* **-cock**) *n.* either of two small ground-dwelling birds related to the snipe, with short legs and rounded wings, a stocky body, and a disproportionately long bill. Genus: *Scolopax*.

woodcraft /wŏŏd kraaft/ *n.* **1.** SKILL IN THINGS CONCERNING WOODS skill in travelling, living, or working in the woods or forests **2.** US SKILL IN MAKING THINGS FROM WOOD skill in carving or making objects from wood —**woodcrafter** *n.* —**woodcraftsman** *n.*

woodcreeper /wŏŏd kreeper/ (*plural* **-ers** *or* **-er**) *n.* a Central or South American forest bird that clings to tree trunks with its short strong legs and probes for insects with its bill. Family: Dendrocolaptidae.

woodcut /wŏŏd kut/ *n.* **1.** BLOCK OF WOOD FOR MAKING PRINTS a block of wood carved with a picture or design and from which prints are made **2.** PRINT MADE WITH WOODCUT a print made by pressing a woodcut into a colouring substance and then onto paper

woodcutter /wŏŏd kuter/ *n.* **1.** OCCUPATIONS LUMBERJACK sb who chops down trees **2.** CRAFT SB WHO MAKES PRINTS sb who makes woodcuts, and prints from woodcuts

wood duck *n.* a crested North American duck that nests in tree cavities near water. The male has black, chestnut, green, purple, and white plumage. Latin name: *Aix sponsa*.

wooded /wŏŏdid/ *adj.* covered with or consisting of woodland or trees

wooden /wŏŏd'n/ *adj.* **1.** MADE OF WOOD made or consisting of wood **2.** UNGAINLY lacking flexibility, relaxation, and grace **3.** INEXPRESSIVE lacking animation, emotion, or responsiveness ○ *a wooden prose style* **4.** DULL IN SOUND making a dull unresonant sound ○ *spoke in a toneless, wooden voice* —**woodenly** *adv.* —**woodenness** *n.*

wood engraving *n.* **1.** ART OF ENGRAVING ON WOOD the art or process of engraving a picture or design with a burin on a block of wood **2.** PRINT FROM ENGRAVING ON WOOD an engraving made with a burin on a block of wood, or a print from one —**wood engraver** *n.*

woodenhead /wŏŏd'n hed/ *n.* sb who is considered very unintelligent (*informal insult*) —**woodenheaded** /wŏŏd'n héddid/ *adj.* —**woodenheadedly** /-héddidli/ *adv.* —**woodenheadedness** *n.*

Wooden Horse *n.* = **Trojan Horse** *n.* 1

wooden spoon *n.* a prize awarded for being last in a race or competition

woodenware /wŏŏd'n wair/ *n.* dishes or utensils made from wood

woodfree /wŏŏd free/ *adj.* used to describe paper made from wood pulp that has been chemically treated to remove impurities

wood frog *n.* an eastern North American frog that lives in woodlands and is light brown with darker markings on the head. Latin name: *Rana sylvatica*.

woodgrain /wŏŏd grayn/ *n.* a material or finish that imitates the natural grain of wood

woodgrouse /wŏŏd growss/ (*plural* **-grouse** *or* **-grouses**) *n.* = **capercaillie**

wood hedgehog *n.* a pale buff fungus that has a spiny underside to the cap and is found in broad-leaved woodlands. Latin name: *Hydnum repandum*.

wood hoopoe /wud hŏŏ poo, -pō/ *n.* a tropical African bird that has dark glossy plumage, a long tail, and a slender curved bill. Genus: *Phoeniculus*.

wood hyacinth *n.* = **bluebell**

wood ibis *n.* **1.** AFRICAN STORK WITH YELLOW BILL an African stork with white plumage, a bare red face, and a yellow bill. Latin name: *Mycteria ibis*. **2.** = **wood stork**

woodland /wŏŏddlənd/ *n.* land that is covered with trees, shrubs, or bushes —**woodlander** *n.*

woodlark /wŏŏd laark/ (*plural* **-larks** *or* **-lark**) *n.* a small Eurasian lark noted for its song in flight. Latin name: *Lullula arborea*.

woodlouse /wŏŏd lowss/ *n.* any of several small land-dwelling crustaceans that live in damp woody places and are capable of rolling into a ball. Genera: *Oniscus* and *Porcellio*.

woodman *n.* = **woodsman**

wood mouse *n.* a small mouse that lives in woodlands in western and central Europe and North Africa. Latin name: *Adopdemus sylvaticus*.

woodnote /wŏŏd nōt/ *n.* a natural musical note, call, or song, e.g. that made by a wild bird (*literary*)

wood nymph *n.* **1.** MYTHOL WOODLAND NYMPH a nymph that lives in woodlands, e.g. a dryad **2.** INSECTS BUTTERFLY any one of several brown butterflies, especially one with a broad yellow band and black-and-white eyespots on each front wing. Family: Satyridae. **3.** HUMMINGBIRD a Central or South American hummingbird. Genus: *Thalurania*.

wood opal *n.* wood impregnated and fossilized by silica and displaying the preserved wood grain

wood owl *n.* = **tawny owl**

Woodpecker

woodpecker /wŏŏd peker/ *n.* a tree-climbing bird that has boldly-patterned plumage, a stiff tail, and a hard bill for hammering against wood and extracting insects. Family: Picidae.

wood pigeon *n.* a pigeon that has a white patch on each side of the neck and lives in woodlands. Latin name: *Columba palumbus*.

woodpile /wŏŏd pīl/ *n.* a heap or stack of firewood

wood pitch *n.* the sticky residue left after wood tar has been distilled

woodprint /wŏŏd print/ *n.* = **woodcut** *n.* 1

wood pulp *n.* wood that has been mechanically and chemically broken down for use in making paper and paper products

wood rat *n.* = **pack rat**

Woodridge /wŏŏdrij/ village in northeastern Illinois, northeast of Naperville. It is a western suburb of Chicago. Population: 28,854 (1996).

Woodroffe, Mount /wŏŏd rof/ mountain in South Australia, the highest peak in the state. Height: 1,439 m/4,721 ft.

woodruff /wŏŏd ruf/ (*plural* **-ruffs** *or* **-ruff**) *n.* any of several plants with sweet-scented flowers used in perfumery and for flavouring wines and liqueurs. Genera: *Asperula* and *Galium*. [Old English *wudurofe*, from *wudu* 'wood' + *rofe*, of unknown meaning and origin]

Woodruff key *n.* a self-aligning key that is semi-circular in cross-section, designed to fit into the recess of a shaft [Late 19thC. Named after the *Woodruff* Manufacturing Co. in Hartford, Connecticut in the United States, which developed the key.]

woodrush /wŏŏd rush/ *n.* a plant that grows in cold and temperate areas of the northern hemisphere and has flat leaves fringed with hairs. Genus: *Luzula*.

woods /wŏŏdz/ *npl.* **1.** FORESTED AREA a forested or wooded area or region **2.** MUSIC WOODWIND the woodwind instruments of an orchestra

Tiger Woods

Woods /wŏŏdz/, **Tiger** (*b.* 1975) US golfer. At 21, he became the youngest player ever to win the US Masters championship (1997). Real name **Eldrick Woods**

wood sage *n.* a downy aromatic European plant found in woods and heaths. Latin name: *Teucrium scordonia*.

woodscrew /wŏŏd skroo/ *n.* a tapered metal screw that can be driven into wood by a screwdriver

woodshed /wŏŏd shed/ *n.* an outbuilding or connected room in which firewood and tools are stored

woodsia /wŏŏdzi ə/ (*plural* **-as** *or* **-a**) *n.* a small fern that has wiry fronds and is found in northern often mountainous regions. Genus: *Woodsia*. [Mid-19thC. From modern Latin, genus name, in honour of the English botanist Joseph *Woods* (1776–1864).]

woodsman /wŏŏdzmən/ (*plural* **-men** /-mən/), **woodman** /wŏŏdmən/ (*plural* **-men** /-mən/) *n.* sb who is skilled at living, working, or travelling in the woods

wood sorrel *n.* an herb that has a creeping stem, heart-shaped leaves, and white flowers with coloured veins. Genus: *Oxalis*. [Translation of obsolete French *sorrel de boys*, from the plant's sour taste, resembling sorrel, and the fact that it grows in woodland]

wood spirit *n.* = **methanol**

Woodstock /wŏŏd stok/ **1.** town in Oxfordshire, England. Blenheim Palace, home of the Dukes of Marlborough, is located there. Population: 2,898 (1991). **2.** city in southern Ontario, Canada, on the River Thames. Population: 30,075 (1991). **3.** town in New York State. It is best known for a rock music festival in 1969, although the site of the festival was moved beforehand to nearby Bethel. Population: 6,290 (1990).

wood stork *n.* a large stork with a long heavy bill, bare head, white plumage, and black wingtips found in wooded marshes in North, Central, and South America. Genus: *Mycteria americana*.

wood sugar *n.* = **xylose**

woodswallow /wŏŏd swollō/ *n.* a medium-sized, long-winged Australian bird that has a black-tipped bill and feeds on insects while on the wing. Genus: *Artamus*. [Mid-19thC]

woodsy /wŏŏdzi/ (**-ier**, **-iest**) *adj.* US, Can relating to or reminiscent of the woods (*informal*)

wood tar *n.* a black viscous tar produced as a by-product in the destructive distillation of wood, used as a protective coating for rope and timber

wood thrush *n.* a large thrush that lives in wooded areas of eastern North America and has a reddish-brown head, a pale spotted breast, and a melodious call. Latin name: *Hylocichla mustelina*.

wood tick *n.* a tick of western North America that transmits the pathogenic microorganism that causes Rocky Mountain spotted fever. Genus: *Dermacentor*.

wood vinegar *n.* = **pyroligneous acid**

wood warbler *n.* **1.** SMALL EUROPEAN WOODLAND WARBLER a small yellowish-green European songbird that lives in woods. Latin name: *Phylloscopus sibilatrix*. **2.** BRIGHTLY COLOURED AMERICAN SONGBIRD a small, insect-eating, often brightly coloured bird found throughout North and South America that has a distinctive song. Family: Parulidae.

Woodward /woŏdwərd/, **Roger Robert** (b. 1944) Australian pianist. He is noted for his renditions of works by Beethoven and Chopin, as well as contemporary composers.

wood wasp n. = **horntail**

woodwaxen /woŏd waks'n/ n. = **dyer's-greenweed**

Tenor shawm (16th century)

Piccolo

Flute

Oboe

Bassoon

Clarinet

Saxophone

Spanish gaita gallega (19th century)

Woodwind instruments

woodwind /woŏd wind/ n. **1.** MUSICAL INSTRUMENT a wind instrument, originally made of wood, belonging to the family of instruments that includes the flute, clarinet, oboe, and bassoon **2.** WOODWINDS OF ORCHESTRA the woodwinds of an orchestra, considered collectively (takes a singular verb) ■ adj. RELATING TO WOODWIND relating to or consisting of a woodwind [Late 19thC]

woodwork /woŏd wurk/ n. **1.** MANUFACTURE OF WOODEN ITEMS the skill or craft of making items out of wood. US term **woodworking** n. **2.** ITEMS MADE FROM WOOD items or components made from wood, especially the in-

terior parts of a building, e.g. the frames of windows, staircases, and doors **3.** FRAME OF SOCCER GOAL the goalposts and crossbar of a soccer goal (informal) ◇ **crawl** or **come out of the woodwork** to appear suddenly and unexpectedly in large numbers (slang) ○ It's amazing how many relatives crawl out of the woodwork when a rich man dies.

woodworking /woŏd wurking/ n. US = **woodwork** ■ adj. RELATING TO WOODWORK relating to woodwork or used in making things from wood

woodworm /woŏd wurm/ n. **1.** INSECTS WOOD-BORING LARVA a worm or insect larva that bores into and weakens wood, e.g. in joists or stairs inside a building **2.** DAMAGE TO WOOD BY WOOD-BORING INSECTS the damaged condition of wood from its infestation by wood-boring insects, especially larvae

woody /woŏdi/ adj. (**-ier, -iest**) **1.** HAVING MANY TREES containing or covered with many trees **2.** RELATING TO WOOD relating to, typical of, or situated in the wood **3.** MADE OF WOOD made of or containing wood or a material resembling wood **4.** RESEMBLING WOOD resembling wood in some way, e.g. in appearance, texture, or smell ■ n. **woody** (plural **-ies**), **woodie** (plural **-ies**) US OFFENSIVE TERM an offensive term for a stiffly erect penis (slang offensive)

woodyard /woŏd yaard/ n. a place where wood is cut and stored

woody nightshade n. a woody Eurasian plant with purple flowers and poisonous red fruits resembling berries. Genus: Solanum dulcamara. US term **bittersweet**

woof[1] /woŏf/ n. SOUND OF BARKING DOG the sound made by a dog when it barks ■ interj. REPRESENTATION OR IMITATION OF BARKING a representation or imitation of the sound made by a barking dog ■ vi. (**woofs, woofing, woofed**) MAKE BARKING SOUND to produce a woof [Early 19thC. An imitation of the sound.]

woof[2] /woŏf/ n. **1.** = **weft 2.** TEXTILES WOVEN FABRIC a woven fabric or its texture [Old English owef, literally 'to weave on', from wefan 'to weave'. Ultimately from an Indo-European word that is also the ancestor of English web and wave.]

woofer /woŏfər/ n. a loudspeaker used to reproduce low-frequency sounds. ◊ **tweeter** [Mid-20thC. As a metaphor from WOOF[1].]

wool /woŏl/ n. **1.** ZOOL SHEEP'S HAIR the short curly overlapping hair of sheep and some other mammals, e.g. the llama and the alpaca **2.** TEXTILES YARN USED TO MAKE CLOTHES yarn spun from the wool of sheep or other mammals, used in knitting or weaving **3.** TEXTILES WOOLLEN MATERIAL material knitted or woven using wool **4.** INSECTS HAIR OF INSECT LARVA the furry hair of some insect larvae, e.g. caterpillars (informal) **5.** BOT HAIRS GROWING ON PLANT a mass of soft hairs that grows on some plants ■ adj. TEXTILES MADE FROM WOOL knitted or woven using wool [Old English wull. Ultimately from an Indo-European word that is also the ancestor of Latin lana (source of English lanolin).] ◇ **pull the wool over sb's eyes** to deceive or trick sb

wool classer n. ANZ sb who grades sheep fleeces — **wool classing** n.

wool clip n. the annual wool yield of a farm, district, or country

wooled adj. US = **woolled**

woolen adj., n. US = **woollen**

Woolf /woŏlf/, **Virginia** (1882–1941) British novelist and

critic. The psychological depth of her stream-of-consciousness technique and the poetic language of novels such as To the Lighthouse (1927) profoundly influenced the 20th-century English novel. Born **Virginia Adeline Stephen**

wool fat n. = **lanolin**

woolgathering /woŏl gathəring/ n. daydreaming or absent-mindedness [Mid-16thC. Originally used to mean 'gathering the bits of wool torn from sheep by bushes', the underlying idea being 'wasting time'.] —**woolgather** vi. —**woolgatherer** n.

wool grease n. a fatty wax that coats the fibres of sheep's wool and yields lanolin

woolgrower /woŏl grō ər/ n. sb who keeps sheep in order to sell their wool —**woolgrowing** n.

woolled /woŏld/ adj. having wool, especially of a particular kind ○ a fine-woolled breed of sheep

woollen /woŏlən/ adj. **1.** MADE FROM WOOL knitted or woven using wool **2.** PRODUCING WOOL OR WOOLLEN ITEMS relating to the production of wool or items made from wool ■ n. WOOLLEN GARMENT a garment made from wool, especially a sweater or cardigan

Woolley /woŏlli/, **Sir Leonard** (1880–1960) British archaeologist. He excavated the royal cemetery and ziggurat at Ur and other sites in Egypt and the Near East. Full name **Charles Leonard Woolley**

woolly /woŏlli/ adj. (**-lier, -liest**) **1.** TEXTILES MADE OF WOOL knitted or woven using wool. ◊ **woollen 2.** INSECTS COVERED WITH INSECT HAIR used to describe an insect larva, e.g. a caterpillar, that is covered with furry hair resembling wool **3.** CONFUSED confused, vague, and lacking focus ○ woolly thinking **4.** BOT COVERED WITH PLANT HAIRS used to describe a stem, leaf, or other plant part that is covered with long, soft, white hairs **5.** US UNCIVILIZED AND UNRULY rough and boisterous in a way that is reminiscent of the frontier days of the American West (informal) ■ n. (plural **-lies**) WOOLLEN GARMENT a garment made from wool (informal) ■ **woolies** npl. US LONG WOOLLEN UNDERWEAR long underwear made of wool —**woollily** adv. —**woolliness** n.

woolly aphid n. a tiny insect that secretes a waxy substance in long filaments that gives it a woolly appearance. Family: Aphididae.

woolly bear n. the caterpillar of various moths, especially the tiger moth, that has a coat of dense woolly hairs

woolly-headed adj. **1.** CONFUSED confused, vague, and lacking focus **2.** HAVING THICK CURLY HAIR having thick curly hair that looks or feels like wool

woolly mammoth n. an extinct mammoth with a shaggy coat that lived in cold regions across North America and Eurasia during the Ice Age. Genus: Mammuthus primigenius.

woolpack /woŏl pak/ n. **1.** MATERIAL FOR WRAPPING BALE OF WOOL the coarse material, usually jute or canvas, used to wrap a bale of wool **2.** CONTAINER FOR BALE OF WOOL a package in which a bale of raw wool is transported

woolsack n. a sack for holding wool

Woolsack /woŏl sak/ n. the seat from which the Lord Chancellor presides over the House of Lords

woolshed /woŏl shed/ n. ANZ a building or group of buildings in which sheep are sheared and their wool is prepared and packed for market

woolskin /woŏlskin/ n. US = **woolfell**

wool-sorter n. sb who sorts wool into different grades

wool-sorter's disease n. pulmonary anthrax resulting from the inhalation of spores of an anthrax bacterium that contaminates wool

wool stapler n. **1.** = **wool-sorter 2.** WOOL DEALER sb who deals in wool

Woolwich /woŏlij, -ich/ n. district of London, England, located on the southern bank of the River Thames. The Thames Barrier, designed to prevent London from being flooded, was completed there in 1982.

woomera /woŏmmərə, woom-/ (plural **-as**), **woomerah** (plural **-ahs**), **womera** n. a wooden stick with a notch at one end, used by Australian Aboriginals to launch a spear. The stick provides extra leverage

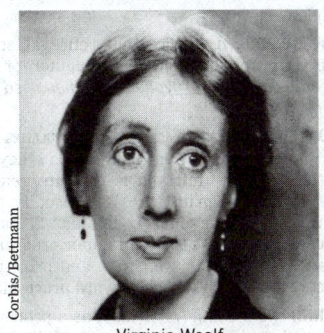

Corbis/Bettmann

Virginia Woolf

and force. [Early 19thC. From Dharvk, the Aboriginal language of the Port Jackson area in Australia.]

Woop Woop /wo͝op woop/ *n. Aus* a remote town or area that is regarded as lacking the facilities and sophistication of the city (*informal humorous*) [Early 20thC. Mock Australian Aboriginal.]

woosh *n., vi.* = **whoosh**

Wootton /wúttən/, **Barbara Frances, Baroness Wootton of Abinger** (1897–1988) British social scientist. Her writings include *Testament for Social Science* (1950), a pioneering study of the nature of social science. Born **Barbara Frances Adam**

woozy /wo͝ozi/ (**-ier, -iest**) *adj.* **1. WEAK AND DIZZY** weak and unsteady or dizzy **2. CONFUSED** confused or unable to think clearly [Late 19thC. Origin uncertain: perhaps coined from OOZY or BOOZY.] —**woozily** *adv.* —**wooziness** *n.*

wop /wop/ *n.* a highly offensive term referring to an Italian person (*slang offensive*) [Early 20thC. Via Italian dialect *guappo* 'tough, bold' from Spanish *guapo* 'dandy', of uncertain origin: perhaps from Middle French *vape* 'insipid', from Latin *vappa* 'wine gone flat'.]

wop-wops /wóp wops/ *n. NZ* an offensive term referring to a rural or isolated region (*insult*)

Worcester /wo͝ostər/ **1.** city and administrative centre of Worcestershire, west-central England. Population: 91,100 (1995). **2.** city in central Massachusetts, west of Boston. Population: 169,759 (1990).

Worcester china, **Worcester porcelain, Worcester** *n.* fine china made in Worcester since 1751, or the articles made from this china

Worcester sauce *n.* = **Worcestershire sauce**

Worcestershire /wo͝ostərshər/ county of west-central England. It was abolished in 1974 but restored as an administrative county in 1998.

Worcestershire sauce *n.* a thin pungent table sauce flavoured with soy, tamarind, and spices, originally made in Worcestershire

Worcs. *abbr.* Worcestershire

word /wurd/ *n.* **1. MEANINGFUL UNIT OF LANGUAGE SOUNDS** a meaningful sound or combination of sounds that is a unit of language or its representation in a text **2. BRIEF UTTERANCE** a brief comment, announcement, discussion, or conversation ○ *Could I have a word with you in my office, please?* **3. INFORMATION** information or news about sb or sth ○ *Is there any word on your daughter?* **4. RUMOUR** rumour or gossip ○ *The word is that she's leaving the company.* **5. PROMISE** a promise, assurance, or guarantee ○ *I give you my word.* **6. COMMAND** a command, order, or authorization ○ *He gave the word to attack.* **7. PASSWORD** a password or verbal signal ○ *Don't let anyone in unless they give the word.* **8.** COMPUT **FIXED NUMBER OF PROCESSED BITS** a number of bits, e.g. 32, 48, or 64, processed as a single unit by a computer ■ **words** *npl.* **1. ANGRY TALK** angry or quarrelsome speech ○ *had words with him over the shoddy merchandise he sold us* **2.** MUSIC **TEXT OF SONG** the text or lyrics of a song, musical, or opera ■ *vt.* (**words, wording, worded**) **PHRASE STH** to express sth in words [Old English. Ultimately from an Indo-European word that is also the ancestor of Latin *verbum* (source of English *verb*) and Greek *rhētôr* 'public speaker' (source of English *rhetoric*.] ◇ **a man of his word, a woman of her word** sb who keeps his or her promise ◇ **be as good as your word** to do as promised ◇ **be the last word in sth** to be the best, greatest, most fashionable, or most up-to-date instance of sth ◇ **eat your words** to admit humbly that you were wrong or mistaken (*informal*) ◇ **in a word** briefly or very concisely expressed ◇ **my word** used to express surprise or astonishment (*dated*) ◇ **put in** *or* **say a good word for sb** to speak well of or recommend sb ◇ **put words in sb's mouth** to say that sb has said sth when in fact he or she did not say it

Word *n.* CHR **1. DIVINE REASON** in Christian theology, the divine rational principle as epitomized by Jesus Christ **2. Word, Word of God CHRISTIAN HOLY SCRIPTURES** in Christianity, the Bible or Scriptures, considered as revealing divine truth

wordage /wúrdij/ *n.* **1. NUMBER OF WORDS** the number of words in a text **2. WORDS COLLECTIVELY** words considered as a group **3. WORDINESS** the use of too many words to express sth **4. WORDING OF STH** the choice of words made by a writer or speaker

word association *n.* a method of assessing sb's mental state or personality by asking the person to respond with the first word that comes to mind when a given word is heard

word blindness *n.* = **alexia** —**word-blind** *adj.*

wordbook /wúrd bo͝ok/ *n.* a dictionary, vocabulary, or lexicon

wordbreak /wúrd brayk/ *n.* the point in a word where it can be divided if there is insufficient room at the end of a line for the entire word

word class *n.* a category of words that have the same form or function, e.g. parts of speech

word count *n.* the calculation of the number of words in a piece of text, or the result of such a calculation

word deafness *n.* the loss of the capacity to understand spoken words, especially when caused by a cerebral lesion —**word-deaf** *adj.*

worded /wúrdid/ *adj.* expressed in words, especially in a particular way ○ *a carefully worded reply*

word finder *n.* a book that lists words according to meaning or subject, designed to help users find the word that best expresses the meaning they want to convey

word for word *adv.* **1. IN SAME WORDS** in exactly the same words as originally used **2. LITERALLY** by translating each word used in a spoken or written piece of foreign language individually ■ *adj.* **word-for-word 1. USING SAME WORDS** using exactly the same words as the original spoken or written text **2. LITERAL** translating each word used in a spoken or written piece of foreign language individually

word game *n.* **1. GAME TO CONSTRUCT OR FIND WORDS** a game in which players have to construct, find, or change the form of words **2. CRAFTY LANGUAGE** disingenuous language intended to mislead, misrepresent, conceal, or put a spin onto a usually awkward situation or issue (*slang; often plural*) ○ *Please stop the word games and give me a truthful answer.*

word-hoard *n.* the total number of words that sb is able to use or understand

wording /wúrding/ *n.* the choice of words made by a writer or speaker

wordless /wúrdləss/ *adj.* **1. NOT USING WORDS** communicating without the use of speech **2. UNABLE TO SPEAK** incapable of speech, especially temporarily —**wordlessly** *adv.* —**wordlessness** *n.*

wordmonger /wúrd mung gər/ *n.* sb who uses words pretentiously or merely for effect (*dated*)

Word of God *n.* = **Word** *n.* 2

word of honour *n.* a solemn promise or undertaking to do sth

word of mouth *n.* communication using the spoken word, as distinct from written communication

word-of-mouth *adj.* made by using oral communication, not written ○ *A small business thrives on word-of-mouth recommendation.*

word-perfect *adj.* **1. KNOWING OR PERFORMING STH PERFECTLY** having memorized, spoken, or sung with total accuracy. US term **letter-perfect 2. KNOWN OR PERFORMED PERFECTLY** memorized, spoken, or sung with total accuracy. US term **letter-perfect 3. ABSOLUTELY CORRECT** accurate in every detail

word picture *n.* a vivid description of sth in words

wordplay /wúrd play/ *n.* the witty, subtle, or ingenious use of words, e.g. in taking advantage of their multiple meanings

word processing *n.* the creation, retrieval, storage, and printing of text using a computer or other electronic equipment (*hyphenated when used before a noun*)

word processor *n.* **1. MACHINE FOR MANIPULATING TEXT** a piece of electronic equipment that has a keyboard and video display unit and is used to create, retrieve, store, and print text. It is usually not as advanced as a personal computer. **2. COMPUTER PROGRAM FOR MANIPULATING TEXT** a computer program that is used to create, retrieve, store, and print text **3. SB PROCESSING WORDS** sb who does word processing

wordsmith /wúrd smith/ *n.* sb such as a professional writer or journalist who uses words skilfully

word square *n.* a puzzle consisting of a square grid to be constructed of words that read the same vertically and horizontally

word stress *n.* the placing of stress on the syllables of a word, or an instance of this

Wordsworth /wúrdzwərth/, **Dorothy** (1771–1855) British writer. She was the sister and companion of William Wordsworth. Her journals are literary documents in their own right as well as shedding light on her brother's life and work.

Wordsworth, William (1770–1850) British poet. *Lyrical Ballads* (1798), written with Samuel Taylor Coleridge, was the seminal work of English romantic poetry. His greatest work is the autobiographical epic *The Prelude* (1850). —**Wordsworthian** *adj.*

word wrap, **word wrapping** *n.* COMPUT a feature of word-processing programs in which a word that causes a preset line length to be exceeded is moved automatically to the beginning of the next line

wordy /wúrdi/ (**-ier, -iest**) *adj.* **1. USING TOO MANY WORDS** using an excessive number of words in writing or speech **2. RELATING TO WORDS** relating to or consisting of words [Old English *wordig*] —**wordily** *adv.* —**wordiness** *n.*

WORD KEY: SYNONYMS

wordy, verbose, long-winded, rambling, prolix, diffuse

CORE MEANING: too long or not concisely expressed

wordy an informal word used to describe speech or writing that is too long, especially when it contains ideas or concepts that are not concisely expressed; **verbose** a more formal word meaning the same as *wordy*; **long-winded** used to describe speech or writing that is excessively long to the point of tedium; **rambling** used to describe speech or writing that is excessively long and badly ordered, making it difficult to follow; **prolix** a formal word meaning the same as *long-winded*; **diffuse** a formal word meaning the same as *rambling*.

wore past tense of **wear**

work /wurk/ *n.* **1. PAID JOB** paid employment at a job ○ *people looking for work* **2. DUTIES OF JOB** the duties or activities that are part of a job or occupation ○ *Much of my work involves talking on the phone.* **3. SB'S PLACE OF EMPLOYMENT** the place where sb is employed ○ *spends all her time at work* **4. TIME SPENT AT PLACE OF EMPLOYMENT** the time that a person spends carrying out his or her job ○ *meet you after work* **5. PURPOSEFUL EFFORT** the physical or mental effort directed at doing or making sth ○ *It was a lot of work, but it was worth it.* **6. STH MADE OR DONE** that which has been made or done as part of a job or as a result of effort or activity requiring skill (*often used in combination*) ○ *Your work is not satisfactory.* **7.** ARTS **ARTISTIC OR INTELLECTUAL CREATION** an artistic or intellectual composition, e.g. a book, treatise, painting, sculpture, film, or piece of music (*often used in the plural*) **8.** PHYS **MEANS FOR ENERGY TRANSFER** the transfer of energy, measured as the product of the force applied to a body and the distance moved by that body in the direction of the force. Symbol *W* **9. STH MANUFACTURED** that which has been or is in the process of being worked on or manufactured ■ *v.* (**works, working, worked** *or* **wrought** *archaic* /rawt/, **worked** *or* **wrought** *archaic*) **1.** *vi.* **HAVE JOB** to have a paid job **2.** *vti.* **EXERT OR CAUSE EFFORT** to exert or make sb exert physical or mental effort in order to do, make, or accomplish sth **3.** *vti.* **FUNCTION** to function or operate or cause sth to function or operate ○ *The television doesn't work.* **4.** *vi.* **BE SUCCESSFUL** to be effective or achieve a desired result ○ *Our relationship just isn't working.* **5.** *vti.* **WORK IN SPECIFIC PLACE** to carry on an operation or activity in a particular place or area ○ *You'll be working the southern region.* **6.** *vi.* **EXERT INFLUENCE** to produce results or exert an influence **7.** *vti.* **SHAPE STH** to shape, bend, form, or forge a material, or to be shaped, bent, formed, or forged in a specified way **8.** *vt.* **CULTIVATE LAND** to cultivate land in order to grow crops on it **9.** *vt.* **ACHIEVE STH** to effect sth or bring sth about **10.** *vti.* **ATTAIN SPECIFIED CONDITION** to attain or cause sth to attain a specified condition slowly or gradually **11.** *vti.* **MOVE SLOWLY AND WITH EFFORT** to move or progress slowly and with effort, or to cause sth to move or progress in this way ○ *He worked his way through the crowd.* **12.** *vt. US, Can* **SOLVE MATHEMATICAL PROBLEM** to solve a mathematical problem or puzzle **13.** *vti.* **EXERCISE** to move or exercise a muscle or part of the body **14.** *vt.* **PROVOKE EMOTIONAL RESPONSE IN SB** to arouse or stir up emotions in sb **15.** *vt.* SEW **MAKE STH IN NEEDLEWORK** to make or decorate sth by hand in needlework or embroidery **16.** *vi.* MECH ENG **MOVE LOOSELY** to move in a loose way that results in friction and wear (*refers to machinery*) **17.** *vt.* **ARRANGE STH** to arrange or exploit sth in order to gain an advantage (*informal*) ○ *He managed to work it so that he got every other Friday off.* **18.** *vt.* **CHARM SB** to use charm and personal influence on sb in order to attain popularity or acclaim **19.** *vti.* **FERMENT** to ferment or cause sth to ferment **20.** *vi.* NAUT **STRAIN SLIGHTLY IN ROUGH WATER** to give slightly in rough water so that the joints move slightly and the fastenings become looser (*refers to ships*) **21.** *vi.* SAILING **SAIL INTO WIND** to sail against the wind [Old English *weorc*. Ultimately from an Indo-European word that is also the ancestor of English *energy, organ,* and *orgy*.] ◇ **at work 1.** engaged in employment **2.** in operation ◇ **do sb's dirty work** to do sth unpleasant, dishonest, or immoral on behalf of sb else ◇ **have your work cut out (for you)** to be faced with a difficult task ◇ **make short work of sb** *or* **sth** to dispose of or deal with sb or sth very quickly

WORD KEY: USAGE

See Usage note at ***wrought***.

WORD KEY: SYNONYMS

work, labour, toil, drudgery

CORE MEANING: sustained effort required to do or produce sth

work the physical and mental effort employed to do or achieve sth. It can be used to talk about animals and machines as well as people; **labour** strenuous work, usually physical; **toil** tiring, often tedious, physical work; **drudgery** work that is strenuous and not at all rewarding. Used especially of work that is sustained over a long period.

work back *vi. Aus* to stay on late at work, with or without payment

work in *vt.* **1. ADD STH GRADUALLY** to add sth gradually while blending it with another substance **2. ARRANGE TO INCLUDE STH** to arrange a time or place for sth in a given situation ○ *I'll see if I can work you in on Friday.*

work off *vt.* **1. work off, work at PAY DEBT BY WORKING** to pay back a debt by doing work rather than by paying the money owed **2. USE STH UP BY WORKING** to use up or get rid of sth by the effort of working

work on, work upon *vt.* **1. AFFECT SB OR STH** to influence or attempt to influence sb or sth **2. MAKE OR FIX STH** to spend time making, improving, or fixing sth **3. USE STH AS BASIS** to use sth as a starting point for further investigation or enquiry

work out *v.* **1.** *vt.* **SOLVE OR CALCULATE STH** to solve a problem or find an answer to a question by reasoning or calculation **2.** *vt.* **RESOLVE DIFFICULTY** to resolve differences or find a way of dealing with a difficulty **3.** *vt.* **THINK STH UP** to devise sth, especially a course of action **4.** *vt.* **COMPREHEND SB OR STH** to understand sb or sth fully **5.** *vt.* **ACHIEVE STH BY EFFORT** to succeed in doing sth after working long and hard at it **6.** *vt.* = **work off** *v.* **1 7.** *vt.* **EXHAUST MINE BY EXTRACTION** to extract all the valuable material from a mine or deposit **8.** *vi.* **END SATISFACTORILY** to have a satisfactory or successful result **9.** *vi.* **END IN PARTICULAR WAY** to have a particular result **10.** *vi.* **EXERCISE** to train or take part in strenuous physical exercise as a way of keeping fit **11.** *vi.* **MAKE TOTAL** to come to a particular amount

WORD KEY: SYNONYMS

See Synonyms at ***deduce***.

work over *vt.* **1. REDO STH** to do sth again **2. EXAMINE STH THOROUGHLY** to work at or examine sth thoroughly and in detail **3. GIVE SB A BEATING** to give sb a severe beating or subject sb to severe physical punishment (*informal*)

work through *vt.* to deal with an emotional problem by thinking about it often until it is understood or its impact is lessened

work up *v.* **1.** *vt.* **EXCITE EMOTIONS IN SB** to arouse or stir up emotions in sb **2.** *vt.* **CREATE STH** to create sth or cause it to grow ○ *working up a sweat* **3.** *vt.* **IMPROVE STH** to develop, refine, or improve sth **4.** *vi.* **BECOME MORE INTENSE** to grow or develop in intensity **5.** *vt.* MED **EXAMINE A PATIENT THOROUGHLY** to subject a patient to a thorough diagnostic examination

work up to *vt.* to gradually reach a particular level by effort

workable /wúrkəb'l/ *adj.* **1. ABLE TO BE DONE** able to be accomplished or carried out ○ *The plan is not workable.* **2. ABLE TO BE WORKED ON** capable of being operated or handled ○ *workable steel* —**workability** /wùrkə bílləti/ *n.* —**workableness** /wúrkəb'lnəss/ *n.* —**workably** /wúrkəbli/ *adv.*

workaday /wúrkə day/, **workday** /wúrk day/ *adj.* **1. ROUTINE AND COMMONPLACE** ordinary or part of the experience of most people **2. APPROPRIATE FOR WORK** suitable for work or for a working day [Mid-16thC. Origin uncertain: perhaps from WORK + DAY.]

workaholic /wúrkə hóllik/ *n.* sb who displays a compulsive need to work hard and for very long hours [Mid-20thC. Coined from WORK + -AHOLIC.]

workbag /wúrk bag/, **workbasket** /wúrk baaskit/ *n.* a bag for holding materials and tools for work, especially sewing or knitting

workbench /wúrk bench/ *n.* a table or surface on which work is done, e.g. by a carpenter or mechanic

workbook /wúrk bòòk/ *n.* **1. STUDENT'S EXERCISE BOOK** a book of exercises and questions for students, usually with spaces for answers to be written in **2. INSTRUCTION BOOK** a book of instructions on how to do or operate sth **3. RECORD OF WORK** a book in which a record is kept of work done or to be done

work camp *n.* **1. CAMP FOR VOLUNTEER WORKERS** a camp where volunteers, especially young people or members of a religious organization, work on a project of benefit to the community **2. PRISON CAMP** a camp in which prisoners are forced to work

workday /wúrk day/ *n. US* = **working day** ■ *adj.* US = **workaday**

worked /wurkt/ *adj.* produced, decorated, or treated with craft and skill [Late 16thC. Originally 'that has been worked on'.]

worked up *adj.* full of anger or other strong emotion (*informal*)

worker /wúrkər/ *n.* **1. PERSON OR THING THAT WORKS** a person, animal, or device that is engaged in or used for a task of some kind **2. EMPLOYEE** sb who is an employee, not an employer or manager **3.** INDUST **MEMBER OF WORKING CLASS** sb who belongs to the working class, especially a factory employee or manual labourer **4.** INSECTS **INSECT THAT WORKS** a member of a colony of social insects, especially sterile females, that carry out all the work, e.g. gathering food or feeding larvae

worker director *n.* an ordinary employee of a business who is given a place on a board of managers to represent the interests of the workers (*dated*)

worker participation *n.* the involvement of ordinary employees in making decisions at all levels in a business

worker-priest *n.* a Roman Catholic priest who also has a secular job

workers' compensation *n.* **1. US PROGRAMME COMPENSATING INJURED WORKERS** in the United States, a form of insurance required from employers that provides money as compensation for workers who are injured at work or who contract an occupational disease **2. COMPENSATION PAID FOR WORK INJURY IN US** in the United States, money paid as compensation to a worker who is injured at work or contracts an occupational disease

workers' cooperative *n.* a business that is owned jointly by those who work in it

work ethic *n.* a dedication to work, or belief in the moral value of hard work ○ *hasn't got much of a work ethic*

workfare /wúrk fair/ *n.* a government scheme that obliges unemployed people to do community work or attend training schemes in return for benefit payments [Mid-20thC. Blend of WORK and WELFARE.]

workflow /wúrkflō/ *n.* the progress or rate of progress of work done by a business, department, or individual

workfolk /wúrkfōk/ *npl.* working people, especially rural or farm workers (*takes a plural verb*)

workforce /wúrk fawrss/ *n.* **1. ALL WORKERS IN COMPANY** all of the workers employed in a company or industry **2. ALL PEOPLE EMPLOYED OR EMPLOYABLE** all of the people who are employed or able to work, e.g. in a country

work function *n.* the minimum energy needed to remove an electron from within a solid to a point outside its surface in a vacuum. Symbol Φ

work-harden *vt.* to increase the hardness or strength of a metal by subjecting it to compression, tension, or another mechanical process

workhorse /wúrk hawrss/ *n.* **1.** AGRIC **HORSE USED FOR HEAVY WORK** a horse used for heavy work such as hauling, rather than for riding **2. HARD-WORKING PERSON** sb who works hard and diligently, often assuming extra duties (*informal*) **3. RELIABLE TOOL OR MACHINE** sth such as a machine that performs well over long periods

workhouse /wúrk howss/ (*plural* **-houses** /-howziz/) *n.* formerly, a publicly run institution in Britain in which people living in poverty were given food and accommodation in return for unpaid work

work-in *n.* a type of industrial action in which the workers of a business that is threatened with closure occupy the premises and continue to work

working /wúrking/ *adj.* **1. FUNCTIONING** capable of being used or operated **2. WORN AT WORK** suitable for use while at work **3. HAVING PAID JOB** engaged in doing paid work **4. SPENT AT WORK** taken up with work ○ *all his working life* **5. GIVEN OVER TO WORK** spent doing work at a time when work is not normally done ○ *a working lunch* **6. ADEQUATE** good enough for a purpose, though not perfect or complete ○ *a working knowledge of Italian* **7. PROVIDING BASIS** usable as a basis for further work ○ *a working theory* ■ *n.* **1. PROCESS OF SHAPING STH** the shaping, bending, forming, or forging of a material **2. JERKING MOTION** the convulsive, involuntary motion of a part of the body, caused by excitement or tension (*formal*) ■ *npl.* **1. workings FUNCTIONING OF STH** the operation of sth or the way in which it operates **2. workings USED PARTS OF MINE** the parts of a mine or quarry in which work is carried on

working capital *n.* **1. MONEY AVAILABLE TO COMPANY** the money that a business has available for use **2. CURRENT ASSETS MINUS LIABILITIES** the amount of current assets that remains after current liabilities are deducted

working class *n.* **1. HOURLY WORKERS** the part of society made up of people who work for hourly wages, not salaries, especially manual or industrial labourers (*often used in the plural*) **2. MARXIST PROLETARIAT** in Marxist theory, the proletariat or revolutionary class

working-class *adj.* relating to or belonging to the part of society made up of people who work for hourly wages, not salaries, especially manual or industrial labourers ○ *a working-class neighbourhood*

working day *n.* US term **workday 1. DAY FOR WORK** a day on which people work, usually but not always a weekday **2. HOURS AT WORK** the part of a day during which sb works

working dog *n.* a dog that is kept in order to do work, e.g. herding, guarding, or guiding. Among breeds of working dog are the collie, Doberman pinscher, German shepherd, and husky.

working drawing *n.* a detailed scale drawing of sth, for use as a guide in building or manufacturing

working girl *n.* **1. YOUNG WOMAN WITH A PAID JOB** a young woman who works for a living (*informal*) **2. WOMAN PROSTITUTE** a woman who is a prostitute (*slang*)

working hours *npl.* the part of the day during which most people normally work and shops and offices are open

working man *n.* a man who works for wages, especially at manual labour

working memory *n.* the contents of a person's consciousness at the present moment

working paper *n.* a document created as a basis for discussion rather than as an authoritative text

working party *n.* a group of people appointed to carry out a specific task

zh vision In foreign words: kh German Bach; aN French vin; aaN French blanc; ö German schön, French feu; öN French bon; ŏN French un; ü French rue Stress marks: ´ as in secret \seek rət\; academic \akə démmik\

working storage *n.* the amount of storage in a computer's memory that is assigned for data stored only while a program is running

working substance *n.* a substance, especially a fluid, that undergoes changes in form or degree that are used to operate sth such as an engine

working title *n.* the provisional title by which a project, especially a film or novel, is known while it is still being worked on

Workington /wúrkingtən/ town and port in Cumbria, northwestern England. Population: 25,579 (1991).

working week *n.* the amount of hours or days worked in a week. US term **workweek**

working woman (*plural* **working women** /-wimmin/) *n.* a woman who works for wages, especially in a manual job

work-in-progress (*plural* **works-in-progress**) *n.* a piece of artistic work, e.g. a novel or musical composition, that has not yet been finished but may be printed, exhibited, or performed

workless /wúrkləss/ *adj.* having no job (*dated*) — **worklessness** *n.*

workload /wúrk lōd/ *n.* **1.** AMOUNT OF WORK FOR SB the amount of work assigned to a person or a group, and that is to be done in a particular period **2.** AMOUNT OF WORK MACHINE DOES the amount of work that a machine does or can do in a particular period

workman /wúrkmən/ (*plural* **-men** /-mən/) *n.* **1.** MAN WORKING FOR WAGES a man who works for hourly wages, not a salary, especially at a manual job **2.** MAN JUDGED ON WORKING ABILITY a man described or judged according to his skill or diligence as a worker ○ *a tidy workman* [Old English]

workmanlike /wúrkmən līk/, **workmanly** /wúrkmənli/ *adj.* done in a way that is thorough and satisfactory, without being imaginative or exciting

workmanship /wúrkmənship/ *n.* **1.** ART OR SKILL OF WORKER the skill or craft of a worker or artisan **2.** QUALITY OF SKILL the level of skill used in making or doing sth **3.** PRODUCT OR RESULT OF WORKER'S SKILL the product or result of the skill of a worker or artisan

workmate /wúrk mayt/ *n.* sb who works with or in the same place as another

work of art *n.* **1.** PAINTING OR SCULPTURE a piece of fine art, e.g. a painting or sculpture **2.** STH MADE OR DONE WELL sth made or done exceptionally well ○ *The second goal was an absolute work of art.*

workout /wúrk owt/ *n.* **1.** STRENUOUS EXERCISE SESSION a session of strenuous physical exercise or the practising of physical skills intended as a way of keeping fit or as practice for a game or athletics competition **2.** RIGOROUS TEST a tough practical test of the capability or performance of a person, animal, or device [Early 20thC]

workpeople /wúrk peep'l/ *npl.* hourly workers, especially those with manual jobs

workpiece /wúrk peess/ *n.* sth that has been, or is in the process of being, worked on or manufactured

workplace /wúrk playss/ *n.* the place where sb works, e.g. a factory or office

work print *n.* a print of a film used in various stages of editing and as a guide in cutting the original negative from which the final commercial prints are made

workroom /wúrk room, -rŏŏm/ *n.* a room in which work is done, especially one equipped for manual work

works /wurks/ *n.* (*plural* **works**) **1.** PLACE FOR INDUSTRIAL PRODUCTION a place where industrial work, especially manufacturing, is done ○ *an engineering works* **2.** SYRINGE FOR INJECTING NARCOTICS a syringe used to inject narcotics (*slang*) **3.** EVERYTHING all things that are available (*informal*) ○ *A hot dog with the works, please.* **4.** *US* BAD BEATING a severe beating or punishment (*slang*) ■ *npl.* **1.** COLLECTED COMPOSITIONS all of the compositions created by an artist, writer, or musician ○ *the complete works of Shakespeare* **2.** INNER MECHANISMS the interior moving parts of a mechanism ○ *the works of the clock are rusty* **3.** ACTS deeds or actions ◇ **in the works** being prepared or worked on

works council, **works committee** *n.* a group of representatives of employers and employees in a company that meet to discuss matters of common interest relating to the running of the business

worksheet /wúrk sheet/ *n.* **1.** SHEET OF QUESTIONS FOR STUDENTS a sheet of questions or tasks for students on a recent lesson **2.** SHEET RECORDING WORK a sheet of paper used for keeping a record of work done or scheduled **3.** SHEET FOR DRAFT a sheet of paper used for making a rough draft or preliminary notes

workshop /wúrk shop/ *n.* **1.** PLACE WHERE MANUAL WORK IS DONE a place where manual work is done, especially manufacturing or repairing **2.** GROUP WORKING TOGETHER a group of people working on a creative project, discussing a topic, or studying a subject ○ *a songwriting workshop*

workshy /wúrk shī/ *adj.* lazy and unwilling to work [Early 20thC. Translation of German *arbeitsscheu*.]

work song *n.* a song sung by people working, usually with a repetitive rhythm that guides the rhythm of the work being done

Worksop /wúrk sop/ town in Nottinghamshire, east-central England. Population: 10,090 (1991).

workspace /wúrk spayss/ *n.* an area set aside for an individual worker or a business

workstation /wúrk staysh'n/ *n.* **1.** WORKING AREA a small area in a workplace assigned to one worker, especially a desk with a computer **2.** COMPUT TERMINAL OF NETWORK OR MAINFRAME a computer terminal, usually connected to a network in a business environment, that runs application programs and serves as an access point to the network **3.** COMPUT POWERFUL SPECIALIZED COMPUTER a powerful stand-alone computer, often with a high-resolution display, used for computer-aided design and other complex and specialized applications

work stoppage *n.* an occasion when a group of employees stop work, often as a protest or as a bargaining tool

work-study *n.* EFFICIENCY INVESTIGATION an investigation into the most efficient way of doing a job ■ *adj. US, Can* COMBINING WORK AND STUDY combining an academic programme with paid employment in which students gain practical experience in the workplace

work surface *n.* a rigid flat area on which work is done, e.g. a tabletop or the top of a kitchen unit

worktable /wúrk tayb'l/ *n.* a table at which work is done, e.g. writing or drawing

worktop /wúrk top/ *n.* a rigid flat surface on which work is done, especially the flat top fitted onto kitchen units, used when preparing food

work to rule (**works to rule**, **working to rule**, **worked to rule**) *vi.* UK, Can to take part in a labour protest in which workers make a point of adhering strictly to the rules of the workplace so that work will slow down

work-to-rule *n.* UK, Can a type of labour protest in which workers make a point of adhering strictly to the rules of the workplace so that work will slow down

workup /wúrk up/ *n.* a complete diagnostic medical examination

workwear /wúrk wair/ *n.* clothes worn at work, especially at manual work

workweek /wúrk week/, **work week** *n.* US = **working week**

world /wurld/ *n.* **1.** PLANET EARTH the planet Earth **2.** EARTH AND EVERYTHING ON IT the Earth, including all of its inhabitants and the things upon it **3.** HUMAN RACE all of the human inhabitants of the Earth ○ *Soon, the world would know the truth.* **4.** SOCIETY human society ○ *in the eyes of the world* **5.** PART OF EARTH a particular part of the Earth, considered in terms of time or space ○ *the western world* **6.** AREA OF ACTIVITY a specified area of human activity and the people involved in it ○ *the world of fashion* **7.** UNIVERSE all the galaxies that are known or thought to exist in space **8.** DOMAIN a sphere, realm, or domain ○ *the world of reptiles* **9.** INHABITED BODY an astronomical body considered to be inhabited, e.g. a planet **10.** EVERYTHING IN SB'S LIFE all that relates to or makes up the life of an individual ○ *Her entire world collapsed.* **11.** CONDITION OF EXISTENCE a condition or state of existence ○ *the world of tomorrow* **12.** GREAT DEAL OR AMOUNT a very large amount, degree, or distance ○ *They're still worlds apart.* ○ *in a world of hurt* **13.** SECULAR EXISTENCE secular life and its ways ○ *a man of the world* ■ *adj.* **1.** OF THE ENTIRE WORLD relating to the entire world ○ *the world champions* **2.** EXERTING INFLUENCE GLOBALLY exerting influence over the whole of the world ○ *a world figure* **3.** AFFECTING WHOLE WORLD involving or affecting the whole of the Earth ○ *a world crisis* [Old English *woruld* 'human existence, age, Earth'. Ultimately from a prehistoric Germanic compound meaning 'age of man' that is also the ancestor of English *old* and *werewolf*.] ◇ **be out of this world** to be extraordinarily good in some way (*informal*) ◇ **for all the world** exactly and in every detail ◇ **have the best of both worlds** to have the advantage of the best features of two different situations ◇ **in the world** used to express puzzlement, surprise, or dismay, or to give emphasis to a statement ○ *What in the world have you done?* ◇ **not for the world** no matter what happens ○ *Not for the world would I think of doing such a thing.* ◇ **think the world of sb** to be extremely fond of sb

World Bank *n.* a specialized agency of the United Nations established in 1944 that guarantees loans to member nations for the purpose of reconstruction and development. Full form **International Bank for Reconstruction and Development**

world-beater *n.* one that is the best in a particular field

world-beating *adj.* surpassing all others in a particular field

world-class *adj.* ranked among the best or most prominent in the world ○ *a world-class downhill racer* ○ *a world-class liar*

World Council of Churches *n.* an international ecumenical organization founded in 1948 that links Protestant and Eastern churches from around the world for the purpose of coordinated and co-operative action in religious and secular areas

World Court *n.* = **International Court of Justice**

World Cup *n.* a sports tournament, especially in football, contested by the national teams of qualifying countries, held every four years on a different continent and in a different country

world economy *n.* the economy of the world, considered as an international exchange of goods and services

World English *n.* the English language in all its varieties as it is spoken and written over the world

World Health Organization *n.* a specialized agency of the United Nations that helps countries to improve their health services and coordinates international action against diseases

World Heritage Site *n.* an area or structure designated by UNESCO as being of global significance and conserved by a country that has signed a United Nations convention pledging its protection

world language *n.* **1.** LANGUAGE USED IN MANY COUNTRIES a language that is used in many countries, e.g. English, Spanish, or Arabic **2.** INTERNATIONAL ARTIFICIAL LANGUAGE a language created for international use, e.g. Esperanto or Interlingua

world leader *n.* **1.** LEADER OF POWERFUL COUNTRY a leader of a politically and economically powerful country **2.** STH BIGGEST OR BEST IN WORLD a company, organization, or country that is the biggest or best in a particular field

world-line *n.* the path of a particle in time and space, which is straight if the particle moves in a uniform way

worldling /wúrldling/ *n.* sb more interested in everyday material things than in spiritual matters

worldly /wúrldli/ *adj.* **1.** BELONGING TO PHYSICAL WORLD relating to everyday material existence **2.** MATERIALISTIC much more interested in everyday material concerns than in the spiritual side of life **3.** EXPERIENCED IN LIFE experienced in and knowledgeable about human society and its ways

worldly-minded *adj.* = **worldly** *adj.* **2**, **worldly** *adj.* **3**

UNESCO WORLD HERITAGE SITES: AUSTRALIA, CANADA, NEW ZEALAND, THE UNITED KINGDOM, AND THE UNITED STATES

Australia

1981	Great Barrier Reef
1981	Kakadu National Park
1981	Willandra Lakes Region
1982	Tasmanian Wilderness
1982	Lord Howe Island Group
1987	Uluru National Park
1987	Central Eastern Australian Rainforest Reserves
1988	Wet Tropics of Queensland
1991	Shark Bay
1992	Fraser Island
1994	Australian Fossil Mammal Sites (Riversleigh/Naracoorte)
1997	Heard and McDonald Islands
1997	Macquarie Island

Canada

1978	L'Anse aux Meadows National Historic Park
1978	Nahanni National Park Reserve
1979	Dinosaur Provincial Park
1981	Anthony Island
1981	Head-Smashed-In Buffalo Jump Complex
1983	Wood Buffalo National Park
1984	Rocky Mountain Park
1985	Québec (Historic Area)
1987	Gros Morne National Park
1995	Lunenburg Old Town

New Zealand

1990	Tongariro National Park
1990	Te Wahipounamu — South West New Zealand
1998	New Zealand Sub-Antarctic Islands

United Kingdom

1986	Giant's Causeway and Causeway Coast
1986	Durham Castle and Cathedral
1986	Ironbridge Gorge
1986	Studley Royal Park, including the Ruins of Fountains Abbey
1986	Stonehenge, Avebury, and Associated Sites
1986	Castles and Town Walls of King Edward in Gwynedd
1986	Saint Kilda
1987	Blenheim Palace
1987	City of Bath
1987	Hadrian's Wall
1987	Westminster Palace, Westminster Abbey, and Saint Margaret's Church
1988	Henderson Island
1988	Canterbury Cathedral, Saint Augustine's Abbey, and Saint Martin's Church
1988	Tower of London
1995	Old and New Towns of Edinburgh
1995	Gough Island Wildlife Reserve
1997	Maritime Greenwich

United States

1978	Mesa Verde National Park
1978	Yellowstone National Park
1979	Grand Canyon National Park
1979	Everglades National Park
1979	Independence National Historic Park
1980	Redwood National Park
1981	Mammoth Cave National Park
1981	Olympic National Park
1982	Cahokia Mounds State Historic Park
1983	Great Smoky Mountains National Park
1983	La Fortaleza and San Juan Historic Site in Puerto Rico
1984	Statue of Liberty
1984	Yosemite National Park
1987	Monticello and University of Virginia in Charlottesville
1987	Chaco Culture National Historical Park
1987	Hawaii Volcanoes National Park
1992	Taos Pueblo
1995	Carlsbad Caverns National Park

---

worldly-wise *adj.* = **worldly** *adj.* 3

world music *n.* popular music from or influenced by countries outside the western world and its traditions

world power *n.* a country or alliance of countries powerful enough to influence events on a global scale

World Series *tdmk.* a trademark for a series of baseball games played in the United States, between the winners of the American League and the National League to decide the major leagues championship

world's fair *n.* an exhibition of commercial and cultural products from many different countries

world-shaking *adj.* = **earthshattering**

world soul *n.* a spirit believed to animate the world in the same way that the human soul animates the body

world-view, **worldview** *n.* a comprehensive interpretation or image of the universe and humanity

world war *n.* a war involving a number of countries on each side, with fighting spread over much of the world

World War I *n.* a war fought in Europe from 1914 to 1918, in which an alliance including Great Britain, France, Russia, Italy, and the United States defeated the alliance of Germany, Austria-Hungary, Turkey, and Bulgaria

World War II *n.* a war fought in Europe, Africa and Asia from 1939 to 1945, in which an alliance including Great Britain, France, the Soviet Union, and the United States defeated the alliance of Germany, Italy, and Japan

world-weary *adj.* tired of or bored with life —**world-weariness** *n.*

worldwide /wúrld wíd/ *adj.* RELATING TO WHOLE WORLD affecting or found throughout the entire world ■ *adv.* OVER WHOLE EARTH all over the world

World Wide Web *n.* the very large set of linked documents and other files located on computers connected through the Internet and used to access, manipulate, and download data and programs

worm /wurm/ *n.* **1.** ZOOL LONG CYLINDRICAL INVERTEBRATE an invertebrate that has a slender, soft, cylindrical or flat body and no apparent appendages, especially an annelid, nematode, or flatworm (*often used in combination*) **2.** INSECTS INSECT LARVA the larva of an insect, e.g. a caterpillar, grub, or maggot **3.** ANIMAL LOOKING OR MOVING LIKE WORM an animal that looks or moves like a worm, e.g. the shipworm or the slowworm **4.** OFFENSIVE TERM an offensive term that deliberately insults sb regarded as contemptible, especially sb who behaves in a grovelling way (*insult offensive*) **5.** STH THAT TORMENTS sth that torments, undermines, or corrupts a person from within ○ *a worm of discontent* **6.** MECH ENG THREADED SHAFT a shaft with a helical thread that is the part of a gear that meshes with a toothed wheel **7.** SPIRAL CONDENSER IN STILL a spiral pipe in a still in which alcohol condenses **8.** COMPUT INVASIVE COMPUTER PROGRAM a computer program that invades computers on a network, replicates itself to prevent deletion, interferes with the host computer's operation, and often carries a virus ■ *v.* (**worms**, **worming**, **wormed**) **1.** *vt.* PROCEED DEVIOUSLY to make progress deviously or obsequiously **2.** *vt.* OBTAIN STH DEVIOUSLY to obtain sth from sb by devious or underhanded means **3.** *vt.* VET, MED TREAT SB FOR PARASITIC WORMS to treat a person or animal in order to prevent or remove an infestation of parasitic worms **4.** *vt.* WIND YARN ROUND ROPE to wind yarn round a rope so as to give it a smooth surface **5.** *vi.* MOVE LIKE WORM to move in a slow, slithering way **6.** *vi.* SEARCH FOR EARTHWORMS to search for earthworms, especially for use as fishing bait [Old English *wurm*. Ultimately from an Indo-European word that is also the ancestor of Latin *vermis* (source of English *vermin*), and English *wrap*, the underlying idea being 'twisting'.] —**wormer** *n.* —**wormish** *adj.*

WORM /wurm/ *n.* a computer storage medium, usually optical, in which data cannot be changed after it is stored but can be read. Full form **write once read many (times)**

wormcast /wúrm kaast/ *n.* a small spiral mound of earth or sand that has been excreted by a burrowing earthworm or lugworm

worm-eaten *adj.* **1.** EATEN INTO BY WORMS weakened by worms burrowing into it **2.** DECAYED affected by decay or rot **3.** DILAPIDATED old or worn-out

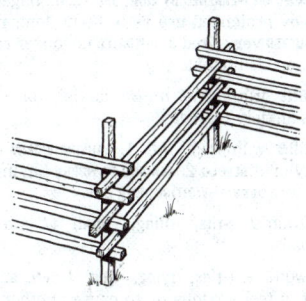

Worm fence

worm fence *n.* a fence consisting of crossed poles that support interlocking rails in a zigzag pattern

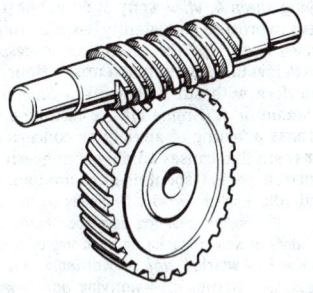

Worm gear

worm gear *n.* **1.** GEAR WITH THREADED SHAFT a gear consisting of a shaft with a helical thread that meshes a toothed wheel to transfer rotary motion between two shafts at right angles to one another **2.** = **worm wheel**

worm grass *n.* = **pinkroot** *n.* 1

wormhole /wúrm hōl/ *n.* **1.** HOLE MADE BY WORM a hole made by a burrowing worm, e.g. in wood **2.** HYPOTHETICAL PASSAGE BETWEEN PARTS OF UNIVERSE a hypothetical passage in space-time connecting widely separated parts of the universe —**wormholed** *adj.*

worm lizard *n.* = **amphisbaena** *n.* 1

worms /wurmz/ *n.* an infestation of parasites, especially pinworms or tapeworms, affecting the intestines or other parts of a person's or animal's body (*takes a singular verb*) [Old English (see WORM)]

Worms /wurmz, vawrmz/ historic city in Rhineland-Palatinate State, southwestern Germany. Population: 78,415 (1993).

wormseed /wúrm seed/ *n.* a plant whose seeds or other parts are used as a treatment for infestation by parasitic worms

worm's-eye view *n.* a view of sb or sth from a lower or inferior position

worm snake *n.* a small nonvenomous snake with vestigial eyes, found in the central and eastern United States. Genus: *Carphophis*.

worm wheel *n.* the toothed wheel that meshes with the threaded shaft in a worm gear

wormwood /wúrm wŏŏd/ *n.* **1.** BITTER-TASTING PLANT a plant that yields a bitter extract used to flavour absinthe and formerly as a medicine for intestinal worms. Genus: *Artemisia*. **2.** CAUSE OF BITTERNESS sth that causes sb to feel bitter (*literary*) ○ *Her ingratitude was wormwood to him.* [14thC. By folk etymology from Old English *wermod*, by association with WORM, because the plant was used as medicine for intestinal worms.]

wormy /wúrmi/ *adj.* **1.** INFESTED BY WORMS full of or eaten into by worms **2.** RESEMBLING WORM resembling or characteristic of a worm —**worminess** *n.*

worn /wawrn/ past participle of **wear** ■ *adj.* **1.** SHOWING EFFECTS OF WEAR weakened or frayed by use **2.** SHOWING EFFECTS OF FATIGUE showing the effects of fatigue, worry, illness, or age **3.** HACKNEYED used so much as to have lost meaning [15thC (see WEAR)] —**wornness** *n.*

worn-out *adj.* (*not hyphenated when used after a verb*) **1.** DAMAGED OR WEAKENED BY LONG USE so damaged or affected by prolonged use as to be no longer usable **2.** EXHAUSTED very tired **3.** OUTDATED no longer relevant, useful, or fashionable

worriment /wúrrimənt/ *n. US* anxiety or sth that causes anxiety (*dated*)

worrisome /wúrrissəm/ *adj.* **1.** CAUSING WORRY causing anxiety or distress **2.** TENDING TO WORRY having a tendency to worry —**worrisomely** *adv.*

worrit /wúrrit/ (**-rits, -riting, -rited**) *vti.* to worry (*regional*)

worry /wúrri/ *v.* (**-ries, -rying, -ried**) **1.** *vti.* BE OR MAKE ANXIOUS to feel anxious or to cause another person to feel anxious about sth unpleasant that may have happened or may happen **2.** *vt.* ANNOY ANOTHER to annoy another person by making insistent demands or complaints **3.** *vt.* TRY TO BITE ANIMAL to try to wound or kill an animal by biting it ○ *a dog suspected of worrying sheep* **4.** *vt.* = **worry at 5.** *vi.* PROCEED DESPITE PROBLEMS to proceed persistently despite problems or obstacles ○ *worried the project along despite continued delays* **6.** *vt.* TOUCH STH REPEATEDLY to touch, move, or interfere with sth repeatedly ○ *Stop worrying that button or it'll come off.* ■ *n.* (*plural* **-ries**) **1.** ANXIOUSNESS a feeling of anxiety or concern **2.** CAUSE OF ANXIETY sth that causes anxiety or concern **3.** PERIOD OF ANXIETY a period spent feeling anxious or concerned [Old English *wyrgan.* Originally in the sense 'to strangle'. Its modern meaning developed perhaps via the idea of dogs or wolves harrassing their prey by seizing it by the throat.] —**worried** *adj.* —**worriedly** *adv.* —**worriedness** *n.* —**worrier** *n.* —**worrying** *adj.* —**worryingly** *adv.* ◇ **not to worry** used to tell sb that sth is not important and need not be a cause of concern ○ *Not to worry. We'll do better next time.* ◇ **no worries** *ANZ* used to say that sth is no trouble or is not worth mentioning (*informal*)

WORD KEY: SYNONYMS

worry, unease, care, anxiety, angst, stress

CORE MEANING: lack of peace of mind

worry describes a troubled state of mind resulting from concern about current or potential difficulties; **unease** is a more formal word meaning the same as ***worry***, often also suggesting discontent or dissatisfaction; **care** is a more formal word meaning the same as ***worry***; **anxiety** describes nervous apprehension about a future event or a general fear of possible misfortune; **angst** describes nonspecific chronic anxiety about the human condition or the state of the world; **stress** describes the worry and nervous apprehension related to a particular situation or event, for example a job or the process of moving house.

worry at, worry *vt.* **1.** TEAR AT STH WITH TEETH to shake or tear at sth with the teeth **2.** KEEP THINKING ABOUT STH to think about a problem repeatedly in an effort to find a solution

worry beads *npl.* a string of beads for fingering or playing with when feeling tense

worryguts /wúrri guts/ (*plural* **-guts**) *n.* sb who tends to worry needlessly (*informal*) US term **worrywart**

worrywart /wúrri wawrt/ *n. US* = **worryguts** (*informal*)

worse /wurss/ comparative of **bad, badly, ill** ■ *adj.* **1.** LESS GOOD THAN STH ELSE less good in quality or effect than before or than sb or sth else ○ *did a worse job on the decorating than the previous workers* **2.** MORE SEVERE more severe than before or than sth else of the same kind ○ *The patient's fever is worse this morning.* **3.** SICKER more ill than before ○ *The patient is worse today.* ■ *adv.* TO A WORSE DEGREE to a degree worse than before ■ *n.* STH WORSE sb or sth that is worse than another ○ *Of the two of them, this one's the worse.* [Old English *wyrsa.* From a prehistoric Germanic word that is also the ancestor of English *war,* the underlying idea being of things thrown into confusion or deteriorating.] ◇ **be none the worse for sth** to experience no harm or ill effects from sth

worsen /wúrss'n/ (**-ens, -ening, -ened**) *vti.* to become or cause sth to become worse

worser /wúrssər/ comparative of **bad** (*nonstandard*) [15thC]

worship /wúrship/ *v.* (**-ships, -shipping, -shipped**) **1.** *vti.* RELIG TREAT SB OR STH AS DEITY to treat sb or sth as divine and show respect by engaging in acts of prayer and devotion **2.** *vt.* LOVE SB DEEPLY to love, admire, or respect sb or sth greatly and perhaps excessively or unquestioningly **3.** *vi.* RELIG TAKE PART IN RELIGIOUS SERVICE to take part in a religious service ■ *n.* **1.** RELIG RELIGIOUS ADORATION the adoration, devotion, and respect given to a deity **2.** RELIG RELIGIOUS RITES the rites or services through which people show their adoration, devotion, and respect for a deity **3.** GREAT DEVOTION great or excessive love, admiration, and respect felt for sb or sth [Old English *weortscipe,* literally 'condition of worth', from *weorth* 'worth' (source of English *worth*)] —**worshippable** *adj.* —**worshipper** *n.* —**worshippingly** *adv.*

Worship *n. UK, Can* a title of respect for a mayor, magistrate, or other similar dignitary ○ *His Worship, the Mayor*

worshipful /wúrshipf'l/ *adj.* **1.** SHOWING WORSHIP showing or expressing deep reverence and devotion **2. worshipful, Worshipful** DISTINGUISHED used as the honouring adjective in the titles of some dignitaries, e.g. mayors, and of the ancient guild companies of the City of London —**worshipfully** *adv.* —**worshipfulness** *n.*

worst /wurst/ superlative of **bad, badly, ill** ■ *adj.* LEAST GOOD least good, most unpleasant, or most unfavourable ○ *your worst enemy* ○ *My worst forebodings were soon realized.* ■ *adv.* LEAST WELL in the least good, most unpleasant, or most unfavourable way ■ *n.* LEAST GOOD THING the least good, least pleasant, or least favourable aspect or part of sth, or the worst thing that could happen or be done ○ *fear the worst* ○ *The worst was over.* ■ *vt.* (**worsts, worsting, worsted**) DEFEAT SB to get the better of or defeat an opponent [Old English *wyrsta.* Ultimately from an Indo-European base meaning 'to confuse', which is also the ancestor of English *wurst.*] ◇ **get the worst of it** to be defeated, or to get the least benefit from sth ◇ **(in) the worst way** *US* very much, very badly, or very intensely

worst case *n.* the least desirable, most disastrous situation or result that can be envisaged (*hyphenated when used before a noun*) ○ *the worst-case scenario*

worsted /wŏŏstid/ *n.* **1.** SMOOTH WOOLLEN CLOTH smooth closely-woven woollen cloth without a nap, made from tightly twisted yarn **2.** SMOOTH WOOLLEN CLOTH the tightly twisted yarn, made from long-fibred wool, from which worsted cloth is made [13thC. Named after the village of *Worstead* in Norfolk, where it was originally made.]

wort[1] /wurt/ *n.* BOT a medicinal plant. This word survives mainly in plant names, e.g. 'liverwort' and 'woundwort'. (*usually used in combination*) [Old English *wyrt.* Ultimately from an Indo-European base meaning 'branch, root', which is also the ancestor of English *root.*]

wort[2] /wurt/ *n.* BEVERAGES a sugary liquid produced from crushed malted grain and water, to which yeast and hops are added in the brewing of beer [Old English *wyrt* (see WORT[1])]

worth /wurth/ *n.* **1.** VALUE IN MONEY the value of sth, especially in terms of money ○ *The necklace has little real worth, but it means a lot to me.* **2.** AMOUNT EQUALLING GIVEN VALUE the amount of sth that can be bought for a particular sum of money or that will last for a particular length of time ○ *twenty pounds' worth of petrol* **3.** MORAL OR SOCIAL VALUE the goodness, usefulness, or importance of sth or sb, irrespective of financial value or wealth ○ *A diploma from that place has little worth.* **4.** WEALTH the wealth of a person, group, organization, or other entity ■ *adj.* **1.** EQUAL IN VALUE TO STATED AMOUNT equivalent in value to the amount stated ○ *How much is it worth?* ○ *a painting worth thousands* **2.** IMPORTANT ENOUGH TO JUSTIFY STH important, large, or good enough to justify sth ○ *His friendship is not worth having.* [Old English *weorþ.* Ultimately from an Indo-European base meaning 'to turn', which is also the ancestor of English *verse*[1].] ◇ **for all you are worth** as fast, energetically, or enthusiastically as possible ◇ **for what it's worth** used to suggest that what you say may not be true or of much value ○ *Here's my opinion on the issue, for what it's worth.*

Worthing /wúrthing/ town and seaside resort in West Sussex, southeastern England. Population: 98,500 (1995).

worthless /wúrthləss/ *adj.* **1.** HAVING NO VALUE having no financial or other value or usefulness **2.** LACKING GOOD, ATTRACTIVE, OR ADMIRABLE QUALITIES bad, incompetent, or totally lacking good, attractive, or admirable qualities —**worthlessly** *adv.* —**worthlessness** *n.*

worthwhile /wúrth wíl/ *adj.* rewarding or beneficial enough to justify the time taken or the effort made [Mid-17thC. Shortening of 'worth the while'.]

WORD KEY: USAGE

One word or two? ***Worthwhile*** is now increasingly commonly written as one word, and the traditional rule that it should be written as two words after a verb (*It seemed worth while* but *It was a worthwhile thing to do*) is largely disappearing.

worthy /wúrthi/ *adj.* (**-thier, -thiest**) **1.** DESERVING fully deserving sth, usually as a suitable reward for merit or importance ○ *That remark is not worthy of a reply.* **2.** RESPECTABLE morally upright, good, and deserving respect **3.** GOOD BUT DULL having good qualities, good intentions, or the best of motives, but being boring and pedestrian ■ *n.* (*plural* **-thies**) SB GOOD OR MORAL sb who is good or morally upright and therefore deserves respect (*often used ironically*) ○ *studied the lives of the colonial governors and other 18th-century worthies* —**worthily** *adv.* —**worthiness** *n.*

wot[1] /wot/ *pron., det., adv.* a humorous or informal spelling of 'what' (*informal or humorous*) ○ *Wot they done then?*

wot[2] 1st person present singular, 3rd person present singular of **wit** (*archaic*)

Wotan /vō taan, -tan/ *n.* in Germanic mythology, the supreme god and the god of war. He corresponds to Odin in Norse mythology.

wotcher /wóchər/, **wotcha** /wóchə/ *interj.* hello (*slang*) [Late 19thC. A contraction of 'what cheer'.]

would /wŏŏd/ CORE MEANING: used to express the sense of 'will' in reported speech or when referring to an event that has not happened yet ○ *Susan didn't think she would pass.* ○ *It would be wrong to suggest otherwise.*

vi. **1.** USED WITH 'IF' CLAUSES used in stating what will, or suggesting what might, happen under the circumstances described in the conditional clause ○ *You would know him if you saw him.* ○ *My mother would be annoyed if I were late.* **2.** POLITE REQUEST used in making polite requests or offers ○ *Would you mind closing the window?* ○ *Would you like more coffee?* **3.** HABITUAL ACTION used to indicate that a past action was habitual ○ *Every Sunday we would drive out to Henley.* ◇ **would that** used to introduce a strong desire or wish, usually one that is not expected to be fulfilled (*formal*) ○ *Would that we had never met.*

WORD KEY: USAGE

See Usage note at ***should.***

would-be *adj.* HOPING TO DO OR BE STH who hopes, or is trying, to do or be sth ○ *a would-be poet* ■ *n.* PERSON ASPIRING TO STH a person who is hoping or trying to become sth or achieve the status of sth (*informal*) ○ *The reception was attended by all the major candidates for office and other would-bes.*

wouldn't /wŏŏdd'nt/ *contr.* would not

would've /wŏŏddəv/ *contr.* would have

Woulfe bottle /wŏŏlf-/ *n.* a vessel with more than one neck, in which gases can be bubbled through liquids [Named after the English chemist Peter Woulfe (1727?–1803)]

wound[1] /woond/ *n.* **1.** INJURY TO BODY an injury in which the skin, tissue, or an organ is broken by some external force, e.g. a blow or surgical incision, with damage to the underlying tissue **2.** EMOTIONAL INJURY a lasting emotional or psychological injury ○ *still*

a at; aa father; aw all; ay day; air hair; ə about, edible, item, common, circus; e egg; ee eel; hw when; i it, happy; ī ice; 'l apple; 'm rhythm; 'n fashion; o odd; ō open; ŏŏ good; oo pool; ow owl; oy oil; th thin; th this; u up; ur urge;

recovering from the wounds of a bitter divorce ■ *vti.* **(wounds, wounding, wounded, wounded) 1.** INJURE to cause a wound in the body of sb or sth, especially using a knife, gun, or other weapon ○ *He was wounded in the leg.* **2.** CAUSE EMOTIONAL WOUND to cause sb emotional or psychological distress by saying or doing sth ○ *cutting remarks intended to wound* [Old English *wund*. Ultimately from an Indo-European base meaning 'to beat', which is also the ancestor of English *wen*[1].] —**woundable** *adj.* —**wounded** *adj.* —**wounder** *n.* —**wounding** *adj.* —**woundingly** *adv.* —**woundless** *adj.*

WORD KEY: SYNONYMS

See Synonyms at ***harm***.

wound[2] /wownd/ past participle, past tense of **wind**[2]

Wounded Knee /wo͝ondid née/ village in South Dakota. In 1890 it was the site of a massacre of Native North Americans in which between 150 and 370 Sioux people were killed, most of them unarmed.

woundwort /wo͝ond wurt/ (*plural* **-worts** *or* **-wort**) *n.* **1.** HEALING PLANT OF MINT FAMILY betony or a related plant of the mint family, formerly used to treat wounds. Genus: *Stachys*. **2.** PLANT FOR TREATING WOUNDS any plant formerly used to treat wounds

wove past tense of **weave**

woven /wōvən/ past participle of **weave** ■ *adj.* CREATED BY WEAVING made or manufactured by the process of weaving ○ *woven synthetic textiles*

wove paper *n.* paper made using a roller with a fine mesh that leaves a faint mesh imprint

wow[1] /wow/ *interj.* EXPRESSING SURPRISE used to express surprise, admiration, wonder, or pleasure (*informal*) ■ *vt.* **(wows, wowing, wowed)** IMPRESS SB GREATLY to impress or delight sb greatly (*informal*) ○ *The acrobats wowed the audience with their daring moves.* ■ *n.* GREAT SUCCESS a great success or an object of great admiration (*informal*) [Early 16thC. A natural interjection.]

wow[2] /wow/ *n.* RECORDING a distortion in recorded sound in the form of slow fluctuations in the pitch of long notes, caused by variations in the speed of the reproducing or recording equipment [Mid-20thC. An imitation of the acoustic effect.]

WOW *abbr.* INDUST waiting on weather

wowser /wówzər/ *n.* ANZ (*informal*) **1.** PURITANICAL PERSON sb with a puritanical disposition who disapproves of activities such as drinking and dancing **2.** KILLJOY sb who disrupts or ruins the fun of others [Late 19thC. Origin uncertain: perhaps from English dialect *wow* 'to waul'.]

WP *abbr.* **1.** weather permitting **2.** word processing **3.** word processor **4.** LAW without prejudice

WPA *abbr.* HIST Work Projects Administration

W particle *n.* an elementary particle with a relatively large mass and either positively or negatively charged, believed to mediate weak interactions between other particles in which the charges on the particles change

WPB, **w.p.b.** *abbr.* waste paper basket

WPC *abbr.* woman police constable

WPGA *abbr.* Women's Professional Golfers' Association

WPI *abbr.* wholesale price index

wpm *abbr.* words per minute

wpn *abbr.* weapon

Wraac /rak/ *n.* a member of the Women's Royal Australian Army Corps

WRAAC /rak/ *abbr.* Women's Royal Australian Army Corps

WRAAF /raf/ *abbr.* Women's Royal Australian Air Force

WRAC /rak/ *abbr.* Women's Royal Army Corps

wrack[1] /rak/ *n.* **1.** MARINE BIOL MARINE VEGETATION seaweed floating in the sea or growing on the shoreline **2.** MARINE BIOL BROWN SEAWEED any brown seaweed, e.g. bladderwrack. Family: Fucaceae. **3.** NAUT WRECKED SHIP a wrecked ship, especially one driven onto the shore (*archaic*) **4.** WRECKAGE wreckage or a piece of wreckage (*archaic*) ■ *vti.* **(wracks, wracking, wracked)** WRECK OR BE WRECKED to wreck sth or be wrecked (*old*) [14thC. From Dutch *wrak* 'wreck'.]

wrack[2] /rak/, **rack** *n.* **1.** DESTRUCTION the complete destruction of sth ○ *wrack and ruin* **2.** REMNANT OF STH DESTROYED a fragment or remnant of sth that has been destroyed (*literary*) [Old English *wræc* 'misery']

WRAF /raf/ *abbr.* Women's Royal Air Force

wraith /rayth/ (*plural* **wraiths**) *n.* PARANORMAL **1.** GHOST the ghost of a dead person, or any ghostly and insubstantial apparition **2.** APPARITION OF SB SOON TO DIE a vision of a person still alive, said to appear as a premonition of that person's death [Early 16thC. Origin unknown.]

Wran /ran/ *n.* a member of the Women's Royal Australian Naval Service

Wrangel Island /ráng g'l-/ island in the Arctic Ocean, northeastern Russia, between the East Siberian Sea and the Chukchi Sea. Area: 4,660 sq. km/ 1,800 sq. mi.

Wrangell Mountains /ráng g'l-/ mountain range in southeastern Alaska, near the border with the Yukon Territory, Canada. The highest peak is Mount Blackburn, 4,996 m/16,390 ft.

wrangle /ráng g'l/ *v.* **(-gles, -gling, -gled) 1.** *vi.* ARGUE NOISILY to argue noisily and persistently ○ *wrangled for hours over the wording of the agreement* **2.** *vt.* GET STH BY PERSISTENT ARGUMENT to obtain sth or persuade sb by arguing persistently (*informal*) ○ *managed to wrangle a commitment to peace out of the opposing side* **3.** *vt.* US, Can AGRIC HERD ANIMALS to herd horses or cattle ■ *n.* LONG ARGUMENT a lengthy or noisy and bad-tempered argument or dispute [14thC. From a prehistoric Germanic word which is related to the ancestor of English *wring*.]

wrangler /ráng glər/ *n.* **1.** Can, US AGRIC SB WHO LOOKS AFTER HORSES sb who takes care of horses kept for riding on a ranch **2.** SB INVOLVED IN LENGTHY ARGUMENT sb who argues noisily and persistently or is involved in a lengthy argument **3.** MATHS STUDENT WITH FIRST CLASS HONOURS at Cambridge University, sb who achieves first class honours in the final undergraduate examinations in mathematics [Early 16thC]

WRANS /ranz/ *abbr.* Women's Royal Australian Naval Service

wrap /rap/ *v.* **(wraps, wrapping, wraps, wrapped) 1.** *vt.* COVER STH UP to cover sth up by winding or folding a pliable material such as cloth or paper around it ○ *The package was wrapped in plain brown paper.* **2.** *vti.* COIL AROUND STH to wind, fold, or clasp sth, oneself, or itself around sb or sth else ○ *He wrapped his arms around the pole and wouldn't let go.* **3.** *vt.* FOLD STH UP to fold or roll sth up into a compact bundle ○ *linen napkins neatly wrapped* **4.** *vt.* ENVELOP STH to envelop and obscure or conceal sth ○ *Fog wrapped the harbour.* **5.** *vt.* GIVE STH AURA to surround sth with a particular type of atmosphere or quality such as secrecy or scandal ○ *The whole affair was wrapped in secrecy.* **6.** *vt.* ENGROSS SB to occupy the mind and attention of sb fully ○ *wrapped in thought* **7.** *vi.* CINEMA FINISH FILMING to finish filming or videotaping sth ○ *We're scheduled to wrap at the end of the month.* **8.** *vi.* US FINISH to come to an end ○ *'The government's antitrust case... was supposed to wrap by the end of the year'.* (*Newsweek*; November 1998) **9.** *vti.* COMPUT TAKE STH OVER TO NEXT LINE to take a word or piece of text over to the next line automatically on reaching the margin, or to be taken over in this way **10. wrap, rap** *vt.* Aus PRAISE SB to sing sb's praises ■ *n.* **1.** CLOTHES OUTER GARMENT an outer garment such as a shawl, cloak, or coat to be wrapped or folded around the wearer **2.** INDUST MATERIAL USED TO WRAP STH material, or a piece of material, used to wrap sth **3.** CINEMA COMPLETION OF FILMING the completion of filming or videotaping sth ○ *All right, everybody, that's a wrap!* **4.** US FOOD FILLED TORTILLA SANDWICH a sandwich consisting of fillings enclosed in a tortilla **5.** Aus PIECE OF PRAISE a praising comment or assessment of sth (*informal*) [14thC. Origin unknown.] ◇ **keep sth under wraps** to keep sth secret ○ *Our new product is being kept under wraps for the moment.*

wrap up *v.* **1.** *vt.* COVER STH WITH MATERIAL to cover sth completely with material such as paper, plastic, or foil **2.** *vi.* DON WARM CLOTHES to put on warm clothes for protection from the cold, wind, or rain ○ *Wrap up well, it's freezing outside.* **3.** *vt.* COMPLETE STH to complete sth or bring it to an end (*informal*) ○ *We'll wrap up the editing phase of the project next week.* **4.** *vt.* US SUMMARIZE STH to give a short final summary of sth such as the news **5.** *vi.* BE SILENT to stop talking and be silent (*informal; usually used as a command*) **6.** *vt.* Aus PRAISE SB to sing sb's praises (*informal*) ◇ **be wrapped up in sb** *or* **sth** to be completely absorbed by or preoccupied with sb or sth ○ *She is completely wrapped up in her career.*

wraparound /ráppə rownd/, **wrapround** /ráp rownd/ *adj.* **1. wrapround, wrapover** CLOTHES DESIGNED FOR WRAPPING AROUND BODY designed to be worn wrapped around the body and tied in position with one edge overlapping the other rather than fastened with buttons or a zip. **2.** CURVING AROUND SIDES curving around the sides of whatever it is fitted to ■ *n.* **1. wrapround, wrapover** CLOTHES WRAPAROUND GARMENT a wraparound skirt or other piece of clothing **2.** WRAPAROUND FITMENT a fitment that is shaped to curve around the sides of sth **3.** COMPUT COMPUTER FUNCTION AUTOMATICALLY STARTING NEW LINE a function of a computer program or visual display unit that makes text automatically begin a new line as soon the last character space in the previous line is filled **4.** PUBL PAPER STRIP AROUND BOOK'S DUST COVER a strip of paper fastened around the dust cover of a book, e.g. to announce a price reduction **5.** PRINTING PLATE FOR ATTACHING TO PRESS CYLINDER a plate of flexible material that can be attached to the cylinder of a rotary press

wrapover /ráppōvər/ *n.* = **wraparound** *adj.* 1

wrapped /rapt/ *adj.* Aus extremely pleased (*informal*) [Mid-20thC. A blend of *wrapped (up in)* and RAPT.]

wrapper /ráppər/ *n.* **1.** MATERIAL WRAPPED AROUND STH the paper, plastic, or other material wrapped around sth that is sold **2.** PUBL = **dust jacket 3.** PAPER AROUND MAGAZINE OR NEWSPAPER a piece of paper wrapped around a magazine or newspaper sent by post **4.** TOBACCO LEAF FORMING OUTSIDE OF CIGAR a tobacco leaf wrapped around a cigar to form its outer skin **5.** CLOTHES LOOSE LOUNGING GARMENT a garment such as a dressing gown that wraps loosely around the body (*dated*)

wrapping /rápping/ *n.* the paper, plastic, or other material used to wrap sth

wrapround *n., adj.* = **wraparound**

wrap-up *n.* **1.** US SHORT FINAL SUMMARY a short summary at the end of sth such as a news bulletin **2.** Aus PIECE OF PRAISE a praising comment or assessment of sth (*informal*)

wrasse /rass/ (*plural* **wrasses** *or* **wrasse**) *n.* a fish with protruding lips and well-developed canine teeth that lives in temperate and tropical seas worldwide. Wrasses are found in various sizes and are often brightly coloured. Family: Labridae. [Late 17thC. From Cornish *wrah* 'old woman'.]

wrath /roth/ *n.* **1.** GREAT ANGER fury often marked by a desire for vengeance **2.** RELIG DIVINE RETRIBUTION God's punishment for sin **3.** VENGEANCE the vengeance, punishment, or destruction wreaked by sb in anger (*literary*) ■ *adj.* FURIOUS full of anger (*archaic or literary*) [Old English *wræþþu*. From *wrāþ* 'angry' (see WROTH).] —**wrathless** *adj.*

WORD KEY: SYNONYMS

See Synonyms at ***anger***.

wrathful /róthf'l/ *adj.* extremely or violently angry, or expressing one's anger —**wrathfully** *adv.* —**wrathfulness** *n.*

Wray /ray/, **Fay** (*b.* 1907) Canadian-born US actor. She starred in several films of the early sound era, most notably *King Kong* (1933). Full name **Vina F. Wray**

wreak /reek/ **(wreaks, wreaking, wreaked)** *vt.* **1.** CAUSE HAVOC OR DESTRUCTION to cause sth violent and destructive ○ *a storm that wreaked vast destruction* **2.** INFLICT REVENGE to inflict sth violent, especially revenge or punishment, on sb **3.** EXPRESS ANGER OR HATRED to express anger, hatred, or another violent emotion in action against sb (*literary*) [Old English *wrecan* 'to drive out'] —**wreaker** *n.*

WORD KEY: USAGE

See Usage note at ***wrought***.

wreath /reeth/ (*plural* **wreaths** /reethz, reeths/) *n.* **1.** CIRCULAR ARRANGEMENT OF FLOWERS a circular arrangement of flowers and greenery placed as a memorial on a grave, hung up as a decoration, or put on sb's head as a sign of honour **2.** REPRESENTATION OF WREATH a representation of a circular arrangement of flowers, vines, or other things, e.g. in a carving or on a coat of arms **3.** CIRCULAR SHAPE a hollow circular shape formed by sth such as smoke [Old English *wriþa*. From *wrīþan* (see WRITHE).] —**wreathless** *adj.*

wreathe /reeth/ (**wreathes, wreathing, wreathed**) *v.* **1.** *vt.* PUT WREATH ON OR AROUND STH to encircle, surround, or cover sth with a wreath or wreaths or a similar type of decoration **2.** *vt.* MAKE STH INTO WREATH BY INTER-TWINING to make things into a wreath by twisting and intertwining them **3.** *vti.* WRITHE OR COIL to move, or to cause sth to move, in coils, curves, or spirals [Mid-16thC. Partly formed from WREATH and partly a back-formation from *wrethen* 'twisted'.]

wreck /rek/ *vt.* (**wrecks, wrecking, wrecked**) **1.** DESTROY OR DAMAGE STH to destroy sth completely or damage it beyond repair **2.** DESTROY SHIP to cause a ship to sink or run aground and be destroyed ■ *n.* **1.** NAUT DESTRUCTION OF SHIP the sinking or destruction at sea of a ship from accidental causes **2.** NAUT BADLY DAMAGED SHIP a very badly damaged or sunken ship **3.** CARGO FROM WRECKED SHIP cargo or other goods that are washed ashore after a shipwreck **4.** REMAINS OF STH DESTROYED sth that has been totally destroyed, or its shattered remains **5.** STH BADLY DAMAGED sth that is in very poor condition, damaged, or dilapidated **6.** SB LOOKING OR FEELING TERRIBLE sb who is physically or emotionally exhausted or broken down **7.** DESTRUCTION the ruin or destruction of sth **8.** *US* = **crash**[1] *n.* 1 [13thC. From Anglo-Norman *wrec*, of Scandinavian origin.]

wreckage /rékij/ *n.* **1.** REMAINS AFTER DESTRUCTION the broken pieces left after sth has been extremely badly damaged or destroyed **2.** PROCESS OF WRECKING the wrecking, ruining, or destruction of sth (*formal*)

wrecker /rékər/ *n.* **1.** SB WHO WRECKS sb who destroys or spoils sth, especially deliberately, maliciously, or with pleasure ○ *He's a wrecker of others' dreams.* **2.** *US, Can* SB DEMOLISHING BUILDINGS OR DISMANTLING CARS sb whose job is to demolish buildings or dismantle old cars for salvage **3.** *US* AUTOMOT = **breakdown lorry 4.** SB LURING SHIPS TO DESTRUCTION sb who, in the past, lured ships onto rocks in order to steal the cargo or other goods on board

wrecker's ball *n. US* = **wrecking ball**

wreckfish /rék fish/ (*plural* **-fish** *or* **-fishes**) *n.* = **stone bass** [Late 19thC. So called from its habit of following wreckage.]

wrecking ball *n.* a heavy ball attached by a cable to a crane and swung to knock down parts of buildings that are being demolished

wrecking bar *n.* a short crowbar forked at one end and bent at the other to provide leverage

Wrekin /reekin/ hill in Shropshire, west-central England, near the River Severn. Height: 407 m/1,335 ft.

Wren

wren /ren/ *n.* **1.** SMALL BROWN SONGBIRD a small songbird found in Europe, Asia, and North and South America with a long slender downturned bill, usually brown feathers, and a short upright tail. Family: Troglodytidae. **2.** = **fairy wren** [Old English *wrenna*]

Wren /ren/ *n.* a member of the Women's Royal Naval Service [Early 20thC. Back-formation from the acronym formed from WRNS.]

Sir Christopher Wren: Portrait medal
by G. D. Gaab

Wren /ren/, **Sir Christopher** (1632–1723) English architect, scientist, and mathematician. The founder of the English baroque style, he designed St Paul's Cathedral, London (1675–1710) and 50 other English churches. He was also a noted mathematician and inventor, and a founding member of the Royal Society.

wrench /rench/ *v.* (**wrenches, wrenching, wrenched**) **1.** *vti.* PULL AND TWIST STH AWAY to pull sth away forcefully, often using a twisting movement ○ *He angrily wrenched the bag away from the cashier and left the shop.* **2.** *vt.* INJURE STH BY TWISTING to injure part of the body by twisting it suddenly and forcibly **3.** *vt.* DISTRESS SB to make sb feel very sad or distressed **4.** *vt.* SKEW MEANING OR FUNCTION to distort sth in order to make it mean or appear to be sth different ■ *n.* **1.** FORCEFUL TWISTING PULL a forceful twisting pull at sth, especially to free it **2.** ADJUSTABLE SPANNER a spanner, especially a large one, with adjustable jaws **3.** *US* = **spanner 4.** SADNESS AND LOSS ON PARTING a difficult parting from a person or place, or the feelings of sadness and loss that accompany such a parting ○ *Leaving New York was a terrible wrench after having lived there for 30 years.* **5.** SURGE OF EMOTION a sudden surge of emotion, e.g. pity or empathy ○ *the wrench we felt when viewing film footage of the flood's devastation* **6.** SPRAIN CAUSED BY TWISTING a sprain caused by a sudden forceful twisting movement of a part of the body [Old English *wrencan*. Ultimately from an Indo-European base meaning 'to turn' that is also the ancestor of English *converge*.]

wrest /rest/ *vt.* (**wrests, wresting, wrested**) **1.** GAIN CONTROL OR POWER to take sth such as control or power from sb in the face of opposition or resistance **2.** PULL STH AWAY FORCIBLY to seize sth with the hands and take it away from sb by using physical force **3.** GET STH WITH EFFORT to get or extract sth with an effort or struggle **4.** ALTER STH'S MEANING to change or twist the meaning of sth ■ *n.* FORCEFUL PULL a sharp wrench or pull at sth [Old English *wræstan*. From a prehistoric Germanic base that is also the ancestor of English *wrist*.] —**wrester** *n.*

wrestle /réss'l/ *v.* (**-tles, -tling, -tled**) **1.** *vti.* FIGHT BY GRIPPING AND PUSHING to fight sb using special holds and moves in an attempt to force his or her shoulders onto a mat **2.** *vti.* HAVE A STRUGGLING FIGHT to fight with sb by gripping and pushing rather than hitting him or her **3.** *vi.* HAVE DIFFICULTY to struggle to deal with sth difficult or intractable ○ *I spent the evening wrestling with my accounts.* **4.** *vti.* MANOEUVRE STH AWKWARD to struggle to lift or move sth ○ *We wrestled the trunk down the hall.* ■ *n.* **1.** FIGHT BETWEEN WRESTLERS a wrestling match or a fight in which people wrestle rather than hit each other **2.** A STRUGGLE WITH STH DIFFICULT a struggle to deal with sth difficult or intractable [Old English. From *wræstan* (see WREST).] —**wrestler** *n.*

wrestling /réssling/ *n.* **1.** SPORT WITH TWO CONTESTANTS FIGHT-ING a sport in which two contestants fight by gripping each other using special holds, each trying to force the other's shoulders onto a mat **2.** ACTION OF STRUGGLING WITH SB the action of having a struggling fight with sb [Old English *wræstlunge*]

wretch /rech/ *n.* **1.** SB MISERABLE sb who is in trouble or distress and evokes pity in others **2.** ANNOYING PERSON sb who provokes mild irritation or annoyance

(*humorous*) **3.** DESPICABLE PERSON sb who provokes contempt or disapproval (*formal*) [Old English *wrecca*. Related to the source of English *wreak*.]

wretched /réchid/ *adj.* **1.** UNHAPPY OR ILL feeling very unhappy or ill **2.** APPEARING MISERABLE OR DEPRIVED in a state of great hardship, deprivation, and hopelessness and arousing sympathy in others ○ *living in wretched conditions* **3.** INADEQUATE OR OF LOW QUALITY seriously inadequate or of very low quality **4.** IR-RITATING provoking irritation or anger ○ *The wretched car won't start!* —**wretchedly** *adv.* —**wretchedness** *n.*

Wrexham /réksəm/ town in northeastern Wales, near the border with England. Population: 41,300 (1995).

wrick *vt., n.* = **rick**

wrier comparative of **wry**

wriest superlative of **wry**

wriggle /rígg'l/ *v.* (**-gles, -gling, -gled**) **1.** *vti.* TWIST AND TURN to make quick small twisting and turning movements with the body, or to cause the body to make these movements **2.** *vi.* MOVE WHILE TWISTING AND TURNING to move by making quick twisting and turning movements ○ *managed to wriggle out of the sleeping bag* ■ *n.* **1.** TWISTING OR TURNING MOVEMENT a short twisting or turning movement **2.** TWISTING PASSAGE OR COURSE a twisting passage or line [14thC. Origin uncertain: probably from Middle Low German *wriggelen*, from *wriggen* 'to turn'.] —**wriggler** *n.* —**wriggly** *adj.*

wriggle out of *vt.* to avoid doing sth or suffering the consequences of sth by making excuses or using deception

Wright /rīt/, **Billy** (1924–94) British footballer. As captain of England, he was the first player to win more than 100 caps. His club was Wolverhampton Wanderers. Real name **William Ambrose Wright**

Frank Lloyd Wright

Wright, Frank Lloyd (1869–1959) US architect. The clean lines of his designs, his use of new materials, and his consideration of the environment around his buildings made him one of the most influential modern architects.

Wright, Joseph (1734–97) British painter. His genre scenes and portraits show the striking effects of light. Known as **Joseph Wright of Derby**

Wright, Joseph (1855–1930) British philologist. He wrote books on philology and was editor of the *English Dialect Dictionary* (1896–1905).

Wright, Judith Arundell (*b.* 1915) Australian poet. Her works display concern for the environment and sympathy with Australia's Aboriginals.

Wright, Peter (*b.* 1916) UK intelligence officer. He worked for MI5 (1955–76). The British government failed to suppress publication of his autobiography *Spy Catcher* (1987).

Wright, Wilbur (1867–1912) US inventor. With his brother **Orville Wright** (1871–1958), he made the first successful flight of a powered aircraft at Kitty Hawk, North Carolina (1903).

wring /ring/ *vt.* (**wrings, wringing, wrung** /rung/, **wrung**) **1.** TWIST AND COMPRESS STH to twist and compress sth in order to force liquid out of it ○ *Wring the towel out and hang it up to dry.* **2.** FORCE OUT LIQUID BY TWISTING to force liquid out of sth by twisting and compressing it **3.** EXTRACT STH WITH DIFFICULTY to extract sth from sb with great difficulty ○ *finally managed to wring an answer out of him* **4.** TWIST STH FORCIBLY AND PAINFULLY to twist sth forcibly, e.g. an animal's neck, usually causing pain or death **5.** CAUSE DISTRESS to cause sb

Library of Congress

Wilbur (right) and Orville Wright

emotional pain and distress ■ *n.* TWIST GIVEN TO WET MATERIAL a twist or squeeze given to wet material in order to force out water or other liquid [Old English *wringen*. Ultimately from a prehistoric Germanic base that is also the ancestor of English *wrong*.]

wringer /ríngər/ ◇ **put sb through the wringer** *US* to subject sb to a very difficult or stressful experience (*informal*)

wringing wet *adj.* extremely wet

wrinkle /ríngk'l/ *n.* **1.** FACIAL LINE FROM AGEING a line or crease between small folds of skin that forms on the face as a result of ageing or exposure to the sun **2.** SMALL FOLD IN MATERIAL a small untidy or unintentional fold in cloth or paper **3.** PROBLEM sth that causes trouble or inconvenience ○ *We need to iron out the wrinkles in the plan before implementing it.* **4.** NEW FEATURE an ingenious trick, method of doing sth, or feature of sth (*informal*) ○ *We've added a couple of new wrinkles to the policy.* ■ *vti.* (**-kles, -kling, -kled**) **1.** MAKE OR GET SMALL UNTIDY FOLDS to make small untidy or unintentional folds in sth, or to come to have untidy folds ○ *This fabric wrinkles easily.* **2.** MAKE OR GET LINES ON SKIN to develop lines or to cause lines to develop in the skin as a result of ageing or exposure to the sun **3.** CONTRACT PART OF FACE to tighten the muscles in part of the face so that it contracts or creases [14thC. Origin uncertain: possible from, ultimately, Old English *gewrinclian* 'to wind'.] —**wrinkled** *adj.* —**wrinkleless** *adj.*

wrinkly /ríngkli/ *adj.* (**-klier, -kliest**) HAVING WRINKLES covered with wrinkles ■ *n.* OFFENSIVE TERM an offensive term referring condescendingly to sb of advanced age (*slang offensive*)

wrist /rist/ *n.* **1.** ANAT JOINT AT BASE OF HAND the lower end of the forearm or the joint between the forearm and the hand together with the tissue surrounding it **2.** CLOTHES PART OF GARMENT OVER WRIST the part of a sleeve or glove that covers the wrist [Old English. Ultimately from a prehistoric Germanic base that is also the ancestor of English *wrest*.]

wristband /ríst band/ *n.* **1.** ABSORBENT BAND WORN ROUND WRIST an absorbent band of material worn round the wrist to keep sweat from running onto the hand **2.** WATCH STRAP the strap of a wristwatch **3.** IDENTIFICATION BAND WORN ROUND WRIST an identification band worn round the wrist, e.g. when in hospital **4.** CLOTHES PART OF STH COVERING WRIST a band of material that fits over the wrist, e.g. at the end of a long sleeve or on a glove

wrist-drop *n.* inability to move the muscles that raise the wrist and move the fingers, caused by damage to or compression of the radial nerve

wristlet /rístlət/ *n.* a close-fitting band of material worn round the wrist, especially a decorative one that is attached to the top of a glove or the end of a sleeve

wristlock /ríst lok/ *n.* a hold in wrestling in which the wrist is held and twisted, rendering an opponent helpless

wrist pin *n. US, Can* = **gudgeon pin**

wristwatch /ríst woch/ *n.* a watch on a band that is worn round the wrist

wristy /rísti/ (**-ier, -iest**) *adj.* using a lot of wrist movement when hitting a ball

writ[1] /rit/ *n.* **1.** LAW WRITTEN COURT ORDER a written court order demanding that the addressee do or stop doing whatever is specified in the order **2.** WRITTEN TEXT a piece of written text (*archaic*) [Old English 'sth written'. Formed from *wrītan* 'to write'.]

writ[2] past tense, past participle of **write** (*archaic*)

write /rīt/ (**writes, writing, wrote** /rōt/ *or* **writ** *archaic*, **written** /rítt'n/ *or* **writ** *archaic* /rit/) *v.* **1.** *vti.* PUT WORDS ON PAPER to put words, letters, numbers, or musical notation on a surface using a pen, pencil, or similar instrument **2.** *vti.* CREATE BOOK, POEM, OR MUSIC to create or compose sth for others to read or listen to, e.g. a letter or note, an article, a poem, or a piece of music **3.** *vti.* COMPOSE AND SEND LETTER to compose and send a letter to sb ○ *I wrote her a long letter.* **4.** *vi.* COMPOSE MATERIAL FOR PUBLICATION to create books, poems, or newspaper articles for publication, often as part of a job **5.** *vt.* FILL IN FORM to fill in the details on a form such as a cheque, prescription, or other document and, usually, sign it ○ *I'll write you a cheque.* **6.** *vt.* TELL STH IN WORDS to say sth in a letter, book, or article ○ *He wrote that he would be home on Tuesday.* **7.** *vt.* SPELL STH to spell a word or words ○ *two words that are written the same but mean different things* **8.** *vi.* WORK AS WRITING TOOL to function as a writing instrument ○ *There's something wrong with this pen: it won't write.* **9.** *vti.* USE CURSIVE SCRIPT to employ a cursive script when setting down words **10.** *vt.* DISPLAY STH to reveal or exhibit sth clearly ○ *She had glee written all over her face.* **11.** *vt.* INSUR = **underwrite** *v.* 1 **12.** *vt.* PREDETERMINE STH to ordain or prophesy what will happen in the future (*usually passive*) ○ *It is written: your future is preordained.* **13.** *vt.* COMPUT STORE COMPUTER DATA to transfer data to a storage medium such as a magnetic or optical disc or tape **14.** *vt.* COMPUT DISPLAY STH ON SCREEN to display text or images on a computer monitor [Old English *wrītan* 'to score, draw, write'. Ultimately from a prehistoric Germanic base meaning 'to tear', of unknown origin.]

WORD KEY: ORIGIN

The notion underlying ***write*** is of 'cutting' or 'scratching' (it is related to German *reissen* 'to tear'). The earliest form of writing involved cutting marks on hard materials such as stone and wood and the same word was carried over when the technique of writing moved on to pen and ink.

write away *vt.* to send off an order for goods of some kind to a distant supplier ○ *wrote away for new upholstery materials*

write down *vt.* **1.** RECORD STH IN WORDS to record sth in writing, usually so that the information is not lost or forgotten ○ *I wrote down her address.* **2.** OVERSIMPLIFY STH FOR UNSOPHISTICATED AUDIENCE to write in simplified language for the benefit of an audience considered to be unsophisticated, inexperienced, or unintelligent **3.** WRITE DISPARAGINGLY ABOUT SB to write slightingly or disparagingly about sb **4.** REDUCE THE ENTERED VALUE OF STH to reduce the price or value of sth, especially the value of an asset as entered in the accounts of a business

write in *v.* **1.** *vt.* WRITE DETAILS IN FORM to write additional words into a text or document ○ *wrote in all the personal health data required* **2.** *vi.* WRITE TO AN ORGANIZATION to send a letter to an organization **3.** *vt. US* POL ADD NAME TO BALLOT to add sb's name to a ballot paper in an election in order to vote for that person

write off *v.* **1.** *vi.* POL WRITE TO AN ORGANIZATION to send a letter to an organization, usually in order to obtain sth from it ○ *I wrote off for a brochure.* **2.** *vt.* DECIDE SB OR STH IS WORTHLESS to dismiss sb or sth as worthless or unsuccessful and not worth continued attention or performance (*informal*) **3.** *vt.* DAMAGE VEHICLE TOO BADLY TO REPAIR to damage a vehicle so badly that it is not economic to repair it **4.** *vt.* ACCT REDUCE VALUE OF STH to reduce the estimated value of an asset for accounting purposes **5.** *vt.* ACCT REMOVE BAD DEBT OR VALUELESS ASSET to remove a debt considered irrecoverable or an asset with no value from the accounts of a business

write out *v.* **1.** *vt.* WRITE STH IN COMPLETE FORM to write sth in its complete form ○ *write out your name* **2.** *vt.* SAY STH IN WRITING to express sth in written form **3.** *vt.* BROADCAST REMOVE A CHARACTER FROM A SERIES to remove a regular character from a radio or television series ○ *He's been written out of the show.* **4.** *vr.* WRITE TO POINT OF EXHAUSTION to write so much that your ideas or stamina are exhausted ○ *By midnight I was written out after 12 hours at the keyboard.*

write up *vt.* **1.** WRITE STH FROM EARLIER NOTES to write a report or account of sth from notes made earlier **2.** WRITE REVIEW OF STH to write a review of sth such as a new play or book **3.** UPDATE JOURNAL OR DIARY to bring sth such as a journal or log up to date by writing additional entries **4.** *US* REPORT SB FOR UNLAWFUL ACT to report sb in writing for violating a law or rule ○ *wrote the motorist up for illegal parking* **5.** *US* ACCT OVERVALUE ASSETS to overvalue corporate assets

write-down *n.* a reduction in the value of an asset as entered in the books of a business

write-in *n. US* POL **1.** VOTE ADDING CANDIDATE TO BALLOT PAPER a vote cast in an election by adding sb's name to the ballot paper **2.** CANDIDATE ADDED TO BALLOT PAPER a candidate added to a ballot paper by a voter

write-off *n.* **1.** AUTOMOT VEHICLE DAMAGED BEYOND REPAIR sth, especially a vehicle, that is so badly damaged that it is not economic to repair it ○ *Nobody was injured but the car was a write-off.* **2.** ACCT REDUCTION IN VALUE a reduction in the estimated value of an asset **3.** ACCT STH REDUCED IN VALUE an asset that has had its estimated value reduced **4.** ACCT AMOUNT OF REDUCTION IN VALUE the monetary amount by which sth such as a corporate asset has been reduced in value

write-protected *adj.* used to describe computer storage space that cannot be altered or erased

writer /rítər/ *n.* **1.** SB WHO WRITES AS PROFESSION sb who writes books or articles as a profession **2.** PERSON WHO WROTE DOCUMENT the person who wrote a particular text or document **3.** SB WHO CAN WRITE sb who is able to write, who writes well, or who enjoys writing **4.** SCRIBE a scribe (*archaic*) [Old English *wrītere*]

writer's block *n.* an inability on the part of a writer to start a new piece of writing or continue an existing one

writer's cramp *n.* a muscular spasm that results from a prolonged period of writing and affects the muscles of the forearm, hand, and fingers, causing temporary cramping and pain

Writer to the Signet (*plural* **Writers to the Signet**) *n. Scotland* a member of a society of solicitors who have the power to prepare crown writs

write-up *n.* **1.** PUBL REVIEW OF MATERIAL a written account of material, especially a published review of a new play, book, or film **2.** *US* ACCT OVERVALUATION OF ASSETS a deliberate overvaluation of company assets

writhe /rīth/ *v.* (**writhes, writhing, writhed**) **1.** *vi.* TWIST OR SQUIRM to make violent twisting and rolling movements with the body, especially as a result of severe pain ○ *writhing in agony* **2.** *vti.* MOVE IN TWISTING WAY to move in a twisting, squirming way, or to cause the body to move in this way **3.** *vi.* EXPERIENCE STRONG EMOTION to feel a particular emotion, especially embarrassment or shame, very strongly, and experience internal stress as a result of it ■ *n.* WRITHING MOVEMENT a twisting or squirming movement [Old English *wrīþan*. Ultimately from a prehistoric Germanic base that is also the ancestor of English *wrest* and *wreath*.] —**writher** *n.*

writing /ríting/ *n.* **1.** WORDS WRITTEN DOWN words or other symbols, e.g. hieroglyphics, written down as a means of communication **2.** WRITTEN MATERIAL written material, especially considered as the product of a writer's skill **3.** ACTIVITY OF CREATING BOOKS the activity of creating written works, especially as a job **4.** STYLE OF LETTERS IN WRITING the letters and words formed on a page by sb using a pen or pencil, or the style in which sb writes ○ *I can't read your writing.* ■ **writings** *npl.* ALL AUTHOR'S WRITTEN OUTPUT all the publications and written work of a writer ○ *Churchill's writings on the war.* ◇ **the writing on the wall** sth that suggests that a disaster of some kind is about to happen ○ *She should have seen the writing on the wall when her boss asked her if she had ever thought of a change of career.*

writing case *n.* a portable case with compartments for holding paper, pens, and other materials for writing

writing paper *n.* paper of a quality good enough to write on with ink

Writings *npl.* = **Hagiographa**

written past participle of **write**

Written Law *n.* JUDAISM = **Torah** *n.* 2

WRNS *abbr.* Women's Royal Naval Service

wrnt *abbr.* warrant

Wroclaw /vrót swaaf/ city and port in southwestern Poland, on the River Oder. Population: 644,000 (1992).

wrong /rong/ *adj.* **1.** INCORRECT not correct or accurate ○ *That's the wrong answer.* **2.** MISTAKEN holding an incorrect opinion about a person, thing, or matter ○ *I thought it would be fun, but I was wrong.* **3.** NOT MEANT not the intended or desired one ○ *It was sent to the wrong address.* **4.** NOT IN NORMAL STATE not in the normal satisfactory state ○ *What's wrong with you today?* **5.** NOT CONFORMING TO ACCEPTED STANDARDS not in accordance with law, morality, or with people's sense of fairness, justice, and what is acceptable behaviour ○ *It's wrong to steal.* **6.** UNSUITABLE unsuitable, or showing poor judgment on the part of the person who chooses, does, or says it ○ *It's the wrong time of year to be planting seeds.* **7.** NOT WORKING not functioning properly ○ *There's something wrong with the washing machine.* **8.** NOT VISIBLE used to describe the side of a fabric or garment that is not intended to be seen ○ *I always iron knitted garments on the wrong side.* **9.** REVERSED OR INVERTED opposite to the normal, proper, or intended side, way or direction ○ *This picture is the wrong way up.* ■ *adv.* **1.** INCORRECTLY incorrectly or in a way that leads to failure or a different result from the one intended ○ *You've spelt that wrong.* **2.** IN WRONG DIRECTION in a direction that is different from or opposite to the right or intended direction ■ *n.* **1.** ACTION NOT CONSIDERED MORAL an action or situation that does not conform to ideas of morality or justice **2.** UNACCEPTABLE BEHAVIOUR behaviour that is morally or socially unacceptable ○ *Children have to be taught the difference between right and wrong.* **3.** LAW = **tort 4.** LAW INFRINGEMENT OF SB'S LEGAL RIGHTS an infringement, abridgment, or violation of another party's rights under the law ■ *vt.* (**wrongs, wronging, wronged**) **1.** TREAT SB UNJUSTLY to judge or treat sb unjustly ○ *He felt he had been wronged.* **2.** DISCREDIT SB to discredit sb by saying malicious but untrue things about him or her **3.** BRING DISHONOR ON A WOMAN to seduce a woman and thereby bring about her dishonour (*archaic*) [Old English *wrange* 'wrongful act'. The adjective *wrang* probably existed in Old English, but is not found before the 12thC. The adjective and probably the noun are of Scandinavian origin.] —**wronger** *n.* —**wrongly** *adv.* —**wrongness** *n.* ◇ **be in the wrong 1.** to be to blame for sth **2.** to be mistaken ◇ **get sth wrong** to make a mistake in an answer or calculation ◇ **get sth wrong, get sb wrong** to misunderstand sth or sb ○ *Don't get me wrong: I'm very grateful for your help.* ◇ **go wrong 1.** to go badly or not according to plan **2.** to make a mistake **3.** to fail to conform to ideas of morality or justice ◇ **go wrong with** to develop a malfunction or error ○ *Something's gone wrong with the television.*

wrongdoing /róng doo ing/ *n.* behaviour or an action that fails to conform to standards of law or morality —**wrongdoer** *n.*

wrong-foot (**wrong-foots, wrong-footing, wrong-footed**) *vt.* **1.** CATCH SB UNAWARES to put sb at a disadvantage or in an embarrassing position by doing or saying sth unexpected **2.** SPORTS CATCH OPPONENT OFF BALANCE to cause an opponent to anticipate wrongly the direction in which a move is going to be made or a ball hit or kicked

wrongful /róngf'l/ *adj.* **1.** UNLAWFUL not done according to the law ○ *wrongful dismissal* **2.** UNJUST not just or fair —**wrongfully** *adv.* —**wrongfulness** *n.*

wrong-headed *adj.* **1.** IRRATIONAL completely contrary to reason or good sense **2.** OBSTINATELY UNREASONABLE obstinately sticking to a false belief, opinion, or course of action —**wrong-headedly** *adv.* —**wrong-headedness** *n.*

wrong number *n.* an incorrectly dialled telephone number that connects the caller with the wrong person

wrong'un /róngən/ *n.* (*informal*) **1.** BAD OR CRIMINAL PERSON sb who is considered to have a bad character or

criminal tendencies **2.** CRICKET GOOGLY a googly [Late 19thC. Contraction of 'wrong one'.]

wrote past tense of **write**

wroth /rōth, roth/ *adj.* extremely angry (*archaic or literary*) [Old English *wrāp*. Ultimately from a prehistoric Germanic base that is also the ancestor of English *wreath* and *wrath*.]

wrought past tense, past participle of **work** (*archaic*) ■ *adj.* **1.** MADE CAREFULLY OR DECORATIVELY made in a skilful or decorative way (*often used in combination*) ○ *a delicately wrought ebony screen* **2.** RELATING TO DECORATIVE METALWORK used to describe decorative metalwork shaped by hammering and welding

──────── **WORD KEY: USAGE** ────────

Correct and incorrect contexts: As the term *wrought iron* suggests, *wrought* is a past tense not of *wreak* but of *work*. Confusion is perhaps inevitable, because *wreak* means 'inflict, vent, cause', and *work*, too, can mean 'cause', among many other things. Furthermore, *work* has the additional, and far more common, past tense *worked*. *Wrought* is seen in only a few, rather specialized situations such as ones relating to metalwork, and the set phrase *What hath God wrought* (used by Samuel Morse in the first successful test of the telegraph). *Wrought havoc*, however, is not correct; it should be *wreaked havoc*.

Wrought iron

wrought iron *n.* a highly refined form of iron that is easy to shape but is strong and fairly resistant to rust, widely used for decorative metalwork. Wrought iron contains only 1 to 3 per cent of silicate slag distributed in fibres within the iron, thus making it very malleable. —**wrought-iron** *adj.*

wrought-up, **wrought up** *adj.* tensely nervous, agitated, or excited

WRP *abbr.* Worker's Revolutionary Party

wrung past tense, past participle of **wring**

WRVS *abbr.* Women's Royal Voluntary Service

wry /rī/ (**wrier** or **wryer, wriest** or **wryest**) *adj.* **1.** AMUSING AND IRONIC combining, or expressing a mixture of, mild amusement and irony ○ *a wry remark* **2.** CHARACTERIZED BY IRONIC ACCEPTANCE characterized by or showing a slightly ironic acceptance of sth not particularly pleasant or desirable ○ *a wry grin* **3.** TWISTED out of shape or twisted to one side [Old English *wrīgian* 'to turn'. Ultimately from an Indo-European base meaning 'to turn' that is also the ancestor of English *invert*.] —**wryly** *adv.* —**wryness** *n.*

wrybill /rī bil/ *n.* a New Zealand shore bird of the plover family whose bill is bent to one side so that it can search for food beneath pebbles. Latin name: *Anarhyncus fontalis.*

wryneck /rī nek/ *n.* **1.** BIRD OF WOODPECKER FAMILY a European and Asian bird of the woodpecker family with mottled brown plumage and a short sharp bill. The wryneck eats insects and lives in holes but does not drill into trees. Latin name: *Jynx torquilla* and *Jynx ruficollis.* **2.** MED = **torticollis**

WS *abbr.* Western Samoa

WSW *abbr.* west-southwest

wt *abbr.* weight

WTO *abbr.* World Trade Organization

Wu /woo/ *n.* LANG a group of Chinese dialects belonging to the Sino-Tibetan language family of the Chinese group. It is spoken mainly in the Jiangsu and Zhe-

jiang provinces of China and is the colloquial language of Shanghai. About 90 million people speak Wu. [Early 20thC. From Chinese *wú.*]

Wuhan /woo hán/ capital city of Hubei Province, central China. Population: 3,860,000 (1993).

wulfenite /woolfə nīt/ *n.* an orange, yellow, or brown mineral consisting of lead molybdate, used as a source of molybdenum [Mid-19thC. Named after the Austrian scientist F. X. von *Wulfen* (1728–1805).]

wunderkind /wundər kind, voondər-/ (*plural* -**kinds** or -**kinder**) *n.* **1.** YOUNG SUCCESSFUL PERSON sb who is extremely successful at a young age **2.** CHILD PRODIGY a child who is unusually talented at sth [Late 19thC. From German, literally 'wonder child'.]

Wundt /voont/, **Wilhelm** (1832–1920) German psychologist. His work established psychology as an independent science. Full name **Wilhelm Max Wundt**

Wuppertal /voopər taal/ city in North Rhine-Westphalia State, northwestern Germany. It is situated about 32 km/20 mi. east of Düsseldorf. Population: 382,400 (1995).

Wurlitzer /wúrlitsər/ *tdmk.* **1.** a trademark for a type of electric organ **2.** a trademark for a type of jukebox

wurst /wurst, woorst, voorst/ *n.* **1.** GERMAN SAUSAGE a type of sausage made in Germany and Austria, especially a large sausage intended to be sliced and eaten cold **2.** US SAUSAGE sausage of any kind [Mid-19thC. From German *Wurst* 'sausage'. Ultimately from an Indo-European base meaning 'to confuse' that is also the ancestor of English *worst.*]

Würzburg /vúrts burg, vürts berk/ city in northeastern Bavaria State, southern Germany. Population: 127,700 (1995).

wushu /woo shoo/, **wu shu** *n.* Chinese martial arts considered collectively [Late 20thC. From Chinese *wǔ shù*, literally 'military technique'.]

wuss /wooss/ *n.* US a term that deliberately insults sb regarded as weak or ineffectual (*slang insult*) [Late 20th C. Origin unknown.] —**wussy** *adj.*

wuthering /wúthəring/ *adj.* N England **1.** BLOWING STRONGLY used to describe a wind that blows strongly and makes a loud roaring sound **2.** HAVING BLUSTERY WINDS subject to persistent blustery or noisy winds [Late 18thC. Formed from obsolete *wuther* 'to rush', of uncertain origin: possibly from Scandinavian.]

WV *abbr.* **1.** West Virginia **2.** (Windward Islands) St Vincent

WVS now called **WRVS**

WWF *abbr.* **1.** World Wide Fund for Nature **2.** World Wrestling Federation

WWI *abbr.* World War One

WWII *abbr.* World War Two

WWW *abbr.* World Wide Web

WY, Wy *abbr.* Wyoming

Wyandot /wī ən dot/ (*plural* -**dot** or -**dots**), **Wyandotte** (*plural* -**dotte** or -**dottes**) *n.* PEOPLES a member of a Native North American people that originally occupied lands in Ohio and parts of neighbouring states, and whose members now live mainly in Oklahoma [Mid-18thC. Via French *Ouendat* from Huron *Wendat.*]

Wyandotte *n.* a medium-sized North American domestic chicken [Late 19thC. Variant of WYANDOT.]

Wyatt /wī ət/, **James** (1746–1813) British architect. He is noted for his restoration of English cathedrals. His work in the Gothic Revival style is exemplified by Fonthill Abbey, Wiltshire (1807).

Wyatt, Sir Thomas (1503–42) English courtier and poet. His service at Henry VIII's court included diplomatic missions. His poems, published in 1557, introduced Italian verse forms into England.

wych elm /wích-/, **witch elm** *n.* an elm with a rounded crown, long pointed leaves, and clusters of winged green fruit. Latin name: *Ulmus glabra.* [Old English *wice.* Ultimately from an Indo-European base meaning 'to bend, be pliant', which is also the ancestor of English *wicker, vetch, weak,* and *vicar.*]

Wycherley /wíchər li/, **William** (1640?–1716) English playwright. His comedies include *The Country Wife* (1675) and *The Plain Dealer* (1677).

wych-hazel *n.* = witch hazel

Wycliffe /wíklif/, **Wyclif, Wiclif, John** (1330?–84) English philosopher and religious reformer. He supervised the first English translation of the Bible, published posthumously in 1388. He rejected the doctrine of transubstantiation and denounced abuses in the Roman Catholic Church, anticipating the Protestant Reformation. —**Wycliffite** *n., adj.*

Wye /wī/ river of southwestern Wales and western England. It flows into the estuary of the River Severn. Length: 209 km/130 mi.

Andrew Wyeth (right)

Wyeth /wī əth/, **Andrew** (*b.* 1917) US artist. The son of N. C. Wyeth, he typically depicted rural scenes with a strong emotional charge in paintings such as *Christina's World* (1948). Full name **Andrew Newell Wyeth**

Wykeham /wíkəm/, **William of** (1324–1404) English statesman. He was bishop of Winchester (1367) and lord chancellor of England (1367–71, 1389–91). He founded New College, Oxford (1379) and Winchester College (1382).

Wykehamist /wíkəmist/ *n.* a pupil or former pupil of Winchester College [Mid-18thC. Named after William of *Wykeham* (1324–1404), who founded the school.]

wynd /wīnd/ *n. Scotland* a narrow lane in a town [15thC. Origin uncertain: Probably formed from WIND[2].]

wynn /win/, **wyn** *n.* a runic letter used in Old English [Old English *wyn*, literally 'joy'. Runes were named using words beginning with their sound.]

Wyvern

Wyo. *abbr.* Wyoming

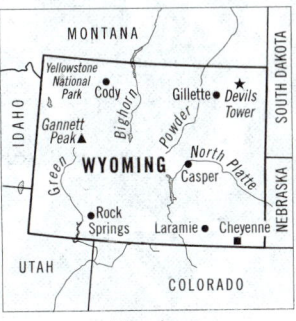

Wyoming

Wyoming /wī ṓming/ state of the northwestern United States, bordered by Montana, South Dakota, Nebraska, Colorado, Utah, and Idaho. Capital: Cheyenne. Population: 528,964 (1997). Area: 253,350 sq. km/97,819 sq. mi. —**Wyomingite** *n.*

WYSIWYG /wízzi wig/ *adj.* used to describe any technology that enables the user to see an image of text and graphics on a computer display exactly as it will appear when printed. Full form **what you see is what you get** [Late 20thC. Acronym.]

wyvern /wívərn, -urn/, **wivern** *n.* in heraldry, a mythical creature depicted as having two legs, a dragon's head, wings, and a long tail [Late 16th C. Via Old French *wivre* from Latin *vipera* (see VIPER).]

Xx

x^1 /eks/, **X** *n.* (*plural* **x's**; *plural* **X's** *or* **Xs**) **1.** **24TH LETTER OF ENGLISH ALPHABET** the twenty-fourth letter of the modern English alphabet **2.** **SPEECH SOUND CORRESPONDING TO LETTER 'X'** the speech sound that corresponds to the letter 'X' **3.** **LETTER 'X' WRITTEN** a written representation of the letter 'X' **4.** **'X'-SHAPED SYMBOLIC MARK** an 'X'-shaped mark used in place of a signature by sb who cannot write, to indicate a vote, to show that sth is incorrect, or to represent a kiss **5.** **SYMBOL USED TO REPRESENT AN UNKNOWN** a letter 'X' or an 'X'-shaped mark used to represent an unknown quantity, an unnamed person, or any unknown or unspecified factor or thing ■ *vt.* (**x-es** *or* **x'es, x-ing** *or* **x'ing, x-ed** *or* **x'ed**; **X-es** *or* **X's, X-ing** *or* **X'ing, X-ed** *or* **X'ed**) **MARK OR SIGN WITH 'X'** to mark or sign sth with an 'X'

X out *vt.* *US* to cross sth out

x^2 *symbol.* **1.** COMM, FIN ex **2.** MATH a Cartesian coordinate along the x-axis **3.** MATH an algebraic variable **4.** BRIDGE any card that is not an honour **5.** by (*used when giving the dimensions of sth*) **6.** MATH multiplied by

x^3 *abbr.* TELECOM, BUSINESS extension

X^1 /eks/, **x** *n.* the Roman numeral for ten

X^2 *adj.* **CLASSIFYING ADULT FILM** used in the United Kingdom until 1982 to classify films that could not be shown publicly to anyone under 18 and until 1990 in the United States to classify films unsuitable for under-17s. Now called **18** ■ *symbol.* PHYS, ELECTRON ENG reactance

Xanadu /zánnə doo, zánnə doó/ (*plural* **-dus**) *n.* an idyllically beautiful place [Mid-20thC. From Samuel Taylor Coleridge's poem *Kubla Khan* (1816), in which it is the name of a residence of Kubla Khan (1216–94). An alteration of *Shang-tu*.]

xanth- *prefix.* = **xantho-**

xanthan gum /zánthən-/ *n.* a natural gum with a high molecular weight that is produced by the fermentation of glucose and is used in the food industry as a stabilizer [Mid-20thC. 'Xanthan' formed from modern Latin *Xanthomonas*, a bacterium, coined from XANTHO- + MONAD.]

xanthate /zán thayt/ *n.* a chemical compound that is a salt or ester of xanthic acid. Xanthates are used in the chemical extraction of metals such as copper and gold and in the manufacture of rayon. [Mid-19thC. Formed from XANTHIC ACID.]

xanthene /zán theen/ *n.* a yellow crystalline compound used as a fungicide. Its structure forms the basis of a range of organic dyes such as fluoroscein. Formula: CH$_2$(C$_6$H$_4$)$_2$O. [Late 19thC]

xanthic acid /zànthik-/ *n.* an unstable organic sulphur-containing acid. Formula: ROC(S)SH where R is an organic group.

xanthine /zán theen, -thīn/ *n.* **1.** **CRYSTALLINE COMPOUND** a yellow-white crystalline compound found in blood and urine and in some plants. It is the precursor of uric acid. Formula: C$_5$H$_4$N$_4$O$_2$. **2.** **XANTHINE DERIVATIVE** a derivative of xanthine such as caffeine, theophylline, or theobromine [Mid-19thC]

xantho- *prefix.* **1.** yellow ○ *xanthopterin* **2.** xanthic acid ○ *xanthate* [From Greek *xanthos* 'yellow']

xanthoma /zan thómə/ (*plural* **-mas** *or* **-mata** /-mətə/) *n.* a yellow lipid-filled lesion on the skin, especially

Xanthine

on the eyelids, that indicates a disorder of fat metabolism —**xanthomatous** *adj.*

xanthomatosis /zànthōmə tóssiss/ *n.* the presence of multiple xanthomas on the skin

xanthophyll /zánthōfil/ *n.* a yellow oxygen-containing pigment found with chlorophyll in the tissue of plants. Some xanthophylls are responsible for the colours of autumn leaves. —**xanthophyllic** /zànthō fíllik/ *adj.*

Xanthus /zánthəss/ ancient capital city of Lycia in southern Asia Minor, in present-day southwestern Turkey. Destroyed by the Persians in 546 BC and the Romans in 42 BC, the remains of the city and numerous artworks were discovered by Sir Charles Fellows in 1838. —**Xanthian** *n.*, *adj.*

Xavier /závvi ər, záyvi ər/, **St Francis** (1506–52) Spanish missionary. He helped St Ignatius of Loyola to found the Jesuits, and established missions in India, Japan, and parts of Southeast Asia. Known as **the Apostle of the Indies**

x-axis *n.* **1.** **AXIS IN TWO-DIMENSIONAL COORDINATE SYSTEM** the horizontal axis in a two-dimensional coordinate system **2.** **AXIS IN THREE-DIMENSIONAL COORDINATE SYSTEM** an axis in the three-dimensional Cartesian coordinate system, conventionally the horizontal one

X-certificate *adj.* containing explicitly sexual or violent material or unsuitable for children, as in the former UK classification for cinema films. US term **X-rated**

X-chromosome, **X chromosome** *n.* a chromosome present in both sexes that plays a role in determining the sex of an individual. Female mammals carry two X chromosomes and males carry one. ◊ **Y chromosome**

x-coordinate *n.* the position of a point in space with reference to the x-axis in the Cartesian coordinate system, defined in conjunction with the y- and z-coordinates

XD, **xdiv** *abbr.* STOCK EXCH ex dividend

Xe *symbol.* xenon

xebec /zeébek, záy-/, **zebec** *n.* a small Mediterranean ship with three masts rigged with both square and triangular sails [Mid-18thC. Via French *chebec* from, ultimately, Arabic *šabbāk*.]

xen- *prefix.* = **xeno-** (*used before vowels*)

Xenakis /ze nákis/, **Yannis** (*b.* 1922) Romanian-born Greek composer. Originally an engineer and archi-

tect, he used mathematical ideas in his 'stochastic music'.

xenia /zeéni ə, zénni ə/ *n.* the effect of genes carried by pollen on the food storage tissue (**endosperm**) of the pollinated seed [Late 19thC. Via modern Latin from Greek, formed from *xenos* (see XENO-).]

xeno- *prefix.* foreign, strange, different ○ *xenophile* ○ *xenolith* [Via modern Latin from Greek *xenos* 'stranger, foreigner']

xenobiotic /zénnō bī óttik, zeénə-/ *adj.* **FOREIGN TO BODY** used to describe a chemical compound, e.g. a drug or pesticide, that is foreign to the body of a living organism ■ *n.* **FOREIGN COMPOUND** a xenobiotic chemical compound

Xenocrates /ze nókrə teez/ (396–314 BC) Greek philosopher. A student of Plato, he is considered the first philosopher to have drawn the distinction between mind, body, and soul.

xenocryst /zénnōkrist/ *n.* a crystal in an igneous rock introduced from an external source and not crystallized from the magma [Late 19thC. Formed from an abbreviation of XENO- + CRYSTAL.]

xenodiagnosis /zénnō dī əg nóssiss/ (*plural* **-noses** /-nō seez/) *n.* the diagnosis of a parasitic infection by allowing a noninfected disease-carrying organism, e.g. a mosquito, to feed on an infected person's blood and then examining the organism for infection —**xenodiagnostic** /-nóstik/ *adj.*

xenogeneic /zénnōjə náy ik/ *adj.* coming from or derived from a different species [Mid-20thC. Modelled on SYNGENEIC.]

xenogenesis /zénnō jénnəssiss/ *n.* BIOL **1.** **PRODUCTION OF OFFSPRING DIFFERENT FROM PARENTS** the supposed production of offspring completely different from either parent **2.** **ALTERNATION OF GENERATIONS** the existence in the life cycle of an organism of two or more alternating forms or reproductive modes, e.g. sexual and asexual cycles —**xenogenetic** /zénnōjə néttik/ *adj.*

xenograft /zénnō graaft/ *n.* = **heterograft**

xenolith /zénnōlith/ *n.* a fragment of rock that is different in origin from the igneous rock in which it occurs —**xenolithic** /zénnō líthik/ *adj.*

xenon /zéen on, zén-/ *n.* a heavy colourless odourless gaseous chemical element that is relatively inert, found in minute quantities in air, and used in electronic tubes and specialized lamps. Symbol **Xe** [Late 19thC. From Greek *xenon*, the neuter of *xenos* (see XENO-).]

Xenophanes /ze nóffə neez/ (*fl.* late 6th–early 5th centuries BC) Greek philosopher and poet. He ridiculed the polytheistic beliefs of earlier Greek poets and is thought to have founded the Eleatic school of philosophy.

xenophile /zénnō fīl/ *n.* sb who likes foreign people, their customs and culture, or foreign things —**xenophilia** /-fílli ə/ *n.* —**xenophilous** /ze nóffiləss/ *adj.*

xenophobe /zénnəfōb/ *n.* sb who fears or dislikes foreign people, their customs and culture, or foreign things

xenophobia /zénnə fóbi ə/ *n.* an intense fear or dislike of foreign people, their customs and culture, or foreign things —**xenophobic** /zénnə fóbik/ *adj.*

Xenophon /zénnəf'n/ (430?–355? BC) Greek historian and soldier. A disciple of Socrates, he participated in the attack on Persia by Cyrus the Younger (401 BC) and led the 10,000-strong Greek force to safety on the Black Sea, an episode he described in his *Anabasis*.

xenopus /zénnəpəss/ *n.* an aquatic frog found in pools and streams in southern Africa. Genus: *Xenopus*. [Late 19thC. Via modern Latin, name of the genus, from Greek *xeno-* (see XENO-) + *pous* 'foot'.]

xenotransplantation /zénnō tránss plaan táysh'n/ *n.* the process of transplanting organs from one species to another, especially from animals to humans [Late 20thC. Coined from XENO- + *transplantation*.]

xer- *prefix.* = xero- (*used before vowels*)

xeric /zéerik/ *adj.* relating to or living in a dry habitat —**xerically** *adv.*

xero- *prefix.* dry, dryness ○ *xerothermic* [From Greek *xēros*]

xeroderma /zéerō dúrmə/, **xerodermia** /-dúrmi ə/ *n.* a mild form of the hereditary disorder ichthyosis, marked by discoloured dry hard scaly skin —**xerodermatic** /zéerō dur máttik/ *adj.* —**xerodermatous** /zéerō dúrmətəss/ *adj.*

xeroderma pigmentosum /-píg mən tṓssəm/ *n.* a rare and often fatal hereditary condition beginning in infancy in which the skin and eyes are damaged by sunlight. It results in freckles, discoloured patches, and skin cancers.

xerography /zeer róggrəfi/ *n.* a method of photocopying in which the image is formed by attracting a resinous powder to an electrostatically charged plate, then transferred to paper and fixed by heating —**xerographer** *n.* —**xerographic** /zéerō gráffik/ *adj.* —**xerographically** /-gráffikli/ *adv.*

xeromorphic /zéerō máwrfik/ *adj.* used to describe plants or plant parts that are adapted for survival in dry conditions, e.g. spiny leaves that reduce surface area and therefore water loss [Early 20thC. Ultimately from Greek *xēros* 'dry'.]

xerophilous /zeer róffiləss/ *adj.* thriving in or adapted for a hot dry habitat —**xerophile** /zéerō fīl/ *n.* —**xerophily** /zeer róffili/ *n.*

xerophthalmia /zéer of thálmi ə/ *n.* an eye disease caused by vitamin A deficiency, marked by dryness and ulceration of the conjunctiva and cornea. If untreated, it may cause blindness. —**xerophthalmic** *adj.*

xerophyte /zéerə fīt/ *n.* a plant that is adapted for a dry habitat, e.g. a cactus —**xerophytic** /zéerō fíttik/ *adj.* —**xerophytically** /-fíttikli/ *adv.* —**xerophytism** /-fītizəm/ *n.*

xeroradiography /zéerō ráydi óggrəfi/ *n.* a type of high-definition X-ray photography in which the image is first made on a specially coated metal plate then transferred to paper. It is often used in screening for breast cancer. [Mid-20thC. Coined from Greek *xēro-* 'dry', from *xēros* + RADIOGRAPHY.]

xerosis /zeer róssiss/ *n.* abnormal dryness of the skin and mucous membranes of the eye, caused by thickening of the membranes —**xerotic** /zeer róttik/ *adj.*

xerostomia /zéerō stṓmi ə/ *n.* an abnormal lack of saliva in the mouth, caused by disease, poisoning, or some drugs

xerothermic /zéerō thúrmik/ *adj.* very hot and having little rainfall ○ *a xerothermic climate*

Xerox /zéer roks/ *tdmk.* a trademark for a photocopying process

Xerxes I /zúrk seez/, **King of Persia** (519?–465 BC). As king (486–465 BC), he led a huge army into Greece (480 BC), defeating the Greeks at Thermopylae and burning Athens, but his fleet was defeated at Salamis. He was assassinated by his palace guard. Known as **Xerxes the Great**

x-height *n.* the height of the lower-case letter x in a particular typeface, used as a measure of the height of the main body of all lower-case letters in that typeface

Xhosa /kóssə, káwssə/ (*plural* **-sa** *or* **-sas**), **Xosa** *n.* **1.** PEOPLES **MEMBER OF A S AFRICAN PEOPLE** a member of a Bantu people of South Africa **2.** LANG **XHOSA LANGUAGE** the language of the Xhosa people, belonging to the Bantu group of the Benue-Congo family of languages. Xhosa is spoken by about 7 million people and is closely related to Zulu. [Early 19thC. From Nguni.] —**Xhosan** *adj.*

xi /zī, sī, ksī, ksee/ (*plural* **xis**) *n.* the 14th letter of the Greek alphabet, represented in the English alphabet as 'x'. See table at **alphabet**

Xiamen /shya͋á mén/ city and seaport on Xiamen Island in Fujian Province, southeastern China. It lies in the Taiwan Strait, west of Taiwan. Population: 470,000 (1993).

Xi'an /shyaan/ capital city of Shaanxi Province in eastern China. One of China's oldest cities, it is home to some major archaeological sites, including one found to contain a vast army of life-sized soldiers made of terracotta. Population: 2,790,000 (1992).

Xiangtan /shyang tán, syang tán/ city in southern China, in Hunan Province. It is an inland port and industrial centre on the River Xiang. Population: 411,000 (1988).

xi hyperon, **xi-particle** *n.* a neutral or negatively charged elementary particle present in cosmic rays and in high-energy collisions in particle accelerators [Mid-20thC. *Xi* is the name of the Greek letter used to represent such a particle.]

Xi Jiang /shee͋ jyáng/ river in southern China that rises in Yunnan Province and flows east to the South China Sea. Length: 2,100 km/1,300 mi.

Xining /shee͋ níng/ capital city of Qinghai Province, in central China, northeast of Lanzhou. Population: 551,776 (1990).

Xinjiang Uygur /shín jyáng wee͋gər/ autonomous region in northwestern China. With one sixth of China's land, it is the country's largest region. Capital: Urumqi. Population: 15,550,000 (1991). Area: 1,600,000 sq. km/618,000 sq. mi.

xiphisternum /zíffi stúrnəm/ (*plural* **-na** /-nə/) *n.* the third and lowest segment of the breastbone (**sternum**) in humans. It consists of a flat plate of cartilage that gradually changes to bone during life.

xiphoid /zíffoyd/ *adj.* **1.** SWORD-SHAPED shaped like a sword **2.** OF THE XIPHISTERNUM relating to the xiphisternum ■ *n.* **xiphoid**, **xiphoid process** = **xiphisternum**

XL *abbr.* extra large (*used of clothing sizes*)

Xmas /kríssməss, éksməss/ *n.* Christmas (*informal*) [Mid-16thC. *X* represents the Greek letter *chi*, an abbreviation of Greek *Khristos* 'Christ'.]

Xn *abbr.* Christian

Xnty *abbr.* Christianity

xoanon /zó͋ ə non/ (*plural* **-na** /-nə/) *n.* an image of a god that has been carved out of wood [Early 18thC. From Greek *xoanon* 'carved statue'.]

X-radiation *n.* **1.** EXPOSURE TO X-RAYS exposure to X-rays or medical treatment by means of X-rays **2.** X-RAY RADIATION radiation in the form of X-rays

X-rated *adj.* **1.** SEXUALLY EXPLICIT containing explicit sex scenes or descriptions of sex (*informal*) **2.** *US* = **X-certificate** [Late 20thC. From 'X' rating given to such material.]

X-ray, **X ray, x-ray, x ray** *n.* **1.** ELECTROMAGNETIC RADIATION

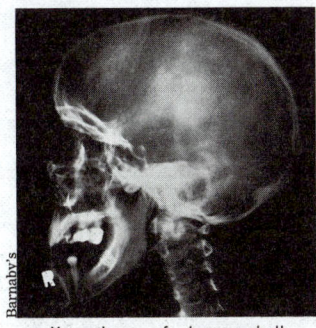

X-ray: Image of a human skull

a high-energy electromagnetic radiation. It has a wavelength between 0.01 and 10 nanometres, which is between gamma rays and ultraviolet light, and can penetrate solids and ionize gas. **2.** PHOTOGRAPHIC IMAGE USING X-RAYS an image produced on photographic film by X-rays passing through objects or parts of the body, often used in medicine and science as a diagnostic tool. Dense parts such as bones absorb the X-rays and so appear as lighter regions on the developed film. **3.** COMMUNICATION **CODE WORD FOR THE LETTER 'X'** the NATO phonetic alphabet code word for the letter 'X', used in international radio communications ■ *vt.* (**X-rays, X-raying, X-rayed**) **1.** PHOTOGRAPH STH USING X-RAYS to expose sth, e.g. a part of the body, to X-rays in order to obtain a photographic image of it **2.** EXAMINE PATIENT USING X-RAYS to examine or treat sb using X-rays [Late 19thC. Translation of German *X-Strahl*, the name given by Röntgen, who discovered the rays, *x* signifying 'unknown'.]

X-ray astronomy *n.* the branch of astronomy in which the properties of celestial bodies are determined using the X-rays they emit. Because the Earth's atmosphere is opaque to X-rays, observations are made using rockets or satellites.

X-ray crystallography *n.* the study of crystal structures using the diffraction patterns produced by scattered X-rays

X-ray diffraction *n.* the diffraction of X-rays produced by the atoms within a crystal, used to determine information about the crystal's structure

X-ray star, **X-ray source** *n.* a celestial object that emits X-rays in addition to other types of radiation

X-ray therapy *n.* the medical application of X-rays in treating illnesses such as cancer

X-ray tube *n.* an evacuated tube in which a stream of high-energy electrons is made to strike a metal target to produce X-rays

XS *abbr.* extra small (*used of clothing sizes*)

Xt. *abbr.* Christ

Xtian *abbr.* Christian

xtn *abbr.* TELECOM, BUSINESS extension

Xty *abbr.* Christianity

xu /soo/ (*plural* **xu**) *n.* **1.** SUB-UNIT OF VIETNAMESE CURRENCY a sub-unit of currency in Vietnam, 100 of which are worth a dong. See table at **currency 2.** COIN WORTH XU coin worth one xu [Mid-20thC. Via Vietnamese from French *sou* (see SOU).]

xyl- *prefix.* = xylo- (*used before vowels*)

xylan /zī́ lan/ *n.* a yellow gummy polysaccharide (**pentosan**) found in plant cell walls and woody tissue such as straw husks that yields xylose when subjected to hydrolysis

xylem /zī́ləm, zī́ lem/ *n.* plant tissue that carries water and dissolved minerals from the roots through the stem and leaves. It also helps to support the plant and is the main constituent of wood. [Late 19thC. From German, formed from Greek *xulon* 'wood'.]

CH$_3$

1,4-Xylene

1,3-Xylene

1,2-Xylene

Xylene

xylene /zī́ leen/ *n.* any of three isomeric hydrocarbons that are flammable volatile colourless liquids obtained from petroleum or natural gas and are used as solvents and in making aviation fuel, resins, and dyes. Formula: C_8H_{10}.

xylidine /zī́li deen, zī́li dīn, zílli-/ *n.* any of six toxic amines derived from xylene and used in dyes and in organic synthesis. Formula: $C_8H_{11}N$.

xylo- *prefix.* **1.** wood ○ *xylograph* **2.** xylene ○ *xyli-dine* [From Greek *xulon* 'wood']

xylogenous /zī lójjənəss/ *adj.* adapted to or living in or on wood [Coined from Greek *xulo-* 'wood', from *xulon* + -GENOUS]

xylograph /zílə graaf, -graf/ *n.* **1.** WOOD ENGRAVING an engraving made on wood **2.** PRINT FROM XYLOGRAPH a print made from an engraving made on wood ■ *vt.* (**-graphs, -graphing, -graphed**) MAKE A XYLOGRAPH to take a print from an engraving made on wood —**xylographer** /zī lóggrəfər/ *n.* —**xylographic** /zílə gráffik/ *adj.* —**xylographical** /-gráffik'l/ *adj.* —**xylographically** /-gráffikli/ *adv.*

xylography /zī lóggrəfi/ *n.* the art of engraving on and printing from wooden blocks

xyloid /zí loyd/ *adj.* relating to or resembling wood

xylol /zí lol/ *n.* = xylene [Mid-19thC. Coined from XYLO- + -OL.]

xylophagous /zī lóffəgəss/ *adj.* feeding on or living in wood —**xylophage** /zílō fayj/ *n.*

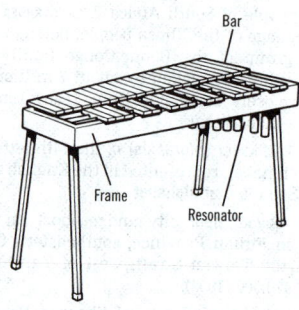

Xylophone

xylophone /zíləfōn/ *n.* a musical instrument consisting of a row of wooden bars of different lengths that are laid out like a keyboard and produce a tone when struck with a mallet —**xylophonist** /zī lóffənist/ *n.*

xylose /zí lōz, -lōss/ *n.* a white crystalline combustible sugar obtained from xylan and used in diabetic foods and in dyeing and tanning. Formula: $C_5H_{10}O_5$.

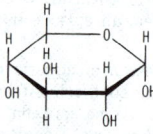

Xylose

xystus /zístəss/ (*plural* **-tuses**), **xyst** /zist/ *n.* **1.** ANCIENT GREEK COVERED EXERCISE AREA in ancient Greece, a long walkway with a roof supported by pillars, used for athletics **2.** ANCIENT ROMAN PATH in ancient Rome, a covered or open path in a garden, lined with trees or pillars [Mid-17thC. Via Latin from Greek *xustos* 'covered colonnade', literally 'smooth' (from its polished floor), from *xuein* 'to scrape'.]

y[1] /wī/ (*plural* **y's**), **Y** (*plural* **Y's** *or* **Ys**) *n.* **1.** 25TH LETTER OF ENGLISH ALPHABET the 25th letter of the modern English alphabet **2.** SPEECH SOUND CORRESPONDING TO LETTER 'Y' the speech sound that corresponds to the letter 'Y' **3.** LETTER 'Y' WRITTEN a written representation of the letter 'Y' **4.** STH SHAPED LIKE Y a Y-shaped object or group of objects

y[2] (*plural* **y's**) *symbol.* **1.** y-axis **2.** a coordinate along the y-axis **3.** an algebraic variable **4.** yocto-

Y[1] *symbol.* **1.** ELEC admittance **2.** an unknown factor **3.** yotta- **4.** yttrium

Y[2] *abbr.* **1.** yen **2.** yuan **3.** YMCA (*informal*) **4.** YWCA (*informal*) **5.** YMHA (*informal*) **6.** YWHA (*informal*)

y. *abbr.* year

-y[1], **-ey** *suffix.* **1.** consisting of or characterized by ○ *muddy* **2.** somewhat, like ○ *chilly* ○ *wintry* **3.** tending toward ○ *sleepy* [Old English *-ig*]

-y[2] *suffix.* **1.** condition, state, or quality ○ *infamy* **2.** an activity ○ *chandlery* **3.** the place where an activity is carried on, or the result or product of an activity ○ *colliery* ○ *laundry* **4.** body or group ○ *soldiery* [Via Old French *-ie* from Latin *-ia*]

-y[3] *suffix.* = **-ie**

Y2K *abbr.* **1.** year 2000 ○ *Y2K-compliant software* **2.** millennium bug

yabber /yábbər/ *vti.* (**-bers**, **-bering**, **-bered**) *Australian* TALK VERY FAST to talk a lot or say sth rapidly, often so that it is incomprehensible (*informal*) ■ *n. Australian* RAPID SPEECH rapid speech that is often incomprehensible (*informal*)

yabby /yábbi/ (*plural* **-bies** *or* **-by**), **yabbie** (*plural* **-bies** *or* **-bie**) *n. Aus* a small freshwater crayfish found in Australia. Genus: *Cherax*. [Late 19thC. From Wergaia (spoken in Victoria, Australia) *yabij*.]

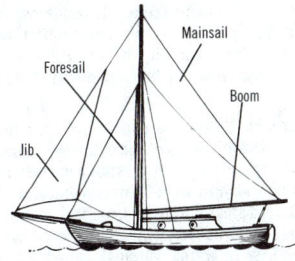

Yacht

yacht /yot/ *n.* **1.** SAILING BOAT a sailing boat, often one that has living quarters and is used for cruising or racing. Most sailing yachts have a motor as an alternative or extra means of power. **2.** MOTORBOAT FOR CRUISING a large motorboat used for cruising ■ *vi.* (**yachts**, **yachting**, **yachted**) SAIL IN YACHT to sail in a yacht for leisure or sport [Mid-16thC. From obsolete Dutch *jaghte*, a shortening of *jaghtschip* 'chasing ship'.]

— WORD KEY: SYNONYMS —
See Synonyms at **boat**.

yachtie /yótti/ *n.* sb who owns a yacht or enjoys sailing, cruising, or racing in yachts (*informal*)

yachting /yótting/ *n.* the sport or pastime of sailing a yacht

yachtsman /yótsmən/ (*plural* **-men** /-mən/) *n.* sb who owns or sails a yacht —**yachtsmanship** *n.*

yachtswoman /yóts wŏomən/ (*plural* **-en** /-wimmin/) *n.* a woman who owns or sails a yacht

yack *vi., n.* = **yak**[2] (*informal*)

yackety-yak /yákəti yák/ *vi.* (**yackety-yaks**, **yackety-yakking**, **yackety-yakked**), *n.* = **yak**[2] (*informal*) [Mid-20thC. An imitation of the sound.]

yadda yadda yadda *n.* US boring, trite, superficial, unending talk (*slang*) ○ *just a lot of yadda yadda yadda on the talk shows tonight* [Late 20thC. Origin uncertain.]

yaffle /yáff'l/ (*plural* **-fles** *or* **-fle**) *n.* a green woodpecker (*regional*) [Late 18thC. An imitation of the bird's call.]

YAG /yag/ *n.* a mineral made synthetically from yttrium, aluminium, and garnet. It is used in infrared lasers and as a gemstone. [Mid-20thC. Acronym formed from *yttrium*, *aluminium* and *garnet*.]

Yagi aerial /yaági-/ *n.* a directional radio or television aerial consisting of several elements arranged in line [Mid-20thC. Named after Hidetsugu Yagi (1886–1976), Japanese electrical engineer.]

yah[1] /yaa/ *interj.* used to express derision or defiance (*dated*) [Early 17thC. A natural exclamation.]

yah[2] *adv.* yes. This is used especially when parodying affected upper-class accents. (*informal*) ○ *Okay, yah, super.* [Mid-19thC. A parody of an affected pronunciation of 'hear! hear!'.]

yahoo[1] /yaa hoó, yə-, yáa hoo/ (*plural* **-hoos**) *n.* an offensively crude or brutish person (*insult*) [Early 18thC. Named after the *Yahoos* in Jonathan Swift's *Gulliver's Travels* (1726).] —**yahooism** /yə hoó izəm/ *n.*

yahoo[2] /yə hoó/ *interj.* EXPRESSING ENTHUSIASM used to express enthusiasm, approval, or celebration (*informal*) ○ *Yahoo! Let's go!* ■ *n.* (*plural* **-hoos**) ENTHUSIASTIC CRY a cry of joy (*informal*)

Yahrzeit /yáwrt sīt/ *n.* in Judaism, the anniversary of sb's death, celebrated by near relatives with the lighting of a memorial candle and the saying of the Kaddish [Mid-19thC. From Yiddish *yortsayt*, literally 'year's time'.]

Yahweh /yaá way/, **Yahveh** /-vay/, **Jahveh, Jahweh** *n.* a name of God, expanded from the four letters, YHWH (**Tetragrammaton**), that form the proper name of God in Hebrew [Late 19thC. From Hebrew.]

Yahwism /yaáwizəm/, **Yahvism** /yaáv-/ *n.* the use of 'Yahweh' to represent the name of God or to worship God

Yahwist /yaáwist/, **Yahvist** /yaáv-/ *n.* the unknown writer of the parts of the Old Testament of the Bible in which a set of four letters (**Tetragrammaton**) is used to refer to God

Yahwistic /yaa wístik/, **Yahvistic** /-víst-/ *adj.* relating to Yahweh, Yahwism, or the Yahwist

Yak

yak[1] /yak/ (*plural* **yaks** *or* **yak**) *n.* a large long-haired ox of the Tibetan highlands that has long curved horns and is found both wild and domesticated. Latin name: *Bos grunniens*. [Late 18thC. From Tibetan *gyag*.]

yak[2] /yak/, **yack** *vi.* (**yaks, yakking, yakked; yacks, yacking, yacked**) CHATTER CONTINUOUSLY to talk continuously, usually about unimportant matters (*informal*) ■ *n.* CONTINUOUS CHATTER continuous talking, usually about unimportant matters, or an instance of this (*informal*) [Mid-20thC. An imitation of the sound.]

Yakama /yákəmə/ (*plural* **-ma** *or* **-mas**) *n.* **1.** PEOPLES MEMBER OF NATIVE N AMERICAN PEOPLE a member of a Native North American people of south-central Washington State **2.** LANG YAKAMA LANGUAGE the Penutian language spoken by the Yakama. It is spoken by about 3,000 people. [Mid-19thC. From Sahaptin.]

yakitori /yáki táwri/ *n.* a dish of Japanese origin consisting of small pieces of grilled chicken that are basted on skewers with a sauce of soy, stock, sugar, and mirin [Mid-20thC. From Japanese, literally 'grilling fowl'.]

yakka /yákə/, **yakker** /yákər/, **yacker** *n.* ANZ work (*informal*) [Late 19thC. Origin unknown.]

Yakut /ya koót/ (*plural* **-kut** *or* **-kuts**) *n.* **1.** PEOPLES MEMBER OF SIBERIAN ETHNIC GROUP a member of an ethnic group that lives in northeastern Siberia, mainly in the Russian republic of Sakha **2.** LANG YAKUT LANGUAGE the language of the Yakut people, belonging to the Turkic branch of the Altaic family of languages. Yakut is spoken by about 300,000 people. [Mid-18thC. Via Russian from Yakut.] —**Yakut** *adj.*

Yakutsk /yə koótsk/ capital city of the autonomous region of Sakha, northeastern Russia. Population: 197,600 (1992).

yakuza /yə koózə/ (*plural* **-za**) *n.* **1.** JAPANESE CRIME SYNDICATE a Japanese criminal organization involved in illegal activities such as drug-dealing, extortion, and prostitution **2.** YAKUZA MEMBER a member the yakuza [Mid-20thC. From Japanese 'gambler', formed from *ya* 'eight' + *ku* 'nine' + *-za* 'three', the worst hand in a card game.]

Yale lock /yáyl lok/ *tdmk.* a trademark for a type of cylindrical lock that is operated using a flat serrated key

y'all *contr. Southern US* = **you all** (*informal*)

Yallourn /yál awrn/ town in southern Victoria, Australia. It is a major coal-mining centre. Population: 15,512 (1996).

Yalta /yáltə, yóltə/ town and resort in Crimea Region, southern Ukraine. Situated on the Black Sea, it was the site of a conference in 1945 between Joseph Stalin, Franklin Roosevelt, and Winston Churchill that determined the areas of Germany that each of the great powers would administer after World War II. Population: 89,000 (1991).

Yalu /yaa loo/ river in East Asia, forming most of the boundary between North Korea and China. Length: 790 km/490 mi.

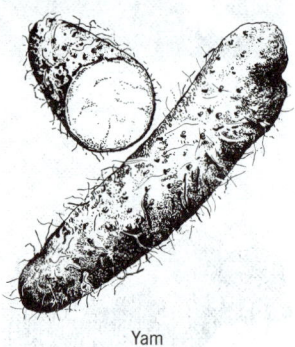

Yam

yam /yam/ n. **1. ROOT VEGETABLE** a vegetable that resembles a large white floury potato and is the root of a tropical vine **2. TROPICAL VINE** a tropical vine that produces yams. Genus: *Dioscorea*. [Late 16thC. Via Portuguese *inhame* or Spanish *iñame*, of West African origin (related to Fulani *nyami* 'to eat').]

yamen /yaáměn, yaá men/ n. in the Chinese Empire, the home or office of a mandarin or other public official [Early 19thC. From Chinese *yámen*, from *yá* 'office' + *mén* 'gate'.]

Yamim Nora'im /yaa mím nawr aa ím/ npl. in Judaism, the period of repentance lasting from Rosh Hashanah to Yom Kippur [From Hebrew, 'Days of Awe']

yammer /yámmər/ vi. (-mers, -mering, -mered) (informal) **1. TALK LOUDLY AND AT LENGTH** to talk, chat, or chatter noisily and continuously sth **2. WHINE** to whine or complain persistently about sth **3. HOWL OR WAIL** to make repeated howling sounds of pain or distress ▪ n. (informal) **1. NOISY CHATTERING** noisy continuous talk, chat, or chattering **2. COMPLAINT** a whining sound or persistent complaint [15thC. Origin uncertain: probably from Middle Dutch *jammeren* 'to mourn'.] —**yammerer** n.

Yamoussoukro /yámmōō sōōkrō/ capital city of Côte d'Ivoire, in the central part of the country. Population: 100,000 (1988).

Yan'an /yán án/ town in northern Shaanxi Province, northeastern China. The terminus of the Long March, Yan'an was used by communist forces as a base between 1936 and 1949. Population: 113,277 (1990).

yancha /yán chaá/ n. Hong Kong the social practice of going to a teahouse. It is the cultural equivalent of going to the pub in the United Kingdom. (dated)

yang /yang/, **Yang** n. the principle of light, heat, motivation and masculinity in Chinese philosophy that is the counterpart to yin. The dual, opposite, and complementary principles of yin and yang are thought to exist in varying proportions in all things. ◊ **yin** [Late 17thC. From Chinese *yáng* 'sun, positive'.]

Yangon /yang gón/ capital city of Myanmar, in the south of the country. Population: 2,513,023 (1983). Former name **Rangoon** (until 1989)

Yangtze /yáng see, yáng ts-/, **Yangzi** the longest river in China. It rises in the Kunlun Mountains, and flows southwards and then eastwards to enter the East China Sea directly north of Shanghai. Length: 5,470 km/3,400 mi.

yank /yangk/ v. (**yanks, yanking, yanked**) **1. vti. PULL SHARPLY** to pull or jerk sb or sth suddenly and sharply **2. vt. REMOVE SB OR STH SWIFTLY** to remove sb or sth suddenly and quickly ▪ n. **SHARP PULL** a sudden sharp pull or jerk [Early 19thC. Origin unknown.]

— WORD KEY: SYNONYMS —
See Synonyms at *pull*.

Yank /yangk/ n. PEOPLES an offensive term referring to sb who is from the United States (informal) [Late 18thC. Shortening of YANKEE.]

Yankee /yángki/ n. **1.** PEOPLES = **Yank** n. (informal; offensive in some contexts) **2.** US PEOPLES **SB FROM A NORTHERN US STATE** sb born or living in a northern state of the United States, especially a soldier fighting on the side of the Union during the American Civil War (offensive in some contexts) **3.** US PEOPLES **SB FROM NEW ENGLAND** sb who was born or brought up in one of the states of New England (offensive in some contexts) **4.** COMMUNICATION **CODE WORD FOR LETTER 'Y'** the NATO phonetic alphabet code word for the letter 'Y', used in international radio communications [Mid-18thC. Origin uncertain: perhaps from Dutch *Janke* 'Johnny'.] —**Yankeedom** n.

Yankee Doodle /-dōŏd'l/ n. **1.** POPULAR AMERICAN SONG a song first popular during the American War of Independence **2.** PEOPLES = **Yank** n. (informal) [In the meaning of 'Yankee', from the idea that the song is typically national]

Yankeeism /yángki izəm/ n. an expression or other characteristic considered typical of Yankees

Yankton /yángktən/ city in southeastern South Dakota, southwest of Sioux Falls and northwest of Sioux City, Iowa. Population: 13,884 (1996).

yanqui /yángki/ n. (plural **-quis**) n. an offensive term used by some members of Spanish-speaking American communities to refer disparagingly to an English-speaking US citizen [Early 20thC. Spanish phonetic spelling of YANKEE.]

Yaoundé /yaa ōónd ay/ capital city of Cameroon, in the southwestern part of the country. Population: 800,000 (1992).

yap /yap/ vi. (**yaps, yapping, yapped**) **1. MAKE HIGH BARKING SOUND** to make a short loud high-pitched barking noise **2. CHATTER ANNOYINGLY** to talk continuously about trivial things, often in a loud or high-pitched voice (informal) ▪ n. **1. SHORT HIGH-PITCHED BARK** a short, loud, high-pitched bark **2. TRIVIAL CONVERSATION** a trivial or meaningless conversation (informal) **3. MOUTH** sb's mouth (slang) [Early 19thC. An imitation of a dog's bark.] —**yapper** n. —**yappy** adj.

Yap /yap/ group of islands, islets, and atolls in the western Pacific Ocean. Part of the Caroline Islands, the group comprises one of the states of Micronesia. Population: 10,886 (1991). Area: 119 sq. km/46 sq. mi.

yapok /yáppok/ (plural **-poks** or **-pok**) n. an amphibious nocturnal opossum of tropical Central and South America that has dense fur, webbed hind feet, a long tail, and feeds on aquatic organisms such as shrimp. Latin name: *Chironectes minimus*. [Early 19thC. Named after the river *Oyapok*, which forms the border between northern Brazil and French Guiana.]

yapon n. = yaupon

Yaqui /yáki/ (plural **-qui** or **-quis**) n. **1.** PEOPLES **MEMBER OF NATIVE N AMERICAN PEOPLE** a member of a Native North American people of Arizona and Sonora, Mexico **2.** LANG **YAQUI LANGUAGE** the Uto-Aztecan language of the Yaqui people. Yaqui is spoken by about 20,000 people. [Early 19thC. Via Spanish from Yaqui *Hiaki*.] —**Yaqui** adj.

yarborough /yaárbərə/ n. a hand in bridge or whist consisting of 13 cards each of which has a value lower than nine [Late 19thC. Named after Charles Anderson Worsley (1809–97), Second Earl of *Yarborough*, who allegedly bet 1000 to 1 against the occurrence of such a hand.]

yard[1] /yaárd/ n. **1. IMPERIAL UNIT OF LENGTH** a unit of length equal to 0.9144 m/3 ft **2.** = **yardstick** n. **2** **3. SPAR SUPPORTING SAIL** a long spar that supports the head of a square sail, lugsail, or lateen [Old English *gerd* 'rod'] ◊ **the whole nine yards** US the totality or full extent of sth (informal)

yard[2] /yaárd/ n. **1. ENCLOSED PAVED PIECE OF LAND** an area of ground that is usually paved and enclosed, and is next to or surrounded by a building or buildings **2.** US, Can = **garden 3. AREA USED FOR BUSINESS OR ACTIVITY** an area of ground, sometimes with associated build-

---

ings, used for a particular purpose (often used in combination) ◊ a builder's yard **4. RAILWAY STORAGE AREA** an area of railway tracks used for storing rolling stock or locomotives and for making up trains **5. LIVESTOCK ENCLOSURE** an enclosed area of land for livestock **6.** US, Can **WINTER GRAZING AREA** an area of land where deer, moose, or other animals graze in winter ▪ vt. (**yards, yarding, yarded**) **KEEP LIVESTOCK IN A YARD** to put or keep livestock in a yard [Old English *geard* 'enclosure, garden']

Yard n. Scotland Yard (informal)

yardage[1] /yaárdij/ n. measurement in yards, or an amount measured in yards

yardage[2] /yaárdij/ n. **1. USE OF A LIVESTOCK YARD** use of a livestock yard for storing animals before transporting them **2. FEE CHARGED FOR USING A YARD** a fee charged for storing livestock in a yard

yardarm /yaárd aarm/ n. an end of the yard used to support a sail

yardbird /yaárd burd/ n. US **1. SOLDIER ASSIGNED MENIAL DUTIES** a soldier who is assigned menial tasks or is confined to a limited area, usually as a punishment (informal) **2. INEPT RECRUIT** an untrained and inept military recruit **3. CONVICT** a convict or prisoner (dated informal) [Mid-19thC. Modelled on JAILBIRD.]

yard goods npl. = piece goods

yard grass n. a coarse annual grass with ground-hugging leaves and grouped spikes that grows widely as a weed. Latin name: *Eleusine indica*.

Yardie /yaárdi/ n. a member of a criminal syndicate that originated in Jamaica

yardman /yaárdmən/ (plural **-men** /-mən/) n. **1. SB EMPLOYED IN A YARD** sb who works in a yard, especially a railway yard or a timberyard **2.** US **GARDENER** sb employed to look after a lawn or garden

yard of ale n. **1. YARD-LONG GLASS** a long narrow drinking glass, sometimes shaped like a horn, approximately one yard long and holding two to three pints of beer **2. CONTENTS OF A YARD OF ALE** the contents of a yard of ale

yard sale n. US a sale at which personal possessions and household items are sold, usually held in the garden of sb's house

yardstick /yaárd stik/ n. **1. YARD-LONG MEASURING STICK** a measuring stick one yard long, usually marked in feet and inches **2. STANDARD OF COMPARISON** a standard used to judge the quality, value, or success of sth

yard work n. US = gardening

yare /yair/ adj. **1. EASY TO HANDLE** used to describe a ship that is easy to handle and responsive **2. READY** ready or prepared (archaic) **3. QUICK** quick or lively (archaic) ▪ adv. **QUICKLY** quickly or nimbly (archaic) [Old English *gearo* 'ready'] —**yarely** adv.

yarmulke /yaármŏŏlkə/, **yarmulka, yarmulkah** n. a small round cap worn by Jewish men and boys. Orthodox Jews wear the yarmulke at all times, while others wear it for prayer or on ceremonial occasions only. [Mid-20thC. Via Yiddish from Polish *jarmułka*, of uncertain origin: probably from, ultimately, Turkish *yağmur* 'rain'.]

yarn /yaárn/ n. **1. THREAD** a continuous twisted strand of wool, cotton, or synthetic fibres, usually used for knitting or weaving **2. STRAND OF GLASS OR METAL** a continuous strand of a material such as glass or metal **3. LONG STORY** a long or involved tale, especially one that relates exciting or incredible events (informal) ▪ vi. (**yarns, yarning, yarned**) **TELL A YARN** to relate a long tale full of incredible events (informal) [Old English *gearn*. Ultimately from an Indo-European base meaning 'entrail' that is also the ancestor of English *hernia* and *cord*.]

yarn-dyed adj. dyed in the form of yarn before being woven or knitted

Yaroslavl /yaáro slaávəl/ city and capital of Yaroslavl Oblast, central European Russia. It is situated on the Volga River. Population: 636,000 (1990).

Yarra /yárrə/ river in southern Victoria, Australia. Length: 250 km/155 mi.

yarrow /yárrō/ (plural **-rows** or **-row**) n. a European and Asian composite plant with leaves resembling ferns

---

and broad flat clusters of flower heads. Latin name: *Achillea millefolium*. [Old English *gearwe*]

yashmak /yásh mak/, **yashmac** n. a veil worn by some Muslim women in public [Mid-19thC. From Turkish *yaşmak*.]

yataghan /yáttəgən/, **yatagan, ataghan** /áttəgən/ n. a Turkish sword with no handle guard and a single-edged blade that curves inwards then outwards [Early 19thC. From Turkish *yatağan*.]

yatra /yáttrə/ n. a holy pilgrimage for Hindus [Early 19thC. From Sanskrit *yātrā*, which was formed from *yā* 'to undertake a trip'.]

yatter /yáttər/ vi. (**-ters, -tering, -tered**) CHATTER CONTINUOUSLY to talk continuously, especially about trivial things (*informal*) ■ n. CONTINUOUS CHATTER continuous talk, especially about trivial things, or an instance of this (*informal*) [Mid-19thC. An imitation of the sound. Perhaps modelled on CHATTER.]

yaup vi., n. US = **yawp**

yaupon /yáwpən/ (*plural* **-pons** *or* **-pon**), **yapon** (*plural* **-pons** *or* **-pon**) n. an evergreen holly of the southeastern United States that has red fruit and smooth bitter leaves that are made into a tea for their emetic and purgative properties. Latin name: *Ilex vomitoria*. [Early 18thC. From Catawba *yápa*, literally 'tree leaf'.]

yautia /yáwti ə/ (*plural* **-as** *or* **-a**) n. 1. PLANT YIELDING EDIBLE TUBERS a West Indian plant of the arum family cultivated for its edible tuber. Genus: *Xanthosoma*. 2. EDIBLE TUBER the brown starchy tuber of the yautia plant, cooked and eaten as a vegetable [Early 20thC. Via Spanish from Taino.]

yaw /yaw/ vti. (**yaws, yawing, yawed**) 1. GO OR PUT OFF COURSE to deviate from a straight course, or to make a boat or ship do this 2. TURN AROUND A VERTICAL AXIS to turn around the vertical axis, or to make an aircraft turn in this way. ◊ **pitch, roll** 3. ZIGZAG to move unsteadily on a zigzag course, or to make sb or sth advance in this way ■ n. 1. DEVIATION FROM COURSE the deviation of a ship from a straight course 2. MOVEMENT ABOUT VERTICAL AXIS the movement of an aircraft about its vertical axis. ◊ **pitch, roll** [Mid-16thC. Origin unknown.]

yawl /yawl/ n. 1. SAILING VESSEL a sailing vessel rigged fore-and-aft with a large mainmast and a smaller mizzenmast towards the stern 2. SHIP'S ROWING BOAT a small boat kept on a ship, rowed by four or six people [Mid-17thC. From Dutch *jol*, of unknown origin.]

yawn /yawn/ v. (**yawns, yawning, yawned**) 1. vi. OPEN MOUTH WIDE to open the mouth wide and take a long deep breath, usually involuntarily, because of tiredness or boredom 2. vt. SAY STH WHILE YAWNING to say sth while yawning, or in a tired or bored voice 3. vi. BE WIDE OPEN to open wide or be wide open, especially in a threatening or alarming manner ■ n. 1. ACT OF YAWNING an involuntary response to tiredness or boredom in which the mouth is opened wide and a long deep breath is taken 2. SB OR STH BORING a boring person, thing, or event (*informal*) [Old English *ginian*] —**yawning** adj. —**yawningly** adv.

yawner /yáwnər/ n. 1. SB YAWNING sb who yawns 2. = **yawn** n. 2 (*informal*)

yawp /yawp/, **yaup** vi. (**yawps, yawping, yawped; yaups, yauping, yauped**) US (*informal*) 1. TALK COARSELY to talk or complain loudly, coarsely, and sometimes meaninglessly 2. UTTER A YELP to utter a sharp loud yelp ■ n. US (*informal*) 1. YELP a sharp, loud yelp 2. COARSE TALK loud, coarse, and sometimes meaningless talk [14thC. Origin uncertain: perhaps related to YELP.] —**yawper** n.

yaws /yawz/ n. an infectious tropical disease marked initially by red skin eruptions and later by joint pains. It mainly affects children and is caused by the bacterium *Treponema pertenue*. (*takes a singular or plural verb*) [Late 17thC. From Carib *yaya*.]

y-axis n. 1. VERTICAL AXIS the vertical axis in a two-dimensional coordinate system such as a graph 2. AXIS IN THREE-DIMENSIONAL COORDINATE SYSTEM one of the axes in the three-dimensional Cartesian coordinate system, conventionally the vertical one

Yb symbol. ytterbium

YC abbr. Young Conservative

Y chromosome, **Y-chromosome** n. the sex chromosome that determines the male sex in humans and other mammals. The body cells of males each possess one Y chromosome paired with one X chromosome. ◊ **X chromosome**

yclept /i klépt/ adj. called by the name of (*archaic or humorous*) [Old English *geclipod*, past participle of *geclipian* 'to call']

yd abbr. MEASURE yard

yea /yay/ adv., n. YES yes (*archaic*) ■ adv. INDEED indeed (*archaic*) ○ '*Yea, though I walk through the valley of the shadow of death, I will fear no evil*' (Psalm 23, King James Bible) [Old English *gēa* 'yes']

yeah /yaa, yair/ interj. yes (*informal*) [Early 20thC. Variant of YEA.]

yean /yeen/ (**yeans, yeaning, yeaned**) vti. to give birth to a young sheep or goat (*archaic*) [14thC. From an assumed Old English *geēanian* 'to give birth to young'.]

yeanling /yéenling/ n. a young sheep or goat (*archaic*)

year /yeer, yur/ n. 1. TWELVE-MONTH PERIOD FROM JANUARY 1 a period of 365 days (or 366 in a leap year), measured from 1 January to 31 December 2. TWELVE-MONTH PERIOD FROM ANY DATE a period of 365 or 366 days, measured exactly or approximately from any date ○ *The company's financial year ends on 31 July.* 3. SOLAR YEAR the time it takes the Earth to orbit the Sun, approximately 365.25 days 4. TIME OF PLANET'S ORBIT AROUND SUN the time taken for a planet to orbit once round the Sun 5. PERIOD OF PARTICULAR ACTIVITY the time occupied by a particular activity within a twelve-month period ○ *academic year* 6. AGE BAND IN SCHOOL OR COLLEGE a group of students, usually of approximately the same age, who start school or college at the same time and study together in one or more classes ■ **years** npl. 1. LONG TIME a very long time (*informal*) ○ *It's years since I last saw him.* ○ *We haven't been back for years.* 2. AGE age, especially advanced age ○ *a man of his years* 3. TIME IN GENERAL time in the past, present, or future ○ *in years to come* 4. PARTICULAR PERIOD OF TIME a particular period of time, usually in the past ○ *her early years* [Old English *gēar*] ◊ **since the year dot** for an extremely long time (*informal*) ◊ **year in, year out** in a regular or repeated way over a long period of time, especially when this is seen as monotonous (*informal*)

yearbook /yéer bōōk, y/ n. 1. ANNUAL RECORD OF EVENTS a book published annually containing details of events in the previous year, usually within a particular organization or field of interest 2. BOOK COMMEMORATING A SCHOOL YEAR in the United States, a book compiled by members of a graduating class of a high school or college, commemorating their school year and usually including photographs of the students

year-end n. END OF A YEAR the end of a financial year or calendar year ■ adj. DONE AT THE YEAR-END occurring or done at the end of a financial year or calendar year

yearling /yéerling, y/ n. 1. YOUNG ANIMAL an animal, e.g. a calf or deer, between one and two years of age 2. YEAR-OLD RACEHORSE a racehorse that is one year old, as reckoned from 1 January in the year after it was born 3. BOND MATURING IN ONE YEAR a bond that comes to term after one year

yearlong /yéer lóng, y/ adj. lasting for a year or continuing throughout a year

yearly /yéerli/ adj. 1. ANNUAL happening, done, appearing, or published once a year or every year 2. RELATING TO ONE YEAR relating to or lasting for a period of twelve months ■ adv. 1. ONCE A YEAR once every year 2. PER YEAR during each year ■ n. (*plural* **yearlies** /yéerliz/) ANNUAL EVENT OR ISSUE sth that happens or appears once a year, especially an annual publication [Old English *gēarlīc*]

yearn /yurn/ vi. (**yearns, yearning, yearned**) 1. LONG FOR to want sb or sth very much, often with a feeling of sadness because of the difficulty or impossibility of fulfilling the desire 2. FEEL AFFECTION to feel affection, tenderness, or compassion [Old English *giernan*. Ultimately from an Indo-European base meaning 'to want' which is also the ancestor of English *greedy* and *charisma*.] —**yearner** n.

yearning /yúrning/ n. a very strong desire, often tinged with sadness [Old English *gierninge*] —**yearningly** adv.

year of grace, **year of our Lord** n. a particular year of the Christian era

year out n. = gap year

year-round adj. LASTING THROUGHOUT THE YEAR existing, continuing, or operating throughout the year ■ adv. THROUGHOUT THE YEAR throughout the year

yea-sayer n. US 1. SB OPTIMISTIC sb who is always confident and optimistic 2. SB AGREEING SUBMISSIVELY sb who always agrees submissively with a superior

yeast /yeest/ n. 1. SMALL SINGLE-CELLED FUNGUS a small single-celled fungus that ferments sugars and other carbohydrates, and reproduces by budding. Genus: *Saccharomyces*. 2. PREPARATION OF YEAST CELLS a commercial preparation of yeast cells, used in brewing, baking, and as a source of vitamins and protein 3. FROTH the yellowish froth that forms on the surface of a fermenting liquid such as beer, contains yeast cells and carbon dioxide, and promotes fermentation 4. FOAM any foam or froth, e.g. on sea waves 5. CAUSE OF FERMENT OR ACTIVITY sb or sth that causes ferment, activity, or unrest ■ vi. (**yeasts, yeasting, yeasted**) FERMENT to ferment, froth, or foam [Old English *gist*]

yeast extract n. a thick sticky brown food obtained from yeast and eaten as a spread or used in cooking

yeast infection n. an overgrowth of a fungus in the vagina, intestines, skin, or mouth, causing irritation and swelling. Technical name **candidiasis**

yeasty /yéesti/ (**-ier, -iest**) adj. 1. RELATING TO YEAST relating to, containing, tasting, or smelling of yeast 2. CAUSING FERMENTATION fermenting, or causing fermentation 3. FROTHY full of foam 4. RESTLESS marked by or causing agitation or restlessness 5. ENERGETIC full of vitality, productivity, or creativity 6. FRIVOLOUS light and frivolous —**yeastily** adv. —**yeastiness** n.

William Butler Yeats

Yeats /yayts/, **William Butler** (1865–1939) Irish poet and dramatist. A leader of the Irish Renaissance, he is considered to be one of the greatest poets of the 20th century. His poetry incorporates a complex personal mythology. He wrote plays for Dublin's Abbey Theatre, which he cofounded. He won the Nobel Prize in literature (1923).

yech /yekh, yek/ interj. US used to express disgust (*informal*) [Mid-20thC. A natural exclamation.]

yegg /yeg/ n. US a burglar, especially a safecracker (*slang*) [Early 20thC. Origin unknown.]

Yekaterinburg /ye kátta réen burg/ industrial city in central Russia, on the River Iset, on the eastern slopes of the Ural Mountains. Population: 1,280,000 (1995).

yell /yel/ vti. (**yells, yelling, yelled**) SHOUT LOUDLY to shout or scream sth, or to speak in a very loud voice ■ n. 1. LOUD CRY a loud shout, scream, or cry 2. US, Can CHEER OF SUPPORT a rhythmic word or phrase chanted together by people to give support or encouragement [Old English *giellan*. Ultimately from an Indo-European base meaning 'to call' which is also the ancestor of English *nightingale*.] —**yeller** n.

Yell /yel/ the second largest of the Shetland Islands of Scotland. Population: 1,075 (1991). Area: 210 sq. km/81 sq. mi.

yellow /yéllō/ adj. **1.** OF THE COLOUR OF BUTTER having or being near the colour of butter or ripe lemons **2.** OFFENSIVE TERM an offensive term referring to people from or born in Asia (offensive) **3.** COWARDLY cowardly or afraid (informal insult) **4.** SENSATIONALIST using scandalous or sensational material, often greatly exaggerating or distorting the truth. ♦ yellow journalism ■ n. **1.** YELLOW COLOUR a colour such as that of butter or ripe lemons that lies between orange and green on the visible spectrum and is one of the three primary colours of pigment. Yellow is also one of the three primary colours used in printing and photographic processing. **2.** YELLOW PIGMENT a yellow pigment or dye ○ using a bright yellow to complement the green **3.** YELLOW FABRIC yellow clothing or fabric ○ dressed in yellow **4.** YELLOW OBJECT a yellow object or substance **5.** YELLOW SNOOKER BALL a yellow ball in a cue game such as snooker ○ pot the yellow **6.** EGG YOLK the yolk of an egg ■ yellows npl. PLANT DISEASE a plant disease marked by a yellowing of foliage that may be caused by a mineral deficiency, virus, or some other infectious agent ■ vti. (-lows, -lowing, -lowed) BECOME YELLOW to become or make sth yellow or yellowish, especially as a result of age [Old English geolu. Ultimately from an Indo-European base meaning 'to shine' which is also the ancestor of English gleam and gold.] —yellowish adj. —yellowishness n. —yellowly adv. —yellowness n. —yellowy adj.

—— WORD KEY: SYNONYMS ——
See Synonyms at **cowardly**.

yellow-bellied adj. **1.** COWARDLY cowardly or afraid (informal insult) **2.** YELLOW UNDERNEATH with a yellow underside

yellow-belly n. a cowardly person (informal insult)

yellow bile n. = **choler** (archaic)

yellowbird /yéllō burd/ n. a bird with yellow plumage, e.g. the goldfinch

yellow brain fungus n. a type of jelly fungus

yellow cake n. the concentrated semirefined oxide of uranium ore

yellow card n. in football, a card shown by the referee to a player guilty of serious or persistent foul play as an indication that the player has been cautioned. ◊ **red card**

yellow cress n. a cress with yellow flowers that is related to watercress, but is not limited to growing at water margins

yellow-dog contract n. US an employment contract in which the employee agrees not to join a trade union. Such contracts are no longer legal.

yellow fever n. an infectious, often fatal viral disease of warm climates, transmitted by mosquitoes and marked by high fever, haemorrhaging, vomiting of blood, liver damage, and jaundice

yellowfin tuna /yéllōfin tyóōnə/, **yellowfin** (plural **-fins** or **-fin**) n. a small, widely distributed tuna inhabiting warm seas. It has yellowish fins and is an important food fish. Latin name: Thunnus albacares.

yellow-green alga n. an alga that lives in soil and other moist environments and contains brown and bright yellow pigments that mask the chlorophyll. Division: Chrysophyta.

yellowhammer /yéllō hamər/ n. a stout-billed European songbird of the bunting family. The male has a bright yellow head, neck, and breast. Latin name: Emberiza citrinella. [Mid-16thC. By folk etymology from earlier yelambre, from yelwe 'yellow' + -amber, of uncertain origin: perhaps from Old English amore, a type of bird.]

yellow jack n. **1.** YELLOW FEVER yellow fever (archaic) **2.** YELLOWISH ATLANTIC FOOD FISH a large yellowish food fish that lives off the Atlantic coast of North, South, and Central America. Latin name: Caranx bartholomaei.

yellow jacket n. US a social wasp with black-and-yellow bands on its body. It nests in the ground or in the hollows of trees, and can sting repeatedly. Family: Vespidae.

yellow jersey n. in the Tour de France, the jersey awarded to the cyclist with the fastest elapsed time at a completed stage of the race

yellow journalism n. a style of journalism that makes unscrupulous use of scandalous, lurid, or sensationalized stories to attract readers [Late 19thC. A reference to the yellow ink of the Yellow Kid cartoons appearing in the sensationalist New York World.]

Yellowknife /yéllō nīf/ capital city of the Northwest Territories, Canada. It is situated on the northern shore of the Great Slave Lake. Population: 15,179 (1991).

yellowlegs /yéllō legz/ (plural **-legs**) n. either of two large American shore birds, the greater yellowlegs or the lesser yellowlegs, of the sandpiper family that have bright yellow legs, mottled brown plumage, and white underparts. Genus: Tringa.

yellow line n. a line painted in yellow at the edge of a road, indicating that parking is allowed only for limited periods or at specified times

yellow ochre n. a yellow-brown inorganic pigment that contains iron and is used in artist's colours

Yellow Pages tdmk. a trademark for a telephone directory printed on yellow paper and containing names, addresses, and telephone numbers of businesses and other organizations listed according to the products or services offered

yellow peril, **Yellow Peril** n. a highly offensive term referring to the perceived threat to Western nations posed by the nations of eastern Asia, especially China (dated offensive)

yellow pine n. the strong yellowish wood of various kinds of pine tree, especially the North American shortleaf and longleaf pines

yellow poplar n. **1.** = **tulip tree 2.** = **tulipwood**

yellow press n. collectively, the newspapers that make unscrupulous use of scandalous, lurid, or sensationalized stories to attract readers. ♦ **yellow journalism**

yellow rain n. a fungal toxin that occurs as a form of precipitation in Southeast Asia. It has been attributed by different sections of the scientific community to residue from chemical warfare or to the excrement of wild honeybees.

yellow rattle n. a plant found in both Europe and North America that has yellow flowers whose seeds rattle in their pouches when they are shaken. Latin name: Rhinanthus minor.

Yellow River /yéllō-/ = **Huang He**

Yellow Sea arm of the Pacific Ocean bordered on the west and north by China and on the east by the Korean Peninsula. It merges with the East China Sea to the south.

yellow spot n. OPHTHALMOL = **macula**

Yellowstone /yéllō stōn/ river in the western United States, rising in northwestern Wyoming, and flowing into the Missouri River in North Dakota. Length: 1,110 km/692 mi.

Yellowstone National Park the world's first national park, established in 1872 in parts of Wyoming, Montana, and Idaho. It is noted for its geysers, hot springs, and the Yellowstone Falls. Area: 8,983 sq. km/3,468 sq. mi.

yellow streak n. a tendency to be cowardly (insult)

yellowtail /yéllō tayl/ (plural **-tails** or **-tail**) n. **1.** MARINE FISH WITH YELLOWISH TAIL a marine game fish with a yellowish tail, found in the coastal waters of California and Mexico. Latin name: Seriola lalandei. **2.** AUSTRALIAN BAIT FISH a small greenish fish with silver underparts and a yellow tail and fins found in southern Australian and New Zealand waters and commonly used as bait. Latin name: Trachurus novaezelandiae.

yellowweed /yéllō weed/ n. a yellow-flowered plant such as the ragwort or the goldenrod

yellowwood /yéllō wŏŏd/ (plural **-woods** or **-wood**) n. **1.** US TREE WITH YELLOW WOOD a tree of the southern United States that has yellow wood, yields a yellow dye, and bears drooping clusters of showy white flowers. Latin name: Cladastris lutea. **2.** WOOD OF YELLOWWOOD

TREE the yellow-coloured wood of the yellowwood tree

yellowwort /yéllō wurt/ (plural **-worts** or **-wort**) n. a perennial plant of the gentian family that has grey waxy foliage and yellow leaves, and is usually found on chalky turf. Latin name: Blackstonia perfoliata.

yellow-yite /yéllō yīt/ (plural **yellow-yites** or **yellow-yite**) n. Scotland a yellowhammer [Early 19thC. The second element is of unknown origin.]

yelp /yelp/ v. (**yelps**, **yelping**, **yelped**) **1.** vi. BARK OR CRY SHARPLY to utter a short sharp high-pitched bark or cry, usually of pain **2.** vt. UTTER STH WITH YELPING SOUND to say sth in a sharp high-pitched voice ■ n. SHORT BARK OR CRY a short high-pitched bark or cry [Old English gelpan 'to boast'. Ultimately from an Indo-European base meaning 'to call' which is also the ancestor of English yell.] —**yelper** n.

Yeltsin /yéltsin/, **Boris** (b. 1931) Russian statesman. He was the first democratically elected Russian president (1991), and was instrumental in planning the country's transition from communism to a market economy. Full name **Boris Nikolayevich Yeltsin**

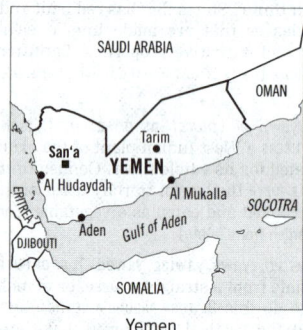

Yemen

Yemen /yémmən/ country on the Arabian peninsula, in southwestern Asia, on the Red Sea. The country was created in 1990 by the unification of the Yemen Arab Republic, or North Yemen, and the People's Democratic Republic of Yemen, or South Yemen. Language: Arabic. Currency: Yemeni riyal. Capital: San'a. Population: 16,600,000 (1996). Area: 536,869 sq. km/207,285 sq. mi. Official name **Republic of Yemen** — **Yemeni** n., adj.

yen[1] /yen/ (plural **yen**) n. **1.** UNIT OF JAPANESE CURRENCY a unit of currency in Japan, worth 100 sen. See table at **currency 2.** NOTE WORTH A YEN a note worth a yen [Late 19thC. Via Japanese en from Chinese yuán, literally 'round'.]

yen[2] /yen/ n. YEARNING a strong yearning for sth ■ vi. (**yens**, **yenning**, **yenned**) HAVE YEARNING to have a strong yearning for sth [Early 20thC. Origin uncertain: probably from Chinese (Cantonese) yǎn.]

Yenisey /yénni say/ river in central Siberian Russia. It is formed in the Sayan Mountains in southern Siberia by the union of the Greater Yenisey and the Little Yenisey, and flows northwards into the Kara Sea. Length: 4.090 km/2,540 mi.

yenta /yéntə/, **yente** n. US an offensive term that deliberately insults a woman's temperament or behaviour (slang insult) [Mid-20thC. Formed from Yiddish yente, from the feminine name Yente, from, ultimately, Latin gentilis 'of the same family'.]

yeoman /yṓmən/ n. (plural **-men** /-mən/) **1.** NAVY SIGNALS OFFICER a noncommissioned or petty officer in the Royal Navy or the Marines who is in charge of signals **2.** FARMER WITH SMALL FREEHOLDING a member of a former class of English commoners who owned and cultivated their own land **3.** SHERIFF'S ASSISTANT an assistant to a sheriff or other official in the past **4.** ATTENDANT TO NOBILITY OR ROYALTY a servant or minor official employed in the past in a royal or noble household **5.** YEOMAN OF THE GUARD a yeoman of the guard ■ adj. PERFORMED DILIGENTLY characterized by loyalty, diligence, and reliability ○ performed yeoman service in completing the task on time [13thC. Origin uncertain: perhaps a contraction of earlier yongman 'young man'.]

yeomanly /yṓmənli/ adj. **1.** RELATING TO YEOMAN relating to or characteristic of a yeoman or yeomen **2.** STAUNCH AND DEPENDABLE dependable, loyal, and brave (*archaic or literary*) ■ *adv.* BRAVELY in a brave and loyal way

yeoman of the guard (*plural* **yeomen of the guard**) *n.* a member of a British royal guard who perform ceremonial duties, especially as guards of the Tower of London

yeomanry /yṓmənri/ *n.* **1.** FARMERS WITH SMALL FREEHOLDINGS a former class of English commoners who owned and cultivated their own land **2.** FORMER BRITISH CAVALRY FORCE a British cavalry force organized as a home guard in 1761 that became part of the Territorial Army in 1907

Yeovil /yṓvil/ town in Somerset, southwestern England. Population: 35,000 (1993).

yep /yep/ *adv.* yes (*informal*) [Late19thC. Alteration of YES, possibly on the model of *nope*.]

YER *abbr.* BANKING yearly effective rate

yerba /yáirbə, yúr-/, **yerba maté** *n.* = **maté** [Early 19thC. From Spanish 'herb'.]

Yerevan /yérrə vaán/ capital and largest city of Armenia, on the River Hrazdan, in the west of the country. Population: 1,202,000 (1990).

Yerkish /yúrkish/ *n.* an artificial language of visual symbols created for experimental communication between chimpanzees and humans [Late 20thC. Named in honour of the US primatologist Robert Meams YERKES (1876–1956).]

yersinia /yur sínni ə/ *n.* any of several gram-negative bacteria, many of which cause disease in humans and animals. One of these bacteria is a common cause of gastric infections while another causes bubonic plague. Genus: *Yersinia.* [Mid-20thC. From modern Latin, genus name, from the name of the Swiss-born French bacteriologist A. E. J. *Yersin* (1863–1943).]

yersiniosis /yur sínni óssiss/ *n.* a condition, mainly found in children and young adults, caused by a bacterium and characterized by intestinal pain and symptoms that resemble appendicitis [Late 20thC. Formed from YERSINIA, the bacterium that causes the disease.]

yes /yess/ *adv.* **1.** ASSENT INDICATOR used especially in speech to indicate assent, agreement, or affirmation ○ *'Do you mean it's all over?' 'Yes, I suppose I do'.* ○ *97 per cent of respondents answered yes, a ringing endorsement of one of his central beliefs.* **2.** INDICATES CONTRADICTION used to indicate contradiction in response to a negative proposition ○ *'He won't believe you'. 'Oh yes he will'.* **3.** MARK OF ATTENTION used to indicate that sb is ready to give his or her attention to sb who has asked for it ○ *'Doctor?' 'Yes?'* **4.** ACCEPTANCE used to accept an offer or a request ○ *'Would you like some tea?' 'Yes, please'.* ■ *n.* **1. yes** (*plural* **yeses** *or* **yesses**) AFFIRMATIVE RESPONSE an affirmative response to a question ○ *Was that a yes or a no?* **2.** AFFIRMATIVE VOTER sb who votes in the affirmative ○ *The yeses have 65 per cent and the noes 35 per cent, so the motion is carried.* [Old English *gēse*, from *gēa* (see YEA) + *sīe* 'may it be (so)', a form of the verb *to be*]

yeshiva /yə sheévə/ (*plural* **-vas** *or* **-vot** /-vot/ *or* **-voth**), **yeshivah** (*plural* **-vahs** *or* **-vot** *or* **-voth**) *n.* a seminary for orthodox Jewish, usually unmarried, men where they study the primary source of Jewish law, the Talmud [Mid-19thC. From Hebrew *yĕšīḇāh*, from *yāšaḇ* 'to sit'.]

yes man, yes-man *n.* sb who agrees enthusiastically with the ideas and views of a superior without offering any criticism

yes/no question *n.* a question that can be answered with 'yes' or 'no' and that in English begins with an actual or implied verb

yessir /yéssər/, **yessiree** /yés surreé/ *interj.* used, often ironically or humorously, to express submissive assent or obedience (*informal*) [Early 20thC. Representing a casual pronunciation of *yes, sir.*]

yester /yéstər/ *adj.* happening or belonging to yesterday (*archaic; usually used in combination*) ○ *yesteryear* [Late 16thC. Backformation for *yesterday.*]

yester- *prefix.* used to refer to a time in the past denoted by the suffix ○ *yestermorning* [Old English *geostran*]

yesterday /yéstərday, -di/ *n.* **1.** DAY BEFORE TODAY the day before this one **2.** PAST a time in the past ■ *adv.* **1.** ON THE PREVIOUS DAY on the day before today **2.** IN THE PAST at a time in the past [Old English *geostran dæg*]

yesterevening /yéstər eevning/ *adv.* DURING YESTERDAY EVENING yesterday in the evening (*archaic or literary*) ■ *n.* YESTERDAY'S EVENING the evening of yesterday (*archaic or literary*)

yestermorning /yéstər mawrning/ *adv.* DURING YESTERDAY MORNING yesterday in the morning (*archaic or literary*) ■ *n.* YESTERDAY'S MORNING the morning of yesterday (*archaic or literary*)

yesternight /yéstər nīt/ *adv.* DURING LAST NIGHT yesterday in the night (*archaic or literary*) ■ *n.* LAST NIGHT the night of yesterday (*archaic or literary*) [Old English *gystran niht*]

yesteryear /yéstər yeer, -yur/ *n.* **1.** THE PAST the not very recent past **2.** LAST YEAR the year before this one [Late 19thC. Coined by the poet Dante Gabriel ROSSETTI to translate French *antan.*]

yet /yet/ *adv.* **1.** SO FAR so far, or up to now (*often used with a negative or interrogative*) ○ *The information has not yet been analysed.* **2.** NOW now, as opposed to later (*often used with a negative*) ○ *I can't come over just yet.* **3.** EVEN even or still (*often used with a comparative*) ○ *He spurred her on to yet greater efforts.* **4.** IN SPITE OF EVERYTHING used to indicate that it is still possible that sth will happen despite everything ○ *We'll solve this problem yet.* **5.** UP TO NOW used with superlatives to indicate that sth is, e.g., the best, worst, or most impressive up to now (*often used after a superlative*) ○ *This study is the largest yet – a 14-year study of 87,000 nurses.* **6.** FOR LONGER used to indicate that sth will go on happening for a specified time ○ *It would take hours yet for the space telescope photos to arrive on Earth and be processed.* **7.** NEVER UP TO NOW used to indicate that sb has not done sth up to now ○ *The largest hotel in the town, the Queen's Head, has yet to welcome a member of the royal family.* ■ *conj.* NEVERTHELESS however or nevertheless ○ *They can't find the cause, yet the researchers agree that one must be found.* [Old English *gīet*, of uncertain origin] ◇ **as yet** up to now or up to the time being spoken about (*often used with a negative*)

WORD KEY: USAGE

Did she go yet? In the simple past tense ***yet*** is not used in this way even in informal British English; the perfect tense (*Has she gone yet?*) is used. In some meanings, ***yet*** and *still* are largely interchangeable: *This has still to be decided* or *This has yet to be decided.*

yeti /yétti/ (*plural* **-tis**) *n.* a mysterious hairy humanoid animal said to live in the Himalayas [Mid-20thC. Origin uncertain: perhaps from Tibetan *yeh-teh* 'small manlike animal', or an alteration of Tibetan *miti*, from *mi* 'person' + *ti* 'kind of animal'.]

Yevtushenko /yévtə shéngkō/, **Yevgeny Aleksandrovich** (*b.* 1933) Russian poet. His works such as *Zima Junction* (1956) and *Babi Yar* (1961) were critical of the post-Stalinist U.S.S.R., and were widely read in the Soviet Union and the West, although officially condemned by Soviet authorities.

Yew

yew /yoo/ *n.* **1.** EVERGREEN TREE an evergreen tree or shrub that has flat dark green needles and red cones that resemble berries. Most parts of the tree are considered poisonous. Genus: *Taxus.* **2.** YEW WOOD the fine-grained wood of the yew **3.** YEW BOW an archer's bow made from yew [Old English *īw*]

Yezidi /yézzidi/ *n.* a member of a Kurdish religious group, founded by an Islamic mystic in the 12th century but incorporating many elements of Iranian myth and tradition. The group has been branded as heretical by orthodox Muslims and has been the object of intense persecution. [Early 19thC. Origin unknown.] —**Yezidism** *n.*

Y-fronts *tdmk.* a trademark for men's or boys' underpants that have an opening at the front with seams in the shape of an inverted Y

Yggdrasil /ígdrə sil/, **Ygdrasil** *n.* in Norse mythology, the great ash tree that overshadows the world, binding together earth, heaven, and hell [From Old Norse]

YHA *abbr.* Youth Hostels Association

YHWH, YHVH, JHVH, JHWH *n.* the transliteration of the four letters (**Tetragrammaton**) representing the name of God in the Bible. This transliteration was only ever pronounced by the high priest in the Temple. ◊ **Adonai, Yahweh**

Yi /yee/ *n.* a Korean dynasty that ruled Korea from 1392, following a period of Mongol invasions, until 1910, and that restored aristocratic dominance and Chinese influence

yid /yid/ *n.* a highly offensive term referring to a Jewish person (*taboo offensive*) [Late 19thC. Via Yiddish from Middle High German *jüde* 'Jew', ultimately from Latin *Judaeus* (see JEW).]

Yiddish /yíddish/ *n.* LANG a language written in Hebrew script and spoken by Jewish people in many European countries, in Israel, and in some parts of North and South America. Mainly derived from medieval German dialect, it includes many elements from Hebrew, Aramaic, and other languages, especially Slavonic languages. [Late 19thC. From Yiddish *yidish (daytsh)*, literally 'Jewish (German)', from Middle High German *jüdisch diutsch*, from *jüde* 'Jewish person', ultimately from Latin *Judaeus.*] —**Yiddish** *adj.*

yield /yeeld/ *v.* (**yields, yielding, yielded**) **1.** *vt.* AGRIC PRODUCE STH to produce sth naturally or as a result of cultivation ○ *The field yields a good crop.* **2.** *vt.* GIVE STH AS RESULT to produce sth as the result of work, activity, or calculation ○ *The research has yielded some interesting results.* **3.** *vt.* FIN GIVE PROFIT to gain an amount as a return on an investment ○ *bonds that yield 9 per cent* **4.** *vi.* GIVE WAY to give way or give up further resistance ○ *She refused to yield despite our pleas.* **5.** *vt.* GIVE STH UP TO SB to give sth up to sb else or concede it ○ *He eventually yielded control of the company to his daughter.* **6.** *vi.* GIVE WAY TO PRESSURE to move or bend under pressure or with the application of force ○ *The window was painted shut and wouldn't yield.* **7.** *vi.* SURRENDER to admit defeat and surrender **8.** *vi.* BE REPLACED BY STH to be replaced by sth else ○ *Older houses and gardens were gradually yielding to modern purpose-built flats.* **9.** *vi.* US TRANSP LET ANOTHER PASS to slow down or stop in order to let another vehicle pass ○ *yield to traffic on the right* ■ *n.* **1.** AGRIC AMOUNT PRODUCED the amount of sth, especially a crop, produced by cultivation or labour ○ *Yields per acre were slightly lower than last year.* **2.** FIN RETURN ON INVESTMENT a part of a return on investment coming from the receipt of interest or dividends ○ *The yield on the account was disappointing.* **3.** CHEM PRODUCT FROM A CHEMICAL REACTION the quantity of product resulting from a chemical reaction or process, often expressed as a percentage of the amount that is theoretically obtainable **4.** PHYS EXPLOSIVE FORCE the amount of energy released in a nuclear explosion expressed as the amount of TNT that would have the same explosive force [Old English *geldan* 'to pay'. Ultimately from a prehistoric Germanic base meaning 'to pay', which is also the ancestor of English *guild.*] —**yieldability** /yeéldə bílləti/ *n.* —**yieldable** /yeéldəb'l/ *adj.* —**yielder** *n.*

WORD KEY: SYNONYMS

yield, capitulate, submit, succumb, surrender

CORE MEANING: to give way

yield to give way to sth such as force, pressure, entreaty, or persuasion; **capitulate** to cease to resist a superior force, especially one that seems invincible, sometimes without having offered much active opposition; **submit**

to accept sb else's authority or will, especially reluctantly or under pressure; **succumb** to give in to sth due to weakness or a failure to offer much active opposition; **surrender** to give way to the power of another and stop offering resistance, usually after active opposition.

yield up *vt.* to reveal sth formerly hidden or secret

yielding /yeélding/ *adj.* **1.** SOFT AND BENDING inclined to give or bend under pressure **2.** COMPLIANT tending to obey others **3.** PRODUCING productive of a good or bad yield or crop —**yieldingly** *adv.* —**yieldingness** *n.*

yikes /yīks/ *interj.* used when suddenly startled (*informal*) [Late 20thC. Origin uncertain: perhaps an alteration of YOICKS.]

yin /yin/ *n.* the principle of darkness, negativity, and femininity in Chinese philosophy that is the counterpart to yang. The dual, opposite, and complementary principles of yin and yang are thought to exist in varying proportions in all things. ◊ **yang** [Late 17thC. From Chinese *yīn* 'shade, feminine, moon'.]

Yinglish /yíng glish/ *n.* LANG a type of English with a heavy overlay of Yiddish words and syntax, as spoken by early Jewish immigrants to the United States [Mid-20thC. Blend of YIDDISH and ENGLISH.] —**Yinglish** *adj.*

yip /yip/ *vi.* (**yips, yipping, yipped**) BARK to give a high-pitched bark ■ *n.* SHRILL BARK a high-pitched bark [15thC. Originally 'to cheep', used of birds; ultimately an imitation of the sound.]

yipe /yīp/ *interj.* US used to express fear or alarm (*informal*) [Mid-20thC. Origin uncertain.]

yippee *interj.* used to express joy and excitement (*usually used by or to children*) [Early 20thC. A natural exclamation.]

yips /yips/ *npl.* nervousness that impairs the performance of a sportsman or sportswoman, especially a golfer [Mid-20thC. Origin unknown.]

Yissus /yíssəss/ *interj.* S Africa used to express astonishment, disbelief, or annoyance [From the Afrikaans pronunciation of *Jesus*]

Yizkor /yíz kawr/ *n.* a memorial prayer for deceased relatives recited in synagogue on Festivals and Yom Kippur [Mid-20thC. From Hebrew *yizkōr*, literally 'may He remember'.]

-yl *suffix.* a group of atoms forming a radical ○ *carbonyl* [Via French *-yle* from Greek *hulē* 'wood, organic matter']

ylang-ylang /eé lang eé lang/, **ilang-ilang** *n.* a tropical tree native to Asia and North Australia with flowers that yield a fragrant oil used in perfumery. Latin name: *Cananga odorata*. [Late 19thC. From Tagalog *ilang-ilang*.]

ylem /fíləm/ *n.* hypothetical matter that, according to the big bang theory of the origin of the universe, was the substance from which the chemical elements were formed. ◊ **big bang theory** [Mid-20thC. Via medieval Latin *hylem* 'universal matter' from, ultimately Greek *hulē* 'wood, matter'.]

Y-level *n.* a rotatable level mounted on a Y-shaped frame, used in surveying

YMCA *abbr.* Young Men's Christian Association ■ *n.* (*plural* **YMCAs**) YMCA CENTRE a building or other centre where social, sports, or educational facilities are provided by the YMCA for its members

YMHA (*plural* **YMHAs**) *abbr.* Young Men's Hebrew Association

Ymir /eé meer/ *n.* the forefather of all the giants of Norse mythology. Ymir was killed by Odin and his brothers, and the world was formed from his body, the heavens from his skull, and the water from his blood.

yo /yō/ *interj.* used as a greeting or to get sb's attention [15thC. Natural exclamation.]

yob /yob/ *n.* a young hooligan (*informal*) [Mid-19thC. Backward spelling of BOY.] —**yobbery** *n.* —**yobbish** *adj.*

YOB *abbr.* year of birth

yobbo /yóbbō/ (*plural* **-bos**) *n.* = **yob** (*informal*) [Early 20thC. Formed from YOB.]

yod /yod/, **yodh** *n.* the tenth letter of the Hebrew

alphabet, represented in the English alphabet as 'y' or 'j'. See table at **alphabet**

yodel /yốd'l/, **yodle** *vi.* (**-dels** /s/, **-delling, -delled; -dles, -dling, -dled**) SING HIGH to sing, changing rapidly between a normal and falsetto voice. It is a feature of Alpine folk music and of some US country and western music. ■ *n.* YODELLING SONG a song or passage that features yodelling [Early 19thC. From German *jodeln*, literally 'to utter JO'; ultimately an imitation of the sound.] —**yodeller** *n.*

yodh *n.* = **yod**

yodle *vi., n.* = **yodel**

Yoga: Half spinal twist position

Tony Arruza/Corbis

yoga /yốgə/ *n.* **1.** HINDU DISCIPLINE any of a group of related Hindu disciplines that promote the unity of the individual with a supreme being through a system of postures and rituals **2.** SYSTEM OF EXERCISE a system or set of breathing exercises and postures derived from or based on Hindu yoga [Late 18thC. From Sanskrit *yogaḥ*, literally 'union'. Ultimately from an Indo-European word meaning 'to join', which is also the ancestor of English *yoke, join,* and *zygo-*.]

yogh /yog/ *n.* a letter ʒ used in Middle English, usually represented in modern English as 'gh' or 'y' [13thC. Origin uncertain.]

yoghurt /yóggərt, yốgərt/, **yogurt, yoghourt** *n.* milk fermented by bacteria to give a tangy or slightly sour flavour and a lightly set or thick and creamy consistency. It is sometimes sweetened and flavoured, usually with fruit. [Early 17thC. From Turkish *yoğurt*.]

yogi /yốgi/ (*plural* **-gis**), **yogin** /yốgin/ *n.* **1.** YOGA PRACTITIONER sb who practises yoga **2.** STUDENT OF GURU sb who studies under a guru or other spiritual teacher of Indian religion [Early 17thC. From Sanskrit *yogī*, from *yogaḥ* 'yoga'.]

yogurt *n.* = **yoghurt**

Yogyakarta /yóggyə kaártə/ *city* in southwestern Indonesia, on the island of Java. Population: 412,059 (1990).

yo-heave-ho *interj.* used formerly by sailors as a rhythmic accompaniment to hauling work

yoicks /yoyks/ *interj.* used to encourage hounds in a foxhunt [Mid-18thC. Origin uncertain.]

Yoke

yoke /yōk/ *n.* **1.** ANIMAL HARNESS a wooden frame for harnessing two draught animals **2.** FRAME FOR CARRYING LOADS a frame designed to fit across sb's shoulders with balanced loads suspended at either end **3.** RESTRICTIVE BURDEN sth that is oppressive and restrictive **4.** CLOTHES FITTED PART OF A GARMENT the fitted part of a garment, usually around the shoulders or waist, from which an unfitted part is suspended **5.**

BOND a bond or tie that keeps people together ○ *the yoke of marriage* **6.** *Ireland, N Ireland* WHATSIT OR THINGUMABOB any gadget or implement whose proper name is not known ○ *I need a yoke to fix this screw in.* **7.** HIST CROSSED SPEARS an archway made of crossed spears under which defeated enemies of the ancient Romans were forced to march **8.** JOINED ANIMALS two animals joined by a yoke **9.** NAUT RUDDER CROSSBAR a crossbar fitted to the top of a rudder and connected to the front of a boat by ropes or cables for steering **10.** ELECTRON ENG CATHODE RAY DEVICE a device fitted to the neck of a cathode ray tube to control the scanning motion of the electron beam **11.** RECORDING EQUIPMENT FOR MULTI-TRACK RECORDING equipment for recording or reproducing sounds or music on more than one track simultaneously, by joining together two or more magnetic recording heads **12.** AIR AIRCRAFT PART the handle of the steering mechanism for an aeroplane's ailerons ■ *vt.* (**yokes, yoking, yoked**) **1.** FIT ANIMALS WITH A YOKE to put a yoke on two draught animals **2.** CONNECT AN ANIMAL TO A VEHICLE to connect a draught animal to a plough or vehicle **3.** LINK THINGS TOGETHER to join or link two things forcibly or surprisingly ○ *Foxhunters were yoked together with farmers on the issue.* [Old English *geoc.* Ultimately from an Indo-European word meaning 'to join', which is also the ancestor of English *join, zygo-,* and *yoga.*]

yokel /yốk'l/ *n.* an offensive term for a country dweller, regarded as lacking sophistication, education, or other qualities thought typical of city dwellers (*insult offensive*) [Early 19thC. Origin uncertain: perhaps from a dialect word meaning 'green woodpecker, yellowhammer'.] —**yokelish** *adj.*

Yokohama /yốkō haámə/ *capital city* and port of Kanagawa Prefecture, in southeastern Honshu Island, Japan. Population: 3,265,000 (1994).

yolk /yōk/ *n.* **1.** YELLOW OF EGG the round yellow portion of a bird's or reptile's egg, containing protein and fats that provide nourishment for the developing young. Yolks are virtually absent from the eggs of mammals, whose embryos absorb nutrients from the mother. **2.** OILY SUBSTANCE IN WOOL a greasy substance from the skin of sheep that collects in wool [Old English *geol(o)ca*, from *geolu* (see YELLOW)] —**yolky** *adj.*

yolk sac *n.* a thin membrane surrounding the embryo in birds, fish, reptiles, and mammals. In birds, fish, and reptiles, it encloses the yolk.

yolk stalk *n.* a narrow tube or duct attaching the yolk sac to an embryo and allowing the passage of yolk to the embryo's elementary digestive tract

Yom Kippur /yom kíppər, -ki poór/ *n.* the holiest day of the Jewish year, falling on the tenth day of Tshiri, in September or October, on which Jewish people fast and say prayers of penitence [From Hebrew *Yōm Kippūr* 'day of atonement']

yomp /yomp/ (**yomps, yomping, yomped**) *vi.* to walk while heavily laden or over difficult terrain (*informal*) [Late 20thC. Origin unknown.]

yom tov /yóm tóv, yómtəv/ (*plural* **yamim tovim** /yaa meém tŏ veém/) *n.* JUDAISM a Jewish term for a religious festival [Directly and via Yiddish *yontef* from Hebrew *yōm ṭōb*, literally 'good day']

yon /yon/ *adv.* YONDER yonder, over there (*regional*) ■ *det. Scotland N England* THAT OR THOSE that or those over there [Partly a shortening of YONDER, and partly from Old English *geon* 'that one']

■ **WORD KEY: REGIONAL NOTE** ■

Yon and *yonder* were once widely used in English. There was thus a tripartite system where *this book* meant 'the book close to the speaker', *that book* meant 'the one close to the listener', and *yon book* meant 'the one close to neither speaker nor listener'. Some dialect speakers linked these words even more closely by combining both and pronouncing **yon** as 'thon' and *yonder* as 'thonder'.

yond /yond/ *adv., det.* yonder, over there (*archaic or literary*) [Old English *geond, geondan* (source of English *beyond*). Ultimately from an Indo-European base meaning 'that one', which is also the ancestor of *yon.*]

yonder /yóndər/ *adv.* OVER THERE over there (*regional*) ■ *det.* THAT that over there (*regional*) [14thC. Formed from YOND.]

yoni /yṓni/ (*plural* **-nis**) *n.* in Hinduism, a re-presentation of the female genitals regarded as a manifestation of the feminine principle [Late 18thC. From Sanskrit *yonih* 'womb', of unknown origin.]

Yonkers /yóngkərz/ city in southeastern New York State, on the Hudson River, north of New York. Population: 190,316 (1996).

yonks /yongks/ *n.* a very long time (*slang*) [Mid-20thC. Origin uncertain.]

yoo-hoo /yoŏ hoŏ/ *interj.* HELLO used to get sb's attention, especially when the speaker is at a distance ■ *vti.* (**yoo-hoos, yoo-hooing, yoo-hooed**) SAY YOO-HOO to say or shout 'yoo-hoo' to attract sb's attention [Early 20thC. Natural exclamation.]

yore /yawr/ *n.* time long past (*literary*) [Old English *geāra*, of uncertain origin: perhaps a variant of *gēara*, literally 'of years', from *gēar* (see YEAR)]

york /yawrk/ (**yorks, yorking, yorked**) *vt.* in cricket, to get a batsman out or to attempt to get a batsman out by bowling a ball so that it pitches immediately under the bat [Late 19thC. Back-formation from *yorker* 'fast ball under the bat', of uncertain origin: probably after the city of YORK, England, because the technique was introduced by players from Yorkshire.]

York[1] /yawrk/ *n.* the branch of the Plantagenet dynasty that ruled England from 1461 to 1485. It was named after its founder, Edward, Duke of York (**Edward IV**).

York[2] /yawrk/ city in Yorkshire, northern England. Originally a Celtic settlement, under the Romans it became an important regional centre. Population: 105,500 (1991).

Yorke Peninsula /yáwrk-/ peninsula in South Australia, situated between the Gulf of St Vincent and the Spencer Gulf

yorker *n.* a ball bowled in cricket so that it pitches on the ground immediately under the bat

yorkie /yáwrki/, **Yorkie** *n.* a Yorkshire Terrier (*informal*) [Early 19thC. Shortening.]

Yorkist /yáwrkist/ *n.* YORK SUPPORTER sb who was loyal to or connected with the House of York that ruled England from 1461 to 1485 ■ *adj.* OF YORK supporting or connected with the House of York

York rite *n.* a masonic ceremony that confers different degrees at different levels of the membership [Late 19thC. Named after the city of YORK in England.]

Yorks. *abbr.* Yorkshire

Yorkshire /yáwrkshər/ former county in northern England, historically divided into East, North, and West Ridings. The largest traditional county in England, in 1974 it was divided into North Yorkshire, South Yorkshire, and West Yorkshire, with some areas becoming parts of Cleveland and Humberside. The last two counties were abolished in 1996, when the districts in them became unitary authorities, and the East Riding of Yorkshire became a county again.

Yorkshire Dales area of wild moorlands divided by fertile valleys in the mid-Pennines, northern England

Yorkshire fog *n.* a common grass of the British Isles that has downy leaves and white or pink flower heads. Latin name: *Holcus lanatus*. [Late 19thC. *Yorkshire* from the plant's origin there; *fog* 'a type of grass'.]

Yorkshire pudding *n.* a flour-based batter that is traditionally cooked in the drippings of roast meat. It was originally served with gravy before roast meat with the intention of satisfying appetites so that a small amount of meat would go a long way. [Mid-18thC. Named after YORKSHIRE.]

Yorkshire terrier *n.* a very small long-haired terrier with a long silky brown and grey coat [Late 19thC. Named after YORKSHIRE, where the breed was developed.]

Yorkton /yáwrktən/ town in Saskatchewan, Canada, northeast of Regina. Population: 17,713 (1996).

Yoruba /yórrŏŏbə/ (*plural* **-ba** *or* **-bas**) *n.* **1.** PEOPLES MEMBER OF WEST AFRICAN PEOPLE a member of a West African people living mostly in Nigeria **2.** LANG YORUBA LANGUAGE a language spoken in southwestern Nigeria, Benin and Togo. It belongs to the Niger-

Yorkshire terrier

Congo language family and is spoken by about 20 million people. **3.** REGION OF CITY-STATES IN NIGERIA a region of city-states that developed in northern Nigeria around AD 1200, notable for the population's animistic religion and their artistic work, in particular wood and bronze pieces [Mid-19thC. From Yoruba.] —**Yoruban** *adj.* —**Yoruban** *adj.*

Yosemite Falls /yə sémməti-, yō-/ waterfall in the Yosemite National Park, California. Consisting of the Upper Yosemite Falls and the Lower Yosemite Falls, it is one of the highest waterfalls in the world, with a total drop of 739 m/2,245 ft.

Yosemite National Park /yō sémməti-/ national park in central California in the Sierra Nevada, established in 1890. It is noted for its giant sequoia trees and waterfalls. Area: 3,079 sq. km/1,189 sq. mi.

you (*stressed*) /yoo/; (*unstressed*) /yŏŏ, yə/ *pron.* **1.** PERSON BEING ADDRESSED refers to the person or people being addressed or written to ○ *I'm fine – how about you?* **2.** PERSON OR PEOPLE UNSPECIFIED refers to an unspecified person or people in general ○ *You have to see it to believe it.* ○ *You mix all the dry ingredients together in a bowl.* **3.** THOSE BEING REFERRED TO used to refer to the person you are talking to, as well as other people of the same type or class (*used before a plural*) ○ *Isn't it time you kids were in bed?* **4.** PERSONALITY OF PERSON ADDRESSED refers to the personality of the person addressed or sth's suitability to express it (*informal*) ○ *Don't buy that suit – it's not really you!* **5.** US YOURSELF yourself (*informal*) ○ *You'll have to get you a job.* [Old English *īow*, from *gē* (see YE)]

—— **WORD KEY: USAGE** ——
See Usage note at **yourself**.

you-all, **y'all** *pron. Southern US* used to address more than one person (*informal*)

you-beaut *adj. Aus* exceptional or outstanding (*informal*) ['Beaut' is a shortening of BEAUTIFUL]

you'd /yood/ *contr.* **1.** you had **2.** you would [Early 17thC. Contraction.]

you'll /yool/ *contr.* **1.** you will **2.** you shall [Late 16thC. Contraction.]

young /yung/ *adj.* **1.** NOT VERY OLD having lived or been in existence a relatively short time **2.** OF YOUTH relating to sb's youth **3.** YOUTHFUL looking or behaving like a young or younger person **4.** FOR YOUNG PEOPLE designed for or appropriate to young people **5.** RECENTLY BEGUN recently begun or in an early stage **6.** GEOL NOT SIGNIFICANTLY ERODED in a relatively early stage of landscape formation and therefore steep and largely uneroded ■ *npl.* **1.** OFFSPRING offspring, especially when still completely dependent on parents **2.** YOUNG PEOPLE young people in general [Old English *geong*. Ultimately from an Indo-European word meaning 'youth, vigor', which is also the ancestor of English *youth* and *juvenile*.] —**youngish** *adj.* —**youngness** *n.*

Young /yung/, **Arthur** (1721–1820) British agriculturist and writer. He is known for his books describing his travels in England, Ireland, and France.

Young, Brigham (1801–77) US religious leader. He succeeded Joseph Smith as the leader of the Church of Jesus Christ of Latter-Day Saints (1844–77). He organized the church members' migration from Illinois to Utah (1845–46), where he founded Salt Lake City.

Young, Cy (1867–1955) US baseball player. He was the first player in major league history to pitch a perfect

game (1904), and an annual award for the best major league pitcher was established in his honour. Real name **Denton True Young**

Young, Nat (*b.* 1947) Australian surfer. He was winner of the world amateur championship (1966), the world pro-am championship (1970), and the world professional longboard championship (1986–87, 1989).

Young, Thomas (1773–1829) British physicist and Egyptologist. He was noted for his work in optics, in particular his discovery of the phenomenon of interference. He helped decipher the Egyptian hieroglyphics on the Rosetta Stone.

young blood *n.* fresh, new, and vigorous ideas or people

young fogy *n.* a young person whose ideas and outlook are old-fashioned and conservative (*disapproving*) [Modelled on FOGY]

young fustic *n.* = fustic *n.* 4

Young Ireland *n.* a movement of Irish nationalists in the 1840s who were prepared to use violence to achieve their ends —**Young Irelander** *n.*

young lady *n.* **1.** YOUNG WOMAN used to refer to or address a girl or young woman, often in annoyance or exasperation **2.** GIRLFRIEND a man's or boy's girlfriend (*dated*)

youngling /yúngling/ *n.* a young person or a young animal [Old English *geongling*]

young man *n.* **1.** BOY used to refer to or address a boy or young man, often in annoyance or exasperation **2.** BOYFRIEND a girl's or woman's boyfriend (*dated*)

young offender *n.* **1.** JUVENILE CRIMINAL in the UK, sb under 18 who has committed a criminal act. US term **youthful offender 2.** *Can* JUVENILE CRIMINAL in Canada, sb between the ages of 12 and 18 who has committed a crime and must be treated according to the terms of the Young Offenders Act, 1984

Young Pretender *n.* ♦ Stuart, Charles Edward

youngster /yúngstər/ *n.* **1.** CHILD a child or young person **2.** YOUNG HORSE a young horse

—— **WORD KEY: SYNONYMS** ——
See Synonyms at **youth**.

Young Turk *n.* **1.** TURKISH NATIONALIST REVOLUTIONARY a member of a liberal pro-democratic Turkish nationalist movement in the early 20th century that brought about a short-lived revolution in 1908 **2.** UPSTART a young person, especially one of a group, who attempts to wrest control of an organization from an older, established, more conservative group

young'un /yúngən/ *n.* an infant or child (*informal*) [Early 20thC. Contraction of *young one*.]

younker /yúngkər/ *n.* (*archaic*) **1.** YOUNG MALE a young man **2.** CHILD a child **3.** YOUNG NOBLE a young nobleman [Early 16thC. From Middle Dutch *jonckher*, from *jonc* 'young' + *hēre* 'lord'.]

your (*stressed*) /yawr, yoor/; (*unstressed*) /yər/ *det.* **1.** BELONGING TO PERSON SPOKEN TO refers to sth that belongs to or relates to an addressee ○ *What's your phone number?* **2.** BELONGING OR RELATING TO SB refers to sth that belongs or relates to an unspecified person or people in general ○ *The house is on your left as you come down the road.* **3.** INDICATES TOPIC refers to sb or sth as an example or topic (*informal*) ○ *Take your Queen, for example.* [Old English *ēower*, from *gē* (see YE)]

Yourcenar /yoŏrsə naar/, **Marguerite** (1903–87) Belgian-

Marguerite Yourcenar

born French and US writer. Many of her works, including *Memoirs of Hadrian* (1951), follow historical themes. Pseudonym of **Marguerite de Crayencour**

you're *(stressed)* /yoor, yawr/; *(unstressed)* /yər/ *contr.* you are [Late 16thC. Contraction.]

yours /yawrz, yoorz/ *pron.* **1.** INDICATES BELONGING refers to sth that belongs or relates to the person or people being addressed ○ *I'm taking my tea through to the sitting-room – shall I take yours as well?* **2. yours, Yours** LETTER ENDING used at the end of letters before sb signs his or her name ○ *Sincerely yours, Marcia Klein* [14thC. Formed from YOUR.] ◇ **Yours sincerely, Yours faithfully, Yours truly** used at the end of a letter before sb signs his or her name ○ *Yours sincerely, John Smith*

yourself /yawr sélf, yoor-, yər-/ *(plural* **-selves** /-sélvz/*) pron.* **1.** SB BEING ADDRESSED refers to the person or people being addressed or written to ○ *Be careful not to hurt yourself.* **2.** MAKING REFERENCE TO SB SPOKEN TO refers emphatically or politely to the person or people being addressed or written to ○ *'Consider', he replied, 'how you yourself really feel about such things.'* **3.** YOUR NORMAL SELF your normal or usual self ○ *You are not yourself tonight.*

— WORD KEY: USAGE —

Grammar: The primary uses of **yourself** are as a reflexive pronoun (*Don't hurt yourself*) and as a reinforcing pronoun (*Can you do it yourself?*). It should not be used as an alternative for *you* in sentences of the type *That's up to you* (not: *That's up to yourself*).

yours truly *pron.* me, myself, or I ○ *Of course, everyone's going to be there except yours truly.*

yous /yooz/, **youse** *pron.* used to address more than one person (*regional nonstandard*) [Late 19thC. Formed from YOU.]

youth /yooth/ *n.* **1.** TIME WHEN SB IS YOUNG the period of human life between childhood and maturity **2.** BEING YOUNG the state of being young **3.** YOUNG PERSON a young person, especially a boy or young man **4.** EARLY STAGE an early stage of sth **5.** GEOL EROSION STAGE the first stage in landscape formation in which fast-flowing streams travel down steep mountain valleys ■ *npl.* YOUNG PEOPLE young people in general [Old English *geoguþ*, from a prehistoric Germanic word]

— WORD KEY: SYNONYMS —

youth, child, kid, teenager, youngster

CORE MEANING: sb who is young

youth a man or boy who is in his teens or early twenties; **child** between birth and the onset of puberty; **kid** an informal word for a child or young person; **teenager** sb between the ages of thirteen and nineteen; **youngster** sb who is young, often, humourously, younger than others mentioned or present.

youth club *n.* a centre that provides organized activities for young people during their leisure time

Youth Court *n.* a provincial court in Canada with jurisdiction over all cases involving offenders under the age of 18

youth custody *n.* in Britain, a custodial sentence of four to eighteen months for an offender aged 15 to 21

Youth Custody Centre *n.* in Britain, a penal institution for young offenders ○ US term **reformatory**

youthful /yooth'f'l/ *adj.* **1.** LIKE YOUTH typical of or possessing youth **2.** VIGOROUS vigorous and energetic **3.** NOT FULLY DEVELOPED in early development and not yet mature **4.** GEOL MILDLY ERODED steep, rugged, relatively uneroded **5.** GEOG NEAR SOURCE used to describe a fast-flowing stream close to its source —**youthfully** *adv.* —**youthfulness** *n.*

youthful offender *n. US* = **young offender**

youth hostel *n.* any of an international group of establishments offering cheap accommodation for travellers, especially young travellers

Youth Training Scheme *n.* in Britain, a former government scheme providing work-related training courses and work experience for jobless school-leavers

you've /yoov/ *contr.* you have [Late 17thC. Contraction.]

yow /yow/ *interj.* used to express pain, surprise, or alarm (*informal*) [Mid-19thC. An imitation of the sound of an involuntary cry.]

yowl /yowl/ *vi.* (**yowls, yowling, yowled**) UTTER A HOWL to cry out mournfully or as an expression of pain ■ *n.* SAD CRY a long mournful wail [12thC. Origin uncertain: probably an imitation of the sound.] —**yowler** *n.*

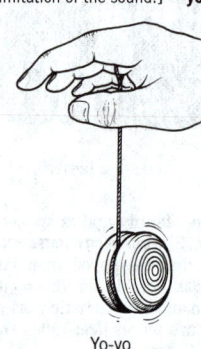

Yo-yo

yo-yo /yṓ yṓ/ *n.* (*plural* **yo-yos**) **1.** TOY WITH STRING WOUND ON SPOOL a toy consisting of a long string wound onto a spool that is dropped and raised repeatedly using the force of gravity and momentum to unwind and rewind the string **2.** FLUCTUATING THING sth that repeatedly goes up and down or fluctuates between one extreme and another **3.** *US, Can* OFFENSIVE TERM an offensive term for sb regarded as silly or unintelligent (*slang insult*) ■ *vi.* (**yo-yos, yo-yoing, yo-yoed**) FLUCTUATE to fluctuate between two extremes or directions [Early 20thC. Earlier a trademark, of uncertain origin: probably the name of a Philippine toy, from a language of the Philippines.]

yo-yo dieting *n.* a situation in which sb repeatedly loses weight through dieting and then regains the weight that he or she has lost

Ypres /eépra/ town in southwestern Belgium, in West Flanders Province, near the border of France. During World War I, the town was the site of several major battles and was almost completely destroyed. Population: 35,100 (1989).

Ypsilanti /ípsə lánti/, **Alexander, Prince** (1792–1828) Greek soldier. In 1821 he led an unsuccessful rebellion against the Turks in the Greek War of Independence.

yr *abbr.* **1.** year **2.** younger **3.** your

Yrs *abbr.* Yours (*used at end of letter*)

YT *abbr.* Yukon Territory

YTD *abbr.* year to date

YTS *abbr.* Youth Training Scheme

ytterbia /i túrbi ə/ *n.* = **ytterbium oxide** [Late 19thC. Named for *Ytterby* (see YTTERBIUM).]

ytterbium /i túrbi əm/ *n.* a soft silvery metal belonging to the lanthanide group of rare earth elements, used to strengthen steel, in laser devices, and in portable X-ray units. Symbol **Yb** [Late 19thC. Formed from earlier *ytterbite*, a mineral containing the element, which was named after *Ytterby*, a Swedish quarry where it was found.] —**ytterbic** *adj.*

ytterbium oxide *n.* a colourless oxide of ytterbium used in certain alloys and ceramics. Formula: Yb_2O_3.

yttria /íttri ə/ *n.* = **yttrium oxide** [Early 19thC. Named after *Ytterby*, a Swedish quarry, because a mineral (gadolinite) was found there from which the compound was obtained.]

yttrium /íttri əm/ *n.* a silvery grey metallic element occurring in many uranium and rare-earth ores, used in superconducting alloys and in permanent magnets. Symbol **Y** [Early 19thC. Formed from YTTRIA.] —**yttric** *adj.*

yttrium metal *n.* a metal in the group that includes yttrium and related rare earth elements such as holmium, erbium, thulium, ytterbium, and lutetium

yttrium oxide *n.* a yellowish powder with several industrial applications, notably in glass, ceramics, lasers, and microwave components. Formula: Y_2O_3.

YU *abbr.* Yugoslavia (*international vehicle registration*)

yuan /yoo án/ (*plural* **-an**) *n.* **1.** UNIT OF CHINESE CURRENCY the main unit of currency in China, worth 10 jiao. See table at **currency 2.** NOTE WORTH ONE YUAN a note worth one yuan [Early 20thC. From Chinese *yuán*, literally 'round' (source of English *yen*).]

Yucatán /yóōkə taán/ peninsula in Central America consisting of three Mexican states, Belize, and part of northern Guatemala. Area: 181,300 sq. km/70,000 sq. mi.

yucca /yúkə/ *n.* an evergreen plant native to the southwestern United States and Mexico but widely grown for its sharp lance-shaped leaves and clusters of white flowers that grow in vertical spikes. Genus: *Yucca.* [Mid-16thC. Via Spanish *yuca* from Taino.]

yuck /yuk/, **yuk** *interj.* used to express disgust or revulsion (*informal*) [Mid-20thC. An imitation of the sound of vomiting.]

yucky /yúki/ (**-ier, -iest**), **yukky** (**-kier, -kiest**) *adj.* disgusting or unpleasant (*informal*) —**yuckiness** *n.*

Yug. *abbr.* Yugoslavia

yuga /yóōgə/ *n.* in Hinduism, any one of the four stages in each cycle of history, each worse than the one before [Late 18thC. From Sanskrit *yugam* 'yoke, era'.]

Yugo. *abbr.* Yugoslavia

Yugoslavia

Yugoslavia /yóōgō slaávi ə/ republic in the Balkans, southeastern Europe, consisting of Serbia and Montenegro, two of the six republics that made up the former Federal People's Republic of Yugoslavia. Language: Serbo-Croat. Currency: Yugoslav new dinar. Capital: Belgrade. Population: 10,574,000 (1996). Area: 102,173 sq. km/39,449 sq. mi. Official name **Federal Republic of Yugoslavia** —**Yugoslav** /yóōgō slaav/ *n., adj.*

yuk *interj.* = **yuck**

yukky *adj.* = **yucky**

Yukon /yóōk on/ river in North America, flowing through Canada and Alaska and into the Bering Sea. Length: 3,185 km/1,979 mi.

Yukon Territory

Yukon Territory /yóōk on térritəri/ territory in northwestern Canada. It was the site of the Klondike gold rush between 1896 and 1899. Capital: Whitehorse. Population: 30,766 (1996). Area: 483,450 sq. km/186,660 sq. mi.

Yukon Time *n.* the time observed in the Yukon Territory and in a section of more or less equivalent longitude extending southwards from there, being nine hours behind Universal Coordinated Time

yulan /yŏŏ lan/ *n.* a deciduous spreading tree or shrub of the magnolia family, native to China, that has masses of fragrant white cup-shaped flowers that appear in spring before the leaves. Latin name: *Magnolia denudata.* [Early 19thC. From Chinese *yùlán*, literally 'jade orchid'.]

Yule /yool/, **yule** *n.* Christmas day or the Christmas season (*archaic literary*) [Old English *gēol* 'mid-winter festival, Christmas', of prehistoric Germanic origin]

yule log *n.* a large log traditionally placed on the hearth fire on Christmas eve

Yuletide /yŏŏl tīd/ *n.* the Christmas season

Yuma /yŏŏmə/ *n.* PEOPLES a member of a Native North American people of southwestern Arizona and neighbouring areas [Early 19thC. From Pima *yumī*.] —**Yuma** *adj.*

Yuman /yŏŏmən/ *n.* LANG a family of languages spoken in the southwestern US and in northern Mexico. Yuman languages are spoken by about 4,000 people. [Late 19thC. Formed from YUMA.] —**Yuman** *adj.*

yummy /yúmmi/ (**-mier, -miest**) *adj.* very appealing to taste or smell [Late 19thC. Formed from *yum*, an imitation of the sound of smacking the lips.] —**yumminess** *n.*

Yunnan /yoo nán/ province in southern China, on the southwestern border of the country. Capital: Kunming. Population: 39,390,000 (1994). Area: 390,000 sq. km/150,600 sq. mi.

Yün Shoup'ing /yŭn shō píng/ (1633–90) Chinese artist. He is known for his landscapes and flower paintings.

yup /yup/ *adv.* yes (*informal*) [Early 20thC. Representing a casual pronunciation of YES.]

Yupik /yŏŏpik/ (*plural* **-pik** *or* **-piks**) *n.* **1.** PEOPLES **INUIT PEOPLE** an Inuit people of Western Alaska and parts of coastal Siberia **2.** LANG **YUPIK LANGUAGE GROUP** the group of languages spoken by the Yupik people [Mid-20thC. From Alaskan Yupik *Yup'ik*, literally 'real person'.] —**Yupik** *adj.*

yuppie /yúppi/ *n.* a young educated city-dwelling professional, especially when regarded as materialistic [Late 20thC. Coined from *y(oung) u(rban) p(rofessional)*, on the model of HIPPIE.]

yuppie flu, **yuppie disease** *n.* ME (*informal*)

yuppify /yúppi fī/ (**-fies, -fying, -fied**) *vt.* to cause an area to be increasingly populated by young educated city-dwelling professionals or to modify sth with the values ascribed to yuppies —**yuppification** /yúppifi káysh'n/ *n.*

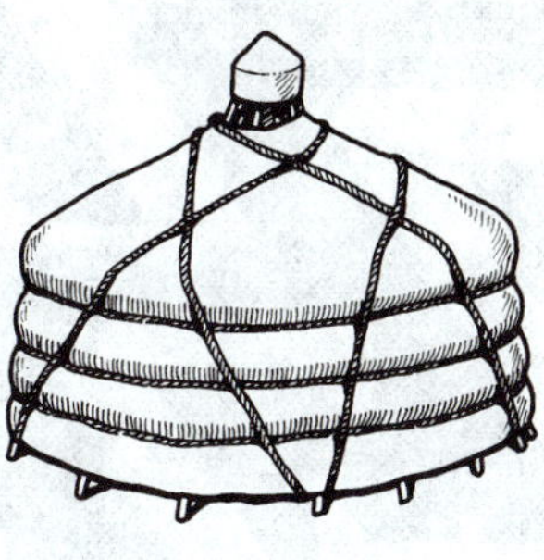

Yurt

yurt /yurt/ *n.* a collapsible circular tent of skins stretched over a pole frame, used by Central Asian nomadic peoples [Late 18thC. Via Russian *yurta* from, ultimately, Turkic *jurt*.]

YV *abbr.* Venezuela (*international vehicle registration*)

YWCA *abbr.* Young Women's Christian Association ■ *n.* **YWCA CENTRE** a building or other centre where social, sports, or educational facilities are provided by the YWCA for its members

YWHA *abbr.* Young Women's Hebrew Association

z¹ /zed/, **Z** *n.* (*plural* **z's**; *plural* **Z's** *or* **Zs**) **1. 26TH LETTER OF ENGLISH ALPHABET** the 26th and final letter of the modern English alphabet **2. SOUND CORRESPONDING TO LETTER 'Z'** the speech sound that corresponds to the letter 'Z' **3. LETTER 'Z' WRITTEN** a written representation of the letter 'Z' **4. STH Z-SHAPED** sth shaped like a 'Z' ■ **z's** *npl.* **SLEEP** sleep, from the traditional transcription of the sound of snoring (*informal*)

───── **WORD KEY: REGIONAL NOTE** ─────
Words beginning with **z** are rare in the dialects. Indeed, the letter is often pronounced 'a-zed', and words such as *zip* and *zoo* are often pronounced 'azip' and 'azoo' (*I broke my azip going to the azoo.*). The exception to this generalization is southwest England, where we find *zart* used as an oath, and *zawster* and *zichel* used for 'seamstress' and 'suchlike'.
─────────────────────────────

z² *symbol.* **1.** MONEY zaire **2.** MATH a Cartesian co-ordinate along the z-axis **3.** MATH an algebraic variable **4.** zepto-

Z¹, z. *abbr.* **1.** GEOG zone **2.** CARS Zambia (*international vehicle registration*)

Z², z. *symbol.* **1.** PHYS impedance **2.** CHEM atomic number **3.** zetta-

ZA *abbr.* South Africa (*international vehicle registration*)

Zaanstad /zaan shtát/ city in North Holland Province, western Netherlands. Population: 133,817 (1996).

zabaglione /zább'l yóni, zábba lyóni/ *n.* a dessert made of egg yolks, sugar, and Marsala wine beaten over hot water until pale and foamy. It is served hot with sponge finger biscuits. [Late 19thC. From Italian, variant of *zabaione*, of uncertain origin.]

Zacynthus /zə sínthəss, -kínth-/ the most southerly of the Ionian Islands, in southwestern Greece. Population: 30,014. Area: 401 sq. km/155 sq. mi.

zaddik *n.* = tzaddik

zaffer /záffər/, **zaffre** *n.* an impure form of cobalt oxide that is added to glass and ceramics to make them blue [Mid-17thC. Directly or via Italian *zaffera* from French *safre*, of uncertain origin.]

zaftig /záftig/, **zoftig** /zóftig/ *adj.* with a full-figured body [Mid-20thC. Via Yiddish from Middle High German *saftec* 'juicy', from *saft* 'juice'.]

zag /zag/ *n.* **OPPOSITE DIRECTION TO ZIG** a direction or segment of a course running opposite to a zig ■ *vi.* (**zags, zagging, zagged**) **TURN ABRUPTLY** to change direction quickly [Late 18thC. From ZIGZAG.]

Zagreb /záa greb/ capital city of Croatia, situated in the north of the country, approximately 25 km/15 mi. from the border with Slovenia. Population: 726,770 (1991).

Zagros Mountains /zág ross/ mountain range in southwestern Iran, extending from the borders with Turkey and Azerbaijan in the north to the Persian Gulf in the south. The highest peak is Zard Kuh, 4,548 m/14,921 ft. Length: 1,600 km/1,000 mi.

Zaharias /zə háiriee əss, -hárriee-/, **Babe Didrikson** (1913–56) US athlete. She excelled in basketball, swimming, athletics, and golf. Born **Mildred Didrikson**

Zaharoff /zə khaárəf/, **Sir Basil** (1849–1936) Turkish-born French arms dealer. He was an Allied agent during World War I, and established chairs at a number of major European universities. Born **Zacharias Basileor Zaharoff**

Babe Didrikson Zaharias

zaibatsu /zí bat soó/ (*plural* -**su**) *n.* a large industrial combine created in Japan in the 1890s, usually by a single family, as part of the process of industrialization [Mid-20thC. From Japanese, from *zai* 'wealth' + *batsu* 'clique'.]

zaikai /zī kí'/ *n.* the business and financial community of Japan [Mid-20thC. From Japanese, from *zai* 'wealth' + *kai* 'world'.]

zaïre /zaa ee'r/ (*plural* -**ïre** *or* -**ïres**) *n.* **1. UNIT OF CONGOLESE CURRENCY** the main unit of currency in the Democratic Republic of Congo, worth 100 makuta **2. NOTE WORTH ONE ZAÏRE** a note worth one zaïre [Mid-20thC. Named for *Zaire*, local name of the Congo River.]

Zaire /zī ee'r, zaa-/ **1.** former name for **Democratic Republic of Congo** (1971–97) **2.** former name for **River Congo**

Zairean /zī ee'rən/ *adj.* PEOPLES relating to Zaire, now the Democratic Republic of Congo, or its people or culture

zakat /zə kaát/ *n.* a tax that goes to charity, obligatory for all Muslims, set traditionally at 2.5 per cent of sb's annual income and capital [Early 19thC. Via Persian and Urdu *zakā(t)* or Turkish *zekât* from Arabic *zakā(t)* 'almsgiving'.]

zakuski /zə koóski/, **zakuska** /zə koóskə/ *npl.* a variety of blinis and breads with savoury toppings, especially caviare and other accompanying titbits, served in Russia with vodka. Traditionally, it is an alternative to the first course of a meal but sometimes it provides a pre-theatre supper, followed by the main meal after the show. [Late 19thC. From Russian, plural of *zakuska* 'hors d'oeuvre'.]

Zambezi /zam beézi/ river in southern Africa, flowing through Zambia, Angola, Zimbabwe, and Mozambique, and into the Indian Ocean. Length: 3,540 km/2,200 mi.

Zambia /zámbi ə/ republic in south-central Africa. It became independent from the United Kingdom in 1964. Language: English. Currency: kwacha. Capital: Lusaka. Population: 9,715,000 (1996). Area: 752,614 sq. km/290,586 sq. mi. Official name **Republic of Zambia** —**Zambian** /zámbi ən/ *n., adj.*

Zamboni /zam bóni/ *tdmk.* US, Can a trademark for a machine that resurfaces the ice on hockey and skating rinks

zamia /záymi ə/ *n.* a small tropical tree (**cycad**) that looks like a palm tree, with a short thick trunk, spiky leaves, and upright woody cones that contain seeds. It is a modern representative of a group of trees that is largely extinct. Genus: *Zamia*. [Early

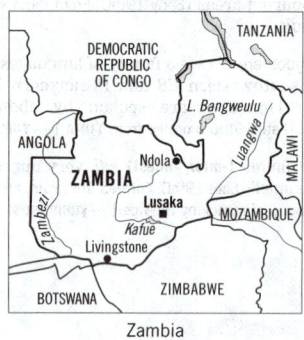
Zambia

19thC. Via modern Latin, genus name, ultimately from a misreading of Latin *azaniae* 'pine cones'.]

zamindar /zə meen daár/, **zemindar**, **jamindar** *n.* **1. TAX COLLECTOR IN MOGUL INDIA** a collector of property taxes in Mogul India **2. TAXPAYER IN BRITISH COLONIAL INDIA** a landlord in British colonial India liable for tax on his holdings **3. LANDOWNER IN INDIA OR PAKISTAN** sb who has traditionally owned land in India or Pakistan [Late 17thC. Via Urdu from Persian *zamīndār*, from *zamīn* 'land' + *dār* 'holder'.]

zamindari /zə meen daári/ (*plural* -**is**), **zemindary** (*plural* -**ies**), **jamindari** (*plural* -**is**) *n.* the system of traditional land ownership in India or Pakistan, or the area of land owned [Mid-18thC. Via Urdu from Persian *zamīndārī*, from *zamīndār* (see ZAMINDAR).]

zanana /zə naánə/ *n.* **1. WOMEN'S QUARTERS IN TRAINS** in southern Asia, an area reserved for women in some trains and waiting rooms in railway stations **2.** = **zenana** [Mid-18thC. From Persian and Urdu *zanānah*, from *zan* 'woman' Ultimately from the Indo-European word for 'woman' that is also the ancestor of English *queen*, *gyno-*, and *banshee*.]

zander /zándər/ (*plural* -**der** *or* -**ders**) *n.* a central European freshwater fish in the perch family, harvested for food. Latin name: *Stizostedion lucioperca*. [Mid-19thC. Via German from Low German *sandāt*, of unknown origin.]

zandoli /zan dóli/ *n.* *Carib* a largish brown and green lizard that lives in holes

ZANU, **Zanu** *abbr.* Zimbabwe African National Union

zany /záyni/ *adj.* (-**nier**, -**niest**) **AMUSINGLY UNCONVENTIONAL** entertainingly strange or amusingly unusual ■ *n.* (*plural* -**nies**) **1. CLOWN** a fool, buffoon, or clown **2.** THEATRE **STOCK CHARACTER** a stock character in Renaissance comedies who mimicked other characters [Late 16thC. Via French *zani* from, ultimately, Italian dialect *Zanni*, a variant of *Gianni*, pet form of *Giovanni*, the character in the commedia dell'arte who tried to mimic the clown.] —**zanily** *adv.* —**zaniness** *n.* —**zanism** *n.*

Zanzibar /zánzi baar/ island of Tanzania, in the Indian Ocean, approximately 35 km/22 mi. off the eastern coast of Africa. Population: 375,539 (1988). Area: 1,650 sq. km/637 sq. mi.

zap /zap/ *v.* (**zaps, zapping, zapped**) (*informal*) **1.** *vt.* **DESTROY SB OR STH** to kill or finish sb or sth off with sudden force **2.** *vti.* **CHANGE TV CHANNELS USING REMOTE CONTROL** to change channels on a television set using a remote control device, especially to change channels rapidly **3.** *vi.* **MOVE QUICKLY** to move about or accomplish sth very rapidly **4.** *vt.* **COOK STH IN MICROWAVE**

a at; aa father; aw all; ay day; air hair; ə about, edible, item, common, circus; e egg; ee eel; hw when; i it, happy; ī ice; 'l apple; 'm rhythm; 'n fashion; o odd; ō open; oo good; oo pool; ow owl; oy oil; th thin; th this; u up; ur urge;

to cook sth in a microwave oven ○ *I'll just zap this for a minute and then we can eat.* **5.** *vt.* Malaysia, Singapore **PHOTOCOPY** to photocopy sth ■ *n.* (*informal*) **1. ENERGY** energy and excitement **2. TIME IN MICROWAVE** a short period of time in a microwave oven ■ *interj.* **EXPRESSION OF FORCEFUL ACTION** used especially in comic books to indicate sudden and violent force (*informal*) [Early 20thC. An imitation of the sound of a lightning strike or electric sparks.]

Zapata /saa páataa, zə-tə/, **Emiliano** (1879–1919) Mexican revolutionary. He took part in a number of uprisings, and redistributed land among the Native Central Americans in southern Mexico.

Zapata moustache *n.* a thick moustache that curves down around the edges of the mouth [Mid-20thC. Named after Emiliano ZAPATA, who wore such a moustache.]

zapateado /záppə tay áadō/ (*plural* **-dos**), **zapateo** /záppə táy ō/ (*plural* **-os**) *n.* a Spanish or Latin American dance involving rhythmic tapping of the feet [Mid-19thC. From Spanish, from *zapatear* 'to tap with the shoe', from *zapato* 'shoe'.]

Zapopan /záapō pan/ city in southwestern Mexico near Guadalajara. Population: 668,323 (1990).

Zaporizhzhya /zə pa rózhyə/ city in southeastern Ukraine. It is situated about 217 km/135 mi. west of Donetsk. Population: 897,000 (1993).

Zapotec /zápə tek/ (*plural* **-tec** *or* **-tecs**) *n.* **1.** **PEOPLES NATIVE CENTRAL AMERICAN PEOPLE** a Native Central American people who before the arrival of the Spanish in the 16th century had developed one of the most advanced civilizations in Mesoamerica. Today, most Zapotec live in the highlands of Oaxaca, Mexico. **2.** **LANG OTO-MANGUEAN LANGUAGE** a language belonging to the Oto-Manguean family that is spoken in Oaxaca, Mexico. About 500,000 people speak Zapotec and it is one of the most widely-spoken Native American languages. [Late 18thC. Via Spanish *zapoteco* from, ultimately, Nahuatl *tzapotecatl*, literally 'person from the place of the sapotilla'.] —**Zapotecan** *adj.*

zapper /záppər/ *n.* US (*informal*) **1.** **REMOTE CONTROL** a remote control for a television or video recorder **2.** **INSECT-KILLING DEVICE** a device that attracts and electrocutes insects

zappy /záppi/ (**-pier, -piest**) *adj.* lively and forcefully impressive (*informal*)

ZAPU /záppoo/, **Zapu** *abbr.* Zimbabwe African People's Union

Zaragoza /zárrə gōzə/ capital of Zaragoza Province in the autonomous region of Aragon, northeastern Spain. Population: 607,900 (1995).

Zarathustra /zárrə thoŏstrə/ = **Zoroaster**

zaratite /zárrə tīt/ *n.* an amorphous green mineral consisting of hydrated nickel carbonate [Mid-19thC. From Spanish *zaratita*, from the surname *Zarate*.]

zareba /zə reébə/ *n.* an outdoor enclosure, especially one made of thorn bushes and used as protection around a campsite or village in various parts of North Africa [Mid-19thC. From Arabic *zarība* 'cattle pen'.]

zarf /zaarf/ *n.* a metal frame for holding a cup, used in the Middle East [Mid-19thC. From Arabic *ẓarf* 'vessel'.]

zari /záari/, **jari** *n.* S Asia gold brocade used to decorate clothes [Mid-20thC. Via Urdu from Persian *zarī*, from *zar* 'gold'.]

Zaria /záari ə/ city in Kaduna State, north-central Nigeria. Population: 345,200 (1992).

zarzuela /zaar zwáylə/ *n.* a type of Spanish musical theatre, usually comic, combining dialogue, music, and dance [Late 19thC. From Spanish, of uncertain origin.]

Zátopek /záataw pek/, **Emile** (*b.* 1922) Czech athlete. He was the Olympic gold medallist in the 10,000 metres (1948 and 1952), 5,000 metres (1952), and marathon (1952).

zax /zaks/ *n.* a tool similar to a hatchet used for cutting and shaping slate [Mid-17thC. Variant of *sax*, from Old English *seax* 'knife'. Ultimately from an Indo-European base meaning 'to cut', that is also the ancestor of English *saw*, *sickle*, and *section*.]

z-axis *n.* one of the axes of the Cartesian coordinate system that provides a reference in three-dimensional space

zayin /záayin/ *n.* the seventh letter of the Hebrew alphabet, represented in the English alphabet as 'Z' [Early 19thC. From Hebrew, literally 'weapon'.]

zazen /zaa zen/ *n.* a form of meditation in Zen, practised sitting in a prescribed position [Early 18thC. From Japanese, 'sitting zen'.]

Z boson *n.* = **Z particle**

ZB station *n.* NZ a commercial radio station

Z chart *n.* a chart used in business and industry to illustrate production data

z-coordinate *n.* one of three numbers that provide a reference to a position in three-dimensional space, conventionally the vertical one

zeal /zeel/ *n.* energetic and unflagging enthusiasm, especially for a cause or idea [14thC. Via late Latin *zelus* from Greek *zēlos* 'eager rivalry' (source also of English *jealous*).]

Zealand /zeélənd/ = **Sjaelland**

zealot /zéllət/ *n.* sb who shows excessive enthusiasm for a cause, particularly a religious cause [Mid-16thC. Via late Latin from Greek *zēlōtēs*, from *zēloun* 'to be jealous', from *zēlos* (see **ZEAL**).] —**zealotry** *n.*

Zealot /zéllət/ *n.* a member of a group of Jewish rebels who attempted the military overthrow of Roman rule in Palestine in the 1st and 2nd centuries AD

zealous /zélləss/ *adj.* actively and unreservedly enthusiastic [Early 16thC. From medieval Latin *zelosus*, from *zelus* (see **ZEAL**).] —**zealously** *adv.* —**zealousness** *n.*

zeatin /zeé ətin/ *n.* a naturally occurring growth promoter found in many plants, first isolated from kernels of Indian corn [Mid-20thC. Coined from modern Latin *Zea*, genus name of maize (see **ZEIN**) + -IN.]

zebec *n.* = **xebec**

Zebedee /zébbəddi/ *n.* in the Bible, a fisherman, and the father of the apostles, James and John (Matthew 4:21)

Zebra

zebra /zébbrə, zeébrə/ *n.* an animal resembling a horse that is native to Africa, has a black-and-white or brown-and-white striped hide, and is found in small family groups that sometimes make up larger herds. Genus: *Equus.* [Early 17thC. From Italian, Spanish, or Portuguese, originally 'wild ass', of uncertain origin.] —**zebraic** /zi bráy ik/ *adj.* —**zebrine** /zéb rīn, zeéb-/ *adj.* —**zebroid** /zéb róyd, zeéb-/ *adj.*

zebra crossing *n.* a pedestrian crossing marked by white stripes in the road, at which drivers of vehicles must stop if a pedestrian is waiting to cross

zebra danio *n.* = **zebra fish**

zebra finch *n.* an Australian finch found throughout inland areas that has a reddish-orange bill, grey head and back, and a black-and-white striped tail. Zebra finches are popular cage birds and now exist in a variety of colours not found in the wild. Latin name: *Poephila guttata.*

zebra fish *n.* a small freshwater fish native to India and popular in aquariums, with a blue body and longitudinal silvery or gold stripes. Latin name: *Brachydanio rerio.*

zebra mussel *n.* a European and Asian freshwater mussel regarded as a nuisance in the Great Lakes in the United States and surrounding waterways where it was accidentally introduced. Latin name: *Dreissena polymorpha.*

zebra plant *n.* a tropical South American evergreen plant with green and purple striped leaves. Latin name: *Calathea zebrina.*

zebrawood /zébbrə wŏod, zeébrə-/ *n.* **1.** **HARDWOOD TREE WITH STRIPED WOOD** a tropical hardwood tree producing wood in distinct dark and light coloured bands, used to make decorative furniture. Latin name: *Connarus guianensis.* **2.** **TREE WITH STRIPED WOOD** any tropical tree producing wood in two distinct colour bands **3.** **STRIPED WOOD** wood from a zebrawood tree

zebu /zeé boo/ (*plural* **-bu** *or* **-bus**) *n.* a domesticated ox of Asia and India with a humped back, curving horns, floppy ears, and a large dewlap. Latin name: *Bos indicus.* [Late 18thC. From French *zébu*, of unknown origin.]

zecchino /ze keénō/ (*plural* **-ni** *or* **-nos**) *n.* = **sequin** [Early 17thC. From Italian (see **SEQUIN**).]

Zechariah /zékə rí ə/ *n.* **1.** **HEBREW PROPHET** in the Bible, a Hebrew priest and prophet of the 6th century BC. He was the husband of Elizabeth, and father of John the Baptist. **2.** **BOOK IN BIBLE** a book in the Bible containing the prophecies of Zechariah, including his visions of the rebuilding of the Temple in a restored Jerusalem. See table at **Bible**

zechin /zékin/ *n.* = **sequin** [Late 16thC. From Italian *zecchino* (see **SEQUIN**).]

zed /zed/ *n.* a written representation of the sound of the letter 'Z'. US term **zee** [15thC. Via French *zède* and Latin *zeta* from Greek *zēta*.]

Zedekiah /zéddi kī ə/ *n.* in the Bible, the last king of Judah (597 BC–586 BC). After rebelling against Nebuchadnezzar, he was imprisoned in Babylon, where he died in captivity (2 Kings 24–25) (2 Chronicles 36).

zedoary /zéddō əri/ (*plural* **-ies**) *n.* **1.** **AROMATIC PLANT** an Indian plant with yellow flowers and starchy aromatic rhizomes that when dried are used as a condiment, in cosmetics, in perfume, and medicinally as a stimulant. Latin name: *Curcuma zedoaria.* **2.** **ZEDOARY POWDER** an aromatic powder obtained from crushing dried zedoary roots [15thC. Via medieval Latin *zedoarium* from Persian *zadwār*.]

zedonk /zeé dónk, zé-/ *n.* the offspring of a male zebra and a female donkey [Late 20thC. Coined from ZEBRA + DONKEY.]

zee /zee/ *n.* US = **zed** [Late 17thC. Alteration of Latin *zeta*, under the influence of *b*, *p*, etc.]

Zeebrugge /zeé brŏogə/ port in northwestern Belgium, in northwestern Flanders Province

Zeeland /zeélənd/ province in the southwestern Netherlands. Population: 367,400 (1996). Area: 1,800 sq. km/695 sq. mi.

Zeeman effect /zeémən-/ *n.* the splitting of single lines in a spectrum into two, three, or more polarized lines when the source of the spectrum is placed in a magnetic field [Late 19thC. Named after the Dutch physicist Pieter *Zeeman* (1865–1943), who described the phenomenon.]

Franco Zeffirelli

Zeffirelli /zéffə rélli/, **Franco** (*b.* 1923) Italian film, stage, and opera director. His films include versions of Shakespeare and adaptations of operas.

Zeil /zīl/ the highest mountain in the Northern Territory of Australia. Height: 1,510 m/4,954 ft.

zein /zee in/ *n.* a powder of proteins obtained from corn, with various applications in industry and manufacturing [Early 19thC. Coined from modern Latin

Zea, genus name of maize, via Latin *zea* 'emmer' from Greek *zeia*, a kind of wheat.]

Zeiss /tsīss, zīss/, **Carl** (1816–88) German manufacturer. In partnership with Ernst Karl Abbe, he produced high-quality optical instruments, notably cameras and microscopes.

Zeitgeist /zít gīst, tsít-/, **zeitgeist** *n.* the ideas prevalent in a period and place, particularly as expressed in literature, philosophy, and religion [Mid-19thC. From German, literally 'spirit of the time'.]

zelkova /zélkəvə/ *n.* an Asian tree especially cultivated for its resistance to Dutch elm disease. Genus: *Zelkova*. [Late 19thC. Via modern Latin, genus name, from, ultimately, a Caucasian source.]

zemindar *n.* = **zamindar**

zemindary *n.* = **zamindari**

zemstvo /zémst vō/ (*plural* **-stvos**) *n.* an elected provincial legislature that existed in Russia between 1864 and 1917 [Mid-19thC. From Russian, from obsolete *zem* 'land'. Ultimately from an Indo-European base meaning 'earth', which is also the ancestor of English *chthonic*, *humble*, and *bridegroom*.]

Zen /zen/, **Zen Buddhism** *n.* a major school of Buddhism originating in 12th century China that emphasizes enlightenment through meditation and insight [Early 18thC. Via Japanese *zen* and Chinese *chán* from, ultimately, Sanskrit *dhyānam* 'meditation', literally 'watching'.]

zenana, **zanana** *n.* in southern Asia, the part of the house reserved for women and girls in a Muslim household [Mid-18thC. From Persian and Urdu *zanānah*, from *zan* 'woman'. Ultimately from an Indo-European word that is also the ancestor of English *queen*, *gyno-*, and *banshee*.]

Zen Buddhism *n.* = **Zen**

Zend /zend/ *n.* **1.** = **Zend-Avesta 2.** LANG = **Avesta**

Zend-Avesta *n.* the canonical writings of Zoroastrianism, preserved in the Pahlavi language [Mid-17thC. Via French from Persian *zand-awastā*, literally 'Avesta with interpretation', from Middle Persian *zend* 'interpretation' + *Awastā* (see AVESTA).]

zener diode /zénər-/ *n.* a type of semiconductor used as a voltage regulator because of its ability to maintain a constant voltage during fluctuating current conditions [Mid-20thC. Named after the US physicist Clarence M. *Zener* (1905–93), whose research led to the device.]

zenith /zénnith/ *n.* **1.** ASTRON **POINT STRAIGHT UP** the point of the celestial sphere that is directly over the observer and 90 degrees from all points on that person's horizon **2. HIGHEST POINT** the high point or climax of sth [14thC. Via Old French and medieval Latin from, ultimately, Arabic *samt (ar-ra's)* 'path (over the head)' (source also of English *azimuth*).] —**zenithal** *adj.*

zenithal projection *n.* a type of map projection of the Earth onto a plane tangential to a point on the surface of the Earth such as the North Pole or the Equator

Zeno of Citium /zeénō uv síshee əm/ (*fl.* late 4th-early 3rd centuries BC) Greek philosopher. He founded his own school of philosophy, stoicism, in Athens in about 300 BC.

Zeno of Elea /zeénō əv eéli ə/ (*fl.* 5th century BC) Greek mathematician and philosopher. The paradoxes for which his philosophy is known were designed to discredit the information conveyed by the senses. Aristotle regarded him as the inventor of dialectical reasoning.

zeolite /zeé ə līt/ *n.* one of a large group of amorphous hydrated aluminium silicate minerals that may also contain sodium, calcium, barium, and potassium, occurring in cavities in weathered igneous rocks and hydrothermal veins. The ion exchange properties of zeolites have application in water purification. [Late 18thC. Coined from Greek *zein* 'to boil' (source of English *eczema*).] —**zeolitic** /zeé ə líttik/ *adj.*

Zephaniah /zəffə nī ə/ *n.* **1. HEBREW PROPHET** in the Bible, a minor Hebrew prophet of the 7th century BC **2. BOOK IN THE BIBLE** a book in the Bible, traditionally attributed to Zephaniah. It urges repentance by the people of Judah, and predicts a day of judgment.

zephyr /zéffər/ *n.* **1. MILD WIND** a light warming breeze **2.** TEXTILES **DELICATE FABRIC** a delicate usually woollen fabric or garment [Pre-12thC. Via Latin from Greek *zephuros* 'west wind'.]

zephyr lily *n.* a tropical American plant with clump-forming bulbs, narrow leaves, and single funnel-shaped colourful flowers. Genus: *Zephyranthes.* [From the fact that the plant is native to warm regions]

Zephyrus /zéffərəss/ *n.* in Greek mythology, the god who personified the west wind and was always mild and gentle in character. ◊ **Boreas**

zeppelin /zéppəlin/ *n.* a rigid cylindrical airship consisting of a covered frame and a suspended compartment for engines and passengers [Early 20thC. Named after Count Ferdinand von *Zeppelin* (1838–1917), who constructed the first such airship.]

Zermatt /tsur mát/ town and ski resort in Valais Canton, southwestern Switzerland. Population: 4,200 (1989).

zero /zeérō/ *n.* (*plural* **-ros** *or* **-roes**) **1. SYMBOL 0** the numerical symbol 0, representing the absence of any quantity or magnitude **2. NUMBER WITH THE VALUE OF 0** the number that, when added to another number, results in that number, e.g. 0 + 4 = 4 **3. STARTING POINT FOR VALUES ON GAUGE** the starting or centre point for values on a counter, scale, or gauge ○ *Set the counter to zero.* **4. LOW TEMPERATURE** the temperature indicated by 0 on a thermometer scale, especially that corresponding to the freezing point of water on the Celsius scale ○ *It got down to zero last night.* **5. LOW POINT** the lowest possible point or degree ○ *Her spirits are at zero.* **6. NOTHING** nothing or nil ○ *They beat us five zero.* **7.** *US* **FAILURE** sb who is regarded as a complete failure (*insult*) **8.** LING **ABSTRACT REALIZATION OF A MORPHEME** a variant form of a morpheme (**allomorph**) that is purely abstract and does not exist in any physical phonetic form. An example of a zero allomorph in English is the plural marker of 'sheep'. Compare 'two cats', 'two dogs', and 'two sheep'. **9.** ARMS **SETTING ON A GUN SIGHT** a setting on a gun sight indicating the centre of a target ■ *vt.* (**-roes, -roing, -roed**) **SET TO ZERO** to set an instrument, gauge, counter, or similar measuring device to zero ■ *adj.* **1. COMPLETELY WITHOUT STH** utterly lacking a particular thing (*informal*) **2.** METEOROL **WITH LIMITED VISIBILITY** used to describe a level of visibility limited to 15 m/50 ft vertically or 50 m/165 ft horizontally [Early 17thC. Via French and Italian from, ultimately, Arabic *ṣifr* 'emptiness' (source of English *cipher*).]

zero in *vi.* **1.** MIL **LOCATE A TARGET AND AIM AT IT** to find the precise position of a target and move towards it or aim a weapon at it, threateningly or inexorably **2. IDENTIFY STH AND CONCENTRATE ON IT** to identify sth precisely and concentrate all efforts on dealing with it ○ *The report zeroed in on the weaknesses inherent in the management structure.* [From the technique of setting a gun sight exactly on a target by cancelling out the effects of elevation and wind deflection]

zero-base, **zero-based** *adj.* relating to a budget or budgeting that considers each item on its merits without reference to previous practice or expenditure

zero-coupon *adj.* FIN not paying interest but sold at a discount and redeemable at maturity ○ *a zero-coupon bond*

zero-defect *adj.* with no defects or flaws

zero gravity *n.* PHYS a condition of apparent weightlessness resulting from the centrifugal force on an object counterbalancing the gravitational force attracting it

zero grazing *n.* a system of feeding cattle or other livestock in which freshly cut forage is brought daily to animals that are permanently housed instead of being allowed to graze

zero growth *n.* no increase in the growth or development of sth, especially when an increase might have been expected and where any increase is measured as a percentage ○ *predictions of zero growth in the economy*

zero hour *n.* **1.** MIL **SCHEDULED START OF A MILITARY OPERATION** the time set for the start of a military operation **2. TIME WHEN STH IMPORTANT WILL OCCUR** the time or date when sth important is due to happen

zero option *n.* an offer to limit the number of short-range nuclear missiles or remove them altogether if an opposing side agrees to do the same

zero population growth *n.* a situation in which the number of new births is no greater than the number of people dying, so that the overall population size remains the same

zero-rate (**-rates, -rating, -rated**) *vt. UK, Can* to make goods or services exempt from a value-added tax — **zero-rated** *adj.* —**zero rating** *n.*

zero-sum *adj.* relating to a situation in which a gain by one side or person requires any other side or person involved in it to sustain a corresponding loss

zeroth /zeér ōth/ *adj.* preceding number one in a series [Late 19thC. Coined from ZERO + -TH.]

zero tolerance *n.* the absence of any leniency or exception in the enforcement of a law, rule, or regulation, especially a law against antisocial behaviour

zero-zero *adj.* AIR used to describe flying conditions in which cloud is so thick and low that the pilot can see nothing ahead and nothing above or below the aircraft [Shortening of *zero ceiling, zero visibility*]

zero-zero option *n.* = **double-zero option**

zest /zest/ *n.* **1. HEARTY ENJOYMENT** lively enjoyment and enthusiasm ○ *zest for life* **2. EXCITING ELEMENT ADDING TO ENJOYMENT** an exciting or interesting quality that makes sth particularly enjoyable **3.** COOK **CITRUS PEEL USED AS FLAVOURING** the thin outer rind of the peel of a citrus fruit that is cut, scraped, or grated to yield a sharp fruity flavouring for foods and drinks **4. PIQUANT FLAVOUR** a pleasantly sharp flavour ■ *vt.* (**zests, zesting, zested**) **1.** COOK **GRATE THE SKIN OF CITRUS FRUIT** to cut, grate, or scrape the rind of a citrus fruit in order to flavour foods and drinks **2. MAKE STH MORE STIMULATING AND ENJOYABLE** to make an experience more enjoyable by adding excitement or interest to it [15thC. Originally in the meaning of 'orange or lemon peel', from French, of unknown origin.] —**zesty** *adj.*

zester /zéstər/ *n.* a small utensil with a row of tiny sharpened holes or edges at its tip for cutting strips of zest from oranges, lemons, or other citrus fruits

zestful /zéstf'l/ *adj.* full of or showing lively enjoyment and enthusiasm —**zestfully** *adv.* —**zestfulness** *n.*

zeta /zeétə/ *n.* the sixth letter of the Greek alphabet, written in the English alphabet as Z [Early 18thC. From Greek *zēta*, of Phoenician origin.]

Zethus /zeéthəss/ *n.* in Greek mythology, a son of Zeus and Antiope and the twin of Amphion. The brothers became joint kings of Thebes.

zeugma /zyoógmə, zoóg-/ *n.* a figure of speech in which an adjective or verb is used with two nouns but is appropriate to only one of them or has a different sense with each. The sentence 'During the race he broke the record and a leg' is a zeugma. [Late 16thC. Via Latin from Greek, literally 'joining'.] —**zeugmatic** /zyoog máttik, zoog-/ *adj.* —**zeugmatically** *adv.*

Zeus *n.* in Greek mythology, the god of the sky, ruler of the Olympian gods, and spiritual father of gods and mortals. Roman equivalent **Jupiter**

Zhangjiakou /jáng jyaá kō/ city in northeastern China in Hebei Province, situated at one of the gates of the Great Wall of China. Population: 529,136 (1990).

Zhejiang /jé jáng/ province in China on the East China Sea. Capital: Hangzhou. Population: 42,940,000 (1994). Area: 100,000 sq. km/38,600 sq. mi.

Zhenghe expeditions /júng húr-/ *npl.* a series of seven overseas trade expeditions under the Ming emperor Yonglo between 1405 and 1423 that were the last Chinese attempt to create a worldwide trading empire [Named after *Zhenghe*, the court eunuch who led the expeditions]

Zhengzhou /júng jṓ/ capital city of Henan Province, located on the Yellow River between Taiyuan and Wuhan, in eastern China. Population: 1,710,000 (1991).

zho *n.* ZOOL = **dzo**

Zhou /jō/ *n.* a Chinese dynasty that ruled from the 12th to the 3rd centuries BC, during which China was divided into feudal states and the religions of

Confucianism and Taoism arose [Late 18thC. From Chinese *zhòu*.]

Zia ul-Haq /zée ə öol haȧk/, **Muhammad** (1924–88) Pakistani statesman and general. He overthrew Prime Minister Zulfikar Ali Bhutto (1977), and as president of Pakistan (1978–88) imposed martial law and introduced the Islamic legal code. He approved Bhutto's execution (1979) over international protests.

zibeline /zíbbə lïn/, **zibelline** *n.* a thick soft fabric with a long nap, made of wool, especially mohair or alpaca, or of the hair of another animal such as a camel [Late 16thC. Via French from Italian *zibellino* 'sable', of Slavic origin.]

zibet /zíbbit/ *n.* a civet native to Southeast Asia. Latin name: *Viverra zibetha*. [Late 16thC. Via medieval Latin *zibethum* or Italian *zibetto* from Arabic *zabād* 'musky perfume obtained from civets' (source of English *civet*).]

zidovudine /zï dóvvyöö deen/ *n.* = AZT [Late 20thC. Origin uncertain: probably an alteration of AZIDOTHYMIDINE.]

Florenz Ziegfeld

Ziegfeld /zíg feld/, **Florenz** (1869–1932) US theatre producer. He launched the Ziegfeld Follies, an annual musical revue (1907), and produced extravagant musicals in New York.

zig /zig/ *n.* ONE DIRECTION OF A ZIGZAG a sharp line, direction, movement, or course that forms part of a zigzag ■ *vi.* (**zigs, zigging, zigged**) FORM PART OF A ZIGZAG to move in a sharp line, direction, movement, or course that forms part of a zigzag [Mid-20thC. Back-formation from ZIGZAG.]

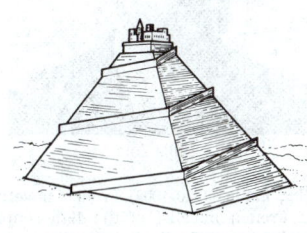
Ziggurat

ziggurat /zíggöö rat/ *n.* an ancient Mesopotamian pyramid-shaped tower with a square base, rising in storeys of ever-decreasing size, with a terrace at each storey and a temple at the very top. It is thought that the Tower of Babel referred to in the Bible was a tower of this kind. [Late 19thC. From Assyrian *ziqquratu* 'pinnacle'.]

zigzag /zíg zag/ *n.* **1.** LINE TAKING ALTERNATING TURNS a line going at an angle first one way, then sharply the opposite way, then back the first way, and so on, like the outline of a saw's teeth **2.** STH REPEATEDLY SWITCHING DIRECTIONS SHARPLY sth that follows a sharply alternating line or course, e.g. a road with sharp bends alternating right and left ■ *adv.* IN SHARPLY ALTERNATING DIRECTIONS along a sharply alternating line or course ■ *v.* (**-zags, -zagging, -zagged**) **1.** *vti.* PROCEED IN A SHARPLY ALTERNATING PATH to follow a sharply alternating line or course, moving rapidly ○ *They zigzagged across the field, dodging enemy bullets.* **2.** *vt.* SEW MAKE A SHARPLY ALTERNATING PATTERN to make a pattern of sharply alternating lines or directions, e.g. by sewing sth with herringbone stitches [Early

18thC. Via French from German *Zickzack*, of uncertain origin: perhaps formed from *Zacke* 'tooth'.] —**zigzaggedness** *n.*

zigzag fence *n. Northeast US* a fence made of split rails each resting on and set at angles to the next, forming a zigzag

zila *n.* = zillah

zila parishad /zíl aa púrrishad/, **zilla parishad, zillah parishad** *n.* a local council that governs an administrative district in India

zilch /zilch/ *pron.* zero or nothing at all (*informal*) ○ *They take all the profits and we're left with zilch.* [Mid-20thC. Origin unknown.]

zill /zil/ *n.* either one of a pair of tiny cymbals that belly dancers hold in their fingers and play in time to their dancing [From Turkish *zil* 'cymbals']

zillah /zíllə, zíllaa/, **zilla, zila** *n.* an administrative district in India when the country was under British rule [Early 19thC. Via Persian and Urdu from Arabic *dila'* 'division'.]

zillion /zíllyən/ *det.* HUGE NUMBER OR QUANTITY a number or quantity so huge it cannot be counted or determined (*informal*) ○ *I had a zillion things to do.* ■ *pron.* HUGE NUMBER OF PEOPLE OR THINGS a number of people or quantity of things so huge it cannot be counted or determined (*informal*) ○ *Zillions preferred the new model to the old one.* [Mid-20thC. Modelled on *million* and *billion*, with *z* representing the last in a series.]

zillionaire /zílyə náir/ *n.* sb who is extremely wealthy (*informal*) [Mid-20thC. Modelled on *millionaire*.]

Zimbabwe

Zimbabwe /zim baȧbwi, -baȧb way/ republic in southern Africa. Language: English. Currency: Zimbabwe dollar. Capital: Harare. Population: 11,515,000 (1996). Area: 390,759 sq. km/150,873 sq. mi. Official name **Republic of Zimbabwe**. Former name **Rhodesia** —**Zimbabwean** *n., adj.*

Zimmer /zímmər/, **Zimmer frame** *tdmk.* a trademark for a lightweight metal tubular frame with four rubber-tipped legs, designed to support sb who needs help in walking

zinc /zingk/ *n.* **1.** BLUISH METALLIC ELEMENT USED AS ANTI-CORROSIVE a bluish-white metallic chemical element that is used in alloys such as brass and nickel-silver and as a protective corrosion-resistant coating for other metals, especially steel and iron. Symbol **Zn 2.** INDUST GALVANIZED IRON corrugated iron with a protective zinc coating (*informal*) ■ *vt.* (**zincs, zincing** *or* **zincking, zinced** *or* **zincked**) INDUST COAT WITH ZINC to cover a metal, especially iron or steel, with a protective corrosion-resistant coating of zinc [Mid-17thC. From German *Zink*, of unknown origin.] —**zincic** *adj.* —**zincky** *adj.* —**zincoid** /zíng k əyd/ *adj.*

zincate /zíng kayt/ *n.* a salt derived from zinc hydroxide

zinc blende *n.* MINERALS = sphalerite

zinc chloride *n.* a poisonous soluble salt used as a wood preservative, an antiseptic, and a catalyst in chemical reactions. Formula: $ZnCl_2$.

zinciferous /zing kíffərəss/ *adj.* containing or yielding zinc, especially as an ore

zincite /zíngk ït/ *n.* a reddish-orange mineral form of zinc oxide

zinckenite *n.* MINERALS = zinkenite

zinco /zíngkö/ *n.* (*plural* **-cos**) *n.* a zincograph (*informal*) [Late 19thC. Shortening.]

zincograph /zíngkə graaf, -graf/ *n.* **1.** ZINC PRINTING PLATE WITH AN ETCHED SURFACE a printing plate made of zinc that has the design to be printed etched into its surface **2.** PRINT TAKEN FROM A ZINC PLATE a print taken from a printing plate made of zinc that has the design to be printed etched into its surface [Late 19thC. Back-formation from ZINCOGRAPHY.]

zincography /zing kóggrəfi/ *n.* the art or business of making zinc printing plates with the designs to be printed etched into their surfaces [Mid-19thC. Coined from modern Latin *zincum* 'zinc' + -GRAPHY.] —**zincographer** *n.* —**zincographic** /zíngkə gráffik/ *adj.*

zinc ointment *n.* a soothing antiseptic ointment containing zinc oxide in a base of petroleum jelly or lanolin, used to treat skin conditions

zinc oxide *n.* an odourless water-insoluble white powder that is used as an astringent in cosmetics, an antiseptic in ointments, and a pigment in paints and inks. Formula: ZnO.

zinc sulphate *n.* a colourless crystalline powder that is used as a pigment in paints and inks, as an emetic in pharmaceuticals, and in wood preservatives and crop sprays. Formula: $ZnSO_4$.

zinc sulphide *n.* a crystalline white or yellowish powder used as a pigment and as a phosphor on X-ray and television screens. Formula: ZnS.

zinc white *n.* zinc oxide used as a white pigment in paint

zindabad /zínd aa baad/ *interj. S Asia* USED TO EXPRESS LOUD ENTHUSIASM used to express loud approval, acclaim, or enthusiasm ■ *n. S Asia* LOUD SHOUT OF ENTHUSIASM a loud shout of approval, acclaim, or enthusiasm [Mid-20thC. From Urdu, literally 'may – live'.]

Zinder /zíndər/ city in south-central Niger. Situated about 113 km/70 mi. north of the border with Nigeria, it was Niger's capital until 1926. Population: 119,838 (1988).

zine /zeen/ *n.* a self-published paper, Internet magazine, or other periodical, issued at irregular intervals with limited means and usually appealing to a specialist readership (*informal*) [Mid-20thC. Shortening of MAGAZINE.]

Zinfandel /zínfan del/ *n.* **1.** PLANTS VARIETY OF GRAPE a variety of black grape used, especially in California, to make a light fruity red or rosé wine **2.** WINE WINE MADE FROM ZINFANDEL GRAPE a light-bodied fruity red or rosé wine, or less commonly a hearty red wine, made from the Zinfandel grape, especially in California [Mid-19thC. Origin unknown.]

zing /zing/ *n.* **1.** SHARP SINGING SOUND a short high-pitched humming or buzzing sound, e.g. the sound of a bullet whizzing through the air **2.** LIVELY AND EXCITING QUALITY a lively exciting aspect of sth that makes it particularly enjoyable (*informal*) ○ *The rhythm guitar gives the tune extra zing.* ■ *v.* (**zings, zinging, zinged**) (*informal*) **1.** *vi.* MAKE A HUMMING NOISE to make or move with a short high-pitched humming or buzzing noise **2.** *vt. US* ATTACK WITH WORDS to criticize sb sharply, especially in a swift and clever way [Early 20thC. An imitation of the sound.] —**zingy** *adj.*

zinger /zíngər/ *n. US* (*informal*) **1.** SB OR STH ENERGETIC AND SURPRISING sb who or sth that is energetic and produces startling results **2.** CLEVER REMARK SKILFULLY DELIVERED a remark delivered with great skill and speed, especially a sharp and perfectly timed witticism or criticism **3.** SHOCKING AND UNEXPECTED HAPPENING a shocking and unexpected turn of events such as an abrupt shift in the plot of a film, play, or book [Early 20thC. Formed from ZING.]

zinjanthropus /zin jánthrəpəss/ (*plural* **-pi** /-pï/ *or* **-puses**) *n.* a hominid fossil found in 1959 at Olduvai Gorge in East Africa. Originally classified as a distinct genus and species, it is now recognized as a australopithecine. [Mid-20thC. From modern Latin, former genus name, from medieval Arabic *Zinj* 'East Africa' + Greek *anthrōpos* 'person'.] —**zinjanthropine** /-thrə peen/ *adj., n.*

zinkenite, **zinckenite** *n.* a dark-grey mineral consisting of antimony and a sulphide of lead [Mid-19thC. Named after the German mineralogist J. K. L. Zincken (1790–1862).]

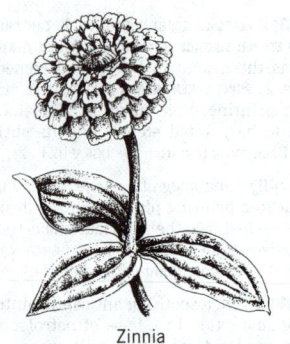

Zinnia

zinnia /zínni ə/ (*plural* **-as** *or* **-a**) *n.* a plant of the daisy family native to Mexico and adjacent areas that is widely grown as a garden plant for its large colourful flower heads. Genus: *Zinnia*. [Mid-18thC. From modern Latin, genus name, named after the German physician and botanist J. G. *Zinn* (1727–59).]

Zinzendorf /tsín tsən dáwrf/, **Nikolaus Ludwig, Graf von** (1700–60) German religious reformer. A founder and leader of the Moravian Church, he established Moravian congregations in Europe and the United States.

Zion /zí ən/ *n.* **1.** JUDAISM **MOUNTAIN NEAR JERUSALEM** one of the hills of Jerusalem, in Biblical times emblematic of the house or household of God and later by extension the Jewish people and their religion **2.** CHR **PLACE OF CHRISTIAN LIFE AND WORSHIP** in Christian belief, the place where God lives and is worshipped on earth or in the kingdom of heaven [Pre-12thC. Via late Latin and Greek from Hebrew *ṣīyôn*.]

Zionism /zí ənizəm/ *n.* a worldwide movement, originating in the 19th century, that sought to establish and develop a Jewish nation in Palestine. Since 1948 its function has been to support the state of Israel.

Zionist /zí ənist/ *n.* **1.** JUDAISM **SUPPORTER OF A JEWISH STATE** a supporter of 19th-century Zionism, or a modern supporter of the state of Israel **2.** *S Africa* CHR **CHRISTIAN WITH TRADITIONAL AFRICAN BELIEFS** a member of an independent Christian church in South Africa that incorporates traditional African beliefs and forms of worship —**Zionist** *adj.* —**Zionistic** /zíə nístik/ *adj.*

zip /zip/ *n.* **1.** *UK, Can* **FASTENER WITH INTERLOCKING TEETH** a fastener for clothes, bags, or other items, consisting of two rows of interlocking metal or plastic teeth with an attached sliding tab pulled to open or close the fastener. US term **zipper 2.** **LIVELY AND EXCITING QUALITY** a lively exciting aspect of sth that makes it particularly enjoyable (*informal*) **3.** **BRIEF HISSING SOUND** a brief sibilant sound such as the sound of a bullet whizzing through the air **4.** = **zip code** ■ *v.* (**zips, zipping, zipped**) **1.** *vti.* **FASTEN WITH ZIP** to fasten sth, or to be fastened, with a zip **2.** *vi.* **MAKE OR MOVE WITH HISSING SOUND** to make or move with a rapid sibilant sound (*informal*) **3.** *vti.* **GO OR MOVE VERY FAST** to go somewhere or move sth somewhere very fast (*informal*) **4.** *vt.* COMPUT **COMPRESS A FILE** to compress a computer file for storage or transmission [Late 19thC. An imitation of the sound.]

ZIP code, **zip code** *n.* *US* = **postcode** [An acronym formed from *Zone Improvement Program*]

zip fastener *n.* = **zip** *n.* 1

zip file *n.* a computer file with the extension .ZIP containing data that has been compressed for storage or transmission.

zip gun *n.* *US, Can* a homemade pistol, especially one that uses a spring or a rubber band as the firing mechanism (*slang*)

zipless /zípləss/ *adj.* **1.** **WITH NO ZIP FASTENER** not fitted with, or fastened using, a zip **2.** **PASSIONATE** passionate and lasting only a short time [Late 20thC. In the sense of 'passionate', from the idea of clothes coming off suddenly, without the awkward undoing of zips.]

zipper /zípər/ *n.* *US* = **zip** [Early 20thC. Originally a trademark.]

zippered /zípərd/ *adj.* *US* fitted with or fastened using a zip. Also called **zip-up**

Zippo /zíppō/ *tdmk.* a trademark for a sturdy metal cigarette lighter [Mid-20thC]

zippy /zíppi/ (**-pier, -piest**) *adj.* (*informal*) **1.** **ENERGETIC** showing or having spirit or energy **2.** **ACCELERATING QUICKLY** with good acceleration

zip-up *adj.* fitted with, or fastened using, a zip. US term **zippered**

zircalloy, **zircaloy** *n.* an alloy of zirconium with tin, chromium, and nickel that is resistant to heat and corrosion, making it a useful material in the nuclear power industry

zircon /zúr kon/ *n.* zirconium silicate, a very hard crystalline mineral that is the main source of zirconium. In its colourless varieties it is used as a substitute for diamonds in jewellery. [Late 18thC. From German *Zirkon*, via Arabic from, ultimately, Persian *āzargūn* 'fire colour'.]

zirconia /zur kóni ə/ *n.* = **zirconium oxide** [Late 18thC. Formed from ZIRCON.]

zirconium /zur kóni əm/ *n.* a greyish-white metallic chemical element used as a coating for the fuel rods in nuclear reactors because of its very high resistance to corrosion and its low absorption of neutrons. Symbol **Zr** —**zirconic** /zur kónnik/ *adj.*

zirconium oxide *n.* a heavy water-insoluble white powder used as a pigment for paints, as an abrasive, and in making heat-resistant materials and ceramics. Formula: ZrO_2.

zit /zit/ *n.* a pimple on the skin (*slang*) [Mid-20thC. Origin unknown.] —**zitty** /zítti/ *adj.*

Zither

zither /zíthər/ *n.* a musical instrument consisting of a flat shallow sound box with up to forty-five metal strings stretched across it that are plucked with the fingers or a plectrum [Mid-19thC. Via German from Latin *cithara* (see CITHARA).] —**zitherist** *n.*

ziti /zeé tee/ *n.* pasta in the form of medium-sized tubes, longer and thicker than macaroni [Mid-19thC. From Italian, plural of *zito*, literally 'boy'.]

zizz /ziz/ *n.* **A NAP** a brief sleep (*informal*) ■ *vi.* (**zizzes, zizzing, zizzed**) **TAKE NAP** to have a brief sleep (*informal*) [Mid-20thC. From ZZZ, representing the sound of a person snoring.]

Zl *abbr.* zloty

Z line *n.* a narrow dark line across striated muscle fibres that marks the boundaries between adjacent segments [Z from the initial letter of German *Zwischenscheibe* 'intervening disc']

zloty /zlótti/ (*plural* **-ties** *or* **-ty**) *n.* **1.** **UNIT OF POLISH CURRENCY** the main unit of currency in Poland, worth 100 groszy. See table at **currency 2.** **COIN WORTH A ZLOTY** a coin worth one zloty [Early 20thC. From Polish *złoty*, literally 'golden', from *złoto* 'gold'. Ultimately from an Indo-European word that is also the ancestor of English *gold* and *guilder*.]

Zn *symbol.* zinc

ZO *n.* = **dzo**

zo- *prefix.* = **zoo-** (*used before vowels*)

zoarium /zō áiri əm/ (*plural* **-ums** *or* **-a** /zō áiri ə/) *n.* a collection of distinct organisms that together form a compound organism [Late 19thC. Formed from Greek *zōion* 'animal' (see -ZOON).]

zod. *abbr.* zodiac

zodiac /zódi ak/ *n.* **1.** ASTRON **PART OF THE SKY CONTAINING THE MAJOR CONSTELLATIONS** a narrow band in the sky in which the movements of the major planets, Sun,

and Moon take place, astrologically divided into twelve sections named after the major constellations **2.** ZODIAC **ASTROLOGER'S CHART** a chart linking twelve constellations to twelve divisions of the year, used as the astrologer's main tool for analysing character and predicting the future **3.** **RECURRING SET** a set of things or sequence of events that repeats itself cyclically (*literary*) [14thC. Via French and Latin from Greek *zōidiakos kuklos*, literally 'circle of animal figures', from *zōidion* 'small animal', from *zōion* 'living being' (see -ZOON).] —**zodiacal** /zō dí ək'l/ *adj.*

zodiacal constellation *n.* any of the twelve constellations that a sign of the zodiac is named after. The constellations are Aries, Taurus, Gemini, Cancer, Leo, Virgo, Libra, Scorpio, Sagittarius, Capricorn, Aquarius, and Pisces.

zodiacal light *n.* a faint glow in the sky, seen before sunrise to the east and after sunset to the west and caused by small particles reflected in sunlight

Zog I /zōg/, **King of Albania** (1895–1961). He was prime minister (1922–24) and president (1925–28) of Albania before proclaiming himself king (1928). He fled when the Italians invaded during World War II (1939), and later abdicated in 1946.

Zohar /zō haar/ *n.* a 13th-century Jewish mystical text that is the primary text of Cabbalistic writings [Late 17thC. From Hebrew *zōhar*, literally 'light, splendour'.]

-zoic *suffix.* **1.** relating to a particular geologic era ○ *Mesozoic* **2.** having a particular kind of animal existence [Formed from Greek *zōē* 'life'. Ultimately from an Indo-European base meaning 'to live', which is also the ancestor of English *quick*, *vital*, and *biology*.]

zoisite /zóy sīt/ *n.* a grey or green hydrated calcium aluminosilicate mineral found in metamorphic rocks [Early 19thC. Named after the Slovenian scholar Baron Sigismund *Zois* von Edelstein (1747–1819), who discovered it.]

zol /zol/ *n.* *S Africa* (*slang*) **1.** **SMOKABLE CANNABIS** cannabis for smoking as a drug **2.** **CANNABIS CIGARETTE** a hand-rolled cannabis cigarette

AKG London

Émile Zola

Zola /zólə/, **Émile** (1840–1902) French novelist. The leading French novelist of the 19th century, he employed a scientifically based technique of naturalism in his epic 20-novel cycle *Les Rougon-Macquart* (1871–93). He is also known for 'J'Accuse' (1898), a defence of Alfred Dreyfus. Full name **Émile Édouard Charles Antoine Zola**

Zollverein /zólfə rīn, tsól-/ *n.* **1.** HISTORY **19C GERMAN CUSTOMS UNION** a customs union formed in the 19th century by a number of German states to establish uniform import tariffs from other countries and free trade among themselves **2.** **CUSTOMS UNION** any customs union formed to establish uniform import tariffs [Mid-19thC. From German, literally 'tariff union'.]

zombie /zómbi/, **zombi** *n.* **1.** SB **UNRESPONSIVE OR UNTHINKING** sb who lacks energy, enthusiasm, or the ability to think independently (*informal*) **2.** **DEAD BODY GIVEN LIFE BY VOODOO** in voodoo, a soul-less dead body brought back to life again **3.** **VOODOO SPIRIT REVIVING A DEAD BODY** in voodoo, a spirit that brings a soul-less dead body back to life again **4.** RELIG **SNAKE GOD OF VOODOO** a snake god of West Indian, Brazilian, and West African voodoo religions **5.** BEVERAGES **VERY STRONG RUM COCKTAIL** a very strong alcoholic cocktail made with various kinds of rum **6.** HIST **ARMY CONSCRIPT ASSIGNED FOR HOME DEFENCE** in Canada, a conscripted soldier assigned to home defence during World War II (*slang*) [Early 19thC. Via Caribbean Creole from Kimbundu *n-zumbi* 'ghost', originally the name of a snake god.] —**zombiism** *n.*

zombify /zómbi fī/ (**-fies, -fying, -fied**) *vt.* to convert sb into a zombie

zonal /zṓn'l/, **zonary** /zṓnəri/ *adj.* **1.** RELATING TO ZONES relating to a zone or zones **2.** SPLIT INTO ZONES divided up into zones —**zonally** *adv.*

zonal soil *n.* soil whose nature is established by the action of the climate and vegetation of the area in which it is found

zona pellucida /zṓnə pə lóossidə/ *n.* a thick transparent envelope that surrounds a developing ovum, allowing only one sperm cell through to fertilize the ovum [From modern Latin, literally 'transparent band']

zonary *adj.* = **zonal**

zonate /zṓ nayt/, **zonated** /zō náytid/ *adj.* **1.** ARRANGED IN ZONES divided up into zones **2.** MARKED BY ZONES distinguished by zones, e.g. of colour or texture

zonation /zō náysh'n/ *n.* the division of sth into separate zones

zone /zōn/ *n.* **1.** SEPARATE AREA WITH A PARTICULAR FUNCTION an area regarded as separate or kept separate, especially one with a particular use or function ○ *a loading zone* **2.** SUBSECTION OF A PARTICULAR AREA one of the smaller, usually named or numbered sections that a particular area is divided into, e.g. those of a transport network or a sportsfield **3.** METEOROL HORIZONTAL CLIMATIC BAND AROUND THE EARTH one of five horizontal bands across the Earth's surface, separated by the Arctic Circle, the Tropic of Cancer, the Tropic of Capricorn, and the Antarctic Circle, that marks climates. The zones are called the North Frigid Zone, the North Temperate Zone, the South Frigid Zone, the South Temperate Zone, and the Torrid Zone. **4.** TIME TIME ZONE a time zone **5.** ECOL AREA WITH DISTINCT PLANTS AND ANIMALS an area with characteristic types of organisms determined largely by its environment, e.g. any of the belts of vegetation on a mountain **6.** GEOL UNIT OF ROCK FORMATION WITH FOSSILS a unit of a rock formation characterized by its fossil content **7.** MATH PART OF A SPHERE the portion of a sphere included between two parallel planes meeting the sphere, one of which may be tangent to the sphere or both of which may intersect it ■ *vti.* (**zones, zoning, zoned**) **1.** SPLIT INTO ZONES to divide up an area into zones **2.** DESIGNATE AREA FOR STH to declare officially that an area is to be used for a particular purpose or to be developed in a particular way (*often passive*) ○ *The canal areas have been zoned for leisure and recreation.* [15thC. Via French and Latin from Greek *zōnē* 'belt, girdle'.] —**zoning** *n.*

zone melting *n.* = **zone refining**

zone of saturation *n.* an area of soil or rock below the level of the water table where all the voids are filled with water

zone refining *n.* a technique for greatly purifying metals in which a molten area is made to pass along an otherwise solid bar so that impurities become concentrated at one end

zonetime /zṓn tīm/ *n.* NAVIG the standard time that exists throughout a particular time zone [Early 20thC]

zonk /zongk/ (**zonks, zonking, zonked**) *vti.* to lose consciousness or become stupefied from exhaustion or an intake of alcohol or narcotic drugs, or to make sb do this (*slang*) [Early 20thC. From *zonk* 'sound of a heavy blow', an imitation of the sound.]

zonked /zongkt/, **zonked out** *adj.* unconscious, stupefied, or sleeping, especially as a result of the effects of alcohol or a drug (*slang*) [Mid-20thC]

zonule /zónnyool/ *n.* a small zone, band, or belt —**zonular** /zónnyōōlər/ *adj.*

zoo /zoo/ (*plural* **zoos**) *n.* **1.** PARK DISPLAYING LIVE ANIMALS IN ENCLOSURES a park where live wild animals from different parts of the world are kept in cages or enclosures for people to come and see, and where they are bred and studied by scientists **2.** CHAOTIC PLACE a place characterized as being full of noisy obstreperous people creating confusion and disorder (*informal*) [Mid-19thC. Shortening of ZOOLOGICAL GARDEN.]

zoo- *prefix.* **1.** animal, animal kingdom ○ *zootoxin* **2.** motile organism ○ *zoospore* [From Greek *zōion* (see -ZOON)]

zooflagellate /zṓ ə flájələt/ *n.* a colourless protozoan that ingests organic matter, is often parasitic, and has one or more flagella

zoogeography /zṓ ə ji óggrəfi/ *n.* the scientific study of the areas where different animals live and the causes and effects of such distribution, especially distributions on a large or global scale —**zoogeographer** *n.* —**zoogeographic** /zṓ ə jée ə gráffik/ *adj.*

zoogloea /zṓ ə glée ə/ (*plural* **-as** *or* **-ae**), **zooglea** (*plural* **-as** *or* **-ae**) *n.* a colony of microbes embedded in a gelatinous matrix [Late 19thC. From modern Latin, from Greek *zōion* 'animal' + *gloios* 'glutinous substance'.] —**zoogloeal** *adj.*

zoography /zō óggrəfi/ *n.* a branch of zoology that deals with describing animals and their habitats —**zoographer** *n.* —**zoographic** /zṓ ə gráffik/ *adj.*

zooid /zṓ oyd/ *n.* an individual invertebrate animal that reproduces nonsexually by budding or splitting, especially one that lives in a colony in which each member is joined to others by living material, e.g. a coral [Mid-19thC. Coined from ZOO- + -OID.] —**zooidal** *adj.*

zookeeper /zóo keepər/ *n.* sb whose job is looking after the animals in a zoo

zool. *abbr.* **1.** zoological **2.** zoology

zoolatry /zō óllətri/ *n.* **1.** ANIMAL WORSHIP in some ancient cultures, the worshipping of animals **2.** EXTREME DEVOTION TO ANIMALS excessive devotion to animals, especially domestic pets (*humorous*) —**zoolater** *n.* —**zoolatrous** *adj.*

zoological /zṓ ə lójjik'l, zóo-/ *adj.* **1.** OF SCIENTIFIC STUDY OF ANIMALS relating to the scientific study of animals **2.** ABOUT ANIMALS relating to or about animals

zoological garden *n.* a zoo (*formal*)

zoologist /zō óllәjist, zoo-/ *n.* sb who studies animals and animal behaviour scientifically

zoology /zō ólləji, zoo-/ (*plural* **-gies**) *n.* **1.** SCIENTIFIC STUDY OF ANIMALS the branch of biology that involves the scientific study of animals and all aspects of animal life **2.** ANIMALS LIVING IN REGION the animal life of a particular region **3.** ANIMAL'S OR ANIMAL GROUP'S CHARACTERISTICS the physical and biological characteristics of a particular animal or group of animals [Mid-17thC. Via modern Latin from Greek *zōologia*, literally 'the study of life', from *zōion* 'life form' (see -ZOON).]

zoom /zoom/ *v.* (**zooms, zooming, zoomed**) **1.** *vi.* MOVE SPEEDILY to move very fast, especially while emitting a loud low-pitched buzzing noise **2.** *vi.* MAKE LOUD BUZZING NOISE to emit a loud low-pitched buzzing or humming noise **3.** *vi.* INCREASE SUDDENLY to rise or increase suddenly and significantly **4.** *vti.* AIR CARRY OUT STEEP CLIMB IN AIRCRAFT to make an aircraft climb rapidly at a very steep angle, or to be piloted in this way ■ *n.* **1.** LOUD BUZZING NOISE a loud low-pitched buzzing noise, especially one caused by rapid movement **2.** PHOTOGRAPHY = **zoom lens 3.** CINEMA SHOT WITH ZOOM LENS a shot in which a zoom lens is used to make the object in focus appear to move closer or farther away while the camera itself stays still [Late 19thC. An imitation of the sound.]

zoom in *vi.* to make an object appear bigger or closer, or to decrease the area in view, by use of a zoom lens or a graphic imaging device

zoom out *vi.* to make an object appear smaller or further away, or to increase the area in view, by use of a zoom lens or a graphic imaging device

zoometry /zō ómmətri/ *n.* the branch of zoology that deals with the sizes and proportions of animals —**zoometric** /zṓ ə méttrik/ *adj.* —**zoometrist** *n.*

zoom lens /zóom lenz/, **zoom** *n.* a camera lens assembly with adjustable focal lengths that make an object being photographed or filmed appear closer or farther away than it really is

zoomorphism /zṓ ə máwrfizəm/ *n.* **1.** ATTRIBUTION OF ANIMAL FORMS TO GODS the representation of gods as animals, or the attributing of animal characteristics to gods **2.** ARTS USE OF ANIMALS IN ART the use of animal figures in art and design, or of animal symbols in literature —**zoomorphic** /zṓ ə máwrfik/ *adj.*

-zoon *suffix.* animal, zooid ○ *epizoon* [Via modern Latin from Greek *zōion* 'living being, animal'. Ultimately from an Indo-European base meaning 'to live', which is also the ancestor of English *quick*, *vital*, *biology*, and *whiskey*.]

zoonosis /zṓ ə nṓsiss, zō ónnəssiss/ (*plural* **-ses** /zṓ ə nṓ seez/) *n.* a disease, e.g. rabies, anthrax, or ringworm that can be transmitted from vertebrate animals to humans [Late 19thC. Coined from ZOO- + Greek *nosos* 'disease'.] —**zoonotic** /zṓ ə nóttik/ *adj.*

zoophagous /zō óffəgəss/ *adj.* feeding on animals

zoophilia /zṓ ə fílli ə/ *n.* a sexual attraction to animals

zoophilic *adj.* = **zoophilous**

zoophilism /zō óffilizəm/ *n.* a strong affinity for animals and a devotion to protecting or rescuing them from human activities, e.g. vivisection, that exploit or endanger them

zoophilous /zō óffiləss/, **zoophilic** /zṓ ə fíllik/ *adj.* **1.** DEVOTED TO ANIMALS very fond of animals **2.** BOT POLLINATED BY ANIMALS using the actions of animals other than insects in pollinating a plant

zoophobia /zṓ ə fṓbi ə/ *n.* an unusually intense fear of animals —**zoophobe** /zṓ əfōb/ *n.* —**zoophobous** /zō óffəbəss/ *adj.*

zoophyte /zṓ ə fīt/ *n.* an invertebrate animal that looks like a plant, e.g. the sea anemone, coral, or sponge [Early 17thC. Via modern Latin from Greek *zōiophuton*, literally 'animal-plant', from *zōion* 'animal' + *phuton* 'plant'.] —**zoophytic** /zṓ ə fíttik/ *adj.*

zooplankton /zṓ ə plángktən/ *n.* plankton that is made up of microscopic animals, e.g. protozoans. ◊ **phytoplankton**

zooplasty /zṓ ə plasti/ *n.* the surgical transplantation of an animal organ, e.g. a pig's heart, into a human body —**zooplastic** /zṓ ə plástik/ *adj.*

zoosperm /zṓ ə spurm/ *n.* = **spermatozoon** —**zoospermatic** /zṓ ə spur máttik/ *adj.*

zoosporangium /zṓ əspə ránji əm/ (*plural* **-a** /-ji ə/) *n.* an organ of a fungus or plant that produces spores that can swim —**zoosporangial** /zṓ əspə ránji əl/ *adj.*

zoospore /zṓ ə spawr/ *n.* a spore of some algae and fungi that is capable of independent movement —**zoosporal** /zṓ ə spáwrəl/ *adj.* —**zoosporic** /-spórrik/ *adj.*

zoosterol /zō óstə rol/ *n.* a sterol that is produced by an animal, e.g. cholesterol

zootomy /zō óttəmi/ *n.* **1.** STUDY OF ANIMAL ANATOMY the study of the anatomy of animals, especially comparative anatomy **2.** ANIMAL DISSECTION the dissection of animals [Mid-17thC. Formed from ZOO-, on the model of 'anatomy'.] —**zootomic** /zṓ ə tómmik/ *adj.* —**zootomically** /-tómmikli/ *adv.* —**zootomist** *n.*

zootoxin /zṓ ə tóksin/ *n.* a poisonous substance produced by an animal, e.g. snake venom —**zootoxic** /zṓ ə tóksik/ *adj.*

zoot suit /zóot-, -/ *n.* a man's suit, popular in the 1940s, that had a long jacket heavily padded at the shoulders and baggy high-waisted trousers tapering to narrow bottoms. A long watch chain was also sometimes worn looping across the trousers. [*Zoot* of uncertain origin: probably a rhyming formation from SUIT] —**zoot suiter** *n.*

zoo TV *n.* a type of television programme that encourages emotional and often uncontrolled reactions from the participants such as those featuring debates or personal disclosures in front of live audiences (*slang*)

zooxanthella /zṓ əzən théllə/ (*plural* **-lae** /-thélli/) *n.* a microscopic yellow-green alga that lives symbiotically within the cells of some marine invertebrates, especially corals [Late 19thC. From modern Latin, literally 'small yellow animal', from Greek *zōion* 'animal' + *xanthos* 'yellow'.]

zori /záwri, zórri/ (*plural* **-ri** *or* **-ris**) *n.* a simple Japanese sandal with a flat sole and a single thong, originally made of straw but now also made of rubber or felt [Early 19thC. From Japanese, literally 'straw sole'.]

zorilla /zo ríllə/, **zorille, zoril** /zórril/ *n.* a carnivorous African mammal of the weasel family that looks like a skunk and has long black-and-white fur. Latin name: *Ictonyx striatus.* [Late 18thC. Via French and modern Latin from Spanish *zorilla*, literally 'little fox', from *zorro* 'fox'.]

Zoroaster /zórrō ástər/ (630?–550? BC) Persian prophet. He founded Zoroastrianism, a religion based on revelations he received from Ahura Mazda, the 'Lord Wisdom'.

Zoroastrianism /zórrō ástri ənizəm/ *n.* an ancient religion founded by the Persian prophet Zoroaster the principal belief of which is in a supreme deity and in a cosmic contest between two spirits, one good and one evil. The sacred writings of Zoroastrianism are collected in the Zend-Avesta. —**Zoroastrian** *n.*, *adj.*

zoster /zóstər/ *n.* **1.** MED SHINGLES shingles (*technical*) **2.** ARCHAEOL ANCIENT GREEK BELT a belt worn by men, especially soldiers, in ancient Greece [Early 18thC. Via Latin from Greek *zōstēr* 'girdle'; from the fact that the blisters often appear in a band across the body.]

Zouave /zoo aáv/ *n.* **1.** ALGERIAN INFANTRYMAN IN FRENCH ARMY UNIT a member of a former French infantry unit composed of Algerian soldiers, noted for their colourful uniforms and precision drill **2.** MEMBER OF UNIT IMITATING FRENCH ZOUAVES a member of an army unit imitating the uniform of the French Zouaves, especially those on the Union side during the US Civil War [Mid-19thC. Via French from Kabyle *Zouaoua*, the name of a tribe in Algeria.]

zouk /zook/ *n.* a style of dance music originating in Guadeloupe and Martinique played with guitars and synthesizers that combines a strong fast disco beat and Caribbean rhythms [Late 20thC. Via French from Antillean Creole.]

zounds /zowndz/ *interj.* a mild expression of surprise or annoyance (*archaic*) [Late 16thC. Shortening of *by God's wounds*!]

zoysia /zóyssi ə/ *n.* a low-growing grass plant often used for lawns in its native Asia and other regions. Genus: *Zoysia*. [Mid-20thC. From modern Latin, genus name, named after the Austrian botanist Carl von *Zoys* zu Laubach (1756–1800?).]

Z particle *n.* a short-lived electrically neutral elementary particle considered to mediate the weak interaction between other elementary particles

ZPG *abbr.* zero population growth

Zr *symbol.* zirconium

zucchetto /zoo kéttō/ *n.* (*plural* **-tos**) a small round skullcap worn by members of the Roman Catholic clergy that varies in colour depending on the rank of the person wearing it. The pope wears a white one, cardinals red, bishops purple, and priests black. [Mid-19thC. Alteration of Italian *zucchetta*, literally 'headlet', from *zucca* 'gourd, head' (see ZUCCHINI).]

zucchini /zoo keéni/ *n.* (*plural* **-ni** *or* **-nis**) *n.* Aus, Can, US **1.** PLANTS = **courgette 2.** ZUCCHINI PLANT the plant on which zucchini grow [Early 20thC. From Italian, plural of *zucchino* 'courgette', literally 'small gourd', from *zucca* 'gourd', from late Latin *cucutia*, a variant of Latin *cucurbita* (source of English *gourd*).]

zugzwang /zoóg zwang/ *n.* DISADVANTAGEOUS CHESS SITUATION a chess situation in which a player is forced into making a disadvantageous move, especially one that involves the loss of a piece ■ *vt.* (**-zwangs, -zwanging, -zwanged**) FORCE INTO BAD CHESS POSITION to force a chess opponent into a disadvantageous situation, especially one that involves the loss of one of the opponent's pieces [Early 20thC. From German, literally 'being forced to move'.]

Zuider Zee /zídər zeé/ former inlet of the North Sea, south of the West Friesian Islands and occupying a deep indentation in the coast of the Netherlands. After completion of the Ijsselmeer Dam in 1932, parts of it were drained, and the remainder now forms the Ijsselmeer.

Zulu /zoó loo/ (*plural* **-lu** *or* **-lus**) *n.* **1.** PEOPLES MEMBER OF SOUTH AFRICAN PEOPLE a member of a people of South Africa who live mainly in the northern part of the province of Natal, where they were the dominant people during the 19th century. They fiercely resisted Boer incursions into their lands and, under their chief, Cetewayo, fought and won several battles against British forces before being comprehensively defeated in 1879. **2.** LANG BENUE-CONGO LANGUAGE a language spoken in eastern South Africa that belongs to the Bantu group of Benue-Congo languages, closely related to Xhosa. Zulu is spoken by about 8 million people. **3.** COMMUNICATION CODE WORD FOR LETTER 'Z' the NATO phonetic alphabet code word for the letter 'Z', used in international radio communications [Early 19thC. From Zulu *umzulu*.] —**Zulu** *adj.*

Zululand /zoóloo land/ historic region in South Africa. Now incorporated into KwaZulu-Natal Province, it is the homeland of the Zulu people.

Zuni /zoóni/ (*plural* **-ni** *or* **-nis**), **Zuñi** /zoónyi/ (*plural* **-ñi** *or* **-ñis**) *n.* **1.** PEOPLES MEMBER OF A NATIVE N AMERICAN PEOPLE a member of a Native North American Pueblo people of western New Mexico **2.** LANG ZUNI LANGUAGE the language spoken by the Zuni people of New Mexico. It is a linguistically isolated language with no identified relatives. Zuni is spoken by about 5,000 people. [Mid-19thC. From American Spanish, of Keresan origin.] —**Zuni** *adj.*

Zurich /zoórik/, **Zürich** the largest city in Switzerland and capital of Zurich Canton. Population: 353,361 (1994).

Zurich, Lake of lake in northern Switzerland, predominantly in Zurich Canton. Area: 88 sq. km/34 sq. mi.

ZW *abbr.* Zimbabwe

Zwickau /zwík ow, tsvík ow/ city in Saxony, eastern Germany. Population: 103,900 (1995).

zwieback /zweé bak/ *n.* a piece of bread, sliced and baked again until crisp and dry [Late 19thC. From German, literally 'twice-bake'.]

Zwinglian /zwín gli ən, zwíngli ən/ *adj.* RELATING TO ZWINGLI OR HIS DOCTRINE relating to the life, works, or beliefs of the Swiss Protestant theologian Ulrich Zwingli, who believed that the Communion wafer and wine were only symbolic of Christ's body and blood ■ *n.* FOLLOWER OF ZWINGLI a follower of the Swiss Protestant theologian Ulrich Zwingli or a believer in his doctrines —**Zwinglianism** *n.*

zwitterion /zwíttər ī ən, tsvíttər-/ *n.* an ion that has both a negative and a positive pole [Early 20thC. From German, literally 'hybrid ion'.]

Zwolle /zwóllə/ capital city of Overijssel Province, in the north-central Netherlands. Population: 100,835 (1996).

zydeco /zídikō/ *n.* a style of dance music originating in Louisiana that is usually played on accordion, guitar, and violin and combines traditional French melodies with Caribbean and blues influences [Mid-20thC. Origin uncertain: probably from Louisiana creole *Les haricots (sont pas salé)*, literally 'the beans (are not salted)', the name of a well-known dance tune.]

zyg- *prefix.* = **zygo-** (*used before vowels*)

zygo- *prefix.* **1.** yoke, pair ○ *zygomorphic* **2.** union, reproduction ○ *zygogenesis* [From Greek *zugon* 'yoke, pair'. Ultimately from an Indo-European word meaning 'to join', which is also the ancestor of English *yoke*, *join*, *adjust*, and *yoga*.]

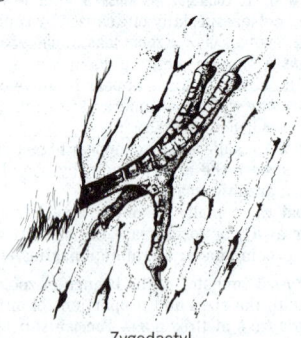
Zygodactyl

zygodactyl /zígō dáktil/ *adj.* zygodactyl, zygodactylous WITH TWO PAIRS OF TOES with toes arranged in pairs, two facing forwards and two backwards, like those found on woodpeckers ■ *n.* BIRD WITH TWO PAIRS OF TOES a bird that has two pairs of toes, e.g. the woodpecker —**zygodactylism** /zígō dáktilizəm/ *n.*

zygogenesis /zígō jénnəssiss/ *n.* reproduction involving the fusion of male and female nuclei —**zygogenetic** /zígōjə néttik/ *adj.*

zygoma /zī gō̌mə/ (*plural* **-mata** /-mə̌tə/) *n.* **1.** CHEEKBONE a cheekbone (*technical*) **2. = zygomatic arch 3. = zygomatic process** [Late 17thC. From Greek *zugōma*, lit-erally 'joining', from *zugoun* 'to join'.] —**zygomatic** /zígə máttik/ *adj.*

zygomatic arch *n.* a slender bar of bone connecting the cheekbone with the temporal bone on the side of the skull

zygomatic bone *n.* a cheekbone (*technical*)

zygomatic process *n.* a bony projection that forms part of the zygomatic arch and is joined to the cheekbone

zygomorphic /zígō máwrfik/ *adj.* producing identical halves only when divided along a vertical axis —**zygomorphism** *n.* —**zygomorphy** /zígō mawrfi/ *n.*

zygosis /zī gṓssiss/ *n.* BIOL = **conjugation** *n.* 6 [Late 19thC. From Greek *zugōsis*, from *zugoun* 'to join'.] —**zygose** /zígōss/ *adj.*

zygosity /zī góssəti/ *n.* a particular characterization of a genetic trait, zygote, or embryo, e.g. whether twins have resulted from the division of one zygote or from two different zygotes (*often used in combination*) [Mid-20thC. Formed from ZYGOSIS.]

zygospore /zígō spawr/ *n.* a thick-walled sexual spore formed from the union of two gametes in some fungi and green algae —**zygosporic** /zígō spórrik/ *adj.*

zygote /zígōt/ *n.* an ovum that has been fertilized by a spermatozoon [Late 19thC. From Greek *zugōtos* 'joined', from *zugoun* 'to join'.] —**zygotic** /zī góttik/ *adj.* —**zy-gotically** /-góttikli/ *adv.*

zygotene /zígə teen/ *n.* a stage of the first meiotic cell division in which homologous chromosomes are paired [Early 20thC. From French *zygotène*, from *zygo-* 'zygo-' and *-tène* 'ribbon' (from Latin *taenia*).]

-zygous *suffix.* having a particular kind of zygotic constitution ○ *hemizygous* [Formed from Greek *zugos* 'yoked, paired', which in turn was formed from *zugon* 'yoke' (see ZYGO-)]

zym- *prefix.* = **zymo-** (*used before vowels*)

zymase /zím ayss, -ayz/ *n.* an enzyme or complex of enzymes obtained from yeast that makes sugars ferment [Late 19thC. Coined from Greek *zumē* 'leaven' (see ZYMO-) + -ASE.]

zymo- *prefix.* **1.** fermentation ○ *zymology* **2.** enzyme ○ *zymogen* [Via modern Latin from Greek *zumē* 'leaven' (source also of English *enzyme*). Ultimately from an Indo-European word meaning 'to mix', which is also the ancestor of English *juice*.]

zymogen /zíməjən/ *n.* = proenzyme

zymogenesis /zímō jénnəssiss/ *n.* the transformation of a zymogen into an enzyme

zymogenic /zímō jénnik/, **zymogenetic** /zíməjə néttik/, **zymogenous** /zī mójjənəss/ *adj.* **1.** RELATING TO ZYMOGENS relating to a zymogen **2.** CAUSING FERMENTATION causing or producing fermentation [Late 19thC]

zymology /zī mólləji/ *n.* a branch of biochemistry that studies fermentation, in particular the behaviour of enzymes during it —**zymologic** /zímə lójjik/ *adj.* —**zymologist** *n.*

zymolysis /zī mólləssiss/ *n.* the action of enzymes in the process of fermentation (*technical*) —**zymolytic** /zímə líttik/ *adj.*

zymometer /zī mómmitər/ *n.* an instrument that measures how much or how efficiently fermentation has taken place, by measuring the level of carbon dioxide produced

zymosis /zī móssiss/ *n.* = **zymolysis** [Early 18thC. From Greek *zumōsis* 'fermentation', from *zumoun* 'to leaven', from *zumē* (see ZYMO-).]

zymotic /zī móttik/ *adj.* relating to, producing, or produced by fermentation [Mid-19thC. From Greek *zumōtikos* 'causing fermentation', from *zumōsis* (see ZYMOSIS).] —**zymotically** *adv.*

zymurgy /zímərji/ *n.* the scientific study of the process of fermentation in brewing and distilling [Mid-19thC. Formed from ZYMO-, on the model of 'metallurgy'.] —**zymur-gic** /zī múrjik/ *adj.*

Zyrian /zírri ən/ *n.*, *adj.* LANG the Komi language, particularly its northern dialect [Late 19thC. From Russian *Zyryanin*.]

zzz /zz/ *n.* (*plural* **zzz's**) a representation of the sound made by sb sleeping or snoring, often used in cartoons (*humorous*)

TABLES, CHARTS, AND COMPOSITE PICTURES

The following tables, charts, and composite pictures can be found at their alphabetical entry:

Airport codes
Aircraft
Alphabets
Angles
Astrological signs
Automobiles
Bible, Books of the
Boats
Braille
Brass instruments
Bridges
Calendars
Cards
Cloud formations
Crosses
Currencies
Deserts
Diacritical marks
Domains (used in e-mail)
El Niño
Emoticons
European Union
Fungi
Geometry
Gulf Stream
Gymnasium equipment
Herbs
Hats
Keyboard instruments
Knots
Lakes
Leaf shapes
Map projections
Measurements
Military ranks
Mountains
Musical notation
National Parks
Oceans and seas
Percussion instruments
Periodic table
Phases of the Moon
Presidents of the United States
Prime ministers of Canada, Britain, Australia, and New Zealand
Proofreaders' marks
Registration of automobiles
Rivers
Roofs
Runes
San Andreas Fault
Semaphore
Shoes
Stars
Stringed instruments
Time zones
Triangles
Trigrams
Volcanoes
Waterfalls
Weather symbols
Woodwind instruments
World Heritage Sites

Illustration Credits